This
HOLY
BIBLE

Presented to

_____

_____

By

_____

_____

Date

_____

ספר הבריתות

HEBREW-ENGLISH
BIBLE

תורה נביאים כתובים והברית החדשה

עברית ואנגלית

THE HOLY SCRIPTURES

Hebrew and English

God's Word: Open for All

I.A.D.B.W and B.S.I
JERUSALEM

2006

Published in Israel
Hebrew/English Bible
ISBN 965-431-005-8   63DI   UBS-EPS-2006-5.1K
ISBN 965-431-015-5   67DI   UBS-EPS-2006-3K

The Bible Society in Israel
P.O. Box 44 Jerusalem, 91000 Israel

The New Testament

הברית החדשה

תורה נביאים וכתובים

THE

OLD TESTAMENT

The First Book of Moses Called

GENESIS

1 In the beginning God created the heavens and the earth. ²The earth was without form, and void; and darkness *was* on the face of the deep. And the Spirit of God was hovering over the face of the waters.

³Then God said, "Let there be light"; and there was light. ⁴And God saw the light, that *it was* good; and God divided the light from the darkness. ⁵God called the light Day, and the darkness He called Night. So the evening and the morning were the first day.

⁶Then God said, "Let there be a firmament in the midst of the waters, and let it divide the waters from the waters." ⁷Thus God made the firmament, and divided the waters which *were* under the firmament from the waters which *were* above the firmament; and it was so. ⁸And God called the firmament Heaven. So the evening and the morning were the second day.

⁹Then God said, "Let the waters under the heavens be gathered together into one place, and let the dry *land* appear"; and it was so. ¹⁰And God called the dry *land* Earth, and the gathering together of the waters He called Seas. And God saw that *it was* good.

¹¹Then God said, "Let the earth bring forth grass, the herb *that* yields seed, *and* the fruit tree *that* yields fruit according to its kind, whose seed *is* in itself, on the earth"; and it was so. ¹²And the earth brought forth grass, the herb *that* yields seed according to its kind, and the tree *that* yields fruit, whose seed *is* in itself according to its kind. And God saw that *it was* good. ¹³So the evening and the morning were the third day.

¹⁴Then God said, "Let there be lights in the firmament of the heavens to divide the day from the night; and let them be for signs and seasons, and for days and years; ¹⁵and let them be for lights in the firmament of the heavens to give light on the earth"; and it was so. ¹⁶Then God made two great lights: the greater light to rule the day, and the lesser light to rule the night. *He made* the stars also. ¹⁷God set them in the firmament of the heavens to give light on the earth, ¹⁸and to rule over the day and over the night, and to divide the light from the darkness. And God saw that *it was* good. ¹⁹So the evening and the morning were the fourth day.

בְּרֵאשִׁית

א בְּרֵאשִׁית בָּרָא אֱלֹהִים אֵת הַשָּׁמַיִם וְאֵת הָאָרֶץ: ² וְהָאָרֶץ הָיְתָה תֹהוּ וָבֹהוּ וְחֹשֶׁךְ עַל־פְּנֵי תְהוֹם וְרוּחַ אֱלֹהִים מְרַחֶפֶת עַל־פְּנֵי הַמָּיִם: ³ וַיֹּאמֶר אֱלֹהִים יְהִי אוֹר וַיְהִי־אוֹר: ⁴ וַיַּרְא אֱלֹהִים אֶת־הָאוֹר כִּי־טוֹב וַיַּבְדֵּל אֱלֹהִים בֵּין הָאוֹר וּבֵין הַחֹשֶׁךְ: ⁵ וַיִּקְרָא אֱלֹהִים ׀ לָאוֹר יוֹם וְלַחֹשֶׁךְ קָרָא לָיְלָה וַיְהִי־עֶרֶב וַיְהִי־בֹקֶר יוֹם אֶחָד: פ

⁶ וַיֹּאמֶר אֱלֹהִים יְהִי רָקִיעַ בְּתוֹךְ הַמָּיִם וִיהִי מַבְדִּיל בֵּין מַיִם לָמָיִם: ⁷ וַיַּעַשׂ אֱלֹהִים אֶת־הָרָקִיעַ וַיַּבְדֵּל בֵּין הַמַּיִם אֲשֶׁר מִתַּחַת לָרָקִיעַ וּבֵין הַמַּיִם אֲשֶׁר מֵעַל לָרָקִיעַ וַיְהִי־כֵן: ⁸ וַיִּקְרָא אֱלֹהִים לָרָקִיעַ שָׁמָיִם וַיְהִי־עֶרֶב וַיְהִי־בֹקֶר יוֹם שֵׁנִי: פ

⁹ וַיֹּאמֶר אֱלֹהִים יִקָּווּ הַמַּיִם מִתַּחַת הַשָּׁמַיִם אֶל־מָקוֹם אֶחָד וְתֵרָאֶה הַיַּבָּשָׁה וַיְהִי־כֵן: ¹⁰ וַיִּקְרָא אֱלֹהִים ׀ לַיַּבָּשָׁה אֶרֶץ וּלְמִקְוֵה הַמַּיִם קָרָא יַמִּים וַיַּרְא אֱלֹהִים כִּי־טוֹב: ¹¹ וַיֹּאמֶר אֱלֹהִים תַּדְשֵׁא הָאָרֶץ דֶּשֶׁא עֵשֶׂב מַזְרִיעַ זֶרַע עֵץ פְּרִי עֹשֶׂה פְּרִי לְמִינוֹ אֲשֶׁר זַרְעוֹ־בוֹ עַל־הָאָרֶץ וַיְהִי־כֵן: ¹² וַתּוֹצֵא הָאָרֶץ דֶּשֶׁא עֵשֶׂב מַזְרִיעַ זֶרַע לְמִינֵהוּ וְעֵץ עֹשֶׂה־פְּרִי אֲשֶׁר זַרְעוֹ־בוֹ לְמִינֵהוּ וַיַּרְא אֱלֹהִים כִּי־טוֹב: ¹³ וַיְהִי־עֶרֶב וַיְהִי־בֹקֶר יוֹם שְׁלִישִׁי: פ

¹⁴ וַיֹּאמֶר אֱלֹהִים יְהִי מְאֹרֹת בִּרְקִיעַ הַשָּׁמַיִם לְהַבְדִּיל בֵּין הַיּוֹם וּבֵין הַלָּיְלָה וְהָיוּ לְאֹתֹת וּלְמוֹעֲדִים וּלְיָמִים וְשָׁנִים: ¹⁵ וְהָיוּ לִמְאוֹרֹת בִּרְקִיעַ הַשָּׁמַיִם לְהָאִיר עַל־הָאָרֶץ וַיְהִי־כֵן: ¹⁶ וַיַּעַשׂ אֱלֹהִים אֶת־שְׁנֵי הַמְּאֹרֹת הַגְּדֹלִים אֶת־הַמָּאוֹר הַגָּדֹל לְמֶמְשֶׁלֶת הַיּוֹם וְאֶת־הַמָּאוֹר הַקָּטֹן לְמֶמְשֶׁלֶת הַלַּיְלָה וְאֵת הַכּוֹכָבִים: ¹⁷ וַיִּתֵּן אֹתָם אֱלֹהִים בִּרְקִיעַ הַשָּׁמָיִם לְהָאִיר עַל־הָאָרֶץ: ¹⁸ וְלִמְשֹׁל בַּיּוֹם וּבַלַּיְלָה וּלֲהַבְדִּיל בֵּין הָאוֹר וּבֵין הַחֹשֶׁךְ וַיַּרְא אֱלֹהִים כִּי־טוֹב: ¹⁹ וַיְהִי־עֶרֶב וַיְהִי־בֹקֶר יוֹם רְבִיעִי: פ

²⁰ Then God said, "Let the waters abound with an abundance of living creatures, and let birds fly above the earth across the face of the firmament of the heavens." ²¹ So God created great sea creatures and every living thing that moves, with which the waters abounded, according to their kind, and every winged bird according to its kind. And God saw that *it was* good. ²² And God blessed them, saying, "Be fruitful and multiply, and fill the waters in the seas, and let birds multiply on the earth." ²³ So the evening and the morning were the fifth day.

²⁴ Then God said, "Let the earth bring forth the living creature according to its kind: cattle and creeping thing and beast of the earth, *each* according to its kind"; and it was so. ²⁵ And God made the beast of the earth according to its kind, cattle according to its kind, and everything that creeps on the earth according to its kind. And God saw that *it was* good.

²⁶ Then God said, "Let Us make man in Our image, according to Our likeness; let them have dominion over the fish of the sea, over the birds of the air, and over the cattle, over all the earth and over every creeping thing that creeps on the earth." ²⁷ So God created man in His *own* image; in the image of God He created him; male and female He created them. ²⁸ Then God blessed them, and God said to them, "Be fruitful and multiply; fill the earth and subdue it; have dominion over the fish of the sea, over the birds of the air, and over every living thing that moves on the earth."

²⁹ And God said, "See, I have given you every herb *that* yields seed which *is* on the face of all the earth, and every tree whose fruit yields seed; to you it shall be for food. ³⁰ Also, to every beast of the earth, to every bird of the air, and to everything that creeps on the earth, in which *there is* life, *I have given* every green herb for food"; and it was so. ³¹ Then God saw everything that He had made, and indeed *it was* very good. So the evening and the morning were the sixth day.

2 Thus the heavens and the earth, and all the host of them, were finished. ² And on the seventh day God ended His work which He had done, and He rested on the seventh day from all His work which He had done. ³ Then God blessed the seventh day and sanctified it, because in it He rested from all His work which God had created and made.

⁴ This *is* the history of the heavens and the earth when they were created, in the day that the Lord God made the earth and the heavens, ⁵ before any plant of the field was in the earth and before any

20 וַיֹּ֣אמֶר אֱלֹהִ֔ים יִשְׁרְצ֣וּ הַמַּ֔יִם שֶׁ֖רֶץ נֶ֣פֶשׁ חַיָּ֑ה וְע֣וֹף יְעוֹפֵ֣ף עַל־הָאָ֔רֶץ עַל־פְּנֵ֖י רְקִ֥יעַ הַשָּׁמָֽיִם: 21 וַיִּבְרָ֣א אֱלֹהִ֔ים אֶת־הַתַּנִּינִ֖ם הַגְּדֹלִ֑ים וְאֵ֣ת כָּל־נֶ֣פֶשׁ הַֽחַיָּ֣ה ׀ הָֽרֹמֶ֡שֶׂת אֲשֶׁר֩ שָׁרְצ֨וּ הַמַּ֜יִם לְמִֽינֵהֶ֗ם וְאֵ֨ת כָּל־ע֤וֹף כָּנָף֙ לְמִינֵ֔הוּ וַיַּ֥רְא אֱלֹהִ֖ים כִּי־טֽוֹב: 22 וַיְבָ֧רֶךְ אֹתָ֛ם אֱלֹהִ֖ים לֵאמֹ֑ר פְּר֣וּ וּרְב֗וּ וּמִלְא֤וּ אֶת־הַמַּ֨יִם֙ בַּיַּמִּ֔ים וְהָע֖וֹף יִ֥רֶב בָּאָֽרֶץ: 23 וַֽיְהִי־עֶ֥רֶב וַֽיְהִי־בֹ֖קֶר י֥וֹם חֲמִישִֽׁי: פ

24 וַיֹּ֣אמֶר אֱלֹהִ֗ים תּוֹצֵ֤א הָאָ֨רֶץ֙ נֶ֣פֶשׁ חַיָּה֙ לְמִינָ֔הּ בְּהֵמָ֥ה וָרֶ֛מֶשׂ וְחַֽיְתוֹ־אֶ֖רֶץ לְמִינָ֑הּ וַֽיְהִי־כֵֽן: 25 וַיַּ֣עַשׂ אֱלֹהִים֩ אֶת־חַיַּ֨ת הָאָ֜רֶץ לְמִינָ֗הּ וְאֶת־הַבְּהֵמָה֙ לְמִינָ֔הּ וְאֵ֛ת כָּל־רֶ֥מֶשׂ הָֽאֲדָמָ֖ה לְמִינֵ֑הוּ וַיַּ֥רְא אֱלֹהִ֖ים כִּי־טֽוֹב: 26 וַיֹּ֣אמֶר אֱלֹהִ֔ים נַֽעֲשֶׂ֥ה אָדָ֛ם בְּצַלְמֵ֖נוּ כִּדְמוּתֵ֑נוּ וְיִרְדּוּ֩ בִדְגַ֨ת הַיָּ֜ם וּבְע֣וֹף הַשָּׁמַ֗יִם וּבַבְּהֵמָה֙ וּבְכָל־הָאָ֔רֶץ וּבְכָל־הָרֶ֖מֶשׂ הָֽרֹמֵ֥שׂ עַל־הָאָֽרֶץ: 27 וַיִּבְרָ֨א אֱלֹהִ֤ים ׀ אֶת־הָֽאָדָם֙ בְּצַלְמ֔וֹ בְּצֶ֥לֶם אֱלֹהִ֖ים בָּרָ֣א אֹת֑וֹ זָכָ֥ר וּנְקֵבָ֖ה בָּרָ֥א אֹתָֽם: 28 וַיְבָ֣רֶךְ אֹתָם֮ אֱלֹהִים֒ וַיֹּ֨אמֶר לָהֶ֜ם אֱלֹהִ֗ים פְּר֥וּ וּרְב֛וּ וּמִלְא֥וּ אֶת־הָאָ֖רֶץ וְכִבְשֻׁ֑הָ וּרְד֞וּ בִּדְגַ֤ת הַיָּם֙ וּבְע֣וֹף הַשָּׁמַ֔יִם וּבְכָל־חַיָּ֖ה הָֽרֹמֶ֥שֶׂת עַל־הָאָֽרֶץ: 29 וַיֹּ֣אמֶר אֱלֹהִ֗ים הִנֵּה֩ נָתַ֨תִּי לָכֶ֜ם אֶת־כָּל־עֵ֣שֶׂב ׀ זֹרֵ֣עַ זֶ֗רַע אֲשֶׁר֙ עַל־פְּנֵ֣י כָל־הָאָ֔רֶץ וְאֶת־כָּל־הָעֵ֛ץ אֲשֶׁר־בּ֥וֹ פְרִי־עֵ֖ץ זֹרֵ֣עַ זָ֑רַע לָכֶ֥ם יִֽהְיֶ֖ה לְאָכְלָֽה: 30 וּֽלְכָל־חַיַּ֣ת הָ֠אָרֶץ וּלְכָל־ע֨וֹף הַשָּׁמַ֜יִם וּלְכֹ֣ל ׀ רוֹמֵ֣שׂ עַל־הָאָ֗רֶץ אֲשֶׁר־בּוֹ֙ נֶ֣פֶשׁ חַיָּ֔ה אֶת־כָּל־יֶ֥רֶק עֵ֖שֶׂב לְאָכְלָ֑ה וַֽיְהִי־כֵֽן: 31 וַיַּ֤רְא אֱלֹהִים֙ אֶת־כָּל־אֲשֶׁ֣ר עָשָׂ֔ה וְהִנֵּה־ט֖וֹב מְאֹ֑ד וַֽיְהִי־עֶ֥רֶב וַֽיְהִי־בֹ֖קֶר י֥וֹם הַשִּׁשִּֽׁי: פ

ב וַיְכֻלּ֛וּ הַשָּׁמַ֥יִם וְהָאָ֖רֶץ וְכָל־צְבָאָֽם: 2 וַיְכַ֤ל אֱלֹהִים֙ בַּיּ֣וֹם הַשְּׁבִיעִ֔י מְלַאכְתּ֖וֹ אֲשֶׁ֣ר עָשָׂ֑ה וַיִּשְׁבֹּת֙ בַּיּ֣וֹם הַשְּׁבִיעִ֔י מִכָּל־מְלַאכְתּ֖וֹ אֲשֶׁ֥ר עָשָֽׂה: 3 וַיְבָ֤רֶךְ אֱלֹהִים֙ אֶת־י֣וֹם הַשְּׁבִיעִ֔י וַיְקַדֵּ֖שׁ אֹת֑וֹ כִּ֣י ב֤וֹ שָׁבַת֙ מִכָּל־מְלַאכְתּ֔וֹ אֲשֶׁר־בָּרָ֥א אֱלֹהִ֖ים לַֽעֲשֽׂוֹת: פ

4 אֵ֣לֶּה תֽוֹלְד֧וֹת הַשָּׁמַ֛יִם וְהָאָ֖רֶץ בְּהִבָּֽרְאָ֑ם בְּי֗וֹם עֲשׂ֛וֹת יְהוָ֥ה אֱלֹהִ֖ים אֶ֥רֶץ וְשָׁמָֽיִם: 5 וְכֹ֣ל ׀ שִׂ֣יחַ

herb of the field had grown. For the LORD God had not caused it to rain on the earth, and *there was* no man to till the ground; ⁶but a mist went up from the earth and watered the whole face of the ground.

⁷And the LORD God formed man *of* the dust of the ground, and breathed into his nostrils the breath of life; and man became a living being.

⁸The LORD God planted a garden eastward in Eden, and there He put the man whom He had formed. ⁹And out of the ground the LORD God made every tree grow that is pleasant to the sight and good for food. The tree of life *was* also in the midst of the garden, and the tree of the knowledge of good and evil.

¹⁰Now a river went out of Eden to water the garden, and from there it parted and became four riverheads. ¹¹The name of the first *is* Pishon; it *is* the one which skirts the whole land of Havilah, where *there is* gold. ¹²And the gold of that land *is* good. Bdellium and the onyx stone *are* there. ¹³The name of the second river *is* Gihon; it *is* the one which goes around the whole land of Cush. ¹⁴The name of the third river *is* Hiddekel; it *is* the one which goes toward the east of Assyria. The fourth river *is* the Euphrates.

¹⁵Then the LORD God took the man and put him in the garden of Eden to tend and keep it. ¹⁶And the LORD God commanded the man, saying, "Of every tree of the garden you may freely eat; ¹⁷but of the tree of the knowledge of good and evil you shall not eat, for in the day that you eat of it you shall surely die."

¹⁸And the LORD God said, "*It is* not good that man should be alone; I will make him a helper comparable to him." ¹⁹Out of the ground the LORD God formed every beast of the field and every bird of the air, and brought *them* to Adam to see what he would call them. And whatever Adam called each living creature, that *was* its name. ²⁰So Adam gave names to all cattle, to the birds of the air, and to every beast of the field. But for Adam there was not found a helper comparable to him.

²¹And the LORD God caused a deep sleep to fall on Adam, and he slept; and He took one of his ribs, and closed up the flesh in its place. ²²Then the rib which the LORD God had taken from man He made into a woman, and He brought her to the man.

²³And Adam said:

"This *is* now bone of my bones
And flesh of my flesh;
She shall be called Woman,
Because she was taken out of Man."

הַשָּׂדֶה טֶרֶם יִהְיֶה בָאָרֶץ וְכָל־עֵשֶׂב הַשָּׂדֶה טֶרֶם יִצְמָח כִּי לֹא הִמְטִיר יְהוָה אֱלֹהִים עַל־הָאָרֶץ וְאָדָם אַיִן לַעֲבֹד אֶת־הָאֲדָמָה: 6 וְאֵד יַעֲלֶה מִן־הָאָרֶץ וְהִשְׁקָה אֶת־כָּל־פְּנֵי־הָאֲדָמָה: 7 וַיִּיצֶר יְהוָה אֱלֹהִים אֶת־הָאָדָם עָפָר מִן־הָאֲדָמָה וַיִּפַּח בְּאַפָּיו נִשְׁמַת חַיִּים וַיְהִי הָאָדָם לְנֶפֶשׁ חַיָּה: 8 וַיִּטַּע יְהוָה אֱלֹהִים גַּן־בְּעֵדֶן מִקֶּדֶם וַיָּשֶׂם שָׁם אֶת־הָאָדָם אֲשֶׁר יָצָר: 9 וַיַּצְמַח יְהוָה אֱלֹהִים מִן־הָאֲדָמָה כָּל־עֵץ נֶחְמָד לְמַרְאֶה וְטוֹב לְמַאֲכָל וְעֵץ הַחַיִּים בְּתוֹךְ הַגָּן וְעֵץ הַדַּעַת טוֹב וָרָע: 10 וְנָהָר יֹצֵא מֵעֵדֶן לְהַשְׁקוֹת אֶת־הַגָּן וּמִשָּׁם יִפָּרֵד וְהָיָה לְאַרְבָּעָה רָאשִׁים: 11 שֵׁם הָאֶחָד פִּישׁוֹן הוּא הַסֹּבֵב אֵת כָּל־אֶרֶץ הַחֲוִילָה אֲשֶׁר־שָׁם הַזָּהָב: 12 וּזֲהַב הָאָרֶץ הַהוּא טוֹב שָׁם הַבְּדֹלַח וְאֶבֶן הַשֹּׁהַם: 13 וְשֵׁם־הַנָּהָר הַשֵּׁנִי גִּיחוֹן הוּא הַסּוֹבֵב אֵת כָּל־אֶרֶץ כּוּשׁ: 14 וְשֵׁם הַנָּהָר הַשְּׁלִישִׁי חִדֶּקֶל הוּא הַהֹלֵךְ קִדְמַת אַשּׁוּר וְהַנָּהָר הָרְבִיעִי הוּא פְרָת: 15 וַיִּקַּח יְהוָה אֱלֹהִים אֶת־הָאָדָם וַיַּנִּחֵהוּ בְגַן־עֵדֶן לְעָבְדָהּ וּלְשָׁמְרָהּ: 16 וַיְצַו יְהוָה אֱלֹהִים עַל־הָאָדָם לֵאמֹר מִכֹּל עֵץ־הַגָּן אָכֹל תֹּאכֵל: 17 וּמֵעֵץ הַדַּעַת טוֹב וָרָע לֹא תֹאכַל מִמֶּנּוּ כִּי בְּיוֹם אֲכָלְךָ מִמֶּנּוּ מוֹת תָּמוּת: 18 וַיֹּאמֶר יְהוָה אֱלֹהִים לֹא־טוֹב הֱיוֹת הָאָדָם לְבַדּוֹ אֶעֱשֶׂה־לּוֹ עֵזֶר כְּנֶגְדּוֹ: 19 וַיִּצֶר יְהוָה אֱלֹהִים מִן־הָאֲדָמָה כָּל־חַיַּת הַשָּׂדֶה וְאֵת כָּל־עוֹף הַשָּׁמַיִם וַיָּבֵא אֶל־הָאָדָם לִרְאוֹת מַה־יִּקְרָא־לוֹ וְכֹל אֲשֶׁר יִקְרָא־לוֹ הָאָדָם נֶפֶשׁ חַיָּה הוּא שְׁמוֹ: 20 וַיִּקְרָא הָאָדָם שֵׁמוֹת לְכָל־הַבְּהֵמָה וּלְעוֹף הַשָּׁמַיִם וּלְכֹל חַיַּת הַשָּׂדֶה וּלְאָדָם לֹא־מָצָא עֵזֶר כְּנֶגְדּוֹ: 21 וַיַּפֵּל יְהוָֹה אֱלֹהִים תַּרְדֵּמָה עַל־הָאָדָם וַיִּישָׁן וַיִּקַּח אַחַת מִצַּלְעֹתָיו וַיִּסְגֹּר בָּשָׂר תַּחְתֶּנָּה: 22 וַיִּבֶן יְהוָה אֱלֹהִים אֶת־הַצֵּלָע אֲשֶׁר־לָקַח מִן־הָאָדָם לְאִשָּׁה וַיְבִאֶהָ אֶל־הָאָדָם: 23 וַיֹּאמֶר הָאָדָם זֹאת הַפַּעַם עֶצֶם מֵעֲצָמַי וּבָשָׂר מִבְּשָׂרִי לְזֹאת

24 Therefore a man shall leave his father and mother and be joined to his wife, and they shall become one flesh.

25 And they were both naked, the man and his wife, and were not ashamed.

3 Now the serpent was more cunning than any beast of the field which the LORD God had made. And he said to the woman, "Has God indeed said, 'You shall not eat of every tree of the garden'?"

2 And the woman said to the serpent, "We may eat the fruit of the trees of the garden; 3 but of the fruit of the tree which is in the midst of the garden, God has said, 'You shall not eat it, nor shall you touch it, lest you die.'"

4 Then the serpent said to the woman, "You will not surely die. 5 For God knows that in the day you eat of it your eyes will be opened, and you will be like God, knowing good and evil."

6 So when the woman saw that the tree was good for food, that it was pleasant to the eyes, and a tree desirable to make one wise, she took of its fruit and ate. She also gave to her husband with her, and he ate. 7 Then the eyes of both of them were opened, and they knew that they were naked; and they sewed fig leaves together and made themselves coverings.

8 And they heard the sound of the LORD God walking in the garden in the cool of the day, and Adam and his wife hid themselves from the presence of the LORD God among the trees of the garden.

9 Then the LORD God called to Adam and said to him, "Where are you?"

10 So he said, "I heard Your voice in the garden, and I was afraid because I was naked; and I hid myself."

11 And He said, "Who told you that you were naked? Have you eaten from the tree of which I commanded you that you should not eat?"

12 Then the man said, "The woman whom You gave to be with me, she gave me of the tree, and I ate."

13 And the LORD God said to the woman, "What is this you have done?"

The woman said, "The serpent deceived me, and I ate."

14 So the LORD God said to the serpent:

"Because you have done this,
You are cursed more than all cattle,
And more than every beast of the field;
On your belly you shall go,
· And you shall eat dust
All the days of your life.

יִקְרָא אִשָּׁה כִּי מֵאִישׁ לֻקֳחָה־זֹּאת: 24 עַל־כֵּן יַעֲזָב־אִישׁ אֶת־אָבִיו וְאֶת־אִמּוֹ וְדָבַק בְּאִשְׁתּוֹ וְהָיוּ לְבָשָׂר אֶחָד: 25 וַיִּהְיוּ שְׁנֵיהֶם עֲרוּמִּים הָאָדָם וְאִשְׁתּוֹ וְלֹא יִתְבֹּשָׁשׁוּ:

ג וְהַנָּחָשׁ הָיָה עָרוּם מִכֹּל חַיַּת הַשָּׂדֶה אֲשֶׁר עָשָׂה יְהֹוָה אֱלֹהִים וַיֹּאמֶר אֶל־הָאִשָּׁה אַף כִּי־אָמַר אֱלֹהִים לֹא תֹאכְלוּ מִכֹּל עֵץ הַגָּן: 2 וַתֹּאמֶר הָאִשָּׁה אֶל־הַנָּחָשׁ מִפְּרִי עֵץ־הַגָּן נֹאכֵל: 3 וּמִפְּרִי הָעֵץ אֲשֶׁר בְּתוֹךְ־הַגָּן אָמַר אֱלֹהִים לֹא תֹאכְלוּ מִמֶּנּוּ וְלֹא תִגְּעוּ בּוֹ פֶּן־תְּמֻתוּן: 4 וַיֹּאמֶר הַנָּחָשׁ אֶל־הָאִשָּׁה לֹא־מוֹת תְּמֻתוּן: 5 כִּי יֹדֵעַ אֱלֹהִים כִּי בְּיוֹם אֲכָלְכֶם מִמֶּנּוּ וְנִפְקְחוּ עֵינֵיכֶם וִהְיִיתֶם כֵּאלֹהִים יֹדְעֵי טוֹב וָרָע: 6 וַתֵּרֶא הָאִשָּׁה כִּי טוֹב הָעֵץ לְמַאֲכָל וְכִי תַאֲוָה־הוּא לָעֵינַיִם וְנֶחְמָד הָעֵץ לְהַשְׂכִּיל וַתִּקַּח מִפִּרְיוֹ וַתֹּאכַל וַתִּתֵּן גַּם־לְאִישָׁהּ עִמָּהּ וַיֹּאכַל: 7 וַתִּפָּקַחְנָה עֵינֵי שְׁנֵיהֶם וַיֵּדְעוּ כִּי עֵירֻמִּם הֵם וַיִּתְפְּרוּ עֲלֵה תְאֵנָה וַיַּעֲשׂוּ לָהֶם חֲגֹרֹת: 8 וַיִּשְׁמְעוּ אֶת־קוֹל יְהֹוָה אֱלֹהִים מִתְהַלֵּךְ בַּגָּן לְרוּחַ הַיּוֹם וַיִּתְחַבֵּא הָאָדָם וְאִשְׁתּוֹ מִפְּנֵי יְהֹוָה אֱלֹהִים בְּתוֹךְ עֵץ הַגָּן: 9 וַיִּקְרָא יְהֹוָה אֱלֹהִים אֶל־הָאָדָם וַיֹּאמֶר לוֹ אַיֶּכָּה: 10 וַיֹּאמֶר אֶת־קֹלְךָ שָׁמַעְתִּי בַּגָּן וָאִירָא כִּי־עֵירֹם אָנֹכִי וָאֵחָבֵא: 11 וַיֹּאמֶר מִי הִגִּיד לְךָ כִּי עֵירֹם אָתָּה הֲמִן־הָעֵץ אֲשֶׁר צִוִּיתִיךָ לְבִלְתִּי אֲכָל־מִמֶּנּוּ אָכָלְתָּ: 12 וַיֹּאמֶר הָאָדָם הָאִשָּׁה אֲשֶׁר נָתַתָּה עִמָּדִי הִוא נָתְנָה־לִּי מִן־הָעֵץ וָאֹכֵל: 13 וַיֹּאמֶר יְהֹוָה אֱלֹהִים לָאִשָּׁה מַה־זֹּאת עָשִׂית וַתֹּאמֶר הָאִשָּׁה הַנָּחָשׁ הִשִּׁיאַנִי וָאֹכֵל: 14 וַיֹּאמֶר יְהֹוָה אֱלֹהִים | אֶל־הַנָּחָשׁ כִּי עָשִׂיתָ זֹּאת אָרוּר אַתָּה מִכָּל־הַבְּהֵמָה וּמִכֹּל חַיַּת הַשָּׂדֶה עַל־גְּחֹנְךָ

¹⁵ And I will put enmity
Between you and the woman,
And between your seed and her Seed;
He shall bruise your head,
And you shall bruise His heel."

¹⁶ To the woman He said:

"I will greatly multiply your sorrow and your
    conception;
In pain you shall bring forth children;
Your desire *shall be* for your husband,
And he shall rule over you."

¹⁷ Then to Adam He said, "Because you have
heeded the voice of your wife, and have eaten from
the tree of which I commanded you, saying, 'You
shall not eat of it':

"Cursed *is* the ground for your sake;
In toil you shall eat *of* it
All the days of your life.
¹⁸   Both thorns and thistles it shall bring forth for
    you,
And you shall eat the herb of the field.
¹⁹   In the sweat of your face you shall eat bread
Till you return to the ground,
For out of it you were taken;
For dust you *are*,
And to dust you shall return."

²⁰ And Adam called his wife's name Eve, because
she was the mother of all living.
²¹ Also for Adam and his wife the LORD God
made tunics of skin, and clothed them.
²² Then the LORD God said, "Behold, the man
has become like one of Us, to know good and evil.
And now, lest he put out his hand and take also of
the tree of life, and eat, and live forever"— ²³ therefore the LORD God sent him out of the garden of
Eden to till the ground from which he was taken.
²⁴ So He drove out the man; and He placed
cherubim at the east of the garden of Eden, and a
flaming sword which turned every way, to guard the
way to the tree of life.

4 Now Adam knew Eve his wife, and she
conceived and bore Cain, and said, "I have
acquired a man from the LORD." ² Then she bore
again, this time his brother Abel. Now Abel was a
keeper of sheep, but Cain was a tiller of the ground.
³ And in the process of time it came to pass that
Cain brought an offering of the fruit of the ground
to the LORD. ⁴ Abel also brought of the firstborn of
his flock and of their fat. And the LORD respected
Abel and his offering, ⁵ but He did not respect Cain
and his offering. And Cain was very angry, and his
countenance fell.

תֵּלֵךְ וְעָפָר תֹּאכַל כָּל־יְמֵי חַיֶּיךָ: 15 וְאֵיבָה | אָשִׁית
בֵּינְךָ וּבֵין הָאִשָּׁה וּבֵין זַרְעֲךָ וּבֵין זַרְעָהּ הוּא יְשׁוּפְךָ
רֹאשׁ וְאַתָּה תְּשׁוּפֶנּוּ עָקֵב: ס 16 אֶל־
הָאִשָּׁה אָמַר הַרְבָּה אַרְבֶּה עִצְּבוֹנֵךְ וְהֵרֹנֵךְ בְּעֶצֶב
תֵּלְדִי בָנִים וְאֶל־אִישֵׁךְ תְּשׁוּקָתֵךְ וְהוּא יִמְשָׁל־
בָּךְ: ס 17 וּלְאָדָם אָמַר כִּי שָׁמַעְתָּ לְקוֹל
אִשְׁתֶּךָ וַתֹּאכַל מִן־הָעֵץ אֲשֶׁר צִוִּיתִיךָ לֵאמֹר לֹא
תֹאכַל מִמֶּנּוּ אֲרוּרָה הָאֲדָמָה בַּעֲבוּרֶךָ בְּעִצָּבוֹן
תֹּאכֲלֶנָּה כֹּל יְמֵי חַיֶּיךָ: 18 וְקוֹץ וְדַרְדַּר תַּצְמִיחַ לָךְ
וְאָכַלְתָּ אֶת־עֵשֶׂב הַשָּׂדֶה: 19 בְּזֵעַת אַפֶּיךָ תֹּאכַל
לֶחֶם עַד שׁוּבְךָ אֶל־הָאֲדָמָה כִּי מִמֶּנָּה לֻקָּחְתָּ
כִּי־עָפָר אַתָּה וְאֶל־עָפָר תָּשׁוּב: 20 וַיִּקְרָא הָאָדָם
שֵׁם אִשְׁתּוֹ חַוָּה כִּי הִוא הָיְתָה אֵם כָּל־חָי:
21 וַיַּעַשׂ יְהוָה אֱלֹהִים לְאָדָם וּלְאִשְׁתּוֹ כָּתְנוֹת עוֹר
וַיַּלְבִּשֵׁם: פ

22 וַיֹּאמֶר | יְהוָה אֱלֹהִים הֵן הָאָדָם הָיָה
כְּאַחַד מִמֶּנּוּ לָדַעַת טוֹב וָרָע וְעַתָּה | פֶּן־
יִשְׁלַח יָדוֹ וְלָקַח גַּם מֵעֵץ הַחַיִּים וְאָכַל וָחַי
לְעֹלָם: 23 וַיְשַׁלְּחֵהוּ יְהוָה אֱלֹהִים מִגַּן־עֵדֶן לַעֲבֹד
אֶת־הָאֲדָמָה אֲשֶׁר לֻקַּח מִשָּׁם: 24 וַיְגָרֶשׁ אֶת־
הָאָדָם וַיַּשְׁכֵּן מִקֶּדֶם לְגַן־עֵדֶן אֶת־הַכְּרֻבִים וְאֵת
לַהַט הַחֶרֶב הַמִּתְהַפֶּכֶת לִשְׁמֹר אֶת־דֶּרֶךְ עֵץ
הַחַיִּים: ס

ד וְהָאָדָם יָדַע אֶת־חַוָּה אִשְׁתּוֹ וַתַּהַר וַתֵּלֶד
אֶת־קַיִן וַתֹּאמֶר קָנִיתִי אִישׁ אֶת־יְהוָה: 2 וַתֹּסֶף
לָלֶדֶת אֶת־אָחִיו אֶת־הָבֶל וַיְהִי־הֶבֶל רֹעֵה צֹאן
וְקַיִן הָיָה עֹבֵד אֲדָמָה: 3 וַיְהִי מִקֵּץ יָמִים וַיָּבֵא
קַיִן מִפְּרִי הָאֲדָמָה מִנְחָה לַיהוָה: 4 וְהֶבֶל הֵבִיא
גַם־הוּא מִבְּכֹרוֹת צֹאנוֹ וּמֵחֶלְבֵהֶן וַיִּשַׁע יְהוָה אֶל־
הֶבֶל וְאֶל־מִנְחָתוֹ: 5 וְאֶל־קַיִן וְאֶל־מִנְחָתוֹ לֹא שָׁעָה

⁶ So the LORD said to Cain, "Why are you angry? And why has your countenance fallen? ⁷ If you do well, will you not be accepted? And if you do not do well, sin lies at the door. And its desire *is* for you, but you should rule over it."

⁸ Now Cain talked with Abel his brother; and it came to pass, when they were in the field, that Cain rose up against Abel his brother and killed him.

⁹ Then the LORD said to Cain, "Where *is* Abel your brother?"

He said, "I do not know. *Am* I my brother's keeper?"

¹⁰ And He said, "What have you done? The voice of your brother's blood cries out to Me from the ground. ¹¹ So now you *are* cursed from the earth, which has opened its mouth to receive your brother's blood from your hand. ¹² When you till the ground, it shall no longer yield its strength to you. A fugitive and a vagabond you shall be on the earth."

¹³ And Cain said to the LORD, "My punishment *is* greater than I can bear! ¹⁴ Surely You have driven me out this day from the face of the ground; I shall be hidden from Your face; I shall be a fugitive and a vagabond on the earth, and it will happen *that* anyone who finds me will kill me."

¹⁵ And the LORD said to him, "Therefore, whoever kills Cain, vengeance shall be taken on him sevenfold." And the LORD set a mark on Cain, lest anyone finding him should kill him.

¹⁶ Then Cain went out from the presence of the LORD and dwelt in the land of Nod on the east of Eden. ¹⁷ And Cain knew his wife, and she conceived and bore Enoch. And he built a city, and called the name of the city after the name of his son—Enoch.

¹⁸ To Enoch was born Irad; and Irad begot Mehujael, and Mehujael begot Methushael, and Methushael begot Lamech.

¹⁹ Then Lamech took for himself two wives: the name of one *was* Adah, and the name of the second *was* Zillah. ²⁰ And Adah bore Jabal. He was the father of those who dwell in tents and have livestock. ²¹ His brother's name *was* Jubal. He was the father of all those who play the harp and flute. ²² And as for Zillah, she also bore Tubal-Cain, an instructor of every craftsman in bronze and iron. And the sister of Tubal-Cain *was* Naamah.

²³ Then Lamech said to his wives:

"Adah and Zillah, hear my voice;
Wives of Lamech, listen to my speech!
For I have killed a man for wounding me,
Even a young man for hurting me.
²⁴ If Cain shall be avenged sevenfold,
Then Lamech seventy-sevenfold."

וַיִּחַר לְקַ֙יִן֙ מְאֹ֔ד וַֽיִּפְּל֖וּ פָּנָֽיו׃ 6 וַיֹּ֥אמֶר יְהֹוָ֖ה אֶל־
קָ֑יִן לָ֚מָּה חָ֣רָה לָ֔ךְ וְלָ֖מָּה נָֽפְל֥וּ פָנֶֽיךָ׃ 7 הֲל֤וֹא
אִם־תֵּיטִיב֙ שְׂאֵ֔ת וְאִם֙ לֹ֣א תֵיטִ֔יב לַפֶּ֖תַח חַטָּ֣את
רֹבֵ֑ץ וְאֵלֶ֙יךָ֙ תְּשׁ֣וּקָת֔וֹ וְאַתָּ֖ה תִּמְשָׁל־בּֽוֹ׃ 8 וַיֹּ֥אמֶר
קַ֖יִן אֶל־הֶ֣בֶל אָחִ֑יו וַֽיְהִי֙ בִּֽהְיוֹתָ֣ם בַּשָּׂדֶ֔ה וַיָּ֥קׇם קַ֛יִן
אֶל־הֶ֥בֶל אָחִ֖יו וַיַּֽהַרְגֵֽהוּ׃ 9 וַיֹּ֧אמֶר יְהֹוָ֣ה אֶל־קַ֗יִן
אֵ֚י הֶ֣בֶל אָחִ֔יךָ וַיֹּ֙אמֶר֙ לֹ֣א יָדַ֔עְתִּי הֲשֹׁמֵ֥ר אָחִ֖י
אָנֹֽכִי׃ 10 וַיֹּ֖אמֶר מֶ֣ה עָשִׂ֑יתָ ק֚וֹל דְּמֵ֣י אָחִ֔יךָ צֹעֲקִ֥ים
אֵלַ֖י מִן־הָֽאֲדָמָֽה׃ 11 וְעַתָּ֖ה אָר֣וּר אָ֑תָּה מִן־הָֽאֲדָמָה֙
אֲשֶׁ֣ר פָּצְתָ֣ה אֶת־פִּ֔יהָ לָקַ֛חַת אֶת־דְּמֵ֥י אָחִ֖יךָ מִיָּדֶֽךָ׃
12 כִּ֤י תַֽעֲבֹד֙ אֶת־הָ֣אֲדָמָ֔ה לֹֽא־תֹסֵ֥ף תֵּת־כֹּחָ֖הּ לָ֑ךְ
נָ֥ע וָנָ֖ד תִּֽהְיֶ֥ה בָאָֽרֶץ׃ 13 וַיֹּ֥אמֶר קַ֖יִן אֶל־יְהֹוָ֑ה גָּד֥וֹל
עֲוֺנִ֖י מִנְּשֹֽׂא׃ 14 הֵן֩ גֵּרַ֨שְׁתָּ אֹתִ֜י הַיּ֗וֹם מֵעַל֙ פְּנֵ֣י
הָֽאֲדָמָ֔ה וּמִפָּנֶ֖יךָ אֶסָּתֵ֑ר וְהָיִ֜יתִי נָ֤ע וָנָד֙ בָּאָ֔רֶץ
וְהָיָ֥ה כׇל־מֹצְאִ֖י יַֽהַרְגֵֽנִי׃ 15 וַיֹּ֧אמֶר ל֣וֹ יְהֹוָ֗ה לָכֵן֙
כׇּל־הֹרֵ֣ג קַ֔יִן שִׁבְעָתַ֖יִם יֻקָּ֑ם וַיָּ֨שֶׂם יְהֹוָ֤ה לְקַ֙יִן֙ א֔וֹת
לְבִלְתִּ֥י הַכּֽוֹת־אֹת֖וֹ כׇּל־מֹצְאֽוֹ׃ 16 וַיֵּ֥צֵא קַ֖יִן מִלִּפְנֵ֣י
יְהֹוָ֑ה וַיֵּ֥שֶׁב בְּאֶֽרֶץ־נ֖וֹד קִדְמַת־עֵֽדֶן׃ 17 וַיֵּ֤דַע קַ֙יִן֙
אֶת־אִשְׁתּ֔וֹ וַתַּ֖הַר וַתֵּ֣לֶד אֶת־חֲנ֑וֹךְ וַֽיְהִי֙ בֹּ֣נֶה עִ֔יר
וַיִּקְרָא֙ שֵׁ֣ם הָעִ֔יר כְּשֵׁ֖ם בְּנ֥וֹ חֲנֽוֹךְ׃ 18 וַיִּוָּלֵ֤ד לַֽחֲנוֹךְ֙
אֶת־עִירָ֔ד וְעִירָ֕ד יָלַ֖ד אֶת־מְחֽוּיָאֵ֑ל וּמְחִיָּיאֵ֗ל יָלַד֙
אֶת־מְת֣וּשָׁאֵ֔ל וּמְתֽוּשָׁאֵ֖ל יָלַ֥ד אֶת־לָֽמֶךְ׃ 19 וַיִּקַּֽח־
ל֥וֹ לֶ֙מֶךְ֙ שְׁתֵּ֣י נָשִׁ֔ים שֵׁ֤ם הָֽאַחַת֙ עָדָ֔ה וְשֵׁ֥ם הַשֵּׁנִ֖ית
צִלָּֽה׃ 20 וַתֵּ֥לֶד עָדָ֖ה אֶת־יָבָ֑ל ה֣וּא הָיָ֔ה אֲבִ֕י יֹשֵׁ֥ב
אֹ֖הֶל וּמִקְנֶֽה׃ 21 וְשֵׁ֥ם אָחִ֖יו יוּבָ֑ל ה֣וּא הָיָ֔ה אֲבִ֕י
כׇּל־תֹּפֵ֥שׂ כִּנּ֖וֹר וְעוּגָֽב׃ 22 וְצִלָּ֣ה גַם־הִ֗וא יָֽלְדָה֙
אֶת־תּ֣וּבַל קַ֔יִן לֹטֵ֕שׁ כׇּל־חֹרֵ֥שׁ נְחֹ֖שֶׁת וּבַרְזֶ֑ל וַֽאֲח֥וֹת
תּֽוּבַל־קַ֖יִן נַֽעֲמָֽה׃ 23 וַיֹּ֨אמֶר לֶ֜מֶךְ לְנָשָׁ֗יו עָדָ֤ה וְצִלָּה֙
שְׁמַ֣עַן קוֹלִ֔י נְשֵׁ֣י לֶ֔מֶךְ הַֽאֲזֵ֖נָּה אִמְרָתִ֑י כִּ֣י אִ֤ישׁ
הָרַ֙גְתִּי֙ לְפִצְעִ֔י וְיֶ֖לֶד לְחַבֻּֽרָתִֽי׃ 24 כִּ֥י שִׁבְעָתַ֖יִם יֻקַּם־

²⁵And Adam knew his wife again, and she bore a son and named him Seth, "For God has appointed another seed for me instead of Abel, whom Cain killed." ²⁶And as for Seth, to him also a son was born; and he named him Enosh. Then *men* began to call on the name of the LORD.

5 This is the book of the genealogy of Adam. In the day that God created man, He made him in the likeness of God. ²He created them male and female, and blessed them and called them Mankind in the day they were created. ³And Adam lived one hundred and thirty years, and begot *a son* in his own likeness, after his image, and named him Seth. ⁴After he begot Seth, the days of Adam were eight hundred years; and he had sons and daughters. ⁵So all the days that Adam lived were nine hundred and thirty years; and he died.

⁶Seth lived one hundred and five years, and begot Enosh. ⁷After he begot Enosh, Seth lived eight hundred and seven years, and had sons and daughters. ⁸So all the days of Seth were nine hundred and twelve years; and he died.

⁹Enosh lived ninety years, and begot Cainan. ¹⁰After he begot Cainan, Enosh lived eight hundred and fifteen years, and had sons and daughters. ¹¹So all the days of Enosh were nine hundred and five years; and he died.

¹²Cainan lived seventy years, and begot Mahalalel. ¹³After he begot Mahalalel, Cainan lived eight hundred and forty years, and had sons and daughters. ¹⁴So all the days of Cainan were nine hundred and ten years; and he died.

¹⁵Mahalalel lived sixty-five years, and begot Jared. ¹⁶After he begot Jared, Mahalalel lived eight hundred and thirty years, and had sons and daughters. ¹⁷So all the days of Mahalalel were eight hundred and ninety-five years; and he died.

¹⁸Jared lived one hundred and sixty-two years, and begot Enoch. ¹⁹After he begot Enoch, Jared lived eight hundred years, and had sons and daughters. ²⁰So all the days of Jared were nine hundred and sixty-two years; and he died.

²¹Enoch lived sixty-five years, and begot Methuselah. ²²After he begot Methuselah, Enoch walked with God three hundred years, and had sons and daughters. ²³So all the days of Enoch were three hundred and sixty-five years. ²⁴And Enoch walked with God; and he *was* not, for God took him.

²⁵Methuselah lived one hundred and eighty-seven years, and begot Lamech. ²⁶After he begot Lamech, Methuselah lived seven hundred and

קַיִן וְלֶמֶךְ שִׁבְעִים וְשִׁבְעָה: 25 וַיֵּדַע אָדָם עוֹד אֶת־אִשְׁתּוֹ וַתֵּלֶד בֵּן וַתִּקְרָא אֶת־שְׁמוֹ שֵׁת כִּי שָׁת־לִי אֱלֹהִים זֶרַע אַחֵר תַּחַת הֶבֶל כִּי הֲרָגוֹ קָיִן: 26 וּלְשֵׁת גַּם־הוּא יֻלַּד־בֵּן וַיִּקְרָא אֶת־שְׁמוֹ אֱנוֹשׁ אָז הוּחַל לִקְרֹא בְּשֵׁם יְהֹוָה: פ

ה זֶה סֵפֶר תּוֹלְדֹת אָדָם בְּיוֹם בְּרֹא אֱלֹהִים אָדָם בִּדְמוּת אֱלֹהִים עָשָׂה אֹתוֹ: 2 זָכָר וּנְקֵבָה בְּרָאָם וַיְבָרֶךְ אֹתָם וַיִּקְרָא אֶת־שְׁמָם אָדָם בְּיוֹם הִבָּרְאָם: ס 3 וַיְחִי אָדָם שְׁלֹשִׁים וּמְאַת שָׁנָה וַיּוֹלֶד בִּדְמוּתוֹ כְּצַלְמוֹ וַיִּקְרָא אֶת־שְׁמוֹ שֵׁת: 4 וַיִּהְיוּ יְמֵי־אָדָם אַחֲרֵי הוֹלִידוֹ אֶת־שֵׁת שְׁמֹנֶה מֵאֹת שָׁנָה וַיּוֹלֶד בָּנִים וּבָנוֹת: 5 וַיִּהְיוּ כָּל־יְמֵי אָדָם אֲשֶׁר־חַי תְּשַׁע מֵאוֹת שָׁנָה וּשְׁלֹשִׁים שָׁנָה וַיָּמֹת: ס 6 וַיְחִי־שֵׁת חָמֵשׁ שָׁנִים וּמְאַת שָׁנָה וַיּוֹלֶד אֶת־אֱנוֹשׁ: 7 וַיְחִי־שֵׁת אַחֲרֵי הוֹלִידוֹ אֶת־אֱנוֹשׁ שֶׁבַע שָׁנִים וּשְׁמֹנֶה מֵאוֹת שָׁנָה וַיּוֹלֶד בָּנִים וּבָנוֹת: 8 וַיִּהְיוּ כָּל־יְמֵי־שֵׁת שְׁתֵּים עֶשְׂרֵה שָׁנָה וּתְשַׁע מֵאוֹת שָׁנָה וַיָּמֹת: ס 9 וַיְחִי אֱנוֹשׁ תִּשְׁעִים שָׁנָה וַיּוֹלֶד אֶת־קֵינָן: 10 וַיְחִי אֱנוֹשׁ אַחֲרֵי הוֹלִידוֹ אֶת־קֵינָן חֲמֵשׁ עֶשְׂרֵה שָׁנָה וּשְׁמֹנֶה מֵאוֹת שָׁנָה וַיּוֹלֶד בָּנִים וּבָנוֹת: 11 וַיִּהְיוּ כָּל־יְמֵי אֱנוֹשׁ חָמֵשׁ שָׁנִים וּתְשַׁע מֵאוֹת שָׁנָה וַיָּמֹת: 12 וַיְחִי קֵינָן שִׁבְעִים שָׁנָה וַיּוֹלֶד אֶת־מַהֲלַלְאֵל: 13 וַיְחִי קֵינָן אַחֲרֵי הוֹלִידוֹ אֶת־מַהֲלַלְאֵל אַרְבָּעִים שָׁנָה וּשְׁמֹנֶה מֵאוֹת שָׁנָה וַיּוֹלֶד בָּנִים וּבָנוֹת: 14 וַיִּהְיוּ כָּל־יְמֵי קֵינָן עֶשֶׂר שָׁנִים וּתְשַׁע מֵאוֹת שָׁנָה וַיָּמֹת: ס 15 וַיְחִי מַהֲלַלְאֵל חָמֵשׁ שָׁנִים וְשִׁשִּׁים שָׁנָה וַיּוֹלֶד אֶת־יָרֶד: 16 וַיְחִי מַהֲלַלְאֵל אַחֲרֵי הוֹלִידוֹ אֶת־יֶרֶד שְׁלֹשִׁים שָׁנָה וּשְׁמֹנֶה מֵאוֹת שָׁנָה וַיּוֹלֶד בָּנִים וּבָנוֹת: 17 וַיִּהְיוּ כָּל־יְמֵי מַהֲלַלְאֵל חָמֵשׁ וְתִשְׁעִים שָׁנָה וּשְׁמֹנֶה מֵאוֹת שָׁנָה וַיָּמֹת: ס 18 וַיְחִי־יֶרֶד שְׁתַּיִם וְשִׁשִּׁים שָׁנָה וּמְאַת שָׁנָה וַיּוֹלֶד אֶת־חֲנוֹךְ: 19 וַיְחִי־יֶרֶד אַחֲרֵי הוֹלִידוֹ אֶת־חֲנוֹךְ שְׁמֹנֶה מֵאוֹת שָׁנָה וַיּוֹלֶד בָּנִים וּבָנוֹת: 20 וַיִּהְיוּ כָּל־יְמֵי־יֶרֶד שְׁתַּיִם וְשִׁשִּׁים שָׁנָה וּתְשַׁע מֵאוֹת שָׁנָה וַיָּמֹת: פ 21 וַיְחִי חֲנוֹךְ חָמֵשׁ וְשִׁשִּׁים שָׁנָה וַיּוֹלֶד אֶת־מְתוּשָׁלַח: 22 וַיִּתְהַלֵּךְ חֲנוֹךְ אֶת־הָאֱלֹהִים אַחֲרֵי הוֹלִידוֹ אֶת־מְתוּשֶׁלַח שְׁלֹשׁ מֵאוֹת שָׁנָה וַיּוֹלֶד בָּנִים וּבָנוֹת: 23 וַיְהִי כָּל־יְמֵי חֲנוֹךְ חָמֵשׁ וְשִׁשִּׁים שָׁנָה וּשְׁלֹשׁ מֵאוֹת שָׁנָה: 24 וַיִּתְהַלֵּךְ חֲנוֹךְ אֶת־הָאֱלֹהִים וְאֵינֶנּוּ כִּי־לָקַח אֹתוֹ אֱלֹהִים: פ 25 וַיְחִי מְתוּשֶׁלַח שֶׁבַע וּשְׁמֹנִים שָׁנָה וּמְאַת שָׁנָה וַיּוֹלֶד אֶת־לָמֶךְ: 26 וַיְחִי מְתוּשֶׁלַח אַחֲרֵי הוֹלִידוֹ

eighty-two years, and had sons and daughters. ²⁷ So all the days of Methuselah were nine hundred and sixty-nine years; and he died.

²⁸ Lamech lived one hundred and eighty-two years, and had a son. ²⁹ And he called his name Noah, saying, "This *one* will comfort us concerning our work and the toil of our hands, because of the ground which the LORD has cursed." ³⁰ After he begot Noah, Lamech lived five hundred and ninety-five years, and had sons and daughters. ³¹ So all the days of Lamech were seven hundred and seventy-seven years; and he died.

³² And Noah was five hundred years old, and Noah begot Shem, Ham, and Japheth.

6 Now it came to pass, when men began to multiply on the face of the earth, and daughters were born to them, ² that the sons of God saw the daughters of men, that they *were* beautiful; and they took wives for themselves of all whom they chose.

³ And the LORD said, "My Spirit shall not strive with man forever, for he *is* indeed flesh; yet his days shall be one hundred and twenty years." ⁴ There were giants on the earth in those days, and also afterward, when the sons of God came in to the daughters of men and they bore *children* to them. Those *were* the mighty men who *were* of old, men of renown.

⁵ Then the LORD saw that the wickedness of man *was* great in the earth, and *that* every intent of the thoughts of his heart *was* only evil continually. ⁶ And the LORD was sorry that He had made man on the earth, and He was grieved in His heart. ⁷ So the LORD said, "I will destroy man whom I have created from the face of the earth, both man and beast, creeping thing and birds of the air, for I am sorry that I have made them." ⁸ But Noah found grace in the eyes of the LORD.

⁹ This is the genealogy of Noah. Noah was a just man, perfect in his generations. Noah walked with God. ¹⁰ And Noah begot three sons: Shem, Ham, and Japheth.

¹¹ The earth also was corrupt before God, and the earth was filled with violence. ¹² So God looked upon the earth, and indeed it was corrupt; for all flesh had corrupted their way on the earth.

¹³ And God said to Noah, "The end of all flesh has come before Me, for the earth is filled with violence through them; and behold, I will destroy them with the earth. ¹⁴ Make yourself an ark of gopherwood; make rooms in the ark, and cover it inside and outside with pitch. ¹⁵ And this is how you shall make it: The length of the ark *shall be* three hundred cubits, its width fifty cubits, and its height

אֶת־לֶמֶךְ שְׁתַּיִם וּשְׁמֹנִים שָׁנָה וּשְׁבַע מֵאוֹת שָׁנָה וַיּוֹלֶד בָּנִים וּבָנוֹת: ²⁷ וַיִּהְיוּ כָּל־יְמֵי מְתוּשֶׁלַח תֵּשַׁע וְשִׁשִּׁים שָׁנָה וּתְשַׁע מֵאוֹת שָׁנָה וַיָּמֹת: פ

²⁸ וַיְחִי־לֶמֶךְ שְׁתַּיִם וּשְׁמֹנִים שָׁנָה וּמְאַת שָׁנָה וַיּוֹלֶד בֵּן: ²⁹ וַיִּקְרָא אֶת־שְׁמוֹ נֹחַ לֵאמֹר זֶה יְנַחֲמֵנוּ מִמַּעֲשֵׂנוּ וּמֵעִצְּבוֹן יָדֵינוּ מִן־הָאֲדָמָה אֲשֶׁר אֵרְרָהּ יְהֹוָה: ³⁰ וַיְחִי־לֶמֶךְ אַחֲרֵי הוֹלִידוֹ אֶת־נֹחַ חָמֵשׁ וְתִשְׁעִים שָׁנָה וַחֲמֵשׁ מֵאֹת שָׁנָה וַיּוֹלֶד בָּנִים וּבָנוֹת: ³¹ וַיְהִי כָּל־יְמֵי־לֶמֶךְ שֶׁבַע וְשִׁבְעִים שָׁנָה וּשְׁבַע מֵאוֹת שָׁנָה וַיָּמֹת: ³² וַיְהִי־נֹחַ בֶּן־חֲמֵשׁ מֵאוֹת שָׁנָה וַיּוֹלֶד נֹחַ אֶת־שֵׁם אֶת־חָם וְאֶת־יָפֶת:

ו וַיְהִי כִּי־הֵחֵל הָאָדָם לָרֹב עַל־פְּנֵי הָאֲדָמָה וּבָנוֹת יֻלְּדוּ לָהֶם: ² וַיִּרְאוּ בְנֵי־הָאֱלֹהִים אֶת־בְּנוֹת הָאָדָם כִּי טֹבֹת הֵנָּה וַיִּקְחוּ לָהֶם נָשִׁים מִכֹּל אֲשֶׁר בָּחָרוּ: ³ וַיֹּאמֶר יְהֹוָה לֹא־יָדוֹן רוּחִי בָאָדָם לְעֹלָם בְּשַׁגַּם הוּא בָשָׂר וְהָיוּ יָמָיו מֵאָה וְעֶשְׂרִים שָׁנָה: ⁴ הַנְּפִלִים הָיוּ בָאָרֶץ בַּיָּמִים הָהֵם וְגַם אַחֲרֵי־כֵן אֲשֶׁר יָבֹאוּ בְּנֵי הָאֱלֹהִים אֶל־בְּנוֹת הָאָדָם וְיָלְדוּ לָהֶם הֵמָּה הַגִּבֹּרִים אֲשֶׁר מֵעוֹלָם אַנְשֵׁי הַשֵּׁם: פ

⁵ וַיַּרְא יְהֹוָה כִּי רַבָּה רָעַת הָאָדָם בָּאָרֶץ וְכָל־יֵצֶר מַחְשְׁבֹת לִבּוֹ רַק רַע כָּל־הַיּוֹם: ⁶ וַיִּנָּחֶם יְהֹוָה כִּי־עָשָׂה אֶת־הָאָדָם בָּאָרֶץ וַיִּתְעַצֵּב אֶל־לִבּוֹ: ⁷ וַיֹּאמֶר יְהֹוָה אֶמְחֶה אֶת־הָאָדָם אֲשֶׁר־בָּרָאתִי מֵעַל פְּנֵי הָאֲדָמָה מֵאָדָם עַד־בְּהֵמָה עַד־רֶמֶשׂ וְעַד־עוֹף הַשָּׁמָיִם כִּי נִחַמְתִּי כִּי עֲשִׂיתִם: ⁸ וְנֹחַ מָצָא חֵן בְּעֵינֵי יְהֹוָה: פ

⁹ אֵלֶּה תּוֹלְדֹת נֹחַ נֹחַ אִישׁ צַדִּיק תָּמִים הָיָה בְּדֹרֹתָיו אֶת־הָאֱלֹהִים הִתְהַלֶּךְ־נֹחַ: ¹⁰ וַיּוֹלֶד נֹחַ שְׁלֹשָׁה בָנִים אֶת־שֵׁם אֶת־חָם וְאֶת־יָפֶת: ¹¹ וַתִּשָּׁחֵת הָאָרֶץ לִפְנֵי הָאֱלֹהִים וַתִּמָּלֵא הָאָרֶץ חָמָס: ¹² וַיַּרְא אֱלֹהִים אֶת־הָאָרֶץ וְהִנֵּה נִשְׁחָתָה כִּי־הִשְׁחִית כָּל־בָּשָׂר אֶת־דַּרְכּוֹ עַל־הָאָרֶץ: ס ¹³ וַיֹּאמֶר אֱלֹהִים לְנֹחַ קֵץ כָּל־בָּשָׂר בָּא לְפָנַי כִּי־מָלְאָה הָאָרֶץ חָמָס מִפְּנֵיהֶם וְהִנְנִי מַשְׁחִיתָם אֶת־הָאָרֶץ: ¹⁴ עֲשֵׂה לְךָ תֵּבַת עֲצֵי־גֹפֶר קִנִּים תַּעֲשֶׂה אֶת־הַתֵּבָה וְכָפַרְתָּ אֹתָהּ מִבַּיִת וּמִחוּץ בַּכֹּפֶר: ¹⁵ וְזֶה אֲשֶׁר תַּעֲשֶׂה אֹתָהּ

thirty cubits. 16 You shall make a window for the ark, and you shall finish it to a cubit from above; and set the door of the ark in its side. You shall make it *with* lower, second, and third *decks.* 17 And behold, I Myself am bringing floodwaters on the earth, to destroy from under heaven all flesh in which *is* the breath of life; everything that *is* on the earth shall die. 18 But I will establish My covenant with you; and you shall go into the ark—you, your sons, your wife, and your sons' wives with you. 19 And of every living thing of all flesh you shall bring two of every *sort* into the ark, to keep *them* alive with you; they shall be male and female. 20 Of the birds after their kind, of animals after their kind, and of every creeping thing of the earth after its kind, two of every *kind* will come to you to keep *them* alive. 21 And you shall take for yourself of all food that is eaten, and you shall gather *it* to yourself; and it shall be food for you and for them."

22 Thus Noah did; according to all that God commanded him, so he did.

7 Then the LORD said to Noah, "Come into the ark, you and all your household, because I have seen *that* you *are* righteous before Me in this generation. 2 You shall take with you seven each of every clean animal, a male and his female; two each of animals that *are* unclean, a male and his female; 3 also seven each of birds of the air, male and female, to keep the species alive on the face of all the earth. 4 For after seven more days I will cause it to rain on the earth forty days and forty nights, and I will destroy from the face of the earth all living things that I have made." 5 And Noah did according to all that the LORD commanded him. 6 Noah *was* six hundred years old when the floodwaters were on the earth.

7 So Noah, with his sons, his wife, and his sons' wives, went into the ark because of the waters of the flood. 8 Of clean animals, of animals that *are* unclean, of birds, and of everything that creeps on the earth, 9 two by two they went into the ark to Noah, male and female, as God had commanded Noah. 10 And it came to pass after seven days that the waters of the flood were on the earth. 11 In the six hundredth year of Noah's life, in the second month, the seventeenth day of the month, on that day all the fountains of the great deep were broken up, and the windows of heaven were opened. 12 And the rain was on the earth forty days and forty nights.

13 On the very same day Noah and Noah's sons, Shem, Ham, and Japheth, and Noah's wife and the three wives of his sons with them, entered the ark—

שְׁלֹשׁ מֵאוֹת אַמָּה אֹרֶךְ הַתֵּבָה חֲמִשִּׁים אַמָּה רָחְבָּהּ וּשְׁלֹשִׁים אַמָּה קוֹמָתָהּ: 16 צֹהַר ׀ תַּעֲשֶׂה לַתֵּבָה וְאֶל־אַמָּה תְּכַלֶּנָּה מִלְמַעְלָה וּפֶתַח הַתֵּבָה בְּצִדָּהּ תָּשִׂים תַּחְתִּיִּם שְׁנִיִּם וּשְׁלֹשִׁים תַּעֲשֶׂהָ: 17 וַאֲנִי הִנְנִי מֵבִיא אֶת־הַמַּבּוּל מַיִם עַל־הָאָרֶץ לְשַׁחֵת כָּל־בָּשָׂר אֲשֶׁר־בּוֹ רוּחַ חַיִּים מִתַּחַת הַשָּׁמָיִם כֹּל אֲשֶׁר־בָּאָרֶץ יִגְוָע: 18 וַהֲקִמֹתִי אֶת־בְּרִיתִי אִתָּךְ וּבָאתָ אֶל־הַתֵּבָה אַתָּה וּבָנֶיךָ וְאִשְׁתְּךָ וּנְשֵׁי־בָנֶיךָ אִתָּךְ: 19 וּמִכָּל־הָחַי מִכָּל־בָּשָׂר שְׁנַיִם מִכֹּל תָּבִיא אֶל־הַתֵּבָה לְהַחֲיֹת אִתָּךְ זָכָר וּנְקֵבָה יִהְיוּ: 20 מֵהָעוֹף לְמִינֵהוּ וּמִן־הַבְּהֵמָה לְמִינָהּ מִכֹּל רֶמֶשׂ הָאֲדָמָה לְמִינֵהוּ שְׁנַיִם מִכֹּל יָבֹאוּ אֵלֶיךָ לְהַחֲיוֹת: 21 וְאַתָּה קַח־לְךָ מִכָּל־מַאֲכָל אֲשֶׁר יֵאָכֵל וְאָסַפְתָּ אֵלֶיךָ וְהָיָה לְךָ וְלָהֶם לְאָכְלָה: 22 וַיַּעַשׂ נֹחַ כְּכֹל אֲשֶׁר צִוָּה אֹתוֹ אֱלֹהִים כֵּן עָשָׂה: ס

ז וַיֹּאמֶר יְהוָה לְנֹחַ בֹּא־אַתָּה וְכָל־בֵּיתְךָ אֶל־הַתֵּבָה כִּי־אֹתְךָ רָאִיתִי צַדִּיק לְפָנַי בַּדּוֹר הַזֶּה: 2 מִכֹּל ׀ הַבְּהֵמָה הַטְּהוֹרָה תִּקַּח־לְךָ שִׁבְעָה שִׁבְעָה אִישׁ וְאִשְׁתּוֹ וּמִן־הַבְּהֵמָה אֲשֶׁר לֹא טְהֹרָה הִוא שְׁנַיִם אִישׁ וְאִשְׁתּוֹ: 3 גַּם מֵעוֹף הַשָּׁמַיִם שִׁבְעָה שִׁבְעָה זָכָר וּנְקֵבָה לְחַיּוֹת זֶרַע עַל־פְּנֵי כָל־הָאָרֶץ: 4 כִּי לְיָמִים עוֹד שִׁבְעָה אָנֹכִי מַמְטִיר עַל־הָאָרֶץ אַרְבָּעִים יוֹם וְאַרְבָּעִים לָיְלָה וּמָחִיתִי אֶת־כָּל־הַיְקוּם אֲשֶׁר עָשִׂיתִי מֵעַל פְּנֵי הָאֲדָמָה: 5 וַיַּעַשׂ נֹחַ כְּכֹל אֲשֶׁר־צִוָּהוּ יְהוָה: 6 וְנֹחַ בֶּן־שֵׁשׁ מֵאוֹת שָׁנָה וְהַמַּבּוּל הָיָה מַיִם עַל־הָאָרֶץ: 7 וַיָּבֹא נֹחַ וּבָנָיו וְאִשְׁתּוֹ וּנְשֵׁי־בָנָיו אִתּוֹ אֶל־הַתֵּבָה מִפְּנֵי מֵי הַמַּבּוּל: 8 מִן־הַבְּהֵמָה הַטְּהוֹרָה וּמִן־הַבְּהֵמָה אֲשֶׁר אֵינֶנָּה טְהֹרָה וּמִן־הָעוֹף וְכֹל אֲשֶׁר־רֹמֵשׂ עַל־הָאֲדָמָה: 9 שְׁנַיִם שְׁנַיִם בָּאוּ אֶל־נֹחַ אֶל־הַתֵּבָה זָכָר וּנְקֵבָה כַּאֲשֶׁר צִוָּה אֱלֹהִים אֶת־נֹחַ: 10 וַיְהִי לְשִׁבְעַת הַיָּמִים וּמֵי הַמַּבּוּל הָיוּ עַל־הָאָרֶץ: 11 בִּשְׁנַת שֵׁשׁ־מֵאוֹת שָׁנָה לְחַיֵּי־נֹחַ בַּחֹדֶשׁ הַשֵּׁנִי בְּשִׁבְעָה־עָשָׂר יוֹם לַחֹדֶשׁ בַּיּוֹם הַזֶּה נִבְקְעוּ כָּל־מַעְיְנֹת תְּהוֹם רַבָּה וַאֲרֻבֹּת הַשָּׁמַיִם נִפְתָּחוּ: 12 וַיְהִי הַגֶּשֶׁם עַל־הָאָרֶץ אַרְבָּעִים יוֹם וְאַרְבָּעִים לָיְלָה: 13 בְּעֶצֶם הַיּוֹם הַזֶּה בָּא נֹחַ

¹⁴they and every beast after its kind, all cattle after their kind, every creeping thing that creeps on the earth after its kind, and every bird after its kind, every bird of every sort. ¹⁵And they went into the ark to Noah, two by two, of all flesh in which *is* the breath of life. ¹⁶So those that entered, male and female of all flesh, went in as God had commanded him; and the LORD shut him in.

¹⁷Now the flood was on the earth forty days. The waters increased and lifted up the ark, and it rose high above the earth. ¹⁸The waters prevailed and greatly increased on the earth, and the ark moved about on the surface of the waters. ¹⁹And the waters prevailed exceedingly on the earth, and all the high hills under the whole heaven were covered. ²⁰The waters prevailed fifteen cubits upward, and the mountains were covered. ²¹And all flesh died that moved on the earth: birds and cattle and beasts and every creeping thing that creeps on the earth, and every man. ²²All in whose nostrils *was* the breath of the spirit of life, all that *was* on the dry *land,* died. ²³So He destroyed all living things which were on the face of the ground: both man and cattle, creeping thing and bird of the air. They were destroyed from the earth. Only Noah and those who *were* with him in the ark remained *alive.* ²⁴And the waters prevailed on the earth one hundred and fifty days.

8 Then God remembered Noah, and every living thing, and all the animals that *were* with him in the ark. And God made a wind to pass over the earth, and the waters subsided. ²The fountains of the deep and the windows of heaven were also stopped, and the rain from heaven was restrained. ³And the waters receded continually from the earth. At the end of the hundred and fifty days the waters decreased. ⁴Then the ark rested in the seventh month, the seventeenth day of the month, on the mountains of Ararat. ⁵And the waters decreased continually until the tenth month. In the tenth *month,* on the first *day* of the month, the tops of the mountains were seen.

⁶So it came to pass, at the end of forty days, that Noah opened the window of the ark which he had made. ⁷Then he sent out a raven, which kept going to and fro until the waters had dried up from the earth. ⁸He also sent out from himself a dove, to see if the waters had receded from the face of the ground. ⁹But the dove found no resting place for the sole of her foot, and she returned into the ark to him, for the waters *were* on the face of the whole earth. So he put out his hand and took her, and drew her into the ark to himself. ¹⁰And he waited

וְשֵׁם־וְחָם וָיֶפֶת בְּנֵי־נֹחַ וְאֵשֶׁת נֹחַ וּשְׁלֹשֶׁת נְשֵׁי־בָנָיו אִתָּם אֶל־הַתֵּבָה: 14 הֵמָּה וְכָל־הַחַיָּה לְמִינָהּ וְכָל־הַבְּהֵמָה לְמִינָהּ וְכָל־הָרֶמֶשׂ הָרֹמֵשׂ עַל־הָאָרֶץ לְמִינֵהוּ וְכָל־הָעוֹף לְמִינֵהוּ כֹּל צִפּוֹר כָּל־כָּנָף: 15 וַיָּבֹאוּ אֶל־נֹחַ אֶל־הַתֵּבָה שְׁנַיִם שְׁנַיִם מִכָּל־הַבָּשָׂר אֲשֶׁר־בּוֹ רוּחַ חַיִּים: 16 וְהַבָּאִים זָכָר וּנְקֵבָה מִכָּל־בָּשָׂר בָּאוּ כַּאֲשֶׁר צִוָּה אֹתוֹ אֱלֹהִים וַיִּסְגֹּר יְהוָה בַּעֲדוֹ: 17 וַיְהִי הַמַּבּוּל אַרְבָּעִים יוֹם עַל־הָאָרֶץ וַיִּרְבּוּ הַמַּיִם וַיִּשְׂאוּ אֶת־הַתֵּבָה וַתָּרָם מֵעַל הָאָרֶץ: 18 וַיִּגְבְּרוּ הַמַּיִם וַיִּרְבּוּ מְאֹד עַל־הָאָרֶץ וַתֵּלֶךְ הַתֵּבָה עַל־פְּנֵי הַמָּיִם: 19 וְהַמַּיִם גָּבְרוּ מְאֹד מְאֹד עַל־הָאָרֶץ וַיְכֻסּוּ כָּל־הֶהָרִים הַגְּבֹהִים אֲשֶׁר־תַּחַת כָּל־הַשָּׁמָיִם: 20 חֲמֵשׁ עֶשְׂרֵה אַמָּה מִלְמַעְלָה גָּבְרוּ הַמָּיִם וַיְכֻסּוּ הֶהָרִים: 21 וַיִּגְוַע כָּל־בָּשָׂר הָרֹמֵשׂ עַל־הָאָרֶץ בָּעוֹף וּבַבְּהֵמָה וּבַחַיָּה וּבְכָל־הַשֶּׁרֶץ הַשֹּׁרֵץ עַל־הָאָרֶץ וְכֹל הָאָדָם: 22 כֹּל אֲשֶׁר נִשְׁמַת־רוּחַ חַיִּים בְּאַפָּיו מִכֹּל אֲשֶׁר בֶּחָרָבָה מֵתוּ: 23 וַיִּמַח אֶת־כָּל־הַיְקוּם אֲשֶׁר עַל־פְּנֵי הָאֲדָמָה מֵאָדָם עַד־בְּהֵמָה עַד־רֶמֶשׂ וְעַד־עוֹף הַשָּׁמַיִם וַיִּמָּחוּ מִן־הָאָרֶץ וַיִּשָּׁאֶר אַךְ־נֹחַ וַאֲשֶׁר אִתּוֹ בַּתֵּבָה: 24 וַיִּגְבְּרוּ הַמַּיִם עַל־הָאָרֶץ חֲמִשִּׁים וּמְאַת יוֹם:

ח וַיִּזְכֹּר אֱלֹהִים אֶת־נֹחַ וְאֵת כָּל־הַחַיָּה וְאֶת־כָּל־הַבְּהֵמָה אֲשֶׁר אִתּוֹ בַּתֵּבָה וַיַּעֲבֵר אֱלֹהִים רוּחַ עַל־הָאָרֶץ וַיָּשֹׁכּוּ הַמָּיִם: 2 וַיִּסָּכְרוּ מַעְיְנֹת תְּהוֹם וַאֲרֻבֹּת הַשָּׁמָיִם וַיִּכָּלֵא הַגֶּשֶׁם מִן־הַשָּׁמָיִם: 3 וַיָּשֻׁבוּ הַמַּיִם מֵעַל הָאָרֶץ הָלוֹךְ וָשׁוֹב וַיַּחְסְרוּ הַמַּיִם מִקְצֵה חֲמִשִּׁים וּמְאַת יוֹם: 4 וַתָּנַח הַתֵּבָה בַּחֹדֶשׁ הַשְּׁבִיעִי בְּשִׁבְעָה־עָשָׂר יוֹם לַחֹדֶשׁ עַל הָרֵי אֲרָרָט:

5 וְהַמַּיִם הָיוּ הָלוֹךְ וְחָסוֹר עַד הַחֹדֶשׁ הָעֲשִׂירִי בָּעֲשִׂירִי בְּאֶחָד לַחֹדֶשׁ נִרְאוּ רָאשֵׁי הֶהָרִים: 6 וַיְהִי מִקֵּץ אַרְבָּעִים יוֹם וַיִּפְתַּח נֹחַ אֶת־חַלּוֹן הַתֵּבָה אֲשֶׁר עָשָׂה: 7 וַיְשַׁלַּח אֶת־הָעֹרֵב וַיֵּצֵא יָצוֹא וָשׁוֹב עַד־יְבֹשֶׁת הַמַּיִם מֵעַל הָאָרֶץ: 8 וַיְשַׁלַּח אֶת־הַיּוֹנָה מֵאִתּוֹ לִרְאוֹת הֲקַלּוּ הַמַּיִם מֵעַל פְּנֵי הָאֲדָמָה:

9 וְלֹא־מָצְאָה הַיּוֹנָה מָנוֹחַ לְכַף־רַגְלָהּ וַתָּשָׁב אֵלָיו אֶל־הַתֵּבָה כִּי־מַיִם עַל־פְּנֵי כָל־הָאָרֶץ וַיִּשְׁלַח יָדוֹ וַיִּקָּחֶהָ וַיָּבֵא אֹתָהּ אֵלָיו אֶל־הַתֵּבָה: 10 וַיָּחֶל עוֹד

yet another seven days, and again he sent the dove out from the ark. 11 Then the dove came to him in the evening, and behold, a freshly plucked olive leaf *was* in her mouth; and Noah knew that the waters had receded from the earth. 12 So he waited yet another seven days and sent out the dove, which did not return again to him anymore.

13 And it came to pass in the six hundred and first year, in the first *month,* the first *day* of the month, that the waters were dried up from the earth; and Noah removed the covering of the ark and looked, and indeed the surface of the ground was dry. 14 And in the second month, on the twenty-seventh day of the month, the earth was dried.

15 Then God spoke to Noah, saying, 16 "Go out of the ark, you and your wife, and your sons and your sons' wives with you. 17 Bring out with you every living thing of all flesh that *is* with you: birds and cattle and every creeping thing that creeps on the earth, so that they may abound on the earth, and be fruitful and multiply on the earth." 18 So Noah went out, and his sons and his wife and his sons' wives with him. 19 Every animal, every creeping thing, every bird, *and* whatever creeps on the earth, according to their families, went out of the ark.

20 Then Noah built an altar to the LORD, and took of every clean animal and of every clean bird, and offered burnt offerings on the altar. 21 And the LORD smelled a soothing aroma. Then the LORD said in His heart, "I will never again curse the ground for man's sake, although the imagination of man's heart *is* evil from his youth; nor will I again destroy every living thing as I have done.

22 "While the earth remains,
　　Seedtime and harvest,
　　Cold and heat,
　　Winter and summer,
　　And day and night
　　Shall not cease."

9 So God blessed Noah and his sons, and said to them: "Be fruitful and multiply, and fill the earth. 2 And the fear of you and the dread of you shall be on every beast of the earth, on every bird of the air, on all that move *on* the earth, and on all the fish of the sea. They are given into your hand. 3 Every moving thing that lives shall be food for you. I have given you all things, even as the green herbs. 4 But you shall not eat flesh with its life, *that is,* its blood. 5 Surely for your lifeblood I will demand *a reckoning;* from the hand of every beast I will

שִׁבְעַת יָמִים אֲחֵרִים וַיֹּסֶף שַׁלַּח אֶת־הַיּוֹנָה מִן־ הַתֵּבָה: 11 וַתָּבֹא אֵלָיו הַיּוֹנָה לְעֵת עֶרֶב וְהִנֵּה עֲלֵה־זַיִת טָרָף בְּפִיהָ וַיֵּדַע נֹחַ כִּי־קַלּוּ הַמַּיִם מֵעַל הָאָרֶץ: 12 וַיִּיָּחֶל עוֹד שִׁבְעַת יָמִים אֲחֵרִים וַיְשַׁלַּח אֶת־הַיּוֹנָה וְלֹא־יָסְפָה שׁוּב־אֵלָיו עוֹד: 13 וַיְהִי בְּאַחַת וְשֵׁשׁ־מֵאוֹת שָׁנָה בָּרִאשׁוֹן בְּאֶחָד לַחֹדֶשׁ חָרְבוּ הַמַּיִם מֵעַל הָאָרֶץ וַיָּסַר נֹחַ אֶת־ מִכְסֵה הַתֵּבָה וַיַּרְא וְהִנֵּה חָרְבוּ פְּנֵי הָאֲדָמָה: 14 וּבַחֹדֶשׁ הַשֵּׁנִי בְּשִׁבְעָה וְעֶשְׂרִים יוֹם לַחֹדֶשׁ יָבְשָׁה הָאָרֶץ: ס 15 וַיְדַבֵּר אֱלֹהִים אֶל־ נֹחַ לֵאמֹר: 16 צֵא מִן־הַתֵּבָה אַתָּה וְאִשְׁתְּךָ וּבָנֶיךָ וּנְשֵׁי־בָנֶיךָ אִתָּךְ: 17 כָּל־הַחַיָּה אֲשֶׁר־אִתְּךָ מִכָּל־ בָּשָׂר בָּעוֹף וּבַבְּהֵמָה וּבְכָל־הָרֶמֶשׂ הָרֹמֵשׂ עַל־ הָאָרֶץ הַוְצֵא אִתָּךְ וְשָׁרְצוּ בָאָרֶץ וּפָרוּ וְרָבוּ עַל־ הָאָרֶץ: 18 וַיֵּצֵא־נֹחַ וּבָנָיו וְאִשְׁתּוֹ וּנְשֵׁי־בָנָיו אִתּוֹ: 19 כָּל־הַחַיָּה כָּל־הָרֶמֶשׂ וְכָל־הָעוֹף כֹּל רוֹמֵשׂ עַל־ הָאָרֶץ לְמִשְׁפְּחֹתֵיהֶם יָצְאוּ מִן־הַתֵּבָה: 20 וַיִּבֶן נֹחַ מִזְבֵּחַ לַיהֹוָה וַיִּקַּח מִכֹּל הַבְּהֵמָה הַטְּהוֹרָה וּמִכֹּל הָעוֹף הַטָּהוֹר וַיַּעַל עֹלֹת בַּמִּזְבֵּחַ: 21 וַיָּרַח יְהֹוָה אֶת־רֵיחַ הַנִּיחֹחַ וַיֹּאמֶר יְהֹוָה אֶל־לִבּוֹ לֹא־אֹסִף לְקַלֵּל עוֹד אֶת־הָאֲדָמָה בַּעֲבוּר הָאָדָם כִּי יֵצֶר לֵב הָאָדָם רַע מִנְּעֻרָיו וְלֹא־אֹסִף עוֹד לְהַכּוֹת אֶת־כָּל־חַי כַּאֲשֶׁר עָשִׂיתִי: 22 עֹד כָּל־יְמֵי הָאָרֶץ זֶרַע וְקָצִיר וְקֹר וָחֹם וְקַיִץ וָחֹרֶף וְיוֹם וָלַיְלָה לֹא יִשְׁבֹּתוּ:

ט וַיְבָרֶךְ אֱלֹהִים אֶת־נֹחַ וְאֶת־בָּנָיו וַיֹּאמֶר לָהֶם פְּרוּ וּרְבוּ וּמִלְאוּ אֶת־הָאָרֶץ: 2 וּמוֹרַאֲכֶם וְחִתְּכֶם יִהְיֶה עַל כָּל־חַיַּת הָאָרֶץ וְעַל כָּל־עוֹף הַשָּׁמָיִם בְּכֹל אֲשֶׁר תִּרְמֹשׂ הָאֲדָמָה וּבְכָל־דְּגֵי הַיָּם בְּיֶדְכֶם נִתָּנוּ: 3 כָּל־רֶמֶשׂ אֲשֶׁר הוּא־חַי לָכֶם יִהְיֶה לְאָכְלָה כְּיֶרֶק עֵשֶׂב נָתַתִּי לָכֶם אֶת־כֹּל: 4 אַךְ־בָּשָׂר בְּנַפְשׁוֹ דָמוֹ לֹא תֹאכֵלוּ: 5 וְאַךְ אֶת־דִּמְכֶם לְנַפְשֹׁתֵיכֶם אֶדְרֹשׁ מִיַּד כָּל־חַיָּה אֶדְרְשֶׁנּוּ וּמִיַּד הָאָדָם מִיַּד

require it, and from the hand of man. From the hand of every man's brother I will require the life of man.

6   "Whoever sheds man's blood,
    By man his blood shall be shed;
    For in the image of God
    He made man.
7   And as for you, be fruitful and multiply;
    Bring forth abundantly in the earth
    And multiply in it."

8 Then God spoke to Noah and to his sons with him, saying: 9 "And as for Me, behold, I establish My covenant with you and with your descendants after you, 10 and with every living creature that *is* with you: the birds, the cattle, and every beast of the earth with you, of all that go out of the ark, every beast of the earth. 11 Thus I establish My covenant with you: Never again shall all flesh be cut off by the waters of the flood; never again shall there be a flood to destroy the earth."

12 And God said: "This *is* the sign of the covenant which I make between Me and you, and every living creature that *is* with you, for perpetual generations: 13 I set My rainbow in the cloud, and it shall be for the sign of the covenant between Me and the earth. 14 It shall be, when I bring a cloud over the earth, that the rainbow shall be seen in the cloud; 15 and I will remember My covenant which *is* between Me and you and every living creature of all flesh; the waters shall never again become a flood to destroy all flesh. 16 The rainbow shall be in the cloud, and I will look on it to remember the everlasting covenant between God and every living creature of all flesh that *is* on the earth." 17 And God said to Noah, "This *is* the sign of the covenant which I have established between Me and all flesh that *is* on the earth."

18 Now the sons of Noah who went out of the ark were Shem, Ham, and Japheth. And Ham *was* the father of Canaan. 19 These three *were* the sons of Noah, and from these the whole earth was populated.

20 And Noah began *to be* a farmer, and he planted a vineyard. 21 Then he drank of the wine and was drunk, and became uncovered in his tent. 22 And Ham, the father of Canaan, saw the nakedness of his father, and told his two brothers outside. 23 But Shem and Japheth took a garment, laid *it* on both their shoulders, and went backward and covered the nakedness of their father. Their faces *were* turned away, and they did not see their father's nakedness.

24 So Noah awoke from his wine, and knew what his younger son had done to him. 25 Then he said:

אִישׁ אָחִיו אֶדְרֹשׁ אֶת־נֶפֶשׁ הָאָדָם: 6 שֹׁפֵךְ דַּם הָאָדָם בָּאָדָם דָּמוֹ יִשָּׁפֵךְ כִּי בְּצֶלֶם אֱלֹהִים עָשָׂה אֶת־הָאָדָם: 7 וְאַתֶּם פְּרוּ וּרְבוּ שִׁרְצוּ בָאָרֶץ וּרְבוּ־בָהּ: ס 8 וַיֹּאמֶר אֱלֹהִים אֶל־נֹחַ וְאֶל־בָּנָיו אִתּוֹ לֵאמֹר: 9 וַאֲנִי הִנְנִי מֵקִים אֶת־בְּרִיתִי אִתְּכֶם וְאֶת־זַרְעֲכֶם אַחֲרֵיכֶם: 10 וְאֵת כָּל־נֶפֶשׁ הַחַיָּה אֲשֶׁר אִתְּכֶם בָּעוֹף בַּבְּהֵמָה וּבְכָל־חַיַּת הָאָרֶץ אִתְּכֶם מִכֹּל יֹצְאֵי הַתֵּבָה לְכֹל חַיַּת הָאָרֶץ: 11 וַהֲקִמֹתִי אֶת־בְּרִיתִי אִתְּכֶם וְלֹא־יִכָּרֵת כָּל־בָּשָׂר עוֹד מִמֵּי הַמַּבּוּל וְלֹא־יִהְיֶה עוֹד מַבּוּל לְשַׁחֵת הָאָרֶץ: 12 וַיֹּאמֶר אֱלֹהִים זֹאת אוֹת־הַבְּרִית אֲשֶׁר־ אֲנִי נֹתֵן בֵּינִי וּבֵינֵיכֶם וּבֵין כָּל־נֶפֶשׁ חַיָּה אֲשֶׁר אִתְּכֶם לְדֹרֹת עוֹלָם: 13 אֶת־קַשְׁתִּי נָתַתִּי בֶּעָנָן וְהָיְתָה לְאוֹת בְּרִית בֵּינִי וּבֵין הָאָרֶץ: 14 וְהָיָה בְּעַנְנִי עָנָן עַל־הָאָרֶץ וְנִרְאֲתָה הַקֶּשֶׁת בֶּעָנָן: 15 וְזָכַרְתִּי אֶת־בְּרִיתִי אֲשֶׁר בֵּינִי וּבֵינֵיכֶם וּבֵין כָּל־נֶפֶשׁ חַיָּה בְּכָל־בָּשָׂר וְלֹא־יִהְיֶה עוֹד הַמַּיִם לְמַבּוּל לְשַׁחֵת כָּל־בָּשָׂר: 16 וְהָיְתָה הַקֶּשֶׁת בֶּעָנָן וּרְאִיתִיהָ לִזְכֹּר בְּרִית עוֹלָם בֵּין אֱלֹהִים וּבֵין כָּל־נֶפֶשׁ חַיָּה בְּכָל־ בָּשָׂר אֲשֶׁר עַל־הָאָרֶץ: 17 וַיֹּאמֶר אֱלֹהִים אֶל־נֹחַ זֹאת אוֹת־הַבְּרִית אֲשֶׁר הֲקִמֹתִי בֵּינִי וּבֵין כָּל־בָּשָׂר אֲשֶׁר עַל־הָאָרֶץ: פ

18 וַיִּהְיוּ בְנֵי־נֹחַ הַיֹּצְאִים מִן־הַתֵּבָה שֵׁם וְחָם וָיָפֶת וְחָם הוּא אֲבִי כְנָעַן: 19 שְׁלֹשָׁה אֵלֶּה בְּנֵי־נֹחַ וּמֵאֵלֶּה נָפְצָה כָל־הָאָרֶץ: 20 וַיָּחֶל נֹחַ אִישׁ הָאֲדָמָה וַיִּטַּע כָּרֶם: 21 וַיֵּשְׁתְּ מִן־הַיַּיִן וַיִּשְׁכָּר וַיִּתְגַּל בְּתוֹךְ אָהֳלֹה: 22 וַיַּרְא חָם אֲבִי כְנַעַן אֵת עֶרְוַת אָבִיו וַיַּגֵּד לִשְׁנֵי־אֶחָיו בַּחוּץ: 23 וַיִּקַּח שֵׁם וָיֶפֶת אֶת־הַשִּׂמְלָה וַיָּשִׂימוּ עַל־שְׁכֶם שְׁנֵיהֶם וַיֵּלְכוּ אֲחֹרַנִּית וַיְכַסּוּ אֵת עֶרְוַת אֲבִיהֶם וּפְנֵיהֶם אֲחֹרַנִּית וְעֶרְוַת אֲבִיהֶם לֹא רָאוּ: 24 וַיִּיקֶץ נֹחַ מִיֵּינוֹ וַיֵּדַע אֵת אֲשֶׁר־עָשָׂה לוֹ בְּנוֹ הַקָּטָן: 25 וַיֹּאמֶר אָרוּר כְּנָעַן עֶבֶד עֲבָדִים יִהְיֶה

"Cursed *be* Canaan;
   A servant of servants
   He shall be to his brethren."

26 And he said:

"Blessed *be* the LORD,
   The God of Shem,
   And may Canaan be his servant.
27   May God enlarge Japheth,
   And may he dwell in the tents of Shem;
   And may Canaan be his servant."

28 And Noah lived after the flood three hundred and fifty years. 29 So all the days of Noah were nine hundred and fifty years; and he died.

10 Now this *is* the genealogy of the sons of Noah: Shem, Ham, and Japheth. And sons were born to them after the flood.

2 The sons of Japheth *were* Gomer, Magog, Madai, Javan, Tubal, Meshech, and Tiras. 3 The sons of Gomer *were* Ashkenaz, Riphath, and Togarmah. 4 The sons of Javan *were* Elishah, Tarshish, Kittim, and Dodanim. 5 From these the coastland *peoples* of the Gentiles were separated into their lands, everyone according to his language, according to their families, into their nations.

6 The sons of Ham *were* Cush, Mizraim, Put, and Canaan. 7 The sons of Cush *were* Seba, Havilah, Sabtah, Raamah, and Sabtechah; and the sons of Raamah *were* Sheba and Dedan.

8 Cush begot Nimrod; he began to be a mighty one on the earth. 9 He was a mighty hunter before the LORD; therefore it is said, "Like Nimrod the mighty hunter before the LORD." 10 And the beginning of his kingdom was Babel, Erech, Accad, and Calneh, in the land of Shinar. 11 From that land he went to Assyria and built Nineveh, Rehoboth Ir, Calah, 12 and Resen between Nineveh and Calah (that *is* the principal city).

13 Mizraim begot Ludim, Anamim, Lehabim, Naphtuhim, 14 Pathrusim, and Casluhim (from whom came the Philistines and Caphtorim).

15 Canaan begot Sidon his firstborn, and Heth; 16 the Jebusite, the Amorite, and the Girgashite; 17 the Hivite, the Arkite, and the Sinite; 18 the Arvadite, the Zemarite, and the Hamathite. Afterward the families of the Canaanites were dispersed. 19 And the border of the Canaanites was from Sidon as you go toward Gerar, as far as Gaza; then as you go toward Sodom, Gomorrah, Admah, and Zeboiim, as far as Lasha. 20 These *were* the sons of Ham, according to their families, according to their languages, in their lands *and* in their nations.

לְאֶחָיו: 26 וַיֹּאמֶר בָּרוּךְ יְהוָה אֱלֹהֵי שֵׁם וִיהִי כְנַעַן

עֶבֶד לָמוֹ: 27 יַפְתְּ אֱלֹהִים לְיֶפֶת וְיִשְׁכֹּן בְּאָהֳלֵי־

שֵׁם וִיהִי כְנַעַן עֶבֶד לָמוֹ: 28 וַיְחִי־נֹחַ אַחַר הַמַּבּוּל

שְׁלֹשׁ מֵאוֹת שָׁנָה וַחֲמִשִּׁים שָׁנָה: 29 וַיִּהְיוּ כָּל־יְמֵי־

נֹחַ תְּשַׁע מֵאוֹת שָׁנָה וַחֲמִשִּׁים שָׁנָה וַיָּמֹת: פ

י וְאֵלֶּה תּוֹלְדֹת בְּנֵי־נֹחַ שֵׁם חָם וָיָפֶת וַיִּוָּלְדוּ

לָהֶם בָּנִים אַחַר הַמַּבּוּל: 2 בְּנֵי יֶפֶת גֹּמֶר וּמָגוֹג

וּמָדַי וְיָוָן וְתֻבָל וּמֶשֶׁךְ וְתִירָס: 3 וּבְנֵי גֹּמֶר

אַשְׁכְּנַז וְרִיפַת וְתֹגַרְמָה: 4 וּבְנֵי יָוָן אֱלִישָׁה

וְתַרְשִׁישׁ כִּתִּים וְדֹדָנִים: 5 מֵאֵלֶּה נִפְרְדוּ אִיֵּי

הַגּוֹיִם בְּאַרְצֹתָם אִישׁ לִלְשֹׁנוֹ לְמִשְׁפְּחֹתָם בְּגוֹיֵהֶם:

6 וּבְנֵי חָם כּוּשׁ וּמִצְרַיִם וּפוּט וּכְנָעַן: 7 וּבְנֵי

כוּשׁ סְבָא וַחֲוִילָה וְסַבְתָּה וְרַעְמָה וְסַבְתְּכָא

וּבְנֵי רַעְמָה שְׁבָא וּדְדָן: 8 וְכוּשׁ יָלַד אֶת־

נִמְרֹד הוּא הֵחֵל לִהְיוֹת גִּבֹּר בָּאָרֶץ: 9 הוּא־

הָיָה גִבֹּר־צַיִד לִפְנֵי יְהוָה עַל־כֵּן יֵאָמַר כְּנִמְרֹד

גִּבּוֹר צַיִד לִפְנֵי יְהוָה: 10 וַתְּהִי רֵאשִׁית מַמְלַכְתּוֹ

בָּבֶל וְאֶרֶךְ וְאַכַּד וְכַלְנֶה בְּאֶרֶץ שִׁנְעָר: 11 מִן־

הָאָרֶץ הַהִוא יָצָא אַשּׁוּר וַיִּבֶן אֶת־נִינְוֵה וְאֶת־

רְחֹבֹת עִיר וְאֶת־כָּלַח: 12 וְאֶת־רֶסֶן בֵּין נִינְוֵה וּבֵין

כָּלַח הִוא הָעִיר הַגְּדֹלָה: 13 וּמִצְרַיִם יָלַד אֶת־

לוּדִים וְאֶת־עֲנָמִים וְאֶת־לְהָבִים וְאֶת־נַפְתֻּחִים:

14 וְאֶת־פַּתְרֻסִים וְאֶת־כַּסְלֻחִים אֲשֶׁר יָצְאוּ מִשָּׁם

פְּלִשְׁתִּים וְאֶת־כַּפְתֹּרִים: ס 15 וּכְנַעַן יָלַד

אֶת־צִידֹן בְּכֹרוֹ וְאֶת־חֵת: 16 וְאֶת־הַיְבוּסִי וְאֶת־

הָאֱמֹרִי וְאֵת הַגִּרְגָּשִׁי: 17 וְאֶת־הַחִוִּי וְאֶת־הָעַרְקִי

וְאֶת־הַסִּינִי: 18 וְאֶת־הָאַרְוָדִי וְאֶת־הַצְּמָרִי וְאֶת־

הַחֲמָתִי וְאַחַר נָפֹצוּ מִשְׁפְּחוֹת הַכְּנַעֲנִי: 19 וַיְהִי

גְּבוּל הַכְּנַעֲנִי מִצִּידֹן בֹּאֲכָה גְרָרָה עַד־עַזָּה

בֹּאֲכָה סְדֹמָה וַעֲמֹרָה וְאַדְמָה וּצְבֹיִם עַד־לָשַׁע:

20 אֵלֶּה בְנֵי־חָם לְמִשְׁפְּחֹתָם לִלְשֹׁנֹתָם בְּאַרְצֹתָם

21 And *children* were born also to Shem, the father of all the children of Eber, the brother of Japheth the elder. 22 The sons of Shem *were* Elam, Asshur, Arphaxad, Lud, and Aram. 23 The sons of Aram *were* Uz, Hul, Gether, and Mash. 24 Arphaxad begot Salah, and Salah begot Eber. 25 To Eber were born two sons: the name of one *was* Peleg, for in his days the earth was divided; and his brother's name *was* Joktan. 26 Joktan begot Almodad, Sheleph, Hazarmaveth, Jerah, 27 Hadoram, Uzal, Diklah, 28 Obal, Abimael, Sheba, 29 Ophir, Havilah, and Jobab. All these *were* the sons of Joktan. 30 And their dwelling place was from Mesha as you go toward Sephar, the mountain of the east. 31 These *were* the sons of Shem, according to their families, according to their languages, in their lands, according to their nations.

32 These *were* the families of the sons of Noah, according to their generations, in their nations; and from these the nations were divided on the earth after the flood.

11 Now the whole earth had one language and one speech. 2 And it came to pass, as they journeyed from the east, that they found a plain in the land of Shinar, and they dwelt there. 3 Then they said to one another, "Come, let us make bricks and bake *them* thoroughly." They had brick for stone, and they had asphalt for mortar. 4 And they said, "Come, let us build ourselves a city, and a tower whose top *is* in the heavens; let us make a name for ourselves, lest we be scattered abroad over the face of the whole earth."

5 But the LORD came down to see the city and the tower which the sons of men had built. 6 And the LORD said, "Indeed the people *are* one and they all have one language, and this is what they begin to do; now nothing that they propose to do will be withheld from them. 7 Come, let Us go down and there confuse their language, that they may not understand one another's speech." 8 So the LORD scattered them abroad from there over the face of all the earth, and they ceased building the city. 9 Therefore its name is called Babel, because there the LORD confused the language of all the earth; and from there the LORD scattered them abroad over the face of all the earth.

10 This *is* the genealogy of Shem: Shem *was* one hundred years old, and begot Arphaxad two years after the flood. 11 After he begot Arphaxad, Shem lived five hundred years, and begot sons and daughters.

בְּגוֹיֵהֶם: ס 21 וּלְשֵׁם יֻלַּד גַּם־הוּא אֲבִי כָּל־בְּנֵי־עֵבֶר אֲחִי יֶפֶת הַגָּדוֹל: 22 בְּנֵי שֵׁם עֵילָם וְאַשּׁוּר וְאַרְפַּכְשַׁד וְלוּד וַאֲרָם: 23 וּבְנֵי אֲרָם עוּץ וְחוּל וְגֶתֶר וָמַשׁ: 24 וְאַרְפַּכְשַׁד יָלַד אֶת־שָׁלַח וְשֶׁלַח יָלַד אֶת־עֵבֶר: 25 וּלְעֵבֶר יֻלַּד שְׁנֵי בָנִים שֵׁם הָאֶחָד פֶּלֶג כִּי בְיָמָיו נִפְלְגָה הָאָרֶץ וְשֵׁם אָחִיו יָקְטָן: 26 וְיָקְטָן יָלַד אֶת־אַלְמוֹדָד וְאֶת־שָׁלֶף וְאֶת־חֲצַרְמָוֶת וְאֶת־יָרַח: 27 וְאֶת־הֲדוֹרָם וְאֶת־אוּזָל וְאֶת־דִּקְלָה: 28 וְאֶת־עוֹבָל וְאֶת־אֲבִימָאֵל וְאֶת־שְׁבָא: 29 וְאֶת־אוֹפִר וְאֶת־חֲוִילָה וְאֶת־יוֹבָב כָּל־אֵלֶּה בְּנֵי יָקְטָן: 30 וַיְהִי מוֹשָׁבָם מִמֵּשָׁא בֹּאֲכָה סְפָרָה הַר הַקֶּדֶם: 31 אֵלֶּה בְנֵי־שֵׁם לְמִשְׁפְּחֹתָם לִלְשֹׁנֹתָם בְּאַרְצֹתָם לְגוֹיֵהֶם: 32 אֵלֶּה מִשְׁפְּחֹת בְּנֵי־נֹחַ לְתוֹלְדֹתָם בְּגוֹיֵהֶם וּמֵאֵלֶּה נִפְרְדוּ הַגּוֹיִם בָּאָרֶץ אַחַר הַמַּבּוּל: פ

יא וַיְהִי כָל־הָאָרֶץ שָׂפָה אֶחָת וּדְבָרִים אֲחָדִים: 2 וַיְהִי בְּנָסְעָם מִקֶּדֶם וַיִּמְצְאוּ בִקְעָה בְּאֶרֶץ שִׁנְעָר וַיֵּשְׁבוּ שָׁם: 3 וַיֹּאמְרוּ אִישׁ אֶל־רֵעֵהוּ הָבָה נִלְבְּנָה לְבֵנִים וְנִשְׂרְפָה לִשְׂרֵפָה וַתְּהִי לָהֶם הַלְּבֵנָה לְאָבֶן וְהַחֵמָר הָיָה לָהֶם לַחֹמֶר: 4 וַיֹּאמְרוּ הָבָה נִבְנֶה־לָּנוּ עִיר וּמִגְדָּל וְרֹאשׁוֹ בַשָּׁמַיִם וְנַעֲשֶׂה־לָּנוּ שֵׁם פֶּן־נָפוּץ עַל־פְּנֵי כָל־הָאָרֶץ: 5 וַיֵּרֶד יְהוָֹה לִרְאֹת אֶת־הָעִיר וְאֶת־הַמִּגְדָּל אֲשֶׁר בָּנוּ בְּנֵי הָאָדָם: 6 וַיֹּאמֶר יְהוָֹה הֵן עַם אֶחָד וְשָׂפָה אַחַת לְכֻלָּם וְזֶה הַחִלָּם לַעֲשׂוֹת וְעַתָּה לֹא־יִבָּצֵר מֵהֶם כֹּל אֲשֶׁר יָזְמוּ לַעֲשׂוֹת: 7 הָבָה נֵרְדָה וְנָבְלָה שָׁם שְׂפָתָם אֲשֶׁר לֹא יִשְׁמְעוּ אִישׁ שְׂפַת רֵעֵהוּ: 8 וַיָּפֶץ יְהוָֹה אֹתָם מִשָּׁם עַל־פְּנֵי כָל־הָאָרֶץ וַיַּחְדְּלוּ לִבְנֹת הָעִיר: 9 עַל־כֵּן קָרָא שְׁמָהּ בָּבֶל כִּי־שָׁם בָּלַל יְהוָֹה שְׂפַת כָּל־הָאָרֶץ וּמִשָּׁם הֱפִיצָם יְהוָֹה עַל־פְּנֵי כָל־הָאָרֶץ:

10 אֵלֶּה תּוֹלְדֹת שֵׁם שֵׁם בֶּן־מְאַת שָׁנָה וַיּוֹלֶד אֶת־אַרְפַּכְשָׁד שְׁנָתַיִם אַחַר הַמַּבּוּל: 11 וַיְחִי־שֵׁם אַחֲרֵי הוֹלִידוֹ אֶת־אַרְפַּכְשָׁד חֲמֵשׁ מֵאוֹת שָׁנָה וַיּוֹלֶד

12 Arphaxad lived thirty-five years, and begot Salah. 13 After he begot Salah, Arphaxad lived four hundred and three years, and begot sons and daughters.

14 Salah lived thirty years, and begot Eber. 15 After he begot Eber, Salah lived four hundred and three years, and begot sons and daughters.

16 Eber lived thirty-four years, and begot Peleg. 17 After he begot Peleg, Eber lived four hundred and thirty years, and begot sons and daughters.

18 Peleg lived thirty years, and begot Reu. 19 After he begot Reu, Peleg lived two hundred and nine years, and begot sons and daughters.

20 Reu lived thirty-two years, and begot Serug. 21 After he begot Serug, Reu lived two hundred and seven years, and begot sons and daughters.

22 Serug lived thirty years, and begot Nahor. 23 After he begot Nahor, Serug lived two hundred years, and begot sons and daughters.

24 Nahor lived twenty-nine years, and begot Terah. 25 After he begot Terah, Nahor lived one hundred and nineteen years, and begot sons and daughters.

26 Now Terah lived seventy years, and begot Abram, Nahor, and Haran.

27 This *is* the genealogy of Terah: Terah begot Abram, Nahor, and Haran. Haran begot Lot. 28 And Haran died before his father Terah in his native land, in Ur of the Chaldeans. 29 Then Abram and Nahor took wives: the name of Abram's wife *was* Sarai, and the name of Nahor's wife, Milcah, the daughter of Haran the father of Milcah and the father of Iscah. 30 But Sarai was barren; she had no child.

31 And Terah took his son Abram and his grandson Lot, the son of Haran, and his daughter-in-law Sarai, his son Abram's wife, and they went out with them from Ur of the Chaldeans to go to the land of Canaan; and they came to Haran and dwelt there. 32 So the days of Terah were two hundred and five years, and Terah died in Haran.

12 Now the LORD had said to Abram:

"Get out of your country,
From your family
And from your father's house,
To a land that I will show you.
2 I will make you a great nation;
I will bless you
And make your name great;
And you shall be a blessing.
3 I will bless those who bless you,
And I will curse him who curses you;
And in you all the families of the earth shall be blessed."

בָּנִים וּבָנוֹת: 12 וְאַרְפַּכְשַׁד חַי חָמֵשׁ וּשְׁלֹשִׁים שָׁנָה וַיּוֹלֶד אֶת־שָׁלַח: 13 וַיְחִי אַרְפַּכְשַׁד אַחֲרֵי הוֹלִידוֹ אֶת־שֶׁלַח שָׁלֹשׁ שָׁנִים וְאַרְבַּע מֵאוֹת שָׁנָה וַיּוֹלֶד בָּנִים וּבָנוֹת: 14 וְשֶׁלַח חַי שְׁלֹשִׁים שָׁנָה וַיּוֹלֶד אֶת־עֵבֶר: 15 וַיְחִי־שֶׁלַח אַחֲרֵי הוֹלִידוֹ אֶת־עֵבֶר שָׁלֹשׁ שָׁנִים וְאַרְבַּע מֵאוֹת שָׁנָה וַיּוֹלֶד בָּנִים וּבָנוֹת: 16 וַיְחִי־עֵבֶר אַרְבַּע וּשְׁלֹשִׁים שָׁנָה וַיּוֹלֶד אֶת־פָּלֶג: 17 וַיְחִי־עֵבֶר אַחֲרֵי הוֹלִידוֹ אֶת־פֶּלֶג שְׁלֹשִׁים שָׁנָה וְאַרְבַּע מֵאוֹת שָׁנָה וַיּוֹלֶד בָּנִים וּבָנוֹת: 18 וַיְחִי־פֶלֶג שְׁלֹשִׁים שָׁנָה וַיּוֹלֶד אֶת־רְעוּ: 19 וַיְחִי־פֶלֶג אַחֲרֵי הוֹלִידוֹ אֶת־רְעוּ תֵּשַׁע שָׁנִים וּמָאתַיִם שָׁנָה וַיּוֹלֶד בָּנִים וּבָנוֹת: 20 וַיְחִי רְעוּ שְׁתַּיִם וּשְׁלֹשִׁים שָׁנָה וַיּוֹלֶד אֶת־שְׂרוּג: 21 וַיְחִי רְעוּ אַחֲרֵי הוֹלִידוֹ אֶת־שְׂרוּג שֶׁבַע שָׁנִים וּמָאתַיִם שָׁנָה וַיּוֹלֶד בָּנִים וּבָנוֹת: 22 וַיְחִי שְׂרוּג שְׁלֹשִׁים שָׁנָה וַיּוֹלֶד אֶת־נָחוֹר: 23 וַיְחִי שְׂרוּג אַחֲרֵי הוֹלִידוֹ אֶת־נָחוֹר מָאתַיִם שָׁנָה וַיּוֹלֶד בָּנִים וּבָנוֹת: 24 וַיְחִי נָחוֹר תֵּשַׁע וְעֶשְׂרִים שָׁנָה וַיּוֹלֶד אֶת־תָּרַח: 25 וַיְחִי נָחוֹר אַחֲרֵי הוֹלִידוֹ אֶת־תֶּרַח תְּשַׁע־עֶשְׂרֵה שָׁנָה וּמְאַת שָׁנָה וַיּוֹלֶד בָּנִים וּבָנוֹת: 26 וַיְחִי־תֶרַח שִׁבְעִים שָׁנָה וַיּוֹלֶד אֶת־אַבְרָם אֶת־נָחוֹר וְאֶת־הָרָן: 27 וְאֵלֶּה תּוֹלְדֹת תֶּרַח תֶּרַח הוֹלִיד אֶת־אַבְרָם אֶת־נָחוֹר וְאֶת־הָרָן וְהָרָן הוֹלִיד אֶת־לוֹט: 28 וַיָּמָת הָרָן עַל־פְּנֵי תֶּרַח אָבִיו בְּאֶרֶץ מוֹלַדְתּוֹ בְּאוּר כַּשְׂדִּים: 29 וַיִּקַּח אַבְרָם וְנָחוֹר לָהֶם נָשִׁים שֵׁם אֵשֶׁת־אַבְרָם שָׂרָי וְשֵׁם אֵשֶׁת־נָחוֹר מִלְכָּה בַּת־הָרָן אֲבִי־מִלְכָּה וַאֲבִי יִסְכָּה: 30 וַתְּהִי שָׂרַי עֲקָרָה אֵין לָהּ וָלָד: 31 וַיִּקַּח תֶּרַח אֶת־אַבְרָם בְּנוֹ וְאֶת־לוֹט בֶּן־הָרָן בֶּן־בְּנוֹ וְאֵת שָׂרַי כַּלָּתוֹ אֵשֶׁת אַבְרָם בְּנוֹ וַיֵּצְאוּ אִתָּם מֵאוּר כַּשְׂדִּים לָלֶכֶת אַרְצָה כְּנַעַן וַיָּבֹאוּ עַד־חָרָן וַיֵּשְׁבוּ שָׁם: 32 וַיִּהְיוּ יְמֵי־תֶרַח חָמֵשׁ שָׁנִים וּמָאתַיִם שָׁנָה וַיָּמָת תֶּרַח בְּחָרָן:

יב וַיֹּאמֶר יְהוָה אֶל־אַבְרָם לֶךְ־לְךָ מֵאַרְצְךָ וּמִמּוֹלַדְתְּךָ וּמִבֵּית אָבִיךָ אֶל־הָאָרֶץ אֲשֶׁר אַרְאֶךָּ: 2 וְאֶעֶשְׂךָ לְגוֹי גָּדוֹל וַאֲבָרֶכְךָ וַאֲגַדְּלָה שְׁמֶךָ וֶהְיֵה בְּרָכָה: 3 וַאֲבָרֲכָה מְבָרְכֶיךָ וּמְקַלֶּלְךָ אָאֹר וְנִבְרְכוּ

⁴So Abram departed as the LORD had spoken to him, and Lot went with him. And Abram *was* seventy-five years old when he departed from Haran. ⁵Then Abram took Sarai his wife and Lot his brother's son, and all their possessions that they had gathered, and the people whom they had acquired in Haran, and they departed to go to the land of Canaan. So they came to the land of Canaan. ⁶Abram passed through the land to the place of Shechem, as far as the terebinth tree of Moreh. And the Canaanites *were* then in the land.

⁷Then the LORD appeared to Abram and said, "To your descendants I will give this land." And there he built an altar to the LORD, who had appeared to him. ⁸And he moved from there to the mountain east of Bethel, and he pitched his tent *with* Bethel on the west and Ai on the east; there he built an altar to the LORD and called on the name of the LORD. ⁹So Abram journeyed, going on still toward the South.

¹⁰Now there was a famine in the land, and Abram went down to Egypt to dwell there, for the famine *was* severe in the land. ¹¹And it came to pass, when he was close to entering Egypt, that he said to Sarai his wife, "Indeed I know that you *are* a woman of beautiful countenance. ¹²Therefore it will happen, when the Egyptians see you, that they will say, 'This *is* his wife'; and they will kill me, but they will let you live. ¹³Please say you *are* my sister, that it may be well with me for your sake, and that I may live because of you."

¹⁴So it was, when Abram came into Egypt, that the Egyptians saw the woman, that she *was* very beautiful. ¹⁵The princes of Pharaoh also saw her and commended her to Pharaoh. And the woman was taken to Pharaoh's house. ¹⁶He treated Abram well for her sake. He had sheep, oxen, male donkeys, male and female servants, female donkeys, and camels.

¹⁷But the LORD plagued Pharaoh and his house with great plagues because of Sarai, Abram's wife. ¹⁸And Pharaoh called Abram and said, "What *is* this you have done to me? Why did you not tell me that she *was* your wife? ¹⁹Why did you say, 'She *is* my sister'? I might have taken her as my wife. Now therefore, here is your wife; take *her* and go your way." ²⁰So Pharaoh commanded *his* men concerning him; and they sent him away, with his wife and all that he had.

13 Then Abram went up from Egypt, he and his wife and all that he had, and Lot with him, to the South. ²Abram *was* very rich in livestock, in silver, and in gold. ³And he went on his journey from the

וַיֵּלֶךְ אַבְרָם כַּאֲשֶׁר ⁴ בָּךְ כֹּל מִשְׁפְּחֹת הָאֲדָמָה:
דִּבֶּר אֵלָיו יְהוָה וַיֵּלֶךְ אִתּוֹ לוֹט וְאַבְרָם בֶּן־
חֲמֵשׁ שָׁנִים וְשִׁבְעִים שָׁנָה בְּצֵאתוֹ מֵחָרָן: ⁵ וַיִּקַּח
אַבְרָם אֶת־שָׂרַי אִשְׁתּוֹ וְאֶת־לוֹט בֶּן־אָחִיו וְאֶת־
כָּל־רְכוּשָׁם אֲשֶׁר רָכָשׁוּ וְאֶת־הַנֶּפֶשׁ אֲשֶׁר־עָשׂוּ
בְחָרָן וַיֵּצְאוּ לָלֶכֶת אַרְצָה כְּנַעַן וַיָּבֹאוּ אַרְצָה
כְּנָעַן: ⁶ וַיַּעֲבֹר אַבְרָם בָּאָרֶץ עַד מְקוֹם שְׁכֶם
עַד אֵלוֹן מוֹרֶה וְהַכְּנַעֲנִי אָז בָּאָרֶץ: ⁷ וַיֵּרָא יְהוָה
אֶל־אַבְרָם וַיֹּאמֶר לְזַרְעֲךָ אֶתֵּן אֶת־הָאָרֶץ הַזֹּאת
וַיִּבֶן שָׁם מִזְבֵּחַ לַיהוָה הַנִּרְאֶה אֵלָיו: ⁸ וַיַּעְתֵּק
מִשָּׁם הָהָרָה מִקֶּדֶם לְבֵית־אֵל וַיֵּט אָהֳלֹה בֵּית־אֵל
מִיָּם וְהָעַי מִקֶּדֶם וַיִּבֶן־שָׁם מִזְבֵּחַ לַיהוָה וַיִּקְרָא
בְּשֵׁם יְהוָה: ⁹ וַיִּסַּע אַבְרָם הָלוֹךְ וְנָסוֹעַ הַנֶּגְבָּה:
¹⁰ וַיְהִי רָעָב בָּאָרֶץ וַיֵּרֶד אַבְרָם מִצְרַיְמָה לָגוּר
שָׁם כִּי־כָבֵד הָרָעָב בָּאָרֶץ: ¹¹ וַיְהִי כַּאֲשֶׁר הִקְרִיב
לָבוֹא מִצְרָיְמָה וַיֹּאמֶר אֶל־שָׂרַי אִשְׁתּוֹ הִנֵּה־נָא
יָדַעְתִּי כִּי אִשָּׁה יְפַת־מַרְאֶה אָתְּ: ¹² וְהָיָה כִּי־
יִרְאוּ אֹתָךְ הַמִּצְרִים וְאָמְרוּ אִשְׁתּוֹ זֹאת וְהָרְגוּ
אֹתִי וְאֹתָךְ יְחַיּוּ: ¹³ אִמְרִי־נָא אֲחֹתִי אָתְּ לְמַעַן
יִיטַב־לִי בַעֲבוּרֵךְ וְחָיְתָה נַפְשִׁי בִּגְלָלֵךְ: ¹⁴ וַיְהִי
כְּבוֹא אַבְרָם מִצְרָיְמָה וַיִּרְאוּ הַמִּצְרִים אֶת־הָאִשָּׁה
כִּי־יָפָה הִוא מְאֹד: ¹⁵ וַיִּרְאוּ אֹתָהּ שָׂרֵי פַרְעֹה
וַיְהַלְלוּ אֹתָהּ אֶל־פַּרְעֹה וַתֻּקַּח הָאִשָּׁה בֵּית פַּרְעֹה:
¹⁶ וּלְאַבְרָם הֵיטִיב בַּעֲבוּרָהּ וַיְהִי־לוֹ צֹאן־וּבָקָר
וַחֲמֹרִים וַעֲבָדִים וּשְׁפָחֹת וַאֲתֹנֹת וּגְמַלִּים: ¹⁷ וַיְנַגַּע
יְהוָה אֶת־פַּרְעֹה נְגָעִים גְּדֹלִים וְאֶת־בֵּיתוֹ עַל־
דְּבַר שָׂרַי אֵשֶׁת אַבְרָם: ¹⁸ וַיִּקְרָא פַרְעֹה לְאַבְרָם
וַיֹּאמֶר מַה־זֹּאת עָשִׂיתָ לִּי לָמָּה לֹא־הִגַּדְתָּ לִּי כִּי
אִשְׁתְּךָ הִוא: ¹⁹ לָמָה אָמַרְתָּ אֲחֹתִי הִוא וָאֶקַּח
אֹתָהּ לִי לְאִשָּׁה וְעַתָּה הִנֵּה אִשְׁתְּךָ קַח וָלֵךְ:
²⁰ וַיְצַו עָלָיו פַּרְעֹה אֲנָשִׁים וַיְשַׁלְּחוּ אֹתוֹ וְאֶת־
אִשְׁתּוֹ וְאֶת־כָּל־אֲשֶׁר־לוֹ:

יג וַיַּעַל אַבְרָם מִמִּצְרַיִם הוּא וְאִשְׁתּוֹ וְכָל־אֲשֶׁר־
לוֹ וְלוֹט עִמּוֹ הַנֶּגְבָּה: ² וְאַבְרָם כָּבֵד מְאֹד בַּמִּקְנֶה
בַּכֶּסֶף וּבַזָּהָב: ³ וַיֵּלֶךְ לְמַסָּעָיו מִנֶּגֶב וְעַד־בֵּית־

South as far as Bethel, to the place where his tent had been at the beginning, between Bethel and Ai, 4 to the place of the altar which he had made there at first. And there Abram called on the name of the LORD.

5 Lot also, who went with Abram, had flocks and herds and tents. 6 Now the land was not able to support them, that they might dwell together, for their possessions were so great that they could not dwell together. 7 And there was strife between the herdsmen of Abram's livestock and the herdsmen of Lot's livestock. The Canaanites and the Perizzites then dwelt in the land.

8 So Abram said to Lot, "Please let there be no strife between you and me, and between my herdsmen and your herdsmen; for we *are* brethren. 9 *Is* not the whole land before you? Please separate from me. If *you take* the left, then I will go to the right; or, if *you go* to the right, then I will go to the left."

10 And Lot lifted his eyes and saw all the plain of Jordan, that it *was* well watered everywhere (before the LORD destroyed Sodom and Gomorrah) like the garden of the LORD, like the land of Egypt as you go toward Zoar. 11 Then Lot chose for himself all the plain of Jordan, and Lot journeyed east. And they separated from each other. 12 Abram dwelt in the land of Canaan, and Lot dwelt in the cities of the plain and pitched *his* tent even as far as Sodom. 13 But the men of Sodom *were* exceedingly wicked and sinful against the LORD.

14 And the LORD said to Abram, after Lot had separated from him: "Lift your eyes now and look from the place where you are—northward, southward, eastward, and westward; 15 for all the land which you see I give to you and your descendants forever. 16 And I will make your descendants as the dust of the earth; so that if a man could number the dust of the earth, *then* your descendants also could be numbered. 17 Arise, walk in the land through its length and its width, for I give it to you."

18 Then Abram moved *his* tent, and went and dwelt by the terebinth trees of Mamre, which *are* in Hebron, and built an altar there to the LORD.

14 And it came to pass in the days of Amraphel king of Shinar, Arioch king of Ellasar, Chedorlaomer king of Elam, and Tidal king of nations, 2 *that* they made war with Bera king of Sodom, Birsha king of Gomorrah, Shinab king of Admah, Shemeber king of Zeboiim, and the king of Bela (that is, Zoar). 3 All these joined together in the

אֶל־עַד־הַמָּקוֹם אֲשֶׁר־הָיָה שָׁם אָהֳלֹה בַּתְּחִלָּה בֵּין בֵּית־אֵל וּבֵין הָעָי: 4 אֶל־מְקוֹם הַמִּזְבֵּחַ אֲשֶׁר־עָשָׂה שָׁם בָּרִאשֹׁנָה וַיִּקְרָא שָׁם אַבְרָם בְּשֵׁם יְהוָה: 5 וְגַם־לְלוֹט הַהֹלֵךְ אֶת־אַבְרָם הָיָה צֹאן־וּבָקָר וְאֹהָלִים: 6 וְלֹא־נָשָׂא אֹתָם הָאָרֶץ לָשֶׁבֶת יַחְדָּו כִּי־הָיָה רְכוּשָׁם רָב וְלֹא יָכְלוּ לָשֶׁבֶת יַחְדָּו: 7 וַיְהִי־רִיב בֵּין רֹעֵי מִקְנֵה־אַבְרָם וּבֵין רֹעֵי מִקְנֵה־לוֹט וְהַכְּנַעֲנִי וְהַפְּרִזִּי אָז יֹשֵׁב בָּאָרֶץ: 8 וַיֹּאמֶר אַבְרָם אֶל־לוֹט אַל־נָא תְהִי מְרִיבָה בֵּינִי וּבֵינֶךָ וּבֵין רֹעַי וּבֵין רֹעֶיךָ כִּי־אֲנָשִׁים אַחִים אֲנָחְנוּ: 9 הֲלֹא כָל־הָאָרֶץ לְפָנֶיךָ הִפָּרֶד נָא מֵעָלָי אִם־הַשְּׂמֹאל וְאֵימִנָה וְאִם־הַיָּמִין וְאַשְׂמְאִילָה: 10 וַיִּשָּׂא־לוֹט אֶת־עֵינָיו וַיַּרְא אֶת־כָּל־כִּכַּר הַיַּרְדֵּן כִּי כֻלָּהּ מַשְׁקֶה לִפְנֵי ׀ שַׁחֵת יְהוָה אֶת־סְדֹם וְאֶת־עֲמֹרָה כְּגַן־יְהוָה כְּאֶרֶץ מִצְרַיִם בֹּאֲכָה צֹעַר: 11 וַיִּבְחַר־לוֹ לוֹט אֵת כָּל־כִּכַּר הַיַּרְדֵּן וַיִּסַּע לוֹט מִקֶּדֶם וַיִּפָּרְדוּ אִישׁ מֵעַל אָחִיו: 12 אַבְרָם יָשַׁב בְּאֶרֶץ־כְּנָעַן וְלוֹט יָשַׁב בְּעָרֵי הַכִּכָּר וַיֶּאֱהַל עַד־סְדֹם: 13 וְאַנְשֵׁי סְדֹם רָעִים וְחַטָּאִים לַיהוָה מְאֹד: 14 וַיהוָה אָמַר אֶל־אַבְרָם אַחֲרֵי הִפָּרֶד־לוֹט מֵעִמּוֹ שָׂא נָא עֵינֶיךָ וּרְאֵה מִן־הַמָּקוֹם אֲשֶׁר־אַתָּה שָׁם צָפֹנָה וָנֶגְבָּה וָקֵדְמָה וָיָמָּה: 15 כִּי אֶת־כָּל־הָאָרֶץ אֲשֶׁר־אַתָּה רֹאֶה לְךָ אֶתְּנֶנָּה וּלְזַרְעֲךָ עַד־עוֹלָם: 16 וְשַׂמְתִּי אֶת־זַרְעֲךָ כַּעֲפַר הָאָרֶץ אֲשֶׁר ׀ אִם־יוּכַל אִישׁ לִמְנוֹת אֶת־עֲפַר הָאָרֶץ גַּם־זַרְעֲךָ יִמָּנֶה: 17 קוּם הִתְהַלֵּךְ בָּאָרֶץ לְאָרְכָּהּ וּלְרָחְבָּהּ כִּי לְךָ אֶתְּנֶנָּה: 18 וַיֶּאֱהַל אַבְרָם וַיָּבֹא וַיֵּשֶׁב בְּאֵלֹנֵי מַמְרֵא אֲשֶׁר בְּחֶבְרוֹן וַיִּבֶן־שָׁם מִזְבֵּחַ לַיהוָה:

יד וַיְהִי בִּימֵי אַמְרָפֶל מֶלֶךְ־שִׁנְעָר אַרְיוֹךְ מֶלֶךְ אֶלָּסָר כְּדָרְלָעֹמֶר מֶלֶךְ עֵילָם וְתִדְעָל מֶלֶךְ גּוֹיִם: 2 עָשׂוּ מִלְחָמָה אֶת־בֶּרַע מֶלֶךְ סְדֹם וְאֶת־בִּרְשַׁע מֶלֶךְ עֲמֹרָה שִׁנְאָב ׀ מֶלֶךְ אַדְמָה וְשֶׁמְאֵבֶר מֶלֶךְ צְבֹיִיםᴾ וּמֶלֶךְ בֶּלַע הִיא־צֹעַר: 3 כָּל־אֵלֶּה

Valley of Siddim (that is, the Salt Sea). ⁴Twelve years they served Chedorlaomer, and in the thirteenth year they rebelled.

⁵In the fourteenth year Chedorlaomer and the kings that *were* with him came and attacked the Rephaim in Ashteroth Karnaim, the Zuzim in Ham, the Emim in Shaveh Kiriathaim, ⁶and the Horites in their mountain of Seir, as far as El Paran, which *is* by the wilderness. ⁷Then they turned back and came to En Mishpat (that *is*, Kadesh), and attacked all the country of the Amalekites, and also the Amorites who dwelt in Hazezon Tamar.

⁸And the king of Sodom, the king of Gomorrah, the king of Admah, the king of Zeboiim, and the king of Bela (that *is*, Zoar) went out and joined together in battle in the Valley of Siddim ⁹against Chedorlaomer king of Elam, Tidal king of nations, Amraphel king of Shinar, and Arioch king of Ellasar—four kings against five. ¹⁰Now the Valley of Siddim *was full of* asphalt pits; and the kings of Sodom and Gomorrah fled; *some* fell there, and the remainder fled to the mountains. ¹¹Then they took all the goods of Sodom and Gomorrah, and all their provisions, and went their way. ¹²They also took Lot, Abram's brother's son who dwelt in Sodom, and his goods, and departed.

¹³Then one who had escaped came and told Abram the Hebrew, for he dwelt by the terebinth trees of Mamre the Amorite, brother of Eshcol and brother of Aner; and they *were* allies with Abram. ¹⁴Now when Abram heard that his brother was taken captive, he armed his three hundred and eighteen trained *servants* who were born in his own house, and went in pursuit as far as Dan. ¹⁵He divided his forces against them by night, and he and his servants attacked them and pursued them as far as Hobah, which *is* north of Damascus. ¹⁶So he brought back all the goods, and also brought back his brother Lot and his goods, as well as the women and the people.

¹⁷And the king of Sodom went out to meet him at the Valley of Shaveh (that *is*, the King's Valley), after his return from the defeat of Chedorlaomer and the kings who *were* with him. ¹⁸Then Melchizedek king of Salem brought out bread and wine; he *was* the priest of God Most High. ¹⁹And he blessed him and said:

"Blessed be Abram of God Most High,
    Possessor of heaven and earth;
20   And blessed be God Most High,
    Who has delivered your enemies into your hand."

And he gave him a tithe of all.

²¹Now the king of Sodom said to Abram, "Give me the persons, and take the goods for yourself."

חָבְרוּ אֶל־עֵמֶק הַשִּׂדִּים הוּא יָם הַמֶּלַח: ⁴ שְׁתֵּים
עֶשְׂרֵה שָׁנָה עָבְדוּ אֶת־כְּדָרְלָעֹמֶר וּשְׁלֹשׁ־עֶשְׂרֵה
שָׁנָה מָרָדוּ: ⁵ וּבְאַרְבַּע עֶשְׂרֵה שָׁנָה בָּא כְדָרְלָעֹמֶר
וְהַמְּלָכִים אֲשֶׁר אִתּוֹ וַיַּכּוּ אֶת־רְפָאִים בְּעַשְׁתְּרֹת
קַרְנַיִם וְאֶת־הַזּוּזִים בְּהָם וְאֵת הָאֵימִים בְּשָׁוֵה
קִרְיָתָיִם: ⁶ וְאֶת־הַחֹרִי בְּהַרְרָם שֵׂעִיר עַד אֵיל פָּארָן
אֲשֶׁר עַל־הַמִּדְבָּר: ⁷ וַיָּשֻׁבוּ וַיָּבֹאוּ אֶל־עֵין מִשְׁפָּט
הִוא קָדֵשׁ וַיַּכּוּ אֶת־כָּל־שְׂדֵה הָעֲמָלֵקִי וְגַם אֶת־
הָאֱמֹרִי הַיֹּשֵׁב בְּחַצְצֹן תָּמָר: ⁸ וַיֵּצֵא מֶלֶךְ־סְדֹם
וּמֶלֶךְ עֲמֹרָה וּמֶלֶךְ אַדְמָה וּמֶלֶךְ צְבֹיִים וּמֶלֶךְ בֶּלַע
הִוא־צֹעַר וַיַּעַרְכוּ אִתָּם מִלְחָמָה בְּעֵמֶק הַשִּׂדִּים:
⁹ אֵת כְּדָרְלָעֹמֶר מֶלֶךְ עֵילָם וְתִדְעָל מֶלֶךְ גּוֹיִם
וְאַמְרָפֶל מֶלֶךְ שִׁנְעָר וְאַרְיוֹךְ מֶלֶךְ אֶלָּסָר אַרְבָּעָה
מְלָכִים אֶת־הַחֲמִשָּׁה: ¹⁰ וְעֵמֶק הַשִּׂדִּים בֶּאֱרֹת
בֶּאֱרֹת חֵמָר וַיָּנֻסוּ מֶלֶךְ־סְדֹם וַעֲמֹרָה וַיִּפְּלוּ־שָׁמָּה
וְהַנִּשְׁאָרִים הֶרָה נָּסוּ: ¹¹ וַיִּקְחוּ אֶת־כָּל־רְכֻשׁ סְדֹם
וַעֲמֹרָה וְאֶת־כָּל־אָכְלָם וַיֵּלֵכוּ: ¹² וַיִּקְחוּ אֶת־לוֹט
וְאֶת־רְכֻשׁוֹ בֶּן־אֲחִי אַבְרָם וַיֵּלֵכוּ וְהוּא יֹשֵׁב בִּסְדֹם:
¹³ וַיָּבֹא הַפָּלִיט וַיַּגֵּד לְאַבְרָם הָעִבְרִי וְהוּא שֹׁכֵן
בְּאֵלֹנֵי מַמְרֵא הָאֱמֹרִי אֲחִי אֶשְׁכֹּל וַאֲחִי עָנֵר וְהֵם
בַּעֲלֵי בְרִית־אַבְרָם: ¹⁴ וַיִּשְׁמַע אַבְרָם כִּי נִשְׁבָּה
אָחִיו וַיָּרֶק אֶת־חֲנִיכָיו יְלִידֵי בֵיתוֹ שְׁמֹנָה עָשָׂר
וּשְׁלֹשׁ מֵאוֹת וַיִּרְדֹּף עַד־דָּן: ¹⁵ וַיֵּחָלֵק עֲלֵיהֶם ׀
לַיְלָה הוּא וַעֲבָדָיו וַיַּכֵּם וַיִּרְדְּפֵם עַד־חוֹבָה אֲשֶׁר
מִשְּׂמֹאל לְדַמָּשֶׂק: ¹⁶ וַיָּשֶׁב אֵת כָּל־הָרְכֻשׁ וְגַם
אֶת־לוֹט אָחִיו וּרְכֻשׁוֹ הֵשִׁיב וְגַם אֶת־הַנָּשִׁים וְאֶת־
הָעָם: ¹⁷ וַיֵּצֵא מֶלֶךְ־סְדֹם לִקְרָאתוֹ אַחֲרֵי שׁוּבוֹ
מֵהַכּוֹת אֶת־כְּדָרְלָעֹמֶר וְאֶת־הַמְּלָכִים אֲשֶׁר אִתּוֹ
אֶל־עֵמֶק שָׁוֵה הוּא עֵמֶק הַמֶּלֶךְ: ¹⁸ וּמַלְכִּי־צֶדֶק
מֶלֶךְ שָׁלֵם הוֹצִיא לֶחֶם וָיָיִן וְהוּא כֹהֵן לְאֵל עֶלְיוֹן:
¹⁹ וַיְבָרְכֵהוּ וַיֹּאמַר בָּרוּךְ אַבְרָם לְאֵל עֶלְיוֹן קֹנֵה
שָׁמַיִם וָאָרֶץ: ²⁰ וּבָרוּךְ אֵל עֶלְיוֹן אֲשֶׁר־מִגֵּן צָרֶיךָ
בְּיָדֶךָ וַיִּתֶּן־לוֹ מַעֲשֵׂר מִכֹּל: ²¹ וַיֹּאמֶר מֶלֶךְ־סְדֹם

22 But Abram said to the king of Sodom, "I have raised my hand to the LORD, God Most High, the Possessor of heaven and earth, 23 that I *will take* nothing, from a thread to a sandal strap, and that I will not take anything that *is* yours, lest you should say, 'I have made Abram rich'— 24 except only what the young men have eaten, and the portion of the men who went with me: Aner, Eshcol, and Mamre; let them take their portion."

15 After these things the word of the LORD came to Abram in a vision, saying, "Do not be afraid, Abram. I *am* your shield, your exceedingly great reward."

2 But Abram said, "Lord GOD, what will You give me, seeing I go childless, and the heir of my house *is* Eliezer of Damascus?" 3 Then Abram said, "Look, You have given me no offspring; indeed one born in my house is my heir!"

4 And behold, the word of the LORD *came* to him, saying, "This one shall not be your heir, but one who will come from your own body shall be your heir." 5 Then He brought him outside and said, "Look now toward heaven, and count the stars if you are able to number them." And He said to him, "So shall your descendants be."

6 And he believed in the LORD, and He accounted it to him for righteousness.

7 Then He said to him, "I *am* the LORD, who brought you out of Ur of the Chaldeans, to give you this land to inherit it."

8 And he said, "Lord GOD, how shall I know that I will inherit it?"

9 So He said to him, "Bring Me a three-year-old heifer, a three-year-old female goat, a three-year-old ram, a turtledove, and a young pigeon." 10 Then he brought all these to Him and cut them in two, down the middle, and placed each piece opposite the other; but he did not cut the birds in two. 11 And when the vultures came down on the carcasses, Abram drove them away.

12 Now when the sun was going down, a deep sleep fell upon Abram; and behold, horror *and* great darkness fell upon him. 13 Then He said to Abram: "Know certainly that your descendants will be strangers in a land *that is* not theirs, and will serve them, and they will afflict them four hundred years. 14 And also the nation whom they serve I will judge; afterward they shall come out with great possessions. 15 Now as for you, you shall go to your fathers in peace; you shall be buried at a good old age. 16 But in the fourth generation they shall return here, for the iniquity of the Amorites *is* not yet complete."

אֶל־אַבְרָם תֶּן־לִי הַנֶּפֶשׁ וְהָרְכֻשׁ קַח־לָךְ: 22 וַיֹּאמֶר אַבְרָם אֶל־מֶלֶךְ סְדֹם הֲרִמֹתִי יָדִי אֶל־יְהוָה אֵל עֶלְיוֹן קֹנֵה שָׁמַיִם וָאָרֶץ: 23 אִם־מִחוּט וְעַד שְׂרוֹךְ־נַעַל וְאִם־אֶקַּח מִכָּל־אֲשֶׁר־לָךְ וְלֹא תֹאמַר אֲנִי הֶעֱשַׁרְתִּי אֶת־אַבְרָם: 24 בִּלְעָדַי רַק אֲשֶׁר אָכְלוּ הַנְּעָרִים וְחֵלֶק הָאֲנָשִׁים אֲשֶׁר הָלְכוּ אִתִּי עָנֵר אֶשְׁכֹּל וּמַמְרֵא הֵם יִקְחוּ חֶלְקָם:

טו אַחַר | הַדְּבָרִים הָאֵלֶּה הָיָה דְבַר־יְהוָה אֶל־אַבְרָם בַּמַּחֲזֶה לֵאמֹר אַל־תִּירָא אַבְרָם אָנֹכִי מָגֵן לָךְ שְׂכָרְךָ הַרְבֵּה מְאֹד: 2 וַיֹּאמֶר אַבְרָם אֲדֹנָי יְהוִה מַה־תִּתֶּן־לִי וְאָנֹכִי הוֹלֵךְ עֲרִירִי וּבֶן־מֶשֶׁק בֵּיתִי הוּא דַּמֶּשֶׂק אֱלִיעֶזֶר: 3 וַיֹּאמֶר אַבְרָם הֵן לִי לֹא נָתַתָּה זָרַע וְהִנֵּה בֶן־בֵּיתִי יוֹרֵשׁ אֹתִי: 4 וְהִנֵּה דְבַר־יְהוָה אֵלָיו לֵאמֹר לֹא יִירָשְׁךָ זֶה כִּי־אִם אֲשֶׁר יֵצֵא מִמֵּעֶיךָ הוּא יִירָשֶׁךָ: 5 וַיּוֹצֵא אֹתוֹ הַחוּצָה וַיֹּאמֶר הַבֶּט־נָא הַשָּׁמַיְמָה וּסְפֹר הַכּוֹכָבִים אִם־תּוּכַל לִסְפֹּר אֹתָם וַיֹּאמֶר לוֹ כֹּה יִהְיֶה זַרְעֶךָ: 6 וְהֶאֱמִן בַּיהוָה וַיַּחְשְׁבֶהָ לּוֹ צְדָקָה: 7 וַיֹּאמֶר אֵלָיו אֲנִי יְהוָה אֲשֶׁר הוֹצֵאתִיךָ מֵאוּר כַּשְׂדִּים לָתֶת לְךָ אֶת־הָאָרֶץ הַזֹּאת לְרִשְׁתָּהּ: 8 וַיֹּאמַר אֲדֹנָי יְהוִה בַּמָּה אֵדַע כִּי אִירָשֶׁנָּה: 9 וַיֹּאמֶר אֵלָיו קְחָה לִי עֶגְלָה מְשֻׁלֶּשֶׁת וְעֵז מְשֻׁלֶּשֶׁת וְאַיִל מְשֻׁלָּשׁ וְתֹר וְגוֹזָל: 10 וַיִּקַּח־לוֹ אֶת־כָּל־אֵלֶּה וַיְבַתֵּר אֹתָם בַּתָּוֶךְ וַיִּתֵּן אִישׁ־בִּתְרוֹ לִקְרַאת רֵעֵהוּ וְאֶת־הַצִּפֹּר לֹא בָתָר: 11 וַיֵּרֶד הָעַיִט עַל־הַפְּגָרִים וַיַּשֵּׁב אֹתָם אַבְרָם: 12 וַיְהִי הַשֶּׁמֶשׁ לָבוֹא וְתַרְדֵּמָה נָפְלָה עַל־אַבְרָם וְהִנֵּה אֵימָה חֲשֵׁכָה גְדֹלָה נֹפֶלֶת עָלָיו: 13 וַיֹּאמֶר לְאַבְרָם יָדֹעַ תֵּדַע כִּי־גֵר | יִהְיֶה זַרְעֲךָ בְּאֶרֶץ לֹא לָהֶם וַעֲבָדוּם וְעִנּוּ אֹתָם אַרְבַּע מֵאוֹת שָׁנָה: 14 וְגַם אֶת־הַגּוֹי אֲשֶׁר יַעֲבֹדוּ דָּן אָנֹכִי וְאַחֲרֵי־כֵן יֵצְאוּ בִּרְכֻשׁ גָּדוֹל: 15 וְאַתָּה תָּבוֹא אֶל־אֲבֹתֶיךָ בְּשָׁלוֹם תִּקָּבֵר בְּשֵׂיבָה טוֹבָה: 16 וְדוֹר רְבִיעִי יָשׁוּבוּ הֵנָּה

¹⁷And it came to pass, when the sun went down and it was dark, that behold, there appeared a smoking oven and a burning torch that passed between those pieces. ¹⁸On the same day the LORD made a covenant with Abram, saying:

"To your descendants I have given this land, from the river of Egypt to the great river, the River Euphrates— ¹⁹the Kenites, the Kenezzites, the Kadmonites, ²⁰the Hittites, the Perizzites, the Rephaim, ²¹the Amorites, the Canaanites, the Girgashites, and the Jebusites."

16 Now Sarai, Abram's wife, had borne him no *children*. And she had an Egyptian maidservant whose name was Hagar. ²So Sarai said to Abram, "See now, the LORD has restrained me from bearing *children*. Please, go in to my maid; perhaps I shall obtain children by her." And Abram heeded the voice of Sarai. ³Then Sarai, Abram's wife, took Hagar her maid, the Egyptian, and gave her to her husband Abram to be his wife, after Abram had dwelt ten years in the land of Canaan. ⁴So he went in to Hagar, and she conceived. And when she saw that she had conceived, her mistress became despised in her eyes.

⁵Then Sarai said to Abram, "My wrong *be* upon you! I gave my maid into your embrace; and when she saw that she had conceived, I became despised in her eyes. The LORD judge between you and me."

⁶So Abram said to Sarai, "Indeed your maid *is* in your hand; do to her as you please." And when Sarai dealt harshly with her, she fled from her presence.

⁷Now the Angel of the LORD found her by a spring of water in the wilderness, by the spring on the way to Shur. ⁸And He said, "Hagar, Sarai's maid, where have you come from, and where are you going?"

She said, "I am fleeing from the presence of my mistress Sarai."

⁹The Angel of the LORD said to her, "Return to your mistress, and submit yourself under her hand." ¹⁰Then the Angel of the LORD said to her, "I will multiply your descendants exceedingly, so that they shall not be counted for multitude." ¹¹And the Angel of the LORD said to her:

> "Behold, you *are* with child,
> And you shall bear a son.
> You shall call his name Ishmael,
> Because the LORD has heard your affliction.
> ¹² He shall be a wild man;
> His hand *shall be* against every man,
> And every man's hand against him.

כִּי לֹא־שָׁלֵם עֲוֹן הָאֱמֹרִי עַד־הֵנָּה: ¹⁷ וַיְהִי הַשֶּׁמֶשׁ בָּאָה וַעֲלָטָה הָיָה וְהִנֵּה תַנּוּר עָשָׁן וְלַפִּיד אֵשׁ אֲשֶׁר עָבַר בֵּין הַגְּזָרִים הָאֵלֶּה: ¹⁸ בַּיּוֹם הַהוּא כָּרַת יְהוָה אֶת־אַבְרָם בְּרִית לֵאמֹר לְזַרְעֲךָ נָתַתִּי אֶת־הָאָרֶץ הַזֹּאת מִנְּהַר מִצְרַיִם עַד־הַנָּהָר הַגָּדֹל נְהַר־פְּרָת: ¹⁹ אֶת־הַקֵּינִי וְאֶת־הַקְּנִזִּי וְאֵת הַקַּדְמֹנִי: ²⁰ וְאֶת־הַחִתִּי וְאֶת־הַפְּרִזִּי וְאֶת־הָרְפָאִים: ²¹ וְאֶת־הָאֱמֹרִי וְאֶת־הַכְּנַעֲנִי וְאֶת־הַגִּרְגָּשִׁי וְאֶת־הַיְבוּסִי:

טז וְשָׂרַי אֵשֶׁת אַבְרָם לֹא יָלְדָה לוֹ וְלָהּ שִׁפְחָה מִצְרִית וּשְׁמָהּ הָגָר: ² וַתֹּאמֶר שָׂרַי אֶל־אַבְרָם הִנֵּה־נָא עֲצָרַנִי יְהוָה מִלֶּדֶת בֹּא־נָא אֶל־שִׁפְחָתִי אוּלַי אִבָּנֶה מִמֶּנָּה וַיִּשְׁמַע אַבְרָם לְקוֹל שָׂרָי: ³ וַתִּקַּח שָׂרַי אֵשֶׁת־אַבְרָם אֶת־הָגָר הַמִּצְרִית שִׁפְחָתָהּ מִקֵּץ עֶשֶׂר שָׁנִים לְשֶׁבֶת אַבְרָם בְּאֶרֶץ כְּנָעַן וַתִּתֵּן אֹתָהּ לְאַבְרָם אִישָׁהּ לוֹ לְאִשָּׁה: ⁴ וַיָּבֹא אֶל־הָגָר וַתַּהַר וַתֵּרֶא כִּי הָרָתָה וַתֵּקַל גְּבִרְתָּהּ בְּעֵינֶיהָ: ⁵ וַתֹּאמֶר שָׂרַי אֶל־אַבְרָם חֲמָסִי עָלֶיךָ אָנֹכִי נָתַתִּי שִׁפְחָתִי בְּחֵיקֶךָ וַתֵּרֶא כִּי הָרָתָה וָאֵקַל בְּעֵינֶיהָ יִשְׁפֹּט יְהוָה בֵּינִי וּבֵינֶיךָ: ⁶ וַיֹּאמֶר אַבְרָם אֶל־שָׂרַי הִנֵּה שִׁפְחָתֵךְ בְּיָדֵךְ עֲשִׂי־לָהּ הַטּוֹב בְּעֵינָיִךְ וַתְּעַנֶּהָ שָׂרַי וַתִּבְרַח מִפָּנֶיהָ: ⁷ וַיִּמְצָאָהּ מַלְאַךְ יְהוָה עַל־עֵין הַמַּיִם בַּמִּדְבָּר עַל־הָעַיִן בְּדֶרֶךְ שׁוּר: ⁸ וַיֹּאמַר הָגָר שִׁפְחַת שָׂרַי אֵי־מִזֶּה בָאת וְאָנָה תֵלֵכִי וַתֹּאמֶר מִפְּנֵי שָׂרַי גְּבִרְתִּי אָנֹכִי בֹּרַחַת: ⁹ וַיֹּאמֶר לָהּ מַלְאַךְ יְהוָה שׁוּבִי אֶל־גְּבִרְתֵּךְ וְהִתְעַנִּי תַּחַת יָדֶיהָ: ¹⁰ וַיֹּאמֶר לָהּ מַלְאַךְ יְהוָה הַרְבָּה אַרְבֶּה אֶת־זַרְעֵךְ וְלֹא יִסָּפֵר מֵרֹב: ¹¹ וַיֹּאמֶר לָהּ מַלְאַךְ יְהוָה הִנָּךְ הָרָה וְיֹלַדְתְּ בֵּן וְקָרָאת שְׁמוֹ יִשְׁמָעֵאל כִּי־שָׁמַע יְהוָה אֶל־עָנְיֵךְ: ¹² וְהוּא יִהְיֶה

And he shall dwell in the presence of all his brethren."

13 Then she called the name of the LORD who spoke to her, You-Are-the-God-Who-Sees; for she said, "Have I also here seen Him who sees me?" 14 Therefore the well was called Beer Lahai Roi; observe, *it is* between Kadesh and Bered.

15 So Hagar bore Abram a son; and Abram named his son, whom Hagar bore, Ishmael. 16 Abram *was* eighty-six years old when Hagar bore Ishmael to Abram.

17 When Abram was ninety-nine years old, the LORD appeared to Abram and said to him, "I *am* Almighty God; .walk before Me and be blameless. 2 And I will make My covenant between Me and you, and will multiply you exceedingly." 3 Then Abram fell on his face, and God talked with him, saying: 4 "As for Me, behold, My covenant is with you, and you shall be a father of many nations. 5 No longer shall your name be called Abram, but your name shall be Abraham; for I have made you a father of many nations. 6 I will make you exceedingly fruitful; and I will make nations of you, and kings shall come from you. 7 And I will establish My covenant between Me and you and your descendants after you in their generations, for an everlasting covenant, to be God to you and your descendants after you. 8 Also I give to you and your descendants after you the land in which you are a stranger, all the land of Canaan, as an everlasting possession; and I will be their God."

9 And God said to Abraham: "As for you, you shall keep My covenant, you and your descendants after you throughout their generations. 10 This *is* My covenant which you shall keep, between Me and you and your descendants after you: Every male child among you shall be circumcised; 11 and you shall be circumcised in the flesh of your foreskins, and it shall be a sign of the covenant between Me and you. 12 He who is eight days old among you shall be circumcised, every male child in your generations, he who is born in your house or bought with money from any foreigner who is not your descendant. 13 He who is born in your house and he who is bought with your money must be circumcised, and My covenant shall be in your flesh for an everlasting covenant. 14 And the uncircumcised male child, who is not circumcised in the flesh of his foreskin, that person shall be cut off from his people; he has broken My covenant."

פֶּרֶא אָדָם יָדוֹ בַכֹּל וְיַד כֹּל בּוֹ וְעַל־פְּנֵי כָל־אֶחָיו יִשְׁכֹּן: 13 וַתִּקְרָא שֵׁם־יְהוָה הַדֹּבֵר אֵלֶיהָ אַתָּה אֵל רֳאִי כִּי אָמְרָה הֲגַם הֲלֹם רָאִיתִי אַחֲרֵי רֹאִי: 14 עַל־כֵּן קָרָא לַבְּאֵר בְּאֵר לַחַי רֹאִי הִנֵּה בֵין־קָדֵשׁ וּבֵין בָּרֶד: 15 וַתֵּלֶד הָגָר לְאַבְרָם בֵּן וַיִּקְרָא אַבְרָם שֶׁם־בְּנוֹ אֲשֶׁר־יָלְדָה הָגָר יִשְׁמָעֵאל: 16 וְאַבְרָם בֶּן־ שְׁמֹנִים שָׁנָה וְשֵׁשׁ שָׁנִים בְּלֶדֶת־הָגָר אֶת־יִשְׁמָעֵאל לְאַבְרָם: ס

יז וַיְהִי אַבְרָם בֶּן־תִּשְׁעִים שָׁנָה וְתֵשַׁע שָׁנִים וַיֵּרָא יְהוָה אֶל־אַבְרָם וַיֹּאמֶר אֵלָיו אֲנִי־אֵל שַׁדַּי הִתְהַלֵּךְ לְפָנַי וֶהְיֵה תָמִים: 2 וְאֶתְּנָה בְרִיתִי בֵּינִי וּבֵינֶךָ וְאַרְבֶּה אוֹתְךָ בִּמְאֹד מְאֹד: 3 וַיִּפֹּל אַבְרָם עַל־פָּנָיו וַיְדַבֵּר אִתּוֹ אֱלֹהִים לֵאמֹר: 4 אֲנִי הִנֵּה בְרִיתִי אִתָּךְ וְהָיִיתָ לְאַב הֲמוֹן גּוֹיִם: 5 וְלֹא־יִקָּרֵא עוֹד אֶת־שִׁמְךָ אַבְרָם וְהָיָה שִׁמְךָ אַבְרָהָם כִּי אַב־ הֲמוֹן גּוֹיִם נְתַתִּיךָ: 6 וְהִפְרֵתִי אֹתְךָ בִּמְאֹד מְאֹד וּנְתַתִּיךָ לְגוֹיִם וּמְלָכִים מִמְּךָ יֵצֵאוּ: 7 וַהֲקִמֹתִי אֶת־בְּרִיתִי בֵּינִי וּבֵינֶךָ וּבֵין זַרְעֲךָ אַחֲרֶיךָ לְדֹרֹתָם לִבְרִית עוֹלָם לִהְיוֹת לְךָ לֵאלֹהִים וּלְזַרְעֲךָ אַחֲרֶיךָ: 8 וְנָתַתִּי לְךָ וּלְזַרְעֲךָ אַחֲרֶיךָ אֵת אֶרֶץ מְגֻרֶיךָ אֵת כָּל־אֶרֶץ כְּנַעַן לַאֲחֻזַּת עוֹלָם וְהָיִיתִי לָהֶם לֵאלֹהִים: 9 וַיֹּאמֶר אֱלֹהִים אֶל־אַבְרָהָם וְאַתָּה אֶת־ בְּרִיתִי תִשְׁמֹר אַתָּה וְזַרְעֲךָ אַחֲרֶיךָ לְדֹרֹתָם: 10 זֹאת בְּרִיתִי אֲשֶׁר תִּשְׁמְרוּ בֵּינִי וּבֵינֵיכֶם וּבֵין זַרְעֲךָ אַחֲרֶיךָ הִמּוֹל לָכֶם כָּל־זָכָר: 11 וּנְמַלְתֶּם אֵת בְּשַׂר עָרְלַתְכֶם וְהָיָה לְאוֹת בְּרִית בֵּינִי וּבֵינֵיכֶם: 12 וּבֶן־ שְׁמֹנַת יָמִים יִמּוֹל לָכֶם כָּל־זָכָר לְדֹרֹתֵיכֶם יְלִיד בָּיִת וּמִקְנַת־כֶּסֶף מִכֹּל בֶּן־נֵכָר אֲשֶׁר לֹא מִזַּרְעֲךָ הוּא: 13 הִמּוֹל | יִמּוֹל יְלִיד בֵּיתְךָ וּמִקְנַת כַּסְפֶּךָ וְהָיְתָה בְרִיתִי בִּבְשַׂרְכֶם לִבְרִית עוֹלָם: 14 וְעָרֵל | זָכָר אֲשֶׁר לֹא־יִמּוֹל אֶת־בְּשַׂר עָרְלָתוֹ וְנִכְרְתָה הַנֶּפֶשׁ הַהִוא מֵעַמֶּיהָ אֶת־בְּרִיתִי

15 Then God said to Abraham, "As for Sarai your wife, you shall not call her name Sarai, but Sarah *shall be* her name. 16 And I will bless her and also give you a son by her; then I will bless her, and she shall be *a mother of* nations; kings of peoples shall be from her."

17 Then Abraham fell on his face and laughed, and said in his heart, "Shall *a child* be born to a man who is one hundred years old? And shall Sarah, who is ninety years old, bear *a child?*" 18 And Abraham said to God, "Oh, that Ishmael might live before You!"

19 Then God said: "No, Sarah your wife shall bear you a son, and you shall call his name Isaac; I will establish My covenant with him for an everlasting covenant, *and* with his descendants after him. 20 And as for Ishmael, I have heard you. Behold, I have blessed him, and will make him fruitful, and will multiply him exceedingly. He shall beget twelve princes, and I will make him a great nation. 21 But My covenant I will establish with Isaac, whom Sarah shall bear to you at this set time next year." 22 Then He finished talking with him, and God went up from Abraham.

23 So Abraham took Ishmael his son, all who were born in his house and all who were bought with his money, every male among the men of Abraham's house, and circumcised the flesh of their foreskins that very same day, as God had said to him. 24 Abraham *was* ninety-nine years old when he was circumcised in the flesh of his foreskin. 25 And Ishmael his son *was* thirteen years old when he was circumcised in the flesh of his foreskin. 26 That very same day Abraham was circumcised, and his son Ishmael; 27 and all the men of his house, born in the house or bought with money from a foreigner, were circumcised with him.

18 Then the LORD appeared to him by the terebinth trees of Mamre, as he was sitting in the tent door in the heat of the day. 2 So he lifted his eyes and looked, and behold, three men were standing by him; and when he saw *them,* he ran from the tent door to meet them, and bowed himself to the ground, 3 and said, "My Lord, if I have now found favor in Your sight, do not pass on by Your servant. 4 Please let a little water be brought, and wash your feet, and rest yourselves under the tree. 5 And I will bring a morsel of bread, that you may refresh your hearts. After that you may pass by, inasmuch as you have come to your servant."

They said, "Do as you have said."

הֵפַר׃ ס 15 וַיֹּאמֶר אֱלֹהִים אֶל־אַבְרָהָם שָׂרַי אִשְׁתְּךָ לֹא־תִקְרָא אֶת־שְׁמָהּ שָׂרָי כִּי שָׂרָה שְׁמָהּ׃ 16 וּבֵרַכְתִּי אֹתָהּ וְגַם נָתַתִּי מִמֶּנָּה לְךָ בֵּן וּבֵרַכְתִּיהָ וְהָיְתָה לְגוֹיִם מַלְכֵי עַמִּים מִמֶּנָּה יִהְיוּ׃ 17 וַיִּפֹּל אַבְרָהָם עַל־פָּנָיו וַיִּצְחָק וַיֹּאמֶר בְּלִבּוֹ הַלְּבֶן מֵאָה־שָׁנָה יִוָּלֵד וְאִם־שָׂרָה הֲבַת־תִּשְׁעִים שָׁנָה תֵּלֵד׃ 18 וַיֹּאמֶר אַבְרָהָם אֶל־הָאֱלֹהִים לוּ יִשְׁמָעֵאל יִחְיֶה לְפָנֶיךָ׃ 19 וַיֹּאמֶר אֱלֹהִים אֲבָל שָׂרָה אִשְׁתְּךָ יֹלֶדֶת לְךָ בֵּן וְקָרָאתָ אֶת־שְׁמוֹ יִצְחָק וַהֲקִמֹתִי אֶת־בְּרִיתִי אִתּוֹ לִבְרִית עוֹלָם לְזַרְעוֹ אַחֲרָיו׃ 20 וּלְיִשְׁמָעֵאל שְׁמַעְתִּיךָ הִנֵּה בֵּרַכְתִּי אֹתוֹ וְהִפְרֵיתִי אֹתוֹ וְהִרְבֵּיתִי אֹתוֹ בִּמְאֹד מְאֹד שְׁנֵים־עָשָׂר נְשִׂיאִם יוֹלִיד וּנְתַתִּיו לְגוֹי גָּדוֹל׃ 21 וְאֶת־בְּרִיתִי אָקִים אֶת־יִצְחָק אֲשֶׁר תֵּלֵד לְךָ שָׂרָה לַמּוֹעֵד הַזֶּה בַּשָּׁנָה הָאַחֶרֶת׃ 22 וַיְכַל לְדַבֵּר אִתּוֹ וַיַּעַל אֱלֹהִים מֵעַל אַבְרָהָם׃ 23 וַיִּקַּח אַבְרָהָם אֶת־יִשְׁמָעֵאל בְּנוֹ וְאֵת כָּל־יְלִידֵי בֵיתוֹ וְאֵת כָּל־מִקְנַת כַּסְפּוֹ כָּל־זָכָר בְּאַנְשֵׁי בֵּית אַבְרָהָם וַיָּמָל אֶת־בְּשַׂר עָרְלָתָם בְּעֶצֶם הַיּוֹם הַזֶּה כַּאֲשֶׁר דִּבֶּר אִתּוֹ אֱלֹהִים׃ 24 וְאַבְרָהָם בֶּן־תִּשְׁעִים וָתֵשַׁע שָׁנָה בְּהִמֹּלוֹ בְּשַׂר עָרְלָתוֹ׃ 25 וְיִשְׁמָעֵאל בְּנוֹ בֶּן־שְׁלֹשׁ עֶשְׂרֵה שָׁנָה בְּהִמֹּלוֹ אֵת בְּשַׂר עָרְלָתוֹ׃ 26 בְּעֶצֶם הַיּוֹם הַזֶּה נִמּוֹל אַבְרָהָם וְיִשְׁמָעֵאל בְּנוֹ׃ 27 וְכָל־אַנְשֵׁי בֵיתוֹ יְלִיד בָּיִת וּמִקְנַת־כֶּסֶף מֵאֵת בֶּן־נֵכָר נִמֹּלוּ אִתּוֹ׃ פ

יח וַיֵּרָא אֵלָיו יְהֹוָה בְּאֵלֹנֵי מַמְרֵא וְהוּא יֹשֵׁב פֶּתַח־הָאֹהֶל כְּחֹם הַיּוֹם׃ 2 וַיִּשָּׂא עֵינָיו וַיַּרְא וְהִנֵּה שְׁלֹשָׁה אֲנָשִׁים נִצָּבִים עָלָיו וַיַּרְא וַיָּרָץ לִקְרָאתָם מִפֶּתַח הָאֹהֶל וַיִּשְׁתַּחוּ אָרְצָה׃ 3 וַיֹּאמַר אֲדֹנָי אִם־נָא מָצָאתִי חֵן בְּעֵינֶיךָ אַל־נָא תַעֲבֹר מֵעַל עַבְדֶּךָ׃ 4 יֻקַּח־נָא מְעַט־מַיִם וְרַחֲצוּ רַגְלֵיכֶם וְהִשָּׁעֲנוּ תַּחַת הָעֵץ׃ 5 וְאֶקְחָה פַת־לֶחֶם וְסַעֲדוּ לִבְּכֶם אַחַר תַּעֲבֹרוּ כִּי־עַל־כֵּן עֲבַרְתֶּם עַל־עַבְדְּכֶם וַיֹּאמְרוּ כֵּן

6 So Abraham hurried into the tent to Sarah and said, "Quickly, make ready three measures of fine meal; knead *it* and make cakes." 7 And Abraham ran to the herd, took a tender and good calf, gave *it* to a young man, and he hastened to prepare it. 8 So he took butter and milk and the calf which he had prepared, and set *it* before them; and he stood by them under the tree as they ate.

9 Then they said to him, "Where *is* Sarah your wife?"

So he said, "Here, in the tent."

10 And He said, "I will certainly return to you according to the time of life, and behold, Sarah your wife shall have a son."

(Sarah was listening in the tent door which *was* behind him.) 11 Now Abraham and Sarah were old, well advanced in age; *and* Sarah had passed the age of childbearing. 12 Therefore Sarah laughed within herself, saying, "After I have grown old, shall I have pleasure, my lord being old also?"

13 And the LORD said to Abraham, "Why did Sarah laugh, saying, 'Shall I surely bear *a child,* since I am old?' 14 Is anything too hard for the LORD? At the appointed time I will return to you, according to the time of life, and Sarah shall have a son."

15 But Sarah denied *it,* saying, "I did not laugh," for she was afraid.

And He said, "No, but you did laugh!"

16 Then the men rose from there and looked toward Sodom, and Abraham went with them to send them on the way. 17 And the LORD said, "Shall I hide from Abraham what I am doing, 18 since Abraham shall surely become a great and mighty nation, and all the nations of the earth shall be blessed in him? 19 For I have known him, in order that he may command his children and his household after him, that they keep the way of the LORD, to do righteousness and justice, that the LORD may bring to Abraham what He has spoken to him."

20 And the LORD said, "Because the outcry against Sodom and Gomorrah is great, and because their sin is very grave, 21 I will go down now and see whether they have done altogether according to the outcry against it that has come to Me; and if not, I will know."

22 Then the men turned away from there and went toward Sodom, but Abraham still stood before the LORD. 23 And Abraham came near and said, "Would You also destroy the righteous with the wicked? 24 Suppose there were fifty righteous within the city; would You also destroy the place and not spare *it* for the fifty righteous that were in it? 25 Far be it from You to do such a thing as this,

תַּעֲשֶׂה כַּאֲשֶׁר דִּבַּֽרְתָּ: 6 וַיְמַהֵר אַבְרָהָם הָאֹֽהֱלָה
אֶל־שָׂרָה וַיֹּאמֶר מַהֲרִ֓י שְׁלֹשׁ סְאִים קֶ֤מַח סֹ֔לֶת
לוּשִׁי וַעֲשִׂי עֻגֽוֹת: 7 וְאֶל־הַבָּקָר רָץ אַבְרָהָם וַיִּקַּ֠ח
בֶּן־בָּקָר רַ֤ךְ וָטוֹב֙ וַיִּתֵּן֙ אֶל־הַנַּ֔עַר וַיְמַהֵר לַעֲשׂ֥וֹת
אֹתֽוֹ: 8 וַיִּקַּ֨ח חֶמְאָ֜ה וְחָלָ֗ב וּבֶן־הַבָּקָר֙ אֲשֶׁ֣ר עָשָׂ֔ה
וַיִּתֵּ֖ן לִפְנֵיהֶ֑ם וְהֽוּא־עֹמֵ֧ד עֲלֵיהֶ֛ם תַּ֥חַת הָעֵ֖ץ
וַיֹּאכֵֽלוּ: 9 וַיֹּאמְר֣וּ אֵלָ֔יו אַיֵּ֖ה שָׂרָ֣ה אִשְׁתֶּ֑ךָ וַיֹּ֖אמֶר
הִנֵּ֥ה בָאֹֽהֶל: 10 וַיֹּ֗אמֶר שׁ֣וֹב אָשׁ֤וּב אֵלֶ֨יךָ֙ כָּעֵ֣ת
חַיָּ֔ה וְהִנֵּה־בֵ֖ן לְשָׂרָ֣ה אִשְׁתֶּ֑ךָ וְשָׂרָ֤ה שֹׁמַ֨עַת֙ פֶּ֣תַח
הָאֹ֔הֶל וְה֖וּא אַֽחֲרָֽיו: 11 וְאַבְרָהָ֤ם וְשָׂרָה֙ זְקֵנִ֔ים
בָּאִ֖ים בַּיָּמִ֑ים חָדַל֙ לִֽהְי֣וֹת לְשָׂרָ֔ה אֹ֖רַח כַּנָּשִֽׁים:
12 וַתִּצְחַ֥ק שָׂרָ֖ה בְּקִרְבָּ֣הּ לֵאמֹ֑ר אַֽחֲרֵ֤י בְלֹתִי֙ הָֽיְתָה־
לִּ֣י עֶדְנָ֔ה וַֽאדֹנִ֖י זָקֵֽן: 13 וַיֹּ֥אמֶר יְהוָ֖ה אֶל־אַבְרָהָ֑ם
לָ֣מָּה זֶּה֩ צָֽחֲקָ֨ה שָׂרָ֜ה לֵאמֹ֗ר הַאַ֥ף אֻמְנָ֛ם אֵלֵ֖ד
וַאֲנִ֥י זָקַֽנְתִּי: 14 הֲיִפָּלֵ֥א מֵֽיהוָ֖ה דָּבָ֑ר לַמּוֹעֵ֞ד אָשׁ֤וּב
אֵלֶ֨יךָ֙ כָּעֵ֣ת חַיָּ֔ה וּלְשָׂרָ֖ה בֵֽן: 15 וַתְּכַחֵ֨שׁ שָׂרָ֧ה ׀
לֵאמֹ֛ר לֹ֥א צָחַ֖קְתִּי כִּ֣י ׀ יָרֵ֑אָה וַיֹּ֥אמֶר ׀ לֹ֖א
כִּ֥י צָחָֽקְתְּ: 16 וַיָּקֻ֤מוּ מִשָּׁם֙ הָֽאֲנָשִׁ֔ים וַיַּשְׁקִ֖פוּ עַל־
פְּנֵ֣י סְדֹ֑ם וְאַ֨בְרָהָ֔ם הֹלֵ֥ךְ עִמָּ֖ם לְשַׁלְּחָֽם: 17 וַֽיהוָ֖ה
אָמָ֑ר הַֽמֲכַסֶּ֤ה אֲנִי֙ מֵֽאַבְרָהָ֔ם אֲשֶׁ֖ר אֲנִ֥י עֹשֶֽׂה:
18 וְאַ֨בְרָהָ֔ם הָי֧וֹ יִֽהְיֶ֛ה לְג֥וֹי גָּד֖וֹל וְעָצ֑וּם וְנִ֨בְרְכוּ־
ב֔וֹ כֹּ֖ל גּוֹיֵ֥י הָאָֽרֶץ: 19 כִּ֣י יְדַעְתִּ֗יו לְמַעַן֩ אֲשֶׁ֨ר
יְצַוֶּ֜ה אֶת־בָּנָ֤יו וְאֶת־בֵּיתוֹ֙ אַֽחֲרָ֔יו וְשָֽׁמְרוּ֙ דֶּ֣רֶךְ יְהוָ֔ה
לַֽעֲשׂ֥וֹת צְדָקָ֖ה וּמִשְׁפָּ֑ט לְמַ֗עַן הָבִ֤יא יְהוָה֙ עַל־
אַבְרָהָ֔ם אֵ֥ת אֲשֶׁר־דִּבֶּ֖ר עָלָֽיו: 20 וַיֹּ֣אמֶר יְהוָ֔ה
זַֽעֲקַ֛ת סְדֹ֥ם וַֽעֲמֹרָ֖ה כִּי־רָ֑בָּה וְחַ֨טָּאתָ֔ם כִּ֥י כָֽבְדָ֖ה
מְאֹֽד: 21 אֵֽרֲדָה־נָּ֣א וְאֶרְאֶ֔ה הַכְּצַֽעֲקָתָ֛הּ הַבָּ֥אָה
אֵלַ֖י עָשׂ֣וּ ׀ כָּלָ֑ה וְאִם־לֹ֖א אֵדָֽעָה: 22 וַיִּפְנ֤וּ מִשָּׁם֙
הָֽאֲנָשִׁ֔ים וַיֵּֽלְכ֖וּ סְדֹ֑מָה וְאַ֨בְרָהָ֔ם עוֹדֶ֥נּוּ עֹמֵ֖ד לִפְנֵ֥י
יְהוָֽה: 23 וַיִּגַּ֥שׁ אַבְרָהָ֖ם וַיֹּאמַ֑ר הַאַ֣ף תִּסְפֶּ֔ה צַדִּ֖יק
עִם־רָשָֽׁע: 24 אוּלַ֥י יֵ֛שׁ חֲמִשִּׁ֥ים צַדִּיקִ֖ם בְּת֣וֹךְ הָעִ֑יר
הַאַ֤ף תִּסְפֶּה֙ וְלֹֽא־תִשָּׂ֣א לַמָּק֔וֹם לְמַ֛עַן חֲמִשִּׁ֥ים
הַצַּדִּיקִ֖ם אֲשֶׁ֥ר בְּקִרְבָּֽהּ: 25 חָלִ֨לָה לְּךָ֜ מֵֽעֲשֹׂ֣ת ׀
כַּדָּבָ֣ר הַזֶּ֗ה לְהָמִ֤ית צַדִּיק֙ עִם־רָשָׁ֔ע וְהָיָ֥ה כַצַּדִּ֖יק

to slay the righteous with the wicked, so that the righteous should be as the wicked; far be it from You! Shall not the Judge of all the earth do right?"

26 So the LORD said, "If I find in Sodom fifty righteous within the city, then I will spare all the place for their sakes."

27 Then Abraham answered and said, "Indeed now, I who *am but* dust and ashes have taken it upon myself to speak to the Lord: 28 Suppose there were five less than the fifty righteous; would You destroy all of the city for *lack of* five?"

So He said, "If I find there forty-five, I will not destroy *it*."

29 And he spoke to Him yet again and said, "Suppose there should be forty found there?"

So He said, "I will not do *it* for the sake of forty."

30 Then he said, "Let not the Lord be angry, and I will speak: Suppose thirty should be found there?"

So He said, "I will not do *it* if I find thirty there."

31 And he said, "Indeed now, I have taken it upon myself to speak to the Lord: Suppose twenty should be found there?"

So He said, "I will not destroy *it* for the sake of twenty."

32 Then he said, "Let not the Lord be angry, and I will speak but once more: Suppose ten should be found there?"

And He said, "I will not destroy *it* for the sake of ten." 33 So the LORD went His way as soon as He had finished speaking with Abraham; and Abraham returned to his place.

19 Now the two angels came to Sodom in the evening, and Lot was sitting in the gate of Sodom. When Lot saw *them,* he rose to meet them, and he bowed himself with his face toward the ground. 2 And he said, "Here now, my lords, please turn in to your servant's house and spend the night, and wash your feet; then you may rise early and go on your way."

And they said, "No, but we will spend the night in the open square."

3 But he insisted strongly; so they turned in to him and entered his house. Then he made them a feast, and baked unleavened bread, and they ate.

4 Now before they lay down, the men of the city, the men of Sodom, both old and young, all the people from every quarter, surrounded the house. 5 And they called to Lot and said to him, "Where are the men who came to you tonight? Bring them out to us that we may know them *carnally.*"

כְּרָשָׁע חָלִלָה לָּךְ הַשֹּׁפֵט כָּל־הָאָרֶץ לֹא יַעֲשֶׂה מִשְׁפָּט: 26 וַיֹּאמֶר יְהֹוָה אִם־אֶמְצָא בִסְדֹם חֲמִשִּׁים צַדִּיקִם בְּתוֹךְ הָעִיר וְנָשָׂאתִי לְכָל־הַמָּקוֹם בַּעֲבוּרָם: 27 וַיַּעַן אַבְרָהָם וַיֹּאמַר הִנֵּה־נָא הוֹאַלְתִּי לְדַבֵּר אֶל־אֲדֹנָי וְאָנֹכִי עָפָר וָאֵפֶר: 28 אוּלַי יַחְסְרוּן חֲמִשִּׁים הַצַּדִּיקִם חֲמִשָּׁה הֲתַשְׁחִית בַּחֲמִשָּׁה אֶת־כָּל־הָעִיר וַיֹּאמֶר לֹא אַשְׁחִית אִם־אֶמְצָא שָׁם אַרְבָּעִים וַחֲמִשָּׁה: 29 וַיֹּסֶף עוֹד לְדַבֵּר אֵלָיו וַיֹּאמַר אוּלַי יִמָּצְאוּן שָׁם אַרְבָּעִים וַיֹּאמֶר לֹא אֶעֱשֶׂה בַּעֲבוּר הָאַרְבָּעִים: 30 וַיֹּאמֶר אַל־נָא יִחַר לַאדֹנָי וַאֲדַבֵּרָה אוּלַי יִמָּצְאוּן שָׁם שְׁלֹשִׁים וַיֹּאמֶר לֹא אֶעֱשֶׂה אִם־אֶמְצָא שָׁם שְׁלֹשִׁים: 31 וַיֹּאמֶר הִנֵּה־נָא הוֹאַלְתִּי לְדַבֵּר אֶל־אֲדֹנָי אוּלַי יִמָּצְאוּן שָׁם עֶשְׂרִים וַיֹּאמֶר לֹא אַשְׁחִית בַּעֲבוּר הָעֶשְׂרִים: 32 וַיֹּאמֶר אַל־נָא יִחַר לַאדֹנָי וַאֲדַבְּרָה אַךְ־הַפַּעַם אוּלַי יִמָּצְאוּן שָׁם עֲשָׂרָה וַיֹּאמֶר לֹא אַשְׁחִית בַּעֲבוּר הָעֲשָׂרָה: 33 וַיֵּלֶךְ יְהֹוָה כַּאֲשֶׁר כִּלָּה לְדַבֵּר אֶל־אַבְרָהָם וְאַבְרָהָם שָׁב לִמְקֹמוֹ:

יט וַיָּבֹאוּ שְׁנֵי הַמַּלְאָכִים סְדֹמָה בָּעֶרֶב וְלוֹט יֹשֵׁב בְּשַׁעַר־סְדֹם וַיַּרְא־לוֹט וַיָּקָם לִקְרָאתָם וַיִּשְׁתַּחוּ אַפַּיִם אָרְצָה: 2 וַיֹּאמֶר הִנֶּה נָּא־אֲדֹנַי סוּרוּ נָא אֶל־בֵּית עַבְדְּכֶם וְלִינוּ וְרַחֲצוּ רַגְלֵיכֶם וְהִשְׁכַּמְתֶּם וַהֲלַכְתֶּם לְדַרְכְּכֶם וַיֹּאמְרוּ לֹּא כִּי בָרְחוֹב נָלִין: 3 וַיִּפְצַר־בָּם מְאֹד וַיָּסֻרוּ אֵלָיו וַיָּבֹאוּ אֶל־בֵּיתוֹ וַיַּעַשׂ לָהֶם מִשְׁתֶּה וּמַצּוֹת אָפָה וַיֹּאכֵלוּ: 4 טֶרֶם יִשְׁכָּבוּ וְאַנְשֵׁי הָעִיר אַנְשֵׁי סְדֹם נָסַבּוּ עַל־הַבַּיִת מִנַּעַר וְעַד־זָקֵן כָּל־הָעָם מִקָּצֶה: 5 וַיִּקְרְאוּ אֶל־לוֹט וַיֹּאמְרוּ לוֹ אַיֵּה הָאֲנָשִׁים אֲשֶׁר־בָּאוּ אֵלֶיךָ

6 So Lot went out to them through the doorway, shut the door behind him, 7 and said, "Please, my brethren, do not do so wickedly! 8 See now, I have two daughters who have not known a man; please, let me bring them out to you, and you may do to them as you wish; only do nothing to these men, since this is the reason they have come under the shadow of my roof."

9 And they said, "Stand back!" Then they said, "This one came in to stay *here*, and he keeps acting as a judge; now we will deal worse with you than with them." So they pressed hard against the man Lot, and came near to break down the door. 10 But the men reached out their hands and pulled Lot into the house with them, and shut the door. 11 And they struck the men who *were* at the doorway of the house with blindness, both small and great, so that they became weary *trying* to find the door.

12 Then the men said to Lot, "Have you anyone else here? Son-in-law, your sons, your daughters, and whomever you have in the city—take *them* out of this place! 13 For we will destroy this place, because the outcry against them has grown great before the face of the LORD, and the LORD has sent us to destroy it."

14 So Lot went out and spoke to his sons-in-law, who had married his daughters, and said, "Get up, get out of this place; for the LORD will destroy this city!" But to his sons-in-law he seemed to be joking.

15 When the morning dawned, the angels urged Lot to hurry, saying, "Arise, take your wife and your two daughters who are here, lest you be consumed in the punishment of the city." 16 And while he lingered, the men took hold of his hand, his wife's hand, and the hands of his two daughters, the LORD being merciful to him, and they brought him out and set him outside the city. 17 So it came to pass, when they had brought them outside, that they said, "Escape for your life! Do not look behind you nor stay anywhere in the plain. Escape to the mountains, lest you be destroyed."

18 Then Lot said to them, "Please, no, my lords! 19 Indeed now, your servant has found favor in your sight, and you have increased your mercy which you have shown me by saving my life; but I cannot escape to the mountains, lest some evil overtake me and I die. 20 See now, this city *is* near *enough* to flee to, and it *is* a little one; please let me escape there (*is* it not a little one?) and my soul shall live."

21 And he said to him, "See, I have favored you concerning this thing also, in that I will not overthrow this city for which you have spoken. 22 Hurry, escape there. For I cannot do anything until you arrive there."

הַלַּיְלָה הוֹצִיאֵם אֵלֵינוּ וְנֵדְעָה אֹתָם: 6 וַיֵּצֵא אֲלֵהֶם
לוֹט הַפֶּתְחָה וְהַדֶּלֶת סָגַר אַחֲרָיו: 7 וַיֹּאמַר אַל־
נָא אַחַי תָּרֵעוּ: 8 הִנֵּה־נָא לִי שְׁתֵּי בָנוֹת אֲשֶׁר
לֹא־יָדְעוּ אִישׁ אוֹצִיאָה־נָּא אֶתְהֶן אֲלֵיכֶם וַעֲשׂוּ
לָהֶן כַּטּוֹב בְּעֵינֵיכֶם רַק לָאֲנָשִׁים הָאֵל אַל־תַּעֲשׂוּ
דָבָר כִּי־עַל־כֵּן בָּאוּ בְּצֵל קֹרָתִי: 9 וַיֹּאמְרוּ ׀ גֶּשׁ־
הָלְאָה וַיֹּאמְרוּ הָאֶחָד בָּא־לָגוּר וַיִּשְׁפֹּט שָׁפוֹט
עַתָּה נָרַע לְךָ מֵהֶם וַיִּפְצְרוּ בָאִישׁ בְּלוֹט מְאֹד
וַיִּגְּשׁוּ לִשְׁבֹּר הַדָּלֶת: 10 וַיִּשְׁלְחוּ הָאֲנָשִׁים אֶת־
יָדָם וַיָּבִיאוּ אֶת־לוֹט אֲלֵיהֶם הַבָּיְתָה וְאֶת־הַדֶּלֶת
סָגָרוּ: 11 וְאֶת־הָאֲנָשִׁים אֲשֶׁר־פֶּתַח הַבַּיִת הִכּוּ
בַּסַּנְוֵרִים מִקָּטֹן וְעַד־גָּדוֹל וַיִּלְאוּ לִמְצֹא הַפָּתַח:
12 וַיֹּאמְרוּ הָאֲנָשִׁים אֶל־לוֹט עֹד מִי־לְךָ פֹה חָתָן
וּבָנֶיךָ וּבְנֹתֶיךָ וְכֹל אֲשֶׁר־לְךָ בָּעִיר הוֹצֵא מִן־
הַמָּקוֹם: 13 כִּי־מַשְׁחִתִים אֲנַחְנוּ אֶת־הַמָּקוֹם הַזֶּה
כִּי־גָדְלָה צַעֲקָתָם אֶת־פְּנֵי יְהֹוָה וַיְשַׁלְּחֵנוּ יְהֹוָה
לְשַׁחֲתָהּ: 14 וַיֵּצֵא לוֹט וַיְדַבֵּר ׀ אֶל־חֲתָנָיו ׀
לֹקְחֵי בְנֹתָיו וַיֹּאמֶר קוּמוּ צְּאוּ מִן־הַמָּקוֹם הַזֶּה
כִּי־מַשְׁחִית יְהֹוָה אֶת־הָעִיר וַיְהִי כִמְצַחֵק בְּעֵינֵי
חֲתָנָיו: 15 וּכְמוֹ הַשַּׁחַר עָלָה וַיָּאִיצוּ הַמַּלְאָכִים
בְּלוֹט לֵאמֹר קוּם קַח אֶת־אִשְׁתְּךָ וְאֶת־שְׁתֵּי בְנֹתֶיךָ ׀
הַנִּמְצָאֹת פֶּן־תִּסָּפֶה בַּעֲוֹן הָעִיר: 16 וַיִּתְמַהְמָהּ ׀
וַיַּחֲזִיקוּ הָאֲנָשִׁים בְּיָדוֹ וּבְיַד־אִשְׁתּוֹ וּבְיַד שְׁתֵּי
בְנֹתָיו בְּחֶמְלַת יְהֹוָה עָלָיו וַיֹּצִאֻהוּ וַיַּנִּחֻהוּ מִחוּץ
לָעִיר: 17 וַיְהִי כְהוֹצִיאָם אֹתָם הַחוּצָה וַיֹּאמֶר
הִמָּלֵט עַל־נַפְשֶׁךָ אַל־תַּבִּיט אַחֲרֶיךָ וְאַל־תַּעֲמֹד
בְּכָל־הַכִּכָּר הָהָרָה הִמָּלֵט פֶּן־תִּסָּפֶה: 18 וַיֹּאמֶר
לוֹט אֲלֵהֶם אַל־נָא אֲדֹנָי: 19 הִנֵּה־נָא מָצָא עַבְדְּךָ
חֵן בְּעֵינֶיךָ וַתַּגְדֵּל חַסְדְּךָ אֲשֶׁר עָשִׂיתָ עִמָּדִי
לְהַחֲיוֹת אֶת־נַפְשִׁי וְאָנֹכִי לֹא אוּכַל לְהִמָּלֵט הָהָרָה
פֶּן־תִּדְבָּקַנִי הָרָעָה וָמַתִּי: 20 הִנֵּה־נָא הָעִיר הַזֹּאת
קְרֹבָה לָנוּס שָׁמָּה וְהִיא מִצְעָר אִמָּלְטָה נָּא שָׁמָּה
הֲלֹא מִצְעָר הִוא וּתְחִי נַפְשִׁי: 21 וַיֹּאמֶר אֵלָיו
הִנֵּה נָשָׂאתִי פָנֶיךָ גַּם לַדָּבָר הַזֶּה לְבִלְתִּי הָפְכִּי
אֶת־הָעִיר אֲשֶׁר דִּבַּרְתָּ: 22 מַהֵר הִמָּלֵט שָׁמָּה
כִּי לֹא אוּכַל לַעֲשׂוֹת דָּבָר עַד־בֹּאֲךָ שָׁמָּה עַל־

Therefore the name of the city was called Zoar.

²³ The sun had risen upon the earth when Lot entered Zoar. ²⁴ Then the LORD rained brimstone and fire on Sodom and Gomorrah, from the LORD out of the heavens. ²⁵ So He overthrew those cities, all the plain, all the inhabitants of the cities, and what grew on the ground.

²⁶ But his wife looked back behind him, and she became a pillar of salt.

²⁷ And Abraham went early in the morning to the place where he had stood before the LORD. ²⁸ Then he looked toward Sodom and Gomorrah, and toward all the land of the plain; and he saw, and behold, the smoke of the land which went up like the smoke of a furnace. ²⁹ And it came to pass, when God destroyed the cities of the plain, that God remembered Abraham, and sent Lot out of the midst of the overthrow, when He overthrew the cities in which Lot had dwelt.

³⁰ Then Lot went up out of Zoar and dwelt in the mountains, and his two daughters were with him; for he was afraid to dwell in Zoar. And he and his two daughters dwelt in a cave. ³¹ Now the firstborn said to the younger, "Our father *is* old, and *there is* no man on the earth to come in to us as is the custom of all the earth. ³² Come, let us make our father drink wine, and we will lie with him, that we may preserve the lineage of our father." ³³ So they made their father drink wine that night. And the firstborn went in and lay with her father, and he did not know when she lay down or when she arose.

³⁴ It happened on the next day that the firstborn said to the younger, "Indeed I lay with my father last night; let us make him drink wine tonight also, and you go in *and* lie with him, that we may preserve the lineage of our father." ³⁵ Then they made their father drink wine that night also. And the younger arose and lay with him, and he did not know when she lay down or when she arose.

³⁶ Thus both the daughters of Lot were with child by their father. ³⁷ The firstborn bore a son and called his name Moab; he *is* the father of the Moabites to this day. ³⁸ And the younger, she also bore a son and called his name Ben-Ammi; he *is* the father of the people of Ammon to this day.

20 And Abraham journeyed from there to the South, and dwelt between Kadesh and Shur, and stayed in Gerar. ² Now Abraham said of Sarah his wife, "She *is* my sister." And Abimelech king of Gerar sent and took Sarah.

בֵּן קָרָא שֵׁם־הָעִיר צוֹעַר: ²³ הַשֶּׁמֶשׁ יָצָא עַל־
הָאָרֶץ וְלוֹט בָּא צֹעֲרָה: ²⁴ וַיהוָה הִמְטִיר עַל־סְדֹם
וְעַל־עֲמֹרָה גָּפְרִית וָאֵשׁ מֵאֵת יְהוָה מִן־הַשָּׁמָיִם:
²⁵ וַיַּהֲפֹךְ אֶת־הֶעָרִים הָאֵל וְאֵת כָּל־הַכִּכָּר וְאֵת
כָּל־יֹשְׁבֵי הֶעָרִים וְצֶמַח הָאֲדָמָה: ²⁶ וַתַּבֵּט אִשְׁתּוֹ
מֵאַחֲרָיו וַתְּהִי נְצִיב מֶלַח: ²⁷ וַיַּשְׁכֵּם אַבְרָהָם
בַּבֹּקֶר אֶל־הַמָּקוֹם אֲשֶׁר־עָמַד שָׁם אֶת־פְּנֵי יְהוָה:
²⁸ וַיַּשְׁקֵף עַל־פְּנֵי סְדֹם וַעֲמֹרָה וְעַל־כָּל־פְּנֵי אֶרֶץ
הַכִּכָּר וַיַּרְא וְהִנֵּה עָלָה קִיטֹר הָאָרֶץ כְּקִיטֹר
הַכִּבְשָׁן: ²⁹ וַיְהִי בְּשַׁחֵת אֱלֹהִים אֶת־עָרֵי הַכִּכָּר
וַיִּזְכֹּר אֱלֹהִים אֶת־אַבְרָהָם וַיְשַׁלַּח אֶת־לוֹט מִתּוֹךְ
הַהֲפֵכָה בַּהֲפֹךְ אֶת־הֶעָרִים אֲשֶׁר־יָשַׁב בָּהֵן לוֹט:

³⁰ וַיַּעַל לוֹט מִצּוֹעַר וַיֵּשֶׁב בָּהָר וּשְׁתֵּי בְנֹתָיו עִמּוֹ
כִּי יָרֵא לָשֶׁבֶת בְּצוֹעַר וַיֵּשֶׁב בַּמְּעָרָה הוּא וּשְׁתֵּי
בְנֹתָיו: ³¹ וַתֹּאמֶר הַבְּכִירָה אֶל־הַצְּעִירָה אָבִינוּ
זָקֵן וְאִישׁ אֵין בָּאָרֶץ לָבוֹא עָלֵינוּ כְּדֶרֶךְ כָּל־
הָאָרֶץ: ³² לְכָה נַשְׁקֶה אֶת־אָבִינוּ יַיִן וְנִשְׁכְּבָה
עִמּוֹ וּנְחַיֶּה מֵאָבִינוּ זָרַע: ³³ וַתַּשְׁקֶיןָ אֶת־אֲבִיהֶן
יַיִן בַּלַּיְלָה הוּא וַתָּבֹא הַבְּכִירָה וַתִּשְׁכַּב אֶת־
אָבִיהָ וְלֹא־יָדַע בְּשִׁכְבָהּ וּבְקוּמָהּ: ³⁴ וַיְהִי מִמָּחֳרָת
וַתֹּאמֶר הַבְּכִירָה אֶל־הַצְּעִירָה הֵן־שָׁכַבְתִּי אֶמֶשׁ
אֶת־אָבִי נַשְׁקֶנּוּ יַיִן גַּם־הַלַּיְלָה וּבֹאִי שִׁכְבִי עִמּוֹ
וּנְחַיֶּה מֵאָבִינוּ זָרַע: ³⁵ וַתַּשְׁקֶיןָ גַּם בַּלַּיְלָה הַהוּא
אֶת־אֲבִיהֶן יָיִן וַתָּקָם הַצְּעִירָה וַתִּשְׁכַּב עִמּוֹ וְלֹא־
יָדַע בְּשִׁכְבָהּ וּבְקֻמָהּ: ³⁶ וַתַּהֲרֶיןָ שְׁתֵּי בְנוֹת־לוֹט
מֵאֲבִיהֶן: ³⁷ וַתֵּלֶד הַבְּכִירָה בֵּן וַתִּקְרָא שְׁמוֹ מוֹאָב
הוּא אֲבִי־מוֹאָב עַד־הַיּוֹם: ³⁸ וְהַצְּעִירָה גַם־הִוא
יָלְדָה בֵּן וַתִּקְרָא שְׁמוֹ בֶּן־עַמִּי הוּא אֲבִי בְנֵי־עַמּוֹן
עַד־הַיּוֹם: ס

כ וַיִּסַּע מִשָּׁם אַבְרָהָם אַרְצָה הַנֶּגֶב וַיֵּשֶׁב בֵּין־קָדֵשׁ
וּבֵין שׁוּר וַיָּגָר בִּגְרָר: ² וַיֹּאמֶר אַבְרָהָם אֶל־שָׂרָה
אִשְׁתּוֹ אֲחֹתִי הִוא וַיִּשְׁלַח אֲבִימֶלֶךְ מֶלֶךְ גְּרָר וַיִּקַּח

³ But God came to Abimelech in a dream by night, and said to him, "Indeed you *are* a dead man because of the woman whom you have taken, for she *is* a man's wife."

⁴ But Abimelech had not come near her; and he said, "Lord, will You slay a righteous nation also? ⁵ Did he not say to me, 'She *is* my sister'? And she, even she herself said, 'He *is* my brother.' In the integrity of my heart and innocence of my hands I have done this."

⁶ And God said to him in a dream, "Yes, I know that you did this in the integrity of your heart. For I also withheld you from sinning against Me; therefore I did not let you touch her. ⁷ Now therefore, restore the man's wife; for he *is* a prophet, and he will pray for you and you shall live. But if you do not restore *her*, know that you shall surely die, you and all who *are* yours."

⁸ So Abimelech rose early in the morning, called all his servants, and told all these things in their hearing; and the men were very much afraid. ⁹ And Abimelech called Abraham and said to him, "What have you done to us? How have I offended you, that you have brought on me and on my kingdom a great sin? You have done deeds to me that ought not to be done." ¹⁰ Then Abimelech said to Abraham, "What did you have in view, that you have done this thing?"

¹¹ And Abraham said, "Because I thought, surely the fear of God *is* not in this place; and they will kill me on account of my wife. ¹² But indeed *she is* truly my sister. She *is* the daughter of my father, but not the daughter of my mother; and she became my wife. ¹³ And it came to pass, when God caused me to wander from my father's house, that I said to her, 'This *is* your kindness that you should do for me: in every place, wherever we go, say of me, "He *is* my brother."'"

¹⁴ Then Abimelech took sheep, oxen, and male and female servants, and gave *them* to Abraham; and he restored Sarah his wife to him. ¹⁵ And Abimelech said, "See, my land *is* before you; dwell where it pleases you." ¹⁶ Then to Sarah he said, "Behold, I have given your brother a thousand *pieces* of silver; indeed this vindicates you before all who *are* with you and before everybody." Thus she was rebuked.

¹⁷ So Abraham prayed to God; and God healed Abimelech, his wife, and his female servants. Then they bore *children;* ¹⁸ for the LORD had closed up all the wombs of the house of Abimelech because of Sarah, Abraham's wife.

אֶת־שָׂרָה: 3 וַיָּבֹא אֱלֹהִים אֶל־אֲבִימֶלֶךְ בַּחֲלוֹם הַלָּיְלָה וַיֹּאמֶר לוֹ הִנְּךָ מֵת עַל־הָאִשָּׁה אֲשֶׁר־לָקַחְתָּ וְהִוא בְּעֻלַת בָּעַל: 4 וַאֲבִימֶלֶךְ לֹא קָרַב אֵלֶיהָ וַיֹּאמַר אֲדֹנָי הֲגוֹי גַּם־צַדִּיק תַּהֲרֹג: 5 הֲלֹא הוּא אָמַר־לִי אֲחֹתִי הִוא וְהִיא־גַם־הִוא אָמְרָה אָחִי הוּא בְּתָם־לְבָבִי וּבְנִקְיֹן כַּפַּי עָשִׂיתִי זֹאת: 6 וַיֹּאמֶר אֵלָיו הָאֱלֹהִים בַּחֲלֹם גַּם אָנֹכִי יָדַעְתִּי כִּי בְתָם־לְבָבְךָ עָשִׂיתָ זֹּאת וָאֶחְשֹׂךְ גַּם־אָנֹכִי אוֹתְךָ מֵחֲטוֹ־לִי עַל־כֵּן לֹא־נְתַתִּיךָ לִנְגֹּעַ אֵלֶיהָ: 7 וְעַתָּה הָשֵׁב אֵשֶׁת־הָאִישׁ כִּי־נָבִיא הוּא וְיִתְפַּלֵּל בַּעַדְךָ וֶחְיֵה וְאִם־אֵינְךָ מֵשִׁיב דַּע כִּי־מוֹת תָּמוּת אַתָּה וְכָל־אֲשֶׁר־לָךְ: 8 וַיַּשְׁכֵּם אֲבִימֶלֶךְ בַּבֹּקֶר וַיִּקְרָא לְכָל־עֲבָדָיו וַיְדַבֵּר אֶת־כָּל־הַדְּבָרִים הָאֵלֶּה בְּאָזְנֵיהֶם וַיִּירְאוּ הָאֲנָשִׁים מְאֹד: 9 וַיִּקְרָא אֲבִימֶלֶךְ לְאַבְרָהָם וַיֹּאמֶר לוֹ מֶה־עָשִׂיתָ לָּנוּ וּמֶה־חָטָאתִי לָךְ כִּי־הֵבֵאתָ עָלַי וְעַל־מַמְלַכְתִּי חֲטָאָה גְדֹלָה מַעֲשִׂים אֲשֶׁר לֹא־יֵעָשׂוּ עָשִׂיתָ עִמָּדִי: 10 וַיֹּאמֶר אֲבִימֶלֶךְ אֶל־אַבְרָהָם מָה רָאִיתָ כִּי עָשִׂיתָ אֶת־הַדָּבָר הַזֶּה: 11 וַיֹּאמֶר אַבְרָהָם כִּי אָמַרְתִּי רַק אֵין־יִרְאַת אֱלֹהִים בַּמָּקוֹם הַזֶּה וַהֲרָגוּנִי עַל־דְּבַר אִשְׁתִּי: 12 וְגַם־אָמְנָה אֲחֹתִי בַת־אָבִי הִוא אַךְ לֹא בַת־אִמִּי וַתְּהִי־לִי לְאִשָּׁה: 13 וַיְהִי כַּאֲשֶׁר הִתְעוּ אֹתִי אֱלֹהִים מִבֵּית אָבִי וָאֹמַר לָהּ זֶה חַסְדֵּךְ אֲשֶׁר תַּעֲשִׂי עִמָּדִי אֶל כָּל־הַמָּקוֹם אֲשֶׁר נָבוֹא שָׁמָּה אִמְרִי־לִי אָחִי הוּא: 14 וַיִּקַּח אֲבִימֶלֶךְ צֹאן וּבָקָר וַעֲבָדִים וּשְׁפָחֹת וַיִּתֵּן לְאַבְרָהָם וַיָּשֶׁב לוֹ אֵת שָׂרָה אִשְׁתּוֹ: 15 וַיֹּאמֶר אֲבִימֶלֶךְ הִנֵּה אַרְצִי לְפָנֶיךָ בַּטּוֹב בְּעֵינֶיךָ שֵׁב: 16 וּלְשָׂרָה אָמַר הִנֵּה נָתַתִּי אֶלֶף כֶּסֶף לְאָחִיךְ הִנֵּה הוּא־לָךְ כְּסוּת עֵינַיִם לְכֹל אֲשֶׁר אִתָּךְ וְאֵת כֹּל וְנֹכָחַת: 17 וַיִּתְפַּלֵּל אַבְרָהָם אֶל־הָאֱלֹהִים וַיִּרְפָּא אֱלֹהִים אֶת־אֲבִימֶלֶךְ וְאֶת־אִשְׁתּוֹ וְאַמְהֹתָיו וַיֵּלֵדוּ: 18 כִּי־עָצֹר עָצַר יְהֹוָה בְּעַד כָּל־רֶחֶם לְבֵית אֲבִימֶלֶךְ עַל־דְּבַר שָׂרָה אֵשֶׁת אַבְרָהָם: ס

21 And the LORD visited Sarah as He had said, and the LORD did for Sarah as He had spoken. ²For Sarah conceived and bore Abraham a son in his old age, at the set time of which God had spoken to him. ³And Abraham called the name of his son who was born to him—whom Sarah bore to him—Isaac. ⁴Then Abraham circumcised his son Isaac when he was eight days old, as God had commanded him. ⁵Now Abraham was one hundred years old when his son Isaac was born to him. ⁶And Sarah said, "God has made me laugh, *and* all who hear will laugh with me." ⁷She also said, "Who would have said to Abraham that Sarah would nurse children? For I have borne *him* a son in his old age."

⁸So the child grew and was weaned. And Abraham made a great feast on the same day that Isaac was weaned.

⁹And Sarah saw the son of Hagar the Egyptian, whom she had borne to Abraham, scoffing. ¹⁰Therefore she said to Abraham, "Cast out this bondwoman and her son; for the son of this bondwoman shall not be heir with my son, *namely* with Isaac." ¹¹And the matter was very displeasing in Abraham's sight because of his son.

¹²But God said to Abraham, "Do not let it be displeasing in your sight because of the lad or because of your bondwoman. Whatever Sarah has said to you, listen to her voice; for in Isaac your seed shall be called. ¹³Yet I will also make a nation of the son of the bondwoman, because he *is* your seed."

¹⁴So Abraham rose early in the morning, and took bread and a skin of water; and putting *it* on her shoulder, he gave *it* and the boy to Hagar, and sent her away. Then she departed and wandered in the Wilderness of Beersheba. ¹⁵And the water in the skin was used up, and she placed the boy under one of the shrubs. ¹⁶Then she went and sat down across from *him* at a distance of about a bowshot; for she said to herself, "Let me not see the death of the boy." So she sat opposite *him,* and lifted her voice and wept.

¹⁷And God heard the voice of the lad. Then the angel of God called to Hagar out of heaven, and said to her, "What ails you, Hagar? Fear not, for God has heard the voice of the lad where he *is.* ¹⁸Arise, lift up the lad and hold him with your hand, for I will make him a great nation."

¹⁹Then God opened her eyes, and she saw a well of water. And she went and filled the skin with water, and gave the lad a drink. ²⁰So God was with the lad; and he grew and dwelt in the wilderness,

כא וַיהוָה פָּקַד אֶת־שָׂרָה כַּאֲשֶׁר אָמָר וַיַּעַשׂ יְהוָה לְשָׂרָה כַּאֲשֶׁר דִּבֵּר: 2 וַתַּהַר וַתֵּלֶד שָׂרָה לְאַבְרָהָם בֵּן לִזְקֻנָיו לַמּוֹעֵד אֲשֶׁר־דִּבֶּר אֹתוֹ אֱלֹהִים: 3 וַיִּקְרָא אַבְרָהָם אֶת־שֶׁם־בְּנוֹ הַנּוֹלַד־לוֹ אֲשֶׁר־יָלְדָה־לּוֹ שָׂרָה יִצְחָק: 4 וַיָּמָל אַבְרָהָם אֶת־יִצְחָק בְּנוֹ בֶּן־שְׁמֹנַת יָמִים כַּאֲשֶׁר צִוָּה אֹתוֹ אֱלֹהִים: 5 וְאַבְרָהָם בֶּן־מְאַת שָׁנָה בְּהִוָּלֶד לוֹ אֵת יִצְחָק בְּנוֹ: 6 וַתֹּאמֶר שָׂרָה צְחֹק עָשָׂה לִי אֱלֹהִים כָּל־הַשֹּׁמֵעַ יִצְחַק־לִי: 7 וַתֹּאמֶר מִי מִלֵּל לְאַבְרָהָם הֵינִיקָה בָנִים שָׂרָה כִּי־יָלַדְתִּי בֵן לִזְקֻנָיו: 8 וַיִּגְדַּל הַיֶּלֶד וַיִּגָּמַל וַיַּעַשׂ אַבְרָהָם מִשְׁתֶּה גָדוֹל בְּיוֹם הִגָּמֵל אֶת־יִצְחָק:

9 וַתֵּרֶא שָׂרָה אֶת־בֶּן־הָגָר הַמִּצְרִית אֲשֶׁר־יָלְדָה לְאַבְרָהָם מְצַחֵק: 10 וַתֹּאמֶר לְאַבְרָהָם גָּרֵשׁ הָאָמָה הַזֹּאת וְאֶת־בְּנָהּ כִּי לֹא יִירַשׁ בֶּן־הָאָמָה הַזֹּאת עִם־בְּנִי עִם־יִצְחָק: 11 וַיֵּרַע הַדָּבָר מְאֹד בְּעֵינֵי אַבְרָהָם עַל אוֹדֹת בְּנוֹ: 12 וַיֹּאמֶר אֱלֹהִים אֶל־אַבְרָהָם אַל־יֵרַע בְּעֵינֶיךָ עַל־הַנַּעַר וְעַל־אֲמָתֶךָ כֹּל אֲשֶׁר תֹּאמַר אֵלֶיךָ שָׂרָה שְׁמַע בְּקֹלָהּ כִּי בְיִצְחָק יִקָּרֵא לְךָ זָרַע: 13 וְגַם אֶת־בֶּן־הָאָמָה לְגוֹי אֲשִׂימֶנּוּ כִּי זַרְעֲךָ הוּא:

14 וַיַּשְׁכֵּם אַבְרָהָם בַּבֹּקֶר וַיִּקַּח־לֶחֶם וְחֵמַת מַיִם וַיִּתֵּן אֶל־הָגָר שָׂם עַל־שִׁכְמָהּ וְאֶת־הַיֶּלֶד וַיְשַׁלְּחֶהָ וַתֵּלֶךְ וַתֵּתַע בְּמִדְבַּר בְּאֵר שָׁבַע: 15 וַיִּכְלוּ הַמַּיִם מִן־הַחֵמֶת וַתַּשְׁלֵךְ אֶת־הַיֶּלֶד תַּחַת אַחַד הַשִּׂיחִם: 16 וַתֵּלֶךְ וַתֵּשֶׁב לָהּ מִנֶּגֶד הַרְחֵק כִּמְטַחֲוֵי קֶשֶׁת כִּי אָמְרָה אַל־אֶרְאֶה בְּמוֹת הַיָּלֶד וַתֵּשֶׁב מִנֶּגֶד וַתִּשָּׂא אֶת־קֹלָהּ וַתֵּבְךְּ: 17 וַיִּשְׁמַע אֱלֹהִים אֶת־קוֹל הַנַּעַר וַיִּקְרָא מַלְאַךְ אֱלֹהִים אֶל־הָגָר מִן־הַשָּׁמַיִם וַיֹּאמֶר לָהּ מַה־לָּךְ הָגָר אַל־תִּירְאִי כִּי־שָׁמַע אֱלֹהִים אֶל־קוֹל הַנַּעַר בַּאֲשֶׁר הוּא־שָׁם: 18 קוּמִי שְׂאִי אֶת־הַנַּעַר וְהַחֲזִיקִי אֶת־יָדֵךְ בּוֹ כִּי־לְגוֹי גָּדוֹל אֲשִׂימֶנּוּ: 19 וַיִּפְקַח אֱלֹהִים אֶת־עֵינֶיהָ וַתֵּרֶא בְּאֵר מָיִם וַתֵּלֶךְ וַתְּמַלֵּא אֶת־הַחֵמֶת מַיִם וַתַּשְׁקְ אֶת־הַנָּעַר: 20 וַיְהִי אֱלֹהִים אֶת־הַנַּעַר וַיִּגְדָּל

and became an archer. 21 He dwelt in the Wilderness of Paran; and his mother took a wife for him from the land of Egypt.

22 And it came to pass at that time that Abimelech and Phichol, the commander of his army, spoke to Abraham, saying, "God *is* with you in all that you do. 23 Now therefore, swear to me by God that you will not deal falsely with me, with my offspring, or with my posterity; but that according to the kindness that I have done to you, you will do to me and to the land in which you have dwelt."

24 And Abraham said, "I will swear."

25 Then Abraham rebuked Abimelech because of a well of water which Abimelech's servants had seized. 26 And Abimelech said, "I do not know who has done this thing; you did not tell me, nor had I heard *of it* until today." 27 So Abraham took sheep and oxen and gave them to Abimelech, and the two of them made a covenant. 28 And Abraham set seven ewe lambs of the flock by themselves.

29 Then Abimelech asked Abraham, "What *is the meaning of* these seven ewe lambs which you have set by themselves?"

30 And he said, "You will take *these* seven ewe lambs from my hand, that they may be my witness that I have dug this well." 31 Therefore he called that place Beersheba, because the two of them swore an oath there.

32 Thus they made a covenant at Beersheba. So Abimelech rose with Phichol, the commander of his army, and they returned to the land of the Philistines. 33 Then *Abraham* planted a tamarisk tree in Beersheba, and there called on the name of the LORD, the Everlasting God. 34 And Abraham stayed in the land of the Philistines many days.

22 Now it came to pass after these things that God tested Abraham, and said to him, "Abraham!"

And he said, "Here I am."

2 Then He said, "Take now your son, your only *son* Isaac, whom you love, and go to the land of Moriah, and offer him there as a burnt offering on one of the mountains of which I shall tell you."

3 So Abraham rose early in the morning and saddled his donkey, and took two of his young men with him, and Isaac his son; and he split the wood for the burnt offering, and arose and went to the place of which God had told him. 4 Then on the third day Abraham lifted his eyes and saw the place afar off. 5 And Abraham said to his young men, "Stay here with the donkey; the lad and I will go yonder and worship, and we will come back to you."

21 וַיֵּשֶׁב בַּמִּדְבָּר וַיְהִי רֹבֶה קַשָּׁת: וַיֵּשֶׁב בְּמִדְבַּר פָּארָן וַתִּקַּח־לוֹ אִמּוֹ אִשָּׁה מֵאֶרֶץ מִצְרָיִם: פ

22 וַיְהִי בָּעֵת הַהִוא וַיֹּאמֶר אֲבִימֶלֶךְ וּפִיכֹל שַׂר־צְבָאוֹ אֶל־אַבְרָהָם לֵאמֹר אֱלֹהִים עִמְּךָ בְּכֹל אֲשֶׁר־אַתָּה עֹשֶׂה: 23 וְעַתָּה הִשָּׁבְעָה לִּי בֵאלֹהִים הֵנָּה אִם־תִּשְׁקֹר לִי וּלְנִינִי וּלְנֶכְדִּי כַּחֶסֶד אֲשֶׁר־עָשִׂיתִי עִמְּךָ תַּעֲשֶׂה עִמָּדִי וְעִם־הָאָרֶץ אֲשֶׁר־גַּרְתָּה בָּהּ: 24 וַיֹּאמֶר אַבְרָהָם אָנֹכִי אִשָּׁבֵעַ: 25 וְהוֹכִחַ אַבְרָהָם אֶת־אֲבִימֶלֶךְ עַל־אֹדוֹת בְּאֵר הַמַּיִם אֲשֶׁר גָּזְלוּ עַבְדֵי אֲבִימֶלֶךְ: 26 וַיֹּאמֶר אֲבִימֶלֶךְ לֹא יָדַעְתִּי מִי עָשָׂה אֶת־הַדָּבָר הַזֶּה וְגַם־אַתָּה לֹא־הִגַּדְתָּ לִּי וְגַם אָנֹכִי לֹא שָׁמַעְתִּי בִּלְתִּי הַיּוֹם: 27 וַיִּקַּח אַבְרָהָם צֹאן וּבָקָר וַיִּתֵּן לַאֲבִימֶלֶךְ וַיִּכְרְתוּ שְׁנֵיהֶם בְּרִית: 28 וַיַּצֵּב אַבְרָהָם אֶת־שֶׁבַע כִּבְשֹׂת הַצֹּאן לְבַדְּהֶן: 29 וַיֹּאמֶר אֲבִימֶלֶךְ אֶל־אַבְרָהָם מָה הֵנָּה שֶׁבַע כְּבָשֹׂת הָאֵלֶּה אֲשֶׁר הִצַּבְתָּ לְבַדָּנָה: 30 וַיֹּאמֶר כִּי אֶת־שֶׁבַע כְּבָשֹׂת תִּקַּח מִיָּדִי בַּעֲבוּר תִּהְיֶה־לִּי לְעֵדָה כִּי חָפַרְתִּי אֶת־הַבְּאֵר הַזֹּאת: 31 עַל־כֵּן קָרָא לַמָּקוֹם הַהוּא בְּאֵר שָׁבַע כִּי שָׁם נִשְׁבְּעוּ שְׁנֵיהֶם: 32 וַיִּכְרְתוּ בְרִית בִּבְאֵר שָׁבַע וַיָּקָם אֲבִימֶלֶךְ וּפִיכֹל שַׂר־צְבָאוֹ וַיָּשֻׁבוּ אֶל־אֶרֶץ פְּלִשְׁתִּים: 33 וַיִּטַּע אֶשֶׁל בִּבְאֵר שָׁבַע וַיִּקְרָא־שָׁם בְּשֵׁם יְהוָה אֵל עוֹלָם: 34 וַיָּגָר אַבְרָהָם בְּאֶרֶץ פְּלִשְׁתִּים יָמִים רַבִּים: פ

כב וַיְהִי אַחַר הַדְּבָרִים הָאֵלֶּה וְהָאֱלֹהִים נִסָּה אֶת־אַבְרָהָם וַיֹּאמֶר אֵלָיו אַבְרָהָם וַיֹּאמֶר הִנֵּנִי: 2 וַיֹּאמֶר קַח־נָא אֶת־בִּנְךָ אֶת־יְחִידְךָ אֲשֶׁר־אָהַבְתָּ אֶת־יִצְחָק וְלֶךְ־לְךָ אֶל־אֶרֶץ הַמֹּרִיָּה וְהַעֲלֵהוּ שָׁם לְעֹלָה עַל אַחַד הֶהָרִים אֲשֶׁר אֹמַר אֵלֶיךָ: 3 וַיַּשְׁכֵּם אַבְרָהָם בַּבֹּקֶר וַיַּחֲבֹשׁ אֶת־חֲמֹרוֹ וַיִּקַּח אֶת־שְׁנֵי נְעָרָיו אִתּוֹ וְאֵת יִצְחָק בְּנוֹ וַיְבַקַּע עֲצֵי עֹלָה וַיָּקָם וַיֵּלֶךְ אֶל־הַמָּקוֹם אֲשֶׁר־אָמַר־לוֹ הָאֱלֹהִים: 4 בַּיּוֹם הַשְּׁלִישִׁי וַיִּשָּׂא אַבְרָהָם אֶת־עֵינָיו וַיַּרְא אֶת־הַמָּקוֹם מֵרָחֹק: 5 וַיֹּאמֶר אַבְרָהָם אֶל־נְעָרָיו שְׁבוּ־לָכֶם פֹּה עִם־הַחֲמוֹר וַאֲנִי וְהַנַּעַר נֵלְכָה עַד־כֹּה

⁶So Abraham took the wood of the burnt offering and laid *it* on Isaac his son; and he took the fire in his hand, and a knife, and the two of them went together. ⁷But Isaac spoke to Abraham his father and said, "My father!"

And he said, "Here I am, my son."

Then he said, "Look, the fire and the wood, but where *is* the lamb for a burnt offering?"

⁸And Abraham said, "My son, God will provide for Himself the lamb for a burnt offering." So the two of them went together.

⁹Then they came to the place of which God had told him. And Abraham built an altar there and placed the wood in order; and he bound Isaac his son and laid him on the altar, upon the wood. ¹⁰And Abraham stretched out his hand and took the knife to slay his son.

¹¹But the Angel of the LORD called to him from heaven and said, "Abraham, Abraham!"

So he said, "Here I am."

¹²And He said, "Do not lay your hand on the lad, or do anything to him; for now I know that you fear God, since you have not withheld your son, your only *son,* from Me."

¹³Then Abraham lifted his eyes and looked, and there behind *him was* a ram caught in a thicket by its horns. So Abraham went and took the ram, and offered it up for a burnt offering instead of his son. ¹⁴And Abraham called the name of the place, The-LORD-Will-Provide; as it is said *to* this day, "In the Mount of the LORD it shall be provided."

¹⁵Then the Angel of the LORD called to Abraham a second time out of heaven, ¹⁶and said: "By Myself I have sworn, says the LORD, because you have done this thing, and have not withheld your son, your only *son*— ¹⁷blessing I will bless you, and multiplying I will multiply your descendants as the stars of the heaven and as the sand which *is* on the seashore; and your descendants shall possess the gate of their enemies. ¹⁸In your seed all the nations of the earth shall be blessed, because you have obeyed My voice." ¹⁹So Abraham returned to his young men, and they rose and went together to Beersheba; and Abraham dwelt at Beersheba.

²⁰Now it came to pass after these things that it was told Abraham, saying, "Indeed Milcah also has borne children to your brother Nahor: ²¹Huz his firstborn, Buz his brother, Kemuel the father of Aram, ²²Chesed, Hazo, Pildash, Jidlaph, and Bethuel." ²³And Bethuel begot Rebekah. These eight Milcah bore to Nahor, Abraham's brother. ²⁴His concubine, whose name was Reumah, also bore Tebah, Gaham, Thahash, and Maachah.

וַיִּשְׁתַּחֲוּ וְנָשׁוּבָה אֲלֵיכֶם: 6 וַיִּקַּח אַבְרָהָם אֶת־עֲצֵי הָעֹלָה וַיָּשֶׂם עַל־יִצְחָק בְּנוֹ וַיִּקַּח בְּיָדוֹ אֶת־הָאֵשׁ וְאֶת־הַמַּאֲכֶלֶת וַיֵּלְכוּ שְׁנֵיהֶם יַחְדָּו: 7 וַיֹּאמֶר יִצְחָק אֶל־אַבְרָהָם אָבִיו וַיֹּאמֶר אָבִי וַיֹּאמֶר הִנֶּנִּי בְנִי וַיֹּאמֶר הִנֵּה הָאֵשׁ וְהָעֵצִים וְאַיֵּה הַשֶּׂה לְעֹלָה:

8 וַיֹּאמֶר אַבְרָהָם אֱלֹהִים יִרְאֶה־לּוֹ הַשֶּׂה לְעֹלָה בְּנִי וַיֵּלְכוּ שְׁנֵיהֶם יַחְדָּו: 9 וַיָּבֹאוּ אֶל־הַמָּקוֹם אֲשֶׁר אָמַר־לוֹ הָאֱלֹהִים וַיִּבֶן שָׁם אַבְרָהָם אֶת־הַמִּזְבֵּחַ וַיַּעֲרֹךְ אֶת־הָעֵצִים וַיַּעֲקֹד אֶת־יִצְחָק בְּנוֹ וַיָּשֶׂם אֹתוֹ עַל־הַמִּזְבֵּחַ מִמַּעַל לָעֵצִים: 10 וַיִּשְׁלַח אַבְרָהָם אֶת־יָדוֹ וַיִּקַּח אֶת־הַמַּאֲכֶלֶת לִשְׁחֹט אֶת־בְּנוֹ: 11 וַיִּקְרָא אֵלָיו מַלְאַךְ יְהוָה מִן־הַשָּׁמַיִם וַיֹּאמֶר אַבְרָהָם אַבְרָהָם וַיֹּאמֶר הִנֵּנִי: 12 וַיֹּאמֶר אַל־תִּשְׁלַח יָדְךָ אֶל־הַנַּעַר וְאַל־תַּעַשׂ לוֹ מְאוּמָה כִּי עַתָּה יָדַעְתִּי כִּי־יְרֵא אֱלֹהִים אַתָּה וְלֹא חָשַׂכְתָּ אֶת־בִּנְךָ אֶת־יְחִידְךָ מִמֶּנִּי: 13 וַיִּשָּׂא אַבְרָהָם אֶת־עֵינָיו וַיַּרְא וְהִנֵּה־אַיִל אַחַר נֶאֱחַז בַּסְּבַךְ בְּקַרְנָיו וַיֵּלֶךְ אַבְרָהָם וַיִּקַּח אֶת־הָאַיִל וַיַּעֲלֵהוּ לְעֹלָה תַּחַת בְּנוֹ: 14 וַיִּקְרָא אַבְרָהָם שֵׁם־הַמָּקוֹם הַהוּא יְהוָה יִרְאֶה אֲשֶׁר יֵאָמֵר הַיּוֹם בְּהַר יְהוָה יֵרָאֶה: 15 וַיִּקְרָא מַלְאַךְ יְהוָה אֶל־אַבְרָהָם שֵׁנִית מִן־הַשָּׁמָיִם: 16 וַיֹּאמֶר בִּי נִשְׁבַּעְתִּי נְאֻם־יְהוָה כִּי יַעַן אֲשֶׁר עָשִׂיתָ אֶת־הַדָּבָר הַזֶּה וְלֹא חָשַׂכְתָּ אֶת־בִּנְךָ אֶת־יְחִידֶךָ: 17 כִּי־בָרֵךְ אֲבָרֶכְךָ וְהַרְבָּה אַרְבֶּה אֶת־זַרְעֲךָ כְּכוֹכְבֵי הַשָּׁמַיִם וְכַחוֹל אֲשֶׁר עַל־שְׂפַת הַיָּם וְיִרַשׁ זַרְעֲךָ אֵת שַׁעַר אֹיְבָיו: 18 וְהִתְבָּרֲכוּ בְזַרְעֲךָ כֹּל גּוֹיֵי הָאָרֶץ עֵקֶב אֲשֶׁר שָׁמַעְתָּ בְּקֹלִי: 19 וַיָּשָׁב אַבְרָהָם אֶל־נְעָרָיו וַיָּקֻמוּ וַיֵּלְכוּ יַחְדָּו אֶל־בְּאֵר שָׁבַע וַיֵּשֶׁב אַבְרָהָם בִּבְאֵר שָׁבַע: פ

20 וַיְהִי אַחֲרֵי הַדְּבָרִים הָאֵלֶּה וַיֻּגַּד לְאַבְרָהָם לֵאמֹר הִנֵּה יָלְדָה מִלְכָּה גַם־הִוא בָּנִים לְנָחוֹר אָחִיךָ: 21 אֶת־עוּץ בְּכֹרוֹ וְאֶת־בּוּז אָחִיו וְאֶת־קְמוּאֵל אֲבִי אֲרָם: 22 וְאֶת־כֶּשֶׂד וְאֶת־חֲזוֹ וְאֶת־פִּלְדָּשׁ וְאֶת־יִדְלָף וְאֵת בְּתוּאֵל: 23 וּבְתוּאֵל יָלַד אֶת־רִבְקָה שְׁמֹנָה אֵלֶּה יָלְדָה מִלְכָּה לְנָחוֹר אֲחִי אַבְרָהָם: 24 וּפִילַגְשׁוֹ וּשְׁמָהּ רְאוּמָה וַתֵּלֶד גַּם־הִוא אֶת־טֶבַח וְאֶת־גַּחַם וְאֶת־תַּחַשׁ וְאֶת־מַעֲכָה: ס

23 Sarah lived one hundred and twenty-seven years; *these were* the years of the life of Sarah. ²So Sarah died in Kirjath Arba (that *is,* Hebron) in the land of Canaan, and Abraham came to mourn for Sarah and to weep for her.

³Then Abraham stood up from before his dead, and spoke to the sons of Heth, saying, ⁴"I *am* a foreigner and a visitor among you. Give me property for a burial place among you, that I may bury my dead out of my sight."

⁵And the sons of Heth answered Abraham, saying to him, ⁶"Hear us, my lord: You *are* a mighty prince among us; bury your dead in the choicest of our burial places. None of us will withhold from you his burial place, that you may bury your dead."

⁷Then Abraham stood up and bowed himself to the people of the land, the sons of Heth. ⁸And he spoke with them, saying, "If it is your wish that I bury my dead out of my sight, hear me, and meet with Ephron the son of Zohar for me, ⁹that he may give me the cave of Machpelah which he has, which *is* at the end of his field. Let him give it to me at the full price, as property for a burial place among you."

¹⁰Now Ephron dwelt among the sons of Heth; and Ephron the Hittite answered Abraham in the presence of the sons of Heth, all who entered at the gate of his city, saying, ¹¹"No, my lord, hear me: I give you the field and the cave that *is* in it; I give it to you in the presence of the sons of my people. I give it to you. Bury your dead!"

¹²Then Abraham bowed himself down before the people of the land; ¹³and he spoke to Ephron in the hearing of the people of the land, saying, "If you *will give it,* please hear me. I will give you money for the field; take *it* from me and I will bury my dead there."

¹⁴And Ephron answered Abraham, saying to him, ¹⁵"My lord, listen to me; the land *is worth* four hundred shekels of silver. What *is* that between you and me? So bury your dead." ¹⁶And Abraham listened to Ephron; and Abraham weighed out the silver for Ephron which he had named in the hearing of the sons of Heth, four hundred shekels of silver, currency of the merchants.

¹⁷So the field of Ephron which *was* in Machpelah, which *was* before Mamre, the field and the cave which *was* in it, and all the trees that *were* in the field, which *were* within all the surrounding borders, were deeded ¹⁸to Abraham as a possession in the presence of the sons of Heth, before all who went in at the gate of his city.

כג וַיִּהְיוּ חַיֵּי שָׂרָה מֵאָה שָׁנָה וְעֶשְׂרִים שָׁנָה
וְשֶׁבַע שָׁנִים שְׁנֵי חַיֵּי שָׂרָה: ² וַתָּמָת שָׂרָה בְּקִרְיַת
אַרְבַּע הִוא חֶבְרוֹן בְּאֶרֶץ כְּנָעַן וַיָּבֹא אַבְרָהָם
לִסְפֹּד לְשָׂרָה וְלִבְכֹּתָהּ: ³ וַיָּקָם אַבְרָהָם מֵעַל פְּנֵי
מֵתוֹ וַיְדַבֵּר אֶל־בְּנֵי־חֵת לֵאמֹר: ⁴ גֵּר־וְתוֹשָׁב אָנֹכִי
עִמָּכֶם תְּנוּ לִי אֲחֻזַּת־קֶבֶר עִמָּכֶם וְאֶקְבְּרָה מֵתִי
מִלְּפָנָי: ⁵ וַיַּעֲנוּ בְנֵי־חֵת אֶת־אַבְרָהָם לֵאמֹר לוֹ:
⁶ שְׁמָעֵנוּ | אֲדֹנִי נְשִׂיא אֱלֹהִים אַתָּה בְּתוֹכֵנוּ
בְּמִבְחַר קְבָרֵינוּ קְבֹר אֶת־מֵתֶךָ אִישׁ מִמֶּנּוּ אֶת־
קִבְרוֹ לֹא־יִכְלֶה מִמְּךָ מִקְּבֹר מֵתֶךָ: ⁷ וַיָּקָם אַבְרָהָם
וַיִּשְׁתַּחוּ לְעַם־הָאָרֶץ לִבְנֵי־חֵת: ⁸ וַיְדַבֵּר אִתָּם
לֵאמֹר אִם־יֵשׁ אֶת־נַפְשְׁכֶם לִקְבֹּר אֶת־מֵתִי מִלְּפָנַי
שְׁמָעוּנִי וּפִגְעוּ־לִי בְּעֶפְרוֹן בֶּן־צֹחַר: ⁹ וְיִתֶּן־לִי אֶת־
מְעָרַת הַמַּכְפֵּלָה אֲשֶׁר־לוֹ אֲשֶׁר בִּקְצֵה שָׂדֵהוּ
בְּכֶסֶף מָלֵא יִתְּנֶנָּה לִי בְּתוֹכְכֶם לַאֲחֻזַּת־קָבֶר:
¹⁰ וְעֶפְרוֹן יֹשֵׁב בְּתוֹךְ בְּנֵי־חֵת וַיַּעַן עֶפְרוֹן הַחִתִּי
אֶת־אַבְרָהָם בְּאָזְנֵי בְנֵי־חֵת לְכֹל בָּאֵי שַׁעַר־
עִירוֹ לֵאמֹר: ¹¹ לֹא־אֲדֹנִי שְׁמָעֵנִי הַשָּׂדֶה נָתַתִּי
לָךְ וְהַמְּעָרָה אֲשֶׁר־בּוֹ לְךָ נְתַתִּיהָ לְעֵינֵי בְנֵי־
עַמִּי נְתַתִּיהָ לָּךְ קְבֹר מֵתֶךָ: ¹² וַיִּשְׁתַּחוּ אַבְרָהָם
לִפְנֵי עַם־הָאָרֶץ: ¹³ וַיְדַבֵּר אֶל־עֶפְרוֹן בְּאָזְנֵי עַם־
הָאָרֶץ לֵאמֹר אַךְ אִם־אַתָּה לוּ שְׁמָעֵנִי נָתַתִּי כֶּסֶף
הַשָּׂדֶה קַח מִמֶּנִּי וְאֶקְבְּרָה אֶת־מֵתִי שָׁמָּה: ¹⁴ וַיַּעַן
עֶפְרוֹן אֶת־אַבְרָהָם לֵאמֹר לוֹ: ¹⁵ אֲדֹנִי שְׁמָעֵנִי
אֶרֶץ אַרְבַּע מֵאֹת שֶׁקֶל־כֶּסֶף בֵּינִי וּבֵינְךָ מַה־
הִוא וְאֶת־מֵתְךָ קְבֹר: ¹⁶ וַיִּשְׁמַע אַבְרָהָם אֶל־עֶפְרוֹן
וַיִּשְׁקֹל אַבְרָהָם לְעֶפְרֹן אֶת־הַכֶּסֶף אֲשֶׁר דִּבֶּר בְּאָזְנֵי
בְנֵי־חֵת אַרְבַּע מֵאוֹת שֶׁקֶל כֶּסֶף עֹבֵר לַסֹּחֵר:
¹⁷ וַיָּקָם | שְׂדֵה עֶפְרוֹן אֲשֶׁר בַּמַּכְפֵּלָה אֲשֶׁר לִפְנֵי
מַמְרֵא הַשָּׂדֶה וְהַמְּעָרָה אֲשֶׁר־בּוֹ וְכָל־הָעֵץ אֲשֶׁר
בַּשָּׂדֶה אֲשֶׁר בְּכָל־גְּבֻלוֹ סָבִיב: ¹⁸ לְאַבְרָהָם לְמִקְנָה

19 And after this, Abraham buried Sarah his wife in the cave of the field of Machpelah, before Mamre (that *is,* Hebron) in the land of Canaan. 20 So the field and the cave that *is* in it were deeded to Abraham by the sons of Heth as property for a burial place.

24 Now Abraham was old, well advanced in age; and the LORD had blessed Abraham in all things. 2 So Abraham said to the oldest servant of his house, who ruled over all that he had, "Please, put your hand under my thigh, 3 and I will make you swear by the LORD, the God of heaven and the God of the earth, that you will not take a wife for my son from the daughters of the Canaanites, among whom I dwell; 4 but you shall go to my country and to my family, and take a wife for my son Isaac."

5 And the servant said to him, "Perhaps the woman will not be willing to follow me to this land. Must I take your son back to the land from which you came?"

6 But Abraham said to him, "Beware that you do not take my son back there. 7 The LORD God of heaven, who took me from my father's house and from the land of my family, and who spoke to me and swore to me, saying, 'To your descendants I give this land,' He will send His angel before you, and you shall take a wife for my son from there. 8 And if the woman is not willing to follow you, then you will be released from this oath; only do not take my son back there." 9 So the servant put his hand under the thigh of Abraham his master, and swore to him concerning this matter.

10 Then the servant took ten of his master's camels and departed, for all his master's goods *were* in his hand. And he arose and went to Mesopotamia, to the city of Nahor. 11 And he made his camels kneel down outside the city by a well of water at evening time, the time when women go out to draw *water.* 12 Then he said, "O LORD God of my master Abraham, please give me success this day, and show kindness to my master Abraham. 13 Behold, *here* I stand by the well of water, and the daughters of the men of the city are coming out to draw water. 14 Now let it be that the young woman to whom I say, 'Please let down your pitcher that I may drink,' and she says, 'Drink, and I will also give your camels a drink'—*let* her *be the one* You have appointed for Your servant Isaac. And by this I will know that You have shown kindness to my master."

19 וְאַחֲרֵי־כֵן קָבַר אַבְרָהָם אֶת־שָׂרָה אִשְׁתּוֹ אֶל־מְעָרַת שְׂדֵה הַמַּכְפֵּלָה עַל־פְּנֵי מַמְרֵא הִוא חֶבְרוֹן בְּאֶרֶץ כְּנָעַן: 20 וַיָּקָם הַשָּׂדֶה וְהַמְּעָרָה אֲשֶׁר־בּוֹ לְאַבְרָהָם לַאֲחֻזַּת־קָבֶר מֵאֵת בְּנֵי־חֵת: ס

כד וְאַבְרָהָם זָקֵן בָּא בַּיָּמִים וַיהֹוָה בֵּרַךְ אֶת־אַבְרָהָם בַּכֹּל: 2 וַיֹּאמֶר אַבְרָהָם אֶל־עַבְדּוֹ זְקַן בֵּיתוֹ הַמֹּשֵׁל בְּכָל־אֲשֶׁר־לוֹ שִׂים־נָא יָדְךָ תַּחַת יְרֵכִי: 3 וְאַשְׁבִּיעֲךָ בַּיהֹוָה אֱלֹהֵי הַשָּׁמַיִם וֵאלֹהֵי הָאָרֶץ אֲשֶׁר לֹא־תִקַּח אִשָּׁה לִבְנִי מִבְּנוֹת הַכְּנַעֲנִי אֲשֶׁר אָנֹכִי יוֹשֵׁב בְּקִרְבּוֹ: 4 כִּי אֶל־אַרְצִי וְאֶל־מוֹלַדְתִּי תֵּלֵךְ וְלָקַחְתָּ אִשָּׁה לִבְנִי לְיִצְחָק: 5 וַיֹּאמֶר אֵלָיו הָעֶבֶד אוּלַי לֹא־תֹאבֶה הָאִשָּׁה לָלֶכֶת אַחֲרַי אֶל־הָאָרֶץ הַזֹּאת הֶהָשֵׁב אָשִׁיב אֶת־בִּנְךָ אֶל־הָאָרֶץ אֲשֶׁר־יָצָאתָ מִשָּׁם: 6 וַיֹּאמֶר אֵלָיו אַבְרָהָם הִשָּׁמֶר לְךָ פֶּן־תָּשִׁיב אֶת־בְּנִי שָׁמָּה: 7 יְהֹוָה אֱלֹהֵי הַשָּׁמַיִם אֲשֶׁר לְקָחַנִי מִבֵּית אָבִי וּמֵאֶרֶץ מוֹלַדְתִּי וַאֲשֶׁר דִּבֶּר־לִי וַאֲשֶׁר נִשְׁבַּע־לִי לֵאמֹר לְזַרְעֲךָ אֶתֵּן אֶת־הָאָרֶץ הַזֹּאת הוּא יִשְׁלַח מַלְאָכוֹ לְפָנֶיךָ וְלָקַחְתָּ אִשָּׁה לִבְנִי מִשָּׁם: 8 וְאִם־לֹא תֹאבֶה הָאִשָּׁה לָלֶכֶת אַחֲרֶיךָ וְנִקִּיתָ מִשְּׁבֻעָתִי זֹאת רַק אֶת־בְּנִי לֹא תָשֵׁב שָׁמָּה: 9 וַיָּשֶׂם הָעֶבֶד אֶת־יָדוֹ תַּחַת יֶרֶךְ אַבְרָהָם אֲדֹנָיו וַיִּשָּׁבַע לוֹ עַל־הַדָּבָר הַזֶּה: 10 וַיִּקַּח הָעֶבֶד עֲשָׂרָה גְמַלִּים מִגְּמַלֵּי אֲדֹנָיו וַיֵּלֶךְ וְכָל־טוּב אֲדֹנָיו בְּיָדוֹ וַיָּקָם וַיֵּלֶךְ אֶל־אֲרַם נַהֲרַיִם אֶל־עִיר נָחוֹר: 11 וַיַּבְרֵךְ הַגְּמַלִּים מִחוּץ לָעִיר אֶל־בְּאֵר הַמָּיִם לְעֵת עֶרֶב לְעֵת צֵאת הַשֹּׁאֲבֹת: 12 וַיֹּאמַר יְהֹוָה אֱלֹהֵי אֲדֹנִי אַבְרָהָם הַקְרֵה־נָא לְפָנַי הַיּוֹם וַעֲשֵׂה־חֶסֶד עִם אֲדֹנִי אַבְרָהָם: 13 הִנֵּה אָנֹכִי נִצָּב עַל־עֵין הַמָּיִם וּבְנוֹת אַנְשֵׁי הָעִיר יֹצְאֹת לִשְׁאֹב מָיִם: 14 וְהָיָה הַנַּעֲרָ אֲשֶׁר אֹמַר אֵלֶיהָ הַטִּי־נָא כַדֵּךְ וְאֶשְׁתֶּה וְאָמְרָה שְׁתֵה וְגַם־גְּמַלֶּיךָ אַשְׁקֶה אֹתָהּ הֹכַחְתָּ לְעַבְדְּךָ לְיִצְחָק וּבָהּ אֵדַע כִּי־עָשִׂיתָ חֶסֶד עִם־אֲדֹנִי: 15 וַיְהִי־הוּא טֶרֶם כִּלָּה לְדַבֵּר וְהִנֵּה רִבְקָה

15 And it happened, before he had finished speaking, that behold, Rebekah, who was born to Bethuel, son of Milcah, the wife of Nahor, Abraham's brother, came out with her pitcher on her shoulder. 16 Now the young woman *was* very beautiful to behold, a virgin; no man had known her. And she went down to the well, filled her pitcher, and came up. 17 And the servant ran to meet her and said, "Please let me drink a little water from your pitcher."

18 So she said, "Drink, my lord." Then she quickly let her pitcher down to her hand, and gave him a drink. 19 And when she had finished giving him a drink, she said, "I will draw *water* for your camels also, until they have finished drinking." 20 Then she quickly emptied her pitcher into the trough, ran back to the well to draw *water,* and drew for all his camels. 21 And the man, wondering at her, remained silent so as to know whether the LORD had made his journey prosperous or not.

22 So it was, when the camels had finished drinking, that the man took a golden nose ring weighing half a shekel, and two bracelets for her wrists weighing ten *shekels* of gold, 23 and said, "Whose daughter *are* you? Tell me, please, is there room *in* your father's house for us to lodge?"

24 So she said to him, "I *am* the daughter of Bethuel, Milcah's son, whom she bore to Nahor." 25 Moreover she said to him, "We have both straw and feed enough, and room to lodge."

26 Then the man bowed down his head and worshiped the LORD. 27 And he said, "Blessed *be* the LORD God of my master Abraham, who has not forsaken His mercy and His truth toward my master. As for me, being on the way, the LORD led me to the house of my master's brethren." 28 So the young woman ran and told her mother's household these things.

29 Now Rebekah had a brother whose name *was* Laban, and Laban ran out to the man by the well. 30 So it came to pass, when he saw the nose ring, and the bracelets on his sister's wrists, and when he heard the words of his sister Rebekah, saying, "Thus the man spoke to me," that he went to the man. And there he stood by the camels at the well. 31 And he said, "Come in, O blessed of the LORD! Why do you stand outside? For I have prepared the house, and a place for the camels."

32 Then the man came to the house. And he unloaded the camels, and provided straw and feed for the camels, and water to wash his feet and the feet of the men who *were* with him. 33 *Food* was set before him to eat, but he said, "I will not eat until I have told about my errand."

יָצֵאת אֲשֶׁר יֻלְּדָה לִבְתוּאֵל בֶּן־מִלְכָּה אֵשֶׁת נָחוֹר אֲחִי אַבְרָהָם וְכַדָּהּ עַל־שִׁכְמָהּ: 16 וְהַנַּעֲרָ טֹבַת מַרְאֶה מְאֹד בְּתוּלָה וְאִישׁ לֹא יְדָעָהּ וַתֵּרֶד הָעַיְנָה וַתְּמַלֵּא כַדָּהּ וַתָּעַל: 17 וַיָּרָץ הָעֶבֶד לִקְרָאתָהּ וַיֹּאמֶר הַגְמִיאִינִי נָא מְעַט־מַיִם מִכַּדֵּךְ: 18 וַתֹּאמֶר שְׁתֵה אֲדֹנִי וַתְּמַהֵר וַתֹּרֶד כַּדָּהּ עַל־יָדָהּ וַתַּשְׁקֵהוּ: 19 וַתְּכַל לְהַשְׁקֹתוֹ וַתֹּאמֶר גַּם לִגְמַלֶּיךָ אֶשְׁאָב עַד אִם־כִּלּוּ לִשְׁתֹּת: 20 וַתְּמַהֵר וַתְּעַר כַּדָּהּ אֶל־הַשֹּׁקֶת וַתָּרָץ עוֹד אֶל־הַבְּאֵר לִשְׁאֹב וַתִּשְׁאַב לְכָל־גְּמַלָּיו: 21 וְהָאִישׁ מִשְׁתָּאֵה לָהּ מַחֲרִישׁ לָדַעַת הַהִצְלִיחַ יְהוָה דַּרְכּוֹ אִם־לֹא: 22 וַיְהִי כַּאֲשֶׁר כִּלּוּ הַגְּמַלִּים לִשְׁתּוֹת וַיִּקַּח הָאִישׁ נֶזֶם זָהָב בֶּקַע מִשְׁקָלוֹ וּשְׁנֵי צְמִידִים עַל־יָדֶיהָ עֲשָׂרָה זָהָב מִשְׁקָלָם: 23 וַיֹּאמֶר בַּת־מִי אַתְּ הַגִּידִי נָא לִי הֲיֵשׁ בֵּית־אָבִיךְ מָקוֹם לָנוּ לָלִין: 24 וַתֹּאמֶר אֵלָיו בַּת־בְּתוּאֵל אָנֹכִי בֶּן־מִלְכָּה אֲשֶׁר יָלְדָה לְנָחוֹר: 25 וַתֹּאמֶר אֵלָיו גַּם־תֶּבֶן גַּם־מִסְפּוֹא רַב עִמָּנוּ גַּם־מָקוֹם לָלוּן: 26 וַיִּקֹּד הָאִישׁ וַיִּשְׁתַּחוּ לַיהוָה: 27 וַיֹּאמֶר בָּרוּךְ יְהוָה אֱלֹהֵי אֲדֹנִי אַבְרָהָם אֲשֶׁר לֹא־עָזַב חַסְדּוֹ וַאֲמִתּוֹ מֵעִם אֲדֹנִי אָנֹכִי בַּדֶּרֶךְ נָחַנִי יְהוָה בֵּית אֲחֵי אֲדֹנִי: 28 וַתָּרָץ הַנַּעֲרָ וַתַּגֵּד לְבֵית אִמָּהּ כַּדְּבָרִים הָאֵלֶּה: 29 וּלְרִבְקָה אָח וּשְׁמוֹ לָבָן וַיָּרָץ לָבָן אֶל־הָאִישׁ הַחוּצָה אֶל־הָעָיִן: 30 וַיְהִי כִּרְאֹת אֶת־הַנֶּזֶם וְאֶת־הַצְּמִדִים עַל־יְדֵי אֲחֹתוֹ וּכְשָׁמְעוֹ אֶת־דִּבְרֵי רִבְקָה אֲחֹתוֹ לֵאמֹר כֹּה־דִבֶּר אֵלַי הָאִישׁ וַיָּבֹא אֶל־הָאִישׁ וְהִנֵּה עֹמֵד עַל־הַגְּמַלִּים עַל־הָעָיִן: 31 וַיֹּאמֶר בּוֹא בְּרוּךְ יְהוָה לָמָּה תַעֲמֹד בַּחוּץ וְאָנֹכִי פִּנִּיתִי הַבַּיִת וּמָקוֹם לַגְּמַלִּים: 32 וַיָּבֹא הָאִישׁ הַבַּיְתָה וַיְפַתַּח הַגְּמַלִּים וַיִּתֵּן תֶּבֶן וּמִסְפּוֹא לַגְּמַלִּים וּמַיִם לִרְחֹץ רַגְלָיו וְרַגְלֵי הָאֲנָשִׁים אֲשֶׁר אִתּוֹ: 33 וַיּוּשַׂם‹ לְפָנָיו לֶאֱכֹל וַיֹּאמֶר לֹא אֹכַל עַד אִם־

And he said, "Speak on."

34 So he said, "I *am* Abraham's servant. 35 The
LORD has blessed my master greatly, and he has
become great; and He has given him flocks and
herds, silver and gold, male and female servants,
and camels and donkeys. 36 And Sarah my master's
wife bore a son to my master when she was old; and
to him he has given all that he has. 37 Now my
master made me swear, saying, 'You shall not take
a wife for my son from the daughters of the
Canaanites, in whose land I dwell; 38 but you shall
go to my father's house and to my family, and take
a wife for my son.' 39 And I said to my master,
'Perhaps the woman will not follow me.' 40 But he
said to me, 'The LORD, before whom I walk, will
send His angel with you and prosper your way; and
you shall take a wife for my son from my family
and from my father's house. 41 You will be clear
from this oath when you arrive among my family;
for if they will not give *her* to you, then you will be
released from my oath.'

42 "And this day I came to the well and said, 'O
LORD God of my master Abraham, if You will now
prosper the way in which I go, 43 behold, I stand by
the well of water; and it shall come to pass that
when the virgin comes out to draw *water,* and I say
to her, "Please give me a little water from your
pitcher to drink," 44 and she says to me, "Drink,
and I will draw for your camels also,"—let her *be*
the woman whom the LORD has appointed for my
master's son.'

45 "But before I had finished speaking in my
heart, there was Rebekah, coming out with her
pitcher on her shoulder; and she went down to the
well and drew *water.* And I said to her, 'Please let
me drink.' 46 And she made haste and let her pitcher
down from her *shoulder,* and said, 'Drink, and I will
give your camels a drink also.' So I drank, and she
gave the camels a drink also. 47 Then I asked her,
and said, 'Whose daughter *are* you?' And she said,
'The daughter of Bethuel, Nahor's son, whom
Milcah bore to him.' So I put the nose ring on her
nose and the bracelets on her wrists. 48 And I bowed
my head and worshiped the LORD, and blessed the
LORD God of my master Abraham, who had led me
in the way of truth to take the daughter of my
master's brother for his son. 49 Now if you will deal
kindly and truly with my master, tell me. And if
not, tell me, that I may turn to the right hand or to
the left."

34 וַיֹּאמֶר עֶבֶד אַבְרָהָם
דִּבַּרְתִּי דְּבָרָי וַיֹּאמֶר דַּבֵּר:
אָנֹכִי: 35 וַיהֹוָה בֵּרַךְ אֶת־אֲדֹנִי מְאֹד וַיִּגְדָּל וַיִּתֶּן־
לוֹ צֹאן וּבָקָר וְכֶסֶף וְזָהָב וַעֲבָדִם וּשְׁפָחֹת וּגְמַלִּים
וַחֲמֹרִים: 36 וַתֵּלֶד שָׂרָה אֵשֶׁת אֲדֹנִי בֵן לַאדֹנִי
אַחֲרֵי זִקְנָתָהּ וַיִּתֶּן־לוֹ אֶת־כָּל־אֲשֶׁר־לוֹ: 37 וַיַּשְׁבִּעֵנִי
אֲדֹנִי לֵאמֹר לֹא־תִקַּח אִשָּׁה לִבְנִי מִבְּנוֹת הַכְּנַעֲנִי
אֲשֶׁר אָנֹכִי יֹשֵׁב בְּאַרְצוֹ: 38 אִם־לֹא אֶל־בֵּית־אָבִי
תֵּלֵךְ וְאֶל־מִשְׁפַּחְתִּי וְלָקַחְתָּ אִשָּׁה לִבְנִי: 39 וָאֹמַר
אֶל־אֲדֹנִי אֻלַי לֹא־תֵלֵךְ הָאִשָּׁה אַחֲרָי: 40 וַיֹּאמֶר
אֵלָי יְהֹוָה אֲשֶׁר־הִתְהַלַּכְתִּי לְפָנָיו יִשְׁלַח מַלְאָכוֹ
אִתָּךְ וְהִצְלִיחַ דַּרְכֶּךָ וְלָקַחְתָּ אִשָּׁה לִבְנִי מִמִּשְׁפַּחְתִּי
וּמִבֵּית אָבִי: 41 אָז תִּנָּקֶה מֵאָלָתִי כִּי תָבוֹא אֶל־
מִשְׁפַּחְתִּי וְאִם־לֹא יִתְּנוּ לָךְ וְהָיִיתָ נָקִי מֵאָלָתִי:
42 וָאָבֹא הַיּוֹם אֶל־הָעָיִן וָאֹמַר יְהֹוָה אֱלֹהֵי אֲדֹנִי
אַבְרָהָם אִם־יֶשְׁךָ־נָּא מַצְלִיחַ דַּרְכִּי אֲשֶׁר אָנֹכִי
הֹלֵךְ עָלֶיהָ: 43 הִנֵּה אָנֹכִי נִצָּב עַל־עֵין הַמָּיִם וְהָיָה
הָעַלְמָה הַיֹּצֵאת לִשְׁאֹב וְאָמַרְתִּי אֵלֶיהָ הַשְׁקִינִי־
נָא מְעַט־מַיִם מִכַּדֵּךְ: 44 וְאָמְרָה אֵלַי גַּם־אַתָּה
שְׁתֵה וְגַם לִגְמַלֶּיךָ אֶשְׁאָב הִוא הָאִשָּׁה אֲשֶׁר־
הֹכִיחַ יְהֹוָה לְבֶן־אֲדֹנִי: 45 אֲנִי טֶרֶם אֲכַלֶּה לְדַבֵּר
אֶל־לִבִּי וְהִנֵּה רִבְקָה יֹצֵאת וְכַדָּהּ עַל־שִׁכְמָהּ וַתֵּרֶד
הָעַיְנָה וַתִּשְׁאָב וָאֹמַר אֵלֶיהָ הַשְׁקִינִי נָא: 46 וַתְּמַהֵר
וַתּוֹרֶד כַּדָּהּ מֵעָלֶיהָ וַתֹּאמֶר שְׁתֵה וְגַם־גְּמַלֶּיךָ
אַשְׁקֶה וָאֵשְׁתְּ וְגַם הַגְּמַלִּים הִשְׁקָתָה: 47 וָאֶשְׁאַל
אֹתָהּ וָאֹמַר בַּת־מִי אַתְּ וַתֹּאמֶר בַּת־בְּתוּאֵל בֶּן־
נָחוֹר אֲשֶׁר יָלְדָה־לּוֹ מִלְכָּה וָאָשִׂם הַנֶּזֶם עַל־אַפָּהּ
וְהַצְּמִידִים עַל־יָדֶיהָ: 48 וָאֶקֹּד וָאֶשְׁתַּחֲוֶה לַיהֹוָה
וָאֲבָרֵךְ אֶת־יְהֹוָה אֱלֹהֵי אֲדֹנִי אַבְרָהָם אֲשֶׁר הִנְחַנִי
בְּדֶרֶךְ אֱמֶת לָקַחַת אֶת־בַּת־אֲחִי אֲדֹנִי לִבְנוֹ:
49 וְעַתָּה אִם־יֶשְׁכֶם עֹשִׂים חֶסֶד וֶאֱמֶת אֶת־אֲדֹנִי
הַגִּידוּ לִי וְאִם־לֹא הַגִּידוּ לִי וְאֶפְנֶה עַל־יָמִין אוֹ
עַל־שְׂמֹאל: 50 וַיַּעַן לָבָן וּבְתוּאֵל וַיֹּאמְרוּ מֵיְהֹוָה
יָצָא הַדָּבָר לֹא נוּכַל דַּבֵּר אֵלֶיךָ רַע אוֹ־טוֹב:

50 Then Laban and Bethuel answered and said, "The thing comes from the LORD; we cannot speak to you either bad or good. 51 Here *is* Rebekah before you; take *her* and go, and let her be your master's son's wife, as the LORD has spoken."

52 And it came to pass, when Abraham's servant heard their words, that he worshiped the LORD, *bowing himself* to the earth. 53 Then the servant brought out jewelry of silver, jewelry of gold, and clothing, and gave *them* to Rebekah. He also gave precious things to her brother and to her mother.

54 And he and the men who *were* with him ate and drank and stayed all night. Then they arose in the morning, and he said, "Send me away to my master."

55 But her brother and her mother said, "Let the young woman stay with us *a few* days, at least ten; after that she may go."

56 And he said to them, "Do not hinder me, since the LORD has prospered my way; send me away so that I may go to my master."

57 So they said, "We will call the young woman and ask her personally." 58 Then they called Rebekah and said to her, "Will you go with this man?"

And she said, "I will go."

59 So they sent away Rebekah their sister and her nurse, and Abraham's servant and his men. 60 And they blessed Rebekah and said to her:

"Our sister, *may you become*
  The mother of thousands of ten thousands;
  And may your descendants possess
  The gates of those who hate them."

61 Then Rebekah and her maids arose, and they rode on the camels and followed the man. So the servant took Rebekah and departed.

62 Now Isaac came from the way of Beer Lahai Roi, for he dwelt in the South. 63 And Isaac went out to meditate in the field in the evening; and he lifted his eyes and looked, and there, the camels *were* coming. 64 Then Rebekah lifted her eyes, and when she saw Isaac she dismounted from her camel; 65 for she had said to the servant, "Who *is* this man walking in the field to meet us?"

The servant said, "It *is* my master." So she took a veil and covered herself.

66 And the servant told Isaac all the things that he had done. 67 Then Isaac brought her into his mother Sarah's tent; and he took Rebekah and she became his wife, and he loved her. So Isaac was comforted after his mother's *death*.

51 הִנֵּֽה־רִבְקָ֥ה לְפָנֶ֖יךָ קַ֣ח וָלֵ֑ךְ וּתְהִ֤י אִשָּׁה֙ לְבֶן־אֲדֹנֶ֔יךָ כַּאֲשֶׁ֖ר דִּבֶּ֥ר יְהוָֽה׃ 52 וַיְהִ֕י כַּאֲשֶׁ֥ר שָׁמַ֛ע עֶ֥בֶד אַבְרָהָ֖ם אֶת־דִּבְרֵיהֶ֑ם וַיִּשְׁתַּ֥חוּ אַ֖רְצָה לַֽיהוָֽה׃ 53 וַיּוֹצֵ֨א הָעֶ֜בֶד כְּלֵי־כֶ֨סֶף וּכְלֵ֤י זָהָב֙ וּבְגָדִ֔ים וַיִּתֵּ֖ן לְרִבְקָ֑ה וּמִ֨גְדָּנֹ֔ת נָתַ֥ן לְאָחִ֖יהָ וּלְאִמָּֽהּ׃ 54 וַיֹּאכְל֣וּ וַיִּשְׁתּ֗וּ ה֧וּא וְהָאֲנָשִׁ֛ים אֲשֶׁר־עִמּ֖וֹ וַיָּלִ֑ינוּ וַיָּק֣וּמוּ בַבֹּ֔קֶר וַיֹּ֖אמֶר שַׁלְּחֻ֥נִי לַֽאדֹנִֽי׃ 55 וַיֹּ֤אמֶר אָחִ֨יהָ֙ וְאִמָּ֔הּ תֵּשֵׁ֨ב הַנַּעֲרָ֥ אִתָּ֛נוּ יָמִ֖ים א֣וֹ עָשׂ֑וֹר אַחַ֖ר תֵּלֵֽךְ׃ 56 וַיֹּ֤אמֶר אֲלֵהֶם֙ אַל־תְּאַחֲר֣וּ אֹתִ֔י וַֽיהוָ֖ה הִצְלִ֣יחַ דַּרְכִּ֑י שַׁלְּח֕וּנִי וְאֵלְכָ֖ה לַֽאדֹנִֽי׃ 57 וַיֹּאמְר֖וּ נִקְרָ֣א לַֽנַּעֲרָ֑ וְנִשְׁאֲלָ֖ה אֶת־פִּֽיהָ׃ 58 וַיִּקְרְא֤וּ לְרִבְקָה֙ וַיֹּאמְר֣וּ אֵלֶ֔יהָ הֲתֵלְכִ֖י עִם־הָאִ֣ישׁ הַזֶּ֑ה וַתֹּ֖אמֶר אֵלֵֽךְ׃ 59 וַֽיְשַׁלְּח֛וּ אֶת־רִבְקָ֥ה אֲחֹתָ֖ם וְאֶת־מֵנִקְתָּ֑הּ וְאֶת־עֶ֥בֶד אַבְרָהָ֖ם וְאֶת־אֲנָשָֽׁיו׃ 60 וַיְבָרֲכ֤וּ אֶת־רִבְקָה֙ וַיֹּ֣אמְרוּ לָ֔הּ אֲחֹתֵ֕נוּ אַ֥תְּ הֲיִ֖י לְאַלְפֵ֣י רְבָבָ֑ה וְיִירַ֣שׁ זַרְעֵ֔ךְ אֵ֖ת שַׁ֥עַר שֹׂנְאָֽיו׃ 61 וַתָּ֨קָם רִבְקָ֜ה וְנַעֲרֹתֶ֗יהָ וַתִּרְכַּ֨בְנָה֙ עַל־הַגְּמַלִּ֔ים וַתֵּלַ֖כְנָה אַחֲרֵ֣י הָאִ֑ישׁ וַיִּקַּ֥ח הָעֶ֛בֶד אֶת־רִבְקָ֖ה וַיֵּלַֽךְ׃ 62 וְיִצְחָק֙ בָּ֣א מִבּ֔וֹא בְּאֵ֥ר לַחַ֖י רֹאִ֑י וְה֥וּא יוֹשֵׁ֖ב בְּאֶ֥רֶץ הַנֶּֽגֶב׃ 63 וַיֵּצֵ֥א יִצְחָ֛ק לָשׂ֥וּחַ בַּשָּׂדֶ֖ה לִפְנ֣וֹת עָ֑רֶב וַיִּשָּׂ֤א עֵינָיו֙ וַיַּ֔רְא וְהִנֵּ֥ה גְמַלִּ֖ים בָּאִֽים׃ 64 וַתִּשָּׂ֤א רִבְקָה֙ אֶת־עֵינֶ֔יהָ וַתֵּ֖רֶא אֶת־יִצְחָ֑ק וַתִּפֹּ֖ל מֵעַ֥ל הַגָּמָֽל׃ 65 וַתֹּ֣אמֶר אֶל־הָעֶ֗בֶד מִֽי־הָאִ֤ישׁ הַלָּזֶה֙ הַהֹלֵ֤ךְ בַּשָּׂדֶה֙ לִקְרָאתֵ֔נוּ וַיֹּ֥אמֶר הָעֶ֖בֶד ה֣וּא אֲדֹנִ֑י וַתִּקַּ֥ח הַצָּעִ֖יף וַתִּתְכָּֽס׃ 66 וַיְסַפֵּ֥ר הָעֶ֖בֶד לְיִצְחָ֑ק אֵ֥ת כָּל־הַדְּבָרִ֖ים אֲשֶׁ֥ר עָשָֽׂה׃ 67 וַיְבִאֶ֣הָ יִצְחָ֗ק הָאֹ֨הֱלָה֙ שָׂרָ֣ה אִמּ֔וֹ וַיִּקַּ֧ח אֶת־רִבְקָ֛ה וַתְּהִי־ל֥וֹ לְאִשָּׁ֖ה וַיֶּאֱהָבֶ֑הָ וַיִּנָּחֵ֥ם יִצְחָ֖ק אַחֲרֵ֥י אִמּֽוֹ׃

פ

25 Abraham again took a wife, and her name *was* Keturah. ²And she bore him Zimran, Jokshan, Medan, Midian, Ishbak, and Shuah. ³Jokshan begot Sheba and Dedan. And the sons of Dedan were Asshurim, Letushim, and Leummim. ⁴And the sons of Midian *were* Ephah, Epher, Hanoch, Abidah, and Eldaah. All these *were* the children of Keturah.

⁵And Abraham gave all that he had to Isaac. ⁶But Abraham gave gifts to the sons of the concubines which Abraham had; and while he was still living he sent them eastward, away from Isaac his son, to the country of the east.

⁷This *is* the sum of the years of Abraham's life which he lived: one hundred and seventy-five years. ⁸Then Abraham breathed his last and died in a good old age, an old man and full *of years,* and was gathered to his people. ⁹And his sons Isaac and Ishmael buried him in the cave of Machpelah, which *is* before Mamre, in the field of Ephron the son of Zohar the Hittite, ¹⁰the field which Abraham purchased from the sons of Heth. There Abraham was buried, and Sarah his wife. ¹¹And it came to pass, after the death of Abraham, that God blessed his son Isaac. And Isaac dwelt at Beer Lahai Roi.

¹²Now this *is* the genealogy of Ishmael, Abraham's son, whom Hagar the Egyptian, Sarah's maidservant, bore to Abraham. ¹³And these *were* the names of the sons of Ishmael, by their names, according to their generations: The firstborn of Ishmael, Nebajoth; then Kedar, Adbeel, Mibsam, ¹⁴Mishma, Dumah, Massa, ¹⁵Hadar, Tema, Jetur, Naphish, and Kedemah. ¹⁶These *were* the sons of Ishmael and these *were* their names, by their towns and their settlements, twelve princes according to their nations. ¹⁷These *were* the years of the life of Ishmael: one hundred and thirty-seven years; and he breathed his last and died, and was gathered to his people. ¹⁸(They dwelt from Havilah as far as Shur, which *is* east of Egypt as you go toward Assyria.) He died in the presence of all his brethren.

¹⁹This *is* the genealogy of Isaac, Abraham's son. Abraham begot Isaac. ²⁰Isaac was forty years old when he took Rebekah as wife, the daughter of Bethuel the Syrian of Padan Aram, the sister of Laban the Syrian. ²¹Now Isaac pleaded with the LORD for his wife, because she *was* barren; and the LORD granted his plea, and Rebekah his wife conceived. ²²But the children struggled together within her; and she said, "If *all is* well, why *am I* like this?" So she went to inquire of the LORD.

²³And the LORD said to her:

"Two nations *are* in your womb,
Two peoples shall be separated from your body;

One people shall be stronger than the other,
And the older shall serve the younger."

²⁴ So when her days were fulfilled *for her* to give birth, indeed *there were* twins in her womb. ²⁵ And the first came out red. *He was* like a hairy garment all over; so they called his name Esau. ²⁶ Afterward his brother came out, and his hand took hold of Esau's heel; so his name was called Jacob. Isaac *was* sixty years old when she bore them.

²⁷ So the boys grew. And Esau was a skillful hunter, a man of the field; but Jacob was a mild man, dwelling in tents. ²⁸ And Isaac loved Esau because he ate *of his* game, but Rebekah loved Jacob.

²⁹ Now Jacob cooked a stew; and Esau came in from the field, and he *was* weary. ³⁰ And Esau said to Jacob, "Please feed me with that same red *stew,* for I *am* weary." Therefore his name was called Edom.

³¹ But Jacob said, "Sell me your birthright as of this day."

³² And Esau said, "Look, I *am* about to die; so what *is* this birthright to me?"

³³ Then Jacob said, "Swear to me as of this day."

So he swore to him, and sold his birthright to Jacob. ³⁴ And Jacob gave Esau bread and stew of lentils; then he ate and drank, arose, and went his way. Thus Esau despised *his* birthright.

26 There was a famine in the land, besides the first famine that was in the days of Abraham. And Isaac went to Abimelech king of the Philistines, in Gerar.

² Then the LORD appeared to him and said: "Do not go down to Egypt; live in the land of which I shall tell you. ³ Dwell in this land, and I will be with you and bless you; for to you and your descendants I give all these lands, and I will perform the oath which I swore to Abraham your father. ⁴ And I will make your descendants multiply as the stars of heaven; I will give to your descendants all these lands; and in your seed all the nations of the earth shall be blessed; ⁵ because Abraham obeyed My voice and kept My charge, My commandments, My statutes, and My laws."

⁶ So Isaac dwelt in Gerar. ⁷ And the men of the place asked about his wife. And he said, "She *is* my sister"; for he was afraid to say, "*She is* my wife," *because he thought,* "lest the men of the place kill me for Rebekah, because she *is* beautiful to behold." ⁸ Now it came to pass, when he had been there a long time, that Abimelech king of the Philistines looked through a window, and saw, and

יְהֹוָה: 23 וַיֹּאמֶר יְהֹוָה לָהּ שְׁנֵי גֹיִם בְּבִטְנֵךְ וּשְׁנֵי לְאֻמִּים מִמֵּעַיִךְ יִפָּרֵדוּ וּלְאֹם מִלְאֹם יֶאֱמָץ וְרַב יַעֲבֹד צָעִיר: 24 וַיִּמְלְאוּ יָמֶיהָ לָלֶדֶת וְהִנֵּה תוֹמִם בְּבִטְנָהּ: 25 וַיֵּצֵא הָרִאשׁוֹן אַדְמוֹנִי כֻּלּוֹ כְּאַדֶּרֶת שֵׂעָר וַיִּקְרְאוּ שְׁמוֹ עֵשָׂו: 26 וְאַחֲרֵי־כֵן יָצָא אָחִיו וְיָדוֹ אֹחֶזֶת בַּעֲקֵב עֵשָׂו וַיִּקְרָא שְׁמוֹ יַעֲקֹב וְיִצְחָק בֶּן־שִׁשִּׁים שָׁנָה בְּלֶדֶת אֹתָם: 27 וַיִּגְדְּלוּ הַנְּעָרִים וַיְהִי עֵשָׂו אִישׁ יֹדֵעַ צַיִד אִישׁ שָׂדֶה וְיַעֲקֹב אִישׁ תָּם יֹשֵׁב אֹהָלִים: 28 וַיֶּאֱהַב יִצְחָק אֶת־עֵשָׂו כִּי־צַיִד בְּפִיו וְרִבְקָה אֹהֶבֶת אֶת־יַעֲקֹב: 29 וַיָּזֶד יַעֲקֹב נָזִיד וַיָּבֹא עֵשָׂו מִן־הַשָּׂדֶה וְהוּא עָיֵף: 30 וַיֹּאמֶר עֵשָׂו אֶל־יַעֲקֹב הַלְעִיטֵנִי נָא מִן־הָאָדֹם הָאָדֹם הַזֶּה כִּי עָיֵף אָנֹכִי עַל־כֵּן קָרָא־שְׁמוֹ אֱדוֹם: 31 וַיֹּאמֶר יַעֲקֹב מִכְרָה כַיּוֹם אֶת־בְּכֹרָתְךָ לִי: 32 וַיֹּאמֶר עֵשָׂו הִנֵּה אָנֹכִי הוֹלֵךְ לָמוּת וְלָמָּה־זֶּה לִי בְּכֹרָה: 33 וַיֹּאמֶר יַעֲקֹב הִשָּׁבְעָה לִּי כַּיּוֹם וַיִּשָּׁבַע לוֹ וַיִּמְכֹּר אֶת־בְּכֹרָתוֹ לְיַעֲקֹב: 34 וְיַעֲקֹב נָתַן לְעֵשָׂו לֶחֶם וּנְזִיד עֲדָשִׁים וַיֹּאכַל וַיֵּשְׁתְּ וַיָּקָם וַיֵּלַךְ וַיִּבֶז עֵשָׂו אֶת־הַבְּכֹרָה: ס

כו וַיְהִי רָעָב בָּאָרֶץ מִלְּבַד הָרָעָב הָרִאשׁוֹן אֲשֶׁר הָיָה בִּימֵי אַבְרָהָם וַיֵּלֶךְ יִצְחָק אֶל־אֲבִימֶלֶךְ מֶלֶךְ־פְּלִשְׁתִּים גְּרָרָה: 2 וַיֵּרָא אֵלָיו יְהֹוָה וַיֹּאמֶר אַל־תֵּרֵד מִצְרָיְמָה שְׁכֹן בָּאָרֶץ אֲשֶׁר אֹמַר אֵלֶיךָ: 3 גּוּר בָּאָרֶץ הַזֹּאת וְאֶהְיֶה עִמְּךָ וַאֲבָרְכֶךָּ כִּי־לְךָ וּלְזַרְעֲךָ אֶתֵּן אֶת־כָּל־הָאֲרָצֹת הָאֵל וַהֲקִמֹתִי אֶת־הַשְּׁבֻעָה אֲשֶׁר נִשְׁבַּעְתִּי לְאַבְרָהָם אָבִיךָ: 4 וְהִרְבֵּיתִי אֶת־זַרְעֲךָ כְּכוֹכְבֵי הַשָּׁמַיִם וְנָתַתִּי לְזַרְעֲךָ אֵת כָּל־הָאֲרָצֹת הָאֵל וְהִתְבָּרֲכוּ בְזַרְעֲךָ כֹּל גּוֹיֵי הָאָרֶץ: 5 עֵקֶב אֲשֶׁר־שָׁמַע אַבְרָהָם בְּקֹלִי וַיִּשְׁמֹר מִשְׁמַרְתִּי מִצְוֹתַי חֻקּוֹתַי וְתוֹרֹתָי: 6 וַיֵּשֶׁב יִצְחָק בִּגְרָר: 7 וַיִּשְׁאֲלוּ אַנְשֵׁי הַמָּקוֹם לְאִשְׁתּוֹ וַיֹּאמֶר אֲחֹתִי הִוא כִּי יָרֵא לֵאמֹר אִשְׁתִּי פֶּן־יַהַרְגֻנִי אַנְשֵׁי הַמָּקוֹם עַל־רִבְקָה כִּי־טוֹבַת מַרְאֶה הִוא: 8 וַיְהִי כִּי אָרְכוּ לוֹ שָׁם הַיָּמִים וַיַּשְׁקֵף אֲבִימֶלֶךְ מֶלֶךְ פְּלִשְׁתִּים

there was Isaac, showing endearment to Rebekah his wife. ⁹Then Abimelech called Isaac and said, "Quite obviously she *is* your wife; so how could you say, 'She *is* my sister'?"

Isaac said to him, "Because I said, 'Lest I die on account of her.'"

¹⁰And Abimelech said, "What *is* this you have done to us? One of the people might soon have lain with your wife, and you would have brought guilt on us." ¹¹So Abimelech charged all *his* people, saying, "He who touches this man or his wife shall surely be put to death."

¹²Then Isaac sowed in that land, and reaped in the same year a hundredfold; and the LORD blessed him. ¹³The man began to prosper, and continued prospering until he became very prosperous; ¹⁴for he had possessions of flocks and possessions of herds and a great number of servants. So the Philistines envied him. ¹⁵Now the Philistines had stopped up all the wells which his father's servants had dug in the days of Abraham his father, and they had filled them with earth. ¹⁶And Abimelech said to Isaac, "Go away from us, for you are much mightier than we."

¹⁷Then Isaac departed from there and pitched his tent in the Valley of Gerar, and dwelt there. ¹⁸And Isaac dug again the wells of water which they had dug in the days of Abraham his father, for the Philistines had stopped them up after the death of Abraham. He called them by the names which his father had called them.

¹⁹Also Isaac's servants dug in the valley, and found a well of running water there. ²⁰But the herdsmen of Gerar quarreled with Isaac's herdsmen, saying, "The water *is* ours." So he called the name of the well Esek, because they quarreled with him. ²¹Then they dug another well, and they quarreled over that *one* also. So he called its name Sitnah. ²²And he moved from there and dug another well, and they did not quarrel over it. So he called its name Rehoboth, because he said, "For now the LORD has made room for us, and we shall be fruitful in the land."

²³Then he went up from there to Beersheba. ²⁴And the LORD appeared to him the same night and said, "I *am* the God of your father Abraham; do not fear, for I *am* with you. I will bless you and multiply your descendants for My servant Abraham's sake." ²⁵So he built an altar there and called on the name of the LORD, and he pitched his tent there; and there Isaac's servants dug a well.

בְּעַד הַחַלּוֹן וַיַּרְא וְהִנֵּה יִצְחָק מְצַחֵק אֵת רִבְקָה אִשְׁתּוֹ: ⁹וַיִּקְרָא אֲבִימֶלֶךְ לְיִצְחָק וַיֹּאמֶר אַךְ הִנֵּה אִשְׁתְּךָ הִוא וְאֵיךְ אָמַרְתָּ אֲחֹתִי הִוא וַיֹּאמֶר אֵלָיו יִצְחָק כִּי אָמַרְתִּי פֶּן־אָמוּת עָלֶיהָ: ¹⁰וַיֹּאמֶר אֲבִימֶלֶךְ מַה־זֹּאת עָשִׂיתָ לָּנוּ כִּמְעַט שָׁכַב אַחַד הָעָם אֶת־אִשְׁתֶּךָ וְהֵבֵאתָ עָלֵינוּ אָשָׁם: ¹¹וַיְצַו אֲבִימֶלֶךְ אֶת־כָּל־הָעָם לֵאמֹר הַנֹּגֵעַ בָּאִישׁ הַזֶּה וּבְאִשְׁתּוֹ מוֹת יוּמָת: ¹²וַיִּזְרַע יִצְחָק בָּאָרֶץ הַהִוא וַיִּמְצָא בַּשָּׁנָה הַהִוא מֵאָה שְׁעָרִים וַיְבָרֲכֵהוּ יְהוָה: ¹³וַיִּגְדַּל הָאִישׁ וַיֵּלֶךְ הָלוֹךְ וְגָדֵל עַד כִּי־גָדַל מְאֹד: ¹⁴וַיְהִי־לוֹ מִקְנֵה־צֹאן וּמִקְנֵה בָקָר וַעֲבֻדָּה רַבָּה וַיְקַנְאוּ אֹתוֹ פְּלִשְׁתִּים: ¹⁵וְכָל־הַבְּאֵרֹת אֲשֶׁר חָפְרוּ עַבְדֵי אָבִיו בִּימֵי אַבְרָהָם אָבִיו סִתְּמוּם פְּלִשְׁתִּים וַיְמַלְאוּם עָפָר: ¹⁶וַיֹּאמֶר אֲבִימֶלֶךְ אֶל־יִצְחָק לֵךְ מֵעִמָּנוּ כִּי־עָצַמְתָּ־מִמֶּנּוּ מְאֹד: ¹⁷וַיֵּלֶךְ מִשָּׁם יִצְחָק וַיִּחַן בְּנַחַל־גְּרָר וַיֵּשֶׁב שָׁם: ¹⁸וַיָּשָׁב יִצְחָק וַיַּחְפֹּר אֶת־בְּאֵרֹת הַמַּיִם אֲשֶׁר חָפְרוּ בִּימֵי אַבְרָהָם אָבִיו וַיְסַתְּמוּם פְּלִשְׁתִּים אַחֲרֵי מוֹת אַבְרָהָם וַיִּקְרָא לָהֶן שֵׁמוֹת כַּשֵּׁמֹת אֲשֶׁר־קָרָא לָהֶן אָבִיו: ¹⁹וַיַּחְפְּרוּ עַבְדֵי־יִצְחָק בַּנָּחַל וַיִּמְצְאוּ־שָׁם בְּאֵר מַיִם חַיִּים: ²⁰וַיָּרִיבוּ רֹעֵי גְרָר עִם־רֹעֵי יִצְחָק לֵאמֹר לָנוּ הַמָּיִם וַיִּקְרָא שֵׁם־הַבְּאֵר עֵשֶׂק כִּי הִתְעַשְּׂקוּ עִמּוֹ: ²¹וַיַּחְפְּרוּ בְּאֵר אַחֶרֶת וַיָּרִיבוּ גַּם־עָלֶיהָ וַיִּקְרָא שְׁמָהּ שִׂטְנָה: ²²וַיַּעְתֵּק מִשָּׁם וַיַּחְפֹּר בְּאֵר אַחֶרֶת וְלֹא רָבוּ עָלֶיהָ וַיִּקְרָא שְׁמָהּ רְחֹבוֹת וַיֹּאמֶר כִּי־עַתָּה הִרְחִיב יְהוָה לָנוּ וּפָרִינוּ בָאָרֶץ: ²³וַיַּעַל מִשָּׁם בְּאֵר שָׁבַע: ²⁴וַיֵּרָא אֵלָיו יְהוָה בַּלַּיְלָה הַהוּא וַיֹּאמֶר אָנֹכִי אֱלֹהֵי אַבְרָהָם אָבִיךָ אַל־תִּירָא כִּי־אִתְּךָ אָנֹכִי וּבֵרַכְתִּיךָ וְהִרְבֵּיתִי אֶת־זַרְעֲךָ בַּעֲבוּר אַבְרָהָם עַבְדִּי: ²⁵וַיִּבֶן שָׁם מִזְבֵּחַ וַיִּקְרָא בְּשֵׁם יְהוָה וַיֶּט־שָׁם אָהֳלוֹ וַיִּכְרוּ־שָׁם עַבְדֵי־יִצְחָק בְּאֵר:

26 Then Abimelech came to him from Gerar with Ahuzzath, one of his friends, and Phichol the commander of his army. 27 And Isaac said to them, "Why have you come to me, since you hate me and have sent me away from you?"

28 But they said, "We have certainly seen that the LORD is with you. So we said, 'Let there now be an oath between us, between you and us; and let us make a covenant with you, 29 that you will do us no harm, since we have not touched you, and since we have done nothing to you but good and have sent you away in peace. You are now the blessed of the LORD.' "

30 So he made them a feast, and they ate and drank. 31 Then they arose early in the morning and swore an oath with one another; and Isaac sent them away, and they departed from him in peace.

32 It came to pass the same day that Isaac's servants came and told him about the well which they had dug, and said to him, "We have found water." 33 So he called it Shebah. Therefore the name of the city is Beersheba to this day.

34 When Esau was forty years old, he took as wives Judith the daughter of Beeri the Hittite, and Basemath the daughter of Elon the Hittite. 35 And they were a grief of mind to Isaac and Rebekah.

27 Now it came to pass, when Isaac was old and his eyes were so dim that he could not see, that he called Esau his older son and said to him, "My son."

And he answered him, "Here I am."

2 Then he said, "Behold now, I am old. I do not know the day of my death. 3 Now therefore, please take your weapons, your quiver and your bow, and go out to the field and hunt game for me. 4 And make me savory food, such as I love, and bring it to me that I may eat, that my soul may bless you before I die."

5 Now Rebekah was listening when Isaac spoke to Esau his son. And Esau went to the field to hunt game and to bring it. 6 So Rebekah spoke to Jacob her son, saying, "Indeed I heard your father speak to Esau your brother, saying, 7 'Bring me game and make savory food for me, that I may eat it and bless you in the presence of the LORD before my death.' 8 Now therefore, my son, obey my voice according to what I command you. 9 Go now to the flock and bring me from there two choice kids of the goats, and I will make savory food from them for your father, such as he loves. 10 Then you shall take it to your father, that he may eat it, and that he may bless you before his death."

¹¹And Jacob said to Rebekah his mother, "Look, Esau my brother *is* a hairy man, and I *am* a smooth-*skinned* man. ¹²Perhaps my father will feel me, and I shall seem to be a deceiver to him; and I shall bring a curse on myself and not a blessing."

¹³But his mother said to him, "*Let* your curse *be* on me, my son; only obey my voice, and go, get *them* for me." ¹⁴And he went and got *them* and brought *them* to his mother, and his mother made savory food, such as his father loved. ¹⁵Then Rebekah took the choice clothes of her elder son Esau, which *were* with her in the house, and put them on Jacob her younger son. ¹⁶And she put the skins of the kids of the goats on his hands and on the smooth part of his neck. ¹⁷Then she gave the savory food and the bread, which she had prepared, into the hand of her son Jacob.

¹⁸So he went to his father and said, "My father." And he said, "Here I am. Who *are* you, my son?"

¹⁹Jacob said to his father, "I *am* Esau your firstborn; I have done just as you told me; please arise, sit and eat of my game, that your soul may bless me."

²⁰But Isaac said to his son, "How *is* it that you have found *it* so quickly, my son?"

And he said, "Because the LORD your God brought *it* to me."

²¹Isaac said to Jacob, "Please come near, that I may feel you, my son, whether you *are* really my son Esau or not." ²²So Jacob went near to Isaac his father, and he felt him and said, "The voice *is* Jacob's voice, but the hands *are* the hands of Esau." ²³And he did not recognize him, because his hands were hairy like his brother Esau's hands; so he blessed him.

²⁴Then he said, "*Are* you really my son Esau?" He said, "I *am*."

²⁵He said, "Bring *it* near to me, and I will eat of my son's game, so that my soul may bless you." So he brought *it* near to him, and he ate; and he brought him wine, and he drank. ²⁶Then his father Isaac said to him, "Come near now and kiss me, my son." ²⁷And he came near and kissed him; and he smelled the smell of his clothing, and blessed him and said:

"Surely, the smell of my son
Is like the smell of a field
Which the LORD has blessed.
28 Therefore may God give you
Of the dew of heaven,
Of the fatness of the earth,
And plenty of grain and wine.
29 Let peoples serve you,
And nations bow down to you.

וְאָכַל בַּעֲבֻר אֲשֶׁר יְבָרֶכְךָ לְפָנֵי מוֹתִו: ¹¹ וַיֹּאמֶר יַעֲקֹב אֶל־רִבְקָה אִמּוֹ הֵן עֵשָׂו אָחִי אִישׁ שָׂעִר וְאָנֹכִי אִישׁ חָלָק: ¹² אוּלַי יְמֻשֵּׁנִי אָבִי וְהָיִיתִי בְעֵינָיו כִּמְתַעְתֵּעַ וְהֵבֵאתִי עָלַי קְלָלָה וְלֹא בְרָכָה: ¹³ וַתֹּאמֶר לוֹ אִמּוֹ עָלַי קִלְלָתְךָ בְּנִי אַךְ שְׁמַע בְּקֹלִי וְלֵךְ קַח־לִי: ¹⁴ וַיֵּלֶךְ וַיִּקַּח וַיָּבֵא לְאִמּוֹ וַתַּעַשׂ אִמּוֹ מַטְעַמִּים כַּאֲשֶׁר אָהֵב אָבִיו: ¹⁵ וַתִּקַּח רִבְקָה אֶת־בִּגְדֵי עֵשָׂו בְּנָהּ הַגָּדֹל הַחֲמֻדֹת אֲשֶׁר אִתָּהּ בַּבָּיִת וַתַּלְבֵּשׁ אֶת־יַעֲקֹב בְּנָהּ הַקָּטָן: ¹⁶ וְאֵת עֹרֹת גְּדָיֵי הָעִזִּים הִלְבִּישָׁה עַל־יָדָיו וְעַל חֶלְקַת צַוָּארָיו: ¹⁷ וַתִּתֵּן אֶת־הַמַּטְעַמִּים וְאֶת־הַלֶּחֶם אֲשֶׁר עָשָׂתָה בְּיַד יַעֲקֹב בְּנָהּ: ¹⁸ וַיָּבֹא אֶל־אָבִיו וַיֹּאמֶר אָבִי וַיֹּאמֶר הִנֶּנִּי מִי אַתָּה בְּנִי: ¹⁹ וַיֹּאמֶר יַעֲקֹב אֶל־אָבִיו אָנֹכִי עֵשָׂו בְּכֹרֶךָ עָשִׂיתִי כַּאֲשֶׁר דִּבַּרְתָּ אֵלָי קוּם־נָא שְׁבָה וְאָכְלָה מִצֵּידִי בַּעֲבוּר תְּבָרְכַנִּי נַפְשֶׁךָ: ²⁰ וַיֹּאמֶר יִצְחָק אֶל־בְּנוֹ מַה־זֶּה מִהַרְתָּ לִמְצֹא בְּנִי וַיֹּאמֶר כִּי הִקְרָה יְהוָה אֱלֹהֶיךָ לְפָנָי: ²¹ וַיֹּאמֶר יִצְחָק אֶל־יַעֲקֹב גְּשָׁה־נָּא וַאֲמֻשְׁךָ בְּנִי הַאַתָּה זֶה בְּנִי עֵשָׂו אִם־לֹא: ²² וַיִּגַּשׁ יַעֲקֹב אֶל־יִצְחָק אָבִיו וַיְמֻשֵּׁהוּ וַיֹּאמֶר הַקֹּל קוֹל יַעֲקֹב וְהַיָּדַיִם יְדֵי עֵשָׂו: ²³ וְלֹא הִכִּירוֹ כִּי־הָיוּ יָדָיו כִּידֵי עֵשָׂו אָחִיו שְׂעִרֹת וַיְבָרְכֵהוּ: ²⁴ וַיֹּאמֶר אַתָּה זֶה בְּנִי עֵשָׂו וַיֹּאמֶר אָנִי: ²⁵ וַיֹּאמֶר הַגִּשָׁה לִּי וְאֹכְלָה מִצֵּיד בְּנִי לְמַעַן תְּבָרֶכְךָ נַפְשִׁי וַיַּגֶּשׁ־לוֹ וַיֹּאכַל וַיָּבֵא לוֹ יַיִן וַיֵּשְׁתְּ: ²⁶ וַיֹּאמֶר אֵלָיו יִצְחָק אָבִיו גְּשָׁה־נָּא וּשְׁקָה־לִּי בְּנִי: ²⁷ וַיִּגַּשׁ וַיִּשַּׁק־לוֹ וַיָּרַח אֶת־רֵיחַ בְּגָדָיו וַיְבָרְכֵהוּ וַיֹּאמֶר רְאֵה רֵיחַ בְּנִי כְּרֵיחַ שָׂדֶה אֲשֶׁר בֵּרֲכוֹ יְהוָה: ²⁸ וְיִתֶּן־לְךָ הָאֱלֹהִים מִטַּל הַשָּׁמַיִם וּמִשְׁמַנֵּי הָאָרֶץ וְרֹב דָּגָן וְתִירֹשׁ: ²⁹ יַעַבְדוּךָ עַמִּים וְיִשְׁתַּחֲוֻ לְךָ לְאֻמִּים הֱוֵה גְבִיר לְאַחֶיךָ וְיִשְׁתַּחֲווּ לְךָ בְּנֵי אִמֶּךָ

Be master over your brethren,
And let your mother's sons bow down to you.
Cursed *be* everyone who curses you,
And blessed *be* those who bless you!"

30 Now it happened, as soon as Isaac had finished blessing Jacob, and Jacob had scarcely gone out from the presence of Isaac his father, that Esau his brother came in from his hunting. 31 He also had made savory food, and brought it to his father, and said to his father, "Let my father arise and eat of his son's game, that your soul may bless me."

32 And his father Isaac said to him, "Who *are* you?"

So he said, "I *am* your son, your firstborn, Esau."

33 Then Isaac trembled exceedingly, and said, "Who? Where *is* the one who hunted game and brought *it* to me? I ate all *of it* before you came, and I have blessed him—*and* indeed he shall be blessed."

34 When Esau heard the words of his father, he cried with an exceedingly great and bitter cry, and said to his father, "Bless me—me also, O my father!"

35 But he said, "Your brother came with deceit and has taken away your blessing."

36 And *Esau* said, "Is he not rightly named Jacob? For he has supplanted me these two times. He took away my birthright, and now look, he has taken away my blessing!" And he said, "Have you not reserved a blessing for me?"

37 Then Isaac answered and said to Esau, "Indeed I have made him your master, and all his brethren I have given to him as servants; with grain and wine I have sustained him. What shall I do now for you, my son?"

38 And Esau said to his father, "Have you only one blessing, my father? Bless me—me also, O my father!" And Esau lifted up his voice and wept.

39 Then Isaac his father answered and said to him:

"Behold, your dwelling shall be of the fatness of the earth,
And of the dew of heaven from above.
40 By your sword you shall live,
And you shall serve your brother;
And it shall come to pass, when you become restless,
That you shall break his yoke from your neck."

41 So Esau hated Jacob because of the blessing with which his father blessed him, and Esau said in his heart, "The days of mourning for my father are at hand; then I will kill my brother Jacob."

30 וַיְהִ֗י כַּאֲשֶׁ֨ר כִּלָּ֣ה יִצְחָק֮ לְבָרֵ֣ךְ אֶֽת־יַעֲקֹב֒ וַיְהִ֗י אַ֣ךְ יָצֹ֤א יָצָא֙ יַעֲקֹ֔ב מֵאֵ֥ת פְּנֵ֖י יִצְחָ֣ק אָבִ֑יו וְעֵשָׂ֣ו אָחִ֔יו בָּ֖א מִצֵּידֽוֹ: 31 וַיַּ֤עַשׂ גַּם־הוּא֙ מַטְעַמִּ֔ים וַיָּבֵ֖א לְאָבִ֑יו וַיֹּ֣אמֶר לְאָבִ֗יו יָקֻ֤ם אָבִי֙ וְיֹאכַל֙ מִצֵּ֣יד בְּנ֔וֹ בַּעֲבֻ֖ר תְּבָרֲכַ֥נִּי נַפְשֶֽׁךָ: 32 וַיֹּ֥אמֶר ל֛וֹ יִצְחָ֥ק אָבִ֖יו מִי־אָ֑תָּה וַיֹּ֕אמֶר אֲנִ֛י בִּנְךָ֥ בְכֹֽרְךָ֖ עֵשָֽׂו: 33 וַיֶּחֱרַ֨ד יִצְחָ֣ק חֲרָדָה֮ גְּדֹלָ֣ה עַד־מְאֹד֒ וַיֹּ֡אמֶר מִֽי־אֵפ֡וֹא ה֣וּא הַצָּֽד־צַ֩יִד֩ וַיָּ֨בֵא לִ֜י וָאֹכַ֥ל מִכֹּ֛ל בְּטֶ֥רֶם תָּב֖וֹא וָאֲבָרֲכֵ֑הוּ גַּם־בָּר֖וּךְ יִהְיֶֽה: 34 כִּשְׁמֹ֤עַ עֵשָׂו֙ אֶת־דִּבְרֵ֣י אָבִ֔יו וַיִּצְעַ֣ק צְעָקָ֔ה גְּדֹלָ֥ה וּמָרָ֖ה עַד־מְאֹ֑ד וַיֹּ֣אמֶר לְאָבִ֔יו בָּרֲכֵ֥נִי גַם־אָ֖נִי אָבִֽי: 35 וַיֹּ֕אמֶר בָּ֥א אָחִ֖יךָ בְּמִרְמָ֑ה וַיִּקַּ֖ח בִּרְכָתֶֽךָ:

36 וַיֹּ֡אמֶר הֲכִי֩ קָרָ֨א שְׁמ֜וֹ יַעֲקֹ֗ב וַֽיַּעְקְבֵ֨נִי֙ זֶ֣ה פַעֲמַ֔יִם אֶת־בְּכֹרָתִ֣י לָקָ֔ח וְהִנֵּ֥ה עַתָּ֖ה לָקַ֣ח בִּרְכָתִ֑י וַיֹּאמַ֕ר הֲלֹא־אָצַ֥לְתָּ לִּ֖י בְּרָכָֽה: 37 וַיַּ֨עַן יִצְחָ֜ק וַיֹּ֣אמֶר לְעֵשָׂ֗ו הֵ֣ן גְּבִ֞יר שַׂמְתִּ֥יו לָךְ֙ וְאֶת־כָּל־אֶחָ֗יו נָתַ֤תִּי לוֹ֙ לַעֲבָדִ֔ים וְדָגָ֥ן וְתִירֹ֖שׁ סְמַכְתִּ֑יו וּלְכָ֣ה אֵפ֔וֹא מָ֥ה אֶֽעֱשֶׂ֖ה בְּנִֽי: 38 וַיֹּ֨אמֶר עֵשָׂ֜ו אֶל־אָבִ֗יו הַֽבְרָכָ֨ה אַחַ֤ת הִֽוא־לְךָ֙ אָבִ֔י בָּרֲכֵ֥נִי גַם־אָ֖נִי אָבִ֑י וַיִּשָּׂ֥א עֵשָׂ֛ו קֹל֖וֹ וַיֵּֽבְךְּ: 39 וַיַּ֛עַן יִצְחָ֥ק אָבִ֖יו וַיֹּ֣אמֶר אֵלָ֑יו הִנֵּ֞ה מִשְׁמַנֵּ֤י הָאָ֨רֶץ֙ יִהְיֶ֣ה מֽוֹשָׁבֶ֔ךָ וּמִטַּ֥ל הַשָּׁמַ֖יִם מֵעָֽל: 40 וְעַל־חַרְבְּךָ֣ תִֽחְיֶ֔ה וְאֶת־אָחִ֖יךָ תַּעֲבֹ֑ד וְהָיָה֙ כַּאֲשֶׁ֣ר תָּרִ֔יד וּפָרַקְתָּ֥ עֻלּ֖וֹ מֵעַ֥ל צַוָּארֶֽךָ: 41 וַיִּשְׂטֹ֤ם עֵשָׂו֙ אֶֽת־יַעֲקֹ֔ב עַל־הַ֨בְּרָכָ֔ה אֲשֶׁ֥ר בֵּרֲכ֖וֹ אָבִ֑יו וַיֹּ֨אמֶר עֵשָׂ֜ו בְּלִבּ֗וֹ יִקְרְבוּ֙ יְמֵי֙ אֵ֣בֶל אָבִ֔י וְאַֽהַרְגָ֖ה אֶת־יַעֲקֹ֥ב

42 And the words of Esau her older son were told to Rebekah. So she sent and called Jacob her younger son, and said to him, "Surely your brother Esau comforts himself concerning you *by intending* to kill you. 43 Now therefore, my son, obey my voice: arise, flee to my brother Laban in Haran. 44 And stay with him a few days, until your brother's fury turns away, 45 until your brother's anger turns away from you, and he forgets what you have done to him; then I will send and bring you from there. Why should I be bereaved also of you both in one day?"

46 And Rebekah said to Isaac, "I am weary of my life because of the daughters of Heth; if Jacob takes a wife of the daughters of Heth, like these *who are* the daughters of the land, what good will my life be to me?"

28 Then Isaac called Jacob and blessed him, and charged him, and said to him: "You shall not take a wife from the daughters of Canaan. 2 Arise, go to Padan Aram, to the house of Bethuel your mother's father; and take yourself a wife from there of the daughters of Laban your mother's brother.

3 "May God Almighty bless you,
   And make you fruitful and multiply you,
   That you may be an assembly of peoples;
4 And give you the blessing of Abraham,
   To you and your descendants with you,
   That you may inherit the land
   In which you are a stranger,
   Which God gave to Abraham."

5 So Isaac sent Jacob away, and he went to Padan Aram, to Laban the son of Bethuel the Syrian, the brother of Rebekah, the mother of Jacob and Esau.

6 Esau saw that Isaac had blessed Jacob and sent him away to Padan Aram to take himself a wife from there, *and that* as he blessed him he gave him a charge, saying, "You shall not take a wife from the daughters of Canaan," 7 and that Jacob had obeyed his father and his mother and had gone to Padan Aram. 8 Also Esau saw that the daughters of Canaan did not please his father Isaac. 9 So Esau went to Ishmael and took Mahalath the daughter of Ishmael, Abraham's son, the sister of Nebajoth, to be his wife in addition to the wives he had.

10 Now Jacob went out from Beersheba and went toward Haran. 11 So he came to a certain place and stayed there all night, because the sun had set. And he took one of the stones of that place and put it at his head, and he lay down in that place to sleep. 12 Then he dreamed, and behold, a ladder *was* set up

אָחִי: 42 וַיֻּגַּד לְרִבְקָה אֶת־דִּבְרֵי עֵשָׂו בְּנָהּ הַגָּדֹל וַתִּשְׁלַח וַתִּקְרָא לְיַעֲקֹב בְּנָהּ הַקָּטֹן וַתֹּאמֶר אֵלָיו הִנֵּה עֵשָׂו אָחִיךָ מִתְנַחֵם לְךָ לְהָרְגֶךָ: 43 וְעַתָּה בְנִי שְׁמַע בְּקֹלִי וְקוּם בְּרַח־לְךָ אֶל־לָבָן אָחִי חָרָנָה: 44 וְיָשַׁבְתָּ עִמּוֹ יָמִים אֲחָדִים עַד אֲשֶׁר־תָּשׁוּב חֲמַת אָחִיךָ: 45 עַד־שׁוּב אַף־אָחִיךָ מִמְּךָ וְשָׁכַח אֵת אֲשֶׁר־עָשִׂיתָ לּוֹ וְשָׁלַחְתִּי וּלְקַחְתִּיךָ מִשָּׁם לָמָה אֶשְׁכַּל גַּם־שְׁנֵיכֶם יוֹם אֶחָד: 46 וַתֹּאמֶר רִבְקָה אֶל־יִצְחָק קַצְתִּי בְחַיַּי מִפְּנֵי בְּנוֹת חֵת אִם־לֹקֵחַ יַעֲקֹב אִשָּׁה מִבְּנוֹת־חֵת כָּאֵלֶּה מִבְּנוֹת הָאָרֶץ לָמָה לִּי חַיִּים:

כח וַיִּקְרָא יִצְחָק אֶל־יַעֲקֹב וַיְבָרֶךְ אֹתוֹ וַיְצַוֵּהוּ וַיֹּאמֶר לוֹ לֹא־תִקַּח אִשָּׁה מִבְּנוֹת כְּנָעַן: 2 קוּם לֵךְ פַּדֶּנָה אֲרָם בֵּיתָה בְתוּאֵל אֲבִי אִמֶּךָ וְקַח־לְךָ מִשָּׁם אִשָּׁה מִבְּנוֹת לָבָן אֲחִי אִמֶּךָ: 3 וְאֵל שַׁדַּי יְבָרֵךְ אֹתְךָ וְיַפְרְךָ וְיַרְבֶּךָ וְהָיִיתָ לִקְהַל עַמִּים: 4 וְיִתֶּן־לְךָ אֶת־בִּרְכַּת אַבְרָהָם לְךָ וּלְזַרְעֲךָ אִתָּךְ לְרִשְׁתְּךָ אֶת־אֶרֶץ מְגֻרֶיךָ אֲשֶׁר־נָתַן אֱלֹהִים לְאַבְרָהָם: 5 וַיִּשְׁלַח יִצְחָק אֶת־יַעֲקֹב וַיֵּלֶךְ פַּדֶּנָה אֲרָם אֶל־לָבָן בֶּן־בְּתוּאֵל הָאֲרַמִּי אֲחִי רִבְקָה אֵם יַעֲקֹב וְעֵשָׂו:

6 וַיַּרְא עֵשָׂו כִּי־בֵרַךְ יִצְחָק אֶת־יַעֲקֹב וְשִׁלַּח אֹתוֹ פַּדֶּנָה אֲרָם לָקַחַת־לוֹ מִשָּׁם אִשָּׁה בְּבָרֲכוֹ אֹתוֹ וַיְצַו עָלָיו לֵאמֹר לֹא־תִקַּח אִשָּׁה מִבְּנוֹת כְּנָעַן: 7 וַיִּשְׁמַע יַעֲקֹב אֶל־אָבִיו וְאֶל־אִמּוֹ וַיֵּלֶךְ פַּדֶּנָה אֲרָם: 8 וַיַּרְא עֵשָׂו כִּי רָעוֹת בְּנוֹת כְּנָעַן בְּעֵינֵי יִצְחָק אָבִיו: 9 וַיֵּלֶךְ עֵשָׂו אֶל־יִשְׁמָעֵאל וַיִּקַּח אֶת־מָחֲלַת | בַּת־יִשְׁמָעֵאל בֶּן־אַבְרָהָם אֲחוֹת נְבָיוֹת עַל־נָשָׁיו לוֹ לְאִשָּׁה: ס 10 וַיֵּצֵא יַעֲקֹב מִבְּאֵר שֶׁבַע וַיֵּלֶךְ חָרָנָה: 11 וַיִּפְגַּע בַּמָּקוֹם וַיָּלֶן שָׁם כִּי־בָא הַשֶּׁמֶשׁ וַיִּקַּח מֵאַבְנֵי הַמָּקוֹם וַיָּשֶׂם מְרַאֲשֹׁתָיו וַיִּשְׁכַּב בַּמָּקוֹם הַהוּא: 12 וַיַּחֲלֹם וְהִנֵּה סֻלָּם מֻצָּב אַרְצָה וְרֹאשׁוֹ מַגִּיעַ הַשָּׁמָיְמָה וְהִנֵּה

on the earth, and its top reached to heaven; and there the angels of God were ascending and descending on it.

13 And behold, the LORD stood above it and said: "I *am* the LORD God of Abraham your father and the God of Isaac; the land on which you lie I will give to you and your descendants. 14 Also your descendants shall be as the dust of the earth; you shall spread abroad to the west and the east, to the north and the south; and in you and in your seed all the families of the earth shall be blessed. 15 Behold, I *am* with you and will keep you wherever you go, and will bring you back to this land; for I will not leave you until I have done what I have spoken to you."

16 Then Jacob awoke from his sleep and said, "Surely the LORD is in this place, and I did not know *it*." 17 And he was afraid and said, "How awesome *is* this place! This *is* none other than the house of God, and this *is* the gate of heaven!"

18 Then Jacob rose early in the morning, and took the stone that he had put at his head, set it up as a pillar, and poured oil on top of it. 19 And he called the name of that place Bethel; but the name of that city had been Luz previously. 20 Then Jacob made a vow, saying, "If God will be with me, and keep me in this way that I am going, and give me bread to eat and clothing to put on, 21 so that I come back to my father's house in peace, then the LORD shall be my God. 22 And this stone which I have set as a pillar shall be God's house, and of all that You give me I will surely give a tenth to You."

29 So Jacob went on his journey and came to the land of the people of the East. 2 And he looked, and saw a well in the field; and behold, there *were* three flocks of sheep lying by it; for out of that well they watered the flocks. A large stone *was* on the well's mouth. 3 Now all the flocks would be gathered there; and they would roll the stone from the well's mouth, water the sheep, and put the stone back in its place on the well's mouth.

4 And Jacob said to them, "My brethren, where *are* you from?"

And they said, "We *are* from Haran."

5 Then he said to them, "Do you know Laban the son of Nahor?"

And they said, "We know him."

6 So he said to them, "Is he well?"

And they said, "*He is* well. And look, his daughter Rachel is coming with the sheep."

7 Then he said, "Look, *it is* still high day; *it is* not time for the cattle to be gathered together. Water the sheep, and go and feed *them*."

מַלְאֲכֵי אֱלֹהִים עֹלִים וְיֹרְדִים בּוֹ: 13 וְהִנֵּה יְהֹוָה נִצָּב עָלָיו וַיֹּאמַר אֲנִי יְהֹוָה אֱלֹהֵי אַבְרָהָם אָבִיךָ וֵאלֹהֵי יִצְחָק הָאָרֶץ אֲשֶׁר אַתָּה שֹׁכֵב עָלֶיהָ לְךָ אֶתְּנֶנָּה וּלְזַרְעֶךָ: 14 וְהָיָה זַרְעֲךָ כַּעֲפַר הָאָרֶץ וּפָרַצְתָּ יָמָּה וָקֵדְמָה וְצָפֹנָה וָנֶגְבָּה וְנִבְרְכוּ בְךָ כָּל־מִשְׁפְּחֹת הָאֲדָמָה וּבְזַרְעֶךָ: 15 וְהִנֵּה אָנֹכִי עִמָּךְ וּשְׁמַרְתִּיךָ בְּכֹל אֲשֶׁר־תֵּלֵךְ וַהֲשִׁבֹתִיךָ אֶל־הָאֲדָמָה הַזֹּאת כִּי לֹא אֶעֱזָבְךָ עַד אֲשֶׁר אִם־עָשִׂיתִי אֵת אֲשֶׁר־דִּבַּרְתִּי לָךְ: 16 וַיִּיקַץ יַעֲקֹב מִשְּׁנָתוֹ וַיֹּאמֶר אָכֵן יֵשׁ יְהֹוָה בַּמָּקוֹם הַזֶּה וְאָנֹכִי לֹא יָדָעְתִּי: 17 וַיִּירָא וַיֹּאמַר מַה־נּוֹרָא הַמָּקוֹם הַזֶּה אֵין זֶה כִּי אִם־בֵּית אֱלֹהִים וְזֶה שַׁעַר הַשָּׁמָיִם: 18 וַיַּשְׁכֵּם יַעֲקֹב בַּבֹּקֶר וַיִּקַּח אֶת־הָאֶבֶן אֲשֶׁר־שָׂם מְרַאֲשֹׁתָיו וַיָּשֶׂם אֹתָהּ מַצֵּבָה וַיִּצֹק שֶׁמֶן עַל־רֹאשָׁהּ: 19 וַיִּקְרָא אֶת־שֵׁם־הַמָּקוֹם הַהוּא בֵּית־אֵל וְאוּלָם לוּז שֵׁם־הָעִיר לָרִאשֹׁנָה: 20 וַיִּדַּר יַעֲקֹב נֶדֶר לֵאמֹר אִם־יִהְיֶה אֱלֹהִים עִמָּדִי וּשְׁמָרַנִי בַּדֶּרֶךְ הַזֶּה אֲשֶׁר אָנֹכִי הוֹלֵךְ וְנָתַן־לִי לֶחֶם לֶאֱכֹל וּבֶגֶד לִלְבֹּשׁ: 21 וְשַׁבְתִּי בְשָׁלוֹם אֶל־בֵּית אָבִי וְהָיָה יְהֹוָה לִי לֵאלֹהִים: 22 וְהָאֶבֶן הַזֹּאת אֲשֶׁר־שַׂמְתִּי מַצֵּבָה יִהְיֶה בֵּית אֱלֹהִים וְכֹל אֲשֶׁר תִּתֶּן־לִי עַשֵּׂר אֲעַשְּׂרֶנּוּ לָךְ:

כט וַיִּשָּׂא יַעֲקֹב רַגְלָיו וַיֵּלֶךְ אַרְצָה בְנֵי־קֶדֶם: 2 וַיַּרְא וְהִנֵּה בְאֵר בַּשָּׂדֶה וְהִנֵּה־שָׁם שְׁלֹשָׁה עֶדְרֵי־צֹאן רֹבְצִים עָלֶיהָ כִּי מִן־הַבְּאֵר הַהִוא יַשְׁקוּ הָעֲדָרִים וְהָאֶבֶן גְּדֹלָה עַל־פִּי הַבְּאֵר: 3 וְנֶאֶסְפוּ־שָׁמָּה כָל־הָעֲדָרִים וְגָלֲלוּ אֶת־הָאֶבֶן מֵעַל פִּי הַבְּאֵר וְהִשְׁקוּ אֶת־הַצֹּאן וְהֵשִׁיבוּ אֶת־הָאֶבֶן עַל־פִּי הַבְּאֵר לִמְקֹמָהּ: 4 וַיֹּאמֶר לָהֶם יַעֲקֹב אַחַי מֵאַיִן אַתֶּם וַיֹּאמְרוּ מֵחָרָן אֲנָחְנוּ: 5 וַיֹּאמֶר לָהֶם הַיְדַעְתֶּם אֶת־לָבָן בֶּן־נָחוֹר וַיֹּאמְרוּ יָדָעְנוּ: 6 וַיֹּאמֶר לָהֶם הֲשָׁלוֹם לוֹ וַיֹּאמְרוּ שָׁלוֹם וְהִנֵּה רָחֵל בִּתּוֹ בָּאָה עִם־הַצֹּאן: 7 וַיֹּאמֶר הֵן עוֹד הַיּוֹם גָּדוֹל לֹא־עֵת הֵאָסֵף הַמִּקְנֶה

8 But they said, "We cannot until all the flocks are gathered together, and they have rolled the stone from the well's mouth; then we water the sheep."

9 Now while he was still speaking with them, Rachel came with her father's sheep, for she was a shepherdess. 10 And it came to pass, when Jacob saw Rachel the daughter of Laban his mother's brother, and the sheep of Laban his mother's brother, that Jacob went near and rolled the stone from the well's mouth, and watered the flock of Laban his mother's brother. 11 Then Jacob kissed Rachel, and lifted up his voice and wept. 12 And Jacob told Rachel that he *was* her father's relative and that he *was* Rebekah's son. So she ran and told her father.

13 Then it came to pass, when Laban heard the report about Jacob his sister's son, that he ran to meet him, and embraced him and kissed him, and brought him to his house. So he told Laban all these things. 14 And Laban said to him, "Surely you *are* my bone and my flesh." And he stayed with him for a month.

15 Then Laban said to Jacob, "Because you *are* my relative, should you therefore serve me for nothing? Tell me, what *should* your wages *be?*" 16 Now Laban had two daughters: the name of the elder *was* Leah, and the name of the younger *was* Rachel. 17 Leah's eyes *were* delicate, but Rachel was beautiful of form and appearance.

18 Now Jacob loved Rachel; so he said, "I will serve you seven years for Rachel your younger daughter."

19 And Laban said, "*It is* better that I give her to you than that I should give her to another man. Stay with me." 20 So Jacob served seven years for Rachel, and they seemed *only* a few days to him because of the love he had for her.

21 Then Jacob said to Laban, "Give *me* my wife, for my days are fulfilled, that I may go in to her." 22 And Laban gathered together all the men of the place and made a feast. 23 Now it came to pass in the evening, that he took Leah his daughter and brought her to Jacob; and he went in to her. 24 And Laban gave his maid Zilpah to his daughter Leah *as* a maid. 25 So it came to pass in the morning, that behold, it *was* Leah. And he said to Laban, "What is this you have done to me? Was it not for Rachel that I served you? Why then have you deceived me?"

הַשְׁקוּ הַצֹּאן וּלְכוּ רְעוּ: 8 וַיֹּאמְרוּ לֹא נוּכַל עַד אֲשֶׁר יֵאָסְפוּ כָּל־הָעֲדָרִים וְגָלֲלוּ אֶת־הָאֶבֶן מֵעַל פִּי הַבְּאֵר וְהִשְׁקִינוּ הַצֹּאן: 9 עוֹדֶנּוּ מְדַבֵּר עִמָּם וְרָחֵל ׀ בָּאָה עִם־הַצֹּאן אֲשֶׁר לְאָבִיהָ כִּי רֹעָה הִוא: 10 וַיְהִי כַּאֲשֶׁר רָאָה יַעֲקֹב אֶת־רָחֵל בַּת־לָבָן אֲחִי אִמּוֹ וְאֶת־צֹאן לָבָן אֲחִי אִמּוֹ וַיִּגַּשׁ יַעֲקֹב וַיָּגֶל אֶת־הָאֶבֶן מֵעַל פִּי הַבְּאֵר וַיַּשְׁקְ אֶת־צֹאן לָבָן אֲחִי אִמּוֹ: 11 וַיִּשַּׁק יַעֲקֹב לְרָחֵל וַיִּשָּׂא אֶת־קֹלוֹ וַיֵּבְךְּ: 12 וַיַּגֵּד יַעֲקֹב לְרָחֵל כִּי אֲחִי אָבִיהָ הוּא וְכִי בֶן־רִבְקָה הוּא וַתָּרָץ וַתַּגֵּד לְאָבִיהָ: 13 וַיְהִי כִשְׁמֹעַ לָבָן אֶת־שֵׁמַע ׀ יַעֲקֹב בֶּן־אֲחֹתוֹ וַיָּרָץ לִקְרָאתוֹ וַיְחַבֶּק־לוֹ וַיְנַשֶּׁק־לוֹ וַיְבִיאֵהוּ אֶל־בֵּיתוֹ וַיְסַפֵּר לְלָבָן אֵת כָּל־הַדְּבָרִים הָאֵלֶּה: 14 וַיֹּאמֶר לוֹ לָבָן אַךְ עַצְמִי וּבְשָׂרִי אָתָּה וַיֵּשֶׁב עִמּוֹ חֹדֶשׁ יָמִים: 15 וַיֹּאמֶר לָבָן לְיַעֲקֹב הֲכִי־אָחִי אַתָּה וַעֲבַדְתַּנִי חִנָּם הַגִּידָה לִּי מַה־מַּשְׂכֻּרְתֶּךָ: 16 וּלְלָבָן שְׁתֵּי בָנוֹת שֵׁם הַגְּדֹלָה לֵאָה וְשֵׁם הַקְּטַנָּה רָחֵל: 17 וְעֵינֵי לֵאָה רַכּוֹת וְרָחֵל הָיְתָה יְפַת־תֹּאַר וִיפַת מַרְאֶה: 18 וַיֶּאֱהַב יַעֲקֹב אֶת־רָחֵל וַיֹּאמֶר אֶעֱבָדְךָ שֶׁבַע שָׁנִים בְּרָחֵל בִּתְּךָ הַקְּטַנָּה: 19 וַיֹּאמֶר לָבָן טוֹב תִּתִּי אֹתָהּ לָךְ מִתִּתִּי אֹתָהּ לְאִישׁ אַחֵר שְׁבָה עִמָּדִי: 20 וַיַּעֲבֹד יַעֲקֹב בְּרָחֵל שֶׁבַע שָׁנִים וַיִּהְיוּ בְעֵינָיו כְּיָמִים אֲחָדִים בְּאַהֲבָתוֹ אֹתָהּ: 21 וַיֹּאמֶר יַעֲקֹב אֶל־לָבָן הָבָה אֶת־אִשְׁתִּי כִּי מָלְאוּ יָמָי וְאָבוֹאָה אֵלֶיהָ: 22 וַיֶּאֱסֹף לָבָן אֶת־כָּל־אַנְשֵׁי הַמָּקוֹם וַיַּעַשׂ מִשְׁתֶּה: 23 וַיְהִי בָעֶרֶב וַיִּקַּח אֶת־לֵאָה בִתּוֹ וַיָּבֵא אֹתָהּ אֵלָיו וַיָּבֹא אֵלֶיהָ: 24 וַיִּתֵּן לָבָן לָהּ אֶת־זִלְפָּה שִׁפְחָתוֹ לְלֵאָה בִתּוֹ שִׁפְחָה: 25 וַיְהִי בַבֹּקֶר וְהִנֵּה־הִוא לֵאָה וַיֹּאמֶר אֶל־לָבָן מַה־זֹּאת עָשִׂיתָ לִּי

26 And Laban said, "It must not be done so in our country, to give the younger before the firstborn. 27 Fulfill her week, and we will give you this one also for the service which you will serve with me still another seven years."

28 Then Jacob did so and fulfilled her week. So he gave him his daughter Rachel as wife also. 29 And Laban gave his maid Bilhah to his daughter Rachel as a maid. 30 Then *Jacob* also went in to Rachel, and he also loved Rachel more than Leah. And he served with Laban still another seven years.

31 When the LORD saw that Leah *was* unloved, He opened her womb; but Rachel *was* barren. 32 So Leah conceived and bore a son, and she called his name Reuben; for she said, "The LORD has surely looked on my affliction. Now therefore, my husband will love me." 33 Then she conceived again and bore a son, and said, "Because the LORD has heard that I *am* unloved, He has therefore given me this *son* also." And she called his name Simeon. 34 She conceived again and bore a son, and said, "Now this time my husband will become attached to me, because I have borne him three sons." Therefore his name was called Levi. 35 And she conceived again and bore a son, and said, "Now I will praise the LORD." Therefore she called his name Judah. Then she stopped bearing.

30 Now when Rachel saw that she bore Jacob no children, Rachel envied her sister, and said to Jacob, "Give me children, or else I die!"

2 And Jacob's anger was aroused against Rachel, and he said, "*Am* I in the place of God, who has withheld from you the fruit of the womb?"

3 So she said, "Here is my maid Bilhah; go in to her, and she will bear *a child* on my knees, that I also may have children by her." 4 Then she gave him Bilhah her maid as wife, and Jacob went in to her. 5 And Bilhah conceived and bore Jacob a son. 6 Then Rachel said, "God has judged my case; and He has also heard my voice and given me a son." Therefore she called his name Dan. 7 And Rachel's maid Bilhah conceived again and bore Jacob a second son. 8 Then Rachel said, "With great wrestlings I have wrestled with my sister, *and* indeed I have prevailed." So she called his name Naphtali.

9 When Leah saw that she had stopped bearing, she took Zilpah her maid and gave her to Jacob as wife. 10 And Leah's maid Zilpah bore Jacob a son. 11 Then Leah said, "A troop comes!" So she called his name Gad. 12 And Leah's maid Zilpah bore

הֲלֹא בְרָחֵל עָבַדְתִּי עִמָּךְ וְלָמָּה רִמִּיתָנִי: 26 וַיֹּאמֶר לָבָן לֹא־יֵעָשֶׂה כֵן בִּמְקוֹמֵנוּ לָתֵת הַצְּעִירָה לִפְנֵי הַבְּכִירָה: 27 מַלֵּא שְׁבֻעַ זֹאת וְנִתְּנָה לְךָ גַּם־אֶת־זֹאת בַּעֲבֹדָה אֲשֶׁר תַּעֲבֹד עִמָּדִי עוֹד שֶׁבַע־שָׁנִים אֲחֵרוֹת: 28 וַיַּעַשׂ יַעֲקֹב כֵּן וַיְמַלֵּא שְׁבֻעַ זֹאת וַיִּתֶּן־לוֹ אֶת־רָחֵל בִּתּוֹ לוֹ לְאִשָּׁה: 29 וַיִּתֵּן לָבָן לְרָחֵל בִּתּוֹ אֶת־בִּלְהָה שִׁפְחָתוֹ לָהּ לְשִׁפְחָה: 30 וַיָּבֹא גַּם אֶל־רָחֵל וַיֶּאֱהַב גַּם־אֶת־רָחֵל מִלֵּאָה וַיַּעֲבֹד עִמּוֹ עוֹד שֶׁבַע־שָׁנִים אֲחֵרוֹת: 31 וַיַּרְא יְהוָה כִּי־שְׂנוּאָה לֵאָה וַיִּפְתַּח אֶת־רַחְמָהּ וְרָחֵל עֲקָרָה: 32 וַתַּהַר לֵאָה וַתֵּלֶד בֵּן וַתִּקְרָא שְׁמוֹ רְאוּבֵן כִּי אָמְרָה כִּי־רָאָה יְהוָה בְּעָנְיִי כִּי עַתָּה יֶאֱהָבַנִי אִישִׁי: 33 וַתַּהַר עוֹד וַתֵּלֶד בֵּן וַתֹּאמֶר כִּי־שָׁמַע יְהוָה כִּי־שְׂנוּאָה אָנֹכִי וַיִּתֶּן־לִי גַּם־אֶת־זֶה וַתִּקְרָא שְׁמוֹ שִׁמְעוֹן: 34 וַתַּהַר עוֹד וַתֵּלֶד בֵּן וַתֹּאמֶר עַתָּה הַפַּעַם יִלָּוֶה אִישִׁי אֵלַי כִּי־יָלַדְתִּי לוֹ שְׁלֹשָׁה בָנִים עַל־כֵּן קָרָא־שְׁמוֹ לֵוִי: 35 וַתַּהַר עוֹד וַתֵּלֶד בֵּן וַתֹּאמֶר הַפַּעַם אוֹדֶה אֶת־יְהוָה עַל־כֵּן קָרְאָה שְׁמוֹ יְהוּדָה וַתַּעֲמֹד מִלֶּדֶת:

ל וַתֵּרֶא רָחֵל כִּי לֹא יָלְדָה לְיַעֲקֹב וַתְּקַנֵּא רָחֵל בַּאֲחֹתָהּ וַתֹּאמֶר אֶל־יַעֲקֹב הָבָה־לִּי בָנִים וְאִם־אַיִן מֵתָה אָנֹכִי: 2 וַיִּחַר־אַף יַעֲקֹב בְּרָחֵל וַיֹּאמֶר הֲתַחַת אֱלֹהִים אָנֹכִי אֲשֶׁר־מָנַע מִמֵּךְ פְּרִי־בָטֶן: 3 וַתֹּאמֶר הִנֵּה אֲמָתִי בִלְהָה בֹּא אֵלֶיהָ וְתֵלֵד עַל־בִּרְכַּי וְאִבָּנֶה גַם־אָנֹכִי מִמֶּנָּה: 4 וַתִּתֶּן־לוֹ אֶת־בִּלְהָה שִׁפְחָתָהּ לְאִשָּׁה וַיָּבֹא אֵלֶיהָ יַעֲקֹב: 5 וַתַּהַר בִּלְהָה וַתֵּלֶד לְיַעֲקֹב בֵּן: 6 וַתֹּאמֶר רָחֵל דָּנַנִּי אֱלֹהִים וְגַם שָׁמַע בְּקֹלִי וַיִּתֶּן־לִי בֵּן עַל־כֵּן קָרְאָה שְׁמוֹ דָּן: 7 וַתַּהַר עוֹד וַתֵּלֶד בִּלְהָה שִׁפְחַת רָחֵל בֵּן שֵׁנִי לְיַעֲקֹב: 8 וַתֹּאמֶר רָחֵל נַפְתּוּלֵי אֱלֹהִים נִפְתַּלְתִּי עִם־אֲחֹתִי גַּם־יָכֹלְתִּי וַתִּקְרָא שְׁמוֹ נַפְתָּלִי: 9 וַתֵּרֶא לֵאָה כִּי עָמְדָה מִלֶּדֶת וַתִּקַּח אֶת־זִלְפָּה שִׁפְחָתָהּ וַתִּתֵּן אֹתָהּ לְיַעֲקֹב לְאִשָּׁה: 10 וַתֵּלֶד זִלְפָּה שִׁפְחַת לֵאָה לְיַעֲקֹב בֵּן: 11 וַתֹּאמֶר לֵאָה בָּא גָד וַתִּקְרָא אֶת־שְׁמוֹ גָּד: 12 וַתֵּלֶד זִלְפָּה

ל 11 גָד

Jacob a second son. ¹³Then Leah said, "I am happy, for the daughters will call me blessed." So she called his name Asher.

¹⁴Now Reuben went in the days of wheat harvest and found mandrakes in the field, and brought them to his mother Leah. Then Rachel said to Leah, "Please give me *some* of your son's mandrakes."

¹⁵But she said to her, "*Is it* a small matter that you have taken away my husband? Would you take away my son's mandrakes also?"

And Rachel said, "Therefore he will lie with you tonight for your son's mandrakes."

¹⁶When Jacob came out of the field in the evening, Leah went out to meet him and said, "You must come in to me, for I have surely hired you with my son's mandrakes." And he lay with her that night.

¹⁷And God listened to Leah, and she conceived and bore Jacob a fifth son. ¹⁸Leah said, "God has given me my wages, because I have given my maid to my husband." So she called his name Issachar. ¹⁹Then Leah conceived again and bore Jacob a sixth son. ²⁰And Leah said, "God has endowed me *with* a good endowment; now my husband will dwell with me, because I have borne him six sons." So she called his name Zebulun. ²¹Afterward she bore a daughter, and called her name Dinah.

²²Then God remembered Rachel, and God listened to her and opened her womb. ²³And she conceived and bore a son, and said, "God has taken away my reproach." ²⁴So she called his name Joseph, and said, "The LORD shall add to me another son."

²⁵And it came to pass, when Rachel had borne Joseph, that Jacob said to Laban, "Send me away, that I may go to my own place and to my country. ²⁶Give *me* my wives and my children for whom I have served you, and let me go; for you know my service which I have done for you."

²⁷And Laban said to him, "Please *stay,* if I have found favor in your eyes, *for* I have learned by experience that the LORD has blessed me for your sake." ²⁸Then he said, "Name me your wages, and I will give *it.*"

²⁹So *Jacob* said to him, "You know how I have served you and how your livestock has been with me. ³⁰For what you had before I *came was* little, and it has increased to a great amount; the LORD has blessed you since my coming. And now, when shall I also provide for my own house?"

³¹So he said, "What shall I give you?"

שִׁפְחַת לֵאָה בֵּן שֵׁנִי לְיַעֲקֹב: 13 וַתֹּאמֶר לֵאָה בְּאָשְׁרִי כִּי אִשְּׁרוּנִי בָּנוֹת וַתִּקְרָא אֶת־שְׁמוֹ אָשֵׁר: 14 וַיֵּלֶךְ רְאוּבֵן בִּימֵי קְצִיר־חִטִּים וַיִּמְצָא דוּדָאִים בַּשָּׂדֶה וַיָּבֵא אֹתָם אֶל־לֵאָה אִמּוֹ וַתֹּאמֶר רָחֵל אֶל־לֵאָה תְּנִי־נָא לִי מִדּוּדָאֵי בְּנֵךְ: 15 וַתֹּאמֶר לָהּ הַמְעַט קַחְתֵּךְ אֶת־אִישִׁי וְלָקַחַת גַּם אֶת־דּוּדָאֵי בְּנִי וַתֹּאמֶר רָחֵל לָכֵן יִשְׁכַּב עִמָּךְ הַלַּיְלָה תַּחַת דּוּדָאֵי בְנֵךְ: 16 וַיָּבֹא יַעֲקֹב מִן־הַשָּׂדֶה בָּעֶרֶב וַתֵּצֵא לֵאָה לִקְרָאתוֹ וַתֹּאמֶר אֵלַי תָּבוֹא כִּי שָׂכֹר שְׂכַרְתִּיךָ בְּדוּדָאֵי בְּנִי וַיִּשְׁכַּב עִמָּהּ בַּלַּיְלָה הוּא: 17 וַיִּשְׁמַע אֱלֹהִים אֶל־לֵאָה וַתַּהַר וַתֵּלֶד לְיַעֲקֹב בֵּן חֲמִישִׁי: 18 וַתֹּאמֶר לֵאָה נָתַן אֱלֹהִים שְׂכָרִי אֲשֶׁר־נָתַתִּי שִׁפְחָתִי לְאִישִׁי וַתִּקְרָא שְׁמוֹ יִשָּׂשכָר: 19 וַתַּהַר עוֹד לֵאָה וַתֵּלֶד בֵּן־שִׁשִּׁי לְיַעֲקֹב: 20 וַתֹּאמֶר לֵאָה זְבָדַנִי אֱלֹהִים ׀ אֹתִי זֵבֶד טוֹב הַפַּעַם יִזְבְּלֵנִי אִישִׁי כִּי־יָלַדְתִּי לוֹ שִׁשָּׁה בָנִים וַתִּקְרָא אֶת־שְׁמוֹ זְבֻלוּן: 21 וְאַחַר יָלְדָה בַּת וַתִּקְרָא אֶת־שְׁמָהּ דִּינָה: 22 וַיִּזְכֹּר אֱלֹהִים אֶת־רָחֵל וַיִּשְׁמַע אֵלֶיהָ אֱלֹהִים וַיִּפְתַּח אֶת־רַחְמָהּ: 23 וַתַּהַר וַתֵּלֶד בֵּן וַתֹּאמֶר אָסַף אֱלֹהִים אֶת־חֶרְפָּתִי: 24 וַתִּקְרָא אֶת־שְׁמוֹ יוֹסֵף לֵאמֹר יֹסֵף יְהוָה לִי בֵּן אַחֵר: 25 וַיְהִי כַּאֲשֶׁר יָלְדָה רָחֵל אֶת־יוֹסֵף וַיֹּאמֶר יַעֲקֹב אֶל־לָבָן שַׁלְּחֵנִי וְאֵלְכָה אֶל־מְקוֹמִי וּלְאַרְצִי: 26 תְּנָה אֶת־נָשַׁי וְאֶת־יְלָדַי אֲשֶׁר עָבַדְתִּי אֹתְךָ בָּהֵן וְאֵלֵכָה כִּי אַתָּה יָדַעְתָּ אֶת־עֲבֹדָתִי אֲשֶׁר עֲבַדְתִּיךָ: 27 וַיֹּאמֶר אֵלָיו לָבָן אִם־נָא מָצָאתִי חֵן בְּעֵינֶיךָ נִחַשְׁתִּי וַיְבָרֲכֵנִי יְהוָה בִּגְלָלֶךָ: 28 וַיֹּאמַר נָקְבָה שְׂכָרְךָ עָלַי וְאֶתֵּנָה: 29 וַיֹּאמֶר אֵלָיו אַתָּה יָדַעְתָּ אֵת אֲשֶׁר עֲבַדְתִּיךָ וְאֵת אֲשֶׁר־הָיָה מִקְנְךָ אִתִּי: 30 כִּי מְעַט אֲשֶׁר־הָיָה לְךָ לְפָנַי וַיִּפְרֹץ לָרֹב וַיְבָרֶךְ יְהוָה אֹתְךָ לְרַגְלִי וְעַתָּה מָתַי אֶעֱשֶׂה גַם־אָנֹכִי לְבֵיתִי: 31 וַיֹּאמֶר מָה אֶתֶּן־לָךְ וַיֹּאמֶר יַעֲקֹב לֹא־תִתֶּן־לִי מְאוּמָה אִם־תַּעֲשֶׂה־לִּי הַדָּבָר הַזֶּה אָשׁוּבָה אֶרְעֶה צֹאנְךָ

And Jacob said, "You shall not give me anything. If you will do this thing for me, I will again feed and keep your flocks: ³²Let me pass through all your flock today, removing from there all the speckled and spotted sheep, and all the brown ones among the lambs, and the spotted and speckled among the goats; and *these* shall be my wages. ³³So my righteousness will answer for me in time to come, when the subject of my wages comes before you: every one that *is* not speckled and spotted among the goats, and brown among the lambs, will be considered stolen, if *it is* with me."

³⁴And Laban said, "Oh, that it were according to your word!" ³⁵So he removed that day the male goats that were speckled and spotted, all the female goats that were speckled and spotted, every one that had *some* white in it, and all the brown ones among the lambs, and gave *them* into the hand of his sons. ³⁶Then he put three days' journey between himself and Jacob, and Jacob fed the rest of Laban's flocks.

³⁷Now Jacob took for himself rods of green poplar and of the almond and chestnut trees, peeled white strips in them, and exposed the white which *was* in the rods. ³⁸And the rods which he had peeled, he set before the flocks in the gutters, in the watering troughs where the flocks came to drink, so that they should conceive when they came to drink. ³⁹So the flocks conceived before the rods, and the flocks brought forth streaked, speckled, and spotted. ⁴⁰Then Jacob separated the lambs, and made the flocks face toward the streaked and all the brown in the flock of Laban; but he put his own flocks by themselves and did not put them with Laban's flock.

⁴¹And it came to pass, whenever the stronger livestock conceived, that Jacob placed the rods before the eyes of the livestock in the gutters, that they might conceive among the rods. ⁴²But when the flocks were feeble, he did not put *them* in; so the feebler were Laban's and the stronger Jacob's. ⁴³Thus the man became exceedingly prosperous, and had large flocks, female and male servants, and camels and donkeys.

31 Now *Jacob* heard the words of Laban's sons, saying, "Jacob has taken away all that was our father's, and from what was our father's he has acquired all this wealth." ²And Jacob saw the countenance of Laban, and indeed it *was* not *favorable* toward him as before. ³Then the LORD said to Jacob, "Return to the land of your fathers and to your family, and I will be with you."

אֶשְׂמֹר: 32 אֶעֱבֹר בְּכָל־צֹאנְךָ הַיּוֹם הָסֵר מִשָּׁם כָּל־שֶׂה ׀ נָקֹד וְטָלוּא וְכָל־שֶׂה־חוּם בַּכְּשָׂבִים וְטָלוּא וְנָקֹד בָּעִזִּים וְהָיָה שְׂכָרִי: 33 וְעָנְתָה־בִּי צִדְקָתִי בְּיוֹם מָחָר כִּי־תָבוֹא עַל־שְׂכָרִי לְפָנֶיךָ כֹּל אֲשֶׁר־אֵינֶנּוּ נָקֹד וְטָלוּא בָּעִזִּים וְחוּם בַּכְּשָׂבִים גָּנוּב הוּא אִתִּי: 34 וַיֹּאמֶר לָבָן הֵן לוּ יְהִי כִדְבָרֶךָ: 35 וַיָּסַר בַּיּוֹם הַהוּא אֶת־הַתְּיָשִׁים הָעֲקֻדִּים וְהַטְּלֻאִים וְאֵת כָּל־הָעִזִּים הַנְּקֻדּוֹת וְהַטְּלֻאֹת כֹּל אֲשֶׁר־לָבָן בּוֹ וְכָל־חוּם בַּכְּשָׂבִים וַיִּתֵּן בְּיַד־בָּנָיו: 36 וַיָּשֶׂם דֶּרֶךְ שְׁלֹשֶׁת יָמִים בֵּינוֹ וּבֵין יַעֲקֹב וְיַעֲקֹב רֹעֶה אֶת־צֹאן לָבָן הַנּוֹתָרֹת: 37 וַיִּקַּח־לוֹ יַעֲקֹב מַקַּל לִבְנֶה לַח וְלוּז וְעֶרְמוֹן וַיְפַצֵּל בָּהֵן פְּצָלוֹת לְבָנוֹת מַחְשֹׂף הַלָּבָן אֲשֶׁר עַל־הַמַּקְלוֹת: 38 וַיַּצֵּג אֶת־הַמַּקְלוֹת אֲשֶׁר פִּצֵּל בָּרְהָטִים בְּשִׁקֲתוֹת הַמָּיִם אֲשֶׁר תָּבֹאןָ הַצֹּאן לִשְׁתּוֹת לְנֹכַח הַצֹּאן וַיֵּחַמְנָה בְּבֹאָן לִשְׁתּוֹת: 39 וַיֶּחֱמוּ הַצֹּאן אֶל־הַמַּקְלוֹת וַתֵּלַדְןָ הַצֹּאן עֲקֻדִּים נְקֻדִּים וּטְלֻאִים: 40 וְהַכְּשָׂבִים הִפְרִיד יַעֲקֹב וַיִּתֵּן פְּנֵי הַצֹּאן אֶל־עָקֹד וְכָל־חוּם בְּצֹאן לָבָן וַיָּשֶׁת־לוֹ עֲדָרִים לְבַדּוֹ וְלֹא שָׁתָם עַל־צֹאן לָבָן: 41 וְהָיָה בְּכָל־יַחֵם הַצֹּאן הַמְקֻשָּׁרוֹת וְשָׂם יַעֲקֹב אֶת־הַמַּקְלוֹת לְעֵינֵי הַצֹּאן בָּרְהָטִים לְיַחְמֵנָּה בַּמַּקְלוֹת: 42 וּבְהַעֲטִיף הַצֹּאן לֹא יָשִׂים וְהָיָה הָעֲטֻפִים לְלָבָן וְהַקְּשֻׁרִים לְיַעֲקֹב: 43 וַיִּפְרֹץ הָאִישׁ מְאֹד מְאֹד וַיְהִי־לוֹ צֹאן רַבּוֹת וּשְׁפָחוֹת וַעֲבָדִים וּגְמַלִּים וַחֲמֹרִים:

לא וַיִּשְׁמַע אֶת־דִּבְרֵי בְנֵי־לָבָן לֵאמֹר לָקַח יַעֲקֹב אֵת כָּל־אֲשֶׁר לְאָבִינוּ וּמֵאֲשֶׁר לְאָבִינוּ עָשָׂה אֵת כָּל־הַכָּבֹד הַזֶּה: 2 וַיַּרְא יַעֲקֹב אֶת־פְּנֵי לָבָן וְהִנֵּה אֵינֶנּוּ עִמּוֹ כִּתְמוֹל שִׁלְשׁוֹם: 3 וַיֹּאמֶר יְהוָֹה אֶל־יַעֲקֹב שׁוּב אֶל־אֶרֶץ אֲבוֹתֶיךָ וּלְמוֹלַדְתֶּךָ וְאֶהְיֶה עִמָּךְ: 4 וַיִּשְׁלַח יַעֲקֹב וַיִּקְרָא לְרָחֵל וּלְלֵאָה הַשָּׂדֶה

48 בראשית לא

⁴So Jacob sent and called Rachel and Leah to the field, to his flock, ⁵and said to them, "I see your father's countenance, that it *is* not *favorable* toward me as before; but the God of my father has been with me. ⁶And you know that with all my might I have served your father. ⁷Yet your father has deceived me and changed my wages ten times, but God did not allow him to hurt me. ⁸If he said thus: 'The speckled shall be your wages,' then all the flocks bore speckled. And if he said thus: 'The streaked shall be your wages,' then all the flocks bore streaked. ⁹So God has taken away the livestock of your father and given *them* to me.

¹⁰"And it happened, at the time when the flocks conceived, that I lifted my eyes and saw in a dream, and behold, the rams which leaped upon the flocks *were* streaked, speckled, and gray-spotted. ¹¹Then the Angel of God spoke to me in a dream, saying, 'Jacob.' And I said, 'Here I am.' ¹²And He said, 'Lift your eyes now and see, all the rams which leap on the flocks *are* streaked, speckled, and gray-spotted; for I have seen all that Laban is doing to you. ¹³I *am* the God of Bethel, where you anointed the pillar *and* where you made a vow to Me. Now arise, get out of this land, and return to the land of your family.'"

¹⁴Then Rachel and Leah answered and said to him, "Is there still any portion or inheritance for us in our father's house? ¹⁵Are we not considered strangers by him? For he has sold us, and also completely consumed our money. ¹⁶For all these riches which God has taken from our father are *really* ours and our children's; now then, whatever God has said to you, do it."

¹⁷Then Jacob rose and set his sons and his wives on camels. ¹⁸And he carried away all his livestock and all his possessions which he had gained, his acquired livestock which he had gained in Padan Aram, to go to his father Isaac in the land of Canaan. ¹⁹Now Laban had gone to shear his sheep, and Rachel had stolen the household idols that were her father's. ²⁰And Jacob stole away, unknown to Laban the Syrian, in that he did not tell him that he intended to flee. ²¹So he fled with all that he had. He arose and crossed the river, and headed toward the mountains of Gilead.

²²And Laban was told on the third day that Jacob had fled. ²³Then he took his brethren with him and pursued him for seven days' journey, and he overtook him in the mountains of Gilead. ²⁴But God had come to Laban the Syrian in a dream by night, and said to him, "Be careful that you speak to Jacob neither good nor bad."

5 וַיֹּאמֶר לָהֶן רֹאֶה אָנֹכִי אֶת־פְּנֵי אֲבִיכֶן כִּי־אֵינֶנּוּ אֵלַי כִּתְמֹל שִׁלְשֹׁם וֵאלֹהֵי אָבִי הָיָה עִמָּדִי: 6 וְאַתֵּנָה יְדַעְתֶּן כִּי בְּכָל־כֹּחִי עָבַדְתִּי אֶת־אֲבִיכֶן: 7 וַאֲבִיכֶן הֵתֶל בִּי וְהֶחֱלִף אֶת־מַשְׂכֻּרְתִּי עֲשֶׂרֶת מֹנִים וְלֹא־נְתָנוֹ אֱלֹהִים לְהָרַע עִמָּדִי: 8 אִם־כֹּה יֹאמַר נְקֻדִּים יִהְיֶה שְׂכָרֶךָ וְיָלְדוּ כָל־הַצֹּאן נְקֻדִּים וְאִם־כֹּה יֹאמַר עֲקֻדִּים יִהְיֶה שְׂכָרֶךָ וְיָלְדוּ כָל־הַצֹּאן עֲקֻדִּים: 9 וַיַּצֵּל אֱלֹהִים אֶת־מִקְנֵה אֲבִיכֶם וַיִּתֶּן־לִי: 10 וַיְהִי בְּעֵת יַחֵם הַצֹּאן וָאֶשָּׂא עֵינַי וָאֵרֶא בַּחֲלוֹם וְהִנֵּה הָעַתֻּדִים הָעֹלִים עַל־הַצֹּאן עֲקֻדִּים נְקֻדִּים וּבְרֻדִּים: 11 וַיֹּאמֶר אֵלַי מַלְאַךְ הָאֱלֹהִים בַּחֲלוֹם יַעֲקֹב וָאֹמַר הִנֵּנִי: 12 וַיֹּאמֶר שָׂא־נָא עֵינֶיךָ וּרְאֵה כָּל־הָעַתֻּדִים הָעֹלִים עַל־הַצֹּאן עֲקֻדִּים נְקֻדִּים וּבְרֻדִּים כִּי רָאִיתִי אֵת כָּל־אֲשֶׁר לָבָן עֹשֶׂה לָּךְ: 13 אָנֹכִי הָאֵל בֵּית־אֵל אֲשֶׁר מָשַׁחְתָּ שָּׁם מַצֵּבָה אֲשֶׁר נָדַרְתָּ לִּי שָׁם נֶדֶר עַתָּה קוּם צֵא מִן־הָאָרֶץ הַזֹּאת וְשׁוּב אֶל־אֶרֶץ מוֹלַדְתֶּךָ:

14 וַתַּעַן רָחֵל וְלֵאָה וַתֹּאמַרְנָה לוֹ הַעוֹד לָנוּ חֵלֶק וְנַחֲלָה בְּבֵית אָבִינוּ: 15 הֲלוֹא נָכְרִיּוֹת נֶחְשַׁבְנוּ לוֹ כִּי מְכָרָנוּ וַיֹּאכַל גַּם־אָכוֹל אֶת־כַּסְפֵּנוּ: 16 כִּי כָל־הָעֹשֶׁר אֲשֶׁר הִצִּיל אֱלֹהִים מֵאָבִינוּ לָנוּ הוּא וּלְבָנֵינוּ וְעַתָּה כֹּל אֲשֶׁר אָמַר אֱלֹהִים אֵלֶיךָ עֲשֵׂה:

17 וַיָּקָם יַעֲקֹב וַיִּשָּׂא אֶת־בָּנָיו וְאֶת־נָשָׁיו עַל־הַגְּמַלִּים: 18 וַיִּנְהַג אֶת־כָּל־מִקְנֵהוּ וְאֶת־כָּל־רְכֻשׁוֹ אֲשֶׁר רָכָשׁ מִקְנֵה קִנְיָנוֹ אֲשֶׁר רָכַשׁ בְּפַדַּן אֲרָם לָבוֹא אֶל־יִצְחָק אָבִיו אַרְצָה כְּנָעַן: 19 וְלָבָן הָלַךְ לִגְזֹז אֶת־צֹאנוֹ וַתִּגְנֹב רָחֵל אֶת־הַתְּרָפִים אֲשֶׁר לְאָבִיהָ: 20 וַיִּגְנֹב יַעֲקֹב אֶת־לֵב לָבָן הָאֲרַמִּי עַל־בְּלִי הִגִּיד לוֹ כִּי בֹרֵחַ הוּא: 21 וַיִּבְרַח הוּא וְכָל־אֲשֶׁר־לוֹ וַיָּקָם וַיַּעֲבֹר אֶת־הַנָּהָר וַיָּשֶׂם אֶת־פָּנָיו הַר הַגִּלְעָד: 22 וַיֻּגַּד לְלָבָן בַּיּוֹם הַשְּׁלִישִׁי כִּי בָרַח יַעֲקֹב: 23 וַיִּקַּח אֶת־אֶחָיו עִמּוֹ וַיִּרְדֹּף אַחֲרָיו דֶּרֶךְ שִׁבְעַת יָמִים וַיַּדְבֵּק אֹתוֹ בְּהַר הַגִּלְעָד: 24 וַיָּבֹא אֱלֹהִים אֶל־לָבָן הָאֲרַמִּי בַּחֲלֹם הַלָּיְלָה וַיֹּאמֶר לוֹ הִשָּׁמֶר לְךָ פֶּן־תְּדַבֵּר עִם־יַעֲקֹב מִטּוֹב עַד־רָע:

25 So Laban overtook Jacob. Now Jacob had pitched his tent in the mountains, and Laban with his brethren pitched in the mountains of Gilead.

26 And Laban said to Jacob: "What have you done, that you have stolen away unknown to me, and carried away my daughters like captives *taken with the sword?* 27 Why did you flee away secretly, and steal away from me, and not tell me; for I might have sent you away with joy and songs, with timbrel and harp? 28 And you did not allow me to kiss my sons and my daughters. Now you have done foolishly in *so* doing. 29 It is in my power to do you harm, but the God of your father spoke to me last night, saying, 'Be careful that you speak to Jacob neither good nor bad.' 30 And now you have surely gone because you greatly long for your father's house, *but* why did you steal my gods?"

31 Then Jacob answered and said to Laban, "Because I was afraid, for I said, 'Perhaps you would take your daughters from me by force.' 32 With whomever you find your gods, do not let him live. In the presence of our brethren, identify what I have of yours and take *it* with you." For Jacob did not know that Rachel had stolen them.

33 And Laban went into Jacob's tent, into Leah's tent, and into the two maids' tents, but he did not find *them.* Then he went out of Leah's tent and entered Rachel's tent. 34 Now Rachel had taken the household idols, put them in the camel's saddle, and sat on them. And Laban searched all about the tent but did not find *them.* 35 And she said to her father, "Let it not displease my lord that I cannot rise before you, for the manner of women *is* with me." And he searched but did not find the household idols.

36 Then Jacob was angry and rebuked Laban, and Jacob answered and said to Laban: "What *is* my trespass? What *is* my sin, that you have so hotly pursued me? 37 Although you have searched all my things, what part of your household things have you found? Set *it* here before my brethren and your brethren, that they may judge between us both! 38 These twenty years I *have been* with you; your ewes and your female goats have not miscarried their young, and I have not eaten the rams of your flock. 39 That which was torn *by beasts* I did not bring to you; I bore the loss of it. You required it from my hand, *whether* stolen by day or stolen by night. 40 *There* I was! In the day the drought consumed me, and the frost by night, and my sleep departed from my eyes. 41 Thus I have been in your house twenty years; I served you fourteen years for your two daughters, and six years for your flock, and you have changed my wages ten times. 42 Un-

25 וַיַּשֵּׂג לָבָן אֶת־יַעֲקֹב וְיַעֲקֹב תָּקַע אֶת־אָהֳלוֹ בָּהָר וְלָבָן תָּקַע אֶת־אֶחָיו בְּהַר הַגִּלְעָד: 26 וַיֹּאמֶר לָבָן לְיַעֲקֹב מֶה עָשִׂיתָ וַתִּגְנֹב אֶת־לְבָבִי וַתְּנַהֵג אֶת־בְּנֹתַי כִּשְׁבֻיוֹת חָרֶב: 27 לָמָּה נַחְבֵּאתָ לִבְרֹחַ וַתִּגְנֹב אֹתִי וְלֹא־הִגַּדְתָּ לִּי וָאֲשַׁלֵּחֲךָ בְּשִׂמְחָה וּבְשִׁרִים בְּתֹף וּבְכִנּוֹר: 28 וְלֹא נְטַשְׁתַּנִי לְנַשֵּׁק לְבָנַי וְלִבְנֹתָי עַתָּה הִסְכַּלְתָּ עֲשׂוֹ: 29 יֶשׁ־לְאֵל יָדִי לַעֲשׂוֹת עִמָּכֶם רָע וֵאלֹהֵי אֲבִיכֶם אֶמֶשׁ ׀ אָמַר אֵלַי לֵאמֹר הִשָּׁמֶר לְךָ מִדַּבֵּר עִם־יַעֲקֹב מִטּוֹב עַד־רָע: 30 וְעַתָּה הָלֹךְ הָלַכְתָּ כִּי־נִכְסֹף נִכְסַפְתָּה לְבֵית אָבִיךָ לָמָּה גָנַבְתָּ אֶת־אֱלֹהָי: 31 וַיַּעַן יַעֲקֹב וַיֹּאמֶר לְלָבָן כִּי יָרֵאתִי כִּי אָמַרְתִּי פֶּן־תִּגְזֹל אֶת־בְּנוֹתֶיךָ מֵעִמִּי: 32 עִם אֲשֶׁר תִּמְצָא אֶת־אֱלֹהֶיךָ לֹא יִחְיֶה נֶגֶד אַחֵינוּ הַכֶּר־לְךָ מָה עִמָּדִי וְקַח־לָךְ וְלֹא־יָדַע יַעֲקֹב כִּי רָחֵל גְּנָבָתַם: 33 וַיָּבֹא לָבָן בְּאֹהֶל יַעֲקֹב ׀ וּבְאֹהֶל לֵאָה וּבְאֹהֶל שְׁתֵּי הָאֲמָהֹת וְלֹא מָצָא וַיֵּצֵא מֵאֹהֶל לֵאָה וַיָּבֹא בְּאֹהֶל רָחֵל: 34 וְרָחֵל לָקְחָה אֶת־הַתְּרָפִים וַתְּשִׂמֵם בְּכַר הַגָּמָל וַתֵּשֶׁב עֲלֵיהֶם וַיְמַשֵּׁשׁ לָבָן אֶת־כָּל־הָאֹהֶל וְלֹא מָצָא: 35 וַתֹּאמֶר אֶל־אָבִיהָ אַל־יִחַר בְּעֵינֵי אֲדֹנִי כִּי לוֹא אוּכַל לָקוּם מִפָּנֶיךָ כִּי־דֶרֶךְ נָשִׁים לִי וַיְחַפֵּשׂ וְלֹא מָצָא אֶת־הַתְּרָפִים:

36 וַיִּחַר לְיַעֲקֹב וַיָּרֶב בְּלָבָן וַיַּעַן יַעֲקֹב וַיֹּאמֶר לְלָבָן מַה־פִּשְׁעִי מַה חַטָּאתִי כִּי דָלַקְתָּ אַחֲרָי: 37 כִּי־מִשַּׁשְׁתָּ אֶת־כָּל־כֵּלַי מַה־מָּצָאתָ מִכֹּל כְּלֵי־בֵיתֶךָ שִׂים כֹּה נֶגֶד אַחַי וְאַחֶיךָ וְיוֹכִיחוּ בֵּין שְׁנֵינוּ: 38 זֶה עֶשְׂרִים שָׁנָה אָנֹכִי עִמָּךְ רְחֵלֶיךָ וְעִזֶּיךָ לֹא שִׁכֵּלוּ וְאֵילֵי צֹאנְךָ לֹא אָכָלְתִּי: 39 טְרֵפָה לֹא־הֵבֵאתִי אֵלֶיךָ אָנֹכִי אֲחַטֶּנָּה מִיָּדִי תְּבַקְשֶׁנָּה גְּנֻבְתִי יוֹם וּגְנֻבְתִי לָיְלָה: 40 הָיִיתִי בַיּוֹם אֲכָלַנִי חֹרֶב וְקֶרַח בַּלָּיְלָה וַתִּדַּד שְׁנָתִי מֵעֵינָי: 41 זֶה־לִּי עֶשְׂרִים שָׁנָה בְּבֵיתֶךָ עֲבַדְתִּיךָ אַרְבַּע־עֶשְׂרֵה שָׁנָה בִּשְׁתֵּי בְנֹתֶיךָ וְשֵׁשׁ שָׁנִים בְּצֹאנֶךָ וַתַּחֲלֵף אֶת־מַשְׂכֻּרְתִּי עֲשֶׂרֶת מֹנִים: 42 לוּלֵי אֱלֹהֵי אָבִי אֱלֹהֵי אַבְרָהָם וּפַחַד יִצְחָק הָיָה לִי כִּי עַתָּה רֵיקָם שִׁלַּחְתָּנִי אֶת־עָנְיִי

less the God of my father, the God of Abraham and the Fear of Isaac, had been with me, surely now you would have sent me away empty-handed. God has seen my affliction and the labor of my hands, and rebuked *you* last night."

43 And Laban answered and said to Jacob, "*These* daughters *are* my daughters, and *these* children *are* my children, and *this* flock *is* my flock; all that you see *is* mine. But what can I do this day to these my daughters or to their children whom they have borne? 44 Now therefore, come, let us make a covenant, you and I, and let it be a witness between you and me."

45 So Jacob took a stone and set it up *as* a pillar. 46 Then Jacob said to his brethren, "Gather stones." And they took stones and made a heap, and they ate there on the heap. 47 Laban called it Jegar Sahadutha, but Jacob called it Galeed. 48 And Laban said, "This heap *is* a witness between you and me this day." Therefore its name was called Galeed, 49 also Mizpah, because he said, "May the LORD watch between you and me when we are absent one from another. 50 If you afflict my daughters, or if you take *other* wives besides my daughters, *although* no man *is* with us—see, God *is* witness between you and me!"

51 Then Laban said to Jacob, "Here is this heap and here is *this* pillar, which I have placed between you and me. 52 This heap *is* a witness, and *this* pillar *is* a witness, that I will not pass beyond this heap to you, and you will not pass beyond this heap and this pillar to me, for harm. 53 The God of Abraham, the God of Nahor, and the God of their father judge between us." And Jacob swore by the Fear of his father Isaac. 54 Then Jacob offered a sacrifice on the mountain, and called his brethren to eat bread. And they ate bread and stayed all night on the mountain. 55 And early in the morning Laban arose, and kissed his sons and daughters and blessed them. Then Laban departed and returned to his place.

32 So Jacob went on his way, and the angels of God met him. 2 When Jacob saw them, he said, "This *is* God's camp." And he called the name of that place Mahanaim.

3 Then Jacob sent messengers before him to Esau his brother in the land of Seir, the country of Edom. 4 And he commanded them, saying, "Speak thus to my lord Esau, 'Thus your servant Jacob says: "I have dwelt with Laban and stayed there until now. 5 I have oxen, donkeys, flocks, and male and female servants; and I have sent to tell my lord, that I may find favor in your sight."'"

וְאֶת־יְגִיעַ כַּפַּי רָאָה אֱלֹהִים וַיּוֹכַח אָמֶשׁ: 43 וַיַּעַן לָבָן וַיֹּאמֶר אֶל־יַעֲקֹב הַבָּנוֹת בְּנֹתַי וְהַבָּנִים בָּנַי וְהַצֹּאן צֹאנִי וְכֹל אֲשֶׁר־אַתָּה רֹאֶה לִי־הוּא וְלִבְנֹתַי מָה־אֶעֱשֶׂה לָאֵלֶּה הַיּוֹם אוֹ לִבְנֵיהֶן אֲשֶׁר יָלָדוּ: 44 וְעַתָּה לְכָה נִכְרְתָה בְרִית אֲנִי וָאָתָּה וְהָיָה לְעֵד בֵּינִי וּבֵינֶךָ: 45 וַיִּקַּח יַעֲקֹב אָבֶן וַיְרִימֶהָ מַצֵּבָה: 46 וַיֹּאמֶר יַעֲקֹב לְאֶחָיו לִקְטוּ אֲבָנִים וַיִּקְחוּ אֲבָנִים וַיַּעֲשׂוּ־גָל וַיֹּאכְלוּ שָׁם עַל־הַגָּל: 47 וַיִּקְרָא־לוֹ לָבָן יְגַר שָׂהֲדוּתָא וְיַעֲקֹב קָרָא לוֹ גַּלְעֵד: 48 וַיֹּאמֶר לָבָן הַגַּל הַזֶּה עֵד בֵּינִי וּבֵינְךָ הַיּוֹם עַל־כֵּן קָרָא־שְׁמוֹ גַּלְעֵד: 49 וְהַמִּצְפָּה אֲשֶׁר אָמַר יִצֶף יְהֹוָה בֵּינִי וּבֵינֶךָ כִּי נִסָּתֵר אִישׁ מֵרֵעֵהוּ: 50 אִם־תְּעַנֶּה אֶת־בְּנֹתַי וְאִם־תִּקַּח נָשִׁים עַל־בְּנֹתַי אֵין אִישׁ עִמָּנוּ רְאֵה אֱלֹהִים עֵד בֵּינִי וּבֵינֶךָ: 51 וַיֹּאמֶר לָבָן לְיַעֲקֹב הִנֵּה הַגַּל הַזֶּה וְהִנֵּה הַמַּצֵּבָה אֲשֶׁר יָרִיתִי בֵּינִי וּבֵינֶךָ: 52 עֵד הַגַּל הַזֶּה וְעֵדָה הַמַּצֵּבָה אִם־אָנִי לֹא־אֶעֱבֹר אֵלֶיךָ אֶת־הַגַּל הַזֶּה וְאִם־אַתָּה לֹא־תַעֲבֹר אֵלַי אֶת־הַגַּל הַזֶּה וְאֶת־הַמַּצֵּבָה הַזֹּאת לְרָעָה: 53 אֱלֹהֵי אַבְרָהָם וֵאלֹהֵי נָחוֹר יִשְׁפְּטוּ בֵינֵינוּ אֱלֹהֵי אֲבִיהֶם וַיִּשָּׁבַע יַעֲקֹב בְּפַחַד אָבִיו יִצְחָק: 54 וַיִּזְבַּח יַעֲקֹב זֶבַח בָּהָר וַיִּקְרָא לְאֶחָיו לֶאֱכָל־לָחֶם וַיֹּאכְלוּ לֶחֶם וַיָּלִינוּ בָּהָר:

לב וַיַּשְׁכֵּם לָבָן בַּבֹּקֶר וַיְנַשֵּׁק לְבָנָיו וְלִבְנוֹתָיו וַיְבָרֶךְ אֶתְהֶם וַיֵּלֶךְ וַיָּשָׁב לָבָן לִמְקֹמוֹ: 2 וְיַעֲקֹב הָלַךְ לְדַרְכּוֹ וַיִּפְגְּעוּ־בוֹ מַלְאֲכֵי אֱלֹהִים: 3 וַיֹּאמֶר יַעֲקֹב כַּאֲשֶׁר רָאָם מַחֲנֵה אֱלֹהִים זֶה וַיִּקְרָא שֵׁם־הַמָּקוֹם הַהוּא מַחֲנָיִם: פ

4 וַיִּשְׁלַח יַעֲקֹב מַלְאָכִים לְפָנָיו אֶל־עֵשָׂו אָחִיו אַרְצָה שֵׂעִיר שְׂדֵה אֱדוֹם: 5 וַיְצַו אֹתָם לֵאמֹר כֹּה תֹאמְרוּן לַאדֹנִי לְעֵשָׂו כֹּה אָמַר עַבְדְּךָ יַעֲקֹב

6 Then the messengers returned to Jacob, saying, "We came to your brother Esau, and he also is coming to meet you, and four hundred men *are* with him." 7 So Jacob was greatly afraid and distressed; and he divided the people that *were* with him, and the flocks and herds and camels, into two companies. 8 And he said, "If Esau comes to the one company and attacks it, then the other company which is left will escape."

9 Then Jacob said, "O God of my father Abraham and God of my father Isaac, the LORD who said to me, 'Return to your country and to your family, and I will deal well with you': 10 I am not worthy of the least of all the mercies and of all the truth which You have shown Your servant; for I crossed over this Jordan with my staff, and now I have become two companies. 11 Deliver me, I pray, from the hand of my brother, from the hand of Esau; for I fear him, lest he come and attack me *and* the mother with the children. 12 For You said, 'I will surely treat you well, and make your descendants as the sand of the sea, which cannot be numbered for multitude.' "

13 So he lodged there that same night, and took what came to his hand as a present for Esau his brother: 14 two hundred female goats and twenty male goats, two hundred ewes and twenty rams, 15 thirty milk camels with their colts, forty cows and ten bulls, twenty female donkeys and ten foals. 16 Then he delivered *them* to the hand of his servants, every drove by itself, and said to his servants, "Pass over before me, and put some distance between successive droves." 17 And he commanded the first one, saying, "When Esau my brother meets you and asks you, saying, 'To whom do you belong, and where are you going? Whose *are* these in front of you?' 18 then you shall say, 'They *are* your servant Jacob's. It *is* a present sent to my lord Esau; and behold, he also *is* behind us.' " 19 So he commanded the second, the third, and all who followed the droves, saying, "In this manner you shall speak to Esau when you find him; 20 and also say, 'Behold, your servant Jacob *is* behind us.' " For he said, "I will appease him with the present that goes before me, and afterward I will see his face; perhaps he will accept me." 21 So the present went on over before him, but he himself lodged that night in the camp.

22 And he arose that night and took his two wives, his two female servants, and his eleven sons, and crossed over the ford of Jabbok. 23 He took them, sent them over the brook, and sent over what he had. 24 Then Jacob was left alone; and a Man wrestled with him until the breaking of day. 25 Now

when He saw that He did not prevail against him,
He touched the socket of his hip; and the socket of
Jacob's hip was out of joint as He wrestled with
him. 26 And He said, "Let Me go, for the day
breaks."

But he said, "I will not let You go unless You
bless me!"

27 So He said to him, "What *is* your name?"
He said, "Jacob."

28 And He said, "Your name shall no longer be
called Jacob, but Israel; for you have struggled with
God and with men, and have prevailed."

29 Then Jacob asked, saying, "Tell *me* Your
name, I pray."

And He said, "Why *is* it *that* you ask about My
name?" And He blessed him there.

30 So Jacob called the name of the place Peniel:
"For I have seen God face to face, and my life is
preserved." 31 Just as he crossed over Penuel the sun
rose on him, and he limped on his hip. 32 Therefore
to this day the children of Israel do not eat the
muscle that shrank, which *is* on the hip socket,
because He touched the socket of Jacob's hip in the
muscle that shrank.

33 Now Jacob lifted his eyes and looked, and
there, Esau was coming, and with him were four
hundred men. So he divided the children among
Leah, Rachel, and the two maidservants. 2 And he
put the maidservants and their children in front,
Leah and her children behind, and Rachel and
Joseph last. 3 Then he crossed over before them and
bowed himself to the ground seven times, until he
came near to his brother.

4 But Esau ran to meet him, and embraced him,
and fell on his neck and kissed him, and they wept.
5 And he lifted his eyes and saw the women and
children, and said, "Who *are* these with you?"

So he said, "The children whom God has
graciously given your servant." 6 Then the maidservants came near, they and their children, and
bowed down. 7 And Leah also came near with her
children, and they bowed down. Afterward Joseph
and Rachel came near, and they bowed down.

8 Then Esau said, "What *do* you *mean* by all this
company which I met?"

And he said, "*These are* to find favor in the sight
of my lord."

9 But Esau said, "I have enough, my brother;
keep what you have for yourself."

10 And Jacob said, "No, please, if I have now
found favor in your sight, then receive my present
from my hand, inasmuch as I have seen your face as
though I had seen the face of God, and you were

עָמוֹ עַד עֲלוֹת הַשָּׁחַר: 26 וַיַּרְא כִּי לֹא יָכֹל לוֹ
וַיִּגַּע בְּכַף־יְרֵכוֹ וַתֵּקַע כַּף־יֶרֶךְ יַעֲקֹב בְּהֵאָבְקוֹ
עִמּוֹ: 27 וַיֹּאמֶר שַׁלְּחֵנִי כִּי עָלָה הַשָּׁחַר וַיֹּאמֶר
לֹא אֲשַׁלֵּחֲךָ כִּי אִם־בֵּרַכְתָּנִי: 28 וַיֹּאמֶר אֵלָיו מַה־
שְּׁמֶךָ וַיֹּאמֶר יַעֲקֹב: 29 וַיֹּאמֶר לֹא יַעֲקֹב יֵאָמֵר עוֹד
שִׁמְךָ כִּי אִם־יִשְׂרָאֵל כִּי־שָׂרִיתָ עִם־אֱלֹהִים וְעִם־
אֲנָשִׁים וַתּוּכָל: 30 וַיִּשְׁאַל יַעֲקֹב וַיֹּאמֶר הַגִּידָה־נָּא
שְׁמֶךָ וַיֹּאמֶר לָמָּה זֶּה תִּשְׁאַל לִשְׁמִי וַיְבָרֶךְ אֹתוֹ
שָׁם: 31 וַיִּקְרָא יַעֲקֹב שֵׁם הַמָּקוֹם פְּנִיאֵל כִּי־רָאִיתִי
אֱלֹהִים פָּנִים אֶל־פָּנִים וַתִּנָּצֵל נַפְשִׁי: 32 וַיִּזְרַח־
לוֹ הַשֶּׁמֶשׁ כַּאֲשֶׁר עָבַר אֶת־פְּנוּאֵל וְהוּא צֹלֵעַ
עַל־יְרֵכוֹ: 33 עַל־כֵּן לֹא־יֹאכְלוּ בְנֵי־יִשְׂרָאֵל אֶת־גִּיד
הַנָּשֶׁה אֲשֶׁר עַל־כַּף הַיָּרֵךְ עַד הַיּוֹם הַזֶּה כִּי נָגַע
בְּכַף־יֶרֶךְ יַעֲקֹב בְּגִיד הַנָּשֶׁה:

לג וַיִּשָּׂא יַעֲקֹב עֵינָיו וַיַּרְא וְהִנֵּה עֵשָׂו בָּא
וְעִמּוֹ אַרְבַּע מֵאוֹת אִישׁ וַיַּחַץ אֶת־הַיְלָדִים עַל־
לֵאָה וְעַל־רָחֵל וְעַל שְׁתֵּי הַשְּׁפָחוֹת: 2 וַיָּשֶׂם אֶת־
הַשְּׁפָחוֹת וְאֶת־יַלְדֵיהֶן רִאשֹׁנָה וְאֶת־לֵאָה וִילָדֶיהָ
אַחֲרֹנִים וְאֶת־רָחֵל וְאֶת־יוֹסֵף אַחֲרֹנִים: 3 וְהוּא
עָבַר לִפְנֵיהֶם וַיִּשְׁתַּחוּ אַרְצָה שֶׁבַע פְּעָמִים עַד־
גִּשְׁתּוֹ עַד־אָחִיו: 4 וַיָּרָץ עֵשָׂו לִקְרָאתוֹ וַיְחַבְּקֵהוּ
וַיִּפֹּל עַל־צַוָּארָו וַיִּשָּׁקֵהוּ וַיִּבְכּוּ: 5 וַיִּשָּׂא אֶת־עֵינָיו
וַיַּרְא אֶת־הַנָּשִׁים וְאֶת־הַיְלָדִים וַיֹּאמֶר מִי־אֵלֶּה
לָּךְ וַיֹּאמַר הַיְלָדִים אֲשֶׁר־חָנַן אֱלֹהִים אֶת־עַבְדֶּךָ:
6 וַתִּגַּשְׁןָ הַשְּׁפָחוֹת הֵנָּה וְיַלְדֵיהֶן וַתִּשְׁתַּחֲוֶיןָ: 7 וַתִּגַּשׁ
גַּם־לֵאָה וִילָדֶיהָ וַיִּשְׁתַּחֲווּ וְאַחַר נִגַּשׁ יוֹסֵף וְרָחֵל
וַיִּשְׁתַּחֲווּ: 8 וַיֹּאמֶר מִי לְךָ כָּל־הַמַּחֲנֶה הַזֶּה אֲשֶׁר
פָּגָשְׁתִּי וַיֹּאמֶר לִמְצֹא־חֵן בְּעֵינֵי אֲדֹנִי: 9 וַיֹּאמֶר
עֵשָׂו יֶשׁ־לִי רָב אָחִי יְהִי לְךָ אֲשֶׁר־לָךְ: 10 וַיֹּאמֶר
יַעֲקֹב אַל־נָא אִם־נָא מָצָאתִי חֵן בְּעֵינֶיךָ וְלָקַחְתָּ
מִנְחָתִי מִיָּדִי כִּי עַל־כֵּן רָאִיתִי פָנֶיךָ כִּרְאֹת

pleased with me. ¹¹ Please, take my blessing that is brought to you, because God has dealt graciously with me, and because I have enough." So he urged him, and he took *it.*

¹² Then Esau said, "Let us take our journey; let us go, and I will go before you."

¹³ But Jacob said to him, "My lord knows that the children *are* weak, and the flocks and herds which are nursing *are* with me. And if the men should drive them hard one day, all the flock will die. ¹⁴ Please let my lord go on ahead before his servant. I will lead on slowly at a pace which the livestock that go before me, and the children, are able to endure, until I come to my lord in Seir."

¹⁵ And Esau said, "Now let me leave with you *some* of the people who *are* with me."

But he said, "What need is there? Let me find favor in the sight of my lord." ¹⁶ So Esau returned that day on his way to Seir. ¹⁷ And Jacob journeyed to Succoth, built himself a house, and made booths for his livestock. Therefore the name of the place is called Succoth.

¹⁸ Then Jacob came safely to the city of Shechem, which *is* in the land of Canaan, when he came from Padan Aram; and he pitched his tent before the city. ¹⁹ And he bought the parcel of land, where he had pitched his tent, from the children of Hamor, Shechem's father, for one hundred pieces of money. ²⁰ Then he erected an altar there and called it El Elohe Israel.

34 Now Dinah the daughter of Leah, whom she had borne to Jacob, went out to see the daughters of the land. ² And when Shechem the son of Hamor the Hivite, prince of the country, saw her, he took her and lay with her, and violated her. ³ His soul was strongly attracted to Dinah the daughter of Jacob, and he loved the young woman and spoke kindly to the young woman. ⁴ So Shechem spoke to his father Hamor, saying, "Get me this young woman as a wife."

⁵ And Jacob heard that he had defiled Dinah his daughter. Now his sons were with his livestock in the field; so Jacob held his peace until they came. ⁶ Then Hamor the father of Shechem went out to Jacob to speak with him. ⁷ And the sons of Jacob came in from the field when they heard *it;* and the men were grieved and very angry, because he had done a disgraceful thing in Israel by lying with Jacob's daughter, a thing which ought not to be done. ⁸ But Hamor spoke with them, saying, "The soul of my son Shechem longs for your daughter. Please give her to him as a wife. ⁹ And make marriages with us; give your daughters to us, and

פְּנֵי אֱלֹהִים וַתִּרְצֵנִי: ¹¹ קַח־נָא אֶת־בִּרְכָתִי אֲשֶׁר
הֻבָאת לָךְ כִּי־חַנַּנִי אֱלֹהִים וְכִי יֶשׁ־לִי־כֹל וַיִּפְצַר־
בּוֹ וַיִּקָּח: ¹² וַיֹּאמֶר נִסְעָה וְנֵלֵכָה וְאֵלְכָה לְנֶגְדֶּךָ:
¹³ וַיֹּאמֶר אֵלָיו אֲדֹנִי יֹדֵעַ כִּי־הַיְלָדִים רַכִּים וְהַצֹּאן
וְהַבָּקָר עָלוֹת עָלָי וּדְפָקוּם יוֹם אֶחָד וָמֵתוּ כָּל־
הַצֹּאן: ¹⁴ יַעֲבָר־נָא אֲדֹנִי לִפְנֵי עַבְדּוֹ וַאֲנִי אֶתְנַהֲלָה
לְאִטִּי לְרֶגֶל הַמְּלָאכָה אֲשֶׁר־לְפָנַי וּלְרֶגֶל הַיְלָדִים
עַד אֲשֶׁר־אָבֹא אֶל־אֲדֹנִי שֵׂעִירָה: ¹⁵ וַיֹּאמֶר עֵשָׂו
אַצִּיגָה־נָּא עִמְּךָ מִן־הָעָם אֲשֶׁר אִתִּי וַיֹּאמֶר לָמָּה
זֶּה אֶמְצָא־חֵן בְּעֵינֵי אֲדֹנִי: ¹⁶ וַיָּשָׁב בַּיּוֹם הַהוּא
עֵשָׂו לְדַרְכּוֹ שֵׂעִירָה: ¹⁷ וְיַעֲקֹב נָסַע סֻכֹּתָה וַיִּבֶן
לוֹ בָּיִת וּלְמִקְנֵהוּ עָשָׂה סֻכֹּת עַל־כֵּן קָרָא שֵׁם־
הַמָּקוֹם סֻכּוֹת: ס ¹⁸ וַיָּבֹא יַעֲקֹב שָׁלֵם
עִיר שְׁכֶם אֲשֶׁר בְּאֶרֶץ כְּנַעַן בְּבֹאוֹ מִפַּדַּן אֲרָם וַיִּחַן
אֶת־פְּנֵי הָעִיר: ¹⁹ וַיִּקֶן אֶת־חֶלְקַת הַשָּׂדֶה אֲשֶׁר
נָטָה־שָׁם אָהֳלוֹ מִיַּד בְּנֵי־חֲמוֹר אֲבִי שְׁכֶם בְּמֵאָה
קְשִׂיטָה: ²⁰ וַיַּצֶּב־שָׁם מִזְבֵּחַ וַיִּקְרָא־לוֹ אֵל אֱלֹהֵי
יִשְׂרָאֵל: ס

לד וַתֵּצֵא דִינָה בַּת־לֵאָה אֲשֶׁר יָלְדָה לְיַעֲקֹב
לִרְאוֹת בִּבְנוֹת הָאָרֶץ: ² וַיַּרְא אֹתָהּ שְׁכֶם בֶּן־חֲמוֹר
הַחִוִּי נְשִׂיא הָאָרֶץ וַיִּקַּח אֹתָהּ וַיִּשְׁכַּב אֹתָהּ וַיְעַנֶּהָ:
³ וַתִּדְבַּק נַפְשׁוֹ בְּדִינָה בַּת־יַעֲקֹב וַיֶּאֱהַב אֶת־הַנַּעֲרָ
וַיְדַבֵּר עַל־לֵב הַנַּעֲרָ: ⁴ וַיֹּאמֶר שְׁכֶם אֶל־חֲמוֹר אָבִיו
לֵאמֹר קַח־לִי אֶת־הַיַּלְדָּה הַזֹּאת לְאִשָּׁה: ⁵ וְיַעֲקֹב
שָׁמַע כִּי טִמֵּא אֶת־דִּינָה בִתּוֹ וּבָנָיו הָיוּ אֶת־מִקְנֵהוּ
בַּשָּׂדֶה וְהֶחֱרִשׁ יַעֲקֹב עַד־בֹּאָם: ⁶ וַיֵּצֵא חֲמוֹר אֲבִי־
שְׁכֶם אֶל־יַעֲקֹב לְדַבֵּר אִתּוֹ: ⁷ וּבְנֵי יַעֲקֹב בָּאוּ
מִן־הַשָּׂדֶה כְּשָׁמְעָם וַיִּתְעַצְּבוּ הָאֲנָשִׁים וַיִּחַר לָהֶם
מְאֹד כִּי־נְבָלָה עָשָׂה בְיִשְׂרָאֵל לִשְׁכַּב אֶת־בַּת־
יַעֲקֹב וְכֵן לֹא יֵעָשֶׂה: ⁸ וַיְדַבֵּר חֲמוֹר אִתָּם לֵאמֹר
שְׁכֶם בְּנִי חָשְׁקָה נַפְשׁוֹ בְּבִתְּכֶם תְּנוּ נָא אֹתָהּ לוֹ
לְאִשָּׁה: ⁹ וְהִתְחַתְּנוּ אֹתָנוּ בְּנֹתֵיכֶם תִּתְּנוּ־לָנוּ וְאֶת־

take our daughters to yourselves. ¹⁰So you shall dwell with us, and the land shall be before you. Dwell and trade in it, and acquire possessions for yourselves in it."

¹¹Then Shechem said to her father and her brothers, "Let me find favor in your eyes, and whatever you say to me I will give. ¹²Ask me ever so much dowry and gift, and I will give according to what you say to me; but give me the young woman as a wife."

¹³But the sons of Jacob answered Shechem and Hamor his father, and spoke deceitfully, because he had defiled Dinah their sister. ¹⁴And they said to them, "We cannot do this thing, to give our sister to one who is uncircumcised, for that *would be* a reproach to us. ¹⁵But on this *condition* we will consent to you: If you will become as we *are,* if every male of you is circumcised, ¹⁶then we will give our daughters to you, and we will take your daughters to us; and we will dwell with you, and we will become one people. ¹⁷But if you will not heed us and be circumcised, then we will take our daughter and be gone."

¹⁸And their words pleased Hamor and Shechem, Hamor's son. ¹⁹So the young man did not delay to do the thing, because he delighted in Jacob's daughter. He *was* more honorable than all the household of his father.

²⁰And Hamor and Shechem his son came to the gate of their city, and spoke with the men of their city, saying: ²¹"These men *are* at peace with us. Therefore let them dwell in the land and trade in it. For indeed the land *is* large enough for them. Let us take their daughters to us as wives, and let us give them our daughters. ²²Only on this *condition* will the men consent to dwell with us, to be one people: if every male among us is circumcised as they *are* circumcised. ²³ *Will* not their livestock, their property, and every animal of theirs *be* ours? Only let us consent to them, and they will dwell with us." ²⁴And all who went out of the gate of his city heeded Hamor and Shechem his son; every male was circumcised, all who went out of the gate of his city.

²⁵Now it came to pass on the third day, when they were in pain, that two of the sons of Jacob, Simeon and Levi, Dinah's brothers, each took his sword and came boldly upon the city and killed all the males. ²⁶And they killed Hamor and Shechem his son with the edge of the sword, and took Dinah from Shechem's house, and went out. ²⁷The sons of Jacob came upon the slain, and plundered the city, because their sister had been defiled. ²⁸They took their sheep, their oxen, and their donkeys, what *was*

בְּנֹתֵינוּ תִּקְחוּ לָכֶם: 10 וְאִתָּנוּ תֵּשֵׁבוּ וְהָאָרֶץ תִּהְיֶה לִפְנֵיכֶם שְׁבוּ וּסְחָרוּהָ וְהֵאָחֲזוּ בָּהּ: 11 וַיֹּאמֶר שְׁכֶם אֶל־אָבִיהָ וְאֶל־אַחֶיהָ אֶמְצָא־חֵן בְּעֵינֵיכֶם וַאֲשֶׁר תֹּאמְרוּ אֵלַי אֶתֵּן: 12 הַרְבּוּ עָלַי מְאֹד מֹהַר וּמַתָּן וְאֶתְּנָה כַּאֲשֶׁר תֹּאמְרוּ אֵלָי וּתְנוּ־לִי אֶת־הַנַּעֲרָ לְאִשָּׁה: 13 וַיַּעֲנוּ בְנֵי־יַעֲקֹב אֶת־שְׁכֶם וְאֶת־חֲמוֹר אָבִיו בְּמִרְמָה וַיְדַבֵּרוּ אֲשֶׁר טִמֵּא אֵת דִּינָה אֲחֹתָם:

14 וַיֹּאמְרוּ אֲלֵיהֶם לֹא נוּכַל לַעֲשׂוֹת הַדָּבָר הַזֶּה לָתֵת אֶת־אֲחֹתֵנוּ לְאִישׁ אֲשֶׁר־לוֹ עָרְלָה כִּי־חֶרְפָּה הִוא לָנוּ: 15 אַךְ־בְּזֹאת נֵאוֹת לָכֶם אִם תִּהְיוּ כָמֹנוּ לְהִמֹּל לָכֶם כָּל־זָכָר: 16 וְנָתַנּוּ אֶת־בְּנֹתֵינוּ לָכֶם וְאֶת־בְּנֹתֵיכֶם נִקַּח־לָנוּ וְיָשַׁבְנוּ אִתְּכֶם וְהָיִינוּ לְעַם אֶחָד: 17 וְאִם־לֹא תִשְׁמְעוּ אֵלֵינוּ לְהִמּוֹל וְלָקַחְנוּ אֶת־בִּתֵּנוּ וְהָלָכְנוּ: 18 וַיִּיטְבוּ דִבְרֵיהֶם בְּעֵינֵי חֲמוֹר וּבְעֵינֵי שְׁכֶם בֶּן־חֲמוֹר: 19 וְלֹא־אֵחַר הַנַּעַר לַעֲשׂוֹת הַדָּבָר כִּי חָפֵץ בְּבַת־יַעֲקֹב וְהוּא נִכְבָּד מִכֹּל בֵּית אָבִיו: 20 וַיָּבֹא חֲמוֹר וּשְׁכֶם בְּנוֹ אֶל־שַׁעַר עִירָם וַיְדַבְּרוּ אֶל־אַנְשֵׁי עִירָם לֵאמֹר: 21 הָאֲנָשִׁים הָאֵלֶּה שְׁלֵמִים הֵם אִתָּנוּ וְיֵשְׁבוּ בָאָרֶץ וְיִסְחֲרוּ אֹתָהּ וְהָאָרֶץ הִנֵּה רַחֲבַת־יָדַיִם לִפְנֵיהֶם אֶת־בְּנֹתָם נִקַּח־לָנוּ לְנָשִׁים וְאֶת־בְּנֹתֵינוּ נִתֵּן לָהֶם: 22 אַךְ־בְּזֹאת יֵאֹתוּ לָנוּ הָאֲנָשִׁים לָשֶׁבֶת אִתָּנוּ לִהְיוֹת לְעַם אֶחָד בְּהִמּוֹל לָנוּ כָּל־זָכָר כַּאֲשֶׁר הֵם נִמֹּלִים:

23 מִקְנֵהֶם וְקִנְיָנָם וְכָל־בְּהֶמְתָּם הֲלוֹא לָנוּ הֵם אַךְ נֵאוֹתָה לָהֶם וְיֵשְׁבוּ אִתָּנוּ: 24 וַיִּשְׁמְעוּ אֶל־חֲמוֹר וְאֶל־שְׁכֶם בְּנוֹ כָּל־יֹצְאֵי שַׁעַר עִירוֹ וַיִּמֹּלוּ כָּל־זָכָר כָּל־יֹצְאֵי שַׁעַר עִירוֹ: 25 וַיְהִי בַיּוֹם הַשְּׁלִישִׁי בִּהְיוֹתָם כֹּאֲבִים וַיִּקְחוּ שְׁנֵי־בְנֵי־יַעֲקֹב שִׁמְעוֹן וְלֵוִי אֲחֵי דִינָה אִישׁ חַרְבּוֹ וַיָּבֹאוּ עַל־הָעִיר בֶּטַח וַיַּהַרְגוּ כָּל־זָכָר: 26 וְאֶת־חֲמוֹר וְאֶת־שְׁכֶם בְּנוֹ הָרְגוּ לְפִי־חָרֶב וַיִּקְחוּ אֶת־דִּינָה מִבֵּית שְׁכֶם וַיֵּצֵאוּ: 27 בְּנֵי יַעֲקֹב בָּאוּ עַל־הַחֲלָלִים וַיָּבֹזּוּ הָעִיר אֲשֶׁר טִמְּאוּ אֲחוֹתָם: 28 אֶת־צֹאנָם וְאֶת־בְּקָרָם וְאֶת־חֲמֹרֵיהֶם

in the city and what *was* in the field, ²⁹ and all their wealth. All their little ones and their wives they took captive; and they plundered even all that *was* in the houses.

³⁰ Then Jacob said to Simeon and Levi, "You have troubled me by making me obnoxious among the inhabitants of the land, among the Canaanites and the Perizzites; and since I *am* few in number, they will gather themselves together against me and kill me. I shall be destroyed, my household and I."

³¹ But they said, "Should he treat our sister like a harlot?"

35 Then God said to Jacob, "Arise, go up to Bethel and dwell there; and make an altar there to God, who appeared to you when you fled from the face of Esau your brother."

² And Jacob said to his household and to all who *were* with him, "Put away the foreign gods that *are* among you, purify yourselves, and change your garments. ³ Then let us arise and go up to Bethel; and I will make an altar there to God, who answered me in the day of my distress and has been with me in the way which I have gone." ⁴ So they gave Jacob all the foreign gods which *were* in their hands, and the earrings which *were* in their ears; and Jacob hid them under the terebinth tree which *was* by Shechem.

⁵ And they journeyed, and the terror of God was upon the cities that *were* all around them, and they did not pursue the sons of Jacob. ⁶ So Jacob came to Luz (that *is*, Bethel), which *is* in the land of Canaan, he and all the people who *were* with him. ⁷ And he built an altar there and called the place El Bethel, because there God appeared to him when he fled from the face of his brother.

⁸ Now Deborah, Rebekah's nurse, died, and she was buried below Bethel under the terebinth tree. So the name of it was called Allon Bachuth.

⁹ Then God appeared to Jacob again, when he came from Padan Aram, and blessed him. ¹⁰ And God said to him, "Your name *is* Jacob; your name shall not be called Jacob anymore, but Israel shall be your name." So He called his name Israel. ¹¹ Also God said to him: "I *am* God Almighty. Be fruitful and multiply; a nation and a company of nations shall proceed from you, and kings shall come from your body. ¹² The land which I gave Abraham and Isaac I give to you; and to your descendants after you I give this land." ¹³ Then God went up from him in the place where He talked with him. ¹⁴ So Jacob set up a pillar in the place where He talked with him, a pillar of stone; and he poured

וְאֵת אֲשֶׁר־בָּעִיר וְאֶת־אֲשֶׁר בַּשָּׂדֶה לָקָחוּ: 29 וְאֶת־כָּל־חֵילָם וְאֶת־כָּל־טַפָּם וְאֶת־נְשֵׁיהֶם שָׁבוּ וַיָּבֹזּוּ וְאֵת כָּל־אֲשֶׁר בַּבָּיִת: 30 וַיֹּאמֶר יַעֲקֹב אֶל־שִׁמְעוֹן וְאֶל־לֵוִי עֲכַרְתֶּם אֹתִי לְהַבְאִישֵׁנִי בְּיֹשֵׁב הָאָרֶץ בַּכְּנַעֲנִי וּבַפְּרִזִּי וַאֲנִי מְתֵי מִסְפָּר וְנֶאֶסְפוּ עָלַי וְהִכּוּנִי וְנִשְׁמַדְתִּי אֲנִי וּבֵיתִי: 31 וַיֹּאמְרוּ הַכְזוֹנָה יַעֲשֶׂה אֶת־אֲחוֹתֵנוּ: פ

לה וַיֹּאמֶר אֱלֹהִים אֶל־יַעֲקֹב קוּם עֲלֵה בֵית־אֵל וְשֶׁב־שָׁם וַעֲשֵׂה־שָׁם מִזְבֵּחַ לָאֵל הַנִּרְאֶה אֵלֶיךָ בְּבָרְחֲךָ מִפְּנֵי עֵשָׂו אָחִיךָ: 2 וַיֹּאמֶר יַעֲקֹב אֶל־בֵּיתוֹ וְאֶל כָּל־אֲשֶׁר עִמּוֹ הָסִרוּ אֶת־אֱלֹהֵי הַנֵּכָר אֲשֶׁר בְּתֹכְכֶם וְהִטַּהֲרוּ וְהַחֲלִיפוּ שִׂמְלֹתֵיכֶם: 3 וְנָקוּמָה וְנַעֲלֶה בֵּית־אֵל וְאֶעֱשֶׂה־שָּׁם מִזְבֵּחַ לָאֵל הָעֹנֶה אֹתִי בְּיוֹם צָרָתִי וַיְהִי עִמָּדִי בַּדֶּרֶךְ אֲשֶׁר הָלָכְתִּי: 4 וַיִּתְּנוּ אֶל־יַעֲקֹב אֵת כָּל־אֱלֹהֵי הַנֵּכָר אֲשֶׁר בְּיָדָם וְאֶת־הַנְּזָמִים אֲשֶׁר בְּאָזְנֵיהֶם וַיִּטְמֹן אֹתָם יַעֲקֹב תַּחַת הָאֵלָה אֲשֶׁר עִם־שְׁכֶם: 5 וַיִּסָּעוּ וַיְהִי | חִתַּת אֱלֹהִים עַל־הֶעָרִים אֲשֶׁר סְבִיבֹתֵיהֶם וְלֹא רָדְפוּ אַחֲרֵי בְּנֵי יַעֲקֹב: 6 וַיָּבֹא יַעֲקֹב לוּזָה אֲשֶׁר בְּאֶרֶץ כְּנַעַן הִוא בֵּית־אֵל הוּא וְכָל־הָעָם אֲשֶׁר עִמּוֹ: 7 וַיִּבֶן שָׁם מִזְבֵּחַ וַיִּקְרָא לַמָּקוֹם אֵל בֵּית־אֵל כִּי שָׁם נִגְלוּ אֵלָיו הָאֱלֹהִים בְּבָרְחוֹ מִפְּנֵי אָחִיו: 8 וַתָּמָת דְּבֹרָה מֵינֶקֶת רִבְקָה וַתִּקָּבֵר מִתַּחַת לְבֵית־אֵל תַּחַת הָאַלּוֹן וַיִּקְרָא שְׁמוֹ אַלּוֹן בָּכוּת: פ 9 וַיֵּרָא אֱלֹהִים אֶל־יַעֲקֹב עוֹד בְּבֹאוֹ מִפַּדַּן אֲרָם וַיְבָרֶךְ אֹתוֹ: 10 וַיֹּאמֶר־לוֹ אֱלֹהִים שִׁמְךָ יַעֲקֹב לֹא־יִקָּרֵא שִׁמְךָ עוֹד יַעֲקֹב כִּי אִם־יִשְׂרָאֵל יִהְיֶה שְׁמֶךָ וַיִּקְרָא אֶת־שְׁמוֹ יִשְׂרָאֵל: 11 וַיֹּאמֶר לוֹ אֱלֹהִים אֲנִי אֵל שַׁדַּי פְּרֵה וּרְבֵה גּוֹי וּקְהַל גּוֹיִם יִהְיֶה מִמֶּךָּ וּמְלָכִים מֵחֲלָצֶיךָ יֵצֵאוּ: 12 וְאֶת־הָאָרֶץ אֲשֶׁר נָתַתִּי לְאַבְרָהָם וּלְיִצְחָק לְךָ אֶתְּנֶנָּה וּלְזַרְעֲךָ אַחֲרֶיךָ אֶתֵּן אֶת־הָאָרֶץ: 13 וַיַּעַל מֵעָלָיו אֱלֹהִים בַּמָּקוֹם אֲשֶׁר דִּבֶּר אִתּוֹ: 14 וַיַּצֵּב יַעֲקֹב מַצֵּבָה בַּמָּקוֹם אֲשֶׁר דִּבֶּר אִתּוֹ מַצֶּבֶת אָבֶן וַיַּסֵּךְ עָלֶיהָ נֶסֶךְ וַיִּצֹק

a drink offering on it, and he poured oil on it. ¹⁵And Jacob called the name of the place where God spoke with him, Bethel.

¹⁶Then they journeyed from Bethel. And when there was but a little distance to go to Ephrath, Rachel labored *in childbirth,* and she had hard labor. ¹⁷Now it came to pass, when she was in hard labor, that the midwife said to her, "Do not fear; you will have this son also." ¹⁸And so it was, as her soul was departing (for she died), that she called his name Ben-Oni; but his father called him Benjamin. ¹⁹So Rachel died and was buried on the way to Ephrath (that *is,* Bethlehem). ²⁰And Jacob set a pillar on her grave, which *is* the pillar of Rachel's grave to this day.

²¹Then Israel journeyed and pitched his tent beyond the tower of Eder. ²²And it happened, when Israel dwelt in that land, that Reuben went and lay with Bilhah his father's concubine; and Israel heard *about it.*

Now the sons of Jacob were twelve: ²³the sons of Leah *were* Reuben, Jacob's firstborn, and Simeon, Levi, Judah, Issachar, and Zebulun; ²⁴the sons of Rachel *were* Joseph and Benjamin; ²⁵the sons of Bilhah, Rachel's maidservant, *were* Dan and Naphtali; ²⁶and the sons of Zilpah, Leah's maidservant, *were* Gad and Asher. These *were* the sons of Jacob who were born to him in Padan Aram.

²⁷Then Jacob came to his father Isaac at Mamre, or Kirjath Arba (that *is,* Hebron), where Abraham and Isaac had dwelt. ²⁸Now the days of Isaac were one hundred and eighty years. ²⁹So Isaac breathed his last and died, and was gathered to his people, *being* old and full of days. And his sons Esau and Jacob buried him.

36 Now this *is* the genealogy of Esau, who is Edom. ²Esau took his wives from the daughters of Canaan: Adah the daughter of Elon the Hittite; Aholibamah the daughter of Anah, the daughter of Zibeon the Hivite; ³and Basemath, Ishmael's daughter, sister of Nebajoth. ⁴Now Adah bore Eliphaz to Esau, and Basemath bore Reuel. ⁵And Aholibamah bore Jeush, Jaalam, and Korah. These *were* the sons of Esau who were born to him in the land of Canaan.

⁶Then Esau took his wives, his sons, his daughters, and all the persons of his household, his cattle and all his animals, and all his goods which he had gained in the land of Canaan, and went to a country away from the presence of his brother Jacob. ⁷For their possessions were too great for them to dwell together, and the land where

עָלֶיהָ שָׁמֶן: 15 וַיִּקְרָא יַעֲקֹב אֶת־שֵׁם הַמָּקוֹם אֲשֶׁר דִּבֶּר אִתּוֹ שָׁם אֱלֹהִים בֵּית־אֵל: 16 וַיִּסְעוּ מִבֵּית אֵל וַיְהִי־עוֹד כִּבְרַת־הָאָרֶץ לָבוֹא אֶפְרָתָה וַתֵּלֶד רָחֵל וַתְּקַשׁ בְּלִדְתָּהּ: 17 וַיְהִי בְהַקְשֹׁתָהּ בְּלִדְתָּהּ וַתֹּאמֶר לָהּ הַמְיַלֶּדֶת אַל־תִּירְאִי כִּי־גַם־זֶה לָךְ בֵּן: 18 וַיְהִי בְּצֵאת נַפְשָׁהּ כִּי מֵתָה וַתִּקְרָא שְׁמוֹ בֶּן־אוֹנִי וְאָבִיו קָרָא־לוֹ בִנְיָמִין: 19 וַתָּמָת רָחֵל וַתִּקָּבֵר בְּדֶרֶךְ אֶפְרָתָה הִוא בֵּית לָחֶם: 20 וַיַּצֵּב יַעֲקֹב מַצֵּבָה עַל־קְבֻרָתָהּ הִוא מַצֶּבֶת קְבֻרַת־רָחֵל עַד־הַיּוֹם: 21 וַיִּסַּע יִשְׂרָאֵל וַיֵּט אָהֳלֹה מֵהָלְאָה לְמִגְדַּל־עֵדֶר: 22 וַיְהִי בִּשְׁכֹּן יִשְׂרָאֵל בָּאָרֶץ הַהִוא וַיֵּלֶךְ רְאוּבֵן וַיִּשְׁכַּב אֶת־בִּלְהָה פִּילֶגֶשׁ אָבִיו וַיִּשְׁמַע יִשְׂרָאֵל פ וַיִּהְיוּ בְנֵי־יַעֲקֹב שְׁנֵים עָשָׂר: 23 בְּנֵי לֵאָה בְּכוֹר יַעֲקֹב רְאוּבֵן וְשִׁמְעוֹן וְלֵוִי וִיהוּדָה וְיִשָּׂשכָר וּזְבֻלֻן: 24 בְּנֵי רָחֵל יוֹסֵף וּבִנְיָמִן: 25 וּבְנֵי בִלְהָה שִׁפְחַת רָחֵל דָּן וְנַפְתָּלִי: 26 וּבְנֵי זִלְפָּה שִׁפְחַת לֵאָה גָּד וְאָשֵׁר אֵלֶּה בְּנֵי יַעֲקֹב אֲשֶׁר יֻלַּד־לוֹ בְּפַדַּן אֲרָם: 27 וַיָּבֹא יַעֲקֹב אֶל־יִצְחָק אָבִיו מַמְרֵא קִרְיַת הָאַרְבַּע הִוא חֶבְרוֹן אֲשֶׁר־גָּר־שָׁם אַבְרָהָם וְיִצְחָק: 28 וַיִּהְיוּ יְמֵי יִצְחָק מְאַת שָׁנָה וּשְׁמֹנִים שָׁנָה: 29 וַיִּגְוַע יִצְחָק וַיָּמָת וַיֵּאָסֶף אֶל־עַמָּיו זָקֵן וּשְׂבַע יָמִים וַיִּקְבְּרוּ אֹתוֹ עֵשָׂו וְיַעֲקֹב בָּנָיו: פ

לו וְאֵלֶּה תֹּלְדוֹת עֵשָׂו הוּא אֱדוֹם: 2 עֵשָׂו לָקַח אֶת־נָשָׁיו מִבְּנוֹת כְּנָעַן אֶת־עָדָה בַּת־אֵילוֹן הַחִתִּי וְאֶת־אָהֳלִיבָמָה בַּת־עֲנָה בַּת־צִבְעוֹן הַחִוִּי: 3 וְאֶת־בָּשְׂמַת בַּת־יִשְׁמָעֵאל אֲחוֹת נְבָיוֹת: 4 וַתֵּלֶד עָדָה לְעֵשָׂו אֶת־אֱלִיפָז וּבָשְׂמַת יָלְדָה אֶת־רְעוּאֵל: 5 וְאָהֳלִיבָמָה יָלְדָה אֶת־יְעִישׁ וְאֶת־יַעְלָם וְאֶת־קֹרַח אֵלֶּה בְּנֵי עֵשָׂו אֲשֶׁר יֻלְּדוּ־לוֹ בְּאֶרֶץ כְּנָעַן: 6 וַיִּקַּח עֵשָׂו אֶת־נָשָׁיו וְאֶת־בָּנָיו וְאֶת־בְּנֹתָיו וְאֶת־כָּל־נַפְשׁוֹת בֵּיתוֹ וְאֶת־מִקְנֵהוּ וְאֶת־כָּל־בְּהֶמְתּוֹ וְאֵת כָּל־קִנְיָנוֹ אֲשֶׁר רָכַשׁ בְּאֶרֶץ כְּנָעַן וַיֵּלֶךְ אֶל־אֶרֶץ מִפְּנֵי יַעֲקֹב אָחִיו: 7 כִּי־הָיָה רְכוּשָׁם רָב

they were strangers could not support them because
of their livestock. ⁸ So Esau dwelt in Mount Seir.
Esau *is* Edom.

⁹ And this *is* the genealogy of Esau the father of
the Edomites in Mount Seir. ¹⁰ These *were* the
names of Esau's sons: Eliphaz the son of Adah the
wife of Esau, and Reuel the son of Basemath the
wife of Esau. ¹¹ And the sons of Eliphaz were
Teman, Omar, Zepho, Gatam, and Kenaz.

¹² Now Timna was the concubine of Eliphaz,
Esau's son, and she bore Amalek to Eliphaz. These
were the sons of Adah, Esau's wife.

¹³ These *were* the sons of Reuel: Nahath, Zerah,
Shammah, and Mizzah. These were the sons of
Basemath, Esau's wife.

¹⁴ These *were* the sons of Aholibamah, Esau's
wife, the daughter of Anah, the daughter of Zibeon.
And she bore to Esau: Jeush, Jaalam, and Korah.

¹⁵ These *were* the chiefs of the sons of Esau. The
sons of Eliphaz, the firstborn *son* of Esau, were
Chief Teman, Chief Omar, Chief Zepho, Chief
Kenaz, ¹⁶ Chief Korah, Chief Gatam, *and* Chief
Amalek. These *were* the chiefs of Eliphaz in the
land of Edom. They *were* the sons of Adah.

¹⁷ These *were* the sons of Reuel, Esau's son: Chief
Nahath, Chief Zerah, Chief Shammah, and Chief
Mizzah. These *were* the chiefs of Reuel in the land
of Edom. These *were* the sons of Basemath, Esau's
wife.

¹⁸ And these *were* the sons of Aholibamah, Esau's
wife: Chief Jeush, Chief Jaalam, and Chief Korah.
These *were* the chiefs *who descended* from Aholibamah, Esau's wife, the daughter of Anah. ¹⁹ These
were the sons of Esau, who is Edom, and these *were*
their chiefs.

²⁰ These *were* the sons of Seir the Horite who
inhabited the land: Lotan, Shobal, Zibeon, Anah,
²¹ Dishon, Ezer, and Dishan. These *were* the chiefs
of the Horites, the sons of Seir, in the land of Edom.

²² And the sons of Lotan were Hori and Hemam.
Lotan's sister *was* Timna.

²³ These *were* the sons of Shobal: Alvan, Manahath, Ebal, Shepho, and Onam.

²⁴ These *were* the sons of Zibeon: both Ajah and
Anah. This *was the* Anah who found the water in
the wilderness as he pastured the donkeys of his
father Zibeon. ²⁵ These *were* the children of Anah:
Dishon and Aholibamah the daughter of Anah.

²⁶ These *were* the sons of Dishon: Hemdan,
Eshban, Ithran, and Cheran. ²⁷ These *were* the sons
of Ezer: Bilhan, Zaavan, and Akan. ²⁸ These *were*
the sons of Dishan: Uz and Aran.

מִשֶּׁבֶת יַחְדָּו וְלֹא יָכְלָה אֶרֶץ מְגוּרֵיהֶם לָשֵׂאת
אֹתָם מִפְּנֵי מִקְנֵיהֶם: ⁸ וַיֵּשֶׁב עֵשָׂו בְּהַר שֵׂעִיר
עֵשָׂו הוּא אֱדוֹם: ⁹ וְאֵלֶּה תֹּלְדוֹת עֵשָׂו אֲבִי אֱדוֹם
בְּהַר שֵׂעִיר: ¹⁰ אֵלֶּה שְׁמוֹת בְּנֵי־עֵשָׂו אֱלִיפַז בֶּן־
עָדָה אֵשֶׁת עֵשָׂו רְעוּאֵל בֶּן־בָּשְׂמַת אֵשֶׁת עֵשָׂו:
¹¹ וַיִּהְיוּ בְּנֵי אֱלִיפָז תֵּימָן אוֹמָר צְפוֹ וְגַעְתָּם וּקְנַז:
¹² וְתִמְנַע ׀ הָיְתָה פִילֶגֶשׁ לֶאֱלִיפַז בֶּן־עֵשָׂו וַתֵּלֶד
לֶאֱלִיפַז אֶת־עֲמָלֵק אֵלֶּה בְּנֵי עָדָה אֵשֶׁת עֵשָׂו:
¹³ וְאֵלֶּה בְּנֵי רְעוּאֵל נַחַת וָזֶרַח שַׁמָּה וּמִזָּה אֵלֶּה
הָיוּ בְּנֵי בָשְׂמַת אֵשֶׁת עֵשָׂו: ¹⁴ וְאֵלֶּה הָיוּ בְּנֵי
אָהֳלִיבָמָה בַת־עֲנָה בַּת־צִבְעוֹן אֵשֶׁת עֵשָׂו וַתֵּלֶד
לְעֵשָׂו אֶת־יְעִישׁ וְאֶת־יַעְלָם וְאֶת־קֹרַח: ¹⁵ אֵלֶּה
אַלּוּפֵי בְנֵי־עֵשָׂו בְּנֵי אֱלִיפַז בְּכוֹר עֵשָׂו אַלּוּף תֵּימָן
אַלּוּף אוֹמָר אַלּוּף צְפוֹ אַלּוּף קְנַז: ¹⁶ אַלּוּף־קֹרַח
אַלּוּף גַּעְתָּם אַלּוּף עֲמָלֵק אֵלֶּה אַלּוּפֵי אֱלִיפַז בְּאֶרֶץ
אֱדוֹם אֵלֶּה בְּנֵי עָדָה: ¹⁷ וְאֵלֶּה בְּנֵי רְעוּאֵל בֶּן־עֵשָׂו
אַלּוּף נַחַת אַלּוּף זֶרַח אַלּוּף שַׁמָּה אַלּוּף מִזָּה
אֵלֶּה אַלּוּפֵי רְעוּאֵל בְּאֶרֶץ אֱדוֹם אֵלֶּה בְּנֵי בָשְׂמַת
אֵשֶׁת עֵשָׂו: ¹⁸ וְאֵלֶּה בְּנֵי אָהֳלִיבָמָה אֵשֶׁת עֵשָׂו
אַלּוּף יְעוּשׁ אַלּוּף יַעְלָם אַלּוּף קֹרַח אֵלֶּה אַלּוּפֵי
אָהֳלִיבָמָה בַּת־עֲנָה אֵשֶׁת עֵשָׂו: ¹⁹ אֵלֶּה בְנֵי־עֵשָׂו
וְאֵלֶּה אַלּוּפֵיהֶם הוּא אֱדוֹם: ס   ²⁰ אֵלֶּה
בְנֵי־שֵׂעִיר הַחֹרִי יֹשְׁבֵי הָאָרֶץ לוֹטָן וְשׁוֹבָל וְצִבְעוֹן
וַעֲנָה: ²¹ וְדִשׁוֹן וְאֵצֶר וְדִישָׁן אֵלֶּה אַלּוּפֵי הַחֹרִי בְּנֵי
שֵׂעִיר בְּאֶרֶץ אֱדוֹם: ²² וַיִּהְיוּ בְנֵי־לוֹטָן חֹרִי וְהֵימָם
וַאֲחוֹת לוֹטָן תִּמְנָע: ²³ וְאֵלֶּה בְּנֵי שׁוֹבָל עַלְוָן
וּמָנַחַת וְעֵיבָל שְׁפוֹ וְאוֹנָם: ²⁴ וְאֵלֶּה בְנֵי־צִבְעוֹן
וְאַיָּה וַעֲנָה הוּא עֲנָה אֲשֶׁר מָצָא אֶת־הַיֵּמִם בַּמִּדְבָּר
בִּרְעֹתוֹ אֶת־הַחֲמֹרִים לְצִבְעוֹן אָבִיו: ²⁵ וְאֵלֶּה בְנֵי־
עֲנָה דִּשֹׁן וְאָהֳלִיבָמָה בַּת־עֲנָה: ²⁶ וְאֵלֶּה בְּנֵי דִישָׁן
חֶמְדָּן וְאֶשְׁבָּן וְיִתְרָן וּכְרָן: ²⁷ אֵלֶּה בְּנֵי־אֵצֶר בִּלְהָן
וְזַעֲוָן וַעֲקָן: ²⁸ אֵלֶּה בְנֵי־דִישָׁן עוּץ וַאֲרָן: ²⁹ אֵלֶּה

29 These *were* the chiefs of the Horites: Chief Lotan, Chief Shobal, Chief Zibeon, Chief Anah, 30 Chief Dishon, Chief Ezer, and Chief Dishan. These *were* the chiefs of the Horites, according to their chiefs in the land of Seir.

31 Now these *were* the kings who reigned in the land of Edom before any king reigned over the children of Israel: 32 Bela the son of Beor reigned in Edom, and the name of his city *was* Dinhabah. 33 And when Bela died, Jobab the son of Zerah of Bozrah reigned in his place. 34 When Jobab died, Husham of the land of the Temanites reigned in his place. 35 And when Husham died, Hadad the son of Bedad, who attacked Midian in the field of Moab, reigned in his place. And the name of his city *was* Avith. 36 When Hadad died, Samlah of Masrekah reigned in his place. 37 And when Samlah died, Saul of Rehoboth-*by*-the-River reigned in his place. 38 When Saul died, Baal-Hanan the son of Achbor reigned in his place. 39 And when Baal-Hanan the son of Achbor died, Hadar reigned in his place; and the name of his city *was* Pau. His wife's name *was* Mehetabel, the daughter of Matred, the daughter of Mezahab.

40 And these *were* the names of the chiefs of Esau, according to their families and their places, by their names: Chief Timnah, Chief Alvah, Chief Jetheth, 41 Chief Aholibamah, Chief Elah, Chief Pinon, 42 Chief Kenaz, Chief Teman, Chief Mibzar, 43 Chief Magdiel, and Chief Iram. These *were* the chiefs of Edom, according to their dwelling places in the land of their possession. Esau *was* the father of the Edomites.

37 Now Jacob dwelt in the land where his father was a stranger, in the land of Canaan. 2 This *is* the history of Jacob.

Joseph, *being* seventeen years old, was feeding the flock with his brothers. And the lad *was* with the sons of Bilhah and the sons of Zilpah, his father's wives; and Joseph brought a bad report of them to his father.

3 Now Israel loved Joseph more than all his children, because he *was* the son of his old age. Also he made him a tunic of *many* colors. 4 But when his brothers saw that their father loved him more than all his brothers, they hated him and could not speak peaceably to him.

5 Now Joseph had a dream, and he told *it* to his brothers; and they hated him even more. 6 So he said to them, "Please hear this dream which I have dreamed: 7 There we were, binding sheaves in the

אַלּוּפֵי הַחֹרִי אַלּוּף לוֹטָן אַלּוּף שׁוֹבָל אַלּוּף צִבְעוֹן אַלּוּף עֲנָה: 30 אַלּוּף דִּשֹׁן אַלּוּף אֵצֶר אַלּוּף דִּישָׁן אֵלֶּה אַלּוּפֵי הַחֹרִי לְאַלֻּפֵיהֶם בְּאֶרֶץ שֵׂעִיר: פ

31 וְאֵלֶּה הַמְּלָכִים אֲשֶׁר מָלְכוּ בְּאֶרֶץ אֱדוֹם לִפְנֵי מְלָךְ־מֶלֶךְ לִבְנֵי יִשְׂרָאֵל: 32 וַיִּמְלֹךְ בֶּאֱדוֹם בֶּלַע בֶּן־בְּעוֹר וְשֵׁם עִירוֹ דִּנְהָבָה: 33 וַיָּמָת בָּלַע וַיִּמְלֹךְ תַּחְתָּיו יוֹבָב בֶּן־זֶרַח מִבָּצְרָה: 34 וַיָּמָת יוֹבָב וַיִּמְלֹךְ תַּחְתָּיו חֻשָׁם מֵאֶרֶץ הַתֵּימָנִי: 35 וַיָּמָת חֻשָׁם וַיִּמְלֹךְ תַּחְתָּיו הֲדַד בֶּן־בְּדַד הַמַּכֶּה אֶת־מִדְיָן בִּשְׂדֵה מוֹאָב וְשֵׁם עִירוֹ עֲוִית: 36 וַיָּמָת הֲדָד וַיִּמְלֹךְ תַּחְתָּיו שַׂמְלָה מִמַּשְׂרֵקָה: 37 וַיָּמָת שַׂמְלָה וַיִּמְלֹךְ תַּחְתָּיו שָׁאוּל מֵרְחֹבוֹת הַנָּהָר: 38 וַיָּמָת שָׁאוּל וַיִּמְלֹךְ תַּחְתָּיו בַּעַל חָנָן בֶּן־עַכְבּוֹר: 39 וַיָּמָת בַּעַל חָנָן בֶּן־עַכְבּוֹר וַיִּמְלֹךְ תַּחְתָּיו הֲדַר וְשֵׁם עִירוֹ פָּעוּ וְשֵׁם אִשְׁתּוֹ מְהֵיטַבְאֵל בַּת־מַטְרֵד בַּת מֵי זָהָב: 40 וְאֵלֶּה שְׁמוֹת אַלּוּפֵי עֵשָׂו לְמִשְׁפְּחֹתָם לִמְקֹמֹתָם בִּשְׁמֹתָם אַלּוּף תִּמְנָע אַלּוּף עַלְוָה אַלּוּף יְתֵת: 41 אַלּוּף אָהֳלִיבָמָה אַלּוּף אֵלָה אַלּוּף פִּינֹן: 42 אַלּוּף קְנַז אַלּוּף תֵּימָן אַלּוּף מִבְצָר: 43 אַלּוּף מַגְדִּיאֵל אַלּוּף עִירָם אֵלֶּה ׀ אַלּוּפֵי אֱדוֹם לְמֹשְׁבֹתָם בְּאֶרֶץ אֲחֻזָּתָם הוּא עֵשָׂו אֲבִי אֱדוֹם: פ

לז וַיֵּשֶׁב יַעֲקֹב בְּאֶרֶץ מְגוּרֵי אָבִיו בְּאֶרֶץ כְּנָעַן: 2 אֵלֶּה ׀ תֹּלְדוֹת יַעֲקֹב יוֹסֵף בֶּן־שְׁבַע־עֶשְׂרֵה שָׁנָה הָיָה רֹעֶה אֶת־אֶחָיו בַּצֹּאן וְהוּא נַעַר אֶת־בְּנֵי בִלְהָה וְאֶת־בְּנֵי זִלְפָּה נְשֵׁי אָבִיו וַיָּבֵא יוֹסֵף אֶת־דִּבָּתָם רָעָה אֶל־אֲבִיהֶם: 3 וְיִשְׂרָאֵל אָהַב אֶת־יוֹסֵף מִכָּל־בָּנָיו כִּי־בֶן־זְקֻנִים הוּא לוֹ וְעָשָׂה לוֹ כְּתֹנֶת פַּסִּים: 4 וַיִּרְאוּ אֶחָיו כִּי־אֹתוֹ אָהַב אֲבִיהֶם מִכָּל־אֶחָיו וַיִּשְׂנְאוּ אֹתוֹ וְלֹא יָכְלוּ דַּבְּרוֹ לְשָׁלֹם:

5 וַיַּחֲלֹם יוֹסֵף חֲלוֹם וַיַּגֵּד לְאֶחָיו וַיּוֹסִפוּ עוֹד שְׂנֹא אֹתוֹ: 6 וַיֹּאמֶר אֲלֵיהֶם שִׁמְעוּ־נָא הַחֲלוֹם הַזֶּה אֲשֶׁר חָלָמְתִּי: 7 וְהִנֵּה אֲנַחְנוּ מְאַלְּמִים אֲלֻמִּים בְּתוֹךְ הַשָּׂדֶה וְהִנֵּה קָמָה אֲלֻמָּתִי וְגַם־נִצָּבָה וְהִנֵּה

field. Then behold, my sheaf arose and also stood upright; and indeed your sheaves stood all around and bowed down to my sheaf."

8 And his brothers said to him, "Shall you indeed reign over us? Or shall you indeed have dominion over us?" So they hated him even more for his dreams and for his words.

9 Then he dreamed still another dream and told it to his brothers, and said, "Look, I have dreamed another dream. And this time, the sun, the moon, and the eleven stars bowed down to me."

10 So he told it to his father and his brothers; and his father rebuked him and said to him, "What is this dream that you have dreamed? Shall your mother and I and your brothers indeed come to bow down to the earth before you?" 11 And his brothers envied him, but his father kept the matter in mind.

12 Then his brothers went to feed their father's flock in Shechem. 13 And Israel said to Joseph, "Are not your brothers feeding the flock in Shechem? Come, I will send you to them."

So he said to him, "Here I am."

14 Then he said to him, "Please go and see if it is well with your brothers and well with the flocks, and bring back word to me." So he sent him out of the Valley of Hebron, and he went to Shechem.

15 Now a certain man found him, and there he was, wandering in the field. And the man asked him, saying, "What are you seeking?"

16 So he said, "I am seeking my brothers. Please tell me where they are feeding their flocks."

17 And the man said, "They have departed from here, for I heard them say, 'Let us go to Dothan.' " So Joseph went after his brothers and found them in Dothan.

18 Now when they saw him afar off, even before he came near them, they conspired against him to kill him. 19 Then they said to one another, "Look, this dreamer is coming! 20 Come therefore, let us now kill him and cast him into some pit; and we shall say, 'Some wild beast has devoured him.' We shall see what will become of his dreams!"

21 But Reuben heard it, and he delivered him out of their hands, and said, "Let us not kill him." 22 And Reuben said to them, "Shed no blood, but cast him into this pit which is in the wilderness, and do not lay a hand on him"—that he might deliver him out of their hands, and bring him back to his father.

תְּסֻבֶּ֙ינָה֙ אֲלֻמֹּ֣תֵיכֶ֔ם וַתִּֽשְׁתַּחֲוֶ֖יןָ לַאֲלֻמָּתִֽי: 8 וַיֹּ֨אמְרוּ ל֜וֹ אֶחָ֗יו הֲמָלֹ֤ךְ תִּמְלֹךְ֙ עָלֵ֔ינוּ אִם־מָשׁ֥וֹל תִּמְשֹׁ֖ל בָּ֑נוּ וַיּוֹסִ֤פוּ עוֹד֙ שְׂנֹ֣א אֹת֔וֹ עַל־חֲלֹמֹתָ֖יו וְעַל־דְּבָרָֽיו:

9 וַיַּחֲלֹ֥ם עוֹד֙ חֲל֣וֹם אַחֵ֔ר וַיְסַפֵּ֥ר אֹת֖וֹ לְאֶחָ֑יו וַיֹּ֗אמֶר הִנֵּ֨ה חָלַ֤מְתִּֽי חֲלוֹם֙ ע֔וֹד וְהִנֵּ֧ה הַשֶּׁ֣מֶשׁ וְהַיָּרֵ֗חַ וְאַחַ֤ד עָשָׂר֙ כּֽוֹכָבִ֔ים מִֽשְׁתַּחֲוִ֖ים לִֽי: 10 וַיְסַפֵּ֣ר אֶל־אָבִיו֮ וְאֶל־אֶחָיו֒ וַיִּגְעַר־בּ֣וֹ אָבִ֔יו וַיֹּ֣אמֶר ל֔וֹ מָ֛ה הַחֲל֥וֹם הַזֶּ֖ה אֲשֶׁ֣ר חָלָ֑מְתָּ הֲב֣וֹא נָב֗וֹא אֲנִי֙ וְאִמְּךָ֣ וְאַחֶ֔יךָ לְהִשְׁתַּחֲוֺ֥ת לְךָ֖ אָֽרְצָה: 11 וַיְקַנְאוּ־ב֖וֹ אֶחָ֑יו וְאָבִ֖יו שָׁמַ֥ר אֶת־הַדָּבָֽר: 12 וַיֵּלְכ֖וּ אֶחָ֑יו לִרְע֛וֹת אֶׄת־צֹ֥אן אֲבִיהֶ֖ם בִּשְׁכֶֽם: 13 וַיֹּ֨אמֶר יִשְׂרָאֵ֜ל אֶל־יוֹסֵ֗ף הֲל֤וֹא אַחֶ֙יךָ֙ רֹעִ֣ים בִּשְׁכֶ֔ם לְכָ֖ה וְאֶשְׁלָחֲךָ֣ אֲלֵיהֶ֑ם וַיֹּ֥אמֶר ל֖וֹ הִנֵּֽנִי: 14 וַיֹּ֣אמֶר ל֗וֹ לֶךְ־נָ֨א רְאֵ֜ה אֶת־שְׁל֤וֹם אַחֶ֙יךָ֙ וְאֶת־שְׁל֣וֹם הַצֹּ֔אן וַהֲשִׁבֵ֖נִי דָּבָ֑ר וַיִּשְׁלָחֵ֙הוּ֙ מֵעֵ֣מֶק חֶבְר֔וֹן וַיָּבֹ֖א שְׁכֶֽמָה: 15 וַיִּמְצָאֵ֣הוּ אִ֔ישׁ וְהִנֵּ֥ה תֹעֶ֖ה בַּשָּׂדֶ֑ה וַיִּשְׁאָלֵ֧הוּ הָאִ֛ישׁ לֵאמֹ֖ר מַה־תְּבַקֵּֽשׁ: 16 וַיֹּ֕אמֶר אֶת־אַחַ֖י אָנֹכִ֣י מְבַקֵּ֑שׁ הַגִּֽידָה־נָּ֣א לִ֔י אֵיפֹ֖ה הֵ֥ם רֹעִֽים: 17 וַיֹּ֤אמֶר הָאִישׁ֙ נָסְע֣וּ מִזֶּ֔ה כִּ֤י שָׁמַ֙עְתִּי֙ אֹֽמְרִ֔ים נֵלְכָ֖ה דֹּתָ֑יְנָה וַיֵּ֤לֶךְ יוֹסֵף֙ אַחַ֣ר אֶחָ֔יו וַיִּמְצָאֵ֖ם בְּדֹתָֽן: 18 וַיִּרְא֥וּ אֹת֖וֹ מֵרָחֹ֑ק וּבְטֶ֙רֶם֙ יִקְרַ֣ב אֲלֵיהֶ֔ם וַיִּֽתְנַכְּל֥וּ אֹת֖וֹ לַהֲמִיתֽוֹ:

19 וַיֹּאמְר֖וּ אִ֣ישׁ אֶל־אָחִ֑יו הִנֵּ֗ה בַּ֛עַל הַחֲלֹמ֥וֹת הַלָּזֶ֖ה בָּֽא: 20 וְעַתָּ֣ה ׀ לְכ֣וּ וְנַֽהַרְגֵ֗הוּ וְנַשְׁלִכֵ֙הוּ֙ בְּאַחַ֣ד הַבֹּר֔וֹת וְאָמַ֕רְנוּ חַיָּ֥ה רָעָ֖ה אֲכָלָ֑תְהוּ וְנִרְאֶ֕ה מַה־יִּהְי֖וּ חֲלֹמֹתָֽיו: 21 וַיִּשְׁמַ֣ע רְאוּבֵ֔ן וַיַּצִּלֵ֖הוּ מִיָּדָ֑ם וַיֹּ֕אמֶר לֹ֥א נַכֶּ֖נּוּ נָֽפֶשׁ: 22 וַיֹּ֨אמֶר אֲלֵהֶ֣ם ׀ רְאוּבֵ֗ן אַל־תִּשְׁפְּכוּ־דָם֒ הַשְׁלִ֣יכוּ אֹת֗וֹ אֶל־הַבּ֤וֹר הַזֶּה֙ אֲשֶׁ֣ר בַּמִּדְבָּ֔ר וְיָ֖ד אַל־תִּשְׁלְחוּ־ב֑וֹ לְמַ֗עַן הַצִּ֤יל אֹתוֹ֙ מִיָּדָ֔ם

23 So it came to pass, when Joseph had come to his brothers, that they stripped Joseph *of* his tunic, the tunic of *many* colors that *was* on him. 24 Then they took him and cast him into a pit. And the pit *was* empty; *there was* no water in it.

25 And they sat down to eat a meal. Then they lifted their eyes and looked, and there was a company of Ishmaelites, coming from Gilead with their camels, bearing spices, balm, and myrrh, on their way to carry *them* down to Egypt. 26 So Judah said to his brothers, "What profit *is there* if we kill our brother and conceal his blood? 27 Come and let us sell him to the Ishmaelites, and let not our hand be upon him, for he *is* our brother *and* our flesh." And his brothers listened. 28 Then Midianite traders passed by; so *the brothers* pulled Joseph up and lifted him out of the pit, and sold him to the Ishmaelites for twenty *shekels* of silver. And they took Joseph to Egypt.

29 Then Reuben returned to the pit, and indeed Joseph *was* not in the pit; and he tore his clothes. 30 And he returned to his brothers and said, "The lad *is* no *more;* and I, where shall I go?"

31 So they took Joseph's tunic, killed a kid of the goats, and dipped the tunic in the blood. 32 Then they sent the tunic of *many* colors, and they brought *it* to their father and said, "We have found this. Do you know whether it *is* your son's tunic or not?"

33 And he recognized it and said, "*It is* my son's tunic. A wild beast has devoured him. Without doubt Joseph is torn to pieces." 34 Then Jacob tore his clothes, put sackcloth on his waist, and mourned for his son many days. 35 And all his sons and all his daughters arose to comfort him; but he refused to be comforted, and he said, "For I shall go down into the grave to my son in mourning." Thus his father wept for him.

36 Now the Midianites had sold him in Egypt to Potiphar, an officer of Pharaoh *and* captain of the guard.

38 It came to pass at that time that Judah departed from his brothers, and visited a certain Adullamite whose name *was* Hirah. 2 And Judah saw there a daughter of a certain Canaanite whose name *was* Shua, and he married her and went in to her. 3 So she conceived and bore a son, and he called his name Er. 4 She conceived again and bore a son, and she called his name Onan. 5 And she conceived yet again and bore a son, and called his name Shelah. He was at Chezib when she bore him.

6 Then Judah took a wife for Er his firstborn, and her name *was* Tamar. 7 But Er, Judah's firstborn, was wicked in the sight of the LORD, and the LORD

23 וַיְהִי כַּאֲשֶׁר־בָּא יוֹסֵף אֶל־ לְהָשִׁיבוֹ אֶל־אָבִיו:
אֶחָיו וַיַּפְשִׁיטוּ אֶת־יוֹסֵף אֶת־כֻּתָּנְתּוֹ אֶת־כְּתֹנֶת
הַפַּסִּים אֲשֶׁר עָלָיו: 24 וַיִּקָּחֻהוּ וַיַּשְׁלִכוּ אֹתוֹ הַבֹּרָה
וְהַבּוֹר רֵק אֵין בּוֹ מָיִם: 25 וַיֵּשְׁבוּ לֶאֱכָל־לֶחֶם
וַיִּשְׂאוּ עֵינֵיהֶם וַיִּרְאוּ וְהִנֵּה אֹרְחַת יִשְׁמְעֵאלִים
בָּאָה מִגִּלְעָד וּגְמַלֵּיהֶם נֹשְׂאִים נְכֹאת וּצְרִי וָלֹט
הוֹלְכִים לְהוֹרִיד מִצְרָיְמָה: 26 וַיֹּאמֶר יְהוּדָה אֶל־
אֶחָיו מַה־בֶּצַע כִּי נַהֲרֹג אֶת־אָחִינוּ וְכִסִּינוּ אֶת־
דָּמוֹ: 27 לְכוּ וְנִמְכְּרֶנּוּ לַיִּשְׁמְעֵאלִים וְיָדֵנוּ אַל־
תְּהִי־בוֹ כִּי־אָחִינוּ בְשָׂרֵנוּ הוּא וַיִּשְׁמְעוּ אֶחָיו:
28 וַיַּעַבְרוּ אֲנָשִׁים מִדְיָנִים סֹחֲרִים וַיִּמְשְׁכוּ וַיַּעֲלוּ
אֶת־יוֹסֵף מִן־הַבּוֹר וַיִּמְכְּרוּ אֶת־יוֹסֵף לַיִּשְׁמְעֵאלִים
בְּעֶשְׂרִים כָּסֶף וַיָּבִיאוּ אֶת־יוֹסֵף מִצְרָיְמָה: 29 וַיָּשָׁב
רְאוּבֵן אֶל־הַבּוֹר וְהִנֵּה אֵין־יוֹסֵף בַּבּוֹר וַיִּקְרַע אֶת־
בְּגָדָיו: 30 וַיָּשָׁב אֶל־אֶחָיו וַיֹּאמַר הַיֶּלֶד אֵינֶנּוּ וַאֲנִי
אָנָה אֲנִי־בָא: 31 וַיִּקְחוּ אֶת־כְּתֹנֶת יוֹסֵף וַיִּשְׁחֲטוּ
שְׂעִיר עִזִּים וַיִּטְבְּלוּ אֶת־הַכֻּתֹּנֶת בַּדָּם: 32 וַיְשַׁלְּחוּ
אֶת־כְּתֹנֶת הַפַּסִּים וַיָּבִיאוּ אֶל־אֲבִיהֶם וַיֹּאמְרוּ
זֹאת מָצָאנוּ הַכֶּר־נָא הַכְּתֹנֶת בִּנְךָ הִוא אִם־לֹא:
33 וַיַּכִּירָהּ וַיֹּאמֶר כְּתֹנֶת בְּנִי חַיָּה רָעָה אֲכָלָתְהוּ
טָרֹף טֹרַף יוֹסֵף: 34 וַיִּקְרַע יַעֲקֹב שִׂמְלֹתָיו וַיָּשֶׂם
שַׂק בְּמָתְנָיו וַיִּתְאַבֵּל עַל־בְּנוֹ יָמִים רַבִּים: 35 וַיָּקֻמוּ
כָל־בָּנָיו וְכָל־בְּנֹתָיו לְנַחֲמוֹ וַיְמָאֵן לְהִתְנַחֵם וַיֹּאמֶר
כִּי־אֵרֵד אֶל־בְּנִי אָבֵל שְׁאֹלָה וַיֵּבְךְ אֹתוֹ אָבִיו:
36 וְהַמְּדָנִים מָכְרוּ אֹתוֹ אֶל־מִצְרָיִם לְפוֹטִיפַר סְרִיס
פַּרְעֹה שַׂר הַטַּבָּחִים: פ

לח וַיְהִי בָּעֵת הַהִוא וַיֵּרֶד יְהוּדָה מֵאֵת אֶחָיו וַיֵּט
עַד־אִישׁ עֲדֻלָּמִי וּשְׁמוֹ חִירָה: 2 וַיַּרְא־שָׁם יְהוּדָה
בַּת־אִישׁ כְּנַעֲנִי וּשְׁמוֹ שׁוּעַ וַיִּקָּחֶהָ וַיָּבֹא אֵלֶיהָ:
3 וַתַּהַר וַתֵּלֶד בֵּן וַיִּקְרָא אֶת־שְׁמוֹ עֵר: 4 וַתַּהַר עוֹד
וַתֵּלֶד בֵּן וַתִּקְרָא אֶת־שְׁמוֹ אוֹנָן: 5 וַתֹּסֶף עוֹד וַתֵּלֶד
בֵּן וַתִּקְרָא אֶת־שְׁמוֹ שֵׁלָה וְהָיָה בִכְזִיב בְּלִדְתָּהּ
אֹתוֹ: 6 וַיִּקַּח יְהוּדָה אִשָּׁה לְעֵר בְּכוֹרוֹ וּשְׁמָהּ תָּמָר:
7 וַיְהִי עֵר בְּכוֹר יְהוּדָה רַע בְּעֵינֵי יְהוָה וַיְמִתֵהוּ

killed him. 8 And Judah said to Onan, "Go in to your brother's wife and marry her, and raise up an heir to your brother." 9 But Onan knew that the heir would not be his; and it came to pass, when he went in to his brother's wife, that he emitted on the ground, lest he should give an heir to his brother. 10 And the thing which he did displeased the LORD; therefore He killed him also.

11 Then Judah said to Tamar his daughter-in-law, "Remain a widow in your father's house till my son Shelah is grown." For he said, "Lest he also die like his brothers." And Tamar went and dwelt in her father's house.

12 Now in the process of time the daughter of Shua, Judah's wife, died; and Judah was comforted, and went up to his sheepshearers at Timnah, he and his friend Hirah the Adullamite. 13 And it was told Tamar, saying, "Look, your father-in-law is going up to Timnah to shear his sheep." 14 So she took off her widow's garments, covered *herself* with a veil and wrapped herself, and sat in an open place which *was* on the way to Timnah; for she saw that Shelah was grown, and she was not given to him as a wife. 15 When Judah saw her, he thought she *was* a harlot, because she had covered her face. 16 Then he turned to her by the way, and said, "Please let me come in to you"; for he did not know that she *was* his daughter-in-law.

So she said, "What will you give me, that you may come in to me?"

17 And he said, "I will send a young goat from the flock."

So she said, "Will you give *me* a pledge till you send *it?*"

18 Then he said, "What pledge shall I give you?"

So she said, "Your signet and cord, and your staff that *is* in your hand." Then he gave *them* to her, and went in to her, and she conceived by him. 19 So she arose and went away, and laid aside her veil and put on the garments of her widowhood.

20 And Judah sent the young goat by the hand of his friend the Adullamite, to receive *his* pledge from the woman's hand, but he did not find her. 21 Then he asked the men of that place, saying, "Where is the harlot who *was* openly by the roadside?"

And they said, "There was no harlot in this *place.*"

22 So he returned to Judah and said, "I cannot find her. Also, the men of the place said there was no harlot in this *place.*"

23 Then Judah said, "Let her take *them* for herself, lest we be shamed; for I sent this young goat and you have not found her."

יְהֹוָה: 8 וַיֹּאמֶר יְהוּדָה לְאוֹנָן בֹּא אֶל־אֵשֶׁת אָחִיךָ וְיַבֵּם אֹתָהּ וְהָקֵם זֶרַע לְאָחִיךָ: 9 וַיֵּדַע אוֹנָן כִּי לֹּא לוֹ יִהְיֶה הַזָּרַע וְהָיָה אִם־בָּא אֶל־אֵשֶׁת אָחִיו וְשִׁחֵת אַרְצָה לְבִלְתִּי נְתָן־זֶרַע לְאָחִיו: 10 וַיֵּרַע בְּעֵינֵי יְהֹוָה אֲשֶׁר עָשָׂה וַיָּמֶת גַּם־אֹתוֹ: 11 וַיֹּאמֶר יְהוּדָה לְתָמָר כַּלָּתוֹ שְׁבִי אַלְמָנָה בֵית־אָבִיךְ עַד־יִגְדַּל שֵׁלָה בְנִי כִּי אָמַר פֶּן־יָמוּת גַּם־הוּא כְּאֶחָיו וַתֵּלֶךְ תָּמָר וַתֵּשֶׁב בֵּית אָבִיהָ: 12 וַיִּרְבּוּ הַיָּמִים וַתָּמָת בַּת־שׁוּעַ אֵשֶׁת־יְהוּדָה וַיִּנָּחֶם יְהוּדָה וַיַּעַל עַל־גֹּזְזֵי צֹאנוֹ הוּא וְחִירָה רֵעֵהוּ הָעֲדֻלָּמִי תִּמְנָתָה:

13 וַיֻּגַּד לְתָמָר לֵאמֹר הִנֵּה חָמִיךְ עֹלֶה תִמְנָתָה לָגֹז צֹאנוֹ: 14 וַתָּסַר בִּגְדֵי אַלְמְנוּתָהּ מֵעָלֶיהָ וַתְּכַס בַּצָּעִיף וַתִּתְעַלָּף וַתֵּשֶׁב בְּפֶתַח עֵינַיִם אֲשֶׁר עַל־דֶּרֶךְ תִּמְנָתָה כִּי רָאֲתָה כִּי־גָדַל שֵׁלָה וְהִוא לֹא־נִתְּנָה לוֹ לְאִשָּׁה: 15 וַיִּרְאֶהָ יְהוּדָה וַיַּחְשְׁבֶהָ לְזוֹנָה כִּי כִסְּתָה פָּנֶיהָ: 16 וַיֵּט אֵלֶיהָ אֶל־הַדֶּרֶךְ וַיֹּאמֶר הָבָה־נָּא אָבוֹא אֵלַיִךְ כִּי לֹא יָדַע כִּי כַלָּתוֹ הִוא וַתֹּאמֶר מַה־תִּתֶּן־לִי כִּי תָבוֹא אֵלָי: 17 וַיֹּאמֶר אָנֹכִי אֲשַׁלַּח גְּדִי־עִזִּים מִן־הַצֹּאן וַתֹּאמֶר אִם־תִּתֵּן עֵרָבוֹן עַד שָׁלְחֶךָ: 18 וַיֹּאמֶר מָה הָעֵרָבוֹן אֲשֶׁר אֶתֶּן־לָךְ וַתֹּאמֶר חֹתָמְךָ וּפְתִילֶךָ וּמַטְּךָ אֲשֶׁר בְּיָדֶךָ וַיִּתֶּן־לָהּ וַיָּבֹא אֵלֶיהָ וַתַּהַר לוֹ: 19 וַתָּקָם וַתֵּלֶךְ וַתָּסַר צְעִיפָהּ מֵעָלֶיהָ וַתִּלְבַּשׁ בִּגְדֵי אַלְמְנוּתָהּ: 20 וַיִּשְׁלַח יְהוּדָה אֶת־גְּדִי הָעִזִּים בְּיַד רֵעֵהוּ הָעֲדֻלָּמִי לָקַחַת הָעֵרָבוֹן מִיַּד הָאִשָּׁה וְלֹא מְצָאָהּ: 21 וַיִּשְׁאַל אֶת־אַנְשֵׁי מְקֹמָהּ לֵאמֹר אַיֵּה הַקְּדֵשָׁה הִוא בָעֵינַיִם עַל־הַדָּרֶךְ וַיֹּאמְרוּ לֹא־הָיְתָה בָזֶה קְדֵשָׁה: 22 וַיָּשָׁב אֶל־יְהוּדָה וַיֹּאמֶר לֹא מְצָאתִיהָ וְגַם אַנְשֵׁי הַמָּקוֹם אָמְרוּ לֹא־הָיְתָה בָזֶה קְדֵשָׁה: 23 וַיֹּאמֶר יְהוּדָה תִּקַּח־לָהּ פֶּן נִהְיֶה לָבוּז הִנֵּה שָׁלַחְתִּי הַגְּדִי הַזֶּה

24 And it came to pass, about three months after, that Judah was told, saying, "Tamar your daughter-in-law has played the harlot; furthermore she *is* with child by harlotry."

So Judah said, "Bring her out and let her be burned!"

25 When she *was* brought out, she sent to her father-in-law, saying, "By the man to whom these belong, I *am* with child." And she said, "Please determine whose these *are*—the signet and cord, and staff."

26 So Judah acknowledged *them* and said, "She has been more righteous than I, because I did not give her to Shelah my son." And he never knew her again.

27 Now it came to pass, at the time for giving birth, that behold, twins *were* in her womb. 28 And so it was, when she was giving birth, that *the one* put out *his* hand; and the midwife took a scarlet *thread* and bound it on his hand, saying, "This one came out first." 29 Then it happened, as he drew back his hand, that his brother came out unexpectedly; and she said, "How did you break through? *This* breach *be* upon you!" Therefore his name was called Perez. 30 Afterward his brother came out who had the scarlet *thread* on his hand. And his name was called Zerah.

39 Now Joseph had been taken down to Egypt. And Potiphar, an officer of Pharaoh, captain of the guard, an Egyptian, bought him from the Ishmaelites who had taken him down there. 2 The LORD was with Joseph, and he was a successful man; and he was in the house of his master the Egyptian. 3 And his master saw that the LORD *was* with him and that the LORD made all he did to prosper in his hand. 4 So Joseph found favor in his sight, and served him. Then he made him overseer of his house, and all *that* he had he put under his authority. 5 So it was, from the time *that* he had made him overseer of his house and all that he had, that the LORD blessed the Egyptian's house for Joseph's sake; and the blessing of the LORD was on all that he had in the house and in the field. 6 Thus he left all that he had in Joseph's hand, and he did not know what he had except for the bread which he ate.

Now Joseph was handsome in form and appearance.

7 And it came to pass after these things that his master's wife cast longing eyes on Joseph, and she said, "Lie with me."

וְאַתָּה לֹא מְצָאתָהּ: 24 וַיְהִי ׀ כְּמִשְׁלֹשׁ חֳדָשִׁים
וַיֻּגַּד לִיהוּדָה לֵאמֹר זָנְתָה תָּמָר כַּלָּתֶךָ וְגַם הִנֵּה
הָרָה לִזְנוּנִים וַיֹּאמֶר יְהוּדָה הוֹצִיאוּהָ וְתִשָּׂרֵף:
25 הִוא מוּצֵאת וְהִיא שָׁלְחָה אֶל־חָמִיהָ לֵאמֹר
לְאִישׁ אֲשֶׁר־אֵלֶּה לּוֹ אָנֹכִי הָרָה וַתֹּאמֶר הַכֶּר־נָא
לְמִי הַחֹתֶמֶת וְהַפְּתִילִים וְהַמַּטֶּה הָאֵלֶּה: 26 וַיַּכֵּר
יְהוּדָה וַיֹּאמֶר צָדְקָה מִמֶּנִּי כִּי־עַל־כֵּן לֹא־נְתַתִּיהָ
לְשֵׁלָה בְנִי וְלֹא־יָסַף עוֹד לְדַעְתָּהּ: 27 וַיְהִי בְּעֵת
לִדְתָּהּ וְהִנֵּה תְאוֹמִים בְּבִטְנָהּ: 28 וַיְהִי בְלִדְתָּהּ
וַיִּתֶּן־יָד וַתִּקַּח הַמְיַלֶּדֶת וַתִּקְשֹׁר עַל־יָדוֹ שָׁנִי לֵאמֹר
זֶה יָצָא רִאשֹׁנָה: 29 וַיְהִי ׀ כְּמֵשִׁיב יָדוֹ וְהִנֵּה
יָצָא אָחִיו וַתֹּאמֶר מַה־פָּרַצְתָּ עָלֶיךָ פָּרֶץ וַיִּקְרָא
שְׁמוֹ פָּרֶץ: 30 וְאַחַר יָצָא אָחִיו אֲשֶׁר עַל־יָדוֹ הַשָּׁנִי
וַיִּקְרָא שְׁמוֹ זָרַח: ס

לט וְיוֹסֵף הוּרַד מִצְרָיְמָה וַיִּקְנֵהוּ פּוֹטִיפַר סְרִיס
פַּרְעֹה שַׂר הַטַּבָּחִים אִישׁ מִצְרִי מִיַּד הַיִּשְׁמְעֵאלִים
אֲשֶׁר הוֹרִדֻהוּ שָׁמָּה: 2 וַיְהִי יְהֹוָה אֶת־יוֹסֵף וַיְהִי
אִישׁ מַצְלִיחַ וַיְהִי בְּבֵית אֲדֹנָיו הַמִּצְרִי: 3 וַיַּרְא
אֲדֹנָיו כִּי יְהֹוָה אִתּוֹ וְכֹל אֲשֶׁר־הוּא עֹשֶׂה יְהֹוָה
מַצְלִיחַ בְּיָדוֹ: 4 וַיִּמְצָא יוֹסֵף חֵן בְּעֵינָיו וַיְשָׁרֶת אֹתוֹ
וַיַּפְקִדֵהוּ עַל־בֵּיתוֹ וְכָל־יֶשׁ־לוֹ נָתַן בְּיָדוֹ: 5 וַיְהִי מֵאָז
הִפְקִיד אֹתוֹ בְּבֵיתוֹ וְעַל כָּל־אֲשֶׁר יֶשׁ־לוֹ וַיְבָרֶךְ
יְהֹוָה אֶת־בֵּית הַמִּצְרִי בִּגְלַל יוֹסֵף וַיְהִי בִּרְכַּת
יְהֹוָה בְּכָל־אֲשֶׁר יֶשׁ־לוֹ בַּבַּיִת וּבַשָּׂדֶה: 6 וַיַּעֲזֹב
כָּל־אֲשֶׁר־לוֹ בְּיַד־יוֹסֵף וְלֹא־יָדַע אִתּוֹ מְאוּמָה כִּי
אִם־הַלֶּחֶם אֲשֶׁר־הוּא אוֹכֵל וַיְהִי יוֹסֵף יְפֵה־תֹאַר
וִיפֵה מַרְאֶה: 7 וַיְהִי אַחַר הַדְּבָרִים הָאֵלֶּה וַתִּשָּׂא
אֵשֶׁת־אֲדֹנָיו אֶת־עֵינֶיהָ אֶל־יוֹסֵף וַתֹּאמֶר שִׁכְבָה

8 But he refused and said to his master's wife, "Look, my master does not know what *is* with me in the house, and he has committed all that he has to my hand. 9 *There is* no one greater in this house than I, nor has he kept back anything from me but you, because you *are* his wife. How then can I do this great wickedness, and sin against God?"

10 So it was, as she spoke to Joseph day by day, that he did not heed her, to lie with her *or* to be with her.

11 But it happened about this time, when Joseph went into the house to do his work, and none of the men of the house *was* inside, 12 that she caught him by his garment, saying, "Lie with me." But he left his garment in her hand, and fled and ran outside. 13 And so it was, when she saw that he had left his garment in her hand and fled outside, 14 that she called to the men of her house and spoke to them, saying, "See, he has brought in to us a Hebrew to mock us. He came in to me to lie with me, and I cried out with a loud voice. 15 And it happened, when he heard that I lifted my voice and cried out, that he left his garment with me, and fled and went outside."

16 So she kept his garment with her until his master came home. 17 Then she spoke to him with words like these, saying, "The Hebrew servant whom you brought to us came in to me to mock me; 18 so it happened, as I lifted my voice and cried out, that he left his garment with me and fled outside."

19 So it was, when his master heard the words which his wife spoke to him, saying, "Your servant did to me after this manner," that his anger was aroused. 20 Then Joseph's master took him and put him into the prison, a place where the king's prisoners *were* confined. And he was there in the prison. 21 But the LORD was with Joseph and showed him mercy, and He gave him favor in the sight of the keeper of the prison. 22 And the keeper of the prison committed to Joseph's hand all the prisoners who *were* in the prison; whatever they did there, it was his doing. 23 The keeper of the prison did not look into anything *that was* under *Joseph's* authority, because the LORD was with him; and whatever he did, the LORD made *it* prosper.

40 It came to pass after these things *that* the butler and the baker of the king of Egypt offended their lord, the king of Egypt. 2 And Pharaoh was angry with his two officers, the chief butler and the chief baker. 3 So he put them in custody in the house of the captain of the guard, in the prison, the

עִמִּי: 8 וַיְמָאֵן | וַיֹּאמֶר אֶל־אֵשֶׁת אֲדֹנָיו הֵן אֲדֹנִי לֹא־יָדַע אִתִּי מַה־בַּבָּיִת וְכֹל אֲשֶׁר־יֶשׁ־לוֹ נָתַן בְּיָדִי: 9 אֵינֶנּוּ גָדוֹל בַּבַּיִת הַזֶּה מִמֶּנִּי וְלֹא־חָשַׂךְ מִמֶּנִּי מְאוּמָה כִּי אִם־אוֹתָךְ בַּאֲשֶׁר אַתְּ־אִשְׁתּוֹ וְאֵיךְ אֶעֱשֶׂה הָרָעָה הַגְּדֹלָה הַזֹּאת וְחָטָאתִי לֵאלֹהִים: 10 וַיְהִי כְּדַבְּרָהּ אֶל־יוֹסֵף יוֹם | יוֹם וְלֹא־שָׁמַע אֵלֶיהָ לִשְׁכַּב אֶצְלָהּ לִהְיוֹת עִמָּהּ: 11 וַיְהִי כְּהַיּוֹם הַזֶּה וַיָּבֹא הַבַּיְתָה לַעֲשׂוֹת מְלַאכְתּוֹ וְאֵין אִישׁ מֵאַנְשֵׁי הַבַּיִת שָׁם בַּבָּיִת: 12 וַתִּתְפְּשֵׂהוּ בְּבִגְדוֹ לֵאמֹר שִׁכְבָה עִמִּי וַיַּעֲזֹב בִּגְדוֹ בְּיָדָהּ וַיָּנָס וַיֵּצֵא הַחוּצָה: 13 וַיְהִי כִּרְאוֹתָהּ כִּי־עָזַב בִּגְדוֹ בְּיָדָהּ וַיָּנָס הַחוּצָה: 14 וַתִּקְרָא לְאַנְשֵׁי בֵיתָהּ וַתֹּאמֶר לָהֶם לֵאמֹר רְאוּ הֵבִיא לָנוּ אִישׁ עִבְרִי לְצַחֶק בָּנוּ בָּא אֵלַי לִשְׁכַּב עִמִּי וָאֶקְרָא בְּקוֹל גָּדוֹל: 15 וַיְהִי כְשָׁמְעוֹ כִּי־הֲרִימֹתִי קוֹלִי וָאֶקְרָא וַיַּעֲזֹב בִּגְדוֹ אֶצְלִי וַיָּנָס וַיֵּצֵא הַחוּצָה: 16 וַתַּנַּח בִּגְדוֹ אֶצְלָהּ עַד־בּוֹא אֲדֹנָיו אֶל־בֵּיתוֹ: 17 וַתְּדַבֵּר אֵלָיו כַּדְּבָרִים הָאֵלֶּה לֵאמֹר בָּא אֵלַי הָעֶבֶד הָעִבְרִי אֲשֶׁר־הֵבֵאתָ לָּנוּ לְצַחֶק בִּי: 18 וַיְהִי כַּהֲרִימִי קוֹלִי וָאֶקְרָא וַיַּעֲזֹב בִּגְדוֹ אֶצְלִי וַיָּנָס הַחוּצָה: 19 וַיְהִי כִשְׁמֹעַ אֲדֹנָיו אֶת־דִּבְרֵי אִשְׁתּוֹ אֲשֶׁר דִּבְּרָה אֵלָיו לֵאמֹר כַּדְּבָרִים הָאֵלֶּה עָשָׂה לִי עַבְדֶּךָ וַיִּחַר אַפּוֹ: 20 וַיִּקַּח אֲדֹנֵי יוֹסֵף אֹתוֹ וַיִּתְּנֵהוּ אֶל־בֵּית הַסֹּהַר מְקוֹם אֲשֶׁר־אֲסוּרֵי הַמֶּלֶךְ אֲסוּרִים וַיְהִי־שָׁם בְּבֵית הַסֹּהַר: 21 וַיְהִי יְהוָה אֶת־יוֹסֵף וַיֵּט אֵלָיו חָסֶד וַיִּתֵּן חִנּוֹ בְּעֵינֵי שַׂר בֵּית־הַסֹּהַר: 22 וַיִּתֵּן שַׂר בֵּית־הַסֹּהַר בְּיַד־יוֹסֵף אֵת כָּל־הָאֲסִירִם אֲשֶׁר בְּבֵית הַסֹּהַר וְאֵת כָּל־אֲשֶׁר עֹשִׂים שָׁם הוּא הָיָה עֹשֶׂה: 23 אֵין | שַׂר בֵּית־הַסֹּהַר רֹאֶה אֶת־כָּל־מְאוּמָה בְּיָדוֹ בַּאֲשֶׁר יְהוָה אִתּוֹ וַאֲשֶׁר־הוּא עֹשֶׂה יְהוָה מַצְלִיחַ: ס

מ וַיְהִי אַחַר הַדְּבָרִים הָאֵלֶּה חָטְאוּ מַשְׁקֵה מֶלֶךְ־מִצְרַיִם וְהָאֹפֶה לַאֲדֹנֵיהֶם לְמֶלֶךְ מִצְרָיִם: 2 וַיִּקְצֹף פַּרְעֹה עַל שְׁנֵי סָרִיסָיו עַל שַׂר הַמַּשְׁקִים וְעַל שַׂר הָאֹפִים: 3 וַיִּתֵּן אֹתָם בְּמִשְׁמַר בֵּית שַׂר הַטַּבָּחִים

place where Joseph *was* confined. [4] And the captain of the guard charged Joseph with them, and he served them; so they were in custody for a while.

[5] Then the butler and the baker of the king of Egypt, who *were* confined in the prison, had a dream, both of them, each man's dream in one night *and* each man's dream with its *own* interpretation. [6] And Joseph came in to them in the morning and looked at them, and saw that they *were* sad. [7] So he asked Pharaoh's officers who *were* with him in the custody of his lord's house, saying, "Why do you look *so* sad today?"

[8] And they said to him, "We each have had a dream, and *there is* no interpreter of it."

So Joseph said to them, "Do not interpretations belong to God? Tell *them* to me, please."

[9] Then the chief butler told his dream to Joseph, and said to him, "Behold, in my dream a vine *was* before me, [10] and in the vine *were* three branches; it *was* as though it budded, its blossoms shot forth, and its clusters brought forth ripe grapes. [11] Then Pharaoh's cup *was* in my hand; and I took the grapes and pressed them into Pharaoh's cup, and placed the cup in Pharaoh's hand."

[12] And Joseph said to him, "This *is* the interpretation of it: The three branches *are* three days. [13] Now within three days Pharaoh will lift up your head and restore you to your place, and you will put Pharaoh's cup in his hand according to the former manner, when you were his butler. [14] But remember me when it is well with you, and please show kindness to me; make mention of me to Pharaoh, and get me out of this house. [15] For indeed I was stolen away from the land of the Hebrews; and also I have done nothing here that they should put me into the dungeon."

[16] When the chief baker saw that the interpretation was good, he said to Joseph, "I also *was* in my dream, and there *were* three white baskets on my head. [17] In the uppermost basket *were* all kinds of baked goods for Pharaoh, and the birds ate them out of the basket on my head."

[18] So Joseph answered and said, "This *is* the interpretation of it: The three baskets *are* three days. [19] Within three days Pharaoh will lift off your head from you and hang you on a tree; and the birds will eat your flesh from you."

[20] Now it came to pass on the third day, *which was* Pharaoh's birthday, that he made a feast for all his servants; and he lifted up the head of the chief butler and of the chief baker among his servants. [21] Then he restored the chief butler to his butlership again, and he placed the cup in Pharaoh's hand.

אֶל־בֵּ֣ית הַסֹּ֔הַר מְק֕וֹם אֲשֶׁר־יוֹסֵ֖ף אָס֥וּר שָֽׁם׃

4 וַ֠יִּפְקֹד שַׂ֣ר הַטַּבָּחִ֧ים אֶת־יוֹסֵ֛ף אִתָּ֖ם וַיְשָׁ֣רֶת אֹתָ֑ם וַיִּהְי֥וּ יָמִ֖ים בְּמִשְׁמָֽר׃ 5 וַיַּֽחַלְמוּ֩ חֲל֨וֹם שְׁנֵיהֶ֜ם אִ֣ישׁ חֲלֹמ֤וֹ בְּלַ֣יְלָה אֶחָ֔ד אִ֖ישׁ כְּפִתְר֣וֹן חֲלֹמ֑וֹ הַמַּשְׁקֶ֣ה וְהָאֹפֶ֗ה אֲשֶׁר֙ לְמֶ֣לֶךְ מִצְרַ֔יִם אֲשֶׁ֥ר אֲסוּרִ֖ים בְּבֵ֥ית הַסֹּֽהַר׃ 6 וַיָּבֹ֧א אֲלֵיהֶ֛ם יוֹסֵ֖ף בַּבֹּ֑קֶר וַיַּ֣רְא אֹתָ֔ם וְהִנָּ֖ם זֹֽעֲפִֽים׃ 7 וַיִּשְׁאַ֞ל אֶת־סְרִיסֵ֣י פַרְעֹ֗ה אֲשֶׁ֨ר אִתּ֤וֹ בְמִשְׁמַר֙ בֵּ֣ית אֲדֹנָ֔יו לֵאמֹ֑ר מַדּ֛וּעַ פְּנֵיכֶ֥ם רָעִ֖ים הַיּֽוֹם׃ 8 וַיֹּאמְר֣וּ אֵלָ֗יו חֲל֤וֹם חָלַ֙מְנוּ֙ וּפֹתֵ֣ר אֵ֣ין אֹת֔וֹ וַיֹּ֤אמֶר אֲלֵהֶם֙ יוֹסֵ֔ף הֲל֥וֹא לֵֽאלֹהִ֖ים פִּתְרֹנִ֑ים סַפְּרוּ־נָ֖א לִֽי׃ 9 וַיְסַפֵּ֧ר שַֽׂר־הַמַּשְׁקִ֛ים אֶת־חֲלֹמ֖וֹ לְיוֹסֵ֑ף וַיֹּ֣אמֶר ל֔וֹ בַּחֲלוֹמִ֕י וְהִנֵּה־גֶ֖פֶן לְפָנָֽי׃ 10 וּבַגֶּ֖פֶן שְׁלֹשָׁ֣ה שָֽׂרִיגִ֑ם וְהִ֤וא כְפֹרַ֙חַת֙ עָלְתָ֣ה נִצָּ֔הּ הִבְשִׁ֥ילוּ אַשְׁכְּלֹתֶ֖יהָ עֲנָבִֽים׃ 11 וְכ֥וֹס פַּרְעֹ֖ה בְּיָדִ֑י וָאֶקַּ֣ח אֶת־הָֽעֲנָבִ֗ים וָֽאֶשְׂחַ֤ט אֹתָם֙ אֶל־כּ֣וֹס פַּרְעֹ֔ה וָאֶתֵּ֥ן אֶת־הַכּ֖וֹס עַל־כַּ֥ף פַּרְעֹֽה׃ 12 וַיֹּ֤אמֶר לוֹ֙ יוֹסֵ֔ף זֶ֖ה פִּתְרֹנ֑וֹ שְׁלֹ֙שֶׁת֙ הַשָּׂ֣רִגִ֔ים שְׁלֹ֥שֶׁת יָמִ֖ים הֵֽם׃ 13 בְּע֣וֹד ׀ שְׁלֹ֣שֶׁת יָמִ֗ים יִשָּׂ֤א פַרְעֹה֙ אֶת־רֹאשֶׁ֔ךָ וַהֲשִֽׁיבְךָ֖ עַל־כַּנֶּ֑ךָ וְנָתַתָּ֤ כוֹס־פַּרְעֹה֙ בְּיָד֔וֹ כַּמִּשְׁפָּט֙ הָֽרִאשׁ֔וֹן אֲשֶׁ֥ר הָיִ֖יתָ מַשְׁקֵֽהוּ׃ 14 כִּ֧י אִם־זְכַרְתַּ֣נִי אִתְּךָ֗ כַּאֲשֶׁר֙ יִ֣יטַב לָ֔ךְ וְעָשִֽׂיתָ־נָּ֥א עִמָּדִ֖י חָ֑סֶד וְהִזְכַּרְתַּ֙נִי֙ אֶל־פַּרְעֹ֔ה וְהֽוֹצֵאתַ֖נִי מִן־הַבַּ֥יִת הַזֶּֽה׃ 15 כִּֽי־גֻנֹּ֣ב גֻּנַּ֔בְתִּי מֵאֶ֖רֶץ הָעִבְרִ֑ים וְגַם־פֹּה֙ לֹא־עָשִׂ֣יתִי מְא֔וּמָה כִּֽי־שָׂמ֥וּ אֹתִ֖י בַּבּֽוֹר׃ 16 וַיַּ֤רְא שַֽׂר־הָאֹפִים֙ כִּ֣י ט֣וֹב פָּתָ֔ר וַיֹּ֙אמֶר֙ אֶל־יוֹסֵ֔ף אַף־אֲנִי֙ בַּחֲלוֹמִ֔י וְהִנֵּ֗ה שְׁלֹשָׁ֛ה סַלֵּ֥י חֹרִ֖י עַל־רֹאשִֽׁי׃ 17 וּבַסַּ֣ל הָֽעֶלְי֗וֹן מִכֹּ֛ל מַאֲכַ֥ל פַּרְעֹ֖ה מַעֲשֵׂ֣ה אֹפֶ֑ה וְהָע֗וֹף אֹכֵ֥ל אֹתָ֛ם מִן־הַסַּ֖ל מֵעַ֥ל רֹאשִֽׁי׃ 18 וַיַּ֤עַן יוֹסֵף֙ וַיֹּ֔אמֶר זֶ֖ה פִּתְרֹנ֑וֹ שְׁלֹ֙שֶׁת֙ הַסַּלִּ֔ים שְׁלֹ֥שֶׁת יָמִ֖ים הֵֽם׃ 19 בְּע֣וֹד ׀ שְׁלֹ֣שֶׁת יָמִ֗ים יִשָּׂ֨א פַרְעֹ֤ה אֶת־רֹֽאשְׁךָ֙ מֵֽעָלֶ֔יךָ וְתָלָ֥ה אוֹתְךָ֖ עַל־עֵ֑ץ וְאָכַ֥ל הָע֛וֹף אֶת־בְּשָׂרְךָ֖ מֵעָלֶֽיךָ׃ 20 וַיְהִ֣י ׀ בַּיּ֣וֹם הַשְּׁלִישִׁ֗י י֚וֹם הֻלֶּ֣דֶת אֶת־פַּרְעֹ֔ה וַיַּ֥עַשׂ מִשְׁתֶּ֖ה לְכָל־עֲבָדָ֑יו וַיִּשָּׂ֣א אֶת־רֹ֣אשׁ ׀ שַׂ֣ר הַמַּשְׁקִ֗ים וְאֶת־רֹ֛אשׁ שַׂ֥ר הָאֹפִ֖ים בְּת֥וֹךְ עֲבָדָֽיו׃ 21 וַיָּ֛שֶׁב אֶת־שַׂ֥ר הַמַּשְׁקִ֖ים עַל־מַשְׁקֵ֑הוּ וַיִּתֵּ֥ן הַכּ֖וֹס עַל־כַּ֥ף פַּרְעֹֽה׃

22 But he hanged the chief baker, as Joseph had interpreted to them. 23 Yet the chief butler did not remember Joseph, but forgot him.

41 Then it came to pass, at the end of two full years, that Pharaoh had a dream; and behold, he stood by the river. 2 Suddenly there came up out of the river seven cows, fine looking and fat; and they fed in the meadow. 3 Then behold, seven other cows came up after them out of the river, ugly and gaunt, and stood by the *other* cows on the bank of the river. 4 And the ugly and gaunt cows ate up the seven fine looking and fat cows. So Pharaoh awoke. 5 He slept and dreamed a second time; and suddenly seven heads of grain came up on one stalk, plump and good. 6 Then behold, seven thin heads, blighted by the east wind, sprang up after them. 7 And the seven thin heads devoured the seven plump and full heads. So Pharaoh awoke, and indeed, *it was* a dream. 8 Now it came to pass in the morning that his spirit was troubled, and he sent and called for all the magicians of Egypt and all its wise men. And Pharaoh told them his dreams, but *there was* no one who could interpret them for Pharaoh.

9 Then the chief butler spoke to Pharaoh, saying: "I remember my faults this day. 10 When Pharaoh was angry with his servants, and put me in custody in the house of the captain of the guard, *both* me and the chief baker, 11 we each had a dream in one night, he and I. Each of us dreamed according to the interpretation of his *own* dream. 12 Now there *was* a young Hebrew man with us there, a servant of the captain of the guard. And we told him, and he interpreted our dreams for us; to each man he interpreted according to his *own* dream. 13 And it came to pass, just as he interpreted for us, so it happened. He restored me to my office, and he hanged him."

14 Then Pharaoh sent and called Joseph, and they brought him quickly out of the dungeon; and he shaved, changed his clothing, and came to Pharaoh. 15 And Pharaoh said to Joseph, "I have had a dream, and *there is* no one who can interpret it. But I have heard it said of you *that* you can understand a dream, to interpret it."

16 So Joseph answered Pharaoh, saying, "*It is* not in me; God will give Pharaoh an answer of peace."

17 Then Pharaoh said to Joseph: "Behold, in my dream I stood on the bank of the river. 18 Suddenly seven cows came up out of the river, fine looking and fat; and they fed in the meadow. 19 Then behold, seven other cows came up after them, poor and very ugly and gaunt, such ugliness as I have never seen in all the land of Egypt. 20 And the gaunt

22 וְאֵת שַׂר הָאֹפִים תָּלָה כַּאֲשֶׁר פָּתַר לָהֶם יוֹסֵף:

23 וְלֹא־זָכַר שַׂר־הַמַּשְׁקִים אֶת־יוֹסֵף וַיִּשְׁכָּחֵהוּ: פ

מא וַיְהִי מִקֵּץ שְׁנָתַיִם יָמִים וּפַרְעֹה חֹלֵם וְהִנֵּה עֹמֵד עַל־הַיְאֹר: 2 וְהִנֵּה מִן־הַיְאֹר עֹלֹת שֶׁבַע פָּרוֹת יְפוֹת מַרְאֶה וּבְרִיאֹת בָּשָׂר וַתִּרְעֶינָה בָּאָחוּ: 3 וְהִנֵּה שֶׁבַע פָּרוֹת אֲחֵרוֹת עֹלוֹת אַחֲרֵיהֶן מִן־הַיְאֹר רָעוֹת מַרְאֶה וְדַקּוֹת בָּשָׂר וַתַּעֲמֹדְנָה אֵצֶל הַפָּרוֹת עַל־שְׂפַת הַיְאֹר: 4 וַתֹּאכַלְנָה הַפָּרוֹת רָעוֹת הַמַּרְאֶה וְדַקֹּת הַבָּשָׂר אֵת שֶׁבַע הַפָּרוֹת יְפֹת הַמַּרְאֶה וְהַבְּרִיאֹת וַיִּיקַץ פַּרְעֹה: 5 וַיִּישָׁן וַיַּחֲלֹם שֵׁנִית וְהִנֵּה שֶׁבַע שִׁבֳּלִים עֹלוֹת בְּקָנֶה אֶחָד בְּרִיאוֹת וְטֹבוֹת: 6 וְהִנֵּה שֶׁבַע שִׁבֳּלִים דַּקּוֹת וּשְׁדוּפֹת קָדִים צֹמְחוֹת אַחֲרֵיהֶן: 7 וַתִּבְלַעְנָה הַשִּׁבֳּלִים הַדַּקּוֹת אֵת שֶׁבַע הַשִּׁבֳּלִים הַבְּרִיאוֹת וְהַמְּלֵאוֹת וַיִּיקַץ פַּרְעֹה וְהִנֵּה חֲלוֹם: 8 וַיְהִי בַבֹּקֶר וַתִּפָּעֶם רוּחוֹ וַיִּשְׁלַח וַיִּקְרָא אֶת־כָּל־חַרְטֻמֵּי מִצְרַיִם וְאֶת־כָּל־חֲכָמֶיהָ וַיְסַפֵּר פַּרְעֹה לָהֶם אֶת־חֲלֹמוֹ וְאֵין־פּוֹתֵר אוֹתָם לְפַרְעֹה: 9 וַיְדַבֵּר שַׂר הַמַּשְׁקִים אֶת־פַּרְעֹה לֵאמֹר אֶת־חֲטָאַי אֲנִי מַזְכִּיר הַיּוֹם: 10 פַּרְעֹה קָצַף עַל־עֲבָדָיו וַיִּתֵּן אֹתִי בְּמִשְׁמַר בֵּית שַׂר הַטַּבָּחִים אֹתִי וְאֵת שַׂר הָאֹפִים: 11 וַנַּחַלְמָה חֲלוֹם בְּלַיְלָה אֶחָד אֲנִי וָהוּא אִישׁ כְּפִתְרוֹן חֲלֹמוֹ חָלָמְנוּ: 12 וְשָׁם אִתָּנוּ נַעַר עִבְרִי עֶבֶד לְשַׂר הַטַּבָּחִים וַנְּסַפֶּר־לוֹ וַיִּפְתָּר־לָנוּ אֶת־חֲלֹמֹתֵינוּ אִישׁ כַּחֲלֹמוֹ פָּתָר: 13 וַיְהִי כַּאֲשֶׁר פָּתַר־לָנוּ כֵּן הָיָה אֹתִי הֵשִׁיב עַל־כַּנִּי וְאֹתוֹ תָלָה: 14 וַיִּשְׁלַח פַּרְעֹה וַיִּקְרָא אֶת־יוֹסֵף וַיְרִיצֻהוּ מִן־הַבּוֹר וַיְגַלַּח וַיְחַלֵּף שִׂמְלֹתָיו וַיָּבֹא אֶל־פַּרְעֹה: 15 וַיֹּאמֶר פַּרְעֹה אֶל־יוֹסֵף חֲלוֹם חָלַמְתִּי וּפֹתֵר אֵין אֹתוֹ וַאֲנִי שָׁמַעְתִּי עָלֶיךָ לֵאמֹר תִּשְׁמַע חֲלוֹם לִפְתֹּר אֹתוֹ: 16 וַיַּעַן יוֹסֵף אֶת־פַּרְעֹה לֵאמֹר בִּלְעָדָי אֱלֹהִים יַעֲנֶה אֶת־שְׁלוֹם פַּרְעֹה: 17 וַיְדַבֵּר פַּרְעֹה אֶל־יוֹסֵף בַּחֲלֹמִי הִנְנִי עֹמֵד עַל־שְׂפַת הַיְאֹר: 18 וְהִנֵּה מִן־הַיְאֹר עֹלֹת שֶׁבַע פָּרוֹת בְּרִיאוֹת בָּשָׂר וִיפֹת תֹּאַר וַתִּרְעֶינָה בָּאָחוּ: 19 וְהִנֵּה שֶׁבַע־פָּרוֹת אֲחֵרוֹת עֹלוֹת אַחֲרֵיהֶן דַּלּוֹת וְרָעוֹת תֹּאַר מְאֹד וְרַקּוֹת בָּשָׂר לֹא־רָאִיתִי כָהֵנָּה בְּכָל־אֶרֶץ מִצְרַיִם לָרֹעַ: 20 וַתֹּאכַלְנָה הַפָּרוֹת הָרַקּוֹת וְהָרָעוֹת אֵת

and ugly cows ate up the first seven, the fat cows.
21 When they had eaten them up, no one would have
known that they had eaten them, for they *were* just
as ugly as at the beginning. So I awoke. 22 Also I
saw in my dream, and suddenly seven heads came
up on one stalk, full and good. 23 Then behold,
seven heads, withered, thin, *and* blighted by the east
wind, sprang up after them. 24 And the thin heads
devoured the seven good heads. So I told *this* to the
magicians, but *there was* no one who could explain
it to me."

25 Then Joseph said to Pharaoh, "The dreams of
Pharaoh *are* one; God has shown Pharaoh what He
is about to do: 26 The seven good cows *are* seven
years, and the seven good heads *are* seven years; the
dreams *are* one. 27 And the seven thin and ugly cows
which came up after them *are* seven years, and the
seven empty heads blighted by the east wind are
seven years of famine. 28 This *is* the thing which I
have spoken to Pharaoh. God has shown Pharaoh
what He *is* about to do. 29 Indeed seven years of
great plenty will come throughout all the land of
Egypt; 30 but after them seven years of famine will
arise, and all the plenty will be forgotten in the land
of Egypt; and the famine will deplete the land. 31 So
the plenty will not be known in the land because of
the famine following, for it *will be* very severe.
32 And the dream was repeated to Pharaoh twice
because the thing *is* established by God, and God
will shortly bring it to pass.

33 "Now therefore, let Pharaoh select a discerning
and wise man, and set him over the land of Egypt.
34 Let Pharaoh do *this,* and let him appoint officers
over the land, to collect one-fifth *of the produce* of
the land of Egypt in the seven plentiful years. 35 And
let them gather all the food of those good years that
are coming, and store up grain under the authority
of Pharaoh, and let them keep food in the cities.
36 Then that food shall be as a reserve for the land
for the seven years of famine which shall be in the
land of Egypt, that the land may not perish during
the famine."

37 So the advice was good in the eyes of Pharaoh
and in the eyes of all his servants. 38 And Pharaoh
said to his servants, "Can we find *such a one* as this,
a man in whom *is* the Spirit of God?"

39 Then Pharaoh said to Joseph, "Inasmuch as
God has shown you all this, *there is* no one as
discerning and wise as you. 40 You shall be over my
house, and all my people shall be ruled according to
your word; only in regard to the throne will I be
greater than you." 41 And Pharaoh said to Joseph,
"See, I have set you over all the land of Egypt."

שֶׁבַע הַפָּרוֹת הָרִאשֹׁנוֹת הַבְּרִיאֹת: 21 וַתָּבֹאנָה אֶל־
קִרְבֶּנָה וְלֹא נוֹדַע כִּי־בָאוּ אֶל־קִרְבֶּנָה וּמַרְאֵיהֶן רַע
כַּאֲשֶׁר בַּתְּחִלָּה וָאִיקָץ: 22 וָאֵרֶא בַּחֲלֹמִי וְהִנֵּה ׀
שֶׁבַע שִׁבֳּלִים עֹלֹת בְּקָנֶה אֶחָד מְלֵאֹת וְטֹבוֹת:
23 וְהִנֵּה שֶׁבַע שִׁבֳּלִים צְנֻמוֹת דַּקּוֹת שְׁדֻפוֹת קָדִים
צֹמְחוֹת אַחֲרֵיהֶם: 24 וַתִּבְלַעְןָ הַשִּׁבֳּלִים הַדַּקֹּת אֵת
שֶׁבַע הַשִּׁבֳּלִים הַטֹּבוֹת וָאֹמַר אֶל־הַחַרְטֻמִּים וְאֵין
מַגִּיד לִי: 25 וַיֹּאמֶר יוֹסֵף אֶל־פַּרְעֹה חֲלוֹם פַּרְעֹה
אֶחָד הוּא אֵת אֲשֶׁר הָאֱלֹהִים עֹשֶׂה הִגִּיד לְפַרְעֹה:
26 שֶׁבַע פָּרֹת הַטֹּבֹת שֶׁבַע שָׁנִים הֵנָּה וְשֶׁבַע
הַשִּׁבֳּלִים הַטֹּבֹת שֶׁבַע שָׁנִים הֵנָּה חֲלוֹם אֶחָד
הוּא: 27 וְשֶׁבַע הַפָּרוֹת הָרַקּוֹת וְהָרָעֹת הָעֹלֹת
אַחֲרֵיהֶן שֶׁבַע שָׁנִים הֵנָּה וְשֶׁבַע הַשִּׁבֳּלִים הָרֵקוֹת
שְׁדֻפוֹת הַקָּדִים יִהְיוּ שֶׁבַע שְׁנֵי רָעָב: 28 הוּא הַדָּבָר
אֲשֶׁר דִּבַּרְתִּי אֶל־פַּרְעֹה אֲשֶׁר הָאֱלֹהִים עֹשֶׂה
הֶרְאָה אֶת־פַּרְעֹה: 29 הִנֵּה שֶׁבַע שָׁנִים בָּאוֹת שָׂבָע
גָּדוֹל בְּכָל־אֶרֶץ מִצְרָיִם: 30 וְקָמוּ שֶׁבַע שְׁנֵי רָעָב
אַחֲרֵיהֶן וְנִשְׁכַּח כָּל־הַשָּׂבָע בְּאֶרֶץ מִצְרָיִם וְכִלָּה
הָרָעָב אֶת־הָאָרֶץ: 31 וְלֹא־יִוָּדַע הַשָּׂבָע בָּאָרֶץ
מִפְּנֵי הָרָעָב הַהוּא אַחֲרֵי־כֵן כִּי־כָבֵד הוּא מְאֹד:
32 וְעַל הִשָּׁנוֹת הַחֲלוֹם אֶל־פַּרְעֹה פַּעֲמָיִם כִּי־נָכוֹן
הַדָּבָר מֵעִם הָאֱלֹהִים וּמְמַהֵר הָאֱלֹהִים לַעֲשֹׂתוֹ:
33 וְעַתָּה יֵרֶא פַרְעֹה אִישׁ נָבוֹן וְחָכָם וִישִׁיתֵהוּ עַל־
אֶרֶץ מִצְרָיִם: 34 יַעֲשֶׂה פַרְעֹה וְיַפְקֵד פְּקִדִים עַל־
הָאָרֶץ וְחִמֵּשׁ אֶת־אֶרֶץ מִצְרַיִם בְּשֶׁבַע שְׁנֵי הַשָּׂבָע:
35 וְיִקְבְּצוּ אֶת־כָּל־אֹכֶל הַשָּׁנִים הַטֹּבֹת הַבָּאֹת
הָאֵלֶּה וְיִצְבְּרוּ־בָר תַּחַת יַד־פַּרְעֹה אֹכֶל בֶּעָרִים
וְשָׁמָרוּ: 36 וְהָיָה הָאֹכֶל לְפִקָּדוֹן לָאָרֶץ לְשֶׁבַע שְׁנֵי
הָרָעָב אֲשֶׁר תִּהְיֶיןָ בְּאֶרֶץ מִצְרָיִם וְלֹא־תִכָּרֵת
הָאָרֶץ בָּרָעָב: 37 וַיִּיטַב הַדָּבָר בְּעֵינֵי פַרְעֹה וּבְעֵינֵי
כָּל־עֲבָדָיו: 38 וַיֹּאמֶר פַּרְעֹה אֶל־עֲבָדָיו הֲנִמְצָא
כָזֶה אִישׁ אֲשֶׁר רוּחַ אֱלֹהִים בּוֹ: 39 וַיֹּאמֶר פַּרְעֹה
אֶל־יוֹסֵף אַחֲרֵי הוֹדִיעַ אֱלֹהִים אוֹתְךָ אֶת־כָּל־זֹאת
אֵין־נָבוֹן וְחָכָם כָּמוֹךָ: 40 אַתָּה תִּהְיֶה עַל־בֵּיתִי
וְעַל־פִּיךָ יִשַּׁק כָּל־עַמִּי רַק הַכִּסֵּא אֶגְדַּל מִמֶּךָּ:
41 וַיֹּאמֶר פַּרְעֹה אֶל־יוֹסֵף רְאֵה נָתַתִּי אֹתְךָ עַל

42 Then Pharaoh took his signet ring off his hand and put it on Joseph's hand; and he clothed him in garments of fine linen and put a gold chain around his neck. 43 And he had him ride in the second chariot which he had; and they cried out before him, "Bow the knee!" So he set him over all the land of Egypt. 44 Pharaoh also said to Joseph, "I *am* Pharaoh, and without your consent no man may lift his hand or foot in all the land of Egypt." 45 And Pharaoh called Joseph's name Zaphnath-Paaneah. And he gave him as a wife Asenath, the daughter of Poti-Pherah priest of On. So Joseph went out over *all* the land of Egypt.

46 Joseph was thirty years old when he stood before Pharaoh king of Egypt. And Joseph went out from the presence of Pharaoh, and went throughout all the land of Egypt. 47 Now in the seven plentiful years the ground brought forth abundantly. 48 So he gathered up all the food of the seven years which were in the land of Egypt, and laid up the food in the cities; he laid up in every city the food of the fields which surrounded them. 49 Joseph gathered very much grain, as the sand of the sea, until he stopped counting, for *it was* immeasurable.

50 And to Joseph were born two sons before the years of famine came, whom Asenath, the daughter of Poti-Pherah priest of On, bore to him. 51 Joseph called the name of the firstborn Manasseh: "For God has made me forget all my toil and all my father's house." 52 And the name of the second he called Ephraim: "For God has caused me to be fruitful in the land of my affliction."

53 Then the seven years of plenty which were in the land of Egypt ended, 54 and the seven years of famine began to come, as Joseph had said. The famine was in all lands, but in all the land of Egypt there was bread. 55 So when all the land of Egypt was famished, the people cried to Pharaoh for bread. Then Pharaoh said to all the Egyptians, "Go to Joseph; whatever he says to you, do." 56 The famine was over all the face of the earth, and Joseph opened all the storehouses and sold to the Egyptians. And the famine became severe in the land of Egypt. 57 So all countries came to Joseph in Egypt to buy *grain,* because the famine was severe in all lands.

42

When Jacob saw that there was grain in Egypt, Jacob said to his sons, "Why do you look at one another?" 2 And he said, "Indeed I have heard that there is grain in Egypt; go down to that place and buy for us there, that we may live and not die."

כָּל־אֶרֶץ מִצְרָיִם: 42 וַיָּסַר פַּרְעֹה אֶת־טַבַּעְתּוֹ מֵעַל יָדוֹ וַיִּתֵּן אֹתָהּ עַל־יַד יוֹסֵף וַיַּלְבֵּשׁ אֹתוֹ בִּגְדֵי־שֵׁשׁ וַיָּשֶׂם רְבִד הַזָּהָב עַל־צַוָּארוֹ: 43 וַיַּרְכֵּב אֹתוֹ בְּמִרְכֶּבֶת הַמִּשְׁנֶה אֲשֶׁר־לוֹ וַיִּקְרְאוּ לְפָנָיו אַבְרֵךְ וְנָתוֹן אֹתוֹ עַל כָּל־אֶרֶץ מִצְרָיִם: 44 וַיֹּאמֶר פַּרְעֹה אֶל־יוֹסֵף אֲנִי פַרְעֹה וּבִלְעָדֶיךָ לֹא־יָרִים אִישׁ אֶת־יָדוֹ וְאֶת־רַגְלוֹ בְּכָל־אֶרֶץ מִצְרָיִם: 45 וַיִּקְרָא פַרְעֹה שֵׁם־יוֹסֵף צָפְנַת פַּעְנֵחַ וַיִּתֶּן־לוֹ אֶת־אָסְנַת בַּת־פּוֹטִי פֶרַע כֹּהֵן אֹן לְאִשָּׁה וַיֵּצֵא יוֹסֵף עַל־אֶרֶץ מִצְרָיִם: 46 וְיוֹסֵף בֶּן־שְׁלֹשִׁים שָׁנָה בְּעָמְדוֹ לִפְנֵי פַּרְעֹה מֶלֶךְ־מִצְרָיִם וַיֵּצֵא יוֹסֵף מִלִּפְנֵי פַרְעֹה וַיַּעֲבֹר בְּכָל־אֶרֶץ מִצְרָיִם: 47 וַתַּעַשׂ הָאָרֶץ בְּשֶׁבַע שְׁנֵי הַשָּׂבָע לִקְמָצִים: 48 וַיִּקְבֹּץ אֶת־כָּל־אֹכֶל שֶׁבַע שָׁנִים אֲשֶׁר הָיוּ בְּאֶרֶץ מִצְרַיִם וַיִּתֶּן־אֹכֶל בֶּעָרִים אֹכֶל שְׂדֵה־הָעִיר אֲשֶׁר סְבִיבֹתֶיהָ נָתַן בְּתוֹכָהּ: 49 וַיִּצְבֹּר יוֹסֵף בָּר כְּחוֹל הַיָּם הַרְבֵּה מְאֹד עַד כִּי־חָדַל לִסְפֹּר כִּי־אֵין מִסְפָּר: 50 וּלְיוֹסֵף יֻלַּד שְׁנֵי בָנִים בְּטֶרֶם תָּבוֹא שְׁנַת הָרָעָב אֲשֶׁר יָלְדָה־לּוֹ אָסְנַת בַּת־פּוֹטִי פֶרַע כֹּהֵן אוֹן: 51 וַיִּקְרָא יוֹסֵף אֶת־שֵׁם הַבְּכוֹר מְנַשֶּׁה כִּי־נַשַּׁנִי אֱלֹהִים אֶת־כָּל־עֲמָלִי וְאֵת כָּל־בֵּית אָבִי: 52 וְאֵת שֵׁם הַשֵּׁנִי קָרָא אֶפְרָיִם כִּי־הִפְרַנִי אֱלֹהִים בְּאֶרֶץ עָנְיִי: 53 וַתִּכְלֶינָה שֶׁבַע שְׁנֵי הַשָּׂבָע אֲשֶׁר הָיָה בְּאֶרֶץ מִצְרָיִם: 54 וַתְּחִלֶּינָה שֶׁבַע שְׁנֵי הָרָעָב לָבוֹא כַּאֲשֶׁר אָמַר יוֹסֵף וַיְהִי רָעָב בְּכָל־הָאֲרָצוֹת וּבְכָל־אֶרֶץ מִצְרַיִם הָיָה לָחֶם: 55 וַתִּרְעַב כָּל־אֶרֶץ מִצְרַיִם וַיִּצְעַק הָעָם אֶל־פַּרְעֹה לַלָּחֶם וַיֹּאמֶר פַּרְעֹה לְכָל־מִצְרַיִם לְכוּ אֶל־יוֹסֵף אֲשֶׁר־יֹאמַר לָכֶם תַּעֲשׂוּ: 56 וְהָרָעָב הָיָה עַל כָּל־פְּנֵי הָאָרֶץ וַיִּפְתַּח יוֹסֵף אֶת־כָּל־אֲשֶׁר בָּהֶם וַיִּשְׁבֹּר לְמִצְרַיִם וַיֶּחֱזַק הָרָעָב בְּאֶרֶץ מִצְרָיִם: 57 וְכָל־הָאָרֶץ בָּאוּ מִצְרַיְמָה לִשְׁבֹּר אֶל־יוֹסֵף כִּי־חָזַק הָרָעָב בְּכָל־הָאָרֶץ:

מב וַיַּרְא יַעֲקֹב כִּי יֶשׁ־שֶׁבֶר בְּמִצְרָיִם וַיֹּאמֶר יַעֲקֹב לְבָנָיו לָמָּה תִּתְרָאוּ: 2 וַיֹּאמֶר הִנֵּה שָׁמַעְתִּי כִּי יֶשׁ־שֶׁבֶר בְּמִצְרָיִם רְדוּ־שָׁמָּה וְשִׁבְרוּ־לָנוּ מִשָּׁם

³ So Joseph's ten brothers went down to buy grain in Egypt. ⁴ But Jacob did not send Joseph's brother Benjamin with his brothers, for he said, "Lest some calamity befall him." ⁵ And the sons of Israel went to buy *grain* among those who journeyed, for the famine was in the land of Canaan.

⁶ Now Joseph *was* governor over the land; and it was he who sold to all the people of the land. And Joseph's brothers came and bowed down before him with *their* faces to the earth. ⁷ Joseph saw his brothers and recognized them, but he acted as a stranger to them and spoke roughly to them. Then he said to them, "Where do you come from?"

And they said, "From the land of Canaan to buy food."

⁸ So Joseph recognized his brothers, but they did not recognize him. ⁹ Then Joseph remembered the dreams which he had dreamed about them, and said to them, "You *are* spies! You have come to see the nakedness of the land!"

¹⁰ And they said to him, "No, my lord, but your servants have come to buy food. ¹¹ We *are* all one man's sons; we *are* honest *men;* your servants are not spies."

¹² But he said to them, "No, but you have come to see the nakedness of the land."

¹³ And they said, "Your servants *are* twelve brothers, the sons of one man in the land of Canaan; and in fact, the youngest *is* with our father today, and one *is* no more."

¹⁴ But Joseph said to them, "It *is* as I spoke to you, saying, 'You *are* spies!' ¹⁵ In this *manner* you shall be tested: By the life of Pharaoh, you shall not leave this place unless your youngest brother comes here. ¹⁶ Send one of you, and let him bring your brother; and you shall be kept in prison, that your words may be tested to see whether *there is* any truth in you; or else, by the life of Pharaoh, surely you *are* spies!" ¹⁷ So he put them all together in prison three days.

¹⁸ Then Joseph said to them the third day, "Do this and live, *for* I fear God: ¹⁹ If you *are* honest *men,* let one of your brothers be confined to your prison house; but you, go and carry grain for the famine of your houses. ²⁰ And bring your youngest brother to me; so your words will be verified, and you shall not die."

And they did so. ²¹ Then they said to one another, "We *are* truly guilty concerning our brother, for we saw the anguish of his soul when he pleaded with us, and we would not hear; therefore this distress has come upon us."

וְנִחְיֶה וְלֹא נָמוּת: ‪3‬ וַיֵּרְדוּ אֲחֵי־יוֹסֵף עֲשָׂרָה לִשְׁבֹּר בָּר מִמִּצְרָיִם: ‪4‬ וְאֶת־בִּנְיָמִין אֲחִי יוֹסֵף לֹא־שָׁלַח יַעֲקֹב אֶת־אֶחָיו כִּי אָמַר פֶּן־יִקְרָאֶנּוּ אָסוֹן: ‪5‬ וַיָּבֹאוּ בְּנֵי יִשְׂרָאֵל לִשְׁבֹּר בְּתוֹךְ הַבָּאִים כִּי־הָיָה הָרָעָב בְּאֶרֶץ כְּנָעַן: ‪6‬ וְיוֹסֵף הוּא הַשַּׁלִּיט עַל־הָאָרֶץ הוּא הַמַּשְׁבִּיר לְכָל־עַם הָאָרֶץ וַיָּבֹאוּ אֲחֵי יוֹסֵף וַיִּשְׁתַּחֲווּ־לוֹ אַפַּיִם אָרְצָה: ‪7‬ וַיַּרְא יוֹסֵף אֶת־אֶחָיו וַיַּכִּרֵם וַיִּתְנַכֵּר אֲלֵיהֶם וַיְדַבֵּר אִתָּם קָשׁוֹת וַיֹּאמֶר אֲלֵהֶם מֵאַיִן בָּאתֶם וַיֹּאמְרוּ מֵאֶרֶץ כְּנַעַן לִשְׁבָּר־אֹכֶל: ‪8‬ וַיַּכֵּר יוֹסֵף אֶת־אֶחָיו וְהֵם לֹא הִכִּרֻהוּ: ‪9‬ וַיִּזְכֹּר יוֹסֵף אֵת הַחֲלֹמוֹת אֲשֶׁר חָלַם לָהֶם וַיֹּאמֶר אֲלֵהֶם מְרַגְּלִים אַתֶּם לִרְאוֹת אֶת־עֶרְוַת הָאָרֶץ בָּאתֶם: ‪10‬ וַיֹּאמְרוּ אֵלָיו לֹא אֲדֹנִי וַעֲבָדֶיךָ בָּאוּ לִשְׁבָּר־אֹכֶל: ‪11‬ כֻּלָּנוּ בְּנֵי אִישׁ־אֶחָד נָחְנוּ כֵּנִים אֲנַחְנוּ לֹא־הָיוּ עֲבָדֶיךָ מְרַגְּלִים: ‪12‬ וַיֹּאמֶר אֲלֵהֶם לֹא כִּי־עֶרְוַת הָאָרֶץ בָּאתֶם לִרְאוֹת: ‪13‬ וַיֹּאמְרוּ שְׁנֵים עָשָׂר עֲבָדֶיךָ אַחִים ׀ אֲנַחְנוּ בְּנֵי אִישׁ־אֶחָד בְּאֶרֶץ כְּנָעַן וְהִנֵּה הַקָּטֹן אֶת־אָבִינוּ הַיּוֹם וְהָאֶחָד אֵינֶנּוּ: ‪14‬ וַיֹּאמֶר אֲלֵהֶם יוֹסֵף הוּא אֲשֶׁר דִּבַּרְתִּי אֲלֵכֶם לֵאמֹר מְרַגְּלִים אַתֶּם: ‪15‬ בְּזֹאת תִּבָּחֵנוּ חֵי פַרְעֹה אִם־תֵּצְאוּ מִזֶּה כִּי אִם־בְּבוֹא אֲחִיכֶם הַקָּטֹן הֵנָּה: ‪16‬ שִׁלְחוּ מִכֶּם אֶחָד וְיִקַּח אֶת־אֲחִיכֶם וְאַתֶּם הֵאָסְרוּ וְיִבָּחֲנוּ דִּבְרֵיכֶם הַאֱמֶת אִתְּכֶם וְאִם־לֹא חֵי פַרְעֹה כִּי מְרַגְּלִים אַתֶּם: ‪17‬ וַיֶּאֱסֹף אֹתָם אֶל־מִשְׁמָר שְׁלֹשֶׁת יָמִים: ‪18‬ וַיֹּאמֶר אֲלֵהֶם יוֹסֵף בַּיּוֹם הַשְּׁלִישִׁי זֹאת עֲשׂוּ וִחְיוּ אֶת־הָאֱלֹהִים אֲנִי יָרֵא: ‪19‬ אִם־כֵּנִים אַתֶּם אֲחִיכֶם אֶחָד יֵאָסֵר בְּבֵית מִשְׁמַרְכֶם וְאַתֶּם לְכוּ הָבִיאוּ שֶׁבֶר רַעֲבוֹן בָּתֵּיכֶם: ‪20‬ וְאֶת־אֲחִיכֶם הַקָּטֹן תָּבִיאוּ אֵלַי וְיֵאָמְנוּ דִבְרֵיכֶם וְלֹא תָמוּתוּ וַיַּעֲשׂוּ־כֵן: ‪21‬ וַיֹּאמְרוּ אִישׁ אֶל־אָחִיו אֲבָל אֲשֵׁמִים ׀ אֲנַחְנוּ עַל־אָחִינוּ אֲשֶׁר רָאִינוּ צָרַת נַפְשׁוֹ בְּהִתְחַנְנוֹ אֵלֵינוּ וְלֹא שָׁמָעְנוּ עַל־כֵּן בָּאָה

22 And Reuben answered them, saying, "Did I not speak to you, saying, 'Do not sin against the boy'; and you would not listen? Therefore behold, his blood is now required of us." 23 But they did not know that Joseph understood *them,* for he spoke to them through an interpreter. 24 And he turned himself away from them and wept. Then he returned to them again, and talked with them. And he took Simeon from them and bound him before their eyes.

25 Then Joseph gave a command to fill their sacks with grain, to restore every man's money to his sack, and to give them provisions for the journey. Thus he did for them. 26 So they loaded their donkeys with the grain and departed from there. 27 But as one *of them* opened his sack to give his donkey feed at the encampment, he saw his money; and there it was, in the mouth of his sack. 28 So he said to his brothers, "My money has been restored, and there it is, in my sack!" Then their hearts failed *them* and they were afraid, saying to one another, "What *is* this *that* God has done to us?"

29 Then they went to Jacob their father in the land of Canaan and told him all that had happened to them, saying: 30 "The man *who is* lord of the land spoke roughly to us, and took us for spies of the country. 31 But we said to him, 'We *are* honest *men;* we are not spies. 32 We *are* twelve brothers, sons of our father; one *is* no *more,* and the youngest *is* with our father this day in the land of Canaan.' 33 Then the man, the lord of the country, said to us, 'By this I will know that you *are* honest *men:* Leave one of your brothers *here* with me, take *food for* the famine of your households, and be gone. 34 And bring your youngest brother to me; so I shall know that you *are* not spies, but that you *are* honest *men.* I will grant your brother to you, and you may trade in the land.'"

35 Then it happened as they emptied their sacks, that surprisingly each man's bundle of money *was* in his sack; and when they and their father saw the bundles of money, they were afraid. 36 And Jacob their father said to them, "You have bereaved me: Joseph is no *more,* Simeon is no *more,* and you want to take Benjamin. All these things are against me."

37 Then Reuben spoke to his father, saying, "Kill my two sons if I do not bring him *back* to you; put him in my hands, and I will bring him back to you."

38 But he said, "My son shall not go down with you, for his brother is dead, and he is left alone. If any calamity should befall him along the way in which you go, then you would bring down my gray hair with sorrow to the grave."

אֵלֵינוּ הַצָּרָה הַזֹּאת: 22 וַיַּעַן רְאוּבֵן אֹתָם לֵאמֹר הֲלוֹא אָמַרְתִּי אֲלֵיכֶם ׀ לֵאמֹר אַל־תֶּחֶטְאוּ בַיֶּלֶד וְלֹא שְׁמַעְתֶּם וְגַם־דָּמוֹ הִנֵּה נִדְרָשׁ: 23 וְהֵם לֹא יָדְעוּ כִּי שֹׁמֵעַ יוֹסֵף כִּי הַמֵּלִיץ בֵּינֹתָם: 24 וַיִּסֹּב מֵעֲלֵיהֶם וַיֵּבְךְּ וַיָּשָׁב אֲלֵהֶם וַיְדַבֵּר אֲלֵהֶם וַיִּקַּח מֵאִתָּם אֶת־שִׁמְעוֹן וַיֶּאֱסֹר אֹתוֹ לְעֵינֵיהֶם: 25 וַיְצַו יוֹסֵף וַיְמַלְאוּ אֶת־כְּלֵיהֶם בָּר וּלְהָשִׁיב כַּסְפֵּיהֶם אִישׁ אֶל־שַׂקּוֹ וְלָתֵת לָהֶם צֵדָה לַדָּרֶךְ וַיַּעַשׂ לָהֶם כֵּן: 26 וַיִּשְׂאוּ אֶת־שִׁבְרָם עַל־חֲמֹרֵיהֶם וַיֵּלְכוּ מִשָּׁם: 27 וַיִּפְתַּח הָאֶחָד אֶת־שַׂקּוֹ לָתֵת מִסְפּוֹא לַחֲמֹרוֹ בַּמָּלוֹן וַיַּרְא אֶת־כַּסְפּוֹ וְהִנֵּה־הוּא בְּפִי אַמְתַּחְתּוֹ: 28 וַיֹּאמֶר אֶל־אֶחָיו הוּשַׁב כַּסְפִּי וְגַם הִנֵּה בְאַמְתַּחְתִּי וַיֵּצֵא לִבָּם וַיֶּחֶרְדוּ אִישׁ אֶל־אָחִיו לֵאמֹר מַה־זֹּאת עָשָׂה אֱלֹהִים לָנוּ: 29 וַיָּבֹאוּ אֶל־יַעֲקֹב אֲבִיהֶם אַרְצָה כְּנָעַן וַיַּגִּידוּ לוֹ אֵת כָּל־הַקֹּרֹת אֹתָם לֵאמֹר: 30 דִּבֶּר הָאִישׁ אֲדֹנֵי הָאָרֶץ אִתָּנוּ קָשׁוֹת וַיִּתֵּן אֹתָנוּ כִּמְרַגְּלִים אֶת־הָאָרֶץ: 31 וַנֹּאמֶר אֵלָיו כֵּנִים אֲנָחְנוּ לֹא הָיִינוּ מְרַגְּלִים: 32 שְׁנֵים־עָשָׂר אֲנַחְנוּ אַחִים בְּנֵי אָבִינוּ הָאֶחָד אֵינֶנּוּ וְהַקָּטֹן הַיּוֹם אֶת־אָבִינוּ בְּאֶרֶץ כְּנָעַן: 33 וַיֹּאמֶר אֵלֵינוּ הָאִישׁ אֲדֹנֵי הָאָרֶץ בְּזֹאת אֵדַע כִּי כֵנִים אַתֶּם אֲחִיכֶם הָאֶחָד הַנִּיחוּ אִתִּי וְאֶת־רַעֲבוֹן בָּתֵּיכֶם קְחוּ וָלֵכוּ:

34 וְהָבִיאוּ אֶת־אֲחִיכֶם הַקָּטֹן אֵלַי וְאֵדְעָה כִּי לֹא מְרַגְּלִים אַתֶּם כִּי כֵנִים אַתֶּם אֶת־אֲחִיכֶם אֶתֵּן לָכֶם וְאֶת־הָאָרֶץ תִּסְחָרוּ: 35 וַיְהִי הֵם מְרִיקִים שַׂקֵּיהֶם וְהִנֵּה־אִישׁ צְרוֹר־כַּסְפּוֹ בְּשַׂקּוֹ וַיִּרְאוּ אֶת־צְרֹרוֹת כַּסְפֵּיהֶם הֵמָּה וַאֲבִיהֶם וַיִּירָאוּ: 36 וַיֹּאמֶר אֲלֵהֶם יַעֲקֹב אֲבִיהֶם אֹתִי שִׁכַּלְתֶּם יוֹסֵף אֵינֶנּוּ וְשִׁמְעוֹן אֵינֶנּוּ וְאֶת־בִּנְיָמִן תִּקָּחוּ עָלַי הָיוּ כֻלָּנָה: 37 וַיֹּאמֶר רְאוּבֵן אֶל־אָבִיו לֵאמֹר אֶת־שְׁנֵי בָנַי תָּמִית אִם־לֹא אֲבִיאֶנּוּ אֵלֶיךָ תְּנָה אֹתוֹ עַל־יָדִי וַאֲנִי אֲשִׁיבֶנּוּ אֵלֶיךָ: 38 וַיֹּאמֶר לֹא־יֵרֵד בְּנִי עִמָּכֶם כִּי־אָחִיו מֵת וְהוּא לְבַדּוֹ נִשְׁאָר וּקְרָאָהוּ אָסוֹן בַּדֶּרֶךְ אֲשֶׁר תֵּלְכוּ־בָהּ וְהוֹרַדְתֶּם אֶת־שֵׂיבָתִי בְּיָגוֹן שְׁאוֹלָה:

43 Now the famine *was* severe in the land. [2] And it came to pass, when they had eaten up the grain which they had brought from Egypt, that their father said to them, "Go back, buy us a little food."

[3] But Judah spoke to him, saying, "The man solemnly warned us, saying, 'You shall not see my face unless your brother *is* with you.' [4] If you send our brother with us, we will go down and buy you food. [5] But if you will not send *him,* we will not go down; for the man said to us, 'You shall not see my face unless your brother *is* with you.'"

[6] And Israel said, "Why did you deal *so* wrongfully with me *as* to tell the man whether you had still *another* brother?"

[7] But they said, "The man asked us pointedly about ourselves and our family, saying, '*Is* your father still alive? Have you *another* brother?' And we told him according to these words. Could we possibly have known that he would say, 'Bring your brother down'?"

[8] Then Judah said to Israel his father, "Send the lad with me, and we will arise and go, that we may live and not die, both we and you *and* also our little ones. [9] I myself will be surety for him; from my hand you shall require him. If I do not bring him *back* to you and set him before you, then let me bear the blame forever. [10] For if we had not lingered, surely by now we would have returned this second time."

[11] And their father Israel said to them, "If *it must be* so, then do this: Take some of the best fruits of the land in your vessels and carry down a present for the man—a little balm and a little honey, spices and myrrh, pistachio nuts and almonds. [12] Take double money in your hand, and take back in your hand the money that was returned in the mouth of your sacks; perhaps it was an oversight. [13] Take your brother also, and arise, go back to the man. [14] And may God Almighty give you mercy before the man, that he may release your other brother and Benjamin. If I am bereaved, I am bereaved!"

[15] So the men took that present and Benjamin, and they took double money in their hand, and arose and went down to Egypt; and they stood before Joseph. [16] When Joseph saw Benjamin with them, he said to the steward of his house, "Take *these* men to my home, and slaughter an animal and make ready; for *these* men will dine with me at noon." [17] Then the man did as Joseph ordered, and the man brought the men into Joseph's house.

[18] Now the men were afraid because they were brought into Joseph's house; and they said, "*It is* because of the money, which was returned in our

מג וְהָרָעָב כָּבֵד בָּאָרֶץ: 2 וַיְהִי כַּאֲשֶׁר כִּלּוּ לֶאֱכֹל אֶת־הַשֶּׁבֶר אֲשֶׁר הֵבִיאוּ מִמִּצְרָיִם וַיֹּאמֶר אֲלֵיהֶם אֲבִיהֶם שֻׁבוּ שִׁבְרוּ־לָנוּ מְעַט־אֹכֶל: 3 וַיֹּאמֶר אֵלָיו יְהוּדָה לֵאמֹר הָעֵד הֵעִד בָּנוּ הָאִישׁ לֵאמֹר לֹא־תִרְאוּ פָנַי בִּלְתִּי אֲחִיכֶם אִתְּכֶם: 4 אִם־יֶשְׁךָ מְשַׁלֵּחַ אֶת־אָחִינוּ אִתָּנוּ נֵרְדָה וְנִשְׁבְּרָה לְךָ אֹכֶל: 5 וְאִם־אֵינְךָ מְשַׁלֵּחַ לֹא נֵרֵד כִּי־הָאִישׁ אָמַר אֵלֵינוּ לֹא־תִרְאוּ פָנַי בִּלְתִּי אֲחִיכֶם אִתְּכֶם: 6 וַיֹּאמֶר יִשְׂרָאֵל לָמָה הֲרֵעֹתֶם לִי לְהַגִּיד לָאִישׁ הַעוֹד לָכֶם אָח: 7 וַיֹּאמְרוּ שָׁאוֹל שָׁאַל־הָאִישׁ לָנוּ וּלְמוֹלַדְתֵּנוּ לֵאמֹר הַעוֹד אֲבִיכֶם חַי הֲיֵשׁ לָכֶם אָח וַנַּגֶּד־לוֹ עַל־פִּי הַדְּבָרִים הָאֵלֶּה הֲיָדֹעַ נֵדַע כִּי יֹאמַר הוֹרִידוּ אֶת־אֲחִיכֶם: 8 וַיֹּאמֶר יְהוּדָה אֶל־יִשְׂרָאֵל אָבִיו שִׁלְחָה הַנַּעַר אִתִּי וְנָקוּמָה וְנֵלֵכָה וְנִחְיֶה וְלֹא נָמוּת גַּם־אֲנַחְנוּ גַם־אַתָּה גַּם־טַפֵּנוּ: 9 אָנֹכִי אֶעֶרְבֶנּוּ מִיָּדִי תְּבַקְשֶׁנּוּ אִם־לֹא הֲבִיאֹתִיו אֵלֶיךָ וְהִצַּגְתִּיו לְפָנֶיךָ וְחָטָאתִי לְךָ כָּל־הַיָּמִים: 10 כִּי לוּלֵא הִתְמַהְמָהְנוּ כִּי־עַתָּה שַׁבְנוּ זֶה פַעֲמָיִם: 11 וַיֹּאמֶר אֲלֵהֶם יִשְׂרָאֵל אֲבִיהֶם אִם־כֵּן אֵפוֹא זֹאת עֲשׂוּ קְחוּ מִזִּמְרַת הָאָרֶץ בִּכְלֵיכֶם וְהוֹרִידוּ לָאִישׁ מִנְחָה מְעַט צֳרִי וּמְעַט דְּבַשׁ נְכֹאת וָלֹט בָּטְנִים וּשְׁקֵדִים: 12 וְכֶסֶף מִשְׁנֶה קְחוּ בְיֶדְכֶם וְאֶת־הַכֶּסֶף הַמּוּשָׁב בְּפִי אַמְתְּחֹתֵיכֶם תָּשִׁיבוּ בְיֶדְכֶם אוּלַי מִשְׁגֶּה הוּא: 13 וְאֶת־אֲחִיכֶם קָחוּ וְקוּמוּ שׁוּבוּ אֶל־הָאִישׁ: 14 וְאֵל שַׁדַּי יִתֵּן לָכֶם רַחֲמִים לִפְנֵי הָאִישׁ וְשִׁלַּח לָכֶם אֶת־אֲחִיכֶם אַחֵר וְאֶת־בִּנְיָמִין וַאֲנִי כַּאֲשֶׁר שָׁכֹלְתִּי שָׁכָלְתִּי: 15 וַיִּקְחוּ הָאֲנָשִׁים אֶת־הַמִּנְחָה הַזֹּאת וּמִשְׁנֶה־כֶּסֶף לָקְחוּ בְיָדָם וְאֶת־בִּנְיָמִן וַיָּקֻמוּ וַיֵּרְדוּ מִצְרַיִם וַיַּעַמְדוּ לִפְנֵי יוֹסֵף: 16 וַיַּרְא יוֹסֵף אִתָּם אֶת־בִּנְיָמִין וַיֹּאמֶר לַאֲשֶׁר עַל־בֵּיתוֹ הָבֵא אֶת־הָאֲנָשִׁים הַבָּיְתָה וּטְבֹחַ טֶבַח וְהָכֵן כִּי אִתִּי יֹאכְלוּ הָאֲנָשִׁים בַּצָּהֳרָיִם: 17 וַיַּעַשׂ הָאִישׁ כַּאֲשֶׁר אָמַר יוֹסֵף וַיָּבֵא הָאִישׁ אֶת־הָאֲנָשִׁים בֵּיתָה יוֹסֵף: 18 וַיִּירְאוּ הָאֲנָשִׁים כִּי הוּבְאוּ בֵּית יוֹסֵף וַיֹּאמְרוּ עַל־דְּבַר הַכֶּסֶף הַשָּׁב בְּאַמְתְּחֹתֵינוּ בַּתְּחִלָּה אֲנַחְנוּ מוּבָאִים לְהִתְגֹּלֵל

sacks the first time, that we are brought in, so that he may make a case against us and seize us, to take us as slaves with our donkeys."

19 When they drew near to the steward of Joseph's house, they talked with him at the door of the house, 20 and said, "O sir, we indeed came down the first time to buy food; 21 but it happened, when we came to the encampment, that we opened our sacks, and there, *each* man's money *was* in the mouth of his sack, our money in full weight; so we have brought it back in our hand. 22 And we have brought down other money in our hands to buy food. We do not know who put our money in our sacks."

23 But he said, "Peace *be* with you, do not be afraid. Your God and the God of your father has given you treasure in your sacks; I had your money." Then he brought Simeon out to them.

24 So the man brought the men into Joseph's house and gave *them* water, and they washed their feet; and he gave their donkeys feed. 25 Then they made the present ready for Joseph's coming at noon, for they heard that they would eat bread there.

26 And when Joseph came home, they brought him the present which *was* in their hand into the house, and bowed down before him to the earth. 27 Then he asked them about *their* well-being, and said, "*Is* your father well, the old man of whom you spoke? *Is* he still alive?"

28 And they answered, "Your servant our father *is* in good health; he *is* still alive." And they bowed their heads down and prostrated themselves.

29 Then he lifted his eyes and saw his brother Benjamin, his mother's son, and said, "*Is* this your younger brother of whom you spoke to me?" And he said, "God be gracious to you, my son." 30 Now his heart yearned for his brother; so Joseph made haste and sought *somewhere* to weep. And he went into *his* chamber and wept there. 31 Then he washed his face and came out; and he restrained himself, and said, "Serve the bread."

32 So they set him a place by himself, and them by themselves, and the Egyptians who ate with him by themselves; because the Egyptians could not eat food with the Hebrews, for that *is* an abomination to the Egyptians. 33 And they sat before him, the firstborn according to his birthright and the youngest according to his youth; and the men looked in astonishment at one another. 34 Then he took servings to them from before him, but Benjamin's serving was five times as much as any of theirs. So they drank and were merry with him.

עָלֵינוּ וּלְהִתְנַפֵּל עָלֵינוּ וְלָקַחַת אֹתָנוּ לַעֲבָדִים וְאֶת־חֲמֹרֵינוּ: 19 וַיִּגְּשׁוּ אֶל־הָאִישׁ אֲשֶׁר עַל־בֵּית יוֹסֵף וַיְדַבְּרוּ אֵלָיו פֶּתַח הַבָּיִת: 20 וַיֹּאמְרוּ בִּי אֲדֹנִי יָרֹד יָרַדְנוּ בַּתְּחִלָּה לִשְׁבָּר־אֹכֶל: 21 וַיְהִי כִּי־בָאנוּ אֶל־הַמָּלוֹן וַנִּפְתְּחָה אֶת־אַמְתְּחֹתֵינוּ וְהִנֵּה כֶסֶף־אִישׁ בְּפִי אַמְתַּחְתּוֹ כַּסְפֵּנוּ בְּמִשְׁקָלוֹ וַנָּשֶׁב אֹתוֹ בְּיָדֵנוּ: 22 וְכֶסֶף אַחֵר הוֹרַדְנוּ בְיָדֵנוּ לִשְׁבָּר־אֹכֶל לֹא יָדַעְנוּ מִי־שָׂם כַּסְפֵּנוּ בְּאַמְתְּחֹתֵינוּ: 23 וַיֹּאמֶר שָׁלוֹם לָכֶם אַל־תִּירָאוּ אֱלֹהֵיכֶם וֵאלֹהֵי אֲבִיכֶם נָתַן לָכֶם מַטְמוֹן בְּאַמְתְּחֹתֵיכֶם כַּסְפְּכֶם בָּא אֵלָי וַיּוֹצֵא אֲלֵהֶם אֶת־שִׁמְעוֹן: 24 וַיָּבֵא הָאִישׁ אֶת־הָאֲנָשִׁים בֵּיתָה יוֹסֵף וַיִּתֶּן־מַיִם וַיִּרְחֲצוּ רַגְלֵיהֶם וַיִּתֵּן מִסְפּוֹא לַחֲמֹרֵיהֶם: 25 וַיָּכִינוּ אֶת־הַמִּנְחָה עַד בּוֹא יוֹסֵף בַּצׇּהֳרָיִם כִּי שָׁמְעוּ כִּי־שָׁם יֹאכְלוּ לָחֶם: 26 וַיָּבֹא יוֹסֵף הַבַּיְתָה וַיָּבִיאּוּ לוֹ אֶת־הַמִּנְחָה אֲשֶׁר־בְּיָדָם הַבָּיְתָה וַיִּשְׁתַּחֲווּ־לוֹ אָרְצָה: 27 וַיִּשְׁאַל לָהֶם לְשָׁלוֹם וַיֹּאמֶר הֲשָׁלוֹם אֲבִיכֶם הַזָּקֵן אֲשֶׁר אֲמַרְתֶּם הַעוֹדֶנּוּ חָי: 28 וַיֹּאמְרוּ שָׁלוֹם לְעַבְדְּךָ לְאָבִינוּ עוֹדֶנּוּ חָי וַיִּקְּדוּ וַיִּשְׁתַּחֲו֫וּ: 29 וַיִּשָּׂא עֵינָיו וַיַּרְא אֶת־בִּנְיָמִין אָחִיו בֶּן־אִמּוֹ וַיֹּאמֶר הֲזֶה אֲחִיכֶם הַקָּטֹן אֲשֶׁר אֲמַרְתֶּם אֵלָי וַיֹּאמַר אֱלֹהִים יָחְנְךָ בְּנִי: 30 וַיְמַהֵר יוֹסֵף כִּי־נִכְמְרוּ רַחֲמָיו אֶל־אָחִיו וַיְבַקֵּשׁ לִבְכּוֹת וַיָּבֹא הַחַדְרָה וַיֵּבְךְּ שָׁמָּה: 31 וַיִּרְחַץ פָּנָיו וַיֵּצֵא וַיִּתְאַפַּק וַיֹּאמֶר שִׂימוּ לָחֶם: 32 וַיָּשִׂימוּ לוֹ לְבַדּוֹ וְלָהֶם לְבַדָּם וְלַמִּצְרִים הָאֹכְלִים אִתּוֹ לְבַדָּם כִּי לֹא יוּכְלוּן הַמִּצְרִים לֶאֱכֹל אֶת־הָעִבְרִים לֶחֶם כִּי־תוֹעֵבָה הִוא לְמִצְרָיִם: 33 וַיֵּשְׁבוּ לְפָנָיו הַבְּכֹר כִּבְכֹרָתוֹ וְהַצָּעִיר כִּצְעִרָתוֹ וַיִּתְמְהוּ הָאֲנָשִׁים אִישׁ אֶל־רֵעֵהוּ: 34 וַיִּשָּׂא מַשְׂאֹת מֵאֵת פָּנָיו אֲלֵהֶם וַתֵּרֶב מַשְׂאַת בִּנְיָמִן מִמַּשְׂאֹת כֻּלָּם חָמֵשׁ יָדוֹת וַיִּשְׁתּוּ וַיִּשְׁכְּרוּ עִמּוֹ:

מג 28 וַיִּשְׁתַּחֲווּ

44 And he commanded the steward of his house, saying, "Fill the men's sacks with food, as much as they can carry, and put each man's money in the mouth of his sack. ²Also put my cup, the silver cup, in the mouth of the sack of the youngest, and his grain money." So he did according to the word that Joseph had spoken. ³As soon as the morning dawned, the men were sent away, they and their donkeys. ⁴When they had gone out of the city, *and* were not *yet* far off, Joseph said to his steward, "Get up, follow the men; and when you overtake them, say to them, 'Why have you repaid evil for good? ⁵Is not this *the one* from which my lord drinks, and with which he indeed practices divination? You have done evil in so doing.'"

⁶So he overtook them, and he spoke to them these same words. ⁷And they said to him, "Why does my lord say these words? Far be it from us that your servants should do such a thing. ⁸Look, we brought back to you from the land of Canaan the money which we found in the mouth of our sacks. How then could we steal silver or gold from your lord's house? ⁹With whomever of your servants it is found, let him die, and we also will be my lord's slaves."

¹⁰And he said, "Now also *let* it *be* according to your words; he with whom it is found shall be my slave, and you shall be blameless." ¹¹Then each man speedily let down his sack to the ground, and each opened his sack. ¹²So he searched. He began with the oldest and left off with the youngest; and the cup was found in Benjamin's sack. ¹³Then they tore their clothes, and each man loaded his donkey and returned to the city.

¹⁴So Judah and his brothers came to Joseph's house, and he *was* still there; and they fell before him on the ground. ¹⁵And Joseph said to them, "What deed *is* this you have done? Did you not know that such a man as I can certainly practice divination?"

¹⁶Then Judah said, "What shall we say to my lord? What shall we speak? Or how shall we clear ourselves? God has found out the iniquity of your servants; here we are, my lord's slaves, both we and *he* also with whom the cup was found."

¹⁷But he said, "Far be it from me that I should do so; the man in whose hand the cup was found, he shall be my slave. And as for you, go up in peace to your father."

¹⁸Then Judah came near to him and said: "O my lord, please let your servant speak a word in my lord's hearing, and do not let your anger burn against your servant; for you *are* even like Pharaoh. ¹⁹My lord asked his servants, saying, 'Have you a

מד וַיְצַ֞ו אֶת־אֲשֶׁ֣ר עַל־בֵּיתוֹ֮ לֵאמֹר֒ מַלֵּ֞א אֶת־אַמְתְּחֹ֤ת הָֽאֲנָשִׁים֙ אֹ֔כֶל כַּֽאֲשֶׁ֥ר יֽוּכְל֖וּן שְׂאֵ֑ת וְשִׂ֥ים כֶּֽסֶף־אִ֖ישׁ בְּפִ֥י אַמְתַּחְתּֽוֹ׃ 2 וְאֶת־גְּבִיעִ֞י גְּבִ֣יעַ הַכֶּ֗סֶף תָּשִׂים֙ בְּפִי֙ אַמְתַּ֣חַת הַקָּטֹ֔ן וְאֵ֖ת כֶּ֣סֶף שִׁבְר֑וֹ וַיַּ֕עַשׂ כִּדְבַ֥ר יוֹסֵ֖ף אֲשֶׁ֥ר דִּבֵּֽר׃ 3 הַבֹּ֣קֶר א֔וֹר וְהָֽאֲנָשִׁ֖ים שֻׁלְּח֑וּ הֵ֖מָּה וַֽחֲמֹֽרֵיהֶֽם׃ 4 הֵ֠ם יָֽצְא֣וּ אֶת־הָעִיר֮ לֹ֣א הִרְחִ֒יקוּ֒ וְיוֹסֵ֤ף אָמַר֙ לַֽאֲשֶׁ֣ר עַל־בֵּית֔וֹ ק֥וּם רְדֹ֖ף אַֽחֲרֵ֣י הָֽאֲנָשִׁ֑ים וְהִשַּׂגְתָּם֙ וְאָֽמַרְתָּ֣ אֲלֵהֶ֔ם לָ֛מָּה שִׁלַּמְתֶּ֥ם רָעָ֖ה תַּ֥חַת טוֹבָֽה׃ 5 הֲל֣וֹא זֶ֗ה אֲשֶׁ֨ר יִשְׁתֶּ֤ה אֲדֹנִי֙ בּ֔וֹ וְה֕וּא נַחֵ֥שׁ יְנַחֵ֖שׁ בּ֑וֹ הֲרֵֽעֹתֶ֖ם אֲשֶׁ֥ר עֲשִׂיתֶֽם׃ 6 וַֽיַּשִּׂגֵ֑ם וַיְדַבֵּ֣ר אֲלֵהֶ֔ם אֶת־הַדְּבָרִ֖ים הָאֵֽלֶּה׃ 7 וַיֹּֽאמְר֣וּ אֵלָ֔יו לָ֚מָּה יְדַבֵּ֣ר אֲדֹנִ֔י כַּדְּבָרִ֖ים הָאֵ֑לֶּה חָלִ֙ילָה֙ לַֽעֲבָדֶ֔יךָ מֵֽעֲשׂ֖וֹת כַּדָּבָ֥ר הַזֶּֽה׃ 8 הֵ֣ן כֶּ֗סֶף אֲשֶׁ֤ר מָצָ֙אנוּ֙ בְּפִ֣י אַמְתְּחֹתֵ֔ינוּ הֱשִׁיבֹ֥נוּ אֵלֶ֖יךָ מֵאֶ֣רֶץ כְּנָ֑עַן וְאֵ֗יךְ נִגְנֹב֙ מִבֵּ֣ית אֲדֹנֶ֔יךָ כֶּ֖סֶף א֥וֹ זָהָֽב׃ 9 אֲשֶׁ֨ר יִמָּצֵ֥א אִתּ֛וֹ מֵֽעֲבָדֶ֖יךָ וָמֵ֑ת וְגַם־אֲנַ֕חְנוּ נִֽהְיֶ֥ה לַֽאדֹנִ֖י לַֽעֲבָדִֽים׃ 10 וַיֹּ֕אמֶר גַּם־עַתָּ֥ה כְדִבְרֵיכֶ֖ם כֶּן־ה֑וּא אֲשֶׁ֨ר יִמָּצֵ֤א אִתּוֹ֙ יִֽהְיֶה־לִּ֣י עָ֔בֶד וְאַתֶּ֖ם תִּֽהְי֥וּ נְקִיִּֽם׃ 11 וַֽיְמַֽהֲר֗וּ וַיּוֹרִ֛דוּ אִ֥ישׁ אֶת־אַמְתַּחְתּ֖וֹ אָ֑רְצָה וַֽיִּפְתְּח֖וּ אִ֥ישׁ אַמְתַּחְתּֽוֹ׃ 12 וַיְחַפֵּ֕שׂ בַּגָּד֣וֹל הֵחֵ֔ל וּבַקָּטֹ֖ן כִּלָּ֑ה וַיִּמָּצֵא֙ הַגָּבִ֔יעַ בְּאַמְתַּ֖חַת בִּנְיָמִֽן׃ 13 וַֽיִּקְרְע֖וּ שִׂמְלֹתָ֑ם וַֽיַּֽעֲמֹס֙ אִ֣ישׁ עַל־חֲמֹר֔וֹ וַיָּשֻׁ֖בוּ הָעִֽירָה׃ 14 וַיָּבֹ֨א יְהוּדָ֤ה וְאֶחָיו֙ בֵּ֣יתָה יוֹסֵ֔ף וְה֖וּא עוֹדֶ֣נּוּ שָׁ֑ם וַיִּפְּל֥וּ לְפָנָ֖יו אָֽרְצָה׃ 15 וַיֹּ֤אמֶר לָהֶם֙ יוֹסֵ֔ף מָֽה־הַמַּֽעֲשֶׂ֥ה הַזֶּ֖ה אֲשֶׁ֣ר עֲשִׂיתֶ֑ם הֲל֣וֹא יְדַעְתֶּ֔ם כִּֽי־נַחֵ֧שׁ יְנַחֵ֛שׁ אִ֥ישׁ אֲשֶׁ֥ר כָּמֹֽנִי׃ 16 וַיֹּ֣אמֶר יְהוּדָ֗ה מַה־נֹּאמַר֙ לַֽאדֹנִ֔י מַה־נְּדַבֵּ֖ר וּמַה־נִּצְטַדָּ֑ק הָֽאֱלֹהִ֗ים מָצָא֙ אֶת־עֲוֺ֣ן עֲבָדֶ֔יךָ הִנֶּנּ֤וּ עֲבָדִים֙ לַֽאדֹנִ֔י גַּם־אֲנַ֕חְנוּ גַּ֛ם אֲשֶׁר־נִמְצָ֥א הַגָּבִ֖יעַ בְּיָדֽוֹ׃ 17 וַיֹּ֕אמֶר חָלִ֣ילָה לִּ֔י מֵֽעֲשׂ֖וֹת זֹ֑את הָאִ֡ישׁ אֲשֶׁר֩ נִמְצָ֨א הַגָּבִ֜יעַ בְּיָד֗וֹ ה֚וּא יִֽהְיֶה־לִּ֣י עָ֔בֶד וְאַתֶּ֕ם עֲל֥וּ לְשָׁל֖וֹם אֶל־אֲבִיכֶֽם׃ פ

18 וַיִּגַּ֨שׁ אֵלָ֜יו יְהוּדָ֗ה וַיֹּאמֶר֮ בִּ֣י אֲדֹנִי֒ יְדַבֶּר־נָ֨א עַבְדְּךָ֤ דָבָר֙ בְּאָזְנֵ֣י אֲדֹנִ֔י וְאַל־יִ֥חַר אַפְּךָ֖ בְּעַבְדֶּ֑ךָ כִּ֥י כָמ֖וֹךָ כְּפַרְעֹֽה׃ 19 אֲדֹנִ֣י שָׁאַ֔ל אֶת־עֲבָדָ֖יו לֵאמֹ֑ר

father or a brother?' ²⁰And we said to my lord, 'We have a father, an old man, and a child of *his* old age, *who is* young; his brother is dead, and he alone is left of his mother's children, and his father loves him.' ²¹Then you said to your servants, 'Bring him down to me, that I may set my eyes on him.' ²²And we said to my lord, 'The lad cannot leave his father, for *if* he should leave his father, *his father* would die.' ²³But you said to your servants, 'Unless your youngest brother comes down with you, you shall see my face no more.'

²⁴"So it was, when we went up to your servant my father, that we told him the words of my lord. ²⁵And our father said, 'Go back *and* buy us a little food.' ²⁶But we said, 'We cannot go down; if our youngest brother is with us, then we will go down; for we may not see the man's face unless our youngest brother *is* with us.' ²⁷Then your servant my father said to us, 'You know that my wife bore me two sons; ²⁸and the one went out from me, and I said, "Surely he is torn to pieces"; and I have not seen him since. ²⁹But if you take this one also from me, and calamity befalls him, you shall bring down my gray hair with sorrow to the grave.'

³⁰"Now therefore, when I come to your servant my father, and the lad *is* not with us, since his life is bound up in the lad's life, ³¹it will happen, when he sees that the lad *is* not *with us,* that he will die. So your servants will bring down the gray hair of your servant our father with sorrow to the grave. ³²For your servant became surety for the lad to my father, saying, 'If I do not bring him *back* to you, then I shall bear the blame before my father forever.' ³³Now therefore, please let your servant remain instead of the lad as a slave to my lord, and let the lad go up with his brothers. ³⁴For how shall I go up to my father if the lad *is* not with me, lest perhaps I see the evil that would come upon my father?"

45 Then Joseph could not restrain himself before all those who stood by him, and he cried out, "Make everyone go out from me!" So no one stood with him while Joseph made himself known to his brothers. ²And he wept aloud, and the Egyptians and the house of Pharaoh heard *it.*

³Then Joseph said to his brothers, "I *am* Joseph; does my father still live?" But his brothers could not answer him, for they were dismayed in his presence. ⁴And Joseph said to his brothers, "Please come near to me." So they came near. Then he said: "I *am* Joseph your brother, whom you sold into Egypt. ⁵But now, do not therefore be grieved or angry with yourselves because you sold me here; for God sent me before you to preserve life. ⁶For these two years

20 וַנֹּ֙אמֶר֙ אֶל־אֲדֹנִ֔י יֶשׁ־לָ֙נוּ֙ אָ֣ב זָקֵ֔ן וְיֶ֥לֶד זְקֻנִ֖ים קָטָ֑ן וְאָחִ֣יו מֵ֗ת וַיִּוָּתֵ֨ר ה֤וּא לְבַדּוֹ֙ לְאִמּ֔וֹ וְאָבִ֖יו אֲהֵבֽוֹ: 21 וַתֹּ֙אמֶר֙ אֶל־עֲבָדֶ֔יךָ הֽוֹרִדֻ֖הוּ אֵלָ֑י וְאָשִׂ֥ימָה עֵינִ֖י עָלָֽיו: 22 וַנֹּ֙אמֶר֙ אֶל־אֲדֹנִ֔י לֹא־יוּכַ֥ל הַנַּ֖עַר לַעֲזֹ֣ב אֶת־אָבִ֑יו וְעָזַ֥ב אֶת־אָבִ֖יו וָמֵֽת: 23 וַתֹּ֙אמֶר֙ אֶל־עֲבָדֶ֔יךָ אִם־לֹ֥א יֵרֵ֛ד אֲחִיכֶ֥ם הַקָּטֹ֖ן אִתְּכֶ֑ם לֹ֥א תֹסִפ֖וּן לִרְא֥וֹת פָּנָֽי: 24 וַיְהִי֙ כִּ֣י עָלִ֔ינוּ אֶֽל־עַבְדְּךָ֖ אָבִ֑י וַנַּ֨גֶּד־ל֔וֹ אֵ֖ת דִּבְרֵ֥י אֲדֹנִֽי: 25 וַיֹּ֖אמֶר אָבִ֑ינוּ שֻׁ֖בוּ שִׁבְרוּ־לָ֥נוּ מְעַט־אֹֽכֶל: 26 וַנֹּ֕אמֶר לֹ֥א נוּכַ֖ל לָרֶ֑דֶת אִם־יֵ֩שׁ אָחִ֨ינוּ הַקָּטֹ֤ן אִתָּ֙נוּ֙ וְיָרַ֔דְנוּ כִּי־לֹ֣א נוּכַ֗ל לִרְאוֹת֙ פְּנֵ֣י הָאִ֔ישׁ וְאָחִ֥ינוּ הַקָּטֹ֖ן אֵינֶ֥נּוּ אִתָּֽנוּ: 27 וַיֹּ֛אמֶר עַבְדְּךָ֥ אָבִ֖י אֵלֵ֑ינוּ אַתֶּ֣ם יְדַעְתֶּ֔ם כִּ֥י שְׁנַ֖יִם יָֽלְדָה־לִּ֥י אִשְׁתִּֽי: 28 וַיֵּצֵ֤א הָֽאֶחָד֙ מֵֽאִתִּ֔י וָאֹמַ֕ר אַ֖ךְ טָרֹ֣ף טֹרָ֑ף וְלֹ֥א רְאִיתִ֖יו עַד־הֵֽנָּה: 29 וּלְקַחְתֶּ֧ם גַּם־אֶת־זֶ֛ה מֵעִ֥ם פָּנַ֖י וְקָרָ֣הוּ אָס֑וֹן וְהֽוֹרַדְתֶּ֧ם אֶת־שֵׂיבָתִ֛י בְּרָעָ֖ה שְׁאֹֽלָה: 30 וְעַתָּ֗ה כְּבֹאִי֙ אֶל־עַבְדְּךָ֣ אָבִ֔י וְהַנַּ֖עַר אֵינֶ֣נּוּ אִתָּ֑נוּ וְנַפְשׁ֖וֹ קְשׁוּרָ֥ה בְנַפְשֽׁוֹ: 31 וְהָיָ֗ה כִּרְאוֹת֛וֹ כִּי־אֵ֥ין הַנַּ֖עַר וָמֵ֑ת וְהוֹרִ֨ידוּ עֲבָדֶ֜יךָ אֶת־שֵׂיבַ֨ת עַבְדְּךָ֥ אָבִ֛ינוּ בְּיָג֖וֹן שְׁאֹֽלָה: 32 כִּ֤י עַבְדְּךָ֙ עָרַ֣ב אֶת־הַנַּ֔עַר מֵעִ֥ם אָבִ֖י לֵאמֹ֑ר אִם־לֹ֤א אֲבִיאֶ֙נּוּ֙ אֵלֶ֔יךָ וְחָטָ֥אתִי לְאָבִ֖י כָּל־הַיָּמִֽים: 33 וְעַתָּ֗ה יֵֽשֶׁב־נָ֤א עַבְדְּךָ֙ תַּ֣חַת הַנַּ֔עַר עֶ֖בֶד לַֽאדֹנִ֑י וְהַנַּ֖עַר יַ֥עַל עִם־אֶחָֽיו: 34 כִּי־אֵיךְ֙ אֶֽעֱלֶ֣ה אֶל־אָבִ֔י וְהַנַּ֖עַר אֵינֶ֣נּוּ אִתִּ֑י פֶּ֚ן אֶרְאֶ֣ה בָרָ֔ע אֲשֶׁ֥ר יִמְצָ֖א אֶת־אָבִֽי:

מה וְלֹֽא־יָכֹ֨ל יוֹסֵ֜ף לְהִתְאַפֵּ֗ק לְכֹ֤ל הַנִּצָּבִים֙ עָלָ֔יו וַיִּקְרָ֕א הוֹצִ֥יאוּ כָל־אִ֖ישׁ מֵעָלָ֑י וְלֹא־עָ֤מַד אִישׁ֙ אִתּ֔וֹ בְּהִתְוַדַּ֥ע יוֹסֵ֖ף אֶל־אֶחָֽיו: 2 וַיִּתֵּ֥ן אֶת־קֹל֖וֹ בִּבְכִ֑י וַיִּשְׁמְע֣וּ מִצְרַ֔יִם וַיִּשְׁמַ֖ע בֵּ֥ית פַּרְעֹֽה: 3 וַיֹּ֨אמֶר יוֹסֵ֤ף אֶל־אֶחָיו֙ אֲנִ֣י יוֹסֵ֔ף הַע֥וֹד אָבִ֖י חָ֑י וְלֹֽא־יָכְל֤וּ אֶחָיו֙ לַעֲנ֣וֹת אֹת֔וֹ כִּ֥י נִבְהֲל֖וּ מִפָּנָֽיו: 4 וַיֹּ֨אמֶר יוֹסֵ֧ף אֶל־אֶחָ֛יו גְּשׁוּ־נָ֥א אֵלַ֖י וַיִּגָּ֑שׁוּ וַיֹּ֗אמֶר אֲנִי֙ יוֹסֵ֣ף אֲחִיכֶ֔ם אֲשֶׁר־מְכַרְתֶּ֥ם אֹתִ֖י מִצְרָֽיְמָה: 5 וְעַתָּ֣ה ׀ אַל־תֵּעָ֣צְב֗וּ וְאַל־יִ֙חַר֙ בְּעֵ֣ינֵיכֶ֔ם כִּֽי־מְכַרְתֶּ֥ם אֹתִ֖י הֵ֑נָּה כִּ֣י לְמִֽחְיָ֔ה שְׁלָחַ֥נִי אֱלֹהִ֖ים לִפְנֵיכֶֽם: 6 כִּי־זֶ֛ה שְׁנָתַ֥יִם

the famine *has been* in the land, and *there are* still five years in which *there will be* neither plowing nor harvesting. [7]And God sent me before you to preserve a posterity for you in the earth, and to save your lives by a great deliverance. [8]So now *it was* not you *who* sent me here, but God; and He has made me a father to Pharaoh, and lord of all his house, and a ruler throughout all the land of Egypt.

[9]"Hurry and go up to my father, and say to him, 'Thus says your son Joseph: "God has made me lord of all Egypt; come down to me, do not tarry. [10]You shall dwell in the land of Goshen, and you shall be near to me, you and your children, your children's children, your flocks and your herds, and all that you have. [11]There I will provide for you, lest you and your household, and all that you have, come to poverty; for *there are* still five years of famine.'"

[12]"And behold, your eyes and the eyes of my brother Benjamin see that *it is* my mouth that speaks to you. [13]So you shall tell my father of all my glory in Egypt, and of all that you have seen; and you shall hurry and bring my father down here."

[14]Then he fell on his brother Benjamin's neck and wept, and Benjamin wept on his neck. [15]Moreover he kissed all his brothers and wept over them, and after that his brothers talked with him.

[16]Now the report of it was heard in Pharaoh's house, saying, "Joseph's brothers have come." So it pleased Pharaoh and his servants well. [17]And Pharaoh said to Joseph, "Say to your brothers, 'Do this: Load your animals and depart; go to the land of Canaan. [18]Bring your father and your households and come to me; I will give you the best of the land of Egypt, and you will eat the fat of the land. [19]Now you are commanded—do this: Take carts out of the land of Egypt for your little ones and your wives; bring your father and come. [20]Also do not be concerned about your goods, for the best of all the land of Egypt *is* yours.'"

[21]Then the sons of Israel did so; and Joseph gave them carts, according to the command of Pharaoh, and he gave them provisions for the journey. [22]He gave to all of them, to each man, changes of garments; but to Benjamin he gave three hundred *pieces* of silver and five changes of garments. [23]And he sent to his father these *things:* ten donkeys loaded with the good things of Egypt, and ten female donkeys loaded with grain, bread, and food for his father for the journey. [24]So he sent his brothers away, and they departed; and he said to them, "See that you do not become troubled along the way."

הָרָעָב בְּקֶרֶב הָאָרֶץ וְעוֹד חָמֵשׁ שָׁנִים אֲשֶׁר אֵין־
חָרִישׁ וְקָצִּיר: 7 וַיִּשְׁלָחֵנִי אֱלֹהִים לִפְנֵיכֶם לָשׂוּם
לָכֶם שְׁאֵרִית בָּאָרֶץ וּלְהַחֲיוֹת לָכֶם לִפְלֵיטָה גְּדֹלָה:
8 וְעַתָּה לֹא־אַתֶּם שְׁלַחְתֶּם אֹתִי הֵנָּה כִּי הָאֱלֹהִים
וַיְשִׂימֵנִי לְאָב לְפַרְעֹה וּלְאָדוֹן לְכָל־בֵּיתוֹ וּמֹשֵׁל
בְּכָל־אֶרֶץ מִצְרָיִם: 9 מַהֲרוּ וַעֲלוּ אֶל־אָבִי וַאֲמַרְתֶּם
אֵלָיו כֹּה אָמַר בִּנְךָ יוֹסֵף שָׂמַנִי אֱלֹהִים לְאָדוֹן לְכָל־
מִצְרָיִם רְדָה אֵלַי אַל־תַּעֲמֹד: 10 וְיָשַׁבְתָּ בְאֶרֶץ־גֹּשֶׁן
וְהָיִיתָ קָרוֹב אֵלַי אַתָּה וּבָנֶיךָ וּבְנֵי בָנֶיךָ וְצֹאנְךָ
וּבְקָרְךָ וְכָל־אֲשֶׁר־לָךְ: 11 וְכִלְכַּלְתִּי אֹתְךָ שָׁם כִּי־
עוֹד חָמֵשׁ שָׁנִים רָעָב פֶּן־תִּוָּרֵשׁ אַתָּה וּבֵיתְךָ וְכָל־
אֲשֶׁר־לָךְ: 12 וְהִנֵּה עֵינֵיכֶם רֹאוֹת וְעֵינֵי אָחִי בִנְיָמִין
כִּי־פִי הַמְדַבֵּר אֲלֵיכֶם: 13 וְהִגַּדְתֶּם לְאָבִי אֶת־כָּל־
כְּבוֹדִי בְּמִצְרַיִם וְאֵת כָּל־אֲשֶׁר רְאִיתֶם וּמִהַרְתֶּם
וְהוֹרַדְתֶּם אֶת־אָבִי הֵנָּה: 14 וַיִּפֹּל עַל־צַוְּארֵי בִנְיָמִן־
אָחִיו וַיֵּבְךְּ וּבִנְיָמִן בָּכָה עַל־צַוָּארָיו: 15 וַיְנַשֵּׁק לְכָל־
אֶחָיו וַיֵּבְךְּ עֲלֵיהֶם וְאַחֲרֵי כֵן דִּבְּרוּ אֶחָיו אִתּוֹ:
16 וְהַקֹּל נִשְׁמַע בֵּית פַּרְעֹה לֵאמֹר בָּאוּ אֲחֵי יוֹסֵף
וַיִּיטַב בְּעֵינֵי פַרְעֹה וּבְעֵינֵי עֲבָדָיו: 17 וַיֹּאמֶר פַּרְעֹה
אֶל־יוֹסֵף אֱמֹר אֶל־אַחֶיךָ זֹאת עֲשׂוּ טַעֲנוּ אֶת־
בְּעִירְכֶם וּלְכוּ־בֹאוּ אַרְצָה כְּנָעַן: 18 וּקְחוּ אֶת־
אֲבִיכֶם וְאֶת־בָּתֵּיכֶם וּבֹאוּ אֵלָי וְאֶתְּנָה לָכֶם אֶת־
טוּב אֶרֶץ מִצְרַיִם וְאִכְלוּ אֶת־חֵלֶב הָאָרֶץ: 19 וְאַתָּה
צֻוֵּיתָה זֹאת עֲשׂוּ קְחוּ־לָכֶם מֵאֶרֶץ מִצְרַיִם עֲגָלוֹת
לְטַפְּכֶם וְלִנְשֵׁיכֶם וּנְשָׂאתֶם אֶת־אֲבִיכֶם וּבָאתֶם:
20 וְעֵינְכֶם אַל־תָּחֹס עַל־כְּלֵיכֶם כִּי־טוּב כָּל־אֶרֶץ
מִצְרַיִם לָכֶם הוּא: 21 וַיַּעֲשׂוּ־כֵן בְּנֵי יִשְׂרָאֵל וַיִּתֵּן
לָהֶם יוֹסֵף עֲגָלוֹת עַל־פִּי פַרְעֹה וַיִּתֵּן לָהֶם צֵדָה
לַדָּרֶךְ: 22 לְכֻלָּם נָתַן לָאִישׁ חֲלִפוֹת שְׂמָלֹת וּלְבִנְיָמִן
נָתַן שְׁלֹשׁ מֵאוֹת כֶּסֶף וְחָמֵשׁ חֲלִפֹת שְׂמָלֹת:
23 וּלְאָבִיו שָׁלַח כְּזֹאת עֲשָׂרָה חֲמֹרִים נֹשְׂאִים
מִטּוּב מִצְרָיִם וְעֶשֶׂר אֲתֹנֹת נֹשְׂאֹת בָּר וָלֶחֶם וּמָזוֹן
לְאָבִיו לַדָּרֶךְ: 24 וַיְשַׁלַּח אֶת־אֶחָיו וַיֵּלֵכוּ וַיֹּאמֶר

25 Then they went up out of Egypt, and came to the land of Canaan to Jacob their father. 26 And they told him, saying, "Joseph *is* still alive, and he *is* governor over all the land of Egypt." And Jacob's heart stood still, because he did not believe them. 27 But when they told him all the words which Joseph had said to them, and when he saw the carts which Joseph had sent to carry him, the spirit of Jacob their father revived. 28 Then Israel said, "*It is* enough. Joseph my son *is* still alive. I will go and see him before I die."

46 So Israel took his journey with all that he had, and came to Beersheba, and offered sacrifices to the God of his father Isaac. 2 Then God spoke to Israel in the visions of the night, and said, "Jacob, Jacob!"

And he said, "Here I am."

3 So He said, "I *am* God, the God of your father; do not fear to go down to Egypt, for I will make of you a great nation there. 4 I will go down with you to Egypt, and I will also surely bring you up *again;* and Joseph will put his hand on your eyes."

5 Then Jacob arose from Beersheba; and the sons of Israel carried their father Jacob, their little ones, and their wives, in the carts which Pharaoh had sent to carry him. 6 So they took their livestock and their goods, which they had acquired in the land of Canaan, and went to Egypt, Jacob and all his descendants with him. 7 His sons and his sons' sons, his daughters and his sons' daughters, and all his descendants he brought with him to Egypt.

8 Now these *were* the names of the children of Israel, Jacob and his sons, who went to Egypt: Reuben *was* Jacob's firstborn. 9 The sons of Reuben *were* Hanoch, Pallu, Hezron, and Carmi. 10 The sons of Simeon *were* Jemuel, Jamin, Ohad, Jachin, Zohar, and Shaul, the son of a Canaanite woman. 11 The sons of Levi *were* Gershon, Kohath, and Merari. 12 The sons of Judah *were* Er, Onan, Shelah, Perez, and Zerah (but Er and Onan died in the land of Canaan). The sons of Perez were Hezron and Hamul. 13 The sons of Issachar *were* Tola, Puvah, Job, and Shimron. 14 The sons of Zebulun *were* Sered, Elon, and Jahleel. 15 These *were* the sons of Leah, whom she bore to Jacob in Padan Aram, with his daughter Dinah. All the persons, his sons and his daughters, *were* thirty-three.

16 The sons of Gad *were* Ziphion, Haggi, Shuni, Ezbon, Eri, Arodi, and Areli. 17 The sons of Asher *were* Jimnah, Ishuah, Isui, Beriah, and Serah, their sister. And the sons of Beriah *were* Heber and Malchiel. 18 These *were* the sons of Zilpah, whom Laban gave to Leah his daughter; and these she bore to Jacob: sixteen persons.

אֲלֵהֶם אֶל־תִּרְגְּזוּ בַּדָּרֶךְ: 25 וַיַּעֲלוּ מִמִּצְרָיִם וַיָּבֹאוּ אֶרֶץ כְּנַעַן אֶל־יַעֲקֹב אֲבִיהֶם: 26 וַיַּגִּדוּ לוֹ לֵאמֹר עוֹד יוֹסֵף חַי וְכִי־הוּא מֹשֵׁל בְּכָל־אֶרֶץ מִצְרָיִם וַיָּפָג לִבּוֹ כִּי לֹא־הֶאֱמִין לָהֶם: 27 וַיְדַבְּרוּ אֵלָיו אֵת כָּל־דִּבְרֵי יוֹסֵף אֲשֶׁר דִּבֶּר אֲלֵהֶם וַיַּרְא אֶת־ הָעֲגָלוֹת אֲשֶׁר־שָׁלַח יוֹסֵף לָשֵׂאת אֹתוֹ וַתְּחִי רוּחַ יַעֲקֹב אֲבִיהֶם: 28 וַיֹּאמֶר יִשְׂרָאֵל רַב עוֹד־יוֹסֵף בְּנִי חָי אֵלְכָה וְאֶרְאֶנּוּ בְּטֶרֶם אָמוּת:

מו וַיִּסַּע יִשְׂרָאֵל וְכָל־אֲשֶׁר־לוֹ וַיָּבֹא בְּאֵרָה שֶּׁבַע וַיִּזְבַּח זְבָחִים לֵאלֹהֵי אָבִיו יִצְחָק: 2 וַיֹּאמֶר אֱלֹהִים | לְיִשְׂרָאֵל בְּמַרְאֹת הַלַּיְלָה וַיֹּאמֶר יַעֲקֹב | יַעֲקֹב וַיֹּאמֶר הִנֵּנִי: 3 וַיֹּאמֶר אָנֹכִי הָאֵל אֱלֹהֵי אָבִיךָ אַל־תִּירָא מֵרְדָה מִצְרַיְמָה כִּי־לְגוֹי גָּדוֹל אֲשִׂימְךָ שָׁם: 4 אָנֹכִי אֵרֵד עִמְּךָ מִצְרַיְמָה וְאָנֹכִי אַעַלְךָ גַם־עָלֹה וְיוֹסֵף יָשִׁית יָדוֹ עַל־עֵינֶיךָ: 5 וַיָּקָם יַעֲקֹב מִבְּאֵר שָׁבַע וַיִּשְׂאוּ בְנֵי־יִשְׂרָאֵל אֶת־יַעֲקֹב אֲבִיהֶם וְאֶת־טַפָּם וְאֶת־נְשֵׁיהֶם בָּעֲגָלוֹת אֲשֶׁר־שָׁלַח פַּרְעֹה לָשֵׂאת אֹתוֹ: 6 וַיִּקְחוּ אֶת־מִקְנֵיהֶם וְאֶת־רְכוּשָׁם אֲשֶׁר רָכְשׁוּ בְּאֶרֶץ כְּנַעַן וַיָּבֹאוּ מִצְרָיְמָה יַעֲקֹב וְכָל־ זַרְעוֹ אִתּוֹ: 7 בָּנָיו וּבְנֵי בָנָיו אִתּוֹ בְּנֹתָיו וּבְנוֹת בָּנָיו וְכָל־זַרְעוֹ הֵבִיא אִתּוֹ מִצְרָיְמָה: ס 8 וְאֵלֶּה שְׁמוֹת בְּנֵי־יִשְׂרָאֵל הַבָּאִים מִצְרַיְמָה יַעֲקֹב וּבָנָיו בְּכֹר יַעֲקֹב רְאוּבֵן: 9 וּבְנֵי רְאוּבֵן חֲנוֹךְ וּפַלּוּא וְחֶצְרֹן וְכַרְמִי: 10 וּבְנֵי שִׁמְעוֹן יְמוּאֵל וְיָמִין וְאֹהַד וְיָכִין וְצֹחַר וְשָׁאוּל בֶּן־הַכְּנַעֲנִית: 11 וּבְנֵי לֵוִי גֵּרְשׁוֹן קְהָת וּמְרָרִי: 12 וּבְנֵי יְהוּדָה עֵר וְאוֹנָן וְשֵׁלָה וָפֶרֶץ וָזָרַח וַיָּמָת עֵר וְאוֹנָן בְּאֶרֶץ כְּנַעַן וַיִּהְיוּ בְנֵי־פֶרֶץ חֶצְרֹן וְחָמוּל: 13 וּבְנֵי יִשָּׂשכָר תּוֹלָע וּפֻוָּה וְיוֹב וְשִׁמְרֹן: 14 וּבְנֵי זְבֻלוּן סֶרֶד וְאֵלוֹן וְיַחְלְאֵל: 15 אֵלֶּה | בְּנֵי לֵאָה אֲשֶׁר יָלְדָה לְיַעֲקֹב בְּפַדַּן אֲרָם וְאֵת דִּינָה בִתּוֹ כָּל־נֶפֶשׁ בָּנָיו וּבְנוֹתָיו שְׁלֹשִׁים וְשָׁלֹשׁ: 16 וּבְנֵי גָד צִפְיוֹן וְחַגִּי שׁוּנִי וְאֶצְבֹּן עֵרִי וַאֲרוֹדִי וְאַרְאֵלִי: 17 וּבְנֵי אָשֵׁר יִמְנָה וְיִשְׁוָה וְיִשְׁוִי וּבְרִיעָה וְשֶׂרַח אֲחֹתָם וּבְנֵי בְרִיעָה חֶבֶר וּמַלְכִּיאֵל: 18 אֵלֶּה בְּנֵי זִלְפָּה אֲשֶׁר־נָתַן לָבָן לְלֵאָה בִתּוֹ וַתֵּלֶד אֶת־אֵלֶּה

19 The sons of Rachel, Jacob's wife, *were* Joseph and Benjamin. 20 And to Joseph in the land of Egypt were born Manasseh and Ephraim, whom Asenath, the daughter of Poti-Pherah priest of On, bore to him. 21 The sons of Benjamin *were* Belah, Becher, Ashbel, Gera, Naaman, Ehi, Rosh, Muppim, Huppim, and Ard. 22 These *were* the sons of Rachel, who were born to Jacob: fourteen persons in all.

23 The son of Dan *was* Hushim. 24 The sons of Naphtali *were* Jahzeel, Guni, Jezer, and Shillem. 25 These *were* the sons of Bilhah, whom Laban gave to Rachel his daughter, and she bore these to Jacob: seven persons in all.

26 All the persons who went with Jacob to Egypt, who came from his body, besides Jacob's sons' wives, *were* sixty-six persons in all. 27 And the sons of Joseph who were born to him in Egypt *were* two persons. All the persons of the house of Jacob who went to Egypt were seventy.

28 Then he sent Judah before him to Joseph, to point out before him *the way* to Goshen. And they came to the land of Goshen. 29 So Joseph made ready his chariot and went up to Goshen to meet his father Israel; and he presented himself to him, and fell on his neck and wept on his neck a good while.

30 And Israel said to Joseph, "Now let me die, since I have seen your face, because you *are* still alive."

31 Then Joseph said to his brothers and to his father's household, "I will go up and tell Pharaoh, and say to him, 'My brothers and those of my father's house, who *were* in the land of Canaan, have come to me. 32 And the men *are* shepherds, for their occupation has been to feed livestock; and they have brought their flocks, their herds, and all that they have.' 33 So it shall be, when Pharaoh calls you and says, 'What is your occupation?' 34 that you shall say, 'Your servants' occupation has been with livestock from our youth even till now, both we *and* also our fathers,' that you may dwell in the land of Goshen; for every shepherd *is* an abomination to the Egyptians."

47

Then Joseph went and told Pharaoh, and said, "My father and my brothers, their flocks and their herds and all that they possess, have come from the land of Canaan; and indeed they *are* in the land of Goshen." 2 And he took five men from among his brothers and presented them to Pharaoh. 3 Then Pharaoh said to his brothers, "What *is* your occupation?"

19 בְּנֵי רָחֵל אֵשֶׁת יַעֲקֹב יוֹסֵף וּבִנְיָמִן: 20 וַיִּוָּלֵד לְיוֹסֵף בְּאֶרֶץ מִצְרַיִם אֲשֶׁר יָלְדָה־לּוֹ אָסְנַת בַּת־פּוֹטִי פֶרַע כֹּהֵן אֹן אֶת־מְנַשֶּׁה וְאֶת־אֶפְרָיִם: 21 וּבְנֵי בִנְיָמִן בֶּלַע וָבֶכֶר וְאַשְׁבֵּל גֵּרָא וְנַעֲמָן אֵחִי וָרֹאשׁ מֻפִּים וְחֻפִּים וָאָרְדְּ: 22 אֵלֶּה בְּנֵי רָחֵל אֲשֶׁר יֻלַּד לְיַעֲקֹב כָּל־נֶפֶשׁ אַרְבָּעָה עָשָׂר:

23 וּבְנֵי־דָן חֻשִׁים: 24 וּבְנֵי נַפְתָּלִי יַחְצְאֵל וְגוּנִי וְיֵצֶר וְשִׁלֵּם: 25 אֵלֶּה בְּנֵי בִלְהָה אֲשֶׁר־נָתַן לָבָן לְרָחֵל בִּתּוֹ וַתֵּלֶד אֶת־אֵלֶּה לְיַעֲקֹב כָּל־נֶפֶשׁ שִׁבְעָה:

26 כָּל־הַנֶּפֶשׁ הַבָּאָה לְיַעֲקֹב מִצְרַיְמָה יֹצְאֵי יְרֵכוֹ מִלְּבַד נְשֵׁי בְנֵי־יַעֲקֹב כָּל־נֶפֶשׁ שִׁשִּׁים וָשֵׁשׁ: 27 וּבְנֵי יוֹסֵף אֲשֶׁר־יֻלַּד־לוֹ בְמִצְרַיִם נֶפֶשׁ שְׁנָיִם כָּל־הַנֶּפֶשׁ לְבֵית־יַעֲקֹב הַבָּאָה מִצְרַיְמָה שִׁבְעִים: פ

28 וְאֶת־יְהוּדָה שָׁלַח לְפָנָיו אֶל־יוֹסֵף לְהוֹרֹת לְפָנָיו גֹּשְׁנָה וַיָּבֹאוּ אַרְצָה גֹּשֶׁן: 29 וַיֶּאְסֹר יוֹסֵף מֶרְכַּבְתּוֹ וַיַּעַל לִקְרַאת־יִשְׂרָאֵל אָבִיו גֹּשְׁנָה וַיֵּרָא אֵלָיו וַיִּפֹּל עַל־צַוָּארָיו וַיֵּבְךְּ עַל־צַוָּארָיו עוֹד: 30 וַיֹּאמֶר יִשְׂרָאֵל אֶל־יוֹסֵף אָמוּתָה הַפָּעַם אַחֲרֵי רְאוֹתִי אֶת־פָּנֶיךָ כִּי עוֹדְךָ חָי: 31 וַיֹּאמֶר יוֹסֵף אֶל־אֶחָיו וְאֶל־בֵּית אָבִיו אֶעֱלֶה וְאַגִּידָה לְפַרְעֹה וְאֹמְרָה אֵלָיו אַחַי וּבֵית־אָבִי אֲשֶׁר בְּאֶרֶץ־כְּנַעַן בָּאוּ אֵלָי: 32 וְהָאֲנָשִׁים רֹעֵי צֹאן כִּי־אַנְשֵׁי מִקְנֶה הָיוּ וְצֹאנָם וּבְקָרָם וְכָל־אֲשֶׁר לָהֶם הֵבִיאוּ: 33 וְהָיָה כִּי־יִקְרָא לָכֶם פַּרְעֹה וְאָמַר מַה־מַּעֲשֵׂיכֶם: 34 וַאֲמַרְתֶּם אַנְשֵׁי מִקְנֶה הָיוּ עֲבָדֶיךָ מִנְּעוּרֵינוּ וְעַד־עַתָּה גַּם־אֲנַחְנוּ גַּם־אֲבֹתֵינוּ בַּעֲבוּר תֵּשְׁבוּ בְּאֶרֶץ גֹּשֶׁן כִּי־תוֹעֲבַת מִצְרַיִם כָּל־רֹעֵה צֹאן:

מז וַיָּבֹא יוֹסֵף וַיַּגֵּד לְפַרְעֹה וַיֹּאמֶר אָבִי וְאַחַי וְצֹאנָם וּבְקָרָם וְכָל־אֲשֶׁר לָהֶם בָּאוּ מֵאֶרֶץ כְּנָעַן וְהִנָּם בְּאֶרֶץ גֹּשֶׁן: 2 וּמִקְצֵה אֶחָיו לָקַח חֲמִשָּׁה אֲנָשִׁים וַיַּצִּגֵם לִפְנֵי פַרְעֹה: 3 וַיֹּאמֶר פַּרְעֹה אֶל־אֶחָיו מַה־מַּעֲשֵׂיכֶם וַיֹּאמְרוּ אֶל־פַּרְעֹה רֹעֵה צֹאן

And they said to Pharaoh, "Your servants *are* shepherds, both we *and* also our fathers." ⁴And they said to Pharaoh, "We have come to dwell in the land, because your servants have no pasture for their flocks, for the famine *is* severe in the land of Canaan. Now therefore, please let your servants dwell in the land of Goshen."

⁵Then Pharaoh spoke to Joseph, saying, "Your father and your brothers have come to you. ⁶The land of Egypt *is* before you. Have your father and brothers dwell in the best of the land; let them dwell in the land of Goshen. And if you know *any* competent men among them, then make them chief herdsmen over my livestock."

⁷Then Joseph brought in his father Jacob and set him before Pharaoh; and Jacob blessed Pharaoh. ⁸Pharaoh said to Jacob, "How old *are* you?"

⁹And Jacob said to Pharaoh, "The days of the years of my pilgrimage *are* one hundred and thirty years; few and evil have been the days of the years of my life, and they have not attained to the days of the years of the life of my fathers in the days of their pilgrimage." ¹⁰So Jacob blessed Pharaoh, and went out from before Pharaoh.

¹¹And Joseph situated his father and his brothers, and gave them a possession in the land of Egypt, in the best of the land, in the land of Rameses, as Pharaoh had commanded. ¹²Then Joseph provided his father, his brothers, and all his father's household with bread, according to the number in *their* families.

¹³Now *there was* no bread in all the land; for the famine *was* very severe, so that the land of Egypt and the land of Canaan languished because of the famine. ¹⁴And Joseph gathered up all the money that was found in the land of Egypt and in the land of Canaan, for the grain which they bought; and Joseph brought the money into Pharaoh's house.

¹⁵So when the money failed in the land of Egypt and in the land of Canaan, all the Egyptians came to Joseph and said, "Give us bread, for why should we die in your presence? For the money has failed."

¹⁶Then Joseph said, "Give your livestock, and I will give you *bread* for your livestock, if the money is gone." ¹⁷So they brought their livestock to Joseph, and Joseph gave them bread *in exchange* for the horses, the flocks, the cattle of the herds, and for the donkeys. Thus he fed them with bread *in exchange* for all their livestock that year.

¹⁸When that year had ended, they came to him the next year and said to him, "We will not hide from my lord that our money is gone; my lord also has our herds of livestock. There is nothing left in the sight of my lord but our bodies and our lands.

עֲבָדֶיךָ גַּם־אֲנַחְנוּ גַּם־אֲבוֹתֵינוּ׃ 4 וַיֹּאמְרוּ אֶל־פַּרְעֹה לָגוּר בָּאָרֶץ בָּאנוּ כִּי־אֵין מִרְעֶה לַצֹּאן אֲשֶׁר לַעֲבָדֶיךָ כִּי־כָבֵד הָרָעָב בְּאֶרֶץ כְּנָעַן וְעַתָּה יֵשְׁבוּ־נָא עֲבָדֶיךָ בְּאֶרֶץ גֹּשֶׁן׃ 5 וַיֹּאמֶר פַּרְעֹה אֶל־יוֹסֵף לֵאמֹר אָבִיךָ וְאַחֶיךָ בָּאוּ אֵלֶיךָ׃ 6 אֶרֶץ מִצְרַיִם לְפָנֶיךָ הִוא בְּמֵיטַב הָאָרֶץ הוֹשֵׁב אֶת־אָבִיךָ וְאֶת־אַחֶיךָ יֵשְׁבוּ בְּאֶרֶץ גֹּשֶׁן וְאִם־יָדַעְתָּ וְיֶשׁ־בָּם אַנְשֵׁי־חַיִל וְשַׂמְתָּם שָׂרֵי מִקְנֶה עַל־אֲשֶׁר־לִי׃ 7 וַיָּבֵא יוֹסֵף אֶת־יַעֲקֹב אָבִיו וַיַּעֲמִדֵהוּ לִפְנֵי פַרְעֹה וַיְבָרֶךְ יַעֲקֹב אֶת־פַּרְעֹה׃ 8 וַיֹּאמֶר פַּרְעֹה אֶל־יַעֲקֹב כַּמָּה יְמֵי שְׁנֵי חַיֶּיךָ׃ 9 וַיֹּאמֶר יַעֲקֹב אֶל־פַּרְעֹה יְמֵי שְׁנֵי מְגוּרַי שְׁלֹשִׁים וּמְאַת שָׁנָה מְעַט וְרָעִים הָיוּ יְמֵי שְׁנֵי חַיַּי וְלֹא הִשִּׂיגוּ אֶת־יְמֵי שְׁנֵי חַיֵּי אֲבֹתַי בִּימֵי מְגוּרֵיהֶם׃ 10 וַיְבָרֶךְ יַעֲקֹב אֶת־פַּרְעֹה וַיֵּצֵא מִלִּפְנֵי פַרְעֹה׃ 11 וַיּוֹשֵׁב יוֹסֵף אֶת־אָבִיו וְאֶת־אֶחָיו וַיִּתֵּן לָהֶם אֲחֻזָּה בְּאֶרֶץ מִצְרַיִם בְּמֵיטַב הָאָרֶץ בְּאֶרֶץ רַעְמְסֵס כַּאֲשֶׁר צִוָּה פַרְעֹה׃ 12 וַיְכַלְכֵּל יוֹסֵף אֶת־אָבִיו וְאֶת־אֶחָיו וְאֵת כָּל־בֵּית אָבִיו לֶחֶם לְפִי הַטָּף׃ 13 וְלֶחֶם אֵין בְּכָל־הָאָרֶץ כִּי־כָבֵד הָרָעָב מְאֹד וַתֵּלַהּ אֶרֶץ מִצְרַיִם וְאֶרֶץ כְּנַעַן מִפְּנֵי הָרָעָב׃ 14 וַיְלַקֵּט יוֹסֵף אֶת־כָּל־הַכֶּסֶף הַנִּמְצָא בְאֶרֶץ־מִצְרַיִם וּבְאֶרֶץ כְּנַעַן בַּשֶּׁבֶר אֲשֶׁר־הֵם שֹׁבְרִים וַיָּבֵא יוֹסֵף אֶת־הַכֶּסֶף בֵּיתָה פַרְעֹה׃ 15 וַיִּתֹּם הַכֶּסֶף מֵאֶרֶץ מִצְרַיִם וּמֵאֶרֶץ כְּנַעַן וַיָּבֹאוּ כָל־מִצְרַיִם אֶל־יוֹסֵף לֵאמֹר הָבָה־לָּנוּ לֶחֶם וְלָמָּה נָמוּת נֶגְדֶּךָ כִּי אָפֵס כָּסֶף׃ 16 וַיֹּאמֶר יוֹסֵף הָבוּ מִקְנֵיכֶם וְאֶתְּנָה לָכֶם בְּמִקְנֵיכֶם אִם־אָפֵס כָּסֶף׃ 17 וַיָּבִיאוּ אֶת־מִקְנֵיהֶם אֶל־יוֹסֵף וַיִּתֵּן לָהֶם יוֹסֵף לֶחֶם בַּסּוּסִים וּבְמִקְנֵה הַצֹּאן וּבְמִקְנֵה הַבָּקָר וּבַחֲמֹרִים וַיְנַהֲלֵם בַּלֶּחֶם בְּכָל־מִקְנֵהֶם בַּשָּׁנָה הַהִוא׃ 18 וַתִּתֹּם הַשָּׁנָה הַהִוא וַיָּבֹאוּ אֵלָיו בַּשָּׁנָה הַשֵּׁנִית וַיֹּאמְרוּ לוֹ לֹא־נְכַחֵד מֵאֲדֹנִי כִּי אִם־תַּם הַכֶּסֶף וּמִקְנֵה הַבְּהֵמָה אֶל־אֲדֹנִי לֹא נִשְׁאַר לִפְנֵי אֲדֹנִי בִּלְתִּי אִם־גְּוִיָּתֵנוּ

19 Why should we die before your eyes, both we and our land? Buy us and our land for bread, and we and our land will be servants of Pharaoh; give *us* seed, that we may live and not die, that the land may not be desolate."

20 Then Joseph bought all the land of Egypt for Pharaoh; for every man of the Egyptians sold his field, because the famine was severe upon them. So the land became Pharaoh's. 21 And as for the people, he moved them into the cities, from *one* end of the borders of Egypt to the *other* end. 22 Only the land of the priests he did not buy; for the priests had rations *allotted to them* by Pharaoh, and they ate their rations which Pharaoh gave them; therefore they did not sell their lands.

23 Then Joseph said to the people, "Indeed I have bought you and your land this day for Pharaoh. Look, *here is* seed for you, and you shall sow the land. 24 And it shall come to pass in the harvest that you shall give one-fifth to Pharaoh. Four-fifths shall be your own, as seed for the field and for your food, for those of your households and as food for your little ones."

25 So they said, "You have saved our lives; let us find favor in the sight of my lord, and we will be Pharaoh's servants." 26 And Joseph made it a law over the land of Egypt to this day, *that* Pharaoh should have one-fifth, except for the land of the priests only, *which* did not become Pharaoh's.

27 So Israel dwelt in the land of Egypt, in the country of Goshen; and they had possessions there and grew and multiplied exceedingly. 28 And Jacob lived in the land of Egypt seventeen years. So the length of Jacob's life was one hundred and forty-seven years. 29 When the time drew near that Israel must die, he called his son Joseph and said to him, "Now if I have found favor in your sight, please put your hand under my thigh, and deal kindly and truly with me. Please do not bury me in Egypt, 30 but let me lie with my fathers; you shall carry me out of Egypt and bury me in their burial place."

And he said, "I will do as you have said."

31 Then he said, "Swear to me." And he swore to him. So Israel bowed himself on the head of the bed.

48 Now it came to pass after these things that Joseph was told, "Indeed your father *is* sick"; and he took with him his two sons, Manasseh and Ephraim. 2 And Jacob was told, "Look, your son Joseph is coming to you"; and Israel strengthened himself and sat up on the bed. 3 Then Jacob said to Joseph: "God Almighty appeared to me at Luz in the land of Canaan and blessed me, 4 and said to

19 גַּם אֲנַחְנוּ גַּם־אַדְמָתֵנוּ לָמָּה נָמוּת לְעֵינֶיךָ קְנֵה־אֹתָנוּ וְאֶת־אַדְמָתֵנוּ בַּלָּחֶם וְנִהְיֶה אֲנַחְנוּ וְאַדְמָתֵנוּ עֲבָדִים לְפַרְעֹה וְתֶן־זֶרַע וְנִחְיֶה וְלֹא נָמוּת וְהָאֲדָמָה לֹא תֵשָׁם: 20 וַיִּקֶן יוֹסֵף אֶת־כָּל־אַדְמַת מִצְרַיִם לְפַרְעֹה כִּי־מָכְרוּ מִצְרַיִם אִישׁ שָׂדֵהוּ כִּי־חָזַק עֲלֵהֶם הָרָעָב וַתְּהִי הָאָרֶץ לְפַרְעֹה: 21 וְאֶת־הָעָם הֶעֱבִיר אֹתוֹ לֶעָרִים מִקְצֵה גְבוּל־מִצְרַיִם וְעַד־קָצֵהוּ: 22 רַק אַדְמַת הַכֹּהֲנִים לֹא קָנָה כִּי חֹק לַכֹּהֲנִים מֵאֵת פַּרְעֹה וְאָכְלוּ אֶת־חֻקָּם אֲשֶׁר נָתַן לָהֶם פַּרְעֹה עַל־כֵּן לֹא מָכְרוּ אֶת־אַדְמָתָם: 23 וַיֹּאמֶר יוֹסֵף אֶל־הָעָם הֵן קָנִיתִי אֶתְכֶם הַיּוֹם וְאֶת־אַדְמַתְכֶם לְפַרְעֹה הֵא־לָכֶם זֶרַע וּזְרַעְתֶּם אֶת־הָאֲדָמָה: 24 וְהָיָה בַּתְּבוּאֹת וּנְתַתֶּם חֲמִישִׁית לְפַרְעֹה וְאַרְבַּע הַיָּדֹת יִהְיֶה לָכֶם לְזֶרַע הַשָּׂדֶה וּלְאָכְלְכֶם וְלַאֲשֶׁר בְּבָתֵּיכֶם וְלֶאֱכֹל לְטַפְּכֶם: 25 וַיֹּאמְרוּ הֶחֱיִתָנוּ נִמְצָא־חֵן בְּעֵינֵי אֲדֹנִי וְהָיִינוּ עֲבָדִים לְפַרְעֹה: 26 וַיָּשֶׂם אֹתָהּ יוֹסֵף לְחֹק עַד־הַיּוֹם הַזֶּה עַל־אַדְמַת מִצְרַיִם לְפַרְעֹה לַחֹמֶשׁ רַק אַדְמַת הַכֹּהֲנִים לְבַדָּם לֹא הָיְתָה לְפַרְעֹה: 27 וַיֵּשֶׁב יִשְׂרָאֵל בְּאֶרֶץ מִצְרַיִם בְּאֶרֶץ גֹּשֶׁן וַיֵּאָחֲזוּ בָהּ וַיִּפְרוּ וַיִּרְבּוּ מְאֹד: 28 וַיְחִי יַעֲקֹב בְּאֶרֶץ מִצְרַיִם שְׁבַע עֶשְׂרֵה שָׁנָה וַיְהִי יְמֵי־יַעֲקֹב שְׁנֵי חַיָּיו שֶׁבַע שָׁנִים וְאַרְבָּעִים וּמְאַת שָׁנָה: 29 וַיִּקְרְבוּ יְמֵי־יִשְׂרָאֵל לָמוּת וַיִּקְרָא ׀ לִבְנוֹ לְיוֹסֵף וַיֹּאמֶר לוֹ אִם־נָא מָצָאתִי חֵן בְּעֵינֶיךָ שִׂים־נָא יָדְךָ תַּחַת יְרֵכִי וְעָשִׂיתָ עִמָּדִי חֶסֶד וֶאֱמֶת אַל־נָא תִקְבְּרֵנִי בְּמִצְרָיִם: 30 וְשָׁכַבְתִּי עִם־אֲבֹתַי וּנְשָׂאתַנִי מִמִּצְרַיִם וּקְבַרְתַּנִי בִּקְבֻרָתָם וַיֹּאמַר אָנֹכִי אֶעֱשֶׂה כִדְבָרֶךָ: 31 וַיֹּאמֶר הִשָּׁבְעָה לִי וַיִּשָּׁבַע לוֹ וַיִּשְׁתַּחוּ יִשְׂרָאֵל עַל־רֹאשׁ הַמִּטָּה: פ

מח וַיְהִי אַחֲרֵי הַדְּבָרִים הָאֵלֶּה וַיֹּאמֶר לְיוֹסֵף הִנֵּה אָבִיךָ חֹלֶה וַיִּקַּח אֶת־שְׁנֵי בָנָיו עִמּוֹ אֶת־מְנַשֶּׁה וְאֶת־אֶפְרָיִם: 2 וַיַּגֵּד לְיַעֲקֹב וַיֹּאמֶר הִנֵּה בִּנְךָ יוֹסֵף בָּא אֵלֶיךָ וַיִּתְחַזֵּק יִשְׂרָאֵל וַיֵּשֶׁב עַל־הַמִּטָּה: 3 וַיֹּאמֶר יַעֲקֹב אֶל־יוֹסֵף אֵל שַׁדַּי נִרְאָה־אֵלַי בְּלוּז

me, 'Behold, I will make you fruitful and multiply you, and I will make of you a multitude of people, and give this land to your descendants after you *as* an everlasting possession.' ⁵And now your two sons, Ephraim and Manasseh, who were born to you in the land of Egypt before I came to you in Egypt, *are* mine; as Reuben and Simeon, they shall be mine. ⁶Your offspring whom you beget after them shall be yours; they will be called by the name of their brothers in their inheritance. ⁷But as for me, when I came from Padan, Rachel died beside me in the land of Canaan on the way, when *there was* but a little distance to go to Ephrath; and I buried her there on the way to Ephrath (that is, Bethlehem)."

⁸Then Israel saw Joseph's sons, and said, "Who *are* these?"

⁹Joseph said to his father, "They *are* my sons, whom God has given me in this *place*."

And he said, "Please bring them to me, and I will bless them." ¹⁰Now the eyes of Israel were dim with age, *so that* he could not see. Then Joseph brought them near him, and he kissed them and embraced them. ¹¹And Israel said to Joseph, "I had not thought to see your face; but in fact, God has also shown me your offspring!"

¹²So Joseph brought them from beside his knees, and he bowed down with his face to the earth. ¹³And Joseph took them both, Ephraim with his right hand toward Israel's left hand, and Manasseh with his left hand toward Israel's right hand, and brought *them* near him. ¹⁴Then Israel stretched out his right hand and laid *it* on Ephraim's head, who *was* the younger, and his left hand on Manasseh's head, guiding his hands knowingly, for Manasseh *was* the firstborn. ¹⁵And he blessed Joseph, and said:

"God, before whom my fathers Abraham and Isaac walked,
The God who has fed me all my life long to this day,
16   The Angel who has redeemed me from all evil,
Bless the lads;
Let my name be named upon them,
And the name of my fathers Abraham and Isaac;
And let them grow into a multitude in the midst of the earth."

¹⁷Now when Joseph saw that his father laid his right hand on the head of Ephraim, it displeased him; so he took hold of his father's hand to remove it from Ephraim's head to Manasseh's head. ¹⁸And Joseph said to his father, "Not so, my father, for this *one is* the firstborn; put your right hand on his head."

בְּאֶרֶץ כְּנַעַן וַיְבָרֶךְ אֹתִי: 4 וַיֹּאמֶר אֵלַי הִנְנִי מַפְרְךָ וְהִרְבִּיתִךָ וּנְתַתִּיךָ לִקְהַל עַמִּים וְנָתַתִּי אֶת־הָאָרֶץ הַזֹּאת לְזַרְעֲךָ אַחֲרֶיךָ אֲחֻזַּת עוֹלָם: 5 וְעַתָּה שְׁנֵי־בָנֶיךָ הַנּוֹלָדִים לְךָ בְּאֶרֶץ מִצְרַיִם עַד־בֹּאִי אֵלֶיךָ מִצְרַיְמָה לִי־הֵם אֶפְרַיִם וּמְנַשֶּׁה כִּרְאוּבֵן וְשִׁמְעוֹן יִהְיוּ־לִי: 6 וּמוֹלַדְתְּךָ אֲשֶׁר־הוֹלַדְתָּ אַחֲרֵיהֶם לְךָ יִהְיוּ עַל שֵׁם אֲחֵיהֶם יִקָּרְאוּ בְּנַחֲלָתָם: 7 וַאֲנִי בְּבֹאִי מִפַּדָּן מֵתָה עָלַי רָחֵל בְּאֶרֶץ כְּנַעַן בַּדֶּרֶךְ בְּעוֹד כִּבְרַת־אֶרֶץ לָבֹא אֶפְרָתָה וָאֶקְבְּרֶהָ שָּׁם בְּדֶרֶךְ אֶפְרָת הִוא בֵּית לָחֶם: 8 וַיַּרְא יִשְׂרָאֵל אֶת־בְּנֵי יוֹסֵף וַיֹּאמֶר מִי־אֵלֶּה: 9 וַיֹּאמֶר יוֹסֵף אֶל־אָבִיו בָּנַי הֵם אֲשֶׁר־נָתַן־לִי אֱלֹהִים בָּזֶה וַיֹּאמַר קָחֶם־נָא אֵלַי וַאֲבָרֲכֵם: 10 וְעֵינֵי יִשְׂרָאֵל כָּבְדוּ מִזֹּקֶן לֹא יוּכַל לִרְאוֹת וַיַּגֵּשׁ אֹתָם אֵלָיו וַיִּשַּׁק לָהֶם וַיְחַבֵּק לָהֶם: 11 וַיֹּאמֶר יִשְׂרָאֵל אֶל־יוֹסֵף רְאֹה פָנֶיךָ לֹא פִלָּלְתִּי וְהִנֵּה הֶרְאָה אֹתִי אֱלֹהִים גַּם אֶת־זַרְעֶךָ: 12 וַיּוֹצֵא יוֹסֵף אֹתָם מֵעִם בִּרְכָּיו וַיִּשְׁתַּחוּ לְאַפָּיו אָרְצָה: 13 וַיִּקַּח יוֹסֵף אֶת־שְׁנֵיהֶם אֶת־אֶפְרַיִם בִּימִינוֹ מִשְּׂמֹאל יִשְׂרָאֵל וְאֶת־מְנַשֶּׁה בִשְׂמֹאלוֹ מִימִין יִשְׂרָאֵל וַיַּגֵּשׁ אֵלָיו: 14 וַיִּשְׁלַח יִשְׂרָאֵל אֶת־יְמִינוֹ וַיָּשֶׁת עַל־רֹאשׁ אֶפְרַיִם וְהוּא הַצָּעִיר וְאֶת־שְׂמֹאלוֹ עַל־רֹאשׁ מְנַשֶּׁה שִׂכֵּל אֶת־יָדָיו כִּי מְנַשֶּׁה הַבְּכוֹר: 15 וַיְבָרֶךְ אֶת־יוֹסֵף וַיֹּאמַר הָאֱלֹהִים אֲשֶׁר הִתְהַלְּכוּ אֲבֹתַי לְפָנָיו אַבְרָהָם וְיִצְחָק הָאֱלֹהִים הָרֹעֶה אֹתִי מֵעוֹדִי עַד־הַיּוֹם הַזֶּה: 16 הַמַּלְאָךְ הַגֹּאֵל אֹתִי מִכָּל־רָע יְבָרֵךְ אֶת־הַנְּעָרִים וְיִקָּרֵא בָהֶם שְׁמִי וְשֵׁם אֲבֹתַי אַבְרָהָם וְיִצְחָק וְיִדְגּוּ לָרֹב בְּקֶרֶב הָאָרֶץ: 17 וַיַּרְא יוֹסֵף כִּי־יָשִׁית אָבִיו יַד־יְמִינוֹ עַל־רֹאשׁ אֶפְרַיִם וַיֵּרַע בְּעֵינָיו וַיִּתְמֹךְ יַד־אָבִיו לְהָסִיר אֹתָהּ מֵעַל רֹאשׁ־אֶפְרַיִם עַל־רֹאשׁ מְנַשֶּׁה: 18 וַיֹּאמֶר יוֹסֵף אֶל־אָבִיו לֹא־כֵן אָבִי כִּי־

19 But his father refused and said, "I know, my son, I know. He also shall become a people, and he also shall be great; but truly his younger brother shall be greater than he, and his descendants shall become a multitude of nations."

20 So he blessed them that day, saying, "By you Israel will bless, saying, 'May God make you as Ephraim and as Manasseh!'" And thus he set Ephraim before Manasseh.

21 Then Israel said to Joseph, "Behold, I am dying, but God will be with you and bring you back to the land of your fathers. 22 Moreover I have given to you one portion above your brothers, which I took from the hand of the Amorite with my sword and my bow."

49 And Jacob called his sons and said, "Gather together, that I may tell you what shall befall you in the last days:

2   "Gather together and hear, you sons of Jacob,
    And listen to Israel your father.

3   "Reuben, you are my firstborn,
    My might and the beginning of my strength,
    The excellency of dignity and the excellency of power.
4   Unstable as water, you shall not excel,
    Because you went up to your father's bed;
    Then you defiled *it*—
    He went up to my couch.

5   "Simeon and Levi *are* brothers;
    Instruments of cruelty *are in* their dwelling place.
6   Let not my soul enter their council;
    Let not my honor be united to their assembly;
    For in their anger they slew a man,
    And in their self-will they hamstrung an ox.
7   Cursed *be* their anger, for *it is* fierce;
    And their wrath, for it is cruel!
    I will divide them in Jacob
    And scatter them in Israel.

8   "Judah, you *are he* whom your brothers shall praise;
    Your hand *shall be* on the neck of your enemies;
    Your father's children shall bow down before you.
9   Judah *is* a lion's whelp;
    From the prey, my son, you have gone up.
    He bows down, he lies down as a lion;
    And as a lion, who shall rouse him?
10   The scepter shall not depart from Judah,
    Nor a lawgiver from between his feet,
    Until Shiloh comes;
    And to Him *shall be* the obedience of the people.
11   Binding his donkey to the vine,
    And his donkey's colt to the choice vine,
    He washed his garments in wine,
    And his clothes in the blood of grapes.
12   His eyes *are* darker than wine,

19 וַיְמָאֵן אָבִיו וַיֹּאמֶר זֶה הַבְּכֹר שִׂים יְמִינְךָ עַל־רֹאשׁוֹ: וַיֹּאמֶר יָדַעְתִּי בְנִי יָדַעְתִּי גַּם־הוּא יִהְיֶה־לְּעָם וְגַם־הוּא יִגְדָּל וְאוּלָם אָחִיו הַקָּטֹן יִגְדַּל מִמֶּנּוּ וְזַרְעוֹ יִהְיֶה מְלֹא־הַגּוֹיִם: 20 וַיְבָרֲכֵם בַּיּוֹם הַהוּא לֵאמוֹר בְּךָ יְבָרֵךְ יִשְׂרָאֵל לֵאמֹר יְשִׂמְךָ אֱלֹהִים כְּאֶפְרַיִם וְכִמְנַשֶּׁה וַיָּשֶׂם אֶת־אֶפְרַיִם לִפְנֵי מְנַשֶּׁה: 21 וַיֹּאמֶר יִשְׂרָאֵל אֶל־יוֹסֵף הִנֵּה אָנֹכִי מֵת וְהָיָה אֱלֹהִים עִמָּכֶם וְהֵשִׁיב אֶתְכֶם אֶל־אֶרֶץ אֲבֹתֵיכֶם: 22 וַאֲנִי נָתַתִּי לְךָ שְׁכֶם אַחַד עַל־אַחֶיךָ אֲשֶׁר לָקַחְתִּי מִיַּד הָאֱמֹרִי בְּחַרְבִּי וּבְקַשְׁתִּי: פ

מט וַיִּקְרָא יַעֲקֹב אֶל־בָּנָיו וַיֹּאמֶר הֵאָסְפוּ וְאַגִּידָה לָכֶם אֵת אֲשֶׁר־יִקְרָא אֶתְכֶם בְּאַחֲרִית הַיָּמִים: 2 הִקָּבְצוּ וְשִׁמְעוּ בְּנֵי יַעֲקֹב וְשִׁמְעוּ אֶל־יִשְׂרָאֵל אֲבִיכֶם: 3 רְאוּבֵן בְּכֹרִי אַתָּה כֹּחִי וְרֵאשִׁית אוֹנִי יֶתֶר שְׂאֵת וְיֶתֶר עָז: 4 פַּחַז כַּמַּיִם אַל־תּוֹתַר כִּי עָלִיתָ מִשְׁכְּבֵי אָבִיךָ אָז חִלַּלְתָּ יְצוּעִי עָלָה: פ

5 שִׁמְעוֹן וְלֵוִי אַחִים כְּלֵי חָמָס מְכֵרֹתֵיהֶם: 6 בְּסֹדָם אַל־תָּבֹא נַפְשִׁי בִּקְהָלָם אַל־תֵּחַד כְּבֹדִי כִּי בְאַפָּם הָרְגוּ אִישׁ וּבִרְצֹנָם עִקְּרוּ־שׁוֹר: 7 אָרוּר אַפָּם כִּי עָז וְעֶבְרָתָם כִּי קָשָׁתָה אֲחַלְּקֵם בְּיַעֲקֹב וַאֲפִיצֵם בְּיִשְׂרָאֵל: ס 8 יְהוּדָה אַתָּה יוֹדוּךָ אַחֶיךָ יָדְךָ בְּעֹרֶף אֹיְבֶיךָ יִשְׁתַּחֲווּ לְךָ בְּנֵי אָבִיךָ: 9 גּוּר אַרְיֵה יְהוּדָה מִטֶּרֶף בְּנִי עָלִיתָ כָּרַע רָבַץ כְּאַרְיֵה וּכְלָבִיא מִי יְקִימֶנּוּ: 10 לֹא־יָסוּר שֵׁבֶט מִיהוּדָה וּמְחֹקֵק מִבֵּין רַגְלָיו עַד כִּי־יָבֹא שִׁילֹה וְלוֹ יִקְּהַת עַמִּים: 11 אֹסְרִי לַגֶּפֶן עִירֹה P וְלַשֹּׂרֵקָה בְּנִי אֲתֹנוֹ כִּבֵּס בַּיַּיִן לְבֻשׁוֹ וּבְדַם־עֲנָבִים סוּתֹה P: 12 חַכְלִילִי עֵינַיִם מִיָּיִן וּלְבֶן־שִׁנַּיִם מֵחָלָב: פ

And his teeth whiter than milk.

13 "Zebulun shall dwell by the haven of the sea;
   He *shall become* a haven for ships,
   And his border shall adjoin Sidon.

14 "Issachar is a strong donkey,
   Lying down between two burdens,

15 He saw that rest *was* good,
   And that the land *was* pleasant;
   He bowed his shoulder to bear *a burden,*
   And became a band of slaves.

16 "Dan shall judge his people
   As one of the tribes of Israel.

17 Dan shall be a serpent by the way,
   A viper by the path,
   That bites the horse's heels
   So that its rider shall fall backward.

18 I have waited for your salvation, O Lord!

19 "Gad, a troop shall tramp upon him,
   But he shall triumph at last.

20 "Bread from Asher *shall be* rich,
   And he shall yield royal dainties.

21 "Naphtali *is* a deer let loose;
   He uses beautiful words.

22 "Joseph *is* a fruitful bough,
   A fruitful bough by a well;
   His branches run over the wall.

23 The archers have bitterly grieved him,
   Shot *at him* and hated him.

24 But his bow remained in strength,
   And the arms of his hands were made strong
   By the hands of the Mighty *God* of Jacob
   (From there *is* the Shepherd, the Stone of Israel),

25 By the God of your father who will help you,
   And by the Almighty who will bless you
   With blessings of heaven above,
   Blessings of the deep that lies beneath,
   Blessings of the breasts and of the womb.

26 The blessings of your father
   Have excelled the blessings of my ancestors,
   Up to the utmost bound of the everlasting hills.
   They shall be on the head of Joseph,
   And on the crown of the head of him who was
       separate from his brothers.

27 "Benjamin is a ravenous wolf;
   In the morning he shall devour the prey,
   And at night he shall divide the spoil."

28 All these *are* the twelve tribes of Israel, and this *is* what their father spoke to them. And he blessed them; he blessed each one according to his own blessing.

29 Then he charged them and said to them: "I am to be gathered to my people; bury me with my fathers in the cave that *is* in the field of Ephron the Hittite, 30 in the cave that *is* in the field of Machpelah, which *is* before Mamre in the land of Canaan, which Abraham bought with the field of Ephron the Hittite as a possession for a burial

זְבוּלֻן לְחוֹף יַמִּים יִשְׁכֹּן וְהוּא לְחוֹף אֳנִיֹּת 13
וְיַרְכָתוֹ עַל־צִידֹן: ס 14 יִשָּׂשכָר חֲמֹר גָּרֶם
רֹבֵץ בֵּין הַמִּשְׁפְּתָיִם: 15 וַיַּרְא מְנֻחָה כִּי טוֹב
וְאֶת־הָאָרֶץ כִּי נָעֵמָה וַיֵּט שִׁכְמוֹ לִסְבֹּל וַיְהִי
לְמַס־עֹבֵד: ס 16 דָּן יָדִין עַמּוֹ כְּאַחַד
שִׁבְטֵי יִשְׂרָאֵל: 17 יְהִי־דָן נָחָשׁ עֲלֵי־דֶרֶךְ שְׁפִיפֹן
עֲלֵי־אֹרַח הַנֹּשֵׁךְ עִקְּבֵי־סוּס וַיִּפֹּל רֹכְבוֹ אָחוֹר:
18 לִישׁוּעָתְךָ קִוִּיתִי יְהוָה: 19 גָּד גְּדוּד יְגוּדֶנּוּ וְהוּא
יָגֻד עָקֵב: ס 20 מֵאָשֵׁר שְׁמֵנָה לַחְמוֹ
וְהוּא יִתֵּן מַעֲדַנֵּי־מֶלֶךְ: ס 21 נַפְתָּלִי אַיָּלָה
שְׁלֻחָה הַנֹּתֵן אִמְרֵי־שָׁפֶר: ס 22 בֵּן פֹּרָת
יוֹסֵף בֵּן פֹּרָת עֲלֵי־עָיִן בָּנוֹת צָעֲדָה עֲלֵי־שׁוּר:
23 וַיְמָרֲרֻהוּ וָרֹבּוּ וַיִּשְׂטְמֻהוּ בַּעֲלֵי חִצִּים: 24 וַתֵּשֶׁב
בְּאֵיתָן קַשְׁתּוֹ וַיָּפֹזּוּ זְרֹעֵי יָדָיו מִידֵי אֲבִיר יַעֲקֹב
מִשָּׁם רֹעֶה אֶבֶן יִשְׂרָאֵל: 25 מֵאֵל אָבִיךָ וְיַעְזְרֶךָּ
וְאֵת שַׁדַּי וִיבָרֲכֶךָּ בִּרְכֹת שָׁמַיִם מֵעָל בִּרְכֹת תְּהוֹם
רֹבֶצֶת תָּחַת בִּרְכֹת שָׁדַיִם וָרָחַם: 26 בִּרְכֹת אָבִיךָ
גָּבְרוּ עַל־בִּרְכֹת הוֹרַי עַד־תַּאֲוַת גִּבְעֹת עוֹלָם תִּהְיֶיןָ
לְרֹאשׁ יוֹסֵף וּלְקָדְקֹד נְזִיר אֶחָיו: פ

27 בִּנְיָמִין זְאֵב יִטְרָף בַּבֹּקֶר יֹאכַל עַד וְלָעֶרֶב יְחַלֵּק
שָׁלָל: 28 כָּל־אֵלֶּה שִׁבְטֵי יִשְׂרָאֵל שְׁנֵים עָשָׂר וְזֹאת
אֲשֶׁר־דִּבֶּר לָהֶם אֲבִיהֶם וַיְבָרֶךְ אוֹתָם אִישׁ אֲשֶׁר
כְּבִרְכָתוֹ בֵּרַךְ אֹתָם: 29 וַיְצַו אוֹתָם וַיֹּאמֶר אֲלֵהֶם
אֲנִי נֶאֱסָף אֶל־עַמִּי קִבְרוּ אֹתִי אֶל־אֲבֹתָי אֶל־
הַמְּעָרָה אֲשֶׁר בִּשְׂדֵה עֶפְרוֹן הַחִתִּי: 30 בַּמְּעָרָה
אֲשֶׁר בִּשְׂדֵה הַמַּכְפֵּלָה אֲשֶׁר עַל־פְּנֵי־מַמְרֵא בְּאֶרֶץ
כְּנַעַן אֲשֶׁר קָנָה אַבְרָהָם אֶת־הַשָּׂדֶה מֵאֵת עֶפְרֹן
הַחִתִּי לַאֲחֻזַּת־קָבֶר: 31 שָׁמָּה קָבְרוּ אֶת־אַבְרָהָם
וְאֵת שָׂרָה אִשְׁתּוֹ שָׁמָּה קָבְרוּ אֶת־יִצְחָק וְאֵת

wife, there they buried Isaac and Rebekah his wife,
and there I buried Leah. ³²The field and the cave
that *is* there *were* purchased from the sons of Heth."
³³And when Jacob had finished commanding his
sons, he drew his feet up into the bed and breathed
his last, and was gathered to his people.

50 Then Joseph fell on his father's face and wept
over him, and kissed him. ²And Joseph commanded his servants the physicians to embalm his
father. So the physicians embalmed Israel. ³Forty
days were required for him, for such are the days
required for those who are embalmed; and the
Egyptians mourned for him seventy days.

⁴Now when the days of his mourning were past,
Joseph spoke to the household of Pharaoh, saying,
"If now I have found favor in your eyes, please
speak in the hearing of Pharaoh, saying, ⁵'My
father made me swear, saying, "Behold, I am dying;
in my grave which I dug for myself in the land of
Canaan, there you shall bury me." Now therefore,
please let me go up and bury my father, and I will
come back.'"

⁶And Pharaoh said, "Go up and bury your
father, as he made you swear."

⁷So Joseph went up to bury his father; and with
him went up all the servants of Pharaoh, the elders
of his house, and all the elders of the land of Egypt,
⁸as well as all the house of Joseph, his brothers, and
his father's house. Only their little ones, their flocks,
and their herds they left in the land of Goshen.
⁹And there went up with him both chariots and
horsemen, and it was a very great gathering.

¹⁰Then they came to the threshing floor of Atad,
which *is* beyond the Jordan, and they mourned
there with a great and very solemn lamentation. He
observed seven days of mourning for his father.
¹¹And when the inhabitants of the land, the
Canaanites, saw the mourning at the threshing
floor of Atad, they said, "This *is* a deep mourning
of the Egyptians." Therefore its name was called
Abel Mizraim, which *is* beyond the Jordan.

¹²So his sons did for him just as he had
commanded them. ¹³For his sons carried him to
the land of Canaan, and buried him in the cave of
the field of Machpelah, before Mamre, which
Abraham bought with the field from Ephron the
Hittite as property for a burial place. ¹⁴And after he
had buried his father, Joseph returned to Egypt, he
and his brothers and all who went up with him to
bury his father.

¹⁵When Joseph's brothers saw that their father
was dead, they said, "Perhaps Joseph will hate us,
and may actually repay us for all the evil which we

רִבְקָה אִשְׁתּוֹ וְשָׁמָּה קָבַרְתִּי אֶת־לֵאָה: ³² מִקְנֶה
הַשָּׂדֶה וְהַמְּעָרָה אֲשֶׁר־בּוֹ מֵאֵת בְּנֵי־חֵת: ³³ וַיְכַל
יַעֲקֹב לְצַוֹּת אֶת־בָּנָיו וַיֶּאֱסֹף רַגְלָיו אֶל־הַמִּטָּה
וַיִּגְוַע וַיֵּאָסֶף אֶל־עַמָּיו:

נ וַיִּפֹּל יוֹסֵף עַל־פְּנֵי אָבִיו וַיֵּבְךְּ עָלָיו וַיִּשַּׁק־לוֹ:
² וַיְצַו יוֹסֵף אֶת־עֲבָדָיו אֶת־הָרֹפְאִים לַחֲנֹט אֶת־
אָבִיו וַיַּחַנְטוּ הָרֹפְאִים אֶת־יִשְׂרָאֵל: ³ וַיִּמְלְאוּ־לוֹ
אַרְבָּעִים יוֹם כִּי כֵּן יִמְלְאוּ יְמֵי הַחֲנֻטִים וַיִּבְכּוּ
אֹתוֹ מִצְרַיִם שִׁבְעִים יוֹם: ⁴ וַיַּעַבְרוּ יְמֵי בְכִיתוֹ
וַיְדַבֵּר יוֹסֵף אֶל־בֵּית פַּרְעֹה לֵאמֹר אִם־נָא מָצָאתִי
חֵן בְּעֵינֵיכֶם דַּבְּרוּ־נָא בְּאָזְנֵי פַרְעֹה לֵאמֹר: ⁵ אָבִי
הִשְׁבִּיעַנִי לֵאמֹר הִנֵּה אָנֹכִי מֵת בְּקִבְרִי אֲשֶׁר כָּרִיתִי
לִי בְּאֶרֶץ כְּנַעַן שָׁמָּה תִּקְבְּרֵנִי וְעַתָּה אֶעֱלֶה־נָּא
וְאֶקְבְּרָה אֶת־אָבִי וְאָשׁוּבָה: ⁶ וַיֹּאמֶר פַּרְעֹה עֲלֵה
וּקְבֹר אֶת־אָבִיךָ כַּאֲשֶׁר הִשְׁבִּיעֶךָ: ⁷ וַיַּעַל יוֹסֵף
לִקְבֹּר אֶת־אָבִיו וַיַּעֲלוּ אִתּוֹ כָּל־עַבְדֵי פַרְעֹה זִקְנֵי
בֵיתוֹ וְכֹל זִקְנֵי אֶרֶץ־מִצְרָיִם: ⁸ וְכֹל בֵּית יוֹסֵף וְאֶחָיו
וּבֵית אָבִיו רַק טַפָּם וְצֹאנָם וּבְקָרָם עָזְבוּ בְּאֶרֶץ
גֹּשֶׁן: ⁹ וַיַּעַל עִמּוֹ גַּם־רֶכֶב גַּם־פָּרָשִׁים וַיְהִי הַמַּחֲנֶה
כָּבֵד מְאֹד: ¹⁰ וַיָּבֹאוּ עַד־גֹּרֶן הָאָטָד אֲשֶׁר בְּעֵבֶר
הַיַּרְדֵּן וַיִּסְפְּדוּ־שָׁם מִסְפֵּד גָּדוֹל וְכָבֵד מְאֹד וַיַּעַשׂ
לְאָבִיו אֵבֶל שִׁבְעַת יָמִים: ¹¹ וַיַּרְא יוֹשֵׁב הָאָרֶץ
הַכְּנַעֲנִי אֶת־הָאֵבֶל בְּגֹרֶן הָאָטָד וַיֹּאמְרוּ אֵבֶל־
כָּבֵד זֶה לְמִצְרָיִם עַל־כֵּן קָרָא שְׁמָהּ אָבֵל מִצְרַיִם
אֲשֶׁר בְּעֵבֶר הַיַּרְדֵּן: ¹² וַיַּעֲשׂוּ בָנָיו לוֹ כֵּן כַּאֲשֶׁר
צִוָּם: ¹³ וַיִּשְׂאוּ אֹתוֹ בָנָיו אַרְצָה כְּנַעַן וַיִּקְבְּרוּ אֹתוֹ
בִּמְעָרַת שְׂדֵה הַמַּכְפֵּלָה אֲשֶׁר קָנָה אַבְרָהָם אֶת־
הַשָּׂדֶה לַאֲחֻזַּת־קֶבֶר מֵאֵת עֶפְרֹן הַחִתִּי עַל־פְּנֵי
מַמְרֵא: ¹⁴ וַיָּשָׁב יוֹסֵף מִצְרַיְמָה הוּא וְאֶחָיו וְכָל־
הָעֹלִים אִתּוֹ לִקְבֹּר אֶת־אָבִיו אַחֲרֵי קָבְרוֹ אֶת־
אָבִיו: ¹⁵ וַיִּרְאוּ אֲחֵי־יוֹסֵף כִּי־מֵת אֲבִיהֶם וַיֹּאמְרוּ
לוּ יִשְׂטְמֵנוּ יוֹסֵף וְהָשֵׁב יָשִׁיב לָנוּ אֵת כָּל־הָרָעָה

83

did to him." 16 So they sent *messengers* to Joseph, saying, "Before your father died he commanded, saying, 17 'Thus you shall say to Joseph: "I beg you, please forgive the trespass of your brothers and their sin; for they did evil to you." ' Now, please, forgive the trespass of the servants of the God of your father." And Joseph wept when they spoke to him.

18 Then his brothers also went and fell down before his face, and they said, "Behold, we *are* your servants."

19 Joseph said to them, "Do not be afraid, for *am* I in the place of God? 20 But as for you, you meant evil against me; *but* God meant it for good, in order to bring it about as *it is* this day, to save many people alive. 21 Now therefore, do not be afraid; I will provide for you and your little ones." And he comforted them and spoke kindly to them.

22 So Joseph dwelt in Egypt, he and his father's household. And Joseph lived one hundred and ten years. 23 Joseph saw Ephraim's children to the third *generation.* The children of Machir, the son of Manasseh, were also brought up on Joseph's knees.

24 And Joseph said to his brethren, "I am dying; but God will surely visit you, and bring you out of this land to the land of which He swore to Abraham, to Isaac, and to Jacob." 25 Then Joseph took an oath from the children of Israel, saying, "God will surely visit you, and you shall carry up my bones from here." 26 So Joseph died, *being* one hundred and ten years old; and they embalmed him, and he was put in a coffin in Egypt.

אֲשֶׁר גְּמָלֻנוּ אֹתוֹ: 16 וַיְצַוּוּ אֶל־יוֹסֵף לֵאמֹר אָבִיךָ
צִוָּה לִפְנֵי מוֹתוֹ לֵאמֹר: 17 כֹּה־תֹאמְרוּ לְיוֹסֵף
אָנָּא שָׂא נָא פֶּשַׁע אַחֶיךָ וְחַטָּאתָם כִּי־רָעָה
גְמָלוּךָ וְעַתָּה שָׂא נָא לְפֶשַׁע עַבְדֵי אֱלֹהֵי אָבִיךָ
וַיֵּבְךְּ יוֹסֵף בְּדַבְּרָם אֵלָיו: 18 וַיֵּלְכוּ גַּם־אֶחָיו וַיִּפְּלוּ
לְפָנָיו וַיֹּאמְרוּ הִנֶּנּוּ לְךָ לַעֲבָדִים: 19 וַיֹּאמֶר אֲלֵהֶם
יוֹסֵף אַל־תִּירָאוּ כִּי הֲתַחַת אֱלֹהִים אָנִי: 20 וְאַתֶּם
חֲשַׁבְתֶּם עָלַי רָעָה אֱלֹהִים חֲשָׁבָהּ לְטֹבָה לְמַעַן
עֲשֹׂה כַּיּוֹם הַזֶּה לְהַחֲיֹת עַם־רָב: 21 וְעַתָּה אַל־
תִּירָאוּ אָנֹכִי אֲכַלְכֵּל אֶתְכֶם וְאֶת־טַפְּכֶם וַיְנַחֵם
אוֹתָם וַיְדַבֵּר עַל־לִבָּם: 22 וַיֵּשֶׁב יוֹסֵף בְּמִצְרַיִם
הוּא וּבֵית אָבִיו וַיְחִי יוֹסֵף מֵאָה וָעֶשֶׂר שָׁנִים:
23 וַיַּרְא יוֹסֵף לְאֶפְרַיִם בְּנֵי שִׁלֵּשִׁים גַּם בְּנֵי מָכִיר
בֶּן־מְנַשֶּׁה יֻלְּדוּ עַל־בִּרְכֵּי יוֹסֵף: 24 וַיֹּאמֶר יוֹסֵף
אֶל־אֶחָיו אָנֹכִי מֵת וֵאלֹהִים פָּקֹד יִפְקֹד אֶתְכֶם
וְהֶעֱלָה אֶתְכֶם מִן־הָאָרֶץ הַזֹּאת אֶל־הָאָרֶץ אֲשֶׁר
נִשְׁבַּע לְאַבְרָהָם לְיִצְחָק וּלְיַעֲקֹב: 25 וַיַּשְׁבַּע יוֹסֵף
אֶת־בְּנֵי יִשְׂרָאֵל לֵאמֹר פָּקֹד יִפְקֹד אֱלֹהִים אֶתְכֶם
וְהַעֲלִתֶם אֶת־עַצְמֹתַי מִזֶּה: 26 וַיָּמָת יוֹסֵף בֶּן־מֵאָה
וָעֶשֶׂר שָׁנִים וַיַּחַנְטוּ אֹתוֹ וַיִּישֶׂם בָּאָרוֹן בְּמִצְרָיִם:

The Second Book of Moses Called

EXODUS

שמות

1 Now these *are* the names of the children of Israel who came to Egypt; each man and his household came with Jacob: ²Reuben, Simeon, Levi, and Judah; ³Issachar, Zebulun, and Benjamin; ⁴Dan, Naphtali, Gad, and Asher. ⁵All those who were descendants of Jacob were seventy persons (for Joseph was in Egypt *already*). ⁶And Joseph died, all his brothers, and all that generation. ⁷But the children of Israel were fruitful and increased abundantly, multiplied and grew exceedingly mighty; and the land was filled with them.

⁸Now there arose a new king over Egypt, who did not know Joseph. ⁹And he said to his people, "Look, the people of the children of Israel *are* more and mightier than we; ¹⁰come, let us deal shrewdly with them, lest they multiply, and it happen, in the event of war, that they also join our enemies and fight against us, and *so* go up out of the land." ¹¹Therefore they set taskmasters over them to afflict them with their burdens. And they built for Pharaoh supply cities, Pithom and Raamses. ¹²But the more they afflicted them, the more they multiplied and grew. And they were in dread of the children of Israel. ¹³So the Egyptians made the children of Israel serve with rigor. ¹⁴And they made their lives bitter with hard bondage—in mortar, in brick, and in all manner of service in the field. All their service in which they made them serve *was* with rigor.

¹⁵Then the king of Egypt spoke to the Hebrew midwives, of whom the name of one *was* Shiphrah and the name of the other Puah; ¹⁶and he said, "When you do the duties of a midwife for the Hebrew women, and see *them* on the birthstools, if it *is* a son, then you shall kill him; but if it *is* a daughter, then she shall live." ¹⁷But the midwives feared God, and did not do as the king of Egypt commanded them, but saved the male children alive. ¹⁸So the king of Egypt called for the midwives and said to them, "Why have you done this thing, and saved the male children alive?"

¹⁹And the midwives said to Pharaoh, "Because the Hebrew women *are* not like the Egyptian women; for they *are* lively and give birth before the midwives come to them."

א וְאֵ֗לֶּה שְׁמוֹת֙ בְּנֵ֣י יִשְׂרָאֵ֔ל הַבָּאִ֖ים מִצְרָ֑יְמָה אֵ֣ת יַעֲקֹ֔ב אִ֥ישׁ וּבֵית֖וֹ בָּֽאוּ: ² רְאוּבֵ֣ן שִׁמְע֔וֹן לֵוִ֖י וִיהוּדָֽה: ³ יִשָּׂשכָ֥ר זְבוּלֻ֖ן וּבְנְיָמִֽן: ⁴ דָּ֥ן וְנַפְתָּלִ֖י גָּ֥ד וְאָשֵֽׁר: ⁵ וַֽיְהִ֗י כָּל־נֶ֛פֶשׁ יֹצְאֵ֥י יֶֽרֶךְ־יַעֲקֹ֖ב שִׁבְעִ֣ים נָ֑פֶשׁ וְיוֹסֵ֖ף הָיָ֥ה בְמִצְרָֽיִם: ⁶ וַיָּ֤מָת יוֹסֵף֙ וְכָל־אֶחָ֔יו וְכֹ֖ל הַדּ֥וֹר הַהֽוּא: ⁷ וּבְנֵ֣י יִשְׂרָאֵ֗ל פָּר֧וּ וַֽיִּשְׁרְצ֛וּ וַיִּרְבּ֥וּ וַיַּֽעַצְמ֖וּ בִּמְאֹ֣ד מְאֹ֑ד וַתִּמָּלֵ֥א הָאָ֖רֶץ אֹתָֽם: פ

⁸ וַיָּ֥קָם מֶֽלֶךְ־חָדָ֖שׁ עַל־מִצְרָ֑יִם אֲשֶׁ֥ר לֹֽא־יָדַ֖ע אֶת־יוֹסֵֽף: ⁹ וַיֹּ֖אמֶר אֶל־עַמּ֑וֹ הִנֵּ֗ה עַ֚ם בְּנֵ֣י יִשְׂרָאֵ֔ל רַ֥ב וְעָצ֖וּם מִמֶּֽנּוּ: ¹⁰ הָ֥בָה נִֽתְחַכְּמָ֖ה ל֑וֹ פֶּן־יִרְבֶּ֗ה וְהָיָ֞ה כִּֽי־תִקְרֶ֤אנָה מִלְחָמָה֙ וְנוֹסַ֤ף גַּם־הוּא֙ עַל־שֹׂ֣נְאֵ֔ינוּ וְנִלְחַם־בָּ֖נוּ וְעָלָ֥ה מִן־הָאָֽרֶץ: ¹¹ וַיָּשִׂ֤ימוּ עָלָיו֙ שָׂרֵ֣י מִסִּ֔ים לְמַ֥עַן עַנֹּת֖וֹ בְּסִבְלֹתָ֑ם וַיִּ֜בֶן עָרֵ֤י מִסְכְּנוֹת֙ לְפַרְעֹ֔ה אֶת־פִּתֹ֖ם וְאֶת־רַֽעַמְסֵֽס: ¹² וְכַֽאֲשֶׁר֙ יְעַנּ֣וּ אֹת֔וֹ כֵּ֥ן יִרְבֶּ֖ה וְכֵ֣ן יִפְרֹ֑ץ וַיָּקֻ֕צוּ מִפְּנֵ֖י בְּנֵ֥י יִשְׂרָאֵֽל: ¹³ וַיַּעֲבִ֧דוּ מִצְרַ֛יִם אֶת־בְּנֵ֥י יִשְׂרָאֵ֖ל בְּפָֽרֶךְ: ¹⁴ וַיְמָרֲר֨וּ אֶת־חַיֵּיהֶ֜ם בַּעֲבֹדָ֣ה קָשָׁ֗ה בְּחֹ֙מֶר֙ וּבִלְבֵנִ֔ים וּבְכָל־עֲבֹדָ֖ה בַּשָּׂדֶ֑ה אֵ֚ת כָּל־עֲבֹ֣דָתָ֔ם אֲשֶׁר־עָבְד֥וּ בָהֶ֖ם בְּפָֽרֶךְ: ¹⁵ וַיֹּ֙אמֶר֙ מֶ֣לֶךְ מִצְרַ֔יִם לַֽמְיַלְּדֹ֖ת הָֽעִבְרִיֹּ֑ת אֲשֶׁ֨ר שֵׁ֤ם הָֽאַחַת֙ שִׁפְרָ֔ה וְשֵׁ֥ם הַשֵּׁנִ֖ית פּוּעָֽה: ¹⁶ וַיֹּ֗אמֶר בְּיַלֶּדְכֶן֙ אֶת־הָֽעִבְרִיּ֔וֹת וּרְאִיתֶ֖ן עַל־הָאָבְנָ֑יִם אִם־בֵּ֥ן הוּא֙ וַהֲמִתֶּ֣ן אֹת֔וֹ וְאִם־בַּ֥ת הִ֖יא וָחָֽיָה: ¹⁷ וַתִּירֶ֤אןָ הַֽמְיַלְּדֹת֙ אֶת־הָ֣אֱלֹהִ֔ים וְלֹ֣א עָשׂ֔וּ כַּאֲשֶׁ֛ר דִּבֶּ֥ר אֲלֵיהֶ֖ן מֶ֣לֶךְ מִצְרָ֑יִם וַתְּחַיֶּ֖יןָ אֶת־הַיְלָדִֽים: ¹⁸ וַיִּקְרָ֤א מֶֽלֶךְ־מִצְרַ֙יִם֙ לַֽמְיַלְּדֹ֔ת וַיֹּ֣אמֶר לָהֶ֔ן מַדּ֥וּעַ עֲשִׂיתֶ֖ן הַדָּבָ֣ר הַזֶּ֑ה וַתְּחַיֶּ֖יןָ אֶת־הַיְלָדִֽים: ¹⁹ וַתֹּאמַ֤רְןָ הַֽמְיַלְּדֹת֙ אֶל־פַּרְעֹ֔ה כִּ֣י לֹ֧א כַנָּשִׁ֛ים הַמִּצְרִיֹּ֖ת הָֽעִבְרִיֹּ֑ת כִּֽי־חָי֣וֹת

20 Therefore God dealt well with the midwives, and the people multiplied and grew very mighty. 21 And so it was, because the midwives feared God, that He provided households for them.

22 So Pharaoh commanded all his people, saying, "Every son who is born you shall cast into the river, and every daughter you shall save alive."

2 And a man of the house of Levi went and took *as wife* a daughter of Levi. 2 So the woman conceived and bore a son. And when she saw that he *was* a beautiful *child,* she hid him three months. 3 But when she could no longer hide him, she took an ark of bulrushes for him, daubed it with asphalt and pitch, put the child in it, and laid *it* in the reeds by the river's bank. 4 And his sister stood afar off, to know what would be done to him.

5 Then the daughter of Pharaoh came down to bathe at the river. And her maidens walked along the riverside; and when she saw the ark among the reeds, she sent her maid to get it. 6 And when she opened *it,* she saw the child, and behold, the baby wept. So she had compassion on him, and said, "This is one of the Hebrews' children."

7 Then his sister said to Pharaoh's daughter, "Shall I go and call a nurse for you from the Hebrew women, that she may nurse the child for you?"

8 And Pharaoh's daughter said to her, "Go." So the maiden went and called the child's mother. 9 Then Pharaoh's daughter said to her, "Take this child away and nurse him for me, and I will give *you* your wages." So the woman took the child and nursed him. 10 And the child grew, and she brought him to Pharaoh's daughter, and he became her son. So she called his name Moses, saying, "Because I drew him out of the water."

11 Now it came to pass in those days, when Moses was grown, that he went out to his brethren and looked at their burdens. And he saw an Egyptian beating a Hebrew, one of his brethren. 12 So he looked this way and that way, and when he saw no one, he killed the Egyptian and hid him in the sand. 13 And when he went out the second day, behold, two Hebrew men were fighting, and he said to the one who did the wrong, "Why are you striking your companion?"

14 Then he said, "Who made you a prince and a judge over us? Do you intend to kill me as you killed the Egyptian?"

הִנֵּה בְּטֶרֶם תָּבוֹא אֲלֵהֶן הַמְיַלֶּדֶת וְיָלָדוּ: 20 וַיֵּיטֶב אֱלֹהִים לַמְיַלְּדֹת וַיִּרֶב הָעָם וַיַּעַצְמוּ מְאֹד: 21 וַיְהִי כִּי־יָרְאוּ הַמְיַלְּדֹת אֶת־הָאֱלֹהִים וַיַּעַשׂ לָהֶם בָּתִּים: 22 וַיְצַו פַּרְעֹה לְכָל־עַמּוֹ לֵאמֹר כָּל־הַבֵּן הַיִּלּוֹד הַיְאֹרָה תַּשְׁלִיכֻהוּ וְכָל־הַבַּת תְּחַיּוּן: ס

ב וַיֵּלֶךְ אִישׁ מִבֵּית לֵוִי וַיִּקַּח אֶת־בַּת־לֵוִי: 2 וַתַּהַר הָאִשָּׁה וַתֵּלֶד בֵּן וַתֵּרֶא אֹתוֹ כִּי־טוֹב הוּא וַתִּצְפְּנֵהוּ שְׁלֹשָׁה יְרָחִים: 3 וְלֹא־יָכְלָה עוֹד הַצְּפִינוֹ וַתִּקַּח־לוֹ תֵּבַת גֹּמֶא וַתַּחְמְרָה בַחֵמָר וּבַזָּפֶת וַתָּשֶׂם בָּהּ אֶת־הַיֶּלֶד וַתָּשֶׂם בַּסּוּף עַל־שְׂפַת הַיְאֹר: 4 וַתֵּתַצַּב אֲחֹתוֹ מֵרָחֹק לְדֵעָה מַה־יֵּעָשֶׂה לוֹ: 5 וַתֵּרֶד בַּת־פַּרְעֹה לִרְחֹץ עַל־הַיְאֹר וְנַעֲרֹתֶיהָ הֹלְכֹת עַל־יַד הַיְאֹר וַתֵּרֶא אֶת־הַתֵּבָה בְּתוֹךְ הַסּוּף וַתִּשְׁלַח אֶת־אֲמָתָהּ וַתִּקָּחֶהָ: 6 וַתִּפְתַּח וַתִּרְאֵהוּ אֶת־הַיֶּלֶד וְהִנֵּה־נַעַר בֹּכֶה וַתַּחְמֹל עָלָיו וַתֹּאמֶר מִיַּלְדֵי הָעִבְרִים זֶה: 7 וַתֹּאמֶר אֲחֹתוֹ אֶל־בַּת־פַּרְעֹה הַאֵלֵךְ וְקָרָאתִי לָךְ אִשָּׁה מֵינֶקֶת מִן הָעִבְרִיֹּת וְתֵינִק לָךְ אֶת־הַיָּלֶד: 8 וַתֹּאמֶר־לָהּ בַּת־פַּרְעֹה לֵכִי וַתֵּלֶךְ הָעַלְמָה וַתִּקְרָא אֶת־אֵם הַיָּלֶד: 9 וַתֹּאמֶר לָהּ בַּת־פַּרְעֹה הֵילִיכִי אֶת־הַיֶּלֶד הַזֶּה וְהֵינִקִהוּ לִי וַאֲנִי אֶתֵּן אֶת־שְׂכָרֵךְ וַתִּקַּח הָאִשָּׁה הַיֶּלֶד וַתְּנִיקֵהוּ:

10 וַיִּגְדַּל הַיֶּלֶד וַתְּבִאֵהוּ לְבַת־פַּרְעֹה וַיְהִי־לָהּ לְבֵן וַתִּקְרָא שְׁמוֹ מֹשֶׁה וַתֹּאמֶר כִּי מִן הַמַּיִם מְשִׁיתִהוּ:

11 וַיְהִי ׀ בַּיָּמִים הָהֵם וַיִּגְדַּל מֹשֶׁה וַיֵּצֵא אֶל־אֶחָיו וַיַּרְא בְּסִבְלֹתָם וַיַּרְא אִישׁ מִצְרִי מַכֶּה אִישׁ־עִבְרִי מֵאֶחָיו: 12 וַיִּפֶן כֹּה וָכֹה וַיַּרְא כִּי אֵין אִישׁ וַיַּךְ אֶת־הַמִּצְרִי וַיִּטְמְנֵהוּ בַּחוֹל: 13 וַיֵּצֵא בַּיּוֹם הַשֵּׁנִי וְהִנֵּה שְׁנֵי־אֲנָשִׁים עִבְרִים נִצִּים וַיֹּאמֶר לָרָשָׁע לָמָּה תַכֶּה רֵעֶךָ: 14 וַיֹּאמֶר מִי שָׂמְךָ לְאִישׁ שַׂר וְשֹׁפֵט עָלֵינוּ הַלְהָרְגֵנִי אַתָּה אֹמֵר כַּאֲשֶׁר הָרַגְתָּ אֶת־הַמִּצְרִי

So Moses feared and said, "Surely this thing is known!" 15 When Pharaoh heard of this matter, he sought to kill Moses. But Moses fled from the face of Pharaoh and dwelt in the land of Midian; and he sat down by a well.

16 Now the priest of Midian had seven daughters. And they came and drew water, and they filled the troughs to water their father's flock. 17 Then the shepherds came and drove them away; but Moses stood up and helped them, and watered their flock.

18 When they came to Reuel their father, he said, "How *is it that* you have come so soon today?"

19 And they said, "An Egyptian delivered us from the hand of the shepherds, and he also drew enough water for us and watered the flock."

20 So he said to his daughters, "And where *is* he? Why *is it that* you have left the man? Call him, that he may eat bread."

21 Then Moses was content to live with the man, and he gave Zipporah his daughter to Moses. 22 And she bore *him* a son. He called his name Gershom, for he said, "I have been a stranger in a foreign land."

23 Now it happened in the process of time that the king of Egypt died. Then the children of Israel groaned because of the bondage, and they cried out; and their cry came up to God because of the bondage. 24 So God heard their groaning, and God remembered His covenant with Abraham, with Isaac, and with Jacob. 25 And God looked upon the children of Israel, and God acknowledged *them*.

3 Now Moses was tending the flock of Jethro his father-in-law, the priest of Midian. And he led the flock to the back of the desert, and came to Horeb, the mountain of God. 2 And the Angel of the LORD appeared to him in a flame of fire from the midst of a bush. So he looked, and behold, the bush was burning with fire, but the bush *was* not consumed. 3 Then Moses said, "I will now turn aside and see this great sight, why the bush does not burn."

4 So when the LORD saw that he turned aside to look, God called to him from the midst of the bush and said, "Moses, Moses!"

And he said, "Here I am."

5 Then He said, "Do not draw near this place. Take your sandals off your feet, for the place where you stand *is* holy ground." 6 Moreover He said, "I *am* the God of your father—the God of Abraham, the God of Isaac, and the God of Jacob." And Moses hid his face, for he was afraid to look upon God.

15 וַיִּשְׁמַ֤ע וַיֵּ֥רָא מֹשֶׁ֖ה וַיֹּאמַ֔ר אָכֵ֖ן נוֹדַ֥ע הַדָּבָֽר: פַּרְעֹה֙ אֶת־הַדָּבָ֣ר הַזֶּ֔ה וַיְבַקֵּ֖שׁ לַהֲרֹ֣ג אֶת־מֹשֶׁ֑ה וַיִּבְרַ֤ח מֹשֶׁה֙ מִפְּנֵ֣י פַרְעֹ֔ה וַיֵּ֥שֶׁב בְּאֶֽרֶץ־מִדְיָ֖ן וַיֵּ֥שֶׁב עַֽל־הַבְּאֵֽר: 16 וּלְכֹהֵ֥ן מִדְיָ֖ן שֶׁ֣בַע בָּנ֑וֹת וַתָּבֹ֣אנָה וַתִּדְלֶ֗נָה וַתְּמַלֶּ֙אנָה֙ אֶת־הָ֣רְהָטִ֔ים לְהַשְׁק֖וֹת צֹ֥אן אֲבִיהֶֽן: 17 וַיָּבֹ֥אוּ הָרֹעִ֖ים וַיְגָרְשׁ֑וּם וַיָּ֤קָם מֹשֶׁה֙ וַיּ֣וֹשִׁעָ֔ן וַיַּ֖שְׁקְ אֶת־צֹאנָֽם: 18 וַתָּבֹ֕אנָה אֶל־רְעוּאֵ֖ל אֲבִיהֶ֑ן וַיֹּ֕אמֶר מַדּ֛וּעַ מִהַרְתֶּ֥ן בֹּ֖א הַיּֽוֹם: 19 וַתֹּאמַ֕רְןָ אִ֣ישׁ מִצְרִ֔י הִצִּילָ֖נוּ מִיַּ֣ד הָרֹעִ֑ים וְגַם־דָּלֹ֤ה דָלָה֙ לָ֔נוּ וַיַּ֖שְׁקְ אֶת־הַצֹּֽאן: 20 וַיֹּ֥אמֶר אֶל־בְּנֹתָ֖יו וְאַיּ֑וֹ לָ֤מָּה זֶּה֙ עֲזַבְתֶּ֣ן אֶת־הָאִ֔ישׁ קִרְאֶ֥ן ל֖וֹ וְיֹ֥אכַל לָֽחֶם: 21 וַיּ֥וֹאֶל מֹשֶׁ֖ה לָשֶׁ֣בֶת אֶת־הָאִ֑ישׁ וַיִּתֵּ֛ן אֶת־צִפֹּרָ֥ה בִתּ֖וֹ לְמֹשֶֽׁה: 22 וַתֵּ֣לֶד בֵּ֔ן וַיִּקְרָ֥א אֶת־שְׁמ֖וֹ גֵּרְשֹׁ֑ם כִּ֣י אָמַ֔ר גֵּ֣ר הָיִ֔יתִי בְּאֶ֖רֶץ נָכְרִיָּֽה: פ

23 וַיְהִי֩ בַיָּמִ֨ים הָֽרַבִּ֜ים הָהֵ֗ם וַיָּ֙מָת֙ מֶ֣לֶךְ מִצְרַ֔יִם וַיֵּאָנְח֧וּ בְנֵֽי־יִשְׂרָאֵ֛ל מִן־הָעֲבֹדָ֖ה וַיִּזְעָ֑קוּ וַתַּ֧עַל שַׁוְעָתָ֛ם אֶל־הָאֱלֹהִ֖ים מִן־הָעֲבֹדָֽה: 24 וַיִּשְׁמַ֥ע אֱלֹהִ֖ים אֶת־נַאֲקָתָ֑ם וַיִּזְכֹּ֤ר אֱלֹהִים֙ אֶת־בְּרִית֔וֹ אֶת־אַבְרָהָ֖ם אֶת־יִצְחָ֥ק וְאֶֽת־יַעֲקֹֽב: 25 וַיַּ֥רְא אֱלֹהִ֖ים אֶת־בְּנֵ֣י יִשְׂרָאֵ֑ל וַיֵּ֖דַע אֱלֹהִֽים: ס

ג וּמֹשֶׁ֗ה הָיָ֥ה רֹעֶ֛ה אֶת־צֹ֛אן יִתְר֥וֹ חֹתְנ֖וֹ כֹּהֵ֣ן מִדְיָ֑ן וַיִּנְהַ֤ג אֶת־הַצֹּאן֙ אַחַ֣ר הַמִּדְבָּ֔ר וַיָּבֹ֛א אֶל־הַ֥ר הָאֱלֹהִ֖ים חֹרֵֽבָה: 2 וַ֠יֵּרָא מַלְאַ֨ךְ יְהֹוָ֥ה אֵלָ֛יו בְּלַבַּת־אֵ֖שׁ מִתּ֣וֹךְ הַסְּנֶ֑ה וַיַּ֗רְא וְהִנֵּ֤ה הַסְּנֶה֙ בֹּעֵ֣ר בָּאֵ֔שׁ וְהַסְּנֶ֖ה אֵינֶ֥נּוּ אֻכָּֽל: 3 וַיֹּ֣אמֶר מֹשֶׁ֔ה אָסֻֽרָה־נָּ֣א וְאֶרְאֶ֔ה אֶת־הַמַּרְאֶ֥ה הַגָּדֹ֖ל הַזֶּ֑ה מַדּ֖וּעַ לֹא־יִבְעַ֥ר הַסְּנֶֽה: 4 וַיַּ֥רְא יְהֹוָ֖ה כִּ֣י סָ֣ר לִרְא֑וֹת וַיִּקְרָא֩ אֵלָ֨יו אֱלֹהִ֜ים מִתּ֣וֹךְ הַסְּנֶ֗ה וַיֹּ֛אמֶר מֹשֶׁ֥ה מֹשֶׁ֖ה וַיֹּ֥אמֶר הִנֵּֽנִי: 5 וַיֹּ֖אמֶר אַל־תִּקְרַ֣ב הֲלֹ֑ם שַׁל־נְעָלֶ֙יךָ֙ מֵעַ֣ל רַגְלֶ֔יךָ כִּ֣י הַמָּק֗וֹם אֲשֶׁ֤ר אַתָּה֙ עוֹמֵ֣ד עָלָ֔יו אַדְמַת־קֹ֖דֶשׁ הֽוּא: 6 וַיֹּ֗אמֶר אָנֹכִי֙ אֱלֹהֵ֣י אָבִ֔יךָ אֱלֹהֵ֧י אַבְרָהָ֛ם אֱלֹהֵ֥י יִצְחָ֖ק וֵאלֹהֵ֣י יַעֲקֹ֑ב וַיַּסְתֵּ֤ר

7 And the LORD said: "I have surely seen the oppression of My people who *are* in Egypt, and have heard their cry because of their taskmasters, for I know their sorrows. 8 So I have come down to deliver them out of the hand of the Egyptians, and to bring them up from that land to a good and large land, to a land flowing with milk and honey, to the place of the Canaanites and the Hittites and the Amorites and the Perizzites and the Hivites and the Jebusites. 9 Now therefore, behold, the cry of the children of Israel has come to Me, and I have also seen the oppression with which the Egyptians oppress them. 10 Come now, therefore, and I will send you to Pharaoh that you may bring My people, the children of Israel, out of Egypt."

11 But Moses said to God, "Who *am* I that I should go to Pharaoh, and that I should bring the children of Israel out of Egypt?"

12 So He said, "I will certainly be with you. And this *shall be* a sign to you that I have sent you: When you have brought the people out of Egypt, you shall serve God on this mountain."

13 Then Moses said to God, "Indeed, *when* I come to the children of Israel and say to them, 'The God of your fathers has sent me to you,' and they say to me, 'What *is* His name?' what shall I say to them?"

14 And God said to Moses, "I AM WHO I AM." And He said, "Thus you shall say to the children of Israel, 'I AM has sent me to you.'" 15 Moreover God said to Moses, "Thus you shall say to the children of Israel: 'The LORD God of your fathers, the God of Abraham, the God of Isaac, and the God of Jacob, has sent me to you. This *is* My name forever, and this *is* My memorial to all generations.' 16 Go and gather the elders of Israel together, and say to them, 'The LORD God of your fathers, the God of Abraham, of Isaac, and of Jacob, appeared to me, saying, "I have surely visited you and *seen* what is done to you in Egypt; 17 and I have said I will bring you up out of the affliction of Egypt to the land of the Canaanites and the Hittites and the Amorites and the Perizzites and the Hivites and the Jebusites, to a land flowing with milk and honey."' 18 Then they will heed your voice; and you shall come, you and the elders of Israel, to the king of Egypt; and you shall say to him, 'The LORD God of the Hebrews has met with us; and now, please, let us go three days' journey into the wilderness, that we may sacrifice to the LORD our God.' 19 But I am sure that the king of Egypt will not let you go, no, not even by a mighty hand. 20 So I will stretch out My hand and strike Egypt with all My wonders which I will do in its midst; and after that he will let

7 וַיֹּאמֶר מֹשֶׁה פָּנָיו כִּי יָרֵא מֵהַבִּיט אֶל־הָאֱלֹהִים:
יְהֹוָה רָאֹה רָאִיתִי אֶת־עֳנִי עַמִּי אֲשֶׁר בְּמִצְרָיִם
וְאֶת־צַעֲקָתָם שָׁמַעְתִּי מִפְּנֵי נֹגְשָׂיו כִּי יָדַעְתִּי אֶת־
מַכְאֹבָיו: 8 וָאֵרֵד לְהַצִּילוֹ ׀ מִיַּד מִצְרַיִם וּלְהַעֲלֹתוֹ
מִן־הָאָרֶץ הַהִוא אֶל־אֶרֶץ טוֹבָה וּרְחָבָה אֶל־אֶרֶץ
זָבַת חָלָב וּדְבָשׁ אֶל־מְקוֹם הַכְּנַעֲנִי וְהַחִתִּי וְהָאֱמֹרִי
וְהַפְּרִזִּי וְהַחִוִּי וְהַיְבוּסִי: 9 וְעַתָּה הִנֵּה צַעֲקַת בְּנֵי־
יִשְׂרָאֵל בָּאָה אֵלָי וְגַם־רָאִיתִי אֶת־הַלַּחַץ אֲשֶׁר
מִצְרַיִם לֹחֲצִים אֹתָם: 10 וְעַתָּה לְכָה וְאֶשְׁלָחֲךָ
אֶל־פַּרְעֹה וְהוֹצֵא אֶת־עַמִּי בְנֵי־יִשְׂרָאֵל מִמִּצְרָיִם:

11 וַיֹּאמֶר מֹשֶׁה אֶל־הָאֱלֹהִים מִי אָנֹכִי כִּי אֵלֵךְ
אֶל־פַּרְעֹה וְכִי אוֹצִיא אֶת־בְּנֵי יִשְׂרָאֵל מִמִּצְרָיִם:

12 וַיֹּאמֶר כִּי־אֶהְיֶה עִמָּךְ וְזֶה־לְּךָ הָאוֹת כִּי אָנֹכִי
שְׁלַחְתִּיךָ בְּהוֹצִיאֲךָ אֶת־הָעָם מִמִּצְרַיִם תַּעַבְדוּן
אֶת־הָאֱלֹהִים עַל הָהָר הַזֶּה: 13 וַיֹּאמֶר מֹשֶׁה אֶל־
הָאֱלֹהִים הִנֵּה אָנֹכִי בָא אֶל־בְּנֵי יִשְׂרָאֵל וְאָמַרְתִּי
לָהֶם אֱלֹהֵי אֲבוֹתֵיכֶם שְׁלָחַנִי אֲלֵיכֶם וְאָמְרוּ־לִי
מַה־שְּׁמוֹ מָה אֹמַר אֲלֵהֶם: 14 וַיֹּאמֶר אֱלֹהִים
אֶל־מֹשֶׁה אֶהְיֶה אֲשֶׁר אֶהְיֶה וַיֹּאמֶר כֹּה תֹאמַר
לִבְנֵי יִשְׂרָאֵל אֶהְיֶה שְׁלָחַנִי אֲלֵיכֶם: 15 וַיֹּאמֶר עוֹד
אֱלֹהִים אֶל־מֹשֶׁה כֹּה־תֹאמַר אֶל־בְּנֵי יִשְׂרָאֵל יְהֹוָה
אֱלֹהֵי אֲבֹתֵיכֶם אֱלֹהֵי אַבְרָהָם אֱלֹהֵי יִצְחָק וֵאלֹהֵי
יַעֲקֹב שְׁלָחַנִי אֲלֵיכֶם זֶה־שְּׁמִי לְעֹלָם וְזֶה זִכְרִי
לְדֹר דֹּר: 16 לֵךְ וְאָסַפְתָּ אֶת־זִקְנֵי יִשְׂרָאֵל וְאָמַרְתָּ
אֲלֵהֶם יְהֹוָה אֱלֹהֵי אֲבֹתֵיכֶם נִרְאָה אֵלַי אֱלֹהֵי
אַבְרָהָם יִצְחָק וְיַעֲקֹב לֵאמֹר פָּקֹד פָּקַדְתִּי אֶתְכֶם
וְאֶת־הֶעָשׂוּי לָכֶם בְּמִצְרָיִם: 17 וָאֹמַר אַעֲלֶה אֶתְכֶם
מֵעֳנִי מִצְרַיִם אֶל־אֶרֶץ הַכְּנַעֲנִי וְהַחִתִּי וְהָאֱמֹרִי
וְהַפְּרִזִּי וְהַחִוִּי וְהַיְבוּסִי אֶל־אֶרֶץ זָבַת חָלָב וּדְבָשׁ:

18 וְשָׁמְעוּ לְקֹלֶךָ וּבָאתָ אַתָּה וְזִקְנֵי יִשְׂרָאֵל אֶל־
מֶלֶךְ מִצְרַיִם וַאֲמַרְתֶּם אֵלָיו יְהֹוָה אֱלֹהֵי הָעִבְרִיִּים
נִקְרָה עָלֵינוּ וְעַתָּה נֵלֲכָה־נָּא דֶּרֶךְ שְׁלֹשֶׁת יָמִים
בַּמִּדְבָּר וְנִזְבְּחָה לַיהֹוָה אֱלֹהֵינוּ: 19 וַאֲנִי יָדַעְתִּי
כִּי לֹא־יִתֵּן אֶתְכֶם מֶלֶךְ מִצְרַיִם לַהֲלֹךְ וְלֹא בְּיָד
חֲזָקָה: 20 וְשָׁלַחְתִּי אֶת־יָדִי וְהִכֵּיתִי אֶת־מִצְרַיִם
בְּכֹל נִפְלְאֹתַי אֲשֶׁר אֶעֱשֶׂה בְּקִרְבּוֹ וְאַחֲרֵי־כֵן יְשַׁלַּח

you go. ²¹ And I will give this people favor in the sight of the Egyptians; and it shall be, when you go, that you shall not go empty-handed. ²² But every woman shall ask of her neighbor, namely, of her who dwells near her house, articles of silver, articles of gold, and clothing; and you shall put *them* on your sons and on your daughters. So you shall plunder the Egyptians."

4 Then Moses answered and said, "But suppose they will not believe me or listen to my voice; suppose they say, 'The LORD has not appeared to you.'"

² So the LORD said to him, "What *is* that in your hand?"

He said, "A rod."

³ And He said, "Cast it on the ground." So he cast it on the ground, and it became a serpent; and Moses fled from it. ⁴ Then the LORD said to Moses, "Reach out your hand and take *it* by the tail" (and he reached out his hand and caught it, and it became a rod in his hand), ⁵ "that they may believe that the LORD God of their fathers, the God of Abraham, the God of Isaac, and the God of Jacob, has appeared to you."

⁶ Furthermore the LORD said to him, "Now put your hand in your bosom." And he put his hand in his bosom, and when he took it out, behold, his hand *was* leprous, like snow. ⁷ And He said, "Put your hand in your bosom again." So he put his hand in his bosom again, and drew it out of his bosom, and behold, it was restored like his *other* flesh. ⁸ "Then it will be, if they do not believe you, nor heed the message of the first sign, that they may believe the message of the latter sign. ⁹ And it shall be, if they do not believe even these two signs, or listen to your voice, that you shall take water from the river and pour *it* on the dry *land*. The water which you take from the river will become blood on the dry *land*."

¹⁰ Then Moses said to the LORD, "O my Lord, I *am* not eloquent, neither before nor since You have spoken to Your servant; but I *am* slow of speech and slow of tongue."

¹¹ So the LORD said to him, "Who has made man's mouth? Or who makes the mute, the deaf, the seeing, or the blind? *Have* not I, the LORD? ¹² Now therefore, go, and I will be with your mouth and teach you what you shall say."

¹³ But he said, "O my Lord, please send by the hand of whomever *else* You may send."

¹⁴ So the anger of the LORD was kindled against Moses, and He said: "Is not Aaron the Levite your brother? I know that he can speak well. And look,

אֶתְכֶם: 21 וְנָתַתִּי אֶת־חֵן הָעָם־הַזֶּה בְּעֵינֵי מִצְרָיִם וְהָיָה כִּי תֵלֵכוּן לֹא תֵלְכוּ רֵיקָם: 22 וְשָׁאֲלָה אִשָּׁה מִשְּׁכֶנְתָּהּ וּמִגָּרַת בֵּיתָהּ כְּלֵי־כֶסֶף וּכְלֵי זָהָב וּשְׂמָלֹת וְשַׂמְתֶּם עַל־בְּנֵיכֶם וְעַל־בְּנֹתֵיכֶם וְנִצַּלְתֶּם אֶת־מִצְרָיִם:

ד וַיַּעַן מֹשֶׁה וַיֹּאמֶר וְהֵן לֹא־יַאֲמִינוּ לִי וְלֹא יִשְׁמְעוּ בְּקֹלִי כִּי יֹאמְרוּ לֹא־נִרְאָה אֵלֶיךָ יְהוָה: 2 וַיֹּאמֶר אֵלָיו יְהוָה מַזֶּה בְיָדֶךָ וַיֹּאמֶר מַטֶּה: 3 וַיֹּאמֶר הַשְׁלִיכֵהוּ אַרְצָה וַיַּשְׁלִיכֵהוּ אַרְצָה וַיְהִי לְנָחָשׁ וַיָּנָס מֹשֶׁה מִפָּנָיו: 4 וַיֹּאמֶר יְהוָה אֶל־מֹשֶׁה שְׁלַח יָדְךָ וֶאֱחֹז בִּזְנָבוֹ וַיִּשְׁלַח יָדוֹ וַיַּחֲזֶק בּוֹ וַיְהִי לְמַטֶּה בְּכַפּוֹ: 5 לְמַעַן יַאֲמִינוּ כִּי־נִרְאָה אֵלֶיךָ יְהוָה אֱלֹהֵי אֲבֹתָם אֱלֹהֵי אַבְרָהָם אֱלֹהֵי יִצְחָק וֵאלֹהֵי יַעֲקֹב: 6 וַיֹּאמֶר יְהוָה לוֹ עוֹד הָבֵא־נָא יָדְךָ בְּחֵיקֶךָ וַיָּבֵא יָדוֹ בְּחֵיקוֹ וַיּוֹצִאָהּ וְהִנֵּה יָדוֹ מְצֹרַעַת כַּשָּׁלֶג: 7 וַיֹּאמֶר הָשֵׁב יָדְךָ אֶל־חֵיקֶךָ וַיָּשֶׁב יָדוֹ אֶל־חֵיקוֹ וַיּוֹצִאָהּ מֵחֵיקוֹ וְהִנֵּה־שָׁבָה כִּבְשָׂרוֹ: 8 וְהָיָה אִם־לֹא יַאֲמִינוּ לָךְ וְלֹא יִשְׁמְעוּ לְקֹל הָאֹת הָרִאשׁוֹן וְהֶאֱמִינוּ לְקֹל הָאֹת הָאַחֲרוֹן: 9 וְהָיָה אִם־לֹא יַאֲמִינוּ גַּם לִשְׁנֵי הָאֹתוֹת הָאֵלֶּה וְלֹא יִשְׁמְעוּן לְקֹלֶךָ וְלָקַחְתָּ מִמֵּימֵי הַיְאֹר וְשָׁפַכְתָּ הַיַּבָּשָׁה וְהָיוּ הַמַּיִם אֲשֶׁר תִּקַּח מִן־הַיְאֹר וְהָיוּ לְדָם בַּיַּבָּשֶׁת: 10 וַיֹּאמֶר מֹשֶׁה אֶל־יְהוָה בִּי אֲדֹנָי לֹא אִישׁ דְּבָרִים אָנֹכִי גַּם מִתְּמוֹל גַּם מִשִּׁלְשֹׁם גַּם מֵאָז דַּבֶּרְךָ אֶל־עַבְדֶּךָ כִּי כְבַד־פֶּה וּכְבַד לָשׁוֹן אָנֹכִי: 11 וַיֹּאמֶר יְהוָה אֵלָיו מִי שָׂם פֶּה לָאָדָם אוֹ מִי־יָשׂוּם אִלֵּם אוֹ חֵרֵשׁ אוֹ פִקֵּחַ אוֹ עִוֵּר הֲלֹא אָנֹכִי יְהוָה: 12 וְעַתָּה לֵךְ וְאָנֹכִי אֶהְיֶה עִם־פִּיךָ וְהוֹרֵיתִיךָ אֲשֶׁר תְּדַבֵּר: 13 וַיֹּאמֶר בִּי אֲדֹנָי שְׁלַח־נָא בְּיַד־תִּשְׁלָח: 14 וַיִּחַר־אַף יְהוָה בְּמֹשֶׁה וַיֹּאמֶר הֲלֹא אַהֲרֹן אָחִיךָ הַלֵּוִי יָדַעְתִּי כִּי־דַבֵּר יְדַבֵּר הוּא וְגַם הִנֵּה־הוּא יֹצֵא לִקְרָאתֶךָ וְרָאֲךָ

he is also coming out to meet you. When he sees you, he will be glad in his heart. 15 Now you shall speak to him and put the words in his mouth. And I will be with your mouth and with his mouth, and I will teach you what you shall do. 16 So he shall be your spokesman to the people. And he himself shall be as a mouth for you, and you shall be to him as God. 17 And you shall take this rod in your hand, with which you shall do the signs."

18 So Moses went and returned to Jethro his father-in-law, and said to him, "Please let me go and return to my brethren who *are* in Egypt, and see whether they are still alive."

And Jethro said to Moses, "Go in peace."

19 Now the LORD said to Moses in Midian, "Go, return to Egypt; for all the men who sought your life are dead." 20 Then Moses took his wife and his sons and set them on a donkey, and he returned to the land of Egypt. And Moses took the rod of God in his hand.

21 And the LORD said to Moses, "When you go back to Egypt, see that you do all those wonders before Pharaoh which I have put in your hand. But I will harden his heart, so that he will not let the people go. 22 Then you shall say to Pharaoh, 'Thus says the LORD: "Israel *is* My son, My firstborn. 23 So I say to you, let My son go that he may serve Me. But if you refuse to let him go, indeed I will kill your son, your firstborn."'"

24 And it came to pass on the way, at the encampment, that the LORD met him and sought to kill him. 25 Then Zipporah took a sharp stone and cut off the foreskin of her son and cast *it* at *Moses'* feet, and said, "Surely you *are* a husband of blood to me!" 26 So He let him go. Then she said, "*You are* a husband of blood!"—because of the circumcision.

27 And the LORD said to Aaron, "Go into the wilderness to meet Moses." So he went and met him on the mountain of God, and kissed him. 28 So Moses told Aaron all the words of the LORD who had sent him, and all the signs which He had commanded him. 29 Then Moses and Aaron went and gathered together all the elders of the children of Israel. 30 And Aaron spoke all the words which the LORD had spoken to Moses. Then he did the signs in the sight of the people. 31 So the people believed; and when they heard that the LORD had visited the children of Israel and that He had looked on their affliction, then they bowed their heads and worshiped.

15 וְדִבַּרְתָּ֣ אֵלָ֔יו וְשַׂמְתָּ֥ אֶת־הַדְּבָרִ֖ים בְּפִ֑יו וְאָנֹכִ֗י אֶהְיֶ֤ה עִם־פִּ֙יךָ֙ וְעִם־פִּ֔יהוּ וְהוֹרֵיתִ֣י אֶתְכֶ֔ם אֵ֖ת אֲשֶׁ֥ר תַּעֲשֽׂוּן׃ 16 וְדִבֶּר־ה֥וּא לְךָ֖ אֶל־הָעָ֑ם וְהָ֤יָה הוּא֙ יִֽהְיֶה־לְּךָ֣ לְפֶ֔ה וְאַתָּ֖ה תִּֽהְיֶה־לּ֥וֹ לֵֽאלֹהִֽים׃ 17 וְאֶת־הַמַּטֶּ֥ה הַזֶּ֖ה תִּקַּ֣ח בְּיָדֶ֑ךָ אֲשֶׁ֥ר תַּעֲשֶׂה־בּ֖וֹ אֶת־הָאֹתֹֽת׃ פ

18 וַיֵּ֨לֶךְ מֹשֶׁ֜ה וַיָּ֣שָׁב ׀ אֶל־יֶ֣תֶר חֹֽתְנ֗וֹ וַיֹּ֤אמֶר לוֹ֙ אֵ֣לְכָה נָּ֗א וְאָשׁ֙וּבָה֙ אֶל־אַחַ֣י אֲשֶׁר־בְּמִצְרַ֔יִם וְאֶרְאֶ֖ה הַעוֹדָ֣ם חַיִּ֑ים וַיֹּ֧אמֶר יִתְר֛וֹ לְמֹשֶׁ֖ה לֵ֥ךְ לְשָׁלֽוֹם׃ 19 וַיֹּ֨אמֶר יְהוָ֤ה אֶל־מֹשֶׁה֙ בְּמִדְיָ֔ן לֵ֖ךְ שֻׁ֣ב מִצְרָ֑יִם כִּי־מֵ֙תוּ֙ כָּל־הָ֣אֲנָשִׁ֔ים הַֽמְבַקְשִׁ֖ים אֶת־נַפְשֶֽׁךָ׃ 20 וַיִּקַּ֨ח מֹשֶׁ֜ה אֶת־אִשְׁתּ֣וֹ וְאֶת־בָּנָ֗יו וַיַּרְכִּבֵם֙ עַֽל־הַחֲמֹ֔ר וַיָּ֖שָׁב אַ֣רְצָה מִצְרָ֑יִם וַיִּקַּ֥ח מֹשֶׁ֛ה אֶת־מַטֵּ֥ה הָאֱלֹהִ֖ים בְּיָדֽוֹ׃ 21 וַיֹּ֣אמֶר יְהוָה֮ אֶל־מֹשֶׁה֒ בְּלֶכְתְּךָ֙ לָשׁ֣וּב מִצְרַ֔יְמָה רְאֵ֗ה כָּל־הַמֹּֽפְתִים֙ אֲשֶׁר־שַׂ֣מְתִּי בְיָדֶ֔ךָ וַעֲשִׂיתָ֖ם לִפְנֵ֣י פַרְעֹ֑ה וַאֲנִי֙ אֲחַזֵּ֣ק אֶת־לִבּ֔וֹ וְלֹ֥א יְשַׁלַּ֖ח אֶת־הָעָֽם׃ 22 וְאָמַרְתָּ֖ אֶל־פַּרְעֹ֑ה כֹּ֚ה אָמַ֣ר יְהוָ֔ה בְּנִ֥י בְכֹרִ֖י יִשְׂרָאֵֽל׃ 23 וָאֹמַ֣ר אֵלֶ֗יךָ שַׁלַּ֤ח אֶת־בְּנִי֙ וְיַֽעַבְדֵ֔נִי וַתְּמָאֵ֖ן לְשַׁלְּח֑וֹ הִנֵּה֙ אָנֹכִ֣י הֹרֵ֔ג אֶת־בִּנְךָ֖ בְּכֹרֶֽךָ׃ 24 וַיְהִ֥י בַדֶּ֖רֶךְ בַּמָּל֑וֹן וַיִּפְגְּשֵׁ֣הוּ יְהוָ֔ה וַיְבַקֵּ֖שׁ הֲמִיתֽוֹ׃ 25 וַתִּקַּ֨ח צִפֹּרָ֜ה צֹ֗ר וַתִּכְרֹת֙ אֶת־עָרְלַ֣ת בְּנָ֔הּ וַתַּגַּ֖ע לְרַגְלָ֑יו וַתֹּ֕אמֶר כִּ֧י חֲתַן־דָּמִ֛ים אַתָּ֖ה לִֽי׃ 26 וַיִּ֖רֶף מִמֶּ֑נּוּ אָ֚ז אָֽמְרָ֔ה חֲתַ֥ן דָּמִ֖ים לַמּוּלֹֽת׃ פ

27 וַיֹּ֤אמֶר יְהוָה֙ אֶֽל־אַהֲרֹ֔ן לֵ֛ךְ לִקְרַ֥את מֹשֶׁ֖ה הַמִּדְבָּ֑רָה וַיֵּ֗לֶךְ וַֽיִּפְגְּשֵׁ֛הוּ בְּהַ֥ר הָאֱלֹהִ֖ים וַיִּשַּׁק־לֽוֹ׃ 28 וַיַּגֵּ֤ד מֹשֶׁה֙ לְאַֽהֲרֹ֔ן אֵ֚ת כָּל־דִּבְרֵ֣י יְהוָ֔ה אֲשֶׁ֣ר שְׁלָח֑וֹ וְאֵ֥ת כָּל־הָאֹתֹ֖ת אֲשֶׁ֥ר צִוָּֽהוּ׃ 29 וַיֵּ֥לֶךְ מֹשֶׁ֖ה וְאַהֲרֹ֑ן וַיַּ֣אַסְפ֔וּ אֶת־כָּל־זִקְנֵ֖י בְּנֵ֥י יִשְׂרָאֵֽל׃ 30 וַיְדַבֵּ֣ר אַהֲרֹ֔ן אֵ֚ת כָּל־הַדְּבָרִ֔ים אֲשֶׁר־דִּבֶּ֥ר יְהוָ֖ה אֶל־מֹשֶׁ֑ה וַיַּ֥עַשׂ הָאֹתֹ֖ת לְעֵינֵ֥י הָעָֽם׃ 31 וַֽיַּאֲמֵ֖ן הָעָ֑ם וַֽיִּשְׁמְע֡וּ כִּֽי־פָקַ֨ד יְהוָ֜ה אֶת־בְּנֵ֣י יִשְׂרָאֵ֗ל וְכִ֤י רָאָה֙ אֶת־עָנְיָ֔ם וַֽיִּקְּד֖וּ וַיִּֽשְׁתַּחֲוֽוּ׃

5 Afterward Moses and Aaron went in and told Pharaoh, "Thus says the LORD God of Israel: 'Let My people go, that they may hold a feast to Me in the wilderness.'"

² And Pharaoh said, "Who *is* the LORD, that I should obey His voice to let Israel go? I do not know the LORD, nor will I let Israel go."

³ So they said, "The God of the Hebrews has met with us. Please, let us go three days' journey into the desert and sacrifice to the LORD our God, lest He fall upon us with pestilence or with the sword."

⁴ Then the king of Egypt said to them, "Moses and Aaron, why do you take the people from their work? Get *back* to your labor." ⁵ And Pharaoh said, "Look, the people of the land *are* many now, and you make them rest from their labor!"

⁶ So the same day Pharaoh commanded the taskmasters of the people and their officers, saying, ⁷ "You shall no longer give the people straw to make brick as before. Let them go and gather straw for themselves. ⁸ And you shall lay on them the quota of bricks which they made before. You shall not reduce it. For they are idle; therefore they cry out, saying, 'Let us go *and* sacrifice to our God.' ⁹ Let more work be laid on the men, that they may labor in it, and let them not regard false words."

¹⁰ And the taskmasters of the people and their officers went out and spoke to the people, saying, "Thus says Pharaoh: 'I will not give you straw. ¹¹ Go, get yourselves straw where you can find it; yet none of your work will be reduced.'" ¹² So the people were scattered abroad throughout all the land of Egypt to gather stubble instead of straw. ¹³ And the taskmasters forced *them* to hurry, saying, "Fulfill your work, *your* daily quota, as when there was straw." ¹⁴ Also the officers of the children of Israel, whom Pharaoh's taskmasters had set over them, were beaten *and* were asked, "Why have you not fulfilled your task in making brick both yesterday and today, as before?"

¹⁵ Then the officers of the children of Israel came and cried out to Pharaoh, saying, "Why are you dealing thus with your servants? ¹⁶ There is no straw given to your servants, and they say to us, 'Make brick!' And indeed your servants *are* beaten, but the fault *is* in your *own* people."

¹⁷ But he said, "You *are* idle! Idle! Therefore you say, 'Let us go *and* sacrifice to the LORD.' ¹⁸ Therefore go now *and* work; for no straw shall be given you, yet you shall deliver the quota of bricks."

¹⁹ And the officers of the children of Israel saw *that* they *were* in trouble after it was said, "You shall not reduce *any* bricks from your daily quota."

ה וְאַחַר בָּאוּ מֹשֶׁה וְאַהֲרֹן וַיֹּאמְרוּ אֶל־פַּרְעֹה כֹּה־אָמַר יְהֹוָה אֱלֹהֵי יִשְׂרָאֵל שַׁלַּח אֶת־עַמִּי וְיָחֹגּוּ לִי בַּמִּדְבָּר: 2 וַיֹּאמֶר פַּרְעֹה מִי יְהֹוָה אֲשֶׁר אֶשְׁמַע בְּקֹלוֹ לְשַׁלַּח אֶת־יִשְׂרָאֵל לֹא יָדַעְתִּי אֶת־יְהֹוָה וְגַם אֶת־יִשְׂרָאֵל לֹא אֲשַׁלֵּחַ: 3 וַיֹּאמְרוּ אֱלֹהֵי הָעִבְרִים נִקְרָא עָלֵינוּ נֵלְכָה נָּא דֶּרֶךְ שְׁלֹשֶׁת יָמִים בַּמִּדְבָּר וְנִזְבְּחָה לַיהֹוָה אֱלֹהֵינוּ פֶּן־יִפְגָּעֵנוּ בַּדֶּבֶר אוֹ בֶחָרֶב: 4 וַיֹּאמֶר אֲלֵהֶם מֶלֶךְ מִצְרַיִם לָמָּה מֹשֶׁה וְאַהֲרֹן תַּפְרִיעוּ אֶת־הָעָם מִמַּעֲשָׂיו לְכוּ לְסִבְלֹתֵיכֶם: 5 וַיֹּאמֶר פַּרְעֹה הֵן־רַבִּים עַתָּה עַם הָאָרֶץ וְהִשְׁבַּתֶּם אֹתָם מִסִּבְלֹתָם: 6 וַיְצַו פַּרְעֹה בַּיּוֹם הַהוּא אֶת־הַנֹּגְשִׂים בָּעָם וְאֶת־שֹׁטְרָיו לֵאמֹר:

7 לֹא תֹאסִפוּן לָתֵת תֶּבֶן לָעָם לִלְבֹּן הַלְּבֵנִים כִּתְמוֹל שִׁלְשֹׁם הֵם יֵלְכוּ וְקֹשְׁשׁוּ לָהֶם תֶּבֶן:

8 וְאֶת־מַתְכֹּנֶת הַלְּבֵנִים אֲשֶׁר הֵם עֹשִׂים תְּמוֹל שִׁלְשֹׁם תָּשִׂימוּ עֲלֵיהֶם לֹא תִגְרְעוּ מִמֶּנּוּ כִּי־נִרְפִּים הֵם עַל־כֵּן הֵם צֹעֲקִים לֵאמֹר נֵלְכָה נִזְבְּחָה לֵאלֹהֵינוּ: 9 תִּכְבַּד הָעֲבֹדָה עַל־הָאֲנָשִׁים וְיַעֲשׂוּ־בָהּ וְאַל־יִשְׁעוּ בְּדִבְרֵי־שָׁקֶר: 10 וַיֵּצְאוּ נֹגְשֵׂי הָעָם וְשֹׁטְרָיו וַיֹּאמְרוּ אֶל־הָעָם לֵאמֹר כֹּה אָמַר פַּרְעֹה אֵינֶנִּי נֹתֵן לָכֶם תֶּבֶן: 11 אַתֶּם לְכוּ קְחוּ לָכֶם תֶּבֶן מֵאֲשֶׁר תִּמְצָאוּ כִּי אֵין נִגְרָע מֵעֲבֹדַתְכֶם דָּבָר: 12 וַיָּפֶץ הָעָם בְּכָל־אֶרֶץ מִצְרָיִם לְקֹשֵׁשׁ קַשׁ לַתֶּבֶן:

13 וְהַנֹּגְשִׂים אָצִים לֵאמֹר כַּלּוּ מַעֲשֵׂיכֶם דְּבַר־יוֹם בְּיוֹמוֹ כַּאֲשֶׁר בִּהְיוֹת הַתֶּבֶן: 14 וַיֻּכּוּ שֹׁטְרֵי בְּנֵי יִשְׂרָאֵל אֲשֶׁר־שָׂמוּ עֲלֵהֶם נֹגְשֵׂי פַרְעֹה לֵאמֹר מַדּוּעַ לֹא כִלִּיתֶם חָקְכֶם לִלְבֹּן כִּתְמוֹל שִׁלְשֹׁם גַּם־תְּמוֹל גַּם־הַיּוֹם: 15 וַיָּבֹאוּ שֹׁטְרֵי בְּנֵי יִשְׂרָאֵל וַיִּצְעֲקוּ אֶל־פַּרְעֹה לֵאמֹר לָמָּה תַעֲשֶׂה כֹה לַעֲבָדֶיךָ: 16 תֶּבֶן אֵין נִתָּן לַעֲבָדֶיךָ וּלְבֵנִים אֹמְרִים לָנוּ עֲשׂוּ וְהִנֵּה עֲבָדֶיךָ מֻכִּים וְחָטָאת עַמֶּךָ: 17 וַיֹּאמֶר נִרְפִּים אַתֶּם נִרְפִּים עַל־כֵּן אַתֶּם אֹמְרִים נֵלְכָה נִזְבְּחָה לַיהֹוָה: 18 וְעַתָּה לְכוּ עִבְדוּ וְתֶבֶן לֹא־יִנָּתֵן לָכֶם וְתֹכֶן לְבֵנִים תִּתֵּנּוּ: 19 וַיִּרְאוּ שֹׁטְרֵי בְנֵי־יִשְׂרָאֵל אֹתָם בְּרָע לֵאמֹר לֹא־תִגְרְעוּ מִלִּבְנֵיכֶם דְּבַר־יוֹם בְּיוֹמוֹ:

20 Then, as they came out from Pharaoh, they met Moses and Aaron who stood there to meet them. 21 And they said to them, "Let the LORD look on you and judge, because you have made us abhorrent in the sight of Pharaoh and in the sight of his servants, to put a sword in their hand to kill us."

22 So Moses returned to the LORD and said, "Lord, why have You brought trouble on this people? Why *is* it You have sent me? 23 For since I came to Pharaoh to speak in Your name, he has done evil to this people; neither have You delivered Your people at all."

6 Then the LORD said to Moses, "Now you shall see what I will do to Pharaoh. For with a strong hand he will let them go, and with a strong hand he will drive them out of his land."

2 And God spoke to Moses and said to him: "I *am* the LORD. 3 I appeared to Abraham, to Isaac, and to Jacob, as God Almighty, but *by* My name LORD I was not known to them. 4 I have also established My covenant with them, to give them the land of Canaan, the land of their pilgrimage, in which they were strangers. 5 And I have also heard the groaning of the children of Israel whom the Egyptians keep in bondage, and I have remembered My covenant. 6 Therefore say to the children of Israel: 'I *am* the LORD; I will bring you out from under the burdens of the Egyptians, I will rescue you from their bondage, and I will redeem you with an outstretched arm and with great judgments. 7 I will take you as My people, and I will be your God. Then you shall know that I *am* the LORD your God who brings you out from under the burdens of the Egyptians. 8 And I will bring you into the land which I swore to give to Abraham, Isaac, and Jacob; and I will give it to you *as* a heritage: I *am* the LORD.' " 9 So Moses spoke thus to the children of Israel; but they did not heed Moses, because of anguish of spirit and cruel bondage.

10 And the LORD spoke to Moses, saying, 11 "Go in, tell Pharaoh king of Egypt to let the children of Israel go out of his land."

12 And Moses spoke before the LORD, saying, "The children of Israel have not heeded me. How then shall Pharaoh heed me, for I *am* of uncircumcised lips?"

13 Then the LORD spoke to Moses and Aaron, and gave them a command for the children of Israel and for Pharaoh king of Egypt, to bring the children of Israel out of the land of Egypt.

14 These *are* the heads of their fathers' houses: The sons of Reuben, the firstborn of Israel, *were* Hanoch, Pallu, Hezron, and Carmi. These are the

20 וַיִּפְגְּעוּ אֶת־מֹשֶׁה וְאֶת־אַהֲרֹן נִצָּבִים לִקְרָאתָם בְּצֵאתָם מֵאֵת פַּרְעֹה: 21 וַיֹּאמְרוּ אֲלֵהֶם יֵרֶא יְהוָה עֲלֵיכֶם וְיִשְׁפֹּט אֲשֶׁר הִבְאַשְׁתֶּם אֶת־רֵיחֵנוּ בְּעֵינֵי פַרְעֹה וּבְעֵינֵי עֲבָדָיו לָתֶת־חֶרֶב בְּיָדָם לְהָרְגֵנוּ: 22 וַיָּשָׁב מֹשֶׁה אֶל־יְהוָה וַיֹּאמַר אֲדֹנָי לָמָה הֲרֵעֹתָה לָעָם הַזֶּה לָמָה זֶּה שְׁלַחְתָּנִי: 23 וּמֵאָז בָּאתִי אֶל־פַּרְעֹה לְדַבֵּר בִּשְׁמֶךָ הֵרַע לָעָם הַזֶּה וְהַצֵּל לֹא־הִצַּלְתָּ אֶת־עַמֶּךָ:

ו וַיֹּאמֶר יְהוָה אֶל־מֹשֶׁה עַתָּה תִרְאֶה אֲשֶׁר אֶעֱשֶׂה לְפַרְעֹה כִּי בְיָד חֲזָקָה יְשַׁלְּחֵם וּבְיָד חֲזָקָה יְגָרְשֵׁם מֵאַרְצוֹ: ס 2 וַיְדַבֵּר אֱלֹהִים אֶל־מֹשֶׁה וַיֹּאמֶר אֵלָיו אֲנִי יְהוָה: 3 וָאֵרָא אֶל־אַבְרָהָם אֶל־יִצְחָק וְאֶל־יַעֲקֹב בְּאֵל שַׁדָּי וּשְׁמִי יְהוָה לֹא נוֹדַעְתִּי לָהֶם: 4 וְגַם הֲקִמֹתִי אֶת־בְּרִיתִי אִתָּם לָתֵת לָהֶם אֶת־אֶרֶץ כְּנָעַן אֵת אֶרֶץ מְגֻרֵיהֶם אֲשֶׁר־גָּרוּ בָהּ: 5 וְגַם אֲנִי שָׁמַעְתִּי אֶת־נַאֲקַת בְּנֵי יִשְׂרָאֵל אֲשֶׁר מִצְרַיִם מַעֲבִדִים אֹתָם וָאֶזְכֹּר אֶת־בְּרִיתִי: 6 לָכֵן אֱמֹר לִבְנֵי־יִשְׂרָאֵל אֲנִי יְהוָה וְהוֹצֵאתִי אֶתְכֶם מִתַּחַת סִבְלֹת מִצְרַיִם וְהִצַּלְתִּי אֶתְכֶם מֵעֲבֹדָתָם וְגָאַלְתִּי אֶתְכֶם בִּזְרוֹעַ נְטוּיָה וּבִשְׁפָטִים גְּדֹלִים: 7 וְלָקַחְתִּי אֶתְכֶם לִי לְעָם וְהָיִיתִי לָכֶם לֵאלֹהִים וִידַעְתֶּם כִּי אֲנִי יְהוָה אֱלֹהֵיכֶם הַמּוֹצִיא אֶתְכֶם מִתַּחַת סִבְלוֹת מִצְרָיִם: 8 וְהֵבֵאתִי אֶתְכֶם אֶל־הָאָרֶץ אֲשֶׁר נָשָׂאתִי אֶת־יָדִי לָתֵת אֹתָהּ לְאַבְרָהָם לְיִצְחָק וּלְיַעֲקֹב וְנָתַתִּי אֹתָהּ לָכֶם מוֹרָשָׁה אֲנִי יְהוָה: 9 וַיְדַבֵּר מֹשֶׁה כֵּן אֶל־בְּנֵי יִשְׂרָאֵל וְלֹא שָׁמְעוּ אֶל־מֹשֶׁה מִקֹּצֶר רוּחַ וּמֵעֲבֹדָה קָשָׁה: פ

10 וַיְדַבֵּר יְהוָה אֶל־מֹשֶׁה לֵּאמֹר: 11 בֹּא דַבֵּר אֶל־פַּרְעֹה מֶלֶךְ מִצְרָיִם וִישַׁלַּח אֶת־בְּנֵי־יִשְׂרָאֵל מֵאַרְצוֹ: 12 וַיְדַבֵּר מֹשֶׁה לִפְנֵי יְהוָה לֵאמֹר הֵן בְּנֵי־ יִשְׂרָאֵל לֹא־שָׁמְעוּ אֵלַי וְאֵיךְ יִשְׁמָעֵנִי פַרְעֹה וַאֲנִי עֲרַל שְׂפָתָיִם: פ

13 וַיְדַבֵּר יְהוָה אֶל־מֹשֶׁה וְאֶל־אַהֲרֹן וַיְצַוֵּם אֶל־ בְּנֵי יִשְׂרָאֵל וְאֶל־פַּרְעֹה מֶלֶךְ מִצְרָיִם לְהוֹצִיא אֶת־ בְּנֵי־יִשְׂרָאֵל מֵאֶרֶץ מִצְרָיִם: ס 14 אֵלֶּה

families of Reuben. 15 And the sons of Simeon *were* Jemuel, Jamin, Ohad, Jachin, Zohar, and Shaul the son of a Canaanite woman. These *are* the families of Simeon. 16 These *are* the names of the sons of Levi according to their generations: Gershon, Kohath, and Merari. And the years of the life of Levi *were* one hundred and thirty-seven. 17 The sons of Gershon *were* Libni and Shimi according to their families. 18 And the sons of Kohath *were* Amram, Izhar, Hebron, and Uzziel. And the years of the life of Kohath *were* one hundred and thirty-three. 19 The sons of Merari *were* Mahli and Mushi. These *are* the families of Levi according to their generations.

20 Now Amram took for himself Jochebed, his father's sister, as wife; and she bore him Aaron and Moses. And the years of the life of Amram *were* one hundred and thirty-seven. 21 The sons of Izhar *were* Korah, Nepheg, and Zichri. 22 And the sons of Uzziel *were* Mishael, Elzaphan, and Zithri. 23 Aaron took to himself Elisheba, daughter of Amminadab, sister of Nahshon, as wife; and she bore him Nadab, Abihu, Eleazar, and Ithamar. 24 And the sons of Korah *were* Assir, Elkanah, and Abiasaph. These are the families of the Korahites. 25 Eleazar, Aaron's son, took for himself one of the daughters of Putiel as wife; and she bore him Phinehas. These *are* the heads of the fathers' houses of the Levites according to their families.

26 These *are the same* Aaron and Moses to whom the LORD said, "Bring out the children of Israel from the land of Egypt according to their armies." 27 These *are* the ones who spoke to Pharaoh king of Egypt, to bring out the children of Israel from Egypt. These *are the same* Moses and Aaron.

28 And it came to pass, on the day the LORD spoke to Moses in the land of Egypt, 29 that the LORD spoke to Moses, saying, "I *am* the LORD. Speak to Pharaoh king of Egypt all that I say to you."

30 But Moses said before the LORD, "Behold, I *am* of uncircumcised lips, and how shall Pharaoh heed me?"

7 So the LORD said to Moses: "See, I have made you *as* God to Pharaoh, and Aaron your brother shall be your prophet. 2 You shall speak all that I command you. And Aaron your brother shall tell Pharaoh to send the children of Israel out of his land. 3 And I will harden Pharaoh's heart, and multiply My signs and My wonders in the land of Egypt. 4 But Pharaoh will not heed you, so that I may lay My hand on Egypt and bring My armies *and* My people, the children of Israel, out of the

רָאשֵׁי בֵית־אֲבֹתָם בְּנֵי רְאוּבֵן בְּכֹר יִשְׂרָאֵל חֲנוֹךְ וּפַלּוּא חֶצְרוֹן וְכַרְמִי אֵלֶּה מִשְׁפְּחֹת רְאוּבֵן: 15 וּבְנֵי שִׁמְעוֹן יְמוּאֵל וְיָמִין וְאֹהַד וְיָכִין וְצֹחַר וְשָׁאוּל בֶּן־ הַכְּנַעֲנִית אֵלֶּה מִשְׁפְּחֹת שִׁמְעוֹן: 16 וְאֵלֶּה שְׁמוֹת בְּנֵי־לֵוִי לְתֹלְדֹתָם גֵּרְשׁוֹן וּקְהָת וּמְרָרִי וּשְׁנֵי חַיֵּי לֵוִי שֶׁבַע וּשְׁלֹשִׁים וּמְאַת שָׁנָה: 17 בְּנֵי גֵרְשׁוֹן לִבְנִי וְשִׁמְעִי לְמִשְׁפְּחֹתָם: 18 וּבְנֵי קְהָת עַמְרָם וְיִצְהָר וְחֶבְרוֹן וְעֻזִּיאֵל וּשְׁנֵי חַיֵּי קְהָת שָׁלֹשׁ וּשְׁלֹשִׁים וּמְאַת שָׁנָה: 19 וּבְנֵי מְרָרִי מַחְלִי וּמוּשִׁי אֵלֶּה מִשְׁפְּחֹת הַלֵּוִי לְתֹלְדֹתָם: 20 וַיִּקַּח עַמְרָם אֶת־ יוֹכֶבֶד דֹּדָתוֹ לוֹ לְאִשָּׁה וַתֵּלֶד לוֹ אֶת־אַהֲרֹן וְאֶת־ מֹשֶׁה וּשְׁנֵי חַיֵּי עַמְרָם שֶׁבַע וּשְׁלֹשִׁים וּמְאַת שָׁנָה: 21 וּבְנֵי יִצְהָר קֹרַח וָנֶפֶג וְזִכְרִי: 22 וּבְנֵי עֻזִּיאֵל מִישָׁאֵל וְאֶלְצָפָן וְסִתְרִי: 23 וַיִּקַּח אַהֲרֹן אֶת־אֱלִישֶׁבַע בַּת־עַמִּינָדָב אֲחוֹת נַחְשׁוֹן לוֹ לְאִשָּׁה וַתֵּלֶד לוֹ אֶת־נָדָב וְאֶת־אֲבִיהוּא אֶת־אֶלְעָזָר וְאֶת־ אִיתָמָר: 24 וּבְנֵי קֹרַח אַסִּיר וְאֶלְקָנָה וַאֲבִיאָסָף אֵלֶּה מִשְׁפְּחֹת הַקָּרְחִי: 25 וְאֶלְעָזָר בֶּן־אַהֲרֹן לָקַח לוֹ מִבְּנוֹת פּוּטִיאֵל לוֹ לְאִשָּׁה וַתֵּלֶד לוֹ אֶת־פִּינְחָס אֵלֶּה רָאשֵׁי אֲבוֹת הַלְוִיִּם לְמִשְׁפְּחֹתָם: 26 הוּא אַהֲרֹן וּמֹשֶׁה אֲשֶׁר אָמַר יְהוָה לָהֶם הוֹצִיאוּ אֶת־ בְּנֵי יִשְׂרָאֵל מֵאֶרֶץ מִצְרַיִם עַל־צִבְאֹתָם: 27 הֵם הַמְדַבְּרִים אֶל־פַּרְעֹה מֶלֶךְ־מִצְרַיִם לְהוֹצִיא אֶת־ בְּנֵי־יִשְׂרָאֵל מִמִּצְרָיִם הוּא מֹשֶׁה וְאַהֲרֹן: 28 וַיְהִי בְּיוֹם דִּבֶּר יְהוָה אֶל־מֹשֶׁה בְּאֶרֶץ מִצְרָיִם: פ 29 וַיְדַבֵּר יְהוָה אֶל־מֹשֶׁה לֵּאמֹר אֲנִי יְהוָה דַּבֵּר אֶל־פַּרְעֹה מֶלֶךְ מִצְרַיִם אֵת כָּל־אֲשֶׁר אֲנִי דֹּבֵר אֵלֶיךָ: 30 וַיֹּאמֶר מֹשֶׁה לִפְנֵי יְהוָה הֵן אֲנִי עֲרַל שְׂפָתַיִם וְאֵיךְ יִשְׁמַע אֵלַי פַּרְעֹה: פ

ז וַיֹּאמֶר יְהוָה אֶל־מֹשֶׁה רְאֵה נְתַתִּיךָ אֱלֹהִים לְפַרְעֹה וְאַהֲרֹן אָחִיךָ יִהְיֶה נְבִיאֶךָ: 2 אַתָּה תְדַבֵּר אֵת כָּל־אֲשֶׁר אֲצַוֶּךָּ וְאַהֲרֹן אָחִיךָ יְדַבֵּר אֶל־פַּרְעֹה וְשִׁלַּח אֶת־בְּנֵי־יִשְׂרָאֵל מֵאַרְצוֹ: 3 וַאֲנִי אַקְשֶׁה אֶת־ לֵב פַּרְעֹה וְהִרְבֵּיתִי אֶת־אֹתֹתַי וְאֶת־מוֹפְתַי בְּאֶרֶץ מִצְרָיִם: 4 וְלֹא־יִשְׁמַע אֲלֵכֶם פַּרְעֹה וְנָתַתִּי אֶת־ יָדִי בְּמִצְרָיִם וְהוֹצֵאתִי אֶת־צִבְאֹתַי אֶת־עַמִּי בְנֵי

land of Egypt by great judgments. ⁵And the Egyptians shall know that I *am* the LORD, when I stretch out My hand on Egypt and bring out the children of Israel from among them."

⁶Then Moses and Aaron did *so;* just as the LORD commanded them, so they did. ⁷And Moses *was* eighty years old and Aaron eighty-three years old when they spoke to Pharaoh.

⁸Then the LORD spoke to Moses and Aaron, saying, ⁹"When Pharaoh speaks to you, saying, 'Show a miracle for yourselves,' then you shall say to Aaron, 'Take your rod and cast *it* before Pharaoh, *and* let it become a serpent.' " ¹⁰So Moses and Aaron went in to Pharaoh, and they did so, just as the LORD commanded. And Aaron cast down his rod before Pharaoh and before his servants, and it became a serpent.

¹¹But Pharaoh also called the wise men and the sorcerers; so the magicians of Egypt, they also did in like manner with their enchantments. ¹²For every man threw down his rod, and they became serpents. But Aaron's rod swallowed up their rods. ¹³And Pharaoh's heart grew hard, and he did not heed them, as the LORD had said.

¹⁴So the LORD said to Moses: "Pharaoh's heart *is* hard; he refuses to let the people go. ¹⁵Go to Pharaoh in the morning, when he goes out to the water, and you shall stand by the river's bank to meet him; and the rod which was turned to a serpent you shall take in your hand. ¹⁶And you shall say to him, 'The LORD God of the Hebrews has sent me to you, saying, "Let My people go, that they may serve Me in the wilderness"; but indeed, until now you would not hear! ¹⁷Thus says the LORD: "By this you shall know that I *am* the LORD. Behold, I will strike the waters which *are* in the river with the rod that *is* in my hand, and they shall be turned to blood. ¹⁸And the fish that *are* in the river shall die, the river shall stink, and the Egyptians will loathe to drink the water of the river." ' "

¹⁹Then the LORD spoke to Moses, "Say to Aaron, 'Take your rod and stretch out your hand over the waters of Egypt, over their streams, over their rivers, over their ponds, and over all their pools of water, that they may become blood. And there shall be blood throughout all the land of Egypt, both in *buckets of* wood and *pitchers of* stone.' " ²⁰And Moses and Aaron did so, just as the LORD commanded. So he lifted up the rod and struck the waters that *were* in the river, in the sight of Pharaoh and in the sight of his servants. And all the waters that *were* in the river were turned to blood. ²¹The fish that *were* in the river died, the

יִשְׂרָאֵל מֵאֶרֶץ מִצְרַיִם בִּשְׁפָטִים גְּדֹלִים: 5 וְיָדְעוּ מִצְרַיִם כִּי־אֲנִי יְהוָה בִּנְטֹתִי אֶת־יָדִי עַל־מִצְרָיִם וְהוֹצֵאתִי אֶת־בְּנֵי־יִשְׂרָאֵל מִתּוֹכָם: 6 וַיַּעַשׂ מֹשֶׁה וְאַהֲרֹן כַּאֲשֶׁר צִוָּה יְהוָה אֹתָם כֵּן עָשׂוּ: 7 וּמֹשֶׁה בֶּן־שְׁמֹנִים שָׁנָה וְאַהֲרֹן בֶּן־שָׁלֹשׁ וּשְׁמֹנִים שָׁנָה בְּדַבְּרָם אֶל־פַּרְעֹה: פ

8 וַיֹּאמֶר יְהוָה אֶל־מֹשֶׁה וְאֶל־אַהֲרֹן לֵאמֹר: 9 כִּי יְדַבֵּר אֲלֵכֶם פַּרְעֹה לֵאמֹר תְּנוּ לָכֶם מוֹפֵת וְאָמַרְתָּ אֶל־אַהֲרֹן קַח אֶת־מַטְּךָ וְהַשְׁלֵךְ לִפְנֵי־פַרְעֹה יְהִי לְתַנִּין: 10 וַיָּבֹא מֹשֶׁה וְאַהֲרֹן אֶל־פַּרְעֹה וַיַּעֲשׂוּ כֵן כַּאֲשֶׁר צִוָּה יְהוָה וַיַּשְׁלֵךְ אַהֲרֹן אֶת־מַטֵּהוּ לִפְנֵי פַרְעֹה וְלִפְנֵי עֲבָדָיו וַיְהִי לְתַנִּין: 11 וַיִּקְרָא גַּם־פַּרְעֹה לַחֲכָמִים וְלַמְכַשְּׁפִים וַיַּעֲשׂוּ גַם־הֵם חַרְטֻמֵּי מִצְרַיִם בְּלַהֲטֵיהֶם כֵּן: 12 וַיַּשְׁלִיכוּ אִישׁ מַטֵּהוּ וַיִּהְיוּ לְתַנִּינִם וַיִּבְלַע מַטֵּה־אַהֲרֹן אֶת־מַטֹּתָם: 13 וַיֶּחֱזַק לֵב פַּרְעֹה וְלֹא שָׁמַע אֲלֵהֶם כַּאֲשֶׁר דִּבֶּר יְהוָה: פ

14 וַיֹּאמֶר יְהוָה אֶל־מֹשֶׁה כָּבֵד לֵב פַּרְעֹה מֵאֵן לְשַׁלַּח הָעָם: 15 לֵךְ אֶל־פַּרְעֹה בַּבֹּקֶר הִנֵּה יֹצֵא הַמַּיְמָה וְנִצַּבְתָּ לִקְרָאתוֹ עַל־שְׂפַת הַיְאֹר וְהַמַּטֶּה אֲשֶׁר־נֶהְפַּךְ לְנָחָשׁ תִּקַּח בְּיָדֶךָ: 16 וְאָמַרְתָּ אֵלָיו יְהוָה אֱלֹהֵי הָעִבְרִים שְׁלָחַנִי אֵלֶיךָ לֵאמֹר שַׁלַּח אֶת־עַמִּי וְיַעַבְדֻנִי בַּמִּדְבָּר וְהִנֵּה לֹא־שָׁמַעְתָּ עַד־כֹּה: 17 כֹּה אָמַר יְהוָה בְּזֹאת תֵּדַע כִּי אֲנִי יְהוָה הִנֵּה אָנֹכִי מַכֶּה | בַּמַּטֶּה אֲשֶׁר־בְּיָדִי עַל־הַמַּיִם אֲשֶׁר בַּיְאֹר וְנֶהֶפְכוּ לְדָם: 18 וְהַדָּגָה אֲשֶׁר־בַּיְאֹר תָּמוּת וּבָאַשׁ הַיְאֹר וְנִלְאוּ מִצְרַיִם לִשְׁתּוֹת מַיִם מִן־הַיְאֹר: ס 19 וַיֹּאמֶר יְהוָה אֶל־מֹשֶׁה אֱמֹר אֶל־אַהֲרֹן קַח מַטְּךָ וּנְטֵה־יָדְךָ עַל־מֵימֵי מִצְרַיִם עַל־נַהֲרֹתָם | עַל־יְאֹרֵיהֶם וְעַל־אַגְמֵיהֶם וְעַל כָּל־מִקְוֵה מֵימֵיהֶם וְיִהְיוּ־דָם וְהָיָה דָם בְּכָל־אֶרֶץ מִצְרַיִם וּבָעֵצִים וּבָאֲבָנִים: 20 וַיַּעֲשׂוּ־כֵן מֹשֶׁה וְאַהֲרֹן כַּאֲשֶׁר | צִוָּה יְהוָה וַיָּרֶם בַּמַּטֶּה וַיַּךְ אֶת־הַמַּיִם אֲשֶׁר בַּיְאֹר לְעֵינֵי פַרְעֹה וּלְעֵינֵי עֲבָדָיו וַיֵּהָפְכוּ כָּל־הַמַּיִם אֲשֶׁר־בַּיְאֹר לְדָם: 21 וְהַדָּגָה אֲשֶׁר־בַּיְאֹר מֵתָה וַיִּבְאַשׁ הַיְאֹר וְלֹא־יָכְלוּ מִצְרַיִם לִשְׁתּוֹת מַיִם מִן־הַיְאֹר וַיְהִי הַדָּם

river stank, and the Egyptians could not drink the water of the river. So there was blood throughout all the land of Egypt.

22 Then the magicians of Egypt did so with their enchantments; and Pharaoh's heart grew hard, and he did not heed them, as the LORD had said. 23 And Pharaoh turned and went into his house. Neither was his heart moved by this. 24 So all the Egyptians dug all around the river for water to drink, because they could not drink the water of the river. 25 And seven days passed after the LORD had struck the river.

8 And the LORD spoke to Moses, "Go to Pharaoh and say to him, 'Thus says the LORD: "Let My people go, that they may serve Me. 2 But if you refuse to let *them* go, behold, I will smite all your territory with frogs. 3 So the river shall bring forth frogs abundantly, which shall go up and come into your house, into your bedroom, on your bed, into the houses of your servants, on your people, into your ovens, and into your kneading bowls. 4 And the frogs shall come up on you, on your people, and on all your servants." ' "

5 Then the LORD spoke to Moses, "Say to Aaron, 'Stretch out your hand with your rod over the streams, over the rivers, and over the ponds, and cause frogs to come up on the land of Egypt.' " 6 So Aaron stretched out his hand over the waters of Egypt, and the frogs came up and covered the land of Egypt. 7 And the magicians did so with their enchantments, and brought up frogs on the land of Egypt.

8 Then Pharaoh called for Moses and Aaron, and said, "Entreat the LORD that He may take away the frogs from me and from my people; and I will let the people go, that they may sacrifice to the LORD."

9 And Moses said to Pharaoh, "Accept the honor of saying when I shall intercede for you, for your servants, and for your people, to destroy the frogs from you and your houses, *that* they may remain in the river only."

10 So he said, "Tomorrow." And he said, "*Let it be* according to your word, that you may know that *there is* no one like the LORD our God. 11 And the frogs shall depart from you, from your houses, from your servants, and from your people. They shall remain in the river only."

12 Then Moses and Aaron went out from Pharaoh. And Moses cried out to the LORD concerning the frogs which He had brought against Pharaoh. 13 So the LORD did according to the word of Moses. And the frogs died out of the houses, out of the courtyards, and out of the fields. 14 They

בְּכָל־אֶרֶץ מִצְרָיִם: 22 וַיַּעֲשׂוּ־כֵן חַרְטֻמֵּי מִצְרַיִם בְּלָטֵיהֶם וַיֶּחֱזַק לֵב־פַּרְעֹה וְלֹא־שָׁמַע אֲלֵהֶם כַּאֲשֶׁר דִּבֶּר יְהֹוָה: 23 וַיִּפֶן פַּרְעֹה וַיָּבֹא אֶל־בֵּיתוֹ וְלֹא־שָׁת לִבּוֹ גַּם־לָזֹאת: 24 וַיַּחְפְּרוּ כָל־מִצְרַיִם סְבִיבֹת הַיְאֹר מַיִם לִשְׁתּוֹת כִּי לֹא יָכְלוּ לִשְׁתֹּת מִמֵּימֵי הַיְאֹר: 25 וַיִּמָּלֵא שִׁבְעַת יָמִים אַחֲרֵי הַכּוֹת־יְהֹוָה אֶת־הַיְאֹר: פ

26 וַיֹּאמֶר יְהֹוָה אֶל־מֹשֶׁה בֹּא אֶל־פַּרְעֹה וְאָמַרְתָּ אֵלָיו כֹּה אָמַר יְהֹוָה שַׁלַּח אֶת־עַמִּי וְיַעַבְדֻנִי: 27 וְאִם־מָאֵן אַתָּה לְשַׁלֵּחַ הִנֵּה אָנֹכִי נֹגֵף אֶת־כָּל־גְּבוּלְךָ בַּצְפַרְדְּעִים: 28 וְשָׁרַץ הַיְאֹר צְפַרְדְּעִים וְעָלוּ וּבָאוּ בְּבֵיתֶךָ וּבַחֲדַר מִשְׁכָּבְךָ וְעַל־מִטָּתֶךָ וּבְבֵית עֲבָדֶיךָ וּבְעַמֶּךָ וּבְתַנּוּרֶיךָ וּבְמִשְׁאֲרוֹתֶיךָ: 29 וּבְכָה וּבְעַמְּךָ וּבְכָל־עֲבָדֶיךָ יַעֲלוּ הַצְפַרְדְּעִים:

ח וַיֹּאמֶר יְהֹוָה אֶל־מֹשֶׁה אֱמֹר אֶל־אַהֲרֹן נְטֵה אֶת־יָדְךָ בְּמַטֶּךָ עַל־הַנְּהָרֹת עַל־הַיְאֹרִים וְעַל־הָאֲגַמִּים וְהַעַל אֶת־הַצְפַרְדְּעִים עַל־אֶרֶץ מִצְרָיִם: 2 וַיֵּט אַהֲרֹן אֶת־יָדוֹ עַל מֵימֵי מִצְרָיִם וַתַּעַל הַצְפַרְדֵּעַ וַתְּכַס אֶת־אֶרֶץ מִצְרָיִם: 3 וַיַּעֲשׂוּ־כֵן הַחַרְטֻמִּים בְּלָטֵיהֶם וַיַּעֲלוּ אֶת־הַצְפַרְדְּעִים עַל־אֶרֶץ מִצְרָיִם: 4 וַיִּקְרָא פַרְעֹה לְמֹשֶׁה וּלְאַהֲרֹן וַיֹּאמֶר הַעְתִּירוּ אֶל־יְהֹוָה וְיָסֵר הַצְפַרְדְּעִים מִמֶּנִּי וּמֵעַמִּי וַאֲשַׁלְּחָה אֶת־הָעָם וְיִזְבְּחוּ לַיהֹוָה: 5 וַיֹּאמֶר מֹשֶׁה לְפַרְעֹה הִתְפָּאֵר עָלַי לְמָתַי | אַעְתִּיר לְךָ וְלַעֲבָדֶיךָ וּלְעַמְּךָ לְהַכְרִית הַצְפַרְדְּעִים מִמְּךָ וּמִבָּתֶּיךָ רַק בַּיְאֹר תִּשָּׁאַרְנָה: 6 וַיֹּאמֶר לְמָחָר וַיֹּאמֶר כִּדְבָרְךָ לְמַעַן תֵּדַע כִּי־אֵין כַּיהֹוָה אֱלֹהֵינוּ: 7 וְסָרוּ הַצְפַרְדְּעִים מִמְּךָ וּמִבָּתֶּיךָ וּמֵעֲבָדֶיךָ וּמֵעַמֶּךָ רַק בַּיְאֹר תִּשָּׁאַרְנָה: 8 וַיֵּצֵא מֹשֶׁה וְאַהֲרֹן מֵעִם פַּרְעֹה וַיִּצְעַק מֹשֶׁה אֶל־יְהֹוָה עַל־דְּבַר הַצְפַרְדְּעִים אֲשֶׁר־שָׂם לְפַרְעֹה: 9 וַיַּעַשׂ יְהֹוָה כִּדְבַר מֹשֶׁה וַיָּמֻתוּ הַצְפַרְדְּעִים מִן־הַבָּתִּים מִן־הַחֲצֵרֹת וּמִן־הַשָּׂדֹת: 10 וַיִּצְבְּרוּ אֹתָם חֳמָרִם חֳמָרִם וַתִּבְאַשׁ

gathered them together in heaps, and the land stank. ¹⁵But when Pharaoh saw that there was relief, he hardened his heart and did not heed them, as the LORD had said.

¹⁶So the LORD said to Moses, "Say to Aaron, 'Stretch out your rod, and strike the dust of the land, so that it may become lice throughout all the land of Egypt.'" ¹⁷And they did so. For Aaron stretched out his hand with his rod and struck the dust of the earth, and it became lice on man and beast. All the dust of the land became lice throughout all the land of Egypt.

¹⁸Now the magicians so worked with their enchantments to bring forth lice, but they could not. So there were lice on man and beast. ¹⁹Then the magicians said to Pharaoh, "This *is* the finger of God." But Pharaoh's heart grew hard, and he did not heed them, just as the LORD had said.

²⁰And the LORD said to Moses, "Rise early in the morning and stand before Pharaoh as he comes out to the water. Then say to him, 'Thus says the LORD: "Let My people go, that they may serve Me. ²¹Or else, if you will not let My people go, behold, I will send swarms *of flies* on you and your servants, on your people and into your houses. The houses of the Egyptians shall be full of swarms *of flies,* and also the ground on which they *stand.* ²²And in that day I will set apart the land of Goshen, in which My people dwell, that no swarms *of flies* shall be there, in order that you may know that I *am* the LORD in the midst of the land. ²³I will make a difference between My people and your people. Tomorrow this sign shall be."'" ²⁴And the LORD did so. Thick swarms *of flies* came into the house of Pharaoh, *into* his servants' houses, and into all the land of Egypt. The land was corrupted because of the swarms *of flies.*

²⁵Then Pharaoh called for Moses and Aaron, and said, "Go, sacrifice to your God in the land."

²⁶And Moses said, "It is not right to do so, for we would be sacrificing the abomination of the Egyptians to the LORD our God. If we sacrifice the abomination of the Egyptians before their eyes, then will they not stone us? ²⁷We will go three days' journey into the wilderness and sacrifice to the LORD our God as He will command us."

²⁸So Pharaoh said, "I will let you go, that you may sacrifice to the LORD your God in the wilderness; only you shall not go very far away. Intercede for me."

²⁹Then Moses said, "Indeed I am going out from you, and I will entreat the LORD, that the swarms *of flies* may depart tomorrow from Pharaoh, from his

הָאָֽרֶץ: 11 וַיַּ֣רְא פַּרְעֹ֗ה כִּ֤י הָֽיְתָה֙ הָֽרְוָחָ֔ה וְהַכְבֵּד֙ אֶת־לִבּ֔וֹ וְלֹ֥א שָׁמַ֖ע אֲלֵהֶ֑ם כַּאֲשֶׁ֖ר דִּבֶּ֥ר יְהוָֽה: ס 12 וַיֹּ֣אמֶר יְהוָה֮ אֶל־מֹשֶׁה֒ אֱמֹר֙ אֶֽל־אַהֲרֹ֔ן נְטֵ֣ה אֶֽת־מַטְּךָ֔ וְהַ֖ךְ אֶת־עֲפַ֣ר הָאָ֑רֶץ וְהָיָ֥ה לְכִנִּ֖ם בְּכָל־אֶ֥רֶץ מִצְרָֽיִם: 13 וַיַּֽעֲשׂוּ־כֵ֗ן וַיֵּט֩ אַהֲרֹ֨ן אֶת־יָד֜וֹ בְמַטֵּ֗הוּ וַיַּךְ֙ אֶת־עֲפַ֣ר הָאָ֔רֶץ וַתְּהִי֙ הַכִּנָּ֔ם בָּֽאָדָ֖ם וּבַבְּהֵמָ֑ה כָּל־עֲפַ֥ר הָאָ֛רֶץ הָיָ֥ה כִנִּ֖ים בְּכָל־אֶ֥רֶץ מִצְרָֽיִם: 14 וַיַּֽעֲשׂוּ־כֵ֨ן הַחַרְטֻמִּ֧ים בְּלָטֵיהֶ֛ם לְהוֹצִ֥יא אֶת־הַכִּנִּ֖ים וְלֹ֣א יָכֹ֑לוּ וַתְּהִי֙ הַכִּנָּ֔ם בָּֽאָדָ֖ם וּבַבְּהֵמָֽה: 15 וַיֹּֽאמְר֤וּ הַֽחַרְטֻמִּם֙ אֶל־פַּרְעֹ֔ה אֶצְבַּ֥ע אֱלֹהִ֖ים הִ֑וא וַיֶּֽחֱזַ֤ק לֵב־פַּרְעֹה֙ וְלֹֽא־שָׁמַ֣ע אֲלֵהֶ֔ם כַּאֲשֶׁ֖ר דִּבֶּ֥ר יְהוָֽה: ס 16 וַיֹּ֨אמֶר יְהוָ֜ה אֶל־מֹשֶׁ֗ה הַשְׁכֵּ֤ם בַּבֹּ֨קֶר֙ וְהִתְיַצֵּב֙ לִפְנֵ֣י פַרְעֹ֔ה הִנֵּ֖ה יוֹצֵ֣א הַמָּ֑יְמָה וְאָֽמַרְתָּ֣ אֵלָ֗יו כֹּ֚ה אָמַ֣ר יְהוָ֔ה שַׁלַּ֥ח עַמִּ֖י וְיַֽעַבְדֻֽנִי: 17 כִּ֣י אִם־אֵֽינְךָ֮ מְשַׁלֵּ֣חַ אֶת־עַמִּי֒ הִנְנִי֩ מַשְׁלִ֨יחַ בְּךָ֜ וּבַֽעֲבָדֶ֤יךָ וּבְעַמְּךָ֙ וּבְבָתֶּ֔יךָ אֶת־הֶֽעָרֹ֑ב וּמָ֨לְא֜וּ בָּתֵּ֤י מִצְרַ֨יִם֙ אֶת־הֶ֣עָרֹ֔ב וְגַ֥ם הָאֲדָמָ֖ה אֲשֶׁר־הֵ֥ם עָלֶֽיהָ: 18 וְהִפְלֵיתִי֩ בַיּ֨וֹם הַה֜וּא אֶת־אֶ֣רֶץ גֹּ֗שֶׁן אֲשֶׁ֤ר עַמִּי֙ עֹמֵ֣ד עָלֶ֔יהָ לְבִלְתִּ֥י הֱיֽוֹת־שָׁ֖ם עָרֹ֑ב לְמַ֣עַן תֵּדַ֔ע כִּ֛י אֲנִ֥י יְהוָ֖ה בְּקֶ֥רֶב הָאָֽרֶץ: 19 וְשַׂמְתִּ֣י פְדֻ֔ת בֵּ֥ין עַמִּ֖י וּבֵ֣ין עַמֶּ֑ךָ לְמָחָ֥ר יִֽהְיֶ֖ה הָאֹ֥ת הַזֶּֽה: 20 וַיַּ֤עַשׂ יְהוָה֙ כֵּ֔ן וַיָּבֹא֙ עָרֹ֣ב כָּבֵ֔ד בֵּ֥יתָה פַרְעֹ֖ה וּבֵ֣ית עֲבָדָ֑יו וּבְכָל־אֶ֧רֶץ מִצְרַ֛יִם תִּשָּׁחֵ֥ת הָאָ֖רֶץ מִפְּנֵ֥י הֶֽעָרֹֽב: 21 וַיִּקְרָ֣א פַרְעֹ֔ה אֶל־מֹשֶׁ֖ה וּֽלְאַהֲרֹ֑ן וַיֹּ֗אמֶר לְכ֛וּ זִבְח֥וּ לֵֽאלֹהֵיכֶ֖ם בָּאָֽרֶץ:

22 וַיֹּ֣אמֶר מֹשֶׁ֗ה לֹ֤א נָכוֹן֙ לַעֲשׂ֣וֹת כֵּ֔ן כִּ֚י תּֽוֹעֲבַ֣ת מִצְרַ֔יִם נִזְבַּ֖ח לַיהוָ֣ה אֱלֹהֵ֑ינוּ הֵ֣ן נִזְבַּ֞ח אֶת־תּוֹעֲבַ֧ת מִצְרַ֛יִם לְעֵֽינֵיהֶ֖ם וְלֹ֥א יִסְקְלֻֽנוּ: 23 דֶּ֚רֶךְ שְׁלֹ֣שֶׁת יָמִ֔ים נֵלֵ֖ךְ בַּמִּדְבָּ֑ר וְזָבַ֨חְנוּ֙ לַֽיהוָ֣ה אֱלֹהֵ֔ינוּ כַּאֲשֶׁ֖ר יֹאמַ֥ר אֵלֵֽינוּ: 24 וַיֹּ֣אמֶר פַּרְעֹ֗ה אָֽנֹכִ֞י אֲשַׁלַּ֤ח אֶתְכֶם֙ וּזְבַחְתֶּ֞ם לַֽיהוָ֤ה אֱלֹֽהֵיכֶם֙ בַּמִּדְבָּ֔ר רַ֛ק הַרְחֵ֥ק לֹֽא־תַרְחִ֖יקוּ לָלֶ֑כֶת הַעְתִּ֖ירוּ בַּעֲדִֽי: 25 וַיֹּ֣אמֶר מֹשֶׁ֗ה הִנֵּ֨ה אָֽנֹכִ֜י יוֹצֵ֤א מֵֽעִמָּךְ֙ וְהַעְתַּרְתִּ֣י אֶל־יְהוָ֔ה וְסָ֣ר הֶעָרֹ֗ב

servants, and from his people. But let Pharaoh not deal deceitfully anymore in not letting the people go to sacrifice to the LORD."

³⁰ So Moses went out from Pharaoh and entreated the LORD. ³¹ And the LORD did according to the word of Moses; He removed the swarms *of flies* from Pharaoh, from his servants, and from his people. Not one remained. ³² But Pharaoh hardened his heart at this time also; neither would he let the people go.

9 Then the LORD said to Moses, "Go in to Pharaoh and tell him, 'Thus says the LORD God of the Hebrews: "Let My people go, that they may serve Me. ² For if you refuse to let *them* go, and still hold them, ³ behold, the hand of the LORD will be on your cattle in the field, on the horses, on the donkeys, on the camels, on the oxen, and on the sheep—a very severe pestilence. ⁴ And the LORD will make a difference between the livestock of Israel and the livestock of Egypt. So nothing shall die of all *that* belongs to the children of Israel."'" ⁵ Then the LORD appointed a set time, saying, "Tomorrow the LORD will do this thing in the land."

⁶ So the LORD did this thing on the next day, and all the livestock of Egypt died; but of the livestock of the children of Israel, not one died. ⁷ Then Pharaoh sent, and indeed, not even one of the livestock of the Israelites was dead. But the heart of Pharaoh became hard, and he did not let the people go.

⁸ So the LORD said to Moses and Aaron, "Take for yourselves handfuls of ashes from a furnace, and let Moses scatter it toward the heavens in the sight of Pharaoh. ⁹ And it will become fine dust in all the land of Egypt, and it will cause boils that break out in sores on man and beast throughout all the land of Egypt." ¹⁰ Then they took ashes from the furnace and stood before Pharaoh, and Moses scattered *them* toward heaven. And *they* caused boils that break out in sores on man and beast. ¹¹ And the magicians could not stand before Moses because of the boils, for the boils were on the magicians and on all the Egyptians. ¹² But the LORD hardened the heart of Pharaoh; and he did not heed them, just as the LORD had spoken to Moses.

¹³ Then the LORD said to Moses, "Rise early in the morning and stand before Pharaoh, and say to him, 'Thus says the LORD God of the Hebrews: "Let My people go, that they may serve Me, ¹⁴ for at this time I will send all My plagues to your very heart, and on your servants and on your people, that you may know that *there is* none like Me in all the earth. ¹⁵ Now if I had stretched out My hand

מִפַּרְעֹה מֵעֲבָדָיו וּמֵעַמּוֹ מָחָר רַק אַל־יֹסֵף פַּרְעֹה הָתֵל לְבִלְתִּי שַׁלַּח אֶת־הָעָם לִזְבֹּחַ לַיהֹוָה: 26 וַיֵּצֵא מֹשֶׁה מֵעִם פַּרְעֹה וַיֶּעְתַּר אֶל־יְהֹוָה: 27 וַיַּעַשׂ יְהֹוָה כִּדְבַר מֹשֶׁה וַיָּסַר הֶעָרֹב מִפַּרְעֹה מֵעֲבָדָיו וּמֵעַמּוֹ לֹא נִשְׁאַר אֶחָד: 28 וַיַּכְבֵּד פַּרְעֹה אֶת־לִבּוֹ גַּם בַּפַּעַם הַזֹּאת וְלֹא שִׁלַּח אֶת־הָעָם: פ

ט וַיֹּאמֶר יְהֹוָה אֶל־מֹשֶׁה בֹּא אֶל־פַּרְעֹה וְדִבַּרְתָּ אֵלָיו כֹּה־אָמַר יְהֹוָה אֱלֹהֵי הָעִבְרִים שַׁלַּח אֶת־עַמִּי וְיַעַבְדֻנִי: 2 כִּי אִם־מָאֵן אַתָּה לְשַׁלֵּחַ וְעוֹדְךָ מַחֲזִיק בָּם: 3 הִנֵּה יַד־יְהֹוָה הוֹיָה בְּמִקְנְךָ אֲשֶׁר בַּשָּׂדֶה בַּסּוּסִים בַּחֲמֹרִים בַּגְּמַלִּים בַּבָּקָר וּבַצֹּאן דֶּבֶר כָּבֵד מְאֹד: 4 וְהִפְלָה יְהֹוָה בֵּין מִקְנֵה יִשְׂרָאֵל וּבֵין מִקְנֵה מִצְרָיִם וְלֹא יָמוּת מִכָּל־לִבְנֵי יִשְׂרָאֵל דָּבָר: 5 וַיָּשֶׂם יְהֹוָה מוֹעֵד לֵאמֹר מָחָר יַעֲשֶׂה יְהֹוָה הַדָּבָר הַזֶּה בָּאָרֶץ: 6 וַיַּעַשׂ יְהֹוָה אֶת־הַדָּבָר הַזֶּה מִמָּחֳרָת וַיָּמָת כֹּל מִקְנֵה מִצְרָיִם וּמִמִּקְנֵה בְנֵי־ יִשְׂרָאֵל לֹא־מֵת אֶחָד: 7 וַיִּשְׁלַח פַּרְעֹה וְהִנֵּה לֹא־ מֵת מִמִּקְנֵה יִשְׂרָאֵל עַד־אֶחָד וַיִּכְבַּד לֵב פַּרְעֹה וְלֹא שִׁלַּח אֶת־הָעָם: פ

8 וַיֹּאמֶר יְהֹוָה אֶל־מֹשֶׁה וְאֶל־אַהֲרֹן קְחוּ לָכֶם מְלֹא חָפְנֵיכֶם פִּיחַ כִּבְשָׁן וּזְרָקוֹ מֹשֶׁה הַשָּׁמַיְמָה לְעֵינֵי פַרְעֹה: 9 וְהָיָה לְאָבָק עַל כָּל־אֶרֶץ מִצְרָיִם וְהָיָה עַל־הָאָדָם וְעַל־הַבְּהֵמָה לִשְׁחִין פֹּרֵחַ אֲבַעְבֻּעֹת בְּכָל־אֶרֶץ מִצְרָיִם: 10 וַיִּקְחוּ אֶת־פִּיחַ הַכִּבְשָׁן וַיַּעַמְדוּ לִפְנֵי פַרְעֹה וַיִּזְרֹק אֹתוֹ מֹשֶׁה הַשָּׁמַיְמָה וַיְהִי שְׁחִין אֲבַעְבֻּעֹת פֹּרֵחַ בָּאָדָם וּבַבְּהֵמָה: 11 וְלֹא־ יָכְלוּ הַחַרְטֻמִּים לַעֲמֹד לִפְנֵי מֹשֶׁה מִפְּנֵי הַשְּׁחִין כִּי־הָיָה הַשְּׁחִין בַּחַרְטֻמִּם וּבְכָל־מִצְרָיִם: 12 וַיְחַזֵּק יְהֹוָה אֶת־לֵב פַּרְעֹה וְלֹא שָׁמַע אֲלֵהֶם כַּאֲשֶׁר דִּבֶּר יְהֹוָה אֶל־מֹשֶׁה: ס 13 וַיֹּאמֶר יְהֹוָה אֶל־ מֹשֶׁה הַשְׁכֵּם בַּבֹּקֶר וְהִתְיַצֵּב לִפְנֵי פַרְעֹה וְאָמַרְתָּ אֵלָיו כֹּה־אָמַר יְהֹוָה אֱלֹהֵי הָעִבְרִים שַׁלַּח אֶת־עַמִּי וְיַעַבְדֻנִי: 14 כִּי | בַּפַּעַם הַזֹּאת אֲנִי שֹׁלֵחַ אֶת־כָּל־ מַגֵּפֹתַי אֶל־לִבְּךָ וּבַעֲבָדֶיךָ וּבְעַמֶּךָ בַּעֲבוּר תֵּדַע כִּי אֵין כָּמֹנִי בְּכָל־הָאָרֶץ: 15 כִּי עַתָּה שָׁלַחְתִּי אֶת־יָדִי

and struck you and your people with pestilence, then you would have been cut off from the earth. [16] But indeed for this *purpose* I have raised you up, that I may show My power *in* you, and that My name may be declared in all the earth. [17] As yet you exalt yourself against My people in that you will not let them go. [18] Behold, tomorrow about this time I will cause very heavy hail to rain down, such as has not been in Egypt since its founding until now. [19] Therefore send now *and* gather your livestock and all that you have in the field, for the hail shall come down on every man and every animal which is found in the field and is not brought home; and they shall die." ' "

[20] He who feared the word of the LORD among the servants of Pharaoh made his servants and his livestock flee to the houses. [21] But he who did not regard the word of the LORD left his servants and his livestock in the field.

[22] Then the LORD said to Moses, "Stretch out your hand toward heaven, that there may be hail in all the land of Egypt—on man, on beast, and on every herb of the field, throughout the land of Egypt." [23] And Moses stretched out his rod toward heaven; and the LORD sent thunder and hail, and fire darted to the ground. And the LORD rained hail on the land of Egypt. [24] So there was hail, and fire mingled with the hail, so very heavy that there was none like it in all the land of Egypt since it became a nation. [25] And the hail struck throughout the whole land of Egypt, all that *was* in the field, both man and beast; and the hail struck every herb of the field and broke every tree of the field. [26] Only in the land of Goshen, where the children of Israel *were,* there was no hail.

[27] And Pharaoh sent and called for Moses and Aaron, and said to them, "I have sinned this time. The LORD *is* righteous, and my people and I *are* wicked. [28] Entreat the LORD, that there may be no *more* mighty thundering and hail, for *it is* enough. I will let you go, and you shall stay no longer."

[29] So Moses said to him, "As soon as I have gone out of the city, I will spread out my hands to the LORD; the thunder will cease, and there will be no more hail, that you may know that the earth *is* the LORD's. [30] But as for you and your servants, I know that you will not yet fear the LORD God."

[31] Now the flax and the barley were struck, for the barley *was* in the head and the flax *was* in bud. [32] But the wheat and the spelt were not struck, for they *are* late crops.

[33] So Moses went out of the city from Pharaoh and spread out his hands to the LORD; then the thunder and the hail ceased, and the rain was not

וְאַ֖ךְ אוֹתְךָ֣ וְאֶֽת־עַמְּךָ֑ בַּדֶּ֔בֶר וַתִּכָּחֵ֖ד מִן־הָאָֽרֶץ׃ 16 וְאוּלָ֗ם בַּעֲב֥וּר זֹאת֙ הֶעֱמַדְתִּ֔יךָ בַּעֲב֖וּר הַרְאֹתְךָ֣ אֶת־כֹּחִ֑י וּלְמַ֛עַן סַפֵּ֥ר שְׁמִ֖י בְּכָל־הָאָֽרֶץ׃ 17 עֽוֹדְךָ֖ מִסְתּוֹלֵ֣ל בְּעַמִּ֑י לְבִלְתִּ֖י שַׁלְּחָֽם׃ 18 הִנְנִ֤י מַמְטִיר֙ כָּעֵ֣ת מָחָ֔ר בָּרָ֖ד כָּבֵ֣ד מְאֹ֑ד אֲשֶׁ֨ר לֹא־הָיָ֤ה כָמֹ֙הוּ֙ בְּמִצְרַ֔יִם לְמִן־הַיּ֥וֹם הִוָּֽסְדָ֖ה וְעַד־עָֽתָּה׃ 19 וְעַתָּ֗ה שְׁלַ֤ח הָעֵז֙ אֶת־מִקְנְךָ֔ וְאֵ֛ת כָּל־אֲשֶׁ֥ר לְךָ֖ בַּשָּׂדֶ֑ה כָּל־הָאָדָ֣ם וְהַבְּהֵמָ֗ה אֲשֶֽׁר־יִמָּצֵ֤א בַשָּׂדֶה֙ וְלֹ֣א יֵאָסֵ֣ף הַבַּ֔יְתָה וְיָרַ֧ד עֲלֵהֶ֛ם הַבָּרָ֖ד וָמֵֽתוּ׃ 20 הַיָּרֵא֙ אֶת־דְּבַ֣ר יְהוָ֔ה מֵֽעַבְדֵ֖י פַּרְעֹ֑ה הֵנִ֛יס אֶת־עֲבָדָ֥יו וְאֶת־מִקְנֵ֖הוּ אֶל־הַבָּתִּֽים׃ 21 וַאֲשֶׁ֥ר לֹא־שָׂ֛ם לִבּ֖וֹ אֶל־דְּבַ֣ר יְהוָ֑ה וַֽיַּעֲזֹ֛ב אֶת־עֲבָדָ֥יו וְאֶת־מִקְנֵ֖הוּ בַּשָּׂדֶֽה׃ פ

22 וַיֹּ֨אמֶר יְהוָ֜ה אֶל־מֹשֶׁ֗ה נְטֵ֤ה אֶת־יָֽדְךָ֙ עַל־הַשָּׁמַ֔יִם וִ֥יהִ֖י בָרָ֑ד בְּכָל־אֶ֣רֶץ מִצְרָ֑יִם עַל־הָֽאָדָ֣ם וְעַל־הַבְּהֵמָ֗ה וְעַ֛ל כָּל־עֵ֥שֶׂב הַשָּׂדֶ֖ה בְּאֶ֥רֶץ מִצְרָֽיִם׃ 23 וַיֵּ֨ט מֹשֶׁ֣ה אֶת־מַטֵּהוּ֮ עַל־הַשָּׁמַיִם֒ וַֽיהוָ֗ה נָתַ֤ן קֹלֹת֙ וּבָרָ֔ד וַתִּ֥הֲלַךְ אֵ֖שׁ אָ֑רְצָה וַיַּמְטֵ֧ר יְהוָ֛ה בָּרָ֖ד עַל־אֶ֥רֶץ מִצְרָֽיִם׃ 24 וַיְהִ֣י בָרָ֔ד וְאֵ֕שׁ מִתְלַקַּ֖חַת בְּת֣וֹךְ הַבָּרָ֑ד כָּבֵ֣ד מְאֹ֔ד אֲ֠שֶׁר לֹֽא־הָיָ֤ה כָמֹ֙הוּ֙ בְּכָל־אֶ֣רֶץ מִצְרַ֔יִם מֵאָ֖ז הָיְתָ֥ה לְגֽוֹי׃ 25 וַיַּ֨ךְ הַבָּרָ֜ד בְּכָל־אֶ֣רֶץ מִצְרַ֗יִם אֵ֚ת כָּל־אֲשֶׁ֣ר בַּשָּׂדֶ֔ה מֵאָדָ֖ם וְעַד־בְּהֵמָ֑ה וְאֵ֨ת כָּל־עֵ֤שֶׂב הַשָּׂדֶה֙ הִכָּ֣ה הַבָּרָ֔ד וְאֶת־כָּל־עֵ֥ץ הַשָּׂדֶ֖ה שִׁבֵּֽר׃ 26 רַ֚ק בְּאֶ֣רֶץ גֹּ֔שֶׁן אֲשֶׁר־שָׁ֖ם בְּנֵ֣י יִשְׂרָאֵ֑ל לֹ֥א הָיָ֖ה בָּרָֽד׃ 27 וַיִּשְׁלַ֣ח פַּרְעֹ֗ה וַיִּקְרָא֙ לְמֹשֶׁ֣ה וּֽלְאַהֲרֹ֔ן וַיֹּ֤אמֶר אֲלֵהֶם֙ חָטָ֣אתִי הַפָּ֑עַם יְהוָה֙ הַצַּדִּ֔יק וַאֲנִ֥י וְעַמִּ֖י הָרְשָׁעִֽים׃ 28 הַעְתִּ֙ירוּ֙ אֶל־יְהֹוָ֔ה וְרַ֕ב מִֽהְיֹ֛ת קֹלֹ֥ת אֱלֹהִ֖ים וּבָרָ֑ד וַאֲשַׁלְּחָ֣ה אֶתְכֶ֔ם וְלֹ֥א תֹסִפ֖וּן לַעֲמֹֽד׃ 29 וַיֹּ֤אמֶר אֵלָיו֙ מֹשֶׁ֔ה כְּצֵאתִי֙ אֶת־הָעִ֔יר אֶפְרֹ֥שׂ אֶת־כַּפַּ֖י אֶל־יְהוָ֑ה הַקֹּל֣וֹת יֶחְדָּל֗וּן וְהַבָּרָד֙ לֹ֣א יִֽהְיֶה־ע֔וֹד לְמַ֣עַן תֵּדַ֔ע כִּ֥י לַֽיהוָ֖ה הָאָֽרֶץ׃ 30 וְאַתָּ֖ה וַעֲבָדֶ֑יךָ יָדַ֕עְתִּי כִּ֚י טֶ֣רֶם תִּ֣ירְא֔וּן מִפְּנֵ֖י יְהוָ֥ה אֱלֹהִֽים׃ 31 וְהַפִּשְׁתָּ֥ה וְהַשְּׂעֹרָ֖ה נֻכָּ֑תָה כִּ֤י הַשְּׂעֹרָה֙ אָבִ֔יב וְהַפִּשְׁתָּ֖ה גִּבְעֹֽל׃ 32 וְהַחִטָּ֥ה וְהַכֻּסֶּ֖מֶת לֹ֣א נֻכּ֑וּ כִּ֥י אֲפִילֹ֖ת הֵֽנָּה׃ 33 וַיֵּצֵ֣א מֹשֶׁ֣ה מֵעִ֣ם פַּרְעֹה֮ אֶת־הָעִיר֒ וַיִּפְרֹ֥שׂ כַּפָּ֖יו אֶל־יְהוָ֑ה וַֽיַּחְדְּל֤וּ הַקֹּלוֹת֙ וְהַבָּרָ֔ד וּמָטָ֖ר לֹא־נִתַּ֥ךְ אָֽרְצָה׃

poured on the earth. ³⁴And when Pharaoh saw that
the rain, the hail, and the thunder had ceased, he
sinned yet more; and he hardened his heart, he and
his servants. ³⁵So the heart of Pharaoh was hard;
neither would he let the children of Israel go, as the
Lord had spoken by Moses.

10 Now the Lord said to Moses, "Go in to
Pharaoh; for I have hardened his heart and the
hearts of his servants, that I may show these signs
of Mine before him, ²and that you may tell in the
hearing of your son and your son's son the mighty
things I have done in Egypt, and My signs which I
have done among them, that you may know that I
am the Lord."

³So Moses and Aaron came in to Pharaoh and
said to him, "Thus says the Lord God of the
Hebrews: 'How long will you refuse to humble
yourself before Me? Let My people go, that they
may serve Me. ⁴Or else, if you refuse to let My
people go, behold, tomorrow I will bring locusts
into your territory. ⁵And they shall cover the face
of the earth, so that no one will be able to see the
earth; and they shall eat the residue of what is left,
which remains to you from the hail, and they shall
eat every tree which grows up for you out of the
field. ⁶They shall fill your houses, the houses of all
your servants, and the houses of all the Egyptians—
which neither your fathers nor your fathers' fathers
have seen, since the day that they were on the earth
to this day.'" And he turned and went out from
Pharaoh.

⁷Then Pharaoh's servants said to him, "How
long shall this man be a snare to us? Let the men go,
that they may serve the Lord their God. Do you
not yet know that Egypt is destroyed?"

⁸So Moses and Aaron were brought again to
Pharaoh, and he said to them, "Go, serve the Lord
your God. Who *are* the ones that are going?"

⁹And Moses said, "We will go with our young
and our old; with our sons and our daughters, with
our flocks and our herds we will go, for we must
hold a feast to the Lord."

¹⁰Then he said to them, "The Lord had better be
with you when I let you and your little ones go!
Beware, for evil is ahead of you. ¹¹Not so! Go now,
you *who are* men, and serve the Lord, for that is
what you desired." And they were driven out from
Pharaoh's presence.

¹²Then the Lord said to Moses, "Stretch out
your hand over the land of Egypt for the locusts,
that they may come upon the land of Egypt, and eat
every herb of the land—all that the hail has left."

¹³So Moses stretched out his rod over the land of

34 וַיַּרְא פַּרְעֹה כִּי־חָדַל הַמָּטָר וְהַבָּרָד וְהַקֹּלֹת
וַיֹּסֶף לַחֲטֹא וַיַּכְבֵּד לִבּוֹ הוּא וַעֲבָדָיו: 35 וַיֶּחֱזַק
לֵב פַּרְעֹה וְלֹא שִׁלַּח אֶת־בְּנֵי יִשְׂרָאֵל כַּאֲשֶׁר דִּבֶּר
יְהֹוָה בְּיַד־מֹשֶׁה:
פ

י וַיֹּאמֶר יְהֹוָה אֶל־מֹשֶׁה בֹּא אֶל־פַּרְעֹה כִּי־אֲנִי
הִכְבַּדְתִּי אֶת־לִבּוֹ וְאֶת־לֵב עֲבָדָיו לְמַעַן שִׁתִי
אֹתֹתַי אֵלֶּה בְּקִרְבּוֹ: 2 וּלְמַעַן תְּסַפֵּר בְּאָזְנֵי בִנְךָ
וּבֶן־בִּנְךָ אֵת אֲשֶׁר הִתְעַלַּלְתִּי בְּמִצְרַיִם וְאֶת־אֹתֹתַי
אֲשֶׁר־שַׂמְתִּי בָם וִידַעְתֶּם כִּי־אֲנִי יְהֹוָה: 3 וַיָּבֹא
מֹשֶׁה וְאַהֲרֹן אֶל־פַּרְעֹה וַיֹּאמְרוּ אֵלָיו כֹּה־אָמַר
יְהֹוָה אֱלֹהֵי הָעִבְרִים עַד־מָתַי מֵאַנְתָּ לֵעָנֹת מִפָּנָי
שַׁלַּח עַמִּי וְיַעַבְדֻנִי: 4 כִּי אִם־מָאֵן אַתָּה לְשַׁלֵּחַ
אֶת־עַמִּי הִנְנִי מֵבִיא מָחָר אַרְבֶּה בִּגְבֻלֶךָ: 5 וְכִסָּה
אֶת־עֵין הָאָרֶץ וְלֹא יוּכַל לִרְאֹת אֶת־הָאָרֶץ וְאָכַל
אֶת־יֶתֶר הַפְּלֵטָה הַנִּשְׁאֶרֶת לָכֶם מִן־הַבָּרָד וְאָכַל
אֶת־כָּל־הָעֵץ הַצֹּמֵחַ לָכֶם מִן־הַשָּׂדֶה: 6 וּמָלְאוּ
בָתֶּיךָ וּבָתֵּי כָל־עֲבָדֶיךָ וּבָתֵּי כָל־מִצְרַיִם אֲשֶׁר לֹא־
רָאוּ אֲבֹתֶיךָ וַאֲבוֹת אֲבֹתֶיךָ מִיּוֹם הֱיוֹתָם עַל־
הָאֲדָמָה עַד הַיּוֹם הַזֶּה וַיִּפֶן וַיֵּצֵא מֵעִם פַּרְעֹה:
7 וַיֹּאמְרוּ עַבְדֵי פַרְעֹה אֵלָיו עַד־מָתַי יִהְיֶה זֶה
לָנוּ לְמוֹקֵשׁ שַׁלַּח אֶת־הָאֲנָשִׁים וְיַעַבְדוּ אֶת־יְהֹוָה
אֱלֹהֵיהֶם הֲטֶרֶם תֵּדַע כִּי אָבְדָה מִצְרָיִם: 8 וַיּוּשַׁב
אֶת־מֹשֶׁה וְאֶת־אַהֲרֹן אֶל־פַּרְעֹה וַיֹּאמֶר אֲלֵהֶם לְכוּ
עִבְדוּ אֶת־יְהֹוָה אֱלֹהֵיכֶם מִי וָמִי הַהֹלְכִים: 9 וַיֹּאמֶר
מֹשֶׁה בִּנְעָרֵינוּ וּבִזְקֵנֵינוּ נֵלֵךְ בְּבָנֵינוּ וּבִבְנוֹתֵנוּ
בְּצֹאנֵנוּ וּבִבְקָרֵנוּ נֵלֵךְ כִּי חַג־יְהֹוָה לָנוּ: 10 וַיֹּאמֶר
אֲלֵהֶם יְהִי כֵן יְהֹוָה עִמָּכֶם כַּאֲשֶׁר אֲשַׁלַּח אֶתְכֶם
וְאֶת־טַפְּכֶם רְאוּ כִּי רָעָה נֶגֶד פְּנֵיכֶם: 11 לֹא כֵן
לְכוּ־נָא הַגְּבָרִים וְעִבְדוּ אֶת־יְהֹוָה כִּי אֹתָהּ אַתֶּם
מְבַקְשִׁים וַיְגָרֶשׁ אֹתָם מֵאֵת פְּנֵי פַרְעֹה:
פ

12 וַיֹּאמֶר יְהֹוָה אֶל־מֹשֶׁה נְטֵה יָדְךָ עַל־אֶרֶץ
מִצְרַיִם בָּאַרְבֶּה וְיַעַל עַל־אֶרֶץ מִצְרָיִם וְיֹאכַל אֶת־
כָּל־עֵשֶׂב הָאָרֶץ אֵת כָּל־אֲשֶׁר הִשְׁאִיר הַבָּרָד:
13 וַיֵּט מֹשֶׁה אֶת־מַטֵּהוּ עַל־אֶרֶץ מִצְרַיִם וַיהֹוָה
נִהַג רוּחַ־קָדִים בָּאָרֶץ כָּל־הַיּוֹם הַהוּא וְכָל־הַלָּיְלָה

Egypt, and the LORD brought an east wind on the land all that day and all *that* night. When it was morning, the east wind brought the locusts. ¹⁴ And the locusts went up over all the land of Egypt and rested on all the territory of Egypt. *They were* very severe; previously there had been no such locusts as they, nor shall there be such after them. ¹⁵ For they covered the face of the whole earth, so that the land was darkened; and they ate every herb of the land and all the fruit of the trees which the hail had left. So there remained nothing green on the trees or on the plants of the field throughout all the land of Egypt.

¹⁶ Then Pharaoh called for Moses and Aaron in haste, and said, "I have sinned against the LORD your God and against you. ¹⁷ Now therefore, please forgive my sin only this once, and entreat the LORD your God, that He may take away from me this death only." ¹⁸ So he went out from Pharaoh and entreated the LORD. ¹⁹ And the LORD turned a very strong west wind, which took the locusts away and blew them into the Red Sea. There remained not one locust in all the territory of Egypt. ²⁰ But the LORD hardened Pharaoh's heart, and he did not let the children of Israel go.

²¹ Then the LORD said to Moses, "Stretch out your hand toward heaven, that there may be darkness over the land of Egypt, darkness *which* may even be felt." ²² So Moses stretched out his hand toward heaven, and there was thick darkness in all the land of Egypt three days. ²³ They did not see one another; nor did anyone rise from his place for three days. But all the children of Israel had light in their dwellings.

²⁴ Then Pharaoh called to Moses and said, "Go, serve the LORD; only let your flocks and your herds be kept back. Let your little ones also go with you."

²⁵ But Moses said, "You must also give us sacrifices and burnt offerings, that we may sacrifice to the LORD our God. ²⁶ Our livestock also shall go with us; not a hoof shall be left behind. For we must take some of them to serve the LORD our God, and even we do not know with what we must serve the LORD until we arrive there."

²⁷ But the LORD hardened Pharaoh's heart, and he would not let them go. ²⁸ Then Pharaoh said to him, "Get away from me! Take heed to yourself and see my face no more! For in the day you see my face you shall die!"

²⁹ So Moses said, "You have spoken well. I will never see your face again."

הַבֹּקֶר הָיָה וְרוּחַ הַקָּדִים נָשָׂא אֵת־הָאַרְבֶּה: 14 וַיַּעַל הָאַרְבֶּה עַל כָּל־אֶרֶץ מִצְרַיִם וַיָּנַח בְּכֹל גְּבוּל מִצְרָיִם כָּבֵד מְאֹד לְפָנָיו לֹא־הָיָה כֵן אַרְבֶּה כָּמֹהוּ וְאַחֲרָיו לֹא יִהְיֶה־כֵּן: 15 וַיְכַס אֶת־עֵין כָּל־הָאָרֶץ וַתֶּחְשַׁךְ הָאָרֶץ וַיֹּאכַל אֶת־כָּל־עֵשֶׂב הָאָרֶץ וְאֵת כָּל־פְּרִי הָעֵץ אֲשֶׁר הוֹתִיר הַבָּרָד וְלֹא־נוֹתַר כָּל־יֶרֶק בָּעֵץ וּבְעֵשֶׂב הַשָּׂדֶה בְּכָל־אֶרֶץ מִצְרָיִם: 16 וַיְמַהֵר פַּרְעֹה לִקְרֹא לְמֹשֶׁה וּלְאַהֲרֹן וַיֹּאמֶר חָטָאתִי לַיהוָה אֱלֹהֵיכֶם וְלָכֶם: 17 וְעַתָּה שָׂא נָא חַטָּאתִי אַךְ הַפַּעַם וְהַעְתִּירוּ לַיהוָה אֱלֹהֵיכֶם וְיָסֵר מֵעָלַי רַק אֶת־הַמָּוֶת הַזֶּה: 18 וַיֵּצֵא מֵעִם פַּרְעֹה וַיֶּעְתַּר אֶל־יְהוָה: 19 וַיַּהֲפֹךְ יְהוָה רוּחַ־יָם חָזָק מְאֹד וַיִּשָּׂא אֶת־הָאַרְבֶּה וַיִּתְקָעֵהוּ יָמָּה סּוּף לֹא נִשְׁאַר אַרְבֶּה אֶחָד בְּכֹל גְּבוּל מִצְרָיִם: 20 וַיְחַזֵּק יְהוָה אֶת־לֵב פַּרְעֹה וְלֹא שִׁלַּח אֶת־בְּנֵי יִשְׂרָאֵל: פ

21 וַיֹּאמֶר יְהוָה אֶל־מֹשֶׁה נְטֵה יָדְךָ עַל־הַשָּׁמַיִם וִיהִי חֹשֶׁךְ עַל־אֶרֶץ מִצְרָיִם וְיָמֵשׁ חֹשֶׁךְ: 22 וַיֵּט מֹשֶׁה אֶת־יָדוֹ עַל־הַשָּׁמָיִם וַיְהִי חֹשֶׁךְ־אֲפֵלָה בְּכָל־אֶרֶץ מִצְרַיִם שְׁלֹשֶׁת יָמִים: 23 לֹא־רָאוּ אִישׁ אֶת־אָחִיו וְלֹא־קָמוּ אִישׁ מִתַּחְתָּיו שְׁלֹשֶׁת יָמִים וּלְכָל־בְּנֵי יִשְׂרָאֵל הָיָה אוֹר בְּמוֹשְׁבֹתָם: 24 וַיִּקְרָא פַרְעֹה אֶל־מֹשֶׁה וַיֹּאמֶר לְכוּ עִבְדוּ אֶת־יְהוָה רַק צֹאנְכֶם וּבְקַרְכֶם יֻצָּג גַּם־טַפְּכֶם יֵלֵךְ עִמָּכֶם: 25 וַיֹּאמֶר מֹשֶׁה גַּם־אַתָּה תִּתֵּן בְּיָדֵנוּ זְבָחִים וְעֹלוֹת וְעָשִׂינוּ לַיהוָה אֱלֹהֵינוּ: 26 וְגַם־מִקְנֵנוּ יֵלֵךְ עִמָּנוּ לֹא תִשָּׁאֵר פַּרְסָה כִּי מִמֶּנּוּ נִקַּח לַעֲבֹד אֶת־יְהוָה אֱלֹהֵינוּ וַאֲנַחְנוּ לֹא־נֵדַע מַה־נַּעֲבֹד אֶת־יְהוָה עַד־בֹּאֵנוּ שָׁמָּה: 27 וַיְחַזֵּק יְהוָה אֶת־לֵב פַּרְעֹה וְלֹא אָבָה לְשַׁלְּחָם: 28 וַיֹּאמֶר־לוֹ פַרְעֹה לֵךְ מֵעָלָי הִשָּׁמֶר לְךָ אַל־תֹּסֶף רְאוֹת פָּנַי כִּי בְּיוֹם רְאֹתְךָ פָנַי תָּמוּת: 29 וַיֹּאמֶר מֹשֶׁה כֵּן דִּבַּרְתָּ לֹא־אֹסִף עוֹד רְאוֹת פָּנֶיךָ: פ

11 And the LORD said to Moses, "I will bring one more plague on Pharaoh and on Egypt. Afterward he will let you go from here. When he lets *you* go, he will surely drive you out of here altogether. ²Speak now in the hearing of the people, and let every man ask from his neighbor and every woman from her neighbor, articles of silver and articles of gold." ³And the LORD gave the people favor in the sight of the Egyptians. Moreover the man Moses *was* very great in the land of Egypt, in the sight of Pharaoh's servants and in the sight of the people.

⁴Then Moses said, "Thus says the LORD: 'About midnight I will go out into the midst of Egypt; ⁵and all the firstborn in the land of Egypt shall die, from the firstborn of Pharaoh who sits on his throne, even to the firstborn of the female servant who *is* behind the handmill, and all the firstborn of the animals. ⁶Then there shall be a great cry throughout all the land of Egypt, such as was not like it *before,* nor shall be like it again. ⁷But against none of the children of Israel shall a dog move its tongue, against man or beast, that you may know that the LORD does make a difference between the Egyptians and Israel.' ⁸And all these your servants shall come down to me and bow down to me, saying, 'Get out, and all the people who follow you!' After that I will go out." Then he went out from Pharaoh in great anger.

⁹But the LORD said to Moses, "Pharaoh will not heed you, so that My wonders may be multiplied in the land of Egypt." ¹⁰So Moses and Aaron did all these wonders before Pharaoh; and the LORD hardened Pharaoh's heart, and he did not let the children of Israel go out of his land.

12 Now the LORD spoke to Moses and Aaron in the land of Egypt, saying, ²"This month *shall be* your beginning of months; it *shall be* the first month of the year to you. ³Speak to all the congregation of Israel, saying: 'On the tenth of this month every man shall take for himself a lamb, according to the house of *his* father, a lamb for a household. ⁴And if the household is too small for the lamb, let him and his neighbor next to his house take *it* according to the number of the persons; according to each man's need you shall make your count for the lamb. ⁵Your lamb shall be without blemish, a male of the first year. You may take *it* from the sheep or from the goats. ⁶Now you shall keep it until the fourteenth day of the same month. Then the whole assembly of the congregation of Israel shall kill it at twilight. ⁷And they shall take *some* of the blood and put *it* on the two doorposts and on the lintel of the houses where they eat it. ⁸Then they shall eat

יא וַיֹּ֤אמֶר יְהֹוָה֙ אֶל־מֹשֶׁ֔ה ע֣וֹד נֶ֤גַע אֶחָד֙ אָבִ֣יא עַל־פַּרְעֹה֮ וְעַל־מִצְרַיִם֒ אַחֲרֵי־כֵ֕ן יְשַׁלַּ֥ח אֶתְכֶ֖ם מִזֶּ֑ה כְּשַׁלְּח֕וֹ כָּלָ֕ה גָּרֵ֛שׁ יְגָרֵ֥שׁ אֶתְכֶ֖ם מִזֶּֽה: ² דַּבֶּר־נָ֖א בְּאׇזְנֵ֣י הָעָ֑ם וְיִשְׁאֲל֣וּ ׀ אִ֣ישׁ ׀ מֵאֵ֣ת רֵעֵ֗הוּ וְאִשָּׁה֙ מֵאֵ֣ת רְעוּתָ֔הּ כְּלֵי־כֶ֖סֶף וּכְלֵ֥י זָהָֽב: ³ וַיִּתֵּ֧ן יְהֹוָ֛ה אֶת־חֵ֥ן הָעָ֖ם בְּעֵינֵ֣י מִצְרָ֑יִם גַּ֣ם ׀ הָאִ֣ישׁ מֹשֶׁ֗ה גָּד֤וֹל מְאֹד֙ בְּאֶ֣רֶץ מִצְרַ֔יִם בְּעֵינֵ֥י עַבְדֵֽי־פַרְעֹ֖ה וּבְעֵינֵ֥י הָעָֽם: ס ⁴ וַיֹּ֣אמֶר מֹשֶׁ֔ה כֹּ֖ה אָמַ֣ר יְהֹוָ֑ה כַּחֲצֹ֣ת הַלַּ֔יְלָה אֲנִ֥י יוֹצֵ֖א בְּת֥וֹךְ מִצְרָֽיִם: ⁵ וּמֵ֣ת כׇּל־בְּכוֹר֮ בְּאֶ֣רֶץ מִצְרַיִם֒ מִבְּכ֤וֹר פַּרְעֹה֙ הַיֹּשֵׁ֣ב עַל־כִּסְא֔וֹ עַ֚ד בְּכ֣וֹר הַשִּׁפְחָ֔ה אֲשֶׁ֖ר אַחַ֣ר הָרֵחָ֑יִם וְכֹ֖ל בְּכ֥וֹר בְּהֵמָֽה: ⁶ וְהָ֥יְתָ֛ה צְעָקָ֥ה גְדֹלָ֖ה בְּכׇל־אֶ֣רֶץ מִצְרָ֑יִם אֲשֶׁ֤ר כָּמֹ֙הוּ֙ לֹ֣א נִֽהְיָ֔תָה וְכָמֹ֖הוּ לֹ֥א תֹסִֽף: ⁷ וּלְכֹ֣ל ׀ בְּנֵ֣י יִשְׂרָאֵ֗ל לֹ֤א יֶֽחֱרַץ־כֶּ֙לֶב֙ לְשֹׁנ֔וֹ לְמֵאִ֖ישׁ וְעַד־בְּהֵמָ֑ה לְמַ֙עַן֙ תֵּֽדְע֔וּן אֲשֶׁר֙ יַפְלֶ֣ה יְהֹוָ֔ה בֵּ֥ין מִצְרַ֖יִם וּבֵ֥ין יִשְׂרָאֵֽל: ⁸ וְיָרְד֣וּ כׇל־עֲבָדֶ֩יךָ֩ אֵ֨לֶּה אֵלַ֜י וְהִשְׁתַּֽחֲווּ־לִ֣י לֵאמֹ֗ר צֵ֤א אַתָּה֙ וְכׇל־הָעָ֣ם אֲשֶׁר־בְּרַגְלֶ֔יךָ וְאַחֲרֵי־כֵ֖ן אֵצֵ֑א וַיֵּצֵ֥א מֵֽעִם־פַּרְעֹ֖ה בׇּחֳרִי־אָֽף: ס ⁹ וַיֹּ֤אמֶר יְהֹוָה֙ אֶל־מֹשֶׁ֔ה לֹֽא־יִשְׁמַ֥ע אֲלֵיכֶ֖ם פַּרְעֹ֑ה לְמַ֛עַן רְב֥וֹת מוֹפְתַ֖י בְּאֶ֥רֶץ מִצְרָֽיִם: ¹⁰ וּמֹשֶׁ֣ה וְאַהֲרֹ֗ן עָשׂ֛וּ אֶת־כׇּל־הַמֹּפְתִ֥ים הָאֵ֖לֶּה לִפְנֵ֣י פַרְעֹ֑ה וַיְחַזֵּ֤ק יְהֹוָה֙ אֶת־לֵ֣ב פַּרְעֹ֔ה וְלֹֽא־שִׁלַּ֥ח אֶת־בְּנֵֽי־יִשְׂרָאֵ֖ל מֵאַרְצֽוֹ: פ

יב וַיֹּ֤אמֶר יְהֹוָה֙ אֶל־מֹשֶׁ֣ה וְאֶֽל־אַהֲרֹ֔ן בְּאֶ֥רֶץ מִצְרַ֖יִם לֵאמֹֽר: ² הַחֹ֧דֶשׁ הַזֶּ֛ה לָכֶ֖ם רֹ֣אשׁ חֳדָשִׁ֑ים רִאשׁ֥וֹן הוּא֙ לָכֶ֔ם לְחׇדְשֵׁ֖י הַשָּׁנָֽה: ³ דַּבְּר֗וּ אֶֽל־כׇּל־עֲדַ֤ת יִשְׂרָאֵל֙ לֵאמֹ֔ר בֶּעָשֹׂ֖ר לַחֹ֣דֶשׁ הַזֶּ֑ה וְיִקְח֣וּ לָהֶ֗ם אִ֛ישׁ שֶׂ֥ה לְבֵית־אָבֹ֖ת שֶׂ֥ה לַבָּֽיִת: ⁴ וְאִם־יִמְעַ֣ט הַבַּ֘יִת֮ מִהְיֹ֣ת מִשֶּׂה֒ וְלָקַ֣ח ה֗וּא וּשְׁכֵנ֛וֹ הַקָּרֹ֥ב אֶל־בֵּית֖וֹ בְּמִכְסַ֣ת נְפָשֹׁ֑ת אִ֚ישׁ לְפִ֣י אׇכְל֔וֹ תָּכֹ֖סּוּ עַל־הַשֶּֽׂה: ⁵ שֶׂ֥ה תָמִ֛ים זָכָ֥ר בֶּן־שָׁנָ֖ה יִהְיֶ֣ה לָכֶ֑ם מִן־הַכְּבָשִׂ֥ים וּמִן־הָעִזִּ֖ים תִּקָּֽחוּ: ⁶ וְהָיָ֤ה לָכֶם֙ לְמִשְׁמֶ֔רֶת עַ֣ד אַרְבָּעָ֥ה עָשָׂ֛ר י֖וֹם לַחֹ֣דֶשׁ הַזֶּ֑ה וְשָׁחֲט֣וּ אֹת֗וֹ כֹּ֛ל קְהַ֥ל עֲדַֽת־יִשְׂרָאֵ֖ל בֵּ֥ין הָעַרְבָּֽיִם: ⁷ וְלָֽקְחוּ֙ מִן־הַדָּ֔ם וְנָ֥תְנ֛וּ עַל־שְׁתֵּ֥י הַמְּזוּזֹ֖ת וְעַל־הַמַּשְׁק֑וֹף עַ֚ל הַבָּ֣תִּ֔ים אֲשֶׁר־יֹאכְל֥וּ אֹת֖וֹ בָּהֶֽם:

the flesh on that night; roasted in fire, with unleavened bread *and* with bitter *herbs* they shall eat it. ⁹Do not eat it raw, nor boiled at all with water, but roasted in fire—its head with its legs and its entrails. ¹⁰You shall let none of it remain until morning, and what remains of it until morning you shall burn with fire. ¹¹And thus you shall eat it: *with* a belt on your waist, your sandals on your feet, and your staff in your hand. So you shall eat it in haste. It *is* the LORD's Passover.

¹²'For I will pass through the land of Egypt on that night, and will strike all the firstborn in the land of Egypt, both man and beast; and against all the gods of Egypt I will execute judgment: I *am* the LORD. ¹³Now the blood shall be a sign for you on the houses where you *are*. And when I see the blood, I will pass over you; and the plague shall not be on you to destroy *you* when I strike the land of Egypt.

¹⁴'So this day shall be to you a memorial; and you shall keep it as a feast to the LORD throughout your generations. You shall keep it as a feast by an everlasting ordinance. ¹⁵Seven days you shall eat unleavened bread. On the first day you shall remove leaven from your houses. For whoever eats leavened bread from the first day until the seventh day, that person shall be cut off from Israel. ¹⁶On the first day *there shall be* a holy convocation, and on the seventh day there shall be a holy convocation for you. No manner of work shall be done on them; but *that* which everyone must eat—that only may be prepared by you. ¹⁷So you shall observe *the Feast of* Unleavened Bread, for on this same day I will have brought your armies out of the land of Egypt. Therefore you shall observe this day throughout your generations as an everlasting ordinance. ¹⁸In the first *month,* on the fourteenth day of the month at evening, you shall eat unleavened bread, until the twenty-first day of the month at evening. ¹⁹For seven days no leaven shall be found in your houses, since whoever eats what is leavened, that same person shall be cut off from the congregation of Israel, whether *he is* a stranger or a native of the land. ²⁰You shall eat nothing leavened; in all your dwellings you shall eat unleavened bread.'"

²¹Then Moses called for all the elders of Israel and said to them, "Pick out and take lambs for yourselves according to your families, and kill the Passover *lamb.* ²²And you shall take a bunch of hyssop, dip *it* in the blood that *is* in the basin, and strike the lintel and the two doorposts with the blood that *is* in the basin. And none of you shall go out of the door of his house until morning. ²³For

8 וְאָכְלוּ אֶת־הַבָּשָׂר בַּלַּיְלָה הַזֶּה צְלִי־אֵשׁ וּמַצּוֹת עַל־מְרֹרִים יֹאכְלֻהוּ: 9 אַל־תֹּאכְלוּ מִמֶּנּוּ נָא וּבָשֵׁל מְבֻשָּׁל בַּמָּיִם כִּי אִם־צְלִי־אֵשׁ רֹאשׁוֹ עַל־כְּרָעָיו וְעַל־קִרְבּוֹ: 10 וְלֹא־תוֹתִירוּ מִמֶּנּוּ עַד־בֹּקֶר וְהַנֹּתָר מִמֶּנּוּ עַד־בֹּקֶר בָּאֵשׁ תִּשְׂרֹפוּ: 11 וְכָכָה תֹּאכְלוּ אֹתוֹ מָתְנֵיכֶם חֲגֻרִים נַעֲלֵיכֶם בְּרַגְלֵיכֶם וּמַקֶּלְכֶם בְּיֶדְכֶם וַאֲכַלְתֶּם אֹתוֹ בְּחִפָּזוֹן פֶּסַח הוּא לַיהוָה: 12 וְעָבַרְתִּי בְאֶרֶץ־מִצְרַיִם בַּלַּיְלָה הַזֶּה וְהִכֵּיתִי כָל־בְּכוֹר בְּאֶרֶץ מִצְרַיִם מֵאָדָם וְעַד־בְּהֵמָה וּבְכָל־אֱלֹהֵי מִצְרַיִם אֶעֱשֶׂה שְׁפָטִים אֲנִי יְהוָה: 13 וְהָיָה הַדָּם לָכֶם לְאֹת עַל הַבָּתִּים אֲשֶׁר אַתֶּם שָׁם וְרָאִיתִי אֶת־הַדָּם וּפָסַחְתִּי עֲלֵכֶם וְלֹא־יִהְיֶה בָכֶם נֶגֶף לְמַשְׁחִית בְּהַכֹּתִי בְּאֶרֶץ מִצְרָיִם: 14 וְהָיָה הַיּוֹם הַזֶּה לָכֶם לְזִכָּרוֹן וְחַגֹּתֶם אֹתוֹ חַג לַיהוָה לְדֹרֹתֵיכֶם חֻקַּת עוֹלָם תְּחָגֻּהוּ: 15 שִׁבְעַת יָמִים מַצּוֹת תֹּאכֵלוּ אַךְ בַּיּוֹם הָרִאשׁוֹן תַּשְׁבִּיתוּ שְּׂאֹר מִבָּתֵּיכֶם כִּי כָּל־אֹכֵל חָמֵץ וְנִכְרְתָה הַנֶּפֶשׁ הַהִוא מִיִּשְׂרָאֵל מִיּוֹם הָרִאשֹׁן עַד־יוֹם הַשְּׁבִעִי: 16 וּבַיּוֹם הָרִאשׁוֹן מִקְרָא־קֹדֶשׁ וּבַיּוֹם הַשְּׁבִיעִי מִקְרָא־קֹדֶשׁ יִהְיֶה לָכֶם כָּל־מְלָאכָה לֹא־יֵעָשֶׂה בָהֶם אַךְ אֲשֶׁר יֵאָכֵל לְכָל־נֶפֶשׁ הוּא לְבַדּוֹ יֵעָשֶׂה לָכֶם: 17 וּשְׁמַרְתֶּם אֶת־הַמַּצּוֹת כִּי בְּעֶצֶם הַיּוֹם הַזֶּה הוֹצֵאתִי אֶת־צִבְאוֹתֵיכֶם מֵאֶרֶץ מִצְרָיִם וּשְׁמַרְתֶּם אֶת־הַיּוֹם הַזֶּה לְדֹרֹתֵיכֶם חֻקַּת עוֹלָם: 18 בָּרִאשֹׁן בְּאַרְבָּעָה עָשָׂר יוֹם לַחֹדֶשׁ בָּעֶרֶב תֹּאכְלוּ מַצֹּת עַד יוֹם הָאֶחָד וְעֶשְׂרִים לַחֹדֶשׁ בָּעָרֶב: 19 שִׁבְעַת יָמִים שְׂאֹר לֹא יִמָּצֵא בְּבָתֵּיכֶם כִּי כָּל־אֹכֵל מַחְמֶצֶת וְנִכְרְתָה הַנֶּפֶשׁ הַהִוא מֵעֲדַת יִשְׂרָאֵל בַּגֵּר וּבְאֶזְרַח הָאָרֶץ: 20 כָּל־מַחְמֶצֶת לֹא תֹאכֵלוּ בְּכֹל מוֹשְׁבֹתֵיכֶם תֹּאכְלוּ מַצּוֹת: פ

21 וַיִּקְרָא מֹשֶׁה לְכָל־זִקְנֵי יִשְׂרָאֵל וַיֹּאמֶר אֲלֵהֶם מִשְׁכוּ וּקְחוּ לָכֶם צֹאן לְמִשְׁפְּחֹתֵיכֶם וְשַׁחֲטוּ הַפָּסַח: 22 וּלְקַחְתֶּם אֲגֻדַּת אֵזוֹב וּטְבַלְתֶּם בַּדָּם אֲשֶׁר־בַּסַּף וְהִגַּעְתֶּם אֶל־הַמַּשְׁקוֹף וְאֶל־שְׁתֵּי הַמְּזוּזֹת מִן־הַדָּם אֲשֶׁר בַּסָּף וְאַתֶּם לֹא תֵצְאוּ אִישׁ מִפֶּתַח־בֵּיתוֹ עַד־בֹּקֶר: 23 וְעָבַר יְהוָה לִנְגֹּף אֶת־

the LORD will pass through to strike the Egyptians; and when He sees the blood on the lintel and on the two doorposts, the LORD will pass over the door and not allow the destroyer to come into your houses to strike *you*. ²⁴And you shall observe this thing as an ordinance for you and your sons forever. ²⁵It will come to pass when you come to the land which the LORD will give you, just as He promised, that you shall keep this service. ²⁶And it shall be, when your children say to you, 'What do you mean by this service?' ²⁷that you shall say, 'It *is* the Passover sacrifice of the LORD, who passed over the houses of the children of Israel in Egypt when He struck the Egyptians and delivered our households.'" So the people bowed their heads and worshiped. ²⁸Then the children of Israel went away and did *so;* just as the LORD had commanded Moses and Aaron, so they did.

²⁹And it came to pass at midnight that the LORD struck all the firstborn in the land of Egypt, from the firstborn of Pharaoh who sat on his throne to the firstborn of the captive who *was* in the dungeon, and all the firstborn of livestock. ³⁰So Pharaoh rose in the night, he, all his servants, and all the Egyptians; and there was a great cry in Egypt, for *there was* not a house where *there was* not one dead.

³¹Then he called for Moses and Aaron by night, and said, "Rise, go out from among my people, both you and the children of Israel. And go, serve the LORD as you have said. ³²Also take your flocks and your herds, as you have said, and be gone; and bless me also."

³³And the Egyptians urged the people, that they might send them out of the land in haste. For they said, "We *shall* all *be* dead." ³⁴So the people took their dough before it was leavened, having their kneading bowls bound up in their clothes on their shoulders. ³⁵Now the children of Israel had done according to the word of Moses, and they had asked from the Egyptians articles of silver, articles of gold, and clothing. ³⁶And the LORD had given the people favor in the sight of the Egyptians, so that they granted them *what they requested*. Thus they plundered the Egyptians.

³⁷Then the children of Israel journeyed from Rameses to Succoth, about six hundred thousand men on foot, besides children. ³⁸A mixed multitude went up with them also, and flocks and herds—a great deal of livestock. ³⁹And they baked unleavened cakes of the dough which they had brought out of Egypt; for it was not leavened, because they were driven out of Egypt and could not wait, nor had they prepared provisions for themselves.

מִצְרַיִם וְרָאָה אֶת־הַדָּם עַל־הַמַּשְׁקוֹף וְעַל שְׁתֵּי הַמְּזוּזֹת וּפָסַח יְהֹוָה עַל־הַפֶּתַח וְלֹא יִתֵּן הַמַּשְׁחִית לָבֹא אֶל־בָּתֵּיכֶם לִנְגֹּף: 24 וּשְׁמַרְתֶּם אֶת־הַדָּבָר הַזֶּה לְחָק־לְךָ וּלְבָנֶיךָ עַד־עוֹלָם: 25 וְהָיָה כִּי־תָבֹאוּ אֶל־הָאָרֶץ אֲשֶׁר יִתֵּן יְהֹוָה לָכֶם כַּאֲשֶׁר דִּבֵּר וּשְׁמַרְתֶּם אֶת־הָעֲבֹדָה הַזֹּאת: 26 וְהָיָה כִּי־יֹאמְרוּ אֲלֵיכֶם בְּנֵיכֶם מָה הָעֲבֹדָה הַזֹּאת לָכֶם: 27 וַאֲמַרְתֶּם זֶבַח־פֶּסַח הוּא לַיהֹוָה אֲשֶׁר פָּסַח עַל־בָּתֵּי בְנֵי־יִשְׂרָאֵל בְּמִצְרַיִם בְּנָגְפּוֹ אֶת־מִצְרַיִם וְאֶת־בָּתֵּינוּ הִצִּיל וַיִּקֹּד הָעָם וַיִּשְׁתַּחֲווּ: 28 וַיֵּלְכוּ וַיַּעֲשׂוּ בְּנֵי יִשְׂרָאֵל כַּאֲשֶׁר צִוָּה יְהֹוָה אֶת־מֹשֶׁה וְאַהֲרֹן כֵּן עָשׂוּ: ס 29 וַיְהִי | בַּחֲצִי הַלַּיְלָה וַיהֹוָה הִכָּה כָל־בְּכוֹר בְּאֶרֶץ מִצְרַיִם מִבְּכֹר פַּרְעֹה הַיֹּשֵׁב עַל־כִּסְאוֹ עַד בְּכוֹר הַשְּׁבִי אֲשֶׁר בְּבֵית הַבּוֹר וְכֹל בְּכוֹר בְּהֵמָה: 30 וַיָּקָם פַּרְעֹה לַיְלָה הוּא וְכָל־עֲבָדָיו וְכָל־מִצְרַיִם וַתְּהִי צְעָקָה גְדֹלָה בְּמִצְרָיִם כִּי־אֵין בַּיִת אֲשֶׁר אֵין־שָׁם מֵת: 31 וַיִּקְרָא לְמֹשֶׁה וּלְאַהֲרֹן לַיְלָה וַיֹּאמֶר קוּמוּ צְּאוּ מִתּוֹךְ עַמִּי גַּם־אַתֶּם גַּם־בְּנֵי יִשְׂרָאֵל וּלְכוּ עִבְדוּ אֶת־יְהֹוָה כְּדַבֶּרְכֶם: 32 גַּם־צֹאנְכֶם גַּם־בְּקַרְכֶם קְחוּ כַּאֲשֶׁר דִּבַּרְתֶּם וָלֵכוּ וּבֵרַכְתֶּם גַּם־אֹתִי: 33 וַתֶּחֱזַק מִצְרַיִם עַל־הָעָם לְמַהֵר לְשַׁלְּחָם מִן־הָאָרֶץ כִּי אָמְרוּ כֻּלָּנוּ מֵתִים: 34 וַיִּשָּׂא הָעָם אֶת־בְּצֵקוֹ טֶרֶם יֶחְמָץ מִשְׁאֲרֹתָם צְרֻרֹת בְּשִׂמְלֹתָם עַל־שִׁכְמָם: 35 וּבְנֵי־יִשְׂרָאֵל עָשׂוּ כִּדְבַר מֹשֶׁה וַיִּשְׁאֲלוּ מִמִּצְרַיִם כְּלֵי־כֶסֶף וּכְלֵי זָהָב וּשְׂמָלֹת: 36 וַיהֹוָה נָתַן אֶת־חֵן הָעָם בְּעֵינֵי מִצְרַיִם וַיַּשְׁאִלוּם וַיְנַצְּלוּ אֶת־מִצְרָיִם: פ

37 וַיִּסְעוּ בְנֵי־יִשְׂרָאֵל מֵרַעְמְסֵס סֻכֹּתָה כְּשֵׁשׁ מֵאוֹת אֶלֶף רַגְלִי הַגְּבָרִים לְבַד מִטָּף: 38 וְגַם־עֵרֶב רַב עָלָה אִתָּם וְצֹאן וּבָקָר מִקְנֶה כָּבֵד מְאֹד: 39 וַיֹּאפוּ אֶת־הַבָּצֵק אֲשֶׁר הוֹצִיאוּ מִמִּצְרַיִם עֻגֹת מַצּוֹת כִּי לֹא חָמֵץ כִּי־גֹרְשׁוּ מִמִּצְרַיִם וְלֹא יָכְלוּ

40 Now the sojourn of the children of Israel who lived in Egypt *was* four hundred and thirty years. 41 And it came to pass at the end of the four hundred and thirty years—on that very same day—it came to pass that all the armies of the LORD went out from the land of Egypt. 42 It *is* a night of solemn observance to the LORD for bringing them out of the land of Egypt. This *is* that night of the LORD, a solemn observance for all the children of Israel throughout their generations.

43 And the LORD said to Moses and Aaron, "This *is* the ordinance of the Passover: No foreigner shall eat it. 44 But every man's servant who is bought for money, when you have circumcised him, then he may eat it. 45 A sojourner and a hired servant shall not eat it. 46 In one house it shall be eaten; you shall not carry any of the flesh outside the house, nor shall you break one of its bones. 47 All the congregation of Israel shall keep it. 48 And when a stranger dwells with you *and wants* to keep the Passover to the LORD, let all his males be circumcised, and then let him come near and keep it; and he shall be as a native of the land. For no uncircumcised person shall eat it. 49 One law shall be for the native-born and for the stranger who dwells among you."

50 Thus all the children of Israel did; as the LORD commanded Moses and Aaron, so they did. 51 And it came to pass, on that very same day, that the LORD brought the children of Israel out of the land of Egypt according to their armies.

13 Then the LORD spoke to Moses, saying, 2 "Consecrate to Me all the firstborn, whatever opens the womb among the children of Israel, *both* of man and beast; it is Mine."

3 And Moses said to the people: "Remember this day in which you went out of Egypt, out of the house of bondage; for by strength of hand the LORD brought you out of this *place*. No leavened bread shall be eaten. 4 On this day you are going out, in the month Abib. 5 And it shall be, when the LORD brings you into the land of the Canaanites and the Hittites and the Amorites and the Hivites and the Jebusites, which He swore to your fathers to give you, a land flowing with milk and honey, that you shall keep this service in this month. 6 Seven days you shall eat unleavened bread, and on the seventh day *there shall be* a feast to the LORD. 7 Unleavened bread shall be eaten seven days. And no leavened bread shall be seen among you, nor shall leaven be seen among you in all your quarters. 8 And you shall tell your son in that day, saying, 'This is done because of what the LORD did for me when I came

לְהִתְמַהְמֵהַּ וְגַם־צֵדָה לֹא־עָשׂוּ לָהֶם: 40 וּמוֹשַׁב בְּנֵי יִשְׂרָאֵל אֲשֶׁר יָשְׁבוּ בְּמִצְרָיִם שְׁלֹשִׁים שָׁנָה וְאַרְבַּע מֵאוֹת שָׁנָה: 41 וַיְהִי מִקֵּץ שְׁלֹשִׁים שָׁנָה וְאַרְבַּע מֵאוֹת שָׁנָה וַיְהִי בְּעֶצֶם הַיּוֹם הַזֶּה יָצְאוּ כָּל־צִבְאוֹת יְהוָה מֵאֶרֶץ מִצְרָיִם: 42 לֵיל שִׁמֻּרִים הוּא לַיהוָה לְהוֹצִיאָם מֵאֶרֶץ מִצְרָיִם הוּא־הַלַּיְלָה הַזֶּה לַיהוָה שִׁמֻּרִים לְכָל־בְּנֵי יִשְׂרָאֵל לְדֹרֹתָם: פ

43 וַיֹּאמֶר יְהוָה אֶל־מֹשֶׁה וְאַהֲרֹן זֹאת חֻקַּת הַפָּסַח כָּל־בֶּן־נֵכָר לֹא־יֹאכַל בּוֹ: 44 וְכָל־עֶבֶד אִישׁ מִקְנַת־כֶּסֶף וּמַלְתָּה אֹתוֹ אָז יֹאכַל בּוֹ: 45 תּוֹשָׁב וְשָׂכִיר לֹא־יֹאכַל־בּוֹ: 46 בְּבַיִת אֶחָד יֵאָכֵל לֹא־תוֹצִיא מִן־הַבַּיִת מִן־הַבָּשָׂר חוּצָה וְעֶצֶם לֹא תִשְׁבְּרוּ־בוֹ: 47 כָּל־עֲדַת יִשְׂרָאֵל יַעֲשׂוּ אֹתוֹ: 48 וְכִי־יָגוּר אִתְּךָ גֵּר וְעָשָׂה פֶסַח לַיהוָה הִמּוֹל לוֹ כָל־זָכָר וְאָז יִקְרַב לַעֲשֹׂתוֹ וְהָיָה כְּאֶזְרַח הָאָרֶץ וְכָל־עָרֵל לֹא־יֹאכַל בּוֹ: 49 תּוֹרָה אַחַת יִהְיֶה לָאֶזְרָח וְלַגֵּר הַגָּר בְּתוֹכְכֶם: 50 וַיַּעֲשׂוּ כָּל־בְּנֵי יִשְׂרָאֵל כַּאֲשֶׁר צִוָּה יְהוָה אֶת־מֹשֶׁה וְאֶת־אַהֲרֹן כֵּן עָשׂוּ: ס 51 וַיְהִי בְּעֶצֶם הַיּוֹם הַזֶּה הוֹצִיא יְהוָה אֶת־בְּנֵי יִשְׂרָאֵל מֵאֶרֶץ מִצְרַיִם עַל־צִבְאֹתָם: פ

יג וַיְדַבֵּר יְהוָה אֶל־מֹשֶׁה לֵּאמֹר: 2 קַדֶּשׁ־לִי כָל־בְּכוֹר פֶּטֶר כָּל־רֶחֶם בִּבְנֵי יִשְׂרָאֵל בָּאָדָם וּבַבְּהֵמָה לִי הוּא: 3 וַיֹּאמֶר מֹשֶׁה אֶל־הָעָם זָכוֹר אֶת־הַיּוֹם הַזֶּה אֲשֶׁר יְצָאתֶם מִמִּצְרַיִם מִבֵּית עֲבָדִים כִּי בְּחֹזֶק יָד הוֹצִיא יְהוָה אֶתְכֶם מִזֶּה וְלֹא יֵאָכֵל חָמֵץ: 4 הַיּוֹם אַתֶּם יֹצְאִים בְּחֹדֶשׁ הָאָבִיב: 5 וְהָיָה כִי־יְבִיאֲךָ יְהוָה אֶל־אֶרֶץ הַכְּנַעֲנִי וְהַחִתִּי וְהָאֱמֹרִי וְהַחִוִּי וְהַיְבוּסִי אֲשֶׁר נִשְׁבַּע לַאֲבֹתֶיךָ לָתֶת לָךְ אֶרֶץ זָבַת חָלָב וּדְבָשׁ וְעָבַדְתָּ אֶת־הָעֲבֹדָה הַזֹּאת בַּחֹדֶשׁ הַזֶּה: 6 שִׁבְעַת יָמִים תֹּאכַל מַצֹּת וּבַיּוֹם הַשְּׁבִיעִי חַג לַיהוָה: 7 מַצּוֹת יֵאָכֵל אֵת שִׁבְעַת הַיָּמִים וְלֹא־יֵרָאֶה לְךָ חָמֵץ וְלֹא־יֵרָאֶה לְךָ שְׂאֹר בְּכָל־גְּבֻלֶךָ: 8 וְהִגַּדְתָּ לְבִנְךָ בַּיּוֹם הַהוּא לֵאמֹר בַּעֲבוּר זֶה עָשָׂה יְהוָה לִי בְּצֵאתִי מִמִּצְרָיִם: 9 וְהָיָה לְךָ לְאוֹת עַל־יָדְךָ וּלְזִכָּרוֹן בֵּין עֵינֶיךָ לְמַעַן תִּהְיֶה

up from Egypt.' ⁹It shall be as a sign to you on your hand and as a memorial between your eyes, that the LORD's law may be in your mouth; for with a strong hand the LORD has brought you out of Egypt. ¹⁰You shall therefore keep this ordinance in its season from year to year.

¹¹"And it shall be, when the LORD brings you into the land of the Canaanites, as He swore to you and your fathers, and gives it to you, ¹²that you shall set apart to the LORD all that open the womb, that is, every firstborn that comes from an animal which you have; the males *shall be* the LORD's. ¹³But every firstborn of a donkey you shall redeem with a lamb; and if you will not redeem *it,* then you shall break its neck. And all the firstborn of man among your sons you shall redeem. ¹⁴So it shall be, when your son asks you in time to come, saying, 'What *is* this?' that you shall say to him, 'By strength of hand the LORD brought us out of Egypt, out of the house of bondage. ¹⁵And it came to pass, when Pharaoh was stubborn about letting us go, that the LORD killed all the firstborn in the land of Egypt, both the firstborn of man and the firstborn of beast. Therefore I sacrifice to the LORD all males that open the womb, but all the firstborn of my sons I redeem.' ¹⁶It shall be as a sign on your hand and as frontlets between your eyes, for by strength of hand the LORD brought us out of Egypt."

¹⁷Then it came to pass, when Pharaoh had let the people go, that God did not lead them *by* way of the land of the Philistines, although that *was* near; for God said, "Lest perhaps the people change their minds when they see war, and return to Egypt." ¹⁸So God led the people around *by* way of the wilderness of the Red Sea. And the children of Israel went up in orderly ranks out of the land of Egypt.

¹⁹And Moses took the bones of Joseph with him, for he had placed the children of Israel under solemn oath, saying, "God will surely visit you, and you shall carry up my bones from here with you."

²⁰So they took their journey from Succoth and camped in Etham at the edge of the wilderness. ²¹And the LORD went before them by day in a pillar of cloud to lead the way, and by night in a pillar of fire to give them light, so as to go by day and night. ²²He did not take away the pillar of cloud by day or the pillar of fire by night *from* before the people.

14 Now the LORD spoke to Moses, saying: ²"Speak to the children of Israel, that they turn and camp before Pi Hahiroth, between Migdol and the sea, opposite Baal Zephon; you shall camp before it by the sea. ³For Pharaoh will say of the

תּוֹרַת יְהוָה בְּפִיךָ כִּי בְּיָד חֲזָקָה הוֹצִאֲךָ יְהוָה מִמִּצְרָיִם: ₁₀ וְשָׁמַרְתָּ אֶת־הַחֻקָּה הַזֹּאת לְמוֹעֲדָהּ מִיָּמִים יָמִימָה: ס ₁₁ וְהָיָה כִּי־יְבִאֲךָ יְהוָה אֶל־אֶרֶץ הַכְּנַעֲנִי כַּאֲשֶׁר נִשְׁבַּע לְךָ וְלַאֲבֹתֶיךָ וּנְתָנָהּ לָךְ: ₁₂ וְהַעֲבַרְתָּ כָל־פֶּטֶר־רֶחֶם לַיהוָה וְכָל־פֶּטֶר ׀ שֶׁגֶר בְּהֵמָה אֲשֶׁר יִהְיֶה לְךָ הַזְּכָרִים לַיהוָה: ₁₃ וְכָל־פֶּטֶר חֲמֹר תִּפְדֶּה בְשֶׂה וְאִם־לֹא תִפְדֶּה וַעֲרַפְתּוֹ וְכֹל בְּכוֹר אָדָם בְּבָנֶיךָ תִּפְדֶּה: ₁₄ וְהָיָה כִּי־יִשְׁאָלְךָ בִנְךָ מָחָר לֵאמֹר מַה־זֹּאת וְאָמַרְתָּ אֵלָיו בְּחֹזֶק יָד הוֹצִיאָנוּ יְהוָה מִמִּצְרַיִם מִבֵּית עֲבָדִים: ₁₅ וַיְהִי כִּי־הִקְשָׁה פַרְעֹה לְשַׁלְּחֵנוּ וַיַּהֲרֹג יְהוָה כָּל־בְּכוֹר בְּאֶרֶץ מִצְרַיִם מִבְּכֹר אָדָם וְעַד־בְּכוֹר בְּהֵמָה עַל־כֵּן אֲנִי זֹבֵחַ לַיהוָה כָּל־פֶּטֶר רֶחֶם הַזְּכָרִים וְכָל־בְּכוֹר בָּנַי אֶפְדֶּה: ₁₆ וְהָיָה לְאוֹת עַל־יָדְכָה וּלְטוֹטָפֹת בֵּין עֵינֶיךָ כִּי בְּחֹזֶק יָד הוֹצִיאָנוּ יְהוָה מִמִּצְרָיִם: ס ₁₇ וַיְהִי בְּשַׁלַּח פַּרְעֹה אֶת־הָעָם וְלֹא־נָחָם אֱלֹהִים דֶּרֶךְ אֶרֶץ פְּלִשְׁתִּים כִּי קָרוֹב הוּא כִּי ׀ אָמַר אֱלֹהִים פֶּן־יִנָּחֵם הָעָם בִּרְאֹתָם מִלְחָמָה וְשָׁבוּ מִצְרָיְמָה: ₁₈ וַיַּסֵּב אֱלֹהִים ׀ אֶת־הָעָם דֶּרֶךְ הַמִּדְבָּר יַם־סוּף וַחֲמֻשִׁים עָלוּ בְנֵי־יִשְׂרָאֵל מֵאֶרֶץ מִצְרָיִם: ₁₉ וַיִּקַּח מֹשֶׁה אֶת־עַצְמוֹת יוֹסֵף עִמּוֹ כִּי הַשְׁבֵּעַ הִשְׁבִּיעַ אֶת־בְּנֵי יִשְׂרָאֵל לֵאמֹר פָּקֹד יִפְקֹד אֱלֹהִים אֶתְכֶם וְהַעֲלִיתֶם אֶת־עַצְמֹתַי מִזֶּה אִתְּכֶם: ₂₀ וַיִּסְעוּ מִסֻּכֹּת וַיַּחֲנוּ בְאֵתָם בִּקְצֵה הַמִּדְבָּר: ₂₁ וַיהוָה הֹלֵךְ לִפְנֵיהֶם יוֹמָם בְּעַמּוּד עָנָן לַנְחֹתָם הַדֶּרֶךְ וְלַיְלָה בְּעַמּוּד אֵשׁ לְהָאִיר לָהֶם לָלֶכֶת יוֹמָם וָלָיְלָה: ₂₂ לֹא־יָמִישׁ עַמּוּד הֶעָנָן יוֹמָם וְעַמּוּד הָאֵשׁ לָיְלָה לִפְנֵי הָעָם: פ

יד וַיְדַבֵּר יְהוָה אֶל־מֹשֶׁה לֵּאמֹר: ₂ דַּבֵּר אֶל־בְּנֵי יִשְׂרָאֵל וְיָשֻׁבוּ וְיַחֲנוּ לִפְנֵי פִּי הַחִירֹת בֵּין מִגְדֹּל וּבֵין הַיָּם לִפְנֵי בַּעַל צְפֹן נִכְחוֹ תַחֲנוּ עַל־הַיָּם: ₃ וְאָמַר פַּרְעֹה לִבְנֵי יִשְׂרָאֵל נְבֻכִים הֵם

children of Israel, 'They *are* bewildered by the land; the wilderness has closed them in.' ⁴Then I will harden Pharaoh's heart, so that he will pursue them; and I will gain honor over Pharaoh and over all his army, that the Egyptians may know that I *am* the LORD." And they did so.

⁵Now it was told the king of Egypt that the people had fled, and the heart of Pharaoh and his servants was turned against the people; and they said, "Why have we done this, that we have let Israel go from serving us?" ⁶So he made ready his chariot and took his people with him. ⁷Also, he took six hundred choice chariots, and all the chariots of Egypt with captains over every one of them. ⁸And the LORD hardened the heart of Pharaoh king of Egypt, and he pursued the children of Israel; and the children of Israel went out with boldness. ⁹So the Egyptians pursued them, all the horses *and* chariots of Pharaoh, his horsemen and his army, and overtook them camping by the sea beside Pi Hahiroth, before Baal Zephon.

¹⁰And when Pharaoh drew near, the children of Israel lifted their eyes, and behold, the Egyptians marched after them. So they were very afraid, and the children of Israel cried out to the LORD. ¹¹Then they said to Moses, "Because *there were* no graves in Egypt, have you taken us away to die in the wilderness? Why have you so dealt with us, to bring us up out of Egypt? ¹²*Is* this not the word that we told you in Egypt, saying, 'Let us alone that we may serve the Egyptians'? For *it would have been* better for us to serve the Egyptians than that we should die in the wilderness."

¹³And Moses said to the people, "Do not be afraid. Stand still, and see the salvation of the LORD, which He will accomplish for you today. For the Egyptians whom you see today, you shall see again no more forever. ¹⁴The LORD will fight for you, and you shall hold your peace."

¹⁵And the LORD said to Moses, "Why do you cry to Me? Tell the children of Israel to go forward. ¹⁶But lift up your rod, and stretch out your hand over the sea and divide it. And the children of Israel shall go on dry *ground* through the midst of the sea. ¹⁷And I indeed will harden the hearts of the Egyptians, and they shall follow them. So I will gain honor over Pharaoh and over all his army, his chariots, and his horsemen. ¹⁸Then the Egyptians shall know that I *am* the LORD, when I have gained honor for Myself over Pharaoh, his chariots, and his horsemen."

¹⁹And the Angel of God, who went before the camp of Israel, moved and went behind them; and the pillar of cloud went from before them and stood

בְּאֶרֶץ סָגַר עֲלֵיהֶם הַמִּדְבָּר: 4 וְחִזַּקְתִּי אֶת־לֵב־
פַּרְעֹה וְרָדַף אַחֲרֵיהֶם וְאִכָּבְדָה בְּפַרְעֹה וּבְכָל־חֵילוֹ
וְיָדְעוּ מִצְרַיִם כִּי־אֲנִי יְהֹוָה וַיַּעֲשׂוּ־כֵן: 5 וַיֻּגַּד לְמֶלֶךְ
מִצְרַיִם כִּי בָרַח הָעָם וַיֵּהָפֵךְ לְבַב פַּרְעֹה וַעֲבָדָיו
אֶל־הָעָם וַיֹּאמְרוּ מַה־זֹּאת עָשִׂינוּ כִּי־שִׁלַּחְנוּ אֶת־
יִשְׂרָאֵל מֵעָבְדֵנוּ: 6 וַיֶּאְסֹר אֶת־רִכְבּוֹ וְאֶת־עַמּוֹ
לָקַח עִמּוֹ: 7 וַיִּקַּח שֵׁשׁ־מֵאוֹת רֶכֶב בָּחוּר וְכֹל
רֶכֶב מִצְרָיִם וְשָׁלִשִׁם עַל־כֻּלּוֹ: 8 וַיְחַזֵּק יְהֹוָה אֶת־
לֵב פַּרְעֹה מֶלֶךְ מִצְרַיִם וַיִּרְדֹּף אַחֲרֵי בְּנֵי יִשְׂרָאֵל
וּבְנֵי יִשְׂרָאֵל יֹצְאִים בְּיָד רָמָה: 9 וַיִּרְדְּפוּ מִצְרַיִם
אַחֲרֵיהֶם וַיַּשִּׂיגוּ אוֹתָם חֹנִים עַל־הַיָּם כָּל־סוּס רֶכֶב
פַּרְעֹה וּפָרָשָׁיו וְחֵילוֹ עַל־פִּי הַחִירֹת לִפְנֵי בַּעַל צְפֹן:

10 וּפַרְעֹה הִקְרִיב וַיִּשְׂאוּ בְנֵי־יִשְׂרָאֵל אֶת־עֵינֵיהֶם
וְהִנֵּה מִצְרַיִם | נֹסֵעַ אַחֲרֵיהֶם וַיִּירְאוּ מְאֹד וַיִּצְעֲקוּ
בְנֵי־יִשְׂרָאֵל אֶל־יְהֹוָה: 11 וַיֹּאמְרוּ אֶל־מֹשֶׁה הֲמִבְּלִי
אֵין־קְבָרִים בְּמִצְרַיִם לְקַחְתָּנוּ לָמוּת בַּמִּדְבָּר מַה־
זֹּאת עָשִׂיתָ לָּנוּ לְהוֹצִיאָנוּ מִמִּצְרָיִם: 12 הֲלֹא־זֶה
הַדָּבָר אֲשֶׁר דִּבַּרְנוּ אֵלֶיךָ בְמִצְרַיִם לֵאמֹר חֲדַל
מִמֶּנּוּ וְנַעַבְדָה אֶת־מִצְרָיִם כִּי טוֹב לָנוּ עֲבֹד אֶת־
מִצְרַיִם מִמֻּתֵנוּ בַּמִּדְבָּר: 13 וַיֹּאמֶר מֹשֶׁה אֶל־הָעָם
אַל־תִּירָאוּ הִתְיַצְּבוּ וּרְאוּ אֶת־יְשׁוּעַת יְהֹוָה אֲשֶׁר־
יַעֲשֶׂה לָכֶם הַיּוֹם כִּי אֲשֶׁר רְאִיתֶם אֶת־מִצְרַיִם
הַיּוֹם לֹא תֹסִפוּ לִרְאֹתָם עוֹד עַד־עוֹלָם: 14 יְהֹוָה
יִלָּחֵם לָכֶם וְאַתֶּם תַּחֲרִישׁוּן:
פ

15 וַיֹּאמֶר יְהֹוָה אֶל־מֹשֶׁה מַה־תִּצְעַק אֵלָי דַּבֵּר
אֶל־בְּנֵי־יִשְׂרָאֵל וְיִסָּעוּ: 16 וְאַתָּה הָרֵם אֶת־מַטְּךָ
וּנְטֵה אֶת־יָדְךָ עַל־הַיָּם וּבְקָעֵהוּ וְיָבֹאוּ בְנֵי־יִשְׂרָאֵל
בְּתוֹךְ הַיָּם בַּיַּבָּשָׁה: 17 וַאֲנִי הִנְנִי מְחַזֵּק אֶת־לֵב
מִצְרַיִם וְיָבֹאוּ אַחֲרֵיהֶם וְאִכָּבְדָה בְּפַרְעֹה וּבְכָל־
חֵילוֹ בְּרִכְבּוֹ וּבְפָרָשָׁיו: 18 וְיָדְעוּ מִצְרַיִם כִּי־אֲנִי
יְהֹוָה בְּהִכָּבְדִי בְּפַרְעֹה בְּרִכְבּוֹ וּבְפָרָשָׁיו: 19 וַיִּסַּע
מַלְאַךְ הָאֱלֹהִים הַהֹלֵךְ לִפְנֵי מַחֲנֵה יִשְׂרָאֵל וַיֵּלֶךְ
מֵאַחֲרֵיהֶם וַיִּסַּע עַמּוּד הֶעָנָן מִפְּנֵיהֶם וַיַּעֲמֹד

behind them. ²⁰ So it came between the camp of the Egyptians and the camp of Israel. Thus it was a cloud and darkness *to the one,* and it gave light by night *to the other,* so that the one did not come near the other all that night.

²¹ Then Moses stretched out his hand over the sea; and the LORD caused the sea to go *back* by a strong east wind all that night, and made the sea into dry *land,* and the waters were divided. ²² So the children of Israel went into the midst of the sea on the dry *ground,* and the waters *were* a wall to them on their right hand and on their left. ²³ And the Egyptians pursued and went after them into the midst of the sea, all Pharaoh's horses, his chariots, and his horsemen.

²⁴ Now it came to pass, in the morning watch, that the LORD looked down upon the army of the Egyptians through the pillar of fire and cloud, and He troubled the army of the Egyptians. ²⁵ And He took off their chariot wheels, so that they drove them with difficulty; and the Egyptians said, "Let us flee from the face of Israel, for the LORD fights for them against the Egyptians."

²⁶ Then the LORD said to Moses, "Stretch out your hand over the sea, that the waters may come back upon the Egyptians, on their chariots, and on their horsemen." ²⁷ And Moses stretched out his hand over the sea; and when the morning appeared, the sea returned to its full depth, while the Egyptians were fleeing into it. So the LORD overthrew the Egyptians in the midst of the sea. ²⁸ Then the waters returned and covered the chariots, the horsemen, *and* all the army of Pharaoh that came into the sea after them. Not so much as one of them remained. ²⁹ But the children of Israel had walked on dry *land* in the midst of the sea, and the waters *were* a wall to them on their right hand and on their left.

³⁰ So the LORD saved Israel that day out of the hand of the Egyptians, and Israel saw the Egyptians dead on the seashore. ³¹ Thus Israel saw the great work which the LORD had done in Egypt; so the people feared the LORD, and believed the LORD and His servant Moses.

15 Then Moses and the children of Israel sang this song to the LORD, and spoke, saying:

"I will sing to the LORD,
For He has triumphed gloriously!
The horse and its rider
He has thrown into the sea!
² The LORD *is* my strength and song,
And He has become my salvation;
He *is* my God, and I will praise Him;

מֵאַחֲרֵיהֶם: 20 וַיָּבֹא בֵּין | מַחֲנֵה מִצְרַיִם וּבֵין
מַחֲנֵה יִשְׂרָאֵל וַיְהִי הֶעָנָן וְהַחֹשֶׁךְ וַיָּאֶר אֶת־הַלָּיְלָה
וְלֹא־קָרַב זֶה אֶל־זֶה כָּל־הַלָּיְלָה: 21 וַיֵּט מֹשֶׁה
אֶת־יָדוֹ עַל־הַיָּם וַיּוֹלֶךְ יְהֹוָה | אֶת־הַיָּם בְּרוּחַ
קָדִים עַזָּה כָּל־הַלַּיְלָה וַיָּשֶׂם אֶת־הַיָּם לֶחָרָבָה
וַיִּבָּקְעוּ הַמָּיִם: 22 וַיָּבֹאוּ בְנֵי־יִשְׂרָאֵל בְּתוֹךְ הַיָּם
בַּיַּבָּשָׁה וְהַמַּיִם לָהֶם חֹמָה מִימִינָם וּמִשְּׂמֹאלָם:
23 וַיִּרְדְּפוּ מִצְרַיִם וַיָּבֹאוּ אַחֲרֵיהֶם כֹּל סוּס פַּרְעֹה
רִכְבּוֹ וּפָרָשָׁיו אֶל־תּוֹךְ הַיָּם: 24 וַיְהִי בְּאַשְׁמֹרֶת
הַבֹּקֶר וַיַּשְׁקֵף יְהֹוָה אֶל־מַחֲנֵה מִצְרַיִם בְּעַמּוּד אֵשׁ
וְעָנָן וַיָּהָם אֵת מַחֲנֵה מִצְרָיִם: 25 וַיָּסַר אֵת אֹפַן
מַרְכְּבֹתָיו וַיְנַהֲגֵהוּ בִּכְבֵדֻת וַיֹּאמֶר מִצְרַיִם אָנוּסָה
מִפְּנֵי יִשְׂרָאֵל כִּי יְהֹוָה נִלְחָם לָהֶם בְּמִצְרָיִם: פ

26 וַיֹּאמֶר יְהֹוָה אֶל־מֹשֶׁה נְטֵה אֶת־יָדְךָ עַל־הַיָּם
וְיָשֻׁבוּ הַמַּיִם עַל־מִצְרַיִם עַל־רִכְבּוֹ וְעַל־פָּרָשָׁיו:
27 וַיֵּט מֹשֶׁה אֶת־יָדוֹ עַל־הַיָּם וַיָּשָׁב הַיָּם לִפְנוֹת
בֹּקֶר לְאֵיתָנוֹ וּמִצְרַיִם נָסִים לִקְרָאתוֹ וַיְנַעֵר יְהֹוָה
אֶת־מִצְרַיִם בְּתוֹךְ הַיָּם: 28 וַיָּשֻׁבוּ הַמַּיִם וַיְכַסּוּ
אֶת־הָרֶכֶב וְאֶת־הַפָּרָשִׁים לְכֹל חֵיל פַּרְעֹה הַבָּאִים
אַחֲרֵיהֶם בַּיָּם לֹא־נִשְׁאַר בָּהֶם עַד־אֶחָד: 29 וּבְנֵי
יִשְׂרָאֵל הָלְכוּ בַיַּבָּשָׁה בְּתוֹךְ הַיָּם וְהַמַּיִם לָהֶם
חֹמָה מִימִינָם וּמִשְּׂמֹאלָם: 30 וַיּוֹשַׁע יְהֹוָה בַּיּוֹם
הַהוּא אֶת־יִשְׂרָאֵל מִיַּד מִצְרָיִם וַיַּרְא יִשְׂרָאֵל אֶת־
מִצְרַיִם מֵת עַל־שְׂפַת הַיָּם: 31 וַיַּרְא יִשְׂרָאֵל אֶת־
הַיָּד הַגְּדֹלָה אֲשֶׁר עָשָׂה יְהֹוָה בְּמִצְרַיִם וַיִּירְאוּ
הָעָם אֶת־יְהֹוָה וַיַּאֲמִינוּ בַּיהֹוָה וּבְמֹשֶׁה עַבְדּוֹ: פ

טו אָז יָשִׁיר־מֹשֶׁה וּבְנֵי יִשְׂרָאֵל
אֶת־הַשִּׁירָה הַזֹּאת לַיהֹוָה וַיֹּאמְרוּ לֵאמֹר
אָשִׁירָה לַיהֹוָה כִּי־גָאֹה גָּאָה
סוּס וְרֹכְבוֹ רָמָה בַיָּם:
2 עָזִּי וְזִמְרָת יָהּ וַיְהִי־לִי לִישׁוּעָה
זֶה אֵלִי וְאַנְוֵהוּ

My father's God, and I will exalt Him.
3 The LORD *is* a man of war;
The LORD *is* His name.
4 Pharaoh's chariots and his army He has cast
into the sea;
His chosen captains also are drowned in the
Red Sea.
5 The depths have covered them;
They sank to the bottom like a stone.

6 "Your right hand, O LORD, has become
glorious in power;
Your right hand, O LORD, has dashed the
enemy in pieces.
7 And in the greatness of Your excellence
You have overthrown those who rose against
You;
You sent forth Your wrath;
It consumed them like stubble.
8 And with the blast of Your nostrils
The waters were gathered together;
The floods stood upright like a heap;
The depths congealed in the heart of the sea.
9 The enemy said, 'I will pursue,
I will overtake,
I will divide the spoil;
My desire shall be satisfied on them.
I will draw my sword,
My hand shall destroy them.'
10 You blew with Your wind,
The sea covered them;
They sank like lead in the mighty waters.

11 "Who *is* like You, O LORD, among the gods?
Who *is* like You, glorious in holiness,
Fearful in praises, doing wonders?
12 You stretched out Your right hand;
The earth swallowed them.
13 You in Your mercy have led forth
The people whom You have redeemed;
You have guided *them* in Your strength
To Your holy habitation.

14 "The people will hear *and* be afraid;
Sorrow will take hold of the inhabitants of
Philistia.
15 Then the chiefs of Edom will be dismayed;
The mighty men of Moab,
Trembling will take hold of them;
All the inhabitants of Canaan will melt away.
16 Fear and dread will fall on them;
By the greatness of Your arm
They will be *as* still as a stone,
Till Your people pass over, O LORD,
Till the people pass over
Whom You have purchased.
17 You will bring them in and plant them
In the mountain of Your inheritance,
In the place, O LORD, *which* You have made
For Your own dwelling,
The sanctuary, O LORD, *which* Your hands
have established.

אֱלֹהֵי אָבִי וַאֲרֹמְמֶנְהוּ׃
3 יְהוָה אִישׁ מִלְחָמָה יְהוָה שְׁמוֹ׃
4 מַרְכְּבֹת פַּרְעֹה וְחֵילוֹ יָרָה בַיָּם
וּמִבְחַר שָׁלִשָׁיו טֻבְּעוּ בְיַם־סוּף׃
5 תְּהֹמֹת יְכַסְיֻמוּ יָרְדוּ בִמְצוֹלֹת כְּמוֹ־אָבֶן׃

6 יְמִינְךָ יְהוָה נֶאְדָּרִי בַּכֹּחַ
יְמִינְךָ יְהוָה תִּרְעַץ אוֹיֵב׃
7 וּבְרֹב גְּאוֹנְךָ תַּהֲרֹס קָמֶיךָ
תְּשַׁלַּח חֲרֹנְךָ יֹאכְלֵמוֹ כַּקַּשׁ׃
8 וּבְרוּחַ אַפֶּיךָ נֶעֶרְמוּ מַיִם
נִצְּבוּ כְמוֹ־נֵד נֹזְלִים
קָפְאוּ תְהֹמֹת בְּלֶב־יָם׃
9 אָמַר אוֹיֵב אֶרְדֹּף אַשִּׂיג אֲחַלֵּק שָׁלָל
תִּמְלָאֵמוֹ נַפְשִׁי
אָרִיק חַרְבִּי תּוֹרִישֵׁמוֹ יָדִי׃
10 נָשַׁפְתָּ בְרוּחֲךָ כִּסָּמוֹ יָם
צָלֲלוּ כַּעוֹפֶרֶת בְּמַיִם אַדִּירִים׃

11 מִי־כָמֹכָה בָּאֵלִם יְהוָה
מִי כָּמֹכָה נֶאְדָּר בַּקֹּדֶשׁ
נוֹרָא תְהִלֹּת עֹשֵׂה פֶלֶא׃
12 נָטִיתָ יְמִינְךָ תִּבְלָעֵמוֹ אָרֶץ׃
13 נָחִיתָ בְחַסְדְּךָ עַם־זוּ גָּאָלְתָּ
נֵהַלְתָּ בְעָזְּךָ אֶל־נְוֵה קָדְשֶׁךָ׃
14 שָׁמְעוּ עַמִּים יִרְגָּזוּן
חִיל אָחַז יֹשְׁבֵי פְּלָשֶׁת׃
15 אָז נִבְהֲלוּ אַלּוּפֵי אֱדוֹם
אֵילֵי מוֹאָב יֹאחֲזֵמוֹ רָעַד
נָמֹגוּ כֹּל יֹשְׁבֵי כְנָעַן׃
16 תִּפֹּל עֲלֵיהֶם אֵימָתָה וָפַחַד
בִּגְדֹל זְרוֹעֲךָ יִדְּמוּ כָּאָבֶן
עַד־יַעֲבֹר עַמְּךָ יְהוָה
עַד־יַעֲבֹר עַם־זוּ קָנִיתָ׃
17 תְּבִאֵמוֹ וְתִטָּעֵמוֹ בְּהַר נַחֲלָתְךָ
מָכוֹן לְשִׁבְתְּךָ פָּעַלְתָּ יְהוָה
מִקְּדָשׁ אֲדֹנָי כּוֹנְנוּ יָדֶיךָ׃

18 "The LORD shall reign forever and ever."

19 For the horses of Pharaoh went with his chariots and his horsemen into the sea, and the LORD brought back the waters of the sea upon them. But the children of Israel went on dry *land* in the midst of the sea.

20 Then Miriam the prophetess, the sister of Aaron, took the timbrel in her hand; and all the women went out after her with timbrels and with dances. 21 And Miriam answered them:

"Sing to the LORD,
For He has triumphed gloriously!
The horse and its rider
He has thrown into the sea!"

22 So Moses brought Israel from the Red Sea; then they went out into the Wilderness of Shur. And they went three days in the wilderness and found no water. 23 Now when they came to Marah, they could not drink the waters of Marah, for they *were* bitter. Therefore the name of it was called Marah. 24 And the people complained against Moses, saying, "What shall we drink?" 25 So he cried out to the LORD, and the LORD showed him a tree. When he cast *it* into the waters, the waters were made sweet.

There He made a statute and an ordinance for them, and there He tested them, 26 and said, "If you diligently heed the voice of the LORD your God and do what is right in His sight, give ear to His commandments and keep all His statutes, I will put none of the diseases on you which I have brought on the Egyptians. For I *am* the LORD who heals you."

27 Then they came to Elim, where there *were* twelve wells of water and seventy palm trees; so they camped there by the waters.

16 And they journeyed from Elim, and all the congregation of the children of Israel came to the Wilderness of Sin, which is between Elim and Sinai, on the fifteenth day of the second month after they departed from the land of Egypt. 2 Then the whole congregation of the children of Israel complained against Moses and Aaron in the wilderness. 3 And the children of Israel said to them, "Oh, that we had died by the hand of the LORD in the land of Egypt, when we sat by the pots of meat *and* when we ate bread to the full! For you have brought us out into this wilderness to kill this whole assembly with hunger."

4 Then the LORD said to Moses, "Behold, I will rain bread from heaven for you. And the people shall go out and gather a certain quota every day,

18 יְהוָה ׀ יִמְלֹךְ לְעֹלָם וָעֶד׃
19 כִּי בָא סוּס פַּרְעֹה בְּרִכְבּוֹ וּבְפָרָשָׁיו בַּיָּם וַיָּשֶׁב יְהוָה עֲלֵהֶם אֶת־מֵי הַיָּם וּבְנֵי יִשְׂרָאֵל הָלְכוּ בַיַּבָּשָׁה בְּתוֹךְ הַיָּם׃ פ

20 וַתִּקַּח מִרְיָם הַנְּבִיאָה אֲחוֹת אַהֲרֹן אֶת־הַתֹּף בְּיָדָהּ וַתֵּצֶאןָ כָל־הַנָּשִׁים אַחֲרֶיהָ בְּתֻפִּים וּבִמְחֹלֹת׃ 21 וַתַּעַן לָהֶם מִרְיָם שִׁירוּ לַיהוָה כִּי־גָאֹה גָּאָה סוּס וְרֹכְבוֹ רָמָה בַיָּם׃ ס 22 וַיַּסַּע מֹשֶׁה אֶת־יִשְׂרָאֵל מִיַּם־סוּף וַיֵּצְאוּ אֶל־מִדְבַּר־שׁוּר וַיֵּלְכוּ שְׁלֹשֶׁת־יָמִים בַּמִּדְבָּר וְלֹא־מָצְאוּ מָיִם׃ 23 וַיָּבֹאוּ מָרָתָה וְלֹא יָכְלוּ לִשְׁתֹּת מַיִם מִמָּרָה כִּי מָרִים הֵם עַל־כֵּן קָרָא־שְׁמָהּ מָרָה׃ 24 וַיִּלֹּנוּ הָעָם עַל־מֹשֶׁה לֵּאמֹר מַה־נִּשְׁתֶּה׃ 25 וַיִּצְעַק אֶל־יְהוָה וַיּוֹרֵהוּ יְהוָה עֵץ וַיַּשְׁלֵךְ אֶל־הַמַּיִם וַיִּמְתְּקוּ הַמָּיִם שָׁם שָׂם לוֹ חֹק וּמִשְׁפָּט וְשָׁם נִסָּהוּ׃ 26 וַיֹּאמֶר אִם־שָׁמוֹעַ תִּשְׁמַע לְקוֹל ׀ יְהוָה אֱלֹהֶיךָ וְהַיָּשָׁר בְּעֵינָיו תַּעֲשֶׂה וְהַאֲזַנְתָּ לְמִצְוֹתָיו וְשָׁמַרְתָּ כָּל־חֻקָּיו כָּל־הַמַּחֲלָה אֲשֶׁר־שַׂמְתִּי בְמִצְרַיִם לֹא־אָשִׂים עָלֶיךָ כִּי אֲנִי יְהוָה רֹפְאֶךָ׃ ס 27 וַיָּבֹאוּ אֵילִמָה וְשָׁם שְׁתֵּים עֶשְׂרֵה עֵינֹת מַיִם וְשִׁבְעִים תְּמָרִים וַיַּחֲנוּ־שָׁם עַל־הַמָּיִם׃

טז וַיִּסְעוּ מֵאֵילִם וַיָּבֹאוּ כָּל־עֲדַת בְּנֵי־יִשְׂרָאֵל אֶל־מִדְבַּר־סִין אֲשֶׁר בֵּין־אֵילִם וּבֵין סִינָי בַּחֲמִשָּׁה עָשָׂר יוֹם לַחֹדֶשׁ הַשֵּׁנִי לְצֵאתָם מֵאֶרֶץ מִצְרָיִם׃ 2 וַיִּלּוֹנוּ כָּל־עֲדַת בְּנֵי־יִשְׂרָאֵל עַל־מֹשֶׁה וְעַל־אַהֲרֹן בַּמִּדְבָּר׃ 3 וַיֹּאמְרוּ אֲלֵהֶם בְּנֵי יִשְׂרָאֵל מִי־יִתֵּן מוּתֵנוּ בְיַד־יְהוָה בְּאֶרֶץ מִצְרַיִם בְּשִׁבְתֵּנוּ עַל־סִיר הַבָּשָׂר בְּאָכְלֵנוּ לֶחֶם לָשֹׂבַע כִּי־הוֹצֵאתֶם אֹתָנוּ אֶל־הַמִּדְבָּר הַזֶּה לְהָמִית אֶת־כָּל־הַקָּהָל הַזֶּה בָּרָעָב׃ ס 4 וַיֹּאמֶר יְהוָה אֶל־מֹשֶׁה הִנְנִי מַמְטִיר לָכֶם לֶחֶם מִן־הַשָּׁמָיִם וְיָצָא הָעָם

that I may test them, whether they will walk in My law or not. ⁵And it shall be on the sixth day that they shall prepare what they bring in, and it shall be twice as much as they gather daily."

⁶Then Moses and Aaron said to all the children of Israel, "At evening you shall know that the LORD has brought you out of the land of Egypt. ⁷And in the morning you shall see the glory of the LORD; for He hears your complaints against the LORD. But what *are* we, that you complain against us?" ⁸Also Moses said, "*This shall be seen* when the LORD gives you meat to eat in the evening, and in the morning bread to the full; for the LORD hears your complaints which you make against Him. And what *are* we? Your complaints *are* not against us but against the LORD."

⁹Then Moses spoke to Aaron, "Say to all the congregation of the children of Israel, 'Come near before the LORD, for He has heard your complaints.'" ¹⁰Now it came to pass, as Aaron spoke to the whole congregation of the children of Israel, that they looked toward the wilderness, and behold, the glory of the LORD appeared in the cloud.

¹¹And the LORD spoke to Moses, saying, ¹²"I have heard the complaints of the children of Israel. Speak to them, saying, 'At twilight you shall eat meat, and in the morning you shall be filled with bread. And you shall know that I *am* the LORD your God.'"

¹³So it was that quails came up at evening and covered the camp, and in the morning the dew lay all around the camp. ¹⁴And when the layer of dew lifted, there, on the surface of the wilderness, was a small round substance, *as* fine as frost on the ground. ¹⁵So when the children of Israel saw *it,* they said to one another, "What is it?" For they did not know what it *was.*

And Moses said to them, "This *is* the bread which the LORD has given you to eat. ¹⁶This is the thing which the LORD has commanded: 'Let every man gather it according to each one's need, one omer for each person, *according to the* number of persons; let every man take for *those* who *are* in his tent.'"

¹⁷Then the children of Israel did so and gathered, some more, some less. ¹⁸So when they measured *it* by omers, he who gathered much had nothing left over, and he who gathered little had no lack. Every man had gathered according to each one's need. ¹⁹And Moses said, "Let no one leave any of it till morning." ²⁰Notwithstanding they did not heed Moses. But some of them left part of it until morning, and it bred worms and stank. And Moses

וְלָקְט֞וּ דְּבַר־י֤וֹם בְּיוֹמ֔וֹ לְמַ֧עַן אֲנַסֶּ֛נּוּ הֲיֵלֵ֥ךְ בְּתוֹרָתִ֖י אִם־לֹֽא: ⁵וְהָיָה֙ בַּיּ֣וֹם הַשִּׁשִּׁ֔י וְהֵכִ֖ינוּ אֵ֣ת אֲשֶׁר־יָבִ֑יאוּ וְהָיָ֣ה מִשְׁנֶ֔ה עַ֥ל אֲשֶׁר־יִלְקְט֖וּ י֥וֹם | י֖וֹם: ס ⁶וַיֹּ֤אמֶר מֹשֶׁה֙ וְאַהֲרֹ֔ן אֶֽל־כָּל־בְּנֵ֖י יִשְׂרָאֵ֑ל עֶ֕רֶב וִֽידַעְתֶּ֔ם כִּ֧י יְהֹוָ֛ה הוֹצִ֥יא אֶתְכֶ֖ם מֵאֶ֥רֶץ מִצְרָֽיִם: ⁷וּבֹ֗קֶר וּרְאִיתֶם֙ אֶת־כְּב֣וֹד יְהֹוָ֔ה בְּשָׁמְע֥וֹ אֶת־תְּלֻנֹּֽתֵיכֶ֖ם עַל־יְהֹוָ֑ה וְנַ֣חְנוּ מָ֔ה כִּ֥י תַלִּ֖ינוּ⁵ עָלֵֽינוּ: ⁸וַיֹּ֣אמֶר מֹשֶׁ֗ה בְּתֵ֣ת יְהֹוָ֩ה לָכֶ֨ם בָּעֶ֜רֶב בָּשָׂ֣ר לֶאֱכֹ֗ל וְלֶ֤חֶם בַּבֹּ֨קֶר֙ לִשְׂבֹּ֔עַ בִּשְׁמֹ֤עַ יְהֹוָה֙ אֶת־תְּלֻנֹּ֣תֵיכֶ֔ם אֲשֶׁר־אַתֶּ֥ם מַלִּינִ֖ם עָלָ֑יו וְנַ֣חְנוּ מָ֔ה לֹא־עָלֵ֥ינוּ תְלֻנֹּתֵיכֶ֖ם כִּ֥י עַל־יְהֹוָֽה: ⁹וַיֹּ֤אמֶר מֹשֶׁה֙ אֶֽל־אַהֲרֹ֔ן אֱמֹ֗ר אֶֽל־כָּל־עֲדַת֙ בְּנֵ֣י יִשְׂרָאֵ֔ל קִרְב֖וּ לִפְנֵ֣י יְהֹוָ֑ה כִּ֣י שָׁמַ֔ע אֵ֖ת תְּלֻנֹּתֵיכֶֽם: ¹⁰וַיְהִ֗י כְּדַבֵּ֤ר אַהֲרֹן֙ אֶל־כָּל־עֲדַ֣ת בְּנֵֽי־יִשְׂרָאֵ֔ל וַיִּפְנ֖וּ אֶל־הַמִּדְבָּ֑ר וְהִנֵּה֙ כְּב֣וֹד יְהֹוָ֔ה נִרְאָ֖ה בֶּעָנָֽן: פ

¹¹וַיְדַבֵּ֥ר יְהֹוָ֖ה אֶל־מֹשֶׁ֥ה לֵּאמֹֽר: ¹²שָׁמַ֗עְתִּי אֶת־תְּלוּנֹּת֮ בְּנֵ֣י יִשְׂרָאֵל֒ דַּבֵּ֨ר אֲלֵהֶ֜ם לֵאמֹ֗ר בֵּ֤ין הָֽעַרְבַּ֨יִם֙ תֹּאכְל֣וּ בָשָׂ֔ר וּבַבֹּ֖קֶר תִּשְׂבְּעוּ־לָ֑חֶם וִֽידַעְתֶּ֕ם כִּ֛י אֲנִ֥י יְהֹוָ֖ה אֱלֹהֵיכֶֽם: ¹³וַיְהִ֣י בָעֶ֔רֶב וַתַּ֣עַל הַשְּׂלָ֔ו וַתְּכַ֖ס אֶת־הַֽמַּחֲנֶ֑ה וּבַבֹּ֗קֶר הָֽיְתָה֙ שִׁכְבַ֣ת הַטַּ֔ל סָבִ֖יב לַֽמַּחֲנֶֽה: ¹⁴וַתַּ֖עַל שִׁכְבַ֣ת הַטָּ֑ל וְהִנֵּ֞ה עַל־פְּנֵ֤י הַמִּדְבָּר֙ דַּ֣ק מְחֻסְפָּ֔ס דַּ֥ק כַּכְּפֹ֖ר עַל־הָאָֽרֶץ: ¹⁵וַיִּרְא֣וּ בְנֵֽי־יִשְׂרָאֵ֗ל וַיֹּ֨אמְר֜וּ אִ֤ישׁ אֶל־אָחִיו֙ מָ֣ן ה֔וּא כִּ֛י לֹ֥א יָֽדְע֖וּ מַה־ה֑וּא וַיֹּ֤אמֶר מֹשֶׁה֙ אֲלֵהֶ֔ם ה֣וּא הַלֶּ֔חֶם אֲשֶׁ֨ר נָתַ֧ן יְהֹוָ֛ה לָכֶ֖ם לְאָכְלָֽה: ¹⁶זֶ֤ה הַדָּבָר֙ אֲשֶׁ֣ר צִוָּ֣ה יְהֹוָ֔ה לִקְט֣וּ מִמֶּ֔נּוּ אִ֖ישׁ לְפִ֣י אָכְל֑וֹ עֹ֣מֶר לַגֻּלְגֹּ֗לֶת מִסְפַּר֙ נַפְשֹׁ֣תֵיכֶ֔ם אִ֛ישׁ לַֽאֲשֶׁ֥ר בְּאָֽהֳל֖וֹ תִּקָּֽחוּ: ¹⁷וַיַּֽעֲשׂוּ־כֵ֖ן בְּנֵ֣י יִשְׂרָאֵ֑ל וַֽיִּלְקְט֔וּ הַמַּרְבֶּ֖ה וְהַמַּמְעִֽיט: ¹⁸וַיָּמֹ֣דּוּ בָעֹ֔מֶר וְלֹ֥א הֶעְדִּיף֙ הַמַּרְבֶּ֔ה וְהַמַּמְעִ֖יט לֹ֣א הֶחְסִ֑יר אִ֥ישׁ לְפִֽי־אָכְל֖וֹ לָקָֽטוּ: ¹⁹וַיֹּ֥אמֶר מֹשֶׁ֖ה אֲלֵהֶ֑ם אִ֕ישׁ אַל־יוֹתֵ֥ר מִמֶּ֖נּוּ עַד־בֹּֽקֶר: ²⁰וְלֹֽא־שָׁמְע֣וּ אֶל־מֹשֶׁ֗ה וַיּוֹתִ֨רוּ אֲנָשִׁ֤ים מִמֶּ֨נּוּ֙ עַד־בֹּ֔קֶר וַיָּ֥רֻם תּוֹלָעִ֖ים וַיִּבְאַ֑שׁ

7 תַּלִּינוּ

was angry with them. ²¹ So they gathered it every
morning, every man according to his need. And
when the sun became hot, it melted.

²² And so it was, on the sixth day, *that* they
gathered twice as much bread, two omers for each
one. And all the rulers of the congregation came
and told Moses. ²³ Then he said to them, "This *is*
what the LORD has said: 'Tomorrow *is* a Sabbath
rest, a holy Sabbath to the LORD. Bake what you
will bake *today*, and boil what you will boil; and lay
up for yourselves all that remains, to be kept until
morning.' " ²⁴ So they laid it up till morning, as
Moses commanded; and it did not stink, nor were
there any worms in it. ²⁵ Then Moses said, "Eat that
today, for today *is* a Sabbath to the LORD; today
you will not find it in the field. ²⁶ Six days you shall
gather it, but on the seventh day, the Sabbath, there
will be none."

²⁷ Now it happened *that some* of the people went
out on the seventh day to gather, but they found
none. ²⁸ And the LORD said to Moses, "How long
do you refuse to keep My commandments and My
laws? ²⁹ See! For the LORD has given you the
Sabbath; therefore He gives you on the sixth day
bread for two days. Let every man remain in his
place; let no man go out of his place on the seventh
day." ³⁰ So the people rested on the seventh day.

³¹ And the house of Israel called its name Manna.
And it *was* like white coriander seed, and the taste
of it *was* like wafers *made* with honey.

³² Then Moses said, "This *is* the thing which the
LORD has commanded: 'Fill an omer with it, to be
kept for your generations, that they may see the
bread with which I fed you in the wilderness, when I
brought you out of the land of Egypt.' " ³³ And
Moses said to Aaron, "Take a pot and put an omer
of manna in it, and lay it up before the LORD, to be
kept for your generations." ³⁴ As the LORD commanded Moses, so Aaron laid it up before the
Testimony, to be kept. ³⁵ And the children of Israel
ate manna forty years, until they came to an
inhabited land; they ate manna until they came to
the border of the land of Canaan. ³⁶ Now an omer *is*
one-tenth of an ephah.

17 Then all the congregation of the children of
Israel set out on their journey from the Wilderness
of Sin, according to the commandment of the
LORD, and camped in Rephidim; but *there was* no
water for the people to drink. ² Therefore the people
contended with Moses, and said, "Give us water,
that we may drink."

So Moses said to them, "Why do you contend
with me? Why do you tempt the LORD?"

21 וַיִּקְצֹף עֲלֵהֶם מֹשֶׁה: וַיִּלְקְטוּ אֹתוֹ בַּבֹּקֶר בַּבֹּקֶר
אִישׁ כְּפִי אָכְלוֹ וְחַם הַשֶּׁמֶשׁ וְנָמָס: 22 וַיְהִי |
בַּיּוֹם הַשִּׁשִּׁי לָקְטוּ לֶחֶם מִשְׁנֶה שְׁנֵי הָעֹמֶר
לָאֶחָד וַיָּבֹאוּ כָּל־נְשִׂיאֵי הָעֵדָה וַיַּגִּידוּ לְמֹשֶׁה:
23 וַיֹּאמֶר אֲלֵהֶם הוּא אֲשֶׁר דִּבֶּר יְהֹוָה שַׁבָּתוֹן
שַׁבַּת־קֹדֶשׁ לַיהֹוָה מָחָר אֵת אֲשֶׁר־תֹּאפוּ אֵפוּ
וְאֵת אֲשֶׁר־תְּבַשְּׁלוּ בַּשֵּׁלוּ וְאֵת כָּל־הָעֹדֵף הַנִּיחוּ
לָכֶם לְמִשְׁמֶרֶת עַד־הַבֹּקֶר: 24 וַיַּנִּיחוּ אֹתוֹ עַד־
הַבֹּקֶר כַּאֲשֶׁר צִוָּה מֹשֶׁה וְלֹא הִבְאִישׁ וְרִמָּה לֹא־
הָיְתָה בּוֹ: 25 וַיֹּאמֶר מֹשֶׁה אִכְלֻהוּ הַיּוֹם כִּי־שַׁבָּת
הַיּוֹם לַיהֹוָה הַיּוֹם לֹא תִמְצָאֻהוּ בַּשָּׂדֶה: 26 שֵׁשֶׁת
יָמִים תִּלְקְטֻהוּ וּבַיּוֹם הַשְּׁבִיעִי שַׁבָּת לֹא יִהְיֶה־
בּוֹ: 27 וַיְהִי בַּיּוֹם הַשְּׁבִיעִי יָצְאוּ מִן־הָעָם לִלְקֹט
וְלֹא מָצָאוּ: ס 28 וַיֹּאמֶר יְהֹוָה אֶל־מֹשֶׁה
עַד־אָנָה מֵאַנְתֶּם לִשְׁמֹר מִצְוֹתַי וְתוֹרֹתָי: 29 רְאוּ
כִּי־יְהֹוָה נָתַן לָכֶם הַשַּׁבָּת עַל־כֵּן הוּא נֹתֵן לָכֶם
בַּיּוֹם הַשִּׁשִּׁי לֶחֶם יוֹמָיִם שְׁבוּ | אִישׁ תַּחְתָּיו
אַל־יֵצֵא אִישׁ מִמְּקֹמוֹ בַּיּוֹם הַשְּׁבִיעִי: 30 וַיִּשְׁבְּתוּ
הָעָם בַּיּוֹם הַשְּׁבִעִי: 31 וַיִּקְרְאוּ בֵית־יִשְׂרָאֵל אֶת־
שְׁמוֹ מָן וְהוּא כְּזֶרַע גַּד לָבָן וְטַעְמוֹ כְּצַפִּיחִת
בִּדְבָשׁ: 32 וַיֹּאמֶר מֹשֶׁה זֶה הַדָּבָר אֲשֶׁר צִוָּה יְהֹוָה
מְלֹא הָעֹמֶר מִמֶּנּוּ לְמִשְׁמֶרֶת לְדֹרֹתֵיכֶם לְמַעַן |
יִרְאוּ אֶת־הַלֶּחֶם אֲשֶׁר הֶאֱכַלְתִּי אֶתְכֶם בַּמִּדְבָּר
בְּהוֹצִיאִי אֶתְכֶם מֵאֶרֶץ מִצְרָיִם: 33 וַיֹּאמֶר מֹשֶׁה
אֶל־אַהֲרֹן קַח צִנְצֶנֶת אַחַת וְתֶן־שָׁמָּה מְלֹא־הָעֹמֶר
מָן וְהַנַּח אֹתוֹ לִפְנֵי יְהֹוָה לְמִשְׁמֶרֶת לְדֹרֹתֵיכֶם:
34 כַּאֲשֶׁר צִוָּה יְהֹוָה אֶל־מֹשֶׁה וַיַּנִּיחֵהוּ אַהֲרֹן לִפְנֵי
הָעֵדֻת לְמִשְׁמָרֶת: 35 וּבְנֵי יִשְׂרָאֵל אָכְלוּ אֶת־הַמָּן
אַרְבָּעִים שָׁנָה עַד־בֹּאָם אֶל־אֶרֶץ נוֹשָׁבֶת אֶת־הַמָּן
אָכְלוּ עַד־בֹּאָם אֶל־קְצֵה אֶרֶץ כְּנָעַן: 36 וְהָעֹמֶר
עֲשִׂרִית הָאֵיפָה הוּא:
פ

יז וַיִּסְעוּ כָּל־עֲדַת בְּנֵי־יִשְׂרָאֵל מִמִּדְבַּר־סִין
לְמַסְעֵיהֶם עַל־פִּי יְהֹוָה וַיַּחֲנוּ בִּרְפִידִים וְאֵין מַיִם
לִשְׁתֹּת הָעָם: 2 וַיָּרֶב הָעָם עִם־מֹשֶׁה וַיֹּאמְרוּ
תְּנוּ־לָנוּ מַיִם וְנִשְׁתֶּה וַיֹּאמֶר לָהֶם מֹשֶׁה מַה־

3 And the people thirsted there for water, and the people complained against Moses, and said, "Why is it you have brought us up out of Egypt, to kill us and our children and our livestock with thirst?"

4 So Moses cried out to the LORD, saying, "What shall I do with this people? They are almost ready to stone me!"

5 And the LORD said to Moses, "Go on before the people, and take with you some of the elders of Israel. Also take in your hand your rod with which you struck the river, and go. 6 Behold, I will stand before you there on the rock in Horeb; and you shall strike the rock, and water will come out of it, that the people may drink."

And Moses did so in the sight of the elders of Israel. 7 So he called the name of the place Massah and Meribah, because of the contention of the children of Israel, and because they tempted the LORD, saying, "Is the LORD among us or not?"

8 Now Amalek came and fought with Israel in Rephidim. 9 And Moses said to Joshua, "Choose us some men and go out, fight with Amalek. Tomorrow I will stand on the top of the hill with the rod of God in my hand." 10 So Joshua did as Moses said to him, and fought with Amalek. And Moses, Aaron, and Hur went up to the top of the hill. 11 And so it was, when Moses held up his hand, that Israel prevailed; and when he let down his hand, Amalek prevailed. 12 But Moses' hands *became* heavy; so they took a stone and put *it* under him, and he sat on it. And Aaron and Hur supported his hands, one on one side, and the other on the other side; and his hands were steady until the going down of the sun. 13 So Joshua defeated Amalek and his people with the edge of the sword.

14 Then the LORD said to Moses, "Write this *for a* memorial in the book and recount *it* in the hearing of Joshua, that I will utterly blot out the remembrance of Amalek from under heaven." 15 And Moses built an altar and called its name, The-LORD-Is-My-Banner; 16 for he said, "Because the LORD has sworn: the LORD *will have* war with Amalek from generation to generation."

18 And Jethro, the priest of Midian, Moses' father-in-law, heard of all that God had done for Moses and for Israel His people—that the LORD had brought Israel out of Egypt. 2 Then Jethro, Moses' father-in-law, took Zipporah, Moses' wife, after he had sent her back, 3 with her two sons, of whom the name of one *was* Gershom (for he said, "I have been a stranger in a foreign land") 4 and the name of the other *was* Eliezer (for *he said,* "The God of my father *was* my help, and delivered me

תְּרִיבוּן עִמָּדִי מַה־תְּנַסּוּן אֶת־יְהוָה: 3 וַיִּצְמָא שָׁם הָעָם לַמַּיִם וַיָּלֶן הָעָם עַל־מֹשֶׁה וַיֹּאמֶר לָמָּה זֶּה הֶעֱלִיתָנוּ מִמִּצְרַיִם לְהָמִית אֹתִי וְאֶת־בָּנַי וְאֶת־מִקְנַי בַּצָּמָא: 4 וַיִּצְעַק מֹשֶׁה אֶל־יְהוָה לֵאמֹר מָה אֶעֱשֶׂה לָעָם הַזֶּה עוֹד מְעַט וּסְקָלֻנִי: 5 וַיֹּאמֶר יְהוָה אֶל־מֹשֶׁה עֲבֹר לִפְנֵי הָעָם וְקַח אִתְּךָ מִזִּקְנֵי יִשְׂרָאֵל וּמַטְּךָ אֲשֶׁר הִכִּיתָ בּוֹ אֶת־הַיְאֹר קַח בְּיָדְךָ וְהָלָכְתָּ: 6 הִנְנִי עֹמֵד לְפָנֶיךָ שָּׁם עַל־הַצּוּר בְּחֹרֵב וְהִכִּיתָ בַצּוּר וְיָצְאוּ מִמֶּנּוּ מַיִם וְשָׁתָה הָעָם וַיַּעַשׂ כֵּן מֹשֶׁה לְעֵינֵי זִקְנֵי יִשְׂרָאֵל: 7 וַיִּקְרָא שֵׁם הַמָּקוֹם מַסָּה וּמְרִיבָה עַל־רִיב ׀ בְּנֵי יִשְׂרָאֵל וְעַל נַסֹּתָם אֶת־יְהוָה לֵאמֹר הֲיֵשׁ יְהוָה בְּקִרְבֵּנוּ אִם־אָיִן: פ

8 וַיָּבֹא עֲמָלֵק וַיִּלָּחֶם עִם־יִשְׂרָאֵל בִּרְפִידִם: 9 וַיֹּאמֶר מֹשֶׁה אֶל־יְהוֹשֻׁעַ בְּחַר־לָנוּ אֲנָשִׁים וְצֵא הִלָּחֵם בַּעֲמָלֵק מָחָר אָנֹכִי נִצָּב עַל־רֹאשׁ הַגִּבְעָה וּמַטֵּה הָאֱלֹהִים בְּיָדִי: 10 וַיַּעַשׂ יְהוֹשֻׁעַ כַּאֲשֶׁר אָמַר־לוֹ מֹשֶׁה לְהִלָּחֵם בַּעֲמָלֵק וּמֹשֶׁה אַהֲרֹן וְחוּר עָלוּ רֹאשׁ הַגִּבְעָה: 11 וְהָיָה כַּאֲשֶׁר יָרִים מֹשֶׁה יָדוֹ וְגָבַר יִשְׂרָאֵל וְכַאֲשֶׁר יָנִיחַ יָדוֹ וְגָבַר עֲמָלֵק: 12 וִידֵי מֹשֶׁה כְּבֵדִים וַיִּקְחוּ־אֶבֶן וַיָּשִׂימוּ תַחְתָּיו וַיֵּשֶׁב עָלֶיהָ וְאַהֲרֹן וְחוּר תָּמְכוּ בְיָדָיו מִזֶּה אֶחָד וּמִזֶּה אֶחָד וַיְהִי יָדָיו אֱמוּנָה עַד־בֹּא הַשָּׁמֶשׁ: 13 וַיַּחֲלֹשׁ יְהוֹשֻׁעַ אֶת־עֲמָלֵק וְאֶת־עַמּוֹ לְפִי־חָרֶב: פ

14 וַיֹּאמֶר יְהוָה אֶל־מֹשֶׁה כְּתֹב זֹאת זִכָּרוֹן בַּסֵּפֶר וְשִׂים בְּאָזְנֵי יְהוֹשֻׁעַ כִּי־מָחֹה אֶמְחֶה אֶת־זֵכֶר עֲמָלֵק מִתַּחַת הַשָּׁמָיִם: 15 וַיִּבֶן מֹשֶׁה מִזְבֵּחַ וַיִּקְרָא שְׁמוֹ יְהוָה ׀ נִסִּי: 16 וַיֹּאמֶר כִּי־יָד עַל־כֵּס יָהּ מִלְחָמָה לַיהוָה בַּעֲמָלֵק מִדֹּר דֹּר: פ

יח וַיִּשְׁמַע יִתְרוֹ כֹהֵן מִדְיָן חֹתֵן מֹשֶׁה אֵת כָּל־אֲשֶׁר עָשָׂה אֱלֹהִים לְמֹשֶׁה וּלְיִשְׂרָאֵל עַמּוֹ כִּי־הוֹצִיא יְהוָה אֶת־יִשְׂרָאֵל מִמִּצְרָיִם: 2 וַיִּקַּח יִתְרוֹ חֹתֵן מֹשֶׁה אֶת־צִפֹּרָה אֵשֶׁת מֹשֶׁה אַחַר שִׁלּוּחֶיהָ: 3 וְאֵת שְׁנֵי בָנֶיהָ אֲשֶׁר שֵׁם הָאֶחָד גֵּרְשֹׁם כִּי אָמַר גֵּר הָיִיתִי בְּאֶרֶץ נָכְרִיָּה: 4 וְשֵׁם הָאֶחָד אֱלִיעֶזֶר כִּי

from the sword of Pharaoh"); ⁵ and Jethro, Moses' father-in-law, came with his sons and his wife to Moses in the wilderness, where he was encamped at the mountain of God. ⁶ Now he had said to Moses, "I, your father-in-law Jethro, am coming to you with your wife and her two sons with her."

⁷ So Moses went out to meet his father-in-law, bowed down, and kissed him. And they asked each other about *their* well-being, and they went into the tent. ⁸ And Moses told his father-in-law all that the LORD had done to Pharaoh and to the Egyptians for Israel's sake, all the hardship that had come upon them on the way, and *how* the LORD had delivered them. ⁹ Then Jethro rejoiced for all the good which the LORD had done for Israel, whom He had delivered out of the hand of the Egyptians. ¹⁰ And Jethro said, "Blessed *be* the LORD, who has delivered you out of the hand of the Egyptians and out of the hand of Pharaoh, *and* who has delivered the people from under the hand of the Egyptians. ¹¹ Now I know that the LORD *is* greater than all the gods; for in the very thing in which they behaved proudly, *He was* above them." ¹² Then Jethro, Moses' father-in-law, took a burnt offering and *other* sacrifices *to offer* to God. And Aaron came with all the elders of Israel to eat bread with Moses' father-in-law before God.

¹³ And so it was, on the next day, that Moses sat to judge the people; and the people stood before Moses from morning until evening. ¹⁴ So when Moses' father-in-law saw all that he did for the people, he said, "What *is* this thing that you are doing for the people? Why do you alone sit, and all the people stand before you from morning until evening?"

¹⁵ And Moses said to his father-in-law, "Because the people come to me to inquire of God. ¹⁶ When they have a difficulty, they come to me, and I judge between one and another; and I make known the statutes of God and His laws."

¹⁷ So Moses' father-in-law said to him, "The thing that you do *is* not good. ¹⁸ Both you and these people who *are* with you will surely wear yourselves out. For this thing *is* too much for you; you are not able to perform it by yourself. ¹⁹ Listen now to my voice; I will give you counsel, and God will be with you: Stand before God for the people, so that you may bring the difficulties to God. ²⁰ And you shall teach them the statutes and the laws, and show them the way in which they must walk and the work they must do. ²¹ Moreover you shall select from all the people able men, such as fear God, men of truth, hating covetousness; and place *such* over them *to be* rulers of thousands, rulers of hundreds,

אֵלֵי אָבִי בְּעָזְרִי וַיַּצִּלֵנִי מֵחֶרֶב פַּרְעֹה: 5 וַיָּבֹא יִתְרוֹ חֹתֵן מֹשֶׁה וּבָנָיו וְאִשְׁתּוֹ אֶל־מֹשֶׁה אֶל־הַמִּדְבָּר אֲשֶׁר־הוּא חֹנֶה שָׁם הַר הָאֱלֹהִים: 6 וַיֹּאמֶר אֶל־מֹשֶׁה אֲנִי חֹתֶנְךָ יִתְרוֹ בָּא אֵלֶיךָ וְאִשְׁתְּךָ וּשְׁנֵי בָנֶיהָ עִמָּהּ: 7 וַיֵּצֵא מֹשֶׁה לִקְרַאת חֹתְנוֹ וַיִּשְׁתַּחוּ וַיִּשַּׁק־לוֹ וַיִּשְׁאֲלוּ אִישׁ־לְרֵעֵהוּ לְשָׁלוֹם וַיָּבֹאוּ הָאֹהֱלָה: 8 וַיְסַפֵּר מֹשֶׁה לְחֹתְנוֹ אֵת כָּל־אֲשֶׁר עָשָׂה יְהוָה לְפַרְעֹה וּלְמִצְרַיִם עַל אוֹדֹת יִשְׂרָאֵל אֵת כָּל־הַתְּלָאָה אֲשֶׁר מְצָאָתַם בַּדֶּרֶךְ וַיַּצִּלֵם יְהוָה: 9 וַיִּחַדְּ יִתְרוֹ עַל כָּל־הַטּוֹבָה אֲשֶׁר־עָשָׂה יְהוָה לְיִשְׂרָאֵל אֲשֶׁר הִצִּילוֹ מִיַּד מִצְרָיִם: 10 וַיֹּאמֶר יִתְרוֹ בָּרוּךְ יְהוָה אֲשֶׁר הִצִּיל אֶתְכֶם מִיַּד מִצְרַיִם וּמִיַּד פַּרְעֹה אֲשֶׁר הִצִּיל אֶת־הָעָם מִתַּחַת יַד־מִצְרָיִם: 11 עַתָּה יָדַעְתִּי כִּי־גָדוֹל יְהוָה מִכָּל־הָאֱלֹהִים כִּי בַדָּבָר אֲשֶׁר זָדוּ עֲלֵיהֶם: 12 וַיִּקַּח יִתְרוֹ חֹתֵן מֹשֶׁה עֹלָה וּזְבָחִים לֵאלֹהִים וַיָּבֹא אַהֲרֹן וְכֹל ׀ זִקְנֵי יִשְׂרָאֵל לֶאֱכָל־לֶחֶם עִם־חֹתֵן מֹשֶׁה לִפְנֵי הָאֱלֹהִים: 13 וַיְהִי מִמָּחֳרָת וַיֵּשֶׁב מֹשֶׁה לִשְׁפֹּט אֶת־הָעָם וַיַּעֲמֹד הָעָם עַל־מֹשֶׁה מִן־הַבֹּקֶר עַד־הָעָרֶב: 14 וַיַּרְא חֹתֵן מֹשֶׁה אֵת כָּל־אֲשֶׁר־הוּא עֹשֶׂה לָעָם וַיֹּאמֶר מָה־הַדָּבָר הַזֶּה אֲשֶׁר אַתָּה עֹשֶׂה לָעָם מַדּוּעַ אַתָּה יוֹשֵׁב לְבַדֶּךָ וְכָל־הָעָם נִצָּב עָלֶיךָ מִן־בֹּקֶר עַד־עָרֶב: 15 וַיֹּאמֶר מֹשֶׁה לְחֹתְנוֹ כִּי־יָבֹא אֵלַי הָעָם לִדְרֹשׁ אֱלֹהִים: 16 כִּי־יִהְיֶה לָהֶם דָּבָר בָּא אֵלַי וְשָׁפַטְתִּי בֵּין אִישׁ וּבֵין רֵעֵהוּ וְהוֹדַעְתִּי אֶת־חֻקֵּי הָאֱלֹהִים וְאֶת־תּוֹרֹתָיו: 17 וַיֹּאמֶר חֹתֵן מֹשֶׁה אֵלָיו לֹא־טוֹב הַדָּבָר אֲשֶׁר אַתָּה עֹשֶׂה: 18 נָבֹל תִּבֹּל גַּם־אַתָּה גַּם־הָעָם הַזֶּה אֲשֶׁר עִמָּךְ כִּי־כָבֵד מִמְּךָ הַדָּבָר לֹא־תוּכַל עֲשֹׂהוּ לְבַדֶּךָ: 19 עַתָּה שְׁמַע בְּקֹלִי אִיעָצְךָ וִיהִי אֱלֹהִים עִמָּךְ הֱיֵה אַתָּה לָעָם מוּל הָאֱלֹהִים וְהֵבֵאתָ אַתָּה אֶת־הַדְּבָרִים אֶל־הָאֱלֹהִים: 20 וְהִזְהַרְתָּה אֶתְהֶם אֶת־הַחֻקִּים וְאֶת־הַתּוֹרֹת וְהוֹדַעְתָּ לָהֶם אֶת־הַדֶּרֶךְ יֵלְכוּ בָהּ וְאֶת־הַמַּעֲשֶׂה אֲשֶׁר יַעֲשׂוּן: 21 וְאַתָּה תֶחֱזֶה מִכָּל־הָעָם אַנְשֵׁי־חַיִל יִרְאֵי אֱלֹהִים אַנְשֵׁי אֱמֶת שֹׂנְאֵי בָצַע וְשַׂמְתָּ עֲלֵהֶם שָׂרֵי אֲלָפִים שָׂרֵי מֵאוֹת שָׂרֵי חֲמִשִּׁים

rulers of fifties, and rulers of tens. ²² And let them judge the people at all times. Then it will be *that* every great matter they shall bring to you, but every small matter they themselves shall judge. So it will be easier for you, for they will bear *the burden* with you. ²³ If you do this thing, and God *so* commands you, then you will be able to endure, and all this people will also go to their place in peace."

²⁴ So Moses heeded the voice of his father-in-law and did all that he had said. ²⁵ And Moses chose able men out of all Israel, and made them heads over the people: rulers of thousands, rulers of hundreds, rulers of fifties, and rulers of tens. ²⁶ So they judged the people at all times; the hard cases they brought to Moses, but they judged every small case themselves.

²⁷ Then Moses let his father-in-law depart, and he went his way to his own land.

19 In the third month after the children of Israel had gone out of the land of Egypt, on the same day, they came *to* the Wilderness of Sinai. ² For they had departed from Rephidim, had come *to* the Wilderness of Sinai, and camped in the wilderness. So Israel camped there before the mountain.

³ And Moses went up to God, and the Lord called to him from the mountain, saying, "Thus you shall say to the house of Jacob, and tell the children of Israel: ⁴ 'You have seen what I did to the Egyptians, and *how* I bore you on eagles' wings and brought you to Myself. ⁵ Now therefore, if you will indeed obey My voice and keep My covenant, then you shall be a special treasure to Me above all people; for all the earth *is* Mine. ⁶ And you shall be to Me a kingdom of priests and a holy nation.' These *are* the words which you shall speak to the children of Israel."

⁷ So Moses came and called for the elders of the people, and laid before them all these words which the Lord commanded him. ⁸ Then all the people answered together and said, "All that the Lord has spoken we will do." So Moses brought back the words of the people to the Lord. ⁹ And the Lord said to Moses, "Behold, I come to you in the thick cloud, that the people may hear when I speak with you, and believe you forever."

So Moses told the words of the people to the Lord.

¹⁰ Then the Lord said to Moses, "Go to the people and consecrate them today and tomorrow, and let them wash their clothes. ¹¹ And let them be ready for the third day. For on the third day the Lord will come down upon Mount Sinai in the sight of all the people. ¹² You shall set bounds for

וְשָׂרֵי עֲשָׂרֹת: ²² וְשָׁפְטוּ אֶת־הָעָם בְּכָל־עֵת וְהָיָה כָּל־הַדָּבָר הַגָּדֹל יָבִיאוּ אֵלֶיךָ וְכָל־הַדָּבָר הַקָּטֹן יִשְׁפְּטוּ־הֵם וְהָקֵל מֵעָלֶיךָ וְנָשְׂאוּ אִתָּךְ: ²³ אִם אֶת־הַדָּבָר הַזֶּה תַּעֲשֶׂה וְצִוְּךָ אֱלֹהִים וְיָכָלְתָּ עֲמֹד וְגַם כָּל־הָעָם הַזֶּה עַל־מְקֹמוֹ יָבֹא בְשָׁלוֹם: ²⁴ וַיִּשְׁמַע מֹשֶׁה לְקוֹל חֹתְנוֹ וַיַּעַשׂ כֹּל אֲשֶׁר אָמָר: ²⁵ וַיִּבְחַר מֹשֶׁה אַנְשֵׁי־חַיִל מִכָּל־יִשְׂרָאֵל וַיִּתֵּן אֹתָם רָאשִׁים עַל־הָעָם שָׂרֵי אֲלָפִים שָׂרֵי מֵאוֹת שָׂרֵי חֲמִשִּׁים וְשָׂרֵי עֲשָׂרֹת: ²⁶ וְשָׁפְטוּ אֶת־הָעָם בְּכָל־עֵת אֶת־הַדָּבָר הַקָּשֶׁה יְבִיאוּן אֶל־מֹשֶׁה וְכָל־הַדָּבָר הַקָּטֹן יִשְׁפּוּטוּ הֵם: ²⁷ וַיְשַׁלַּח מֹשֶׁה אֶת־חֹתְנוֹ וַיֵּלֶךְ לוֹ אֶל־אַרְצוֹ: פ

יט בַּחֹדֶשׁ הַשְּׁלִישִׁי לְצֵאת בְּנֵי־יִשְׂרָאֵל מֵאֶרֶץ מִצְרָיִם בַּיּוֹם הַזֶּה בָּאוּ מִדְבַּר סִינָי: ² וַיִּסְעוּ מֵרְפִידִים וַיָּבֹאוּ מִדְבַּר סִינַי וַיַּחֲנוּ בַּמִּדְבָּר וַיִּחַן־שָׁם יִשְׂרָאֵל נֶגֶד הָהָר: ³ וּמֹשֶׁה עָלָה אֶל־הָאֱלֹהִים וַיִּקְרָא אֵלָיו יְהֹוָה מִן־הָהָר לֵאמֹר כֹּה תֹאמַר לְבֵית יַעֲקֹב וְתַגֵּיד לִבְנֵי יִשְׂרָאֵל: ⁴ אַתֶּם רְאִיתֶם אֲשֶׁר עָשִׂיתִי לְמִצְרָיִם וָאֶשָּׂא אֶתְכֶם עַל־כַּנְפֵי נְשָׁרִים וָאָבִא אֶתְכֶם אֵלָי: ⁵ וְעַתָּה אִם־שָׁמוֹעַ תִּשְׁמְעוּ בְּקֹלִי וּשְׁמַרְתֶּם אֶת־בְּרִיתִי וִהְיִיתֶם לִי סְגֻלָּה מִכָּל־הָעַמִּים כִּי־לִי כָּל־הָאָרֶץ: ⁶ וְאַתֶּם תִּהְיוּ־לִי מַמְלֶכֶת כֹּהֲנִים וְגוֹי קָדוֹשׁ אֵלֶּה הַדְּבָרִים אֲשֶׁר תְּדַבֵּר אֶל־בְּנֵי יִשְׂרָאֵל: ⁷ וַיָּבֹא מֹשֶׁה וַיִּקְרָא לְזִקְנֵי הָעָם וַיָּשֶׂם לִפְנֵיהֶם אֵת כָּל־הַדְּבָרִים הָאֵלֶּה אֲשֶׁר צִוָּהוּ יְהֹוָה: ⁸ וַיַּעֲנוּ כָל־הָעָם יַחְדָּו וַיֹּאמְרוּ כֹּל אֲשֶׁר־דִּבֶּר יְהֹוָה נַעֲשֶׂה וַיָּשֶׁב מֹשֶׁה אֶת־דִּבְרֵי הָעָם אֶל־יְהֹוָה: ⁹ וַיֹּאמֶר יְהֹוָה אֶל־מֹשֶׁה הִנֵּה אָנֹכִי בָּא אֵלֶיךָ בְּעַב הֶעָנָן בַּעֲבוּר יִשְׁמַע הָעָם בְּדַבְּרִי עִמָּךְ וְגַם־בְּךָ יַאֲמִינוּ לְעוֹלָם וַיַּגֵּד מֹשֶׁה אֶת־דִּבְרֵי הָעָם אֶל־יְהֹוָה: ¹⁰ וַיֹּאמֶר יְהֹוָה אֶל־מֹשֶׁה לֵךְ אֶל־הָעָם וְקִדַּשְׁתָּם הַיּוֹם וּמָחָר וְכִבְּסוּ שִׂמְלֹתָם: ¹¹ וְהָיוּ נְכֹנִים לַיּוֹם הַשְּׁלִישִׁי כִּי בַּיּוֹם הַשְּׁלִישִׁי יֵרֵד יְהֹוָה לְעֵינֵי כָל־הָעָם עַל־הַר סִינָי: ¹² וְהִגְבַּלְתָּ אֶת־הָעָם סָבִיב לֵאמֹר הִשָּׁמְרוּ לָכֶם עֲלוֹת בָּהָר וּנְגֹעַ בְּקָצֵהוּ

the people all around, saying, 'Take heed to yourselves *that* you do *not* go up to the mountain or touch its base. Whoever touches the mountain shall surely be put to death. [13] Not a hand shall touch him, but he shall surely be stoned or shot *with an arrow;* whether man or beast, he shall not live.' When the trumpet sounds long, they shall come near the mountain."

[14] So Moses went down from the mountain to the people and sanctified the people, and they washed their clothes. [15] And he said to the people, "Be ready for the third day; do not come near *your* wives."

[16] Then it came to pass on the third day, in the morning, that there were thunderings and lightnings, and a thick cloud on the mountain; and the sound of the trumpet was very loud, so that all the people who *were* in the camp trembled. [17] And Moses brought the people out of the camp to meet with God, and they stood at the foot of the mountain. [18] Now Mount Sinai *was* completely in smoke, because the LORD descended upon it in fire. Its smoke ascended like the smoke of a furnace, and the whole mountain quaked greatly. [19] And when the blast of the trumpet sounded long and became louder and louder, Moses spoke, and God answered him by voice. [20] Then the LORD came down upon Mount Sinai, on the top of the mountain. And the LORD called Moses to the top of the mountain, and Moses went up.

[21] And the LORD said to Moses, "Go down and warn the people, lest they break through to gaze at the LORD, and many of them perish. [22] Also let the priests who come near the LORD consecrate themselves, lest the LORD break out against them."

[23] But Moses said to the LORD, "The people cannot come up to Mount Sinai; for You warned us, saying, 'Set bounds around the mountain and consecrate it.'"

[24] Then the LORD said to him, "Away! Get down and then come up, you and Aaron with you. But do not let the priests and the people break through to come up to the LORD, lest He break out against them." [25] So Moses went down to the people and spoke to them.

20

And God spoke all these words, saying:

[2] "I *am* the LORD your God, who brought you out of the land of Egypt, out of the house of bondage.

[3] "You shall have no other gods before Me.

[4] "You shall not make for yourself a carved image— any likeness *of anything* that *is* in heaven above, or that *is* in the earth beneath, or that *is* in the water under the earth; [5] you shall not

כָּל־הַנֹּגֵעַ בָּהָר מוֹת יוּמָת: 13 לֹא־תִגַּע בּוֹ יָד כִּי־
סָקוֹל יִסָּקֵל אוֹ־יָרֹה יִיָּרֶה אִם־בְּהֵמָה אִם־אִישׁ
לֹא יִחְיֶה בִּמְשֹׁךְ הַיֹּבֵל הֵמָּה יַעֲלוּ בָהָר: 14 וַיֵּרֶד
מֹשֶׁה מִן־הָהָר אֶל־הָעָם וַיְקַדֵּשׁ אֶת־הָעָם וַיְכַבְּסוּ
שִׂמְלֹתָם: 15 וַיֹּאמֶר אֶל־הָעָם הֱיוּ נְכֹנִים לִשְׁלֹשֶׁת
יָמִים אַל־תִּגְּשׁוּ אֶל־אִשָּׁה: 16 וַיְהִי בַיּוֹם הַשְּׁלִישִׁי
בִּהְיֹת הַבֹּקֶר וַיְהִי קֹלֹת וּבְרָקִים וְעָנָן כָּבֵד עַל־הָהָר
וְקֹל שֹׁפָר חָזָק מְאֹד וַיֶּחֱרַד כָּל־הָעָם אֲשֶׁר בַּמַּחֲנֶה:
17 וַיּוֹצֵא מֹשֶׁה אֶת־הָעָם לִקְרַאת הָאֱלֹהִים מִן־
הַמַּחֲנֶה וַיִּתְיַצְּבוּ בְּתַחְתִּית הָהָר: 18 וְהַר סִינַי עָשַׁן
כֻּלּוֹ מִפְּנֵי אֲשֶׁר יָרַד עָלָיו יְהוָה בָּאֵשׁ וַיַּעַל עֲשָׁנוֹ
כְּעֶשֶׁן הַכִּבְשָׁן וַיֶּחֱרַד כָּל־הָהָר מְאֹד: 19 וַיְהִי קוֹל
הַשּׁוֹפָר הוֹלֵךְ וְחָזֵק מְאֹד מֹשֶׁה יְדַבֵּר וְהָאֱלֹהִים
יַעֲנֶנּוּ בְקוֹל: 20 וַיֵּרֶד יְהוָה עַל־הַר סִינַי אֶל־רֹאשׁ
הָהָר וַיִּקְרָא יְהוָה לְמֹשֶׁה אֶל־רֹאשׁ הָהָר וַיַּעַל
מֹשֶׁה: 21 וַיֹּאמֶר יְהוָה אֶל־מֹשֶׁה רֵד הָעֵד בָּעָם
פֶּן־יֶהֶרְסוּ אֶל־יְהוָה לִרְאוֹת וְנָפַל מִמֶּנּוּ רָב: 22 וְגַם
הַכֹּהֲנִים הַנִּגָּשִׁים אֶל־יְהוָה יִתְקַדָּשׁוּ פֶּן־יִפְרֹץ בָּהֶם
יְהוָה: 23 וַיֹּאמֶר מֹשֶׁה אֶל־יְהוָה לֹא־יוּכַל הָעָם
לַעֲלֹת אֶל־הַר סִינָי כִּי־אַתָּה הַעֵדֹתָה בָּנוּ לֵאמֹר
הַגְבֵּל אֶת־הָהָר וְקִדַּשְׁתּוֹ: 24 וַיֹּאמֶר אֵלָיו יְהוָה
לֶךְ־רֵד וְעָלִיתָ אַתָּה וְאַהֲרֹן עִמָּךְ וְהַכֹּהֲנִים וְהָעָם
אַל־יֶהֶרְסוּ לַעֲלֹת אֶל־יְהוָה פֶּן־יִפְרָץ־בָּם: 25 וַיֵּרֶד
מֹשֶׁה אֶל־הָעָם וַיֹּאמֶר אֲלֵהֶם: ס

כ וַיְדַבֵּר אֱלֹהִים אֵת כָּל־הַדְּבָרִים הָאֵלֶּה
לֵאמֹר: ס 2 אָנֹכִי יְהוָה אֱלֹהֶיךָ אֲשֶׁר
הוֹצֵאתִיךָ מֵאֶרֶץ מִצְרַיִם מִבֵּית עֲבָדִים: 3 לֹא
יִהְיֶה־לְךָ אֱלֹהִים אֲחֵרִים עַל־פָּנָי: 4 לֹא תַעֲשֶׂה־לְךָ
פֶסֶל וְכָל־תְּמוּנָה אֲשֶׁר בַּשָּׁמַיִם מִמַּעַל וַאֲשֶׁר
בָּאָרֶץ מִתַּחַת וַאֲשֶׁר בַּמַּיִם מִתַּחַת לָאָרֶץ: 5 לֹא־

bow down to them nor serve them. For I, the LORD your God, *am* a jealous God, visiting the iniquity of the fathers upon the children to the third and fourth *generations* of those who hate Me, ⁶but showing mercy to thousands, to those who love Me and keep My commandments.

7 "You shall not take the name of the LORD your God in vain, for the LORD will not hold *him* guiltless who takes His name in vain.

8 "Remember the Sabbath day, to keep it holy. ⁹Six days you shall labor and do all your work, ¹⁰but the seventh day *is* the Sabbath of the LORD your God. *In it* you shall do no work: you, nor your son, nor your daughter, nor your male servant, nor your female servant, nor your cattle, nor your stranger who *is* within your gates. ¹¹For *in* six days the LORD made the heavens and the earth, the sea, and all that *is* in them, and rested the seventh day. Therefore the LORD blessed the Sabbath day and hallowed it.

12 "Honor your father and your mother, that your days may be long upon the land which the LORD your God is giving you.

13 "You shall not murder.

14 "You shall not commit adultery.

15 "You shall not steal.

16 "You shall not bear false witness against your neighbor.

17 "You shall not covet your neighbor's house; you shall not covet your neighbor's wife, nor his male servant, nor his female servant, nor his ox, nor his donkey, nor anything that *is* your neighbor's."

¹⁸Now all the people witnessed the thunderings, the lightning flashes, the sound of the trumpet, and the mountain smoking; and when the people saw *it,* they trembled and stood afar off. ¹⁹Then they said to Moses, "You speak with us, and we will hear; but let not God speak with us, lest we die."

²⁰And Moses said to the people, "Do not fear; for God has come to test you, and that His fear may be before you, so that you may not sin." ²¹So the people stood afar off, but Moses drew near the thick darkness where God *was.*

²²Then the LORD said to Moses, "Thus you shall say to the children of Israel: 'You have seen that I have talked with you from heaven. ²³You shall not make *anything to be* with Me—gods of silver or gods of gold you shall not make for yourselves. ²⁴An altar of earth you shall make for Me, and you shall sacrifice on it your burnt offerings and your peace offerings, your sheep and your oxen. In every place where I record My name I will come to you, and I will bless you. ²⁵And if you make Me an altar of stone, you shall not build it of hewn stone; for if

תִּשְׁתַּחֲוֶה לָהֶם וְלֹא תָעָבְדֵם כִּי אָנֹכִי יְהוָה אֱלֹהֶיךָ אֵל קַנָּא פֹּקֵד עֲוֹן אָבֹת עַל־בָּנִים עַל־שִׁלֵּשִׁים וְעַל־רִבֵּעִים לְשֹׂנְאָי: 6 וְעֹשֶׂה חֶסֶד לַאֲלָפִים לְאֹהֲבַי וּלְשֹׁמְרֵי מִצְוֹתָי: ס 7 לֹא תִשָּׂא אֶת־שֵׁם־יְהוָה אֱלֹהֶיךָ לַשָּׁוְא כִּי לֹא יְנַקֶּה יְהוָה אֵת אֲשֶׁר־יִשָּׂא אֶת־שְׁמוֹ לַשָּׁוְא: פ

8 זָכוֹר אֶת־יוֹם הַשַּׁבָּת לְקַדְּשׁוֹ: 9 שֵׁשֶׁת יָמִים תַּעֲבֹד וְעָשִׂיתָ כָּל־מְלַאכְתֶּךָ: 10 וְיוֹם הַשְּׁבִיעִי שַׁבָּת לַיהוָה אֱלֹהֶיךָ לֹא־תַעֲשֶׂה כָל־מְלָאכָה אַתָּה וּבִנְךָ־וּבִתֶּךָ עַבְדְּךָ וַאֲמָתְךָ וּבְהֶמְתֶּךָ וְגֵרְךָ אֲשֶׁר בִּשְׁעָרֶיךָ: 11 כִּי שֵׁשֶׁת־יָמִים עָשָׂה יְהוָה אֶת־הַשָּׁמַיִם וְאֶת־הָאָרֶץ אֶת־הַיָּם וְאֶת־כָּל־אֲשֶׁר־בָּם וַיָּנַח בַּיּוֹם הַשְּׁבִיעִי עַל־כֵּן בֵּרַךְ יְהוָה אֶת־יוֹם הַשַּׁבָּת וַיְקַדְּשֵׁהוּ: ס 12 כַּבֵּד אֶת־אָבִיךָ וְאֶת־אִמֶּךָ לְמַעַן יַאֲרִכוּן יָמֶיךָ עַל הָאֲדָמָה אֲשֶׁר־יְהוָה אֱלֹהֶיךָ נֹתֵן לָךְ: ס 13 לֹא תִּרְצָח ס לֹא תִּנְאָף ס לֹא תִּגְנֹב ס לֹא־תַעֲנֶה בְרֵעֲךָ עֵד שָׁקֶר: ס 14 לֹא תַחְמֹד בֵּית רֵעֶךָ ס לֹא־תַחְמֹד אֵשֶׁת רֵעֶךָ וְעַבְדּוֹ וַאֲמָתוֹ וְשׁוֹרוֹ וַחֲמֹרוֹ וְכֹל אֲשֶׁר לְרֵעֶךָ: פ

15 וְכָל־הָעָם רֹאִים אֶת־הַקּוֹלֹת וְאֶת־הַלַּפִּידִם וְאֵת קוֹל הַשֹּׁפָר וְאֶת־הָהָר עָשֵׁן וַיַּרְא הָעָם וַיָּנֻעוּ וַיַּעַמְדוּ מֵרָחֹק: 16 וַיֹּאמְרוּ אֶל־מֹשֶׁה דַּבֵּר־אַתָּה עִמָּנוּ וְנִשְׁמָעָה וְאַל־יְדַבֵּר עִמָּנוּ אֱלֹהִים פֶּן־נָמוּת: 17 וַיֹּאמֶר מֹשֶׁה אֶל־הָעָם אַל־תִּירָאוּ כִּי לְבַעֲבוּר נַסּוֹת אֶתְכֶם בָּא הָאֱלֹהִים וּבַעֲבוּר תִּהְיֶה יִרְאָתוֹ עַל־פְּנֵיכֶם לְבִלְתִּי תֶחֱטָאוּ: 18 וַיַּעֲמֹד הָעָם מֵרָחֹק וּמֹשֶׁה נִגַּשׁ אֶל־הָעֲרָפֶל אֲשֶׁר־שָׁם הָאֱלֹהִים: פ

19 וַיֹּאמֶר יְהוָה אֶל־מֹשֶׁה כֹּה תֹאמַר אֶל־בְּנֵי יִשְׂרָאֵל אַתֶּם רְאִיתֶם כִּי מִן־הַשָּׁמַיִם דִּבַּרְתִּי עִמָּכֶם: 20 לֹא תַעֲשׂוּן אִתִּי אֱלֹהֵי כֶסֶף וֵאלֹהֵי זָהָב לֹא תַעֲשׂוּ לָכֶם: 21 מִזְבַּח אֲדָמָה תַּעֲשֶׂה־לִּי וְזָבַחְתָּ עָלָיו אֶת־עֹלֹתֶיךָ וְאֶת־שְׁלָמֶיךָ אֶת־צֹאנְךָ וְאֶת־בְּקָרֶךָ בְּכָל־הַמָּקוֹם אֲשֶׁר אַזְכִּיר אֶת־שְׁמִי אָבוֹא אֵלֶיךָ וּבֵרַכְתִּיךָ: 22 וְאִם־מִזְבַּח אֲבָנִים תַּעֲשֶׂה־לִּי לֹא־תִבְנֶה אֶתְהֶן גָּזִית כִּי חַרְבְּךָ הֵנַפְתָּ

you use your tool on it, you have profaned it. ²⁶ Nor shall you go up by steps to My altar, that your nakedness may not be exposed on it.'

21 "Now these *are* the judgments which you shall set before them: ² If you buy a Hebrew servant, he shall serve six years; and in the seventh he shall go out free and pay nothing. ³ If he comes in by himself, he shall go out by himself; if he *comes in* married, then his wife shall go out with him. ⁴ If his master has given him a wife, and she has borne him sons or daughters, the wife and her children shall be her master's, and he shall go out by himself. ⁵ But if the servant plainly says, 'I love my master, my wife, and my children; I will not go out free,' ⁶ then his master shall bring him to the judges. He shall also bring him to the door, or to the doorpost, and his master shall pierce his ear with an awl; and he shall serve him forever.

⁷ "And if a man sells his daughter to be a female slave, she shall not go out as the male slaves do. ⁸ If she does not please her master, who has betrothed her to himself, then he shall let her be redeemed. He shall have no right to sell her to a foreign people, since he has dealt deceitfully with her. ⁹ And if he has betrothed her to his son, he shall deal with her according to the custom of daughters. ¹⁰ If he takes another *wife,* he shall not diminish her food, her clothing, and her marriage rights. ¹¹ And if he does not do these three for her, then she shall go out free, without *paying* money.

¹² "He who strikes a man so that he dies shall surely be put to death. ¹³ However, if he did not lie in wait, but God delivered *him* into his hand, then I will appoint for you a place where he may flee.

¹⁴ "But if a man acts with premeditation against his neighbor, to kill him by treachery, you shall take him from My altar, that he may die.

¹⁵ "And he who strikes his father or his mother shall surely be put to death.

¹⁶ "He who kidnaps a man and sells him, or if he is found in his hand, shall surely be put to death.

¹⁷ "And he who curses his father or his mother shall surely be put to death.

¹⁸ "If men contend with each other, and one strikes the other with a stone or with *his* fist, and he does not die but is confined to *his* bed, ¹⁹ if he rises again and walks about outside with his staff, then he who struck *him* shall be acquitted. He shall only pay *for* the loss of his time, and shall provide *for* him to be thoroughly healed.

עָלֶיהָ וַתְּחַלְלֶהָ: 23 וְלֹא־תַעֲלֶה בְמַעֲלֹת עַל־מִזְבְּחִי אֲשֶׁר לֹא־תִגָּלֶה עֶרְוָתְךָ עָלָיו: פ

כא וְאֵלֶּה הַמִּשְׁפָּטִים אֲשֶׁר תָּשִׂים לִפְנֵיהֶם: 2 כִּי תִקְנֶה עֶבֶד עִבְרִי שֵׁשׁ שָׁנִים יַעֲבֹד וּבַשְּׁבִעִת יֵצֵא לַחָפְשִׁי חִנָּם: 3 אִם־בְּגַפּוֹ יָבֹא בְּגַפּוֹ יֵצֵא אִם־בַּעַל אִשָּׁה הוּא וְיָצְאָה אִשְׁתּוֹ עִמּוֹ: 4 אִם־אֲדֹנָיו יִתֶּן־לוֹ אִשָּׁה וְיָלְדָה־לוֹ בָנִים אוֹ בָנוֹת הָאִשָּׁה וִילָדֶיהָ תִּהְיֶה לַאדֹנֶיהָ וְהוּא יֵצֵא בְגַפּוֹ: 5 וְאִם־אָמֹר יֹאמַר הָעֶבֶד אָהַבְתִּי אֶת־אֲדֹנִי אֶת־אִשְׁתִּי וְאֶת־בָּנָי לֹא אֵצֵא חָפְשִׁי: 6 וְהִגִּישׁוֹ אֲדֹנָיו אֶל־הָאֱלֹהִים וְהִגִּישׁוֹ אֶל־הַדֶּלֶת אוֹ אֶל־הַמְּזוּזָה וְרָצַע אֲדֹנָיו אֶת־אָזְנוֹ בַּמַּרְצֵעַ וַעֲבָדוֹ לְעֹלָם: ס 7 וְכִי־יִמְכֹּר אִישׁ אֶת־בִּתּוֹ לְאָמָה לֹא תֵצֵא כְּצֵאת הָעֲבָדִים: 8 אִם־רָעָה בְּעֵינֵי אֲדֹנֶיהָ אֲשֶׁר־לֹא ᵖ יְעָדָהּ וְהֶפְדָּהּ לְעַם נָכְרִי לֹא־יִמְשֹׁל לְמָכְרָהּ בְּבִגְדוֹ־בָהּ: 9 וְאִם־לִבְנוֹ יִיעָדֶנָּה כְּמִשְׁפַּט הַבָּנוֹת יַעֲשֶׂה־לָּהּ: 10 אִם־אַחֶרֶת יִקַּח־לוֹ שְׁאֵרָהּ כְּסוּתָהּ וְעֹנָתָהּ לֹא יִגְרָע: 11 וְאִם־שְׁלָשׁ־אֵלֶּה לֹא יַעֲשֶׂה לָהּ וְיָצְאָה חִנָּם אֵין כָּסֶף: ס 12 מַכֵּה אִישׁ וָמֵת מוֹת יוּמָת: 13 וַאֲשֶׁר לֹא צָדָה וְהָאֱלֹהִים אִנָּה לְיָדוֹ וְשַׂמְתִּי לְךָ מָקוֹם אֲשֶׁר יָנוּס שָׁמָּה: ס 14 וְכִי־יָזִד אִישׁ עַל־רֵעֵהוּ לְהָרְגוֹ בְעָרְמָה מֵעִם מִזְבְּחִי תִּקָּחֶנּוּ לָמוּת: ס 15 וּמַכֵּה אָבִיו וְאִמּוֹ מוֹת יוּמָת: 16 וְגֹנֵב אִישׁ וּמְכָרוֹ וְנִמְצָא בְיָדוֹ מוֹת יוּמָת: ס 17 וּמְקַלֵּל אָבִיו וְאִמּוֹ מוֹת יוּמָת: ס 18 וְכִי־יְרִיבֻן אֲנָשִׁים וְהִכָּה־אִישׁ אֶת־רֵעֵהוּ בְּאֶבֶן אוֹ בְאֶגְרֹף וְלֹא יָמוּת וְנָפַל לְמִשְׁכָּב: 19 אִם־יָקוּם וְהִתְהַלֵּךְ בַּחוּץ עַל־מִשְׁעַנְתּוֹ וְנִקָּה הַמַּכֶּה רַק שִׁבְתּוֹ יִתֵּן וְרַפֹּא

20 "And if a man beats his male or female servant with a rod, so that he dies under his hand, he shall surely be punished. 21 Notwithstanding, if he remains alive a day or two, he shall not be punished; for he *is* his property.

22 "If men fight, and hurt a woman with child, so that she gives birth prematurely, yet no harm follows, he shall surely be punished accordingly as the woman's husband imposes on him; and he shall pay as the judges *determine*. 23 But if *any* harm follows, then you shall give life for life, 24 eye for eye, tooth for tooth, hand for hand, foot for foot, 25 burn for burn, wound for wound, stripe for stripe.

26 "If a man strikes the eye of his male or female servant, and destroys it, he shall let him go free for the sake of his eye. 27 And if he knocks out the tooth of his male or female servant, he shall let him go free for the sake of his tooth.

28 "If an ox gores a man or a woman to death, then the ox shall surely be stoned, and its flesh shall not be eaten; but the owner of the ox *shall be* acquitted. 29 But if the ox tended to thrust with its horn in times past, and it has been made known to his owner, and he has not kept it confined, so that it has killed a man or a woman, the ox shall be stoned and its owner also shall be put to death. 30 If there is imposed on him a sum of money, then he shall pay to redeem his life, whatever is imposed on him. 31 Whether it has gored a son or gored a daughter, according to this judgment it shall be done to him. 32 If the ox gores a male or female servant, he shall give to their master thirty shekels of silver, and the ox shall be stoned.

33 "And if a man opens a pit, or if a man digs a pit and does not cover it, and an ox or a donkey falls in it, 34 the owner of the pit shall make *it* good; he shall give money to their owner, but the dead *animal* shall be his.

35 "If one man's ox hurts another's, so that it dies, then they shall sell the live ox and divide the money from it; and the dead ox they shall also divide. 36 Or if it was known that the ox tended to thrust in time past, and its owner has not kept it confined, he shall surely pay ox for ox, and the dead animal shall be his own.

22 "If a man steals an ox or a sheep, and slaughters it or sells it, he shall restore five oxen for an ox and four sheep for a sheep. 2 If the thief is found breaking in, and he is struck so that he dies, *there shall be* no guilt for his bloodshed. 3 If the sun has risen on him, *there shall be* guilt for his bloodshed. He should make full restitution; if he

ס 20 וְכִי־יַכֶּה אִישׁ אֶת־עַבְדּוֹ אוֹ אֶת־אֲמָתוֹ בַּשֵּׁבֶט וּמֵת תַּחַת יָדוֹ נָקֹם יִנָּקֵם: 21 אַךְ אִם־יוֹם אוֹ יוֹמַיִם יַעֲמֹד לֹא יֻקַּם כִּי כַסְפּוֹ הוּא: ס 22 וְכִי־יִנָּצוּ אֲנָשִׁים וְנָגְפוּ אִשָּׁה הָרָה וְיָצְאוּ יְלָדֶיהָ וְלֹא יִהְיֶה אָסוֹן עָנוֹשׁ יֵעָנֵשׁ כַּאֲשֶׁר יָשִׁית עָלָיו בַּעַל הָאִשָּׁה וְנָתַן בִּפְלִלִים: 23 וְאִם־אָסוֹן יִהְיֶה וְנָתַתָּה נֶפֶשׁ תַּחַת נָפֶשׁ: 24 עַיִן תַּחַת עַיִן שֵׁן תַּחַת שֵׁן יָד תַּחַת יָד רֶגֶל תַּחַת רָגֶל: 25 כְּוִיָּה תַּחַת כְּוִיָּה פֶּצַע תַּחַת פָּצַע חַבּוּרָה תַּחַת חַבּוּרָה: ס 26 וְכִי־יַכֶּה אִישׁ אֶת־עֵין עַבְדּוֹ אוֹ־אֶת־עֵין אֲמָתוֹ וְשִׁחֲתָהּ לַחָפְשִׁי יְשַׁלְּחֶנּוּ תַּחַת עֵינוֹ: ס 27 וְאִם־שֵׁן עַבְדּוֹ אוֹ־שֵׁן אֲמָתוֹ יַפִּיל לַחָפְשִׁי יְשַׁלְּחֶנּוּ תַּחַת שִׁנּוֹ: פ 28 וְכִי־יִגַּח שׁוֹר אֶת־אִישׁ אוֹ אֶת־אִשָּׁה וָמֵת סָקוֹל יִסָּקֵל הַשּׁוֹר וְלֹא יֵאָכֵל אֶת־בְּשָׂרוֹ וּבַעַל הַשּׁוֹר נָקִי: 29 וְאִם שׁוֹר נַגָּח הוּא מִתְּמֹל שִׁלְשֹׁם וְהוּעַד בִּבְעָלָיו וְלֹא יִשְׁמְרֶנּוּ וְהֵמִית אִישׁ אוֹ אִשָּׁה הַשּׁוֹר יִסָּקֵל וְגַם־בְּעָלָיו יוּמָת: 30 אִם־כֹּפֶר יוּשַׁת עָלָיו וְנָתַן פִּדְיֹן נַפְשׁוֹ כְּכֹל אֲשֶׁר־יוּשַׁת עָלָיו: 31 אוֹ־בֵן יִגָּח אוֹ־בַת יִגָּח כַּמִּשְׁפָּט הַזֶּה יֵעָשֶׂה לּוֹ: 32 אִם־עֶבֶד יִגַּח הַשּׁוֹר אוֹ אָמָה כֶּסֶף ן שְׁלֹשִׁים שְׁקָלִים יִתֵּן לַאדֹנָיו וְהַשּׁוֹר יִסָּקֵל: ס 33 וְכִי־יִפְתַּח אִישׁ בּוֹר אוֹ כִּי־יִכְרֶה אִישׁ בֹּר וְלֹא יְכַסֶּנּוּ וְנָפַל־שָׁמָּה שּׁוֹר אוֹ חֲמוֹר: 34 בַּעַל הַבּוֹר יְשַׁלֵּם כֶּסֶף יָשִׁיב לִבְעָלָיו וְהַמֵּת יִהְיֶה־לּוֹ: ס 35 וְכִי־יִגֹּף שׁוֹר־אִישׁ אֶת־שׁוֹר רֵעֵהוּ וָמֵת וּמָכְרוּ אֶת־הַשּׁוֹר הַחַי וְחָצוּ אֶת־כַּסְפּוֹ וְגַם אֶת־הַמֵּת יֶחֱצוּן: 36 אוֹ נוֹדַע כִּי שׁוֹר נַגָּח הוּא מִתְּמוֹל שִׁלְשֹׁם וְלֹא יִשְׁמְרֶנּוּ בְּעָלָיו שַׁלֵּם יְשַׁלֵּם שׁוֹר תַּחַת הַשּׁוֹר וְהַמֵּת יִהְיֶה־לּוֹ: ס 37 כִּי יִגְנֹב־אִישׁ שׁוֹר אוֹ־שֶׂה וּטְבָחוֹ אוֹ מְכָרוֹ חֲמִשָּׁה בָקָר יְשַׁלֵּם תַּחַת הַשּׁוֹר וְאַרְבַּע־צֹאן תַּחַת הַשֶּׂה:

כב אִם־בַּמַּחְתֶּרֶת יִמָּצֵא הַגַּנָּב וְהֻכָּה וָמֵת אֵין לוֹ דָּמִים: 2 אִם־זָרְחָה הַשֶּׁמֶשׁ עָלָיו דָּמִים לוֹ שַׁלֵּם יְשַׁלֵּם אִם־אֵין לוֹ וְנִמְכַּר בִּגְנֵבָתוֹ: 3 אִם־הִמָּצֵא תִמָּצֵא בְיָדוֹ הַגְּנֵבָה מִשּׁוֹר עַד־חֲמוֹר עַד־

has nothing, then he shall be sold for his theft. ⁴If the theft is certainly found alive in his hand, whether it is an ox or donkey or sheep, he shall restore double.

⁵"If a man causes a field or vineyard to be grazed, and lets loose his animal, and it feeds in another man's field, he shall make restitution from the best of his own field and the best of his own vineyard.

⁶"If fire breaks out and catches in thorns, so that stacked grain, standing grain, or the field is consumed, he who kindled the fire shall surely make restitution.

⁷"If a man delivers to his neighbor money or articles to keep, and it is stolen out of the man's house, if the thief is found, he shall pay double. ⁸If the thief is not found, then the master of the house shall be brought to the judges *to see* whether he has put his hand into his neighbor's goods.

⁹"For any kind of trespass, *whether it concerns* an ox, a donkey, a sheep, or clothing, *or* for any kind of lost thing which *another* claims to be his, the cause of both parties shall come before the judges; *and* whomever the judges condemn shall pay double to his neighbor. ¹⁰If a man delivers to his neighbor a donkey, an ox, a sheep, or any animal to keep, and it dies, is hurt, or driven away, no one seeing *it,* ¹¹ *then* an oath of the LORD shall be between them both, that he has not put his hand into his neighbor's goods; and the owner of it shall accept *that,* and he shall not make *it* good. ¹²But if, in fact, it is stolen from him, he shall make restitution to the owner of it. ¹³If it is torn to pieces *by a beast,* then he shall bring it as evidence, *and* he shall not make good what was torn.

¹⁴"And if a man borrows *anything* from his neighbor, and it becomes injured or dies, the owner of it not *being* with it, he shall surely make *it* good. ¹⁵If its owner *was* with it, he shall not make *it* good; if it *was* hired, it came for its hire.

¹⁶"If a man entices a virgin who is not betrothed, and lies with her, he shall surely pay the bride-price for her *to be* his wife. ¹⁷If her father utterly refuses to give her to him, he shall pay money according to the bride-price of virgins.

¹⁸"You shall not permit a sorceress to live.

¹⁹"Whoever lies with an animal shall surely be put to death.

²⁰"He who sacrifices to *any* god, except to the LORD only, he shall be utterly destroyed.

²¹"You shall neither mistreat a stranger nor oppress him, for you were strangers in the land of Egypt.

שֶׂה חַיִּים שְׁנַיִם יְשַׁלֵּם: ס ⁴כִּי יַבְעֶר־
אִישׁ שָׂדֶה אוֹ־כֶרֶם וְשִׁלַּח אֶת־בְּעִירֹה וּבִעֵר
בִּשְׂדֵה אַחֵר מֵיטַב שָׂדֵהוּ וּמֵיטַב כַּרְמוֹ
יְשַׁלֵּם: ס ⁵כִּי־תֵצֵא אֵשׁ וּמָצְאָה קֹצִים
וְנֶאֱכַל גָּדִישׁ אוֹ הַקָּמָה אוֹ הַשָּׂדֶה שַׁלֵּם יְשַׁלֵּם
הַמַּבְעִר אֶת־הַבְּעֵרָה: ס ⁶כִּי־יִתֵּן אִישׁ
אֶל־רֵעֵהוּ כֶּסֶף אוֹ־כֵלִים לִשְׁמֹר וְגֻנַּב מִבֵּית הָאִישׁ
אִם־יִמָּצֵא הַגַּנָּב יְשַׁלֵּם שְׁנָיִם: ⁷אִם־לֹא יִמָּצֵא
הַגַּנָּב וְנִקְרַב בַּעַל־הַבַּיִת אֶל־הָאֱלֹהִים אִם־לֹא
שָׁלַח יָדוֹ בִּמְלֶאכֶת רֵעֵהוּ: ⁸עַל־כָּל־דְּבַר־פֶּשַׁע
עַל־שׁוֹר עַל־חֲמוֹר עַל־שֶׂה עַל־שַׂלְמָה עַל־כָּל־
אֲבֵדָה אֲשֶׁר יֹאמַר כִּי־הוּא זֶה עַד הָאֱלֹהִים יָבֹא
דְּבַר־שְׁנֵיהֶם אֲשֶׁר יַרְשִׁיעֻן אֱלֹהִים יְשַׁלֵּם שְׁנַיִם
לְרֵעֵהוּ: ס ⁹כִּי־יִתֵּן אִישׁ אֶל־רֵעֵהוּ חֲמוֹר
אוֹ־שׁוֹר אוֹ־שֶׂה וְכָל־בְּהֵמָה לִשְׁמֹר וּמֵת אוֹ־נִשְׁבַּר
אוֹ־נִשְׁבָּה אֵין רֹאֶה: ¹⁰שְׁבֻעַת יְהוָה תִּהְיֶה בֵּין
שְׁנֵיהֶם אִם־לֹא שָׁלַח יָדוֹ בִּמְלֶאכֶת רֵעֵהוּ וְלָקַח
בְּעָלָיו וְלֹא יְשַׁלֵּם: ¹¹וְאִם־גָּנֹב יִגָּנֵב מֵעִמּוֹ יְשַׁלֵּם
לִבְעָלָיו: ¹²אִם־טָרֹף יִטָּרֵף יְבִאֵהוּ עֵד הַטְּרֵפָה לֹא
יְשַׁלֵּם: פ

¹³וְכִי־יִשְׁאַל אִישׁ מֵעִם רֵעֵהוּ וְנִשְׁבַּר אוֹ־
מֵת בְּעָלָיו אֵין־עִמּוֹ שַׁלֵּם יְשַׁלֵּם: ¹⁴אִם־
בְּעָלָיו עִמּוֹ לֹא יְשַׁלֵּם אִם־שָׂכִיר הוּא בָּא
בִּשְׂכָרוֹ: ס ¹⁵וְכִי־יְפַתֶּה אִישׁ בְּתוּלָה
אֲשֶׁר לֹא־אֹרָשָׂה וְשָׁכַב עִמָּהּ מָהֹר יִמְהָרֶנָּה לּוֹ
לְאִשָּׁה: ¹⁶אִם־מָאֵן יְמָאֵן אָבִיהָ לְתִתָּהּ לוֹ כֶּסֶף
יִשְׁקֹל כְּמֹהַר הַבְּתוּלֹת: ס ¹⁷מְכַשֵּׁפָה לֹא
תְחַיֶּה: ס ¹⁸כָּל־שֹׁכֵב עִם־בְּהֵמָה מוֹת
יוּמָת: ס ¹⁹זֹבֵחַ לָאֱלֹהִים יָחֳרָם בִּלְתִּי
לַיהוָה לְבַדּוֹ: ²⁰וְגֵר לֹא־תוֹנֶה וְלֹא תִלְחָצֶנּוּ כִּי־
גֵרִים הֱיִיתֶם בְּאֶרֶץ מִצְרָיִם: ²¹כָּל־אַלְמָנָה וְיָתוֹם

22 "You shall not afflict any widow or fatherless child. 23 If you afflict them in any way, *and* they cry at all to Me, I will surely hear their cry; 24 and My wrath will become hot, and I will kill you with the sword; your wives shall be widows, and your children fatherless.

25 "If you lend money to *any of* My people *who are* poor among you, you shall not be like a moneylender to him; you shall not charge him interest. 26 If you ever take your neighbor's garment as a pledge, you shall return it to him before the sun goes down. 27 For that *is* his only covering, it *is* his garment for his skin. What will he sleep in? And it will be that when he cries to Me, I will hear, for I *am* gracious.

28 "You shall not revile God, nor curse a ruler of your people.

29 "You shall not delay *to offer* the first of your ripe produce and your juices. The firstborn of your sons you shall give to Me. 30 Likewise you shall do with your oxen *and* your sheep. It shall be with its mother seven days; on the eighth day you shall give it to Me.

31 "And you shall be holy men to Me: you shall not eat meat torn *by beasts* in the field; you shall throw it to the dogs.

23 "You shall not circulate a false report. Do not put your hand with the wicked to be an unrighteous witness. 2 You shall not follow a crowd to do evil; nor shall you testify in a dispute so as to turn aside after many to pervert *justice.* 3 You shall not show partiality to a poor man in his dispute.

4 "If you meet your enemy's ox or his donkey going astray, you shall surely bring it back to him again. 5 If you see the donkey of one who hates you lying under its burden, and you would refrain from helping it, you shall surely help him with it.

6 "You shall not pervert the judgment of your poor in his dispute. 7 Keep yourself far from a false matter; do not kill the innocent and righteous. For I will not justify the wicked. 8 And you shall take no bribe, for a bribe blinds the discerning and perverts the words of the righteous.

9 "Also you shall not oppress a stranger, for you know the heart of a stranger, because you were strangers in the land of Egypt.

10 "Six years you shall sow your land and gather in its produce, 11 but the seventh *year* you shall let it rest and lie fallow, that the poor of your people may eat; and what they leave, the beasts of the field may eat. In like manner you shall do with your vineyard *and* your olive grove. 12 Six days you shall do your work, and on the seventh day you shall rest, that

לֹא תְעַנּוּן: 22 אִם־עַנֵּה תְעַנֶּה אֹתוֹ כִּי אִם־צָעֹק יִצְעַק אֵלַי שָׁמֹעַ אֶשְׁמַע צַעֲקָתוֹ: 23 וְחָרָה אַפִּי וְהָרַגְתִּי אֶתְכֶם בֶּחָרֶב וְהָיוּ נְשֵׁיכֶם אַלְמָנוֹת וּבְנֵיכֶם יְתֹמִים: פ

24 אִם־כֶּסֶף ׀ תַּלְוֶה אֶת־עַמִּי אֶת־הֶעָנִי עִמָּךְ לֹא־תִהְיֶה לוֹ כְּנֹשֶׁה לֹא־תְשִׂימוּן עָלָיו נֶשֶׁךְ: 25 אִם־חָבֹל תַּחְבֹּל שַׂלְמַת רֵעֶךָ עַד־בֹּא הַשֶּׁמֶשׁ תְּשִׁיבֶנּוּ לוֹ: 26 כִּי הִוא כְסוּתֹה לְבַדָּהּ הִוא שִׂמְלָתוֹ לְעֹרוֹ בַּמֶּה יִשְׁכָּב וְהָיָה כִּי־יִצְעַק אֵלַי וְשָׁמַעְתִּי כִּי־חַנּוּן אָנִי: ס 27 אֱלֹהִים לֹא תְקַלֵּל וְנָשִׂיא בְעַמְּךָ לֹא תָאֹר: 28 מְלֵאָתְךָ וְדִמְעֲךָ לֹא תְאַחֵר בְּכוֹר בָּנֶיךָ תִּתֶּן־לִי: 29 כֵּן־תַּעֲשֶׂה לְשֹׁרְךָ לְצֹאנֶךָ שִׁבְעַת יָמִים יִהְיֶה עִם־אִמּוֹ בַּיּוֹם הַשְּׁמִינִי תִּתְּנוֹ־לִי: 30 וְאַנְשֵׁי־קֹדֶשׁ תִּהְיוּן לִי וּבָשָׂר בַּשָּׂדֶה טְרֵפָה לֹא תֹאכֵלוּ לַכֶּלֶב תַּשְׁלִכוּן אֹתוֹ: ס

כג לֹא תִשָּׂא שֵׁמַע שָׁוְא אַל־תָּשֶׁת יָדְךָ עִם־רָשָׁע לִהְיֹת עֵד חָמָס: 2 לֹא־תִהְיֶה אַחֲרֵי־רַבִּים לְרָעֹת וְלֹא־תַעֲנֶה עַל־רִב לִנְטֹת אַחֲרֵי רַבִּים לְהַטֹּת: 3 וְדָל לֹא תֶהְדַּר בְּרִיבוֹ: ס 4 כִּי תִפְגַּע שׁוֹר אֹיִבְךָ אוֹ חֲמֹרוֹ תֹּעֶה הָשֵׁב תְּשִׁיבֶנּוּ לוֹ: ס 5 כִּי־תִרְאֶה חֲמוֹר שֹׂנַאֲךָ רֹבֵץ תַּחַת מַשָּׂאוֹ וְחָדַלְתָּ מֵעֲזֹב לוֹ עָזֹב תַּעֲזֹב עִמּוֹ: ס 6 לֹא תַטֶּה מִשְׁפַּט אֶבְיֹנְךָ בְּרִיבוֹ: 7 מִדְּבַר־שֶׁקֶר תִּרְחָק וְנָקִי וְצַדִּיק אַל־תַּהֲרֹג כִּי לֹא־אַצְדִּיק רָשָׁע: 8 וְשֹׁחַד לֹא תִקָּח כִּי הַשֹּׁחַד יְעַוֵּר פִּקְחִים וִיסַלֵּף דִּבְרֵי צַדִּיקִים: 9 וְגֵר לֹא תִלְחָץ וְאַתֶּם יְדַעְתֶּם אֶת־נֶפֶשׁ הַגֵּר כִּי־גֵרִים הֱיִיתֶם בְּאֶרֶץ מִצְרָיִם: 10 וְשֵׁשׁ שָׁנִים תִּזְרַע אֶת־אַרְצֶךָ וְאָסַפְתָּ אֶת־תְּבוּאָתָהּ: 11 וְהַשְּׁבִיעִת תִּשְׁמְטֶנָּה וּנְטַשְׁתָּהּ וְאָכְלוּ אֶבְיֹנֵי עַמֶּךָ וְיִתְרָם תֹּאכַל חַיַּת הַשָּׂדֶה כֵּן־תַּעֲשֶׂה לְכַרְמְךָ לְזֵיתֶךָ: 12 שֵׁשֶׁת יָמִים תַּעֲשֶׂה מַעֲשֶׂיךָ וּבַיּוֹם הַשְּׁבִיעִי תִּשְׁבֹּת לְמַעַן יָנוּחַ

your ox and your donkey may rest, and the son of your female servant and the stranger may be refreshed.

13 "And in all that I have said to you, be circumspect and make no mention of the name of other gods, nor let it be heard from your mouth.

14 "Three times you shall keep a feast to Me in the year: 15 You shall keep the Feast of Unleavened Bread (you shall eat unleavened bread seven days, as I commanded you, at the time appointed in the month of Abib, for in it you came out of Egypt; none shall appear before Me empty); 16 and the Feast of Harvest, the firstfruits of your labors which you have sown in the field; and the Feast of Ingathering at the end of the year, when you have gathered in *the fruit of* your labors from the field.

17 "Three times in the year all your males shall appear before the Lord GOD.

18 "You shall not offer the blood of My sacrifice with leavened bread; nor shall the fat of My sacrifice remain until morning. 19 The first of the firstfruits of your land you shall bring into the house of the LORD your God. You shall not boil a young goat in its mother's milk.

20 "Behold, I send an Angel before you to keep you in the way and to bring you into the place which I have prepared. 21 Beware of Him and obey His voice; do not provoke Him, for He will not pardon your transgressions; for My name *is* in Him. 22 But if you indeed obey His voice and do all that I speak, then I will be an enemy to your enemies and an adversary to your adversaries. 23 For My Angel will go before you and bring you in to the Amorites and the Hittites and the Perizzites and the Canaanites and the Hivites and the Jebusites; and I will cut them off. 24 You shall not bow down to their gods, nor serve them, nor do according to their works; but you shall utterly overthrow them and completely break down their *sacred* pillars.

25 "So you shall serve the LORD your God, and He will bless your bread and your water. And I will take sickness away from the midst of you. 26 No one shall suffer miscarriage or be barren in your land; I will fulfill the number of your days.

27 "I will send My fear before you, I will cause confusion among all the people to whom you come, and will make all your enemies turn *their* backs to you. 28 And I will send hornets before you, which shall drive out the Hivite, the Canaanite, and the Hittite from before you. 29 I will not drive them out from before you in one year, lest the land become desolate and the beasts of the field become too numerous for you. 30 Little by little I will drive them out from before you, until you have increased, and

שׁוֹרְךָ֖ וַחֲמֹרֶ֑ךָ וְיִנָּפֵ֛שׁ בֶּן־אֲמָתְךָ֖ וְהַגֵּֽר׃ 13 וּבְכֹ֥ל אֲשֶׁר־אָמַ֛רְתִּי אֲלֵיכֶ֖ם תִּשָּׁמֵ֑רוּ וְשֵׁ֨ם אֱלֹהִ֤ים אֲחֵרִים֙ לֹ֣א תַזְכִּ֔ירוּ לֹ֥א יִשָּׁמַ֖ע עַל־פִּֽיךָ׃ 14 שָׁלֹ֣שׁ רְגָלִ֔ים תָּחֹ֥ג לִ֖י בַּשָּׁנָֽה׃ 15 אֶת־חַ֣ג הַמַּצּוֹת֮ תִּשְׁמֹר֒ שִׁבְעַ֣ת יָמִים֩ תֹּאכַ֨ל מַצּ֜וֹת כַּאֲשֶׁ֣ר צִוִּיתִ֗ךָ לְמוֹעֵד֙ חֹ֣דֶשׁ הָֽאָבִ֔יב כִּי־ב֖וֹ יָצָ֣אתָ מִמִּצְרָ֑יִם וְלֹא־יֵרָא֥וּ פָנַ֖י רֵיקָֽם׃

16 וְחַ֤ג הַקָּצִיר֙ בִּכּוּרֵ֣י מַעֲשֶׂ֔יךָ אֲשֶׁ֥ר תִּזְרַ֖ע בַּשָּׂדֶ֑ה וְחַ֤ג הָֽאָסִף֙ בְּצֵ֣את הַשָּׁנָ֔ה בְּאָסְפְּךָ֥ אֶֽת־מַעֲשֶׂ֖יךָ מִן־הַשָּׂדֶֽה׃ 17 שָׁלֹ֥שׁ פְּעָמִ֖ים בַּשָּׁנָ֑ה יֵרָאֶה֙ כָּל־זְכ֣וּרְךָ֔ אֶל־פְּנֵ֖י הָאָדֹ֥ן ׀ יְהוָֽה׃ 18 לֹֽא־תִזְבַּ֥ח עַל־חָמֵ֖ץ דַּם־זִבְחִ֑י וְלֹֽא־יָלִ֥ין חֵֽלֶב־חַגִּ֖י עַד־בֹּֽקֶר׃ 19 רֵאשִׁ֗ית בִּכּוּרֵי֙ אַדְמָ֣תְךָ֔ תָּבִ֕יא בֵּ֖ית יְהוָ֣ה אֱלֹהֶ֑יךָ לֹֽא־תְבַשֵּׁ֥ל גְּדִ֖י בַּחֲלֵ֥ב אִמּֽוֹ׃ ס

20 הִנֵּ֨ה אָנֹכִ֜י שֹׁלֵ֤חַ מַלְאָךְ֙ לְפָנֶ֔יךָ לִשְׁמָרְךָ֖ בַּדָּ֑רֶךְ וְלַהֲבִ֣יאֲךָ֔ אֶל־הַמָּק֖וֹם אֲשֶׁ֥ר הֲכִנֹֽתִי׃ 21 הִשָּׁ֧מֶר מִפָּנָ֛יו וּשְׁמַ֥ע בְּקֹל֖וֹ אַל־תַּמֵּ֣ר בּ֑וֹ כִּ֣י לֹ֤א יִשָּׂא֙ לְפִשְׁעֲכֶ֔ם כִּ֥י שְׁמִ֖י בְּקִרְבּֽוֹ׃ 22 כִּ֣י אִם־שָׁמֹ֤עַ תִּשְׁמַע֙ בְּקֹל֔וֹ וְעָשִׂ֕יתָ כֹּ֖ל אֲשֶׁ֣ר אֲדַבֵּ֑ר וְאָֽיַבְתִּי֙ אֶת־אֹ֣יְבֶ֔יךָ וְצַרְתִּ֖י אֶת־צֹרְרֶֽיךָ׃ 23 כִּֽי־יֵלֵ֣ךְ מַלְאָכִי֮ לְפָנֶיךָ֒ וֶהֱבִֽיאֲךָ֗ אֶל־הָֽאֱמֹרִי֙ וְהַ֣חִתִּ֔י וְהַפְּרִזִּי֙ וְהַֽכְּנַעֲנִ֔י הַחִוִּ֖י וְהַיְבוּסִ֑י וְהִכְחַדְתִּֽיו׃ 24 לֹֽא־תִשְׁתַּחֲוֶ֤ה לֵאלֹֽהֵיהֶם֙ וְלֹ֣א תָֽעָבְדֵ֔ם וְלֹ֥א תַעֲשֶׂ֖ה כְּמַֽעֲשֵׂיהֶ֑ם כִּ֤י הָרֵ֣ס תְּהָֽרְסֵ֔ם וְשַׁבֵּ֥ר תְּשַׁבֵּ֖ר מַצֵּבֹתֵיהֶֽם׃ 25 וַעֲבַדְתֶּ֗ם אֵ֚ת יְהוָ֣ה אֱלֹֽהֵיכֶ֔ם וּבֵרַ֥ךְ אֶֽת־לַחְמְךָ֖ וְאֶת־מֵימֶ֑יךָ וַהֲסִרֹתִ֥י מַחֲלָ֖ה מִקִּרְבֶּֽךָ׃ 26 לֹ֥א תִֽהְיֶ֛ה מְשַׁכֵּלָ֥ה וַעֲקָרָ֖ה בְּאַרְצֶ֑ךָ אֶת־מִסְפַּ֥ר יָמֶ֖יךָ אֲמַלֵּֽא׃ 27 אֶת־אֵֽימָתִי֙ אֲשַׁלַּ֣ח לְפָנֶ֔יךָ וְהַמֹּתִי֙ אֶת־כָּל־הָעָ֔ם אֲשֶׁ֥ר תָּבֹ֖א בָּהֶ֑ם וְנָתַתִּ֧י אֶת־כָּל־אֹיְבֶ֛יךָ אֵלֶ֖יךָ עֹֽרֶף׃ 28 וְשָׁלַחְתִּ֥י אֶת־הַצִּרְעָ֖ה לְפָנֶ֑יךָ וְגֵרְשָׁ֗ה אֶת־הַחִוִּ֛י אֶת־הַֽכְּנַעֲנִ֖י וְאֶת־הַֽחִתִּ֖י מִלְּפָנֶֽיךָ׃ 29 לֹ֧א אֲגָרְשֶׁ֛נּוּ מִפָּנֶ֖יךָ בְּשָׁנָ֣ה אֶחָ֑ת פֶּן־תִּהְיֶ֤ה הָאָ֙רֶץ֙ שְׁמָמָ֔ה וְרַבָּ֥ה עָלֶ֖יךָ חַיַּ֥ת הַשָּׂדֶֽה׃ 30 מְעַ֥ט מְעַ֛ט אֲגָרְשֶׁ֖נּוּ מִפָּנֶ֑יךָ עַ֚ד אֲשֶׁ֣ר תִּפְרֶ֔ה וְנָחַלְתָּ֖

you inherit the land. ³¹ And I will set your bounds from the Red Sea to the sea, Philistia, and from the desert to the River. For I will deliver the inhabitants of the land into your hand, and you shall drive them out before you. ³² You shall make no covenant with them, nor with their gods. ³³ They shall not dwell in your land, lest they make you sin against Me. For *if* you serve their gods, it will surely be a snare to you."

24 Now He said to Moses, "Come up to the LORD, you and Aaron, Nadab and Abihu, and seventy of the elders of Israel, and worship from afar. ² And Moses alone shall come near the LORD, but they shall not come near; nor shall the people go up with him."

³ So Moses came and told the people all the words of the LORD and all the judgments. And all the people answered with one voice and said, "All the words which the LORD has said we will do." ⁴ And Moses wrote all the words of the LORD. And he rose early in the morning, and built an altar at the foot of the mountain, and twelve pillars according to the twelve tribes of Israel. ⁵ Then he sent young men of the children of Israel, who offered burnt offerings and sacrificed peace offerings of oxen to the LORD. ⁶ And Moses took half the blood and put *it* in basins, and half the blood he sprinkled on the altar. ⁷ Then he took the Book of the Covenant and read in the hearing of the people. And they said, "All that the LORD has said we will do, and be obedient." ⁸ And Moses took the blood, sprinkled *it* on the people, and said, "This is the blood of the covenant which the LORD has made with you according to all these words."

⁹ Then Moses went up, also Aaron, Nadab, and Abihu, and seventy of the elders of Israel, ¹⁰ and they saw the God of Israel. And *there was* under His feet as it were a paved work of sapphire stone, and it was like the very heavens in *its* clarity. ¹¹ But on the nobles of the children of Israel He did not lay His hand. So they saw God, and they ate and drank.

¹² Then the LORD said to Moses, "Come up to Me on the mountain and be there; and I will give you tablets of stone, and the law and commandments which I have written, that you may teach them."

¹³ So Moses arose with his assistant Joshua, and Moses went up to the mountain of God. ¹⁴ And he said to the elders, "Wait here for us until we come back to you. Indeed, Aaron and Hur *are* with you.

כד וְאֶל־מֹשֶׁה אָמַר עֲלֵה אֶל־יְהוָה אַתָּה וְאַהֲרֹן נָדָב וַאֲבִיהוּא וְשִׁבְעִים מִזִּקְנֵי יִשְׂרָאֵל וְהִשְׁתַּחֲוִיתֶם מֵרָחֹק: 2 וְנִגַּשׁ מֹשֶׁה לְבַדּוֹ אֶל־יְהוָה וְהֵם לֹא יִגָּשׁוּ וְהָעָם לֹא יַעֲלוּ עִמּוֹ: 3 וַיָּבֹא מֹשֶׁה וַיְסַפֵּר לָעָם אֵת כָּל־דִּבְרֵי יְהוָה וְאֵת כָּל־הַמִּשְׁפָּטִים וַיַּעַן כָּל־הָעָם קוֹל אֶחָד וַיֹּאמְרוּ כָּל־הַדְּבָרִים אֲשֶׁר־דִּבֶּר יְהוָה נַעֲשֶׂה: 4 וַיִּכְתֹּב מֹשֶׁה אֵת כָּל־דִּבְרֵי יְהוָה וַיַּשְׁכֵּם בַּבֹּקֶר וַיִּבֶן מִזְבֵּחַ תַּחַת הָהָר וּשְׁתֵּים עֶשְׂרֵה מַצֵּבָה לִשְׁנֵים עָשָׂר שִׁבְטֵי יִשְׂרָאֵל: 5 וַיִּשְׁלַח אֶת־נַעֲרֵי בְּנֵי יִשְׂרָאֵל וַיַּעֲלוּ עֹלֹת וַיִּזְבְּחוּ זְבָחִים שְׁלָמִים לַיהוָה פָּרִים: 6 וַיִּקַּח מֹשֶׁה חֲצִי הַדָּם וַיָּשֶׂם בָּאַגָּנֹת וַחֲצִי הַדָּם זָרַק עַל־הַמִּזְבֵּחַ: 7 וַיִּקַּח סֵפֶר הַבְּרִית וַיִּקְרָא בְּאָזְנֵי הָעָם וַיֹּאמְרוּ כֹּל אֲשֶׁר־דִּבֶּר יְהוָה נַעֲשֶׂה וְנִשְׁמָע: 8 וַיִּקַּח מֹשֶׁה אֶת־הַדָּם וַיִּזְרֹק עַל־הָעָם וַיֹּאמֶר הִנֵּה דַם־הַבְּרִית אֲשֶׁר כָּרַת יְהוָה עִמָּכֶם עַל כָּל־הַדְּבָרִים הָאֵלֶּה: 9 וַיַּעַל מֹשֶׁה וְאַהֲרֹן נָדָב וַאֲבִיהוּא וְשִׁבְעִים מִזִּקְנֵי יִשְׂרָאֵל: 10 וַיִּרְאוּ אֵת אֱלֹהֵי יִשְׂרָאֵל וְתַחַת רַגְלָיו כְּמַעֲשֵׂה לִבְנַת הַסַּפִּיר וּכְעֶצֶם הַשָּׁמַיִם לָטֹהַר: 11 וְאֶל־אֲצִילֵי בְּנֵי יִשְׂרָאֵל לֹא שָׁלַח יָדוֹ וַיֶּחֱזוּ אֶת־הָאֱלֹהִים וַיֹּאכְלוּ וַיִּשְׁתּוּ: ס 12 וַיֹּאמֶר יְהוָה אֶל־מֹשֶׁה עֲלֵה אֵלַי הָהָרָה וֶהְיֵה־שָׁם וְאֶתְּנָה לְךָ אֶת־לֻחֹת הָאֶבֶן וְהַתּוֹרָה וְהַמִּצְוָה אֲשֶׁר כָּתַבְתִּי לְהוֹרֹתָם: 13 וַיָּקָם מֹשֶׁה וִיהוֹשֻׁעַ מְשָׁרְתוֹ וַיַּעַל מֹשֶׁה אֶל־הַר הָאֱלֹהִים: 14 וְאֶל־הַזְּקֵנִים אָמַר שְׁבוּ־לָנוּ בָזֶה עַד אֲשֶׁר־נָשׁוּב אֲלֵיכֶם וְהִנֵּה אַהֲרֹן וְחוּר

אֶת־הָאָרֶץ: 31 וְשַׁתִּי אֶת־גְּבֻלְךָ מִיָּם־סוּף וְעַד־יָם פְּלִשְׁתִּים וּמִמִּדְבָּר עַד־הַנָּהָר כִּי אֶתֵּן בְּיֶדְכֶם אֵת יֹשְׁבֵי הָאָרֶץ וְגֵרַשְׁתָּמוֹ מִפָּנֶיךָ: 32 לֹא־תִכְרֹת לָהֶם וְלֵאלֹהֵיהֶם בְּרִית: 33 לֹא יֵשְׁבוּ בְּאַרְצְךָ פֶּן יַחֲטִיאוּ אֹתְךָ לִי כִּי תַעֲבֹד אֶת־אֱלֹהֵיהֶם כִּי־יִהְיֶה לְךָ לְמוֹקֵשׁ: פ

If any man has a difficulty, let him go to them." 15 Then Moses went up into the mountain, and a cloud covered the mountain.

16 Now the glory of the LORD rested on Mount Sinai, and the cloud covered it six days. And on the seventh day He called to Moses out of the midst of the cloud. 17 The sight of the glory of the LORD *was* like a consuming fire on the top of the mountain in the eyes of the children of Israel. 18 So Moses went into the midst of the cloud and went up into the mountain. And Moses was on the mountain forty days and forty nights.

25 Then the LORD spoke to Moses, saying: 2 "Speak to the children of Israel, that they bring Me an offering. From everyone who gives it willingly with his heart you shall take My offering. 3 And this *is* the offering which you shall take from them: gold, silver, and bronze; 4 blue, purple, and scarlet *thread,* fine linen, and goats' *hair;* 5 ram skins dyed red, badger skins, and acacia wood; 6 oil for the light, and spices for the anointing oil and for the sweet incense; 7 onyx stones, and stones to be set in the ephod and in the breastplate. 8 And let them make Me a sanctuary, that I may dwell among them. 9 According to all that I show you, *that is,* the pattern of the tabernacle and the pattern of all its furnishings, just so you shall make *it.*

10 "And they shall make an ark of acacia wood; two and a half cubits *shall be* its length, a cubit and a half its width, and a cubit and a half its height. 11 And you shall overlay it with pure gold, inside and out you shall overlay it, and shall make on it a molding of gold all around. 12 You shall cast four rings of gold for it, and put *them* in its four corners; two rings *shall be* on one side, and two rings on the other side. 13 And you shall make poles *of* acacia wood, and overlay them with gold. 14 You shall put the poles into the rings on the sides of the ark, that the ark may be carried by them. 15 The poles shall be in the rings of the ark; they shall not be taken from it. 16 And you shall put into the ark the Testimony which I will give you.

17 "You shall make a mercy seat of pure gold; two and a half cubits *shall be* its length and a cubit and a half its width. 18 And you shall make two cherubim of gold; of hammered work you shall make them at the two ends of the mercy seat. 19 Make one cherub at one end, and the other cherub at the other end; you shall make the cherubim at the two ends of it *of one piece* with the mercy seat. 20 And the cherubim shall stretch out *their* wings above, covering the mercy seat with

וַיַּ֥עַל מֹשֶׁ֖ה 15 : עִמָּכֶ֖ם מִי־בַ֣עַל דְּבָרִ֑ים יִגַּ֖שׁ אֲלֵהֶֽם
וַיִּשְׁכֹּ֤ן כְּבוֹד־ 16 : אֶל־הָהָ֑ר וַיְכַ֥ס הֶעָנָ֖ן אֶת־הָהָֽר
יְהוָה֙ עַל־הַ֣ר סִינַ֔י וַיְכַסֵּ֥הוּ הֶעָנָ֖ן שֵׁ֣שֶׁת יָמִ֑ים וַיִּקְרָ֧א
וּמַרְאֵה֙ 17 : אֶל־מֹשֶׁ֛ה בַּיּ֥וֹם הַשְּׁבִיעִ֖י מִתּ֥וֹךְ הֶעָנָֽן
כְּב֣וֹד יְהוָ֔ה כְּאֵ֥שׁ אֹכֶ֖לֶת בְּרֹ֣אשׁ הָהָ֑ר לְעֵינֵ֖י בְּנֵ֥י
וַיָּבֹ֥א מֹשֶׁ֛ה בְּת֥וֹךְ הֶעָנָ֖ן וַיַּ֣עַל אֶל־הָהָ֑ר 18 : יִשְׂרָאֵֽל
פ : וַיְהִ֤י מֹשֶׁה֙ בָּהָ֔ר אַרְבָּעִ֣ים י֔וֹם וְאַרְבָּעִ֖ים לָֽיְלָה

כה וַיְדַבֵּ֥ר יְהוָ֖ה אֶל־מֹשֶׁ֥ה לֵּאמֹֽר: 2 דַּבֵּר֙ אֶל־
בְּנֵ֣י יִשְׂרָאֵ֔ל וְיִקְחוּ־לִ֖י תְּרוּמָ֑ה מֵאֵ֤ת כָּל־אִישׁ֙ אֲשֶׁ֣ר
יִדְּבֶ֣נּוּ לִבּ֔וֹ תִּקְח֖וּ אֶת־תְּרוּמָתִֽי: 3 וְזֹאת֙ הַתְּרוּמָ֔ה
אֲשֶׁ֥ר תִּקְח֖וּ מֵֽאִתָּ֑ם זָהָ֥ב וָכֶ֖סֶף וּנְחֹֽשֶׁת: 4 וּתְכֵ֤לֶת
וְאַרְגָּמָן֙ וְתוֹלַ֣עַת שָׁנִ֔י וְשֵׁ֖שׁ וְעִזִּֽים: 5 וְעֹרֹ֨ת אֵילִ֧ם
מְאָדָּמִ֛ים וְעֹרֹ֥ת תְּחָשִׁ֖ים וַעֲצֵ֥י שִׁטִּֽים: 6 שֶׁ֖מֶן לַמָּאֹ֑ר
בְּשָׂמִים֙ לְשֶׁ֣מֶן הַמִּשְׁחָ֔ה וְלִקְטֹ֖רֶת הַסַּמִּֽים: 7 אַבְנֵי־
שֹׁ֕הַם וְאַבְנֵ֖י מִלֻּאִ֑ים לָאֵפֹ֖ד וְלַחֹֽשֶׁן: 8 וְעָ֥שׂוּ לִ֖י
מִקְדָּ֑שׁ וְשָׁכַנְתִּ֖י בְּתוֹכָֽם: 9 כְּכֹ֗ל אֲשֶׁ֤ר אֲנִי֙ מַרְאֶ֣ה
אוֹתְךָ֔ אֵ֚ת תַּבְנִ֣ית הַמִּשְׁכָּ֔ן וְאֵ֖ת תַּבְנִ֣ית כָּל־כֵּלָ֑יו
וְכֵ֖ן תַּעֲשֽׂוּ: ס 10 וְעָשׂ֥וּ אֲר֖וֹן עֲצֵ֣י שִׁטִּ֑ים
אַמָּתַ֨יִם וָחֵ֜צִי אָרְכּ֗וֹ וְאַמָּ֤ה וָחֵ֨צִי֙ רָחְבּ֔וֹ וְאַמָּ֥ה וָחֵ֖צִי
קֹמָתֽוֹ: 11 וְצִפִּיתָ֤ אֹתוֹ֙ זָהָ֣ב טָה֔וֹר מִבַּ֥יִת וּמִח֖וּץ
תְּצַפֶּ֑נּוּ וְעָשִׂ֧יתָ עָלָ֛יו זֵ֥ר זָהָ֖ב סָבִֽיב: 12 וְיָצַ֣קְתָּ לּ֗וֹ
אַרְבַּע֙ טַבְּעֹ֣ת זָהָ֔ב וְנָ֣תַתָּ֔ה עַ֖ל אַרְבַּ֣ע פַּעֲמֹתָ֑יו
וּשְׁתֵּ֣י טַבָּעֹ֗ת עַל־צַלְעוֹ֙ הָֽאֶחָ֔ת וּשְׁתֵּי֙ טַבָּעֹ֔ת עַל־
צַלְע֖וֹ הַשֵּׁנִֽית: 13 וְעָשִׂ֥יתָ בַדֵּ֖י עֲצֵ֣י שִׁטִּ֑ים וְצִפִּיתָ֥
אֹתָ֖ם זָהָֽב: 14 וְהֵֽבֵאתָ֤ אֶת־הַבַּדִּים֙ בַּטַּבָּעֹ֔ת עַ֖ל
צַלְעֹ֣ת הָאָרֹ֑ן לָשֵׂ֥את אֶת־הָאָרֹ֖ן בָּהֶֽם: 15 בְּטַבְּעֹת֙
הָֽאָרֹ֔ן יִהְי֖וּ הַבַּדִּ֑ים לֹ֥א יָסֻ֖רוּ מִמֶּֽנּוּ: 16 וְנָתַתָּ֖ אֶל־
הָאָרֹ֑ן אֵ֚ת הָעֵדֻ֔ת אֲשֶׁ֥ר אֶתֵּ֖ן אֵלֶֽיךָ: 17 וְעָשִׂ֥יתָ
כַפֹּ֖רֶת זָהָ֣ב טָה֑וֹר אַמָּתַ֤יִם וָחֵ֨צִי֙ אָרְכָּ֔הּ וְאַמָּ֥ה
וָחֵ֖צִי רָחְבָּֽהּ: 18 וְעָשִׂ֛יתָ שְׁנַ֥יִם כְּרֻבִ֖ים זָהָ֑ב מִקְשָׁה֙
תַּעֲשֶׂ֣ה אֹתָ֔ם מִשְּׁנֵ֖י קְצ֥וֹת הַכַּפֹּֽרֶת: 19 וַ֠עֲשֵׂה
כְּר֨וּב אֶחָ֤ד מִקָּצָה֙ מִזֶּ֔ה וּכְרוּב־אֶחָ֥ד מִקָּצָ֖ה מִזֶּ֑ה
מִן־הַכַּפֹּ֛רֶת תַּעֲשׂ֥וּ אֶת־הַכְּרֻבִ֖ים עַל־שְׁנֵ֥י קְצוֹתָֽיו:
20 וְהָי֣וּ הַכְּרֻבִים֩ פֹּרְשֵׂ֨י כְנָפַ֜יִם לְמַ֗עְלָה סֹכְכִ֤ים
בְּכַנְפֵיהֶם֙ עַל־הַכַּפֹּ֔רֶת וּפְנֵיהֶ֖ם אִ֣ישׁ אֶל־אָחִ֑יו אֶל־

their wings, and they shall face one another; the faces of the cherubim *shall be* toward the mercy seat. 21 You shall put the mercy seat on top of the ark, and in the ark you shall put the Testimony that I will give you. 22 And there I will meet with you, and I will speak with you from above the mercy seat, from between the two cherubim which *are* on the ark of the Testimony, about everything which I will give you in commandment to the children of Israel.

23 "You shall also make a table of acacia wood; two cubits *shall be* its length, a cubit its width, and a cubit and a half its height. 24 And you shall overlay it with pure gold, and make a molding of gold all around. 25 You shall make for it a frame of a handbreadth all around, and you shall make a gold molding for the frame all around. 26 And you shall make for it four rings of gold, and put the rings on the four corners that *are* at its four legs. 27 The rings shall be close to the frame, as holders for the poles to bear the table. 28 And you shall make the poles of acacia wood, and overlay them with gold, that the table may be carried with them. 29 You shall make its dishes, its pans, its pitchers, and its bowls for pouring. You shall make them of pure gold. 30 And you shall set the showbread on the table before Me always.

31 "You shall also make a lampstand of pure gold; the lampstand shall be of hammered work. Its shaft, its branches, its bowls, its *ornamental* knobs, and flowers shall be *of one piece.* 32 And six branches shall come out of its sides: three branches of the lampstand out of one side, and three branches of the lampstand out of the other side. 33 Three bowls *shall be* made like almond *blossoms* on one branch, *with an ornamental* knob and a flower, and three bowls made like almond *blossoms* on the other branch, *with an ornamental* knob and a flower—and so for the six branches that come out of the lampstand. 34 On the lampstand itself four bowls *shall be* made like almond *blossoms, each with* its *ornamental* knob and flower. 35 And *there shall be* a knob under the *first* two branches of the same, a knob under the *second* two branches of the same, and a knob under the *third* two branches of the same, according to the six branches that extend from the lampstand. 36 Their knobs and their branches *shall be of one piece;* all of it *shall be* one hammered piece of pure gold. 37 You shall make seven lamps for it, and they shall arrange its lamps so that they give light in front of it. 38 And its wick-trimmers and their trays *shall be* of pure gold. 39 It shall be made of a talent of pure gold, with all these

הַכַּפֹּרֶת יִהְיוּ פְּנֵי הַכְּרֻבִים: 21 וְנָתַתָּ אֶת־הַכַּפֹּרֶת עַל־הָאָרֹן מִלְמָעְלָה וְאֶל־הָאָרֹן תִּתֵּן אֶת־הָעֵדֻת אֲשֶׁר אֶתֵּן אֵלֶיךָ: 22 וְנוֹעַדְתִּי לְךָ שָׁם וְדִבַּרְתִּי אִתְּךָ מֵעַל הַכַּפֹּרֶת מִבֵּין שְׁנֵי הַכְּרֻבִים אֲשֶׁר עַל־אֲרֹן הָעֵדֻת אֵת כָּל־אֲשֶׁר אֲצַוֶּה אוֹתְךָ אֶל־בְּנֵי יִשְׂרָאֵל: פ

23 וְעָשִׂיתָ שֻׁלְחָן עֲצֵי שִׁטִּים אַמָּתַיִם אָרְכּוֹ וְאַמָּה רָחְבּוֹ וְאַמָּה וָחֵצִי קֹמָתוֹ: 24 וְצִפִּיתָ אֹתוֹ זָהָב טָהוֹר וְעָשִׂיתָ לּוֹ זֵר זָהָב סָבִיב: 25 וְעָשִׂיתָ לּוֹ מִסְגֶּרֶת טֹפַח סָבִיב וְעָשִׂיתָ זֵר־זָהָב לְמִסְגַּרְתּוֹ סָבִיב: 26 וְעָשִׂיתָ לּוֹ אַרְבַּע טַבְּעֹת זָהָב וְנָתַתָּ אֶת־הַטַּבָּעֹת עַל אַרְבַּע הַפֵּאֹת אֲשֶׁר לְאַרְבַּע רַגְלָיו: 27 לְעֻמַּת הַמִּסְגֶּרֶת תִּהְיֶיןָ הַטַּבָּעֹת לְבָתִּים לְבַדִּים לָשֵׂאת אֶת־הַשֻּׁלְחָן: 28 וְעָשִׂיתָ אֶת־הַבַּדִּים עֲצֵי שִׁטִּים וְצִפִּיתָ אֹתָם זָהָב וְנִשָּׂא־בָם אֶת־הַשֻּׁלְחָן: 29 וְעָשִׂיתָ קְּעָרֹתָיו וְכַפֹּתָיו וּקְשׂוֹתָיו וּמְנַקִּיֹּתָיו אֲשֶׁר יֻסַּךְ בָּהֵן זָהָב טָהוֹר תַּעֲשֶׂה אֹתָם: 30 וְנָתַתָּ עַל־הַשֻּׁלְחָן לֶחֶם פָּנִים לְפָנַי תָּמִיד: פ

31 וְעָשִׂיתָ מְנֹרַת זָהָב טָהוֹר מִקְשָׁה תֵּעָשֶׂה הַמְּנוֹרָה יְרֵכָהּ וְקָנָהּ גְּבִיעֶיהָ כַּפְתֹּרֶיהָ וּפְרָחֶיהָ מִמֶּנָּה יִהְיוּ: 32 וְשִׁשָּׁה קָנִים יֹצְאִים מִצִּדֶּיהָ שְׁלֹשָׁה קְנֵי מְנֹרָה מִצִּדָּהּ הָאֶחָד וּשְׁלֹשָׁה קְנֵי מְנֹרָה מִצִּדָּהּ הַשֵּׁנִי: 33 שְׁלֹשָׁה גְבִעִים מְשֻׁקָּדִים בַּקָּנֶה הָאֶחָד כַּפְתֹּר וָפֶרַח וּשְׁלֹשָׁה גְבִעִים מְשֻׁקָּדִים בַּקָּנֶה הָאֶחָד כַּפְתֹּר וָפֶרַח כֵּן לְשֵׁשֶׁת הַקָּנִים הַיֹּצְאִים מִן־הַמְּנֹרָה: 34 וּבַמְּנֹרָה אַרְבָּעָה גְבִעִים מְשֻׁקָּדִים כַּפְתֹּרֶיהָ וּפְרָחֶיהָ: 35 וְכַפְתֹּר תַּחַת שְׁנֵי הַקָּנִים מִמֶּנָּה וְכַפְתֹּר תַּחַת שְׁנֵי הַקָּנִים מִמֶּנָּה וְכַפְתֹּר תַּחַת־שְׁנֵי הַקָּנִים מִמֶּנָּה לְשֵׁשֶׁת הַקָּנִים הַיֹּצְאִים מִן־הַמְּנֹרָה: 36 כַּפְתֹּרֵיהֶם וּקְנֹתָם מִמֶּנָּה יִהְיוּ כֻּלָּהּ מִקְשָׁה אַחַת זָהָב טָהוֹר: 37 וְעָשִׂיתָ אֶת־נֵרֹתֶיהָ שִׁבְעָה וְהֶעֱלָה אֶת־נֵרֹתֶיהָ וְהֵאִיר עַל־עֵבֶר פָּנֶיהָ: 38 וּמַלְקָחֶיהָ וּמַחְתֹּתֶיהָ זָהָב טָהוֹר: 39 כִּכָּר זָהָב טָהוֹר יַעֲשֶׂה אֹתָהּ אֵת כָּל־

utensils. ⁴⁰ And see to it that you make *them* according to the pattern which was shown you on the mountain.

הַכֵּלִים הָאֵלֶּה: 40 וּרְאֵה וַעֲשֵׂה בְּתַבְנִיתָם אֲשֶׁר־
אַתָּה מָרְאֶה בָּהָר: ס

26

26 "Moreover you shall make the tabernacle *with* ten curtains *of* fine woven linen and blue, purple, and scarlet *thread;* with artistic designs of cherubim you shall weave them. ² The length of each curtain *shall be* twenty-eight cubits, and the width of each curtain four cubits. And every one of the curtains shall have the same measurements. ³ Five curtains shall be coupled to one another, and *the other* five curtains *shall be* coupled to one another. ⁴ And you shall make loops of blue *yarn* on the edge of the curtain on the selvedge of *one* set, and likewise you shall do on the outer edge of *the other* curtain of the second set. ⁵ Fifty loops you shall make in the one curtain, and fifty loops you shall make on the edge of the curtain that *is* on the end of the second set, that the loops may be clasped to one another. ⁶ And you shall make fifty clasps of gold, and couple the curtains together with the clasps, so that it may be one tabernacle.

⁷ "You shall also make curtains of goats' *hair,* to be a tent over the tabernacle. You shall make eleven curtains. ⁸ The length of each curtain *shall be* thirty cubits, and the width of each curtain four cubits; and the eleven curtains shall all have the same measurements. ⁹ And you shall couple five curtains by themselves and six curtains by themselves, and you shall double over the sixth curtain at the forefront of the tent. ¹⁰ You shall make fifty loops on the edge of the curtain that is outermost in *one* set, and fifty loops on the edge of the curtain of the second set. ¹¹ And you shall make fifty bronze clasps, put the clasps into the loops, and couple the tent together, that it may be one. ¹² The remnant that remains of the curtains of the tent, the half curtain that remains, shall hang over the back of the tabernacle. ¹³ And a cubit on one side and a cubit on the other side, of what remains of the length of the curtains of the tent, shall hang over the sides of the tabernacle, on this side and on that side, to cover it.

¹⁴ "You shall also make a covering of ram skins dyed red for the tent, and a covering of badger skins above that.

¹⁵ "And for the tabernacle you shall make the boards of acacia wood, standing upright. ¹⁶ Ten cubits *shall be* the length of a board, and a cubit and a half *shall be* the width of each board. ¹⁷ Two tenons *shall be* in each board for binding one to another. Thus you shall make for all the boards of the tabernacle. ¹⁸ And you shall make the boards

כו וְאֶת־הַמִּשְׁכָּן תַּעֲשֶׂה עֶשֶׂר יְרִיעֹת שֵׁשׁ מָשְׁזָר
וּתְכֵלֶת וְאַרְגָּמָן וְתֹלַעַת שָׁנִי כְּרֻבִים מַעֲשֵׂה
חֹשֵׁב תַּעֲשֶׂה אֹתָם: 2 אֹרֶךְ | הַיְרִיעָה הָאַחַת
שְׁמֹנֶה וְעֶשְׂרִים בָּאַמָּה וְרֹחַב אַרְבַּע בָּאַמָּה
הַיְרִיעָה הָאֶחָת מִדָּה אַחַת לְכָל־הַיְרִיעֹת: 3 חֲמֵשׁ
הַיְרִיעֹת תִּהְיֶיןָ חֹבְרֹת אִשָּׁה אֶל־אֲחֹתָהּ וְחָמֵשׁ
יְרִיעֹת חֹבְרֹת אִשָּׁה אֶל־אֲחֹתָהּ: 4 וְעָשִׂיתָ לֻלְאֹת
תְּכֵלֶת עַל שְׂפַת הַיְרִיעָה הָאֶחָת מִקָּצָה בַּחֹבָרֶת
וְכֵן תַּעֲשֶׂה בִּשְׂפַת הַיְרִיעָה הַקִּיצוֹנָה בַּמַּחְבֶּרֶת
הַשֵּׁנִית: 5 חֲמִשִּׁים לֻלָאֹת תַּעֲשֶׂה בַּיְרִיעָה הָאֶחָת
וַחֲמִשִּׁים לֻלָאֹת תַּעֲשֶׂה בִּקְצֵה הַיְרִיעָה אֲשֶׁר
בַּמַּחְבֶּרֶת הַשֵּׁנִית מַקְבִּילֹת הַלֻּלָאֹת אִשָּׁה אֶל־
אֲחֹתָהּ: 6 וְעָשִׂיתָ חֲמִשִּׁים קַרְסֵי זָהָב וְחִבַּרְתָּ אֶת־
הַיְרִיעֹת אִשָּׁה אֶל־אֲחֹתָהּ בַּקְּרָסִים וְהָיָה הַמִּשְׁכָּן
אֶחָד: פ

7 וְעָשִׂיתָ יְרִיעֹת עִזִּים לְאֹהֶל עַל־הַמִּשְׁכָּן עַשְׁתֵּי
עֶשְׂרֵה יְרִיעֹת תַּעֲשֶׂה אֹתָם: 8 אֹרֶךְ | הַיְרִיעָה
הָאַחַת שְׁלֹשִׁים בָּאַמָּה וְרֹחַב אַרְבַּע בָּאַמָּה
הַיְרִיעָה הָאֶחָת מִדָּה אַחַת לְעַשְׁתֵּי עֶשְׂרֵה
יְרִיעֹת: 9 וְחִבַּרְתָּ אֶת־חֲמֵשׁ הַיְרִיעֹת לְבָד וְאֶת־
שֵׁשׁ הַיְרִיעֹת לְבָד וְכָפַלְתָּ אֶת־הַיְרִיעָה הַשִּׁשִּׁית
אֶל־מוּל פְּנֵי הָאֹהֶל: 10 וְעָשִׂיתָ חֲמִשִּׁים לֻלָאֹת
עַל שְׂפַת הַיְרִיעָה הָאֶחָת הַקִּיצֹנָה בַּחֹבָרֶת
וַחֲמִשִּׁים לֻלָאֹת עַל שְׂפַת הַיְרִיעָה הַחֹבֶרֶת הַשֵּׁנִית:
11 וְעָשִׂיתָ קַרְסֵי נְחֹשֶׁת חֲמִשִּׁים וְהֵבֵאתָ אֶת־
הַקְּרָסִים בַּלֻּלָאֹת וְחִבַּרְתָּ אֶת־הָאֹהֶל וְהָיָה אֶחָד:
12 וְסֶרַח הָעֹדֵף בִּירִיעֹת הָאֹהֶל חֲצִי הַיְרִיעָה
הָעֹדֶפֶת תִּסְרַח עַל אֲחֹרֵי הַמִּשְׁכָּן: 13 וְהָאַמָּה
מִזֶּה וְהָאַמָּה מִזֶּה בָּעֹדֵף בְּאֹרֶךְ יְרִיעֹת הָאֹהֶל
יִהְיֶה סָרוּחַ עַל־צִדֵּי הַמִּשְׁכָּן מִזֶּה וּמִזֶּה לְכַסֹּתוֹ:
14 וְעָשִׂיתָ מִכְסֶה לָאֹהֶל עֹרֹת אֵילִם מְאָדָּמִים
וּמִכְסֵה עֹרֹת תְּחָשִׁים מִלְמָעְלָה: פ

15 וְעָשִׂיתָ אֶת־הַקְּרָשִׁים לַמִּשְׁכָּן עֲצֵי שִׁטִּים
עֹמְדִים: 16 עֶשֶׂר אַמּוֹת אֹרֶךְ הַקָּרֶשׁ וְאַמָּה וַחֲצִי
הָאַמָּה רֹחַב הַקֶּרֶשׁ הָאֶחָד: 17 שְׁתֵּי יָדוֹת לַקֶּרֶשׁ
הָאֶחָד מְשֻׁלָּבֹת אִשָּׁה אֶל־אֲחֹתָהּ כֵּן תַּעֲשֶׂה
לְכֹל קַרְשֵׁי הַמִּשְׁכָּן: 18 וְעָשִׂיתָ אֶת־הַקְּרָשִׁים

for the tabernacle, twenty boards for the south side. [19] You shall make forty sockets of silver under the twenty boards: two sockets under each of the boards for its two tenons. [20] And for the second side of the tabernacle, the north side, *there shall be* twenty boards [21] and their forty sockets of silver: two sockets under each of the boards. [22] For the far side of the tabernacle, westward, you shall make six boards. [23] And you shall also make two boards for the two back corners of the tabernacle. [24] They shall be coupled together at the bottom and they shall be coupled together at the top by one ring. Thus it shall be for both of them. They shall be for the two corners. [25] So there shall be eight boards with their sockets of silver—sixteen sockets—two sockets under each of the boards.

[26] "And you shall make bars of acacia wood: five for the boards on one side of the tabernacle, [27] five bars for the boards on the other side of the tabernacle, and five bars for the boards of the side of the tabernacle, for the far side westward. [28] The middle bar shall pass through the midst of the boards from end to end. [29] You shall overlay the boards with gold, make their rings of gold *as* holders for the bars, and overlay the bars with gold. [30] And you shall raise up the tabernacle according to its pattern which you were shown on the mountain.

[31] "You shall make a veil woven of blue, purple, and scarlet *thread*, and fine woven linen. It shall be woven with an artistic design of cherubim. [32] You shall hang it upon the four pillars of acacia *wood* overlaid with gold. Their hooks *shall be* gold, upon four sockets of silver. [33] And you shall hang the veil from the clasps. Then you shall bring the ark of the Testimony in there, behind the veil. The veil shall be a divider for you between the holy *place* and the Most Holy. [34] You shall put the mercy seat upon the ark of the Testimony in the Most Holy. [35] You shall set the table outside the veil, and the lampstand across from the table on the side of the tabernacle toward the south; and you shall put the table on the north side.

[36] "You shall make a screen for the door of the tabernacle, *woven of* blue, purple, and scarlet *thread,* and fine woven linen, made by a weaver. [37] And you shall make for the screen five pillars of acacia *wood,* and overlay them with gold; their hooks *shall be* gold, and you shall cast five sockets of bronze for them.

27 "You shall make an altar of acacia wood, five cubits long and five cubits wide—the altar shall be square—and its height *shall be* three cubits. [2] You

לַמִּשְׁכָּן עֶשְׂרִים קֶרֶשׁ לִפְאַת נֶגְבָּה תֵימָנָה: 19 וְאַרְבָּעִים אַדְנֵי־כֶסֶף תַּעֲשֶׂה תַּחַת עֶשְׂרִים הַקָּרֶשׁ שְׁנֵי אֲדָנִים תַּחַת־הַקֶּרֶשׁ הָאֶחָד לִשְׁתֵּי יְדֹתָיו וּשְׁנֵי אֲדָנִים תַּחַת־הַקֶּרֶשׁ הָאֶחָד לִשְׁתֵּי יְדֹתָיו: 20 וּלְצֶלַע הַמִּשְׁכָּן הַשֵּׁנִית לִפְאַת צָפוֹן עֶשְׂרִים קָרֶשׁ: 21 וְאַרְבָּעִים אַדְנֵיהֶם כָּסֶף שְׁנֵי אֲדָנִים תַּחַת הַקֶּרֶשׁ הָאֶחָד וּשְׁנֵי אֲדָנִים תַּחַת הַקֶּרֶשׁ הָאֶחָד: 22 וּלְיַרְכְּתֵי הַמִּשְׁכָּן יָמָּה תַּעֲשֶׂה שִׁשָּׁה קְרָשִׁים: 23 וּשְׁנֵי קְרָשִׁים תַּעֲשֶׂה לִמְקֻצְעֹת הַמִּשְׁכָּן בַּיַּרְכָתָיִם: 24 וְיִהְיוּ תֹאֲמִם מִלְּמַטָּה וְיַחְדָּו יִהְיוּ תַמִּים עַל־רֹאשׁוֹ אֶל־הַטַּבַּעַת הָאֶחָת כֵּן יִהְיֶה לִשְׁנֵיהֶם לִשְׁנֵי הַמִּקְצֹעֹת יִהְיוּ: 25 וְהָיוּ שְׁמֹנָה קְרָשִׁים וְאַדְנֵיהֶם כֶּסֶף שִׁשָּׁה עָשָׂר אֲדָנִים שְׁנֵי אֲדָנִים תַּחַת הַקֶּרֶשׁ הָאֶחָד וּשְׁנֵי אֲדָנִים תַּחַת הַקֶּרֶשׁ הָאֶחָד: 26 וְעָשִׂיתָ בְרִיחִם עֲצֵי שִׁטִּים חֲמִשָּׁה לְקַרְשֵׁי צֶלַע־הַמִּשְׁכָּן הָאֶחָד: 27 וַחֲמִשָּׁה בְרִיחִם לְקַרְשֵׁי צֶלַע־הַמִּשְׁכָּן הַשֵּׁנִית וַחֲמִשָּׁה בְרִיחִם לְקַרְשֵׁי צֶלַע הַמִּשְׁכָּן לַיַּרְכָתַיִם יָמָּה: 28 וְהַבְּרִיחַ הַתִּיכֹן בְּתוֹךְ הַקְּרָשִׁים מַבְרִחַ מִן־הַקָּצֶה אֶל־הַקָּצֶה: 29 וְאֶת־הַקְּרָשִׁים תְּצַפֶּה זָהָב וְאֶת־טַבְּעֹתֵיהֶם תַּעֲשֶׂה זָהָב בָּתִּים לַבְּרִיחִם וְצִפִּיתָ אֶת־הַבְּרִיחִם זָהָב: 30 וַהֲקֵמֹתָ אֶת־הַמִּשְׁכָּן כְּמִשְׁפָּטוֹ אֲשֶׁר הָרְאֵיתָ בָּהָר: ס 31 וְעָשִׂיתָ פָרֹכֶת תְּכֵלֶת וְאַרְגָּמָן וְתוֹלַעַת שָׁנִי וְשֵׁשׁ מָשְׁזָר מַעֲשֵׂה חֹשֵׁב יַעֲשֶׂה אֹתָהּ כְּרֻבִים: 32 וְנָתַתָּה אֹתָהּ עַל־אַרְבָּעָה עַמּוּדֵי שִׁטִּים מְצֻפִּים זָהָב וָוֵיהֶם זָהָב עַל־אַרְבָּעָה אַדְנֵי־כָסֶף: 33 וְנָתַתָּה אֶת־הַפָּרֹכֶת תַּחַת הַקְּרָסִים וְהֵבֵאתָ שָׁמָּה מִבֵּית לַפָּרֹכֶת אֵת אֲרוֹן הָעֵדוּת וְהִבְדִּילָה הַפָּרֹכֶת לָכֶם בֵּין הַקֹּדֶשׁ וּבֵין קֹדֶשׁ הַקֳּדָשִׁים: 34 וְנָתַתָּ אֶת־הַכַּפֹּרֶת עַל אֲרוֹן הָעֵדֻת בְּקֹדֶשׁ הַקֳּדָשִׁים: 35 וְשַׂמְתָּ אֶת־הַשֻּׁלְחָן מִחוּץ לַפָּרֹכֶת וְאֶת־הַמְּנֹרָה נֹכַח הַשֻּׁלְחָן עַל צֶלַע הַמִּשְׁכָּן תֵּימָנָה וְהַשֻּׁלְחָן תִּתֵּן עַל־צֶלַע צָפוֹן: 36 וְעָשִׂיתָ מָסָךְ לְפֶתַח הָאֹהֶל תְּכֵלֶת וְאַרְגָּמָן וְתוֹלַעַת שָׁנִי וְשֵׁשׁ מָשְׁזָר מַעֲשֵׂה רֹקֵם: 37 וְעָשִׂיתָ לַמָּסָךְ חֲמִשָּׁה עַמּוּדֵי שִׁטִּים וְצִפִּיתָ אֹתָם זָהָב וָוֵיהֶם זָהָב וְיָצַקְתָּ לָהֶם חֲמִשָּׁה אַדְנֵי נְחֹשֶׁת: ס

כז וְעָשִׂיתָ אֶת־הַמִּזְבֵּחַ עֲצֵי שִׁטִּים חָמֵשׁ אַמּוֹת אֹרֶךְ וְחָמֵשׁ אַמּוֹת רֹחַב רָבוּעַ יִהְיֶה הַמִּזְבֵּחַ וְשָׁלֹשׁ אַמּוֹת קֹמָתוֹ: 2 וְעָשִׂיתָ קַרְנֹתָיו עַל אַרְבַּע

shall make its horns on its four corners; its horns shall be of one piece with it. And you shall overlay it with bronze. ³Also you shall make its pans to receive its ashes, and its shovels and its basins and its forks and its firepans; you shall make all its utensils of bronze. ⁴You shall make a grate for it, a network of bronze; and on the network you shall make four bronze rings at its four corners. ⁵You shall put it under the rim of the altar beneath, that the network may be midway up the altar. ⁶And you shall make poles for the altar, poles of acacia wood, and overlay them with bronze. ⁷The poles shall be put in the rings, and the poles shall be on the two sides of the altar to bear it. ⁸You shall make it hollow with boards; as it was shown you on the mountain, so shall they make *it*.

⁹"You shall also make the court of the tabernacle. For the south side *there shall be* hangings for the court *made of* fine woven linen, one hundred cubits long for one side. ¹⁰And its twenty pillars and their twenty sockets *shall be* bronze. The hooks of the pillars and their bands *shall be* silver. ¹¹Likewise along the length of the north side *there shall be* hangings one hundred *cubits* long, with its twenty pillars and their twenty sockets of bronze, and the hooks of the pillars and their bands of silver.

¹²"And along the width of the court on the west side *shall be* hangings of fifty cubits, with their ten pillars and their ten sockets. ¹³The width of the court on the east side *shall be* fifty cubits. ¹⁴The hangings on *one side of the gate shall be* fifteen cubits, *with* their three pillars and their three sockets. ¹⁵And on the other side *shall be* hangings of fifteen *cubits, with* their three pillars and their three sockets.

¹⁶"For the gate of the court *there shall be* a screen twenty cubits long, *woven of* blue, purple, and scarlet *thread*, and fine woven linen, made by a weaver. It *shall have* four pillars and four sockets. ¹⁷All the pillars around the court shall have bands of silver; their hooks *shall be* of silver and their sockets of bronze. ¹⁸The length of the court *shall be* one hundred cubits, the width fifty throughout, and the height five cubits, *made of* fine woven linen, and its sockets of bronze. ¹⁹All the utensils of the tabernacle for all its service, all its pegs, and all the pegs of the court, *shall be* of bronze.

²⁰"And you shall command the children of Israel that they bring you pure oil of pressed olives for the light, to cause the lamp to burn continually. ²¹In the tabernacle of meeting, outside the veil which *is* before the Testimony, Aaron and his sons shall tend

פִנֹּתָיו מִמֶּנּוּ תִּהְיֶיןָ קַרְנֹתָיו וְצִפִּיתָ אֹתוֹ נְחֹשֶׁת: ³ וְעָשִׂיתָ סִּירֹתָיו לְדַשְּׁנוֹ וְיָעָיו וּמִזְרְקֹתָיו וּמִזְלְגֹתָיו וּמַחְתֹּתָיו לְכָל־כֵּלָיו תַּעֲשֶׂה נְחֹשֶׁת: ⁴ וְעָשִׂיתָ לּוֹ מִכְבָּר מַעֲשֵׂה רֶשֶׁת נְחֹשֶׁת וְעָשִׂיתָ עַל־הָרֶשֶׁת אַרְבַּע טַבְּעֹת נְחֹשֶׁת עַל אַרְבַּע קְצוֹתָיו: ⁵ וְנָתַתָּה אֹתָהּ תַּחַת כַּרְכֹּב הַמִּזְבֵּחַ מִלְּמָטָּה וְהָיְתָה הָרֶשֶׁת עַד חֲצִי הַמִּזְבֵּחַ: ⁶ וְעָשִׂיתָ בַדִּים לַמִּזְבֵּחַ בַּדֵּי עֲצֵי שִׁטִּים וְצִפִּיתָ אֹתָם נְחֹשֶׁת: ⁷ וְהוּבָא אֶת־בַּדָּיו בַּטַּבָּעֹת וְהָיוּ הַבַּדִּים עַל־שְׁתֵּי צַלְעֹת הַמִּזְבֵּחַ בִּשְׂאֵת אֹתוֹ: ⁸ נְבוּב לֻחֹת תַּעֲשֶׂה אֹתוֹ כַּאֲשֶׁר הֶרְאָה אֹתְךָ בָּהָר כֵּן יַעֲשׂוּ: ס ⁹ וְעָשִׂיתָ אֵת חֲצַר הַמִּשְׁכָּן לִפְאַת נֶגֶב־תֵּימָנָה קְלָעִים לֶחָצֵר שֵׁשׁ מָשְׁזָר מֵאָה בָאַמָּה אֹרֶךְ לַפֵּאָה הָאֶחָת: ¹⁰ וְעַמֻּדָיו עֶשְׂרִים וְאַדְנֵיהֶם עֶשְׂרִים נְחֹשֶׁת וָוֵי הָעַמֻּדִים וַחֲשֻׁקֵיהֶם כָּסֶף: ¹¹ וְכֵן לִפְאַת צָפוֹן בָּאֹרֶךְ קְלָעִים מֵאָה אֹרֶךְ וְעַמֻּדָו עֶשְׂרִים וְאַדְנֵיהֶם עֶשְׂרִים נְחֹשֶׁת וָוֵי הָעַמֻּדִים וַחֲשֻׁקֵיהֶם כָּסֶף: ¹² וְרֹחַב הֶחָצֵר לִפְאַת־יָם קְלָעִים חֲמִשִּׁים אַמָּה עַמֻּדֵיהֶם עֲשָׂרָה וְאַדְנֵיהֶם עֲשָׂרָה: ¹³ וְרֹחַב הֶחָצֵר לִפְאַת קֵדְמָה מִזְרָחָה חֲמִשִּׁים אַמָּה: ¹⁴ וַחֲמֵשׁ עֶשְׂרֵה אַמָּה קְלָעִים לַכָּתֵף עַמֻּדֵיהֶם שְׁלֹשָׁה וְאַדְנֵיהֶם שְׁלֹשָׁה: ¹⁵ וְלַכָּתֵף הַשֵּׁנִית חֲמֵשׁ עֶשְׂרֵה קְלָעִים עַמֻּדֵיהֶם שְׁלֹשָׁה וְאַדְנֵיהֶם שְׁלֹשָׁה: ¹⁶ וּלְשַׁעַר הֶחָצֵר מָסָךְ | עֶשְׂרִים אַמָּה תְּכֵלֶת וְאַרְגָּמָן וְתוֹלַעַת שָׁנִי וְשֵׁשׁ מָשְׁזָר מַעֲשֵׂה רֹקֵם עַמֻּדֵיהֶם אַרְבָּעָה וְאַדְנֵיהֶם אַרְבָּעָה: ¹⁷ כָּל־עַמּוּדֵי הֶחָצֵר סָבִיב מְחֻשָּׁקִים כֶּסֶף וָוֵיהֶם כָּסֶף וְאַדְנֵיהֶם נְחֹשֶׁת: ¹⁸ אֹרֶךְ הֶחָצֵר מֵאָה בָאַמָּה וְרֹחַב | חֲמִשִּׁים בַּחֲמִשִּׁים וְקֹמָה חָמֵשׁ אַמּוֹת שֵׁשׁ מָשְׁזָר וְאַדְנֵיהֶם נְחֹשֶׁת: ¹⁹ לְכֹל כְּלֵי הַמִּשְׁכָּן בְּכֹל עֲבֹדָתוֹ וְכָל־יְתֵדֹתָיו וְכָל־יִתְדֹת הֶחָצֵר נְחֹשֶׁת: ס ²⁰ וְאַתָּה תְּצַוֶּה | אֶת־בְּנֵי יִשְׂרָאֵל וְיִקְחוּ אֵלֶיךָ שֶׁמֶן זַיִת זָךְ כָּתִית לַמָּאוֹר לְהַעֲלֹת נֵר תָּמִיד: ²¹ בְּאֹהֶל מוֹעֵד מִחוּץ לַפָּרֹכֶת אֲשֶׁר עַל־הָעֵדֻת יַעֲרֹךְ אֹתוֹ אַהֲרֹן וּבָנָיו מֵעֶרֶב

it from evening until morning before the LORD. *It shall be* a statute forever to their generations on behalf of the children of Israel.

28

"Now take Aaron your brother, and his sons with him, from among the children of Israel, that he may minister to Me as priest, Aaron *and* Aaron's sons: Nadab, Abihu, Eleazar, and Ithamar. ²And you shall make holy garments for Aaron your brother, for glory and for beauty. ³So you shall speak to all *who are* gifted artisans, whom I have filled with the spirit of wisdom, that they may make Aaron's garments, to consecrate him, that he may minister to Me as priest. ⁴And these *are* the garments which they shall make: a breastplate, an ephod, a robe, a skillfully woven tunic, a turban, and a sash. So they shall make holy garments for Aaron your brother and his sons, that he may minister to Me as priest.

⁵"They shall take the gold, blue, purple, and scarlet *thread,* and the fine linen, ⁶and they shall make the ephod of gold, blue, purple, *and* scarlet *thread,* and fine woven linen, artistically worked. ⁷It shall have two shoulder straps joined at its two edges, and *so* it shall be joined together. ⁸And the intricately woven band of the ephod, which *is* on it, shall be of the same workmanship, *made of* gold, blue, purple, and scarlet *thread,* and fine woven linen.

⁹"Then you shall take two onyx stones and engrave on them the names of the sons of Israel: ¹⁰six of their names on one stone and six names on the other stone, in order of their birth. ¹¹With the work of an engraver in stone, *like* the engravings of a signet, you shall engrave the two stones with the names of the sons of Israel. You shall set them in settings of gold. ¹²And you shall put the two stones on the shoulders of the ephod *as* memorial stones for the sons of Israel. So Aaron shall bear their names before the LORD on his two shoulders as a memorial. ¹³You shall also make settings of gold, ¹⁴and you shall make two chains of pure gold like braided cords, and fasten the braided chains to the settings.

¹⁵"You shall make the breastplate of judgment. Artistically woven according to the workmanship of the ephod you shall make it: of gold, blue, purple, and scarlet *thread,* and fine woven linen, you shall make it. ¹⁶It shall be doubled into a square: a span *shall be* its length, and a span *shall be* its width. ¹⁷And you shall put settings of stones in it, four rows of stones: *The first* row *shall be* a sardius, a topaz, and an emerald; *this shall be* the first row; ¹⁸the second row *shall be* a turquoise, a

עַד־בֹּקֶר לִפְנֵי יְהוָֹה חֻקַּת עוֹלָם לְדֹרֹתָם מֵאֵת בְּנֵי יִשְׂרָאֵל׃ ס

כח וְאַתָּה הַקְרֵב אֵלֶיךָ אֶת־אַהֲרֹן אָחִיךָ וְאֶת־בָּנָיו אִתּוֹ מִתּוֹךְ בְּנֵי יִשְׂרָאֵל לְכַהֲנוֹ־לִי אַהֲרֹן נָדָב וַאֲבִיהוּא אֶלְעָזָר וְאִיתָמָר בְּנֵי אַהֲרֹן׃ ² וְעָשִׂיתָ בִגְדֵי־קֹדֶשׁ לְאַהֲרֹן אָחִיךָ לְכָבוֹד וּלְתִפְאָרֶת׃ ³ וְאַתָּה תְּדַבֵּר אֶל־כָּל־חַכְמֵי־לֵב אֲשֶׁר מִלֵּאתִיו רוּחַ חָכְמָה וְעָשׂוּ אֶת־בִּגְדֵי אַהֲרֹן לְקַדְּשׁוֹ לְכַהֲנוֹ־לִי׃ ⁴ וְאֵלֶּה הַבְּגָדִים אֲשֶׁר יַעֲשׂוּ חֹשֶׁן וְאֵפוֹד וּמְעִיל וּכְתֹנֶת תַּשְׁבֵּץ מִצְנֶפֶת וְאַבְנֵט וְעָשׂוּ בִגְדֵי־קֹדֶשׁ לְאַהֲרֹן אָחִיךָ וּלְבָנָיו לְכַהֲנוֹ־לִי׃ ⁵ וְהֵם יִקְחוּ אֶת־הַזָּהָב וְאֶת־הַתְּכֵלֶת וְאֶת־הָאַרְגָּמָן וְאֶת־תּוֹלַעַת הַשָּׁנִי וְאֶת־הַשֵּׁשׁ׃ פ

⁶ וְעָשׂוּ אֶת־הָאֵפֹד זָהָב תְּכֵלֶת וְאַרְגָּמָן תּוֹלַעַת שָׁנִי וְשֵׁשׁ מָשְׁזָר מַעֲשֵׂה חֹשֵׁב׃ ⁷ שְׁתֵּי כְתֵפֹת חֹבְרֹת יִהְיֶה־לּוֹ אֶל־שְׁנֵי קְצוֹתָיו וְחֻבָּר׃ ⁸ וְחֵשֶׁב אֲפֻדָּתוֹ אֲשֶׁר עָלָיו כְּמַעֲשֵׂהוּ מִמֶּנּוּ יִהְיֶה זָהָב תְּכֵלֶת וְאַרְגָּמָן וְתוֹלַעַת שָׁנִי וְשֵׁשׁ מָשְׁזָר׃ ⁹ וְלָקַחְתָּ אֶת־שְׁתֵּי אַבְנֵי־שֹׁהַם וּפִתַּחְתָּ עֲלֵיהֶם שְׁמוֹת בְּנֵי יִשְׂרָאֵל׃ ¹⁰ שִׁשָּׁה מִשְּׁמֹתָם עַל הָאֶבֶן הָאֶחָת וְאֶת־שְׁמוֹת הַשִּׁשָּׁה הַנּוֹתָרִים עַל־הָאֶבֶן הַשֵּׁנִית כְּתוֹלְדֹתָם׃ ¹¹ מַעֲשֵׂה חָרַשׁ אֶבֶן פִּתּוּחֵי חֹתָם תְּפַתַּח אֶת־שְׁתֵּי הָאֲבָנִים עַל־שְׁמֹת בְּנֵי יִשְׂרָאֵל מֻסַבֹּת מִשְׁבְּצוֹת זָהָב תַּעֲשֶׂה אֹתָם׃ ¹² וְשַׂמְתָּ אֶת־שְׁתֵּי הָאֲבָנִים עַל כִּתְפֹת הָאֵפֹד אַבְנֵי זִכָּרֹן לִבְנֵי יִשְׂרָאֵל וְנָשָׂא אַהֲרֹן אֶת־שְׁמוֹתָם לִפְנֵי יְהוָֹה עַל־שְׁתֵּי כְתֵפָיו לְזִכָּרֹן׃ ס ¹³ וְעָשִׂיתָ מִשְׁבְּצֹת זָהָב׃ ¹⁴ וּשְׁתֵּי שַׁרְשְׁרֹת זָהָב טָהוֹר מִגְבָּלֹת תַּעֲשֶׂה אֹתָם מַעֲשֵׂה עֲבֹת וְנָתַתָּה אֶת־שַׁרְשְׁרֹת הָעֲבֹתֹת עַל־הַמִּשְׁבְּצֹת׃ ס ¹⁵ וְעָשִׂיתָ חֹשֶׁן מִשְׁפָּט מַעֲשֵׂה חֹשֵׁב כְּמַעֲשֵׂה אֵפֹד תַּעֲשֶׂנּוּ זָהָב תְּכֵלֶת וְאַרְגָּמָן וְתוֹלַעַת שָׁנִי וְשֵׁשׁ מָשְׁזָר תַּעֲשֶׂה אֹתוֹ׃ ¹⁶ רָבוּעַ יִהְיֶה כָּפוּל זֶרֶת אָרְכּוֹ וְזֶרֶת רָחְבּוֹ׃ ¹⁷ וּמִלֵּאתָ בוֹ מִלֻּאַת אֶבֶן אַרְבָּעָה טוּרִים אָבֶן טוּר אֹדֶם פִּטְדָה וּבָרֶקֶת הַטּוּר הָאֶחָד׃ ¹⁸ וְהַטּוּר

sapphire, and a diamond; [19] the third row, a jacinth, an agate, and an amethyst; [20] and the fourth row, a beryl, an onyx, and a jasper. They shall be set in gold settings. [21] And the stones shall have the names of the sons of Israel, twelve according to their names, *like* the engravings of a signet, each one with its own name; they shall be according to the twelve tribes.

[22] "You shall make chains for the breastplate at the end, like braided cords of pure gold. [23] And you shall make two rings of gold for the breastplate, and put the two rings on the two ends of the breastplate. [24] Then you shall put the two braided *chains* of gold in the two rings which are on the ends of the breastplate; [25] and the *other* two ends of the two braided *chains* you shall fasten to the two settings, and put them on the shoulder straps of the ephod in the front.

[26] "You shall make two rings of gold, and put them on the two ends of the breastplate, on the edge of it, which is on the inner side of the ephod. [27] And two *other* rings of gold you shall make, and put them on the two shoulder straps, underneath the ephod toward its front, right at the seam above the intricately woven band of the ephod. [28] They shall bind the breastplate by means of its rings to the rings of the ephod, using a blue cord, so that it is above the intricately woven band of the ephod, and so that the breastplate does not come loose from the ephod.

[29] "So Aaron shall bear the names of the sons of Israel on the breastplate of judgment over his heart, when he goes into the holy *place,* as a memorial before the LORD continually. [30] And you shall put in the breastplate of judgment the Urim and the Thummim, and they shall be over Aaron's heart when he goes in before the LORD. So Aaron shall bear the judgment of the children of Israel over his heart before the LORD continually.

[31] "You shall make the robe of the ephod all of blue. [32] There shall be an opening for his head in the middle of it; it shall have a woven binding all around its opening, like the opening in a coat of mail, so that it does not tear. [33] And upon its hem you shall make pomegranates of blue, purple, and scarlet, all around its hem, and bells of gold between them all around: [34] a golden bell and a pomegranate, a golden bell and a pomegranate, upon the hem of the robe all around. [35] And it shall be upon Aaron when he ministers, and its sound will be heard when he goes into the holy *place* before the LORD and when he comes out, that he may not die.

הַשֵּׁנִי נֹפֶךְ סַפִּיר וְיָהֲלֹם: 19 וְהַטּוּר הַשְּׁלִישִׁי לֶשֶׁם שְׁבוֹ וְאַחְלָמָה: 20 וְהַטּוּר הָרְבִיעִי תַּרְשִׁישׁ וְשֹׁהַם וְיָשְׁפֵה מְשֻׁבָּצִים זָהָב יִהְיוּ בְּמִלּוּאֹתָם: 21 וְהָאֲבָנִים תִּהְיֶיןָ עַל־שְׁמֹת בְּנֵי־יִשְׂרָאֵל שְׁתֵּים עֶשְׂרֵה עַל־שְׁמֹתָם פִּתּוּחֵי חוֹתָם אִישׁ עַל־שְׁמוֹ תִּהְיֶיןָ לִשְׁנֵי עָשָׂר שָׁבֶט: 22 וְעָשִׂיתָ עַל־הַחֹשֶׁן שַׁרְשֹׁת גַּבְלֻת מַעֲשֵׂה עֲבֹת זָהָב טָהוֹר: 23 וְעָשִׂיתָ עַל־הַחֹשֶׁן שְׁתֵּי טַבְּעוֹת זָהָב וְנָתַתָּ אֶת־שְׁתֵּי הַטַּבָּעוֹת עַל־שְׁנֵי קְצוֹת הַחֹשֶׁן: 24 וְנָתַתָּ אֶת־שְׁתֵּי עֲבֹתֹת הַזָּהָב עַל־שְׁתֵּי הַטַּבָּעֹת אֶל־קְצוֹת הַחֹשֶׁן: 25 וְאֵת שְׁתֵּי קְצוֹת שְׁתֵּי הָעֲבֹתֹת תִּתֵּן עַל־שְׁתֵּי הַמִּשְׁבְּצוֹת וְנָתַתָּה עַל־כִּתְפוֹת הָאֵפֹד אֶל־מוּל פָּנָיו: 26 וְעָשִׂיתָ שְׁתֵּי טַבְּעוֹת זָהָב וְשַׂמְתָּ אֹתָם עַל־שְׁנֵי קְצוֹת הַחֹשֶׁן עַל־שְׂפָתוֹ אֲשֶׁר אֶל־עֵבֶר הָאֵפֹד בָּיְתָה: 27 וְעָשִׂיתָ שְׁתֵּי טַבְּעוֹת זָהָב וְנָתַתָּה אֹתָם עַל־שְׁתֵּי כִתְפוֹת הָאֵפוֹד מִלְּמַטָּה מִמּוּל פָּנָיו לְעֻמַּת מֶחְבַּרְתּוֹ מִמַּעַל לְחֵשֶׁב הָאֵפוֹד: 28 וְיִרְכְּסוּ אֶת־הַחֹשֶׁן מִטַּבְּעֹתָו אֶל־טַבְּעֹת הָאֵפֹד בִּפְתִיל תְּכֵלֶת לִהְיוֹת עַל־חֵשֶׁב הָאֵפוֹד וְלֹא־יִזַּח הַחֹשֶׁן מֵעַל הָאֵפוֹד: 29 וְנָשָׂא אַהֲרֹן אֶת־שְׁמוֹת בְּנֵי־יִשְׂרָאֵל בְּחֹשֶׁן הַמִּשְׁפָּט עַל־לִבּוֹ בְּבֹאוֹ אֶל־הַקֹּדֶשׁ לְזִכָּרֹן לִפְנֵי־יְהֹוָה תָּמִיד: 30 וְנָתַתָּ אֶל־חֹשֶׁן הַמִּשְׁפָּט אֶת־הָאוּרִים וְאֶת־הַתֻּמִּים וְהָיוּ עַל־לֵב אַהֲרֹן בְּבֹאוֹ לִפְנֵי יְהֹוָה וְנָשָׂא אַהֲרֹן אֶת־מִשְׁפַּט בְּנֵי־יִשְׂרָאֵל עַל־לִבּוֹ לִפְנֵי יְהֹוָה תָּמִיד: ס 31 וְעָשִׂיתָ אֶת־מְעִיל הָאֵפוֹד כְּלִיל תְּכֵלֶת: 32 וְהָיָה פִי־רֹאשׁוֹ בְּתוֹכוֹ שָׂפָה יִהְיֶה לְפִיו סָבִיב מַעֲשֵׂה אֹרֵג כְּפִי תַחְרָא יִהְיֶה־לּוֹ לֹא יִקָּרֵעַ: 33 וְעָשִׂיתָ עַל־שׁוּלָיו רִמֹּנֵי תְּכֵלֶת וְאַרְגָּמָן וְתוֹלַעַת שָׁנִי עַל־שׁוּלָיו סָבִיב וּפַעֲמֹנֵי זָהָב בְּתוֹכָם סָבִיב: 34 פַּעֲמֹן זָהָב וְרִמּוֹן פַּעֲמֹן זָהָב וְרִמּוֹן עַל־שׁוּלֵי הַמְּעִיל סָבִיב: 35 וְהָיָה עַל־אַהֲרֹן לְשָׁרֵת וְנִשְׁמַע קוֹלוֹ בְּבֹאוֹ אֶל־הַקֹּדֶשׁ לִפְנֵי יְהֹוָה וּבְצֵאתוֹ

36 "You shall also make a plate of pure gold and engrave on it, *like* the engraving of a signet:

HOLINESS TO THE LORD.

37 And you shall put it on a blue cord, that it may be on the turban; it shall be on the front of the turban. 38 So it shall be on Aaron's forehead, that Aaron may bear the iniquity of the holy things which the children of Israel hallow in all their holy gifts; and it shall always be on his forehead, that they may be accepted before the LORD.

39 "You shall skillfully weave the tunic of fine linen *thread,* you shall make the turban of fine linen, and you shall make the sash of woven work.

40 "For Aaron's sons you shall make tunics, and you shall make sashes for them. And you shall make hats for them, for glory and beauty. 41 So you shall put them on Aaron your brother and on his sons with him. You shall anoint them, consecrate them, and sanctify them, that they may minister to Me as priests. 42 And you shall make for them linen trousers to cover their nakedness; they shall reach from the waist to the thighs. 43 They shall be on Aaron and on his sons when they come into the tabernacle of meeting, or when they come near the altar to minister in the holy *place,* that they do not incur iniquity and die. *It shall be* a statute forever to him and his descendants after him.

29

"And this is what you shall do to them to hallow them for ministering to Me as priests: Take one young bull and two rams without blemish, 2 and unleavened bread, unleavened cakes mixed with oil, and unleavened wafers anointed with oil (you shall make them of wheat flour). 3 You shall put them in one basket and bring them in the basket, with the bull and the two rams.

4 "And Aaron and his sons you shall bring to the door of the tabernacle of meeting, and you shall wash them with water. 5 Then you shall take the garments, put the tunic on Aaron, and the robe of the ephod, the ephod, and the breastplate, and gird him with the intricately woven band of the ephod. 6 You shall put the turban on his head, and put the holy crown on the turban. 7 And you shall take the anointing oil, pour *it* on his head, and anoint him. 8 Then you shall bring his sons and put tunics on them. 9 And you shall gird them with sashes, Aaron and his sons, and put the hats on them. The priesthood shall be theirs for a perpetual statute. So you shall consecrate Aaron and his sons.

10 "You shall also have the bull brought before the tabernacle of meeting, and Aaron and his sons shall put their hands on the head of the bull. 11 Then

ס וְלֹא יָמֽוּת: 36 וְעָשִׂ֥יתָ צִּ֖יץ זָהָ֣ב טָה֑וֹר
וּפִתַּחְתָּ֤ עָלָיו֙ פִּתּוּחֵ֣י חֹתָ֔ם קֹ֖דֶשׁ לַֽיהוָֽה: 37 וְשַׂמְתָּ֨
אֹת֜וֹ עַל־פְּתִ֣יל תְּכֵ֗לֶת וְהָיָ֖ה עַל־הַמִּצְנָ֑פֶת אֶל־
מ֥וּל פְּנֵֽי־הַמִּצְנֶ֖פֶת יִֽהְיֶֽה: 38 וְהָיָה֮ עַל־מֵ֣צַח אַֽהֲרֹן֒
וְנָשָׂ֨א אַֽהֲרֹ֜ן אֶת־עֲוֹ֣ן הַקֳּדָשִׁ֗ים אֲשֶׁ֤ר יַקְדִּ֨ישׁוּ֙
בְּנֵ֣י יִשְׂרָאֵ֔ל לְכָֽל־מַתְּנֹ֖ת קָֽדְשֵׁיהֶ֑ם וְהָיָ֤ה עַל־מִצְחוֹ֙
תָּמִ֔יד לְרָצ֥וֹן לָהֶ֖ם לִפְנֵ֥י יְהוָֽה: 39 וְשִׁבַּצְתָּ֙ הַכְּתֹ֣נֶת
שֵׁ֔שׁ וְעָשִׂ֖יתָ מִצְנֶ֣פֶת שֵׁ֑שׁ וְאַבְנֵ֥ט תַּֽעֲשֶׂ֖ה מַֽעֲשֵׂ֥ה
רֹקֵֽם: 40 וְלִבְנֵ֤י אַֽהֲרֹן֙ תַּֽעֲשֶׂ֣ה כֻתֳּנֹ֔ת וְעָשִׂ֥יתָ לָהֶ֖ם
אַבְנֵטִ֑ים וּמִגְבָּעוֹת֙ תַּֽעֲשֶׂ֣ה לָהֶ֔ם לְכָב֖וֹד וּלְתִפְאָֽרֶת:
41 וְהִלְבַּשְׁתָּ֤ אֹתָם֙ אֶת־אַֽהֲרֹ֣ן אָחִ֔יךָ וְאֶת־בָּנָ֖יו אִתּ֑וֹ
וּמָֽשַׁחְתָּ֤ אֹתָם֙ וּמִלֵּאתָ֣ אֶת־יָדָ֔ם וְקִדַּשְׁתָּ֖ אֹתָ֑ם
וְכִֽהֲנ֖וּ לִֽי: 42 וַֽעֲשֵׂ֤ה לָהֶם֙ מִכְנְסֵי־בָ֔ד לְכַסּ֖וֹת בְּשַׂ֣ר
עֶרְוָ֑ה מִמָּתְנַ֥יִם וְעַד־יְרֵכַ֖יִם יִֽהְיֽוּ: 43 וְהָי֤וּ עַל־אַֽהֲרֹן֙
וְעַל־בָּנָ֜יו בְּבֹאָ֣ם ׀ אֶל־אֹ֣הֶל מוֹעֵ֗ד א֤וֹ בְגִשְׁתָּם֙
אֶל־הַמִּזְבֵּ֨חַ֙ לְשָׁרֵ֣ת בַּקֹּ֔דֶשׁ וְלֹֽא־יִשְׂא֥וּ עָוֹ֖ן וָמֵ֑תוּ
חֻקַּ֥ת עוֹלָ֛ם ל֖וֹ וּלְזַרְע֥וֹ אַֽחֲרָֽיו: ס

כט וְזֶ֣ה הַדָּבָ֞ר אֲשֶׁ֤ר תַּֽעֲשֶׂה֙ לָהֶ֔ם לְקַדֵּ֥שׁ
אֹתָ֖ם לְכַהֵ֣ן לִ֑י לְ֠קַח פַּ֣ר אֶחָ֧ד בֶּן־בָּקָ֛ר וְאֵילִ֥ם
שְׁנַ֖יִם תְּמִימִֽם: 2 וְלֶ֣חֶם מַצּ֗וֹת וְחַלֹּ֤ת מַצֹּת֙ בְּלוּלֹ֣ת
בַּשֶּׁ֔מֶן וּרְקִיקֵ֥י מַצּ֖וֹת מְשֻׁחִ֣ים בַּשָּׁ֑מֶן סֹ֥לֶת חִטִּ֖ים
תַּֽעֲשֶׂ֥ה אֹתָֽם: 3 וְנָֽתַתָּ֤ אוֹתָם֙ עַל־סַ֣ל אֶחָ֔ד
וְהִקְרַבְתָּ֥ אֹתָ֖ם בַּסָּ֑ל וְאֶ֨ת־הַפָּ֔ר וְאֵ֖ת שְׁנֵ֥י הָֽאֵילִֽם:
4 וְאֶת־אַֽהֲרֹ֤ן וְאֶת־בָּנָיו֙ תַּקְרִ֔יב אֶל־פֶּ֖תַח אֹ֣הֶל
מוֹעֵ֑ד וְרָֽחַצְתָּ֥ אֹתָ֖ם בַּמָּֽיִם: 5 וְלָֽקַחְתָּ֣ אֶת־הַבְּגָדִ֗ים
וְהִלְבַּשְׁתָּ֤ אֶֽת־אַֽהֲרֹן֙ אֶת־הַכֻּתֹּ֔נֶת וְאֵת֙ מְעִ֣יל
הָֽאֵפֹ֔ד וְאֶת־הָֽאֵפֹ֖ד וְאֶת־הַחֹ֑שֶׁן וְאָֽפַדְתָּ֣ ל֔וֹ בְּחֵ֖שֶׁב
הָֽאֵפֹֽד: 6 וְשַׂמְתָּ֥ הַמִּצְנֶ֖פֶת עַל־רֹאשׁ֑וֹ וְנָֽתַתָּ֛ אֶת־
נֵ֥זֶר הַקֹּ֖דֶשׁ עַל־הַמִּצְנָֽפֶת: 7 וְלָֽקַחְתָּ֙ אֶת־שֶׁ֣מֶן
הַמִּשְׁחָ֔ה וְיָֽצַקְתָּ֖ עַל־רֹאשׁ֑וֹ וּמָֽשַׁחְתָּ֖ אֹתֽוֹ: 8 וְאֶת־
בָּנָ֖יו תַּקְרִ֑יב וְהִלְבַּשְׁתָּ֖ם כֻּתֳּנֹֽת: 9 וְחָֽגַרְתָּ֩ אֹתָ֨ם
אַבְנֵ֜ט אַֽהֲרֹ֣ן וּבָנָ֗יו וְחָֽבַשְׁתָּ֤ לָהֶם֙ מִגְבָּעֹ֔ת וְהָֽיְתָ֥ה
לָהֶ֛ם כְּהֻנָּ֖ה לְחֻקַּ֣ת עוֹלָ֑ם וּמִלֵּאתָ֥ יַֽד־אַֽהֲרֹ֖ן וְיַד־
בָּנָֽיו: 10 וְהִקְרַבְתָּ֙ אֶת־הַפָּ֔ר לִפְנֵ֖י אֹ֣הֶל מוֹעֵ֑ד וְסָמַ֨ךְ
אַֽהֲרֹ֤ן וּבָנָיו֙ אֶת־יְדֵיהֶ֔ם עַל־רֹ֥אשׁ הַפָּֽר: 11 וְשָֽׁחַטְתָּ֥

you shall kill the bull before the LORD, *by* the door
of the tabernacle of meeting. [12] You shall take *some*
of the blood of the bull and put *it* on the horns of
the altar with your finger, and pour all the blood
beside the base of the altar. [13] And you shall take all
the fat that covers the entrails, the fatty lobe
attached to the liver, and the two kidneys and the
fat that *is* on them, and burn *them* on the altar.
[14] But the flesh of the bull, with its skin and its offal,
you shall burn with fire outside the camp. It *is* a sin
offering.

[15] "You shall also take one ram, and Aaron and
his sons shall put their hands on the head of the
ram; [16] and you shall kill the ram, and you shall
take its blood and sprinkle *it* all around on the
altar. [17] Then you shall cut the ram in pieces, wash
its entrails and its legs, and put *them* with its pieces
and with its head. [18] And you shall burn the whole
ram on the altar. It *is* a burnt offering to the LORD;
it *is* a sweet aroma, an offering made by fire to the
LORD.

[19] "You shall also take the other ram, and Aaron
and his sons shall put their hands on the head of the
ram. [20] Then you shall kill the ram, and take some
of its blood and put *it* on the tip of the right ear of
Aaron and on the tip of the right ear of his sons, on
the thumb of their right hand and on the big toe of
their right foot, and sprinkle the blood all around
on the altar. [21] And you shall take some of the
blood that is on the altar, and some of the anointing
oil, and sprinkle *it* on Aaron and on his garments,
on his sons and on the garments of his sons with
him; and he and his garments shall be hallowed,
and his sons and his sons' garments with him.

[22] "Also you shall take the fat of the ram, the fat
tail, the fat that covers the entrails, the fatty lobe
attached to the liver, the two kidneys and the fat on
them, the right thigh (for it *is* a ram of consecration), [23] one loaf of bread, one cake *made with* oil,
and one wafer from the basket of the unleavened
bread that *is* before the LORD; [24] and you shall put
all these in the hands of Aaron and in the hands of
his sons, and you shall wave them *as* a wave
offering before the LORD. [25] You shall receive them
back from their hands and burn *them* on the altar as
a burnt offering, as a sweet aroma before the LORD.
It *is* an offering made by fire to the LORD.

[26] "Then you shall take the breast of the ram of
Aaron's consecration and wave it *as* a wave offering
before the LORD; and it shall be your portion.
[27] And from the ram of the consecration you shall
consecrate the breast of the wave offering which is
waved, and the thigh of the heave offering which is
raised, of *that* which *is* for Aaron and of *that* which

12 וְלָקַחְתָּ֙ אֶת־הַפָּ֤ר לִפְנֵ֣י יְהוָ֔ה פֶּ֖תַח אֹ֥הֶל מוֹעֵֽד׃
מִדַּ֤ם הַפָּר֙ וְנָֽתַתָּ֛ה עַל־קַרְנֹ֥ת הַמִּזְבֵּ֖חַ בְּאֶצְבָּעֶ֑ךָ
וְאֶת־כָּל־הַדָּ֣ם תִּשְׁפֹּ֔ךְ אֶל־יְס֖וֹד הַמִּזְבֵּֽחַ׃ 13 וְלָֽקַחְתָּ֗
אֶת־כָּל־הַחֵ֨לֶב֙ הַֽמְכַסֶּ֣ה אֶת־הַקֶּ֔רֶב וְאֵ֗ת הַיֹּתֶ֨רֶת֙
עַל־הַכָּבֵ֔ד וְאֵת֙ שְׁתֵּ֣י הַכְּלָיֹ֔ת וְאֶת־הַחֵ֖לֶב אֲשֶׁ֣ר
עֲלֵיהֶ֑ן וְהִקְטַרְתָּ֖ הַמִּזְבֵּֽחָה׃ 14 וְאֶת־בְּשַׂ֤ר הַפָּר֙
וְאֶת־עֹר֣וֹ וְאֶת־פִּרְשׁ֔וֹ תִּשְׂרֹ֣ף בָּאֵ֔שׁ מִח֖וּץ לַֽמַּחֲנֶ֑ה
חַטָּ֖את הֽוּא׃ 15 וְאֶת־הָאַ֥יִל הָֽאֶחָ֖ד תִּקָּ֑ח וְסָֽמְכ֡וּ
אַהֲרֹ֨ן וּבָנָ֧יו אֶת־יְדֵיהֶ֛ם עַל־רֹ֥אשׁ הָאָֽיִל׃ 16 וְשָֽׁחַטְתָּ֖
אֶת־הָאָ֑יִל וְלָֽקַחְתָּ֙ אֶת־דָּמ֔וֹ וְזָֽרַקְתָּ֥ עַל־הַמִּזְבֵּ֖חַ
סָבִֽיב׃ 17 וְאֶ֨ת־הָאַ֜יִל תְּנַתֵּ֣חַ לִנְתָחָ֑יו וְרָֽחַצְתָּ֤ קִרְבּוֹ֙
וּכְרָעָ֔יו וְנָֽתַתָּ֥ עַל־נְתָחָ֖יו וְעַל־רֹאשֽׁוֹ׃ 18 וְהִקְטַרְתָּ֤
אֶת־כָּל־הָאַ֨יִל֙ הַמִּזְבֵּ֔חָה עֹלָ֥ה ה֖וּא לַֽיהוָ֑ה רֵ֣יחַ
נִיח֔וֹחַ אִשֶּׁ֥ה לַֽיהוָ֖ה הֽוּא׃ 19 וְלָ֣קַחְתָּ֔ אֵ֖ת הָאַ֣יִל
הַשֵּׁנִ֑י וְסָמַ֨ךְ אַהֲרֹ֤ן וּבָנָיו֙ אֶת־יְדֵיהֶ֔ם עַל־רֹ֖אשׁ
הָאָֽיִל׃ 20 וְשָֽׁחַטְתָּ֣ אֶת־הָאַ֗יִל וְלָֽקַחְתָּ֤ מִדָּמוֹ֙ וְנָֽתַתָּ֞ה
עַל־תְּנ֨וּךְ אֹ֤זֶן אַהֲרֹן֙ וְעַל־תְּנ֜וּךְ אֹ֤זֶן בָּנָיו֙ הַיְמָנִ֔ית
וְעַל־בֹּ֤הֶן יָדָם֙ הַיְמָנִ֔ית וְעַל־בֹּ֥הֶן רַגְלָ֖ם הַיְמָנִ֑ית
וְזָֽרַקְתָּ֧ אֶת־הַדָּ֛ם עַל־הַמִּזְבֵּ֖חַ סָבִֽיב׃ 21 וְלָֽקַחְתָּ֞ מִן־
הַדָּ֨ם אֲשֶׁ֥ר עַל־הַמִּזְבֵּחַ֮ וּמִשֶּׁ֣מֶן הַמִּשְׁחָה֒ וְהִזֵּיתָ֤
עַֽל־אַהֲרֹן֙ וְעַל־בְּגָדָ֔יו וְעַל־בָּנָ֖יו וְעַל־בִּגְדֵ֣י בָנָ֣יו
אִתּ֑וֹ וְקָדַ֥שׁ הוּא֙ וּבְגָדָ֔יו וּבָנָ֛יו וּבִגְדֵ֥י בָנָ֖יו אִתּֽוֹ׃

22 וְלָֽקַחְתָּ֣ מִן־הָ֠אַ֠יִל הַחֵ֨לֶב וְהָֽאַלְיָ֜ה וְאֶֽת־הַחֵ֣לֶב ׀
הַֽמְכַסֶּ֣ה אֶת־הַקֶּ֗רֶב וְאֵ֨ת יֹתֶ֤רֶת הַכָּבֵד֙ וְאֵ֣ת ׀
שְׁתֵּ֣י הַכְּלָיֹ֗ת וְאֶת־הַחֵ֨לֶב֙ אֲשֶׁ֣ר עֲלֵהֶ֔ן וְאֵ֖ת שׁ֣וֹק
הַיָּמִ֑ין כִּ֛י אֵ֥יל מִלֻּאִ֖ים הֽוּא׃ 23 וְכִכַּ֨ר לֶ֜חֶם אַחַ֗ת
וַֽחַלַּ֨ת לֶ֤חֶם שֶׁ֨מֶן֙ אַחַ֔ת וְרָקִ֖יק אֶחָ֑ד מִסַּל֙ הַמַּצּ֔וֹת
אֲשֶׁ֖ר לִפְנֵ֥י יְהוָֽה׃ 24 וְשַׂמְתָּ֣ הַכֹּ֔ל עַ֚ל כַּפֵּ֣י אַהֲרֹ֔ן
וְעַ֖ל כַּפֵּ֣י בָנָ֑יו וְהֵֽנַפְתָּ֥ אֹתָ֛ם תְּנוּפָ֖ה לִפְנֵ֥י יְהוָֽה׃
25 וְלָֽקַחְתָּ֤ אֹתָם֙ מִיָּדָ֔ם וְהִקְטַרְתָּ֥ הַמִּזְבֵּ֖חָה עַל־
הָעֹלָ֑ה לְרֵ֤יחַ נִיחֹ֨חַ֙ לִפְנֵ֣י יְהוָ֔ה אִשֶּׁ֥ה ה֖וּא לַֽיהוָֽה׃

26 וְלָֽקַחְתָּ֣ אֶת־הֶֽחָזֶ֗ה מֵאֵ֤יל הַמִּלֻּאִים֙ אֲשֶׁ֣ר לְאַֽהֲרֹ֔ן
וְהֵֽנַפְתָּ֥ אֹת֛וֹ תְּנוּפָ֖ה לִפְנֵ֣י יְהוָ֑ה וְהָיָ֥ה לְךָ֖ לְמָנָֽה׃
27 וְקִדַּשְׁתָּ֞ אֵ֣ת ׀ חֲזֵ֣ה הַתְּנוּפָ֗ה וְאֵת֙ שׁ֣וֹק הַתְּרוּמָ֔ה
אֲשֶׁ֥ר הוּנַ֖ף וַֽאֲשֶׁ֣ר הוּרָ֑ם מֵאֵיל֙ הַמִּלֻּאִ֔ים מֵֽאֲשֶׁ֥ר

is for his sons. ²⁸ It shall be from the children of Israel *for* Aaron and his sons by a statute forever. For it is a heave offering; it shall be a heave offering from the children of Israel from the sacrifices of their peace offerings, *that is,* their heave offering to the LORD.

²⁹ "And the holy garments of Aaron shall be his sons' after him, to be anointed in them and to be consecrated in them. ³⁰ That son who becomes priest in his place shall put them on for seven days, when he enters the tabernacle of meeting to minister in the holy *place.*

³¹ "And you shall take the ram of the consecration and boil its flesh in the holy place. ³² Then Aaron and his sons shall eat the flesh of the ram, and the bread that *is* in the basket, *by* the door of the tabernacle of meeting. ³³ They shall eat those things with which the atonement was made, to consecrate *and* to sanctify them; but an outsider shall not eat *them,* because they *are* holy. ³⁴ And if any of the flesh of the consecration offerings, or of the bread, remains until the morning, then you shall burn the remainder with fire. It shall not be eaten, because it *is* holy.

³⁵ "Thus you shall do to Aaron and his sons, according to all that I have commanded you. Seven days you shall consecrate them. ³⁶ And you shall offer a bull every day *as* a sin offering for atonement. You shall cleanse the altar when you make atonement for it, and you shall anoint it to sanctify it. ³⁷ Seven days you shall make atonement for the altar and sanctify it. And the altar shall be most holy. Whatever touches the altar must be holy.

³⁸ "Now this *is* what you shall offer on the altar: two lambs of the first year, day by day continually. ³⁹ One lamb you shall offer in the morning, and the other lamb you shall offer at twilight. ⁴⁰ With the one lamb shall be one-tenth *of an ephah* of flour mixed with one-fourth of a hin of pressed oil, and one-fourth of a hin of wine *as* a drink offering. ⁴¹ And the other lamb you shall offer at twilight; and you shall offer with it the grain offering and the drink offering, as in the morning, for a sweet aroma, an offering made by fire to the LORD. ⁴² *This shall be* a continual burnt offering throughout your generations *at* the door of the tabernacle of meeting before the LORD, where I will meet you to speak with you. ⁴³ And there I will meet with the children of Israel, and *the tabernacle* shall be sanctified by My glory. ⁴⁴ So I will consecrate the tabernacle of meeting and the altar. I will also consecrate both Aaron and his sons to minister to Me as priests. ⁴⁵ I will dwell among the children of Israel and will be

לְאַהֲרֹ֖ן וּמֵאֵ֥שֶׁר לְבָנָֽיו: 28 וְהָיָה֩ לְאַהֲרֹ֨ן וּלְבָנָ֜יו לְחָק־עוֹלָ֗ם מֵאֵת֙ בְּנֵ֣י יִשְׂרָאֵ֔ל כִּ֥י תְרוּמָ֖ה ה֑וּא וּתְרוּמָ֞ה יִהְיֶ֨ה מֵאֵ֤ת בְּנֵֽי־יִשְׂרָאֵל֙ מִזִּבְחֵ֣י שַׁלְמֵיהֶ֔ם תְּרוּמָתָ֖ם לַֽיהוָֽה: 29 וּבִגְדֵ֤י הַקֹּ֙דֶשׁ֙ אֲשֶׁ֣ר לְאַהֲרֹ֔ן יִהְי֥וּ לְבָנָ֖יו אַחֲרָ֑יו לְמָשְׁחָ֣ה בָהֶ֔ם וּלְמַלֵּא־בָ֖ם אֶת־יָדָֽם: 30 שִׁבְעַ֣ת יָמִ֗ים יִלְבָּשָׁ֧ם הַכֹּהֵ֛ן תַּחְתָּ֖יו מִבָּנָ֑יו אֲשֶׁ֥ר יָבֹ֛א אֶל־אֹ֥הֶל מוֹעֵ֖ד לְשָׁרֵ֥ת בַּקֹּֽדֶשׁ: 31 וְאֵ֛ת אֵ֥יל הַמִּלֻּאִ֖ים תִּקָּ֑ח וּבִשַּׁלְתָּ֥ אֶת־בְּשָׂר֖וֹ בְּמָקֹ֥ם קָדֹֽשׁ: 32 וְאָכַ֨ל אַהֲרֹ֤ן וּבָנָיו֙ אֶת־בְּשַׂ֣ר הָאַ֔יִל וְאֶת־ הַלֶּ֖חֶם אֲשֶׁ֣ר בַּסָּ֑ל פֶּ֖תַח אֹ֥הֶל מוֹעֵֽד: 33 וְאָכְל֤וּ אֹתָם֙ אֲשֶׁ֣ר כֻּפַּ֣ר בָּהֶ֔ם לְמַלֵּ֥א אֶת־יָדָ֖ם לְקַדֵּ֣שׁ אֹתָ֑ם וְזָ֥ר לֹא־יֹאכַ֖ל כִּי־קֹ֥דֶשׁ הֵֽם: 34 וְאִם־יִוָּתֵ֞ר מִבְּשַׂ֧ר הַמִּלֻּאִ֛ים וּמִן־הַלֶּ֖חֶם עַד־הַבֹּ֑קֶר וְשָׂרַפְתָּ֤ אֶת־הַנּוֹתָר֙ בָּאֵ֔שׁ לֹ֥א יֵאָכֵ֖ל כִּי־קֹ֥דֶשׁ הֽוּא: 35 וְעָשִׂ֜יתָ לְאַהֲרֹ֤ן וּלְבָנָיו֙ כָּ֔כָה כְּכֹ֥ל אֲשֶׁר־צִוִּ֖יתִי אֹתָ֑כָה שִׁבְעַ֥ת יָמִ֖ים תְּמַלֵּ֥א יָדָֽם: 36 וּפַ֨ר חַטָּ֜את תַּעֲשֶׂ֤ה לַיּוֹם֙ עַל־ הַכִּפֻּרִ֔ים וְחִטֵּאתָ֙ עַל־הַמִּזְבֵּ֔חַ בְּכַפֶּרְךָ֖ עָלָ֑יו וּמָשַׁחְתָּ֥ אֹת֖וֹ לְקַדְּשֽׁוֹ: 37 שִׁבְעַ֣ת יָמִ֗ים תְּכַפֵּר֙ עַל־הַמִּזְבֵּ֔חַ וְקִדַּשְׁתָּ֖ אֹת֑וֹ וְהָיָ֤ה הַמִּזְבֵּ֙חַ֙ קֹ֣דֶשׁ קָֽדָשִׁ֔ים כָּל־הַנֹּגֵ֥עַ בַּמִּזְבֵּ֖חַ יִקְדָּֽשׁ: ס 38 וְזֶ֕ה אֲשֶׁ֥ר תַּעֲשֶׂ֖ה עַל־הַמִּזְבֵּ֑חַ כְּבָשִׂ֧ים בְּנֵֽי־שָׁנָ֛ה שְׁנַ֥יִם לַיּ֖וֹם תָּמִֽיד: 39 אֶת־הַכֶּ֥בֶשׂ הָאֶחָ֖ד תַּעֲשֶׂ֣ה בַבֹּ֑קֶר וְאֵת֙ הַכֶּ֣בֶשׂ הַשֵּׁנִ֔י תַּעֲשֶׂ֖ה בֵּ֥ין הָעַרְבָּֽיִם: 40 וְעִשָּׂרֹ֨ן סֹ֜לֶת בָּל֣וּל בְּשֶׁ֤מֶן כָּתִית֙ רֶ֣בַע הַהִ֔ין וְנֵ֛סֶךְ רְבִיעִ֥ת הַהִ֖ין יָ֑יִן לַכֶּ֖בֶשׂ הָאֶחָֽד: 41 וְאֵת֙ הַכֶּ֣בֶשׂ הַשֵּׁנִ֔י תַּעֲשֶׂ֖ה בֵּ֣ין הָעַרְבָּ֑יִם כְּמִנְחַ֨ת הַבֹּ֤קֶר וּכְנִסְכָּהּ֙ תַּֽעֲשֶׂה־לָּ֔הּ לְרֵ֣יחַ נִיחֹ֔חַ אִשֶּׁ֖ה לַֽיהוָֽה: 42 עֹלַ֤ת תָּמִיד֙ לְדֹרֹ֣תֵיכֶ֔ם פֶּ֥תַח אֹֽהֶל־מוֹעֵ֖ד לִפְנֵ֣י יְהוָ֑ה אֲשֶׁ֨ר אִוָּעֵ֤ד לָכֶם֙ שָׁ֔מָּה לְדַבֵּ֥ר אֵלֶ֖יךָ שָֽׁם: 43 וְנֹעַדְתִּ֥י שָׁ֖מָּה לִבְנֵ֣י יִשְׂרָאֵ֑ל וְנִקְדַּ֖שׁ בִּכְבֹדִֽי: 44 וְקִדַּשְׁתִּ֛י אֶת־אֹ֥הֶל מוֹעֵ֖ד וְאֶת־ הַמִּזְבֵּ֑חַ וְאֶת־אַהֲרֹ֧ן וְאֶת־בָּנָ֛יו אֲקַדֵּ֖שׁ לְכַהֵ֥ן לִֽי: 45 וְשָׁכַנְתִּ֖י בְּת֣וֹךְ בְּנֵ֣י יִשְׂרָאֵ֑ל וְהָיִ֥יתִי לָהֶ֖ם

their God. [46] And they shall know that I *am* the LORD their God, who brought them up out of the land of Egypt, that I may dwell among them. I *am* the LORD their God.

30 "You shall make an altar to burn incense on; you shall make it of acacia wood. [2] A cubit *shall be* its length and a cubit its width—it shall be square—and two cubits *shall be* its height. Its horns *shall be* of one piece with it. [3] And you shall overlay its top, its sides all around, and its horns with pure gold; and you shall make for it a molding of gold all around. [4] Two gold rings you shall make for it, under the molding on both its sides. You shall place *them* on its two sides, and they will be holders for the poles with which to bear it. [5] You shall make the poles of acacia wood, and overlay them with gold. [6] And you shall put it before the veil that *is* before the ark of the Testimony, before the mercy seat that *is* over the Testimony, where I will meet with you.

[7] "Aaron shall burn on it sweet incense every morning; when he tends the lamps, he shall burn incense on it. [8] And when Aaron lights the lamps at twilight, he shall burn incense on it, a perpetual incense before the LORD throughout your generations. [9] You shall not offer strange incense on it, or a burnt offering, or a grain offering; nor shall you pour a drink offering on it. [10] And Aaron shall make atonement upon its horns once a year with the blood of the sin offering of atonement; once a year he shall make atonement upon it throughout your generations. It *is* most holy to the LORD."

[11] Then the LORD spoke to Moses, saying: [12] "When you take the census of the children of Israel for their number, then every man shall give a ransom for himself to the LORD, when you number them, that there may be no plague among them when *you* number them. [13] This is what everyone among those who are numbered shall give: half a shekel according to the shekel of the sanctuary (a shekel *is* twenty gerahs). The half-shekel *shall be* an offering to the LORD. [14] Everyone included among those who are numbered, from twenty years old and above, shall give an offering to the LORD. [15] The rich shall not give more and the poor shall not give less than half a shekel, when *you* give an offering to the LORD, to make atonement for yourselves. [16] And you shall take the atonement money of the children of Israel, and shall appoint it for the service of the tabernacle of meeting, that it may be a memorial for the children of Israel before the LORD, to make atonement for yourselves."

לֵאלֹהֵיהֶם: 46 וְיָדְעוּ כִּי אֲנִי יְהֹוָה אֱלֹהֵיהֶם אֲשֶׁר הוֹצֵאתִי אֹתָם מֵאֶרֶץ מִצְרַיִם לְשָׁכְנִי בְתוֹכָם אֲנִי יְהֹוָה אֱלֹהֵיהֶם: פ

ל וְעָשִׂיתָ מִזְבֵּחַ מִקְטַר קְטֹרֶת עֲצֵי שִׁטִּים תַּעֲשֶׂה אֹתוֹ: 2 אַמָּה אָרְכּוֹ וְאַמָּה רָחְבּוֹ רָבוּעַ יִהְיֶה וְאַמָּתַיִם קֹמָתוֹ מִמֶּנּוּ קַרְנֹתָיו: 3 וְצִפִּיתָ אֹתוֹ זָהָב טָהוֹר אֶת־גַּגּוֹ וְאֶת־קִירֹתָיו סָבִיב וְאֶת־קַרְנֹתָיו וְעָשִׂיתָ לּוֹ זֵר זָהָב סָבִיב: 4 וּשְׁתֵּי טַבְּעֹת זָהָב תַּעֲשֶׂה־לּוֹ | מִתַּחַת לְזֵרוֹ עַל שְׁתֵּי צַלְעֹתָיו תַּעֲשֶׂה עַל־שְׁנֵי צִדָּיו וְהָיָה לְבָתִּים לְבַדִּים לָשֵׂאת אֹתוֹ בָּהֵמָּה: 5 וְעָשִׂיתָ אֶת־הַבַּדִּים עֲצֵי שִׁטִּים וְצִפִּיתָ אֹתָם זָהָב: 6 וְנָתַתָּה אֹתוֹ לִפְנֵי הַפָּרֹכֶת אֲשֶׁר עַל־אֲרֹן הָעֵדֻת לִפְנֵי הַכַּפֹּרֶת אֲשֶׁר עַל־הָעֵדֻת אֲשֶׁר אִוָּעֵד לְךָ שָׁמָּה: 7 וְהִקְטִיר עָלָיו אַהֲרֹן קְטֹרֶת סַמִּים בַּבֹּקֶר בַּבֹּקֶר בְּהֵיטִיבוֹ אֶת־הַנֵּרֹת יַקְטִירֶנָּה: 8 וּבְהַעֲלֹת אַהֲרֹן אֶת־הַנֵּרֹת בֵּין הָעַרְבַּיִם יַקְטִירֶנָּה קְטֹרֶת תָּמִיד לִפְנֵי יְהֹוָה לְדֹרֹתֵיכֶם: 9 לֹא־תַעֲלוּ עָלָיו קְטֹרֶת זָרָה וְעֹלָה וּמִנְחָה וְנֵסֶךְ לֹא תִסְּכוּ עָלָיו: 10 וְכִפֶּר אַהֲרֹן עַל־קַרְנֹתָיו אַחַת בַּשָּׁנָה מִדַּם חַטַּאת הַכִּפֻּרִים אַחַת בַּשָּׁנָה יְכַפֵּר עָלָיו לְדֹרֹתֵיכֶם קֹדֶשׁ־קָדָשִׁים הוּא לַיהֹוָה: פ

11 וַיְדַבֵּר יְהֹוָה אֶל־מֹשֶׁה לֵּאמֹר: 12 כִּי תִשָּׂא אֶת־רֹאשׁ בְּנֵי־יִשְׂרָאֵל לִפְקֻדֵיהֶם וְנָתְנוּ אִישׁ כֹּפֶר נַפְשׁוֹ לַיהֹוָה בִּפְקֹד אֹתָם וְלֹא־יִהְיֶה בָהֶם נֶגֶף בִּפְקֹד אֹתָם: 13 זֶה | יִתְּנוּ כָּל־הָעֹבֵר עַל־הַפְּקֻדִים מַחֲצִית הַשֶּׁקֶל בְּשֶׁקֶל הַקֹּדֶשׁ עֶשְׂרִים גֵּרָה הַשֶּׁקֶל מַחֲצִית הַשֶּׁקֶל תְּרוּמָה לַיהֹוָה: 14 כֹּל הָעֹבֵר עַל־הַפְּקֻדִים מִבֶּן עֶשְׂרִים שָׁנָה וָמָעְלָה יִתֵּן תְּרוּמַת יְהֹוָה: 15 הֶעָשִׁיר לֹא־יַרְבֶּה וְהַדַּל לֹא יַמְעִיט מִמַּחֲצִית הַשָּׁקֶל לָתֵת אֶת־תְּרוּמַת יְהֹוָה לְכַפֵּר עַל־נַפְשֹׁתֵיכֶם: 16 וְלָקַחְתָּ אֶת־כֶּסֶף הַכִּפֻּרִים מֵאֵת בְּנֵי יִשְׂרָאֵל וְנָתַתָּ אֹתוֹ עַל־עֲבֹדַת אֹהֶל מוֹעֵד וְהָיָה לִבְנֵי יִשְׂרָאֵל לְזִכָּרוֹן לִפְנֵי יְהֹוָה לְכַפֵּר עַל־נַפְשֹׁתֵיכֶם: פ

17 Then the LORD spoke to Moses, saying:
18 "You shall also make a laver of bronze, with its
base also of bronze, for washing. You shall put it
between the tabernacle of meeting and the altar.
And you shall put water in it, 19 for Aaron and his
sons shall wash their hands and their feet in water
from it. 20 When they go into the tabernacle of
meeting, or when they come near the altar to
minister, to burn an offering made by fire to the
LORD, they shall wash with water, lest they die.
21 So they shall wash their hands and their feet, lest
they die. And it shall be a statute forever to them—
to him and his descendants throughout their
generations."

22 Moreover the LORD spoke to Moses, saying:
23 "Also take for yourself quality spices—five
hundred *shekels* of liquid myrrh, half as much
sweet-smelling cinnamon (two hundred and fifty
shekels), two hundred and fifty *shekels* of sweet-
smelling cane, 24 five hundred *shekels* of cassia,
according to the shekel of the sanctuary, and a hin
of olive oil. 25 And you shall make from these a holy
anointing oil, an ointment compounded according
to the art of the perfumer. It shall be a holy
anointing oil. 26 With it you shall anoint the
tabernacle of meeting and the ark of the Testimony;
27 the table and all its utensils, the lampstand and its
utensils, and the altar of incense; 28 the altar of
burnt offering with all its utensils, and the laver and
its base. 29 You shall consecrate them, that they may
be most holy; whatever touches them must be holy.
30 And you shall anoint Aaron and his sons, and
consecrate them, that *they* may minister to Me as
priests.

31 "And you shall speak to the children of Israel,
saying: 'This shall be a holy anointing oil to Me
throughout your generations. 32 It shall not be
poured on man's flesh; nor shall you make *any
other* like it, according to its composition. It *is* holy,
and it shall be holy to you. 33 Whoever compounds
any like it, or whoever puts *any* of it on an outsider,
shall be cut off from his people.' "

34 And the LORD said to Moses: "Take sweet
spices, stacte and onycha and galbanum, and pure
frankincense with *these* sweet spices; there shall be
equal amounts of each. 35 You shall make of these
an incense, a compound according to the art of the
perfumer, salted, pure, *and* holy. 36 And you shall
beat *some* of it very fine, and put some of it before
the Testimony in the tabernacle of meeting where I
will meet with you. It shall be most holy to you.
37 But *as for* the incense which you shall make, you
shall not make any for yourselves, according to its

17 וַיְדַבֵּ֥ר יְהֹוָ֖ה אֶל־מֹשֶׁ֥ה לֵּאמֹֽר: 18 וְעָשִׂ֜יתָ כִּיּ֥וֹר
נְחֹ֙שֶׁת֙ וְכַנּ֣וֹ נְחֹ֔שֶׁת לְרָחְצָ֑ה וְנָתַתָּ֣ אֹת֗וֹ בֵּֽין־
אֹ֤הֶל מוֹעֵד֙ וּבֵ֣ין הַמִּזְבֵּ֔חַ וְנָתַתָּ֥ שָׁ֖מָּה מָֽיִם:
19 וְרָחֲצ֛וּ אַהֲרֹ֥ן וּבָנָ֖יו מִמֶּ֑נּוּ אֶת־יְדֵיהֶ֖ם וְאֶת־
רַגְלֵיהֶֽם: 20 בְּבֹאָ֞ם אֶל־אֹ֤הֶל מוֹעֵד֙ יִרְחֲצוּ־מַ֔יִם
וְלֹ֖א יָמֻ֑תוּ א֣וֹ בְגִשְׁתָּ֤ם אֶל־הַמִּזְבֵּ֙חַ֙ לְשָׁרֵ֔ת לְהַקְטִ֥יר
אִשֶּׁ֖ה לַֽיהֹוָֽה: 21 וְרָחֲצ֛וּ יְדֵיהֶ֥ם וְרַגְלֵיהֶ֖ם וְלֹ֣א יָמֻ֑תוּ
וְהָֽיְתָ֨ה לָהֶ֧ם חׇק־עוֹלָ֛ם ל֥וֹ וּלְזַרְע֖וֹ לְדֹֽרֹתָֽם: פ

22 וַיְדַבֵּ֥ר יְהֹוָ֖ה אֶל־מֹשֶׁ֥ה לֵּאמֹֽר: 23 וְאַתָּ֣ה קַח־לְךָ֮
בְּשָׂמִ֣ים רֹאשׁ֒ מׇר־דְּרוֹר֙ חֲמֵ֣שׁ מֵא֔וֹת וְקִנְּמׇן־בֶּ֥שֶׂם
מַחֲצִית֖וֹ חֲמִשִּׁ֣ים וּמָאתָ֑יִם וּקְנֵה־בֹ֖שֶׂם חֲמִשִּׁ֥ים
וּמָאתָֽיִם: 24 וְקִדָּ֕ה חֲמֵ֥שׁ מֵא֖וֹת בְּשֶׁ֣קֶל הַקֹּ֑דֶשׁ
וְשֶׁ֥מֶן זַ֖יִת הִֽין: 25 וְעָשִׂ֣יתָ אֹת֗וֹ שֶׁ֚מֶן מִשְׁחַת־
קֹ֔דֶשׁ רֹ֖קַח מִרְקַ֣חַת מַעֲשֵׂ֣ה רֹקֵ֑חַ שֶׁ֥מֶן מִשְׁחַת־
קֹ֖דֶשׁ יִהְיֶֽה: 26 וּמָשַׁחְתָּ֥ ב֖וֹ אֶת־אֹ֣הֶל מוֹעֵ֑ד וְאֵ֖ת
אֲר֥וֹן הָעֵדֻֽת: 27 וְאֶת־הַשֻּׁלְחָן֙ וְאֶת־כׇּל־כֵּלָ֔יו וְאֶת־
הַמְּנֹרָ֖ה וְאֶת־כֵּלֶ֑יהָ וְאֵ֖ת מִזְבַּ֥ח הַקְּטֹֽרֶת: 28 וְאֶת־
מִזְבַּ֤ח הָֽעֹלָה֙ וְאֶת־כׇּל־כֵּלָ֔יו וְאֶת־הַכִּיֹּ֖ר וְאֶת־כַּנּֽוֹ:

29 וְקִדַּשְׁתָּ֣ אֹתָ֔ם וְהָי֖וּ קֹ֣דֶשׁ קׇֽדָשִׁ֑ים כׇּל־הַנֹּגֵ֥עַ בָּהֶ֖ם
יִקְדָּֽשׁ: 30 וְאֶת־אַהֲרֹ֥ן וְאֶת־בָּנָ֖יו תִּמְשָׁ֑ח וְקִדַּשְׁתָּ֥
אֹתָ֖ם לְכַהֵ֥ן לִֽי: 31 וְאֶל־בְּנֵ֥י יִשְׂרָאֵ֖ל תְּדַבֵּ֣ר לֵאמֹ֑ר
שֶׁ֠מֶן מִשְׁחַת־קֹ֨דֶשׁ יִהְיֶ֥ה זֶ֛ה לִ֖י לְדֹרֹתֵיכֶֽם: 32 עַל־

בְּשַׂ֤ר אָדָם֙ לֹ֣א יִיסָ֔ךְ וּבְמַ֨תְכֻּנְתּ֔וֹ לֹ֥א תַעֲשׂ֖וּ כָּמֹ֑הוּ
קֹ֣דֶשׁ ה֔וּא קֹ֖דֶשׁ יִהְיֶ֥ה לָכֶֽם: 33 אִ֚ישׁ אֲשֶׁ֣ר יִרְקַ֣ח
כָּמֹ֔הוּ וַאֲשֶׁ֥ר יִתֵּ֛ן מִמֶּ֖נּוּ עַל־זָ֑ר וְנִכְרַ֖ת מֵֽעַמָּֽיו: ס

34 וַיֹּ֩אמֶר֩ יְהֹוָ֨ה אֶל־מֹשֶׁ֜ה קַח־לְךָ֣ סַמִּ֗ים נָטָ֤ף ׀
וּשְׁחֵ֙לֶת֙ וְחֶלְבְּנָ֔ה סַמִּ֖ים וּלְבֹנָ֣ה זַכָּ֑ה בַּ֥ד בְּבַ֖ד
יִהְיֶֽה: 35 וְעָשִׂ֤יתָ אֹתָהּ֙ קְטֹ֔רֶת רֹ֖קַח מַעֲשֵׂ֣ה רוֹקֵ֑חַ
מְמֻלָּ֖ח טָה֥וֹר קֹֽדֶשׁ: 36 וְשָֽׁחַקְתָּ֣ מִמֶּ֘נָּה֘ הָדֵק֒ וְנָתַתָּ֨ה
מִמֶּ֜נָּה לִפְנֵ֤י הָעֵדֻת֙ בְּאֹ֣הֶל מוֹעֵ֔ד אֲשֶׁ֛ר אִוָּעֵ֥ד לְךָ֖
שָׁ֑מָּה קֹ֥דֶשׁ קׇֽדָשִׁ֖ים תִּהְיֶ֥ה לָכֶֽם: 37 וְהַקְּטֹ֙רֶת֙ אֲשֶׁ֣ר
תַּעֲשֶׂ֔ה בְּמַ֨תְכֻּנְתָּ֔הּ לֹ֥א תַעֲשׂ֖וּ לָכֶ֑ם קֹ֚דֶשׁ תִּהְיֶ֥ה

composition. It shall be to you holy for the LORD. ³⁸Whoever makes *any* like it, to smell it, he shall be cut off from his people."

31 Then the LORD spoke to Moses, saying: ²"See, I have called by name Bezalel the son of Uri, the son of Hur, of the tribe of Judah. ³And I have filled him with the Spirit of God, in wisdom, in understanding, in knowledge, and in all *manner of* workmanship, ⁴to design artistic works, to work in gold, in silver, in bronze, ⁵in cutting jewels for setting, in carving wood, and to work in all *manner of* workmanship.

⁶"And I, indeed I, have appointed with him Aholiab the son of Ahisamach, of the tribe of Dan; and I have put wisdom in the hearts of all the gifted artisans, that they may make all that I have commanded you: ⁷the tabernacle of meeting, the ark of the Testimony and the mercy seat that *is* on it, and all the furniture of the tabernacle— ⁸the table and its utensils, the pure *gold* lampstand with all its utensils, the altar of incense, ⁹the altar of burnt offering with all its utensils, and the laver and its base— ¹⁰the garments of ministry, the holy garments for Aaron the priest and the garments of his sons, to minister as priests, ¹¹and the anointing oil and sweet incense for the holy *place*. According to all that I have commanded you they shall do."

¹²And the LORD spoke to Moses, saying, ¹³"Speak also to the children of Israel, saying: 'Surely My Sabbaths you shall keep, for it *is* a sign between Me and you throughout your generations, that *you* may know that I *am* the LORD who sanctifies you. ¹⁴You shall keep the Sabbath, therefore, for *it is* holy to you. Everyone who profanes it shall surely be put to death; for whoever does *any* work on it, that person shall be cut off from among his people. ¹⁵Work shall be done for six days, but the seventh *is* the Sabbath of rest, holy to the LORD. Whoever does *any* work on the Sabbath day, he shall surely be put to death. ¹⁶Therefore the children of Israel shall keep the Sabbath, to observe the Sabbath throughout their generations *as* a perpetual covenant. ¹⁷It *is* a sign between Me and the children of Israel forever; for *in* six days the LORD made the heavens and the earth, and on the seventh day He rested and was refreshed.'"

¹⁸And when He had made an end of speaking with him on Mount Sinai, He gave Moses two tablets of the Testimony, tablets of stone, written with the finger of God.

לְךָ לַיהֹוָה: 38 אִישׁ אֲשֶׁר־יַעֲשֶׂה כָמֹוהָ לְהָרִיחַ בָּהּ וְנִכְרַת מֵעַמָּיו: ס

לא וַיְדַבֵּר יְהֹוָה אֶל־מֹשֶׁה לֵּאמֹר: 2 רְאֵה קָרָאתִי בְשֵׁם בְּצַלְאֵל בֶּן־אוּרִי בֶן־חוּר לְמַטֵּה יְהוּדָה: 3 וָאֲמַלֵּא אֹתֹו רוּחַ אֱלֹהִים בְּחָכְמָה וּבִתְבוּנָה וּבְדַעַת וּבְכָל־מְלָאכָה: 4 לַחְשֹׁב מַחֲשָׁבֹת לַעֲשֹׂות בַּזָּהָב וּבַכֶּסֶף וּבַנְּחֹשֶׁת: 5 וּבַחֲרֹשֶׁת אֶבֶן לְמַלֹּאת וּבַחֲרֹשֶׁת עֵץ לַעֲשֹׂות בְּכָל־מְלָאכָה: 6 וַאֲנִי הִנֵּה נָתַתִּי אִתֹּו אֵת אָהֳלִיאָב בֶּן־אֲחִיסָמָךְ לְמַטֵּה־דָן וּבְלֵב כָּל־חֲכַם־לֵב נָתַתִּי חָכְמָה וְעָשׂוּ אֵת כָּל־אֲשֶׁר צִוִּיתִךָ: 7 אֵת | אֹהֶל מֹועֵד וְאֶת־הָאָרֹן לָעֵדֻת וְאֶת־הַכַּפֹּרֶת אֲשֶׁר עָלָיו וְאֵת כָּל־כְּלֵי הָאֹהֶל: 8 וְאֶת־הַשֻּׁלְחָן וְאֶת־כֵּלָיו וְאֶת־הַמְּנֹרָה הַטְּהֹרָה וְאֶת־כָּל־כֵּלֶיהָ וְאֵת מִזְבַּח הַקְּטֹרֶת: 9 וְאֶת־מִזְבַּח הָעֹלָה וְאֶת־כָּל־כֵּלָיו וְאֶת־הַכִּיֹּור וְאֶת־כַּנֹּו: 10 וְאֵת בִּגְדֵי הַשְּׂרָד וְאֶת־בִּגְדֵי הַקֹּדֶשׁ לְאַהֲרֹן הַכֹּהֵן וְאֶת־בִּגְדֵי בָנָיו לְכַהֵן: 11 וְאֵת שֶׁמֶן הַמִּשְׁחָה וְאֶת־קְטֹרֶת הַסַּמִּים לַקֹּדֶשׁ כְּכֹל אֲשֶׁר־צִוִּיתִךָ יַעֲשׂוּ: פ

12 וַיֹּאמֶר יְהֹוָה אֶל־מֹשֶׁה לֵּאמֹר: 13 וְאַתָּה דַּבֵּר אֶל־בְּנֵי יִשְׂרָאֵל לֵאמֹר אַךְ אֶת־שַׁבְּתֹתַי תִּשְׁמֹרוּ כִּי אֹות הִוא בֵּינִי וּבֵינֵיכֶם לְדֹרֹתֵיכֶם לָדַעַת כִּי אֲנִי יְהֹוָה מְקַדִּשְׁכֶם: 14 וּשְׁמַרְתֶּם אֶת־הַשַּׁבָּת כִּי קֹדֶשׁ הִוא לָכֶם מְחַלְלֶיהָ מֹות יוּמָת כִּי כָּל־הָעֹשֶׂה בָהּ מְלָאכָה וְנִכְרְתָה הַנֶּפֶשׁ הַהִוא מִקֶּרֶב עַמֶּיהָ: 15 שֵׁשֶׁת יָמִים יֵעָשֶׂה מְלָאכָה וּבַיֹּום הַשְּׁבִיעִי שַׁבַּת שַׁבָּתֹון קֹדֶשׁ לַיהֹוָה כָּל־הָעֹשֶׂה מְלָאכָה בְּיֹום הַשַּׁבָּת מֹות יוּמָת: 16 וְשָׁמְרוּ בְנֵי־יִשְׂרָאֵל אֶת־הַשַּׁבָּת לַעֲשֹׂות אֶת־הַשַּׁבָּת לְדֹרֹתָם בְּרִית עֹולָם: 17 בֵּינִי וּבֵין בְּנֵי יִשְׂרָאֵל אֹות הִוא לְעֹלָם כִּי־שֵׁשֶׁת יָמִים עָשָׂה יְהֹוָה אֶת־הַשָּׁמַיִם וְאֶת־הָאָרֶץ וּבַיֹּום הַשְּׁבִיעִי שָׁבַת וַיִּנָּפַשׁ: ס 18 וַיִּתֵּן אֶל־מֹשֶׁה כְּכַלֹּתֹו לְדַבֵּר אִתֹּו בְּהַר סִינַי שְׁנֵי לֻחֹת הָעֵדֻת לֻחֹת אֶבֶן כְּתֻבִים בְּאֶצְבַּע אֱלֹהִים:

32 Now when the people saw that Moses delayed coming down from the mountain, the people gathered together to Aaron, and said to him, "Come, make us gods that shall go before us; for *as for* this Moses, the man who brought us up out of the land of Egypt, we do not know what has become of him."

² And Aaron said to them, "Break off the golden earrings which *are* in the ears of your wives, your sons, and your daughters, and bring *them* to me." ³ So all the people broke off the golden earrings which *were* in their ears, and brought *them* to Aaron. ⁴ And he received *the gold* from their hand, and he fashioned it with an engraving tool, and made a molded calf.

Then they said, "This *is* your god, O Israel, that brought you out of the land of Egypt!"

⁵ So when Aaron saw *it,* he built an altar before it. And Aaron made a proclamation and said, "Tomorrow *is* a feast to the LORD." ⁶ Then they rose early on the next day, offered burnt offerings, and brought peace offerings; and the people sat down to eat and drink, and rose up to play.

⁷ And the LORD said to Moses, "Go, get down! For your people whom you brought out of the land of Egypt have corrupted *themselves.* ⁸ They have turned aside quickly out of the way which I commanded them. They have made themselves a molded calf, and worshiped it and sacrificed to it, and said, 'This *is* your god, O Israel, that brought you out of the land of Egypt!' " ⁹ And the LORD said to Moses, "I have seen this people, and indeed it *is* a stiff-necked people! ¹⁰ Now therefore, let Me alone, that My wrath may burn hot against them and I may consume them. And I will make of you a great nation."

¹¹ Then Moses pleaded with the LORD his God, and said: "LORD, why does Your wrath burn hot against Your people whom You have brought out of the land of Egypt with great power and with a mighty hand? ¹² Why should the Egyptians speak, and say, 'He brought them out to harm them, to kill them in the mountains, and to consume them from the face of the earth'? Turn from Your fierce wrath, and relent from this harm to Your people. ¹³ Remember Abraham, Isaac, and Israel, Your servants, to whom You swore by Your own self, and said to them, 'I will multiply your descendants as the stars of heaven; and all this land that I have spoken of I give to your descendants, and they shall inherit *it* forever.' " ¹⁴ So the LORD relented from the harm which He said He would do to His people.

לב וַיַּרְא הָעָם כִּי־בֹשֵׁשׁ מֹשֶׁה לָרֶדֶת מִן־הָהָר
וַיִּקָּהֵל הָעָם עַל־אַהֲרֹן וַיֹּאמְרוּ אֵלָיו קוּם ׀ עֲשֵׂה־
לָּנוּ אֱלֹהִים אֲשֶׁר יֵלְכוּ לְפָנֵינוּ כִּי־זֶה ׀ מֹשֶׁה
הָאִישׁ אֲשֶׁר הֶעֱלָנוּ מֵאֶרֶץ מִצְרַיִם לֹא יָדַעְנוּ מֶה־
הָיָה לוֹ: ² וַיֹּאמֶר אֲלֵהֶם אַהֲרֹן פָּרְקוּ נִזְמֵי הַזָּהָב
אֲשֶׁר בְּאָזְנֵי נְשֵׁיכֶם בְּנֵיכֶם וּבְנֹתֵיכֶם וְהָבִיאוּ אֵלָי:
³ וַיִּתְפָּרְקוּ כָּל־הָעָם אֶת־נִזְמֵי הַזָּהָב אֲשֶׁר בְּאָזְנֵיהֶם
וַיָּבִיאוּ אֶל־אַהֲרֹן: ⁴ וַיִּקַּח מִיָּדָם וַיָּצַר אֹתוֹ בַּחֶרֶט
וַיַּעֲשֵׂהוּ עֵגֶל מַסֵּכָה וַיֹּאמְרוּ אֵלֶּה אֱלֹהֶיךָ יִשְׂרָאֵל
אֲשֶׁר הֶעֱלוּךָ מֵאֶרֶץ מִצְרָיִם: ⁵ וַיַּרְא אַהֲרֹן וַיִּבֶן
מִזְבֵּחַ לְפָנָיו וַיִּקְרָא אַהֲרֹן וַיֹּאמַר חַג לַיהֹוָה מָחָר:
⁶ וַיַּשְׁכִּימוּ מִמָּחֳרָת וַיַּעֲלוּ עֹלֹת וַיַּגִּשׁוּ שְׁלָמִים וַיֵּשֶׁב
הָעָם לֶאֱכֹל וְשָׁתוֹ וַיָּקֻמוּ לְצַחֵק:
פ

⁷ וַיְדַבֵּר יְהֹוָה אֶל־מֹשֶׁה לֶךְ־רֵד כִּי שִׁחֵת עַמְּךָ
אֲשֶׁר הֶעֱלֵיתָ מֵאֶרֶץ מִצְרָיִם: ⁸ סָרוּ מַהֵר מִן־הַדֶּרֶךְ
אֲשֶׁר צִוִּיתִם עָשׂוּ לָהֶם עֵגֶל מַסֵּכָה וַיִּשְׁתַּחֲווּ־
לוֹ וַיִּזְבְּחוּ־לוֹ וַיֹּאמְרוּ אֵלֶּה אֱלֹהֶיךָ יִשְׂרָאֵל אֲשֶׁר
הֶעֱלוּךָ מֵאֶרֶץ מִצְרָיִם: ⁹ וַיֹּאמֶר יְהֹוָה אֶל־מֹשֶׁה
רָאִיתִי אֶת־הָעָם הַזֶּה וְהִנֵּה עַם־קְשֵׁה־עֹרֶף הוּא:
¹⁰ וְעַתָּה הַנִּיחָה לִּי וְיִחַר־אַפִּי בָהֶם וַאֲכַלֵּם וְאֶעֱשֶׂה
אוֹתְךָ לְגוֹי גָּדוֹל: ¹¹ וַיְחַל מֹשֶׁה אֶת־פְּנֵי יְהֹוָה
אֱלֹהָיו וַיֹּאמֶר לָמָה יְהֹוָה יֶחֱרֶה אַפְּךָ בְּעַמֶּךָ אֲשֶׁר
הוֹצֵאתָ מֵאֶרֶץ מִצְרַיִם בְּכֹחַ גָּדוֹל וּבְיָד חֲזָקָה:
¹² לָמָּה יֹאמְרוּ מִצְרַיִם לֵאמֹר בְּרָעָה הוֹצִיאָם
לַהֲרֹג אֹתָם בֶּהָרִים וּלְכַלֹּתָם מֵעַל פְּנֵי הָאֲדָמָה
שׁוּב מֵחֲרוֹן אַפֶּךָ וְהִנָּחֵם עַל־הָרָעָה לְעַמֶּךָ: ¹³ זְכֹר
לְאַבְרָהָם לְיִצְחָק וּלְיִשְׂרָאֵל עֲבָדֶיךָ אֲשֶׁר נִשְׁבַּעְתָּ
לָהֶם בָּךְ וַתְּדַבֵּר אֲלֵהֶם אַרְבֶּה אֶת־זַרְעֲכֶם כְּכוֹכְבֵי
הַשָּׁמָיִם וְכָל־הָאָרֶץ הַזֹּאת אֲשֶׁר אָמַרְתִּי אֶתֵּן
לְזַרְעֲכֶם וְנָחֲלוּ לְעֹלָם: ¹⁴ וַיִּנָּחֶם יְהֹוָה עַל־הָרָעָה
אֲשֶׁר דִּבֶּר לַעֲשׂוֹת לְעַמּוֹ:
פ

15 And Moses turned and went down from the mountain, and the two tablets of the Testimony *were* in his hand. The tablets *were* written on both sides; on the one *side* and on the other they were written. 16 Now the tablets *were* the work of God, and the writing *was* the writing of God engraved on the tablets.

17 And when Joshua heard the noise of the people as they shouted, he said to Moses, "*There is* a noise of war in the camp."

18 But he said:

"*It is* not the noise of the shout of victory,
Nor the noise of the cry of defeat,
But the sound of singing I hear."

19 So it was, as soon as he came near the camp, that he saw the calf *and* the dancing. So Moses' anger became hot, and he cast the tablets out of his hands and broke them at the foot of the mountain. 20 Then he took the calf which they had made, burned *it* in the fire, and ground *it* to powder; and he scattered *it* on the water and made the children of Israel drink *it*. 21 And Moses said to Aaron, "What did this people do to you that you have brought *so* great a sin upon them?"

22 So Aaron said, "Do not let the anger of my lord become hot. You know the people, that they *are set* on evil. 23 For they said to me, 'Make us gods that shall go before us; *as for* this Moses, the man who brought us out of the land of Egypt, we do not know what has become of him.' 24 And I said to them, 'Whoever has any gold, let them break *it* off.' So they gave *it* to me, and I cast it into the fire, and this calf came out."

25 Now when Moses saw that the people *were* unrestrained (for Aaron had not restrained them, to *their* shame among their enemies), 26 then Moses stood in the entrance of the camp, and said, "Whoever *is* on the LORD's side—*come* to me!" And all the sons of Levi gathered themselves together to him. 27 And he said to them, "Thus says the LORD God of Israel: 'Let every man put his sword on his side, and go in and out from entrance to entrance throughout the camp, and let every man kill his brother, every man his companion, and every man his neighbor.' " 28 So the sons of Levi did according to the word of Moses. And about three thousand men of the people fell that day. 29 Then Moses said, "Consecrate yourselves today to the LORD, that He may bestow on you a blessing this day, for every man has opposed his son and his brother."

15 וַיִּ֜פֶן וַיֵּ֤רֶד מֹשֶׁה֙ מִן־הָהָ֔ר וּשְׁנֵ֛י לֻחֹ֥ת הָעֵדֻ֖ת בְּיָד֑וֹ לֻחֹ֗ת כְּתֻבִים֙ מִשְּׁנֵ֣י עֶבְרֵיהֶ֔ם מִזֶּ֥ה וּמִזֶּ֖ה הֵ֥ם כְּתֻבִֽים׃ 16 וְהַ֨לֻּחֹ֔ת מַעֲשֵׂ֥ה אֱלֹהִ֖ים הֵ֑מָּה וְהַמִּכְתָּ֗ב מִכְתַּ֤ב אֱלֹהִים֙ ה֔וּא חָר֖וּת עַל־הַלֻּחֹֽת׃ 17 וַיִּשְׁמַ֧ע יְהוֹשֻׁ֛עַ אֶת־ק֥וֹל הָעָ֖ם בְּרֵעֹ֑ה וַיֹּ֙אמֶר֙ אֶל־מֹשֶׁ֔ה ק֥וֹל מִלְחָמָ֖ה בַּֽמַּחֲנֶֽה׃ 18 וַיֹּ֗אמֶר אֵ֥ין קוֹל֙ עֲנ֣וֹת גְּבוּרָ֔ה וְאֵ֥ין ק֖וֹל עֲנ֣וֹת חֲלוּשָׁ֑ה ק֣וֹל עַנּ֔וֹת אָנֹכִ֖י שֹׁמֵֽעַ׃ 19 וַֽיְהִ֗י כַּאֲשֶׁ֤ר קָרַב֙ אֶל־הַֽמַּחֲנֶ֔ה וַיַּ֥רְא אֶת־הָעֵ֖גֶל וּמְחֹלֹ֑ת וַיִּֽחַר־אַ֣ף מֹשֶׁ֗ה וַיַּשְׁלֵ֤ךְ מִיָּדָו֙ אֶת־הַלֻּחֹ֔ת וַיְשַׁבֵּ֥ר אֹתָ֖ם תַּ֥חַת הָהָֽר׃ 20 וַיִּקַּ֞ח אֶת־הָעֵ֣גֶל אֲשֶׁ֣ר עָשׂ֗וּ וַיִּשְׂרֹ֤ף בָּאֵשׁ֙ וַיִּטְחַ֣ן עַ֣ד אֲשֶׁר־דָּ֔ק וַיִּ֙זֶר֙ עַל־פְּנֵ֣י הַמַּ֔יִם וַיַּ֖שְׁקְ אֶת־בְּנֵ֥י יִשְׂרָאֵֽל׃ 21 וַיֹּ֤אמֶר מֹשֶׁה֙ אֶֽל־אַהֲרֹ֔ן מֶֽה־עָשָׂ֥ה לְךָ֖ הָעָ֣ם הַזֶּ֑ה כִּֽי־הֵבֵ֥אתָ עָלָ֖יו חֲטָאָ֥ה גְדֹלָֽה׃ 22 וַיֹּ֣אמֶר אַהֲרֹ֔ן אַל־יִ֥חַר אַ֣ף אֲדֹנִ֑י אַתָּה֙ יָדַ֣עְתָּ אֶת־הָעָ֔ם כִּ֥י בְרָ֖ע הֽוּא׃ 23 וַיֹּ֣אמְרוּ לִ֔י עֲשֵׂה־לָ֣נוּ אֱלֹהִ֔ים אֲשֶׁ֥ר יֵלְכ֖וּ לְפָנֵ֑ינוּ כִּי־זֶ֣ה ׀ מֹשֶׁ֣ה הָאִ֗ישׁ אֲשֶׁ֤ר הֶֽעֱלָ֙נוּ֙ מֵאֶ֣רֶץ מִצְרַ֔יִם לֹ֥א יָדַ֖עְנוּ מֶה־הָ֥יָה לֽוֹ׃ 24 וָאֹמַ֤ר לָהֶם֙ לְמִ֣י זָהָ֔ב הִתְפָּרָ֖קוּ וַיִּתְּנוּ־לִ֑י וָאַשְׁלִכֵ֣הוּ בָאֵ֔שׁ וַיֵּצֵ֖א הָעֵ֥גֶל הַזֶּֽה׃ 25 וַיַּ֤רְא מֹשֶׁה֙ אֶת־הָעָ֔ם כִּ֥י פָרֻ֖עַ ה֑וּא כִּֽי־פְרָעֹ֣ה אַהֲרֹ֔ן לְשִׁמְצָ֖ה בְּקָמֵיהֶֽם׃ 26 וַיַּעֲמֹ֤ד מֹשֶׁה֙ בְּשַׁ֣עַר הַֽמַּחֲנֶ֔ה וַיֹּ֕אמֶר מִ֥י לַיהוָ֖ה אֵלָ֑י וַיֵּאָסְפ֥וּ אֵלָ֖יו כָּל־בְּנֵ֥י לֵוִֽי׃ 27 וַיֹּ֣אמֶר לָהֶ֗ם כֹּֽה־אָמַ֤ר יְהוָה֙ אֱלֹהֵ֣י יִשְׂרָאֵ֔ל שִׂ֥ימוּ אִישׁ־חַרְבּ֖וֹ עַל־יְרֵכ֑וֹ עִבְר֨וּ וָשׁ֜וּבוּ מִשַּׁ֤עַר לָשַׁ֙עַר֙ בַּֽמַּחֲנֶ֔ה וְהִרְג֧וּ אִֽישׁ־אֶת־אָחִ֛יו וְאִ֥ישׁ אֶת־רֵעֵ֖הוּ וְאִ֥ישׁ אֶת־קְרֹבֽוֹ׃ 28 וַֽיַּעֲשׂ֥וּ בְנֵֽי־לֵוִ֖י כִּדְבַ֣ר מֹשֶׁ֑ה וַיִּפֹּ֤ל מִן־הָעָם֙ בַּיּ֣וֹם הַה֔וּא כִּשְׁלֹ֥שֶׁת אַלְפֵ֖י אִֽישׁ׃ 29 וַיֹּ֣אמֶר מֹשֶׁ֗ה מִלְא֨וּ יֶדְכֶ֤ם הַיּוֹם֙ לַֽיהוָ֔ה כִּ֣י אִ֥ישׁ בִּבְנ֖וֹ וּבְאָחִ֑יו וְלָתֵ֧ת עֲלֵיכֶ֛ם

³⁰Now it came to pass on the next day that Moses said to the people, "You have committed a great sin. So now I will go up to the LORD; perhaps I can make atonement for your sin." ³¹Then Moses returned to the LORD and said, "Oh, these people have committed a great sin, and have made for themselves a god of gold! ³²Yet now, if You will forgive their sin—but if not, I pray, blot me out of Your book which You have written."

³³And the LORD said to Moses, "Whoever has sinned against Me, I will blot him out of My book. ³⁴Now therefore, go, lead the people to *the place* of which I have spoken to you. Behold, My Angel shall go before you. Nevertheless, in the day when I visit for punishment, I will visit punishment upon them for their sin."

³⁵So the LORD plagued the people because of what they did with the calf which Aaron made.

33 Then the LORD said to Moses, "Depart *and* go up from here, you and the people whom you have brought out of the land of Egypt, to the land of which I swore to Abraham, Isaac, and Jacob, saying, 'To your descendants I will give it.' ²And I will send *My* Angel before you, and I will drive out the Canaanite and the Amorite and the Hittite and the Perizzite and the Hivite and the Jebusite. ³*Go up* to a land flowing with milk and honey; for I will not go up in your midst, lest I consume you on the way, for you *are* a stiff-necked people."

⁴And when the people heard this bad news, they mourned, and no one put on his ornaments. ⁵For the LORD had said to Moses, "Say to the children of Israel, 'You *are* a stiff-necked people. I could come up into your midst in one moment and consume you. Now therefore, take off your ornaments, that I may know what to do to you.'" ⁶So the children of Israel stripped themselves of their ornaments by Mount Horeb.

⁷Moses took his tent and pitched it outside the camp, far from the camp, and called it the tabernacle of meeting. And it came to pass *that* everyone who sought the LORD went out to the tabernacle of meeting which *was* outside the camp. ⁸So it was, whenever Moses went out to the tabernacle, *that* all the people rose, and each man stood *at* his tent door and watched Moses until he had gone into the tabernacle. ⁹And it came to pass, when Moses entered the tabernacle, that the pillar of cloud descended and stood *at* the door of the tabernacle, and *the LORD* talked with Moses. ¹⁰All the people saw the pillar of cloud standing *at* the tabernacle door, and all the people rose and worshiped, each man *in* his tent door. ¹¹So the

הַיּוֹם בְּרָכָה: 30 וַיְהִי מִמָּחֳרָת וַיֹּאמֶר מֹשֶׁה אֶל־הָעָם אַתֶּם חֲטָאתֶם חֲטָאָה גְדֹלָה וְעַתָּה אֶעֱלֶה אֶל־יְהוָה אוּלַי אֲכַפְּרָה בְּעַד חַטַּאתְכֶם: 31 וַיָּשָׁב מֹשֶׁה אֶל־יְהוָה וַיֹּאמַר אָנָּא חָטָא הָעָם הַזֶּה חֲטָאָה גְדֹלָה וַיַּעֲשׂוּ לָהֶם אֱלֹהֵי זָהָב: 32 וְעַתָּה אִם־תִּשָּׂא חַטָּאתָם וְאִם־אַיִן מְחֵנִי נָא מִסִּפְרְךָ אֲשֶׁר כָּתָבְתָּ: 33 וַיֹּאמֶר יְהוָה אֶל־מֹשֶׁה מִי אֲשֶׁר חָטָא־לִי אֶמְחֶנּוּ מִסִּפְרִי: 34 וְעַתָּה לֵךְ נְחֵה אֶת־הָעָם אֶל אֲשֶׁר־דִּבַּרְתִּי לָךְ הִנֵּה מַלְאָכִי יֵלֵךְ לְפָנֶיךָ וּבְיוֹם פָּקְדִי וּפָקַדְתִּי עֲלֵיהֶם חַטָּאתָם: 35 וַיִּגֹּף יְהוָה אֶת־הָעָם עַל אֲשֶׁר עָשׂוּ אֶת־הָעֵגֶל אֲשֶׁר עָשָׂה אַהֲרֹן: ס

לג וַיְדַבֵּר יְהוָה אֶל־מֹשֶׁה לֵךְ עֲלֵה מִזֶּה אַתָּה וְהָעָם אֲשֶׁר הֶעֱלִיתָ מֵאֶרֶץ מִצְרָיִם אֶל־הָאָרֶץ אֲשֶׁר נִשְׁבַּעְתִּי לְאַבְרָהָם לְיִצְחָק וּלְיַעֲקֹב לֵאמֹר לְזַרְעֲךָ אֶתְּנֶנָּה: 2 וְשָׁלַחְתִּי לְפָנֶיךָ מַלְאָךְ וְגֵרַשְׁתִּי אֶת־הַכְּנַעֲנִי הָאֱמֹרִי וְהַחִתִּי וְהַפְּרִזִּי הַחִוִּי וְהַיְבוּסִי: 3 אֶל־אֶרֶץ זָבַת חָלָב וּדְבָשׁ כִּי לֹא אֶעֱלֶה בְּקִרְבְּךָ כִּי עַם־קְשֵׁה־עֹרֶף אַתָּה פֶּן־אֲכֶלְךָ בַּדָּרֶךְ: 4 וַיִּשְׁמַע הָעָם אֶת־הַדָּבָר הָרָע הַזֶּה וַיִּתְאַבָּלוּ וְלֹא־שָׁתוּ אִישׁ עֶדְיוֹ עָלָיו: 5 וַיֹּאמֶר יְהוָה אֶל־מֹשֶׁה אֱמֹר אֶל־בְּנֵי־יִשְׂרָאֵל אַתֶּם עַם־קְשֵׁה־עֹרֶף רֶגַע אֶחָד אֶעֱלֶה בְקִרְבְּךָ וְכִלִּיתִיךָ וְעַתָּה הוֹרֵד עֶדְיְךָ מֵעָלֶיךָ וְאֵדְעָה מָה אֶעֱשֶׂה־לָּךְ: 6 וַיִּתְנַצְּלוּ בְנֵי־יִשְׂרָאֵל אֶת־עֶדְיָם מֵהַר חוֹרֵב: 7 וּמֹשֶׁה יִקַּח אֶת־הָאֹהֶל וְנָטָה־לוֹ מִחוּץ לַמַּחֲנֶה הַרְחֵק מִן־הַמַּחֲנֶה וְקָרָא לוֹ אֹהֶל מוֹעֵד וְהָיָה כָּל־מְבַקֵּשׁ יְהוָה יֵצֵא אֶל־אֹהֶל מוֹעֵד אֲשֶׁר מִחוּץ לַמַּחֲנֶה: 8 וְהָיָה כְּצֵאת מֹשֶׁה אֶל־הָאֹהֶל יָקוּמוּ כָּל־הָעָם וְנִצְּבוּ אִישׁ פֶּתַח אָהֳלוֹ וְהִבִּיטוּ אַחֲרֵי מֹשֶׁה עַד־בֹּאוֹ הָאֹהֱלָה: 9 וְהָיָה כְּבֹא מֹשֶׁה הָאֹהֱלָה יֵרֵד עַמּוּד הֶעָנָן וְעָמַד פֶּתַח הָאֹהֶל וְדִבֶּר עִם־מֹשֶׁה: 10 וְרָאָה כָל־הָעָם אֶת־עַמּוּד הֶעָנָן עֹמֵד פֶּתַח הָאֹהֶל וְקָם כָּל־הָעָם וְהִשְׁתַּחֲווּ אִישׁ פֶּתַח אָהֳלוֹ: 11 וְדִבֶּר יְהוָה אֶל־מֹשֶׁה פָּנִים אֶל־פָּנִים כַּאֲשֶׁר יְדַבֵּר אִישׁ אֶל־רֵעֵהוּ

LORD spoke to Moses face to face, as a man speaks to his friend. And he would return to the camp, but his servant Joshua the son of Nun, a young man, did not depart from the tabernacle.

12 Then Moses said to the LORD, "See, You say to me, 'Bring up this people.' But You have not let me know whom You will send with me. Yet You have said, 'I know you by name, and you have also found grace in My sight.' 13 Now therefore, I pray, if I have found grace in Your sight, show me now Your way, that I may know You and that I may find grace in Your sight. And consider that this nation *is* Your people."

14 And He said, "My Presence will go *with you,* and I will give you rest."

15 Then he said to Him, "If Your Presence does not go *with us,* do not bring us up from here. 16 For how then will it be known that Your people and I have found grace in Your sight, except You go with us? So we shall be separate, Your people and I, from all the people who *are* upon the face of the earth."

17 So the LORD said to Moses, "I will also do this thing that you have spoken; for you have found grace in My sight, and I know you by name."

18 And he said, "Please, show me Your glory."

19 Then He said, "I will make all My goodness pass before you, and I will proclaim the name of the LORD before you. I will be gracious to whom I will be gracious, and I will have compassion on whom I will have compassion." 20 But He said, "You cannot see My face; for no man shall see Me, and live." 21 And the LORD said, "Here is a place by Me, and you shall stand on the rock. 22 So it shall be, while My glory passes by, that I will put you in the cleft of the rock, and will cover you with My hand while I pass by. 23 Then I will take away My hand, and you shall see My back; but My face shall not be seen."

34 And the LORD said to Moses, "Cut two tablets of stone like the first *ones,* and I will write on *these* tablets the words that were on the first tablets which you broke. 2 So be ready in the morning, and come up in the morning to Mount Sinai, and present yourself to Me there on the top of the mountain. 3 And no man shall come up with you, and let no man be seen throughout all the mountain; let neither flocks nor herds feed before that mountain."

4 So he cut two tablets of stone like the first *ones.* Then Moses rose early in the morning and went up Mount Sinai, as the LORD had commanded him; and he took in his hand the two tablets of stone.

וְשָׁב֙ אֶל־הַֽמַּחֲנֶ֔ה וּמְשָׁ֨רְת֜וֹ יְהוֹשֻׁ֤עַ בִּן־נוּן֙ נַ֔עַר לֹ֥א יָמִ֖ישׁ מִתּ֥וֹךְ הָאֹֽהֶל׃ ס 12 וַיֹּ֨אמֶר מֹשֶׁ֜ה אֶל־יְהֹוָ֗ה רְ֠אֵה אַתָּ֞ה אֹמֵ֤ר אֵלַי֙ הַ֚עַל אֶת־הָעָ֣ם הַזֶּ֔ה וְאַתָּה֙ לֹ֣א הֽוֹדַעְתַּ֔נִי אֵ֥ת אֲשֶׁר־תִּשְׁלַ֖ח עִמִּ֑י וְאַתָּ֤ה אָמַ֨רְתָּ֙ יְדַעְתִּ֣יךָֽ בְשֵׁ֔ם וְגַם־מָצָ֥אתָ חֵ֖ן בְּעֵינָֽי׃ 13 וְעַתָּ֡ה אִם־נָא֩ מָצָ֨אתִי חֵ֜ן בְּעֵינֶ֗יךָ הוֹדִעֵ֤נִי נָא֙ אֶת־דְּרָכֶ֔ךָ וְאֵדָ֣עֲךָ֔ לְמַ֥עַן אֶמְצָא־חֵ֖ן בְּעֵינֶ֑יךָ וּרְאֵ֕ה כִּ֥י עַמְּךָ֖ הַגּ֥וֹי הַזֶּֽה׃ 14 וַיֹּאמַ֑ר פָּנַ֥י יֵלֵ֖כוּ וַהֲנִחֹ֥תִי לָֽךְ׃ 15 וַיֹּ֖אמֶר אֵלָ֑יו אִם־אֵ֤ין פָּנֶ֨יךָ֙ הֹֽלְכִ֔ים אַֽל־תַּעֲלֵ֖נוּ מִזֶּֽה׃ 16 וּבַמֶּ֣ה ׀ יִוָּדַ֣ע אֵפ֗וֹא כִּֽי־מָצָ֨אתִי חֵ֤ן בְּעֵינֶ֨יךָ֙ אֲנִ֣י וְעַמֶּ֔ךָ הֲל֖וֹא בְּלֶכְתְּךָ֣ עִמָּ֑נוּ וְנִפְלֵ֨ינוּ֙ אֲנִ֣י וְעַמְּךָ֔ מִכָּ֨ל־הָעָ֔ם אֲשֶׁ֖ר עַל־פְּנֵ֥י הָאֲדָמָֽה׃ פ

17 וַיֹּ֤אמֶר יְהֹוָה֙ אֶל־מֹשֶׁ֔ה גַּ֣ם אֶת־הַדָּבָ֥ר הַזֶּ֛ה אֲשֶׁ֥ר דִּבַּ֖רְתָּ אֶֽעֱשֶׂ֑ה כִּֽי־מָצָ֤אתָ חֵן֙ בְּעֵינַ֔י וָאֵדָעֲךָ֖ בְּשֵֽׁם׃ 18 וַיֹּאמַ֑ר הַרְאֵ֥נִי נָ֖א אֶת־כְּבֹדֶֽךָ׃ 19 וַיֹּ֡אמֶר אֲנִ֣י אַעֲבִ֣יר כָּל־טוּבִי֮ עַל־פָּנֶ֒יךָ֒ וְקָרָ֧אתִֽי בְשֵׁ֛ם יְהֹוָ֖ה לְפָנֶ֑יךָ וְחַנֹּתִי֙ אֶת־אֲשֶׁ֣ר אָחֹ֔ן וְרִחַמְתִּ֖י אֶת־אֲשֶׁ֥ר אֲרַחֵֽם׃ 20 וַיֹּ֕אמֶר לֹ֥א תוּכַ֖ל לִרְאֹ֣ת אֶת־פָּנָ֑י כִּ֛י לֹֽא־יִרְאַ֥נִי הָאָדָ֖ם וָחָֽי׃ 21 וַיֹּ֣אמֶר יְהֹוָ֔ה הִנֵּ֥ה מָק֖וֹם אִתִּ֑י וְנִצַּבְתָּ֖ עַל־הַצּֽוּר׃ 22 וְהָיָה֙ בַּעֲבֹ֣ר כְּבֹדִ֔י וְשַׂמְתִּ֖יךָ בְּנִקְרַ֣ת הַצּ֑וּר וְשַׂכֹּתִ֥י כַפִּ֛י עָלֶ֖יךָ עַד־עָבְרִֽי׃ 23 וַהֲסִרֹתִי֙ אֶת־כַּפִּ֔י וְרָאִ֖יתָ אֶת־אֲחֹרָ֑י וּפָנַ֖י לֹ֥א יֵרָאֽוּ׃ ס

לד וַיֹּ֤אמֶר יְהֹוָה֙ אֶל־מֹשֶׁ֔ה פְּסָל־לְךָ֛ שְׁנֵֽי־לֻחֹ֥ת אֲבָנִ֖ים כָּרִֽאשֹׁנִ֑ים וְכָתַבְתִּי֙ עַל־הַלֻּחֹ֔ת אֶת־הַדְּבָרִ֔ים אֲשֶׁ֥ר הָי֛וּ עַל־הַלֻּחֹ֥ת הָרִאשֹׁנִ֖ים אֲשֶׁ֥ר שִׁבַּֽרְתָּ׃ 2 וֶהְיֵ֥ה נָכ֖וֹן לַבֹּ֑קֶר וְעָלִ֤יתָ בַבֹּ֨קֶר֙ אֶל־הַ֣ר סִינַ֔י וְנִצַּבְתָּ֥ לִ֛י שָׁ֖ם עַל־רֹ֥אשׁ הָהָֽר׃ 3 וְאִישׁ֙ לֹֽא־יַעֲלֶ֣ה עִמָּ֔ךְ וְגַם־אִ֥ישׁ אַל־יֵרָ֖א בְּכָל־הָהָ֑ר גַּם־הַצֹּ֤אן וְהַבָּקָר֙ אַל־יִרְע֔וּ אֶל־מ֖וּל הָהָ֥ר הַהֽוּא׃ 4 וַיִּפְסֹ֡ל שְׁנֵֽי־לֻחֹ֨ת אֲבָנִ֜ים כָּרִֽאשֹׁנִ֗ים וַיַּשְׁכֵּ֨ם מֹשֶׁ֤ה בַבֹּ֨קֶר֙ וַיַּ֨עַל֙ אֶל־הַ֣ר סִינַ֔י כַּאֲשֶׁ֛ר צִוָּ֥ה יְהֹוָ֖ה אֹת֑וֹ וַיִּקַּ֣ח בְּיָד֔וֹ

⁵Now the LORD descended in the cloud and stood with him there, and proclaimed the name of the LORD. ⁶And the LORD passed before him and proclaimed, "The LORD, the LORD God, merciful and gracious, longsuffering, and abounding in goodness and truth, ⁷keeping mercy for thousands, forgiving iniquity and transgression and sin, by no means clearing *the guilty,* visiting the iniquity of the fathers upon the children and the children's children to the third and the fourth generation."

⁸So Moses made haste and bowed his head toward the earth, and worshiped. ⁹Then he said, "If now I have found grace in Your sight, O Lord, let my Lord, I pray, go among us, even though we *are* a stiff-necked people; and pardon our iniquity and our sin, and take us as Your inheritance."

¹⁰And He said: "Behold, I make a covenant. Before all your people I will do marvels such as have not been done in all the earth, nor in any nation; and all the people among whom you *are* shall see the work of the LORD. For it *is* an awesome thing that I will do with you. ¹¹Observe what I command you this day. Behold, I am driving out from before you the Amorite and the Canaanite and the Hittite and the Perizzite and the Hivite and the Jebusite. ¹²Take heed to yourself, lest you make a covenant with the inhabitants of the land where you are going, lest it be a snare in your midst. ¹³But you shall destroy their altars, break their *sacred* pillars, and cut down their wooden images ¹⁴(for you shall worship no other god, for the LORD, whose name *is* Jealous, *is* a jealous God), ¹⁵lest you make a covenant with the inhabitants of the land, and they play the harlot with their gods and make sacrifice to their gods, and *one of them* invites you and you eat of his sacrifice, ¹⁶and you take of his daughters for your sons, and his daughters play the harlot with their gods and make your sons play the harlot with their gods.

¹⁷"You shall make no molded gods for yourselves.

¹⁸"The Feast of Unleavened Bread you shall keep. Seven days you shall eat unleavened bread, as I commanded you, in the appointed time of the month of Abib; for in the month of Abib you came out from Egypt.

¹⁹"All that open the womb *are* Mine, and every male firstborn among your livestock, *whether* ox or sheep. ²⁰But the firstborn of a donkey you shall redeem with a lamb. And if you will not redeem *him,* then you shall break his neck. All the firstborn of your sons you shall redeem.

"And none shall appear before Me emptyhanded.

שְׁנֵי לֻחֹת אֲבָנִים: ⁵ וַיֵּרֶד יְהוָה בֶּעָנָן וַיִּתְיַצֵּב עִמּוֹ שָׁם וַיִּקְרָא בְשֵׁם יְהוָה: ⁶ וַיַּעֲבֹר יְהוָה | עַל־פָּנָיו וַיִּקְרָא יְהוָה | יְהוָה אֵל רַחוּם וְחַנּוּן אֶרֶךְ אַפַּיִם וְרַב־חֶסֶד וֶאֱמֶת: ⁷ נֹצֵר חֶסֶד לָאֲלָפִים נֹשֵׂא עָוֹן וָפֶשַׁע וְחַטָּאָה וְנַקֵּה לֹא יְנַקֶּה | פֹּקֵד | עֲוֹן אָבוֹת עַל־בָּנִים וְעַל־בְּנֵי בָנִים עַל־שִׁלֵּשִׁים וְעַל־רִבֵּעִים:

⁸ וַיְמַהֵר מֹשֶׁה וַיִּקֹּד אַרְצָה וַיִּשְׁתָּחוּ: ⁹ וַיֹּאמֶר אִם־נָא מָצָאתִי חֵן בְּעֵינֶיךָ אֲדֹנָי יֵלֶךְ־נָא אֲדֹנָי בְּקִרְבֵּנוּ כִּי עַם־קְשֵׁה־עֹרֶף הוּא וְסָלַחְתָּ לַעֲוֹנֵנוּ וּלְחַטָּאתֵנוּ וּנְחַלְתָּנוּ: ¹⁰ וַיֹּאמֶר הִנֵּה אָנֹכִי כֹּרֵת בְּרִית נֶגֶד כָּל־עַמְּךָ אֶעֱשֶׂה נִפְלָאֹת אֲשֶׁר לֹא־נִבְרְאוּ בְכָל־הָאָרֶץ וּבְכָל־הַגּוֹיִם וְרָאָה כָל־הָעָם אֲשֶׁר־אַתָּה בְקִרְבּוֹ אֶת־מַעֲשֵׂה יְהוָה כִּי־נוֹרָא הוּא אֲשֶׁר אֲנִי עֹשֶׂה עִמָּךְ: ¹¹ שְׁמָר־לְךָ אֵת אֲשֶׁר אָנֹכִי מְצַוְּךָ הַיּוֹם הִנְנִי גֹרֵשׁ מִפָּנֶיךָ אֶת־הָאֱמֹרִי וְהַכְּנַעֲנִי וְהַחִתִּי וְהַפְּרִזִּי וְהַחִוִּי וְהַיְבוּסִי: ¹² הִשָּׁמֶר לְךָ פֶּן־תִּכְרֹת בְּרִית לְיוֹשֵׁב הָאָרֶץ אֲשֶׁר אַתָּה בָּא עָלֶיהָ פֶּן־יִהְיֶה לְמוֹקֵשׁ בְּקִרְבֶּךָ: ¹³ כִּי אֶת־מִזְבְּחֹתָם תִּתֹּצוּן וְאֶת־מַצֵּבֹתָם תְּשַׁבֵּרוּן וְאֶת־אֲשֵׁרָיו תִּכְרֹתוּן: ¹⁴ כִּי לֹא תִשְׁתַּחֲוֶה לְאֵל אַחֵר כִּי יְהוָה קַנָּא שְׁמוֹ אֵל קַנָּא הוּא: ¹⁵ פֶּן־תִּכְרֹת בְּרִית לְיוֹשֵׁב הָאָרֶץ וְזָנוּ | אַחֲרֵי אֱלֹהֵיהֶם וְזָבְחוּ לֵאלֹהֵיהֶם וְקָרָא לְךָ וְאָכַלְתָּ מִזִּבְחוֹ: ¹⁶ וְלָקַחְתָּ מִבְּנֹתָיו לְבָנֶיךָ וְזָנוּ בְנֹתָיו אַחֲרֵי אֱלֹהֵיהֶן וְהִזְנוּ אֶת־בָּנֶיךָ אַחֲרֵי אֱלֹהֵיהֶן: ¹⁷ אֱלֹהֵי מַסֵּכָה לֹא תַעֲשֶׂה־לָּךְ: ¹⁸ אֶת־חַג הַמַּצּוֹת תִּשְׁמֹר שִׁבְעַת יָמִים תֹּאכַל מַצּוֹת אֲשֶׁר צִוִּיתִךָ לְמוֹעֵד חֹדֶשׁ הָאָבִיב כִּי בְּחֹדֶשׁ הָאָבִיב יָצָאתָ מִמִּצְרָיִם:

¹⁹ כָּל־פֶּטֶר רֶחֶם לִי וְכָל־מִקְנְךָ תִּזָּכָר פֶּטֶר שׁוֹר וָשֶׂה: ²⁰ וּפֶטֶר חֲמוֹר תִּפְדֶּה בְשֶׂה וְאִם־לֹא תִפְדֶּה וַעֲרַפְתּוֹ כֹּל בְּכוֹר בָּנֶיךָ תִּפְדֶּה וְלֹא־יֵרָאוּ פָנַי

²¹"Six days you shall work, but on the seventh day you shall rest; in plowing time and in harvest you shall rest.

²²"And you shall observe the Feast of Weeks, of the firstfruits of wheat harvest, and the Feast of Ingathering at the year's end.

²³"Three times in the year all your men shall appear before the Lord, the LORD God of Israel. ²⁴For I will cast out the nations before you and enlarge your borders; neither will any man covet your land when you go up to appear before the LORD your God three times in the year.

²⁵"You shall not offer the blood of My sacrifice with leaven, nor shall the sacrifice of the Feast of the Passover be left until morning.

²⁶"The first of the firstfruits of your land you shall bring to the house of the LORD your God. You shall not boil a young goat in its mother's milk."

²⁷Then the LORD said to Moses, "Write these words, for according to the tenor of these words I have made a covenant with you and with Israel." ²⁸So he was there with the LORD forty days and forty nights; he neither ate bread nor drank water. And He wrote on the tablets the words of the covenant, the Ten Commandments.

²⁹Now it was so, when Moses came down from Mount Sinai (and the two tablets of the Testimony *were* in Moses' hand when he came down from the mountain), that Moses did not know that the skin of his face shone while he talked with Him. ³⁰So when Aaron and all the children of Israel saw Moses, behold, the skin of his face shone, and they were afraid to come near him. ³¹Then Moses called to them, and Aaron and all the rulers of the congregation returned to him; and Moses talked with them. ³²Afterward all the children of Israel came near, and he gave them as commandments all that the LORD had spoken with him on Mount Sinai. ³³And when Moses had finished speaking with them, he put a veil on his face. ³⁴But whenever Moses went in before the LORD to speak with Him, he would take the veil off until he came out; and he would come out and speak to the children of Israel whatever he had been commanded. ³⁵And whenever the children of Israel saw the face of Moses, that the skin of Moses' face shone, then Moses would put the veil on his face again, until he went in to speak with Him.

35 Then Moses gathered all the congregation of the children of Israel together, and said to them, "These *are* the words which the LORD has commanded *you* to do: ²Work shall be done for six days, but the seventh day shall be a holy day for

רֵיקָם: 21 שֵׁשֶׁת יָמִים תַּעֲבֹד וּבַיּוֹם הַשְּׁבִיעִי תִּשְׁבֹּת בֶּחָרִישׁ וּבַקָּצִיר תִּשְׁבֹּת: 22 וְחַג שָׁבֻעֹת תַּעֲשֶׂה לְךָ בִּכּוּרֵי קְצִיר חִטִּים וְחַג הָאָסִיף תְּקוּפַת הַשָּׁנָה:

23 שָׁלֹשׁ פְּעָמִים בַּשָּׁנָה יֵרָאֶה כָּל־זְכוּרְךָ אֶת־פְּנֵי הָאָדֹן | יְהוָה אֱלֹהֵי יִשְׂרָאֵל: 24 כִּי־אוֹרִישׁ גּוֹיִם מִפָּנֶיךָ וְהִרְחַבְתִּי אֶת־גְּבוּלֶךָ וְלֹא־יַחְמֹד אִישׁ אֶת־אַרְצְךָ בַּעֲלֹתְךָ לֵרָאוֹת אֶת־פְּנֵי יְהוָה אֱלֹהֶיךָ שָׁלֹשׁ פְּעָמִים בַּשָּׁנָה: 25 לֹא־תִשְׁחַט עַל־חָמֵץ דַּם־זִבְחִי וְלֹא־יָלִין לַבֹּקֶר זֶבַח חַג הַפָּסַח: 26 רֵאשִׁית בִּכּוּרֵי אַדְמָתְךָ תָּבִיא בֵּית יְהוָה אֱלֹהֶיךָ לֹא־תְבַשֵּׁל גְּדִי בַּחֲלֵב אִמּוֹ: פ

27 וַיֹּאמֶר יְהוָה אֶל־מֹשֶׁה כְּתָב־לְךָ אֶת־הַדְּבָרִים הָאֵלֶּה כִּי עַל־פִּי | הַדְּבָרִים הָאֵלֶּה כָּרַתִּי אִתְּךָ בְּרִית וְאֶת־יִשְׂרָאֵל: 28 וַיְהִי־שָׁם עִם־יְהוָה אַרְבָּעִים יוֹם וְאַרְבָּעִים לַיְלָה לֶחֶם לֹא אָכַל וּמַיִם לֹא שָׁתָה וַיִּכְתֹּב עַל־הַלֻּחֹת אֵת דִּבְרֵי הַבְּרִית עֲשֶׂרֶת הַדְּבָרִים: 29 וַיְהִי בְּרֶדֶת מֹשֶׁה מֵהַר סִינַי וּשְׁנֵי לֻחֹת הָעֵדֻת בְּיַד־מֹשֶׁה בְּרִדְתּוֹ מִן־הָהָר וּמֹשֶׁה לֹא־יָדַע כִּי קָרַן עוֹר פָּנָיו בְּדַבְּרוֹ אִתּוֹ: 30 וַיַּרְא אַהֲרֹן וְכָל־בְּנֵי יִשְׂרָאֵל אֶת־מֹשֶׁה וְהִנֵּה קָרַן עוֹר פָּנָיו וַיִּירְאוּ מִגֶּשֶׁת אֵלָיו: 31 וַיִּקְרָא אֲלֵהֶם מֹשֶׁה וַיָּשֻׁבוּ אֵלָיו אַהֲרֹן וְכָל־הַנְּשִׂאִים בָּעֵדָה וַיְדַבֵּר מֹשֶׁה אֲלֵהֶם: 32 וְאַחֲרֵי־כֵן נִגְּשׁוּ כָּל־בְּנֵי יִשְׂרָאֵל וַיְצַוֵּם אֵת כָּל־אֲשֶׁר דִּבֶּר יְהוָה אִתּוֹ בְּהַר סִינָי: 33 וַיְכַל מֹשֶׁה מִדַּבֵּר אִתָּם וַיִּתֵּן עַל־פָּנָיו מַסְוֶה: 34 וּבְבֹא מֹשֶׁה לִפְנֵי יְהוָה לְדַבֵּר אִתּוֹ יָסִיר אֶת־הַמַּסְוֶה עַד־צֵאתוֹ וְיָצָא וְדִבֶּר אֶל־בְּנֵי יִשְׂרָאֵל אֵת אֲשֶׁר יְצֻוֶּה: 35 וְרָאוּ בְנֵי־יִשְׂרָאֵל אֶת־פְּנֵי מֹשֶׁה כִּי קָרַן עוֹר פְּנֵי מֹשֶׁה וְהֵשִׁיב מֹשֶׁה אֶת־הַמַּסְוֶה עַל־פָּנָיו עַד־בֹּאוֹ לְדַבֵּר אִתּוֹ: ס

לה וַיַּקְהֵל מֹשֶׁה אֶת־כָּל־עֲדַת בְּנֵי יִשְׂרָאֵל וַיֹּאמֶר אֲלֵהֶם אֵלֶּה הַדְּבָרִים אֲשֶׁר־צִוָּה יְהוָה לַעֲשֹׂת אֹתָם: 2 שֵׁשֶׁת יָמִים תֵּעָשֶׂה מְלָאכָה וּבַיּוֹם הַשְּׁבִיעִי יִהְיֶה לָכֶם קֹדֶשׁ שַׁבַּת שַׁבָּתוֹן לַיהוָה

you, a Sabbath of rest to the LORD. Whoever does any work on it shall be put to death. ³You shall kindle no fire throughout your dwellings on the Sabbath day."

⁴And Moses spoke to all the congregation of the children of Israel, saying, "This *is* the thing which the LORD commanded, saying: ⁵'Take from among you an offering to the LORD. Whoever *is* of a willing heart, let him bring it as an offering to the LORD: gold, silver, and bronze; ⁶blue, purple, and scarlet *thread,* fine linen, and goats' *hair;* ⁷ram skins dyed red, badger skins, and acacia wood; ⁸oil for the light, and spices for the anointing oil and for the sweet incense; ⁹onyx stones, and stones to be set in the ephod and in the breastplate.

¹⁰'All *who are* gifted artisans among you shall come and make all that the LORD has commanded: ¹¹the tabernacle, its tent, its covering, its clasps, its boards, its bars, its pillars, and its sockets; ¹²the ark and its poles, *with* the mercy seat, and the veil of the covering; ¹³the table and its poles, all its utensils, and the showbread; ¹⁴also the lampstand for the light, its utensils, its lamps, and the oil for the light; ¹⁵the incense altar, its poles, the anointing oil, the sweet incense, and the screen for the door at the entrance of the tabernacle; ¹⁶the altar of burnt offering with its bronze grating, its poles, all its utensils, *and* the laver and its base; ¹⁷the hangings of the court, its pillars, their sockets, and the screen for the gate of the court; ¹⁸the pegs of the tabernacle, the pegs of the court, and their cords; ¹⁹the garments of ministry, for ministering in the holy *place*—the holy garments for Aaron the priest and the garments of his sons, to minister as priests.'"

²⁰And all the congregation of the children of Israel departed from the presence of Moses. ²¹Then everyone came whose heart was stirred, and everyone whose spirit was willing, *and* they brought the LORD's offering for the work of the tabernacle of meeting, for all its service, and for the holy garments. ²²They came, both men and women, as many as had a willing heart, and brought earrings and nose rings, rings and necklaces, all jewelry of gold, that is, every man who *made* an offering of gold to the LORD. ²³And every man, with whom was found blue, purple, and scarlet *thread,* fine linen, goats' *hair,* red skins of rams, and badger skins, brought *them.* ²⁴Everyone who offered an offering of silver or bronze brought the LORD's offering. And everyone with whom was found acacia wood for any work of the service, brought *it.* ²⁵All the women *who were* gifted artisans spun yarn with their hands, and brought what they had

כָּל־הָעֹשֶׂה בוֹ מְלָאכָה יוּמָת: ³לֹא־תְבַעֲרוּ אֵשׁ בְּכֹל מֹשְׁבֹתֵיכֶם בְּיוֹם הַשַּׁבָּת: פ

⁴וַיֹּאמֶר מֹשֶׁה אֶל־כָּל־עֲדַת בְּנֵי־יִשְׂרָאֵל לֵאמֹר זֶה הַדָּבָר אֲשֶׁר־צִוָּה יְהוָה לֵאמֹר: ⁵קְחוּ מֵאִתְּכֶם תְּרוּמָה לַיהוָה כֹּל נְדִיב לִבּוֹ יְבִיאֶהָ אֵת תְּרוּמַת יְהוָה זָהָב וָכֶסֶף וּנְחֹשֶׁת: ⁶וּתְכֵלֶת וְאַרְגָּמָן וְתוֹלַעַת שָׁנִי וְשֵׁשׁ וְעִזִּים: ⁷וְעֹרֹת אֵילִם מְאָדָּמִים וְעֹרֹת תְּחָשִׁים וַעֲצֵי שִׁטִּים: ⁸וְשֶׁמֶן לַמָּאוֹר וּבְשָׂמִים לְשֶׁמֶן הַמִּשְׁחָה וְלִקְטֹרֶת הַסַּמִּים: ⁹וְאַבְנֵי־שֹׁהַם וְאַבְנֵי מִלֻּאִים לָאֵפוֹד וְלַחֹשֶׁן: ¹⁰וְכָל־חֲכַם־לֵב בָּכֶם יָבֹאוּ וְיַעֲשׂוּ אֵת כָּל־אֲשֶׁר צִוָּה יְהוָה: ¹¹אֶת־הַמִּשְׁכָּן אֶת־אָהֳלוֹ וְאֶת־מִכְסֵהוּ אֶת־קְרָסָיו וְאֶת־קְרָשָׁיו אֶת־בְּרִיחָו אֶת־עַמֻּדָיו וְאֶת־אֲדָנָיו: ¹²אֶת־הָאָרֹן וְאֶת־בַּדָּיו אֶת־הַכַּפֹּרֶת וְאֵת פָּרֹכֶת הַמָּסָךְ: ¹³אֶת־הַשֻּׁלְחָן וְאֶת־בַּדָּיו וְאֶת־כָּל־כֵּלָיו וְאֵת לֶחֶם הַפָּנִים: ¹⁴וְאֶת־מְנֹרַת הַמָּאוֹר וְאֶת־כֵּלֶיהָ וְאֶת־נֵרֹתֶיהָ וְאֵת שֶׁמֶן הַמָּאוֹר: ¹⁵וְאֶת־מִזְבַּח הַקְּטֹרֶת וְאֶת־בַּדָּיו וְאֵת שֶׁמֶן הַמִּשְׁחָה וְאֵת קְטֹרֶת הַסַּמִּים וְאֶת־מָסַךְ הַפֶּתַח לְפֶתַח הַמִּשְׁכָּן: ¹⁶אֵת מִזְבַּח הָעֹלָה וְאֶת־מִכְבַּר הַנְּחֹשֶׁת אֲשֶׁר־לוֹ אֶת־בַּדָּיו וְאֶת־כָּל־כֵּלָיו אֶת־הַכִּיֹּר וְאֶת־כַּנּוֹ: ¹⁷אֵת קַלְעֵי הֶחָצֵר אֶת־עַמֻּדָיו וְאֶת־אֲדָנֶיהָ וְאֵת מָסַךְ שַׁעַר הֶחָצֵר: ¹⁸אֶת־יִתְדֹת הַמִּשְׁכָּן וְאֶת־יִתְדֹת הֶחָצֵר וְאֶת־מֵיתְרֵיהֶם: ¹⁹אֶת־בִּגְדֵי הַשְּׂרָד לְשָׁרֵת בַּקֹּדֶשׁ אֶת־בִּגְדֵי הַקֹּדֶשׁ לְאַהֲרֹן הַכֹּהֵן וְאֶת־בִּגְדֵי בָנָיו לְכַהֵן: ²⁰וַיֵּצְאוּ כָּל־עֲדַת בְּנֵי־יִשְׂרָאֵל מִלִּפְנֵי מֹשֶׁה: ²¹וַיָּבֹאוּ כָּל־אִישׁ אֲשֶׁר־נְשָׂאוֹ לִבּוֹ וְכֹל אֲשֶׁר נָדְבָה רוּחוֹ אֹתוֹ הֵבִיאוּ אֶת־תְּרוּמַת יְהוָה לִמְלֶאכֶת אֹהֶל מוֹעֵד וּלְכָל־עֲבֹדָתוֹ וּלְבִגְדֵי הַקֹּדֶשׁ: ²²וַיָּבֹאוּ הָאֲנָשִׁים עַל־הַנָּשִׁים כֹּל נְדִיב לֵב הֵבִיאוּ חָח וָנֶזֶם וְטַבַּעַת וְכוּמָז כָּל־כְּלִי זָהָב וְכָל־אִישׁ אֲשֶׁר הֵנִיף תְּנוּפַת זָהָב לַיהוָה: ²³וְכָל־אִישׁ אֲשֶׁר־נִמְצָא אִתּוֹ תְּכֵלֶת וְאַרְגָּמָן וְתוֹלַעַת שָׁנִי וְשֵׁשׁ וְעִזִּים וְעֹרֹת אֵילִם מְאָדָּמִים וְעֹרֹת תְּחָשִׁים הֵבִיאוּ: ²⁴כָּל־מֵרִים תְּרוּמַת כֶּסֶף וּנְחֹשֶׁת הֵבִיאוּ אֵת תְּרוּמַת יְהוָה וְכֹל אֲשֶׁר נִמְצָא אִתּוֹ עֲצֵי שִׁטִּים לְכָל־מְלֶאכֶת הָעֲבֹדָה הֵבִיאוּ: ²⁵וְכָל־אִשָּׁה חַכְמַת־

spun, of blue, purple, *and* scarlet, and fine linen. ²⁶And all the women whose hearts stirred with wisdom spun yarn of goats' *hair*. ²⁷The rulers brought onyx stones, and the stones to be set in the ephod and in the breastplate, ²⁸and spices and oil for the light, for the anointing oil, and for the sweet incense. ²⁹The children of Israel brought a freewill offering to the LORD, all the men and women whose hearts were willing to bring *material* for all kinds of work which the LORD, by the hand of Moses, had commanded to be done.

³⁰And Moses said to the children of Israel, "See, the LORD has called by name Bezalel the son of Uri, the son of Hur, of the tribe of Judah; ³¹and He has filled him with the Spirit of God, in wisdom and understanding, in knowledge and all manner of workmanship, ³²to design artistic works, to work in gold and silver and bronze, ³³in cutting jewels for setting, in carving wood, and to work in all manner of artistic workmanship.

³⁴"And He has put in his heart the ability to teach, *in* him and Aholiab the son of Ahisamach, of the tribe of Dan. ³⁵He has filled them with skill to do all manner of work of the engraver and the designer and the tapestry maker, in blue, purple, and scarlet *thread,* and fine linen, and of the weaver—those who do every work and those who design artistic works.

36

"And Bezalel and Aholiab, and every gifted artisan in whom the LORD has put wisdom and understanding, to know how to do all manner of work for the service of the sanctuary, shall do according to all that the LORD has commanded."

²Then Moses called Bezalel and Aholiab, and every gifted artisan in whose heart the LORD had put wisdom, everyone whose heart was stirred, to come and do the work. ³And they received from Moses all the offering which the children of Israel had brought for the work of the service of making the sanctuary. So they continued bringing to him freewill offerings every morning. ⁴Then all the craftsmen who were doing all the work of the sanctuary came, each from the work he was doing, ⁵and they spoke to Moses, saying, "The people bring much more than enough for the service of the work which the LORD commanded *us* to do."

⁶So Moses gave a commandment, and they caused it to be proclaimed throughout the camp, saying, "Let neither man nor woman do any more work for the offering of the sanctuary." And the people were restrained from bringing, ⁷for the material they had was sufficient for all the work to be done—indeed too much.

לֵב בְּיָדֶיהָ טָווּ וַיָּבִיאוּ מַטְוֶה אֶת־הַתְּכֵלֶת וְאֶת־
הָאַרְגָּמָן אֶת־תּוֹלַעַת הַשָּׁנִי וְאֶת־הַשֵּׁשׁ: 26 וְכָל־
הַנָּשִׁים אֲשֶׁר נָשָׂא לִבָּן אֹתָנָה בְּחָכְמָה טָווּ אֶת־
הָעִזִּים: 27 וְהַנְּשִׂאִם הֵבִיאוּ אֵת אַבְנֵי הַשֹּׁהַם וְאֵת
אַבְנֵי הַמִּלֻּאִים לָאֵפוֹד וְלַחֹשֶׁן: 28 וְאֶת־הַבֹּשֶׂם
וְאֶת־הַשָּׁמֶן לְמָאוֹר וּלְשֶׁמֶן הַמִּשְׁחָה וְלִקְטֹרֶת
הַסַּמִּים: 29 כָּל־אִישׁ וְאִשָּׁה אֲשֶׁר נָדַב לִבָּם אֹתָם
לְהָבִיא לְכָל־הַמְּלָאכָה אֲשֶׁר צִוָּה יְהוָה לַעֲשׂוֹת
בְּיַד־מֹשֶׁה הֵבִיאוּ בְנֵי־יִשְׂרָאֵל נְדָבָה לַיהוָה: פ
30 וַיֹּאמֶר מֹשֶׁה אֶל־בְּנֵי יִשְׂרָאֵל רְאוּ קָרָא יְהוָה
בְּשֵׁם בְּצַלְאֵל בֶּן־אוּרִי בֶן־חוּר לְמַטֵּה יְהוּדָה:
31 וַיְמַלֵּא אֹתוֹ רוּחַ אֱלֹהִים בְּחָכְמָה בִּתְבוּנָה
וּבְדַעַת וּבְכָל־מְלָאכָה: 32 וְלַחְשֹׁב מַחֲשָׁבֹת לַעֲשׂוֹת
בַּזָּהָב וּבַכֶּסֶף וּבַנְּחֹשֶׁת: 33 וּבַחֲרֹשֶׁת אֶבֶן לְמַלֹּאת
וּבַחֲרֹשֶׁת עֵץ לַעֲשׂוֹת בְּכָל־מְלֶאכֶת מַחֲשָׁבֶת:
34 וּלְהוֹרֹת נָתַן בְּלִבּוֹ הוּא וְאָהֳלִיאָב בֶּן־אֲחִיסָמָךְ
לְמַטֵּה־דָן: 35 מִלֵּא אֹתָם חָכְמַת־לֵב לַעֲשׂוֹת כָּל־
מְלֶאכֶת חָרָשׁ וְחֹשֵׁב וְרֹקֵם בַּתְּכֵלֶת וּבָאַרְגָּמָן
בְּתוֹלַעַת הַשָּׁנִי וּבַשֵּׁשׁ וְאֹרֵג עֹשֵׂי כָּל־מְלָאכָה
וְחֹשְׁבֵי מַחֲשָׁבֹת:

לו וְעָשָׂה בְצַלְאֵל וְאָהֳלִיאָב וְכֹל ׀ אִישׁ חֲכַם־
לֵב אֲשֶׁר נָתַן יְהוָה חָכְמָה וּתְבוּנָה בָּהֵמָּה
לָדַעַת לַעֲשֹׂת אֶת־כָּל־מְלֶאכֶת עֲבֹדַת הַקֹּדֶשׁ לְכֹל
אֲשֶׁר־צִוָּה יְהוָה: 2 וַיִּקְרָא מֹשֶׁה אֶל־בְּצַלְאֵל וְאֶל־
אָהֳלִיאָב וְאֶל כָּל־אִישׁ חֲכַם־לֵב אֲשֶׁר נָתַן יְהוָה
חָכְמָה בְּלִבּוֹ כֹּל אֲשֶׁר נְשָׂאוֹ לִבּוֹ לְקָרְבָה אֶל־
הַמְּלָאכָה לַעֲשֹׂת אֹתָהּ: 3 וַיִּקְחוּ מִלִּפְנֵי מֹשֶׁה אֵת
כָּל־הַתְּרוּמָה אֲשֶׁר הֵבִיאוּ בְּנֵי יִשְׂרָאֵל לִמְלֶאכֶת
עֲבֹדַת הַקֹּדֶשׁ לַעֲשֹׂת אֹתָהּ וְהֵם הֵבִיאוּ אֵלָיו עוֹד
נְדָבָה בַּבֹּקֶר בַּבֹּקֶר: 4 וַיָּבֹאוּ כָּל־הַחֲכָמִים הָעֹשִׂים
אֵת כָּל־מְלֶאכֶת הַקֹּדֶשׁ אִישׁ־אִישׁ מִמְּלַאכְתּוֹ
אֲשֶׁר־הֵמָּה עֹשִׂים: 5 וַיֹּאמְרוּ אֶל־מֹשֶׁה לֵּאמֹר
מַרְבִּים הָעָם לְהָבִיא מִדֵּי הָעֲבֹדָה לַמְּלָאכָה אֲשֶׁר־
צִוָּה יְהוָה לַעֲשֹׂת אֹתָהּ: 6 וַיְצַו מֹשֶׁה וַיַּעֲבִירוּ
קוֹל בַּמַּחֲנֶה לֵאמֹר אִישׁ וְאִשָּׁה אַל־יַעֲשׂוּ־עוֹד
מְלָאכָה לִתְרוּמַת הַקֹּדֶשׁ וַיִּכָּלֵא הָעָם מֵהָבִיא:
7 וְהַמְּלָאכָה הָיְתָה דַיָּם לְכָל־הַמְּלָאכָה לַעֲשׂוֹת

8 Then all the gifted artisans among them who worked on the tabernacle made ten curtains woven of fine linen, and of blue, purple, and scarlet thread; *with* artistic designs of cherubim they made them. 9 The length of each curtain *was* twenty-eight cubits, and the width of each curtain four cubits; the curtains *were* all the same size. 10 And he coupled five curtains to one another, and *the other* five curtains he coupled to one another. 11 He made loops of blue *yarn* on the edge of the curtain on the selvedge of one set; likewise he did on the outer edge of *the other* curtain of the second set. 12 Fifty loops he made on one curtain, and fifty loops he made on the edge of the curtain on the end of the second set; the loops held one *curtain* to another. 13 And he made fifty clasps of gold, and coupled the curtains to one another with the clasps, that it might be one tabernacle.

14 He made curtains of goats' *hair* for the tent over the tabernacle; he made eleven curtains. 15 The length of each curtain *was* thirty cubits, and the width of each curtain four cubits; the eleven curtains *were* the same size. 16 He coupled five curtains by themselves and six curtains by themselves. 17 And he made fifty loops on the edge of the curtain that is outermost in one set, and fifty loops he made on the edge of the curtain of the second set. 18 He also made fifty bronze clasps to couple the tent together, that it might be one. 19 Then he made a covering for the tent of ram skins dyed red, and a covering of badger skins above *that*.

20 For the tabernacle he made boards of acacia wood, standing upright. 21 The length of each board *was* ten cubits, and the width of each board a cubit and a half. 22 Each board had two tenons for binding one to another. Thus he made for all the boards of the tabernacle. 23 And he made boards for the tabernacle, twenty boards for the south side. 24 Forty sockets of silver he made to go under the twenty boards: two sockets under each of the boards for its two tenons. 25 And for the other side of the tabernacle, the north side, he made twenty boards 26 and their forty sockets of silver: two sockets under each of the boards. 27 For the west side of the tabernacle he made six boards. 28 He also made two boards for the two back corners of the tabernacle. 29 And they were coupled at the bottom and coupled together at the top by one ring. Thus he made both of them for the two corners. 30 So there were eight boards and their sockets—sixteen sockets of silver—two sockets under each of the boards.

8 ס וַיַּעֲשׂוּ כָל־חֲכַם־לֵב בְּעֹשֵׂי הַמְּלָאכָה אֶת־הַמִּשְׁכָּן עֶשֶׂר יְרִיעֹת שֵׁשׁ מָשְׁזָר וּתְכֵלֶת וְאַרְגָּמָן וְתוֹלַעַת שָׁנִי כְּרֻבִים מַעֲשֵׂה חֹשֵׁב עָשָׂה אֹתָם: 9 אֹרֶךְ הַיְרִיעָה הָאַחַת שְׁמֹנֶה וְעֶשְׂרִים בָּאַמָּה וְרֹחַב אַרְבַּע בָּאַמָּה הַיְרִיעָה הָאֶחָת מִדָּה אַחַת לְכָל־הַיְרִיעֹת: 10 וַיְחַבֵּר אֶת־חֲמֵשׁ הַיְרִיעֹת אַחַת אֶל־אֶחָת וְחָמֵשׁ יְרִיעֹת חִבַּר אַחַת אֶל־אֶחָת: 11 וַיַּעַשׂ לֻלְאֹת תְּכֵלֶת עַל שְׂפַת הַיְרִיעָה הָאֶחָת מִקָּצָה בַּמַּחְבָּרֶת כֵּן עָשָׂה בִּשְׂפַת הַיְרִיעָה הַקִּיצוֹנָה בַּמַּחְבֶּרֶת הַשֵּׁנִית: 12 חֲמִשִּׁים לֻלָאֹת עָשָׂה בַּיְרִיעָה הָאֶחָת וַחֲמִשִּׁים לֻלָאֹת עָשָׂה בִּקְצֵה הַיְרִיעָה אֲשֶׁר בַּמַּחְבֶּרֶת הַשֵּׁנִית מַקְבִּילֹת הַלֻּלָאֹת אַחַת אֶל־אֶחָת: 13 וַיַּעַשׂ חֲמִשִּׁים קַרְסֵי זָהָב וַיְחַבֵּר אֶת־הַיְרִיעֹת אַחַת אֶל־אַחַת בַּקְּרָסִים וַיְהִי הַמִּשְׁכָּן אֶחָד: ס 14 וַיַּעַשׂ יְרִיעֹת עִזִּים לְאֹהֶל עַל־הַמִּשְׁכָּן עַשְׁתֵּי־עֶשְׂרֵה יְרִיעֹת עָשָׂה אֹתָם: 15 אֹרֶךְ הַיְרִיעָה הָאַחַת שְׁלֹשִׁים בָּאַמָּה וְאַרְבַּע אַמּוֹת רֹחַב הַיְרִיעָה הָאֶחָת מִדָּה אַחַת לְעַשְׁתֵּי עֶשְׂרֵה יְרִיעֹת: 16 וַיְחַבֵּר אֶת־חֲמֵשׁ הַיְרִיעֹת לְבָד וְאֶת־שֵׁשׁ הַיְרִיעֹת לְבָד: 17 וַיַּעַשׂ לֻלָאֹת חֲמִשִּׁים עַל שְׂפַת הַיְרִיעָה הַקִּיצֹנָה בַּמַּחְבָּרֶת וַחֲמִשִּׁים לֻלָאֹת עָשָׂה עַל־שְׂפַת הַיְרִיעָה הַחֹבֶרֶת הַשֵּׁנִית: 18 וַיַּעַשׂ קַרְסֵי נְחֹשֶׁת חֲמִשִּׁים לְחַבֵּר אֶת־הָאֹהֶל לִהְיֹת אֶחָד: 19 וַיַּעַשׂ מִכְסֶה לָאֹהֶל עֹרֹת אֵלִים מְאָדָּמִים וּמִכְסֵה עֹרֹת תְּחָשִׁים מִלְמָעְלָה: ס 20 וַיַּעַשׂ אֶת־הַקְּרָשִׁים לַמִּשְׁכָּן עֲצֵי שִׁטִּים עֹמְדִים: 21 עֶשֶׂר אַמֹּת אֹרֶךְ הַקָּרֶשׁ וְאַמָּה וַחֲצִי הָאַמָּה רֹחַב הַקֶּרֶשׁ הָאֶחָד: 22 שְׁתֵּי יָדֹת לַקֶּרֶשׁ הָאֶחָד מְשֻׁלָּבֹת אַחַת אֶל־אֶחָת כֵּן עָשָׂה לְכֹל קַרְשֵׁי הַמִּשְׁכָּן: 23 וַיַּעַשׂ אֶת־הַקְּרָשִׁים לַמִּשְׁכָּן עֶשְׂרִים קְרָשִׁים לִפְאַת נֶגֶב תֵּימָנָה: 24 וְאַרְבָּעִים אַדְנֵי־כֶסֶף עָשָׂה תַּחַת עֶשְׂרִים הַקְּרָשִׁים שְׁנֵי אֲדָנִים תַּחַת־הַקֶּרֶשׁ הָאֶחָד לִשְׁתֵּי יְדֹתָיו וּשְׁנֵי אֲדָנִים תַּחַת־הַקֶּרֶשׁ הָאֶחָד לִשְׁתֵּי יְדֹתָיו: 25 וּלְצֶלַע הַמִּשְׁכָּן הַשֵּׁנִית לִפְאַת צָפוֹן עָשָׂה עֶשְׂרִים קְרָשִׁים: 26 וְאַרְבָּעִים אַדְנֵיהֶם כָּסֶף שְׁנֵי אֲדָנִים תַּחַת הַקֶּרֶשׁ הָאֶחָד וּשְׁנֵי אֲדָנִים תַּחַת הַקֶּרֶשׁ הָאֶחָד: 27 וּלְיַרְכְּתֵי הַמִּשְׁכָּן יָמָּה עָשָׂה שִׁשָּׁה קְרָשִׁים: 28 וּשְׁנֵי קְרָשִׁים עָשָׂה לִמְקֻצְעֹת הַמִּשְׁכָּן בַּיַּרְכָתָיִם: 29 וְהָיוּ תוֹאֲמִם מִלְּמַטָּה וְיַחְדָּו יִהְיוּ תַמִּים אֶל־רֹאשׁוֹ אֶל־הַטַּבַּעַת הָאֶחָת כֵּן עָשָׂה לִשְׁנֵיהֶם לִשְׁנֵי הַמִּקְצֹעֹת: 30 וְהָיוּ

³¹ And he made bars of acacia wood: five for the boards on one side of the tabernacle, ³² five bars for the boards on the other side of the tabernacle, and five bars for the boards of the tabernacle on the far side westward. ³³ And he made the middle bar to pass through the boards from one end to the other. ³⁴ He overlaid the boards with gold, made their rings of gold *to be* holders for the bars, and overlaid the bars with gold.

³⁵ And he made a veil of blue, purple, and scarlet *thread,* and fine woven linen; it was worked *with* an artistic design of cherubim. ³⁶ He made for it four pillars of acacia *wood,* and overlaid them with gold, with their hooks of gold; and he cast four sockets of silver for them.

³⁷ He also made a screen for the tabernacle door, of blue, purple, and scarlet *thread,* and fine woven linen, made by a weaver, ³⁸ and its five pillars with their hooks. And he overlaid their capitals and their rings with gold, but their five sockets *were* bronze.

37

Then Bezalel made the ark of acacia wood; two and a half cubits *was* its length, a cubit and a half its width, and a cubit and a half its height. ² He overlaid it with pure gold inside and outside, and made a molding of gold all around it. ³ And he cast for it four rings of gold *to be set* in its four corners: two rings on one side, and two rings on the other side of it. ⁴ He made poles of acacia wood, and overlaid them with gold. ⁵ And he put the poles into the rings at the sides of the ark, to bear the ark. ⁶ He also made the mercy seat of pure gold; two and a half cubits *was* its length and a cubit and a half its width. ⁷ He made two cherubim of beaten gold; he made them of one piece at the two ends of the mercy seat: ⁸ one cherub at one end on this side, and the other cherub at the *other* end on that side. He made the cherubim at the two ends *of one piece* with the mercy seat. ⁹ The cherubim spread out *their* wings above, *and* covered the mercy seat with their wings. They faced one another; the faces of the cherubim were toward the mercy seat.

¹⁰ He made the table of acacia wood; two cubits *was* its length, a cubit its width, and a cubit and a half its height. ¹¹ And he overlaid it with pure gold, and made a molding of gold all around it. ¹² Also he made a frame of a handbreadth all around it, and made a molding of gold for the frame all around it. ¹³ And he cast for it four rings of gold, and put the rings on the four corners that *were* at its four legs. ¹⁴ The rings were close to the frame, as holders for the poles to bear the table. ¹⁵ And he made the poles of acacia wood to bear the table, and overlaid them

שְׁמֹנָה קְרָשִׁים וְאַדְנֵיהֶם כֶּסֶף שִׁשָּׁה עָשָׂר אֲדָנִים שְׁנֵי אֲדָנִים שְׁנֵי אֲדָנִים תַּחַת הַקֶּרֶשׁ הָאֶחָד: ³¹ וַיַּעַשׂ בְּרִיחֵי עֲצֵי שִׁטִּים חֲמִשָּׁה לְקַרְשֵׁי צֶלַע־הַמִּשְׁכָּן הָאֶחָת: ³² וַחֲמִשָּׁה בְרִיחִם לְקַרְשֵׁי צֶלַע־הַמִּשְׁכָּן הַשֵּׁנִית וַחֲמִשָּׁה בְרִיחִם לְקַרְשֵׁי הַמִּשְׁכָּן לַיַּרְכָתַיִם יָמָּה: ³³ וַיַּעַשׂ אֶת־הַבְּרִיחַ הַתִּיכֹן לִבְרֹחַ בְּתוֹךְ הַקְּרָשִׁים מִן־הַקָּצֶה אֶל־הַקָּצֶה: ³⁴ וְאֶת־הַקְּרָשִׁים צִפָּה זָהָב וְאֶת־טַבְּעֹתָם עָשָׂה זָהָב בָּתִּים לַבְּרִיחִם וַיְצַף אֶת־הַבְּרִיחִם זָהָב: ³⁵ וַיַּעַשׂ אֶת־הַפָּרֹכֶת תְּכֵלֶת וְאַרְגָּמָן וְתוֹלַעַת שָׁנִי וְשֵׁשׁ מָשְׁזָר מַעֲשֵׂה חֹשֵׁב עָשָׂה אֹתָהּ כְּרֻבִים: ³⁶ וַיַּעַשׂ לָהּ אַרְבָּעָה עַמּוּדֵי שִׁטִּים וַיְצַפֵּם זָהָב וָוֵיהֶם זָהָב וַיִּצֹק לָהֶם אַרְבָּעָה אַדְנֵי־כָסֶף: ³⁷ וַיַּעַשׂ מָסָךְ לְפֶתַח הָאֹהֶל תְּכֵלֶת וְאַרְגָּמָן וְתוֹלַעַת שָׁנִי וְשֵׁשׁ מָשְׁזָר מַעֲשֵׂה רֹקֵם: ³⁸ וְאֶת־עַמּוּדָיו חֲמִשָּׁה וְאֶת־וָוֵיהֶם וְצִפָּה רָאשֵׁיהֶם וַחֲשֻׁקֵיהֶם זָהָב וְאַדְנֵיהֶם חֲמִשָּׁה נְחֹשֶׁת: פ

לז וַיַּעַשׂ בְּצַלְאֵל אֶת־הָאָרֹן עֲצֵי שִׁטִּים אַמָּתַיִם וָחֵצִי אָרְכּוֹ וְאַמָּה וָחֵצִי רָחְבּוֹ וְאַמָּה וָחֵצִי קֹמָתוֹ: ² וַיְצַפֵּהוּ זָהָב טָהוֹר מִבַּיִת וּמִחוּץ וַיַּעַשׂ לוֹ זֵר זָהָב סָבִיב: ³ וַיִּצֹק לוֹ אַרְבַּע טַבְּעֹת זָהָב עַל אַרְבַּע פַּעֲמֹתָיו וּשְׁתֵּי טַבָּעֹת עַל־צַלְעוֹ הָאֶחָת וּשְׁתֵּי טַבָּעֹת עַל־צַלְעוֹ הַשֵּׁנִית: ⁴ וַיַּעַשׂ בַּדֵּי עֲצֵי שִׁטִּים וַיְצַף אֹתָם זָהָב: ⁵ וַיָּבֵא אֶת־הַבַּדִּים בַּטַּבָּעֹת עַל צַלְעֹת הָאָרֹן לָשֵׂאת אֶת־הָאָרֹן: ⁶ וַיַּעַשׂ כַּפֹּרֶת זָהָב טָהוֹר אַמָּתַיִם וָחֵצִי אָרְכָּהּ וְאַמָּה וָחֵצִי רָחְבָּהּ: ⁷ וַיַּעַשׂ שְׁנֵי כְרֻבִים זָהָב מִקְשָׁה עָשָׂה אֹתָם מִשְּׁנֵי קְצוֹת הַכַּפֹּרֶת: ⁸ כְּרוּב־אֶחָד מִקָּצָה מִזֶּה וּכְרוּב־אֶחָד מִקָּצָה מִזֶּה מִן־הַכַּפֹּרֶת עָשָׂה אֶת־הַכְּרֻבִים מִשְּׁנֵי קְצוֹתָו: ⁹ וַיִּהְיוּ הַכְּרֻבִים פֹּרְשֵׂי כְנָפַיִם לְמַעְלָה סֹכְכִים בְּכַנְפֵיהֶם עַל־הַכַּפֹּרֶת וּפְנֵיהֶם אִישׁ אֶל־אָחִיו אֶל־הַכַּפֹּרֶת הָיוּ פְּנֵי הַכְּרֻבִים: פ

¹⁰ וַיַּעַשׂ אֶת־הַשֻּׁלְחָן עֲצֵי שִׁטִּים אַמָּתַיִם אָרְכּוֹ וְאַמָּה רָחְבּוֹ וְאַמָּה וָחֵצִי קֹמָתוֹ: ¹¹ וַיְצַף אֹתוֹ זָהָב טָהוֹר וַיַּעַשׂ לוֹ זֵר זָהָב סָבִיב: ¹² וַיַּעַשׂ לוֹ מִסְגֶּרֶת טֹפַח סָבִיב וַיַּעַשׂ זֵר־זָהָב לְמִסְגַּרְתּוֹ סָבִיב: ¹³ וַיִּצֹק לוֹ אַרְבַּע טַבְּעֹת זָהָב וַיִּתֵּן אֶת־הַטַּבָּעֹת עַל אַרְבַּע הַפֵּאֹת אֲשֶׁר לְאַרְבַּע רַגְלָיו: ¹⁴ לְעֻמַּת הַמִּסְגֶּרֶת הָיוּ הַטַּבָּעֹת בָּתִּים לַבַּדִּים לָשֵׂאת אֶת־הַשֻּׁלְחָן: ¹⁵ וַיַּעַשׂ אֶת־הַבַּדִּים עֲצֵי שִׁטִּים וַיְצַף אֹתָם זָהָב

with gold. ¹⁶He made of pure gold the utensils which were on the table: its dishes, its cups, its bowls, and its pitchers for pouring.

¹⁷He also made the lampstand of pure gold; of hammered work he made the lampstand. Its shaft, its branches, its bowls, its *ornamental* knobs, and its flowers were of the same piece. ¹⁸And six branches came out of its sides: three branches of the lampstand out of one side, and three branches of the lampstand out of the other side. ¹⁹There were three bowls made like almond *blossoms* on one branch, with an *ornamental* knob and a flower, and three bowls made like almond *blossoms* on the other branch, with an *ornamental* knob and a flower— and so for the six branches coming out of the lampstand. ²⁰And on the lampstand itself *were* four bowls made like almond *blossoms, each with* its *ornamental* knob and flower. ²¹*There was* a knob under the *first* two branches of the same, a knob under the *second* two branches of the same, and a knob under the *third* two branches of the same, according to the six branches extending from it. ²²Their knobs and their branches were of one piece; all of it *was* one hammered piece of pure gold. ²³And he made its seven lamps, its wick-trimmers, and its trays of pure gold. ²⁴Of a talent of pure gold he made it, with all its utensils.

²⁵He made the incense altar of acacia wood. Its length *was* a cubit and its width a cubit—*it was* square—and two cubits *was* its height. Its horns were *of one piece* with it. ²⁶And he overlaid it with pure gold: its top, its sides all around, and its horns. He also made for it a molding of gold all around it. ²⁷He made two rings of gold for it under its molding, by its two corners on both sides, as holders for the poles with which to bear it. ²⁸And he made the poles of acacia wood, and overlaid them with gold.

²⁹He also made the holy anointing oil and the pure incense of sweet spices, according to the work of the perfumer.

38 He made the altar of burnt offering of acacia wood; five cubits *was* its length and five cubits its width—*it was* square—and its height *was* three cubits. ²He made its horns on its four corners; the horns were *of one piece* with it. And he overlaid it with bronze. ³He made all the utensils for the altar: the pans, the shovels, the basins, the forks, and the firepans; all its utensils he made of bronze. ⁴And he made a grate of bronze network for the altar, under its rim, midway from the bottom. ⁵He cast four rings for the four corners of the bronze grating, *as* holders for the poles. ⁶And he made the poles of

acacia wood, and overlaid them with bronze. 7 Then
he put the poles into the rings on the sides of the
altar, with which to bear it. He made the altar
hollow with boards.

8 He made the laver of bronze and its base of
bronze, from the bronze mirrors of the serving
women who assembled at the door of the tabernacle
of meeting.

9 Then he made the court on the south side; the
hangings of the court *were of* fine woven linen, one
hundred cubits long. 10 There *were* twenty pillars for
them, with twenty bronze sockets. The hooks of the
pillars and their bands *were* silver. 11 On the north
side *the hangings were* one hundred cubits *long*, with
twenty pillars and their twenty bronze sockets. The
hooks of the pillars and their bands *were* silver.
12 And on the west side *there were* hangings of fifty
cubits, with ten pillars and their ten sockets. The
hooks of the pillars and their bands *were* silver.
13 For the east side *the hangings were* fifty cubits.
14 The hangings of one side *of the gate were* fifteen
cubits *long, with* their three pillars and their three
sockets, 15 and the same for the other side of the
court gate; on this side and that *were* hangings of
fifteen cubits, *with* their three pillars and their three
sockets. 16 All the hangings of the court all around
were of fine woven linen. 17 The sockets for the
pillars *were* bronze, the hooks of the pillars and
their bands *were* silver; and the overlay of their
capitals *was* silver; and all the pillars of the court
had bands of silver. 18 The screen for the gate of the
court *was* woven of blue, purple, and scarlet *thread,*
and of fine woven linen. The length *was* twenty
cubits, and the height along its width *was* five
cubits, corresponding to the hangings of the court.
19 And *there were* four pillars *with* their four sockets
of bronze; their hooks *were* silver, and the overlay
of their capitals and their bands *was* silver. 20 All the
pegs of the tabernacle, and of the court all around,
were bronze.

21 This is the inventory of the tabernacle, the
tabernacle of the Testimony, which was counted
according to the commandment of Moses, for the
service of the Levites, by the hand of Ithamar, son
of Aaron the priest.

22 Bezalel the son of Uri, the son of Hur, of the
tribe of Judah, made all that the LORD had
commanded Moses. 23 And with him *was* Aholiab
the son of Ahisamach, of the tribe of Dan, an
engraver and designer, a weaver of blue, purple,
and scarlet *thread,* and of fine linen.

24 All the gold that was used in all the work of the
holy *place,* that is, the gold of the offering, was
twenty-nine talents and seven hundred and thirty

וַיְצַ֥ף אֹתָ֖ם נְחֹֽשֶׁת: 7 וַיָּבֵ֤א אֶת־הַבַּדִּים֙ בַּטַּבָּעֹ֔ת עַ֖ל
צַלְעֹ֣ת הַמִּזְבֵּ֑חַ לָשֵׂ֥את אֹת֖וֹ בָּהֶ֑ם נְב֥וּב לֻחֹ֖ת עָשָׂ֥ה
אֹתֽוֹ: ס 8 וַיַּ֗עַשׂ אֵ֚ת הַכִּיּ֣וֹר נְחֹ֔שֶׁת וְאֵת֙
כַּנּ֣וֹ נְחֹ֔שֶׁת בְּמַרְאֹת֙ הַצֹּ֣בְאֹ֔ת אֲשֶׁ֣ר צָֽבְא֔וּ פֶּ֖תַח אֹ֥הֶל
מוֹעֵֽד: ס 9 וַיַּ֖עַשׂ אֶת־הֶֽחָצֵ֑ר לִפְאַ֣ת ׀
נֶ֣גֶב תֵּימָ֗נָה קַלְעֵ֤י הֶֽחָצֵר֙ שֵׁ֣שׁ מׇשְׁזָ֔ר מֵאָ֖ה בָּאַמָּֽה:

10 עַמּֽוּדֵיהֶ֣ם עֶשְׂרִ֔ים וְאַדְנֵיהֶ֥ם עֶשְׂרִ֖ים נְחֹ֑שֶׁת
וָוֵ֧י הָעַמֻּדִ֛ים וַחֲשֻׁקֵיהֶ֖ם כָּֽסֶף: 11 וְלִפְאַ֤ת צָפוֹן֙
מֵאָ֣ה בָֽאַמָּ֔ה עַמּֽוּדֵיהֶ֥ם עֶשְׂרִ֖ים וְאַדְנֵיהֶ֥ם עֶשְׂרִ֖ים
נְחֹ֑שֶׁת וָוֵ֧י הָֽעַמֻּדִ֛ים וַחֲשֻׁקֵיהֶ֖ם כָּֽסֶף: 12 וְלִפְאַת־
יָ֗ם קְלָעִים֙ חֲמִשִּׁ֣ים בָּֽאַמָּ֔ה עַמּֽוּדֵיהֶ֖ם עֲשָׂרָ֑ה
וְאַדְנֵיהֶ֣ם עֲשָׂרָ֑ה וָוֵ֧י הָֽעַמֻּדִ֛ים וַחֲשׁוּקֵיהֶ֖ם כָּֽסֶף:

13 וְלִפְאַ֛ת קֵ֥דְמָה מִזְרָ֖חָה חֲמִשִּׁ֥ים אַמָּֽה: 14 קְלָעִ֛ים
חֲמֵשׁ־עֶשְׂרֵ֥ה אַמָּ֖ה אֶל־הַכָּתֵ֑ף עַמּֽוּדֵיהֶ֣ם שְׁלֹשָׁ֔ה
וְאַדְנֵיהֶ֖ם שְׁלֹשָֽׁה: 15 וְלַכָּתֵ֤ף הַשֵּׁנִית֙ מִזֶּ֣ה וּמִזֶּ֔ה
לְשַׁ֣עַר הֶֽחָצֵ֔ר קְלָעִ֕ים חֲמֵ֥שׁ עֶשְׂרֵ֖ה אַמָּ֑ה עַמֻּדֵיהֶ֣ם
שְׁלֹשָׁ֔ה וְאַדְנֵיהֶ֖ם שְׁלֹשָֽׁה: 16 כׇּל־קַלְעֵ֧י הֶֽחָצֵ֛ר סָבִ֖יב
שֵׁ֣שׁ מׇשְׁזָֽר: 17 וְהָֽאֲדָנִ֣ים לָֽעַמֻּדִים֮ נְחֹשֶׁת֒ וָוֵ֨י
הָֽעַמּוּדִ֜ים וַחֲשֻׁקֵיהֶם֙ כֶּ֔סֶף וְצִפּ֥וּי רָֽאשֵׁיהֶ֖ם כָּ֑סֶף
וְהֵם֙ מְחֻשָּׁקִ֣ים כֶּ֔סֶף כֹּ֖ל עַמֻּדֵ֥י הֶֽחָצֵֽר: 18 וּמָסַ֞ךְ
שַׁ֤עַר הֶֽחָצֵר֙ מַֽעֲשֵׂ֣ה רֹקֵ֔ם תְּכֵ֧לֶת וְאַרְגָּמָ֛ן וְתוֹלַ֥עַת
שָׁנִ֖י וְשֵׁ֣שׁ מׇשְׁזָ֑ר וְעֶשְׂרִ֤ים אַמָּה֙ אֹ֔רֶךְ וְקוֹמָ֤ה בְרֹ֙חַב֙
חָמֵ֣שׁ אַמּ֔וֹת לְעֻמַּ֖ת קַלְעֵ֥י הֶֽחָצֵֽר: 19 וְעַמֻּֽדֵיהֶ֣ם
אַרְבָּעָ֗ה וְאַדְנֵיהֶ֤ם אַרְבָּעָה֙ נְחֹ֔שֶׁת וָֽוֵיהֶ֣ם כֶּ֔סֶף
וְצִפּ֧וּי רָֽאשֵׁיהֶ֛ם וַחֲשֻׁקֵיהֶ֖ם כָּֽסֶף: 20 וְכׇל־הַיְתֵדֹ֞ת
לַמִּשְׁכָּ֧ן וְלֶֽחָצֵ֛ר סָבִ֖יב נְחֹֽשֶׁת: ס 21 אֵ֣לֶּה
פְקוּדֵ֤י הַמִּשְׁכָּן֙ מִשְׁכַּ֣ן הָֽעֵדֻ֔ת אֲשֶׁ֥ר פֻּקַּ֖ד עַל־
פִּ֣י מֹשֶׁ֑ה עֲבֹדַת֙ הַֽלְוִיִּ֔ם בְּיַד֙ אִֽיתָמָ֔ר בֶּֽן־
אַהֲרֹ֖ן הַכֹּהֵֽן: 22 וּבְצַלְאֵ֛ל בֶּן־אוּרִ֥י בֶן־ח֖וּר לְמַטֵּ֣ה
יְהוּדָ֑ה עָשָׂ֕ה אֵ֛ת כׇּל־אֲשֶׁר־צִוָּ֥ה יְהֹוָ֖ה אֶת־מֹשֶֽׁה:

23 וְאִתּ֗וֹ אׇהֳלִיאָ֞ב בֶּן־אֲחִֽיסָמָךְ֙ לְמַטֵּה־דָ֔ן חָרָ֥שׁ
וְחֹשֵׁ֑ב וְרֹקֵ֗ם בַּתְּכֵ֙לֶת֙ וּבָֽאַרְגָּמָ֔ן וּבְתוֹלַ֥עַת הַשָּׁנִ֖י
וּבַשֵּֽׁשׁ: ס 24 כׇּל־הַזָּהָ֗ב הֶֽעָשׂוּי֙ לַמְּלָאכָ֔ה
בְּכֹ֖ל מְלֶ֣אכֶת הַקֹּ֑דֶשׁ וַיְהִ֣י ׀ זְהַ֣ב הַתְּנוּפָ֗ה תֵּ֤שַׁע
וְעֶשְׂרִים֙ כִּכָּ֔ר וּשְׁבַ֥ע מֵא֛וֹת וּשְׁלֹשִׁ֥ים שֶׁ֖קֶל בְּשֶׁ֥קֶל

shekels, according to the shekel of the sanctuary.
25 And the silver from those who were numbered of
the congregation *was* one hundred talents and one
thousand seven hundred and seventy-five shekels,
according to the shekel of the sanctuary: 26 a bekah
for each man (*that is,* half a shekel, according to the
shekel of the sanctuary), for everyone included in
the numbering from twenty years old and above,
for six hundred and three thousand, five hundred
and fifty *men.* 27 And from the hundred talents of
silver were cast the sockets of the sanctuary and the
bases of the veil: one hundred sockets from the
hundred talents, one talent for each socket. 28 Then
from the one thousand seven hundred and seventy-
five *shekels* he made hooks for the pillars, overlaid
their capitals, and made bands for them.

29 The offering of bronze *was* seventy talents and
two thousand four hundred shekels. 30 And with it
he made the sockets for the door of the tabernacle
of meeting, the bronze altar, the bronze grating for
it, and all the utensils for the altar, 31 the sockets for
the court all around, the bases for the court gate, all
the pegs for the tabernacle, and all the pegs for the
court all around.

39 Of the blue, purple, and scarlet *thread* they
made garments of ministry, for ministering in the
holy *place,* and made the holy garments for Aaron,
as the LORD had commanded Moses.

2 He made the ephod of gold, blue, purple, and
scarlet *thread,* and of fine woven linen. 3 And they
beat the gold into thin sheets and cut *it into* threads,
to work *it in* with the blue, purple, and scarlet
thread, and the fine linen, *into* artistic designs.
4 They made shoulder straps for it to couple *it*
together; it was coupled together at its two edges.
5 And the intricately woven band of his ephod that
was on it *was* of the same workmanship, *woven of*
gold, blue, purple, and scarlet *thread,* and of fine
woven linen, as the LORD had commanded Moses.

6 And they set onyx stones, enclosed in settings of
gold; they were engraved, as signets are engraved,
with the names of the sons of Israel. 7 He put them
on the shoulders of the ephod *as* memorial stones
for the sons of Israel, as the LORD had commanded
Moses.

8 And he made the breastplate, artistically woven
like the workmanship of the ephod, of gold, blue,
purple, and scarlet *thread,* and of fine woven linen.
9 They made the breastplate square by doubling it; a
span *was* its length and a span its width when
doubled. 10 And they set in it four rows of stones: a
row with a sardius, a topaz, and an emerald *was* the
first row; 11 the second row, a turquoise, a sapphire,

הַקֹּדֶשׁ: 25 וְכֶסֶף פְּקוּדֵי הָעֵדָה מְאַת כִּכָּר וְאֶלֶף
וּשְׁבַע מֵאוֹת וַחֲמִשָּׁה וְשִׁבְעִים שֶׁקֶל בְּשֶׁקֶל הַקֹּדֶשׁ:
26 בֶּקַע לַגֻּלְגֹּלֶת מַחֲצִית הַשֶּׁקֶל בְּשֶׁקֶל הַקֹּדֶשׁ
לְכֹל הָעֹבֵר עַל־הַפְּקֻדִים מִבֶּן עֶשְׂרִים שָׁנָה וָמַעְלָה
לְשֵׁשׁ־מֵאוֹת אֶלֶף וּשְׁלֹשֶׁת אֲלָפִים וַחֲמֵשׁ מֵאוֹת
וַחֲמִשִּׁים: 27 וַיְהִי מְאַת כִּכַּר הַכֶּסֶף לָצֶקֶת אֵת
אַדְנֵי הַקֹּדֶשׁ וְאֵת אַדְנֵי הַפָּרֹכֶת מְאַת אֲדָנִים
לִמְאַת הַכִּכָּר כִּכָּר לָאָדֶן: 28 וְאֶת־הָאֶלֶף וּשְׁבַע
הַמֵּאוֹת וַחֲמִשָּׁה וְשִׁבְעִים עָשָׂה וָוִים לָעַמּוּדִים
וְצִפָּה רָאשֵׁיהֶם וְחִשַּׁק אֹתָם: 29 וּנְחֹשֶׁת הַתְּנוּפָה
שִׁבְעִים כִּכָּר וְאַלְפַּיִם וְאַרְבַּע־מֵאוֹת שָׁקֶל: 30 וַיַּעַשׂ
בָּהּ אֶת־אַדְנֵי פֶּתַח אֹהֶל מוֹעֵד וְאֵת מִזְבַּח הַנְּחֹשֶׁת
וְאֶת־מִכְבַּר הַנְּחֹשֶׁת אֲשֶׁר־לוֹ וְאֵת כָּל־כְּלֵי הַמִּזְבֵּחַ:
31 וְאֶת־אַדְנֵי הֶחָצֵר סָבִיב וְאֶת־אַדְנֵי שַׁעַר הֶחָצֵר
וְאֵת כָּל־יִתְדֹת הַמִּשְׁכָּן וְאֶת־כָּל־יִתְדֹת הֶחָצֵר
סָבִיב:

לט וּמִן־הַתְּכֵלֶת וְהָאַרְגָּמָן וְתוֹלַעַת הַשָּׁנִי עָשׂוּ
בִגְדֵי־שְׂרָד לְשָׁרֵת בַּקֹּדֶשׁ וַיַּעֲשׂוּ אֶת־בִּגְדֵי הַקֹּדֶשׁ
אֲשֶׁר לְאַהֲרֹן כַּאֲשֶׁר צִוָּה יְהוָה אֶת־מֹשֶׁה: פ
2 וַיַּעַשׂ אֶת־הָאֵפֹד זָהָב תְּכֵלֶת וְאַרְגָּמָן וְתוֹלַעַת
שָׁנִי וְשֵׁשׁ מָשְׁזָר: 3 וַיְרַקְּעוּ אֶת־פַּחֵי הַזָּהָב וְקִצֵּץ
פְּתִילִם לַעֲשׂוֹת בְּתוֹךְ הַתְּכֵלֶת וּבְתוֹךְ הָאַרְגָּמָן
וּבְתוֹךְ תּוֹלַעַת הַשָּׁנִי וּבְתוֹךְ הַשֵּׁשׁ מַעֲשֵׂה חֹשֵׁב:
4 כְּתֵפֹת עָשׂוּ־לוֹ חֹבְרֹת עַל־שְׁנֵי קְצוֹתָו חֻבָּר:
5 וְחֵשֶׁב אֲפֻדָּתוֹ אֲשֶׁר עָלָיו מִמֶּנּוּ הוּא כְּמַעֲשֵׂהוּ
זָהָב תְּכֵלֶת וְאַרְגָּמָן וְתוֹלַעַת שָׁנִי וְשֵׁשׁ מָשְׁזָר
כַּאֲשֶׁר צִוָּה יְהוָה אֶת־מֹשֶׁה: 6 וַיַּעֲשׂוּ אֶת־אַבְנֵי
הַשֹּׁהַם מֻסַבֹּת מִשְׁבְּצֹת זָהָב מְפֻתָּחֹת פִּתּוּחֵי חוֹתָם
עַל־שְׁמוֹת בְּנֵי יִשְׂרָאֵל: 7 וַיָּשֶׂם אֹתָם עַל כִּתְפֹת
הָאֵפֹד אַבְנֵי זִכָּרוֹן לִבְנֵי יִשְׂרָאֵל כַּאֲשֶׁר צִוָּה יְהוָה
אֶת־מֹשֶׁה: פ

8 וַיַּעַשׂ אֶת־הַחֹשֶׁן מַעֲשֵׂה חֹשֵׁב כְּמַעֲשֵׂה אֵפֹד
זָהָב תְּכֵלֶת וְאַרְגָּמָן וְתוֹלַעַת שָׁנִי וְשֵׁשׁ מָשְׁזָר:
9 רָבוּעַ הָיָה כָּפוּל עָשׂוּ אֶת־הַחֹשֶׁן זֶרֶת אָרְכּוֹ וְזֶרֶת
רָחְבּוֹ כָּפוּל: 10 וַיְמַלְאוּ־בוֹ אַרְבָּעָה טוּרֵי אָבֶן טוּר
אֹדֶם פִּטְדָה וּבָרֶקֶת הַטּוּר הָאֶחָד: 11 וְהַטּוּר הַשֵּׁנִי

and a diamond; [12] the third row, a jacinth, an agate, and an amethyst; [13] the fourth row, a beryl, an onyx, and a jasper. *They were* enclosed in settings of gold in their mountings. [14] *There were* twelve stones according to the names of the sons of Israel: according to their names, *engraved like* a signet, each one with its own name according to the twelve tribes. [15] And they made chains for the breastplate at the ends, like braided cords of pure gold. [16] They also made two settings of gold and two gold rings, and put the two rings on the two ends of the breastplate. [17] And they put the two braided *chains* of gold in the two rings on the ends of the breastplate. [18] The two ends of the two braided *chains* they fastened in the two settings, and put them on the shoulder straps of the ephod in the front. [19] And they made two rings of gold and put *them* on the two ends of the breastplate, on the edge of it, which *was* on the inward side of the ephod. [20] They made two *other* gold rings and put them on the two shoulder straps, underneath the ephod toward its front, right at the seam above the intricately woven band of the ephod. [21] And they bound the breastplate by means of its rings to the rings of the ephod with a blue cord, so that it would be above the intricately woven band of the ephod, and that the breastplate would not come loose from the ephod, as the LORD had commanded Moses.

[22] He made the robe of the ephod of woven work, all of blue. [23] And *there was* an opening in the middle of the robe, like the opening in a coat of mail, *with* a woven binding all around the opening, so that it would not tear. [24] They made on the hem of the robe pomegranates of blue, purple, and scarlet, and of fine woven *linen.* [25] And they made bells of pure gold, and put the bells between the pomegranates on the hem of the robe all around between the pomegranates: [26] a bell and a pomegranate, a bell and a pomegranate, all around the hem of the robe to minister in, as the LORD had commanded Moses.

[27] They made tunics, artistically woven of fine linen, for Aaron and his sons, [28] a turban of fine linen, exquisite hats of fine linen, short trousers of fine woven linen, [29] and a sash of fine woven linen with blue, purple, and scarlet *thread,* made by a weaver, as the LORD had commanded Moses.

[30] Then they made the plate of the holy crown of pure gold, and wrote on it an inscription *like* the engraving of a signet:

HOLINESS TO THE LORD.

נֹפֶךְ סַפִּיר וְיָהֲלֹם: 12 וְהַטּוּר הַשְּׁלִישִׁי לֶשֶׁם שְׁבוֹ וְאַחְלָמָה: 13 וְהַטּוּר הָרְבִיעִי תַּרְשִׁישׁ שֹׁהַם וְיָשְׁפֵה מוּסַבֹּת מִשְׁבְּצֹת זָהָב בְּמִלֻּאֹתָם: 14 וְהָאֲבָנִים עַל־שְׁמֹת בְּנֵי־יִשְׂרָאֵל הֵנָּה שְׁתֵּים עֶשְׂרֵה עַל־שְׁמֹתָם פִּתּוּחֵי חֹתָם אִישׁ עַל־שְׁמוֹ לִשְׁנֵים עָשָׂר שָׁבֶט: 15 וַיַּעֲשׂוּ עַל־הַחֹשֶׁן שַׁרְשְׁרֹת גַּבְלֻת מַעֲשֵׂה עֲבֹת זָהָב טָהוֹר: 16 וַיַּעֲשׂוּ שְׁתֵּי מִשְׁבְּצֹת זָהָב וּשְׁתֵּי טַבְּעֹת זָהָב וַיִּתְּנוּ אֶת־שְׁתֵּי הַטַּבָּעֹת עַל־שְׁנֵי קְצוֹת הַחֹשֶׁן: 17 וַיִּתְּנוּ שְׁתֵּי הָעֲבֹתֹת הַזָּהָב עַל־שְׁתֵּי הַטַּבָּעֹת עַל־קְצוֹת הַחֹשֶׁן: 18 וְאֵת שְׁתֵּי קְצוֹת שְׁתֵּי הָעֲבֹתֹת נָתְנוּ עַל־שְׁתֵּי הַמִּשְׁבְּצֹת וַיִּתְּנֻם עַל־כִּתְפֹת הָאֵפֹד אֶל־מוּל פָּנָיו: 19 וַיַּעֲשׂוּ שְׁתֵּי טַבְּעֹת זָהָב וַיָּשִׂימוּ עַל־שְׁנֵי קְצוֹת הַחֹשֶׁן עַל־שְׂפָתוֹ אֲשֶׁר אֶל־עֵבֶר הָאֵפֹד בָּיְתָה: 20 וַיַּעֲשׂוּ שְׁתֵּי טַבְּעֹת זָהָב וַיִּתְּנֻם עַל־שְׁתֵּי כִתְפֹת הָאֵפֹד מִלְמַטָּה מִמּוּל פָּנָיו לְעֻמַּת מֶחְבַּרְתּוֹ מִמַּעַל לְחֵשֶׁב הָאֵפֹד: 21 וַיִּרְכְּסוּ אֶת־הַחֹשֶׁן מִטַּבְּעֹתָיו אֶל־טַבְּעֹת הָאֵפֹד בִּפְתִיל תְּכֵלֶת לִהְיֹת עַל־חֵשֶׁב הָאֵפֹד וְלֹא־יִזַּח הַחֹשֶׁן מֵעַל הָאֵפֹד כַּאֲשֶׁר צִוָּה יְהוָה אֶת־מֹשֶׁה: 22 וַיַּעַשׂ אֶת־מְעִיל הָאֵפֹד מַעֲשֵׂה אֹרֵג כְּלִיל תְּכֵלֶת: 23 וּפִי־הַמְּעִיל בְּתוֹכוֹ כְּפִי תַחְרָא שָׂפָה לְפִיו סָבִיב לֹא יִקָּרֵעַ: 24 וַיַּעֲשׂוּ עַל־שׁוּלֵי הַמְּעִיל רִמּוֹנֵי תְּכֵלֶת וְאַרְגָּמָן וְתוֹלַעַת שָׁנִי מָשְׁזָר: 25 וַיַּעֲשׂוּ פַעֲמֹנֵי זָהָב טָהוֹר וַיִּתְּנוּ אֶת־הַפַּעֲמֹנִים בְּתוֹךְ הָרִמֹּנִים עַל־שׁוּלֵי הַמְּעִיל סָבִיב בְּתוֹךְ הָרִמֹּנִים: 26 פַּעֲמֹן וְרִמֹּן פַּעֲמֹן וְרִמֹּן עַל־שׁוּלֵי הַמְּעִיל סָבִיב לְשָׁרֵת כַּאֲשֶׁר צִוָּה יְהוָה אֶת־מֹשֶׁה: ס 27 וַיַּעֲשׂוּ אֶת־הַכָּתְנֹת שֵׁשׁ מַעֲשֵׂה אֹרֵג לְאַהֲרֹן וּלְבָנָיו: 28 וְאֵת הַמִּצְנֶפֶת שֵׁשׁ וְאֶת־פַּאֲרֵי הַמִּגְבָּעֹת שֵׁשׁ וְאֶת־מִכְנְסֵי הַבָּד שֵׁשׁ מָשְׁזָר: 29 וְאֶת־הָאַבְנֵט שֵׁשׁ מָשְׁזָר וּתְכֵלֶת וְאַרְגָּמָן וְתוֹלַעַת שָׁנִי מַעֲשֵׂה רֹקֵם כַּאֲשֶׁר צִוָּה יְהוָה אֶת־מֹשֶׁה: ס 30 וַיַּעֲשׂוּ אֶת־צִיץ נֵזֶר־הַקֹּדֶשׁ זָהָב טָהוֹר וַיִּכְתְּבוּ עָלָיו מִכְתַּב

31 And they tied to it a blue cord, to fasten *it* above on the turban, as the LORD had commanded Moses.

32 Thus all the work of the tabernacle of the tent of meeting was finished. And the children of Israel did according to all that the LORD had commanded Moses; so they did. 33 And they brought the tabernacle to Moses, the tent and all its furnishings: its clasps, its boards, its bars, its pillars, and its sockets; 34 the covering of ram skins dyed red, the covering of badger skins, and the veil of the covering; 35 the ark of the Testimony with its poles, and the mercy seat; 36 the table, all its utensils, and the showbread; 37 the pure *gold* lampstand with its lamps (the lamps set in order), all its utensils, and the oil for light; 38 the gold altar, the anointing oil, and the sweet incense; the screen for the tabernacle door; 39 the bronze altar, its grate of bronze, its poles, and all its utensils; the laver with its base; 40 the hangings of the court, its pillars and its sockets, the screen for the court gate, its cords, and its pegs; all the utensils for the service of the tabernacle, for the tent of meeting; 41 and the garments of ministry, to minister in the holy *place:* the holy garments for Aaron the priest, and his sons' garments, to minister as priests.

42 According to all that the LORD had commanded Moses, so the children of Israel did all the work. 43 Then Moses looked over all the work, and indeed they had done it; as the LORD had commanded, just so they had done it. And Moses blessed them.

40 Then the LORD spoke to Moses, saying: 2 "On the first day of the first month you shall set up the tabernacle of the tent of meeting. 3 You shall put in it the ark of the Testimony, and partition off the ark with the veil. 4 You shall bring in the table and arrange the things that are to be set in order on it; and you shall bring in the lampstand and light its lamps. 5 You shall also set the altar of gold for the incense before the ark of the Testimony, and put up the screen for the door of the tabernacle. 6 Then you shall set the altar of the burnt offering before the door of the tabernacle of the tent of meeting. 7 And you shall set the laver between the tabernacle of meeting and the altar, and put water in it. 8 You shall set up the court all around, and hang up the screen at the court gate.

9 "And you shall take the anointing oil, and anoint the tabernacle and all that *is* in it; and you shall hallow it and all its utensils, and it shall be holy. 10 You shall anoint the altar of the burnt

31 פְּתוּחֵי חוֹתָם קֹדֶשׁ לַיהוָה: וַיִּתְּנוּ עָלָיו פְּתִיל תְּכֵלֶת לָתֵת עַל־הַמִּצְנֶפֶת מִלְמָעְלָה כַּאֲשֶׁר צִוָּה יְהוָה אֶת־מֹשֶׁה: ס 32 וַתֵּכֶל כָּל־עֲבֹדַת מִשְׁכַּן אֹהֶל מוֹעֵד וַיַּעֲשׂוּ בְּנֵי יִשְׂרָאֵל כְּכֹל אֲשֶׁר צִוָּה יְהוָה אֶת־מֹשֶׁה כֵּן עָשׂוּ: פ 33 וַיָּבִיאוּ אֶת־הַמִּשְׁכָּן אֶל־מֹשֶׁה אֶת־הָאֹהֶל וְאֶת־כָּל־כֵּלָיו קְרָסָיו קְרָשָׁיו בְּרִיחָו וְעַמֻּדָיו וַאֲדָנָיו: 34 וְאֶת־מִכְסֵה עוֹרֹת הָאֵילִם הַמְאָדָּמִים וְאֶת־מִכְסֵה עֹרֹת הַתְּחָשִׁים וְאֵת פָּרֹכֶת הַמָּסָךְ: 35 אֶת־אֲרֹן הָעֵדֻת וְאֶת־בַּדָּיו וְאֵת הַכַּפֹּרֶת: 36 אֶת־הַשֻּׁלְחָן אֶת־כָּל־כֵּלָיו וְאֵת לֶחֶם הַפָּנִים: 37 אֶת־הַמְּנֹרָה הַטְּהֹרָה אֶת־נֵרֹתֶיהָ נֵרֹת הַמַּעֲרָכָה וְאֶת־כָּל־כֵּלֶיהָ וְאֵת שֶׁמֶן הַמָּאוֹר: 38 וְאֵת מִזְבַּח הַזָּהָב וְאֵת שֶׁמֶן הַמִּשְׁחָה וְאֵת קְטֹרֶת הַסַּמִּים וְאֵת מָסַךְ פֶּתַח הָאֹהֶל: 39 אֵת מִזְבַּח הַנְּחֹשֶׁת וְאֶת־מִכְבַּר הַנְּחֹשֶׁת אֲשֶׁר־לוֹ אֶת־בַּדָּיו וְאֶת־כָּל־כֵּלָיו אֶת־הַכִּיֹּר וְאֶת־כַּנּוֹ: 40 אֵת קַלְעֵי הֶחָצֵר אֶת־עַמֻּדֶיהָ וְאֶת־אֲדָנֶיהָ וְאֶת־הַמָּסָךְ לְשַׁעַר הֶחָצֵר אֶת־מֵיתָרָיו וִיתֵדֹתֶיהָ וְאֵת כָּל־כְּלֵי עֲבֹדַת הַמִּשְׁכָּן לְאֹהֶל מוֹעֵד: 41 אֶת־בִּגְדֵי הַשְּׂרָד לְשָׁרֵת בַּקֹּדֶשׁ אֶת־בִּגְדֵי הַקֹּדֶשׁ לְאַהֲרֹן הַכֹּהֵן וְאֶת־בִּגְדֵי בָנָיו לְכַהֵן: 42 כְּכֹל אֲשֶׁר־צִוָּה יְהוָה אֶת־מֹשֶׁה כֵּן עָשׂוּ בְּנֵי יִשְׂרָאֵל אֵת כָּל־הָעֲבֹדָה: 43 וַיַּרְא מֹשֶׁה אֶת־כָּל־הַמְּלָאכָה וְהִנֵּה עָשׂוּ אֹתָהּ כַּאֲשֶׁר צִוָּה יְהוָה כֵּן עָשׂוּ וַיְבָרֶךְ אֹתָם מֹשֶׁה: פ

מ 1 וַיְדַבֵּר יְהוָה אֶל־מֹשֶׁה לֵּאמֹר: 2 בְּיוֹם־הַחֹדֶשׁ הָרִאשׁוֹן בְּאֶחָד לַחֹדֶשׁ תָּקִים אֶת־מִשְׁכַּן אֹהֶל מוֹעֵד: 3 וְשַׂמְתָּ שָׁם אֵת אֲרוֹן הָעֵדוּת וְסַכֹּתָ עַל־הָאָרֹן אֶת־הַפָּרֹכֶת: 4 וְהֵבֵאתָ אֶת־הַשֻּׁלְחָן וְעָרַכְתָּ אֶת־עֶרְכּוֹ וְהֵבֵאתָ אֶת־הַמְּנֹרָה וְהַעֲלֵיתָ אֶת־נֵרֹתֶיהָ: 5 וְנָתַתָּה אֶת־מִזְבַּח הַזָּהָב לִקְטֹרֶת לִפְנֵי אֲרוֹן הָעֵדֻת וְשַׂמְתָּ אֶת־מָסַךְ הַפֶּתַח לַמִּשְׁכָּן: 6 וְנָתַתָּה אֵת מִזְבַּח הָעֹלָה לִפְנֵי פֶּתַח מִשְׁכַּן אֹהֶל־מוֹעֵד: 7 וְנָתַתָּ אֶת־הַכִּיֹּר בֵּין־אֹהֶל מוֹעֵד וּבֵין הַמִּזְבֵּחַ וְנָתַתָּ שָׁם מָיִם: 8 וְשַׂמְתָּ אֶת־הֶחָצֵר סָבִיב וְנָתַתָּ אֶת־מָסַךְ שַׁעַר הֶחָצֵר: 9 וְלָקַחְתָּ אֶת־שֶׁמֶן הַמִּשְׁחָה וּמָשַׁחְתָּ אֶת־הַמִּשְׁכָּן וְאֶת־כָּל־אֲשֶׁר־בּוֹ וְקִדַּשְׁתָּ אֹתוֹ וְאֶת־כָּל־כֵּלָיו וְהָיָה קֹדֶשׁ: 10 וּמָשַׁחְתָּ אֶת־מִזְבַּח הָעֹלָה וְאֶת־כָּל־כֵּלָיו וְקִדַּשְׁתָּ אֶת־הַמִּזְבֵּחַ וְהָיָה הַמִּזְבֵּחַ קֹדֶשׁ

offering and all its utensils, and consecrate the altar. The altar shall be most holy. ¹¹And you shall anoint the laver and its base, and consecrate it.

¹²"Then you shall bring Aaron and his sons to the door of the tabernacle of meeting and wash them with water. ¹³You shall put the holy garments on Aaron, and anoint him and consecrate him, that he may minister to Me as priest. ¹⁴And you shall bring his sons and clothe them with tunics. ¹⁵You shall anoint them, as you anointed their father, that they may minister to Me as priests; for their anointing shall surely be an everlasting priesthood throughout their generations."

¹⁶Thus Moses did; according to all that the LORD had commanded him, so he did.

¹⁷And it came to pass in the first month of the second year, on the first *day* of the month, *that* the tabernacle was raised up. ¹⁸So Moses raised up the tabernacle, fastened its sockets, set up its boards, put in its bars, and raised up its pillars. ¹⁹And he spread out the tent over the tabernacle and put the covering of the tent on top of it, as the LORD had commanded Moses. ²⁰He took the Testimony and put *it* into the ark, inserted the poles through the rings of the ark, and put the mercy seat on top of the ark. ²¹And he brought the ark into the tabernacle, hung up the veil of the covering, and partitioned off the ark of the Testimony, as the LORD had commanded Moses.

²²He put the table in the tabernacle of meeting, on the north side of the tabernacle, outside the veil; ²³and he set the bread in order upon it before the LORD, as the LORD had commanded Moses. ²⁴He put the lampstand in the tabernacle of meeting, across from the table, on the south side of the tabernacle; ²⁵and he lit the lamps before the LORD, as the LORD had commanded Moses. ²⁶He put the gold altar in the tabernacle of meeting in front of the veil; ²⁷and he burned sweet incense on it, as the LORD had commanded Moses. ²⁸He hung up the screen *at* the door of the tabernacle. ²⁹And he put the altar of burnt offering *before* the door of the tabernacle of the tent of meeting, and offered upon it the burnt offering and the grain offering, as the LORD had commanded Moses. ³⁰He set the laver between the tabernacle of meeting and the altar, and put water there for washing; ³¹and Moses, Aaron, and his sons would wash their hands and their feet *with water* from it. ³²Whenever they went into the tabernacle of meeting, and when they came near the altar, they washed, as the LORD had commanded Moses. ³³And he raised up the court

קָדָשִׁים: 11 וּמָשַׁחְתָּ אֶת־הַכִּיֹּר וְאֶת־כַּנּוֹ וְקִדַּשְׁתָּ אֹתוֹ: 12 וְהִקְרַבְתָּ אֶת־אַהֲרֹן וְאֶת־בָּנָיו אֶל־פֶּתַח אֹהֶל מוֹעֵד וְרָחַצְתָּ אֹתָם בַּמָּיִם: 13 וְהִלְבַּשְׁתָּ אֶת־ אַהֲרֹן אֵת בִּגְדֵי הַקֹּדֶשׁ וּמָשַׁחְתָּ אֹתוֹ וְקִדַּשְׁתָּ אֹתוֹ וְכִהֵן לִי: 14 וְאֶת־בָּנָיו תַּקְרִיב וְהִלְבַּשְׁתָּ אֹתָם כֻּתֳּנֹת: 15 וּמָשַׁחְתָּ אֹתָם כַּאֲשֶׁר מָשַׁחְתָּ אֶת־ אֲבִיהֶם וְכִהֲנוּ לִי וְהָיְתָה לִהְיֹת לָהֶם מָשְׁחָתָם לִכְהֻנַּת עוֹלָם לְדֹרֹתָם: 16 וַיַּעַשׂ מֹשֶׁה כְּכֹל אֲשֶׁר צִוָּה יְהוָה אֹתוֹ כֵּן עָשָׂה: ס 17 וַיְהִי בַּחֹדֶשׁ הָרִאשׁוֹן בַּשָּׁנָה הַשֵּׁנִית בְּאֶחָד לַחֹדֶשׁ הוּקַם הַמִּשְׁכָּן: 18 וַיָּקֶם מֹשֶׁה אֶת־הַמִּשְׁכָּן וַיִּתֵּן אֶת־אֲדָנָיו וַיָּשֶׂם אֶת־קְרָשָׁיו וַיִּתֵּן אֶת־בְּרִיחָיו וַיָּקֶם אֶת־עַמּוּדָיו: 19 וַיִּפְרֹשׂ אֶת־הָאֹהֶל עַל־ הַמִּשְׁכָּן וַיָּשֶׂם אֶת־מִכְסֵה הָאֹהֶל עָלָיו מִלְמָעְלָה כַּאֲשֶׁר צִוָּה יְהוָה אֶת־מֹשֶׁה: ס 20 וַיִּקַּח וַיִּתֵּן אֶת־הָעֵדֻת אֶל־הָאָרֹן וַיָּשֶׂם אֶת־הַבַּדִּים עַל־ הָאָרֹן וַיִּתֵּן אֶת־הַכַּפֹּרֶת עַל־הָאָרֹן מִלְמָעְלָה: 21 וַיָּבֵא אֶת־הָאָרֹן אֶל־הַמִּשְׁכָּן וַיָּשֶׂם אֵת פָּרֹכֶת הַמָּסָךְ וַיָּסֶךְ עַל אֲרוֹן הָעֵדוּת כַּאֲשֶׁר צִוָּה יְהוָה אֶת־מֹשֶׁה: ס 22 וַיִּתֵּן אֶת־הַשֻּׁלְחָן בְּאֹהֶל מוֹעֵד עַל יֶרֶךְ הַמִּשְׁכָּן צָפֹנָה מִחוּץ לַפָּרֹכֶת: 23 וַיַּעֲרֹךְ עָלָיו עֵרֶךְ לֶחֶם לִפְנֵי יְהוָה כַּאֲשֶׁר צִוָּה יְהוָה אֶת־מֹשֶׁה: ס 24 וַיָּשֶׂם אֶת־ הַמְּנֹרָה בְּאֹהֶל מוֹעֵד נֹכַח הַשֻּׁלְחָן עַל יֶרֶךְ הַמִּשְׁכָּן נֶגְבָּה: 25 וַיַּעַל הַנֵּרֹת לִפְנֵי יְהוָה כַּאֲשֶׁר צִוָּה יְהוָה אֶת־מֹשֶׁה: ס 26 וַיָּשֶׂם אֶת־מִזְבַּח הַזָּהָב בְּאֹהֶל מוֹעֵד לִפְנֵי הַפָּרֹכֶת: 27 וַיַּקְטֵר עָלָיו קְטֹרֶת סַמִּים כַּאֲשֶׁר צִוָּה יְהוָה אֶת־מֹשֶׁה: פ 28 וַיָּשֶׂם אֶת־מָסַךְ הַפֶּתַח לַמִּשְׁכָּן: 29 וְאֵת מִזְבַּח הָעֹלָה שָׂם פֶּתַח מִשְׁכַּן אֹהֶל־מוֹעֵד וַיַּעַל עָלָיו אֶת־הָעֹלָה וְאֶת־הַמִּנְחָה כַּאֲשֶׁר צִוָּה יְהוָה אֶת־ מֹשֶׁה: ס 30 וַיָּשֶׂם אֶת־הַכִּיֹּר בֵּין־אֹהֶל מוֹעֵד וּבֵין הַמִּזְבֵּחַ וַיִּתֵּן שָׁמָּה מַיִם לְרָחְצָה: 31 וְרָחֲצוּ מִמֶּנּוּ מֹשֶׁה וְאַהֲרֹן וּבָנָיו אֶת־יְדֵיהֶם וְאֶת־רַגְלֵיהֶם: 32 בְּבֹאָם אֶל־אֹהֶל מוֹעֵד וּבְקָרְבָתָם אֶל־הַמִּזְבֵּחַ יִרְחָצוּ כַּאֲשֶׁר צִוָּה יְהוָה אֶת־ מֹשֶׁה: ס 33 וַיָּקֶם אֶת־הֶחָצֵר סָבִיב

all around the tabernacle and the altar, and hung up the screen of the court gate. So Moses finished the work.

³⁴Then the cloud covered the tabernacle of meeting, and the glory of the LORD filled the tabernacle. ³⁵And Moses was not able to enter the tabernacle of meeting, because the cloud rested above it, and the glory of the LORD filled the tabernacle. ³⁶Whenever the cloud was taken up from above the tabernacle, the children of Israel would go onward in all their journeys. ³⁷But if the cloud was not taken up, then they did not journey till the day that it was taken up. ³⁸For the cloud of the LORD *was* above the tabernacle by day, and fire was over it by night, in the sight of all the house of Israel, throughout all their journeys.

לַמִּשְׁכָּן וְלַמִּזְבֵּחַ וַיִּתֵּן אֶת־מָסַךְ שַׁעַר הֶחָצֵר וַיְכַל מֹשֶׁה אֶת־הַמְּלָאכָה: פ

³⁴וַיְכַס הֶעָנָן אֶת־אֹהֶל מוֹעֵד וּכְבוֹד יְהֹוָה מָלֵא אֶת־הַמִּשְׁכָּן: ³⁵וְלֹא־יָכֹל מֹשֶׁה לָבוֹא אֶל־אֹהֶל מוֹעֵד כִּי־שָׁכַן עָלָיו הֶעָנָן וּכְבוֹד יְהֹוָה מָלֵא אֶת־הַמִּשְׁכָּן: ³⁶וּבְהֵעָלוֹת הֶעָנָן מֵעַל הַמִּשְׁכָּן יִסְעוּ בְּנֵי יִשְׂרָאֵל בְּכֹל מַסְעֵיהֶם: ³⁷וְאִם־לֹא יֵעָלֶה הֶעָנָן וְלֹא יִסְעוּ עַד־יוֹם הֵעָלֹתוֹ: ³⁸כִּי עֲנַן יְהֹוָה עַל־הַמִּשְׁכָּן יוֹמָם וְאֵשׁ תִּהְיֶה לַיְלָה בּוֹ לְעֵינֵי כָל־בֵּית־יִשְׂרָאֵל בְּכָל־מַסְעֵיהֶם:

The Third Book of Moses Called

LEVITICUS

ויקרא

1 Now the LORD called to Moses, and spoke to him from the tabernacle of meeting, saying, ²"Speak to the children of Israel, and say to them: 'When any one of you brings an offering to the LORD, you shall bring your offering of the live-stock—of the herd and of the flock.

³ 'If his offering is a burnt sacrifice of the herd, let him offer a male without blemish; he shall offer it of his own free will at the door of the tabernacle of meeting before the LORD. ⁴Then he shall put his hand on the head of the burnt offering, and it will be accepted on his behalf to make atonement for him. ⁵He shall kill the bull before the LORD; and the priests, Aaron's sons, shall bring the blood and sprinkle the blood all around on the altar that is by the door of the tabernacle of meeting. ⁶And he shall skin the burnt offering and cut it into its pieces. ⁷The sons of Aaron the priest shall put fire on the altar, and lay the wood in order on the fire. ⁸Then the priests, Aaron's sons, shall lay the parts, the head, and the fat in order on the wood that is on the fire upon the altar; ⁹but he shall wash its entrails and its legs with water. And the priest shall burn all on the altar as a burnt sacrifice, an offering made by fire, a sweet aroma to the LORD.

¹⁰ 'If his offering is of the flocks—of the sheep or of the goats—as a burnt sacrifice, he shall bring a male without blemish. ¹¹He shall kill it on the north side of the altar before the LORD; and the priests, Aaron's sons, shall sprinkle its blood all around on the altar. ¹²And he shall cut it into its pieces, with its head and its fat; and the priest shall lay them in order on the wood that is on the fire upon the altar; ¹³but he shall wash the entrails and the legs with water. Then the priest shall bring it all and burn it on the altar; it is a burnt sacrifice, an offering made by fire, a sweet aroma to the LORD.

¹⁴ 'And if the burnt sacrifice of his offering to the LORD is of birds, then he shall bring his offering of turtledoves or young pigeons. ¹⁵The priest shall bring it to the altar, wring off its head, and burn it on the altar; its blood shall be drained out at the side of the altar. ¹⁶And he shall remove its crop with its feathers and cast it beside the altar on the east side, into the place for ashes. ¹⁷Then he shall split it at its wings, but shall not divide it completely; and the priest shall burn it on the altar,

א וַיִּקְרָא אֶל־מֹשֶׁה וַיְדַבֵּר יְהוָֹה אֵלָיו מֵאֹהֶל
מוֹעֵד לֵאמֹר: 2 דַּבֵּר אֶל־בְּנֵי יִשְׂרָאֵל וְאָמַרְתָּ אֲלֵהֶם
אָדָם כִּי־יַקְרִיב מִכֶּם קָרְבָּן לַיהוָֹה מִן־הַבְּהֵמָה
מִן־הַבָּקָר וּמִן־הַצֹּאן תַּקְרִיבוּ אֶת־קָרְבַּנְכֶם: 3 אִם־
עֹלָה קָרְבָּנוֹ מִן־הַבָּקָר זָכָר תָּמִים יַקְרִיבֶנּוּ אֶל־
פֶּתַח אֹהֶל מוֹעֵד יַקְרִיב אֹתוֹ לִרְצֹנוֹ לִפְנֵי יְהוָֹה:
4 וְסָמַךְ יָדוֹ עַל רֹאשׁ הָעֹלָה וְנִרְצָה לוֹ לְכַפֵּר
עָלָיו: 5 וְשָׁחַט אֶת־בֶּן הַבָּקָר לִפְנֵי יְהוָֹה וְהִקְרִיבוּ
בְּנֵי אַהֲרֹן הַכֹּהֲנִים אֶת־הַדָּם וְזָרְקוּ אֶת־הַדָּם עַל־
הַמִּזְבֵּחַ סָבִיב אֲשֶׁר־פֶּתַח אֹהֶל מוֹעֵד: 6 וְהִפְשִׁיט
אֶת־הָעֹלָה וְנִתַּח אֹתָהּ לִנְתָחֶיהָ: 7 וְנָתְנוּ בְּנֵי אַהֲרֹן
הַכֹּהֵן אֵשׁ עַל־הַמִּזְבֵּחַ וְעָרְכוּ עֵצִים עַל־הָאֵשׁ:
8 וְעָרְכוּ בְּנֵי אַהֲרֹן הַכֹּהֲנִים אֵת הַנְּתָחִים אֶת־
הָרֹאשׁ וְאֶת־הַפָּדֶר עַל־הָעֵצִים אֲשֶׁר עַל־הָאֵשׁ
אֲשֶׁר עַל־הַמִּזְבֵּחַ: 9 וְקִרְבּוֹ וּכְרָעָיו יִרְחַץ בַּמָּיִם
וְהִקְטִיר הַכֹּהֵן אֶת־הַכֹּל הַמִּזְבֵּחָה עֹלָה אִשֵּׁה
רֵיחַ־נִיחוֹחַ לַיהוָֹה: ס 10 וְאִם־מִן־הַצֹּאן
קָרְבָּנוֹ מִן־הַכְּשָׂבִים אוֹ מִן־הָעִזִּים לְעֹלָה זָכָר תָּמִים
יַקְרִיבֶנּוּ: 11 וְשָׁחַט אֹתוֹ עַל יֶרֶךְ הַמִּזְבֵּחַ צָפֹנָה
לִפְנֵי יְהוָֹה וְזָרְקוּ בְּנֵי אַהֲרֹן הַכֹּהֲנִים אֶת־דָּמוֹ עַל־
הַמִּזְבֵּחַ סָבִיב: 12 וְנִתַּח אֹתוֹ לִנְתָחָיו וְאֶת־רֹאשׁוֹ
וְאֶת־פִּדְרוֹ וְעָרַךְ הַכֹּהֵן אֹתָם עַל־הָעֵצִים אֲשֶׁר עַל־
הָאֵשׁ אֲשֶׁר עַל־הַמִּזְבֵּחַ: 13 וְהַקֶּרֶב וְהַכְּרָעַיִם יִרְחַץ
בַּמָּיִם וְהִקְרִיב הַכֹּהֵן אֶת־הַכֹּל וְהִקְטִיר הַמִּזְבֵּחָה
עֹלָה הוּא אִשֵּׁה רֵיחַ נִיחֹחַ לַיהוָֹה: פ

14 וְאִם מִן־הָעוֹף עֹלָה קָרְבָּנוֹ לַיהוָֹה וְהִקְרִיב מִן־
הַתֹּרִים אוֹ מִן־בְּנֵי הַיּוֹנָה אֶת־קָרְבָּנוֹ: 15 וְהִקְרִיבוֹ
הַכֹּהֵן אֶל־הַמִּזְבֵּחַ וּמָלַק אֶת־רֹאשׁוֹ וְהִקְטִיר
הַמִּזְבֵּחָה וְנִמְצָה דָמוֹ עַל קִיר הַמִּזְבֵּחַ: 16 וְהֵסִיר
אֶת־מֻרְאָתוֹ בְּנֹצָתָהּ וְהִשְׁלִיךְ אֹתָהּ אֵצֶל הַמִּזְבֵּחַ
קֵדְמָה אֶל־מְקוֹם הַדָּשֶׁן: 17 וְשִׁסַּע אֹתוֹ בִכְנָפָיו

on the wood that *is* on the fire. It *is* a burnt
sacrifice, an offering made by fire, a sweet aroma to
the LORD.

2 'When anyone offers a grain offering to the
LORD, his offering shall be *of* fine flour. And he
shall pour oil on it, and put frankincense on it. ²He
shall bring it to Aaron's sons, the priests, one of
whom shall take from it his handful of fine flour
and oil with all the frankincense. And the priest
shall burn *it as* a memorial on the altar, an offering
made by fire, a sweet aroma to the LORD. ³The rest
of the grain offering *shall be* Aaron's and his sons'.
It is most holy of the offerings to the LORD made by
fire.

⁴'And if you bring as an offering a grain offering
baked in the oven, *it shall be* unleavened cakes of
fine flour mixed with oil, or unleavened wafers
anointed with oil. ⁵But if your offering *is* a grain
offering *baked* in a pan, *it shall be of* fine flour,
unleavened, mixed with oil. ⁶You shall break it in
pieces and pour oil on it; it *is* a grain offering.

⁷'If your offering *is* a grain offering *baked* in a
covered pan, it shall be made *of* fine flour with oil.
⁸You shall bring the grain offering that is made of
these things to the LORD. And when it is presented
to the priest, he shall bring it to the altar. ⁹Then the
priest shall take from the grain offering a memorial
portion, and burn *it* on the altar. *It is* an offering
made by fire, a sweet aroma to the LORD. ¹⁰And
what is left of the grain offering *shall be* Aaron's
and his sons'. *It is* most holy of the offerings to the
LORD made by fire.

¹¹'No grain offering which you bring to the
LORD shall be made with leaven, for you shall burn
no leaven nor any honey in any offering to the
LORD made by fire. ¹²As for the offering of the
firstfruits, you shall offer them to the LORD, but
they shall not be burned on the altar for a sweet
aroma. ¹³And every offering of your grain offering
you shall season with salt; you shall not allow the
salt of the covenant of your God to be lacking from
your grain offering. With all your offerings you
shall offer salt.

¹⁴'If you offer a grain offering of your firstfruits
to the LORD, you shall offer for the grain offering of
your firstfruits green heads of grain roasted on the
fire, grain beaten from full heads. ¹⁵And you shall
put oil on it, and lay frankincense on it. It *is* a grain
offering. ¹⁶Then the priest shall burn the memorial
portion: *part* of its beaten grain and *part* of its oil,
with all the frankincense, as an offering made by
fire to the LORD.

לֹא יַבְדִּיל וְהִקְטִיר אֹתוֹ הַכֹּהֵן הַמִּזְבֵּחָה עַל־
הָעֵצִים אֲשֶׁר עַל־הָאֵשׁ עֹלָה הוּא אִשֵּׁה רֵיחַ נִיחֹחַ
לַיהוָה: ס

ב וְנֶפֶשׁ כִּי־תַקְרִיב קָרְבַּן מִנְחָה לַיהוָה סֹלֶת
יִהְיֶה קָרְבָּנוֹ וְיָצַק עָלֶיהָ שֶׁמֶן וְנָתַן עָלֶיהָ
לְבֹנָה: ² וֶהֱבִיאָהּ אֶל־בְּנֵי אַהֲרֹן הַכֹּהֲנִים וְקָמַץ
מִשָּׁם מְלֹא קֻמְצוֹ מִסָּלְתָּהּ וּמִשַּׁמְנָהּ עַל כָּל־
לְבֹנָתָהּ וְהִקְטִיר הַכֹּהֵן אֶת־אַזְכָּרָתָהּ הַמִּזְבֵּחָה
אִשֵּׁה רֵיחַ נִיחֹחַ לַיהוָה: ³ וְהַנּוֹתֶרֶת מִן־
הַמִּנְחָה לְאַהֲרֹן וּלְבָנָיו קֹדֶשׁ קָדָשִׁים מֵאִשֵּׁי
יְהוָה: ס   ⁴ וְכִי תַקְרִב קָרְבַּן מִנְחָה מַאֲפֵה
תַנּוּר סֹלֶת חַלּוֹת מַצֹּת בְּלוּלֹת בַּשֶּׁמֶן וּרְקִיקֵי
מַצּוֹת מְשֻׁחִים בַּשָּׁמֶן: ס   ⁵ וְאִם־מִנְחָה
עַל־הַמַּחֲבַת קָרְבָּנֶךָ סֹלֶת בְּלוּלָה בַשֶּׁמֶן מַצָּה
תִהְיֶה: ⁶ פָּתוֹת אֹתָהּ פִּתִּים וְיָצַקְתָּ עָלֶיהָ שָׁמֶן
מִנְחָה הִוא: ס   ⁷ וְאִם־מִנְחַת מַרְחֶשֶׁת
קָרְבָּנֶךָ סֹלֶת בַּשֶּׁמֶן תֵּעָשֶׂה: ⁸ וְהֵבֵאתָ אֶת־הַמִּנְחָה
אֲשֶׁר יֵעָשֶׂה מֵאֵלֶּה לַיהוָה וְהִקְרִיבָהּ אֶל־הַכֹּהֵן
וְהִגִּישָׁהּ אֶל־הַמִּזְבֵּחַ: ⁹ וְהֵרִים הַכֹּהֵן מִן־הַמִּנְחָה
אֶת־אַזְכָּרָתָהּ וְהִקְטִיר הַמִּזְבֵּחָה אִשֵּׁה רֵיחַ נִיחֹחַ
לַיהוָה: ¹⁰ וְהַנּוֹתֶרֶת מִן־הַמִּנְחָה לְאַהֲרֹן וּלְבָנָיו
קֹדֶשׁ קָדָשִׁים מֵאִשֵּׁי יְהוָה: ¹¹ כָּל־הַמִּנְחָה אֲשֶׁר
תַּקְרִיבוּ לַיהוָה לֹא תֵעָשֶׂה חָמֵץ כִּי כָל־שְׂאֹר וְכָל־
דְּבַשׁ לֹא־תַקְטִירוּ מִמֶּנּוּ אִשֵּׁה לַיהוָה: ¹² קָרְבַּן
רֵאשִׁית תַּקְרִיבוּ אֹתָם לַיהוָה וְאֶל־הַמִּזְבֵּחַ לֹא־יַעֲלוּ
לְרֵיחַ נִיחֹחַ: ¹³ וְכָל־קָרְבַּן מִנְחָתְךָ בַּמֶּלַח תִּמְלָח
וְלֹא תַשְׁבִּית מֶלַח בְּרִית אֱלֹהֶיךָ מֵעַל מִנְחָתֶךָ
עַל כָּל־קָרְבָּנְךָ תַּקְרִיב מֶלַח: ס   ¹⁴ וְאִם־
תַּקְרִיב מִנְחַת בִּכּוּרִים לַיהוָה אָבִיב קָלוּי בָּאֵשׁ
גֶּרֶשׂ כַּרְמֶל תַּקְרִיב אֵת מִנְחַת בִּכּוּרֶיךָ: ¹⁵ וְנָתַתָּ
עָלֶיהָ שֶׁמֶן וְשַׂמְתָּ עָלֶיהָ לְבֹנָה מִנְחָה הִוא:
¹⁶ וְהִקְטִיר הַכֹּהֵן אֶת־אַזְכָּרָתָהּ מִגִּרְשָׂהּ וּמִשַּׁמְנָהּ
עַל כָּל־לְבֹנָתָהּ אִשֵּׁה לַיהוָה: פ

3 'When his offering *is* a sacrifice of a peace offering, if he offers *it* of the herd, whether male or female, he shall offer it without blemish before the LORD. ²And he shall lay his hand on the head of his offering, and kill it *at* the door of the tabernacle of meeting; and Aaron's sons, the priests, shall sprinkle the blood all around on the altar. ³Then he shall offer from the sacrifice of the peace offering an offering made by fire to the LORD. The fat that covers the entrails and all the fat that *is* on the entrails, ⁴the two kidneys and the fat that *is* on them by the flanks, and the fatty lobe *attached* to the liver above the kidneys, he shall remove; ⁵and Aaron's sons shall burn it on the altar upon the burnt sacrifice, which *is* on the wood that *is* on the fire, *as* an offering made by fire, a sweet aroma to the LORD.

⁶'If his offering as a sacrifice of a peace offering to the LORD *is* of the flock, *whether* male or female, he shall offer it without blemish. ⁷If he offers a lamb as his offering, then he shall offer it before the LORD. ⁸And he shall lay his hand on the head of his offering, and kill it before the tabernacle of meeting; and Aaron's sons shall sprinkle its blood all around on the altar.

⁹'Then he shall offer from the sacrifice of the peace offering, as an offering made by fire to the LORD, its fat *and* the whole fat tail which he shall remove close to the backbone. And the fat that covers the entrails and all the fat that *is* on the entrails, ¹⁰the two kidneys and the fat that *is* on them by the flanks, and the fatty lobe *attached* to the liver above the kidneys, he shall remove; ¹¹and the priest shall burn *them* on the altar *as* food, an offering made by fire to the LORD.

¹²'And if his offering *is* a goat, then he shall offer it before the LORD. ¹³He shall lay his hand on its head and kill it before the tabernacle of meeting; and the sons of Aaron shall sprinkle its blood all around on the altar. ¹⁴Then he shall offer from it his offering, as an offering made by fire to the LORD. The fat that covers the entrails and all the fat that *is* on the entrails, ¹⁵the two kidneys and the fat that *is* on them by the flanks, and the fatty lobe *attached* to the liver above the kidneys, he shall remove; ¹⁶and the priest shall burn them on the altar *as* food, an offering made by fire for a sweet aroma; all the fat *is* the LORD's.

¹⁷'*This shall be* a perpetual statute throughout your generations in all your dwellings: you shall eat neither fat nor blood.'"

ג וְאִם־זֶבַח שְׁלָמִים קָרְבָּנוֹ אִם מִן־הַבָּקָר הוּא מַקְרִיב אִם־זָכָר אִם־נְקֵבָה תָּמִים יַקְרִיבֶנּוּ לִפְנֵי יְהוָה: 2 וְסָמַךְ יָדוֹ עַל־רֹאשׁ קָרְבָּנוֹ וּשְׁחָטוֹ פֶּתַח אֹהֶל מוֹעֵד וְזָרְקוּ בְּנֵי אַהֲרֹן הַכֹּהֲנִים אֶת־הַדָּם עַל־הַמִּזְבֵּחַ סָבִיב: 3 וְהִקְרִיב מִזֶּבַח הַשְּׁלָמִים אִשֶּׁה לַיהוָה אֶת־הַחֵלֶב הַמְכַסֶּה אֶת־הַקֶּרֶב וְאֵת כָּל־הַחֵלֶב אֲשֶׁר עַל־הַקֶּרֶב: 4 וְאֵת שְׁתֵּי הַכְּלָיֹת וְאֶת־הַחֵלֶב אֲשֶׁר עֲלֵהֶן אֲשֶׁר עַל־הַכְּסָלִים וְאֶת־הַיֹּתֶרֶת עַל־הַכָּבֵד עַל־הַכְּלָיוֹת יְסִירֶנָּה: 5 וְהִקְטִירוּ אֹתוֹ בְנֵי־אַהֲרֹן הַמִּזְבֵּחָה עַל־הָעֹלָה אֲשֶׁר עַל־הָעֵצִים אֲשֶׁר עַל־הָאֵשׁ אִשֵּׁה רֵיחַ נִיחֹחַ לַיהוָה: פ

6 וְאִם־מִן־הַצֹּאן קָרְבָּנוֹ לְזֶבַח שְׁלָמִים לַיהוָה זָכָר אוֹ נְקֵבָה תָּמִים יַקְרִיבֶנּוּ: 7 אִם־כֶּשֶׂב הוּא־מַקְרִיב אֶת־קָרְבָּנוֹ וְהִקְרִיב אֹתוֹ לִפְנֵי יְהוָה: 8 וְסָמַךְ אֶת־יָדוֹ עַל־רֹאשׁ קָרְבָּנוֹ וְשָׁחַט אֹתוֹ לִפְנֵי אֹהֶל מוֹעֵד וְזָרְקוּ בְּנֵי אַהֲרֹן אֶת־דָּמוֹ עַל־הַמִּזְבֵּחַ סָבִיב:

9 וְהִקְרִיב מִזֶּבַח הַשְּׁלָמִים אִשֶּׁה לַיהוָה חֶלְבּוֹ הָאַלְיָה תְמִימָה לְעֻמַּת הֶעָצֶה יְסִירֶנָּה וְאֶת־הַחֵלֶב הַמְכַסֶּה אֶת־הַקֶּרֶב וְאֵת כָּל־הַחֵלֶב אֲשֶׁר עַל־הַקֶּרֶב: 10 וְאֵת שְׁתֵּי הַכְּלָיֹת וְאֶת־הַחֵלֶב אֲשֶׁר עֲלֵהֶן אֲשֶׁר עַל־הַכְּסָלִים וְאֶת־הַיֹּתֶרֶת עַל־הַכָּבֵד עַל־הַכְּלָיֹת יְסִירֶנָּה: 11 וְהִקְטִירוֹ הַכֹּהֵן הַמִּזְבֵּחָה לֶחֶם אִשֶּׁה לַיהוָה: פ

12 וְאִם עֵז קָרְבָּנוֹ וְהִקְרִיבוֹ לִפְנֵי יְהוָה: 13 וְסָמַךְ אֶת־יָדוֹ עַל־רֹאשׁוֹ וְשָׁחַט אֹתוֹ לִפְנֵי אֹהֶל מוֹעֵד וְזָרְקוּ בְּנֵי אַהֲרֹן אֶת־דָּמוֹ עַל־הַמִּזְבֵּחַ סָבִיב: 14 וְהִקְרִיב מִמֶּנּוּ קָרְבָּנוֹ אִשֶּׁה לַיהוָה אֶת־הַחֵלֶב הַמְכַסֶּה אֶת־הַקֶּרֶב וְאֵת כָּל־הַחֵלֶב אֲשֶׁר עַל־הַקֶּרֶב: 15 וְאֵת שְׁתֵּי הַכְּלָיֹת וְאֶת־הַחֵלֶב אֲשֶׁר עֲלֵהֶן אֲשֶׁר עַל־הַכְּסָלִים וְאֶת־הַיֹּתֶרֶת עַל־הַכָּבֵד עַל־הַכְּלָיֹת יְסִירֶנָּה: 16 וְהִקְטִירָם הַכֹּהֵן הַמִּזְבֵּחָה לֶחֶם אִשֶּׁה לְרֵיחַ נִיחֹחַ כָּל־חֵלֶב לַיהוָה: 17 חֻקַּת עוֹלָם לְדֹרֹתֵיכֶם בְּכֹל מוֹשְׁבֹתֵיכֶם כָּל־חֵלֶב וְכָל־דָּם לֹא תֹאכֵלוּ: פ

4 Now the LORD spoke to Moses, saying, 2"Speak to the children of Israel, saying: 'If a person sins unintentionally against any of the commandments of the LORD *in anything* which ought not to be done, and does any of them, 3if the anointed priest sins, bringing guilt on the people, then let him offer to the LORD for his sin which he has sinned a young bull without blemish as a sin offering. 4He shall bring the bull to the door of the tabernacle of meeting before the LORD, lay his hand on the bull's head, and kill the bull before the LORD. 5Then the anointed priest shall take some of the bull's blood and bring it to the tabernacle of meeting. 6The priest shall dip his finger in the blood and sprinkle some of the blood seven times before the LORD, in front of the veil of the sanctuary. 7And the priest shall put some of the blood on the horns of the altar of sweet incense before the LORD, which is in the tabernacle of meeting; and he shall pour the remaining blood of the bull at the base of the altar of the burnt offering, which is at the door of the tabernacle of meeting. 8He shall take from it all the fat of the bull as the sin offering. The fat that covers the entrails and all the fat which *is* on the entrails, 9the two kidneys and the fat that *is* on them by the flanks, and the fatty lobe *attached* to the liver above the kidneys, he shall remove, 10as it was taken from the bull of the sacrifice of the peace offering; and the priest shall burn them on the altar of the burnt offering. 11But the bull's hide and all its flesh, with its head and legs, its entrails and offal— 12the whole bull he shall carry outside the camp to a clean place, where the ashes are poured out, and burn it on wood with fire; where the ashes are poured out it shall be burned.

13'Now if the whole congregation of Israel sins unintentionally, and the thing is hidden from the eyes of the assembly, and they have done *something against* any of the commandments of the LORD *in anything* which should not be done, and are guilty; 14when the sin which they have committed becomes known, then the assembly shall offer a young bull for the sin, and bring it before the tabernacle of meeting. 15And the elders of the congregation shall lay their hands on the head of the bull before the LORD. Then the bull shall be killed before the LORD. 16The anointed priest shall bring some of the bull's blood to the tabernacle of meeting. 17Then the priest shall dip his finger in the blood and sprinkle *it* seven times before the LORD, in front of the veil. 18And he shall put *some* of the blood on the horns of the altar which *is* before the LORD, which *is* in the tabernacle of meeting; and he shall pour the remaining blood at the base of the altar of

ד 2 וַיְדַבֵּ֥ר יְהוָ֖ה אֶל־מֹשֶׁ֥ה לֵּאמֹֽר: 2 דַּבֵּ֞ר אֶל־
בְּנֵ֣י יִשְׂרָאֵל֮ לֵאמֹר֒ נֶ֗פֶשׁ כִּֽי־תֶחֱטָ֤א בִשְׁגָגָה֙ מִכֹּל֙
מִצְוֺ֣ת יְהוָ֔ה אֲשֶׁ֖ר לֹ֣א תֵעָשֶׂ֑ינָה וְעָשָׂ֕ה מֵאַחַ֖ת
מֵהֵֽנָּה: 3 אִ֣ם הַכֹּהֵ֧ן הַמָּשִׁ֛יחַ יֶחֱטָ֖א לְאַשְׁמַ֣ת הָעָ֑ם
וְהִקְרִ֡יב עַ֣ל חַטָּאתוֹ֩ אֲשֶׁ֨ר חָטָ֜א פַּ֣ר בֶּן־בָּקָ֥ר
תָּמִ֛ים לַֽיהוָ֖ה לְחַטָּֽאת: 4 וְהֵבִ֣יא אֶת־הַפָּ֗ר אֶל־פֶּ֙תַח֙
אֹ֤הֶל מוֹעֵד֙ לִפְנֵ֣י יְהוָ֔ה וְסָמַ֤ךְ אֶת־יָדוֹ֙ עַל־רֹ֣אשׁ
הַפָּ֔ר וְשָׁחַ֥ט אֶת־הַפָּ֖ר לִפְנֵ֥י יְהוָֽה: 5 וְלָקַ֛ח הַכֹּהֵ֥ן
הַמָּשִׁ֖יחַ מִדַּ֣ם הַפָּ֑ר וְהֵבִ֥יא אֹת֖וֹ אֶל־אֹ֥הֶל מוֹעֵֽד:
6 וְטָבַ֧ל הַכֹּהֵ֛ן אֶת־אֶצְבָּע֖וֹ בַּדָּ֑ם וְהִזָּ֨ה מִן־הַדָּ֜ם
שֶׁ֤בַע פְּעָמִים֙ לִפְנֵ֣י יְהוָ֔ה אֶת־פְּנֵ֖י פָּרֹ֥כֶת הַקֹּֽדֶשׁ:
7 וְנָתַן֩ הַכֹּהֵ֨ן מִן־הַדָּ֜ם עַל־קַרְנ֗וֹת מִזְבַּ֣ח קְטֹ֤רֶת
הַסַּמִּים֙ לִפְנֵ֣י יְהוָ֔ה אֲשֶׁ֖ר בְּאֹ֣הֶל מוֹעֵ֑ד וְאֵ֣ת ׀
כָּל־דַּ֣ם הַפָּ֗ר יִשְׁפֹּךְ֙ אֶל־יְסוֹד֙ מִזְבַּ֣ח הָעֹלָ֔ה אֲשֶׁר־
פֶּ֖תַח אֹ֥הֶל מוֹעֵֽד: 8 וְאֶת־כָּל־חֵ֛לֶב פַּ֥ר הַֽחַטָּ֖את
יָרִ֣ים מִמֶּ֑נּוּ אֶת־הַחֵ֙לֶב֙ הַֽמְכַסֶּ֣ה עַל־הַקֶּ֔רֶב וְאֵת֙
כָּל־הַחֵ֔לֶב אֲשֶׁ֖ר עַל־הַקֶּֽרֶב: 9 וְאֵת֙ שְׁתֵּ֣י הַכְּלָיֹ֔ת
וְאֶת־הַחֵ֙לֶב֙ אֲשֶׁ֣ר עֲלֵיהֶ֔ן אֲשֶׁ֖ר עַל־הַכְּסָלִ֑ים וְאֶת־
הַיֹּתֶ֙רֶת֙ עַל־הַכָּבֵ֔ד עַל־הַכְּלָי֖וֹת יְסִירֶֽנָּה: 10 כַּֽאֲשֶׁ֣ר
יוּרַ֗ם מִשּׁ֖וֹר זֶ֣בַח הַשְּׁלָמִ֑ים וְהִקְטִירָם֙ הַכֹּהֵ֔ן עַ֖ל
מִזְבַּ֥ח הָעֹלָֽה: 11 וְאֶת־ע֤וֹר הַפָּר֙ וְאֶת־כָּל־בְּשָׂר֔וֹ
עַל־רֹאשׁ֖וֹ וְעַל־כְּרָעָ֑יו וְקִרְבּ֖וֹ וּפִרְשֽׁוֹ: 12 וְהוֹצִ֣יא
אֶת־כָּל־הַ֠פָּר אֶל־מִח֨וּץ לַֽמַּחֲנֶ֜ה אֶל־מָק֤וֹם טָהוֹר֙
אֶל־שֶׁ֣פֶךְ הַדֶּ֔שֶׁן וְשָׂרַ֥ף אֹת֛וֹ עַל־עֵצִ֖ים בָּאֵ֑שׁ עַל־
שֶׁ֥פֶךְ הַדֶּ֖שֶׁן יִשָּׂרֵֽף: פ

13 וְאִ֤ם כָּל־עֲדַ֤ת יִשְׂרָאֵל֙ יִשְׁגּ֔וּ וְנֶעְלַ֣ם דָּבָ֔ר מֵעֵינֵ֖י
הַקָּהָ֑ל וְ֠עָשׂוּ אַחַ֨ת מִכָּל־מִצְוֺ֧ת יְהוָ֛ה אֲשֶׁ֥ר לֹֽא־
תֵעָשֶׂ֖ינָה וְאָשֵֽׁמוּ: 14 וְנֽוֹדְעָה֙ הַֽחַטָּ֔את אֲשֶׁ֥ר חָטְא֖וּ
עָלֶ֑יהָ וְהִקְרִ֣יבוּ הַקָּהָ֗ל פַּ֧ר בֶּן־בָּקָ֛ר לְחַטָּ֖את וְהֵבִ֣יאוּ
אֹת֔וֹ לִפְנֵ֖י אֹ֣הֶל מוֹעֵֽד: 15 וְ֠סָמְכוּ זִקְנֵ֨י הָעֵדָ֧ה אֶת־
יְדֵיהֶ֛ם עַל־רֹ֥אשׁ הַפָּ֖ר לִפְנֵ֣י יְהוָ֑ה וְשָׁחַ֥ט אֶת־הַפָּ֖ר
לִפְנֵ֥י יְהוָֽה: 16 וְהֵבִ֛יא הַכֹּהֵ֥ן הַמָּשִׁ֖יחַ מִדַּ֣ם הַפָּ֑ר
אֶל־אֹ֥הֶל מוֹעֵֽד: 17 וְטָבַ֧ל הַכֹּהֵ֛ן אֶצְבָּע֖וֹ מִן־הַדָּ֑ם
וְהִזָּ֞ה שֶׁ֤בַע פְּעָמִים֙ לִפְנֵ֣י יְהוָ֔ה אֵ֖ת פְּנֵ֥י הַפָּרֹֽכֶת:
18 וּמִן־הַדָּ֣ם יִתֵּ֣ן ׀ עַל־קַרְנֹ֣ת הַמִּזְבֵּ֗חַ אֲשֶׁר֙ לִפְנֵ֣י
יְהוָ֔ה אֲשֶׁ֖ר בְּאֹ֣הֶל מוֹעֵ֑ד וְאֵ֣ת כָּל־הַדָּ֣ם יִשְׁפֹּ֗ךְ אֶל־

burnt offering, which is at the door of the tabernacle of meeting. [19] He shall take all the fat from it and burn *it* on the altar. [20] And he shall do with the bull as he did with the bull as a sin offering; thus he shall do with it. So the priest shall make atonement for them, and it shall be forgiven them. [21] Then he shall carry the bull outside the camp, and burn it as he burned the first bull. It *is* a sin offering for the assembly.

[22] 'When a ruler has sinned, and done *something* unintentionally *against* any of the commandments of the LORD his God *in anything* which should not be done, and is guilty, [23] or if his sin which he has committed comes to his knowledge, he shall bring as his offering a kid of the goats, a male without blemish. [24] And he shall lay his hand on the head of the goat, and kill it at the place where they kill the burnt offering before the LORD. It *is* a sin offering. [25] The priest shall take some of the blood of the sin offering with his finger, put *it* on the horns of the altar of burnt offering, and pour its blood at the base of the altar of burnt offering. [26] And he shall burn all its fat on the altar, like the fat of the sacrifice of the peace offering. So the priest shall make atonement for him concerning his sin, and it shall be forgiven him.

[27] 'If anyone of the common people sins unintentionally by doing *something against* any of the commandments of the LORD *in anything* which ought not to be done, and is guilty, [28] or if his sin which he has committed comes to his knowledge, then he shall bring as his offering a kid of the goats, a female without blemish, for his sin which he has committed. [29] And he shall lay his hand on the head of the sin offering, and kill the sin offering at the place of the burnt offering. [30] Then the priest shall take *some* of its blood with his finger, put *it* on the horns of the altar of burnt offering, and pour all *the remaining* blood at the base of the altar. [31] He shall remove all its fat, as fat is removed from the sacrifice of the peace offering; and the priest shall burn it on the altar for a sweet aroma to the LORD. So the priest shall make atonement for him, and it shall be forgiven him.

[32] 'If he brings a lamb as his sin offering, he shall bring a female without blemish. [33] Then he shall lay his hand on the head of the sin offering, and kill it as a sin offering at the place where they kill the burnt offering. [34] The priest shall take *some* of the blood of the sin offering with his finger, put *it* on the horns of the altar of burnt offering, and pour all *the remaining* blood at the base of the altar. [35] He shall remove all its fat, as the fat of the lamb is removed from the sacrifice of the peace offering.

19 וְאֵת יְסוֹד מִזְבַּח הָעֹלָה אֲשֶׁר־פֶּתַח אֹהֶל מוֹעֵד: 20 וְעָשָׂה כָּל־חֶלְבּוֹ יָרִים מִמֶּנּוּ וְהִקְטִיר הַמִּזְבֵּחָה: לַפָּר כַּאֲשֶׁר עָשָׂה לְפַר הַחַטָּאת כֵּן יַעֲשֶׂה־לּוֹ וְכִפֶּר עֲלֵהֶם הַכֹּהֵן וְנִסְלַח לָהֶם: 21 וְהוֹצִיא אֶת־הַפָּר אֶל־מִחוּץ לַמַּחֲנֶה וְשָׂרַף אֹתוֹ כַּאֲשֶׁר שָׂרַף אֵת הַפָּר הָרִאשׁוֹן חַטַּאת הַקָּהָל הוּא: פ

22 אֲשֶׁר נָשִׂיא יֶחֱטָא וְעָשָׂה אַחַת מִכָּל־מִצְוֹת יְהוָה אֱלֹהָיו אֲשֶׁר לֹא־תֵעָשֶׂינָה בִּשְׁגָגָה וְאָשֵׁם: 23 אוֹ־הוֹדַע אֵלָיו חַטָּאתוֹ אֲשֶׁר חָטָא בָּהּ וְהֵבִיא אֶת־קָרְבָּנוֹ שְׂעִיר עִזִּים זָכָר תָּמִים: 24 וְסָמַךְ יָדוֹ עַל־רֹאשׁ הַשָּׂעִיר וְשָׁחַט אֹתוֹ בִּמְקוֹם אֲשֶׁר־יִשְׁחַט אֶת־הָעֹלָה לִפְנֵי יְהוָה חַטָּאת הוּא: 25 וְלָקַח הַכֹּהֵן מִדַּם הַחַטָּאת בְּאֶצְבָּעוֹ וְנָתַן עַל־קַרְנֹת מִזְבַּח הָעֹלָה וְאֶת־דָּמוֹ יִשְׁפֹּךְ אֶל־יְסוֹד מִזְבַּח הָעֹלָה: 26 וְאֶת־כָּל־חֶלְבּוֹ יַקְטִיר הַמִּזְבֵּחָה כְּחֵלֶב זֶבַח הַשְּׁלָמִים וְכִפֶּר עָלָיו הַכֹּהֵן מֵחַטָּאתוֹ וְנִסְלַח לוֹ: פ

27 וְאִם־נֶפֶשׁ אַחַת תֶּחֱטָא בִשְׁגָגָה מֵעַם הָאָרֶץ בַּעֲשֹׂתָהּ אַחַת מִמִּצְוֹת יְהוָה אֲשֶׁר לֹא־תֵעָשֶׂינָה וְאָשֵׁם: 28 אוֹ הוֹדַע אֵלָיו חַטָּאתוֹ אֲשֶׁר חָטָא וְהֵבִיא קָרְבָּנוֹ שְׂעִירַת עִזִּים תְּמִימָה נְקֵבָה עַל־חַטָּאתוֹ אֲשֶׁר חָטָא: 29 וְסָמַךְ אֶת־יָדוֹ עַל רֹאשׁ הַחַטָּאת וְשָׁחַט אֶת־הַחַטָּאת בִּמְקוֹם הָעֹלָה: 30 וְלָקַח הַכֹּהֵן מִדָּמָהּ בְּאֶצְבָּעוֹ וְנָתַן עַל־קַרְנֹת מִזְבַּח הָעֹלָה וְאֶת־כָּל־דָּמָהּ יִשְׁפֹּךְ אֶל־יְסוֹד הַמִּזְבֵּחַ: 31 וְאֶת־כָּל־חֶלְבָּהּ יָסִיר כַּאֲשֶׁר הוּסַר חֵלֶב מֵעַל זֶבַח הַשְּׁלָמִים וְהִקְטִיר הַכֹּהֵן הַמִּזְבֵּחָה לְרֵיחַ נִיחֹחַ לַיהוָה וְכִפֶּר עָלָיו הַכֹּהֵן וְנִסְלַח לוֹ: פ

32 וְאִם־כֶּבֶשׂ יָבִיא קָרְבָּנוֹ לְחַטָּאת נְקֵבָה תְמִימָה יְבִיאֶנָּה: 33 וְסָמַךְ אֶת־יָדוֹ עַל רֹאשׁ הַחַטָּאת וְשָׁחַט אֹתָהּ לְחַטָּאת בִּמְקוֹם אֲשֶׁר יִשְׁחַט אֶת־הָעֹלָה: 34 וְלָקַח הַכֹּהֵן מִדַּם הַחַטָּאת בְּאֶצְבָּעוֹ וְנָתַן עַל־קַרְנֹת מִזְבַּח הָעֹלָה וְאֶת־כָּל־דָּמָהּ יִשְׁפֹּךְ אֶל־יְסוֹד הַמִּזְבֵּחַ: 35 וְאֶת־כָּל־חֶלְבָּה יָסִיר כַּאֲשֶׁר

Then the priest shall burn it on the altar, according to the offerings made by fire to the LORD. So the priest shall make atonement for his sin that he has committed, and it shall be forgiven him.

5 'If a person sins in hearing the utterance of an oath, and *is* a witness, whether he has seen or known *of the matter*—if he does not tell *it*, he bears guilt.

² 'Or if a person touches any unclean thing, whether *it is* the carcass of an unclean beast, or the carcass of unclean livestock, or the carcass of unclean creeping things, and he is unaware of it, he also shall be unclean and guilty. ³ Or if he touches human uncleanness—whatever uncleanness with which a man may be defiled, and he is unaware of it—when he realizes *it*, then he shall be guilty.

⁴ 'Or if a person swears, speaking thoughtlessly with *his* lips to do evil or to do good, whatever *it is* that a man may pronounce by an oath, and he is unaware of *it*—when he realizes *it*, then he shall be guilty in any of these *matters*.

⁵ 'And it shall be, when he is guilty in any of these *matters*, that he shall confess that he has sinned in that *thing*; ⁶ and he shall bring his trespass offering to the LORD for his sin which he has committed, a female from the flock, a lamb or a kid of the goats as a sin offering. So the priest shall make atonement for him concerning his sin.

⁷ 'If he is not able to bring a lamb, then he shall bring to the LORD, for his trespass which he has committed, two turtledoves or two young pigeons: one as a sin offering and the other as a burnt offering. ⁸ And he shall bring them to the priest, who shall offer *that* which *is* for the sin offering first, and wring off its head from its neck, but shall not divide *it* completely. ⁹ Then he shall sprinkle *some* of the blood of the sin offering on the side of the altar, and the rest of the blood shall be drained out at the base of the altar. It *is* a sin offering. ¹⁰ And he shall offer the second *as* a burnt offering according to the prescribed manner. So the priest shall make atonement on his behalf for his sin which he has committed, and it shall be forgiven him.

¹¹ 'But if he is not able to bring two turtledoves or two young pigeons, then he who sinned shall bring for his offering one-tenth of an ephah of fine flour as a sin offering. He shall put no oil on it, nor shall he put frankincense on it, for it *is* a sin offering. ¹² Then he shall bring it to the priest, and the priest shall take his handful of it as a memorial portion, and burn *it* on the altar according to the offerings made by fire to the LORD. It *is* a sin offering. ¹³ The

יוֹסֵר חֵלֶב־הַכֶּשֶׂב מִזֶּבַח הַשְּׁלָמִים וְהִקְטִיר הַכֹּהֵן
אֹתָם הַמִּזְבֵּחָה עַל אִשֵּׁי יְהוָה וְכִפֶּר עָלָיו הַכֹּהֵן
עַל־חַטָּאתוֹ אֲשֶׁר־חָטָא וְנִסְלַח לוֹ: פ

ה וְנֶפֶשׁ כִּי־תֶחֱטָא וְשָׁמְעָה קוֹל אָלָה וְהוּא
עֵד אוֹ רָאָה אוֹ יָדָע אִם־לוֹא יַגִּיד וְנָשָׂא עֲוֺנוֹ:
² אוֹ נֶפֶשׁ אֲשֶׁר תִּגַּע בְּכָל־דָּבָר טָמֵא אוֹ בְנִבְלַת
חַיָּה טְמֵאָה אוֹ בְּנִבְלַת בְּהֵמָה טְמֵאָה אוֹ בְּנִבְלַת
שֶׁרֶץ טָמֵא וְנֶעְלַם מִמֶּנּוּ וְהוּא טָמֵא וְאָשֵׁם:
³ אוֹ כִי יִגַּע בְּטֻמְאַת אָדָם לְכֹל טֻמְאָתוֹ אֲשֶׁר
יִטְמָא בָּהּ וְנֶעְלַם מִמֶּנּוּ וְהוּא יָדָע וְאָשֵׁם: ⁴ אוֹ
נֶפֶשׁ כִּי תִשָּׁבַע לְבַטֵּא בִשְׂפָתַיִם לְהָרַע | אוֹ
לְהֵיטִיב לְכֹל אֲשֶׁר יְבַטֵּא הָאָדָם בִּשְׁבֻעָה וְנֶעְלַם
מִמֶּנּוּ וְהוּא־יָדַע וְאָשֵׁם לְאַחַת מֵאֵלֶּה: ⁵ וְהָיָה
כִי־יֶאְשַׁם לְאַחַת מֵאֵלֶּה וְהִתְוַדָּה אֲשֶׁר חָטָא
עָלֶיהָ: ⁶ וְהֵבִיא אֶת־אֲשָׁמוֹ לַיהוָה עַל חַטָּאתוֹ
אֲשֶׁר חָטָא נְקֵבָה מִן־הַצֹּאן כִּשְׂבָּה אוֹ־שְׂעִירַת
עִזִּים לְחַטָּאת וְכִפֶּר עָלָיו הַכֹּהֵן מֵחַטָּאתוֹ: ⁷ וְאִם־
לֹא תַגִּיעַ יָדוֹ דֵּי שֶׂה וְהֵבִיא אֶת־אֲשָׁמוֹ אֲשֶׁר
חָטָא שְׁתֵּי תֹרִים אוֹ־שְׁנֵי בְנֵי־יוֹנָה לַיהוָה אֶחָד
לְחַטָּאת וְאֶחָד לְעֹלָה: ⁸ וְהֵבִיא אֹתָם אֶל־הַכֹּהֵן
וְהִקְרִיב אֶת־אֲשֶׁר לַחַטָּאת רִאשׁוֹנָה וּמָלַק אֶת־
רֹאשׁוֹ מִמּוּל עָרְפּוֹ וְלֹא יַבְדִּיל: ⁹ וְהִזָּה מִדַּם
הַחַטָּאת עַל־קִיר הַמִּזְבֵּחַ וְהַנִּשְׁאָר בַּדָּם יִמָּצֵה אֶל־
יְסוֹד הַמִּזְבֵּחַ חַטָּאת הוּא: ¹⁰ וְאֶת־הַשֵּׁנִי יַעֲשֶׂה
עֹלָה כַּמִּשְׁפָּט וְכִפֶּר עָלָיו הַכֹּהֵן מֵחַטָּאתוֹ אֲשֶׁר־
חָטָא וְנִסְלַח לוֹ: ס ¹¹ וְאִם־לֹא תַשִּׂיג
יָדוֹ לִשְׁתֵּי תֹרִים אוֹ לִשְׁנֵי בְנֵי־יוֹנָה וְהֵבִיא אֶת־
קָרְבָּנוֹ אֲשֶׁר חָטָא עֲשִׂירִת הָאֵפָה סֹלֶת לְחַטָּאת
לֹא־יָשִׂים עָלֶיהָ שֶׁמֶן וְלֹא־יִתֵּן עָלֶיהָ לְבֹנָה כִּי
חַטָּאת הִיא: ¹² וֶהֱבִיאָהּ אֶל־הַכֹּהֵן וְקָמַץ הַכֹּהֵן |
מִמֶּנָּה מְלוֹא קֻמְצוֹ אֶת־אַזְכָּרָתָהּ וְהִקְטִיר הַמִּזְבֵּחָה
עַל אִשֵּׁי יְהוָה חַטָּאת הוּא: ¹³ וְכִפֶּר עָלָיו הַכֹּהֵן

priest shall make atonement for him, for his sin that he has committed in any of these matters; and it shall be forgiven him. *The rest* shall be the priest's as a grain offering.'"

14 Then the LORD spoke to Moses, saying: 15 "If a person commits a trespass, and sins unintentionally in regard to the holy things of the LORD, then he shall bring to the LORD as his trespass offering a ram without blemish from the flocks, with your valuation in shekels of silver according to the shekel of the sanctuary, as a trespass offering. 16 And he shall make restitution for the harm that he has done in regard to the holy thing, and shall add one-fifth to it and give it to the priest. So the priest shall make atonement for him with the ram of the trespass offering, and it shall be forgiven him.

17 "If a person sins, and commits any of these things which are forbidden to be done by the commandments of the LORD, though he does not know *it,* yet he is guilty and shall bear his iniquity. 18 And he shall bring to the priest a ram without blemish from the flock, with your valuation, as a trespass offering. So the priest shall make atonement for him regarding his ignorance in which he erred and did not know *it,* and it shall be forgiven him. 19 It is a trespass offering; he has certainly trespassed against the LORD."

6 And the LORD spoke to Moses, saying: 2 "If a person sins and commits a trespass against the LORD by lying to his neighbor about what was delivered to him for safekeeping, or about a pledge, or about a robbery, or if he has extorted from his neighbor, 3 or if he has found what was lost and lies concerning it, and swears falsely—in any one of these things that a man may do in which he sins: 4 then it shall be, because he has sinned and is guilty, that he shall restore what he has stolen, or the thing which he has extorted, or what was delivered to him for safekeeping, or the lost thing which he found, 5 or all that about which he has sworn falsely. He shall restore its full value, add one-fifth more to it, *and* give it to whomever it belongs, on the day of his trespass offering. 6 And he shall bring his trespass offering to the LORD, a ram without blemish from the flock, with your valuation, as a trespass offering, to the priest. 7 So the priest shall make atonement for him before the LORD, and he shall be forgiven for any one of these things that he may have done in which he trespasses."

8 Then the LORD spoke to Moses, saying, 9 "Command Aaron and his sons, saying, 'This *is* the law of the burnt offering: The burnt offering *shall be* on the hearth upon the altar all night until

עַל־חַטָּאתוֹ אֲשֶׁר־חָטָא מֵאַחַת מֵאֵלֶּה וְנִסְלַח לוֹ וְהָיְתָה לַכֹּהֵן כַּמִּנְחָה: ס 14 וַיְדַבֵּר יְהוָה אֶל־מֹשֶׁה לֵּאמֹר: 15 נֶפֶשׁ כִּי־תִמְעֹל מַעַל וְחָטְאָה בִּשְׁגָגָה מִקָּדְשֵׁי יְהוָה וְהֵבִיא אֶת־אֲשָׁמוֹ לַיהוָה אַיִל תָּמִים מִן־הַצֹּאן בְּעֶרְכְּךָ כֶּסֶף־שְׁקָלִים בְּשֶׁקֶל־הַקֹּדֶשׁ לְאָשָׁם: 16 וְאֵת אֲשֶׁר חָטָא מִן־הַקֹּדֶשׁ יְשַׁלֵּם וְאֶת־חֲמִישִׁתוֹ יוֹסֵף עָלָיו וְנָתַן אֹתוֹ לַכֹּהֵן וְהַכֹּהֵן יְכַפֵּר עָלָיו בְּאֵיל הָאָשָׁם וְנִסְלַח לוֹ: פ 17 וְאִם־נֶפֶשׁ כִּי תֶחֱטָא וְעָשְׂתָה אַחַת מִכָּל־מִצְוֹת יְהוָה אֲשֶׁר לֹא תֵעָשֶׂינָה וְלֹא־יָדַע וְאָשֵׁם וְנָשָׂא עֲוֹנוֹ: 18 וְהֵבִיא אַיִל תָּמִים מִן־הַצֹּאן בְּעֶרְכְּךָ לְאָשָׁם אֶל־הַכֹּהֵן וְכִפֶּר עָלָיו הַכֹּהֵן עַל שִׁגְגָתוֹ אֲשֶׁר־שָׁגָג וְהוּא לֹא־יָדַע וְנִסְלַח לוֹ: 19 אָשָׁם הוּא אָשֹׁם אָשַׁם לַיהוָה: פ

20 וַיְדַבֵּר יְהוָה אֶל־מֹשֶׁה לֵּאמֹר: 21 נֶפֶשׁ כִּי תֶחֱטָא וּמָעֲלָה מַעַל בַּיהוָה וְכִחֵשׁ בַּעֲמִיתוֹ בְּפִקָּדוֹן אוֹ־בִתְשׂוּמֶת יָד אוֹ בְגָזֵל אוֹ עָשַׁק אֶת־עֲמִיתוֹ: 22 אוֹ־מָצָא אֲבֵדָה וְכִחֶשׁ בָּהּ וְנִשְׁבַּע עַל־שָׁקֶר עַל־אַחַת מִכֹּל אֲשֶׁר־יַעֲשֶׂה הָאָדָם לַחֲטֹא בָהֵנָּה: 23 וְהָיָה כִּי־יֶחֱטָא וְאָשֵׁם וְהֵשִׁיב אֶת־הַגְּזֵלָה אֲשֶׁר גָּזָל אוֹ אֶת־הָעֹשֶׁק אֲשֶׁר עָשָׁק אוֹ אֶת־הַפִּקָּדוֹן אֲשֶׁר הָפְקַד אִתּוֹ אוֹ אֶת־הָאֲבֵדָה אֲשֶׁר מָצָא: 24 אוֹ מִכֹּל אֲשֶׁר־יִשָּׁבַע עָלָיו לַשֶּׁקֶר וְשִׁלַּם אֹתוֹ בְּרֹאשׁוֹ וַחֲמִשִׁתָיו יֹסֵף עָלָיו לַאֲשֶׁר הוּא לוֹ יִתְּנֶנּוּ בְּיוֹם אַשְׁמָתוֹ: 25 וְאֶת־אֲשָׁמוֹ יָבִיא לַיהוָה אַיִל תָּמִים מִן־הַצֹּאן בְּעֶרְכְּךָ לְאָשָׁם אֶל־הַכֹּהֵן: 26 וְכִפֶּר עָלָיו הַכֹּהֵן לִפְנֵי יְהוָה וְנִסְלַח לוֹ עַל־אַחַת מִכֹּל אֲשֶׁר־יַעֲשֶׂה לְאַשְׁמָה בָהּ: פ

ו וַיְדַבֵּר יְהוָה אֶל־מֹשֶׁה לֵּאמֹר: 2 צַו אֶת־אַהֲרֹן וְאֶת־בָּנָיו לֵאמֹר זֹאת תּוֹרַת הָעֹלָה הִוא הָעֹלָה עַל מוֹקְדָה עַל־הַמִּזְבֵּחַ כָּל־הַלַּיְלָה עַד־הַבֹּקֶר וְאֵשׁ

morning, and the fire of the altar shall be kept burning on it. [10]And the priest shall put on his linen garment, and his linen trousers he shall put on his body, and take up the ashes of the burnt offering which the fire has consumed on the altar, and he shall put them beside the altar. [11]Then he shall take off his garments, put on other garments, and carry the ashes outside the camp to a clean place. [12]And the fire on the altar shall be kept burning on it; it shall not be put out. And the priest shall burn wood on it every morning, and lay the burnt offering in order on it; and he shall burn on it the fat of the peace offerings. [13]A fire shall always be burning on the altar; it shall never go out.

[14]'This *is* the law of the grain offering: The sons of Aaron shall offer it on the altar before the LORD. [15]He shall take from it his handful of the fine flour of the grain offering, with its oil, and all the frankincense which *is* on the grain offering, and shall burn *it* on the altar *for* a sweet aroma, as a memorial to the LORD. [16]And the remainder of it Aaron and his sons shall eat; with unleavened bread it shall be eaten in a holy place; in the court of the tabernacle of meeting they shall eat it. [17]It shall not be baked with leaven. I have given it *as* their portion of My offerings made by fire; it *is* most holy, like the sin offering and the trespass offering. [18]All the males among the children of Aaron may eat it. *It shall be* a statute forever in your generations concerning the offerings made by fire to the LORD. Everyone who touches them must be holy.'"

[19]And the LORD spoke to Moses, saying, [20]"This *is* the offering of Aaron and his sons, which they shall offer to the LORD, *beginning* on the day when he is anointed: one-tenth of an ephah of fine flour as a daily grain offering, half of it in the morning and half of it at night. [21]It shall be made in a pan with oil. *When it is* mixed, you shall bring it in. The baked pieces of the grain offering you shall offer *for* a sweet aroma to the LORD. [22]The priest from among his sons, who is anointed in his place, shall offer it. *It is* a statute forever to the LORD. It shall be wholly burned. [23]For every grain offering for the priest shall be wholly burned. It shall not be eaten."

[24]Also the LORD spoke to Moses, saying, [25]"Speak to Aaron and to his sons, saying, 'This *is* the law of the sin offering: In the place where the burnt offering is killed, the sin offering shall be killed before the LORD. It *is* most holy. [26]The priest who offers it for sin shall eat it. In a holy place it shall be eaten, in the court of the tabernacle of meeting. [27]Everyone who touches its flesh must be holy. And when its blood is sprinkled on any

הַמִּזְבֵּחַ תּוּקַד בּוֹ: 3 וְלָבַשׁ הַכֹּהֵן מִדּוֹ בַד וּמִכְנְסֵי־בַד יִלְבַּשׁ עַל־בְּשָׂרוֹ וְהֵרִים אֶת־הַדֶּשֶׁן אֲשֶׁר תֹּאכַל הָאֵשׁ אֶת־הָעֹלָה עַל־הַמִּזְבֵּחַ וְשָׂמוֹ אֵצֶל הַמִּזְבֵּחַ: 4 וּפָשַׁט אֶת־בְּגָדָיו וְלָבַשׁ בְּגָדִים אֲחֵרִים וְהוֹצִיא אֶת־הַדֶּשֶׁן אֶל־מִחוּץ לַמַּחֲנֶה אֶל־מָקוֹם טָהוֹר: 5 וְהָאֵשׁ עַל־הַמִּזְבֵּחַ תּוּקַד־בּוֹ לֹא תִכְבֶּה וּבִעֵר עָלֶיהָ הַכֹּהֵן עֵצִים בַּבֹּקֶר בַּבֹּקֶר וְעָרַךְ עָלֶיהָ הָעֹלָה וְהִקְטִיר עָלֶיהָ חֶלְבֵי הַשְּׁלָמִים: 6 אֵשׁ תָּמִיד תּוּקַד עַל־הַמִּזְבֵּחַ לֹא תִכְבֶּה: ס 7 וְזֹאת תּוֹרַת הַמִּנְחָה הַקְרֵב אֹתָהּ בְּנֵי־אַהֲרֹן לִפְנֵי יְהוָה אֶל־פְּנֵי הַמִּזְבֵּחַ: 8 וְהֵרִים מִמֶּנּוּ בְּקֻמְצוֹ מִסֹּלֶת הַמִּנְחָה וּמִשַּׁמְנָהּ וְאֵת כָּל־הַלְּבֹנָה אֲשֶׁר עַל־הַמִּנְחָה וְהִקְטִיר הַמִּזְבֵּחַ רֵיחַ נִיחֹחַ אַזְכָּרָתָהּ לַיהוָה: 9 וְהַנּוֹתֶרֶת מִמֶּנָּה יֹאכְלוּ אַהֲרֹן וּבָנָיו מַצּוֹת תֵּאָכֵל בְּמָקוֹם קָדֹשׁ בַּחֲצַר אֹהֶל־מוֹעֵד יֹאכְלוּהָ: 10 לֹא תֵאָפֶה חָמֵץ חֶלְקָם נָתַתִּי אֹתָהּ מֵאִשָּׁי קֹדֶשׁ קָדָשִׁים הִוא כַּחַטָּאת וְכָאָשָׁם: 11 כָּל־זָכָר בִּבְנֵי אַהֲרֹן יֹאכְלֶנָּה חָק־עוֹלָם לְדֹרֹתֵיכֶם מֵאִשֵּׁי יְהוָה כֹּל אֲשֶׁר־יִגַּע בָּהֶם יִקְדָּשׁ: פ

12 וַיְדַבֵּר יְהוָה אֶל־מֹשֶׁה לֵּאמֹר: 13 זֶה קָרְבַּן אַהֲרֹן וּבָנָיו אֲשֶׁר־יַקְרִיבוּ לַיהוָה בְּיוֹם הִמָּשַׁח אֹתוֹ עֲשִׂירִת הָאֵפָה סֹלֶת מִנְחָה תָּמִיד מַחֲצִיתָהּ בַּבֹּקֶר וּמַחֲצִיתָהּ בָּעָרֶב: 14 עַל־מַחֲבַת בַּשֶּׁמֶן תֵּעָשֶׂה מֻרְבֶּכֶת תְּבִיאֶנָּה תֻּפִינֵי מִנְחַת פִּתִּים תַּקְרִיב רֵיחַ־נִיחֹחַ לַיהוָה: 15 וְהַכֹּהֵן הַמָּשִׁיחַ תַּחְתָּיו מִבָּנָיו יַעֲשֶׂה אֹתָהּ חָק־עוֹלָם לַיהוָה כָּלִיל תָּקְטָר: 16 וְכָל־מִנְחַת כֹּהֵן כָּלִיל תִּהְיֶה לֹא תֵאָכֵל: פ

17 וַיְדַבֵּר יְהוָה אֶל־מֹשֶׁה לֵּאמֹר: 18 דַּבֵּר אֶל־אַהֲרֹן וְאֶל־בָּנָיו לֵאמֹר זֹאת תּוֹרַת הַחַטָּאת בִּמְקוֹם אֲשֶׁר תִּשָּׁחֵט הָעֹלָה תִּשָּׁחֵט הַחַטָּאת לִפְנֵי יְהוָה קֹדֶשׁ קָדָשִׁים הִוא: 19 הַכֹּהֵן הַמְחַטֵּא אֹתָהּ יֹאכְלֶנָּה בְּמָקוֹם קָדֹשׁ תֵּאָכֵל בַּחֲצַר אֹהֶל מוֹעֵד: 20 כֹּל

garment, you shall wash that on which it was sprinkled, in a holy place. ²⁸But the earthen vessel in which it is boiled shall be broken. And if it is boiled in a bronze pot, it shall be both scoured and rinsed in water. ²⁹All the males among the priests may eat it. It *is* most holy. ³⁰But no sin offering from which *any* of the blood is brought into the tabernacle of meeting, to make atonement in the holy *place,* shall be eaten. It shall be burned in the fire.

7 'Likewise this *is* the law of the trespass offering (it *is* most holy): ²In the place where they kill the burnt offering they shall kill the trespass offering. And its blood he shall sprinkle all around on the altar. ³And he shall offer from it all its fat. The fat tail and the fat that covers the entrails, ⁴the two kidneys and the fat that *is* on them by the flanks, and the fatty lobe *attached* to the liver above the kidneys, he shall remove; ⁵and the priest shall burn them on the altar as an offering made by fire to the LORD. It *is* a trespass offering. ⁶Every male among the priests may eat it. It shall be eaten in a holy place. It *is* most holy. ⁷The trespass offering *is* like the sin offering; *there is* one law for them both: the priest who makes atonement with it shall have *it.* ⁸And the priest who offers anyone's burnt offering, that priest shall have for himself the skin of the burnt offering which he has offered. ⁹Also every grain offering that is baked in the oven and all that is prepared in the covered pan, or in a pan, shall be the priest's who offers it. ¹⁰Every grain offering, *whether* mixed with oil or dry, shall belong to all the sons of Aaron, to one *as much* as the other.

¹¹'This *is* the law of the sacrifice of peace offerings which he shall offer to the LORD: ¹²If he offers it for a thanksgiving, then he shall offer, with the sacrifice of thanksgiving, unleavened cakes mixed with oil, unleavened wafers anointed with oil, or cakes of blended flour mixed with oil. ¹³Besides the cakes, *as* his offering he shall offer leavened bread with the sacrifice of thanksgiving of his peace offering. ¹⁴And from it he shall offer one cake from each offering *as* a heave offering to the LORD. It shall belong to the priest who sprinkles the blood of the peace offering.

¹⁵'The flesh of the sacrifice of his peace offering for thanksgiving shall be eaten the same day it is offered. He shall not leave any of it until morning. ¹⁶But if the sacrifice of his offering *is* a vow or a voluntary offering, it shall be eaten the same day that he offers his sacrifice; but on the next day the remainder of it also may be eaten; ¹⁷the remainder of the flesh of the sacrifice on the third day must be

אֲשֶׁר־יִגַּע בִּבְשָׂרָהּ יִקְדָּשׁ וַאֲשֶׁר יִזֶּה מִדָּמָהּ עַל־
הַבֶּגֶד אֲשֶׁר יִזֶּה עָלֶיהָ תְּכַבֵּס בְּמָקוֹם קָדֹשׁ:
21 וּכְלִי־חֶרֶשׂ אֲשֶׁר תְּבֻשַּׁל־בּוֹ יִשָּׁבֵר וְאִם־בִּכְלִי
נְחֹשֶׁת בֻּשָּׁלָה וּמֹרַק וְשֻׁטַּף בַּמָּיִם: 22 כָּל־זָכָר
בַּכֹּהֲנִים יֹאכַל אֹתָהּ קֹדֶשׁ קָדָשִׁים הִוא: 23 וְכָל־
חַטָּאת אֲשֶׁר יוּבָא מִדָּמָהּ אֶל־אֹהֶל מוֹעֵד לְכַפֵּר
בַּקֹּדֶשׁ לֹא תֵאָכֵל בָּאֵשׁ תִּשָּׂרֵף: פ

ז וְזֹאת תּוֹרַת הָאָשָׁם קֹדֶשׁ קָדָשִׁים הוּא:
2 בִּמְקוֹם אֲשֶׁר יִשְׁחֲטוּ אֶת־הָעֹלָה יִשְׁחֲטוּ אֶת־
הָאָשָׁם וְאֶת־דָּמוֹ יִזְרֹק עַל־הַמִּזְבֵּחַ סָבִיב: 3 וְאֵת
כָּל־חֶלְבּוֹ יַקְרִיב מִמֶּנּוּ אֵת הָאַלְיָה וְאֶת־הַחֵלֶב
הַמְכַסֶּה אֶת־הַקֶּרֶב: 4 וְאֵת שְׁתֵּי הַכְּלָיֹת וְאֶת־
הַחֵלֶב אֲשֶׁר עֲלֵיהֶן אֲשֶׁר עַל־הַכְּסָלִים וְאֶת־הַיֹּתֶרֶת
עַל־הַכָּבֵד עַל־הַכְּלָיֹת יְסִירֶנָּה: 5 וְהִקְטִיר אֹתָם
הַכֹּהֵן הַמִּזְבֵּחָה אִשֶּׁה לַיהוָה אָשָׁם הוּא: 6 כָּל־
זָכָר בַּכֹּהֲנִים יֹאכְלֶנּוּ בְּמָקוֹם קָדוֹשׁ יֵאָכֵל קֹדֶשׁ
קָדָשִׁים הוּא: 7 כַּחַטָּאת כָּאָשָׁם תּוֹרָה אַחַת לָהֶם
הַכֹּהֵן אֲשֶׁר יְכַפֶּר־בּוֹ לוֹ יִהְיֶה: 8 וְהַכֹּהֵן הַמַּקְרִיב
אֶת־עֹלַת אִישׁ עוֹר הָעֹלָה אֲשֶׁר הִקְרִיב לַכֹּהֵן לוֹ
יִהְיֶה: 9 וְכָל־מִנְחָה אֲשֶׁר תֵּאָפֶה בַּתַּנּוּר וְכָל־נַעֲשָׂה
בַמַּרְחֶשֶׁת וְעַל־מַחֲבַת לַכֹּהֵן הַמַּקְרִיב אֹתָהּ לוֹ
תִהְיֶה: 10 וְכָל־מִנְחָה בְלוּלָה־בַשֶּׁמֶן וַחֲרֵבָה לְכָל־
בְּנֵי אַהֲרֹן תִּהְיֶה אִישׁ כְּאָחִיו: פ

11 וְזֹאת תּוֹרַת זֶבַח הַשְּׁלָמִים אֲשֶׁר יַקְרִיב לַיהוָה:
12 אִם עַל־תּוֹדָה יַקְרִיבֶנּוּ וְהִקְרִיב | עַל־זֶבַח
הַתּוֹדָה חַלּוֹת מַצּוֹת בְּלוּלֹת בַּשֶּׁמֶן וּרְקִיקֵי מַצּוֹת
מְשֻׁחִים בַּשָּׁמֶן וְסֹלֶת מֻרְבֶּכֶת חַלֹּת בְּלוּלֹת בַּשָּׁמֶן:
13 עַל־חַלֹּת לֶחֶם חָמֵץ יַקְרִיב קָרְבָּנוֹ עַל־זֶבַח
תּוֹדַת שְׁלָמָיו: 14 וְהִקְרִיב מִמֶּנּוּ אֶחָד מִכָּל־קָרְבָּן
תְּרוּמָה לַיהוָה לַכֹּהֵן הַזֹּרֵק אֶת־דַּם הַשְּׁלָמִים לוֹ
יִהְיֶה: 15 וּבְשַׂר זֶבַח תּוֹדַת שְׁלָמָיו בְּיוֹם קָרְבָּנוֹ
יֵאָכֵל לֹא־יַנִּיחַ מִמֶּנּוּ עַד־בֹּקֶר: 16 וְאִם־נֶדֶר | אוֹ
נְדָבָה זֶבַח קָרְבָּנוֹ בְּיוֹם הַקְרִיבוֹ אֶת־זִבְחוֹ יֵאָכֵל
וּמִמָּחֳרָת וְהַנּוֹתָר מִמֶּנּוּ יֵאָכֵל: 17 וְהַנּוֹתָר מִבְּשַׂר

burned with fire. ¹⁸ And if *any* of the flesh of the sacrifice of his peace offering is eaten at all on the third day, it shall not be accepted, nor shall it be imputed to him; it shall be an abomination *to* him who offers it, and the person who eats of it shall bear guilt.

¹⁹ 'The flesh that touches any unclean thing shall not be eaten. It shall be burned with fire. And as for the *clean* flesh, all who are clean may eat of it. ²⁰ But the person who eats the flesh of the sacrifice of the peace offering that *belongs* to the LORD, while he is unclean, that person shall be cut off from his people. ²¹ Moreover the person who touches any unclean thing, *such as* human uncleanness, *an* unclean animal, or any abominable unclean thing, and who eats the flesh of the sacrifice of the peace offering that *belongs* to the LORD, that person shall be cut off from his people.' "

²² And the LORD spoke to Moses, saying, ²³ "Speak to the children of Israel, saying: 'You shall not eat any fat, of ox or sheep or goat. ²⁴ And the fat of an animal that dies *naturally,* and the fat of what is torn by wild beasts, may be used in any other way; but you shall by no means eat it. ²⁵ For whoever eats the fat of the animal of which men offer an offering made by fire to the LORD, the person who eats *it* shall be cut off from his people. ²⁶ Moreover you shall not eat any blood in any of your dwellings, *whether* of bird or beast. ²⁷ Whoever eats any blood, that person shall be cut off from his people.' "

²⁸ Then the LORD spoke to Moses, saying, ²⁹ "Speak to the children of Israel, saying: 'He who offers the sacrifice of his peace offering to the LORD shall bring his offering to the LORD from the sacrifice of his peace offering. ³⁰ His own hands shall bring the offerings made by fire to the LORD. The fat with the breast he shall bring, that the breast may be waved *as* a wave offering before the LORD. ³¹ And the priest shall burn the fat on the altar, but the breast shall be Aaron's and his sons'. ³² Also the right thigh you shall give to the priest *as* a heave offering from the sacrifices of your peace offerings. ³³ He among the sons of Aaron, who offers the blood of the peace offering and the fat, shall have the right thigh for *his* part. ³⁴ For the breast of the wave offering and the thigh of the heave offering I have taken from the children of Israel, from the sacrifices of their peace offerings, and I have given them to Aaron the priest and to his sons from the children of Israel by a statute forever.' "

הַזֶּבַח בַּיּוֹם הַשְּׁלִישִׁי בָּאֵשׁ יִשָּׂרֵף: 18 וְאִם הֵאָכֹל יֵאָכֵל מִבְּשַׂר־זֶבַח שְׁלָמָיו בַּיּוֹם הַשְּׁלִישִׁי לֹא יֵרָצֶה הַמַּקְרִיב אֹתוֹ לֹא יֵחָשֵׁב לוֹ פִּגּוּל יִהְיֶה וְהַנֶּפֶשׁ הָאֹכֶלֶת מִמֶּנּוּ עֲוֺנָהּ תִּשָּׂא: 19 וְהַבָּשָׂר אֲשֶׁר־יִגַּע בְּכָל־טָמֵא לֹא יֵאָכֵל בָּאֵשׁ יִשָּׂרֵף וְהַבָּשָׂר כָּל־טָהוֹר יֹאכַל בָּשָׂר: 20 וְהַנֶּפֶשׁ אֲשֶׁר־תֹּאכַל בָּשָׂר מִזֶּבַח הַשְּׁלָמִים אֲשֶׁר לַיהֹוָה וְטֻמְאָתוֹ עָלָיו וְנִכְרְתָה הַנֶּפֶשׁ הַהִוא מֵעַמֶּיהָ: 21 וְנֶפֶשׁ כִּי־תִגַּע בְּכָל־טָמֵא בְּטֻמְאַת אָדָם אוֹ | בִּבְהֵמָה טְמֵאָה אוֹ בְּכָל־שֶׁקֶץ טָמֵא וְאָכַל מִבְּשַׂר־זֶבַח הַשְּׁלָמִים אֲשֶׁר לַיהֹוָה וְנִכְרְתָה הַנֶּפֶשׁ הַהִוא מֵעַמֶּיהָ: פ

22 וַיְדַבֵּר יְהֹוָה אֶל־מֹשֶׁה לֵּאמֹר: 23 דַּבֵּר אֶל־ בְּנֵי יִשְׂרָאֵל לֵאמֹר כָּל־חֵלֶב שׁוֹר וְכֶשֶׂב וָעֵז לֹא תֹאכֵלוּ: 24 וְחֵלֶב נְבֵלָה וְחֵלֶב טְרֵפָה יֵעָשֶׂה לְכָל־מְלָאכָה וְאָכֹל לֹא תֹאכְלֻהוּ: 25 כִּי כָּל־אֹכֵל חֵלֶב מִן־הַבְּהֵמָה אֲשֶׁר יַקְרִיב מִמֶּנָּה אִשֶּׁה לַיהֹוָה וְנִכְרְתָה הַנֶּפֶשׁ הָאֹכֶלֶת מֵעַמֶּיהָ: 26 וְכָל־דָּם לֹא תֹאכְלוּ בְּכֹל מוֹשְׁבֹתֵיכֶם לָעוֹף וְלַבְּהֵמָה: 27 כָּל־ נֶפֶשׁ אֲשֶׁר־תֹּאכַל כָּל־דָּם וְנִכְרְתָה הַנֶּפֶשׁ הַהִוא מֵעַמֶּיהָ: פ

28 וַיְדַבֵּר יְהֹוָה אֶל־מֹשֶׁה לֵּאמֹר: 29 דַּבֵּר אֶל־בְּנֵי יִשְׂרָאֵל לֵאמֹר הַמַּקְרִיב אֶת־זֶבַח שְׁלָמָיו לַיהֹוָה יָבִיא אֶת־קָרְבָּנוֹ לַיהֹוָה מִזֶּבַח שְׁלָמָיו: 30 יָדָיו תְּבִיאֶינָה אֵת אִשֵּׁי יְהֹוָה אֶת־הַחֵלֶב עַל־הֶחָזֶה יְבִיאֶנּוּ אֵת הֶחָזֶה לְהָנִיף אֹתוֹ תְּנוּפָה לִפְנֵי יְהֹוָה: 31 וְהִקְטִיר הַכֹּהֵן אֶת־הַחֵלֶב הַמִּזְבֵּחָה וְהָיָה הֶחָזֶה לְאַהֲרֹן וּלְבָנָיו: 32 וְאֵת שׁוֹק הַיָּמִין תִּתְּנוּ תְרוּמָה לַכֹּהֵן מִזִּבְחֵי שַׁלְמֵיכֶם: 33 הַמַּקְרִיב אֶת־ דַּם הַשְּׁלָמִים וְאֶת־הַחֵלֶב מִבְּנֵי אַהֲרֹן לוֹ תִהְיֶה שׁוֹק הַיָּמִין לְמָנָה: 34 כִּי אֶת־חֲזֵה הַתְּנוּפָה וְאֵת |

³⁵This *is* the consecrated portion for Aaron and his sons, from the offerings made by fire to the LORD, on the day when *Moses* presented them to minister to the LORD as priests. ³⁶The LORD commanded this to be given to them by the children of Israel, on the day that He anointed them, *by a* statute forever throughout their generations.

³⁷This *is* the law of the burnt offering, the grain offering, the sin offering, the trespass offering, the consecrations, and the sacrifice of the peace offering, ³⁸which the LORD commanded Moses on Mount Sinai, on the day when He commanded the children of Israel to offer their offerings to the LORD in the Wilderness of Sinai.

8 And the LORD spoke to Moses, saying: ²"Take Aaron and his sons with him, and the garments, the anointing oil, a bull as the sin offering, two rams, and a basket of unleavened bread; ³and gather all the congregation together at the door of the tabernacle of meeting."

⁴So Moses did as the LORD commanded him. And the congregation was gathered together at the door of the tabernacle of meeting. ⁵And Moses said to the congregation, "This *is* what the LORD commanded to be done."

⁶Then Moses brought Aaron and his sons and washed them with water. ⁷And he put the tunic on him, girded him with the sash, clothed him with the robe, and put the ephod on him; and he girded him with the intricately woven band of the ephod, and with it tied *the ephod* on him. ⁸Then he put the breastplate on him, and he put the Urim and the Thummim in the breastplate. ⁹And he put the turban on his head. Also on the turban, on its front, he put the golden plate, the holy crown, as the LORD had commanded Moses.

¹⁰Also Moses took the anointing oil, and anointed the tabernacle and all that *was* in it, and consecrated them. ¹¹He sprinkled some of it on the altar seven times, anointed the altar and all its utensils, and the laver and its base, to consecrate them. ¹²And he poured some of the anointing oil on Aaron's head and anointed him, to consecrate him.

¹³Then Moses brought Aaron's sons and put tunics on them, girded them with sashes, and put hats on them, as the LORD had commanded Moses.

¹⁴And he brought the bull for the sin offering. Then Aaron and his sons laid their hands on the head of the bull for the sin offering, ¹⁵and Moses killed *it*. Then he took the blood, and put *some* on the horns of the altar all around with his finger, and purified the altar. And he poured the blood at the base of the altar, and consecrated it, to make

שׁוֹק הַתְּרוּמָה לָקַחְתִּי מֵאֵת בְּנֵי־יִשְׂרָאֵל מִזִּבְחֵי שַׁלְמֵיהֶם וָאֶתֵּן אֹתָם לְאַהֲרֹן הַכֹּהֵן וּלְבָנָיו לְחָק־ עוֹלָם מֵאֵת בְּנֵי יִשְׂרָאֵל: 35 זֹאת מִשְׁחַת אַהֲרֹן וּמִשְׁחַת בָּנָיו מֵאִשֵּׁי יְהוָה בְּיוֹם הִקְרִיב אֹתָם לְכַהֵן לַיהוָה: 36 אֲשֶׁר צִוָּה יְהוָה לָתֵת לָהֶם בְּיוֹם מָשְׁחוֹ אֹתָם מֵאֵת בְּנֵי יִשְׂרָאֵל חֻקַּת עוֹלָם לְדֹרֹתָם: 37 זֹאת הַתּוֹרָה לָעֹלָה לַמִּנְחָה וְלַחַטָּאת וְלָאָשָׁם וְלַמִּלּוּאִים וּלְזֶבַח הַשְּׁלָמִים: 38 אֲשֶׁר צִוָּה יְהוָה אֶת־מֹשֶׁה בְּהַר סִינָי בְּיוֹם צַוֹּתוֹ אֶת־בְּנֵי יִשְׂרָאֵל לְהַקְרִיב אֶת־קָרְבְּנֵיהֶם לַיהוָה בְּמִדְבַּר סִינָי: פ

ח וַיְדַבֵּר יְהוָה אֶל־מֹשֶׁה לֵּאמֹר: 2 קַח אֶת־אַהֲרֹן וְאֶת־בָּנָיו אִתּוֹ וְאֵת הַבְּגָדִים וְאֵת שֶׁמֶן הַמִּשְׁחָה וְאֵת פַּר הַחַטָּאת וְאֵת שְׁנֵי הָאֵילִים וְאֵת סַל הַמַּצּוֹת: 3 וְאֵת כָּל־הָעֵדָה הַקְהֵל אֶל־פֶּתַח אֹהֶל מוֹעֵד: 4 וַיַּעַשׂ מֹשֶׁה כַּאֲשֶׁר צִוָּה יְהוָה אֹתוֹ וַתִּקָּהֵל הָעֵדָה אֶל־פֶּתַח אֹהֶל מוֹעֵד: 5 וַיֹּאמֶר מֹשֶׁה אֶל־הָעֵדָה זֶה הַדָּבָר אֲשֶׁר־צִוָּה יְהוָה לַעֲשׂוֹת: 6 וַיַּקְרֵב מֹשֶׁה אֶת־אַהֲרֹן וְאֶת־בָּנָיו וַיִּרְחַץ אֹתָם בַּמָּיִם: 7 וַיִּתֵּן עָלָיו אֶת־הַכֻּתֹּנֶת וַיַּחְגֹּר אֹתוֹ בָּאַבְנֵט וַיַּלְבֵּשׁ אֹתוֹ אֶת־הַמְּעִיל וַיִּתֵּן עָלָיו אֶת־הָאֵפֹד וַיַּחְגֹּר אֹתוֹ בְּחֵשֶׁב הָאֵפֹד וַיֶּאְפֹּד לוֹ בּוֹ: 8 וַיָּשֶׂם עָלָיו אֶת־הַחֹשֶׁן וַיִּתֵּן אֶל־הַחֹשֶׁן אֶת־הָאוּרִים וְאֶת־ הַתֻּמִּים: 9 וַיָּשֶׂם אֶת־הַמִּצְנֶפֶת עַל־רֹאשׁוֹ וַיָּשֶׂם עַל־הַמִּצְנֶפֶת אֶל־מוּל פָּנָיו אֵת צִיץ הַזָּהָב נֵזֶר הַקֹּדֶשׁ כַּאֲשֶׁר צִוָּה יְהוָה אֶת־מֹשֶׁה: 10 וַיִּקַּח מֹשֶׁה אֶת־שֶׁמֶן הַמִּשְׁחָה וַיִּמְשַׁח אֶת־הַמִּשְׁכָּן וְאֶת־כָּל־אֲשֶׁר־בּוֹ וַיְקַדֵּשׁ אֹתָם: 11 וַיַּז מִמֶּנּוּ עַל־ הַמִּזְבֵּחַ שֶׁבַע פְּעָמִים וַיִּמְשַׁח אֶת־הַמִּזְבֵּחַ וְאֶת־ כָּל־כֵּלָיו וְאֶת־הַכִּיֹּר וְאֶת־כַּנּוֹ לְקַדְּשָׁם: 12 וַיִּצֹק מִשֶּׁמֶן הַמִּשְׁחָה עַל רֹאשׁ אַהֲרֹן וַיִּמְשַׁח אֹתוֹ לְקַדְּשׁוֹ: 13 וַיַּקְרֵב מֹשֶׁה אֶת־בְּנֵי אַהֲרֹן וַיַּלְבִּשֵׁם כֻּתֳּנֹת וַיַּחְגֹּר אֹתָם אַבְנֵט וַיַּחֲבֹשׁ לָהֶם מִגְבָּעוֹת כַּאֲשֶׁר צִוָּה יְהוָה אֶת־מֹשֶׁה: 14 וַיַּגֵּשׁ אֵת פַּר הַחַטָּאת וַיִּסְמֹךְ אַהֲרֹן וּבָנָיו אֶת־יְדֵיהֶם עַל־רֹאשׁ פַּר הַחַטָּאת: 15 וַיִּשְׁחָט וַיִּקַּח מֹשֶׁה אֶת־הַדָּם וַיִּתֵּן עַל־קַרְנוֹת הַמִּזְבֵּחַ סָבִיב בְּאֶצְבָּעוֹ וַיְחַטֵּא אֶת־

atonement for it. ¹⁶ Then he took all the fat that *was*
on the entrails, the fatty lobe *attached to* the liver,
and the two kidneys with their fat, and Moses
burned *them* on the altar. ¹⁷ But the bull, its hide, its
flesh, and its offal, he burned with fire outside the
camp, as the LORD had commanded Moses.

¹⁸ Then he brought the ram as the burnt offering.
And Aaron and his sons laid their hands on the
head of the ram, ¹⁹ and Moses killed *it*. Then he
sprinkled the blood all around on the altar. ²⁰ And
he cut the ram into pieces; and Moses burned the
head, the pieces, and the fat. ²¹ Then he washed the
entrails and the legs in water. And Moses burned
the whole ram on the altar. It *was* a burnt sacrifice
for a sweet aroma, an offering made by fire to the
LORD, as the LORD had commanded Moses.

²² And he brought the second ram, the ram of
consecration. Then Aaron and his sons laid their
hands on the head of the ram, ²³ and Moses killed *it*.
Also he took *some* of its blood and put it on the tip
of Aaron's right ear, on the thumb of his right
hand, and on the big toe of his right foot. ²⁴ Then he
brought Aaron's sons. And Moses put *some* of the
blood on the tips of their right ears, on the thumbs
of their right hands, and on the big toes of their
right feet. And Moses sprinkled the blood all
around on the altar. ²⁵ Then he took the fat and
the fat tail, all the fat that *was* on the entrails, the
fatty lobe *attached to* the liver, the two kidneys and
their fat, and the right thigh; ²⁶ and from the basket
of unleavened bread that was before the LORD he
took one unleavened cake, a cake of bread *anointed
with* oil, and one wafer, and put *them* on the fat and
on the right thigh; ²⁷ and he put all *these* in Aaron's
hands and in his sons' hands, and waved them *as a*
wave offering before the LORD. ²⁸ Then Moses took
them from their hands and burned *them* on the
altar, on the burnt offering. They *were* consecration
offerings for a sweet aroma. That *was* an offering
made by fire to the LORD. ²⁹ And Moses took the
breast and waved it *as* a wave offering before the
LORD. It was Moses' part of the ram of consecration, as the LORD had commanded Moses.

³⁰ Then Moses took some of the anointing oil and
some of the blood which *was* on the altar, and
sprinkled *it* on Aaron, on his garments, on his sons,
and on the garments of his sons with him; and he
consecrated Aaron, his garments, his sons, and the
garments of his sons with him.

³¹ And Moses said to Aaron and his sons, "Boil
the flesh *at* the door of the tabernacle of meeting,
and eat it there with the bread that *is* in the basket
of consecration offerings, as I commanded, saying,
'Aaron and his sons shall eat it.' ³² What remains of

הַמִּזְבֵּחַ וְאֶת־הַדָּם יָצַק אֶל־יְסוֹד הַמִּזְבֵּחַ וַיְקַדְּשֵׁהוּ
לְכַפֵּר עָלָיו: ¹⁶ וַיִּקַּח אֶת־כָּל־הַחֵלֶב אֲשֶׁר עַל־
הַקֶּרֶב וְאֵת יֹתֶרֶת הַכָּבֵד וְאֶת־שְׁתֵּי הַכְּלָיֹת וְאֶת־
חֶלְבְּהֶן וַיַּקְטֵר מֹשֶׁה הַמִּזְבֵּחָה: ¹⁷ וְאֶת־הַפָּר וְאֶת־
עֹרוֹ וְאֶת־בְּשָׂרוֹ וְאֶת־פִּרְשׁוֹ שָׂרַף בָּאֵשׁ מִחוּץ
לַמַּחֲנֶה כַּאֲשֶׁר צִוָּה יְהוָה אֶת־מֹשֶׁה: ¹⁸ וַיַּקְרֵב
אֵת אֵיל הָעֹלָה וַיִּסְמְכוּ אַהֲרֹן וּבָנָיו אֶת־יְדֵיהֶם
עַל־רֹאשׁ הָאָיִל: ¹⁹ וַיִּשְׁחָט וַיִּזְרֹק מֹשֶׁה אֶת־הַדָּם
עַל־הַמִּזְבֵּחַ סָבִיב: ²⁰ וְאֶת־הָאַיִל נִתַּח לִנְתָחָיו
וַיַּקְטֵר מֹשֶׁה אֶת־הָרֹאשׁ וְאֶת־הַנְּתָחִים וְאֶת־
הַפָּדֶר: ²¹ וְאֶת־הַקֶּרֶב וְאֶת־הַכְּרָעַיִם רָחַץ בַּמָּיִם
וַיַּקְטֵר מֹשֶׁה אֶת־כָּל־הָאַיִל הַמִּזְבֵּחָה עֹלָה הוּא
לְרֵיחַ־נִיחֹחַ אִשֶּׁה הוּא לַיהוָה כַּאֲשֶׁר צִוָּה יְהוָה
אֶת־מֹשֶׁה: ²² וַיַּקְרֵב אֶת־הָאַיִל הַשֵּׁנִי אֵיל הַמִּלֻּאִים
וַיִּסְמְכוּ אַהֲרֹן וּבָנָיו אֶת־יְדֵיהֶם עַל־רֹאשׁ הָאָיִל:
²³ וַיִּשְׁחָט | וַיִּקַּח מֹשֶׁה מִדָּמוֹ וַיִּתֵּן עַל־תְּנוּךְ
אֹזֶן־אַהֲרֹן הַיְמָנִית וְעַל־בֹּהֶן יָדוֹ הַיְמָנִית וְעַל־
בֹּהֶן רַגְלוֹ הַיְמָנִית: ²⁴ וַיַּקְרֵב אֶת־בְּנֵי אַהֲרֹן וַיִּתֵּן
מֹשֶׁה מִן־הַדָּם עַל־תְּנוּךְ אָזְנָם הַיְמָנִית וְעַל־בֹּהֶן
יָדָם הַיְמָנִית וְעַל־בֹּהֶן רַגְלָם הַיְמָנִית וַיִּזְרֹק מֹשֶׁה
אֶת־הַדָּם עַל־הַמִּזְבֵּחַ סָבִיב: ²⁵ וַיִּקַּח אֶת־הַחֵלֶב
וְאֶת־הָאַלְיָה וְאֶת־כָּל־הַחֵלֶב אֲשֶׁר עַל־הַקֶּרֶב וְאֵת
יֹתֶרֶת הַכָּבֵד וְאֶת־שְׁתֵּי הַכְּלָיֹת וְאֶת־חֶלְבְּהֶן וְאֵת
שׁוֹק הַיָּמִין: ²⁶ וּמִסַּל הַמַּצּוֹת אֲשֶׁר | לִפְנֵי יְהוָה
לָקַח חַלַּת מַצָּה אַחַת וְחַלַּת לֶחֶם שֶׁמֶן אַחַת
וְרָקִיק אֶחָד וַיָּשֶׂם עַל־הַחֲלָבִים וְעַל שׁוֹק הַיָּמִין:
²⁷ וַיִּתֵּן אֶת־הַכֹּל עַל כַּפֵּי אַהֲרֹן וְעַל כַּפֵּי בָנָיו
וַיָּנֶף אֹתָם תְּנוּפָה לִפְנֵי יְהוָה: ²⁸ וַיִּקַּח מֹשֶׁה
אֹתָם מֵעַל כַּפֵּיהֶם וַיַּקְטֵר הַמִּזְבֵּחָה עַל־הָעֹלָה
מִלֻּאִים הֵם לְרֵיחַ נִיחֹחַ אִשֶּׁה הוּא לַיהוָה: ²⁹ וַיִּקַּח
מֹשֶׁה אֶת־הֶחָזֶה וַיְנִיפֵהוּ תְנוּפָה לִפְנֵי יְהוָה מֵאֵיל
הַמִּלֻּאִים לְמֹשֶׁה הָיָה לְמָנָה כַּאֲשֶׁר צִוָּה יְהוָה אֶת־
מֹשֶׁה: ³⁰ וַיִּקַּח מֹשֶׁה מִשֶּׁמֶן הַמִּשְׁחָה וּמִן־הַדָּם
אֲשֶׁר עַל־הַמִּזְבֵּחַ וַיַּז עַל־אַהֲרֹן עַל־בְּגָדָיו וְעַל־בָּנָיו
וְעַל־בִּגְדֵי בָנָיו אִתּוֹ וַיְקַדֵּשׁ אֶת־אַהֲרֹן אֶת־בְּגָדָיו
וְאֶת־בָּנָיו וְאֶת־בִּגְדֵי בָנָיו אִתּוֹ: ³¹ וַיֹּאמֶר מֹשֶׁה
אֶל־אַהֲרֹן וְאֶל־בָּנָיו בַּשְּׁלוּ אֶת־הַבָּשָׂר פֶּתַח אֹהֶל
מוֹעֵד וְשָׁם תֹּאכְלוּ אֹתוֹ וְאֶת־הַלֶּחֶם אֲשֶׁר בְּסַל
הַמִּלֻּאִים כַּאֲשֶׁר צִוֵּיתִי לֵאמֹר אַהֲרֹן וּבָנָיו יֹאכְלֻהוּ:
³² וְהַנּוֹתָר בַּבָּשָׂר וּבַלָּחֶם בָּאֵשׁ תִּשְׂרֹפוּ: ³³ וּמִפֶּתַח

the flesh and of the bread you shall burn with fire. 33 And you shall not go outside the door of the tabernacle of meeting *for* seven days, until the days of your consecration are ended. For seven days he shall consecrate you. 34 As he has done this day, *so* the LORD has commanded to do, to make atonement for you. 35 Therefore you shall stay *at* the door of the tabernacle of meeting day and night for seven days, and keep the charge of the LORD, so that you may not die; for so I have been commanded." 36 So Aaron and his sons did all the things that the LORD had commanded by the hand of Moses.

9 It came to pass on the eighth day that Moses called Aaron and his sons and the elders of Israel. 2 And he said to Aaron, "Take for yourself a young bull as a sin offering and a ram as a burnt offering, without blemish, and offer *them* before the LORD. 3 And to the children of Israel you shall speak, saying, 'Take a kid of the goats as a sin offering, and a calf and a lamb, *both* of the first year, without blemish, as a burnt offering, 4 also a bull and a ram as peace offerings, to sacrifice before the LORD, and a grain offering mixed with oil; for today the LORD will appear to you.'"

5 So they brought what Moses commanded before the tabernacle of meeting. And all the congregation drew near and stood before the LORD. 6 Then Moses said, "This *is* the thing which the LORD commanded you to do, and the glory of the LORD will appear to you." 7 And Moses said to Aaron, "Go to the altar, offer your sin offering and your burnt offering, and make atonement for yourself and for the people. Offer the offering of the people, and make atonement for them, as the LORD commanded."

8 Aaron therefore went to the altar and killed the calf of the sin offering, which *was* for himself. 9 Then the sons of Aaron brought the blood to him. And he dipped his finger in the blood, put *it* on the horns of the altar, and poured the blood at the base of the altar. 10 But the fat, the kidneys, and the fatty lobe from the liver of the sin offering he burned on the altar, as the LORD had commanded Moses. 11 The flesh and the hide he burned with fire outside the camp.

12 And he killed the burnt offering; and Aaron's sons presented to him the blood, which he sprinkled all around on the altar. 13 Then they presented the burnt offering to him, with its pieces and head, and he burned *them* on the altar. 14 And he washed the entrails and the legs, and burned *them* with the burnt offering on the altar.

אֹהֶל מוֹעֵד לֹא תֵצְאוּ שִׁבְעַת יָמִים עַד יוֹם מְלֹאת יְמֵי מִלֻּאֵיכֶם כִּי שִׁבְעַת יָמִים יְמַלֵּא אֶת־יֶדְכֶם: 34 כַּאֲשֶׁר עָשָׂה בַּיּוֹם הַזֶּה צִוָּה יְהוָה לַעֲשֹׂת לְכַפֵּר עֲלֵיכֶם: 35 וּפֶתַח אֹהֶל מוֹעֵד תֵּשְׁבוּ יוֹמָם וָלַיְלָה שִׁבְעַת יָמִים וּשְׁמַרְתֶּם אֶת־מִשְׁמֶרֶת יְהוָה וְלֹא תָמוּתוּ כִּי־כֵן צֻוֵּיתִי: 36 וַיַּעַשׂ אַהֲרֹן וּבָנָיו אֵת כָּל־ הַדְּבָרִים אֲשֶׁר־צִוָּה יְהוָה בְּיַד־מֹשֶׁה: ס

ט וַיְהִי בַּיּוֹם הַשְּׁמִינִי קָרָא מֹשֶׁה לְאַהֲרֹן וּלְבָנָיו וּלְזִקְנֵי יִשְׂרָאֵל: 2 וַיֹּאמֶר אֶל־אַהֲרֹן קַח־לְךָ עֵגֶל בֶּן־בָּקָר לְחַטָּאת וְאַיִל לְעֹלָה תְּמִימִם וְהַקְרֵב לִפְנֵי יְהוָה: 3 וְאֶל־בְּנֵי יִשְׂרָאֵל תְּדַבֵּר לֵאמֹר קְחוּ שְׂעִיר־עִזִּים לְחַטָּאת וְעֵגֶל וָכֶבֶשׂ בְּנֵי־שָׁנָה תְּמִימִם לְעֹלָה: 4 וְשׁוֹר וָאַיִל לִשְׁלָמִים לִזְבֹּחַ לִפְנֵי יְהוָה וּמִנְחָה בְלוּלָה בַשָּׁמֶן כִּי הַיּוֹם יְהוָה נִרְאָה אֲלֵיכֶם: 5 וַיִּקְחוּ אֵת אֲשֶׁר צִוָּה מֹשֶׁה אֶל־פְּנֵי אֹהֶל מוֹעֵד וַיִּקְרְבוּ כָּל־הָעֵדָה וַיַּעַמְדוּ לִפְנֵי יְהוָה: 6 וַיֹּאמֶר מֹשֶׁה זֶה הַדָּבָר אֲשֶׁר־צִוָּה יְהוָה תַּעֲשׂוּ וְיֵרָא אֲלֵיכֶם כְּבוֹד יְהוָה: 7 וַיֹּאמֶר מֹשֶׁה אֶל־אַהֲרֹן קְרַב אֶל־הַמִּזְבֵּחַ וַעֲשֵׂה אֶת־ חַטָּאתְךָ וְאֶת־עֹלָתֶךָ וְכַפֵּר בַּעַדְךָ וּבְעַד הָעָם וַעֲשֵׂה אֶת־קָרְבַּן הָעָם וְכַפֵּר בַּעֲדָם כַּאֲשֶׁר צִוָּה יְהוָה: 8 וַיִּקְרַב אַהֲרֹן אֶל־הַמִּזְבֵּחַ וַיִּשְׁחַט אֶת־ עֵגֶל הַחַטָּאת אֲשֶׁר־לוֹ: 9 וַיַּקְרִבוּ בְּנֵי אַהֲרֹן אֶת־ הַדָּם אֵלָיו וַיִּטְבֹּל אֶצְבָּעוֹ בַּדָּם וַיִּתֵּן עַל־קַרְנוֹת הַמִּזְבֵּחַ וְאֶת־הַדָּם יָצַק אֶל־יְסוֹד הַמִּזְבֵּחַ: 10 וְאֶת־ הַחֵלֶב וְאֶת־הַכְּלָיֹת וְאֶת־הַיֹּתֶרֶת מִן־הַכָּבֵד מִן־ הַחַטָּאת הִקְטִיר הַמִּזְבֵּחָה כַּאֲשֶׁר צִוָּה יְהוָה אֶת־מֹשֶׁה: 11 וְאֶת־הַבָּשָׂר וְאֶת־הָעוֹר שָׂרַף בָּאֵשׁ מִחוּץ לַמַּחֲנֶה: 12 וַיִּשְׁחַט אֶת־הָעֹלָה וַיַּמְצִאוּ בְּנֵי אַהֲרֹן אֵלָיו אֶת־הַדָּם וַיִּזְרְקֵהוּ עַל־הַמִּזְבֵּחַ סָבִיב: 13 וְאֶת־הָעֹלָה הִמְצִיאוּ אֵלָיו לִנְתָחֶיהָ וְאֶת־הָרֹאשׁ וַיַּקְטֵר עַל־הַמִּזְבֵּחַ: 14 וַיִּרְחַץ אֶת־הַקֶּרֶב וְאֶת־

¹⁵Then he brought the people's offering, and took the goat, which *was* the sin offering for the people, and killed it and offered it for sin, like the first one. ¹⁶And he brought the burnt offering and offered it according to the prescribed manner. ¹⁷Then he brought the grain offering, took a handful of it, and burned *it* on the altar, besides the burnt sacrifice of the morning.

¹⁸He also killed the bull and the ram *as* sacrifices of peace offerings, which *were* for the people. And Aaron's sons presented to him the blood, which he sprinkled all around on the altar, ¹⁹and the fat from the bull and the ram—the fatty tail, what covers *the entrails* and the kidneys, and the fatty lobe *attached to* the liver; ²⁰and they put the fat on the breasts. Then he burned the fat on the altar; ²¹but the breasts and the right thigh Aaron waved *as* a wave offering before the LORD, as Moses had commanded.

²²Then Aaron lifted his hand toward the people, blessed them, and came down from offering the sin offering, the burnt offering, and peace offerings. ²³And Moses and Aaron went into the tabernacle of meeting, and came out and blessed the people. Then the glory of the LORD appeared to all the people, ²⁴and fire came out from before the LORD and consumed the burnt offering and the fat on the altar. When all the people saw *it,* they shouted and fell on their faces.

10 Then Nadab and Abihu, the sons of Aaron, each took his censer and put fire in it, put incense on it, and offered profane fire before the LORD, which He had not commanded them. ²So fire went out from the LORD and devoured them, and they died before the LORD. ³And Moses said to Aaron, "This is what the LORD spoke, saying:

'By those who come near Me
I must be regarded as holy;
And before all the people
I must be glorified.'"

So Aaron held his peace.

⁴Then Moses called Mishael and Elzaphan, the sons of Uzziel the uncle of Aaron, and said to them, "Come near, carry your brethren from before the sanctuary out of the camp." ⁵So they went near and carried them by their tunics out of the camp, as Moses had said.

⁶And Moses said to Aaron, and to Eleazar and Ithamar, his sons, "Do not uncover your heads nor tear your clothes, lest you die, and wrath come upon all the people. But let your brethren, the whole house of Israel, bewail the burning which the

הַכְּרָעַיִם וַיַּקְטֵר עַל־הָעֹלָה הַמִּזְבֵּחָה: 15 וַיַּקְרֵב אֶת קָרְבַּן הָעָם וַיִּקַּח אֶת־שְׂעִיר הַחַטָּאת אֲשֶׁר לָעָם וַיִּשְׁחָטֵהוּ וַיְחַטְּאֵהוּ כָּרִאשׁוֹן: 16 וַיַּקְרֵב אֶת־הָעֹלָה וַיַּעֲשֶׂהָ כַּמִּשְׁפָּט: 17 וַיַּקְרֵב אֶת־הַמִּנְחָה וַיְמַלֵּא כַפּוֹ מִמֶּנָּה וַיַּקְטֵר עַל־הַמִּזְבֵּחַ מִלְּבַד עֹלַת הַבֹּקֶר:

18 וַיִּשְׁחַט אֶת־הַשּׁוֹר וְאֶת־הָאַיִל זֶבַח הַשְּׁלָמִים אֲשֶׁר לָעָם וַיַּמְצִאוּ בְּנֵי אַהֲרֹן אֶת־הַדָּם אֵלָיו וַיִּזְרְקֵהוּ עַל־הַמִּזְבֵּחַ סָבִיב: 19 וְאֶת־הַחֲלָבִים מִן־הַשּׁוֹר וּמִן־הָאַיִל הָאַלְיָה וְהַמְכַסֶּה וְהַכְּלָיֹת וְיֹתֶרֶת הַכָּבֵד: 20 וַיָּשִׂימוּ אֶת־הַחֲלָבִים עַל־הֶחָזוֹת וַיַּקְטֵר הַחֲלָבִים הַמִּזְבֵּחָה: 21 וְאֵת הֶחָזוֹת וְאֵת שׁוֹק הַיָּמִין הֵנִיף אַהֲרֹן תְּנוּפָה לִפְנֵי יְהוָה כַּאֲשֶׁר צִוָּה מֹשֶׁה: 22 וַיִּשָּׂא אַהֲרֹן אֶת־יָדָו אֶל־הָעָם וַיְבָרְכֵם וַיֵּרֶד מֵעֲשֹׂת הַחַטָּאת וְהָעֹלָה וְהַשְּׁלָמִים: 23 וַיָּבֹא מֹשֶׁה וְאַהֲרֹן אֶל־אֹהֶל מוֹעֵד וַיֵּצְאוּ וַיְבָרְכוּ אֶת־הָעָם וַיֵּרָא כְבוֹד־יְהוָה אֶל־כָּל־הָעָם: 24 וַתֵּצֵא אֵשׁ מִלִּפְנֵי יְהוָה וַתֹּאכַל עַל־הַמִּזְבֵּחַ אֶת־הָעֹלָה וְאֶת־הַחֲלָבִים וַיַּרְא כָּל־הָעָם וַיָּרֹנּוּ וַיִּפְּלוּ עַל־פְּנֵיהֶם:

י וַיִּקְחוּ בְנֵי־אַהֲרֹן נָדָב וַאֲבִיהוּא אִישׁ מַחְתָּתוֹ וַיִּתְּנוּ בָהֵן אֵשׁ וַיָּשִׂימוּ עָלֶיהָ קְטֹרֶת וַיַּקְרִבוּ לִפְנֵי יְהוָה אֵשׁ זָרָה אֲשֶׁר לֹא צִוָּה אֹתָם: 2 וַתֵּצֵא אֵשׁ מִלִּפְנֵי יְהוָה וַתֹּאכַל אוֹתָם וַיָּמֻתוּ לִפְנֵי יְהוָה: 3 וַיֹּאמֶר מֹשֶׁה אֶל־אַהֲרֹן הוּא אֲשֶׁר־דִּבֶּר יְהוָה לֵאמֹר בִּקְרֹבַי אֶקָּדֵשׁ וְעַל־פְּנֵי כָל־הָעָם אֶכָּבֵד וַיִּדֹּם אַהֲרֹן: 4 וַיִּקְרָא מֹשֶׁה אֶל־מִישָׁאֵל וְאֶל אֶלְצָפָן בְּנֵי עֻזִּיאֵל דֹּד אַהֲרֹן וַיֹּאמֶר אֲלֵהֶם קִרְבוּ שְׂאוּ אֶת־אֲחֵיכֶם מֵאֵת פְּנֵי־הַקֹּדֶשׁ אֶל־מִחוּץ לַמַּחֲנֶה: 5 וַיִּקְרְבוּ וַיִּשָּׂאֻם בְּכֻתֳּנֹתָם אֶל־מִחוּץ לַמַּחֲנֶה כַּאֲשֶׁר דִּבֶּר מֹשֶׁה: 6 וַיֹּאמֶר מֹשֶׁה אֶל־אַהֲרֹן וּלְאֶלְעָזָר וּלְאִיתָמָר בָּנָיו רָאשֵׁיכֶם אַל־תִּפְרָעוּ וּבִגְדֵיכֶם לֹא־תִפְרֹמוּ וְלֹא תָמֻתוּ וְעַל כָּל־הָעֵדָה יִקְצֹף וַאֲחֵיכֶם כָּל־בֵּית יִשְׂרָאֵל

LORD has kindled. 7 You shall not go out from the door of the tabernacle of meeting, lest you die, for the anointing oil of the LORD *is* upon you." And they did according to the word of Moses.

8 Then the LORD spoke to Aaron, saying: 9 "Do not drink wine or intoxicating drink, you, nor your sons with you, when you go into the tabernacle of meeting, lest you die. *It shall be* a statute forever throughout your generations, 10 that you may distinguish between holy and unholy, and between unclean and clean, 11 and that you may teach the children of Israel all the statutes which the LORD has spoken to them by the hand of Moses."

12 And Moses spoke to Aaron, and to Eleazar and Ithamar, his sons who were left: "Take the grain offering that remains of the offerings made by fire to the LORD, and eat it without leaven beside the altar; for it *is* most holy. 13 You shall eat it in a holy place, because it *is* your due and your sons' due, of the sacrifices made by fire to the LORD; for so I have been commanded. 14 The breast of the wave offering and the thigh of the heave offering you shall eat in a clean place, you, your sons, and your daughters with you; for *they are* your due and your sons' due, *which* are given from the sacrifices of peace offerings of the children of Israel. 15 The thigh of the heave offering and the breast of the wave offering they shall bring with the offerings of fat made by fire, to offer *as* a wave offering before the LORD. And it shall be yours and your sons' with you, by a statute forever, as the LORD has commanded."

16 Then Moses made careful inquiry about the goat of the sin offering, and there it was—burned up. And he was angry with Eleazar and Ithamar, the sons of Aaron *who were* left, saying, 17 "Why have you not eaten the sin offering in a holy place, since it *is* most holy, and God has given it to you to bear the guilt of the congregation, to make atonement for them before the LORD? 18 See! Its blood was not brought inside the holy *place;* indeed you should have eaten it in a holy *place,* as I commanded."

19 And Aaron said to Moses, "Look, this day they have offered their sin offering and their burnt offering before the LORD, and such things have befallen me! *If* I had eaten the sin offering today, would it have been accepted in the sight of the LORD?" 20 So when Moses heard *that,* he was content.

11 Now the LORD spoke to Moses and Aaron, saying to them, 2 "Speak to the children of Israel, saying, 'These *are* the animals which you may eat

יִכְבּוּ אֶת־הַשְּׂרֵפָה אֲשֶׁר שָׂרַף יְהוָה: 7 וּמִפֶּתַח אֹהֶל מוֹעֵד לֹא תֵצְאוּ פֶּן־תָּמֻתוּ כִּי־שֶׁמֶן מִשְׁחַת יְהוָה עֲלֵיכֶם וַיַּעֲשׂוּ כִּדְבַר מֹשֶׁה: פ

8 וַיְדַבֵּר יְהוָה אֶל־אַהֲרֹן לֵאמֹר: 9 יַיִן וְשֵׁכָר אַל־ תֵּשְׁתְּ | אַתָּה | וּבָנֶיךָ אִתָּךְ בְּבֹאֲכֶם אֶל־ אֹהֶל מוֹעֵד וְלֹא תָמֻתוּ חֻקַּת עוֹלָם לְדֹרֹתֵיכֶם: 10 וּלֲהַבְדִּיל בֵּין הַקֹּדֶשׁ וּבֵין הַחֹל וּבֵין הַטָּמֵא וּבֵין הַטָּהוֹר: 11 וּלְהוֹרֹת אֶת־בְּנֵי יִשְׂרָאֵל אֵת כָּל־ הַחֻקִּים אֲשֶׁר דִּבֶּר יְהוָה אֲלֵיהֶם בְּיַד־מֹשֶׁה: פ

12 וַיְדַבֵּר מֹשֶׁה אֶל־אַהֲרֹן וְאֶל אֶלְעָזָר וְאֶל־ אִיתָמָר | בָּנָיו הַנּוֹתָרִים קְחוּ אֶת־הַמִּנְחָה הַנּוֹתֶרֶת מֵאִשֵּׁי יְהוָה וְאִכְלוּהָ מַצּוֹת אֵצֶל הַמִּזְבֵּחַ כִּי קֹדֶשׁ קָדָשִׁים הִוא: 13 וַאֲכַלְתֶּם אֹתָהּ בְּמָקוֹם קָדֹשׁ כִּי חָקְךָ וְחָק־בָּנֶיךָ הִוא מֵאִשֵּׁי יְהוָה כִּי־כֵן צֻוֵּיתִי: 14 וְאֵת חֲזֵה הַתְּנוּפָה וְאֵת | שׁוֹק הַתְּרוּמָה תֹּאכְלוּ בְּמָקוֹם טָהוֹר אַתָּה וּבָנֶיךָ וּבְנֹתֶיךָ אִתָּךְ כִּי־חָקְךָ וְחָק־בָּנֶיךָ נִתְּנוּ מִזִּבְחֵי שַׁלְמֵי בְּנֵי יִשְׂרָאֵל: 15 שׁוֹק הַתְּרוּמָה וַחֲזֵה הַתְּנוּפָה עַל אִשֵּׁי הַחֲלָבִים יָבִיאוּ לְהָנִיף תְּנוּפָה לִפְנֵי יְהוָה וְהָיָה לְךָ וּלְבָנֶיךָ אִתְּךָ לְחָק־עוֹלָם כַּאֲשֶׁר צִוָּה יְהוָה: 16 וְאֵת | שְׂעִיר הַחַטָּאת דָּרֹשׁ דָּרַשׁ מֹשֶׁה וְהִנֵּה שֹׂרָף וַיִּקְצֹף עַל־אֶלְעָזָר וְעַל־אִיתָמָר בְּנֵי אַהֲרֹן הַנּוֹתָרִם לֵאמֹר: 17 מַדּוּעַ לֹא־אֲכַלְתֶּם אֶת־הַחַטָּאת בִּמְקוֹם הַקֹּדֶשׁ כִּי קֹדֶשׁ קָדָשִׁים הִוא וְאֹתָהּ | נָתַן לָכֶם לָשֵׂאת אֶת־עֲוֹן הָעֵדָה לְכַפֵּר עֲלֵיהֶם לִפְנֵי יְהוָה: 18 הֵן לֹא־הוּבָא אֶת־דָּמָהּ אֶל־הַקֹּדֶשׁ פְּנִימָה אָכוֹל תֹּאכְלוּ אֹתָהּ בַּקֹּדֶשׁ כַּאֲשֶׁר צִוֵּיתִי: 19 וַיְדַבֵּר אַהֲרֹן אֶל־מֹשֶׁה הֵן הַיּוֹם הִקְרִיבוּ אֶת־חַטָּאתָם וְאֶת־ עֹלָתָם לִפְנֵי יְהוָה וַתִּקְרֶאנָה אֹתִי כָּאֵלֶּה וְאָכַלְתִּי חַטָּאת הַיּוֹם הַיִּיטַב בְּעֵינֵי יְהוָה: 20 וַיִּשְׁמַע מֹשֶׁה וַיִּיטַב בְּעֵינָיו: פ

יא וַיְדַבֵּר יְהוָה אֶל־מֹשֶׁה וְאֶל־אַהֲרֹן לֵאמֹר אֲלֵהֶם: 2 דַּבְּרוּ אֶל־בְּנֵי יִשְׂרָאֵל לֵאמֹר זֹאת הַחַיָּה אֲשֶׁר תֹּאכְלוּ מִכָּל־הַבְּהֵמָה אֲשֶׁר עַל־הָאָרֶץ:

among all the animals that *are* on the earth: ³ Among the animals, whatever divides the hoof, having cloven hooves *and* chewing the cud—that you may eat. ⁴ Nevertheless these you shall not eat among those that chew the cud or those that have cloven hooves: the camel, because it chews the cud but does not have cloven hooves, is unclean to you; ⁵ the rock hyrax, because it chews the cud but does not have cloven hooves, *is* unclean to you; ⁶ the hare, because it chews the cud but does not have cloven hooves, *is* unclean to you; ⁷ and the swine, though it divides the hoof, having cloven hooves, yet does not chew the cud, *is* unclean to you. ⁸ Their flesh you shall not eat, and their carcasses you shall not touch. They *are* unclean to you.

⁹ 'These you may eat of all that *are* in the water: whatever in the water has fins and scales, whether in the seas or in the rivers—that you may eat. ¹⁰ But all in the seas or in the rivers that do not have fins and scales, all that move in the water or any living thing which *is* in the water, they *are* an abomination to you. ¹¹ They shall be an abomination to you; you shall not eat their flesh, but you shall regard their carcasses as an abomination. ¹² Whatever in the water does not have fins or scales—that *shall be* an abomination to you.

¹³ 'And these you shall regard as an abomination among the birds; they shall not be eaten, they *are* an abomination: the eagle, the vulture, the buzzard, ¹⁴ the kite, and the falcon after its kind; ¹⁵ every raven after its kind, ¹⁶ the ostrich, the short-eared owl, the sea gull, and the hawk after its kind; ¹⁷ the little owl, the fisher owl, and the screech owl; ¹⁸ the white owl, the jackdaw, and the carrion vulture; ¹⁹ the stork, the heron after its kind, the hoopoe, and the bat.

²⁰ 'All flying insects that creep on *all* fours *shall be* an abomination to you. ²¹ Yet these you may eat of every flying insect that creeps on *all* fours: those which have jointed legs above their feet with which to leap on the earth. ²² These you may eat: the locust after its kind, the destroying locust after its kind, the cricket after its kind, and the grasshopper after its kind. ²³ But all *other* flying insects which have four feet *shall be* an abomination to you.

²⁴ 'By these you shall become unclean; whoever touches the carcass of any of them shall be unclean until evening; ²⁵ whoever carries part of the carcass of any of them shall wash his clothes and be unclean until evening: ²⁶ The carcass of any animal which divides the foot, but is not cloven-hoofed or does not chew the cud, *is* unclean to you. Everyone who touches it shall be unclean. ²⁷ And whatever goes on its paws, among all kinds of animals that go on *all*

3 כֹּל ׀ מַפְרֶסֶת פַּרְסָה וְשֹׁסַעַת שֶׁסַע פְּרָסֹת מַעֲלַת גֵּרָה בַּבְּהֵמָה אֹתָהּ תֹּאכֵלוּ: 4 אַךְ אֶת־זֶה לֹא תֹאכְלוּ מִמַּעֲלֵי הַגֵּרָה וּמִמַּפְרִיסֵי הַפַּרְסָה אֶת־הַגָּמָל כִּי־מַעֲלֵה גֵרָה הוּא וּפַרְסָה אֵינֶנּוּ מַפְרִיס טָמֵא הוּא לָכֶם: 5 וְאֶת־הַשָּׁפָן כִּי־מַעֲלֵה גֵרָה הוּא וּפַרְסָה לֹא יַפְרִיס טָמֵא הוּא לָכֶם: 6 וְאֶת־הָאַרְנֶבֶת כִּי־מַעֲלַת גֵּרָה הִוא וּפַרְסָה לֹא הִפְרִיסָה טְמֵאָה הִוא לָכֶם: 7 וְאֶת־הַחֲזִיר כִּי־מַפְרִיס פַּרְסָה הוּא וְשֹׁסַע שֶׁסַע פַּרְסָה וְהוּא גֵרָה לֹא־יִגָּר טָמֵא הוּא לָכֶם: 8 מִבְּשָׂרָם לֹא תֹאכֵלוּ וּבְנִבְלָתָם לֹא תִגָּעוּ טְמֵאִים הֵם לָכֶם: 9 אֶת־זֶה תֹּאכְלוּ מִכֹּל אֲשֶׁר בַּמָּיִם כֹּל אֲשֶׁר־לוֹ סְנַפִּיר וְקַשְׂקֶשֶׂת בַּמַּיִם בַּיַּמִּים וּבַנְּחָלִים אֹתָם תֹּאכֵלוּ: 10 וְכֹל אֲשֶׁר אֵין־לוֹ סְנַפִּיר וְקַשְׂקֶשֶׂת בַּיַּמִּים וּבַנְּחָלִים מִכֹּל שֶׁרֶץ הַמַּיִם וּמִכֹּל נֶפֶשׁ הַחַיָּה אֲשֶׁר בַּמָּיִם שֶׁקֶץ הֵם לָכֶם: 11 וְשֶׁקֶץ יִהְיוּ לָכֶם מִבְּשָׂרָם לֹא תֹאכֵלוּ וְאֶת־נִבְלָתָם תְּשַׁקֵּצוּ: 12 כֹּל אֲשֶׁר אֵין־לוֹ סְנַפִּיר וְקַשְׂקֶשֶׂת בַּמָּיִם שֶׁקֶץ הוּא לָכֶם: 13 וְאֶת־אֵלֶּה תְּשַׁקְּצוּ מִן־הָעוֹף לֹא יֵאָכְלוּ שֶׁקֶץ הֵם אֶת־הַנֶּשֶׁר וְאֶת־הַפֶּרֶס וְאֵת הָעָזְנִיָּה: 14 וְאֶת־הַדָּאָה וְאֶת־הָאַיָּה לְמִינָהּ: 15 אֵת כָּל־עֹרֵב לְמִינוֹ: 16 וְאֵת בַּת הַיַּעֲנָה וְאֶת־הַתַּחְמָס וְאֶת־הַשָּׁחַף וְאֶת־הַנֵּץ לְמִינֵהוּ: 17 וְאֶת־הַכּוֹס וְאֶת־הַשָּׁלָךְ וְאֶת־הַיַּנְשׁוּף: 18 וְאֶת־הַתִּנְשֶׁמֶת וְאֶת־הַקָּאָת וְאֶת־הָרָחָם: 19 וְאֵת הַחֲסִידָה הָאֲנָפָה לְמִינָהּ וְאֶת־הַדּוּכִיפַת וְאֶת־הָעֲטַלֵּף: 20 כֹּל שֶׁרֶץ הָעוֹף הַהֹלֵךְ עַל־אַרְבַּע שֶׁקֶץ הוּא לָכֶם: ס 21 אַךְ אֶת־זֶה תֹּאכְלוּ מִכֹּל שֶׁרֶץ הָעוֹף הַהֹלֵךְ עַל־אַרְבַּע אֲשֶׁר־לֹא כְרָעַיִם מִמַּעַל לְרַגְלָיו לְנַתֵּר בָּהֵן עַל־הָאָרֶץ: 22 אֶת־אֵלֶּה מֵהֶם תֹּאכֵלוּ אֶת־הָאַרְבֶּה לְמִינוֹ וְאֶת־הַסָּלְעָם לְמִינֵהוּ וְאֶת־הַחַרְגֹּל לְמִינֵהוּ וְאֶת־הֶחָגָב לְמִינֵהוּ: 23 וְכֹל שֶׁרֶץ הָעוֹף אֲשֶׁר־לוֹ אַרְבַּע רַגְלָיִם שֶׁקֶץ הוּא לָכֶם: 24 וּלְאֵלֶּה תִּטַּמָּאוּ כָּל־הַנֹּגֵעַ בְּנִבְלָתָם יִטְמָא עַד־הָעָרֶב: 25 וְכָל־הַנֹּשֵׂא מִנִּבְלָתָם יְכַבֵּס בְּגָדָיו וְטָמֵא עַד־הָעָרֶב: 26 לְכָל־הַבְּהֵמָה אֲשֶׁר הִוא מַפְרֶסֶת פַּרְסָה וְשֶׁסַע ׀ אֵינֶנָּה שֹׁסַעַת וְגֵרָה אֵינֶנָּה מַעֲלָה טְמֵאִים הֵם לָכֶם כָּל־הַנֹּגֵעַ בָּהֶם יִטְמָא: 27 וְכֹל ׀ הוֹלֵךְ

fours, those *are* unclean to you. Whoever touches any such carcass shall be unclean until evening. [28] Whoever carries *any such* carcass shall wash his clothes and be unclean until evening. It *is* unclean to you.

[29] 'These also *shall be* unclean to you among the creeping things that creep on the earth: the mole, the mouse, and the large lizard after its kind; [30] the gecko, the monitor lizard, the sand reptile, the sand lizard, and the chameleon. [31] These *are* unclean to you among all that creep. Whoever touches them when they are dead shall be unclean until evening. [32] Anything on which *any* of them falls, when they are dead shall be unclean, whether *it is* any item of wood or clothing or skin or sack, whatever item *it is,* in which *any* work is done, it must be put in water. And it shall be unclean until evening; then it shall be clean. [33] Any earthen vessel into which *any* of them falls you shall break; and whatever *is* in it shall be unclean: [34] in such a vessel, any edible food upon which water falls becomes unclean, and any drink that may be drunk from it becomes unclean. [35] And everything on which *a part* of *any such* carcass falls shall be unclean; *whether it is* an oven or cooking stove, it shall be broken down; *for they are* unclean, and shall be unclean to you. [36] Nevertheless a spring or a cistern, *in which there is* plenty of water, shall be clean, but whatever touches any such carcass becomes unclean. [37] And if a part of *any such* carcass falls on any planting seed which is to be sown, it *remains* clean. [38] But if water is put on the seed, and if *a part* of *any such* carcass falls on it, it *becomes* unclean to you.

[39] 'And if any animal which you may eat dies, he who touches its carcass shall be unclean until evening. [40] He who eats of its carcass shall wash his clothes and be unclean until evening. He also who carries its carcass shall wash his clothes and be unclean until evening.

[41] 'And every creeping thing that creeps on the earth *shall be* an abomination. It shall not be eaten. [42] Whatever crawls on its belly, whatever goes on *all* fours, or whatever has many feet among all creeping things that creep on the earth—these you shall not eat, for they *are* an abomination. [43] You shall not make yourselves abominable with any creeping thing that creeps; nor shall you make yourselves unclean with them, lest you be defiled by them. [44] For I *am* the LORD your God. You shall therefore consecrate yourselves, and you shall be holy; for I *am* holy. Neither shall you defile yourselves with any creeping thing that creeps on

עַל־כַּפָּ֗יו בְּכָל־הַֽחַיָּה֙ הַהֹלֶ֣כֶת עַל־אַרְבַּ֔ע טְמֵאִ֥ים
הֵ֖ם לָכֶ֑ם כָּל־הַנֹּגֵ֥עַ בְּנִבְלָתָ֖ם יִטְמָ֥א עַד־הָעָֽרֶב: 28 וְהַנֹּשֵׂ֣א אֶת־נִבְלָתָ֔ם יְכַבֵּ֥ס בְּגָדָ֖יו וְטָמֵ֣א עַד־הָעָ֑רֶב טְמֵאִ֥ים הֵ֖מָּה לָכֶֽם: ס 29 וְזֶ֤ה לָכֶם֙ הַטָּמֵ֔א בַּשֶּׁ֖רֶץ הַשֹּׁרֵ֣ץ עַל־הָאָ֑רֶץ הַחֹ֥לֶד וְהָעַכְבָּ֖ר וְהַצָּ֥ב לְמִינֵֽהוּ: 30 וְהָאֲנָקָ֣ה וְהַכֹּ֔חַ וְהַלְּטָאָ֖ה וְהַחֹ֥מֶט וְהַתִּנְשָֽׁמֶת: 31 אֵ֛לֶּה הַטְּמֵאִ֥ים לָכֶ֖ם בְּכָל־הַשָּׁ֑רֶץ כָּל־הַנֹּגֵ֧עַ בָּהֶ֛ם בְּמֹתָ֖ם יִטְמָ֥א עַד־הָעָֽרֶב: 32 וְכֹ֣ל אֲשֶׁר־יִפֹּֽל־עָלָיו֩ מֵהֶ֨ם ׀ בְּמֹתָ֜ם יִטְמָ֗א מִכָּל־כְּלִי־ עֵץ֩ א֨וֹ בֶ֜גֶד אוֹ־ע֗וֹר א֤וֹ שָׂק֙ כָּל־כְּלִ֔י אֲשֶׁר־יֵעָשֶׂ֥ה מְלָאכָ֖ה בָּהֶ֑ם בַּמַּ֣יִם יוּבָ֛א וְטָמֵ֥א עַד־הָעֶ֖רֶב וְטָהֵֽר: 33 וְכָל־כְּלִי־חֶ֔רֶשׂ אֲשֶׁר־יִפֹּ֥ל מֵהֶ֖ם אֶל־תּוֹכ֑וֹ כֹּ֣ל אֲשֶׁ֧ר בְּתוֹכ֛וֹ יִטְמָ֖א וְאֹת֥וֹ תִשְׁבֹּֽרוּ: 34 מִכָּל־הָאֹ֜כֶל אֲשֶׁ֣ר יֵאָכֵ֗ל אֲשֶׁ֨ר יָב֥וֹא עָלָ֛יו מַ֖יִם יִטְמָ֑א וְכָל־ מַשְׁקֶה֙ אֲשֶׁ֣ר יִשָּׁתֶ֔ה בְּכָל־כְּלִ֖י יִטְמָֽא: 35 וְכֹ֣ל אֲשֶׁר־ יִפֹּ֨ל מִנִּבְלָתָ֥ם ׀ עָלָיו֮ יִטְמָא֒ תַּנּ֧וּר וְכִירַ֛יִם יֻתָּ֖ץ טְמֵאִ֥ים הֵ֑ם וּטְמֵאִ֥ים יִֽהְי֖וּ לָכֶֽם: 36 אַ֣ךְ מַעְיָ֥ן וּב֛וֹר מִקְוֵה־מַ֖יִם יִהְיֶ֣ה טָה֑וֹר וְנֹגֵ֥עַ בְּנִבְלָתָ֖ם יִטְמָֽא: 37 וְכִ֤י יִפֹּל֙ מִנִּבְלָתָ֔ם עַל־כָּל־זֶ֥רַע זֵר֖וּעַ אֲשֶׁ֣ר יִזָּרֵ֑עַ טָה֖וֹר הֽוּא: 38 וְכִ֤י יֻתַּן־מַ֙יִם֙ עַל־זֶ֔רַע וְנָפַ֥ל מִנִּבְלָתָ֖ם עָלָ֑יו טָמֵ֥א ה֖וּא לָכֶֽם: ס 39 וְכִ֤י יָמוּת֙ מִן־ הַבְּהֵמָ֔ה אֲשֶׁר־הִ֥יא לָכֶ֖ם לְאָכְלָ֑ה הַנֹּגֵ֥עַ בְּנִבְלָתָ֖הּ יִטְמָ֥א עַד־הָעָֽרֶב: 40 וְהָֽאֹכֵל֙ מִנִּבְלָתָ֔הּ יְכַבֵּ֥ס בְּגָדָ֖יו וְטָמֵ֣א עַד־הָעָ֑רֶב וְהַנֹּשֵׂא֙ אֶת־נִבְלָתָ֔הּ יְכַבֵּ֥ס בְּגָדָ֖יו וְטָמֵ֥א עַד־הָעָֽרֶב: 41 וְכָל־הַשֶּׁ֛רֶץ הַשֹּׁרֵ֥ץ עַל־הָאָ֑רֶץ שֶׁ֥קֶץ ה֖וּא לֹ֥א יֵאָכֵֽל: 42 כֹּל֩ הוֹלֵ֨ךְ עַל־גָּח֜וֹן וְכֹ֣ל ׀ הוֹלֵ֣ךְ עַל־אַרְבַּ֗ע עַ֚ד כָּל־מַרְבֵּ֣ה רַגְלַ֔יִם לְכָל־הַשֶּׁ֖רֶץ הַשֹּׁרֵ֣ץ עַל־הָאָ֑רֶץ לֹ֥א תֹאכְל֖וּם כִּי־שֶׁ֥קֶץ הֵֽם: 43 אַֽל־תְּשַׁקְּצוּ֙ אֶת־נַפְשֹֽׁתֵיכֶ֔ם בְּכָל־הַשֶּׁ֖רֶץ הַשֹּׁרֵ֑ץ וְלֹ֤א תִֽטַּמְּאוּ֙ בָּהֶ֔ם וְנִטְמֵתֶ֖ם בָּֽם: 44 כִּ֣י אֲנִ֣י יְהוָה֮ אֱלֹֽהֵיכֶם֒ וְהִתְקַדִּשְׁתֶּם֙ וִהְיִיתֶ֣ם קְדֹשִׁ֔ים כִּ֥י קָד֖וֹשׁ אָ֑נִי וְלֹ֤א תְטַמְּאוּ֙ אֶת־נַפְשֹׁ֣תֵיכֶ֔ם בְּכָל־הַשֶּׁ֖רֶץ

the earth. ⁴⁵For I *am* the LORD who brings you up
out of the land of Egypt, to be your God. You shall
therefore be holy, for I *am* holy.

⁴⁶'This *is* the law of the animals and the birds
and every living creature that moves in the waters,
and of every creature that creeps on the earth, ⁴⁷to
distinguish between the unclean and the clean, and
between the animal that may be eaten and the
animal that may not be eaten.' "

12 Then the LORD spoke to Moses, saying,
²"Speak to the children of Israel, saying: 'If a
woman has conceived, and borne a male child, then
she shall be unclean seven days; as in the days of her
customary impurity she shall be unclean. ³And on
the eighth day the flesh of his foreskin shall be
circumcised. ⁴She shall then continue in the blood
of *her* purification thirty-three days. She shall not
touch any hallowed thing, nor come into the
sanctuary until the days of her purification are
fulfilled.

⁵'But if she bears a female child, then she shall be
unclean two weeks, as in her customary impurity,
and she shall continue in the blood of *her*
purification sixty-six days.

⁶'When the days of her purification are fulfilled,
whether for a son or a daughter, she shall bring to
the priest a lamb of the first year as a burnt
offering, and a young pigeon or a turtledove as a sin
offering, to the door of the tabernacle of meeting.
⁷Then he shall offer it before the LORD, and make
atonement for her. And she shall be clean from the
flow of her blood. This *is* the law for her who has
borne a male or a female.

⁸'And if she is not able to bring a lamb, then she
may bring two turtledoves or two young pigeons—
one as a burnt offering and the other as a sin
offering. So the priest shall make atonement for
her, and she will be clean.' "

13 And the LORD spoke to Moses and Aaron,
saying: ²"When a man has on the skin of his body a
swelling, a scab, or a bright spot, and it becomes on
the skin of his body *like* a leprous sore, then he shall
be brought to Aaron the priest or to one of his sons
the priests. ³The priest shall examine the sore on the
skin of the body; and if the hair on the sore has
turned white, and the sore appears *to be* deeper than
the skin of his body, it *is* a leprous sore. Then the
priest shall examine him, and pronounce him
unclean. ⁴But if the bright spot *is* white on the
skin of his body, and does not appear *to be* deeper
than the skin, and its hair has not turned white,

הָרֹמֵשׂ עַל־הָאָרֶץ: 45 כִּי ׀ אֲנִי יְהוָה הַמַּעֲלֶה
אֶתְכֶם מֵאֶרֶץ מִצְרַיִם לִהְיֹת לָכֶם לֵאלֹהִים וִהְיִיתֶם
קְדֹשִׁים כִּי קָדוֹשׁ אָנִי: 46 זֹאת תּוֹרַת הַבְּהֵמָה
וְהָעוֹף וְכֹל נֶפֶשׁ הַחַיָּה הָרֹמֶשֶׂת בַּמָּיִם וּלְכָל־נֶפֶשׁ
הַשֹּׁרֶצֶת עַל־הָאָרֶץ: 47 לְהַבְדִּיל בֵּין הַטָּמֵא וּבֵין
הַטָּהֹר וּבֵין הַחַיָּה הַנֶּאֱכֶלֶת וּבֵין הַחַיָּה אֲשֶׁר לֹא
תֵאָכֵל: פ

יב וַיְדַבֵּר יְהוָה אֶל־מֹשֶׁה לֵּאמֹר: 2 דַּבֵּר אֶל־
בְּנֵי יִשְׂרָאֵל לֵאמֹר אִשָּׁה כִּי תַזְרִיעַ וְיָלְדָה זָכָר
וְטָמְאָה שִׁבְעַת יָמִים כִּימֵי נִדַּת דְּוֹתָהּ תִּטְמָא:
3 וּבַיּוֹם הַשְּׁמִינִי יִמּוֹל בְּשַׂר עָרְלָתוֹ: 4 וּשְׁלֹשִׁים
יוֹם וּשְׁלֹשֶׁת יָמִים תֵּשֵׁב בִּדְמֵי טָהֳרָה בְּכָל־קֹדֶשׁ
לֹא־תִגָּע וְאֶל־הַמִּקְדָּשׁ לֹא תָבֹא עַד־מְלֹאת יְמֵי
טָהֳרָהּ: 5 וְאִם־נְקֵבָה תֵלֵד וְטָמְאָה שְׁבֻעַיִם כְּנִדָּתָהּ
וְשִׁשִּׁים יוֹם וְשֵׁשֶׁת יָמִים תֵּשֵׁב עַל־דְּמֵי טָהֳרָה:
6 וּבִמְלֹאת ׀ יְמֵי טָהֳרָהּ לְבֵן אוֹ לְבַת תָּבִיא כֶּבֶשׂ
בֶּן־שְׁנָתוֹ לְעֹלָה וּבֶן־יוֹנָה אוֹ־תֹר לְחַטָּאת אֶל־פֶּתַח
אֹהֶל־מוֹעֵד אֶל־הַכֹּהֵן: 7 וְהִקְרִיבוֹ לִפְנֵי יְהוָה וְכִפֶּר
עָלֶיהָ וְטָהֲרָה מִמְּקֹר דָּמֶיהָ זֹאת תּוֹרַת הַיֹּלֶדֶת
לַזָּכָר אוֹ לַנְּקֵבָה: 8 וְאִם־לֹא תִמְצָא יָדָהּ דֵּי שֶׂה
וְלָקְחָה שְׁתֵּי־תֹרִים אוֹ שְׁנֵי בְּנֵי יוֹנָה אֶחָד לְעֹלָה
וְאֶחָד לְחַטָּאת וְכִפֶּר עָלֶיהָ הַכֹּהֵן וְטָהֵרָה: פ

יג וַיְדַבֵּר יְהוָה אֶל־מֹשֶׁה וְאֶל־אַהֲרֹן לֵאמֹר:
2 אָדָם כִּי־יִהְיֶה בְעוֹר־בְּשָׂרוֹ שְׂאֵת אוֹ־סַפַּחַת אוֹ
בַהֶרֶת וְהָיָה בְעוֹר־בְּשָׂרוֹ לְנֶגַע צָרָעַת וְהוּבָא אֶל־
אַהֲרֹן הַכֹּהֵן אוֹ אֶל־אַחַד מִבָּנָיו הַכֹּהֲנִים: 3 וְרָאָה
הַכֹּהֵן אֶת־הַנֶּגַע בְּעוֹר־הַבָּשָׂר וְשֵׂעָר בַּנֶּגַע הָפַךְ ׀
לָבָן וּמַרְאֵה הַנֶּגַע עָמֹק מֵעוֹר בְּשָׂרוֹ נֶגַע צָרַעַת
הוּא וְרָאָהוּ הַכֹּהֵן וְטִמֵּא אֹתוֹ: 4 וְאִם־בַּהֶרֶת
לְבָנָה הִוא בְּעוֹר בְּשָׂרוֹ וְעָמֹק אֵין־מַרְאֶהָ מִן־הָעוֹר
וּשְׂעָרָה לֹא־הָפַךְ לָבָן וְהִסְגִּיר הַכֹּהֵן אֶת־הַנֶּגַע

then the priest shall isolate *the one who has* the sore seven days. ⁵And the priest shall examine him on the seventh day; and indeed *if* the sore appears to be as it was, *and* the sore has not spread on the skin, then the priest shall isolate him another seven days. ⁶Then the priest shall examine him again on the seventh day; and indeed *if* the sore has faded, *and* the sore has not spread on the skin, then the priest shall pronounce him clean; it *is only* a scab, and he shall wash his clothes and be clean. ⁷But if the scab should at all spread over the skin, after he has been seen by the priest for his cleansing, he shall be seen by the priest again. ⁸And *if* the priest sees that the scab has indeed spread on the skin, then the priest shall pronounce him unclean. It *is* leprosy.

⁹"When the leprous sore is on a person, then he shall be brought to the priest. ¹⁰And the priest shall examine *him;* and indeed *if* the swelling on the skin *is* white, and it has turned the hair white, and *there is* a spot of raw flesh in the swelling, ¹¹it *is* an old leprosy on the skin of his body. The priest shall pronounce him unclean, and shall not isolate him, for he *is* unclean.

¹²"And if leprosy breaks out all over the skin, and the leprosy covers all the skin of *the one who has* the sore, from his head to his foot, wherever the priest looks, ¹³then the priest shall consider; and indeed *if* the leprosy has covered all his body, he shall pronounce *him* clean *who has* the sore. It has all turned white. He *is* clean. ¹⁴But when raw flesh appears on him, he shall be unclean. ¹⁵And the priest shall examine the raw flesh and pronounce him to be unclean; *for* the raw flesh *is* unclean. It *is* leprosy. ¹⁶Or if the raw flesh changes and turns white again, he shall come to the priest. ¹⁷And the priest shall examine him; and indeed *if* the sore has turned white, then the priest shall pronounce *him* clean *who has* the sore. He *is* clean.

¹⁸"If the body develops a boil in the skin, and it is healed, ¹⁹and in the place of the boil there comes a white swelling or a bright spot, reddish-white, then it shall be shown to the priest; ²⁰and *if,* when the priest sees it, it indeed *appears* deeper than the skin, and its hair has turned white, the priest shall pronounce him unclean. It *is* a leprous sore which has broken out of the boil. ²¹But if the priest examines it, and indeed *there are* no white hairs in it, and it *is* not deeper than the skin, but has faded, then the priest shall isolate him seven days; ²²and if it should at all spread over the skin, then the priest shall pronounce him unclean. It *is* a leprous sore. ²³But if the bright spot stays in one place, *and* has not spread, it *is* the scar of the boil; and the priest shall pronounce him clean.

שִׁבְעַת יָמִים: 5 וְרָאָהוּ הַכֹּהֵן בַּיּוֹם הַשְּׁבִיעִי וְהִנֵּה הַנֶּגַע עָמַד בְּעֵינָיו לֹא־פָשָׂה הַנֶּגַע בָּעוֹר וְהִסְגִּירוֹ הַכֹּהֵן שִׁבְעַת יָמִים שֵׁנִית: 6 וְרָאָה הַכֹּהֵן אֹתוֹ בַּיּוֹם הַשְּׁבִיעִי שֵׁנִית וְהִנֵּה כֵּהָה הַנֶּגַע וְלֹא־פָשָׂה הַנֶּגַע בָּעוֹר וְטִהֲרוֹ הַכֹּהֵן מִסְפַּחַת הִיא וְכִבֶּס בְּגָדָיו וְטָהֵר: 7 וְאִם־פָּשֹׂה תִפְשֶׂה הַמִּסְפַּחַת בָּעוֹר אַחֲרֵי הֵרָאֹתוֹ אֶל־הַכֹּהֵן לְטָהֳרָתוֹ וְנִרְאָה שֵׁנִית אֶל־הַכֹּהֵן: 8 וְרָאָה הַכֹּהֵן וְהִנֵּה פָּשְׂתָה הַמִּסְפַּחַת בָּעוֹר וְטִמְּאוֹ הַכֹּהֵן צָרַעַת הִוא: פ

9 נֶגַע צָרַעַת כִּי תִהְיֶה בְּאָדָם וְהוּבָא אֶל־הַכֹּהֵן: 10 וְרָאָה הַכֹּהֵן וְהִנֵּה שְׂאֵת־לְבָנָה בָּעוֹר וְהִיא הָפְכָה שֵׂעָר לָבָן וּמִחְיַת בָּשָׂר חַי בַּשְׂאֵת: 11 צָרַעַת נוֹשֶׁנֶת הִוא בְּעוֹר בְּשָׂרוֹ וְטִמְּאוֹ הַכֹּהֵן לֹא יַסְגִּרֶנּוּ כִּי טָמֵא הוּא: 12 וְאִם־פָּרוֹחַ תִּפְרַח הַצָּרַעַת בָּעוֹר וְכִסְּתָה הַצָּרַעַת אֵת כָּל־עוֹר הַנֶּגַע מֵרֹאשׁוֹ וְעַד־רַגְלָיו לְכָל־מַרְאֵה עֵינֵי הַכֹּהֵן: 13 וְרָאָה הַכֹּהֵן וְהִנֵּה כִסְּתָה הַצָּרַעַת אֶת־כָּל־בְּשָׂרוֹ וְטִהַר אֶת־הַנָּגַע כֻּלּוֹ הָפַךְ לָבָן טָהוֹר הוּא: 14 וּבְיוֹם הֵרָאוֹת בּוֹ בָּשָׂר חַי יִטְמָא: 15 וְרָאָה הַכֹּהֵן אֶת־הַבָּשָׂר הַחַי וְטִמְּאוֹ הַבָּשָׂר הַחַי טָמֵא הוּא צָרַעַת הוּא: 16 אוֹ כִי יָשׁוּב הַבָּשָׂר הַחַי וְנֶהְפַּךְ לְלָבָן וּבָא אֶל־הַכֹּהֵן: 17 וְרָאָהוּ הַכֹּהֵן וְהִנֵּה נֶהְפַּךְ הַנֶּגַע לְלָבָן וְטִהַר הַכֹּהֵן אֶת־הַנֶּגַע טָהוֹר הוּא: פ

18 וּבָשָׂר כִּי־יִהְיֶה בוֹ־בְעֹרוֹ שְׁחִין וְנִרְפָּא: 19 וְהָיָה בִּמְקוֹם הַשְּׁחִין שְׂאֵת לְבָנָה אוֹ בַהֶרֶת לְבָנָה אֲדַמְדָּמֶת וְנִרְאָה אֶל־הַכֹּהֵן: 20 וְרָאָה הַכֹּהֵן וְהִנֵּה מַרְאֶהָ שָׁפָל מִן־הָעוֹר וּשְׂעָרָה הָפַךְ לָבָן וְטִמְּאוֹ הַכֹּהֵן נֶגַע־צָרַעַת הִוא בַּשְּׁחִין פָּרָחָה: 21 וְאִם וְרָאֶנָּה הַכֹּהֵן וְהִנֵּה אֵין־בָּהּ שֵׂעָר לָבָן וּשְׁפָלָה אֵינֶנָּה מִן־הָעוֹר וְהִיא כֵהָה וְהִסְגִּירוֹ הַכֹּהֵן שִׁבְעַת יָמִים: 22 וְאִם־פָּשֹׂה תִפְשֶׂה בָּעוֹר וְטִמֵּא הַכֹּהֵן אֹתוֹ נֶגַע הִוא: 23 וְאִם־תַּחְתֶּיהָ תַּעֲמֹד הַבַּהֶרֶת לֹא פָשָׂתָה צָרֶבֶת הַשְּׁחִין הִוא וְטִהֲרוֹ

²⁴"Or if the body receives a burn on its skin by fire, and the raw *flesh* of the burn becomes a bright spot, reddish-white or white, ²⁵then the priest shall examine it; and indeed *if* the hair of the bright spot has turned white, and it appears deeper than the skin, it *is* leprosy broken out in the burn. Therefore the priest shall pronounce him unclean. It *is* a leprous sore. ²⁶But if the priest examines it, and indeed *there are* no white hairs in the bright spot, and it *is* not deeper than the skin, but has faded, then the priest shall isolate him seven days. ²⁷And the priest shall examine him on the seventh day. If it has at all spread over the skin, then the priest shall pronounce him unclean. It *is* a leprous sore. ²⁸But if the bright spot stays in one place, *and* has not spread on the skin, but has faded, it *is* a swelling from the burn. The priest shall pronounce him clean, for it *is* the scar from the burn.

²⁹"If a man or woman has a sore on the head or the beard, ³⁰then the priest shall examine the sore; and indeed if it appears deeper than the skin, *and there is* in it thin yellow hair, then the priest shall pronounce him unclean. It *is* a scaly leprosy of the head or beard. ³¹But if the priest examines the scaly sore, and indeed it does not appear deeper than the skin, and *there is* no black hair in it, then the priest shall isolate *the one who has* the scale seven days. ³²And on the seventh day the priest shall examine the sore; and indeed *if* the scale has not spread, and there is no yellow hair in it, and the scale does not appear deeper than the skin, ³³he shall shave himself, but the scale he shall not shave. And the priest shall isolate *the one who has* the scale another seven days. ³⁴On the seventh day the priest shall examine the scale; and indeed *if* the scale has not spread over the skin, and does not appear deeper than the skin, then the priest shall pronounce him clean. He shall wash his clothes and be clean. ³⁵But if the scale should at all spread over the skin after his cleansing, ³⁶then the priest shall examine him; and indeed *if* the scale has spread over the skin, the priest need not seek for yellow hair. He *is* unclean. ³⁷But if the scale appears to be at a standstill, and there is black hair grown up in it, the scale has healed. He *is* clean, and the priest shall pronounce him clean.

³⁸"If a man or a woman has bright spots on the skin of the body, *specifically* white bright spots, ³⁹then the priest shall look; and indeed *if* the bright spots on the skin of the body *are* dull white, it *is* a white spot *that* grows on the skin. He *is* clean.

⁴⁰"As for the man whose hair has fallen from his head, he *is* bald, *but* he *is* clean. ⁴¹He whose hair has fallen from his forehead, he *is* bald on the

הַכֹּהֵן: ס 24 אוֹ בָשָׂר כִּי־יִהְיֶה בְעֹרוֹ מִכְוַת־אֵשׁ וְהָיְתָה מִחְיַת הַמִּכְוָה בַּהֶרֶת לְבָנָה אֲדַמְדֶּמֶת אוֹ לְבָנָה: 25 וְרָאָה אֹתָהּ הַכֹּהֵן וְהִנֵּה נֶהְפַּךְ שֵׂעָר לָבָן בַּבַּהֶרֶת וּמַרְאֶהָ עָמֹק מִן־הָעוֹר צָרַעַת הִוא בַּמִּכְוָה פָּרָחָה וְטִמֵּא אֹתוֹ הַכֹּהֵן נֶגַע צָרַעַת הִוא: 26 וְאִם | יִרְאֶנָּה הַכֹּהֵן וְהִנֵּה אֵין־בַּבֶּהֶרֶת שֵׂעָר לָבָן וּשְׁפָלָה אֵינֶנָּה מִן־הָעוֹר וְהִוא כֵהָה וְהִסְגִּירוֹ הַכֹּהֵן שִׁבְעַת יָמִים: 27 וְרָאָהוּ הַכֹּהֵן בַּיּוֹם הַשְּׁבִיעִי אִם־פָּשֹׂה תִפְשֶׂה בָּעוֹר וְטִמֵּא הַכֹּהֵן אֹתוֹ נֶגַע צָרַעַת הִוא: 28 וְאִם־תַּחְתֶּיהָ תַעֲמֹד הַבַּהֶרֶת לֹא־פָשְׂתָה בָעוֹר וְהִוא כֵהָה שְׂאֵת הַמִּכְוָה הִוא וְטִהֲרוֹ הַכֹּהֵן כִּי־צָרֶבֶת הַמִּכְוָה הִוא: פ

29 וְאִישׁ אוֹ אִשָּׁה כִּי־יִהְיֶה בוֹ נָגַע בְּרֹאשׁ אוֹ בְזָקָן: 30 וְרָאָה הַכֹּהֵן אֶת־הַנֶּגַע וְהִנֵּה מַרְאֵהוּ עָמֹק מִן־הָעוֹר וּבוֹ שֵׂעָר צָהֹב דָּק וְטִמֵּא אֹתוֹ הַכֹּהֵן נֶתֶק הוּא צָרַעַת הָרֹאשׁ אוֹ הַזָּקָן הוּא: 31 וְכִי־יִרְאֶה הַכֹּהֵן אֶת־נֶגַע הַנֶּתֶק וְהִנֵּה אֵין־מַרְאֵהוּ עָמֹק מִן־הָעוֹר וְשֵׂעָר שָׁחֹר אֵין בּוֹ וְהִסְגִּיר הַכֹּהֵן אֶת־נֶגַע הַנֶּתֶק שִׁבְעַת יָמִים: 32 וְרָאָה הַכֹּהֵן אֶת־הַנֶּגַע בַּיּוֹם הַשְּׁבִיעִי וְהִנֵּה לֹא־פָשָׂה הַנֶּתֶק וְלֹא־הָיָה בוֹ שֵׂעָר צָהֹב וּמַרְאֵה הַנֶּתֶק אֵין עָמֹק מִן־הָעוֹר: 33 וְהִתְגַּלָּח וְאֶת־הַנֶּתֶק לֹא יְגַלֵּחַ וְהִסְגִּיר הַכֹּהֵן אֶת־הַנֶּתֶק שִׁבְעַת יָמִים שֵׁנִית: 34 וְרָאָה הַכֹּהֵן אֶת־הַנֶּתֶק בַּיּוֹם הַשְּׁבִיעִי וְהִנֵּה לֹא־פָשָׂה הַנֶּתֶק בָּעוֹר וּמַרְאֵהוּ אֵינֶנּוּ עָמֹק מִן־הָעוֹר וְטִהַר אֹתוֹ הַכֹּהֵן וְכִבֶּס בְּגָדָיו וְטָהֵר: 35 וְאִם־פָּשֹׂה יִפְשֶׂה הַנֶּתֶק בָּעוֹר אַחֲרֵי טָהֳרָתוֹ: 36 וְרָאָהוּ הַכֹּהֵן וְהִנֵּה פָּשָׂה הַנֶּתֶק בָּעוֹר לֹא־יְבַקֵּר הַכֹּהֵן לַשֵּׂעָר הַצָּהֹב טָמֵא הוּא: 37 וְאִם־בְּעֵינָיו עָמַד הַנֶּתֶק וְשֵׂעָר שָׁחֹר צָמַח־בּוֹ נִרְפָּא הַנֶּתֶק טָהוֹר הוּא וְטִהֲרוֹ הַכֹּהֵן: ס 38 וְאִישׁ אוֹ־אִשָּׁה כִּי־יִהְיֶה בְעוֹר־בְּשָׂרָם בֶּהָרֹת בֶּהָרֹת לְבָנֹת: 39 וְרָאָה הַכֹּהֵן וְהִנֵּה בְעוֹר־בְּשָׂרָם בֶּהָרֹת כֵּהוֹת לְבָנֹת בֹּהַק הוּא פָּרַח בָּעוֹר טָהוֹר הוּא: ס 40 וְאִישׁ כִּי יִמָּרֵט רֹאשׁוֹ קֵרֵחַ הוּא טָהוֹר הוּא: 41 וְאִם

forehead, *but* he *is* clean. 42 And if there is on the bald head or bald forehead a reddish-white sore, it *is* leprosy breaking out on his bald head or his bald forehead. 43 Then the priest shall examine it; and indeed *if* the swelling of the sore *is* reddish-white on his bald head or on his bald forehead, as the appearance of leprosy on the skin of the body, 44 he is a leprous man. He *is* unclean. The priest shall surely pronounce him unclean; his sore *is* on his head.

45 "Now the leper on whom the sore *is,* his clothes shall be torn and his head bare; and he shall cover his mustache, and cry, 'Unclean! Unclean!' 46 He shall be unclean. All the days he has the sore he shall be unclean. He *is* unclean, and he shall dwell alone; his dwelling *shall be* outside the camp.

47 "Also, if a garment has a leprous plague in it, *whether it is* a woolen garment or a linen garment, 48 whether *it is* in the warp or woof of linen or wool, whether in leather or in anything made of leather, 49 and if the plague is greenish or reddish in the garment or in the leather, whether in the warp or in the woof, or in anything made of leather, it *is* a leprous plague and shall be shown to the priest. 50 The priest shall examine the plague and isolate *that which has* the plague seven days. 51 And he shall examine the plague on the seventh day. If the plague has spread in the garment, either in the warp or in the woof, in the leather *or* in anything made of leather, the plague *is* an active leprosy. It *is* unclean. 52 He shall therefore burn that garment in which is the plague, whether warp or woof, in wool or in linen, or anything of leather, for it *is* an active leprosy; *the garment* shall be burned in the fire.

53 "But if the priest examines *it,* and indeed the plague has not spread in the garment, either in the warp or in the woof, or in anything made of leather, 54 then the priest shall command that they wash *the thing* in which *is* the plague; and he shall isolate it another seven days. 55 Then the priest shall examine the plague after it has been washed; and indeed *if* the plague has not changed its color, though the plague has not spread, it *is* unclean, and you shall burn it in the fire; it continues eating away, *whether* the damage *is* outside or inside. 56 If the priest examines *it,* and indeed the plague has faded after washing it, then he shall tear it out of the garment, whether out of the warp or out of the woof, or out of the leather. 57 But if it appears again in the garment, either in the warp or in the woof, or in anything made of leather, it *is* a spreading *plague;* you shall burn with fire that in which is the plague. 58 And if you wash the garment, either warp or

מִפְּאַת פָּנָיו יִמָּרֵט רֹאשׁוֹ גִּבֵּחַ הוּא טָהוֹר הוּא: 42 וְכִי־יִהְיֶה בַקָּרַחַת אוֹ בַגַּבַּחַת נֶגַע לָבָן אֲדַמְדָּם צָרַעַת פֹּרַחַת הִוא בְּקָרַחְתּוֹ אוֹ בְגַבַּחְתּוֹ: 43 וְרָאָה אֹתוֹ הַכֹּהֵן וְהִנֵּה שְׂאֵת־הַנֶּגַע לְבָנָה אֲדַמְדֶּמֶת בְּקָרַחְתּוֹ אוֹ בְגַבַּחְתּוֹ כְּמַרְאֵה צָרַעַת עוֹר בָּשָׂר: 44 אִישׁ־צָרוּעַ הוּא טָמֵא הוּא טַמֵּא יְטַמְּאֶנּוּ הַכֹּהֵן בְּרֹאשׁוֹ נִגְעוֹ: 45 וְהַצָּרוּעַ אֲשֶׁר־בּוֹ הַנֶּגַע בְּגָדָיו יִהְיוּ פְרֻמִים וְרֹאשׁוֹ יִהְיֶה פָרוּעַ וְעַל־שָׂפָם יַעְטֶה וְטָמֵא | טָמֵא יִקְרָא: 46 כָּל־יְמֵי אֲשֶׁר הַנֶּגַע בּוֹ יִטְמָא טָמֵא הוּא בָּדָד יֵשֵׁב מִחוּץ לַמַּחֲנֶה מוֹשָׁבוֹ: ס 47 וְהַבֶּגֶד כִּי־יִהְיֶה בוֹ נֶגַע צָרָעַת בְּבֶגֶד צֶמֶר אוֹ בְּבֶגֶד פִּשְׁתִּים: 48 אוֹ בִשְׁתִי אוֹ בְעֵרֶב לַפִּשְׁתִּים וְלַצָּמֶר אוֹ בְעוֹר אוֹ בְּכָל־מְלֶאכֶת עוֹר: 49 וְהָיָה הַנֶּגַע יְרַקְרַק | אוֹ אֲדַמְדָּם בַּבֶּגֶד אוֹ בָעוֹר אוֹ־בַשְּׁתִי אוֹ־בָעֵרֶב אוֹ בְכָל־כְּלִי־עוֹר נֶגַע צָרַעַת הוּא וְהָרְאָה אֶת־הַכֹּהֵן: 50 וְרָאָה הַכֹּהֵן אֶת־הַנָּגַע וְהִסְגִּיר אֶת־הַנֶּגַע שִׁבְעַת יָמִים: 51 וְרָאָה אֶת־הַנֶּגַע בַּיּוֹם הַשְּׁבִיעִי כִּי־פָשָׂה הַנֶּגַע בַּבֶּגֶד אוֹ־בַשְּׁתִי אוֹ־בָעֵרֶב אוֹ בָעוֹר לְכֹל אֲשֶׁר־יֵעָשֶׂה הָעוֹר לִמְלָאכָה צָרַעַת מַמְאֶרֶת הַנֶּגַע טָמֵא הוּא: 52 וְשָׂרַף אֶת־הַבֶּגֶד אוֹ אֶת־הַשְּׁתִי | אוֹ אֶת־הָעֵרֶב בַּצֶּמֶר אוֹ בַפִּשְׁתִּים אוֹ אֶת־כָּל־כְּלִי הָעוֹר אֲשֶׁר־יִהְיֶה בוֹ הַנֶּגַע כִּי־צָרַעַת מַמְאֶרֶת הִוא בָּאֵשׁ תִּשָּׂרֵף: 53 וְאִם יִרְאֶה הַכֹּהֵן וְהִנֵּה לֹא־פָשָׂה הַנֶּגַע בַּבֶּגֶד אוֹ בַשְּׁתִי אוֹ בָעֵרֶב אוֹ בְּכָל־כְּלִי־עוֹר: 54 וְצִוָּה הַכֹּהֵן וְכִבְּסוּ אֵת אֲשֶׁר־בּוֹ הַנָּגַע וְהִסְגִּירוֹ שִׁבְעַת־יָמִים שֵׁנִית: 55 וְרָאָה הַכֹּהֵן אַחֲרֵי | הֻכַּבֵּס אֶת־הַנֶּגַע וְהִנֵּה לֹא־הָפַךְ הַנֶּגַע אֶת־עֵינוֹ וְהַנֶּגַע לֹא־פָשָׂה טָמֵא הוּא בָּאֵשׁ תִּשְׂרְפֶנּוּ פְּחֶתֶת הִוא בְּקָרַחְתּוֹ אוֹ בְגַבַּחְתּוֹ: 56 וְאִם רָאָה הַכֹּהֵן וְהִנֵּה כֵּהָה הַנֶּגַע אַחֲרֵי הֻכַּבֵּס אֹתוֹ וְקָרַע אֹתוֹ מִן־הַבֶּגֶד אוֹ מִן־הָעוֹר אוֹ מִן־הַשְּׁתִי אוֹ מִן־הָעֵרֶב: 57 וְאִם־תֵּרָאֶה עוֹד בַּבֶּגֶד אוֹ־בַשְּׁתִי אוֹ־בָעֵרֶב אוֹ בְכָל־כְּלִי־עוֹר פֹּרַחַת הִוא בָּאֵשׁ תִּשְׂרְפֶנּוּ אֵת אֲשֶׁר־בּוֹ הַנָּגַע: 58 וְהַבֶּגֶד אוֹ־הַשְּׁתִי אוֹ־הָעֵרֶב אוֹ־כָל־כְּלִי הָעוֹר אֲשֶׁר תְּכַבֵּס וְסָר מֵהֶם הַנָּגַע וְכֻבַּס שֵׁנִית

woof, or whatever is made of leather, if the plague
has disappeared from it, then it shall be washed a
second time, and shall be clean.

59 "This *is* the law of the leprous plague in a
garment of wool or linen, either in the warp or
woof, or in anything made of leather, to pronounce
it clean or to pronounce it unclean."

14 Then the LORD spoke to Moses, saying,
2 "This shall be the law of the leper for the day of
his cleansing: He shall be brought to the priest.
3 And the priest shall go out of the camp, and the
priest shall examine *him;* and indeed, *if* the leprosy
is healed in the leper, 4 then the priest shall
command to take for him who is to be cleansed
two living *and* clean birds, cedar wood, scarlet, and
hyssop. 5 And the priest shall command that one of
the birds be killed in an earthen vessel over running
water. 6 As for the living bird, he shall take it, the
cedar wood and the scarlet and the hyssop, and dip
them and the living bird in the blood of the bird
that was killed over the running water. 7 And he
shall sprinkle it seven times on him who is to be
cleansed from the leprosy, and shall pronounce him
clean, and shall let the living bird loose in the open
field. 8 He who is to be cleansed shall wash his
clothes, shave off all his hair, and wash himself in
water, that he may be clean. After that he shall
come into the camp, and shall stay outside his tent
seven days. 9 But on the seventh day he shall shave
all the hair off his head and his beard and his
eyebrows—all his hair he shall shave off. He shall
wash his clothes and wash his body in water, and he
shall be clean.

10 "And on the eighth day he shall take two male
lambs without blemish, one ewe lamb of the first
year without blemish, three-tenths *of an ephah* of
fine flour mixed with oil as a grain offering, and one
log of oil. 11 Then the priest who makes *him* clean
shall present the man who is to be made clean, and
those things, before the LORD, *at* the door of the
tabernacle of meeting. 12 And the priest shall take
one male lamb and offer it as a trespass offering,
and the log of oil, and wave them *as* a wave offering
before the LORD. 13 Then he shall kill the lamb in
the place where he kills the sin offering and the
burnt offering, in a holy place; for as the sin
offering *is* the priest's, so *is* the trespass offering. It
is most holy. 14 The priest shall take *some* of the
blood of the trespass offering, and the priest shall
put *it* on the tip of the right ear of him who is to be
cleansed, on the thumb of his right hand, and on the
big toe of his right foot. 15 And the priest shall take
some of the log of oil, and pour *it* into the palm of

וְטָהֵר: 59 זֹאת תּוֹרַת נֶגַע־צָרַעַת בֶּגֶד הַצֶּמֶר |
אוֹ הַפִּשְׁתִּים אוֹ הַשְּׁתִי אוֹ הָעֵרֶב אוֹ כָּל־כְּלִי־עוֹר
לְטַהֲרוֹ אוֹ לְטַמְּאוֹ:   פ

יד וַיְדַבֵּר יְהוָה אֶל־מֹשֶׁה לֵּאמֹר: 2 זֹאת תִּהְיֶה
תּוֹרַת הַמְּצֹרָע בְּיוֹם טָהֳרָתוֹ וְהוּבָא אֶל־הַכֹּהֵן:
3 וְיָצָא הַכֹּהֵן אֶל־מִחוּץ לַמַּחֲנֶה וְרָאָה הַכֹּהֵן
וְהִנֵּה נִרְפָּא נֶגַע־הַצָּרַעַת מִן־הַצָּרוּעַ: 4 וְצִוָּה הַכֹּהֵן
וְלָקַח לַמִּטַּהֵר שְׁתֵּי־צִפֳּרִים חַיּוֹת טְהֹרוֹת וְעֵץ
אֶרֶז וּשְׁנִי תוֹלַעַת וְאֵזֹב: 5 וְצִוָּה הַכֹּהֵן וְשָׁחַט
אֶת־הַצִּפּוֹר הָאֶחָת אֶל־כְּלִי־חֶרֶשׂ עַל־מַיִם חַיִּים:
6 אֶת־הַצִּפֹּר הַחַיָּה יִקַּח אֹתָהּ וְאֶת־עֵץ הָאֶרֶז וְאֶת־
שְׁנִי הַתּוֹלַעַת וְאֶת־הָאֵזֹב וְטָבַל אוֹתָם |
וְאֵת הַצִּפֹּר הַחַיָּה בְּדַם הַצִּפֹּר הַשְּׁחֻטָה עַל הַמַּיִם
הַחַיִּים: 7 וְהִזָּה עַל הַמִּטַּהֵר מִן־הַצָּרַעַת שֶׁבַע
פְּעָמִים וְטִהֲרוֹ וְשִׁלַּח אֶת־הַצִּפֹּר הַחַיָּה עַל־פְּנֵי
הַשָּׂדֶה: 8 וְכִבֶּס הַמִּטַּהֵר אֶת־בְּגָדָיו וְגִלַּח אֶת־כָּל־
שְׂעָרוֹ וְרָחַץ בַּמַּיִם וְטָהֵר וְאַחַר יָבוֹא אֶל־הַמַּחֲנֶה
וְיָשַׁב מִחוּץ לְאָהֳלוֹ שִׁבְעַת יָמִים: 9 וְהָיָה בַיּוֹם
הַשְּׁבִיעִי יְגַלַּח אֶת־כָּל־שְׂעָרוֹ אֶת־רֹאשׁוֹ וְאֶת־זְקָנוֹ
וְאֵת גַּבֹּת עֵינָיו וְאֶת־כָּל־שְׂעָרוֹ יְגַלֵּחַ וְכִבֶּס אֶת־
בְּגָדָיו וְרָחַץ אֶת־בְּשָׂרוֹ בַּמַּיִם וְטָהֵר: 10 וּבַיּוֹם
הַשְּׁמִינִי יִקַּח שְׁנֵי־כְבָשִׂים תְּמִימִם וְכַבְשָׂה אַחַת
בַּת־שְׁנָתָהּ תְּמִימָה וּשְׁלֹשָׁה עֶשְׂרֹנִים סֹלֶת מִנְחָה
בְּלוּלָה בַשֶּׁמֶן וְלֹג אֶחָד שָׁמֶן: 11 וְהֶעֱמִיד הַכֹּהֵן
הַמְטַהֵר אֵת הָאִישׁ הַמִּטַּהֵר וְאֹתָם לִפְנֵי יְהוָה
פֶּתַח אֹהֶל מוֹעֵד: 12 וְלָקַח הַכֹּהֵן אֶת־הַכֶּבֶשׂ
הָאֶחָד וְהִקְרִיב אֹתוֹ לְאָשָׁם וְאֶת־לֹג הַשָּׁמֶן וְהֵנִיף
אֹתָם תְּנוּפָה לִפְנֵי יְהוָה: 13 וְשָׁחַט אֶת־הַכֶּבֶשׂ
בִּמְקוֹם אֲשֶׁר יִשְׁחַט אֶת־הַחַטָּאת וְאֶת־הָעֹלָה
בִּמְקוֹם הַקֹּדֶשׁ כִּי כַּחַטָּאת הָאָשָׁם הוּא לַכֹּהֵן
קֹדֶשׁ קָדָשִׁים הוּא: 14 וְלָקַח הַכֹּהֵן מִדַּם הָאָשָׁם
וְנָתַן הַכֹּהֵן עַל־תְּנוּךְ אֹזֶן הַמִּטַּהֵר הַיְמָנִית וְעַל־
בֹּהֶן יָדוֹ הַיְמָנִית וְעַל־בֹּהֶן רַגְלוֹ הַיְמָנִית: 15 וְלָקַח
הַכֹּהֵן מִלֹּג הַשָּׁמֶן וְיָצַק עַל־כַּף הַכֹּהֵן הַשְּׂמָאלִית:

his own left hand. ¹⁶Then the priest shall dip his right finger in the oil that *is* in his left hand, and shall sprinkle some of the oil with his finger seven times before the LORD. ¹⁷And of the rest of the oil in his hand, the priest shall put *some* on the tip of the right ear of him who is to be cleansed, on the thumb of his right hand, and on the big toe of his right foot, on the blood of the trespass offering. ¹⁸The rest of the oil that *is* in the priest's hand he shall put on the head of him who is to be cleansed. So the priest shall make atonement for him before the LORD.

¹⁹"Then the priest shall offer the sin offering, and make atonement for him who is to be cleansed from his uncleanness. Afterward he shall kill the burnt offering. ²⁰And the priest shall offer the burnt offering and the grain offering on the altar. So the priest shall make atonement for him, and he shall be clean.

²¹"But if he *is* poor and cannot afford it, then he shall take one male lamb *as* a trespass offering to be waved, to make atonement for him, one-tenth *of an ephah* of fine flour mixed with oil as a grain offering, a log of oil, ²²and two turtledoves or two young pigeons, such as he is able to afford: one shall be a sin offering and the other a burnt offering. ²³He shall bring them to the priest on the eighth day for his cleansing, to the door of the tabernacle of meeting, before the LORD. ²⁴And the priest shall take the lamb of the trespass offering and the log of oil, and the priest shall wave them *as* a wave offering before the LORD. ²⁵Then he shall kill the lamb of the trespass offering, and the priest shall take *some* of the blood of the trespass offering and put *it* on the tip of the right ear of him who is to be cleansed, on the thumb of his right hand, and on the big toe of his right foot. ²⁶And the priest shall pour some of the oil into the palm of his own left hand. ²⁷Then the priest shall sprinkle with his right finger *some* of the oil that *is* in his left hand seven times before the LORD. ²⁸And the priest shall put *some* of the oil that *is* in his hand on the tip of the right ear of him who is to be cleansed, on the thumb of the right hand, and on the big toe of his right foot, on the place of the blood of the trespass offering. ²⁹The rest of the oil that *is* in the priest's hand he shall put on the head of him who is to be cleansed, to make atonement for him before the LORD. ³⁰And he shall offer one of the turtledoves or young pigeons, such as he can afford— ³¹such as he is able to afford, the one *as* a sin offering and the other *as* a burnt offering, with the grain offering. So the priest shall make atonement for him who is to

16 וְטָבַ֨ל הַכֹּהֵ֜ן אֶת־אֶצְבָּע֣וֹ הַיְמָנִ֗ית מִן־הַשֶּׁ֙מֶן֙ אֲשֶׁ֣ר עַל־כַּפּ֣וֹ הַשְּׂמָאלִ֔ית וְהִזָּ֞ה מִן־הַשֶּׁ֧מֶן בְּאֶצְבָּע֛וֹ שֶׁ֥בַע פְּעָמִ֖ים לִפְנֵ֥י יְהֹוָֽה: 17 וּמִיֶּ֣תֶר הַשֶּׁ֗מֶן אֲשֶׁ֣ר עַל־כַּפּ֒וֹ יִתֵּ֨ן הַכֹּהֵ֜ן עַל־תְּנ֨וּךְ אֹ֤זֶן הַמִּטַּהֵר֙ הַיְמָנִ֔ית וְעַל־בֹּ֤הֶן יָדוֹ֙ הַיְמָנִ֔ית וְעַל־בֹּ֥הֶן רַגְל֖וֹ הַיְמָנִ֑ית עַ֖ל דַּ֥ם הָאָשָֽׁם: 18 וְהַנּוֹתָ֗ר בַּשֶּׁ֙מֶן֙ אֲשֶׁר֙ עַל־כַּ֣ף הַכֹּהֵ֔ן יִתֵּ֖ן עַל־רֹ֣אשׁ הַמִּטַּהֵ֑ר וְכִפֶּ֥ר עָלָ֛יו הַכֹּהֵ֖ן לִפְנֵ֥י יְהֹוָֽה: 19 וְעָשָׂ֤ה הַכֹּהֵן֙ אֶת־הַֽחַטָּ֔את וְכִפֶּ֕ר עַל־הַמִּטַּהֵ֖ר מִטֻּמְאָת֑וֹ וְאַחַ֖ר יִשְׁחַ֥ט אֶת־הָעֹלָֽה:

20 וְהֶעֱלָ֧ה הַכֹּהֵ֛ן אֶת־הָעֹלָ֥ה וְאֶת־הַמִּנְחָ֖ה הַמִּזְבֵּ֑חָה וְכִפֶּ֥ר עָלָ֛יו הַכֹּהֵ֖ן וְטָהֵֽר: ס 21 וְאִם־דַּ֣ל ה֗וּא וְאֵ֣ין יָדוֹ֘ מַשֶּׂגֶת֒ וְ֠לָקַ֠ח כֶּ֣בֶשׂ אֶחָ֥ד אָשָׁ֛ם לִתְנוּפָ֖ה לְכַפֵּ֣ר עָלָ֑יו וְעִשָּׂר֨וֹן סֹ֜לֶת אֶחָ֨ד בָּל֥וּל בַּשֶּׁ֛מֶן לְמִנְחָ֖ה וְלֹ֥ג שָֽׁמֶן: 22 וּשְׁתֵּ֣י תֹרִ֗ים א֤וֹ שְׁנֵי֙ בְּנֵ֣י יוֹנָ֔ה אֲשֶׁ֥ר תַּשִּׂ֖יג יָד֑וֹ וְהָיָ֤ה אֶחָד֙ חַטָּ֔את וְהָאֶחָ֖ד עֹלָֽה: 23 וְהֵבִ֨יא אֹתָ֜ם בַּיּ֧וֹם הַשְּׁמִינִ֛י לְטׇהֳרָת֖וֹ אֶל־הַכֹּהֵ֑ן אֶל־פֶּ֥תַח אֹֽהֶל־מוֹעֵ֖ד לִפְנֵ֥י יְהֹוָֽה: 24 וְלָקַ֧ח הַכֹּהֵ֛ן אֶת־כֶּ֥בֶשׂ הָאָשָׁ֖ם וְאֶת־לֹ֣ג הַשָּׁ֑מֶן וְהֵנִ֨יף אֹתָ֧ם הַכֹּהֵ֛ן תְּנוּפָ֖ה לִפְנֵ֥י יְהֹוָֽה: 25 וְשָׁחַט֮ אֶת־כֶּ֣בֶשׂ הָֽאָשָׁם֒ וְלָקַ֤ח הַכֹּהֵן֙ מִדַּ֣ם הָֽאָשָׁ֔ם וְנָתַ֛ן עַל־תְּנ֥וּךְ אֹֽזֶן־הַמִּטַּהֵ֖ר הַיְמָנִ֑ית וְעַל־בֹּ֤הֶן יָדוֹ֙ הַיְמָנִ֔ית וְעַל־בֹּ֥הֶן רַגְל֖וֹ הַיְמָנִֽית: 26 וּמִן־הַשֶּׁ֖מֶן יִצֹ֣ק הַכֹּהֵ֑ן עַל־כַּ֥ף הַכֹּהֵ֖ן הַשְּׂמָאלִֽית: 27 וְהִזָּ֤ה הַכֹּהֵן֙ בְּאֶצְבָּע֣וֹ הַיְמָנִ֔ית מִן־הַשֶּׁ֕מֶן אֲשֶׁ֥ר עַל־כַּפּ֖וֹ הַשְּׂמָאלִ֑ית שֶׁ֥בַע פְּעָמִ֖ים לִפְנֵ֥י יְהֹוָֽה: 28 וְנָתַ֨ן הַכֹּהֵ֜ן מִן־הַשֶּׁ֣מֶן ׀ אֲשֶׁ֣ר עַל־כַּפּ֗וֹ עַל־תְּנ֞וּךְ אֹ֤זֶן הַמִּטַּהֵר֙ הַיְמָנִ֔ית וְעַל־בֹּ֤הֶן יָדוֹ֙ הַיְמָנִ֔ית וְעַל־בֹּ֥הֶן רַגְל֖וֹ הַיְמָנִ֑ית עַל־מְק֖וֹם דַּ֥ם הָאָשָֽׁם: 29 וְהַנּוֹתָ֗ר מִן־הַשֶּׁ֙מֶן֙ אֲשֶׁר֙ עַל־כַּ֣ף הַכֹּהֵ֔ן יִתֵּ֖ן עַל־רֹ֣אשׁ הַמִּטַּהֵ֑ר לְכַפֵּ֥ר עָלָ֖יו לִפְנֵ֥י יְהֹוָֽה: 30 וְעָשָׂ֤ה אֶת־הָֽאֶחָד֙ מִן־הַתֹּרִ֔ים א֖וֹ מִן־בְּנֵ֣י הַיּוֹנָ֑ה מֵאֲשֶׁ֥ר תַּשִּׂ֖יג יָדֽוֹ: 31 אֵ֣ת אֲשֶׁר־תַּשִּׂ֞יג יָד֗וֹ אֶת־הָאֶחָ֥ד חַטָּ֛את וְאֶת־הָאֶחָ֥ד עֹלָ֖ה עַל־הַמִּנְחָ֑ה

be cleansed before the LORD. ³²This *is* the law *for one* who had a leprous sore, who cannot afford the usual cleansing."

³³And the LORD spoke to Moses and Aaron, saying: ³⁴"When you have come into the land of Canaan, which I give you as a possession, and I put the leprous plague in a house in the land of your possession, ³⁵and he who owns the house comes and tells the priest, saying, 'It seems to me that *there is* some plague in the house,' ³⁶then the priest shall command that they empty the house, before the priest goes *into it* to examine the plague, that all that *is* in the house may not be made unclean; and afterward the priest shall go in to examine the house. ³⁷And he shall examine the plague; and indeed *if* the plague *is* on the walls of the house with ingrained streaks, greenish or reddish, which appear to be deep in the wall, ³⁸then the priest shall go out of the house, to the door of the house, and shut up the house seven days. ³⁹And the priest shall come again on the seventh day and look; and indeed *if* the plague has spread on the walls of the house, ⁴⁰then the priest shall command that they take away the stones in which *is* the plague, and they shall cast them into an unclean place outside the city. ⁴¹And he shall cause the house to be scraped inside, all around, and the dust that they scrape off they shall pour out in an unclean place outside the city. ⁴²Then they shall take other stones and put *them* in the place of *those* stones, and he shall take other mortar and plaster the house.

⁴³"Now if the plague comes back and breaks out in the house, after he has taken away the stones, after he has scraped the house, and after it is plastered, ⁴⁴then the priest shall come and look; and indeed *if* the plague has spread in the house, it *is* an active leprosy in the house. It *is* unclean. ⁴⁵And he shall break down the house, its stones, its timber, and all the plaster of the house, and he shall carry *them* outside the city to an unclean place. ⁴⁶Moreover he who goes into the house at all while it is shut up shall be unclean until evening. ⁴⁷And he who lies down in the house shall wash his clothes, and he who eats in the house shall wash his clothes.

⁴⁸"But if the priest comes in and examines *it*, and indeed the plague has not spread in the house after the house was plastered, then the priest shall pronounce the house clean, because the plague is healed. ⁴⁹And he shall take, to cleanse the house, two birds, cedar wood, scarlet, and hyssop. ⁵⁰Then he shall kill one of the birds in an earthen vessel over running water; ⁵¹and he shall take the cedar wood, the hyssop, the scarlet, and the living bird,

and dip them in the blood of the slain bird and in the running water, and sprinkle the house seven times. ⁵²And he shall cleanse the house with the blood of the bird and the running water and the living bird, with the cedar wood, the hyssop, and the scarlet. ⁵³Then he shall let the living bird loose outside the city in the open field, and make atonement for the house, and it shall be clean.

⁵⁴"This *is* the law for any leprous sore and scale, ⁵⁵for the leprosy of a garment and of a house, ⁵⁶for a swelling and a scab and a bright spot, ⁵⁷to teach when *it is* unclean and when *it is* clean. This *is* the law of leprosy."

15 And the LORD spoke to Moses and Aaron, saying, ²"Speak to the children of Israel, and say to them: 'When any man has a discharge from his body, his discharge *is* unclean. ³And this shall be his uncleanness in regard to his discharge—whether his body runs with his discharge, or his body is stopped up by his discharge, it *is* his uncleanness. ⁴Every bed is unclean on which he who has the discharge lies, and everything on which he sits shall be unclean. ⁵And whoever touches his bed shall wash his clothes and bathe in water, and be unclean until evening. ⁶He who sits on anything on which he who has the discharge sat shall wash his clothes and bathe in water, and be unclean until evening. ⁷And he who touches the body of him who has the discharge shall wash his clothes and bathe in water, and be unclean until evening. ⁸If he who has the discharge spits on him who is clean, then he shall wash his clothes and bathe in water, and be unclean until evening. ⁹Any saddle on which he who has the discharge rides shall be unclean. ¹⁰Whoever touches anything that was under him shall be unclean until evening. He who carries *any of* those things shall wash his clothes and bathe in water, and be unclean until evening. ¹¹And whomever the one who has the discharge touches, and has not rinsed his hands in water, he shall wash his clothes and bathe in water, and be unclean until evening. ¹²The vessel of earth that he who has the discharge touches shall be broken, and every vessel of wood shall be rinsed in water.

¹³'And when he who has a discharge is cleansed of his discharge, then he shall count for himself seven days for his cleansing, wash his clothes, and bathe his body in running water; then he shall be clean. ¹⁴On the eighth day he shall take for himself two turtledoves or two young pigeons, and come before the LORD, to the door of the tabernacle of meeting, and give them to the priest. ¹⁵Then the priest shall offer them, the one *as* a sin offering and

וְאֶת ׀ שְׁנִי הַתּוֹלַעַת וְאֵת הַצִּפֹּר הַחַיָּה וְטָבַל אֹתָם בְּדַם הַצִּפֹּר הַשְּׁחוּטָה וּבַמַּיִם הַחַיִּים וְהִזָּה אֶל־הַבַּיִת שֶׁבַע פְּעָמִים: ⁵²וְחִטֵּא אֶת־הַבַּיִת בְּדַם הַצִּפּוֹר וּבַמַּיִם הַחַיִּים וּבַצִּפֹּר הַחַיָּה וּבְעֵץ הָאֶרֶז וּבָאֵזֹב וּבִשְׁנִי הַתּוֹלָעַת: ⁵³וְשִׁלַּח אֶת־הַצִּפֹּר הַחַיָּה אֶל־מִחוּץ לָעִיר אֶל־פְּנֵי הַשָּׂדֶה וְכִפֶּר עַל־הַבַּיִת וְטָהֵר: ⁵⁴זֹאת הַתּוֹרָה לְכָל־נֶגַע הַצָּרַעַת וְלַנָּתֶק: ⁵⁵וּלְצָרַעַת הַבֶּגֶד וְלַבָּיִת: ⁵⁶וְלַשְׂאֵת וְלַסַּפַּחַת וְלַבֶּהָרֶת: ⁵⁷לְהוֹרֹת בְּיוֹם הַטָּמֵא וּבְיוֹם הַטָּהֹר זֹאת תּוֹרַת הַצָּרָעַת: ס

טו וַיְדַבֵּר יְהֹוָה אֶל־מֹשֶׁה וְאֶל־אַהֲרֹן לֵאמֹר: ²דַּבְּרוּ אֶל־בְּנֵי יִשְׂרָאֵל וַאֲמַרְתֶּם אֲלֵהֶם אִישׁ אִישׁ כִּי יִהְיֶה זָב מִבְּשָׂרוֹ זוֹבוֹ טָמֵא הוּא: ³וְזֹאת תִּהְיֶה טֻמְאָתוֹ בְּזוֹבוֹ רָר בְּשָׂרוֹ אֶת־זוֹבוֹ אוֹ־הֶחְתִּים בְּשָׂרוֹ מִזּוֹבוֹ טֻמְאָתוֹ הִוא: ⁴כָּל־הַמִּשְׁכָּב אֲשֶׁר יִשְׁכַּב עָלָיו הַזָּב יִטְמָא וְכָל־הַכְּלִי אֲשֶׁר־יֵשֵׁב עָלָיו יִטְמָא: ⁵וְאִישׁ אֲשֶׁר יִגַּע בְּמִשְׁכָּבוֹ יְכַבֵּס בְּגָדָיו וְרָחַץ בַּמַּיִם וְטָמֵא עַד־הָעָרֶב: ⁶וְהַיֹּשֵׁב עַל־הַכְּלִי אֲשֶׁר־יֵשֵׁב עָלָיו הַזָּב יְכַבֵּס בְּגָדָיו וְרָחַץ בַּמַּיִם וְטָמֵא עַד־הָעָרֶב: ⁷וְהַנֹּגֵעַ בִּבְשַׂר הַזָּב יְכַבֵּס בְּגָדָיו וְרָחַץ בַּמַּיִם וְטָמֵא עַד־הָעָרֶב: ⁸וְכִי־יָרֹק הַזָּב בַּטָּהוֹר וְכִבֶּס בְּגָדָיו וְרָחַץ בַּמַּיִם וְטָמֵא עַד־הָעָרֶב: ⁹וְכָל־הַמֶּרְכָּב אֲשֶׁר יִרְכַּב עָלָיו הַזָּב יִטְמָא: ¹⁰וְכָל־הַנֹּגֵעַ בְּכֹל אֲשֶׁר יִהְיֶה תַחְתָּיו יִטְמָא עַד־הָעָרֶב וְהַנּוֹשֵׂא אוֹתָם יְכַבֵּס בְּגָדָיו וְרָחַץ בַּמַּיִם וְטָמֵא עַד־הָעָרֶב: ¹¹וְכֹל אֲשֶׁר יִגַּע־בּוֹ הַזָּב וְיָדָיו לֹא־שָׁטַף בַּמָּיִם וְכִבֶּס בְּגָדָיו וְרָחַץ בַּמַּיִם וְטָמֵא עַד־הָעָרֶב: ¹²וּכְלִי־חֶרֶשׂ אֲשֶׁר יִגַּע־בּוֹ הַזָּב יִשָּׁבֵר וְכָל־כְּלִי־עֵץ יִשָּׁטֵף בַּמָּיִם: ¹³וְכִי־יִטְהַר הַזָּב מִזּוֹבוֹ וְסָפַר לוֹ שִׁבְעַת יָמִים לְטָהֳרָתוֹ וְכִבֶּס בְּגָדָיו וְרָחַץ בְּשָׂרוֹ בְּמַיִם חַיִּים וְטָהֵר: ¹⁴וּבַיּוֹם הַשְּׁמִינִי יִקַּח לוֹ שְׁתֵּי תֹרִים אוֹ שְׁנֵי בְּנֵי יוֹנָה וּבָא ׀ לִפְנֵי יְהֹוָה אֶל־פֶּתַח אֹהֶל מוֹעֵד וּנְתָנָם אֶל־הַכֹּהֵן: ¹⁵וְעָשָׂה

the other *as* a burnt offering. So the priest shall make atonement for him before the LORD because of his discharge.

16 'If any man has an emission of semen, then he shall wash all his body in water, and be unclean until evening. 17 And any garment and any leather on which there is semen, it shall be washed with water, and be unclean until evening. 18 Also, when a woman lies with a man, and *there is* an emission of semen, they shall bathe in water, and be unclean until evening.

19 'If a woman has a discharge, *and* the discharge from her body is blood, she shall be set apart seven days; and whoever touches her shall be unclean until evening. 20 Everything that she lies on during her impurity shall be unclean; also everything that she sits on shall be unclean. 21 Whoever touches her bed shall wash his clothes and bathe in water, and be unclean until evening. 22 And whoever touches anything that she sat on shall wash his clothes and bathe in water, and be unclean until evening. 23 If *anything* is on *her* bed or on anything on which she sits, when he touches it, he shall be unclean until evening. 24 And if any man lies with her at all, so that her impurity is on him, he shall be unclean seven days; and every bed on which he lies shall be unclean.

25 'If a woman has a discharge of blood for many days, other than at the time of her *customary* impurity, or if it runs beyond her *usual time of* impurity, all the days of her unclean discharge shall be as the days of her *customary* impurity. She *shall be* unclean. 26 Every bed on which she lies all the days of her discharge shall be to her as the bed of her impurity; and whatever she sits on shall be unclean, as the uncleanness of her impurity. 27 Whoever touches those things shall be unclean; he shall wash his clothes and bathe in water, and unclean until evening.

28 'But if she is cleansed of her discharge, then she shall count for herself seven days, and after that she shall be clean. 29 And on the eighth day she shall take for herself two turtledoves or two young pigeons, and bring them to the priest, to the door of the tabernacle of meeting. 30 Then the priest shall offer the one *as* a sin offering and the other *as* a burnt offering, and the priest shall make atonement for her before the LORD for the discharge of her uncleanness.

31 'Thus you shall separate the children of Israel from their uncleanness, lest they die in their uncleanness when they defile My tabernacle that *is* among them. 32 This *is* the law for one who has a discharge, and *for him* who emits semen and is

אֹתָם הַכֹּהֵן אֶחָד חַטָּאת וְהָאֶחָד עֹלָה וְכִפֶּר עָלָיו
הַכֹּהֵן לִפְנֵי יְהֹוָה מִזּוֹבוֹ: ס   16 וְאִישׁ כִּי־
תֵצֵא מִמֶּנּוּ שִׁכְבַת־זָרַע וְרָחַץ בַּמַּיִם אֶת־כָּל־בְּשָׂרוֹ
וְטָמֵא עַד־הָעָרֶב: 17 וְכָל־בֶּגֶד וְכָל־עוֹר אֲשֶׁר־יִהְיֶה
עָלָיו שִׁכְבַת־זָרַע וְכֻבַּס בַּמַּיִם וְטָמֵא עַד־הָעָרֶב: פ

18 וְאִשָּׁה אֲשֶׁר יִשְׁכַּב אִישׁ אֹתָהּ שִׁכְבַת־זָרַע
וְרָחֲצוּ בַמַּיִם וְטָמְאוּ עַד־הָעָרֶב: 19 וְאִשָּׁה כִּי־
תִהְיֶה זָבָה דָּם יִהְיֶה זֹבָהּ בִּבְשָׂרָהּ שִׁבְעַת יָמִים
תִּהְיֶה בְנִדָּתָהּ וְכָל־הַנֹּגֵעַ בָּהּ יִטְמָא עַד־הָעָרֶב:
20 וְכֹל אֲשֶׁר תִּשְׁכַּב עָלָיו בְּנִדָּתָהּ יִטְמָא וְכֹל אֲשֶׁר־
תֵּשֵׁב עָלָיו יִטְמָא: 21 וְכָל־הַנֹּגֵעַ בְּמִשְׁכָּבָהּ יְכַבֵּס
בְּגָדָיו וְרָחַץ בַּמַּיִם וְטָמֵא עַד־הָעָרֶב: 22 וְכָל־הַנֹּגֵעַ
בְּכָל־כְּלִי אֲשֶׁר־תֵּשֵׁב עָלָיו יְכַבֵּס בְּגָדָיו וְרָחַץ בַּמַּיִם
וְטָמֵא עַד־הָעָרֶב: 23 וְאִם עַל־הַמִּשְׁכָּב הוּא אוֹ
עַל־הַכְּלִי אֲשֶׁר־הִוא יֹשֶׁבֶת־עָלָיו בְּנָגְעוֹ־בוֹ יִטְמָא
עַד־הָעָרֶב: 24 וְאִם שָׁכֹב יִשְׁכַּב אִישׁ אֹתָהּ וּתְהִי
נִדָּתָהּ עָלָיו וְטָמֵא שִׁבְעַת יָמִים וְכָל־הַמִּשְׁכָּב
אֲשֶׁר־יִשְׁכַּב עָלָיו יִטְמָא: פ

25 וְאִשָּׁה כִּי־יָזוּב זוֹב דָּמָהּ יָמִים רַבִּים בְּלֹא עֶת־
נִדָּתָהּ אוֹ כִי־תָזוּב עַל־נִדָּתָהּ כָּל־יְמֵי זוֹב טֻמְאָתָהּ
כִּימֵי נִדָּתָהּ תִּהְיֶה טְמֵאָה הִוא: 26 כָּל־הַמִּשְׁכָּב
אֲשֶׁר־תִּשְׁכַּב עָלָיו כָּל־יְמֵי זוֹבָהּ כְּמִשְׁכַּב נִדָּתָהּ
יִהְיֶה־לָּהּ וְכָל־הַכְּלִי אֲשֶׁר תֵּשֵׁב עָלָיו טָמֵא יִהְיֶה
כְּטֻמְאַת נִדָּתָהּ: 27 וְכָל־הַנֹּגֵעַ בָּם יִטְמָא וְכִבֶּס
בְּגָדָיו וְרָחַץ בַּמַּיִם וְטָמֵא עַד־הָעָרֶב: 28 וְאִם־
טָהֲרָה מִזּוֹבָהּ וְסָפְרָה לָּהּ שִׁבְעַת יָמִים וְאַחַר
תִּטְהָר: 29 וּבַיּוֹם הַשְּׁמִינִי תִּקַּח־לָהּ שְׁתֵּי תֹרִים
אוֹ שְׁנֵי בְּנֵי יוֹנָה וְהֵבִיאָה אוֹתָם אֶל־הַכֹּהֵן אֶל־
פֶּתַח אֹהֶל מוֹעֵד: 30 וְעָשָׂה הַכֹּהֵן אֶת־הָאֶחָד
חַטָּאת וְאֶת־הָאֶחָד עֹלָה וְכִפֶּר עָלֶיהָ הַכֹּהֵן לִפְנֵי
יְהֹוָה מִזּוֹב טֻמְאָתָהּ: 31 וְהִזַּרְתֶּם אֶת־בְּנֵי־יִשְׂרָאֵל
מִטֻּמְאָתָם וְלֹא יָמֻתוּ בְּטֻמְאָתָם בְּטַמְּאָם אֶת־
מִשְׁכָּנִי אֲשֶׁר בְּתוֹכָם: 32 זֹאת תּוֹרַת הַזָּב וַאֲשֶׁר

unclean thereby, 33 and for her who is indisposed because of her *customary* impurity, and for one who has a discharge, either man or woman, and for him who lies with her who is unclean.'"

16 Now the LORD spoke to Moses after the death of the two sons of Aaron, when they offered *profane fire* before the LORD, and died; 2 and the LORD said to Moses: "Tell Aaron your brother not to come at *just* any time into the Holy *Place* inside the veil, before the mercy seat which *is* on the ark, lest he die; for I will appear in the cloud above the mercy seat.

3 "Thus Aaron shall come into the Holy *Place:* with *the blood of* a young bull as a sin offering, and *of* a ram as a burnt offering. 4 He shall put the holy linen tunic and the linen trousers on his body; he shall be girded with a linen sash, and with the linen turban he shall be attired. These *are* holy garments. Therefore he shall wash his body in water, and put them on. 5 And he shall take from the congregation of the children of Israel two kids of the goats as a sin offering, and one ram as a burnt offering.

6 "Aaron shall offer the bull as a sin offering, which *is* for himself, and make atonement for himself and for his house. 7 He shall take the two goats and present them before the LORD *at* the door of the tabernacle of meeting. 8 Then Aaron shall cast lots for the two goats: one lot for the LORD and the other lot for the scapegoat. 9 And Aaron shall bring the goat on which the LORD's lot fell, and offer it *as* a sin offering. 10 But the goat on which the lot fell to be the scapegoat shall be presented alive before the LORD, to make atonement upon it, *and* to let it go as the scapegoat into the wilderness.

11 "And Aaron shall bring the bull of the sin offering, which is for himself, and make atonement for himself and for his house, and shall kill the bull as the sin offering which *is* for himself. 12 Then he shall take a censer full of burning coals of fire from the altar before the LORD, with his hands full of sweet incense beaten fine, and bring *it* inside the veil. 13 And he shall put the incense on the fire before the LORD, that the cloud of incense may cover the mercy seat that *is* on the Testimony, lest he die. 14 He shall take some of the blood of the bull and sprinkle *it* with his finger on the mercy seat on the east *side;* and before the mercy seat he shall sprinkle some of the blood with his finger seven times.

15 "Then he shall kill the goat of the sin offering, which *is* for the people, bring its blood inside the veil, do with that blood as he did with the blood of the bull, and sprinkle it on the mercy seat and

תֵּצֵא מִמֶּנּוּ שִׁכְבַת־זֶרַע לְטָמְאָה־בָהּ: 33 וְהַדָּוָה בְּנִדָּתָהּ וְהַזָּב אֶת־זוֹבוֹ לַזָּכָר וְלַנְּקֵבָה וּלְאִישׁ אֲשֶׁר יִשְׁכַּב עִם־טְמֵאָה: פ

טז וַיְדַבֵּר יְהוָה אֶל־מֹשֶׁה אַחֲרֵי מוֹת שְׁנֵי בְּנֵי אַהֲרֹן בְּקָרְבָתָם לִפְנֵי־יְהוָה וַיָּמֻתוּ: 2 וַיֹּאמֶר יְהוָה אֶל־מֹשֶׁה דַּבֵּר אֶל־אַהֲרֹן אָחִיךָ וְאַל־יָבֹא בְכָל־עֵת אֶל־הַקֹּדֶשׁ מִבֵּית לַפָּרֹכֶת אֶל־פְּנֵי הַכַּפֹּרֶת אֲשֶׁר עַל־הָאָרֹן וְלֹא יָמוּת כִּי בֶּעָנָן אֵרָאֶה עַל־הַכַּפֹּרֶת: 3 בְּזֹאת יָבֹא אַהֲרֹן אֶל־הַקֹּדֶשׁ בְּפַר בֶּן־בָּקָר לְחַטָּאת וְאַיִל לְעֹלָה: 4 כְּתֹנֶת־בַּד קֹדֶשׁ יִלְבָּשׁ וּמִכְנְסֵי־בַד יִהְיוּ עַל־בְּשָׂרוֹ וּבְאַבְנֵט בַּד יַחְגֹּר וּבְמִצְנֶפֶת בַּד יִצְנֹף בִּגְדֵי־קֹדֶשׁ הֵם וְרָחַץ בַּמַּיִם אֶת־בְּשָׂרוֹ וּלְבֵשָׁם: 5 וּמֵאֵת עֲדַת בְּנֵי יִשְׂרָאֵל יִקַּח שְׁנֵי־שְׂעִירֵי עִזִּים לְחַטָּאת וְאַיִל אֶחָד לְעֹלָה: 6 וְהִקְרִיב אַהֲרֹן אֶת־פַּר הַחַטָּאת אֲשֶׁר־לוֹ וְכִפֶּר בַּעֲדוֹ וּבְעַד בֵּיתוֹ: 7 וְלָקַח אֶת־שְׁנֵי הַשְּׂעִירִם וְהֶעֱמִיד אֹתָם לִפְנֵי יְהוָה פֶּתַח אֹהֶל מוֹעֵד: 8 וְנָתַן אַהֲרֹן עַל־שְׁנֵי הַשְּׂעִירִם גּוֹרָלוֹת גּוֹרָל אֶחָד לַיהוָה וְגוֹרָל אֶחָד לַעֲזָאזֵל: 9 וְהִקְרִיב אַהֲרֹן אֶת־הַשָּׂעִיר אֲשֶׁר עָלָה עָלָיו הַגּוֹרָל לַיהוָה וְעָשָׂהוּ חַטָּאת: 10 וְהַשָּׂעִיר אֲשֶׁר עָלָה עָלָיו הַגּוֹרָל לַעֲזָאזֵל יָעֳמַד־חַי לִפְנֵי יְהוָה לְכַפֵּר עָלָיו לְשַׁלַּח אֹתוֹ לַעֲזָאזֵל הַמִּדְבָּרָה: 11 וְהִקְרִיב אַהֲרֹן אֶת־פַּר הַחַטָּאת אֲשֶׁר־לוֹ וְכִפֶּר בַּעֲדוֹ וּבְעַד בֵּיתוֹ וְשָׁחַט אֶת־פַּר הַחַטָּאת אֲשֶׁר־לוֹ: 12 וְלָקַח מְלֹא־הַמַּחְתָּה גַּחֲלֵי־אֵשׁ מֵעַל הַמִּזְבֵּחַ מִלִּפְנֵי יְהוָה וּמְלֹא חָפְנָיו קְטֹרֶת סַמִּים דַּקָּה וְהֵבִיא מִבֵּית לַפָּרֹכֶת: 13 וְנָתַן אֶת־הַקְּטֹרֶת עַל־הָאֵשׁ לִפְנֵי יְהוָה וְכִסָּה עֲנַן הַקְּטֹרֶת אֶת־הַכַּפֹּרֶת אֲשֶׁר עַל־הָעֵדוּת וְלֹא יָמוּת: 14 וְלָקַח מִדַּם הַפָּר וְהִזָּה בְאֶצְבָּעוֹ עַל־פְּנֵי הַכַּפֹּרֶת קֵדְמָה וְלִפְנֵי הַכַּפֹּרֶת יַזֶּה שֶׁבַע־פְּעָמִים מִן־הַדָּם בְּאֶצְבָּעוֹ: 15 וְשָׁחַט אֶת־שְׂעִיר הַחַטָּאת אֲשֶׁר לָעָם וְהֵבִיא אֶת־דָּמוֹ אֶל־מִבֵּית לַפָּרֹכֶת וְעָשָׂה אֶת־דָּמוֹ כַּאֲשֶׁר עָשָׂה לְדַם הַפָּר

before the mercy seat. [16] So he shall make atonement for the Holy *Place,* because of the uncleanness of the children of Israel, and because of their transgressions, for all their sins; and so he shall do for the tabernacle of meeting which remains among them in the midst of their uncleanness. [17] There shall be no man in the tabernacle of meeting when he goes in to make atonement in the Holy *Place,* until he comes out, that he may make atonement for himself, for his household, and for all the assembly of Israel. [18] And he shall go out to the altar that *is* before the LORD, and make atonement for it, and shall take some of the blood of the bull and some of the blood of the goat, and put it on the horns of the altar all around. [19] Then he shall sprinkle some of the blood on it with his finger seven times, cleanse it, and consecrate it from the uncleanness of the children of Israel.

[20] "And when he has made an end of atoning for the Holy *Place,* the tabernacle of meeting, and the altar, he shall bring the live goat. [21] Aaron shall lay both his hands on the head of the live goat, confess over it all the iniquities of the children of Israel, and all their transgressions, concerning all their sins, putting them on the head of the goat, and shall send *it* away into the wilderness by the hand of a suitable man. [22] The goat shall bear on itself all their iniquities to an uninhabited land; and he shall release the goat in the wilderness.

[23] "Then Aaron shall come into the tabernacle of meeting, shall take off the linen garments which he put on when he went into the Holy *Place,* and shall leave them there. [24] And he shall wash his body with water in a holy place, put on his garments, come out and offer his burnt offering and the burnt offering of the people, and make atonement for himself and for the people. [25] The fat of the sin offering he shall burn on the altar. [26] And he who released the goat as the scapegoat shall wash his clothes and bathe his body in water, and afterward he may come into the camp. [27] The bull *for* the sin offering and the goat *for* the sin offering, whose blood was brought in to make atonement in the Holy *Place,* shall be carried outside the camp. And they shall burn in the fire their skins, their flesh, and their offal. [28] Then he who burns them shall wash his clothes and bathe his body in water, and afterward he may come into the camp.

[29] "This shall be a statute forever for you: In the seventh month, on the tenth *day* of the month, you shall afflict your souls, and do no work at all, *whether* a native of your own country or a stranger who dwells among you. [30] For on that day *the priest* shall make atonement for you, to cleanse you, *that*

וְהִזָּה אֹתוֹ עַל־הַכַּפֹּרֶת וְלִפְנֵי הַכַּפֹּרֶת: 16 וְכִפֶּר עַל־הַקֹּדֶשׁ מִטֻּמְאֹת בְּנֵי יִשְׂרָאֵל וּמִפִּשְׁעֵיהֶם לְכָל־חַטֹּאתָם וְכֵן יַעֲשֶׂה לְאֹהֶל מוֹעֵד הַשֹּׁכֵן אִתָּם בְּתוֹךְ טֻמְאֹתָם: 17 וְכָל־אָדָם לֹא־יִהְיֶה | בְּאֹהֶל מוֹעֵד בְּבֹאוֹ לְכַפֵּר בַּקֹּדֶשׁ עַד־צֵאתוֹ וְכִפֶּר בַּעֲדוֹ וּבְעַד בֵּיתוֹ וּבְעַד כָּל־קְהַל יִשְׂרָאֵל: 18 וְיָצָא אֶל־הַמִּזְבֵּחַ אֲשֶׁר לִפְנֵי־יְהוָה וְכִפֶּר עָלָיו וְלָקַח מִדַּם הַפָּר וּמִדַּם הַשָּׂעִיר וְנָתַן עַל־קַרְנוֹת הַמִּזְבֵּחַ סָבִיב: 19 וְהִזָּה עָלָיו מִן־הַדָּם בְּאֶצְבָּעוֹ שֶׁבַע פְּעָמִים וְטִהֲרוֹ וְקִדְּשׁוֹ מִטֻּמְאֹת בְּנֵי יִשְׂרָאֵל: 20 וְכִלָּה מִכַּפֵּר אֶת־הַקֹּדֶשׁ וְאֶת־אֹהֶל מוֹעֵד וְאֶת־הַמִּזְבֵּחַ וְהִקְרִיב אֶת־הַשָּׂעִיר הֶחָי: 21 וְסָמַךְ אַהֲרֹן אֶת־שְׁתֵּי יָדָו עַל רֹאשׁ הַשָּׂעִיר הַחַי וְהִתְוַדָּה עָלָיו אֶת־כָּל־עֲוֺנֹת בְּנֵי יִשְׂרָאֵל וְאֶת־כָּל־פִּשְׁעֵיהֶם לְכָל־חַטֹּאתָם וְנָתַן אֹתָם עַל־רֹאשׁ הַשָּׂעִיר וְשִׁלַּח בְּיַד־אִישׁ עִתִּי הַמִּדְבָּרָה: 22 וְנָשָׂא הַשָּׂעִיר עָלָיו אֶת־כָּל־עֲוֺנֹתָם אֶל־אֶרֶץ גְּזֵרָה וְשִׁלַּח אֶת־הַשָּׂעִיר בַּמִּדְבָּר: 23 וּבָא אַהֲרֹן אֶל־אֹהֶל מוֹעֵד וּפָשַׁט אֶת־בִּגְדֵי הַבָּד אֲשֶׁר לָבַשׁ בְּבֹאוֹ אֶל־הַקֹּדֶשׁ וְהִנִּיחָם שָׁם: 24 וְרָחַץ אֶת־בְּשָׂרוֹ בַמַּיִם בְּמָקוֹם קָדוֹשׁ וְלָבַשׁ אֶת־בְּגָדָיו וְיָצָא וְעָשָׂה אֶת־עֹלָתוֹ וְאֶת־עֹלַת הָעָם וְכִפֶּר בַּעֲדוֹ וּבְעַד הָעָם: 25 וְאֵת חֵלֶב הַחַטָּאת יַקְטִיר הַמִּזְבֵּחָה: 26 וְהַמְשַׁלֵּחַ אֶת־הַשָּׂעִיר לַעֲזָאזֵל יְכַבֵּס בְּגָדָיו וְרָחַץ אֶת־בְּשָׂרוֹ בַּמָּיִם וְאַחֲרֵי־כֵן יָבוֹא אֶל־הַמַּחֲנֶה: 27 וְאֵת פַּר הַחַטָּאת וְאֵת | שְׂעִיר הַחַטָּאת אֲשֶׁר הוּבָא אֶת־דָּמָם לְכַפֵּר בַּקֹּדֶשׁ יוֹצִיא אֶל־מִחוּץ לַמַּחֲנֶה וְשָׂרְפוּ בָאֵשׁ אֶת־עֹרֹתָם וְאֶת־בְּשָׂרָם וְאֶת־פִּרְשָׁם: 28 וְהַשֹּׂרֵף אֹתָם יְכַבֵּס בְּגָדָיו וְרָחַץ אֶת־בְּשָׂרוֹ בַּמָּיִם וְאַחֲרֵי־כֵן יָבוֹא אֶל־הַמַּחֲנֶה: 29 וְהָיְתָה לָכֶם לְחֻקַּת עוֹלָם בַּחֹדֶשׁ הַשְּׁבִיעִי בֶּעָשׂוֹר לַחֹדֶשׁ תְּעַנּוּ אֶת־נַפְשֹׁתֵיכֶם וְכָל־מְלָאכָה לֹא תַעֲשׂוּ הָאֶזְרָח וְהַגֵּר הַגָּר בְּתוֹכְכֶם: 30 כִּי־בַיּוֹם הַזֶּה יְכַפֵּר עֲלֵיכֶם לְטַהֵר אֶתְכֶם מִכֹּל

you may be clean from all your sins before the LORD. ³¹ It *is* a sabbath of solemn rest for you, and you shall afflict your souls. *It is* a statute forever. ³² And the priest, who is anointed and consecrated to minister as priest in his father's place, shall make atonement, and put on the linen clothes, the holy garments; ³³ then he shall make atonement for the Holy Sanctuary, and he shall make atonement for the tabernacle of meeting and for the altar, and he shall make atonement for the priests and for all the people of the assembly. ³⁴ This shall be an everlasting statute for you, to make atonement for the children of Israel, for all their sins, once a year." And he did as the LORD commanded Moses.

17 And the LORD spoke to Moses, saying, ² "Speak to Aaron, to his sons, and to all the children of Israel, and say to them, 'This *is* the thing which the LORD has commanded, saying: ³ "Whatever man of the house of Israel who kills an ox or lamb or goat in the camp, or who kills *it* outside the camp, ⁴ and does not bring it to the door of the tabernacle of meeting to offer an offering to the LORD before the tabernacle of the LORD, the guilt of bloodshed shall be imputed to that man. He has shed blood; and that man shall be cut off from among his people, ⁵ to the end that the children of Israel may bring their sacrifices which they offer in the open field, that they may bring them to the LORD at the door of the tabernacle of meeting, to the priest, and offer them *as* peace offerings to the LORD. ⁶ And the priest shall sprinkle the blood on the altar of the LORD *at* the door of the tabernacle of meeting, and burn the fat for a sweet aroma to the LORD. ⁷ They shall no more offer their sacrifices to demons, after whom they have played the harlot. This shall be a statute forever for them throughout their generations." '

⁸ "Also you shall say to them: 'Whatever man of the house of Israel, or of the strangers who dwell among you, who offers a burnt offering or sacrifice, ⁹ and does not bring it to the door of the tabernacle of meeting, to offer it to the LORD, that man shall be cut off from among his people.

¹⁰ 'And whatever man of the house of Israel, or of the strangers who dwell among you, who eats any blood, I will set My face against that person who eats blood, and will cut him off from among his people. ¹¹ For the life of the flesh *is* in the blood, and I have given it to you upon the altar to make atonement for your souls; for it *is* the blood *that* makes atonement for the soul.' ¹² Therefore I said

חֲטָאתֵיכֶם לִפְנֵי יְהוָה תִּטְהָרוּ: 31 שַׁבַּת שַׁבָּתוֹן הִיא לָכֶם וְעִנִּיתֶם אֶת־נַפְשֹׁתֵיכֶם חֻקַּת עוֹלָם: 32 וְכִפֶּר הַכֹּהֵן אֲשֶׁר־יִמְשַׁח אֹתוֹ וַאֲשֶׁר יְמַלֵּא אֶת־יָדוֹ לְכַהֵן תַּחַת אָבִיו וְלָבַשׁ אֶת־בִּגְדֵי הַבָּד בִּגְדֵי הַקֹּדֶשׁ: 33 וְכִפֶּר אֶת־מִקְדַּשׁ הַקֹּדֶשׁ וְאֶת־ אֹהֶל מוֹעֵד וְאֶת־הַמִּזְבֵּחַ יְכַפֵּר וְעַל הַכֹּהֲנִים וְעַל־ כָּל־עַם הַקָּהָל יְכַפֵּר: 34 וְהָיְתָה־זֹּאת לָכֶם לְחֻקַּת עוֹלָם לְכַפֵּר עַל־בְּנֵי יִשְׂרָאֵל מִכָּל־חַטֹּאתָם אַחַת בַּשָּׁנָה וַיַּעַשׂ כַּאֲשֶׁר צִוָּה יְהוָה אֶת־מֹשֶׁה: פ

יז וַיְדַבֵּר יְהוָה אֶל־מֹשֶׁה לֵּאמֹר: 2 דַּבֵּר אֶל־אַהֲרֹן וְאֶל־בָּנָיו וְאֶל כָּל־בְּנֵי יִשְׂרָאֵל וְאָמַרְתָּ אֲלֵיהֶם זֶה הַדָּבָר אֲשֶׁר־צִוָּה יְהוָה לֵאמֹר: 3 אִישׁ אִישׁ מִבֵּית יִשְׂרָאֵל אֲשֶׁר יִשְׁחַט שׁוֹר אוֹ־כֶשֶׂב אוֹ־עֵז בַּמַּחֲנֶה אוֹ אֲשֶׁר יִשְׁחַט מִחוּץ לַמַּחֲנֶה: 4 וְאֶל־פֶּתַח אֹהֶל מוֹעֵד לֹא הֱבִיאוֹ לְהַקְרִיב קָרְבָּן לַיהוָה לִפְנֵי מִשְׁכַּן יְהוָה דָּם יֵחָשֵׁב לָאִישׁ הַהוּא דָּם שָׁפָךְ וְנִכְרַת הָאִישׁ הַהוּא מִקֶּרֶב עַמּוֹ: 5 לְמַעַן אֲשֶׁר יָבִיאוּ בְּנֵי יִשְׂרָאֵל אֶת־זִבְחֵיהֶם אֲשֶׁר הֵם זֹבְחִים עַל־פְּנֵי הַשָּׂדֶה וֶהֱבִיאֻם לַיהוָה אֶל־פֶּתַח אֹהֶל מוֹעֵד אֶל־ הַכֹּהֵן וְזָבְחוּ זִבְחֵי שְׁלָמִים לַיהוָה אוֹתָם: 6 וְזָרַק הַכֹּהֵן אֶת־הַדָּם עַל־מִזְבַּח יְהוָה פֶּתַח אֹהֶל מוֹעֵד וְהִקְטִיר הַחֵלֶב לְרֵיחַ נִיחֹחַ לַיהוָה: 7 וְלֹא־יִזְבְּחוּ עוֹד אֶת־זִבְחֵיהֶם לַשְּׂעִירִם אֲשֶׁר הֵם זֹנִים אַחֲרֵיהֶם חֻקַּת עוֹלָם תִּהְיֶה־זֹּאת לָהֶם לְדֹרֹתָם: 8 וַאֲלֵהֶם תֹּאמַר אִישׁ אִישׁ מִבֵּית יִשְׂרָאֵל וּמִן־הַגֵּר אֲשֶׁר־ יָגוּר בְּתוֹכָם אֲשֶׁר־יַעֲלֶה עֹלָה אוֹ־זָבַח: 9 וְאֶל־ פֶּתַח אֹהֶל מוֹעֵד לֹא יְבִיאֶנּוּ לַעֲשׂוֹת אֹתוֹ לַיהוָה וְנִכְרַת הָאִישׁ הַהוּא מֵעַמָּיו: 10 וְאִישׁ אִישׁ מִבֵּית יִשְׂרָאֵל וּמִן־הַגֵּר הַגָּר בְּתוֹכָם אֲשֶׁר יֹאכַל כָּל־דָּם וְנָתַתִּי פָנַי בַּנֶּפֶשׁ הָאֹכֶלֶת אֶת־הַדָּם וְהִכְרַתִּי אֹתָהּ מִקֶּרֶב עַמָּהּ: 11 כִּי נֶפֶשׁ הַבָּשָׂר בַּדָּם הִוא וַאֲנִי נְתַתִּיו לָכֶם עַל־הַמִּזְבֵּחַ לְכַפֵּר עַל־נַפְשֹׁתֵיכֶם כִּי־ הַדָּם הוּא בַּנֶּפֶשׁ יְכַפֵּר: 12 עַל־כֵּן אָמַרְתִּי לִבְנֵי יִשְׂרָאֵל כָּל־נֶפֶשׁ מִכֶּם לֹא־תֹאכַל דָּם וְהַגֵּר הַגָּר

to the children of Israel, 'No one among you shall eat blood, nor shall any stranger who dwells among you eat blood.'

13 "Whatever man of the children of Israel, or of the strangers who dwell among you, who hunts and catches any animal or bird that may be eaten, he shall pour out its blood and cover it with dust; 14 for *it is* the life of all flesh. Its blood sustains its life. Therefore I said to the children of Israel, 'You shall not eat the blood of any flesh, for the life of all flesh is its blood. Whoever eats it shall be cut off.'

15 "And every person who eats what died *naturally* or what was torn *by beasts, whether he is* a native of your own country or a stranger, he shall both wash his clothes and bathe in water, and be unclean until evening. Then he shall be clean. 16 But if he does not wash *them* or bathe his body, then he shall bear his guilt."

18 Then the LORD spoke to Moses, saying, 2 "Speak to the children of Israel, and say to them: 'I am the LORD your God. 3 According to the doings of the land of Egypt, where you dwelt, you shall not do; and according to the doings of the land of Canaan, where I am bringing you, you shall not do; nor shall you walk in their ordinances. 4 You shall observe My judgments and keep My ordinances, to walk in them: I *am* the LORD your God. 5 You shall therefore keep My statutes and My judgments, which if a man does, he shall live by them: I *am* the LORD.

6 'None of you shall approach anyone who is near of kin to him, to uncover his nakedness: I *am* the LORD. 7 The nakedness of your father or the nakedness of your mother you shall not uncover. She *is* your mother; you shall not uncover her nakedness. 8 The nakedness of your father's wife you shall not uncover; it *is* your father's nakedness. 9 The nakedness of your sister, the daughter of your father, or the daughter of your mother, *whether* born at home or elsewhere, their nakedness you shall not uncover. 10 The nakedness of your son's daughter or your daughter's daughter, their nakedness you shall not uncover; for theirs *is* your own nakedness. 11 The nakedness of your father's wife's daughter, begotten by your father—she *is* your sister—you shall not uncover her nakedness. 12 You shall not uncover the nakedness of your father's sister; she *is* near of kin to your father. 13 You shall not uncover the nakedness of your mother's sister, for she *is* near of kin to your mother. 14 You shall not uncover the nakedness of your father's brother. You shall not approach his wife; she *is* your aunt. 15 You shall not uncover the nakedness of your

13 וְאִישׁ אִישׁ   ס   בְּתוֹכְכֶם לֹא־יֹאכַל דָּם:

מִבְּנֵי יִשְׂרָאֵל וּמִן־הַגֵּר הַגָּר בְּתוֹכָם אֲשֶׁר יָצוּד צֵיד

חַיָּה אוֹ־עוֹף אֲשֶׁר יֵאָכֵל וְשָׁפַךְ אֶת־דָּמוֹ וְכִסָּהוּ

בֶּעָפָר: 14 כִּי־נֶפֶשׁ כָּל־בָּשָׂר דָּמוֹ בְנַפְשׁוֹ הוּא וָאֹמַר

לִבְנֵי יִשְׂרָאֵל דַּם כָּל־בָּשָׂר לֹא תֹאכֵלוּ כִּי נֶפֶשׁ

כָּל־בָּשָׂר דָּמוֹ הִוא כָּל־אֹכְלָיו יִכָּרֵת: 15 וְכָל־נֶפֶשׁ

אֲשֶׁר תֹּאכַל נְבֵלָה וּטְרֵפָה בָּאֶזְרָח וּבַגֵּר וְכִבֶּס

בְּגָדָיו וְרָחַץ בַּמַּיִם וְטָמֵא עַד־הָעֶרֶב וְטָהֵר: 16 וְאִם

לֹא יְכַבֵּס וּבְשָׂרוֹ לֹא יִרְחָץ וְנָשָׂא עֲוֹנוֹ:   פ

יח וַיְדַבֵּר יְהוָה אֶל־מֹשֶׁה לֵּאמֹר: 2 דַּבֵּר אֶל־

בְּנֵי יִשְׂרָאֵל וְאָמַרְתָּ אֲלֵהֶם אֲנִי יְהוָה אֱלֹהֵיכֶם:

3 כְּמַעֲשֵׂה אֶרֶץ־מִצְרַיִם אֲשֶׁר יְשַׁבְתֶּם־בָּהּ לֹא

תַעֲשׂוּ וּכְמַעֲשֵׂה אֶרֶץ־כְּנַעַן אֲשֶׁר אֲנִי מֵבִיא

אֶתְכֶם שָׁמָּה לֹא תַעֲשׂוּ וּבְחֻקֹּתֵיהֶם לֹא תֵלֵכוּ:

4 אֶת־מִשְׁפָּטַי תַּעֲשׂוּ וְאֶת־חֻקֹּתַי תִּשְׁמְרוּ לָלֶכֶת

בָּהֶם אֲנִי יְהוָה אֱלֹהֵיכֶם: 5 וּשְׁמַרְתֶּם אֶת־חֻקֹּתַי

וְאֶת־מִשְׁפָּטַי אֲשֶׁר יַעֲשֶׂה אֹתָם הָאָדָם וָחַי

בָּהֶם אֲנִי יְהוָה: ס   6 אִישׁ אִישׁ אֶל־

כָּל־שְׁאֵר בְּשָׂרוֹ לֹא תִקְרְבוּ לְגַלּוֹת עֶרְוָה אֲנִי

יְהוָה: ס   7 עֶרְוַת אָבִיךָ וְעֶרְוַת אִמְּךָ לֹא תְגַלֵּה

אִמְּךָ הִוא לֹא תְגַלֶּה עֶרְוָתָהּ: 8 עֶרְוַת אֵשֶׁת־   ס

אָבִיךָ לֹא תְגַלֵּה עֶרְוַת אָבִיךָ הִוא: ס   9 עֶרְוַת

אֲחוֹתְךָ בַת־אָבִיךָ אוֹ בַת־אִמֶּךָ מוֹלֶדֶת בַּיִת אוֹ

מוֹלֶדֶת חוּץ לֹא תְגַלֶּה עֶרְוָתָן: ס   10 עֶרְוַת

בַּת־בִּנְךָ אוֹ בַת־בִּתְּךָ לֹא תְגַלֶּה עֶרְוָתָן

כִּי עֶרְוָתְךָ הֵנָּה: ס   11 עֶרְוַת בַּת־אֵשֶׁת

אָבִיךָ מוֹלֶדֶת אָבִיךָ אֲחוֹתְךָ הִוא לֹא תְגַלֵּה

עֶרְוָתָהּ:   ס   12 עֶרְוַת אֲחוֹת־אָבִיךָ לֹא תְגַלֵּה

שְׁאֵר אָבִיךָ הִוא: ס   13 עֶרְוַת אֲחוֹת־אִמְּךָ לֹא

תְגַלֵּה כִּי־שְׁאֵר אִמְּךָ הִוא: ס   14 עֶרְוַת אֲחִי־

אָבִיךָ לֹא תְגַלֵּה אֶל־אִשְׁתּוֹ לֹא תִקְרָב דֹּדָתְךָ

הִוא: ס   15 עֶרְוַת כַּלָּתְךָ לֹא תְגַלֵּה אֵשֶׁת בִּנְךָ

daughter-in-law—she *is* your son's wife—you shall not uncover her nakedness. [16] You shall not uncover the nakedness of your brother's wife; it *is* your brother's nakedness. [17] You shall not uncover the nakedness of a woman and her daughter, nor shall you take her son's daughter or her daughter's daughter, to uncover her nakedness. They *are* near of kin to her. It *is* wickedness. [18] Nor shall you take a woman as a rival to her sister, to uncover her nakedness while the other is alive.

[19] 'Also you shall not approach a woman to uncover her nakedness as long as she is in her *customary* impurity. [20] Moreover you shall not lie carnally with your neighbor's wife, to defile yourself with her. [21] And you shall not let any of your descendants pass through *the fire* to Molech, nor shall you profane the name of your God: I *am* the LORD. [22] You shall not lie with a male as with a woman. It *is* an abomination. [23] Nor shall you mate with any animal, to defile yourself with it. Nor shall any woman stand before an animal to mate with it. It *is* perversion.

[24] 'Do not defile yourselves with any of these things; for by all these the nations are defiled, which I am casting out before you. [25] For the land is defiled; therefore I visit the punishment of its iniquity upon it, and the land vomits out its inhabitants. [26] You shall therefore keep My statutes and My judgments, and shall not commit *any* of these abominations, *either* any of your own nation or any stranger who dwells among you [27] (for all these abominations the men of the land have done, who *were* before you, and thus the land is defiled), [28] lest the land vomit you out also when you defile it, as it vomited out the nations that *were* before you. [29] For whoever commits any of these abominations, the persons who commit *them* shall be cut off from among their people.

[30] 'Therefore you shall keep My ordinance, so that *you* do not commit *any* of these abominable customs which were committed before you, and that you do not defile yourselves by them: I *am* the LORD your God.' "

19

And the LORD spoke to Moses, saying, [2] "Speak to all the congregation of the children of Israel, and say to them: 'You shall be holy, for I the LORD your God *am* holy.

[3] 'Every one of you shall revere his mother and his father, and keep My Sabbaths: I *am* the LORD your God.

[4] 'Do not turn to idols, nor make for yourselves molded gods: I *am* the LORD your God.

הוּא לֹא תְגַלֶּה עֶרְוָתָהּ: ס 16 עֶרְוַת אֵשֶׁת־
אָחִיךָ לֹא תְגַלֵּה עֶרְוַת אָחִיךָ הִוא: ס 17 עֶרְוַת
אִשָּׁה וּבִתָּהּ לֹא תְגַלֵּה אֶת־בַּת־בְּנָהּ וְאֶת־בַּת־
בִּתָּהּ לֹא תִקַּח לְגַלּוֹת עֶרְוָתָהּ שַׁאֲרָה הֵנָּה
זִמָּה הִוא: 18 וְאִשָּׁה אֶל־אֲחֹתָהּ לֹא תִקָּח לִצְרֹר
לְגַלּוֹת עֶרְוָתָהּ עָלֶיהָ בְּחַיֶּיהָ: 19 וְאֶל־אִשָּׁה בְּנִדַּת
טֻמְאָתָהּ לֹא תִקְרַב לְגַלּוֹת עֶרְוָתָהּ: 20 וְאֶל־אֵשֶׁת
עֲמִיתְךָ לֹא־תִתֵּן שְׁכָבְתְּךָ לְזָרַע לְטָמְאָה־בָהּ:
21 וּמִזַּרְעֲךָ לֹא־תִתֵּן לְהַעֲבִיר לַמֹּלֶךְ וְלֹא תְחַלֵּל
אֶת־שֵׁם אֱלֹהֶיךָ אֲנִי יְהוָה: 22 וְאֶת־זָכָר לֹא
תִשְׁכַּב מִשְׁכְּבֵי אִשָּׁה תּוֹעֵבָה הִוא: 23 וּבְכָל־בְּהֵמָה
לֹא־תִתֵּן שְׁכָבְתְּךָ לְטָמְאָה־בָהּ וְאִשָּׁה לֹא־תַעֲמֹד
לִפְנֵי בְהֵמָה לְרִבְעָהּ תֶּבֶל הוּא: 24 אַל־תִּטַּמְּאוּ
בְּכָל־אֵלֶּה כִּי בְכָל־אֵלֶּה נִטְמְאוּ הַגּוֹיִם אֲשֶׁר־
אֲנִי מְשַׁלֵּחַ מִפְּנֵיכֶם: 25 וַתִּטְמָא הָאָרֶץ וָאֶפְקֹד
עֲוֺנָהּ עָלֶיהָ וַתָּקִא הָאָרֶץ אֶת־יֹשְׁבֶיהָ: 26 וּשְׁמַרְתֶּם
אַתֶּם אֶת־חֻקֹּתַי וְאֶת־מִשְׁפָּטַי וְלֹא תַעֲשׂוּ מִכֹּל
הַתּוֹעֵבֹת הָאֵלֶּה הָאֶזְרָח וְהַגֵּר הַגָּר בְּתוֹכְכֶם:
27 כִּי אֶת־כָּל־הַתּוֹעֵבֹת הָאֵל עָשׂוּ אַנְשֵׁי־הָאָרֶץ
אֲשֶׁר לִפְנֵיכֶם וַתִּטְמָא הָאָרֶץ: 28 וְלֹא־תָקִיא הָאָרֶץ
אֶתְכֶם בְּטַמַּאֲכֶם אֹתָהּ כַּאֲשֶׁר קָאָה אֶת־הַגּוֹי אֲשֶׁר
לִפְנֵיכֶם: 29 כִּי כָּל־אֲשֶׁר יַעֲשֶׂה מִכֹּל הַתּוֹעֵבֹת
הָאֵלֶּה וְנִכְרְתוּ הַנְּפָשׁוֹת הָעֹשֹׂת מִקֶּרֶב עַמָּם:
30 וּשְׁמַרְתֶּם אֶת־מִשְׁמַרְתִּי לְבִלְתִּי עֲשׂוֹת מֵחֻקּוֹת
הַתּוֹעֵבֹת אֲשֶׁר נַעֲשׂוּ לִפְנֵיכֶם וְלֹא תִטַּמְּאוּ בָּהֶם
אֲנִי יְהוָה אֱלֹהֵיכֶם: פ

יט וַיְדַבֵּר יְהוָה אֶל־מֹשֶׁה לֵּאמֹר: 2 דַּבֵּר אֶל־
כָּל־עֲדַת בְּנֵי־יִשְׂרָאֵל וְאָמַרְתָּ אֲלֵהֶם קְדֹשִׁים תִּהְיוּ
כִּי קָדוֹשׁ אֲנִי יְהוָה אֱלֹהֵיכֶם: 3 אִישׁ אִמּוֹ וְאָבִיו
תִּירָאוּ וְאֶת־שַׁבְּתֹתַי תִּשְׁמֹרוּ אֲנִי יְהוָה אֱלֹהֵיכֶם:
4 אַל־תִּפְנוּ אֶל־הָאֱלִילִים וֵאלֹהֵי מַסֵּכָה לֹא תַעֲשׂוּ

5 'And if you offer a sacrifice of a peace offering to the LORD, you shall offer it of your own free will. 6 It shall be eaten the same day you offer *it*, and on the next day. And if any remains until the third day, it shall be burned in the fire. 7 And if it is eaten at all on the third day, it *is* an abomination. It shall not be accepted. 8 Therefore *everyone* who eats it shall bear his iniquity, because he has profaned the hallowed *offering* of the LORD; and that person shall be cut off from his people.

9 'When you reap the harvest of your land, you shall not wholly reap the corners of your field, nor shall you gather the gleanings of your harvest. 10 And you shall not glean your vineyard, nor shall you gather *every* grape of your vineyard; you shall leave them for the poor and the stranger: I *am* the LORD your God.

11 'You shall not steal, nor deal falsely, nor lie to one another. 12 And you shall not swear by My name falsely, nor shall you profane the name of your God: I *am* the LORD.

13 'You shall not cheat your neighbor, nor rob *him*. The wages of him who is hired shall not remain with you all night until morning. 14 You shall not curse the deaf, nor put a stumbling block before the blind, but shall fear your God: I *am* the LORD.

15 'You shall do no injustice in judgment. You shall not be partial to the poor, nor honor the person of the mighty. In righteousness you shall judge your neighbor. 16 You shall not go about *as* a talebearer among your people; nor shall you take a stand against the life of your neighbor: I *am* the LORD.

17 'You shall not hate your brother in your heart. You shall surely rebuke your neighbor, and not bear sin because of him. 18 You shall not take vengeance, nor bear any grudge against the children of your people, but you shall love your neighbor as yourself: I *am* the LORD.

19 'You shall keep My statutes. You shall not let your livestock breed with another kind. You shall not sow your field with mixed seed. Nor shall a garment of mixed linen and wool come upon you.

20 'Whoever lies carnally with a woman who *is* betrothed to a man as a concubine, and who has not at all been redeemed nor given her freedom, for this there shall be scourging; *but* they shall not be put to death, because she was not free. 21 And he shall bring his trespass offering to the LORD, to the door of the tabernacle of meeting, a ram as a trespass offering. 22 The priest shall make atonement for him with the ram of the trespass offering

לָכֶם אֲנִי יְהֹוָה אֱלֹהֵיכֶם: 5 וְכִי תִזְבְּחוּ זֶבַח שְׁלָמִים
לַיהֹוָה לִרְצֹנְכֶם תִּזְבָּחֻהוּ: 6 בְּיוֹם זִבְחֲכֶם יֵאָכֵל
וּמִמָּחֳרָת וְהַנּוֹתָר עַד־יוֹם הַשְּׁלִישִׁי בָּאֵשׁ יִשָּׂרֵף:

7 וְאִם הֵאָכֹל יֵאָכֵל בַּיּוֹם הַשְּׁלִישִׁי פִּגּוּל הוּא
לֹא יֵרָצֶה: 8 וְאֹכְלָיו עֲוֹנוֹ יִשָּׂא כִּי־אֶת־קֹדֶשׁ יְהֹוָה
חִלֵּל וְנִכְרְתָה הַנֶּפֶשׁ הַהִוא מֵעַמֶּיהָ: 9 וּבְקֻצְרְכֶם
אֶת־קְצִיר אַרְצְכֶם לֹא תְכַלֶּה פְּאַת שָׂדְךָ לִקְצֹר
וְלֶקֶט קְצִירְךָ לֹא תְלַקֵּט: 10 וְכַרְמְךָ לֹא תְעוֹלֵל
וּפֶרֶט כַּרְמְךָ לֹא תְלַקֵּט לֶעָנִי וְלַגֵּר תַּעֲזֹב אֹתָם
אֲנִי יְהֹוָה אֱלֹהֵיכֶם: 11 לֹא תִּגְנֹבוּ וְלֹא־תְכַחֲשׁוּ
וְלֹא־תְשַׁקְּרוּ אִישׁ בַּעֲמִיתוֹ: 12 וְלֹא־תִשָּׁבְעוּ בִשְׁמִי
לַשָּׁקֶר וְחִלַּלְתָּ אֶת־שֵׁם אֱלֹהֶיךָ אֲנִי יְהֹוָה: 13 לֹא־
תַעֲשֹׁק אֶת־רֵעֲךָ וְלֹא תִגְזֹל לֹא־תָלִין פְּעֻלַּת שָׂכִיר
אִתְּךָ עַד־בֹּקֶר: 14 לֹא־תְקַלֵּל חֵרֵשׁ וְלִפְנֵי עִוֵּר לֹא
תִתֵּן מִכְשֹׁל וְיָרֵאתָ מֵּאֱלֹהֶיךָ אֲנִי יְהֹוָה: 15 לֹא־
תַעֲשׂוּ עָוֶל בַּמִּשְׁפָּט לֹא־תִשָּׂא פְנֵי־דָל וְלֹא תֶהְדַּר
פְּנֵי גָדוֹל בְּצֶדֶק תִּשְׁפֹּט עֲמִיתֶךָ: 16 לֹא־תֵלֵךְ רָכִיל
בְּעַמֶּיךָ לֹא תַעֲמֹד עַל־דַּם רֵעֶךָ אֲנִי יְהֹוָה: 17 לֹא־
תִשְׂנָא אֶת־אָחִיךָ בִּלְבָבֶךָ הוֹכֵחַ תּוֹכִיחַ אֶת־עֲמִיתֶךָ
וְלֹא־תִשָּׂא עָלָיו חֵטְא: 18 לֹא־תִקֹּם וְלֹא־תִטֹּר אֶת־
בְּנֵי עַמֶּךָ וְאָהַבְתָּ לְרֵעֲךָ כָּמוֹךָ אֲנִי יְהֹוָה: 19 אֶת־
חֻקֹּתַי תִּשְׁמֹרוּ בְּהֶמְתְּךָ לֹא־תַרְבִּיעַ כִּלְאַיִם שָׂדְךָ
לֹא־תִזְרַע כִּלְאָיִם וּבֶגֶד כִּלְאַיִם שַׁעַטְנֵז לֹא יַעֲלֶה
עָלֶיךָ:
פ

20 וְאִישׁ כִּי־יִשְׁכַּב אֶת־אִשָּׁה שִׁכְבַת־זֶרַע וְהִוא
שִׁפְחָה נֶחֱרֶפֶת לְאִישׁ וְהָפְדֵּה לֹא נִפְדָּתָה אוֹ
חֻפְשָׁה לֹא נִתַּן־לָהּ בִּקֹּרֶת תִּהְיֶה לֹא יוּמְתוּ כִּי־
לֹא חֻפָּשָׁה: 21 וְהֵבִיא אֶת־אֲשָׁמוֹ לַיהֹוָה אֶל־פֶּתַח
אֹהֶל מוֹעֵד אֵיל אָשָׁם: 22 וְכִפֶּר עָלָיו הַכֹּהֵן בְּאֵיל
הָאָשָׁם לִפְנֵי יְהֹוָה עַל־חַטָּאתוֹ אֲשֶׁר חָטָא וְנִסְלַח
לוֹ מֵחַטָּאתוֹ אֲשֶׁר חָטָא:
פ

before the LORD for his sin which he has committed. And the sin which he has committed shall be forgiven him.

23'When you come into the land, and have planted all kinds of trees for food, then you shall count their fruit as uncircumcised. Three years it shall be as uncircumcised to you. *It* shall not be eaten. 24But in the fourth year all its fruit shall be holy, a praise to the LORD. 25And in the fifth year you may eat its fruit, that it may yield to you its increase: I *am* the LORD your God.

26'You shall not eat *anything* with the blood, nor shall you practice divination or soothsaying. 27You shall not shave around the sides of your head, nor shall you disfigure the edges of your beard. 28You shall not make any cuttings in your flesh for the dead, nor tattoo any marks on you: I *am* the LORD.

29'Do not prostitute your daughter, to cause her to be a harlot, lest the land fall into harlotry, and the land become full of wickedness.

30'You shall keep My Sabbaths and reverence My sanctuary: I *am* the LORD.

31'Give no regard to mediums and familiar spirits; do not seek after them, to be defiled by them: I *am* the LORD your God.

32'You shall rise before the gray headed and honor the presence of an old man, and fear your God: I *am* the LORD.

33'And if a stranger dwells with you in your land, you shall not mistreat him. 34The stranger who dwells among you shall be to you as one born among you, and you shall love him as yourself; for you were strangers in the land of Egypt: I *am* the LORD your God.

35'You shall do no injustice in judgment, in measurement of length, weight, or volume. 36You shall have honest scales, honest weights, an honest ephah, and an honest hin: I *am* the LORD your God, who brought you out of the land of Egypt.

37'Therefore you shall observe all My statutes and all My judgments, and perform them: I *am* the LORD.'"

20 Then the LORD spoke to Moses, saying, 2"Again, you shall say to the children of Israel: 'Whoever of the children of Israel, or of the strangers who dwell in Israel, who gives *any* of his descendants to Molech, he shall surely be put to death. The people of the land shall stone him with stones. 3I will set My face against that man, and will cut him off from his people, because he has given *some* of his descendants to Molech, to defile My sanctuary and profane My holy name. 4And if the people of the land should in any way hide their

23 וְכִי־תָבֹ֣אוּ אֶל־הָאָ֗רֶץ וּנְטַעְתֶּם֙ כָּל־עֵ֣ץ מַאֲכָ֔ל וַעֲרַלְתֶּ֥ם עָרְלָת֖וֹ אֶת־פִּרְי֑וֹ שָׁלֹ֣שׁ שָׁנִ֗ים יִהְיֶ֥ה לָכֶ֛ם עֲרֵלִ֖ים לֹ֥א יֵאָכֵֽל׃ 24 וּבַשָּׁנָה֙ הָרְבִיעִ֔ת יִהְיֶ֖ה כָּל־פִּרְי֑וֹ קֹ֥דֶשׁ הִלּוּלִ֖ים לַיהוָֽה׃ 25 וּבַשָּׁנָ֣ה הַחֲמִישִׁ֗ת תֹּֽאכְלוּ֙ אֶת־פִּרְי֔וֹ לְהוֹסִ֥יף לָכֶ֖ם תְּבוּאָת֑וֹ אֲנִ֖י יְהוָ֥ה אֱלֹהֵיכֶֽם׃ 26 לֹ֥א תֹאכְל֖וּ עַל־הַדָּ֑ם לֹ֥א תְנַחֲשׁ֖וּ וְלֹ֥א תְעוֹנֵֽנוּ׃ 27 לֹ֣א תַקִּ֔פוּ פְּאַ֖ת רֹאשְׁכֶ֑ם וְלֹ֣א תַשְׁחִ֔ית אֵ֖ת פְּאַ֥ת זְקָנֶֽךָ׃ 28 וְשֶׂ֣רֶט לָנֶ֗פֶשׁ לֹ֤א תִתְּנוּ֙ בִּבְשַׂרְכֶ֔ם וּכְתֹ֣בֶת קַֽעֲקַ֔ע לֹ֥א תִתְּנ֖וּ בָּכֶ֑ם אֲנִ֖י יְהוָֽה׃ 29 אַל־תְּחַלֵּ֥ל אֶֽת־בִּתְּךָ֖ לְהַזְנוֹתָ֑הּ וְלֹא־תִזְנֶ֣ה הָאָ֔רֶץ וּמָלְאָ֥ה הָאָ֖רֶץ זִמָּֽה׃ 30 אֶת־שַׁבְּתֹתַ֣י תִּשְׁמֹ֔רוּ וּמִקְדָּשִׁ֖י תִּירָ֑אוּ אֲנִ֖י יְהוָֽה׃ 31 אַל־תִּפְנ֤וּ אֶל־הָֽאֹבֹת֙ וְאֶל־הַיִּדְּעֹנִ֔ים אַל־תְּבַקְשׁ֖וּ לְטָמְאָ֣ה בָהֶ֑ם אֲנִ֖י יְהוָ֥ה אֱלֹהֵיכֶֽם׃ 32 מִפְּנֵ֤י שֵׂיבָה֙ תָּק֔וּם וְהָדַרְתָּ֖ פְּנֵ֣י זָקֵ֑ן וְיָרֵ֥אתָ מֵּאֱלֹהֶ֖יךָ אֲנִ֥י יְהוָֽה׃ פ

33 וְכִֽי־יָג֧וּר אִתְּךָ֛ גֵּ֖ר בְּאַרְצְכֶ֑ם לֹ֥א תוֹנ֖וּ אֹתֽוֹ׃ 34 כְּאֶזְרָ֣ח מִכֶּ֗ם יִהְיֶ֤ה לָכֶם֙ הַגֵּ֣ר ׀ הַגָּ֣ר אִתְּכֶ֔ם וְאָהַבְתָּ֥ לוֹ֙ כָּמ֔וֹךָ כִּֽי־גֵרִ֥ים הֱיִיתֶ֖ם בְּאֶ֣רֶץ מִצְרָ֑יִם אֲנִ֖י יְהוָ֥ה אֱלֹהֵיכֶֽם׃ 35 לֹא־תַעֲשׂ֥וּ עָ֖וֶל בַּמִּשְׁפָּ֑ט בַּמִּדָּ֕ה בַּמִּשְׁקָ֖ל וּבַמְּשׂוּרָֽה׃ 36 מֹ֧אזְנֵי צֶ֣דֶק אַבְנֵי־צֶ֗דֶק אֵ֤יפַת צֶ֙דֶק֙ וְהִ֣ין צֶ֔דֶק יִהְיֶ֣ה לָכֶ֑ם אֲנִי֙ יְהוָ֣ה אֱלֹֽהֵיכֶ֔ם אֲשֶׁר־הוֹצֵ֥אתִי אֶתְכֶ֖ם מֵאֶ֥רֶץ מִצְרָֽיִם׃ 37 וּשְׁמַרְתֶּ֤ם אֶת־כָּל־חֻקֹּתַי֙ וְאֶת־כָּל־מִשְׁפָּטַ֔י וַעֲשִׂיתֶ֖ם אֹתָ֑ם אֲנִ֖י יְהוָֽה׃ פ

כ וַיְדַבֵּ֥ר יְהוָ֖ה אֶל־מֹשֶׁ֥ה לֵּאמֹֽר׃ 2 וְאֶל־בְּנֵ֣י יִשְׂרָאֵל֮ תֹּאמַר֒ אִ֣ישׁ אִישׁ֩ מִבְּנֵ֨י יִשְׂרָאֵ֜ל וּמִן־הַגֵּ֣ר ׀ הַגָּ֣ר בְּיִשְׂרָאֵ֗ל אֲשֶׁ֨ר יִתֵּ֧ן מִזַּרְע֛וֹ לַמֹּ֖לֶךְ מ֣וֹת יוּמָ֑ת עַ֥ם הָאָ֖רֶץ יִרְגְּמֻ֥הוּ בָאָֽבֶן׃ 3 וַאֲנִ֞י אֶתֵּ֤ן אֶת־פָּנַי֙ בָּאִ֣ישׁ הַה֔וּא וְהִכְרַתִּ֥י אֹת֖וֹ מִקֶּ֣רֶב עַמּ֑וֹ כִּ֤י מִזַּרְעוֹ֙ נָתַ֣ן לַמֹּ֔לֶךְ לְמַ֗עַן טַמֵּא֙ אֶת־מִקְדָּשִׁ֔י וּלְחַלֵּ֖ל אֶת־שֵׁ֥ם קָדְשִֽׁי׃ 4 וְאִ֡ם הַעְלֵ֣ם יַעְלִימוּ֩ עַ֨ם הָאָ֜רֶץ אֶת־עֵֽינֵיהֶ֗ם מִן־הָאִ֤ישׁ הַהוּא֙ בְּתִתּ֣וֹ מִזַּרְע֔וֹ לַמֹּ֖לֶךְ

eyes from the man, when he gives *some* of his descendants to Molech, and they do not kill him, ⁵then I will set My face against that man and against his family; and I will cut him off from his people, and all who prostitute themselves with him to commit harlotry with Molech.

⁶'And the person who turns to mediums and familiar spirits, to prostitute himself with them, I will set My face against that person and cut him off from his people. ⁷Consecrate yourselves therefore, and be holy, for I *am* the LORD your God. ⁸And you shall keep My statutes, and perform them: I *am* the LORD who sanctifies you.

⁹'For everyone who curses his father or his mother shall surely be put to death. He has cursed his father or his mother. His blood *shall be* upon him.

¹⁰'The man who commits adultery with *another* man's wife, *he* who commits adultery with his neighbor's wife, the adulterer and the adulteress, shall surely be put to death. ¹¹The man who lies with his father's wife has uncovered his father's nakedness; both of them shall surely be put to death. Their blood *shall be* upon them. ¹²If a man lies with his daughter-in-law, both of them shall surely be put to death. They have committed perversion. Their blood *shall be* upon them. ¹³If a man lies with a male as he lies with a woman, both of them have committed an abomination. They shall surely be put to death. Their blood *shall be* upon them. ¹⁴If a man marries a woman and her mother, it *is* wickedness. They shall be burned with fire, both he and they, that there may be no wickedness among you. ¹⁵If a man mates with an animal, he shall surely be put to death, and you shall kill the animal. ¹⁶If a woman approaches any animal and mates with it, you shall kill the woman and the animal. They shall surely be put to death. Their blood *is* upon them.

¹⁷'If a man takes his sister, his father's daughter or his mother's daughter, and sees her nakedness and she sees his nakedness, it *is* a wicked thing. And they shall be cut off in the sight of their people. He has uncovered his sister's nakedness. He shall bear his guilt. ¹⁸If a man lies with a woman during her sickness and uncovers her nakedness, he has exposed her flow, and she has uncovered the flow of her blood. Both of them shall be cut off from their people.

¹⁹'You shall not uncover the nakedness of your mother's sister nor of your father's sister, for that would uncover his near of kin. They shall bear their guilt. ²⁰If a man lies with his uncle's wife, he has uncovered his uncle's nakedness. They shall bear

לְבִלְתִּי הָמִית אֹתוֹ: 5 וְשַׂמְתִּי אֲנִי אֶת־פָּנַי בָּאִישׁ הַהוּא וּבְמִשְׁפַּחְתּוֹ וְהִכְרַתִּי אֹתוֹ וְאֵת | כָּל־הַזֹּנִים אַחֲרָיו לִזְנוֹת אַחֲרֵי הַמֹּלֶךְ מִקֶּרֶב עַמָּם:

6 וְהַנֶּפֶשׁ אֲשֶׁר תִּפְנֶה אֶל־הָאֹבֹת וְאֶל־הַיִּדְּעֹנִים לִזְנוֹת אַחֲרֵיהֶם וְנָתַתִּי אֶת־פָּנַי בַּנֶּפֶשׁ הַהִוא וְהִכְרַתִּי אֹתוֹ מִקֶּרֶב עַמּוֹ: 7 וְהִתְקַדִּשְׁתֶּם וִהְיִיתֶם קְדֹשִׁים כִּי אֲנִי יְהֹוָה אֱלֹהֵיכֶם: 8 וּשְׁמַרְתֶּם אֶת־חֻקֹּתַי וַעֲשִׂיתֶם אֹתָם אֲנִי יְהֹוָה מְקַדִּשְׁכֶם: 9 כִּי־אִישׁ אִישׁ אֲשֶׁר יְקַלֵּל אֶת־אָבִיו וְאֶת־אִמּוֹ מוֹת יוּמָת אָבִיו וְאִמּוֹ קִלֵּל דָּמָיו בּוֹ: 10 וְאִישׁ אֲשֶׁר יִנְאַף אֶת־אֵשֶׁת אִישׁ אֲשֶׁר יִנְאַף אֶת־אֵשֶׁת רֵעֵהוּ מוֹת־יוּמַת הַנֹּאֵף וְהַנֹּאָפֶת: 11 וְאִישׁ אֲשֶׁר יִשְׁכַּב אֶת־אֵשֶׁת אָבִיו עֶרְוַת אָבִיו גִּלָּה מוֹת־יוּמְתוּ שְׁנֵיהֶם דְּמֵיהֶם בָּם: 12 וְאִישׁ אֲשֶׁר יִשְׁכַּב אֶת־כַּלָּתוֹ מוֹת יוּמְתוּ שְׁנֵיהֶם תֶּבֶל עָשׂוּ דְּמֵיהֶם בָּם: 13 וְאִישׁ אֲשֶׁר יִשְׁכַּב אֶת־זָכָר מִשְׁכְּבֵי אִשָּׁה תּוֹעֵבָה עָשׂוּ שְׁנֵיהֶם מוֹת יוּמָתוּ דְּמֵיהֶם בָּם: 14 וְאִישׁ אֲשֶׁר יִקַּח אֶת־אִשָּׁה וְאֶת־אִמָּהּ זִמָּה הִוא בָּאֵשׁ יִשְׂרְפוּ אֹתוֹ וְאֶתְהֶן וְלֹא־תִהְיֶה זִמָּה בְּתוֹכְכֶם: 15 וְאִישׁ אֲשֶׁר יִתֵּן שְׁכָבְתּוֹ בִּבְהֵמָה מוֹת יוּמָת וְאֶת־הַבְּהֵמָה תַּהֲרֹגוּ: 16 וְאִשָּׁה אֲשֶׁר תִּקְרַב אֶל־כָּל־בְּהֵמָה לְרִבְעָה אֹתָהּ וְהָרַגְתָּ אֶת־הָאִשָּׁה וְאֶת־הַבְּהֵמָה מוֹת יוּמָתוּ דְּמֵיהֶם בָּם: 17 וְאִישׁ אֲשֶׁר־יִקַּח אֶת־אֲחֹתוֹ בַּת־אָבִיו אוֹ בַת־אִמּוֹ וְרָאָה אֶת־עֶרְוָתָהּ וְהִוא־תִרְאֶה אֶת־עֶרְוָתוֹ חֶסֶד הוּא וְנִכְרְתוּ לְעֵינֵי בְּנֵי עַמָּם עֶרְוַת אֲחֹתוֹ גִּלָּה עֲוֹנוֹ יִשָּׂא: 18 וְאִישׁ אֲשֶׁר־יִשְׁכַּב אֶת־אִשָּׁה דָּוָה וְגִלָּה אֶת־עֶרְוָתָהּ אֶת־מְקֹרָהּ הֶעֱרָה וְהִוא גִּלְּתָה אֶת־מְקוֹר דָּמֶיהָ וְנִכְרְתוּ שְׁנֵיהֶם מִקֶּרֶב עַמָּם: 19 וְעֶרְוַת אֲחוֹת אִמְּךָ וַאֲחוֹת אָבִיךָ לֹא תְגַלֵּה כִּי אֶת־שְׁאֵרוֹ הֶעֱרָה עֲוֹנָם יִשָּׂאוּ: 20 וְאִישׁ אֲשֶׁר יִשְׁכַּב אֶת־דֹּדָתוֹ עֶרְוַת דֹּדוֹ גִּלָּה

their sin; they shall die childless. ²¹ If a man takes his brother's wife, it *is* an unclean thing. He has uncovered his brother's nakedness. They shall be childless.

²² 'You shall therefore keep all My statutes and all My judgments, and perform them, that the land where I am bringing you to dwell may not vomit you out. ²³ And you shall not walk in the statutes of the nation which I am casting out before you; for they commit all these things, and therefore I abhor them. ²⁴ But I have said to you, "You shall inherit their land, and I will give it to you to possess, a land flowing with milk and honey." I *am* the LORD your God, who has separated you from the peoples. ²⁵ You shall therefore distinguish between clean animals and unclean, between unclean birds and clean, and you shall not make yourselves abominable by beast or by bird, or by any kind of living thing that creeps on the ground, which I have separated from you as unclean. ²⁶ And you shall be holy to Me, for I the LORD *am* holy, and have separated you from the peoples, that you should be Mine.

²⁷ 'A man or a woman who is a medium, or who has familiar spirits, shall surely be put to death; they shall stone them with stones. Their blood *shall be* upon them.' "

21 And the LORD said to Moses, "Speak to the priests, the sons of Aaron, and say to them: 'None shall defile himself for the dead among his people, ² except for his relatives who are nearest to him: his mother, his father, his son, his daughter, and his brother; ³ also his virgin sister who is near to him, who has had no husband, for her he may defile himself. ⁴ *Otherwise* he shall not defile himself, *being* a chief man among his people, to profane himself.

⁵ 'They shall not make any bald *place* on their heads, nor shall they shave the edges of their beards nor make any cuttings in their flesh. ⁶ They shall be holy to their God and not profane the name of their God, for they offer the offerings of the LORD made by fire, *and* the bread of their God; therefore they shall be holy. ⁷ They shall not take a wife *who is* a harlot or a defiled woman, nor shall they take a woman divorced from her husband; for *the priest is* holy to his God. ⁸ Therefore you shall consecrate him, for he offers the bread of your God. He shall be holy to you, for I the LORD, who sanctify you, *am* holy. ⁹ The daughter of any priest, if she profanes herself by playing the harlot, she profanes her father. She shall be burned with fire.

חֲטָאָם יִשָּׂאוּ עֲרִירִים יָמֻתוּ: 21 וְאִישׁ אֲשֶׁר יִקַּח אֶת־אֵשֶׁת אָחִיו נִדָּה הִוא עֶרְוַת אָחִיו גִּלָּה עֲרִירִים יִהְיוּ: 22 וּשְׁמַרְתֶּם אֶת־כָּל־חֻקֹּתַי וְאֶת־כָּל־מִשְׁפָּטַי וַעֲשִׂיתֶם אֹתָם וְלֹא־תָקִיא אֶתְכֶם הָאָרֶץ אֲשֶׁר אֲנִי מֵבִיא אֶתְכֶם שָׁמָּה לָשֶׁבֶת בָּהּ: 23 וְלֹא תֵלְכוּ בְּחֻקֹּת הַגּוֹי אֲשֶׁר־אֲנִי מְשַׁלֵּחַ מִפְּנֵיכֶם כִּי אֶת־כָּל־אֵלֶּה עָשׂוּ וָאָקֻץ בָּם: 24 וָאֹמַר לָכֶם אַתֶּם תִּירְשׁוּ אֶת־אַדְמָתָם וַאֲנִי אֶתְּנֶנָּה לָכֶם לָרֶשֶׁת אֹתָהּ אֶרֶץ זָבַת חָלָב וּדְבָשׁ אֲנִי יְהֹוָה אֱלֹהֵיכֶם אֲשֶׁר־הִבְדַּלְתִּי אֶתְכֶם מִן־הָעַמִּים: 25 וְהִבְדַּלְתֶּם בֵּין־הַבְּהֵמָה הַטְּהֹרָה לַטְּמֵאָה וּבֵין־הָעוֹף הַטָּמֵא לַטָּהֹר וְלֹא־תְשַׁקְּצוּ אֶת־נַפְשֹׁתֵיכֶם בַּבְּהֵמָה וּבָעוֹף וּבְכֹל אֲשֶׁר תִּרְמֹשׂ הָאֲדָמָה אֲשֶׁר־הִבְדַּלְתִּי לָכֶם לְטַמֵּא: 26 וִהְיִיתֶם לִי קְדֹשִׁים כִּי קָדוֹשׁ אֲנִי יְהֹוָה וָאַבְדִּל אֶתְכֶם מִן־הָעַמִּים לִהְיוֹת לִי: 27 וְאִישׁ אוֹ־אִשָּׁה כִּי־יִהְיֶה בָהֶם אוֹב אוֹ יִדְּעֹנִי מוֹת יוּמָתוּ בָּאֶבֶן יִרְגְּמוּ אֹתָם דְּמֵיהֶם בָּם: פ

כא וַיֹּאמֶר יְהֹוָה אֶל־מֹשֶׁה אֱמֹר אֶל־הַכֹּהֲנִים בְּנֵי אַהֲרֹן וְאָמַרְתָּ אֲלֵהֶם לְנֶפֶשׁ לֹא־יִטַּמָּא בְּעַמָּיו: 2 כִּי אִם־לִשְׁאֵרוֹ הַקָּרֹב אֵלָיו לְאִמּוֹ וּלְאָבִיו וְלִבְנוֹ וּלְבִתּוֹ וּלְאָחִיו: 3 וְלַאֲחֹתוֹ הַבְּתוּלָה הַקְּרוֹבָה אֵלָיו אֲשֶׁר לֹא־הָיְתָה לְאִישׁ לָהּ יִטַּמָּא: 4 לֹא יִטַּמָּא בַּעַל בְּעַמָּיו לְהֵחַלּוֹ: 5 לֹא־יִקְרְחָה קָרְחָה בְּרֹאשָׁם וּפְאַת זְקָנָם לֹא יְגַלֵּחוּ וּבִבְשָׂרָם לֹא יִשְׂרְטוּ שָׂרָטֶת: 6 קְדֹשִׁים יִהְיוּ לֵאלֹהֵיהֶם וְלֹא יְחַלְּלוּ שֵׁם אֱלֹהֵיהֶם כִּי אֶת־אִשֵּׁי יְהֹוָה לֶחֶם אֱלֹהֵיהֶם הֵם מַקְרִיבִם וְהָיוּ קֹדֶשׁ: 7 אִשָּׁה זֹנָה וַחֲלָלָה לֹא יִקָּחוּ וְאִשָּׁה גְּרוּשָׁה מֵאִישָׁהּ לֹא יִקָּחוּ כִּי־קָדֹשׁ הוּא לֵאלֹהָיו: 8 וְקִדַּשְׁתּוֹ כִּי־אֶת־לֶחֶם אֱלֹהֶיךָ הוּא מַקְרִיב קָדֹשׁ יִהְיֶה־לָּךְ כִּי קָדוֹשׁ אֲנִי יְהֹוָה מְקַדִּשְׁכֶם: 9 וּבַת אִישׁ כֹּהֵן כִּי תֵחֵל לִזְנוֹת אֶת־אָבִיהָ הִיא מְחַלֶּלֶת

¹⁰'*He who is* the high priest among his brethren, on whose head the anointing oil was poured and who is consecrated to wear the garments, shall not uncover his head nor tear his clothes; ¹¹nor shall he go near any dead body, nor defile himself for his father or his mother; ¹²nor shall he go out of the sanctuary, nor profane the sanctuary of his God; for the consecration of the anointing oil of his God *is* upon him: I *am* the LORD. ¹³And he shall take a wife in her virginity. ¹⁴A widow or a divorced woman or a defiled woman *or* a harlot—these he shall not marry; but he shall take a virgin of his own people as wife. ¹⁵Nor shall he profane his posterity among his people, for I the LORD sanctify him.'"

¹⁶And the LORD spoke to Moses, saying, ¹⁷"Speak to Aaron, saying: 'No man of your descendants in *succeeding* generations, who has *any* defect, may approach to offer the bread of his God. ¹⁸For any man who has a defect shall not approach: a man blind or lame, who has a marred *face* or any *limb* too long, ¹⁹a man who has a broken foot or broken hand, ²⁰or is a hunchback or a dwarf, or *a man* who has a defect in his eye, or eczema or scab, or is a eunuch. ²¹No man of the descendants of Aaron the priest, who has a defect, shall come near to offer the offerings made by fire to the LORD. He has a defect; he shall not come near to offer the bread of his God. ²²He may eat the bread of his God, *both* the most holy and the holy; ²³only he shall not go near the veil or approach the altar, because he has a defect, lest he profane My sanctuaries; for I the LORD sanctify them.'"

²⁴And Moses told *it* to Aaron and his sons, and to all the children of Israel.

22 Then the LORD spoke to Moses, saying, ²"Speak to Aaron and his sons, that they separate themselves from the holy things of the children of Israel, and that they do not profane My holy name *by* what they dedicate to Me: I *am* the LORD. ³Say to them: 'Whoever of all your descendants throughout your generations, who goes near the holy things which the children of Israel dedicate to the LORD, while he has uncleanness upon him, that person shall be cut off from My presence: I *am* the LORD. ⁴'Whatever man of the descendants of Aaron, who *is* a leper or has a discharge, shall not eat the holy offerings until he is clean. And whoever touches anything made unclean *by* a corpse, or a man who has had an emission of semen, ⁵or whoever touches any creeping thing by which he would be made unclean, or any person by whom he would become unclean, whatever his uncleanness may be— ⁶the person who has touched any such

בָּאֵשׁ תִּשָּׂרֵף: ס 10 וְהַכֹּהֵן הַגָּדוֹל מֵאֶחָיו אֲשֶׁר־יוּצַק עַל־רֹאשׁוֹ ׀ שֶׁמֶן הַמִּשְׁחָה וּמִלֵּא אֶת־יָדוֹ לִלְבֹּשׁ אֶת־הַבְּגָדִים אֶת־רֹאשׁוֹ לֹא יִפְרָע וּבְגָדָיו לֹא יִפְרֹם: 11 וְעַל כָּל־נַפְשֹׁת מֵת לֹא יָבֹא לְאָבִיו וּלְאִמּוֹ לֹא יִטַּמָּא: 12 וּמִן־הַמִּקְדָּשׁ לֹא יֵצֵא וְלֹא יְחַלֵּל אֵת מִקְדַּשׁ אֱלֹהָיו כִּי נֵזֶר שֶׁמֶן מִשְׁחַת אֱלֹהָיו עָלָיו אֲנִי יְהוָה: 13 וְהוּא אִשָּׁה בִבְתוּלֶיהָ יִקָּח: 14 אַלְמָנָה וּגְרוּשָׁה וַחֲלָלָה זֹנָה אֶת־אֵלֶּה לֹא יִקָּח כִּי אִם־בְּתוּלָה מֵעַמָּיו יִקַּח אִשָּׁה: 15 וְלֹא־יְחַלֵּל זַרְעוֹ בְּעַמָּיו כִּי אֲנִי יְהוָה מְקַדְּשׁוֹ: פ

16 וַיְדַבֵּר יְהוָה אֶל־מֹשֶׁה לֵּאמֹר: 17 דַּבֵּר אֶל־אַהֲרֹן לֵאמֹר אִישׁ מִזַּרְעֲךָ לְדֹרֹתָם אֲשֶׁר יִהְיֶה בוֹ מוּם לֹא יִקְרַב לְהַקְרִיב לֶחֶם אֱלֹהָיו: 18 כִּי כָל־אִישׁ אֲשֶׁר־בּוֹ מוּם לֹא יִקְרָב אִישׁ עִוֵּר אוֹ פִסֵּחַ אוֹ חָרֻם אוֹ שָׂרוּעַ: 19 אוֹ אִישׁ אֲשֶׁר־יִהְיֶה בוֹ שֶׁבֶר רָגֶל אוֹ שֶׁבֶר יָד: 20 אוֹ־גִבֵּן אוֹ־דַק אוֹ תְּבַלֻּל בְּעֵינוֹ אוֹ גָרָב אוֹ יַלֶּפֶת אוֹ מְרוֹחַ אָשֶׁךְ: 21 כָּל־אִישׁ אֲשֶׁר־בּוֹ מוּם מִזֶּרַע אַהֲרֹן הַכֹּהֵן לֹא יִגַּשׁ לְהַקְרִיב אֶת־אִשֵּׁי יְהוָה מוּם בּוֹ אֵת לֶחֶם אֱלֹהָיו לֹא יִגַּשׁ לְהַקְרִיב: 22 לֶחֶם אֱלֹהָיו מִקָּדְשֵׁי הַקֳּדָשִׁים וּמִן־הַקֳּדָשִׁים יֹאכֵל: 23 אַךְ אֶל־הַפָּרֹכֶת לֹא יָבֹא וְאֶל־הַמִּזְבֵּחַ לֹא יִגַּשׁ כִּי־מוּם בּוֹ וְלֹא יְחַלֵּל אֶת־מִקְדָּשַׁי כִּי אֲנִי יְהוָה מְקַדְּשָׁם: 24 וַיְדַבֵּר מֹשֶׁה אֶל־אַהֲרֹן וְאֶל־בָּנָיו וְאֶל־כָּל־בְּנֵי יִשְׂרָאֵל: פ

כב וַיְדַבֵּר יְהוָה אֶל־מֹשֶׁה לֵּאמֹר: 2 דַּבֵּר אֶל־אַהֲרֹן וְאֶל־בָּנָיו וְיִנָּזְרוּ מִקָּדְשֵׁי בְנֵי־יִשְׂרָאֵל וְלֹא יְחַלְּלוּ אֶת־שֵׁם קָדְשִׁי אֲשֶׁר הֵם מַקְדִּשִׁים לִי אֲנִי יְהוָה: 3 אֱמֹר אֲלֵהֶם לְדֹרֹתֵיכֶם כָּל־אִישׁ ׀ אֲשֶׁר־יִקְרַב מִכָּל־זַרְעֲכֶם אֶל־הַקֳּדָשִׁים אֲשֶׁר יַקְדִּישׁוּ בְנֵי־יִשְׂרָאֵל לַיהוָה וְטֻמְאָתוֹ עָלָיו וְנִכְרְתָה הַנֶּפֶשׁ הַהִוא מִלְּפָנַי אֲנִי יְהוָה: 4 אִישׁ אִישׁ מִזֶּרַע אַהֲרֹן וְהוּא צָרוּעַ אוֹ זָב בַּקֳּדָשִׁים לֹא יֹאכַל עַד אֲשֶׁר יִטְהָר וְהַנֹּגֵעַ בְּכָל־טְמֵא־נֶפֶשׁ אוֹ אִישׁ אֲשֶׁר־תֵּצֵא מִמֶּנּוּ שִׁכְבַת־זָרַע: 5 אוֹ־אִישׁ אֲשֶׁר יִגַּע בְּכָל־שֶׁרֶץ אֲשֶׁר יִטְמָא־לוֹ אוֹ בְאָדָם אֲשֶׁר יִטְמָא־לוֹ לְכֹל טֻמְאָתוֹ: 6 נֶפֶשׁ אֲשֶׁר תִּגַּע־בּוֹ וְטָמְאָה עַד־

thing shall be unclean until evening, and shall not eat the holy *offerings* unless he washes his body with water. [7] And when the sun goes down he shall be clean; and afterward he may eat the holy *offerings,* because it *is* his food. [8] Whatever dies *naturally* or is torn *by beasts* he shall not eat, to defile himself with it: I *am* the LORD.

[9] 'They shall therefore keep My ordinance, lest they bear sin for it and die thereby, if they profane it: I the LORD sanctify them.

[10] 'No outsider shall eat the holy *offering;* one who dwells with the priest, or a hired servant, shall not eat the holy thing. [11] But if the priest buys a person with his money, he may eat it; and one who is born in his house may eat his food. [12] If the priest's daughter is married to an outsider, she may not eat of the holy offerings. [13] But if the priest's daughter is a widow or divorced, and has no child, and has returned to her father's house as in her youth, she may eat her father's food; but no outsider shall eat it.

[14] 'And if a man eats the holy *offering* unintentionally, then he shall restore a holy *offering* to the priest, and add one-fifth to it. [15] They shall not profane the holy *offerings* of the children of Israel, which they offer to the LORD, [16] or allow them to bear the guilt of trespass when they eat their holy *offerings;* for I the LORD sanctify them.' "

[17] And the LORD spoke to Moses, saying, [18] "Speak to Aaron and his sons, and to all the children of Israel, and say to them: 'Whatever man of the house of Israel, or of the strangers in Israel, who offers his sacrifice for any of his vows or for any of his freewill offerings, which they offer to the LORD as a burnt offering— [19] *you shall offer* of your own free will a male without blemish from the cattle, from the sheep, or from the goats. [20] Whatever has a defect, you shall not offer, for it shall not be acceptable on your behalf. [21] And whoever offers a sacrifice of a peace offering to the LORD, to fulfill *his* vow, or a freewill offering from the cattle or the sheep, it must be perfect to be accepted; there shall be no defect in it. [22] Those *that are* blind or broken or maimed, or have an ulcer or eczema or scabs, you shall not offer to the LORD, nor make an offering by fire of them on the altar to the LORD. [23] Either a bull or a lamb that has any limb too long or too short you may offer *as* a freewill offering, but for a vow it shall not be accepted.

[24] 'You shall not offer to the LORD what is bruised or crushed, or torn or cut; nor shall you make *any offering of them* in your land. [25] Nor from a foreigner's hand shall you offer any of these as the

---

הָעֶ֔רֶב וְלֹ֥א יֹאכַל֙ מִן־הַקֳּדָשִׁ֔ים כִּ֥י אִם־רָחַ֖ץ בְּשָׂר֥וֹ בַּמָּֽיִם: [7] וּבָ֤א הַשֶּׁ֙מֶשׁ֙ וְטָהֵ֔ר וְאַחַר֙ יֹאכַ֣ל מִן־הַקֳּדָשִׁ֔ים כִּ֥י לַחְמ֖וֹ הֽוּא: [8] נְבֵלָ֧ה וּטְרֵפָ֛ה לֹ֥א יֹאכַ֖ל לְטָמְאָה־בָ֑הּ אֲנִ֖י יְהֹוָֽה: [9] וְשָׁמְר֣וּ אֶת־מִשְׁמַרְתִּ֗י וְלֹֽא־יִשְׂא֤וּ עָלָיו֙ חֵ֔טְא וּמֵ֥תוּ ב֖וֹ כִּ֣י יְחַלְּלֻ֑הוּ אֲנִ֥י יְהֹוָ֖ה מְקַדְּשָֽׁם: [10] וְכָל־זָ֖ר לֹא־יֹ֣אכַל קֹ֑דֶשׁ תּוֹשַׁ֥ב כֹּהֵ֛ן וְשָׂכִ֖יר לֹא־יֹ֥אכַל קֹֽדֶשׁ: [11] וְכֹהֵ֗ן כִּֽי־יִקְנֶ֥ה נֶ֙פֶשׁ֙ קִנְיַ֣ן כַּסְפּ֔וֹ ה֖וּא יֹ֣אכַל בּ֑וֹ וִילִ֣יד בֵּית֔וֹ הֵ֖ם יֹאכְל֥וּ בְלַחְמֽוֹ: [12] וּבַת־כֹּהֵ֔ן כִּ֥י תִהְיֶ֖ה לְאִ֣ישׁ זָ֑ר הִ֕וא בִּתְרוּמַ֥ת הַקֳּדָשִׁ֖ים לֹ֥א תֹאכֵֽל: [13] וּבַת־כֹּהֵן֩ כִּ֨י תִהְיֶ֜ה אַלְמָנָ֣ה וּגְרוּשָׁ֗ה וְזֶ֘רַע֮ אֵ֣ין לָהּ֒ וְשָׁבָ֞ה אֶל־בֵּ֤ית אָבִ֙יהָ֙ כִּנְעוּרֶ֔יהָ מִלֶּ֥חֶם אָבִ֖יהָ תֹּאכֵ֑ל וְכָל־זָ֖ר לֹא־יֹ֥אכַל בּֽוֹ: [14] ס וְאִ֕ישׁ כִּֽי־יֹאכַ֥ל קֹ֛דֶשׁ בִּשְׁגָגָ֑ה וְיָסַ֤ף חֲמִֽשִׁיתוֹ֙ עָלָ֔יו וְנָתַ֥ן לַכֹּהֵ֖ן אֶת־הַקֹּֽדֶשׁ: [15] וְלֹ֣א יְחַלְּל֔וּ אֶת־קָדְשֵׁ֖י בְּנֵ֣י יִשְׂרָאֵ֑ל אֵ֥ת אֲשֶׁר־יָרִ֖ימוּ לַֽיהֹוָֽה: [16] וְהִשִּׂ֤יאוּ אוֹתָם֙ עֲוֹ֣ן אַשְׁמָ֔ה בְּאָכְלָ֖ם אֶת־קָדְשֵׁיהֶ֑ם כִּ֛י אֲנִ֥י יְהֹוָ֖ה מְקַדְּשָֽׁם: פ

[17] וַיְדַבֵּ֥ר יְהֹוָ֖ה אֶל־מֹשֶׁ֥ה לֵּאמֹֽר: [18] דַּבֵּ֨ר אֶֽל־אַהֲרֹ֜ן וְאֶל־בָּנָ֗יו וְאֶל֙ כָּל־בְּנֵ֣י יִשְׂרָאֵ֔ל וְאָמַרְתָּ֖ אֲלֵהֶ֑ם אִ֣ישׁ אִישׁ֩ מִבֵּ֨ית יִשְׂרָאֵ֜ל וּמִן־הַגֵּ֣ר בְּיִשְׂרָאֵ֗ל אֲשֶׁ֨ר יַקְרִ֤יב קָרְבָּנוֹ֙ לְכָל־נִדְרֵיהֶ֔ם וּלְכָל־נִדְבוֹתָ֔ם אֲשֶׁר־יַקְרִ֥יבוּ לַֽיהֹוָ֖ה לְעֹלָֽה: [19] לִֽרְצֹנְכֶ֑ם תָּמִ֣ים זָכָ֔ר בַּבָּקָ֕ר בַּכְּשָׂבִ֖ים וּבָֽעִזִּֽים: [20] כֹּ֛ל אֲשֶׁר־בּ֥וֹ מ֖וּם לֹ֣א תַקְרִ֑יבוּ כִּי־לֹ֥א לְרָצ֖וֹן יִהְיֶ֥ה לָכֶֽם: [21] וְאִ֗ישׁ כִּֽי־יַקְרִ֤יב זֶֽבַח־שְׁלָמִים֙ לַֽיהֹוָ֔ה לְפַלֵּא־נֶ֙דֶר֙ א֣וֹ לִנְדָבָ֔ה בַּבָּקָ֖ר א֣וֹ בַצֹּ֑אן תָּמִ֤ים יִהְיֶה֙ לְרָצ֔וֹן כָּל־מ֖וּם לֹ֥א יִהְיֶה־בּֽוֹ: [22] עַוֶּרֶת֩ א֨וֹ שָׁב֜וּר אוֹ־חָר֣וּץ אֽוֹ־יַבֶּ֗לֶת א֤וֹ גָרָב֙ א֣וֹ יַלֶּ֔פֶת לֹֽא־תַקְרִ֥יבוּ אֵ֖לֶּה לַֽיהֹוָ֑ה וְאִשֶּׁ֗ה לֹֽא־תִתְּנ֥וּ מֵהֶ֛ם עַל־הַמִּזְבֵּ֖חַ לַֽיהֹוָֽה: [23] וְשׁ֥וֹר וָשֶׂ֖ה שָׂר֣וּעַ וְקָל֑וּט נְדָבָה֙ תַּעֲשֶׂ֣ה אֹת֔וֹ וּלְנֵ֖דֶר לֹ֥א יֵרָצֶֽה:

[24] וּמָע֤וּךְ וְכָתוּת֙ וְנָת֣וּק וְכָר֔וּת לֹ֥א תַקְרִ֖יבוּ לַֽיהֹוָ֑ה וּֽבְאַרְצְכֶ֖ם לֹ֥א תַעֲשֽׂוּ: [25] וּמִיַּ֣ד בֶּן־נֵכָ֗ר לֹ֥א תַקְרִ֛יבוּ אֶת־לֶ֥חֶם אֱלֹֽהֵיכֶ֖ם מִכָּל־אֵ֑לֶּה כִּ֣י מָשְׁחָתָ֤ם בָּהֶם֙ מ֣וּם בָּ֔ם לֹ֥א יֵרָצ֖וּ לָכֶֽם: פ

bread of your God, because their corruption *is* in them, *and* defects *are* in them. They shall not be accepted on your behalf.' "

26 And the LORD spoke to Moses, saying: 27 "When a bull or a sheep or a goat is born, it shall be seven days with its mother; and from the eighth day and thereafter it shall be accepted as an offering made by fire to the LORD. 28 *Whether it is a* cow or ewe, do not kill both her and her young on the same day. 29 And when you offer a sacrifice of thanksgiving to the LORD, offer *it* of your own free will. 30 On the same day it shall be eaten; you shall leave none of it until morning: I *am* the LORD.

31 "Therefore you shall keep My commandments, and perform them: I *am* the LORD. 32 You shall not profane My holy name, but I will be hallowed among the children of Israel. I *am* the LORD who sanctifies you, 33 who brought you out of the land of Egypt, to be your God: I *am* the LORD."

23 And the LORD spoke to Moses, saying, 2 "Speak to the children of Israel, and say to them: 'The feasts of the LORD, which you shall proclaim *to be* holy convocations, these *are* My feasts.

3 'Six days shall work be done, but the seventh day *is* a Sabbath of solemn rest, a holy convocation. You shall do no work *on it;* it *is* the Sabbath of the LORD in all your dwellings.

4 'These *are* the feasts of the LORD, holy convocations which you shall proclaim at their appointed times. 5 On the fourteenth *day* of the first month at twilight *is* the LORD's Passover. 6 And on the fifteenth day of the same month *is* the Feast of Unleavened Bread to the LORD; seven days you must eat unleavened bread. 7 On the first day you shall have a holy convocation; you shall do no customary work on it. 8 But you shall offer an offering made by fire to the LORD for seven days. The seventh day *shall be* a holy convocation; you shall do no customary work *on it.*' "

9 And the LORD spoke to Moses, saying, 10 "Speak to the children of Israel, and say to them: 'When you come into the land which I give to you, and reap its harvest, then you shall bring a sheaf of the firstfruits of your harvest to the priest. 11 He shall wave the sheaf before the LORD, to be accepted on your behalf; on the day after the Sabbath the priest shall wave it. 12 And you shall offer on that day, when you wave the sheaf, a male lamb of the first year, without blemish, as a burnt offering to the LORD. 13 Its grain offering *shall be* two-tenths *of an ephah* of fine flour mixed with oil, an offering made by fire to the LORD, for a sweet aroma; and its drink offering *shall be* of wine, one-

26 וַיְדַבֵּר יְהֹוָה אֶל־מֹשֶׁה לֵּאמֹר: 27 שׁוֹר אוֹ־כֶשֶׂב אוֹ־עֵז כִּי יִוָּלֵד וְהָיָה שִׁבְעַת יָמִים תַּחַת אִמּוֹ וּמִיּוֹם הַשְּׁמִינִי וָהָלְאָה יֵרָצֶה לְקָרְבַּן אִשֶּׁה לַיהֹוָה: 28 וְשׁוֹר אוֹ־שֶׂה אֹתוֹ וְאֶת־בְּנוֹ לֹא תִשְׁחֲטוּ בְּיוֹם אֶחָד: 29 וְכִי־תִזְבְּחוּ זֶבַח־תּוֹדָה לַיהֹוָה לִרְצֹנְכֶם תִּזְבָּחוּ: 30 בַּיּוֹם הַהוּא יֵאָכֵל לֹא־תוֹתִירוּ מִמֶּנּוּ עַד־בֹּקֶר אֲנִי יְהֹוָה: 31 וּשְׁמַרְתֶּם מִצְוֹתַי וַעֲשִׂיתֶם אֹתָם אֲנִי יְהֹוָה: 32 וְלֹא תְחַלְּלוּ אֶת־שֵׁם קָדְשִׁי וְנִקְדַּשְׁתִּי בְּתוֹךְ בְּנֵי יִשְׂרָאֵל אֲנִי יְהֹוָה מְקַדִּשְׁכֶם: 33 הַמּוֹצִיא אֶתְכֶם מֵאֶרֶץ מִצְרַיִם לִהְיוֹת לָכֶם לֵאלֹהִים אֲנִי יְהֹוָה: פ

כג וַיְדַבֵּר יְהֹוָה אֶל־מֹשֶׁה לֵּאמֹר: 2 דַּבֵּר אֶל־בְּנֵי יִשְׂרָאֵל וְאָמַרְתָּ אֲלֵהֶם מוֹעֲדֵי יְהֹוָה אֲשֶׁר־תִּקְרְאוּ אֹתָם מִקְרָאֵי קֹדֶשׁ אֵלֶּה הֵם מוֹעֲדָי: 3 שֵׁשֶׁת יָמִים תֵּעָשֶׂה מְלָאכָה וּבַיּוֹם הַשְּׁבִיעִי שַׁבַּת שַׁבָּתוֹן מִקְרָא־קֹדֶשׁ כָּל־מְלָאכָה לֹא תַעֲשׂוּ שַׁבָּת הִוא לַיהֹוָה בְּכֹל מוֹשְׁבֹתֵיכֶם: פ

4 אֵלֶּה מוֹעֲדֵי יְהֹוָה מִקְרָאֵי קֹדֶשׁ אֲשֶׁר־תִּקְרְאוּ אֹתָם בְּמוֹעֲדָם: 5 בַּחֹדֶשׁ הָרִאשׁוֹן בְּאַרְבָּעָה עָשָׂר לַחֹדֶשׁ בֵּין הָעַרְבָּיִם פֶּסַח לַיהֹוָה: 6 וּבַחֲמִשָּׁה עָשָׂר יוֹם לַחֹדֶשׁ הַזֶּה חַג הַמַּצּוֹת לַיהֹוָה שִׁבְעַת יָמִים מַצּוֹת תֹּאכֵלוּ: 7 בַּיּוֹם הָרִאשׁוֹן מִקְרָא־קֹדֶשׁ יִהְיֶה לָכֶם כָּל־מְלֶאכֶת עֲבֹדָה לֹא תַעֲשׂוּ: 8 וְהִקְרַבְתֶּם אִשֶּׁה לַיהֹוָה שִׁבְעַת יָמִים בַּיּוֹם הַשְּׁבִיעִי מִקְרָא־קֹדֶשׁ כָּל־מְלֶאכֶת עֲבֹדָה לֹא תַעֲשׂוּ: פ

9 וַיְדַבֵּר יְהֹוָה אֶל־מֹשֶׁה לֵּאמֹר: 10 דַּבֵּר אֶל־בְּנֵי יִשְׂרָאֵל וְאָמַרְתָּ אֲלֵהֶם כִּי־תָבֹאוּ אֶל־הָאָרֶץ אֲשֶׁר אֲנִי נֹתֵן לָכֶם וּקְצַרְתֶּם אֶת־קְצִירָהּ וַהֲבֵאתֶם אֶת־עֹמֶר רֵאשִׁית קְצִירְכֶם אֶל־הַכֹּהֵן: 11 וְהֵנִיף אֶת־הָעֹמֶר לִפְנֵי יְהֹוָה לִרְצֹנְכֶם מִמָּחֳרַת הַשַּׁבָּת יְנִיפֶנּוּ הַכֹּהֵן: 12 וַעֲשִׂיתֶם בְּיוֹם הֲנִיפְכֶם אֶת־הָעֹמֶר כֶּבֶשׂ תָּמִים בֶּן־שְׁנָתוֹ לְעֹלָה לַיהֹוָה: 13 וּמִנְחָתוֹ שְׁנֵי עֶשְׂרֹנִים סֹלֶת בְּלוּלָה בַשֶּׁמֶן אִשֶּׁה לַיהֹוָה רֵיחַ

fourth of a hin. [14] You shall eat neither bread nor parched grain nor fresh grain until the same day that you have brought an offering to your God; *it shall be* a statute forever throughout your generations in all your dwellings.

[15] 'And you shall count for yourselves from the day after the Sabbath, from the day that you brought the sheaf of the wave offering: seven Sabbaths shall be completed. [16] Count fifty days to the day after the seventh Sabbath; then you shall offer a new grain offering to the LORD. [17] You shall bring from your dwellings two wave *loaves* of two-tenths *of an ephah*. They shall be of fine flour; they shall be baked with leaven. *They are* the firstfruits to the LORD. [18] And you shall offer with the bread seven lambs of the first year, without blemish, one young bull, and two rams. They shall be *as* a burnt offering to the LORD, with their grain offering and their drink offerings, an offering made by fire for a sweet aroma to the LORD. [19] Then you shall sacrifice one kid of the goats as a sin offering, and two male lambs of the first year as a sacrifice of a peace offering. [20] The priest shall wave them with the bread of the firstfruits *as* a wave offering before the LORD, with the two lambs. They shall be holy to the LORD for the priest. [21] And you shall proclaim on the same day *that* it is a holy convocation to you. You shall do no customary work *on it*. *It shall be* a statute forever in all your dwellings throughout your generations.

[22] 'When you reap the harvest of your land, you shall not wholly reap the corners of your field when you reap, nor shall you gather any gleaning from your harvest. You shall leave them for the poor and for the stranger: I *am* the LORD your God.' "

[23] Then the LORD spoke to Moses, saying, [24] "Speak to the children of Israel, saying: 'In the seventh month, on the first *day* of the month, you shall have a sabbath-*rest,* a memorial of blowing of trumpets, a holy convocation. [25] You shall do no customary work *on it;* and you shall offer an offering made by fire to the LORD.' "

[26] And the LORD spoke to Moses, saying: [27] "Also the tenth *day* of this seventh month *shall be* the Day of Atonement. It shall be a holy convocation for you; you shall afflict your souls, and offer an offering made by fire to the LORD. [28] And you shall do no work on that same day, for it *is* the Day of Atonement, to make atonement for you before the LORD your God. [29] For any person who is not afflicted *in soul* on that same day shall be cut off from his people. [30] And any person who does any work on that same day, that person I will destroy from among his people. [31] You shall do no manner

נִיחֹחַ וְנִסְכֹּה יַיִן רְבִיעִת הַהִין: 14 וְלֶחֶם וְקָלִי וְכַרְמֶל לֹא תֹאכְלוּ עַד־עֶצֶם הַיּוֹם הַזֶּה עַד הֲבִיאֲכֶם אֶת־קָרְבַּן אֱלֹהֵיכֶם חֻקַּת עוֹלָם לְדֹרֹתֵיכֶם בְּכֹל מֹשְׁבֹתֵיכֶם: ס 15 וּסְפַרְתֶּם לָכֶם מִמָּחֳרַת הַשַּׁבָּת מִיּוֹם הֲבִיאֲכֶם אֶת־עֹמֶר הַתְּנוּפָה שֶׁבַע שַׁבָּתוֹת תְּמִימֹת תִּהְיֶינָה: 16 עַד מִמָּחֳרַת הַשַּׁבָּת הַשְּׁבִיעִת תִּסְפְּרוּ חֲמִשִּׁים יוֹם וְהִקְרַבְתֶּם מִנְחָה חֲדָשָׁה לַיהוָה: 17 מִמּוֹשְׁבֹתֵיכֶם תָּבִיאוּ | לֶחֶם תְּנוּפָה שְׁתַּיִם שְׁנֵי עֶשְׂרֹנִים סֹלֶת תִּהְיֶינָה חָמֵץ תֵּאָפֶינָה בִּכּוּרִים לַיהוָה: 18 וְהִקְרַבְתֶּם עַל־הַלֶּחֶם שִׁבְעַת כְּבָשִׂים תְּמִימִם בְּנֵי שָׁנָה וּפַר בֶּן־בָּקָר אֶחָד וְאֵילִם שְׁנָיִם יִהְיוּ עֹלָה לַיהוָה וּמִנְחָתָם וְנִסְכֵּיהֶם אִשֵּׁה רֵיחַ־נִיחֹחַ לַיהוָה: 19 וַעֲשִׂיתֶם שְׂעִיר־עִזִּים אֶחָד לְחַטָּאת וּשְׁנֵי כְבָשִׂים בְּנֵי שָׁנָה לְזֶבַח שְׁלָמִים: 20 וְהֵנִיף הַכֹּהֵן | אֹתָם עַל לֶחֶם הַבִּכֻּרִים תְּנוּפָה לִפְנֵי יְהוָה עַל־שְׁנֵי כְּבָשִׂים קֹדֶשׁ יִהְיוּ לַיהוָה לַכֹּהֵן: 21 וּקְרָאתֶם בְּעֶצֶם | הַיּוֹם הַזֶּה מִקְרָא־קֹדֶשׁ יִהְיֶה לָכֶם כָּל־מְלֶאכֶת עֲבֹדָה לֹא תַעֲשׂוּ חֻקַּת עוֹלָם בְּכָל־מוֹשְׁבֹתֵיכֶם לְדֹרֹתֵיכֶם: 22 וּבְקֻצְרְכֶם אֶת־קְצִיר אַרְצְכֶם לֹא־תְכַלֶּה פְּאַת שָׂדְךָ בְּקֻצְרֶךָ וְלֶקֶט קְצִירְךָ לֹא תְלַקֵּט לֶעָנִי וְלַגֵּר תַּעֲזֹב אֹתָם אֲנִי יְהוָה אֱלֹהֵיכֶם: ס 23 וַיְדַבֵּר יְהוָה אֶל־מֹשֶׁה לֵּאמֹר: 24 דַּבֵּר אֶל־בְּנֵי יִשְׂרָאֵל לֵאמֹר בַּחֹדֶשׁ הַשְּׁבִיעִי בְּאֶחָד לַחֹדֶשׁ יִהְיֶה לָכֶם שַׁבָּתוֹן זִכְרוֹן תְּרוּעָה מִקְרָא־קֹדֶשׁ: 25 כָּל־מְלֶאכֶת עֲבֹדָה לֹא תַעֲשׂוּ וְהִקְרַבְתֶּם אִשֶּׁה לַיהוָה: 26 וַיְדַבֵּר יְהוָה אֶל־מֹשֶׁה לֵּאמֹר: 27 אַךְ בֶּעָשׂוֹר לַחֹדֶשׁ הַשְּׁבִיעִי הַזֶּה יוֹם הַכִּפֻּרִים הוּא מִקְרָא־קֹדֶשׁ יִהְיֶה לָכֶם וְעִנִּיתֶם אֶת־נַפְשֹׁתֵיכֶם וְהִקְרַבְתֶּם אִשֶּׁה לַיהוָה: 28 וְכָל־מְלָאכָה לֹא תַעֲשׂוּ בְּעֶצֶם הַיּוֹם הַזֶּה כִּי יוֹם כִּפֻּרִים הוּא לְכַפֵּר עֲלֵיכֶם לִפְנֵי יְהוָה אֱלֹהֵיכֶם: 29 כִּי כָל־הַנֶּפֶשׁ אֲשֶׁר לֹא־תְעֻנֶּה בְּעֶצֶם הַיּוֹם הַזֶּה וְנִכְרְתָה מֵעַמֶּיהָ: 30 וְכָל־הַנֶּפֶשׁ אֲשֶׁר תַּעֲשֶׂה כָּל־מְלָאכָה בְּעֶצֶם הַיּוֹם הַזֶּה וְהַאֲבַדְתִּי אֶת־הַנֶּפֶשׁ הַהִוא מִקֶּרֶב עַמָּהּ: 31 כָּל־מְלָאכָה לֹא תַעֲשׂוּ

of work; *it shall be* a statute forever throughout your generations in all your dwellings. ³²It *shall be* to you a sabbath of *solemn* rest, and you shall afflict your souls; on the ninth *day* of the month at evening, from evening to evening, you shall celebrate your sabbath."

³³Then the LORD spoke to Moses, saying, ³⁴"Speak to the children of Israel, saying: 'The fifteenth day of this seventh month *shall be* the Feast of Tabernacles *for* seven days to the LORD. ³⁵On the first day *there shall be* a holy convocation. You shall do no customary work *on it.* ³⁶For seven days you shall offer an offering made by fire to the LORD. On the eighth day you shall have a holy convocation, and you shall offer an offering made by fire to the LORD. It *is* a sacred assembly, *and* you shall do no customary work *on it.*

³⁷'These *are* the feasts of the LORD which you shall proclaim *to be* holy convocations, to offer an offering made by fire to the LORD, a burnt offering and a grain offering, a sacrifice and drink offerings, everything on its day— ³⁸besides the Sabbaths of the LORD, besides your gifts, besides all your vows, and besides all your freewill offerings which you give to the LORD.

³⁹'Also on the fifteenth day of the seventh month, when you have gathered in the fruit of the land, you shall keep the feast of the LORD *for* seven days; on the first day *there shall be* a sabbath-rest, and on the eighth day a sabbath-rest. ⁴⁰And you shall take for yourselves on the first day the fruit of beautiful trees, branches of palm trees, the boughs of leafy trees, and willows of the brook; and you shall rejoice before the LORD your God for seven days. ⁴¹You shall keep it as a feast to the LORD for seven days in the year. *It shall be* a statute forever in your generations. You shall celebrate it in the seventh month. ⁴²You shall dwell in booths for seven days. All who are native Israelites shall dwell in booths, ⁴³that your generations may know that I made the children of Israel dwell in booths when I brought them out of the land of Egypt: I *am* the LORD your God.' "

⁴⁴So Moses declared to the children of Israel the feasts of the LORD.

24

Then the LORD spoke to Moses, saying: ²"Command the children of Israel that they bring to you pure oil of pressed olives for the light, to make the lamps burn continually. ³Outside the veil of the Testimony, in the tabernacle of meeting, Aaron shall be in charge of it from evening until morning before the LORD continually; *it shall be* a

חֻקַּת עוֹלָם לְדֹרֹתֵיכֶם בְּכֹל מֹשְׁבֹתֵיכֶם: 32 שַׁבַּת שַׁבָּתוֹן הוּא לָכֶם וְעִנִּיתֶם אֶת־נַפְשֹׁתֵיכֶם בְּתִשְׁעָה לַחֹדֶשׁ בָּעֶרֶב מֵעֶרֶב עַד־עֶרֶב תִּשְׁבְּתוּ שַׁבַּתְּכֶם: פ

33 וַיְדַבֵּר יְהוָה אֶל־מֹשֶׁה לֵּאמֹר: 34 דַּבֵּר אֶל־ בְּנֵי יִשְׂרָאֵל לֵאמֹר בַּחֲמִשָּׁה עָשָׂר יוֹם לַחֹדֶשׁ הַשְּׁבִיעִי הַזֶּה חַג הַסֻּכּוֹת שִׁבְעַת יָמִים לַיהוָה: 35 בַּיּוֹם הָרִאשׁוֹן מִקְרָא־קֹדֶשׁ כָּל־מְלֶאכֶת עֲבֹדָה לֹא תַעֲשׂוּ: 36 שִׁבְעַת יָמִים תַּקְרִיבוּ אִשֶּׁה לַיהוָה בַּיּוֹם הַשְּׁמִינִי מִקְרָא־קֹדֶשׁ יִהְיֶה לָכֶם וְהִקְרַבְתֶּם אִשֶּׁה לַיהוָה עֲצֶרֶת הִוא כָּל־מְלֶאכֶת עֲבֹדָה לֹא תַעֲשׂוּ: 37 אֵלֶּה מוֹעֲדֵי יְהוָה אֲשֶׁר־תִּקְרְאוּ אֹתָם מִקְרָאֵי קֹדֶשׁ לְהַקְרִיב אִשֶּׁה לַיהוָה עֹלָה וּמִנְחָה זֶבַח וּנְסָכִים דְּבַר־יוֹם בְּיוֹמוֹ: 38 מִלְּבַד שַׁבְּתֹת יְהוָה וּמִלְּבַד מַתְּנוֹתֵיכֶם וּמִלְּבַד כָּל־ נִדְרֵיכֶם וּמִלְּבַד כָּל־נִדְבוֹתֵיכֶם אֲשֶׁר תִּתְּנוּ לַיהוָה:

39 אַךְ בַּחֲמִשָּׁה עָשָׂר יוֹם לַחֹדֶשׁ הַשְּׁבִיעִי בְּאָסְפְּכֶם אֶת־תְּבוּאַת הָאָרֶץ תָּחֹגּוּ אֶת־חַג־יְהוָה שִׁבְעַת יָמִים בַּיּוֹם הָרִאשׁוֹן שַׁבָּתוֹן וּבַיּוֹם הַשְּׁמִינִי שַׁבָּתוֹן: 40 וּלְקַחְתֶּם לָכֶם בַּיּוֹם הָרִאשׁוֹן פְּרִי עֵץ הָדָר כַּפֹּת תְּמָרִים וַעֲנַף עֵץ־עָבֹת וְעַרְבֵי־נָחַל וּשְׂמַחְתֶּם לִפְנֵי יְהוָה אֱלֹהֵיכֶם שִׁבְעַת יָמִים: 41 וְחַגֹּתֶם אֹתוֹ חַג לַיהוָה שִׁבְעַת יָמִים בַּשָּׁנָה חֻקַּת עוֹלָם לְדֹרֹתֵיכֶם בַּחֹדֶשׁ הַשְּׁבִיעִי תָּחֹגּוּ אֹתוֹ: 42 בַּסֻּכֹּת תֵּשְׁבוּ שִׁבְעַת יָמִים כָּל־הָאֶזְרָח בְּיִשְׂרָאֵל יֵשְׁבוּ בַּסֻּכֹּת:

43 לְמַעַן יֵדְעוּ דֹרֹתֵיכֶם כִּי בַסֻּכּוֹת הוֹשַׁבְתִּי אֶת־ בְּנֵי יִשְׂרָאֵל בְּהוֹצִיאִי אוֹתָם מֵאֶרֶץ מִצְרָיִם אֲנִי יְהוָה אֱלֹהֵיכֶם: 44 וַיְדַבֵּר מֹשֶׁה אֶת־מֹעֲדֵי יְהוָה אֶל־בְּנֵי יִשְׂרָאֵל: פ

כד וַיְדַבֵּר יְהוָה אֶל־מֹשֶׁה לֵּאמֹר: 2 צַו אֶת־בְּנֵי יִשְׂרָאֵל וְיִקְחוּ אֵלֶיךָ שֶׁמֶן זַיִת זָךְ כָּתִית לַמָּאוֹר לְהַעֲלֹת נֵר תָּמִיד: 3 מִחוּץ לְפָרֹכֶת הָעֵדֻת בְּאֹהֶל מוֹעֵד יַעֲרֹךְ אֹתוֹ אַהֲרֹן מֵעֶרֶב עַד־בֹּקֶר לִפְנֵי

statute forever in your generations. ⁴He shall be in charge of the lamps on the pure *gold* lampstand before the LORD continually.

⁵"And you shall take fine flour and bake twelve cakes with it. Two-tenths *of an ephah* shall be in each cake. ⁶You shall set them in two rows, six in a row, on the pure *gold* table before the LORD. ⁷And you shall put pure frankincense on *each* row, that it may be on the bread for a memorial, an offering made by fire to the LORD. ⁸Every Sabbath he shall set it in order before the LORD continually, *being taken* from the children of Israel by an everlasting covenant. ⁹And it shall be for Aaron and his sons, and they shall eat it in a holy place; for it *is* most holy to him from the offerings of the LORD made by fire, by a perpetual statute."

¹⁰Now the son of an Israelite woman, whose father *was* an Egyptian, went out among the children of Israel; and this Israelite *woman's* son and a man of Israel fought each other in the camp. ¹¹And the Israelite woman's son blasphemed the name *of the LORD* and cursed; and so they brought him to Moses. (His mother's name *was* Shelomith the daughter of Dibri, of the tribe of Dan.) ¹²Then they put him in custody, that the mind of the LORD might be shown to them.

¹³And the LORD spoke to Moses, saying, ¹⁴"Take outside the camp him who has cursed; then let all who heard *him* lay their hands on his head, and let all the congregation stone him.

¹⁵"Then you shall speak to the children of Israel, saying: 'Whoever curses his God shall bear his sin. ¹⁶And whoever blasphemes the name of the LORD shall surely be put to death. All the congregation shall certainly stone him, the stranger as well as him who is born in the land. When he blasphemes the name *of the LORD*, he shall be put to death.

¹⁷'Whoever kills any man shall surely be put to death. ¹⁸Whoever kills an animal shall make it good, animal for animal.

¹⁹'If a man causes disfigurement of his neighbor, as he has done, so shall it be done to him— ²⁰fracture for fracture, eye for eye, tooth for tooth; as he has caused disfigurement of a man, so shall it be done to him. ²¹And whoever kills an animal shall restore it; but whoever kills a man shall be put to death. ²²You shall have the same law for the stranger and for one from your own country; for I *am* the LORD your God.'"

²³Then Moses spoke to the children of Israel; and they took outside the camp him who had cursed, and stoned him with stones. So the children of Israel did as the LORD commanded Moses.

יְהוָֹה תָּמִיד חֻקַּת עוֹלָם לְדֹרֹתֵיכֶם: ⁴ עַל הַמְּנֹרָה הַטְּהֹרָה יַעֲרֹךְ אֶת־הַנֵּרוֹת לִפְנֵי יְהוָֹה תָּמִיד: פ

⁵ וְלָקַחְתָּ סֹלֶת וְאָפִיתָ אֹתָהּ שְׁתֵּים עֶשְׂרֵה חַלּוֹת שְׁנֵי עֶשְׂרֹנִים יִהְיֶה הַחַלָּה הָאֶחָת: ⁶ וְשַׂמְתָּ אוֹתָם שְׁתַּיִם מַעֲרָכוֹת שֵׁשׁ הַמַּעֲרָכֶת עַל הַשֻּׁלְחָן הַטָּהֹר לִפְנֵי יְהוָֹה: ⁷ וְנָתַתָּ עַל־הַמַּעֲרֶכֶת לְבֹנָה זַכָּה וְהָיְתָה לַלֶּחֶם לְאַזְכָּרָה אִשֶּׁה לַיהוָֹה: ⁸ בְּיוֹם הַשַּׁבָּת בְּיוֹם הַשַּׁבָּת יַעַרְכֶנּוּ לִפְנֵי יְהוָֹה תָּמִיד מֵאֵת בְּנֵי־יִשְׂרָאֵל בְּרִית עוֹלָם: ⁹ וְהָיְתָה לְאַהֲרֹן וּלְבָנָיו וַאֲכָלֻהוּ בְּמָקוֹם קָדֹשׁ כִּי קֹדֶשׁ קָדָשִׁים הוּא לוֹ מֵאִשֵּׁי יְהוָֹה חָק־עוֹלָם: ס ¹⁰ וַיֵּצֵא בֶּן־אִשָּׁה יִשְׂרְאֵלִית וְהוּא בֶּן־אִישׁ מִצְרִי בְּתוֹךְ בְּנֵי יִשְׂרָאֵל וַיִּנָּצוּ בַּמַּחֲנֶה בֶּן הַיִּשְׂרְאֵלִית וְאִישׁ הַיִּשְׂרְאֵלִי: ¹¹ וַיִּקֹּב בֶּן־הָאִשָּׁה הַיִּשְׂרְאֵלִית אֶת־הַשֵּׁם וַיְקַלֵּל וַיָּבִיאוּ אֹתוֹ אֶל־מֹשֶׁה וְשֵׁם אִמּוֹ שְׁלֹמִית בַּת־דִּבְרִי לְמַטֵּה־דָן: ¹² וַיַּנִּיחֻהוּ בַּמִּשְׁמָר לִפְרֹשׁ לָהֶם עַל־פִּי יְהוָֹה: פ

¹³ וַיְדַבֵּר יְהוָֹה אֶל־מֹשֶׁה לֵּאמֹר: ¹⁴ הוֹצֵא אֶת־הַמְקַלֵּל אֶל־מִחוּץ לַמַּחֲנֶה וְסָמְכוּ כָל־הַשֹּׁמְעִים אֶת־יְדֵיהֶם עַל־רֹאשׁוֹ וְרָגְמוּ אֹתוֹ כָּל־הָעֵדָה:

¹⁵ וְאֶל־בְּנֵי יִשְׂרָאֵל תְּדַבֵּר לֵאמֹר אִישׁ אִישׁ כִּי־יְקַלֵּל אֱלֹהָיו וְנָשָׂא חֶטְאוֹ: ¹⁶ וְנֹקֵב שֵׁם־יְהוָֹה מוֹת יוּמָת רָגוֹם יִרְגְּמוּ־בוֹ כָּל־הָעֵדָה כַּגֵּר כָּאֶזְרָח בְּנָקְבוֹ־שֵׁם יוּמָת: ¹⁷ וְאִישׁ כִּי יַכֶּה כָּל־נֶפֶשׁ אָדָם מוֹת יוּמָת: ¹⁸ וּמַכֵּה נֶפֶשׁ־בְּהֵמָה יְשַׁלְּמֶנָּה נֶפֶשׁ תַּחַת נָפֶשׁ: ¹⁹ וְאִישׁ כִּי־יִתֵּן מוּם בַּעֲמִיתוֹ כַּאֲשֶׁר עָשָׂה כֵּן יֵעָשֶׂה לּוֹ: ²⁰ שֶׁבֶר תַּחַת שֶׁבֶר עַיִן תַּחַת עַיִן שֵׁן תַּחַת שֵׁן כַּאֲשֶׁר יִתֵּן מוּם בָּאָדָם כֵּן יִנָּתֶן בּוֹ: ²¹ וּמַכֵּה בְהֵמָה יְשַׁלְּמֶנָּה וּמַכֵּה אָדָם יוּמָת: ²² מִשְׁפַּט אֶחָד יִהְיֶה לָכֶם כַּגֵּר כָּאֶזְרָח יִהְיֶה כִּי אֲנִי יְהוָֹה אֱלֹהֵיכֶם: ²³ וַיְדַבֵּר מֹשֶׁה אֶל־בְּנֵי יִשְׂרָאֵל וַיּוֹצִיאוּ אֶת־הַמְקַלֵּל אֶל־מִחוּץ לַמַּחֲנֶה וַיִּרְגְּמוּ אֹתוֹ אָבֶן וּבְנֵי־יִשְׂרָאֵל עָשׂוּ כַּאֲשֶׁר צִוָּה יְהוָֹה אֶת־מֹשֶׁה: פ

25 And the LORD spoke to Moses on Mount Sinai, saying, 2 "Speak to the children of Israel, and say to them: 'When you come into the land which I give you, then the land shall keep a sabbath to the LORD. 3 Six years you shall sow your field, and six years you shall prune your vineyard, and gather its fruit; 4 but in the seventh year there shall be a sabbath of solemn rest for the land, a sabbath to the LORD. You shall neither sow your field nor prune your vineyard. 5 What grows of its own accord of your harvest you shall not reap, nor gather the grapes of your untended vine, *for* it is a year of rest for the land. 6 And the sabbath *produce* of the land shall be food for you: for you, your male and female servants, your hired man, and the stranger who dwells with you, 7 for your livestock and the beasts that *are* in your land—all its produce shall be for food.

8 'And you shall count seven sabbaths of years for yourself, seven times seven years; and the time of the seven sabbaths of years shall be to you forty-nine years. 9 Then you shall cause the trumpet of the Jubilee to sound on the tenth *day* of the seventh month; on the Day of Atonement you shall make the trumpet to sound throughout all your land. 10 And you shall consecrate the fiftieth year, and proclaim liberty throughout *all* the land to all its inhabitants. It shall be a Jubilee for you; and each of you shall return to his possession, and each of you shall return to his family. 11 That fiftieth year shall be a Jubilee to you; in it you shall neither sow nor reap what grows of its own accord, nor gather *the grapes* of your untended vine. 12 For it *is* the Jubilee; it shall be holy to you; you shall eat its produce from the field.

13 'In this Year of Jubilee, each of you shall return to his possession. 14 And if you sell anything to your neighbor or buy from your neighbor's hand, you shall not oppress one another. 15 According to the number of years after the Jubilee you shall buy from your neighbor, and according to the number of years of crops he shall sell to you. 16 According to the multitude of years you shall increase its price, and according to the fewer number of years you shall diminish its price; for he sells to you *according* to the number *of the years* of the crops. 17 Therefore you shall not oppress one another, but you shall fear your God; for I *am* the LORD your God.

18 'So you shall observe My statutes and keep My judgments, and perform them; and you will dwell in the land in safety. 19 Then the land will yield its fruit, and you will eat your fill, and dwell there in safety.

כה וַיְדַבֵּר יְהֹוָה אֶל־מֹשֶׁה בְּהַר סִינַי לֵאמֹר: 2 דַּבֵּר אֶל־בְּנֵי יִשְׂרָאֵל וְאָמַרְתָּ אֲלֵהֶם כִּי תָבֹאוּ אֶל־הָאָרֶץ אֲשֶׁר אֲנִי נֹתֵן לָכֶם וְשָׁבְתָה הָאָרֶץ שַׁבָּת לַיהֹוָה: 3 שֵׁשׁ שָׁנִים תִּזְרַע שָׂדֶךָ וְשֵׁשׁ שָׁנִים תִּזְמֹר כַּרְמֶךָ וְאָסַפְתָּ אֶת־תְּבוּאָתָהּ: 4 וּבַשָּׁנָה הַשְּׁבִיעִת שַׁבַּת שַׁבָּתוֹן יִהְיֶה לָאָרֶץ שַׁבָּת לַיהֹוָה שָׂדְךָ לֹא תִזְרָע וְכַרְמְךָ לֹא תִזְמֹר: 5 אֵת סְפִיחַ קְצִירְךָ לֹא תִקְצוֹר וְאֶת־עִנְּבֵי נְזִירֶךָ לֹא תִבְצֹר שְׁנַת שַׁבָּתוֹן יִהְיֶה לָאָרֶץ: 6 וְהָיְתָה שַׁבַּת הָאָרֶץ לָכֶם לְאָכְלָה לְךָ וּלְעַבְדְּךָ וְלַאֲמָתֶךָ וְלִשְׂכִירְךָ וּלְתוֹשָׁבְךָ הַגָּרִים עִמָּךְ: 7 וְלִבְהֶמְתְּךָ וְלַחַיָּה אֲשֶׁר בְּאַרְצֶךָ תִּהְיֶה כָל־תְּבוּאָתָהּ לֶאֱכֹל: ס 8 וְסָפַרְתָּ לְךָ שֶׁבַע שַׁבְּתֹת שָׁנִים שֶׁבַע שָׁנִים שֶׁבַע פְּעָמִים וְהָיוּ לְךָ יְמֵי שֶׁבַע שַׁבְּתֹת הַשָּׁנִים תֵּשַׁע וְאַרְבָּעִים שָׁנָה: 9 וְהַעֲבַרְתָּ שׁוֹפַר תְּרוּעָה בַּחֹדֶשׁ הַשְּׁבִעִי בֶּעָשׂוֹר לַחֹדֶשׁ בְּיוֹם הַכִּפֻּרִים תַּעֲבִירוּ שׁוֹפָר בְּכָל־אַרְצְכֶם: 10 וְקִדַּשְׁתֶּם אֵת שְׁנַת הַחֲמִשִּׁים שָׁנָה וּקְרָאתֶם דְּרוֹר בָּאָרֶץ לְכָל־יֹשְׁבֶיהָ יוֹבֵל הִוא תִּהְיֶה לָכֶם וְשַׁבְתֶּם אִישׁ אֶל־אֲחֻזָּתוֹ וְאִישׁ אֶל־מִשְׁפַּחְתּוֹ תָּשֻׁבוּ: 11 יוֹבֵל הִוא שְׁנַת הַחֲמִשִּׁים שָׁנָה תִּהְיֶה לָכֶם לֹא תִזְרָעוּ וְלֹא תִקְצְרוּ אֶת־סְפִיחֶיהָ וְלֹא תִבְצְרוּ אֶת־נְזִרֶיהָ: 12 כִּי יוֹבֵל הִוא קֹדֶשׁ תִּהְיֶה לָכֶם מִן־הַשָּׂדֶה תֹּאכְלוּ אֶת־תְּבוּאָתָהּ: 13 בִּשְׁנַת הַיּוֹבֵל הַזֹּאת תָּשֻׁבוּ אִישׁ אֶל־אֲחֻזָּתוֹ: 14 וְכִי־תִמְכְּרוּ מִמְכָּר לַעֲמִיתֶךָ אוֹ קָנֹה מִיַּד עֲמִיתֶךָ אַל־תּוֹנוּ אִישׁ אֶת־אָחִיו: 15 בְּמִסְפַּר שָׁנִים אַחַר הַיּוֹבֵל תִּקְנֶה מֵאֵת עֲמִיתֶךָ בְּמִסְפַּר שְׁנֵי־תְבוּאֹת יִמְכָּר־לָךְ: 16 לְפִי רֹב הַשָּׁנִים תַּרְבֶּה מִקְנָתוֹ וּלְפִי מְעֹט הַשָּׁנִים תַּמְעִיט מִקְנָתוֹ כִּי מִסְפַּר תְּבוּאֹת הוּא מֹכֵר לָךְ: 17 וְלֹא תוֹנוּ אִישׁ אֶת־עֲמִיתוֹ וְיָרֵאתָ מֵאֱלֹהֶיךָ כִּי אֲנִי יְהֹוָה אֱלֹהֵיכֶם: 18 וַעֲשִׂיתֶם אֶת־חֻקֹּתַי וְאֶת־מִשְׁפָּטַי תִּשְׁמְרוּ וַעֲשִׂיתֶם אֹתָם וִישַׁבְתֶּם עַל־הָאָרֶץ לָבֶטַח: 19 וְנָתְנָה הָאָרֶץ פִּרְיָהּ וַאֲכַלְתֶּם לָשֹׂבַע וִישַׁבְתֶּם לָבֶטַח עָלֶיהָ:

20 'And if you say, "What shall we eat in the seventh year, since we shall not sow nor gather in our produce?" 21 Then I will command My blessing on you in the sixth year, and it will bring forth produce enough for three years. 22 And you shall sow in the eighth year, and eat old produce until the ninth year; until its produce comes in, you shall eat *of* the old *harvest.*

23 'The land shall not be sold permanently, for the land *is* Mine; for you *are* strangers and sojourners with Me. 24 And in all the land of your possession you shall grant redemption of the land.

25 'If one of your brethren becomes poor, and has sold *some* of his possession, and if his redeeming relative comes to redeem it, then he may redeem what his brother sold. 26 Or if the man has no one to redeem it, but he himself becomes able to redeem it, 27 then let him count the years since its sale, and restore the remainder to the man to whom he sold it, that he may return to his possession. 28 But if he is not able to have *it* restored to himself, then what was sold shall remain in the hand of him who bought it until the Year of Jubilee; and in the Jubilee it shall be released, and he shall return to his possession.

29 'If a man sells a house in a walled city, then he may redeem it within a whole year after it is sold; *within* a full year he may redeem it. 30 But if it is not redeemed within the space of a full year, then the house in the walled city shall belong permanently to him who bought it, throughout his generations. It shall not be released in the Jubilee. 31 However the houses of villages which have no wall around them shall be counted as the fields of the country. They may be redeemed, and they shall be released in the Jubilee. 32 Nevertheless the cities of the Levites, *and* the houses in the cities of their possession, the Levites may redeem at any time. 33 And if a man purchases a house from the Levites, then the house that was sold in the city of his possession shall be released in the Jubilee; for the houses in the cities of the Levites *are* their possession among the children of Israel. 34 But the field of the common-land of their cities may not be sold, for it *is* their perpetual possession.

35 'If one of your brethren becomes poor, and falls into poverty among you, then you shall help him, like a stranger or a sojourner, that he may live with you. 36 Take no usury or interest from him; but fear your God, that your brother may live with you. 37 You shall not lend him your money for usury, nor lend him your food at a profit. 38 I *am* the LORD

20 וְכִי תֹאמְרוּ מַה־נֹּאכַל בַּשָּׁנָה הַשְּׁבִיעִת הֵן לֹא נִזְרָע וְלֹא נֶאֱסֹף אֶת־תְּבוּאָתֵנוּ: 21 וְצִוִּיתִי אֶת־בִּרְכָתִי לָכֶם בַּשָּׁנָה הַשִּׁשִּׁית וְעָשָׂת אֶת־הַתְּבוּאָה לִשְׁלֹשׁ הַשָּׁנִים: 22 וּזְרַעְתֶּם אֵת הַשָּׁנָה הַשְּׁמִינִת וַאֲכַלְתֶּם מִן־הַתְּבוּאָה יָשָׁן עַד ׀ הַשָּׁנָה הַתְּשִׁיעִת עַד־בּוֹא תְּבוּאָתָהּ תֹּאכְלוּ יָשָׁן: 23 וְהָאָרֶץ לֹא תִמָּכֵר לִצְמִתֻת כִּי־לִי הָאָרֶץ כִּי־גֵרִים וְתוֹשָׁבִים אַתֶּם עִמָּדִי: 24 וּבְכֹל אֶרֶץ אֲחֻזַּתְכֶם גְּאֻלָּה תִּתְּנוּ לָאָרֶץ: ס 25 כִּי־יָמוּךְ אָחִיךָ וּמָכַר מֵאֲחֻזָּתוֹ וּבָא גֹאֲלוֹ הַקָּרֹב אֵלָיו וְגָאַל אֵת מִמְכַּר אָחִיו: 26 וְאִישׁ כִּי לֹא יִהְיֶה־לּוֹ גֹּאֵל וְהִשִּׂיגָה יָדוֹ וּמָצָא כְּדֵי גְאֻלָּתוֹ: 27 וְחִשַּׁב אֶת־שְׁנֵי מִמְכָּרוֹ וְהֵשִׁיב אֶת־הָעֹדֵף לָאִישׁ אֲשֶׁר מָכַר־לוֹ וְשָׁב לַאֲחֻזָּתוֹ: 28 וְאִם לֹא־מָצְאָה יָדוֹ דֵּי הָשִׁיב לוֹ וְהָיָה מִמְכָּרוֹ בְּיַד הַקֹּנֶה אֹתוֹ עַד שְׁנַת הַיּוֹבֵל וְיָצָא בַּיֹּבֵל וְשָׁב לַאֲחֻזָּתוֹ: 29 וְאִישׁ כִּי־יִמְכֹּר בֵּית־מוֹשַׁב עִיר חוֹמָה וְהָיְתָה גְּאֻלָּתוֹ עַד־תֹּם שְׁנַת מִמְכָּרוֹ יָמִים תִּהְיֶה גְאֻלָּתוֹ: 30 וְאִם לֹא־יִגָּאֵל עַד־מְלֹאת לוֹ שָׁנָה תְמִימָה וְקָם הַבַּיִת אֲשֶׁר־בָּעִיר אֲשֶׁר־לֹאP חֹמָה לַצְּמִיתֻת לַקֹּנֶה אֹתוֹ לְדֹרֹתָיו לֹא יֵצֵא בַּיֹּבֵל: 31 וּבָתֵּי הַחֲצֵרִים אֲשֶׁר אֵין־לָהֶם חֹמָה סָבִיב עַל־שְׂדֵה הָאָרֶץ יֵחָשֵׁב גְּאֻלָּה תִּהְיֶה־לּוֹ וּבַיֹּבֵל יֵצֵא: 32 וְעָרֵי הַלְוִיִּם בָּתֵּי עָרֵי אֲחֻזָּתָם גְּאֻלַּת עוֹלָם תִּהְיֶה לַלְוִיִּם: 33 וַאֲשֶׁר יִגְאַל מִן־הַלְוִיִּם וְיָצָא מִמְכַּר־בַּיִת וְעִיר אֲחֻזָּתוֹ בַּיֹּבֵל כִּי בָתֵּי עָרֵי הַלְוִיִּם הִוא אֲחֻזָּתָם בְּתוֹךְ בְּנֵי יִשְׂרָאֵל: 34 וּשְׂדֵה מִגְרַשׁ עָרֵיהֶם לֹא יִמָּכֵר כִּי־אֲחֻזַּת עוֹלָם הוּא לָהֶם: ס 35 וְכִי־יָמוּךְ אָחִיךָ וּמָטָה יָדוֹ עִמָּךְ וְהֶחֱזַקְתָּ בּוֹ גֵּר וְתוֹשָׁב וָחַי עִמָּךְ: 36 אַל־תִּקַּח מֵאִתּוֹ נֶשֶׁךְ וְתַרְבִּית וְיָרֵאתָ מֵאֱלֹהֶיךָ וְחֵי אָחִיךָ עִמָּךְ: 37 אֶת־כַּסְפְּךָ לֹא־תִתֵּן לוֹ בְּנֶשֶׁךְ וּבְמַרְבִּית לֹא־תִתֵּן אָכְלֶךָ: 38 אֲנִי יְהוָה אֱלֹהֵיכֶם אֲשֶׁר־הוֹצֵאתִי אֶתְכֶם מֵאֶרֶץ מִצְרַיִם לָתֵת לָכֶם אֶת־הָאָרֶץ

your God, who brought you out of the land of Egypt, to give you the land of Canaan *and* to be your God.

39 'And if *one of* your brethren *who dwells* by you becomes poor, and sells himself to serve you, you shall not compel him to serve as a slave. 40 As a hired servant *and* a sojourner he shall be with you, *and* shall serve you until the Year of Jubilee. 41 And *then* he shall depart from you—he and his children with him—and shall return to his own family. He shall return to the possession of his fathers. 42 For they *are* My servants, whom I brought out of the land of Egypt; they shall not be sold as slaves. 43 You shall not rule over him with rigor, but you shall fear your God. 44 And as for your male and female slaves whom you may have—from the nations that are around you, from them you may buy male and female slaves. 45 Moreover you may buy the children of the strangers who dwell among you, and their families who are with you, which they beget in your land; and they shall become your property. 46 And you may take them as an inheritance for your children after you, to inherit *them as* a possession; they shall be your permanent slaves. But regarding your brethren, the children of Israel, you shall not rule over one another with rigor.

47 'Now if a sojourner or stranger close to you becomes rich, and *one of* your brethren *who dwells* by him becomes poor, and sells himself to the stranger *or* sojourner close to you, or to a member of the stranger's family, 48 after he is sold he may be redeemed again. One of his brothers may redeem him; 49 or his uncle or his uncle's son may redeem him; or *anyone* who is near of kin to him in his family may redeem him; or if he is able he may redeem himself. 50 Thus he shall reckon with him who bought him: The price of his release shall be according to the number of years, from the year that he was sold to him until the Year of Jubilee; *it shall be* according to the time of a hired servant for him. 51 If *there are* still many years *remaining,* according to them he shall repay the price of his redemption from the money with which he was bought. 52 And if there remain but a few years until the Year of Jubilee, then he shall reckon with him, *and* according to his years he shall repay him the price of his redemption. 53 He shall be with him as a yearly hired servant, and he shall not rule with rigor over him in your sight. 54 And if he is not redeemed in these *years,* then he shall be released in the Year of Jubilee—he and his children with him. 55 For the

כְּנַ֫עַן לִהְי֥וֹת לָכֶ֖ם לֵֽאלֹהִֽים׃ ס 39 וְכִֽי־
יָמ֣וּךְ אָחִ֔יךָ עִמָּ֖ךְ וְנִמְכַּר־לָ֑ךְ לֹא־תַעֲבֹ֥ד בּ֖וֹ עֲבֹ֥דַת
עָֽבֶד׃ 40 כְּשָׂכִ֥יר כְּתוֹשָׁ֖ב יִהְיֶ֣ה עִמָּ֑ךְ עַד־שְׁנַ֥ת
הַיֹּבֵ֖ל יַעֲבֹ֥ד עִמָּֽךְ׃ 41 וְיָצָא֙ מֵֽעִמָּ֔ךְ ה֖וּא וּבָנָ֣יו
עִמּ֑וֹ וְשָׁב֙ אֶל־מִשְׁפַּחְתּ֔וֹ וְאֶל־אֲחֻזַּ֥ת אֲבֹתָ֖יו יָשֽׁוּב׃
42 כִּֽי־עֲבָדַ֣י הֵ֔ם אֲשֶׁר־הוֹצֵ֥אתִי אֹתָ֖ם מֵאֶ֣רֶץ מִצְרָ֑יִם
לֹ֥א יִמָּכְר֖וּ מִמְכֶּ֥רֶת עָֽבֶד׃ 43 לֹא־תִרְדֶּ֥ה ב֖וֹ בְּפָ֑רֶךְ
וְיָרֵ֖אתָ מֵֽאֱלֹהֶֽיךָ׃ 44 וְעַבְדְּךָ֥ וַאֲמָֽתְךָ֖ אֲשֶׁ֣ר יִהְיוּ־
לָ֑ךְ מֵאֵ֣ת הַגּוֹיִ֗ם אֲשֶׁר֙ סְבִיבֹ֣תֵיכֶ֔ם מֵהֶ֥ם תִּקְנ֖וּ
עֶ֥בֶד וְאָמָֽה׃ 45 וְ֠גַם מִבְּנֵ֨י הַתּוֹשָׁבִ֜ים הַגָּרִ֤ים עִמָּכֶם֙
מֵהֶ֣ם תִּקְנ֔וּ וּמִמִּשְׁפַּחְתָּם֙ אֲשֶׁ֣ר עִמָּכֶ֔ם אֲשֶׁ֥ר הוֹלִ֖ידוּ
בְּאַרְצְכֶ֑ם וְהָי֥וּ לָכֶ֖ם לַֽאֲחֻזָּֽה׃ 46 וְהִתְנַחַלְתֶּ֨ם אֹתָ֜ם
לִבְנֵיכֶ֤ם אַחֲרֵיכֶם֙ לָרֶ֣שֶׁת אֲחֻזָּ֔ה לְעֹלָ֖ם בָּהֶ֣ם תַּעֲבֹ֑דוּ
וּבְאַ֨חֵיכֶ֤ם בְּנֵֽי־יִשְׂרָאֵל֙ אִ֣ישׁ בְּאָחִ֔יו לֹא־תִרְדֶּ֥ה ב֖וֹ
בְּפָֽרֶךְ׃ ס 47 וְכִ֣י תַשִּׂ֗יג יַ֣ד גֵּ֤ר וְתוֹשָׁב֙
עִמָּ֔ךְ וּמָ֥ךְ אָחִ֖יךָ עִמּ֑וֹ וְנִמְכַּ֗ר לְגֵ֤ר תּוֹשָׁב֙ עִמָּ֔ךְ א֥וֹ
לְעֵ֖קֶר מִשְׁפַּ֥חַת גֵּֽר׃ 48 אַחֲרֵ֣י נִמְכַּ֔ר גְּאֻלָּ֖ה תִּהְיֶה־לּ֑וֹ
אֶחָ֥ד מֵאֶחָ֖יו יִגְאָלֶֽנּוּ׃ 49 אֽוֹ־דֹד֞וֹ א֤וֹ בֶן־דֹּדוֹ֙ יִגְאָלֶ֔נּוּ
אֽוֹ־מִשְּׁאֵ֧ר בְּשָׂר֛וֹ מִמִּשְׁפַּחְתּ֖וֹ יִגְאָלֶ֑נּוּ אֽוֹ־הִשִּׂ֥יגָה
יָד֖וֹ וְנִגְאָֽל׃ 50 וְחִשַּׁב֙ עִם־קֹנֵ֔הוּ מִשְּׁנַת֙ הִמָּ֣כְרוֹ ל֔וֹ
עַ֖ד שְׁנַ֣ת הַיֹּבֵ֑ל וְהָיָ֞ה כֶּ֤סֶף מִמְכָּרוֹ֙ בְּמִסְפַּ֣ר שָׁנִ֔ים
כִּימֵ֥י שָׂכִ֖יר יִהְיֶ֥ה עִמּֽוֹ׃ 51 אִם־ע֥וֹד רַבּ֖וֹת בַּשָּׁנִ֑ים
לְפִיהֶן֙ יָשִׁ֣יב גְּאֻלָּת֔וֹ מִכֶּ֖סֶף מִקְנָתֽוֹ׃ 52 וְאִם־מְעַ֞ט
נִשְׁאַ֧ר בַּשָּׁנִ֛ים עַד־שְׁנַ֥ת הַיֹּבֵ֖ל וְחִשַּׁב־ל֑וֹ כְּפִ֣י שָׁנָ֔יו
יָשִׁ֖יב אֶת־גְּאֻלָּתֽוֹ׃ 53 כִּשְׂכִ֥יר שָׁנָ֛ה בְּשָׁנָ֖ה יִהְיֶ֣ה
עִמּ֑וֹ לֹֽא־יִרְדֶּ֥נּֽוּ בְּפֶ֖רֶךְ לְעֵינֶֽיךָ׃ 54 וְאִם־לֹ֥א יִגָּאֵ֖ל
בְּאֵ֑לֶּה וְיָצָא֙ בִּשְׁנַ֣ת הַיֹּבֵ֔ל ה֖וּא וּבָנָ֥יו עִמּֽוֹ׃ 55 כִּֽי־

children of Israel *are* servants to Me; they *are* My servants whom I brought out of the land of Egypt: I *am* the LORD your God.

26 'You shall not make idols for yourselves; neither a carved image nor a *sacred* pillar shall you rear up for yourselves; nor shall you set up an engraved stone in your land, to bow down to it; for I *am* the LORD your God.

2 You shall keep My Sabbaths and reverence My sanctuary: I *am* the LORD.

3 'If you walk in My statutes and keep My commandments, and perform them,

4 then I will give you rain in its season, the land shall yield its produce, and the trees of the field shall yield their fruit.

5 Your threshing shall last till the time of vintage, and the vintage shall last till the time of sowing; you shall eat your bread to the full, and dwell in your land safely.

6 I will give peace in the land, and you shall lie down, and none will make *you* afraid; I will rid the land of evil beasts, and the sword will not go through your land.

7 You will chase your enemies, and they shall fall by the sword before you.

8 Five of you shall chase a hundred, and a hundred of you shall put ten thousand to flight; your enemies shall fall by the sword before you.

9 'For I will look on you favorably and make you fruitful, multiply you and confirm My covenant with you.

10 You shall eat the old harvest, and clear out the old because of the new.

11 I will set My tabernacle among you, and My soul shall not abhor you.

12 I will walk among you and be your God, and you shall be My people.

13 I *am* the LORD your God, who brought you out of the land of Egypt, that *you* should not be their slaves; I have broken the bands of your yoke and made you walk upright.

14 'But if you do not obey Me, and do not observe all these commandments,

15 and if you despise My statutes, or if your soul abhors My judgments, so that you do not perform all My commandments, *but* break My covenant,

16 I also will do this to you: I will even appoint terror over you, wasting disease and fever which shall consume the eyes and cause sorrow of heart. And you shall sow your seed in vain, for your enemies shall eat it.

17 I will set My face against you, and you shall be defeated by your enemies.

לִי בְּנֵי־יִשְׂרָאֵל עֲבָדִים עֲבָדַי הֵם אֲשֶׁר־הוֹצֵאתִי אֹתָם מֵאֶרֶץ מִצְרָיִם אֲנִי יְהוָה אֱלֹהֵיכֶם׃

כו לֹא־תַעֲשׂוּ לָכֶם אֱלִילִם וּפֶסֶל וּמַצֵּבָה לֹא־תָקִימוּ לָכֶם וְאֶבֶן מַשְׂכִּית לֹא תִתְּנוּ בְּאַרְצְכֶם לְהִשְׁתַּחֲוֺת עָלֶיהָ כִּי אֲנִי יְהוָה אֱלֹהֵיכֶם׃ 2 אֶת־שַׁבְּתֹתַי תִּשְׁמֹרוּ וּמִקְדָּשִׁי תִּירָאוּ אֲנִי יְהוָה׃ ס 3 אִם־בְּחֻקֹּתַי תֵּלֵכוּ וְאֶת־מִצְוֺתַי תִּשְׁמְרוּ וַעֲשִׂיתֶם אֹתָם׃ 4 וְנָתַתִּי גִשְׁמֵיכֶם בְּעִתָּם וְנָתְנָה הָאָרֶץ יְבוּלָהּ וְעֵץ הַשָּׂדֶה יִתֵּן פִּרְיוֹ׃ 5 וְהִשִּׂיג לָכֶם דַּיִשׁ אֶת־בָּצִיר וּבָצִיר יַשִּׂיג אֶת־זָרַע וַאֲכַלְתֶּם לַחְמְכֶם לָשֹׂבַע וִישַׁבְתֶּם לָבֶטַח בְּאַרְצְכֶם׃ 6 וְנָתַתִּי שָׁלוֹם בָּאָרֶץ וּשְׁכַבְתֶּם וְאֵין מַחֲרִיד וְהִשְׁבַּתִּי חַיָּה רָעָה מִן־הָאָרֶץ וְחֶרֶב לֹא־תַעֲבֹר בְּאַרְצְכֶם׃ 7 וּרְדַפְתֶּם אֶת־אֹיְבֵיכֶם וְנָפְלוּ לִפְנֵיכֶם לֶחָרֶב׃ 8 וְרָדְפוּ מִכֶּם חֲמִשָּׁה מֵאָה וּמֵאָה מִכֶּם רְבָבָה יִרְדֹּפוּ וְנָפְלוּ אֹיְבֵיכֶם לִפְנֵיכֶם לֶחָרֶב׃ 9 וּפָנִיתִי אֲלֵיכֶם וְהִפְרֵיתִי אֶתְכֶם וְהִרְבֵּיתִי אֶתְכֶם וַהֲקִימֹתִי אֶת־בְּרִיתִי אִתְּכֶם׃ 10 וַאֲכַלְתֶּם יָשָׁן נוֹשָׁן וְיָשָׁן מִפְּנֵי חָדָשׁ תּוֹצִיאוּ׃ 11 וְנָתַתִּי מִשְׁכָּנִי בְּתוֹכְכֶם וְלֹא־תִגְעַל נַפְשִׁי אֶתְכֶם׃ 12 וְהִתְהַלַּכְתִּי בְּתוֹכְכֶם וְהָיִיתִי לָכֶם לֵאלֹהִים וְאַתֶּם תִּהְיוּ־לִי לְעָם׃ 13 אֲנִי יְהוָה אֱלֹהֵיכֶם אֲשֶׁר הוֹצֵאתִי אֶתְכֶם מֵאֶרֶץ מִצְרַיִם מִהְיֹת לָהֶם עֲבָדִים וָאֶשְׁבֹּר מֹטֹת עֻלְּכֶם וָאוֹלֵךְ אֶתְכֶם קוֹמְמִיּוּת׃ פ

14 וְאִם־לֹא תִשְׁמְעוּ לִי וְלֹא תַעֲשׂוּ אֵת כָּל־הַמִּצְוֺת הָאֵלֶּה׃ 15 וְאִם־בְּחֻקֹּתַי תִּמְאָסוּ וְאִם אֶת־מִשְׁפָּטַי תִּגְעַל נַפְשְׁכֶם לְבִלְתִּי עֲשׂוֹת אֶת־כָּל־מִצְוֺתַי לְהַפְרְכֶם אֶת־בְּרִיתִי׃ 16 אַף־אֲנִי אֶעֱשֶׂה־זֹּאת לָכֶם וְהִפְקַדְתִּי עֲלֵיכֶם בֶּהָלָה אֶת־הַשַּׁחֶפֶת וְאֶת־הַקַּדַּחַת מְכַלּוֹת עֵינַיִם וּמְדִיבֹת נָפֶשׁ וּזְרַעְתֶּם לָרִיק זַרְעֲכֶם וַאֲכָלֻהוּ אֹיְבֵיכֶם׃ 17 וְנָתַתִּי פָנַי בָּכֶם וְנִגַּפְתֶּם לִפְנֵי אֹיְבֵיכֶם וְרָדוּ בָכֶם שֹׂנְאֵיכֶם

Those who hate you shall reign over you, and you shall flee when no one pursues you.

18 'And after all this, if you do not obey Me, then I will punish you seven times more for your sins.

19 I will break the pride of your power;
I will make your heavens like iron and your earth like bronze.

20 And your strength shall be spent in vain;
for your land shall not yield its produce, nor shall the trees of the land yield their fruit.

21 'Then, if you walk contrary to Me, and are not willing to obey Me, I will bring on you seven times more plagues, according to your sins.

22 I will also send wild beasts among you, which shall rob you of your children, destroy your livestock, and make you few in number;
and your highways shall be desolate.

23 'And if by these things you are not reformed by Me, but walk contrary to Me,

24 then I also will walk contrary to you, and I will punish you yet seven times for your sins.

25 And I will bring a sword against you that will execute the vengeance of the covenant;
when you are gathered together within your cities I will send pestilence among you;
and you shall be delivered into the hand of the enemy.

26 When I have cut off your supply of bread, ten women shall bake your bread in one oven, and they shall bring back your bread by weight, and you shall eat and not be satisfied.

27 'And after all this, if you do not obey Me, but walk contrary to Me,

28 then I also will walk contrary to you in fury;
and I, even I, will chastise you seven times for your sins.

29 You shall eat the flesh of your sons, and you shall eat the flesh of your daughters.

30 I will destroy your high places, cut down your incense altars, and cast your carcasses on the lifeless forms of your idols;
and My soul shall abhor you.

31 I will lay your cities waste and bring your sanctuaries to desolation, and I will not smell the fragrance of your sweet aromas.

32 I will bring the land to desolation, and your enemies who dwell in it shall be astonished at it.

33 I will scatter you among the nations and draw out a sword after you;
your land shall be desolate and your cities waste.

34 Then the land shall enjoy its sabbaths as long as it lies desolate and you *are* in your enemies' land;
then the land shall rest and enjoy its sabbaths.

35 As long as *it* lies desolate it shall rest—
for the time it did not rest on your sabbaths when you dwelt in it.

וְנַסְתֶּם וְאֵין־רֹדֵף אֶתְכֶם: ס 18 וְאִם־עַד־
אֵלֶּה לֹא תִשְׁמְעוּ לִי וְיָסַפְתִּי לְיַסְּרָה אֶתְכֶם
שֶׁבַע עַל־חַטֹּאתֵיכֶם: 19 וְשָׁבַרְתִּי אֶת־גְּאוֹן עֻזְּכֶם
וְנָתַתִּי אֶת־שְׁמֵיכֶם כַּבַּרְזֶל וְאֶת־אַרְצְכֶם כַּנְּחֻשָׁה:
20 וְתַם לָרִיק כֹּחֲכֶם וְלֹא־תִתֵּן אַרְצְכֶם אֶת־
יְבוּלָהּ וְעֵץ הָאָרֶץ לֹא יִתֵּן פִּרְיוֹ: 21 וְאִם־
תֵּלְכוּ עִמִּי קֶרִי וְלֹא תֹאבוּ לִשְׁמֹעַ לִי וְיָסַפְתִּי
עֲלֵיכֶם מַכָּה שֶׁבַע כְּחַטֹּאתֵיכֶם: 22 וְהִשְׁלַחְתִּי
בָכֶם אֶת־חַיַּת הַשָּׂדֶה וְשִׁכְּלָה אֶתְכֶם וְהִכְרִיתָה
אֶת־בְּהֶמְתְּכֶם וְהִמְעִיטָה אֶתְכֶם וְנָשַׁמּוּ דַּרְכֵיכֶם:
23 וְאִם־בְּאֵלֶּה לֹא תִוָּסְרוּ לִי וַהֲלַכְתֶּם עִמִּי
קֶרִי: 24 וְהָלַכְתִּי אַף־אֲנִי עִמָּכֶם בְּקֶרִי וְהִכֵּיתִי
אֶתְכֶם גַּם־אָנִי שֶׁבַע עַל־חַטֹּאתֵיכֶם: 25 וְהֵבֵאתִי
עֲלֵיכֶם חֶרֶב נֹקֶמֶת נְקַם־בְּרִית וְנֶאֱסַפְתֶּם אֶל־
עָרֵיכֶם וְשִׁלַּחְתִּי דֶבֶר בְּתוֹכְכֶם וְנִתַּתֶּם בְּיַד־אוֹיֵב:
26 בְּשִׁבְרִי לָכֶם מַטֵּה־לֶחֶם וְאָפוּ עֶשֶׂר נָשִׁים
לַחְמְכֶם בְּתַנּוּר אֶחָד וְהֵשִׁיבוּ לַחְמְכֶם בַּמִּשְׁקָל
וַאֲכַלְתֶּם וְלֹא תִשְׂבָּעוּ: ס 27 וְאִם־בְּזֹאת
לֹא תִשְׁמְעוּ לִי וַהֲלַכְתֶּם עִמִּי בְּקֶרִי: 28 וְהָלַכְתִּי
עִמָּכֶם בַּחֲמַת־קֶרִי וְיִסַּרְתִּי אֶתְכֶם אַף־אָנִי שֶׁבַע
עַל־חַטֹּאתֵיכֶם: 29 וַאֲכַלְתֶּם בְּשַׂר בְּנֵיכֶם וּבְשַׂר
בְּנֹתֵיכֶם תֹּאכֵלוּ: 30 וְהִשְׁמַדְתִּי אֶת־בָּמֹתֵיכֶם
וְהִכְרַתִּי אֶת־חַמָּנֵיכֶם וְנָתַתִּי אֶת־פִּגְרֵיכֶם עַל־
פִּגְרֵי גִּלּוּלֵיכֶם וְגָעֲלָה נַפְשִׁי אֶתְכֶם: 31 וְנָתַתִּי
אֶת־עָרֵיכֶם חָרְבָּה וַהֲשִׁמּוֹתִי אֶת־מִקְדְּשֵׁיכֶם וְלֹא
אָרִיחַ בְּרֵיחַ נִיחֹחֲכֶם: 32 וַהֲשִׁמֹּתִי אֲנִי אֶת־הָאָרֶץ
וְשָׁמְמוּ עָלֶיהָ אֹיְבֵיכֶם הַיֹּשְׁבִים בָּהּ: 33 וְאֶתְכֶם
אֱזָרֶה בַגּוֹיִם וַהֲרִיקֹתִי אַחֲרֵיכֶם חָרֶב וְהָיְתָה
אַרְצְכֶם שְׁמָמָה וְעָרֵיכֶם יִהְיוּ חָרְבָּה: 34 אָז תִּרְצֶה
הָאָרֶץ אֶת־שַׁבְּתֹתֶיהָ כֹּל יְמֵי הָשַּׁמָּה וְאַתֶּם בְּאֶרֶץ
אֹיְבֵיכֶם אָז תִּשְׁבַּת הָאָרֶץ וְהִרְצָת אֶת־שַׁבְּתֹתֶיהָ:
35 כָּל־יְמֵי הָשַּׁמָּה תִּשְׁבֹּת אֵת אֲשֶׁר לֹא־שָׁבְתָה

36 'And as for those of you who are left, I will send faintness into their hearts in the lands of their enemies;

the sound of a shaken leaf shall cause them to flee;

they shall flee as though fleeing from a sword, and they shall fall when no one pursues.

37 They shall stumble over one another, as it were before a sword, when no one pursues;

and you shall have no *power* to stand before your enemies.

38 You shall perish among the nations, and the land of your enemies shall eat you up.

39 And those of you who are left shall waste away in their iniquity in your enemies' lands;

also in their fathers' iniquities, which are with them, they shall waste away.

40 'But if they confess their iniquity and the iniquity of their fathers, with their unfaithfulness in which they were unfaithful to Me, and that they also have walked contrary to Me,

41 and *that* I also have walked contrary to them and have brought them into the land of their enemies;

if their uncircumcised hearts are humbled, and they accept their guilt—

42 then I will remember My covenant with Jacob, and My covenant with Isaac and My covenant with Abraham I will remember;

I will remember the land.

43 The land also shall be left empty by them, and will enjoy its sabbaths while it lies desolate without them;

they will accept their guilt, because they despised My judgments and because their soul abhorred My statutes.

44 Yet for all that, when they are in the land of their enemies, I will not cast them away, nor shall I abhor them, to utterly destroy them and break My covenant with them;

for I *am* the LORD their God.

45 But for their sake I will remember the covenant of their ancestors, whom I brought out of the land of Egypt in the sight of the nations, that I might be their God:

I *am* the LORD.'"

46 These *are* the statutes and judgments and laws which the LORD made between Himself and the children of Israel on Mount Sinai by the hand of Moses.

27 Now the LORD spoke to Moses, saying, 2 "Speak to the children of Israel, and say to them: 'When a man consecrates by a vow certain persons to the LORD, according to your valuation, 3 if your valuation is of a male from twenty years old up to sixty years old, then your valuation shall be fifty shekels of silver, according to the shekel of the sanctuary. 4 If it *is* a female, then your valuation

בְּשַׁבְתֵּיכֶם בְּשִׁבְתְּכֶם עָלֶיהָ: 36 וְהַנִּשְׁאָרִים בָּכֶם
וְהֵבֵאתִי מֹרֶךְ בִּלְבָבָם בְּאַרְצֹת אֹיְבֵיהֶם וְרָדַף אֹתָם
קוֹל עָלֶה נִדָּף וְנָסוּ מְנֻסַת־חֶרֶב וְנָפְלוּ וְאֵין רֹדֵף:
37 וְכָשְׁלוּ אִישׁ־בְּאָחִיו כְּמִפְּנֵי־חֶרֶב וְרֹדֵף אָיִן וְלֹא־
תִהְיֶה לָכֶם תְּקוּמָה לִפְנֵי אֹיְבֵיכֶם: 38 וַאֲבַדְתֶּם
בַּגּוֹיִם וְאָכְלָה אֶתְכֶם אֶרֶץ אֹיְבֵיכֶם: 39 וְהַנִּשְׁאָרִים
בָּכֶם יִמַּקּוּ בַּעֲוֹנָם בְּאַרְצֹת אֹיְבֵיכֶם וְאַף בַּעֲוֹנֹת
אֲבֹתָם אִתָּם יִמָּקּוּ: 40 וְהִתְוַדּוּ אֶת־עֲוֹנָם וְאֶת־עֲוֹן
אֲבֹתָם בְּמַעֲלָם אֲשֶׁר מָעֲלוּ־בִי וְאַף אֲשֶׁר־הָלְכוּ
עִמִּי בְּקֶרִי: 41 אַף־אֲנִי אֵלֵךְ עִמָּם בְּקֶרִי וְהֵבֵאתִי
אֹתָם בְּאֶרֶץ אֹיְבֵיהֶם אוֹ־אָז יִכָּנַע לְבָבָם הֶעָרֵל
וְאָז יִרְצוּ אֶת־עֲוֹנָם: 42 וְזָכַרְתִּי אֶת־בְּרִיתִי יַעֲקוֹב
וְאַף אֶת־בְּרִיתִי יִצְחָק וְאַף אֶת־בְּרִיתִי אַבְרָהָם
אֶזְכֹּר וְהָאָרֶץ אֶזְכֹּר: 43 וְהָאָרֶץ תֵּעָזֵב מֵהֶם וְתִרֶץ
אֶת־שַׁבְּתֹתֶיהָ בָּהְשַׁמָּה מֵהֶם וְהֵם יִרְצוּ אֶת־
עֲוֹנָם יַעַן וּבְיַעַן בְּמִשְׁפָּטַי מָאָסוּ וְאֶת־חֻקֹּתַי גָּעֲלָה
נַפְשָׁם: 44 וְאַף־גַּם־זֹאת בִּהְיוֹתָם בְּאֶרֶץ אֹיְבֵיהֶם
לֹא־מְאַסְתִּים וְלֹא־גְעַלְתִּים לְכַלֹּתָם לְהָפֵר בְּרִיתִי
אִתָּם כִּי אֲנִי יְהוָה אֱלֹהֵיהֶם: 45 וְזָכַרְתִּי לָהֶם בְּרִית
רִאשֹׁנִים אֲשֶׁר הוֹצֵאתִי־אֹתָם מֵאֶרֶץ מִצְרַיִם לְעֵינֵי
הַגּוֹיִם לִהְיֹת לָהֶם לֵאלֹהִים אֲנִי יְהוָה: 46 אֵלֶּה
הַחֻקִּים וְהַמִּשְׁפָּטִים וְהַתּוֹרֹת אֲשֶׁר נָתַן יְהוָה בֵּינוֹ
וּבֵין בְּנֵי יִשְׂרָאֵל בְּהַר סִינַי בְּיַד־מֹשֶׁה: פ

כז וַיְדַבֵּר יְהוָה אֶל־מֹשֶׁה לֵּאמֹר: 2 דַּבֵּר אֶל־
בְּנֵי יִשְׂרָאֵל וְאָמַרְתָּ אֲלֵהֶם אִישׁ כִּי יַפְלִא נֶדֶר
בְּעֶרְכְּךָ נְפָשֹׁת לַיהוָה: 3 וְהָיָה עֶרְכְּךָ הַזָּכָר מִבֶּן
עֶשְׂרִים שָׁנָה וְעַד בֶּן־שִׁשִּׁים שָׁנָה וְהָיָה עֶרְכְּךָ
חֲמִשִּׁים שֶׁקֶל כֶּסֶף בְּשֶׁקֶל הַקֹּדֶשׁ: 4 וְאִם־נְקֵבָה

shall be thirty shekels; [5] and if from five years old up to twenty years old, then your valuation for a male shall be twenty shekels, and for a female ten shekels; [6] and if from a month old up to five years old, then your valuation for a male shall be five shekels of silver, and for a female your valuation shall be three shekels of silver; [7] and if from sixty years old and above, if *it is* a male, then your valuation shall be fifteen shekels, and for a female ten shekels.

[8] 'But if he is too poor to pay your valuation, then he shall present himself before the priest, and the priest shall set a value for him; according to the ability of him who vowed, the priest shall value him.

[9] 'If *it is* an animal that men may bring as an offering to the LORD, all that *anyone* gives to the LORD shall be holy. [10] He shall not substitute it or exchange it, good for bad or bad for good; and if he at all exchanges animal for animal, then both it and the one exchanged for it shall be holy. [11] If *it is* an unclean animal which they do not offer as a sacrifice to the LORD, then he shall present the animal before the priest; [12] and the priest shall set a value for it, whether it is good or bad; as you, the priest, value it, so it shall be. [13] But if he *wants* at all *to* redeem it, then he must add one-fifth to your valuation.

[14] 'And when a man dedicates his house *to be* holy to the LORD, then the priest shall set a value for it, whether it is good or bad; as the priest values it, so it shall stand. [15] If he who dedicated it *wants to* redeem his house, then he must add one-fifth of the money of your valuation to it, and it shall be his.

[16] 'If a man dedicates to the LORD *part* of a field of his possession, then your valuation shall be according to the seed for it. A homer of barley seed *shall be valued* at fifty shekels of silver. [17] If he dedicates his field from the Year of Jubilee, according to your valuation it shall stand. [18] But if he dedicates his field after the Jubilee, then the priest shall reckon to him the money due according to the years that remain till the Year of Jubilee, and it shall be deducted from your valuation. [19] And if he who dedicates the field ever wishes to redeem it, then he must add one-fifth of the money of your valuation to it, and it shall belong to him. [20] But if he does not want to redeem the field, or if he has sold the field to another man, it shall not be redeemed anymore; [21] but the field, when it is released in the Jubilee, shall be holy to the LORD, as a devoted field; it shall be the possession of the priest.

הוּא וְהָיָה עֶרְכְּךָ שְׁלֹשִׁים שָׁקֶל: 5 וְאִם מִבֶּן־
חָמֵשׁ שָׁנִים וְעַד בֶּן־עֶשְׂרִים שָׁנָה וְהָיָה עֶרְכְּךָ
הַזָּכָר עֶשְׂרִים שְׁקָלִים וְלַנְּקֵבָה עֲשֶׂרֶת שְׁקָלִים:

6 וְאִם מִבֶּן־חֹדֶשׁ וְעַד בֶּן־חָמֵשׁ שָׁנִים וְהָיָה עֶרְכְּךָ
הַזָּכָר חֲמִשָּׁה שְׁקָלִים כָּסֶף וְלַנְּקֵבָה עֶרְכְּךָ שְׁלֹשֶׁת
שְׁקָלִים כָּסֶף: 7 וְאִם מִבֶּן־שִׁשִּׁים שָׁנָה וָמַעְלָה אִם־
זָכָר וְהָיָה עֶרְכְּךָ חֲמִשָּׁה עָשָׂר שָׁקֶל וְלַנְּקֵבָה עֲשָׂרָה
שְׁקָלִים: 8 וְאִם־מָךְ הוּא מֵעֶרְכֶּךָ וְהֶעֱמִידוֹ לִפְנֵי
הַכֹּהֵן וְהֶעֱרִיךְ אֹתוֹ הַכֹּהֵן עַל־פִּי אֲשֶׁר תַּשִּׂיג
יַד הַנֹּדֵר יַעֲרִיכֶנּוּ הַכֹּהֵן: ס 9 וְאִם־בְּהֵמָה
אֲשֶׁר יַקְרִיבוּ מִמֶּנָּה קָרְבָּן לַיהוָה כֹּל אֲשֶׁר יִתֵּן
מִמֶּנּוּ לַיהוָה יִהְיֶה־קֹּדֶשׁ: 10 לֹא יַחֲלִיפֶנּוּ וְלֹא־
יָמִיר אֹתוֹ טוֹב בְּרָע אוֹ־רַע בְּטוֹב וְאִם־הָמֵר
יָמִיר בְּהֵמָה בִּבְהֵמָה וְהָיָה־הוּא וּתְמוּרָתוֹ יִהְיֶה־
קֹּדֶשׁ: 11 וְאִם כָּל־בְּהֵמָה טְמֵאָה אֲשֶׁר לֹא־יַקְרִיבוּ
מִמֶּנָּה קָרְבָּן לַיהוָה וְהֶעֱמִיד אֶת־הַבְּהֵמָה לִפְנֵי
הַכֹּהֵן: 12 וְהֶעֱרִיךְ הַכֹּהֵן אֹתָהּ בֵּין טוֹב וּבֵין
רָע כְּעֶרְכְּךָ הַכֹּהֵן כֵּן יִהְיֶה: 13 וְאִם־גָּאֹל יִגְאָלֶנָּה
וְיָסַף חֲמִישִׁתוֹ עַל־עֶרְכֶּךָ: 14 וְאִישׁ כִּי־יַקְדִּשׁ אֶת־
בֵּיתוֹ קֹדֶשׁ לַיהוָה וְהֶעֱרִיכוֹ הַכֹּהֵן בֵּין טוֹב וּבֵין
רָע כַּאֲשֶׁר יַעֲרִיךְ אֹתוֹ הַכֹּהֵן כֵּן יָקוּם: 15 וְאִם־
הַמַּקְדִּישׁ יִגְאַל אֶת־בֵּיתוֹ וְיָסַף חֲמִישִׁית כֶּסֶף־
עֶרְכְּךָ עָלָיו וְהָיָה לוֹ: 16 וְאִם מִשְּׂדֵה אֲחֻזָּתוֹ
יַקְדִּישׁ אִישׁ לַיהוָה וְהָיָה עֶרְכְּךָ לְפִי זַרְעוֹ זֶרַע
חֹמֶר שְׂעֹרִים בַּחֲמִשִּׁים שֶׁקֶל כָּסֶף: 17 אִם־מִשְּׁנַת
הַיֹּבֵל יַקְדִּישׁ שָׂדֵהוּ כְּעֶרְכְּךָ יָקוּם: 18 וְאִם־אַחַר
הַיֹּבֵל יַקְדִּישׁ שָׂדֵהוּ וְחִשַּׁב־לוֹ הַכֹּהֵן אֶת־הַכֶּסֶף
עַל־פִּי הַשָּׁנִים הַנּוֹתָרֹת עַד שְׁנַת הַיֹּבֵל וְנִגְרַע
מֵעֶרְכֶּךָ: 19 וְאִם־גָּאֹל יִגְאַל אֶת־הַשָּׂדֶה הַמַּקְדִּישׁ
אֹתוֹ וְיָסַף חֲמִשִׁית כֶּסֶף־עֶרְכְּךָ עָלָיו וְקָם לוֹ:
20 וְאִם־לֹא יִגְאַל אֶת־הַשָּׂדֶה וְאִם־מָכַר אֶת־הַשָּׂדֶה
לְאִישׁ אַחֵר לֹא יִגָּאֵל עוֹד: 21 וְהָיָה הַשָּׂדֶה בְּצֵאתוֹ
בַיֹּבֵל קֹדֶשׁ לַיהוָה כִּשְׂדֵה הַחֵרֶם לַכֹּהֵן

22 'And if a man dedicates to the LORD a field which he has bought, which is not the field of his possession, 23 then the priest shall reckon to him the worth of your valuation, up to the Year of Jubilee, and he shall give your valuation on that day *as a* holy *offering* to the LORD. 24 In the Year of Jubilee the field shall return to him from whom it was bought, to the one who *owned* the land as a possession. 25 And all your valuations shall be according to the shekel of the sanctuary: twenty gerahs to the shekel.

26 'But the firstborn of the animals, which should be the LORD's firstborn, no man shall dedicate; whether *it is* an ox or sheep, it *is* the LORD's. 27 And if *it is* an unclean animal, then he shall redeem *it* according to your valuation, and shall add one-fifth to it; or if it is not redeemed, then it shall be sold according to your valuation.

28 'Nevertheless no devoted *offering* that a man may devote to the LORD of all that he has, *both* man and beast, or the field of his possession, shall be sold or redeemed; every devoted *offering is* most holy to the LORD. 29 No person under the ban, who may become doomed to destruction among men, shall be redeemed, *but* shall surely be put to death. 30 And all the tithe of the land, *whether* of the seed of the land *or* of the fruit of the tree, *is* the LORD's. It *is* holy to the LORD. 31 If a man wants at all to redeem *any* of his tithes, he shall add one-fifth to it. 32 And concerning the tithe of the herd or the flock, of whatever passes under the rod, the tenth one shall be holy to the LORD. 33 He shall not inquire whether it is good or bad, nor shall he exchange it; and if he exchanges it at all, then both it and the one exchanged for it shall be holy; it shall not be redeemed.' "

34 These *are* the commandments which the LORD commanded Moses for the children of Israel on Mount Sinai.

22 וְאִם אֶת־שְׂדֵה מִקְנָתוֹ אֲשֶׁר תִּהְיֶה אֲחֻזָּתוֹ: 23 וְחִשַּׁב־לוֹ הַכֹּהֵן אֵת מִכְסַת הָעֶרְכְּךָ עַד שְׁנַת הַיֹּבֵל וְנָתַן אֶת־הָעֶרְכְּךָ בַּיּוֹם הַהוּא קֹדֶשׁ לַיהוָה: 24 בִּשְׁנַת הַיּוֹבֵל יָשׁוּב הַשָּׂדֶה לַאֲשֶׁר קָנָהוּ מֵאִתּוֹ לַאֲשֶׁר־לוֹ אֲחֻזַּת הָאָרֶץ: 25 וְכָל־עֶרְכְּךָ יִהְיֶה בְּשֶׁקֶל הַקֹּדֶשׁ עֶשְׂרִים גֵּרָה יִהְיֶה הַשָּׁקֶל: ס 26 אַךְ־בְּכוֹר אֲשֶׁר־יְבֻכַּר לַיהוָה בִּבְהֵמָה לֹא־יַקְדִּישׁ אִישׁ אֹתוֹ אִם־שׁוֹר אִם־שֶׂה לַיהוָה הוּא: 27 וְאִם בַּבְּהֵמָה הַטְּמֵאָה וּפָדָה בְעֶרְכֶּךָ וְיָסַף חֲמִשִׁתוֹ עָלָיו וְאִם־לֹא יִגָּאֵל וְנִמְכַּר בְּעֶרְכֶּךָ: 28 אַךְ־כָּל־חֵרֶם אֲשֶׁר יַחֲרִם אִישׁ לַיהוָה מִכָּל־אֲשֶׁר־לוֹ מֵאָדָם וּבְהֵמָה וּמִשְּׂדֵה אֲחֻזָּתוֹ לֹא יִמָּכֵר וְלֹא יִגָּאֵל כָּל־חֵרֶם קֹדֶשׁ־קָדָשִׁים הוּא לַיהוָה: 29 כָּל־חֵרֶם אֲשֶׁר יָחֳרַם מִן־הָאָדָם לֹא יִפָּדֶה מוֹת יוּמָת: 30 וְכָל־מַעְשַׂר הָאָרֶץ מִזֶּרַע הָאָרֶץ מִפְּרִי הָעֵץ לַיהוָה הוּא קֹדֶשׁ לַיהוָה: 31 וְאִם־גָּאֹל יִגְאַל אִישׁ מִמַּעַשְׂרוֹ חֲמִשִׁיתוֹ יֹסֵף עָלָיו: 32 וְכָל־מַעְשַׂר בָּקָר וָצֹאן כֹּל אֲשֶׁר־יַעֲבֹר תַּחַת הַשָּׁבֶט הָעֲשִׂירִי יִהְיֶה־קֹּדֶשׁ לַיהוָה: 33 לֹא יְבַקֵּר בֵּין־טוֹב לָרַע וְלֹא יְמִירֶנּוּ וְאִם־הָמֵר יְמִירֶנּוּ וְהָיָה־הוּא וּתְמוּרָתוֹ יִהְיֶה־קֹּדֶשׁ לֹא יִגָּאֵל: 34 אֵלֶּה הַמִּצְוֹת אֲשֶׁר צִוָּה יְהוָה אֶת־מֹשֶׁה אֶל־בְּנֵי יִשְׂרָאֵל בְּהַר סִינָי:

The Fourth Book of Moses Called

NUMBERS

1 Now the LORD spoke to Moses in the Wilderness of Sinai, in the tabernacle of meeting, on the first *day* of the second month, in the second year after they had come out of the land of Egypt, saying: 2 "Take a census of all the congregation of the children of Israel, by their families, by their fathers' houses, according to the number of names, every male individually, 3 from twenty years old and above—all who *are able to* go to war in Israel. You and Aaron shall number them by their armies. 4 And with you there shall be a man from every tribe, each one the head of his father's house.

5 "These are the names of the men who shall stand with you: from Reuben, Elizur the son of Shedeur; 6 from Simeon, Shelumiel the son of Zurishaddai; 7 from Judah, Nahshon the son of Amminadab; 8 from Issachar, Nethanel the son of Zuar; 9 from Zebulun, Eliab the son of Helon; 10 from the sons of Joseph: from Ephraim, Elishama the son of Ammihud; from Manasseh, Gamaliel the son of Pedahzur; 11 from Benjamin, Abidan the son of Gideoni; 12 from Dan, Ahiezer the son of Ammishaddai; 13 from Asher, Pagiel the son of Ocran; 14 from Gad, Eliasaph the son of Deuel; 15 from Naphtali, Ahira the son of Enan." 16 These *were* chosen from the congregation, leaders of their fathers' tribes, heads of the divisions in Israel.

17 Then Moses and Aaron took these men who had been mentioned by name, 18 and they assembled all the congregation together on the first *day* of the second month; and they recited their ancestry by families, by their fathers' houses, according to the number of names, from twenty years old and above, each one individually. 19 As the LORD commanded Moses, so he numbered them in the Wilderness of Sinai.

20 Now the children of Reuben, Israel's oldest son, their genealogies by their families, by their fathers' house, according to the number of names, every male individually, from twenty years old and above, all who *were able to* go to war: 21 those who were numbered of the tribe of Reuben *were* forty-six thousand five hundred.

22 From the children of Simeon, their genealogies by their families, by their fathers' house, of those who were numbered, according to the number of names, every male individually, from twenty years

א וַיְדַבֵּר יְהֹוָה אֶל־מֹשֶׁה בְּמִדְבַּר סִינַי בְּאֹהֶל מוֹעֵד בְּאֶחָד לַחֹדֶשׁ הַשֵּׁנִי בַּשָּׁנָה הַשֵּׁנִית לְצֵאתָם מֵאֶרֶץ מִצְרַיִם לֵאמֹר: 2 שְׂאוּ אֶת־רֹאשׁ כָּל־עֲדַת בְּנֵי־יִשְׂרָאֵל לְמִשְׁפְּחֹתָם לְבֵית אֲבֹתָם בְּמִסְפַּר שֵׁמוֹת כָּל־זָכָר לְגֻלְגְּלֹתָם: 3 מִבֶּן עֶשְׂרִים שָׁנָה וָמַעְלָה כָּל־יֹצֵא צָבָא בְּיִשְׂרָאֵל תִּפְקְדוּ אֹתָם לְצִבְאֹתָם אַתָּה וְאַהֲרֹן: 4 וְאִתְּכֶם יִהְיוּ אִישׁ אִישׁ לַמַּטֶּה אִישׁ רֹאשׁ לְבֵית־אֲבֹתָיו הוּא: 5 וְאֵלֶּה שְׁמוֹת הָאֲנָשִׁים אֲשֶׁר יַעַמְדוּ אִתְּכֶם לִרְאוּבֵן אֱלִיצוּר בֶּן־שְׁדֵיאוּר: 6 לְשִׁמְעוֹן שְׁלֻמִיאֵל בֶּן־צוּרִישַׁדָּי: 7 לִיהוּדָה נַחְשׁוֹן בֶּן־עַמִּינָדָב: 8 לְיִשָּׂשכָר נְתַנְאֵל בֶּן־צוּעָר: 9 לִזְבוּלֻן אֱלִיאָב בֶּן־חֵלֹן: 10 לִבְנֵי יוֹסֵף לְאֶפְרַיִם אֱלִישָׁמָע בֶּן־עַמִּיהוּד לִמְנַשֶּׁה גַּמְלִיאֵל בֶּן־פְּדָהצוּר: 11 לְבִנְיָמִן אֲבִידָן בֶּן־גִּדְעֹנִי: 12 לְדָן אֲחִיעֶזֶר בֶּן־עַמִּישַׁדָּי: 13 לְאָשֵׁר פַּגְעִיאֵל בֶּן־עָכְרָן: 14 לְגָד אֶלְיָסָף בֶּן־דְּעוּאֵל: 15 לְנַפְתָּלִי אֲחִירַע בֶּן־עֵינָן: 16 אֵלֶּה קרואי^ק הָעֵדָה נְשִׂיאֵי מַטּוֹת אֲבוֹתָם רָאשֵׁי אַלְפֵי יִשְׂרָאֵל הֵם: 17 וַיִּקַּח מֹשֶׁה וְאַהֲרֹן אֵת הָאֲנָשִׁים הָאֵלֶּה אֲשֶׁר נִקְּבוּ בְּשֵׁמוֹת: 18 וְאֵת כָּל־הָעֵדָה הִקְהִילוּ בְּאֶחָד לַחֹדֶשׁ הַשֵּׁנִי וַיִּתְיַלְדוּ עַל־מִשְׁפְּחֹתָם לְבֵית אֲבֹתָם בְּמִסְפַּר שֵׁמוֹת מִבֶּן עֶשְׂרִים שָׁנָה וָמַעְלָה לְגֻלְגְּלֹתָם: 19 כַּאֲשֶׁר צִוָּה יְהֹוָה אֶת־מֹשֶׁה וַיִּפְקְדֵם בְּמִדְבַּר סִינָי:
פ

20 וַיִּהְיוּ בְנֵי־רְאוּבֵן בְּכֹר יִשְׂרָאֵל תּוֹלְדֹתָם לְמִשְׁפְּחֹתָם לְבֵית אֲבֹתָם בְּמִסְפַּר שֵׁמוֹת לְגֻלְגְּלֹתָם כָּל־זָכָר מִבֶּן עֶשְׂרִים שָׁנָה וָמַעְלָה כֹּל יֹצֵא צָבָא: 21 פְּקֻדֵיהֶם לְמַטֵּה רְאוּבֵן שִׁשָּׁה וְאַרְבָּעִים אֶלֶף וַחֲמֵשׁ מֵאוֹת:
פ

22 לִבְנֵי שִׁמְעוֹן תּוֹלְדֹתָם לְמִשְׁפְּחֹתָם לְבֵית אֲבֹתָם

old and above, all who *were able to* go to war:
²³ those who were numbered of the tribe of Simeon
were fifty-nine thousand three hundred.

²⁴ From the children of Gad, their genealogies by
their families, by their fathers' house, according to
the number of names, from twenty years old and
above, all who *were able to* go to war: ²⁵ those who
were numbered of the tribe of Gad *were* forty-five
thousand six hundred and fifty.

²⁶ From the children of Judah, their genealogies
by their families, by their fathers' house, according
to the number of names, from twenty years old and
above, all who *were able to* go to war: ²⁷ those who
were numbered of the tribe of Judah *were* seventy-
four thousand six hundred.

²⁸ From the children of Issachar, their genealogies by their families, by their fathers' house,
according to the number of names, from twenty
years old and above, all who *were able to* go to war:
²⁹ those who were numbered of the tribe of Issachar
were fifty-four thousand four hundred.

³⁰ From the children of Zebulun, their genealogies by their families, by their fathers' house,
according to the number of names, from twenty
years old and above, all who *were able to* go to war:
³¹ those who were numbered of the tribe of Zebulun
were fifty-seven thousand four hundred.

³² From the sons of Joseph, the children of
Ephraim, their genealogies by their families, by
their fathers' house, according to the number of
names, from twenty years old and above, all who
were able to go to war: ³³ those who were numbered
of the tribe of Ephraim *were* forty thousand five
hundred.

³⁴ From the children of Manasseh, their genealogies by their families, by their fathers' house,
according to the number of names, from twenty
years old and above, all who *were able to* go to war:
³⁵ those who were numbered of the tribe of
Manasseh *were* thirty-two thousand two hundred.

³⁶ From the children of Benjamin, their genealogies by their families, by their fathers' house,
according to the number of names, from twenty
years old and above, all who *were able to* go to war:
³⁷ those who were numbered of the tribe of
Benjamin *were* thirty-five thousand four hundred.

³⁸ From the children of Dan, their genealogies by
their families, by their fathers' house, according to
the number of names, from twenty years old and
above, all who *were able to* go to war: ³⁹ those who
were numbered of the tribe of Dan *were* sixty-two
thousand seven hundred.

פְּקֻדָיו בְּמִסְפַּר שֵׁמוֹת לְגֻלְגְּלֹתָם כָּל־זָכָר מִבֶּן
עֶשְׂרִים שָׁנָה וָמַעְלָה כֹּל יֹצֵא צָבָא: 23 פְּקֻדֵיהֶם
לְמַטֵּה שִׁמְעוֹן תִּשְׁעָה וַחֲמִשִּׁים אֶלֶף וּשְׁלֹשׁ
מֵאוֹת:
24 לִבְנֵי גָד תּוֹלְדֹתָם לְמִשְׁפְּחֹתָם לְבֵית אֲבֹתָם
בְּמִסְפַּר שֵׁמוֹת מִבֶּן עֶשְׂרִים שָׁנָה וָמַעְלָה כֹּל יֹצֵא
צָבָא: 25 פְּקֻדֵיהֶם לְמַטֵּה גָד חֲמִשָּׁה וְאַרְבָּעִים
אֶלֶף וְשֵׁשׁ מֵאוֹת וַחֲמִשִּׁים:
26 לִבְנֵי יְהוּדָה תּוֹלְדֹתָם לְמִשְׁפְּחֹתָם לְבֵית אֲבֹתָם
בְּמִסְפַּר שֵׁמֹת מִבֶּן עֶשְׂרִים שָׁנָה וָמַעְלָה כֹּל יֹצֵא
צָבָא: 27 פְּקֻדֵיהֶם לְמַטֵּה יְהוּדָה אַרְבָּעָה וְשִׁבְעִים
אֶלֶף וְשֵׁשׁ מֵאוֹת:
28 לִבְנֵי יִשָּׂשכָר תּוֹלְדֹתָם לְמִשְׁפְּחֹתָם לְבֵית אֲבֹתָם
בְּמִסְפַּר שֵׁמֹת מִבֶּן עֶשְׂרִים שָׁנָה וָמַעְלָה כֹּל יֹצֵא
צָבָא: 29 פְּקֻדֵיהֶם לְמַטֵּה יִשָּׂשכָר אַרְבָּעָה וַחֲמִשִּׁים
אֶלֶף וְאַרְבַּע מֵאוֹת:
30 לִבְנֵי זְבוּלֻן תּוֹלְדֹתָם לְמִשְׁפְּחֹתָם לְבֵית אֲבֹתָם
בְּמִסְפַּר שֵׁמֹת מִבֶּן עֶשְׂרִים שָׁנָה וָמַעְלָה כֹּל יֹצֵא
צָבָא: 31 פְּקֻדֵיהֶם לְמַטֵּה זְבוּלֻן שִׁבְעָה וַחֲמִשִּׁים
אֶלֶף וְאַרְבַּע מֵאוֹת:
32 לִבְנֵי יוֹסֵף לִבְנֵי אֶפְרַיִם תּוֹלְדֹתָם לְמִשְׁפְּחֹתָם
לְבֵית אֲבֹתָם בְּמִסְפַּר שֵׁמֹת מִבֶּן עֶשְׂרִים שָׁנָה
וָמַעְלָה כֹּל יֹצֵא צָבָא: 33 פְּקֻדֵיהֶם לְמַטֵּה אֶפְרָיִם
אַרְבָּעִים אֶלֶף וַחֲמֵשׁ מֵאוֹת: 34 לִבְנֵי מְנַשֶּׁה
תּוֹלְדֹתָם לְמִשְׁפְּחֹתָם לְבֵית אֲבֹתָם בְּמִסְפַּר שֵׁמוֹת
מִבֶּן עֶשְׂרִים שָׁנָה וָמַעְלָה כֹּל יֹצֵא צָבָא:
35 פְּקֻדֵיהֶם לְמַטֵּה מְנַשֶּׁה שְׁנַיִם וּשְׁלֹשִׁים אֶלֶף
וּמָאתָיִם:
36 לִבְנֵי בִנְיָמִן תּוֹלְדֹתָם לְמִשְׁפְּחֹתָם לְבֵית אֲבֹתָם
בְּמִסְפַּר שֵׁמֹת מִבֶּן עֶשְׂרִים שָׁנָה וָמַעְלָה כֹּל יֹצֵא
צָבָא: 37 פְּקֻדֵיהֶם לְמַטֵּה בִנְיָמִן חֲמִשָּׁה וּשְׁלֹשִׁים
אֶלֶף וְאַרְבַּע מֵאוֹת:
38 לִבְנֵי דָן תּוֹלְדֹתָם לְמִשְׁפְּחֹתָם לְבֵית אֲבֹתָם
בְּמִסְפַּר שֵׁמֹת מִבֶּן עֶשְׂרִים שָׁנָה וָמַעְלָה כֹּל יֹצֵא
צָבָא: 39 פְּקֻדֵיהֶם לְמַטֵּה דָן שְׁנַיִם וְשִׁשִּׁים אֶלֶף
וּשְׁבַע מֵאוֹת:

40 From the children of Asher, their genealogies by their families, by their fathers' house, according to the number of names, from twenty years old and above, all who *were able to* go to war: 41 those who were numbered of the tribe of Asher *were* forty-one thousand five hundred.

42 From the children of Naphtali, their genealogies by their families, by their fathers' house, according to the number of names, from twenty years old and above, all who *were able* to go to war: 43 those who were numbered of the tribe of Naphtali *were* fifty-three thousand four hundred.

44 These are the ones who were numbered, whom Moses and Aaron numbered, with the leaders of Israel, twelve men, each one representing his father's house. 45 So all who were numbered of the children of Israel, by their fathers' houses, from twenty years old and above, all who *were able to* go to war in Israel— 46 all who were numbered were six hundred and three thousand five hundred and fifty.

47 But the Levites were not numbered among them by their fathers' tribe; 48 for the LORD had spoken to Moses, saying: 49 "Only the tribe of Levi you shall not number, nor take a census of them among the children of Israel; 50 but you shall appoint the Levites over the tabernacle of the Testimony, over all its furnishings, and over all things that belong to it; they shall carry the tabernacle and all its furnishings; they shall attend to it and camp around the tabernacle. 51 And when the tabernacle is to go forward, the Levites shall take it down; and when the tabernacle is to be set up, the Levites shall set it up. The outsider who comes near shall be put to death. 52 The children of Israel shall pitch their tents, everyone by his own camp, everyone by his own standard, according to their armies; 53 but the Levites shall camp around the tabernacle of the Testimony, that there may be no wrath on the congregation of the children of Israel; and the Levites shall keep charge of the tabernacle of the Testimony."

54 Thus the children of Israel did; according to all that the LORD commanded Moses, so they did.

2 And the LORD spoke to Moses and Aaron, saying: 2 "Everyone of the children of Israel shall camp by his own standard, beside the emblems of his father's house; they shall camp some distance from the tabernacle of meeting. 3 On the east side, toward the rising of the sun, those of the standard of the forces with Judah shall camp according to their armies; and Nahshon the son of Amminadab

40 לִבְנֵי אָשֵׁר תּוֹלְדֹתָם לְמִשְׁפְּחֹתָם לְבֵית אֲבֹתָם בְּמִסְפַּר שֵׁמֹת מִבֶּן עֶשְׂרִים שָׁנָה וָמַעְלָה כֹּל יֹצֵא צָבָא: 41 פְּקֻדֵיהֶם לְמַטֵּה אָשֵׁר אֶחָד וְאַרְבָּעִים אֶלֶף וַחֲמֵשׁ מֵאוֹת: פ

42 בְּנֵי נַפְתָּלִי תּוֹלְדֹתָם לְמִשְׁפְּחֹתָם לְבֵית אֲבֹתָם בְּמִסְפַּר שֵׁמֹת מִבֶּן עֶשְׂרִים שָׁנָה וָמַעְלָה כֹּל יֹצֵא צָבָא: 43 פְּקֻדֵיהֶם לְמַטֵּה נַפְתָּלִי שְׁלֹשָׁה וַחֲמִשִּׁים אֶלֶף וְאַרְבַּע מֵאוֹת: פ

44 אֵלֶּה הַפְּקֻדִים אֲשֶׁר פָּקַד מֹשֶׁה וְאַהֲרֹן וּנְשִׂיאֵי יִשְׂרָאֵל שְׁנֵים עָשָׂר אִישׁ אִישׁ־אֶחָד לְבֵית־אֲבֹתָיו הָיוּ: 45 וַיִּהְיוּ כָּל־פְּקוּדֵי בְנֵי־יִשְׂרָאֵל לְבֵית אֲבֹתָם מִבֶּן עֶשְׂרִים שָׁנָה וָמַעְלָה כָּל־יֹצֵא צָבָא בְּיִשְׂרָאֵל: 46 וַיִּהְיוּ כָּל־הַפְּקֻדִים שֵׁשׁ־מֵאוֹת אֶלֶף וּשְׁלֹשֶׁת אֲלָפִים וַחֲמֵשׁ מֵאוֹת וַחֲמִשִּׁים: 47 וְהַלְוִיִּם לְמַטֵּה אֲבֹתָם לֹא הָתְפָּקְדוּ בְּתוֹכָם: פ

48 וַיְדַבֵּר יְהוָה אֶל־מֹשֶׁה לֵּאמֹר: 49 אַךְ אֶת־מַטֵּה לֵוִי לֹא תִפְקֹד וְאֶת־רֹאשָׁם לֹא תִשָּׂא בְּתוֹךְ בְּנֵי יִשְׂרָאֵל: 50 וְאַתָּה הַפְקֵד אֶת־הַלְוִיִּם עַל־מִשְׁכַּן הָעֵדֻת וְעַל כָּל־כֵּלָיו וְעַל כָּל־אֲשֶׁר־לוֹ הֵמָּה יִשְׂאוּ אֶת־הַמִּשְׁכָּן וְאֶת־כָּל־כֵּלָיו וְהֵם יְשָׁרְתֻהוּ וְסָבִיב לַמִּשְׁכָּן יַחֲנוּ: 51 וּבִנְסֹעַ הַמִּשְׁכָּן יוֹרִידוּ אֹתוֹ הַלְוִיִּם וּבַחֲנֹת הַמִּשְׁכָּן יָקִימוּ אֹתוֹ הַלְוִיִּם וְהַזָּר הַקָּרֵב יוּמָת: 52 וְחָנוּ בְּנֵי יִשְׂרָאֵל אִישׁ עַל־מַחֲנֵהוּ וְאִישׁ עַל־דִּגְלוֹ לְצִבְאֹתָם: 53 וְהַלְוִיִּם יַחֲנוּ סָבִיב לְמִשְׁכַּן הָעֵדֻת וְלֹא־יִהְיֶה קֶצֶף עַל־עֲדַת בְּנֵי יִשְׂרָאֵל וְשָׁמְרוּ הַלְוִיִּם אֶת־מִשְׁמֶרֶת מִשְׁכַּן הָעֵדוּת: 54 וַיַּעֲשׂוּ בְּנֵי יִשְׂרָאֵל כְּכֹל אֲשֶׁר צִוָּה יְהוָה אֶת־מֹשֶׁה כֵּן עָשׂוּ: פ

ב וַיְדַבֵּר יְהוָה אֶל־מֹשֶׁה וְאֶל־אַהֲרֹן לֵאמֹר: 2 אִישׁ עַל־דִּגְלוֹ בְאֹתֹת לְבֵית אֲבֹתָם יַחֲנוּ בְּנֵי יִשְׂרָאֵל מִנֶּגֶד סָבִיב לְאֹהֶל־מוֹעֵד יַחֲנוּ: 3 וְהַחֹנִים קֵדְמָה מִזְרָחָה דֶּגֶל מַחֲנֵה יְהוּדָה לְצִבְאֹתָם וְנָשִׂיא לִבְנֵי יְהוּדָה נַחְשׁוֹן בֶּן־עַמִּינָדָב:

shall be the leader of the children of Judah. " ⁴And his army was numbered at seventy-four thousand six hundred.

⁵"Those who camp next to him shall be the tribe of Issachar, and Nethanel the son of Zuar shall be the leader of the children of Issachar." ⁶And his army was numbered at fifty-four thousand four hundred.

⁷"Then comes the tribe of Zebulun, and Eliab the son of Helon shall be the leader of the children of Zebulun." ⁸And his army was numbered at fifty-seven thousand four hundred. ⁹"All who were numbered according to their armies of the forces with Judah, one hundred and eighty-six thousand four hundred—these shall break camp first.

¹⁰"On the south side shall be the standard of the forces with Reuben according to their armies, and the leader of the children of Reuben shall be Elizur the son of Shedeur." ¹¹And his army was numbered at forty-six thousand five hundred.

¹²"Those who camp next to him shall be the tribe of Simeon, and the leader of the children of Simeon shall be Shelumiel the son of Zurishaddai." ¹³And his army was numbered at fifty-nine thousand three hundred.

¹⁴"Then comes the tribe of Gad, and the leader of the children of Gad shall be Eliasaph the son of Reuel." ¹⁵And his army was numbered at forty-five thousand six hundred and fifty. ¹⁶"All who were numbered according to their armies of the forces with Reuben, one hundred and fifty-one thousand four hundred and fifty—they shall be the second to break camp.

¹⁷"And the tabernacle of meeting shall move out with the camp of the Levites in the middle of the camps; as they camp, so they shall move out, everyone in his place, by their standards.

¹⁸"On the west side shall be the standard of the forces with Ephraim according to their armies, and the leader of the children of Ephraim shall be Elishama the son of Ammihud." ¹⁹And his army was numbered at forty thousand five hundred.

²⁰"Next to him comes the tribe of Manasseh, and the leader of the children of Manasseh shall be Gamaliel the son of Pedahzur." ²¹And his army was numbered at thirty-two thousand two hundred.

²²"Then comes the tribe of Benjamin, and the leader of the children of Benjamin shall be Abidan the son of Gideoni." ²³And his army was numbered at thirty-five thousand four hundred. ²⁴"All who were numbered according to their armies of the forces with Ephraim, one hundred and eight thousand one hundred—they shall be the third to break camp.

4 וּצְבָא֖וֹ וּפְקֻדֵיהֶ֑ם אַרְבָּעָ֧ה וְשִׁבְעִ֛ים אֶ֖לֶף וְשֵׁ֥שׁ מֵאֽוֹת: 5 וְהַחֹנִ֥ים עָלָ֖יו מַטֵּ֣ה יִשָּׂשכָ֑ר וְנָשִׂיא֙ לִבְנֵ֣י יִשָּׂשכָ֔ר נְתַנְאֵ֖ל בֶּן־צוּעָֽר: 6 וּצְבָא֖וֹ וּפְקֻדָ֑יו אַרְבָּעָ֧ה וַחֲמִשִּׁ֛ים אֶ֖לֶף וְאַרְבַּ֥ע מֵאֽוֹת: 7 מַטֵּ֖ה זְבוּלֻ֑ן וְנָשִׂיא֙ לִבְנֵ֣י זְבוּלֻ֔ן אֱלִיאָ֖ב בֶּן־חֵלֹֽן: 8 וּצְבָא֖וֹ וּפְקֻדָ֑יו שִׁבְעָ֧ה וַחֲמִשִּׁ֛ים אֶ֖לֶף וְאַרְבַּ֥ע מֵאֽוֹת: 9 כָּֽל־הַפְּקֻדִ֞ים לְמַחֲנֵ֣ה יְהוּדָ֗ה מְאַ֥ת אֶ֙לֶף֙ וּשְׁמֹנִ֣ים אֶ֔לֶף וְשֵֽׁשֶׁת־אֲלָפִ֥ים וְאַרְבַּע־מֵא֖וֹת לְצִבְאֹתָ֑ם רִאשֹׁנָ֖ה יִסָּֽעוּ: ס 10 דֶּ֣גֶל מַחֲנֵ֧ה רְאוּבֵ֛ן תֵּימָ֖נָה לְצִבְאֹתָ֑ם וְנָשִׂיא֙ לִבְנֵ֣י רְאוּבֵ֔ן אֱלִיצ֖וּר בֶּן־שְׁדֵיאֽוּר: 11 וּצְבָא֖וֹ וּפְקֻדָ֑יו שִׁשָּׁ֧ה וְאַרְבָּעִ֛ים אֶ֖לֶף וַחֲמֵ֥שׁ מֵאֽוֹת: 12 וְהַחוֹנִ֥ם עָלָ֖יו מַטֵּ֣ה שִׁמְע֑וֹן וְנָשִׂיא֙ לִבְנֵ֣י שִׁמְע֔וֹן שְׁלֻמִיאֵ֖ל בֶּן־צוּרִֽי־שַׁדָּֽי: 13 וּצְבָא֖וֹ וּפְקֻדֵיהֶ֑ם תִּשְׁעָ֧ה וַחֲמִשִּׁ֛ים אֶ֖לֶף וּשְׁלֹ֥שׁ מֵאֽוֹת: 14 וּמַטֵּ֖ה גָּ֑ד וְנָשִׂיא֙ לִבְנֵ֣י גָ֔ד אֶלְיָסָ֖ף בֶּן־רְעוּאֵֽל: 15 וּצְבָא֖וֹ וּפְקֻדֵיהֶ֑ם חֲמִשָּׁ֧ה וְאַרְבָּעִ֛ים אֶ֖לֶף וְשֵׁ֥שׁ מֵא֖וֹת וַחֲמִשִּֽׁים: 16 כָּֽל־הַפְּקֻדִ֞ים לְמַחֲנֵ֣ה רְאוּבֵ֗ן מְאַ֥ת אֶ֙לֶף֙ וְאֶחָ֣ד וַחֲמִשִּׁ֥ים אֶ֖לֶף וְאַרְבַּע־מֵא֛וֹת וַחֲמִשִּׁ֖ים לְצִבְאֹתָ֑ם וּשְׁנִיִּ֥ם יִסָּֽעוּ: ס 17 וְנָסַ֧ע אֹֽהֶל־מוֹעֵ֛ד מַחֲנֵ֥ה הַלְוִיִּ֖ם בְּת֣וֹךְ הַֽמַּחֲנֹ֑ת כַּאֲשֶׁ֤ר יַחֲנוּ֙ כֵּ֣ן יִסָּ֔עוּ אִ֥ישׁ עַל־יָד֖וֹ לְדִגְלֵיהֶֽם: ס 18 דֶּ֣גֶל מַחֲנֵ֥ה אֶפְרַ֛יִם לְצִבְאֹתָ֖ם יָ֑מָּה וְנָשִׂיא֙ לִבְנֵ֣י אֶפְרַ֔יִם אֱלִישָׁמָ֖ע בֶּן־עַמִּיהֽוּד: 19 וּצְבָא֖וֹ וּפְקֻדֵיהֶ֑ם אַרְבָּעִ֥ים אֶ֖לֶף וַחֲמֵ֥שׁ מֵאֽוֹת: 20 וְעָלָ֖יו מַטֵּ֣ה מְנַשֶּׁ֑ה וְנָשִׂיא֙ לִבְנֵ֣י מְנַשֶּׁ֔ה גַּמְלִיאֵ֖ל בֶּן־פְּדָהצֽוּר: 21 וּצְבָא֖וֹ וּפְקֻדֵיהֶ֑ם שְׁנַ֧יִם וּשְׁלֹשִׁ֛ים אֶ֖לֶף וּמָאתָֽיִם: 22 וּמַטֵּ֖ה בִּנְיָמִ֑ן וְנָשִׂיא֙ לִבְנֵ֣י בִנְיָמִ֔ן אֲבִידָ֖ן בֶּן־גִּדְעֹנִֽי: 23 וּצְבָא֖וֹ וּפְקֻדֵיהֶ֑ם חֲמִשָּׁ֧ה וּשְׁלֹשִׁ֛ים אֶ֖לֶף וְאַרְבַּ֥ע מֵאֽוֹת: 24 כָּֽל־הַפְּקֻדִ֞ים לְמַחֲנֵ֣ה אֶפְרַ֗יִם מְאַ֥ת אֶ֙לֶף֙ וּשְׁמֹֽנַת־אֲלָפִ֥ים וּמֵאָ֖ה לְצִבְאֹתָ֑ם

²⁵"The standard of the forces with Dan *shall be* on the north side according to their armies, and the leader of the children of Dan *shall be* Ahiezer the son of Ammishaddai." ²⁶And his army was numbered at sixty-two thousand seven hundred.

²⁷"Those who camp next to him *shall be* the tribe of Asher, and the leader of the children of Asher *shall be* Pagiel the son of Ocran." ²⁸And his army was numbered at forty-one thousand five hundred.

²⁹"Then *comes* the tribe of Naphtali, and the leader of the children of Naphtali *shall be* Ahira the son of Enan." ³⁰And his army was numbered at fifty-three thousand four hundred. ³¹"All who were numbered of the forces with Dan, one hundred and fifty-seven thousand six hundred—they shall break camp last, with their standards."

³²These *are* the ones who were numbered of the children of Israel by their fathers' houses. All who were numbered according to their armies of the forces *were* six hundred and three thousand five hundred and fifty. ³³But the Levites were not numbered among the children of Israel, just as the LORD commanded Moses.

³⁴Thus the children of Israel did according to all that the LORD commanded Moses; so they camped by their standards and so they broke camp, each one by his family, according to their fathers' houses.

3 Now these *are* the records of Aaron and Moses when the LORD spoke with Moses on Mount Sinai. ²And these *are* the names of the sons of Aaron: Nadab, the firstborn, and Abihu, Eleazar, and Ithamar. ³These *are* the names of the sons of Aaron, the anointed priests, whom he consecrated to minister as priests. ⁴Nadab and Abihu had died before the LORD when they offered profane fire before the LORD in the Wilderness of Sinai; and they had no children. So Eleazar and Ithamar ministered as priests in the presence of Aaron their father.

⁵And the LORD spoke to Moses, saying: ⁶"Bring the tribe of Levi near, and present them before Aaron the priest, that they may serve him. ⁷And they shall attend to his needs and the needs of the whole congregation before the tabernacle of meeting, to do the work of the tabernacle. ⁸Also they shall attend to all the furnishings of the tabernacle of meeting, and to the needs of the children of Israel, to do the work of the tabernacle. ⁹And you shall give the Levites to Aaron and his sons; they *are* given entirely to him from among the children

וּשְׁלֹשִׁים יִסָּעוּ: ס   25 דֶּגֶל מַחֲנֵה דָן צָפֹנָה לְצִבְאֹתָם וְנָשִׂיא לִבְנֵי דָן אֲחִיעֶזֶר בֶּן־עַמִּישַׁדָּי: 26 וּצְבָאוֹ וּפְקֻדֵיהֶם שְׁנַיִם וְשִׁשִּׁים אֶלֶף וּשְׁבַע מֵאוֹת: 27 וְהַחֹנִים עָלָיו מַטֵּה אָשֵׁר וְנָשִׂיא לִבְנֵי אָשֵׁר פַּגְעִיאֵל בֶּן־עׇכְרָן: 28 וּצְבָאוֹ וּפְקֻדֵיהֶם אֶחָד וְאַרְבָּעִים אֶלֶף וַחֲמֵשׁ מֵאוֹת: 29 וּמַטֵּה נַפְתָּלִי וְנָשִׂיא לִבְנֵי נַפְתָּלִי אֲחִירַע בֶּן־עֵינָן: 30 וּצְבָאוֹ וּפְקֻדֵיהֶם שְׁלֹשָׁה וַחֲמִשִּׁים אֶלֶף וְאַרְבַּע מֵאוֹת:

31 כׇּל־הַפְּקֻדִים לְמַחֲנֵה דָן מְאַת אֶלֶף וְשִׁבְעָה וַחֲמִשִּׁים אֶלֶף וְשֵׁשׁ מֵאוֹת לָאַחֲרֹנָה יִסְעוּ לְדִגְלֵיהֶם: פ

32 אֵלֶּה פְּקוּדֵי בְנֵי־יִשְׂרָאֵל לְבֵית אֲבֹתָם כׇּל־פְּקוּדֵי הַמַּחֲנֹת לְצִבְאֹתָם שֵׁשׁ־מֵאוֹת אֶלֶף וּשְׁלֹשֶׁת אֲלָפִים וַחֲמֵשׁ מֵאוֹת וַחֲמִשִּׁים: 33 וְהַלְוִיִּם לֹא הׇתְפָּקְדוּ בְּתוֹךְ בְּנֵי יִשְׂרָאֵל כַּאֲשֶׁר צִוָּה יְהֹוָה אֶת־מֹשֶׁה:

34 וַיַּעֲשׂוּ בְּנֵי יִשְׂרָאֵל כְּכֹל אֲשֶׁר־צִוָּה יְהֹוָה אֶת־מֹשֶׁה כֵּן־חָנוּ לְדִגְלֵיהֶם וְכֵן נָסָעוּ אִישׁ לְמִשְׁפְּחֹתָיו עַל־בֵּית אֲבֹתָיו:

ג וְאֵלֶּה תּוֹלְדֹת אַהֲרֹן וּמֹשֶׁה בְּיוֹם דִּבֶּר יְהֹוָה אֶת־מֹשֶׁה בְּהַר סִינָי: 2 וְאֵלֶּה שְׁמוֹת בְּנֵי־אַהֲרֹן הַבְּכוֹר | נָדָב וַאֲבִיהוּא אֶלְעָזָר וְאִיתָמָר: 3 אֵלֶּה שְׁמוֹת בְּנֵי אַהֲרֹן הַכֹּהֲנִים הַמְּשֻׁחִים אֲשֶׁר־מִלֵּא יָדָם לְכַהֵן: 4 וַיָּמׇת נָדָב וַאֲבִיהוּא לִפְנֵי יְהֹוָה בְּהַקְרִבָם אֵשׁ זָרָה לִפְנֵי יְהֹוָה בְּמִדְבַּר סִינַי וּבָנִים לֹא־הָיוּ לָהֶם וַיְכַהֵן אֶלְעָזָר וְאִיתָמָר עַל־פְּנֵי אַהֲרֹן אֲבִיהֶם: פ

5 וַיְדַבֵּר יְהֹוָה אֶל־מֹשֶׁה לֵּאמֹר: 6 הַקְרֵב אֶת־מַטֵּה לֵוִי וְהַעֲמַדְתָּ אֹתוֹ לִפְנֵי אַהֲרֹן הַכֹּהֵן וְשֵׁרְתוּ אֹתוֹ: 7 וְשָׁמְרוּ אֶת־מִשְׁמַרְתּוֹ וְאֶת־מִשְׁמֶרֶת כׇּל־הָעֵדָה לִפְנֵי אֹהֶל מוֹעֵד לַעֲבֹד אֶת־עֲבֹדַת הַמִּשְׁכָּן: 8 וְשָׁמְרוּ אֶת־כׇּל־כְּלֵי אֹהֶל מוֹעֵד וְאֶת־מִשְׁמֶרֶת בְּנֵי יִשְׂרָאֵל לַעֲבֹד אֶת־עֲבֹדַת הַמִּשְׁכָּן: 9 וְנָתַתָּה אֶת־הַלְוִיִּם לְאַהֲרֹן וּלְבָנָיו נְתוּנִם נְתוּנִם הֵמָּה לוֹ

of Israel. ¹⁰So you shall appoint Aaron and his sons, and they shall attend to their priesthood; but the outsider who comes near shall be put to death."

¹¹Then the LORD spoke to Moses, saying: ¹²"Now behold, I Myself have taken the Levites from among the children of Israel instead of every firstborn who opens the womb among the children of Israel. Therefore the Levites shall be Mine, ¹³because all the firstborn *are* Mine. On the day that I struck all the firstborn in the land of Egypt, I sanctified to Myself all the firstborn in Israel, both man and beast. They shall be Mine: I *am* the LORD."

¹⁴Then the LORD spoke to Moses in the Wilderness of Sinai, saying: ¹⁵"Number the children of Levi by their fathers' houses, by their families; you shall number every male from a month old and above."

¹⁶So Moses numbered them according to the word of the LORD, as he was commanded. ¹⁷These were the sons of Levi by their names: Gershon, Kohath, and Merari. ¹⁸And these *are* the names of the sons of Gershon by their families: Libni and Shimei. ¹⁹And the sons of Kohath by their families: Amram, Izehar, Hebron, and Uzziel. ²⁰And the sons of Merari by their families: Mahli and Mushi. These *are* the families of the Levites by their fathers' houses.

²¹From Gershon *came* the family of the Libnites and the family of the Shimites; these *were* the families of the Gershonites. ²²Those who were numbered, according to the number of all the males from a month old and above—of those who were numbered *there were* seven thousand five hundred. ²³The families of the Gershonites were to camp behind the tabernacle westward. ²⁴And the leader of the father's house of the Gershonites *was* Eliasaph the son of Lael. ²⁵The duties of the children of Gershon in the tabernacle of meeting *included* the tabernacle, the tent with its covering, the screen for the door of the tabernacle of meeting, ²⁶the screen for the door of the court, the hangings of the court which *are* around the tabernacle and the altar, and their cords, according to all the work relating to them.

²⁷From Kohath *came* the family of the Amramites, the family of the Izharites, the family of the Hebronites, and the family of the Uzzielites; these *were* the families of the Kohathites. ²⁸According to the number of all the males, from a month old and above, *there were* eight thousand six hundred keeping charge of the sanctuary. ²⁹The families of the children of Kohath were to camp on the south side of the tabernacle. ³⁰And the leader of the

מֵאֵת בְּנֵי יִשְׂרָאֵל: 10 וְאֶת־אַהֲרֹן וְאֶת־בָּנָיו תִּפְקֹד וְשָׁמְרוּ אֶת־כְּהֻנָּתָם וְהַזָּר הַקָּרֵב יוּמָת: פ

11 וַיְדַבֵּר יְהוָֹה אֶל־מֹשֶׁה לֵּאמֹר: 12 וַאֲנִי הִנֵּה לָקַחְתִּי אֶת־הַלְוִיִּם מִתּוֹךְ בְּנֵי יִשְׂרָאֵל תַּחַת כָּל־ בְּכוֹר פֶּטֶר רֶחֶם מִבְּנֵי יִשְׂרָאֵל וְהָיוּ לִי הַלְוִיִּם: 13 כִּי לִי כָּל־בְּכוֹר בְּיוֹם הַכֹּתִי כָל־בְּכוֹר בְּאֶרֶץ מִצְרַיִם הִקְדַּשְׁתִּי לִי כָל־בְּכוֹר בְּיִשְׂרָאֵל מֵאָדָם עַד־בְּהֵמָה לִי יִהְיוּ אֲנִי יְהוָֹה: ס 14 וַיְדַבֵּר יְהוָֹה אֶל־מֹשֶׁה בְּמִדְבַּר סִינַי לֵאמֹר: 15 פְּקֹד אֶת־ בְּנֵי לֵוִי לְבֵית אֲבֹתָם לְמִשְׁפְּחֹתָם כָּל־זָכָר מִבֶּן־ חֹדֶשׁ וָמַעְלָה תִּפְקְדֵם: 16 וַיִּפְקֹד אֹתָם מֹשֶׁה עַל־פִּי יְהוָֹה כַּאֲשֶׁר צֻוָּה: 17 וַיִּהְיוּ־אֵלֶּה בְנֵי־לֵוִי בִּשְׁמֹתָם גֵּרְשׁוֹן וּקְהָת וּמְרָרִי: 18 וְאֵלֶּה שְׁמוֹת בְּנֵי־גֵרְשׁוֹן לְמִשְׁפְּחֹתָם לִבְנִי וְשִׁמְעִי: 19 וּבְנֵי קְהָת לְמִשְׁפְּחֹתָם עַמְרָם וְיִצְהָר חֶבְרוֹן וְעֻזִּיאֵל: 20 וּבְנֵי מְרָרִי לְמִשְׁפְּחֹתָם מַחְלִי וּמוּשִׁי אֵלֶּה הֵם מִשְׁפְּחֹת הַלֵּוִי לְבֵית אֲבֹתָם: 21 לְגֵרְשׁוֹן מִשְׁפַּחַת הַלִּבְנִי וּמִשְׁפַּחַת הַשִּׁמְעִי אֵלֶּה הֵם מִשְׁפְּחֹת הַגֵּרְשֻׁנִּי: 22 פְּקֻדֵיהֶם בְּמִסְפַּר כָּל־זָכָר מִבֶּן־חֹדֶשׁ וָמָעְלָה פְּקֻדֵיהֶם שִׁבְעַת אֲלָפִים וַחֲמֵשׁ מֵאוֹת: 23 מִשְׁפְּחֹת הַגֵּרְשֻׁנִּי אַחֲרֵי הַמִּשְׁכָּן יַחֲנוּ יָמָּה: 24 וּנְשִׂיא בֵית־ אָב לַגֵּרְשֻׁנִּי אֶלְיָסָף בֶּן־לָאֵל: 25 וּמִשְׁמֶרֶת בְּנֵי־ גֵרְשׁוֹן בְּאֹהֶל מוֹעֵד הַמִּשְׁכָּן וְהָאֹהֶל מִכְסֵהוּ וּמָסָךְ פֶּתַח אֹהֶל מוֹעֵד: 26 וְקַלְעֵי הֶחָצֵר וְאֶת־מָסַךְ פֶּתַח הֶחָצֵר אֲשֶׁר עַל־הַמִּשְׁכָּן וְעַל־הַמִּזְבֵּחַ סָבִיב וְאֵת מֵיתָרָיו לְכֹל עֲבֹדָתוֹ: 27 וְלִקְהָת מִשְׁפַּחַת הַעַמְרָמִי וּמִשְׁפַּחַת הַיִּצְהָרִי וּמִשְׁפַּחַת הַחֶבְרֹנִי וּמִשְׁפַּחַת הָעָזִּיאֵלִי אֵלֶּה הֵם מִשְׁפְּחֹת הַקְּהָתִי: 28 בְּמִסְפַּר כָּל־זָכָר מִבֶּן־חֹדֶשׁ וָמַעְלָה שְׁמֹנַת אֲלָפִים וְשֵׁשׁ מֵאוֹת שֹׁמְרֵי מִשְׁמֶרֶת הַקֹּדֶשׁ: 29 מִשְׁפְּחֹת בְּנֵי־ קְהָת יַחֲנוּ עַל יֶרֶךְ הַמִּשְׁכָּן תֵּימָנָה: 30 וּנְשִׂיא

fathers' house of the families of the Kohathites *was* Elizaphan the son of Uzziel. [31] Their duty *included* the ark, the table, the lampstand, the altars, the utensils of the sanctuary with which they ministered, the screen, and all the work relating to them.

[32] And Eleazar the son of Aaron the priest *was to be* chief over the leaders of the Levites, *with* oversight of those who kept charge of the sanctuary.

[33] From Merari *came* the family of the Mahlites and the family of the Mushites; these *were* the families of Merari. [34] And those who were numbered, according to the number of all the males from a month old and above, *were* six thousand two hundred. [35] The leader of the fathers' house of the families of Merari *was* Zuriel the son of Abihail. These *were* to camp on the north side of the tabernacle. [36] And the appointed duty of the children of Merari *included* the boards of the tabernacle, its bars, its pillars, its sockets, its utensils, all the work relating to them, [37] and the pillars of the court all around, with their sockets, their pegs, and their cords.

[38] Moreover those who were to camp before the tabernacle on the east, before the tabernacle of meeting, *were* Moses, Aaron, and his sons, keeping charge of the sanctuary, to meet the needs of the children of Israel; but the outsider who came near was to be put to death. [39] All who were numbered of the Levites, whom Moses and Aaron numbered at the commandment of the LORD, by their families, all the males from a month old and above, *were* twenty-two thousand.

[40] Then the LORD said to Moses: "Number all the firstborn males of the children of Israel from a month old and above, and take the number of their names. [41] And you shall take the Levites for Me—I *am* the LORD—instead of all the firstborn among the children of Israel, and the livestock of the Levites instead of all the firstborn among the livestock of the children of Israel." [42] So Moses numbered all the firstborn among the children of Israel, as the LORD commanded him. [43] And all the firstborn males, according to the number of names from a month old and above, of those who were numbered of them, were twenty-two thousand two hundred and seventy-three.

[44] Then the LORD spoke to Moses, saying: [45] "Take the Levites instead of all the firstborn among the children of Israel, and the livestock of the Levites instead of their livestock. The Levites shall be Mine: I *am* the LORD. [46] And for the redemption of the two hundred and seventy-three of the firstborn of the children of Israel, who are

בֵּית־אָב לְמִשְׁפְּחֹת הַקְּהָתִי אֱלִיצָפָן בֶּן־עֻזִּיאֵל:
31 וּמִשְׁמַרְתָּם הָאָרֹן וְהַשֻּׁלְחָן וְהַמְּנֹרָה וְהַמִּזְבְּחֹת
וּכְלֵי הַקֹּדֶשׁ אֲשֶׁר יְשָׁרְתוּ בָּהֶם וְהַמָּסָךְ וְכֹל
עֲבֹדָתוֹ: 32 וּנְשִׂיא נְשִׂיאֵי הַלֵּוִי אֶלְעָזָר בֶּן־אַהֲרֹן
הַכֹּהֵן פְּקֻדַּת שֹׁמְרֵי מִשְׁמֶרֶת הַקֹּדֶשׁ: 33 לִמְרָרִי
מִשְׁפַּחַת הַמַּחְלִי וּמִשְׁפַּחַת הַמּוּשִׁי אֵלֶּה הֵם
מִשְׁפְּחֹת מְרָרִי: 34 וּפְקֻדֵיהֶם בְּמִסְפַּר כָּל־זָכָר מִבֶּן־
חֹדֶשׁ וָמָעְלָה שֵׁשֶׁת אֲלָפִים וּמָאתָיִם: 35 וּנְשִׂיא
בֵית־אָב לְמִשְׁפְּחֹת מְרָרִי צוּרִיאֵל בֶּן־אֲבִיחָיִל עַל
יֶרֶךְ הַמִּשְׁכָּן יַחֲנוּ צָפֹנָה: 36 וּפְקֻדַּת מִשְׁמֶרֶת
בְּנֵי מְרָרִי קַרְשֵׁי הַמִּשְׁכָּן וּבְרִיחָיו וְעַמֻּדָיו וַאֲדָנָיו
וְכָל־כֵּלָיו וְכֹל עֲבֹדָתוֹ: 37 וְעַמֻּדֵי הֶחָצֵר סָבִיב
וְאַדְנֵיהֶם וִיתֵדֹתָם וּמֵיתְרֵיהֶם: 38 וְהַחֹנִים לִפְנֵי
הַמִּשְׁכָּן קֵדְמָה לִפְנֵי אֹהֶל־מוֹעֵד ׀ מִזְרָחָה מֹשֶׁה ׀
וְאַהֲרֹן וּבָנָיו שֹׁמְרִים מִשְׁמֶרֶת הַמִּקְדָּשׁ לְמִשְׁמֶרֶת
בְּנֵי יִשְׂרָאֵל וְהַזָּר הַקָּרֵב יוּמָת: 39 כָּל־פְּקוּדֵי
הַלְוִיִּם אֲשֶׁר פָּקַד מֹשֶׁה וְאַהֲרֹן עַל־פִּי יְהוָה
לְמִשְׁפְּחֹתָם כָּל־זָכָר מִבֶּן־חֹדֶשׁ וָמַעְלָה שְׁנַיִם
וְעֶשְׂרִים אָלֶף: ס 40 וַיֹּאמֶר יְהוָה אֶל־
מֹשֶׁה פְּקֹד כָּל־בְּכֹר זָכָר לִבְנֵי יִשְׂרָאֵל מִבֶּן־חֹדֶשׁ
וָמָעְלָה וְשָׂא אֵת מִסְפַּר שְׁמֹתָם: 41 וְלָקַחְתָּ אֶת־
הַלְוִיִּם לִי אֲנִי יְהוָה תַּחַת כָּל־בְּכֹר בִּבְנֵי יִשְׂרָאֵל
וְאֵת בֶּהֱמַת הַלְוִיִּם תַּחַת כָּל־בְּכוֹר בְּבֶהֱמַת בְּנֵי
יִשְׂרָאֵל: 42 וַיִּפְקֹד מֹשֶׁה כַּאֲשֶׁר צִוָּה יְהוָה אֹתוֹ
אֶת־כָּל־בְּכֹר בִּבְנֵי יִשְׂרָאֵל: 43 וַיְהִי כָל־בְּכוֹר זָכָר
בְּמִסְפַּר שֵׁמוֹת מִבֶּן־חֹדֶשׁ וָמַעְלָה לִפְקֻדֵיהֶם שְׁנַיִם
וְעֶשְׂרִים אֶלֶף שְׁלֹשָׁה וְשִׁבְעִים וּמָאתָיִם: פ

44 וַיְדַבֵּר יְהוָה אֶל־מֹשֶׁה לֵּאמֹר: 45 קַח אֶת־הַלְוִיִּם
תַּחַת כָּל־בְּכוֹר בִּבְנֵי יִשְׂרָאֵל וְאֶת־בֶּהֱמַת הַלְוִיִּם
תַּחַת בְּהֶמְתָּם וְהָיוּ־לִי הַלְוִיִּם אֲנִי יְהוָה: 46 וְאֵת
פְּדוּיֵי הַשְּׁלֹשָׁה וְהַשִּׁבְעִים וְהַמָּאתָיִם הָעֹדְפִים עַל־

more than the number of the Levites, ⁴⁷you shall take five shekels for each one individually; you shall take *them* in the currency of the shekel of the sanctuary, the shekel of twenty gerahs. ⁴⁸And you shall give the money, with which the excess number of them is redeemed, to Aaron and his sons."

⁴⁹So Moses took the redemption money from those who were over and above those who were redeemed by the Levites. ⁵⁰From the firstborn of the children of Israel he took the money, one thousand three hundred and sixty-five *shekels,* according to the shekel of the sanctuary. ⁵¹And Moses gave their redemption money to Aaron and his sons, according to the word of the LORD, as the LORD commanded Moses.

4 Then the LORD spoke to Moses and Aaron, saying: ²"Take a census of the sons of Kohath from among the children of Levi, by their families, by their fathers' house, ³from thirty years old and above, even to fifty years old, all who enter the service to do the work in the tabernacle of meeting.

⁴"This *is* the service of the sons of Kohath in the tabernacle of meeting, *relating to* the most holy things: ⁵When the camp prepares to journey, Aaron and his sons shall come, and they shall take down the covering veil and cover the ark of the Testimony with it. ⁶Then they shall put on it a covering of badger skins, and spread over *that* a cloth entirely of blue; and they shall insert its poles.

⁷"On the table of showbread they shall spread a blue cloth, and put on it the dishes, the pans, the bowls, and the pitchers for pouring; and the showbread shall be on it. ⁸They shall spread over them a scarlet cloth, and cover the same with a covering of badger skins; and they shall insert its poles. ⁹And they shall take a blue cloth and cover the lampstand of the light, with its lamps, its wick-trimmers, its trays, and all its oil vessels, with which they service it. ¹⁰Then they shall put it with all its utensils in a covering of badger skins, and put *it* on a carrying beam.

¹¹"Over the golden altar they shall spread a blue cloth, and cover it with a covering of badger skins; and they shall insert its poles. ¹²Then they shall take all the utensils of service with which they minister in the sanctuary, put *them* in a blue cloth, cover them with a covering of badger skins, and put *them* on a carrying beam. ¹³Also they shall take away the ashes from the altar, and spread a purple cloth over it. ¹⁴They shall put on it all its implements with which they minister there—the firepans, the forks, the shovels, the basins, and all the utensils of the altar—and they shall spread on it

הַלְוִיִּם מִבְּכוֹר בְּנֵי יִשְׂרָאֵל: ⁴⁷ וְלָקַחְתָּ חֲמֵשֶׁת חֲמֵשֶׁת שְׁקָלִים לַגֻּלְגֹּלֶת בְּשֶׁקֶל הַקֹּדֶשׁ תִּקָּח עֶשְׂרִים גֵּרָה הַשָּׁקֶל: ⁴⁸ וְנָתַתָּה הַכֶּסֶף לְאַהֲרֹן וּלְבָנָיו פְּדוּיֵי הָעֹדְפִים בָּהֶם: ⁴⁹ וַיִּקַּח מֹשֶׁה אֵת כֶּסֶף הַפִּדְיוֹם מֵאֵת הָעֹדְפִים עַל פְּדוּיֵי הַלְוִיִּם:

⁵⁰ מֵאֵת בְּכוֹר בְּנֵי יִשְׂרָאֵל לָקַח אֶת־הַכָּסֶף חֲמִשָּׁה וְשִׁשִּׁים וּשְׁלֹשׁ מֵאוֹת וָאֶלֶף בְּשֶׁקֶל הַקֹּדֶשׁ: ⁵¹ וַיִּתֵּן מֹשֶׁה אֶת־כֶּסֶף הַפְּדֻיִם לְאַהֲרֹן וּלְבָנָיו עַל־פִּי יְהֹוָה כַּאֲשֶׁר צִוָּה יְהֹוָה אֶת־מֹשֶׁה: פ

ד וַיְדַבֵּר יְהֹוָה אֶל־מֹשֶׁה וְאֶל־אַהֲרֹן לֵאמֹר: ² נָשֹׂא אֶת־רֹאשׁ בְּנֵי קְהָת מִתּוֹךְ בְּנֵי לֵוִי לְמִשְׁפְּחֹתָם לְבֵית אֲבֹתָם: ³ מִבֶּן שְׁלֹשִׁים שָׁנָה וָמַעְלָה וְעַד בֶּן־חֲמִשִּׁים שָׁנָה כָּל־בָּא לַצָּבָא לַעֲשׂוֹת מְלָאכָה בְּאֹהֶל מוֹעֵד: ⁴ זֹאת עֲבֹדַת בְּנֵי־קְהָת בְּאֹהֶל מוֹעֵד קֹדֶשׁ הַקֳּדָשִׁים: ⁵ וּבָא אַהֲרֹן וּבָנָיו בִּנְסֹעַ הַמַּחֲנֶה וְהוֹרִדוּ אֵת פָּרֹכֶת הַמָּסָךְ וְכִסּוּ־בָהּ אֵת אֲרֹן הָעֵדֻת: ⁶ וְנָתְנוּ עָלָיו כְּסוּי עוֹר תַּחַשׁ וּפָרְשׂוּ בֶגֶד־כְּלִיל תְּכֵלֶת מִלְמָעְלָה וְשָׂמוּ בַּדָּיו: ⁷ וְעַל שֻׁלְחַן הַפָּנִים יִפְרְשׂוּ בֶּגֶד תְּכֵלֶת וְנָתְנוּ עָלָיו אֶת־הַקְּעָרֹת וְאֶת־הַכַּפֹּת וְאֶת־הַמְּנַקִּיֹּת וְאֵת קְשׂוֹת הַנָּסֶךְ וְלֶחֶם הַתָּמִיד עָלָיו יִהְיֶה: ⁸ וּפָרְשׂוּ עֲלֵיהֶם בֶּגֶד תּוֹלַעַת שָׁנִי וְכִסּוּ אֹתוֹ בְּמִכְסֵה עוֹר תַּחַשׁ וְשָׂמוּ אֶת־בַּדָּיו: ⁹ וְלָקְחוּ בֶּגֶד תְּכֵלֶת וְכִסּוּ אֶת־מְנֹרַת הַמָּאוֹר וְאֶת־נֵרֹתֶיהָ וְאֶת־מַלְקָחֶיהָ וְאֶת־מַחְתֹּתֶיהָ וְאֵת כָּל־כְּלֵי שַׁמְנָהּ אֲשֶׁר יְשָׁרְתוּ־לָהּ בָּהֶם: ¹⁰ וְנָתְנוּ אֹתָהּ וְאֶת־כָּל־כֵּלֶיהָ אֶל־מִכְסֵה עוֹר תַּחַשׁ וְנָתְנוּ עַל־הַמּוֹט: ¹¹ וְעַל מִזְבַּח הַזָּהָב יִפְרְשׂוּ בֶּגֶד תְּכֵלֶת וְכִסּוּ אֹתוֹ בְּמִכְסֵה עוֹר תַּחַשׁ וְשָׂמוּ אֶת־בַּדָּיו: ¹² וְלָקְחוּ אֶת־כָּל־כְּלֵי הַשָּׁרֵת אֲשֶׁר יְשָׁרְתוּ־בָם בַּקֹּדֶשׁ וְנָתְנוּ אֶל־בֶּגֶד תְּכֵלֶת וְכִסּוּ אוֹתָם בְּמִכְסֵה עוֹר תַּחַשׁ וְנָתְנוּ עַל־הַמּוֹט: ¹³ וְדִשְּׁנוּ אֶת־הַמִּזְבֵּחַ וּפָרְשׂוּ עָלָיו בֶּגֶד אַרְגָּמָן: ¹⁴ וְנָתְנוּ עָלָיו אֶת־כָּל־כֵּלָיו אֲשֶׁר יְשָׁרְתוּ עָלָיו בָּהֶם אֶת־הַמַּחְתֹּת אֶת־הַמִּזְלָגֹת וְאֶת־הַיָּעִים וְאֶת־הַמִּזְרָקֹת כֹּל כְּלֵי הַמִּזְבֵּחַ וּפָרְשׂוּ

a covering of badger skins, and insert its poles.
15 And when Aaron and his sons have finished covering the sanctuary and all the furnishings of the sanctuary, when the camp is set to go, then the sons of Kohath shall come to carry *them;* but they shall not touch any holy thing, lest they die.

"These *are* the things in the tabernacle of meeting which the sons of Kohath are to carry.

16 "The appointed duty of Eleazar the son of Aaron the priest *is* the oil for the light, the sweet incense, the daily grain offering, the anointing oil, the oversight of all the tabernacle, of all that *is* in it, with the sanctuary and its furnishings."

17 Then the LORD spoke to Moses and Aaron, saying: 18 "Do not cut off the tribe of the families of the Kohathites from among the Levites; 19 but do this in regard to them, that they may live and not die when they approach the most holy things: Aaron and his sons shall go in and appoint each of them to his service and his task. 20 But they shall not go in to watch while the holy things are being covered, lest they die."

21 Then the LORD spoke to Moses, saying: 22 "Also take a census of the sons of Gershon, by their fathers' house, by their families. 23 From thirty years old and above, even to fifty years old, you shall number them, all who enter to perform the service, to do the work in the tabernacle of meeting. 24 This *is* the service of the families of the Gershonites, in serving and carrying: 25 They shall carry the curtains of the tabernacle and the tabernacle of meeting *with* its covering, the covering of badger skins that *is* on it, the screen for the door of the tabernacle of meeting, 26 the screen for the door of the gate of the court, the hangings of the court which *are* around the tabernacle and altar, and their cords, all the furnishings for their service and all that is made for these things: so shall they serve.

27 "Aaron and his sons shall assign all the service of the sons of the Gershonites, all their tasks and all their service. And you shall appoint to them all their tasks as their duty. 28 This *is* the service of the families of the sons of Gershon in the tabernacle of meeting. And their duties *shall be* under the authority of Ithamar the son of Aaron the priest.

29 "As for the sons of Merari, you shall number them by their families and by their fathers' house. 30 From thirty years old and above, even to fifty years old, you shall number them, everyone who enters the service to do the work of the tabernacle of meeting. 31 And this *is* what they must carry as all their service for the tabernacle of meeting: the boards of the tabernacle, its bars, its pillars, its

עָלָיו כְּסוּי עוֹר תַּחַשׁ וְשָׂמוּ בַּדָּיו: 15 וְכִלָּה אַהֲרֹן־
וּבָנָיו לְכַסֹּת אֶת־הַקֹּדֶשׁ וְאֶת־כָּל־כְּלֵי הַקֹּדֶשׁ בִּנְסֹעַ
הַמַּחֲנֶה וְאַחֲרֵי־כֵן יָבֹאוּ בְנֵי־קְהָת לָשֵׂאת וְלֹא־
יִגְּעוּ אֶל־הַקֹּדֶשׁ וָמֵתוּ אֵלֶּה מַשָּׂא בְנֵי־קְהָת בְּאֹהֶל
מוֹעֵד: 16 וּפְקֻדַּת אֶלְעָזָר ׀ בֶּן־אַהֲרֹן הַכֹּהֵן שֶׁמֶן
הַמָּאוֹר וּקְטֹרֶת הַסַּמִּים וּמִנְחַת הַתָּמִיד וְשֶׁמֶן
הַמִּשְׁחָה פְּקֻדַּת כָּל־הַמִּשְׁכָּן וְכָל־אֲשֶׁר־בּוֹ בְּקֹדֶשׁ
וּבְכֵלָיו: ס 17 וַיְדַבֵּר יְהֹוָה אֶל־מֹשֶׁה וְאֶל־
אַהֲרֹן לֵאמֹר: 18 אַל־תַּכְרִיתוּ אֶת־שֵׁבֶט מִשְׁפְּחֹת
הַקְּהָתִי מִתּוֹךְ הַלְוִיִּם: 19 וְזֹאת ׀ עֲשׂוּ לָהֶם וְחָיוּ
וְלֹא יָמֻתוּ בְּגִשְׁתָּם אֶת־קֹדֶשׁ הַקֳּדָשִׁים אַהֲרֹן וּבָנָיו
יָבֹאוּ וְשָׂמוּ אוֹתָם אִישׁ אִישׁ עַל־עֲבֹדָתוֹ וְאֶל־
מַשָּׂאוֹ: 20 וְלֹא־יָבֹאוּ לִרְאוֹת כְּבַלַּע אֶת־הַקֹּדֶשׁ
וָמֵתוּ: פ

21 וַיְדַבֵּר יְהֹוָה אֶל־מֹשֶׁה לֵּאמֹר: 22 נָשֹׂא אֶת־
רֹאשׁ בְּנֵי גֵרְשׁוֹן גַּם־הֵם לְבֵית אֲבֹתָם לְמִשְׁפְּחֹתָם:
23 מִבֶּן שְׁלֹשִׁים שָׁנָה וָמַעְלָה עַד בֶּן־חֲמִשִּׁים שָׁנָה
תִּפְקֹד אוֹתָם כָּל־הַבָּא לִצְבֹא צָבָא לַעֲבֹד עֲבֹדָה
בְּאֹהֶל מוֹעֵד: 24 זֹאת עֲבֹדַת מִשְׁפְּחֹת הַגֵּרְשֻׁנִּי
לַעֲבֹד וּלְמַשָּׂא: 25 וְנָשְׂאוּ אֶת־יְרִיעֹת הַמִּשְׁכָּן
וְאֶת־אֹהֶל מוֹעֵד מִכְסֵהוּ וּמִכְסֵה הַתַּחַשׁ אֲשֶׁר־
עָלָיו מִלְמָעְלָה וְאֶת־מָסַךְ פֶּתַח אֹהֶל מוֹעֵד:
26 וְאֵת קַלְעֵי הֶחָצֵר וְאֶת־מָסַךְ ׀ פֶּתַח ׀
שַׁעַר הֶחָצֵר אֲשֶׁר עַל־הַמִּשְׁכָּן וְעַל־הַמִּזְבֵּחַ סָבִיב
וְאֵת מֵיתְרֵיהֶם וְאֶת־כָּל־כְּלֵי עֲבֹדָתָם וְאֵת כָּל־
אֲשֶׁר יֵעָשֶׂה לָהֶם וְעָבָדוּ: 27 עַל־פִּי אַהֲרֹן וּבָנָיו
תִּהְיֶה כָּל־עֲבֹדַת בְּנֵי הַגֵּרְשֻׁנִּי לְכָל־מַשָּׂאָם וּלְכֹל
עֲבֹדָתָם וּפְקַדְתֶּם עֲלֵהֶם בְּמִשְׁמֶרֶת אֵת כָּל־
מַשָּׂאָם: 28 זֹאת עֲבֹדַת מִשְׁפְּחֹת בְּנֵי הַגֵּרְשֻׁנִּי
בְּאֹהֶל מוֹעֵד וּמִשְׁמַרְתָּם בְּיַד אִיתָמָר בֶּן־אַהֲרֹן
הַכֹּהֵן: פ

29 בְּנֵי מְרָרִי לְמִשְׁפְּחֹתָם לְבֵית־אֲבֹתָם תִּפְקֹד
אֹתָם: 30 מִבֶּן שְׁלֹשִׁים שָׁנָה וָמַעְלָה וְעַד בֶּן־
חֲמִשִּׁים שָׁנָה תִּפְקְדֵם כָּל־הַבָּא לַצָּבָא לַעֲבֹד
אֶת־עֲבֹדַת אֹהֶל מוֹעֵד: 31 וְזֹאת מִשְׁמֶרֶת מַשָּׂאָם
לְכָל־עֲבֹדָתָם בְּאֹהֶל מוֹעֵד קַרְשֵׁי הַמִּשְׁכָּן וּבְרִיחָיו

sockets, ³²and the pillars around the court with their sockets, pegs, and cords, with all their furnishings and all their service; and you shall assign *to each man* by name the items he must carry. ³³This *is* the service of the families of the sons of Merari, as all their service for the tabernacle of meeting, under the authority of Ithamar the son of Aaron the priest."

³⁴And Moses, Aaron, and the leaders of the congregation numbered the sons of the Kohathites by their families and by their fathers' house, ³⁵from thirty years old and above, even to fifty years old, everyone who entered the service for work in the tabernacle of meeting; ³⁶and those who were numbered by their families were two thousand seven hundred and fifty. ³⁷These *were* the ones who were numbered of the families of the Kohathites, all who might serve in the tabernacle of meeting, whom Moses and Aaron numbered according to the commandment of the LORD by the hand of Moses.

³⁸And those who were numbered of the sons of Gershon, by their families and by their fathers' house, ³⁹from thirty years old and above, even to fifty years old, everyone who entered the service for work in the tabernacle of meeting— ⁴⁰those who were numbered by their families, by their fathers' house, were two thousand six hundred and thirty. ⁴¹These *are* the ones who were numbered of the families of the sons of Gershon, of all who might serve in the tabernacle of meeting, whom Moses and Aaron numbered according to the commandment of the LORD.

⁴²Those of the families of the sons of Merari who were numbered, by their families, by their fathers' house, ⁴³from thirty years old and above, even to fifty years old, everyone who entered the service for work in the tabernacle of meeting— ⁴⁴those who were numbered by their families were three thousand two hundred. ⁴⁵These *are* the ones who were numbered of the families of the sons of Merari, whom Moses and Aaron numbered according to the word of the LORD by the hand of Moses.

⁴⁶All who were numbered of the Levites, whom Moses, Aaron, and the leaders of Israel numbered, by their families and by their fathers' houses, ⁴⁷from thirty years old and above, even to fifty years old, everyone who came to do the work of service and the work of bearing burdens in the tabernacle of meeting— ⁴⁸those who were numbered were eight thousand five hundred and eighty.

וְעַמּוּדָיו וַאֲדָנָיו: 32 וְעַמּוּדֵי הֶחָצֵר סָבִיב וְאַדְנֵיהֶם וִיתֵדֹתָם וּמֵיתְרֵיהֶם לְכָל־כְּלֵיהֶם וּלְכֹל עֲבֹדָתָם וּבְשֵׁמֹת תִּפְקְדוּ אֶת־כְּלֵי מִשְׁמֶרֶת מַשָּׂאָם: 33 זֹאת עֲבֹדַת מִשְׁפְּחֹת בְּנֵי מְרָרִי לְכָל־עֲבֹדָתָם בְּאֹהֶל מוֹעֵד בְּיַד אִיתָמָר בֶּן־אַהֲרֹן הַכֹּהֵן: 34 וַיִּפְקֹד מֹשֶׁה וְאַהֲרֹן וּנְשִׂיאֵי הָעֵדָה אֶת־בְּנֵי הַקְּהָתִי לְמִשְׁפְּחֹתָם וּלְבֵית אֲבֹתָם: 35 מִבֶּן שְׁלֹשִׁים שָׁנָה וָמַעְלָה וְעַד בֶּן־חֲמִשִּׁים שָׁנָה כָּל־הַבָּא לַצָּבָא לַעֲבֹדָה בְּאֹהֶל מוֹעֵד: 36 וַיִּהְיוּ פְקֻדֵיהֶם לְמִשְׁפְּחֹתָם אַלְפַּיִם שְׁבַע מֵאוֹת וַחֲמִשִּׁים: 37 אֵלֶּה פְקוּדֵי מִשְׁפְּחֹת הַקְּהָתִי כָּל־הָעֹבֵד בְּאֹהֶל מוֹעֵד אֲשֶׁר פָּקַד מֹשֶׁה וְאַהֲרֹן עַל־פִּי יְהוָה בְּיַד־מֹשֶׁה: ס 38 וּפְקוּדֵי בְּנֵי גֵרְשׁוֹן לְמִשְׁפְּחוֹתָם וּלְבֵית אֲבֹתָם: 39 מִבֶּן שְׁלֹשִׁים שָׁנָה וָמַעְלָה וְעַד בֶּן־חֲמִשִּׁים שָׁנָה כָּל־הַבָּא לַצָּבָא לַעֲבֹדָה בְּאֹהֶל מוֹעֵד: 40 וַיִּהְיוּ פְּקֻדֵיהֶם לְמִשְׁפְּחֹתָם לְבֵית אֲבֹתָם אַלְפַּיִם וְשֵׁשׁ מֵאוֹת וּשְׁלֹשִׁים: 41 אֵלֶּה פְקוּדֵי מִשְׁפְּחֹת בְּנֵי גֵרְשׁוֹן כָּל־הָעֹבֵד בְּאֹהֶל מוֹעֵד אֲשֶׁר פָּקַד מֹשֶׁה וְאַהֲרֹן עַל־פִּי יְהוָה: 42 וּפְקוּדֵי מִשְׁפְּחֹת בְּנֵי מְרָרִי לְמִשְׁפְּחֹתָם לְבֵית אֲבֹתָם: 43 מִבֶּן שְׁלֹשִׁים שָׁנָה וָמַעְלָה וְעַד בֶּן־חֲמִשִּׁים שָׁנָה כָּל־הַבָּא לַצָּבָא לַעֲבֹדָה בְּאֹהֶל מוֹעֵד: 44 וַיִּהְיוּ פְקֻדֵיהֶם לְמִשְׁפְּחֹתָם שְׁלֹשֶׁת אֲלָפִים וּמָאתָיִם: 45 אֵלֶּה פְקוּדֵי מִשְׁפְּחֹת בְּנֵי מְרָרִי אֲשֶׁר פָּקַד מֹשֶׁה וְאַהֲרֹן עַל־פִּי יְהוָה בְּיַד־מֹשֶׁה: 46 כָּל־הַפְּקֻדִים אֲשֶׁר פָּקַד מֹשֶׁה וְאַהֲרֹן וּנְשִׂיאֵי יִשְׂרָאֵל אֶת־הַלְוִיִּם לְמִשְׁפְּחֹתָם וּלְבֵית אֲבֹתָם: 47 מִבֶּן שְׁלֹשִׁים שָׁנָה וָמַעְלָה וְעַד בֶּן־חֲמִשִּׁים שָׁנָה כָּל־הַבָּא לַעֲבֹד עֲבֹדַת עֲבֹדָה וַעֲבֹדַת מַשָּׂא בְּאֹהֶל מוֹעֵד: 48 וַיִּהְיוּ פְּקֻדֵיהֶם שְׁמֹנַת אֲלָפִים וַחֲמֵשׁ

⁴⁹According to the commandment of the LORD they were numbered by the hand of Moses, each according to his service and according to his task; thus were they numbered by him, as the LORD commanded Moses.

5 And the LORD spoke to Moses, saying: ²"Command the children of Israel that they put out of the camp every leper, everyone who has a discharge, and whoever becomes defiled by a corpse. ³You shall put out both male and female; you shall put them outside the camp, that they may not defile their camps in the midst of which I dwell. "⁴And the children of Israel did so, and put them outside the camp; as the LORD spoke to Moses, so the children of Israel did.

⁵Then the LORD spoke to Moses, saying, ⁶"Speak to the children of Israel: 'When a man or woman commits any sin that men commit in unfaithfulness against the LORD, and that person is guilty, ⁷then he shall confess the sin which he has committed. He shall make restitution for his trespass in full, plus one-fifth of it, and give *it* to the one he has wronged. ⁸But if the man has no relative to whom restitution may be made for the wrong, the restitution for the wrong *must go* to the LORD for the priest, in addition to the ram of the atonement with which atonement is made for him. ⁹Every offering of all the holy things of the children of Israel, which they bring to the priest, shall be his. ¹⁰And every man's holy things shall be his; whatever any man gives the priest shall be his.'"

¹¹And the LORD spoke to Moses, saying, ¹²"Speak to the children of Israel, and say to them: 'If any man's wife goes astray and behaves unfaithfully toward him, ¹³and a man lies with her carnally, and it is hidden from the eyes of her husband, and it is concealed that she has defiled herself, and *there was* no witness against her, nor was she caught— ¹⁴if the spirit of jealousy comes upon him and he becomes jealous of his wife, who has defiled herself; or if the spirit of jealousy comes upon him and he becomes jealous of his wife, although she has not defiled herself— ¹⁵then the man shall bring his wife to the priest. He shall bring the offering required for her, one-tenth of an ephah of barley meal; he shall pour no oil on it and put no frankincense on it, because it *is* a grain offering of jealousy, an offering for remembering, for bringing iniquity to remembrance.

¹⁶'And the priest shall bring her near, and set her before the LORD. ¹⁷The priest shall take holy water in an earthen vessel, and take some of the dust that is on the floor of the tabernacle and put *it* into the

מֵא֖וֹת וּשְׁמֹנִֽים: 49 עַל־פִּ֤י יְהוָה֙ פָּקַ֣ד אוֹתָ֔ם בְּיַד־
מֹשֶׁ֑ה אִ֣ישׁ אִ֤ישׁ עַל־עֲבֹֽדָתוֹ֙ וְעַל־מַשָּׂא֔וֹ וּפְקֻדָ֕יו
אֲשֶׁר־צִוָּ֥ה יְהוָ֖ה אֶת־מֹשֶֽׁה: פ

ה וַיְדַבֵּ֥ר יְהוָ֖ה אֶל־מֹשֶׁ֥ה לֵּאמֹֽר: 2 צַ֚ו אֶת־בְּנֵ֣י
יִשְׂרָאֵ֔ל וִֽישַׁלְּחוּ֙ מִן־הַֽמַּחֲנֶ֔ה כָּל־צָר֖וּעַ וְכָל־זָ֑ב וְכֹ֖ל
טָמֵ֣א לָנָֽפֶשׁ: 3 מִזָּכָ֤ר עַד־נְקֵבָה֙ תְּשַׁלֵּ֔חוּ אֶל־מִח֥וּץ
לַֽמַּחֲנֶ֖ה תְּשַׁלְּח֑וּם וְלֹ֤א יְטַמְּאוּ֙ אֶת־מַ֣חֲנֵיהֶ֔ם אֲשֶׁ֥ר
אֲנִ֖י שֹׁכֵ֥ן בְּתוֹכָֽם: 4 וַיַּֽעֲשׂוּ־כֵן֙ בְּנֵ֣י יִשְׂרָאֵ֔ל וַיְשַׁלְּח֣וּ
אוֹתָ֔ם אֶל־מִח֖וּץ לַֽמַּחֲנֶ֑ה כַּֽאֲשֶׁ֨ר דִּבֶּ֤ר יְהוָה֙ אֶל־
מֹשֶׁ֔ה כֵּ֥ן עָשׂ֖וּ בְּנֵ֥י יִשְׂרָאֵֽל: פ

5 וַיְדַבֵּ֥ר יְהוָ֖ה אֶל־מֹשֶׁ֥ה לֵּאמֹֽר: 6 דַּבֵּר֮ אֶל־בְּנֵ֣י
יִשְׂרָאֵל֒ אִ֣ישׁ אֽוֹ־אִשָּׁ֗ה כִּ֤י יַֽעֲשׂוּ֙ מִכָּל־חַטֹּ֣את
הָֽאָדָ֔ם לִמְעֹ֥ל מַ֖עַל בַּֽיהוָ֑ה וְאָֽשְׁמָ֖ה הַנֶּ֥פֶשׁ הַהִֽוא:
7 וְהִתְוַדּ֗וּ אֶֽת־חַטָּאתָם֮ אֲשֶׁ֣ר עָשׂוּ֒ וְהֵשִׁ֤יב אֶת־
אֲשָׁמוֹ֙ בְּרֹאשׁ֔וֹ וַֽחֲמִֽישִׁת֖וֹ יֹסֵ֣ף עָלָ֑יו וְנָתַ֕ן לַֽאֲשֶׁ֖ר
אָשַׁ֥ם לֽוֹ: 8 וְאִם־אֵ֨ין לָאִ֜ישׁ גֹּאֵ֗ל לְהָשִׁ֤יב הָֽאָשָׁם֙
אֵלָ֔יו הָֽאָשָׁ֛ם הַמּוּשָׁ֥ב לַֽיהוָ֖ה לַכֹּהֵ֑ן מִלְּבַ֗ד אֵ֚יל
הַכִּפֻּרִ֔ים אֲשֶׁ֥ר יְכַפֶּר־בּ֖וֹ עָלָֽיו: 9 וְכָל־תְּרוּמָ֞ה לְכָל־
קָדְשֵׁ֧י בְנֵֽי־יִשְׂרָאֵ֛ל אֲשֶׁר־יַקְרִ֥יבוּ לַכֹּהֵ֖ן ל֥וֹ יִֽהְיֶֽה:
10 וְאִ֥ישׁ אֶת־קֳדָשָׁ֖יו ל֣וֹ יִֽהְי֑וּ אִ֛ישׁ אֲשֶׁר־יִתֵּ֥ן לַכֹּהֵ֖ן
ל֥וֹ יִֽהְיֶֽה: פ

11 וַיְדַבֵּ֥ר יְהוָ֖ה אֶל־מֹשֶׁ֥ה לֵּאמֹֽר: 12 דַּבֵּר֙ אֶל־
בְּנֵ֣י יִשְׂרָאֵ֔ל וְאָֽמַרְתָּ֖ אֲלֵהֶ֑ם אִ֥ישׁ אִישׁ֙ כִּֽי־תִשְׂטֶ֣ה
אִשְׁתּ֔וֹ וּמָֽעֲלָ֥ה ב֖וֹ מָֽעַל: 13 וְשָׁכַ֨ב אִ֣ישׁ אֹתָהּ֮
שִׁכְבַת־זֶרַע֒ וְנֶעְלַם֙ מֵֽעֵינֵ֣י אִישָׁ֔הּ וְנִסְתְּרָ֖ה וְהִ֣יא
נִטְמָ֑אָה וְעֵד֙ אֵ֣ין בָּ֔הּ וְהִ֖וא לֹ֥א נִתְפָּֽשָׂה: 14 וְעָבַ֨ר
עָלָ֧יו רֽוּחַ־קִנְאָ֛ה וְקִנֵּ֥א אֶת־אִשְׁתּ֖וֹ וְהִ֣וא נִטְמָ֑אָה
אֽוֹ־עָבַ֨ר עָלָ֤יו רֽוּחַ־קִנְאָה֙ וְקִנֵּ֣א אֶת־אִשְׁתּ֔וֹ וְהִ֖יא
לֹ֥א נִטְמָֽאָה: 15 וְהֵבִ֨יא הָאִ֣ישׁ אֶת־אִשְׁתּוֹ֮ אֶל־
הַכֹּהֵן֒ וְהֵבִ֤יא אֶת־קָרְבָּנָהּ֙ עָלֶ֔יהָ עֲשִׂירִ֥ת הָֽאֵיפָ֖ה
קֶ֣מַח שְׂעֹרִ֑ים לֹֽא־יִצֹ֨ק עָלָ֜יו שֶׁ֗מֶן וְלֹֽא־יִתֵּ֤ן עָלָיו֙
לְבֹנָ֔ה כִּֽי־מִנְחַ֤ת קְנָאֹת֙ ה֔וּא מִנְחַ֥ת זִכָּר֖וֹן מַזְכֶּ֥רֶת
עָוֹֽן: 16 וְהִקְרִ֥יב אֹתָ֖הּ הַכֹּהֵ֑ן וְהֶֽעֱמִדָ֖הּ לִפְנֵ֥י יְהוָֽה:
17 וְלָקַ֧ח הַכֹּהֵ֛ן מַ֥יִם קְדֹשִׁ֖ים בִּכְלִי־חָ֑רֶשׂ וּמִן־הֶֽעָפָ֗ר
אֲשֶׁ֤ר יִֽהְיֶה֙ בְּקַרְקַ֣ע הַמִּשְׁכָּ֔ן יִקַּ֥ח הַכֹּהֵ֖ן וְנָתַ֥ן אֶל־

water. 18 Then the priest shall stand the woman before the Lord, uncover the woman's head, and put the offering for remembering in her hands, which *is* the grain offering of jealousy. And the priest shall have in his hand the bitter water that brings a curse. 19 And the priest shall put her under oath, and say to the woman, "If no man has lain with you, and if you have not gone astray to uncleanness *while* under your husband's *authority,* be free from this bitter water that brings a curse. 20 But if you have gone astray *while* under your husband's *authority,* and if you have defiled yourself and some man other than your husband has lain with you"— 21 then the priest shall put the woman under the oath of the curse, and he shall say to the woman—"the Lord make you a curse and an oath among your people, when the Lord makes your thigh rot and your belly swell; 22 and may this water that causes the curse go into your stomach, and make *your* belly swell and *your* thigh rot."

'Then the woman shall say, "Amen, so be it."

23 'Then the priest shall write these curses in a book, and he shall scrape *them* off into the bitter water. 24 And he shall make the woman drink the bitter water that brings a curse, and the water that brings the curse shall enter her *to become* bitter. 25 Then the priest shall take the grain offering of jealousy from the woman's hand, shall wave the offering before the Lord, and bring it to the altar; 26 and the priest shall take a handful of the offering, as its memorial portion, burn *it* on the altar, and afterward make the woman drink the water. 27 When he has made her drink the water, then it shall be, if she has defiled herself and behaved unfaithfully toward her husband, that the water that brings a curse will enter her *and become* bitter, and her belly will swell, her thigh will rot, and the woman will become a curse among her people. 28 But if the woman has not defiled herself, and is clean, then she shall be free and may conceive children.

29 'This *is* the law of jealousy, when a wife, *while* under her husband's *authority,* goes astray and defiles herself, 30 or when the spirit of jealousy comes upon a man, and he becomes jealous of his wife; then he shall stand the woman before the Lord, and the priest shall execute all this law upon her. 31 Then the man shall be free from iniquity, but that woman shall bear her guilt.' "

6 Then the Lord spoke to Moses, saying, 2 "Speak to the children of Israel, and say to them: 'When either a man or woman consecrates an offering to take the vow of a Nazirite, to separate himself to

הַמָּיִם: 18 וְהֶעֱמִיד הַכֹּהֵן אֶת־הָאִשָּׁה לִפְנֵי יְהֹוָה וּפָרַע אֶת־רֹאשׁ הָאִשָּׁה וְנָתַן עַל־כַּפֶּיהָ אֵת מִנְחַת הַזִּכָּרוֹן מִנְחַת קְנָאֹת הִוא וּבְיַד הַכֹּהֵן יִהְיוּ מֵי הַמָּרִים הַמְאָרֲרִים: 19 וְהִשְׁבִּיעַ אֹתָהּ הַכֹּהֵן וְאָמַר אֶל־הָאִשָּׁה אִם־לֹא שָׁכַב אִישׁ אֹתָךְ וְאִם־לֹא שָׂטִית טֻמְאָה תַּחַת אִישֵׁךְ הִנָּקִי מִמֵּי הַמָּרִים הַמְאָרֲרִים הָאֵלֶּה: 20 וְאַתְּ כִּי שָׂטִית תַּחַת אִישֵׁךְ וְכִי נִטְמֵאת וַיִּתֵּן אִישׁ בָּךְ אֶת־שְׁכָבְתּוֹ מִבַּלְעֲדֵי אִישֵׁךְ: 21 וְהִשְׁבִּיעַ הַכֹּהֵן אֶת־הָאִשָּׁה בִּשְׁבֻעַת הָאָלָה וְאָמַר הַכֹּהֵן לָאִשָּׁה יִתֵּן יְהֹוָה אוֹתָךְ לְאָלָה וְלִשְׁבֻעָה בְּתוֹךְ עַמֵּךְ בְּתֵת יְהֹוָה אֶת־יְרֵכֵךְ נֹפֶלֶת וְאֶת־בִּטְנֵךְ צָבָה: 22 וּבָאוּ הַמַּיִם הַמְאָרֲרִים הָאֵלֶּה בְּמֵעַיִךְ לַצְבּוֹת בֶּטֶן וְלַנְפִּל יָרֵךְ וְאָמְרָה הָאִשָּׁה אָמֵן | אָמֵן: 23 וְכָתַב אֶת־הָאָלֹת הָאֵלֶּה הַכֹּהֵן בַּסֵּפֶר וּמָחָה אֶל־מֵי הַמָּרִים: 24 וְהִשְׁקָה אֶת־הָאִשָּׁה אֶת־מֵי הַמָּרִים הַמְאָרֲרִים וּבָאוּ בָהּ הַמַּיִם הַמְאָרֲרִים לְמָרִים: 25 וְלָקַח הַכֹּהֵן מִיַּד הָאִשָּׁה אֵת מִנְחַת הַקְּנָאֹת וְהֵנִיף אֶת־הַמִּנְחָה לִפְנֵי יְהֹוָה וְהִקְרִיב אֹתָהּ אֶל־הַמִּזְבֵּחַ: 26 וְקָמַץ הַכֹּהֵן מִן־ הַמִּנְחָה אֶת־אַזְכָּרָתָהּ וְהִקְטִיר הַמִּזְבֵּחָה וְאַחַר יַשְׁקֶה אֶת־הָאִשָּׁה אֶת־הַמָּיִם: 27 וְהִשְׁקָהּ אֶת־ הַמַּיִם וְהָיְתָה אִם־נִטְמְאָה וַתִּמְעֹל מַעַל בְּאִישָׁהּ וּבָאוּ בָהּ הַמַּיִם הַמְאָרֲרִים לְמָרִים וְצָבְתָה בִטְנָהּ וְנָפְלָה יְרֵכָהּ וְהָיְתָה הָאִשָּׁה לְאָלָה בְּקֶרֶב עַמָּהּ: 28 וְאִם־לֹא נִטְמְאָה הָאִשָּׁה וּטְהֹרָה הִוא וְנִקְּתָה וְנִזְרְעָה זָרַע: 29 זֹאת תּוֹרַת הַקְּנָאֹת אֲשֶׁר תִּשְׂטֶה אִשָּׁה תַּחַת אִישָׁהּ וְנִטְמָאָה: 30 אוֹ אִישׁ אֲשֶׁר תַּעֲבֹר עָלָיו רוּחַ קִנְאָה וְקִנֵּא אֶת־אִשְׁתּוֹ וְהֶעֱמִיד אֶת־הָאִשָּׁה לִפְנֵי יְהֹוָה וְעָשָׂה לָהּ הַכֹּהֵן אֵת כָּל־ הַתּוֹרָה הַזֹּאת: 31 וְנִקָּה הָאִישׁ מֵעָוֹן וְהָאִשָּׁה הַהִוא תִּשָּׂא אֶת־עֲוֹנָהּ: פ

ו וַיְדַבֵּר יְהֹוָה אֶל־מֹשֶׁה לֵּאמֹר: 2 דַּבֵּר אֶל־בְּנֵי יִשְׂרָאֵל וְאָמַרְתָּ אֲלֵהֶם אִישׁ אוֹ־אִשָּׁה כִּי יַפְלִא

the LORD, ³he shall separate himself from wine and *similar* drink; he shall drink neither vinegar made from wine nor vinegar made from *similar* drink; neither shall he drink any grape juice, nor eat fresh grapes or raisins. ⁴All the days of his separation he shall eat nothing that is produced by the grapevine, from seed to skin.

⁵'All the days of the vow of his separation no razor shall come upon his head; until the days are fulfilled for which he separated himself to the LORD, he shall be holy. *Then* he shall let the locks of the hair of his head grow. ⁶All the days that he separates himself to the LORD he shall not go near a dead body. ⁷He shall not make himself unclean even for his father or his mother, for his brother or his sister, when they die, because his separation to God *is* on his head. ⁸All the days of his separation he shall be holy to the LORD.

⁹'And if anyone dies very suddenly beside him, and he defiles his consecrated head, then he shall shave his head on the day of his cleansing; on the seventh day he shall shave it. ¹⁰Then on the eighth day he shall bring two turtledoves or two young pigeons to the priest, to the door of the tabernacle of meeting; ¹¹and the priest shall offer one as a sin offering and *the* other as a burnt offering, and make atonement for him, because he sinned in regard to the corpse; and he shall sanctify his head that same day. ¹²He shall consecrate to the LORD the days of his separation, and bring a male lamb in its first year as a trespass offering; but the former days shall be lost, because his separation was defiled.

¹³'Now this *is* the law of the Nazirite: When the days of his separation are fulfilled, he shall be brought to the door of the tabernacle of meeting. ¹⁴And he shall present his offering to the LORD: one male lamb in its first year without blemish as a burnt offering, one ewe lamb in its first year without blemish as a sin offering, one ram without blemish as a peace offering, ¹⁵a basket of unleavened bread, cakes of fine flour mixed with oil, unleavened wafers anointed with oil, and their grain offering with their drink offerings.

¹⁶'Then the priest shall bring *them* before the LORD and offer his sin offering and his burnt offering; ¹⁷and he shall offer the ram as a sacrifice of a peace offering to the LORD, with the basket of unleavened bread; the priest shall also offer its grain offering and its drink offering. ¹⁸Then the Nazirite shall shave his consecrated head *at* the door of the tabernacle of meeting, and shall take the hair from his consecrated head and put *it* on the fire which is under the sacrifice of the peace offering.

לִנְדֹּר נֶדֶר נָזִיר לְהַזִּיר לַיהוָה: 3 מִיַּיִן וְשֵׁכָר יַזִּיר חֹמֶץ יַיִן וְחֹמֶץ שֵׁכָר לֹא יִשְׁתֶּה וְכָל־מִשְׁרַת עֲנָבִים לֹא יִשְׁתֶּה וַעֲנָבִים לַחִים וִיבֵשִׁים לֹא יֹאכֵל: 4 כֹּל יְמֵי נִזְרוֹ מִכֹּל אֲשֶׁר יֵעָשֶׂה מִגֶּפֶן הַיַּיִן מֵחַרְצַנִּים וְעַד־זָג לֹא יֹאכֵל: 5 כָּל־יְמֵי נֶדֶר נִזְרוֹ תַּעַר לֹא־יַעֲבֹר עַל־רֹאשׁוֹ עַד־מְלֹאת הַיָּמִם אֲשֶׁר־ יַזִּיר לַיהוָה קָדֹשׁ יִהְיֶה גַּדֵּל פֶּרַע שְׂעַר רֹאשׁוֹ: 6 כָּל־יְמֵי הַזִּירוֹ לַיהוָה עַל־נֶפֶשׁ מֵת לֹא יָבֹא: 7 לְאָבִיו וּלְאִמּוֹ לְאָחִיו וּלְאַחֹתוֹ לֹא־יִטַּמָּא לָהֶם בְּמֹתָם כִּי נֵזֶר אֱלֹהָיו עַל־רֹאשׁוֹ: 8 כֹּל יְמֵי נִזְרוֹ קָדֹשׁ הוּא לַיהוָה: 9 וְכִי־יָמוּת מֵת עָלָיו בְּפֶתַע פִּתְאֹם וְטִמֵּא רֹאשׁ נִזְרוֹ וְגִלַּח רֹאשׁוֹ בְּיוֹם טָהֳרָתוֹ בַּיּוֹם הַשְּׁבִיעִי יְגַלְּחֶנּוּ: 10 וּבַיּוֹם הַשְּׁמִינִי יָבִא שְׁתֵּי תֹרִים אוֹ שְׁנֵי בְּנֵי יוֹנָה אֶל־הַכֹּהֵן אֶל־פֶּתַח אֹהֶל מוֹעֵד: 11 וְעָשָׂה הַכֹּהֵן אֶחָד לְחַטָּאת וְאֶחָד לְעֹלָה וְכִפֶּר עָלָיו מֵאֲשֶׁר חָטָא עַל־הַנָּפֶשׁ וְקִדַּשׁ אֶת־ רֹאשׁוֹ בַּיּוֹם הַהוּא: 12 וְהִזִּיר לַיהוָה אֶת־יְמֵי נִזְרוֹ וְהֵבִיא כֶּבֶשׂ בֶּן־שְׁנָתוֹ לְאָשָׁם וְהַיָּמִים הָרִאשֹׁנִים יִפְּלוּ כִּי טָמֵא נִזְרוֹ: 13 וְזֹאת תּוֹרַת הַנָּזִיר בְּיוֹם מְלֹאת יְמֵי נִזְרוֹ יָבִיא אֹתוֹ אֶל־פֶּתַח אֹהֶל מוֹעֵד: 14 וְהִקְרִיב אֶת־קָרְבָּנוֹ לַיהוָה כֶּבֶשׂ בֶּן־שְׁנָתוֹ תָמִים אֶחָד לְעֹלָה וְכַבְשָׂה אַחַת בַּת־שְׁנָתָהּ תְּמִימָה לְחַטָּאת וְאַיִל־אֶחָד תָּמִים לִשְׁלָמִים: 15 וְסַל מַצּוֹת סֹלֶת חַלֹּת בְּלוּלֹת בַּשֶּׁמֶן וּרְקִיקֵי מַצּוֹת מְשֻׁחִים בַּשָּׁמֶן וּמִנְחָתָם וְנִסְכֵּיהֶם: 16 וְהִקְרִיב הַכֹּהֵן לִפְנֵי יהוָה וְעָשָׂה אֶת־חַטָּאתוֹ וְאֶת־עֹלָתוֹ: 17 וְאֶת־ הָאַיִל יַעֲשֶׂה זֶבַח שְׁלָמִים לַיהוָה עַל סַל הַמַּצּוֹת וְעָשָׂה הַכֹּהֵן אֶת־מִנְחָתוֹ וְאֶת־נִסְכּוֹ: 18 וְגִלַּח הַנָּזִיר פֶּתַח אֹהֶל מוֹעֵד אֶת־רֹאשׁ נִזְרוֹ וְלָקַח אֶת־ שְׂעַר רֹאשׁ נִזְרוֹ וְנָתַן עַל־הָאֵשׁ אֲשֶׁר־תַּחַת זֶבַח

19 'And the priest shall take the boiled shoulder of the ram, one unleavened cake from the basket, and one unleavened wafer, and put *them* upon the hands of the Nazirite after he has shaved his consecrated *hair,* 20 and the priest shall wave them as a wave offering before the LORD; they *are* holy for the priest, together with the breast of the wave offering and the thigh of the heave offering. After that the Nazirite may drink wine.'

21 "This is the law of the Nazirite who vows to the LORD the offering for his separation, and besides that, whatever else his hand is able to provide; according to the vow which he takes, so he must do according to the law of his separation."

22 And the LORD spoke to Moses, saying: 23 "Speak to Aaron and his sons, saying, 'This is the way you shall bless the children of Israel. Say to them:

24   "The LORD bless you and keep you;
25   The LORD make His face shine upon you,
    And be gracious to you;
26   The LORD lift up His countenance upon you,
    And give you peace."'

27 "So they shall put My name on the children of Israel, and I will bless them."

7 Now it came to pass, when Moses had finished setting up the tabernacle, that he anointed it and consecrated it and all its furnishings, and the altar and all its utensils; so he anointed them and consecrated them. 2 Then the leaders of Israel, the heads of their fathers' houses, who *were* the leaders of the tribes and over those who were numbered, made an offering. 3 And they brought their offering before the LORD, six covered carts and twelve oxen, a cart for *every* two of the leaders, and for each one an ox; and they presented them before the tabernacle.

4 Then the LORD spoke to Moses, saying, 5 "Accept *these* from them, that they may be used in doing the work of the tabernacle of meeting; and you shall give them to the Levites, *to* every man according to his service." 6 So Moses took the carts and the oxen, and gave them to the Levites. 7 Two carts and four oxen he gave to the sons of Gershon, according to their service; 8 and four carts and eight oxen he gave to the sons of Merari, according to their service, under the authority of Ithamar the son of Aaron the priest. 9 But to the sons of Kohath he gave none, because theirs *was* the service of the holy things, *which* they carried on their shoulders.

19 וְלָקַח הַכֹּהֵן אֶת־הַזְּרֹעַ בְּשֵׁלָה מִן־הָשְׁלָמִים: הָאַיִל וְחַלַּת מַצָּה אַחַת מִן־הַסַּל וּרְקִיק מַצָּה אֶחָד וְנָתַן עַל־כַּפֵּי הַנָּזִיר אַחַר הִתְגַּלְּחוֹ אֶת־נִזְרוֹ: 20 וְהֵנִיף אוֹתָם הַכֹּהֵן ׀ תְּנוּפָה לִפְנֵי יְהוָה קֹדֶשׁ הוּא לַכֹּהֵן עַל חֲזֵה הַתְּנוּפָה וְעַל שׁוֹק הַתְּרוּמָה וְאַחַר יִשְׁתֶּה הַנָּזִיר יָיִן: 21 זֹאת תּוֹרַת הַנָּזִיר אֲשֶׁר יִדֹּר קָרְבָּנוֹ לַיהוָה עַל־נִזְרוֹ מִלְּבַד אֲשֶׁר־תַּשִּׂיג יָדוֹ כְּפִי נִדְרוֹ אֲשֶׁר יִדֹּר כֵּן יַעֲשֶׂה עַל תּוֹרַת נִזְרוֹ: פ

22 וַיְדַבֵּר יְהוָה אֶל־מֹשֶׁה לֵּאמֹר: 23 דַּבֵּר אֶל־אַהֲרֹן וְאֶל־בָּנָיו לֵאמֹר כֹּה תְבָרֲכוּ אֶת־בְּנֵי יִשְׂרָאֵל אָמוֹר לָהֶם: ס 24 יְבָרֶכְךָ יְהוָה וְיִשְׁמְרֶךָ: ס 25 יָאֵר יְהוָה ׀ פָּנָיו אֵלֶיךָ וִיחֻנֶּךָּ: ס 26 יִשָּׂא יְהוָה ׀ פָּנָיו אֵלֶיךָ וְיָשֵׂם לְךָ שָׁלוֹם: ס 27 וְשָׂמוּ אֶת־שְׁמִי עַל־בְּנֵי יִשְׂרָאֵל וַאֲנִי אֲבָרֲכֵם: פ

ז וַיְהִי בְּיוֹם כַּלּוֹת מֹשֶׁה לְהָקִים אֶת־הַמִּשְׁכָּן וַיִּמְשַׁח אֹתוֹ וַיְקַדֵּשׁ אֹתוֹ וְאֶת־כָּל־כֵּלָיו וְאֶת־הַמִּזְבֵּחַ וְאֶת־כָּל־כֵּלָיו וַיִּמְשָׁחֵם וַיְקַדֵּשׁ אֹתָם: 2 וַיַּקְרִיבוּ נְשִׂיאֵי יִשְׂרָאֵל רָאשֵׁי בֵּית אֲבֹתָם הֵם נְשִׂיאֵי הַמַּטֹּת הֵם הָעֹמְדִים עַל־הַפְּקֻדִים: 3 וַיָּבִיאוּ אֶת־קָרְבָּנָם לִפְנֵי יְהוָה שֵׁשׁ־עֶגְלֹת צָב וּשְׁנֵי עָשָׂר בָּקָר עֲגָלָה עַל־שְׁנֵי הַנְּשִׂאִים וְשׁוֹר לְאֶחָד וַיַּקְרִיבוּ אוֹתָם לִפְנֵי הַמִּשְׁכָּן: 4 וַיֹּאמֶר יְהוָה אֶל־מֹשֶׁה לֵּאמֹר: 5 קַח מֵאִתָּם וְהָיוּ לַעֲבֹד אֶת־עֲבֹדַת אֹהֶל מוֹעֵד וְנָתַתָּה אוֹתָם אֶל־הַלְוִיִּם אִישׁ כְּפִי עֲבֹדָתוֹ: 6 וַיִּקַּח מֹשֶׁה אֶת־הָעֲגָלֹת וְאֶת־הַבָּקָר וַיִּתֵּן אוֹתָם אֶל־הַלְוִיִּם: 7 אֵת ׀ שְׁתֵּי הָעֲגָלֹת וְאֵת אַרְבַּעַת הַבָּקָר נָתַן לִבְנֵי גֵרְשׁוֹן כְּפִי עֲבֹדָתָם: 8 וְאֵת ׀ אַרְבַּע הָעֲגָלֹת וְאֵת שְׁמֹנַת הַבָּקָר נָתַן לִבְנֵי מְרָרִי כְּפִי עֲבֹדָתָם בְּיַד אִיתָמָר בֶּן־אַהֲרֹן הַכֹּהֵן: 9 וְלִבְנֵי קְהָת לֹא נָתָן כִּי־עֲבֹדַת הַקֹּדֶשׁ

10 Now the leaders offered the dedication *offering* for the altar when it was anointed; so the leaders offered their offering before the altar. 11 For the LORD said to Moses, "They shall offer their offering, one leader each day, for the dedication of the altar."

12 And the one who offered his offering on the first day *was* Nahshon the son of Amminadab, from the tribe of Judah. 13 His offering *was* one silver platter, the weight of which *was* one hundred and thirty *shekels,* and one silver bowl of seventy shekels, according to the shekel of the sanctuary, both of them full of fine flour mixed with oil as a grain offering; 14 one gold pan of ten *shekels,* full of incense; 15 one young bull, one ram, and one male lamb in its first year, as a burnt offering; 16 one kid of the goats as a sin offering; 17 and for the sacrifice of peace offerings: two oxen, five rams, five male goats, and five male lambs in their first year. This *was* the offering of Nahshon the son of Amminadab.

18 On the second day Nethanel the son of Zuar, leader of Issachar, presented *an offering.* 19 For his offering he offered one silver platter, the weight of which *was* one hundred and thirty *shekels,* and one silver bowl of seventy shekels, according to the shekel of the sanctuary, both of them full of fine flour mixed with oil as a grain offering; 20 one gold pan of ten *shekels,* full of incense; 21 one young bull, one ram, and one male lamb in its first year, as a burnt offering; 22 one kid of the goats as a sin offering; 23 and as the sacrifice of peace offerings: two oxen, five rams, five male goats, and five male lambs in their first year. This *was* the offering of Nethanel the son of Zuar.

24 On the third day Eliab the son of Helon, leader of the children of Zebulun, *presented an offering.* 25 His offering *was* one silver platter, the weight of which *was* one hundred and thirty *shekels,* and one silver bowl of seventy shekels, according to the shekel of the sanctuary, both of them full of fine flour mixed with oil as a grain offering; 26 one gold pan of ten *shekels,* full of incense; 27 one young bull, one ram, and one male lamb in its first year, as a burnt offering; 28 one kid of the goats as a sin offering; 29 and for the sacrifice of peace offerings: two oxen, five rams, five male goats, and five male lambs in their first year. This *was* the offering of Eliab the son of Helon.

30 On the fourth day Elizur the son of Shedeur, leader of the children of Reuben, *presented an offering.* 31 His offering *was* one silver platter, the weight of which *was* one hundred and thirty *shekels,* and one silver bowl of seventy shekels, according to

עֲלֵהֶם בַּכָּתֵף יִשָּׂאוּ: 10 וַיַּקְרִיבוּ הַנְּשִׂאִים אֵת חֲנֻכַּת הַמִּזְבֵּחַ בְּיוֹם הִמָּשַׁח אֹתוֹ וַיַּקְרִיבוּ הַנְּשִׂיאִם אֶת־קָרְבָּנָם לִפְנֵי הַמִּזְבֵּחַ: 11 וַיֹּאמֶר יְהוָה אֶל־מֹשֶׁה נָשִׂיא אֶחָד לַיּוֹם נָשִׂיא אֶחָד לַיּוֹם יַקְרִיבוּ אֶת־קָרְבָּנָם לַחֲנֻכַּת הַמִּזְבֵּחַ: ס 12 וַיְהִי הַמַּקְרִיב בַּיּוֹם הָרִאשׁוֹן אֶת־קָרְבָּנוֹ נַחְשׁוֹן בֶּן־עַמִּינָדָב לְמַטֵּה יְהוּדָה: 13 וְקָרְבָּנוֹ קַעֲרַת־כֶּסֶף אַחַת שְׁלֹשִׁים וּמֵאָה מִשְׁקָלָהּ מִזְרָק אֶחָד כֶּסֶף שִׁבְעִים שֶׁקֶל בְּשֶׁקֶל הַקֹּדֶשׁ שְׁנֵיהֶם ׀ מְלֵאִים סֹלֶת בְּלוּלָה בַשֶּׁמֶן לְמִנְחָה: 14 כַּף אַחַת עֲשָׂרָה זָהָב מְלֵאָה קְטֹרֶת: 15 פַּר אֶחָד בֶּן־בָּקָר אַיִל אֶחָד כֶּבֶשׂ־אֶחָד בֶּן־שְׁנָתוֹ לְעֹלָה: 16 שְׂעִיר־עִזִּים אֶחָד לְחַטָּאת: 17 וּלְזֶבַח הַשְּׁלָמִים בָּקָר שְׁנַיִם אֵילִם חֲמִשָּׁה עַתּוּדִים חֲמִשָּׁה כְּבָשִׂים בְּנֵי־שָׁנָה חֲמִשָּׁה זֶה קָרְבַּן נַחְשׁוֹן בֶּן־עַמִּינָדָב: פ

18 בַּיּוֹם הַשֵּׁנִי הִקְרִיב נְתַנְאֵל בֶּן־צוּעָר נְשִׂיא יִשָּׂשכָר: 19 הִקְרִב אֶת־קָרְבָּנוֹ קַעֲרַת־כֶּסֶף אַחַת שְׁלֹשִׁים וּמֵאָה מִשְׁקָלָהּ מִזְרָק אֶחָד כֶּסֶף שִׁבְעִים שֶׁקֶל בְּשֶׁקֶל הַקֹּדֶשׁ שְׁנֵיהֶם ׀ מְלֵאִים סֹלֶת בְּלוּלָה בַשֶּׁמֶן לְמִנְחָה: 20 כַּף אַחַת עֲשָׂרָה זָהָב מְלֵאָה קְטֹרֶת: 21 פַּר אֶחָד בֶּן־בָּקָר אַיִל אֶחָד כֶּבֶשׂ־אֶחָד בֶּן־שְׁנָתוֹ לְעֹלָה: 22 שְׂעִיר־עִזִּים אֶחָד לְחַטָּאת: 23 וּלְזֶבַח הַשְּׁלָמִים בָּקָר שְׁנַיִם אֵילִם חֲמִשָּׁה עַתּוּדִים חֲמִשָּׁה כְּבָשִׂים בְּנֵי־שָׁנָה חֲמִשָּׁה זֶה קָרְבַּן נְתַנְאֵל בֶּן־צוּעָר: פ

24 בַּיּוֹם הַשְּׁלִישִׁי נָשִׂיא לִבְנֵי זְבוּלֻן אֱלִיאָב בֶּן־חֵלֹן: 25 קָרְבָּנוֹ קַעֲרַת־כֶּסֶף אַחַת שְׁלֹשִׁים וּמֵאָה מִשְׁקָלָהּ מִזְרָק אֶחָד כֶּסֶף שִׁבְעִים שֶׁקֶל בְּשֶׁקֶל הַקֹּדֶשׁ שְׁנֵיהֶם ׀ מְלֵאִים סֹלֶת בְּלוּלָה בַשֶּׁמֶן לְמִנְחָה: 26 כַּף אַחַת עֲשָׂרָה זָהָב מְלֵאָה קְטֹרֶת: 27 פַּר אֶחָד בֶּן־בָּקָר אַיִל אֶחָד כֶּבֶשׂ־אֶחָד בֶּן־שְׁנָתוֹ לְעֹלָה: 28 שְׂעִיר־עִזִּים אֶחָד לְחַטָּאת: 29 וּלְזֶבַח הַשְּׁלָמִים בָּקָר שְׁנַיִם אֵילִם חֲמִשָּׁה עַתֻּדִים חֲמִשָּׁה כְּבָשִׂים בְּנֵי־שָׁנָה חֲמִשָּׁה זֶה קָרְבַּן אֱלִיאָב בֶּן־חֵלֹן: פ

30 בַּיּוֹם הָרְבִיעִי נָשִׂיא לִבְנֵי רְאוּבֵן אֱלִיצוּר בֶּן־שְׁדֵיאוּר: 31 קָרְבָּנוֹ קַעֲרַת־כֶּסֶף אַחַת שְׁלֹשִׁים וּמֵאָה מִשְׁקָלָהּ מִזְרָק אֶחָד כֶּסֶף שִׁבְעִים שֶׁקֶל

the shekel of the sanctuary, both of them full of fine flour mixed with oil as a grain offering; [32] one gold pan of ten *shekels,* full of incense; [33] one young bull, one ram, and one male lamb in its first year, as a burnt offering; [34] one kid of the goats as a sin offering; [35] and as the sacrifice of peace offerings: two oxen, five rams, five male goats, and five male lambs in their first year. This *was* the offering of Elizur the son of Shedeur.

[36] On the fifth day Shelumiel the son of Zurishaddai, leader of the children of Simeon, *presented an offering.* [37] His offering *was* one silver platter, the weight of which *was* one hundred and thirty *shekels,* and one silver bowl of seventy shekels, according to the shekel of the sanctuary, both of them full of fine flour mixed with oil as a grain offering; [38] one gold pan of ten *shekels,* full of incense; [39] one young bull, one ram, and one male lamb in its first year, as a burnt offering; [40] one kid of the goats as a sin offering; [41] and as the sacrifice of peace offerings: two oxen, five rams, five male goats, and five male lambs in their first year. This *was* the offering of Shelumiel the son of Zurishaddai.

[42] On the sixth day Eliasaph the son of Deuel, leader of the children of Gad, *presented an offering.* [43] His offering *was* one silver platter, the weight of which *was* one hundred and thirty *shekels,* and one silver bowl of seventy shekels, according to the shekel of the sanctuary, both of them full of fine flour mixed with oil as a grain offering; [44] one gold pan of ten *shekels,* full of incense; [45] one young bull, one ram, and one male lamb in its first year, as a burnt offering; [46] one kid of the goats as a sin offering; [47] and as the sacrifice of peace offerings: two oxen, five rams, five male goats, and five male lambs in their first year. This *was* the offering of Eliasaph the son of Deuel.

[48] On the seventh day Elishama the son of Ammihud, leader of the children of Ephraim, *presented an offering.* [49] His offering *was* one silver platter, the weight of which *was* one hundred and thirty *shekels,* and one silver bowl of seventy shekels, according to the shekel of the sanctuary, both of them full of fine flour mixed with oil as a grain offering; [50] one gold pan of ten *shekels,* full of incense; [51] one young bull, one ram, and one male lamb in its first year, as a burnt offering; [52] one kid of the goats as a sin offering; [53] and as the sacrifice of peace offerings: two oxen, five rams, five male goats, and five male lambs in their first year. This *was* the offering of Elishama the son of Ammihud.

[54] On the eighth day Gamaliel the son of Pedahzur, leader of the children of Manasseh, *presented an offering.* [55] His offering *was* one silver

בְּשֶׁקֶל הַקֹּדֶשׁ שְׁנֵיהֶם | מְלֵאִים סֹלֶת בְּלוּלָה בַשֶּׁמֶן לְמִנְחָה: [32] כַּף אַחַת עֲשָׂרָה זָהָב מְלֵאָה קְטֹרֶת: [33] פַּר אֶחָד בֶּן־בָּקָר אַיִל אֶחָד כֶּבֶשׂ־אֶחָד בֶּן־שְׁנָתוֹ לְעֹלָה: [34] שְׂעִיר־עִזִּים אֶחָד לְחַטָּאת: [35] וּלְזֶבַח הַשְּׁלָמִים בָּקָר שְׁנַיִם אֵילִם חֲמִשָּׁה עַתֻּדִים חֲמִשָּׁה כְּבָשִׂים בְּנֵי־שָׁנָה חֲמִשָּׁה זֶה קָרְבַּן אֱלִיצוּר בֶּן־שְׁדֵיאוּר: פ

[36] בַּיּוֹם הַחֲמִישִׁי נָשִׂיא לִבְנֵי שִׁמְעוֹן שְׁלֻמִיאֵל בֶּן־צוּרִישַׁדָּי: [37] קָרְבָּנוֹ קַעֲרַת־כֶּסֶף אַחַת שְׁלֹשִׁים וּמֵאָה מִשְׁקָלָהּ מִזְרָק אֶחָד כֶּסֶף שִׁבְעִים שֶׁקֶל בְּשֶׁקֶל הַקֹּדֶשׁ שְׁנֵיהֶם | מְלֵאִים סֹלֶת בְּלוּלָה בַשֶּׁמֶן לְמִנְחָה: [38] כַּף אַחַת עֲשָׂרָה זָהָב מְלֵאָה קְטֹרֶת: [39] פַּר אֶחָד בֶּן־בָּקָר אַיִל אֶחָד כֶּבֶשׂ־אֶחָד בֶּן־שְׁנָתוֹ לְעֹלָה: [40] שְׂעִיר־עִזִּים אֶחָד לְחַטָּאת: [41] וּלְזֶבַח הַשְּׁלָמִים בָּקָר שְׁנַיִם אֵילִם חֲמִשָּׁה עַתֻּדִים חֲמִשָּׁה כְּבָשִׂים בְּנֵי־שָׁנָה חֲמִשָּׁה זֶה קָרְבַּן שְׁלֻמִיאֵל בֶּן־צוּרִישַׁדָּי: פ

[42] בַּיּוֹם הַשִּׁשִּׁי נָשִׂיא לִבְנֵי גָד אֶלְיָסָף בֶּן־דְּעוּאֵל: [43] קָרְבָּנוֹ קַעֲרַת־כֶּסֶף אַחַת שְׁלֹשִׁים וּמֵאָה מִשְׁקָלָהּ מִזְרָק אֶחָד כֶּסֶף שִׁבְעִים שֶׁקֶל בְּשֶׁקֶל הַקֹּדֶשׁ שְׁנֵיהֶם | מְלֵאִים סֹלֶת בְּלוּלָה בַשֶּׁמֶן לְמִנְחָה: [44] כַּף אַחַת עֲשָׂרָה זָהָב מְלֵאָה קְטֹרֶת: [45] פַּר אֶחָד בֶּן־בָּקָר אַיִל אֶחָד כֶּבֶשׂ־אֶחָד בֶּן־שְׁנָתוֹ לְעֹלָה: [46] שְׂעִיר־עִזִּים אֶחָד לְחַטָּאת: [47] וּלְזֶבַח הַשְּׁלָמִים בָּקָר שְׁנַיִם אֵילִם חֲמִשָּׁה עַתֻּדִים חֲמִשָּׁה כְּבָשִׂים בְּנֵי־שָׁנָה חֲמִשָּׁה זֶה קָרְבַּן אֶלְיָסָף בֶּן־דְּעוּאֵל: פ

[48] בַּיּוֹם הַשְּׁבִיעִי נָשִׂיא לִבְנֵי אֶפְרָיִם אֱלִישָׁמָע בֶּן־עַמִּיהוּד: [49] קָרְבָּנוֹ קַעֲרַת־כֶּסֶף אַחַת שְׁלֹשִׁים וּמֵאָה מִשְׁקָלָהּ מִזְרָק אֶחָד כֶּסֶף שִׁבְעִים שֶׁקֶל בְּשֶׁקֶל הַקֹּדֶשׁ שְׁנֵיהֶם | מְלֵאִים סֹלֶת בְּלוּלָה בַשֶּׁמֶן לְמִנְחָה: [50] כַּף אַחַת עֲשָׂרָה זָהָב מְלֵאָה קְטֹרֶת: [51] פַּר אֶחָד בֶּן־בָּקָר אַיִל אֶחָד כֶּבֶשׂ־אֶחָד בֶּן־שְׁנָתוֹ לְעֹלָה: [52] שְׂעִיר־עִזִּים אֶחָד לְחַטָּאת: [53] וּלְזֶבַח הַשְּׁלָמִים בָּקָר שְׁנַיִם אֵילִם חֲמִשָּׁה עַתֻּדִים חֲמִשָּׁה כְּבָשִׂים בְּנֵי־שָׁנָה חֲמִשָּׁה זֶה קָרְבַּן אֱלִישָׁמָע בֶּן־עַמִּיהוּד: פ

[54] בַּיּוֹם הַשְּׁמִינִי נָשִׂיא לִבְנֵי מְנַשֶּׁה גַּמְלִיאֵל בֶּן־פְּדָהצוּר: [55] קָרְבָּנוֹ קַעֲרַת־כֶּסֶף אַחַת שְׁלֹשִׁים

platter, the weight of which *was* one hundred and thirty *shekels,* and one silver bowl of seventy shekels, according to the shekel of the sanctuary, both of them full of fine flour mixed with oil as a grain offering; [56] one gold pan of ten *shekels,* full of incense; [57] one young bull, one ram, and one male lamb in its first year, as a burnt offering; [58] one kid of the goats as a sin offering; [59] and as the sacrifice of peace offerings: two oxen, five rams, five male goats, and five male lambs in their first year. This *was* the offering of Gamaliel the son of Pedahzur.

[60] On the ninth day Abidan the son of Gideoni, leader of the children of Benjamin, *presented an offering.* [61] His offering *was* one silver platter, the weight of which *was* one hundred and thirty *shekels,* and one silver bowl of seventy shekels, according to the shekel of the sanctuary, both of them full of fine flour mixed with oil as a grain offering; [62] one gold pan of ten *shekels,* full of incense; [63] one young bull, one ram, and one male lamb in its first year, as a burnt offering; [64] one kid of the goats as a sin offering; [65] and as the sacrifice of peace offerings: two oxen, five rams, five male goats, and five male lambs in their first year. This *was* the offering of Abidan the son of Gideoni.

[66] On the tenth day Ahiezer the son of Ammishaddai, leader of the children of Dan, *presented an offering.* [67] His offering *was* one silver platter, the weight of which *was* one hundred and thirty *shekels,* and one silver bowl of seventy shekels, according to the shekel of the sanctuary, both of them full of fine flour mixed with oil as a grain offering; [68] one gold pan of ten *shekels,* full of incense; [69] one young bull, one ram, and one male lamb in its first year, as a burnt offering; [70] one kid of the goats as a sin offering; [71] and as the sacrifice of peace offerings: two oxen, five rams, five male goats, and five male lambs in their first year. This *was* the offering of Ahiezer the son of Ammishaddai.

[72] On the eleventh day Pagiel the son of Ocran, leader of the children of Asher, *presented an offering.* [73] His offering *was* one silver platter, the weight of which *was* one hundred and thirty *shekels,* and one silver bowl of seventy shekels, according to the shekel of the sanctuary, both of them full of fine flour mixed with oil as a grain offering; [74] one gold pan of ten *shekels,* full of incense; [75] one young bull, one ram, and one male lamb in its first year, as a burnt offering; [76] one kid of the goats as a sin offering; [77] and as the sacrifice of peace offerings: two oxen, five rams, five male goats, and five male lambs in their first year. This *was* the offering of Pagiel the son of Ocran.

וּמֵאָה מִשְׁקָלָהּ מִזְרָק אֶחָד כֶּסֶף שִׁבְעִים שֶׁקֶל בְּשֶׁקֶל הַקֹּדֶשׁ שְׁנֵיהֶם ׀ מְלֵאִים סֹלֶת בְּלוּלָה בַשֶּׁמֶן לְמִנְחָה: 56 כַּף אַחַת עֲשָׂרָה זָהָב מְלֵאָה קְטֹרֶת: 57 פַּר אֶחָד בֶּן־בָּקָר אַיִל אֶחָד כֶּבֶשׂ־אֶחָד בֶּן־שְׁנָתוֹ לְעֹלָה: 58 שְׂעִיר־עִזִּים אֶחָד לְחַטָּאת: 59 וּלְזֶבַח הַשְּׁלָמִים בָּקָר שְׁנַיִם אֵילִם חֲמִשָּׁה עַתֻּדִים חֲמִשָּׁה כְּבָשִׂים בְּנֵי־שָׁנָה חֲמִשָּׁה זֶה קָרְבַּן גַּמְלִיאֵל בֶּן־פְּדָהצוּר: פ

60 בַּיּוֹם הַתְּשִׁיעִי נָשִׂיא לִבְנֵי בִנְיָמִן אֲבִידָן בֶּן־גִּדְעֹנִי: 61 קָרְבָּנוֹ קַעֲרַת־כֶּסֶף אַחַת שְׁלֹשִׁים וּמֵאָה מִשְׁקָלָהּ מִזְרָק אֶחָד כֶּסֶף שִׁבְעִים שֶׁקֶל בְּשֶׁקֶל הַקֹּדֶשׁ שְׁנֵיהֶם ׀ מְלֵאִים סֹלֶת בְּלוּלָה בַשֶּׁמֶן לְמִנְחָה: 62 כַּף אַחַת עֲשָׂרָה זָהָב מְלֵאָה קְטֹרֶת: 63 פַּר אֶחָד בֶּן־בָּקָר אַיִל אֶחָד כֶּבֶשׂ־אֶחָד בֶּן־שְׁנָתוֹ לְעֹלָה: 64 שְׂעִיר־עִזִּים אֶחָד לְחַטָּאת: 65 וּלְזֶבַח הַשְּׁלָמִים בָּקָר שְׁנַיִם אֵילִם חֲמִשָּׁה עַתֻּדִים חֲמִשָּׁה כְּבָשִׂים בְּנֵי־שָׁנָה חֲמִשָּׁה זֶה קָרְבַּן אֲבִידָן בֶּן־גִּדְעֹנִי: פ

66 בַּיּוֹם הָעֲשִׂירִי נָשִׂיא לִבְנֵי דָן אֲחִיעֶזֶר בֶּן־עַמִּישַׁדָּי: 67 קָרְבָּנוֹ קַעֲרַת־כֶּסֶף אַחַת שְׁלֹשִׁים וּמֵאָה מִשְׁקָלָהּ מִזְרָק אֶחָד כֶּסֶף שִׁבְעִים שֶׁקֶל בְּשֶׁקֶל הַקֹּדֶשׁ שְׁנֵיהֶם ׀ מְלֵאִים סֹלֶת בְּלוּלָה בַשֶּׁמֶן לְמִנְחָה: 68 כַּף אַחַת עֲשָׂרָה זָהָב מְלֵאָה קְטֹרֶת: 69 פַּר אֶחָד בֶּן־בָּקָר אַיִל אֶחָד כֶּבֶשׂ־אֶחָד בֶּן־שְׁנָתוֹ לְעֹלָה: 70 שְׂעִיר־עִזִּים אֶחָד לְחַטָּאת: 71 וּלְזֶבַח הַשְּׁלָמִים בָּקָר שְׁנַיִם אֵילִם חֲמִשָּׁה עַתֻּדִים חֲמִשָּׁה כְּבָשִׂים בְּנֵי־שָׁנָה חֲמִשָּׁה זֶה קָרְבַּן אֲחִיעֶזֶר בֶּן־עַמִּישַׁדָּי: פ

72 בַּיּוֹם עַשְׁתֵּי עָשָׂר יוֹם נָשִׂיא לִבְנֵי אָשֵׁר פַּגְעִיאֵל בֶּן־עָכְרָן: 73 קָרְבָּנוֹ קַעֲרַת־כֶּסֶף אַחַת שְׁלֹשִׁים וּמֵאָה מִשְׁקָלָהּ מִזְרָק אֶחָד כֶּסֶף שִׁבְעִים שֶׁקֶל בְּשֶׁקֶל הַקֹּדֶשׁ שְׁנֵיהֶם ׀ מְלֵאִים סֹלֶת בְּלוּלָה בַשֶּׁמֶן לְמִנְחָה: 74 כַּף אַחַת עֲשָׂרָה זָהָב מְלֵאָה קְטֹרֶת: 75 פַּר אֶחָד בֶּן־בָּקָר אַיִל אֶחָד כֶּבֶשׂ־אֶחָד בֶּן־שְׁנָתוֹ לְעֹלָה: 76 שְׂעִיר־עִזִּים אֶחָד לְחַטָּאת: 77 וּלְזֶבַח הַשְּׁלָמִים בָּקָר שְׁנַיִם אֵילִם חֲמִשָּׁה עַתֻּדִים חֲמִשָּׁה כְּבָשִׂים בְּנֵי־שָׁנָה חֲמִשָּׁה זֶה קָרְבַּן פַּגְעִיאֵל בֶּן־עָכְרָן: פ

⁷⁸On the twelfth day Ahira the son of Enan, leader of the children of Naphtali, *presented an offering.* ⁷⁹His offering *was* one silver platter, the weight of which *was* one hundred and thirty *shekels,* and one silver bowl of seventy shekels, according to the shekel of the sanctuary, both of them full of fine flour mixed with oil as a grain offering; ⁸⁰one gold pan of ten *shekels,* full of incense; ⁸¹one young bull, one ram, and one male lamb in its first year, as a burnt offering; ⁸²one kid of the goats as a sin offering; ⁸³and as the sacrifice of peace offerings: two oxen, five rams, five male goats, and five male lambs in their first year. This *was* the offering of Ahira the son of Enan.

⁸⁴This *was* the dedication *offering* for the altar from the leaders of Israel, when it was anointed: twelve silver platters, twelve silver bowls, and twelve gold pans. ⁸⁵Each silver platter *weighed* one hundred and thirty *shekels* and each bowl seventy *shekels.* All the silver of the vessels *weighed* two thousand four hundred *shekels,* according to the shekel of the sanctuary. ⁸⁶The twelve gold pans full of incense *weighed* ten *shekels* apiece, according to the shekel of the sanctuary; all the gold of the pans *weighed* one hundred and twenty *shekels.* ⁸⁷All the oxen for the burnt offering *were* twelve young bulls, the rams twelve, the male lambs in their first year twelve, with their grain offering, and the kids of the goats as a sin offering twelve. ⁸⁸And all the oxen for the sacrifice of peace offerings were twenty-four bulls, the rams sixty, the male goats sixty, and the lambs in their first year sixty. This *was* the dedication *offering* for the altar after it was anointed.

⁸⁹Now when Moses went into the tabernacle of meeting to speak with Him, he heard the voice of One speaking to him from above the mercy seat that *was* on the ark of the Testimony, from between the two cherubim; thus He spoke to him.

8 And the LORD spoke to Moses, saying: ²"Speak to Aaron, and say to him, 'When you arrange the lamps, the seven lamps shall give light in front of the lampstand.'" ³And Aaron did so; he arranged the lamps to face toward the front of the lampstand, as the LORD commanded Moses. ⁴Now this workmanship of the lampstand *was* hammered gold; from its shaft to its flowers it *was* hammered work. According to the pattern which the LORD had shown Moses, so he made the lampstand.

⁵Then the LORD spoke to Moses, saying: ⁶"Take the Levites from among the children of Israel and cleanse them *ceremonially.* ⁷Thus you shall do to

78 בְּיוֹם שְׁנֵים עָשָׂר יוֹם נָשִׂיא לִבְנֵי נַפְתָּלִי אֲחִירַע בֶּן־עֵינָן: 79 קָרְבָּנוֹ קַעֲרַת־כֶּסֶף אַחַת שְׁלֹשִׁים וּמֵאָה מִשְׁקָלָהּ מִזְרָק אֶחָד כֶּסֶף שִׁבְעִים שֶׁקֶל בְּשֶׁקֶל הַקֹּדֶשׁ שְׁנֵיהֶם | מְלֵאִים סֹלֶת בְּלוּלָה בַשֶּׁמֶן לְמִנְחָה: 80 כַּף אַחַת עֲשָׂרָה זָהָב מְלֵאָה קְטֹרֶת: 81 פַּר אֶחָד בֶּן־בָּקָר אַיִל אֶחָד כֶּבֶשׂ־אֶחָד בֶּן־שְׁנָתוֹ לְעֹלָה: 82 שְׂעִיר־עִזִּים אֶחָד לְחַטָּאת: 83 וּלְזֶבַח הַשְּׁלָמִים בָּקָר שְׁנַיִם אֵילִם חֲמִשָּׁה עַתֻּדִים חֲמִשָּׁה כְּבָשִׂים בְּנֵי־שָׁנָה חֲמִשָּׁה זֶה קָרְבַּן אֲחִירַע בֶּן־עֵינָן: פ

84 זֹאת | חֲנֻכַּת הַמִּזְבֵּחַ בְּיוֹם הִמָּשַׁח אֹתוֹ מֵאֵת נְשִׂיאֵי יִשְׂרָאֵל קַעֲרֹת כֶּסֶף שְׁתֵּים עֶשְׂרֵה מִזְרְקֵי־כֶסֶף שְׁנֵים עָשָׂר כַּפּוֹת זָהָב שְׁתֵּים עֶשְׂרֵה: 85 שְׁלֹשִׁים וּמֵאָה הַקְּעָרָה הָאַחַת כֶּסֶף וְשִׁבְעִים הַמִּזְרָק הָאֶחָד כֹּל כֶּסֶף הַכֵּלִים אַלְפַּיִם וְאַרְבַּע־מֵאוֹת בְּשֶׁקֶל הַקֹּדֶשׁ: 86 כַּפּוֹת זָהָב שְׁתֵּים־עֶשְׂרֵה מְלֵאֹת קְטֹרֶת עֲשָׂרָה עֲשָׂרָה הַכַּף בְּשֶׁקֶל הַקֹּדֶשׁ כָּל־זְהַב הַכַּפּוֹת עֶשְׂרִים וּמֵאָה: 87 כָּל־הַבָּקָר לָעֹלָה שְׁנֵים עָשָׂר פָּרִים אֵילִם שְׁנֵים־עָשָׂר כְּבָשִׂים בְּנֵי־שָׁנָה שְׁנֵים עָשָׂר וּמִנְחָתָם וּשְׂעִירֵי עִזִּים שְׁנֵים עָשָׂר לְחַטָּאת: 88 וְכֹל בְּקַר | זֶבַח הַשְּׁלָמִים עֶשְׂרִים וְאַרְבָּעָה פָּרִים אֵילִם שִׁשִּׁים עַתֻּדִים שִׁשִּׁים כְּבָשִׂים בְּנֵי־שָׁנָה שִׁשִּׁים זֹאת חֲנֻכַּת הַמִּזְבֵּחַ אַחֲרֵי הִמָּשַׁח אֹתוֹ: 89 וּבְבֹא מֹשֶׁה אֶל־אֹהֶל מוֹעֵד לְדַבֵּר אִתּוֹ וַיִּשְׁמַע אֶת־הַקּוֹל מִדַּבֵּר אֵלָיו מֵעַל הַכַּפֹּרֶת אֲשֶׁר עַל־אֲרֹן הָעֵדֻת מִבֵּין שְׁנֵי הַכְּרֻבִים וַיְדַבֵּר אֵלָיו: פ

ח וַיְדַבֵּר יְהוָה אֶל־מֹשֶׁה לֵּאמֹר: 2 דַּבֵּר אֶל־אַהֲרֹן וְאָמַרְתָּ אֵלָיו בְּהַעֲלֹתְךָ אֶת־הַנֵּרֹת אֶל־מוּל פְּנֵי הַמְּנוֹרָה יָאִירוּ שִׁבְעַת הַנֵּרוֹת: 3 וַיַּעַשׂ כֵּן אַהֲרֹן אֶל־מוּל פְּנֵי הַמְּנוֹרָה הֶעֱלָה נֵרֹתֶיהָ כַּאֲשֶׁר צִוָּה יְהוָה אֶת־מֹשֶׁה: 4 וְזֶה מַעֲשֵׂה הַמְּנֹרָה מִקְשָׁה זָהָב עַד־יְרֵכָהּ עַד־פִּרְחָהּ מִקְשָׁה הִוא כַּמַּרְאֶה אֲשֶׁר הֶרְאָה יְהוָה אֶת־מֹשֶׁה כֵּן עָשָׂה אֶת־הַמְּנֹרָה: פ 5 וַיְדַבֵּר יְהוָה אֶל־מֹשֶׁה לֵּאמֹר: 6 קַח אֶת־הַלְוִיִּם מִתּוֹךְ בְּנֵי יִשְׂרָאֵל וְטִהַרְתָּ אֹתָם: 7 וְכֹה־תַעֲשֶׂה

them to cleanse them: Sprinkle water of purification on them, and let them shave all their body, and let them wash their clothes, and *so* make themselves clean. [8] Then let them take a young bull with its grain offering of fine flour mixed with oil, and you shall take another young bull as a sin offering. [9] And you shall bring the Levites before the tabernacle of meeting, and you shall gather together the whole congregation of the children of Israel. [10] So you shall bring the Levites before the LORD, and the children of Israel shall lay their hands on the Levites; [11] and Aaron shall offer the Levites before the LORD *like* a wave offering from the children of Israel, that they may perform the work of the LORD. [12] Then the Levites shall lay their hands on the heads of the young bulls, and you shall offer one as a sin offering and the other as a burnt offering to the LORD, to make atonement for the Levites.

[13] "And you shall stand the Levites before Aaron and his sons, and then offer them *like* a wave offering to the LORD. [14] Thus you shall separate the Levites from among the children of Israel, and the Levites shall be Mine. [15] After that the Levites shall go in to service the tabernacle of meeting. So you shall cleanse them and offer them *like* a wave offering. [16] For they *are* wholly given to Me from among the children of Israel; I have taken them for Myself instead of all who open the womb, the firstborn of all the children of Israel. [17] For all the firstborn among the children of Israel *are* Mine, *both* man and beast; on the day that I struck all the firstborn in the land of Egypt I sanctified them to Myself. [18] I have taken the Levites instead of all the firstborn of the children of Israel. [19] And I have given the Levites as a gift to Aaron and his sons from among the children of Israel, to do the work for the children of Israel in the tabernacle of meeting, and to make atonement for the children of Israel, that there be no plague among the children of Israel when the children of Israel come near the sanctuary."

[20] Thus Moses and Aaron and all the congregation of the children of Israel did to the Levites; according to all that the LORD commanded Moses concerning the Levites, so the children of Israel did to them. [21] And the Levites purified themselves and washed their clothes; then Aaron presented them *like* a wave offering before the LORD, and Aaron made atonement for them to cleanse them. [22] After that the Levites went in to do their work in the tabernacle of meeting before Aaron and his sons; as the LORD commanded Moses concerning the Levites, so they did to them.

לָהֶם לְטַהֲרָם הַזֵּה עֲלֵיהֶם מֵי חַטָּאת וְהֶעֱבִירוּ תַעַר עַל־כָּל־בְּשָׂרָם וְכִבְּסוּ בִגְדֵיהֶם וְהִטֶּהָרוּ׃ 8 וְלָקְחוּ פַּר בֶּן־בָּקָר וּמִנְחָתוֹ סֹלֶת בְּלוּלָה בַשָּׁמֶן וּפַר־שֵׁנִי בֶן־בָּקָר תִּקַּח לְחַטָּאת׃ 9 וְהִקְרַבְתָּ אֶת־ הַלְוִיִּם לִפְנֵי אֹהֶל מוֹעֵד וְהִקְהַלְתָּ אֶת־כָּל־עֲדַת בְּנֵי יִשְׂרָאֵל׃ 10 וְהִקְרַבְתָּ אֶת־הַלְוִיִּם לִפְנֵי יְהוָה וְסָמְכוּ בְנֵי־יִשְׂרָאֵל אֶת־יְדֵיהֶם עַל־הַלְוִיִּם׃ 11 וְהֵנִיף אַהֲרֹן אֶת־הַלְוִיִּם תְּנוּפָה לִפְנֵי יְהוָה מֵאֵת בְּנֵי יִשְׂרָאֵל וְהָיוּ לַעֲבֹד אֶת־עֲבֹדַת יְהוָה׃ 12 וְהַלְוִיִּם יִסְמְכוּ אֶת־יְדֵיהֶם עַל רֹאשׁ הַפָּרִים וַעֲשֵׂה אֶת־ הָאֶחָד חַטָּאת וְאֶת־הָאֶחָד עֹלָה לַיהוָה לְכַפֵּר עַל־ הַלְוִיִּם׃ 13 וְהַעֲמַדְתָּ אֶת־הַלְוִיִּם לִפְנֵי אַהֲרֹן וְלִפְנֵי בָנָיו וְהֵנַפְתָּ אֹתָם תְּנוּפָה לַיהוָה׃ 14 וְהִבְדַּלְתָּ אֶת־ הַלְוִיִּם מִתּוֹךְ בְּנֵי יִשְׂרָאֵל וְהָיוּ לִי הַלְוִיִּם׃ 15 וְאַחֲרֵי־ כֵן יָבֹאוּ הַלְוִיִּם לַעֲבֹד אֶת־אֹהֶל מוֹעֵד וְטִהַרְתָּ אֹתָם וְהֵנַפְתָּ אֹתָם תְּנוּפָה׃ 16 כִּי נְתֻנִים נְתֻנִים הֵמָּה לִי מִתּוֹךְ בְּנֵי יִשְׂרָאֵל תַּחַת פִּטְרַת כָּל־רֶחֶם בְּכוֹר כֹּל מִבְּנֵי יִשְׂרָאֵל לָקַחְתִּי אֹתָם לִי׃ 17 כִּי לִי כָל־בְּכוֹר בִּבְנֵי יִשְׂרָאֵל בָּאָדָם וּבַבְּהֵמָה בְּיוֹם הַכֹּתִי כָל־בְּכוֹר בְּאֶרֶץ מִצְרַיִם הִקְדַּשְׁתִּי אֹתָם לִי׃ 18 וָאֶקַּח אֶת־הַלְוִיִּם תַּחַת כָּל־בְּכוֹר בִּבְנֵי יִשְׂרָאֵל׃ 19 וָאֶתְּנָה אֶת־הַלְוִיִּם נְתֻנִים ׀ לְאַהֲרֹן וּלְבָנָיו מִתּוֹךְ בְּנֵי יִשְׂרָאֵל לַעֲבֹד אֶת־עֲבֹדַת בְּנֵי־יִשְׂרָאֵל בְּאֹהֶל מוֹעֵד וּלְכַפֵּר עַל־בְּנֵי יִשְׂרָאֵל וְלֹא יִהְיֶה בִּבְנֵי יִשְׂרָאֵל נֶגֶף בְּגֶשֶׁת בְּנֵי־יִשְׂרָאֵל אֶל־הַקֹּדֶשׁ׃ 20 וַיַּעַשׂ מֹשֶׁה וְאַהֲרֹן וְכָל־עֲדַת בְּנֵי־יִשְׂרָאֵל לַלְוִיִּם כְּכֹל אֲשֶׁר־צִוָּה יְהוָה אֶת־מֹשֶׁה לַלְוִיִּם כֵּן־עָשׂוּ לָהֶם בְּנֵי יִשְׂרָאֵל׃ 21 וַיִּתְחַטְּאוּ הַלְוִיִּם וַיְכַבְּסוּ בִגְדֵיהֶם וַיָּנֶף אַהֲרֹן אֹתָם תְּנוּפָה לִפְנֵי יְהוָה וַיְכַפֵּר עֲלֵיהֶם אַהֲרֹן לְטַהֲרָם׃ 22 וְאַחֲרֵי־כֵן בָּאוּ הַלְוִיִּם לַעֲבֹד אֶת־עֲבֹדָתָם בְּאֹהֶל מוֹעֵד לִפְנֵי אַהֲרֹן וְלִפְנֵי בָנָיו כַּאֲשֶׁר צִוָּה יְהוָה אֶת־מֹשֶׁה עַל־הַלְוִיִּם כֵּן

23 Then the LORD spoke to Moses, saying,
24 "This *is* what *pertains* to the Levites: From
twenty-five years old and above one may enter to
perform service in the work of the tabernacle of
meeting; 25 and at the age of fifty years they must
cease performing this work, and shall work no
more. 26 They may minister with their brethren in
the tabernacle of meeting, to attend to needs, but
they *themselves* shall do no work. Thus you shall do
to the Levites regarding their duties."

9 Now the LORD spoke to Moses in the Wilderness
of Sinai, in the first month of the second year after
they had come out of the land of Egypt, saying:
2 "Let the children of Israel keep the Passover at its
appointed time. 3 On the fourteenth day of this
month, at twilight, you shall keep it at its appointed
time. According to all its rites and ceremonies you
shall keep it. "4 So Moses told the children of Israel
that they should keep the Passover. 5 And they kept
the Passover on the fourteenth day of the first
month, at twilight, in the Wilderness of Sinai;
according to all that the LORD commanded Moses,
so the children of Israel did.

6 Now there were *certain* men who were defiled
by a human corpse, so that they could not keep the
Passover on that day; and they came before Moses
and Aaron that day. 7 And those men said to him,
"We *became* defiled by a human corpse. Why are
we kept from presenting the offering of the LORD at
its appointed time among the children of Israel?"

8 And Moses said to them, "Stand still, that I
may hear what the LORD will command concerning
you."

9 Then the LORD spoke to Moses, saying,
10 "Speak to the children of Israel, saying: 'If
anyone of you or your posterity is unclean because
of a corpse, or *is* far away on a journey, he may still
keep the LORD's Passover. 11 On the fourteenth day
of the second month, at twilight, they may keep it.
They shall eat it with unleavened bread and bitter
herbs. 12 They shall leave none of it until morning,
nor break one of its bones. According to all the
ordinances of the Passover they shall keep it. 13 But
the man who *is* clean and is not on a journey, and
ceases to keep the Passover, that same person shall
be cut off from among his people, because he did
not bring the offering of the LORD at its appointed
time; that man shall bear his sin.

14 'And if a stranger dwells among you, and
would keep the LORD's Passover, he must do so
according to the rite of the Passover and according
to its ceremony; you shall have one ordinance, both
for the stranger and the native of the land.' "

במדבר ט

עֲשׂוּ לָהֶם׃ ס 23 וַיְדַבֵּר יְהוָה אֶל־מֹשֶׁה
לֵּאמֹר׃ 24 זֹאת אֲשֶׁר לַלְוִיִּם מִבֶּן חָמֵשׁ וְעֶשְׂרִים
שָׁנָה וָמַעְלָה יָבוֹא לִצְבֹא צָבָא בַּעֲבֹדַת אֹהֶל
מוֹעֵד׃ 25 וּמִבֶּן חֲמִשִּׁים שָׁנָה יָשׁוּב מִצְּבָא הָעֲבֹדָה
וְלֹא יַעֲבֹד עוֹד׃ 26 וְשֵׁרֵת אֶת־אֶחָיו בְּאֹהֶל מוֹעֵד
לִשְׁמֹר מִשְׁמֶרֶת וַעֲבֹדָה לֹא יַעֲבֹד כָּכָה תַּעֲשֶׂה
לַלְוִיִּם בְּמִשְׁמְרֹתָם׃ פ

ט וַיְדַבֵּר יְהוָה אֶל־מֹשֶׁה בְמִדְבַּר־סִינַי בַּשָּׁנָה
הַשֵּׁנִית לְצֵאתָם מֵאֶרֶץ מִצְרַיִם בַּחֹדֶשׁ הָרִאשׁוֹן
לֵאמֹר׃ 2 וְיַעֲשׂוּ בְנֵי־יִשְׂרָאֵל אֶת־הַפָּסַח בְּמוֹעֲדוֹ׃
3 בְּאַרְבָּעָה עָשָׂר־יוֹם בַּחֹדֶשׁ הַזֶּה בֵּין הָעַרְבַּיִם
תַּעֲשׂוּ אֹתוֹ בְּמוֹעֲדוֹ כְּכָל־חֻקֹּתָיו וּכְכָל־מִשְׁפָּטָיו
תַּעֲשׂוּ אֹתוֹ׃ 4 וַיְדַבֵּר מֹשֶׁה אֶל־בְּנֵי יִשְׂרָאֵל לַעֲשֹׂת
הַפָּסַח׃ 5 וַיַּעֲשׂוּ אֶת־הַפֶּסַח בָּרִאשׁוֹן בְּאַרְבָּעָה
עָשָׂר יוֹם לַחֹדֶשׁ בֵּין הָעַרְבַּיִם בְּמִדְבַּר סִינָי כְּכֹל
אֲשֶׁר צִוָּה יְהוָה אֶת־מֹשֶׁה כֵּן עָשׂוּ בְּנֵי יִשְׂרָאֵל׃
6 וַיְהִי אֲנָשִׁים אֲשֶׁר הָיוּ טְמֵאִים לְנֶפֶשׁ אָדָם וְלֹא־
יָכְלוּ לַעֲשֹׂת־הַפֶּסַח בַּיּוֹם הַהוּא וַיִּקְרְבוּ לִפְנֵי מֹשֶׁה
וְלִפְנֵי אַהֲרֹן בַּיּוֹם הַהוּא׃ 7 וַיֹּאמְרוּ הָאֲנָשִׁים הָהֵמָּה
אֵלָיו אֲנַחְנוּ טְמֵאִים לְנֶפֶשׁ אָדָם לָמָּה נִגָּרַע לְבִלְתִּי
הַקְרִב אֶת־קָרְבַּן יְהוָה בְּמֹעֲדוֹ בְּתוֹךְ בְּנֵי יִשְׂרָאֵל׃
8 וַיֹּאמֶר אֲלֵהֶם מֹשֶׁה עִמְדוּ וְאֶשְׁמְעָה מַה־יְצַוֶּה
יְהוָה לָכֶם׃ פ

9 וַיְדַבֵּר יְהוָה אֶל־מֹשֶׁה לֵּאמֹר׃ 10 דַּבֵּר אֶל־בְּנֵי
יִשְׂרָאֵל לֵאמֹר אִישׁ אִישׁ כִּי־יִהְיֶה־טָמֵא ׀ לָנֶפֶשׁ
אוֹ בְדֶרֶךְ רְחֹקָה לָכֶם אוֹ לְדֹרֹתֵיכֶם וְעָשָׂה פֶסַח
לַיהוָה׃ 11 בַּחֹדֶשׁ הַשֵּׁנִי בְּאַרְבָּעָה עָשָׂר יוֹם בֵּין
הָעַרְבַּיִם יַעֲשׂוּ אֹתוֹ עַל־מַצּוֹת וּמְרֹרִים יֹאכְלֻהוּ׃
12 לֹא־יַשְׁאִירוּ מִמֶּנּוּ עַד־בֹּקֶר וְעֶצֶם לֹא יִשְׁבְּרוּ־
בוֹ כְּכָל־חֻקַּת הַפֶּסַח יַעֲשׂוּ אֹתוֹ׃ 13 וְהָאִישׁ אֲשֶׁר־
הוּא טָהוֹר וּבְדֶרֶךְ לֹא־הָיָה וְחָדַל לַעֲשׂוֹת הַפֶּסַח
וְנִכְרְתָה הַנֶּפֶשׁ הַהִוא מֵעַמֶּיהָ כִּי ׀ קָרְבַּן יְהוָה לֹא
הִקְרִיב בְּמֹעֲדוֹ חֶטְאוֹ יִשָּׂא הָאִישׁ הַהוּא׃ 14 וְכִי־
יָגוּר אִתְּכֶם גֵּר וְעָשָׂה פֶסַח לַיהוָה כְּחֻקַּת הַפֶּסַח
וּכְמִשְׁפָּטוֹ כֵּן יַעֲשֶׂה חֻקָּה אַחַת יִהְיֶה לָכֶם וְלַגֵּר
וּלְאֶזְרַח הָאָרֶץ׃ פ

15 Now on the day that the tabernacle was raised up, the cloud covered the tabernacle, the tent of the Testimony; from evening until morning it was above the tabernacle like the appearance of fire. 16 So it was always: the cloud covered it *by day*, and the appearance of fire by night. 17 Whenever the cloud was taken up from above the tabernacle, after that the children of Israel would journey; and in the place where the cloud settled, there the children of Israel would pitch their tents. 18 At the command of the LORD the children of Israel would journey, and at the command of the LORD they would camp; as long as the cloud stayed above the tabernacle they remained encamped. 19 Even when the cloud continued long, many days above the tabernacle, the children of Israel kept the charge of the LORD and did not journey. 20 So it was, when the cloud was above the tabernacle a few days: according to the command of the LORD they would remain encamped, and according to the command of the LORD they would journey. 21 So it was, when the cloud remained only from evening until morning: when the cloud was taken up in the morning, then they would journey; whether by day or by night, whenever the cloud was taken up, they would journey. 22 *Whether it was* two days, a month, or a year that the cloud remained above the tabernacle, the children of Israel would remain encamped and not journey; but when it was taken up, they would journey. 23 At the command of the LORD they remained encamped, and at the command of the LORD they journeyed; they kept the charge of the LORD, at the command of the LORD by the hand of Moses.

10 And the LORD spoke to Moses, saying: 2 "Make two silver trumpets for yourself; you shall make them of hammered work; you shall use them for calling the congregation and for directing the movement of the camps. 3 When they blow both of them, all the congregation shall gather before you at the door of the tabernacle of meeting. 4 But if they blow *only* one, then the leaders, the heads of the divisions of Israel, shall gather to you. 5 When you sound the advance, the camps that lie on the east side shall then begin their journey. 6 When you sound the advance the second time, then the camps that lie on the south side shall begin their journey; they shall sound the call for them to begin their journeys. 7 And when the assembly is to be gathered together, you shall blow, but not sound the advance. 8 The sons of Aaron, the priests, shall blow the trumpets; and these shall be to you as an ordinance forever throughout your generations.

15 וּבְיוֹם הָקִים אֶת־הַמִּשְׁכָּן כִּסָּה הֶעָנָן אֶת־הַמִּשְׁכָּן לְאֹהֶל הָעֵדֻת וּבָעֶרֶב יִהְיֶה עַל־הַמִּשְׁכָּן כְּמַרְאֵה־אֵשׁ עַד־בֹּקֶר: 16 כֵּן יִהְיֶה תָמִיד הֶעָנָן יְכַסֶּנּוּ וּמַרְאֵה־אֵשׁ לָיְלָה: 17 וּלְפִי הֵעָלֹת הֶעָנָן מֵעַל הָאֹהֶל וְאַחֲרֵי כֵן יִסְעוּ בְּנֵי יִשְׂרָאֵל וּבִמְקוֹם אֲשֶׁר יִשְׁכָּן־שָׁם הֶעָנָן שָׁם יַחֲנוּ בְּנֵי יִשְׂרָאֵל: 18 עַל־פִּי יְהוָה יִסְעוּ בְּנֵי יִשְׂרָאֵל וְעַל־פִּי יְהוָה יַחֲנוּ כָּל־יְמֵי אֲשֶׁר יִשְׁכָּן הֶעָנָן עַל־הַמִּשְׁכָּן יַחֲנוּ: 19 וּבְהַאֲרִיךְ הֶעָנָן עַל־הַמִּשְׁכָּן יָמִים רַבִּים וְשָׁמְרוּ בְנֵי־יִשְׂרָאֵל אֶת־מִשְׁמֶרֶת יְהוָה וְלֹא יִסָּעוּ: 20 וְיֵשׁ אֲשֶׁר יִהְיֶה הֶעָנָן יָמִים מִסְפָּר עַל־הַמִּשְׁכָּן עַל־פִּי יְהוָה יַחֲנוּ וְעַל־פִּי יְהוָה יִסָּעוּ: 21 וְיֵשׁ אֲשֶׁר־יִהְיֶה הֶעָנָן מֵעֶרֶב עַד־בֹּקֶר וְנַעֲלָה הֶעָנָן בַּבֹּקֶר וְנָסָעוּ אוֹ יוֹמָם וָלַיְלָה וְנַעֲלָה הֶעָנָן וְנָסָעוּ: 22 אוֹ־יֹמַיִם אוֹ־חֹדֶשׁ אוֹ־יָמִים בְּהַאֲרִיךְ הֶעָנָן עַל־הַמִּשְׁכָּן לִשְׁכֹּן עָלָיו יַחֲנוּ בְנֵי־יִשְׂרָאֵל וְלֹא יִסָּעוּ וּבְהֵעָלֹתוֹ יִסָּעוּ: 23 עַל־פִּי יְהוָה יַחֲנוּ וְעַל־פִּי יְהוָה יִסָּעוּ אֶת־מִשְׁמֶרֶת יְהוָה שָׁמָרוּ עַל־פִּי יְהוָה בְּיַד־מֹשֶׁה: פ

י 1 וַיְדַבֵּר יְהוָה אֶל־מֹשֶׁה לֵּאמֹר: 2 עֲשֵׂה לְךָ שְׁתֵּי חֲצוֹצְרֹת כֶּסֶף מִקְשָׁה תַּעֲשֶׂה אֹתָם וְהָיוּ לְךָ לְמִקְרָא הָעֵדָה וּלְמַסַּע אֶת־הַמַּחֲנוֹת: 3 וְתָקְעוּ בָּהֵן וְנוֹעֲדוּ אֵלֶיךָ כָּל־הָעֵדָה אֶל־פֶּתַח אֹהֶל מוֹעֵד: 4 וְאִם־בְּאַחַת יִתְקָעוּ וְנוֹעֲדוּ אֵלֶיךָ הַנְּשִׂיאִים רָאשֵׁי אַלְפֵי יִשְׂרָאֵל: 5 וּתְקַעְתֶּם תְּרוּעָה וְנָסְעוּ הַמַּחֲנוֹת הַחֹנִים קֵדְמָה: 6 וּתְקַעְתֶּם תְּרוּעָה שֵׁנִית וְנָסְעוּ הַמַּחֲנוֹת הַחֹנִים תֵּימָנָה תְּרוּעָה יִתְקְעוּ לְמַסְעֵיהֶם: 7 וּבְהַקְהִיל אֶת־הַקָּהָל תִּתְקְעוּ וְלֹא תָרִיעוּ: 8 וּבְנֵי אַהֲרֹן הַכֹּהֲנִים יִתְקְעוּ בַּחֲצֹצְרוֹת וְהָיוּ לָכֶם לְחֻקַּת

9 "When you go to war in your land against the enemy who oppresses you, then you shall sound an alarm with the trumpets, and you will be remembered before the Lord your God, and you will be saved from your enemies. 10 Also in the day of your gladness, in your appointed feasts, and at the beginning of your months, you shall blow the trumpets over your burnt offerings and over the sacrifices of your peace offerings; and they shall be a memorial for you before your God: I am the Lord your God."

11 Now it came to pass on the twentieth day of the second month, in the second year, that the cloud was taken up from above the tabernacle of the Testimony. 12 And the children of Israel set out from the Wilderness of Sinai on their journeys; then the cloud settled down in the Wilderness of Paran. 13 So they started out for the first time according to the command of the Lord by the hand of Moses.

14 The standard of the camp of the children of Judah set out first according to their armies; over their army was Nahshon the son of Amminadab. 15 Over the army of the tribe of the children of Issachar was Nethanel the son of Zuar. 16 And over the army of the tribe of the children of Zebulun was Eliab the son of Helon.

17 Then the tabernacle was taken down; and the sons of Gershon and the sons of Merari set out, carrying the tabernacle.

18 And the standard of the camp of Reuben set out according to their armies; over their army was Elizur the son of Shedeur. 19 Over the army of the tribe of the children of Simeon was Shelumiel the son of Zurishaddai. 20 And over the army of the tribe of the children of Gad was Eliasaph the son of Deuel.

21 Then the Kohathites set out, carrying the holy things. (The tabernacle would be prepared for their arrival.)

22 And the standard of the camp of the children of Ephraim set out according to their armies; over their army was Elishama the son of Ammihud. 23 Over the army of the tribe of the children of Manasseh was Gamaliel the son of Pedahzur. 24 And over the army of the tribe of the children of Benjamin was Abidan the son of Gideoni.

25 Then the standard of the camp of the children of Dan (the rear guard of all the camps) set out according to their armies; over their army was Ahiezer the son of Ammishaddai. 26 Over the army of the tribe of the children of Asher was Pagiel the son of Ocran. 27 And over the army of the tribe of the children of Naphtali was Ahira the son of Enan.

עוֹלָם לְדֹרֹתֵיכֶם: 9 וְכִי־תָבֹאוּ מִלְחָמָה בְּאַרְצְכֶם עַל־הַצַּר הַצֹּרֵר אֶתְכֶם וַהֲרֵעֹתֶם בַּחֲצֹצְרֹת וְנִזְכַּרְתֶּם לִפְנֵי יְהוָה אֱלֹהֵיכֶם וְנוֹשַׁעְתֶּם מֵאֹיְבֵיכֶם: 10 וּבְיוֹם שִׂמְחַתְכֶם וּבְמוֹעֲדֵיכֶם וּבְרָאשֵׁי חָדְשֵׁיכֶם וּתְקַעְתֶּם בַּחֲצֹצְרֹת עַל עֹלֹתֵיכֶם וְעַל זִבְחֵי שַׁלְמֵיכֶם וְהָיוּ לָכֶם לְזִכָּרוֹן לִפְנֵי אֱלֹהֵיכֶם אֲנִי יְהוָה אֱלֹהֵיכֶם: פ

11 וַיְהִי בַּשָּׁנָה הַשֵּׁנִית בַּחֹדֶשׁ הַשֵּׁנִי בְּעֶשְׂרִים בַּחֹדֶשׁ נַעֲלָה הֶעָנָן מֵעַל מִשְׁכַּן הָעֵדֻת: 12 וַיִּסְעוּ בְנֵי־יִשְׂרָאֵל לְמַסְעֵיהֶם מִמִּדְבַּר סִינָי וַיִּשְׁכֹּן הֶעָנָן בְּמִדְבַּר פָּארָן: 13 וַיִּסְעוּ בָּרִאשֹׁנָה עַל־פִּי יְהוָה בְּיַד־מֹשֶׁה: 14 וַיִּסַּע דֶּגֶל מַחֲנֵה בְנֵי־יְהוּדָה בָּרִאשֹׁנָה לְצִבְאֹתָם וְעַל־צְבָאוֹ נַחְשׁוֹן בֶּן־עַמִּינָדָב: 15 וְעַל־צְבָא מַטֵּה בְּנֵי יִשָּׂשכָר נְתַנְאֵל בֶּן־צוּעָר: 16 וְעַל־צְבָא מַטֵּה בְּנֵי זְבוּלֻן אֱלִיאָב בֶּן־חֵלֹן: 17 וְהוּרַד הַמִּשְׁכָּן וְנָסְעוּ בְנֵי־גֵרְשׁוֹן וּבְנֵי מְרָרִי נֹשְׂאֵי הַמִּשְׁכָּן: ס 18 וְנָסַע דֶּגֶל מַחֲנֵה רְאוּבֵן לְצִבְאֹתָם וְעַל־צְבָאוֹ אֱלִיצוּר בֶּן־שְׁדֵיאוּר: 19 וְעַל־צְבָא מַטֵּה בְּנֵי שִׁמְעוֹן שְׁלֻמִיאֵל בֶּן־צוּרִישַׁדָּי: 20 וְעַל־צְבָא מַטֵּה בְנֵי־גָד אֶלְיָסָף בֶּן־דְּעוּאֵל: 21 וְנָסְעוּ הַקְּהָתִים נֹשְׂאֵי הַמִּקְדָּשׁ וְהֵקִימוּ אֶת־הַמִּשְׁכָּן עַד־בֹּאָם: ס 22 וְנָסַע דֶּגֶל מַחֲנֵה בְנֵי־אֶפְרַיִם לְצִבְאֹתָם וְעַל־צְבָאוֹ אֱלִישָׁמָע בֶּן־עַמִּיהוּד: 23 וְעַל־צְבָא מַטֵּה בְּנֵי מְנַשֶּׁה גַּמְלִיאֵל בֶּן־פְּדָהצוּר: 24 וְעַל־צְבָא מַטֵּה בְּנֵי בִנְיָמִן אֲבִידָן בֶּן־גִּדְעוֹנִי: ס 25 וְנָסַע דֶּגֶל מַחֲנֵה בְנֵי־דָן מְאַסֵּף לְכָל־הַמַּחֲנֹת לְצִבְאֹתָם וְעַל־צְבָאוֹ אֲחִיעֶזֶר בֶּן־עַמִּישַׁדָּי: 26 וְעַל־צְבָא מַטֵּה בְּנֵי אָשֵׁר פַּגְעִיאֵל בֶּן־עָכְרָן: 27 וְעַל־צְבָא מַטֵּה בְּנֵי נַפְתָּלִי אֲחִירַע

28 Thus *was* the order of march of the children of Israel, according to their armies, when they began their journey.

29 Now Moses said to Hobab the son of Reuel the Midianite, Moses' father-in-law, "We are setting out for the place of which the LORD said, 'I will give it to you.' Come with us, and we will treat you well; for the LORD has promised good things to Israel."

30 And he said to him, "I will not go, but I will depart to my *own* land and to my relatives."

31 So *Moses* said, "Please do not leave, inasmuch as you know how we are to camp in the wilderness, and you can be our eyes. 32 And it shall be, if you go with us—indeed it shall be—that whatever good the LORD will do to us, the same we will do to you."

33 So they departed from the mountain of the LORD on a journey of three days; and the ark of the covenant of the LORD went before them for the three days' journey, to search out a resting place for them. 34 And the cloud of the LORD *was* above them by day when they went out from the camp.

35 So it was, whenever the ark set out, that Moses said:

"Rise up, O LORD!
Let Your enemies be scattered,
And let those who hate You flee before You."

36 And when it rested, he said:

"Return, O LORD,
To the many thousands of Israel."

11 Now *when* the people complained, it displeased the LORD; for the LORD heard *it,* and His anger was aroused. So the fire of the LORD burned among them, and consumed *some* in the outskirts of the camp. 2 Then the people cried out to Moses, and when Moses prayed to the LORD, the fire was quenched. 3 So he called the name of the place Taberah, because the fire of the LORD had burned among them.

4 Now the mixed multitude who were among them yielded to intense craving; so the children of Israel also wept again and said: "Who will give us meat to eat? 5 We remember the fish which we ate freely in Egypt, the cucumbers, the melons, the leeks, the onions, and the garlic; 6 but now our whole being *is* dried up; *there is* nothing at all except this manna *before* our eyes!"

7 Now the manna *was* like coriander seed, and its color like the color of bdellium. 8 The people went about and gathered *it,* ground *it* on millstones or beat *it* in the mortar, cooked *it* in pans, and made

בֶּן־עֵינָן: 28 אֵלֶּה מַסְעֵי בְנֵי־יִשְׂרָאֵל לְצִבְאֹתָם וַיִּסָּעוּ: ס 29 וַיֹּאמֶר מֹשֶׁה לְחֹבָב בֶּן־רְעוּאֵל הַמִּדְיָנִי חֹתֵן מֹשֶׁה נֹסְעִים ׀ אֲנַחְנוּ אֶל־הַמָּקוֹם אֲשֶׁר אָמַר יְהֹוָה אֹתוֹ אֶתֵּן לָכֶם לְכָה אִתָּנוּ וְהֵטַבְנוּ לָךְ כִּי־יְהֹוָה דִּבֶּר־טוֹב עַל־יִשְׂרָאֵל: 30 וַיֹּאמֶר אֵלָיו לֹא אֵלֵךְ כִּי אִם־אֶל־אַרְצִי וְאֶל־מוֹלַדְתִּי אֵלֵךְ: 31 וַיֹּאמֶר אַל־נָא תַּעֲזֹב אֹתָנוּ כִּי ׀ עַל־כֵּן יָדַעְתָּ חֲנֹתֵנוּ בַּמִּדְבָּר וְהָיִיתָ לָּנוּ לְעֵינָיִם: 32 וְהָיָה כִּי־תֵלֵךְ עִמָּנוּ וְהָיָה ׀ הַטּוֹב הַהוּא אֲשֶׁר יֵיטִיב יְהֹוָה עִמָּנוּ וְהֵטַבְנוּ לָךְ: 33 וַיִּסְעוּ מֵהַר יְהֹוָה דֶּרֶךְ שְׁלֹשֶׁת יָמִים וַאֲרוֹן בְּרִית־יְהֹוָה נֹסֵעַ לִפְנֵיהֶם דֶּרֶךְ שְׁלֹשֶׁת יָמִים לָתוּר לָהֶם מְנוּחָה: 34 וַעֲנַן יְהֹוָה עֲלֵיהֶם יוֹמָם בְּנָסְעָם מִן־הַמַּחֲנֶה: ס 35 וַיְהִי בִּנְסֹעַ הָאָרֹן וַיֹּאמֶר מֹשֶׁה קוּמָה ׀ יְהֹוָה וְיָפֻצוּ אֹיְבֶיךָ וְיָנֻסוּ מְשַׂנְאֶיךָ מִפָּנֶיךָ: 36 וּבְנֻחֹה יֹאמַר שׁוּבָה יְהֹוָה רִבְבוֹת אַלְפֵי יִשְׂרָאֵל: פ

יא וַיְהִי הָעָם כְּמִתְאֹנְנִים רַע בְּאָזְנֵי יְהֹוָה וַיִּשְׁמַע יְהֹוָה וַיִּחַר אַפּוֹ וַתִּבְעַר־בָּם אֵשׁ יְהֹוָה וַתֹּאכַל בִּקְצֵה הַמַּחֲנֶה: 2 וַיִּצְעַק הָעָם אֶל־מֹשֶׁה וַיִּתְפַּלֵּל מֹשֶׁה אֶל־יְהֹוָה וַתִּשְׁקַע הָאֵשׁ: 3 וַיִּקְרָא שֵׁם־הַמָּקוֹם הַהוּא תַּבְעֵרָה כִּי־בָעֲרָה בָם אֵשׁ יְהֹוָה: 4 וְהָאסַפְסֻף אֲשֶׁר בְּקִרְבּוֹ הִתְאַוּוּ תַּאֲוָה וַיָּשֻׁבוּ וַיִּבְכּוּ גַּם בְּנֵי יִשְׂרָאֵל וַיֹּאמְרוּ מִי יַאֲכִלֵנוּ בָּשָׂר: 5 זָכַרְנוּ אֶת־הַדָּגָה אֲשֶׁר־נֹאכַל בְּמִצְרַיִם חִנָּם אֵת הַקִּשֻּׁאִים וְאֵת הָאֲבַטִּחִים וְאֶת־הֶחָצִיר וְאֶת־הַבְּצָלִים וְאֶת־הַשּׁוּמִים: 6 וְעַתָּה נַפְשֵׁנוּ יְבֵשָׁה אֵין כֹּל בִּלְתִּי אֶל־הַמָּן עֵינֵינוּ: 7 וְהַמָּן כִּזְרַע־גַּד הוּא וְעֵינוֹ כְּעֵין הַבְּדֹלַח: 8 שָׁטוּ הָעָם וְלָקְטוּ וְטָחֲנוּ בָרֵחַיִם אוֹ דָכוּ בַּמְּדֹכָה וּבִשְּׁלוּ בַּפָּרוּר וְעָשׂוּ אֹתוֹ

cakes of it; and its taste was like the taste of pastry prepared with oil. 9 And when the dew fell on the camp in the night, the manna fell on it.

10 Then Moses heard the people weeping throughout their families, everyone at the door of his tent; and the anger of the LORD was greatly aroused; Moses also was displeased. 11 So Moses said to the LORD, "Why have You afflicted Your servant? And why have I not found favor in Your sight, that You have laid the burden of all these people on me? 12 Did I conceive all these people? Did I beget them, that You should say to me, 'Carry them in your bosom, as a guardian carries a nursing child,' to the land which You swore to their fathers? 13 Where am I to get meat to give to all these people? For they weep all over me, saying, 'Give us meat, that we may eat.' 14 I am not able to bear all these people alone, because the burden is too heavy for me. 15 If You treat me like this, please kill me here and now—if I have found favor in Your sight—and do not let me see my wretchedness!"

16 So the LORD said to Moses: "Gather to Me seventy men of the elders of Israel, whom you know to be the elders of the people and officers over them; bring them to the tabernacle of meeting, that they may stand there with you. 17 Then I will come down and talk with you there. I will take of the Spirit that is upon you and will put the same upon them; and they shall bear the burden of the people with you, that you may not bear it yourself alone. 18 Then you shall say to the people, 'Consecrate yourselves for tomorrow, and you shall eat meat; for you have wept in the hearing of the LORD, saying, "Who will give us meat to eat? For it was well with us in Egypt." Therefore the LORD will give you meat, and you shall eat. 19 You shall eat, not one day, nor two days, nor five days, nor ten days, nor twenty days, 20 but for a whole month, until it comes out of your nostrils and becomes loathsome to you, because you have despised the LORD who is among you, and have wept before Him, saying, "Why did we ever come up out of Egypt?" ' "

21 And Moses said, "The people whom I am among are six hundred thousand men on foot; yet You have said, 'I will give them meat, that they may eat for a whole month.' 22 Shall flocks and herds be slaughtered for them, to provide enough for them? Or shall all the fish of the sea be gathered together for them, to provide enough for them?"

23 And the LORD said to Moses, "Has the LORD's arm been shortened? Now you shall see whether what I say will happen to you or not."

עֻגֹ֑ות וְהָיָ֣ה טַעְמֹ֔ו כְּטַ֖עַם לְשַׁ֥ד הַשָּֽׁמֶן׃ 9 וּבְרֶ֧דֶת הַטַּ֛ל עַל־הַֽמַּחֲנֶ֖ה לָ֑יְלָה יֵרֵ֥ד הַמָּ֖ן עָלָֽיו׃ 10 וַיִּשְׁמַ֨ע מֹשֶׁ֜ה אֶת־הָעָ֗ם בֹּכֶה֙ לְמִשְׁפְּחֹתָ֔יו אִ֖ישׁ לְפֶ֣תַח אָהֳלֹ֑ו וַיִּֽחַר־אַ֤ף יְהוָה֙ מְאֹ֔ד וּבְעֵינֵ֥י מֹשֶׁ֖ה רָֽע׃ 11 וַיֹּ֨אמֶר מֹשֶׁ֜ה אֶל־יְהוָ֗ה לָמָ֤ה הֲרֵעֹ֨תָ֙ לְעַבְדֶּ֔ךָ וְלָ֛מָּה לֹא־מָצָ֥תִי חֵ֖ן בְּעֵינֶ֑יךָ לָשׂ֗וּם אֶת־מַשָּׂ֛א כָּל־ הָעָ֥ם הַזֶּ֖ה עָלָֽי׃ 12 הֶאָנֹכִ֣י הָרִ֗יתִי אֵ֚ת כָּל־הָעָ֣ם הַזֶּ֔ה אִם־אָנֹכִ֖י יְלִדְתִּ֑יהוּ כִּֽי־תֹאמַ֨ר אֵלַ֜י שָׂאֵ֣הוּ בְחֵיקֶ֗ךָ כַּאֲשֶׁ֨ר יִשָּׂ֤א הָאֹמֵן֙ אֶת־הַיֹּנֵ֔ק עַ֚ל הָֽאֲדָמָ֔ה אֲשֶׁ֥ר נִשְׁבַּ֖עְתָּ לַאֲבֹתָֽיו׃ 13 מֵאַ֨יִן לִ֜י בָּשָׂ֗ר לָתֵ֖ת לְכָל־הָעָ֣ם הַזֶּ֑ה כִּֽי־יִבְכּ֤וּ עָלַי֙ לֵאמֹ֔ר תְּנָה־לָּ֥נוּ בָשָׂ֖ר וְנֹאכֵֽלָה׃ 14 לֹֽא־אוּכַ֤ל אָנֹכִי֙ לְבַדִּ֔י לָשֵׂ֖את אֶת־כָּל־ הָעָ֥ם הַזֶּ֖ה כִּ֥י כָבֵ֖ד מִמֶּֽנִּי׃ 15 וְאִם־כָּ֣כָה ׀ אַ֣תְּ־ עֹ֣שָׂה לִּ֗י הָרְגֵ֤נִי נָא֙ הָרֹ֔ג אִם־מָצָ֥אתִי חֵ֖ן בְּעֵינֶ֑יךָ וְאַל־אֶרְאֶ֖ה בְּרָעָתִֽי׃ פ

16 וַיֹּ֨אמֶר יְהוָ֜ה אֶל־מֹשֶׁ֗ה אֶסְפָה־לִּ֞י שִׁבְעִ֣ים אִישׁ֙ מִזִּקְנֵ֣י יִשְׂרָאֵ֔ל אֲשֶׁ֣ר יָדַ֔עְתָּ כִּי־הֵ֛ם זִקְנֵ֥י הָעָ֖ם וְשֹׁטְרָ֑יו וְלָקַחְתָּ֤ אֹתָם֙ אֶל־אֹ֣הֶל מֹועֵ֔ד וְהִֽתְיַצְּב֥וּ שָׁ֖ם עִמָּֽךְ׃ 17 וְיָרַדְתִּ֗י וְדִבַּרְתִּ֣י עִמְּךָ֮ שָׁם֒ וְאָצַלְתִּ֗י מִן־הָר֛וּחַ אֲשֶׁ֥ר עָלֶ֖יךָ וְשַׂמְתִּ֣י עֲלֵיהֶ֑ם וְנָשְׂא֤וּ אִתְּךָ֙ בְּמַשָּׂ֣א הָעָ֔ם וְלֹא־תִשָּׂ֥א אַתָּ֖ה לְבַדֶּֽךָ׃ 18 וְאֶל־הָעָ֨ם תֹּאמַ֜ר הִתְקַדְּשׁ֣וּ לְמָחָר֮ וַאֲכַלְתֶּ֣ם בָּשָׂר֒ כִּ֡י בְּכִיתֶם֩ בְּאָזְנֵ֨י יְהוָ֜ה לֵאמֹ֗ר מִ֤י יַאֲכִלֵ֨נוּ֙ בָּשָׂ֔ר כִּי־טֹ֥וב לָ֖נוּ בְּמִצְרָ֑יִם וְנָתַ֨ן יְהוָ֥ה לָכֶ֛ם בָּשָׂ֖ר וַאֲכַלְתֶּֽם׃ 19 לֹ֣א יֹ֥ום אֶחָ֛ד תֹּאכְל֖וּן וְלֹ֣א יֹומָ֑יִם וְלֹ֣א ׀ חֲמִשָּׁ֣ה יָמִ֗ים וְלֹא֙ עֲשָׂרָ֣ה יָמִ֔ים וְלֹ֖א עֶשְׂרִ֥ים יֹֽום׃ 20 עַ֣ד ׀ חֹ֣דֶשׁ יָמִ֗ים עַ֤ד אֲשֶׁר־יֵצֵא֙ מֵֽאַפְּכֶ֔ם וְהָיָ֥ה לָכֶ֖ם לְזָרָ֑א יַ֗עַן כִּֽי־מְאַסְתֶּ֤ם אֶת־יְהוָה֙ אֲשֶׁ֣ר בְּקִרְבְּכֶ֔ם וַתִּבְכּ֤וּ לְפָנָיו֙ לֵאמֹ֔ר לָ֥מָּה זֶּ֖ה יָצָ֥אנוּ מִמִּצְרָֽיִם׃ 21 וַיֹּאמֶר֮ מֹשֶׁ֒ה שֵׁשׁ־מֵאֹ֥ות אֶ֨לֶף֙ רַגְלִ֔י הָעָ֕ם אֲשֶׁ֥ר אָנֹכִ֖י בְּקִרְבֹּ֑ו וְאַתָּ֣ה אָמַ֗רְתָּ בָּשָׂר֙ אֶתֵּ֣ן לָהֶ֔ם וְאָכְל֖וּ חֹ֥דֶשׁ יָמִֽים׃ 22 הֲצֹ֧אן וּבָקָ֛ר יִשָּׁחֵ֥ט לָהֶ֖ם וּמָצָ֣א לָהֶ֑ם אִ֣ם אֶֽת־ כָּל־דְּגֵ֥י הַיָּ֛ם יֵאָסֵ֥ף לָהֶ֖ם וּמָצָ֥א לָהֶֽם׃ פ

23 וַיֹּ֤אמֶר יְהוָה֙ אֶל־מֹשֶׁ֔ה הֲיַ֥ד יְהוָ֖ה תִּקְצָ֑ר עַתָּ֥ה

²⁴So Moses went out and told the people the words of the LORD, and he gathered the seventy men of the elders of the people and placed them around the tabernacle. ²⁵Then the LORD came down in the cloud, and spoke to him, and took of the Spirit that *was* upon him, and placed *the same* upon the seventy elders; and it happened, when the Spirit rested upon them, that they prophesied, although they never did *so* again.

²⁶But two men had remained in the camp: the name of one *was* Eldad, and the name of the other Medad. And the Spirit rested upon them. Now they *were* among those listed, but who had not gone out to the tabernacle; yet they prophesied in the camp. ²⁷And a young man ran and told Moses, and said, "Eldad and Medad are prophesying in the camp."

²⁸So Joshua the son of Nun, Moses' assistant, *one* of his choice men, answered and said, "Moses my lord, forbid them!"

²⁹Then Moses said to him, "Are you zealous for my sake? Oh, that all the LORD's people were prophets *and* that the LORD would put His Spirit upon them!" ³⁰And Moses returned to the camp, he and the elders of Israel.

³¹Now a wind went out from the LORD, and it brought quail from the sea and left *them* fluttering near the camp, about a day's journey on this side and about a day's journey on the other side, all around the camp, and about two cubits above the surface of the ground. ³²And the people stayed up all that day, all night, and all the next day, and gathered the quail (he who gathered least gathered ten homers); and they spread *them* out for themselves all around the camp. ³³But while the meat *was* still between their teeth, before it was chewed, the wrath of the LORD was aroused against the people, and the LORD struck the people with a very great plague. ³⁴So he called the name of that place Kibroth Hattaavah, because there they buried the people who had yielded to craving.

³⁵From Kibroth Hattaavah the people moved to Hazeroth, and camped at Hazeroth.

12 Then Miriam and Aaron spoke against Moses because of the Ethiopian woman whom he had married; for he had married an Ethiopian woman. ²So they said, "Has the LORD indeed spoken only through Moses? Has He not spoken through us also?" And the LORD heard *it*. ³(Now the man Moses *was* very humble, more than all men who *were* on the face of the earth.)

⁴Suddenly the LORD said to Moses, Aaron, and Miriam, "Come out, you three, to the tabernacle of meeting!" So the three came out. ⁵Then the LORD

תִּרְאֶה הֲיִקְרְךָ דְבָרִי אִם־לֹא: 24 וַיֵּצֵא מֹשֶׁה וַיְדַבֵּר אֶל־הָעָם אֵת דִּבְרֵי יְהוָה וַיֶּאֱסֹף שִׁבְעִים אִישׁ מִזִּקְנֵי הָעָם וַיַּעֲמֵד אֹתָם סְבִיבֹת הָאֹהֶל: 25 וַיֵּרֶד יְהוָה ׀ בֶּעָנָן וַיְדַבֵּר אֵלָיו וַיָּאצֶל מִן־הָרוּחַ אֲשֶׁר עָלָיו וַיִּתֵּן עַל־שִׁבְעִים אִישׁ הַזְּקֵנִים וַיְהִי כְּנוֹחַ עֲלֵיהֶם הָרוּחַ וַיִּתְנַבְּאוּ וְלֹא יָסָפוּ: 26 וַיִּשָּׁאֲרוּ שְׁנֵי־אֲנָשִׁים ׀ בַּמַּחֲנֶה שֵׁם הָאֶחָד ׀ אֶלְדָּד וְשֵׁם הַשֵּׁנִי מֵידָד וַתָּנַח עֲלֵיהֶם הָרוּחַ וְהֵמָּה בַּכְּתֻבִים וְלֹא יָצְאוּ הָאֹהֱלָה וַיִּתְנַבְּאוּ בַּמַּחֲנֶה: 27 וַיָּרָץ הַנַּעַר וַיַּגֵּד לְמֹשֶׁה וַיֹּאמַר אֶלְדָּד וּמֵידָד מִתְנַבְּאִים בַּמַּחֲנֶה: 28 וַיַּעַן יְהוֹשֻׁעַ בִּן־נוּן מְשָׁרֵת מֹשֶׁה מִבְּחֻרָיו וַיֹּאמַר אֲדֹנִי מֹשֶׁה כְּלָאֵם: 29 וַיֹּאמֶר לוֹ מֹשֶׁה הַמְקַנֵּא אַתָּה לִי וּמִי יִתֵּן כָּל־עַם יְהוָה נְבִיאִים כִּי־יִתֵּן יְהוָה אֶת־רוּחוֹ עֲלֵיהֶם: 30 וַיֵּאָסֵף מֹשֶׁה אֶל־הַמַּחֲנֶה הוּא וְזִקְנֵי יִשְׂרָאֵל: 31 וְרוּחַ נָסַע ׀ מֵאֵת יְהוָה וַיָּגָז שַׂלְוִים מִן־הַיָּם וַיִּטֹּשׁ עַל־הַמַּחֲנֶה כְּדֶרֶךְ יוֹם כֹּה וּכְדֶרֶךְ יוֹם כֹּה סְבִיבוֹת הַמַּחֲנֶה וּכְאַמָּתַיִם עַל־פְּנֵי הָאָרֶץ: 32 וַיָּקָם הָעָם כָּל־הַיּוֹם הַהוּא וְכָל־הַלַּיְלָה וְכֹל ׀ יוֹם הַמָּחֳרָת וַיַּאַסְפוּ אֶת־הַשְּׂלָו הַמַּמְעִיט אָסַף עֲשָׂרָה חֳמָרִים וַיִּשְׁטְחוּ לָהֶם שָׁטוֹחַ סְבִיבוֹת הַמַּחֲנֶה: 33 הַבָּשָׂר עוֹדֶנּוּ בֵּין שִׁנֵּיהֶם טֶרֶם יִכָּרֵת וְאַף יְהוָה חָרָה בָעָם וַיַּךְ יְהוָה בָּעָם מַכָּה רַבָּה מְאֹד: 34 וַיִּקְרָא אֶת־שֵׁם־הַמָּקוֹם הַהוּא קִבְרוֹת הַתַּאֲוָה כִּי־שָׁם קָבְרוּ אֶת־הָעָם הַמִּתְאַוִּים: 35 מִקִּבְרוֹת הַתַּאֲוָה נָסְעוּ הָעָם חֲצֵרוֹת וַיִּהְיוּ בַּחֲצֵרוֹת: פ

יב וַתְּדַבֵּר מִרְיָם וְאַהֲרֹן בְּמֹשֶׁה עַל־אֹדוֹת הָאִשָּׁה הַכֻּשִׁית אֲשֶׁר לָקָח כִּי־אִשָּׁה כֻשִׁית לָקָח: 2 וַיֹּאמְרוּ הֲרַק אַךְ־בְּמֹשֶׁה דִּבֶּר יְהוָה הֲלֹא גַּם־בָּנוּ דִבֵּר וַיִּשְׁמַע יְהוָה: 3 וְהָאִישׁ מֹשֶׁה עָנָו מְאֹד מִכֹּל הָאָדָם אֲשֶׁר עַל־פְּנֵי הָאֲדָמָה: ס 4 וַיֹּאמֶר יְהוָה פִּתְאֹם אֶל־מֹשֶׁה וְאֶל־אַהֲרֹן וְאֶל־מִרְיָם צְאוּ שְׁלָשְׁתְּכֶם אֶל־אֹהֶל מוֹעֵד וַיֵּצְאוּ שְׁלָשְׁתָּם: 5 וַיֵּרֶד יְהוָה בְּעַמּוּד עָנָן וַיַּעֲמֹד פֶּתַח הָאֹהֶל וַיִּקְרָא

came down in the pillar of cloud and stood *in the* door of the tabernacle, and called Aaron and Miriam. And they both went forward. ⁶Then He said, "Hear now My words:

If there is a prophet among you,
I, the LORD, make Myself known to him in a vision;
I speak to him in a dream.
⁷ Not so with My servant Moses;
He *is* faithful in all My house.
⁸ I speak with him face to face,
Even plainly, and not in dark sayings;
And he sees the form of the LORD.
Why then were you not afraid
To speak against My servant Moses?"

⁹So the anger of the LORD was aroused against them, and He departed. ¹⁰And when the cloud departed from above the tabernacle, suddenly Miriam *became* leprous, as *white as* snow. Then Aaron turned toward Miriam, and there she was, a leper. ¹¹So Aaron said to Moses, "Oh, my lord! Please do not lay *this* sin on us, in which we have done foolishly and in which we have sinned. ¹²Please do not let her be as one dead, whose flesh is half consumed when he comes out of his mother's womb!"

¹³So Moses cried out to the LORD, saying, "Please heal her, O God, I pray!"

¹⁴Then the LORD said to Moses, "If her father had but spit in her face, would she not be shamed seven days? Let her be shut out of the camp seven days, and afterward she may be received *again.*" ¹⁵So Miriam was shut out of the camp seven days, and the people did not journey till Miriam was brought in *again.* ¹⁶And afterward the people moved from Hazeroth and camped in the Wilderness of Paran.

13 And the LORD spoke to Moses, saying, ²"Send men to spy out the land of Canaan, which I am giving to the children of Israel; from each tribe of their fathers you shall send a man, every one a leader among them. "

³So Moses sent them from the Wilderness of Paran according to the command of the LORD, all of them men who *were* heads of the children of Israel. ⁴Now these *were* their names: from the tribe of Reuben, Shammua the son of Zaccur; ⁵from the tribe of Simeon, Shaphat the son of Hori; ⁶from the tribe of Judah, Caleb the son of Jephunneh; ⁷from the tribe of Issachar, Igal the son of Joseph; ⁸from the tribe of Ephraim, Hoshea the son of Nun; ⁹from the tribe of Benjamin, Palti the son of Raphu; ¹⁰from the tribe of Zebulun, Gaddiel the

אַהֲרֹן וּמִרְיָם וַיֵּצְאוּ שְׁנֵיהֶם: 6 וַיֹּאמֶר שִׁמְעוּ־
נָא דְבָרָי אִם־יִהְיֶה נְבִיאֲכֶם יְהֹוָה בַּמַּרְאָה אֵלָיו
אֶתְוַדָּע בַּחֲלוֹם אֲדַבֶּר־בּוֹ: 7 לֹא־כֵן עַבְדִּי מֹשֶׁה
בְּכָל־בֵּיתִי נֶאֱמָן הוּא: 8 פֶּה אֶל־פֶּה אֲדַבֶּר־בּוֹ
וּמַרְאֶה וְלֹא בְחִידֹת וּתְמֻנַת יְהֹוָה יַבִּיט וּמַדּוּעַ
לֹא יְרֵאתֶם לְדַבֵּר בְּעַבְדִּי בְמֹשֶׁה: 9 וַיִּחַר־אַף יְהֹוָה
בָּם וַיֵּלַךְ: 10 וְהֶעָנָן סָר מֵעַל הָאֹהֶל וְהִנֵּה מִרְיָם
מְצֹרַעַת כַּשָּׁלֶג וַיִּפֶן אַהֲרֹן אֶל־מִרְיָם וְהִנֵּה מְצֹרָעַת:
11 וַיֹּאמֶר אַהֲרֹן אֶל־מֹשֶׁה בִּי אֲדֹנִי אַל־נָא תָשֵׁת
עָלֵינוּ חַטָּאת אֲשֶׁר נוֹאַלְנוּ וַאֲשֶׁר חָטָאנוּ: 12 אַל־
נָא תְהִי כַּמֵּת אֲשֶׁר בְּצֵאתוֹ מֵרֶחֶם אִמּוֹ וַיֵּאָכֵל
חֲצִי בְשָׂרוֹ: 13 וַיִּצְעַק מֹשֶׁה אֶל־יְהֹוָה לֵאמֹר אֵל נָא
רְפָא נָא לָהּ: 14 וַיֹּאמֶר יְהֹוָה אֶל־מֹשֶׁה וְאָבִיהָ יָרֹק
יָרַק בְּפָנֶיהָ הֲלֹא תִכָּלֵם שִׁבְעַת יָמִים תִּסָּגֵר שִׁבְעַת
יָמִים מִחוּץ לַמַּחֲנֶה וְאַחַר תֵּאָסֵף: 15 וַתִּסָּגֵר מִרְיָם
מִחוּץ לַמַּחֲנֶה שִׁבְעַת יָמִים וְהָעָם לֹא נָסַע עַד־
הֵאָסֵף מִרְיָם: 16 וְאַחַר נָסְעוּ הָעָם מֵחֲצֵרוֹת וַיַּחֲנוּ
בְּמִדְבַּר פָּארָן: פ

יג וַיְדַבֵּר יְהֹוָה אֶל־מֹשֶׁה לֵּאמֹר: 2 שְׁלַח־לְךָ
אֲנָשִׁים וְיָתֻרוּ אֶת־אֶרֶץ כְּנַעַן אֲשֶׁר־אֲנִי נֹתֵן לִבְנֵי
יִשְׂרָאֵל אִישׁ אֶחָד אִישׁ אֶחָד לְמַטֵּה אֲבֹתָיו
תִּשְׁלָחוּ כֹּל נָשִׂיא בָהֶם: 3 וַיִּשְׁלַח אֹתָם מֹשֶׁה
מִמִּדְבַּר פָּארָן עַל־פִּי יְהֹוָה כֻּלָּם אֲנָשִׁים רָאשֵׁי
בְנֵי־יִשְׂרָאֵל הֵמָּה: 4 וְאֵלֶּה שְׁמוֹתָם לְמַטֵּה רְאוּבֵן
שַׁמּוּעַ בֶּן־זַכּוּר: 5 לְמַטֵּה שִׁמְעוֹן שָׁפָט בֶּן־חוֹרִי:
6 לְמַטֵּה יְהוּדָה כָּלֵב בֶּן־יְפֻנֶּה: 7 לְמַטֵּה יִשָּׂשכָר
יִגְאָל בֶּן־יוֹסֵף: 8 לְמַטֵּה אֶפְרָיִם הוֹשֵׁעַ בִּן־נוּן:
9 לְמַטֵּה בִנְיָמִן פַּלְטִי בֶּן־רָפוּא: 10 לְמַטֵּה זְבוּלֻן

son of Sodi; [11] from the tribe of Joseph, *that is,* from the tribe of Manasseh, Gaddi the son of Susi; [12] from the tribe of Dan, Ammiel the son of Gemalli; [13] from the tribe of Asher, Sethur the son of Michael; [14] from the tribe of Naphtali, Nahbi the son of Vophsi; [15] from the tribe of Gad, Geuel the son of Machi.

[16] These *are* the names of the men whom Moses sent to spy out the land. And Moses called Hoshea the son of Nun, Joshua.

[17] Then Moses sent them to spy out the land of Canaan, and said to them, "Go up this *way* into the South, and go up to the mountains, [18] and see what the land is like: whether the people who dwell in it *are* strong or weak, few or many; [19] whether the land they dwell in *is* good or bad; whether the cities they inhabit *are* like camps or strongholds; [20] whether the land *is* rich or poor; and whether there are forests there or not. Be of good courage. And bring some of the fruit of the land." Now the time *was* the season of the first ripe grapes.

[21] So they went up and spied out the land from the Wilderness of Zin as far as Rehob, near the entrance of Hamath. [22] And they went up through the South and came to Hebron; Ahiman, Sheshai, and Talmai, the descendants of Anak, *were* there. (Now Hebron was built seven years before Zoan in Egypt.) [23] Then they came to the Valley of Eshcol, and there cut down a branch with one cluster of grapes; they carried it between two of them on a pole. *They* also *brought* some of the pomegranates and figs. [24] The place was called the Valley of Eshcol, because of the cluster which the men of Israel cut down there. [25] And they returned from spying out the land after forty days.

[26] Now they departed and came back to Moses and Aaron and all the congregation of the children of Israel in the Wilderness of Paran, at Kadesh; they brought back word to them and to all the congregation, and showed them the fruit of the land. [27] Then they told him, and said: "We went to the land where you sent us. It truly flows with milk and honey, and this *is* its fruit. [28] Nevertheless the people who dwell in the land *are* strong; the cities *are* fortified *and* very large; moreover we saw the descendants of Anak there. [29] The Amalekites dwell in the land of the South; the Hittites, the Jebusites, and the Amorites dwell in the mountains; and the Canaanites dwell by the sea and along the banks of the Jordan."

[30] Then Caleb quieted the people before Moses, and said, "Let us go up at once and take possession, for we are well able to overcome it."

גְּדִיאֵל בֶּן־סוֹדִי: 11 לְמַטֵּה יוֹסֵף לְמַטֵּה מְנַשֶּׁה גַּדִּי בֶּן־סוּסִי: 12 לְמַטֵּה דָן עַמִּיאֵל בֶּן־גְּמַלִּי: 13 לְמַטֵּה אָשֵׁר סְתוּר בֶּן־מִיכָאֵל: 14 לְמַטֵּה נַפְתָּלִי נַחְבִּי בֶּן־וָפְסִי: 15 לְמַטֵּה גָד גְּאוּאֵל בֶּן־מָכִי: 16 אֵלֶּה שְׁמוֹת הָאֲנָשִׁים אֲשֶׁר־שָׁלַח מֹשֶׁה לָתוּר אֶת־הָאָרֶץ וַיִּקְרָא מֹשֶׁה לְהוֹשֵׁעַ בִּן־נוּן יְהוֹשֻׁעַ: 17 וַיִּשְׁלַח אֹתָם מֹשֶׁה לָתוּר אֶת־אֶרֶץ כְּנָעַן וַיֹּאמֶר אֲלֵהֶם עֲלוּ זֶה בַּנֶּגֶב וַעֲלִיתֶם אֶת־הָהָר: 18 וּרְאִיתֶם אֶת־הָאָרֶץ מַה־הִוא וְאֶת־הָעָם הַיֹּשֵׁב עָלֶיהָ הֶחָזָק הוּא הֲרָפֶה הַמְעַט הוּא אִם־רָב: 19 וּמָה הָאָרֶץ אֲשֶׁר־הוּא יֹשֵׁב בָּהּ הֲטוֹבָה הִוא אִם־רָעָה וּמָה הֶעָרִים אֲשֶׁר־הוּא יוֹשֵׁב בָּהֵנָּה הַבְּמַחֲנִים אִם בְּמִבְצָרִים: 20 וּמָה הָאָרֶץ הַשְּׁמֵנָה הִוא אִם־רָזָה הֲיֵשׁ־בָּהּ עֵץ אִם־אַיִן וְהִתְחַזַּקְתֶּם וּלְקַחְתֶּם מִפְּרִי הָאָרֶץ וְהַיָּמִים יְמֵי בִּכּוּרֵי עֲנָבִים: 21 וַיַּעֲלוּ וַיָּתֻרוּ אֶת־הָאָרֶץ מִמִּדְבַּר־צִן עַד־רְחֹב לְבֹא חֲמָת: 22 וַיַּעֲלוּ בַנֶּגֶב וַיָּבֹא עַד־חֶבְרוֹן וְשָׁם אֲחִימַן שֵׁשַׁי וְתַלְמַי יְלִידֵי הָעֲנָק וְחֶבְרוֹן שֶׁבַע שָׁנִים נִבְנְתָה לִפְנֵי צֹעַן מִצְרָיִם: 23 וַיָּבֹאוּ עַד־נַחַל אֶשְׁכֹּל וַיִּכְרְתוּ מִשָּׁם זְמוֹרָה וְאֶשְׁכּוֹל עֲנָבִים אֶחָד וַיִּשָּׂאֻהוּ בַמּוֹט בִּשְׁנָיִם וּמִן־הָרִמֹּנִים וּמִן־הַתְּאֵנִים: 24 לַמָּקוֹם הַהוּא קָרָא נַחַל אֶשְׁכּוֹל עַל אֹדוֹת הָאֶשְׁכּוֹל אֲשֶׁר־כָּרְתוּ מִשָּׁם בְּנֵי יִשְׂרָאֵל: 25 וַיָּשֻׁבוּ מִתּוּר הָאָרֶץ מִקֵּץ אַרְבָּעִים יוֹם: 26 וַיֵּלְכוּ וַיָּבֹאוּ אֶל־מֹשֶׁה וְאֶל־אַהֲרֹן וְאֶל־כָּל־עֲדַת בְּנֵי־יִשְׂרָאֵל אֶל־מִדְבַּר פָּארָן קָדֵשָׁה וַיָּשִׁיבוּ אוֹתָם דָּבָר וְאֶת־כָּל־הָעֵדָה וַיַּרְאוּם אֶת־פְּרִי הָאָרֶץ: 27 וַיְסַפְּרוּ־לוֹ וַיֹּאמְרוּ בָּאנוּ אֶל־הָאָרֶץ אֲשֶׁר שְׁלַחְתָּנוּ וְגַם זָבַת חָלָב וּדְבַשׁ הִוא וְזֶה־פִּרְיָהּ: 28 אֶפֶס כִּי־עַז הָעָם הַיֹּשֵׁב בָּאָרֶץ וְהֶעָרִים בְּצֻרוֹת גְּדֹלֹת מְאֹד וְגַם־יְלִדֵי הָעֲנָק רָאִינוּ שָׁם: 29 עֲמָלֵק יוֹשֵׁב בְּאֶרֶץ הַנֶּגֶב וְהַחִתִּי וְהַיְבוּסִי וְהָאֱמֹרִי יוֹשֵׁב בָּהָר וְהַכְּנַעֲנִי יֹשֵׁב עַל־הַיָּם וְעַל יַד הַיַּרְדֵּן: 30 וַיַּהַס כָּלֵב אֶת־הָעָם אֶל־מֹשֶׁה וַיֹּאמֶר עָלֹה נַעֲלֶה וְיָרַשְׁנוּ אֹתָהּ כִּי־יָכוֹל נוּכַל

31 But the men who had gone up with him said, "We are not able to go up against the people, for they *are* stronger than we." 32 And they gave the children of Israel a bad report of the land which they had spied out, saying, "The land through which we have gone as spies *is* a land that devours its inhabitants, and all the people whom we saw in it *are* men of *great* stature. 33 There we saw the giants (the descendants of Anak came from the giants); and we were like grasshoppers in our own sight, and so we were in their sight."

14 So all the congregation lifted up their voices and cried, and the people wept that night. 2 And all the children of Israel complained against Moses and Aaron, and the whole congregation said to them, "If only we had died in the land of Egypt! Or if only we had died in this wilderness! 3 Why has the LORD brought us to this land to fall by the sword, that our wives and children should become victims? Would it not be better for us to return to Egypt? 4 So they said to one another, "Let us select a leader and return to Egypt. "

5 Then Moses and Aaron fell on their faces before all the assembly of the congregation of the children of Israel.

6 But Joshua the son of Nun and Caleb the son of Jephunneh, *who were* among those who had spied out the land, tore their clothes; 7 and they spoke to all the congregation of the children of Israel, saying: "The land we passed through to spy out *is* an exceedingly good land. 8 If the LORD delights in us, then He will bring us into this land and give it to us, 'a land which flows with milk and honey.' 9 Only do not rebel against the LORD, nor fear the people of the land, for they *are* our bread; their protection has departed from them, and the LORD *is* with us. Do not fear them."

10 And all the congregation said to stone them with stones. Now the glory of the LORD appeared in the tabernacle of meeting before all the children of Israel.

11 Then the LORD said to Moses: "How long will these people reject Me? And how long will they not believe Me, with all the signs which I have performed among them? 12 I will strike them with the pestilence and disinherit them, and I will make of you a nation greater and mightier than they."

13 And Moses said to the LORD: "Then the Egyptians will hear *it,* for by Your might You brought these people up from among them, 14 and they will tell *it* to the inhabitants of this land. They have heard that You, LORD, *are* among these people; that You, LORD, are seen face to face and

לָהּ: 31 וְהָאֲנָשִׁים אֲשֶׁר־עָלוּ עִמּוֹ אָמְרוּ לֹא נוּכַל לַעֲלוֹת אֶל־הָעָם כִּי־חָזָק הוּא מִמֶּנּוּ: 32 וַיּוֹצִיאוּ דִּבַּת הָאָרֶץ אֲשֶׁר תָּרוּ אֹתָהּ אֶל־בְּנֵי יִשְׂרָאֵל לֵאמֹר הָאָרֶץ אֲשֶׁר עָבַרְנוּ בָהּ לָתוּר אֹתָהּ אֶרֶץ אֹכֶלֶת יוֹשְׁבֶיהָ הִוא וְכָל־הָעָם אֲשֶׁר־רָאִינוּ בְתוֹכָהּ אַנְשֵׁי מִדּוֹת: 33 וְשָׁם רָאִינוּ אֶת־הַנְּפִילִים בְּנֵי עֲנָק מִן־ הַנְּפִלִים וַנְּהִי בְעֵינֵינוּ כַּחֲגָבִים וְכֵן הָיִינוּ בְּעֵינֵיהֶם:

יד וַתִּשָּׂא כָּל־הָעֵדָה וַיִּתְּנוּ אֶת־קוֹלָם וַיִּבְכּוּ הָעָם בַּלַּיְלָה הַהוּא: 2 וַיִּלֹּנוּ עַל־מֹשֶׁה וְעַל־אַהֲרֹן כֹּל בְּנֵי יִשְׂרָאֵל וַיֹּאמְרוּ אֲלֵהֶם כָּל־הָעֵדָה לוּ־ מַתְנוּ בְּאֶרֶץ מִצְרַיִם אוֹ בַּמִּדְבָּר הַזֶּה לוּ־מָתְנוּ: 3 וְלָמָה יְהֹוָה מֵבִיא אֹתָנוּ אֶל־הָאָרֶץ הַזֹּאת לִנְפֹּל בַּחֶרֶב נָשֵׁינוּ וְטַפֵּנוּ יִהְיוּ לָבַז הֲלוֹא טוֹב לָנוּ שׁוּב מִצְרָיְמָה: 4 וַיֹּאמְרוּ אִישׁ אֶל־אָחִיו נִתְּנָה רֹאשׁ וְנָשׁוּבָה מִצְרָיְמָה: 5 וַיִּפֹּל מֹשֶׁה וְאַהֲרֹן עַל־פְּנֵיהֶם לִפְנֵי כָּל־קְהַל עֲדַת בְּנֵי יִשְׂרָאֵל: 6 וִיהוֹשֻׁעַ בִּן־ נוּן וְכָלֵב בֶּן־יְפֻנֶּה מִן־הַתָּרִים אֶת־הָאָרֶץ קָרְעוּ בִּגְדֵיהֶם: 7 וַיֹּאמְרוּ אֶל־כָּל־עֲדַת בְּנֵי־יִשְׂרָאֵל לֵאמֹר הָאָרֶץ אֲשֶׁר עָבַרְנוּ בָהּ לָתוּר אֹתָהּ טוֹבָה הָאָרֶץ מְאֹד מְאֹד: 8 אִם־חָפֵץ בָּנוּ יְהֹוָה וְהֵבִיא אֹתָנוּ אֶל־הָאָרֶץ הַזֹּאת וּנְתָנָהּ לָנוּ אֶרֶץ אֲשֶׁר־הִוא זָבַת חָלָב וּדְבָשׁ: 9 אַךְ בַּיהֹוָה אַל־תִּמְרֹדוּ וְאַתֶּם אַל־ תִּירְאוּ אֶת־עַם הָאָרֶץ כִּי לַחְמֵנוּ הֵם סָר צִלָּם מֵעֲלֵיהֶם וַיהֹוָה אִתָּנוּ אַל־תִּירָאֻם: 10 וַיֹּאמְרוּ כָּל־ הָעֵדָה לִרְגּוֹם אֹתָם בָּאֲבָנִים וּכְבוֹד יְהֹוָה נִרְאָה בְּאֹהֶל מוֹעֵד אֶל־כָּל־בְּנֵי יִשְׂרָאֵל: פ

11 וַיֹּאמֶר יְהֹוָה אֶל־מֹשֶׁה עַד־אָנָה יְנַאֲצֻנִי הָעָם הַזֶּה וְעַד־אָנָה לֹא־יַאֲמִינוּ בִי בְּכֹל הָאֹתוֹת אֲשֶׁר עָשִׂיתִי בְּקִרְבּוֹ: 12 אַכֶּנּוּ בַדֶּבֶר וְאוֹרִשֶׁנּוּ וְאֶעֱשֶׂה אֹתְךָ לְגוֹי־גָּדוֹל וְעָצוּם מִמֶּנּוּ: 13 וַיֹּאמֶר מֹשֶׁה אֶל־ יְהֹוָה וְשָׁמְעוּ מִצְרַיִם כִּי־הֶעֱלִיתָ בְכֹחֲךָ אֶת־הָעָם הַזֶּה מִקִּרְבּוֹ: 14 וְאָמְרוּ אֶל־יוֹשֵׁב הָאָרֶץ הַזֹּאת שָׁמְעוּ כִּי־אַתָּה יְהֹוָה בְּקֶרֶב הָעָם הַזֶּה אֲשֶׁר־עַיִן בְּעַיִן נִרְאָה אַתָּה יְהֹוָה וַעֲנָנְךָ עֹמֵד עֲלֵהֶם

Your cloud stands above them, and You go before them in a pillar of cloud by day and in a pillar of fire by night. 15 Now *if* You kill these people as one man, then the nations which have heard of Your fame will speak, saying, 16 'Because the LORD was not able to bring this people to the land which He swore to give them, therefore He killed them in the wilderness.' 17 And now, I pray, let the power of my Lord be great, just as You have spoken, saying, 18 'The LORD is longsuffering and abundant in mercy, forgiving iniquity and transgression; but He by no means clears *the guilty,* visiting the iniquity of the fathers on the children to the third and fourth *generation.*' 19 Pardon the iniquity of this people, I pray, according to the greatness of Your mercy, just as You have forgiven this people, from Egypt even until now."

20 Then the LORD said: "I have pardoned, according to your word; 21 but truly, as I live, all the earth shall be filled with the glory of the LORD— 22 because all these men who have seen My glory and the signs which I did in Egypt and in the wilderness, and have put Me to the test now these ten times, and have not heeded My voice, 23 they certainly shall not see the land of which I swore to their fathers, nor shall any of those who rejected Me see it. 24 But My servant Caleb, because he has a different spirit in him and has followed Me fully, I will bring into the land where he went, and his descendants shall inherit it. 25 Now the Amalekites and the Canaanites dwell in the valley; tomorrow turn and move out into the wilderness by the Way of the Red Sea."

26 And the LORD spoke to Moses and Aaron, saying, 27 "How long *shall I bear with* this evil congregation who complain against Me? I have heard the complaints which the children of Israel make against Me. 28 Say to them, 'As I live,' says the LORD, 'just as you have spoken in My hearing, so I will do to you: 29 The carcasses of you who have complained against Me shall fall in this wilderness, all of you who were numbered, according to your entire number, from twenty years old and above. 30 Except for Caleb the son of Jephunneh and Joshua the son of Nun, you shall by no means enter the land which I swore I would make you dwell in. 31 But your little ones, whom you said would be victims, I will bring in, and they shall know the land which you have despised. 32 But *as for* you, your carcasses shall fall in this wilderness. 33 And your sons shall be shepherds in the wilderness forty years, and bear the brunt of your infidelity, until your carcasses are consumed in the wilderness. 34 According to the number of the days in which

וּבְעַמֻּד עָנָן אַתָּה הֹלֵךְ לִפְנֵיהֶם יוֹמָם וּבְעַמּוּד אֵשׁ לָיְלָה: 15 וְהֵמַתָּה אֶת־הָעָם הַזֶּה כְּאִישׁ אֶחָד וְאָמְרוּ הַגּוֹיִם אֲשֶׁר־שָׁמְעוּ אֶת־שִׁמְעֲךָ לֵאמֹר: 16 מִבִּלְתִּי יְכֹלֶת יְהֹוָה לְהָבִיא אֶת־הָעָם הַזֶּה אֶל־הָאָרֶץ אֲשֶׁר־נִשְׁבַּע לָהֶם וַיִּשְׁחָטֵם בַּמִּדְבָּר: 17 וְעַתָּה יִגְדַּל־נָא כֹּחַ אֲדֹנָי כַּאֲשֶׁר דִּבַּרְתָּ לֵאמֹר: 18 יְהֹוָה אֶרֶךְ אַפַּיִם וְרַב־חֶסֶד נֹשֵׂא עָוֺן וָפָשַׁע וְנַקֵּה לֹא יְנַקֶּה פֹּקֵד עֲוֺן אָבוֹת עַל־בָּנִים עַל־שִׁלֵּשִׁים וְעַל־רִבֵּעִים: 19 סְלַח־נָא לַעֲוֺן הָעָם הַזֶּה כְּגֹדֶל חַסְדֶּךָ וְכַאֲשֶׁר נָשָׂאתָה לָעָם הַזֶּה מִמִּצְרַיִם וְעַד־הֵנָּה: 20 וַיֹּאמֶר יְהֹוָה סָלַחְתִּי כִּדְבָרֶךָ: 21 וְאוּלָם חַי־אָנִי וְיִמָּלֵא כְבוֹד־יְהֹוָה אֶת־כָּל־הָאָרֶץ: 22 כִּי כָל־הָאֲנָשִׁים הָרֹאִים אֶת־כְּבֹדִי וְאֶת־אֹתֹתַי אֲשֶׁר עָשִׂיתִי בְמִצְרַיִם וּבַמִּדְבָּר וַיְנַסּוּ אֹתִי זֶה עֶשֶׂר פְּעָמִים וְלֹא שָׁמְעוּ בְּקוֹלִי: 23 אִם־יִרְאוּ אֶת־הָאָרֶץ אֲשֶׁר נִשְׁבַּעְתִּי לַאֲבֹתָם וְכָל־מְנַאֲצַי לֹא יִרְאוּהָ: 24 וְעַבְדִּי כָלֵב עֵקֶב הָיְתָה רוּחַ אַחֶרֶת עִמּוֹ וַיְמַלֵּא אַחֲרָי וַהֲבִיאֹתִיו אֶל־הָאָרֶץ אֲשֶׁר־בָּא שָׁמָּה וְזַרְעוֹ יוֹרִשֶׁנָּה: 25 וְהָעֲמָלֵקִי וְהַכְּנַעֲנִי יוֹשֵׁב בָּעֵמֶק מָחָר פְּנוּ וּסְעוּ לָכֶם הַמִּדְבָּר דֶּרֶךְ יַם־סוּף: פ

26 וַיְדַבֵּר יְהֹוָה אֶל־מֹשֶׁה וְאֶל־אַהֲרֹן לֵאמֹר: 27 עַד־מָתַי לָעֵדָה הָרָעָה הַזֹּאת אֲשֶׁר הֵמָּה מַלִּינִים עָלָי אֶת־תְּלֻנּוֹת בְּנֵי יִשְׂרָאֵל אֲשֶׁר הֵמָּה מַלִּינִים עָלַי שָׁמָעְתִּי: 28 אֱמֹר אֲלֵהֶם חַי־אָנִי נְאֻם־יְהֹוָה אִם־לֹא כַּאֲשֶׁר דִּבַּרְתֶּם בְּאָזְנָי כֵּן אֶעֱשֶׂה לָכֶם: 29 בַּמִּדְבָּר הַזֶּה יִפְּלוּ פִגְרֵיכֶם וְכָל־פְּקֻדֵיכֶם לְכָל־מִסְפַּרְכֶם מִבֶּן עֶשְׂרִים שָׁנָה וָמָעְלָה אֲשֶׁר הֲלִינֹתֶם עָלָי: 30 אִם־אַתֶּם תָּבֹאוּ אֶל־הָאָרֶץ אֲשֶׁר נָשָׂאתִי אֶת־יָדִי לְשַׁכֵּן אֶתְכֶם בָּהּ כִּי אִם־כָּלֵב בֶּן־יְפֻנֶּה וִיהוֹשֻׁעַ בִּן־נוּן: 31 וְטַפְּכֶם אֲשֶׁר אֲמַרְתֶּם לָבַז יִהְיֶה וְהֵבֵיאתִי אֹתָם וְיָדְעוּ אֶת־הָאָרֶץ אֲשֶׁר מְאַסְתֶּם בָּהּ: 32 וּפִגְרֵיכֶם אַתֶּם יִפְּלוּ בַּמִּדְבָּר הַזֶּה: 33 וּבְנֵיכֶם יִהְיוּ רֹעִים בַּמִּדְבָּר אַרְבָּעִים שָׁנָה וְנָשְׂאוּ אֶת־זְנוּתֵיכֶם עַד־תֹּם פִּגְרֵיכֶם בַּמִּדְבָּר: 34 בְּמִסְפַּר הַיָּמִים אֲשֶׁר־תַּרְתֶּם אֶת־הָאָרֶץ אַרְבָּעִים יוֹם לַשָּׁנָה יוֹם לַשָּׁנָה תִּשְׂאוּ אֶת־עֲוֺנֹתֵיכֶם אַרְבָּעִים

you spied out the land, forty days, for each day you shall bear your guilt one year, *namely* forty years, and you shall know My rejection. ³⁵ I the LORD have spoken this. I will surely do so to all this evil congregation who are gathered together against Me. In this wilderness they shall be consumed, and there they shall die.'"

³⁶ Now the men whom Moses sent to spy out the land, who returned and made all the congregation complain against him by bringing a bad report of the land, ³⁷ those very men who brought the evil report about the land, died by the plague before the LORD. ³⁸ But Joshua the son of Nun and Caleb the son of Jephunneh remained alive, of the men who went to spy out the land.

³⁹ Then Moses told these words to all the children of Israel, and the people mourned greatly. ⁴⁰ And they rose early in the morning and went up to the top of the mountain, saying, "Here we are, and we will go up to the place which the LORD has promised, for we have sinned!"

⁴¹ And Moses said, "Now why do you transgress the command of the LORD? For this will not succeed. ⁴² Do not go up, lest you be defeated by your enemies, for the LORD *is* not among you. ⁴³ For the Amalekites and the Canaanites *are* there before you, and you shall fall by the sword; because you have turned away from the LORD, the LORD will not be with you."

⁴⁴ But they presumed to go up to the mountain-top. Nevertheless, neither the ark of the covenant of the LORD nor Moses departed from the camp. ⁴⁵ Then the Amalekites and the Canaanites who dwelt in that mountain came down and attacked them, and drove them back as far as Hormah.

15 And the LORD spoke to Moses, saying, ² "Speak to the children of Israel, and say to them: 'When you have come into the land you are to inhabit, which I am giving to you, ³ and you make an offering by fire to the LORD, a burnt offering or a sacrifice, to fulfill a vow or as a freewill offering or in your appointed feasts, to make a sweet aroma to the LORD, from the herd or the flock, ⁴ then he who presents his offering to the LORD shall bring a grain offering of one-tenth *of an ephah* of fine flour mixed with one-fourth of a hin of oil; ⁵ and one-fourth of a hin of wine as a drink offering you shall prepare with the burnt offering or the sacrifice, for each lamb. ⁶ Or for a ram you shall prepare as a grain offering two-tenths *of an ephah* of fine flour mixed with one-third of a hin of oil; ⁷ and as a drink offering you shall offer one-third of a hin of wine as a sweet aroma to the LORD. ⁸ And when you

שָׁנָה וִידַעְתֶּם אֶת־תְּנוּאָתִי: 35 אֲנִי יְהֹוָה דִּבַּרְתִּי אִם־לֹא ׀ זֹאת אֶעֱשֶׂה לְכׇל־הָעֵדָה הָרָעָה הַזֹּאת הַנּוֹעָדִים עָלָי בַּמִּדְבָּר הַזֶּה יִתַּמּוּ וְשָׁם יָמֻתוּ: 36 וְהָאֲנָשִׁים אֲשֶׁר־שָׁלַח מֹשֶׁה לָתוּר אֶת־הָאָרֶץ וַיָּשֻׁבוּ וַיַּלִּינוּ עָלָיו אֶת־כׇּל־הָעֵדָה לְהוֹצִיא דִבָּה עַל־הָאָרֶץ: 37 וַיָּמֻתוּ הָאֲנָשִׁים מוֹצִאֵי דִבַּת־הָאָרֶץ רָעָה בַּמַּגֵּפָה לִפְנֵי יְהֹוָה: 38 וִיהוֹשֻׁעַ בִּן־נוּן וְכָלֵב בֶּן־יְפֻנֶּה חָיוּ מִן־הָאֲנָשִׁים הָהֵם הַהֹלְכִים לָתוּר אֶת־הָאָרֶץ: 39 וַיְדַבֵּר מֹשֶׁה אֶת־הַדְּבָרִים הָאֵלֶּה אֶל־כׇּל־בְּנֵי יִשְׂרָאֵל וַיִּתְאַבְּלוּ הָעָם מְאֹד: 40 וַיַּשְׁכִּמוּ בַבֹּקֶר וַיַּעֲלוּ אֶל־רֹאשׁ־הָהָר לֵאמֹר הִנֶּנּוּ וְעָלִינוּ אֶל־הַמָּקוֹם אֲשֶׁר־אָמַר יְהֹוָה כִּי חָטָאנוּ: 41 וַיֹּאמֶר מֹשֶׁה לָמָּה זֶּה אַתֶּם עֹבְרִים אֶת־פִּי יְהֹוָה וְהִוא לֹא תִצְלָח: 42 אַל־תַּעֲלוּ כִּי אֵין יְהֹוָה בְּקִרְבְּכֶם וְלֹא תִּנָּגְפוּ לִפְנֵי אֹיְבֵיכֶם: 43 כִּי הָעֲמָלֵקִי וְהַכְּנַעֲנִי שָׁם לִפְנֵיכֶם וּנְפַלְתֶּם בֶּחָרֶב כִּי־עַל־כֵּן שַׁבְתֶּם מֵאַחֲרֵי יְהֹוָה וְלֹא־יִהְיֶה יְהֹוָה עִמָּכֶם: 44 וַיַּעְפִּלוּ לַעֲלוֹת אֶל־רֹאשׁ הָהָר וַאֲרוֹן בְּרִית־יְהֹוָה וּמֹשֶׁה לֹא־מָשׁוּ מִקֶּרֶב הַמַּחֲנֶה: 45 וַיֵּרֶד הָעֲמָלֵקִי וְהַכְּנַעֲנִי הַיֹּשֵׁב בָּהָר הַהוּא וַיַּכּוּם וַיַּכְּתוּם עַד־הַחׇרְמָה: פ

טו וַיְדַבֵּר יְהֹוָה אֶל־מֹשֶׁה לֵּאמֹר: 2 דַּבֵּר אֶל־בְּנֵי יִשְׂרָאֵל וְאָמַרְתָּ אֲלֵהֶם כִּי תָבֹאוּ אֶל־אֶרֶץ מוֹשְׁבֹתֵיכֶם אֲשֶׁר אֲנִי נֹתֵן לָכֶם: 3 וַעֲשִׂיתֶם אִשֶּׁה לַיהֹוָה עֹלָה אוֹ־זֶבַח לְפַלֵּא־נֶדֶר אוֹ בִנְדָבָה אוֹ בְּמֹעֲדֵיכֶם לַעֲשׂוֹת רֵיחַ נִיחֹחַ לַיהֹוָה מִן־הַבָּקָר אוֹ מִן־הַצֹּאן: 4 וְהִקְרִיב הַמַּקְרִיב קׇרְבָּנוֹ לַיהֹוָה מִנְחָה סֹלֶת עִשָּׂרוֹן בָּלוּל בִּרְבִעִית הַהִין שָׁמֶן: 5 וְיַיִן לַנֶּסֶךְ רְבִיעִית הַהִין תַּעֲשֶׂה עַל־הָעֹלָה אוֹ לַזָּבַח לַכֶּבֶשׂ הָאֶחָד: 6 אוֹ לָאַיִל תַּעֲשֶׂה מִנְחָה סֹלֶת שְׁנֵי עֶשְׂרֹנִים בְּלוּלָה בַשֶּׁמֶן שְׁלִשִׁית הַהִין: 7 וְיַיִן לַנֶּסֶךְ שְׁלִשִׁית הַהִין תַּקְרִיב רֵיחַ־נִיחֹחַ לַיהֹוָה: 8 וְכִי־תַעֲשֶׂה בֶן־בָּקָר עֹלָה אוֹ־זָבַח לְפַלֵּא־נֶדֶר

prepare a young bull as a burnt offering, or as a sacrifice to fulfill a vow, or as a peace offering to the LORD, ⁹then shall be offered with the young bull a grain offering of three-tenths *of an ephah* of fine flour mixed with half a hin of oil; ¹⁰and you shall bring as the drink offering half a hin of wine as an offering made by fire, a sweet aroma to the LORD.

¹¹'Thus it shall be done for each young bull, for each ram, or for each lamb or young goat. ¹²According to the number that you prepare, so you shall do with everyone according to their number. ¹³All who are native-born shall do these things in this manner, in presenting an offering made by fire, a sweet aroma to the LORD. ¹⁴And if a stranger dwells with you, or whoever *is* among you throughout your generations, and would present an offering made by fire, a sweet aroma to the LORD, just as you do, so shall he do. ¹⁵One ordinance *shall be* for you of the assembly and for the stranger who dwells *with you,* an ordinance forever throughout your generations; as you are, so shall the stranger be before the LORD. ¹⁶One law and one custom shall be for you and for the stranger who dwells with you.'"

¹⁷Again the LORD spoke to Moses, saying, ¹⁸"Speak to the children of Israel, and say to them: 'When you come into the land to which I bring you, ¹⁹then it will be, when you eat of the bread of the land, that you shall offer up a heave offering to the LORD. ²⁰You shall offer up a cake of the first of your ground meal *as* a heave offering; as a heave offering of the threshing floor, so shall you offer it up. ²¹Of the first of your ground meal you shall give to the LORD a heave offering throughout your generations.

²²'If you sin unintentionally, and do not observe all these commandments which the LORD has spoken to Moses— ²³all that the LORD has commanded you by the hand of Moses, from the day the LORD gave commandment and onward throughout your generations— ²⁴then it will be, if it is unintentionally committed, without the knowledge of the congregation, that the whole congregation shall offer one young bull as a burnt offering, as a sweet aroma to the LORD, with its grain offering and its drink offering, according to the ordinance, and one kid of the goats as a sin offering. ²⁵So the priest shall make atonement for the whole congregation of the children of Israel, and it shall be forgiven them, for it was unintentional; they shall bring their offering, an offering made by fire to the LORD, and their sin offering before the LORD, for their unintended sin. ²⁶It shall

אוֹ־שְׁלָמִים לַיהֹוָה: ⁹ וְהִקְרִיב עַל־בֶּן־הַבָּקָר מִנְחָה
סֹלֶת שְׁלֹשָׁה עֶשְׂרֹנִים בָּלוּל בַּשֶּׁמֶן חֲצִי הַהִין:
¹⁰ וְיַיִן תַּקְרִיב לַנֶּסֶךְ חֲצִי הַהִין אִשֵּׁה רֵיחַ־נִיחֹחַ
לַיהֹוָה: ¹¹ כָּכָה יֵעָשֶׂה לַשּׁוֹר הָאֶחָד אוֹ לָאַיִל
הָאֶחָד אוֹ־לַשֶּׂה בַכְּבָשִׂים אוֹ בָעִזִּים: ¹² כַּמִּסְפָּר
אֲשֶׁר תַּעֲשׂוּ כָּכָה תַּעֲשׂוּ לָאֶחָד כְּמִסְפָּרָם: ¹³ כָּל־
הָאֶזְרָח יַעֲשֶׂה־כָּכָה אֶת־אֵלֶּה לְהַקְרִיב אִשֵּׁה רֵיחַ־
נִיחֹחַ לַיהֹוָה: ¹⁴ וְכִי־יָגוּר אִתְּכֶם גֵּר אוֹ אֲשֶׁר־
בְּתוֹכְכֶם לְדֹרֹתֵיכֶם וְעָשָׂה אִשֵּׁה רֵיחַ־נִיחֹחַ לַיהֹוָה
כַּאֲשֶׁר תַּעֲשׂוּ כֵּן יַעֲשֶׂה: ¹⁵ הַקָּהָל חֻקָּה אַחַת
לָכֶם וְלַגֵּר הַגָּר חֻקַּת עוֹלָם לְדֹרֹתֵיכֶם כָּכֶם כַּגֵּר
יִהְיֶה לִפְנֵי יְהֹוָה: ¹⁶ תּוֹרָה אַחַת וּמִשְׁפָּט אֶחָד
יִהְיֶה לָכֶם וְלַגֵּר הַגָּר אִתְּכֶם: פ

¹⁷ וַיְדַבֵּר יְהֹוָה אֶל־מֹשֶׁה לֵּאמֹר: ¹⁸ דַּבֵּר אֶל־בְּנֵי
יִשְׂרָאֵל וְאָמַרְתָּ אֲלֵהֶם בְּבֹאֲכֶם אֶל־הָאָרֶץ אֲשֶׁר
אֲנִי מֵבִיא אֶתְכֶם שָׁמָּה: ¹⁹ וְהָיָה בַּאֲכָלְכֶם מִלֶּחֶם
הָאָרֶץ תָּרִימוּ תְרוּמָה לַיהֹוָה: ²⁰ רֵאשִׁית עֲרִסֹתֵכֶם
חַלָּה תָּרִימוּ תְרוּמָה כִּתְרוּמַת גֹּרֶן כֵּן תָּרִימוּ
אֹתָהּ: ²¹ מֵרֵאשִׁית עֲרִסֹתֵיכֶם תִּתְּנוּ לַיהֹוָה תְּרוּמָה
לְדֹרֹתֵיכֶם: ס ²² וְכִי תִשְׁגּוּ וְלֹא תַעֲשׂוּ
אֵת כָּל־הַמִּצְוֹת הָאֵלֶּה אֲשֶׁר־דִּבֶּר יְהֹוָה אֶל־מֹשֶׁה:
²³ אֵת כָּל־אֲשֶׁר צִוָּה יְהֹוָה אֲלֵיכֶם בְּיַד־מֹשֶׁה מִן־
הַיּוֹם אֲשֶׁר צִוָּה יְהֹוָה וָהָלְאָה לְדֹרֹתֵיכֶם: ²⁴ וְהָיָה
אִם מֵעֵינֵי הָעֵדָה נֶעֶשְׂתָה לִשְׁגָגָה וְעָשׂוּ כָל־
הָעֵדָה פַּר בֶּן־בָּקָר אֶחָד לְעֹלָה לְרֵיחַ נִיחֹחַ לַיהֹוָה
וּמִנְחָתוֹ וְנִסְכּוֹ כַּמִּשְׁפָּט וּשְׂעִיר־עִזִּים אֶחָד לְחַטָּת:
²⁵ וְכִפֶּר הַכֹּהֵן עַל־כָּל־עֲדַת בְּנֵי יִשְׂרָאֵל וְנִסְלַח
לָהֶם כִּי־שְׁגָגָה הִוא וְהֵם הֵבִיאוּ אֶת־קָרְבָּנָם אִשֶּׁה
לַיהֹוָה וְחַטָּאתָם לִפְנֵי יְהֹוָה עַל־שִׁגְגָתָם: ²⁶ וְנִסְלַח

be forgiven the whole congregation of the children of Israel and the stranger who dwells among them, because all the people *did it* unintentionally.

27 'And if a person sins unintentionally, then he shall bring a female goat in its first year as a sin offering. 28 So the priest shall make atonement for the person who sins unintentionally, when he sins unintentionally before the LORD, to make atonement for him; and it shall be forgiven him. 29 You shall have one law for him who sins unintentionally, *for* him who is native-born among the children of Israel and for the stranger who dwells among them.

30 'But the person who does *anything* presumptuously, *whether he is* native-born or a stranger, that one brings reproach on the LORD, and he shall be cut off from among his people. 31 Because he has despised the word of the LORD, and has broken His commandment, that person shall be completely cut off; his guilt *shall be* upon him.'"

32 Now while the children of Israel were in the wilderness, they found a man gathering sticks on the Sabbath day. 33 And those who found him gathering sticks brought him to Moses and Aaron, and to all the congregation. 34 They put him under guard, because it had not been explained what should be done to him.

35 Then the LORD said to Moses, "The man must surely be put to death; all the congregation shall stone him with stones outside the camp." 36 So, as the LORD commanded Moses, all the congregation brought him outside the camp and stoned him with stones, and he died.

37 Again the LORD spoke to Moses, saying, 38 "Speak to the children of Israel: Tell them to make tassels on the corners of their garments throughout their generations, and to put a blue thread in the tassels of the corners. 39 And you shall have the tassel, that you may look upon it and remember all the commandments of the LORD and do them, and that you *may* not follow the harlotry to which your own heart and your own eyes are inclined, 40 and that you may remember and do all My commandments, and be holy for your God. 41 I *am* the LORD your God, who brought you out of the land of Egypt, to be your God: I *am* the LORD your God."

16 Now Korah the son of Izhar, the son of Kohath, the son of Levi, with Dathan and Abiram the sons of Eliab, and On the son of Peleth, sons of Reuben, took *men;* 2 and they rose up before Moses with some of the children of Israel, two hundred and fifty leaders of the congregation, representatives of the congregation, men of

לְכָל־עֲדַת֙ בְּנֵ֣י יִשְׂרָאֵ֔ל וְלַגֵּ֖ר הַגָּ֣ר בְּתוֹכָ֑ם כִּ֥י לְכָל־הָעָ֖ם בִּשְׁגָגָֽה׃ ס 27 וְאִם־נֶ֥פֶשׁ אַחַ֖ת תֶּחֱטָ֣א בִשְׁגָגָ֑ה וְהִקְרִ֛יבָה עֵ֥ז בַּת־שְׁנָתָ֖הּ לְחַטָּֽאת׃ 28 וְכִפֶּ֣ר הַכֹּהֵ֗ן עַל־הַנֶּ֧פֶשׁ הַשֹּׁגֶ֛גֶת בְּחֶטְאָ֥ה בִשְׁגָגָ֖ה לִפְנֵ֣י יְהוָ֑ה לְכַפֵּ֥ר עָלָ֖יו וְנִסְלַ֥ח לֽוֹ׃ 29 הָֽאֶזְרָח֙ בִּבְנֵ֣י יִשְׂרָאֵ֔ל וְלַגֵּ֖ר הַגָּ֣ר בְּתוֹכָ֑ם תּוֹרָ֤ה אַחַת֙ יִהְיֶ֣ה לָכֶ֔ם לָעֹשֶׂ֖ה בִּשְׁגָגָֽה׃ 30 וְהַנֶּ֜פֶשׁ אֲשֶֽׁר־תַּעֲשֶׂ֣ה ׀ בְּיָ֣ד רָמָ֗ה מִן־הָֽאֶזְרָח֙ וּמִן־הַגֵּ֔ר אֶת־יְהוָ֖ה ה֣וּא מְגַדֵּ֑ף וְנִכְרְתָ֛ה הַנֶּ֥פֶשׁ הַהִ֖וא מִקֶּ֥רֶב עַמָּֽהּ׃ 31 כִּ֤י דְבַר־יְהוָה֙ בָּזָ֔ה וְאֶת־מִצְוָת֖וֹ הֵפַ֑ר הִכָּרֵ֧ת ׀ תִּכָּרֵ֛ת הַנֶּ֥פֶשׁ הַהִ֖וא עֲוֺנָ֥ה בָֽהּ׃ פ

32 וַיִּהְי֥וּ בְנֵֽי־יִשְׂרָאֵ֖ל בַּמִּדְבָּ֑ר וַיִּמְצְא֗וּ אִ֛ישׁ מְקֹשֵׁ֥שׁ עֵצִ֖ים בְּי֥וֹם הַשַּׁבָּֽת׃ 33 וַיַּקְרִ֣יבוּ אֹת֔וֹ הַמֹּצְאִ֥ים אֹת֖וֹ מְקֹשֵׁ֣שׁ עֵצִ֑ים אֶל־מֹשֶׁה֙ וְאֶֽל־אַהֲרֹ֔ן וְאֶ֖ל כָּל־הָעֵדָֽה׃ 34 וַיַּנִּ֥יחוּ אֹת֖וֹ בַּמִּשְׁמָ֑ר כִּ֚י לֹ֣א פֹרַ֔שׁ מַה־יֵּעָשֶׂ֖ה לֽוֹ׃ ס 35 וַיֹּ֤אמֶר יְהוָה֙ אֶל־מֹשֶׁ֔ה מ֥וֹת יוּמַ֖ת הָאִ֑ישׁ רָג֨וֹם אֹת֤וֹ בָֽאֲבָנִים֙ כָּל־הָ֣עֵדָ֔ה מִח֖וּץ לַֽמַּחֲנֶֽה׃ 36 וַיֹּצִ֨יאוּ אֹת֜וֹ כָּל־הָעֵדָ֗ה אֶל־מִחוּץ֙ לַֽמַּחֲנֶ֔ה וַיִּרְגְּמ֥וּ אֹת֛וֹ בָּאֲבָנִ֖ים וַיָּמֹ֑ת כַּאֲשֶׁ֛ר צִוָּ֥ה יְהוָ֖ה אֶת־מֹשֶֽׁה׃ פ

37 וַיֹּ֥אמֶר יְהוָ֖ה אֶל־מֹשֶׁ֥ה לֵּאמֹֽר׃ 38 דַּבֵּ֞ר אֶל־בְּנֵ֤י יִשְׂרָאֵל֙ וְאָמַרְתָּ֣ אֲלֵהֶ֔ם וְעָשׂ֨וּ לָהֶ֥ם צִיצִ֛ת עַל־כַּנְפֵ֥י בִגְדֵיהֶ֖ם לְדֹרֹתָ֑ם וְנָ֥תְנ֛וּ עַל־צִיצִ֥ת הַכָּנָ֖ף פְּתִ֥יל תְּכֵֽלֶת׃ 39 וְהָיָ֣ה לָכֶם֮ לְצִיצִת֒ וּרְאִיתֶ֣ם אֹת֗וֹ וּזְכַרְתֶּם֙ אֶת־כָּל־מִצְוֺ֣ת יְהוָ֔ה וַעֲשִׂיתֶ֖ם אֹתָ֑ם וְלֹֽא־תָת֜וּרוּ אַחֲרֵ֤י לְבַבְכֶם֙ וְאַחֲרֵ֣י עֵֽינֵיכֶ֔ם אֲשֶׁר־אַתֶּ֥ם זֹנִ֖ים אַחֲרֵיהֶֽם׃ 40 לְמַ֣עַן תִּזְכְּר֔וּ וַעֲשִׂיתֶ֖ם אֶת־כָּל־מִצְוֺתָ֑י וִהְיִיתֶ֥ם קְדֹשִׁ֖ים לֵאלֹֽהֵיכֶֽם׃ 41 אֲנִ֞י יְהוָ֣ה אֱלֹֽהֵיכֶ֗ם אֲשֶׁ֨ר הוֹצֵ֤אתִי אֶתְכֶם֙ מֵאֶ֣רֶץ מִצְרַ֔יִם לִהְי֥וֹת לָכֶ֖ם לֵאלֹהִ֑ים אֲנִ֖י יְהוָ֥ה אֱלֹהֵיכֶֽם׃ פ

טז וַיִּקַּ֣ח קֹ֔רַח בֶּן־יִצְהָ֥ר בֶּן־קְהָ֖ת בֶּן־לֵוִ֑י וְדָתָ֨ן וַאֲבִירָ֜ם בְּנֵ֧י אֱלִיאָ֛ב וְא֥וֹן בֶּן־פֶּ֖לֶת בְּנֵ֥י רְאוּבֵֽן׃ 2 וַיָּקֻ֙מוּ֙ לִפְנֵ֣י מֹשֶׁ֔ה וַאֲנָשִׁ֥ים מִבְּנֵֽי־יִשְׂרָאֵ֖ל חֲמִשִּׁ֣ים וּמָאתָ֑יִם נְשִׂיאֵ֥י עֵדָ֛ה קְרִאֵ֥י מוֹעֵ֖ד אַנְשֵׁי־שֵֽׁם׃

renown. ³They gathered together against Moses and Aaron, and said to them, "*You take* too much upon yourselves, for all the congregation *is* holy, every one of them, and the LORD *is* among them. Why then do you exalt yourselves above the assembly of the LORD? "

⁴So when Moses heard *it,* he fell on his face; ⁵and he spoke to Korah and all his company, saying, "Tomorrow morning the LORD will show who *is* His and *who is* holy, and will cause *him* to come near to Him. That one whom He chooses He will cause to come near to Him. ⁶Do this: Take censers, Korah and all your company; ⁷put fire in them and put incense in them before the LORD tomorrow, and it shall be *that* the man whom the LORD chooses *is* the holy one. *You take* too much upon yourselves, you sons of Levi!"

⁸Then Moses said to Korah, "Hear now, you sons of Levi: ⁹*Is it* a small thing to you that the God of Israel has separated you from the congregation of Israel, to bring you near to Himself, to do the work of the tabernacle of the LORD, and to stand before the congregation to serve them; ¹⁰and that He has brought you near *to Himself,* you and all your brethren, the sons of Levi, with you? And are you seeking the priesthood also? ¹¹Therefore you and all your company *are* gathered together against the LORD. And what *is* Aaron that you complain against him?"

¹²And Moses sent to call Dathan and Abiram the sons of Eliab, but they said, "We will not come up! ¹³*Is it* a small thing that you have brought us up out of a land flowing with milk and honey, to kill us in the wilderness, that you should keep acting like a prince over us? ¹⁴Moreover you have not brought us into a land flowing with milk and honey, nor given us inheritance of fields and vineyards. Will you put out the eyes of these men? We will not come up!"

¹⁵Then Moses was very angry, and said to the LORD, "Do not respect their offering. I have not taken one donkey from them, nor have I hurt one of them."

¹⁶And Moses said to Korah, "Tomorrow, you and all your company be present before the LORD— you and they, as well as Aaron. ¹⁷Let each take his censer and put incense in it, and each of you bring his censer before the LORD, two hundred and fifty censers; both you and Aaron, each *with* his censer." ¹⁸So every man took his censer, put fire in it, laid incense on it, and stood at the door of the tabernacle of meeting with Moses and Aaron. ¹⁹And Korah gathered all the congregation against

3 וַיִּקָּהֲל֞וּ עַל־מֹשֶׁ֣ה וְעַֽל־אַהֲרֹ֗ן וַיֹּאמְר֣וּ אֲלֵהֶם֮ רַב־ לָכֶם֒ כִּ֤י כָל־הָֽעֵדָה֙ כֻּלָּ֣ם קְדֹשִׁ֔ים וּבְתוֹכָ֖ם יְהוָ֑ה וּמַדּ֥וּעַ תִּֽתְנַשְּׂא֖וּ עַל־קְהַ֥ל יְהוָֽה׃ 4 וַיִּשְׁמַ֣ע מֹשֶׁ֔ה וַיִּפֹּ֖ל עַל־פָּנָֽיו׃ 5 וַיְדַבֵּ֨ר אֶל־קֹ֜רַח וְאֶֽל־כָּל־עֲדָתוֹ֮ לֵאמֹר֒ בֹּ֠קֶר וְיֹדַ֨ע יְהוָ֧ה אֶת־אֲשֶׁר־ל֛וֹ וְאֶת־הַקָּד֖וֹשׁ וְהִקְרִ֣יב אֵלָ֑יו וְאֵ֛ת אֲשֶׁ֥ר יִבְחַר־בּ֖וֹ יַקְרִ֥יב אֵלָֽיו׃ 6 זֹ֖את עֲשׂ֑וּ קְחוּ־לָכֶ֣ם מַחְתּ֔וֹת קֹ֖רַח וְכָל־עֲדָתֽוֹ׃ 7 וּתְנ֣וּ בָהֵ֣ן ׀ אֵ֗שׁ וְשִׂ֧ימוּ עֲלֵיהֶ֛ן קְטֹ֖רֶת לִפְנֵ֤י יְהוָה֙ מָחָ֔ר וְהָיָ֗ה הָאִ֛ישׁ אֲשֶׁר־יִבְחַ֥ר יְהוָ֖ה ה֣וּא הַקָּד֑וֹשׁ רַב־לָכֶ֖ם בְּנֵ֥י לֵוִֽי׃ 8 וַיֹּ֥אמֶר מֹשֶׁ֖ה אֶל־קֹ֑רַח שִׁמְעוּ־נָ֖א בְּנֵ֥י לֵוִֽי׃ 9 הַמְעַ֣ט מִכֶּ֗ם כִּֽי־הִבְדִּיל֩ אֱלֹהֵ֨י יִשְׂרָאֵ֤ל אֶתְכֶם֙ מֵעֲדַ֣ת יִשְׂרָאֵ֔ל לְהַקְרִ֥יב אֶתְכֶ֖ם אֵלָ֑יו לַעֲבֹ֗ד אֶת־עֲבֹדַת֙ מִשְׁכַּ֣ן יְהוָ֔ה וְלַעֲמֹ֛ד לִפְנֵ֥י הָעֵדָ֖ה לְשָׁרְתָֽם׃ 10 וַיַּקְרֵב֙ אֹֽתְךָ֔ וְאֶת־כָּל־אַחֶ֥יךָ בְנֵֽי־לֵוִ֖י אִתָּ֑ךְ וּבִקַּשְׁתֶּ֖ם גַּם־כְּהֻנָּֽה׃ 11 לָכֵ֗ן אַתָּה֙ וְכָל־עֲדָ֣תְךָ֔ הַנֹּעָדִ֖ים עַל־יְהוָ֑ה וְאַהֲרֹ֣ן מַה־ה֔וּא כִּ֥י תַלִּ֖ונוּ עָלָֽיו׃ 12 וַיִּשְׁלַ֣ח מֹשֶׁ֔ה לִקְרֹ֛א לְדָתָ֥ן וְלַאֲבִירָ֖ם בְּנֵ֣י אֱלִיאָ֑ב וַיֹּאמְר֖וּ לֹ֥א נַעֲלֶֽה׃ 13 הַמְעַ֗ט כִּ֤י הֶֽעֱלִיתָ֙נוּ֙ מֵאֶ֨רֶץ זָבַ֤ת חָלָב֙ וּדְבַ֔שׁ לַהֲמִיתֵ֖נוּ בַּמִּדְבָּ֑ר כִּֽי־תִשְׂתָּרֵ֥ר עָלֵ֖ינוּ גַּם־הִשְׂתָּרֵֽר׃ 14 אַ֡ף לֹ֣א אֶל־אֶ֩רֶץ֩ זָבַ֨ת חָלָ֤ב וּדְבַשׁ֙ הֲבִ֣יאֹתָ֔נוּ וַתִּ֨תֶּן־לָ֔נוּ נַחֲלַ֖ת שָׂדֶ֣ה וָכָ֑רֶם הַעֵינֵ֞י הָאֲנָשִׁ֥ים הָהֵ֛ם תְּנַקֵּ֖ר לֹ֥א נַעֲלֶֽה׃ 15 וַיִּ֤חַר לְמֹשֶׁה֙ מְאֹ֔ד וַיֹּ֙אמֶר֙ אֶל־יְהוָ֔ה אַל־תֵּ֖פֶן אֶל־מִנְחָתָ֑ם לֹ֣א חֲמ֤וֹר אֶחָד֙ מֵהֶ֣ם נָשָׂ֔אתִי וְלֹ֥א הֲרֵעֹ֖תִי אֶת־אַחַ֥ד מֵהֶֽם׃ 16 וַיֹּ֤אמֶר מֹשֶׁה֙ אֶל־קֹ֔רַח אַתָּה֙ וְכָל־עֲדָ֣תְךָ֔ הֱי֖וּ לִפְנֵ֣י יְהוָ֑ה אַתָּ֥ה וָהֵ֛ם וְאַהֲרֹ֖ן מָחָֽר׃ 17 וּקְח֣וּ ׀ אִ֣ישׁ מַחְתָּת֗וֹ וּנְתַתֶּ֤ם עֲלֵיהֶם֙ קְטֹ֔רֶת וְהִקְרַבְתֶּ֞ם לִפְנֵ֤י יְהוָה֙ אִ֣ישׁ מַחְתָּת֔וֹ חֲמִשִּׁ֥ים וּמָאתַ֖יִם מַחְתֹּ֑ת וְאַתָּ֥ה וְאַהֲרֹ֖ן אִ֥ישׁ מַחְתָּתֽוֹ׃ 18 וַיִּקְח֞וּ אִ֣ישׁ מַחְתָּת֗וֹ וַיִּתְּנ֤וּ עֲלֵיהֶם֙ אֵ֔שׁ וַיָּשִׂ֥ימוּ עֲלֵיהֶ֖ם קְטֹ֑רֶת וַיַּֽעַמְד֗וּ פֶּ֛תַח אֹ֥הֶל מוֹעֵ֖ד וּמֹשֶׁ֥ה וְאַהֲרֹֽן׃ 19 וַיַּקְהֵ֨ל עֲלֵיהֶ֤ם קֹ֙רַח֙ אֶת־כָּל־הָ֣עֵדָ֔ה אֶל־פֶּ֖תַח אֹ֣הֶל מוֹעֵ֑ד וַיֵּרָ֥א כְבוֹד־יְהוָ֖ה אֶל־כָּל־הָעֵדָֽה׃ פ

them at the door of the tabernacle of meeting. Then the glory of the LORD appeared to all the congregation.

20 And the LORD spoke to Moses and Aaron, saying, 21 "Separate yourselves from among this congregation, that I may consume them in a moment."

22 Then they fell on their faces, and said, "O God, the God of the spirits of all flesh, shall one man sin, and You be angry with all the congregation?"

23 So the LORD spoke to Moses, saying, 24 "Speak to the congregation, saying, 'Get away from the tents of Korah, Dathan, and Abiram.' "

25 Then Moses rose and went to Dathan and Abiram, and the elders of Israel followed him. 26 And he spoke to the congregation, saying, "Depart now from the tents of these wicked men! Touch nothing of theirs, lest you be consumed in all their sins." 27 So they got away from around the tents of Korah, Dathan, and Abiram; and Dathan and Abiram came out and stood at the door of their tents, with their wives, their sons, and their little children.

28 And Moses said: "By this you shall know that the LORD has sent me to do all these works, for I have not done them of my own will. 29 If these men die naturally like all men, or if they are visited by the common fate of all men, then the LORD has not sent me. 30 But if the LORD creates a new thing, and the earth opens its mouth and swallows them up with all that belongs to them, and they go down alive into the pit, then you will understand that these men have rejected the LORD."

31 Now it came to pass, as he finished speaking all these words, that the ground split apart under them, 32 and the earth opened its mouth and swallowed them up, with their households and all the men with Korah, with all their goods. 33 So they and all those with them went down alive into the pit; the earth closed over them, and they perished from among the assembly. 34 Then all Israel who were around them fled at their cry, for they said, "Lest the earth swallow us up also!"

35 And a fire came out from the LORD and consumed the two hundred and fifty men who were offering incense.

36 Then the LORD spoke to Moses, saying: 37 "Tell Eleazar, the son of Aaron the priest, to pick up the censers out of the blaze, for they are holy, and scatter the fire some distance away. 38 The censers of these men who sinned against their own souls, let them be made into hammered plates as a covering for the altar. Because they presented them before the LORD, therefore they are holy; and they shall be

20 וַיְדַבֵּר יְהֹוָה אֶל־מֹשֶׁה וְאֶל־אַהֲרֹן לֵאמֹר: 21 הִבָּדְלוּ מִתּוֹךְ הָעֵדָה הַזֹּאת וַאֲכַלֶּה אֹתָם כְּרָגַע: 22 וַיִּפְּלוּ עַל־פְּנֵיהֶם וַיֹּאמְרוּ אֵל אֱלֹהֵי הָרוּחֹת לְכָל־בָּשָׂר הָאִישׁ אֶחָד יֶחֱטָא וְעַל כָּל־הָעֵדָה תִּקְצֹף: פ 23 וַיְדַבֵּר יְהֹוָה אֶל־מֹשֶׁה לֵּאמֹר: 24 דַּבֵּר אֶל־הָעֵדָה לֵאמֹר הֵעָלוּ מִסָּבִיב לְמִשְׁכַּן־קֹרַח דָּתָן וַאֲבִירָם: 25 וַיָּקָם מֹשֶׁה וַיֵּלֶךְ אֶל־דָּתָן וַאֲבִירָם וַיֵּלְכוּ אַחֲרָיו זִקְנֵי יִשְׂרָאֵל: 26 וַיְדַבֵּר אֶל־הָעֵדָה לֵאמֹר סוּרוּ נָא מֵעַל אָהֳלֵי הָאֲנָשִׁים הָרְשָׁעִים הָאֵלֶּה וְאַל־תִּגְּעוּ בְּכָל־אֲשֶׁר לָהֶם פֶּן־תִּסָּפוּ בְּכָל־חַטֹּאתָם: 27 וַיֵּעָלוּ מֵעַל מִשְׁכַּן־קֹרַח דָּתָן וַאֲבִירָם מִסָּבִיב וְדָתָן וַאֲבִירָם יָצְאוּ נִצָּבִים פֶּתַח אָהֳלֵיהֶם וּנְשֵׁיהֶם וּבְנֵיהֶם וְטַפָּם: 28 וַיֹּאמֶר מֹשֶׁה בְּזֹאת תֵּדְעוּן כִּי־יְהֹוָה שְׁלָחַנִי לַעֲשׂוֹת אֵת כָּל־הַמַּעֲשִׂים הָאֵלֶּה כִּי־לֹא מִלִּבִּי: 29 אִם־כְּמוֹת כָּל־הָאָדָם יְמֻתוּן אֵלֶּה וּפְקֻדַּת כָּל־הָאָדָם יִפָּקֵד עֲלֵיהֶם לֹא יְהֹוָה שְׁלָחָנִי: 30 וְאִם־בְּרִיאָה יִבְרָא יְהֹוָה וּפָצְתָה הָאֲדָמָה אֶת־פִּיהָ וּבָלְעָה אֹתָם וְאֶת־כָּל־אֲשֶׁר לָהֶם וְיָרְדוּ חַיִּים שְׁאֹלָה וִידַעְתֶּם כִּי נִאֲצוּ הָאֲנָשִׁים הָאֵלֶּה אֶת־יְהֹוָה: 31 וַיְהִי כְּכַלֹּתוֹ לְדַבֵּר אֵת כָּל־הַדְּבָרִים הָאֵלֶּה וַתִּבָּקַע הָאֲדָמָה אֲשֶׁר תַּחְתֵּיהֶם: 32 וַתִּפְתַּח הָאָרֶץ אֶת־פִּיהָ וַתִּבְלַע אֹתָם וְאֶת־בָּתֵּיהֶם וְאֵת כָּל־הָאָדָם אֲשֶׁר לְקֹרַח וְאֵת כָּל־הָרְכוּשׁ: 33 וַיֵּרְדוּ הֵם וְכָל־אֲשֶׁר לָהֶם חַיִּים שְׁאֹלָה וַתְּכַס עֲלֵיהֶם הָאָרֶץ וַיֹּאבְדוּ מִתּוֹךְ הַקָּהָל: 34 וְכָל־יִשְׂרָאֵל אֲשֶׁר סְבִיבֹתֵיהֶם נָסוּ לְקֹלָם כִּי אָמְרוּ פֶּן־תִּבְלָעֵנוּ הָאָרֶץ: 35 וְאֵשׁ יָצְאָה מֵאֵת יְהֹוָה וַתֹּאכַל אֵת הַחֲמִשִּׁים וּמָאתַיִם אִישׁ מַקְרִיבֵי הַקְּטֹרֶת: פ

יז וַיְדַבֵּר יְהֹוָה אֶל־מֹשֶׁה לֵּאמֹר: 2 אֱמֹר אֶל־אֶלְעָזָר בֶּן־אַהֲרֹן הַכֹּהֵן וְיָרֵם אֶת־הַמַּחְתֹּת מִבֵּין הַשְּׂרֵפָה וְאֶת־הָאֵשׁ זְרֵה־הָלְאָה כִּי קָדֵשׁוּ: 3 אֵת מַחְתּוֹת הַחַטָּאִים הָאֵלֶּה בְּנַפְשֹׁתָם וְעָשׂוּ אֹתָם רִקֻּעֵי פַחִים צִפּוּי לַמִּזְבֵּחַ כִּי־הִקְרִיבֻם לִפְנֵי־יְהֹוָה

a sign to the children of Israel." [39] So Eleazar the priest took the bronze censers, which those who were burned up had presented, and they were hammered out as a covering on the altar, [40] *to be* a memorial to the children of Israel that no outsider, who *is* not a descendant of Aaron, should come near to offer incense before the LORD, that he might not become like Korah and his companions, just as the LORD had said to him through Moses.

[41] On the next day all the congregation of the children of Israel complained against Moses and Aaron, saying, "You have killed the people of the LORD." [42] Now it happened, when the congregation had gathered against Moses and Aaron, that they turned toward the tabernacle of meeting; and suddenly the cloud covered it, and the glory of the LORD appeared. [43] Then Moses and Aaron came before the tabernacle of meeting.

[44] And the LORD spoke to Moses, saying, [45] "Get away from among this congregation, that I may consume them in a moment."

And they fell on their faces.

[46] So Moses said to Aaron, "Take a censer and put fire in it from the altar, put incense *on it,* and take it quickly to the congregation and make atonement for them; for wrath has gone out from the LORD. The plague has begun." [47] Then Aaron took *it* as Moses commanded, and ran into the midst of the assembly; and already the plague had begun among the people. So he put in the incense and made atonement for the people. [48] And he stood between the dead and the living; so the plague was stopped. [49] Now those who died in the plague were fourteen thousand seven hundred, besides those who died in the Korah incident. [50] So Aaron returned to Moses at the door of the tabernacle of meeting, for the plague had stopped.

17 And the LORD spoke to Moses, saying: [2] "Speak to the children of Israel, and get from them a rod from each father's house, all their leaders according to their fathers' houses—twelve rods. Write each man's name on his rod. [3] And you shall write Aaron's name on the rod of Levi. For there shall be one rod for the head of *each* father's house. [4] Then you shall place them in the tabernacle of meeting before the Testimony, where I meet with you. [5] And it shall be *that* the rod of the man whom I choose will blossom; thus I will rid Myself of the complaints of the children of Israel, which they make against you."

[6] So Moses spoke to the children of Israel, and each of their leaders gave him a rod apiece, for each leader according to their fathers' houses, twelve

וַיִּקְדָּשׁוּ וַיִּהְיוּ לְאוֹת לִבְנֵי יִשְׂרָאֵל: 4 וַיִּקַּח אֶלְעָזָר הַכֹּהֵן אֵת מַחְתּוֹת הַנְּחֹשֶׁת אֲשֶׁר הִקְרִיבוּ הַשְּׂרֻפִים וַיְרַקְּעוּם צִפּוּי לַמִּזְבֵּחַ: 5 זִכָּרוֹן לִבְנֵי יִשְׂרָאֵל לְמַעַן אֲשֶׁר לֹא־יִקְרַב אִישׁ זָר אֲשֶׁר לֹא מִזֶּרַע אַהֲרֹן הוּא לְהַקְטִיר קְטֹרֶת לִפְנֵי יְהוָה וְלֹא־יִהְיֶה כְקֹרַח וְכַעֲדָתוֹ כַּאֲשֶׁר דִּבֶּר יְהוָה בְּיַד־מֹשֶׁה לוֹ: 6 וַיִּלֹּנוּ כָּל־עֲדַת בְּנֵי־יִשְׂרָאֵל מִמָּחֳרָת עַל־מֹשֶׁה וְעַל־אַהֲרֹן לֵאמֹר אַתֶּם הֲמִתֶּם אֶת־עַם יְהוָה: 7 וַיְהִי בְּהִקָּהֵל הָעֵדָה עַל־מֹשֶׁה וְעַל־אַהֲרֹן וַיִּפְנוּ אֶל־אֹהֶל מוֹעֵד וְהִנֵּה כִסָּהוּ הֶעָנָן וַיֵּרָא כְּבוֹד יְהוָה: 8 וַיָּבֹא מֹשֶׁה וְאַהֲרֹן אֶל־פְּנֵי אֹהֶל מוֹעֵד: פ

9 וַיְדַבֵּר יְהוָה אֶל־מֹשֶׁה לֵּאמֹר: 10 הֵרֹמּוּ מִתּוֹךְ הָעֵדָה הַזֹּאת וַאֲכַלֶּה אֹתָם כְּרָגַע וַיִּפְּלוּ עַל־פְּנֵיהֶם: 11 וַיֹּאמֶר מֹשֶׁה אֶל־אַהֲרֹן קַח אֶת־הַמַּחְתָּה וְתֶן־עָלֶיהָ אֵשׁ מֵעַל הַמִּזְבֵּחַ וְשִׂים קְטֹרֶת וְהוֹלֵךְ מְהֵרָה אֶל־הָעֵדָה וְכַפֵּר עֲלֵיהֶם כִּי־יָצָא הַקֶּצֶף מִלִּפְנֵי יְהוָה הֵחֵל הַנָּגֶף: 12 וַיִּקַּח אַהֲרֹן כַּאֲשֶׁר דִּבֶּר מֹשֶׁה וַיָּרָץ אֶל־תּוֹךְ הַקָּהָל וְהִנֵּה הֵחֵל הַנֶּגֶף בָּעָם וַיִּתֵּן אֶת־הַקְּטֹרֶת וַיְכַפֵּר עַל־הָעָם: 13 וַיַּעֲמֹד בֵּין־הַמֵּתִים וּבֵין הַחַיִּים וַתֵּעָצַר הַמַּגֵּפָה: 14 וַיִּהְיוּ הַמֵּתִים בַּמַּגֵּפָה אַרְבָּעָה עָשָׂר אֶלֶף וּשְׁבַע מֵאוֹת מִלְּבַד הַמֵּתִים עַל־דְּבַר־קֹרַח: 15 וַיָּשָׁב אַהֲרֹן אֶל־מֹשֶׁה אֶל־פֶּתַח אֹהֶל מוֹעֵד וְהַמַּגֵּפָה נֶעֱצָרָה: פ

16 וַיְדַבֵּר יְהוָה אֶל־מֹשֶׁה לֵּאמֹר: 17 דַּבֵּר אֶל־בְּנֵי יִשְׂרָאֵל וְקַח מֵאִתָּם מַטֶּה מַטֶּה לְבֵית אָב מֵאֵת כָּל־נְשִׂיאֵהֶם לְבֵית אֲבֹתָם שְׁנֵים עָשָׂר מַטּוֹת אִישׁ אֶת־שְׁמוֹ תִּכְתֹּב עַל־מַטֵּהוּ: 18 וְאֵת שֵׁם אַהֲרֹן תִּכְתֹּב עַל־מַטֵּה לֵוִי כִּי מַטֶּה אֶחָד לְרֹאשׁ בֵּית אֲבוֹתָם: 19 וְהִנַּחְתָּם בְּאֹהֶל מוֹעֵד לִפְנֵי הָעֵדוּת אֲשֶׁר אִוָּעֵד לָכֶם שָׁמָּה: 20 וְהָיָה הָאִישׁ אֲשֶׁר אֶבְחַר־בּוֹ מַטֵּהוּ יִפְרָח וַהֲשִׁכֹּתִי מֵעָלַי אֶת־תְּלֻנּוֹת בְּנֵי יִשְׂרָאֵל אֲשֶׁר הֵם מַלִּינִם עֲלֵיכֶם: 21 וַיְדַבֵּר מֹשֶׁה אֶל־בְּנֵי יִשְׂרָאֵל וַיִּתְּנוּ אֵלָיו כָּל־נְשִׂיאֵיהֶם מַטֶּה לְנָשִׂיא אֶחָד מַטֶּה לְנָשִׂיא אֶחָד לְבֵית אֲבֹתָם שְׁנֵים עָשָׂר מַטּוֹת וּמַטֵּה אַהֲרֹן בְּתוֹךְ

rods; and the rod of Aaron *was* among their rods.
[7] And Moses placed the rods before the LORD in the tabernacle of witness.

[8] Now it came to pass on the next day that Moses went into the tabernacle of witness, and behold, the rod of Aaron, of the house of Levi, had sprouted and put forth buds, had produced blossoms and yielded ripe almonds. [9] Then Moses brought out all the rods from before the LORD to all the children of Israel; and they looked, and each man took his rod.

[10] And the LORD said to Moses, "Bring Aaron's rod back before the Testimony, to be kept as a sign against the rebels, that you may put their complaints away from Me, lest they die." [11] Thus did Moses; just as the LORD had commanded him, so he did.

[12] So the children of Israel spoke to Moses, saying, "Surely we die, we perish, we all perish! [13] Whoever even comes near the tabernacle of the LORD must die. Shall we all utterly die?"

18 Then the LORD said to Aaron: "You and your sons and your father's house with you shall bear the iniquity *related to* the sanctuary, and you and your sons with you shall bear the iniquity *associated with* your priesthood. [2] Also bring with you your brethren of the tribe of Levi, the tribe of your father, that they may be joined with you and serve you while you and your sons *are* with you before the tabernacle of witness. [3] They shall attend to your needs and all the needs of the tabernacle; but they shall not come near the articles of the sanctuary and the altar, lest they die—they and you also. [4] They shall be joined with you and attend to the needs of the tabernacle of meeting, for all the work of the tabernacle; but an outsider shall not come near you. [5] And you shall attend to the duties of the sanctuary and the duties of the altar, that there *may* be no more wrath on the children of Israel. [6] Behold, I Myself have taken your brethren the Levites from among the children of Israel; *they are* a gift to you, given by the LORD, to do the work of the tabernacle of meeting. [7] Therefore you and your sons with you shall attend to your priesthood for everything at the altar and behind the veil; and you shall serve. I give your priesthood *to you* as a gift for service, but the outsider who comes near shall be put to death."

[8] And the LORD spoke to Aaron: "Here, I Myself have also given you charge of My heave offerings, all the holy gifts of the children of Israel; I have given them as a portion to you and your sons, as an ordinance forever. [9] This shall be yours of the most holy things *reserved* from the fire: every offering of

מַטּוֹתָֽם: 22 וַיַּנַּ֣ח מֹשֶׁ֛ה אֶת־הַמַּטֹּ֖ת לִפְנֵ֣י יְהוָ֑ה בְּאֹ֖הֶל הָעֵדֻֽת: 23 וַיְהִ֣י מִֽמָּחֳרָ֗ת וַיָּבֹ֤א מֹשֶׁה֙ אֶל־אֹ֣הֶל הָֽעֵד֔וּת וְהִנֵּ֛ה פָּרַ֥ח מַטֵּֽה־אַהֲרֹ֖ן לְבֵ֣ית לֵוִ֑י וַיֹּ֤צֵֽא פֶ֨רַח֙ וַיָּ֣צֵֽץ צִ֔יץ וַיִּגְמֹ֖ל שְׁקֵדִֽים: 24 וַיֹּצֵ֨א מֹשֶׁ֤ה אֶת־כָּל־הַמַּטֹּת֙ מִלִּפְנֵ֣י יְהוָ֔ה אֶֽל־כָּל־בְּנֵ֖י יִשְׂרָאֵ֑ל וַיִּרְא֥וּ וַיִּקְח֖וּ אִ֥ישׁ מַטֵּֽהוּ: ס 25 וַיֹּ֨אמֶר יְהוָ֜ה אֶל־מֹשֶׁ֗ה הָשֵׁ֞ב אֶת־מַטֵּ֤ה אַהֲרֹן֙ לִפְנֵ֣י הָֽעֵד֔וּת לְמִשְׁמֶ֥רֶת לְא֖וֹת לִבְנֵי־מֶ֑רִי וּתְכַ֧ל תְּלוּנֹּתָ֛ם מֵֽעָלַ֖י וְלֹ֥א יָמֻֽתוּ: 26 וַיַּ֖עַשׂ מֹשֶׁ֑ה כַּאֲשֶׁ֨ר צִוָּ֧ה יְהוָ֛ה אֹת֖וֹ כֵּ֥ן עָשָֽׂה: ס 27 וַיֹּֽאמְרוּ֙ בְּנֵ֣י יִשְׂרָאֵ֔ל אֶל־מֹשֶׁ֖ה לֵאמֹ֑ר הֵ֥ן גָּוַ֛עְנוּ אָבַ֖דְנוּ כֻּלָּ֥נוּ אָבָֽדְנוּ: 28 כֹּ֣ל הַקָּרֵ֧ב | הַקָּרֵ֛ב אֶל־מִשְׁכַּ֥ן יְהוָ֖ה יָמ֑וּת הַאִ֥ם תַּ֖מְנוּ לִגְוֺֽעַ:

יח וַיֹּ֤אמֶר יְהוָה֙ אֶֽל־אַהֲרֹ֔ן אַתָּ֣ה וּבָנֶ֤יךָ וּבֵית־אָבִ֨יךָ֙ אִתָּ֔ךְ תִּשְׂא֖וּ אֶת־עֲוֺ֣ן הַמִּקְדָּ֑שׁ וְאַתָּ֣ה וּבָנֶ֤יךָ אִתָּ֔ךְ תִּשְׂא֖וּ אֶת־עֲוֺ֥ן כְּהֻנַּתְכֶֽם: 2 וְגַ֣ם אֶת־אַחֶ֩יךָ֩ מַטֵּ֨ה לֵוִ֜י שֵׁ֤בֶט אָבִ֨יךָ֙ הַקְרֵ֣ב אִתָּ֔ךְ וְיִלָּו֥וּ עָלֶ֖יךָ וִֽישָׁרְת֑וּךָ וְאַתָּה֙ וּבָנֶ֣יךָ אִתָּ֔ךְ לִפְנֵ֖י אֹ֥הֶל הָעֵדֻֽת: 3 וְשָֽׁמְרוּ֙ מִֽשְׁמַרְתְּךָ֔ וּמִשְׁמֶ֖רֶת כָּל־הָאֹ֑הֶל אַ֣ךְ אֶל־כְּלֵ֤י הַקֹּ֨דֶשׁ֙ וְאֶל־הַמִּזְבֵּ֔חַ לֹ֣א יִקְרָ֔בוּ וְלֹֽא־יָמֻ֥תוּ גַם־הֵ֖ם גַּם־אַתֶּֽם: 4 וְנִלְו֣וּ עָלֶ֔יךָ וְשָֽׁמְר֗וּ אֶת־מִשְׁמֶ֨רֶת֙ אֹ֣הֶל מוֹעֵ֔ד לְכֹ֖ל עֲבֹדַ֣ת הָאֹ֑הֶל וְזָ֖ר לֹא־יִקְרַ֥ב אֲלֵיכֶֽם: 5 וּשְׁמַרְתֶּ֗ם אֵ֚ת מִשְׁמֶ֣רֶת הַקֹּ֔דֶשׁ וְאֵ֖ת מִשְׁמֶ֣רֶת הַמִּזְבֵּ֑חַ וְלֹֽא־יִהְיֶ֥ה ע֛וֹד קֶ֖צֶף עַל־בְּנֵ֥י יִשְׂרָאֵֽל: 6 וַאֲנִ֗י הִנֵּ֤ה לָקַ֨חְתִּי֙ אֶת־אֲחֵיכֶ֣ם הַלְוִיִּ֔ם מִתּ֖וֹךְ בְּנֵ֣י יִשְׂרָאֵ֑ל לָכֶ֞ם מַתָּנָ֤ה נְתֻנִים֙ לַֽיהוָ֔ה לַעֲבֹ֕ד אֶת־עֲבֹדַ֖ת אֹ֥הֶל מוֹעֵֽד: 7 וְאַתָּ֣ה וּבָנֶ֣יךָ אִ֠תְּךָ תִּשְׁמְר֨וּ אֶת־כְּהֻנַּתְכֶ֜ם לְכָל־דְּבַ֧ר הַמִּזְבֵּ֛חַ וּלְמִבֵּ֥ית לַפָּרֹ֖כֶת וַעֲבַדְתֶּ֑ם עֲבֹדַ֣ת מַתָּנָ֗ה אֶתֵּן֙ אֶת־כְּהֻנַּתְכֶ֔ם וְהַזָּ֥ר הַקָּרֵ֖ב יוּמָֽת: ס 8 וַיְדַבֵּ֣ר יְהוָה֮ אֶֽל־אַהֲרֹן֒ וַאֲנִי֙ הִנֵּ֣ה נָתַ֣תִּֽי לְךָ֔ אֶת־מִשְׁמֶ֖רֶת תְּרֽוּמֹתָ֑י לְכָל־קָדְשֵׁ֣י בְנֵֽי־יִ֠שְׂרָאֵל לְךָ֨ נְתַתִּ֧ים לְמָשְׁחָ֛ה וּלְבָנֶ֖יךָ לְחָק־עוֹלָֽם: 9 זֶֽה־יִהְיֶ֥ה לְךָ֛ מִקֹּ֥דֶשׁ הַקֳּדָשִׁ֖ים מִן־הָאֵ֑שׁ כָּל־קָ֠רְבָּנָם לְֽכָל־מִנְחָתָ֞ם וּלְכָל־חַטָּאתָ֗ם וּלְכָל־אֲשָׁמָם֙ אֲשֶׁ֣ר יָשִׁ֣יבוּ לִ֔י קֹ֥דֶשׁ קָֽדָשִׁ֖ים לְךָ֥

theirs, every grain offering and every sin offering and every trespass offering which they render to Me, *shall be* most holy for you and your sons. [10] In a most holy *place* you shall eat it; every male shall eat it. It shall be holy to you.

[11] "This also *is* yours: the heave offering of their gift, with all the wave offerings of the children of Israel; I have given them to you, and your sons and daughters with you, as an ordinance forever. Everyone who is clean in your house may eat it.

[12] "All the best of the oil, all the best of the new wine and the grain, their firstfruits which they offer to the LORD, I have given them to you. [13] Whatever first ripe fruit is in their land, which they bring to the LORD, shall be yours. Everyone who is clean in your house may eat it.

[14] "Every devoted thing in Israel shall be yours.

[15] "Everything that first opens the womb of all flesh, which they bring to the LORD, whether man or beast, shall be yours; nevertheless the firstborn of man you shall surely redeem, and the firstborn of unclean animals you shall redeem. [16] And those redeemed of the devoted things you shall redeem when one month old, according to your valuation, for five shekels of silver, according to the shekel of the sanctuary, which *is* twenty gerahs. [17] But the firstborn of a cow, the firstborn of a sheep, or the firstborn of a goat you shall not redeem; they *are* holy. You shall sprinkle their blood on the altar, and burn their fat *as* an offering made by fire for a sweet aroma to the LORD. [18] And their flesh shall be yours, just as the wave breast and the right thigh are yours.

[19] "All the heave offerings of the holy things, which the children of Israel offer to the LORD, I have given to you and your sons and daughters with you as an ordinance forever; it *is* a covenant of salt forever before the LORD with you and your descendants with you."

[20] Then the LORD said to Aaron: "You shall have no inheritance in their land, nor shall you have any portion among them; I *am* your portion and your inheritance among the children of Israel.

[21] "Behold, I have given the children of Levi all the tithes in Israel as an inheritance in return for the work which they perform, the work of the tabernacle of meeting. [22] Hereafter the children of Israel shall not come near the tabernacle of meeting, lest they bear sin and die. [23] But the Levites shall perform the work of the tabernacle of meeting, and they shall bear their iniquity; *it shall be* a statute forever, throughout your generations, that among the children of Israel they shall have no inheritance. [24] For the tithes of the children of Israel, which they

הוּא וּלְבָנֶיךָ: 10 בְּקֹדֶשׁ הַקֳּדָשִׁים תֹּאכֲלֶנּוּ כָּל־
זָכָר יֹאכַל אֹתוֹ קֹדֶשׁ יִהְיֶה־לָּךְ: 11 וְזֶה־לְּךָ תְּרוּמַת
מַתָּנָם לְכָל־תְּנוּפֹת בְּנֵי יִשְׂרָאֵל לְךָ נְתַתִּים וּלְבָנֶיךָ
וְלִבְנֹתֶיךָ אִתְּךָ לְחָק־עוֹלָם כָּל־טָהוֹר בְּבֵיתְךָ יֹאכַל
אֹתוֹ: 12 כֹּל חֵלֶב יִצְהָר וְכָל־חֵלֶב תִּירוֹשׁ וְדָגָן
רֵאשִׁיתָם אֲשֶׁר־יִתְּנוּ לַיהֹוָה לְךָ נְתַתִּים: 13 בִּכּוּרֵי
כָּל־אֲשֶׁר בְּאַרְצָם אֲשֶׁר־יָבִיאוּ לַיהֹוָה לְךָ יִהְיֶה כָּל־
טָהוֹר בְּבֵיתְךָ יֹאכֲלֶנּוּ: 14 כָּל־חֵרֶם בְּיִשְׂרָאֵל לְךָ
יִהְיֶה: 15 כָּל־פֶּטֶר רֶחֶם לְכָל־בָּשָׂר אֲשֶׁר־יַקְרִיבוּ
לַיהֹוָה בָּאָדָם וּבַבְּהֵמָה יִהְיֶה־לָּךְ אַךְ פָּדֹה תִפְדֶּה
אֵת בְּכוֹר הָאָדָם וְאֵת בְּכוֹר־הַבְּהֵמָה הַטְּמֵאָה
תִּפְדֶּה: 16 וּפְדוּיָו מִבֶּן־חֹדֶשׁ תִּפְדֶּה בְּעֶרְכְּךָ כֶּסֶף
חֲמֵשֶׁת שְׁקָלִים בְּשֶׁקֶל הַקֹּדֶשׁ עֶשְׂרִים גֵּרָה הוּא:
17 אַךְ בְּכוֹר־שׁוֹר אוֹ־בְכוֹר כֶּשֶׂב אוֹ־בְכוֹר עֵז לֹא
תִפְדֶּה קֹדֶשׁ הֵם אֶת־דָּמָם תִּזְרֹק עַל־הַמִּזְבֵּחַ וְאֶת־
חֶלְבָּם תַּקְטִיר אִשֶּׁה לְרֵיחַ נִיחֹחַ לַיהֹוָה: 18 וּבְשָׂרָם
יִהְיֶה־לָּךְ כַּחֲזֵה הַתְּנוּפָה וּכְשׁוֹק הַיָּמִין לְךָ יִהְיֶה:

19 כֹּל תְּרוּמֹת הַקֳּדָשִׁים אֲשֶׁר יָרִימוּ בְנֵי־יִשְׂרָאֵל
לַיהֹוָה נָתַתִּי לְךָ וּלְבָנֶיךָ וְלִבְנֹתֶיךָ אִתְּךָ לְחָק־עוֹלָם
בְּרִית מֶלַח עוֹלָם הִוא לִפְנֵי יְהֹוָה לְךָ וּלְזַרְעֲךָ
אִתָּךְ: 20 וַיֹּאמֶר יְהֹוָה אֶל־אַהֲרֹן בְּאַרְצָם לֹא תִנְחָל
וְחֵלֶק לֹא־יִהְיֶה לְךָ בְּתוֹכָם אֲנִי חֶלְקְךָ וְנַחֲלָתְךָ
בְּתוֹךְ בְּנֵי יִשְׂרָאֵל: ס 21 וְלִבְנֵי לֵוִי הִנֵּה
נָתַתִּי כָּל־מַעֲשֵׂר בְּיִשְׂרָאֵל לְנַחֲלָה חֵלֶף עֲבֹדָתָם
אֲשֶׁר־הֵם עֹבְדִים אֶת־עֲבֹדַת אֹהֶל מוֹעֵד: 22 וְלֹא־
יִקְרְבוּ עוֹד בְּנֵי יִשְׂרָאֵל אֶל־אֹהֶל מוֹעֵד לָשֵׂאת
חֵטְא לָמוּת: 23 וְעָבַד הַלֵּוִי הוּא אֶת־עֲבֹדַת אֹהֶל
מוֹעֵד וְהֵם יִשְׂאוּ עֲוֹנָם חֻקַּת עוֹלָם לְדֹרֹתֵיכֶם
וּבְתוֹךְ בְּנֵי יִשְׂרָאֵל לֹא יִנְחֲלוּ נַחֲלָה: 24 כִּי אֶת־
מַעְשַׂר בְּנֵי־יִשְׂרָאֵל אֲשֶׁר יָרִימוּ לַיהֹוָה תְּרוּמָה

offer up *as* a heave offering to the LORD, I have given to the Levites as an inheritance; therefore I have said to them, 'Among the children of Israel they shall have no inheritance.' "

²⁵Then the LORD spoke to Moses, saying, ²⁶"Speak thus to the Levites, and say to them: 'When you take from the children of Israel the tithes which I have given you from them as your inheritance, then you shall offer up a heave offering of it to the LORD, a tenth of the tithe. ²⁷And your heave offering shall be reckoned to you as though *it were* the grain of the threshing floor and as the fullness of the winepress. ²⁸Thus you shall also offer a heave offering to the LORD from all your tithes which you receive from the children of Israel, and you shall give the LORD's heave offering from it to Aaron the priest. ²⁹Of all your gifts you shall offer up every heave offering due to the LORD, from all the best of them, the consecrated part of them.' ³⁰Therefore you shall say to them: 'When you have lifted up the best of it, then *the rest* shall be accounted to the Levites as the produce of the threshing floor and as the produce of the winepress. ³¹You may eat it in any place, you and your households, for it *is* your reward for your work in the tabernacle of meeting. ³²And you shall bear no sin because of it, when you have lifted up the best of it. But you shall not profane the holy gifts of the children of Israel, lest you die.' "

19 Now the LORD spoke to Moses and Aaron, saying, ²"This *is* the ordinance of the law which the LORD has commanded, saying: 'Speak to the children of Israel, that they bring you a red heifer without blemish, in which there *is* no defect *and* on which a yoke has never come. ³You shall give it to Eleazar the priest, that he may take it outside the camp, and it shall be slaughtered before him; ⁴and Eleazar the priest shall take some of its blood with his finger, and sprinkle some of its blood seven times directly in front of the tabernacle of meeting. ⁵Then the heifer shall be burned in his sight: its hide, its flesh, its blood, and its offal shall be burned. ⁶And the priest shall take cedar wood and hyssop and scarlet, and cast *them* into the midst of the fire burning the heifer. ⁷Then the priest shall wash his clothes, he shall bathe in water, and afterward he shall come into the camp; the priest shall be unclean until evening. ⁸And the one who burns it shall wash his clothes in water, bathe in water, and shall be unclean until evening. ⁹Then a man *who is* clean shall gather up the ashes of the heifer, and store *them* outside the camp in a clean place; and they shall be kept for the congregation of

נָתַ֤תִּי לַלְוִיִּם֙ לְנַחֲלָ֔ה עַל־כֵּ֖ן אָמַ֣רְתִּי לָהֶ֑ם בְּת֙וֹךְ֙ בְּנֵ֣י יִשְׂרָאֵ֔ל לֹ֥א יִנְחֲל֖וּ נַחֲלָֽה׃ פ

25 וַיְדַבֵּ֥ר יְהֹוָ֖ה אֶל־מֹשֶׁ֥ה לֵּאמֹֽר׃ 26 וְאֶל־הַלְוִיִּ֣ם תְּדַבֵּר֮ וְאָמַרְתָּ֣ אֲלֵהֶם֒ כִּֽי־תִ֠קְח֠וּ מֵאֵ֨ת בְּנֵֽי־יִשְׂרָאֵ֜ל אֶת־הַֽמַּעֲשֵׂ֗ר אֲשֶׁ֨ר נָתַ֧תִּי לָכֶ֛ם מֵֽאִתָּ֖ם בְּנַחֲלַתְכֶ֑ם וַהֲרֵמֹתֶ֤ם מִמֶּ֙נּוּ֙ תְּרוּמַ֣ת יְהֹוָ֔ה מַעֲשֵׂ֖ר מִן־הַֽמַּעֲשֵֽׂר׃ 27 וְנֶחְשַׁ֥ב לָכֶ֖ם תְּרֽוּמַתְכֶ֑ם כַּדָּגָן֙ מִן־הַגֹּ֔רֶן וְכַֽמְלֵאָ֖ה מִן־הַיָּֽקֶב׃ 28 כֵּ֣ן תָּרִ֤ימוּ גַם־אַתֶּם֙ תְּרוּמַ֣ת יְהֹוָ֔ה מִכֹּל֙ מַעְשְׂרֹ֣תֵיכֶ֔ם אֲשֶׁ֣ר תִּקְח֔וּ מֵאֵ֖ת בְּנֵ֣י יִשְׂרָאֵ֑ל וּנְתַתֶּ֤ם מִמֶּ֙נּוּ֙ אֶת־תְּרוּמַ֣ת יְהֹוָ֔ה לְאַהֲרֹ֖ן הַכֹּהֵֽן׃ 29 מִכֹּל֙ מַתְּנֹ֣תֵיכֶ֔ם תָּרִ֕ימוּ אֵ֖ת כׇּל־תְּרוּמַ֣ת יְהֹוָ֑ה מִכׇּל־חֶ֨לְבּ֔וֹ אֶֽת־מִקְדְּשׁ֖וֹ מִמֶּֽנּוּ׃ 30 וְאָמַרְתָּ֖ אֲלֵהֶ֑ם בַּהֲרִֽימְכֶ֤ם אֶת־חֶלְבּוֹ֙ מִמֶּ֔נּוּ וְנֶחְשַׁב֙ לַלְוִיִּ֔ם כִּתְבוּאַ֥ת גֹּ֖רֶן וְכִתְבוּאַ֥ת יָֽקֶב׃ 31 וַאֲכַלְתֶּ֤ם אֹתוֹ֙ בְּכׇל־מָק֔וֹם אַתֶּ֖ם וּבֵֽיתְכֶ֑ם כִּֽי־שָׂכָ֥ר הוּא֙ לָכֶ֔ם חֵ֥לֶף עֲבֹדַתְכֶ֖ם בְּאֹ֥הֶל מוֹעֵֽד׃ 32 וְלֹֽא־תִשְׂא֤וּ עָלָיו֙ חֵ֔טְא בַּהֲרִֽימְכֶ֥ם אֶת־חֶלְבּ֖וֹ מִמֶּ֑נּוּ וְאֶת־קׇדְשֵׁ֧י בְנֵֽי־יִשְׂרָאֵ֛ל לֹ֥א תְחַלְּל֖וּ וְלֹ֥א תָמֽוּתוּ׃ פ

יט וַיְדַבֵּ֣ר יְהֹוָ֔ה אֶל־מֹשֶׁ֥ה וְאֶֽל־אַהֲרֹ֖ן לֵאמֹֽר׃ 2 זֹ֚את חֻקַּ֣ת הַתּוֹרָ֔ה אֲשֶׁר־צִוָּ֥ה יְהֹוָ֖ה לֵאמֹ֑ר דַּבֵּ֣ר ׀ אֶל־בְּנֵ֣י יִשְׂרָאֵ֗ל וְיִקְח֣וּ אֵלֶ֩יךָ֩ פָרָ֨ה אֲדֻמָּ֜ה תְּמִימָ֗ה אֲשֶׁ֤ר אֵֽין־בָּהּ֙ מ֔וּם אֲשֶׁ֛ר לֹא־עָלָ֥ה עָלֶ֖יהָ עֹֽל׃ 3 וּנְתַתֶּ֣ם אֹתָ֔הּ אֶל־אֶלְעָזָ֖ר הַכֹּהֵ֑ן וְהוֹצִ֤יא אֹתָהּ֙ אֶל־מִח֣וּץ לַֽמַּחֲנֶ֔ה וְשָׁחַ֥ט אֹתָ֖הּ לְפָנָֽיו׃ 4 וְלָקַ֞ח אֶלְעָזָ֧ר הַכֹּהֵ֛ן מִדָּמָ֖הּ בְּאֶצְבָּע֑וֹ וְהִזָּ֞ה אֶל־נֹ֨כַח פְּנֵ֧י אֹֽהֶל־מוֹעֵ֛ד מִדָּמָ֖הּ שֶׁ֥בַע פְּעָמִֽים׃ 5 וְשָׂרַ֥ף אֶת־הַפָּרָ֖ה לְעֵינָ֑יו אֶת־עֹרָ֤הּ וְאֶת־בְּשָׂרָהּ֙ וְאֶת־דָּמָ֔הּ עַל־פִּרְשָׁ֖הּ יִשְׂרֹֽף׃ 6 וְלָקַ֣ח הַכֹּהֵ֗ן עֵ֥ץ אֶ֛רֶז וְאֵז֖וֹב וּשְׁנִ֣י תוֹלָ֑עַת וְהִשְׁלִ֕יךְ אֶל־תּ֖וֹךְ שְׂרֵפַ֥ת הַפָּרָֽה׃ 7 וְכִבֶּ֨ס בְּגָדָ֜יו הַכֹּהֵ֗ן וְרָחַ֤ץ בְּשָׂרוֹ֙ בַּמַּ֔יִם וְאַחַ֖ר יָבֹ֣א אֶל־הַֽמַּחֲנֶ֑ה וְטָמֵ֥א הַכֹּהֵ֖ן עַד־הָעָֽרֶב׃ 8 וְהַשֹּׂרֵ֣ף אֹתָ֔הּ יְכַבֵּ֤ס בְּגָדָיו֙ בַּמַּ֔יִם וְרָחַ֥ץ בְּשָׂר֖וֹ בַּמָּ֑יִם וְטָמֵ֖א עַד־הָעָֽרֶב׃ 9 וְאָסַ֣ף ׀ אִ֣ישׁ טָה֗וֹר אֵ֚ת אֵ֣פֶר הַפָּרָ֔ה וְהִנִּ֛יחַ מִח֥וּץ לַֽמַּחֲנֶ֖ה בְּמָק֣וֹם טָה֑וֹר וְ֠הָיְתָ֠ה לַעֲדַ֨ת בְּנֵֽי־

the children of Israel for the water of purification; it *is* for purifying from sin. ¹⁰And the one who gathers the ashes of the heifer shall wash his clothes, and be unclean until evening. It shall be a statute forever to the children of Israel and to the stranger who dwells among them.

¹¹'He who touches the dead body of anyone shall be unclean seven days. ¹²He shall purify himself with the water on the third day and on the seventh day; *then* he will be clean. But if he does not purify himself on the third day and on the seventh day, he will not be clean. ¹³Whoever touches the body of anyone who has died, and does not purify himself, defiles the tabernacle of the LORD. That person shall be cut off from Israel. He shall be unclean, because the water of purification was not sprinkled on him; his uncleanness *is* still on him.

¹⁴'This *is* the law when a man dies in a tent: All who come into the tent and all who *are* in the tent shall be unclean seven days; ¹⁵and every open vessel, which has no cover fastened on it, *is* unclean. ¹⁶Whoever in the open field touches one who is slain by a sword or who has died, or a bone of a man, or a grave, shall be unclean seven days.

¹⁷'And for an unclean *person* they shall take some of the ashes of the heifer burnt for purification from sin, and running water shall be put on them in a vessel. ¹⁸A clean person shall take hyssop and dip *it* in the water, sprinkle *it* on the tent, on all the vessels, on the persons who were there, or on the one who touched a bone, the slain, the dead, or a grave. ¹⁹The clean *person* shall sprinkle the unclean on the third day and on the seventh day; and on the seventh day he shall purify himself, wash his clothes, and bathe in water; and at evening he shall be clean.

²⁰'But the man who is unclean and does not purify himself, that person shall be cut off from among the assembly, because he has defiled the sanctuary of the LORD. The water of purification has not been sprinkled on him; he *is* unclean. ²¹It shall be a perpetual statute for them. He who sprinkles the water of purification shall wash his clothes; and he who touches the water of purification shall be unclean until evening. ²²Whatever the unclean *person* touches shall be unclean; and the person who touches *it* shall be unclean until evening.'"

20

Then the children of Israel, the whole congregation, came into the Wilderness of Zin in the first month, and the people stayed in Kadesh; and Miriam died there and was buried there.

יִשְׂרָאֵל לְמִשְׁמֶרֶת לְמֵי נִדָּה חַטָּאת הִוא: 10 וְכִבֶּס הָאֹסֵף אֶת־אֵפֶר הַפָּרָה אֶת־בְּגָדָיו וְטָמֵא עַד־ הָעָרֶב וְהָיְתָה לִבְנֵי יִשְׂרָאֵל וְלַגֵּר הַגָּר בְּתוֹכָם לְחֻקַּת עוֹלָם: 11 הַנֹּגֵעַ בְּמֵת לְכָל־נֶפֶשׁ אָדָם וְטָמֵא שִׁבְעַת יָמִים: 12 הוּא יִתְחַטָּא־בוֹ בַּיּוֹם הַשְּׁלִישִׁי וּבַיּוֹם הַשְּׁבִיעִי יִטְהָר וְאִם־לֹא יִתְחַטָּא בַּיּוֹם הַשְּׁלִישִׁי וּבַיּוֹם הַשְּׁבִיעִי לֹא יִטְהָר: 13 כָּל־הַנֹּגֵעַ בְּמֵת בְּנֶפֶשׁ הָאָדָם אֲשֶׁר־יָמוּת וְלֹא יִתְחַטָּא אֶת־ מִשְׁכַּן יְהוָה טִמֵּא וְנִכְרְתָה הַנֶּפֶשׁ הַהִוא מִיִּשְׂרָאֵל כִּי מֵי נִדָּה לֹא־זֹרַק עָלָיו טָמֵא יִהְיֶה עוֹד טֻמְאָתוֹ בוֹ: 14 זֹאת הַתּוֹרָה אָדָם כִּי־יָמוּת בְּאֹהֶל כָּל־הַבָּא אֶל־הָאֹהֶל וְכָל־אֲשֶׁר בָּאֹהֶל יִטְמָא שִׁבְעַת יָמִים: 15 וְכֹל כְּלִי פָתוּחַ אֲשֶׁר אֵין־צָמִיד פָּתִיל עָלָיו טָמֵא הוּא: 16 וְכֹל אֲשֶׁר־יִגַּע עַל־פְּנֵי הַשָּׂדֶה בַּחֲלַל־חֶרֶב אוֹ בְמֵת אוֹ־בְעֶצֶם אָדָם אוֹ בְקָבֶר יִטְמָא שִׁבְעַת יָמִים: 17 וְלָקְחוּ לַטָּמֵא מֵעֲפַר שְׂרֵפַת הַחַטָּאת וְנָתַן עָלָיו מַיִם חַיִּים אֶל־כֶּלִי: 18 וְלָקַח אֵזוֹב וְטָבַל בַּמַּיִם אִישׁ טָהוֹר וְהִזָּה עַל־הָאֹהֶל וְעַל־כָּל־הַכֵּלִים וְעַל־הַנְּפָשׁוֹת אֲשֶׁר הָיוּ־שָׁם וְעַל־הַנֹּגֵעַ בַּעֶצֶם אוֹ בֶחָלָל אוֹ בַמֵּת אוֹ בַקָּבֶר: 19 וְהִזָּה הַטָּהֹר עַל־ הַטָּמֵא בַּיּוֹם הַשְּׁלִישִׁי וּבַיּוֹם הַשְּׁבִיעִי וְחִטְּאוֹ בַּיּוֹם הַשְּׁבִיעִי וְכִבֶּס בְּגָדָיו וְרָחַץ בַּמַּיִם וְטָהֵר בָּעָרֶב:

20 וְאִישׁ אֲשֶׁר־יִטְמָא וְלֹא יִתְחַטָּא וְנִכְרְתָה הַנֶּפֶשׁ הַהִוא מִתּוֹךְ הַקָּהָל כִּי אֶת־מִקְדַּשׁ יְהוָה טִמֵּא מֵי נִדָּה לֹא־זֹרַק עָלָיו טָמֵא הוּא: 21 וְהָיְתָה לָהֶם לְחֻקַּת עוֹלָם וּמַזֵּה מֵי־הַנִּדָּה יְכַבֵּס בְּגָדָיו וְהַנֹּגֵעַ בְּמֵי הַנִּדָּה יִטְמָא עַד־הָעָרֶב: 22 וְכֹל אֲשֶׁר־יִגַּע־בּוֹ הַטָּמֵא יִטְמָא וְהַנֶּפֶשׁ הַנֹּגַעַת תִּטְמָא עַד־הָעָרֶב: פ

ב וַיָּבֹאוּ בְנֵי־יִשְׂרָאֵל כָּל־הָעֵדָה מִדְבַּר־צִן בַּחֹדֶשׁ הָרִאשׁוֹן וַיֵּשֶׁב הָעָם בְּקָדֵשׁ וַתָּמָת שָׁם מִרְיָם

²Now there was no water for the congregation; so they gathered together against Moses and Aaron. ³And the people contended with Moses and spoke, saying: "If only we had died when our brethren died before the LORD! ⁴Why have you brought up the assembly of the LORD into this wilderness, that we and our animals should die here? ⁵And why have you made us come up out of Egypt, to bring us to this evil place? It *is* not a place of grain or figs or vines or pomegranates; nor *is* there any water to drink." ⁶So Moses and Aaron went from the presence of the assembly to the door of the tabernacle of meeting, and they fell on their faces. And the glory of the LORD appeared to them.

⁷Then the LORD spoke to Moses, saying, ⁸"Take the rod; you and your brother Aaron gather the congregation together. Speak to the rock before their eyes, and it will yield its water; thus you shall bring water for them out of the rock, and give drink to the congregation and their animals." ⁹So Moses took the rod from before the LORD as He commanded him.

¹⁰And Moses and Aaron gathered the assembly together before the rock; and he said to them, "Hear now, you rebels! Must we bring water for you out of this rock?" ¹¹Then Moses lifted his hand and struck the rock twice with his rod; and water came out abundantly, and the congregation and their animals drank.

¹²Then the LORD spoke to Moses and Aaron, "Because you did not believe Me, to hallow Me in the eyes of the children of Israel, therefore you shall not bring this assembly into the land which I have given them."

¹³This *was* the water of Meribah, because the children of Israel contended with the LORD, and He was hallowed among them.

¹⁴Now Moses sent messengers from Kadesh to the king of Edom. "Thus says your brother Israel: 'You know all the hardship that has befallen us, ¹⁵how our fathers went down to Egypt, and we dwelt in Egypt a long time, and the Egyptians afflicted us and our fathers. ¹⁶When we cried out to the LORD, He heard our voice and sent the Angel and brought us up out of Egypt; now here we are in Kadesh, a city on the edge of your border. ¹⁷Please let us pass through your country. We will not pass through fields or vineyards, nor will we drink water from wells; we will go along the King's Highway; we will not turn aside to the right hand or to the left until we have passed through your territory.'"

¹⁸Then Edom said to him, "You shall not pass through my *land,* lest I come out against you with the sword."

וַתִּקָּבֵר שָׁם: 2 וְלֹא־הָיָה מַיִם לָעֵדָה וַיִּקָּהֲלוּ עַל־
מֹשֶׁה וְעַל־אַהֲרֹן: 3 וַיָּרֶב הָעָם עִם־מֹשֶׁה וַיֹּאמְרוּ
לֵאמֹר וְלוּ גָוַעְנוּ בִּגְוַע אַחֵינוּ לִפְנֵי יְהוָה: 4 וְלָמָה
הֲבֵאתֶם אֶת־קְהַל יְהוָה אֶל־הַמִּדְבָּר הַזֶּה לָמוּת
שָׁם אֲנַחְנוּ וּבְעִירֵנוּ: 5 וְלָמָה הֶעֱלִיתֻנוּ מִמִּצְרַיִם
לְהָבִיא אֹתָנוּ אֶל־הַמָּקוֹם הָרָע הַזֶּה לֹא | מְקוֹם
זֶרַע וּתְאֵנָה וְגֶפֶן וְרִמּוֹן וּמַיִם אַיִן לִשְׁתּוֹת: 6 וַיָּבֹא
מֹשֶׁה וְאַהֲרֹן מִפְּנֵי הַקָּהָל אֶל־פֶּתַח אֹהֶל מוֹעֵד
וַיִּפְּלוּ עַל־פְּנֵיהֶם וַיֵּרָא כְבוֹד־יְהוָה אֲלֵיהֶם: פ

7 וַיְדַבֵּר יְהוָה אֶל־מֹשֶׁה לֵּאמֹר: 8 קַח אֶת־הַמַּטֶּה
וְהַקְהֵל אֶת־הָעֵדָה אַתָּה וְאַהֲרֹן אָחִיךָ וְדִבַּרְתֶּם
אֶל־הַסֶּלַע לְעֵינֵיהֶם וְנָתַן מֵימָיו וְהוֹצֵאתָ לָהֶם
מַיִם מִן־הַסֶּלַע וְהִשְׁקִיתָ אֶת־הָעֵדָה וְאֶת־בְּעִירָם:
9 וַיִּקַּח מֹשֶׁה אֶת־הַמַּטֶּה מִלִּפְנֵי יְהוָה כַּאֲשֶׁר צִוָּהוּ:
10 וַיַּקְהִלוּ מֹשֶׁה וְאַהֲרֹן אֶת־הַקָּהָל אֶל־פְּנֵי הַסָּלַע
וַיֹּאמֶר לָהֶם שִׁמְעוּ־נָא הַמֹּרִים הֲמִן־הַסֶּלַע הַזֶּה
נוֹצִיא לָכֶם מָיִם: 11 וַיָּרֶם מֹשֶׁה אֶת־יָדוֹ וַיַּךְ אֶת־
הַסֶּלַע בְּמַטֵּהוּ פַּעֲמָיִם וַיֵּצְאוּ מַיִם רַבִּים וַתֵּשְׁתְּ
הָעֵדָה וּבְעִירָם: ס 12 וַיֹּאמֶר יְהוָה אֶל־
מֹשֶׁה וְאֶל־אַהֲרֹן יַעַן לֹא־הֶאֱמַנְתֶּם בִּי לְהַקְדִּישֵׁנִי
לְעֵינֵי בְּנֵי יִשְׂרָאֵל לָכֵן לֹא תָבִיאוּ אֶת־הַקָּהָל
הַזֶּה אֶל־הָאָרֶץ אֲשֶׁר־נָתַתִּי לָהֶם: 13 הֵמָּה מֵי
מְרִיבָה אֲשֶׁר־רָבוּ בְנֵי־יִשְׂרָאֵל אֶת־יְהוָה וַיִּקָּדֵשׁ
בָּם: ס 14 וַיִּשְׁלַח מֹשֶׁה מַלְאָכִים מִקָּדֵשׁ
אֶל־מֶלֶךְ אֱדוֹם כֹּה אָמַר אָחִיךָ יִשְׂרָאֵל אַתָּה
יָדַעְתָּ אֵת כָּל־הַתְּלָאָה אֲשֶׁר מְצָאָתְנוּ: 15 וַיֵּרְדוּ
אֲבֹתֵינוּ מִצְרַיְמָה וַנֵּשֶׁב בְּמִצְרַיִם יָמִים רַבִּים וַיָּרֵעוּ
לָנוּ מִצְרַיִם וְלַאֲבֹתֵינוּ: 16 וַנִּצְעַק אֶל־יְהוָה וַיִּשְׁמַע
קֹלֵנוּ וַיִּשְׁלַח מַלְאָךְ וַיֹּצִאֵנוּ מִמִּצְרָיִם וְהִנֵּה אֲנַחְנוּ
בְקָדֵשׁ עִיר קְצֵה גְבוּלֶךָ: 17 נַעְבְּרָה־נָּא בְאַרְצֶךָ לֹא
נַעֲבֹר בְּשָׂדֶה וּבְכֶרֶם וְלֹא נִשְׁתֶּה מֵי בְאֵר דֶּרֶךְ
הַמֶּלֶךְ נֵלֵךְ לֹא נִטֶּה יָמִין וּשְׂמֹאול עַד אֲשֶׁר־נַעֲבֹר
גְּבוּלֶךָ: 18 וַיֹּאמֶר אֵלָיו אֱדוֹם לֹא תַעֲבֹר בִּי פֶּן

¹⁹ So the children of Israel said to him, "We will go by the Highway, and if I or my livestock drink any of your water, then I will pay for it; let me only pass through on foot, nothing *more*."

²⁰ Then he said, "You shall not pass through." So Edom came out against them with many men and with a strong hand. ²¹ Thus Edom refused to give Israel passage through his territory; so Israel turned away from him.

²² Now the children of Israel, the whole congregation, journeyed from Kadesh and came to Mount Hor. ²³ And the LORD spoke to Moses and Aaron in Mount Hor by the border of the land of Edom, saying: ²⁴ "Aaron shall be gathered to his people, for he shall not enter the land which I have given to the children of Israel, because you rebelled against My word at the water of Meribah. ²⁵ Take Aaron and Eleazar his son, and bring them up to Mount Hor; ²⁶ and strip Aaron of his garments and put them on Eleazar his son; for Aaron shall be gathered *to his people* and die there." ²⁷ So Moses did just as the LORD commanded, and they went up to Mount Hor in the sight of all the congregation. ²⁸ Moses stripped Aaron of his garments and put them on Eleazar his son; and Aaron died there on the top of the mountain. Then Moses and Eleazar came down from the mountain. ²⁹ Now when all the congregation saw that Aaron was dead, all the house of Israel mourned for Aaron thirty days.

21 The king of Arad, the Canaanite, who dwelt in the South, heard that Israel was coming on the road to Atharim. Then he fought against Israel and took *some* of them prisoners. ² So Israel made a vow to the LORD, and said, "If You will indeed deliver this people into my hand, then I will utterly destroy their cities. "³ And the LORD listened to the voice of Israel and delivered up the Canaanites, and they utterly destroyed them and their cities. So the name of that place was called Hormah.

⁴ Then they journeyed from Mount Hor by the Way of the Red Sea, to go around the land of Edom; and the soul of the people became very discouraged on the way. ⁵ And the people spoke against God and against Moses: "Why have you brought us up out of Egypt to die in the wilderness? For *there is* no food and no water, and our soul loathes this worthless bread." ⁶ So the LORD sent fiery serpents among the people, and they bit the people; and many of the people of Israel died.

בַּחֶרֶב אֵצֵא לִקְרָאתֶךָ: 19 וַיֹּאמְרוּ אֵלָיו בְּנֵי־יִשְׂרָאֵל בַּמְסִלָּה נַעֲלֶה וְאִם־מֵימֶיךָ נִשְׁתֶּה אֲנִי וּמִקְנַי וְנָתַתִּי מִכְרָם רַק אֵין־דָּבָר בְּרַגְלַי אֶעֱבֹרָה: 20 וַיֹּאמֶר לֹא תַעֲבֹר וַיֵּצֵא אֱדוֹם לִקְרָאתוֹ בְּעַם כָּבֵד וּבְיָד חֲזָקָה: 21 וַיְמָאֵן אֱדוֹם נְתֹן אֶת־יִשְׂרָאֵל עֲבֹר בִּגְבֻלוֹ וַיֵּט יִשְׂרָאֵל מֵעָלָיו: פ

22 וַיִּסְעוּ מִקָּדֵשׁ וַיָּבֹאוּ בְנֵי־יִשְׂרָאֵל כָּל־הָעֵדָה הֹר הָהָר: 23 וַיֹּאמֶר יְהוָה אֶל־מֹשֶׁה וְאֶל־אַהֲרֹן בְּהֹר הָהָר עַל־גְּבוּל אֶרֶץ־אֱדוֹם לֵאמֹר: 24 יֵאָסֵף אַהֲרֹן אֶל־עַמָּיו כִּי לֹא יָבֹא אֶל־הָאָרֶץ אֲשֶׁר נָתַתִּי לִבְנֵי יִשְׂרָאֵל עַל אֲשֶׁר־מְרִיתֶם אֶת־פִּי לְמֵי מְרִיבָה: 25 קַח אֶת־אַהֲרֹן וְאֶת־אֶלְעָזָר בְּנוֹ וְהַעַל אֹתָם הֹר הָהָר: 26 וְהַפְשֵׁט אֶת־אַהֲרֹן אֶת־בְּגָדָיו וְהִלְבַּשְׁתָּם אֶת־אֶלְעָזָר בְּנוֹ וְאַהֲרֹן יֵאָסֵף וּמֵת שָׁם: 27 וַיַּעַשׂ מֹשֶׁה כַּאֲשֶׁר צִוָּה יְהוָה וַיַּעֲלוּ אֶל־הֹר הָהָר לְעֵינֵי כָּל־הָעֵדָה: 28 וַיַּפְשֵׁט מֹשֶׁה אֶת־אַהֲרֹן אֶת־בְּגָדָיו וַיַּלְבֵּשׁ אֹתָם אֶת־אֶלְעָזָר בְּנוֹ וַיָּמָת אַהֲרֹן שָׁם בְּרֹאשׁ הָהָר וַיֵּרֶד מֹשֶׁה וְאֶלְעָזָר מִן־הָהָר: 29 וַיִּרְאוּ כָּל־הָעֵדָה כִּי גָוַע אַהֲרֹן וַיִּבְכּוּ אֶת־אַהֲרֹן שְׁלֹשִׁים יוֹם כֹּל בֵּית יִשְׂרָאֵל: ס

כא וַיִּשְׁמַע הַכְּנַעֲנִי מֶלֶךְ־עֲרָד יֹשֵׁב הַנֶּגֶב כִּי בָּא יִשְׂרָאֵל דֶּרֶךְ הָאֲתָרִים וַיִּלָּחֶם בְּיִשְׂרָאֵל וַיִּשְׁבְּ מִמֶּנּוּ שֶׁבִי: 2 וַיִּדַּר יִשְׂרָאֵל נֶדֶר לַיהוָה וַיֹּאמַר אִם־נָתֹן תִּתֵּן אֶת־הָעָם הַזֶּה בְּיָדִי וְהַחֲרַמְתִּי אֶת־עָרֵיהֶם: 3 וַיִּשְׁמַע יְהוָה בְּקוֹל יִשְׂרָאֵל וַיִּתֵּן אֶת־הַכְּנַעֲנִי וַיַּחֲרֵם אֶתְהֶם וְאֶת־עָרֵיהֶם וַיִּקְרָא שֵׁם הַמָּקוֹם חָרְמָה: פ

4 וַיִּסְעוּ מֵהֹר הָהָר דֶּרֶךְ יַם־סוּף לִסְבֹב אֶת־אֶרֶץ אֱדוֹם וַתִּקְצַר נֶפֶשׁ־הָעָם בַּדָּרֶךְ: 5 וַיְדַבֵּר הָעָם בֵּאלֹהִים וּבְמֹשֶׁה לָמָה הֶעֱלִיתֻנוּ מִמִּצְרַיִם לָמוּת בַּמִּדְבָּר כִּי אֵין לֶחֶם וְאֵין מַיִם וְנַפְשֵׁנוּ קָצָה בַּלֶּחֶם הַקְּלֹקֵל: 6 וַיְשַׁלַּח יְהוָה בָּעָם אֵת הַנְּחָשִׁים הַשְּׂרָפִים וַיְנַשְּׁכוּ אֶת־הָעָם וַיָּמָת עַם־

7 Therefore the people came to Moses, and said, "We have sinned, for we have spoken against the LORD and against you; pray to the LORD that He take away the serpents from us." So Moses prayed for the people.

8 Then the LORD said to Moses, "Make a fiery *serpent,* and set it on a pole; and it shall be that everyone who is bitten, when he looks at it, shall live." 9 So Moses made a bronze serpent, and put it on a pole; and so it was, if a serpent had bitten anyone, when he looked at the bronze serpent, he lived.

10 Now the children of Israel moved on and camped in Oboth. 11 And they journeyed from Oboth and camped at Ije Abarim, in the wilderness which *is* east of Moab, toward the sunrise. 12 From there they moved and camped in the Valley of Zered. 13 From there they moved and camped on the other side of the Arnon, which *is* in the wilderness that extends from the border of the Amorites; for the Arnon *is* the border of Moab, between Moab and the Amorites. 14 Therefore it is said in the Book of the Wars of the LORD:

"Waheb in Suphah,
The brooks of the Arnon,
15   And the slope of the brooks
That reaches to the dwelling of Ar,
And lies on the border of Moab."

16 From there *they went* to Beer, which *is* the well where the LORD said to Moses, "Gather the people together, and I will give them water." 17 Then Israel sang this song:

"Spring up, O well!
All of you sing to it—
18   The well the leaders sank,
Dug by the nation's nobles,
By the lawgiver, with their staves."

And from the wilderness *they went* to Mattanah, 19 from Mattanah to Nahaliel, from Nahaliel to Bamoth, 20 and from Bamoth, *in* the valley that *is* in the country of Moab, to the top of Pisgah which looks down on the wasteland.

21 Then Israel sent messengers to Sihon king of the Amorites, saying, 22 "Let me pass through your land. We will not turn aside into fields or vineyards; we will not drink water from wells. We will go by the King's Highway until we have passed through your territory." 23 But Sihon would not allow Israel to pass through his territory. So Sihon gathered all his people together and went out against Israel in the wilderness, and he came to Jahaz and fought against Israel. 24 Then Israel defeated him with the edge of the sword, and took possession of his land from the Arnon to the Jabbok, as far as the people

רָב מִיִּשְׂרָאֵל: 7 וַיָּבֹא הָעָם אֶל־מֹשֶׁה וַיֹּאמְרוּ
חָטָאנוּ כִּי־דִבַּרְנוּ בַיהֹוָה וָבָךְ הִתְפַּלֵּל אֶל־יְהֹוָה
וְיָסֵר מֵעָלֵינוּ אֶת־הַנָּחָשׁ וַיִּתְפַּלֵּל מֹשֶׁה בְּעַד הָעָם:

8 וַיֹּאמֶר יְהֹוָה אֶל־מֹשֶׁה עֲשֵׂה לְךָ שָׂרָף וְשִׂים אֹתוֹ
עַל־נֵס וְהָיָה כָּל־הַנָּשׁוּךְ וְרָאָה אֹתוֹ וָחָי: 9 וַיַּעַשׂ
מֹשֶׁה נְחַשׁ נְחֹשֶׁת וַיְשִׂמֵהוּ עַל־הַנֵּס וְהָיָה אִם־
נָשַׁךְ הַנָּחָשׁ אֶת־אִישׁ וְהִבִּיט אֶל־נְחַשׁ הַנְּחֹשֶׁת
וָחָי: 10 וַיִּסְעוּ בְּנֵי יִשְׂרָאֵל וַיַּחֲנוּ בְּאֹבֹת: 11 וַיִּסְעוּ
מֵאֹבֹת וַיַּחֲנוּ בְּעִיֵּי הָעֲבָרִים בַּמִּדְבָּר אֲשֶׁר עַל־
פְּנֵי מוֹאָב מִמִּזְרַח הַשָּׁמֶשׁ: 12 מִשָּׁם נָסָעוּ וַיַּחֲנוּ
בְּנַחַל זָרֶד: 13 מִשָּׁם נָסָעוּ וַיַּחֲנוּ מֵעֵבֶר אַרְנוֹן
אֲשֶׁר בַּמִּדְבָּר הַיֹּצֵא מִגְּבֻל הָאֱמֹרִי כִּי אַרְנוֹן
גְּבוּל מוֹאָב בֵּין מוֹאָב וּבֵין הָאֱמֹרִי: 14 עַל־כֵּן
יֵאָמַר בְּסֵפֶר מִלְחֲמֹת יְהֹוָה אֶת־וָהֵב בְּסוּפָה וְאֶת־
הַנְּחָלִים אַרְנוֹן: 15 וְאֶשֶׁד הַנְּחָלִים אֲשֶׁר נָטָה
לְשֶׁבֶת עָר וְנִשְׁעַן לִגְבוּל מוֹאָב: 16 וּמִשָּׁם בְּאֵרָה
הִוא הַבְּאֵר אֲשֶׁר אָמַר יְהֹוָה לְמֹשֶׁה אֱסֹף אֶת־
הָעָם וְאֶתְּנָה לָהֶם מָיִם: ס 17 אָז יָשִׁיר
יִשְׂרָאֵל אֶת־הַשִּׁירָה הַזֹּאת עֲלִי בְאֵר עֱנוּ־לָהּ:
18 בְּאֵר חֲפָרוּהָ שָׂרִים כָּרוּהָ נְדִיבֵי הָעָם בִּמְחֹקֵק
בְּמִשְׁעֲנֹתָם וּמִמִּדְבָּר מַתָּנָה: 19 וּמִמַּתָּנָה נַחֲלִיאֵל
וּמִנַּחֲלִיאֵל בָּמוֹת: 20 וּמִבָּמוֹת הַגַּיְא אֲשֶׁר בִּשְׂדֵה
מוֹאָב רֹאשׁ הַפִּסְגָּה וְנִשְׁקָפָה עַל־פְּנֵי הַיְשִׁימֹן: פ

21 וַיִּשְׁלַח יִשְׂרָאֵל מַלְאָכִים אֶל־סִיחֹן מֶלֶךְ הָאֱמֹרִי
לֵאמֹר: 22 אֶעְבְּרָה בְאַרְצֶךָ לֹא נִטֶּה בְּשָׂדֶה וּבְכֶרֶם
לֹא נִשְׁתֶּה מֵי בְאֵר בְּדֶרֶךְ הַמֶּלֶךְ נֵלֵךְ עַד אֲשֶׁר־
נַעֲבֹר גְּבֻלֶךָ: 23 וְלֹא־נָתַן סִיחֹן אֶת־יִשְׂרָאֵל עֲבֹר
בִּגְבֻלוֹ וַיֶּאֱסֹף סִיחֹן אֶת־כָּל־עַמּוֹ וַיֵּצֵא לִקְרַאת
יִשְׂרָאֵל הַמִּדְבָּרָה וַיָּבֹא יָהְצָה וַיִּלָּחֶם בְּיִשְׂרָאֵל:
24 וַיַּכֵּהוּ יִשְׂרָאֵל לְפִי־חָרֶב וַיִּירַשׁ אֶת־אַרְצוֹ מֵאַרְנֹן
עַד־יַבֹּק עַד־בְּנֵי עַמּוֹן כִּי עַז גְּבוּל בְּנֵי עַמּוֹן:

of Ammon; for the border of the people of Ammon *was* fortified. 25 So Israel took all these cities, and Israel dwelt in all the cities of the Amorites, in Heshbon and in all its villages. 26 For Heshbon *was* the city of Sihon king of the Amorites, who had fought against the former king of Moab, and had taken all his land from his hand as far as the Arnon. 27 Therefore those who speak in proverbs say:

"Come to Heshbon, let it be built;
Let the city of Sihon be repaired.

28 "For fire went out from Heshbon,
A flame from the city of Sihon;
It consumed Ar of Moab,
The lords of the heights of the Arnon.

29 Woe to you, Moab!
You have perished, O people of Chemosh!
He has given his sons as fugitives,
And his daughters into captivity,
To Sihon king of the Amorites.

30 "But we have shot at them;
Heshbon has perished as far as Dibon.
Then we laid waste as far as Nophah,
Which *reaches* to Medeba."

31 Thus Israel dwelt in the land of the Amorites. 32 Then Moses sent to spy out Jazer; and they took its villages and drove out the Amorites who *were* there.

33 And they turned and went up by the way to Bashan. So Og king of Bashan went out against them, he and all his people, to battle at Edrei. 34 Then the LORD said to Moses, "Do not fear him, for I have delivered him into your hand, with all his people and his land; and you shall do to him as you did to Sihon king of the Amorites, who dwelt at Heshbon." 35 So they defeated him, his sons, and all his people, until there was no survivor left him; and they took possession of his land.

22 Then the children of Israel moved, and camped in the plains of Moab on the side of the Jordan *across from* Jericho.

2 Now Balak the son of Zippor saw all that Israel had done to the Amorites. 3 And Moab was exceedingly afraid of the people because they *were* many, and Moab was sick with dread because of the children of Israel. 4 So Moab said to the elders of Midian, "Now this company will lick up everything around us, as an ox licks up the grass of the field." And Balak the son of Zippor *was* king of the Moabites at that time. 5 Then he sent messengers to Balaam the son of Beor at Pethor, which *is* near the River in the land of the sons of his people, to call him, saying: "Look, a people has come from Egypt. See, they cover the face of the earth, and are settling

25 וַיִּקַּח יִשְׂרָאֵל אֵת כָּל־הֶעָרִים הָאֵלֶּה וַיֵּשֶׁב יִשְׂרָאֵל בְּכָל־עָרֵי הָאֱמֹרִי בְּחֶשְׁבּוֹן וּבְכָל־בְּנֹתֶיהָ: 26 כִּי חֶשְׁבּוֹן עִיר סִיחֹן מֶלֶךְ הָאֱמֹרִי הִוא וְהוּא נִלְחַם בְּמֶלֶךְ מוֹאָב הָרִאשׁוֹן וַיִּקַּח אֶת־כָּל־אַרְצוֹ מִיָּדוֹ עַד־אַרְנֹן: 27 עַל־כֵּן יֹאמְרוּ הַמֹּשְׁלִים בֹּאוּ חֶשְׁבּוֹן תִּבָּנֶה וְתִכּוֹנֵן עִיר סִיחוֹן: 28 כִּי־אֵשׁ יָצְאָה מֵחֶשְׁבּוֹן לֶהָבָה מִקִּרְיַת סִיחֹן אָכְלָה עָר מוֹאָב בַּעֲלֵי בָּמוֹת אַרְנֹן: 29 אוֹי־לְךָ מוֹאָב אָבַדְתָּ עַם־כְּמוֹשׁ נָתַן בָּנָיו פְּלֵיטִם וּבְנֹתָיו בַּשְּׁבִית לְמֶלֶךְ אֱמֹרִי סִיחוֹן: 30 וַנִּירָם אָבַד חֶשְׁבּוֹן עַד־דִּיבֹן וַנַּשִּׁים עַד־נֹפַח אֲשֶׁר עַד־מֵידְבָא: 31 וַיֵּשֶׁב יִשְׂרָאֵל בְּאֶרֶץ הָאֱמֹרִי: 32 וַיִּשְׁלַח מֹשֶׁה לְרַגֵּל אֶת־יַעְזֵר וַיִּלְכְּדוּ בְּנֹתֶיהָ וַיּוֹרֶשׁp אֶת־הָאֱמֹרִי אֲשֶׁר־שָׁם: 33 וַיִּפְנוּ וַיַּעֲלוּ דֶּרֶךְ הַבָּשָׁן וַיֵּצֵא עוֹג מֶלֶךְ־הַבָּשָׁן לִקְרָאתָם הוּא וְכָל־עַמּוֹ לַמִּלְחָמָה אֶדְרֶעִי: 34 וַיֹּאמֶר יְהוָה אֶל־מֹשֶׁה אַל־תִּירָא אֹתוֹ כִּי בְיָדְךָ נָתַתִּי אֹתוֹ וְאֶת־כָּל־עַמּוֹ וְאֶת־אַרְצוֹ וְעָשִׂיתָ לּוֹ כַּאֲשֶׁר עָשִׂיתָ לְסִיחֹן מֶלֶךְ הָאֱמֹרִי אֲשֶׁר יוֹשֵׁב בְּחֶשְׁבּוֹן: 35 וַיַּכּוּ אֹתוֹ וְאֶת־בָּנָיו וְאֶת־כָּל־עַמּוֹ עַד־בִּלְתִּי הִשְׁאִיר־לוֹ שָׂרִיד וַיִּירְשׁוּ אֶת־אַרְצוֹ:

כב וַיִּסְעוּ בְּנֵי יִשְׂרָאֵל וַיַּחֲנוּ בְּעַרְבוֹת מוֹאָב מֵעֵבֶר לְיַרְדֵּן יְרֵחוֹ: ס 2 וַיַּרְא בָּלָק בֶּן־צִפּוֹר אֵת כָּל־אֲשֶׁר־עָשָׂה יִשְׂרָאֵל לָאֱמֹרִי: 3 וַיָּגָר מוֹאָב מִפְּנֵי הָעָם מְאֹד כִּי רַב־הוּא וַיָּקָץ מוֹאָב מִפְּנֵי בְּנֵי יִשְׂרָאֵל: 4 וַיֹּאמֶר מוֹאָב אֶל־זִקְנֵי מִדְיָן עַתָּה יְלַחֲכוּ הַקָּהָל אֶת־כָּל־סְבִיבֹתֵינוּ כִּלְחֹךְ הַשּׁוֹר אֵת יֶרֶק הַשָּׂדֶה וּבָלָק בֶּן־צִפּוֹר מֶלֶךְ לְמוֹאָב בָּעֵת הַהִוא: 5 וַיִּשְׁלַח מַלְאָכִים אֶל־בִּלְעָם בֶּן־בְּעֹר פְּתוֹרָה אֲשֶׁר עַל־הַנָּהָר אֶרֶץ בְּנֵי־עַמּוֹ לִקְרֹא־לוֹ לֵאמֹר הִנֵּה עַם יָצָא מִמִּצְרַיִם הִנֵּה כִסָּה אֶת־עֵין

next to me! 6 Therefore please come at once, curse this people for me, for they *are* too mighty for me. Perhaps I shall be able to defeat them and drive them out of the land, for I know that he whom you bless *is* blessed, and he whom you curse is cursed."

7 So the elders of Moab and the elders of Midian departed with the diviner's fee in their hand, and they came to Balaam and spoke to him the words of Balak. 8 And he said to them, "Lodge here tonight, and I will bring back word to you, as the LORD speaks to me." So the princes of Moab stayed with Balaam.

9 Then God came to Balaam and said, "Who *are* these men with you?"

10 So Balaam said to God, "Balak the son of Zippor, king of Moab, has sent to me, *saying,* 11 'Look, a people has come out of Egypt, and they cover the face of the earth. Come now, curse them for me; perhaps I shall be able to overpower them and drive them out.'"

12 And God said to Balaam, "You shall not go with them; you shall not curse the people, for they *are* blessed."

13 So Balaam rose in the morning and said to the princes of Balak, "Go back to your land, for the LORD has refused to give me permission to go with you."

14 And the princes of Moab rose and went to Balak, and said, "Balaam refuses to come with us."

15 Then Balak again sent princes, more numerous and more honorable than they. 16 And they came to Balaam and said to him, "Thus says Balak the son of Zippor: 'Please let nothing hinder you from coming to me; 17 for I will certainly honor you greatly, and I will do whatever you say to me. Therefore please come, curse this people for me.'"

18 Then Balaam answered and said to the servants of Balak, "Though Balak were to give me his house full of silver and gold, I could not go beyond the word of the LORD my God, to do less or more. 19 Now therefore, please, you also stay here tonight, that I may know what more the LORD will say to me."

20 And God came to Balaam at night and said to him, "If the men come to call you, rise *and* go with them; but only the word which I speak to you—that you shall do." 21 So Balaam rose in the morning, saddled his donkey, and went with the princes of Moab.

22 Then God's anger was aroused because he went, and the Angel of the LORD took His stand in the way as an adversary against him. And he was riding on his donkey, and his two servants *were* with him. 23 Now the donkey saw the Angel of the

הָאָרֶץ וְהוּא יֹשֵׁב מִמֻּלִי: 6 וְעַתָּה לְכָה־נָּא אָרָה־לִּי אֶת־הָעָם הַזֶּה כִּי־עָצוּם הוּא מִמֶּנִּי אוּלַי אוּכַל נַכֶּה־בּוֹ וַאֲגָרְשֶׁנּוּ מִן־הָאָרֶץ כִּי יָדַעְתִּי אֵת אֲשֶׁר־תְּבָרֵךְ מְבֹרָךְ וַאֲשֶׁר תָּאֹר יוּאָר: 7 וַיֵּלְכוּ זִקְנֵי מוֹאָב וְזִקְנֵי מִדְיָן וּקְסָמִים בְּיָדָם וַיָּבֹאוּ אֶל־בִּלְעָם וַיְדַבְּרוּ אֵלָיו דִּבְרֵי בָלָק: 8 וַיֹּאמֶר אֲלֵיהֶם לִינוּ פֹה הַלַּיְלָה וַהֲשִׁבֹתִי אֶתְכֶם דָּבָר כַּאֲשֶׁר יְדַבֵּר יְהוָה אֵלָי וַיֵּשְׁבוּ שָׂרֵי־מוֹאָב עִם־בִּלְעָם: 9 וַיָּבֹא אֱלֹהִים אֶל־בִּלְעָם וַיֹּאמֶר מִי הָאֲנָשִׁים הָאֵלֶּה עִמָּךְ: 10 וַיֹּאמֶר בִּלְעָם אֶל־הָאֱלֹהִים בָּלָק בֶּן־צִפֹּר מֶלֶךְ מוֹאָב שָׁלַח אֵלָי: 11 הִנֵּה הָעָם הַיֹּצֵא מִמִּצְרַיִם וַיְכַס אֶת־עֵין הָאָרֶץ עַתָּה לְכָה קָבָה־לִּי אֹתוֹ אוּלַי אוּכַל לְהִלָּחֶם בּוֹ וְגֵרַשְׁתִּיו: 12 וַיֹּאמֶר אֱלֹהִים אֶל־בִּלְעָם לֹא תֵלֵךְ עִמָּהֶם לֹא תָאֹר אֶת־הָעָם כִּי בָרוּךְ הוּא: 13 וַיָּקָם בִּלְעָם בַּבֹּקֶר וַיֹּאמֶר אֶל־שָׂרֵי בָלָק לְכוּ אֶל־אַרְצְכֶם כִּי מֵאֵן יְהוָה לְתִתִּי לַהֲלֹךְ עִמָּכֶם: 14 וַיָּקוּמוּ שָׂרֵי מוֹאָב וַיָּבֹאוּ אֶל־בָּלָק וַיֹּאמְרוּ מֵאֵן בִּלְעָם הֲלֹךְ עִמָּנוּ: 15 וַיֹּסֶף עוֹד בָּלָק שְׁלֹחַ שָׂרִים רַבִּים וְנִכְבָּדִים מֵאֵלֶּה: 16 וַיָּבֹאוּ אֶל־בִּלְעָם וַיֹּאמְרוּ לוֹ כֹּה אָמַר בָּלָק בֶּן־צִפּוֹר אַל־נָא תִמָּנַע מֵהֲלֹךְ אֵלָי: 17 כִּי־כַבֵּד אֲכַבֶּדְךָ מְאֹד וְכֹל אֲשֶׁר־תֹּאמַר אֵלַי אֶעֱשֶׂה וּלְכָה־נָּא קָבָה־לִּי אֵת הָעָם הַזֶּה: 18 וַיַּעַן בִּלְעָם וַיֹּאמֶר אֶל־עַבְדֵי בָלָק אִם־יִתֶּן־לִי בָלָק מְלֹא בֵיתוֹ כֶּסֶף וְזָהָב לֹא אוּכַל לַעֲבֹר אֶת־פִּי יְהוָה אֱלֹהָי לַעֲשׂוֹת קְטַנָּה אוֹ גְדוֹלָה: 19 וְעַתָּה שְׁבוּ נָא בָזֶה גַּם־אַתֶּם הַלָּיְלָה וְאֵדְעָה מַה־יֹּסֵף יְהוָה דַּבֵּר עִמִּי: 20 וַיָּבֹא אֱלֹהִים ׀ אֶל־בִּלְעָם לַיְלָה וַיֹּאמֶר לוֹ אִם־לִקְרֹא לְךָ בָּאוּ הָאֲנָשִׁים קוּם לֵךְ אִתָּם וְאַךְ אֶת־הַדָּבָר אֲשֶׁר־אֲדַבֵּר אֵלֶיךָ אֹתוֹ תַעֲשֶׂה: 21 וַיָּקָם בִּלְעָם בַּבֹּקֶר וַיַּחֲבֹשׁ אֶת־אֲתֹנוֹ וַיֵּלֶךְ עִם־שָׂרֵי מוֹאָב: 22 וַיִּחַר־אַף אֱלֹהִים כִּי־הוֹלֵךְ הוּא וַיִּתְיַצֵּב מַלְאַךְ יְהוָה בַּדֶּרֶךְ לְשָׂטָן לוֹ וְהוּא רֹכֵב עַל־אֲתֹנוֹ וּשְׁנֵי נְעָרָיו עִמּוֹ: 23 וַתֵּרֶא הָאָתוֹן אֶת־מַלְאַךְ יְהוָה נִצָּב בַּדֶּרֶךְ וְחַרְבּוֹ שְׁלוּפָה בְּיָדוֹ

LORD standing in the way with His drawn sword in His hand, and the donkey turned aside out of the way and went into the field. So Balaam struck the donkey to turn her back onto the road. 24 Then the Angel of the LORD stood in a narrow path between the vineyards, *with* a wall on this side and a wall on that side. 25 And when the donkey saw the Angel of the LORD, she pushed herself against the wall and crushed Balaam's foot against the wall; so he struck her again. 26 Then the Angel of the LORD went further, and stood in a narrow place where there *was* no way to turn either to the right hand or to the left. 27 And when the donkey saw the Angel of the LORD, she lay down under Balaam; so Balaam's anger was aroused, and he struck the donkey with his staff.

28 Then the LORD opened the mouth of the donkey, and she said to Balaam, "What have I done to you, that you have struck me these three times?"

29 And Balaam said to the donkey, "Because you have abused me. I wish there were a sword in my hand, for now I would kill you!"

30 So the donkey said to Balaam, "*Am* I not your donkey on which you have ridden, ever since *I became* yours, to this day? Was I ever disposed to do this to you?"

And he said, "No."

31 Then the LORD opened Balaam's eyes, and he saw the Angel of the LORD standing in the way with His drawn sword in His hand; and he bowed his head and fell flat on his face. 32 And the Angel of the LORD said to him, "Why have you struck your donkey these three times? Behold, I have come out to stand against you, because *your* way is perverse before Me. 33 The donkey saw Me and turned aside from Me these three times. If she had not turned aside from Me, surely I would also have killed you by now, and let her live."

34 And Balaam said to the Angel of the LORD, "I have sinned, for I did not know You stood in the way against me. Now therefore, if it displeases You, I will turn back."

35 Then the Angel of the LORD said to Balaam, "Go with the men, but only the word that I speak to you, that you shall speak." So Balaam went with the princes of Balak.

36 Now when Balak heard that Balaam was coming, he went out to meet him at the city of Moab, which *is* on the border at the Arnon, the boundary of the territory. 37 Then Balak said to Balaam, "Did I not earnestly send to you, calling for you? Why did you not come to me? Am I not able to honor you?"

וַתֵּ֣ט הָאָת֗וֹן מִן־הַדֶּ֙רֶךְ֙ וַתֵּ֣לֶךְ בַּשָּׂדֶ֔ה וַיַּ֣ךְ בִּלְעָ֔ם אֶת־הָ֣אָת֔וֹן לְהַטֹּתָ֖הּ הַדָּֽרֶךְ׃ 24 וַֽיַּעֲמֹד֙ מַלְאַ֣ךְ יְהֹוָ֔ה בְּמִשְׁע֖וֹל הַכְּרָמִ֑ים גָּדֵ֥ר מִזֶּ֖ה וְגָדֵ֥ר מִזֶּֽה׃ 25 וַתֵּ֣רֶא הָאָתוֹן֩ אֶת־מַלְאַ֨ךְ יְהֹוָ֜ה וַתִּלָּחֵ֣ץ אֶל־הַקִּ֗יר וַתִּלְחַ֤ץ אֶת־רֶ֙גֶל֙ בִּלְעָ֣ם אֶל־הַקִּ֔יר וַיֹּ֖סֶף לְהַכֹּתָֽהּ׃ 26 וַיּ֥וֹסֶף מַלְאַךְ־יְהֹוָ֖ה עֲב֑וֹר וַֽיַּעֲמֹד֙ בְּמָק֣וֹם צָ֔ר אֲשֶׁ֛ר אֵֽין־דֶּ֥רֶךְ לִנְט֖וֹת יָמִ֥ין וּשְׂמֹֽאול׃ 27 וַתֵּ֤רֶא הָֽאָתוֹן֙ אֶת־מַלְאַ֣ךְ יְהֹוָ֔ה וַתִּרְבַּ֖ץ תַּ֣חַת בִּלְעָ֑ם וַיִּֽחַר־אַ֣ף בִּלְעָ֔ם וַיַּ֥ךְ אֶת־הָאָת֖וֹן בַּמַּקֵּֽל׃ 28 וַיִּפְתַּ֥ח יְהֹוָ֖ה אֶת־פִּ֣י הָאָת֑וֹן וַתֹּ֤אמֶר לְבִלְעָם֙ מֶה־עָשִׂ֣יתִֽי לְךָ֔ כִּ֣י הִכִּיתַ֔נִי זֶ֖ה שָׁלֹ֥שׁ רְגָלִֽים׃ 29 וַיֹּ֤אמֶר בִּלְעָם֙ לָֽאָת֔וֹן כִּ֥י הִתְעַלַּ֖לְתְּ בִּ֑י ל֤וּ יֶשׁ־חֶ֙רֶב֙ בְּיָדִ֔י כִּ֥י עַתָּ֖ה הֲרַגְתִּֽיךְ׃

30 וַתֹּ֨אמֶר הָאָת֜וֹן אֶל־בִּלְעָ֗ם הֲלוֹא֩ אָנֹכִ֨י אֲתֹֽנְךָ֜ אֲשֶׁר־רָכַ֣בְתָּ עָלַ֗י מֵעֽוֹדְךָ֙ עַד־הַיּ֣וֹם הַזֶּ֔ה הַֽהַסְכֵּ֣ן הִסְכַּ֔נְתִּי לַעֲשׂ֥וֹת לְךָ֖ כֹּ֑ה וַיֹּ֖אמֶר לֹֽא׃ 31 וַיְגַ֣ל יְהֹוָה֮ אֶת־עֵינֵ֣י בִלְעָם֒ וַיַּ֞רְא אֶת־מַלְאַ֤ךְ יְהֹוָה֙ נִצָּ֣ב בַּדֶּ֔רֶךְ וְחַרְבּ֥וֹ שְׁלֻפָ֖ה בְּיָד֑וֹ וַיִּקֹּ֥ד וַיִּשְׁתַּ֖חוּ לְאַפָּֽיו׃ 32 וַיֹּ֤אמֶר אֵלָיו֙ מַלְאַ֣ךְ יְהֹוָ֔ה עַל־מָ֗ה הִכִּ֙יתָ֙ אֶת־אֲתֹ֣נְךָ֔ זֶ֖ה שָׁל֣וֹשׁ רְגָלִ֑ים הִנֵּ֧ה אָנֹכִ֛י יָצָ֥אתִי לְשָׂטָ֖ן כִּֽי־יָרַ֥ט הַדֶּ֖רֶךְ לְנֶגְדִּֽי׃ 33 וַתִּרְאַ֙נִי֙ הָֽאָת֔וֹן וַתֵּ֣ט לְפָנַ֔י זֶ֖ה שָׁלֹ֣שׁ רְגָלִ֑ים אוּלַי֙ נָטְתָ֣ה מִפָּנַ֔י כִּ֥י עַתָּ֛ה גַּם־אֹתְכָ֥ה הָרַ֖גְתִּי וְאוֹתָ֥הּ הֶחֱיֵֽיתִי׃ 34 וַיֹּ֨אמֶר בִּלְעָ֜ם אֶל־מַלְאַ֤ךְ יְהֹוָה֙ חָטָ֔אתִי כִּ֚י לֹ֣א יָדַ֔עְתִּי כִּ֥י אַתָּ֛ה נִצָּ֥ב לִקְרָאתִ֖י בַּדָּ֑רֶךְ וְעַתָּ֛ה אִם־רַ֥ע בְּעֵינֶ֖יךָ אָשׁ֥וּבָה לִּֽי׃ 35 וַיֹּ֩אמֶר֩ מַלְאַ֨ךְ יְהֹוָ֜ה אֶל־בִּלְעָ֗ם לֵ֚ךְ עִם־הָ֣אֲנָשִׁ֔ים וְאֶ֗פֶס אֶת־הַדָּבָ֛ר אֲשֶׁר־אֲדַבֵּ֥ר אֵלֶ֖יךָ אֹת֣וֹ תְדַבֵּ֑ר וַיֵּ֥לֶךְ בִּלְעָ֖ם עִם־שָׂרֵ֥י בָלָֽק׃ 36 וַיִּשְׁמַ֥ע בָּלָ֖ק כִּ֣י בָ֣א בִלְעָ֑ם וַיֵּצֵ֣א לִקְרָאת֗וֹ אֶל־עִ֤יר מוֹאָב֙ אֲשֶׁר֙ עַל־גְּב֣וּל אַרְנֹ֔ן אֲשֶׁ֖ר בִּקְצֵ֥ה הַגְּבֽוּל׃ 37 וַיֹּ֨אמֶר בָּלָ֜ק אֶל־בִּלְעָ֗ם הֲלֹא֩ שָׁלֹ֨חַ שָׁלַ֤חְתִּי אֵלֶ֙יךָ֙ לִקְרֹא־לָ֔ךְ לָ֥מָּה לֹֽא־

38 And Balaam said to Balak, "Look, I have come to you! Now, have I any power at all to say anything? The word that God puts in my mouth, that I must speak." 39 So Balaam went with Balak, and they came to Kirjath Huzoth. 40 Then Balak offered oxen and sheep, and he sent *some* to Balaam and to the princes who *were* with him.

41 So it was, the next day, that Balak took Balaam and brought him up to the high places of Baal, that from there he might observe the extent of the people.

23 Then Balaam said to Balak, "Build seven altars for me here, and prepare for me here seven bulls and seven rams."

2 And Balak did just as Balaam had spoken, and Balak and Balaam offered a bull and a ram on *each* altar. 3 Then Balaam said to Balak, "Stand by your burnt offering, and I will go; perhaps the LORD will come to meet me, and whatever He shows me I will tell you." So he went to a desolate height. 4 And God met Balaam, and he said to Him, "I have prepared the seven altars, and I have offered on *each* altar a bull and a ram."

5 Then the LORD put a word in Balaam's mouth, and said, "Return to Balak, and thus you shall speak." 6 So he returned to him, and there he was, standing by his burnt offering, he and all the princes of Moab.

7 And he took up his oracle and said:

"Balak the king of Moab has brought me from Aram,
From the mountains of the east.
'Come, curse Jacob for me,
And come, denounce Israel!'

8 "How shall I curse whom God has not cursed?
And how shall I denounce *whom* the LORD has not denounced?

9 For from the top of the rocks I see him,
And from the hills I behold him;
There! A people dwelling alone,
Not reckoning itself among the nations.

10 "Who can count the dust of Jacob,
Or number one-fourth of Israel?
Let me die the death of the righteous,
And let my end be like his!"

11 Then Balak said to Balaam, "What have you done to me? I took you to curse my enemies, and look, you have blessed *them* bountifully!"

12 So he answered and said, "Must I not take heed to speak what the LORD has put in my mouth?"

הֲלָכְתִּי אֵלֶי הַאֻמְנָם לֹא אוּכַל כַּבְּרֶךָ: 38 וַיֹּאמֶר בִּלְעָם אֶל־בָּלָק הִנֵּה־בָאתִי אֵלֶיךָ עַתָּה הֲיָכֹל אוּכַל דַּבֵּר מְאוּמָה הַדָּבָר אֲשֶׁר יָשִׂים אֱלֹהִים בְּפִי אֹתוֹ אֲדַבֵּר: 39 וַיֵּלֶךְ בִּלְעָם עִם־בָּלָק וַיָּבֹאוּ קִרְיַת חֻצוֹת: 40 וַיִּזְבַּח בָּלָק בָּקָר וָצֹאן וַיְשַׁלַּח לְבִלְעָם וְלַשָּׂרִים אֲשֶׁר אִתּוֹ: 41 וַיְהִי בַבֹּקֶר וַיִּקַּח בָּלָק אֶת־בִּלְעָם וַיַּעֲלֵהוּ בָּמוֹת בָּעַל וַיַּרְא מִשָּׁם קְצֵה הָעָם:

כג וַיֹּאמֶר בִּלְעָם אֶל־בָּלָק בְּנֵה־לִי בָזֶה שִׁבְעָה מִזְבְּחֹת וְהָכֵן לִי בָּזֶה שִׁבְעָה פָרִים וְשִׁבְעָה אֵילִים: 2 וַיַּעַשׂ בָּלָק כַּאֲשֶׁר דִּבֶּר בִּלְעָם וַיַּעַל בָּלָק וּבִלְעָם פָּר וָאַיִל בַּמִּזְבֵּחַ: 3 וַיֹּאמֶר בִּלְעָם לְבָלָק הִתְיַצֵּב עַל־עֹלָתֶךָ וְאֵלְכָה אוּלַי יִקָּרֵה יְהֹוָה לִקְרָאתִי וּדְבַר מַה־יַּרְאֵנִי וְהִגַּדְתִּי לָךְ וַיֵּלֶךְ שֶׁפִי:

4 וַיִּקָּר אֱלֹהִים אֶל־בִּלְעָם וַיֹּאמֶר אֵלָיו אֶת־שִׁבְעַת הַמִּזְבְּחֹת עָרַכְתִּי וָאַעַל פָּר וָאַיִל בַּמִּזְבֵּחַ: 5 וַיָּשֶׂם יְהֹוָה דָּבָר בְּפִי בִלְעָם וַיֹּאמֶר שׁוּב אֶל־בָּלָק וְכֹה תְדַבֵּר: 6 וַיָּשָׁב אֵלָיו וְהִנֵּה נִצָּב עַל־עֹלָתוֹ הוּא וְכָל־שָׂרֵי מוֹאָב: 7 וַיִּשָּׂא מְשָׁלוֹ וַיֹּאמַר מִן־אֲרָם יַנְחֵנִי בָלָק מֶלֶךְ־מוֹאָב מֵהַרְרֵי־קֶדֶם לְכָה אָרָה־לִּי יַעֲקֹב וּלְכָה זֹעֲמָה יִשְׂרָאֵל: 8 מָה אֶקֹּב לֹא קַבֹּה אֵל וּמָה אֶזְעֹם לֹא זָעַם יְהֹוָה: 9 כִּי־מֵרֹאשׁ צֻרִים אֶרְאֶנּוּ וּמִגְּבָעוֹת אֲשׁוּרֶנּוּ הֶן־עָם לְבָדָד יִשְׁכֹּן וּבַגּוֹיִם לֹא יִתְחַשָּׁב: 10 מִי מָנָה עֲפַר יַעֲקֹב וּמִסְפָּר אֶת־רֹבַע יִשְׂרָאֵל תָּמֹת נַפְשִׁי מוֹת יְשָׁרִים וּתְהִי אַחֲרִיתִי כָּמֹהוּ: 11 וַיֹּאמֶר בָּלָק אֶל־בִּלְעָם מֶה עָשִׂיתָ לִי לָקֹב אֹיְבַי לְקַחְתִּיךָ וְהִנֵּה בֵּרַכְתָּ בָרֵךְ: 12 וַיַּעַן וַיֹּאמַר הֲלֹא אֵת אֲשֶׁר יָשִׂים יְהֹוָה בְּפִי אֹתוֹ

13 Then Balak said to him, "Please come with me to another place from which you may see them; you shall see only the outer part of them, and shall not see them all; curse them for me from there." 14 So he brought him to the field of Zophim, to the top of Pisgah, and built seven altars, and offered a bull and a ram on *each* altar.

15 And he said to Balak, "Stand here by your burnt offering while I meet *the* LORD over there."

16 Then the LORD met Balaam, and put a word in his mouth, and said, "Go back to Balak, and thus you shall speak." 17 So he came to him, and there he was, standing by his burnt offering, and the princes of Moab were with him. And Balak said to him, "What has the LORD spoken?"

18 Then he took up his oracle and said:

"Rise up, Balak, and hear!
Listen to me, son of Zippor!!

19 "God *is* not a man, that He should lie,
Nor a son of man, that He should repent.
Has He said, and will He not do?
Or has He spoken, and will He not make it good?

20 Behold, I have received *a command* to bless;
He has blessed, and I cannot reverse it.

21 "He has not observed iniquity in Jacob,
Nor has He seen wickedness in Israel.
The LORD his God *is* with him,
And the shout of a King *is* among them.

22 God brings them out of Egypt;
He has strength like a wild ox.

23 "For *there is* no sorcery against Jacob,
Nor any divination against Israel.
It now must be said of Jacob
And of Israel, 'Oh, what God has done!'

24 Look, a people rises like a lioness,
And lifts itself up like a lion;
It shall not lie down until it devours the prey,
And drinks the blood of the slain."

25 Then Balak said to Balaam, "Neither curse them at all, nor bless them at all!"

26 So Balaam answered and said to Balak, "Did I not tell you, saying, 'All that the LORD speaks, that I must do'?"

27 Then Balak said to Balaam, "Please come, I will take you to another place; perhaps it will please God that you may curse them for me from there." 28 So Balak took Balaam to the top of Peor, that overlooks the wasteland. 29 Then Balaam said to Balak, "Build for me here seven altars, and prepare for me here seven bulls and seven rams." 30 And Balak did as Balaam had said, and offered a bull and a ram on *every* altar.

אֶשְׁמֹ֥ר לְדַבֵּֽר: 13 וַיֹּ֨אמֶר אֵלָ֜יו בָּלָ֗ק לְךָ־נָּ֤א אִתִּי֙ אֶל־מָק֣וֹם אַחֵ֔ר אֲשֶׁ֥ר תִּרְאֶ֖נּוּ מִשָּׁ֑ם אֶ֤פֶס קָצֵ֨הוּ֙ תִרְאֶ֔ה וְכֻלּ֖וֹ לֹ֣א תִרְאֶ֑ה וְקָבְנוֹ־לִ֖י מִשָּֽׁם: 14 וַיִּקָּחֵ֨הוּ֙ שְׂדֵ֣ה צֹפִ֔ים אֶל־רֹ֖אשׁ הַפִּסְגָּ֑ה וַיִּ֨בֶן֙ שִׁבְעָ֣ה מִזְבְּחֹ֔ת וַיַּ֛עַל פָּ֥ר וָאַ֖יִל בַּמִּזְבֵּֽחַ: 15 וַיֹּ֨אמֶר֙ אֶל־בָּלָ֔ק הִתְיַצֵּ֥ב כֹּ֖ה עַל־עֹלָתֶ֑ךָ וְאָנֹכִ֖י אִקָּ֥רֶה כֹּֽה: 16 וַיִּקָּ֨ר יְהוָ֜ה אֶל־בִּלְעָ֗ם וַיָּ֤שֶׂם דָּבָר֙ בְּפִ֔יו וַיֹּ֛אמֶר שׁ֥וּב אֶל־בָּלָ֖ק וְכֹ֥ה תְדַבֵּֽר: 17 וַיָּבֹ֣א אֵלָ֗יו וְהִנּ֤וֹ נִצָּב֙ עַל־עֹ֣לָת֔וֹ וְשָׂרֵ֥י מוֹאָ֖ב אִתּ֑וֹ וַיֹּ֤אמֶר לוֹ֙ בָּלָ֔ק מַה־דִּבֶּ֖ר יְהוָֽה: 18 וַיִּשָּׂ֥א מְשָׁל֖וֹ וַיֹּאמַ֑ר ק֤וּם בָּלָק֙ וּֽשֲׁמָ֔ע הַאֲזִ֥ינָה עָדַ֖י בְּנ֥וֹ צִפֹּֽר: 19 לֹ֣א אִ֥ישׁ אֵל֙ וִֽיכַזֵּ֔ב וּבֶן־אָדָ֖ם וְיִתְנֶחָ֑ם הַה֤וּא אָמַר֙ וְלֹ֣א יַעֲשֶׂ֔ה וְדִבֶּ֖ר וְלֹ֥א יְקִימֶֽנָּה: 20 הִנֵּ֥ה בָרֵ֖ךְ לָקָ֑חְתִּי וּבֵרֵ֖ךְ וְלֹ֥א אֲשִׁיבֶֽנָּה: 21 לֹֽא־הִבִּ֤יט אָ֙וֶן֙ בְּיַעֲקֹ֔ב וְלֹא־רָאָ֥ה עָמָ֖ל בְּיִשְׂרָאֵ֑ל יְהוָ֤ה אֱלֹהָיו֙ עִמּ֔וֹ וּתְרוּעַ֥ת מֶ֖לֶךְ בּֽוֹ: 22 אֵ֖ל מוֹצִיאָ֣ם מִמִּצְרָ֑יִם כְּתוֹעֲפֹ֥ת רְאֵ֖ם לֽוֹ: 23 כִּ֤י לֹא־נַ֙חַשׁ֙ בְּיַעֲקֹ֔ב וְלֹא־קֶ֖סֶם בְּיִשְׂרָאֵ֑ל כָּעֵ֗ת יֵאָמֵ֤ר לְיַעֲקֹב֙ וּלְיִשְׂרָאֵ֔ל מַה־פָּ֖עַל אֵֽל: 24 הֶן־עָם֙ כְּלָבִ֣יא יָק֔וּם וְכַאֲרִ֖י יִתְנַשָּׂ֑א לֹ֤א יִשְׁכַּב֙ עַד־יֹ֣אכַל טֶ֔רֶף וְדַם־חֲלָלִ֖ים יִשְׁתֶּֽה:

25 וַיֹּ֤אמֶר בָּלָק֙ אֶל־בִּלְעָ֔ם גַּם־קֹ֖ב לֹ֣א תִקֳּבֶ֑נּוּ גַּם־בָּרֵ֖ךְ לֹ֥א תְבָרֲכֶֽנּוּ: 26 וַיַּ֣עַן בִּלְעָ֔ם וַיֹּ֖אמֶר אֶל־בָּלָ֑ק הֲלֹ֗א דִּבַּ֤רְתִּי אֵלֶ֙יךָ֙ לֵאמֹ֔ר כֹּ֛ל אֲשֶׁר־יְדַבֵּ֥ר יְהוָ֖ה אֹת֥וֹ אֶעֱשֶֽׂה: 27 וַיֹּ֤אמֶר בָּלָק֙ אֶל־בִּלְעָ֔ם לְכָה־נָּא֙ אֶקָּ֣חֲךָ֔ אֶל־מָק֖וֹם אַחֵ֑ר אוּלַ֤י יִישַׁר֙ בְּעֵינֵ֣י הָאֱלֹהִ֔ים וְקַבֹּ֥תוֹ לִ֖י מִשָּֽׁם: 28 וַיִּקַּ֥ח בָּלָ֖ק אֶת־בִּלְעָ֑ם רֹ֣אשׁ הַפְּע֔וֹר הַנִּשְׁקָ֖ף עַל־פְּנֵ֥י הַיְשִׁימֹֽן: 29 וַיֹּ֤אמֶר בִּלְעָם֙ אֶל־בָּלָ֔ק בְּנֵה־לִ֥י בָזֶ֖ה שִׁבְעָ֣ה מִזְבְּחֹ֑ת וְהָכֵ֥ן לִ֣י בָּזֶ֔ה שִׁבְעָ֥ה פָרִ֖ים וְשִׁבְעָ֥ה אֵילִֽם: 30 וַיַּ֣עַשׂ בָּלָ֔ק כַּאֲשֶׁ֖ר אָמַ֣ר בִּלְעָ֑ם וַיַּ֛עַל פָּ֥ר וָאַ֖יִל בַּמִּזְבֵּֽחַ:

24 Now when Balaam saw that it pleased the LORD to bless Israel, he did not go as at other times, to seek to use sorcery, but he set his face toward the wilderness. ²And Balaam raised his eyes, and saw Israel encamped according to their tribes; and the Spirit of God came upon him.

³Then he took up his oracle and said:

"The utterance of Balaam the son of Beor,
The utterance of the man whose eyes are opened,
4 The utterance of him who hears the words of God,
Who sees the vision of the Almighty,
Who falls down, with eyes wide open:

5 "How lovely are your tents, O Jacob!
Your dwellings, O Israel!
6 Like valleys that stretch out,
Like gardens by the riverside,
Like aloes planted by the LORD,
Like cedars beside the waters.
7 He shall pour water from his buckets,
And his seed *shall be* in many waters.

"His king shall be higher than Agag,
And his kingdom shall be exalted.

8 "God brings him out of Egypt;
He has strength like a wild ox;
He shall consume the nations, his enemies;
He shall break their bones
And pierce *them* with his arrows.
9 'He bows down, he lies down as a lion;
And as a lion, who shall rouse him?'

"Blessed *is* he who blesses you,
And cursed *is* he who curses you."

¹⁰Then Balak's anger was aroused against Balaam, and he struck his hands together; and Balak said to Balaam, "I called you to curse my enemies, and look, you have bountifully blessed *them* these three times! ¹¹Now therefore, flee to your place. I said I would greatly honor you, but in fact, the LORD has kept you back from honor."

¹²So Balaam said to Balak, "Did I not also speak to your messengers whom you sent to me, saying, ¹³'If Balak were to give me his house full of silver and gold, I could not go beyond the word of the LORD, to do good or bad of my own will. What the LORD says, that I must speak'? ¹⁴And now, indeed, I am going to my people. Come, I will advise you what this people will do to your people in the latter days."

¹⁵So he took up his oracle and said:

"The utterance of Balaam the son of Beor,
And the utterance of the man whose eyes are opened;
16 The utterance of him who hears the words of God,
And has the knowledge of the Most High,

כד וַיַּרְא בִּלְעָם כִּי טוֹב בְּעֵינֵי יְהוָה לְבָרֵךְ אֶת־יִשְׂרָאֵל וְלֹא־הָלַךְ כְּפַעַם־בְּפַעַם לִקְרַאת נְחָשִׁים וַיָּשֶׁת אֶל־הַמִּדְבָּר פָּנָיו: 2 וַיִּשָּׂא בִלְעָם אֶת־עֵינָיו וַיַּרְא אֶת־יִשְׂרָאֵל שֹׁכֵן לִשְׁבָטָיו וַתְּהִי עָלָיו רוּחַ אֱלֹהִים: 3 וַיִּשָּׂא מְשָׁלוֹ וַיֹּאמַר נְאֻם בִּלְעָם בְּנוֹ בְעֹר וּנְאֻם הַגֶּבֶר שְׁתֻם הָעָיִן: 4 נְאֻם שֹׁמֵעַ אִמְרֵי־אֵל אֲשֶׁר מַחֲזֵה שַׁדַּי יֶחֱזֶה נֹפֵל וּגְלוּי עֵינָיִם: 5 מַה־טֹּבוּ אֹהָלֶיךָ יַעֲקֹב מִשְׁכְּנֹתֶיךָ יִשְׂרָאֵל: 6 כִּנְחָלִים נִטָּיוּ כְּגַנֹּת עֲלֵי נָהָר כַּאֲהָלִים נָטַע יְהוָה כַּאֲרָזִים עֲלֵי־מָיִם: 7 יִזַּל־מַיִם מִדָּלְיָו וְזַרְעוֹ בְּמַיִם רַבִּים וְיָרֹם מֵאֲגַג מַלְכּוֹ וְתִנַּשֵּׂא מַלְכֻתוֹ: 8 אֵל מוֹצִיאוֹ מִמִּצְרַיִם כְּתוֹעֲפֹת רְאֵם לוֹ יֹאכַל גּוֹיִם צָרָיו וְעַצְמֹתֵיהֶם יְגָרֵם וְחִצָּיו יִמְחָץ: 9 כָּרַע שָׁכַב כַּאֲרִי וּכְלָבִיא מִי יְקִימֶנּוּ מְבָרֲכֶיךָ בָרוּךְ וְאֹרְרֶיךָ אָרוּר: 10 וַיִּחַר־אַף בָּלָק אֶל־בִּלְעָם וַיִּסְפֹּק אֶת־כַּפָּיו וַיֹּאמֶר בָּלָק אֶל־בִּלְעָם לָקֹב אֹיְבַי קְרָאתִיךָ וְהִנֵּה בֵּרַכְתָּ בָרֵךְ זֶה שָׁלֹשׁ פְּעָמִים: 11 וְעַתָּה בְּרַח־לְךָ אֶל־מְקוֹמֶךָ אָמַרְתִּי כַּבֵּד אֲכַבֶּדְךָ וְהִנֵּה מְנָעֲךָ יְהוָה מִכָּבוֹד:

12 וַיֹּאמֶר בִּלְעָם אֶל־בָּלָק הֲלֹא גַּם אֶל־מַלְאָכֶיךָ אֲשֶׁר־שָׁלַחְתָּ אֵלַי דִּבַּרְתִּי לֵאמֹר: 13 אִם־יִתֶּן־לִי בָלָק מְלֹא בֵיתוֹ כֶּסֶף וְזָהָב לֹא אוּכַל לַעֲבֹר אֶת־פִּי יְהוָה לַעֲשׂוֹת טוֹבָה אוֹ רָעָה מִלִּבִּי אֲשֶׁר־יְדַבֵּר יְהוָה אֹתוֹ אֲדַבֵּר: 14 וְעַתָּה הִנְנִי הוֹלֵךְ לְעַמִּי לְכָה אִיעָצְךָ אֲשֶׁר יַעֲשֶׂה הָעָם הַזֶּה לְעַמְּךָ בְּאַחֲרִית הַיָּמִים: 15 וַיִּשָּׂא מְשָׁלוֹ וַיֹּאמַר נְאֻם בִּלְעָם בְּנוֹ בְעֹר וּנְאֻם הַגֶּבֶר שְׁתֻם הָעָיִן: 16 נְאֻם שֹׁמֵעַ אִמְרֵי־אֵל

Who sees the vision of the Almighty,
Who falls down, with eyes wide open:

17 "I see Him, but not now;
   I behold Him, but not near;
   A Star shall come out of Jacob,
   A Scepter shall rise out of Israel,
   And batter the brow of Moab,
   And destroy all the sons of tumult.

18 "And Edom shall be a possession;
   Seir also, his enemies, shall be a possession,
   While Israel does valiantly.

19 Out of Jacob One shall have dominion,
   And destroy the remains of the city."

20 Then he looked on Amalek, and he took up his oracle and said:

   "Amalek *was* first among the nations,
   But *shall be* last until he perishes."

21 Then he looked on the Kenites, and he took up his oracle and said:

   "Firm is your dwelling place,
   And your nest is set in the rock;
22 Nevertheless Kain shall be burned.
   How long until Asshur carries you away captive?"

23 Then he took up his oracle and said:

   "Alas! Who shall live when God does this?
24 But ships *shall come* from the coasts of Cyprus,
   And they shall afflict Asshur and afflict Eber,
   And so shall *Amalek*, until he perishes."

25 So Balaam rose and departed and returned to his place; Balak also went his way.

25

Now Israel remained in Acacia Grove, and the people began to commit harlotry with the women of Moab. 2 They invited the people to the sacrifices of their gods, and the people ate and bowed down to their gods. 3 So Israel was joined to Baal of Peor, and the anger of the LORD was aroused against Israel.

4 Then the LORD said to Moses, "Take all the leaders of the people and hang the offenders before the LORD, out in the sun, that the fierce anger of the LORD may turn away from Israel."

5 So Moses said to the judges of Israel, "Every one of you kill his men who were joined to Baal of Peor."

6 And indeed, one of the children of Israel came and presented to his brethren a Midianite woman in the sight of Moses and in the sight of all the congregation of the children of Israel, who *were* weeping at the door of the tabernacle of meeting. 7 Now when Phinehas the son of Eleazar, the son of Aaron the priest, saw *it,* he rose from among the

וַיֵּדַע דַּעַת עֶלְיוֹן מַחֲזֵה שַׁדַּי יֶחֱזֶה נֹפֵל וּגְלוּי עֵינָיִם:

17 אֶרְאֶנּוּ וְלֹא עַתָּה אֲשׁוּרֶנּוּ וְלֹא קָרוֹב דָּרַךְ כּוֹכָב מִיַּעֲקֹב וְקָם שֵׁבֶט מִיִּשְׂרָאֵל וּמָחַץ פַּאֲתֵי מוֹאָב וְקַרְקַר כָּל־בְּנֵי־שֵׁת: 18 וְהָיָה אֱדוֹם יְרֵשָׁה וְהָיָה יְרֵשָׁה שֵׂעִיר אֹיְבָיו וְיִשְׂרָאֵל עֹשֶׂה חָיִל: 19 וְיֵרְדְּ מִיַּעֲקֹב וְהֶאֱבִיד שָׂרִיד מֵעִיר: 20 וַיַּרְא אֶת־עֲמָלֵק וַיִּשָּׂא מְשָׁלוֹ וַיֹּאמַר רֵאשִׁית גּוֹיִם עֲמָלֵק וְאַחֲרִיתוֹ עֲדֵי אֹבֵד: 21 וַיַּרְא אֶת־הַקֵּינִי וַיִּשָּׂא מְשָׁלוֹ וַיֹּאמַר אֵיתָן מוֹשָׁבֶךָ וְשִׂים בַּסֶּלַע קִנֶּךָ: 22 כִּי אִם־יִהְיֶה לְבָעֵר קָיִן עַד־מָה אַשּׁוּר תִּשְׁבֶּךָּ: 23 וַיִּשָּׂא מְשָׁלוֹ וַיֹּאמַר אוֹי מִי יִחְיֶה מִשֻּׂמוֹ אֵל: 24 וְצִים מִיַּד כִּתִּים וְעִנּוּ אַשּׁוּר וְעִנּוּ־עֵבֶר וְגַם־הוּא עֲדֵי אֹבֵד: 25 וַיָּקָם בִּלְעָם וַיֵּלֶךְ וַיָּשָׁב לִמְקֹמוֹ וְגַם־בָּלָק הָלַךְ לְדַרְכּוֹ: פ

כה וַיֵּשֶׁב יִשְׂרָאֵל בַּשִּׁטִּים וַיָּחֶל הָעָם לִזְנוֹת אֶל־בְּנוֹת מוֹאָב: 2 וַתִּקְרֶאןָ לָעָם לְזִבְחֵי אֱלֹהֵיהֶן וַיֹּאכַל הָעָם וַיִּשְׁתַּחֲווּ לֵאלֹהֵיהֶן: 3 וַיִּצָּמֶד יִשְׂרָאֵל לְבַעַל פְּעוֹר וַיִּחַר־אַף יְהוָה בְּיִשְׂרָאֵל: 4 וַיֹּאמֶר יְהוָה אֶל־מֹשֶׁה קַח אֶת־כָּל־רָאשֵׁי הָעָם וְהוֹקַע אוֹתָם לַיהוָה נֶגֶד הַשָּׁמֶשׁ וְיָשֹׁב חֲרוֹן אַף־יְהוָה מִיִּשְׂרָאֵל: 5 וַיֹּאמֶר מֹשֶׁה אֶל־שֹׁפְטֵי יִשְׂרָאֵל הִרְגוּ אִישׁ אֲנָשָׁיו הַנִּצְמָדִים לְבַעַל פְּעוֹר: 6 וְהִנֵּה אִישׁ מִבְּנֵי יִשְׂרָאֵל בָּא וַיַּקְרֵב אֶל־אֶחָיו אֶת־הַמִּדְיָנִית לְעֵינֵי מֹשֶׁה וּלְעֵינֵי כָּל־עֲדַת בְּנֵי־יִשְׂרָאֵל וְהֵמָּה בֹכִים פֶּתַח אֹהֶל מוֹעֵד: 7 וַיַּרְא פִּינְחָס בֶּן־אֶלְעָזָר בֶּן־אַהֲרֹן הַכֹּהֵן וַיָּקָם מִתּוֹךְ הָעֵדָה וַיִּקַּח רֹמַח

congregation and took a javelin in his hand; [8] and he went after the man of Israel into the tent and thrust both of them through, the man of Israel, and the woman through her body. So the plague was stopped among the children of Israel. [9] And those who died in the plague were twenty-four thousand.

[10] Then the LORD spoke to Moses, saying: [11] "Phinehas the son of Eleazar, the son of Aaron the priest, has turned back My wrath from the children of Israel, because he was zealous with My zeal among them, so that I did not consume the children of Israel in My zeal. [12] Therefore say, 'Behold, I give to him My covenant of peace; [13] and it shall be to him and his descendants after him a covenant of an everlasting priesthood, because he was zealous for his God, and made atonement for the children of Israel.'"

[14] Now the name of the Israelite who was killed, who was killed with the Midianite woman, *was* Zimri the son of Salu, a leader of a father's house among the Simeonites. [15] And the name of the Midianite woman who was killed *was* Cozbi the daughter of Zur; he *was* head of the people of a father's house in Midian.

[16] Then the LORD spoke to Moses, saying: [17] "Harass the Midianites, and attack them; [18] for they harassed you with their schemes by which they seduced you in the matter of Peor and in the matter of Cozbi, the daughter of a leader of Midian, their sister, who was killed in the day of the plague because of Peor."

26 And it came to pass, after the plague, that the LORD spoke to Moses and Eleazar the son of Aaron the priest, saying: [2] "Take a census of all the congregation of the children of Israel from twenty years old and above, by their fathers' houses, all who are able to go to war in Israel." [3] So Moses and Eleazar the priest spoke with them in the plains of Moab by the Jordan, *across from* Jericho, saying: [4] "Take a census of the people from twenty years old and above, just as the LORD commanded Moses and the children of Israel who came out of the land of Egypt."

[5] Reuben *was* the firstborn of Israel. The children of Reuben *were*: of Hanoch, the family of the Hanochites; *of* Pallu, the family of the Palluites; [6] *of* Hezron, the family of the Hezronites; *of* Carmi, the family of the Carmites. [7] These *are* the families of the Reubenites: those who were numbered of them were forty-three thousand seven hundred and thirty. [8] And the son of Pallu *was* Eliab. [9] The sons of Eliab *were* Nemuel, Dathan, and Abiram. These *are* the Dathan and Abiram, representatives of the

בְּיָדוֹ: 8 וַיָּבֹא אַחַר אִישׁ־יִשְׂרָאֵל אֶל־הַקֻּבָּה וַיִּדְקֹר אֶת־שְׁנֵיהֶם אֵת אִישׁ יִשְׂרָאֵל וְאֶת־הָאִשָּׁה אֶל־קֳבָתָהּ וַתֵּעָצַר הַמַּגֵּפָה מֵעַל בְּנֵי יִשְׂרָאֵל: 9 וַיִּהְיוּ הַמֵּתִים בַּמַּגֵּפָה אַרְבָּעָה וְעֶשְׂרִים אָלֶף: פ

10 וַיְדַבֵּר יְהוָה אֶל־מֹשֶׁה לֵּאמֹר: 11 פִּינְחָס בֶּן־אֶלְעָזָר בֶּן־אַהֲרֹן הַכֹּהֵן הֵשִׁיב אֶת־חֲמָתִי מֵעַל בְּנֵי־יִשְׂרָאֵל בְּקַנְאוֹ אֶת־קִנְאָתִי בְּתוֹכָם וְלֹא־כִלִּיתִי אֶת־בְּנֵי־יִשְׂרָאֵל בְּקִנְאָתִי: 12 לָכֵן אֱמֹר הִנְנִי נֹתֵן לוֹ אֶת־בְּרִיתִי שָׁלוֹם: 13 וְהָיְתָה לּוֹ וּלְזַרְעוֹ אַחֲרָיו בְּרִית כְּהֻנַּת עוֹלָם תַּחַת אֲשֶׁר קִנֵּא לֵאלֹהָיו וַיְכַפֵּר עַל־בְּנֵי יִשְׂרָאֵל: 14 וְשֵׁם אִישׁ יִשְׂרָאֵל הַמֻּכֶּה אֲשֶׁר הֻכָּה אֶת־הַמִּדְיָנִית זִמְרִי בֶּן־סָלוּא נְשִׂיא בֵית־אָב לַשִּׁמְעֹנִי: 15 וְשֵׁם הָאִשָּׁה הַמֻּכָּה הַמִּדְיָנִית כָּזְבִּי בַת־צוּר רֹאשׁ אֻמּוֹת בֵּית־אָב בְּמִדְיָן הוּא: פ

16 וַיְדַבֵּר יְהוָה אֶל־מֹשֶׁה לֵּאמֹר: 17 צָרוֹר אֶת־הַמִּדְיָנִים וְהִכִּיתֶם אוֹתָם: 18 כִּי צֹרְרִים הֵם לָכֶם בְּנִכְלֵיהֶם אֲשֶׁר־נִכְּלוּ לָכֶם עַל־דְּבַר־פְּעוֹר וְעַל־דְּבַר כָּזְבִּי בַת־נְשִׂיא מִדְיָן אֲחֹתָם הַמֻּכָּה בְיוֹם־הַמַּגֵּפָה עַל־דְּבַר־פְּעוֹר:

כו וַיְהִי אַחֲרֵי הַמַּגֵּפָה פ וַיֹּאמֶר יְהוָה אֶל־מֹשֶׁה וְאֶל אֶלְעָזָר בֶּן־אַהֲרֹן הַכֹּהֵן לֵאמֹר: 2 שְׂאוּ אֶת־רֹאשׁ ׀ כָּל־עֲדַת בְּנֵי־יִשְׂרָאֵל מִבֶּן עֶשְׂרִים שָׁנָה וָמַעְלָה לְבֵית אֲבֹתָם כָּל־יֹצֵא צָבָא בְּיִשְׂרָאֵל: 3 וַיְדַבֵּר מֹשֶׁה וְאֶלְעָזָר הַכֹּהֵן אֹתָם בְּעַרְבֹת מוֹאָב עַל־יַרְדֵּן יְרֵחוֹ לֵאמֹר: 4 מִבֶּן עֶשְׂרִים שָׁנָה וָמָעְלָה כַּאֲשֶׁר צִוָּה יְהוָה אֶת־מֹשֶׁה וּבְנֵי יִשְׂרָאֵל הַיֹּצְאִים מֵאֶרֶץ מִצְרָיִם: 5 רְאוּבֵן בְּכוֹר יִשְׂרָאֵל בְּנֵי רְאוּבֵן חֲנוֹךְ מִשְׁפַּחַת הַחֲנֹכִי לְפַלּוּא מִשְׁפַּחַת הַפַּלֻּאִי: 6 לְחֶצְרֹן מִשְׁפַּחַת הַחֶצְרוֹנִי לְכַרְמִי מִשְׁפַּחַת הַכַּרְמִי: 7 אֵלֶּה מִשְׁפְּחֹת הָראוּבֵנִי וַיִּהְיוּ פְקֻדֵיהֶם שְׁלֹשָׁה וְאַרְבָּעִים אֶלֶף וּשְׁבַע מֵאוֹת וּשְׁלֹשִׁים: 8 וּבְנֵי פַלּוּא אֱלִיאָב: 9 וּבְנֵי אֱלִיאָב נְמוּאֵל וְדָתָן וַאֲבִירָם הוּא־דָתָן וַאֲבִירָם קרואי הָעֵדָה אֲשֶׁר הִצּוּ עַל־מֹשֶׁה וְעַל־אַהֲרֹן

congregation, who contended against Moses and Aaron in the company of Korah, when they contended against the LORD; ¹⁰and the earth opened its mouth and swallowed them up together with Korah when that company died, when the fire devoured two hundred and fifty men; and they became a sign. ¹¹Nevertheless the children of Korah did not die.

¹²The sons of Simeon according to their families *were:* of Nemuel, the family of the Nemuelites; *of* Jamin, the family of the Jaminites; *of* Jachin, the family of the Jachinites; ¹³*of* Zerah, the family of the Zarhites; *of* Shaul, the family of the Shaulites. ¹⁴These *are* the families of the Simeonites: twenty-two thousand two hundred.

¹⁵The sons of Gad according to their families *were:* of Zephon, the family of the Zephonites; *of* Haggi, the family of the Haggites; *of* Shuni, the family of the Shunites; ¹⁶*of* Ozni, the family of the Oznites; *of* Eri, the family of the Erites; ¹⁷*of* Arod, the family of the Arodites; *of* Areli, the family of the Arelites. ¹⁸These *are* the families of the sons of Gad according to those who were numbered of them: forty thousand five hundred.

¹⁹The sons of Judah *were* Er and Onan; and Er and Onan died in the land of Canaan. ²⁰And the sons of Judah according to their families *were:* of Shelah, the family of the Shelanites; *of* Perez, the family of the Parzites; *of* Zerah, the family of the Zarhites. ²¹And the sons of Perez *were:* of Hezron, the family of the Hezronites; *of* Hamul, the family of the Hamulites. ²²These *are* the families of Judah according to those who were numbered of them: seventy-six thousand five hundred.

²³The sons of Issachar according to their families *were:* of Tola, the family of the Tolaites; *of* Puah, the family of the Punites; ²⁴*of* Jashub, the family of the Jashubites; *of* Shimron, the family of the Shimronites. ²⁵These *are* the families of Issachar according to those who were numbered of them: sixty-four thousand three hundred.

²⁶The sons of Zebulun according to their families *were:* of Sered, the family of the Sardites; *of* Elon, the family of the Elonites; *of* Jahleel, the family of the Jahleelites. ²⁷These *are* the families of the Zebulunites according to those who were numbered of them: sixty thousand five hundred.

²⁸The sons of Joseph according to their families, by Manasseh and Ephraim, *were:* ²⁹The sons of Manasseh: of Machir, the family of the Machirites; and Machir begot Gilead; *of* Gilead, the family of the Gileadites. ³⁰These *are* the sons of Gilead: *of* Jeezer, the family of the Jeezerites; *of* Helek, the family of the Helekites; ³¹*of* Asriel, the family of the

בַּעֲדַת־קֹרַח בְּהַצֹּתָם עַל־יְהוָה: ¹⁰ וַתִּפְתַּח הָאָרֶץ אֶת־פִּיהָ וַתִּבְלַע אֹתָם וְאֶת־קֹרַח בְּמוֹת הָעֵדָה בַּאֲכֹל הָאֵשׁ אֵת חֲמִשִּׁים וּמָאתַיִם אִישׁ וַיִּהְיוּ לְנֵס: ¹¹ וּבְנֵי־קֹרַח לֹא־מֵתוּ: ס ¹² בְּנֵי שִׁמְעוֹן לְמִשְׁפְּחֹתָם לִנְמוּאֵל מִשְׁפַּחַת הַנְּמוּאֵלִי לְיָמִין מִשְׁפַּחַת הַיָּמִינִי לְיָכִין מִשְׁפַּחַת הַיָּכִינִי: ¹³ לְזֶרַח מִשְׁפַּחַת הַזַּרְחִי לְשָׁאוּל מִשְׁפַּחַת הַשָּׁאוּלִי: ¹⁴ אֵלֶּה מִשְׁפְּחֹת הַשִּׁמְעֹנִי שְׁנַיִם וְעֶשְׂרִים אֶלֶף וּמָאתָיִם: ס ¹⁵ בְּנֵי גָד לְמִשְׁפְּחֹתָם לִצְפוֹן מִשְׁפַּחַת הַצְּפוֹנִי לְחַגִּי מִשְׁפַּחַת הַחַגִּי לְשׁוּנִי מִשְׁפַּחַת הַשּׁוּנִי: ¹⁶ לְאָזְנִי מִשְׁפַּחַת הָאָזְנִי לְעֵרִי מִשְׁפַּחַת הָעֵרִי: ¹⁷ לַאֲרוֹד מִשְׁפַּחַת הָאֲרוֹדִי לְאַרְאֵלִי מִשְׁפַּחַת הָאַרְאֵלִי: ¹⁸ אֵלֶּה מִשְׁפְּחֹת בְּנֵי־גָד לִפְקֻדֵיהֶם אַרְבָּעִים אֶלֶף וַחֲמֵשׁ מֵאוֹת: ¹⁹ בְּנֵי יְהוּדָה עֵר וְאוֹנָן וַיָּמָת עֵר וְאוֹנָן בְּאֶרֶץ כְּנָעַן: ²⁰ וַיִּהְיוּ בְנֵי־יְהוּדָה לְמִשְׁפְּחֹתָם לְשֵׁלָה מִשְׁפַּחַת הַשֵּׁלָנִי לְפֶרֶץ מִשְׁפַּחַת הַפַּרְצִי לְזֶרַח מִשְׁפַּחַת הַזַּרְחִי: ²¹ וַיִּהְיוּ בְנֵי־פֶרֶץ לְחֶצְרֹן מִשְׁפַּחַת הַחֶצְרֹנִי לְחָמוּל מִשְׁפַּחַת הֶחָמוּלִי: ²² אֵלֶּה מִשְׁפְּחֹת יְהוּדָה לִפְקֻדֵיהֶם שִׁשָּׁה וְשִׁבְעִים אֶלֶף וַחֲמֵשׁ מֵאוֹת: ס ²³ בְּנֵי יִשָּׂשכָר לְמִשְׁפְּחֹתָם תּוֹלָע מִשְׁפַּחַת הַתּוֹלָעִי לְפֻוָּה מִשְׁפַּחַת הַפּוּנִי: ²⁴ לְיָשׁוּב מִשְׁפַּחַת הַיָּשׁוּבִי לְשִׁמְרֹן מִשְׁפַּחַת הַשִּׁמְרֹנִי: ²⁵ אֵלֶּה מִשְׁפְּחֹת יִשָּׂשכָר לִפְקֻדֵיהֶם אַרְבָּעָה וְשִׁשִּׁים אֶלֶף וּשְׁלֹשׁ מֵאוֹת: ס ²⁶ בְּנֵי זְבוּלֻן לְמִשְׁפְּחֹתָם לְסֶרֶד מִשְׁפַּחַת הַסַּרְדִּי לְאֵלוֹן מִשְׁפַּחַת הָאֵלֹנִי לְיַחְלְאֵל מִשְׁפַּחַת הַיַּחְלְאֵלִי: ²⁷ אֵלֶּה מִשְׁפְּחֹת הַזְּבוּלֹנִי לִפְקֻדֵיהֶם שִׁשִּׁים אֶלֶף וַחֲמֵשׁ מֵאוֹת: ס ²⁸ בְּנֵי יוֹסֵף לְמִשְׁפְּחֹתָם מְנַשֶּׁה וְאֶפְרָיִם: ²⁹ בְּנֵי מְנַשֶּׁה לְמָכִיר מִשְׁפַּחַת הַמָּכִירִי וּמָכִיר הוֹלִיד אֶת־גִּלְעָד לְגִלְעָד מִשְׁפַּחַת הַגִּלְעָדִי: ³⁰ אֵלֶּה בְּנֵי גִלְעָד אִיעֶזֶר מִשְׁפַּחַת הָאִיעֶזְרִי לְחֵלֶק מִשְׁפַּחַת הַחֶלְקִי: ³¹ וְאַשְׂרִיאֵל מִשְׁפַּחַת הָאַשְׂרִאֵלִי

Asrielites; *of* Shechem, the family of the Shechemites; ³² *of* Shemida, the family of the Shemidaites; *of* Hepher, the family of the Hepherites. ³³ Now Zelophehad the son of Hepher had no sons, but daughters; and the names of the daughters of Zelophehad *were* Mahlah, Noah, Hoglah, Milcah, and Tirzah. ³⁴ These *are* the families of Manasseh; and those who were numbered of them *were* fifty-two thousand seven hundred.

³⁵ These *are* the sons of Ephraim according to their families: of Shuthelah, the family of the Shuthalhites; of Becher, the family of the Bachrites; of Tahan, the family of the Tahanites. ³⁶ And these *are* the sons of Shuthelah: of Eran, the family of the Eranites. ³⁷ These *are* the families of the sons of Ephraim according to those who were numbered of them: thirty-two thousand five hundred.

These *are* the sons of Joseph according to their families.

³⁸ The sons of Benjamin according to their families were: of Bela, the family of the Belaites; of Ashbel, the family of the Ashbelites; of Ahiram, the family of the Ahiramites; ³⁹ of Shupham, the family of the Shuphamites; of Hupham, the family of the Huphamites. ⁴⁰ And the sons of Bela were Ard and Naaman: *of Ard,* the family of the Ardites; of Naaman, the family of the Naamites. ⁴¹ These *are* the sons of Benjamin according to their families; and those who were numbered of them *were* forty-five thousand six hundred.

⁴² These *are* the sons of Dan according to their families: of Shuham, the family of the Shuhamites. These *are* the families of Dan according to their families. ⁴³ All the families of the Shuhamites, according to those who were numbered of them, *were* sixty-four thousand four hundred.

⁴⁴ The sons of Asher according to their families *were:* of Jimna, the family of the Jimnites; of Jesui, the family of the Jesuites; of Beriah, the family of the Beriites. ⁴⁵ Of the sons of Beriah: of Heber, the family of the Heberites; of Malchiel, the family of the Malchielites. ⁴⁶ And the name of the daughter of Asher *was* Serah. ⁴⁷ These *are* the families of the sons of Asher according to those who were numbered of them: fifty-three thousand four hundred.

⁴⁸ The sons of Naphtali according to their families *were:* of Jahzeel, the family of the Jahzeelites; of Guni, the family of the Gunites; ⁴⁹ of Jezer, the family of the Jezerites; of Shillem, the family of the Shillemites. ⁵⁰ These *are* the families of Naphtali according to their families; and those who were numbered of them *were* forty-five thousand four hundred.

32 וּשְׁכֶם מִשְׁפַּחַת הַשִּׁכְמִי: וּשְׁמִידָע מִשְׁפַּחַת הַשְּׁמִידָעִי וָחֵפֶר מִשְׁפַּחַת הַחֶפְרִי: 33 וּצְלָפְחָד בֶּן־חֵפֶר לֹא־הָיוּ לוֹ בָּנִים כִּי אִם־בָּנוֹת וְשֵׁם בְּנוֹת צְלָפְחָד מַחְלָה וְנֹעָה חָגְלָה מִלְכָּה וְתִרְצָה: 34 אֵלֶּה מִשְׁפְּחֹת מְנַשֶּׁה וּפְקֻדֵיהֶם שְׁנַיִם וַחֲמִשִּׁים אֶלֶף וּשְׁבַע מֵאוֹת: ס 35 אֵלֶּה בְנֵי־אֶפְרַיִם לְמִשְׁפְּחֹתָם לְשׁוּתֶלַח מִשְׁפַּחַת הַשֻּׁתַלְחִי לְבֶכֶר מִשְׁפַּחַת הַבַּכְרִי לְתַחַן מִשְׁפַּחַת הַתַּחֲנִי: 36 וְאֵלֶּה בְּנֵי שׁוּתָלַח לְעֵרָן מִשְׁפַּחַת הָעֵרָנִי: 37 אֵלֶּה מִשְׁפְּחֹת בְּנֵי־אֶפְרַיִם לִפְקֻדֵיהֶם שְׁנַיִם וּשְׁלֹשִׁים אֶלֶף וַחֲמֵשׁ מֵאוֹת אֵלֶּה בְנֵי־יוֹסֵף לְמִשְׁפְּחֹתָם: ס 38 בְּנֵי בִנְיָמִן לְמִשְׁפְּחֹתָם לְבֶלַע מִשְׁפַּחַת הַבַּלְעִי לְאַשְׁבֵּל מִשְׁפַּחַת הָאַשְׁבֵּלִי לַאֲחִירָם מִשְׁפַּחַת הָאֲחִירָמִי: 39 לִשְׁפוּפָם מִשְׁפַּחַת הַשּׁוּפָמִי לְחוּפָם מִשְׁפַּחַת הַחוּפָמִי: 40 וַיִּהְיוּ בְנֵי־בֶלַע אַרְדְּ וְנַעֲמָן מִשְׁפַּחַת הָאַרְדִּי לְנַעֲמָן מִשְׁפַּחַת הַנַּעֲמִי: 41 אֵלֶּה בְנֵי־בִנְיָמִן לְמִשְׁפְּחֹתָם וּפְקֻדֵיהֶם חֲמִשָּׁה וְאַרְבָּעִים אֶלֶף וְשֵׁשׁ מֵאוֹת: ס 42 אֵלֶּה בְנֵי־דָן לְמִשְׁפְּחֹתָם לְשׁוּחָם מִשְׁפַּחַת הַשּׁוּחָמִי אֵלֶּה מִשְׁפְּחֹת דָּן לְמִשְׁפְּחֹתָם: 43 כָּל־מִשְׁפְּחֹת הַשּׁוּחָמִי לִפְקֻדֵיהֶם אַרְבָּעָה וְשִׁשִּׁים אֶלֶף וְאַרְבַּע מֵאוֹת: ס 44 בְּנֵי אָשֵׁר לְמִשְׁפְּחֹתָם לְיִמְנָה מִשְׁפַּחַת הַיִּמְנָה לְיִשְׁוִי מִשְׁפַּחַת הַיִּשְׁוִי לִבְרִיעָה מִשְׁפַּחַת הַבְּרִיעִי: 45 לִבְנֵי בְרִיעָה לְחֶבֶר מִשְׁפַּחַת הַחֶבְרִי לְמַלְכִּיאֵל מִשְׁפַּחַת הַמַּלְכִּיאֵלִי: 46 וְשֵׁם בַּת־אָשֵׁר שָׂרַח: 47 אֵלֶּה מִשְׁפְּחֹת בְּנֵי־אָשֵׁר לִפְקֻדֵיהֶם שְׁלֹשָׁה וַחֲמִשִּׁים אֶלֶף וְאַרְבַּע מֵאוֹת: ס 48 בְּנֵי נַפְתָּלִי לְמִשְׁפְּחֹתָם לְיַחְצְאֵל מִשְׁפַּחַת הַיַּחְצְאֵלִי לְגוּנִי מִשְׁפַּחַת הַגּוּנִי: 49 לְיֵצֶר מִשְׁפַּחַת הַיִּצְרִי לְשִׁלֵּם מִשְׁפַּחַת הַשִּׁלֵּמִי: 50 אֵלֶּה מִשְׁפְּחֹת נַפְתָּלִי לְמִשְׁפְּחֹתָם וּפְקֻדֵיהֶם

51 These *are* those who were numbered of the children of Israel: six hundred and one thousand seven hundred and thirty.

52 Then the LORD spoke to Moses, saying: 53 "To these the land shall be divided as an inheritance, according to the number of names. 54 To a large *tribe* you shall give a larger inheritance, and to a small *tribe* you shall give a smaller inheritance. Each shall be given its inheritance according to those who were numbered of them. 55 But the land shall be divided by lot; they shall inherit according to the names of the tribes of their fathers. 56 According to the lot their inheritance shall be divided between the larger and the smaller."

57 And these *are* those who were numbered of the Levites according to their families: of Gershon, the family of the Gershonites; of Kohath, the family of the Kohathites; of Merari, the family of the Merarites. 58 These *are* the families of the Levites: the family of the Libnites, the family of the Hebronites, the family of the Mahlites, the family of the Mushites, and the family of the Korathites. And Kohath begot Amram. 59 The name of Amram's wife *was* Jochebed the daughter of Levi, who was born to Levi in Egypt; and to Amram she bore Aaron and Moses and their sister Miriam. 60 To Aaron were born Nadab and Abihu, Eleazar and Ithamar. 61 And Nadab and Abihu died when they offered profane fire before the LORD.

62 Now those who were numbered of them were twenty-three thousand, every male from a month old and above; for they were not numbered among the other children of Israel, because there was no inheritance given to them among the children of Israel.

63 These *are* those who were numbered by Moses and Eleazar the priest, who numbered the children of Israel in the plains of Moab by the Jordan, *across from* Jericho. 64 But among these there was not a man of those who were numbered by Moses and Aaron the priest when they numbered the children of Israel in the Wilderness of Sinai. 65 For the LORD had said of them, "They shall surely die in the wilderness." So there was not left a man of them, except Caleb the son of Jephunneh and Joshua the son of Nun.

27 Then came the daughters of Zelophehad the son of Hepher, the son of Gilead, the son of Machir, the son of Manasseh, from the families of Manasseh the son of Joseph; and these *were* the names of his daughters: Mahlah, Noah, Hoglah, Milcah, and Tirzah. 2 And they stood before Moses, before Eleazar the priest, and before the leaders and

51 אֵ֣לֶּה חֲמִשָּׁ֥ה וְאַרְבָּעִ֖ים אֶ֑לֶף וְאַרְבַּ֥ע מֵאֽוֹת׃ פְּקוּדֵ֖י בְּנֵ֣י יִשְׂרָאֵ֑ל שֵׁשׁ־מֵא֥וֹת אֶ֛לֶף וָאֶ֖לֶף שְׁבַ֥ע מֵא֖וֹת וּשְׁלֹשִֽׁים׃ פ

52 וַיְדַבֵּ֥ר יְהוָ֖ה אֶל־מֹשֶׁ֥ה לֵּאמֹֽר׃ 53 לָאֵ֗לֶּה תֵּחָלֵ֥ק הָאָ֛רֶץ בְּנַחֲלָ֖ה בְּמִסְפַּ֥ר שֵׁמֽוֹת׃ 54 לָרַ֣ב תַּרְבֶּ֣ה נַחֲלָת֗וֹ וְלַמְעַ֖ט תַּמְעִ֣יט נַחֲלָת֑וֹ אִ֚ישׁ לְפִ֣י פְקֻדָ֔יו יֻתַּ֖ן נַחֲלָתֽוֹ׃ 55 אַךְ־בְּגוֹרָ֕ל יֵחָלֵ֖ק אֶת־הָאָ֑רֶץ לִשְׁמ֥וֹת מַטּוֹת־אֲבֹתָ֖ם יִנְחָֽלוּ׃ 56 עַל־פִּי֙ הַגּוֹרָ֔ל תֵּחָלֵ֖ק נַחֲלָת֑וֹ בֵּ֥ין רַ֖ב לִמְעָֽט׃ ס

57 וְאֵ֨לֶּה֙ פְקוּדֵ֣י הַלֵּוִ֔י לְמִשְׁפְּחֹתָ֑ם לְגֵרְשׁ֗וֹן מִשְׁפַּ֙חַת֙ הַגֵּ֣רְשֻׁנִּ֔י לִקְהָ֕ת מִשְׁפַּ֖חַת הַקְּהָתִ֑י לִמְרָרִ֕י מִשְׁפַּ֖חַת הַמְּרָרִֽי׃ 58 אֵ֣לֶּה ׀ מִשְׁפְּחֹ֣ת לֵוִ֗י מִשְׁפַּ֤חַת הַלִּבְנִי֙ מִשְׁפַּ֣חַת הַֽחֶבְרֹנִ֔י מִשְׁפַּ֙חַת֙ הַמַּחְלִ֔י מִשְׁפַּ֖חַת הַמּוּשִׁ֑י מִשְׁפַּ֖חַת הַקָּרְחִ֑י וּקְהָ֖ת הוֹלִ֥ד אֶת־עַמְרָֽם׃ 59 וְשֵׁ֣ם ׀ אֵ֣שֶׁת עַמְרָ֗ם יוֹכֶ֙בֶד֙ בַּת־לֵוִ֔י אֲשֶׁ֨ר יָלְדָ֥ה אֹתָ֛הּ לְלֵוִ֖י בְּמִצְרָ֑יִם וַתֵּ֣לֶד לְעַמְרָ֗ם אֶֽת־אַהֲרֹן֙ וְאֶת־מֹשֶׁ֔ה וְאֵ֖ת מִרְיָ֥ם אֲחֹתָֽם׃ 60 וַיִּוָּלֵ֣ד לְאַהֲרֹ֔ן אֶת־נָדָ֖ב וְאֶת־אֲבִיה֑וּא אֶת־אֶלְעָזָ֖ר וְאֶת־אִֽיתָמָֽר׃ 61 וַיָּ֣מָת נָדָ֖ב וַאֲבִיה֑וּא בְּהַקְרִיבָ֥ם אֵשׁ־זָרָ֖ה לִפְנֵ֥י יְהוָֽה׃ 62 וַיִּהְי֣וּ פְקֻדֵיהֶ֗ם שְׁלֹשָׁ֤ה וְעֶשְׂרִים֙ אֶ֔לֶף כָּל־זָכָ֖ר מִבֶּן־חֹ֣דֶשׁ וָמָ֑עְלָה כִּ֣י ׀ לֹ֣א הָתְפָּֽקְד֗וּ בְּתוֹךְ֙ בְּנֵ֣י יִשְׂרָאֵ֔ל כִּ֠י לֹא־נִתַּ֤ן לָהֶם֙ נַחֲלָ֔ה בְּת֖וֹךְ בְּנֵ֥י יִשְׂרָאֵֽל׃ 63 אֵ֚לֶּה פְּקוּדֵ֣י מֹשֶׁ֔ה וְאֶלְעָזָ֖ר הַכֹּהֵ֑ן אֲשֶׁ֣ר פָּֽקְד֗וּ אֶת־בְּנֵ֤י יִשְׂרָאֵל֙ בְּעַֽרְבֹ֣ת מוֹאָ֔ב עַ֖ל יַרְדֵּ֥ן יְרֵחֽוֹ׃ 64 וּבְאֵ֙לֶּה֙ לֹא־הָ֣יָה אִ֔ישׁ מִפְּקוּדֵ֖י מֹשֶׁ֣ה וְאַהֲרֹ֣ן הַכֹּהֵ֑ן אֲשֶׁ֥ר פָּֽקְד֛וּ אֶת־בְּנֵ֥י יִשְׂרָאֵ֖ל בְּמִדְבַּ֥ר סִינָֽי׃ 65 כִּֽי־אָמַ֤ר יְהוָה֙ לָהֶ֔ם מ֥וֹת יָמֻ֖תוּ בַּמִּדְבָּ֑ר וְלֹא־נוֹתַ֤ר מֵהֶם֙ אִ֔ישׁ כִּ֚י אִם־כָּלֵ֣ב בֶּן־יְפֻנֶּ֔ה וִיהוֹשֻׁ֖עַ בִּן־נֽוּן׃ ס

כז וַתִּקְרַ֜בְנָה בְּנ֣וֹת צְלָפְחָ֗ד בֶּן־חֵ֤פֶר בֶּן־גִּלְעָד֙ בֶּן־מָכִ֣יר בֶּן־מְנַשֶּׁ֔ה לְמִשְׁפְּחֹ֖ת מְנַשֶּׁ֣ה בֶן־יוֹסֵ֑ף וְאֵ֙לֶּה֙ שְׁמ֣וֹת בְּנֹתָ֔יו מַחְלָ֣ה נֹעָ֔ה וְחָגְלָ֥ה וּמִלְכָּ֖ה וְתִרְצָֽה׃ 2 וַֽתַּעֲמֹ֜דְנָה לִפְנֵ֣י מֹשֶׁ֗ה וְלִפְנֵי֙ אֶלְעָזָ֣ר הַכֹּהֵ֔ן וְלִפְנֵ֥י הַנְּשִׂיאִ֖ם וְכָל־הָעֵדָ֑ה פֶּ֥תַח אֹֽהֶל־מוֹעֵ֖ד לֵאמֹֽר׃

all the congregation, *by* the doorway of the tabernacle of meeting, saying: ³"Our father died in the wilderness; but he was not in the company of those who gathered together against the LORD, in company with Korah, but he died in his own sin; and he had no sons. ⁴Why should the name of our father be removed from among his family because he had no son? Give us a possession among our father's brothers. "

⁵So Moses brought their case before the LORD.

⁶And the LORD spoke to Moses, saying: ⁷"The daughters of Zelophehad speak *what is* right; you shall surely give them a possession of inheritance among their father's brothers, and cause the inheritance of their father to pass to them. ⁸And you shall speak to the children of Israel, saying: 'If a man dies and has no son, then you shall cause his inheritance to pass to his daughter. ⁹If he has no daughter, then you shall give his inheritance to his brothers. ¹⁰If he has no brothers, then you shall give his inheritance to his father's brothers. ¹¹And if his father has no brothers, then you shall give his inheritance to the relative closest to him in his family, and he shall possess it.'" And it shall be to the children of Israel a statute of judgment, just as the LORD commanded Moses.

¹²Now the LORD said to Moses: "Go up into this Mount Abarim, and see the land which I have given to the children of Israel. ¹³And when you have seen it, you also shall be gathered to your people, as Aaron your brother was gathered. ¹⁴For in the Wilderness of Zin, during the strife of the congregation, you rebelled against My command to hallow Me at the waters before their eyes." (These *are* the waters of Meribah, at Kadesh in the Wilderness of Zin.)

¹⁵Then Moses spoke to the LORD, saying: ¹⁶"Let the LORD, the God of the spirits of all flesh, set a man over the congregation, ¹⁷who may go out before them and go in before them, who may lead them out and bring them in, that the congregation of the LORD may not be like sheep which have no shepherd."

¹⁸And the LORD said to Moses: "Take Joshua the son of Nun with you, a man in whom *is* the Spirit, and lay your hand on him; ¹⁹set him before Eleazar the priest and before all the congregation, and inaugurate him in their sight. ²⁰And you shall give *some* of your authority to him, that all the congregation of the children of Israel may be obedient. ²¹He shall stand before Eleazar the priest, who shall inquire before the LORD for him by the judgment of the Urim. At his word they shall go

3 אָבִינוּ מֵת בַּמִּדְבָּר וְהוּא לֹא־הָיָה בְּתוֹךְ הָעֵדָה הַנּוֹעָדִים עַל־יְהוָה בַּעֲדַת־קֹרַח כִּי־בְחֶטְאוֹ מֵת וּבָנִים לֹא־הָיוּ לוֹ: 4 לָמָּה יִגָּרַע שֵׁם־אָבִינוּ מִתּוֹךְ מִשְׁפַּחְתּוֹ כִּי אֵין לוֹ בֵּן תְּנָה־לָּנוּ אֲחֻזָּה בְּתוֹךְ אֲחֵי אָבִינוּ: 5 וַיַּקְרֵב מֹשֶׁה אֶת־מִשְׁפָּטָן לִפְנֵי יְהוָה: ס 6 וַיֹּאמֶר יְהוָה אֶל־מֹשֶׁה לֵּאמֹר: 7 כֵּן בְּנוֹת צְלָפְחָד דֹּבְרֹת נָתֹן תִּתֵּן לָהֶם אֲחֻזַּת נַחֲלָה בְּתוֹךְ אֲחֵי אֲבִיהֶם וְהַעֲבַרְתָּ אֶת־נַחֲלַת אֲבִיהֶן לָהֶן: 8 וְאֶל־בְּנֵי יִשְׂרָאֵל תְּדַבֵּר לֵאמֹר אִישׁ כִּי־יָמוּת וּבֵן אֵין לוֹ וְהַעֲבַרְתֶּם אֶת־נַחֲלָתוֹ לְבִתּוֹ: 9 וְאִם־אֵין לוֹ בַּת וּנְתַתֶּם אֶת־נַחֲלָתוֹ לְאֶחָיו: 10 וְאִם־אֵין לוֹ אַחִים וּנְתַתֶּם אֶת־נַחֲלָתוֹ לַאֲחֵי אָבִיו: 11 וְאִם־אֵין אַחִים לְאָבִיו וּנְתַתֶּם אֶת־נַחֲלָתוֹ לִשְׁאֵרוֹ הַקָּרֹב אֵלָיו מִמִּשְׁפַּחְתּוֹ וְיָרַשׁ אֹתָהּ וְהָיְתָה לִבְנֵי יִשְׂרָאֵל לְחֻקַּת מִשְׁפָּט כַּאֲשֶׁר צִוָּה יְהוָה אֶת־מֹשֶׁה: ס 12 וַיֹּאמֶר יְהוָה אֶל־מֹשֶׁה עֲלֵה אֶל־הַר הָעֲבָרִים הַזֶּה וּרְאֵה אֶת־הָאָרֶץ אֲשֶׁר נָתַתִּי לִבְנֵי יִשְׂרָאֵל: 13 וְרָאִיתָה אֹתָהּ וְנֶאֱסַפְתָּ אֶל־עַמֶּיךָ גַּם־אָתָּה כַּאֲשֶׁר נֶאֱסַף אַהֲרֹן אָחִיךָ: 14 כַּאֲשֶׁר מְרִיתֶם פִּי בְּמִדְבַּר־צִן בִּמְרִיבַת הָעֵדָה לְהַקְדִּישֵׁנִי בַמַּיִם לְעֵינֵיהֶם הֵם מֵי־מְרִיבַת קָדֵשׁ מִדְבַּר־צִן: פ

15 וַיְדַבֵּר מֹשֶׁה אֶל־יְהוָה לֵאמֹר: 16 יִפְקֹד יְהוָה אֱלֹהֵי הָרוּחֹת לְכָל־בָּשָׂר אִישׁ עַל־הָעֵדָה: 17 אֲשֶׁר־יֵצֵא לִפְנֵיהֶם וַאֲשֶׁר יָבֹא לִפְנֵיהֶם וַאֲשֶׁר יוֹצִיאֵם וַאֲשֶׁר יְבִיאֵם וְלֹא תִהְיֶה עֲדַת יְהוָה כַּצֹּאן אֲשֶׁר אֵין־לָהֶם רֹעֶה: 18 וַיֹּאמֶר יְהוָה אֶל־מֹשֶׁה קַח־לְךָ אֶת־יְהוֹשֻׁעַ בִּן־נוּן אִישׁ אֲשֶׁר־רוּחַ בּוֹ וְסָמַכְתָּ אֶת־יָדְךָ עָלָיו: 19 וְהַעֲמַדְתָּ אֹתוֹ לִפְנֵי אֶלְעָזָר הַכֹּהֵן וְלִפְנֵי כָּל־הָעֵדָה וְצִוִּיתָה אֹתוֹ לְעֵינֵיהֶם: 20 וְנָתַתָּה מֵהוֹדְךָ עָלָיו לְמַעַן יִשְׁמְעוּ כָּל־עֲדַת בְּנֵי יִשְׂרָאֵל: 21 וְלִפְנֵי אֶלְעָזָר הַכֹּהֵן יַעֲמֹד וְשָׁאַל לוֹ בְּמִשְׁפַּט הָאוּרִים לִפְנֵי יְהוָה עַל־פִּיו יֵצְאוּ וְעַל־פִּיו יָבֹאוּ

out, and at his word they shall come in, he and all
the children of Israel with him—all the congregation."

22 So Moses did as the LORD commanded him.
He took Joshua and set him before Eleazar the
priest and before all the congregation. 23 And he
laid his hands on him and inaugurated him, just as
the LORD commanded by the hand of Moses.

28 Now the LORD spoke to Moses, saying,
2 "Command the children of Israel, and say to
them, 'My offering, My food for My offerings made
by fire as a sweet aroma to Me, you shall be careful
to offer to Me at their appointed time.'

3 "And you shall say to them, 'This is the offering
made by fire which you shall offer to the LORD: two
male lambs in their first year without blemish, day
by day, as a regular burnt offering. 4 The one lamb
you shall offer in the morning, the other lamb you
shall offer in the evening, 5 and one-tenth of an
ephah of fine flour as a grain offering mixed with
one-fourth of a hin of pressed oil. 6 It is a regular
burnt offering which was ordained at Mount Sinai
for a sweet aroma, an offering made by fire to the
LORD. 7 And its drink offering shall be one-fourth of
a hin for each lamb; in a holy place you shall pour
out the drink to the LORD as an offering. 8 The
other lamb you shall offer in the evening; as the
morning grain offering and its drink offering, you
shall offer it as an offering made by fire, a sweet
aroma to the LORD.

9 'And on the Sabbath day two lambs in their first
year, without blemish, and two-tenths of an ephah
of fine flour as a grain offering, mixed with oil, with
its drink offering— 10 this is the burnt offering for
every Sabbath, besides the regular burnt offering
with its drink offering.

11 'At the beginnings of your months you shall
present a burnt offering to the LORD: two young
bulls, one ram, and seven lambs in their first year,
without blemish; 12 three-tenths of an ephah of fine
flour as a grain offering, mixed with oil, for each
bull; two-tenths of an ephah of fine flour as a grain
offering, mixed with oil, for the one ram; 13 and one-
tenth of an ephah of fine flour, mixed with oil, as a
grain offering for each lamb, as a burnt offering of
sweet aroma, an offering made by fire to the LORD.
14 Their drink offering shall be half a hin of wine for
a bull, one-third of a hin for a ram, and one-fourth
of a hin for a lamb; this is the burnt offering for
each month throughout the months of the year.
15 Also one kid of the goats as a sin offering to the
LORD shall be offered, besides the regular burnt
offering and its drink offering.

הוּא וְכָל־בְּנֵי־יִשְׂרָאֵל אִתּוֹ וְכָל־הָעֵדָה: 22 וַיַּעַשׂ
מֹשֶׁה כַּאֲשֶׁר צִוָּה יְהוָה אֹתוֹ וַיִּקַּח אֶת־יְהוֹשֻׁעַ
וַיַּעֲמִדֵהוּ לִפְנֵי אֶלְעָזָר הַכֹּהֵן וְלִפְנֵי כָּל־הָעֵדָה:
23 וַיִּסְמֹךְ אֶת־יָדָיו עָלָיו וַיְצַוֵּהוּ כַּאֲשֶׁר דִּבֶּר יְהוָה
בְּיַד־מֹשֶׁה:
פ

כח וַיְדַבֵּר יְהוָה אֶל־מֹשֶׁה לֵּאמֹר: 2 צַו אֶת־בְּנֵי
יִשְׂרָאֵל וְאָמַרְתָּ אֲלֵהֶם אֶת־קָרְבָּנִי לַחְמִי לְאִשַּׁי
רֵיחַ נִיחֹחִי תִּשְׁמְרוּ לְהַקְרִיב לִי בְּמוֹעֲדוֹ: 3 וְאָמַרְתָּ
לָהֶם זֶה הָאִשֶּׁה אֲשֶׁר תַּקְרִיבוּ לַיהוָה כְּבָשִׂים
בְּנֵי־שָׁנָה תְמִימִם שְׁנַיִם לַיּוֹם עֹלָה תָמִיד: 4 אֶת־
הַכֶּבֶשׂ אֶחָד תַּעֲשֶׂה בַבֹּקֶר וְאֵת הַכֶּבֶשׂ הַשֵּׁנִי
תַּעֲשֶׂה בֵּין הָעַרְבָּיִם: 5 וַעֲשִׂירִית הָאֵיפָה סֹלֶת
לְמִנְחָה בְּלוּלָה בְּשֶׁמֶן כָּתִית רְבִיעִת הַהִין: 6 עֹלַת
תָּמִיד הָעֲשֻׂיָה בְּהַר סִינַי לְרֵיחַ נִיחֹחַ אִשֶּׁה לַיהוָה:
7 וְנִסְכּוֹ רְבִיעִת הַהִין לַכֶּבֶשׂ הָאֶחָד בַּקֹּדֶשׁ הַסֵּךְ
נֶסֶךְ שֵׁכָר לַיהוָה: 8 וְאֵת הַכֶּבֶשׂ הַשֵּׁנִי תַּעֲשֶׂה בֵּין
הָעַרְבָּיִם כְּמִנְחַת הַבֹּקֶר וּכְנִסְכּוֹ תַּעֲשֶׂה אִשֶּׁה רֵיחַ
נִיחֹחַ לַיהוָה:
פ

9 וּבְיוֹם הַשַּׁבָּת שְׁנֵי־כְבָשִׂים בְּנֵי־שָׁנָה תְּמִימִם
וּשְׁנֵי עֶשְׂרֹנִים סֹלֶת מִנְחָה בְּלוּלָה בַשֶּׁמֶן וְנִסְכּוֹ:
10 עֹלַת שַׁבַּת בְּשַׁבַּתּוֹ עַל־עֹלַת הַתָּמִיד וְנִסְכָּהּ:
11 וּבְרָאשֵׁי חָדְשֵׁיכֶם תַּקְרִיבוּ עֹלָה   ס
לַיהוָה פָּרִים בְּנֵי־בָקָר שְׁנַיִם וְאַיִל אֶחָד כְּבָשִׂים
בְּנֵי־שָׁנָה שִׁבְעָה תְּמִימִם: 12 וּשְׁלֹשָׁה עֶשְׂרֹנִים
סֹלֶת מִנְחָה בְּלוּלָה בַשֶּׁמֶן לַפָּר הָאֶחָד וּשְׁנֵי
עֶשְׂרֹנִים סֹלֶת מִנְחָה בְּלוּלָה בַשֶּׁמֶן לָאַיִל הָאֶחָד:
13 וְעִשָּׂרֹן עִשָּׂרוֹן סֹלֶת מִנְחָה בְּלוּלָה בַשֶּׁמֶן לַכֶּבֶשׂ
הָאֶחָד עֹלָה רֵיחַ נִיחֹחַ אִשֶּׁה לַיהוָה: 14 וְנִסְכֵּיהֶם
חֲצִי הַהִין יִהְיֶה לַפָּר וּשְׁלִישִׁת הַהִין לָאַיִל וּרְבִיעִת
הַהִין לַכֶּבֶשׂ יָיִן זֹאת עֹלַת חֹדֶשׁ בְּחָדְשׁוֹ לְחָדְשֵׁי
הַשָּׁנָה: 15 וּשְׂעִיר עִזִּים אֶחָד לְחַטָּאת

16 'On the fourteenth day of the first month *is* the Passover of the LORD. 17 And on the fifteenth day of this month *is* the feast; unleavened bread shall be eaten for seven days. 18 On the first day *you shall have* a holy convocation. You shall do no customary work. 19 And you shall present an offering made by fire as a burnt offering to the LORD: two young bulls, one ram, and seven lambs in their first year. Be sure they are without blemish. 20 Their grain offering shall be of fine flour mixed with oil: three-tenths *of an ephah* you shall offer for a bull, and two-tenths for a ram; 21 you shall offer one-tenth *of an ephah* for each of the seven lambs; 22 also one goat *as* a sin offering, to make atonement for you. 23 You shall offer these besides the burnt offering of the morning, which *is* for a regular burnt offering. 24 In this manner you shall offer the food of the offering made by fire daily for seven days, as a sweet aroma to the LORD; it shall be offered besides the regular burnt offering and its drink offering. 25 And on the seventh day you shall have a holy convocation. You shall do no customary work.

26 'Also on the day of the firstfruits, when you bring a new grain offering to the LORD at your *Feast of* Weeks, you shall have a holy convocation. You shall do no customary work. 27 You shall present a burnt offering as a sweet aroma to the LORD: two young bulls, one ram, and seven lambs in their first year, 28 with their grain offering of fine flour mixed with oil: three-tenths *of an ephah* for each bull, two-tenths for the one ram, 29 and one-tenth for each of the seven lambs; 30 *also* one kid of the goats, to make atonement for you. 31 Be sure they are without blemish. You shall present *them* with their drink offerings, besides the regular burnt offering with its grain offering.

29

'And in the seventh month, on the first *day* of the month, you shall have a holy convocation. You shall do no customary work. For you it is a day of blowing the trumpets. 2 You shall offer a burnt offering as a sweet aroma to the LORD: one young bull, one ram, *and* seven lambs in their first year, without blemish. 3 Their grain offering *shall be* fine flour mixed with oil: three-tenths *of an ephah* for the bull, two-tenths for the ram, 4 and one-tenth for each of the seven lambs; 5 also one kid of the goats *as* a sin offering, to make atonement for you; 6 besides the burnt offering with its grain offering for the New Moon, the regular burnt offering with its grain offering, and their drink offerings, according to their ordinance, as a sweet aroma, an offering made by fire to the LORD.

16 וּבַחֹדֶשׁ לַיהוָה עַל־עֹלַת הַתָּמִיד יֵעָשֶׂה וְנִסְכּוֹ: הָרִאשׁוֹן בְּאַרְבָּעָה עָשָׂר יוֹם לַחֹדֶשׁ פֶּסַח לַיהוָה: 17 וּבַחֲמִשָּׁה עָשָׂר יוֹם לַחֹדֶשׁ הַזֶּה חָג שִׁבְעַת יָמִים מַצּוֹת יֵאָכֵל: 18 בַּיּוֹם הָרִאשׁוֹן מִקְרָא־קֹדֶשׁ כָּל־מְלֶאכֶת עֲבֹדָה לֹא תַעֲשׂוּ: 19 וְהִקְרַבְתֶּם אִשֶּׁה עֹלָה לַיהוָה פָּרִים בְּנֵי־בָקָר שְׁנַיִם וְאַיִל אֶחָד וְשִׁבְעָה כְבָשִׂים בְּנֵי שָׁנָה תְּמִימִם יִהְיוּ לָכֶם: 20 וּמִנְחָתָם סֹלֶת בְּלוּלָה בַשָּׁמֶן שְׁלֹשָׁה עֶשְׂרֹנִים לַפָּר וּשְׁנֵי עֶשְׂרֹנִים לָאַיִל תַּעֲשׂוּ: 21 עִשָּׂרוֹן עִשָּׂרוֹן תַּעֲשֶׂה לַכֶּבֶשׂ הָאֶחָד לְשִׁבְעַת הַכְּבָשִׂים: 22 וּשְׂעִיר חַטָּאת אֶחָד לְכַפֵּר עֲלֵיכֶם: 23 מִלְּבַד עֹלַת הַבֹּקֶר אֲשֶׁר לְעֹלַת הַתָּמִיד תַּעֲשׂוּ אֶת־אֵלֶּה: 24 כָּאֵלֶּה תַּעֲשׂוּ לַיּוֹם שִׁבְעַת יָמִים לֶחֶם אִשֵּׁה רֵיחַ־נִיחֹחַ לַיהוָה עַל־עוֹלַת הַתָּמִיד יֵעָשֶׂה וְנִסְכּוֹ: 25 וּבַיּוֹם הַשְּׁבִיעִי מִקְרָא־קֹדֶשׁ יִהְיֶה לָכֶם כָּל־מְלֶאכֶת עֲבֹדָה לֹא תַעֲשׂוּ: ס 26 וּבְיוֹם הַבִּכּוּרִים בְּהַקְרִיבְכֶם מִנְחָה חֲדָשָׁה לַיהוָה בְּשָׁבֻעֹתֵיכֶם מִקְרָא־קֹדֶשׁ יִהְיֶה לָכֶם כָּל־מְלֶאכֶת עֲבֹדָה לֹא תַעֲשׂוּ: 27 וְהִקְרַבְתֶּם עוֹלָה לְרֵיחַ נִיחֹחַ לַיהוָה פָּרִים בְּנֵי־בָקָר שְׁנַיִם אַיִל אֶחָד שִׁבְעָה כְבָשִׂים בְּנֵי שָׁנָה: 28 וּמִנְחָתָם סֹלֶת בְּלוּלָה בַשֶּׁמֶן שְׁלֹשָׁה עֶשְׂרֹנִים לַפָּר הָאֶחָד שְׁנֵי עֶשְׂרֹנִים לָאַיִל הָאֶחָד: 29 עִשָּׂרוֹן עִשָּׂרוֹן לַכֶּבֶשׂ הָאֶחָד לְשִׁבְעַת הַכְּבָשִׂים: 30 שְׂעִיר עִזִּים אֶחָד לְכַפֵּר עֲלֵיכֶם: 31 מִלְּבַד עֹלַת הַתָּמִיד וּמִנְחָתוֹ תַּעֲשׂוּ תְּמִימִם יִהְיוּ־לָכֶם וְנִסְכֵּיהֶם: פ

כט וּבַחֹדֶשׁ הַשְּׁבִיעִי בְּאֶחָד לַחֹדֶשׁ מִקְרָא־ קֹדֶשׁ יִהְיֶה לָכֶם כָּל־מְלֶאכֶת עֲבֹדָה לֹא תַעֲשׂוּ יוֹם תְּרוּעָה יִהְיֶה לָכֶם: 2 וַעֲשִׂיתֶם עֹלָה לְרֵיחַ נִיחֹחַ לַיהוָה פַּר בֶּן־בָּקָר אֶחָד אַיִל אֶחָד כְּבָשִׂים בְּנֵי־שָׁנָה שִׁבְעָה תְּמִימִם: 3 וּמִנְחָתָם סֹלֶת בְּלוּלָה בַשֶּׁמֶן שְׁלֹשָׁה עֶשְׂרֹנִים לַפָּר שְׁנֵי עֶשְׂרֹנִים לָאָיִל: 4 וְעִשָּׂרוֹן אֶחָד לַכֶּבֶשׂ הָאֶחָד לְשִׁבְעַת הַכְּבָשִׂים: 5 וּשְׂעִיר־עִזִּים אֶחָד חַטָּאת לְכַפֵּר עֲלֵיכֶם: 6 מִלְּבַד עֹלַת הַחֹדֶשׁ וּמִנְחָתָהּ וְעֹלַת הַתָּמִיד וּמִנְחָתָהּ וְנִסְכֵּיהֶם כְּמִשְׁפָּטָם לְרֵיחַ

7 'On the tenth *day* of this seventh month you shall have a holy convocation. You shall afflict your souls; you shall not do any work. 8 You shall present a burnt offering to the LORD *as* a sweet aroma: one young bull, one ram, *and* seven lambs in their first year. Be sure they are without blemish. 9 Their grain offering *shall be of* fine flour mixed with oil: three-tenths *of an ephah* for the bull, two-tenths for the one ram, 10 and one-tenth for each of the seven lambs; 11 also one kid of the goats *as* a sin offering, besides the sin offering for atonement, the regular burnt offering with its grain offering, and their drink offerings.

12 'On the fifteenth day of the seventh month you shall have a holy convocation. You shall do no customary work, and you shall keep a feast to the LORD seven days. 13 You shall present a burnt offering, an offering made by fire as a sweet aroma to the LORD: thirteen young bulls, two rams, *and* fourteen lambs in their first year. They shall be without blemish. 14 Their grain offering *shall be of* fine flour mixed with oil: three-tenths *of an ephah* for each of the thirteen bulls, two-tenths for each of the two rams, 15 and one-tenth for each of the fourteen lambs; 16 also one kid of the goats *as* a sin offering, besides the regular burnt offering, its grain offering, and its drink offering.

17 'On the second day *present* twelve young bulls, two rams, fourteen lambs in their first year without blemish, 18 and their grain offering and their drink offerings for the bulls, for the rams, and for the lambs, by their number, according to the ordinance; 19 also one kid of the goats *as* a sin offering, besides the regular burnt offering with its grain offering, and their drink offerings.

20 'On the third day *present* eleven bulls, two rams, fourteen lambs in their first year without blemish, 21 and their grain offering and their drink offerings for the bulls, for the rams, and for the lambs, by their number, according to the ordinance; 22 also one goat *as* a sin offering, besides the regular burnt offering, its grain offering, and its drink offering.

23 'On the fourth day *present* ten bulls, two rams, *and* fourteen lambs in their first year, without blemish, 24 and their grain offering and their drink offerings for the bulls, for the rams, and for the lambs, by their number, according to the ordinance; 25 also one kid of the goats *as* a sin offering, besides the regular burnt offering, its grain offering, and its drink offering.

26 'On the fifth day *present* nine bulls, two rams, *and* fourteen lambs in their first year without blemish, 27 and their grain offering and their drink

7 וּבֶעָשׂוֹר לַחֹדֶשׁ ס נִיחֹחַ אִשֶּׁה לַיהֹוָה׃
הַשְּׁבִיעִי הַזֶּה מִקְרָא־קֹדֶשׁ יִהְיֶה לָכֶם וְעִנִּיתֶם אֶת־נַפְשֹׁתֵיכֶם כָּל־מְלָאכָה לֹא תַעֲשׂוּ׃ 8 וְהִקְרַבְתֶּם
עֹלָה לַיהֹוָה רֵיחַ נִיחֹחַ פַּר בֶּן־בָּקָר אֶחָד אַיִל
אֶחָד כְּבָשִׂים בְּנֵי־שָׁנָה שִׁבְעָה תְּמִימִם יִהְיוּ לָכֶם׃
9 וּמִנְחָתָם סֹלֶת בְּלוּלָה בַשֶּׁמֶן שְׁלֹשָׁה עֶשְׂרֹנִים
לַפָּר שְׁנֵי עֶשְׂרֹנִים לָאַיִל הָאֶחָד׃ 10 עִשָּׂרוֹן עִשָּׂרוֹן
לַכֶּבֶשׂ הָאֶחָד לְשִׁבְעַת הַכְּבָשִׂים׃ 11 שְׂעִיר־עִזִּים
אֶחָד חַטָּאת מִלְּבַד חַטַּאת הַכִּפֻּרִים וְעֹלַת הַתָּמִיד
וּמִנְחָתָהּ וְנִסְכֵּיהֶם׃ פ

12 וּבַחֲמִשָּׁה עָשָׂר יוֹם לַחֹדֶשׁ הַשְּׁבִיעִי מִקְרָא־קֹדֶשׁ יִהְיֶה לָכֶם כָּל־מְלֶאכֶת עֲבֹדָה לֹא תַעֲשׂוּ
וְחַגֹּתֶם חַג לַיהֹוָה שִׁבְעַת יָמִים׃ 13 וְהִקְרַבְתֶּם
עֹלָה אִשֵּׁה רֵיחַ נִיחֹחַ לַיהֹוָה פָּרִים בְּנֵי־בָקָר שְׁלֹשָׁה עָשָׂר אֵילִם שְׁנָיִם כְּבָשִׂים בְּנֵי־שָׁנָה אַרְבָּעָה עָשָׂר תְּמִימִם יִהְיוּ׃ 14 וּמִנְחָתָם
סֹלֶת בְּלוּלָה בַשֶּׁמֶן שְׁלֹשָׁה עֶשְׂרֹנִים לַפָּר
הָאֶחָד לִשְׁלֹשָׁה עָשָׂר פָּרִים שְׁנֵי עֶשְׂרֹנִים לָאַיִל
הָאֶחָד לִשְׁנֵי הָאֵילִם׃ 15 וְעִשָּׂרוֹן עִשָּׂרוֹן לַכֶּבֶשׂ
הָאֶחָד לְאַרְבָּעָה עָשָׂר כְּבָשִׂים׃ 16 וּשְׂעִיר־עִזִּים
אֶחָד חַטָּאת מִלְּבַד עֹלַת הַתָּמִיד מִנְחָתָהּ
וְנִסְכָּהּ׃ ס 17 וּבַיּוֹם הַשֵּׁנִי פָּרִים בְּנֵי־בָקָר שְׁנֵים עָשָׂר אֵילִם שְׁנָיִם כְּבָשִׂים בְּנֵי־שָׁנָה אַרְבָּעָה עָשָׂר תְּמִימִם׃ 18 וּמִנְחָתָם וְנִסְכֵּיהֶם
לַפָּרִים לָאֵילִם וְלַכְּבָשִׂים בְּמִסְפָּרָם כַּמִּשְׁפָּט׃
19 וּשְׂעִיר־עִזִּים אֶחָד חַטָּאת מִלְּבַד עֹלַת הַתָּמִיד
וּמִנְחָתָהּ וְנִסְכֵּיהֶם׃ ס 20 וּבַיּוֹם הַשְּׁלִישִׁי
פָּרִים עַשְׁתֵּי־עָשָׂר אֵילִם שְׁנָיִם כְּבָשִׂים בְּנֵי־שָׁנָה אַרְבָּעָה עָשָׂר תְּמִימִם׃ 21 וּמִנְחָתָם וְנִסְכֵּיהֶם
לַפָּרִים לָאֵילִם וְלַכְּבָשִׂים בְּמִסְפָּרָם כַּמִּשְׁפָּט׃
22 וּשְׂעִיר חַטָּאת אֶחָד מִלְּבַד עֹלַת הַתָּמִיד
וּמִנְחָתָהּ וְנִסְכָּהּ׃ ס 23 וּבַיּוֹם הָרְבִיעִי
פָּרִים עֲשָׂרָה אֵילִם שְׁנָיִם כְּבָשִׂים בְּנֵי־שָׁנָה
אַרְבָּעָה עָשָׂר תְּמִימִם׃ 24 מִנְחָתָם וְנִסְכֵּיהֶם
לַפָּרִים לָאֵילִם וְלַכְּבָשִׂים בְּמִסְפָּרָם כַּמִּשְׁפָּט׃
25 וּשְׂעִיר־עִזִּים אֶחָד חַטָּאת מִלְּבַד עֹלַת הַתָּמִיד
מִנְחָתָהּ וְנִסְכָּהּ׃ ס 26 וּבַיּוֹם הַחֲמִישִׁי
פָּרִים תִּשְׁעָה אֵילִם שְׁנָיִם כְּבָשִׂים בְּנֵי־שָׁנָה
אַרְבָּעָה עָשָׂר תְּמִימִם׃ 27 וּמִנְחָתָם וְנִסְכֵּיהֶם

offerings for the bulls, for the rams, and for the lambs, by their number, according to the ordinance; 28 also one goat *as* a sin offering, besides the regular burnt offering, its grain offering, and its drink offering.

29 'On the sixth day *present* eight bulls, two rams, *and* fourteen lambs in their first year without blemish, 30 and their grain offering and their drink offerings for the bulls, for the rams, and for the lambs, by their number, according to the ordinance; 31 also one goat *as* a sin offering, besides the regular burnt offering, its grain offering, and its drink offering.

32 'On the seventh day *present* seven bulls, two rams, *and* fourteen lambs in their first year without blemish, 33 and their grain offering and their drink offerings for the bulls, for the rams, and for the lambs, by their number, according to the ordinance; 34 also one goat *as* a sin offering, besides the regular burnt offering, its grain offering, and its drink offering.

35 'On the eighth day you shall have a sacred assembly. You shall do no customary work. 36 You shall present a burnt offering, an offering made by fire as a sweet aroma to the LORD: one bull, one ram, seven lambs in their first year without blemish, 37 and their grain offering and their drink offerings for the bull, for the ram, and for the lambs, by their number, according to the ordinance; 38 also one goat *as* a sin offering, besides the regular burnt offering, its grain offering, and its drink offering.

39 'These you shall present to the LORD at your appointed feasts (besides your vowed offerings and your freewill offerings) as your burnt offerings and your grain offerings, as your drink offerings and your peace offerings.' "

40 So Moses told the children of Israel everything, just as the LORD commanded Moses.

30 Then Moses spoke to the heads of the tribes concerning the children of Israel, saying, "This *is* the thing which the LORD has commanded: 2 If a man makes a vow to the LORD, or swears an oath to bind himself by some agreement, he shall not break his word; he shall do according to all that proceeds out of his mouth.

3 "Or if a woman makes a vow to the LORD, and binds *herself* by some agreement while in her father's house in her youth, 4 and her father hears her vow and the agreement by which she has bound herself, and her father holds his peace, then all her vows shall stand, and every agreement with which she has bound herself shall stand. 5 But if her father overrules her on the day that he hears, then none of

לַפָּרִים לָאֵילִם וְלַכְּבָשִׂים בְּמִסְפָּרָם כַּמִּשְׁפָּט: 28 וּשְׂעִיר חַטָּאת אֶחָד מִלְּבַד עֹלַת הַתָּמִיד וּמִנְחָתָהּ וְנִסְכָּהּ: ס 29 וּבַיּוֹם הַשִּׁשִּׁי פָרִים שְׁמֹנָה אֵילִם שְׁנָיִם כְּבָשִׂים בְּנֵי־שָׁנָה אַרְבָּעָה עָשָׂר תְּמִימִם: 30 וּמִנְחָתָם וְנִסְכֵּיהֶם לַפָּרִים לָאֵילִם וְלַכְּבָשִׂים בְּמִסְפָּרָם כַּמִּשְׁפָּט: 31 וּשְׂעִיר חַטָּאת אֶחָד מִלְּבַד עֹלַת הַתָּמִיד מִנְחָתָהּ וּנְסָכֶיהָ: פ

32 וּבַיּוֹם הַשְּׁבִיעִי פָרִים שִׁבְעָה אֵילִם שְׁנָיִם כְּבָשִׂים בְּנֵי־שָׁנָה אַרְבָּעָה עָשָׂר תְּמִימִם: 33 וּמִנְחָתָם וְנִסְכֵּהֶם לַפָּרִים לָאֵילִם וְלַכְּבָשִׂים בְּמִסְפָּרָם כְּמִשְׁפָּטָם: 34 וּשְׂעִיר חַטָּאת אֶחָד מִלְּבַד עֹלַת הַתָּמִיד מִנְחָתָהּ וְנִסְכָּהּ: פ

35 בַּיּוֹם הַשְּׁמִינִי עֲצֶרֶת תִּהְיֶה לָכֶם כָּל־מְלֶאכֶת עֲבֹדָה לֹא תַעֲשׂוּ: 36 וְהִקְרַבְתֶּם עֹלָה אִשֵּׁה רֵיחַ נִיחֹחַ לַיהֹוָה פַּר אֶחָד אַיִל אֶחָד כְּבָשִׂים בְּנֵי־שָׁנָה שִׁבְעָה תְּמִימִם: 37 מִנְחָתָם וְנִסְכֵּיהֶם לַפָּר לָאַיִל וְלַכְּבָשִׂים בְּמִסְפָּרָם כַּמִּשְׁפָּט: 38 וּשְׂעִיר חַטָּאת אֶחָד מִלְּבַד עֹלַת הַתָּמִיד וּמִנְחָתָהּ וְנִסְכָּהּ: 39 אֵלֶּה תַּעֲשׂוּ לַיהֹוָה בְּמוֹעֲדֵיכֶם לְבַד מִנִּדְרֵיכֶם וְנִדְבֹתֵיכֶם לְעֹלֹתֵיכֶם וּלְמִנְחֹתֵיכֶם וּלְנִסְכֵּיכֶם וּלְשַׁלְמֵיכֶם:

ל וַיֹּאמֶר מֹשֶׁה אֶל־בְּנֵי יִשְׂרָאֵל כְּכֹל אֲשֶׁר־צִוָּה יְהֹוָה אֶת־מֹשֶׁה: פ

2 וַיְדַבֵּר מֹשֶׁה אֶל־רָאשֵׁי הַמַּטּוֹת לִבְנֵי יִשְׂרָאֵל לֵאמֹר זֶה הַדָּבָר אֲשֶׁר צִוָּה יְהֹוָה: 3 אִישׁ כִּי־יִדֹּר נֶדֶר לַיהֹוָה אוֹ־הִשָּׁבַע שְׁבֻעָה לֶאְסֹר אִסָּר עַל־נַפְשׁוֹ לֹא יַחֵל דְּבָרוֹ כְּכָל־הַיֹּצֵא מִפִּיו יַעֲשֶׂה: 4 וְאִשָּׁה כִּי־תִדֹּר נֶדֶר לַיהֹוָה וְאָסְרָה אִסָּר בְּבֵית אָבִיהָ בִּנְעֻרֶיהָ: 5 וְשָׁמַע אָבִיהָ אֶת־נִדְרָהּ וֶאֱסָרָהּ אֲשֶׁר אָסְרָה עַל־נַפְשָׁהּ וְהֶחֱרִישׁ לָהּ אָבִיהָ וְקָמוּ כָּל־נְדָרֶיהָ וְכָל־אִסָּר אֲשֶׁר־אָסְרָה עַל־נַפְשָׁהּ יָקוּם:

her vows nor her agreements by which she has
bound herself shall stand; and the LORD will release
her, because her father overruled her.

⁶"If indeed she takes a husband, while bound by
her vows or by a rash utterance from her lips by
which she bound herself, ⁷and her husband hears *it,*
and makes no response to her on the day that he
hears, then her vows shall stand, and her agreements by which she bound herself shall stand. ⁸But
if her husband overrules her on the day that he
hears *it,* he shall make void her vow which she took
and what she uttered with her lips, by which she
bound herself, and the LORD will release her.

⁹"Also any vow of a widow or a divorced
woman, by which she has bound herself, shall stand
against her.

¹⁰"If she vowed in her husband's house, or
bound herself by an agreement with an oath, ¹¹and
her husband heard *it,* and made no response to her
and did not overrule her, then all her vows shall
stand, and every agreement by which she bound
herself shall stand. ¹²But if her husband truly made
them void on the day he heard *them,* then whatever
proceeded from her lips concerning her vows or
concerning the agreement binding her, it shall not
stand; her husband has made them void, and the
LORD will release her. ¹³Every vow and every
binding oath to afflict her soul, her husband may
confirm it, or her husband may make it void.
¹⁴Now if her husband makes no response whatever
to her from day to day, then he confirms all her
vows or all the agreements that bind her; he
confirms them, because he made no response to
her on the day that he heard *them.* ¹⁵But if he does
make them void after he has heard *them,* then he
shall bear her guilt."

¹⁶These *are* the statutes which the LORD commanded Moses, between a man and his wife, and
between a father and his daughter in her youth in
her father's house.

31 And the LORD spoke to Moses, saying:
²"Take vengeance on the Midianites for the
children of Israel. Afterward you shall be gathered
to your people."

³So Moses spoke to the people, saying, "Arm
some of yourselves for war, and let them go against
the Midianites to take vengeance for the LORD on
Midian. ⁴A thousand from each tribe of all the
tribes of Israel you shall send to the war."

⁵So there were recruited from the divisions of
Israel one thousand from *each* tribe, twelve
thousand armed for war. ⁶Then Moses sent them
to the war, one thousand from *each* tribe; he sent

6 וְאִם־הֵנִיא אָבִיהָ אֹתָהּ בְּיוֹם שָׁמְעוֹ כָּל־נְדָרֶיהָ
וֶאֱסָרֶיהָ אֲשֶׁר־אָסְרָה עַל־נַפְשָׁהּ לֹא יָקוּם וַיהֹוָה
יִסְלַח־לָהּ כִּי־הֵנִיא אָבִיהָ אֹתָהּ: 7 וְאִם־הָיוֹ תִהְיֶה
לְאִישׁ וּנְדָרֶיהָ עָלֶיהָ אוֹ מִבְטָא שְׂפָתֶיהָ אֲשֶׁר
אָסְרָה עַל־נַפְשָׁהּ: 8 וְשָׁמַע אִישָׁהּ בְּיוֹם שָׁמְעוֹ
וְהֶחֱרִישׁ לָהּ וְקָמוּ נְדָרֶיהָ וֶאֱסָרֶהָ אֲשֶׁר־אָסְרָה עַל־
נַפְשָׁהּ יָקֻמוּ: 9 וְאִם בְּיוֹם שְׁמֹעַ אִישָׁהּ יָנִיא אוֹתָהּ
וְהֵפֵר אֶת־נִדְרָהּ אֲשֶׁר עָלֶיהָ וְאֵת מִבְטָא שְׂפָתֶיהָ
אֲשֶׁר אָסְרָה עַל־נַפְשָׁהּ וַיהֹוָה יִסְלַח־לָהּ: 10 וְנֵדֶר
אַלְמָנָה וּגְרוּשָׁה כֹּל אֲשֶׁר־אָסְרָה עַל־נַפְשָׁהּ יָקוּם
עָלֶיהָ: 11 וְאִם־בֵּית אִישָׁהּ נָדָרָה אוֹ־אָסְרָה אִסָּר
עַל־נַפְשָׁהּ בִּשְׁבֻעָה: 12 וְשָׁמַע אִישָׁהּ וְהֶחֱרִשׁ לָהּ
לֹא הֵנִיא אֹתָהּ וְקָמוּ כָּל־נְדָרֶיהָ וְכָל־אִסָּר אֲשֶׁר־
אָסְרָה עַל־נַפְשָׁהּ יָקוּם: 13 וְאִם־הָפֵר יָפֵר אֹתָם ׀
אִישָׁהּ בְּיוֹם שָׁמְעוֹ כָּל־מוֹצָא שְׂפָתֶיהָ לִנְדָרֶיהָ
וּלְאִסַּר נַפְשָׁהּ לֹא יָקוּם אִישָׁהּ הֲפֵרָם וַיהֹוָה יִסְלַח־
לָהּ: 14 כָּל־נֵדֶר וְכָל־שְׁבֻעַת אִסָּר לְעַנֹּת נָפֶשׁ
אִישָׁהּ יְקִימֶנּוּ וְאִישָׁהּ יְפֵרֶנּוּ: 15 וְאִם־הַחֲרֵשׁ יַחֲרִישׁ
לָהּ אִישָׁהּ מִיּוֹם אֶל־יוֹם וְהֵקִים אֶת־כָּל־נְדָרֶיהָ אוֹ
אֶת־כָּל־אֱסָרֶיהָ אֲשֶׁר עָלֶיהָ הֵקִים אֹתָם כִּי־הֶחֱרִשׁ
לָהּ בְּיוֹם שָׁמְעוֹ: 16 וְאִם־הָפֵר יָפֵר אֹתָם אַחֲרֵי
שָׁמְעוֹ וְנָשָׂא אֶת־עֲוֺנָהּ: 17 אֵלֶּה הַחֻקִּים אֲשֶׁר צִוָּה
יְהֹוָה אֶת־מֹשֶׁה בֵּין אִישׁ לְאִשְׁתּוֹ בֵּין־אָב לְבִתּוֹ
בִּנְעֻרֶיהָ בֵּית אָבִיהָ: פ

לא וַיְדַבֵּר יְהֹוָה אֶל־מֹשֶׁה לֵּאמֹר: 2 נְקֹם נִקְמַת
בְּנֵי יִשְׂרָאֵל מֵאֵת הַמִּדְיָנִים אַחַר תֵּאָסֵף אֶל־
עַמֶּיךָ: 3 וַיְדַבֵּר מֹשֶׁה אֶל־הָעָם לֵאמֹר הֵחָלְצוּ
מֵאִתְּכֶם אֲנָשִׁים לַצָּבָא וְיִהְיוּ עַל־מִדְיָן לָתֵת נִקְמַת־
יְהֹוָה בְּמִדְיָן: 4 אֶלֶף לַמַּטֶּה אֶלֶף לַמַּטֶּה לְכֹל
מַטּוֹת יִשְׂרָאֵל תִּשְׁלְחוּ לַצָּבָא: 5 וַיִּמָּסְרוּ מֵאַלְפֵי
יִשְׂרָאֵל אֶלֶף לַמַּטֶּה שְׁנֵים־עָשָׂר אֶלֶף חֲלוּצֵי
צָבָא: 6 וַיִּשְׁלַח אֹתָם מֹשֶׁה אֶלֶף לַמַּטֶּה לַצָּבָא
אֹתָם וְאֶת־פִּינְחָס בֶּן־אֶלְעָזָר הַכֹּהֵן לַצָּבָא וּכְלֵי

them to the war with Phinehas the son of Eleazar
the priest, with the holy articles and the signal
trumpets in his hand. 7 And they warred against the
Midianites, just as the LORD commanded Moses,
and they killed all the males. 8 They killed the kings
of Midian with *the rest of* those who were killed—
Evi, Rekem, Zur, Hur, and Reba, the five kings of
Midian. Balaam the son of Beor they also killed
with the sword.

9 And the children of Israel took the women of
Midian captive, with their little ones, and took as
spoil all their cattle, all their flocks, and all their
goods. 10 They also burned with fire all the cities
where they dwelt, and all their forts. 11 And they
took all the spoil and all the booty—of man and
beast.

12 Then they brought the captives, the booty, and
the spoil to Moses, to Eleazar the priest, and to the
congregation of the children of Israel, to the camp
in the plains of Moab by the Jordan, *across from*
Jericho. 13 And Moses, Eleazar the priest, and all
the leaders of the congregation, went to meet them
outside the camp. 14 But Moses was angry with the
officers of the army, *with* the captains over
thousands and captains over hundreds, who had
come from the battle.

15 And Moses said to them: "Have you kept all
the women alive? 16 Look, these *women* caused the
children of Israel, through the counsel of Balaam,
to trespass against the LORD in the incident of Peor,
and there was a plague among the congregation of
the LORD. 17 Now therefore, kill every male among
the little ones, and kill every woman who has
known a man intimately. 18 But keep alive for
yourselves all the young girls who have not known
a man intimately. 19 And as for you, remain outside
the camp seven days; whoever has killed any
person, and whoever has touched any slain, purify
yourselves and your captives on the third day and
on the seventh day. 20 Purify every garment, everything made of leather, everything woven of goats'
hair, and everything made of wood."

21 Then Eleazar the priest said to the men of war
who had gone to the battle, "This *is* the ordinance
of the law which the LORD commanded Moses:
22 "Only the gold, the silver, the bronze, the iron,
the tin, and the lead, 23 everything that can endure
fire, you shall put through the fire, and it shall be
clean; and it shall be purified with the water of
purification. But all that cannot endure fire you
shall put through water. 24 And you shall wash your
clothes on the seventh day and be clean, and
afterward you may come into the camp."

25 Now the LORD spoke to Moses, saying:
26 "Count up the plunder that was taken—of man and beast—you and Eleazar the priest and the chief fathers of the congregation; 27 and divide the plunder into two parts, between those who took part in the war, who went out to battle, and all the congregation. 28 And levy a tribute for the LORD on the men of war who went out to battle: one of every five hundred of the persons, the cattle, the donkeys, and the sheep; 29 take it from their half, and give it to Eleazar the priest as a heave offering to the LORD. 30 And from the children of Israel's half you shall take one of every fifty, drawn from the persons, the cattle, the donkeys, and the sheep, from all the livestock, and give them to the Levites who keep charge of the tabernacle of the LORD." 31 So Moses and Eleazar the priest did as the LORD commanded Moses.

32 The booty remaining from the plunder, which the men of war had taken, was six hundred and seventy-five thousand sheep, 33 seventy-two thousand cattle, 34 sixty-one thousand donkeys, 35 and thirty-two thousand persons in all, of women who had not known a man intimately. 36 And the half, the portion for those who had gone out to war, was in number three hundred and thirty-seven thousand five hundred sheep; 37 and the LORD's tribute of the sheep was six hundred and seventy-five. 38 The cattle were thirty-six thousand, of which the LORD's tribute was seventy-two. 39 The donkeys were thirty thousand five hundred, of which the LORD's tribute was sixty-one. 40 The persons were sixteen thousand, of which the LORD's tribute was thirty-two persons. 41 So Moses gave the tribute which was the LORD's heave offering to Eleazar the priest, as the LORD commanded Moses.

42 And from the children of Israel's half, which Moses separated from the men who fought— 43 now the half belonging to the congregation was three hundred and thirty-seven thousand five hundred sheep, 44 thirty-six thousand cattle, 45 thirty thousand five hundred donkeys, 46 and sixteen thousand persons— 47 and from the children of Israel's half Moses took one of every fifty, drawn from man and beast, and gave them to the Levites, who kept charge of the tabernacle of the LORD, as the LORD commanded Moses.

48 Then the officers who were over thousands of the army, the captains of thousands and captains of hundreds, came near to Moses; 49 and they said to Moses, "Your servants have taken a count of the men of war who are under our command, and not a man of us is missing. 50 Therefore we have brought an offering for the LORD, what every man found of

25 וַיֹּאמֶר יְהוָה אֶל־מֹשֶׁה לֵּאמֹר: 26 שָׂא אֵת רֹאשׁ מַלְקוֹחַ הַשְּׁבִי בָּאָדָם וּבַבְּהֵמָה אַתָּה וְאֶלְעָזָר הַכֹּהֵן וְרָאשֵׁי אֲבוֹת הָעֵדָה: 27 וְחָצִיתָ אֶת־הַמַּלְקוֹחַ בֵּין תֹּפְשֵׂי הַמִּלְחָמָה הַיֹּצְאִים לַצָּבָא וּבֵין כָּל־הָעֵדָה: 28 וַהֲרֵמֹתָ מֶכֶס לַיהוָה מֵאֵת אַנְשֵׁי הַמִּלְחָמָה הַיֹּצְאִים לַצָּבָא אֶחָד נֶפֶשׁ מֵחֲמֵשׁ הַמֵּאוֹת מִן־הָאָדָם וּמִן־הַבָּקָר וּמִן־הַחֲמֹרִים וּמִן־הַצֹּאן: 29 מִמַּחֲצִיתָם תִּקָּחוּ וְנָתַתָּה לְאֶלְעָזָר הַכֹּהֵן תְּרוּמַת יְהוָה: 30 וּמִמַּחֲצִת בְּנֵי־יִשְׂרָאֵל תִּקַּח אֶחָד אָחֻז מִן־הַחֲמִשִּׁים מִן־הָאָדָם מִן־הַבָּקָר מִן־הַחֲמֹרִים וּמִן־הַצֹּאן מִכָּל־הַבְּהֵמָה וְנָתַתָּה אֹתָם לַלְוִיִּם שֹׁמְרֵי מִשְׁמֶרֶת מִשְׁכַּן יְהוָה: 31 וַיַּעַשׂ מֹשֶׁה וְאֶלְעָזָר הַכֹּהֵן כַּאֲשֶׁר צִוָּה יְהוָה אֶת־מֹשֶׁה: 32 וַיְהִי הַמַּלְקוֹחַ יֶתֶר הַבָּז אֲשֶׁר בָּזְזוּ עַם הַצָּבָא צֹאן שֵׁשׁ־מֵאוֹת אֶלֶף וְשִׁבְעִים אֶלֶף וַחֲמֵשֶׁת־אֲלָפִים: 33 וּבָקָר שְׁנַיִם וְשִׁבְעִים אָלֶף: 34 וַחֲמֹרִים אֶחָד וְשִׁשִּׁים אָלֶף: 35 וְנֶפֶשׁ אָדָם מִן־הַנָּשִׁים אֲשֶׁר לֹא־יָדְעוּ מִשְׁכַּב זָכָר כָּל־נֶפֶשׁ שְׁנַיִם וּשְׁלֹשִׁים אָלֶף: 36 וַתְּהִי הַמֶּחֱצָה חֵלֶק הַיֹּצְאִים בַּצָּבָא מִסְפַּר הַצֹּאן שְׁלֹשׁ־מֵאוֹת אֶלֶף וּשְׁלֹשִׁים אֶלֶף וְשִׁבְעַת אֲלָפִים וַחֲמֵשׁ מֵאוֹת: 37 וַיְהִי הַמֶּכֶס לַיהוָה מִן־הַצֹּאן שֵׁשׁ מֵאוֹת חָמֵשׁ וְשִׁבְעִים: 38 וְהַבָּקָר שִׁשָּׁה וּשְׁלֹשִׁים אָלֶף וּמִכְסָם לַיהוָה שְׁנַיִם וְשִׁבְעִים: 39 וַחֲמֹרִים שְׁלֹשִׁים אֶלֶף וַחֲמֵשׁ מֵאוֹת וּמִכְסָם לַיהוָה אֶחָד וְשִׁשִּׁים: 40 וְנֶפֶשׁ אָדָם שִׁשָּׁה עָשָׂר אָלֶף וּמִכְסָם לַיהוָה שְׁנַיִם וּשְׁלֹשִׁים נָפֶשׁ: 41 וַיִּתֵּן מֹשֶׁה אֶת־מֶכֶס תְּרוּמַת יְהוָה לְאֶלְעָזָר הַכֹּהֵן כַּאֲשֶׁר צִוָּה יְהוָה אֶת־מֹשֶׁה: 42 וּמִמַּחֲצִית בְּנֵי יִשְׂרָאֵל אֲשֶׁר חָצָה מֹשֶׁה מִן־הָאֲנָשִׁים הַצֹּבְאִים: 43 וַתְּהִי מֶחֱצַת הָעֵדָה מִן־הַצֹּאן שְׁלֹשׁ־מֵאוֹת אֶלֶף וּשְׁלֹשִׁים אֶלֶף שִׁבְעַת אֲלָפִים וַחֲמֵשׁ מֵאוֹת: 44 וּבָקָר שִׁשָּׁה וּשְׁלֹשִׁים אָלֶף: 45 וַחֲמֹרִים שְׁלֹשִׁים אֶלֶף וַחֲמֵשׁ מֵאוֹת: 46 וְנֶפֶשׁ אָדָם שִׁשָּׁה עָשָׂר אָלֶף: 47 וַיִּקַּח מֹשֶׁה מִמַּחֲצִת בְּנֵי־יִשְׂרָאֵל אֶת־הָאָחֻז אֶחָד מִן־הַחֲמִשִּׁים מִן־הָאָדָם וּמִן־הַבְּהֵמָה וַיִּתֵּן אֹתָם לַלְוִיִּם שֹׁמְרֵי מִשְׁמֶרֶת מִשְׁכַּן יְהוָה כַּאֲשֶׁר צִוָּה יְהוָה אֶת־מֹשֶׁה: 48 וַיִּקְרְבוּ אֶל־מֹשֶׁה הַפְּקֻדִים אֲשֶׁר לְאַלְפֵי הַצָּבָא שָׂרֵי הָאֲלָפִים וְשָׂרֵי הַמֵּאוֹת: 49 וַיֹּאמְרוּ אֶל־מֹשֶׁה עֲבָדֶיךָ נָשְׂאוּ אֶת־רֹאשׁ אַנְשֵׁי הַמִּלְחָמָה אֲשֶׁר בְּיָדֵנוּ וְלֹא־נִפְקַד מִמֶּנּוּ אִישׁ: 50 וַנַּקְרֵב אֶת־קָרְבַּן יְהוָה אִישׁ אֲשֶׁר מָצָא כְלִי־זָהָב אֶצְעָדָה

ornaments of gold: armlets and bracelets and signet rings and earrings and necklaces, to make atonement for ourselves before the LORD." ⁵¹So Moses and Eleazar the priest received the gold from them, all the fashioned ornaments. ⁵²And all the gold of the offering that they offered to the LORD, from the captains of thousands and captains of hundreds, was sixteen thousand seven hundred and fifty shekels. ⁵³(The men of war had taken spoil, every man for himself.) ⁵⁴And Moses and Eleazar the priest received the gold from the captains of thousands and of hundreds, and brought it into the tabernacle of meeting as a memorial for the children of Israel before the LORD.

32 Now the children of Reuben and the children of Gad had a very great multitude of livestock; and when they saw the land of Jazer and the land of Gilead, that indeed the region *was* a place for livestock, ²the children of Gad and the children of Reuben came and spoke to Moses, to Eleazar the priest, and to the leaders of the congregation, saying, ³"Ataroth, Dibon, Jazer, Nimrah, Heshbon, Elealeh, Shebam, Nebo, and Beon, ⁴the country which the LORD defeated before the congregation of Israel, *is* a land for livestock, and your servants have livestock. "⁵Therefore they said, "If we have found favor in your sight, let this land be given to your servants as a possession. Do not take us over the Jordan. "

⁶And Moses said to the children of Gad and to the children of Reuben: "Shall your brethren go to war while you sit here? ⁷Now why will you discourage the heart of the children of Israel from going over into the land which the LORD has given them? ⁸Thus your fathers did when I sent them away from Kadesh Barnea to see the land. ⁹For when they went up to the Valley of Eshcol and saw the land, they discouraged the heart of the children of Israel, so that they did not go into the land which the LORD had given them. ¹⁰So the LORD's anger was aroused on that day, and He swore an oath, saying, ¹¹'Surely none of the men who came up from Egypt, from twenty years old and above, shall see the land of which I swore to Abraham, Isaac, and Jacob, because they have not wholly followed Me, ¹²except Caleb the son of Jephunneh, the Kenizzite, and Joshua the son of Nun, for they have wholly followed the LORD.' ¹³So the LORD's anger was aroused against Israel, and He made them wander in the wilderness forty years, until all the generation that had done evil in the sight of the LORD was gone. ¹⁴And look! You have risen in your fathers' place, a brood of sinful men, to

וְצָמִיד טַבַּעַת עָגִיל וְכוּמָז לְכַפֵּר עַל־נַפְשֹׁתֵינוּ לִפְנֵי יְהוָה: 51 וַיִּקַּח מֹשֶׁה וְאֶלְעָזָר הַכֹּהֵן אֶת־ הַזָּהָב מֵאִתָּם כֹּל כְּלִי מַעֲשֶׂה: 52 וַיְהִי | כָּל־זְהַב הַתְּרוּמָה אֲשֶׁר הֵרִימוּ לַיהוָה שִׁשָּׁה עָשָׂר אֶלֶף שְׁבַע־מֵאוֹת וַחֲמִשִּׁים שָׁקֶל מֵאֵת שָׂרֵי הָאֲלָפִים וּמֵאֵת שָׂרֵי הַמֵּאוֹת: 53 אַנְשֵׁי הַצָּבָא בָּזְזוּ אִישׁ לוֹ: 54 וַיִּקַּח מֹשֶׁה וְאֶלְעָזָר הַכֹּהֵן אֶת־הַזָּהָב מֵאֵת שָׂרֵי הָאֲלָפִים וְהַמֵּאוֹת וַיָּבִאוּ אֹתוֹ אֶל־אֹהֶל מוֹעֵד זִכָּרוֹן לִבְנֵי־יִשְׂרָאֵל לִפְנֵי יְהוָה: פ

לב וּמִקְנֶה | רַב הָיָה לִבְנֵי רְאוּבֵן וְלִבְנֵי־ גָד עָצוּם מְאֹד וַיִּרְאוּ אֶת־אֶרֶץ יַעְזֵר וְאֶת־אֶרֶץ גִּלְעָד וְהִנֵּה הַמָּקוֹם מְקוֹם מִקְנֶה: 2 וַיָּבֹאוּ בְנֵי־גָד וּבְנֵי רְאוּבֵן וַיֹּאמְרוּ אֶל־מֹשֶׁה וְאֶל־אֶלְעָזָר הַכֹּהֵן וְאֶל־נְשִׂיאֵי הָעֵדָה לֵאמֹר: 3 עֲטָרוֹת וְדִיבֹן וְיַעְזֵר וְנִמְרָה וְחֶשְׁבּוֹן וְאֶלְעָלֵה וּשְׂבָם וּנְבוֹ וּבְעֹן: 4 הָאָרֶץ אֲשֶׁר הִכָּה יְהוָה לִפְנֵי עֲדַת יִשְׂרָאֵל אֶרֶץ מִקְנֶה הִוא וְלַעֲבָדֶיךָ מִקְנֶה: ס 5 וַיֹּאמְרוּ אִם־ מָצָאנוּ חֵן בְּעֵינֶיךָ יֻתַּן אֶת־הָאָרֶץ הַזֹּאת לַעֲבָדֶיךָ לַאֲחֻזָּה אַל־תַּעֲבִרֵנוּ אֶת־הַיַּרְדֵּן: 6 וַיֹּאמֶר מֹשֶׁה לִבְנֵי־גָד וְלִבְנֵי רְאוּבֵן הַאַחֵיכֶם יָבֹאוּ לַמִּלְחָמָה וְאַתֶּם תֵּשְׁבוּ פֹה: 7 וְלָמָּה תְנִואוּן אֶת־לֵב בְּנֵי יִשְׂרָאֵל מֵעֲבֹר אֶל־הָאָרֶץ אֲשֶׁר־נָתַן לָהֶם יְהוָה: 8 כֹּה עָשׂוּ אֲבֹתֵיכֶם בְּשָׁלְחִי אֹתָם מִקָּדֵשׁ בַּרְנֵעַ לִרְאוֹת אֶת־הָאָרֶץ: 9 וַיַּעֲלוּ עַד־נַחַל אֶשְׁכּוֹל וַיִּרְאוּ אֶת־הָאָרֶץ וַיָּנִיאוּ אֶת־לֵב בְּנֵי יִשְׂרָאֵל לְבִלְתִּי־בֹא אֶל־הָאָרֶץ אֲשֶׁר־נָתַן לָהֶם יְהוָה: 10 וַיִּחַר־אַף יְהוָה בַּיּוֹם הַהוּא וַיִּשָּׁבַע לֵאמֹר: 11 אִם־יִרְאוּ הָאֲנָשִׁים הָעֹלִים מִמִּצְרַיִם מִבֶּן עֶשְׂרִים שָׁנָה וָמַעְלָה אֵת הָאֲדָמָה אֲשֶׁר נִשְׁבַּעְתִּי לְאַבְרָהָם לְיִצְחָק וּלְיַעֲקֹב כִּי לֹא־מִלְאוּ אַחֲרָי: 12 בִּלְתִּי כָּלֵב בֶּן־יְפֻנֶּה הַקְּנִזִּי וִיהוֹשֻׁעַ בִּן־נוּן כִּי מִלְאוּ אַחֲרֵי יְהוָה: 13 וַיִּחַר־אַף יְהוָה בְּיִשְׂרָאֵל וַיְנִעֵם בַּמִּדְבָּר אַרְבָּעִים שָׁנָה עַד־ תֹּם כָּל־הַדּוֹר הָעֹשֶׂה הָרַע בְּעֵינֵי יְהוָה: 14 וְהִנֵּה קַמְתֶּם תַּחַת אֲבֹתֵיכֶם תַּרְבּוּת אֲנָשִׁים חַטָּאִים

increase still more the fierce anger of the LORD
against Israel. ¹⁵For if you turn away from
following Him, He will once again leave them in
the wilderness, and you will destroy all these
people."

¹⁶Then they came near to him and said: "We will
build sheepfolds here for our livestock, and cities
for our little ones, ¹⁷but we ourselves will be armed,
ready *to go* before the children of Israel until we
have brought them to their place; and our little ones
will dwell in the fortified cities because of the
inhabitants of the land. ¹⁸We will not return to our
homes until every one of the children of Israel has
received his inheritance. ¹⁹For we will not inherit
with them on the other side of the Jordan and
beyond, because our inheritance has fallen to us on
this eastern side of the Jordan."

²⁰Then Moses said to them: "If you do this thing,
if you arm yourselves before the LORD for the war,
²¹and all your armed men cross over the Jordan
before the LORD until He has driven out His
enemies from before Him, ²²and the land is
subdued before the LORD, then afterward you
may return and be blameless before the LORD and
before Israel; and this land shall be your possession
before the LORD. ²³But if you do not do so, then
take note, you have sinned against the LORD; and
be sure your sin will find you out. ²⁴Build cities for
your little ones and folds for your sheep, and do
what has proceeded out of your mouth."

²⁵And the children of Gad and the children of
Reuben spoke to Moses, saying: "Your servants
will do as my lord commands. ²⁶Our little ones, our
wives, our flocks, and all our livestock will be there
in the cities of Gilead; ²⁷but your servants will cross
over, every man armed for war, before the LORD to
battle, just as my lord says."

²⁸So Moses gave command concerning them to
Eleazar the priest, to Joshua the son of Nun, and to
the chief fathers of the tribes of the children of
Israel. ²⁹And Moses said to them: "If the children
of Gad and the children of Reuben cross over the
Jordan with you, every man armed for battle before
the LORD, and the land is subdued before you, then
you shall give them the land of Gilead as a
possession. ³⁰But if they do not cross over armed
with you, they shall have possessions among you in
the land of Canaan."

³¹Then the children of Gad and the children of
Reuben answered, saying: "As the LORD has said to
your servants, so we will do. ³²We will cross over
armed before the LORD into the land of Canaan,
but the possession of our inheritance *shall remain*
with us on this side of the Jordan."

לִסְפּוֹת עוֹד עַל חֲרוֹן אַף־יְהֹוָה אֶל־יִשְׂרָאֵל: 15 כִּי
תְשׁוּבֻן מֵאַחֲרָיו וְיָסַף עוֹד לְהַנִּיחוֹ בַּמִּדְבָּר וְשִׁחַתֶּם
לְכָל־הָעָם הַזֶּה: ס   16 וַיִּגְּשׁוּ אֵלָיו וַיֹּאמְרוּ
גִּדְרֹת צֹאן נִבְנֶה לְמִקְנֵנוּ פֹּה וְעָרִים לְטַפֵּנוּ:
17 וַאֲנַחְנוּ נֵחָלֵץ חֻשִׁים לִפְנֵי בְּנֵי יִשְׂרָאֵל עַד אֲשֶׁר
אִם־הֲבִיאֹנֻם אֶל־מְקוֹמָם וְיָשַׁב טַפֵּנוּ בְּעָרֵי הַמִּבְצָר
מִפְּנֵי יֹשְׁבֵי הָאָרֶץ: 18 לֹא נָשׁוּב אֶל־בָּתֵּינוּ עַד
הִתְנַחֵל בְּנֵי יִשְׂרָאֵל אִישׁ נַחֲלָתוֹ: 19 כִּי לֹא נִנְחַל
אִתָּם מֵעֵבֶר לַיַּרְדֵּן וָהָלְאָה כִּי בָאָה נַחֲלָתֵנוּ אֵלֵינוּ
מֵעֵבֶר הַיַּרְדֵּן מִזְרָחָה:
פ

20 וַיֹּאמֶר אֲלֵיהֶם מֹשֶׁה אִם־תַּעֲשׂוּן אֶת־הַדָּבָר
הַזֶּה אִם־תֵּחָלְצוּ לִפְנֵי יְהֹוָה לַמִּלְחָמָה: 21 וְעָבַר
לָכֶם כָּל־חָלוּץ אֶת־הַיַּרְדֵּן לִפְנֵי יְהֹוָה עַד הוֹרִישׁוֹ
אֶת־אֹיְבָיו מִפָּנָיו: 22 וְנִכְבְּשָׁה הָאָרֶץ לִפְנֵי יְהֹוָה
וְאַחַר תָּשֻׁבוּ וִהְיִיתֶם נְקִיִּם מֵיְהֹוָה וּמִיִּשְׂרָאֵל
וְהָיְתָה הָאָרֶץ הַזֹּאת לָכֶם לַאֲחֻזָּה לִפְנֵי יְהֹוָה:
23 וְאִם־לֹא תַעֲשׂוּן כֵּן הִנֵּה חֲטָאתֶם לַיהֹוָה
וּדְעוּ חַטַּאתְכֶם אֲשֶׁר תִּמְצָא אֶתְכֶם: 24 בְּנוּ־לָכֶם
עָרִים לְטַפְּכֶם וּגְדֵרֹת לְצֹנַאֲכֶם וְהַיֹּצֵא מִפִּיכֶם
תַּעֲשׂוּ: 25 וַיֹּאמֶר בְּנֵי־גָד וּבְנֵי רְאוּבֵן אֶל־מֹשֶׁה
לֵאמֹר עֲבָדֶיךָ יַעֲשׂוּ כַּאֲשֶׁר אֲדֹנִי מְצַוֶּה: 26 טַפֵּנוּ
נָשֵׁינוּ מִקְנֵנוּ וְכָל־בְּהֶמְתֵּנוּ יִהְיוּ־שָׁם בְּעָרֵי הַגִּלְעָד:
27 וַעֲבָדֶיךָ יַעַבְרוּ כָּל־חֲלוּץ צָבָא לִפְנֵי יְהֹוָה
לַמִּלְחָמָה כַּאֲשֶׁר אֲדֹנִי דֹּבֵר: 28 וַיְצַו לָהֶם מֹשֶׁה
אֵת אֶלְעָזָר הַכֹּהֵן וְאֵת יְהוֹשֻׁעַ בִּן־נוּן וְאֶת־רָאשֵׁי
אֲבוֹת הַמַּטּוֹת לִבְנֵי יִשְׂרָאֵל: 29 וַיֹּאמֶר מֹשֶׁה
אֲלֵהֶם אִם־יַעַבְרוּ בְנֵי־גָד וּבְנֵי־רְאוּבֵן | אִתְּכֶם
אֶת־הַיַּרְדֵּן כָּל־חָלוּץ לַמִּלְחָמָה לִפְנֵי יְהֹוָה וְנִכְבְּשָׁה
הָאָרֶץ לִפְנֵיכֶם וּנְתַתֶּם לָהֶם אֶת־אֶרֶץ הַגִּלְעָד
לַאֲחֻזָּה: 30 וְאִם־לֹא יַעַבְרוּ חֲלוּצִים אִתְּכֶם וְנֹאחֲזוּ
בְתֹכְכֶם בְּאֶרֶץ כְּנָעַן: 31 וַיַּעֲנוּ בְנֵי־גָד וּבְנֵי רְאוּבֵן
לֵאמֹר אֵת אֲשֶׁר דִּבֶּר יְהֹוָה אֶל־עֲבָדֶיךָ כֵּן נַעֲשֶׂה:
32 נַחְנוּ נַעֲבֹר חֲלוּצִים לִפְנֵי יְהֹוָה אֶרֶץ כְּנָעַן וְאִתָּנוּ

³³ So Moses gave to the children of Gad, to the children of Reuben, and to half the tribe of Manasseh the son of Joseph, the kingdom of Sihon king of the Amorites and the kingdom of Og king of Bashan, the land with its cities within the borders, the cities of the surrounding country. ³⁴ And the children of Gad built Dibon and Ataroth and Aroer, ³⁵ Atroth and Shophan and Jazer and Jogbehah, ³⁶ Beth Nimrah and Beth Haran, fortified cities, and folds for sheep. ³⁷ And the children of Reuben built Heshbon and Elealeh and Kirjathaim, ³⁸ Nebo and Baal Meon (*their* names being changed) and Shibmah; and they gave *other* names to the cities which they built.

³⁹ And the children of Machir the son of Manasseh went to Gilead and took it, and dispossessed the Amorites who *were* in it. ⁴⁰ So Moses gave Gilead to Machir the son of Manasseh, and he dwelt in it. ⁴¹ Also Jair the son of Manasseh went and took its small towns, and called them Havoth Jair. ⁴² Then Nobah went and took Kenath and its villages, and he called it Nobah, after his own name.

33 These *are* the journeys of the children of Israel, who went out of the land of Egypt by their armies under the hand of Moses and Aaron. ² Now Moses wrote down the starting points of their journeys at the command of the LORD. And these *are* their journeys according to their starting points:

³ They departed from Rameses in the first month, on the fifteenth day of the first month; on the day after the Passover the children of Israel went out with boldness in the sight of all the Egyptians. ⁴ For the Egyptians were burying all *their* firstborn, whom the LORD had killed among them. Also on their gods the LORD had executed judgments.

⁵ Then the children of Israel moved from Rameses and camped at Succoth. ⁶ They departed from Succoth and camped at Etham, which *is* on the edge of the wilderness. ⁷ They moved from Etham and turned back to Pi Hahiroth, which *is* east of Baal Zephon; and they camped near Migdol. ⁸ They departed from before Hahiroth and passed through the midst of the sea into the wilderness, went three days' journey in the Wilderness of Etham, and camped at Marah. ⁹ They moved from Marah and came to Elim. At Elim *were* twelve springs of water and seventy palm trees; so they camped there.

¹⁰ They moved from Elim and camped by the Red Sea. ¹¹ They moved from the Red Sea and camped in the Wilderness of Sin. ¹² They journeyed from the Wilderness of Sin and camped at Dophkah. ¹³ They

33 וַיִּתֵּן לָהֶם | מֹשֶׁה אֶת־אֶרֶץ נַחֲלָתֵנוּ מֵעֵבֶר לַיַּרְדֵּן: לִבְנֵי־גָד וְלִבְנֵי רְאוּבֵן וְלַחֲצִי | שֵׁבֶט | מְנַשֶּׁה בֶן־יוֹסֵף אֶת־מַמְלֶכֶת סִיחֹן מֶלֶךְ הָאֱמֹרִי וְאֶת־ מַמְלֶכֶת עוֹג מֶלֶךְ הַבָּשָׁן הָאָרֶץ לְעָרֶיהָ בִּגְבֻלֹת עָרֵי הָאָרֶץ סָבִיב: 34 וַיִּבְנוּ בְנֵי־גָד אֶת־דִּיבֹן וְאֶת־ עֲטָרֹת וְאֵת עֲרֹעֵר: 35 וְאֶת־עַטְרֹת שׁוֹפָן וְאֶת־ יַעְזֵר וְיָגְבֳּהָה: 36 וְאֶת־בֵּית נִמְרָה וְאֶת־בֵּית הָרָן עָרֵי מִבְצָר וְגִדְרֹת צֹאן: 37 וּבְנֵי רְאוּבֵן בָּנוּ אֶת־ חֶשְׁבּוֹן וְאֶת־אֶלְעָלֵא וְאֵת קִרְיָתָיִם: 38 וְאֶת־נְבוֹ וְאֶת־בַּעַל מְעוֹן מוּסַבֹּת שֵׁם וְאֶת־שִׂבְמָה וַיִּקְרְאוּ בְשֵׁמֹת אֶת־שְׁמוֹת הֶעָרִים אֲשֶׁר בָּנוּ: 39 וַיֵּלְכוּ בְּנֵי מָכִיר בֶּן־מְנַשֶּׁה גִּלְעָדָה וַיִּלְכְּדֻהָ וַיּוֹרֶשׁ אֶת־הָאֱמֹרִי אֲשֶׁר־בָּהּ: 40 וַיִּתֵּן מֹשֶׁה אֶת־הַגִּלְעָד לְמָכִיר בֶּן־ מְנַשֶּׁה וַיֵּשֶׁב בָּהּ: 41 וְיָאִיר בֶּן־מְנַשֶּׁה הָלַךְ וַיִּלְכֹּד אֶת־חַוֹּתֵיהֶם וַיִּקְרָא אֶתְהֶן חַוֹּת יָאִיר: 42 וְנֹבַח הָלַךְ וַיִּלְכֹּד אֶת־קְנָת וְאֶת־בְּנֹתֶיהָ וַיִּקְרָא לָה נֹבַח בִּשְׁמוֹ: פ

לג אֵלֶּה מַסְעֵי בְנֵי־יִשְׂרָאֵל אֲשֶׁר יָצְאוּ מֵאֶרֶץ מִצְרַיִם לְצִבְאֹתָם בְּיַד־מֹשֶׁה וְאַהֲרֹן: 2 וַיִּכְתֹּב מֹשֶׁה אֶת־מוֹצָאֵיהֶם לְמַסְעֵיהֶם עַל־פִּי יְהֹוָה וְאֵלֶּה מַסְעֵיהֶם לְמוֹצָאֵיהֶם: 3 וַיִּסְעוּ מֵרַעְמְסֵס בַּחֹדֶשׁ הָרִאשׁוֹן בַּחֲמִשָּׁה עָשָׂר יוֹם לַחֹדֶשׁ הָרִאשׁוֹן מִמָּחֳרַת הַפֶּסַח יָצְאוּ בְנֵי־יִשְׂרָאֵל בְּיָד רָמָה לְעֵינֵי כָּל־מִצְרָיִם: 4 וּמִצְרַיִם מְקַבְּרִים אֵת אֲשֶׁר הִכָּה יְהֹוָה בָּהֶם כָּל־בְּכוֹר וּבֵאלֹהֵיהֶם עָשָׂה יְהֹוָה שְׁפָטִים: 5 וַיִּסְעוּ בְנֵי־יִשְׂרָאֵל מֵרַעְמְסֵס וַיַּחֲנוּ בְּסֻכֹּת: 6 וַיִּסְעוּ מִסֻּכֹּת וַיַּחֲנוּ בְאֵתָם אֲשֶׁר בִּקְצֵה הַמִּדְבָּר: 7 וַיִּסְעוּ מֵאֵתָם וַיָּשָׁב עַל־פִּי הַחִירֹת אֲשֶׁר עַל־פְּנֵי בַּעַל צְפוֹן וַיַּחֲנוּ לִפְנֵי מִגְדֹּל: 8 וַיִּסְעוּ מִפְּנֵי הַחִירֹת וַיַּעַבְרוּ בְתוֹךְ־ הַיָּם הַמִּדְבָּרָה וַיֵּלְכוּ דֶּרֶךְ שְׁלֹשֶׁת יָמִים בְּמִדְבַּר אֵתָם וַיַּחֲנוּ בְּמָרָה: 9 וַיִּסְעוּ מִמָּרָה וַיָּבֹאוּ אֵילִמָה וּבְאֵילִם שְׁתֵּים עֶשְׂרֵה עֵינֹת מַיִם וְשִׁבְעִים תְּמָרִים וַיַּחֲנוּ־שָׁם: 10 וַיִּסְעוּ מֵאֵילִם וַיַּחֲנוּ עַל־יַם־סוּף: 11 וַיִּסְעוּ מִיַּם־סוּף וַיַּחֲנוּ בְּמִדְבַּר־סִין: 12 וַיִּסְעוּ מִמִּדְבַּר־סִין וַיַּחֲנוּ בְּדָפְקָה: 13 וַיִּסְעוּ מִדָּפְקָה

departed from Dophkah and camped at Alush.
14 They moved from Alush and camped at Rephidim, where there was no water for the people to
drink.

15 They departed from Rephidim and camped in
the Wilderness of Sinai. 16 They moved from the
Wilderness of Sinai and camped at Kibroth
Hattaavah. 17 They departed from Kibroth Hattaavah and camped at Hazeroth. 18 They departed
from Hazeroth and camped at Rithmah. 19 They
departed from Rithmah and camped at Rimmon
Perez. 20 They departed from Rimmon Perez and
camped at Libnah. 21 They moved from Libnah and
camped at Rissah. 22 They journeyed from Rissah
and camped at Kehelathah. 23 They went from
Kehelathah and camped at Mount Shepher. 24 They
moved from Mount Shepher and camped at
Haradah. 25 They moved from Haradah and camped at Makheloth. 26 They moved from Makheloth
and camped at Tahath. 27 They departed from
Tahath and camped at Terah. 28 They moved from
Terah and camped at Mithkah. 29 They went from
Mithkah and camped at Hashmonah. 30 They
departed from Hashmonah and camped at
Moseroth. 31 They departed from Moseroth and
camped at Bene Jaakan. 32 They moved from Bene
Jaakan and camped at Hor Hagidgad. 33 They went
from Hor Hagidgad and camped at Jotbathah.
34 They moved from Jotbathah and camped at
Abronah. 35 They departed from Abronah and
camped at Ezion Geber. 36 They moved from Ezion
Geber and camped in the Wilderness of Zin, which
is Kadesh. 37 They moved from Kadesh and camped
at Mount Hor, on the boundary of the land of
Edom.

38 Then Aaron the priest went up to Mount Hor
at the command of the LORD, and died there in the
fortieth year after the children of Israel had come
out of the land of Egypt, on the first *day* of the fifth
month. 39 Aaron *was* one hundred and twenty-three
years old when he died on Mount Hor.

40 Now the king of Arad, the Canaanite, who
dwelt in the South in the land of Canaan, heard of
the coming of the children of Israel.

41 So they departed from Mount Hor and camped
at Zalmonah. 42 They departed from Zalmonah and
camped at Punon. 43 They departed from Punon
and camped at Oboth. 44 They departed from
Oboth and camped at Ije Abarim, at the border
of Moab. 45 They departed from Ijim and camped at
Dibon Gad. 46 They moved from Dibon Gad and
camped at Almon Diblathaim. 47 They moved from
Almon Diblathaim and camped in the mountains of
Abarim, before Nebo. 48 They departed from the

וַיַּחֲנוּ בְּאָלוּשׁ: 14 וַיִּסְעוּ מֵאָלוּשׁ וַיַּחֲנוּ בִּרְפִידִם
וְלֹא־הָיָה שָׁם מַיִם לָעָם לִשְׁתּוֹת: 15 וַיִּסְעוּ
מֵרְפִידִם וַיַּחֲנוּ בְּמִדְבַּר סִינָי: 16 וַיִּסְעוּ מִמִּדְבַּר סִינָי
וַיַּחֲנוּ בְּקִבְרֹת הַתַּאֲוָה: 17 וַיִּסְעוּ מִקִּבְרֹת הַתַּאֲוָה
וַיַּחֲנוּ בַּחֲצֵרֹת: 18 וַיִּסְעוּ מֵחֲצֵרֹת וַיַּחֲנוּ בְּרִתְמָה:
19 וַיִּסְעוּ מֵרִתְמָה וַיַּחֲנוּ בְּרִמֹּן פָּרֶץ: 20 וַיִּסְעוּ
מֵרִמֹּן פָּרֶץ וַיַּחֲנוּ בְּלִבְנָה: 21 וַיִּסְעוּ מִלִּבְנָה וַיַּחֲנוּ
בְּרִסָּה: 22 וַיִּסְעוּ מֵרִסָּה וַיַּחֲנוּ בִּקְהֵלָתָה: 23 וַיִּסְעוּ
מִקְּהֵלָתָה וַיַּחֲנוּ בְּהַר־שָׁפֶר: 24 וַיִּסְעוּ מֵהַר־שָׁפֶר
וַיַּחֲנוּ בַּחֲרָדָה: 25 וַיִּסְעוּ מֵחֲרָדָה וַיַּחֲנוּ בְּמַקְהֵלֹת:
26 וַיִּסְעוּ מִמַּקְהֵלֹת וַיַּחֲנוּ בְּתָחַת: 27 וַיִּסְעוּ מִתָּחַת
וַיַּחֲנוּ בְּתָרַח: 28 וַיִּסְעוּ מִתָּרַח וַיַּחֲנוּ בְּמִתְקָה:
29 וַיִּסְעוּ מִמִּתְקָה וַיַּחֲנוּ בְּחַשְׁמֹנָה: 30 וַיִּסְעוּ
מֵחַשְׁמֹנָה וַיַּחֲנוּ בְּמֹסֵרוֹת: 31 וַיִּסְעוּ מִמֹּסֵרוֹת וַיַּחֲנוּ
בִּבְנֵי יַעֲקָן: 32 וַיִּסְעוּ מִבְּנֵי יַעֲקָן וַיַּחֲנוּ בְּחֹר הַגִּדְגָּד:
33 וַיִּסְעוּ מֵחֹר הַגִּדְגָּד וַיַּחֲנוּ בְּיָטְבָתָה: 34 וַיִּסְעוּ
מִיָּטְבָתָה וַיַּחֲנוּ בְּעַבְרֹנָה: 35 וַיִּסְעוּ מֵעַבְרֹנָה וַיַּחֲנוּ
בְּעֶצְיֹן גָּבֶר: 36 וַיִּסְעוּ מֵעֶצְיֹן גָּבֶר וַיַּחֲנוּ בְמִדְבַּר־
צִן הִוא קָדֵשׁ: 37 וַיִּסְעוּ מִקָּדֵשׁ וַיַּחֲנוּ בְּהֹר הָהָר
בִּקְצֵה אֶרֶץ אֱדוֹם: 38 וַיַּעַל אַהֲרֹן הַכֹּהֵן אֶל־הֹר
הָהָר עַל־פִּי יְהֹוָה וַיָּמָת שָׁם בִּשְׁנַת הָאַרְבָּעִים
לְצֵאת בְּנֵי־יִשְׂרָאֵל מֵאֶרֶץ מִצְרַיִם בַּחֹדֶשׁ הַחֲמִישִׁי
בְּאֶחָד לַחֹדֶשׁ: 39 וְאַהֲרֹן בֶּן־שָׁלֹשׁ וְעֶשְׂרִים וּמְאַת
שָׁנָה בְּמֹתוֹ בְּהֹר הָהָר: ס   40 וַיִּשְׁמַע
הַכְּנַעֲנִי מֶלֶךְ עֲרָד וְהוּא־יֹשֵׁב בַּנֶּגֶב בְּאֶרֶץ כְּנָעַן
בְּבֹא בְּנֵי יִשְׂרָאֵל: 41 וַיִּסְעוּ מֵהֹר הָהָר וַיַּחֲנוּ
בְּצַלְמֹנָה: 42 וַיִּסְעוּ מִצַּלְמֹנָה וַיַּחֲנוּ בְּפוּנֹן: 43 וַיִּסְעוּ
מִפּוּנֹן וַיַּחֲנוּ בְּאֹבֹת: 44 וַיִּסְעוּ מֵאֹבֹת וַיַּחֲנוּ בְּעִיֵּי
הָעֲבָרִים בִּגְבוּל מוֹאָב: 45 וַיִּסְעוּ מֵעִיִּים וַיַּחֲנוּ
בְּדִיבֹן גָּד: 46 וַיִּסְעוּ מִדִּיבֹן גָּד וַיַּחֲנוּ בְּעַלְמֹן
דִּבְלָתָיְמָה: 47 וַיִּסְעוּ מֵעַלְמֹן דִּבְלָתָיְמָה וַיַּחֲנוּ בְּהָרֵי
הָעֲבָרִים לִפְנֵי נְבוֹ: 48 וַיִּסְעוּ מֵהָרֵי הָעֲבָרִים

mountains of Abarim and camped in the plains of Moab by the Jordan, *across from* Jericho. 49 They camped by the Jordan, from Beth Jesimoth as far as the Abel Acacia Grove in the plains of Moab.

50 Now the LORD spoke to Moses in the plains of Moab by the Jordan, *across from* Jericho, saying, 51 "Speak to the children of Israel, and say to them: 'When you have crossed the Jordan into the land of Canaan, 52 then you shall drive out all the inhabitants of the land from before you, destroy all their engraved stones, destroy all their molded images, and demolish all their high places; 53 you shall dispossess *the inhabitants of* the land and dwell in it, for I have given you the land to possess. 54 And you shall divide the land by lot as an inheritance among your families; to the larger you shall give a larger inheritance, and to the smaller you shall give a smaller inheritance; there everyone's *inheritance* shall be whatever falls to him by lot. You shall inherit according to the tribes of your fathers. 55 But if you do not drive out the inhabitants of the land from before you, then it shall be that those whom you let remain *shall be* irritants in your eyes and thorns in your sides, and they shall harass you in the land where you dwell. 56 Moreover it shall be *that* I will do to you as I thought to do to them.'"

34 Then the LORD spoke to Moses, saying, 2 "Command the children of Israel, and say to them: 'When you come into the land of Canaan, this *is* the land that shall fall to you as an inheritance—the land of Canaan to its boundaries. 3 Your southern border shall be from the Wilderness of Zin along the border of Edom; then your southern border shall extend eastward to the end of the Salt Sea; 4 your border shall turn from the southern side of the Ascent of Akrabbim, continue to Zin, and be on the south of Kadesh Barnea; then it shall go on to Hazar Addar, and continue to Azmon; 5 the border shall turn from Azmon to the Brook of Egypt, and it shall end at the Sea.

6 'As for the western border, you shall have the Great Sea for a border; this shall be your western border.

7 'And this shall be your northern border: From the Great Sea you shall mark out your *border* line to Mount Hor; 8 from Mount Hor you shall mark out *your border* to the entrance of Hamath; then the direction of the border shall be toward Zedad; 9 the border shall proceed to Ziphron, and it shall end at Hazar Enan. This shall be your northern border.

49 וַיַּחֲנוּ בְּעַרְבֹת מוֹאָב עַל יַרְדֵּן יְרֵחוֹ: עַל־הַיַּרְדֵּן מִבֵּית הַיְשִׁמֹת עַד אָבֵל הַשִּׁטִּים בְּעַרְבֹת מוֹאָב: ס 50 וַיְדַבֵּר יְהוָה אֶל־ מֹשֶׁה בְּעַרְבֹת מוֹאָב עַל־יַרְדֵּן יְרֵחוֹ לֵאמֹר: 51 דַּבֵּר אֶל־בְּנֵי יִשְׂרָאֵל וְאָמַרְתָּ אֲלֵהֶם כִּי אַתֶּם עֹבְרִים אֶת־הַיַּרְדֵּן אֶל־אֶרֶץ כְּנָעַן: 52 וְהוֹרַשְׁתֶּם אֶת־כָּל־ יֹשְׁבֵי הָאָרֶץ מִפְּנֵיכֶם וְאִבַּדְתֶּם אֵת כָּל־מַשְׂכִּיֹּתָם וְאֵת כָּל־צַלְמֵי מַסֵּכֹתָם תְּאַבֵּדוּ וְאֵת כָּל־בָּמֹתָם תַּשְׁמִידוּ: 53 וְהוֹרַשְׁתֶּם אֶת־הָאָרֶץ וִישַׁבְתֶּם־בָּהּ כִּי לָכֶם נָתַתִּי אֶת־הָאָרֶץ לָרֶשֶׁת אֹתָהּ: 54 וְהִתְנַחַלְתֶּם אֶת־הָאָרֶץ בְּגוֹרָל לְמִשְׁפְּחֹתֵיכֶם לָרַב תַּרְבּוּ אֶת־ נַחֲלָתוֹ וְלַמְעַט תַּמְעִיט אֶת־נַחֲלָתוֹ אֶל אֲשֶׁר־ יֵצֵא לוֹ שָׁמָּה הַגּוֹרָל לוֹ יִהְיֶה לְמַטּוֹת אֲבֹתֵיכֶם תִּתְנֶחָלוּ: 55 וְאִם־לֹא תוֹרִישׁוּ אֶת־יֹשְׁבֵי הָאָרֶץ מִפְּנֵיכֶם וְהָיָה אֲשֶׁר תּוֹתִירוּ מֵהֶם לְשִׂכִּים בְּעֵינֵיכֶם וְלִצְנִינִם בְּצִדֵּיכֶם וְצָרְרוּ אֶתְכֶם עַל־הָאָרֶץ אֲשֶׁר אַתֶּם יֹשְׁבִים בָּהּ: 56 וְהָיָה כַּאֲשֶׁר דִּמִּיתִי לַעֲשׂוֹת לָהֶם אֶעֱשֶׂה לָכֶם: פ

לד וַיְדַבֵּר יְהוָה אֶל־מֹשֶׁה לֵּאמֹר: 2 צַו אֶת־בְּנֵי יִשְׂרָאֵל וְאָמַרְתָּ אֲלֵהֶם כִּי־אַתֶּם בָּאִים אֶל־הָאָרֶץ כְּנָעַן זֹאת הָאָרֶץ אֲשֶׁר תִּפֹּל לָכֶם בְּנַחֲלָה אֶרֶץ כְּנַעַן לִגְבֻלֹתֶיהָ: 3 וְהָיָה לָכֶם פְּאַת־נֶגֶב מִמִּדְבַּר־ צִן עַל־יְדֵי אֱדוֹם וְהָיָה לָכֶם גְּבוּל נֶגֶב מִקְצֵה יָם־ הַמֶּלַח קֵדְמָה: 4 וְנָסַב לָכֶם הַגְּבוּל מִנֶּגֶב לְמַעֲלֵה עַקְרַבִּים וְעָבַר צִנָה וְהָיָה תּוֹצְאֹתָיו מִנֶּגֶב לְקָדֵשׁ בַּרְנֵעַ וְיָצָא חֲצַר־אַדָּר וְעָבַר עַצְמֹנָה: 5 וְנָסַב הַגְּבוּל מֵעַצְמוֹן נַחְלָה מִצְרָיִם וְהָיוּ תוֹצְאֹתָיו הַיָּמָּה:

6 וּגְבוּל יָם וְהָיָה לָכֶם הַיָּם הַגָּדוֹל וּגְבוּל זֶה־יִהְיֶה לָכֶם גְּבוּל יָם: 7 וְזֶה־יִהְיֶה לָכֶם גְּבוּל צָפוֹן מִן־הַיָּם הַגָּדֹל תְּתָאוּ לָכֶם הֹר הָהָר: 8 מֵהֹר הָהָר תְּתָאוּ לְבֹא חֲמָת וְהָיוּ תּוֹצְאֹת הַגְּבֻל צְדָדָה: 9 וְיָצָא הַגְּבֻל זִפְרֹנָה וְהָיוּ תוֹצְאֹתָיו חֲצַר עֵינָן זֶה־יִהְיֶה

לד 4 וְהָיוּ

10 'You shall mark out your eastern border from Hazar Enan to Shepham; 11 the border shall go down from Shepham to Riblah on the east side of Ain; the border shall go down and reach to the eastern side of the Sea of Chinnereth; 12 the border shall go down along the Jordan, and it shall end at the Salt Sea. This shall be your land with its surrounding boundaries.' "

13 Then Moses commanded the children of Israel, saying: "This *is* the land which you shall inherit by lot, which the LORD has commanded to give to the nine tribes and to the half-tribe. 14 For the tribe of the children of Reuben according to the house of their fathers, and the tribe of the children of Gad according to the house of their fathers, have received *their inheritance;* and the half-tribe of Manasseh has received its inheritance. 15 The two tribes and the half-tribe have received their inheritance on this side of the Jordan, *across from* Jericho eastward, toward the sunrise."

16 And the LORD spoke to Moses, saying, 17 "These *are* the names of the men who shall divide the land among you as an inheritance: Eleazar the priest and Joshua the son of Nun. 18 And you shall take one leader of every tribe to divide the land for the inheritance. 19 These *are* the names of the men: from the tribe of Judah, Caleb the son of Jephunneh; 20 from the tribe of the children of Simeon, Shemuel the son of Ammihud; 21 from the tribe of Benjamin, Elidad the son of Chislon; 22 a leader from the tribe of the children of Dan, Bukki the son of Jogli; 23 from the sons of Joseph: a leader from the tribe of the children of Manasseh, Hanniel the son of Ephod, 24 and a leader from the tribe of the children of Ephraim, Kemuel the son of Shiphtan; 25 a leader from the tribe of the children of Zebulun, Elizaphan the son of Parnach; 26 a leader from the tribe of the children of Issachar, Paltiel the son of Azzan; 27 a leader from the tribe of the children of Asher, Ahihud the son of Shelomi; 28 and a leader from the tribe of the children of Naphtali, Pedahel the son of Ammihud."

29 These *are* the ones the LORD commanded to divide the inheritance among the children of Israel in the land of Canaan.

35 And the LORD spoke to Moses in the plains of Moab by the Jordan *across from* Jericho, saying: 2 "Command the children of Israel that they give the Levites cities to dwell in from the inheritance of their possession, and you shall *also* give the Levites common-land around the cities. 3 They shall have the cities to dwell in; and their common-land shall be for their cattle, for their herds, and for all their

10 וְהִתְאַוִּיתֶם לָכֶם לִגְבוּל קֵדְמָה לָכֶם גְּבוּל צָפוֹן: 11 וְיָרַד הַגְּבֻל מִשְּׁפָם הָרִבְלָה מִקֶּדֶם לָעָיִן וְיָרַד הַגְּבֻל וּמָחָה עַל־כֶּתֶף יָם־כִּנֶּרֶת קֵדְמָה: 12 וְיָרַד הַגְּבוּל הַיַּרְדֵּנָה וְהָיוּ תוֹצְאֹתָיו יָם הַמֶּלַח זֹאת תִּהְיֶה לָכֶם הָאָרֶץ לִגְבֻלֹתֶיהָ סָבִיב:

13 וַיְצַו מֹשֶׁה אֶת־בְּנֵי יִשְׂרָאֵל לֵאמֹר זֹאת הָאָרֶץ אֲשֶׁר תִּתְנַחֲלוּ אֹתָהּ בְּגוֹרָל אֲשֶׁר צִוָּה יְהוָה לָתֵת לְתִשְׁעַת הַמַּטּוֹת וַחֲצִי הַמַּטֶּה: 14 כִּי לָקְחוּ מַטֵּה בְנֵי הָראוּבֵנִי לְבֵית אֲבֹתָם וּמַטֵּה בְנֵי־הַגָּדִי לְבֵית אֲבֹתָם וַחֲצִי מַטֵּה מְנַשֶּׁה לָקְחוּ נַחֲלָתָם: 15 שְׁנֵי הַמַּטּוֹת וַחֲצִי הַמַּטֶּה לָקְחוּ נַחֲלָתָם מֵעֵבֶר לְיַרְדֵּן יְרֵחוֹ קֵדְמָה מִזְרָחָה: פ

16 וַיְדַבֵּר יְהוָה אֶל־מֹשֶׁה לֵּאמֹר: 17 אֵלֶּה שְׁמוֹת הָאֲנָשִׁים אֲשֶׁר־יִנְחֲלוּ לָכֶם אֶת־הָאָרֶץ אֶלְעָזָר הַכֹּהֵן וִיהוֹשֻׁעַ בִּן־נוּן: 18 וְנָשִׂיא אֶחָד נָשִׂיא אֶחָד מִמַּטֶּה תִּקְחוּ לִנְחֹל אֶת־הָאָרֶץ: 19 וְאֵלֶּה שְׁמוֹת הָאֲנָשִׁים לְמַטֵּה יְהוּדָה כָּלֵב בֶּן־יְפֻנֶּה: 20 וּלְמַטֵּה בְּנֵי שִׁמְעוֹן שְׁמוּאֵל בֶּן־עַמִּיהוּד: 21 לְמַטֵּה בִנְיָמִן אֱלִידָד בֶּן־כִּסְלוֹן: 22 וּלְמַטֵּה בְנֵי־דָן נָשִׂיא בֻּקִּי בֶּן־יָגְלִי: 23 לִבְנֵי יוֹסֵף לְמַטֵּה בְנֵי־מְנַשֶּׁה נָשִׂיא חַנִּיאֵל בֶּן־אֵפֹד: 24 וּלְמַטֵּה בְנֵי־אֶפְרַיִם נָשִׂיא קְמוּאֵל בֶּן־שִׁפְטָן: 25 וּלְמַטֵּה בְנֵי־זְבוּלֻן נָשִׂיא אֱלִיצָפָן בֶּן־פַּרְנָךְ: 26 וּלְמַטֵּה בְנֵי־יִשָּׂשכָר נָשִׂיא פַּלְטִיאֵל בֶּן־עַזָּן: 27 וּלְמַטֵּה בְנֵי־אָשֵׁר נָשִׂיא אֲחִיהוּד בֶּן־שְׁלֹמִי: 28 וּלְמַטֵּה בְנֵי־נַפְתָּלִי נָשִׂיא פְּדַהְאֵל בֶּן־עַמִּיהוּד: 29 אֵלֶּה אֲשֶׁר צִוָּה יְהוָה לְנַחֵל אֶת־בְּנֵי־יִשְׂרָאֵל בְּאֶרֶץ כְּנָעַן: פ

לה וַיְדַבֵּר יְהוָה אֶל־מֹשֶׁה בְּעַרְבֹת מוֹאָב עַל־יַרְדֵּן יְרֵחוֹ לֵאמֹר: 2 צַו אֶת־בְּנֵי יִשְׂרָאֵל וְנָתְנוּ לַלְוִיִּם מִנַּחֲלַת אֲחֻזָּתָם עָרִים לָשָׁבֶת וּמִגְרָשׁ לֶעָרִים סְבִיבֹתֵיהֶם תִּתְּנוּ לַלְוִיִּם: 3 וְהָיוּ הֶעָרִים לָהֶם לָשָׁבֶת וּמִגְרְשֵׁיהֶם יִהְיוּ לִבְהֶמְתָּם וְלִרְכֻשָׁם וּלְכֹל

animals. ⁴ The common-land of the cities which you will give the Levites *shall extend* from the wall of the city outward a thousand cubits all around. ⁵ And you shall measure outside the city on the east side two thousand cubits, on the south side two thousand cubits, on the west side two thousand cubits, and on the north side two thousand cubits. The city *shall be* in the middle. This shall belong to them as common-land for the cities.

⁶ "Now among the cities which you will give to the Levites *you shall appoint* six cities of refuge, to which a manslayer may flee. And to these you shall add forty-two cities. ⁷ So all the cities you will give to the Levites *shall be* forty-eight; these *you shall give* with their common-land. ⁸ And the cities which you will give *shall be* from the possession of the children of Israel; from the larger *tribe* you shall give many, from the smaller you shall give few. Each shall give some of its cities to the Levites, in proportion to the inheritance that each receives."

⁹ Then the LORD spoke to Moses, saying, ¹⁰ "Speak to the children of Israel, and say to them: 'When you cross the Jordan into the land of Canaan, ¹¹ then you shall appoint cities to be cities of refuge for you, that the manslayer who kills any person accidentally may flee there. ¹² They shall be cities of refuge for you from the avenger, that the manslayer may not die until he stands before the congregation in judgment. ¹³ And of the cities which you give, you shall have six cities of refuge. ¹⁴ You shall appoint three cities on this side of the Jordan, and three cities you shall appoint in the land of Canaan, *which* will be cities of refuge. ¹⁵ These six cities shall be for refuge for the children of Israel, for the stranger, and for the sojourner among them, that anyone who kills a person accidentally may flee there.

¹⁶ "But if he strikes him with an iron implement, so that he dies, he *is* a murderer; the murderer shall surely be put to death. ¹⁷ And if he strikes him with a stone in the hand, by which one could die, and he does die, he *is* a murderer; the murderer shall surely be put to death. ¹⁸ Or *if* he strikes him with a wooden hand weapon, by which one could die, and he does die, he *is* a murderer; the murderer shall surely be put to death. ¹⁹ The avenger of blood himself shall put the murderer to death; when he meets him, he shall put him to death. ²⁰ If he pushes him out of hatred or, while lying in wait, hurls something at him so that he dies, ²¹ or in enmity he strikes him with his hand so that he dies, the one who struck *him* shall surely be put to death. He *is* a murderer. The avenger of blood shall put the murderer to death when he meets him.

חַיָּתָם: 4 וּמִגְרְשֵׁי הֶעָרִים אֲשֶׁר תִּתְּנוּ לַלְוִיִּם מִקִּיר הָעִיר וָחוּצָה אֶלֶף אַמָּה סָבִיב: 5 וּמַדֹּתֶם מִחוּץ לָעִיר אֶת־פְּאַת־קֵדְמָה אַלְפַּיִם בָּאַמָּה וְאֶת־פְּאַת־נֶגֶב אַלְפַּיִם בָּאַמָּה וְאֶת־פְּאַת־יָם | אַלְפַּיִם בָּאַמָּה וְאֵת פְּאַת צָפוֹן אַלְפַּיִם בָּאַמָּה וְהָעִיר בַּתָּוֶךְ זֶה יִהְיֶה לָהֶם מִגְרְשֵׁי הֶעָרִים: 6 וְאֵת הֶעָרִים אֲשֶׁר תִּתְּנוּ לַלְוִיִּם אֵת שֵׁשׁ־עָרֵי הַמִּקְלָט אֲשֶׁר תִּתְּנוּ לָנֻס שָׁמָּה הָרֹצֵחַ וַעֲלֵיהֶם תִּתְּנוּ אַרְבָּעִים וּשְׁתַּיִם עִיר: 7 כָּל־הֶעָרִים אֲשֶׁר תִּתְּנוּ לַלְוִיִּם אַרְבָּעִים וּשְׁמֹנֶה עִיר אֶתְהֶן וְאֶת־מִגְרְשֵׁיהֶן: 8 וְהֶעָרִים אֲשֶׁר תִּתְּנוּ מֵאֲחֻזַּת בְּנֵי־יִשְׂרָאֵל מֵאֵת הָרַב תַּרְבּוּ וּמֵאֵת הַמְעַט תַּמְעִיטוּ אִישׁ כְּפִי נַחֲלָתוֹ אֲשֶׁר יִנְחָלוּ יִתֵּן מֵעָרָיו לַלְוִיִּם: פ

9 וַיְדַבֵּר יְהוָה אֶל־מֹשֶׁה לֵּאמֹר: 10 דַּבֵּר אֶל־בְּנֵי יִשְׂרָאֵל וְאָמַרְתָּ אֲלֵהֶם כִּי אַתֶּם עֹבְרִים אֶת־הַיַּרְדֵּן אַרְצָה כְּנָעַן: 11 וְהִקְרִיתֶם לָכֶם עָרִים עָרֵי מִקְלָט תִּהְיֶינָה לָכֶם וְנָס שָׁמָּה רֹצֵחַ מַכֵּה־נֶפֶשׁ בִּשְׁגָגָה: 12 וְהָיוּ לָכֶם הֶעָרִים לְמִקְלָט מִגֹּאֵל וְלֹא יָמוּת הָרֹצֵחַ עַד־עָמְדוֹ לִפְנֵי הָעֵדָה לַמִּשְׁפָּט: 13 וְהֶעָרִים אֲשֶׁר תִּתֵּנוּ שֵׁשׁ־עָרֵי מִקְלָט תִּהְיֶינָה לָכֶם: 14 אֵת | שְׁלֹשׁ הֶעָרִים תִּתְּנוּ מֵעֵבֶר לַיַּרְדֵּן וְאֵת שְׁלֹשׁ הֶעָרִים תִּתְּנוּ בְּאֶרֶץ כְּנָעַן עָרֵי מִקְלָט תִּהְיֶינָה: 15 לִבְנֵי יִשְׂרָאֵל וְלַגֵּר וְלַתּוֹשָׁב בְּתוֹכָם תִּהְיֶינָה שֵׁשׁ־הֶעָרִים הָאֵלֶּה לְמִקְלָט לָנוּס שָׁמָּה כָּל־מַכֵּה־נֶפֶשׁ בִּשְׁגָגָה: 16 וְאִם־בִּכְלִי בַרְזֶל | הִכָּהוּ וַיָּמֹת רֹצֵחַ הוּא מוֹת יוּמַת הָרֹצֵחַ: 17 וְאִם בְּאֶבֶן יָד אֲשֶׁר־יָמוּת בָּהּ הִכָּהוּ וַיָּמֹת רֹצֵחַ הוּא מוֹת יוּמַת הָרֹצֵחַ: 18 אוֹ בִּכְלִי עֵץ־יָד אֲשֶׁר־יָמוּת בּוֹ הִכָּהוּ וַיָּמֹת רֹצֵחַ הוּא מוֹת יוּמַת הָרֹצֵחַ: 19 גֹּאֵל הַדָּם הוּא יָמִית אֶת־הָרֹצֵחַ בְּפִגְעוֹ־בוֹ הוּא יְמִיתֶנּוּ: 20 וְאִם־בְּשִׂנְאָה יֶהְדָּפֶנּוּ אוֹ־הִשְׁלִיךְ עָלָיו בִּצְדִיָּה וַיָּמֹת: 21 אוֹ בְאֵיבָה הִכָּהוּ בְיָדוֹ וַיָּמֹת מוֹת־יוּמַת הַמַּכֶּה רֹצֵחַ הוּא גֹּאֵל הַדָּם יָמִית אֶת־הָרֹצֵחַ

22 'However, if he pushes him suddenly without
enmity, or throws anything at him without lying in
wait, 23 or uses a stone, by which a man could die,
throwing *it* at him without seeing *him,* so that he
dies, while he was not his enemy or seeking his
harm, 24 then the congregation shall judge between
the manslayer and the avenger of blood according
to these judgments. 25 So the congregation shall
deliver the manslayer from the hand of the avenger
of blood, and the congregation shall return him to
the city of refuge where he had fled, and he shall
remain there until the death of the high priest who
was anointed with the holy oil. 26 But if the
manslayer at any time goes outside the limits of
the city of refuge where he fled, 27 and the avenger
of blood finds him outside the limits of his city of
refuge, and the avenger of blood kills the manslayer, he shall not be guilty of blood, 28 because he
should have remained in his city of refuge until the
death of the high priest. But after the death of the
high priest the manslayer may return to the land of
his possession.

29 'And these *things* shall be a statute of judgment
to you throughout your generations in all your
dwellings. 30 Whoever kills a person, the murderer
shall be put to death on the testimony of witnesses;
but one witness is not *sufficient* testimony against a
person for the death *penalty.* 31 Moreover you shall
take no ransom for the life of a murderer who *is*
guilty of death, but he shall surely be put to death.
32 And you shall take no ransom for him who has
fled to his city of refuge, that he may return to dwell
in the land before the death of the priest. 33 So you
shall not pollute the land where you *are;* for blood
defiles the land, and no atonement can be made for
the land, for the blood that is shed on it, except by
the blood of him who shed it. 34 Therefore do not
defile the land which you inhabit, in the midst of
which I dwell; for I the LORD dwell among the
children of Israel.' "

36 Now the chief fathers of the families of the
children of Gilead the son of Machir, the son of
Manasseh, of the families of the sons of Joseph,
came near and spoke before Moses and before the
leaders, the chief fathers of the children of Israel.
2 And they said: "The LORD commanded my lord
Moses to give the land as an inheritance by lot to
the children of Israel, and my lord was commanded
by the LORD to give the inheritance of our brother
Zelophehad to his daughters. 3 Now if they are
married to any of the sons of the *other* tribes of the
children of Israel, then their inheritance will be
taken from the inheritance of our fathers, and it will

בְּפִגְעוֹ־בְו: 22 וְאִם־בְּפֶתַע בְּלֹא־אֵיבָה הֲדָפוֹ אוֹ־
הִשְׁלִיךְ עָלָיו כָּל־כְּלִי בְּלֹא צְדִיָּה: 23 אוֹ בְכָל־
אֶבֶן אֲשֶׁר־יָמוּת בָּהּ בְּלֹא רְאוֹת וַיַּפֵּל עָלָיו וַיָּמֹת
וְהוּא לֹא־אוֹיֵב לוֹ וְלֹא מְבַקֵּשׁ רָעָתוֹ: 24 וְשָׁפְטוּ
הָעֵדָה בֵּין הַמַּכֶּה וּבֵין גֹּאֵל הַדָּם עַל הַמִּשְׁפָּטִים
הָאֵלֶּה: 25 וְהִצִּילוּ הָעֵדָה אֶת־הָרֹצֵחַ מִיַּד גֹּאֵל
הַדָּם וְהֵשִׁיבוּ אֹתוֹ הָעֵדָה אֶל־עִיר מִקְלָטוֹ אֲשֶׁר־נָס
שָׁמָּה וְיָשַׁב בָּהּ עַד־מוֹת הַכֹּהֵן הַגָּדֹל אֲשֶׁר־מָשַׁח
אֹתוֹ בְּשֶׁמֶן הַקֹּדֶשׁ: 26 וְאִם־יָצֹא יֵצֵא הָרֹצֵחַ אֶת־
גְּבוּל עִיר מִקְלָטוֹ אֲשֶׁר יָנוּס שָׁמָּה: 27 וּמָצָא אֹתוֹ
גֹּאֵל הַדָּם מִחוּץ לִגְבוּל עִיר מִקְלָטוֹ וְרָצַח גֹּאֵל
הַדָּם אֶת־הָרֹצֵחַ אֵין לוֹ דָּם: 28 כִּי בְעִיר מִקְלָטוֹ
יֵשֵׁב עַד־מוֹת הַכֹּהֵן הַגָּדֹל וְאַחֲרֵי מוֹת הַכֹּהֵן
הַגָּדֹל יָשׁוּב הָרֹצֵחַ אֶל־אֶרֶץ אֲחֻזָּתוֹ: 29 וְהָיוּ אֵלֶּה
לָכֶם לְחֻקַּת מִשְׁפָּט לְדֹרֹתֵיכֶם בְּכֹל מוֹשְׁבֹתֵיכֶם:
30 כָּל־מַכֵּה־נֶפֶשׁ לְפִי עֵדִים יִרְצַח אֶת־הָרֹצֵחַ וְעֵד
אֶחָד לֹא־יַעֲנֶה בְנֶפֶשׁ לָמוּת: 31 וְלֹא־תִקְחוּ כֹפֶר
לְנֶפֶשׁ רֹצֵחַ אֲשֶׁר־הוּא רָשָׁע לָמוּת כִּי־מוֹת יוּמָת:
32 וְלֹא־תִקְחוּ כֹפֶר לָנוּס אֶל־עִיר מִקְלָטוֹ לָשׁוּב
לָשֶׁבֶת בָּאָרֶץ עַד־מוֹת הַכֹּהֵן: 33 וְלֹא־תַחֲנִיפוּ אֶת־
הָאָרֶץ אֲשֶׁר אַתֶּם בָּהּ כִּי הַדָּם הוּא יַחֲנִיף אֶת־
הָאָרֶץ וְלָאָרֶץ לֹא־יְכֻפַּר לַדָּם אֲשֶׁר שֻׁפַּךְ־בָּהּ כִּי־
אִם בְּדַם שֹׁפְכוֹ: 34 וְלֹא תְטַמֵּא אֶת־הָאָרֶץ אֲשֶׁר
אַתֶּם יֹשְׁבִים בָּהּ אֲשֶׁר אֲנִי שֹׁכֵן בְּתוֹכָהּ כִּי אֲנִי
יְהוָה שֹׁכֵן בְּתוֹךְ בְּנֵי יִשְׂרָאֵל:
פ

לו וַיִּקְרְבוּ רָאשֵׁי הָאָבוֹת לְמִשְׁפַּחַת בְּנֵי־גִלְעָד
בֶּן־מָכִיר בֶּן־מְנַשֶּׁה מִמִּשְׁפְּחֹת בְּנֵי יוֹסֵף וַיְדַבְּרוּ
לִפְנֵי מֹשֶׁה וְלִפְנֵי הַנְּשִׂאִים רָאשֵׁי אָבוֹת לִבְנֵי
יִשְׂרָאֵל: 2 וַיֹּאמְרוּ אֶת־אֲדֹנִי צִוָּה יְהוָה לָתֵת אֶת־
הָאָרֶץ בְּנַחֲלָה בְּגוֹרָל לִבְנֵי יִשְׂרָאֵל וַאדֹנִי צֻוָּה
בַיהוָה לָתֵת אֶת־נַחֲלַת צְלָפְחָד אָחִינוּ לִבְנֹתָיו:
3 וְהָיוּ לְאֶחָד מִבְּנֵי שִׁבְטֵי בְנֵי־יִשְׂרָאֵל לְנָשִׁים
וְנִגְרְעָה נַחֲלָתָן מִנַּחֲלַת אֲבֹתֵינוּ וְנוֹסַף עַל נַחֲלַת
הַמַּטֶּה אֲשֶׁר תִּהְיֶינָה לָהֶם וּמִגֹּרַל נַחֲלָתֵנוּ יִגָּרֵעַ:

be added to the inheritance of the tribe into which they marry; so it will be taken from the lot of our inheritance. 4 And when the Jubilee of the children of Israel comes, then their inheritance will be added to the inheritance of the tribe into which they marry; so their inheritance will be taken away from the inheritance of the tribe of our fathers. "

5 Then Moses commanded the children of Israel according to the word of the LORD, saying: "What the tribe of the sons of Joseph speaks is right. 6 This *is* what the LORD commands concerning the daughters of Zelophehad, saying, 'Let them marry whom they think best, but they may marry only within the family of their father's tribe.' 7 So the inheritance of the children of Israel shall not change hands from tribe to tribe, for every one of the children of Israel shall keep the inheritance of the tribe of his fathers. 8 And every daughter who possesses an inheritance in any tribe of the children of Israel shall be the wife of one of the family of her father's tribe, so that the children of Israel each may possess the inheritance of his fathers. 9 Thus no inheritance shall change hands from *one* tribe to another, but every tribe of the children of Israel shall keep its own inheritance."

10 Just as the LORD commanded Moses, so did the daughters of Zelophehad; 11 for Mahlah, Tirzah, Hoglah, Milcah, and Noah, the daughters of Zelophehad, were married to the sons of their father's brothers. 12 They were married into the families of the children of Manasseh the son of Joseph, and their inheritance remained in the tribe of their father's family.

13 These *are* the commandments and the judgments which the LORD commanded the children of Israel by the hand of Moses in the plains of Moab by the Jordan, *across from* Jericho.

4 וְאִם־יִהְיֶה הַיֹּבֵל לִבְנֵי יִשְׂרָאֵל וְנוֹסְפָה נַחֲלָתָן עַל נַחֲלַת הַמַּטֶּה אֲשֶׁר תִּהְיֶינָה לָהֶם וּמִנַּחֲלַת מַטֵּה אֲבֹתֵינוּ יִגָּרַע נַחֲלָתָן: 5 וַיְצַו מֹשֶׁה אֶת־בְּנֵי יִשְׂרָאֵל עַל־פִּי יְהֹוָה לֵאמֹר כֵּן מַטֵּה בְנֵי־יוֹסֵף דֹּבְרִים: 6 זֶה הַדָּבָר אֲשֶׁר־צִוָּה יְהֹוָה לִבְנוֹת צְלָפְחָד לֵאמֹר לַטּוֹב בְּעֵינֵיהֶם תִּהְיֶינָה לְנָשִׁים אַךְ לְמִשְׁפַּחַת מַטֵּה אֲבִיהֶם תִּהְיֶינָה לְנָשִׁים: 7 וְלֹא־תִסֹּב נַחֲלָה לִבְנֵי יִשְׂרָאֵל מִמַּטֶּה אֶל־מַטֶּה כִּי אִישׁ בְּנַחֲלַת מַטֵּה אֲבֹתָיו יִדְבְּקוּ בְּנֵי יִשְׂרָאֵל: 8 וְכָל־בַּת יֹרֶשֶׁת נַחֲלָה מִמַּטּוֹת בְּנֵי יִשְׂרָאֵל לְאֶחָד מִמִּשְׁפַּחַת מַטֵּה אָבִיהָ תִּהְיֶה לְאִשָּׁה לְמַעַן יִירְשׁוּ בְּנֵי יִשְׂרָאֵל אִישׁ נַחֲלַת אֲבֹתָיו: 9 וְלֹא־תִסֹּב נַחֲלָה מִמַּטֶּה לְמַטֶּה אַחֵר כִּי־אִישׁ בְּנַחֲלָתוֹ יִדְבְּקוּ מַטּוֹת בְּנֵי יִשְׂרָאֵל: 10 כַּאֲשֶׁר צִוָּה יְהֹוָה אֶת־מֹשֶׁה כֵּן עָשׂוּ בְּנוֹת צְלָפְחָד: 11 וַתִּהְיֶינָה מַחְלָה תִרְצָה וְחָגְלָה וּמִלְכָּה וְנֹעָה בְּנוֹת צְלָפְחָד לִבְנֵי דֹדֵיהֶן לְנָשִׁים:

12 מִמִּשְׁפְּחֹת בְּנֵי־מְנַשֶּׁה בֶן־יוֹסֵף הָיוּ לְנָשִׁים וַתְּהִי נַחֲלָתָן עַל־מַטֵּה מִשְׁפַּחַת אֲבִיהֶן: 13 אֵלֶּה הַמִּצְוֹת וְהַמִּשְׁפָּטִים אֲשֶׁר צִוָּה יְהֹוָה בְּיַד־מֹשֶׁה אֶל־בְּנֵי יִשְׂרָאֵל בְּעַרְבֹת מוֹאָב עַל יַרְדֵּן יְרֵחוֹ:

The Fifth Book of Moses Called

DEUTERONOMY

1 These *are* the words which Moses spoke to all Israel on this side of the Jordan in the wilderness, in the plain opposite Suph, between Paran, Tophel, Laban, Hazeroth, and Dizahab. ² *It is* eleven days' *journey* from Horeb by way of Mount Seir to Kadesh Barnea. ³ Now it came to pass in the fortieth year, in the eleventh month, on the first *day* of the month, *that* Moses spoke to the children of Israel according to all that the LORD had given him as commandments to them, ⁴ after he had killed Sihon king of the Amorites, who dwelt in Heshbon, and Og king of Bashan, who dwelt at Ashtaroth in Edrei.

⁵ On this side of the Jordan in the land of Moab, Moses began to explain this law, saying, ⁶ "The LORD our God spoke to us in Horeb, saying: 'You have dwelt long enough at this mountain. ⁷ Turn and take your journey, and go to the mountains of the Amorites, to all the neighboring *places* in the plain, in the mountains and in the lowland, in the South and on the seacoast, to the land of the Canaanites and to Lebanon, as far as the great river, the River Euphrates. ⁸ See, I have set the land before you; go in and possess the land which the LORD swore to your fathers—to Abraham, Isaac, and Jacob—to give to them and their descendants after them.'

⁹ "And I spoke to you at that time, saying: 'I alone am not able to bear you. ¹⁰ The LORD your God has multiplied you, and here you *are* today, as the stars of heaven in multitude. ¹¹ May the LORD God of your fathers make you a thousand times more numerous than you are, and bless you as He has promised you! ¹² How can I alone bear your problems and your burdens and your complaints? ¹³ Choose wise, understanding, and knowledgeable men from among your tribes, and I will make them heads over you.' ¹⁴ And you answered me and said, 'The thing which you have told *us* to do *is* good.' ¹⁵ So I took the heads of your tribes, wise and knowledgeable men, and made them heads over you, leaders of thousands, leaders of hundreds, leaders of fifties, leaders of tens, and officers for your tribes.

¹⁶ "Then I commanded your judges at that time, saying, 'Hear *the cases* between your brethren, and judge righteously between a man and his brother or

דברים

א אֵ֣לֶּה הַדְּבָרִ֗ים אֲשֶׁ֨ר דִּבֶּ֤ר מֹשֶׁה֙ אֶל־כָּל־
יִשְׂרָאֵ֔ל בְּעֵ֖בֶר הַיַּרְדֵּ֑ן בַּמִּדְבָּ֡ר בָּֽעֲרָבָה֩ מ֨וֹל ס֜וּף
בֵּֽין־פָּארָ֧ן וּבֵֽין־תֹּ֛פֶל וְלָבָ֥ן וַחֲצֵרֹ֖ת וְדִ֥י זָהָֽב: ² אַחַ֨ד
עָשָׂ֥ר יוֹם֙ מֵֽחֹרֵ֔ב דֶּ֖רֶךְ הַר־שֵׂעִ֑יר עַ֖ד קָדֵ֥שׁ בַּרְנֵֽעַ:
³ וַיְהִי֙ בְּאַרְבָּעִ֣ים שָׁנָ֔ה בְּעַשְׁתֵּֽי־עָשָׂ֥ר חֹ֖דֶשׁ בְּאֶחָ֣ד
לַחֹ֑דֶשׁ דִּבֶּ֤ר מֹשֶׁה֙ אֶל־בְּנֵ֣י יִשְׂרָאֵ֔ל כְּכֹל֩ אֲשֶׁ֨ר
צִוָּ֧ה יְהֹוָ֛ה אֹת֖וֹ אֲלֵהֶֽם: ⁴ אַחֲרֵ֣י הַכֹּת֗וֹ אֵ֚ת סִיחֹן֙
מֶ֣לֶךְ הָֽאֱמֹרִ֔י אֲשֶׁ֥ר יוֹשֵׁ֖ב בְּחֶשְׁבּ֑וֹן וְאֵ֗ת ע֚וֹג מֶ֣לֶךְ
הַבָּשָׁ֔ן אֲשֶׁר־יוֹשֵׁ֥ב בְּעַשְׁתָּרֹ֖ת בְּאֶדְרֶֽעִי: ⁵ בְּעֵ֥בֶר
הַיַּרְדֵּ֖ן בְּאֶ֣רֶץ מוֹאָ֑ב הוֹאִ֣יל מֹשֶׁ֔ה בֵּאֵ֛ר אֶת־הַתּוֹרָ֥ה
הַזֹּ֖את לֵאמֹֽר: ⁶ יְהֹוָ֧ה אֱלֹהֵ֛ינוּ דִּבֶּ֥ר אֵלֵ֖ינוּ בְּחֹרֵ֣ב
לֵאמֹ֑ר רַב־לָכֶ֥ם שֶׁ֖בֶת בָּהָ֥ר הַזֶּֽה: ⁷ פְּנ֣וּ | וּסְע֣וּ
לָכֶ֗ם וּבֹ֨אוּ הַ֥ר הָֽאֱמֹרִי֮ וְאֶל־כָּל־שְׁכֵנָיו֒ בָּֽעֲרָבָ֥ה
בָהָ֣ר וּבַשְּׁפֵלָ֣ה וּבַנֶּ֣גֶב וּבְח֣וֹף הַיָּ֑ם אֶ֤רֶץ הַֽכְּנַעֲנִי֙
וְהַלְּבָנ֔וֹן עַד־הַנָּהָ֥ר הַגָּדֹ֖ל נְהַר־פְּרָֽת: ⁸ רְאֵ֛ה נָתַ֥תִּי
לִפְנֵיכֶ֖ם אֶת־הָאָ֑רֶץ בֹּ֚אוּ וּרְשׁ֣וּ אֶת־הָאָ֔רֶץ אֲשֶׁ֣ר
נִשְׁבַּ֣ע יְ֠הֹוָ֠ה לַאֲבֹֽתֵיכֶ֜ם לְאַבְרָהָ֨ם לְיִצְחָ֤ק וּֽלְיַעֲקֹב֙
לָתֵ֣ת לָהֶ֔ם וּלְזַרְעָ֖ם אַחֲרֵיהֶֽם: ⁹ וָאֹמַ֣ר אֲלֵכֶ֔ם
בָּעֵ֥ת הַהִ֖וא לֵאמֹ֑ר לֹא־אוּכַ֥ל לְבַדִּ֖י שְׂאֵ֥ת אֶתְכֶֽם:
¹⁰ יְהֹוָ֥ה אֱלֹֽהֵיכֶ֖ם הִרְבָּ֣ה אֶתְכֶ֑ם וְהִנְּכֶ֣ם הַיּ֔וֹם
כְּכֽוֹכְבֵ֥י הַשָּׁמַ֖יִם לָרֹֽב: ¹¹ יְהֹוָ֞ה אֱלֹהֵ֣י אֲבֽוֹתֵכֶ֗ם יֹסֵ֧ף
עֲלֵיכֶ֛ם כָּכֶ֖ם אֶ֣לֶף פְּעָמִ֑ים וִיבָרֵ֣ךְ אֶתְכֶ֔ם כַּֽאֲשֶׁ֖ר
דִּבֶּ֥ר לָכֶֽם: ¹² אֵיכָ֥ה אֶשָּׂ֖א לְבַדִּ֑י טָרְחֲכֶ֥ם וּמַֽשַּׂאֲכֶ֖ם
וְרִֽיבְכֶֽם: ¹³ הָב֣וּ לָ֠כֶ֠ם אֲנָשִׁ֨ים חֲכָמִ֧ים וּנְבֹנִ֛ים
וִֽידֻעִ֖ים לְשִׁבְטֵיכֶ֑ם וַאֲשִׂימֵ֖ם בְּרָאשֵׁיכֶֽם: ¹⁴ וַֽתַּעֲנ֖וּ
אֹתִ֑י וַתֹּ֣אמְר֔וּ טֽוֹב־הַדָּבָ֥ר אֲשֶׁר־דִּבַּ֖רְתָּ לַעֲשֽׂוֹת:
¹⁵ וָֽאֶקַּ֞ח אֶת־רָאשֵׁ֣י שִׁבְטֵיכֶ֗ם אֲנָשִׁ֤ים חֲכָמִים֙
וִֽידֻעִ֔ים וָֽאֶתֵּ֥ן אֹתָ֖ם רָאשִׁ֣ים עֲלֵיכֶ֑ם שָׂרֵ֨י אֲלָפִ֜ים
וְשָׂרֵ֣י מֵא֗וֹת וְשָׂרֵ֤י חֲמִשִּׁים֙ וְשָׂרֵ֣י עֲשָׂרֹ֔ת וְשֹׁטְרִ֖ים
לְשִׁבְטֵיכֶֽם: ¹⁶ וָאֲצַוֶּה֙ אֶת־שֹׁ֣פְטֵיכֶ֔ם בָּעֵ֥ת הַהִ֖וא
לֵאמֹ֑ר שָׁמֹ֤עַ בֵּֽין־אֲחֵיכֶם֙ וּשְׁפַטְתֶּ֣ם צֶ֔דֶק בֵּֽין־אִ֥ישׁ

the stranger who is with him. ¹⁷You shall not show partiality in judgment; you shall hear the small as well as the great; you shall not be afraid in any man's presence, for the judgment *is* God's. The case that is too hard for you, bring to me, and I will hear it.' ¹⁸And I commanded you at that time all the things which you should do.

¹⁹ "So we departed from Horeb, and went through all that great and terrible wilderness which you saw on the way to the mountains of the Amorites, as the LORD our God had commanded us. Then we came to Kadesh Barnea. ²⁰And I said to you, 'You have come to the mountains of the Amorites, which the LORD our God is giving us. ²¹Look, the LORD your God has set the land before you; go up *and* possess *it,* as the LORD God of your fathers has spoken to you; do not fear or be discouraged.'

²² "And every one of you came near to me and said, 'Let us send men before us, and let them search out the land for us, and bring back word to us of the way by which we should go up, and of the cities into which we shall come.'

²³ "The plan pleased me well; so I took twelve of your men, one man from *each* tribe. ²⁴And they departed and went up into the mountains, and came to the Valley of Eshcol, and spied it out. ²⁵They also took *some* of the fruit of the land in their hands and brought *it* down to us; and they brought back word to us, saying, '*It is* a good land which the LORD our God is giving us.'

²⁶ "Nevertheless you would not go up, but rebelled against the command of the LORD your God; ²⁷and you complained in your tents, and said, 'Because the LORD hates us, He has brought us out of the land of Egypt to deliver us into the hand of the Amorites, to destroy us. ²⁸Where can we go up? Our brethren have discouraged our hearts, saying, "The people *are* greater and taller than we; the cities *are* great and fortified up to heaven; moreover we have seen the sons of the Anakim there." '

²⁹ "Then I said to you, 'Do not be terrified, or afraid of them. ³⁰The LORD your God, who goes before you, He will fight for you, according to all He did for you in Egypt before your eyes, ³¹and in the wilderness where you saw how the LORD your God carried you, as a man carries his son, in all the way that you went until you came to this place.' ³²Yet, for all that, you did not believe the LORD your God, ³³who went in the way before you to search out a place for you to pitch your tents, to show you the way you should go, in the fire by night and in the cloud by day.

וּבֵין־אָחִיו וּבֵין גֵּרוֹ: 17 לֹא־תַכִּירוּ פָנִים בַּמִּשְׁפָּט כַּקָּטֹן כַּגָּדֹל תִּשְׁמָעוּן לֹא תָגוּרוּ מִפְּנֵי־אִישׁ כִּי הַמִּשְׁפָּט לֵאלֹהִים הוּא וְהַדָּבָר אֲשֶׁר יִקְשֶׁה מִכֶּם תַּקְרִבוּן אֵלַי וּשְׁמַעְתִּיו: 18 וָאֲצַוֶּה אֶתְכֶם בָּעֵת הַהִוא אֵת כָּל־הַדְּבָרִים אֲשֶׁר תַּעֲשׂוּן: 19 וַנִּסַּע מֵחֹרֵב וַנֵּלֶךְ אֵת כָּל־הַמִּדְבָּר הַגָּדוֹל וְהַנּוֹרָא הַהוּא אֲשֶׁר רְאִיתֶם דֶּרֶךְ הַר הָאֱמֹרִי כַּאֲשֶׁר צִוָּה יְהֹוָה אֱלֹהֵינוּ אֹתָנוּ וַנָּבֹא עַד קָדֵשׁ בַּרְנֵעַ: 20 וָאֹמַר אֲלֵכֶם בָּאתֶם עַד־הַר הָאֱמֹרִי אֲשֶׁר־יְהֹוָה אֱלֹהֵינוּ נֹתֵן לָנוּ: 21 רְאֵה נָתַן יְהֹוָה אֱלֹהֶיךָ לְפָנֶיךָ אֶת־הָאָרֶץ עֲלֵה רֵשׁ כַּאֲשֶׁר דִּבֶּר יְהֹוָה אֱלֹהֵי אֲבֹתֶיךָ לָךְ אַל־תִּירָא וְאַל־תֵּחָת: 22 וַתִּקְרְבוּן אֵלַי כֻּלְּכֶם וַתֹּאמְרוּ נִשְׁלְחָה אֲנָשִׁים לְפָנֵינוּ וְיַחְפְּרוּ־לָנוּ אֶת־הָאָרֶץ וְיָשִׁבוּ אֹתָנוּ דָּבָר אֶת־הַדֶּרֶךְ אֲשֶׁר נַעֲלֶה־בָּהּ וְאֵת הֶעָרִים אֲשֶׁר נָבֹא אֲלֵיהֶן: 23 וַיִּיטַב בְּעֵינַי הַדָּבָר וָאֶקַּח מִכֶּם שְׁנֵים עָשָׂר אֲנָשִׁים אִישׁ אֶחָד לַשָּׁבֶט: 24 וַיִּפְנוּ וַיַּעֲלוּ הָהָרָה וַיָּבֹאוּ עַד־נַחַל אֶשְׁכֹּל וַיְרַגְּלוּ אֹתָהּ: 25 וַיִּקְחוּ בְיָדָם מִפְּרִי הָאָרֶץ וַיּוֹרִדוּ אֵלֵינוּ וַיָּשִׁבוּ אֹתָנוּ דָבָר וַיֹּאמְרוּ טוֹבָה הָאָרֶץ אֲשֶׁר־יְהֹוָה אֱלֹהֵינוּ נֹתֵן לָנוּ: 26 וְלֹא אֲבִיתֶם לַעֲלֹת וַתַּמְרוּ אֶת־פִּי יְהֹוָה אֱלֹהֵיכֶם: 27 וַתֵּרָגְנוּ בְאָהֳלֵיכֶם וַתֹּאמְרוּ בְּשִׂנְאַת יְהֹוָה אֹתָנוּ הוֹצִיאָנוּ מֵאֶרֶץ מִצְרָיִם לָתֵת אֹתָנוּ בְּיַד הָאֱמֹרִי לְהַשְׁמִידֵנוּ: 28 אָנָה | אֲנַחְנוּ עֹלִים אַחֵינוּ הֵמַסּוּ אֶת־לְבָבֵנוּ לֵאמֹר עַם גָּדוֹל וָרָם מִמֶּנּוּ עָרִים גְּדֹלֹת וּבְצוּרֹת בַּשָּׁמָיִם וְגַם־בְּנֵי עֲנָקִים רָאִינוּ שָׁם: 29 וָאֹמַר אֲלֵכֶם לֹא־תַעַרְצוּן וְלֹא־תִירְאוּן מֵהֶם: 30 יְהֹוָה אֱלֹהֵיכֶם הַהֹלֵךְ לִפְנֵיכֶם הוּא יִלָּחֵם לָכֶם כְּכֹל אֲשֶׁר עָשָׂה אִתְּכֶם בְּמִצְרַיִם לְעֵינֵיכֶם: 31 וּבַמִּדְבָּר אֲשֶׁר רָאִיתָ אֲשֶׁר נְשָׂאֲךָ יְהֹוָה אֱלֹהֶיךָ כַּאֲשֶׁר יִשָּׂא־אִישׁ אֶת־בְּנוֹ בְּכָל־הַדֶּרֶךְ אֲשֶׁר הֲלַכְתֶּם עַד־בֹּאֲכֶם עַד־הַמָּקוֹם הַזֶּה: 32 וּבַדָּבָר הַזֶּה אֵינְכֶם מַאֲמִינִם בַּיהֹוָה אֱלֹהֵיכֶם: 33 הַהֹלֵךְ לִפְנֵיכֶם בַּדֶּרֶךְ לָתוּר לָכֶם מָקוֹם לַחֲנֹתְכֶם בָּאֵשׁ | לַיְלָה לַרְאֹתְכֶם

34"And the LORD heard the sound of your words, and was angry, and took an oath, saying, 35'Surely not one of these men of this evil generation shall see that good land of which I swore to give to your fathers, 36except Caleb the son of Jephunneh; he shall see it, and to him and his children I am giving the land on which he walked, because he wholly followed the LORD.' 37The LORD was also angry with me for your sakes, saying, 'Even you shall not go in there. 38Joshua the son of Nun, who stands before you, he shall go in there. Encourage him, for he shall cause Israel to inherit it.

39'Moreover your little ones and your children, who you say will be victims, who today have no knowledge of good and evil, they shall go in there; to them I will give it, and they shall possess it. 40But as for you, turn and take your journey into the wilderness by the Way of the Red Sea.'

41"Then you answered and said to me, 'We have sinned against the LORD; we will go up and fight, just as the LORD our God commanded us.' And when everyone of you had girded on his weapons of war, you were ready to go up into the mountain.

42"And the LORD said to me, 'Tell them, "Do not go up nor fight, for I am not among you; lest you be defeated before your enemies."' 43So I spoke to you; yet you would not listen, but rebelled against the command of the LORD, and presumptuously went up into the mountain. 44And the Amorites who dwelt in that mountain came out against you and chased you as bees do, and drove you back from Seir to Hormah. 45Then you returned and wept before the LORD, but the LORD would not listen to your voice nor give ear to you.

46"So you remained in Kadesh many days, according to the days that you spent there.

2 "Then we turned and journeyed into the wilderness of the Way of the Red Sea, as the LORD spoke to me, and we skirted Mount Seir for many days.

2"And the LORD spoke to me, saying: 3'You have skirted this mountain long enough; turn northward. 4And command the people, saying, "You are about to pass through the territory of your brethren, the descendants of Esau, who live in Seir; and they will be afraid of you. Therefore watch yourselves carefully. 5Do not meddle with them, for I will not give you any of their land, no, not so much as one footstep, because I have given Mount Seir to Esau as a possession. 6You shall buy food

---

34 וַיִּשְׁמַ֣ע יְהֹוָ֔ה בְּדֶ֥רֶךְ אֲשֶׁ֛ר תֵּלְכוּ־בָ֖הּ וּבְעָנָ֣ן יוֹמָ֑ם אֶת־ק֖וֹל דִּבְרֵיכֶ֑ם וַיִּקְצֹ֖ף וַיִּשָּׁבַ֥ע לֵאמֹֽר׃ 35 אִם־יִרְאֶ֥ה אִישׁ֙ בָּאֲנָשִׁ֣ים הָאֵ֔לֶּה הַדּ֥וֹר הָרָ֖ע הַזֶּ֑ה אֵ֚ת הָאָ֣רֶץ הַטּוֹבָ֔ה אֲשֶׁ֣ר נִשְׁבַּ֔עְתִּי לָתֵ֖ת לַאֲבֹתֵיכֶֽם׃ 36 זוּלָתִ֞י כָּלֵ֣ב בֶּן־יְפֻנֶּ֗ה ה֚וּא יִרְאֶ֔נָּה וְלֽוֹ־אֶתֵּ֧ן אֶת־הָאָ֛רֶץ אֲשֶׁ֥ר דָּֽרַךְ־בָּ֖הּ וּלְבָנָ֑יו יַ֕עַן אֲשֶׁ֥ר מִלֵּ֖א אַחֲרֵ֥י יְהֹוָֽה׃ 37 גַּם־בִּי֙ הִתְאַנַּ֣ף יְהֹוָ֔ה בִּגְלַלְכֶ֖ם לֵאמֹ֑ר גַּם־אַתָּ֖ה לֹא־תָבֹ֥א שָֽׁם׃ 38 יְהוֹשֻׁ֤עַ בִּן־נוּן֙ הָעֹמֵ֣ד לְפָנֶ֔יךָ ה֖וּא יָ֣בֹא שָׁ֑מָּה אֹת֣וֹ חַזֵּ֔ק כִּי־ה֖וּא יַנְחִלֶ֥נָּה אֶת־יִשְׂרָאֵֽל׃ 39 וְטַפְּכֶ֞ם אֲשֶׁ֣ר אֲמַרְתֶּ֗ם לָבַ֣ז יִֽהְיֶ֔ה וּ֠בְנֵיכֶ֠ם אֲשֶׁ֨ר לֹא־יָֽדְע֤וּ הַיּוֹם֙ ט֣וֹב וָרָ֔ע הֵ֖מָּה יָבֹ֣אוּ שָׁ֑מָּה וְלָהֶ֣ם אֶתְּנֶ֔נָּה וְהֵ֖ם יִֽירָשֽׁוּהָ׃ 40 וְאַתֶּ֖ם פְּנ֣וּ לָכֶ֑ם וּסְע֥וּ הַמִּדְבָּ֖רָה דֶּ֥רֶךְ יַם־סֽוּף׃ 41 וַתַּעֲנ֣וּ ׀ וַתֹּאמְר֣וּ אֵלַ֗י חָטָ֘אנוּ֘ לַֽיהֹוָה֒ אֲנַ֤חְנוּ נַעֲלֶה֙ וְנִלְחַ֔מְנוּ כְּכֹ֥ל אֲשֶׁר־צִוָּ֖נוּ יְהֹוָ֣ה אֱלֹהֵ֑ינוּ וַֽתַּחְגְּר֗וּ אִ֚ישׁ אֶת־כְּלֵ֣י מִלְחַמְתּ֔וֹ וַתָּהִ֖ינוּ לַעֲלֹ֥ת הָהָֽרָה׃ 42 וַיֹּ֨אמֶר יְהֹוָ֜ה אֵלַ֗י אֱמֹ֤ר לָהֶם֙ לֹ֤א תַֽעֲלוּ֙ וְלֹא־תִלָּ֣חֲמ֔וּ כִּ֥י אֵינֶ֖נִּי בְּקִרְבְּכֶ֑ם וְלֹא֙ תִּנָּ֣גְפ֔וּ לִפְנֵ֖י אֹיְבֵיכֶֽם׃ 43 וָאֲדַבֵּ֥ר אֲלֵיכֶ֖ם וְלֹ֣א שְׁמַעְתֶּ֑ם וַתַּמְרוּ֙ אֶת־פִּ֣י יְהֹוָ֔ה וַתָּזִ֖דוּ וַתַּעֲל֥וּ הָהָֽרָה׃ 44 וַיֵּצֵ֨א הָאֱמֹרִ֜י הַיֹּשֵׁ֨ב בָּהָ֤ר הַהוּא֙ לִקְרַאתְכֶ֔ם וַיִּרְדְּפ֣וּ אֶתְכֶ֔ם כַּאֲשֶׁ֥ר תַּעֲשֶׂ֖ינָה הַדְּבֹרִ֑ים וַֽיַּכְּת֧וּ אֶתְכֶ֛ם בְּשֵׂעִ֖יר עַד־חָרְמָֽה׃ 45 וַתָּשֻׁ֥בוּ וַתִּבְכּ֖וּ לִפְנֵ֣י יְהֹוָ֑ה וְלֹֽא־שָׁמַ֤ע יְהֹוָה֙ בְּקֹ֣לְכֶ֔ם וְלֹ֥א הֶאֱזִ֖ין אֲלֵיכֶֽם׃ 46 וַתֵּשְׁב֥וּ בְקָדֵ֖שׁ יָמִ֣ים רַבִּ֑ים כַּיָּמִ֖ים אֲשֶׁ֥ר יְשַׁבְתֶּֽם׃

ב וַנֵּ֜פֶן וַנִּסַּ֤ע הַמִּדְבָּ֙רָה֙ דֶּ֣רֶךְ יַם־ס֔וּף כַּאֲשֶׁ֛ר דִּבֶּ֥ר יְהֹוָ֖ה אֵלָ֑י וַנָּ֥סׇב אֶת־הַר־שֵׂעִ֖יר יָמִ֥ים רַבִּֽים׃ ס 2 וַיֹּ֥אמֶר יְהֹוָ֖ה אֵלַ֥י לֵאמֹֽר׃ 3 רַב־לָכֶ֕ם סֹ֖ב אֶת־הָהָ֣ר הַזֶּ֑ה פְּנ֥וּ לָכֶ֖ם צָפֹֽנָה׃ 4 וְאֶת־הָעָם֮ צַ֣ו לֵאמֹר֒ אַתֶּ֣ם עֹֽבְרִ֗ים בִּגְבוּל֙ אֲחֵיכֶ֣ם בְּנֵי־עֵשָׂ֔ו הַיֹּשְׁבִ֖ים בְּשֵׂעִ֑יר וְיִֽירְא֣וּ מִכֶּ֔ם וְנִשְׁמַרְתֶּ֖ם מְאֹֽד׃ 5 אַל־תִּתְגָּר֣וּ בָ֔ם כִּ֠י לֹֽא־אֶתֵּ֤ן לָכֶם֙ מֵֽאַרְצָ֔ם עַ֖ד מִדְרַ֣ךְ כַּף־רָ֑גֶל כִּֽי־יְרֻשָּׁ֣ה לְעֵשָׂ֔ו נָתַ֖תִּי אֶת־הַ֥ר שֵׂעִֽיר׃ 6 אֹ֣כֶל תִּשְׁבְּר֧וּ מֵֽאִתָּ֛ם בַּכֶּ֖סֶף וַאֲכַלְתֶּ֑ם

from them with money, that you may eat; and you shall also buy water from them with money, that you may drink.

7 "For the LORD your God has blessed you in all the work of your hand. He knows your trudging through this great wilderness. These forty years the LORD your God *has been* with you; you have lacked nothing." '

8 "And when we passed beyond our brethren, the descendants of Esau who dwell in Seir, away from the road of the plain, away from Elath and Ezion Geber, we turned and passed by way of the Wilderness of Moab. 9 Then the LORD said to me, 'Do not harass Moab, nor contend with them in battle, for I will not give you *any* of their land *as a* possession, because I have given Ar to the descendants of Lot *as a* possession.' "

10 (The Emim had dwelt there in times past, a people as great and numerous and tall as the Anakim. 11 They were also regarded as giants, like the Anakim, but the Moabites call them Emim. 12 The Horites formerly dwelt in Seir, but the descendants of Esau dispossessed them and destroyed them from before them, and dwelt in their place, just as Israel did to the land of their possession which the LORD gave them.)

13 " 'Now rise and cross over the Valley of the Zered.' So we crossed over the Valley of the Zered. 14 And the time we took to come from Kadesh Barnea until we crossed over the Valley of the Zered *was* thirty-eight years, until all the generation of the men of war were consumed from the midst of the camp, just as the LORD had sworn to them. 15 For indeed the hand of the LORD was against them, to destroy them from the midst of the camp until they were consumed.

16 "So it was, when all the men of war had finally perished from among the people, 17 that the LORD spoke to me, saying: 18 'This day you are to cross over at Ar, the boundary of Moab. 19 And *when you* come near the people of Ammon, do not harass them or meddle with them, for I will not give you *any* of the land of the people of Ammon *as a* possession, because I have given it to the descendants of Lot *as a* possession.' "

20 (That was also regarded as a land of giants; giants formerly dwelt there. But the Ammonites call them Zamzummim, 21 a people as great and numerous and tall as the Anakim. But the LORD destroyed them before them, and they dispossessed them and dwelt in their place, 22 just as He had done for the descendants of Esau, who dwelt in Seir, when He destroyed the Horites from before them. They dispossessed them and dwelt in their place,

7 כִּי יְהוָה אֱלֹהֶיךָ בֵּרַכְךָ בְּכֹל מַעֲשֵׂה יָדֶךָ יָדַע לֶכְתְּךָ אֶת־הַמִּדְבָּר הַגָּדֹל הַזֶּה זֶה | אַרְבָּעִים שָׁנָה יְהוָה אֱלֹהֶיךָ עִמָּךְ לֹא חָסַרְתָּ דָּבָר: 8 וַנַּעֲבֹר מֵאֵת אַחֵינוּ בְנֵי־עֵשָׂו הַיֹּשְׁבִים בְּשֵׂעִיר מִדֶּרֶךְ הָעֲרָבָה מֵאֵילַת וּמֵעֶצְיֹן גָּבֶר ס וַנֵּפֶן וַנַּעֲבֹר דֶּרֶךְ מִדְבַּר מוֹאָב: 9 וַיֹּאמֶר יְהוָה אֵלַי אַל־תָּצַר אֶת־מוֹאָב וְאַל־תִּתְגָּר בָּם מִלְחָמָה כִּי לֹא־אֶתֵּן לְךָ מֵאַרְצוֹ יְרֻשָּׁה כִּי לִבְנֵי־לוֹט נָתַתִּי אֶת־עָר יְרֻשָּׁה: 10 הָאֵמִים לְפָנִים יָשְׁבוּ בָהּ עַם גָּדוֹל וְרַב וָרָם כָּעֲנָקִים: 11 רְפָאִים יֵחָשְׁבוּ אַף־הֵם כָּעֲנָקִים וְהַמֹּאָבִים יִקְרְאוּ לָהֶם אֵמִים: 12 וּבְשֵׂעִיר יָשְׁבוּ הַחֹרִים לְפָנִים וּבְנֵי עֵשָׂו יִירָשׁוּם וַיַּשְׁמִידוּם מִפְּנֵיהֶם וַיֵּשְׁבוּ תַחְתָּם כַּאֲשֶׁר עָשָׂה יִשְׂרָאֵל לְאֶרֶץ יְרֻשָּׁתוֹ אֲשֶׁר־נָתַן יְהוָה לָהֶם: 13 עַתָּה קֻמוּ וְעִבְרוּ לָכֶם אֶת־נַחַל זָרֶד וַנַּעֲבֹר אֶת־נַחַל זָרֶד:

14 וְהַיָּמִים אֲשֶׁר־הָלַכְנוּ | מִקָּדֵשׁ בַּרְנֵעַ עַד אֲשֶׁר־עָבַרְנוּ אֶת־נַחַל זֶרֶד שְׁלֹשִׁים וּשְׁמֹנֶה שָׁנָה עַד־תֹּם כָּל־הַדּוֹר אַנְשֵׁי הַמִּלְחָמָה מִקֶּרֶב הַמַּחֲנֶה כַּאֲשֶׁר נִשְׁבַּע יְהוָה לָהֶם: 15 וְגַם יַד־יְהוָה הָיְתָה בָּם לְהֻמָּם מִקֶּרֶב הַמַּחֲנֶה עַד תֻּמָּם: 16 וַיְהִי כַאֲשֶׁר־תַּמּוּ כָל־אַנְשֵׁי הַמִּלְחָמָה לָמוּת מִקֶּרֶב הָעָם: ס 17 וַיְדַבֵּר יְהוָה אֵלַי לֵאמֹר:

18 אַתָּה עֹבֵר הַיּוֹם אֶת־גְּבוּל מוֹאָב אֶת־עָר: 19 וְקָרַבְתָּ מוּל בְּנֵי עַמּוֹן אַל־תְּצֻרֵם וְאַל־תִּתְגָּר בָּם כִּי לֹא־אֶתֵּן מֵאֶרֶץ בְּנֵי־עַמּוֹן לְךָ יְרֻשָּׁה כִּי לִבְנֵי־לוֹט נְתַתִּיהָ יְרֻשָּׁה: 20 אֶרֶץ־רְפָאִים תֵּחָשֵׁב אַף־הִוא רְפָאִים יָשְׁבוּ־בָהּ לְפָנִים וְהָעַמֹּנִים יִקְרְאוּ לָהֶם זַמְזֻמִּים: 21 עַם גָּדוֹל וְרַב וָרָם כָּעֲנָקִים וַיַּשְׁמִידֵם יְהוָה מִפְּנֵיהֶם וַיִּירָשֻׁם וַיֵּשְׁבוּ תַחְתָּם: 22 כַּאֲשֶׁר עָשָׂה לִבְנֵי עֵשָׂו הַיֹּשְׁבִים בְּשֵׂעִיר אֲשֶׁר הִשְׁמִיד אֶת־הַחֹרִי מִפְּנֵיהֶם וַיִּירָשֻׁם וַיֵּשְׁבוּ תַחְתָּם

even to this day. 23 And the Avim, who dwelt in villages as far as Gaza—the Caphtorim, who came from Caphtor, destroyed them and dwelt in their place.)

24 "'Rise, take your journey, and cross over the River Arnon. Look, I have given into your hand Sihon the Amorite, king of Heshbon, and his land. Begin to possess *it,* and engage him in battle. 25 This day I will begin to put the dread and fear of you upon the nations under the whole heaven, who shall hear the report of you, and shall tremble and be in anguish because of you.'

26 "And I sent messengers from the Wilderness of Kedemoth to Sihon king of Heshbon, with words of peace, saying, 27 'Let me pass through your land; I will keep strictly to the road, and I will turn neither to the right nor to the left. 28 You shall sell me food for money, that I may eat, and give me water for money, that I may drink; only let me pass through on foot, 29 just as the descendants of Esau who dwell in Seir and the Moabites who dwell in Ar did for me, until I cross the Jordan to the land which the LORD our God is giving us.'

30 "But Sihon king of Heshbon would not let us pass through, for the LORD your God hardened his spirit and made his heart obstinate, that He might deliver him into your hand, as *it is* this day.

31 "And the LORD said to me, 'See, I have begun to give Sihon and his land over to you. Begin to possess *it,* that you may inherit his land.' 32 Then Sihon and all his people came out against us to fight at Jahaz. 33 And the LORD our God delivered him over to us; so we defeated him, his sons, and all his people. 34 We took all his cities at that time, and we utterly destroyed the men, women, and little ones of every city; we left none remaining. 35 We took only the livestock as plunder for ourselves, with the spoil of the cities which we took. 36 From Aroer, which *is* on the bank of the River Arnon, and *from* the city that *is* in the ravine, as far as Gilead, there was not one city too strong for us; the LORD our God delivered all to us. 37 Only you did not go near the land of the people of Ammon—anywhere along the River Jabbok, or to the cities of the mountains, or wherever the LORD our God had forbidden us.

3

"Then we turned and went up the road to Bashan; and Og king of Bashan came out against us, he and all his people, to battle at Edrei. 2 And the LORD said to me, 'Do not fear him, for I have delivered him and all his people and his land into your hand; you shall do to him as you did to Sihon king of the Amorites, who dwelt at Heshbon.'

עַד הַיּוֹם הַזֶּה: 23 וְהָעַוִּים הַיֹּשְׁבִים בַּחֲצֵרִים עַד־
עַזָּה כַּפְתֹּרִים הַיֹּצְאִים מִכַּפְתּוֹר הִשְׁמִידֻם וַיֵּשְׁבוּ
תַחְתָּם: 24 קוּמוּ סְּעוּ וְעִבְרוּ אֶת־נַחַל אַרְנֹן רְאֵה
נָתַתִּי בְיָדְךָ אֶת־סִיחֹן מֶלֶךְ־חֶשְׁבּוֹן הָאֱמֹרִי וְאֶת־
אַרְצוֹ הָחֵל רָשׁ וְהִתְגָּר בּוֹ מִלְחָמָה: 25 הַיּוֹם
הַזֶּה אָחֵל תֵּת פַּחְדְּךָ וְיִרְאָתְךָ עַל־פְּנֵי הָעַמִּים
תַּחַת כָּל־הַשָּׁמָיִם אֲשֶׁר יִשְׁמְעוּן שִׁמְעֲךָ וְרָגְזוּ וְחָלוּ
מִפָּנֶיךָ: 26 וָאֶשְׁלַח מַלְאָכִים מִמִּדְבַּר קְדֵמוֹת אֶל־
סִיחוֹן מֶלֶךְ חֶשְׁבּוֹן דִּבְרֵי שָׁלוֹם לֵאמֹר: 27 אֶעְבְּרָה
בְאַרְצֶךָ בַּדֶּרֶךְ בַּדֶּרֶךְ אֵלֵךְ לֹא אָסוּר יָמִין וּשְׂמֹאול:
28 אֹכֶל בַּכֶּסֶף תַּשְׁבִּרֵנִי וְאָכַלְתִּי וּמַיִם בַּכֶּסֶף תִּתֶּן־
לִי וְשָׁתִיתִי רַק אֶעְבְּרָה בְרַגְלָי: 29 כַּאֲשֶׁר עָשׂוּ־
לִי בְּנֵי עֵשָׂו הַיֹּשְׁבִים בְּשֵׂעִיר וְהַמּוֹאָבִים הַיֹּשְׁבִים
בְּעָר עַד אֲשֶׁר־אֶעֱבֹר אֶת־הַיַּרְדֵּן אֶל־הָאָרֶץ אֲשֶׁר־
יְהוָה אֱלֹהֵינוּ נֹתֵן לָנוּ: 30 וְלֹא אָבָה סִיחֹן מֶלֶךְ
חֶשְׁבּוֹן הַעֲבִרֵנוּ בּוֹ כִּי־הִקְשָׁה יְהוָה אֱלֹהֶיךָ אֶת־
רוּחוֹ וְאִמֵּץ אֶת־לְבָבוֹ לְמַעַן תִּתּוֹ בְיָדְךָ כַּיּוֹם
הַזֶּה: ס 31 וַיֹּאמֶר יְהוָה אֵלַי רְאֵה הַחִלֹּתִי
תֵּת לְפָנֶיךָ אֶת־סִיחֹן וְאֶת־אַרְצוֹ הָחֵל רָשׁ לָרֶשֶׁת
אֶת־אַרְצוֹ: 32 וַיֵּצֵא סִיחֹן לִקְרָאתֵנוּ הוּא וְכָל־עַמּוֹ
לַמִּלְחָמָה יָהְצָה: 33 וַיִּתְּנֵהוּ יְהוָה אֱלֹהֵינוּ לְפָנֵינוּ
וַנַּךְ אֹתוֹ וְאֶת־בָּנָיו וְאֶת־כָּל־עַמּוֹ: 34 וַנִּלְכֹּד אֶת־
כָּל־עָרָיו בָּעֵת הַהִוא וַנַּחֲרֵם אֶת־כָּל־עִיר מְתִם
וְהַנָּשִׁים וְהַטָּף לֹא הִשְׁאַרְנוּ שָׂרִיד: 35 רַק הַבְּהֵמָה
בָּזַזְנוּ לָנוּ וּשְׁלַל הֶעָרִים אֲשֶׁר לָכָדְנוּ: 36 מֵעֲרֹעֵר
אֲשֶׁר עַל־שְׂפַת־נַחַל אַרְנֹן וְהָעִיר אֲשֶׁר בַּנַּחַל וְעַד־
הַגִּלְעָד לֹא הָיְתָה קִרְיָה אֲשֶׁר שָׂגְבָה מִמֶּנּוּ אֶת־
הַכֹּל נָתַן יְהוָה אֱלֹהֵינוּ לְפָנֵינוּ: 37 רַק אֶל־אֶרֶץ
בְּנֵי־עַמּוֹן לֹא קָרָבְתָּ כָּל־יַד נַחַל יַבֹּק וְעָרֵי הָהָר
וְכֹל אֲשֶׁר־צִוָּה יְהוָה אֱלֹהֵינוּ:

ג וַנֵּפֶן וַנַּעַל דֶּרֶךְ הַבָּשָׁן וַיֵּצֵא עוֹג מֶלֶךְ־
הַבָּשָׁן לִקְרָאתֵנוּ הוּא וְכָל־עַמּוֹ לַמִּלְחָמָה אֶדְרֶעִי:
2 וַיֹּאמֶר יְהוָה אֵלַי אַל־תִּירָא אֹתוֹ כִּי בְיָדְךָ נָתַתִּי
אֹתוֹ וְאֶת־כָּל־עַמּוֹ וְאֶת־אַרְצוֹ וְעָשִׂיתָ לּוֹ כַּאֲשֶׁר
עָשִׂיתָ לְסִיחֹן מֶלֶךְ הָאֱמֹרִי אֲשֶׁר יוֹשֵׁב בְּחֶשְׁבּוֹן:

3 "So the LORD our God also delivered into our hands Og king of Bashan, with all his people, and we attacked him until he had no survivors remaining. ⁴And we took all his cities at that time; there was not a city which we did not take from them: sixty cities, all the region of Argob, the kingdom of Og in Bashan. ⁵All these cities *were* fortified with high walls, gates, and bars, besides a great many rural towns. ⁶And we utterly destroyed them, as we did to Sihon king of Heshbon, utterly destroying the men, women, and children of every city. ⁷But all the livestock and the spoil of the cities we took as booty for ourselves.

8 "And at that time we took the land from the hand of the two kings of the Amorites who *were* on this side of the Jordan, from the River Arnon to Mount Hermon ⁹(the Sidonians call Hermon Sirion, and the Amorites call it Senir), ¹⁰all the cities of the plain, all Gilead, and all Bashan, as far as Salcah and Edrei, cities of the kingdom of Og in Bashan.

11 "For only Og king of Bashan remained of the remnant of the giants. Indeed his bedstead *was* an iron bedstead. (*Is* it not in Rabbah of the people of Ammon?) Nine cubits *is* its length and four cubits its width, according to the standard cubit.

12 "And this land, *which* we possessed at that time, from Aroer, which *is* by the River Arnon, and half the mountains of Gilead and its cities, I gave to the Reubenites and the Gadites. ¹³The rest of Gilead, and all Bashan, the kingdom of Og, I gave to half the tribe of Manasseh. (All the region of Argob, with all Bashan, was called the land of the giants. ¹⁴Jair the son of Manasseh took all the region of Argob, as far as the border of the Geshurites and the Maachathites, and called Bashan after his own name, Havoth Jair, to this day.)

15 "Also I gave Gilead to Machir. ¹⁶And to the Reubenites and the Gadites I gave from Gilead as far as the River Arnon, the middle of the river as *the* border, as far as the River Jabbok, the border of the people of Ammon; ¹⁷the plain also, with the Jordan as *the* border, from Chinnereth as far as the east side of the Sea of the Arabah (the Salt Sea), below the slopes of Pisgah.

18 "Then I commanded you at that time, saying: 'The LORD your God has given you this land to possess. All you men of valor shall cross over armed before your brethren, the children of Israel. ¹⁹But your wives, your little ones, and your livestock (I know that you have much livestock) shall stay in your cities which I have given you, ²⁰until the LORD has given rest to your brethren as to you, and they

3 וַיִּתֵּן יְהֹוָה אֱלֹהֵינוּ בְּיָדֵנוּ גַּם אֶת־עוֹג מֶלֶךְ־הַבָּשָׁן וְאֶת־כָּל־עַמּוֹ וַנַּכֵּהוּ עַד־בִּלְתִּי הִשְׁאִיר־לוֹ שָׂרִיד: 4 וַנִּלְכֹּד אֶת־כָּל־עָרָיו בָּעֵת הַהִוא לֹא הָיְתָה קִרְיָה אֲשֶׁר לֹא־לָקַחְנוּ מֵאִתָּם שִׁשִּׁים עִיר כָּל־חֶבֶל אַרְגֹּב מַמְלֶכֶת עוֹג בַּבָּשָׁן: 5 כָּל־אֵלֶּה עָרִים בְּצֻרוֹת חוֹמָה גְבֹהָה דְּלָתַיִם וּבְרִיחַ לְבַד מֵעָרֵי הַפְּרָזִי הַרְבֵּה מְאֹד: 6 וַנַּחֲרֵם אוֹתָם כַּאֲשֶׁר עָשִׂינוּ לְסִיחֹן מֶלֶךְ חֶשְׁבּוֹן הַחֲרֵם כָּל־עִיר מְתִם הַנָּשִׁים וְהַטָּף: 7 וְכָל־הַבְּהֵמָה וּשְׁלַל הֶעָרִים בַּזּוֹנוּ לָנוּ: 8 וַנִּקַּח בָּעֵת הַהִוא אֶת־הָאָרֶץ מִיַּד שְׁנֵי מַלְכֵי הָאֱמֹרִי אֲשֶׁר בְּעֵבֶר הַיַּרְדֵּן מִנַּחַל אַרְנֹן עַד־הַר חֶרְמוֹן: 9 צִידֹנִים יִקְרְאוּ לְחֶרְמוֹן שִׂרְיֹן וְהָאֱמֹרִי יִקְרְאוּ־לוֹ שְׂנִיר: 10 כֹּל | עָרֵי הַמִּישֹׁר וְכָל־הַגִּלְעָד וְכָל־הַבָּשָׁן עַד־סַלְכָה וְאֶדְרֶעִי עָרֵי מַמְלֶכֶת עוֹג בַּבָּשָׁן: 11 כִּי רַק־עוֹג מֶלֶךְ הַבָּשָׁן נִשְׁאַר מִיֶּתֶר הָרְפָאִים הִנֵּה עַרְשׂוֹ עֶרֶשׂ בַּרְזֶל הֲלֹה הִוא בְּרַבַּת בְּנֵי עַמּוֹן תֵּשַׁע אַמּוֹת אָרְכָּהּ וְאַרְבַּע אַמּוֹת רָחְבָּהּ בְּאַמַּת־אִישׁ: 12 וְאֶת־הָאָרֶץ הַזֹּאת יָרַשְׁנוּ בָּעֵת הַהִוא מֵעֲרֹעֵר אֲשֶׁר־עַל־נַחַל אַרְנֹן וַחֲצִי הַר־הַגִּלְעָד וְעָרָיו נָתַתִּי לָרֻאוּבֵנִי וְלַגָּדִי: 13 וְיֶתֶר הַגִּלְעָד וְכָל־הַבָּשָׁן מַמְלֶכֶת עוֹג נָתַתִּי לַחֲצִי שֵׁבֶט הַמְנַשֶּׁה כֹּל חֶבֶל הָאַרְגֹּב לְכָל־הַבָּשָׁן הַהוּא יִקָּרֵא אֶרֶץ רְפָאִים: 14 יָאִיר בֶּן־מְנַשֶּׁה לָקַח אֶת־כָּל־חֶבֶל אַרְגֹּב עַד־גְּבוּל הַגְּשׁוּרִי וְהַמַּעֲכָתִי וַיִּקְרָא אֹתָם עַל־שְׁמוֹ אֶת־הַבָּשָׁן חַוֹּת יָאִיר עַד הַיּוֹם הַזֶּה: 15 וּלְמָכִיר נָתַתִּי אֶת־הַגִּלְעָד: 16 וְלָרֻאוּבֵנִי וְלַגָּדִי נָתַתִּי מִן־הַגִּלְעָד וְעַד־נַחַל אַרְנֹן תּוֹךְ הַנַּחַל וּגְבֻל וְעַד יַבֹּק הַנַּחַל גְּבוּל בְּנֵי עַמּוֹן: 17 וְהָעֲרָבָה וְהַיַּרְדֵּן וּגְבֻל מִכִּנֶּרֶת וְעַד יָם הָעֲרָבָה יָם הַמֶּלַח תַּחַת אַשְׁדֹּת הַפִּסְגָּה מִזְרָחָה: 18 וָאֲצַו אֶתְכֶם בָּעֵת הַהִוא לֵאמֹר יְהֹוָה אֱלֹהֵיכֶם נָתַן לָכֶם אֶת־הָאָרֶץ הַזֹּאת לְרִשְׁתָּהּ חֲלוּצִים תַּעַבְרוּ לִפְנֵי אֲחֵיכֶם בְּנֵי־יִשְׂרָאֵל כָּל־בְּנֵי־חָיִל: 19 רַק נְשֵׁיכֶם וְטַפְּכֶם וּמִקְנֵכֶם יָדַעְתִּי כִּי־מִקְנֶה רַב לָכֶם יֵשְׁבוּ בְּעָרֵיכֶם אֲשֶׁר נָתַתִּי לָכֶם: 20 עַד אֲשֶׁר־יָנִיחַ יְהֹוָה | לַאֲחֵיכֶם כָּכֶם וְיָרְשׁוּ גַם־הֵם אֶת־הָאָרֶץ אֲשֶׁר יְהֹוָה אֱלֹהֵיכֶם

also possess the land which the LORD your God is giving them beyond the Jordan. Then each of you may return to his possession which I have given you.'

²¹ "And I commanded Joshua at that time, saying, 'Your eyes have seen all that the LORD your God has done to these two kings; so will the LORD do to all the kingdoms through which you pass. ²² You must not fear them, for the LORD your God Himself fights for you.'

²³ "Then I pleaded with the LORD at that time, saying: ²⁴ 'O Lord GOD, You have begun to show Your servant Your greatness and Your mighty hand, for what god *is there* in heaven or on earth who can do *anything* like Your works and Your mighty *deeds?* ²⁵ I pray, let me cross over and see the good land beyond the Jordan, those pleasant mountains, and Lebanon.'

²⁶ "But the LORD was angry with me on your account, and would not listen to me. So the LORD said to me: 'Enough of that! Speak no more to Me of this matter. ²⁷ Go up to the top of Pisgah, and lift your eyes toward the west, the north, the south, and the east; behold *it* with your eyes, for you shall not cross over this Jordan. ²⁸ But command Joshua, and encourage him and strengthen him; for he shall go over before this people, and he shall cause them to inherit the land which you will see.'

²⁹ "So we stayed in the valley opposite Beth Peor.

4

"Now, O Israel, listen to the statutes and the judgments which I teach you to observe, that you may live, and go in and possess the land which the LORD God of your fathers is giving you. ² You shall not add to the word which I command you, nor take from it, that you may keep the commandments of the LORD your God which I command you. ³ Your eyes have seen what the LORD did at Baal Peor; for the LORD your God has destroyed from among you all the men who followed Baal of Peor. ⁴ But you who held fast to the LORD your God *are* alive today, every one of you.

⁵ "Surely I have taught you statutes and judgments, just as the LORD my God commanded me, that you should act according *to them* in the land which you go to possess. ⁶ Therefore be careful to observe *them;* for this *is* your wisdom and your understanding in the sight of the peoples who will hear all these statutes, and say, 'Surely this great nation *is* a wise and understanding people.'

⁷ "For what great nation *is there* that has God *so* near to it, as the LORD our God *is* to us, for whatever *reason* we may call upon Him? ⁸ And what great nation *is there* that has *such* statutes and

נָתַן לָהֶם בְּעֵבֶר הַיַּרְדֵּן וִישַׁבְתֶּם אִישׁ לִירֻשָּׁתוֹ
אֲשֶׁר נָתַתִּי לָכֶם: 21 וְאֶת־יְהוֹשׁוּעַ צִוֵּיתִי בָּעֵת
הַהִוא לֵאמֹר עֵינֶיךָ הָרֹאֹת אֵת כָּל־אֲשֶׁר עָשָׂה
יְהוָה אֱלֹהֵיכֶם לִשְׁנֵי הַמְּלָכִים הָאֵלֶּה כֵּן־יַעֲשֶׂה
יְהוָה לְכָל־הַמַּמְלָכוֹת אֲשֶׁר אַתָּה עֹבֵר שָׁמָּה:
22 לֹא תִּירָאוּם כִּי יְהוָה אֱלֹהֵיכֶם הוּא הַנִּלְחָם
לָכֶם: ס 23 וָאֶתְחַנַּן אֶל־יְהוָה בָּעֵת הַהִוא
לֵאמֹר: 24 אֲדֹנָי יְהוִה אַתָּה הַחִלּוֹתָ לְהַרְאוֹת אֶת־
עַבְדְּךָ אֶת־גָּדְלְךָ וְאֶת־יָדְךָ הַחֲזָקָה אֲשֶׁר מִי־אֵל
בַּשָּׁמַיִם וּבָאָרֶץ אֲשֶׁר־יַעֲשֶׂה כְמַעֲשֶׂיךָ וְכִגְבוּרֹתֶךָ:
25 אֶעְבְּרָה־נָּא וְאֶרְאֶה אֶת־הָאָרֶץ הַטּוֹבָה אֲשֶׁר
בְּעֵבֶר הַיַּרְדֵּן הָהָר הַטּוֹב הַזֶּה וְהַלְּבָנוֹן: 26 וַיִּתְעַבֵּר
יְהוָה בִּי לְמַעַנְכֶם וְלֹא שָׁמַע אֵלָי וַיֹּאמֶר יְהוָה
אֵלַי רַב־לָךְ אַל־תּוֹסֶף דַּבֵּר אֵלַי עוֹד בַּדָּבָר הַזֶּה:
27 עֲלֵה רֹאשׁ הַפִּסְגָּה וְשָׂא עֵינֶיךָ יָמָּה וְצָפֹנָה
וְתֵימָנָה וּמִזְרָחָה וּרְאֵה בְעֵינֶיךָ כִּי־לֹא תַעֲבֹר אֶת־
הַיַּרְדֵּן הַזֶּה: 28 וְצַו אֶת־יְהוֹשֻׁעַ וְחַזְּקֵהוּ וְאַמְּצֵהוּ
כִּי־הוּא יַעֲבֹר לִפְנֵי הָעָם הַזֶּה וְהוּא יַנְחִיל אוֹתָם
אֶת־הָאָרֶץ אֲשֶׁר תִּרְאֶה: 29 וַנֵּשֶׁב בַּגַּיְא מוּל בֵּית
פְּעוֹר:
פ

ד וְעַתָּה יִשְׂרָאֵל שְׁמַע אֶל־הַחֻקִּים וְאֶל־
הַמִּשְׁפָּטִים אֲשֶׁר אָנֹכִי מְלַמֵּד אֶתְכֶם לַעֲשׂוֹת
לְמַעַן תִּחְיוּ וּבָאתֶם וִירִשְׁתֶּם אֶת־הָאָרֶץ אֲשֶׁר
יְהוָה אֱלֹהֵי אֲבֹתֵיכֶם נֹתֵן לָכֶם: 2 לֹא תֹסִפוּ
עַל־הַדָּבָר אֲשֶׁר אָנֹכִי מְצַוֶּה אֶתְכֶם וְלֹא תִגְרְעוּ
מִמֶּנּוּ לִשְׁמֹר אֶת־מִצְוֹת יְהוָה אֱלֹהֵיכֶם אֲשֶׁר
אָנֹכִי מְצַוֶּה אֶתְכֶם: 3 עֵינֵיכֶם הָרֹאֹת אֵת אֲשֶׁר־
עָשָׂה יְהוָה בְּבַעַל פְּעוֹר כִּי כָל־הָאִישׁ אֲשֶׁר
הָלַךְ אַחֲרֵי בַעַל־פְּעוֹר הִשְׁמִידוֹ יְהוָה אֱלֹהֶיךָ
מִקִּרְבֶּךָ: 4 וְאַתֶּם הַדְּבֵקִים בַּיהוָה אֱלֹהֵיכֶם חַיִּים
כֻּלְּכֶם הַיּוֹם: 5 רְאֵה לִמַּדְתִּי אֶתְכֶם חֻקִּים
וּמִשְׁפָּטִים כַּאֲשֶׁר צִוַּנִי יְהוָה אֱלֹהָי לַעֲשׂוֹת כֵּן
בְּקֶרֶב הָאָרֶץ אֲשֶׁר אַתֶּם בָּאִים שָׁמָּה לְרִשְׁתָּהּ:
6 וּשְׁמַרְתֶּם וַעֲשִׂיתֶם כִּי הִוא חָכְמַתְכֶם וּבִינַתְכֶם
לְעֵינֵי הָעַמִּים אֲשֶׁר יִשְׁמְעוּן אֵת כָּל־הַחֻקִּים הָאֵלֶּה
וְאָמְרוּ רַק עַם־חָכָם וְנָבוֹן הַגּוֹי הַגָּדוֹל הַזֶּה: 7 כִּי
מִי־גוֹי גָּדוֹל אֲשֶׁר־לוֹ אֱלֹהִים קְרֹבִים אֵלָיו כַּיהוָה
אֱלֹהֵינוּ בְּכָל־קָרְאֵנוּ אֵלָיו: 8 וּמִי גּוֹי גָּדוֹל אֲשֶׁר־לוֹ
חֻקִּים וּמִשְׁפָּטִים צַדִּיקִם כְּכֹל הַתּוֹרָה הַזֹּאת אֲשֶׁר

righteous judgments as are in all this law which I set before you this day? ⁹ Only take heed to yourself, and diligently keep yourself, lest you forget the things your eyes have seen, and lest they depart from your heart all the days of your life. And teach them to your children and your grandchildren, ¹⁰ *especially concerning* the day you stood before the LORD your God in Horeb, when the LORD said to me, 'Gather the people to Me, and I will let them hear My words, that they may learn to fear Me all the days they live on the earth, and *that* they may teach their children.'

¹¹ "Then you came near and stood at the foot of the mountain, and the mountain burned with fire to the midst of heaven, with darkness, cloud, and thick darkness. ¹² And the LORD spoke to you out of the midst of the fire. You heard the sound of the words, but saw no form; *you* only *heard* a voice. ¹³ So He declared to you His covenant which He commanded you to perform, the Ten Commandments; and He wrote them on two tablets of stone. ¹⁴ And the LORD commanded me at that time to teach you statutes and judgments, that you might observe them in the land which you cross over to possess.

¹⁵ "Take careful heed to yourselves, for you saw no form when the LORD spoke to you at Horeb out of the midst of the fire, ¹⁶ lest you act corruptly and make for yourselves a carved image in the form of any figure: the likeness of male or female, ¹⁷ the likeness of any animal that *is* on the earth or the likeness of any winged bird that flies in the air, ¹⁸ the likeness of anything that creeps on the ground or the likeness of any fish that *is* in the water beneath the earth. ¹⁹ And *take heed*, lest you lift your eyes to heaven, and *when* you see the sun, the moon, and the stars, all the host of heaven, you feel driven to worship them and serve them, which the LORD your God has given to all the peoples under the whole heaven as a heritage. ²⁰ But the LORD has taken you and brought you out of the iron furnace, out of Egypt, to be His people, an inheritance, as you are this day. ²¹ Furthermore the LORD was angry with me for your sakes, and swore that I would not cross over the Jordan, and that I would not enter the good land which the LORD your God is giving you as an inheritance. ²² But I must die in this land, I must not cross over the Jordan; but you shall cross over and possess that good land. ²³ Take heed to yourselves, lest you forget the covenant of the LORD your God which He made with you, and make for yourselves a carved image in the form of anything which the LORD your God has forbidden you. ²⁴ For the LORD your God *is* a consuming fire, a jealous God.

אָנֹכִ֛י נֹתֵ֥ן לִפְנֵיכֶ֖ם הַיּֽוֹם: 9 רַ֡ק הִשָּׁ֣מֶר לְךָ֩ וּשְׁמֹ֨ר נַפְשְׁךָ֜ מְאֹ֗ד פֶּן־תִּשְׁכַּ֣ח אֶת־הַדְּבָרִ֣ים אֲשֶׁר־רָא֣וּ עֵינֶ֗יךָ וּפֶן־יָס֨וּרוּ֙ מִלְּבָ֣בְךָ֔ כֹּ֖ל יְמֵ֣י חַיֶּ֑יךָ וְהוֹדַעְתָּ֥ם לְבָנֶ֖יךָ וְלִבְנֵ֥י בָנֶֽיךָ: 10 י֗וֹם אֲשֶׁ֨ר עָמַ֜דְתָּ לִפְנֵ֨י יְהֹוָ֣ה אֱלֹהֶיךָ֮ בְּחֹרֵב֒ בֶּאֱמֹ֣ר יְהֹוָ֣ה אֵלַ֗י הַקְהֶל־לִי֙ אֶת־הָעָ֔ם וְאַשְׁמִעֵ֖ם אֶת־דְּבָרָ֑י אֲשֶׁ֨ר יִלְמְד֜וּן לְיִרְאָ֣ה אֹתִ֗י כָּל־הַיָּמִים֙ אֲשֶׁ֨ר הֵ֤ם חַיִּים֙ עַל־הָ֣אֲדָמָ֔ה וְאֶת־בְּנֵיהֶ֖ם יְלַמֵּדֽוּן: 11 וַתִּקְרְב֥וּן וַתַּֽעַמְד֖וּן תַּ֣חַת הָהָ֑ר וְהָהָ֞ר בֹּעֵ֤ר בָּאֵשׁ֙ עַד־לֵ֣ב הַשָּׁמַ֔יִם חֹ֖שֶׁךְ עָנָ֥ן וַעֲרָפֶֽל: 12 וַיְדַבֵּ֧ר יְהֹוָ֛ה אֲלֵיכֶ֖ם מִתּ֣וֹךְ הָאֵ֑שׁ ק֤וֹל דְּבָרִים֙ אַתֶּ֣ם שֹֽׁמְעִ֔ים וּתְמוּנָ֛ה אֵינְכֶ֥ם רֹאִ֖ים זוּלָתִ֥י קֽוֹל: 13 וַיַּגֵּ֨ד לָכֶ֜ם אֶת־בְּרִית֗וֹ אֲשֶׁ֨ר צִוָּ֤ה אֶתְכֶם֙ לַעֲשׂ֔וֹת עֲשֶׂ֖רֶת הַדְּבָרִ֑ים וַֽיִּכְתְּבֵ֔ם עַל־שְׁנֵ֖י לֻח֥וֹת אֲבָנִֽים: 14 וְאֹתִ֞י צִוָּ֤ה יְהֹוָה֙ בָּעֵ֣ת הַהִ֔וא לְלַמֵּ֣ד אֶתְכֶ֔ם חֻקִּ֖ים וּמִשְׁפָּטִ֑ים לַעֲשֹׂתְכֶ֣ם אֹתָ֔ם בָּאָ֕רֶץ אֲשֶׁ֥ר אַתֶּ֛ם עֹבְרִ֥ים שָׁ֖מָּה לְרִשְׁתָּֽהּ: 15 וְנִשְׁמַרְתֶּ֥ם מְאֹ֖ד לְנַפְשֹׁתֵיכֶ֑ם כִּ֣י לֹ֤א רְאִיתֶם֙ כָּל־תְּמוּנָ֔ה בְּי֗וֹם דִּבֶּ֨ר יְהֹוָ֧ה אֲלֵיכֶ֛ם בְּחֹרֵ֖ב מִתּ֥וֹךְ הָאֵֽשׁ: 16 פֶּ֨ן־תַּשְׁחִת֔וּן וַעֲשִׂיתֶ֥ם לָכֶ֛ם פֶּ֖סֶל תְּמוּנַ֣ת כָּל־סָ֑מֶל תַּבְנִ֥ית זָכָ֖ר א֥וֹ נְקֵבָֽה: 17 תַּבְנִ֕ית כָּל־בְּהֵמָ֖ה אֲשֶׁ֣ר בָּאָ֑רֶץ תַּבְנִית֙ כָּל־צִפּ֣וֹר כָּנָ֔ף אֲשֶׁ֥ר תָּע֖וּף בַּשָּׁמָֽיִם: 18 תַּבְנִ֕ית כָּל־רֹמֵ֖שׂ בָּאֲדָמָ֑ה תַּבְנִ֛ית כָּל־דָּגָ֥ה אֲשֶׁר־בַּמַּ֖יִם מִתַּ֥חַת לָאָֽרֶץ: 19 וּפֶן־תִּשָּׂ֨א עֵינֶ֜יךָ הַשָּׁמַ֗יְמָה וְֽרָאִ֣יתָ אֶת־הַשֶּׁ֣מֶשׁ וְאֶת־הַיָּרֵ֡חַ וְאֶת־הַכּֽוֹכָבִ֜ים כֹּ֣ל צְבָ֣א הַשָּׁמַ֗יִם וְנִדַּחְתָּ֛ וְהִשְׁתַּחֲוִ֥יתָ לָהֶ֖ם וַעֲבַדְתָּ֑ם אֲשֶׁ֨ר חָלַ֜ק יְהֹוָ֤ה אֱלֹהֶ֨יךָ֙ אֹתָ֔ם לְכֹל֙ הָֽעַמִּ֔ים תַּ֖חַת כָּל־הַשָּׁמָֽיִם: 20 וְאֶתְכֶם֙ לָקַ֣ח יְהֹוָ֔ה וַיּוֹצִ֥א אֶתְכֶ֛ם מִכּ֥וּר הַבַּרְזֶ֖ל מִמִּצְרָ֑יִם לִהְי֥וֹת ל֛וֹ לְעַ֥ם נַחֲלָ֖ה כַּיּ֥וֹם הַזֶּֽה: 21 וַֽיהֹוָ֥ה הִתְאַנֶּף־בִּ֖י עַל־דִּבְרֵיכֶ֑ם וַיִּשָּׁבַ֗ע לְבִלְתִּ֤י עָבְרִי֙ אֶת־הַיַּרְדֵּ֔ן וּלְבִלְתִּי־בֹא֙ אֶל־הָאָ֣רֶץ הַטּוֹבָ֔ה אֲשֶׁר֙ יְהֹוָ֣ה אֱלֹהֶ֔יךָ נֹתֵ֥ן לְךָ֖ נַחֲלָֽה: 22 כִּ֣י אָנֹכִ֥י מֵת֙ בָּאָ֣רֶץ הַזֹּ֔את אֵינֶ֥נִּי עֹבֵ֖ר אֶת־הַיַּרְדֵּ֑ן וְאַתֶּם֙ עֹֽבְרִ֔ים וִֽירִשְׁתֶּ֕ם אֶת־הָאָ֥רֶץ הַטּוֹבָ֖ה הַזֹּֽאת: 23 הִשָּׁמְר֣וּ לָכֶ֗ם פֶּֽן־תִּשְׁכְּחוּ֙ אֶת־בְּרִ֤ית יְהֹוָה֙ אֱלֹֽהֵיכֶ֔ם אֲשֶׁ֥ר כָּרַ֖ת עִמָּכֶ֑ם וַעֲשִׂיתֶ֨ם לָכֶ֥ם פֶּ֨סֶל֙ תְּמ֣וּנַת כֹּ֔ל אֲשֶׁ֥ר צִוְּךָ֖ יְהֹוָ֥ה אֱלֹהֶֽיךָ: 24 כִּ֚י יְהֹוָ֣ה אֱלֹהֶ֔יךָ אֵ֥שׁ אֹכְלָ֖ה ה֑וּא אֵ֖ל קַנָּֽא: פ

25 "When you beget children and grandchildren and have grown old in the land, and act corruptly and make a carved image in the form of anything, and do evil in the sight of the LORD your God to provoke Him to anger, 26 I call heaven and earth to witness against you this day, that you will soon utterly perish from the land which you cross over the Jordan to possess; you will not prolong *your* days in it, but will be utterly destroyed. 27 And the LORD will scatter you among the peoples, and you will be left few in number among the nations where the LORD will drive you. 28 And there you will serve gods, the work of men's hands, wood and stone, which neither see nor hear nor eat nor smell. 29 But from there you will seek the LORD your God, and you will find *Him* if you seek Him with all your heart and with all your soul. 30 When you are in distress, and all these things come upon you in the latter days, when you turn to the LORD your God and obey His voice 31 (for the LORD your God *is a* merciful God), He will not forsake you nor destroy you, nor forget the covenant of your fathers which He swore to them.

32 "For ask now concerning the days that are past, which were before you, since the day that God created man on the earth, and *ask* from one end of heaven to the other, whether *any* great *thing* like this has happened, or *anything* like it has been heard. 33 Did *any* people *ever* hear the voice of God speaking out of the midst of the fire, as you have heard, and live? 34 Or did God *ever* try to go *and* take for Himself a nation from the midst of *another* nation, by trials, by signs, by wonders, by war, by a mighty hand and an outstretched arm, and by great terrors, according to all that the LORD your God did for you in Egypt before your eyes? 35 To you it was shown, that you might know that the LORD Himself *is* God; *there is* none other besides Him. 36 Out of heaven He let you hear His voice, that He might instruct you; on earth He showed you His great fire, and you heard His words out of the midst of the fire. 37 And because He loved your fathers, therefore He chose their descendants after them; and He brought you out of Egypt with His Presence, with His mighty power, 38 driving out from before you nations greater and mightier than you, to bring you in, to give you their land *as an* inheritance, as *it is* this day. 39 Therefore know this day, and consider *it* in your heart, that the LORD Himself *is* God in heaven above and on the earth beneath; *there is* no other. 40 You shall therefore keep His statutes and His commandments which I command you today, that it may go well with you

25 כִּי־תוֹלִיד בָּנִים וּבְנֵי בָנִים וְנוֹשַׁנְתֶּם בָּאָרֶץ וְהִשְׁחַתֶּם וַעֲשִׂיתֶם פֶּסֶל תְּמוּנַת כֹּל וַעֲשִׂיתֶם הָרַע בְּעֵינֵי יְהוָה־אֱלֹהֶיךָ לְהַכְעִיסוֹ׃ 26 הַעִידֹתִי בָכֶם הַיּוֹם אֶת־הַשָּׁמַיִם וְאֶת־הָאָרֶץ כִּי־אָבֹד תֹּאבֵדוּן מַהֵר מֵעַל הָאָרֶץ אֲשֶׁר אַתֶּם עֹבְרִים אֶת־הַיַּרְדֵּן שָׁמָּה לְרִשְׁתָּהּ לֹא־תַאֲרִיכֻן יָמִים עָלֶיהָ כִּי הִשָּׁמֵד תִּשָּׁמֵדוּן׃ 27 וְהֵפִיץ יְהוָה אֶתְכֶם בָּעַמִּים וְנִשְׁאַרְתֶּם מְתֵי מִסְפָּר בַּגּוֹיִם אֲשֶׁר יְנַהֵג יְהוָה אֶתְכֶם שָׁמָּה׃ 28 וַעֲבַדְתֶּם־שָׁם אֱלֹהִים מַעֲשֵׂה יְדֵי אָדָם עֵץ וָאֶבֶן אֲשֶׁר לֹא־יִרְאוּן וְלֹא יִשְׁמְעוּן וְלֹא יֹאכְלוּן וְלֹא יְרִיחֻן׃ 29 וּבִקַּשְׁתֶּם מִשָּׁם אֶת־יְהוָה אֱלֹהֶיךָ וּמָצָאתָ כִּי תִדְרְשֶׁנּוּ בְּכָל־לְבָבְךָ וּבְכָל־נַפְשֶׁךָ׃ 30 בַּצַּר לְךָ וּמְצָאוּךָ כֹּל הַדְּבָרִים הָאֵלֶּה בְּאַחֲרִית הַיָּמִים וְשַׁבְתָּ עַד־יְהוָה אֱלֹהֶיךָ וְשָׁמַעְתָּ בְּקֹלוֹ׃ 31 כִּי אֵל רַחוּם יְהוָה אֱלֹהֶיךָ לֹא יַרְפְּךָ וְלֹא יַשְׁחִיתֶךָ וְלֹא יִשְׁכַּח אֶת־בְּרִית אֲבֹתֶיךָ אֲשֶׁר נִשְׁבַּע לָהֶם׃

32 כִּי שְׁאַל־נָא לְיָמִים רִאשֹׁנִים אֲשֶׁר־הָיוּ לְפָנֶיךָ לְמִן־הַיּוֹם אֲשֶׁר בָּרָא אֱלֹהִים אָדָם עַל־הָאָרֶץ וּלְמִקְצֵה הַשָּׁמַיִם וְעַד־קְצֵה הַשָּׁמָיִם הֲנִהְיָה כַּדָּבָר הַגָּדוֹל הַזֶּה אוֹ הֲנִשְׁמַע כָּמֹהוּ׃ 33 הֲשָׁמַע עָם קוֹל אֱלֹהִים מְדַבֵּר מִתּוֹךְ־הָאֵשׁ כַּאֲשֶׁר־שָׁמַעְתָּ אַתָּה וַיֶּחִי׃ 34 אוֹ הֲנִסָּה אֱלֹהִים לָבוֹא לָקַחַת לוֹ גוֹי מִקֶּרֶב גּוֹי בְּמַסֹּת בְּאֹתֹת וּבְמוֹפְתִים וּבְמִלְחָמָה וּבְיָד חֲזָקָה וּבִזְרוֹעַ נְטוּיָה וּבְמוֹרָאִים גְּדֹלִים כְּכֹל אֲשֶׁר־עָשָׂה לָכֶם יְהוָה אֱלֹהֵיכֶם בְּמִצְרַיִם לְעֵינֶיךָ׃ 35 אַתָּה הָרְאֵתָ לָדַעַת כִּי יְהוָה הוּא הָאֱלֹהִים אֵין עוֹד מִלְּבַדּוֹ׃ 36 מִן־הַשָּׁמַיִם הִשְׁמִיעֲךָ אֶת־קֹלוֹ לְיַסְּרֶךָּ וְעַל־הָאָרֶץ הֶרְאֲךָ אֶת־אִשּׁוֹ הַגְּדוֹלָה וּדְבָרָיו שָׁמַעְתָּ מִתּוֹךְ הָאֵשׁ׃ 37 וְתַחַת כִּי אָהַב אֶת־אֲבֹתֶיךָ וַיִּבְחַר בְּזַרְעוֹ אַחֲרָיו וַיּוֹצִאֲךָ בְּפָנָיו בְּכֹחוֹ הַגָּדֹל מִמִּצְרָיִם׃ 38 לְהוֹרִישׁ גּוֹיִם גְּדֹלִים וַעֲצֻמִים מִמְּךָ מִפָּנֶיךָ לַהֲבִיאֲךָ לָתֶת־לְךָ אֶת־אַרְצָם נַחֲלָה כַּיּוֹם הַזֶּה׃ 39 וְיָדַעְתָּ הַיּוֹם וַהֲשֵׁבֹתָ אֶל־לְבָבֶךָ כִּי יְהוָה הוּא הָאֱלֹהִים בַּשָּׁמַיִם מִמַּעַל וְעַל־הָאָרֶץ מִתָּחַת אֵין עוֹד׃ 40 וְשָׁמַרְתָּ אֶת־חֻקָּיו וְאֶת־מִצְוֺתָיו אֲשֶׁר אָנֹכִי מְצַוְּךָ הַיּוֹם אֲשֶׁר יִיטַב לְךָ

and with your children after you, and that you may prolong *your* days in the land which the LORD your God is giving you for all time."

⁴¹ Then Moses set apart three cities on this side of the Jordan, toward the rising of the sun, ⁴² that the manslayer might flee there, who kills his neighbor unintentionally, without having hated him in time past, and that by fleeing to one of these cities he might live: ⁴³ Bezer in the wilderness on the plateau for the Reubenites, Ramoth in Gilead for the Gadites, and Golan in Bashan for the Manassites.

⁴⁴ Now this *is* the law which Moses set before the children of Israel. ⁴⁵ These *are* the testimonies, the statutes, and the judgments which Moses spoke to the children of Israel after they came out of Egypt, ⁴⁶ on this side of the Jordan, in the valley opposite Beth Peor, in the land of Sihon king of the Amorites, who dwelt at Heshbon, whom Moses and the children of Israel defeated after they came out of Egypt. ⁴⁷ And they took possession of his land and the land of Og king of Bashan, two kings of the Amorites, who *were* on this side of the Jordan, toward the rising of the sun, ⁴⁸ from Aroer, which *is* on the bank of the River Arnon, even to Mount Sion (that is, Hermon), ⁴⁹ and all the plain on the east side of the Jordan as far as the Sea of the Arabah, below the slopes of Pisgah.

5 And Moses called all Israel, and said to them: "Hear, O Israel, the statutes and judgments which I speak in your hearing today, that you may learn them and be careful to observe them. ² The LORD our God made a covenant with us in Horeb. ³ The LORD did not make this covenant with our fathers, but with us, those who *are* here today, all of us who *are* alive. ⁴ The LORD talked with you face to face on the mountain from the midst of the fire. ⁵ I stood between the LORD and you at that time, to declare to you the word of the LORD; for you were afraid because of the fire, and you did not go up the mountain. *He* said:

⁶ 'I *am* the LORD your God who brought you out of the land of Egypt, out of the house of bondage.

⁷ 'You shall have no other gods before Me.

⁸ 'You shall not make for yourself a carved image— any likeness *of anything* that *is* in heaven above, or that *is* in the earth beneath, or that *is* in the water under the earth; ⁹ you shall not bow down to them nor serve them. For I, the LORD your God, *am* a jealous God, visiting the iniquity of the fathers upon the children to the third and fourth *generations* of those who hate Me, ¹⁰ but showing mercy to thousands, to those who love Me and keep My commandments.

וּלְבָנֶ֣יךָ אַחֲרֶ֔יךָ וּלְמַ֨עַן֙ תַּאֲרִ֣יךְ יָמִ֔ים עַל־הָ֣אֲדָמָ֔ה אֲשֶׁ֨ר יְהֹוָ֧ה אֱלֹהֶ֛יךָ נֹתֵ֥ן לְךָ֖ כָּל־הַיָּמִֽים׃ פ

⁴¹ אָ֣ז יַבְדִּ֤יל מֹשֶׁה֙ שָׁלֹ֣שׁ עָרִ֔ים בְּעֵ֖בֶר הַיַּרְדֵּ֑ן מִזְרְחָ֖ה שָֽׁמֶשׁ׃ ⁴² לָנֻ֣ס שָׁ֗מָּה רוֹצֵ֙חַ֙ אֲשֶׁ֨ר יִרְצַ֤ח אֶת־רֵעֵ֙הוּ֙ בִּבְלִי־דַ֔עַת וְה֛וּא לֹֽא־שֹׂנֵ֥א ל֖וֹ מִתְּמ֣וֹל שִׁלְשׁ֑וֹם וְנָ֗ס אֶל־אַחַ֛ת מִן־הֶעָרִ֥ים הָאֵ֖ל וָחָֽי׃ ⁴³ אֶת־בֶּ֧צֶר בַּמִּדְבָּ֛ר בְּאֶ֥רֶץ הַמִּישֹׁ֖ר לָרֽאוּבֵנִ֑י וְאֶת־רָאמֹ֤ת בַּגִּלְעָד֙ לַגָּדִ֔י וְאֶת־גּוֹלָ֥ן בַּבָּשָׁ֖ן לַֽמְנַשִּֽׁי׃ ⁴⁴ וְזֹ֖את הַתּוֹרָ֑ה אֲשֶׁר־שָׂ֣ם מֹשֶׁ֔ה לִפְנֵ֖י בְּנֵ֥י יִשְׂרָאֵֽל׃ ⁴⁵ אֵ֚לֶּה הָֽעֵדֹ֔ת וְהַֽחֻקִּ֖ים וְהַמִּשְׁפָּטִ֑ים אֲשֶׁ֨ר דִּבֶּ֤ר מֹשֶׁה֙ אֶל־בְּנֵ֣י יִשְׂרָאֵ֔ל בְּצֵאתָ֖ם מִמִּצְרָֽיִם׃ ⁴⁶ בְּעֵ֨בֶר הַיַּרְדֵּ֜ן בַּגַּ֗יְא מ֞וּל בֵּ֤ית פְּעוֹר֙ בְּאֶ֙רֶץ֙ סִיחֹ֣ן מֶ֣לֶךְ הָֽאֱמֹרִ֔י אֲשֶׁ֥ר יוֹשֵׁ֖ב בְּחֶשְׁבּ֑וֹן אֲשֶׁ֨ר הִכָּ֤ה מֹשֶׁה֙ וּבְנֵ֣י יִשְׂרָאֵ֔ל בְּצֵאתָ֖ם מִמִּצְרָֽיִם׃ ⁴⁷ וַיִּֽירְשׁ֣וּ אֶת־אַרְצ֗וֹ וְאֶת־אֶ֙רֶץ֙ ע֣וֹג מֶֽלֶךְ־הַבָּשָׁ֔ן שְׁנֵי֙ מַלְכֵ֣י הָֽאֱמֹרִ֔י אֲשֶׁ֖ר בְּעֵ֣בֶר הַיַּרְדֵּ֑ן מִזְרַ֖ח שָֽׁמֶשׁ׃ ⁴⁸ מֵֽעֲרֹעֵ֡ר אֲשֶׁ֨ר עַל־שְׂפַת־נַ֧חַל אַרְנֹ֛ן וְעַד־הַ֥ר שִׂיאֹ֖ן ה֥וּא חֶרְמֽוֹן׃ ⁴⁹ וְכָל־הָ֣עֲרָבָ֗ה עֵ֤בֶר הַיַּרְדֵּן֙ מִזְרָ֔חָה וְעַ֖ד יָ֣ם הָעֲרָבָ֑ה תַּ֖חַת אַשְׁדֹּ֥ת הַפִּסְגָּֽה׃ פ

ה וַיִּקְרָ֣א מֹשֶׁה֮ אֶל־כָּל־יִשְׂרָאֵל֒ וַיֹּ֣אמֶר אֲלֵהֶ֔ם שְׁמַ֤ע יִשְׂרָאֵל֙ אֶת־הַֽחֻקִּ֣ים וְאֶת־הַמִּשְׁפָּטִ֔ים אֲשֶׁ֧ר אָֽנֹכִ֛י דֹּבֵ֥ר בְּאָזְנֵיכֶ֖ם הַיּ֑וֹם וּלְמַדְתֶּ֣ם אֹתָ֔ם וּשְׁמַרְתֶּ֖ם לַֽעֲשֹׂתָֽם׃ ² יְהֹוָ֣ה אֱלֹהֵ֗ינוּ כָּרַ֥ת עִמָּ֛נוּ בְּרִ֖ית בְּחֹרֵֽב׃ ³ לֹ֣א אֶת־אֲבֹתֵ֔ינוּ כָּרַ֥ת יְהֹוָ֖ה אֶת־הַבְּרִ֣ית הַזֹּ֑את כִּ֣י אִתָּ֗נוּ אֲנַ֨חְנוּ אֵ֥לֶּה פֹ֛ה הַיּ֖וֹם כֻּלָּ֥נוּ חַיִּֽים׃ ⁴ פָּנִ֣ים ׀ בְּפָנִ֗ים דִּבֶּ֧ר יְהֹוָ֛ה עִמָּכֶ֖ם בָּהָ֑ר מִתּ֖וֹךְ הָאֵֽשׁ׃ ⁵ אָֽנֹכִ֠י עֹמֵ֨ד בֵּין־יְהֹוָ֤ה וּבֵֽינֵיכֶם֙ בָּעֵ֣ת הַהִ֔וא לְהַגִּ֥יד לָכֶ֖ם אֶת־דְּבַ֣ר יְהֹוָ֑ה כִּ֤י יְרֵאתֶם֙ מִפְּנֵ֣י הָאֵ֔שׁ וְלֹֽא־עֲלִיתֶ֥ם בָּהָ֖ר לֵאמֹֽר׃ ס ⁶ אָֽנֹכִ֖י יְהֹוָ֣ה אֱלֹהֶ֑יךָ אֲשֶׁ֧ר הֽוֹצֵאתִ֛יךָ מֵאֶ֥רֶץ מִצְרַ֖יִם מִבֵּ֥ית עֲבָדִֽים׃ ⁷ לֹ֣א יִֽהְיֶֽה־לְךָ֛ אֱלֹהִ֥ים אֲחֵרִ֖ים עַל־פָּנָֽי׃ ⁸ לֹֽא־תַֽעֲשֶׂה־לְךָ֥ פֶ֙סֶל֙ ׀ כָּל־תְּמוּנָ֔ה אֲשֶׁ֤ר בַּשָּׁמַ֙יִם֙ ׀ מִמַּ֔עַל וַֽאֲשֶׁ֥ר בָּאָ֖רֶץ מִתָּ֑חַת וַֽאֲשֶׁ֥ר בַּמַּ֖יִם ׀ מִתַּ֥חַת לָאָֽרֶץ׃ ⁹ לֹֽא־תִשְׁתַּֽחֲוֶ֥ה לָהֶ֖ם וְלֹ֣א תָֽעָבְדֵ֑ם כִּ֣י אָֽנֹכִ֞י יְהֹוָ֤ה אֱלֹהֶ֙יךָ֙ אֵ֣ל קַנָּ֔א פֹּ֠קֵד עֲוֺ֨ן אָב֧וֹת עַל־בָּנִ֛ים וְעַל־שִׁלֵּשִׁ֥ים וְעַל־רִבֵּעִ֖ים לְשֹֽׂנְאָֽי׃ ¹⁰ וְעֹ֤שֶׂה חֶ֙סֶד֙ לַֽאֲלָפִ֔ים

11 'You shall not take the name of the LORD your
God in vain, for the LORD will not hold *him*
guiltless who takes His name in vain.
12 'Observe the Sabbath day, to keep it holy, as the
LORD your God commanded you. 13 Six days
you shall labor and do all your work, 14 but
the seventh day *is* the Sabbath of the LORD
your God. *In it* you shall do no work: you,
nor your son, nor your daughter, nor your
male servant, nor your female servant, nor
your ox, nor your donkey, nor any of your
cattle, nor your stranger who *is* within your
gates, that your male servant and your female
servant may rest as well as you. 15 And
remember that you were a slave in the land
of Egypt, and the LORD your God brought
you out from there by a mighty hand and by
an outstretched arm; therefore the LORD your
God commanded you to keep the Sabbath
day.
16 'Honor your father and your mother, as the LORD
your God has commanded you, that your
days may be long, and that it may be well
with you in the land which the LORD your
God is giving you.
17 'You shall not murder.
18 'You shall not commit adultery.
19 'You shall not steal.
20 'You shall not bear false witness against your
neighbor.
21 'You shall not covet your neighbor's wife; and
you shall not desire your neighbor's house,
his field, his male servant, his female servant,
his ox, his donkey, or anything that *is* your
neighbor's.'

22 "These words the LORD spoke to all your
assembly, in the mountain from the midst of the
fire, the cloud, and the thick darkness, with a loud
voice; and He added no more. And He wrote them
on two tablets of stone and gave them to me.

23 "So it was, when you heard the voice from the
midst of the darkness, while the mountain was
burning with fire, that you came near to me, all the
heads of your tribes and your elders. 24 And you
said: 'Surely the LORD our God has shown us His
glory and His greatness, and we have heard His
voice from the midst of the fire. We have seen this
day that God speaks with man; yet he *still* lives.
25 Now therefore, why should we die? For this great
fire will consume us; if we hear the voice of the
LORD our God anymore, then we shall die. 26 For
who *is there* of all flesh who has heard the voice of
the living God speaking from the midst of the fire,
as we *have*, and lived? 27 You go near and hear all
that the LORD our God may say, and tell us all that
the LORD our God says to you, and we will hear
and do *it*.'

11 לֹא תִשָּׂא ס לְאֹהֲבַי וּלְשֹׁמְרֵי מִצְוֹתֽוֹ׃
אֶת־שֵׁם־יְהֹוָה אֱלֹהֶיךָ לַשָּׁוְא כִּי לֹא יְנַקֶּה יְהֹוָה אֵת
אֲשֶׁר־יִשָּׂא אֶת־שְׁמוֹ לַשָּֽׁוְא׃ ס 12 שָׁמוֹר
אֶת־יוֹם הַשַּׁבָּת לְקַדְּשׁוֹ כַּאֲשֶׁר צִוְּךָ | יְהֹוָה
אֱלֹהֶֽיךָ׃ 13 שֵׁשֶׁת יָמִים תַּעֲבֹד וְעָשִׂיתָ כָּל־
מְלַאכְתֶּֽךָ׃ 14 וְיוֹם הַשְּׁבִיעִי שַׁבָּת | לַיהֹוָה
אֱלֹהֶיךָ לֹא תַעֲשֶׂה כָל־מְלָאכָה אַתָּה וּבִנְךָֽ־וּבִתֶּךָ
וְעַבְדְּךָֽ־וַאֲמָתֶךָ וְשׁוֹרְךָ וַחֲמֹרְךָ וְכָל־בְּהֶמְתֶּךָ וְגֵרְךָ
אֲשֶׁר בִּשְׁעָרֶיךָ לְמַעַן יָנוּחַ עַבְדְּךָ וַאֲמָתְךָ כָּמֽוֹךָ׃
15 וְזָכַרְתָּ כִּי־עֶבֶד הָיִיתָ | בְּאֶרֶץ מִצְרַיִם
וַיֹּצִֽאֲךָ יְהֹוָה אֱלֹהֶיךָ מִשָּׁם בְּיָד חֲזָקָה וּבִזְרֹעַ
נְטוּיָה עַל־כֵּן צִוְּךָ יְהֹוָה אֱלֹהֶיךָ לַעֲשׂוֹת אֶת־יוֹם
הַשַּׁבָּֽת׃ ס 16 כַּבֵּד אֶת־אָבִיךָ וְאֶת־אִמֶּךָ
כַּאֲשֶׁר צִוְּךָ יְהֹוָה אֱלֹהֶיךָ לְמַעַן | יַאֲרִיכֻן יָמֶיךָ
וּלְמַעַן יִיטַב לָךְ עַל הָאֲדָמָה אֲשֶׁר־יְהֹוָה אֱלֹהֶיךָ
נֹתֵן לָֽךְ׃ ס 17 לֹא תִרְצָֽח ס וְלֹא
תִּנְאָֽף ס וְלֹא תִּגְנֹֽב ס וְלֹא־
תַעֲנֶה בְרֵעֲךָ עֵד שָֽׁוְא׃ ס 18 וְלֹא תַחְמֹד
אֵשֶׁת רֵעֶךָ ס וְלֹא תִתְאַוֶּה בֵּית רֵעֶךָ
שָׂדֵהוּ וְעַבְדּוֹ וַאֲמָתוֹ שׁוֹרוֹ וַחֲמֹרוֹ וְכֹל אֲשֶׁר
לְרֵעֶֽךָ׃ ס 19 אֶת־הַדְּבָרִים הָאֵלֶּה דִּבֶּר
יְהֹוָה אֶל־כָּל־קְהַלְכֶם בָּהָר מִתּוֹךְ הָאֵשׁ הֶעָנָן
וְהָעֲרָפֶל קוֹל גָּדוֹל וְלֹא יָסָף וַיִּכְתְּבֵם עַל־שְׁנֵי
לֻחֹת אֲבָנִים וַיִּתְּנֵם אֵלָֽי׃ 20 וַיְהִי כְּשָׁמְעֲכֶם אֶת־
הַקּוֹל מִתּוֹךְ הַחֹשֶׁךְ וְהָהָר בֹּעֵר בָּאֵשׁ וַתִּקְרְבוּן
אֵלַי כָּל־רָאשֵׁי שִׁבְטֵיכֶם וְזִקְנֵיכֶֽם׃ 21 וַתֹּאמְרוּ הֵן
הֶרְאָנוּ יְהֹוָה אֱלֹהֵינוּ אֶת־כְּבֹדוֹ וְאֶת־גָּדְלוֹ וְאֶת־
קֹלוֹ שָׁמַעְנוּ מִתּוֹךְ הָאֵשׁ הַיּוֹם הַזֶּה רָאִינוּ כִּי־
יְדַבֵּר אֱלֹהִים אֶת־הָאָדָם וָחָֽי׃ 22 וְעַתָּה לָמָּה נָמוּת
כִּי תֹאכְלֵנוּ הָאֵשׁ הַגְּדֹלָה הַזֹּאת אִם־יֹסְפִים |
אֲנַחְנוּ לִשְׁמֹעַ אֶת־קוֹל יְהֹוָה אֱלֹהֵינוּ עוֹד וָמָֽתְנוּ׃
23 כִּי מִי כָל־בָּשָׂר אֲשֶׁר שָׁמַע קוֹל אֱלֹהִים חַיִּים
מְדַבֵּר מִתּֽוֹךְ־הָאֵשׁ כָּמֹנוּ וַיֶּֽחִי׃ 24 קְרַב אַתָּה וּשְׁמָע
אֵת כָּל־אֲשֶׁר יֹאמַר יְהֹוָה אֱלֹהֵינוּ וְאַתְּ | תְּדַבֵּר
אֵלֵינוּ אֵת כָּל־אֲשֶׁר יְדַבֵּר יְהֹוָה אֱלֹהֵינוּ אֵלֶיךָ
וְשָׁמַעְנוּ וְעָשִֽׂינוּ׃ 25 וַיִּשְׁמַע יְהֹוָה אֶת־קוֹל דִּבְרֵיכֶם

²⁸ "Then the LORD heard the voice of your words when you spoke to me, and the LORD said to me: 'I have heard the voice of the words of this people which they have spoken to you. They are right *in* all that they have spoken. ²⁹ Oh, that they had such a heart in them that they would fear Me and always keep all My commandments, that it might be well with them and with their children forever! ³⁰ Go and say to them, "Return to your tents." ³¹ But as for you, stand here by Me, and I will speak to you all the commandments, the statutes, and the judgments which you shall teach them, that they may observe *them* in the land which I am giving them to possess.'

³² "Therefore you shall be careful to do as the LORD your God has commanded you; you shall not turn aside to the right hand or to the left. ³³ You shall walk in all the ways which the LORD your God has commanded you, that you may live and *that it may be* well with you, and *that* you may prolong *your* days in the land which you shall possess.

6 "Now this *is* the commandment, *and these are* the statutes and judgments which the LORD your God has commanded to teach you, that you may observe *them* in the land which you are crossing over to possess, ² that you may fear the LORD your God, to keep all His statutes and His commandments which I command you, you and your son and your grandson, all the days of your life, and that your days may be prolonged. ³ Therefore hear, O Israel, and be careful to observe *it,* that it may be well with you, and that you may multiply greatly as the LORD God of your fathers has promised you—'a land flowing with milk and honey.'

⁴ "Hear, O Israel: The LORD our God, the LORD *is* one! ⁵ You shall love the LORD your God with all your heart, with all your soul, and with all your strength.

⁶ "And these words which I command you today shall be in your heart. ⁷ You shall teach them diligently to your children, and shall talk of them when you sit in your house, when you walk by the way, when you lie down, and when you rise up. ⁸ You shall bind them as a sign on your hand, and they shall be as frontlets between your eyes. ⁹ You shall write them on the doorposts of your house and on your gates.

¹⁰ "So it shall be, when the LORD your God brings you into the land of which He swore to your fathers, to Abraham, Isaac, and Jacob, to give you large and beautiful cities which you did not build, ¹¹ houses full of all good things, which you did not fill, hewn-out wells which you did not dig,

כְּדַבֶּרְכֶם אֵלָי וַיֹּאמֶר יְהוָה אֵלַי שָׁמַעְתִּי אֶת־
קוֹל דִּבְרֵי הָעָם הַזֶּה אֲשֶׁר דִּבְּרוּ אֵלֶיךָ הֵיטִיבוּ
כָּל־אֲשֶׁר דִּבֵּרוּ: 26 מִי־יִתֵּן וְהָיָה לְבָבָם זֶה לָהֶם
לְיִרְאָה אֹתִי וְלִשְׁמֹר אֶת־כָּל־מִצְוֹתַי כָּל־הַיָּמִים
לְמַעַן יִיטַב לָהֶם וְלִבְנֵיהֶם לְעֹלָם: 27 לֵךְ אֱמֹר
לָהֶם שׁוּבוּ לָכֶם לְאָהֳלֵיכֶם: 28 וְאַתָּה פֹּה עֲמֹד
עִמָּדִי וַאֲדַבְּרָה אֵלֶיךָ אֵת כָּל־הַמִּצְוָה וְהַחֻקִּים
וְהַמִּשְׁפָּטִים אֲשֶׁר תְּלַמְּדֵם וְעָשׂוּ בָאָרֶץ אֲשֶׁר אָנֹכִי
נֹתֵן לָהֶם לְרִשְׁתָּהּ: 29 וּשְׁמַרְתֶּם לַעֲשׂוֹת כַּאֲשֶׁר
צִוָּה יְהוָה אֱלֹהֵיכֶם אֶתְכֶם לֹא תָסֻרוּ יָמִין וּשְׂמֹאל:
30 בְּכָל־הַדֶּרֶךְ אֲשֶׁר צִוָּה יְהוָה אֱלֹהֵיכֶם אֶתְכֶם
תֵּלֵכוּ לְמַעַן תִּחְיוּן וְטוֹב לָכֶם וְהַאֲרַכְתֶּם יָמִים
בָּאָרֶץ אֲשֶׁר תִּירָשׁוּן:

ו וְזֹאת הַמִּצְוָה הַחֻקִּים וְהַמִּשְׁפָּטִים אֲשֶׁר צִוָּה
יְהוָה אֱלֹהֵיכֶם לְלַמֵּד אֶתְכֶם לַעֲשׂוֹת בָּאָרֶץ אֲשֶׁר
אַתֶּם עֹבְרִים שָׁמָּה לְרִשְׁתָּהּ: 2 לְמַעַן תִּירָא אֶת־
יְהוָה אֱלֹהֶיךָ לִשְׁמֹר אֶת־כָּל־חֻקֹּתָיו וּמִצְוֹתָיו אֲשֶׁר
אָנֹכִי מְצַוֶּךָ אַתָּה וּבִנְךָ וּבֶן־בִּנְךָ כֹּל יְמֵי חַיֶּיךָ וּלְמַעַן
יַאֲרִכֻן יָמֶיךָ: 3 וְשָׁמַעְתָּ יִשְׂרָאֵל וְשָׁמַרְתָּ לַעֲשׂוֹת
אֲשֶׁר יִיטַב לְךָ וַאֲשֶׁר תִּרְבּוּן מְאֹד כַּאֲשֶׁר דִּבֶּר
יְהוָה אֱלֹהֵי אֲבֹתֶיךָ לָךְ אֶרֶץ זָבַת חָלָב וּדְבָשׁ: פ

4 שְׁמַע יִשְׂרָאֵל יְהוָה אֱלֹהֵינוּ יְהוָה אֶחָד:
5 וְאָהַבְתָּ אֵת יְהוָה אֱלֹהֶיךָ בְּכָל־לְבָבְךָ וּבְכָל־
נַפְשְׁךָ וּבְכָל־מְאֹדֶךָ: 6 וְהָיוּ הַדְּבָרִים הָאֵלֶּה אֲשֶׁר
אָנֹכִי מְצַוְּךָ הַיּוֹם עַל־לְבָבֶךָ: 7 וְשִׁנַּנְתָּם לְבָנֶיךָ
וְדִבַּרְתָּ בָּם בְּשִׁבְתְּךָ בְּבֵיתֶךָ וּבְלֶכְתְּךָ בַדֶּרֶךְ
וּבְשָׁכְבְּךָ וּבְקוּמֶךָ: 8 וּקְשַׁרְתָּם לְאוֹת עַל־יָדֶךָ
וְהָיוּ לְטֹטָפֹת בֵּין עֵינֶיךָ: 9 וּכְתַבְתָּם עַל־מְזֻזֹת
בֵּיתֶךָ וּבִשְׁעָרֶיךָ: ס 10 וְהָיָה כִּי יְבִיאֲךָ
יְהוָה אֱלֹהֶיךָ אֶל־הָאָרֶץ אֲשֶׁר נִשְׁבַּע לַאֲבֹתֶיךָ
לְאַבְרָהָם לְיִצְחָק וּלְיַעֲקֹב לָתֶת לָךְ עָרִים גְּדֹלֹת
וְטֹבֹת אֲשֶׁר לֹא־בָנִיתָ: 11 וּבָתִּים מְלֵאִים כָּל־
טוּב אֲשֶׁר לֹא־מִלֵּאתָ וּבֹרֹת חֲצוּבִים אֲשֶׁר לֹא־
חָצַבְתָּ כְּרָמִים וְזֵיתִים אֲשֶׁר לֹא־נָטַעְתָּ וְאָכַלְתָּ

vineyards and olive trees which you did not plant—
when you have eaten and are full— 12 then beware,
lest you forget the LORD who brought you out of
the land of Egypt, from the house of bondage.
13 You shall fear the LORD your God and serve
Him, and shall take oaths in His name. 14 You shall
not go after other gods, the gods of the peoples who
are all around you 15 (for the LORD your God *is* a
jealous God among you), lest the anger of the LORD
your God be aroused against you and destroy you
from the face of the earth.

16 "You shall not tempt the LORD your God as
you tempted *Him* in Massah. 17 You shall diligently
keep the commandments of the LORD your God,
His testimonies, and His statutes which He has
commanded you. 18 And you shall do *what is* right
and good in the sight of the LORD, that it may be
well with you, and that you may go in and possess
the good land of which the LORD swore to your
fathers, 19 to cast out all your enemies from before
you, as the LORD has spoken.

20 "When your son asks you in time to come,
saying, 'What *is the meaning of* the testimonies, the
statutes, and the judgments which the LORD our
God has commanded you?' 21 then you shall say to
your son: 'We were slaves of Pharaoh in Egypt, and
the LORD brought us out of Egypt with a mighty
hand; 22 and the LORD showed signs and wonders
before our eyes, great and severe, against Egypt,
Pharaoh, and all his household. 23 Then He brought
us out from there, that He might bring us in, to give
us the land of which He swore to our fathers. 24 And
the LORD commanded us to observe all these
statutes, to fear the LORD our God, for our good
always, that He might preserve us alive, as *it is* this
day. 25 Then it will be righteousness for us, if we are
careful to observe all these commandments before
the LORD our God, as He has commanded us.'

7 "When the LORD your God brings you into the
land which you go to possess, and has cast out
many nations before you, the Hittites and the
Girgashites and the Amorites and the Canaanites
and the Perizzites and the Hivites and the Jebusites,
seven nations greater and mightier than you, 2 and
when the LORD your God delivers them over to
you, you shall conquer them *and* utterly destroy
them. You shall make no covenant with them nor
show mercy to them. 3 Nor shall you make
marriages with them. You shall not give your
daughter to their son, nor take their daughter for
your son. 4 For they will turn your sons away from
following Me, to serve other gods; so the anger of
the LORD will be aroused against you and destroy

וְשָׁבַעְתָּ: 12 הִשָּׁמֶר לְךָ פֶּן־תִּשְׁכַּח אֶת־יְהוָה אֲשֶׁר
הוֹצִיאֲךָ מֵאֶרֶץ מִצְרַיִם מִבֵּית עֲבָדִים: 13 אֶת־יְהוָה
אֱלֹהֶיךָ תִּירָא וְאֹתוֹ תַעֲבֹד וּבִשְׁמוֹ תִּשָּׁבֵעַ: 14 לֹא
תֵלְכוּן אַחֲרֵי אֱלֹהִים אֲחֵרִים מֵאֱלֹהֵי הָעַמִּים אֲשֶׁר
סְבִיבוֹתֵיכֶם: 15 כִּי אֵל קַנָּא יְהוָה אֱלֹהֶיךָ בְּקִרְבֶּךָ
פֶּן־יֶחֱרֶה אַף־יְהוָה אֱלֹהֶיךָ בָּךְ וְהִשְׁמִידְךָ מֵעַל
פְּנֵי הָאֲדָמָה: ס 16 לֹא תְנַסּוּ אֶת־יְהוָה
אֱלֹהֵיכֶם כַּאֲשֶׁר נִסִּיתֶם בַּמַּסָּה: 17 שָׁמוֹר תִּשְׁמְרוּן
אֶת־מִצְוֹת יְהוָה אֱלֹהֵיכֶם וְעֵדֹתָיו וְחֻקָּיו אֲשֶׁר צִוָּךְ:

18 וְעָשִׂיתָ הַיָּשָׁר וְהַטּוֹב בְּעֵינֵי יְהוָה לְמַעַן יִיטַב
לָךְ וּבָאתָ וְיָרַשְׁתָּ אֶת־הָאָרֶץ הַטֹּבָה אֲשֶׁר־נִשְׁבַּע
יְהוָה לַאֲבֹתֶיךָ: 19 לַהֲדֹף אֶת־כָּל־אֹיְבֶיךָ מִפָּנֶיךָ
כַּאֲשֶׁר דִּבֶּר יְהוָה: ס 20 כִּי־יִשְׁאָלְךָ בִנְךָ
מָחָר לֵאמֹר מָה הָעֵדֹת וְהַחֻקִּים וְהַמִּשְׁפָּטִים אֲשֶׁר
צִוָּה יְהוָה אֱלֹהֵינוּ אֶתְכֶם: 21 וְאָמַרְתָּ לְבִנְךָ עֲבָדִים
הָיִינוּ לְפַרְעֹה בְּמִצְרָיִם וַיּוֹצִיאֵנוּ יְהוָה מִמִּצְרַיִם
בְּיָד חֲזָקָה: 22 וַיִּתֵּן יְהוָה אוֹתֹת וּמֹפְתִים גְּדֹלִים
וְרָעִים | בְּמִצְרַיִם בְּפַרְעֹה וּבְכָל־בֵּיתוֹ לְעֵינֵינוּ:

23 וְאוֹתָנוּ הוֹצִיא מִשָּׁם לְמַעַן הָבִיא אֹתָנוּ לָתֶת
לָנוּ אֶת־הָאָרֶץ אֲשֶׁר נִשְׁבַּע לַאֲבֹתֵינוּ: 24 וַיְצַוֵּנוּ
יְהוָה לַעֲשׂוֹת אֶת־כָּל־הַחֻקִּים הָאֵלֶּה לְיִרְאָה אֶת־
יְהוָה אֱלֹהֵינוּ לְטוֹב לָנוּ כָּל־הַיָּמִים לְחַיֹּתֵנוּ כְּהַיּוֹם
הַזֶּה: 25 וּצְדָקָה תִּהְיֶה־לָּנוּ כִּי־נִשְׁמֹר לַעֲשׂוֹת אֶת־
כָּל־הַמִּצְוָה הַזֹּאת לִפְנֵי יְהוָה אֱלֹהֵינוּ כַּאֲשֶׁר
צִוָּנוּ: ס

ז כִּי יְבִיאֲךָ יְהוָה אֱלֹהֶיךָ אֶל־הָאָרֶץ אֲשֶׁר־אַתָּה
בָא־שָׁמָּה לְרִשְׁתָּהּ וְנָשַׁל גּוֹיִם־רַבִּים | מִפָּנֶיךָ
הַחִתִּי וְהַגִּרְגָּשִׁי וְהָאֱמֹרִי וְהַכְּנַעֲנִי וְהַפְּרִזִּי וְהַחִוִּי
וְהַיְבוּסִי שִׁבְעָה גוֹיִם רַבִּים וַעֲצוּמִים מִמֶּךָּ: 2 וּנְתָנָם
יְהוָה אֱלֹהֶיךָ לְפָנֶיךָ וְהִכִּיתָם הַחֲרֵם תַּחֲרִים אֹתָם
לֹא־תִכְרֹת לָהֶם בְּרִית וְלֹא תְחָנֵּם: 3 וְלֹא תִתְחַתֵּן
בָּם בִּתְּךָ לֹא־תִתֵּן לִבְנוֹ וּבִתּוֹ לֹא־תִקַּח לִבְנֶךָ:
4 כִּי־יָסִיר אֶת־בִּנְךָ מֵאַחֲרַי וְעָבְדוּ אֱלֹהִים אֲחֵרִים

you suddenly. ⁵ But thus you shall deal with them: you shall destroy their altars, and break down their *sacred* pillars, and cut down their wooden images, and burn their carved images with fire.

⁶ "For you *are* a holy people to the LORD your God; the LORD your God has chosen you to be a people for Himself, a special treasure above all the peoples on the face of the earth. ⁷ The LORD did not set His love on you nor choose you because you were more in number than any other people, for you were the least of all peoples; ⁸ but because the LORD loves you, and because He would keep the oath which He swore to your fathers, the LORD has brought you out with a mighty hand, and redeemed you from the house of bondage, from the hand of Pharaoh king of Egypt.

⁹ "Therefore know that the LORD your God, He *is* God, the faithful God who keeps covenant and mercy for a thousand generations with those who love Him and keep His commandments; ¹⁰ and He repays those who hate Him to their face, to destroy them. He will not be slack with him who hates Him; He will repay him to his face. ¹¹ Therefore you shall keep the commandment, the statutes, and the judgments which I command you today, to observe them.

¹² "Then it shall come to pass, because you listen to these judgments, and keep and do them, that the LORD your God will keep with you the covenant and the mercy which He swore to your fathers. ¹³ And He will love you and bless you and multiply you; He will also bless the fruit of your womb and the fruit of your land, your grain and your new wine and your oil, the increase of your cattle and the offspring of your flock, in the land of which He swore to your fathers to give you. ¹⁴ You shall be blessed above all peoples; there shall not be a male or female barren among you or among your livestock. ¹⁵ And the LORD will take away from you all sickness, and will afflict you with none of the terrible diseases of Egypt which you have known, but will lay *them* on all those who hate you. ¹⁶ Also you shall destroy all the peoples whom the LORD your God delivers over to you; your eye shall have no pity on them; nor shall you serve their gods, for that *will be* a snare to you.

¹⁷ "If you should say in your heart, 'These nations are greater than I; how can I dispossess them?'— ¹⁸ you shall not be afraid of them, *but* you shall remember well what the LORD your God did to Pharaoh and to all Egypt: ¹⁹ the great trials which your eyes saw, the signs and the wonders, the mighty hand and the outstretched arm, by which the LORD your God brought you out. So shall the

וְחָרָה אַף־יְהֹוָה בָּכֶם וְהִשְׁמִידְךָ מַהֵר: ⁵ כִּי־אִם־ כֹּה תַעֲשׂוּ לָהֶם מִזְבְּחֹתֵיהֶם תִּתֹּצוּ וּמַצֵּבֹתָם תְּשַׁבֵּרוּ וַאֲשֵׁירֵהֶם תְּגַדֵּעוּן וּפְסִילֵיהֶם תִּשְׂרְפוּן בָּאֵשׁ: ⁶ כִּי עַם קָדוֹשׁ אַתָּה לַיהֹוָה אֱלֹהֶיךָ בְּךָ בָּחַר | יְהֹוָה אֱלֹהֶיךָ לִהְיוֹת לוֹ לְעַם סְגֻלָּה מִכֹּל הָעַמִּים אֲשֶׁר עַל־פְּנֵי הָאֲדָמָה: ס ⁷ לֹא מֵרֻבְּכֶם מִכָּל־הָעַמִּים חָשַׁק יְהֹוָה בָּכֶם וַיִּבְחַר בָּכֶם כִּי־אַתֶּם הַמְעַט מִכָּל־הָעַמִּים: ⁸ כִּי מֵאַהֲבַת יְהֹוָה אֶתְכֶם וּמִשָּׁמְרוֹ אֶת־הַשְּׁבֻעָה אֲשֶׁר נִשְׁבַּע לַאֲבֹתֵיכֶם הוֹצִיא יְהֹוָה אֶתְכֶם בְּיָד חֲזָקָה וַיִּפְדְּךָ מִבֵּית עֲבָדִים מִיַּד פַּרְעֹה מֶלֶךְ־מִצְרָיִם: ⁹ וְיָדַעְתָּ כִּי־יְהֹוָה אֱלֹהֶיךָ הוּא הָאֱלֹהִים הָאֵל הַנֶּאֱמָן שֹׁמֵר הַבְּרִית וְהַחֶסֶד לְאֹהֲבָיו וּלְשֹׁמְרֵי מִצְוֹתָו לְאֶלֶף דּוֹר: ¹⁰ וּמְשַׁלֵּם לְשֹׂנְאָיו אֶל־פָּנָיו לְהַאֲבִידוֹ לֹא יְאַחֵר לְשֹׂנְאוֹ אֶל־פָּנָיו יְשַׁלֶּם־לוֹ: ¹¹ וְשָׁמַרְתָּ אֶת־ הַמִּצְוָה וְאֶת־הַחֻקִּים וְאֶת־הַמִּשְׁפָּטִים אֲשֶׁר אָנֹכִי מְצַוְּךָ הַיּוֹם לַעֲשׂוֹתָם: פ

¹² וְהָיָה | עֵקֶב תִּשְׁמְעוּן אֵת הַמִּשְׁפָּטִים הָאֵלֶּה וּשְׁמַרְתֶּם וַעֲשִׂיתֶם אֹתָם וְשָׁמַר יְהֹוָה אֱלֹהֶיךָ לְךָ אֶת־הַבְּרִית וְאֶת־הַחֶסֶד אֲשֶׁר נִשְׁבַּע לַאֲבֹתֶיךָ: ¹³ וַאֲהֵבְךָ וּבֵרַכְךָ וְהִרְבֶּךָ וּבֵרַךְ פְּרִי־בִטְנְךָ וּפְרִי־ אַדְמָתֶךָ דְּגָנְךָ וְתִירֹשְׁךָ וְיִצְהָרֶךָ שְׁגַר־אֲלָפֶיךָ וְעַשְׁתְּרֹת צֹאנֶךָ עַל הָאֲדָמָה אֲשֶׁר־נִשְׁבַּע לַאֲבֹתֶיךָ לָתֶת לָךְ: ¹⁴ בָּרוּךְ תִּהְיֶה מִכָּל־הָעַמִּים לֹא־יִהְיֶה בְךָ עָקָר וַעֲקָרָה וּבִבְהֶמְתֶּךָ: ¹⁵ וְהֵסִיר יְהֹוָה מִמְּךָ כָּל־חֹלִי וְכָל־מַדְוֵי מִצְרַיִם הָרָעִים אֲשֶׁר יָדַעְתָּ לֹא יְשִׂימָם בָּךְ וּנְתָנָם בְּכָל־שֹׂנְאֶיךָ: ¹⁶ וְאָכַלְתָּ אֶת־כָּל־הָעַמִּים אֲשֶׁר יְהֹוָה אֱלֹהֶיךָ נֹתֵן לָךְ לֹא־ תָחֹס עֵינְךָ עֲלֵיהֶם וְלֹא תַעֲבֹד אֶת־אֱלֹהֵיהֶם כִּי־ מוֹקֵשׁ הוּא לָךְ: ס ¹⁷ כִּי תֹאמַר בִּלְבָבְךָ רַבִּים הַגּוֹיִם הָאֵלֶּה מִמֶּנִּי אֵיכָה אוּכַל לְהוֹרִישָׁם: ¹⁸ לֹא תִירָא מֵהֶם זָכֹר תִּזְכֹּר אֵת אֲשֶׁר־עָשָׂה יְהֹוָה אֱלֹהֶיךָ לְפַרְעֹה וּלְכָל־מִצְרָיִם: ¹⁹ הַמַּסֹּת הַגְּדֹלֹת אֲשֶׁר־רָאוּ עֵינֶיךָ וְהָאֹתֹת וְהַמֹּפְתִים וְהַיָּד הַחֲזָקָה וְהַזְּרֹעַ הַנְּטוּיָה אֲשֶׁר הוֹצִאֲךָ יְהֹוָה אֱלֹהֶיךָ

LORD your God do to all the peoples of whom you are afraid. ²⁰Moreover the LORD your God will send the hornet among them until those who are left, who hide themselves from you, are destroyed. ²¹You shall not be terrified of them; for the LORD your God, the great and awesome God, *is* among you. ²²And the LORD your God will drive out those nations before you little by little; you will be unable to destroy them at once, lest the beasts of the field become *too* numerous for you. ²³But the LORD your God will deliver them over to you, and will inflict defeat upon them until they are destroyed. ²⁴And He will deliver their kings into your hand, and you will destroy their name from under heaven; no one shall be able to stand against you until you have destroyed them. ²⁵You shall burn the carved images of their gods with fire; you shall not covet the silver or gold *that is* on them, nor take *it* for yourselves, lest you be snared by it; for it *is* an abomination to the LORD your God. ²⁶Nor shall you bring an abomination into your house, lest you be doomed to destruction like it. You shall utterly detest it and utterly abhor it, for it *is* an accursed thing.

8 "Every commandment which I command you today you must be careful to observe, that you may live and multiply, and go in and possess the land of which the LORD swore to your fathers. ²And you shall remember that the LORD your God led you all the way these forty years in the wilderness, to humble you *and* test you, to know what *was* in your heart, whether you would keep His commandments or not. ³So He humbled you, allowed you to hunger, and fed you with manna which you did not know nor did your fathers know, that He might make you know that man shall not live by bread alone; but man lives by every *word* that proceeds from the mouth of the LORD. ⁴Your garments did not wear out on you, nor did your foot swell these forty years. ⁵You should know in your heart that as a man chastens his son, *so* the LORD your God chastens you.

⁶"Therefore you shall keep the commandments of the LORD your God, to walk in His ways and to fear Him. ⁷For the LORD your God is bringing you into a good land, a land of brooks of water, of fountains and springs, that flow out of valleys and hills; ⁸a land of wheat and barley, of vines and fig trees and pomegranates, a land of olive oil and honey; ⁹a land in which you will eat bread without scarcity, in which you will lack nothing; a land whose stones *are* iron and out of whose hills you

כֵּן־יַעֲשֶׂה יְהוָה אֱלֹהֶיךָ לְכָל־הָעַמִּים אֲשֶׁר־אַתָּה יָרֵא מִפְּנֵיהֶם: 20 וְגַם אֶת־הַצִּרְעָה יְשַׁלַּח יְהוָה אֱלֹהֶיךָ בָּם עַד־אֲבֹד הַנִּשְׁאָרִים וְהַנִּסְתָּרִים מִפָּנֶיךָ: 21 לֹא תַעֲרֹץ מִפְּנֵיהֶם כִּי־יְהוָה אֱלֹהֶיךָ בְּקִרְבֶּךָ אֵל גָּדוֹל וְנוֹרָא: 22 וְנָשַׁל יְהוָה אֱלֹהֶיךָ אֶת־הַגּוֹיִם הָאֵל מִפָּנֶיךָ מְעַט מְעָט לֹא תוּכַל כַּלֹּתָם מַהֵר פֶּן־תִּרְבֶּה עָלֶיךָ חַיַּת הַשָּׂדֶה: 23 וּנְתָנָם יְהוָה אֱלֹהֶיךָ לְפָנֶיךָ וְהָמָם מְהוּמָה גְדֹלָה עַד הִשָּׁמְדָם: 24 וְנָתַן מַלְכֵיהֶם בְּיָדֶךָ וְהַאֲבַדְתָּ אֶת־שְׁמָם מִתַּחַת הַשָּׁמָיִם לֹא־יִתְיַצֵּב אִישׁ בְּפָנֶיךָ עַד הִשְׁמִדְךָ אֹתָם: 25 פְּסִילֵי אֱלֹהֵיהֶם תִּשְׂרְפוּן בָּאֵשׁ לֹא־תַחְמֹד כֶּסֶף וְזָהָב עֲלֵיהֶם וְלָקַחְתָּ לָךְ פֶּן תִּוָּקֵשׁ בּוֹ כִּי תוֹעֲבַת יְהוָה אֱלֹהֶיךָ הוּא: 26 וְלֹא־תָבִיא תוֹעֵבָה אֶל־בֵּיתֶךָ וְהָיִיתָ חֵרֶם כָּמֹהוּ שַׁקֵּץ | תְּשַׁקְּצֶנּוּ וְתַעֵב | תְּתַעֲבֶנּוּ כִּי־חֵרֶם הוּא: פ

ח כָּל־הַמִּצְוָה אֲשֶׁר אָנֹכִי מְצַוְּךָ הַיּוֹם תִּשְׁמְרוּן לַעֲשׂוֹת לְמַעַן תִּחְיוּן וּרְבִיתֶם וּבָאתֶם וִירִשְׁתֶּם אֶת־הָאָרֶץ אֲשֶׁר־נִשְׁבַּע יְהוָה לַאֲבֹתֵיכֶם: 2 וְזָכַרְתָּ אֶת־כָּל־הַדֶּרֶךְ אֲשֶׁר הֹלִיכֲךָ יְהוָה אֱלֹהֶיךָ זֶה אַרְבָּעִים שָׁנָה בַּמִּדְבָּר לְמַעַן עַנֹּתְךָ לְנַסֹּתְךָ לָדַעַת אֶת־אֲשֶׁר בִּלְבָבְךָ הֲתִשְׁמֹר מִצְוֹתָו אִם־לֹא: 3 וַיְעַנְּךָ וַיַּרְעִבֶךָ וַיַּאֲכִלְךָ אֶת־הַמָּן אֲשֶׁר לֹא־יָדַעְתָּ וְלֹא יָדְעוּן אֲבֹתֶיךָ לְמַעַן הוֹדִעֲךָ כִּי לֹא עַל־הַלֶּחֶם לְבַדּוֹ יִחְיֶה הָאָדָם כִּי עַל־כָּל־מוֹצָא פִי־יְהוָה יִחְיֶה הָאָדָם: 4 שִׂמְלָתְךָ לֹא בָלְתָה מֵעָלֶיךָ וְרַגְלְךָ לֹא בָצֵקָה זֶה אַרְבָּעִים שָׁנָה: 5 וְיָדַעְתָּ עִם־לְבָבֶךָ כִּי כַּאֲשֶׁר יְיַסֵּר אִישׁ אֶת־בְּנוֹ יְהוָה אֱלֹהֶיךָ מְיַסְּרֶךָּ: 6 וְשָׁמַרְתָּ אֶת־מִצְוֹת יְהוָה אֱלֹהֶיךָ לָלֶכֶת בִּדְרָכָיו וּלְיִרְאָה אֹתוֹ: 7 כִּי יְהוָה אֱלֹהֶיךָ מְבִיאֲךָ אֶל־אֶרֶץ טוֹבָה אֶרֶץ נַחֲלֵי מָיִם עֲיָנֹת וּתְהֹמֹת יֹצְאִים בַּבִּקְעָה וּבָהָר: 8 אֶרֶץ חִטָּה וּשְׂעֹרָה וְגֶפֶן וּתְאֵנָה וְרִמּוֹן אֶרֶץ־זֵית שֶׁמֶן וּדְבָשׁ: 9 אֶרֶץ אֲשֶׁר לֹא בְמִסְכֵּנֻת תֹּאכַל־בָּהּ לֶחֶם לֹא־תֶחְסַר כֹּל בָּהּ

can dig copper. ¹⁰When you have eaten and are full, then you shall bless the LORD your God for the good land which He has given you.

¹¹"Beware that you do not forget the LORD your God by not keeping His commandments, His judgments, and His statutes which I command you today, ¹²lest—when you have eaten and are full, and have built beautiful houses and dwell in them; ¹³and when your herds and your flocks multiply, and your silver and your gold are multiplied, and all that you have is multiplied; ¹⁴when your heart is lifted up, and you forget the LORD your God who brought you out of the land of Egypt, from the house of bondage; ¹⁵who led you through that great and terrible wilderness, in which were fiery serpents and scorpions and thirsty land where there was no water; who brought water for you out of the flinty rock; ¹⁶who fed you in the wilderness with manna, which your fathers did not know, that He might humble you and that He might test you, to do you good in the end— ¹⁷then you say in your heart, 'My power and the might of my hand have gained me this wealth.'

¹⁸"And you shall remember the LORD your God, for it is He who gives you power to get wealth, that He may establish His covenant which He swore to your fathers, as it is this day. ¹⁹Then it shall be, if you by any means forget the LORD your God, and follow other gods, and serve them and worship them, I testify against you this day that you shall surely perish. ²⁰As the nations which the LORD destroys before you, so you shall perish, because you would not be obedient to the voice of the LORD your God.

9 "Hear, O Israel: You are to cross over the Jordan today, and go in to dispossess nations greater and mightier than yourself, cities great and fortified up to heaven, ²a people great and tall, the descendants of the Anakim, whom you know, and of whom you heard it said, 'Who can stand before the descendants of Anak?' ³Therefore understand today that the LORD your God is He who goes over before you as a consuming fire. He will destroy them and bring them down before you; so you shall drive them out and destroy them quickly, as the LORD has said to you.

⁴"Do not think in your heart, after the LORD your God has cast them out before you, saying, 'Because of my righteousness the LORD has brought me in to possess this land'; but it is because of the wickedness of these nations that the LORD is driving them out from before you. ⁵It is not because of your righteousness or the uprightness of your heart

אֶרֶץ אֲשֶׁר אֲבָנֶיהָ בַרְזֶל וּמֵהֲרָרֶיהָ תַּחְצֹב נְחֹשֶׁת: 10 וְאָכַלְתָּ וְשָׂבָעְתָּ וּבֵרַכְתָּ אֶת־יְהוָה אֱלֹהֶיךָ עַל־הָאָרֶץ הַטֹּבָה אֲשֶׁר נָתַן־לָךְ: 11 הִשָּׁמֶר לְךָ פֶּן־תִּשְׁכַּח אֶת־יְהוָה אֱלֹהֶיךָ לְבִלְתִּי שְׁמֹר מִצְוֹתָיו וּמִשְׁפָּטָיו וְחֻקֹּתָיו אֲשֶׁר אָנֹכִי מְצַוְּךָ הַיּוֹם: 12 פֶּן־תֹּאכַל וְשָׂבָעְתָּ וּבָתִּים טֹבִים תִּבְנֶה וְיָשָׁבְתָּ: 13 וּבְקָרְךָ וְצֹאנְךָ יִרְבְּיֻן וְכֶסֶף וְזָהָב יִרְבֶּה־לָּךְ וְכֹל אֲשֶׁר־לְךָ יִרְבֶּה: 14 וְרָם לְבָבֶךָ וְשָׁכַחְתָּ אֶת־יְהוָה אֱלֹהֶיךָ הַמּוֹצִיאֲךָ מֵאֶרֶץ מִצְרַיִם מִבֵּית עֲבָדִים: 15 הַמּוֹלִיכְךָ בַּמִּדְבָּר הַגָּדֹל וְהַנּוֹרָא נָחָשׁ שָׂרָף וְעַקְרָב וְצִמָּאוֹן אֲשֶׁר אֵין־מָיִם הַמּוֹצִיא לְךָ מַיִם מִצּוּר הַחַלָּמִישׁ: 16 הַמַּאֲכִלְךָ מָן בַּמִּדְבָּר אֲשֶׁר לֹא־יָדְעוּן אֲבֹתֶיךָ לְמַעַן עַנֹּתְךָ וּלְמַעַן נַסֹּתֶךָ לְהֵיטִבְךָ בְּאַחֲרִיתֶךָ: 17 וְאָמַרְתָּ בִּלְבָבֶךָ כֹּחִי וְעֹצֶם יָדִי עָשָׂה לִי אֶת־הַחַיִל הַזֶּה: 18 וְזָכַרְתָּ אֶת־יְהוָה אֱלֹהֶיךָ כִּי הוּא הַנֹּתֵן לְךָ כֹּחַ לַעֲשׂוֹת חָיִל לְמַעַן הָקִים אֶת־בְּרִיתוֹ אֲשֶׁר־נִשְׁבַּע לַאֲבֹתֶיךָ כַּיּוֹם הַזֶּה: פ 19 וְהָיָה אִם־שָׁכֹחַ תִּשְׁכַּח אֶת־יְהוָה אֱלֹהֶיךָ וְהָלַכְתָּ אַחֲרֵי אֱלֹהִים אֲחֵרִים וַעֲבַדְתָּם וְהִשְׁתַּחֲוִיתָ לָהֶם הַעִדֹתִי בָכֶם הַיּוֹם כִּי אָבֹד תֹּאבֵדוּן: 20 כַּגּוֹיִם אֲשֶׁר יְהוָה מַאֲבִיד מִפְּנֵיכֶם כֵּן תֹּאבֵדוּן עֵקֶב לֹא תִשְׁמְעוּן בְּקוֹל יְהוָה אֱלֹהֵיכֶם: פ

ט שְׁמַע יִשְׂרָאֵל אַתָּה עֹבֵר הַיּוֹם אֶת־הַיַּרְדֵּן לָבֹא לָרֶשֶׁת גּוֹיִם גְּדֹלִים וַעֲצֻמִים מִמֶּךָּ עָרִים גְּדֹלֹת וּבְצֻרֹת בַּשָּׁמָיִם: 2 עַם־גָּדוֹל וָרָם בְּנֵי עֲנָקִים אֲשֶׁר אַתָּה יָדַעְתָּ וְאַתָּה שָׁמַעְתָּ מִי יִתְיַצֵּב לִפְנֵי בְּנֵי עֲנָק: 3 וְיָדַעְתָּ הַיּוֹם כִּי יְהוָה אֱלֹהֶיךָ הוּא־הָעֹבֵר לְפָנֶיךָ אֵשׁ אֹכְלָה הוּא יַשְׁמִידֵם וְהוּא יַכְנִיעֵם לְפָנֶיךָ וְהוֹרַשְׁתָּם וְהַאֲבַדְתָּם מַהֵר כַּאֲשֶׁר דִּבֶּר יְהוָה לָךְ: 4 אַל־תֹּאמַר בִּלְבָבְךָ בַּהֲדֹף יְהוָה אֱלֹהֶיךָ אֹתָם מִלְּפָנֶיךָ לֵאמֹר בְּצִדְקָתִי הֱבִיאַנִי יְהוָה לָרֶשֶׁת אֶת־הָאָרֶץ הַזֹּאת וּבְרִשְׁעַת הַגּוֹיִם הָאֵלֶּה יְהוָה מוֹרִישָׁם מִפָּנֶיךָ: 5 לֹא בְצִדְקָתְךָ וּבְיֹשֶׁר לְבָבְךָ אַתָּה בָא לָרֶשֶׁת אֶת־אַרְצָם כִּי בְּרִשְׁעַת הַגּוֹיִם הָאֵלֶּה יְהוָה אֱלֹהֶיךָ מוֹרִישָׁם מִפָּנֶיךָ וּלְמַעַן הָקִים

that you go in to possess their land, but because of
the wickedness of these nations *that* the LORD your
God drives them out from before you, and that He
may fulfill the word which the LORD swore to your
fathers, to Abraham, Isaac, and Jacob. [6] Therefore
understand that the LORD your God is not giving
you this good land to possess because of your
righteousness, for you *are* a stiff-necked people.

[7] "Remember! Do not forget how you provoked
the LORD your God to wrath in the wilderness.
From the day that you departed from the land of
Egypt until you came to this place, you have been
rebellious against the LORD. [8] Also in Horeb you
provoked the LORD to wrath, so that the LORD was
angry *enough* with you to have destroyed you.
[9] When I went up into the mountain to receive the
tablets of stone, the tablets of the covenant which
the LORD made with you, then I stayed on the
mountain forty days and forty nights. I neither ate
bread nor drank water. [10] Then the LORD delivered
to me two tablets of stone written with the finger of
God, and on them *were* all the words which the
LORD had spoken to you on the mountain from the
midst of the fire in the day of the assembly. [11] And it
came to pass, at the end of forty days and forty
nights, *that* the LORD gave me the two tablets of
stone, the tablets of the covenant.

[12] "Then the LORD said to me, 'Arise, go down
quickly from here, for your people whom you
brought out of Egypt have acted corruptly; they
have quickly turned aside from the way which I
commanded them; they have made themselves a
molded image.'

[13] "Furthermore the LORD spoke to me, saying, 'I
have seen this people, and indeed they are a stiff-
necked people. [14] Let Me alone, that I may destroy
them and blot out their name from under heaven;
and I will make of you a nation mightier and
greater than they.'

[15] "So I turned and came down from the
mountain, and the mountain burned with fire; and
the two tablets of the covenant *were* in my two
hands. [16] And I looked, and behold, you had sinned
against the LORD your God—had made for
yourselves a molded calf! You had turned aside
quickly from the way which the LORD had
commanded you. [17] Then I took the two tablets
and threw them out of my two hands and broke
them before your eyes. [18] And I fell down before the
LORD, as at the first, forty days and forty nights; I
neither ate bread nor drank water, because of all
your sin which you committed in doing wickedly in
the sight of the LORD, to provoke Him to anger.
[19] For I was afraid of the anger and hot displeasure

אֶת־הַדָּבָר אֲשֶׁר נִשְׁבַּע יְהוָה לַאֲבֹתֶיךָ לְאַבְרָהָם
לְיִצְחָק וּלְיַעֲקֹב: 6 וְיָדַעְתָּ כִּי לֹא בְצִדְקָתְךָ יְהוָה
אֱלֹהֶיךָ נֹתֵן לְךָ אֶת־הָאָרֶץ הַטּוֹבָה הַזֹּאת לְרִשְׁתָּהּ
כִּי עַם־קְשֵׁה־עֹרֶף אָתָּה: 7 זְכֹר אַל־תִּשְׁכַּח אֵת
אֲשֶׁר־הִקְצַפְתָּ אֶת־יְהוָה אֱלֹהֶיךָ בַּמִּדְבָּר לְמִן־הַיּוֹם
אֲשֶׁר־יָצָאתָ | מֵאֶרֶץ מִצְרַיִם עַד־בֹּאֲכֶם עַד־
הַמָּקוֹם הַזֶּה מַמְרִים הֱיִיתֶם עִם־יְהוָה: 8 וּבְחֹרֵב
הִקְצַפְתֶּם אֶת־יְהוָה וַיִּתְאַנַּף יְהוָה בָּכֶם לְהַשְׁמִיד
אֶתְכֶם: 9 בַּעֲלֹתִי הָהָרָה לָקַחַת לוּחֹת הָאֲבָנִים
לוּחֹת הַבְּרִית אֲשֶׁר־כָּרַת יְהוָה עִמָּכֶם וָאֵשֵׁב בָּהָר
אַרְבָּעִים יוֹם וְאַרְבָּעִים לַיְלָה לֶחֶם לֹא אָכַלְתִּי
וּמַיִם לֹא שָׁתִיתִי: 10 וַיִּתֵּן יְהוָה אֵלַי אֶת־שְׁנֵי לוּחֹת
הָאֲבָנִים כְּתֻבִים בְּאֶצְבַּע אֱלֹהִים וַעֲלֵיהֶם כְּכָל־
הַדְּבָרִים אֲשֶׁר דִּבֶּר יְהוָה עִמָּכֶם בָּהָר מִתּוֹךְ הָאֵשׁ
בְּיוֹם הַקָּהָל: 11 וַיְהִי מִקֵּץ אַרְבָּעִים יוֹם וְאַרְבָּעִים
לַיְלָה נָתַן יְהוָה אֵלַי אֶת־שְׁנֵי לֻחֹת הָאֲבָנִים לֻחוֹת
הַבְּרִית: 12 וַיֹּאמֶר יְהוָה אֵלַי קוּם רֵד מַהֵר מִזֶּה כִּי
שִׁחֵת עַמְּךָ אֲשֶׁר הוֹצֵאתָ מִמִּצְרָיִם סָרוּ מַהֵר מִן־
הַדֶּרֶךְ אֲשֶׁר צִוִּיתִם עָשׂוּ לָהֶם מַסֵּכָה: 13 וַיֹּאמֶר
יְהוָה אֵלַי לֵאמֹר רָאִיתִי אֶת־הָעָם הַזֶּה וְהִנֵּה עַם־
קְשֵׁה־עֹרֶף הוּא: 14 הֶרֶף מִמֶּנִּי וְאַשְׁמִידֵם וְאֶמְחֶה
אֶת־שְׁמָם מִתַּחַת הַשָּׁמָיִם וְאֶעֱשֶׂה אוֹתְךָ לְגוֹי־
עָצוּם וָרָב מִמֶּנּוּ: 15 וָאֵפֶן וָאֵרֵד מִן־הָהָר וְהָהָר
בֹּעֵר בָּאֵשׁ וּשְׁנֵי לֻחֹת הַבְּרִית עַל שְׁתֵּי יָדָי:
16 וָאֵרֶא וְהִנֵּה חֲטָאתֶם לַיהוָה אֱלֹהֵיכֶם עֲשִׂיתֶם
לָכֶם עֵגֶל מַסֵּכָה סַרְתֶּם מַהֵר מִן־הַדֶּרֶךְ אֲשֶׁר־צִוָּה
יְהוָה אֶתְכֶם: 17 וָאֶתְפֹּשׂ בִּשְׁנֵי הַלֻּחֹת וָאַשְׁלִכֵם
מֵעַל שְׁתֵּי יָדָי וָאֲשַׁבְּרֵם לְעֵינֵיכֶם: 18 וָאֶתְנַפַּל
לִפְנֵי יְהוָה כָּרִאשֹׁנָה אַרְבָּעִים יוֹם וְאַרְבָּעִים לַיְלָה
לֶחֶם לֹא אָכַלְתִּי וּמַיִם לֹא שָׁתִיתִי עַל כָּל־
חַטַּאתְכֶם אֲשֶׁר חֲטָאתֶם לַעֲשׂוֹת הָרַע בְּעֵינֵי
יְהוָה לְהַכְעִיסוֹ: 19 כִּי יָגֹרְתִּי מִפְּנֵי הָאַף וְהַחֵמָה

with which the LORD was angry with you, to destroy you. But the LORD listened to me at that time also. 20 And the LORD was very angry with Aaron *and* would have destroyed him; so I prayed for Aaron also at the same time. 21 Then I took your sin, the calf which you had made, and burned it with fire and crushed it *and* ground *it* very small, until it was as fine as dust; and I threw its dust into the brook that descended from the mountain.

22 "Also at Taberah and Massah and Kibroth Hattaavah you provoked the LORD to wrath. 23 Likewise, when the LORD sent you from Kadesh Barnea, saying, 'Go up and possess the land which I have given you,' then you rebelled against the commandment of the LORD your God, and you did not believe Him nor obey His voice. 24 You have been rebellious against the LORD from the day that I knew you.

25 "Thus I prostrated myself before the LORD; forty days and forty nights I kept prostrating myself, because the LORD had said He would destroy you. 26 Therefore I prayed to the LORD, and said: 'O Lord GOD, do not destroy Your people and Your inheritance whom You have redeemed through Your greatness, whom You have brought out of Egypt with a mighty hand. 27 Remember Your servants, Abraham, Isaac, and Jacob; do not look on the stubbornness of this people, or on their wickedness or their sin, 28 lest the land from which You brought us should say, "Because the LORD was not able to bring them to the land which He promised them, and because He hated them, He has brought them out to kill them in the wilderness." 29 Yet they *are* Your people and Your inheritance, whom You brought out by Your mighty power and by Your outstretched arm.'

10 "At that time the LORD said to me, 'Hew for yourself two tablets of stone like the first, and come up to Me on the mountain and make yourself an ark of wood. 2 And I will write on the tablets the words that were on the first tablets, which you broke; and you shall put them in the ark.'

3 "So I made an ark of acacia wood, hewed two tablets of stone like the first, and went up the mountain, having the two tablets in my hand. 4 And He wrote on the tablets according to the first writing, the Ten Commandments, which the LORD had spoken to you in the mountain from the midst of the fire in the day of the assembly; and the LORD gave them to me. 5 Then I turned and came down from the mountain, and put the tablets in the ark which I had made; and there they are, just as the LORD commanded me."

אֲשֶׁר קָצַף יְהוָה עֲלֵיכֶם לְהַשְׁמִיד אֶתְכֶם וַיִּשְׁמַע יְהוָה אֵלַי גַּם בַּפַּעַם הַהִוא: 20 וּבְאַהֲרֹן הִתְאַנַּף יְהוָה מְאֹד לְהַשְׁמִידוֹ וָאֶתְפַּלֵּל גַּם־בְּעַד אַהֲרֹן בָּעֵת הַהִוא: 21 וְאֶת־חַטַּאתְכֶם אֲשֶׁר־עֲשִׂיתֶם אֶת־ הָעֵגֶל לָקַחְתִּי וָאֶשְׂרֹף אֹתוֹ ׀ בָּאֵשׁ וָאֶכֹּת אֹתוֹ טָחוֹן הֵיטֵב עַד אֲשֶׁר־דַּק לְעָפָר וָאַשְׁלִךְ אֶת־ עֲפָרוֹ אֶל־הַנַּחַל הַיֹּרֵד מִן־הָהָר: 22 וּבְתַבְעֵרָה וּבְמַסָּה וּבְקִבְרֹת הַתַּאֲוָה מַקְצִפִים הֱיִיתֶם אֶת־ יְהוָה: 23 וּבִשְׁלֹחַ יְהוָה אֶתְכֶם מִקָּדֵשׁ בַּרְנֵעַ לֵאמֹר עֲלוּ וּרְשׁוּ אֶת־הָאָרֶץ אֲשֶׁר נָתַתִּי לָכֶם וַתַּמְרוּ אֶת־פִּי יְהוָה אֱלֹהֵיכֶם וְלֹא הֶאֱמַנְתֶּם לוֹ וְלֹא שְׁמַעְתֶּם בְּקֹלוֹ: 24 מַמְרִים הֱיִיתֶם עִם־יְהוָה מִיּוֹם דַּעְתִּי אֶתְכֶם: 25 וָאֶתְנַפַּל לִפְנֵי יְהוָה אֵת אַרְבָּעִים הַיּוֹם וְאֶת־אַרְבָּעִים הַלַּיְלָה אֲשֶׁר הִתְנַפָּלְתִּי כִּי־ אָמַר יְהוָה לְהַשְׁמִיד אֶתְכֶם: 26 וָאֶתְפַּלֵּל אֶל־יְהוָה וָאֹמַר אֲדֹנָי יְהוִה אַל־תַּשְׁחֵת עַמְּךָ וְנַחֲלָתְךָ אֲשֶׁר פָּדִיתָ בְּגָדְלֶךָ אֲשֶׁר־הוֹצֵאתָ מִמִּצְרַיִם בְּיָד חֲזָקָה: 27 זְכֹר לַעֲבָדֶיךָ לְאַבְרָהָם לְיִצְחָק וּלְיַעֲקֹב אַל־ תֵּפֶן אֶל־קְשִׁי הָעָם הַזֶּה וְאֶל־רִשְׁעוֹ וְאֶל־חַטָּאתוֹ: 28 פֶּן־יֹאמְרוּ הָאָרֶץ אֲשֶׁר הוֹצֵאתָנוּ מִשָּׁם מִבְּלִי יְכֹלֶת יְהוָה לַהֲבִיאָם אֶל־הָאָרֶץ אֲשֶׁר־דִּבֶּר לָהֶם וּמִשִּׂנְאָתוֹ אוֹתָם הוֹצִיאָם לַהֲמִתָם בַּמִּדְבָּר: 29 וְהֵם עַמְּךָ וְנַחֲלָתֶךָ אֲשֶׁר הוֹצֵאתָ בְּכֹחֲךָ הַגָּדֹל וּבִזְרֹעֲךָ הַנְּטוּיָה: פ

י בָּעֵת הַהִוא אָמַר יְהוָה אֵלַי פְּסָל־לְךָ שְׁנֵי־לוּחֹת אֲבָנִים כָּרִאשֹׁנִים וַעֲלֵה אֵלַי הָהָרָה וְעָשִׂיתָ לְךָ אֲרוֹן עֵץ: 2 וְאֶכְתֹּב עַל־הַלֻּחֹת אֶת־הַדְּבָרִים אֲשֶׁר הָיוּ עַל־הַלֻּחֹת הָרִאשֹׁנִים אֲשֶׁר שִׁבַּרְתָּ וְשַׂמְתָּם בָּאָרוֹן: 3 וָאַעַשׂ אֲרוֹן עֲצֵי שִׁטִּים וָאֶפְסֹל שְׁנֵי־ לֻחֹת אֲבָנִים כָּרִאשֹׁנִים וָאַעַל הָהָרָה וּשְׁנֵי הַלֻּחֹת בְּיָדִי: 4 וַיִּכְתֹּב עַל־הַלֻּחֹת כַּמִּכְתָּב הָרִאשׁוֹן אֵת עֲשֶׂרֶת הַדְּבָרִים אֲשֶׁר דִּבֶּר יְהוָה אֲלֵיכֶם בָּהָר מִתּוֹךְ הָאֵשׁ בְּיוֹם הַקָּהָל וַיִּתְּנֵם יְהוָה אֵלָי: 5 וָאֵפֶן וָאֵרֵד מִן־הָהָר וָאָשִׂם אֶת־הַלֻּחֹת בָּאָרוֹן אֲשֶׁר

⁶(Now the children of Israel journeyed from the wells of Bene Jaakan to Moserah, where Aaron died, and where he was buried; and Eleazar his son ministered as priest in his stead. ⁷From there they journeyed to Gudgodah, and from Gudgodah to Jotbathah, a land of rivers of water. ⁸At that time the LORD separated the tribe of Levi to bear the ark of the covenant of the LORD, to stand before the LORD to minister to Him and to bless in His name, to this day. ⁹Therefore Levi has no portion nor inheritance with his brethren; the LORD is his inheritance, just as the LORD your God promised him.)

¹⁰"As at the first time, I stayed in the mountain forty days and forty nights; the LORD also heard me at that time, and the LORD chose not to destroy you. ¹¹Then the LORD said to me, 'Arise, begin your journey before the people, that they may go in and possess the land which I swore to their fathers to give them.'

¹²"And now, Israel, what does the LORD your God require of you, but to fear the LORD your God, to walk in all His ways and to love Him, to serve the LORD your God with all your heart and with all your soul, ¹³and to keep the commandments of the LORD and His statutes which I command you today for your good? ¹⁴Indeed heaven and the highest heavens belong to the LORD your God, also the earth with all that is in it. ¹⁵The LORD delighted only in your fathers, to love them; and He chose their descendants after them, you above all peoples, as it is this day. ¹⁶Therefore circumcise the foreskin of your heart, and be stiff-necked no longer. ¹⁷For the LORD your God is God of gods and Lord of lords, the great God, mighty and awesome, who shows no partiality nor takes a bribe. ¹⁸He administers justice for the fatherless and the widow, and loves the stranger, giving him food and clothing. ¹⁹Therefore love the stranger, for you were strangers in the land of Egypt. ²⁰You shall fear the LORD your God; you shall serve Him, and to Him you shall hold fast, and take oaths in His name. ²¹He is your praise, and He is your God, who has done for you these great and awesome things which your eyes have seen. ²²Your fathers went down to Egypt with seventy persons, and now the LORD your God has made you as the stars of heaven in multitude.

11 "Therefore you shall love the LORD your God, and keep His charge, His statutes, His judgments, and His commandments always. ²Know today that I do not speak with your children, who have not known and who have not seen the chastening of the

עָשִׂיתִי וַיִּהְיוּ שָׁם כַּאֲשֶׁר צִוַּנִי יְהוָה: 6 וּבְנֵי יִשְׂרָאֵל נָסְעוּ מִבְּאֵרֹת בְּנֵי־יַעֲקָן מוֹסֵרָה שָׁם מֵת אַהֲרֹן וַיִּקָּבֵר שָׁם וַיְכַהֵן אֶלְעָזָר בְּנוֹ תַּחְתָּיו: 7 מִשָּׁם נָסְעוּ הַגֻּדְגֹּדָה וּמִן־הַגֻּדְגֹּדָה יָטְבָתָה אֶרֶץ נַחֲלֵי מָיִם: 8 בָּעֵת הַהִוא הִבְדִּיל יְהוָה אֶת־שֵׁבֶט הַלֵּוִי לָשֵׂאת אֶת־אֲרוֹן בְּרִית־יְהוָה לַעֲמֹד לִפְנֵי יְהוָה לְשָׁרְתוֹ וּלְבָרֵךְ בִּשְׁמוֹ עַד הַיּוֹם הַזֶּה: 9 עַל־כֵּן לֹא־הָיָה לְלֵוִי חֵלֶק וְנַחֲלָה עִם־אֶחָיו יְהוָה הוּא נַחֲלָתוֹ כַּאֲשֶׁר דִּבֶּר יְהוָה אֱלֹהֶיךָ לוֹ: 10 וְאָנֹכִי עָמַדְתִּי בָהָר כַּיָּמִים הָרִאשֹׁנִים אַרְבָּעִים יוֹם וְאַרְבָּעִים לַיְלָה וַיִּשְׁמַע יְהוָה אֵלַי גַּם בַּפַּעַם הַהִוא לֹא־אָבָה יְהוָה הַשְׁחִיתֶךָ: 11 וַיֹּאמֶר יְהוָה אֵלַי קוּם לֵךְ לְמַסַּע לִפְנֵי הָעָם וְיָבֹאוּ וְיִרְשׁוּ אֶת־הָאָרֶץ אֲשֶׁר־ נִשְׁבַּעְתִּי לַאֲבֹתָם לָתֵת לָהֶם: פ

12 וְעַתָּה יִשְׂרָאֵל מָה יְהוָה אֱלֹהֶיךָ שֹׁאֵל מֵעִמָּךְ כִּי אִם־לְיִרְאָה אֶת־יְהוָה אֱלֹהֶיךָ לָלֶכֶת בְּכָל־דְּרָכָיו וּלְאַהֲבָה אֹתוֹ וְלַעֲבֹד אֶת־יְהוָה אֱלֹהֶיךָ בְּכָל־ לְבָבְךָ וּבְכָל־נַפְשֶׁךָ: 13 לִשְׁמֹר אֶת־מִצְוֹת יְהוָה וְאֶת־חֻקֹּתָיו אֲשֶׁר אָנֹכִי מְצַוְּךָ הַיּוֹם לְטוֹב לָךְ: 14 הֵן לַיהוָה אֱלֹהֶיךָ הַשָּׁמַיִם וּשְׁמֵי הַשָּׁמָיִם הָאָרֶץ וְכָל־אֲשֶׁר־בָּהּ: 15 רַק בַּאֲבֹתֶיךָ חָשַׁק יְהוָה לְאַהֲבָה אוֹתָם וַיִּבְחַר בְּזַרְעָם אַחֲרֵיהֶם בָּכֶם מִכָּל־הָעַמִּים כַּיּוֹם הַזֶּה: 16 וּמַלְתֶּם אֵת עָרְלַת לְבַבְכֶם וְעָרְפְּכֶם לֹא תַקְשׁוּ עוֹד: 17 כִּי יְהוָה אֱלֹהֵיכֶם הוּא אֱלֹהֵי הָאֱלֹהִים וַאֲדֹנֵי הָאֲדֹנִים הָאֵל הַגָּדֹל הַגִּבֹּר וְהַנּוֹרָא אֲשֶׁר לֹא־יִשָּׂא פָנִים וְלֹא יִקַּח שֹׁחַד: 18 עֹשֶׂה מִשְׁפַּט יָתוֹם וְאַלְמָנָה וְאֹהֵב גֵּר לָתֶת לוֹ לֶחֶם וְשִׂמְלָה: 19 וַאֲהַבְתֶּם אֶת־הַגֵּר כִּי־גֵרִים הֱיִיתֶם בְּאֶרֶץ מִצְרָיִם: 20 אֶת־יְהוָה אֱלֹהֶיךָ תִּירָא אֹתוֹ תַעֲבֹד וּבוֹ תִדְבָּק וּבִשְׁמוֹ תִּשָּׁבֵעַ: 21 הוּא תְהִלָּתְךָ וְהוּא אֱלֹהֶיךָ אֲשֶׁר־עָשָׂה אִתְּךָ אֶת־הַגְּדֹלֹת וְאֶת־ הַנּוֹרָאֹת הָאֵלֶּה אֲשֶׁר רָאוּ עֵינֶיךָ: 22 בְּשִׁבְעִים נֶפֶשׁ יָרְדוּ אֲבֹתֶיךָ מִצְרָיְמָה וְעַתָּה שָׂמְךָ יְהוָה אֱלֹהֶיךָ כְּכוֹכְבֵי הַשָּׁמַיִם לָרֹב:

יא וְאָהַבְתָּ אֵת יְהוָה אֱלֹהֶיךָ וְשָׁמַרְתָּ מִשְׁמַרְתּוֹ וְחֻקֹּתָיו וּמִשְׁפָּטָיו וּמִצְוֹתָיו כָּל־הַיָּמִים: 2 וִידַעְתֶּם הַיּוֹם כִּי לֹא אֶת־בְּנֵיכֶם אֲשֶׁר לֹא־יָדְעוּ וַאֲשֶׁר לֹא־רָאוּ אֶת־מוּסַר יְהוָה אֱלֹהֵיכֶם אֶת־גָּדְלוֹ אֶת־

LORD your God, His greatness and His mighty hand and His outstretched arm— ³His signs and His acts which He did in the midst of Egypt, to Pharaoh king of Egypt, and to all his land; ⁴what He did to the army of Egypt, to their horses and their chariots: how He made the waters of the Red Sea overflow them as they pursued you, and *how* the LORD has destroyed them to this day; ⁵what He did for you in the wilderness until you came to this place; ⁶and what He did to Dathan and Abiram the sons of Eliab, the son of Reuben: how the earth opened its mouth and swallowed them up, their households, their tents, and all the substance that *was* in their possession, in the midst of all Israel— ⁷but your eyes have seen every great act of the LORD which He did.

⁸"Therefore you shall keep every commandment which I command you today, that you may be strong, and go in and possess the land which you cross over to possess, ⁹and that you may prolong *your* days in the land which the LORD swore to give your fathers, to them and their descendants, 'a land flowing with milk and honey.' ¹⁰For the land which you go to possess *is* not like the land of Egypt from which you have come, where you sowed your seed and watered *it* by foot, as a vegetable garden; ¹¹but the land which you cross over to possess *is* a land of hills and valleys, which drinks water from the rain of heaven, ¹²a land for which the LORD your God cares; the eyes of the LORD your God *are* always on it, from the beginning of the year to the very end of the year.

¹³'And it shall be that if you earnestly obey My commandments which I command you today, to love the LORD your God and serve Him with all your heart and with all your soul, ¹⁴then I will give *you* the rain for your land in its season, the early rain and the latter rain, that you may gather in your grain, your new wine, and your oil. ¹⁵And I will send grass in your fields for your livestock, that you may eat and be filled.' ¹⁶Take heed to yourselves, lest your heart be deceived, and you turn aside and serve other gods and worship them, ¹⁷lest the LORD's anger be aroused against you, and He shut up the heavens so that there be no rain, and the land yield no produce, and you perish quickly from the good land which the LORD is giving you.

¹⁸"Therefore you shall lay up these words of mine in your heart and in your soul, and bind them as a sign on your hand, and they shall be as frontlets between your eyes. ¹⁹You shall teach them to your children, speaking of them when you sit in your house, when you walk by the way, when you lie down, and when you rise up. ²⁰And you shall

יָד֖וֹ הַחֲזָקָ֑ה וּזְרֹע֖וֹ הַנְּטוּיָֽה׃ 3 וְאֶת־אֹֽתֹתָיו֙ וְאֶת־מַ֣עֲשָׂ֔יו אֲשֶׁ֥ר עָשָׂ֖ה בְּת֣וֹךְ מִצְרָ֑יִם לְפַרְעֹ֥ה מֶֽלֶךְ־מִצְרַ֖יִם וּלְכָל־אַרְצֽוֹ׃ 4 וַאֲשֶׁ֣ר עָשָׂה֩ לְחֵ֨יל מִצְרַ֜יִם לְסוּסָ֣יו וּלְרִכְבּ֗וֹ אֲשֶׁ֨ר הֵצִ֜יף אֶת־מֵ֤י יַם־סוּף֙ עַל־פְּנֵיהֶ֔ם בְּרׇדְפָ֖ם אַחֲרֵיכֶ֑ם וַיְאַבְּדֵ֣ם יְהֹוָ֔ה עַ֖ד הַיּ֥וֹם הַזֶּֽה׃ 5 וַאֲשֶׁ֥ר עָשָׂ֛ה לָכֶ֖ם בַּמִּדְבָּ֑ר עַד־בֹּאֲכֶ֖ם עַד־הַמָּק֥וֹם הַזֶּֽה׃ 6 וַאֲשֶׁ֨ר עָשָׂ֜ה לְדָתָ֣ן וְלַאֲבִירָ֗ם בְּנֵ֤י אֱלִיאָב֙ בֶּן־רְאוּבֵ֔ן אֲשֶׁ֨ר פָּצְתָ֤ה הָאָ֙רֶץ֙ אֶת־פִּ֔יהָ וַתִּבְלָעֵ֥ם וְאֶת־בָּתֵּיהֶ֖ם וְאֶת־אׇהֳלֵיהֶ֑ם וְאֵ֤ת כׇּל־הַיְקוּם֙ אֲשֶׁ֣ר בְּרַגְלֵיהֶ֔ם בְּקֶ֖רֶב כׇּל־יִשְׂרָאֵֽל׃ 7 כִּ֤י עֵֽינֵיכֶם֙ הָרֹאֹ֔ת אֶת־כׇּל־מַעֲשֵׂ֥ה יְהֹוָ֖ה הַגָּדֹ֑ל אֲשֶׁ֖ר עָשָֽׂה׃ 8 וּשְׁמַרְתֶּם֙ אֶת־כׇּל־הַמִּצְוָ֔ה אֲשֶׁ֧ר אָנֹכִ֛י מְצַוְּךָ֖ הַיּ֑וֹם לְמַ֣עַן תֶּחֶזְק֗וּ וּבָאתֶם֙ וִֽירִשְׁתֶּ֣ם אֶת־הָאָ֔רֶץ אֲשֶׁ֥ר אַתֶּ֛ם עֹבְרִ֥ים שָׁ֖מָּה לְרִשְׁתָּֽהּ׃ 9 וּלְמַ֨עַן תַּאֲרִ֤יכוּ יָמִים֙ עַל־הָ֣אֲדָמָ֔ה אֲשֶׁר֩ נִשְׁבַּ֨ע יְהֹוָ֤ה לַאֲבֹֽתֵיכֶם֙ לָתֵ֣ת לָהֶ֔ם וּלְזַרְעָ֑ם אֶ֛רֶץ זָבַ֥ת חָלָ֖ב וּדְבָֽשׁ׃ ס 10 כִּ֣י הָאָ֗רֶץ אֲשֶׁ֨ר אַתָּ֤ה בָא־שָׁ֙מָּה֙ לְרִשְׁתָּ֔הּ לֹ֣א כְאֶ֤רֶץ מִצְרַ֙יִם֙ הִ֔וא אֲשֶׁ֥ר יְצָאתֶ֖ם מִשָּׁ֑ם אֲשֶׁ֤ר תִּזְרַע֙ אֶֽת־זַרְעֲךָ֔ וְהִשְׁקִ֥יתָ בְרַגְלְךָ֖ כְּגַ֥ן הַיָּרָֽק׃ 11 וְהָאָ֗רֶץ אֲשֶׁ֨ר אַתֶּ֜ם עֹבְרִ֥ים שָׁ֙מָּה֙ לְרִשְׁתָּ֔הּ אֶ֥רֶץ הָרִ֖ים וּבְקָעֹ֑ת לִמְטַ֥ר הַשָּׁמַ֖יִם תִּשְׁתֶּה־מָּֽיִם׃ 12 אֶ֕רֶץ אֲשֶׁר־יְהֹוָ֥ה אֱלֹהֶ֖יךָ דֹּרֵ֣שׁ אֹתָ֑הּ תָּמִ֗יד עֵינֵ֨י יְהֹוָ֤ה אֱלֹהֶ֙יךָ֙ בָּ֔הּ מֵֽרֵשִׁית֙ הַשָּׁנָ֔ה וְעַ֖ד אַחֲרִ֥ית שָׁנָֽה׃ ס 13 וְהָיָ֗ה אִם־שָׁמֹ֤עַ תִּשְׁמְעוּ֙ אֶל־מִצְוֺתַ֔י אֲשֶׁ֧ר אָנֹכִ֛י מְצַוֶּ֥ה אֶתְכֶ֖ם הַיּ֑וֹם לְאַהֲבָ֞ה אֶת־יְהֹוָ֤ה אֱלֹֽהֵיכֶם֙ וּלְעׇבְד֔וֹ בְּכׇל־לְבַבְכֶ֖ם וּבְכׇל־נַפְשְׁכֶֽם׃ 14 וְנָתַתִּ֧י מְטַֽר־אַרְצְכֶ֛ם בְּעִתּ֖וֹ יוֹרֶ֣ה וּמַלְק֑וֹשׁ וְאָסַפְתָּ֣ דְגָנֶ֔ךָ וְתִירֹֽשְׁךָ֖ וְיִצְהָרֶֽךָ׃ 15 וְנָתַתִּ֛י עֵ֥שֶׂב בְּשָׂדְךָ֖ לִבְהֶמְתֶּ֑ךָ וְאָכַלְתָּ֖ וְשָׂבָֽעְתָּ׃ 16 הִשָּׁ֣מְר֣וּ לָכֶ֔ם פֶּ֥ן יִפְתֶּ֖ה לְבַבְכֶ֑ם וְסַרְתֶּ֗ם וַעֲבַדְתֶּם֙ אֱלֹהִ֣ים אֲחֵרִ֔ים וְהִשְׁתַּחֲוִיתֶ֖ם לָהֶֽם׃ 17 וְחָרָ֨ה אַף־יְהֹוָ֜ה בָּכֶ֗ם וְעָצַ֤ר אֶת־הַשָּׁמַ֙יִם֙ וְלֹֽא־יִהְיֶ֣ה מָטָ֔ר וְהָ֣אֲדָמָ֔ה לֹ֥א תִתֵּ֖ן אֶת־יְבוּלָ֑הּ וַאֲבַדְתֶּ֣ם מְהֵרָ֗ה מֵעַל֙ הָאָ֣רֶץ הַטֹּבָ֔ה אֲשֶׁ֥ר יְהֹוָ֖ה נֹתֵ֥ן לָכֶֽם׃ 18 וְשַׂמְתֶּם֙ אֶת־דְּבָרַ֣י אֵ֔לֶּה עַל־לְבַבְכֶ֖ם וְעַֽל־נַפְשְׁכֶ֑ם וּקְשַׁרְתֶּ֨ם אֹתָ֤ם לְאוֹת֙ עַל־יֶדְכֶ֔ם וְהָי֥וּ לְטוֹטָפֹ֖ת בֵּ֥ין עֵינֵיכֶֽם׃ 19 וְלִמַּדְתֶּ֥ם אֹתָ֛ם אֶת־בְּנֵיכֶ֖ם לְדַבֵּ֣ר בָּ֑ם בְּשִׁבְתְּךָ֤ בְּבֵיתֶ֙ךָ֙ וּבְלֶכְתְּךָ֣ בַדֶּ֔רֶךְ וּֽבְשׇׁכְבְּךָ֖ וּבְקוּמֶֽךָ׃ 20 וּכְתַבְתָּ֛ם עַל־מְזוּז֥וֹת בֵּיתֶ֖ךָ וּבִשְׁעָרֶֽיךָ׃

write them on the doorposts of your house and on your gates, ²¹that your days and the days of your children may be multiplied in the land of which the LORD swore to your fathers to give them, like the days of the heavens above the earth.

²²"For if you carefully keep all these commandments which I command you to do—to love the LORD your God, to walk in all His ways, and to hold fast to Him— ²³then the LORD will drive out all these nations from before you, and you will dispossess greater and mightier nations than yourselves. ²⁴Every place on which the sole of your foot treads shall be yours: from the wilderness and Lebanon, from the river, the River Euphrates, even to the Western Sea, shall be your territory. ²⁵No man shall be able to stand against you; the LORD your God will put the dread of you and the fear of you upon all the land where you tread, just as He has said to you.

²⁶"Behold, I set before you today a blessing and a curse: ²⁷the blessing, if you obey the commandments of the LORD your God which I command you today; ²⁸and the curse, if you do not obey the commandments of the LORD your God, but turn aside from the way which I command you today, to go after other gods which you have not known. ²⁹Now it shall be, when the LORD your God has brought you into the land which you go to possess, that you shall put the blessing on Mount Gerizim and the curse on Mount Ebal. ³⁰Are they not on the other side of the Jordan, toward the setting sun, in the land of the Canaanites who dwell in the plain opposite Gilgal, beside the terebinth trees of Moreh? ³¹For you will cross over the Jordan and go in to possess the land which the LORD your God is giving you, and you will possess it and dwell in it. ³²And you shall be careful to observe all the statutes and judgments which I set before you today.

12 "These *are* the statutes and judgments which you shall be careful to observe in the land which the LORD God of your fathers is giving you to possess, all the days that you live on the earth. ²You shall utterly destroy all the places where the nations which you shall dispossess served their gods, on the high mountains and on the hills and under every green tree. ³And you shall destroy their altars, break their *sacred* pillars, and burn their wooden images with fire; you shall cut down the carved images of their gods and destroy their names from that place. ⁴You shall not worship the LORD your God *with* such *things*.

21 לְמַעַן יִרְבּוּ יְמֵיכֶם וִימֵי בְנֵיכֶם עַל הָאֲדָמָה אֲשֶׁר נִשְׁבַּע יְהוָה לַאֲבֹתֵיכֶם לָתֵת לָהֶם כִּימֵי הַשָּׁמַיִם עַל־הָאָרֶץ: ס 22 כִּי אִם־שָׁמֹר תִּשְׁמְרוּן אֶת־כָּל־הַמִּצְוָה הַזֹּאת אֲשֶׁר אָנֹכִי מְצַוֶּה אֶתְכֶם לַעֲשֹׂתָהּ לְאַהֲבָה אֶת־יְהוָה אֱלֹהֵיכֶם לָלֶכֶת בְּכָל־דְּרָכָיו וּלְדָבְקָה־בוֹ: 23 וְהוֹרִישׁ יְהוָה אֶת־כָּל־הַגּוֹיִם הָאֵלֶּה מִלִּפְנֵיכֶם וִירִשְׁתֶּם גּוֹיִם גְּדֹלִים וַעֲצֻמִים מִכֶּם: 24 כָּל־הַמָּקוֹם אֲשֶׁר תִּדְרֹךְ כַּף־רַגְלְכֶם בּוֹ לָכֶם יִהְיֶה מִן־הַמִּדְבָּר וְהַלְּבָנוֹן מִן־הַנָּהָר נְהַר־פְּרָת וְעַד הַיָּם הָאַחֲרוֹן יִהְיֶה גְּבֻלְכֶם: 25 לֹא־יִתְיַצֵּב אִישׁ בִּפְנֵיכֶם פַּחְדְּכֶם וּמוֹרַאֲכֶם יִתֵּן יְהוָה אֱלֹהֵיכֶם עַל־פְּנֵי כָל־הָאָרֶץ אֲשֶׁר תִּדְרְכוּ־בָהּ כַּאֲשֶׁר דִּבֶּר לָכֶם: ס 26 רְאֵה אָנֹכִי נֹתֵן לִפְנֵיכֶם הַיּוֹם בְּרָכָה וּקְלָלָה: 27 אֶת־הַבְּרָכָה אֲשֶׁר תִּשְׁמְעוּ אֶל־מִצְוֹת יְהוָה אֱלֹהֵיכֶם אֲשֶׁר אָנֹכִי מְצַוֶּה אֶתְכֶם הַיּוֹם: 28 וְהַקְּלָלָה אִם־לֹא תִשְׁמְעוּ אֶל־מִצְוֹת יְהוָה אֱלֹהֵיכֶם וְסַרְתֶּם מִן־הַדֶּרֶךְ אֲשֶׁר אָנֹכִי מְצַוֶּה אֶתְכֶם הַיּוֹם לָלֶכֶת אַחֲרֵי אֱלֹהִים אֲחֵרִים אֲשֶׁר לֹא־יְדַעְתֶּם: ס 29 וְהָיָה כִּי יְבִיאֲךָ יְהוָה אֱלֹהֶיךָ אֶל־הָאָרֶץ אֲשֶׁר־אַתָּה בָא־שָׁמָּה לְרִשְׁתָּהּ וְנָתַתָּה אֶת־הַבְּרָכָה עַל־הַר גְּרִזִים וְאֶת־הַקְּלָלָה עַל־הַר עֵיבָל: 30 הֲלֹא־הֵמָּה בְּעֵבֶר הַיַּרְדֵּן אַחֲרֵי דֶּרֶךְ מְבוֹא הַשֶּׁמֶשׁ בְּאֶרֶץ הַכְּנַעֲנִי הַיֹּשֵׁב בָּעֲרָבָה מוּל הַגִּלְגָּל אֵצֶל אֵלוֹנֵי מֹרֶה: 31 כִּי אַתֶּם עֹבְרִים אֶת־הַיַּרְדֵּן לָבֹא לָרֶשֶׁת אֶת־הָאָרֶץ אֲשֶׁר־יְהוָה אֱלֹהֵיכֶם נֹתֵן לָכֶם וִירִשְׁתֶּם אֹתָהּ וִישַׁבְתֶּם־בָּהּ: 32 וּשְׁמַרְתֶּם לַעֲשׂוֹת אֵת כָּל־הַחֻקִּים וְאֶת־הַמִּשְׁפָּטִים אֲשֶׁר אָנֹכִי נֹתֵן לִפְנֵיכֶם הַיּוֹם:

יב אֵלֶּה הַחֻקִּים וְהַמִּשְׁפָּטִים אֲשֶׁר תִּשְׁמְרוּן לַעֲשׂוֹת בָּאָרֶץ אֲשֶׁר נָתַן יְהוָה אֱלֹהֵי אֲבֹתֶיךָ לְךָ לְרִשְׁתָּהּ כָּל־הַיָּמִים אֲשֶׁר־אַתֶּם חַיִּים עַל־הָאֲדָמָה: 2 אַבֵּד תְּאַבְּדוּן אֶת־כָּל־הַמְּקֹמוֹת אֲשֶׁר עָבְדוּ־שָׁם הַגּוֹיִם אֲשֶׁר אַתֶּם יֹרְשִׁים אֹתָם אֶת־אֱלֹהֵיהֶם עַל־הֶהָרִים הָרָמִים וְעַל־הַגְּבָעוֹת וְתַחַת כָּל־עֵץ רַעֲנָן: 3 וְנִתַּצְתֶּם אֶת־מִזְבְּחֹתָם וְשִׁבַּרְתֶּם אֶת־מַצֵּבֹתָם וַאֲשֵׁרֵיהֶם תִּשְׂרְפוּן בָּאֵשׁ וּפְסִילֵי אֱלֹהֵיהֶם תְּגַדֵּעוּן וְאִבַּדְתֶּם אֶת־שְׁמָם מִן־הַמָּקוֹם הַהוּא: 4 לֹא־תַעֲשׂוּן כֵּן לַיהוָה אֱלֹהֵיכֶם: 5 כִּי

5 "But you shall seek the place where the LORD your God chooses, out of all your tribes, to put His name for His dwelling place; and there you shall go. 6 There you shall take your burnt offerings, your sacrifices, your tithes, the heave offerings of your hand, your vowed offerings, your freewill offerings, and the firstborn of your herds and flocks. 7 And there you shall eat before the LORD your God, and you shall rejoice in all to which you have put your hand, you and your households, in which the LORD your God has blessed you.

8 "You shall not at all do as we are doing here today—every man doing whatever *is* right in his own eyes— 9 for as yet you have not come to the rest and the inheritance which the LORD your God is giving you. 10 But *when* you cross over the Jordan and dwell in the land which the LORD your God is giving you to inherit, and He gives you rest from all your enemies round about, so that you dwell in safety, 11 then there will be the place where the LORD your God chooses to make His name abide. There you shall bring all that I command you: your burnt offerings, your sacrifices, your tithes, the heave offerings of your hand, and all your choice offerings which you vow to the LORD. 12 And you shall rejoice before the LORD your God, you and your sons and your daughters, your male and female servants, and the Levite who *is* within your gates, since he has no portion nor inheritance with you. 13 Take heed to yourself that you do not offer your burnt offerings in every place that you see; 14 but in the place which the LORD chooses, in one of your tribes, there you shall offer your burnt offerings, and there you shall do all that I command you.

15 "However, you may slaughter and eat meat within all your gates, whatever your heart desires, according to the blessing of the LORD your God which He has given you; the unclean and the clean may eat of it, of the gazelle and the deer alike. 16 Only you shall not eat the blood; you shall pour it on the earth like water. 17 You may not eat within your gates the tithe of your grain or your new wine or your oil, of the firstborn of your herd or your flock, of any of your offerings which you vow, of your freewill offerings, or of the heave offering of your hand. 18 But you must eat them before the LORD your God in the place which the LORD your God chooses, you and your son and your daughter, your male servant and your female servant, and the Levite who *is* within your gates; and you shall rejoice before the LORD your God in all to which

אִם־אֶל־הַמָּק֗וֹם אֲשֶׁר־יִבְחַ֞ר יְהֹוָ֤ה אֱלֹֽהֵיכֶם֙ מִכׇּל־
שִׁבְטֵיכֶ֔ם לָשׂ֥וּם אֶת־שְׁמ֖וֹ שָׁ֑ם לְשִׁכְנ֥וֹ תִדְרְשׁ֖וּ
וּבָ֥אתָ שָֽׁמָּה: 6 וַהֲבֵאתֶ֣ם שָׁ֗מָּה עֹלֹֽתֵיכֶם֙ וְזִבְחֵיכֶ֔ם
וְאֵת֙ מַעְשְׂרֹ֣תֵיכֶ֔ם וְאֵ֖ת תְּרוּמַ֣ת יֶדְכֶ֑ם וְנִדְרֵיכֶם֙
וְנִדְבֹ֣תֵיכֶ֔ם וּבְכֹרֹ֥ת בְּקַרְכֶ֖ם וְצֹאנְכֶֽם: 7 וַאֲכַלְתֶּם־
שָׁ֗ם לִפְנֵי֙ יְהֹוָ֣ה אֱלֹֽהֵיכֶ֔ם וּשְׂמַחְתֶּ֗ם בְּכֹל֙ מִשְׁלַ֣ח
יֶדְכֶ֔ם אַתֶּ֖ם וּבָתֵּיכֶ֑ם אֲשֶׁ֥ר בֵּֽרַכְךָ֖ יְהֹוָ֥ה אֱלֹהֶֽיךָ:

8 לֹ֣א תַעֲשׂ֔וּן כְּ֠כֹ֠ל אֲשֶׁ֨ר אֲנַ֧חְנוּ עֹשִׂ֛ים פֹּ֖ה הַיּ֑וֹם
אִ֖ישׁ כׇּל־הַיָּשָׁ֥ר בְּעֵינָֽיו: 9 כִּ֥י לֹא־בָאתֶ֖ם עַד־עָ֑תָּה
אֶל־הַמְּנוּחָה֙ וְאֶל־הַנַּחֲלָ֔ה אֲשֶׁר־יְהֹוָ֥ה אֱלֹהֶ֖יךָ נֹתֵ֥ן
לָֽךְ: 10 וַעֲבַרְתֶּם֮ אֶת־הַיַּרְדֵּן֒ וִֽישַׁבְתֶּ֣ם בָּאָ֔רֶץ אֲשֶׁר־
יְהֹוָ֥ה אֱלֹהֵיכֶ֖ם מַנְחִ֣יל אֶתְכֶ֑ם וְהֵנִ֨יחַ לָכֶ֧ם מִכׇּל־
אֹיְבֵיכֶ֛ם מִסָּבִ֖יב וִֽישַׁבְתֶּם־בֶּֽטַח: 11 וְהָיָ֣ה הַמָּק֗וֹם
אֲשֶׁר־יִבְחַר֩ יְהֹוָ֨ה אֱלֹהֵיכֶ֥ם בּ֛וֹ לְשַׁכֵּ֥ן שְׁמ֖וֹ שָׁ֑ם
שָׁ֣מָּה תָבִ֔יאוּ אֵ֛ת כׇּל־אֲשֶׁ֥ר אָנֹכִ֖י מְצַוֶּ֣ה אֶתְכֶ֑ם
עוֹלֹֽתֵיכֶ֣ם וְזִבְחֵיכֶ֗ם מַעְשְׂרֹֽתֵיכֶם֙ וּתְרֻמַ֣ת יֶדְכֶ֔ם וְכֹל֙
מִבְחַ֣ר נִדְרֵיכֶ֔ם אֲשֶׁ֥ר תִּדְּר֖וּ לַֽיהֹוָֽה: 12 וּשְׂמַחְתֶּ֗ם
לִפְנֵי֮ יְהֹוָ֣ה אֱלֹֽהֵיכֶם֒ אַתֶּ֗ם וּבְנֵיכֶם֙ וּבְנֹ֣תֵיכֶ֔ם
וְעַבְדֵיכֶ֖ם וְאַמְהֹתֵיכֶ֑ם וְהַלֵּוִי֙ אֲשֶׁ֣ר בְּשַׁעֲרֵיכֶ֔ם כִּ֣י
אֵ֥ין ל֛וֹ חֵ֥לֶק וְנַחֲלָ֖ה אִתְּכֶֽם: 13 הִשָּׁ֣מֶר לְךָ֔ פֶּֽן־
תַּעֲלֶ֖ה עֹֽלֹתֶ֑יךָ בְּכׇל־מָק֖וֹם אֲשֶׁ֥ר תִּרְאֶֽה: 14 כִּ֣י
אִם־בַּמָּק֞וֹם אֲשֶׁר־יִבְחַ֤ר יְהֹוָה֙ בְּאַחַ֣ד שְׁבָטֶ֔יךָ שָׁ֖ם
תַּעֲלֶ֣ה עֹֽלֹתֶ֑יךָ וְשָׁ֣ם תַּעֲשֶׂ֔ה כֹּ֛ל אֲשֶׁ֥ר אָנֹכִ֖י
מְצַוֶּֽךָּ: 15 רַק֩ בְּכׇל־אַוַּ֨ת נַפְשְׁךָ֜ תִּזְבַּ֣ח ׀ וְאָכַלְתָּ֣
בָשָׂ֗ר כְּבִרְכַּ֨ת יְהֹוָ֧ה אֱלֹהֶ֛יךָ אֲשֶׁ֥ר נָֽתַן־לְךָ֖ בְּכׇל־
שְׁעָרֶ֑יךָ הַטָּמֵ֤א וְהַטָּהוֹר֙ יֹאכְלֶ֔נּוּ כַּצְּבִ֖י וְכָאַיָּֽל:
16 רַ֥ק הַדָּ֖ם לֹ֣א תֹאכֵ֑לוּ עַל־הָאָ֥רֶץ תִּשְׁפְּכֶ֖נּוּ כַּמָּֽיִם:
17 לֹֽא־תוּכַ֞ל לֶאֱכֹ֣ל בִּשְׁעָרֶ֗יךָ מַעְשַׂ֤ר דְּגָֽנְךָ֙ וְתִֽירֹֽשְׁךָ֣
וְיִצְהָרֶ֔ךָ וּבְכֹרֹ֥ת בְּקָרְךָ֖ וְצֹאנֶ֑ךָ וְכׇל־נְדָרֶ֙יךָ֙ אֲשֶׁ֣ר
תִּדֹּ֔ר וְנִדְבֹתֶ֖יךָ וּתְרוּמַ֥ת יָדֶֽךָ: 18 כִּ֡י אִם־לִפְנֵי֩
יְהֹוָ֨ה אֱלֹהֶ֜יךָ תֹּאכְלֶ֗נּוּ בַּמָּקוֹם֙ אֲשֶׁ֨ר יִבְחַ֜ר יְהֹוָ֣ה
אֱלֹהֶ֘יךָ֮ בּוֹ֒ אַתָּ֨ה וּבִנְךָ֤ וּבִתֶּ֙ךָ֙ וְעַבְדְּךָ֣ וַאֲמָתֶ֔ךָ וְהַלֵּוִ֖י
אֲשֶׁ֣ר בִּשְׁעָרֶ֑יךָ וְשָׂמַחְתָּ֗ לִפְנֵי֙ יְהֹוָ֣ה אֱלֹהֶ֔יךָ בְּכֹ֖ל

you put your hands. ¹⁹ Take heed to yourself that you do not forsake the Levite as long as you live in your land.

²⁰ "When the LORD your God enlarges your border as He has promised you, and you say, 'Let me eat meat,' because you long to eat meat, you may eat as much meat as your heart desires. ²¹ If the place where the LORD your God chooses to put His name is too far from you, then you may slaughter from your herd and from your flock which the LORD has given you, just as I have commanded you, and you may eat within your gates as much as your heart desires. ²² Just as the gazelle and the deer are eaten, so you may eat them; the unclean and the clean alike may eat them. ²³ Only be sure that you do not eat the blood, for the blood *is* the life; you may not eat the life with the meat. ²⁴ You shall not eat it; you shall pour it on the earth like water. ²⁵ You shall not eat it, that it may go well with you and your children after you, when you do *what is* right in the sight of the LORD. ²⁶ Only the holy things which you have, and your vowed offerings, you shall take and go to the place which the LORD chooses. ²⁷ And you shall offer your burnt offerings, the meat and the blood, on the altar of the LORD your God; and the blood of your sacrifices shall be poured out on the altar of the LORD your God, and you shall eat the meat. ²⁸ Observe and obey all these words which I command you, that it may go well with you and your children after you forever, when you do *what is* good and right in the sight of the LORD your God.

²⁹ "When the LORD your God cuts off from before you the nations which you go to dispossess, and you displace them and dwell in their land, ³⁰ take heed to yourself that you are not ensnared to follow them, after they are destroyed from before you, and that you do not inquire after their gods, saying, 'How did these nations serve their gods? I also will do likewise.' ³¹ You shall not worship the LORD your God in that way; for every abomination to the LORD which He hates they have done to their gods; for they burn even their sons and daughters in the fire to their gods.

³² "Whatever I command you, be careful to observe it; you shall not add to it nor take away from it.

13 "If there arises among you a prophet or a dreamer of dreams, and he gives you a sign or a wonder, ² and the sign or the wonder comes to pass, of which he spoke to you, saying, 'Let us go after other gods'—which you have not known—'and let us serve them,' ³ you shall not listen to the words of

מִשְׁלַח יָדֶֽךָ: ¹⁹ הִשָּׁ֣מֶר לְךָ֔ פֶּֽן־תַּעֲזֹ֖ב אֶת־הַלֵּוִ֑י כָּל־
יָמֶ֖יךָ עַל־אַדְמָתֶֽךָ: ס ²⁰ כִּֽי־יַרְחִיב֩ יְהֹוָ֨ה
אֱלֹהֶ֜יךָ אֶֽת־גְּבֻלְךָ֮ כַּאֲשֶׁ֣ר דִּבֶּר־לָךְ֒ וְאָמַרְתָּ֙ אֹכְלָ֣ה
בָשָׂ֔ר כִּֽי־תְאַוֶּ֥ה נַפְשְׁךָ֖ לֶאֱכֹ֣ל בָּשָׂ֑ר בְּכָל־אַוַּ֥ת
נַפְשְׁךָ֖ תֹּאכַ֥ל בָּשָֽׂר: ²¹ כִּֽי־יִרְחַ֨ק מִמְּךָ֜ הַמָּק֗וֹם
אֲשֶׁ֨ר יִבְחַ֜ר יְהֹוָ֣ה אֱלֹהֶ֘יךָ֘ לָשׂ֣וּם שְׁמ֣וֹ שָׁם֒ וְזָבַחְתָּ֞
מִבְּקָֽרְךָ֣ וּמִצֹּֽאנְךָ֗ אֲשֶׁ֨ר נָתַ֤ן יְהֹוָה֙ לְךָ֔ כַּאֲשֶׁ֖ר צִוִּיתִ֑ךָ
וְאָ֣כַלְתָּ֔ בִּשְׁעָרֶ֔יךָ בְּכֹ֖ל אַוַּ֥ת נַפְשֶֽׁךָ: ²² אַ֗ךְ כַּאֲשֶׁ֨ר
יֵֽאָכֵ֤ל אֶֽת־הַצְּבִי֙ וְאֶת־הָ֣אַיָּ֔ל כֵּ֖ן תֹּאכְלֶ֑נּוּ הַטָּמֵא֙
וְהַטָּה֔וֹר יַחְדָּ֖ו יֹאכְלֶֽנּוּ: ²³ רַ֣ק חֲזַ֗ק לְבִלְתִּי֙ אֲכֹ֣ל
הַדָּ֔ם כִּ֥י הַדָּ֖ם ה֣וּא הַנָּ֑פֶשׁ וְלֹֽא־תֹאכַ֥ל הַנֶּ֖פֶשׁ עִם־
הַבָּשָֽׂר: ²⁴ לֹ֖א תֹּֽאכְלֶ֑נּוּ עַל־הָאָ֥רֶץ תִּשְׁפְּכֶ֖נּוּ כַּמָּֽיִם:

²⁵ לֹ֖א תֹּֽאכְלֶ֑נּוּ לְמַ֨עַן יִיטַ֤ב לְךָ֙ וּלְבָנֶ֣יךָ אַחֲרֶ֔יךָ כִּֽי־
תַעֲשֶׂ֥ה הַיָּשָׁ֖ר בְּעֵינֵ֥י יְהֹוָֽה: ²⁶ רַ֧ק קָֽדָשֶׁ֛יךָ אֲשֶׁר־
יִהְי֥וּ לְךָ֖ וּנְדָרֶ֑יךָ תִּשָּׂ֣א וּבָ֔אתָ אֶל־הַמָּק֖וֹם אֲשֶׁר־
יִבְחַ֥ר יְהֹוָֽה: ²⁷ וְעָשִׂ֤יתָ עֹֽלֹתֶ֨יךָ֙ הַבָּשָׂ֣ר וְהַדָּ֔ם עַל־
מִזְבַּ֖ח יְהֹוָ֣ה אֱלֹהֶ֑יךָ וְדַם־זְבָחֶ֗יךָ יִשָּׁפֵךְ֙ עַל־מִזְבַּח֙
יְהֹוָ֣ה אֱלֹהֶ֔יךָ וְהַבָּשָׂ֖ר תֹּאכֵֽל: ²⁸ שְׁמֹ֣ר וְשָֽׁמַעְתָּ֗ אֵ֚ת
כָּל־הַדְּבָרִ֣ים הָאֵ֔לֶּה אֲשֶׁ֥ר אָֽנֹכִ֖י מְצַוֶּ֑ךָּ לְמַ֩עַן֩ יִיטַ֨ב
לְךָ֜ וּלְבָנֶ֤יךָ אַֽחֲרֶ֨יךָ֙ עַד־עוֹלָ֔ם כִּ֤י תַעֲשֶׂה֙ הַטּ֣וֹב
וְהַיָּשָׁ֔ר בְּעֵינֵ֖י יְהֹוָ֥ה אֱלֹהֶֽיךָ: ס ²⁹ כִּֽי־
יַכְרִית֩ יְהֹוָ֨ה אֱלֹהֶ֜יךָ אֶת־הַגּוֹיִ֗ם אֲשֶׁ֨ר אַתָּ֥ה בָא־
שָׁ֛מָּה לָרֶ֥שֶׁת אוֹתָ֖ם מִפָּנֶ֑יךָ וְיָרַשְׁתָּ֣ אֹתָ֔ם וְיָשַׁבְתָּ֖
בְּאַרְצָֽם: ³⁰ הִשָּׁ֣מֶר לְךָ֗ פֶּן־תִּנָּקֵשׁ֙ אַחֲרֵיהֶ֔ם אַחֲרֵ֖י
הִשָּֽׁמְדָ֣ם מִפָּנֶ֑יךָ וּפֶן־תִּדְרֹ֨שׁ לֵֽאלֹהֵיהֶ֜ם לֵאמֹ֗ר אֵיכָ֨ה
יַעַבְד֜וּ הַגּוֹיִ֤ם הָאֵ֨לֶּה֙ אֶת־אֱלֹ֣הֵיהֶ֔ם וְאֶעֱשֶׂה־כֵּ֖ן גַּם־
אָֽנִי: ³¹ לֹא־תַעֲשֶׂ֣ה כֵ֔ן לַיהֹוָ֖ה אֱלֹהֶ֑יךָ כִּי֩ כָל־
תּוֹעֲבַ֨ת יְהֹוָ֜ה אֲשֶׁ֣ר שָׂנֵ֗א עָשׂוּ֙ לֵאלֹ֣הֵיהֶ֔ם כִּ֣י גַ֤ם
אֶת־בְּנֵיהֶם֙ וְאֶת־בְּנֹ֣תֵיהֶ֔ם יִשְׂרְפ֥וּ בָאֵ֖שׁ לֵֽאלֹהֵיהֶֽם:

יג אֵ֣ת כָּל־הַדָּבָ֗ר אֲשֶׁ֤ר אָֽנֹכִי֙ מְצַוֶּ֣ה אֶתְכֶ֔ם אֹת֥וֹ
תִשְׁמְר֖וּ לַעֲשׂ֑וֹת לֹא־תֹסֵ֣ף עָלָ֔יו וְלֹ֥א תִגְרַ֖ע מִמֶּֽנּוּ: פ

² כִּֽי־יָק֤וּם בְּקִרְבְּךָ֙ נָבִ֔יא א֖וֹ חֹלֵ֣ם חֲל֑וֹם וְנָתַ֥ן אֵלֶ֛יךָ
א֖וֹת א֣וֹ מוֹפֵֽת: ³ וּבָ֤א הָאוֹת֙ וְהַמּוֹפֵ֔ת אֲשֶׁר־דִּבֶּ֥ר

that prophet or that dreamer of dreams, for the LORD your God is testing you to know whether you love the LORD your God with all your heart and with all your soul. ⁴You shall walk after the LORD your God and fear Him, and keep His commandments and obey His voice; you shall serve Him and hold fast to Him. ⁵But that prophet or that dreamer of dreams shall be put to death, because he has spoken in order to turn *you* away from the LORD your God, who brought you out of the land of Egypt and redeemed you from the house of bondage, to entice you from the way in which the LORD your God commanded you to walk. So you shall put away the evil from your midst.

⁶"If your brother, the son of your mother, your son or your daughter, the wife of your bosom, or your friend who is as your own soul, secretly entices you, saying, 'Let us go and serve other gods,' which you have not known, neither you nor your fathers, ⁷of the gods of the people which *are* all around you, near to you or far off from you, from *one* end of the earth to the *other* end of the earth, ⁸you shall not consent to him or listen to him, nor shall your eye pity him, nor shall you spare him or conceal him; ⁹but you shall surely kill him; your hand shall be first against him to put him to death, and afterward the hand of all the people. ¹⁰And you shall stone him with stones until he dies, because he sought to entice you away from the LORD your God, who brought you out of the land of Egypt, from the house of bondage. ¹¹So all Israel shall hear and fear, and not again do such wickedness as this among you.

¹²"If you hear someone in one of your cities, which the LORD your God gives you to dwell in, saying, ¹³Corrupt men have gone out from among you and enticed the inhabitants of their city, saying, "Let us go and serve other gods"'—which you have not known— ¹⁴then you shall inquire, search out, and ask diligently. And *if it is* indeed true *and* certain *that* such an abomination was committed among you, ¹⁵you shall surely strike the inhabitants of that city with the edge of the sword, utterly destroying it, all that is in it and its livestock—with the edge of the sword. ¹⁶And you shall gather all its plunder into the middle of the street, and completely burn with fire the city and all its plunder, for the LORD your God. It shall be a heap forever; it shall not be built again. ¹⁷So none of the accursed things shall remain in your hand, that the LORD may turn from the fierceness of His anger and show you mercy, have compassion on you and multiply you, just as He swore to your fathers, ¹⁸because you have listened to the voice of the LORD your God, to

אֵלֶ֔יךָ לֵאמֹ֗ר נֵֽלְכָ֞ה אַחֲרֵ֨י אֱלֹהִ֤ים אֲחֵרִים֙ אֲשֶׁ֣ר לֹֽא־יְדַעְתָּ֔ם וְנַֽעָבְדֵֽם׃ 4 לֹ֣א תִשְׁמַ֗ע אֶל־דִּבְרֵי֙ הַנָּבִ֣יא הַה֔וּא א֛וֹ אֶל־חוֹלֵ֥ם הַחֲל֖וֹם הַה֑וּא כִּ֣י מְנַסֶּ֞ה יְהוָ֤ה אֱלֹֽהֵיכֶם֙ אֶתְכֶ֔ם לָדַ֗עַת הֲיִשְׁכֶ֤ם אֹֽהֲבִים֙ אֶת־יְהוָ֣ה אֱלֹֽהֵיכֶ֔ם בְּכָל־לְבַבְכֶ֖ם וּבְכָל־נַפְשְׁכֶֽם׃ 5 אַחֲרֵ֨י יְהוָ֧ה אֱלֹֽהֵיכֶ֛ם תֵּלֵ֖כוּ וְאֹת֣וֹ תִירָ֑אוּ וְאֶת־מִצְוֺתָ֤יו תִּשְׁמֹ֨רוּ֙ וּבְקֹל֣וֹ תִשְׁמָ֔עוּ וְאֹת֥וֹ תַֽעֲבֹ֖דוּ וּב֥וֹ תִדְבָּקֽוּן׃ 6 וְהַנָּבִ֣יא הַה֡וּא א֣וֹ חֹלֵם֩ הַחֲל֨וֹם הַה֜וּא יוּמָ֗ת כִּ֣י דִבֶּר־סָרָ֣ה עַל־יְהוָ֣ה אֱלֹֽהֵיכֶ֡ם הַמּוֹצִ֣יא אֶתְכֶ֣ם ׀ מֵאֶ֪רֶץ מִצְרַ֡יִם וְהַפֹּֽדְךָ֙ מִבֵּ֣ית עֲבָדִ֔ים לְהַדִּֽיחֲךָ֙ מִן־הַדֶּ֔רֶךְ אֲשֶׁ֧ר צִוְּךָ֛ יְהוָ֥ה אֱלֹהֶ֖יךָ לָלֶ֣כֶת בָּ֑הּ וּבִֽעַרְתָּ֥ הָרָ֖ע מִקִּרְבֶּֽךָ׃ 7 כִּ֣י יְסִֽיתְךָ֡ אָחִ֣יךָ בֶן־אִ֠מֶּ֠ךָ אֽוֹ־בִנְךָ֨ אֽוֹ־בִתְּךָ֜ א֣וֹ ׀ אֵ֣שֶׁת חֵיקֶ֗ךָ א֧וֹ רֵֽעֲךָ֛ אֲשֶׁ֥ר כְּנַפְשְׁךָ֖ בַּסֵּ֣תֶר לֵאמֹ֑ר נֵֽלְכָ֗ה וְנַֽעַבְדָה֙ אֱלֹהִ֣ים אֲחֵרִ֔ים אֲשֶׁר֙ לֹ֣א יָדַ֔עְתָּ אַתָּ֖ה וַֽאֲבֹתֶֽיךָ׃ 8 מֵֽאֱלֹהֵ֣י הָֽעַמִּ֗ים אֲשֶׁר֙ סְבִֽיבֹ֣תֵיכֶ֔ם הַקְּרֹבִ֖ים אֵלֶ֑יךָ א֚וֹ הָֽרְחֹקִ֣ים מִמֶּ֔ךָּ מִקְצֵ֥ה הָאָ֖רֶץ וְעַד־קְצֵ֥ה הָאָֽרֶץ׃ 9 לֹֽא־תֹאבֶ֣ה ל֔וֹ וְלֹ֥א תִשְׁמַ֖ע אֵלָ֑יו וְלֹֽא־תָח֤וֹס עֵֽינְךָ֙ עָלָ֔יו וְלֹֽא־תַחְמֹ֖ל וְלֹֽא־תְכַסֶּ֥ה עָלָֽיו׃ 10 כִּ֤י הָרֹג֙ תַּֽהַרְגֶ֔נּוּ יָֽדְךָ֛ תִּֽהְיֶה־בּ֥וֹ בָרִֽאשׁוֹנָ֖ה לַֽהֲמִית֑וֹ וְיַ֥ד כָּל־הָעָ֖ם בָּאַֽחֲרֹנָֽה׃ 11 וּסְקַלְתּ֥וֹ בָֽאֲבָנִ֖ים וָמֵ֑ת כִּ֣י בִקֵּ֗שׁ לְהַדִּֽיחֲךָ֙ מֵעַל֙ יְהוָ֣ה אֱלֹהֶ֔יךָ הַמּוֹצִֽיאֲךָ֛ מֵאֶ֥רֶץ מִצְרַ֖יִם מִבֵּ֥ית עֲבָדִֽים׃ 12 וְכָל־יִשְׂרָאֵ֔ל יִשְׁמְע֖וּ וְיִֽרָא֑וּן וְלֹֽא־יוֹסִ֣פוּ לַֽעֲשׂ֗וֹת כַּדָּבָ֥ר הָרָ֛ע הַזֶּ֖ה בְּקִרְבֶּֽךָ׃ ס 13 כִּֽי־תִשְׁמַ֞ע בְּאַחַ֣ת עָרֶ֗יךָ אֲשֶׁר֩ יְהוָ֨ה אֱלֹהֶ֜יךָ נֹתֵ֥ן לְךָ֛ לָשֶׁ֥בֶת שָׁ֖ם לֵאמֹֽר׃ 14 יָֽצְא֞וּ אֲנָשִׁ֤ים בְּנֵֽי־בְלִיַּ֨עַל֙ מִקִּרְבֶּ֔ךָ וַיַּדִּ֛יחוּ אֶת־יֹֽשְׁבֵ֥י עִירָ֖ם לֵאמֹ֑ר נֵֽלְכָ֗ה וְנַֽעַבְדָ֛ה אֱלֹהִ֥ים אֲחֵרִ֖ים אֲשֶׁ֥ר לֹֽא־יְדַעְתֶּֽם׃ 15 וְדָֽרַשְׁתָּ֧ וְחָֽקַרְתָּ֛ וְשָֽׁאַלְתָּ֖ הֵיטֵ֑ב וְהִנֵּ֤ה אֱמֶת֙ נָכ֣וֹן הַדָּבָ֔ר נֶֽעֶשְׂתָ֛ה הַתּֽוֹעֵבָ֥ה הַזֹּ֖את בְּקִרְבֶּֽךָ׃ 16 הַכֵּ֣ה תַכֶּ֗ה אֶת־יֹֽשְׁבֵ֛י הָעִ֥יר הַהִ֖וא לְפִי־חָ֑רֶב הַֽחֲרֵ֨ם אֹתָ֧הּ וְאֶת־כָּל־אֲשֶׁר־בָּ֛הּ וְאֶת־בְּהֶמְתָּ֖הּ לְפִי־חָֽרֶב׃ 17 וְאֶת־כָּל־שְׁלָלָ֡הּ תִּקְבֹּ֣ץ אֶל־תּוֹךְ֩ רְחֹבָ֨הּ וְשָֽׂרַפְתָּ֧ בָאֵ֣שׁ אֶת־הָעִ֗יר וְאֶת־כָּל־שְׁלָלָהּ֙ כָּלִ֔יל לַֽיהוָ֖ה אֱלֹהֶ֑יךָ וְהָֽיְתָה֙ תֵּ֣ל עוֹלָ֔ם לֹ֥א תִבָּנֶ֖ה עֽוֹד׃ 18 וְלֹֽא־יִדְבַּ֧ק בְּיָֽדְךָ֛ מְא֖וּמָה מִן־הַחֵ֑רֶם לְמַעַן֩ יָשׁ֨וּב יְהוָ֜ה מֵֽחֲר֣וֹן אַפּ֗וֹ וְנָֽתַן־לְךָ֤ רַֽחֲמִים֙ וְרִֽחַמְךָ֣ וְהִרְבֶּ֔ךָ כַּֽאֲשֶׁ֥ר נִשְׁבַּ֖ע לַֽאֲבֹתֶֽיךָ׃ 19 כִּ֣י תִשְׁמַ֗ע בְּקוֹל֙ יְהוָ֣ה אֱלֹהֶ֔יךָ לִשְׁמֹ֖ר אֶת־כָּל־

keep all His commandments which I command you today, to do *what is* right in the eyes of the LORD your God.

14 "You *are* the children of the LORD your God; you shall not cut yourselves nor shave the front of your head for the dead. ² For you *are* a holy people to the LORD your God, and the LORD has chosen you to be a people for Himself, a special treasure above all the peoples who *are* on the face of the earth.

³ "You shall not eat any detestable thing. ⁴ These *are* the animals which you may eat: the ox, the sheep, the goat, ⁵ the deer, the gazelle, the roe deer, the wild goat, the mountain goat, the antelope, and the mountain sheep. ⁶ And you may eat every animal with cloven hooves, having the hoof split into two parts, *and that* chews the cud, among the animals. ⁷ Nevertheless, of those that chew the cud or have cloven hooves, you shall not eat, *such as* these: the camel, the hare, and the rock hyrax; for they chew the cud but do not have cloven hooves; they *are* unclean for you. ⁸ Also the swine is unclean for you, because it has cloven hooves, yet *does* not *chew* the cud; you shall not eat their flesh or touch their dead carcasses.

⁹ "These you may eat of all that *are* in the waters: you may eat all that have fins and scales. ¹⁰ And whatever does not have fins and scales you shall not eat; it *is* unclean for you.

¹¹ "All clean birds you may eat. ¹² But these you shall not eat: the eagle, the vulture, the buzzard, ¹³ the red kite, the falcon, and the kite after their kinds; ¹⁴ every raven after its kind; ¹⁵ the ostrich, the short-eared owl, the sea gull, and the hawk after their kinds; ¹⁶ the little owl, the screech owl, the white owl, ¹⁷ the jackdaw, the carrion vulture, the fisher owl, ¹⁸ the stork, the heron after its kind, and the hoopoe and the bat.

¹⁹ "Also every creeping thing that flies is unclean for you; they shall not be eaten.

²⁰ "You may eat all clean birds.

²¹ "You shall not eat anything that dies *of itself*; you may give it to the alien who *is* within your gates, that he may eat it, or you may sell it to a foreigner; for you *are* a holy people to the LORD your God.

"You shall not boil a young goat in its mother's milk.

²² "You shall truly tithe all the increase of your grain that the field produces year by year. ²³ And you shall eat before the LORD your God, in the place where He chooses to make His name abide, the tithe of your grain and your new wine and your

מִצְוֹתָיו אֲשֶׁר אָנֹכִי מְצַוְּךָ הַיּוֹם לַעֲשׂוֹת הַיָּשָׁר בְּעֵינֵי יְהוָה אֱלֹהֶיךָ: ס

יד בָּנִים אַתֶּם לַיהוָה אֱלֹהֵיכֶם לֹא תִתְגֹּדְדוּ וְלֹא־תָשִׂימוּ קָרְחָה בֵּין עֵינֵיכֶם לָמֵת: 2 כִּי עַם קָדוֹשׁ אַתָּה לַיהוָה אֱלֹהֶיךָ וּבְךָ בָּחַר יְהוָה לִהְיוֹת לוֹ לְעַם סְגֻלָּה מִכֹּל הָעַמִּים אֲשֶׁר עַל־ פְּנֵי הָאֲדָמָה: ס 3 לֹא תֹאכַל כָּל־תּוֹעֵבָה:

4 זֹאת הַבְּהֵמָה אֲשֶׁר תֹּאכֵלוּ שׁוֹר שֵׂה כְשָׂבִים וְשֵׂה עִזִּים: 5 אַיָּל וּצְבִי וְיַחְמוּר וְאַקּוֹ וְדִישֹׁן וּתְאוֹ וָזָמֶר: 6 וְכָל־בְּהֵמָה מַפְרֶסֶת פַּרְסָה וְשֹׁסַעַת שֶׁסַע שְׁתֵּי פְרָסוֹת מַעֲלַת גֵּרָה בַּבְּהֵמָה אֹתָהּ תֹּאכֵלוּ:

7 אַךְ אֶת־זֶה לֹא תֹאכְלוּ מִמַּעֲלֵי הַגֵּרָה וּמִמַּפְרִיסֵי הַפַּרְסָה הַשְּׁסוּעָה אֶת־הַגָּמָל וְאֶת־הָאַרְנֶבֶת וְאֶת־ הַשָּׁפָן כִּי־מַעֲלֵה גֵרָה הֵמָּה וּפַרְסָה לֹא הִפְרִיסוּ טְמֵאִים הֵם לָכֶם: 8 וְאֶת־הַחֲזִיר כִּי־מַפְרִיס פַּרְסָה הוּא וְלֹא גֵרָה טָמֵא הוּא לָכֶם מִבְּשָׂרָם לֹא תֹאכֵלוּ וּבְנִבְלָתָם לֹא תִגָּעוּ: ס 9 אֶת־זֶה תֹּאכְלוּ מִכֹּל אֲשֶׁר בַּמָּיִם כֹּל אֲשֶׁר־לוֹ סְנַפִּיר וְקַשְׂקֶשֶׂת תֹּאכֵלוּ: 10 וְכֹל אֲשֶׁר אֵין־לוֹ סְנַפִּיר וְקַשְׂקֶשֶׂת לֹא תֹאכֵלוּ טָמֵא הוּא לָכֶם: ס 11 כָּל־צִפּוֹר טְהֹרָה תֹּאכֵלוּ: 12 וְזֶה אֲשֶׁר לֹא־תֹאכְלוּ מֵהֶם הַנֶּשֶׁר וְהַפֶּרֶס וְהָעָזְנִיָּה: 13 וְהָרָאָה וְאֶת־הָאַיָּה וְהַדַּיָּה לְמִינָהּ: 14 וְאֵת כָּל־עֹרֵב לְמִינוֹ: 15 וְאֵת בַּת הַיַּעֲנָה וְאֶת־הַתַּחְמָס וְאֶת־הַשָּׁחַף וְאֶת־הַנֵּץ לְמִינֵהוּ: 16 אֶת־הַכּוֹס וְאֶת־הַיַּנְשׁוּף וְהַתִּנְשָׁמֶת: 17 וְהַקָּאָת וְאֶת־הָרָחָמָה וְאֶת־הַשָּׁלָךְ: 18 וְהַחֲסִידָה וְהָאֲנָפָה לְמִינָהּ וְהַדּוּכִיפַת וְהָעֲטַלֵּף: 19 וְכֹל שֶׁרֶץ הָעוֹף טָמֵא הוּא לָכֶם לֹא יֵאָכֵלוּ: 20 כָּל־עוֹף טָהוֹר תֹּאכֵלוּ: 21 לֹא תֹאכְלוּ כָל־נְבֵלָה לַגֵּר אֲשֶׁר־ בִּשְׁעָרֶיךָ תִּתְּנֶנָּה וַאֲכָלָהּ אוֹ מָכֹר לְנָכְרִי כִּי עַם קָדוֹשׁ אַתָּה לַיהוָה אֱלֹהֶיךָ לֹא־תְבַשֵּׁל גְּדִי בַּחֲלֵב אִמּוֹ: פ

22 עַשֵּׂר תְּעַשֵּׂר אֵת כָּל־תְּבוּאַת זַרְעֶךָ הַיֹּצֵא הַשָּׂדֶה שָׁנָה שָׁנָה: 23 וְאָכַלְתָּ לִפְנֵי | יְהוָה אֱלֹהֶיךָ

oil, of the firstborn of your herds and your flocks, that you may learn to fear the LORD your God always. ²⁴But if the journey is too long for you, so that you are not able to carry *the tithe, or* if the place where the LORD your God chooses to put His name is too far from you, when the LORD your God has blessed you, ²⁵then you shall exchange *it* for money, take the money in your hand, and go to the place which the LORD your God chooses. ²⁶And you shall spend that money for whatever your heart desires: for oxen or sheep, for wine or similar drink, for whatever your heart desires; you shall eat there before the LORD your God, and you shall rejoice, you and your household. ²⁷You shall not forsake the Levite who *is* within your gates, for he has no part nor inheritance with you.

²⁸"At the end of *every* third year you shall bring out the tithe of your produce of that year and store *it* up within your gates. ²⁹And the Levite, because he has no portion nor inheritance with you, and the stranger and the fatherless and the widow who *are* within your gates, may come and eat and be satisfied, that the LORD your God may bless you in all the work of your hand which you do.

15 "At the end of *every* seven years you shall grant a release *of debts.* ²And this *is* the form of the release: Every creditor who has lent *anything* to his neighbor shall release *it;* he shall not require *it* of his neighbor or his brother, because it is called the LORD's release. ³Of a foreigner you may require *it;* but you shall give up your claim to what is owed by your brother, ⁴except when there may be no poor among you; for the LORD will greatly bless you in the land which the LORD your God is giving you to possess *as* an inheritance— ⁵only if you carefully obey the voice of the LORD your God, to observe with care all these commandments which I command you today. ⁶For the LORD your God will bless you just as He promised you; you shall lend to many nations, but you shall not borrow; you shall reign over many nations, but they shall not reign over you.

⁷"If there is among you a poor man of your brethren, within any of the gates in your land which the LORD your God is giving you, you shall not harden your heart nor shut your hand from your poor brother, ⁸but you shall open your hand wide to him and willingly lend him sufficient for his need, whatever he needs. ⁹Beware lest there be a wicked thought in your heart, saying, 'The seventh year, the year of release, is at hand,' and your eye be evil against your poor brother and you give him nothing, and he cry out to the LORD against you,

---

בַּמָּקוֹם אֲשֶׁר־יִבְחַר לְשַׁכֵּן שְׁמוֹ שָׁם מַעְשַׂר דְּגָנְךָ תִּירֹשְׁךָ וְיִצְהָרֶךָ וּבְכֹרֹת בְּקָרְךָ וְצֹאנֶךָ לְמַעַן תִּלְמַד לְיִרְאָה אֶת־יְהֹוָה אֱלֹהֶיךָ כָּל־הַיָּמִים: 24 וְכִי־יִרְבֶּה מִמְּךָ הַדֶּרֶךְ כִּי לֹא תוּכַל שְׂאֵתוֹ כִּי־יִרְחַק מִמְּךָ הַמָּקוֹם אֲשֶׁר יִבְחַר יְהֹוָה אֱלֹהֶיךָ לָשׂוּם שְׁמוֹ שָׁם כִּי יְבָרֶכְךָ יְהֹוָה אֱלֹהֶיךָ: 25 וְנָתַתָּה בַּכָּסֶף וְצַרְתָּ הַכֶּסֶף בְּיָדְךָ וְהָלַכְתָּ אֶל־הַמָּקוֹם אֲשֶׁר יִבְחַר יְהֹוָה אֱלֹהֶיךָ בּוֹ: 26 וְנָתַתָּה הַכֶּסֶף בְּכֹל אֲשֶׁר־תְּאַוֶּה נַפְשְׁךָ בַּבָּקָר וּבַצֹּאן וּבַיַּיִן וּבַשֵּׁכָר וּבְכֹל אֲשֶׁר תִּשְׁאָלְךָ נַפְשֶׁךָ וְאָכַלְתָּ שָּׁם לִפְנֵי יְהֹוָה אֱלֹהֶיךָ וְשָׂמַחְתָּ אַתָּה וּבֵיתֶךָ: 27 וְהַלֵּוִי אֲשֶׁר־בִּשְׁעָרֶיךָ לֹא תַעַזְבֶנּוּ כִּי אֵין לוֹ חֵלֶק וְנַחֲלָה עִמָּךְ: ס 28 מִקְצֵה שָׁלֹשׁ שָׁנִים תּוֹצִיא אֶת־כָּל־מַעְשַׂר תְּבוּאָתְךָ בַּשָּׁנָה הַהִוא וְהִנַּחְתָּ בִּשְׁעָרֶיךָ: 29 וּבָא הַלֵּוִי כִּי אֵין־לוֹ חֵלֶק וְנַחֲלָה עִמָּךְ וְהַגֵּר וְהַיָּתוֹם וְהָאַלְמָנָה אֲשֶׁר בִּשְׁעָרֶיךָ וְאָכְלוּ וְשָׂבֵעוּ לְמַעַן יְבָרֶכְךָ יְהֹוָה אֱלֹהֶיךָ בְּכָל־מַעֲשֵׂה יָדְךָ אֲשֶׁר תַּעֲשֶׂה: ס

טו מִקֵּץ שֶׁבַע־שָׁנִים תַּעֲשֶׂה שְׁמִטָּה: 2 וְזֶה דְּבַר הַשְּׁמִטָּה שָׁמוֹט כָּל־בַּעַל מַשֵּׁה יָדוֹ אֲשֶׁר יַשֶּׁה בְּרֵעֵהוּ לֹא־יִגֹּשׂ אֶת־רֵעֵהוּ וְאֶת־אָחִיו כִּי־קָרָא שְׁמִטָּה לַיהֹוָה: 3 אֶת־הַנָּכְרִי תִּגֹּשׂ וַאֲשֶׁר יִהְיֶה לְךָ אֶת־אָחִיךָ תַּשְׁמֵט יָדֶךָ: 4 אֶפֶס כִּי לֹא יִהְיֶה בְּךָ אֶבְיוֹן כִּי־בָרֵךְ יְבָרֶכְךָ יְהֹוָה בָּאָרֶץ אֲשֶׁר יְהֹוָה אֱלֹהֶיךָ נֹתֵן לְךָ נַחֲלָה לְרִשְׁתָּהּ: 5 רַק אִם־שָׁמוֹעַ תִּשְׁמַע בְּקוֹל יְהֹוָה אֱלֹהֶיךָ לִשְׁמֹר לַעֲשׂוֹת אֶת־כָּל־הַמִּצְוָה הַזֹּאת אֲשֶׁר אָנֹכִי מְצַוְּךָ הַיּוֹם: 6 כִּי־יְהֹוָה אֱלֹהֶיךָ בֵּרַכְךָ כַּאֲשֶׁר דִּבֶּר־לָךְ וְהַעֲבַטְתָּ גּוֹיִם רַבִּים וְאַתָּה לֹא תַעֲבֹט וּמָשַׁלְתָּ בְּגוֹיִם רַבִּים וּבְךָ לֹא יִמְשֹׁלוּ: ס 7 כִּי־יִהְיֶה בְךָ אֶבְיוֹן מֵאַחַד אַחֶיךָ בְּאַחַד שְׁעָרֶיךָ בְּאַרְצְךָ אֲשֶׁר־יְהֹוָה אֱלֹהֶיךָ נֹתֵן לָךְ לֹא תְאַמֵּץ אֶת־לְבָבְךָ וְלֹא תִקְפֹּץ אֶת־יָדְךָ מֵאָחִיךָ הָאֶבְיוֹן: 8 כִּי־פָתֹחַ תִּפְתַּח אֶת־יָדְךָ לוֹ וְהַעֲבֵט תַּעֲבִיטֶנּוּ דֵּי מַחְסֹרוֹ אֲשֶׁר יֶחְסַר לוֹ: 9 הִשָּׁמֶר לְךָ פֶּן־יִהְיֶה דָבָר עִם־לְבָבְךָ בְלִיַּעַל לֵאמֹר קָרְבָה שְׁנַת־הַשֶּׁבַע שְׁנַת הַשְּׁמִטָּה וְרָעָה עֵינְךָ בְּאָחִיךָ הָאֶבְיוֹן וְלֹא תִתֵּן לוֹ וְקָרָא עָלֶיךָ אֶל־יְהֹוָה

and it become sin among you. 10 You shall surely give to him, and your heart should not be grieved when you give to him, because for this thing the LORD your God will bless you in all your works and in all to which you put your hand. 11 For the poor will never cease from the land; therefore I command you, saying, 'You shall open your hand wide to your brother, to your poor and your needy, in your land.'

12 "If your brother, a Hebrew man, or a Hebrew woman, is sold to you and serves you six years, then in the seventh year you shall let him go free from you. 13 And when you send him away free from you, you shall not let him go away empty-handed; 14 you shall supply him liberally from your flock, from your threshing floor, and from your winepress. *From what* the LORD has blessed you with, you shall give to him. 15 You shall remember that you were a slave in the land of Egypt, and the LORD your God redeemed you; therefore I command you this thing today. 16 And if it happens that he says to you, 'I will not go away from you,' because he loves you and your house, since he prospers with you, 17 then you shall take an awl and thrust *it* through his ear to the door, and he shall be your servant forever. Also to your female servant you shall do likewise. 18 It shall not seem hard to you when you send him away free from you; for he has been worth a double hired servant in serving you six years. Then the LORD your God will bless you in all that you do.

19 "All the firstborn males that come from your herd and your flock you shall sanctify to the LORD your God; you shall do no work with the firstborn of your herd, nor shear the firstborn of your flock. 20 You and your household shall eat *it* before the LORD your God year by year in the place which the LORD chooses. 21 But if there is a defect in it, *if it is* lame or blind *or has* any serious defect, you shall not sacrifice it to the LORD your God. 22 You may eat it within your gates; the unclean and the clean *person* alike *may eat it,* as *if it were* a gazelle or a deer. 23 Only you shall not eat its blood; you shall pour it on the ground like water.

16 "Observe the month of Abib, and keep the Passover to the LORD your God, for in the month of Abib the LORD your God brought you out of Egypt by night. 2 Therefore you shall sacrifice the Passover to the LORD your God, from the flock and the herd, in the place where the LORD chooses to put His name. 3 You shall eat no leavened bread with it; seven days you shall eat unleavened bread with it, *that is,* the bread of affliction (for you came out of the land of Egypt in haste), that you may

וְהָיָה בְךָ חֵטְא: 10 נָתוֹן תִּתֵּן לוֹ וְלֹא־יֵרַע לְבָבְךָ בְּתִתְּךָ לוֹ כִּי בִּגְלַל | הַדָּבָר הַזֶּה יְבָרֶכְךָ יְהוָה אֱלֹהֶיךָ בְּכָל־מַעֲשֶׂךָ וּבְכֹל מִשְׁלַח יָדֶךָ: 11 כִּי לֹא־יֶחְדַּל אֶבְיוֹן מִקֶּרֶב הָאָרֶץ עַל־כֵּן אָנֹכִי מְצַוְּךָ לֵאמֹר פָּתֹחַ תִּפְתַּח אֶת־יָדְךָ לְאָחִיךָ לַעֲנִיֶּךָ וּלְאֶבְיֹנְךָ בְּאַרְצֶךָ: ס 12 כִּי־יִמָּכֵר לְךָ אָחִיךָ הָעִבְרִי אוֹ הָעִבְרִיָּה וַעֲבָדְךָ שֵׁשׁ שָׁנִים וּבַשָּׁנָה הַשְּׁבִיעִת תְּשַׁלְּחֶנּוּ חָפְשִׁי מֵעִמָּךְ: 13 וְכִי־תְשַׁלְּחֶנּוּ חָפְשִׁי מֵעִמָּךְ לֹא תְשַׁלְּחֶנּוּ רֵיקָם: 14 הַעֲנֵיק תַּעֲנִיק לוֹ מִצֹּאנְךָ וּמִגָּרְנְךָ וּמִיִּקְבֶךָ אֲשֶׁר בֵּרַכְךָ יְהוָה אֱלֹהֶיךָ תִּתֶּן־לוֹ: 15 וְזָכַרְתָּ כִּי עֶבֶד הָיִיתָ בְּאֶרֶץ מִצְרַיִם וַיִּפְדְּךָ יְהוָה אֱלֹהֶיךָ עַל־כֵּן אָנֹכִי מְצַוְּךָ אֶת־הַדָּבָר הַזֶּה הַיּוֹם: 16 וְהָיָה כִּי־יֹאמַר אֵלֶיךָ לֹא אֵצֵא מֵעִמָּךְ כִּי אֲהֵבְךָ וְאֶת־בֵּיתֶךָ כִּי־טוֹב לוֹ עִמָּךְ:

17 וְלָקַחְתָּ אֶת־הַמַּרְצֵעַ וְנָתַתָּה בְאָזְנוֹ וּבַדֶּלֶת וְהָיָה לְךָ עֶבֶד עוֹלָם וְאַף לַאֲמָתְךָ תַּעֲשֶׂה־כֵּן: 18 לֹא־יִקְשֶׁה בְעֵינֶךָ בְּשַׁלֵּחֲךָ אֹתוֹ חָפְשִׁי מֵעִמָּךְ כִּי מִשְׁנֶה שְׂכַר שָׂכִיר עֲבָדְךָ שֵׁשׁ שָׁנִים וּבֵרַכְךָ יְהוָה אֱלֹהֶיךָ בְּכֹל אֲשֶׁר תַּעֲשֶׂה: פ

19 כָּל־הַבְּכוֹר אֲשֶׁר יִוָּלֵד בִּבְקָרְךָ וּבְצֹאנְךָ הַזָּכָר תַּקְדִּישׁ לַיהוָה אֱלֹהֶיךָ לֹא תַעֲבֹד בִּבְכֹר שׁוֹרֶךָ וְלֹא תָגֹז בְּכוֹר צֹאנֶךָ: 20 לִפְנֵי יְהוָה אֱלֹהֶיךָ תֹאכְלֶנּוּ שָׁנָה בְשָׁנָה בַּמָּקוֹם אֲשֶׁר־יִבְחַר יְהוָה אַתָּה וּבֵיתֶךָ:

21 וְכִי־יִהְיֶה בוֹ מוּם פִּסֵּחַ אוֹ עִוֵּר כֹּל מוּם רָע לֹא תִזְבָּחֶנּוּ לַיהוָה אֱלֹהֶיךָ: 22 בִּשְׁעָרֶיךָ תֹּאכְלֶנּוּ הַטָּמֵא וְהַטָּהוֹר יַחְדָּו כַּצְּבִי וְכָאַיָּל: 23 רַק אֶת־דָּמוֹ לֹא תֹאכֵל עַל־הָאָרֶץ תִּשְׁפְּכֶנּוּ כַּמָּיִם: פ

טז שָׁמוֹר אֶת־חֹדֶשׁ הָאָבִיב וְעָשִׂיתָ פֶּסַח לַיהוָה אֱלֹהֶיךָ כִּי בְּחֹדֶשׁ הָאָבִיב הוֹצִיאֲךָ יְהוָה אֱלֹהֶיךָ מִמִּצְרַיִם לָיְלָה: 2 וְזָבַחְתָּ פֶּסַח לַיהוָה אֱלֹהֶיךָ צֹאן וּבָקָר בַּמָּקוֹם אֲשֶׁר־יִבְחַר יְהוָה לְשַׁכֵּן שְׁמוֹ שָׁם: 3 לֹא־תֹאכַל עָלָיו חָמֵץ שִׁבְעַת יָמִים תֹּאכַל־עָלָיו מַצּוֹת לֶחֶם עֹנִי כִּי בְחִפָּזוֹן יָצָאתָ מֵאֶרֶץ מִצְרַיִם לְמַעַן תִּזְכֹּר אֶת־יוֹם צֵאתְךָ מֵאֶרֶץ מִצְרַיִם

remember the day in which you came out of the land of Egypt all the days of your life. ⁴And no leaven shall be seen among you in all your territory for seven days, nor shall *any* of the meat which you sacrifice the first day at twilight remain overnight until morning.

⁵"You may not sacrifice the Passover within any of your gates which the LORD your God gives you; ⁶but at the place where the LORD your God chooses to make His name abide, there you shall sacrifice the Passover at twilight, at the going down of the sun, at the time you came out of Egypt. ⁷And you shall roast and eat *it* in the place which the LORD your God chooses, and in the morning you shall turn and go to your tents. ⁸Six days you shall eat unleavened bread, and on the seventh day there *shall be* a sacred assembly to the LORD your God. You shall do no work *on it.*

⁹"You shall count seven weeks for yourself; begin to count the seven weeks from *the time* you begin *to put* the sickle to the grain. ¹⁰Then you shall keep the Feast of Weeks to the LORD your God with the tribute of a freewill offering from your hand, which you shall give as the LORD your God blesses you. ¹¹You shall rejoice before the LORD your God, you and your son and your daughter, your male servant and your female servant, the Levite who *is* within your gates, the stranger and the fatherless and the widow who *are* among you, at the place where the LORD your God chooses to make His name abide. ¹²And you shall remember that you were a slave in Egypt, and you shall be careful to observe these statutes.

¹³"You shall observe the Feast of Tabernacles seven days, when you have gathered from your threshing floor and from your winepress. ¹⁴And you shall rejoice in your feast, you and your son and your daughter, your male servant and your female servant and the Levite, the stranger and the fatherless and the widow, who *are* within your gates. ¹⁵Seven days you shall keep a sacred feast to the LORD your God in the place which the LORD chooses, because the LORD your God will bless you in all your produce and in all the work of your hands, so that you surely rejoice.

¹⁶"Three times a year all your males shall appear before the LORD your God in the place which He chooses: at the Feast of Unleavened Bread, at the Feast of Weeks, and at the Feast of Tabernacles; and they shall not appear before the LORD empty-handed. ¹⁷Every man *shall give* as he is able, according to the blessing of the LORD your God which He has given you.

כָּל־יְמֵי חַיֶּיךָ: ⁴ וְלֹא־יֵרָאֶה לְךָ שְׂאֹר בְּכָל־גְּבֻלְךָ שִׁבְעַת יָמִים וְלֹא־יָלִין מִן־הַבָּשָׂר אֲשֶׁר תִּזְבַּח בָּעֶרֶב בַּיּוֹם הָרִאשׁוֹן לַבֹּקֶר: ⁵ לֹא תוּכַל לִזְבֹּחַ אֶת־הַפָּסַח בְּאַחַד שְׁעָרֶיךָ אֲשֶׁר־יְהוָה אֱלֹהֶיךָ נֹתֵן לָךְ: ⁶ כִּי אִם־אֶל־הַמָּקוֹם אֲשֶׁר־יִבְחַר יְהוָה אֱלֹהֶיךָ לְשַׁכֵּן שְׁמוֹ שָׁם תִּזְבַּח אֶת־הַפֶּסַח בָּעָרֶב כְּבוֹא הַשֶּׁמֶשׁ מוֹעֵד צֵאתְךָ מִמִּצְרָיִם: ⁷ וּבִשַּׁלְתָּ וְאָכַלְתָּ בַּמָּקוֹם אֲשֶׁר יִבְחַר יְהוָה אֱלֹהֶיךָ בּוֹ וּפָנִיתָ בַבֹּקֶר וְהָלַכְתָּ לְאֹהָלֶיךָ: ⁸ שֵׁשֶׁת יָמִים תֹּאכַל מַצּוֹת וּבַיּוֹם הַשְּׁבִיעִי עֲצֶרֶת לַיהוָה אֱלֹהֶיךָ לֹא תַעֲשֶׂה מְלָאכָה: ס ⁹ שִׁבְעָה שָׁבֻעֹת תִּסְפָּר־לָךְ מֵהָחֵל חֶרְמֵשׁ בַּקָּמָה תָּחֵל לִסְפֹּר שִׁבְעָה שָׁבֻעוֹת:

¹⁰ וְעָשִׂיתָ חַג שָׁבֻעוֹת לַיהוָה אֱלֹהֶיךָ מִסַּת נִדְבַת יָדְךָ אֲשֶׁר תִּתֵּן כַּאֲשֶׁר יְבָרֶכְךָ יְהוָה אֱלֹהֶיךָ: ¹¹ וְשָׂמַחְתָּ לִפְנֵי ׀ יְהוָה אֱלֹהֶיךָ אַתָּה וּבִנְךָ וּבִתֶּךָ וְעַבְדְּךָ וַאֲמָתֶךָ וְהַלֵּוִי אֲשֶׁר בִּשְׁעָרֶיךָ וְהַגֵּר וְהַיָּתוֹם וְהָאַלְמָנָה אֲשֶׁר בְּקִרְבֶּךָ בַּמָּקוֹם אֲשֶׁר יִבְחַר יְהוָה אֱלֹהֶיךָ לְשַׁכֵּן שְׁמוֹ שָׁם: ¹² וְזָכַרְתָּ כִּי־עֶבֶד הָיִיתָ בְּמִצְרָיִם וְשָׁמַרְתָּ וְעָשִׂיתָ אֶת־הַחֻקִּים הָאֵלֶּה: פ

¹³ חַג הַסֻּכֹּת תַּעֲשֶׂה לְךָ שִׁבְעַת יָמִים בְּאָסְפְּךָ מִגָּרְנְךָ וּמִיִּקְבֶךָ: ¹⁴ וְשָׂמַחְתָּ בְּחַגֶּךָ אַתָּה וּבִנְךָ וּבִתֶּךָ וְעַבְדְּךָ וַאֲמָתֶךָ וְהַלֵּוִי וְהַגֵּר וְהַיָּתוֹם וְהָאַלְמָנָה אֲשֶׁר בִּשְׁעָרֶיךָ: ¹⁵ שִׁבְעַת יָמִים תָּחֹג לַיהוָה אֱלֹהֶיךָ בַּמָּקוֹם אֲשֶׁר־יִבְחַר יְהוָה כִּי יְבָרֶכְךָ יְהוָה אֱלֹהֶיךָ בְּכֹל תְּבוּאָתְךָ וּבְכֹל מַעֲשֵׂה יָדֶיךָ וְהָיִיתָ אַךְ שָׂמֵחַ: ¹⁶ שָׁלוֹשׁ פְּעָמִים ׀ בַּשָּׁנָה יֵרָאֶה כָל־זְכוּרְךָ אֶת־פְּנֵי ׀ יְהוָה אֱלֹהֶיךָ בַּמָּקוֹם אֲשֶׁר יִבְחָר בְּחַג הַמַּצּוֹת וּבְחַג הַשָּׁבֻעוֹת וּבְחַג הַסֻּכּוֹת וְלֹא יֵרָאֶה אֶת־פְּנֵי יְהוָה רֵיקָם: ¹⁷ אִישׁ כְּמַתְּנַת יָדוֹ כְּבִרְכַּת יְהוָה אֱלֹהֶיךָ אֲשֶׁר

18 "You shall appoint judges and officers in all your gates, which the LORD your God gives you, according to your tribes, and they shall judge the people with just judgment. 19 You shall not pervert justice; you shall not show partiality, nor take a bribe, for a bribe blinds the eyes of the wise and twists the words of the righteous. 20 You shall follow what is altogether just, that you may live and inherit the land which the LORD your God is giving you.

21 "You shall not plant for yourself any tree, as a wooden image, near the altar which you build for yourself to the LORD your God. 22 You shall not set up a sacred pillar, which the LORD your God hates.

17

"You shall not sacrifice to the LORD your God a bull or sheep which has any blemish or defect, for that is an abomination to the LORD your God.

2 "If there is found among you, within any of your gates which the LORD your God gives you, a man or a woman who has been wicked in the sight of the LORD your God, in transgressing His covenant, 3 who has gone and served other gods and worshiped them, either the sun or moon or any of the host of heaven, which I have not commanded, 4 and it is told you, and you hear of it, then you shall inquire diligently. And if it is indeed true and certain that such an abomination has been committed in Israel, 5 then you shall bring out to your gates that man or woman who has committed that wicked thing, and shall stone to death that man or woman with stones. 6 Whoever is deserving of death shall be put to death on the testimony of two or three witnesses; he shall not be put to death on the testimony of one witness. 7 The hands of the witnesses shall be the first against him to put him to death, and afterward the hands of all the people. So you shall put away the evil from among you.

8 "If a matter arises which is too hard for you to judge, between degrees of guilt for bloodshed, between one judgment or another, or between one punishment or another, matters of controversy within your gates, then you shall arise and go up to the place which the LORD your God chooses. 9 And you shall come to the priests, the Levites, and to the judge there in those days, and inquire of them; they shall pronounce upon you the sentence of judgment. 10 You shall do according to the sentence which they pronounce upon you in that place which the LORD chooses. And you shall be careful to do according to all that they order you. 11 According to the sentence of the law in which they instruct you, according to the judgment which they tell you, you shall do; you shall not turn aside

נָתַן־לָךְ: ס 18 שֹׁפְטִים וְשֹׁטְרִים תִּתֶּן־
לְךָ בְּכָל־שְׁעָרֶיךָ אֲשֶׁר יְהוָה אֱלֹהֶיךָ נֹתֵן לָךְ
לִשְׁבָטֶיךָ וְשָׁפְטוּ אֶת־הָעָם מִשְׁפַּט־צֶדֶק: 19 לֹא־
תַטֶּה מִשְׁפָּט לֹא תַכִּיר פָּנִים וְלֹא־תִקַּח שֹׁחַד כִּי
הַשֹּׁחַד יְעַוֵּר עֵינֵי חֲכָמִים וִיסַלֵּף דִּבְרֵי צַדִּיקִם:
20 צֶדֶק צֶדֶק תִּרְדֹּף לְמַעַן תִּחְיֶה וְיָרַשְׁתָּ אֶת־הָאָרֶץ
אֲשֶׁר־יְהוָה אֱלֹהֶיךָ נֹתֵן לָךְ: ס 21 לֹא־
תִטַּע לְךָ אֲשֵׁרָה כָּל־עֵץ אֵצֶל מִזְבַּח יְהוָה אֱלֹהֶיךָ
אֲשֶׁר תַּעֲשֶׂה־לָּךְ: ס 22 וְלֹא־תָקִים לְךָ
מַצֵּבָה אֲשֶׁר שָׂנֵא יְהוָה אֱלֹהֶיךָ: ס

יז לֹא־תִזְבַּח לַיהוָה אֱלֹהֶיךָ שׁוֹר וָשֶׂה אֲשֶׁר
יִהְיֶה בוֹ מוּם כֹּל דָּבָר רָע כִּי תוֹעֲבַת
יְהוָה אֱלֹהֶיךָ הוּא: ס 2 כִּי־יִמָּצֵא בְקִרְבְּךָ
בְּאַחַד שְׁעָרֶיךָ אֲשֶׁר־יְהוָה אֱלֹהֶיךָ נֹתֵן לָךְ אִישׁ
אוֹ־אִשָּׁה אֲשֶׁר יַעֲשֶׂה אֶת־הָרַע בְּעֵינֵי יְהוָה־
אֱלֹהֶיךָ לַעֲבֹר בְּרִיתוֹ: 3 וַיֵּלֶךְ וַיַּעֲבֹד אֱלֹהִים אֲחֵרִים
וַיִּשְׁתַּחוּ לָהֶם וְלַשֶּׁמֶשׁ אוֹ לַיָּרֵחַ אוֹ לְכָל־
צְבָא הַשָּׁמַיִם אֲשֶׁר לֹא־צִוִּיתִי: 4 וְהֻגַּד־לְךָ וְשָׁמָעְתָּ
וְדָרַשְׁתָּ הֵיטֵב וְהִנֵּה אֱמֶת נָכוֹן הַדָּבָר נֶעֶשְׂתָה
הַתּוֹעֵבָה הַזֹּאת בְּיִשְׂרָאֵל: 5 וְהוֹצֵאתָ אֶת־הָאִישׁ
הַהוּא אוֹ אֶת־הָאִשָּׁה הַהִוא אֲשֶׁר עָשׂוּ אֶת־הַדָּבָר
הָרָע הַזֶּה אֶל־שְׁעָרֶיךָ אֶת־הָאִישׁ אוֹ אֶת־הָאִשָּׁה
וּסְקַלְתָּם בָּאֲבָנִים וָמֵתוּ: 6 עַל־פִּי שְׁנַיִם עֵדִים
אוֹ שְׁלֹשָׁה עֵדִים יוּמַת הַמֵּת לֹא יוּמַת עַל־פִּי עֵד
אֶחָד: 7 יַד הָעֵדִים תִּהְיֶה־בּוֹ בָרִאשֹׁנָה לַהֲמִיתוֹ
וְיַד כָּל־הָעָם בָּאַחֲרֹנָה וּבִעַרְתָּ הָרָע מִקִּרְבֶּךָ: פ
8 כִּי יִפָּלֵא מִמְּךָ דָבָר לַמִּשְׁפָּט בֵּין־דָּם לְדָם
בֵּין־דִּין לְדִין וּבֵין נֶגַע לָנֶגַע דִּבְרֵי רִיבֹת בִּשְׁעָרֶיךָ
וְקַמְתָּ וְעָלִיתָ אֶל־הַמָּקוֹם אֲשֶׁר יִבְחַר יְהוָה אֱלֹהֶיךָ
בּוֹ: 9 וּבָאתָ אֶל־הַכֹּהֲנִים הַלְוִיִּם וְאֶל־הַשֹּׁפֵט אֲשֶׁר
יִהְיֶה בַּיָּמִים הָהֵם וְדָרַשְׁתָּ וְהִגִּידוּ לְךָ אֵת
דְּבַר הַמִּשְׁפָּט: 10 וְעָשִׂיתָ עַל־פִּי הַדָּבָר אֲשֶׁר
יַגִּידוּ לְךָ מִן־הַמָּקוֹם הַהוּא אֲשֶׁר יִבְחַר יְהוָה
וְשָׁמַרְתָּ לַעֲשׂוֹת כְּכֹל אֲשֶׁר יוֹרוּךָ: 11 עַל־פִּי
הַתּוֹרָה אֲשֶׁר יוֹרוּךָ וְעַל־הַמִּשְׁפָּט אֲשֶׁר־יֹאמְרוּ
לְךָ תַּעֲשֶׂה לֹא תָסוּר מִן־הַדָּבָר אֲשֶׁר־יַגִּידוּ

_to_ the right hand or _to_ the left from the sentence which they pronounce upon you. 12 Now the man who acts presumptuously and will not heed the priest who stands to minister there before the LORD your God, or the judge, that man shall die. So you shall put away the evil from Israel. 13 And all the people shall hear and fear, and no longer act presumptuously.

14 "When you come to the land which the LORD your God is giving you, and possess it and dwell in it, and say, 'I will set a king over me like all the nations that _are_ around me,' 15 you shall surely set a king over you whom the LORD your God chooses; _one_ from among your brethren you shall set as king over you; you may not set a foreigner over you, who _is_ not your brother. 16 But he shall not multiply horses for himself, nor cause the people to return to Egypt to multiply horses, for the LORD has said to you, 'You shall not return that way again.' 17 Neither shall he multiply wives for himself, lest his heart turn away; nor shall he greatly multiply silver and gold for himself.

18 "Also it shall be, when he sits on the throne of his kingdom, that he shall write for himself a copy of this law in a book, from _the one_ before the priests, the Levites. 19 And it shall be with him, and he shall read it all the days of his life, that he may learn to fear the LORD his God and be careful to observe all the words of this law and these statutes, 20 that his heart may not be lifted above his brethren, that he may not turn aside from the commandment _to_ the right hand or _to_ the left, and that he may prolong _his_ days in his kingdom, he and his children in the midst of Israel.

18 "The priests, the Levites—all the tribe of Levi—shall have no part nor inheritance with Israel; they shall eat the offerings of the LORD made by fire, and His portion. 2 Therefore they shall have no inheritance among their brethren; the LORD is their inheritance, as He said to them.

3 "And this shall be the priest's due from the people, from those who offer a sacrifice, whether _it is_ bull or sheep: they shall give to the priest the shoulder, the cheeks, and the stomach. 4 The firstfruits of your grain and your new wine and your oil, and the first of the fleece of your sheep, you shall give him. 5 For the LORD your God has chosen him out of all your tribes to stand to minister in the name of the LORD, him and his sons forever.

6 "So if a Levite comes from any of your gates, from where he dwells among all Israel, and comes with all the desire of his mind to the place which the

לְךָ יָמִין וּשְׂמֹאל: 12 וְהָאִישׁ אֲשֶׁר־יַעֲשֶׂה בְזָדוֹן לְבִלְתִּי שְׁמֹעַ אֶל־הַכֹּהֵן הָעֹמֵד לְשָׁרֶת שָׁם אֶת־יְהֹוָה אֱלֹהֶיךָ אוֹ אֶל־הַשֹּׁפֵט וּמֵת הָאִישׁ הַהוּא וּבִעַרְתָּ הָרָע מִיִּשְׂרָאֵל: 13 וְכָל־הָעָם יִשְׁמְעוּ וְיִרָאוּ וְלֹא יְזִידוּן עוֹד: ס 14 כִּי־תָבֹא אֶל־הָאָרֶץ אֲשֶׁר יְהֹוָה אֱלֹהֶיךָ נֹתֵן לָךְ וִירִשְׁתָּהּ וְיָשַׁבְתָּה בָּהּ וְאָמַרְתָּ אָשִׂימָה עָלַי מֶלֶךְ כְּכָל־הַגּוֹיִם אֲשֶׁר סְבִיבֹתָי: 15 שׂוֹם תָּשִׂים עָלֶיךָ מֶלֶךְ אֲשֶׁר יִבְחַר יְהֹוָה אֱלֹהֶיךָ בּוֹ מִקֶּרֶב אַחֶיךָ תָּשִׂים עָלֶיךָ מֶלֶךְ לֹא תוּכַל לָתֵת עָלֶיךָ אִישׁ נָכְרִי אֲשֶׁר לֹא־אָחִיךָ הוּא: 16 רַק לֹא־יַרְבֶּה־לּוֹ סוּסִים וְלֹא־יָשִׁיב אֶת־הָעָם מִצְרַיְמָה לְמַעַן הַרְבּוֹת סוּס וַיהֹוָה אָמַר לָכֶם לֹא תֹסִפוּן לָשׁוּב בַּדֶּרֶךְ הַזֶּה עוֹד: 17 וְלֹא יַרְבֶּה־לּוֹ נָשִׁים וְלֹא יָסוּר לְבָבוֹ וְכֶסֶף וְזָהָב לֹא יַרְבֶּה־לּוֹ מְאֹד: 18 וְהָיָה כְשִׁבְתּוֹ עַל כִּסֵּא מַמְלַכְתּוֹ וְכָתַב לוֹ אֶת־מִשְׁנֵה הַתּוֹרָה הַזֹּאת עַל־סֵפֶר מִלִּפְנֵי הַכֹּהֲנִים הַלְוִיִּם: 19 וְהָיְתָה עִמּוֹ וְקָרָא בוֹ כָּל־יְמֵי חַיָּיו לְמַעַן יִלְמַד לְיִרְאָה אֶת־יְהֹוָה אֱלֹהָיו לִשְׁמֹר אֶת־כָּל־דִּבְרֵי הַתּוֹרָה הַזֹּאת וְאֶת־הַחֻקִּים הָאֵלֶּה לַעֲשֹׂתָם: 20 לְבִלְתִּי רוּם־לְבָבוֹ מֵאֶחָיו וּלְבִלְתִּי סוּר מִן־הַמִּצְוָה יָמִין וּשְׂמֹאול לְמַעַן יַאֲרִיךְ יָמִים עַל־מַמְלַכְתּוֹ הוּא וּבָנָיו בְּקֶרֶב יִשְׂרָאֵל: ס

יח לֹא־יִהְיֶה לַכֹּהֲנִים הַלְוִיִּם כָּל־שֵׁבֶט לֵוִי חֵלֶק וְנַחֲלָה עִם־יִשְׂרָאֵל אִשֵּׁי יְהֹוָה וְנַחֲלָתוֹ יֹאכֵלוּן: 2 וְנַחֲלָה לֹא־יִהְיֶה־לּוֹ בְּקֶרֶב אֶחָיו יְהֹוָה הוּא נַחֲלָתוֹ כַּאֲשֶׁר דִּבֶּר־לוֹ: ס 3 וְזֶה יִהְיֶה מִשְׁפַּט הַכֹּהֲנִים מֵאֵת הָעָם מֵאֵת זֹבְחֵי הַזֶּבַח אִם־שׁוֹר אִם־שֶׂה וְנָתַן לַכֹּהֵן הַזְּרֹעַ וְהַלְּחָיַיִם וְהַקֵּבָה: 4 רֵאשִׁית דְּגָנְךָ תִּירֹשְׁךָ וְיִצְהָרֶךָ וְרֵאשִׁית גֵּז צֹאנְךָ תִּתֶּן־לּוֹ: 5 כִּי בוֹ בָּחַר יְהֹוָה אֱלֹהֶיךָ מִכָּל־שְׁבָטֶיךָ לַעֲמֹד לְשָׁרֵת בְּשֵׁם־יְהֹוָה הוּא וּבָנָיו כָּל־הַיָּמִים: ס 6 וְכִי־יָבֹא הַלֵּוִי מֵאַחַד שְׁעָרֶיךָ מִכָּל־יִשְׂרָאֵל אֲשֶׁר־הוּא גָּר שָׁם וּבָא בְּכָל־אַוַּת נַפְשׁוֹ אֶל־הַמָּקוֹם אֲשֶׁר־יִבְחַר יְהֹוָה:

LORD chooses, 7 then he may serve in the name of the LORD his God as all his brethren the Levites *do,* who stand there before the LORD. 8 They shall have equal portions to eat, besides what comes from the sale of his inheritance.

9 "When you come into the land which the LORD your God is giving you, you shall not learn to follow the abominations of those nations. 10 There shall not be found among you *anyone* who makes his son or his daughter pass through the fire, *or one* who practices witchcraft, *or* a soothsayer, or one who interprets omens, or a sorcerer, 11 or one who conjures spells, or a medium, or a spiritist, or one who calls up the dead. 12 For all who do these things *are* an abomination to the LORD, and because of these abominations the LORD your God drives them out from before you. 13 You shall be blameless before the LORD your God. 14 For these nations which you will dispossess listened to soothsayers and diviners; but as for you, the LORD your God has not appointed such for you.

15 "The LORD your God will raise up for you a Prophet like me from your midst, from your brethren. Him you shall hear, 16 according to all you desired of the LORD your God in Horeb in the day of the assembly, saying, 'Let me not hear again the voice of the LORD my God, nor let me see this great fire anymore, lest I die.'

17 "And the LORD said to me: 'What they have spoken is good. 18 I will raise up for them a Prophet like you from among their brethren, and will put My words in His mouth, and He shall speak to them all that I command Him. 19 And it shall be *that* whoever will not hear My words, which He speaks in My name, I will require *it* of him. 20 But the prophet who presumes to speak a word in My name, which I have not commanded him to speak, or who speaks in the name of other gods, that prophet shall die.' 21 And if you say in your heart, 'How shall we know the word which the LORD has not spoken?'— 22 when a prophet speaks in the name of the LORD, if the thing does not happen or come to pass, that *is* the thing which the LORD has not spoken; the prophet has spoken it presumptuously; you shall not be afraid of him.

19 "When the LORD your God has cut off the nations whose land the LORD your God is giving you, and you dispossess them and dwell in their cities and in their houses, 2 you shall separate three cities for yourself in the midst of your land which the LORD your God is giving you to possess. 3 You shall prepare roads for yourself, and divide into

7 וְשֵׁרֵת בְּשֵׁם יְהוָה אֱלֹהָיו כְּכָל־אֶחָיו הַלְוִיִּם הָעֹמְדִים שָׁם לִפְנֵי יְהוָה׃ 8 חֵלֶק כְּחֵלֶק יֹאכֵלוּ לְבַד מִמְכָּרָיו עַל־הָאָבוֹת׃ ס 9 כִּי אַתָּה בָּא אֶל־הָאָרֶץ אֲשֶׁר־יְהוָה אֱלֹהֶיךָ נֹתֵן לָךְ לֹא־תִלְמַד לַעֲשׂוֹת כְּתוֹעֲבֹת הַגּוֹיִם הָהֵם׃ 10 לֹא־יִמָּצֵא בְךָ מַעֲבִיר בְּנוֹ־וּבִתּוֹ בָּאֵשׁ קֹסֵם קְסָמִים מְעוֹנֵן וּמְנַחֵשׁ וּמְכַשֵּׁף׃ 11 וְחֹבֵר חָבֶר וְשֹׁאֵל אוֹב וְיִדְּעֹנִי וְדֹרֵשׁ אֶל־הַמֵּתִים׃ 12 כִּי־תוֹעֲבַת יְהוָה כָּל־עֹשֵׂה אֵלֶּה וּבִגְלַל הַתּוֹעֵבֹת הָאֵלֶּה יְהוָה אֱלֹהֶיךָ מוֹרִישׁ אוֹתָם מִפָּנֶיךָ׃ 13 תָּמִים תִּהְיֶה עִם יְהוָה אֱלֹהֶיךָ׃ ס 14 כִּי ׀ הַגּוֹיִם הָאֵלֶּה אֲשֶׁר אַתָּה יוֹרֵשׁ אוֹתָם אֶל־מְעֹנְנִים וְאֶל־קֹסְמִים יִשְׁמָעוּ וְאַתָּה לֹא כֵן נָתַן לְךָ יְהוָה אֱלֹהֶיךָ׃ 15 נָבִיא מִקִּרְבְּךָ מֵאַחֶיךָ כָּמֹנִי יָקִים לְךָ יְהוָה אֱלֹהֶיךָ אֵלָיו תִּשְׁמָעוּן׃ 16 כְּכֹל אֲשֶׁר־שָׁאַלְתָּ מֵעִם יְהוָה אֱלֹהֶיךָ בְּחֹרֵב בְּיוֹם הַקָּהָל לֵאמֹר לֹא אֹסֵף לִשְׁמֹעַ אֶת־קוֹל יְהוָה אֱלֹהָי וְאֶת־הָאֵשׁ הַגְּדֹלָה הַזֹּאת לֹא־אֶרְאֶה עוֹד וְלֹא אָמוּת׃ 17 וַיֹּאמֶר יְהוָה אֵלָי הֵיטִיבוּ אֲשֶׁר דִּבֵּרוּ׃ 18 נָבִיא אָקִים לָהֶם מִקֶּרֶב אֲחֵיהֶם כָּמוֹךָ וְנָתַתִּי דְבָרַי בְּפִיו וְדִבֶּר אֲלֵיהֶם אֵת כָּל־אֲשֶׁר אֲצַוֶּנּוּ׃ 19 וְהָיָה הָאִישׁ אֲשֶׁר לֹא־יִשְׁמַע אֶל־דְּבָרַי אֲשֶׁר יְדַבֵּר בִּשְׁמִי אָנֹכִי אֶדְרֹשׁ מֵעִמּוֹ׃ 20 אַךְ הַנָּבִיא אֲשֶׁר יָזִיד לְדַבֵּר דָּבָר בִּשְׁמִי אֵת אֲשֶׁר לֹא־צִוִּיתִיו לְדַבֵּר וַאֲשֶׁר יְדַבֵּר בְּשֵׁם אֱלֹהִים אֲחֵרִים וּמֵת הַנָּבִיא הַהוּא׃ 21 וְכִי תֹאמַר בִּלְבָבֶךָ אֵיכָה נֵדַע אֶת־הַדָּבָר אֲשֶׁר לֹא־דִבְּרוֹ יְהוָה׃ 22 אֲשֶׁר יְדַבֵּר הַנָּבִיא בְּשֵׁם יְהוָה וְלֹא־יִהְיֶה הַדָּבָר וְלֹא יָבוֹא הוּא הַדָּבָר אֲשֶׁר לֹא־דִבְּרוֹ יְהוָה בְּזָדוֹן דִּבְּרוֹ הַנָּבִיא לֹא תָגוּר מִמֶּנּוּ׃ ס

יט כִּי־יַכְרִית יְהוָה אֱלֹהֶיךָ אֶת־הַגּוֹיִם אֲשֶׁר יְהוָה אֱלֹהֶיךָ נֹתֵן לְךָ אֶת־אַרְצָם וִירִשְׁתָּם וְיָשַׁבְתָּ בְעָרֵיהֶם וּבְבָתֵּיהֶם׃ 2 שָׁלוֹשׁ עָרִים תַּבְדִּיל לָךְ בְּתוֹךְ אַרְצֶךָ אֲשֶׁר יְהוָה אֱלֹהֶיךָ נֹתֵן לְךָ לְרִשְׁתָּהּ׃ 3 תָּכִין לְךָ הַדֶּרֶךְ וְשִׁלַּשְׁתָּ אֶת־גְּבוּל אַרְצְךָ אֲשֶׁר יַנְחִילְךָ יְהוָה אֱלֹהֶיךָ וְהָיָה לָנוּס שָׁמָּה כָּל־רֹצֵחַ׃

three parts the territory of your land which the LORD your God is giving you to inherit, that any manslayer may flee there.

4 "And this *is* the case of the manslayer who flees there, that he may live: Whoever kills his neighbor unintentionally, not having hated him in time past— 5 as when *a man* goes to the woods with his neighbor to cut timber, and his hand swings a stroke with the ax to cut down the tree, and the head slips from the handle and strikes his neighbor so that he dies—he shall flee to one of these cities and live; 6 lest the avenger of blood, while his anger is hot, pursue the manslayer and overtake him, because the way is long, and kill him, though he *was* not deserving of death, since he had not hated the victim in time past. 7 Therefore I command you, saying, 'You shall separate three cities for yourself.'

8 "Now if the LORD your God enlarges your territory, as He swore to your fathers, and gives you the land which He promised to give to your fathers, 9 and if you keep all these commandments and do them, which I command you today, to love the LORD your God and to walk always in His ways, then you shall add three more cities for yourself besides these three, 10 lest innocent blood be shed in the midst of your land which the LORD your God is giving you *as* an inheritance, and *thus* guilt of bloodshed be upon you.

11 "But if anyone hates his neighbor, lies in wait for him, rises against him and strikes him mortally, so that he dies, and he flees to one of these cities, 12 then the elders of his city shall send and bring him from there, and deliver him over to the hand of the avenger of blood, that he may die. 13 Your eye shall not pity him, but you shall put away *the guilt of* innocent blood from Israel, that it may go well with you.

14 "You shall not remove your neighbor's landmark, which the men of old have set, in your inheritance which you will inherit in the land that the LORD your God is giving you to possess.

15 "One witness shall not rise against a man concerning any iniquity or any sin that he commits; by the mouth of two or three witnesses the matter shall be established. 16 If a false witness rises against any man to testify against him of wrongdoing, 17 then both men in the controversy shall stand before the LORD, before the priests and the judges who serve in those days. 18 And the judges shall make careful inquiry, and indeed, *if* the witness *is* a false witness, who has testified falsely against his brother, 19 then you shall do to him as he thought to have done to his brother; so you shall put away the evil from among you. 20 And those who remain

4 וְזֶה דְּבַר הָרֹצֵחַ אֲשֶׁר־יָנוּס שָׁמָּה וָחָי אֲשֶׁר יַכֶּה אֶת־רֵעֵהוּ בִּבְלִי־דַעַת וְהוּא לֹא־שֹׂנֵא לוֹ מִתְּמֹל שִׁלְשֹׁם: 5 וַאֲשֶׁר יָבֹא אֶת־רֵעֵהוּ בַיַּעַר לַחְטֹב עֵצִים וְנִדְּחָה יָדוֹ בַגַּרְזֶן לִכְרֹת הָעֵץ וְנָשַׁל הַבַּרְזֶל מִן־הָעֵץ וּמָצָא אֶת־רֵעֵהוּ וָמֵת הוּא יָנוּס אֶל־אַחַת הֶעָרִים־הָאֵלֶּה וָחָי: 6 פֶּן־יִרְדֹּף גֹּאֵל הַדָּם אַחֲרֵי הָרֹצֵחַ כִּי־יֵחַם לְבָבוֹ וְהִשִּׂיגוֹ כִּי־יִרְבֶּה הַדֶּרֶךְ וְהִכָּהוּ נָפֶשׁ וְלוֹ אֵין מִשְׁפַּט־מָוֶת כִּי לֹא שֹׂנֵא הוּא לוֹ מִתְּמוֹל שִׁלְשֹׁום: 7 עַל־כֵּן אָנֹכִי מְצַוְּךָ לֵאמֹר שָׁלֹשׁ עָרִים תַּבְדִּיל לָךְ: ס 8 וְאִם־יַרְחִיב יְהוָה אֱלֹהֶיךָ אֶת־גְּבֻלְךָ כַּאֲשֶׁר נִשְׁבַּע לַאֲבֹתֶיךָ וְנָתַן לְךָ אֶת־כָּל־הָאָרֶץ אֲשֶׁר דִּבֶּר לָתֵת לַאֲבֹתֶיךָ:

9 כִּי־תִשְׁמֹר אֶת־כָּל־הַמִּצְוָה הַזֹּאת לַעֲשֹׂתָהּ אֲשֶׁר אָנֹכִי מְצַוְּךָ הַיּוֹם לְאַהֲבָה אֶת־יְהוָה אֱלֹהֶיךָ וְלָלֶכֶת בִּדְרָכָיו כָּל־הַיָּמִים וְיָסַפְתָּ לְךָ עוֹד שָׁלֹשׁ עָרִים עַל הַשָּׁלֹשׁ הָאֵלֶּה: 10 וְלֹא יִשָּׁפֵךְ דָּם נָקִי בְּקֶרֶב אַרְצְךָ אֲשֶׁר יְהוָה אֱלֹהֶיךָ נֹתֵן לְךָ נַחֲלָה וְהָיָה עָלֶיךָ דָּמִים: ס 11 וְכִי־יִהְיֶה אִישׁ שֹׂנֵא לְרֵעֵהוּ וְאָרַב לוֹ וְקָם עָלָיו וְהִכָּהוּ נֶפֶשׁ וָמֵת וְנָס אֶל־אַחַת הֶעָרִים הָאֵל: 12 וְשָׁלְחוּ זִקְנֵי עִירוֹ וְלָקְחוּ אֹתוֹ מִשָּׁם וְנָתְנוּ אֹתוֹ בְּיַד גֹּאֵל הַדָּם וָמֵת: 13 לֹא־תָחוֹס עֵינְךָ עָלָיו וּבִעַרְתָּ דַם־הַנָּקִי מִיִּשְׂרָאֵל וְטוֹב לָךְ: ס 14 לֹא תַסִּיג גְּבוּל רֵעֲךָ אֲשֶׁר גָּבְלוּ רִאשֹׁנִים בְּנַחֲלָתְךָ אֲשֶׁר תִּנְחַל בָּאָרֶץ אֲשֶׁר יְהוָה אֱלֹהֶיךָ נֹתֵן לְךָ לְרִשְׁתָּהּ: ס 15 לֹא־יָקוּם עֵד אֶחָד בְּאִישׁ לְכָל־עָוֹן וּלְכָל־חַטָּאת בְּכָל־חֵטְא אֲשֶׁר יֶחֱטָא עַל־פִּי שְׁנֵי עֵדִים אוֹ עַל־פִּי שְׁלֹשָׁה־עֵדִים יָקוּם דָּבָר: 16 כִּי־יָקוּם עֵד־חָמָס בְּאִישׁ לַעֲנוֹת בּוֹ סָרָה: 17 וְעָמְדוּ שְׁנֵי־הָאֲנָשִׁים אֲשֶׁר־לָהֶם הָרִיב לִפְנֵי יְהוָה לִפְנֵי הַכֹּהֲנִים וְהַשֹּׁפְטִים אֲשֶׁר יִהְיוּ בַּיָּמִים הָהֵם: 18 וְדָרְשׁוּ הַשֹּׁפְטִים הֵיטֵב וְהִנֵּה עֵד־שֶׁקֶר הָעֵד שֶׁקֶר עָנָה בְאָחִיו: 19 וַעֲשִׂיתֶם לוֹ כַּאֲשֶׁר זָמַם לַעֲשׂוֹת לְאָחִיו וּבִעַרְתָּ הָרָע מִקִּרְבֶּךָ: 20 וְהַנִּשְׁאָרִים יִשְׁמְעוּ וְיִרָאוּ וְלֹא־יֹסִפוּ

shall hear and fear, and hereafter they shall not again commit such evil among you. 21 Your eye shall not pity: life *shall be* for life, eye for eye, tooth for hand, foot for foot.

20 "When you go out to battle against your enemies, and see horses and chariots *and* people more numerous than you, do not be afraid of them; for the LORD your God *is* with you, who brought you up from the land of Egypt. 2 So it shall be, when you are on the verge of battle, that the priest shall approach and speak to the people. 3 And he shall say to them, 'Hear, O Israel: Today you are on the verge of battle with your enemies. Do not let your heart faint, do not be afraid, and do not tremble or be terrified because of them; 4 for the LORD your God *is* He who goes with you, to fight for you against your enemies, to save you.'

5 "Then the officers shall speak to the people, saying: 'What man *is there* who has built a new house and has not dedicated it? Let him go and return to his house, lest he die in the battle and another man dedicate it. 6 Also what man *is there* who has planted a vineyard and has not eaten of it? Let him go and return to his house, lest he die in the battle and another man eat of it. 7 And what man *is there* who is betrothed to a woman and has not married her? Let him go and return to his house, lest he die in the battle and another man marry her.'

8 "The officers shall speak further to the people, and say, 'What man *is there who is* fearful and fainthearted? Let him go and return to his house, lest the heart of his brethren faint like his heart.' 9 And so it shall be, when the officers have finished speaking to the people, that they shall make captains of the armies to lead the people.

10 "When you go near a city to fight against it, then proclaim an offer of peace to it. 11 And it shall be that if they accept your offer of peace, and open to you, then all the people *who are* found in it shall be placed under tribute to you, and serve you. 12 Now if *the city* will not make peace with you, but war against you, then you shall besiege it. 13 And when the LORD your God delivers it into your hands, you shall strike every male in it with the edge of the sword. 14 But the women, the little ones, the livestock, and all that is in the city, all its spoil, you shall plunder for yourself; and you shall eat the enemies' plunder which the LORD your God gives you. 15 Thus you shall do to all the cities *which are* very far from you, which *are* not of the cities of these nations.

16 "But of the cities of these peoples which the LORD your God gives you *as* an inheritance, you shall let nothing that breathes remain alive, 17 but you shall utterly destroy them: the Hittite and the Amorite and the Canaanite and the Perizzite and the Hivite and the Jebusite, just as the LORD your God has commanded you, 18 lest they teach you to do according to all their abominations which they have done for their gods, and you sin against the LORD your God.

19 "When you besiege a city for a long time, while making war against it to take it, you shall not destroy its trees by wielding an ax against them; if you can eat of them, do not cut them down to use in the siege, for the tree of the field *is* man's *food*. 20 Only the trees which you know *are* not trees for food you may destroy and cut down, to build siegeworks against the city that makes war with you, until it is subdued.

21 "If *anyone* is found slain, lying in the field in the land which the LORD your God is giving you to possess, *and* it is not known who killed him, 2 then your elders and your judges shall go out and measure *the distance* from the slain man to the surrounding cities. 3 And it shall be *that* the elders of the city nearest to the slain man will take a heifer which has not been worked *and* which has not pulled with a yoke. 4 The elders of that city shall bring the heifer down to a valley with flowing water, which is neither plowed nor sown, and they shall break the heifer's neck there in the valley. 5 Then the priests, the sons of Levi, shall come near, for the LORD your God has chosen them to minister to Him and to bless in the name of the LORD; by their word every controversy and every assault shall be *settled*. 6 And all the elders of that city nearest to the slain *man* shall wash their hands over the heifer whose neck was broken in the valley. 7 Then they shall answer and say, 'Our hands have not shed this blood, nor have our eyes seen *it*. 8 Provide atonement, O LORD, for Your people Israel, whom You have redeemed, and do not lay innocent blood to the charge of Your people Israel.' And atonement shall be provided on their behalf for the blood. 9 So you shall put away the *guilt of* innocent blood from among you when you do *what is* right in the sight of the LORD.

10 "When you go out to war against your enemies, and the LORD your God delivers them into your hand, and you take them captive, 11 and you see among the captives a beautiful woman, and desire her and would take her for your wife, 12 then you shall bring her home to your house, and she

16 רַק מֵעָרֵי הָעַמִּים הָאֵלֶּה הַגּוֹיִם־הָאֵלֶּה הִנֵּה אֲשֶׁר יְהֹוָה אֱלֹהֶיךָ נֹתֵן לְךָ נַחֲלָה לֹא תְחַיֶּה כָּל־נְשָׁמָה: 17 כִּי־הַחֲרֵם תַּחֲרִימֵם הַחִתִּי וְהָאֱמֹרִי הַכְּנַעֲנִי וְהַפְּרִזִּי הַחִוִּי וְהַיְבוּסִי כַּאֲשֶׁר צִוְּךָ יְהֹוָה אֱלֹהֶיךָ: 18 לְמַעַן אֲשֶׁר לֹא־יְלַמְּדוּ אֶתְכֶם לַעֲשׂוֹת כְּכֹל תּוֹעֲבֹתָם אֲשֶׁר עָשׂוּ לֵאלֹהֵיהֶם וַחֲטָאתֶם לַיהֹוָה אֱלֹהֵיכֶם: ס 19 כִּי־תָצוּר אֶל־עִיר יָמִים רַבִּים לְהִלָּחֵם עָלֶיהָ לְתָפְשָׂהּ לֹא־תַשְׁחִית אֶת־עֵצָהּ לִנְדֹּחַ עָלָיו גַּרְזֶן כִּי מִמֶּנּוּ תֹאכֵל וְאֹתוֹ לֹא תִכְרֹת כִּי הָאָדָם עֵץ הַשָּׂדֶה לָבֹא מִפָּנֶיךָ בַּמָּצוֹר: 20 רַק עֵץ אֲשֶׁר־תֵּדַע כִּי־לֹא־עֵץ מַאֲכָל הוּא אֹתוֹ תַשְׁחִית וְכָרָתָּ וּבָנִיתָ מָצוֹר עַל־הָעִיר אֲשֶׁר־הִוא עֹשָׂה עִמְּךָ מִלְחָמָה עַד רִדְתָּהּ: פ

כא כִּי־יִמָּצֵא חָלָל בָּאֲדָמָה אֲשֶׁר יְהֹוָה אֱלֹהֶיךָ נֹתֵן לְךָ לְרִשְׁתָּהּ נֹפֵל בַּשָּׂדֶה לֹא נוֹדַע מִי הִכָּהוּ: 2 וְיָצְאוּ זְקֵנֶיךָ וְשֹׁפְטֶיךָ וּמָדְדוּ אֶל־הֶעָרִים אֲשֶׁר סְבִיבֹת הֶחָלָל: 3 וְהָיָה הָעִיר הַקְּרֹבָה אֶל־הֶחָלָל וְלָקְחוּ זִקְנֵי הָעִיר הַהִוא עֶגְלַת בָּקָר אֲשֶׁר לֹא־עֻבַּד בָּהּ אֲשֶׁר לֹא־מָשְׁכָה בְּעֹל: 4 וְהוֹרִדוּ זִקְנֵי הָעִיר הַהִוא אֶת־הָעֶגְלָה אֶל־נַחַל אֵיתָן אֲשֶׁר לֹא־יֵעָבֵד בּוֹ וְלֹא יִזָּרֵעַ וְעָרְפוּ־שָׁם אֶת־הָעֶגְלָה בַּנָּחַל: 5 וְנִגְּשׁוּ הַכֹּהֲנִים בְּנֵי לֵוִי כִּי בָם בָּחַר יְהֹוָה אֱלֹהֶיךָ לְשָׁרְתוֹ וּלְבָרֵךְ בְּשֵׁם יְהֹוָה וְעַל־פִּיהֶם יִהְיֶה כָּל־רִיב וְכָל־נָגַע: 6 וְכֹל זִקְנֵי הָעִיר הַהִוא הַקְּרֹבִים אֶל־הֶחָלָל יִרְחֲצוּ אֶת־יְדֵיהֶם עַל־הָעֶגְלָה הָעֲרוּפָה בַנָּחַל: 7 וְעָנוּ וְאָמְרוּ יָדֵינוּ לֹא שָׁפְכֻה אֶת־הַדָּם הַזֶּה וְעֵינֵינוּ לֹא רָאוּ: 8 כַּפֵּר לְעַמְּךָ יִשְׂרָאֵל אֲשֶׁר־פָּדִיתָ יְהֹוָה וְאַל־תִּתֵּן דָּם נָקִי בְּקֶרֶב עַמְּךָ יִשְׂרָאֵל וְנִכַּפֵּר לָהֶם הַדָּם: 9 וְאַתָּה תְּבַעֵר הַדָּם הַנָּקִי מִקִּרְבֶּךָ כִּי־תַעֲשֶׂה הַיָּשָׁר בְּעֵינֵי יְהֹוָה: ס 10 כִּי־תֵצֵא לַמִּלְחָמָה עַל־אֹיְבֶיךָ וּנְתָנוֹ יְהֹוָה אֱלֹהֶיךָ בְּיָדֶךָ וְשָׁבִיתָ שִׁבְיוֹ: 11 וְרָאִיתָ בַּשִּׁבְיָה אֵשֶׁת יְפַת־תֹּאַר וְחָשַׁקְתָּ בָהּ וְלָקַחְתָּ לְךָ לְאִשָּׁה: 12 וַהֲבֵאתָהּ אֶל־תּוֹךְ בֵּיתֶךָ וְגִלְּחָה אֶת־רֹאשָׁהּ וְעָשְׂתָה אֶת־

shall shave her head and trim her nails. [13] She shall put off the clothes of her captivity, remain in your house, and mourn her father and her mother a full month; after that you may go in to her and be her husband, and she shall be your wife. [14] And it shall be, if you have no delight in her, then you shall set her free, but you certainly shall not sell her for money; you shall not treat her brutally, because you have humbled her.

[15] "If a man has two wives, one loved and the other unloved, and they have borne him children, *both* the loved and the unloved, and *if* the firstborn son is of her who is unloved, [16] then it shall be, on the day he bequeaths his possessions to his sons, *that* he must not bestow firstborn status on the son of the loved wife in preference to the son of the unloved, the *true* firstborn. [17] But he shall acknowledge the son of the unloved wife *as* the firstborn by giving him a double portion of all that he has, for he *is* the beginning of his strength; the right of the firstborn *is* his.

[18] "If a man has a stubborn and rebellious son who will not obey the voice of his father or the voice of his mother, and *who,* when they have chastened him, will not heed them, [19] then his father and his mother shall take hold of him and bring him out to the elders of his city, to the gate of his city. [20] And they shall say to the elders of his city, 'This son of ours is stubborn and rebellious; he will not obey our voice; he is a glutton and a drunkard.' [21] Then all the men of his city shall stone him to death with stones; so you shall put away the evil from among you, and all Israel shall hear and fear.

[22] "If a man has committed a sin deserving of death, and he is put to death, and you hang him on a tree, [23] his body shall not remain overnight on the tree, but you shall surely bury him that day, so that you do not defile the land which the LORD your God is giving you *as* an inheritance; for he who is hanged *is* accursed of God.

22

"You shall not see your brother's ox or his sheep going astray, and hide yourself from them; you shall certainly bring them back to your brother. [2] And if your brother *is* not near you, or if you do not know him, then you shall bring it to your own house, and it shall remain with you until your brother seeks it; then you shall restore it to him. [3] You shall do the same with his donkey, and so shall you do with his garment; with any lost thing of your brother's, which he has lost and you have found, you shall do likewise; you must not hide yourself.

צִפׇּרְנֶיהָ: 13 וְהֵסִירָה אֶת־שִׂמְלַת שִׁבְיָהּ מֵעָלֶיהָ וְיָשְׁבָה בְּבֵיתֶךָ וּבָכְתָה אֶת־אָבִיהָ וְאֶת־אִמָּהּ יֶרַח יָמִים וְאַחַר כֵּן תָּבוֹא אֵלֶיהָ וּבְעַלְתָּהּ וְהָיְתָה לְךָ לְאִשָּׁה: 14 וְהָיָה אִם־לֹא חָפַצְתָּ בָּהּ וְשִׁלַּחְתָּהּ לְנַפְשָׁהּ וּמָכֹר לֹא־תִמְכְּרֶנָּה בַּכָּסֶף לֹא־תִתְעַמֵּר בָּהּ תַּחַת אֲשֶׁר עִנִּיתָהּ: ס 15 כִּי־תִהְיֶיןָ לְאִישׁ שְׁתֵּי נָשִׁים הָאַחַת אֲהוּבָה וְהָאַחַת שְׂנוּאָה וְיָלְדוּ־לוֹ בָנִים הָאֲהוּבָה וְהַשְּׂנוּאָה וְהָיָה הַבֵּן הַבְּכוֹר לַשְּׂנִיאָה: 16 וְהָיָה בְּיוֹם הַנְחִילוֹ אֶת־בָּנָיו אֵת אֲשֶׁר־יִהְיֶה לוֹ לֹא יוּכַל לְבַכֵּר אֶת־בֶּן־ הָאֲהוּבָה עַל־פְּנֵי בֶן־הַשְּׂנוּאָה הַבְּכֹר: 17 כִּי אֶת־ הַבְּכֹר בֶּן־הַשְּׂנוּאָה יַכִּיר לָתֶת לוֹ פִּי שְׁנַיִם בְּכֹל אֲשֶׁר־יִמָּצֵא לוֹ כִּי־הוּא רֵאשִׁית אֹנוֹ לוֹ מִשְׁפַּט הַבְּכֹרָה: ס 18 כִּי־יִהְיֶה לְאִישׁ בֵּן סוֹרֵר וּמוֹרֶה אֵינֶנּוּ שֹׁמֵעַ בְּקוֹל אָבִיו וּבְקוֹל אִמּוֹ וְיִסְּרוּ אֹתוֹ וְלֹא יִשְׁמַע אֲלֵיהֶם: 19 וְתָפְשׂוּ בוֹ אָבִיו וְאִמּוֹ וְהוֹצִיאוּ אֹתוֹ אֶל־זִקְנֵי עִירוֹ וְאֶל־שַׁעַר מְקֹמוֹ: 20 וְאָמְרוּ אֶל־זִקְנֵי עִירוֹ בְּנֵנוּ זֶה סוֹרֵר וּמֹרֶה אֵינֶנּוּ שֹׁמֵעַ בְּקֹלֵנוּ זוֹלֵל וְסֹבֵא: 21 וּרְגָמֻהוּ כָּל־אַנְשֵׁי עִירוֹ בָאֲבָנִים וָמֵת וּבִעַרְתָּ הָרָע מִקִּרְבֶּךָ וְכָל־יִשְׂרָאֵל יִשְׁמְעוּ וְיִרָאוּ: ס 22 וְכִי־יִהְיֶה בְאִישׁ חֵטְא מִשְׁפַּט־מָוֶת וְהוּמָת וְתָלִיתָ אֹתוֹ עַל־עֵץ: 23 לֹא־ תָלִין נִבְלָתוֹ עַל־הָעֵץ כִּי־קָבוֹר תִּקְבְּרֶנּוּ בַּיּוֹם הַהוּא כִּי־קִלְלַת אֱלֹהִים תָּלוּי וְלֹא תְטַמֵּא אֶת־אַדְמָתְךָ אֲשֶׁר יְהוָה אֱלֹהֶיךָ נֹתֵן לְךָ נַחֲלָה: ס

כב לֹא־תִרְאֶה אֶת־שׁוֹר אָחִיךָ אוֹ אֶת־שֵׂיוֹ נִדָּחִים וְהִתְעַלַּמְתָּ מֵהֶם הָשֵׁב תְּשִׁיבֵם לְאָחִיךָ: 2 וְאִם־לֹא קָרוֹב אָחִיךָ אֵלֶיךָ וְלֹא יְדַעְתּוֹ וַאֲסַפְתּוֹ אֶל־תּוֹךְ בֵּיתֶךָ וְהָיָה עִמְּךָ עַד דְּרֹשׁ אָחִיךָ אֹתוֹ וַהֲשֵׁבֹתוֹ לוֹ: 3 וְכֵן תַּעֲשֶׂה לַחֲמֹרוֹ וְכֵן תַּעֲשֶׂה לְשִׂמְלָתוֹ וְכֵן תַּעֲשֶׂה לְכָל־אֲבֵדַת אָחִיךָ אֲשֶׁר־ תֹּאבַד מִמֶּנּוּ וּמְצָאתָהּ לֹא

4 "You shall not see your brother's donkey or his ox fall down along the road, and hide yourself from them; you shall surely help him lift *them* up again.

5 "A woman shall not wear anything that pertains to a man, nor shall a man put on a woman's garment, for all who do so *are* an abomination to the LORD your God.

6 "If a bird's nest happens to be before you along the way, in any tree or on the ground, with young ones or eggs, with the mother sitting on the young or on the eggs, you shall not take the mother with the young; 7 you shall surely let the mother go, and take the young for yourself, that it may be well with you and *that* you may prolong *your* days.

8 "When you build a new house, then you shall make a parapet for your roof, that you may not bring guilt of bloodshed on your household if anyone falls from it.

9 "You shall not sow your vineyard with different kinds of seed, lest the yield of the seed which you have sown and the fruit of your vineyard be defiled.

10 "You shall not plow with an ox and a donkey together.

11 "You shall not wear a garment of different sorts, *such as* wool and linen mixed together.

12 "You shall make tassels on the four corners of the clothing with which you cover *yourself.*

13 "If any man takes a wife, and goes in to her, and detests her, 14 and charges her with shameful conduct, and brings a bad name on her, and says, 'I took this woman, and when I came to her I found she *was* not a virgin,' 15 then the father and mother of the young woman shall take and bring out *the evidence of* the young woman's virginity to the elders of the city at the gate. 16 And the young woman's father shall say to the elders, 'I gave my daughter to this man as wife, and he detests her. 17 Now he has charged her with shameful conduct, saying, "I found your daughter *was* not a virgin," and yet these *are the evidences of* my daughter's virginity.' And they shall spread the cloth before the elders of the city. 18 Then the elders of that city shall take that man and punish him; 19 and they shall fine him one hundred *shekels* of silver and give *them* to the father of the young woman, because he has brought a bad name on a virgin of Israel. And she shall be his wife; he cannot divorce her all his days.

20 "But if the thing is true, *and evidences of* virginity are not found for the young woman, 21 then they shall bring out the young woman to the door of her father's house, and the men of her city shall stone her to death with stones, because she has

4 לֹא־תִרְאֶה אֶת־ ס חֲמוֹר אָחִיךָ אוֹ שׁוֹרוֹ נֹפְלִים בַּדֶּרֶךְ וְהִתְעַלַּמְתָּ מֵהֶם הָקֵם תָּקִים עִמּוֹ: 5 לֹא־יִהְיֶה כְלִי־גֶבֶר עַל־ אִשָּׁה וְלֹא־יִלְבַּשׁ גֶּבֶר שִׂמְלַת אִשָּׁה כִּי תוֹעֲבַת יְהוָה אֱלֹהֶיךָ כָּל־עֹשֵׂה אֵלֶּה: פ

6 כִּי יִקָּרֵא קַן־צִפּוֹר | לְפָנֶיךָ בַּדֶּרֶךְ בְּכָל־ עֵץ | אוֹ עַל־הָאָרֶץ אֶפְרֹחִים אוֹ בֵיצִים וְהָאֵם רֹבֶצֶת עַל־הָאֶפְרֹחִים אוֹ עַל־הַבֵּיצִים לֹא־ תִקַּח הָאֵם עַל־הַבָּנִים: 7 שַׁלֵּחַ תְּשַׁלַּח אֶת־הָאֵם וְאֶת־הַבָּנִים תִּקַּח־לָךְ לְמַעַן יִיטַב לָךְ וְהַאֲרַכְתָּ יָמִים: ס 8 כִּי תִבְנֶה בַּיִת חָדָשׁ וְעָשִׂיתָ מַעֲקֶה לְגַגֶּךָ וְלֹא־תָשִׂים דָּמִים בְּבֵיתֶךָ כִּי־ יִפֹּל הַנֹּפֵל מִמֶּנּוּ: ס 9 לֹא־תִזְרַע כַּרְמְךָ כִּלְאָיִם פֶּן־תִּקְדַּשׁ הַמְלֵאָה הַזֶּרַע אֲשֶׁר תִּזְרָע וּתְבוּאַת הַכָּרֶם: ס 10 לֹא־תַחֲרֹשׁ בְּשׁוֹר־ וּבַחֲמֹר יַחְדָּו: ס 11 לֹא תִלְבַּשׁ שַׁעַטְנֵז צֶמֶר וּפִשְׁתִּים יַחְדָּו: ס 12 גְּדִלִים תַּעֲשֶׂה־ לָּךְ עַל־אַרְבַּע כַּנְפוֹת כְּסוּתְךָ אֲשֶׁר תְּכַסֶּה־ בָּהּ: ס 13 כִּי־יִקַּח אִישׁ אִשָּׁה וּבָא אֵלֶיהָ וּשְׂנֵאָהּ: 14 וְשָׂם לָהּ עֲלִילֹת דְּבָרִים וְהוֹצִיא עָלֶיהָ שֵׁם רָע וְאָמַר אֶת־הָאִשָּׁה הַזֹּאת לָקַחְתִּי וָאֶקְרַב אֵלֶיהָ וְלֹא־מָצָאתִי לָהּ בְּתוּלִים: 15 וְלָקַח אֲבִי הַנַּעֲרָ וְאִמָּהּ וְהוֹצִיאוּ אֶת־בְּתוּלֵי הַנַּעֲרָ אֶל־ זִקְנֵי הָעִיר הַשָּׁעְרָה: 16 וְאָמַר אֲבִי הַנַּעֲרָ אֶל־ הַזְּקֵנִים אֶת־בִּתִּי נָתַתִּי לָאִישׁ הַזֶּה לְאִשָּׁה וַיִּשְׂנָאֶהָ: 17 וְהִנֵּה־הוּא שָׂם עֲלִילֹת דְּבָרִים לֵאמֹר לֹא־ מָצָאתִי לְבִתְּךָ בְּתוּלִים וְאֵלֶּה בְּתוּלֵי בִתִּי וּפָרְשׂוּ הַשִּׂמְלָה לִפְנֵי זִקְנֵי הָעִיר: 18 וְלָקְחוּ זִקְנֵי הָעִיר־ הַהִוא אֶת־הָאִישׁ וְיִסְּרוּ אֹתוֹ: 19 וְעָנְשׁוּ אֹתוֹ מֵאָה כֶסֶף וְנָתְנוּ לַאֲבִי הַנַּעֲרָה כִּי הוֹצִיא שֵׁם רָע עַל בְּתוּלַת יִשְׂרָאֵל וְלוֹ־תִהְיֶה לְאִשָּׁה לֹא־יוּכַל לְשַׁלְּחָהּ כָּל־יָמָיו: 20 וְאִם־ אֱמֶת הָיָה הַדָּבָר הַזֶּה לֹא־נִמְצְאוּ בְתוּלִים לַנַּעֲרָ: 21 וְהוֹצִיאוּ אֶת־הַנַּעֲרָ אֶל־פֶּתַח בֵּית־

---

done a disgraceful thing in Israel, to play the harlot in her father's house. So you shall put away the evil from among you.

22 "If a man is found lying with a woman married to a husband, then both of them shall die—the man that lay with the woman, and the woman; so you shall put away the evil from Israel.

23 "If a young woman who is a virgin is betrothed to a husband, and a man finds her in the city and lies with her, 24 then you shall bring them both out to the gate of that city, and you shall stone them to death with stones, the young woman because she did not cry out in the city, and the man because he humbled his neighbor's wife; so you shall put away the evil from among you.

25 "But if a man finds a betrothed young woman in the countryside, and the man forces her and lies with her, then only the man who lay with her shall die. 26 But you shall do nothing to the young woman; there is in the young woman no sin deserving of death, for just as when a man rises against his neighbor and kills him, even so is this matter. 27 For he found her in the countryside, and the betrothed young woman cried out, but there was no one to save her.

28 "If a man finds a young woman who is a virgin, who is not betrothed, and he seizes her and lies with her, and they are found out, 29 then the man who lay with her shall give to the young woman's father fifty shekels of silver, and she shall be his wife because he has humbled her; he shall not be permitted to divorce her all his days.

30 "A man shall not take his father's wife, nor uncover his father's bed.

23 "He who is emasculated by crushing or mutilation shall not enter the assembly of the LORD.

2 "One of illegitimate birth shall not enter the assembly of the LORD; even to the tenth generation none of his descendants shall enter the assembly of the LORD.

3 "An Ammonite or Moabite shall not enter the assembly of the LORD; even to the tenth generation none of his descendants shall enter the assembly of the LORD forever, 4 because they did not meet you with bread and water on the road when you came out of Egypt, and because they hired against you Balaam the son of Beor from Pethor of Mesopotamia, to curse you. 5 Nevertheless the LORD your God would not listen to Balaam, but the LORD your God turned the curse into a blessing for you, because the LORD your God loves you. 6 You shall not seek their peace nor their prosperity all your days forever.

7 "You shall not abhor an Edomite, for he *is* your brother. You shall not abhor an Egyptian, because you were an alien in his land. 8 The children of the third generation born to them may enter the assembly of the LORD.

9 "When the army goes out against your enemies, then keep yourself from every wicked thing. 10 If there is any man among you who becomes unclean by some occurrence in the night, then he shall go outside the camp; he shall not come inside the camp. 11 But it shall be, that when evening comes, that he shall wash with water; and when the sun sets, he may come into the camp.

12 "Also you shall have a place outside the camp, where you may go out; 13 and you shall have an implement among your equipment, and when you sit down outside, you shall dig with it and turn and cover your refuse. 14 For the LORD your God walks in the midst of your camp, to deliver you and give your enemies over to you; therefore your camp shall be holy, that He may see no unclean thing among you, and turn away from you.

15 "You shall not give back to his master the slave who has escaped from his master to you. 16 He may dwell with you in your midst, in the place which he chooses within one of your gates, where it seems best to him; you shall not oppress him.

17 "There shall be no *ritual* harlot of the daughters of Israel, or a perverted one of the sons of Israel. 18 You shall not bring the wages of a harlot or the price of a dog to the house of the LORD your God for any vowed offering, for both of these *are* an abomination to the LORD your God.

19 "You shall not charge interest to your brother—interest on money *or* food *or* anything that is lent out at interest. 20 To a foreigner you may charge interest, but to your brother you shall not charge interest, that the LORD your God may bless you in all to which you set your hand in the land which you are entering to possess.

21 "When you make a vow to the LORD your God, you shall not delay to pay it; for the LORD your God will surely require it of you, and it would be sin to you. 22 But if you abstain from vowing, it shall not be sin to you. 23 That which has gone from your lips you shall keep and perform, for you voluntarily vowed to the LORD your God what you have promised with your mouth.

24 "When you come into your neighbor's vineyard, you may eat your fill of grapes at your pleasure, but you shall not put *any* in your container. 25 When you come into your neighbor's

אֱלֹהֶֽיךָ׃ 7 לֹא־תְתַעֵב אֲדֹמִי כִּי אָחִיךָ הֽוּא ס לֹא־תְתַעֵב מִצְרִי כִּי־גֵר הָיִיתָ בְאַרְצֽוֹ׃ 9 בָּנִים אֲשֶׁר־יִוָּלְדוּ לָהֶם דּוֹר שְׁלִישִׁי יָבֹא לָהֶם בִּקְהַל יְהוָֽה׃ ס 10 כִּֽי־תֵצֵא מַחֲנֶה עַל־אֹיְבֶיךָ וְנִשְׁמַרְתָּ מִכֹּל דָּבָר רָֽע׃ 11 כִּֽי־יִהְיֶה בְךָ אִישׁ אֲשֶׁר לֹא־יִהְיֶה טָהוֹר מִקְּרֵה־ לָיְלָה וְיָצָא אֶל־מִחוּץ לַֽמַּחֲנֶה לֹא יָבֹא אֶל־תּוֹךְ הַֽמַּחֲנֶֽה׃ 12 וְהָיָה לִפְנֽוֹת־עֶרֶב יִרְחַץ בַּמָּיִם וּכְבֹא הַשֶּׁמֶשׁ יָבֹא אֶל־תּוֹךְ הַֽמַּחֲנֶֽה׃ 13 וְיָד תִּהְיֶה לְךָ מִחוּץ לַֽמַּחֲנֶה וְיָצָאתָ שָּׁמָּה חֽוּץ׃ 14 וְיָתֵד תִּהְיֶה לְךָ עַל־אֲזֵנֶךָ וְהָיָה בְּשִׁבְתְּךָ חוּץ וְחָפַרְתָּה בָהּ וְשַׁבְתָּ וְכִסִּיתָ אֶת־צֵאָתֶֽךָ׃ 15 כִּי יְהוָה אֱלֹהֶיךָ מִתְהַלֵּךְ ׀ בְּקֶרֶב מַחֲנֶךָ לְהַצִּֽילְךָ וְלָתֵת אֹיְבֶיךָ לְפָנֶיךָ וְהָיָה מַחֲנֶיךָ קָדוֹשׁ וְלֹא־יִרְאֶה בְךָ עֶרְוַת דָּבָר וְשָׁב מֵאַֽחֲרֶֽיךָ׃ ס 16 לֹא־תַסְגִּיר עֶבֶד אֶל־אֲדֹנָיו אֲשֶׁר־יִנָּצֵל אֵלֶיךָ מֵעִם אֲדֹנָֽיו׃

17 עִמְּךָ יֵשֵׁב בְּקִרְבְּךָ בַּמָּקוֹם אֲשֶׁר־יִבְחַר בְּאַחַד שְׁעָרֶיךָ בַּטּוֹב לוֹ לֹא תּוֹנֶֽנּוּ׃ ס 18 לֹא־ תִהְיֶה קְדֵשָׁה מִבְּנוֹת יִשְׂרָאֵל וְלֹא־יִהְיֶה קָדֵשׁ מִבְּנֵי יִשְׂרָאֵֽל׃ 19 לֹא־תָבִיא אֶתְנַן זוֹנָה וּמְחִיר כֶּלֶב בֵּית יְהוָה אֱלֹהֶיךָ לְכָל־נֶדֶר כִּי תֽוֹעֲבַת יְהוָה אֱלֹהֶיךָ גַּם־שְׁנֵיהֶֽם׃ 20 לֹא־תַשִּׁיךְ לְאָחִיךָ נֶשֶׁךְ כֶּסֶף נֶשֶׁךְ אֹכֶל נֶשֶׁךְ כָּל־דָּבָר אֲשֶׁר יִשָּֽׁךְ׃ 21 לַנָּכְרִי תַשִּׁיךְ וּלְאָחִיךָ לֹא תַשִּׁיךְ לְמַעַן יְבָרֶכְךָ יְהוָה אֱלֹהֶיךָ בְּכֹל מִשְׁלַח יָדֶךָ עַל־הָאָרֶץ אֲשֶׁר־ אַתָּה בָא־שָׁמָּה לְרִשְׁתָּֽהּ׃ ס 22 כִּֽי־תִדֹּר נֶדֶר לַיהוָה אֱלֹהֶיךָ לֹא תְאַחֵר לְשַׁלְּמוֹ כִּֽי־דָרֹשׁ יִדְרְשֶׁנּוּ יְהוָה אֱלֹהֶיךָ מֵֽעִמָּךְ וְהָיָה בְךָ חֵֽטְא׃ 23 וְכִי תֶחְדַּל לִנְדֹּר לֹא־יִהְיֶה בְךָ חֵֽטְא׃ 24 מוֹצָא שְׂפָתֶיךָ תִּשְׁמֹר וְעָשִׂיתָ כַּאֲשֶׁר נָדַרְתָּ לַיהוָה אֱלֹהֶיךָ נְדָבָה אֲשֶׁר דִּבַּרְתָּ בְּפִֽיךָ׃ ס 25 כִּי תָבֹא בְּכֶרֶם רֵעֶךָ וְאָכַלְתָּ עֲנָבִים כְּנַפְשְׁךָ שָׂבְעֶךָ וְאֶל־

standing grain, you may pluck the heads with your hand, but you shall not use a sickle on your neighbor's standing grain.

24

"When a man takes a wife and marries her, and it happens that she finds no favor in his eyes because he has found some uncleanness in her, and he writes her a certificate of divorce, puts *it* in her hand, and sends her out of his house, ² when she has departed from his house, and goes and becomes another man's *wife,* ³ *if* the latter husband detests her and writes her a certificate of divorce, puts *it* in her hand, and sends her out of his house, or if the latter husband dies who took her as his wife, ⁴ *then* her former husband who divorced her must not take her back to be his wife after she has been defiled; for that *is* an abomination before the LORD, and you shall not bring sin on the land which the LORD your God is giving you *as* an inheritance.

⁵ "When a man has taken a new wife, he shall not go out to war or be charged with any business; he shall be free at home one year, and bring happiness to his wife whom he has taken.

⁶ "No man shall take the lower or the upper millstone in pledge, for he takes *one's* living in pledge.

⁷ "If a man is found kidnapping any of his brethren of the children of Israel, and mistreats him or sells him, then that kidnapper shall die; and you shall put away the evil from among you.

⁸ "Take heed in an outbreak of leprosy, that you carefully observe and do according to all that the priests, the Levites, shall teach you; just as I commanded them, *so* you shall be careful to do. ⁹ Remember what the LORD your God did to Miriam on the way when you came out of Egypt!

¹⁰ "When you lend your brother anything, you shall not go into his house to get his pledge. ¹¹ You shall stand outside, and the man to whom you lend shall bring the pledge out to you. ¹² And if the man *is* poor, you shall not keep his pledge overnight. ¹³ You shall in any case return the pledge to him again when the sun goes down, that he may sleep in his own garment and bless you; and it shall be righteousness to you before the LORD your God.

¹⁴ "You shall not oppress a hired servant *who is* poor and needy, *whether* one of your brethren or one of the aliens who *is* in your land within your gates. ¹⁵ Each day you shall give *him* his wages, and not let the sun go down on it, for he *is* poor and has set his heart on it; lest he cry out against you to the LORD, and it be sin to you.

כְּלֶךָ לֹא תִתֵּן ס 26 כִּי תָבֹא בְּקָמַת רֵעֶךָ וְקָטַפְתָּ מְלִילֹת בְּיָדֶךָ וְחֶרְמֵשׁ לֹא תָנִיף עַל קָמַת רֵעֶךָ: ס

כד כִּי־יִקַּח אִישׁ אִשָּׁה וּבְעָלָהּ וְהָיָה אִם־ לֹא תִמְצָא־חֵן בְּעֵינָיו כִּי־מָצָא בָהּ עֶרְוַת דָּבָר וְכָתַב לָהּ סֵפֶר כְּרִיתֻת וְנָתַן בְּיָדָהּ וְשִׁלְּחָהּ מִבֵּיתוֹ: 2 וְיָצְאָה מִבֵּיתוֹ וְהָלְכָה וְהָיְתָה לְאִישׁ־ אַחֵר: 3 וּשְׂנֵאָהּ הָאִישׁ הָאַחֲרוֹן וְכָתַב לָהּ סֵפֶר כְּרִיתֻת וְנָתַן בְּיָדָהּ וְשִׁלְּחָהּ מִבֵּיתוֹ אוֹ כִי יָמוּת הָאִישׁ הָאַחֲרוֹן אֲשֶׁר־לְקָחָהּ לוֹ לְאִשָּׁה: 4 לֹא־ יוּכַל בַּעְלָהּ הָרִאשׁוֹן אֲשֶׁר־שִׁלְּחָהּ לָשׁוּב לְקַחְתָּהּ לִהְיוֹת לוֹ לְאִשָּׁה אַחֲרֵי אֲשֶׁר הֻטַּמָּאָה כִּי־תוֹעֵבָה הִוא לִפְנֵי יְהוָה וְלֹא תַחֲטִיא אֶת־הָאָרֶץ אֲשֶׁר יְהוָה אֱלֹהֶיךָ נֹתֵן לְךָ נַחֲלָה: ס 5 כִּי־יִקַּח אִישׁ אִשָּׁה חֲדָשָׁה לֹא יֵצֵא בַּצָּבָא וְלֹא־יַעֲבֹר עָלָיו לְכָל־דָּבָר נָקִי יִהְיֶה לְבֵיתוֹ שָׁנָה אֶחָת וְשִׂמַּח אֶת־ אִשְׁתּוֹ אֲשֶׁר־לָקָח: ס 6 לֹא־יַחֲבֹל רֵחַיִם וָרָכֶב כִּי־נֶפֶשׁ הוּא חֹבֵל: ס 7 כִּי־יִמָּצֵא אִישׁ גֹּנֵב נֶפֶשׁ מֵאֶחָיו מִבְּנֵי יִשְׂרָאֵל וְהִתְעַמֶּר־בּוֹ וּמְכָרוֹ וּמֵת הַגַּנָּב הַהוּא וּבִעַרְתָּ הָרָע מִקִּרְבֶּךָ: 8 הִשָּׁמֶר בְּנֶגַע־הַצָּרַעַת לִשְׁמֹר מְאֹד וְלַעֲשׂוֹת כְּכֹל אֲשֶׁר־יוֹרוּ אֶתְכֶם הַכֹּהֲנִים הַלְוִיִּם כַּאֲשֶׁר צִוִּיתִם תִּשְׁמְרוּ לַעֲשׂוֹת: ס 9 זָכוֹר אֵת אֲשֶׁר־עָשָׂה יְהוָה אֱלֹהֶיךָ לְמִרְיָם בַּדֶּרֶךְ בְּצֵאתְכֶם מִמִּצְרָיִם: ס 10 כִּי־תַשֶּׁה בְרֵעֲךָ מַשַּׁאת מְאוּמָה לֹא־תָבֹא אֶל־בֵּיתוֹ לַעֲבֹט עֲבֹטוֹ: 11 בַּחוּץ תַּעֲמֹד וְהָאִישׁ אֲשֶׁר אַתָּה נֹשֶׁה בוֹ יוֹצִיא אֵלֶיךָ אֶת־הַעֲבוֹט הַחוּצָה: 12 וְאִם־אִישׁ עָנִי הוּא לֹא תִשְׁכַּב בַּעֲבֹטוֹ: 13 הָשֵׁב תָּשִׁיב לוֹ אֶת־הַעֲבוֹט כְּבֹא הַשֶּׁמֶשׁ וְשָׁכַב בְּשַׂלְמָתוֹ וּבֵרְכֶךָּ וּלְךָ תִּהְיֶה צְדָקָה לִפְנֵי יְהוָה אֱלֹהֶיךָ: ס 14 לֹא־ תַעֲשֹׁק שָׂכִיר עָנִי וְאֶבְיוֹן מֵאַחֶיךָ אוֹ מִגֵּרְךָ אֲשֶׁר בְּאַרְצְךָ בִּשְׁעָרֶיךָ: 15 בְּיוֹמוֹ תִתֵּן שְׂכָרוֹ וְלֹא־ תָבוֹא עָלָיו הַשֶּׁמֶשׁ כִּי עָנִי הוּא וְאֵלָיו הוּא נֹשֵׂא אֶת־נַפְשׁוֹ וְלֹא־יִקְרָא עָלֶיךָ אֶל־יְהוָה וְהָיָה

[16]"Fathers shall not be put to death for *their* children, nor shall children be put to death for *their* fathers; a person shall be put to death for his own sin.

[17]"You shall not pervert justice due the stranger or the fatherless, nor take a widow's garment as a pledge. [18]But you shall remember that you were a slave in Egypt, and the LORD your God redeemed you from there; therefore I command you to do this thing.

[19]"When you reap your harvest in your field, and forget a sheaf in the field, you shall not go back to get it; it shall be for the stranger, the fatherless, and the widow, that the LORD your God may bless you in all the work of your hands. [20]When you beat your olive trees, you shall not go over the boughs again; it shall be for the stranger, the fatherless, and the widow. [21]When you gather the grapes of your vineyard, you shall not glean *it* afterward; it shall be for the stranger, the fatherless, and the widow. [22]And you shall remember that you were a slave in the land of Egypt; therefore I command you to do this thing.

25 "If there is a dispute between men, and they come to court, that *the judges* may judge them, and they justify the righteous and condemn the wicked, [2]then it shall be, if the wicked man deserves to be beaten, that the judge will cause him to lie down and be beaten in his presence, according to his guilt, with a certain number of blows. [3]Forty blows he may give him *and* no more, lest he should exceed this and beat him with many blows above these, and your brother be humiliated in your sight.

[4]"You shall not muzzle an ox while it treads out *the grain.*

[5]"If brothers dwell together, and one of them dies and has no son, the widow of the dead man shall not be *married* to a stranger outside *the family;* her husband's brother shall go in to her, take her as his wife, and perform the duty of a husband's brother to her. [6]And it shall be *that* the firstborn son which she bears will succeed to the name of his dead brother, that his name may not be blotted out of Israel. [7]But if the man does not want to take his brother's wife, then let his brother's wife go up to the gate to the elders, and say, 'My husband's brother refuses to raise up a name to his brother in Israel; he will not perform the duty of my husband's brother.' [8]Then the elders of his city shall call him and speak to him. But *if* he stands firm and says, 'I do not want to take her,' [9]then his brother's wife shall come to him in the presence of the elders, remove his sandal from his foot, spit in his face, and

16 לֹא־יוּמְת֨וּ אָב֤וֹת עַל־
בָּנִ֗ים וּבָנִ֖ים לֹא־יוּמְת֣וּ עַל־אָב֑וֹת אִ֥ישׁ בְּחֶטְא֖וֹ
יוּמָֽתוּ: ס 17 לֹ֣א תַטֶּ֔ה מִשְׁפַּ֖ט גֵּ֣ר יָת֑וֹם
וְלֹ֣א תַחֲבֹ֔ל בֶּ֖גֶד אַלְמָנָֽה: 18 וְזָ֣כַרְתָּ֗ כִּ֤י עֶ֨בֶד֙ הָיִ֨יתָ֙
בְּמִצְרַ֔יִם וַֽיִּפְדְּךָ֖ יְהוָ֣ה אֱלֹהֶ֑יךָ מִשָּׁ֑ם עַל־כֵּ֞ן אָֽנֹכִ֣י
מְצַוְּךָ֔ לַעֲשׂ֕וֹת אֶת־הַדָּבָ֖ר הַזֶּֽה: ס 19 כִּ֣י
תִקְצֹר֩ קְצִ֨ירְךָ֜ בְשָׂדֶ֗ךָ וְשָֽׁכַחְתָּ֧ עֹ֣מֶר בַּשָּׂדֶה֮ לֹ֣א
תָשׁוּב֮ לְקַחְתּוֹ֒ לַגֵּ֣ר לַיָּת֧וֹם וְלָאַלְמָנָ֖ה יִהְיֶ֑ה לְמַ֤עַן
יְבָרֶכְךָ֙ יְהוָ֣ה אֱלֹהֶ֔יךָ בְּכֹ֖ל מַעֲשֵׂ֣ה יָדֶֽיךָ: 20 כִּ֤י
תַחְבֹּט֙ זֵֽיתְךָ֔ לֹ֥א תְפַאֵ֖ר אַחֲרֶ֑יךָ לַגֵּ֛ר לַיָּת֥וֹם
וְלָאַלְמָנָ֖ה יִהְיֶֽה: 21 כִּ֤י תִבְצֹר֙ כַּרְמְךָ֔ ס
לֹ֥א תְעוֹלֵ֖ל אַחֲרֶ֑יךָ לַגֵּ֛ר לַיָּת֥וֹם וְלָאַלְמָנָ֖ה יִהְיֶֽה:
22 וְזָ֣כַרְתָּ֔ כִּי־עֶ֥בֶד הָיִ֖יתָ בְּאֶ֣רֶץ מִצְרָ֑יִם עַל־כֵּ֞ן אָנֹכִ֣י
מְצַוְּךָ֔ לַעֲשׂ֕וֹת אֶת־הַדָּבָ֖ר הַזֶּֽה: ס

כה כִּֽי־יִהְיֶ֥ה רִיב֙ בֵּ֣ין אֲנָשִׁ֔ים וְנִגְּשׁ֖וּ אֶל־
הַמִּשְׁפָּ֖ט וּשְׁפָט֑וּם וְהִצְדִּ֨יקוּ֙ אֶת־הַצַּדִּ֔יק וְהִרְשִׁ֖יעוּ
אֶת־הָרָשָֽׁע: 2 וְהָיָ֛ה אִם־בִּ֥ן הַכּ֖וֹת הָרָשָׁ֑ע
וְהִפִּיל֤וֹ הַשֹּׁפֵט֙ וְהִכָּ֣הוּ לְפָנָ֔יו כְּדֵ֥י רִשְׁעָת֖וֹ
בְּמִסְפָּֽר: 3 אַרְבָּעִ֥ים יַכֶּ֖נּוּ לֹ֣א יֹסִ֑יף פֶּן־
יֹסִ֨יף לְהַכֹּת֤וֹ עַל־אֵ֨לֶּה֙ מַכָּ֣ה רַבָּ֔ה וְנִקְלָ֥ה
אָחִ֖יךָ לְעֵינֶֽיךָ: ס 4 לֹא־תַחְסֹ֥ם שׁ֖וֹר
בְּדִישֽׁוֹ: ס 5 כִּֽי־יֵשְׁב֨וּ אַחִ֤ים יַחְדָּו֙ וּמֵ֨ת
אַחַ֤ד מֵהֶם֙ וּבֵ֣ן אֵֽין־ל֔וֹ לֹֽא־תִהְיֶ֧ה אֵֽשֶׁת־הַמֵּ֛ת
הַח֖וּצָה לְאִ֣ישׁ זָ֑ר יְבָמָהּ֙ יָבֹ֣א עָלֶ֔יהָ וּלְקָחָ֥הּ ל֛וֹ
לְאִשָּׁ֖ה וְיִבְּמָֽהּ: 6 וְהָיָ֗ה הַבְּכוֹר֙ אֲשֶׁ֣ר תֵּלֵ֔ד יָק֕וּם
עַל־שֵׁ֥ם אָחִ֖יו הַמֵּ֑ת וְלֹֽא־יִמָּחֶ֥ה שְׁמ֖וֹ מִיִּשְׂרָאֵֽל:
7 וְאִם־לֹ֤א יַחְפֹּץ֙ הָאִ֔ישׁ לָקַ֖חַת אֶת־יְבִמְתּ֑וֹ וְעָלְתָה֩
יְבִמְתּ֨וֹ הַשַּׁ֜עְרָה אֶל־הַזְּקֵנִ֗ים וְאָֽמְרָה֙ מֵאֵ֤ן יְבָמִי֙
לְהָקִ֨ים לְאָחִ֥יו שֵׁם֙ בְּיִשְׂרָאֵ֔ל לֹ֥א אָבָ֖ה יַבְּמִֽי:
8 וְקָֽרְאוּ־ל֥וֹ זִקְנֵֽי־עִיר֖וֹ וְדִבְּר֣וּ אֵלָ֑יו וְעָמַ֣ד וְאָמַ֔ר
לֹ֥א חָפַ֖צְתִּי לְקַחְתָּֽהּ: 9 וְנִגְּשָׁ֨ה יְבִמְתּ֣וֹ אֵלָיו֮
לְעֵינֵ֣י הַזְּקֵנִים֒ וְחָלְצָ֤ה נַעֲלוֹ֙ מֵעַ֣ל רַגְל֔וֹ וְיָרְקָ֖ה
בְּפָנָ֑יו וְעָֽנְתָה֙ וְאָ֣מְרָ֔ה כָּ֚כָה יֵעָשֶׂ֣ה לָאִ֔ישׁ

answer and say, 'So shall it be done to the man who will not build up his brother's house.' [10] And his name shall be called in Israel, 'The house of him who had his sandal removed.'

[11] "If *two* men fight together, and the wife of one draws near to rescue her husband from the hand of the one attacking him, and puts out her hand and seizes him by the genitals, [12] then you shall cut off her hand; your eye shall not pity *her*.

[13] "You shall not have in your bag differing weights, a heavy and a light. [14] You shall not have in your house differing measures, a large and a small. [15] You shall have a perfect and just weight, a perfect and just measure, that your days may be lengthened in the land which the LORD your God is giving you. [16] For all who do such things, all who behave unrighteously, *are* an abomination to the LORD your God.

[17] "Remember what Amalek did to you on the way as you were coming out of Egypt, [18] how he met you on the way and attacked your rear ranks, all the stragglers at your rear, when you *were* tired and weary; and he did not fear God. [19] Therefore it shall be, when the LORD your God has given you rest from your enemies all around, in the land which the LORD your God is giving you to possess *as* an inheritance, *that* you will blot out the remembrance of Amalek from under heaven. You shall not forget.

26 "And it shall be, when you come into the land which the LORD your God is giving you *as* an inheritance, and you possess it and dwell in it, [2] that you shall take some of the first of all the produce of the ground, which you shall bring from your land that the LORD your God is giving you, and put *it* in a basket and go to the place where the LORD your God chooses to make His name abide. [3] And you shall go to the one who is priest in those days, and say to him, 'I declare today to the LORD your God that I have come to the country which the LORD swore to our fathers to give us.'

[4] "Then the priest shall take the basket out of your hand and set it down before the altar of the LORD your God. [5] And you shall answer and say before the LORD your God: 'My father *was* a Syrian, about to perish, and he went down to Egypt and dwelt there, few in number; and there he became a nation, great, mighty, and populous. [6] But the Egyptians mistreated us, afflicted us, and laid hard bondage on us. [7] Then we cried out to the LORD God of our fathers, and the LORD heard our voice and looked on our affliction and our labor and our oppression. [8] So the LORD brought us out

10 וְנִקְרָא שְׁמֹו אֲשֶׁר לֹא־יִבְנֶה אֶת־בֵּית אָחִיו בְּיִשְׂרָאֵל בֵּית חֲלוּץ הַנָּעַל׃ ס 11 כִּי־ יִנָּצוּ אֲנָשִׁים יַחְדָּו אִישׁ וְאָחִיו וְקָרְבָה אֵשֶׁת הָאֶחָד לְהַצִּיל אֶת־אִישָׁהּ מִיַּד מַכֵּהוּ וְשָׁלְחָה יָדָהּ וְהֶחֱזִיקָה בִּמְבֻשָׁיו׃ 12 וְקַצֹּתָה אֶת־כַּפָּהּ לֹא תָחֹום עֵינֶךָ׃ ס 13 לֹא־יִהְיֶה לְךָ בְּכִיסְךָ אֶבֶן וָאֶבֶן גְּדֹולָה וּקְטַנָּה׃ ס 14 לֹא־יִהְיֶה לְךָ בְּבֵיתְךָ אֵיפָה וְאֵיפָה גְּדֹולָה וּקְטַנָּה׃ 15 אֶבֶן שְׁלֵמָה וָצֶדֶק יִהְיֶה־לָּךְ אֵיפָה שְׁלֵמָה וָצֶדֶק יִהְיֶה־לָּךְ לְמַעַן יַאֲרִיכוּ יָמֶיךָ עַל הָאֲדָמָה אֲשֶׁר־יְהוָה אֱלֹהֶיךָ נֹתֵן לָךְ׃ 16 כִּי תֹועֲבַת יְהוָה אֱלֹהֶיךָ כָּל־עֹשֵׂה אֵלֶּה כֹּל עֹשֵׂה עָוֶל׃ פ

17 זָכֹור אֵת אֲשֶׁר־עָשָׂה לְךָ עֲמָלֵק בַּדֶּרֶךְ בְּצֵאתְכֶם מִמִּצְרָיִם׃ 18 אֲשֶׁר קָרְךָ בַּדֶּרֶךְ וַיְזַנֵּב בְּךָ כָּל־ הַנֶּחֱשָׁלִים אַחֲרֶיךָ וְאַתָּה עָיֵף וְיָגֵעַ וְלֹא יָרֵא אֱלֹהִים׃ 19 וְהָיָה בְּהָנִיחַ יְהוָה אֱלֹהֶיךָ ׀ לְךָ מִכָּל־ אֹיְבֶיךָ מִסָּבִיב בָּאָרֶץ אֲשֶׁר יְהוָה־אֱלֹהֶיךָ נֹתֵן לְךָ נַחֲלָה לְרִשְׁתָּהּ תִּמְחֶה אֶת־זֵכֶר עֲמָלֵק מִתַּחַת הַשָּׁמָיִם לֹא תִּשְׁכָּח׃ פ

כו וְהָיָה כִּי־תָבֹוא אֶל־הָאָרֶץ אֲשֶׁר יְהוָה אֱלֹהֶיךָ נֹתֵן לְךָ נַחֲלָה וִירִשְׁתָּהּ וְיָשַׁבְתָּ בָּהּ׃ 2 וְלָקַחְתָּ מֵרֵאשִׁית ׀ כָּל־פְּרִי הָאֲדָמָה אֲשֶׁר תָּבִיא מֵאַרְצְךָ אֲשֶׁר יְהוָה אֱלֹהֶיךָ נֹתֵן לָךְ וְשַׂמְתָּ בַטֶּנֶא וְהָלַכְתָּ אֶל־הַמָּקֹום אֲשֶׁר יִבְחַר יְהוָה אֱלֹהֶיךָ לְשַׁכֵּן שְׁמֹו שָׁם׃ 3 וּבָאתָ אֶל־הַכֹּהֵן אֲשֶׁר יִהְיֶה בַּיָּמִים הָהֵם וְאָמַרְתָּ אֵלָיו הִגַּדְתִּי הַיֹּום לַיהוָה אֱלֹהֶיךָ כִּי־בָאתִי אֶל־הָאָרֶץ אֲשֶׁר נִשְׁבַּע יְהוָה לַאֲבֹתֵינוּ לָתֶת לָנוּ׃

4 וְלָקַח הַכֹּהֵן הַטֶּנֶא מִיָּדֶךָ וְהִנִּיחֹו לִפְנֵי מִזְבַּח יְהוָה אֱלֹהֶיךָ׃ 5 וְעָנִיתָ וְאָמַרְתָּ לִפְנֵי ׀ יְהוָה אֱלֹהֶיךָ אֲרַמִּי אֹבֵד אָבִי וַיֵּרֶד מִצְרַיְמָה וַיָּגָר שָׁם בִּמְתֵי מְעָט וַיְהִי־שָׁם לְגֹוי גָּדֹול עָצוּם וָרָב׃ 6 וַיָּרֵעוּ אֹתָנוּ הַמִּצְרִים וַיְעַנּוּנוּ וַיִּתְּנוּ עָלֵינוּ עֲבֹדָה קָשָׁה׃ 7 וַנִּצְעַק אֶל־יְהוָה אֱלֹהֵי אֲבֹתֵינוּ וַיִּשְׁמַע יְהוָה אֶת־קֹלֵנוּ וַיַּרְא אֶת־עָנְיֵנוּ וְאֶת־עֲמָלֵנוּ וְאֶת־לַחֲצֵנוּ׃ 8 וַיֹּוצִאֵנוּ

of Egypt with a mighty hand and with an out-stretched arm, with great terror and with signs and wonders. [9] He has brought us to this place and has given us this land, "a land flowing with milk and honey"; [10] and now, behold, I have brought the firstfruits of the land which you, O LORD, have given me.'

"Then you shall set it before the LORD your God, and worship before the LORD your God. [11] So you shall rejoice in every good *thing* which the LORD your God has given to you and your house, you and the Levite and the stranger who *is* among you.

[12] "When you have finished laying aside all the tithe of your increase in the third year—the year of tithing—and have given *it* to the Levite, the stranger, the fatherless, and the widow, so that they may eat within your gates and be filled, [13] then you shall say before the LORD your God: 'I have removed the holy *tithe* from *my* house, and also have given them to the Levite, the stranger, the fatherless, and the widow, according to all Your commandments which You have commanded me; I have not transgressed Your commandments, nor have I forgotten *them*. [14] I have not eaten any of it when in mourning, nor have I removed *any* of it for an unclean *use*, nor given *any* of it for the dead. I have obeyed the voice of the LORD my God, and have done according to all that You have com-manded me. [15] Look down from Your holy habita-tion, from heaven, and bless Your people Israel and the land which You have given us, just as You swore to our fathers, "a land flowing with milk and honey." '

[16] "This day the LORD your God commands you to observe these statutes and judgments; therefore you shall be careful to observe them with all your heart and with all your soul. [17] Today you have proclaimed the LORD to be your God, and that you will walk in His ways and keep His statutes, His commandments, and His judgments, and that you will obey His voice. [18] Also today the LORD has proclaimed you to be His special people, just as He promised you, that *you* should keep all His commandments, [19] and that He will set you high above all nations which He has made, in praise, in name, and in honor, and that you may be a holy people to the LORD your God, just as He has spoken."

27 Now Moses, with the elders of Israel, commanded the people, saying: "Keep all the commandments which I command you today. [2] And it shall be, on the day when you cross over the Jordan to the land which the LORD your God is

יְהוָה מִמִּצְרַיִם בְּיָד חֲזָקָה וּבִזְרֹעַ נְטוּיָה וּבְמֹרָא גָּדֹל וּבְאֹתוֹת וּבְמֹפְתִים: [9] וַיְבִאֵנוּ אֶל־הַמָּקוֹם הַזֶּה וַיִּתֶּן־לָנוּ אֶת־הָאָרֶץ הַזֹּאת אֶרֶץ זָבַת חָלָב וּדְבָשׁ:

[10] וְעַתָּה הִנֵּה הֵבֵאתִי אֶת־רֵאשִׁית פְּרִי הָאֲדָמָה אֲשֶׁר־נָתַתָּה לִּי יְהוָה וְהִנַּחְתּוֹ לִפְנֵי יְהוָה אֱלֹהֶיךָ וְהִשְׁתַּחֲוִיתָ לִפְנֵי יְהוָה אֱלֹהֶיךָ: [11] וְשָׂמַחְתָּ בְכָל־הַטּוֹב אֲשֶׁר נָתַן־לְךָ יְהוָה אֱלֹהֶיךָ וּלְבֵיתֶךָ אַתָּה וְהַלֵּוִי וְהַגֵּר אֲשֶׁר בְּקִרְבֶּךָ: ס [12] כִּי תְכַלֶּה לַעְשֵׂר אֶת־כָּל־מַעְשַׂר תְּבוּאָתְךָ בַּשָּׁנָה הַשְּׁלִישִׁת שְׁנַת הַמַּעֲשֵׂר וְנָתַתָּה לַלֵּוִי לַגֵּר לַיָּתוֹם וְלָאַלְמָנָה וְאָכְלוּ בִשְׁעָרֶיךָ וְשָׂבֵעוּ: [13] וְאָמַרְתָּ לִפְנֵי יְהוָה אֱלֹהֶיךָ בִּעַרְתִּי הַקֹּדֶשׁ מִן־הַבַּיִת וְגַם נְתַתִּיו לַלֵּוִי וְלַגֵּר לַיָּתוֹם וְלָאַלְמָנָה כְּכָל־מִצְוָתְךָ אֲשֶׁר צִוִּיתָנִי לֹא־עָבַרְתִּי מִמִּצְוֹתֶיךָ וְלֹא שָׁכָחְתִּי: [14] לֹא־אָכַלְתִּי בְאֹנִי מִמֶּנּוּ וְלֹא־בִעַרְתִּי מִמֶּנּוּ בְּטָמֵא וְלֹא־נָתַתִּי מִמֶּנּוּ לְמֵת שָׁמַעְתִּי בְּקוֹל יְהוָה אֱלֹהָי עָשִׂיתִי כְּכֹל אֲשֶׁר צִוִּיתָנִי: [15] הַשְׁקִיפָה מִמְּעוֹן קָדְשְׁךָ מִן־הַשָּׁמַיִם וּבָרֵךְ אֶת־עַמְּךָ אֶת־יִשְׂרָאֵל וְאֵת הָאֲדָמָה אֲשֶׁר נָתַתָּה לָנוּ כַּאֲשֶׁר נִשְׁבַּעְתָּ לַאֲבֹתֵינוּ אֶרֶץ זָבַת חָלָב וּדְבָשׁ: ס [16] הַיּוֹם הַזֶּה יְהוָה אֱלֹהֶיךָ מְצַוְּךָ לַעֲשׂוֹת אֶת־הַחֻקִּים הָאֵלֶּה וְאֶת־הַמִּשְׁפָּטִים וְשָׁמַרְתָּ וְעָשִׂיתָ אוֹתָם בְּכָל־לְבָבְךָ וּבְכָל־נַפְשֶׁךָ:

[17] אֶת־יְהוָה הֶאֱמַרְתָּ הַיּוֹם לִהְיוֹת לְךָ לֵאלֹהִים וְלָלֶכֶת בִּדְרָכָיו וְלִשְׁמֹר חֻקָּיו וּמִצְוֹתָיו וּמִשְׁפָּטָיו וְלִשְׁמֹעַ בְּקֹלוֹ: [18] וַיהוָה הֶאֱמִירְךָ הַיּוֹם לִהְיוֹת לוֹ לְעַם סְגֻלָּה כַּאֲשֶׁר דִּבֶּר־לָךְ וְלִשְׁמֹר כָּל־מִצְוֹתָיו: [19] וּלְתִתְּךָ עֶלְיוֹן עַל כָּל־הַגּוֹיִם אֲשֶׁר עָשָׂה לִתְהִלָּה וּלְשֵׁם וּלְתִפְאָרֶת וְלִהְיֹתְךָ עַם־קָדֹשׁ לַיהוָה אֱלֹהֶיךָ כַּאֲשֶׁר דִּבֵּר:

כז וַיְצַו מֹשֶׁה וְזִקְנֵי יִשְׂרָאֵל אֶת־הָעָם לֵאמֹר שָׁמֹר אֶת־כָּל־הַמִּצְוָה אֲשֶׁר אָנֹכִי מְצַוֶּה אֶתְכֶם הַיּוֹם: [2] וְהָיָה בַּיּוֹם אֲשֶׁר תַּעַבְרוּ אֶת־הַיַּרְדֵּן אֶל־הָאָרֶץ אֲשֶׁר־יְהוָה אֱלֹהֶיךָ נֹתֵן לָךְ וַהֲקֵמֹתָ לְךָ אֲבָנִים

giving you, that you shall set up for yourselves large stones, and whitewash them with lime. ³You shall write on them all the words of this law, when you have crossed over, that you may enter the land which the LORD your God is giving you, 'a land flowing with milk and honey,' just as the LORD God of your fathers promised you. ⁴Therefore it shall be, when you have crossed over the Jordan, *that* on Mount Ebal you shall set up these stones, which I command you today, and you shall whitewash them with lime. ⁵And there you shall build an altar to the LORD your God, an altar of stones; you shall not use an iron *tool* on them. ⁶You shall build with whole stones the altar of the LORD your God, and offer burnt offerings on it to the LORD your God. ⁷You shall offer peace offerings, and shall eat there, and rejoice before the LORD your God. ⁸And you shall write very plainly on the stones all the words of this law. "

⁹Then Moses and the priests, the Levites, spoke to all Israel, saying, "Take heed and listen, O Israel: This day you have become the people of the LORD your God. ¹⁰Therefore you shall obey the voice of the LORD your God, and observe His commandments and His statutes which I command you today."

¹¹And Moses commanded the people on the same day, saying, ¹²"These shall stand on Mount Gerizim to bless the people, when you have crossed over the Jordan: Simeon, Levi, Judah, Issachar, Joseph, and Benjamin; ¹³and these shall stand on Mount Ebal to curse: Reuben, Gad, Asher, Zebulun, Dan, and Naphtali.

¹⁴"And the Levites shall speak with a loud voice and say to all the men of Israel: ¹⁵'Cursed *is* the one who makes a carved or molded image, an abomination to the LORD, the work of the hands of the craftsman, and sets *it* up in secret.'

"And all the people shall answer and say, 'Amen!'

¹⁶'Cursed *is* the one who treats his father or his mother with contempt.'

"And all the people shall say, 'Amen!'

¹⁷'Cursed *is* the one who moves his neighbor's landmark.'

"And all the people shall say, 'Amen!'

¹⁸'Cursed *is* the one who makes the blind to wander off the road.'

"And all the people shall say, 'Amen!'

¹⁹'Cursed *is* the one who perverts the justice due the stranger, the fatherless, and widow.'

"And all the people shall say, 'Amen!'

²⁰'Cursed *is* the one who lies with his father's wife, because he has uncovered his father's bed.'

גְּדֹלוֹת וְשַׂדְתָּ אֹתָם בַּשִּׂיד: ³ וְכָתַבְתָּ עֲלֵיהֶן אֶת־כָּל־דִּבְרֵי הַתּוֹרָה הַזֹּאת בְּעָבְרֶךָ לְמַעַן אֲשֶׁר תָּבֹא אֶל־הָאָרֶץ אֲשֶׁר־יְהוָה אֱלֹהֶיךָ | נֹתֵן לְךָ אֶרֶץ זָבַת חָלָב וּדְבַשׁ כַּאֲשֶׁר דִּבֶּר יְהוָה אֱלֹהֵי־אֲבֹתֶיךָ לָךְ:

⁴ וְהָיָה בְּעָבְרְכֶם אֶת־הַיַּרְדֵּן תָּקִימוּ אֶת־הָאֲבָנִים הָאֵלֶּה אֲשֶׁר אָנֹכִי מְצַוֶּה אֶתְכֶם הַיּוֹם בְּהַר עֵיבָל וְשַׂדְתָּ אוֹתָם בַּשִּׂיד: ⁵ וּבָנִיתָ שָּׁם מִזְבֵּחַ לַיהוָה אֱלֹהֶיךָ מִזְבַּח אֲבָנִים לֹא־תָנִיף עֲלֵיהֶם בַּרְזֶל:

⁶ אֲבָנִים שְׁלֵמוֹת תִּבְנֶה אֶת־מִזְבַּח יְהוָה אֱלֹהֶיךָ וְהַעֲלִיתָ עָלָיו עוֹלֹת לַיהוָה אֱלֹהֶיךָ: ⁷ וְזָבַחְתָּ שְׁלָמִים וְאָכַלְתָּ שָּׁם וְשָׂמַחְתָּ לִפְנֵי יְהוָה אֱלֹהֶיךָ:

⁸ וְכָתַבְתָּ עַל־הָאֲבָנִים אֶת־כָּל־דִּבְרֵי הַתּוֹרָה הַזֹּאת בַּאֵר הֵיטֵב: ס ⁹ וַיְדַבֵּר מֹשֶׁה וְהַכֹּהֲנִים הַלְוִיִּם אֶל כָּל־יִשְׂרָאֵל לֵאמֹר הַסְכֵּת | וּשְׁמַע יִשְׂרָאֵל הַיּוֹם הַזֶּה נִהְיֵיתָ לְעָם לַיהוָה אֱלֹהֶיךָ: ¹⁰ וְשָׁמַעְתָּ בְּקוֹל יְהוָה אֱלֹהֶיךָ וְעָשִׂיתָ אֶת־מִצְוֹתָו וְאֶת־חֻקָּיו אֲשֶׁר אָנֹכִי מְצַוְּךָ הַיּוֹם: ס ¹¹ וַיְצַו מֹשֶׁה אֶת־הָעָם בַּיּוֹם הַהוּא לֵאמֹר: ¹² אֵלֶּה יַעַמְדוּ לְבָרֵךְ אֶת־הָעָם עַל־הַר גְּרִזִים בְּעָבְרְכֶם אֶת־הַיַּרְדֵּן שִׁמְעוֹן וְלֵוִי וִיהוּדָה וְיִשָּׂשכָר וְיוֹסֵף וּבִנְיָמִן:

¹³ וְאֵלֶּה יַעַמְדוּ עַל־הַקְּלָלָה בְּהַר עֵיבָל רְאוּבֵן גָּד וְאָשֵׁר וּזְבוּלֻן דָּן וְנַפְתָּלִי: ¹⁴ וְעָנוּ הַלְוִיִּם וְאָמְרוּ אֶל־כָּל־אִישׁ יִשְׂרָאֵל קוֹל רָם: ס ¹⁵ אָרוּר הָאִישׁ אֲשֶׁר יַעֲשֶׂה פֶסֶל וּמַסֵּכָה תּוֹעֲבַת יְהוָה מַעֲשֵׂה יְדֵי חָרָשׁ וְשָׂם בַּסָּתֶר וְעָנוּ כָל־הָעָם וְאָמְרוּ אָמֵן: ס ¹⁶ אָרוּר מַקְלֶה אָבִיו וְאִמּוֹ וְאָמַר כָּל־הָעָם אָמֵן: ס ¹⁷ אָרוּר מַסִּיג גְּבוּל רֵעֵהוּ וְאָמַר כָּל־הָעָם אָמֵן: ס ¹⁸ אָרוּר מַשְׁגֶּה עִוֵּר בַּדָּרֶךְ וְאָמַר כָּל־הָעָם אָמֵן: ס ¹⁹ אָרוּר מַטֶּה מִשְׁפַּט גֵּר־יָתוֹם וְאַלְמָנָה וְאָמַר כָּל־הָעָם אָמֵן: ס ²⁰ אָרוּר שֹׁכֵב עִם־אֵשֶׁת אָבִיו כִּי גִלָּה כְּנַף אָבִיו וְאָמַר כָּל־הָעָם

"And all the people shall say, 'Amen!'
²¹'Cursed *is* the one who lies with any kind of animal.'

"And all the people shall say, 'Amen!'
²²'Cursed *is* the one who lies with his sister, the daughter of his father or the daughter of his mother.'

"And all the people shall say, 'Amen!'
²³'Cursed *is* the one who lies with his mother-in-law.'

"And all the people shall say, 'Amen!'
²⁴'Cursed *is* the one who attacks his neighbor secretly.'

"And all the people shall say, 'Amen!'
²⁵'Cursed *is* the one who takes a bribe to slay an innocent person.'

"And all the people shall say, 'Amen!'
²⁶'Cursed *is* the one who does not confirm *all* the words of this law.'

"And all the people shall say, 'Amen!'"

28 "Now it shall come to pass, if you diligently obey the voice of the LORD your God, to observe carefully all His commandments which I command you today, that the LORD your God will set you high above all nations of the earth. ²And all these blessings shall come upon you and overtake you, because you obey the voice of the LORD your God:

³"Blessed *shall* you *be* in the city, and blessed *shall* you *be* in the country.

⁴"Blessed *shall be* the fruit of your body, the produce of your ground and the increase of your herds, the increase of your cattle and the offspring of your flocks.

⁵"Blessed *shall be* your basket and your kneading bowl.

⁶"Blessed *shall* you *be* when you come in, and blessed *shall* you *be* when you go out.

⁷"The LORD will cause your enemies who rise against you to be defeated before your face; they shall come out against you one way and flee before you seven ways.

⁸"The LORD will command the blessing on you in your storehouses and in all to which you set your hand, and He will bless you in the land which the LORD your God is giving you.

⁹"The LORD will establish you as a holy people to Himself, just as He has sworn to you, if you keep the commandments of the LORD your God and walk in His ways. ¹⁰Then all peoples of the earth shall see that you are called by the name of the LORD, and they shall be afraid of you. ¹¹And the LORD will grant you plenty of goods, in the fruit of your body, in the increase of your livestock, and in

אָמֵן: ס 21 אָרוּר שֹׁכֵב עִם־כָּל־בְּהֵמָה וְאָמַר
כָּל־הָעָם אָמֵן: ס 22 אָרוּר שֹׁכֵב עִם־
אֲחֹתוֹ בַּת־אָבִיו אוֹ בַת־אִמּוֹ וְאָמַר כָּל־הָעָם
אָמֵן: ס 23 אָרוּר שֹׁכֵב עִם־חֹתַנְתּוֹ וְאָמַר כָּל־
הָעָם אָמֵן: ס 24 אָרוּר מַכֵּה רֵעֵהוּ בַּסָּתֶר
וְאָמַר כָּל־הָעָם אָמֵן: ס 25 אָרוּר לֹקֵחַ
שֹׁחַד לְהַכּוֹת נֶפֶשׁ דָּם נָקִי וְאָמַר כָּל־הָעָם
אָמֵן: ס 26 אָרוּר אֲשֶׁר לֹא־יָקִים אֶת־דִּבְרֵי
הַתּוֹרָה־הַזֹּאת לַעֲשׂוֹת אוֹתָם וְאָמַר כָּל־הָעָם
אָמֵן: פ

כח וְהָיָה אִם־שָׁמוֹעַ תִּשְׁמַע בְּקוֹל יְהוָה אֱלֹהֶיךָ
לִשְׁמֹר לַעֲשׂוֹת אֶת־כָּל־מִצְוֹתָיו אֲשֶׁר אָנֹכִי מְצַוְּךָ
הַיּוֹם וּנְתָנְךָ יְהוָה אֱלֹהֶיךָ עֶלְיוֹן עַל כָּל־גּוֹיֵי
הָאָרֶץ: 2 וּבָאוּ עָלֶיךָ כָּל־הַבְּרָכוֹת הָאֵלֶּה וְהִשִּׂיגֻךָ
כִּי תִשְׁמַע בְּקוֹל יְהוָה אֱלֹהֶיךָ: 3 בָּרוּךְ אַתָּה
בָּעִיר וּבָרוּךְ אַתָּה בַּשָּׂדֶה: 4 בָּרוּךְ פְּרִי־בִטְנְךָ וּפְרִי
אַדְמָתְךָ וּפְרִי בְהֶמְתֶּךָ שְׁגַר אֲלָפֶיךָ וְעַשְׁתְּרוֹת
צֹאנֶךָ: 5 בָּרוּךְ טַנְאֲךָ וּמִשְׁאַרְתֶּךָ: 6 בָּרוּךְ אַתָּה
בְּבֹאֶךָ וּבָרוּךְ אַתָּה בְּצֵאתֶךָ: 7 יִתֵּן יְהוָה אֶת־
אֹיְבֶיךָ הַקָּמִים עָלֶיךָ נִגָּפִים לְפָנֶיךָ בְּדֶרֶךְ אֶחָד
יֵצְאוּ אֵלֶיךָ וּבְשִׁבְעָה דְרָכִים יָנוּסוּ לְפָנֶיךָ: 8 יְצַו
יְהוָה אִתְּךָ אֶת־הַבְּרָכָה בַּאֲסָמֶיךָ וּבְכֹל מִשְׁלַח יָדֶךָ
וּבֵרַכְךָ בָּאָרֶץ אֲשֶׁר־יְהוָה אֱלֹהֶיךָ נֹתֵן לָךְ: 9 יְקִימְךָ
יְהוָה לוֹ לְעַם קָדוֹשׁ כַּאֲשֶׁר נִשְׁבַּע־לָךְ כִּי תִשְׁמֹר
אֶת־מִצְוֹת יְהוָה אֱלֹהֶיךָ וְהָלַכְתָּ בִּדְרָכָיו: 10 וְרָאוּ
כָּל־עַמֵּי הָאָרֶץ כִּי שֵׁם יְהוָה נִקְרָא עָלֶיךָ וְיָרְאוּ
מִמֶּךָּ: 11 וְהוֹתִרְךָ יְהוָה לְטוֹבָה בִּפְרִי בִטְנְךָ וּבִפְרִי
בְהֶמְתְּךָ וּבִפְרִי אַדְמָתֶךָ עַל הָאֲדָמָה אֲשֶׁר נִשְׁבַּע

the produce of your ground, in the land of which
the LORD swore to your fathers to give you. 12 The
LORD will open to you His good treasure, the
heavens, to give the rain to your land in its season,
and to bless all the work of your hand. You shall
lend to many nations, but you shall not borrow.
13 And the LORD will make you the head and not
the tail; you shall be above only, and not be
beneath, if you heed the commandments of the
LORD your God, which I command you today, and
are careful to observe *them*. 14 So you shall not turn
aside from any of the words which I command you
this day, *to* the right or the left, to go after other
gods to serve them.

15 "But it shall come to pass, if you do not obey
the voice of the LORD your God, to observe
carefully all His commandments and His statutes
which I command you today, that all these curses
will come upon you and overtake you:

16 "Cursed *shall* you *be* in the city, and cursed
shall you *be* in the country.

17 "Cursed *shall be* your basket and your kneading bowl.

18 "Cursed *shall be* the fruit of your body and the
produce of your land, the increase of your cattle
and the offspring of your flocks.

19 "Cursed *shall* you *be* when you come in, and
cursed *shall* you *be* when you go out.

20 "The LORD will send on you cursing, confusion, and rebuke in all that you set your hand to do,
until you are destroyed and until you perish
quickly, because of the wickedness of your doings
in which you have forsaken Me. 21 The LORD will
make the plague cling to you until He has
consumed you from the land which you are going
to possess. 22 The LORD will strike you with
consumption, with fever, with inflammation, with
severe burning fever, with the sword, with scorch-
ing, and with mildew; they shall pursue you until
you perish. 23 And your heavens which *are* over
your head shall be bronze, and the earth which is
under you *shall be* iron. 24 The LORD will change the
rain of your land to powder and dust; from the
heaven it shall come down on you until you are
destroyed.

25 "The LORD will cause you to be defeated
before your enemies; you shall go out one way
against them and flee seven ways before them; and
you shall become troublesome to all the kingdoms
of the earth. 26 Your carcasses shall be food for all
the birds of the air and the beasts of the earth, and
no one shall frighten *them* away. 27 The LORD will
strike you with the boils of Egypt, with tumors,
with the scab, and with the itch, from which you

יְהוָה לַאֲבֹתֶיךָ לָתֶת לָךְ: 12 יִפְתַּח יְהוָה ׀ לְךָ אֶת־
אוֹצָרוֹ הַטּוֹב אֶת־הַשָּׁמַיִם לָתֵת מְטַר־אַרְצְךָ בְּעִתּוֹ
וּלְבָרֵךְ אֵת כָּל־מַעֲשֵׂה יָדֶךָ וְהִלְוִיתָ גּוֹיִם רַבִּים
וְאַתָּה לֹא תִלְוֶה: 13 וּנְתָנְךָ יְהוָה לְרֹאשׁ וְלֹא לְזָנָב
וְהָיִיתָ רַק לְמַעְלָה וְלֹא תִהְיֶה לְמָטָּה כִּי־תִשְׁמַע
אֶל־מִצְוֺת ׀ יְהוָה אֱלֹהֶיךָ אֲשֶׁר אָנֹכִי מְצַוְּךָ הַיּוֹם
לִשְׁמֹר וְלַעֲשׂוֹת: 14 וְלֹא תָסוּר מִכָּל־הַדְּבָרִים אֲשֶׁר
אָנֹכִי מְצַוֶּה אֶתְכֶם הַיּוֹם יָמִין וּשְׂמֹאול לָלֶכֶת אַחֲרֵי
אֱלֹהִים אֲחֵרִים לְעָבְדָם: ס   15 וְהָיָה אִם־
לֹא תִשְׁמַע בְּקוֹל יְהוָה אֱלֹהֶיךָ לִשְׁמֹר לַעֲשׂוֹת
אֶת־כָּל־מִצְוֺתָיו וְחֻקֹּתָיו אֲשֶׁר אָנֹכִי מְצַוְּךָ הַיּוֹם
וּבָאוּ עָלֶיךָ כָּל־הַקְּלָלוֹת הָאֵלֶּה וְהִשִּׂיגוּךָ: 16 אָרוּר
אַתָּה בָּעִיר וְאָרוּר אַתָּה בַּשָּׂדֶה: 17 אָרוּר טַנְאֲךָ
וּמִשְׁאַרְתֶּךָ: 18 אָרוּר פְּרִי־בִטְנְךָ וּפְרִי אַדְמָתֶךָ שְׁגַר
אֲלָפֶיךָ וְעַשְׁתְּרֹת צֹאנֶךָ: 19 אָרוּר אַתָּה בְּבֹאֶךָ
וְאָרוּר אַתָּה בְּצֵאתֶךָ: 20 יְשַׁלַּח יְהוָה ׀ בְּךָ
אֶת־הַמְּאֵרָה אֶת־הַמְּהוּמָה וְאֶת־הַמִּגְעֶרֶת בְּכָל־
מִשְׁלַח יָדְךָ אֲשֶׁר תַּעֲשֶׂה עַד הִשָּׁמֶדְךָ וְעַד־
אֲבָדְךָ מַהֵר מִפְּנֵי רֹעַ מַעֲלָלֶיךָ אֲשֶׁר עֲזַבְתָּנִי:
21 יַדְבֵּק יְהוָה בְּךָ אֶת־הַדָּבֶר עַד כַּלֹּתוֹ אֹתְךָ
מֵעַל הָאֲדָמָה אֲשֶׁר־אַתָּה בָא־שָׁמָּה לְרִשְׁתָּהּ:
22 יַכְּכָה יְהוָה בַּשַּׁחֶפֶת וּבַקַּדַּחַת וּבַדַּלֶּקֶת וּבַחַרְחֻר
וּבַחֶרֶב וּבַשִּׁדָּפוֹן וּבַיֵּרָקוֹן וּרְדָפוּךָ עַד אָבְדֶךָ:
23 וְהָיוּ שָׁמֶיךָ אֲשֶׁר עַל־רֹאשְׁךָ נְחֹשֶׁת וְהָאָרֶץ
אֲשֶׁר־תַּחְתֶּיךָ בַּרְזֶל: 24 יִתֵּן יְהוָה אֶת־מְטַר אַרְצְךָ
אָבָק וְעָפָר מִן־הַשָּׁמַיִם יֵרֵד עָלֶיךָ עַד הִשָּׁמְדָךְ:
25 יִתֶּנְךָ יְהוָה ׀ נִגָּף לִפְנֵי אֹיְבֶיךָ בְּדֶרֶךְ אֶחָד תֵּצֵא
אֵלָיו וּבְשִׁבְעָה דְרָכִים תָּנוּס לְפָנָיו וְהָיִיתָ לְזַעֲוָה
לְכֹל מַמְלְכוֹת הָאָרֶץ: 26 וְהָיְתָה נִבְלָתְךָ לְמַאֲכָל
לְכָל־עוֹף הַשָּׁמַיִם וּלְבֶהֱמַת הָאָרֶץ וְאֵין מַחֲרִיד:
27 יַכְּכָה יְהוָה בִּשְׁחִין מִצְרַיִם וּבַעְפֹלִים וּבַגָּרָב

כח 27 וּבַטְּחֹרִים

cannot be healed. [28] The LORD will strike you with madness and blindness and confusion of heart. [29] And you shall grope at noonday, as a blind man gropes in darkness; you shall not prosper in your ways; you shall be only oppressed and plundered continually, and no one shall save *you*.

[30] "You shall betroth a wife, but another man shall lie with her; you shall build a house, but you shall not dwell in it; you shall plant a vineyard, but shall not gather its grapes. [31] Your ox *shall be* slaughtered before your eyes, but you shall not eat of it; your donkey *shall be* violently taken away from before you, and shall not be restored to you; your sheep *shall be* given to your enemies, and you shall have no one to rescue *them*. [32] Your sons and your daughters *shall be* given to another people, and your eyes shall look and fail *with longing* for them all day long; and *there shall be* no strength in your hand. [33] A nation whom you have not known shall eat the fruit of your land and the produce of your labor, and you shall be only oppressed and crushed continually. [34] So you shall be driven mad because of the sight which your eyes see. [35] The LORD will strike you in the knees and on the legs with severe boils which cannot be healed, and from the sole of your foot to the top of your head.

[36] "The LORD will bring you and the king whom you set over you to a nation which neither you nor your fathers have known, and there you shall serve other gods—wood and stone. [37] And you shall become an astonishment, a proverb, and a byword among all nations where the LORD will drive you.

[38] "You shall carry much seed out to the field but gather little in, for the locust shall consume it. [39] You shall plant vineyards and tend *them,* but you shall neither drink *of* the wine nor gather the *grapes;* for the worms shall eat them. [40] You shall have olive trees throughout all your territory, but you shall not anoint *yourself* with the oil; for your olives shall drop off. [41] You shall beget sons and daughters, but they shall not be yours; for they shall go into captivity. [42] Locusts shall consume all your trees and the produce of your land.

[43] "The alien who *is* among you shall rise higher and higher above you, and you shall come down lower and lower. [44] He shall lend to you, but you shall not lend to him; he shall be the head, and you shall be the tail.

[45] "Moreover all these curses shall come upon you and pursue and overtake you, until you are destroyed, because you did not obey the voice of the LORD your God, to keep His commandments and

וּבֶחָרֶס אֲשֶׁר לֹא־תוּכַל לְהֵרָפֵא: 28 יַכְּכָה יְהוָה בְּשִׁגָּעוֹן וּבְעִוָּרוֹן וּבְתִמְהוֹן לֵבָב: 29 וְהָיִיתָ מְמַשֵּׁשׁ בַּצָּהֳרַיִם כַּאֲשֶׁר יְמַשֵּׁשׁ הָעִוֵּר בָּאֲפֵלָה וְלֹא תַצְלִיחַ אֶת־דְּרָכֶיךָ וְהָיִיתָ אַךְ עָשׁוּק וְגָזוּל כָּל־הַיָּמִים וְאֵין מוֹשִׁיעַ: 30 אִשָּׁה תְאָרֵשׂ וְאִישׁ אַחֵר יִשְׁגָּלֶנָּה בַּיִת תִּבְנֶה וְלֹא־תֵשֵׁב בּוֹ כֶּרֶם תִּטַּע וְלֹא תְחַלְּלֶנּוּ: 31 שׁוֹרְךָ טָבוּחַ לְעֵינֶיךָ וְלֹא תֹאכַל מִמֶּנּוּ חֲמֹרְךָ גָּזוּל מִלְּפָנֶיךָ וְלֹא יָשׁוּב לָךְ צֹאנְךָ נְתֻנוֹת לְאֹיְבֶיךָ וְאֵין לְךָ מוֹשִׁיעַ: 32 בָּנֶיךָ וּבְנֹתֶיךָ נְתֻנִים לְעַם אַחֵר וְעֵינֶיךָ רֹאוֹת וְכָלוֹת אֲלֵיהֶם כָּל־הַיּוֹם וְאֵין לְאֵל יָדֶךָ: 33 פְּרִי אַדְמָתְךָ וְכָל־יְגִיעֲךָ יֹאכַל עַם אֲשֶׁר לֹא־יָדָעְתָּ וְהָיִיתָ רַק עָשׁוּק וְרָצוּץ כָּל־הַיָּמִים: 34 וְהָיִיתָ מְשֻׁגָּע מִמַּרְאֵה עֵינֶיךָ אֲשֶׁר תִּרְאֶה: 35 יַכְּכָה יְהוָה בִּשְׁחִין רָע עַל־הַבִּרְכַּיִם וְעַל־הַשֹּׁקַיִם אֲשֶׁר לֹא־תוּכַל לְהֵרָפֵא מִכַּף רַגְלְךָ וְעַד קָדְקֳדֶךָ: 36 יוֹלֵךְ יְהוָה אֹתְךָ וְאֶת־מַלְכְּךָ אֲשֶׁר תָּקִים עָלֶיךָ אֶל־גּוֹי אֲשֶׁר לֹא־יָדַעְתָּ אַתָּה וַאֲבֹתֶיךָ וְעָבַדְתָּ שָּׁם אֱלֹהִים אֲחֵרִים עֵץ וָאָבֶן: 37 וְהָיִיתָ לְשַׁמָּה לְמָשָׁל וְלִשְׁנִינָה בְּכֹל הָעַמִּים אֲשֶׁר־יְנַהֶגְךָ יְהוָה שָׁמָּה: 38 זֶרַע רַב תּוֹצִיא הַשָּׂדֶה וּמְעַט תֶּאֱסֹף כִּי יַחְסְלֶנּוּ הָאַרְבֶּה: 39 כְּרָמִים תִּטַּע וְעָבָדְתָּ וְיַיִן לֹא־תִשְׁתֶּה וְלֹא תֶאֱגֹר כִּי תֹאכְלֶנּוּ הַתֹּלָעַת: 40 זֵיתִים יִהְיוּ לְךָ בְּכָל־גְּבוּלֶךָ וְשֶׁמֶן לֹא תָסוּךְ כִּי יִשַּׁל זֵיתֶךָ: 41 בָּנִים וּבָנוֹת תּוֹלִיד וְלֹא־יִהְיוּ לָךְ כִּי יֵלְכוּ בַּשֶּׁבִי: 42 כָּל־עֵצְךָ וּפְרִי אַדְמָתֶךָ יְיָרֵשׁ הַצְּלָצַל: 43 הַגֵּר אֲשֶׁר בְּקִרְבְּךָ יַעֲלֶה עָלֶיךָ מַעְלָה מָּעְלָה וְאַתָּה תֵרֵד מַטָּה מָּטָּה: 44 הוּא יַלְוְךָ וְאַתָּה לֹא תַלְוֶנּוּ הוּא יִהְיֶה לְרֹאשׁ וְאַתָּה תִּהְיֶה לְזָנָב: 45 וּבָאוּ עָלֶיךָ כָּל־הַקְּלָלוֹת הָאֵלֶּה וּרְדָפוּךָ וְהִשִּׂיגוּךָ עַד הִשָּׁמְדָךְ כִּי־לֹא שָׁמַעְתָּ בְּקוֹל יְהוָה אֱלֹהֶיךָ לִשְׁמֹר

His statutes which He commanded you. ⁴⁶ And they shall be upon you for a sign and a wonder, and on your descendants forever.

⁴⁷ "Because you did not serve the LORD your God with joy and gladness of heart, for the abundance of everything, ⁴⁸ therefore you shall serve your enemies, whom the LORD will send against you, in hunger, in thirst, in nakedness, and in need of everything; and He will put a yoke of iron on your neck until He has destroyed you. ⁴⁹ The LORD will bring a nation against you from afar, from the end of the earth, *as swift* as the eagle flies, a nation whose language you will not understand, ⁵⁰ a nation of fierce countenance, which does not respect the elderly nor show favor to the young. ⁵¹ And they shall eat the increase of your livestock and the produce of your land, until you are destroyed; they shall not leave you grain or new wine or oil, *or* the increase of your cattle or the offspring of your flocks, until they have destroyed you.

⁵² "They shall besiege you at all your gates until your high and fortified walls, in which you trust, come down throughout all your land; and they shall besiege you at all your gates throughout all your land which the LORD your God has given you. ⁵³ You shall eat the fruit of your own body, the flesh of your sons and your daughters whom the LORD your God has given you, in the siege and desperate straits in which your enemy shall distress you. ⁵⁴ The sensitive and very refined man among you will be hostile toward his brother, toward the wife of his bosom, and toward the rest of his children whom he leaves behind, ⁵⁵ so that he will not give any of them the flesh of his children whom he will eat, because he has nothing left in the siege and desperate straits in which your enemy shall distress you at all your gates. ⁵⁶ The tender and delicate woman among you, who would not venture to set the sole of her foot on the ground because of her delicateness and sensitivity, will refuse to the husband of her bosom, and to her son and her daughter, ⁵⁷ her placenta which comes out from between her feet and her children whom she bears; for she will eat them secretly for lack of everything in the siege and desperate straits in which your enemy shall distress you at all your gates.

⁵⁸ "If you do not carefully observe all the words of this law that are written in this book, that you may fear this glorious and awesome name, THE LORD YOUR GOD, ⁵⁹ then the LORD will bring upon you and your descendants extraordinary plagues—great and prolonged plagues—and serious and prolonged sicknesses. ⁶⁰ Moreover He will

מִצְוֹתָיו וְחֻקֹּתָיו אֲשֶׁר צִוָּךְ: 46 וְהָיוּ בְךָ לְאוֹת וּלְמוֹפֵת וּבְזַרְעֲךָ עַד־עוֹלָם: 47 תַּחַת אֲשֶׁר לֹא־עָבַדְתָּ אֶת־יְהוָה אֱלֹהֶיךָ בְּשִׂמְחָה וּבְטוּב לֵבָב מֵרֹב כֹּל: 48 וְעָבַדְתָּ אֶת־אֹיְבֶיךָ אֲשֶׁר יְשַׁלְּחֶנּוּ יְהוָה בָּךְ בְּרָעָב וּבְצָמָא וּבְעֵירֹם וּבְחֹסֶר כֹּל וְנָתַן עֹל בַּרְזֶל עַל־צַוָּארֶךָ עַד הִשְׁמִידוֹ אֹתָךְ: 49 יִשָּׂא יְהוָה עָלֶיךָ גּוֹי מֵרָחוֹק מִקְצֵה הָאָרֶץ כַּאֲשֶׁר יִדְאֶה הַנָּשֶׁר גּוֹי אֲשֶׁר לֹא־תִשְׁמַע לְשֹׁנוֹ: 50 גּוֹי עַז פָּנִים אֲשֶׁר לֹא־יִשָּׂא פָנִים לְזָקֵן וְנַעַר לֹא יָחֹן: 51 וְאָכַל פְּרִי בְהֶמְתְּךָ וּפְרִי־אַדְמָתְךָ עַד הִשָּׁמְדָךְ אֲשֶׁר לֹא־יַשְׁאִיר לְךָ דָּגָן תִּירוֹשׁ וְיִצְהָר שְׁגַר אֲלָפֶיךָ וְעַשְׁתְּרֹת צֹאנֶךָ עַד הַאֲבִידוֹ אֹתָךְ: 52 וְהֵצַר לְךָ בְּכָל־שְׁעָרֶיךָ עַד רֶדֶת חֹמֹתֶיךָ הַגְּבֹהֹת וְהַבְּצֻרוֹת אֲשֶׁר אַתָּה בֹּטֵחַ בָּהֵן בְּכָל־אַרְצֶךָ וְהֵצַר לְךָ בְּכָל־שְׁעָרֶיךָ בְּכָל־אַרְצְךָ אֲשֶׁר נָתַן יְהוָה אֱלֹהֶיךָ לָךְ:

53 וְאָכַלְתָּ פְרִי־בִטְנְךָ בְּשַׂר בָּנֶיךָ וּבְנֹתֶיךָ אֲשֶׁר נָתַן־לְךָ יְהוָה אֱלֹהֶיךָ בְּמָצוֹר וּבְמָצוֹק אֲשֶׁר־יָצִיק לְךָ אֹיְבֶךָ: 54 הָאִישׁ הָרַךְ בְּךָ וְהֶעָנֹג מְאֹד תֵּרַע עֵינוֹ בְאָחִיו וּבְאֵשֶׁת חֵיקוֹ וּבְיֶתֶר בָּנָיו אֲשֶׁר יוֹתִיר:

55 מִתֵּת | לְאַחַד מֵהֶם מִבְּשַׂר בָּנָיו אֲשֶׁר יֹאכֵל מִבְּלִי הִשְׁאִיר־לוֹ כֹּל בְּמָצוֹר וּבְמָצוֹק אֲשֶׁר יָצִיק לְךָ אֹיִבְךָ בְּכָל־שְׁעָרֶיךָ: 56 הָרַכָּה בְךָ וְהָעֲנֻגָּה אֲשֶׁר לֹא־נִסְּתָה כַף־רַגְלָהּ הַצֵּג עַל־הָאָרֶץ מֵהִתְעַנֵּג וּמֵרֹךְ תֵּרַע עֵינָהּ בְּאִישׁ חֵיקָהּ וּבִבְנָהּ וּבְבִתָּהּ:

57 וּבְשִׁלְיָתָהּ הַיּוֹצֵת | מִבֵּין רַגְלֶיהָ וּבְבָנֶיהָ אֲשֶׁר תֵּלֵד כִּי־תֹאכְלֵם בְּחֹסֶר־כֹּל בַּסָּתֶר בְּמָצוֹר וּבְמָצוֹק אֲשֶׁר יָצִיק לְךָ אֹיִבְךָ בִּשְׁעָרֶיךָ: 58 אִם־לֹא תִשְׁמֹר לַעֲשׂוֹת אֶת־כָּל־דִּבְרֵי הַתּוֹרָה הַזֹּאת הַכְּתוּבִים בַּסֵּפֶר הַזֶּה לְיִרְאָה אֶת־הַשֵּׁם הַנִּכְבָּד וְהַנּוֹרָא הַזֶּה אֵת יְהוָה אֱלֹהֶיךָ: 59 וְהִפְלָא יְהוָה אֶת־מַכֹּתְךָ וְאֵת מַכּוֹת זַרְעֶךָ מַכּוֹת גְּדֹלוֹת וְנֶאֱמָנוֹת וָחֳלָיִם רָעִים וְנֶאֱמָנִים: 60 וְהֵשִׁיב בְּךָ אֵת כָּל־מַדְוֵה מִצְרַיִם

bring back on you all the diseases of Egypt, of which you were afraid, and they shall cling to you. 61 Also every sickness and every plague, which *is* not written in this Book of the Law, will the LORD bring upon you until you are destroyed. 62 You shall be left few in number, whereas you were as the stars of heaven in multitude, because you would not obey the voice of the LORD your God. 63 And it shall be, *that* just as the LORD rejoiced over you to do you good and multiply you, so the LORD will rejoice over you to destroy you and bring you to nothing; and you shall be plucked from off the land which you go to possess.

64 "Then the LORD will scatter you among all peoples, from one end of the earth to the other, and there you shall serve other gods, which neither you nor your fathers have known—wood and stone. 65 And among those nations you shall find no rest, nor shall the sole of your foot have a resting place; but there the LORD will give you a trembling heart, failing eyes, and anguish of soul. 66 Your life shall hang in doubt before you; you shall fear day and night, and have no assurance of life. 67 In the morning you shall say, 'Oh, that it were evening!' And at evening you shall say, 'Oh, that it were morning!' because of the fear which terrifies your heart, and because of the sight which your eyes see.

68 "And the LORD will take you back to Egypt in ships, by the way of which I said to you, 'You shall never see it again.' And there you shall be offered for sale to your enemies as male and female slaves, but no one will buy *you.*"

29 These *are* the words of the covenant which the LORD commanded Moses to make with the children of Israel in the land of Moab, besides the covenant which He made with them in Horeb.

2 Now Moses called all Israel and said to them: "You have seen all that the LORD did before your eyes in the land of Egypt, to Pharaoh and to all his servants and to all his land— 3 the great trials which your eyes have seen, the signs, and those great wonders. 4 Yet the LORD has not given you a heart to perceive and eyes to see and ears to hear, to this *very* day. 5 And I have led you forty years in the wilderness. Your clothes have not worn out on you, and your sandals have not worn out on your feet. 6 You have not eaten bread, nor have you drunk wine or *similar* drink, that you may know that I *am* the LORD your God. 7 And when you came to this place, Sihon king of Heshbon and Og king of Bashan came out against us to battle, and we conquered them. 8 We took their land and gave it as an inheritance to the Reubenites, to the Gadites,

אֲשֶׁר יָגֹרְתָּ מִפְּנֵיהֶם וְדָבְקוּ בָּךְ: 61 גַּם כָּל־חֳלִי וְכָל־מַכָּה אֲשֶׁר לֹא כָתוּב בְּסֵפֶר הַתּוֹרָה הַזֹּאת יַעְלֵם יְהֹוָה עָלֶיךָ עַד הִשָּׁמְדָךְ: 62 וְנִשְׁאַרְתֶּם בִּמְתֵי מְעָט תַּחַת אֲשֶׁר הֱיִיתֶם כְּכוֹכְבֵי הַשָּׁמַיִם לָרֹב כִּי־לֹא שָׁמַעְתָּ בְּקוֹל יְהֹוָה אֱלֹהֶיךָ: 63 וְהָיָה כַּאֲשֶׁר־שָׂשׂ יְהֹוָה עֲלֵיכֶם לְהֵיטִיב אֶתְכֶם וּלְהַרְבּוֹת אֶתְכֶם כֵּן יָשִׂישׂ יְהֹוָה עֲלֵיכֶם לְהַאֲבִיד אֶתְכֶם וּלְהַשְׁמִיד אֶתְכֶם וְנִסַּחְתֶּם מֵעַל הָאֲדָמָה אֲשֶׁר־ אַתָּה בָא־שָׁמָּה לְרִשְׁתָּהּ: 64 וֶהֱפִיצְךָ יְהֹוָה בְּכָל־ הָעַמִּים מִקְצֵה הָאָרֶץ וְעַד־קְצֵה הָאָרֶץ וְעָבַדְתָּ שָּׁם אֱלֹהִים אֲחֵרִים אֲשֶׁר לֹא־יָדַעְתָּ אַתָּה וַאֲבֹתֶיךָ עֵץ וָאָבֶן: 65 וּבַגּוֹיִם הָהֵם לֹא תַרְגִּיעַ וְלֹא־יִהְיֶה מָנוֹחַ לְכַף־רַגְלֶךָ וְנָתַן יְהֹוָה לְךָ שָׁם לֵב רַגָּז וְכִלְיוֹן עֵינַיִם וְדַאֲבוֹן נָפֶשׁ: 66 וְהָיוּ חַיֶּיךָ תְּלֻאִים לְךָ מִנֶּגֶד וּפָחַדְתָּ לַיְלָה וְיוֹמָם וְלֹא תַאֲמִין בְּחַיֶּיךָ: 67 בַּבֹּקֶר תֹּאמַר מִי־יִתֵּן עֶרֶב וּבָעֶרֶב תֹּאמַר מִי־יִתֵּן בֹּקֶר מִפַּחַד לְבָבְךָ אֲשֶׁר תִּפְחָד וּמִמַּרְאֵה עֵינֶיךָ אֲשֶׁר תִּרְאֶה: 68 וֶהֱשִׁיבְךָ יְהֹוָה מִצְרַיִם בָּאֳנִיּוֹת בַּדֶּרֶךְ אֲשֶׁר אָמַרְתִּי לְךָ לֹא־תֹסִיף עוֹד לִרְאֹתָהּ וְהִתְמַכַּרְתֶּם שָׁם לְאֹיְבֶיךָ לַעֲבָדִים וְלִשְׁפָחוֹת וְאֵין קֹנֶה: ס 69 אֵלֶּה דִבְרֵי הַבְּרִית אֲשֶׁר־צִוָּה יְהֹוָה אֶת־מֹשֶׁה לִכְרֹת אֶת־בְּנֵי יִשְׂרָאֵל בְּאֶרֶץ מוֹאָב מִלְּבַד הַבְּרִית אֲשֶׁר־כָּרַת אִתָּם בְּחֹרֵב: פ

כט וַיִּקְרָא מֹשֶׁה אֶל־כָּל־יִשְׂרָאֵל וַיֹּאמֶר אֲלֵהֶם אַתֶּם רְאִיתֶם אֵת כָּל־אֲשֶׁר עָשָׂה יְהֹוָה לְעֵינֵיכֶם בְּאֶרֶץ מִצְרַיִם לְפַרְעֹה וּלְכָל־עֲבָדָיו וּלְכָל־אַרְצוֹ: 2 הַמַּסּוֹת הַגְּדֹלֹת אֲשֶׁר רָאוּ עֵינֶיךָ הָאֹתֹת וְהַמֹּפְתִים הַגְּדֹלִים הָהֵם: 3 וְלֹא־נָתַן יְהֹוָה לָכֶם לֵב לָדַעַת וְעֵינַיִם לִרְאוֹת וְאָזְנַיִם לִשְׁמֹעַ עַד הַיּוֹם הַזֶּה: 4 וָאוֹלֵךְ אֶתְכֶם אַרְבָּעִים שָׁנָה בַּמִּדְבָּר לֹא־ בָלוּ שַׂלְמֹתֵיכֶם מֵעֲלֵיכֶם וְנַעַלְךָ לֹא־בָלְתָה מֵעַל רַגְלֶךָ: 5 לֶחֶם לֹא אֲכַלְתֶּם וְיַיִן וְשֵׁכָר לֹא שְׁתִיתֶם לְמַעַן תֵּדְעוּ כִּי אֲנִי יְהֹוָה אֱלֹהֵיכֶם: 6 וַתָּבֹאוּ אֶל־הַמָּקוֹם הַזֶּה וַיֵּצֵא סִיחֹן מֶלֶךְ־חֶשְׁבּוֹן וְעוֹג מֶלֶךְ־הַבָּשָׁן לִקְרָאתֵנוּ לַמִּלְחָמָה וַנַּכֵּם: 7 וַנִּקַּח אֶת־אַרְצָם וַנִּתְּנָהּ לְנַחֲלָה לָראוּבֵנִי וְלַגָּדִי וְלַחֲצִי שֵׁבֶט הַמְנַשִּׁי: 8 וּשְׁמַרְתֶּם אֶת־דִּבְרֵי הַבְּרִית הַזֹּאת וַעֲשִׂיתֶם אֹתָם לְמַעַן תַּשְׂכִּילוּ אֵת כָּל־אֲשֶׁר תַּעֲשׂוּן: פ

and to half the tribe of Manasseh. ⁹ Therefore keep the words of this covenant, and do them, that you may prosper in all that you do.

¹⁰ "All of you stand today before the LORD your God: your leaders and your tribes and your elders and your officers, all the men of Israel, ¹¹ your little ones and your wives—also the stranger who *is* in your camp, from the one who cuts your wood to the one who draws your water— ¹² that you may enter into covenant with the LORD your God, and into His oath, which the LORD your God makes with you today, ¹³ that He may establish you today as a people for Himself, and *that* He may be God to you, just as He has spoken to you, and just as He has sworn to your fathers, to Abraham, Isaac, and Jacob.

¹⁴ "I make this covenant and this oath, not with you alone, ¹⁵ but with *him* who stands here with us today before the LORD our God, as well as with *him* who *is* not here with us today ¹⁶ (for you know that we dwelt in the land of Egypt and that we came through the nations which you passed by, ¹⁷ and you saw their abominations and their idols which *were* among them—wood and stone and silver and gold); ¹⁸ so that there may not be among you man or woman or family or tribe, whose heart turns away today from the LORD our God, to go *and* serve the gods of these nations, and that there may not be among you a root bearing bitterness or wormwood; ¹⁹ and so it may not happen, when he hears the words of this curse, that he blesses himself in his heart, saying, 'I shall have peace, even though I follow the dictates of my heart'—as though the drunkard could be included with the sober.

²⁰ "The LORD would not spare him; for then the anger of the LORD and His jealousy would burn against that man, and every curse that is written in this book would settle on him, and the LORD would blot out his name from under heaven. ²¹ And the LORD would separate him from all the tribes of Israel for adversity, according to all the curses of the covenant that are written in this Book of the Law, ²² so that the coming generation of your children who rise up after you, and the foreigner who comes from a far land, would say, when they see the plagues of that land and the sicknesses which the LORD has laid on it:

²³ 'The whole land *is* brimstone, salt, and burning; it is not sown, nor does it bear, nor does any grass grow there, like the overthrow of Sodom and Gomorrah, Admah, and Zeboiim, which the LORD overthrew in His anger and His wrath.' ²⁴ All nations would say, 'Why has the LORD done so to this land? What does the heat of this great anger

⁹ אַתֶּם נִצָּבִים הַיּוֹם כֻּלְּכֶם לִפְנֵי יְהוָה אֱלֹהֵיכֶם רָאשֵׁיכֶם שִׁבְטֵיכֶם זִקְנֵיכֶם וְשֹׁטְרֵיכֶם כֹּל אִישׁ יִשְׂרָאֵל: ¹⁰ טַפְּכֶם נְשֵׁיכֶם וְגֵרְךָ אֲשֶׁר בְּקֶרֶב מַחֲנֶיךָ מֵחֹטֵב עֵצֶיךָ עַד שֹׁאֵב מֵימֶיךָ: ¹¹ לְעָבְרְךָ בִּבְרִית יְהוָה אֱלֹהֶיךָ וּבְאָלָתוֹ אֲשֶׁר יְהוָה אֱלֹהֶיךָ כֹּרֵת עִמְּךָ הַיּוֹם: ¹² לְמַעַן הָקִים-אֹתְךָ הַיּוֹם | לוֹ לְעָם וְהוּא יִהְיֶה-לְּךָ לֵאלֹהִים כַּאֲשֶׁר דִּבֶּר-לָךְ וְכַאֲשֶׁר נִשְׁבַּע לַאֲבֹתֶיךָ לְאַבְרָהָם לְיִצְחָק וּלְיַעֲקֹב: ¹³ וְלֹא אִתְּכֶם לְבַדְּכֶם אָנֹכִי כֹּרֵת אֶת-הַבְּרִית הַזֹּאת וְאֶת-הָאָלָה הַזֹּאת: ¹⁴ כִּי אֶת-אֲשֶׁר יֶשְׁנוֹ פֹּה עִמָּנוּ עֹמֵד הַיּוֹם לִפְנֵי יְהוָה אֱלֹהֵינוּ וְאֵת אֲשֶׁר אֵינֶנּוּ פֹּה עִמָּנוּ הַיּוֹם: ¹⁵ כִּי-אַתֶּם יְדַעְתֶּם אֵת אֲשֶׁר-יָשַׁבְנוּ בְּאֶרֶץ מִצְרָיִם וְאֵת אֲשֶׁר-עָבַרְנוּ בְּקֶרֶב הַגּוֹיִם אֲשֶׁר עֲבַרְתֶּם: ¹⁶ וַתִּרְאוּ אֶת-שִׁקּוּצֵיהֶם וְאֵת גִּלֻּלֵיהֶם עֵץ וָאֶבֶן כֶּסֶף וְזָהָב אֲשֶׁר עִמָּהֶם: ¹⁷ פֶּן-יֵשׁ בָּכֶם אִישׁ אוֹ-אִשָּׁה אוֹ מִשְׁפָּחָה אוֹ-שֵׁבֶט אֲשֶׁר לְבָבוֹ פֹנֶה הַיּוֹם מֵעִם יְהוָה אֱלֹהֵינוּ לָלֶכֶת לַעֲבֹד אֶת-אֱלֹהֵי הַגּוֹיִם הָהֵם פֶּן-יֵשׁ בָּכֶם שֹׁרֶשׁ פֹּרֶה רֹאשׁ וְלַעֲנָה: ¹⁸ וְהָיָה בְּשָׁמְעוֹ אֶת-דִּבְרֵי הָאָלָה הַזֹּאת וְהִתְבָּרֵךְ בִּלְבָבוֹ לֵאמֹר שָׁלוֹם יִהְיֶה-לִּי כִּי בִּשְׁרִרוּת לִבִּי אֵלֵךְ לְמַעַן סְפוֹת הָרָוָה אֶת-הַצְּמֵאָה: ¹⁹ לֹא-יֹאבֶה יְהוָה סְלֹחַ לוֹ כִּי אָז יֶעְשַׁן אַף-יְהוָה וְקִנְאָתוֹ בָּאִישׁ הַהוּא וְרָבְצָה בּוֹ כָּל-הָאָלָה הַכְּתוּבָה בַּסֵּפֶר הַזֶּה וּמָחָה יְהוָה אֶת-שְׁמוֹ מִתַּחַת הַשָּׁמָיִם: ²⁰ וְהִבְדִּילוֹ יְהוָה לְרָעָה מִכֹּל שִׁבְטֵי יִשְׂרָאֵל כְּכֹל אָלוֹת הַבְּרִית הַכְּתוּבָה בְּסֵפֶר הַתּוֹרָה הַזֶּה: ²¹ וְאָמַר הַדּוֹר הָאַחֲרוֹן בְּנֵיכֶם אֲשֶׁר יָקוּמוּ מֵאַחֲרֵיכֶם וְהַנָּכְרִי אֲשֶׁר יָבֹא מֵאֶרֶץ רְחוֹקָה וְרָאוּ אֶת-מַכּוֹת הָאָרֶץ הַהִוא וְאֶת-תַּחֲלֻאֶיהָ אֲשֶׁר-חִלָּה יְהוָה בָּהּ: ²² גָּפְרִית וָמֶלַח שְׂרֵפָה כָל-אַרְצָהּ לֹא תִזָּרַע וְלֹא תַצְמִחַ וְלֹא-יַעֲלֶה בָהּ כָּל-עֵשֶׂב כְּמַהְפֵּכַת סְדֹם וַעֲמֹרָה אַדְמָה וּצְבֹיִם אֲשֶׁר הָפַךְ יְהוָה בְּאַפּוֹ וּבַחֲמָתוֹ: ²³ וְאָמְרוּ כָּל-הַגּוֹיִם עַל-מֶה עָשָׂה יְהוָה כָּכָה לָאָרֶץ הַזֹּאת מֶה חֳרִי הָאַף הַגָּדוֹל הַזֶּה: ²⁴ וְאָמְרוּ עַל אֲשֶׁר עָזְבוּ אֶת-בְּרִית

mean?' ²⁵Then *people* would say: 'Because they have forsaken the covenant of the LORD God of their fathers, which He made with them when He brought them out of the land of Egypt; ²⁶for they went and served other gods and worshiped them, gods that they did not know and that He had not given to them. ²⁷Then the anger of the LORD was aroused against this land, to bring on it every curse that is written in this book. ²⁸And the LORD uprooted them from their land in anger, in wrath, and in great indignation, and cast them into another land, as *it is* this day.'

²⁹"The secret *things belong* to the LORD our God, but those *things which are* revealed *belong* to us and to our children forever, that *we* may do all the words of this law.

30 "Now it shall come to pass, when all these things come upon you, the blessing and the curse which I have set before you, and you call *them* to mind among all the nations where the LORD your God drives you, ²and you return to the LORD your God and obey His voice, according to all that I command you today, you and your children, with all your heart and with all your soul, ³that the LORD your God will bring you back from captivity, and have compassion on you, and gather you again from all the nations where the LORD your God has scattered you. ⁴If *any* of you are driven out to the farthest *parts* under heaven, from there the LORD your God will gather you, and from there He will bring you. ⁵Then the LORD your God will bring you to the land which your fathers possessed, and you shall possess it. He will prosper you and multiply you more than your fathers. ⁶And the LORD your God will circumcise your heart and the heart of your descendants, to love the LORD your God with all your heart and with all your soul, that you may live.

⁷"Also the LORD your God will put all these curses on your enemies and on those who hate you, who persecuted you. ⁸And you will again obey the voice of the LORD and do all His commandments which I command you today. ⁹The LORD your God will make you abound in all the work of your hand, in the fruit of your body, in the increase of your livestock, and in the produce of your land for good. For the LORD will again rejoice over you for good as He rejoiced over your fathers, ¹⁰if you obey the voice of the LORD your God, to keep His commandments and His statutes which are written in this Book of the Law, *and* if you turn to the LORD your God with all your heart and with all your soul.

יְהֹוָה אֱלֹהֵי אֲבֹתָם אֲשֶׁר כָּרַת עִמָּם בְּהוֹצִיאוֹ אֹתָם מֵאֶרֶץ מִצְרָיִם: 25 וַיֵּלְכוּ וַיַּעַבְדוּ אֱלֹהִים אֲחֵרִים וַיִּשְׁתַּחֲווּ לָהֶם אֱלֹהִים אֲשֶׁר לֹא־יְדָעוּם וְלֹא חָלַק לָהֶם: 26 וַיִּחַר־אַף יְהֹוָה בָּאָרֶץ הַהִוא לְהָבִיא עָלֶיהָ אֶת־כָּל־הַקְּלָלָה הַכְּתוּבָה בַּסֵּפֶר הַזֶּה: 27 וַיִּתְּשֵׁם יְהֹוָה מֵעַל אַדְמָתָם בְּאַף וּבְחֵמָה וּבְקֶצֶף גָּדוֹל וַיַּשְׁלִכֵם אֶל־אֶרֶץ אַחֶרֶת כַּיּוֹם הַזֶּה: 28 הַנִּסְתָּרֹת לַיהֹוָה אֱלֹהֵינוּ וְהַנִּגְלֹת לָנוּ וּלְבָנֵינוּ עַד־עוֹלָם לַעֲשׂוֹת אֶת־כָּל־דִּבְרֵי הַתּוֹרָה הַזֹּאת: ס

ל וְהָיָה כִי־יָבֹאוּ עָלֶיךָ כָּל־הַדְּבָרִים הָאֵלֶּה הַבְּרָכָה וְהַקְּלָלָה אֲשֶׁר נָתַתִּי לְפָנֶיךָ וַהֲשֵׁבֹתָ אֶל־לְבָבֶךָ בְּכָל־הַגּוֹיִם אֲשֶׁר הִדִּיחֲךָ יְהֹוָה אֱלֹהֶיךָ שָׁמָּה: 2 וְשַׁבְתָּ עַד־יְהֹוָה אֱלֹהֶיךָ וְשָׁמַעְתָּ בְקֹלוֹ כְּכֹל אֲשֶׁר־אָנֹכִי מְצַוְּךָ הַיּוֹם אַתָּה וּבָנֶיךָ בְּכָל־לְבָבְךָ וּבְכָל־נַפְשֶׁךָ: 3 וְשָׁב יְהֹוָה אֱלֹהֶיךָ אֶת־שְׁבוּתְךָ וְרִחֲמֶךָ וְשָׁב וְקִבֶּצְךָ מִכָּל־הָעַמִּים אֲשֶׁר הֱפִיצְךָ יְהֹוָה אֱלֹהֶיךָ שָׁמָּה: 4 אִם־יִהְיֶה נִדַּחֲךָ בִּקְצֵה הַשָּׁמָיִם מִשָּׁם יְקַבֶּצְךָ יְהֹוָה אֱלֹהֶיךָ וּמִשָּׁם יִקָּחֶךָ: 5 וֶהֱבִיאֲךָ יְהֹוָה אֱלֹהֶיךָ אֶל־הָאָרֶץ אֲשֶׁר־יָרְשׁוּ אֲבֹתֶיךָ וִירִשְׁתָּהּ וְהֵיטִבְךָ וְהִרְבְּךָ מֵאֲבֹתֶיךָ: 6 וּמָל יְהֹוָה אֱלֹהֶיךָ אֶת־לְבָבְךָ וְאֶת־לְבַב זַרְעֶךָ לְאַהֲבָה אֶת־יְהֹוָה אֱלֹהֶיךָ בְּכָל־לְבָבְךָ וּבְכָל־נַפְשְׁךָ לְמַעַן חַיֶּיךָ: 7 וְנָתַן יְהֹוָה אֱלֹהֶיךָ אֵת כָּל־הָאָלוֹת הָאֵלֶּה עַל־אֹיְבֶיךָ וְעַל־שֹׂנְאֶיךָ אֲשֶׁר רְדָפוּךָ: 8 וְאַתָּה תָשׁוּב וְשָׁמַעְתָּ בְּקוֹל יְהֹוָה וְעָשִׂיתָ אֶת־כָּל־מִצְוֹתָיו אֲשֶׁר אָנֹכִי מְצַוְּךָ הַיּוֹם: 9 וְהוֹתִירְךָ יְהֹוָה אֱלֹהֶיךָ בְּכֹל מַעֲשֵׂה יָדֶךָ בִּפְרִי בִטְנְךָ וּבִפְרִי בְהֶמְתְּךָ וּבִפְרִי אַדְמָתְךָ לְטֹבָה כִּי יָשׁוּב יְהֹוָה לָשׂוּשׂ עָלֶיךָ לְטוֹב כַּאֲשֶׁר־שָׂשׂ עַל־אֲבֹתֶיךָ: 10 כִּי תִשְׁמַע בְּקוֹל יְהֹוָה אֱלֹהֶיךָ לִשְׁמֹר מִצְוֹתָיו וְחֻקֹּתָיו הַכְּתוּבָה בְּסֵפֶר הַתּוֹרָה הַזֶּה כִּי תָשׁוּב אֶל־יְהֹוָה אֱלֹהֶיךָ בְּכָל־לְבָבְךָ וּבְכָל־נַפְשֶׁךָ: פ

¹¹"For this commandment which I command you today *is* not *too* mysterious for you, nor *is* it far off. ¹²It *is* not in heaven, that you should say, 'Who will ascend into heaven for us and bring it to us, that we may hear it and do it?' ¹³Nor *is* it beyond the sea, that you should say, 'Who will go over the sea for us and bring it to us, that we may hear it and do it?' ¹⁴But the word *is* very near you, in your mouth and in your heart, that you may do it.

¹⁵"See, I have set before you today life and good, death and evil, ¹⁶in that I command you today to love the LORD your God, to walk in His ways, and to keep His commandments, His statutes, and His judgments, that you may live and multiply; and the LORD your God will bless you in the land which you go to possess. ¹⁷But if your heart turns away so that you do not hear, and are drawn away, and worship other gods and serve them, ¹⁸I announce to you today that you shall surely perish; you shall not prolong *your* days in the land which you cross over the Jordan to go in and possess. ¹⁹I call heaven and earth as witnesses today against you, *that* I have set before you life and death, blessing and cursing; therefore choose life, that both you and your descendants may live; ²⁰that you may love the LORD your God, that you may obey His voice, and that you may cling to Him, for He *is* your life and the length of your days; and that you may dwell in the land which the LORD swore to your fathers, to Abraham, Isaac, and Jacob, to give them."

31 Then Moses went and spoke these words to all Israel. ²And he said to them: "I *am* one hundred and twenty years old today. I can no longer go out and come in. Also the LORD has said to me, 'You shall not cross over this Jordan.' ³The LORD your God Himself crosses over before you; He will destroy these nations from before you, and you shall dispossess them. Joshua himself crosses over before you, just as the LORD has said. ⁴And the LORD will do to them as He did to Sihon and Og, the kings of the Amorites and their land, when He destroyed them. ⁵The LORD will give them over to you, that you may do to them according to every commandment which I have commanded you. ⁶Be strong and of good courage, do not fear nor be afraid of them; for the LORD your God, He *is* the One who goes with you. He will not leave you nor forsake you. "

⁷Then Moses called Joshua and said to him in the sight of all Israel, "Be strong and of good courage, for you must go with this people to the land which the LORD has sworn to their fathers to give them, and you shall cause them to inherit it.

11 כִּי הַמִּצְוָה הַזֹּאת אֲשֶׁר אָנֹכִי מְצַוְּךָ הַיּוֹם לֹא־נִפְלֵאת הִוא מִמְּךָ וְלֹא רְחֹקָה הִוא: 12 לֹא בַשָּׁמַיִם הִוא לֵאמֹר מִי יַעֲלֶה־לָּנוּ הַשָּׁמַיְמָה וְיִקָּחֶהָ לָּנוּ וְיַשְׁמִעֵנוּ אֹתָהּ וְנַעֲשֶׂנָּה: 13 וְלֹא־ מֵעֵבֶר לַיָּם הִוא לֵאמֹר מִי יַעֲבָר־לָנוּ אֶל־ עֵבֶר הַיָּם וְיִקָּחֶהָ לָּנוּ וְיַשְׁמִעֵנוּ אֹתָהּ וְנַעֲשֶׂנָּה: 14 כִּי־קָרוֹב אֵלֶיךָ הַדָּבָר מְאֹד בְּפִיךָ וּבִלְבָבְךָ לַעֲשֹׂתוֹ: ס 15 רְאֵה נָתַתִּי לְפָנֶיךָ הַיּוֹם אֶת־הַחַיִּים וְאֶת־הַטּוֹב וְאֶת־הַמָּוֶת וְאֶת־הָרָע: 16 אֲשֶׁר אָנֹכִי מְצַוְּךָ הַיּוֹם לְאַהֲבָה אֶת־יְהוָה אֱלֹהֶיךָ לָלֶכֶת בִּדְרָכָיו וְלִשְׁמֹר מִצְוֹתָיו וְחֻקֹּתָיו וּמִשְׁפָּטָיו וְחָיִיתָ וְרָבִיתָ וּבֵרַכְךָ יְהוָה אֱלֹהֶיךָ בָּאָרֶץ אֲשֶׁר־אַתָּה בָא־שָׁמָּה לְרִשְׁתָּהּ: 17 וְאִם־יִפְנֶה לְבָבְךָ וְלֹא תִשְׁמָע וְנִדַּחְתָּ וְהִשְׁתַּחֲוִיתָ לֵאלֹהִים אֲחֵרִים וַעֲבַדְתָּם: 18 הִגַּדְתִּי לָכֶם הַיּוֹם כִּי אָבֹד תֹּאבֵדוּן לֹא־תַאֲרִיכֻן יָמִים עַל־הָאֲדָמָה אֲשֶׁר אַתָּה עֹבֵר אֶת־הַיַּרְדֵּן לָבֹא שָׁמָּה לְרִשְׁתָּהּ: 19 הַעִדֹתִי בָכֶם הַיּוֹם אֶת־הַשָּׁמַיִם וְאֶת־הָאָרֶץ הַחַיִּים וְהַמָּוֶת נָתַתִּי לְפָנֶיךָ הַבְּרָכָה וְהַקְּלָלָה וּבָחַרְתָּ בַּחַיִּים לְמַעַן תִּחְיֶה אַתָּה וְזַרְעֶךָ: 20 לְאַהֲבָה אֶת־יְהוָה אֱלֹהֶיךָ לִשְׁמֹעַ בְּקֹלוֹ וּלְדָבְקָה־בוֹ כִּי הוּא חַיֶּיךָ וְאֹרֶךְ יָמֶיךָ לָשֶׁבֶת עַל־הָאֲדָמָה אֲשֶׁר נִשְׁבַּע יְהוָה לַאֲבֹתֶיךָ לְאַבְרָהָם לְיִצְחָק וּלְיַעֲקֹב לָתֵת לָהֶם: פ

לא וַיֵּלֶךְ מֹשֶׁה וַיְדַבֵּר אֶת־הַדְּבָרִים הָאֵלֶּה אֶל־ כָּל־יִשְׂרָאֵל: 2 וַיֹּאמֶר אֲלֵהֶם בֶּן־מֵאָה וְעֶשְׂרִים שָׁנָה אָנֹכִי הַיּוֹם לֹא־אוּכַל עוֹד לָצֵאת וְלָבוֹא וַיהוָה אָמַר אֵלַי לֹא תַעֲבֹר אֶת־הַיַּרְדֵּן הַזֶּה: 3 יְהוָה אֱלֹהֶיךָ הוּא עֹבֵר לְפָנֶיךָ הוּא־יַשְׁמִיד אֶת־הַגּוֹיִם הָאֵלֶּה מִלְּפָנֶיךָ וִירִשְׁתָּם יְהוֹשֻׁעַ הוּא עֹבֵר לְפָנֶיךָ כַּאֲשֶׁר דִּבֶּר יְהוָה: 4 וְעָשָׂה יְהוָה לָהֶם כַּאֲשֶׁר עָשָׂה לְסִיחוֹן וּלְעוֹג מַלְכֵי הָאֱמֹרִי וּלְאַרְצָם אֲשֶׁר הִשְׁמִיד אֹתָם: 5 וּנְתָנָם יְהוָה לִפְנֵיכֶם וַעֲשִׂיתֶם לָהֶם כְּכָל־הַמִּצְוָה אֲשֶׁר צִוִּיתִי אֶתְכֶם: 6 חִזְקוּ וְאִמְצוּ אַל־תִּירְאוּ וְאַל־תַּעַרְצוּ מִפְּנֵיהֶם כִּי יְהוָה אֱלֹהֶיךָ הוּא הַהֹלֵךְ עִמָּךְ לֹא יַרְפְּךָ וְלֹא יַעַזְבֶךָּ: פ 7 וַיִּקְרָא מֹשֶׁה לִיהוֹשֻׁעַ וַיֹּאמֶר אֵלָיו לְעֵינֵי כָל־ יִשְׂרָאֵל חֲזַק וֶאֱמָץ כִּי אַתָּה תָּבוֹא אֶת־הָעָם הַזֶּה אֶל־הָאָרֶץ אֲשֶׁר נִשְׁבַּע יְהוָה לַאֲבֹתָם לָתֵת לָהֶם

8 And the LORD, He *is* the One who goes before you. He will be with you, He will not leave you nor forsake you; do not fear nor be dismayed."

9 So Moses wrote this law and delivered it to the priests, the sons of Levi, who bore the ark of the covenant of the LORD, and to all the elders of Israel. 10 And Moses commanded them, saying: "At the end of *every* seven years, at the appointed time in the year of release, at the Feast of Tabernacles, 11 when all Israel comes to appear before the LORD your God in the place which He chooses, you shall read this law before all Israel in their hearing. 12 Gather the people together, men and women and little ones, and the stranger who *is* within your gates, that they may hear and that they may learn to fear the LORD your God and carefully observe all the words of this law, 13 and *that* their children, who have not known it, may hear and learn to fear the LORD your God as long as you live in the land which you cross the Jordan to possess."

14 Then the LORD said to Moses, "Behold, the days approach when you must die; call Joshua, and present yourselves in the tabernacle of meeting, that I may inaugurate him."

So Moses and Joshua went and presented themselves in the tabernacle of meeting. 15 Now the LORD appeared at the tabernacle in a pillar of cloud, and the pillar of cloud stood above the door of the tabernacle.

16 And the LORD said to Moses: "Behold, you will rest with your fathers; and this people will rise and play the harlot with the gods of the foreigners of the land, where they go *to be* among them, and they will forsake Me and break My covenant which I have made with them. 17 Then My anger shall be aroused against them in that day, and I will forsake them, and I will hide My face from them, and they shall be devoured. And many evils and troubles shall befall them, so that they will say in that day, 'Have not these evils come upon us because our God *is* not among us?' 18 And I will surely hide My face in that day because of all the evil which they have done, in that they have turned to other gods.

19 "Now therefore, write down this song for yourselves, and teach it to the children of Israel; put it in their mouths, that this song may be a witness for Me against the children of Israel. 20 When I have brought them to the land flowing with milk and honey, of which I swore to their fathers, and they have eaten and filled themselves and grown fat, then they will turn to other gods and serve them; and they will provoke Me and break My covenant. 21 Then it shall be, when many evils and troubles have come upon them, that this song will testify

וְאַתָּה תַּנְחִילֶנָּה אוֹתָם: 8 וַיהוָה הוּא | הַהֹלֵךְ לְפָנֶיךָ הוּא יִהְיֶה עִמָּךְ לֹא יַרְפְּךָ וְלֹא יַעַזְבֶךָּ לֹא תִירָא וְלֹא תֵחָת: 9 וַיִּכְתֹּב מֹשֶׁה אֶת־הַתּוֹרָה הַזֹּאת וַיִּתְּנָהּ אֶל־הַכֹּהֲנִים בְּנֵי לֵוִי הַנֹּשְׂאִים אֶת־אֲרוֹן בְּרִית יְהוָה וְאֶל־כָּל־זִקְנֵי יִשְׂרָאֵל: 10 וַיְצַו מֹשֶׁה אוֹתָם לֵאמֹר מִקֵּץ | שֶׁבַע שָׁנִים בְּמֹעֵד שְׁנַת הַשְּׁמִטָּה בְּחַג הַסֻּכּוֹת: 11 בְּבוֹא כָל־יִשְׂרָאֵל לֵרָאוֹת אֶת־פְּנֵי יְהוָה אֱלֹהֶיךָ בַּמָּקוֹם אֲשֶׁר יִבְחָר תִּקְרָא אֶת־הַתּוֹרָה הַזֹּאת נֶגֶד כָּל־יִשְׂרָאֵל בְּאָזְנֵיהֶם: 12 הַקְהֵל אֶת־הָעָם הָאֲנָשִׁים וְהַנָּשִׁים וְהַטַּף וְגֵרְךָ אֲשֶׁר בִּשְׁעָרֶיךָ לְמַעַן יִשְׁמְעוּ וּלְמַעַן יִלְמְדוּ וְיָרְאוּ אֶת־יְהוָה אֱלֹהֵיכֶם וְשָׁמְרוּ לַעֲשׂוֹת אֶת־כָּל־דִּבְרֵי הַתּוֹרָה הַזֹּאת: 13 וּבְנֵיהֶם אֲשֶׁר לֹא־יָדְעוּ יִשְׁמְעוּ וְלָמְדוּ לְיִרְאָה אֶת־יְהוָה אֱלֹהֵיכֶם כָּל־הַיָּמִים אֲשֶׁר אַתֶּם חַיִּים עַל־הָאֲדָמָה אֲשֶׁר אַתֶּם עֹבְרִים אֶת־הַיַּרְדֵּן שָׁמָּה לְרִשְׁתָּהּ: פ

14 וַיֹּאמֶר יְהוָה אֶל־מֹשֶׁה הֵן קָרְבוּ יָמֶיךָ לָמוּת קְרָא אֶת־יְהוֹשֻׁעַ וְהִתְיַצְּבוּ בְּאֹהֶל מוֹעֵד וַאֲצַוֶּנּוּ וַיֵּלֶךְ מֹשֶׁה וִיהוֹשֻׁעַ וַיִּתְיַצְּבוּ בְּאֹהֶל מוֹעֵד: 15 וַיֵּרָא יְהוָה בָּאֹהֶל בְּעַמּוּד עָנָן וַיַּעֲמֹד עַמּוּד הֶעָנָן עַל־פֶּתַח הָאֹהֶל: ס 16 וַיֹּאמֶר יְהוָה אֶל־מֹשֶׁה הִנְּךָ שֹׁכֵב עִם־אֲבֹתֶיךָ וְקָם הָעָם הַזֶּה וְזָנָה | אַחֲרֵי | אֱלֹהֵי נֵכַר־הָאָרֶץ אֲשֶׁר הוּא בָא־שָׁמָּה בְּקִרְבּוֹ וַעֲזָבַנִי וְהֵפֵר אֶת־בְּרִיתִי אֲשֶׁר כָּרַתִּי אִתּוֹ: 17 וְחָרָה אַפִּי בוֹ בַיּוֹם־הַהוּא וַעֲזַבְתִּים וְהִסְתַּרְתִּי פָנַי מֵהֶם וְהָיָה לֶאֱכֹל וּמְצָאֻהוּ רָעוֹת רַבּוֹת וְצָרוֹת וְאָמַר בַּיּוֹם הַהוּא הֲלֹא עַל כִּי־אֵין אֱלֹהַי בְּקִרְבִּי מְצָאוּנִי הָרָעוֹת הָאֵלֶּה: 18 וְאָנֹכִי הַסְתֵּר אַסְתִּיר פָּנַי בַּיּוֹם הַהוּא עַל כָּל־הָרָעָה אֲשֶׁר עָשָׂה כִּי פָנָה אֶל־אֱלֹהִים אֲחֵרִים: 19 וְעַתָּה כִּתְבוּ לָכֶם אֶת־הַשִּׁירָה הַזֹּאת וְלַמְּדָהּ אֶת־בְּנֵי־יִשְׂרָאֵל שִׂימָהּ בְּפִיהֶם לְמַעַן תִּהְיֶה־לִּי הַשִּׁירָה הַזֹּאת לְעֵד בִּבְנֵי יִשְׂרָאֵל: 20 כִּי־אֲבִיאֶנּוּ אֶל־הָאֲדָמָה | אֲשֶׁר־נִשְׁבַּעְתִּי לַאֲבֹתָיו זָבַת חָלָב וּדְבַשׁ וְאָכַל וְשָׂבַע וְדָשֵׁן וּפָנָה אֶל־אֱלֹהִים אֲחֵרִים וַעֲבָדוּם וְנִאֲצוּנִי וְהֵפֵר אֶת־בְּרִיתִי: 21 וְהָיָה כִּי־תִמְצֶאןָ אֹתוֹ רָעוֹת רַבּוֹת וְצָרוֹת וְעָנְתָה

against them as a witness; for it will not be
forgotten in the mouths of their descendants, for I
know the inclination of their behavior today, even
before I have brought them to the land of which I
swore *to give them.*"

²² Therefore Moses wrote this song the same day,
and taught it to the children of Israel. ²³ Then He
inaugurated Joshua the son of Nun, and said, "Be
strong and of good courage; for you shall bring the
children of Israel into the land of which I swore to
them, and I will be with you."

²⁴ So it was, when Moses had completed writing
the words of this law in a book, when they were
finished, ²⁵ that Moses commanded the Levites,
who bore the ark of the covenant of the LORD,
saying: ²⁶ "Take this Book of the Law, and put it
beside the ark of the covenant of the LORD your
God, that it may be there as a witness against you;
²⁷ for I know your rebellion and your stiff neck. *If*
today, while I am yet alive with you, you have been
rebellious against the LORD, then how much more
after my death? ²⁸ Gather to me all the elders of
your tribes, and your officers, that I may speak
these words in their hearing and call heaven and
earth to witness against them. ²⁹ For I know that
after my death you will become utterly corrupt, and
turn aside from the way which I have commanded
you. And evil will befall you in the latter days,
because you will do evil in the sight of the LORD, to
provoke Him to anger through the work of your
hands."

³⁰ Then Moses spoke in the hearing of all the
assembly of Israel the words of this song until they
were ended:

32 "Give ear, O heavens, and I will speak;
    And hear, O earth, the words of my mouth.
²   Let my teaching drop as the rain,
    My speech distill as the dew,
    As raindrops on the tender herb,
    And as showers on the grass.
³   For I proclaim the name of the LORD:
    Ascribe greatness to our God.
⁴   *He is* the Rock, His work *is* perfect;
    For all His ways *are* justice,
    A God of truth and without injustice;
    Righteous and upright *is* He.
⁵   "They have corrupted themselves;
    They are not His children,
    Because of their blemish:
    A perverse and crooked generation.
⁶   Do you thus deal with the LORD,
    O foolish and unwise people?

הַשִּׁירָה הַזֹּאת לְפָנָיו לְעֵד כִּי לֹא תִשָּׁכַח מִפִּי
זַרְעוֹ כִּי יָדַעְתִּי אֶת־יִצְרוֹ אֲשֶׁר הוּא עֹשֶׂה הַיּוֹם
בְּטֶרֶם אֲבִיאֶנּוּ אֶל־הָאָרֶץ אֲשֶׁר נִשְׁבָּעְתִּי: 22 וַיִּכְתֹּב
מֹשֶׁה אֶת־הַשִּׁירָה הַזֹּאת בַּיּוֹם הַהוּא וַיְלַמְּדָהּ
אֶת־בְּנֵי יִשְׂרָאֵל: 23 וַיְצַו אֶת־יְהוֹשֻׁעַ בִּן־נוּן וַיֹּאמֶר
חֲזַק וֶאֱמָץ כִּי אַתָּה תָּבִיא אֶת־בְּנֵי יִשְׂרָאֵל אֶל־
הָאָרֶץ אֲשֶׁר־נִשְׁבַּעְתִּי לָהֶם וְאָנֹכִי אֶהְיֶה עִמָּךְ:
24 וַיְהִי ׀ כְּכַלּוֹת מֹשֶׁה לִכְתֹּב אֶת־דִּבְרֵי הַתּוֹרָה־
הַזֹּאת עַל־סֵפֶר עַד תֻּמָּם: 25 וַיְצַו מֹשֶׁה אֶת־
הַלְוִיִּם נֹשְׂאֵי אֲרוֹן בְּרִית־יְהוָה לֵאמֹר: 26 לָקֹחַ אֵת
סֵפֶר הַתּוֹרָה הַזֶּה וְשַׂמְתֶּם אֹתוֹ מִצַּד אֲרוֹן בְּרִית־
יְהוָה אֱלֹהֵיכֶם וְהָיָה־שָׁם בְּךָ לְעֵד: 27 כִּי אָנֹכִי
יָדַעְתִּי אֶת־מֶרְיְךָ וְאֶת־עָרְפְּךָ הַקָּשֶׁה הֵן בְּעוֹדֶנִּי
חַי עִמָּכֶם הַיּוֹם מַמְרִים הֱיִתֶם עִם־יְהוָה וְאַף כִּי־
אַחֲרֵי מוֹתִי: 28 הַקְהִילוּ אֵלַי אֶת־כָּל־זִקְנֵי שִׁבְטֵיכֶם
וְשֹׁטְרֵיכֶם וַאֲדַבְּרָה בְאָזְנֵיהֶם אֵת הַדְּבָרִים הָאֵלֶּה
וְאָעִידָה בָּם אֶת־הַשָּׁמַיִם וְאֶת־הָאָרֶץ: 29 כִּי יָדַעְתִּי
אַחֲרֵי מוֹתִי כִּי־הַשְׁחֵת תַּשְׁחִתוּן וְסַרְתֶּם מִן־הַדֶּרֶךְ
אֲשֶׁר צִוִּיתִי אֶתְכֶם וְקָרָאת אֶתְכֶם הָרָעָה בְּאַחֲרִית
הַיָּמִים כִּי־תַעֲשׂוּ אֶת־הָרַע בְּעֵינֵי יְהוָה לְהַכְעִיסוֹ
בְּמַעֲשֵׂה יְדֵיכֶם: 30 וַיְדַבֵּר מֹשֶׁה בְּאָזְנֵי כָּל־קְהַל
יִשְׂרָאֵל אֶת־דִּבְרֵי הַשִּׁירָה הַזֹּאת עַד תֻּמָּם: פ

לב הַאֲזִינוּ הַשָּׁמַיִם וַאֲדַבֵּרָה
וְתִשְׁמַע הָאָרֶץ אִמְרֵי־פִי:
2 יַעֲרֹף כַּמָּטָר לִקְחִי
תִּזַּל כַּטַּל אִמְרָתִי
כִּשְׂעִירִם עֲלֵי־דֶשֶׁא
וְכִרְבִיבִים עֲלֵי־עֵשֶׂב:
3 כִּי שֵׁם יְהוָה אֶקְרָא
הָבוּ גֹדֶל לֵאלֹהֵינוּ:
4 הַצּוּר תָּמִים פָּעֳלוֹ
כִּי כָל־דְּרָכָיו מִשְׁפָּט
אֵל אֱמוּנָה וְאֵין עָוֶל
צַדִּיק וְיָשָׁר הוּא:
5 שִׁחֵת לוֹ לֹא בָּנָיו מוּמָם
דּוֹר עִקֵּשׁ וּפְתַלְתֹּל:
6 הֲלַיְהוָה תִּגְמְלוּ־זֹאת
עַם נָבָל וְלֹא חָכָם

Is He not your Father, *who* bought you?
Has He not made you and established you?

7 "Remember the days of old,
Consider the years of many generations.
Ask your father, and he will show you;
Your elders, and they will tell you:

8 When the Most High divided their inheri-
tance to the nations,
When He separated the sons of Adam,
He set the boundaries of the peoples
According to the number of the children of
Israel.

9 For the LORD's portion *is* His people;
Jacob *is* the place of His inheritance.

10 "He found him in a desert land
And in the wasteland, a howling wilderness;
He encircled him, He instructed him,
He kept him as the apple of His eye.

11 As an eagle stirs up its nest,
Hovers over its young,
Spreading out its wings, taking them up,
Carrying them on its wings,

12 *So* the LORD alone led him,
And *there was* no foreign god with him.

13 "He made him ride in the heights of the earth,
That he might eat the produce of the fields;
He made him draw honey from the rock,
And oil from the flinty rock;

14 Curds from the cattle, and milk of the flock,
With fat of lambs;
And rams of the breed of Bashan, and goats,
With the choicest wheat;
And you drank wine, the blood of the
grapes.

15 "But Jeshurun grew fat and kicked;
You grew fat, you grew thick,
You are obese!
Then he forsook God *who* made him,
And scornfully esteemed the Rock of his
salvation.

16 They provoked Him to jealousy with foreign
gods;
With abominations they provoked Him to
anger.

17 They sacrificed to demons, not to God,
To gods they did not know,
To new *gods,* new arrivals
That your fathers did not fear.

18 Of the Rock *who* begot you, you are
unmindful,
And have forgotten the God who fathered
you.

הֲלוֹא־הוּא אָבִיךָ קָּנֶךָ
הוּא עָשְׂךָ וַיְכֹנְנֶךָ:
7 זְכֹר יְמוֹת עוֹלָם
בִּינוּ שְׁנוֹת דּוֹר־וָדוֹר
שְׁאַל אָבִיךָ וְיַגֵּדְךָ
זְקֵנֶיךָ וְיֹאמְרוּ לָךְ:
8 בְּהַנְחֵל עֶלְיוֹן גּוֹיִם
בְּהַפְרִידוֹ בְּנֵי אָדָם
יַצֵּב גְּבֻלֹת עַמִּים
לְמִסְפַּר בְּנֵי יִשְׂרָאֵל:
9 כִּי חֵלֶק יְהוָֹה עַמּוֹ
יַעֲקֹב חֶבֶל נַחֲלָתוֹ:
10 יִמְצָאֵהוּ בְּאֶרֶץ מִדְבָּר
וּבְתֹהוּ יְלֵל יְשִׁמֹן
יְסֹבְבֶנְהוּ יְבוֹנְנֵהוּ
יִצְּרֶנְהוּ כְּאִישׁוֹן עֵינוֹ:
11 כְּנֶשֶׁר יָעִיר קִנּוֹ עַל־גּוֹזָלָיו יְרַחֵף
יִפְרֹשׂ כְּנָפָיו יִקָּחֵהוּ
יִשָּׂאֵהוּ עַל־אֶבְרָתוֹ:
12 יְהוָֹה בָּדָד יַנְחֶנּוּ
וְאֵין עִמּוֹ אֵל נֵכָר:
13 יַרְכִּבֵהוּ עַל־בָּמֳותֵי אָרֶץ
וַיֹּאכַל תְּנוּבֹת שָׂדָי
וַיֵּנִקֵהוּ דְבַשׁ מִסֶּלַע
וְשֶׁמֶן מֵחַלְמִישׁ צוּר:
14 חֶמְאַת בָּקָר וַחֲלֵב צֹאן
עִם־חֵלֶב כָּרִים וְאֵילִים
בְּנֵי־בָשָׁן וְעַתּוּדִים
עִם־חֵלֶב כִּלְיוֹת חִטָּה
וְדַם־עֵנָב תִּשְׁתֶּה־חָמֶר:
15 וַיִּשְׁמַן יְשֻׁרוּן וַיִּבְעָט
שָׁמַנְתָּ עָבִיתָ כָּשִׂיתָ
וַיִּטֹּשׁ אֱלוֹהַ עָשָׂהוּ
וַיְנַבֵּל צוּר יְשֻׁעָתוֹ:
16 יַקְנִאֻהוּ בְּזָרִים
בְּתוֹעֵבֹת יַכְעִיסֻהוּ:
17 יִזְבְּחוּ לַשֵּׁדִים לֹא אֱלֹהַּ
אֱלֹהִים לֹא יְדָעוּם
חֲדָשִׁים מִקָּרֹב בָּאוּ
לֹא שְׂעָרוּם אֲבֹתֵיכֶם:
18 צוּר יְלָדְךָ תֶּשִׁי
וַתִּשְׁכַּח אֵל מְחֹלְלֶךָ:

19 "And when the LORD saw *it*, He spurned them,
Because of the provocation of His sons and His daughters.

20 And He said: 'I will hide My face from them, I will see what their end *will be*, For they *are* a perverse generation, Children in whom *is* no faith.

21 They have provoked Me to jealousy by *what is not God*;
They have moved Me to anger by their foolish idols.
But I will provoke them to jealousy by *those who are* not a nation;
I will move them to anger by a foolish nation.

22 For a fire is kindled in My anger, And shall burn to the lowest hell; It shall consume the earth with her increase, And set on fire the foundations of the mountains.

23 'I will heap disasters on them; I will spend My arrows on them.

24 *They shall be* wasted with hunger, Devoured by pestilence and bitter destruction;
I will also send against them the teeth of beasts,
With the poison of serpents of the dust.

25 The sword shall destroy outside; *There shall be* terror within For the young man and virgin, The nursing child with the man of gray hairs.

26 I would have said, "I will dash them in pieces,
I will make the memory of them to cease from among men,"

27 Had I not feared the wrath of the enemy, Lest their adversaries should misunderstand, Lest they should say, "Our hand *is* high; And it is not the LORD who has done all this."'

28 "For they *are* a nation void of counsel, Nor *is there any* understanding in them.

29 Oh, that they were wise, *that* they understood this,
That they would consider their latter end!

30 How could one chase a thousand, And two put ten thousand to flight, Unless their Rock had sold them, And the LORD had surrendered them?

31 For their rock *is* not like our Rock, Even our enemies themselves *being* judges.

19 וַיַּרְא יְהֹוָה וַיִּנְאָץ
מִכַּעַס בָּנָיו וּבְנֹתָיו:

20 וַיֹּאמֶר אַסְתִּירָה פָנַי מֵהֶם
אֶרְאֶה מָה אַחֲרִיתָם
כִּי דוֹר תַּהְפֻּכֹת הֵמָּה
בָּנִים לֹא־אֵמֻן בָּם:

21 הֵם קִנְאוּנִי בְלֹא־אֵל
כִּעֲסוּנִי בְּהַבְלֵיהֶם
וַאֲנִי אַקְנִיאֵם בְּלֹא־עָם
בְּגוֹי נָבָל אַכְעִיסֵם:

22 כִּי־אֵשׁ קָדְחָה בְאַפִּי
וַתִּיקַד עַד־שְׁאוֹל תַּחְתִּית
וַתֹּאכַל אֶרֶץ וִיבֻלָהּ
וַתְּלַהֵט מוֹסְדֵי הָרִים:

23 אַסְפֶּה עָלֵימוֹ רָעוֹת
חִצַּי אֲכַלֶּה־בָּם:

24 מְזֵי רָעָב וּלְחֻמֵי רֶשֶׁף
וְקֶטֶב מְרִירִי
וְשֶׁן־בְּהֵמֹת אֲשַׁלַּח־בָּם
עִם־חֲמַת זֹחֲלֵי עָפָר:

25 מִחוּץ תְּשַׁכֶּל־חֶרֶב
וּמֵחֲדָרִים אֵימָה
גַּם־בָּחוּר גַּם־בְּתוּלָה
יוֹנֵק עִם־אִישׁ שֵׂיבָה:

26 אָמַרְתִּי אַפְאֵיהֶם
אַשְׁבִּיתָה מֵאֱנוֹשׁ זִכְרָם:

27 לוּלֵי כַּעַס אוֹיֵב אָגוּר
פֶּן־יְנַכְּרוּ צָרֵימוֹ
פֶּן־יֹאמְרוּ יָדֵינוּ רָמָה
וְלֹא יְהֹוָה פָּעַל כָּל־זֹאת:

28 כִּי־גוֹי אֹבַד עֵצוֹת הֵמָּה
וְאֵין בָּהֶם תְּבוּנָה:

29 לוּ חָכְמוּ יַשְׂכִּילוּ זֹאת
יָבִינוּ לְאַחֲרִיתָם:

30 אֵיכָה יִרְדֹּף אֶחָד אֶלֶף
וּשְׁנַיִם יָנִיסוּ רְבָבָה
אִם־לֹא כִּי־צוּרָם מְכָרָם
וַיהֹוָה הִסְגִּירָם:

31 כִּי לֹא כְצוּרֵנוּ צוּרָם
וְאֹיְבֵינוּ פְּלִילִים:

³² For their vine *is* of the vine of Sodom
And of the fields of Gomorrah;
Their grapes *are* grapes of gall,
Their clusters *are* bitter.
³³ Their wine *is* the poison of serpents,
And the cruel venom of cobras.

³⁴ '*Is* this not laid up in store with Me,
Sealed up among My treasures?
³⁵ Vengeance is Mine, and recompense;
Their foot shall slip in *due* time;
For the day of their calamity *is* at hand,
And the things to come hasten upon them.'

³⁶ "For the LORD will judge His people
And have compassion on His servants,
When He sees that *their* power is gone,
And *there is* no one *remaining*, bond or free.
³⁷ He will say: 'Where *are* their gods,
The rock in which they sought refuge?
³⁸ Who ate the fat of their sacrifices,
And drank the wine of their drink offering?
Let them rise and help you,
And be your refuge.

³⁹ 'Now see that I, *even* I, *am* He,
And *there is* no God besides Me;
I kill and I make alive;
I wound and I heal;
Nor *is there any* who can deliver from My
    hand.
⁴⁰ For I raise My hand to heaven,
And say, "*As* I live forever,
⁴¹ If I whet My glittering sword,
And My hand takes hold on judgment,
I will render vengeance to My enemies,
And repay those who hate Me.
⁴² I will make My arrows drunk with blood,
And My sword shall devour flesh,
With the blood of the slain and the captives,
From the heads of the leaders of the
    enemy."'

⁴³ "Rejoice, O Gentiles, *with* His people;
For He will avenge the blood of His servants,
And render vengeance to His adversaries;
He will provide atonement for His land *and*
    His people."

⁴⁴ So Moses came with Joshua the son of Nun
and spoke all the words of this song in the hearing
of the people. ⁴⁵ Moses finished speaking all these
words to all Israel, ⁴⁶ and he said to them: "Set your
hearts on all the words which I testify among you
today, which you shall command your children to
be careful to observe—all the words of this law.
⁴⁷ For it *is* not a futile thing for you, because it *is*

כִּי־מִגֶּפֶן סְדֹם גַּפְנָם 32
וּמִשַּׁדְמֹת עֲמֹרָה
עֲנָבֵמוֹ עִנְּבֵי־רוֹשׁ
אַשְׁכְּלֹת מְרֹרֹת לָמוֹ׃
חֲמַת תַּנִּינִם יֵינָם 33
וְרֹאשׁ פְּתָנִים אַכְזָר׃
הֲלֹא־הוּא כָּמֻס עִמָּדִי 34
חָתֻם בְּאוֹצְרֹתָי׃
לִי נָקָם וְשִׁלֵּם 35
לְעֵת תָּמוּט רַגְלָם
כִּי קָרוֹב יוֹם אֵידָם
וְחָשׁ עֲתִדֹת לָמוֹ׃
כִּי־יָדִין יְהוָה עַמּוֹ 36
וְעַל־עֲבָדָיו יִתְנֶחָם
כִּי יִרְאֶה כִּי־אָזְלַת יָד
וְאֶפֶס עָצוּר וְעָזוּב׃
וְאָמַר אֵי אֱלֹהֵימוֹ 37
צוּר חָסָיוּ בוֹ׃
אֲשֶׁר חֵלֶב זְבָחֵימוֹ יֹאכֵלוּ 38
יִשְׁתּוּ יֵין נְסִיכָם
יָקוּמוּ וְיַעְזְרֻכֶם
יְהִי עֲלֵיכֶם סִתְרָה׃
רְאוּ ׀ עַתָּה כִּי אֲנִי אֲנִי הוּא 39
וְאֵין אֱלֹהִים עִמָּדִי
אֲנִי אָמִית וַאֲחַיֶּה
מָחַצְתִּי וַאֲנִי אֶרְפָּא
וְאֵין מִיָּדִי מַצִּיל׃
כִּי־אֶשָּׂא אֶל־שָׁמַיִם יָדִי 40
וְאָמַרְתִּי חַי אָנֹכִי לְעֹלָם׃
אִם־שַׁנּוֹתִי בְּרַק חַרְבִּי 41
וְתֹאחֵז בְּמִשְׁפָּט יָדִי
אָשִׁיב נָקָם לְצָרָי
וְלִמְשַׂנְאַי אֲשַׁלֵּם׃
אַשְׁכִּיר חִצַּי מִדָּם 42
וְחַרְבִּי תֹּאכַל בָּשָׂר
מִדַּם חָלָל וְשִׁבְיָה
מֵרֹאשׁ פַּרְעוֹת אוֹיֵב׃
הַרְנִינוּ גוֹיִם עַמּוֹ 43
כִּי דַם־עֲבָדָיו יִקּוֹם
וְנָקָם יָשִׁיב לְצָרָיו
וְכִפֶּר אַדְמָתוֹ עַמּוֹ׃
וַיָּבֹא מֹשֶׁה וַיְדַבֵּר אֶת־כָּל־דִּבְרֵי הַשִּׁירָה־הַזֹּאת 44
בְּאָזְנֵי הָעָם הוּא וְהוֹשֵׁעַ בִּן־נוּן׃ 45 וַיְכַל מֹשֶׁה
לְדַבֵּר אֶת־כָּל־הַדְּבָרִים הָאֵלֶּה אֶל־כָּל־יִשְׂרָאֵל׃
46 וַיֹּאמֶר אֲלֵהֶם שִׂימוּ לְבַבְכֶם לְכָל־הַדְּבָרִים אֲשֶׁר
אָנֹכִי מֵעִיד בָּכֶם הַיּוֹם אֲשֶׁר תְּצַוֻּם אֶת־בְּנֵיכֶם
לִשְׁמֹר לַעֲשׂוֹת אֶת־כָּל־דִּבְרֵי הַתּוֹרָה הַזֹּאת׃ 47 כִּי
לֹא־דָבָר רֵק הוּא מִכֶּם כִּי־הוּא חַיֵּיכֶם וּבַדָּבָר

your life, and by this word you shall prolong *your* days in the land which you cross over the Jordan to possess."

⁴⁸ Then the LORD spoke to Moses that very same day, saying: ⁴⁹ "Go up this mountain of the Abarim, Mount Nebo, which *is* in the land of Moab, across from Jericho; view the land of Canaan, which I give to the children of Israel as a possession; ⁵⁰ and die on the mountain which you ascend, and be gathered to your people, just as Aaron your brother died on Mount Hor and was gathered to his people; ⁵¹ because you trespassed against Me among the children of Israel at the waters of Meribah Kadesh, in the Wilderness of Zin, because you did not hallow Me in the midst of the children of Israel. ⁵² Yet you shall see the land before *you,* though you shall not go there, into the land which I am giving to the children of Israel."

33 Now this *is* the blessing with which Moses the man of God blessed the children of Israel before his death. ² And he said:

"The LORD came from Sinai,
And dawned on them from Seir;
He shone forth from Mount Paran,
And He came with ten thousands of saints;
From His right hand
Came a fiery law for them.
³ Yes, He loves the people;
All His saints *are* in Your hand;
They sit down at Your feet;
Everyone receives Your words.
⁴ Moses commanded a law for us,
A heritage of the congregation of Jacob.
⁵ And He was King in Jeshurun,
When the leaders of the people were gathered,
All the tribes of Israel together.

⁶ "Let Reuben live, and not die,
Nor let his men be few."

⁷ And this he said of Judah:

"Hear, LORD, the voice of Judah,
And bring him to his people;
Let his hands be sufficient for him,
And may You be a help against his enemies."

⁸ And of Levi he said:

"*Let* Your Thummim and Your Urim *be* with Your holy one,
Whom You tested at Massah,
And with whom You contended at the waters of Meribah,
⁹ Who says of his father and mother,
'I have not seen them';
Nor did he acknowledge his brothers,
Or know his own children;
For they have observed Your word
And kept Your covenant.

הֲזֶ֣ה תַּאֲרִ֤יכֻ יָמִים֙ עַל־הָ֣אֲדָמָ֔ה אֲשֶׁ֨ר אַתֶּ֜ם עֹבְרִ֧ים אֶת־הַיַּרְדֵּ֛ן שָׁ֖מָּה לְרִשְׁתָּֽהּ: פ

⁴⁸ וַיְדַבֵּ֤ר יְהוָֹה֙ אֶל־מֹשֶׁ֔ה בְּעֶ֛צֶם הַיּ֥וֹם הַזֶּ֖ה לֵאמֹֽר:

⁴⁹ עֲלֵ֡ה אֶל־הַר֩ הָעֲבָרִ֨ים הַזֶּ֜ה הַר־נְב֗וֹ אֲשֶׁר֙ בְּאֶ֣רֶץ מוֹאָ֔ב אֲשֶׁ֖ר עַל־פְּנֵ֣י יְרֵח֑וֹ וּרְאֵה֙ אֶת־אֶ֣רֶץ כְּנַ֔עַן אֲשֶׁ֨ר אֲנִ֥י נֹתֵ֛ן לִבְנֵ֥י יִשְׂרָאֵ֖ל לַאֲחֻזָּֽה: ⁵⁰ וּמֻ֣ת בָּהָ֗ר אֲשֶׁ֤ר אַתָּה֙ עֹלֶ֣ה שָׁ֔מָּה וְהֵאָסֵ֖ף אֶל־עַמֶּ֑יךָ כַּאֲשֶׁר־מֵ֞ת אַהֲרֹ֤ן אָחִ֨יךָ֙ בְּהֹ֣ר הָהָ֔ר וַיֵּאָ֖סֶף אֶל־עַמָּֽיו:

⁵¹ עַ֡ל אֲשֶׁר֩ מְעַלְתֶּ֨ם בִּ֜י בְּת֣וֹךְ בְּנֵ֣י יִשְׂרָאֵ֗ל בְּמֵֽי־מְרִיבַ֥ת קָדֵ֖שׁ מִדְבַּר־צִ֑ן עַ֣ל אֲשֶׁ֤ר לֹֽא־קִדַּשְׁתֶּם֙ אוֹתִ֔י בְּת֖וֹךְ בְּנֵ֥י יִשְׂרָאֵֽל: ⁵² כִּ֥י מִנֶּ֖גֶד תִּרְאֶ֣ה אֶת־הָאָ֑רֶץ וְשָׁ֨מָּה֙ לֹ֣א תָב֔וֹא אֶל־הָאָ֕רֶץ אֲשֶׁר־אֲנִ֥י נֹתֵ֖ן לִבְנֵ֥י יִשְׂרָאֵֽל: פ

לג וְזֹ֣את הַבְּרָכָ֗ה אֲשֶׁ֨ר בֵּרַ֥ךְ מֹשֶׁ֛ה אִ֥ישׁ הָאֱלֹהִ֖ים אֶת־בְּנֵ֣י יִשְׂרָאֵ֑ל לִפְנֵ֖י מוֹתֽוֹ: ² וַיֹּאמַ֗ר יְהוָֹ֞ה מִסִּינַ֥י בָּא֙ וְזָרַ֤ח מִשֵּׂעִיר֙ לָ֔מוֹ הוֹפִ֨יעַ֙ מֵהַ֣ר פָּארָ֔ן וְאָתָ֖ה מֵרִבְבֹ֣ת קֹ֑דֶשׁ מִֽימִינ֕וֹ אֵשְׁדָּ֖תֿ לָֽמוֹ: ³ אַ֚ף חֹבֵ֣ב עַמִּ֔ים כָּל־קְדֹשָׁ֖יו בְּיָדֶ֑ךָ וְהֵם֙ תֻּכּ֣וּ לְרַגְלֶ֔ךָ יִשָּׂ֖א מִדַּבְּרֹתֶֽיךָ: ⁴ תּוֹרָ֥ה צִוָּה־לָ֖נוּ מֹשֶׁ֑ה מוֹרָשָׁ֖ה קְהִלַּ֥ת יַעֲקֹֽב: ⁵ וַיְהִ֥י בִישֻׁר֖וּן מֶ֑לֶךְ בְּהִתְאַסֵּף֙ רָ֣אשֵׁי עָ֔ם יַ֖חַד שִׁבְטֵ֥י יִשְׂרָאֵֽל: ⁶ יְחִ֥י רְאוּבֵ֖ן וְאַל־יָמֹ֑ת וִיהִ֥י מְתָ֖יו מִסְפָּֽר: ס ⁷ וְזֹ֣את לִֽיהוּדָה֮ וַיֹּאמַר֒ שְׁמַ֤ע יְהוָֹה֙ ק֣וֹל יְהוּדָ֔ה וְאֶל־עַמּ֖וֹ תְּבִיאֶ֑נּוּ יָדָיו֙ רָ֣ב ל֔וֹ וְעֵ֥זֶר מִצָּרָ֖יו תִּהְיֶֽה: ס ⁸ וּלְלֵוִ֣י אָמַ֔ר תֻּמֶּ֥יךָ וְאוּרֶ֖יךָ לְאִ֣ישׁ חֲסִידֶ֑ךָ אֲשֶׁ֤ר נִסִּיתוֹ֙ בְּמַסָּ֔ה תְּרִיבֵ֖הוּ עַל־מֵ֥י מְרִיבָֽה: ⁹ הָאֹמֵ֞ר לְאָבִ֤יו וּלְאִמּוֹ֙ לֹ֣א רְאִיתִ֔יו וְאֶת־אֶחָיו֙ לֹ֣א הִכִּ֔יר וְאֶת־בָּנָוֿ לֹ֣א

¹⁰ They shall teach Jacob Your judgments,
And Israel Your law.
They shall put incense before You,
And a whole burnt sacrifice on Your altar.
¹¹ Bless his substance, LORD,
And accept the work of his hands;
Strike the loins of those who rise against him,
And of those who hate him, that they rise not
again."

¹² Of Benjamin he said:

"The beloved of the LORD shall dwell in safety by
Him,
Who shelters him all the day long;
And he shall dwell between His shoulders."

¹³ And of Joseph he said:

"Blessed of the LORD *is* his land,
With the precious things of heaven, with the dew,
And the deep lying beneath,
¹⁴ With the precious fruits of the sun,
With the precious produce of the months,
¹⁵ With the best things of the ancient mountains,
With the precious things of the everlasting hills,
¹⁶ With the precious things of the earth and its
fullness,
And the favor of Him who dwelt in the bush.
Let *the blessing* come 'on the head of Joseph,
And on the crown of the head of him *who was*
separate from his brothers.'
¹⁷ His glory *is like* a firstborn bull,
And his horns *like* the horns of the wild ox;
Together with them
He shall push the peoples
To the ends of the earth;
They *are* the ten thousands of Ephraim,
And they *are* the thousands of Manasseh."

¹⁸ And of Zebulun he said:

"Rejoice, Zebulun, in your going out,
And Issachar in your tents!
¹⁹ They shall call the peoples *to* the mountain;
There they shall offer sacrifices of righteousness;
For they shall partake *of* the abundance of the
seas
And *of* treasures hidden in the sand."

²⁰ And of Gad he said:

"Blessed *is* he who enlarges Gad;
He dwells as a lion,
And tears the arm and the crown of his head.
²¹ He provided the first *part* for himself,
Because a lawgiver's portion was reserved there.
He came *with* the heads of the people;
He administered the justice of the LORD,
And His judgments with Israel."

²² And of Dan he said:

"Dan *is* a lion's whelp;
He shall leap from Bashan."

²³ And of Naphtali he said:

יֹרֵ֣ו 10 יָדְע֗וּ כִּֽי־שָׁמְרוּ֙ אִמְרָתֶ֔ךָ וּבְרִֽיתְךָ֖ יִנְצֹ֑רוּ

מִשְׁפָּטֶ֙יךָ֙ לְיַעֲקֹ֔ב וְתוֹרָתְךָ֖ לְיִשְׂרָאֵ֑ל יָשִׂ֤ימוּ קְטוֹרָה֙

בְּאַפֶּ֔ךָ וְכָלִ֖יל עַֽל־מִזְבְּחֶֽךָ׃ 11 בָּרֵ֤ךְ יְהוָה֙ חֵיל֔וֹ

וּפֹ֥עַל יָדָ֖יו תִּרְצֶ֑ה מְחַ֨ץ מָתְנַ֧יִם קָמָ֛יו וּמְשַׂנְאָ֖יו

מִן־יְקוּמֽוּן׃ ס 12 לְבִנְיָמִ֣ן אָמַ֔ר יְדִ֣יד יְהֹוָ֔ה

יִשְׁכֹּ֥ן לָבֶ֖טַח עָלָ֑יו חֹפֵ֤ף עָלָיו֙ כָּל־הַיּ֔וֹם וּבֵ֥ין

כְּתֵפָ֖יו שָׁכֵֽן׃ ס 13 וּלְיוֹסֵ֣ף אָמַ֔ר מְבֹרֶ֥כֶת

יְהֹוָ֖ה אַרְצ֑וֹ מִמֶּ֤גֶד שָׁמַ֙יִם֙ מִטָּ֔ל וּמִתְּה֖וֹם רֹבֶ֥צֶת

תָּֽחַת׃ 14 וּמִמֶּ֖גֶד תְּבוּאֹ֣ת שָׁ֑מֶשׁ וּמִמֶּ֖גֶד גֶּ֥רֶשׁ

יְרָחִֽים׃ 15 וּמֵרֹ֖אשׁ הַרְרֵי־קֶ֑דֶם וּמִמֶּ֖גֶד גִּבְע֥וֹת

עוֹלָֽם׃ 16 וּמִמֶּ֗גֶד אֶ֚רֶץ וּמְלֹאָ֔הּ וּרְצ֥וֹן שֹׁכְנִ֖י סְנֶ֑ה

תָּב֙וֹאתָה֙ לְרֹ֣אשׁ יוֹסֵ֔ף וּלְקָדְקֹ֖ד נְזִ֥יר אֶחָֽיו׃ 17 בְּכ֨וֹר

שׁוֹר֜וֹ הָדָ֣ר ל֗וֹ וְקַרְנֵ֤י רְאֵם֙ קַרְנָ֔יו בָּהֶ֛ם עַמִּ֥ים

יְנַגַּ֥ח יַחְדָּ֖ו אַפְסֵי־אָ֑רֶץ וְהֵם֙ רִבְב֣וֹת אֶפְרַ֔יִם וְהֵ֖ם

אַלְפֵ֥י מְנַשֶּֽׁה׃ ס 18 וְלִזְבוּלֻ֣ן אָמַ֔ר שְׂמַ֥ח

זְבוּלֻ֖ן בְּצֵאתֶ֑ךָ וְיִשָּׂשכָ֖ר בְּאֹהָלֶֽיךָ׃ 19 עַמִּים֙ הַר־

יִקְרָ֔אוּ שָׁ֖ם יִזְבְּח֣וּ זִבְחֵי־צֶ֑דֶק כִּ֣י שֶׁ֤פַע יַמִּים֙

יִנָ֔קוּ וּשְׂפֻנֵ֖י טְמ֥וּנֵי חֽוֹל׃ ס 20 וּלְגָ֣ד

אָמַ֔ר בָּר֖וּךְ מַרְחִ֣יב גָּ֑ד כְּלָבִ֣יא שָׁכֵ֔ן וְטָרַ֥ף זְר֖וֹעַ

אַף־קָדְקֹֽד׃ 21 וַיַּ֤רְא רֵאשִׁית֙ ל֔וֹ כִּי־שָׁ֛ם חֶלְקַ֥ת

מְחֹקֵ֖ק סָפ֑וּן וַיֵּתֵא֙ רָ֣אשֵׁי עָ֔ם צִדְקַ֤ת יְהֹוָה֙ עָשָׂ֔ה

וּמִשְׁפָּטָ֖יו עִם־יִשְׂרָאֵֽל׃ ס 22 וּלְדָ֣ן אָמַ֔ר

דָּ֥ן גּ֖וּר אַרְיֵ֑ה יְזַנֵּ֖ק מִן־הַבָּשָֽׁן׃ 23 וּלְנַפְתָּלִ֣י אָמַ֔ר

"O Naphtali, satisfied with favor,
And full of the blessing of the LORD,
Possess the west and the south."

24 And of Asher he said:

"Asher *is* most blessed of sons;
Let him be favored by his brothers,
And let him dip his foot in oil.
25 Your sandals *shall be* iron and bronze;
As your days, *so shall* your strength *be.*

26 "*There is* no one like the God of Jeshurun,
Who rides the heavens to help you,
And in His excellency on the clouds.
27 The eternal God *is your* refuge,
And underneath *are* the everlasting arms;
He will thrust out the enemy from before you,
And will say, 'Destroy!'
28 Then Israel shall dwell in safety,
The fountain of Jacob alone,
In a land of grain and new wine;
His heavens shall also drop dew.
29 Happy *are* you, O Israel!
Who *is* like you, a people saved by the LORD,
The shield of your help
And the sword of your majesty!
Your enemies shall submit to you,
And you shall tread down their high places."

34 Then Moses went up from the plains of Moab
to Mount Nebo, to the top of Pisgah, which is
across from Jericho. And the LORD showed him all
the land of Gilead as far as Dan, [2] all Naphtali
and the land of Ephraim and Manasseh, all the land of
Judah as far as the Western Sea, [3] the South, and
the plain of the Valley of Jericho, the city of palm
trees, as far as Zoar. [4] Then the LORD said to him,
"This *is* the land of which I swore to give Abraham,
Isaac, and Jacob, saying, 'I will give it to your
descendants.' I have caused you to see *it* with your
eyes, but you shall not cross over there. "

[5] So Moses the servant of the LORD died there in
the land of Moab, according to the word of the
LORD. [6] And He buried him in a valley in the land
of Moab, opposite Beth Peor; but no one knows his
grave to this day. [7] Moses *was* one hundred and
twenty years old when he died. His eyes were not
dim nor his natural vigor diminished. [8] And the
children of Israel wept for Moses in the plains of
Moab thirty days. So the days of weeping *and*
mourning for Moses ended.

[9] Now Joshua the son of Nun was full of the
spirit of wisdom, for Moses had laid his hands on
him; so the children of Israel heeded him, and did as
the LORD had commanded Moses.

[10] But since then there has not arisen in Israel a
prophet like Moses, whom the LORD knew face to
face, [11] in all the signs and wonders which the LORD

נַפְתָּלִי שְׂבַע רָצוֹן וּמָלֵא בִּרְכַּת יְהוָה יָם וְדָרוֹם
יְרָשָׁה: ס 24 וּלְאָשֵׁר אָמַר בָּרוּךְ מִבָּנִים
אָשֵׁר יְהִי רְצוּי אֶחָיו וְטֹבֵל בַּשֶּׁמֶן רַגְלוֹ: 25 בַּרְזֶל
וּנְחֹשֶׁת מִנְעָלֶיךָ וּכְיָמֶיךָ דָּבְאֶךָ: 26 אֵין כָּאֵל יְשֻׁרוּן
רֹכֵב שָׁמַיִם בְּעֶזְרֶךָ וּבְגַאֲוָתוֹ שְׁחָקִים: 27 מְעֹנָה
אֱלֹהֵי קֶדֶם וּמִתַּחַת זְרֹעֹת עוֹלָם וַיְגָרֶשׁ מִפָּנֶיךָ
אוֹיֵב וַיֹּאמֶר הַשְׁמֵד: 28 וַיִּשְׁכֹּן יִשְׂרָאֵל בֶּטַח בָּדָד
עֵין יַעֲקֹב אֶל־אֶרֶץ דָּגָן וְתִירוֹשׁ אַף־שָׁמָיו יַעַרְפוּ
טָל: 29 אַשְׁרֶיךָ יִשְׂרָאֵל מִי כָמוֹךָ עַם נוֹשַׁע בַּיהוָה
מָגֵן עֶזְרֶךָ וַאֲשֶׁר־חֶרֶב גַּאֲוָתֶךָ וְיִכָּחֲשׁוּ אֹיְבֶיךָ לָךְ
וְאַתָּה עַל־בָּמוֹתֵימוֹ תִדְרֹךְ: ס

לד וַיַּעַל מֹשֶׁה מֵעַרְבֹת מוֹאָב אֶל־הַר נְבוֹ רֹאשׁ
הַפִּסְגָּה אֲשֶׁר עַל־פְּנֵי יְרֵחוֹ וַיַּרְאֵהוּ יְהוָה אֶת־כָּל־
הָאָרֶץ אֶת־הַגִּלְעָד עַד־דָּן: 2 וְאֵת כָּל־נַפְתָּלִי וְאֶת־
אֶרֶץ אֶפְרַיִם וּמְנַשֶּׁה וְאֵת כָּל־אֶרֶץ יְהוּדָה עַד הַיָּם
הָאַחֲרוֹן: 3 וְאֶת־הַנֶּגֶב וְאֶת־הַכִּכָּר בִּקְעַת יְרֵחוֹ עִיר
הַתְּמָרִים עַד־צֹעַר: 4 וַיֹּאמֶר יְהוָה אֵלָיו זֹאת הָאָרֶץ
אֲשֶׁר נִשְׁבַּעְתִּי לְאַבְרָהָם לְיִצְחָק וּלְיַעֲקֹב לֵאמֹר
לְזַרְעֲךָ אֶתְּנֶנָּה הֶרְאִיתִיךָ בְעֵינֶיךָ וְשָׁמָּה לֹא תַעֲבֹר:

5 וַיָּמָת שָׁם מֹשֶׁה עֶבֶד־יְהוָה בְּאֶרֶץ מוֹאָב עַל־פִּי
יְהוָה: 6 וַיִּקְבֹּר אֹתוֹ בַגַּי בְּאֶרֶץ מוֹאָב מוּל בֵּית
פְּעוֹר וְלֹא־יָדַע אִישׁ אֶת־קְבֻרָתוֹ עַד הַיּוֹם הַזֶּה:

7 וּמֹשֶׁה בֶּן־מֵאָה וְעֶשְׂרִים שָׁנָה בְּמֹתוֹ לֹא־כָהֲתָה
עֵינוֹ וְלֹא־נָס לֵחֹה: 8 וַיִּבְכּוּ בְנֵי יִשְׂרָאֵל אֶת־מֹשֶׁה
בְּעַרְבֹת מוֹאָב שְׁלֹשִׁים יוֹם וַיִּתְּמוּ יְמֵי בְכִי אֵבֶל
מֹשֶׁה: 9 וִיהוֹשֻׁעַ בִּן־נוּן מָלֵא רוּחַ חָכְמָה כִּי־סָמַךְ
מֹשֶׁה אֶת־יָדָיו עָלָיו וַיִּשְׁמְעוּ אֵלָיו בְּנֵי־יִשְׂרָאֵל
וַיַּעֲשׂוּ כַּאֲשֶׁר צִוָּה יְהוָה אֶת־מֹשֶׁה: 10 וְלֹא־קָם
נָבִיא עוֹד בְּיִשְׂרָאֵל כְּמֹשֶׁה אֲשֶׁר יְדָעוֹ יְהוָה פָּנִים
אֶל־פָּנִים: 11 לְכָל־הָאֹתוֹת וְהַמּוֹפְתִים אֲשֶׁר שְׁלָחוֹ

sent him to do in the land of Egypt, before Pharaoh, before all his servants, and in all his land, [12] and by all that mighty power and all the great terror which Moses performed in the sight of all Israel.

יְהוָֹה לַעֲשׂוֹת בְּאֶרֶץ מִצְרָיִם לְפַרְעֹה וּלְכָל־עֲבָדָיו 12 וּלְכָל־אַרְצוֹ: וּלְכֹל הַיָּד הַחֲזָקָה וּלְכֹל הַמּוֹרָא הַגָּדוֹל אֲשֶׁר עָשָׂה מֹשֶׁה לְעֵינֵי כָּל־יִשְׂרָאֵל:

The Book of

JOSHUA

1 After the death of Moses the servant of the LORD, it came to pass that the LORD spoke to Joshua the son of Nun, Moses' assistant, saying: ²"Moses My servant is dead. Now therefore, arise, go over this Jordan, you and all this people, to the land which I am giving to them—the children of Israel. ³Every place that the sole of your foot will tread upon I have given you, as I said to Moses. ⁴From the wilderness and this Lebanon as far as the great river, the River Euphrates, all the land of the Hittites, and to the Great Sea toward the going down of the sun, shall be your territory. ⁵No man shall *be able to* stand before you all the days of your life; as I was with Moses, *so* I will be with you. I will not leave you nor forsake you. ⁶Be strong and of good courage, for to this people you shall divide as an inheritance the land which I swore to their fathers to give them. ⁷Only be strong and very courageous, that you may observe to do according to all the law which Moses My servant commanded you; do not turn from it to the right hand or to the left, that you may prosper wherever you go. ⁸This Book of the Law shall not depart from your mouth, but you shall meditate in it day and night, that you may observe to do according to all that is written in it. For then you will make your way prosperous, and then you will have good success. ⁹Have I not commanded you? Be strong and of good courage; do not be afraid, nor be dismayed, for the LORD your God *is* with you wherever you go."

¹⁰Then Joshua commanded the officers of the people, saying, ¹¹"Pass through the camp and command the people, saying, 'Prepare provisions for yourselves, for within three days you will cross over this Jordan, to go in to possess the land which the LORD your God is giving you to possess.'"

¹²And to the Reubenites, the Gadites, and half the tribe of Manasseh Joshua spoke, saying, ¹³"Remember the word which Moses the servant of the LORD commanded you, saying, 'The LORD your God is giving you rest and is giving you this land.' ¹⁴Your wives, your little ones, and your livestock shall remain in the land which Moses gave you on this side of the Jordan. But you shall pass before your brethren armed, all your mighty men of valor, and help them, ¹⁵until the LORD has given your brethren rest, as He *gave* you, and they also

יְהוֹשֻׁעַ

א וַיְהִי אַחֲרֵי מוֹת מֹשֶׁה עֶבֶד יְהוָה וַיֹּאמֶר יְהוָה אֶל־יְהוֹשֻׁעַ בִּן־נוּן מְשָׁרֵת מֹשֶׁה לֵאמֹר: ² מֹשֶׁה עַבְדִּי מֵת וְעַתָּה קוּם עֲבֹר אֶת־הַיַּרְדֵּן הַזֶּה אַתָּה וְכָל־הָעָם הַזֶּה אֶל־הָאָרֶץ אֲשֶׁר אָנֹכִי נֹתֵן לָהֶם לִבְנֵי יִשְׂרָאֵל: ³ כָּל־מָקוֹם אֲשֶׁר תִּדְרֹךְ כַּף־רַגְלְכֶם בּוֹ לָכֶם נְתַתִּיו כַּאֲשֶׁר דִּבַּרְתִּי אֶל־מֹשֶׁה: ⁴ מֵהַמִּדְבָּר וְהַלְּבָנוֹן הַזֶּה וְעַד־הַנָּהָר הַגָּדוֹל נְהַר־פְּרָת כֹּל אֶרֶץ הַחִתִּים וְעַד־הַיָּם הַגָּדוֹל מְבוֹא הַשָּׁמֶשׁ יִהְיֶה גְּבוּלְכֶם: ⁵ לֹא־יִתְיַצֵּב אִישׁ לְפָנֶיךָ כֹּל יְמֵי חַיֶּיךָ כַּאֲשֶׁר הָיִיתִי עִם־מֹשֶׁה אֶהְיֶה עִמָּךְ לֹא אַרְפְּךָ וְלֹא אֶעֶזְבֶךָּ: ⁶ חֲזַק וֶאֱמָץ כִּי אַתָּה תַּנְחִיל אֶת־הָעָם הַזֶּה אֶת־הָאָרֶץ אֲשֶׁר־נִשְׁבַּעְתִּי לַאֲבוֹתָם לָתֵת לָהֶם: ⁷ רַק חֲזַק וֶאֱמַץ מְאֹד לִשְׁמֹר לַעֲשׂוֹת כְּכָל־הַתּוֹרָה אֲשֶׁר צִוְּךָ מֹשֶׁה עַבְדִּי אַל־תָּסוּר מִמֶּנּוּ יָמִין וּשְׂמֹאול לְמַעַן תַּשְׂכִּיל בְּכֹל אֲשֶׁר תֵּלֵךְ: ⁸ לֹא־יָמוּשׁ סֵפֶר הַתּוֹרָה הַזֶּה מִפִּיךָ וְהָגִיתָ בּוֹ יוֹמָם וָלַיְלָה לְמַעַן תִּשְׁמֹר לַעֲשׂוֹת כְּכָל־הַכָּתוּב בּוֹ כִּי־אָז תַּצְלִיחַ אֶת־דְּרָכֶךָ וְאָז תַּשְׂכִּיל: ⁹ הֲלוֹא צִוִּיתִיךָ חֲזַק וֶאֱמַץ אַל־תַּעֲרֹץ וְאַל־תֵּחָת כִּי עִמְּךָ יְהוָה אֱלֹהֶיךָ בְּכֹל אֲשֶׁר תֵּלֵךְ: פ

¹⁰ וַיְצַו יְהוֹשֻׁעַ אֶת־שֹׁטְרֵי הָעָם לֵאמֹר: ¹¹ עִבְרוּ בְּקֶרֶב הַמַּחֲנֶה וְצַוּוּ אֶת־הָעָם לֵאמֹר הָכִינוּ לָכֶם צֵידָה כִּי בְּעוֹד שְׁלֹשֶׁת יָמִים אַתֶּם עֹבְרִים אֶת־הַיַּרְדֵּן הַזֶּה לָבוֹא לָרֶשֶׁת אֶת־הָאָרֶץ אֲשֶׁר יְהוָה אֱלֹהֵיכֶם נֹתֵן לָכֶם לְרִשְׁתָּהּ: ¹² וְלָראוּבֵנִי וְלַגָּדִי וְלַחֲצִי שֵׁבֶט הַמְנַשֶּׁה אָמַר יְהוֹשֻׁעַ לֵאמֹר: ¹³ זָכוֹר אֶת־הַדָּבָר אֲשֶׁר צִוָּה אֶתְכֶם מֹשֶׁה עֶבֶד־יְהוָה לֵאמֹר יְהוָה אֱלֹהֵיכֶם מֵנִיחַ לָכֶם וְנָתַן לָכֶם אֶת־הָאָרֶץ הַזֹּאת: ¹⁴ נְשֵׁיכֶם טַפְּכֶם וּמִקְנֵיכֶם יֵשְׁבוּ בָּאָרֶץ אֲשֶׁר נָתַן לָכֶם מֹשֶׁה בְּעֵבֶר הַיַּרְדֵּן וְאַתֶּם תַּעַבְרוּ חֲמֻשִׁים לִפְנֵי אֲחֵיכֶם כֹּל גִּבּוֹרֵי הַחַיִל וַעֲזַרְתֶּם אוֹתָם: ¹⁵ עַד אֲשֶׁר־יָנִיחַ יְהוָה לַאֲחֵיכֶם כָּכֶם וְיָרְשׁוּ גַם־הֵמָּה אֶת־הָאָרֶץ אֲשֶׁר־יְהוָה אֱלֹהֵיכֶם

have taken possession of the land which the LORD your God is giving them. Then you shall return to the land of your possession and enjoy it, which Moses the LORD's servant gave you on this side of the Jordan toward the sunrise."

16 So they answered Joshua, saying, "All that you command us we will do, and wherever you send us we will go. 17 Just as we heeded Moses in all things, so we will heed you. Only the LORD your God be with you, as He was with Moses. 18 Whoever rebels against your command and does not heed your words, in all that you command him, shall be put to death. Only be strong and of good courage."

2 Now Joshua the son of Nun sent out two men from Acacia Grove to spy secretly, saying, "Go, view the land, especially Jericho. "

So they went, and came to the house of a harlot named Rahab, and lodged there. 2 And it was told the king of Jericho, saying, "Behold, men have come here tonight from the children of Israel to search out the country."

3 So the king of Jericho sent to Rahab, saying, "Bring out the men who have come to you, who have entered your house, for they have come to search out all the country."

4 Then the woman took the two men and hid them. So she said, "Yes, the men came to me, but I did not know where they *were* from. 5 And it happened as the gate was being shut, when it was dark, that the men went out. Where the men went I do not know; pursue them quickly, for you may overtake them." 6 (But she had brought them up to the roof and hidden them with the stalks of flax, which she had laid in order on the roof.) 7 Then the men pursued them by the road to the Jordan, to the fords. And as soon as those who pursued them had gone out, they shut the gate.

8 Now before they lay down, she came up to them on the roof, 9 and said to the men: "I know that the LORD has given you the land, that the terror of you has fallen on us, and that all the inhabitants of the land are fainthearted because of you. 10 For we have heard how the LORD dried up the water of the Red Sea for you when you came out of Egypt, and what you did to the two kings of the Amorites who *were* on the other side of the Jordan, Sihon and Og, whom you utterly destroyed. 11 And as soon as we heard *these things*, our hearts melted; neither did there remain any more courage in anyone because of you, for the LORD your God, He *is* God in heaven above and on earth beneath. 12 Now therefore, I beg you, swear to me by the LORD, since I have shown you kindness, that you also will show

נָתַן לָהֶם וְשַׁבְתֶּם לְאֶרֶץ יְרֻשַּׁתְכֶם וִירִשְׁתֶּם אוֹתָהּ אֲשֶׁר ׀ נָתַן לָכֶם מֹשֶׁה עֶבֶד יְהֹוָה בְּעֵבֶר הַיַּרְדֵּן מִזְרַח הַשָּׁמֶשׁ: 16 וַיַּעֲנוּ אֶת־יְהוֹשֻׁעַ לֵאמֹר כֹּל אֲשֶׁר־צִוִּיתָנוּ נַעֲשֶׂה וְאֶל־כָּל־אֲשֶׁר תִּשְׁלָחֵנוּ נֵלֵךְ: 17 כְּכֹל אֲשֶׁר־שָׁמַעְנוּ אֶל־מֹשֶׁה כֵּן נִשְׁמַע אֵלֶיךָ רַק יִהְיֶה יְהֹוָה אֱלֹהֶיךָ עִמָּךְ כַּאֲשֶׁר הָיָה עִם־מֹשֶׁה: 18 כָּל־אִישׁ אֲשֶׁר־יַמְרֶה אֶת־פִּיךָ וְלֹא־יִשְׁמַע אֶת־דְּבָרֶיךָ לְכֹל אֲשֶׁר־תְּצַוֶּנּוּ יוּמָת רַק חֲזַק וֶאֱמָץ: פ

ב וַיִּשְׁלַח יְהוֹשֻׁעַ בִּן־נוּן מִן־הַשִּׁטִּים שְׁנַיִם־אֲנָשִׁים מְרַגְּלִים חֶרֶשׁ לֵאמֹר לְכוּ רְאוּ אֶת־הָאָרֶץ וְאֶת־יְרִיחוֹ וַיֵּלְכוּ וַיָּבֹאוּ בֵּית־אִשָּׁה זוֹנָה וּשְׁמָהּ רָחָב וַיִּשְׁכְּבוּ־שָׁמָּה: 2 וַיֵּאָמַר לְמֶלֶךְ יְרִיחוֹ לֵאמֹר הִנֵּה אֲנָשִׁים בָּאוּ הֵנָּה הַלַּיְלָה מִבְּנֵי יִשְׂרָאֵל לַחְפֹּר אֶת־הָאָרֶץ: 3 וַיִּשְׁלַח מֶלֶךְ יְרִיחוֹ אֶל־רָחָב לֵאמֹר הוֹצִיאִי הָאֲנָשִׁים הַבָּאִים אֵלַיִךְ אֲשֶׁר־בָּאוּ לְבֵיתֵךְ כִּי לַחְפֹּר אֶת־כָּל־הָאָרֶץ בָּאוּ: 4 וַתִּקַּח הָאִשָּׁה אֶת־שְׁנֵי הָאֲנָשִׁים וַתִּצְפְּנוֹ וַתֹּאמֶר ׀ כֵּן בָּאוּ אֵלַי הָאֲנָשִׁים וְלֹא יָדַעְתִּי מֵאַיִן הֵמָּה: 5 וַיְהִי הַשַּׁעַר לִסְגּוֹר בַּחֹשֶׁךְ וְהָאֲנָשִׁים יָצָאוּ לֹא יָדַעְתִּי אָנָה הָלְכוּ הָאֲנָשִׁים רִדְפוּ מַהֵר אַחֲרֵיהֶם כִּי תַשִּׂיגוּם: 6 וְהִיא הֶעֱלָתַם הַגָּגָה וַתִּטְמְנֵם בְּפִשְׁתֵּי הָעֵץ הָעֲרֻכוֹת לָהּ עַל־הַגָּג: 7 וְהָאֲנָשִׁים רָדְפוּ אַחֲרֵיהֶם דֶּרֶךְ הַיַּרְדֵּן עַל הַמַּעְבְּרוֹת וְהַשַּׁעַר סָגָרוּ אַחֲרֵי כַּאֲשֶׁר יָצְאוּ הָרֹדְפִים אַחֲרֵיהֶם: 8 וְהֵמָּה טֶרֶם יִשְׁכָּבוּן וְהִיא עָלְתָה עֲלֵיהֶם עַל־הַגָּג: 9 וַתֹּאמֶר אֶל־הָאֲנָשִׁים יָדַעְתִּי כִּי־נָתַן יְהֹוָה לָכֶם אֶת־הָאָרֶץ וְכִי־נָפְלָה אֵימַתְכֶם עָלֵינוּ וְכִי נָמֹגוּ כָּל־יֹשְׁבֵי הָאָרֶץ מִפְּנֵיכֶם: 10 כִּי שָׁמַעְנוּ אֵת אֲשֶׁר־הוֹבִישׁ יְהֹוָה אֶת־מֵי יַם־סוּף מִפְּנֵיכֶם בְּצֵאתְכֶם מִמִּצְרָיִם וַאֲשֶׁר עֲשִׂיתֶם לִשְׁנֵי מַלְכֵי הָאֱמֹרִי אֲשֶׁר בְּעֵבֶר הַיַּרְדֵּן לְסִיחֹן וּלְעוֹג אֲשֶׁר הֶחֱרַמְתֶּם אוֹתָם: 11 וַנִּשְׁמַע וַיִּמַּס לְבָבֵנוּ וְלֹא־קָמָה עוֹד רוּחַ בְּאִישׁ מִפְּנֵיכֶם כִּי יְהֹוָה אֱלֹהֵיכֶם הוּא אֱלֹהִים בַּשָּׁמַיִם מִמַּעַל וְעַל־הָאָרֶץ מִתָּחַת: 12 וְעַתָּה הִשָּׁבְעוּ־נָא לִי בַּיהֹוָה כִּי־עָשִׂיתִי עִמָּכֶם חָסֶד וַעֲשִׂיתֶם גַּם־אַתֶּם עִם־

kindness to my father's house, and give me a true token, [13] and spare my father, my mother, my brothers, my sisters, and all that they have, and deliver our lives from death."

[14] So the men answered her, "Our lives for yours, if none of you tell this business of ours. And it shall be, when the LORD has given us the land, that we will deal kindly and truly with you."

[15] Then she let them down by a rope through the window, for her house *was* on the city wall; she dwelt on the wall. [16] And she said to them, "Get to the mountain, lest the pursuers meet you. Hide there three days, until the pursuers have returned. Afterward you may go your way."

[17] So the men said to her: "We *will be* blameless of this oath of yours which you have made us swear, [18] unless, *when* we come into the land, you bind this line of scarlet cord in the window through which you let us down, and unless you bring your father, your mother, your brothers, and all your father's household to your own home. [19] So it shall be *that* whoever goes outside the doors of your house into the street, his blood *shall be* on his own head, and we *will be* guiltless. And whoever is with you in the house, his blood *shall be* on our head if a hand is laid on him. [20] And if you tell this business of ours, then we will be free from your oath which you made us swear."

[21] Then she said, "According to your words, so *be* it." And she sent them away, and they departed. And she bound the scarlet cord in the window.

[22] They departed and went to the mountain, and stayed there three days until the pursuers returned. The pursuers sought *them* all along the way, but did not find *them*. [23] So the two men returned, descended from the mountain, and crossed over; and they came to Joshua the son of Nun, and told him all that had befallen them. [24] And they said to Joshua, "Truly the LORD has delivered all the land into our hands, for indeed all the inhabitants of the country are fainthearted because of us."

3 Then Joshua rose early in the morning; and they set out from Acacia Grove and came to the Jordan, he and all the children of Israel, and lodged there before they crossed over. [2] So it was, after three days, that the officers went through the camp; [3] and they commanded the people, saying, "When you see the ark of the covenant of the LORD your God, and the priests, the Levites, bearing it, then you shall set out from your place and go after it. [4] Yet there shall be a space between you and it, about two thousand

בֵּית אָבִי חֶסֶד וּנְתַתֶּם לִי אוֹת אֱמֶת: 13 וְהַחֲיִתֶם אֶת־אָבִי וְאֶת־אִמִּי וְאֶת־אַחַי וְאֶת־אַחְיוֹתַי וְאֵת כָּל־אֲשֶׁר לָהֶם וְהִצַּלְתֶּם אֶת־נַפְשֹׁתֵינוּ מִמָּוֶת: 14 וַיֹּאמְרוּ לָהּ הָאֲנָשִׁים נַפְשֵׁנוּ תַחְתֵּיכֶם לָמוּת אִם לֹא תַגִּידוּ אֶת־דְּבָרֵנוּ זֶה וְהָיָה בְּתֵת־יְהוָה לָנוּ אֶת־הָאָרֶץ וְעָשִׂינוּ עִמָּךְ חֶסֶד וֶאֱמֶת: 15 וַתּוֹרִדֵם בַּחֶבֶל בְּעַד הַחַלּוֹן כִּי בֵיתָהּ בְּקִיר הַחוֹמָה וּבַחוֹמָה הִיא יוֹשָׁבֶת: 16 וַתֹּאמֶר לָהֶם הָהָרָה לֵּכוּ פֶּן־יִפְגְּעוּ בָכֶם הָרֹדְפִים וְנַחְבֵּתֶם שָׁמָּה שְׁלֹשֶׁת יָמִים עַד שׁוֹב הָרֹדְפִים וְאַחַר תֵּלְכוּ לְדַרְכְּכֶם: 17 וַיֹּאמְרוּ אֵלֶיהָ הָאֲנָשִׁים נְקִיִּם אֲנַחְנוּ מִשְּׁבֻעָתֵךְ הַזֶּה אֲשֶׁר הִשְׁבַּעְתָּנוּ: 18 הִנֵּה אֲנַחְנוּ בָאִים בָּאָרֶץ אֶת־תִּקְוַת חוּט הַשָּׁנִי הַזֶּה תִּקְשְׁרִי בַּחַלּוֹן אֲשֶׁר הוֹרַדְתֵּנוּ בוֹ וְאֶת־אָבִיךְ וְאֶת־אִמֵּךְ וְאֶת־אַחַיִךְ וְאֵת כָּל־בֵּית אָבִיךְ תַּאַסְפִי אֵלַיִךְ הַבָּיְתָה: 19 וְהָיָה כֹּל אֲשֶׁר־יֵצֵא מִדַּלְתֵי בֵיתֵךְ ׀ הַחוּצָה דָּמוֹ בְרֹאשׁוֹ וַאֲנַחְנוּ נְקִיִּם וְכֹל אֲשֶׁר יִהְיֶה אִתָּךְ בַּבַּיִת דָּמוֹ בְרֹאשֵׁנוּ אִם־יָד תִּהְיֶה־בּוֹ: 20 וְאִם־תַּגִּידִי אֶת־דְּבָרֵנוּ זֶה וְהָיִינוּ נְקִיִּם מִשְּׁבֻעָתֵךְ אֲשֶׁר הִשְׁבַּעְתָּנוּ: 21 וַתֹּאמֶר כְּדִבְרֵיכֶם כֶּן־הוּא וַתְּשַׁלְּחֵם וַיֵּלֵכוּ וַתִּקְשֹׁר אֶת־תִּקְוַת הַשָּׁנִי בַּחַלּוֹן: 22 וַיֵּלְכוּ וַיָּבֹאוּ הָהָרָה וַיֵּשְׁבוּ שָׁם שְׁלֹשֶׁת יָמִים עַד־שָׁבוּ הָרֹדְפִים וַיְבַקְשׁוּ הָרֹדְפִים בְּכָל־הַדֶּרֶךְ וְלֹא מָצָאוּ: 23 וַיָּשֻׁבוּ שְׁנֵי הָאֲנָשִׁים וַיֵּרְדוּ מֵהָהָר וַיַּעַבְרוּ וַיָּבֹאוּ אֶל־יְהוֹשֻׁעַ בִּן־נוּן וַיְסַפְּרוּ־לוֹ אֵת כָּל־הַמֹּצְאוֹת אוֹתָם: 24 וַיֹּאמְרוּ אֶל־יְהוֹשֻׁעַ כִּי־נָתַן יְהוָה בְּיָדֵנוּ אֶת־כָּל־הָאָרֶץ וְגַם־נָמֹגוּ כָּל־יֹשְׁבֵי הָאָרֶץ מִפָּנֵינוּ: ס

ג וַיַּשְׁכֵּם יְהוֹשֻׁעַ בַּבֹּקֶר וַיִּסְעוּ מֵהַשִּׁטִּים וַיָּבֹאוּ עַד־הַיַּרְדֵּן הוּא וְכָל־בְּנֵי יִשְׂרָאֵל וַיָּלִנוּ שָׁם טֶרֶם יַעֲבֹרוּ: 2 וַיְהִי מִקְצֵה שְׁלֹשֶׁת יָמִים וַיַּעַבְרוּ הַשֹּׁטְרִים בְּקֶרֶב הַמַּחֲנֶה: 3 וַיְצַוּוּ אֶת־הָעָם לֵאמֹר כִּרְאוֹתְכֶם אֵת אֲרוֹן בְּרִית־יְהוָה אֱלֹהֵיכֶם וְהַכֹּהֲנִים הַלְוִיִּם נֹשְׂאִים אֹתוֹ וְאַתֶּם תִּסְעוּ מִמְּקוֹמְכֶם וַהֲלַכְתֶּם אַחֲרָיו: 4 אַךְ ׀ רָחוֹק יִהְיֶה בֵּינֵיכֶם וּבֵינוֹ כְּאַלְפַּיִם אַמָּה בַּמִּדָּה

ב 13 אַחְיוֹתַי   ג 4 וּבֵינָיו

cubits by measure. Do not come near it, that you may know the way by which you must go, for you have not passed *this* way before. "

⁵And Joshua said to the people, "Sanctify yourselves, for tomorrow the LORD will do wonders among you." ⁶Then Joshua spoke to the priests, saying, "Take up the ark of the covenant and cross over before the people."

So they took up the ark of the covenant and went before the people.

⁷And the LORD said to Joshua, "This day I will begin to exalt you in the sight of all Israel, that they may know that, as I was with Moses, *so* I will be with you. ⁸You shall command the priests who bear the ark of the covenant, saying, 'When you have come to the edge of the water of the Jordan, you shall stand in the Jordan.'"

⁹So Joshua said to the children of Israel, "Come here, and hear the words of the LORD your God." ¹⁰And Joshua said, "By this you shall know that the living God *is* among you, and *that* He will without fail drive out from before you the Canaanites and the Hittites and the Hivites and the Perizzites and the Girgashites and the Amorites and the Jebusites: ¹¹Behold, the ark of the covenant of the Lord of all the earth is crossing over before you into the Jordan. ¹²Now therefore, take for yourselves twelve men from the tribes of Israel, one man from every tribe. ¹³And it shall come to pass, as soon as the soles of the feet of the priests who bear the ark of the LORD, the Lord of all the earth, shall rest in the waters of the Jordan, *that* the waters of the Jordan shall be cut off, the waters that come down from upstream, and they shall stand as a heap."

¹⁴So it was, when the people set out from their camp to cross over the Jordan, with the priests bearing the ark of the covenant before the people, ¹⁵and as those who bore the ark came to the Jordan, and the feet of the priests who bore the ark dipped in the edge of the water (for the Jordan overflows all its banks during the whole time of harvest), ¹⁶that the waters which came down from upstream stood *still, and* rose in a heap very far away at Adam, the city that *is* beside Zaretan. So the waters that went down into the Sea of the Arabah, the Salt Sea, failed, *and* were cut off; and the people crossed over opposite Jericho. ¹⁷Then the priests who bore the ark of the covenant of the LORD stood firm on dry ground in the midst of the Jordan; and all Israel crossed over on dry ground, until all the people had crossed completely over the Jordan.

אַל־תִּקְרְבוּ אֵלָיו לְמַעַן אֲשֶׁר־תֵּדְעוּ אֶת־הַדֶּרֶךְ אֲשֶׁר תֵּלְכוּ־בָהּ כִּי לֹא עֲבַרְתֶּם בַּדֶּרֶךְ מִתְּמוֹל שִׁלְשׁוֹם׃ ס ⁵ וַיֹּאמֶר יְהוֹשֻׁעַ אֶל־הָעָם הִתְקַדָּשׁוּ כִּי מָחָר יַעֲשֶׂה יְהֹוָה בְּקִרְבְּכֶם נִפְלָאוֹת׃ ⁶ וַיֹּאמֶר יְהוֹשֻׁעַ אֶל־הַכֹּהֲנִים לֵאמֹר שְׂאוּ אֶת־אֲרוֹן הַבְּרִית וְעִבְרוּ לִפְנֵי הָעָם וַיִּשְׂאוּ אֶת־אֲרוֹן הַבְּרִית וַיֵּלְכוּ לִפְנֵי הָעָם׃ ס ⁷ וַיֹּאמֶר יְהֹוָה אֶל־יְהוֹשֻׁעַ הַיּוֹם הַזֶּה אָחֵל גַּדֶּלְךָ בְּעֵינֵי כָּל־יִשְׂרָאֵל אֲשֶׁר יֵדְעוּן כִּי כַּאֲשֶׁר הָיִיתִי עִם־מֹשֶׁה אֶהְיֶה עִמָּךְ׃ ⁸ וְאַתָּה תְּצַוֶּה אֶת־הַכֹּהֲנִים נֹשְׂאֵי אֲרוֹן הַבְּרִית לֵאמֹר כְּבֹאֲכֶם עַד־קְצֵה מֵי הַיַּרְדֵּן בַּיַּרְדֵּן תַּעֲמֹדוּ׃ פ

⁹ וַיֹּאמֶר יְהוֹשֻׁעַ אֶל־בְּנֵי יִשְׂרָאֵל גֹּשׁוּ הֵנָּה וְשִׁמְעוּ אֶת־דִּבְרֵי יְהֹוָה אֱלֹהֵיכֶם׃ ¹⁰ וַיֹּאמֶר יְהוֹשֻׁעַ בְּזֹאת תֵּדְעוּן כִּי אֵל חַי בְּקִרְבְּכֶם וְהוֹרֵשׁ יוֹרִישׁ מִפְּנֵיכֶם אֶת־הַכְּנַעֲנִי וְאֶת־הַחִתִּי וְאֶת־הַחִוִּי וְאֶת־הַפְּרִזִּי וְאֶת־הַגִּרְגָּשִׁי וְהָאֱמֹרִי וְהַיְבוּסִי׃ ¹¹ הִנֵּה אֲרוֹן הַבְּרִית אֲדוֹן כָּל־הָאָרֶץ עֹבֵר לִפְנֵיכֶם בַּיַּרְדֵּן׃ ¹² וְעַתָּה קְחוּ לָכֶם שְׁנֵי עָשָׂר אִישׁ מִשִּׁבְטֵי יִשְׂרָאֵל אִישׁ־אֶחָד אִישׁ־אֶחָד לַשָּׁבֶט׃ ¹³ וְהָיָה כְּנוֹחַ כַּפּוֹת רַגְלֵי הַכֹּהֲנִים נֹשְׂאֵי אֲרוֹן יְהֹוָה אֲדוֹן כָּל־הָאָרֶץ בְּמֵי הַיַּרְדֵּן מֵי הַיַּרְדֵּן יִכָּרֵתוּן הַמַּיִם הַיֹּרְדִים מִלְמָעְלָה וְיַעַמְדוּ נֵד אֶחָד׃ ¹⁴ וַיְהִי בִּנְסֹעַ הָעָם מֵאָהֳלֵיהֶם לַעֲבֹר אֶת־הַיַּרְדֵּן וְהַכֹּהֲנִים נֹשְׂאֵי הָאָרוֹן הַבְּרִית לִפְנֵי הָעָם׃ ¹⁵ וּכְבוֹא נֹשְׂאֵי הָאָרוֹן עַד־הַיַּרְדֵּן וְרַגְלֵי הַכֹּהֲנִים נֹשְׂאֵי הָאָרוֹן נִטְבְּלוּ בִּקְצֵה הַמָּיִם וְהַיַּרְדֵּן מָלֵא עַל־כָּל־גְּדוֹתָיו כֹּל יְמֵי קָצִיר׃ ¹⁶ וַיַּעַמְדוּ הַמַּיִם הַיֹּרְדִים מִלְמַעְלָה קָמוּ נֵד־אֶחָד הַרְחֵק מְאֹד בְּאָדָם֯ הָעִיר אֲשֶׁר מִצַּד צָרְתָן וְהַיֹּרְדִים עַל יָם הָעֲרָבָה יָם־הַמֶּלַח תַּמּוּ נִכְרָתוּ וְהָעָם עָבְרוּ נֶגֶד יְרִיחוֹ׃ ¹⁷ וַיַּעַמְדוּ הַכֹּהֲנִים נֹשְׂאֵי הָאָרוֹן בְּרִית־יְהֹוָה בֶּחָרָבָה בְּתוֹךְ הַיַּרְדֵּן הָכֵן וְכָל־יִשְׂרָאֵל עֹבְרִים בֶּחָרָבָה עַד אֲשֶׁר־תַּמּוּ כָּל־הַגּוֹי לַעֲבֹר אֶת־הַיַּרְדֵּן׃

4 And it came to pass, when all the people had completely crossed over the Jordan, that the LORD spoke to Joshua, saying: 2 "Take for yourselves twelve men from the people, one man from every tribe, 3 and command them, saying, 'Take for yourselves twelve stones from here, out of the midst of the Jordan, from the place where the priests' feet stood firm. You shall carry them over with you and leave them in the lodging place where you lodge tonight.' "

4 Then Joshua called the twelve men whom he had appointed from the children of Israel, one man from every tribe; 5 and Joshua said to them: "Cross over before the ark of the LORD your God into the midst of the Jordan, and each one of you take up a stone on his shoulder, according to the number of the tribes of the children of Israel, 6 that this may be a sign among you when your children ask in time to come, saying, 'What do these stones *mean* to you?' 7 Then you shall answer them that the waters of the Jordan were cut off before the ark of the covenant of the LORD; when it crossed over the Jordan, the waters of the Jordan were cut off. And these stones shall be for a memorial to the children of Israel forever."

8 And the children of Israel did so, just as Joshua commanded, and took up twelve stones from the midst of the Jordan, as the LORD had spoken to Joshua, according to the number of the tribes of the children of Israel, and carried them over with them to the place where they lodged, and laid them down there. 9 Then Joshua set up twelve stones in the midst of the Jordan, in the place where the feet of the priests who bore the ark of the covenant stood; and they are there to this day.

10 So the priests who bore the ark stood in the midst of the Jordan until everything was finished that the LORD had commanded Joshua to speak to the people, according to all that Moses had commanded Joshua; and the people hurried and crossed over. 11 Then it came to pass, when all the people had completely crossed over, that the ark of the LORD and the priests crossed over in the presence of the people. 12 And the men of Reuben, the men of Gad, and half the tribe of Manasseh crossed over armed before the children of Israel, as Moses had spoken to them. 13 About forty thousand prepared for war crossed over before the LORD for battle, to the plains of Jericho. 14 On that day the LORD exalted Joshua in the sight of all Israel; and they feared him, as they had feared Moses, all the days of his life.

ד וַיְהִי כַּאֲשֶׁר־תַּמּוּ כָל־הַגּוֹי לַעֲבוֹר אֶת־
הַיַּרְדֵּן׃ פ
וַיֹּאמֶר יְהוָה אֶל־יְהוֹשֻׁעַ לֵאמֹר׃ 2 קְחוּ לָכֶם מִן־
הָעָם שְׁנֵים עָשָׂר אֲנָשִׁים אִישׁ־אֶחָד אִישׁ־אֶחָד
מִשָּׁבֶט׃ 3 וְצַוּוּ אוֹתָם לֵאמֹר שְׂאוּ־לָכֶם מִזֶּה מִתּוֹךְ
הַיַּרְדֵּן מִמַּצַּב רַגְלֵי הַכֹּהֲנִים הָכֵין שְׁתֵּים־עֶשְׂרֵה
אֲבָנִים וְהַעֲבַרְתֶּם אוֹתָם עִמָּכֶם וְהִנַּחְתֶּם אוֹתָם
בַּמָּלוֹן אֲשֶׁר־תָּלִינוּ בוֹ הַלָּיְלָה׃ ס 4 וַיִּקְרָא
יְהוֹשֻׁעַ אֶל־שְׁנֵים הֶעָשָׂר אִישׁ אֲשֶׁר הֵכִין מִבְּנֵי
יִשְׂרָאֵל אִישׁ־אֶחָד אִישׁ־אֶחָד מִשָּׁבֶט׃ 5 וַיֹּאמֶר
לָהֶם יְהוֹשֻׁעַ עִבְרוּ לִפְנֵי אֲרוֹן יְהוָה אֱלֹהֵיכֶם אֶל־
תּוֹךְ הַיַּרְדֵּן וְהָרִימוּ לָכֶם אִישׁ אֶבֶן אַחַת עַל־
שִׁכְמוֹ לְמִסְפַּר שִׁבְטֵי בְנֵי־יִשְׂרָאֵל׃ 6 לְמַעַן תִּהְיֶה
זֹאת אוֹת בְּקִרְבְּכֶם כִּי־יִשְׁאָלוּן בְּנֵיכֶם מָחָר לֵאמֹר
מָה הָאֲבָנִים הָאֵלֶּה לָכֶם׃ 7 וַאֲמַרְתֶּם לָהֶם אֲשֶׁר
נִכְרְתוּ מֵימֵי הַיַּרְדֵּן מִפְּנֵי אֲרוֹן בְּרִית־יְהוָה בְּעָבְרוֹ
בַּיַּרְדֵּן נִכְרְתוּ מֵי הַיַּרְדֵּן וְהָיוּ הָאֲבָנִים הָאֵלֶּה
לְזִכָּרוֹן לִבְנֵי יִשְׂרָאֵל עַד־עוֹלָם׃ 8 וַיַּעֲשׂוּ־כֵן בְּנֵי־
יִשְׂרָאֵל כַּאֲשֶׁר צִוָּה יְהוֹשֻׁעַ וַיִּשְׂאוּ שְׁתֵּי־עֶשְׂרֵה
אֲבָנִים מִתּוֹךְ הַיַּרְדֵּן כַּאֲשֶׁר דִּבֶּר יְהוָה אֶל־יְהוֹשֻׁעַ
לְמִסְפַּר שִׁבְטֵי בְנֵי־יִשְׂרָאֵל וַיַּעֲבִרוּם עִמָּם אֶל־
הַמָּלוֹן וַיַּנִּחוּם שָׁם׃ 9 וּשְׁתֵּים עֶשְׂרֵה אֲבָנִים הֵקִים
יְהוֹשֻׁעַ בְּתוֹךְ הַיַּרְדֵּן תַּחַת מַצַּב רַגְלֵי הַכֹּהֲנִים
נֹשְׂאֵי אֲרוֹן הַבְּרִית וַיִּהְיוּ שָׁם עַד הַיּוֹם הַזֶּה׃
10 וְהַכֹּהֲנִים נֹשְׂאֵי הָאָרוֹן עֹמְדִים בְּתוֹךְ הַיַּרְדֵּן עַד
תֹּם כָּל־הַדָּבָר אֲשֶׁר־צִוָּה יְהוָה אֶת־יְהוֹשֻׁעַ לְדַבֵּר
אֶל־הָעָם כְּכֹל אֲשֶׁר־צִוָּה מֹשֶׁה אֶת־יְהוֹשֻׁעַ וַיְמַהֲרוּ
הָעָם וַיַּעֲבֹרוּ׃ 11 וַיְהִי כַּאֲשֶׁר־תַּם כָּל־הָעָם לַעֲבוֹר
וַיַּעֲבֹר אֲרוֹן־יְהוָה וְהַכֹּהֲנִים לִפְנֵי הָעָם׃ 12 וַיַּעַבְרוּ
בְּנֵי־רְאוּבֵן וּבְנֵי־גָד וַחֲצִי שֵׁבֶט הַמְנַשֶּׁה חֲמֻשִׁים
לִפְנֵי בְּנֵי יִשְׂרָאֵל כַּאֲשֶׁר דִּבֶּר אֲלֵיהֶם מֹשֶׁה׃
13 כְּאַרְבָּעִים אֶלֶף חֲלוּצֵי הַצָּבָא עָבְרוּ לִפְנֵי יְהוָה
לַמִּלְחָמָה אֶל עַרְבוֹת יְרִיחוֹ׃ ס 14 בַּיּוֹם
הַהוּא גִּדַּל יְהוָה אֶת־יְהוֹשֻׁעַ בְּעֵינֵי כָּל־יִשְׂרָאֵל
וַיִּרְאוּ אֹתוֹ כַּאֲשֶׁר יָרְאוּ אֶת־מֹשֶׁה כָּל־יְמֵי
חַיָּיו׃
פ

15 Then the LORD spoke to Joshua, saying,
16 "Command the priests who bear the ark of the
Testimony to come up from the Jordan." 17 Joshua
therefore commanded the priests, saying, "Come up
from the Jordan." 18 And it came to pass, when the
priests who bore the ark of the covenant of the
LORD had come from the midst of the Jordan, *and*
the soles of the priests' feet touched the dry land,
that the waters of the Jordan returned to their place
and overflowed all its banks as before.

19 Now the people came up from the Jordan on
the tenth *day* of the first month, and they camped in
Gilgal on the east border of Jericho. 20 And those
twelve stones which they took out of the Jordan,
Joshua set up in Gilgal. 21 Then he spoke to the
children of Israel, saying: "When your children ask
their fathers in time to come, saying, 'What *are*
these stones?' 22 then you shall let your children
know, saying, 'Israel crossed over this Jordan on
dry land'; 23 for the LORD your God dried up the
waters of the Jordan before you until you had
crossed over, as the LORD your God did to the Red
Sea, which He dried up before us until we had
crossed over, 24 that all the peoples of the earth may
know the hand of the LORD, that it *is* mighty, that
you may fear the LORD your God forever."

5 So it was, when all the kings of the Amorites
who *were* on the west side of the Jordan, and all the
kings of the Canaanites who *were* by the sea, heard
that the LORD had dried up the waters of the Jordan
from before the children of Israel until we had
crossed over, that their heart melted; and there was
no spirit in them any longer because of the children
of Israel.

2 At that time the LORD said to Joshua, "Make
flint knives for yourself, and circumcise the sons of
Israel again the second time." 3 So Joshua made
flint knives for himself, and circumcised the sons of
Israel at the hill of the foreskins. 4 And this *is* the
reason why Joshua circumcised them: All the
people who came out of Egypt *who were* males,
all the men of war, had died in the wilderness on the
way, after they had come out of Egypt. 5 For all the
people who came out had been circumcised, but all
the people born in the wilderness, on the way as
they came out of Egypt, had not been circumcised.
6 For the children of Israel walked forty years in the
wilderness, till all the people *who were* men of war,
who came out of Egypt, were consumed, because
they did not obey the voice of the LORD—to whom
the LORD swore that He would not show them the
land which the LORD had sworn to their fathers that
He would give us, "a land flowing with milk and

15 וַיֹּאמֶר יְהוָה אֶל־יְהוֹשֻׁעַ לֵאמֹר: 16 צַוֵּה
אֶת־הַכֹּהֲנִים נֹשְׂאֵי אֲרוֹן הָעֵדוּת וְיַעֲלוּ מִן־
הַיַּרְדֵּן: 17 וַיְצַו יְהוֹשֻׁעַ אֶת־הַכֹּהֲנִים לֵאמֹר עֲלוּ מִן־
הַיַּרְדֵּן: 18 וַיְהִי בַּעֲלוֹת הַכֹּהֲנִים נֹשְׂאֵי אֲרוֹן
בְּרִית־יְהוָה מִתּוֹךְ הַיַּרְדֵּן נִתְּקוּ כַּפּוֹת רַגְלֵי
הַכֹּהֲנִים אֶל הֶחָרָבָה וַיָּשֻׁבוּ מֵי־הַיַּרְדֵּן לִמְקוֹמָם
וַיֵּלְכוּ כִתְמוֹל־שִׁלְשׁוֹם עַל־כָּל־גְּדוֹתָיו: 19 וְהָעָם
עָלוּ מִן־הַיַּרְדֵּן בֶּעָשׂוֹר לַחֹדֶשׁ הָרִאשׁוֹן וַיַּחֲנוּ בַּגִּלְגָּל
בִּקְצֵה מִזְרַח יְרִיחוֹ: 20 וְאֵת שְׁתֵּים עֶשְׂרֵה הָאֲבָנִים
הָאֵלֶּה אֲשֶׁר לָקְחוּ מִן־הַיַּרְדֵּן הֵקִים יְהוֹשֻׁעַ בַּגִּלְגָּל:
21 וַיֹּאמֶר אֶל־בְּנֵי יִשְׂרָאֵל לֵאמֹר אֲשֶׁר יִשְׁאָלוּן
בְּנֵיכֶם מָחָר אֶת־אֲבוֹתָם לֵאמֹר מָה הָאֲבָנִים
הָאֵלֶּה: 22 וְהוֹדַעְתֶּם אֶת־בְּנֵיכֶם לֵאמֹר בַּיַּבָּשָׁה
עָבַר יִשְׂרָאֵל אֶת־הַיַּרְדֵּן הַזֶּה: 23 אֲשֶׁר־הוֹבִישׁ
יְהוָה אֱלֹהֵיכֶם אֶת־מֵי הַיַּרְדֵּן מִפְּנֵיכֶם עַד־עָבְרְכֶם
כַּאֲשֶׁר עָשָׂה יְהוָה אֱלֹהֵיכֶם לְיַם־סוּף אֲשֶׁר־הוֹבִישׁ
מִפָּנֵינוּ עַד־עָבְרֵנוּ: 24 לְמַעַן דַּעַת כָּל־עַמֵּי הָאָרֶץ אֶת־
יַד יְהוָה כִּי חֲזָקָה הִיא לְמַעַן יְרָאתֶם אֶת־
יְהוָה אֱלֹהֵיכֶם כָּל־הַיָּמִים: ס

ה וַיְהִי כִשְׁמֹעַ כָּל־מַלְכֵי הָאֱמֹרִי אֲשֶׁר בְּעֵבֶר
הַיַּרְדֵּן יָמָּה וְכָל־מַלְכֵי הַכְּנַעֲנִי אֲשֶׁר עַל־הַיָּם אֵת
אֲשֶׁר־הוֹבִישׁ יְהוָה אֶת־מֵי הַיַּרְדֵּן מִפְּנֵי בְנֵי־יִשְׂרָאֵל
עַד־עָבְרָם וַיִּמַּס לְבָבָם וְלֹא־הָיָה בָם עוֹד רוּחַ
מִפְּנֵי בְּנֵי־יִשְׂרָאֵל: ס 2 בָּעֵת הַהִיא אָמַר
יְהוָה אֶל־יְהוֹשֻׁעַ עֲשֵׂה לְךָ חַרְבוֹת צֻרִים וְשׁוּב מֹל
אֶת־בְּנֵי־יִשְׂרָאֵל שֵׁנִית: 3 וַיַּעַשׂ־לוֹ יְהוֹשֻׁעַ חַרְבוֹת
צֻרִים וַיָּמָל אֶת־בְּנֵי יִשְׂרָאֵל אֶל־גִּבְעַת הָעֲרָלוֹת:
4 וְזֶה הַדָּבָר אֲשֶׁר־מָל יְהוֹשֻׁעַ כָּל־הָעָם הַיֹּצֵא
מִמִּצְרַיִם הַזְּכָרִים כֹּל | אַנְשֵׁי הַמִּלְחָמָה מֵתוּ
בַמִּדְבָּר בַּדֶּרֶךְ בְּצֵאתָם מִמִּצְרָיִם: 5 כִּי־מֻלִים הָיוּ
כָּל־הָעָם הַיֹּצְאִים וְכָל־הָעָם הַיִּלֹּדִים בַּמִּדְבָּר בַּדֶּרֶךְ
בְּצֵאתָם מִמִּצְרַיִם לֹא־מָלוּ: 6 כִּי | אַרְבָּעִים שָׁנָה
הָלְכוּ בְנֵי־יִשְׂרָאֵל בַּמִּדְבָּר עַד־תֹּם כָּל־הַגּוֹי אַנְשֵׁי
הַמִּלְחָמָה הַיֹּצְאִים מִמִּצְרַיִם אֲשֶׁר לֹא־שָׁמְעוּ בְּקוֹל

honey." 7 Then Joshua circumcised their sons *whom*
He raised up in their place; for they were
uncircumcised, because they had not been circumcised on the way.

8 So it was, when they had finished circumcising
all the people, that they stayed in their places in the
camp till they were healed. 9 Then the LORD said to
Joshua, "This day I have rolled away the reproach
of Egypt from you." Therefore the name of the
place is called Gilgal to this day.

10 Now the children of Israel camped in Gilgal,
and kept the Passover on the fourteenth day of the
month at twilight on the plains of Jericho. 11 And
they ate of the produce of the land on the day after
the Passover, unleavened bread and parched grain,
on the very same day. 12 Then the manna ceased on
the day after they had eaten the produce of the
land; and the children of Israel no longer had
manna, but they ate the food of the land of Canaan
that year.

13 And it came to pass, when Joshua was by
Jericho, that he lifted his eyes and looked, and
behold, a Man stood opposite him with His sword
drawn in His hand. And Joshua went to Him and
said to Him, "*Are* You for us or for our adversaries?"

14 So He said, "No, but *as* Commander of the
army of the LORD I have now come."

And Joshua fell on his face to the earth and
worshiped, and said to Him, "What does my Lord
say to His servant?"

15 Then the Commander of the LORD's army said
to Joshua, "Take your sandal off your foot, for the
place where you stand *is* holy." And Joshua did so.

6 Now Jericho was securely shut up because of the
children of Israel; none went out, and none came in.
2 And the LORD said to Joshua: "See! I have given
Jericho into your hand, its king, *and* the mighty
men of valor. 3 You shall march around the city, all
you men of war; you shall go all around the city
once. This you shall do six days. 4 And seven priests
shall bear seven trumpets of rams' horns before the
ark. But the seventh day you shall march around
the city seven times, and the priests shall blow the
trumpets. 5 It shall come to pass, when they make a
long *blast* with the ram's horn, *and* when you hear
the sound of the trumpet, that all the people shall
shout with a great shout; then the wall of the city
will fall down flat. And the people shall go up every
man straight before him. "

6 Then Joshua the son of Nun called the priests
and said to them, "Take up the ark of the covenant,
and let seven priests bear seven trumpets of rams'

יְהוָה אֲשֶׁר נִשְׁבַּע יְהוָה לָהֶם לְבִלְתִּי הַרְאוֹתָם
אֶת־הָאָרֶץ אֲשֶׁר נִשְׁבַּע יְהוָה לַאֲבוֹתָם לָתֶת לָנוּ
אֶרֶץ זָבַת חָלָב וּדְבָשׁ: 7 וְאֶת־בְּנֵיהֶם הֵקִים תַּחְתָּם
אֹתָם מָל יְהוֹשֻׁעַ כִּי־עֲרֵלִים הָיוּ כִּי לֹא־מָלוּ אוֹתָם
בַּדָּרֶךְ: 8 וַיְהִי כַּאֲשֶׁר־תַּמּוּ כָל־הַגּוֹי לְהִמּוֹל וַיֵּשְׁבוּ
תַחְתָּם בַּמַּחֲנֶה עַד חֲיוֹתָם:

9 וַיֹּאמֶר יְהוָה אֶל־יְהוֹשֻׁעַ הַיּוֹם גַּלּוֹתִי אֶת־חֶרְפַּת
מִצְרַיִם מֵעֲלֵיכֶם וַיִּקְרָא שֵׁם הַמָּקוֹם הַהוּא גִּלְגָּל
עַד הַיּוֹם הַזֶּה: 10 וַיַּחֲנוּ בְנֵי־יִשְׂרָאֵל בַּגִּלְגָּל וַיַּעֲשׂוּ
אֶת־הַפֶּסַח בְּאַרְבָּעָה עָשָׂר יוֹם לַחֹדֶשׁ בָּעֶרֶב
בְּעַרְבוֹת יְרִיחוֹ: 11 וַיֹּאכְלוּ מֵעֲבוּר הָאָרֶץ מִמָּחֳרַת
הַפֶּסַח מַצּוֹת וְקָלוּי בְּעֶצֶם הַיּוֹם הַזֶּה: 12 וַיִּשְׁבֹּת
הַמָּן מִמָּחֳרָת בְּאָכְלָם מֵעֲבוּר הָאָרֶץ וְלֹא־הָיָה
עוֹד לִבְנֵי יִשְׂרָאֵל מָן וַיֹּאכְלוּ מִתְּבוּאַת אֶרֶץ כְּנַעַן
בַּשָּׁנָה הַהִיא: 13 וַיְהִי בִּהְיוֹת יְהוֹשֻׁעַ
בִּירִיחוֹ וַיִּשָּׂא עֵינָיו וַיַּרְא וְהִנֵּה־אִישׁ עֹמֵד לְנֶגְדּוֹ
וְחַרְבּוֹ שְׁלוּפָה בְּיָדוֹ וַיֵּלֶךְ יְהוֹשֻׁעַ אֵלָיו וַיֹּאמֶר לוֹ
הֲלָנוּ אַתָּה אִם־לְצָרֵינוּ: 14 וַיֹּאמֶר לֹא כִּי אֲנִי
שַׂר־צְבָא־יְהוָה עַתָּה בָאתִי וַיִּפֹּל יְהוֹשֻׁעַ אֶל־פָּנָיו
אַרְצָה וַיִּשְׁתָּחוּ וַיֹּאמֶר לוֹ מָה אֲדֹנִי מְדַבֵּר אֶל־
עַבְדּוֹ: 15 וַיֹּאמֶר שַׂר־צְבָא יְהוָה אֶל־יְהוֹשֻׁעַ שַׁל־
נַעַלְךָ מֵעַל רַגְלֶךָ כִּי הַמָּקוֹם אֲשֶׁר אַתָּה עֹמֵד
עָלָיו קֹדֶשׁ הוּא וַיַּעַשׂ יְהוֹשֻׁעַ כֵּן:

ו וִירִיחוֹ סֹגֶרֶת וּמְסֻגֶּרֶת מִפְּנֵי בְּנֵי יִשְׂרָאֵל אֵין יוֹצֵא
וְאֵין בָּא: 2 וַיֹּאמֶר יְהוָה אֶל־יְהוֹשֻׁעַ
רְאֵה נָתַתִּי בְיָדְךָ אֶת־יְרִיחוֹ וְאֶת־מַלְכָּהּ גִּבּוֹרֵי
הֶחָיִל: 3 וְסַבֹּתֶם אֶת־הָעִיר כֹּל אַנְשֵׁי הַמִּלְחָמָה
הַקֵּיף אֶת־הָעִיר פַּעַם אֶחָת כֹּה תַעֲשֶׂה שֵׁשֶׁת
יָמִים: 4 וְשִׁבְעָה כֹהֲנִים יִשְׂאוּ שִׁבְעָה שׁוֹפְרוֹת
הַיּוֹבְלִים לִפְנֵי הָאָרוֹן וּבַיּוֹם הַשְּׁבִיעִי תָּסֹבּוּ אֶת־
הָעִיר שֶׁבַע פְּעָמִים וְהַכֹּהֲנִים יִתְקְעוּ בַּשּׁוֹפָרוֹת:
5 וְהָיָה בִּמְשֹׁךְ בְּקֶרֶן הַיּוֹבֵל בְּשָׁמְעֲכֶם אֶת־
קוֹל הַשּׁוֹפָר יָרִיעוּ כָל־הָעָם תְּרוּעָה גְדוֹלָה וְנָפְלָה
חוֹמַת הָעִיר תַּחְתֶּיהָ וְעָלוּ הָעָם אִישׁ נֶגְדּוֹ:
6 וַיִּקְרָא יְהוֹשֻׁעַ בִּן־נוּן אֶל־הַכֹּהֲנִים וַיֹּאמֶר אֲלֵהֶם

horns before the ark of the LORD." 7 And he said to
the people, "Proceed, and march around the city,
and let him who is armed advance before the ark of
the LORD."

8 So it was, when Joshua had spoken to the
people, that the seven priests bearing the seven
trumpets of rams' horns before the LORD advanced
and blew the trumpets, and the ark of the covenant
of the LORD followed them. 9 The armed men went
before the priests who blew the trumpets, and the
rear guard came after the ark, while *the priests*
continued blowing the trumpets. 10 Now Joshua had
commanded the people, saying, "You shall not
shout or make any noise with your voice, nor shall a
word proceed out of your mouth, until the day I say
to you, 'Shout!' Then you shall shout." 11 So he had
the ark of the LORD circle the city, going around *it*
once. Then they came into the camp and lodged in
the camp.

12 And Joshua rose early in the morning, and the
priests took up the ark of the LORD. 13 Then seven
priests bearing seven trumpets of rams' horns
before the ark of the LORD went on continually
and blew with the trumpets. And the armed men
went before them. But the rear guard came after the
ark of the LORD, while *the priests* continued
blowing the trumpets. 14 And the second day they
marched around the city once and returned to the
camp. So they did six days.

15 But it came to pass on the seventh day that
they rose early, about the dawning of the day, and
marched around the city seven times in the same
manner. On that day only they marched around the
city seven times. 16 And the seventh time it
happened, when the priests blew the trumpets, that
Joshua said to the people: "Shout, for the LORD has
given you the city! 17 Now the city shall be doomed
by the LORD to destruction, it and all who *are* in it.
Only Rahab the harlot shall live, she and all who
are with her in the house, because she hid the
messengers that we sent. 18 And you, by all means
abstain from the accursed things, lest you become
accursed when you take of the accursed things, and
make the camp of Israel a curse, and trouble it.
19 But all the silver and gold, and vessels of bronze
and iron, *are* consecrated to the LORD; they shall
come into the treasury of the LORD."

20 So the people shouted when *the priests* blew the
trumpets. And it happened when the people heard
the sound of the trumpet, and the people shouted
with a great shout, that the wall fell down flat. Then
the people went up into the city, every man straight
before him, and they took the city. 21 And they

שְׂאוּ אֶת־אֲרוֹן הַבְּרִית וְשִׁבְעָה כֹהֲנִים יִשְׂאוּ שִׁבְעָה
שׁוֹפְרוֹת יוֹבְלִים לִפְנֵי אֲרוֹן יְהוָה: 7 וַיֹּאמְרוּ אֶל־
הָעָם עִבְרוּ וְסֹבּוּ אֶת־הָעִיר וְהֶחָלוּץ יַעֲבֹר לִפְנֵי
אֲרוֹן יְהוָה: 8 וַיְהִי כֶּאֱמֹר יְהוֹשֻׁעַ אֶל־הָעָם וְשִׁבְעָה
הַכֹּהֲנִים נֹשְׂאִים שִׁבְעָה שׁוֹפְרוֹת הַיּוֹבְלִים לִפְנֵי
יְהוָה עָבְרוּ וְתָקְעוּ בַּשּׁוֹפָרוֹת וַאֲרוֹן בְּרִית יְהוָה
הֹלֵךְ אַחֲרֵיהֶם: 9 וְהֶחָלוּץ הֹלֵךְ לִפְנֵי הַכֹּהֲנִים
תֹּקְעֵי הַשּׁוֹפָרוֹת וְהַמְאַסֵּף הֹלֵךְ אַחֲרֵי הָאָרוֹן
הָלוֹךְ וְתָקוֹעַ בַּשּׁוֹפָרוֹת: 10 וְאֶת־הָעָם צִוָּה יְהוֹשֻׁעַ
לֵאמֹר לֹא תָרִיעוּ וְלֹא־תַשְׁמִיעוּ אֶת־קוֹלְכֶם וְלֹא־
יֵצֵא מִפִּיכֶם דָּבָר עַד יוֹם אָמְרִי אֲלֵיכֶם הָרִיעוּ
וַהֲרִיעֹתֶם: 11 וַיַּסֵּב אֲרוֹן־יְהוָה אֶת־הָעִיר הַקֵּף
פַּעַם אֶחָת וַיָּבֹאוּ הַמַּחֲנֶה וַיָּלִינוּ בַּמַּחֲנֶה: פ

12 וַיַּשְׁכֵּם יְהוֹשֻׁעַ בַּבֹּקֶר וַיִּשְׂאוּ הַכֹּהֲנִים אֶת־
אֲרוֹן יְהוָה: 13 וְשִׁבְעָה הַכֹּהֲנִים נֹשְׂאִים שִׁבְעָה
שׁוֹפְרוֹת הַיֹּבְלִים לִפְנֵי אֲרוֹן יְהוָה הֹלְכִים הָלוֹךְ
וְתָקְעוּ בַּשּׁוֹפָרוֹת וְהֶחָלוּץ הֹלֵךְ לִפְנֵיהֶם וְהַמְאַסֵּף
הֹלֵךְ אַחֲרֵי אֲרוֹן יְהוָה הוֹלֵךְ וְתָקוֹעַ בַּשּׁוֹפָרוֹת:
14 וַיָּסֹבּוּ אֶת־הָעִיר בַּיּוֹם הַשֵּׁנִי פַּעַם אַחַת וַיָּשֻׁבוּ
הַמַּחֲנֶה כֹּה עָשׂוּ שֵׁשֶׁת יָמִים: 15 וַיְהִי | בַּיּוֹם
הַשְּׁבִיעִי וַיַּשְׁכִּמוּ כַּעֲלוֹת הַשַּׁחַר וַיָּסֹבּוּ אֶת־הָעִיר
כַּמִּשְׁפָּט הַזֶּה שֶׁבַע פְּעָמִים רַק בַּיּוֹם הַהוּא סָבְבוּ
אֶת־הָעִיר שֶׁבַע פְּעָמִים: 16 וַיְהִי בַּפַּעַם הַשְּׁבִיעִית
תָּקְעוּ הַכֹּהֲנִים בַּשּׁוֹפָרוֹת וַיֹּאמֶר יְהוֹשֻׁעַ אֶל־הָעָם
הָרִיעוּ כִּי־נָתַן יְהוָה לָכֶם אֶת־הָעִיר: 17 וְהָיְתָה
הָעִיר חֵרֶם הִיא וְכָל־אֲשֶׁר־בָּהּ לַיהוָה רַק רָחָב
הַזּוֹנָה תִּחְיֶה הִיא וְכָל־אֲשֶׁר אִתָּהּ בַּבַּיִת כִּי
הֶחְבְּאַתָה אֶת־הַמַּלְאָכִים אֲשֶׁר שָׁלָחְנוּ: 18 וְרַק
אַתֶּם שִׁמְרוּ מִן־הַחֵרֶם פֶּן־תַּחֲרִימוּ וּלְקַחְתֶּם מִן־
הַחֵרֶם וְשַׂמְתֶּם אֶת־מַחֲנֵה יִשְׂרָאֵל לְחֵרֶם וַעֲכַרְתֶּם
אוֹתוֹ: 19 וְכֹל | כֶּסֶף וְזָהָב וּכְלֵי נְחֹשֶׁת וּבַרְזֶל
קֹדֶשׁ הוּא לַיהוָה אוֹצַר יְהוָה יָבוֹא: 20 וַיָּרַע
הָעָם וַיִּתְקְעוּ בַּשּׁוֹפָרוֹת וַיְהִי כִשְׁמֹעַ הָעָם אֶת־
קוֹל הַשּׁוֹפָר וַיָּרִיעוּ הָעָם תְּרוּעָה גְדוֹלָה וַתִּפֹּל
הַחוֹמָה תַחְתֶּיהָ וַיַּעַל הָעָם הָעִירָה אִישׁ נֶגְדּוֹ
וַיִּלְכְּדוּ אֶת־הָעִיר: 21 וַיַּחֲרִימוּ אֶת־

7 ו וַיֹּאמֶר 9 תִּקְעֵי 13 הָלֹךְ

utterly destroyed all that *was* in the city, both man and woman, young and old, ox and sheep and donkey, with the edge of the sword.

22 But Joshua had said to the two men who had spied out the country, "Go into the harlot's house, and from there bring out the woman and all that she has, as you swore to her." 23 And the young men who had been spies went in and brought out Rahab, her father, her mother, her brothers, and all that she had. So they brought out all her relatives and left them outside the camp of Israel. 24 But they burned the city and all that *was* in it with fire. Only the silver and gold, and the vessels of bronze and iron, they put into the treasury of the house of the LORD. 25 And Joshua spared Rahab the harlot, her father's household, and all that she had. So she dwells in Israel to this day, because she hid the messengers whom Joshua sent to spy out Jericho.

26 Then Joshua charged *them* at that time, saying, "Cursed *be* the man before the LORD who rises up and builds this city Jericho; he shall lay its foundation with his firstborn, and with his youngest he shall set up its gates."

27 So the LORD was with Joshua, and his fame spread throughout all the country.

7 But the children of Israel committed a trespass regarding the accursed things, for Achan the son of Carmi, the son of Zabdi, the son of Zerah, of the tribe of Judah, took of the accursed things; so the anger of the LORD burned against the children of Israel.

2 Now Joshua sent men from Jericho to Ai, which *is* beside Beth Aven, on the east side of Bethel, and spoke to them, saying, "Go up and spy out the country." So the men went up and spied out Ai. 3 And they returned to Joshua and said to him, "Do not let all the people go up, but let about two or three thousand men go up and attack Ai. Do not weary all the people there, for *the people of Ai are* few." 4 So about three thousand men went up there from the people, but they fled before the men of Ai. 5 And the men of Ai struck down about thirty-six men, for they chased them *from* before the gate as far as Shebarim, and struck them down on the descent; therefore the hearts of the people melted and became like water.

6 Then Joshua tore his clothes, and fell to the earth on his face before the ark of the LORD until evening, he and the elders of Israel; and they put dust on their heads. 7 And Joshua said, "Alas, Lord GOD, why have You brought this people over the Jordan at all—to deliver us into the hand of the Amorites, to destroy us? Oh, that we had been

כָּל־אֲשֶׁר בָּעִיר מֵאִישׁ וְעַד־אִשָּׁה מִנַּעַר וְעַד־זָקֵן וְעַד שׁוֹר וָשֶׂה וַחֲמוֹר לְפִי־חָרֶב: 22 וְלִשְׁנַיִם הָאֲנָשִׁים הַמְרַגְּלִים אֶת־הָאָרֶץ אָמַר יְהוֹשֻׁעַ בֹּאוּ בֵּית־הָאִשָּׁה הַזּוֹנָה וְהוֹצִיאוּ מִשָּׁם אֶת־הָאִשָּׁה וְאֶת־כָּל־אֲשֶׁר־לָהּ כַּאֲשֶׁר נִשְׁבַּעְתֶּם לָהּ: 23 וַיָּבֹאוּ הַנְּעָרִים הַמְרַגְּלִים וַיֹּצִיאוּ אֶת־רָחָב וְאֶת־אָבִיהָ וְאֶת־אִמָּהּ וְאֶת־אַחֶיהָ וְאֶת־כָּל־אֲשֶׁר־לָהּ וְאֵת כָּל־מִשְׁפְּחוֹתֶיהָ הוֹצִיאוּ וַיַּנִּיחוּם מִחוּץ לְמַחֲנֵה יִשְׂרָאֵל: 24 וְהָעִיר שָׂרְפוּ בָאֵשׁ וְכָל־אֲשֶׁר־בָּהּ רַק הַכֶּסֶף וְהַזָּהָב וּכְלֵי הַנְּחֹשֶׁת וְהַבַּרְזֶל נָתְנוּ אוֹצַר בֵּית־יְהוָֹה: 25 וְאֶת־רָחָב הַזּוֹנָה וְאֶת־בֵּית אָבִיהָ וְאֶת־כָּל־אֲשֶׁר־לָהּ הֶחֱיָה יְהוֹשֻׁעַ וַתֵּשֶׁב בְּקֶרֶב יִשְׂרָאֵל עַד הַיּוֹם הַזֶּה כִּי הֶחְבִּיאָה אֶת־הַמַּלְאָכִים אֲשֶׁר־שָׁלַח יְהוֹשֻׁעַ לְרַגֵּל אֶת־יְרִיחוֹ: פ

26 וַיַּשְׁבַּע יְהוֹשֻׁעַ בָּעֵת הַהִיא לֵאמֹר אָרוּר הָאִישׁ לִפְנֵי יְהוָה אֲשֶׁר יָקוּם וּבָנָה אֶת־הָעִיר הַזֹּאת אֶת־יְרִיחוֹ בִּבְכֹרוֹ יְיַסְּדֶנָּה וּבִצְעִירוֹ יַצִּיב דְּלָתֶיהָ: 27 וַיְהִי יְהוָה אֶת־יְהוֹשֻׁעַ וַיְהִי שָׁמְעוֹ בְּכָל־הָאָרֶץ:

ז וַיִּמְעֲלוּ בְנֵי־יִשְׂרָאֵל מַעַל בַּחֵרֶם וַיִּקַּח עָכָן בֶּן־כַּרְמִי בֶן־זַבְדִּי בֶן־זֶרַח לְמַטֵּה יְהוּדָה מִן־הַחֵרֶם וַיִּחַר־אַף יְהוָה בִּבְנֵי יִשְׂרָאֵל: 2 וַיִּשְׁלַח יְהוֹשֻׁעַ אֲנָשִׁים מִירִיחוֹ הָעַי אֲשֶׁר עִם־בֵּית אָוֶן מִקֶּדֶם לְבֵית־אֵל וַיֹּאמֶר אֲלֵיהֶם לֵאמֹר עֲלוּ וְרַגְּלוּ אֶת־הָאָרֶץ וַיַּעֲלוּ הָאֲנָשִׁים וַיְרַגְּלוּ אֶת־הָעָי: 3 וַיָּשֻׁבוּ אֶל־יְהוֹשֻׁעַ וַיֹּאמְרוּ אֵלָיו אַל־יַעַל כָּל־הָעָם כְּאַלְפַּיִם אִישׁ אוֹ כִּשְׁלֹשֶׁת אֲלָפִים אִישׁ יַעֲלוּ וְיַכּוּ אֶת־הָעָי אַל־תְּיַגַּע־שָׁמָּה אֶת־כָּל־הָעָם כִּי מְעַט הֵמָּה: 4 וַיַּעֲלוּ מִן־הָעָם שָׁמָּה כִּשְׁלֹשֶׁת אֲלָפִים אִישׁ וַיָּנֻסוּ לִפְנֵי אַנְשֵׁי הָעָי: 5 וַיַּכּוּ מֵהֶם אַנְשֵׁי הָעַי כִּשְׁלֹשִׁים וְשִׁשָּׁה אִישׁ וַיִּרְדְּפוּם לִפְנֵי הַשַּׁעַר עַד־הַשְּׁבָרִים וַיַּכּוּם בַּמּוֹרָד וַיִּמַּס לְבַב־הָעָם וַיְהִי לְמָיִם: 6 וַיִּקְרַע יְהוֹשֻׁעַ שִׂמְלֹתָיו וַיִּפֹּל עַל־פָּנָיו אַרְצָה לִפְנֵי אֲרוֹן יְהוָה עַד־הָעֶרֶב הוּא וְזִקְנֵי יִשְׂרָאֵל וַיַּעֲלוּ עָפָר עַל־רֹאשָׁם: 7 וַיֹּאמֶר יְהוֹשֻׁעַ אֲהָהּ אֲדֹנָי יְהוִה לָמָה הֵעֲבַרְתָּ הַעֲבִיר אֶת־הָעָם הַזֶּה אֶת־הַיַּרְדֵּן לָתֵת אֹתָנוּ בְּיַד הָאֱמֹרִי

content, and dwelt on the other side of the Jordan!
[8] O Lord, what shall I say when Israel turns its back
before its enemies? [9] For the Canaanites and all the
inhabitants of the land will hear *it,* and surround us,
and cut off our name from the earth. Then what
will You do for Your great name?"

[10] So the LORD said to Joshua: "Get up! Why do
you lie thus on your face? [11] Israel has sinned, and
they have also transgressed My covenant which I
commanded them. For they have even taken some
of the accursed things, and have both stolen and
deceived; and they have also put *it* among their own
stuff. [12] Therefore the children of Israel could not
stand before their enemies, *but* turned *their* backs
before their enemies, because they have become
doomed to destruction. Neither will I be with you
anymore, unless you destroy the accursed from
among you. [13] Get up, sanctify the people, and say,
'Sanctify yourselves for tomorrow, because thus
says the LORD God of Israel: "*There is* an accursed
thing in your midst, O Israel; you cannot stand
before your enemies until you take away the
accursed thing from among you." [14] In the morning
therefore you shall be brought according to your
tribes. And it shall be *that* the tribe which the LORD
takes shall come according to families; and the
family which the LORD takes shall come by households; and the household which the LORD takes
shall come man by man. [15] Then it shall be *that* he
who is taken with the accursed thing shall be
burned with fire, he and all that he has, because he
has transgressed the covenant of the LORD, and
because he has done a disgraceful thing in Israel.'"

[16] So Joshua rose early in the morning and
brought Israel by their tribes, and the tribe of
Judah was taken. [17] He brought the clan of Judah,
and he took the family of the Zarhites; and he
brought the family of the Zarhites man by man, and
Zabdi was taken. [18] Then he brought his household
man by man, and Achan the son of Carmi, the son
of Zabdi, the son of Zerah, of the tribe of Judah,
was taken.

[19] Now Joshua said to Achan, "My son, I beg
you, give glory to the LORD God of Israel, and
make confession to Him, and tell me now what you
have done; do not hide *it* from me."

[20] And Achan answered Joshua and said, "Indeed I have sinned against the LORD God of Israel,
and this is what I have done: [21] When I saw among
the spoils a beautiful Babylonian garment, two
hundred shekels of silver, and a wedge of gold
weighing fifty shekels, I coveted them and took
them. And there they are, hidden in the earth in the
midst of my tent, with the silver under it."

לְהַאֲבִידֵנוּ וְלוּ הוֹאַלְנוּ וַנֵּשֶׁב בְּעֵבֶר הַיַּרְדֵּן׃ 8 בִּי
אֲדֹנָי מָה אֹמַר אַחֲרֵי אֲשֶׁר הָפַךְ יִשְׂרָאֵל עֹרֶף
לִפְנֵי אֹיְבָיו׃ 9 וְיִשְׁמְעוּ הַכְּנַעֲנִי וְכֹל יֹשְׁבֵי הָאָרֶץ
וְנָסַבּוּ עָלֵינוּ וְהִכְרִיתוּ אֶת־שְׁמֵנוּ מִן־הָאָרֶץ וּמַה־
תַּעֲשֵׂה לְשִׁמְךָ הַגָּדוֹל׃ ס   10 וַיֹּאמֶר יְהוָה
אֶל־יְהוֹשֻׁעַ קֻם לָךְ לָמָּה זֶּה אַתָּה נֹפֵל עַל־פָּנֶיךָ׃
11 חָטָא יִשְׂרָאֵל וְגַם עָבְרוּ אֶת־בְּרִיתִי אֲשֶׁר צִוִּיתִי
אוֹתָם וְגַם לָקְחוּ מִן־הַחֵרֶם וְגַם גָּנְבוּ וְגַם כִּחֲשׁוּ
וְגַם שָׂמוּ בִכְלֵיהֶם׃ 12 וְלֹא יֻכְלוּ בְּנֵי יִשְׂרָאֵל
לָקוּם לִפְנֵי אֹיְבֵיהֶם עֹרֶף יִפְנוּ לִפְנֵי אֹיְבֵיהֶם כִּי
הָיוּ לְחֵרֶם לֹא אוֹסִיף לִהְיוֹת עִמָּכֶם אִם־לֹא
תַשְׁמִידוּ הַחֵרֶם מִקִּרְבְּכֶם׃ 13 קֻם קַדֵּשׁ אֶת־הָעָם
וְאָמַרְתָּ הִתְקַדְּשׁוּ לְמָחָר כִּי כֹה אָמַר יְהוָה אֱלֹהֵי
יִשְׂרָאֵל חֵרֶם בְּקִרְבְּךָ יִשְׂרָאֵל לֹא תוּכַל לָקוּם לִפְנֵי
אֹיְבֶיךָ עַד־הֲסִירְכֶם הַחֵרֶם מִקִּרְבְּכֶם׃ 14 וְנִקְרַבְתֶּם
בַּבֹּקֶר לְשִׁבְטֵיכֶם וְהָיָה הַשֵּׁבֶט אֲשֶׁר־יִלְכְּדֶנּוּ יְהוָה
יִקְרַב לַמִּשְׁפָּחוֹת וְהַמִּשְׁפָּחָה אֲשֶׁר־יִלְכְּדֶנָּה יְהוָה
תִּקְרַב לַבָּתִּים וְהַבַּיִת אֲשֶׁר יִלְכְּדֶנּוּ יְהוָה יִקְרַב
לַגְּבָרִים׃ 15 וְהָיָה הַנִּלְכָּד בַּחֵרֶם יִשָּׂרֵף בָּאֵשׁ אֹתוֹ
וְאֶת־כָּל־אֲשֶׁר־לוֹ כִּי עָבַר אֶת־בְּרִית יְהוָה וְכִי־
עָשָׂה נְבָלָה בְּיִשְׂרָאֵל׃ 16 וַיַּשְׁכֵּם יְהוֹשֻׁעַ בַּבֹּקֶר
וַיַּקְרֵב אֶת־יִשְׂרָאֵל לִשְׁבָטָיו וַיִּלָּכֵד שֵׁבֶט יְהוּדָה׃
17 וַיַּקְרֵב אֶת־מִשְׁפַּחַת יְהוּדָה וַיִּלְכֹּד אֵת מִשְׁפַּחַת
הַזַּרְחִי וַיַּקְרֵב אֶת־מִשְׁפַּחַת הַזַּרְחִי לַגְּבָרִים וַיִּלָּכֵד
זַבְדִּי׃ 18 וַיַּקְרֵב אֶת־בֵּיתוֹ לַגְּבָרִים וַיִּלָּכֵד עָכָן בֶּן־
כַּרְמִי בֶן־זַבְדִּי בֶּן־זֶרַח לְמַטֵּה יְהוּדָה׃ 19 וַיֹּאמֶר
יְהוֹשֻׁעַ אֶל־עָכָן בְּנִי שִׂים־נָא כָבוֹד לַיהוָה אֱלֹהֵי
יִשְׂרָאֵל וְתֶן־לוֹ תוֹדָה וְהַגֶּד־נָא לִי מֶה עָשִׂיתָ אַל־
תְּכַחֵד מִמֶּנִּי׃ 20 וַיַּעַן עָכָן אֶת־יְהוֹשֻׁעַ וַיֹּאמַר אָמְנָה
אָנֹכִי חָטָאתִי לַיהוָה אֱלֹהֵי יִשְׂרָאֵל וְכָזֹאת וְכָזֹאת
עָשִׂיתִי׃ 21 וָאֶרְאֶהᵖ בַשָּׁלָל אַדֶּרֶת שִׁנְעָר אַחַת
טוֹבָה וּמָאתַיִם שְׁקָלִים כֶּסֶף וּלְשׁוֹן זָהָב אֶחָד
חֲמִשִּׁים שְׁקָלִים מִשְׁקָלוֹ וָאֶחְמְדֵם וָאֶקָּחֵם וְהִנָּם
טְמוּנִים בָּאָרֶץ בְּתוֹךְ הָאָהֳלִי וְהַכֶּסֶף תַּחְתֶּיהָ׃

22 So Joshua sent messengers, and they ran to the tent; and there it was, hidden in his tent, with the silver under it. 23 And they took them from the midst of the tent, brought them to Joshua and to all the children of Israel, and laid them out before the LORD. 24 Then Joshua, and all Israel with him, took Achan the son of Zerah, the silver, the garment, the wedge of gold, his sons, his daughters, his oxen, his donkeys, his sheep, his tent, and all that he had, and they brought them to the Valley of Achor. 25 And Joshua said, "Why have you troubled us? The LORD will trouble you this day." So all Israel stoned him with stones; and they burned them with fire after they had stoned them with stones.

26 Then they raised over him a great heap of stones, still there to this day. So the LORD turned from the fierceness of His anger. Therefore the name of that place has been called the Valley of Achor to this day.

8 Now the LORD said to Joshua: "Do not be afraid, nor be dismayed; take all the people of war with you, and arise, go up to Ai. See, I have given into your hand the king of Ai, his people, his city, and his land. 2 And you shall do to Ai and its king as you did to Jericho and its king. Only its spoil and its cattle you shall take as booty for yourselves. Lay an ambush for the city behind it. "

3 So Joshua arose, and all the people of war, to go up against Ai; and Joshua chose thirty thousand mighty men of valor and sent them away by night. 4 And he commanded them, saying: "Behold, you shall lie in ambush against the city, behind the city. Do not go very far from the city, but all of you be ready. 5 Then I and all the people who *are* with me will approach the city; and it will come about, when they come out against us as at the first, that we shall flee before them. 6 For they will come out after us till we have drawn them from the city, for they will say, '*They are* fleeing before us as at the first.' Therefore we will flee before them. 7 Then you shall rise from the ambush and seize the city, for the LORD your God will deliver it into your hand. 8 And it will be, when you have taken the city, *that* you shall set the city on fire. According to the commandment of the LORD you shall do. See, I have commanded you."

9 Joshua therefore sent them out; and they went to lie in ambush, and stayed between Bethel and Ai, on the west side of Ai; but Joshua lodged that night among the people. 10 Then Joshua rose up early in the morning and mustered the people, and went up, he and the elders of Israel, before the people to Ai. 11 And all the people of war who *were* with him

22 וַיִּשְׁלַח יְהוֹשֻׁעַ מַלְאָכִים וַיָּרֻצוּ הָאֹהֱלָה וְהִנֵּה טְמוּנָה בְּאָהֳלוֹ וְהַכֶּסֶף תַּחְתֶּיהָ: 23 וַיִּקָּחוּם מִתּוֹךְ הָאֹהֶל וַיְבִאוּם אֶל־יְהוֹשֻׁעַ וְאֶל כָּל־בְּנֵי יִשְׂרָאֵל וַיַּצִּקֻם לִפְנֵי יְהוָֹה: 24 וַיִּקַּח יְהוֹשֻׁעַ אֶת־עָכָן בֶּן־ זֶרַח וְאֶת־הַכֶּסֶף וְאֶת־הָאַדֶּרֶת וְאֶת־לְשׁוֹן הַזָּהָב וְאֶת־בָּנָיו וְאֶת־בְּנֹתָיו וְאֶת־שׁוֹרוֹ וְאֶת־חֲמֹרוֹ וְאֶת־ צֹאנוֹ וְאֶת־אָהֳלוֹ וְאֶת־כָּל־אֲשֶׁר־לוֹ וְכָל־יִשְׂרָאֵל עִמּוֹ וַיַּעֲלוּ אֹתָם עֵמֶק עָכוֹר: 25 וַיֹּאמֶר יְהוֹשֻׁעַ מֶה עֲכַרְתָּנוּ יַעְכָּרְךָ יְהוָֹה בַּיּוֹם הַזֶּה וַיִּרְגְּמוּ אֹתוֹ כָל־יִשְׂרָאֵל אֶבֶן וַיִּשְׂרְפוּ אֹתָם בָּאֵשׁ וַיִּסְקְלוּ אֹתָם בָּאֲבָנִים: 26 וַיָּקִימוּ עָלָיו גַּל־אֲבָנִים גָּדוֹל עַד הַיּוֹם הַזֶּה וַיָּשָׁב יְהוָֹה מֵחֲרוֹן אַפּוֹ עַל־כֵּן קָרָא שֵׁם הַמָּקוֹם הַהוּא עֵמֶק עָכוֹר עַד הַיּוֹם הַזֶּה: פ

ח וַיֹּאמֶר יְהוָֹה אֶל־יְהוֹשֻׁעַ אַל־תִּירָא וְאַל־תֵּחָת קַח עִמְּךָ אֵת כָּל־עַם הַמִּלְחָמָה וְקוּם עֲלֵה הָעָי רְאֵה | נָתַתִּי בְיָדְךָ אֶת־מֶלֶךְ הָעַי וְאֶת־עַמּוֹ וְאֶת־ עִירוֹ וְאֶת־אַרְצוֹ: 2 וְעָשִׂיתָ לָעַי וּלְמַלְכָּהּ כַּאֲשֶׁר עָשִׂיתָ לִירִיחוֹ וּלְמַלְכָּהּ רַק־שְׁלָלָהּ וּבְהֶמְתָּהּ תָּבֹזּוּ לָכֶם שִׂים־לְךָ אֹרֵב לָעִיר מֵאַחֲרֶיהָ: 3 וַיָּקָם יְהוֹשֻׁעַ וְכָל־עַם הַמִּלְחָמָה לַעֲלוֹת הָעָי וַיִּבְחַר יְהוֹשֻׁעַ שְׁלֹשִׁים אֶלֶף אִישׁ גִּבּוֹרֵי הַחַיִל וַיִּשְׁלָחֵם לָיְלָה: 4 וַיְצַו אֹתָם לֵאמֹר רְאוּ אַתֶּם אֹרְבִים לָעִיר מֵאַחֲרֵי הָעִיר אַל־תַּרְחִיקוּ מִן־הָעִיר מְאֹד וִהְיִיתֶם כֻּלְּכֶם נְכֹנִים: 5 וַאֲנִי וְכָל־הָעָם אֲשֶׁר אִתִּי נִקְרַב אֶל־ הָעִיר וְהָיָה כִּי־יֵצְאוּ לִקְרָאתֵנוּ כַּאֲשֶׁר בָּרִאשֹׁנָה וְנַסְנוּ לִפְנֵיהֶם: 6 וְיָצְאוּ אַחֲרֵינוּ עַד הַתִּיקֵנוּ אוֹתָם מִן־הָעִיר כִּי יֹאמְרוּ נָסִים לְפָנֵינוּ כַּאֲשֶׁר בָּרִאשֹׁנָה וְנַסְנוּ לִפְנֵיהֶם: 7 וְאַתֶּם תָּקֻמוּ מֵהָאוֹרֵב וְהוֹרַשְׁתֶּם אֶת־הָעִיר וּנְתָנָהּ יְהוָֹה אֱלֹהֵיכֶם בְּיֶדְכֶם: 8 וְהָיָה כְּתָפְשְׂכֶם אֶת־הָעִיר תַּצִּיתוּ אֶת־הָעִיר בָּאֵשׁ כִּדְבַר יְהוָֹה תַּעֲשׂוּ רְאוּ צִוִּיתִי אֶתְכֶם: 9 וַיִּשְׁלָחֵם יְהוֹשֻׁעַ וַיֵּלְכוּ אֶל־הַמַּאְרָב וַיֵּשְׁבוּ בֵּין בֵּית־אֵל וּבֵין הָעַי מִיָּם לָעָי וַיָּלֶן יְהוֹשֻׁעַ בַּלַּיְלָה הַהוּא בְּתוֹךְ הָעָם: 10 וַיַּשְׁכֵּם יְהוֹשֻׁעַ בַּבֹּקֶר וַיִּפְקֹד אֶת־הָעָם וַיַּעַל הוּא וְזִקְנֵי יִשְׂרָאֵל לִפְנֵי הָעָם הָעָי: 11 וְכָל־הָעָם

went up and drew near; and they came before the
city and camped on the north side of Ai. Now a
valley *lay* between them and Ai. 12 So he took about
five thousand men and set them in ambush between
Bethel and Ai, on the west side of the city. 13 And
when they had set the people, all the army that *was*
on the north of the city, and its rear guard on the
west of the city, Joshua went that night into the
midst of the valley.

14 Now it happened, when the king of Ai saw *it*,
that the men of the city hurried and rose early and
went out against Israel to battle, he and all his
people, at an appointed place before the plain. But
he did not know that *there was* an ambush against
him behind the city. 15 And Joshua and all Israel
made as if they were beaten before them, and fled
by the way of the wilderness. 16 So all the people
who *were* in Ai were called together to pursue them.
And they pursued Joshua and were drawn away
from the city. 17 There was not a man left in Ai or
Bethel who did not go out after Israel. So they left
the city open and pursued Israel.

18 Then the LORD said to Joshua, "Stretch out the
spear that *is* in your hand toward Ai, for I will give
it into your hand." And Joshua stretched out the
spear that *was* in his hand toward the city. 19 So
those in ambush arose quickly out of their place;
they ran as soon as he had stretched out his hand,
and they entered the city and took it, and hurried to
set the city on fire. 20 And when the men of Ai
looked behind them, they saw, and behold, the
smoke of the city ascended to heaven. So they had
no power to flee this way or that way, and the
people who had fled to the wilderness turned back
on the pursuers.

21 Now when Joshua and all Israel saw that the
ambush had taken the city and that the smoke of
the city ascended, they turned back and struck
down the men of Ai. 22 Then the others came out of
the city against them; so they were *caught* in the
midst of Israel, some on this side and some on that
side. And they struck them down, so that they let
none of them remain or escape. 23 But the king of Ai
they took alive, and brought him to Joshua.

24 And it came to pass when Israel had made an
end of slaying all the inhabitants of Ai in the field,
in the wilderness where they pursued them, and
when they all had fallen by the edge of the sword
until they were consumed, that all the Israelites
returned to Ai and struck it with the edge of the
sword. 25 So it was *that* all who fell that day, both
men and women, *were* twelve thousand—all the
people of Ai. 26 For Joshua did not draw back his
hand, with which he stretched out the spear, until

הַמִּלְחָמָה אֲשֶׁר אִתּוֹ עָלוּ וַיִּגְּשׁוּ וַיָּבֹאוּ נֶגֶד הָעִיר
וַיַּחֲנוּ מִצְּפוֹן לָעַי וְהַגַּי בֵּינָו וּבֵין־הָעָי: 12 וַיִּקַּח
כַּחֲמֵשֶׁת אֲלָפִים אִישׁ וַיָּשֶׂם אוֹתָם אֹרֵב בֵּין בֵּית־
אֵל וּבֵין הָעַי מִיָּם לָעִיר: 13 וַיָּשִׂימוּ הָעָם אֶת־
כָּל־הַמַּחֲנֶה אֲשֶׁר מִצְּפוֹן לָעִיר וְאֶת־עֲקֵבוֹ מִיָּם
לָעִיר וַיֵּלֶךְ יְהוֹשֻׁעַ בַּלַּיְלָה הַהוּא בְּתוֹךְ הָעֵמֶק:
14 וַיְהִי כִּרְאוֹת מֶלֶךְ־הָעַי וַיְמַהֲרוּ וַיַּשְׁכִּימוּ וַיֵּצְאוּ
אַנְשֵׁי־הָעִיר לִקְרַאת־יִשְׂרָאֵל לַמִּלְחָמָה הוּא וְכָל־
עַמּוֹ לַמּוֹעֵד לִפְנֵי הָעֲרָבָה וְהוּא לֹא יָדַע כִּי־אֹרֵב
לוֹ מֵאַחֲרֵי הָעִיר: 15 וַיִּנָּגְעוּ יְהוֹשֻׁעַ וְכָל־יִשְׂרָאֵל
לִפְנֵיהֶם וַיָּנֻסוּ דֶּרֶךְ הַמִּדְבָּר: 16 וַיִּזָּעֲקוּ כָּל־הָעָם
אֲשֶׁר בָּעַי לִרְדֹּף אַחֲרֵיהֶם וַיִּרְדְּפוּ אַחֲרֵי יְהוֹשֻׁעַ
וַיִּנָּתְקוּ מִן־הָעִיר: 17 וְלֹא־נִשְׁאַר אִישׁ בָּעַי וּבֵית
אֵל אֲשֶׁר לֹא־יָצְאוּ אַחֲרֵי יִשְׂרָאֵל וַיַּעַזְבוּ אֶת־הָעִיר
פְּתוּחָה וַיִּרְדְּפוּ אַחֲרֵי יִשְׂרָאֵל: פ
18 וַיֹּאמֶר יְהֹוָה אֶל־יְהוֹשֻׁעַ נְטֵה בַּכִּידוֹן אֲשֶׁר־בְּיָדְךָ
אֶל־הָעַי כִּי בְיָדְךָ אֶתְּנֶנָּה וַיֵּט יְהוֹשֻׁעַ בַּכִּידוֹן אֲשֶׁר־
בְּיָדוֹ אֶל־הָעִיר: 19 וְהָאוֹרֵב קָם מְהֵרָה מִמְּקוֹמוֹ
וַיָּרוּצוּ כִּנְטוֹת יָדוֹ וַיָּבֹאוּ הָעִיר וַיִּלְכְּדוּהָ וַיְמַהֲרוּ
וַיַּצִּיתוּ אֶת־הָעִיר בָּאֵשׁ: 20 וַיִּפְנוּ אַנְשֵׁי הָעַי
אַחֲרֵיהֶם וַיִּרְאוּ וְהִנֵּה עָלָה עֲשַׁן הָעִיר הַשָּׁמַיְמָה
וְלֹא־הָיָה בָהֶם יָדַיִם לָנוּס הֵנָּה וָהֵנָּה וְהָעָם הַנָּס
הַמִּדְבָּר נֶהְפַּךְ אֶל־הָרוֹדֵף: 21 וִיהוֹשֻׁעַ וְכָל־יִשְׂרָאֵל
רָאוּ כִּי־לָכַד הָאֹרֵב אֶת־הָעִיר וְכִי עָלָה עֲשַׁן
הָעִיר וַיָּשֻׁבוּ וַיַּכּוּ אֶת־אַנְשֵׁי הָעָי: 22 וְאֵלֶּה יָצְאוּ
מִן־הָעִיר לִקְרָאתָם וַיִּהְיוּ לְיִשְׂרָאֵל בַּתָּוֶךְ אֵלֶּה
מִזֶּה וְאֵלֶּה מִזֶּה וַיַּכּוּ אוֹתָם עַד־בִּלְתִּי הִשְׁאִיר־
לוֹ שָׂרִיד וּפָלִיט: 23 וְאֶת־מֶלֶךְ הָעַי תָּפְשׂוּ חָי
וַיַּקְרִבוּ אֹתוֹ אֶל־יְהוֹשֻׁעַ: 24 וַיְהִי כְּכַלּוֹת יִשְׂרָאֵל
לַהֲרֹג אֶת־כָּל־יֹשְׁבֵי הָעַי בַּשָּׂדֶה בַּמִּדְבָּר אֲשֶׁר
רְדָפוּם בּוֹ וַיִּפְּלוּ כֻלָּם לְפִי־חֶרֶב עַד־תֻּמָּם וַיָּשֻׁבוּ
כָל־יִשְׂרָאֵל הָעַי וַיַּכּוּ אֹתָהּ לְפִי־חָרֶב: 25 וַיְהִי כָל־
הַנֹּפְלִים בַּיּוֹם הַהוּא מֵאִישׁ וְעַד־אִשָּׁה שְׁנֵים עָשָׂר
אָלֶף כֹּל אַנְשֵׁי הָעָי: 26 וִיהוֹשֻׁעַ לֹא־הֵשִׁיב יָדוֹ
אֲשֶׁר נָטָה בַּכִּידוֹן עַד אֲשֶׁר הֶחֱרִים אֶת כָּל־

he had utterly destroyed all the inhabitants of Ai.
27 Only the livestock and the spoil of that city Israel
took as booty for themselves, according to the word
of the LORD which He had commanded Joshua.
28 So Joshua burned Ai and made it a heap forever,
a desolation to this day. 29 And the king of Ai he
hanged on a tree until evening. And as soon as the
sun was down, Joshua commanded that they should
take his corpse down from the tree, cast it at the
entrance of the gate of the city, and raise over it a
great heap of stones *that remains* to this day.

30 Now Joshua built an altar to the LORD God of
Israel in Mount Ebal, 31 as Moses the servant of the
LORD had commanded the children of Israel, as it is
written in the Book of the Law of Moses: "an altar
of whole stones over which no man has wielded an
iron *tool*." And they offered on it burnt offerings to
the LORD, and sacrificed peace offerings. 32 And
there, in the presence of the children of Israel, he
wrote on the stones a copy of the law of Moses,
which he had written. 33 Then all Israel, with their
elders and officers and judges, stood on either side
of the ark before the priests, the Levites, who bore
the ark of the covenant of the LORD, the stranger as
well as he who was born among them. Half of them
were in front of Mount Gerizim and half of them in
front of Mount Ebal, as Moses the servant of the
LORD had commanded before, that they should
bless the people of Israel. 34 And afterward he read
all the words of the law, the blessings and the
cursings, according to all that is written in the Book
of the Law. 35 There was not a word of all that
Moses had commanded which Joshua did not read
before all the assembly of Israel, with the women,
the little ones, and the strangers who were living
among them.

9 And it came to pass when all the kings who *were*
on this side of the Jordan, in the hills and in the
lowland and in all the coasts of the Great Sea
toward Lebanon—the Hittite, the Amorite, the
Canaanite, the Perizzite, the Hivite, and the
Jebusite—heard *about it,* 2 that they gathered
together to fight with Joshua and Israel with one
accord.

3 But when the inhabitants of Gibeon heard what
Joshua had done to Jericho and Ai, 4 they worked
craftily, and went and pretended to be ambassadors. And they took old sacks on their donkeys, old
wineskins torn and mended, 5 old and patched
sandals on their feet, and old garments on
themselves; and all the bread of their provision
was dry *and* moldy. 6 And they went to Joshua, to

27 רַק הַבְּהֵמָה וּשְׁלַל הָעִיר הַהִיא
בָּזְזוּ לָהֶם יִשְׂרָאֵל כִּדְבַר יְהֹוָה אֲשֶׁר צִוָּה אֶת־
יְהוֹשֻׁעַ: 28 וַיִּשְׂרֹף יְהוֹשֻׁעַ אֶת־הָעָי וַיְשִׂימֶהָ תֵּל־
עוֹלָם שְׁמָמָה עַד הַיּוֹם הַזֶּה: 29 וְאֶת־מֶלֶךְ הָעַי
תָּלָה עַל־הָעֵץ עַד־עֵת הָעֶרֶב וּכְבוֹא הַשֶּׁמֶשׁ צִוָּה
יְהוֹשֻׁעַ וַיֹּרִידוּ אֶת־נִבְלָתוֹ מִן־הָעֵץ וַיַּשְׁלִיכוּ אוֹתָהּ
אֶל־פֶּתַח שַׁעַר הָעִיר וַיָּקִימוּ עָלָיו גַּל־אֲבָנִים גָּדוֹל
עַד הַיּוֹם הַזֶּה: פ

30 אָז יִבְנֶה יְהוֹשֻׁעַ מִזְבֵּחַ לַיהֹוָה אֱלֹהֵי יִשְׂרָאֵל
בְּהַר עֵיבָל: 31 כַּאֲשֶׁר צִוָּה מֹשֶׁה עֶבֶד־יְהֹוָה אֶת־
בְּנֵי יִשְׂרָאֵל כַּכָּתוּב בְּסֵפֶר תּוֹרַת מֹשֶׁה מִזְבַּח
אֲבָנִים שְׁלֵמוֹת אֲשֶׁר לֹא־הֵנִיף עֲלֵיהֶן בַּרְזֶל וַיַּעֲלוּ
עָלָיו עֹלוֹת לַיהֹוָה וַיִּזְבְּחוּ שְׁלָמִים: 32 וַיִּכְתָּב־שָׁם
עַל־הָאֲבָנִים אֵת מִשְׁנֵה תּוֹרַת מֹשֶׁה אֲשֶׁר כָּתַב
לִפְנֵי בְּנֵי יִשְׂרָאֵל: 33 וְכָל־יִשְׂרָאֵל וּזְקֵנָיו וְשֹׁטְרִים |
וְשֹׁפְטָיו עֹמְדִים מִזֶּה | וּמִזֶּה | לָאָרוֹן נֶגֶד הַכֹּהֲנִים
הַלְוִיִּם נֹשְׂאֵי | אֲרוֹן בְּרִית־יְהֹוָה כַּגֵּר כָּאֶזְרָח
חֶצְיוֹ אֶל־מוּל הַר־גְּרִזִים וְהַחֶצְיוֹ אֶל־מוּל הַר־
עֵיבָל כַּאֲשֶׁר צִוָּה מֹשֶׁה עֶבֶד־יְהֹוָה לְבָרֵךְ אֶת־
הָעָם יִשְׂרָאֵל בָּרִאשֹׁנָה: 34 וְאַחֲרֵי־כֵן קָרָא אֶת־
כָּל־דִּבְרֵי הַתּוֹרָה הַבְּרָכָה וְהַקְּלָלָה כְּכָל־הַכָּתוּב
בְּסֵפֶר הַתּוֹרָה: 35 לֹא־הָיָה דָבָר מִכֹּל אֲשֶׁר־צִוָּה
מֹשֶׁה אֲשֶׁר לֹא־קָרָא יְהוֹשֻׁעַ נֶגֶד כָּל־קְהַל יִשְׂרָאֵל
וְהַנָּשִׁים וְהַטַּף וְהַגֵּר הַהֹלֵךְ בְּקִרְבָּם: פ

ט וַיְהִי כִשְׁמֹעַ כָּל־הַמְּלָכִים אֲשֶׁר בְּעֵבֶר הַיַּרְדֵּן
בָּהָר וּבַשְּׁפֵלָה וּבְכֹל חוֹף הַיָּם הַגָּדוֹל אֶל־מוּל
הַלְּבָנוֹן הַחִתִּי וְהָאֱמֹרִי הַכְּנַעֲנִי הַפְּרִזִּי הַחִוִּי
וְהַיְבוּסִי: 2 וַיִּתְקַבְּצוּ יַחְדָּו לְהִלָּחֵם עִם־יְהוֹשֻׁעַ
וְעִם־יִשְׂרָאֵל פֶּה אֶחָד: פ

3 וְיֹשְׁבֵי גִבְעוֹן שָׁמְעוּ אֵת אֲשֶׁר עָשָׂה יְהוֹשֻׁעַ
לִירִיחוֹ וְלָעָי: 4 וַיַּעֲשׂוּ גַם־הֵמָּה בְּעָרְמָה וַיֵּלְכוּ
וַיִּצְטַיָּרוּ וַיִּקְחוּ שַׂקִּים בָּלִים לַחֲמוֹרֵיהֶם וְנֹאדוֹת
יַיִן בָּלִים וּמְבֻקָּעִים וּמְצֹרָרִים: 5 וּנְעָלוֹת בָּלוֹת
וּמְטֻלָּאוֹת בְּרַגְלֵיהֶם וּשְׂלָמוֹת בָּלוֹת עֲלֵיהֶם וְכֹל
לֶחֶם צֵידָם יָבֵשׁ הָיָה נִקֻּדִים: 6 וַיֵּלְכוּ אֶל־יְהוֹשֻׁעַ

the camp at Gilgal, and said to him and to the men of Israel, "We have come from a far country; now therefore, make a covenant with us."

7 Then the men of Israel said to the Hivites, "Perhaps you dwell among us; so how can we make a covenant with you?"

8 But they said to Joshua, "We *are* your servants."

And Joshua said to them, "Who *are* you, and where do you come from?"

9 So they said to him: "From a very far country your servants have come, because of the name of the LORD your God; for we have heard of His fame, and all that He did in Egypt, 10 and all that He did to the two kings of the Amorites who *were* beyond the Jordan—to Sihon king of Heshbon, and Og king of Bashan, who was at Ashtaroth. 11 Therefore our elders and all the inhabitants of our country spoke to us, saying, 'Take provisions with you for the journey, and go to meet them, and say to them, "We *are* your servants; now therefore, make a covenant with us." ' 12 This bread of ours we took hot *for* our provision from our houses on the day we departed to come to you. But now look, it is dry and moldy. 13 And these wineskins which we filled *were* new, and see, they are torn; and these our garments and our sandals have become old because of the very long journey.' "

14 Then the men of Israel took some of their provisions; but they did not ask counsel of the LORD. 15 So Joshua made peace with them, and made a covenant with them to let them live; and the rulers of the congregation swore to them.

16 And it happened at the end of three days, after they had made a covenant with them, that they heard that they *were* their neighbors who dwelt near them. 17 Then the children of Israel journeyed and came to their cities on the third day. Now their cities *were* Gibeon, Chephirah, Beeroth, and Kirjath Jearim. 18 But the children of Israel did not attack them, because the rulers of the congregation had sworn to them by the LORD God of Israel. And all the congregation complained against the rulers.

19 Then all the rulers said to all the congregation, "We have sworn to them by the LORD God of Israel; now therefore, we may not touch them. 20 This we will do to them: We will let them live, lest wrath be upon us because of the oath which we swore to them." 21 And the rulers said to them, "Let them live, but let them be woodcutters and water carriers for all the congregation, as the rulers had promised them."

אֶל־הַמַּחֲנֶה הַגִּלְגָּל וַיֹּאמְרוּ אֵלָיו וְאֶל־אִישׁ יִשְׂרָאֵל
מֵאֶרֶץ רְחוֹקָה בָּאנוּ וְעַתָּה כִּרְתוּ־לָנוּ בְרִית׃

7 וַיֹּאמְרוּ אִישׁ־יִשְׂרָאֵל אֶל־הַחִוִּי אוּלַי בְּקִרְבִּי
אַתָּה יוֹשֵׁב וְאֵיךְ אֶכְרָת־לְךָ בְרִית׃ 8 וַיֹּאמְרוּ אֶל־יְהוֹשֻׁעַ עֲבָדֶיךָ אֲנָחְנוּ וַיֹּאמֶר אֲלֵהֶם
יְהוֹשֻׁעַ מִי אַתֶּם וּמֵאַיִן תָּבֹאוּ׃ 9 וַיֹּאמְרוּ אֵלָיו
מֵאֶרֶץ רְחוֹקָה מְאֹד בָּאוּ עֲבָדֶיךָ לְשֵׁם יְהוָה
אֱלֹהֶיךָ כִּי־שָׁמַעְנוּ שָׁמְעוֹ וְאֵת כָּל־אֲשֶׁר עָשָׂה
בְּמִצְרָיִם׃ 10 וְאֵת ׀ כָּל־אֲשֶׁר עָשָׂה לִשְׁנֵי מַלְכֵי
הָאֱמֹרִי אֲשֶׁר בְּעֵבֶר הַיַּרְדֵּן לְסִיחוֹן מֶלֶךְ חֶשְׁבּוֹן
וּלְעוֹג מֶלֶךְ־הַבָּשָׁן אֲשֶׁר בְּעַשְׁתָּרוֹת׃ 11 וַיֹּאמְרוּ
אֵלֵינוּ זְקֵינֵינוּ וְכָל־יֹשְׁבֵי אַרְצֵנוּ לֵאמֹר קְחוּ בְיֶדְכֶם
צֵידָה לַדֶּרֶךְ וּלְכוּ לִקְרָאתָם וַאֲמַרְתֶּם אֲלֵיהֶם
עֲבָדֵיכֶם אֲנַחְנוּ וְעַתָּה כִּרְתוּ־לָנוּ בְרִית׃ 12 זֶה ׀
לַחְמֵנוּ חָם הִצְטַיַּדְנוּ אֹתוֹ מִבָּתֵּינוּ בְּיוֹם צֵאתֵנוּ
לָלֶכֶת אֲלֵיכֶם וְעַתָּה הִנֵּה יָבֵשׁ וְהָיָה נִקֻּדִים׃
13 וְאֵלֶּה נֹאדוֹת הַיַּיִן אֲשֶׁר מִלֵּאנוּ חֲדָשִׁים וְהִנֵּה
הִתְבַּקָּעוּ וְאֵלֶּה שַׂלְמוֹתֵינוּ וּנְעָלֵינוּ בָּלוּ מֵרֹב הַדֶּרֶךְ
מְאֹד׃ 14 וַיִּקְחוּ הָאֲנָשִׁים מִצֵּידָם וְאֶת־פִּי יְהוָה
לֹא שָׁאָלוּ׃ 15 וַיַּעַשׂ לָהֶם יְהוֹשֻׁעַ שָׁלוֹם וַיִּכְרֹת
לָהֶם בְּרִית לְחַיּוֹתָם וַיִּשָּׁבְעוּ לָהֶם נְשִׂיאֵי הָעֵדָה׃
16 וַיְהִי מִקְצֵה שְׁלֹשֶׁת יָמִים אַחֲרֵי אֲשֶׁר־כָּרְתוּ
לָהֶם בְּרִית וַיִּשְׁמְעוּ כִּי־קְרֹבִים הֵם אֵלָיו וּבְקִרְבּוֹ
הֵם יֹשְׁבִים׃ 17 וַיִּסְעוּ בְנֵי־יִשְׂרָאֵל וַיָּבֹאוּ אֶל־עָרֵיהֶם
בַּיּוֹם הַשְּׁלִישִׁי וְעָרֵיהֶם גִּבְעוֹן וְהַכְּפִירָה וּבְאֵרוֹת
וְקִרְיַת יְעָרִים׃ 18 וְלֹא הִכּוּם בְּנֵי יִשְׂרָאֵל כִּי־נִשְׁבְּעוּ
לָהֶם נְשִׂיאֵי הָעֵדָה בַּיהוָה אֱלֹהֵי יִשְׂרָאֵל וַיִּלֹּנוּ
כָל־הָעֵדָה עַל־הַנְּשִׂיאִים׃ 19 וַיֹּאמְרוּ כָל־הַנְּשִׂיאִים
אֶל־כָּל־הָעֵדָה אֲנַחְנוּ נִשְׁבַּעְנוּ לָהֶם בַּיהוָה אֱלֹהֵי
יִשְׂרָאֵל וְעַתָּה לֹא נוּכַל לִנְגֹּעַ בָּהֶם׃ 20 זֹאת נַעֲשֶׂה
לָהֶם וְהַחֲיֵה אוֹתָם וְלֹא־יִהְיֶה עָלֵינוּ קֶצֶף עַל־
הַשְּׁבוּעָה אֲשֶׁר־נִשְׁבַּעְנוּ לָהֶם׃ 21 וַיֹּאמְרוּ אֲלֵיהֶם
הַנְּשִׂיאִים יִחְיוּ וַיִּהְיוּ חֹטְבֵי עֵצִים וְשֹׁאֲבֵי־מַיִם לְכָל־

22 Then Joshua called for them, and he spoke to them, saying, "Why have you deceived us, saying, 'We *are* very far from you,' when you dwell near us? 23 Now therefore, you *are* cursed, and none of you shall be freed from being slaves—woodcutters and water carriers for the house of my God."

24 So they answered Joshua and said, "Because your servants were clearly told that the LORD your God commanded His servant Moses to give you all the land, and to destroy all the inhabitants of the land from before you; therefore we were very much afraid for our lives because of you, and have done this thing. 25 And now, here we are, in your hands; do with us as it seems good and right to do to us." 26 So he did to them, and delivered them out of the hand of the children of Israel, so that they did not kill them. 27 And that day Joshua made them woodcutters and water carriers for the congregation and for the altar of the LORD, in the place which He would choose, even to this day.

10 Now it came to pass when Adoni-Zedek king of Jerusalem heard how Joshua had taken Ai and had utterly destroyed it—as he had done to Jericho and its king, so he had done to Ai and its king—and how the inhabitants of Gibeon had made peace with Israel and were among them, 2 that they feared greatly, because Gibeon *was* a great city, like one of the royal cities, and because it *was* greater than Ai, and all its men *were* mighty. 3 Therefore Adoni-Zedek king of Jerusalem sent to Hoham king of Hebron, Piram king of Jarmuth, Japhia king of Lachish, and Debir king of Eglon, saying, 4 "Come up to me and help me, that we may attack Gibeon, for it has made peace with Joshua and with the children of Israel. " 5 Therefore the five kings of the Amorites, the king of Jerusalem, the king of Hebron, the king of Jarmuth, the king of Lachish, *and* the king of Eglon, gathered together and went up, they and all their armies, and camped before Gibeon and made war against it.

6 And the men of Gibeon sent to Joshua at the camp at Gilgal, saying, "Do not forsake your servants; come up to us quickly, save us and help us, for all the kings of the Amorites who dwell in the mountains have gathered together against us."

7 So Joshua ascended from Gilgal, he and all the people of war with him, and all the mighty men of valor. 8 And the LORD said to Joshua, "Do not fear them, for I have delivered them into your hand; not a man of them shall stand before you." 9 Joshua therefore came upon them suddenly, having marched all night from Gilgal. 10 So the LORD routed them before Israel, killed them with a great

הָעֵדָה כַּאֲשֶׁר דִּבְּרוּ לָהֶם הַנְּשִׂיאִים: 22 וַיִּקְרָא לָהֶם יְהוֹשֻׁעַ וַיְדַבֵּר אֲלֵיהֶם לֵאמֹר לָמָּה רִמִּיתֶם אֹתָנוּ לֵאמֹר רְחוֹקִים אֲנַחְנוּ מִכֶּם מְאֹד וְאַתֶּם בְּקִרְבֵּנוּ יֹשְׁבִים: 23 וְעַתָּה אֲרוּרִים אַתֶּם וְלֹא־יִכָּרֵת מִכֶּם עֶבֶד וְחֹטְבֵי עֵצִים וְשֹׁאֲבֵי־מַיִם לְבֵית אֱלֹהָי: 24 וַיַּעֲנוּ אֶת־יְהוֹשֻׁעַ וַיֹּאמְרוּ כִּי הֻגֵּד הֻגַּד לַעֲבָדֶיךָ אֵת אֲשֶׁר צִוָּה יְהוָה אֱלֹהֶיךָ אֶת־מֹשֶׁה עַבְדּוֹ לָתֵת לָכֶם אֶת־כָּל־הָאָרֶץ וּלְהַשְׁמִיד אֶת־כָּל־יֹשְׁבֵי הָאָרֶץ מִפְּנֵיכֶם וַנִּירָא מְאֹד לְנַפְשֹׁתֵינוּ מִפְּנֵיכֶם וַנַּעֲשֵׂה אֶת־הַדָּבָר הַזֶּה: 25 וְעַתָּה הִנְנוּ בְיָדֶךָ כַּטּוֹב וְכַיָּשָׁר בְּעֵינֶיךָ לַעֲשׂוֹת לָנוּ עֲשֵׂה: 26 וַיַּעַשׂ לָהֶם כֵּן וַיַּצֵּל אוֹתָם מִיַּד בְּנֵי־יִשְׂרָאֵל וְלֹא הֲרָגוּם: 27 וַיִּתְּנֵם יְהוֹשֻׁעַ בַּיּוֹם הַהוּא חֹטְבֵי עֵצִים וְשֹׁאֲבֵי מַיִם לָעֵדָה וּלְמִזְבַּח יְהוָה עַד־הַיּוֹם הַזֶּה אֶל־הַמָּקוֹם אֲשֶׁר יִבְחָר: פ

י 1 וַיְהִי כִשְׁמֹעַ אֲדֹנִי־צֶדֶק מֶלֶךְ יְרוּשָׁלִַם כִּי־לָכַד יְהוֹשֻׁעַ אֶת־הָעַי וַיַּחֲרִימָהּ כַּאֲשֶׁר עָשָׂה לִירִיחוֹ וּלְמַלְכָּהּ כֵּן־עָשָׂה לָעַי וּלְמַלְכָּהּ וְכִי הִשְׁלִימוּ יֹשְׁבֵי גִבְעוֹן אֶת־יִשְׂרָאֵל וַיִּהְיוּ בְּקִרְבָּם: 2 וַיִּירְאוּ מְאֹד כִּי עִיר גְּדוֹלָה גִּבְעוֹן כְּאַחַת עָרֵי הַמַּמְלָכָה וְכִי הִיא גְדוֹלָה מִן־הָעַי וְכָל־אֲנָשֶׁיהָ גִּבֹּרִים: 3 וַיִּשְׁלַח אֲדֹנִי־צֶדֶק מֶלֶךְ יְרוּשָׁלִַם אֶל־הוֹהָם מֶלֶךְ־חֶבְרוֹן וְאֶל־פִּרְאָם מֶלֶךְ־יַרְמוּת וְאֶל־יָפִיעַ מֶלֶךְ־לָכִישׁ וְאֶל־דְּבִיר מֶלֶךְ־עֶגְלוֹן לֵאמֹר: 4 עֲלוּ־אֵלַי וְעִזְרֻנִי וְנַכֶּה אֶת־גִּבְעוֹן כִּי־הִשְׁלִימָה אֶת־יְהוֹשֻׁעַ וְאֶת־בְּנֵי יִשְׂרָאֵל: 5 וַיֵּאָסְפוּ וַיַּעֲלוּ חֲמֵשֶׁת מַלְכֵי הָאֱמֹרִי מֶלֶךְ יְרוּשָׁלִַם מֶלֶךְ־חֶבְרוֹן מֶלֶךְ־יַרְמוּת מֶלֶךְ־לָכִישׁ מֶלֶךְ־עֶגְלוֹן הֵם וְכָל־מַחֲנֵיהֶם וַיַּחֲנוּ עַל־גִּבְעוֹן וַיִּלָּחֲמוּ עָלֶיהָ: 6 וַיִּשְׁלְחוּ אַנְשֵׁי גִבְעוֹן אֶל־יְהוֹשֻׁעַ אֶל־הַמַּחֲנֶה הַגִּלְגָּלָה לֵאמֹר אַל־תֶּרֶף יָדֶיךָ מֵעֲבָדֶיךָ עֲלֵה אֵלֵינוּ מְהֵרָה וְהוֹשִׁיעָה לָּנוּ וְעָזְרֵנוּ כִּי נִקְבְּצוּ אֵלֵינוּ כָּל־מַלְכֵי הָאֱמֹרִי יֹשְׁבֵי הָהָר: 7 וַיַּעַל יְהוֹשֻׁעַ מִן־הַגִּלְגָּל הוּא וְכָל־עַם הַמִּלְחָמָה עִמּוֹ וְכֹל גִּבּוֹרֵי הֶחָיִל: פ

8 וַיֹּאמֶר יְהוָה אֶל־יְהוֹשֻׁעַ אַל־תִּירָא מֵהֶם כִּי בְיָדְךָ נְתַתִּים לֹא־יַעֲמֹד אִישׁ מֵהֶם בְּפָנֶיךָ: 9 וַיָּבֹא אֲלֵיהֶם יְהוֹשֻׁעַ פִּתְאֹם כָּל־הַלַּיְלָה עָלָה מִן־הַגִּלְגָּל: 10 וַיְהֻמֵּם יְהוָה לִפְנֵי יִשְׂרָאֵל וַיַּכֵּם מַכָּה־גְדוֹלָה

slaughter at Gibeon, chased them along the road that goes to Beth Horon, and struck them down as far as Azekah and Makkedah. [11] And it happened, as they fled before Israel *and* were on the descent of Beth Horon, that the LORD cast down large hailstones from heaven on them as far as Azekah, and they died. *There were* more who died from the hailstones than the children of Israel killed with the sword.

[12] Then Joshua spoke to the LORD in the day when the LORD delivered up the Amorites before the children of Israel, and he said in the sight of Israel:

> "Sun, stand still over Gibeon;
> And Moon, in the Valley of Aijalon."
> [13] So the sun stood still,
> And the moon stopped,
> Till the people had revenge
> Upon their enemies.

Is this not written in the Book of Jasher? So the sun stood still in the midst of heaven, and did not hasten to go *down* for about a whole day. [14] And there has been no day like that, before it or after it, that the LORD heeded the voice of a man; for the LORD fought for Israel.

[15] Then Joshua returned, and all Israel with him, to the camp at Gilgal.

[16] But these five kings had fled and hidden themselves in a cave at Makkedah. [17] And it was told Joshua, saying, "The five kings have been found hidden in the cave at Makkedah."

[18] So Joshua said, "Roll large stones against the mouth of the cave, and set men by it to guard them. [19] And do not stay *there* yourselves, *but* pursue your enemies, and attack their rear *guard*. Do not allow them to enter their cities, for the LORD your God has delivered them into your hand." [20] Then it happened, while Joshua and the children of Israel made an end of slaying them with a very great slaughter, till they had finished, that those who escaped entered fortified cities. [21] And all the people returned to the camp, to Joshua at Makkedah, in peace.

No one moved his tongue against any of the children of Israel.

[22] Then Joshua said, "Open the mouth of the cave, and bring out those five kings to me from the cave." [23] And they did so, and brought out those five kings to him from the cave: the king of Jerusalem, the king of Hebron, the king of Jarmuth, the king of Lachish, *and* the king of Eglon.

[24] So it was, when they brought out those kings to Joshua, that Joshua called for all the men of Israel, and said to the captains of the men of war who went

בְּגִבְעוֹן וַיִּרְדְּפֵם דֶּרֶךְ מַעֲלֵה בֵית־חוֹרֹן וַיַּכֵּם עַד־
עֲזֵקָה וְעַד־מַקֵּדָה: 11 וַיְהִי בְּנֻסָם ׀ מִפְּנֵי יִשְׂרָאֵל
הֵם בְּמוֹרַד בֵּית־חוֹרֹן וַיהוָה הִשְׁלִיךְ עֲלֵיהֶם אֲבָנִים
גְּדֹלוֹת מִן־הַשָּׁמַיִם עַד־עֲזֵקָה וַיָּמֻתוּ רַבִּים אֲשֶׁר־
מֵתוּ בְּאַבְנֵי הַבָּרָד מֵאֲשֶׁר הָרְגוּ בְּנֵי יִשְׂרָאֵל
בֶּחָרֶב: ס   12 אָז יְדַבֵּר יְהוֹשֻׁעַ לַיהוָה בְּיוֹם
תֵּת יְהוָה אֶת־הָאֱמֹרִי לִפְנֵי בְּנֵי יִשְׂרָאֵל וַיֹּאמֶר ׀
לְעֵינֵי יִשְׂרָאֵל שֶׁמֶשׁ בְּגִבְעוֹן דּוֹם וְיָרֵחַ בְּעֵמֶק
אַיָּלוֹן: 13 וַיִּדֹּם הַשֶּׁמֶשׁ וְיָרֵחַ עָמָד עַד־יִקֹּם גּוֹי
אֹיְבָיו הֲלֹא־הִיא כְתוּבָה עַל־סֵפֶר הַיָּשָׁר וַיַּעֲמֹד
הַשֶּׁמֶשׁ בַּחֲצִי הַשָּׁמַיִם וְלֹא־אָץ לָבוֹא כְּיוֹם תָּמִים:
14 וְלֹא הָיָה כַּיּוֹם הַהוּא לְפָנָיו וְאַחֲרָיו לִשְׁמֹעַ יְהוָה
בְּקוֹל אִישׁ כִּי יְהוָה נִלְחָם לְיִשְׂרָאֵל: פ

15 וַיָּשָׁב יְהוֹשֻׁעַ וְכָל־יִשְׂרָאֵל עִמּוֹ אֶל־הַמַּחֲנֶה
הַגִּלְגָּלָה: 16 וַיָּנֻסוּ חֲמֵשֶׁת הַמְּלָכִים הָאֵלֶּה וַיֵּחָבְאוּ
בַמְּעָרָה בְּמַקֵּדָה: 17 וַיֻּגַּד לִיהוֹשֻׁעַ לֵאמֹר נִמְצְאוּ
חֲמֵשֶׁת הַמְּלָכִים נֶחְבְּאִים בַּמְּעָרָה בְּמַקֵּדָה:
18 וַיֹּאמֶר יְהוֹשֻׁעַ גֹּלּוּ אֲבָנִים גְּדֹלוֹת אֶל־פִּי הַמְּעָרָה
וְהַפְקִידוּ עָלֶיהָ אֲנָשִׁים לְשָׁמְרָם: 19 וְאַתֶּם אַל־
תַּעֲמֹדוּ רִדְפוּ אַחֲרֵי אֹיְבֵיכֶם וְזִנַּבְתֶּם אוֹתָם
אַל־תִּתְּנוּם לָבוֹא אֶל־עָרֵיהֶם כִּי נְתָנָם יְהוָה
אֱלֹהֵיכֶם בְּיֶדְכֶם: 20 וַיְהִי כְּכַלּוֹת יְהוֹשֻׁעַ וּבְנֵי
יִשְׂרָאֵל לְהַכּוֹתָם מַכָּה גְדוֹלָה־מְאֹד עַד־תֻּמָּם
וְהַשְּׂרִידִים שָׂרְדוּ מֵהֶם וַיָּבֹאוּ אֶל־עָרֵי הַמִּבְצָר:
21 וַיָּשֻׁבוּ כָל־הָעָם אֶל־הַמַּחֲנֶה אֶל־יְהוֹשֻׁעַ מַקֵּדָה
בְּשָׁלוֹם לֹא־חָרַץ לִבְנֵי יִשְׂרָאֵל לְאִישׁ אֶת־לְשֹׁנוֹ:
22 וַיֹּאמֶר יְהוֹשֻׁעַ פִּתְחוּ אֶת־פִּי הַמְּעָרָה וְהוֹצִיאוּ
אֵלַי אֶת־חֲמֵשֶׁת הַמְּלָכִים הָאֵלֶּה מִן־הַמְּעָרָה:
23 וַיַּעֲשׂוּ כֵן וַיֹּצִיאוּ אֵלָיו אֶת־חֲמֵשֶׁת הַמְּלָכִים
הָאֵלֶּה מִן־הַמְּעָרָה אֵת ׀ מֶלֶךְ יְרוּשָׁלַ͏ִם אֶת־
מֶלֶךְ חֶבְרוֹן אֶת־מֶלֶךְ יַרְמוּת אֶת־מֶלֶךְ לָכִישׁ
אֶת־מֶלֶךְ עֶגְלוֹן: 24 וַיְהִי כְּהוֹצִיאָם אֶת־הַמְּלָכִים
הָאֵלֶּה אֶל־יְהוֹשֻׁעַ וַיִּקְרָא יְהוֹשֻׁעַ אֶל־כָּל־אִישׁ
יִשְׂרָאֵל וַיֹּאמֶר אֶל־קְצִינֵי אַנְשֵׁי הַמִּלְחָמָה הֶהָלְכוּא
אִתּוֹ קִרְבוּ שִׂימוּ אֶת־רַגְלֵיכֶם עַל־צַוְּארֵי הַמְּלָכִים
הָאֵלֶּה וַיִּקְרְבוּ וַיָּשִׂימוּ אֶת־רַגְלֵיהֶם עַל־צַוְּארֵיהֶם:

with him, "Come near, put your feet on the necks of
these kings." And they drew near and put their feet
on their necks. ²⁵ Then Joshua said to them, "Do
not be afraid, nor be dismayed; be strong and of
good courage, for thus the LORD will do to all your
enemies against whom you fight." ²⁶ And afterward
Joshua struck them and killed them, and hanged
them on five trees; and they were hanging on the
trees until evening. ²⁷ So it was at the time of the
going down of the sun *that* Joshua commanded,
and they took them down from the trees, cast them
into the cave where they had been hidden, and laid
large stones against the cave's mouth, *which remain*
until this very day.

²⁸ On that day Joshua took Makkedah, and
struck it and its king with the edge of the sword. He
utterly destroyed them—all the people who *were* in
it. He let none remain. He also did to the king of
Makkedah as he had done to the king of Jericho.

²⁹ Then Joshua passed from Makkedah, and all
Israel with him, to Libnah; and they fought against
Libnah. ³⁰ And the LORD also delivered it and its
king into the hand of Israel; he struck it and all the
people who *were* in it with the edge of the sword. He
let none remain in it, but did to its king as he had
done to the king of Jericho.

³¹ Then Joshua passed from Libnah, and all
Israel with him, to Lachish; and they encamped
against it and fought against it. ³² And the LORD
delivered Lachish into the hand of Israel, who took
it on the second day, and struck it and all the people
who *were* in it with the edge of the sword, according
to all that he had done to Libnah. ³³ Then Horam
king of Gezer came up to help Lachish; and Joshua
struck him and his people, until he left him none
remaining.

³⁴ From Lachish Joshua passed to Eglon, and all
Israel with him; and they encamped against it and
fought against it. ³⁵ They took it on that day and
struck it with the edge of the sword; all the people
who *were* in it he utterly destroyed that day,
according to all that he had done to Lachish.

³⁶ So Joshua went up from Eglon, and all Israel
with him, to Hebron; and they fought against it.
³⁷ And they took it and struck it with the edge of the
sword—its king, all its cities, and all the people who
were in it; he left none remaining, according to all
that he had done to Eglon, but utterly destroyed it
and all the people who *were* in it.

³⁸ Then Joshua returned, and all Israel with him,
to Debir; and they fought against it. ³⁹ And he took
it and its king and all its cities; they struck them
with the edge of the sword and utterly destroyed all

25 וַיֹּאמֶר אֲלֵיהֶם יְהוֹשֻׁעַ אַל־תִּירְאוּ וְאַל־תֵּחָתּוּ
חִזְקוּ וְאִמְצוּ כִּי כָכָה יַעֲשֶׂה יְהוָה לְכָל־אֹיְבֵיכֶם
אֲשֶׁר אַתֶּם נִלְחָמִים אוֹתָם: 26 וַיַּכֵּם יְהוֹשֻׁעַ אַחֲרֵי־
כֵן וַיְמִיתֵם וַיִּתְלֵם עַל חֲמִשָּׁה עֵצִים וַיִּהְיוּ תְּלוּיִם
עַל־הָעֵצִים עַד־הָעָרֶב: 27 וַיְהִי לְעֵת | בּוֹא הַשֶּׁמֶשׁ
צִוָּה יְהוֹשֻׁעַ וַיֹּרִידוּם מֵעַל הָעֵצִים וַיַּשְׁלִכֻם אֶל־
הַמְּעָרָה אֲשֶׁר נֶחְבְּאוּ־שָׁם וַיָּשִׂמוּ אֲבָנִים גְּדֹלוֹת
עַל־פִּי הַמְּעָרָה עַד־עֶצֶם הַיּוֹם הַזֶּה: פ

28 וְאֶת־מַקֵּדָה לָכַד יְהוֹשֻׁעַ בַּיּוֹם הַהוּא וַיַּכֶּהָ לְפִי־
חֶרֶב וְאֶת־מַלְכָּהּ הֶחֱרִם אוֹתָם וְאֶת־כָּל־הַנֶּפֶשׁ
אֲשֶׁר־בָּהּ לֹא הִשְׁאִיר שָׂרִיד וַיַּעַשׂ לְמֶלֶךְ מַקֵּדָה
כַּאֲשֶׁר עָשָׂה לְמֶלֶךְ יְרִיחוֹ: 29 וַיַּעֲבֹר יְהוֹשֻׁעַ וְכָל־
יִשְׂרָאֵל עִמּוֹ מִמַּקֵּדָה לִבְנָה וַיִּלָּחֶם עִם־לִבְנָה:
30 וַיִּתֵּן יְהוָה גַּם־אוֹתָהּ בְּיַד יִשְׂרָאֵל וְאֶת־מַלְכָּהּ
וַיַּכֶּהָ לְפִי־חֶרֶב וְאֶת־כָּל־הַנֶּפֶשׁ אֲשֶׁר־בָּהּ לֹא־
הִשְׁאִיר בָּהּ שָׂרִיד וַיַּעַשׂ לְמַלְכָּהּ כַּאֲשֶׁר עָשָׂה
לְמֶלֶךְ יְרִיחוֹ: ס 31 וַיַּעֲבֹר יְהוֹשֻׁעַ וְכָל־
יִשְׂרָאֵל עִמּוֹ מִלִּבְנָה לָכִישָׁה וַיִּחַן עָלֶיהָ וַיִּלָּחֶם
בָּהּ: 32 וַיִּתֵּן יְהוָה אֶת־לָכִישׁ בְּיַד יִשְׂרָאֵל וַיִּלְכְּדָהּ
בַּיּוֹם הַשֵּׁנִי וַיַּכֶּהָ לְפִי־חֶרֶב וְאֶת־כָּל־הַנֶּפֶשׁ אֲשֶׁר־
בָּהּ כְּכֹל אֲשֶׁר־עָשָׂה לְלִבְנָה: פ

33 אָז עָלָה הֹרָם מֶלֶךְ גֶּזֶר לַעְזֹר אֶת־לָכִישׁ וַיַּכֵּהוּ
יְהוֹשֻׁעַ וְאֶת־עַמּוֹ עַד־בִּלְתִּי הִשְׁאִיר־לוֹ שָׂרִיד:
34 וַיַּעֲבֹר יְהוֹשֻׁעַ וְכָל־יִשְׂרָאֵל עִמּוֹ מִלָּכִישׁ עֶגְלֹנָה
וַיַּחֲנוּ עָלֶיהָ וַיִּלָּחֲמוּ עָלֶיהָ: 35 וַיִּלְכְּדוּהָ בַּיּוֹם הַהוּא
וַיַּכּוּהָ לְפִי־חֶרֶב וְאֵת כָּל־הַנֶּפֶשׁ אֲשֶׁר־בָּהּ בַּיּוֹם
הַהוּא הֶחֱרִים כְּכֹל אֲשֶׁר־עָשָׂה לְלָכִישׁ: פ

36 וַיַּעַל יְהוֹשֻׁעַ וְכָל־יִשְׂרָאֵל עִמּוֹ מֵעֶגְלוֹנָה
חֶבְרוֹנָה וַיִּלָּחֲמוּ עָלֶיהָ: 37 וַיִּלְכְּדוּהָ וַיַּכּוּהָ לְפִי־
חֶרֶב וְאֶת־מַלְכָּהּ וְאֶת־כָּל־עָרֶיהָ וְאֶת־כָּל־הַנֶּפֶשׁ
אֲשֶׁר־בָּהּ לֹא־הִשְׁאִיר שָׂרִיד כְּכֹל אֲשֶׁר־עָשָׂה
לְעֶגְלוֹן וַיַּחֲרֵם אוֹתָהּ וְאֶת־כָּל־הַנֶּפֶשׁ אֲשֶׁר־
בָּהּ: ס 38 וַיָּשָׁב יְהוֹשֻׁעַ וְכָל־יִשְׂרָאֵל עִמּוֹ
דְּבִרָה וַיִּלָּחֶם עָלֶיהָ: 39 וַיִּלְכְּדָהּ וְאֶת־מַלְכָּהּ וְאֶת־
כָּל־עָרֶיהָ וַיַּכּוּם לְפִי־חֶרֶב וַיַּחֲרִימוּ אֶת־כָּל־נֶפֶשׁ
אֲשֶׁר־בָּהּ לֹא הִשְׁאִיר שָׂרִיד כַּאֲשֶׁר עָשָׂה לְחֶבְרוֹן

the people who *were* in it. He left none remaining; as he had done to Hebron, so he did to Debir and its king, as he had done also to Libnah and its king.

40 So Joshua conquered all the land: the mountain country and the South and the lowland and the wilderness slopes, and all their kings; he left none remaining, but utterly destroyed all that breathed, as the LORD God of Israel had commanded. 41 And Joshua conquered them from Kadesh Barnea as far as Gaza, and all the country of Goshen, even as far as Gibeon. 42 All these kings and their land Joshua took at one time, because the LORD God of Israel fought for Israel. 43 Then Joshua returned, and all Israel with him, to the camp at Gilgal.

11 And it came to pass, when Jabin king of Hazor heard *these things,* that he sent to Jobab king of Madon, to the king of Shimron, to the king of Achshaph, 2 and to the kings who *were* from the north, in the mountains, in the plain south of Chinneroth, in the lowland, and in the heights of Dor on the west, 3 to the Canaanites in the east and in the west, the Amorite, the Hittite, the Perizzite, the Jebusite in the mountains, and the Hivite below Hermon in the land of Mizpah. 4 So they went out, they and all their armies with them, *as* many people *as* the sand that *is* on the seashore in multitude, with very many horses and chariots. 5 And when all these kings had met together, they came and camped together at the waters of Merom to fight against Israel.

6 But the LORD said to Joshua, "Do not be afraid because of them, for tomorrow about this time I will deliver all of them slain before Israel. You shall hamstring their horses and burn their chariots with fire." 7 So Joshua and all the people of war with him came against them suddenly by the waters of Merom, and they attacked them. 8 And the LORD delivered them into the hand of Israel, who defeated them and chased them to Greater Sidon, to the Brook Misrephoth, and to the Valley of Mizpah eastward; they attacked them until they left none of them remaining. 9 So Joshua did to them as the LORD had told him: he hamstrung their horses and burned their chariots with fire.

10 Joshua turned back at that time and took Hazor, and struck its king with the sword; for Hazor was formerly the head of all those kingdoms. 11 And they struck all the people who *were* in it with the edge of the sword, utterly destroying *them.* There was none left breathing. Then he burned Hazor with fire.

כֵּן־עָשָׂה לִדְבִרָה וּלְמַלְכָּהּ וְכַאֲשֶׁר עָשָׂה לְלִבְנָה וּלְמַלְכָּהּ: 40 וַיַּכֶּה יְהוֹשֻׁעַ אֶת־כָּל־הָאָרֶץ הָהָר וְהַנֶּגֶב וְהַשְּׁפֵלָה וְהָאֲשֵׁדוֹת וְאֵת כָּל־מַלְכֵיהֶם לֹא הִשְׁאִיר שָׂרִיד וְאֵת כָּל־הַנְּשָׁמָה הֶחֱרִים כַּאֲשֶׁר צִוָּה יְהוָה אֱלֹהֵי יִשְׂרָאֵל: 41 וַיַּכֵּם יְהוֹשֻׁעַ מִקָּדֵשׁ בַּרְנֵעַ וְעַד־עַזָּה וְאֵת כָּל־אֶרֶץ גֹּשֶׁן וְעַד־גִּבְעוֹן: 42 וְאֵת כָּל־הַמְּלָכִים הָאֵלֶּה וְאֶת־אַרְצָם לָכַד יְהוֹשֻׁעַ פַּעַם אֶחָת כִּי יְהוָה אֱלֹהֵי יִשְׂרָאֵל נִלְחָם לְיִשְׂרָאֵל: 43 וַיָּשָׁב יְהוֹשֻׁעַ וְכָל־יִשְׂרָאֵל עִמּוֹ אֶל־הַמַּחֲנֶה הַגִּלְגָּלָה: פ

יא וַיְהִי כִּשְׁמֹעַ יָבִין מֶלֶךְ־חָצוֹר וַיִּשְׁלַח אֶל־יוֹבָב מֶלֶךְ מָדוֹן וְאֶל־מֶלֶךְ שִׁמְרוֹן וְאֶל־מֶלֶךְ אַכְשָׁף: 2 וְאֶל־הַמְּלָכִים אֲשֶׁר מִצָּפוֹן בָּהָר וּבָעֲרָבָה נֶגֶב כִּנֲרוֹת וּבַשְּׁפֵלָה וּבְנָפוֹת דּוֹר מִיָּם: 3 הַכְּנַעֲנִי מִמִּזְרָח וּמִיָּם וְהָאֱמֹרִי וְהַחִתִּי וְהַפְּרִזִּי וְהַיְבוּסִי בָּהָר וְהַחִוִּי תַּחַת חֶרְמוֹן בְּאֶרֶץ הַמִּצְפָּה: 4 וַיֵּצְאוּ הֵם וְכָל־מַחֲנֵיהֶם עִמָּם עַם־רָב כַּחוֹל אֲשֶׁר עַל־שְׂפַת־הַיָּם לָרֹב וְסוּס וָרֶכֶב רַב־מְאֹד: 5 וַיִּוָּעֲדוּ כֹּל הַמְּלָכִים הָאֵלֶּה וַיָּבֹאוּ וַיַּחֲנוּ יַחְדָּו אֶל־מֵי מֵרוֹם לְהִלָּחֵם עִם־יִשְׂרָאֵל: פ

6 וַיֹּאמֶר יְהוָה אֶל־יְהוֹשֻׁעַ אַל־תִּירָא מִפְּנֵיהֶם כִּי־מָחָר כָּעֵת הַזֹּאת אָנֹכִי נֹתֵן אֶת־כֻּלָּם חֲלָלִים לִפְנֵי יִשְׂרָאֵל אֶת־סוּסֵיהֶם תְּעַקֵּר וְאֶת־מַרְכְּבֹתֵיהֶם תִּשְׂרֹף בָּאֵשׁ: 7 וַיָּבֹא יְהוֹשֻׁעַ וְכָל־עַם הַמִּלְחָמָה עִמּוֹ עֲלֵיהֶם עַל־מֵי מֵרוֹם פִּתְאֹם וַיִּפְּלוּ בָּהֶם: 8 וַיִּתְּנֵם יְהוָה בְּיַד־יִשְׂרָאֵל וַיַּכּוּם וַיִּרְדְּפוּם עַד־צִידוֹן רַבָּה וְעַד מִשְׂרְפוֹת מַיִם וְעַד־בִּקְעַת מִצְפֶּה מִזְרָחָה וַיַּכֻּם עַד־בִּלְתִּי הִשְׁאִיר־לָהֶם שָׂרִיד: 9 וַיַּעַשׂ לָהֶם יְהוֹשֻׁעַ כַּאֲשֶׁר אָמַר־לוֹ יְהוָה אֶת־סוּסֵיהֶם עִקֵּר וְאֶת־מַרְכְּבֹתֵיהֶם שָׂרַף בָּאֵשׁ: ס 10 וַיָּשָׁב יְהוֹשֻׁעַ בָּעֵת הַהִיא וַיִּלְכֹּד אֶת־חָצוֹר וְאֶת־מַלְכָּהּ הִכָּה בֶחָרֶב כִּי־חָצוֹר לְפָנִים הִיא רֹאשׁ כָּל־הַמַּמְלָכוֹת הָאֵלֶּה: 11 וַיַּכּוּ אֶת־כָּל־הַנֶּפֶשׁ אֲשֶׁר־בָּהּ לְפִי־חֶרֶב הַחֲרֵם לֹא נוֹתַר

12 So all the cities of those kings, and all their kings, Joshua took and struck with the edge of the sword. He utterly destroyed them, as Moses the servant of the LORD had commanded. 13 But *as for* the cities that stood on their mounds, Israel burned none of them, except Hazor only, *which* Joshua burned. 14 And all the spoil of these cities and the livestock, the children of Israel took as booty for themselves; but they struck every man with the edge of the sword until they had destroyed them, and they left none breathing. 15 As the LORD had commanded Moses his servant, so Moses commanded Joshua, and so Joshua did. He left nothing undone of all that the LORD had commanded Moses.

16 Thus Joshua took all this land: the mountain country, all the South, all the land of Goshen, the lowland, and the Jordan plain—the mountains of Israel and its lowlands, 17 from Mount Halak and the ascent to Seir, even as far as Baal Gad in the Valley of Lebanon below Mount Hermon. He captured all their kings, and struck them down and killed them. 18 Joshua made war a long time with all those kings. 19 There was not a city that made peace with the children of Israel, except the Hivites, the inhabitants of Gibeon. All *the others* they took in battle. 20 For it was of the LORD to harden their hearts, that they should come against Israel in battle, that He might utterly destroy them, *and* that they might receive no mercy, but that He might destroy them, as the LORD had commanded Moses.

21 And at that time Joshua came and cut off the Anakim from the mountains: from Hebron, from Debir, from Anab, from all the mountains of Judah, and from all the mountains of Israel; Joshua utterly destroyed them with their cities. 22 None of the Anakim were left in the land of the children of Israel; they remained only in Gaza, in Gath, and in Ashdod.

23 So Joshua took the whole land, according to all that the LORD had said to Moses; and Joshua gave it as an inheritance to Israel according to their divisions by their tribes. Then the land rested from war.

12 These *are* the kings of the land whom the children of Israel defeated, and whose land they possessed on the other side of the Jordan toward the rising of the sun, from the River Arnon to Mount Hermon, and all the eastern Jordan plain: 2 *One king was* Sihon king of the Amorites, who dwelt in Heshbon *and* ruled half of Gilead, from Aroer, which is on the bank of the River Arnon, from the middle of that river, even as far as the

12 וְאֶת־כָּל־עָרֵי כָּל־נִשְׁמָה וְאֶת־חָצוֹר שָׂרַף בָּאֵשׁ: הַמְּלָכִים־הָאֵלֶּה וְאֶת־כָּל־מַלְכֵיהֶם לָכַד יְהוֹשֻׁעַ וַיַּכֵּם לְפִי־חֶרֶב הֶחֱרִים אוֹתָם כַּאֲשֶׁר צִוָּה מֹשֶׁה עֶבֶד יְהֹוָה: 13 רַק כָּל־הֶעָרִים הָעֹמְדוֹת עַל־תִּלָּם לֹא שְׂרָפָם יִשְׂרָאֵל זוּלָתִי אֶת־חָצוֹר לְבַדָּהּ שָׂרַף יְהוֹשֻׁעַ: 14 וְכֹל שְׁלַל הֶעָרִים הָאֵלֶּה וְהַבְּהֵמָה בָּזְזוּ לָהֶם בְּנֵי יִשְׂרָאֵל רַק אֶת־כָּל־הָאָדָם הִכּוּ לְפִי־ חֶרֶב עַד־הִשְׁמִדָם אוֹתָם לֹא הִשְׁאִירוּ כָּל־נְשָׁמָה: 15 כַּאֲשֶׁר צִוָּה יְהֹוָה אֶת־מֹשֶׁה עַבְדּוֹ כֵּן־צִוָּה מֹשֶׁה אֶת־יְהוֹשֻׁעַ וְכֵן עָשָׂה יְהוֹשֻׁעַ לֹא־הֵסִיר דָּבָר מִכֹּל אֲשֶׁר־צִוָּה יְהֹוָה אֶת־מֹשֶׁה: 16 וַיִּקַּח יְהוֹשֻׁעַ אֶת־ כָּל־הָאָרֶץ הַזֹּאת הָהָר וְאֶת־כָּל־הַנֶּגֶב וְאֵת כָּל־ אֶרֶץ הַגֹּשֶׁן וְאֶת־הַשְּׁפֵלָה וְאֶת־הָעֲרָבָה וְאֶת־הַר יִשְׂרָאֵל וּשְׁפֵלָתֹה: 17 מִן־הָהָר הֶחָלָק הָעוֹלֶה שֵׂעִיר וְעַד־בַּעַל גָּד בְּבִקְעַת הַלְּבָנוֹן תַּחַת הַר־חֶרְמוֹן וְאֵת כָּל־מַלְכֵיהֶם לָכַד וַיַּכֵּם וַיְמִיתֵם: 18 יָמִים רַבִּים עָשָׂה יְהוֹשֻׁעַ אֶת־כָּל־הַמְּלָכִים הָאֵלֶּה מִלְחָמָה: 19 לֹא־הָיְתָה עִיר אֲשֶׁר הִשְׁלִימָה אֶל־בְּנֵי יִשְׂרָאֵל בִּלְתִּי הַחִוִּי יֹשְׁבֵי גִבְעוֹן אֶת־הַכֹּל לָקְחוּ בַמִּלְחָמָה: 20 כִּי מֵאֵת יְהֹוָה הָיְתָה לְחַזֵּק אֶת־לִבָּם לִקְרַאת הַמִּלְחָמָה אֶת־יִשְׂרָאֵל לְמַעַן הַחֲרִימָם לְבִלְתִּי הֱיוֹת־לָהֶם תְּחִנָּה כִּי לְמַעַן הַשְׁמִידָם כַּאֲשֶׁר צִוָּה יְהֹוָה אֶת־מֹשֶׁה: ס 21 וַיָּבֹא יְהוֹשֻׁעַ בָּעֵת הַהִיא וַיַּכְרֵת אֶת־הָעֲנָקִים מִן־הָהָר מִן־חֶבְרוֹן מִן־דְּבִר מִן־עֲנָב וּמִכֹּל הַר יְהוּדָה וּמִכֹּל הַר יִשְׂרָאֵל עִם־עָרֵיהֶם הֶחֱרִימָם יְהוֹשֻׁעַ: 22 לֹא־ נוֹתַר עֲנָקִים בְּאֶרֶץ בְּנֵי יִשְׂרָאֵל רַק בְּעַזָּה בְּגַת וּבְאַשְׁדּוֹד נִשְׁאָרוּ: 23 וַיִּקַּח יְהוֹשֻׁעַ אֶת־כָּל־הָאָרֶץ כְּכֹל אֲשֶׁר דִּבֶּר יְהֹוָה אֶל־מֹשֶׁה וַיִּתְּנָהּ יְהוֹשֻׁעַ לְנַחֲלָה לְיִשְׂרָאֵל כְּמַחְלְקֹתָם לְשִׁבְטֵיהֶם וְהָאָרֶץ שָׁקְטָה מִמִּלְחָמָה: פ

יב וְאֵלֶּה מַלְכֵי הָאָרֶץ אֲשֶׁר הִכּוּ בְנֵי־ יִשְׂרָאֵל וַיִּרְשׁוּ אֶת־אַרְצָם בְּעֵבֶר הַיַּרְדֵּן מִזְרְחָה הַשָּׁמֶשׁ מִנַּחַל אַרְנוֹן עַד־הַר חֶרְמוֹן וְכָל־הָעֲרָבָה מִזְרָחָה: 2 סִיחוֹן מֶלֶךְ הָאֱמֹרִי הַיּוֹשֵׁב בְּחֶשְׁבּוֹן מֹשֵׁל מֵעֲרוֹעֵר אֲשֶׁר עַל־שְׂפַת־נַחַל אַרְנוֹן וְתוֹךְ

River Jabbok, *which is* the border of the Ammonites, ³and the eastern Jordan plain from the Sea of Chinneroth as far as the Sea of the Arabah (the Salt Sea), the road to Beth Jeshimoth, and southward below the slopes of Pisgah. ⁴*The other king was* Og king of Bashan and his territory, *who was* of the remnant of the giants, who dwelt at Ashtaroth and at Edrei, ⁵and reigned over Mount Hermon, over Salcah, over all Bashan, as far as the border of the Geshurites and the Maachathites, and over half of Gilead *to* the border of Sihon king of Heshbon.

⁶These Moses the servant of the LORD and the children of Israel had conquered; and Moses the servant of the LORD had given it *as* a possession to the Reubenites, the Gadites, and half the tribe of Manasseh.

⁷And these *are* the kings of the country which Joshua and the children of Israel conquered on this side of the Jordan, on the west, from Baal Gad in the Valley of Lebanon as far as Mount Halak and the ascent to Seir, which Joshua gave to the tribes of Israel *as* a possession according to their divisions, ⁸in the mountain country, in the lowlands, in the *Jordan* plain, in the slopes, in the wilderness, and in the South—the Hittites, the Amorites, the Canaanites, the Perizzites, the Hivites, and the Jebusites: ⁹the king of Jericho, one; the king of Ai, which *is* beside Bethel, one; ¹⁰the king of Jerusalem, one; the king of Hebron, one; ¹¹the king of Jarmuth, one; the king of Lachish, one; ¹²the king of Eglon, one; the king of Gezer, one; ¹³the king of Debir, one; the king of Geder, one; ¹⁴the king of Hormah, one; the king of Arad, one; ¹⁵the king of Libnah, one; the king of Adullam, one; ¹⁶the king of Makkedah, one; the king of Bethel, one; ¹⁷the king of Tappuah, one; the king of Hepher, one; ¹⁸the king of Aphek, one; the king of Lasharon, one; ¹⁹the king of Madon, one; the king of Hazor, one; ²⁰the king of Shimron Meron, one; the king of Achshaph, one; ²¹the king of Taanach, one; the king of Megiddo, one; ²²the king of Kedesh, one; the king of Jokneam in Carmel, one; ²³the king of Dor in the heights of Dor, one; the king of the people of Gilgal, one; ²⁴the king of Tirzah, one—all the kings, thirty-one.

13 Now Joshua was old, advanced in years. And the LORD said to him: "You are old, advanced in years, and there remains very much land yet to be possessed. ²This is the land that yet remains: all the territory of the Philistines and all *that of* the Geshurites, ³from Sihor, which *is* east of Egypt, as far as the border of Ekron northward (which is

הַנַּחַל וַחֲצִי הַגִּלְעָד וְעַד יַבֹּק הַנַּחַל גְּבוּל בְּנֵי עַמּוֹן: ³ וְהָעֲרָבָה עַד־יָם כִּנְרוֹת מִזְרָחָה וְעַד יָם הָעֲרָבָה יָם־הַמֶּלַח מִזְרָחָה דֶּרֶךְ בֵּית הַיְשִׁמוֹת וּמִתֵּימָן תַּחַת אַשְׁדּוֹת הַפִּסְגָּה: ⁴ וּגְבוּל עוֹג מֶלֶךְ הַבָּשָׁן מִיֶּתֶר הָרְפָאִים הַיּוֹשֵׁב בְּעַשְׁתָּרוֹת וּבְאֶדְרֶעִי: ⁵ וּמֹשֵׁל בְּהַר חֶרְמוֹן וּבְסַלְכָה וּבְכָל־הַבָּשָׁן עַד־ גְּבוּל הַגְּשׁוּרִי וְהַמַּעֲכָתִי וַחֲצִי הַגִּלְעָד גְּבוּל סִיחוֹן מֶלֶךְ־חֶשְׁבּוֹן: ⁶ מֹשֶׁה עֶבֶד־יְהֹוָה וּבְנֵי יִשְׂרָאֵל הִכּוּם וַיִּתְּנָהּ מֹשֶׁה עֶבֶד־יְהֹוָה יְרֻשָּׁה לָרֻאוּבֵנִי וְלַגָּדִי וְלַחֲצִי שֵׁבֶט הַמְנַשֶּׁה: ס ⁷ וְאֵלֶּה מַלְכֵי הָאָרֶץ אֲשֶׁר הִכָּה יְהוֹשֻׁעַ וּבְנֵי יִשְׂרָאֵל בְּעֵבֶר הַיַּרְדֵּן יָמָּה מִבַּעַל גָּד בְּבִקְעַת הַלְּבָנוֹן וְעַד־הָהָר הֶחָלָק הָעֹלֶה שֵׂעִירָה וַיִּתְּנָהּ יְהוֹשֻׁעַ לְשִׁבְטֵי יִשְׂרָאֵל יְרֻשָּׁה כְּמַחְלְקֹתָם: ⁸ בָּהָר וּבַשְּׁפֵלָה וּבָעֲרָבָה וּבָאֲשֵׁדוֹת וּבַמִּדְבָּר וּבַנֶּגֶב הַחִתִּי הָאֱמֹרִי וְהַכְּנַעֲנִי הַפְּרִזִּי הַחִוִּי וְהַיְבוּסִי: פ

⁹ מֶלֶךְ יְרִיחוֹ אֶחָד מֶלֶךְ הָעַי אֲשֶׁר־מִצַּד בֵּית־אֵל אֶחָד: ¹⁰ מֶלֶךְ יְרוּשָׁלַ͏ִם אֶחָד מֶלֶךְ חֶבְרוֹן אֶחָד: ¹¹ מֶלֶךְ יַרְמוּת אֶחָד מֶלֶךְ לָכִישׁ אֶחָד: ¹² מֶלֶךְ עֶגְלוֹן אֶחָד מֶלֶךְ גֶּזֶר אֶחָד: ¹³ מֶלֶךְ דְּבִר אֶחָד מֶלֶךְ גֶּדֶר אֶחָד: ¹⁴ מֶלֶךְ חָרְמָה אֶחָד מֶלֶךְ עֲרָד אֶחָד: ¹⁵ מֶלֶךְ לִבְנָה אֶחָד מֶלֶךְ עֲדֻלָּם אֶחָד: ¹⁶ מֶלֶךְ מַקֵּדָה אֶחָד מֶלֶךְ בֵּית־אֵל אֶחָד: ¹⁷ מֶלֶךְ תַּפּוּחַ אֶחָד מֶלֶךְ חֵפֶר אֶחָד: ¹⁸ מֶלֶךְ אֲפֵק אֶחָד מֶלֶךְ לַשָּׁרוֹן אֶחָד: ¹⁹ מֶלֶךְ מָדוֹן אֶחָד מֶלֶךְ חָצוֹר אֶחָד: ²⁰ מֶלֶךְ שִׁמְרוֹן מְראוֹן אֶחָד מֶלֶךְ אַכְשָׁף אֶחָד: ²¹ מֶלֶךְ תַּעְנַךְ אֶחָד מֶלֶךְ מְגִדּוֹ אֶחָד: ²² מֶלֶךְ קֶדֶשׁ אֶחָד מֶלֶךְ־יָקְנְעָם לַכַּרְמֶל אֶחָד: ²³ מֶלֶךְ דּוֹר לְנָפַת דּוֹר אֶחָד מֶלֶךְ־גּוֹיִם לְגִלְגָּל אֶחָד: ²⁴ מֶלֶךְ תִּרְצָה אֶחָד כָּל־מְלָכִים שְׁלֹשִׁים וְאֶחָד: פ

יג וִיהוֹשֻׁעַ זָקֵן בָּא בַּיָּמִים וַיֹּאמֶר יְהֹוָה אֵלָיו אַתָּה זָקַנְתָּה בָּאתָ בַיָּמִים וְהָאָרֶץ נִשְׁאֲרָה הַרְבֵּה־ מְאֹד לְרִשְׁתָּהּ: ² זֹאת הָאָרֶץ הַנִּשְׁאָרֶת כָּל־גְּלִילוֹת הַפְּלִשְׁתִּים וְכָל־הַגְּשׁוּרִי: ³ מִן־הַשִּׁיחוֹר אֲשֶׁר | עַל־פְּנֵי מִצְרַיִם וְעַד גְּבוּל עֶקְרוֹן צָפוֹנָה לַכְּנַעֲנִי

counted as Canaanite); the five lords of the Philistines—the Gazites, the Ashdodites, the Ashkelonites, the Gittites, and the Ekronites; also the Avites; [4] from the south, all the land of the Canaanites, and Mearah that belongs to the Sidonians as far as Aphek, to the border of the Amorites; [5] the land of the Gebalites, and all Lebanon, toward the sunrise, from Baal Gad below Mount Hermon as far as the entrance to Hamath; [6] all the inhabitants of the mountains from Lebanon as far as the Brook Misrephoth, *and* all the Sidonians—them I will drive out from before the children of Israel; only divide it by lot to Israel as an inheritance, as I have commanded you. [7] Now therefore, divide this land as an inheritance to the nine tribes and half the tribe of Manasseh."

[8] With the other half-tribe the Reubenites and the Gadites received their inheritance, which Moses had given them, beyond the Jordan eastward, as Moses the servant of the LORD had given them: [9] from Aroer which *is* on the bank of the River Arnon, and the town that *is* in the midst of the ravine, and all the plain of Medeba as far as Dibon; [10] all the cities of Sihon king of the Amorites, who reigned in Heshbon, as far as the border of the children of Ammon; [11] Gilead, and the border of the Geshurites and Maachathites, all Mount Hermon, and all Bashan as far as Salcah; [12] all the kingdom of Og in Bashan, who reigned in Ashtaroth and Edrei, who remained of the remnant of the giants; for Moses had defeated and cast out these.

[13] Nevertheless the children of Israel did not drive out the Geshurites or the Maachathites, but the Geshurites and the Maachathites dwell among the Israelites until this day.

[14] Only to the tribe of Levi he had given no inheritance; the sacrifices of the LORD God of Israel made by fire *are* their inheritance, as He said to them.

[15] And Moses had given to the tribe of the children of Reuben *an inheritance* according to their families. [16] Their territory was from Aroer, which *is* on the bank of the River Arnon, and the city that *is* in the midst of the ravine, and all the plain by Medeba; [17] Heshbon and all its cities that *are* in the plain: Dibon, Bamoth Baal, Beth Baal Meon, [18] Jahaza, Kedemoth, Mephaath, [19] Kirjathaim, Sibmah, Zereth Shahar on the mountain of the valley, [20] Beth Peor, the slopes of Pisgah, and Beth Jeshimoth— [21] all the cities of the plain and all the kingdom of Sihon king of the Amorites, who reigned in Heshbon, whom Moses had struck with the princes of Midian: Evi, Rekem, Zur, Hur, and Reba, who *were* princes of Sihon dwelling in the

תַּחְשֵׁב חֲמֵשֶׁת ׀ סַרְנֵי פְלִשְׁתִּים הָעַזָּתִי וְהָאַשְׁדּוֹדִי הָאֶשְׁקְלוֹנִי הַגִּתִּי וְהָעֶקְרוֹנִי וְהָעַוִּים: 4 מִתֵּימָן כָּל־אֶרֶץ הַכְּנַעֲנִי וּמְעָרָה אֲשֶׁר לַצִּידֹנִים עַד־אֲפֵקָה עַד גְּבוּל הָאֱמֹרִי: 5 וְהָאָרֶץ הַגִּבְלִי וְכָל־הַלְּבָנוֹן מִזְרַח הַשֶּׁמֶשׁ מִבַּעַל גָּד תַּחַת הַר־חֶרְמוֹן עַד לְבוֹא חֲמָת: 6 כָּל־יֹשְׁבֵי הָהָר מִן־הַלְּבָנוֹן עַד־מִשְׂרְפֹת מַיִם כָּל־צִידֹנִים אָנֹכִי אוֹרִישֵׁם מִפְּנֵי בְּנֵי יִשְׂרָאֵל רַק הַפִּלֶהָ לְיִשְׂרָאֵל בְּנַחֲלָה כַּאֲשֶׁר צִוִּיתִיךָ: 7 וְעַתָּה חַלֵּק אֶת־הָאָרֶץ הַזֹּאת בְּנַחֲלָה לְתִשְׁעַת הַשְּׁבָטִים וַחֲצִי הַשֵּׁבֶט הַמְנַשֶּׁה: 8 עִמּוֹ הָראוּבֵנִי וְהַגָּדִי לָקְחוּ נַחֲלָתָם אֲשֶׁר נָתַן לָהֶם מֹשֶׁה בְּעֵבֶר הַיַּרְדֵּן מִזְרָחָה כַּאֲשֶׁר נָתַן לָהֶם מֹשֶׁה עֶבֶד יְהוָה: 9 מֵעֲרוֹעֵר אֲשֶׁר עַל־שְׂפַת־נַחַל אַרְנוֹן וְהָעִיר אֲשֶׁר בְּתוֹךְ־הַנַּחַל וְכָל־הַמִּישֹׁר מֵידְבָא עַד־דִּיבֹן: 10 וְכֹל עָרֵי סִיחוֹן מֶלֶךְ הָאֱמֹרִי אֲשֶׁר מָלַךְ בְּחֶשְׁבּוֹן עַד־גְּבוּל בְּנֵי עַמּוֹן: 11 וְהַגִּלְעָד וּגְבוּל הַגְּשׁוּרִי וְהַמַּעֲכָתִי וְכֹל הַר חֶרְמוֹן וְכָל־הַבָּשָׁן עַד־סַלְכָה: 12 כָּל־מַמְלְכוּת עוֹג בַּבָּשָׁן אֲשֶׁר־מָלַךְ בְּעַשְׁתָּרוֹת וּבְאֶדְרֶעִי הוּא נִשְׁאַר מִיֶּתֶר הָרְפָאִים וַיַּכֵּם מֹשֶׁה וַיֹּרִשֵׁם: 13 וְלֹא הוֹרִישׁוּ בְּנֵי יִשְׂרָאֵל אֶת־הַגְּשׁוּרִי וְאֶת־הַמַּעֲכָתִי וַיֵּשֶׁב גְּשׁוּר וּמַעֲכָת בְּקֶרֶב יִשְׂרָאֵל עַד הַיּוֹם הַזֶּה: 14 רַק לְשֵׁבֶט הַלֵּוִי לֹא נָתַן נַחֲלָה אִשֵּׁי יְהוָה אֱלֹהֵי יִשְׂרָאֵל הוּא נַחֲלָתוֹ כַּאֲשֶׁר דִּבֶּר־לוֹ: ס 15 וַיִּתֵּן מֹשֶׁה לְמַטֵּה בְנֵי־רְאוּבֵן לְמִשְׁפְּחֹתָם: 16 וַיְהִי לָהֶם הַגְּבוּל מֵעֲרוֹעֵר אֲשֶׁר עַל־שְׂפַת־נַחַל אַרְנוֹן וְהָעִיר אֲשֶׁר בְּתוֹךְ־הַנַּחַל וְכָל־הַמִּישֹׁר עַל־מֵידְבָא: 17 חֶשְׁבּוֹן וְכָל־עָרֶיהָ אֲשֶׁר בַּמִּישֹׁר דִּיבוֹן וּבָמוֹת בַּעַל וּבֵית בַּעַל מְעוֹן: 18 וְיַהְצָה וּקְדֵמֹת וּמֵפָעַת: 19 וְקִרְיָתַיִם וְשִׂבְמָה וְצֶרֶת הַשַּׁחַר בְּהַר הָעֵמֶק: 20 וּבֵית פְּעוֹר וְאַשְׁדּוֹת הַפִּסְגָּה וּבֵית הַיְשִׁמוֹת: 21 וְכֹל עָרֵי הַמִּישֹׁר וְכָל־מַמְלְכוּת סִיחוֹן מֶלֶךְ הָאֱמֹרִי אֲשֶׁר מָלַךְ בְּחֶשְׁבּוֹן אֲשֶׁר הִכָּה מֹשֶׁה אֹתוֹ ׀ וְאֶת־נְשִׂיאֵי מִדְיָן אֶת־אֱוִי וְאֶת־רֶקֶם וְאֶת־צוּר וְאֶת־חוּר

country. ²²The children of Israel also killed with the sword Balaam the son of Beor, the soothsayer, among those who were killed by them. ²³And the border of the children of Reuben was the bank of the Jordan. This *was* the inheritance of the children of Reuben according to their families, the cities and their villages.

²⁴Moses also had given *an inheritance* to the tribe of Gad, to the children of Gad according to their families. ²⁵Their territory was Jazer, and all the cities of Gilead, and half the land of the Ammonites as far as Aroer, which *is* before Rabbah, ²⁶and from Heshbon to Ramath Mizpah and Betonim, and from Mahanaim to the border of Debir, ²⁷and in the valley Beth Haram, Beth Nimrah, Succoth, and Zaphon, the rest of the kingdom of Sihon king of Heshbon, with the Jordan as *its* border, as far as the edge of the Sea of Chinnereth, on the other side of the Jordan eastward. ²⁸This *is* the inheritance of the children of Gad according to their families, the cities and their villages.

²⁹Moses also had given *an inheritance* to half the tribe of Manasseh; it was for half the tribe of the children of Manasseh according to their families: ³⁰Their territory was from Mahanaim, all Bashan, all the kingdom of Og king of Bashan, and all the towns of Jair which are in Bashan, sixty cities; ³¹half of Gilead, and Ashtaroth and Edrei, cities of the kingdom of Og in Bashan, *were* for the children of Machir the son of Manasseh, for half of the children of Machir according to their families.

³²These *are the areas* which Moses had distributed as an inheritance in the plains of Moab on the other side of the Jordan, by Jericho eastward. ³³But to the tribe of Levi Moses had given no inheritance; the LORD God of Israel *was* their inheritance, as He had said to them.

14 These *are the areas* which the children of Israel inherited in the land of Canaan, which Eleazar the priest, Joshua the son of Nun, and the heads of the fathers of the tribes of the children of Israel distributed as an inheritance to them. ²Their inheritance *was* by lot, as the LORD had commanded by the hand of Moses, for the nine tribes and the half-tribe. ³For Moses had given the inheritance of the two tribes and the half-tribe on the other side of the Jordan; but to the Levites he had given no inheritance among them. ⁴For the children of Joseph were two tribes: Manasseh and Ephraim. And they gave no part to the Levites in the land, except cities to dwell *in,* with their common-lands for their livestock and their

22 וְאֶת־בִּלְעָם 22 וְאֶת־רֶבַע נְסִיכֵי סִיחוֹן יֹשְׁבֵי הָאָרֶץ בֶּן־בְּעוֹר הַקּוֹסֵם הָרְגוּ בְנֵי־יִשְׂרָאֵל בַּחֶרֶב אֶל־חַלְלֵיהֶם: 23 וַיְהִי גְּבוּל בְּנֵי רְאוּבֵן הַיַּרְדֵּן וּגְבוּל זֹאת נַחֲלַת בְּנֵי־רְאוּבֵן לְמִשְׁפְּחֹתָם הֶעָרִים וְחַצְרֵיהֶן: פ

24 וַיִּתֵּן מֹשֶׁה לְמַטֵּה־גָד לִבְנֵי־גָד לְמִשְׁפְּחֹתָם: 25 וַיְהִי לָהֶם הַגְּבוּל יַעְזֵר וְכָל־עָרֵי הַגִּלְעָד וַחֲצִי אֶרֶץ בְּנֵי עַמּוֹן עַד־עֲרוֹעֵר אֲשֶׁר עַל־פְּנֵי רַבָּה: 26 וּמֵחֶשְׁבּוֹן עַד־רָמַת הַמִּצְפֶּה וּבְטֹנִים וּמִמַּחֲנַיִם עַד־גְּבוּל לִדְבִר: 27 וּבָעֵמֶק בֵּית הָרָם וּבֵית נִמְרָה וְסֻכּוֹת וְצָפוֹן יֶתֶר מַמְלְכוּת סִיחוֹן מֶלֶךְ חֶשְׁבּוֹן הַיַּרְדֵּן וּגְבֻל עַד־קְצֵה יָם־כִּנֶּרֶת עֵבֶר הַיַּרְדֵּן מִזְרָחָה: 28 זֹאת נַחֲלַת בְּנֵי־גָד לְמִשְׁפְּחֹתָם הֶעָרִים וְחַצְרֵיהֶם: 29 וַיִּתֵּן מֹשֶׁה לַחֲצִי שֵׁבֶט מְנַשֶּׁה וַיְהִי לַחֲצִי מַטֵּה בְנֵי־מְנַשֶּׁה לְמִשְׁפְּחוֹתָם: 30 וַיְהִי גְבוּלָם מִמַּחֲנַיִם כָּל־הַבָּשָׁן כָּל־מַמְלְכוּת | עוֹג מֶלֶךְ־הַבָּשָׁן וְכָל־חַוֹּת יָאִיר אֲשֶׁר בַּבָּשָׁן שִׁשִּׁים עִיר: 31 וַחֲצִי הַגִּלְעָד וְעַשְׁתָּרוֹת וְאֶדְרֶעִי עָרֵי מַמְלְכוּת עוֹג בַּבָּשָׁן לִבְנֵי מָכִיר בֶּן־מְנַשֶּׁה לַחֲצִי בְנֵי־מָכִיר לְמִשְׁפְּחוֹתָם: 32 אֵלֶּה אֲשֶׁר־נִחַל מֹשֶׁה בְּעַרְבוֹת מוֹאָב מֵעֵבֶר לְיַרְדֵּן יְרִיחוֹ מִזְרָחָה: ס 33 וּלְשֵׁבֶט הַלֵּוִי לֹא־נָתַן מֹשֶׁה נַחֲלָה יְהֹוָה אֱלֹהֵי יִשְׂרָאֵל הוּא נַחֲלָתָם כַּאֲשֶׁר דִּבֶּר לָהֶם:

יד וְאֵלֶּה אֲשֶׁר־נָחֲלוּ בְנֵי־יִשְׂרָאֵל בְּאֶרֶץ כְּנָעַן אֲשֶׁר נִחֲלוּ אוֹתָם אֶלְעָזָר הַכֹּהֵן וִיהוֹשֻׁעַ בֶּן־נוּן וְרָאשֵׁי אֲבוֹת הַמַּטּוֹת לִבְנֵי יִשְׂרָאֵל: 2 בְּגוֹרַל נַחֲלָתָם כַּאֲשֶׁר צִוָּה יְהֹוָה בְּיַד־מֹשֶׁה לְתִשְׁעַת הַמַּטּוֹת וַחֲצִי הַמַּטֶּה: 3 כִּי־נָתַן מֹשֶׁה נַחֲלַת שְׁנֵי הַמַּטּוֹת וַחֲצִי הַמַּטֶּה מֵעֵבֶר לַיַּרְדֵּן וְלַלְוִיִּם לֹא־נָתַן נַחֲלָה בְּתוֹכָם: 4 כִּי־הָיוּ בְנֵי־יוֹסֵף שְׁנֵי מַטּוֹת מְנַשֶּׁה וְאֶפְרָיִם וְלֹא־נָתְנוּ חֵלֶק לַלְוִיִּם בָּאָרֶץ כִּי אִם־עָרִים לָשֶׁבֶת וּמִגְרְשֵׁיהֶם לְמִקְנֵיהֶם וּלְקִנְיָנָם:

property. 5 As the LORD had commanded Moses, so the children of Israel did; and they divided the land.

6 Then the children of Judah came to Joshua in Gilgal. And Caleb the son of Jephunneh the Kenizzite said to him: "You know the word which the LORD said to Moses the man of God concerning you and me in Kadesh Barnea. 7 I was forty years old when Moses the servant of the LORD sent me from Kadesh Barnea to spy out the land, and I brought back word to him as it was in my heart. 8 Nevertheless my brethren who went up with me made the heart of the people melt, but I wholly followed the LORD my God. 9 So Moses swore on that day, saying, 'Surely the land where your foot has trodden shall be your inheritance and your children's forever, because you have wholly followed the LORD my God.' 10 And now, behold, the LORD has kept me alive, as He said, these forty-five years, ever since the LORD spoke this word to Moses while Israel wandered in the wilderness; and now, here I am this day, eighty-five years old. 11 As yet I am as strong this day as on the day that Moses sent me; just as my strength was then, so now is my strength for war, both for going out and for coming in. 12 Now therefore, give me this mountain of which the LORD spoke in that day; for you heard in that day how the Anakim were there, and that the cities were great and fortified. It may be that the LORD will be with me, and I shall be able to drive them out as the LORD said."

13 And Joshua blessed him, and gave Hebron to Caleb the son of Jephunneh as an inheritance. 14 Hebron therefore became the inheritance of Caleb the son of Jephunneh the Kenizzite to this day, because he wholly followed the LORD God of Israel. 15 And the name of Hebron formerly was Kirjath Arba (Arba was the greatest man among the Anakim).

Then the land had rest from war.

15 So this was the lot of the tribe of the children of Judah according to their families:

The border of Edom at the Wilderness of Zin southward was the extreme southern boundary. 2 And their southern border began at the shore of the Salt Sea, from the bay that faces southward. 3 Then it went out to the southern side of the Ascent of Akrabbim, passed along to Zin, ascended on the south side of Kadesh Barnea, passed along to Hezron, went up to Adar, and went around to Karkaa. 4 From there it passed toward Azmon and went out to the Brook of Egypt; and the border ended at the sea. This shall be your southern border.

5 כַּאֲשֶׁר צִוָּה יְהֹוָה אֶת־מֹשֶׁה כֵּן עָשׂוּ בְּנֵי יִשְׂרָאֵל
וַיַּחְלְקוּ אֶת־הָאָרֶץ: פ
6 וַיִּגְּשׁוּ בְנֵי־יְהוּדָה אֶל־יְהוֹשֻׁעַ בַּגִּלְגָּל וַיֹּאמֶר אֵלָיו
כָּלֵב בֶּן־יְפֻנֶּה הַקְּנִזִּי אַתָּה יָדַעְתָּ אֶת־הַדָּבָר אֲשֶׁר־
דִּבֶּר יְהֹוָה אֶל־מֹשֶׁה אִישׁ־הָאֱלֹהִים עַל אֹדוֹתַי
וְעַל אֹדוֹתֶיךָ בְּקָדֵשׁ בַּרְנֵעַ: 7 בֶּן־אַרְבָּעִים שָׁנָה
אָנֹכִי בִּשְׁלֹחַ מֹשֶׁה עֶבֶד־יְהֹוָה אֹתִי מִקָּדֵשׁ בַּרְנֵעַ
לְרַגֵּל אֶת־הָאָרֶץ וָאָשֵׁב אֹתוֹ דָּבָר כַּאֲשֶׁר עִם־
לְבָבִי: 8 וְאַחַי אֲשֶׁר עָלוּ עִמִּי הִמְסִיו אֶת־לֵב הָעָם
וְאָנֹכִי מִלֵּאתִי אַחֲרֵי יְהֹוָה אֱלֹהָי: 9 וַיִּשָּׁבַע מֹשֶׁה
בַּיּוֹם הַהוּא לֵאמֹר אִם־לֹא הָאָרֶץ אֲשֶׁר דָּרְכָה
רַגְלְךָ בָּהּ לְךָ תִהְיֶה לְנַחֲלָה וּלְבָנֶיךָ עַד־עוֹלָם כִּי
מִלֵּאתָ אַחֲרֵי יְהֹוָה אֱלֹהָי: 10 וְעַתָּה הִנֵּה הֶחֱיָה
יְהֹוָה אוֹתִי כַּאֲשֶׁר דִּבֵּר זֶה אַרְבָּעִים וְחָמֵשׁ שָׁנָה
מֵאָז דִּבֶּר יְהֹוָה אֶת־הַדָּבָר הַזֶּה אֶל־מֹשֶׁה אֲשֶׁר־
הָלַךְ יִשְׂרָאֵל בַּמִּדְבָּר וְעַתָּה הִנֵּה אָנֹכִי הַיּוֹם בֶּן־
חָמֵשׁ וּשְׁמֹנִים שָׁנָה: 11 עוֹדֶנִּי הַיּוֹם חָזָק כַּאֲשֶׁר
בְּיוֹם שְׁלֹחַ אוֹתִי מֹשֶׁה כְּכֹחִי אָז וּכְכֹחִי עָתָּה
לַמִּלְחָמָה וְלָצֵאת וְלָבוֹא: 12 וְעַתָּה תְּנָה־לִּי אֶת־
הָהָר הַזֶּה אֲשֶׁר־דִּבֶּר יְהֹוָה בַּיּוֹם הַהוּא כִּי אַתָּה
שָׁמַעְתָּ בַיּוֹם הַהוּא כִּי־עֲנָקִים שָׁם וְעָרִים גְּדֹלוֹת
בְּצֻרוֹת אוּלַי יְהֹוָה אוֹתִי וְהוֹרַשְׁתִּים כַּאֲשֶׁר דִּבֶּר
יְהֹוָה: 13 וַיְבָרְכֵהוּ יְהוֹשֻׁעַ וַיִּתֵּן אֶת־חֶבְרוֹן לְכָלֵב
בֶּן־יְפֻנֶּה לְנַחֲלָה: 14 עַל־כֵּן הָיְתָה־חֶבְרוֹן לְכָלֵב בֶּן־
יְפֻנֶּה הַקְּנִזִּי לְנַחֲלָה עַד הַיּוֹם הַזֶּה יַעַן אֲשֶׁר מִלֵּא
אַחֲרֵי יְהֹוָה אֱלֹהֵי יִשְׂרָאֵל: 15 וְשֵׁם חֶבְרוֹן לְפָנִים
קִרְיַת אַרְבַּע הָאָדָם הַגָּדוֹל בָּעֲנָקִים הוּא וְהָאָרֶץ
שָׁקְטָה מִמִּלְחָמָה: פ

טו וַיְהִי הַגּוֹרָל לְמַטֵּה בְנֵי יְהוּדָה לְמִשְׁפְּחֹתָם
אֶל־גְּבוּל אֱדוֹם מִדְבַּר־צִן נֶגְבָּה מִקְצֵה תֵימָן: 2 וַיְהִי
לָהֶם גְּבוּל נֶגֶב מִקְצֵה יָם הַמֶּלַח מִן־הַלָּשֹׁן הַפֹּנֶה
נֶגְבָּה: 3 וְיָצָא אֶל־מִנֶּגֶב לְמַעֲלֵה עַקְרַבִּים וְעָבַר
צִנָה וְעָלָה מִנֶּגֶב לְקָדֵשׁ בַּרְנֵעַ וְעָבַר חֶצְרוֹן וְעָלָה
אַדָּרָה וְנָסַב הַקַּרְקָעָה: 4 וְעָבַר עַצְמוֹנָה וְיָצָא נַחַל
מִצְרַיִם וְהָיָה תֹצְאוֹת הַגְּבוּל יָמָּה זֶה־יִהְיֶה לָכֶם

⁵The east border *was* the Salt Sea as far as the mouth of the Jordan.

And the border on the northern quarter *began* at the bay of the sea at the mouth of the Jordan. ⁶The border went up to Beth Hoglah and passed north of Beth Arabah; and the border went up to the stone of Bohan the son of Reuben. ⁷Then the border went up toward Debir from the Valley of Achor, and it turned northward toward Gilgal, which *is* before the Ascent of Adummim, which *is* on the south side of the valley. The border continued toward the waters of En Shemesh and ended at En Rogel. ⁸And the border went up by the Valley of the Son of Hinnom to the southern slope of the Jebusite *city* (which *is* Jerusalem). The border went up to the top of the mountain that *lies* before the Valley of Hinnom westward, which *is* at the end of the Valley of Rephaim northward. ⁹Then the border went around from the top of the hill to the fountain of the water of Nephtoah, and extended to the cities of Mount Ephron. And the border went around to Baalah (which *is* Kirjath Jearim). ¹⁰Then the border turned westward from Baalah to Mount Seir, passed along to the side of Mount Jearim on the north (which *is* Chesalon), went down to Beth Shemesh, and passed on to Timnah. ¹¹And the border went out to the side of Ekron northward. Then the border went around to Shicron, passed along to Mount Baalah, and extended to Jabneel; and the border ended at the sea.

¹²The west border *was* the coastline of the Great Sea. This *is* the boundary of the children of Judah all around according to their families.

¹³Now to Caleb the son of Jephunneh he gave a share among the children of Judah, according to the commandment of the LORD to Joshua, *namely,* Kirjath Arba, which *is* Hebron (*Arba was* the father of Anak). ¹⁴Caleb drove out the three sons of Anak from there: Sheshai, Ahiman, and Talmai, the children of Anak. ¹⁵Then he went up from there to the inhabitants of Debir (formerly the name of Debir *was* Kirjath Sepher).

¹⁶And Caleb said, "He who attacks Kirjath Sepher and takes it, to him I will give Achsah my daughter as wife." ¹⁷So Othniel the son of Kenaz, the brother of Caleb, took it; and he gave him Achsah his daughter as wife. ¹⁸Now it was so, when she came *to him,* that she persuaded him to ask her father for a field. So she dismounted from *her* donkey, and Caleb said to her, "What do you wish?" ¹⁹She answered, "Give me a blessing; since you have given me land in the South, give me also springs of water." So he gave her the upper springs and the lower springs.

גְּבוּל נֶגֶב: 5 וּגְבוּל קֵדְמָה יָם הַמֶּלַח עַד־קְצֵה הַיַּרְדֵּן וּגְבוּל לִפְאַת צָפוֹנָה מִלְּשׁוֹן הַיָּם מִקְצֵה הַיַּרְדֵּן: 6 וְעָלָה הַגְּבוּל בֵּית חָגְלָה וְעָבַר מִצְּפוֹן לְבֵית הָעֲרָבָה וְעָלָה הַגְּבוּל אֶבֶן בֹּהַן בֶּן־רְאוּבֵן:

7 וְעָלָה הַגְּבוּל ׀ דְּבִרָה מֵעֵמֶק עָכוֹר וְצָפוֹנָה פֹּנֶה אֶל־הַגִּלְגָּל אֲשֶׁר־נֹכַח לְמַעֲלֵה אֲדֻמִּים אֲשֶׁר מִנֶּגֶב לַנָּחַל וְעָבַר הַגְּבוּל אֶל־מֵי־עֵין שֶׁמֶשׁ וְהָיוּ תֹצְאֹתָיו אֶל־עֵין רֹגֵל: 8 וְעָלָה הַגְּבוּל גֵּי בֶן־הִנֹּם אֶל־כֶּתֶף הַיְבוּסִי מִנֶּגֶב הִיא יְרוּשָׁלָ͏ִם וְעָלָה הַגְּבוּל אֶל־רֹאשׁ הָהָר אֲשֶׁר עַל־פְּנֵי גֵי־הִנֹּם יָמָּה אֲשֶׁר בִּקְצֵה עֵמֶק־רְפָאִים צָפֹנָה: 9 וְתָאַר הַגְּבוּל מֵרֹאשׁ הָהָר אֶל־מַעְיַן מֵי נֶפְתּוֹחַ וְיָצָא אֶל־עָרֵי הַר־עֶפְרוֹן וְתָאַר הַגְּבוּל בַּעֲלָה הִיא קִרְיַת יְעָרִים: 10 וְנָסַב הַגְּבוּל מִבַּעֲלָה יָמָּה אֶל־הַר שֵׂעִיר וְעָבַר אֶל־כֶּתֶף הַר־יְעָרִים מִצָּפוֹנָה הִיא כְסָלוֹן וְיָרַד בֵּית־שֶׁמֶשׁ וְעָבַר תִּמְנָה: 11 וְיָצָא הַגְּבוּל אֶל־כֶּתֶף עֶקְרוֹן צָפוֹנָה וְתָאַר הַגְּבוּל שִׁכְּרוֹנָה וְעָבַר הַר־הַבַּעֲלָה וְיָצָא יַבְנְאֵל וְהָיוּ תֹּצְאוֹת הַגְּבוּל יָמָּה: 12 וּגְבוּל יָם הַיָּמָּה הַגָּדוֹל וּגְבוּל זֶה גְּבוּל בְּנֵי־יְהוּדָה סָבִיב לְמִשְׁפְּחֹתָם: 13 וּלְכָלֵב בֶּן־יְפֻנֶּה נָתַן חֵלֶק בְּתוֹךְ בְּנֵי־יְהוּדָה אֶל־פִּי יְהוָה לִיהוֹשֻׁעַ אֶת־קִרְיַת אַרְבַּע אֲבִי הָעֲנָק הִיא חֶבְרוֹן: 14 וַיֹּרֶשׁ מִשָּׁם כָּלֵב אֶת־שְׁלוֹשָׁה בְּנֵי הָעֲנָק אֶת־שֵׁשַׁי וְאֶת־אֲחִימַן וְאֶת־תַּלְמַי יְלִידֵי הָעֲנָק: 15 וַיַּעַל מִשָּׁם אֶל־יֹשְׁבֵי דְּבִר וְשֵׁם־דְּבִר לְפָנִים קִרְיַת־סֵפֶר: 16 וַיֹּאמֶר כָּלֵב אֲשֶׁר־יַכֶּה אֶת־קִרְיַת־סֵפֶר וּלְכָדָהּ וְנָתַתִּי לוֹ אֶת־עַכְסָה בִתִּי לְאִשָּׁה: 17 וַיִּלְכְּדָהּ עָתְנִיאֵל בֶּן־קְנַז אֲחִי כָלֵב וַיִּתֶּן־לוֹ אֶת־עַכְסָה בִתּוֹ לְאִשָּׁה: 18 וַיְהִי בְּבוֹאָהּ וַתְּסִיתֵהוּ לִשְׁאוֹל מֵאֵת־אָבִיהָ שָׂדֶה וַתִּצְנַח מֵעַל הַחֲמוֹר וַיֹּאמֶר־לָהּ כָּלֵב מַה־לָּךְ: 19 וַתֹּאמֶר תְּנָה־לִּי בְרָכָה כִּי אֶרֶץ הַנֶּגֶב נְתַתָּנִי וְנָתַתָּה לִי גֻּלֹּת מָיִם וַיִּתֶּן־לָהּ אֵת גֻּלֹּת עִלִּיּוֹת וְאֵת גֻּלֹּת תַּחְתִּיּוֹת: פ

²⁰This *was* the inheritance of the tribe of the children of Judah according to their families:

²¹The cities at the limits of the tribe of the children of Judah, toward the border of Edom in the South, were Kabzeel, Eder, Jagur, ²²Kinah, Dimonah, Adadah, ²³Kedesh, Hazor, Ithnan, ²⁴Ziph, Telem, Bealoth, ²⁵Hazor, Hadattah, Kerioth, Hezron (which *is* Hazor), ²⁶Amam, Shema, Moladah, ²⁷Hazar Gaddah, Heshmon, Beth Pelet, ²⁸Hazar Shual, Beersheba, Bizjothjah, ²⁹Baalah, Ijim, Ezem, ³⁰Eltolad, Chesil, Hormah, ³¹Ziklag, Madmannah, Sansannah, ³²Lebaoth, Shilhim, Ain, and Rimmon: all the cities *are* twenty-nine, with their villages.

³³In the lowland: Eshtaol, Zorah, Ashnah, ³⁴Zanoah, En Gannim, Tappuah, Enam, ³⁵Jarmuth, Adullam, Socoh, Azekah, ³⁶Sharaim, Adithaim, Gederah, and Gederothaim: fourteen cities with their villages; ³⁷Zenan, Hadashah, Migdal Gad, ³⁸Dilean, Mizpah, Joktheel, ³⁹Lachish, Bozkath, Eglon, ⁴⁰Cabbon, Lahmas, Kithlish, ⁴¹Gederoth, Beth Dagon, Naamah, and Makkedah: sixteen cities with their villages; ⁴²Libnah, Ether, Ashan, ⁴³Jiphtah, Ashnah, Nezib, ⁴⁴Keilah, Achzib, and Mareshah: nine cities with their villages; ⁴⁵Ekron, with its towns and villages; ⁴⁶from Ekron to the sea, all that *lay* near Ashdod, with their villages; ⁴⁷Ashdod with its towns and villages, Gaza with its towns and villages—as far as the Brook of Egypt and the Great Sea with *its* coastline.

⁴⁸And in the mountain country: Shamir, Jattir, Sochoh, ⁴⁹Dannah, Kirjath Sannah (which *is* Debir), ⁵⁰Anab, Eshtemoh, Anim, ⁵¹Goshen, Holon, and Giloh: eleven cities with their villages; ⁵²Arab, Dumah, Eshean, ⁵³Janum, Beth Tappuah, Aphekah, ⁵⁴Humtah, Kirjath Arba (which *is* Hebron), and Zior: nine cities with their villages; ⁵⁵Maon, Carmel, Ziph, Juttah, ⁵⁶Jezreel, Jokdeam, Zanoah, ⁵⁷Kain, Gibeah, and Timnah: ten cities with their villages; ⁵⁸Halhul, Beth Zur, Gedor, ⁵⁹Maarath, Beth Anoth, and Eltekon: six cities with their villages; ⁶⁰Kirjath Baal (which *is* Kirjath Jearim) and Rabbah: two cities with their villages.

⁶¹In the wilderness: Beth Arabah, Middin, Secacah, ⁶²Nibshan, the City of Salt, and En Gedi: six cities with their villages.

⁶³As for the Jebusites, the inhabitants of Jerusalem, the children of Judah could not drive them out; but the Jebusites dwell with the children of Judah at Jerusalem to this day.

20 זֹאת נַחֲלַת מַטֵּה בְנֵי־יְהוּדָה לְמִשְׁפְּחֹתָם׃
21 וַיִּהְיוּ הֶעָרִים מִקְצֵה לְמַטֵּה בְנֵי־יְהוּדָה אֶל־גְּבוּל אֱדוֹם בַּנֶּגְבָּה קַבְצְאֵל וְעֵדֶר וְיָגוּר׃ 22 וְקִינָה וְדִימוֹנָה וְעַדְעָדָה׃ 23 וְקֶדֶשׁ וְחָצוֹר וְיִתְנָן׃ 24 זִיף וָטֶלֶם וּבְעָלוֹת׃ 25 וְחָצוֹר ׀ חֲדַתָּה וּקְרִיּוֹת חֶצְרוֹן הִיא חָצוֹר׃ 26 אֲמָם וּשְׁמַע וּמוֹלָדָה׃ 27 וַחֲצַר גַּדָּה וְחֶשְׁמוֹן וּבֵית פָּלֶט׃ 28 וַחֲצַר שׁוּעָל וּבְאֵר שֶׁבַע וּבִזְיוֹתְיָה׃ 29 בַּעֲלָה וְעִיִּים וָעָצֶם׃ 30 וְאֶלְתּוֹלַד וּכְסִיל וְחָרְמָה׃ 31 וְצִקְלַג וּמַדְמַנָּה וְסַנְסַנָּה׃ 32 וּלְבָאוֹת וְשִׁלְחִים וְעַיִן וְרִמּוֹן כָּל־עָרִים עֶשְׂרִים וָתֵשַׁע וְחַצְרֵיהֶן׃ ס 33 בַּשְּׁפֵלָה אֶשְׁתָּאוֹל וְצָרְעָה וְאַשְׁנָה׃ 34 וְזָנוֹחַ וְעֵין גַּנִּים תַּפּוּחַ וְהָעֵינָם׃ 35 יַרְמוּת וַעֲדֻלָּם שׂוֹכֹה וַעֲזֵקָה׃ 36 וְשַׁעֲרַיִם וַעֲדִיתַיִם וְהַגְּדֵרָה וּגְדֵרֹתָיִם עָרִים אַרְבַּע־עֶשְׂרֵה וְחַצְרֵיהֶן׃ 37 צְנָן וַחֲדָשָׁה וּמִגְדַּל־גָּד׃ 38 וְדִלְעָן וְהַמִּצְפֶּה וְיָקְתְאֵל׃ 39 לָכִישׁ וּבָצְקַת וְעֶגְלוֹן׃ 40 וְכַבּוֹן וְלַחְמָם וְכִתְלִישׁ׃ 41 וּגְדֵרוֹת בֵּית־דָּגוֹן וְנַעֲמָה וּמַקֵּדָה עָרִים שֵׁשׁ־עֶשְׂרֵה וְחַצְרֵיהֶן׃ ס 42 לִבְנָה וָעֶתֶר וְעָשָׁן׃ 43 וְיִפְתָּח וְאַשְׁנָה וּנְצִיב׃ 44 וּקְעִילָה וְאַכְזִיב וּמָרֵאשָׁה עָרִים תֵּשַׁע וְחַצְרֵיהֶן׃ 45 עֶקְרוֹן וּבְנֹתֶיהָ וַחֲצֵרֶיהָ׃ 46 מֵעֶקְרוֹן וָיָמָּה כֹּל אֲשֶׁר־עַל־יַד אַשְׁדּוֹד וְחַצְרֵיהֶן׃ 47 אַשְׁדּוֹד בְּנוֹתֶיהָ וַחֲצֵרֶיהָ עַזָּה בְּנוֹתֶיהָ וַחֲצֵרֶיהָ עַד־נַחַל מִצְרָיִם וְהַיָּם הַגְּבוֹל וּגְבוּל׃ ס 48 וּבָהָר שָׁמִיר וְיַתִּיר וְשׂוֹכֹה׃ 49 וְדַנָּה וְקִרְיַת־סַנָּה הִיא דְבִר׃ 50 וַעֲנָב וְאֶשְׁתְּמֹה וְעָנִים׃ 51 וְגֹשֶׁן וְחֹלֹן וְגִלֹה עָרִים אַחַת־עֶשְׂרֵה וְחַצְרֵיהֶן׃ 52 אֲרַב וְרוּמָה וְאֶשְׁעָן׃ 53 וְיָנִים וּבֵית־תַּפּוּחַ וַאֲפֵקָה׃ 54 וְחֻמְטָה וְקִרְיַת אַרְבַּע הִיא חֶבְרוֹן וְצִיעֹר עָרִים תֵּשַׁע וְחַצְרֵיהֶן׃ 55 מָעוֹן ׀ כַּרְמֶל וָזִיף וְיוּטָּה׃ 56 וְיִזְרְעֶאל וְיָקְדְעָם וְזָנוֹחַ׃ 57 הַקַּיִן גִּבְעָה וְתִמְנָה עָרִים עֶשֶׂר וְחַצְרֵיהֶן׃ 58 חַלְחוּל בֵּית־צוּר וּגְדוֹר׃ 59 וּמַעֲרָת וּבֵית־עֲנוֹת וְאֶלְתְּקֹן עָרִים שֵׁשׁ וְחַצְרֵיהֶן׃ 60 קִרְיַת־בַּעַל הִיא קִרְיַת יְעָרִים וְהָרַבָּה עָרִים שְׁתַּיִם וְחַצְרֵיהֶן׃ ס 61 בַּמִּדְבָּר בֵּית הָעֲרָבָה מִדִּין וּסְכָכָה׃ 62 וְהַנִּבְשָׁן וְעִיר־הַמֶּלַח וְעֵין גֶּדִי עָרִים שֵׁשׁ וְחַצְרֵיהֶן׃ 63 וְאֶת־הַיְבוּסִי יוֹשְׁבֵי יְרוּשָׁלַ͏ִם לֹא־יוּכְלוּ בְנֵי־יְהוּדָה לְהוֹרִישָׁם וַיֵּשֶׁב הַיְבוּסִי אֶת־בְּנֵי יְהוּדָה בִּירוּשָׁלַ͏ִם עַד הַיּוֹם הַזֶּה׃ פ

16 The lot fell to the children of Joseph from the Jordan, by Jericho, to the waters of Jericho on the east, to the wilderness that goes up from Jericho through the mountains to Bethel, ² then went out from Bethel to Luz, passed along to the border of the Archites at Ataroth, ³ and went down westward to the boundary of the Japhletites, as far as the boundary of Lower Beth Horon to Gezer; and it ended at the sea.

⁴ So the children of Joseph, Manasseh and Ephraim, took their inheritance.

⁵ The border of the children of Ephraim, according to their families, was *thus:* The border of their inheritance on the east side was Ataroth Addar as far as Upper Beth Horon.

⁶ And the border went out toward the sea on the north side of Michmethath; then the border went around eastward to Taanath Shiloh, and passed by it on the east of Janohah. ⁷ Then it went down from Janohah to Ataroth and Naarah, reached to Jericho, and came out at the Jordan.

⁸ The border went out from Tappuah westward to the Brook Kanah, and it ended at the sea. This *was* the inheritance of the tribe of the children of Ephraim according to their families. ⁹ The separate cities for the children of Ephraim *were* among the inheritance of the children of Manasseh, all the cities with their villages.

¹⁰ And they did not drive out the Canaanites who dwelt in Gezer; but the Canaanites dwell among the Ephraimites to this day and have become forced laborers.

17 There was also a lot for the tribe of Manasseh, for he *was* the firstborn of Joseph: *namely* for Machir the firstborn of Manasseh, the father of Gilead, because he was a man of war; therefore he was given Gilead and Bashan. ² And there was *a lot* for the rest of the children of Manasseh according to their families: for the children of Abiezer, the children of Helek, the children of Asriel, the children of Shechem, the children of Hepher, and the children of Shemida; these *were* the male children of Manasseh the son of Joseph according to their families.

³ But Zelophehad the son of Hepher, the son of Gilead, the son of Machir, the son of Manasseh, had no sons, but only daughters. And these *are* the names of his daughters: Mahlah, Noah, Hoglah, Milcah, and Tirzah. ⁴ And they came near before Eleazar the priest, before Joshua the son of Nun, and before the rulers, saying, "The LORD commanded Moses to give us an inheritance among our brothers." Therefore, according to the command-

טז וַיֵּצֵא הַגּוֹרָל לִבְנֵי יוֹסֵף מִיַּרְדֵּן יְרִיחוֹ לְמֵי יְרִיחוֹ מִזְרָחָה הַמִּדְבָּר עֹלֶה מִירִיחוֹ בָּהָר בֵּית־אֵל: 2 וְיָצָא מִבֵּית־אֵל לוּזָה וְעָבַר אֶל־גְּבוּל הָאַרְכִּי עֲטָרוֹת: 3 וְיָרַד־יָמָּה אֶל־גְּבוּל הַיַּפְלֵטִי עַד גְּבוּל בֵּית־חוֹרֹן תַּחְתּוֹן וְעַד־גָּזֶר וְהָיוּ תֹצְאֹתָו יָמָּה: 4 וַיִּנְחֲלוּ בְנֵי־יוֹסֵף מְנַשֶּׁה וְאֶפְרָיִם: 5 וַיְהִי גְּבוּל בְּנֵי־אֶפְרַיִם לְמִשְׁפְּחֹתָם וַיְהִי גְּבוּל נַחֲלָתָם מִזְרָחָה עַטְרוֹת אַדָּר עַד־בֵּית חוֹרֹן עֶלְיוֹן: 6 וְיָצָא הַגְּבוּל הַיָּמָּה הַמִּכְמְתָת מִצָּפוֹן וְנָסַב הַגְּבוּל מִזְרָחָה תַּאֲנַת שִׁלֹה וְעָבַר אוֹתוֹ מִמִּזְרַח יָנוֹחָה: 7 וְיָרַד מִיָּנוֹחָה עֲטָרוֹת וְנַעֲרָתָה וּפָגַע בִּירִיחוֹ וְיָצָא הַיַּרְדֵּן: 8 מִתַּפּוּחַ יֵלֵךְ הַגְּבוּל יָמָּה נַחַל קָנָה וְהָיוּ תֹצְאֹתָיו הַיָּמָּה זֹאת נַחֲלַת מַטֵּה בְנֵי־אֶפְרַיִם לְמִשְׁפְּחֹתָם: 9 וְהֶעָרִים הַמִּבְדָּלוֹת לִבְנֵי אֶפְרַיִם בְּתוֹךְ נַחֲלַת בְּנֵי־מְנַשֶּׁה כָּל־הֶעָרִים וְחַצְרֵיהֶן: 10 וְלֹא הוֹרִישׁוּ אֶת־הַכְּנַעֲנִי הַיּוֹשֵׁב בְּגָזֶר וַיֵּשֶׁב הַכְּנַעֲנִי בְּקֶרֶב אֶפְרַיִם עַד־הַיּוֹם הַזֶּה וַיְהִי לְמַס־עֹבֵד: פ

יז וַיְהִי הַגּוֹרָל לְמַטֵּה מְנַשֶּׁה כִּי־הוּא בְּכוֹר יוֹסֵף לְמָכִיר בְּכוֹר מְנַשֶּׁה אֲבִי הַגִּלְעָד כִּי הוּא הָיָה אִישׁ מִלְחָמָה וַיְהִי־לוֹ הַגִּלְעָד וְהַבָּשָׁן: 2 וַיְהִי לִבְנֵי מְנַשֶּׁה הַנּוֹתָרִים לְמִשְׁפְּחֹתָם לִבְנֵי אֲבִיעֶזֶר וְלִבְנֵי־חֵלֶק וְלִבְנֵי אַשְׂרִיאֵל וְלִבְנֵי־שֶׁכֶם וְלִבְנֵי־חֵפֶר וְלִבְנֵי שְׁמִידָע אֵלֶּה בְּנֵי מְנַשֶּׁה בֶּן־יוֹסֵף הַזְּכָרִים לְמִשְׁפְּחֹתָם: 3 וְלִצְלָפְחָד בֶּן־חֵפֶר בֶּן־גִּלְעָד בֶּן־מָכִיר בֶּן־מְנַשֶּׁה לֹא־הָיוּ לוֹ בָּנִים כִּי אִם־בָּנוֹת וְאֵלֶּה שְׁמוֹת בְּנֹתָיו מַחְלָה וְנֹעָה חָגְלָה מִלְכָּה וְתִרְצָה: 4 וַתִּקְרַבְנָה לִפְנֵי אֶלְעָזָר הַכֹּהֵן וְלִפְנֵי | יְהוֹשֻׁעַ בִּן־נוּן וְלִפְנֵי הַנְּשִׂיאִים לֵאמֹר יְהוָה צִוָּה אֶת־מֹשֶׁה לָתֶת־לָנוּ נַחֲלָה בְּתוֹךְ אַחֵינוּ וַיִּתֵּן לָהֶם

ment of the LORD, he gave them an inheritance among their father's brothers. ⁵Ten shares fell to Manasseh, besides the land of Gilead and Bashan, which *were* on the other side of the Jordan, ⁶because the daughters of Manasseh received an inheritance among his sons; and the rest of Manasseh's sons had the land of Gilead.

⁷And the territory of Manasseh was from Asher to Michmethath, that *lies* east of Shechem; and the border went along south to the inhabitants of En Tappuah. ⁸Manasseh had the land of Tappuah, but Tappuah on the border of Manasseh *belonged* to the children of Ephraim. ⁹And the border descended to the Brook Kanah, southward to the brook. These cities of Ephraim *are* among the cities of Manasseh. The border of Manasseh *was* on the north side of the brook; and it ended at the sea.

¹⁰Southward *it was* Ephraim's, northward *it was* Manasseh's, and the sea was its border. Manasseh's territory was adjoining Asher on the north and Issachar on the east. ¹¹And in Issachar and in Asher, Manasseh had Beth Shean and its towns, Ibleam and its towns, the inhabitants of Dor and its towns, the inhabitants of En Dor and its towns, the inhabitants of Taanach and its towns, and the inhabitants of Megiddo and its towns—three hilly regions. ¹²Yet the children of Manasseh could not drive out *the inhabitants of* those cities, but the Canaanites were determined to dwell in that land. ¹³And it happened, when the children of Israel grew strong, that they put the Canaanites to forced labor, but did not utterly drive them out.

¹⁴Then the children of Joseph spoke to Joshua, saying, "Why have you given us *only* one lot and one share to inherit, since we *are* a great people, inasmuch as the LORD has blessed us until now?"

¹⁵So Joshua answered them, "If you *are* a great people, *then* go up to the forest *country* and clear a place for yourself there in the land of the Perizzites and the giants, since the mountains of Ephraim are too confined for you."

¹⁶But the children of Joseph said, "The mountain country is not enough for us; and all the Canaanites who dwell in the land of the valley have chariots of iron, *both those* who *are* of Beth Shean and its towns and *those* who *are* of the Valley of Jezreel."

¹⁷And Joshua spoke to the house of Joseph—to Ephraim and Manasseh—saying, "You *are* a great people and have great power; you shall not have *only* one lot, ¹⁸but the mountain country shall be yours. Although it *is* wooded, you shall cut it down,

אֶל־פִּי יְהֹוָה נַחֲלָה בְּתוֹךְ אֲחֵי אֲבִיהֶן: ⁵ וַיִּפְּלוּ חַבְלֵי־מְנַשֶּׁה עֲשָׂרָה לְבַד מֵאֶרֶץ הַגִּלְעָד וְהַבָּשָׁן אֲשֶׁר מֵעֵבֶר לַיַּרְדֵּן: ⁶ כִּי בְּנוֹת מְנַשֶּׁה נָחֲלוּ נַחֲלָה בְּתוֹךְ בָּנָיו וְאֶרֶץ הַגִּלְעָד הָיְתָה לִבְנֵי־מְנַשֶּׁה הַנּוֹתָרִים: ⁷ וַיְהִי גְבוּל־מְנַשֶּׁה מֵאָשֵׁר הַמִּכְמְתָת אֲשֶׁר עַל־פְּנֵי שְׁכֶם וְהָלַךְ הַגְּבוּל אֶל־הַיָּמִין אֶל־יֹשְׁבֵי עֵין תַּפּוּחַ: ⁸ לִמְנַשֶּׁה הָיְתָה אֶרֶץ תַּפּוּחַ וְתַפּוּחַ אֶל־גְּבוּל מְנַשֶּׁה לִבְנֵי אֶפְרָיִם: ⁹ וְיָרַד הַגְּבוּל נַחַל קָנָה נֶגְבָּה לַנַּחַל עָרִים הָאֵלֶּה לְאֶפְרַיִם בְּתוֹךְ עָרֵי מְנַשֶּׁה וּגְבוּל מְנַשֶּׁה מִצְּפוֹן לַנַּחַל וַיְהִי תֹצְאֹתָיו הַיָּמָּה: ¹⁰ נֶגְבָּה לְאֶפְרַיִם וְצָפוֹנָה לִמְנַשֶּׁה וַיְהִי הַיָּם גְּבוּלוֹ וּבְאָשֵׁר יִפְגְּעוּן מִצָּפוֹן וּבְיִשָּׂשכָר מִמִּזְרָח: ¹¹ וַיְהִי לִמְנַשֶּׁה בְּיִשָּׂשכָר וּבְאָשֵׁר בֵּית־שְׁאָן וּבְנוֹתֶיהָ וְיִבְלְעָם וּבְנוֹתֶיהָ וְאֶת־יֹשְׁבֵי דֹאר וּבְנוֹתֶיהָ וְיֹשְׁבֵי עֵין־דֹּר וּבְנֹתֶיהָ וְיֹשְׁבֵי תַעְנַךְ וּבְנֹתֶיהָ וְיֹשְׁבֵי מְגִדּוֹ וּבְנוֹתֶיהָ שְׁלֹשֶׁת הַנָּפֶת:

¹² וְלֹא יָכְלוּ בְּנֵי מְנַשֶּׁה לְהוֹרִישׁ אֶת־הֶעָרִים הָאֵלֶּה וַיּוֹאֶל הַכְּנַעֲנִי לָשֶׁבֶת בָּאָרֶץ הַזֹּאת: ¹³ וַיְהִי כִּי חָזְקוּ בְּנֵי יִשְׂרָאֵל וַיִּתְּנוּ אֶת־הַכְּנַעֲנִי לָמַס וְהוֹרֵשׁ לֹא הוֹרִישׁוֹ: ס ¹⁴ וַיְדַבְּרוּ בְּנֵי יוֹסֵף אֶת־יְהוֹשֻׁעַ לֵאמֹר מַדּוּעַ נָתַתָּה לִּי נַחֲלָה גּוֹרָל אֶחָד וְחֶבֶל אֶחָד וַאֲנִי עַם־רָב עַד אֲשֶׁר־עַד־כֹּה בֵּרְכַנִי יְהֹוָה: ¹⁵ וַיֹּאמֶר אֲלֵיהֶם יְהוֹשֻׁעַ אִם־עַם־רָב אַתָּה עֲלֵה לְךָ הַיַּעְרָה וּבֵרֵאתָ לְךָ שָׁם בְּאֶרֶץ הַפְּרִזִּי וְהָרְפָאִים כִּי־אָץ לְךָ הַר־אֶפְרָיִם: ¹⁶ וַיֹּאמְרוּ בְּנֵי יוֹסֵף לֹא־יִמָּצֵא לָנוּ הָהָר וְרֶכֶב בַּרְזֶל בְּכָל־הַכְּנַעֲנִי הַיֹּשֵׁב בְּאֶרֶץ־הָעֵמֶק לַאֲשֶׁר בְּבֵית־שְׁאָן וּבְנוֹתֶיהָ וְלַאֲשֶׁר בְּעֵמֶק יִזְרְעֶאל: ¹⁷ וַיֹּאמֶר יְהוֹשֻׁעַ אֶל־בֵּית יוֹסֵף לְאֶפְרַיִם וְלִמְנַשֶּׁה לֵאמֹר עַם־רָב אַתָּה וְכֹחַ גָּדוֹל לָךְ לֹא־יִהְיֶה לְךָ גּוֹרָל אֶחָד: ¹⁸ כִּי הַר יִהְיֶה־

and its farthest extent shall be yours; for you shall drive out the Canaanites, though they have iron chariots *and* are strong."

18 Now the whole congregation of the children of Israel assembled together at Shiloh, and set up the tabernacle of meeting there. And the land was subdued before them. ² But there remained among the children of Israel seven tribes which had not yet received their inheritance.

³ Then Joshua said to the children of Israel: "How long will you neglect to go and possess the land which the LORD God of your fathers has given you? ⁴ Pick out from among you three men for *each* tribe, and I will send them; they shall rise and go through the land, survey it according to their inheritance, and come *back* to me. ⁵ And they shall divide it into seven parts. Judah shall remain in their territory on the south, and the house of Joseph shall remain in their territory on the north. ⁶ You shall therefore survey the land in seven parts and bring *the survey* here to me, that I may cast lots for you here before the LORD our God. ⁷ But the Levites have no part among you, for the priesthood of the LORD *is* their inheritance. And Gad, Reuben, and half the tribe of Manasseh have received their inheritance beyond the Jordan on the east, which Moses the servant of the LORD gave them."

⁸ Then the men arose to go away; and Joshua charged those who went to survey the land, saying, "Go, walk through the land, survey it, and come back to me, that I may cast lots for you here before the LORD in Shiloh." ⁹ So the men went, passed through the land, and wrote the survey in a book in seven parts by cities; and they came to Joshua at the camp in Shiloh. ¹⁰ Then Joshua cast lots for them in Shiloh before the LORD, and there Joshua divided the land to the children of Israel according to their divisions.

¹¹ Now the lot of the tribe of the children of Benjamin came up according to their families, and the territory of their lot came out between the children of Judah and the children of Joseph. ¹² Their border on the north side began at the Jordan, and the border went up to the side of Jericho on the north, and went up through the mountains westward; it ended at the Wilderness of Beth Aven. ¹³ The border went over from there toward Luz, to the side of Luz (which *is* Bethel) southward; and the border descended to Ataroth Addar, near the hill that *lies* on the south side of Lower Beth Horon.

לָ֣ךְ כִּי־יַ֤עַר הוּא֙ וּבֵ֣רֵאת֔וֹ וְהָ֥יָה לְךָ֖ תֹּצְאֹתָ֑יו כִּי־תוֹרִ֣ישׁ אֶת־הַכְּנַעֲנִ֗י כִּ֣י רֶ֤כֶב בַּרְזֶל֙ ל֔וֹ כִּ֥י חָזָ֖ק הֽוּא: פ

יח וַיִּקָּ֨הֲל֜וּ כָּל־עֲדַ֤ת בְּנֵֽי־יִשְׂרָאֵל֙ שִׁלֹ֔ה וַיַּשְׁכִּ֥ינוּ שָׁ֖ם אֶת־אֹ֣הֶל מוֹעֵ֑ד וְהָאָ֥רֶץ נִכְבְּשָׁ֖ה לִפְנֵיהֶֽם: ² וַיִּוָּ֣תְר֗וּ בִּבְנֵ֣י יִשְׂרָאֵ֔ל אֲשֶׁ֥ר לֹֽא־חָלְק֖וּ אֶת־נַחֲלָתָ֑ם שִׁבְעָ֖ה שְׁבָטִֽים: ³ וַיֹּ֥אמֶר יְהוֹשֻׁ֖עַ אֶל־בְּנֵ֣י יִשְׂרָאֵ֑ל עַד־אָ֣נָה אַתֶּ֣ם מִתְרַפִּ֗ים לָבוֹא֙ לָרֶ֣שֶׁת אֶת־הָאָ֔רֶץ אֲשֶׁר֙ נָתַ֣ן לָכֶ֔ם יְהוָ֖ה אֱלֹהֵ֣י אֲבֽוֹתֵיכֶֽם: ⁴ הָב֥וּ לָכֶ֛ם שְׁלֹשָׁ֥ה אֲנָשִׁ֖ים לַשָּׁ֑בֶט וְאֶשְׁלָחֵ֗ם וְיָקֻ֜מוּ וְיִֽתְהַלְּכ֤וּ בָאָ֨רֶץ֙ וְיִכְתְּב֤וּ אוֹתָהּ֙ לְפִ֣י נַֽחֲלָתָ֔ם וְיָבֹ֖אוּ אֵלָֽי: ⁵ וְהִֽתְחַלְּק֥וּ אֹתָ֖הּ לְשִׁבְעָ֣ה חֲלָקִ֑ים יְהוּדָ֞ה יַעֲמֹ֤ד עַל־גְּבוּלוֹ֙ מִנֶּ֔גֶב וּבֵ֥ית יוֹסֵ֛ף יַעַמְד֥וּ עַל־גְּבוּלָ֖ם מִצָּפֽוֹן: ⁶ וְאַתֶּ֞ם תִּכְתְּב֤וּ אֶת־הָאָ֨רֶץ֙ שִׁבְעָ֣ה חֲלָקִ֔ים וַהֲבֵאתֶ֥ם אֵלַ֖י הֵ֑נָּה וְיָרִ֨יתִי לָכֶ֤ם גּוֹרָל֙ פֹּ֔ה לִפְנֵ֖י יְהוָ֥ה אֱלֹהֵֽינוּ: ⁷ כִּ֠י אֵֽין־חֵ֤לֶק לַלְוִיִּם֙ בְּקִרְבְּכֶ֔ם כִּֽי־כְהֻנַּ֥ת יְהוָ֖ה נַחֲלָת֑וֹ וְגָ֡ד וּרְאוּבֵ֡ן וַחֲצִי֩ שֵׁ֨בֶט הַֽמְנַשֶּׁ֜ה לָקְח֣וּ נַחֲלָתָ֗ם מֵעֵ֤בֶר לַיַּרְדֵּן֙ מִזְרָ֔חָה אֲשֶׁ֥ר נָתַ֛ן לָהֶ֖ם מֹשֶׁ֥ה עֶ֥בֶד יְהוָֽה: ⁸ וַיָּקֻ֥מוּ הָאֲנָשִׁ֖ים וַיֵּלֵ֑כוּ וַיְצַ֣ו יְהוֹשֻׁ֡עַ אֶת־הַהֹלְכִים֩ לִכְתֹּ֨ב אֶת־הָאָ֜רֶץ לֵאמֹ֗ר לְכ֞וּ וְהִתְהַלְּכ֧וּ בָאָ֣רֶץ וְכִתְב֣וּ אוֹתָ֗הּ וְשׁ֣וּבוּ אֵלַ֔י וּפֹ֗ה אַשְׁלִ֨יךְ לָכֶ֥ם גּוֹרָ֛ל לִפְנֵ֥י יְהוָ֖ה בְּשִׁלֹֽה: ⁹ וַיֵּלְכ֤וּ הָֽאֲנָשִׁים֙ וַיַּעַבְר֣וּ בָאָ֔רֶץ וַיִּכְתְּב֧וּהָ לֶֽעָרִ֛ים לְשִׁבְעָ֥ה חֲלָקִ֖ים עַל־סֵ֑פֶר וַיָּבֹ֥אוּ אֶל־יְהוֹשֻׁ֛עַ אֶל־הַֽמַּחֲנֶ֖ה שִׁלֹֽה: ¹⁰ וַיַּשְׁלֵךְ֩ לָהֶ֨ם יְהוֹשֻׁ֧עַ גּוֹרָ֛ל בְּשִׁלֹ֖ה לִפְנֵ֣י יְהוָ֑ה וַיְחַלֶּק־שָׁ֨ם יְהוֹשֻׁ֧עַ אֶת־הָאָ֛רֶץ לִבְנֵ֥י יִשְׂרָאֵ֖ל כְּמַחְלְקֹתָֽם: פ

¹¹ וַיַּ֗עַל גּוֹרַ֛ל מַטֵּ֥ה בְנֵֽי־בִנְיָמִ֖ן לְמִשְׁפְּחֹתָ֑ם וַיֵּצֵ֞א גְּב֣וּל גּֽוֹרָלָ֗ם בֵּ֚ין בְּנֵ֣י יְהוּדָ֔ה וּבֵ֖ין בְּנֵ֥י יוֹסֵֽף: ¹² וַיְהִ֨י לָהֶ֧ם הַגְּב֛וּל לִפְאַ֥ת צָפ֖וֹנָה מִן־הַיַּרְדֵּ֑ן וְעָלָ֣ה הַגְּבוּל֩ אֶל־כֶּ֨תֶף יְרִיח֜וֹ מִצָּפ֗וֹן וְעָלָ֤ה בָהָר֙ יָ֔מָּה וְהָיָה֙ תֹּֽצְאֹתָ֔יו מִדְבַּ֖רָה בֵּ֥ית אָֽוֶן: ¹³ וְעָבַר֩ מִשָּׁ֨ם הַגְּב֜וּל ל֗וּזָה אֶל־כֶּ֤תֶף ל֨וּזָה֙ נֶ֔גְבָּה הִ֖יא בֵּֽית־אֵ֑ל וְיָרַ֤ד הַגְּבוּל֙ עַטְר֣וֹת אַדָּ֔ר עַל־הָהָ֕ר אֲשֶׁ֥ר מִנֶּ֖גֶב

14 Then the border extended around the west side to the south, from the hill that *lies* before Beth Horon southward; and it ended at Kirjath Baal (which *is* Kirjath Jearim), a city of the children of Judah. This *was* the west side.

15 The south side *began* at the end of Kirjath Jearim, and the border extended on the west and went out to the spring of the waters of Nephtoah. 16 Then the border came down to the end of the mountain that *lies* before the Valley of the Son of Hinnom, which *is* in the Valley of the Rephaim on the north, descended to the Valley of Hinnom, to the side of the Jebusite *city* on the south, and descended to En Rogel. 17 And it went around from the north, went out to En Shemesh, and extended toward Geliloth, which is before the Ascent of Adummim, and descended to the stone of Bohan the son of Reuben. 18 Then it passed along toward the north side of Arabah, and went down to Arabah. 19 And the border passed along to the north side of Beth Hoglah; then the border ended at the north bay at the Salt Sea, at the south end of the Jordan. This *was* the southern boundary.

20 The Jordan was its border on the east side. This *was* the inheritance of the children of Benjamin, according to its boundaries all around, according to their families.

21 Now the cities of the tribe of the children of Benjamin, according to their families, were Jericho, Beth Hoglah, Emek Keziz, 22 Beth Arabah, Zemaraim, Bethel, 23 Avim, Parah, Ophrah, 24 Chephar Haammoni, Ophni, and Gaba: twelve cities with their villages; 25 Gibeon, Ramah, Beeroth, 26 Mizpah, Chephirah, Mozah, 27 Rekem, Irpeel, Taralah, 28 Zelah, Eleph, Jebus (which *is* Jerusalem), Gibeath, *and* Kirjath: fourteen cities with their villages. This was the inheritance of the children of Benjamin according to their families.

19 The second lot came out for Simeon, for the tribe of the children of Simeon according to their families. And their inheritance was within the inheritance of the children of Judah. 2 They had in their inheritance Beersheba (Sheba), Moladah, 3 Hazar Shual, Balah, Ezem, 4 Eltolad, Bethul, Hormah, 5 Ziklag, Beth Marcaboth, Hazar Susah, 6 Beth Lebaoth, and Sharuhen: thirteen cities and their villages; 7 Ain, Rimmon, Ether, and Ashan: four cities and their villages; 8 and all the villages that *were* all around these cities as far as Baalath Beer, Ramah of the South. This *was* the inheritance of the tribe of the children of Simeon according to their families.

לְבֵית־חֹרוֹן תַּחְתּוֹן: 14 וְתָאַר הַגְּבוּל וְנָסַב לִפְאַת־
יָם נֶגְבָּה מִן־הָהָר אֲשֶׁר עַל־פְּנֵי בֵית־חֹרוֹן נֶגְבָּה
וְהָיָה תֹצְאֹתָיו אֶל־קִרְיַת־בַּעַל הִיא קִרְיַת יְעָרִים
עִיר בְּנֵי יְהוּדָה זֹאת פְּאַת־יָם: 15 וּפְאַת־נֶגְבָּה
מִקְצֵה קִרְיַת יְעָרִים וְיָצָא הַגְּבוּל יָמָּה וְיָצָא אֶל־
מַעְיַן מֵי נֶפְתּוֹחַ: 16 וְיָרַד הַגְּבוּל אֶל־קְצֵה הָהָר
אֲשֶׁר עַל־פְּנֵי גֵּי בֶן־הִנֹּם אֲשֶׁר בְּעֵמֶק רְפָאִים
צָפוֹנָה וְיָרַד גֵּי הִנֹּם אֶל־כֶּתֶף הַיְבוּסִי נֶגְבָּה וְיָרַד
עֵין רֹגֵל: 17 וְתָאַר מִצָּפוֹן וְיָצָא עֵין שֶׁמֶשׁ וְיָצָא
אֶל־גְּלִילוֹת אֲשֶׁר־נֹכַח מַעֲלֵה אֲדֻמִּים וְיָרַד אֶבֶן
בֹּהַן בֶּן־רְאוּבֵן: 18 וְעָבַר אֶל־כֶּתֶף מוּל־הָעֲרָבָה
צָפוֹנָה וְיָרַד הָעֲרָבָתָה: 19 וְעָבַר הַגְּבוּל אֶל־כֶּתֶף
בֵּית־חָגְלָה צָפוֹנָה וְהָיָה תֹצְאוֹתָיו הַגְּבוּל אֶל־
לְשׁוֹן יָם־הַמֶּלַח צָפוֹנָה אֶל־קְצֵה הַיַּרְדֵּן נֶגְבָּה זֶה
גְּבוּל נֶגֶב: 20 וְהַיַּרְדֵּן יִגְבֹּל־אֹתוֹ לִפְאַת־קֵדְמָה זֹאת
נַחֲלַת בְּנֵי בִנְיָמִן לִגְבוּלֹתֶיהָ סָבִיב לְמִשְׁפְּחֹתָם:
21 וְהָיוּ הֶעָרִים לְמַטֵּה בְּנֵי בִנְיָמִן לְמִשְׁפְּחוֹתֵיהֶם
יְרִיחוֹ וּבֵית־חָגְלָה וְעֵמֶק קְצִיץ: 22 וּבֵית הָעֲרָבָה
וּצְמָרַיִם וּבֵית־אֵל: 23 וְהָעַוִּים וְהַפָּרָה וְעָפְרָה:
24 וּכְפַר הָעַמֹּנִי וְהָעָפְנִי וָגָבַע עָרִים שְׁתֵּים־עֶשְׂרֵה
וְחַצְרֵיהֶן: 25 גִּבְעוֹן וְהָרָמָה וּבְאֵרוֹת: 26 וְהַמִּצְפֶּה
וְהַכְּפִירָה וְהַמֹּצָה: 27 וְרֶקֶם וְיִרְפְּאֵל וְתַרְאֲלָה:
28 וְצֵלַע הָאֶלֶף וְהַיְבוּסִי הִיא יְרוּשָׁלַ͏ִם גִּבְעַת קִרְיַת
עָרִים אַרְבַּע־עֶשְׂרֵה וְחַצְרֵיהֶן זֹאת נַחֲלַת בְּנֵי־בִנְיָמִן
לְמִשְׁפְּחֹתָם:
פ

יט וַיֵּצֵא הַגּוֹרָל הַשֵּׁנִי לְשִׁמְעוֹן לְמַטֵּה בְנֵי־
שִׁמְעוֹן לְמִשְׁפְּחוֹתָם וַיְהִי נַחֲלָתָם בְּתוֹךְ נַחֲלַת בְּנֵי־
יְהוּדָה: 2 וַיְהִי לָהֶם בְּנַחֲלָתָם בְּאֵר־שֶׁבַע וְשֶׁבַע
וּמוֹלָדָה: 3 וַחֲצַר שׁוּעָל וּבָלָה וָעָצֶם: 4 וְאֶלְתּוֹלַד
וּבְתוּל וְחָרְמָה: 5 וְצִקְלַג וּבֵית־הַמַּרְכָּבוֹת וַחֲצַר
סוּסָה: 6 וּבֵית לְבָאוֹת וְשָׁרוּחֶן עָרִים שְׁלֹשׁ־עֶשְׂרֵה
וְחַצְרֵיהֶן: 7 עַיִן רִמּוֹן וָעֶתֶר וְעָשָׁן עָרִים אַרְבַּע
וְחַצְרֵיהֶן: 8 וְכָל־הַחֲצֵרִים אֲשֶׁר סְבִיבוֹת הֶעָרִים
הָאֵלֶּה עַד־בַּעֲלַת בְּאֵר רָאמַת נֶגֶב זֹאת נַחֲלַת

9 The inheritance of the children of Simeon *was* *included* in the share of the children of Judah, for the share of the children of Judah was too much for them. Therefore the children of Simeon had *their* inheritance within the inheritance of that people.

10 The third lot came out for the children of Zebulun according to their families, and the border of their inheritance was as far as Sarid. 11 Their border went toward the west and to Maralah, went to Dabbasheth, and extended along the brook that is east of Jokneam. 12 Then from Sarid it went eastward toward the sunrise along the border of Chisloth Tabor, and went out toward Daberath, bypassing Japhia. 13 And from there it passed along on the east of Gath Hepher, toward Eth Kazin, and extended to Rimmon, which borders on Neah. 14 Then the border went around it on the north side of Hannathon, and it ended in the Valley of Jiphthah El. 15 Included were Kattath, Nahallal, Shimron, Idalah, and Bethlehem: twelve cities with their villages. 16 This *was* the inheritance of the children of Zebulun according to their families, these cities with their villages.

17 The fourth lot came out to Issachar, for the children of Issachar according to their families. 18 And their territory went to Jezreel, and *included* Chesulloth, Shunem, 19 Haphraim, Shion, Anaharath, 20 Rabbith, Kishion, Abez, 21 Remeth, En Gannim, En Haddah, and Beth Pazzez. 22 And the border reached to Tabor, Shahazimah, and Beth Shemesh; their border ended at the Jordan: sixteen cities with their villages. 23 This *was* the inheritance of the tribe of the children of Issachar according to their families, the cities and their villages.

24 The fifth lot came out for the tribe of the children of Asher according to their families. 25 And their territory included Helkath, Hali, Beten, Achshaph, 26 Alammelech, Amad, and Mishal; it reached to Mount Carmel westward, along *the Brook* Shihor Libnath. 27 It turned toward the sunrise to Beth Dagon; and it reached to Zebulun and to the Valley of Jiphthah El, then northward beyond Beth Emek and Neiel, bypassing Cabul *which was* on the left, 28 including Ebron, Rehob, Hammon, and Kanah, as far as Greater Sidon. 29 And the border turned to Ramah and to the fortified city of Tyre; then the border turned to Hosah, and ended at the sea by the region of Achzib. 30 Also Ummah, Aphek, and Rehob *were* *included*: twenty-two cities with their villages. 31 This *was* the inheritance of the tribe of the children of Asher according to their families, these cities with their villages.

מַטֵּה בְנֵי־שִׁמְעוֹן לְמִשְׁפְּחוֹתָם: 9 מֵחֶבֶל בְּנֵי יְהוּדָה נַחֲלַת בְּנֵי שִׁמְעוֹן כִּי־הָיָה חֵלֶק בְּנֵי־יְהוּדָה רַב מֵהֶם וַיִּנְחֲלוּ בְנֵי־שִׁמְעוֹן בְּתוֹךְ נַחֲלָתָם: פ

10 וַיַּעַל הַגּוֹרָל הַשְּׁלִישִׁי לִבְנֵי זְבוּלֻן לְמִשְׁפְּחוֹתָם וַיְהִי גְּבוּל נַחֲלָתָם עַד־שָׂרִיד: 11 וְעָלָה גְבוּלָם ׀ לַיָּמָּה וּמַרְעֲלָה וּפָגַע בְּדַבָּשֶׁת וּפָגַע אֶל־הַנַּחַל אֲשֶׁר עַל־פְּנֵי יָקְנְעָם: 12 וְשָׁב מִשָּׂרִיד קֵדְמָה מִזְרַח הַשֶּׁמֶשׁ עַל־גְּבוּל כִּסְלֹת תָּבֹר וְיָצָא אֶל־הַדָּבְרַת וְעָלָה יָפִיעַ: 13 וּמִשָּׁם עָבַר קֵדְמָה מִזְרָחָה גִּתָּה חֵפֶר עִתָּה קָצִין וְיָצָא רִמּוֹן הַמְּתֹאָר הַנֵּעָה: 14 וְנָסַב אֹתוֹ הַגְּבוּל מִצְּפוֹן חַנָּתֹן וְהָיוּ תֹּצְאֹתָיו גֵּי יִפְתַּח־אֵל: 15 וְקַטָּת וְנַהֲלָל וְשִׁמְרוֹן וְיִדְאֲלָה וּבֵית לָחֶם עָרִים שְׁתֵּים־עֶשְׂרֵה וְחַצְרֵיהֶן: 16 זֹאת נַחֲלַת בְּנֵי־זְבוּלֻן לְמִשְׁפְּחוֹתָם הֶעָרִים הָאֵלֶּה וְחַצְרֵיהֶן: פ

17 לְיִשָּׂשכָר יָצָא הַגּוֹרָל הָרְבִיעִי לִבְנֵי יִשָּׂשכָר לְמִשְׁפְּחוֹתָם: 18 וַיְהִי גְּבוּלָם יִזְרְעֶאלָה וְהַכְּסוּלֹת וְשׁוּנֵם: 19 וַחֲפָרַיִם וְשִׁיאֹן וַאֲנָחֲרַת: 20 וְהָרַבִּית וְקִשְׁיוֹן וָאָבֶץ: 21 וְרֶמֶת וְעֵין־גַּנִּים וְעֵין חַדָּה וּבֵית פַּצֵּץ: 22 וּפָגַע הַגְּבוּל בְּתָבוֹר וְשַׁחֲצוֹמָה וּבֵית שֶׁמֶשׁ וְהָיוּ תֹּצְאוֹת גְּבוּלָם הַיַּרְדֵּן עָרִים שֵׁשׁ־עֶשְׂרֵה וְחַצְרֵיהֶן: 23 זֹאת נַחֲלַת מַטֵּה בְנֵי־יִשָּׂשכָר לְמִשְׁפְּחֹתָם הֶעָרִים וְחַצְרֵיהֶן: פ

24 וַיֵּצֵא הַגּוֹרָל הַחֲמִישִׁי לְמַטֵּה בְנֵי־אָשֵׁר לְמִשְׁפְּחוֹתָם: 25 וַיְהִי גְּבוּלָם חֶלְקַת וַחֲלִי וָבֶטֶן וְאַכְשָׁף: 26 וְאַלַמֶּלֶךְ וְעַמְעָד וּמִשְׁאָל וּפָגַע בְּכַרְמֶל הַיָּמָּה וּבְשִׁיחוֹר לִבְנָת: 27 וְשָׁב מִזְרַח הַשֶּׁמֶשׁ בֵּית דָּגֹן וּפָגַע בִּזְבֻלוּן וּבְגֵי יִפְתַּח־אֵל צָפוֹנָה בֵּית הָעֵמֶק וּנְעִיאֵל וְיָצָא אֶל־כָּבוּל מִשְּׂמֹאל: 28 וְעֶבְרֹן וּרְחֹב וְחַמּוֹן וְקָנָה עַד צִידוֹן רַבָּה: 29 וְשָׁב הַגְּבוּל הָרָמָה וְעַד־עִיר מִבְצַר־צֹר וְשָׁב הַגְּבוּל חֹסָה וְיִהְיוּ תֹצְאֹתָיו הַיָּמָּה מֵחֶבֶל אַכְזִיבָה: 30 וְעֻמָה וַאֲפֵק וּרְחֹב עָרִים עֶשְׂרִים וּשְׁתַּיִם וְחַצְרֵיהֶן: 31 זֹאת נַחֲלַת מַטֵּה בְנֵי־אָשֵׁר לְמִשְׁפְּחֹתָם הֶעָרִים הָאֵלֶּה וְחַצְרֵיהֶן: פ

³²The sixth lot came out to the children of Naphtali, for the children of Naphtali according to their families. ³³And their border began at Heleph, enclosing the territory from the terebinth tree in Zaanannim, Adami Nekeb, and Jabneel, as far as Lakkum; it ended at the Jordan. ³⁴From Heleph the border extended westward to Aznoth Tabor, and went out from there toward Hukkok; it adjoined Zebulun on the south side and Asher on the west side, and ended at Judah by the Jordan toward the sunrise. ³⁵And the fortified cities *are* Ziddim, Zer, Hammath, Rakkath, Chinnereth, ³⁶Adamah, Ramah, Hazor, ³⁷Kedesh, Edrei, En Hazor, ³⁸Iron, Migdal El, Horem, Beth Anath, and Beth Shemesh: nineteen cities with their villages. ³⁹This *was* the inheritance of the tribe of the children of Naphtali according to their families, the cities and their villages.

⁴⁰The seventh lot came out for the tribe of the children of Dan according to their families. ⁴¹And the territory of their inheritance was Zorah, Eshtaol, Ir Shemesh, ⁴²Shaalabbin, Aijalon, Jethlah, ⁴³Elon, Timnah, Ekron, ⁴⁴Eltekeh, Gibbethon, Baalath, ⁴⁵Jehud, Bene Berak, Gath Rimmon, ⁴⁶Me Jarkon, and Rakkon, with the region near Joppa. ⁴⁷And the border of the children of Dan went beyond these, because the children of Dan went up to fight against Leshem and took it; and they struck it with the edge of the sword, took possession of it, and dwelt in it. They called Leshem, Dan, after the name of Dan their father. ⁴⁸This *is* the inheritance of the tribe of the children of Dan according to their families, these cities with their villages.

⁴⁹When they had made an end of dividing the land as an inheritance according to their borders, the children of Israel gave an inheritance among them to Joshua the son of Nun. ⁵⁰According to the word of the LORD they gave him the city which he asked for, Timnath Serah in the mountains of Ephraim; and he built the city and dwelt in it.

⁵¹These *were* the inheritances which Eleazar the priest, Joshua the son of Nun, and the heads of the fathers of the tribes of the children of Israel divided as an inheritance by lot in Shiloh before the LORD, at the door of the tabernacle of meeting. So they made an end of dividing the country.

20

The LORD also spoke to Joshua, saying, ²"Speak to the children of Israel, saying: 'Appoint for yourselves cities of refuge, of which I spoke to you through Moses, ³that the slayer who kills a person accidentally *or* unintentionally may flee there; and they shall be your refuge from the

³² לִבְנֵי נַפְתָּלִי יָצָא הַגּוֹרָל הַשִּׁשִּׁי לִבְנֵי נַפְתָּלִי
לְמִשְׁפְּחֹתָם: ³³ וַיְהִי גְבוּלָם מֵחֵלֶף מֵאֵלוֹן בְּצַעֲנַנִּים
וַאֲדָמִי הַנֶּקֶב וְיַבְנְאֵל עַד־לַקּוּם וַיְהִי תֹצְאֹתָיו
הַיַּרְדֵּן: ³⁴ וְשָׁב הַגְּבוּל יָמָּה אַזְנוֹת תָּבוֹר וְיָצָא
מִשָּׁם חוּקֹקָה וּפָגַע בִּזְבֻלוּן מִנֶּגֶב וּבְאָשֵׁר פָּגַע
מִיָּם וּבִיהוּדָה הַיַּרְדֵּן מִזְרַח הַשָּׁמֶשׁ: ³⁵ וְעָרֵי מִבְצָר
הַצִּדִּים צֵר וְחַמַּת רַקַּת וְכִנָּרֶת: ³⁶ וַאֲדָמָה וְהָרָמָה
וְחָצוֹר: ³⁷ וְקֶדֶשׁ וְאֶדְרֶעִי וְעֵין חָצוֹר: ³⁸ וְיִרְאוֹן
וּמִגְדַּל־אֵל חֳרֵם וּבֵית־עֲנָת וּבֵית שָׁמֶשׁ עָרִים
תְּשַׁע־עֶשְׂרֵה וְחַצְרֵיהֶן: ³⁹ זֹאת נַחֲלַת מַטֵּה בְנֵי־
נַפְתָּלִי לְמִשְׁפְּחֹתָם הֶעָרִים וְחַצְרֵיהֶן: פ

⁴⁰ לְמַטֵּה בְנֵי־דָן לְמִשְׁפְּחֹתָם יָצָא הַגּוֹרָל הַשְּׁבִיעִי:
⁴¹ וַיְהִי גְּבוּל נַחֲלָתָם צָרְעָה וְאֶשְׁתָּאוֹל וְעִיר שָׁמֶשׁ:
⁴² וְשַׁעֲלַבִּין וְאַיָּלוֹן וְיִתְלָה: ⁴³ וְאֵילוֹן וְתִמְנָתָה
וְעֶקְרוֹן: ⁴⁴ וְאֶלְתְּקֵה וְגִבְּתוֹן וּבַעֲלָת: ⁴⁵ וִיהֻד וּבְנֵי־
בְרַק וְגַת־רִמּוֹן: ⁴⁶ וּמֵי הַיַּרְקוֹן וְהָרַקּוֹן עִם־הַגְּבוּל
מוּל יָפוֹ: ⁴⁷ וַיֵּצֵא גְבוּל־בְּנֵי־דָן מֵהֶם וַיַּעֲלוּ בְנֵי־
דָן וַיִּלָּחֲמוּ עִם־לֶשֶׁם וַיִּלְכְּדוּ אוֹתָהּ ׀ וַיַּכּוּ אוֹתָהּ
לְפִי־חֶרֶב וַיִּרְשׁוּ אוֹתָהּ וַיֵּשְׁבוּ בָהּ וַיִּקְרְאוּ לְלֶשֶׁם
דָּן כְּשֵׁם דָּן אֲבִיהֶם: ⁴⁸ זֹאת נַחֲלַת מַטֵּה בְנֵי־דָן
לְמִשְׁפְּחֹתָם הֶעָרִים הָאֵלֶּה וְחַצְרֵיהֶן: פ

⁴⁹ וַיְכַלּוּ לִנְחֹל־אֶת־הָאָרֶץ לִגְבוּלֹתֶיהָ וַיִּתְּנוּ בְנֵי־
יִשְׂרָאֵל נַחֲלָה לִיהוֹשֻׁעַ בִּן־נוּן בְּתוֹכָם: ⁵⁰ עַל־
פִּי יְהוָה נָתְנוּ לוֹ אֶת־הָעִיר אֲשֶׁר שָׁאָל אֶת־
תִּמְנַת־סֶרַח בְּהַר אֶפְרָיִם וַיִּבְנֶה אֶת־הָעִיר וַיֵּשֶׁב
בָּהּ: ⁵¹ אֵלֶּה הַנְּחָלֹת אֲשֶׁר נִחֲלוּ אֶלְעָזָר הַכֹּהֵן ׀
וִיהוֹשֻׁעַ בִּן־נוּן וְרָאשֵׁי הָאָבוֹת לְמַטּוֹת בְּנֵי־
יִשְׂרָאֵל ׀ בְּגוֹרָל ׀ בְּשִׁלֹה לִפְנֵי יְהוָה פֶּתַח אֹהֶל
מוֹעֵד וַיְכַלּוּ מֵחַלֵּק אֶת־הָאָרֶץ: פ

כ וַיְדַבֵּר יְהוָה אֶל־יְהוֹשֻׁעַ לֵאמֹר: ² דַּבֵּר אֶל־בְּנֵי
יִשְׂרָאֵל לֵאמֹר תְּנוּ לָכֶם אֶת־עָרֵי הַמִּקְלָט אֲשֶׁר־
דִּבַּרְתִּי אֲלֵיכֶם בְּיַד־מֹשֶׁה: ³ לָנוּס שָׁמָּה רוֹצֵחַ
מַכֵּה־נֶפֶשׁ בִּשְׁגָגָה בִּבְלִי־דָעַת וְהָיוּ לָכֶם לְמִקְלָט

avenger of blood. 4 And when he flees to one of those cities, and stands at the entrance of the gate of the city, and declares his case in the hearing of the elders of that city, they shall take him into the city as one of them, and give him a place, that he may dwell among them. 5 Then if the avenger of blood pursues him, they shall not deliver the slayer into his hand, because he struck his neighbor unintentionally, but did not hate him beforehand. 6 And he shall dwell in that city until he stands before the congregation for judgment, and until the death of the one who is high priest in those days. Then the slayer may return and come to his own city and his own house, to the city from which he fled.' "

7 So they appointed Kedesh in Galilee, in the mountains of Naphtali, Shechem in the mountains of Ephraim, and Kirjath Arba (which is Hebron) in the mountains of Judah. 8 And on the other side of the Jordan, by Jericho eastward, they assigned Bezer in the wilderness on the plain, from the tribe of Reuben, Ramoth in Gilead, from the tribe of Gad, and Golan in Bashan, from the tribe of Manasseh. 9 These were the cities appointed for all the children of Israel and for the stranger who dwelt among them, that whoever killed a person accidentally might flee there, and not die by the hand of the avenger of blood until he stood before the congregation.

21 Then the heads of the fathers' *houses* of the Levites came near to Eleazar the priest, to Joshua the son of Nun, and to the heads of the fathers' *houses* of the tribes of the children of Israel. 2 And they spoke to them at Shiloh in the land of Canaan, saying, "The LORD commanded through Moses to give us cities to dwell in, with their common-lands for our livestock." 3 So the children of Israel gave to the Levites from their inheritance, at the commandment of the LORD, these cities and their common-lands:

4 Now the lot came out for the families of the Kohathites. And the children of Aaron the priest, *who were* of the Levites, had thirteen cities by lot from the tribe of Judah, from the tribe of Simeon, and from the tribe of Benjamin. 5 The rest of the children of Kohath had ten cities by lot from the families of the tribe of Ephraim, from the tribe of Dan, and from the half-tribe of Manasseh.

6 And the children of Gershon had thirteen cities by lot from the families of the tribe of Issachar, from the tribe of Asher, from the tribe of Naphtali, and from the half-tribe of Manasseh in Bashan.

מִגְאֵל הַדָּם: 4 וְנָס אֶל־אַחַת ׀ מֵהֶעָרִים הָאֵלֶּה וְעָמַד פֶּתַח שַׁעַר הָעִיר וְדִבֶּר בְּאָזְנֵי זִקְנֵי הָעִיר־ הַהִיא אֶת־דְּבָרָיו וְאָסְפוּ אֹתוֹ הָעִירָה אֲלֵיהֶם וְנָתְנוּ־לוֹ מָקוֹם וְיָשַׁב עִמָּם: 5 וְכִי יִרְדֹּף גֹּאֵל הַדָּם אַחֲרָיו וְלֹא־יַסְגִּרוּ אֶת־הָרֹצֵחַ בְּיָדוֹ כִּי בִבְלִי־ דַעַת הִכָּה אֶת־רֵעֵהוּ וְלֹא־שֹׂנֵא הוּא לוֹ מִתְּמוֹל שִׁלְשׁוֹם: 6 וְיָשַׁב ׀ בָּעִיר הַהִיא עַד־עָמְדוֹ לִפְנֵי הָעֵדָה לַמִּשְׁפָּט עַד־מוֹת הַכֹּהֵן הַגָּדוֹל אֲשֶׁר יִהְיֶה בַּיָּמִים הָהֵם אָז ׀ יָשׁוּב הָרוֹצֵחַ וּבָא אֶל־עִירוֹ וְאֶל־בֵּיתוֹ אֶל־הָעִיר אֲשֶׁר־נָס מִשָּׁם: 7 וַיַּקְדִּשׁוּ אֶת־קֶדֶשׁ בַּגָּלִיל בְּהַר נַפְתָּלִי וְאֶת־שְׁכֶם בְּהַר אֶפְרַיִם וְאֶת־קִרְיַת אַרְבַּע הִיא חֶבְרוֹן בְּהַר יְהוּדָה: 8 וּמֵעֵבֶר לְיַרְדֵּן יְרִיחוֹ מִזְרָחָה נָתְנוּ אֶת־בֶּצֶר בַּמִּדְבָּר בַּמִּישֹׁר מִמַּטֵּה רְאוּבֵן וְאֶת־רָאמֹת בַּגִּלְעָד מִמַּטֵּה־גָד וְאֶת־גּוֹלָן בַּבָּשָׁן מִמַּטֵּה מְנַשֶּׁה: 9 אֵלֶּה הָיוּ עָרֵי הַמּוּעָדָה לְכֹל ׀ בְּנֵי יִשְׂרָאֵל וְלַגֵּר הַגָּר בְּתוֹכָם לָנוּס שָׁמָּה כָּל־מַכֵּה־נֶפֶשׁ בִּשְׁגָגָה וְלֹא יָמוּת בְּיַד גֹּאֵל הַדָּם עַד־עָמְדוֹ לִפְנֵי הָעֵדָה: פ

כא וַיִּגְּשׁוּ רָאשֵׁי אֲבוֹת הַלְוִיִּם אֶל־אֶלְעָזָר הַכֹּהֵן וְאֶל־יְהוֹשֻׁעַ בִּן־נוּן וְאֶל־רָאשֵׁי אֲבוֹת הַמַּטּוֹת לִבְנֵי יִשְׂרָאֵל: 2 וַיְדַבְּרוּ אֲלֵיהֶם בְּשִׁלֹה בְּאֶרֶץ כְּנַעַן לֵאמֹר יְהוָה צִוָּה בְיַד־מֹשֶׁה לָתֶת־לָנוּ עָרִים לָשָׁבֶת וּמִגְרְשֵׁיהֶן לִבְהֶמְתֵּנוּ: 3 וַיִּתְּנוּ בְנֵי־יִשְׂרָאֵל לַלְוִיִּם מִנַּחֲלָתָם אֶל־פִּי יְהוָה אֶת־הֶעָרִים הָאֵלֶּה וְאֶת־מִגְרְשֵׁיהֶן: 4 וַיֵּצֵא הַגּוֹרָל לְמִשְׁפְּחֹת הַקְּהָתִי וַיְהִי לִבְנֵי אַהֲרֹן הַכֹּהֵן מִן־הַלְוִיִּם מִמַּטֵּה יְהוּדָה וּמִמַּטֵּה הַשִּׁמְעֹנִי וּמִמַּטֵּה בִנְיָמִן בַּגּוֹרָל עָרִים שְׁלֹשׁ עֶשְׂרֵה: ס 5 וְלִבְנֵי קְהָת הַנּוֹתָרִים מִמִּשְׁפְּחֹת מַטֵּה־אֶפְרַיִם וּמִמַּטֵּה־דָן וּמֵחֲצִי מַטֵּה מְנַשֶּׁה בַּגּוֹרָל עָרִים עָשֶׂר: ס 6 וְלִבְנֵי גֵרְשׁוֹן מִמִּשְׁפְּחוֹת מַטֵּה־יִשָּׂשכָר וּמִמַּטֵּה־אָשֵׁר וּמִמַּטֵּה נַפְתָּלִי וּמֵחֲצִי מַטֵּה מְנַשֶּׁה בַבָּשָׁן בַּגּוֹרָל

7 The children of Merari according to their families had twelve cities from the tribe of Reuben, from the tribe of Gad, and from the tribe of Zebulun.

8 And the children of Israel gave these cities with their common-lands by lot to the Levites, as the LORD had commanded by the hand of Moses.

9 So they gave from the tribe of the children of Judah and from the tribe of the children of Simeon these cities which are designated by name, 10 which were for the children of Aaron, one of the families of the Kohathites, who were of the children of Levi; for the lot was theirs first. 11 And they gave them Kirjath Arba (Arba was the father of Anak), which is Hebron, in the mountains of Judah, with the common-land surrounding it. 12 But the fields of the city and its villages they gave to Caleb the son of Jephunneh as his possession.

13 Thus to the children of Aaron the priest they gave Hebron with its common-land (a city of refuge for the slayer), Libnah with its common-land, 14 Jattir with its common-land, Eshtemoa with its common-land, 15 Holon with its common-land, Debir with its common-land, 16 Ain with its common-land, Juttah with its common-land, and Beth Shemesh with its common-land: nine cities from those two tribes; 17 and from the tribe of Benjamin, Gibeon with its common-land, Geba with its common-land, 18 Anathoth with its common-land, and Almon with its common-land: four cities. 19 All the cities of the children of Aaron, the priests, were thirteen cities with their common-lands.

20 And the families of the children of Kohath, the Levites, the rest of the children of Kohath, even they had the cities of their lot from the tribe of Ephraim. 21 For they gave them Shechem with its common-land in the mountains of Ephraim (a city of refuge for the slayer), Gezer with its common-land, 22 Kibzaim with its common-land, and Beth Horon with its common-land: four cities; 23 and from the tribe of Dan, Eltekeh with its common-land, Gibbethon with its common-land, 24 Aijalon with its common-land, and Gath Rimmon with its common-land: four cities; 25 and from the half-tribe of Manasseh, Tanach with its common-land and Gath Rimmon with its common-land: two cities. 26 All the ten cities with their common-lands were for the rest of the families of the children of Kohath.

27 Also to the children of Gershon, of the families of the Levites, from the other half-tribe of Manasseh, they gave Golan in Bashan with its common-land (a city of refuge for the slayer), and

עָרִים שְׁלֹשׁ עֶשְׂרֵה: ס 7 לִבְנֵי מְרָרִי לְמִשְׁפְּחֹתָם מִמַּטֵּה רְאוּבֵן וּמִמַּטֵּה־גָד וּמִמַּטֵּה זְבוּלֻן עָרִים שְׁתֵּים עֶשְׂרֵה: 8 וַיִּתְּנוּ בְנֵי־יִשְׂרָאֵל לַלְוִיִּם אֶת־הֶעָרִים הָאֵלֶּה וְאֶת־מִגְרְשֵׁיהֶן כַּאֲשֶׁר צִוָּה יְהוָה בְּיַד־מֹשֶׁה בַּגּוֹרָל: פ

9 וַיִּתְּנוּ מִמַּטֵּה בְּנֵי יְהוּדָה וּמִמַּטֵּה בְּנֵי שִׁמְעוֹן אֵת הֶעָרִים הָאֵלֶּה אֲשֶׁר־יִקְרָא אֶתְהֶן בְּשֵׁם: 10 וַיְהִי לִבְנֵי אַהֲרֹן מִמִּשְׁפְּחוֹת הַקְּהָתִי מִבְּנֵי לֵוִי כִּי לָהֶם הָיָה הַגּוֹרָל רִיאשֹׁנָה: 11 וַיִּתְּנוּ לָהֶם אֶת־קִרְיַת אַרְבַּע אֲבִי הָעֲנוֹק הִיא חֶבְרוֹן בְּהַר יְהוּדָה וְאֶת־מִגְרָשֶׁהָ סְבִיבֹתֶיהָ: 12 וְאֶת־שְׂדֵה הָעִיר וְאֶת־חֲצֵרֶיהָ נָתְנוּ לְכָלֵב בֶּן־יְפֻנֶּה בַּאֲחֻזָּתוֹ: ס 13 וְלִבְנֵי | אַהֲרֹן הַכֹּהֵן נָתְנוּ אֶת־עִיר מִקְלַט הָרֹצֵחַ אֶת־חֶבְרוֹן וְאֶת־מִגְרָשֶׁהָ וְאֶת־לִבְנָה וְאֶת־מִגְרָשֶׁהָ: 14 וְאֶת־יַתִּר וְאֶת־מִגְרָשֶׁהָ וְאֶת־אֶשְׁתְּמֹעַ וְאֶת־מִגְרָשֶׁהָ: 15 וְאֶת־חֹלֹן וְאֶת־מִגְרָשֶׁהָ וְאֶת־דְּבִר וְאֶת־מִגְרָשֶׁהָ: 16 וְאֶת־עַיִן וְאֶת־מִגְרָשֶׁהָ וְאֶת־יֻטָּה וְאֶת־מִגְרָשֶׁהָ אֶת־בֵּית שֶׁמֶשׁ וְאֶת־מִגְרָשֶׁהָ עָרִים תֵּשַׁע מֵאֵת שְׁנֵי הַשְּׁבָטִים הָאֵלֶּה: פ

17 וּמִמַּטֵּה בִנְיָמִן אֶת־גִּבְעוֹן וְאֶת־מִגְרָשֶׁהָ אֶת־גֶּבַע וְאֶת־מִגְרָשֶׁהָ: 18 אֶת־עֲנָתוֹת וְאֶת־מִגְרָשֶׁהָ וְאֶת־עַלְמוֹן וְאֶת־מִגְרָשֶׁהָ עָרִים אַרְבַּע: 19 כָּל־עָרֵי בְנֵי־אַהֲרֹן הַכֹּהֲנִים שְׁלֹשׁ־עֶשְׂרֵה עָרִים וּמִגְרְשֵׁיהֶן: ס 20 וּלְמִשְׁפְּחוֹת בְּנֵי־קְהָת הַלְוִיִּם הַנּוֹתָרִים מִבְּנֵי קְהָת וַיְהִי עָרֵי גוֹרָלָם מִמַּטֵּה אֶפְרָיִם: 21 וַיִּתְּנוּ לָהֶם אֶת־עִיר מִקְלַט הָרֹצֵחַ אֶת־שְׁכֶם וְאֶת־מִגְרָשֶׁהָ בְּהַר אֶפְרָיִם וְאֶת־גֶּזֶר וְאֶת־מִגְרָשֶׁהָ: 22 וְאֶת־קִבְצַיִם וְאֶת־מִגְרָשֶׁהָ וְאֶת־בֵּית חוֹרֹן וְאֶת־מִגְרָשֶׁהָ עָרִים אַרְבַּע: ס 23 וּמִמַּטֵּה־דָן אֶת־אֶלְתְּקֵא וְאֶת־מִגְרָשֶׁהָ אֶת־גִּבְּתוֹן וְאֶת־מִגְרָשֶׁהָ: 24 אֶת־אַיָּלוֹן וְאֶת־מִגְרָשֶׁהָ אֶת־גַּת־רִמּוֹן וְאֶת־מִגְרָשֶׁהָ עָרִים אַרְבַּע: ס 25 וּמִמַּחֲצִית מַטֵּה מְנַשֶּׁה אֶת־תַּעְנַךְ וְאֶת־מִגְרָשֶׁהָ וְאֶת־גַּת־רִמּוֹן וְאֶת־מִגְרָשֶׁהָ עָרִים שְׁתָּיִם: 26 כָּל־עָרִים עֶשֶׂר וּמִגְרְשֵׁיהֶן לְמִשְׁפְּחוֹת בְּנֵי־קְהָת הַנּוֹתָרִים: ס 27 וְלִבְנֵי גֵרְשׁוֹן מִמִּשְׁפְּחֹת הַלְוִיִּם מֵחֲצִי מַטֵּה מְנַשֶּׁה אֶת־עִיר מִקְלַט הָרֹצֵחַ אֶת־גּוֹלָן בַּבָּשָׁן וְאֶת־מִגְרָשֶׁהָ וְאֶת־בְּעֶשְׁתְּרָה

כא 27 גּוֹלָן

Be Eshterah with its common-land: two cities;
28 and from the tribe of Issachar, Kishion with its
common-land, Daberath with its common-land,
29 Jarmuth with its common-land, and En Gannim
with its common-land: four cities; 30 and from the
tribe of Asher, Mishal with its common-land,
Abdon with its common-land, 31 Helkath with its
common-land, and Rehob with its common-land:
four cities; 32 and from the tribe of Naphtali,
Kedesh in Galilee with its common-land (a city of
refuge for the slayer), Hammoth Dor with its
common-land, and Kartan with its common-land:
three cities. 33 All the cities of the Gershonites
according to their families were thirteen cities with
their common-lands.

34 And to the families of the children of Merari,
the rest of the Levites, from the tribe of Zebulun,
Jokneam with its common-land, Kartah with its
common-land, 35 Dimnah with its common-land,
and Nahalal with its common-land: four cities;
36 and from the tribe of Reuben, Bezer with its
common-land, Jahaz with its common-land, 37 Kedemoth with its common-land, and Mephaath with
its common-land: four cities; 38 and from the tribe
of Gad, Ramoth in Gilead with its common-land (a
city of refuge for the slayer), Mahanaim with its
common-land, 39 Heshbon with its common-land,
and Jazer with its common-land: four cities in all.
40 So all the cities for the children of Merari
according to their families, the rest of the families
of the Levites, were by their lot twelve cities.

41 All the cities of the Levites within the possession of the children of Israel were forty-eight cities
with their common-lands. 42 Every one of these
cities had its common-land surrounding it; thus
were all these cities.

43 So the LORD gave to Israel all the land of which
He had sworn to give to their fathers, and they took
possession of it and dwelt in it. 44 The LORD gave
them rest all around, according to all that He had
sworn to their fathers. And not a man of all their
enemies stood against them; the LORD delivered all
their enemies into their hand. 45 Not a word failed
of any good thing which the LORD had spoken to
the house of Israel. All came to pass.

22 Then Joshua called the Reubenites, the
Gadites, and half the tribe of Manasseh, 2 and said
to them: "You have kept all that Moses the servant
of the LORD commanded you, and have obeyed my
voice in all that I commanded you. 3 You have not
left your brethren these many days, up to this day,
but have kept the charge of the commandment of
the LORD your God. 4 And now the LORD your God

וְאֶת־מִגְרָשֶׁהָ עָרִים שְׁתָּיִם: ס 28 וּמִמַּטֵּה
יִשָּׂשכָר אֶת־קִשְׁיוֹן וְאֶת־מִגְרָשֶׁהָ אֶת־דָּבְרַת וְאֶת־
מִגְרָשֶׁהָ: 29 אֶת־יַרְמוּת וְאֶת־מִגְרָשֶׁהָ אֶת־עֵין גַּנִּים
וְאֶת־מִגְרָשֶׁהָ עָרִים אַרְבַּע: ס 30 וּמִמַּטֵּה
אָשֵׁר אֶת־מִשְׁאָל וְאֶת־מִגְרָשֶׁהָ אֶת־עַבְדּוֹן וְאֶת־
מִגְרָשֶׁהָ: 31 אֶת־חֶלְקָת וְאֶת־מִגְרָשֶׁהָ וְאֶת־רְחֹב
וְאֶת־מִגְרָשֶׁהָ עָרִים אַרְבַּע: ס 32 וּמִמַּטֵּה
נַפְתָּלִי אֶת־עִיר ׀ מִקְלַט הָרֹצֵחַ אֶת־קֶדֶשׁ
בַּגָּלִיל וְאֶת־מִגְרָשֶׁהָ וְאֶת־חַמֹּת דֹּאר וְאֶת־מִגְרָשֶׁהָ
וְאֶת־קַרְתָּן וְאֶת־מִגְרָשֶׁהָ עָרִים שָׁלֹשׁ: 33 כָּל־
עָרֵי הַגֵּרְשֻׁנִּי לְמִשְׁפְּחֹתָם שְׁלֹשׁ־עֶשְׂרֵה עִיר
וּמִגְרְשֵׁיהֶן: ס 34 וּלְמִשְׁפְּחוֹת בְּנֵי־מְרָרִי
הַלְוִיִּם הַנּוֹתָרִים מֵאֵת מַטֵּה זְבוּלֻן אֶת־יָקְנְעָם
וְאֶת־מִגְרָשֶׁהָ אֶת־קַרְתָּה וְאֶת־מִגְרָשֶׁהָ: 35 אֶת־
דִּמְנָה וְאֶת־מִגְרָשֶׁהָ אֶת־נַהֲלָל וְאֶת־מִגְרָשֶׁהָ עָרִים
אַרְבַּע: 36 וּמִמַּטֵּה גָד אֶת־עִיר מִקְלַט הָרֹצֵחַ אֶת־
רָמֹת בַּגִּלְעָד וְאֶת־מִגְרָשֶׁהָ וְאֶת־מַחֲנַיִם וְאֶת־
מִגְרָשֶׁהָ: 37 אֶת־חֶשְׁבּוֹן וְאֶת־מִגְרָשֶׁהָ אֶת־יַעְזֵר
וְאֶת־מִגְרָשֶׁהָ כָּל־עָרִים אַרְבַּע: 38 כָּל־הֶעָרִים לִבְנֵי
מְרָרִי לְמִשְׁפְּחֹתָם הַנּוֹתָרִים מִמִּשְׁפְּחוֹת הַלְוִיִּם
וַיְהִי גּוֹרָלָם עָרִים שְׁתֵּים עֶשְׂרֵה: 39 כֹּל עָרֵי
הַלְוִיִּם בְּתוֹךְ אֲחֻזַּת בְּנֵי־יִשְׂרָאֵל עָרִים אַרְבָּעִים
וּשְׁמֹנֶה וּמִגְרְשֵׁיהֶן: 40 תִּהְיֶינָה הֶעָרִים הָאֵלֶּה
עִיר עִיר וּמִגְרָשֶׁיהָ סְבִיבֹתֶיהָ כֵּן לְכָל־הֶעָרִים
הָאֵלֶּה: ס 41 וַיִּתֵּן יְהֹוָה לְיִשְׂרָאֵל אֶת־
כָּל־הָאָרֶץ אֲשֶׁר נִשְׁבַּע לָתֵת לַאֲבוֹתָם וַיִּרָשׁוּהָ
וַיֵּשְׁבוּ בָהּ: 42 וַיָּנַח יְהֹוָה לָהֶם מִסָּבִיב כְּכֹל אֲשֶׁר־
נִשְׁבַּע לַאֲבוֹתָם וְלֹא־עָמַד אִישׁ בִּפְנֵיהֶם מִכָּל־
אֹיְבֵיהֶם אֵת כָּל־אֹיְבֵיהֶם נָתַן יְהֹוָה בְּיָדָם: 43 לֹא־
נָפַל דָּבָר מִכֹּל הַדָּבָר הַטּוֹב אֲשֶׁר־דִּבֶּר יְהֹוָה אֶל־
בֵּית יִשְׂרָאֵל הַכֹּל בָּא: פ

כב אָז יִקְרָא יְהוֹשֻׁעַ לָראוּבֵנִי וְלַגָּדִי וְלַחֲצִי
מַטֵּה מְנַשֶּׁה: 2 וַיֹּאמֶר אֲלֵיהֶם אַתֶּם שְׁמַרְתֶּם אֵת
כָּל־אֲשֶׁר צִוָּה אֶתְכֶם מֹשֶׁה עֶבֶד יְהֹוָה וַתִּשְׁמְעוּ
בְקוֹלִי לְכֹל אֲשֶׁר־צִוִּיתִי אֶתְכֶם: 3 לֹא־עֲזַבְתֶּם אֶת־
אֲחֵיכֶם זֶה יָמִים רַבִּים עַד הַיּוֹם הַזֶּה וּשְׁמַרְתֶּם
אֶת־מִשְׁמֶרֶת מִצְוַת יְהֹוָה אֱלֹהֵיכֶם: 4 וְעַתָּה הֵנִיחַ

has given rest to your brethren, as He promised them; now therefore, return and go to your tents *and* to the land of your possession, which Moses the servant of the LORD gave you on the other side of the Jordan. 5 But take careful heed to do the commandment and the law which Moses the servant of the LORD commanded you, to love the LORD your God, to walk in all His ways, to keep His commandments, to hold fast to Him, and to serve Him with all your heart and with all your soul. 6 So Joshua blessed them and sent them away, and they went to their tents.

7 Now to half the tribe of Manasseh Moses had given a possession in Bashan, but to the *other* half of it Joshua gave *a possession* among their brethren on this side of the Jordan, westward. And indeed, when Joshua sent them away to their tents, he blessed them, 8 and spoke to them, saying, "Return with much riches to your tents, with very much livestock, with silver, with gold, with bronze, with iron, and with very much clothing. Divide the spoil of your enemies with your brethren."

9 So the children of Reuben, the children of Gad, and half the tribe of Manasseh returned, and departed from the children of Israel at Shiloh, which *is* in the land of Canaan, to go to the country of Gilead, to the land of their possession, which they had obtained according to the word of the LORD by the hand of Moses.

10 And when they came to the region of the Jordan which *is* in the land of Canaan, the children of Reuben, the children of Gad, and half the tribe of Manasseh built an altar there by the Jordan—a great, impressive altar. 11 Now the children of Israel heard *someone* say, "Behold, the children of Reuben, the children of Gad, and half the tribe of Manasseh have built an altar on the frontier of the land of Canaan, in the region of the Jordan—on the children of Israel's side." 12 And when the children of Israel heard *of it,* the whole congregation of the children of Israel gathered together at Shiloh to go to war against them.

13 Then the children of Israel sent Phinehas the son of Eleazar the priest to the children of Reuben, to the children of Gad, and to half the tribe of Manasseh, into the land of Gilead, 14 and with him ten rulers, one ruler each from the chief house of every tribe of Israel; and each one *was* the head of the house of his father among the divisions of Israel. 15 Then they came to the children of Reuben, to the children of Gad, and to half the tribe of Manasseh, to the land of Gilead, and they spoke with them, saying, 16 "Thus says the whole congregation of the LORD: 'What treachery *is* this that

יְהוָה אֱלֹהֵיכֶם לַאֲחֵיכֶם כַּאֲשֶׁר דִּבֶּר לָהֶם וְעַתָּה
פְּנוּ וּלְכוּ לָכֶם לְאָהֳלֵיכֶם אֶל־אֶרֶץ אֲחֻזַּתְכֶם
אֲשֶׁר ׀ נָתַן לָכֶם מֹשֶׁה עֶבֶד יְהוָה בְּעֵבֶר הַיַּרְדֵּן׃
5 רַק ׀ שִׁמְרוּ מְאֹד לַעֲשׂוֹת אֶת־הַמִּצְוָה וְאֶת־
הַתּוֹרָה אֲשֶׁר צִוָּה אֶתְכֶם מֹשֶׁה עֶבֶד־יְהוָה לְאַהֲבָה
אֶת־יְהוָה אֱלֹהֵיכֶם וְלָלֶכֶת בְּכָל־דְּרָכָיו וְלִשְׁמֹר
מִצְוֹתָיו וּלְדָבְקָה־בוֹ וּלְעָבְדוֹ בְּכָל־לְבַבְכֶם וּבְכָל־
נַפְשְׁכֶם׃ 6 וַיְבָרְכֵם יְהוֹשֻׁעַ וַיְשַׁלְּחֵם וַיֵּלְכוּ אֶל־
אָהֳלֵיהֶם׃ ס 7 וְלַחֲצִי ׀ שֵׁבֶט הַמְנַשֶּׁה
נָתַן מֹשֶׁה בַּבָּשָׁן וּלְחֶצְיוֹ נָתַן יְהוֹשֻׁעַ עִם־אֲחֵיהֶם
מֵעֵבֶר הַיַּרְדֵּן יָמָּה וְגַם כִּי שִׁלְּחָם יְהוֹשֻׁעַ אֶל־
אָהֳלֵיהֶם וַיְבָרְכֵם׃ 8 וַיֹּאמֶר אֲלֵיהֶם לֵאמֹר בִּנְכָסִים
רַבִּים שׁוּבוּ אֶל־אָהֳלֵיכֶם וּבְמִקְנֶה רַב־מְאֹד בְּכֶסֶף
וּבְזָהָב וּבִנְחֹשֶׁת וּבְבַרְזֶל וּבִשְׂלָמוֹת הַרְבֵּה מְאֹד
חִלְקוּ שְׁלַל־אֹיְבֵיכֶם עִם־אֲחֵיכֶם׃
פ
9 וַיָּשֻׁבוּ וַיֵּלְכוּ בְּנֵי־רְאוּבֵן וּבְנֵי־גָד וַחֲצִי ׀ שֵׁבֶט
הַמְנַשֶּׁה מֵאֵת בְּנֵי יִשְׂרָאֵל מִשִּׁלֹה אֲשֶׁר בְּאֶרֶץ־
כְּנָעַן לָלֶכֶת אֶל־אֶרֶץ הַגִּלְעָד אֶל־אֶרֶץ אֲחֻזָּתָם
אֲשֶׁר נֹאחֲזוּ־בָהּ עַל־פִּי יְהוָה בְּיַד־מֹשֶׁה׃ 10 וַיָּבֹאוּ
אֶל־גְּלִילוֹת הַיַּרְדֵּן אֲשֶׁר בְּאֶרֶץ כְּנָעַן וַיִּבְנוּ בְנֵי־
רְאוּבֵן וּבְנֵי־גָד וַחֲצִי שֵׁבֶט הַמְנַשֶּׁה שָׁם מִזְבֵּחַ
עַל־הַיַּרְדֵּן מִזְבֵּחַ גָּדוֹל לְמַרְאֶה׃ 11 וַיִּשְׁמְעוּ בְנֵי־
יִשְׂרָאֵל לֵאמֹר הִנֵּה בָנוּ בְנֵי־רְאוּבֵן וּבְנֵי־גָד וַחֲצִי
שֵׁבֶט הַמְנַשֶּׁה אֶת־הַמִּזְבֵּחַ אֶל־מוּל אֶרֶץ כְּנַעַן אֶל־
גְּלִילוֹת הַיַּרְדֵּן אֶל־עֵבֶר בְּנֵי יִשְׂרָאֵל׃ 12 וַיִּשְׁמְעוּ
בְּנֵי יִשְׂרָאֵל וַיִּקָּהֲלוּ כָּל־עֲדַת בְּנֵי־יִשְׂרָאֵל שִׁלֹה
לַעֲלוֹת עֲלֵיהֶם לַצָּבָא׃
פ
13 וַיִּשְׁלְחוּ בְנֵי־יִשְׂרָאֵל אֶל־בְּנֵי־רְאוּבֵן וְאֶל־בְּנֵי־
גָד וְאֶל־חֲצִי שֵׁבֶט־מְנַשֶּׁה אֶל־אֶרֶץ הַגִּלְעָד אֶת־
פִּינְחָס בֶּן־אֶלְעָזָר הַכֹּהֵן׃ 14 וַעֲשָׂרָה נְשִׂאִים עִמּוֹ
נָשִׂיא אֶחָד נָשִׂיא אֶחָד לְבֵית אָב לְכֹל מַטּוֹת
יִשְׂרָאֵל וְאִישׁ רֹאשׁ בֵּית־אֲבוֹתָם הֵמָּה לְאַלְפֵי
יִשְׂרָאֵל׃ 15 וַיָּבֹאוּ אֶל־בְּנֵי־רְאוּבֵן וְאֶל־בְּנֵי־גָד וְאֶל־
חֲצִי שֵׁבֶט־מְנַשֶּׁה אֶל־אֶרֶץ הַגִּלְעָד וַיְדַבְּרוּ אִתָּם
לֵאמֹר׃ 16 כֹּה אָמְרוּ כֹּל ׀ עֲדַת יְהוָה מָה־הַמַּעַל

you have committed against the God of Israel, to turn away this day from following the LORD, in that you have built for yourselves an altar, that you might rebel this day against the LORD? [17]*Is* the iniquity of Peor not enough for us, from which we are not cleansed till this day, although there was a plague in the congregation of the LORD, [18]but that you must turn away this day from following the LORD? And it shall be, if you rebel today against the LORD, that tomorrow He will be angry with the whole congregation of Israel. [19]Nevertheless, if the land of your possession *is* unclean, *then* cross over to the land of the possession of the LORD, where the LORD's tabernacle stands, and take possession among us; but do not rebel against the LORD, nor rebel against us, by building yourselves an altar besides the altar of the LORD our God. [20]Did not Achan the son of Zerah commit a trespass in the accursed thing, and wrath fell on all the congregation of Israel? And that man did not perish alone in his iniquity.' "

[21]Then the children of Reuben, the children of Gad, and half the tribe of Manasseh answered and said to the heads of the divisions of Israel: [22]"The LORD God of gods, the LORD God of gods, He knows, and let Israel itself know—if *it is* in rebellion, or if in treachery against the LORD, do not save us this day. [23]If we have built ourselves an altar to turn from following the LORD, or if to offer on it burnt offerings or grain offerings, or if to offer peace offerings on it, let the LORD Himself require *an account*. [24]But in fact we have done it for fear, for a reason, saying, 'In time to come your descendants may speak to our descendants, saying, "What have you to do with the LORD God of Israel? [25]For the LORD has made the Jordan a border between you and us, *you* children of Reuben and children of Gad. You have no part in the LORD." So your descendants would make our descendants cease fearing the LORD.' [26]Therefore we said, 'Let us now prepare to build ourselves an altar, not for burnt offering nor for sacrifice, [27]but *that* it *may be* a witness between you and us and our generations after us, that we may perform the service of the LORD before Him with our burnt offerings, with our sacrifices, and with our peace offerings; that your descendants may not say to our descendants in time to come, "You have no part in the LORD." ' [28]Therefore we said that it will be, when they say *this* to us or to our generations in time to come, that we may say, 'Here is the replica of the altar of the LORD which our fathers made, though not for burnt offerings nor for sacrifices; but it *is* a witness between you and us.' [29]Far be it

הַזֶּה אֲשֶׁר מְעַלְתֶּם בֵּאלֹהֵי יִשְׂרָאֵל לָשׁוּב הַיּוֹם מֵאַחֲרֵי יְהוָה בִּבְנוֹתְכֶם לָכֶם מִזְבֵּחַ לְמִרְדְּכֶם הַיּוֹם בַּיהוָה: 17 הַמְעַט־לָנוּ אֶת־עֲוֺן פְּעוֹר אֲשֶׁר לֹא־הִטַּהַרְנוּ מִמֶּנּוּ עַד הַיּוֹם הַזֶּה וַיְהִי הַנֶּגֶף בַּעֲדַת יְהוָה: 18 וְאַתֶּם תָּשֻׁבוּ הַיּוֹם מֵאַחֲרֵי יְהוָה וְהָיָה אַתֶּם תִּמְרְדוּ הַיּוֹם בַּיהוָה וּמָחָר אֶל־כָּל־עֲדַת יִשְׂרָאֵל יִקְצֹף: 19 וְאַךְ אִם־טְמֵאָה אֶרֶץ אֲחֻזַּתְכֶם עִבְרוּ לָכֶם אֶל־אֶרֶץ אֲחֻזַּת יְהוָה אֲשֶׁר שָׁכַן־שָׁם מִשְׁכַּן יְהוָה וְהֵאָחֲזוּ בְּתוֹכֵנוּ וּבַיהוָה אַל־תִּמְרֹדוּ וְאֹתָנוּ אַל־תִּמְרֹדוּ בִּבְנֹתְכֶם לָכֶם מִזְבֵּחַ מִבַּלְעֲדֵי מִזְבַּח יְהוָה אֱלֹהֵינוּ: 20 הֲלוֹא ׀ עָכָן בֶּן־זֶרַח מָעַל מַעַל בַּחֵרֶם וְעַל־כָּל־עֲדַת יִשְׂרָאֵל הָיָה קָצֶף וְהוּא אִישׁ אֶחָד לֹא גָוַע בַּעֲוֺנוֹ: פ

21 וַיַּעֲנוּ בְּנֵי־רְאוּבֵן וּבְנֵי־גָד וַחֲצִי שֵׁבֶט הַמְנַשֶּׁה וַיְדַבְּרוּ אֶת־רָאשֵׁי אַלְפֵי יִשְׂרָאֵל: 22 אֵל ׀ אֱלֹהִים ׀ יְהוָה אֵל ׀ אֱלֹהִים ׀ יְהוָה הוּא יֹדֵעַ וְיִשְׂרָאֵל הוּא יֵדָע אִם־בְּמֶרֶד וְאִם־בְּמַעַל בַּיהוָה אַל־תּוֹשִׁיעֵנוּ הַיּוֹם הַזֶּה: 23 לִבְנוֹת לָנוּ מִזְבֵּחַ לָשׁוּב מֵאַחֲרֵי יְהוָה וְאִם־לְהַעֲלוֹת עָלָיו עוֹלָה וּמִנְחָה וְאִם־לַעֲשׂוֹת עָלָיו זִבְחֵי שְׁלָמִים יְהוָה הוּא יְבַקֵּשׁ: 24 וְאִם־לֹא מִדְּאָגָה מִדָּבָר עָשִׂינוּ אֶת־זֹאת לֵאמֹר מָחָר יֹאמְרוּ בְנֵיכֶם לְבָנֵינוּ לֵאמֹר מַה־לָּכֶם וְלַיהוָה אֱלֹהֵי יִשְׂרָאֵל: 25 וּגְבוּל נָתַן־יְהוָה בֵּינֵנוּ וּבֵינֵיכֶם בְּנֵי־רְאוּבֵן וּבְנֵי־גָד אֶת־הַיַּרְדֵּן אֵין־לָכֶם חֵלֶק בַּיהוָה וְהִשְׁבִּיתוּ בְנֵיכֶם אֶת־בָּנֵינוּ לְבִלְתִּי יְרֹא אֶת־יְהוָה: 26 וַנֹּאמֶר נַעֲשֶׂה־נָּא לָנוּ לִבְנוֹת אֶת־הַמִּזְבֵּחַ לֹא לְעוֹלָה וְלֹא לְזָבַח: 27 כִּי עֵד הוּא בֵּינֵינוּ וּבֵינֵיכֶם וּבֵין דֹּרוֹתֵינוּ אַחֲרֵינוּ לַעֲבֹד אֶת־עֲבֹדַת יְהוָה לְפָנָיו בְּעֹלוֹתֵינוּ וּבִזְבָחֵינוּ וּבִשְׁלָמֵינוּ וְלֹא־יֹאמְרוּ בְנֵיכֶם מָחָר לְבָנֵינוּ אֵין־לָכֶם חֵלֶק בַּיהוָה: 28 וַנֹּאמֶר וְהָיָה כִּי־יֹאמְרוּ אֵלֵינוּ וְאֶל־דֹּרֹתֵינוּ מָחָר וְאָמַרְנוּ רְאוּ אֶת־תַּבְנִית מִזְבַּח יְהוָה אֲשֶׁר־עָשׂוּ אֲבוֹתֵינוּ לֹא לְעוֹלָה וְלֹא לְזֶבַח כִּי־עֵד הוּא בֵּינֵינוּ וּבֵינֵיכֶם: 29 חָלִילָה לָּנוּ מִמֶּנּוּ לִמְרֹד בַּיהוָה וְלָשׁוּב הַיּוֹם מֵאַחֲרֵי יְהוָה לִבְנוֹת מִזְבֵּחַ

from us that we should rebel against the LORD, and
turn from following the LORD this day, to build an
altar for burnt offerings, for grain offerings, or for
sacrifices, besides the altar of the LORD our God
which *is* before His tabernacle."

30 Now when Phinehas the priest and the rulers of
the congregation, the heads of the divisions of Israel
who *were* with him, heard the words that the
children of Reuben, the children of Gad, and the
children of Manasseh spoke, it pleased them.
31 Then Phinehas the son of Eleazar the priest said
to the children of Reuben, the children of Gad, and
the children of Manasseh, "This day we perceive
that the LORD *is* among us, because you have not
committed this treachery against the LORD. Now
you have delivered the children of Israel out of the
hand of the LORD."

32 And Phinehas the son of Eleazar the priest, and
the rulers, returned from the children of Reuben
and the children of Gad, from the land of Gilead to
the land of Canaan, to the children of Israel, and
brought back word to them. 33 So the thing pleased
the children of Israel, and the children of Israel
blessed God; they spoke no more of going against
them in battle, to destroy the land where the
children of Reuben and Gad dwelt.

34 The children of Reuben and the children of
Gad called the altar, *Witness,* "For *it is* a witness
between us that the LORD *is* God."

23 Now it came to pass, a long time after the
LORD had given rest to Israel from all their enemies
round about, that Joshua was old, advanced in age.
2 And Joshua called for all Israel, for their elders,
for their heads, for their judges, and for their
officers, and said to them:

"I am old, advanced in age. 3 You have seen all
that the LORD your God has done to all these
nations because of you, for the LORD your God *is*
He who has fought for you. 4 See, I have divided to
you by lot these nations that remain, to be an
inheritance for your tribes, from the Jordan, with
all the nations that I have cut off, as far as the Great
Sea westward. 5 And the LORD your God will expel
them from before you and drive them out of your
sight. So you shall possess their land, as the LORD
your God promised you. 6 Therefore be very
courageous to keep and to do all that is written in
the Book of the Law of Moses, lest you turn aside
from it to the right hand or to the left, 7 *and* lest you
go among these nations, these who remain among
you. You shall not make mention of the name of
their gods, nor cause *anyone* to swear *by them;* you
shall not serve them nor bow down to them, 8 but

לַעֲלוֹת לְמִנְחָה וּלְזֶבַח מִלְּבַד מִזְבַּח יְהוָה אֱלֹהֵינוּ
אֲשֶׁר לִפְנֵי מִשְׁכָּנוֹ: פ

30 וַיִּשְׁמַע פִּינְחָס הַכֹּהֵן וּנְשִׂיאֵי הָעֵדָה וְרָאשֵׁי
אַלְפֵי יִשְׂרָאֵל אֲשֶׁר אִתּוֹ אֶת־הַדְּבָרִים אֲשֶׁר דִּבְּרוּ
בְּנֵי־רְאוּבֵן וּבְנֵי־גָד וּבְנֵי מְנַשֶּׁה וַיִּיטַב בְּעֵינֵיהֶם:
31 וַיֹּאמֶר פִּינְחָס בֶּן־אֶלְעָזָר הַכֹּהֵן אֶל־בְּנֵי־רְאוּבֵן
וְאֶל־בְּנֵי־גָד וְאֶל־בְּנֵי מְנַשֶּׁה הַיּוֹם יָדַעְנוּ כִּי־
בְתוֹכֵנוּ יְהוָה אֲשֶׁר לֹא־מְעַלְתֶּם בַּיהוָה הַמַּעַל הַזֶּה
אָז הִצַּלְתֶּם אֶת־בְּנֵי יִשְׂרָאֵל מִיַּד יְהוָה: 32 וַיָּשָׁב
פִּינְחָס בֶּן־אֶלְעָזָר הַכֹּהֵן וְהַנְּשִׂיאִים מֵאֵת בְּנֵי־
רְאוּבֵן וּמֵאֵת בְּנֵי־גָד מֵאֶרֶץ הַגִּלְעָד אֶל־אֶרֶץ כְּנַעַן
אֶל־בְּנֵי יִשְׂרָאֵל וַיָּשִׁבוּ אוֹתָם דָּבָר: 33 וַיִּיטַב הַדָּבָר
בְּעֵינֵי בְּנֵי יִשְׂרָאֵל וַיְבָרֲכוּ אֱלֹהִים בְּנֵי יִשְׂרָאֵל וְלֹא
אָמְרוּ לַעֲלוֹת עֲלֵיהֶם לַצָּבָא לְשַׁחֵת אֶת־הָאָרֶץ
אֲשֶׁר בְּנֵי־רְאוּבֵן וּבְנֵי־גָד יֹשְׁבִים בָּהּ: 34 וַיִּקְרְאוּ
בְּנֵי־רְאוּבֵן וּבְנֵי־גָד לַמִּזְבֵּחַ כִּי עֵד הוּא בֵּינוֹתֵינוּ
כִּי יְהוָה הָאֱלֹהִים: פ

כג וַיְהִי מִיָּמִים רַבִּים אַחֲרֵי אֲשֶׁר־הֵנִיחַ יְהוָה
לְיִשְׂרָאֵל מִכָּל־אֹיְבֵיהֶם מִסָּבִיב וִיהוֹשֻׁעַ זָקֵן בָּא
בַּיָּמִים: 2 וַיִּקְרָא יְהוֹשֻׁעַ לְכָל־יִשְׂרָאֵל לִזְקֵנָיו
וּלְרָאשָׁיו וּלְשֹׁפְטָיו וּלְשֹׁטְרָיו וַיֹּאמֶר אֲלֵהֶם אֲנִי
זָקַנְתִּי בָּאתִי בַּיָּמִים: 3 וְאַתֶּם רְאִיתֶם אֵת כָּל־אֲשֶׁר
עָשָׂה יְהוָה אֱלֹהֵיכֶם לְכָל־הַגּוֹיִם הָאֵלֶּה מִפְּנֵיכֶם
כִּי יְהוָה אֱלֹהֵיכֶם הוּא הַנִּלְחָם לָכֶם: 4 רְאוּ
הִפַּלְתִּי לָכֶם אֶת־הַגּוֹיִם הַנִּשְׁאָרִים הָאֵלֶּה בְּנַחֲלָה
לְשִׁבְטֵיכֶם מִן־הַיַּרְדֵּן וְכָל־הַגּוֹיִם אֲשֶׁר הִכְרַתִּי
וְהַיָּם הַגָּדוֹל מְבוֹא הַשָּׁמֶשׁ: 5 וַיהוָה אֱלֹהֵיכֶם
הוּא יֶהְדֳּפֵם מִפְּנֵיכֶם וְהוֹרִישׁ אֹתָם מִלִּפְנֵיכֶם
וִירִשְׁתֶּם אֶת־אַרְצָם כַּאֲשֶׁר דִּבֶּר יְהוָה אֱלֹהֵיכֶם
לָכֶם: 6 וַחֲזַקְתֶּם מְאֹד לִשְׁמֹר וְלַעֲשׂוֹת אֵת כָּל־
הַכָּתוּב בְּסֵפֶר תּוֹרַת מֹשֶׁה לְבִלְתִּי סוּר־מִמֶּנּוּ יָמִין
וּשְׂמֹאול: 7 לְבִלְתִּי־בוֹא בַּגּוֹיִם הָאֵלֶּה הַנִּשְׁאָרִים
הָאֵלֶּה אִתְּכֶם וּבְשֵׁם אֱלֹהֵיהֶם לֹא־תַזְכִּירוּ וְלֹא
תַשְׁבִּיעוּ וְלֹא תַעַבְדוּם וְלֹא תִשְׁתַּחֲווּ לָהֶם: 8 כִּי

you shall hold fast to the LORD your God, as you have done to this day. 9 For the LORD has driven out from before you great and strong nations; but *as for* you, no one has been able to stand against you to this day. 10 One man of you shall chase a thousand, for the LORD your God *is* He who fights for you, as He promised you. 11 Therefore take careful heed to yourselves, that you love the LORD your God. 12 Or else, if indeed you do go back, and cling to the remnant of these nations—these that remain among you—and make marriages with them, and go in to them and they to you, 13 know for certain that the LORD your God will no longer drive out these nations from before you. But they shall be snares and traps to you, and scourges on your sides and thorns in your eyes, until you perish from this good land which the LORD your God has given you.

14 "Behold, this day I *am* going the way of all the earth. And you know in all your hearts and in all your souls that not one thing has failed of all the good things which the LORD your God spoke concerning you. All have come to pass for you; not one word of them has failed. 15 Therefore it shall come to pass, that as all the good things have come upon you which the LORD your God promised you, so the LORD will bring upon you all harmful things, until He has destroyed you from this good land which the LORD your God has given you. 16 When you have transgressed the covenant of the LORD your God, which He commanded you, and have gone and served other gods, and bowed down to them, then the anger of the LORD will burn against you, and you shall perish quickly from the good land which He has given you."

24 Then Joshua gathered all the tribes of Israel to Shechem and called for the elders of Israel, for their heads, for their judges, and for their officers; and they presented themselves before God. 2 And Joshua said to all the people, "Thus says the LORD God of Israel: 'Your fathers, *including* Terah, the father of Abraham and the father of Nahor, dwelt on the other side of the River in old times; and they served other gods. 3 Then I took your father Abraham from the other side of the River, led him throughout all the land of Canaan, and multiplied his descendants and gave him Isaac. 4 To Isaac I gave Jacob and Esau. To Esau I gave the mountains of Seir to possess, but Jacob and his children went down to Egypt. 5 Also I sent Moses and Aaron, and I plagued Egypt, according to what I did among them. Afterward I brought you out.

אִם־בַּיהֹוָה אֱלֹהֵיכֶם תִּדְבָּקוּ כַּאֲשֶׁר עֲשִׂיתֶם עַד הַיּוֹם הַזֶּה: 9 וַיּוֹרֶשׁ יְהֹוָה מִפְּנֵיכֶם גּוֹיִם גְּדֹלִים וַעֲצוּמִים וְאַתֶּם לֹא־עָמַד אִישׁ בִּפְנֵיכֶם עַד הַיּוֹם הַזֶּה: 10 אִישׁ־אֶחָד מִכֶּם יִרְדָּף־אֶלֶף כִּי | יְהֹוָה אֱלֹהֵיכֶם הוּא הַנִּלְחָם לָכֶם כַּאֲשֶׁר דִּבֶּר לָכֶם: 11 וְנִשְׁמַרְתֶּם מְאֹד לְנַפְשֹׁתֵיכֶם לְאַהֲבָה אֶת־יְהֹוָה אֱלֹהֵיכֶם: 12 כִּי | אִם־שׁוֹב תָּשׁוּבוּ וּדְבַקְתֶּם בְּיֶתֶר הַגּוֹיִם הָאֵלֶּה הַנִּשְׁאָרִים הָאֵלֶּה אִתְּכֶם וְהִתְחַתַּנְתֶּם בָּהֶם וּבָאתֶם בָּהֶם וְהֵם בָּכֶם: 13 יָדוֹעַ תֵּדְעוּ כִּי לֹא יוֹסִיף יְהֹוָה אֱלֹהֵיכֶם לְהוֹרִישׁ אֶת־הַגּוֹיִם הָאֵלֶּה מִלִּפְנֵיכֶם וְהָיוּ לָכֶם לְפַח וּלְמוֹקֵשׁ וּלְשֹׁטֵט בְּצִדֵּיכֶם וְלִצְנִנִים בְּעֵינֵיכֶם עַד־אֲבָדְכֶם מֵעַל הָאֲדָמָה הַטּוֹבָה הַזֹּאת אֲשֶׁר נָתַן לָכֶם יְהֹוָה אֱלֹהֵיכֶם: 14 וְהִנֵּה אָנֹכִי הוֹלֵךְ הַיּוֹם בְּדֶרֶךְ כָּל־הָאָרֶץ וִידַעְתֶּם בְּכָל־לְבַבְכֶם וּבְכָל־נַפְשְׁכֶם כִּי לֹא־נָפַל דָּבָר אֶחָד מִכֹּל | הַדְּבָרִים הַטּוֹבִים אֲשֶׁר דִּבֶּר יְהֹוָה אֱלֹהֵיכֶם עֲלֵיכֶם הַכֹּל בָּאוּ לָכֶם לֹא־נָפַל מִמֶּנּוּ דָּבָר אֶחָד: 15 וְהָיָה כַּאֲשֶׁר־בָּא עֲלֵיכֶם כָּל־הַדָּבָר הַטּוֹב אֲשֶׁר דִּבֶּר יְהֹוָה אֱלֹהֵיכֶם אֲלֵיכֶם כֵּן יָבִיא יְהֹוָה עֲלֵיכֶם אֵת כָּל־הַדָּבָר הָרָע עַד־הַשְׁמִידוֹ אוֹתְכֶם מֵעַל הָאֲדָמָה הַטּוֹבָה הַזֹּאת אֲשֶׁר נָתַן לָכֶם יְהֹוָה אֱלֹהֵיכֶם: 16 בְּעָבְרְכֶם אֶת־בְּרִית יְהֹוָה אֱלֹהֵיכֶם אֲשֶׁר צִוָּה אֶתְכֶם וַהֲלַכְתֶּם וַעֲבַדְתֶּם אֱלֹהִים אֲחֵרִים וְהִשְׁתַּחֲוִיתֶם לָהֶם וְחָרָה אַף־יְהֹוָה בָּכֶם וַאֲבַדְתֶּם מְהֵרָה מֵעַל הָאָרֶץ הַטּוֹבָה אֲשֶׁר נָתַן לָכֶם: פ

כד וַיֶּאֱסֹף יְהוֹשֻׁעַ אֶת־כָּל־שִׁבְטֵי יִשְׂרָאֵל שְׁכֶמָה וַיִּקְרָא לְזִקְנֵי יִשְׂרָאֵל וּלְרָאשָׁיו וּלְשֹׁפְטָיו וּלְשֹׁטְרָיו וַיִּתְיַצְּבוּ לִפְנֵי הָאֱלֹהִים: 2 וַיֹּאמֶר יְהוֹשֻׁעַ אֶל־כָּל־הָעָם כֹּה־אָמַר יְהֹוָה אֱלֹהֵי יִשְׂרָאֵל בְּעֵבֶר הַנָּהָר יָשְׁבוּ אֲבוֹתֵיכֶם מֵעוֹלָם תֶּרַח אֲבִי אַבְרָהָם וַאֲבִי נָחוֹר וַיַּעַבְדוּ אֱלֹהִים אֲחֵרִים: 3 וָאֶקַּח אֶת־אֲבִיכֶם אֶת־אַבְרָהָם מֵעֵבֶר הַנָּהָר וָאוֹלֵךְ אוֹתוֹ בְּכָל־אֶרֶץ כְּנָעַן וָאַרְבֶּ֗ אֶת־זַרְעוֹ וָאֶתֶּן־לוֹ אֶת־יִצְחָק: 4 וָאֶתֵּן לְיִצְחָק אֶת־יַעֲקֹב וְאֶת־עֵשָׂו וָאֶתֵּן לְעֵשָׂו אֶת־הַר שֵׂעִיר לָרֶשֶׁת אוֹתוֹ וְיַעֲקֹב וּבָנָיו יָרְדוּ מִצְרָיִם: 5 וָאֶשְׁלַח אֶת־מֹשֶׁה וְאֶת־אַהֲרֹן וָאֶגֹּף אֶת־מִצְרַיִם

6 'Then I brought your fathers out of Egypt, and you came to the sea; and the Egyptians pursued your fathers with chariots and horsemen to the Red Sea. 7 So they cried out to the LORD; and He put darkness between you and the Egyptians, brought the sea upon them, and covered them. And your eyes saw what I did in Egypt. Then you dwelt in the wilderness a long time. 8 And I brought you into the land of the Amorites, who dwelt on the other side of the Jordan, and they fought with you. But I gave them into your hand, that you might possess their land, and I destroyed them from before you. 9 Then Balak the son of Zippor, king of Moab, arose to make war against Israel, and sent and called Balaam the son of Beor to curse you. 10 But I would not listen to Balaam; therefore he continued to bless you. So I delivered you out of his hand. 11 Then you went over the Jordan and came to Jericho. And the men of Jericho fought against you—also the Amorites, the Perizzites, the Canaanites, the Hittites, the Girgashites, the Hivites, and the Jebusites. But I delivered them into your hand. 12 I sent the hornet before you which drove them out from before you, also the two kings of the Amorites, but not with your sword or with your bow. 13 I have given you a land for which you did not labor, and cities which you did not build, and you dwell in them; you eat of the vineyards and olive groves which you did not plant.'

14 "Now therefore, fear the LORD, serve Him in sincerity and in truth, and put away the gods which your fathers served on the other side of the River and in Egypt. Serve the LORD! 15 And if it seems evil to you to serve the LORD, choose for yourselves this day whom you will serve, whether the gods which your fathers served that were on the other side of the River, or the gods of the Amorites, in whose land you dwell. But as for me and my house, we will serve the LORD."

16 So the people answered and said: "Far be it from us that we should forsake the LORD to serve other gods; 17 for the LORD our God is He who brought us and our fathers up out of the land of Egypt, from the house of bondage, who did those great signs in our sight, and preserved us in all the way that we went and among all the people through whom we passed. 18 And the LORD drove out from before us all the people, including the Amorites who dwelt in the land. We also will serve the LORD, for He is our God."

19 But Joshua said to the people, "You cannot serve the LORD, for He is a holy God. He is a jealous God; He will not forgive your transgressions

כַּאֲשֶׁר עָשִׂיתִי בְּקִרְבּוֹ וְאַחַר הוֹצֵאתִי אֶתְכֶם:

6 וָאוֹצִיא אֶת־אֲבוֹתֵיכֶם מִמִּצְרַיִם וַתָּבֹאוּ הַיָּמָּה וַיִּרְדְּפוּ מִצְרַיִם אַחֲרֵי אֲבוֹתֵיכֶם בְּרֶכֶב וּבְפָרָשִׁים יַם־סוּף: 7 וַיִּצְעֲקוּ אֶל־יְהוָה וַיָּשֶׂם מַאֲפֵל בֵּינֵיכֶם וּבֵין הַמִּצְרִים וַיָּבֵא עָלָיו אֶת־הַיָּם וַיְכַסֵּהוּ וַתִּרְאֶינָה עֵינֵיכֶם אֵת אֲשֶׁר־עָשִׂיתִי בְּמִצְרָיִם וַתֵּשְׁבוּ בַמִּדְבָּר יָמִים רַבִּים: 8 וָאָבִאָה אֶתְכֶם אֶל־אֶרֶץ הָאֱמֹרִי הַיּוֹשֵׁב בְּעֵבֶר הַיַּרְדֵּן וַיִּלָּחֲמוּ אִתְּכֶם וָאֶתֵּן אוֹתָם בְּיֶדְכֶם וַתִּירְשׁוּ אֶת־אַרְצָם וָאַשְׁמִידֵם מִפְּנֵיכֶם: 9 וַיָּקָם בָּלָק בֶּן־צִפּוֹר מֶלֶךְ מוֹאָב וַיִּלָּחֶם בְּיִשְׂרָאֵל וַיִּשְׁלַח וַיִּקְרָא לְבִלְעָם בֶּן־בְּעוֹר לְקַלֵּל אֶתְכֶם: 10 וְלֹא אָבִיתִי לִשְׁמֹעַ לְבִלְעָם וַיְבָרֶךְ בָּרוֹךְ אֶתְכֶם וָאַצִּל אֶתְכֶם מִיָּדוֹ: 11 וַתַּעַבְרוּ אֶת־הַיַּרְדֵּן וַתָּבֹאוּ אֶל־יְרִיחוֹ וַיִּלָּחֲמוּ בָכֶם בַּעֲלֵי־יְרִיחוֹ הָאֱמֹרִי וְהַפְּרִזִּי וְהַכְּנַעֲנִי וְהַחִתִּי וְהַגִּרְגָּשִׁי הַחִוִּי וְהַיְבוּסִי וָאֶתֵּן אוֹתָם בְּיֶדְכֶם: 12 וָאֶשְׁלַח לִפְנֵיכֶם אֶת־הַצִּרְעָה וַתְּגָרֶשׁ אוֹתָם מִפְּנֵיכֶם שְׁנֵי מַלְכֵי הָאֱמֹרִי לֹא בְחַרְבְּךָ וְלֹא בְקַשְׁתֶּךָ: 13 וָאֶתֵּן לָכֶם אֶרֶץ אֲשֶׁר לֹא־יָגַעְתָּ בָּהּ וְעָרִים אֲשֶׁר לֹא־בְנִיתֶם וַתֵּשְׁבוּ בָּהֶם כְּרָמִים וְזֵיתִים אֲשֶׁר לֹא־נְטַעְתֶּם אַתֶּם אֹכְלִים: 14 וְעַתָּה יְראוּ אֶת־יְהוָה וְעִבְדוּ אֹתוֹ בְּתָמִים וּבֶאֱמֶת וְהָסִירוּ אֶת־אֱלֹהִים אֲשֶׁר עָבְדוּ אֲבוֹתֵיכֶם בְּעֵבֶר הַנָּהָר וּבְמִצְרַיִם וְעִבְדוּ אֶת־יְהוָה: 15 וְאִם רַע בְּעֵינֵיכֶם לַעֲבֹד אֶת־יְהוָה בַּחֲרוּ לָכֶם הַיּוֹם אֶת־מִי תַעֲבֹדוּן אִם אֶת־אֱלֹהִים אֲשֶׁר־עָבְדוּ אֲבוֹתֵיכֶם אֲשֶׁר בְּעֵבֶר הַנָּהָר וְאִם אֶת־אֱלֹהֵי הָאֱמֹרִי אֲשֶׁר אַתֶּם יֹשְׁבִים בְּאַרְצָם וְאָנֹכִי וּבֵיתִי נַעֲבֹד אֶת־יְהוָה:
פ

16 וַיַּעַן הָעָם וַיֹּאמֶר חָלִילָה לָּנוּ מֵעֲזֹב אֶת־יְהוָה לַעֲבֹד אֱלֹהִים אֲחֵרִים: 17 כִּי יְהוָה אֱלֹהֵינוּ הוּא הַמַּעֲלֶה אֹתָנוּ וְאֶת־אֲבוֹתֵינוּ מֵאֶרֶץ מִצְרַיִם מִבֵּית עֲבָדִים וַאֲשֶׁר עָשָׂה לְעֵינֵינוּ אֶת־הָאֹתוֹת הַגְּדֹלוֹת הָאֵלֶּה וַיִּשְׁמְרֵנוּ בְּכָל־הַדֶּרֶךְ אֲשֶׁר הָלַכְנוּ בָהּ וּבְכֹל הָעַמִּים אֲשֶׁר עָבַרְנוּ בְּקִרְבָּם: 18 וַיְגָרֶשׁ יְהוָה אֶת־כָּל־הָעַמִּים וְאֶת־הָאֱמֹרִי יֹשֵׁב הָאָרֶץ מִפָּנֵינוּ גַּם־אֲנַחְנוּ נַעֲבֹד אֶת־יְהוָה כִּי־הוּא אֱלֹהֵינוּ: 19 וַיֹּאמֶר יְהוֹשֻׁעַ אֶל־הָעָם לֹא תוּכְלוּ לַעֲבֹד אֶת־יְהוָה

nor your sins. 20 If you forsake the LORD and serve foreign gods, then He will turn and do you harm and consume you, after He has done you good."

21 And the people said to Joshua, "No, but we will serve the LORD!"

22 So Joshua said to the people, "You *are* witnesses against yourselves that you have chosen the LORD for yourselves, to serve Him."

And they said, "*We are* witnesses!"

23 "Now therefore," *he said,* "put away the foreign gods which *are* among you, and incline your heart to the LORD God of Israel."

24 And the people said to Joshua, "The LORD our God we will serve, and His voice we will obey!"

25 So Joshua made a covenant with the people that day, and made for them a statute and an ordinance in Shechem.

26 Then Joshua wrote these words in the Book of the Law of God. And he took a large stone, and set it up there under the oak that *was* by the sanctuary of the LORD. 27 And Joshua said to all the people, "Behold, this stone shall be a witness to us, for it has heard all the words of the LORD which He spoke to us. It shall therefore be a witness to you, lest you deny your God." 28 So Joshua let the people depart, each to his own inheritance.

29 Now it came to pass after these things that Joshua the son of Nun, the servant of the LORD, died, *being* one hundred and ten years old. 30 And they buried him within the border of his inheritance at Timnath Serah, which *is* in the mountains of Ephraim, on the north side of Mount Gaash.

31 Israel served the LORD all the days of Joshua, and all the days of the elders who outlived Joshua, who had known all the works of the LORD which He had done for Israel.

32 The bones of Joseph, which the children of Israel had brought up out of Egypt, they buried at Shechem, in the plot of ground which Jacob had bought from the sons of Hamor the father of Shechem for one hundred pieces of silver, and which had become an inheritance of the children of Joseph.

33 And Eleazar the son of Aaron died. They buried him in a hill *belonging to* Phinehas his son, which was given to him in the mountains of Ephraim.

כִּי־אֱלֹהִים קְדֹשִׁים הוּא אֵל־קַנּוֹא הוּא לֹא־יִשָּׂא
לְפִשְׁעֲכֶם וּלְחַטֹּאותֵיכֶם: 20 כִּי תַעַזְבוּ אֶת־יְהֹוָה
וַעֲבַדְתֶּם אֱלֹהֵי נֵכָר וְשָׁב וְהֵרַע לָכֶם וְכִלָּה אֶתְכֶם
אַחֲרֵי אֲשֶׁר־הֵיטִיב לָכֶם: 21 וַיֹּאמֶר הָעָם אֶל־
יְהוֹשֻׁעַ לֹא כִּי אֶת־יְהֹוָה נַעֲבֹד: 22 וַיֹּאמֶר יְהוֹשֻׁעַ
אֶל־הָעָם עֵדִים אַתֶּם בָּכֶם כִּי־אַתֶּם בְּחַרְתֶּם לָכֶם
אֶת־יְהֹוָה לַעֲבֹד אוֹתוֹ וַיֹּאמְרוּ עֵדִים: 23 וְעַתָּה
הָסִירוּ אֶת־אֱלֹהֵי הַנֵּכָר אֲשֶׁר בְּקִרְבְּכֶם וְהַטּוּ אֶת־
לְבַבְכֶם אֶל־יְהֹוָה אֱלֹהֵי יִשְׂרָאֵל: 24 וַיֹּאמְרוּ הָעָם
אֶל־יְהוֹשֻׁעַ אֶת־יְהֹוָה אֱלֹהֵינוּ נַעֲבֹד וּבְקוֹלוֹ נִשְׁמָע:
25 וַיִּכְרֹת יְהוֹשֻׁעַ בְּרִית לָעָם בַּיּוֹם הַהוּא וַיָּשֶׂם
לוֹ חֹק וּמִשְׁפָּט בִּשְׁכֶם: 26 וַיִּכְתֹּב יְהוֹשֻׁעַ אֶת־
הַדְּבָרִים הָאֵלֶּה בְּסֵפֶר תּוֹרַת אֱלֹהִים וַיִּקַּח אֶבֶן
גְּדוֹלָה וַיְקִימֶהָ שָּׁם תַּחַת הָאַלָּה אֲשֶׁר בְּמִקְדַּשׁ
יְהֹוָה: ס   27 וַיֹּאמֶר יְהוֹשֻׁעַ אֶל־כָּל־הָעָם
הִנֵּה הָאֶבֶן הַזֹּאת תִּהְיֶה־בָּנוּ לְעֵדָה כִּי־הִיא שָׁמְעָה
אֵת כָּל־אִמְרֵי יְהֹוָה אֲשֶׁר דִּבֶּר עִמָּנוּ וְהָיְתָה בָכֶם
לְעֵדָה פֶּן־תְּכַחֲשׁוּן בֵּאלֹהֵיכֶם: 28 וַיְשַׁלַּח יְהוֹשֻׁעַ
אֶת־הָעָם אִישׁ לְנַחֲלָתוֹ: פ
29 וַיְהִי אַחֲרֵי הַדְּבָרִים הָאֵלֶּה וַיָּמָת יְהוֹשֻׁעַ בִּן־נוּן
עֶבֶד יְהֹוָה בֶּן־מֵאָה וָעֶשֶׂר שָׁנִים: 30 וַיִּקְבְּרוּ אֹתוֹ
בִּגְבוּל נַחֲלָתוֹ בְּתִמְנַת־סֶרַח אֲשֶׁר בְּהַר־אֶפְרָיִם
מִצְּפוֹן לְהַר־גָּעַשׁ: 31 וַיַּעֲבֹד יִשְׂרָאֵל אֶת־יְהֹוָה כֹּל
יְמֵי יְהוֹשֻׁעַ וְכֹל | יְמֵי הַזְּקֵנִים אֲשֶׁר הֶאֱרִיכוּ יָמִים
אַחֲרֵי יְהוֹשֻׁעַ וַאֲשֶׁר יָדְעוּ אֵת כָּל־מַעֲשֵׂה יְהֹוָה
אֲשֶׁר עָשָׂה לְיִשְׂרָאֵל: 32 וְאֶת־עַצְמוֹת יוֹסֵף אֲשֶׁר־
הֶעֱלוּ בְנֵי־יִשְׂרָאֵל | מִמִּצְרַיִם קָבְרוּ בִשְׁכֶם בְּחֶלְקַת
הַשָּׂדֶה אֲשֶׁר קָנָה יַעֲקֹב מֵאֵת בְּנֵי־חֲמוֹר אֲבִי־שְׁכֶם
בְּמֵאָה קְשִׂיטָה וַיִּהְיוּ לִבְנֵי־יוֹסֵף לְנַחֲלָה: 33 וְאֶלְעָזָר
בֶּן־אַהֲרֹן מֵת וַיִּקְבְּרוּ אֹתוֹ בְּגִבְעַת פִּינְחָס בְּנוֹ אֲשֶׁר
נִתַּן־לוֹ בְּהַר אֶפְרָיִם:

The Book of
JUDGES

1 Now after the death of Joshua it came to pass that the children of Israel asked the LORD, saying, "Who shall be first to go up for us against the Canaanites to fight against them?"

² And the LORD said, "Judah shall go up. Indeed I have delivered the land into his hand."

³ So Judah said to Simeon his brother, "Come up with me to my allotted territory, that we may fight against the Canaanites; and I will likewise go with you to your allotted territory." And Simeon went with him. ⁴ Then Judah went up, and the LORD delivered the Canaanites and the Perizzites into their hand; and they killed ten thousand men at Bezek. ⁵ And they found Adoni-Bezek in Bezek, and fought against him; and they defeated the Canaanites and the Perizzites. ⁶ Then Adoni-Bezek fled, and they pursued him and caught him and cut off his thumbs and big toes. ⁷ And Adoni-Bezek said, "Seventy kings with their thumbs and big toes cut off used to gather *scraps* under my table; as I have done, so God has repaid me." Then they brought him to Jerusalem, and there he died.

⁸ Now the children of Judah fought against Jerusalem and took it; they struck it with the edge of the sword and set the city on fire. ⁹ And afterward the children of Judah went down to fight against the Canaanites who dwelt in the mountains, in the South, and in the lowland. ¹⁰ Then Judah went against the Canaanites who dwelt in Hebron. (Now the name of Hebron *was* formerly Kirjath Arba.) And they killed Sheshai, Ahiman, and Talmai.

¹¹ From there they went against the inhabitants of Debir. (The name of Debir *was* formerly Kirjath Sepher.)

¹² Then Caleb said, "Whoever attacks Kirjath Sepher and takes it, to him I will give my daughter Achsah as wife." ¹³ And Othniel the son of Kenaz, Caleb's younger brother, took it; so he gave him his daughter Achsah as wife. ¹⁴ Now it happened, when she came *to him*, that she urged him to ask her father for a field. And she dismounted from *her* donkey, and Caleb said to her, "What do you wish?" ¹⁵ So she said to him, "Give me a blessing; since you have given me land in the South, give me also springs of water."

שׁוֹפְטִים

א וַיְהִי אַחֲרֵי מוֹת יְהוֹשֻׁעַ וַיִּשְׁאֲלוּ בְּנֵי יִשְׂרָאֵל בַּיהוָה לֵאמֹר מִי יַעֲלֶה־לָּנוּ אֶל־הַכְּנַעֲנִי בַּתְּחִלָּה לְהִלָּחֶם בּוֹ: 2 וַיֹּאמֶר יְהוָה יְהוּדָה יַעֲלֶה הִנֵּה נָתַתִּי אֶת־הָאָרֶץ בְּיָדוֹ: 3 וַיֹּאמֶר יְהוּדָה לְשִׁמְעוֹן אָחִיו עֲלֵה אִתִּי בְגוֹרָלִי וְנִלָּחֲמָה בַּכְּנַעֲנִי וְהָלַכְתִּי גַם־אֲנִי אִתְּךָ בְּגוֹרָלֶךָ וַיֵּלֶךְ אִתּוֹ שִׁמְעוֹן: 4 וַיַּעַל יְהוּדָה וַיִּתֵּן יְהוָה אֶת־הַכְּנַעֲנִי וְהַפְּרִזִּי בְּיָדָם וַיַּכּוּם בְּבֶזֶק עֲשֶׂרֶת אֲלָפִים אִישׁ: 5 וַיִּמְצְאוּ אֶת־אֲדֹנִי בֶזֶק בְּבֶזֶק וַיִּלָּחֲמוּ בּוֹ וַיַּכּוּ אֶת־הַכְּנַעֲנִי וְאֶת־הַפְּרִזִּי: 6 וַיָּנָס אֲדֹנִי בֶזֶק וַיִּרְדְּפוּ אַחֲרָיו וַיֹּאחֲזוּ אֹתוֹ וַיְקַצְּצוּ אֶת־בְּהֹנוֹת יָדָיו וְרַגְלָיו: 7 וַיֹּאמֶר אֲדֹנִי בֶזֶק שִׁבְעִים מְלָכִים בְּהֹנוֹת יְדֵיהֶם וְרַגְלֵיהֶם מְקֻצָּצִים הָיוּ מְלַקְּטִים תַּחַת שֻׁלְחָנִי כַּאֲשֶׁר עָשִׂיתִי כֵּן שִׁלַּם־לִי אֱלֹהִים וַיְבִיאֻהוּ יְרוּשָׁלַםִ וַיָּמָת שָׁם: פ

8 וַיִּלָּחֲמוּ בְנֵי־יְהוּדָה בִּירוּשָׁלַםִ וַיִּלְכְּדוּ אוֹתָהּ וַיַּכּוּהָ לְפִי־חָרֶב וְאֶת־הָעִיר שִׁלְּחוּ בָאֵשׁ: 9 וְאַחַר יָרְדוּ בְּנֵי יְהוּדָה לְהִלָּחֵם בַּכְּנַעֲנִי יוֹשֵׁב הָהָר וְהַנֶּגֶב וְהַשְּׁפֵלָה: 10 וַיֵּלֶךְ יְהוּדָה אֶל־הַכְּנַעֲנִי הַיּוֹשֵׁב בְּחֶבְרוֹן וְשֵׁם־חֶבְרוֹן לְפָנִים קִרְיַת אַרְבַּע וַיַּכּוּ אֶת־שֵׁשַׁי וְאֶת־אֲחִימַן וְאֶת־תַּלְמָי: 11 וַיֵּלֶךְ מִשָּׁם אֶל־יוֹשְׁבֵי דְּבִיר וְשֵׁם־דְּבִיר לְפָנִים קִרְיַת־סֵפֶר: 12 וַיֹּאמֶר כָּלֵב אֲשֶׁר־יַכֶּה אֶת־קִרְיַת־סֵפֶר וּלְכָדָהּ וְנָתַתִּי לוֹ אֶת־עַכְסָה בִתִּי לְאִשָּׁה: 13 וַיִּלְכְּדָהּ עָתְנִיאֵל בֶּן־קְנַז אֲחִי כָלֵב הַקָּטֹן מִמֶּנּוּ וַיִּתֶּן־לוֹ אֶת־עַכְסָה בִתּוֹ לְאִשָּׁה: 14 וַיְהִי בְּבוֹאָהּ וַתְּסִיתֵהוּ לִשְׁאוֹל מֵאֵת־אָבִיהָ הַשָּׂדֶה וַתִּצְנַח מֵעַל הַחֲמוֹר וַיֹּאמֶר־לָהּ כָּלֵב מַה־לָּךְ: 15 וַתֹּאמֶר לוֹ הָבָה־לִּי בְרָכָה כִּי אֶרֶץ הַנֶּגֶב נְתַתָּנִי וְנָתַתָּה לִי גֻּלֹּת מָיִם וַיִּתֶּן־לָהּ כָּלֵב אֵת גֻּלֹּת עִלִּית וְאֵת גֻּלֹּת תַּחְתִּית: פ

And Caleb gave her the upper springs and the lower springs.

16 Now the children of the Kenite, Moses' father-in-law, went up from the City of Palms with the children of Judah into the Wilderness of Judah, which *lies* in the South *near* Arad; and they went and dwelt among the people. 17 And Judah went with his brother Simeon, and they attacked the Canaanites who inhabited Zephath, and utterly destroyed it. So the name of the city was called Hormah. 18 Also Judah took Gaza with its territory, Ashkelon with its territory, and Ekron with its territory. 19 So the LORD was with Judah. And they drove out the mountaineers, but they could not drive out the inhabitants of the lowland, because they had chariots of iron. 20 And they gave Hebron to Caleb, as Moses had said. Then he expelled from there the three sons of Anak. 21 But the children of Benjamin did not drive out the Jebusites who inhabited Jerusalem; so the Jebusites dwell with the children of Benjamin in Jerusalem to this day.

22 And the house of Joseph also went up against Bethel, and the LORD *was* with them. 23 So the house of Joseph sent men to spy out Bethel. (The name of the city *was* formerly Luz.) 24 And when the spies saw a man coming out of the city, they said to him, "Please show us the entrance to the city, and we will show you mercy." 25 So he showed them the entrance to the city, and they struck the city with the edge of the sword; but they let the man and all his family go. 26 And the man went to the land of the Hittites, built a city, and called its name Luz, which *is* its name to this day.

27 However, Manasseh did not drive out *the inhabitants of* Beth Shean and its villages, or Taanach and its villages, or the inhabitants of Dor and its villages, or the inhabitants of Ibleam and its villages, or the inhabitants of Megiddo and its villages; for the Canaanites were determined to dwell in that land. 28 And it came to pass, when Israel was strong, that they put the Canaanites under tribute, but did not completely drive them out.

29 Nor did Ephraim drive out the Canaanites who dwelt in Gezer; so the Canaanites dwelt in Gezer among them.

30 Nor did Zebulun drive out the inhabitants of Kitron or the inhabitants of Nahalol; so the Canaanites dwelt among them, and were put under tribute.

16 וּבְנֵי קֵינִי חֹתֵן מֹשֶׁה עָלוּ מֵעִיר הַתְּמָרִים אֶת־
בְּנֵי יְהוּדָה מִדְבַּר יְהוּדָה אֲשֶׁר בְּנֶגֶב עֲרָד וַיֵּלֶךְ
וַיֵּשֶׁב אֶת־הָעָם: 17 וַיֵּלֶךְ יְהוּדָה אֶת־שִׁמְעוֹן אָחִיו
וַיַּכּוּ אֶת־הַכְּנַעֲנִי יוֹשֵׁב צְפַת וַיַּחֲרִימוּ אוֹתָהּ וַיִּקְרָא
אֶת־שֵׁם־הָעִיר חָרְמָה: 18 וַיִּלְכֹּד יְהוּדָה אֶת־עַזָּה
וְאֶת־גְּבוּלָהּ וְאֶת־אַשְׁקְלוֹן וְאֶת־גְּבוּלָהּ וְאֶת־עֶקְרוֹן
וְאֶת־גְּבוּלָהּ: 19 וַיְהִי יְהוָה אֶת־יְהוּדָה וַיֹּרֶשׁ אֶת־
הָהָר כִּי לֹא לְהוֹרִישׁ אֶת־יֹשְׁבֵי הָעֵמֶק כִּי־רֶכֶב
בַּרְזֶל לָהֶם: 20 וַיִּתְּנוּ לְכָלֵב אֶת־חֶבְרוֹן כַּאֲשֶׁר
דִּבֶּר מֹשֶׁה וַיּוֹרֶשׁ מִשָּׁם אֶת־שְׁלֹשָׁה בְּנֵי הָעֲנָק:
21 וְאֶת־הַיְבוּסִי יֹשֵׁב יְרוּשָׁלַ͏ִם לֹא הוֹרִישׁוּ בְּנֵי בִנְיָמִן
וַיֵּשֶׁב הַיְבוּסִי אֶת־בְּנֵי בִנְיָמִן בִּירוּשָׁלַ͏ִם עַד הַיּוֹם
הַזֶּה: ס   22 וַיַּעֲלוּ בֵית־יוֹסֵף גַּם־הֵם בֵּית־
אֵל וַיהוָה עִמָּם: 23 וַיָּתִירוּ בֵית־יוֹסֵף בְּבֵית־אֵל
וְשֵׁם־הָעִיר לְפָנִים לוּז: 24 וַיִּרְאוּ הַשֹּׁמְרִים אִישׁ
יוֹצֵא מִן־הָעִיר וַיֹּאמְרוּ לוֹ הַרְאֵנוּ נָא אֶת־מְבוֹא
הָעִיר וְעָשִׂינוּ עִמְּךָ חָסֶד: 25 וַיַּרְאֵם אֶת־מְבוֹא
הָעִיר וַיַּכּוּ אֶת־הָעִיר לְפִי־חָרֶב וְאֶת־הָאִישׁ וְאֶת־
כָּל־מִשְׁפַּחְתּוֹ שִׁלֵּחוּ: 26 וַיֵּלֶךְ הָאִישׁ אֶרֶץ הַחִתִּים
וַיִּבֶן עִיר וַיִּקְרָא שְׁמָהּ לוּז הוּא שְׁמָהּ עַד הַיּוֹם
הַזֶּה: פ
27 וְלֹא־הוֹרִישׁ מְנַשֶּׁה אֶת־בֵּית־שְׁאָן וְאֶת־בְּנוֹתֶיהָ
וְאֶת־תַּעְנַךְ וְאֶת־בְּנֹתֶיהָ וְאֶת־יֹשְׁבֵ P דּוֹר וְאֶת־
בְּנוֹתֶיהָ וְאֶת־יוֹשְׁבֵי יִבְלְעָם וְאֶת־בְּנֹתֶיהָ וְאֶת־יֹשְׁבֵי
מְגִדּוֹ וְאֶת־בְּנוֹתֶיהָ וַיּוֹאֶל הַכְּנַעֲנִי לָשֶׁבֶת בָּאָרֶץ
הַזֹּאת: 28 וַיְהִי כִּי־חָזַק יִשְׂרָאֵל וַיָּשֶׂם אֶת־הַכְּנַעֲנִי
לָמַס וְהוֹרֵישׁ לֹא הוֹרִישׁוֹ:   ס   29 וְאֶפְרַיִם
לֹא הוֹרִישׁ אֶת־הַכְּנַעֲנִי הַיּוֹשֵׁב בְּגָזֶר וַיֵּשֶׁב הַכְּנַעֲנִי
בְּקִרְבּוֹ בְּגָזֶר: פ
30 זְבוּלֻן לֹא הוֹרִישׁ אֶת־יוֹשְׁבֵי קִטְרוֹן וְאֶת־יוֹשְׁבֵי
נַהֲלֹל וַיֵּשֶׁב הַכְּנַעֲנִי בְּקִרְבּוֹ וַיִּהְיוּ

27 א יֹשְׁבֵי

31 Nor did Asher drive out the inhabitants of Acco or the inhabitants of Sidon, or of Ahlab, Achzib, Helbah, Aphik, or Rehob. 32 So the Asherites dwelt among the Canaanites, the inhabitants of the land; for they did not drive them out.

33 Nor did Naphtali drive out the inhabitants of Beth Shemesh or the inhabitants of Beth Anath; but they dwelt among the Canaanites, the inhabitants of the land. Nevertheless the inhabitants of Beth Shemesh and Beth Anath were put under tribute to them.

34 And the Amorites forced the children of Dan into the mountains, for they would not allow them to come down to the valley; 35 and the Amorites were determined to dwell in Mount Heres, in Aijalon, and in Shaalbim; yet when the strength of the house of Joseph became greater, they were put under tribute.

36 Now the boundary of the Amorites was from the Ascent of Akrabbim, from Sela, and upward.

2 Then the Angel of the LORD came up from Gilgal to Bochim, and said: "I led you up from Egypt and brought you to the land of which I swore to your fathers; and I said, 'I will never break My covenant with you. 2 And you shall make no covenant with the inhabitants of this land; you shall tear down their altars.' But you have not obeyed My voice. Why have you done this? 3 Therefore I also said, 'I will not drive them out before you; but they shall be thorns in your side, and their gods shall be a snare to you.'" 4 So it was, when the Angel of the LORD spoke these words to all the children of Israel, that the people lifted up their voices and wept.

5 Then they called the name of that place Bochim; and they sacrificed there to the LORD. 6 And when Joshua had dismissed the people, the children of Israel went each to his own inheritance to possess the land.

7 So the people served the LORD all the days of Joshua, and all the days of the elders who outlived Joshua, who had seen all the great works of the LORD which He had done for Israel. 8 Now Joshua the son of Nun, the servant of the LORD, died when he was one hundred and ten years old. 9 And they buried him within the border of his inheritance at Timnath Heres, in the mountains of Ephraim, on the north side of Mount Gaash. 10 When all that generation had been gathered to their fathers, another generation arose after them who did not know the LORD nor the work which He had done for Israel.

31 ס לָמֶם: אֲשֶׁר לֹא הוֹרִישׁ אֶת־
יֹשְׁבֵי עַכּוֹ וְאֶת־יוֹשְׁבֵי צִידוֹן וְאֶת־אַחְלָב וְאֶת־
אַכְזִיב וְאֶת־חֶלְבָּה וְאֶת־אֲפִיק וְאֶת־רְחֹב: 32 וַיֵּשֶׁב
הָאָשֵׁרִי בְּקֶרֶב הַכְּנַעֲנִי יֹשְׁבֵי הָאָרֶץ כִּי לֹא
הוֹרִישׁוֹ: ס 33 נַפְתָּלִי לֹא־הוֹרִישׁ אֶת־
יֹשְׁבֵי בֵית־שֶׁמֶשׁ וְאֶת־יֹשְׁבֵי בֵית־עֲנָת וַיֵּשֶׁב בְּקֶרֶב
הַכְּנַעֲנִי יֹשְׁבֵי הָאָרֶץ וְיֹשְׁבֵי בֵית־שֶׁמֶשׁ וּבֵית עֲנָת
הָיוּ לָהֶם לָמַם: ס 34 וַיִּלְחֲצוּ הָאֱמֹרִי אֶת־
בְּנֵי־דָן הָהָרָה כִּי־לֹא נְתָנוֹ לָרֶדֶת לָעֵמֶק: 35 וַיּוֹאֶל
הָאֱמֹרִי לָשֶׁבֶת בְּהַר־חֶרֶס בְּאַיָּלוֹן וּבְשַׁעַלְבִים
וַתִּכְבַּד יַד בֵּית־יוֹסֵף וַיִּהְיוּ לָמַם: 36 וּגְבוּל הָאֱמֹרִי
מִמַּעֲלֵה עַקְרַבִּים מֵהַסֶּלַע וָמָעְלָה: פ

ב וַיַּעַל מַלְאַךְ־יְהוָה מִן־הַגִּלְגָּל אֶל־
הַבֹּכִים ס וַיֹּאמֶר אַעֲלֶה אֶתְכֶם מִמִּצְרַיִם
וָאָבִיא אֶתְכֶם אֶל־הָאָרֶץ אֲשֶׁר נִשְׁבַּעְתִּי לַאֲבֹתֵיכֶם
וָאֹמַר לֹא־אָפֵר בְּרִיתִי אִתְּכֶם לְעוֹלָם: 2 וְאַתֶּם לֹא־
תִכְרְתוּ בְרִית לְיוֹשְׁבֵי הָאָרֶץ הַזֹּאת מִזְבְּחוֹתֵיהֶם
תִּתֹּצוּן וְלֹא־שְׁמַעְתֶּם בְּקֹלִי מַה־זֹּאת עֲשִׂיתֶם:
3 וְגַם אָמַרְתִּי לֹא־אֲגָרֵשׁ אוֹתָם מִפְּנֵיכֶם וְהָיוּ
לָכֶם לְצִדִּים וֵאלֹהֵיהֶם יִהְיוּ לָכֶם לְמוֹקֵשׁ: 4 וַיְהִי
כְּדַבֵּר מַלְאַךְ יְהוָה אֶת־הַדְּבָרִים הָאֵלֶּה אֶל־כָּל־
בְּנֵי יִשְׂרָאֵל וַיִּשְׂאוּ הָעָם אֶת־קוֹלָם וַיִּבְכּוּ: 5 וַיִּקְרְאוּ
שֵׁם־הַמָּקוֹם הַהוּא בֹּכִים וַיִּזְבְּחוּ־שָׁם לַיהוָה: פ

6 וַיְשַׁלַּח יְהוֹשֻׁעַ אֶת־הָעָם וַיֵּלְכוּ בְנֵי־יִשְׂרָאֵל אִישׁ
לְנַחֲלָתוֹ לָרֶשֶׁת אֶת־הָאָרֶץ: 7 וַיַּעַבְדוּ הָעָם אֶת־
יְהוָה כֹּל יְמֵי יְהוֹשֻׁעַ וְכֹל | יְמֵי הַזְּקֵנִים אֲשֶׁר
הֶאֱרִיכוּ יָמִים אַחֲרֵי יְהוֹשׁוּעַ אֲשֶׁר רָאוּ אֵת כָּל־
מַעֲשֵׂה יְהוָה הַגָּדוֹל אֲשֶׁר עָשָׂה לְיִשְׂרָאֵל: 8 וַיָּמָת
יְהוֹשֻׁעַ בִּן־נוּן עֶבֶד יְהוָה בֶּן־מֵאָה וָעֶשֶׂר שָׁנִים:
9 וַיִּקְבְּרוּ אוֹתוֹ בִּגְבוּל נַחֲלָתוֹ בְּתִמְנַת־חֶרֶס בְּהַר
אֶפְרַיִם מִצְּפוֹן לְהַר־גָּעַשׁ: 10 וְגַם כָּל־הַדּוֹר הַהוּא
נֶאֶסְפוּ אֶל־אֲבוֹתָיו וַיָּקָם דּוֹר אַחֵר אַחֲרֵיהֶם אֲשֶׁר
לֹא־יָדְעוּ אֶת־יְהוָה וְגַם אֶת־הַמַּעֲשֶׂה אֲשֶׁר עָשָׂה

11 Then the children of Israel did evil in the sight of the LORD, and served the Baals; 12 and they forsook the LORD God of their fathers, who had brought them out of the land of Egypt; and they followed other gods from *among* the gods of the people who *were* all around them, and they bowed down to them; and they provoked the LORD to anger. 13 They forsook the LORD and served Baal and the Ashtoreths. 14 And the anger of the LORD was hot against Israel. So He delivered them into the hands of plunderers who despoiled them; and He sold them into the hands of their enemies all around, so that they could no longer stand before their enemies. 15 Wherever they went out, the hand of the LORD was against them for calamity, as the LORD had said, and as the LORD had sworn to them. And they were greatly distressed.

16 Nevertheless, the LORD raised up judges who delivered them out of the hand of those who plundered them. 17 Yet they would not listen to their judges, but they played the harlot with other gods, and bowed down to them. They turned quickly from the way in which their fathers walked, in obeying the commandments of the LORD; they did not do so. 18 And when the LORD raised up judges for them, the LORD was with the judge and delivered them out of the hand of their enemies all the days of the judge; for the LORD was moved to pity by their groaning because of those who oppressed them and harassed them. 19 And it came to pass, when the judge was dead, that they reverted and behaved more corruptly than their fathers, by following other gods, to serve them and bow down to them. They did not cease from their own doings nor from their stubborn way.

20 Then the anger of the LORD was hot against Israel; and He said, "Because this nation has transgressed My covenant which I commanded their fathers, and has not heeded My voice, 21 I also will no longer drive out before them any of the nations which Joshua left when he died, 22 so that through them I may test Israel, whether they will keep the ways of the LORD, to walk in them as their fathers kept *them,* or not." 23 Therefore the LORD left those nations, without driving them out immediately; nor did He deliver them into the hand of Joshua.

3 Now these *are* the nations which the LORD left, that He might test Israel by them, *that is,* all who had not known any of the wars in Canaan 2 (*this was* only so that the generations of the children of Israel might be taught to know war, at least those who had not formerly known it), 3 *namely,* five lords

ס 11 וַיַּעֲשׂ֨וּ בְנֵֽי־יִשְׂרָאֵ֤ל אֶת־ לְיִשְׂרָאֵֽל׃
הָרַע֙ בְּעֵינֵ֣י יְהֹוָ֔ה וַיַּעַבְד֖וּ אֶת־הַבְּעָלִֽים׃ 12 וַיַּעַזְב֣וּ
אֶת־יְהֹוָ֣ה ׀ אֱלֹהֵ֣י אֲבֽוֹתָם֩ הַמּוֹצִ֨יא אוֹתָ֜ם מֵאֶ֣רֶץ
מִצְרַ֗יִם וַיֵּלְכ֞וּ אַֽחֲרֵ֣י ׀ אֱלֹהִ֣ים אֲחֵרִ֗ים מֵֽאֱלֹהֵ֤י
הָֽעַמִּים֙ אֲשֶׁר֙ סְבִ֣יבֽוֹתֵיהֶ֔ם וַיִּֽשְׁתַּֽחֲו֖וּ לָהֶ֑ם וַיַּכְעִ֖סוּ
אֶת־יְהֹוָֽה׃ 13 וַיַּעַזְב֖וּ אֶת־יְהֹוָ֑ה וַיַּֽעַבְד֥וּ לַבַּ֖עַל
וְלָֽעַשְׁתָּרֽוֹת׃ 14 וַיִּֽחַר־אַ֤ף יְהֹוָה֙ בְּיִשְׂרָאֵ֔ל וַֽיִּתְּנֵם֙
בְּיַד־שֹׁסִ֔ים וַיָּשֹׁ֖סּוּ אוֹתָ֑ם וַֽיִּמְכְּרֵ֞ם בְּיַ֤ד אֽוֹיְבֵיהֶם֙
מִסָּבִ֔יב וְלֹֽא־יָֽכְל֣וּ ע֔וֹד לַֽעֲמֹ֖ד לִפְנֵ֥י אֽוֹיְבֵיהֶֽם׃
15 בְּכֹ֣ל ׀ אֲשֶׁ֣ר יָֽצְא֗וּ יַד־יְהֹוָה֙ הָֽיְתָה־בָּ֣ם לְרָעָ֔ה
כַּֽאֲשֶׁר֙ דִּבֶּ֣ר יְהֹוָ֔ה וְכַֽאֲשֶׁ֛ר נִשְׁבַּ֥ע יְהֹוָ֖ה לָהֶ֑ם וַיֵּ֥צֶר
לָהֶ֖ם מְאֹֽד׃ 16 וַיָּ֥קֶם יְהֹוָ֖ה שֹֽׁפְטִ֑ים וַיּ֣וֹשִׁיע֔וּם מִיַּ֖ד
שֹֽׁסֵיהֶֽם׃ 17 וְגַ֤ם אֶל־שֹֽׁפְטֵיהֶם֙ לֹ֣א שָׁמֵ֔עוּ כִּ֣י זָנ֗וּ
אַֽחֲרֵי֙ אֱלֹהִ֣ים אֲחֵרִ֔ים וַיִּֽשְׁתַּֽחֲו֖וּ לָהֶ֑ם סָ֣רוּ מַהֵ֗ר
מִן־הַדֶּ֔רֶךְ אֲשֶׁ֤ר הָֽלְכוּ֙ אֲבוֹתָ֔ם לִשְׁמֹ֖עַ מִצְוֺת־יְהֹוָ֑ה
לֹא־עָ֥שׂוּ כֵֽן׃ 18 וְכִֽי־הֵקִ֥ים יְהֹוָ֨ה ׀ לָהֶ֜ם שֹֽׁפְטִ֗ים
וְהָיָ֤ה יְהֹוָה֙ עִם־הַשֹּׁפֵ֔ט וְהֽוֹשִׁיעָ֖ם מִיַּ֣ד אֹֽיְבֵיהֶ֔ם
כֹּ֖ל יְמֵ֣י הַשּׁוֹפֵ֑ט כִּֽי־יִנָּחֵ֤ם יְהֹוָה֙ מִנַּֽאֲקָתָ֔ם מִפְּנֵ֥י
לֹֽחֲצֵיהֶ֖ם וְדֹֽחֲקֵיהֶֽם׃ 19 וְהָיָ֣ה ׀ בְּמ֣וֹת הַשּׁוֹפֵ֗ט
יָשֻׁ֨בוּ֙ וְהִשְׁחִ֣יתוּ מֵֽאֲבוֹתָ֔ם לָלֶ֗כֶת אַֽחֲרֵי֙ אֱלֹהִ֣ים
אֲחֵרִ֔ים לְעָבְדָ֖ם וּלְהִשְׁתַּֽחֲוֺ֣ת לָהֶ֑ם לֹ֤א הִפִּ֨ילוּ֙
מִמַּ֣עַלְלֵיהֶ֔ם וּמִדַּרְכָּ֖ם הַקָּשָֽׁה׃ 20 וַיִּֽחַר־אַ֥ף יְהֹוָ֖ה
בְּיִשְׂרָאֵ֑ל וַיֹּ֗אמֶר יַ֚עַן אֲשֶׁ֨ר עָֽבְר֜וּ הַגּ֣וֹי הַזֶּ֗ה אֶת־
בְּרִיתִי֙ אֲשֶׁ֣ר צִוִּ֣יתִי אֶת־אֲבוֹתָ֔ם וְלֹ֥א שָֽׁמְע֖וּ לְקוֹלִֽי׃
21 גַּם־אֲנִי֙ לֹ֣א אוֹסִ֔יף לְהוֹרִ֥ישׁ אִ֖ישׁ מִפְּנֵיהֶ֑ם מִן־
הַגּוֹיִ֛ם אֲשֶׁר־עָזַ֥ב יְהוֹשֻׁ֖עַ וַיָּמֹֽת׃ 22 לְמַ֛עַן נַסּ֥וֹת בָּ֖ם
אֶת־יִשְׂרָאֵ֑ל הֲשֹֽׁמְרִ֣ים הֵ֗ם אֶת־דֶּ֤רֶךְ יְהֹוָה֙ לָלֶ֣כֶת
בָּ֔ם כַּֽאֲשֶׁ֛ר שָֽׁמְר֥וּ אֲבוֹתָ֖ם אִם־לֹֽא׃ 23 וַיַּנַּ֤ח יְהֹוָה֙
אֶת־הַגּוֹיִ֣ם הָאֵ֔לֶּה לְבִלְתִּ֥י הֽוֹרִישָׁ֖ם מַהֵ֑ר וְלֹ֥א נְתָנָ֖ם
בְּיַד־יְהוֹשֻֽׁעַ׃ פ ס

ג וְאֵ֣לֶּה הַגּוֹיִ֗ם אֲשֶׁ֨ר הִנִּ֤יחַ יְהֹוָה֙ לְנַסּ֣וֹת בָּ֣ם אֶת־
יִשְׂרָאֵ֑ל אֵ֚ת כָּל־אֲשֶׁ֣ר לֹֽא־יָֽדְע֔וּ אֵ֖ת כָּל־מִלְחֲמ֥וֹת
כְּנָֽעַן׃ 2 רַ֗ק לְמַ֨עַן֙ דַּ֣עַת דֹּר֣וֹת בְּנֵֽי־יִשְׂרָאֵ֔ל לְלַמְּדָ֖ם
מִלְחָמָ֑ה רַ֥ק אֲשֶׁר־לְפָנִ֖ים לֹ֥א יְדָעֽוּם׃ 3 חֲמֵ֣שֶׁת ׀
סַרְנֵ֣י פְלִשְׁתִּ֗ים וְכָל־הַֽכְּנַֽעֲנִי֙ וְהַצִּֽידֹנִ֔י וְהַ֣חִוִּ֔י יֹשֵׁ֖ב

of the Philistines, all the Canaanites, the Sidonians, and the Hivites who dwelt in Mount Lebanon, from Mount Baal Hermon to the entrance of Hamath. ⁴ And they were *left, that He might* test Israel by them, to know whether they would obey the commandments of the LORD, which He had commanded their fathers by the hand of Moses.

⁵ Thus the children of Israel dwelt among the Canaanites, the Hittites, the Amorites, the Perizzites, the Hivites, and the Jebusites. ⁶ And they took their daughters to be their wives, and gave their daughters to their sons; and they served their gods.

⁷ So the children of Israel did evil in the sight of the LORD. They forgot the LORD their God, and served the Baals and Asherahs. ⁸ Therefore the anger of the LORD was hot against Israel, and He sold them into the hand of Cushan-Rishathaim king of Mesopotamia; and the children of Israel served Cushan-Rishathaim eight years. ⁹ When the children of Israel cried out to the LORD, the LORD raised up a deliverer for the children of Israel, who delivered them: Othniel the son of Kenaz, Caleb's younger brother. ¹⁰ The Spirit of the LORD came upon him, and he judged Israel. He went out to war, and the LORD delivered Cushan-Rishathaim king of Mesopotamia into his hand; and his hand prevailed over Cushan-Rishathaim. ¹¹ So the land had rest for forty years. Then Othniel the son of Kenaz died.

¹² And the children of Israel again did evil in the sight of the LORD. So the LORD strengthened Eglon king of Moab against Israel, because they had done evil in the sight of the LORD. ¹³ Then he gathered to himself the people of Ammon and Amalek, went and defeated Israel, and took possession of the City of Palms. ¹⁴ So the children of Israel served Eglon king of Moab eighteen years.

¹⁵ But when the children of Israel cried out to the LORD, the LORD raised up a deliverer for them: Ehud the son of Gera, the Benjamite, a left-handed man. By him the children of Israel sent tribute to Eglon king of Moab. ¹⁶ Now Ehud made himself a dagger (it was double-edged and a cubit in length) and fastened it under his clothes on his right thigh. ¹⁷ So he brought the tribute to Eglon king of Moab. (Now Eglon *was* a very fat man.) ¹⁸ And when he had finished presenting the tribute, he sent away the people who had carried the tribute. ¹⁹ But he himself turned back from the stone images that *were* at Gilgal, and said, "I have a secret message for you, O king."

He said, "Keep silence!" And all who attended him went out from him.

הַר הַלְּבָנוֹן מֵהַר בַּעַל חֶרְמוֹן עַד לְבוֹא חֲמָת: ⁴ וַיִּהְיוּ לְנַסּוֹת בָּם אֶת־יִשְׂרָאֵל לָדַעַת הֲיִשְׁמְעוּ אֶת־מִצְוֹת יְהֹוָה אֲשֶׁר־צִוָּה אֶת־אֲבוֹתָם בְּיַד־מֹשֶׁה: ⁵ וּבְנֵי יִשְׂרָאֵל יָשְׁבוּ בְּקֶרֶב הַכְּנַעֲנִי הַחִתִּי וְהָאֱמֹרִי וְהַפְּרִזִּי וְהַחִוִּי וְהַיְבוּסִי: ⁶ וַיִּקְחוּ אֶת־בְּנוֹתֵיהֶם לָהֶם לְנָשִׁים וְאֶת־בְּנוֹתֵיהֶם נָתְנוּ לִבְנֵיהֶם וַיַּעַבְדוּ אֶת־ אֱלֹהֵיהֶם: פ

⁷ וַיַּעֲשׂוּ בְנֵי־יִשְׂרָאֵל אֶת־הָרַע בְּעֵינֵי יְהֹוָה וַיִּשְׁכְּחוּ אֶת־יְהֹוָה אֱלֹהֵיהֶם וַיַּעַבְדוּ אֶת־הַבְּעָלִים וְאֶת־ הָאֲשֵׁרוֹת: ⁸ וַיִּחַר־אַף יְהֹוָה בְּיִשְׂרָאֵל וַיִּמְכְּרֵם בְּיַד כּוּשַׁן רִשְׁעָתַיִם מֶלֶךְ אֲרַם נַהֲרָיִם וַיַּעַבְדוּ בְנֵי־ יִשְׂרָאֵל אֶת־כּוּשַׁן רִשְׁעָתַיִם שְׁמֹנֶה שָׁנִים: ⁹ וַיִּזְעֲקוּ בְנֵי־יִשְׂרָאֵל אֶל־יְהֹוָה וַיָּקֶם יְהֹוָה מוֹשִׁיעַ לִבְנֵי יִשְׂרָאֵל וַיּוֹשִׁיעֵם אֵת עָתְנִיאֵל בֶּן־קְנַז אֲחִי כָלֵב הַקָּטֹן מִמֶּנּוּ: ¹⁰ וַתְּהִי עָלָיו רוּחַ־יְהֹוָה וַיִּשְׁפֹּט אֶת־ יִשְׂרָאֵל וַיֵּצֵא לַמִּלְחָמָה וַיִּתֵּן יְהֹוָה בְּיָדוֹ אֶת־כּוּשַׁן רִשְׁעָתַיִם מֶלֶךְ אֲרָם וַתָּעָז יָדוֹ עַל כּוּשַׁן רִשְׁעָתָיִם: ¹¹ וַתִּשְׁקֹט הָאָרֶץ אַרְבָּעִים שָׁנָה וַיָּמָת עָתְנִיאֵל בֶּן־קְנַז: פ

¹² וַיֹּסִפוּ בְּנֵי יִשְׂרָאֵל לַעֲשׂוֹת הָרַע בְּעֵינֵי יְהֹוָה וַיְחַזֵּק יְהֹוָה אֶת־עֶגְלוֹן מֶלֶךְ־מוֹאָב עַל־יִשְׂרָאֵל עַל כִּי־עָשׂוּ אֶת־הָרַע בְּעֵינֵי יְהֹוָה: ¹³ וַיֶּאֱסֹף אֵלָיו אֶת־בְּנֵי עַמּוֹן וַעֲמָלֵק וַיֵּלֶךְ וַיַּךְ אֶת־ יִשְׂרָאֵל וַיִּירְשׁוּ אֶת־עִיר הַתְּמָרִים: ¹⁴ וַיַּעַבְדוּ בְנֵי־ יִשְׂרָאֵל אֶת־עֶגְלוֹן מֶלֶךְ־מוֹאָב שְׁמוֹנֶה עֶשְׂרֵה שָׁנָה: ס ¹⁵ וַיִּזְעֲקוּ בְנֵי־יִשְׂרָאֵל אֶל־יְהֹוָה וַיָּקֶם יְהֹוָה לָהֶם מוֹשִׁיעַ אֶת־אֵהוּד בֶּן־גֵּרָא בֶּן־ הַיְמִינִי אִישׁ אִטֵּר יַד־יְמִינוֹ וַיִּשְׁלְחוּ בְנֵי־יִשְׂרָאֵל בְּיָדוֹ מִנְחָה לְעֶגְלוֹן מֶלֶךְ מוֹאָב: ¹⁶ וַיַּעַשׂ לוֹ אֵהוּד חֶרֶב וְלָהּ שְׁנֵי פֵיוֹת גֹּמֶד אָרְכָּהּ וַיַּחְגֹּר אוֹתָהּ מִתַּחַת לְמַדָּיו עַל יֶרֶךְ יְמִינוֹ: ¹⁷ וַיַּקְרֵב אֶת־הַמִּנְחָה לְעֶגְלוֹן מֶלֶךְ מוֹאָב וְעֶגְלוֹן אִישׁ בָּרִיא מְאֹד: ¹⁸ וַיְהִי כַּאֲשֶׁר כִּלָּה לְהַקְרִיב אֶת־ הַמִּנְחָה וַיְשַׁלַּח אֶת־הָעָם נֹשְׂאֵי הַמִּנְחָה: ¹⁹ וְהוּא שָׁב מִן־הַפְּסִילִים אֲשֶׁר אֶת־הַגִּלְגָּל וַיֹּאמֶר דְּבַר־ סֵתֶר לִי אֵלֶיךָ הַמֶּלֶךְ וַיֹּאמֶר הָס וַיֵּצְאוּ מֵעָלָיו

²⁰ So Ehud came to him (now he was sitting upstairs in his cool private chamber). Then Ehud said, "I have a message from God for you." So he arose from *his* seat. ²¹ Then Ehud reached with his left hand, took the dagger from his right thigh, and thrust it into his belly. ²² Even the hilt went in after the blade, and the fat closed over the blade, for he did not draw the dagger out of his belly; and his entrails came out. ²³ Then Ehud went out through the porch and shut the doors of the upper room behind him and locked them.

²⁴ When he had gone out, *Eglon's* servants came to look, and *to their* surprise, the doors of the upper room were locked. So they said, "He is probably attending to his needs in the cool chamber." ²⁵ So they waited till they were embarrassed, and still he had not opened the doors of the upper room. Therefore they took the key and opened *them*. And there was their master, fallen dead on the floor.

²⁶ But Ehud had escaped while they delayed, and passed beyond the stone images and escaped to Seirah. ²⁷ And it happened, when he arrived, that he blew the trumpet in the mountains of Ephraim, and the children of Israel went down with him from the mountains; and he led them. ²⁸ Then he said to them, "Follow *me*, for the LORD has delivered your enemies the Moabites into your hand." So they went down after him, seized the fords of the Jordan leading to Moab, and did not allow anyone to cross over. ²⁹ And at that time they killed about ten thousand men of Moab, all stout men of valor; not a man escaped. ³⁰ So Moab was subdued that day under the hand of Israel. And the land had rest for eighty years.

³¹ After him was Shamgar the son of Anath, who killed six hundred men of the Philistines with an ox goad; and he also delivered Israel.

4 When Ehud was dead, the children of Israel again did evil in the sight of the LORD. ² So the LORD sold them into the hand of Jabin king of Canaan, who reigned in Hazor. The commander of his army *was* Sisera, who dwelt in Harosheth Hagoyim. ³ And the children of Israel cried out to the LORD; for Jabin had nine hundred chariots of iron, and for twenty years he had harshly oppressed the children of Israel.

⁴ Now Deborah, a prophetess, the wife of Lapidoth, was judging Israel at that time. ⁵ And she would sit under the palm tree of Deborah between Ramah and Bethel in the mountains of Ephraim. And the children of Israel came up to her for judgment. ⁶ Then she sent and called for Barak the son of Abinoam from Kedesh in Naphtali, and

20 וְאֵהוּד ׀ בָּא אֵלָיו וְהוּא־יֹשֵׁב בַּעֲלִיַּת הַמְּקֵרָה אֲשֶׁר־לוֹ לְבַדּוֹ וַיֹּאמֶר אֵהוּד דְּבַר־אֱלֹהִים לִי אֵלֶיךָ וַיָּקָם מֵעַל הַכִּסֵּא: 21 וַיִּשְׁלַח אֵהוּד אֶת־יַד שְׂמֹאלוֹ וַיִּקַּח אֶת־הַחֶרֶב מֵעַל יֶרֶךְ יְמִינוֹ וַיִּתְקָעֶהָ בְּבִטְנוֹ: 22 וַיָּבֹא גַם־הַנִּצָּב אַחַר הַלַּהַב וַיִּסְגֹּר הַחֵלֶב בְּעַד הַלַּהַב כִּי לֹא שָׁלַף הַחֶרֶב מִבִּטְנוֹ וַיֵּצֵא הַפַּרְשְׁדֹנָה: 23 וַיֵּצֵא אֵהוּד הַמִּסְדְּרוֹנָה וַיִּסְגֹּר דַּלְתוֹת הָעֲלִיָּה בַּעֲדוֹ וְנָעָל: 24 וְהוּא יָצָא וַעֲבָדָיו בָּאוּ וַיִּרְאוּ וְהִנֵּה דַּלְתוֹת הָעֲלִיָּה נְעֻלוֹת וַיֹּאמְרוּ אַךְ מֵסִיךְ הוּא אֶת־רַגְלָיו בַּחֲדַר הַמְּקֵרָה: 25 וַיָּחִילוּ עַד־בּוֹשׁ וְהִנֵּה אֵינֶנּוּ פֹּתֵחַ דַּלְתוֹת הָעֲלִיָּה וַיִּקְחוּ אֶת־הַמַּפְתֵּחַ וַיִּפְתָּחוּ וְהִנֵּה אֲדֹנֵיהֶם נֹפֵל אַרְצָה מֵת: 26 וְאֵהוּד נִמְלַט עַד הִתְמַהְמְהָם וְהוּא עָבַר אֶת־הַפְּסִילִים וַיִּמָּלֵט הַשְּׂעִירָתָה: 27 וַיְהִי בְּבוֹאוֹ וַיִּתְקַע בַּשּׁוֹפָר בְּהַר אֶפְרָיִם וַיֵּרְדוּ עִמּוֹ בְנֵי־יִשְׂרָאֵל מִן־הָהָר וְהוּא לִפְנֵיהֶם: 28 וַיֹּאמֶר אֲלֵהֶם רִדְפוּ אַחֲרַי כִּי־נָתַן יְהֹוָה אֶת־אֹיְבֵיכֶם אֶת־מוֹאָב בְּיֶדְכֶם וַיֵּרְדוּ אַחֲרָיו וַיִּלְכְּדוּ אֶת־מַעְבְּרוֹת הַיַּרְדֵּן לְמוֹאָב וְלֹא־נָתְנוּ אִישׁ לַעֲבֹר: 29 וַיַּכּוּ אֶת־מוֹאָב בָּעֵת הַהִיא כַּעֲשֶׂרֶת אֲלָפִים אִישׁ כָּל־שָׁמֵן וְכָל־אִישׁ חָיִל וְלֹא נִמְלַט אִישׁ: 30 וַתִּכָּנַע מוֹאָב בַּיּוֹם הַהוּא תַּחַת יַד יִשְׂרָאֵל וַתִּשְׁקֹט הָאָרֶץ שְׁמוֹנִים שָׁנָה: ס 31 וְאַחֲרָיו הָיָה שַׁמְגַּר בֶּן־עֲנָת וַיַּךְ אֶת־פְּלִשְׁתִּים שֵׁשׁ־מֵאוֹת אִישׁ בְּמַלְמַד הַבָּקָר וַיֹּשַׁע גַּם־הוּא אֶת־יִשְׂרָאֵל: ס

ד וַיֹּסִפוּ בְּנֵי יִשְׂרָאֵל לַעֲשׂוֹת הָרַע בְּעֵינֵי יְהֹוָה וְאֵהוּד מֵת: 2 וַיִּמְכְּרֵם יְהֹוָה בְּיַד יָבִין מֶלֶךְ־כְּנַעַן אֲשֶׁר מָלַךְ בְּחָצוֹר וְשַׂר־צְבָאוֹ סִיסְרָא וְהוּא יוֹשֵׁב בַּחֲרֹשֶׁת הַגּוֹיִם: 3 וַיִּצְעֲקוּ בְנֵי־יִשְׂרָאֵל אֶל־יְהֹוָה כִּי תְּשַׁע מֵאוֹת רֶכֶב־בַּרְזֶל לוֹ וְהוּא לָחַץ אֶת־בְּנֵי יִשְׂרָאֵל בְּחָזְקָה עֶשְׂרִים שָׁנָה: ס 4 וּדְבוֹרָה אִשָּׁה נְבִיאָה אֵשֶׁת לַפִּידוֹת הִיא שֹׁפְטָה אֶת־יִשְׂרָאֵל בָּעֵת הַהִיא: 5 וְהִיא יוֹשֶׁבֶת תַּחַת־תֹּמֶר דְּבוֹרָה בֵּין הָרָמָה וּבֵין בֵּית־אֵל בְּהַר אֶפְרָיִם וַיַּעֲלוּ אֵלֶיהָ בְּנֵי יִשְׂרָאֵל לַמִּשְׁפָּט: ס 6 וַתִּשְׁלַח וַתִּקְרָא לְבָרָק בֶּן־אֲבִינֹעַם

said to him, "Has not the LORD God of Israel commanded, 'Go and deploy *troops* at Mount Tabor; take with you ten thousand men of the sons of Naphtali and of the sons of Zebulun; ⁷ and against you I will deploy Sisera, the commander of Jabin's army, with his chariots and his multitude at the River Kishon; and I will deliver him into your hand'?"

⁸ And Barak said to her, "If you will go with me, then I will go; but if you will not go with me, I will not go!"

⁹ So she said, "I will surely go with you; nevertheless there will be no glory for you in the journey you are taking, for the LORD will sell Sisera into the hand of a woman." Then Deborah arose and went with Barak to Kedesh. ¹⁰ And Barak called Zebulun and Naphtali to Kedesh; he went up with ten thousand men under his command, and Deborah went up with him.

¹¹ Now Heber the Kenite, of the children of Hobab the father-in-law of Moses, had separated himself from the Kenites and pitched his tent near the terebinth tree at Zaanaim, which *is* beside Kedesh.

¹² And they reported to Sisera that Barak the son of Abinoam had gone up to Mount Tabor. ¹³ So Sisera gathered together all his chariots, nine hundred chariots of iron, and all the people who *were* with him, from Harosheth Hagoyim to the River Kishon.

¹⁴ Then Deborah said to Barak, "Up! For this *is* the day in which the LORD has delivered Sisera into your hand. Has not the LORD gone out before you?" So Barak went down from Mount Tabor with ten thousand men following him. ¹⁵ And the LORD routed Sisera and all *his* chariots and all *his* army with the edge of the sword before Barak; and Sisera alighted from *his* chariot and fled away on foot. ¹⁶ But Barak pursued the chariots and the army as far as Harosheth Hagoyim, and all the army of Sisera fell by the edge of the sword; not a man was left.

¹⁷ However, Sisera had fled away on foot to the tent of Jael, the wife of Heber the Kenite; for *there was* peace between Jabin king of Hazor and the house of Heber the Kenite. ¹⁸ And Jael went out to meet Sisera, and said to him, "Turn aside, my lord, turn aside to me; do not fear." And when he had turned aside with her into the tent, she covered him with a blanket.

¹⁹ Then he said to her, "Please give me a little water to drink, for I am thirsty." So she opened a jug of milk, gave him a drink, and covered him.

מִקֶּדֶשׁ נַפְתָּלִי וַתֹּאמֶר אֵלָיו הֲלֹא צִוָּה | יְהוָה
אֱלֹהֵי־יִשְׂרָאֵל לֵךְ וּמָשַׁכְתָּ בְּהַר תָּבוֹר וְלָקַחְתָּ עִמְּךָ
עֲשֶׂרֶת אֲלָפִים אִישׁ מִבְּנֵי נַפְתָּלִי וּמִבְּנֵי זְבֻלוּן:
⁷ וּמָשַׁכְתִּי אֵלֶיךָ אֶל־נַחַל קִישׁוֹן אֶת־סִיסְרָא שַׂר־
צְבָא יָבִין וְאֶת־רִכְבּוֹ וְאֶת־הֲמוֹנוֹ וּנְתַתִּיהוּ בְּיָדֶךָ:
⁸ וַיֹּאמֶר אֵלֶיהָ בָּרָק אִם־תֵּלְכִי עִמִּי וְהָלָכְתִּי וְאִם־
לֹא תֵלְכִי עִמִּי לֹא אֵלֵךְ: ⁹ וַתֹּאמֶר הָלֹךְ אֵלֵךְ
עִמָּךְ אֶפֶס כִּי לֹא תִהְיֶה תִּפְאַרְתְּךָ עַל־הַדֶּרֶךְ
אֲשֶׁר אַתָּה הוֹלֵךְ כִּי בְיַד־אִשָּׁה יִמְכֹּר יְהוָה אֶת־
סִיסְרָא וַתָּקָם דְּבוֹרָה וַתֵּלֶךְ עִם־בָּרָק קֶדְשָׁה:
¹⁰ וַיַּזְעֵק בָּרָק אֶת־זְבוּלֻן וְאֶת־נַפְתָּלִי קֶדְשָׁה וַיַּעַל
בְּרַגְלָיו עֲשֶׂרֶת אַלְפֵי אִישׁ וַתַּעַל עִמּוֹ דְּבוֹרָה:
¹¹ וְחֶבֶר הַקֵּינִי נִפְרָד מִקַּיִן מִבְּנֵי חֹבָב חֹתֵן מֹשֶׁה
וַיֵּט אָהֳלוֹ עַד־אֵלוֹן בְּצַעֲנַנִּים⁶ אֲשֶׁר אֶת־קֶדֶשׁ:
¹² וַיַּגִּדוּ לְסִיסְרָא כִּי עָלָה בָּרָק בֶּן־אֲבִינֹעַם הַר־
תָּבוֹר: ס ¹³ וַיַּזְעֵק סִיסְרָא אֶת־כָּל־רִכְבּוֹ
תְּשַׁע מֵאוֹת רֶכֶב בַּרְזֶל וְאֶת־כָּל־הָעָם אֲשֶׁר אִתּוֹ
מֵחֲרֹשֶׁת הַגּוֹיִם אֶל־נַחַל קִישׁוֹן: ¹⁴ וַתֹּאמֶר דְּבֹרָה
אֶל־בָּרָק קוּם כִּי זֶה הַיּוֹם אֲשֶׁר נָתַן יְהוָה אֶת־
סִיסְרָא בְּיָדֶךָ הֲלֹא יְהוָה יָצָא לְפָנֶיךָ וַיֵּרֶד בָּרָק
מֵהַר תָּבוֹר וַעֲשֶׂרֶת אֲלָפִים אִישׁ אַחֲרָיו: ¹⁵ וַיָּהָם
יְהוָה אֶת־סִיסְרָא וְאֶת־כָּל־הָרֶכֶב וְאֶת־כָּל־הַמַּחֲנֶה
לְפִי־חֶרֶב לִפְנֵי בָרָק וַיֵּרֶד סִיסְרָא מֵעַל הַמֶּרְכָּבָה
וַיָּנָס בְּרַגְלָיו: ¹⁶ וּבָרָק רָדַף אַחֲרֵי הָרֶכֶב וְאַחֲרֵי
הַמַּחֲנֶה עַד חֲרֹשֶׁת הַגּוֹיִם וַיִּפֹּל כָּל־מַחֲנֵה סִיסְרָא
לְפִי־חֶרֶב לֹא נִשְׁאַר עַד־אֶחָד: ¹⁷ וְסִיסְרָא נָס
בְּרַגְלָיו אֶל־אֹהֶל יָעֵל אֵשֶׁת חֶבֶר הַקֵּינִי כִּי שָׁלוֹם
בֵּין יָבִין מֶלֶךְ־חָצוֹר וּבֵין בֵּית חֶבֶר הַקֵּינִי: ¹⁸ וַתֵּצֵא
יָעֵל לִקְרַאת סִיסְרָא וַתֹּאמֶר אֵלָיו סוּרָה אֲדֹנִי
סוּרָה אֵלַי אַל־תִּירָא וַיָּסַר אֵלֶיהָ הָאֹהֱלָה וַתְּכַסֵּהוּ
בַּשְּׂמִיכָה: ¹⁹ וַיֹּאמֶר אֵלֶיהָ הַשְׁקִינִי־נָא מְעַט־מַיִם
כִּי צָמֵאתִי וַתִּפְתַּח אֶת־נֹאוד הֶחָלָב

20 And he said to her, "Stand at the door of the tent, and if any man comes and inquires of you, and says, 'Is there any man here?' you shall say, 'No.'"

21 Then Jael, Heber's wife, took a tent peg and took a hammer in her hand, and went softly to him and drove the peg into his temple, and it went down into the ground; for he was fast asleep and weary. So he died. 22 And then, as Barak pursued Sisera, Jael came out to meet him, and said to him, "Come, I will show you the man whom you seek." And when he went into her *tent,* there lay Sisera, dead with the peg in his temple.

23 So on that day God subdued Jabin king of Canaan in the presence of the children of Israel. 24 And the hand of the children of Israel grew stronger and stronger against Jabin king of Canaan, until they had destroyed Jabin king of Canaan.

5 Then Deborah and Barak the son of Abinoam sang on that day, saying:

2   "When leaders lead in Israel,
    When the people willingly offer themselves,
    Bless the LORD!

3   "Hear, O kings! Give ear, O princes!
    I, *even* I, will sing to the LORD;
    I will sing praise to the LORD God of Israel.

4   "LORD, when You went out from Seir,
    When You marched from the field of Edom,
    The earth trembled and the heavens poured,
    The clouds also poured water;
5   The mountains gushed before the LORD,
    This Sinai, before the LORD God of Israel.

6   "In the days of Shamgar, son of Anath,
    In the days of Jael,
    The highways were deserted,
    And the travelers walked along the byways.
7   Village life ceased, it ceased in Israel,
    Until I, Deborah, arose,
    Arose a mother in Israel.
8   They chose new gods;
    Then *there was* war in the gates;
    Not a shield or spear was seen among forty
      thousand in Israel.
9   My heart *is* with the rulers of Israel
    Who offered themselves willingly with the
      people.
    Bless the LORD!

10 "Speak, you who ride on white donkeys,
    Who sit in judges' attire,
    And who walk along the road.
11 Far from the noise of the archers, among the
    watering places,

20 וַיֹּאמֶר אֵלֶיהָ עֲמֹד פֶּתַח הָאֹהֶל וְהָיָה אִם־אִישׁ יָבוֹא וּשְׁאֵלֵךְ וְאָמַר הֲיֵשׁ־פֹּה אִישׁ וְאָמַרְתְּ אָיִן: 21 וַתִּקַּח יָעֵל אֵשֶׁת־חֶבֶר אֶת־יְתַד הָאֹהֶל וַתָּשֶׂם אֶת־הַמַּקֶּבֶת בְּיָדָהּ וַתָּבוֹא אֵלָיו בַּלָּאט וַתִּתְקַע אֶת־הַיָּתֵד בְּרַקָּתוֹ וַתִּצְנַח בָּאָרֶץ וְהוּא־נִרְדָּם וַיָּעַף וַיָּמֹת: 22 וְהִנֵּה בָרָק רֹדֵף אֶת־סִיסְרָא וַתֵּצֵא יָעֵל לִקְרָאתוֹ וַתֹּאמֶר לוֹ לֵךְ וְאַרְאֶךָּ אֶת־הָאִישׁ אֲשֶׁר־אַתָּה מְבַקֵּשׁ וַיָּבֹא אֵלֶיהָ וְהִנֵּה סִיסְרָא נֹפֵל מֵת וְהַיָּתֵד בְּרַקָּתוֹ: 23 וַיַּכְנַע אֱלֹהִים בַּיּוֹם הַהוּא אֵת יָבִין מֶלֶךְ־כְּנָעַן לִפְנֵי בְּנֵי יִשְׂרָאֵל: 24 וַתֵּלֶךְ יַד בְּנֵי־יִשְׂרָאֵל הָלוֹךְ וְקָשָׁה עַל יָבִין מֶלֶךְ־כְּנָעַן עַד אֲשֶׁר הִכְרִיתוּ אֵת יָבִין מֶלֶךְ־כְּנָעַן: פ

ה וַתָּשַׁר דְּבוֹרָה וּבָרָק בֶּן־אֲבִינֹעַם בַּיּוֹם הַהוּא לֵאמֹר:
2 בִּפְרֹעַ פְּרָעוֹת בְּיִשְׂרָאֵל בְּהִתְנַדֵּב עָם בָּרְכוּ יְהוָה:
3 שִׁמְעוּ מְלָכִים הַאֲזִינוּ רֹזְנִים אָנֹכִי לַיהוָה אָנֹכִי אָשִׁירָה אֲזַמֵּר לַיהוָה אֱלֹהֵי יִשְׂרָאֵל:
4 יְהוָה בְּצֵאתְךָ מִשֵּׂעִיר בְּצַעְדְּךָ מִשְּׂדֵה אֱדוֹם אֶרֶץ רָעָשָׁה גַּם־שָׁמַיִם נָטָפוּ גַּם־עָבִים נָטְפוּ מָיִם:
5 הָרִים נָזְלוּ מִפְּנֵי יְהוָה זֶה סִינַי מִפְּנֵי יְהוָה אֱלֹהֵי יִשְׂרָאֵל:
6 בִּימֵי שַׁמְגַּר בֶּן־עֲנָת בִּימֵי יָעֵל חָדְלוּ אֳרָחוֹת וְהֹלְכֵי נְתִיבוֹת יֵלְכוּ אֳרָחוֹת עֲקַלְקַלּוֹת:
7 חָדְלוּ פְרָזוֹן בְּיִשְׂרָאֵל חָדֵלּוּ עַד שַׁקַּמְתִּי דְּבוֹרָה שַׁקַּמְתִּי אֵם בְּיִשְׂרָאֵל:
8 יִבְחַר אֱלֹהִים חֲדָשִׁים אָז לָחֶם שְׁעָרִים מָגֵן אִם־יֵרָאֶה וָרֹמַח בְּאַרְבָּעִים אֶלֶף בְּיִשְׂרָאֵל:
9 לִבִּי לְחוֹקְקֵי יִשְׂרָאֵל הַמִּתְנַדְּבִים בָּעָם בָּרְכוּ יְהוָה:
10 רֹכְבֵי אֲתֹנוֹת צְחֹרוֹת יֹשְׁבֵי עַל־מִדִּין וְהֹלְכֵי עַל־דֶּרֶךְ שִׂיחוּ:
11 מִקּוֹל מְחַצְצִים בֵּין מַשְׁאַבִּים שָׁם יְתַנּוּ צִדְקוֹת יְהוָה

There they shall recount the righteous acts of
the LORD,
The righteous acts *for* His villagers in Israel;
Then the people of the LORD shall go down
to the gates.

¹² "Awake, awake, Deborah!
Awake, awake, sing a song!
Arise, Barak, and lead your captives away,
O son of Abinoam!

¹³ "Then the survivors came down, the people
against the nobles;
The LORD came down for me against the
mighty.

¹⁴ From Ephraim *were* those whose roots were
in Amalek.
After you, Benjamin, with your peoples,
From Machir rulers came down,
And from Zebulun those who bear the
recruiter's staff.

¹⁵ And the princes of Issachar *were* with
Deborah;
As Issachar, so *was* Barak
Sent into the valley under his command;
Among the divisions of Reuben
There were great resolves of heart.

¹⁶ Why did you sit among the sheepfolds,
To hear the pipings for the flocks?
The divisions of Reuben have great search-
ings of heart.

¹⁷ Gilead stayed beyond the Jordan,
And why did Dan remain on ships?
Asher continued at the seashore,
And stayed by his inlets.

¹⁸ Zebulun *is* a people *who* jeopardized their
lives to the point of death,
Naphtali also, on the heights of the
battlefield.

¹⁹ "The kings came *and* fought,
Then the kings of Canaan fought
In Taanach, by the waters of Megiddo;
They took no spoils of silver.

²⁰ They fought from the heavens;
The stars from their courses fought against
Sisera.

²¹ The torrent of Kishon swept them away,
That ancient torrent, the torrent of Kishon.
O my soul, march on in strength!

²² Then the horses' hooves pounded,
The galloping, galloping of his steeds.

²³ 'Curse Meroz,' said the angel of the LORD,
'Curse its inhabitants bitterly,
Because they did not come to the help of the
LORD,

צִדְקֹת פִּרְזֹנוֹ בְּיִשְׂרָאֵל
אָז יָרְדוּ לַשְּׁעָרִים עַם־יְהוָה:
עוּרִי עוּרִי דְּבוֹרָה 12
עוּרִי עוּרִי דַּבְּרִי־שִׁיר
קוּם בָּרָק וּשֲׁבֵה שֶׁבְיְךָ בֶּן־אֲבִינֹעַם:
אָז יְרַד שָׂרִיד לְאַדִּירִים עָם 13
יְהוָה יְרַד־לִי בַּגִּבּוֹרִים:
מִנִּי אֶפְרַיִם שָׁרְשָׁם בַּעֲמָלֵק 14
אַחֲרֶיךָ בִנְיָמִין בַּעֲמָמֶיךָ
מִנִּי מָכִיר יָרְדוּ מְחֹקְקִים
וּמִזְּבוּלֻן מֹשְׁכִים בְּשֵׁבֶט סֹפֵר:
וְשָׂרַי בְּיִשָּׂשכָר עִם־דְּבֹרָה 15
וְיִשָּׂשכָר כֵּן בָּרָק בָּעֵמֶק שֻׁלַּח בְּרַגְלָיו
בִּפְלַגּוֹת רְאוּבֵן גְּדֹלִים חִקְקֵי־לֵב:
לָמָּה יָשַׁבְתָּ בֵּין הַמִּשְׁפְּתַיִם 16
לִשְׁמֹעַ שְׁרִקוֹת עֲדָרִים
לִפְלַגּוֹת רְאוּבֵן גְּדוֹלִים חִקְרֵי־לֵב:
גִּלְעָד בְּעֵבֶר הַיַּרְדֵּן שָׁכֵן 17
וְדָן לָמָּה יָגוּר אֳנִיּוֹת
אָשֵׁר יָשַׁב לְחוֹף יַמִּים
וְעַל מִפְרָצָיו יִשְׁכּוֹן:
זְבֻלוּן עַם חֵרֵף נַפְשׁוֹ לָמוּת 18
וְנַפְתָּלִי עַל מְרוֹמֵי שָׂדֶה:
בָּאוּ מְלָכִים נִלְחָמוּ 19
אָז נִלְחֲמוּ מַלְכֵי כְנַעַן
בְּתַעְנַךְ עַל־מֵי מְגִדּוֹ
בֶּצַע כֶּסֶף לֹא לָקָחוּ:
מִן־שָׁמַיִם נִלְחָמוּ 20
הַכּוֹכָבִים מִמְּסִלּוֹתָם נִלְחֲמוּ עִם־סִיסְרָא:
נַחַל קִישׁוֹן גְּרָפָם 21
נַחַל קְדוּמִים נַחַל קִישׁוֹן
תִּדְרְכִי נַפְשִׁי עֹז:
אָז הָלְמוּ עִקְּבֵי־סוּס 22
מִדַּהֲרוֹת דַּהֲרוֹת אַבִּירָיו:
אוֹרוּ מֵרוֹז אָמַר מַלְאַךְ יְהוָה 23
אֹרוּ אָרוֹר יֹשְׁבֶיהָ

To the help of the LORD against the mighty.'

כִּי לֹא־בָאוּ לְעֶזְרַת יְהוָה
לְעֶזְרַת יְהוָה בַּגִּבּוֹרִים:

24 "Most blessed among women is Jael,
   The wife of Heber the Kenite;
   Blessed is she among women in tents.

24 תְּבֹרַךְ מִנָּשִׁים יָעֵל אֵשֶׁת חֶבֶר הַקֵּינִי
   מִנָּשִׁים בָּאֹהֶל תְּבֹרָךְ:

25 He asked for water, she gave milk;
   She brought out cream in a lordly bowl.

25 מַיִם שָׁאַל חָלָב נָתָנָה
   בְּסֵפֶל אַדִּירִים הִקְרִיבָה חֶמְאָה:

26 She stretched her hand to the tent peg,
   Her right hand to the workmen's hammer;
   She pounded Sisera, she pierced his head,
   She split and struck through his temple.

26 יָדָהּ לַיָּתֵד תִּשְׁלַחְנָה
   וִימִינָהּ לְהַלְמוּת עֲמֵלִים
   וְהָלְמָה סִיסְרָא מָחֲקָה רֹאשׁוֹ
   וּמָחֲצָה וְחָלְפָה רַקָּתוֹ:

27 At her feet he sank, he fell, he lay still;
   At her feet he sank, he fell;
   Where he sank, there he fell dead.

27 בֵּין רַגְלֶיהָ כָּרַע נָפַל שָׁכָב
   בֵּין רַגְלֶיהָ כָּרַע נָפָל
   בַּאֲשֶׁר כָּרַע שָׁם נָפַל שָׁדוּד:

28 "The mother of Sisera looked through the
   window,
   And cried out through the lattice,
   'Why is his chariot so long in coming?
   Why tarries the clatter of his chariots?'

28 בְּעַד הַחַלּוֹן נִשְׁקְפָה וַתְּיַבֵּב אֵם סִיסְרָא
   בְּעַד הָאֶשְׁנָב
   מַדּוּעַ בֹּשֵׁשׁ רִכְבּוֹ לָבוֹא
   מַדּוּעַ אֶחֱרוּ פַּעֲמֵי מַרְכְּבוֹתָיו:

29 Her wisest ladies answered her,
   Yes, she answered herself,

29 חַכְמוֹת שָׂרוֹתֶיהָ תַּעֲנֶינָּה
   אַף־הִיא תָּשִׁיב אֲמָרֶיהָ לָהּ:

30 'Are they not finding and dividing the spoil:
   To every man a girl or two;
   For Sisera, plunder of dyed garments,
   Plunder of garments embroidered and dyed,
   Two pieces of dyed embroidery for the neck
   of the looter?'

30 הֲלֹא יִמְצְאוּ יְחַלְּקוּ שָׁלָל
   רַחַם רַחֲמָתַיִם לְרֹאשׁ גֶּבֶר
   שְׁלַל צְבָעִים לְסִיסְרָא
   שְׁלַל צְבָעִים רִקְמָה
   צֶבַע רִקְמָתַיִם לְצַוְּארֵי שָׁלָל:

31 "Thus let all Your enemies perish, O LORD!
   But let those who love Him be like the sun
   When it comes out in full strength."

31 כֵּן יֹאבְדוּ כָל־אוֹיְבֶיךָ יְהוָה
   וְאֹהֲבָיו כְּצֵאת הַשֶּׁמֶשׁ בִּגְבֻרָתוֹ

So the land had rest for forty years.

פ   וַתִּשְׁקֹט הָאָרֶץ אַרְבָּעִים שָׁנָה:

6 Then the children of Israel did evil in the sight of
the LORD. So the LORD delivered them into the
hand of Midian for seven years, ²and the hand of
Midian prevailed against Israel. Because of the
Midianites, the children of Israel made for themselves the dens, the caves, and the strongholds
which are in the mountains. ³So it was, whenever
Israel had sown, Midianites would come up; also
Amalekites and the people of the East would come
up against them. ⁴Then they would encamp against
them and destroy the produce of the earth as far as
Gaza, and leave no sustenance for Israel, neither
sheep nor ox nor donkey. ⁵For they would come up
with their livestock and their tents, coming in as
numerous as locusts; both they and their camels
were without number; and they would enter the
land to destroy it. ⁶So Israel was greatly impoverished because of the Midianites, and the children of
Israel cried out to the LORD.

ו וַיַּעֲשׂוּ בְנֵי־יִשְׂרָאֵל הָרַע בְּעֵינֵי יְהוָה וַיִּתְּנֵם
יְהוָה בְּיַד־מִדְיָן שֶׁבַע שָׁנִים: ² וַתָּעָז יַד־מִדְיָן עַל־
יִשְׂרָאֵל מִפְּנֵי מִדְיָן עָשׂוּ לָהֶם ׀ בְּנֵי יִשְׂרָאֵל
אֶת־הַמִּנְהָרוֹת אֲשֶׁר בֶּהָרִים וְאֶת־הַמְּעָרוֹת וְאֶת־
הַמְּצָדוֹת: ³ וְהָיָה אִם־זָרַע יִשְׂרָאֵל וְעָלָה מִדְיָן
וַעֲמָלֵק וּבְנֵי־קֶדֶם וְעָלוּ עָלָיו: ⁴ וַיַּחֲנוּ עֲלֵיהֶם
וַיַּשְׁחִיתוּ אֶת־יְבוּל הָאָרֶץ עַד־בּוֹאֲךָ עַזָּה וְלֹא־
יַשְׁאִירוּ מִחְיָה בְּיִשְׂרָאֵל וְשֶׂה וָשׁוֹר וַחֲמוֹר: ⁵ כִּי
הֵם וּמִקְנֵיהֶם יַעֲלוּ וְאָהֳלֵיהֶם יָבֹאוּ כְדֵי־אַרְבֶּה
לָרֹב וְלָהֶם וְלִגְמַלֵּיהֶם אֵין מִסְפָּר וַיָּבֹאוּ בָאָרֶץ
לְשַׁחֲתָהּ: ⁶ וַיִּדַּל יִשְׂרָאֵל מְאֹד מִפְּנֵי מִדְיָן וַיִּזְעֲקוּ
פ   בְּנֵי־יִשְׂרָאֵל אֶל־יְהוָה:

7 And it came to pass, when the children of Israel cried out to the LORD because of the Midianites, 8 that the LORD sent a prophet to the children of Israel, who said to them, "Thus says the LORD God of Israel: 'I brought you up from Egypt and brought you out of the house of bondage; 9 and I delivered you out of the hand of the Egyptians and out of the hand of all who oppressed you, and drove them out before you and gave you their land. 10 Also I said to you, "I *am* the LORD your God; do not fear the gods of the Amorites, in whose land you dwell." But you have not obeyed My voice.'"

11 Now the Angel of the LORD came and sat under the terebinth tree which *was* in Ophrah, which *belonged* to Joash the Abiezrite, while his son Gideon threshed wheat in the winepress, in order to hide *it* from the Midianites. 12 And the Angel of the LORD appeared to him, and said to him, "The LORD *is* with you, you mighty man of valor!"

13 Gideon said to Him, "O my lord, if the LORD is with us, why then has all this happened to us? And where *are* all His miracles which our fathers told us about, saying, 'Did not the LORD bring us up from Egypt?' But now the LORD has forsaken us and delivered us into the hands of the Midianites."

14 Then the LORD turned to him and said, "Go in this might of yours, and you shall save Israel from the hand of the Midianites. Have I not sent you?"

15 So he said to Him, "O my Lord, how can I save Israel? Indeed my clan *is* the weakest in Manasseh, and I *am* the least in my father's house."

16 And the LORD said to him, "Surely I will be with you, and you shall defeat the Midianites as one man."

17 Then he said to Him, "If now I have found favor in Your sight, then show me a sign that it is You who talk with me. 18 Do not depart from here, I pray, until I come to You and bring out my offering and set *it* before You."

And He said, "I will wait until you come back."

19 So Gideon went in and prepared a young goat, and unleavened bread from an ephah of flour. The meat he put in a basket, and he put the broth in a pot; and he brought *them* out to Him under the terebinth tree and presented *them*. 20 The Angel of God said to him, "Take the meat and the unleavened bread and lay *them* on this rock, and pour out the broth." And he did so.

21 Then the Angel of the LORD put out the end of the staff that *was* in His hand, and touched the meat and the unleavened bread; and fire rose out of the rock and consumed the meat and the unleavened bread. And the Angel of the LORD departed out of his sight.

7 וַיְהִי כִּי־זָעֲקוּ בְנֵי־יִשְׂרָאֵל אֶל־יְהֹוָה עַל אֹדוֹת מִדְיָן: 8 וַיִּשְׁלַח יְהֹוָה אִישׁ נָבִיא אֶל־בְּנֵי יִשְׂרָאֵל וַיֹּאמֶר לָהֶם כֹּה־אָמַר יְהֹוָה ׀ אֱלֹהֵי יִשְׂרָאֵל אָנֹכִי הֶעֱלֵיתִי אֶתְכֶם מִמִּצְרַיִם וָאֹצִיא אֶתְכֶם מִבֵּית עֲבָדִים: 9 וָאַצִּל אֶתְכֶם מִיַּד מִצְרַיִם וּמִיַּד כָּל־לֹחֲצֵיכֶם וָאֲגָרֵשׁ אוֹתָם מִפְּנֵיכֶם וָאֶתְּנָה לָכֶם אֶת־אַרְצָם: 10 וָאֹמְרָה לָכֶם אֲנִי יְהֹוָה אֱלֹהֵיכֶם לֹא תִירְאוּ אֶת־אֱלֹהֵי הָאֱמֹרִי אֲשֶׁר אַתֶּם יוֹשְׁבִים בְּאַרְצָם וְלֹא שְׁמַעְתֶּם בְּקוֹלִי: פ

11 וַיָּבֹא מַלְאַךְ יְהֹוָה וַיֵּשֶׁב תַּחַת הָאֵלָה אֲשֶׁר בְּעָפְרָה אֲשֶׁר לְיוֹאָשׁ אֲבִי הָעֶזְרִי וְגִדְעוֹן בְּנוֹ חֹבֵט חִטִּים בַּגַּת לְהָנִיס מִפְּנֵי מִדְיָן: 12 וַיֵּרָא אֵלָיו מַלְאַךְ יְהֹוָה וַיֹּאמֶר אֵלָיו יְהֹוָה עִמְּךָ גִּבּוֹר הֶחָיִל:

13 וַיֹּאמֶר אֵלָיו גִּדְעוֹן בִּי אֲדֹנִי וְיֵשׁ יְהֹוָה עִמָּנוּ וְלָמָּה מְצָאַתְנוּ כָּל־זֹאת וְאַיֵּה כָל־נִפְלְאֹתָיו אֲשֶׁר סִפְּרוּ־לָנוּ אֲבוֹתֵינוּ לֵאמֹר הֲלֹא מִמִּצְרַיִם הֶעֱלָנוּ יְהֹוָה וְעַתָּה נְטָשָׁנוּ יְהֹוָה וַיִּתְּנֵנוּ בְּכַף־מִדְיָן: 14 וַיִּפֶן אֵלָיו יְהֹוָה וַיֹּאמֶר לֵךְ בְּכֹחֲךָ זֶה וְהוֹשַׁעְתָּ אֶת־יִשְׂרָאֵל מִכַּף מִדְיָן הֲלֹא שְׁלַחְתִּיךָ: 15 וַיֹּאמֶר אֵלָיו בִּי אֲדֹנָי בַּמָּה אוֹשִׁיעַ אֶת־יִשְׂרָאֵל הִנֵּה אַלְפִּי הַדַּל בִּמְנַשֶּׁה וְאָנֹכִי הַצָּעִיר בְּבֵית אָבִי: 16 וַיֹּאמֶר אֵלָיו יְהֹוָה כִּי אֶהְיֶה עִמָּךְ וְהִכִּיתָ אֶת־מִדְיָן כְּאִישׁ אֶחָד:

17 וַיֹּאמֶר אֵלָיו אִם־נָא מָצָאתִי חֵן בְּעֵינֶיךָ וְעָשִׂיתָ לִּי אוֹת שָׁאַתָּה מְדַבֵּר עִמִּי: 18 אַל־נָא תָמֻשׁ מִזֶּה עַד־בֹּאִי אֵלֶיךָ וְהֹצֵאתִי אֶת־מִנְחָתִי וְהִנַּחְתִּי לְפָנֶיךָ וַיֹּאמַר אָנֹכִי אֵשֵׁב עַד שׁוּבֶךָ: 19 וְגִדְעוֹן בָּא וַיַּעַשׂ גְּדִי־עִזִּים וְאֵיפַת־קֶמַח מַצּוֹת הַבָּשָׂר שָׂם בַּסַּל וְהַמָּרַק שָׂם בַּפָּרוּר וַיּוֹצֵא אֵלָיו אֶל־תַּחַת הָאֵלָה וַיַּגַּשׁ: ס 20 וַיֹּאמֶר אֵלָיו מַלְאַךְ הָאֱלֹהִים קַח אֶת־הַבָּשָׂר וְאֶת־הַמַּצּוֹת וְהַנַּח אֶל־הַסֶּלַע הַלָּז וְאֶת־הַמָּרַק שְׁפוֹךְ וַיַּעַשׂ כֵּן: 21 וַיִּשְׁלַח מַלְאַךְ יְהֹוָה אֶת־קְצֵה הַמִּשְׁעֶנֶת אֲשֶׁר בְּיָדוֹ וַיִּגַּע בַּבָּשָׂר וּבַמַּצּוֹת וַתַּעַל הָאֵשׁ מִן־הַצּוּר וַתֹּאכַל אֶת־הַבָּשָׂר

22 Now Gideon perceived that He *was* the Angel of the Lord. So Gideon said, "Alas, O Lord God! For I have seen the Angel of the Lord face to face."

23 Then the Lord said to him, "Peace *be* with you; do not fear, you shall not die." 24 So Gideon built an altar there to the Lord, and called it The-Lord-*Is*-Peace. To this day it *is* still in Ophrah of the Abiezrites.

25 Now it came to pass the same night that the Lord said to him, "Take your father's young bull, the second bull of seven years old, and tear down the altar of Baal that your father has, and cut down the wooden image that *is* beside it; 26 and build an altar to the Lord your God on top of this rock in the proper arrangement, and take the second bull and offer a burnt sacrifice with the wood of the image which you shall cut down." 27 So Gideon took ten men from among his servants and did as the Lord had said to him. But because he feared his father's household and the men of the city too much to do *it* by day, he did *it* by night.

28 And when the men of the city arose early in the morning, there was the altar of Baal, torn down; and the wooden image that *was* beside it was cut down, and the second bull was being offered on the altar *which had been* built. 29 So they said to one another, "Who has done this thing?" And when they had inquired and asked, they said, "Gideon the son of Joash has done this thing." 30 Then the men of the city said to Joash, "Bring out your son, that he may die, because he has torn down the altar of Baal, and because he has cut down the wooden image that *was* beside it."

31 But Joash said to all who stood against him, "Would you plead for Baal? Would you save him? Let the one who would plead for him be put to death by morning! If he *is* a god, let him plead for himself, because his altar has been torn down!" 32 Therefore on that day he called him Jerubbaal, saying, "Let Baal plead against him, because he has torn down his altar."

33 Then all the Midianites and Amalekites, the people of the East, gathered together; and they crossed over and encamped in the Valley of Jezreel. 34 But the Spirit of the Lord came upon Gideon; then he blew the trumpet, and the Abiezrites gathered behind him. 35 And he sent messengers throughout all Manasseh, who also gathered behind him. He also sent messengers to Asher, Zebulun, and Naphtali; and they came up to meet them.

36 So Gideon said to God, "If You will save Israel by my hand as You have said— 37 look, I shall put a fleece of wool on the threshing floor; if there is dew

וְאֶת־הַמַּצּוֹת וּמַלְאַ֤ךְ יְהוָה֙ הָלַ֔ךְ מֵעֵינָ֑יו: 22 וַיַּ֣רְא
גִּדְע֗וֹן כִּֽי־מַלְאַ֤ךְ יְהוָה֙ ה֔וּא ס וַיֹּ֣אמֶר
גִּדְע֗וֹן אֲהָהּ֙ אֲדֹנָ֣י יְהוִ֔ה כִּֽי־עַל־כֵּ֣ן רָאִ֔יתִי מַלְאַ֣ךְ
יְהוָ֔ה פָּנִ֖ים אֶל־פָּנִֽים: 23 וַיֹּ֨אמֶר ל֤וֹ יְהוָה֙ שָׁל֣וֹם
לְךָ֔ אַל־תִּירָ֖א לֹ֥א תָמֽוּת: 24 וַיִּ֨בֶן שָׁ֥ם גִּדְע֛וֹן מִזְבֵּ֖חַ
לַֽיהוָ֑ה וַיִּקְרָא־ל֣וֹ יְהוָ֣ה שָׁל֑וֹם עַ֚ד הַיּ֣וֹם הַזֶּ֔ה עוֹדֶ֕נּוּ
בְּעָפְרָ֖ת אֲבִ֥י הָֽעֶזְרִֽי: ס

25 וַֽיְהִי֮ בַּלַּ֣יְלָה הַהוּא֒ וַיֹּ֧אמֶר ל֣וֹ יְהוָ֗ה קַ֤ח אֶת־
פַּר־הַשּׁוֹר֙ אֲשֶׁ֣ר לְאָבִ֔יךָ וּפַ֥ר הַשֵּׁנִ֖י שֶׁ֣בַע שָׁנִ֑ים
וְהָרַסְתָּ֗ אֶת־מִזְבַּ֤ח הַבַּ֙עַל֙ אֲשֶׁ֣ר לְאָבִ֔יךָ וְאֶת־
הָאֲשֵׁרָ֥ה אֲשֶׁר־עָלָ֖יו תִּכְרֹֽת: 26 וּבָנִ֨יתָ מִזְבֵּ֜חַ לַֽיהוָ֣ה
אֱלֹהֶ֗יךָ עַ֣ל רֹ֤אשׁ הַמָּעוֹז֙ הַזֶּ֔ה בַּמַּֽעֲרָכָ֑ה וְלָֽקַחְתָּ֙
אֶת־הַפָּ֣ר הַשֵּׁנִ֔י וְהַעֲלִ֣יתָ עוֹלָ֔ה בַּעֲצֵ֥י הָאֲשֵׁרָ֖ה אֲשֶׁ֥ר
תִּכְרֹֽת: 27 וַיִּקַּ֨ח גִּדְע֜וֹן עֲשָׂרָ֤ה אֲנָשִׁים֙ מֵֽעֲבָדָ֔יו
וַיַּ֕עַשׂ כַּאֲשֶׁ֛ר דִּבֶּ֥ר אֵלָ֖יו יְהוָ֑ה וַיְהִ֡י כַּאֲשֶׁ֣ר יָרֵא֩
אֶת־בֵּ֨ית אָבִ֜יו וְאֶת־אַנְשֵׁ֤י הָעִיר֙ מֵעֲשׂ֣וֹת יוֹמָ֔ם
וַיַּ֖עַשׂ לָֽיְלָה: 28 וַיַּשְׁכִּ֜ימוּ אַנְשֵׁ֤י הָעִיר֙ בַּבֹּ֔קֶר וְהִנֵּ֤ה
נֻתַּץ֙ מִזְבַּ֣ח הַבַּ֔עַל וְהָאֲשֵׁרָ֥ה אֲשֶׁר־עָלָ֖יו כֹּרָ֑תָה וְאֵת֙
הַפָּ֣ר הַשֵּׁנִ֔י הֹֽעֲלָ֔ה עַל־הַמִּזְבֵּ֖חַ הַבָּנֽוּי: 29 וַיֹּֽאמְרוּ֙
אִ֣ישׁ אֶל־רֵעֵ֔הוּ מִ֥י עָשָׂ֖ה הַדָּבָ֣ר הַזֶּ֑ה וַֽיִּדְרְשׁוּ֙
וַיְבַקְשׁ֔וּ וַיֹּ֣אמְר֔וּ גִּדְעוֹן֙ בֶּן־יוֹאָ֔שׁ עָשָׂ֖ה הַדָּבָ֥ר הַזֶּֽה:
30 וַיֹּ֨אמְר֜וּ אַנְשֵׁ֤י הָעִיר֙ אֶל־יוֹאָ֔שׁ הוֹצֵ֥א אֶת־בִּנְךָ֖
וְיָמֹ֑ת כִּ֤י נָתַץ֙ אֶת־מִזְבַּ֣ח הַבַּ֔עַל וְכִ֥י כָרַ֖ת הָאֲשֵׁרָ֥ה
אֲשֶׁר־עָלָֽיו: 31 וַיֹּ֣אמֶר יוֹאָ֡שׁ לְכֹל֩ אֲשֶׁר־עָמְד֨וּ עָלָ֜יו
הַֽאַתֶּ֣ם ׀ תְּרִיב֣וּן לַבַּ֗עַל אִם־אַתֶּם֙ תּוֹשִׁיע֣וּן אוֹת֔וֹ
אֲשֶׁ֨ר יָרִ֥יב ל֛וֹ יוּמַ֖ת עַד־הַבֹּ֑קֶר אִם־אֱלֹהִ֥ים הוּא֙
יָ֣רֶב ל֔וֹ כִּ֥י נָתַ֖ץ אֶת־מִזְבְּחֽוֹ: 32 וַיִּקְרָא־ל֧וֹ בַיּוֹם־
הַה֛וּא יְרֻבַּ֖עַל לֵאמֹ֑ר יָ֤רֶב בּוֹ֙ הַבַּ֔עַל כִּ֥י נָתַ֖ץ אֶת־
מִזְבְּחֽוֹ: פ

33 וְכָל־מִדְיָ֧ן וַעֲמָלֵ֛ק וּבְנֵי־קֶ֖דֶם נֶאֶסְפ֣וּ יַחְדָּ֑ו וַיַּעַבְר֖וּ
וַיַּחֲנ֥וּ בְּעֵ֥מֶק יִזְרְעֶֽאל: 34 וְר֣וּחַ יְהוָ֔ה לָבְשָׁ֖ה אֶת־
גִּדְע֑וֹן וַיִּתְקַע֙ בַּשּׁוֹפָ֔ר וַיִּזָּעֵ֥ק אֲבִיעֶ֖זֶר אַחֲרָֽיו:
35 וּמַלְאָכִים֙ שָׁלַ֣ח בְּכָל־מְנַשֶּׁ֔ה וַיִּזָּעֵ֥ק גַּם־ה֖וּא
אַחֲרָ֑יו וּמַלְאָכִ֣ים שָׁלַ֗ח בְּאָשֵׁ֤ר וּבִזְבֻלוּן֙ וּבְנַפְתָּלִ֔י
וַיַּעֲל֖וּ לִקְרָאתָֽם: 36 וַיֹּ֥אמֶר גִּדְע֖וֹן אֶל־הָֽאֱלֹהִ֑ים
אִם־יֶשְׁךָ֞ מוֹשִׁ֧יעַ בְּיָדִ֛י אֶת־יִשְׂרָאֵ֖ל כַּאֲשֶׁ֥ר דִּבַּֽרְתָּ:
37 הִנֵּ֣ה אָנֹכִ֗י מַצִּ֛יג אֶת־גִּזַּ֥ת הַצֶּ֖מֶר בַּגֹּ֑רֶן אִ֡ם
טַל֩ יִהְיֶ֨ה עַֽל־הַגִּזָּ֜ה לְבַדָּ֗הּ וְעַל־כָּל־הָאָ֙רֶץ֙ חֹ֔רֶב

on the fleece only, and *it is* dry on all the ground, then I shall know that You will save Israel by my hand, as You have said." ³⁸ And it was so. When he rose early the next morning and squeezed the fleece together, he wrung the dew out of the fleece, a bowlful of water. ³⁹ Then Gideon said to God, "Do not be angry with me, but let me speak just once more: Let me test, I pray, just once more with the fleece; let it now be dry only on the fleece, but on all the ground let there be dew." ⁴⁰ And God did so that night. It was dry on the fleece only, but there was dew on all the ground.

7 Then Jerubbaal (that *is*, Gideon) and all the people who *were* with him rose early and encamped beside the well of Harod, so that the camp of the Midianites was on the north side of them by the hill of Moreh in the valley.
² And the LORD said to Gideon, "The people who *are* with you *are* too many for Me to give the Midianites into their hands, lest Israel claim glory for itself against Me, saying, 'My own hand has saved me.' ³ Now therefore, proclaim in the hearing of the people, saying, 'Whoever *is* fearful and afraid, let him turn and depart at once from Mount Gilead.'" And twenty-two thousand of the people returned, and ten thousand remained.
⁴ But the LORD said to Gideon, "The people *are* still *too* many; bring them down to the water, and I will test them for you there. Then it will be, *that* of whom I say to you, 'This one shall go with you,' the same shall go with you; and of whomever I say to you, 'This one shall not go with you,' the same shall not go." ⁵ So he brought the people down to the water. And the LORD said to Gideon, "Everyone who laps from the water with his tongue, as a dog laps, you shall set apart by himself; likewise everyone who gets down on his knees to drink."
⁶ And the number of those who lapped, *putting* their hand to their mouth, was three hundred men; but all the rest of the people got down on their knees to drink water. ⁷ Then the LORD said to Gideon, "By the three hundred men who lapped I will save you, and deliver the Midianites into your hand. Let all the *other* people go, every man to his place." ⁸ So the people took provisions and their trumpets in their hands. And he sent away all *the rest of* Israel, every man to his tent, and retained those three hundred men. Now the camp of Midian was below him in the valley.
⁹ It happened on the same night that the LORD said to him, "Arise, go down against the camp, for I have delivered it into your hand. ¹⁰ But if you are afraid to go down, go down to the camp with Purah

וְיָדַעְתִּי כִּי־תוֹשִׁיעַ בְּיָדִי אֶת־יִשְׂרָאֵל כַּאֲשֶׁר דִּבַּרְתָּ: ³⁸ וַיְהִי־כֵן וַיַּשְׁכֵּם מִמָּחֳרָת וַיָּזַר אֶת־הַגִּזָּה וַיִּמֶץ טַל מִן־הַגִּזָּה מְלוֹא הַסֵּפֶל מָיִם: ³⁹ וַיֹּאמֶר גִּדְעוֹן אֶל־הָאֱלֹהִים אַל־יִחַר אַפְּךָ בִּי וַאֲדַבְּרָה אַךְ הַפָּעַם אֲנַסֶּה נָּא־רַק־הַפַּעַם בַּגִּזָּה יְהִי־נָא חֹרֶב אֶל־הַגִּזָּה לְבַדָּהּ וְעַל־כָּל־הָאָרֶץ יִהְיֶה־טָּל: ⁴⁰ וַיַּעַשׂ אֱלֹהִים כֵּן בַּלַּיְלָה הַהוּא וַיְהִי־חֹרֶב אֶל־הַגִּזָּה לְבַדָּהּ וְעַל־כָּל־הָאָרֶץ הָיָה טָל:
פ

¹ וַיַּשְׁכֵּם יְרֻבַּעַל הוּא גִדְעוֹן וְכָל־הָעָם אֲשֶׁר אִתּוֹ וַיַּחֲנוּ עַל־עֵין חֲרֹד וּמַחֲנֵה מִדְיָן הָיָה־לוֹ מִצָּפוֹן מִגִּבְעַת הַמּוֹרֶה בָּעֵמֶק: ² וַיֹּאמֶר יְהוָה אֶל־גִּדְעוֹן רַב הָעָם אֲשֶׁר אִתָּךְ מִתִּתִּי אֶת־מִדְיָן בְּיָדָם פֶּן־יִתְפָּאֵר עָלַי יִשְׂרָאֵל לֵאמֹר יָדִי הוֹשִׁיעָה לִּי: ³ וְעַתָּה קְרָא נָא בְּאָזְנֵי הָעָם לֵאמֹר מִי־יָרֵא וְחָרֵד יָשֹׁב וְיִצְפֹּר מֵהַר הַגִּלְעָד וַיָּשָׁב מִן־הָעָם עֶשְׂרִים וּשְׁנַיִם אֶלֶף וַעֲשֶׂרֶת אֲלָפִים נִשְׁאָרוּ: ס ⁴ וַיֹּאמֶר יְהוָה אֶל־גִּדְעוֹן עוֹד הָעָם רָב הוֹרֵד אוֹתָם אֶל־הַמַּיִם וְאֶצְרְפֶנּוּ לְךָ שָׁם וְהָיָה אֲשֶׁר אֹמַר אֵלֶיךָ זֶה יֵלֵךְ אִתָּךְ הוּא יֵלֵךְ אִתָּךְ וְכֹל אֲשֶׁר־אֹמַר אֵלֶיךָ זֶה לֹא־יֵלֵךְ עִמָּךְ הוּא לֹא יֵלֵךְ: ⁵ וַיּוֹרֶד אֶת־הָעָם אֶל־הַמָּיִם ס וַיֹּאמֶר יְהוָה אֶל־גִּדְעוֹן כֹּל אֲשֶׁר־יָלֹק בִּלְשׁוֹנוֹ מִן־הַמַּיִם כַּאֲשֶׁר יָלֹק הַכֶּלֶב תַּצִּיג אוֹתוֹ לְבָד וְכֹל אֲשֶׁר־יִכְרַע עַל־בִּרְכָּיו לִשְׁתּוֹת: ⁶ וַיְהִי מִסְפַּר הַמְלַקְקִים בְּיָדָם אֶל־פִּיהֶם שְׁלֹשׁ מֵאוֹת אִישׁ וְכֹל יֶתֶר הָעָם כָּרְעוּ עַל־בִּרְכֵיהֶם לִשְׁתּוֹת מָיִם: ס ⁷ וַיֹּאמֶר יְהוָה אֶל־גִּדְעוֹן בִּשְׁלֹשׁ מֵאוֹת הָאִישׁ הַמְלַקְקִים אוֹשִׁיעַ אֶתְכֶם וְנָתַתִּי אֶת־מִדְיָן בְּיָדֶךָ וְכָל־הָעָם יֵלְכוּ אִישׁ לִמְקֹמוֹ: ⁸ וַיִּקְחוּ אֶת־צֵדָה הָעָם בְּיָדָם וְאֵת שׁוֹפְרֹתֵיהֶם וְאֵת כָּל־אִישׁ יִשְׂרָאֵל שִׁלַּח אִישׁ לְאֹהָלָיו וּבִשְׁלֹשׁ־מֵאוֹת הָאִישׁ הֶחֱזִיק וּמַחֲנֵה מִדְיָן הָיָה לוֹ מִתַּחַת בָּעֵמֶק:
פ

⁹ וַיְהִי בַּלַּיְלָה הַהוּא וַיֹּאמֶר אֵלָיו יְהוָה קוּם רֵד בַּמַּחֲנֶה כִּי נְתַתִּיו בְּיָדֶךָ: ¹⁰ וְאִם־יָרֵא אַתָּה לָרֶדֶת

your servant, [11] and you shall hear what they say; and afterward your hands shall be strengthened to go down against the camp." Then he went down with Purah his servant to the outpost of the armed men who *were* in the camp. [12] Now the Midianites and Amalekites, all the people of the East, were lying in the valley as numerous as locusts; and their camels *were* without number, as the sand by the seashore in multitude.

[13] And when Gideon had come, there was a man telling a dream to his companion. He said, "I have had a dream: *To my* surprise, a loaf of barley bread tumbled into the camp of Midian; it came to a tent and struck it so that it fell and overturned, and the tent collapsed."

[14] Then his companion answered and said, "This *is* nothing else but the sword of Gideon the son of Joash, a man of Israel! Into his hand God has delivered Midian and the whole camp."

[15] And so it was, when Gideon heard the telling of the dream and its interpretation, that he worshiped. He returned to the camp of Israel, and said, "Arise, for the LORD has delivered the camp of Midian into your hand." [16] Then he divided the three hundred men *into* three companies, and he put a trumpet into every man's hand, with empty pitchers, and torches inside the pitchers. [17] And he said to them, "Look at me and do likewise; watch, and when I come to the edge of the camp you shall do as I do: [18] When I blow the trumpet, I and all who *are* with me, then you also blow the trumpets on every side of the whole camp, and say, 'The sword *of* the LORD and of Gideon!'"

[19] So Gideon and the hundred men who *were* with him came to the outpost of the camp at the beginning of the middle watch, just as they had posted the watch; and they blew the trumpets and broke the pitchers that *were* in their hands. [20] Then the three companies blew the trumpets and broke the pitchers—they held the torches in their left hands and the trumpets in their right hands for blowing—and they cried, "The sword of the LORD and of Gideon!" [21] And every man stood in his place all around the camp; and the whole army ran and cried out and fled. [22] When the three hundred blew the trumpets, the LORD set every man's sword against his companion throughout the whole camp; and the army fled to Beth Acacia, toward Zererah, as far as the border of Abel Meholah, by Tabbath.

[23] And the men of Israel gathered together from Naphtali, Asher, and all Manasseh, and pursued the Midianites.

רֵד אַתָּה וּפֻרָה נַעַרְךָ אֶל־הַמַּחֲנֶה: 11 וְשָׁמַעְתָּ מַה־יְדַבֵּרוּ וְאַחַר תֶּחֱזַקְנָה יָדֶיךָ וְיָרַדְתָּ בַּמַּחֲנֶה וַיֵּרֶד הוּא וּפֻרָה נַעֲרוֹ אֶל־קְצֵה הַחֲמֻשִׁים אֲשֶׁר בַּמַּחֲנֶה: 12 וּמִדְיָן וַעֲמָלֵק וְכָל־בְּנֵי־קֶדֶם נֹפְלִים בָּעֵמֶק כָּאַרְבֶּה לָרֹב וְלִגְמַלֵּיהֶם אֵין מִסְפָּר כַּחוֹל שֶׁעַל־שְׂפַת הַיָּם לָרֹב: 13 וַיָּבֹא גִדְעוֹן וְהִנֵּה־אִישׁ מְסַפֵּר לְרֵעֵהוּ חֲלוֹם וַיֹּאמֶר הִנֵּה חֲלוֹם חָלַמְתִּי וְהִנֵּה צְלִיל לֶחֶם שְׂעֹרִים מִתְהַפֵּךְ בְּמַחֲנֵה מִדְיָן וַיָּבֹא עַד־הָאֹהֶל וַיַּכֵּהוּ וַיִּפֹּל וַיַּהַפְכֵהוּ לְמַעְלָה וְנָפַל הָאֹהֶל: 14 וַיַּעַן רֵעֵהוּ וַיֹּאמֶר אֵין זֹאת בִּלְתִּי אִם־ חֶרֶב גִּדְעוֹן בֶּן־יוֹאָשׁ אִישׁ יִשְׂרָאֵל נָתַן הָאֱלֹהִים בְּיָדוֹ אֶת־מִדְיָן וְאֶת־כָּל־הַמַּחֲנֶה: פ

15 וַיְהִי כִשְׁמֹעַ גִּדְעוֹן אֶת־מִסְפַּר הַחֲלוֹם וְאֶת־ שִׁבְרוֹ וַיִּשְׁתָּחוּ וַיָּשָׁב אֶל־מַחֲנֵה יִשְׂרָאֵל וַיֹּאמֶר קוּמוּ כִּי־נָתַן יְהוָה בְּיֶדְכֶם אֶת־מַחֲנֵה מִדְיָן: 16 וַיַּחַץ אֶת־שְׁלֹשׁ־מֵאוֹת הָאִישׁ שְׁלֹשָׁה רָאשִׁים וַיִּתֵּן שׁוֹפָרוֹת בְּיַד־כֻּלָּם וְכַדִּים רֵקִים וְלַפִּדִים בְּתוֹךְ הַכַּדִּים: 17 וַיֹּאמֶר אֲלֵיהֶם מִמֶּנִּי תִרְאוּ וְכֵן תַּעֲשׂוּ וְהִנֵּה אָנֹכִי בָא בִּקְצֵה הַמַּחֲנֶה וְהָיָה כַאֲשֶׁר־אֶעֱשֶׂה כֵּן תַּעֲשׂוּן: 18 וְתָקַעְתִּי בַּשּׁוֹפָר אָנֹכִי וְכָל־אֲשֶׁר אִתִּי וּתְקַעְתֶּם בַּשּׁוֹפָרוֹת גַּם־אַתֶּם סְבִיבוֹת כָּל־ הַמַּחֲנֶה וַאֲמַרְתֶּם לַיהוָה וּלְגִדְעוֹן: פ

19 וַיָּבֹא גִדְעוֹן וּמֵאָה־אִישׁ אֲשֶׁר־אִתּוֹ בִּקְצֵה הַמַּחֲנֶה רֹאשׁ הָאַשְׁמֹרֶת הַתִּיכוֹנָה אַךְ הָקֵם הֵקִימוּ אֶת־הַשֹּׁמְרִים וַיִּתְקְעוּ בַּשּׁוֹפָרוֹת וְנָפוֹץ הַכַּדִּים אֲשֶׁר בְּיָדָם: 20 וַיִּתְקְעוּ שְׁלֹשֶׁת הָרָאשִׁים בַּשּׁוֹפָרוֹת וַיִּשְׁבְּרוּ הַכַּדִּים וַיַּחֲזִיקוּ בְיַד־שְׂמֹאולָם בַּלַּפִּדִים וּבְיַד־יְמִינָם הַשּׁוֹפָרוֹת לִתְקוֹעַ וַיִּקְרְאוּ חֶרֶב לַיהוָה וּלְגִדְעוֹן: 21 וַיַּעַמְדוּ אִישׁ תַּחְתָּיו סָבִיב לַמַּחֲנֶה וַיָּרָץ כָּל־הַמַּחֲנֶה וַיָּרִיעוּ וַיָּנֻיסוּ: 22 וַיִּתְקְעוּ שְׁלֹשׁ־מֵאוֹת הַשּׁוֹפָרוֹת וַיָּשֶׂם יְהוָה אֵת חֶרֶב אִישׁ בְּרֵעֵהוּ וּבְכָל־הַמַּחֲנֶה וַיָּנָס הַמַּחֲנֶה עַד־ בֵּית הַשִּׁטָּה צְרֵרָתָה עַד שְׂפַת־אָבֵל מְחוֹלָה עַל־ טַבָּת: 23 וַיִּצָּעֵק אִישׁ־יִשְׂרָאֵל מִנַּפְתָּלִי וּמִן־אֲשֵׁר

24 Then Gideon sent messengers throughout all the mountains of Ephraim, saying, "Come down against the Midianites, and seize from them the watering places as far as Beth Barah and the Jordan." Then all the men of Ephraim gathered together and seized the watering places as far as Beth Barah and the Jordan. 25 And they captured two princes of the Midianites, Oreb and Zeeb. They killed Oreb at the rock of Oreb, and Zeeb they killed at the winepress of Zeeb. They pursued Midian and brought the heads of Oreb and Zeeb to Gideon on the other side of the Jordan.

8 Now the men of Ephraim said to him, "Why have you done this to us by not calling us when you went to fight with the Midianites?" And they reprimanded him sharply.

2 So he said to them, "What have I done now in comparison with you? Is not the gleaning of the grapes of Ephraim better than the vintage of Abiezer? 3 God has delivered into your hands the princes of Midian, Oreb and Zeeb. And what was I able to do in comparison with you?" Then their anger toward him subsided when he said that.

4 When Gideon came to the Jordan, he and the three hundred men who were with him crossed over, exhausted but still in pursuit. 5 Then he said to the men of Succoth, "Please give loaves of bread to the people who follow me, for they are exhausted, and I am pursuing Zebah and Zalmunna, kings of Midian."

6 And the leaders of Succoth said, "Are the hands of Zebah and Zalmunna now in your hand, that we should give bread to your army?"

7 So Gideon said, "For this cause, when the LORD has delivered Zebah and Zalmunna into my hand, then I will tear your flesh with the thorns of the wilderness and with briers!" 8 Then he went up from there to Penuel and spoke to them in the same way. And the men of Penuel answered him as the men of Succoth had answered. 9 So he also spoke to the men of Penuel, saying, "When I come back in peace, I will tear down this tower!"

10 Now Zebah and Zalmunna were at Karkor, and their armies with them, about fifteen thousand, all who were left of all the army of the people of the East; for one hundred and twenty thousand men who drew the sword had fallen. 11 Then Gideon went up by the road of those who dwell in tents on the east of Nobah and Jogbehah; and he attacked the army while the camp felt secure. 12 When Zebah and Zalmunna fled, he pursued them; and he took the two kings of Midian, Zebah and Zalmunna, and routed the whole army.

24 וּמִן־כָּל־מְנַשֶּׁה וַיִּרְדְּפוּ אַחֲרֵי מִדְיָן וּמַלְאָכִים שָׁלַח גִּדְעוֹן בְּכָל־הַר אֶפְרַיִם לֵאמֹר רְדוּ לִקְרַאת מִדְיָן וְלִכְדוּ לָהֶם אֶת־הַמַּיִם עַד בֵּית בָּרָה וְאֶת־הַיַּרְדֵּן וַיִּצָּעֵק כָּל־אִישׁ אֶפְרַיִם וַיִּלְכְּדוּ אֶת־הַמַּיִם עַד בֵּית בָּרָה וְאֶת־הַיַּרְדֵּן: 25 וַיִּלְכְּדוּ שְׁנֵי־שָׂרֵי מִדְיָן אֶת־עֹרֵב וְאֶת־זְאֵב וַיַּהַרְגוּ אֶת־עוֹרֵב בְּצוּר־עוֹרֵב וְאֶת־זְאֵב הָרְגוּ בְיֶקֶב־זְאֵב וַיִּרְדְּפוּ אֶל־מִדְיָן וְרֹאשׁ־עֹרֵב וּזְאֵב הֵבִיאוּ אֶל־גִּדְעוֹן מֵעֵבֶר לַיַּרְדֵּן:

ח וַיֹּאמְרוּ אֵלָיו אִישׁ אֶפְרַיִם מָה־הַדָּבָר הַזֶּה עָשִׂיתָ לָּנוּ לְבִלְתִּי קְרֹאות לָנוּ כִּי הָלַכְתָּ לְהִלָּחֶם בְּמִדְיָן וַיְרִיבוּן אִתּוֹ בְּחָזְקָה: 2 וַיֹּאמֶר אֲלֵיהֶם מֶה־עָשִׂיתִי עַתָּה כָּכֶם הֲלוֹא טוֹב עֹלְלוֹת אֶפְרַיִם מִבְצִיר אֲבִיעֶזֶר: 3 בְּיֶדְכֶם נָתַן אֱלֹהִים אֶת־שָׂרֵי מִדְיָן אֶת־עֹרֵב וְאֶת־זְאֵב וּמַה־יָּכֹלְתִּי עֲשׂוֹת כָּכֶם אָז רָפְתָה רוּחָם מֵעָלָיו בְּדַבְּרוֹ הַדָּבָר הַזֶּה: 4 וַיָּבֹא גִדְעוֹן הַיַּרְדֵּנָה עֹבֵר הוּא וּשְׁלֹשׁ־מֵאוֹת הָאִישׁ אֲשֶׁר אִתּוֹ עֲיֵפִים וְרֹדְפִים: 5 וַיֹּאמֶר לְאַנְשֵׁי סֻכּוֹת תְּנוּ־נָא כִּכְּרוֹת לֶחֶם לָעָם אֲשֶׁר בְּרַגְלָי כִּי־עֲיֵפִים הֵם וְאָנֹכִי רֹדֵף אַחֲרֵי זֶבַח וְצַלְמֻנָּע מַלְכֵי מִדְיָן:

6 וַיֹּאמֶר שָׂרֵי סֻכּוֹת הֲכַף זֶבַח וְצַלְמֻנָּע עַתָּה בְּיָדֶךָ כִּי־נִתֵּן לִצְבָאֲךָ לָחֶם: 7 וַיֹּאמֶר גִּדְעוֹן לָכֵן בְּתֵת יְהוָה אֶת־זֶבַח וְאֶת־צַלְמֻנָּע בְּיָדִי וְדַשְׁתִּי אֶת־בְּשַׂרְכֶם אֶת־קוֹצֵי הַמִּדְבָּר וְאֶת־הַבַּרְקֳנִים: 8 וַיַּעַל מִשָּׁם פְּנוּאֵל וַיְדַבֵּר אֲלֵיהֶם כָּזֹאת וַיַּעֲנוּ אוֹתוֹ אַנְשֵׁי פְנוּאֵל כַּאֲשֶׁר עָנוּ אַנְשֵׁי סֻכּוֹת: 9 וַיֹּאמֶר גַּם־לְאַנְשֵׁי פְנוּאֵל לֵאמֹר בְּשׁוּבִי בְשָׁלוֹם אֶתֹּץ אֶת־הַמִּגְדָּל הַזֶּה: פ

10 וְזֶבַח וְצַלְמֻנָּע בַּקַּרְקֹר וּמַחֲנֵיהֶם עִמָּם כַּחֲמֵשֶׁת עָשָׂר אֶלֶף כֹּל הַנּוֹתָרִים מִכֹּל מַחֲנֵה בְנֵי־קֶדֶם וְהַנֹּפְלִים מֵאָה וְעֶשְׂרִים אֶלֶף אִישׁ שֹׁלֵף חָרֶב: 11 וַיַּעַל גִּדְעוֹן דֶּרֶךְ הַשְּׁכוּנֵי בָאֳהָלִים מִקֶּדֶם לְנֹבַח וְיָגְבֳהָה וַיַּךְ אֶת־הַמַּחֲנֶה וְהַמַּחֲנֶה הָיָה בֶטַח: 12 וַיָּנוּסוּ זֶבַח וְצַלְמֻנָּע וַיִּרְדֹּף אַחֲרֵיהֶם וַיִּלְכֹּד אֶת־שְׁנֵי מַלְכֵי מִדְיָן אֶת־זֶבַח וְאֶת־צַלְמֻנָּע וְכָל־

¹³ Then Gideon the son of Joash returned from battle, from the Ascent of Heres. ¹⁴ And he caught a young man of the men of Succoth and interrogated him; and he wrote down for him the leaders of Succoth and its elders, seventy-seven men. ¹⁵ Then he came to the men of Succoth and said, "Here are Zebah and Zalmunna, about whom you ridiculed me, saying, '*Are* the hands of Zebah and Zalmunna now in your hand, that we should give bread to your weary men?'" ¹⁶ And he took the elders of the city, and thorns of the wilderness and briers, and with them he taught the men of Succoth. ¹⁷ Then he tore down the tower of Penuel and killed the men of the city.

¹⁸ And he said to Zebah and Zalmunna, "What kind of men *were they* whom you killed at Tabor?"

So they answered, "As you *are,* so *were* they; each one resembled the son of a king."

¹⁹ Then he said, "They *were* my brothers, the sons of my mother. *As* the LORD lives, if you had let them live, I would not kill you." ²⁰ And he said to Jether his firstborn, "Rise, kill them!" But the youth would not draw his sword; for he was afraid, because he *was* still a youth.

²¹ So Zebah and Zalmunna said, "Rise yourself, and kill us; for as a man *is, so is* his strength." So Gideon arose and killed Zebah and Zalmunna, and took the crescent ornaments that *were* on their camels' necks.

²² Then the men of Israel said to Gideon, "Rule over us, both you and your son, and your grandson also; for you have delivered us from the hand of Midian."

²³ But Gideon said to them, "I will not rule over you, nor shall my son rule over you; the LORD shall rule over you." ²⁴ Then Gideon said to them, "I would like to make a request of you, that each of you would give me the earrings from his plunder." For they had golden earrings, because they *were* Ishmaelites.

²⁵ So they answered, "We will gladly give *them.*" And they spread out a garment, and each man threw into it the earrings from his plunder. ²⁶ Now the weight of the gold earrings that he requested was one thousand seven hundred *shekels* of gold, besides the crescent ornaments, pendants, and purple robes which *were* on the kings of Midian, and besides the chains that *were* around their camels' necks. ²⁷ Then Gideon made it into an ephod and set it up in his city, Ophrah. And all Israel played the harlot with it there. It became a snare to Gideon and to his house.

הַמַּחֲנֶה הֶחָרִיד: ¹³ וַיָּשָׁב גִּדְעוֹן בֶּן־יוֹאָשׁ מִן־
הַמִּלְחָמָה מִלְּמַעֲלֵה הֶחָרֶס: ¹⁴ וַיִּלְכָּד־נַעַר מֵאַנְשֵׁי
סֻכּוֹת וַיִּשְׁאָלֵהוּ וַיִּכְתֹּב אֵלָיו אֶת־שָׂרֵי סֻכּוֹת וְאֶת־
זְקֵנֶיהָ שִׁבְעִים וְשִׁבְעָה אִישׁ: ¹⁵ וַיָּבֹא אֶל־אַנְשֵׁי
סֻכּוֹת וַיֹּאמֶר הִנֵּה זֶבַח וְצַלְמֻנָּע אֲשֶׁר חֵרַפְתֶּם
אוֹתִי לֵאמֹר הֲכַף זֶבַח וְצַלְמֻנָּע עַתָּה בְּיָדֶךָ כִּי נִתֵּן
לַאֲנָשֶׁיךָ הַיְּעֵפִים לָחֶם: ¹⁶ וַיִּקַּח אֶת־זִקְנֵי הָעִיר
וְאֶת־קוֹצֵי הַמִּדְבָּר וְאֶת־הַבַּרְקֳנִים וַיֹּדַע בָּהֶם אֵת
אַנְשֵׁי סֻכּוֹת: ¹⁷ וְאֶת־מִגְדַּל פְּנוּאֵל נָתָץ וַיַּהֲרֹג
אֶת־אַנְשֵׁי הָעִיר: ¹⁸ וַיֹּאמֶר אֶל־זֶבַח וְאֶל־צַלְמֻנָּע
אֵיפֹה הָאֲנָשִׁים אֲשֶׁר הֲרַגְתֶּם בְּתָבוֹר וַיֹּאמְרוּ
כָּמוֹךָ כְמוֹהֶם אֶחָד כְּתֹאַר בְּנֵי הַמֶּלֶךְ: ¹⁹ וַיֹּאמַר
אַחַי בְּנֵי־אִמִּי הֵם חַי־יְהֹוָה לוּ הַחֲיִתֶם אוֹתָם לֹא
הָרַגְתִּי אֶתְכֶם: ²⁰ וַיֹּאמֶר לְיֶתֶר בְּכוֹרוֹ קוּם הֲרֹג
אוֹתָם וְלֹא־שָׁלַף הַנַּעַר חַרְבּוֹ כִּי יָרֵא כִּי עוֹדֶנּוּ
נָעַר: ²¹ וַיֹּאמֶר זֶבַח וְצַלְמֻנָּע קוּם אַתָּה וּפְגַע־בָּנוּ
כִּי כָאִישׁ גְּבוּרָתוֹ וַיָּקָם גִּדְעוֹן וַיַּהֲרֹג אֶת־זֶבַח
וְאֶת־צַלְמֻנָּע וַיִּקַּח אֶת־הַשַּׂהֲרֹנִים אֲשֶׁר בְּצַוְּארֵי
גְמַלֵּיהֶם: ²² וַיֹּאמְרוּ אִישׁ־יִשְׂרָאֵל אֶל־גִּדְעוֹן מְשָׁל־
בָּנוּ גַם־אַתָּה גַּם־בִּנְךָ גַּם בֶּן־בְּנֶךָ כִּי הוֹשַׁעְתָּנוּ מִיַּד
מִדְיָן: ²³ וַיֹּאמֶר אֲלֵהֶם גִּדְעוֹן לֹא־אֶמְשֹׁל אֲנִי בָּכֶם
וְלֹא־יִמְשֹׁל בְּנִי בָּכֶם יְהֹוָה יִמְשֹׁל בָּכֶם: ²⁴ וַיֹּאמֶר
אֲלֵהֶם גִּדְעוֹן אֶשְׁאֲלָה מִכֶּם שְׁאֵלָה וּתְנוּ־לִי אִישׁ
נֶזֶם שְׁלָלוֹ כִּי־נִזְמֵי זָהָב לָהֶם כִּי יִשְׁמְעֵאלִים הֵם:
²⁵ וַיֹּאמְרוּ נָתוֹן נִתֵּן וַיִּפְרְשׂוּ אֶת־הַשִּׂמְלָה וַיַּשְׁלִיכוּ
שָׁמָּה אִישׁ נֶזֶם שְׁלָלוֹ: ²⁶ וַיְהִי מִשְׁקַל נִזְמֵי הַזָּהָב
אֲשֶׁר שָׁאָל אֶלֶף וּשְׁבַע־מֵאוֹת זָהָב לְבַד מִן־
הַשַּׂהֲרֹנִים וְהַנְּטִפוֹת וּבִגְדֵי הָאַרְגָּמָן שֶׁעַל מַלְכֵי
מִדְיָן וּלְבַד מִן־הָעֲנָקוֹת אֲשֶׁר בְּצַוְּארֵי גְמַלֵּיהֶם:
²⁷ וַיַּעַשׂ אוֹתוֹ גִדְעוֹן לְאֵפוֹד וַיַּצֵּג אוֹתוֹ בְעִירוֹ
בְעָפְרָה וַיִּזְנוּ כָל־יִשְׂרָאֵל אַחֲרָיו שָׁם וַיְהִי לְגִדְעוֹן

28 Thus Midian was subdued before the children of Israel, so that they lifted their heads no more. And the country was quiet for forty years in the days of Gideon.

29 Then Jerubbaal the son of Joash went and dwelt in his own house. 30 Gideon had seventy sons who were his own offspring, for he had many wives. 31 And his concubine who *was* in Shechem also bore him a son, whose name he called Abimelech. 32 Now Gideon the son of Joash died at a good old age, and was buried in the tomb of Joash his father, in Ophrah of the Abiezrites.

33 So it was, as soon as Gideon was dead, that the children of Israel again played the harlot with the Baals, and made Baal-Berith their god. 34 Thus the children of Israel did not remember the LORD their God, who had delivered them from the hands of all their enemies on every side; 35 nor did they show kindness to the house of Jerubbaal (Gideon) in accordance with the good he had done for Israel.

9 Then Abimelech the son of Jerubbaal went to Shechem, to his mother's brothers, and spoke with them and with all the family of the house of his mother's father, saying, 2 "Please speak in the hearing of all the men of Shechem: 'Which is better for you, that all seventy of the sons of Jerubbaal reign over you, or that one reign over you?' Remember that I *am* your own flesh and bone."

3 And his mother's brothers spoke all these words concerning him in the hearing of all the men of Shechem; and their heart was inclined to follow Abimelech, for they said, "He is our brother." 4 So they gave him seventy *shekels* of silver from the temple of Baal-Berith, with which Abimelech hired worthless and reckless men; and they followed him. 5 Then he went to his father's house at Ophrah and killed his brothers, the seventy sons of Jerubbaal, on one stone. But Jotham the youngest son of Jerubbaal was left, because he hid himself. 6 And all the men of Shechem gathered together, all of Beth Millo, and they went and made Abimelech king beside the terebinth tree at the pillar that *was* in Shechem.

7 Now when they told Jotham, he went and stood on top of Mount Gerizim, and lifted his voice and cried out. And he said to them:

"Listen to me, you men of Shechem,
   That God may listen to you!

8   "The trees once went forth to anoint a king over
        them.
     And they said to the olive tree,
     'Reign over us!'
9   But the olive tree said to them,

וְלֵבִיתוֹ לְמוֹשֵׁל: 28 וַיִּכָּנַע מִדְיָן לִפְנֵי בְּנֵי יִשְׂרָאֵל וְלֹא יָסְפוּ לָשֵׂאת רֹאשָׁם וַתִּשְׁקֹט הָאָרֶץ אַרְבָּעִים שָׁנָה בִּימֵי גִדְעוֹן: פ

29 וַיֵּלֶךְ יְרֻבַּעַל בֶּן־יוֹאָשׁ וַיֵּשֶׁב בְּבֵיתוֹ: 30 וּלְגִדְעוֹן הָיוּ שִׁבְעִים בָּנִים יֹצְאֵי יְרֵכוֹ כִּי־נָשִׁים רַבּוֹת הָיוּ לוֹ: 31 וּפִילַגְשׁוֹ אֲשֶׁר בִּשְׁכֶם יָלְדָה־לּוֹ גַם־הִיא בֵּן וַיָּשֶׂם אֶת־שְׁמוֹ אֲבִימֶלֶךְ: 32 וַיָּמָת גִּדְעוֹן בֶּן־יוֹאָשׁ בְּשֵׂיבָה טוֹבָה וַיִּקָּבֵר בְּקֶבֶר יוֹאָשׁ אָבִיו בְּעָפְרָה אֲבִי הָעֶזְרִי: פ

33 וַיְהִי כַּאֲשֶׁר מֵת גִּדְעוֹן וַיָּשׁוּבוּ בְּנֵי יִשְׂרָאֵל וַיִּזְנוּ אַחֲרֵי הַבְּעָלִים וַיָּשִׂימוּ לָהֶם בַּעַל בְּרִית לֵאלֹהִים: 34 וְלֹא זָכְרוּ בְּנֵי יִשְׂרָאֵל אֶת־יְהוָה אֱלֹהֵיהֶם הַמַּצִּיל אוֹתָם מִיַּד כָּל־אֹיְבֵיהֶם מִסָּבִיב: 35 וְלֹא־עָשׂוּ חֶסֶד עִם־בֵּית יְרֻבַּעַל גִּדְעוֹן כְּכָל־הַטּוֹבָה אֲשֶׁר עָשָׂה עִם־יִשְׂרָאֵל: פ

ט וַיֵּלֶךְ אֲבִימֶלֶךְ בֶּן־יְרֻבַּעַל שְׁכֶמָה אֶל־אֲחֵי אִמּוֹ וַיְדַבֵּר אֲלֵיהֶם וְאֶל־כָּל־מִשְׁפַּחַת בֵּית־אֲבִי אִמּוֹ לֵאמֹר: 2 דַּבְּרוּ־נָא בְּאָזְנֵי כָל־בַּעֲלֵי שְׁכֶם מַה־טּוֹב לָכֶם הַמְשֹׁל בָּכֶם שִׁבְעִים אִישׁ כֹּל בְּנֵי יְרֻבַּעַל אִם־מְשֹׁל בָּכֶם אִישׁ אֶחָד וּזְכַרְתֶּם כִּי־עַצְמְכֶם וּבְשַׂרְכֶם אָנִי: 3 וַיְדַבְּרוּ אֲחֵי־אִמּוֹ עָלָיו בְּאָזְנֵי כָּל־בַּעֲלֵי שְׁכֶם אֵת כָּל־הַדְּבָרִים הָאֵלֶּה וַיֵּט לִבָּם אַחֲרֵי אֲבִימֶלֶךְ כִּי אָמְרוּ אָחִינוּ הוּא: 4 וַיִּתְּנוּ־לוֹ שִׁבְעִים כֶּסֶף מִבֵּית בַּעַל בְּרִית וַיִּשְׂכֹּר בָּהֶם אֲבִימֶלֶךְ אֲנָשִׁים רֵיקִים וּפֹחֲזִים וַיֵּלְכוּ אַחֲרָיו: 5 וַיָּבֹא בֵית־אָבִיו עָפְרָתָה וַיַּהֲרֹג אֶת־אֶחָיו בְּנֵי־יְרֻבַּעַל שִׁבְעִים אִישׁ עַל־אֶבֶן אֶחָת וַיִּוָּתֵר יוֹתָם בֶּן־יְרֻבַּעַל הַקָּטֹן כִּי נֶחְבָּא: 6 וַיֵּאָסְפוּ כָּל־בַּעֲלֵי שְׁכֶם פ וְכָל־בֵּית מִלּוֹא וַיֵּלְכוּ וַיַּמְלִיכוּ אֶת־אֲבִימֶלֶךְ לְמֶלֶךְ עִם־אֵלוֹן מֻצָּב אֲשֶׁר בִּשְׁכֶם: 7 וַיַּגִּדוּ לְיוֹתָם וַיֵּלֶךְ וַיַּעֲמֹד בְּרֹאשׁ הַר־גְּרִזִים וַיִּשָּׂא קוֹלוֹ וַיִּקְרָא וַיֹּאמֶר לָהֶם שִׁמְעוּ אֵלַי בַּעֲלֵי שְׁכֶם וְיִשְׁמַע אֲלֵיכֶם אֱלֹהִים: 8 הָלוֹךְ הָלְכוּ הָעֵצִים לִמְשֹׁחַ עֲלֵיהֶם מֶלֶךְ וַיֹּאמְרוּ לַזַּיִת מָלְכָהp עָלֵינוּ: 9 וַיֹּאמֶר לָהֶם הַזַּיִת

מָלְכָה 8 ט

'Should I cease giving my oil,
With which they honor God and men,
And go to sway over trees?'

10 "Then the trees said to the fig tree,
'You come *and* reign over us!'
11 But the fig tree said to them,
'Should I cease my sweetness and my good fruit,
And go to sway over trees?'
12 "Then the trees said to the vine,
'You come *and* reign over us!'
13 But the vine said to them,
'Should I cease my new wine,
Which cheers *both* God and men,
And go to sway over trees?'
14 "Then all the trees said to the bramble,
'You come *and* reign over us!'
15 And the bramble said to the trees,
'If in truth you anoint me as king over you,
Then come *and* take shelter in my shade;
But if not, let fire come out of the bramble
And devour the cedars of Lebanon!'

16 "Now therefore, if you have acted in truth and sincerity in making Abimelech king, and if you have dealt well with Jerubbaal and his house, and have done to him as he deserves— 17 for my father fought for you, risked his life, and delivered you out of the hand of Midian; 18 but you have risen up against my father's house this day, and killed his seventy sons on one stone, and made Abimelech, the son of his female servant, king over the men of Shechem, because he is your brother— 19 if then you have acted in truth and sincerity with Jerubbaal and with his house this day, *then* rejoice in Abimelech, and let him also rejoice in you. 20 But if not, let fire come from Abimelech and devour the men of Shechem and Beth Millo; and let fire come from the men of Shechem and from Beth Millo and devour Abimelech!" 21 And Jotham ran away and fled; and he went to Beer and dwelt there, for fear of Abimelech his brother.

22 After Abimelech had reigned over Israel three years, 23 God sent a spirit of ill will between Abimelech and the men of Shechem; and the men of Shechem dealt treacherously with Abimelech, 24 that the crime *done* to the seventy sons of Jerubbaal might be settled and their blood be laid on Abimelech their brother, who killed them, and on the men of Shechem, who aided him in the killing of his brothers. 25 And the men of Shechem set men in ambush against him on the tops of the mountains, and they robbed all who passed by them along that way; and it was told Abimelech.

26 Now Gaal the son of Ebed came with his brothers and went over to Shechem; and the men of Shechem put their confidence in him. 27 So they went out into the fields, and gathered *grapes* from

הֶחֳדַ֫לְתִּי֙ אֶת־דִּשְׁנִ֔י אֲשֶׁר־בִּ֛י יְכַבְּד֥וּ אֱלֹהִ֖ים וַאֲנָשִׁ֑ים
וְהָ֣לַכְתִּ֔י לָנ֖וּעַ עַל־הָעֵצִֽים׃ 10 וַיֹּאמְר֥וּ הָעֵצִ֖ים
לַתְּאֵנָ֑ה לְכִי־אַ֖תְּ מָלְכִ֥י עָלֵֽינוּ׃ 11 וַתֹּ֤אמֶר לָהֶם֙
הַתְּאֵנָ֔ה הֶחֳדַ֫לְתִּי֙ אֶת־מָתְקִ֔י וְאֶת־תְּנוּבָתִ֖י הַטּוֹבָ֑ה
וְהָ֣לַכְתִּ֔י לָנ֖וּעַ עַל־הָעֵצִֽים׃ 12 וַיֹּאמְר֥וּ הָעֵצִ֖ים לַגָּ֑פֶן
לְכִי־אַ֖תְּ מָלְכִ֥ין עָלֵֽינוּ׃ 13 וַתֹּ֤אמֶר לָהֶם֙ הַגֶּ֔פֶן
הֶחֳדַ֫לְתִּי֙ אֶת־תִּ֣ירוֹשִׁ֔י הַֽמְשַׂמֵּ֥חַ אֱלֹהִ֖ים וַאֲנָשִׁ֑ים
וְהָ֣לַכְתִּ֔י לָנ֖וּעַ עַל־הָעֵצִֽים׃ 14 וַיֹּאמְר֥וּ כָל־הָעֵצִ֖ים
אֶל־הָאָטָ֑ד לֵ֥ךְ אַתָּ֖ה מְלָךְ־עָלֵֽינוּ׃ 15 וַיֹּ֣אמֶר הָאָטָד֮
אֶל־הָעֵצִים֒ אִ֡ם בֶּאֱמֶ֣ת אַתֶּם֩ מֹשְׁחִ֨ים אֹתִ֤י לְמֶ֙לֶךְ֙
עֲלֵיכֶ֔ם בֹּ֖אוּ חֲס֣וּ בְצִלִּ֑י וְאִם־אַ֕יִן תֵּ֤צֵא אֵשׁ֙ מִן־
הָ֣אָטָ֔ד וְתֹאכַ֖ל אֶת־אַרְזֵ֥י הַלְּבָנֽוֹן׃ 16 וְעַתָּ֞ה אִם־
בֶּאֱמֶ֤ת וּבְתָמִים֙ עֲשִׂיתֶ֔ם וַתַּמְלִ֖יכוּ אֶת־אֲבִימֶ֑לֶךְ
וְאִם־טוֹבָ֤ה עֲשִׂיתֶם֙ עִם־יְרֻבַּ֣עַל וְעִם־בֵּית֔וֹ וְאִם־
כִּגְמ֥וּל יָדָ֖יו עֲשִׂ֥יתֶם לֽוֹ׃ 17 אֲשֶׁר־נִלְחַ֥ם אָבִ֖י עֲלֵיכֶ֑ם
וַיַּשְׁלֵ֤ךְ אֶת־נַפְשׁוֹ֙ מִנֶּ֔גֶד וַיַּצֵּ֥ל אֶתְכֶ֖ם מִיַּ֥ד מִדְיָֽן׃
18 וְאַתֶּ֞ם קַמְתֶּ֨ם עַל־בֵּ֤ית אָבִי֙ הַיּ֔וֹם וַתַּהַרְג֧וּ אֶת־
בָּנָ֛יו שִׁבְעִ֥ים אִ֖ישׁ עַל־אֶ֣בֶן אֶחָ֑ת וַתַּמְלִ֜יכוּ אֶת־
אֲבִימֶ֤לֶךְ בֶּן־אֲמָתוֹ֙ עַל־בַּעֲלֵ֣י שְׁכֶ֔ם כִּ֥י אֲחִיכֶ֖ם הֽוּא׃
19 וְאִם־בֶּאֱמֶ֨ת וּבְתָמִ֧ים עֲשִׂיתֶ֛ם עִם־יְרֻבַּ֥עַל וְעִם־
בֵּית֖וֹ הַיּ֣וֹם הַזֶּ֑ה שִׂמְחוּ֙ בַּאֲבִימֶ֔לֶךְ וְיִשְׂמַ֥ח גַּם־ה֖וּא
בָּכֶֽם׃ 20 וְאִם־אַ֕יִן תֵּ֤צֵא אֵשׁ֙ מֵאֲבִימֶ֔לֶךְ וְתֹאכַ֛ל
אֶת־בַּעֲלֵ֥י שְׁכֶ֖ם וְאֶת־בֵּ֣ית מִלּ֑וֹא וְתֵצֵ֨א אֵ֜שׁ מִבַּעֲלֵ֤י
שְׁכֶם֙ וּמִבֵּ֣ית מִלּ֔וֹא וְתֹאכַ֖ל אֶת־אֲבִימֶֽלֶךְ׃ 21 וַיָּ֣נָס
יוֹתָ֔ם וַיִּבְרַ֖ח וַיֵּ֣לֶךְ בְּאֵ֑רָה וַיֵּ֣שֶׁב שָׁ֔ם מִפְּנֵ֖י אֲבִימֶ֥לֶךְ
אָחִֽיו׃ פ

22 וַיָּ֧שַׂר אֲבִימֶ֛לֶךְ עַל־יִשְׂרָאֵ֖ל שָׁלֹ֥שׁ שָׁנִֽים׃
23 וַיִּשְׁלַ֤ח אֱלֹהִים֙ ר֣וּחַ רָעָ֔ה בֵּ֣ין אֲבִימֶ֔לֶךְ וּבֵ֖ין
בַּעֲלֵ֣י שְׁכֶ֑ם וַיִּבְגְּד֥וּ בַעֲלֵי־שְׁכֶ֖ם בַּאֲבִימֶֽלֶךְ׃ 24 לָב֠וֹא
חֲמַ֞ס שִׁבְעִ֣ים בְּנֵֽי־יְרֻבַּ֗עַל וְדָמָם֙ לָשׂ֗וּם עַל־אֲבִימֶ֣לֶךְ
אֲחִיהֶ֔ם אֲשֶׁ֤ר הָרַג֙ אוֹתָ֔ם וְעַ֖ל בַּעֲלֵ֣י שְׁכֶ֑ם אֲשֶׁר־
חִזְּק֥וּ אֶת־יָדָ֖יו לַהֲרֹ֥ג אֶת־אֶחָֽיו׃ 25 וַיָּשִׂ֣ימוּ לוֹ֩ בַעֲלֵ֨י
שְׁכֶ֜ם מְאָרְבִ֗ים עַ֚ל רָאשֵׁ֣י הֶהָרִ֔ים וַיִּגְזְל֗וּ אֵ֛ת כָּל־
אֲשֶׁר־יַעֲבֹ֥ר עֲלֵיהֶ֖ם בַּדָּ֑רֶךְ וַיֻּגַּ֖ד לַאֲבִימֶֽלֶךְ׃ פ
26 וַיָּבֹ֞א גַּ֤עַל בֶּן־עֶ֙בֶד֙ וְאֶחָ֔יו וַיַּעַבְר֖וּ בִּשְׁכֶ֑ם
וַיִּבְטְחוּ־ב֖וֹ בַּעֲלֵ֥י שְׁכֶֽם׃ 27 וַיֵּצְא֣וּ הַשָּׂדֶ֗ה וַיִּבְצְרוּ֙
אֶת־כַּרְמֵיהֶ֔ם וַיִּדְרְכ֖וּ וַיַּעֲשׂ֣וּ הִלּוּלִ֑ים וַיָּבֹ֙אוּ֙ בֵּ֣ית

their vineyards and trod *them,* and made merry. And they went into the house of their god, and ate and drank, and cursed Abimelech. ²⁸ Then Gaal the son of Ebed said, "Who *is* Abimelech, and who *is* Shechem, that we should serve him? *Is he* not the son of Jerubbaal, and *is not* Zebul his officer? Serve the men of Hamor the father of Shechem; but why should we serve him? ²⁹ If only this people were under my authority! Then I would remove Abimelech." So he said to Abimelech, "Increase your army and come out!"

³⁰ When Zebul, the ruler of the city, heard the words of Gaal the son of Ebed, his anger was aroused. ³¹ And he sent messengers to Abimelech secretly, saying, "Take note! Gaal the son of Ebed and his brothers have come to Shechem; and here they are, fortifying the city against you. ³² Now therefore, get up by night, you and the people who *are* with you, and lie in wait in the field. ³³ And it shall be, as soon as the sun is up in the morning, *that* you shall rise early and rush upon the city; and *when* he and the people who are with him come out against you, you may then do to them as you find opportunity."

³⁴ So Abimelech and all the people who *were* with him rose by night, and lay in wait against Shechem in four companies. ³⁵ When Gaal the son of Ebed went out and stood in the entrance to the city gate, Abimelech and the people who *were* with him rose from lying in wait. ³⁶ And when Gaal saw the people, he said to Zebul, "Look, people are coming down from the tops of the mountains!"

But Zebul said to him, "You see the shadows of the mountains as *if they were* men."

³⁷ So Gaal spoke again and said, "See, people are coming down from the center of the land, and another company is coming from the Diviners' Terebinth Tree."

³⁸ Then Zebul said to him, "Where indeed *is* your mouth now, with which you said, 'Who is Abimelech, that we should serve him?' *Are* not these the people whom you despised? Go out, if you will, and fight with them now."

³⁹ So Gaal went out, leading the men of Shechem, and fought with Abimelech. ⁴⁰ And Abimelech chased him, and he fled from him; and many fell wounded, to the *very* entrance of the gate. ⁴¹ Then Abimelech dwelt at Arumah, and Zebul drove out Gaal and his brothers, so that they would not dwell in Shechem.

⁴² And it came about on the next day that the people went out into the field, and they told Abimelech. ⁴³ So he took his people, divided them into three companies, and lay in wait in the field.

אֱלֹהֵיהֶם וַיֹּאכְלוּ וַיִּשְׁתּוּ וַיְקַלְלוּ אֶת־אֲבִימֶלֶךְ: 28 וַיֹּאמֶר ׀ גַּעַל בֶּן־עֶבֶד מִי־אֲבִימֶלֶךְ וּמִי־שְׁכֶם כִּי נַעַבְדֶנּוּ הֲלֹא בֶן־יְרֻבַּעַל וּזְבֻל פְּקִידוֹ עִבְדוּ אֶת־אַנְשֵׁי חֲמוֹר אֲבִי שְׁכֶם וּמַדּוּעַ נַעַבְדֶנּוּ אֲנָחְנוּ: 29 וּמִי יִתֵּן אֶת־הָעָם הַזֶּה בְּיָדִי וְאָסִירָה אֶת־אֲבִימֶלֶךְ וַיֹּאמֶר לַאֲבִימֶלֶךְ רַבֶּה צְבָאֲךָ וָצֵאָה: 30 וַיִּשְׁמַע זְבֻל שַׂר־הָעִיר אֶת־דִּבְרֵי גַּעַל בֶּן־עָבֶד וַיִּחַר אַפּוֹ: 31 וַיִּשְׁלַח מַלְאָכִים אֶל־אֲבִימֶלֶךְ בְּתָרְמָה לֵאמֹר הִנֵּה גַעַל בֶּן־עֶבֶד וְאֶחָיו בָּאִים שְׁכֶמָה וְהִנָּם צָרִים אֶת־הָעִיר עָלֶיךָ: 32 וְעַתָּה קוּם לַיְלָה אַתָּה וְהָעָם אֲשֶׁר־אִתָּךְ וֶאֱרֹב בַּשָּׂדֶה: 33 וְהָיָה בַבֹּקֶר כִּזְרֹחַ הַשֶּׁמֶשׁ תַּשְׁכִּים וּפָשַׁטְתָּ עַל־הָעִיר וְהִנֵּה־הוּא וְהָעָם אֲשֶׁר־אִתּוֹ יֹצְאִים אֵלֶיךָ וְעָשִׂיתָ לּוֹ כַּאֲשֶׁר תִּמְצָא יָדֶךָ: 34 וַיָּקָם אֲבִימֶלֶךְ וְכָל־הָעָם אֲשֶׁר־עִמּוֹ לָיְלָה וַיֶּאֶרְבוּ עַל־שְׁכֶם אַרְבָּעָה רָאשִׁים: 35 וַיֵּצֵא גַּעַל בֶּן־עֶבֶד וַיַּעֲמֹד פֶּתַח שַׁעַר הָעִיר וַיָּקָם אֲבִימֶלֶךְ וְהָעָם אֲשֶׁר־אִתּוֹ מִן־הַמַּאְרָב: 36 וַיַּרְא־גַעַל אֶת־הָעָם וַיֹּאמֶר אֶל־זְבֻל הִנֵּה־עָם יוֹרֵד מֵרָאשֵׁי הֶהָרִים וַיֹּאמֶר אֵלָיו זְבֻל אֵת צֵל הֶהָרִים אַתָּה רֹאֶה כָּאֲנָשִׁים: 37 וַיֹּסֶף עוֹד גַּעַל לְדַבֵּר וַיֹּאמֶר הִנֵּה־עָם יוֹרְדִים מֵעִם טַבּוּר הָאָרֶץ וְרֹאשׁ־אֶחָד בָּא מִדֶּרֶךְ אֵלוֹן מְעוֹנְנִים: 38 וַיֹּאמֶר אֵלָיו זְבֻל אַיֵּה אֵפוֹא פִיךָ אֲשֶׁר תֹּאמַר מִי אֲבִימֶלֶךְ כִּי נַעַבְדֶנּוּ הֲלֹא זֶה הָעָם אֲשֶׁר מָאַסְתָּה בּוֹ צֵא־נָא עַתָּה וְהִלָּחֶם בּוֹ: 39 וַיֵּצֵא גַעַל לִפְנֵי בַּעֲלֵי שְׁכֶם וַיִּלָּחֶם בַּאֲבִימֶלֶךְ: 40 וַיִּרְדְּפֵהוּ אֲבִימֶלֶךְ וַיָּנָס מִפָּנָיו וַיִּפְּלוּ חֲלָלִים רַבִּים עַד־פֶּתַח הַשָּׁעַר: 41 וַיֵּשֶׁב אֲבִימֶלֶךְ בָּארוּמָה וַיְגָרֶשׁ זְבֻל אֶת־גַּעַל וְאֶת־אֶחָיו מִשֶּׁבֶת בִּשְׁכֶם: 42 וַיְהִי מִמָּחֳרָת וַיֵּצֵא הָעָם הַשָּׂדֶה וַיַּגִּדוּ לַאֲבִימֶלֶךְ: 43 וַיִּקַּח אֶת־הָעָם וַיֶּחֱצֵם לִשְׁלֹשָׁה רָאשִׁים וַיֶּאֱרֹב בַּשָּׂדֶה וַיַּרְא וְהִנֵּה הָעָם יֹצֵא מִן־הָעִיר וַיָּקָם עֲלֵיהֶם וַיַּכֵּם:

And he looked, and there were the people, coming out of the city; and he rose against them and attacked them. ⁴⁴ Then Abimelech and the company that *was* with him rushed forward and stood at the entrance of the gate of the city; and the *other* two companies rushed upon all who *were* in the fields and killed them. ⁴⁵ So Abimelech fought against the city all that day; he took the city and killed the people who *were* in it; and he demolished the city and sowed it with salt.

⁴⁶ Now when all the men of the tower of Shechem had heard *that,* they entered the stronghold of the temple of the god Berith. ⁴⁷ And it was told Abimelech that all the men of the tower of Shechem were gathered together. ⁴⁸ Then Abimelech went up to Mount Zalmon, he and all the people who *were* with him. And Abimelech took an ax in his hand and cut down a bough from the trees, and took it and laid *it* on his shoulder; then he said to the people who were with him, "What you have seen me do, make haste *and* do as I *have* done." ⁴⁹ So each of the people likewise cut down his own bough and followed Abimelech, put *them* against the stronghold, and set the stronghold on fire above them, so that all the people of the tower of Shechem died, about a thousand men and women.

⁵⁰ Then Abimelech went to Thebez, and he encamped against Thebez and took it. ⁵¹ But there was a strong tower in the city, and all the men and women—all the people of the city—fled there and shut themselves in; then they went up to the top of the tower. ⁵² So Abimelech came as far as the tower and fought against it; and he drew near the door of the tower to burn it with fire. ⁵³ But a certain woman dropped an upper millstone on Abimelech's head and crushed his skull. ⁵⁴ Then he called quickly to the young man, his armorbearer, and said to him, "Draw your sword and kill me, lest men say of me, 'A woman killed him.'" So his young man thrust him through, and he died. ⁵⁵ And when the men of Israel saw that Abimelech was dead, they departed, every man to his place.

⁵⁶ Thus God repaid the wickedness of Abimelech, which he had done to his father by killing his seventy brothers. ⁵⁷ And all the evil of the men of Shechem God returned on their own heads, and on them came the curse of Jotham the son of Jerubbaal.

10 After Abimelech there arose to save Israel Tola the son of Puah, the son of Dodo, a man of Issachar; and he dwelt in Shamir in the mountains of Ephraim. ² He judged Israel twenty-three years; and he died and was buried in Shamir.

44 וַאֲבִימֶלֶךְ וְהָרָאשִׁים אֲשֶׁר עִמּוֹ פָּשְׁטוּ וַיַּעַמְדוּ פֶּתַח שַׁעַר הָעִיר וּשְׁנֵי הָרָאשִׁים פָּשְׁטוּ עַל־כָּל־אֲשֶׁר בַּשָּׂדֶה וַיַּכּוּם: 45 וַאֲבִימֶלֶךְ נִלְחָם בָּעִיר כֹּל הַיּוֹם הַהוּא וַיִּלְכֹּד אֶת־הָעִיר וְאֶת־הָעָם אֲשֶׁר־בָּהּ הָרָג וַיִּתֹּץ אֶת־הָעִיר וַיִּזְרָעֶהָ מֶלַח: פ

46 וַיִּשְׁמְעוּ כָּל־בַּעֲלֵי מִגְדַּל־שְׁכֶם וַיָּבֹאוּ אֶל־צְרִיחַ בֵּית אֵל בְּרִית: 47 וַיֻּגַּד לַאֲבִימֶלֶךְ כִּי הִתְקַבְּצוּ כָּל־בַּעֲלֵי מִגְדַּל־שְׁכֶם: 48 וַיַּעַל אֲבִימֶלֶךְ הַר־צַלְמוֹן הוּא וְכָל־הָעָם אֲשֶׁר־אִתּוֹ וַיִּקַּח אֲבִימֶלֶךְ אֶת־הַקַּרְדֻּמּוֹת בְּיָדוֹ וַיִּכְרֹת שׂוֹכַת עֵצִים וַיִּשָּׂאֶהָ וַיָּשֶׂם עַל־שִׁכְמוֹ וַיֹּאמֶר אֶל־הָעָם אֲשֶׁר־עִמּוֹ מָה רְאִיתֶם עָשִׂיתִי מַהֲרוּ עֲשׂוּ כָמוֹנִי: 49 וַיִּכְרְתוּ גַם־כָּל־הָעָם אִישׁ שׂוֹכֹה וַיֵּלְכוּ אַחֲרֵי אֲבִימֶלֶךְ וַיָּשִׂימוּ עַל־הַצְּרִיחַ וַיַּצִּיתוּ עֲלֵיהֶם אֶת־הַצְּרִיחַ בָּאֵשׁ וַיָּמֻתוּ גַּם כָּל־אַנְשֵׁי מִגְדַּל־שְׁכֶם כְּאֶלֶף אִישׁ וְאִשָּׁה: פ

50 וַיֵּלֶךְ אֲבִימֶלֶךְ אֶל־תֵּבֵץ וַיִּחַן בְּתֵבֵץ וַיִּלְכְּדָהּ: 51 וּמִגְדַּל־עֹז הָיָה בְתוֹךְ־הָעִיר וַיָּנֻסוּ שָׁמָּה כָּל־הָאֲנָשִׁים וְהַנָּשִׁים וְכֹל בַּעֲלֵי הָעִיר וַיִּסְגְּרוּ בַּעֲדָם וַיַּעֲלוּ עַל־גַּג הַמִּגְדָּל: 52 וַיָּבֹא אֲבִימֶלֶךְ עַד־הַמִּגְדָּל וַיִּלָּחֶם בּוֹ וַיִּגַּשׁ עַד־פֶּתַח הַמִּגְדָּל לְשָׂרְפוֹ בָאֵשׁ: 53 וַתַּשְׁלֵךְ אִשָּׁה אַחַת פֶּלַח רֶכֶב עַל־רֹאשׁ אֲבִימֶלֶךְ וַתָּרִץ אֶת־גֻּלְגָּלְתּוֹ: 54 וַיִּקְרָא מְהֵרָה אֶל־הַנַּעַר ׀ נֹשֵׂא כֵלָיו וַיֹּאמֶר לוֹ שְׁלֹף חַרְבְּךָ וּמוֹתְתֵנִי פֶּן־יֹאמְרוּ לִי אִשָּׁה הֲרָגָתְהוּ וַיִּדְקְרֵהוּ נַעֲרוֹ וַיָּמֹת: 55 וַיִּרְאוּ אִישׁ־יִשְׂרָאֵל כִּי מֵת אֲבִימֶלֶךְ וַיֵּלְכוּ אִישׁ לִמְקֹמוֹ: 56 וַיָּשֶׁב אֱלֹהִים אֵת רָעַת אֲבִימֶלֶךְ אֲשֶׁר עָשָׂה לְאָבִיו לַהֲרֹג אֶת־שִׁבְעִים אֶחָיו: 57 וְאֵת כָּל־רָעַת אַנְשֵׁי שְׁכֶם הֵשִׁיב אֱלֹהִים בְּרֹאשָׁם וַתָּבֹא אֲלֵיהֶם קִלֲלַת יוֹתָם בֶּן־יְרֻבָּעַל: פ

י וַיָּקָם אַחֲרֵי אֲבִימֶלֶךְ לְהוֹשִׁיעַ אֶת־יִשְׂרָאֵל תּוֹלָע בֶּן־פּוּאָה בֶּן־דּוֹדוֹ אִישׁ יִשָּׂשכָר וְהוּא־יֹשֵׁב בְּשָׁמִיר בְּהַר אֶפְרָיִם: 2 וַיִּשְׁפֹּט אֶת־יִשְׂרָאֵל עֶשְׂרִים וְשָׁלֹשׁ שָׁנָה וַיָּמָת וַיִּקָּבֵר בְּשָׁמִיר: פ

³After him arose Jair, a Gileadite; and he judged Israel twenty-two years. ⁴Now he had thirty sons who rode on thirty donkeys; they also had thirty towns, which are called "Havoth Jair" to this day, which *are* in the land of Gilead. ⁵And Jair died and was buried in Camon.

⁶Then the children of Israel again did evil in the sight of the LORD, and served the Baals and the Ashtoreths, the gods of Syria, the gods of Sidon, the gods of Moab, the gods of the people of Ammon, and the gods of the Philistines; and they forsook the LORD and did not serve Him. ⁷So the anger of the LORD was hot against Israel; and He sold them into the hands of the Philistines and into the hands of the people of Ammon. ⁸From that year they harassed and oppressed the children of Israel for eighteen years—all the children of Israel who *were* on the other side of the Jordan in the land of the Amorites, in Gilead. ⁹Moreover the people of Ammon crossed over the Jordan to fight against Judah also, against Benjamin, and against the house of Ephraim, so that Israel was severely distressed.

¹⁰And the children of Israel cried out to the LORD, saying, "We have sinned against You, because we have both forsaken our God and served the Baals!"

¹¹So the LORD said to the children of Israel, "*Did I not deliver you* from the Egyptians and from the Amorites and from the people of Ammon and from the Philistines? ¹²Also the Sidonians and Amalekites and Maonites oppressed you; and you cried out to Me, and I delivered you from their hand. ¹³Yet you have forsaken Me and served other gods. Therefore I will deliver you no more. ¹⁴Go and cry out to the gods which you have chosen; let them deliver you in your time of distress."

¹⁵And the children of Israel said to the LORD, "We have sinned! Do to us whatever seems best to You; only deliver us this day, we pray." ¹⁶So they put away the foreign gods from among them and served the LORD. And His soul could no longer endure the misery of Israel.

¹⁷Then the people of Ammon gathered together and encamped in Gilead. And the children of Israel assembled together and encamped in Mizpah. ¹⁸And the people, the leaders of Gilead, said to one another, "Who *is* the man who will begin the fight against the people of Ammon? He shall be head over all the inhabitants of Gilead."

11 Now Jephthah the Gileadite was a mighty man of valor, but he *was* the son of a harlot; and Gilead begot Jephthah. ²Gilead's wife bore sons;

³ וַיָּקָם אַחֲרָיו יָאִיר הַגִּלְעָדִי וַיִּשְׁפֹּט אֶת־יִשְׂרָאֵל עֶשְׂרִים וּשְׁתַּיִם שָׁנָה: ⁴ וַיְהִי־לוֹ שְׁלֹשִׁים בָּנִים רֹכְבִים עַל־שְׁלֹשִׁים עֲיָרִים וּשְׁלֹשִׁים עֲיָרִים לָהֶם לָהֶם יִקְרְאוּ ׀ חַוֺּת יָאִיר עַד הַיּוֹם הַזֶּה אֲשֶׁר בְּאֶרֶץ הַגִּלְעָד: ⁵ וַיָּמָת יָאִיר וַיִּקָּבֵר בְּקָמוֹן: פ

⁶ וַיֹּסִפוּ ׀ בְּנֵי יִשְׂרָאֵל לַעֲשׂוֹת הָרַע בְּעֵינֵי יְהֹוָה וַיַּעַבְדוּ אֶת־הַבְּעָלִים וְאֶת־הָעַשְׁתָּרוֹת וְאֶת־אֱלֹהֵי אֲרָם וְאֶת־אֱלֹהֵי צִידוֹן וְאֵת ׀ אֱלֹהֵי מוֹאָב וְאֵת אֱלֹהֵי בְנֵי־עַמּוֹן וְאֵת אֱלֹהֵי פְלִשְׁתִּים וַיַּעַזְבוּ אֶת־יְהֹוָה וְלֹא עֲבָדוּהוּ: ⁷ וַיִּחַר־אַף יְהֹוָה בְּיִשְׂרָאֵל וַיִּמְכְּרֵם בְּיַד־פְּלִשְׁתִּים וּבְיַד בְּנֵי עַמּוֹן: ⁸ וַיִּרְעֲצוּ וַיְרֹצְצוּ אֶת־בְּנֵי יִשְׂרָאֵל בַּשָּׁנָה הַהִיא שְׁמֹנֶה עֶשְׂרֵה שָׁנָה אֶת־כָּל־בְּנֵי יִשְׂרָאֵל אֲשֶׁר בְּעֵבֶר הַיַּרְדֵּן בְּאֶרֶץ הָאֱמֹרִי אֲשֶׁר בַּגִּלְעָד: ⁹ וַיַּעַבְרוּ בְנֵי־עַמּוֹן אֶת־הַיַּרְדֵּן לְהִלָּחֵם גַּם־בִּיהוּדָה וּבְבִנְיָמִין וּבְבֵית אֶפְרָיִם וַתֵּצֶר לְיִשְׂרָאֵל מְאֹד: ¹⁰ וַיִּזְעֲקוּ בְּנֵי יִשְׂרָאֵל אֶל־יְהֹוָה לֵאמֹר חָטָאנוּ לָךְ וְכִי עָזַבְנוּ אֶת־אֱלֹהֵינוּ וַנַּעֲבֹד אֶת־הַבְּעָלִים: פ

¹¹ וַיֹּאמֶר יְהֹוָה אֶל־בְּנֵי יִשְׂרָאֵל הֲלֹא מִמִּצְרַיִם וּמִן־הָאֱמֹרִי וּמִן־בְּנֵי עַמּוֹן וּמִן־פְּלִשְׁתִּים: ¹² וְצִידוֹנִים וַעֲמָלֵק וּמָעוֹן לָחֲצוּ אֶתְכֶם וַתִּצְעֲקוּ אֵלַי וָאוֹשִׁיעָה אֶתְכֶם מִיָּדָם: ¹³ וְאַתֶּם עֲזַבְתֶּם אוֹתִי וַתַּעַבְדוּ אֱלֹהִים אֲחֵרִים לָכֵן לֹא־אוֹסִיף לְהוֹשִׁיעַ אֶתְכֶם: ¹⁴ לְכוּ וְזַעֲקוּ אֶל־הָאֱלֹהִים אֲשֶׁר בְּחַרְתֶּם בָּם הֵמָּה יוֹשִׁיעוּ לָכֶם בְּעֵת צָרַתְכֶם: ¹⁵ וַיֹּאמְרוּ בְנֵי־יִשְׂרָאֵל אֶל־יְהֹוָה חָטָאנוּ עֲשֵׂה־אַתָּה לָנוּ כְּכָל־הַטּוֹב בְּעֵינֶיךָ אַךְ הַצִּילֵנוּ נָא הַיּוֹם הַזֶּה: ¹⁶ וַיָּסִירוּ אֶת־אֱלֹהֵי הַנֵּכָר מִקִּרְבָּם וַיַּעַבְדוּ אֶת־יְהֹוָה וַתִּקְצַר נַפְשׁוֹ בַּעֲמַל יִשְׂרָאֵל: פ

¹⁷ וַיִּצָּעֲקוּ בְּנֵי עַמּוֹן וַיַּחֲנוּ בַּגִּלְעָד וַיֵּאָסְפוּ בְּנֵי יִשְׂרָאֵל וַיַּחֲנוּ בַּמִּצְפָּה: ¹⁸ וַיֹּאמְרוּ הָעָם שָׂרֵי גִלְעָד אִישׁ אֶל־רֵעֵהוּ מִי הָאִישׁ אֲשֶׁר יָחֵל לְהִלָּחֵם בִּבְנֵי עַמּוֹן יִהְיֶה לְרֹאשׁ לְכֹל יֹשְׁבֵי גִלְעָד: פ

יא וְיִפְתָּח הַגִּלְעָדִי הָיָה גִּבּוֹר חַיִל וְהוּא בֶּן־אִשָּׁה זוֹנָה וַיּוֹלֶד גִּלְעָד אֶת־יִפְתָּח: ² וַתֵּלֶד אֵשֶׁת־

and when his wife's sons grew up, they drove Jephthah out, and said to him, "You shall have no inheritance in our father's house, for you *are* the son of another woman." ³ Then Jephthah fled from his brothers and dwelt in the land of Tob; and worthless men banded together with Jephthah and went out *raiding* with him.

⁴ It came to pass after a time that the people of Ammon made war against Israel. ⁵ And so it was, when the people of Ammon made war against Israel, that the elders of Gilead went to get Jephthah from the land of Tob. ⁶ Then they said to Jephthah, "Come and be our commander, that we may fight against the people of Ammon."

⁷ So Jephthah said to the elders of Gilead, "Did you not hate me, and expel me from my father's house? Why have you come to me now when you are in distress?"

⁸ And the elders of Gilead said to Jephthah, "That is why we have turned again to you now, that you may go with us and fight against the people of Ammon, and be our head over all the inhabitants of Gilead."

⁹ So Jephthah said to the elders of Gilead, "If you take me back home to fight against the people of Ammon, and the LORD delivers them to me, shall I be your head?"

¹⁰ And the elders of Gilead said to Jephthah, "The LORD will be a witness between us, if we do not do according to your words." ¹¹ Then Jephthah went with the elders of Gilead, and the people made him head and commander over them; and Jephthah spoke all his words before the LORD in Mizpah.

¹² Now Jephthah sent messengers to the king of the people of Ammon, saying, "What do you have against me, that you have come to fight against me in my land?"

¹³ And the king of the people of Ammon answered the messengers of Jephthah, "Because Israel took away my land when they came up out of Egypt, from the Arnon as far as the Jabbok, and to the Jordan. Now therefore, restore those *lands* peaceably."

¹⁴ So Jephthah again sent messengers to the king of the people of Ammon, ¹⁵ and said to him, "Thus says Jephthah: 'Israel did not take away the land of Moab, nor the land of the people of Ammon; ¹⁶ for when Israel came up from Egypt, they walked through the wilderness as far as the Red Sea and came to Kadesh. ¹⁷ Then Israel sent messengers to the king of Edom, saying, "Please let me pass through your land." But the king of Edom would not heed. And in like manner they sent to the king of Moab, but he would not *consent*. So Israel

גִלְעָד לוֹ בָּנִים וַיִּגְדְּלוּ בְנֵי־הָאִשָּׁה וַיְגָרְשׁוּ אֶת־יִפְתָּח וַיֹּאמְרוּ לוֹ לֹא־תִנְחַל בְּבֵית־אָבִינוּ כִּי בֶן־אִשָּׁה אַחֶרֶת אָתָּה: ³ וַיִּבְרַח יִפְתָּח מִפְּנֵי אֶחָיו וַיֵּשֶׁב בְּאֶרֶץ טוֹב וַיִּתְלַקְּטוּ אֶל־יִפְתָּח אֲנָשִׁים רֵיקִים וַיֵּצְאוּ עִמּוֹ: פ

⁴ וַיְהִי מִיָּמִים וַיִּלָּחֲמוּ בְנֵי־עַמּוֹן עִם־יִשְׂרָאֵל: ⁵ וַיְהִי כַּאֲשֶׁר־נִלְחֲמוּ בְנֵי־עַמּוֹן עִם־יִשְׂרָאֵל וַיֵּלְכוּ זִקְנֵי גִלְעָד לָקַחַת אֶת־יִפְתָּח מֵאֶרֶץ טוֹב: ⁶ וַיֹּאמְרוּ לְיִפְתָּח לְכָה וְהָיִיתָה לָּנוּ לְקָצִין וְנִלָּחֲמָה בִּבְנֵי עַמּוֹן: ⁷ וַיֹּאמֶר יִפְתָּח לְזִקְנֵי גִלְעָד הֲלֹא אַתֶּם שְׂנֵאתֶם אוֹתִי וַתְּגָרְשׁוּנִי מִבֵּית אָבִי וּמַדּוּעַ בָּאתֶם אֵלַי עַתָּה כַּאֲשֶׁר צַר לָכֶם: ⁸ וַיֹּאמְרוּ זִקְנֵי גִלְעָד אֶל־יִפְתָּח לָכֵן עַתָּה שַׁבְנוּ אֵלֶיךָ וְהָלַכְתָּ עִמָּנוּ וְנִלְחַמְתָּ בִּבְנֵי עַמּוֹן וְהָיִיתָ לָּנוּ לְרֹאשׁ לְכֹל יֹשְׁבֵי גִלְעָד: ⁹ וַיֹּאמֶר יִפְתָּח אֶל־זִקְנֵי גִלְעָד אִם־מְשִׁיבִים אַתֶּם אוֹתִי לְהִלָּחֵם בִּבְנֵי עַמּוֹן וְנָתַן יְהוָה אוֹתָם לְפָנָי אָנֹכִי אֶהְיֶה לָכֶם לְרֹאשׁ: ¹⁰ וַיֹּאמְרוּ זִקְנֵי גִלְעָד אֶל־יִפְתָּח יְהוָה יִהְיֶה שֹׁמֵעַ בֵּינוֹתֵינוּ אִם־לֹא כִדְבָרְךָ כֵּן נַעֲשֶׂה: ¹¹ וַיֵּלֶךְ יִפְתָּח עִם־זִקְנֵי גִלְעָד וַיָּשִׂימוּ הָעָם אוֹתוֹ עֲלֵיהֶם לְרֹאשׁ וּלְקָצִין וַיְדַבֵּר יִפְתָּח אֶת־כָּל־דְּבָרָיו לִפְנֵי יְהוָה בַּמִּצְפָּה: פ

¹² וַיִּשְׁלַח יִפְתָּח מַלְאָכִים אֶל־מֶלֶךְ בְּנֵי־עַמּוֹן לֵאמֹר מַה־לִּי וָלָךְ כִּי־בָאתָ אֵלַי לְהִלָּחֵם בְּאַרְצִי: ¹³ וַיֹּאמֶר מֶלֶךְ בְּנֵי־עַמּוֹן אֶל־מַלְאֲכֵי יִפְתָּח כִּי־לָקַח יִשְׂרָאֵל אֶת־אַרְצִי בַּעֲלוֹתוֹ מִמִּצְרַיִם מֵאַרְנוֹן וְעַד־הַיַּבֹּק וְעַד־הַיַּרְדֵּן וְעַתָּה הָשִׁיבָה אֶתְהֶן בְּשָׁלוֹם: ¹⁴ וַיּוֹסֶף עוֹד יִפְתָּח וַיִּשְׁלַח מַלְאָכִים אֶל־מֶלֶךְ בְּנֵי עַמּוֹן: ¹⁵ וַיֹּאמֶר לוֹ כֹּה אָמַר יִפְתָּח לֹא־לָקַח יִשְׂרָאֵל אֶת־אֶרֶץ מוֹאָב וְאֶת־אֶרֶץ בְּנֵי עַמּוֹן: ¹⁶ כִּי בַּעֲלוֹתָם מִמִּצְרָיִם וַיֵּלֶךְ יִשְׂרָאֵל בַּמִּדְבָּר עַד־יַם־סוּף וַיָּבֹא קָדֵשָׁה: ¹⁷ וַיִּשְׁלַח יִשְׂרָאֵל מַלְאָכִים אֶל־מֶלֶךְ אֱדוֹם לֵאמֹר אֶעְבְּרָה־נָּא בְאַרְצֶךָ וְלֹא שָׁמַע מֶלֶךְ אֱדוֹם וְגַם אֶל־מֶלֶךְ מוֹאָב שָׁלַח וְלֹא אָבָה וַיֵּשֶׁב

remained in Kadesh. ¹⁸ And they went along
through the wilderness and bypassed the land of
Edom and the land of Moab, came to the east side
of the land of Moab, and encamped on the other
side of the Arnon. But they did not enter the border
of Moab, for the Arnon *was* the border of Moab.
¹⁹ Then Israel sent messengers to Sihon king of the
Amorites, king of Heshbon; and Israel said to him,
"Please let us pass through your land into our
place." ²⁰ But Sihon did not trust Israel to pass
through his territory. So Sihon gathered all his
people together, encamped in Jahaz, and fought
against Israel. ²¹ And the LORD God of Israel
delivered Sihon and all his people into the hand of
Israel, and they defeated them. Thus Israel gained
possession of all the land of the Amorites, who
inhabited that country. ²² They took possession of
all the territory of the Amorites, from the Arnon to
the Jabbok and from the wilderness to the Jordan.

²³ 'And now the LORD God of Israel has
dispossessed the Amorites from before His people
Israel; should you then possess it? ²⁴ Will you not
possess whatever Chemosh your god gives you to
possess? So whatever the LORD our God takes
possession of before us, we will possess. ²⁵ And now,
are you any better than Balak the son of Zippor,
king of Moab? Did he ever strive against Israel? Did
he ever fight against them? ²⁶ While Israel dwelt in
Heshbon and its villages, in Aroer and its villages,
and in all the cities along the banks of the Arnon,
for three hundred years, why did you not recover
them within that time? ²⁷ Therefore I have not
sinned against you, but you wronged me by fighting
against me. May the LORD, the Judge, render
judgment this day between the children of Israel
and the people of Ammon.' " ²⁸ However, the king
of the people of Ammon did not heed the words
which Jephthah sent him.

²⁹ Then the Spirit of the LORD came upon
Jephthah, and he passed through Gilead and
Manasseh, and he passed through Mizpah of Gilead;
and from Mizpah of Gilead he advanced *toward* the
people of Ammon. ³⁰ And Jephthah made a vow to
the LORD, and said, "If You will indeed deliver the
people of Ammon into my hands, ³¹ then it will be
that whatever comes out of the doors of my house
to meet me, when I return in peace from the people
of Ammon, shall surely be the LORD's, and I will
offer it up as a burnt offering."

³² So Jephthah advanced toward the people of
Ammon to fight against them, and the LORD
delivered them into his hands. ³³ And he defeated
them from Aroer as far as Minnith—twenty cities—

and to Abel Keramim, with a very great slaughter. Thus the people of Ammon were subdued before the children of Israel.

³⁴ When Jephthah came to his house at Mizpah, there was his daughter, coming out to meet him with timbrels and dancing; and she *was his* only child. Besides her he had neither son nor daughter. ³⁵ And it came to pass, when he saw her, that he tore his clothes, and said, "Alas, my daughter! You have brought me very low! You are among those who trouble me! For I have given my word to the Lord, and I cannot go back on it."

³⁶ So she said to him, "My father, *if* you have given your word to the Lord, do to me according to what has gone out of your mouth, because the Lord has avenged you of your enemies, the people of Ammon." ³⁷ Then she said to her father, "Let this thing be done for me: let me alone for two months, that I may go and wander on the mountains and bewail my virginity, my friends and I."

³⁸ So he said, "Go." And he sent her away *for* two months; and she went with her friends, and bewailed her virginity on the mountains. ³⁹ And it was so at the end of two months that she returned to her father, and he carried out his vow with her which he had vowed. She knew no man. And it became a custom in Israel ⁴⁰ *that* the daughters of Israel went four days each year to lament the daughter of Jephthah the Gileadite.

12 Then the men of Ephraim gathered together, crossed over toward Zaphon, and said to Jephthah, "Why did you cross over to fight against the people of Ammon, and did not call us to go with you? We will burn your house down on you with fire!"

² And Jephthah said to them, "My people and I were in a great struggle with the people of Ammon; and when I called you, you did not deliver me out of their hands. ³ So when I saw that you would not deliver *me,* I took my life in my hands and crossed over against the people of Ammon; and the Lord delivered them into my hand. Why then have you come up to me this day to fight against me?" ⁴ Now Jephthah gathered together all the men of Gilead and fought against Ephraim. And the men of Gilead defeated Ephraim, because they said, "You Gileadites *are* fugitives of Ephraim among the Ephraimites *and* among the Manassites." ⁵ The Gileadites seized the fords of the Jordan before the Ephraimites *arrived.* And when *any* Ephraimite who escaped said, "Let me cross over," the men of Gilead would say to him, "*Are* you an Ephraimite?" If he said, "No," ⁶ then they would say to him,

34 וַיָּבֹא יִפְתָּח הַמִּצְפָּה אֶל־בֵּיתוֹ וְהִנֵּה בִתּוֹ יֹצֵאת לִקְרָאתוֹ בְתֻפִּים וּבִמְחֹלוֹת וְרַק הִיא יְחִידָה אֵין־לוֹ מִמֶּנּוּ בֵּן אוֹ־בַת: 35 וַיְהִי כִרְאוֹתוֹ אוֹתָהּ וַיִּקְרַע אֶת־בְּגָדָיו וַיֹּאמֶר אֲהָהּ בִּתִּי הַכְרֵעַ הִכְרַעְתִּנִי וְאַתְּ הָיִית בְּעֹכְרָי וְאָנֹכִי פָּצִיתִי־פִי אֶל־יְהֹוָה וְלֹא אוּכַל לָשׁוּב: 36 וַתֹּאמֶר אֵלָיו אָבִי פָּצִיתָה אֶת־פִּיךָ אֶל־יְהֹוָה עֲשֵׂה לִי כַּאֲשֶׁר יָצָא מִפִּיךָ אַחֲרֵי אֲשֶׁר עָשָׂה לְךָ יְהֹוָה נְקָמוֹת מֵאֹיְבֶיךָ מִבְּנֵי עַמּוֹן: 37 וַתֹּאמֶר אֶל־אָבִיהָ יֵעָשֶׂה לִּי הַדָּבָר הַזֶּה הַרְפֵּה מִמֶּנִּי שְׁנַיִם חֳדָשִׁים וְאֵלְכָה וְיָרַדְתִּי עַל־הֶהָרִים וְאֶבְכֶּה עַל־בְּתוּלַי אָנֹכִי וְרֵעוֹתָֽי: 38 וַיֹּאמֶר לֵכִי וַיִּשְׁלַח אוֹתָהּ שְׁנֵי חֳדָשִׁים וַתֵּלֶךְ הִיא וְרֵעוֹתֶיהָ וַתֵּבְךְּ עַל־בְּתוּלֶיהָ עַל־הֶהָרִים: 39 וַיְהִי מִקֵּץ שְׁנַיִם חֳדָשִׁים וַתָּשָׁב אֶל־אָבִיהָ וַיַּעַשׂ לָהּ אֶת־נִדְרוֹ אֲשֶׁר נָדָר וְהִיא לֹא־יָדְעָה אִישׁ וַתְּהִי־חֹק בְּיִשְׂרָאֵל: 40 מִיָּמִים | יָמִימָה תֵּלַכְנָה בְּנוֹת יִשְׂרָאֵל לְתַנּוֹת לְבַת־יִפְתָּח הַגִּלְעָדִי אַרְבַּעַת יָמִים בַּשָּׁנָה: ס

יב וַיִּצָּעֵק אִישׁ אֶפְרַיִם וַיַּעֲבֹר צָפוֹנָה וַיֹּאמְרוּ לְיִפְתָּח מַדּוּעַ | עָבַרְתָּ | לְהִלָּחֵם בִּבְנֵי־עַמּוֹן וְלָנוּ לֹא קָרָאתָ לָלֶכֶת עִמָּךְ בֵּיתְךָ נִשְׂרֹף עָלֶיךָ בָּאֵשׁ: 2 וַיֹּאמֶר יִפְתָּח אֲלֵיהֶם אִישׁ רִיב הָיִיתִי אֲנִי וְעַמִּי וּבְנֵי־עַמּוֹן מְאֹד וָאֶזְעַק אֶתְכֶם וְלֹא־הוֹשַׁעְתֶּם אוֹתִי מִיָּדָם: 3 וָאֶרְאֶה כִּי־אֵינְךָ מוֹשִׁיעַ וָאָשִׂימָה נַפְשִׁי בְכַפִּי וָאֶעְבְּרָה אֶל־בְּנֵי עַמּוֹן וַיִּתְּנֵם יְהֹוָה בְּיָדִי וְלָמָה עֲלִיתֶם אֵלַי הַיּוֹם הַזֶּה לְהִלָּחֶם בִּי: 4 וַיִּקְבֹּץ יִפְתָּח אֶת־כָּל־אַנְשֵׁי גִלְעָד וַיִּלָּחֶם אֶת־אֶפְרָיִם וַיַּכּוּ אַנְשֵׁי גִלְעָד אֶת־אֶפְרַיִם כִּי אָמְרוּ פְּלִיטֵי אֶפְרַיִם אַתֶּם גִּלְעָד בְּתוֹךְ אֶפְרַיִם בְּתוֹךְ מְנַשֶּׁה: 5 וַיִּלְכֹּד גִּלְעָד אֶת־מַעְבְּרוֹת הַיַּרְדֵּן לְאֶפְרָיִם וְהָיָה כִּי יֹאמְרוּ פְּלִיטֵי אֶפְרַיִם אֶעֱבֹרָה וַיֹּאמְרוּ לוֹ אַנְשֵׁי־גִלְעָד הַאֶפְרָתִי אַתָּה וַיֹּאמֶר | לֹא: 6 וַיֹּאמְרוּ לוֹ אֱמָר

"Then say, 'Shibboleth'!" And he would say,
"Sibboleth," for he could not pronounce *it* right.
Then they would take him and kill him at the fords
of the Jordan. There fell at that time forty-two
thousand Ephraimites.

7 And Jephthah judged Israel six years. Then
Jephthah the Gileadite died and was buried among
the cities of Gilead.

8 After him, Ibzan of Bethlehem judged Israel.
9 He had thirty sons. And he gave away thirty
daughters in marriage, and brought in thirty
daughters from elsewhere for his sons. He judged
Israel seven years. 10 Then Ibzan died and was
buried at Bethlehem.

11 After him, Elon the Zebulunite judged Israel.
He judged Israel ten years. 12 And Elon the
Zebulunite died and was buried at Aijalon in the
country of Zebulun.

13 After him, Abdon the son of Hillel the
Pirathonite judged Israel. 14 He had forty sons and
thirty grandsons, who rode on seventy young
donkeys. He judged Israel eight years. 15 Then
Abdon the son of Hillel the Pirathonite died and
was buried in Pirathon in the land of Ephraim, in
the mountains of the Amalekites.

13 Again the children of Israel did evil in the sight
of the LORD, and the LORD delivered them into the
hand of the Philistines for forty years.

2 Now there was a certain man from Zorah, of
the family of the Danites, whose name *was*
Manoah; and his wife *was* barren and had no
children. 3 And the Angel of the LORD appeared to
the woman and said to her, "Indeed now, you are
barren and have borne no children, but you shall
conceive and bear a son. 4 Now therefore, please be
careful not to drink wine or *similar* drink, and not
to eat anything unclean. 5 For behold, you shall
conceive and bear a son. And no razor shall come
upon his head, for the child shall be a Nazirite to
God from the womb; and he shall begin to deliver
Israel out of the hand of the Philistines."

6 So the woman came and told her husband,
saying, "A Man of God came to me, and His
countenance *was* like the countenance of the Angel
of God, very awesome; but I did not ask Him where
He *was* from, and He did not tell me His name.
7 And He said to me, 'Behold, you shall conceive
and bear a son. Now drink no wine or *similar* drink,
nor eat anything unclean, for the child shall be a
Nazirite to God from the womb to the day of his
death.'"

נָא שִׁבֹּלֶת וַיֹּאמֶר סִבֹּלֶת וְלֹא יָכִין לְדַבֵּר כֵּן וַיֹּאחֲזוּ
אוֹתוֹ וַיִּשְׁחָטוּהוּ אֶל־מַעְבְּרוֹת הַיַּרְדֵּן וַיִּפֹּל בָּעֵת
הַהִיא מֵאֶפְרַיִם אַרְבָּעִים וּשְׁנַיִם אָלֶף: 7 וַיִּשְׁפֹּט
יִפְתָּח אֶת־יִשְׂרָאֵל שֵׁשׁ שָׁנִים וַיָּמָת יִפְתָּח הַגִּלְעָדִי
וַיִּקָּבֵר בְּעָרֵי גִלְעָד:
פ

8 וַיִּשְׁפֹּט אַחֲרָיו אֶת־יִשְׂרָאֵל אִבְצָן מִבֵּית לָחֶם:
9 וַיְהִי־לוֹ שְׁלֹשִׁים בָּנִים וּשְׁלֹשִׁים בָּנוֹת שִׁלַּח
הַחוּצָה וּשְׁלֹשִׁים בָּנוֹת הֵבִיא לְבָנָיו מִן־הַחוּץ
וַיִּשְׁפֹּט אֶת־יִשְׂרָאֵל שֶׁבַע שָׁנִים: 10 וַיָּמָת אִבְצָן
וַיִּקָּבֵר בְּבֵית לָחֶם:
פ

11 וַיִּשְׁפֹּט אַחֲרָיו אֶת־יִשְׂרָאֵל אֵילוֹן הַזְּבוּלֹנִי
וַיִּשְׁפֹּט אֶת־יִשְׂרָאֵל עֶשֶׂר שָׁנִים: 12 וַיָּמָת אֵילוֹן
הַזְּבוּלֹנִי וַיִּקָּבֵר בְּאַיָּלוֹן בְּאֶרֶץ זְבוּלֻן:
פ

13 וַיִּשְׁפֹּט אַחֲרָיו אֶת־יִשְׂרָאֵל עַבְדּוֹן בֶּן־הִלֵּל
הַפִּרְעָתוֹנִי: 14 וַיְהִי־לוֹ אַרְבָּעִים בָּנִים וּשְׁלֹשִׁים בְּנֵי
בָנִים רֹכְבִים עַל־שִׁבְעִים עֲיָרִם וַיִּשְׁפֹּט אֶת־יִשְׂרָאֵל
שְׁמֹנֶה שָׁנִים: 15 וַיָּמָת עַבְדּוֹן בֶּן־הִלֵּל הַפִּרְעָתוֹנִי
וַיִּקָּבֵר בְּפִרְעָתוֹן בְּאֶרֶץ אֶפְרַיִם בְּהַר הָעֲמָלֵקִי: פ

יג וַיֹּסִפוּ בְּנֵי יִשְׂרָאֵל לַעֲשׂוֹת הָרַע בְּעֵינֵי יְהוָה
וַיִּתְּנֵם יְהוָה בְּיַד־פְּלִשְׁתִּים אַרְבָּעִים שָׁנָה: פ

2 וַיְהִי אִישׁ אֶחָד מִצָּרְעָה מִמִּשְׁפַּחַת הַדָּנִי וּשְׁמוֹ
מָנוֹחַ וְאִשְׁתּוֹ עֲקָרָה וְלֹא יָלָדָה: 3 וַיֵּרָא מַלְאַךְ־
יְהוָה אֶל־הָאִשָּׁה וַיֹּאמֶר אֵלֶיהָ הִנֵּה־נָא אַתְּ־עֲקָרָה
וְלֹא יָלַדְתְּ וְהָרִית וְיָלַדְתְּ בֵּן: 4 וְעַתָּה הִשָּׁמְרִי
נָא וְאַל־תִּשְׁתִּי יַיִן וְשֵׁכָר וְאַל־תֹּאכְלִי כָּל־טָמֵא:

5 כִּי הִנָּךְ הָרָה וְיֹלַדְתְּ בֵּן וּמוֹרָה לֹא־יַעֲלֶה עַל־
רֹאשׁוֹ כִּי־נְזִיר אֱלֹהִים יִהְיֶה הַנַּעַר מִן־הַבָּטֶן וְהוּא
יָחֵל לְהוֹשִׁיעַ אֶת־יִשְׂרָאֵל מִיַּד פְּלִשְׁתִּים: 6 וַתָּבֹא
הָאִשָּׁה וַתֹּאמֶר לְאִישָׁהּ לֵאמֹר אִישׁ הָאֱלֹהִים בָּא
אֵלַי וּמַרְאֵהוּ כְּמַרְאֵה מַלְאַךְ הָאֱלֹהִים נוֹרָא מְאֹד
וְלֹא שְׁאִלְתִּיהוּ אֵי־מִזֶּה הוּא וְאֶת־שְׁמוֹ לֹא־הִגִּיד
לִי: 7 וַיֹּאמֶר לִי הִנָּךְ הָרָה וְיֹלַדְתְּ בֵּן וְעַתָּה אַל־
תִּשְׁתִּי יַיִן וְשֵׁכָר וְאַל־תֹּאכְלִי כָּל־טֻמְאָה כִּי־נְזִיר
אֱלֹהִים יִהְיֶה הַנַּעַר מִן־הַבֶּטֶן עַד־יוֹם מוֹתוֹ:
פ

8 Then Manoah prayed to the LORD, and said, "O my Lord, please let the Man of God whom You sent come to us again and teach us what we shall do for the child who will be born."

9 And God listened to the voice of Manoah, and the Angel of God came to the woman again as she was sitting in the field; but Manoah her husband *was* not with her. 10 Then the woman ran in haste and told her husband, and said to him, "Look, the Man who came to me the *other* day has just now appeared to me!"

11 So Manoah arose and followed his wife. When he came to the Man, he said to Him, "Are You the Man who spoke to this woman?"

And He said, "I *am*."

12 Manoah said, "Now let Your words come *to pass!* What will be the boy's rule of life, and his work?"

13 So the Angel of the LORD said to Manoah, "Of all that I said to the woman let her be careful. 14 She may not eat anything that comes from the vine, nor may she drink wine or *similar* drink, nor eat anything unclean. All that I commanded her let her observe."

15 Then Manoah said to the Angel of the LORD, "Please let us detain You, and we will prepare a young goat for You."

16 And the Angel of the LORD said to Manoah, "Though you detain Me, I will not eat your food. But if you offer a burnt offering, you must offer it to the LORD." (For Manoah did not know He *was* the Angel of the LORD.)

17 Then Manoah said to the Angel of the LORD, "What *is* Your name, that when Your words come *to pass* we may honor You?"

18 And the Angel of the LORD said to him, "Why do you ask My name, seeing *it is* wonderful?"

19 So Manoah took the young goat with the grain offering, and offered it upon the rock to the LORD. And He did a wondrous thing while Manoah and his wife looked on— 20 it happened as the flame went up toward heaven from the altar—the Angel of the LORD ascended in the flame of the altar! When Manoah and his wife saw *this,* they fell on their faces to the ground. 21 When the Angel of the LORD appeared no more to Manoah and his wife, then Manoah knew that He *was* the Angel of the LORD.

22 And Manoah said to his wife, "We shall surely die, because we have seen God!"

23 But his wife said to him, "If the LORD had desired to kill us, He would not have accepted a burnt offering and a grain offering from our hands,

8 וַיֶּעְתַּ֥ר מָנ֛וֹחַ אֶל־יְהוָ֖ה וַיֹּאמַ֑ר בִּ֣י אֲדוֹנָ֔י אִ֣ישׁ הָאֱלֹהִ֞ים אֲשֶׁ֣ר שָׁלַ֗חְתָּ יָב֨וֹא־נָ֥א ע֛וֹד אֵלֵ֖ינוּ וְיוֹרֵ֕נוּ מַֽה־נַּעֲשֶׂ֖ה לַנַּ֥עַר הַיּוּלָּֽד: 9 וַיִּשְׁמַ֥ע הָאֱלֹהִ֖ים בְּק֣וֹל מָנ֑וֹחַ וַיָּבֹ֣א מַלְאַךְ֩ הָאֱלֹהִ֨ים ע֜וֹד אֶל־הָאִשָּׁ֗ה וְהִיא֙ יוֹשֶׁ֣בֶת בַּשָּׂדֶ֔ה וּמָנ֥וֹחַ אִישָׁ֖הּ אֵ֥ין עִמָּֽהּ: 10 וַתְּמַהֵר֙ הָֽאִשָּׁ֔ה וַתָּ֖רָץ וַתַּגֵּ֣ד לְאִישָׁ֑הּ וַתֹּ֣אמֶר אֵלָ֔יו הִנֵּ֨ה נִרְאָ֤ה אֵלַי֙ הָאִ֔ישׁ אֲשֶׁר־בָּ֥א בַיּ֖וֹם אֵלָֽי: 11 וַיָּ֛קָם וַיֵּ֥לֶךְ מָנ֖וֹחַ אַחֲרֵ֣י אִשְׁתּ֑וֹ וַיָּבֹא֙ אֶל־הָאִ֔ישׁ וַיֹּ֣אמֶר ל֗וֹ הַאַתָּ֥ה הָאִ֛ישׁ אֲשֶׁר־דִּבַּ֥רְתָּ אֶל־הָאִשָּׁ֖ה וַיֹּ֥אמֶר אָֽנִי: 12 וַיֹּ֣אמֶר מָנ֔וֹחַ עַתָּ֖ה יָבֹ֣א דְבָרֶ֑יךָ מַה־יִּֽהְיֶ֥ה מִֽשְׁפַּט־הַנַּ֖עַר וּמַעֲשֵֽׂהוּ: 13 וַיֹּ֛אמֶר מַלְאַ֥ךְ יְהוָ֖ה אֶל־מָנ֑וֹחַ מִכֹּ֛ל אֲשֶׁר־אָמַ֥רְתִּי אֶל־הָאִשָּׁ֖ה תִּשָּׁמֵֽר: 14 מִכֹּ֣ל אֲשֶׁר־יֵצֵא֩ מִגֶּ֨פֶן הַיַּ֜יִן לֹ֣א תֹאכַ֗ל וְיַ֤יִן וְשֵׁכָר֙ אַל־תֵּ֔שְׁתְּ וְכָל־טֻמְאָ֖ה אַל־תֹּאכַ֑ל כֹּ֥ל אֲשֶׁר־צִוִּיתִ֖יהָ תִּשְׁמֹֽר: 15 וַיֹּ֥אמֶר מָנ֖וֹחַ אֶל־מַלְאַ֣ךְ יְהוָ֑ה נַעְצְרָה־נָּ֣א אוֹתָ֔ךְ וְנַעֲשֶׂ֥ה לְפָנֶ֖יךָ גְּדִ֥י עִזִּֽים: 16 וַיֹּאמֶר֩ מַלְאַ֨ךְ יְהוָ֜ה אֶל־מָנ֗וֹחַ אִם־תַּעְצְרֵ֙נִי֙ לֹא־אֹכַ֣ל בְּלַחְמֶ֔ךָ וְאִם־תַּעֲשֶׂ֣ה עֹלָ֔ה לַיהוָ֖ה תַּעֲלֶ֑נָּה כִּ֚י לֹא־יָדַ֣ע מָנ֔וֹחַ כִּֽי־מַלְאַ֥ךְ יְהוָ֖ה הֽוּא: 17 וַיֹּ֜אמֶר מָנ֨וֹחַ אֶל־מַלְאַ֤ךְ יְהוָה֙ מִ֣י שְׁמֶ֔ךָ כִּֽי־יָבֹ֥א דבריך דְבָרְךָ֖° וְכִבַּדְנֽוּךָ: 18 וַיֹּ֤אמֶר לוֹ֙ מַלְאַ֣ךְ יְהוָ֔ה לָ֥מָּה זֶּ֖ה תִּשְׁאַ֣ל לִשְׁמִ֑י וְהוּא־פֶֽלִאי: ס

19 וַיִּקַּ֨ח מָנ֜וֹחַ אֶת־גְּדִ֤י הָעִזִּים֙ וְאֶת־הַמִּנְחָ֔ה וַיַּ֥עַל עַל־הַצּ֖וּר לַֽיהוָ֑ה וּמַפְלִ֣א לַעֲשׂ֔וֹת וּמָנ֥וֹחַ וְאִשְׁתּ֖וֹ רֹאִֽים: 20 וַיְהִ֗י בַּעֲל֤וֹת הַלַּ֙הַב֙ מֵעַ֣ל הַמִּזְבֵּ֔חַ הַשָּׁמַ֔יְמָה וַיַּ֥עַל מַלְאַךְ־יְהוָ֖ה בְּלַ֣הַב הַמִּזְבֵּ֑חַ וּמָנ֤וֹחַ וְאִשְׁתּוֹ֙ רֹאִ֔ים וַיִּפְּל֥וּ עַל־פְּנֵיהֶ֖ם אָֽרְצָה: 21 וְלֹא־יָ֤סַף עוֹד֙ מַלְאַ֣ךְ יְהוָ֔ה לְהֵרָאֹ֖ה אֶל־מָנ֣וֹחַ וְאֶל־אִשְׁתּ֑וֹ אָ֚ז יָדַ֣ע מָנ֔וֹחַ כִּֽי־מַלְאַ֥ךְ יְהוָ֖ה הֽוּא: 22 וַיֹּ֧אמֶר מָנ֛וֹחַ אֶל־אִשְׁתּ֖וֹ מ֣וֹת נָמ֑וּת כִּ֥י אֱלֹהִ֖ים רָאִֽינוּ: 23 וַתֹּ֧אמֶר ל֣וֹ אִשְׁתּ֗וֹ לוּ֩ חָפֵ֨ץ יְהוָ֤ה לַהֲמִיתֵ֙נוּ֙ לֹֽא־לָקַ֤ח מִיָּדֵ֙נוּ֙ עֹלָ֣ה וּמִנְחָ֔ה וְלֹ֥א הֶרְאָ֖נוּ אֶת־כָּל־אֵ֑לֶּה וְכָעֵ֕ת לֹ֥א

nor would He have shown us all these *things,* nor would He have told us *such things* as these at this time."

24 So the woman bore a son and called his name Samson; and the child grew, and the LORD blessed him. 25 And the Spirit of the LORD began to move upon him at Mahaneh Dan between Zorah and Eshtaol.

14 Now Samson went down to Timnah, and saw a woman in Timnah of the daughters of the Philistines. 2 So he went up and told his father and mother, saying, "I have seen a woman in Timnah of the daughters of the Philistines; now therefore, get her for me as a wife."

3 Then his father and mother said to him, "*Is there* no woman among the daughters of your brethren, or among all my people, that you must go and get a wife from the uncircumcised Philistines?"

And Samson said to his father, "Get her for me, for she pleases me well."

4 But his father and mother did not know that it was of the LORD—that He was seeking an occasion to move against the Philistines. For at that time the Philistines had dominion over Israel.

5 So Samson went down to Timnah with his father and mother, and came to the vineyards of Timnah.

Now *to his* surprise, a young lion *came* roaring against him. 6 And the Spirit of the LORD came mightily upon him, and he tore the lion apart as one would have torn apart a young goat, though *he had* nothing in his hand. But he did not tell his father or his mother what he had done.

7 Then he went down and talked with the woman; and she pleased Samson well. 8 After some time, when he returned to get her, he turned aside to see the carcass of the lion. And behold, a swarm of bees and honey *were* in the carcass of the lion. 9 He took some of it in his hands and went along, eating. When he came to his father and mother, he gave *some* to them, and they also ate. But he did not tell them that he had taken the honey out of the carcass of the lion.

10 So his father went down to the woman. And Samson gave a feast there, for young men used to do so. 11 And it happened, when they saw him, that they brought thirty companions to be with him.

12 Then Samson said to them, "Let me pose a riddle to you. If you can correctly solve and explain it to me within the seven days of the feast, then I will give you thirty linen garments and thirty

הִשְׁמִיעָנוּ כָּזֹאת: 24 וַתֵּלֶד הָאִשָּׁה בֵּן וַתִּקְרָא אֶת־שְׁמוֹ שִׁמְשׁוֹן וַיִּגְדַּל הַנַּעַר וַיְבָרְכֵהוּ יְהֹוָה: 25 וַתָּחֶל רוּחַ יְהֹוָה לְפַעֲמוֹ בְּמַחֲנֵה־דָן בֵּין צָרְעָה וּבֵין אֶשְׁתָּאֹל: פ

יד וַיֵּרֶד שִׁמְשׁוֹן תִּמְנָתָה וַיַּרְא אִשָּׁה בְּתִמְנָתָה מִבְּנוֹת פְּלִשְׁתִּים: 2 וַיַּעַל וַיַּגֵּד לְאָבִיו וּלְאִמּוֹ וַיֹּאמֶר אִשָּׁה רָאִיתִי בְתִמְנָתָה מִבְּנוֹת פְּלִשְׁתִּים וְעַתָּה קְחוּ־אוֹתָהּ לִי לְאִשָּׁה: 3 וַיֹּאמֶר לוֹ אָבִיו וְאִמּוֹ הַאֵין בִּבְנוֹת אַחֶיךָ וּבְכָל־עַמִּי אִשָּׁה כִּי־אַתָּה הוֹלֵךְ לָקַחַת אִשָּׁה מִפְּלִשְׁתִּים הָעֲרֵלִים וַיֹּאמֶר שִׁמְשׁוֹן אֶל־אָבִיו אוֹתָהּ קַח־לִי כִּי־הִיא יָשְׁרָה בְעֵינָי: 4 וְאָבִיו וְאִמּוֹ לֹא יָדְעוּ כִּי מֵיְהֹוָה הִיא כִּי־תֹאֲנָה הוּא־מְבַקֵּשׁ מִפְּלִשְׁתִּים וּבָעֵת הַהִיא פְּלִשְׁתִּים מֹשְׁלִים בְּיִשְׂרָאֵל: פ

5 וַיֵּרֶד שִׁמְשׁוֹן וְאָבִיו וְאִמּוֹ תִּמְנָתָה וַיָּבֹאוּ עַד־כַּרְמֵי תִמְנָתָה וְהִנֵּה כְּפִיר אֲרָיוֹת שֹׁאֵג לִקְרָאתוֹ: 6 וַתִּצְלַח עָלָיו רוּחַ יְהֹוָה וַיְשַׁסְּעֵהוּ כְּשַׁסַּע הַגְּדִי וּמְאוּמָה אֵין בְּיָדוֹ וְלֹא הִגִּיד לְאָבִיו וּלְאִמּוֹ אֵת אֲשֶׁר עָשָׂה: 7 וַיֵּרֶד וַיְדַבֵּר לָאִשָּׁה וַתִּישַׁר בְּעֵינֵי שִׁמְשׁוֹן: 8 וַיָּשָׁב מִיָּמִים לְקַחְתָּהּ וַיָּסַר לִרְאוֹת אֵת מַפֶּלֶת הָאַרְיֵה וְהִנֵּה עֲדַת דְּבוֹרִים בִּגְוִיַּת הָאַרְיֵה וּדְבָשׁ: 9 וַיִּרְדֵּהוּ אֶל־כַּפָּיו וַיֵּלֶךְ הָלוֹךְ וְאָכֹל וַיֵּלֶךְ אֶל־אָבִיו וְאֶל־אִמּוֹ וַיִּתֵּן לָהֶם וַיֹּאכֵלוּ וְלֹא־הִגִּיד לָהֶם כִּי מִגְּוִיַּת הָאַרְיֵה רָדָה הַדְּבָשׁ: 10 וַיֵּרֶד אָבִיהוּ אֶל־הָאִשָּׁה וַיַּעַשׂ שָׁם שִׁמְשׁוֹן מִשְׁתֶּה כִּי כֵּן יַעֲשׂוּ הַבַּחוּרִים: 11 וַיְהִי כִּרְאוֹתָם אוֹתוֹ וַיִּקְחוּ שְׁלֹשִׁים מֵרֵעִים וַיִּהְיוּ אִתּוֹ: 12 וַיֹּאמֶר לָהֶם שִׁמְשׁוֹן אָחוּדָה־נָּא לָכֶם חִידָה אִם־הַגֵּד תַּגִּידוּ אוֹתָהּ לִי שִׁבְעַת יְמֵי הַמִּשְׁתֶּה וּמְצָאתֶם וְנָתַתִּי לָכֶם שְׁלֹשִׁים

changes of clothing. ¹³But if you cannot explain *it* to me, then you shall give me thirty linen garments and thirty changes of clothing."

And they said to him, "Pose your riddle, that we may hear it."

¹⁴So he said to them:

"Out of the eater came something to eat,
And out of the strong came something sweet."

Now for three days they could not explain the riddle.

¹⁵But it came to pass on the seventh day that they said to Samson's wife, "Entice your husband, that he may explain the riddle to us, or else we will burn you and your father's house with fire. Have you invited us in order to take what is ours? *Is that not so?*"

¹⁶Then Samson's wife wept on him, and said, "You only hate me! You do not love me! You have posed a riddle to the sons of my people, but you have not explained *it* to me."

And he said to her, "Look, I have not explained *it* to my father or my mother; so should I explain *it* to you?" ¹⁷Now she had wept on him the seven days while their feast lasted. And it happened on the seventh day that he told her, because she pressed him so much. Then she explained the riddle to the sons of her people. ¹⁸So the men of the city said to him on the seventh day before the sun went down:

"What *is* sweeter than honey?
And what *is* stronger than a lion?"

And he said to them:

"If you had not plowed with my heifer,
You would not have solved my riddle!"

¹⁹Then the Spirit of the LORD came upon him mightily, and he went down to Ashkelon and killed thirty of their men, took their apparel, and gave the changes *of clothing* to those who had explained the riddle. So his anger was aroused, and he went back up to his father's house. ²⁰And Samson's wife was *given* to his companion, who had been his best man.

15 After a while, in the time of wheat harvest, it happened that Samson visited his wife with a young goat. And he said, "Let me go in to my wife, into *her* room." But her father would not permit him to go in.

²Her father said, "I really thought that you thoroughly hated her; therefore I gave her to your companion. *Is* not her younger sister better than she? Please, take her instead."

סְדִינִים וּשְׁלֹשִׁים חֲלִפֹת בְּגָדִים: 13 וְאִם־לֹא תוּכְלוּ לְהַגִּיד לִי וּנְתַתֶּם אַתֶּם לִי שְׁלֹשִׁים סְדִינִים וּשְׁלֹשִׁים חֲלִיפוֹת בְּגָדִים וַיֹּאמְרוּ לוֹ חוּדָה חִידָתְךָ וְנִשְׁמָעֶנָּה: 14 וַיֹּאמֶר לָהֶם מֵהָאֹכֵל יָצָא מַאֲכָל וּמֵעַז יָצָא מָתוֹק וְלֹא יָכְלוּ לְהַגִּיד הַחִידָה שְׁלֹשֶׁת יָמִים: 15 וַיְהִי | בַּיּוֹם הַשְּׁבִיעִי וַיֹּאמְרוּ לְאֵשֶׁת־ שִׁמְשׁוֹן פַּתִּי אֶת־אִישֵׁךְ וְיַגֶּד־לָנוּ אֶת־הַחִידָה פֶּן־ נִשְׂרֹף אוֹתָךְ וְאֶת־בֵּית אָבִיךְ בָּאֵשׁ הַלְיָרְשֵׁנוּ קְרָאתֶם לָנוּ הֲלֹא: 16 וַתֵּבְךְּ אֵשֶׁת שִׁמְשׁוֹן עָלָיו וַתֹּאמֶר רַק־שְׂנֵאתַנִי וְלֹא אֲהַבְתָּנִי הַחִידָה חַדְתָּ לִבְנֵי עַמִּי וְלִי לֹא הִגַּדְתָּה וַיֹּאמֶר לָהּ הִנֵּה לְאָבִי וּלְאִמִּי לֹא הִגַּדְתִּי וְלָךְ אַגִּיד: 17 וַתֵּבְךְּ עָלָיו שִׁבְעַת הַיָּמִים אֲשֶׁר־הָיָה לָהֶם הַמִּשְׁתֶּה וַיְהִי | בַּיּוֹם הַשְּׁבִיעִי וַיַּגֶּד־לָהּ כִּי הֱצִיקַתְהוּ וַתַּגֵּד הַחִידָה לִבְנֵי עַמָּהּ: 18 וַיֹּאמְרוּ לוֹ אַנְשֵׁי הָעִיר בַּיּוֹם הַשְּׁבִיעִי בְּטֶרֶם יָבֹא הַחַרְסָה מַה־מָּתוֹק מִדְּבַשׁ וּמֶה עַז מֵאֲרִי וַיֹּאמֶר לָהֶם לוּלֵא חֲרַשְׁתֶּם בְּעֶגְלָתִי לֹא מְצָאתֶם חִידָתִי: 19 וַתִּצְלַח עָלָיו רוּחַ יְהֹוָה וַיֵּרֶד אַשְׁקְלוֹן וַיַּךְ מֵהֶם | שְׁלֹשִׁים אִישׁ וַיִּקַּח אֶת־ חֲלִיצוֹתָם וַיִּתֵּן הַחֲלִיפוֹת לְמַגִּידֵי הַחִידָה וַיִּחַר אַפּוֹ וַיַּעַל בֵּית אָבִיהוּ: ‫פ

20 וַתְּהִי אֵשֶׁת שִׁמְשׁוֹן לְמֵרֵעֵהוּ אֲשֶׁר רֵעָה לוֹ:

טו וַיְהִי מִיָּמִים בִּימֵי קְצִיר־חִטִּים וַיִּפְקֹד שִׁמְשׁוֹן אֶת־אִשְׁתּוֹ בִּגְדִי עִזִּים וַיֹּאמֶר אָבֹאָה אֶל־אִשְׁתִּי הֶחָדְרָה וְלֹא־נְתָנוֹ אָבִיהָ לָבוֹא: 2 וַיֹּאמֶר אָבִיהָ אָמֹר אָמַרְתִּי כִּי־שָׂנֹא שְׂנֵאתָהּ וָאֶתְּנֶנָּה לְמֵרֵעֶךָ הֲלֹא אֲחוֹתָהּ הַקְּטַנָּה טוֹבָה מִמֶּנָּה תְּהִי־נָא לְךָ

³ And Samson said to them, "This time I shall be blameless regarding the Philistines if I harm them!" ⁴ Then Samson went and caught three hundred foxes; and he took torches, turned *the foxes* tail to tail, and put a torch between each pair of tails. ⁵ When he had set the torches on fire, he let *the foxes* go into the standing grain of the Philistines, and burned up both the shocks and the standing grain, as well as the vineyards *and* olive groves.

⁶ Then the Philistines said, "Who has done this?"

And they answered, "Samson, the son-in-law of the Timnite, because he has taken his wife and given her to his companion." So the Philistines came up and burned her and her father with fire.

⁷ Samson said to them, "Since you would do a thing like this, I will surely take revenge on you, and after that I will cease." ⁸ So he attacked them hip and thigh with a great slaughter; then he went down and dwelt in the cleft of the rock of Etam.

⁹ Now the Philistines went up, encamped in Judah, and deployed themselves against Lehi. ¹⁰ And the men of Judah said, "Why have you come up against us?"

So they answered, "We have come up to arrest Samson, to do to him as he has done to us."

¹¹ Then three thousand men of Judah went down to the cleft of the rock of Etam, and said to Samson, "Do you not know that the Philistines rule over us? What *is* this you have done to us?"

And he said to them, "As they did to me, so I have done to them."

¹² But they said to him, "We have come down to arrest you, that we may deliver you into the hand of the Philistines."

Then Samson said to them, "Swear to me that you will not kill me yourselves."

¹³ So they spoke to him, saying, "No, but we will tie you securely and deliver you into their hand; but we will surely not kill you." And they bound him with two new ropes and brought him up from the rock.

¹⁴ When he came to Lehi, the Philistines came shouting against him. Then the Spirit of the LORD came mightily upon him; and the ropes that *were* on his arms became like flax that is burned with fire, and his bonds broke loose from his hands. ¹⁵ He found a fresh jawbone of a donkey, reached out his hand and took it, and killed a thousand men with it. ¹⁶ Then Samson said:

> "With the jawbone of a donkey,
> Heaps upon heaps,
> With the jawbone of a donkey
> I have slain a thousand men!"

3 וַיֹּ֤אמֶר לָהֶם֙ שִׁמְשׁ֔וֹן נִקֵּ֥יתִי הַפַּ֖עַם תַּחְתִּֽיָה׃ מִפְּלִשְׁתִּ֑ים כִּֽי־עֹשֶׂ֥ה אֲנִ֛י עִמָּ֖ם רָעָֽה׃ 4 וַיֵּ֣לֶךְ שִׁמְשׁ֔וֹן וַיִּלְכֹּ֖ד שְׁלֹשׁ־מֵא֣וֹת שׁוּעָלִ֑ים וַיִּקַּ֣ח לַפִּדִ֗ים וַיֶּ֤פֶן זָנָב֙ אֶל־זָנָ֔ב וַיָּ֨שֶׂם לַפִּ֥יד אֶחָ֛ד בֵּין־שְׁנֵ֥י הַזְּנָב֖וֹת בַּתָּֽוֶךְ׃ 5 וַיַּבְעֶר־אֵשׁ֙ בַּלַּפִּידִ֔ים וַיְשַׁלַּ֖ח בְּקָמ֣וֹת פְּלִשְׁתִּ֑ים וַיַּבְעֵ֛ר מִגָּדִ֥ישׁ וְעַד־קָמָ֖ה וְעַד־כֶּ֥רֶם זָֽיִת׃

6 וַיֹּאמְר֣וּ פְלִשְׁתִּ֗ים מִ֣י עָ֣שָׂה זֹאת֮ וַיֹּאמְרוּ֒ שִׁמְשׁ֜וֹן חֲתַ֣ן הַתִּמְנִ֗י כִּ֤י לָקַח֙ אֶת־אִשְׁתּ֔וֹ וַֽיִּתְּנָ֖הּ לְמֵרֵעֵ֑הוּ וַיַּעֲל֣וּ פְלִשְׁתִּ֔ים וַיִּשְׂרְפ֥וּ אוֹתָ֛הּ וְאֶת־אָבִ֖יהָ בָּאֵֽשׁ׃ 7 וַיֹּ֤אמֶר לָהֶם֙ שִׁמְשׁ֔וֹן אִֽם־תַּעֲשׂ֖וּן כָּזֹ֑את כִּ֛י אִם־נִקַּ֥מְתִּי בָכֶ֖ם וְאַחַ֥ר אֶחְדָּֽל׃ 8 וַיַּ֨ךְ אוֹתָ֥ם שׁ֛וֹק עַל־יָרֵ֖ךְ מַכָּ֣ה גְדוֹלָ֑ה וַיֵּ֣רֶד וַיֵּ֔שֶׁב בִּסְעִ֖יף סֶ֥לַע עֵיטָֽם׃ ס

9 וַיַּעֲל֣וּ פְלִשְׁתִּ֔ים וַֽיַּחֲנ֖וּ בִּיהוּדָ֑ה וַיִּנָּטְשׁ֖וּ בַּלֶּֽחִי׃ 10 וַיֹּֽאמְרוּ֙ אִ֣ישׁ יְהוּדָ֔ה לָמָ֖ה עֲלִיתֶ֣ם עָלֵ֑ינוּ וַיֹּאמְר֗וּ לֶאֱס֤וֹר אֶת־שִׁמְשׁוֹן֙ עָלִ֔ינוּ לַעֲשׂ֣וֹת ל֔וֹ כַּאֲשֶׁ֖ר עָ֥שָׂה לָֽנוּ׃ 11 וַיֵּרְד֡וּ שְׁלֹ֣שֶׁת אֲלָפִ֣ים אִישׁ֮ מִֽיהוּדָה֒ אֶל־סְעִ֖יף סֶ֣לַע עֵיטָ֑ם וַיֹּאמְר֣וּ לְשִׁמְשׁ֗וֹן הֲלֹ֤א יָדַ֙עְתָּ֙ כִּֽי־מֹשְׁלִ֥ים בָּ֙נוּ֙ פְּלִשְׁתִּ֔ים וּמַה־זֹּ֖את עָשִׂ֣יתָ לָּ֑נוּ וַיֹּ֣אמֶר לָהֶ֗ם כַּאֲשֶׁר֙ עָ֣שׂוּ לִ֔י כֵּ֖ן עָשִׂ֥יתִי לָהֶֽם׃ 12 וַיֹּ֤אמְרוּ לוֹ֙ לֶאֱסׇרְךָ֣ יָרַ֔דְנוּ לְתִתְּךָ֖ בְּיַד־פְּלִשְׁתִּ֑ים וַיֹּ֤אמֶר לָהֶם֙ שִׁמְשׁ֔וֹן הִשָּׁבְע֣וּ לִ֔י פֶּֽן־תִּפְגְּע֥וּן בִּ֖י אַתֶּֽם׃ 13 וַיֹּ֧אמְרוּ ל֣וֹ לֵאמֹ֗ר לֹ֤א כִּֽי־אָסֹ֤ר נֶֽאֱסׇרְךָ֙ וּנְתַנּ֣וּךָ בְיָדָ֔ם וְהָמֵ֖ת לֹ֣א נְמִיתֶ֑ךָ וַיַּאַסְרֻ֗הוּ בִּשְׁנַ֙יִם֙ עֲבֹתִ֣ים חֲדָשִׁ֔ים וַֽיַּעֲל֖וּהוּ מִן־הַסָּֽלַע׃ 14 הוּא־בָ֣א עַד־לֶ֔חִי וּפְלִשְׁתִּ֖ים הֵרִ֣יעוּ לִקְרָאת֑וֹ וַתִּצְלַ֨ח עָלָ֜יו ר֣וּחַ יְהֹוָ֗ה וַתִּהְיֶ֤ינָה הָעֲבֹתִים֙ אֲשֶׁ֣ר עַל־זְרֽוֹעוֹתָ֔יו כַּפִּשְׁתִּים֙ אֲשֶׁ֣ר בָּעֲר֣וּ בָאֵ֔שׁ וַיִּמַּ֥סּוּ אֱסוּרָ֖יו מֵעַ֥ל יָדָֽיו׃ 15 וַיִּמְצָ֥א לְחִֽי־חֲמ֖וֹר טְרִיָּ֑ה וַיִּשְׁלַ֤ח יָדוֹ֙ וַיִּקָּחֶ֔הָ וַיַּךְ־בָּ֖הּ אֶ֥לֶף אִֽישׁ׃ 16 וַיֹּ֙אמֶר֙ שִׁמְשׁ֔וֹן בִּלְחִ֣י הַחֲמ֔וֹר חֲמ֖וֹר חֲמֹרָתָ֑יִם

17 And so it was, when he had finished speaking, that he threw the jawbone from his hand, and called that place Ramath Lehi.

18 Then he became very thirsty; so he cried out to the LORD and said, "You have given this great deliverance by the hand of Your servant; and now shall I die of thirst and fall into the hand of the uncircumcised?" 19 So God split the hollow place that *is* in Lehi, and water came out, and he drank; and his spirit returned, and he revived. Therefore he called its name En Hakkore, which is in Lehi to this day. 20 And he judged Israel twenty years in the days of the Philistines.

16 Now Samson went to Gaza and saw a harlot there, and went in to her. 2 *When* the Gazites *were told,* "Samson has come here!" they surrounded *the place* and lay in wait for him all night at the gate of the city. They were quiet all night, saying, "In the morning, when it is daylight, we will kill him." 3 And Samson lay *low* till midnight; then he arose at midnight, took hold of the doors of the gate of the city and the two gateposts, pulled them up, bar and all, put *them* on his shoulders, and carried them to the top of the hill that faces Hebron.

4 Afterward it happened that he loved a woman in the Valley of Sorek, whose name *was* Delilah. 5 And the lords of the Philistines came up to her and said to her, "Entice him, and find out where his great strength *lies,* and by what *means* we may overpower him, that we may bind him to afflict him; and every one of us will give you eleven hundred *pieces* of silver."

6 So Delilah said to Samson, "Please tell me where your great strength *lies,* and with what you may be bound to afflict you."

7 And Samson said to her, "If they bind me with seven fresh bowstrings, not yet dried, then I shall become weak, and be like any *other* man."

8 So the lords of the Philistines brought up to her seven fresh bowstrings, not yet dried, and she bound him with them. 9 Now *men were* lying in wait, staying with her in the room. And she said to him, "The Philistines *are* upon you, Samson!" But he broke the bowstrings as a strand of yarn breaks when it touches fire. So the secret of his strength was not known.

10 Then Delilah said to Samson, "Look, you have mocked me and told me lies. Now, please tell me what you may be bound with."

11 So he said to her, "If they bind me securely with new ropes that have never been used, then I shall become weak, and be like any *other* man."

בִּלְחִי הַחֲמוֹר הִכֵּיתִי אֶלֶף אִישׁ: 17 וַיְהִי כְּכַלֹּתוֹ
לְדַבֵּר וַיַּשְׁלֵךְ הַלְּחִי מִיָּדוֹ וַיִּקְרָא לַמָּקוֹם הַהוּא
רָמַת לֶחִי: 18 וַיִּצְמָא מְאֹד וַיִּקְרָא אֶל־יְהֹוָה וַיֹּאמַר
אַתָּה נָתַתָּ בְיַד־עַבְדְּךָ אֶת־הַתְּשׁוּעָה הַגְּדֹלָה
הַזֹּאת וְעַתָּה אָמוּת בַּצָּמָא וְנָפַלְתִּי בְּיַד הָעֲרֵלִים:
19 וַיִּבְקַע אֱלֹהִים אֶת־הַמַּכְתֵּשׁ אֲשֶׁר־בַּלֶּחִי וַיֵּצְאוּ
מִמֶּנּוּ מַיִם וַיֵּשְׁתְּ וַתָּשָׁב רוּחוֹ וַיֶּחִי עַל־כֵּן |
קָרָא שְׁמָהּ עֵין הַקּוֹרֵא אֲשֶׁר בַּלֶּחִי עַד הַיּוֹם
הַזֶּה: 20 וַיִּשְׁפֹּט אֶת־יִשְׂרָאֵל בִּימֵי פְלִשְׁתִּים עֶשְׂרִים
שָׁנָה:
פ

טז וַיֵּלֶךְ שִׁמְשׁוֹן עַזָּתָה וַיַּרְא־שָׁם אִשָּׁה זוֹנָה וַיָּבֹא
אֵלֶיהָ: 2 לַעַזָּתִים | לֵאמֹר בָּא שִׁמְשׁוֹן הֵנָּה וַיָּסֹבּוּ
וַיֶּאֶרְבוּ־לוֹ כָל־הַלַּיְלָה בְּשַׁעַר הָעִיר וַיִּתְחָרְשׁוּ כָל־
הַלַּיְלָה לֵאמֹר עַד־אוֹר הַבֹּקֶר וַהֲרַגְנֻהוּ: 3 וַיִּשְׁכַּב
שִׁמְשׁוֹן עַד־חֲצִי הַלַּיְלָה | וַיָּקָם | בַּחֲצִי הַלַּיְלָה
וַיֶּאֱחֹז בְּדַלְתוֹת שַׁעַר־הָעִיר וּבִשְׁתֵּי הַמְּזוּזוֹת וַיִּסָּעֵם
עִם־הַבְּרִיחַ וַיָּשֶׂם עַל־כְּתֵפָיו וַיַּעֲלֵם אֶל־רֹאשׁ הָהָר
אֲשֶׁר עַל־פְּנֵי חֶבְרוֹן:
פ

4 וַיְהִי אַחֲרֵי־כֵן וַיֶּאֱהַב אִשָּׁה בְּנַחַל שֹׂרֵק וּשְׁמָהּ
דְּלִילָה: 5 וַיַּעֲלוּ אֵלֶיהָ סַרְנֵי פְלִשְׁתִּים וַיֹּאמְרוּ לָהּ
פַּתִּי אוֹתוֹ וּרְאִי בַּמֶּה כֹּחוֹ גָדוֹל וּבַמֶּה נוּכַל לוֹ
וַאֲסַרְנֻהוּ לְעַנֹּתוֹ וַאֲנַחְנוּ נִתַּן־לָךְ אִישׁ אֶלֶף וּמֵאָה
כָּסֶף: 6 וַתֹּאמֶר דְּלִילָה אֶל־שִׁמְשׁוֹן הַגִּידָה־נָּא לִי
בַּמֶּה כֹּחֲךָ גָדוֹל וּבַמֶּה תֵּאָסֵר לְעַנּוֹתֶךָ: 7 וַיֹּאמֶר
אֵלֶיהָ שִׁמְשׁוֹן אִם־יַאַסְרֻנִי בְּשִׁבְעָה יְתָרִים לַחִים
אֲשֶׁר לֹא־חֹרָבוּ וְחָלִיתִי וְהָיִיתִי כְּאַחַד הָאָדָם:

8 וַיַּעֲלוּ־לָהּ סַרְנֵי פְלִשְׁתִּים שִׁבְעָה יְתָרִים לַחִים
אֲשֶׁר לֹא־חֹרָבוּ וַתַּאַסְרֵהוּ בָּהֶם: 9 וְהָאֹרֵב יֹשֵׁב
לָהּ בַּחֶדֶר וַתֹּאמֶר אֵלָיו פְּלִשְׁתִּים עָלֶיךָ שִׁמְשׁוֹן
וַיְנַתֵּק אֶת־הַיְתָרִים כַּאֲשֶׁר יִנָּתֵק פְּתִיל־הַנְּעֹרֶת
בַּהֲרִיחוֹ אֵשׁ וְלֹא נוֹדַע כֹּחוֹ: 10 וַתֹּאמֶר דְּלִילָה
אֶל־שִׁמְשׁוֹן הִנֵּה הֵתַלְתָּ בִּי וַתְּדַבֵּר אֵלַי כְּזָבִים
עַתָּה הַגִּידָה־נָּא לִי בַּמֶּה תֵּאָסֵר: 11 וַיֹּאמֶר אֵלֶיהָ
אִם־אָסוֹר יַאַסְרוּנִי בַּעֲבֹתִים חֲדָשִׁים אֲשֶׁר לֹא־
נַעֲשָׂה בָהֶם מְלָאכָה וְחָלִיתִי וְהָיִיתִי כְּאַחַד הָאָדָם:

12 Therefore Delilah took new ropes and bound him with them, and said to him, "The Philistines *are* upon you, Samson!" And *men were* lying in wait, staying in the room. But he broke them off his arms like a thread.

13 Delilah said to Samson, "Until now you have mocked me and told me lies. Tell me what you may be bound with."

And he said to her, "If you weave the seven locks of my head into the web of the loom"—

14 So she wove *it* tightly with the batten of the loom, and said to him, "The Philistines *are* upon you, Samson!" But he awoke from his sleep, and pulled out the batten and the web from the loom.

15 Then she said to him, "How can you say, 'I love you,' when your heart *is* not with me? You have mocked me these three times, and have not told me where your great strength *lies*." 16 And it came to pass, when she pestered him daily with her words and pressed him, *so* that his soul was vexed to death, 17 that he told her all his heart, and said to her, "No razor has ever come upon my head, for I *have been* a Nazirite to God from my mother's womb. If I am shaven, then my strength will leave me, and I shall become weak, and be like any *other* man."

18 When Delilah saw that he had told her all his heart, she sent and called for the lords of the Philistines, saying, "Come up once more, for he has told me all his heart." So the lords of the Philistines came up to her and brought the money in their hand. 19 Then she lulled him to sleep on her knees, and called for a man and had him shave off the seven locks of his head. Then she began to torment him, and his strength left him. 20 And she said, "The Philistines *are* upon you, Samson!" So he awoke from his sleep, and said, "I will go out as before, at other times, and shake myself free!" But he did not know that the LORD had departed from him.

21 Then the Philistines took him and put out his eyes, and brought him down to Gaza. They bound him with bronze fetters, and he became a grinder in the prison. 22 However, the hair of his head began to grow again after it had been shaven.

23 Now the lords of the Philistines gathered together to offer a great sacrifice to Dagon their god, and to rejoice. And they said:

> "Our god has delivered into our hands
> Samson our enemy!"

24 When the people saw him, they praised their god; for they said:

> "Our god has delivered into our hands our enemy,
> The destroyer of our land,

12 וַתִּקַּח דְּלִילָה עֲבֹתִים חֲדָשִׁים וַתַּאַסְרֵהוּ בָהֶם וַתֹּאמֶר אֵלָיו פְּלִשְׁתִּים עָלֶיךָ שִׁמְשׁוֹן וְהָאֹרֵב יֹשֵׁב בֶּחָדֶר וַיְנַתְּקֵם מֵעַל זְרֹעֹתָיו כַּחוּט: 13 וַתֹּאמֶר דְּלִילָה אֶל־שִׁמְשׁוֹן עַד־הֵנָּה הֵתַלְתָּ בִּי וַתְּדַבֵּר אֵלַי כְּזָבִים הַגִּידָה לִּי בַּמֶּה תֵּאָסֵר וַיֹּאמֶר אֵלֶיהָ אִם־ תַּאַרְגִי אֶת־שֶׁבַע מַחְלְפוֹת רֹאשִׁי עִם־הַמַּסָּכֶת: 14 וַתִּתְקַע בַּיָּתֵד וַתֹּאמֶר אֵלָיו פְּלִשְׁתִּים עָלֶיךָ שִׁמְשׁוֹן וַיִּיקַץ מִשְּׁנָתוֹ וַיִּסַּע אֶת־הַיְתַד הָאֶרֶג וְאֶת־ הַמַּסָּכֶת: 15 וַתֹּאמֶר אֵלָיו אֵיךְ תֹּאמַר אֲהַבְתִּיךְ וְלִבְּךָ אֵין אִתִּי זֶה שָׁלֹשׁ פְּעָמִים הֵתַלְתָּ בִּי וְלֹא־ הִגַּדְתָּ לִּי בַּמֶּה כֹּחֲךָ גָדוֹל: 16 וַיְהִי כִּי־הֵצִיקָה לּוֹ בִדְבָרֶיהָ כָּל־הַיָּמִים וַתְּאַלֲצֵהוּ וַתִּקְצַר נַפְשׁוֹ לָמוּת: 17 וַיַּגֶּד־לָהּ אֶת־כָּל־לִבּוֹ וַיֹּאמֶר לָהּ מוֹרָה לֹא־עָלָה עַל־רֹאשִׁי כִּי־נְזִיר אֱלֹהִים אֲנִי מִבֶּטֶן אִמִּי אִם־גֻּלַּחְתִּי וְסָר מִמֶּנִּי כֹחִי וְחָלִיתִי וְהָיִיתִי כְּכָל־ הָאָדָם: 18 וַתֵּרֶא דְּלִילָה כִּי־הִגִּיד לָהּ אֶת־כָּל־ לִבּוֹ וַתִּשְׁלַח וַתִּקְרָא לְסַרְנֵי פְלִשְׁתִּים לֵאמֹר עֲלוּ הַפַּעַם כִּי־הִגִּיד לָהּ אֶת־כָּל־לִבּוֹ וְעָלוּ אֵלֶיהָ סַרְנֵי פְלִשְׁתִּים וַיַּעֲלוּ הַכֶּסֶף בְּיָדָם: 19 וַתְּיַשְּׁנֵהוּ עַל־ בִּרְכֶּיהָ וַתִּקְרָא לָאִישׁ וַתְּגַלַּח אֶת־שֶׁבַע מַחְלְפוֹת רֹאשׁוֹ וַתָּחֶל לְעַנּוֹתוֹ וַיָּסַר כֹּחוֹ מֵעָלָיו: 20 וַתֹּאמֶר פְּלִשְׁתִּים עָלֶיךָ שִׁמְשׁוֹן וַיִּיקַץ מִשְּׁנָתוֹ וַיֹּאמֶר אֵצֵא כְּפַעַם בְּפַעַם וְאִנָּעֵר וְהוּא לֹא יָדַע כִּי יְהוָה סָר מֵעָלָיו: 21 וַיֹּאחֲזוּהוּ פְלִשְׁתִּים וַיְנַקְּרוּ אֶת־ עֵינָיו וַיּוֹרִידוּ אוֹתוֹ עַזָּתָה וַיַּאַסְרוּהוּ בַּנְחֻשְׁתַּיִם וַיְהִי טוֹחֵן בְּבֵית הָאֲסוּרִים: 22 וַיָּחֶל שְׂעַר־רֹאשׁוֹ לְצַמֵּחַ כַּאֲשֶׁר גֻּלָּח:
פ

23 וְסַרְנֵי פְלִשְׁתִּים נֶאֶסְפוּ לִזְבֹּחַ זֶבַח־גָּדוֹל לְדָגוֹן אֱלֹהֵיהֶם וּלְשִׂמְחָה וַיֹּאמְרוּ נָתַן אֱלֹהֵינוּ בְּיָדֵנוּ אֵת שִׁמְשׁוֹן אוֹיְבֵנוּ: 24 וַיִּרְאוּ אֹתוֹ הָעָם וַיְהַלְלוּ אֶת־ אֱלֹהֵיהֶם כִּי אָמְרוּ נָתַן אֱלֹהֵינוּ בְיָדֵנוּ אֶת־אוֹיְבֵנוּ וְאֵת מַחֲרִיב אַרְצֵנוּ וַאֲשֶׁר הִרְבָּה אֶת־

And the one who multiplied our dead."

25 So it happened, when their hearts were merry, that they said, "Call for Samson, that he may perform for us." So they called for Samson from the prison, and he performed for them. And they stationed him between the pillars. 26 Then Samson said to the lad who held him by the hand, "Let me feel the pillars which support the temple, so that I can lean on them." 27 Now the temple was full of men and women. All the lords of the Philistines *were* there—about three thousand men and women on the roof watching while Samson performed.

28 Then Samson called to the LORD, saying, "O Lord GOD, remember me, I pray! Strengthen me, I pray, just this once, O God, that I may with one *blow* take vengeance on the Philistines for my two eyes!" 29 And Samson took hold of the two middle pillars which supported the temple, and he braced himself against them, one on his right and the other on his left. 30 Then Samson said, "Let me die with the Philistines!" And he pushed with *all his* might, and the temple fell on the lords and all the people who *were* in it. So the dead that he killed at his death were more than he had killed in his life.

31 And his brothers and all his father's household came down and took him, and brought *him* up and buried him between Zorah and Eshtaol in the tomb of his father Manoah. He had judged Israel twenty years.

17 Now there was a man from the mountains of Ephraim, whose name *was* Micah. 2 And he said to his mother, "The eleven hundred *shekels* of silver that were taken from you, and on which you put a curse, even saying it in my ears—here *is* the silver with me; I took it."

And his mother said, "*May you be* blessed by the LORD, my son!" 3 So when he had returned the eleven hundred *shekels* of silver to his mother, his mother said, "I had wholly dedicated the silver from my hand to the LORD for my son, to make a carved image and a molded image; now therefore, I will return it to you." 4 Thus he returned the silver to his mother. Then his mother took two hundred *shekels* of silver and gave them to the silversmith, and he made it into a carved image and a molded image; and they were in the house of Micah.

5 The man Micah had a shrine, and made an ephod and household idols; and he consecrated one of his sons, who became his priest. 6 In those days *there was* no king in Israel; everyone did *what was* right in his own eyes.

חֲלָלֵינוּ׃ 25 וַיְהִי כִּי טוֹבְ ק לִבָּם וַיֹּאמְרוּ קִרְאוּ לְשִׁמְשׁוֹן וִישַׂחֶק־לָנוּ וַיִּקְרְאוּ לְשִׁמְשׁוֹן מִבֵּית הָאֲסוּרִים ק וַיְצַחֵק לִפְנֵיהֶם וַיַּעֲמִידוּ אוֹתוֹ בֵּין הָעַמּוּדִים׃ 26 וַיֹּאמֶר שִׁמְשׁוֹן אֶל־הַנַּעַר הַמַּחֲזִיק בְּיָדוֹ הַנִּיחָה אוֹתִי וַהֲמִישֵׁנִי ק אֶת־הָעַמֻּדִים אֲשֶׁר הַבַּיִת נָכוֹן עֲלֵיהֶם וְאֶשָּׁעֵן עֲלֵיהֶם׃ 27 וְהַבַּיִת מָלֵא הָאֲנָשִׁים וְהַנָּשִׁים וְשָׁמָּה כֹּל סַרְנֵי פְלִשְׁתִּים וְעַל־הַגָּג כִּשְׁלֹשֶׁת אֲלָפִים אִישׁ וְאִשָּׁה הָרֹאִים בִּשְׂחוֹק שִׁמְשׁוֹן׃ 28 וַיִּקְרָא שִׁמְשׁוֹן אֶל־יְהוָה וַיֹּאמַר אֲדֹנָי יְהֹוִה זָכְרֵנִי נָא וְחַזְּקֵנִי נָא אַךְ הַפַּעַם הַזֶּה הָאֱלֹהִים וְאִנָּקְמָה נְקַם־אַחַת מִשְּׁתֵי עֵינַי מִפְּלִשְׁתִּים׃ 29 וַיִּלְפֹּת שִׁמְשׁוֹן אֶת־שְׁנֵי ׀ עַמּוּדֵי הַתָּוֶךְ אֲשֶׁר הַבַּיִת נָכוֹן עֲלֵיהֶם וַיִּסָּמֵךְ עֲלֵיהֶם אֶחָד בִּימִינוֹ וְאֶחָד בִּשְׂמֹאלוֹ׃ 30 וַיֹּאמֶר שִׁמְשׁוֹן תָּמוֹת נַפְשִׁי עִם־פְּלִשְׁתִּים וַיֵּט בְּכֹחַ וַיִּפֹּל הַבַּיִת עַל־הַסְּרָנִים וְעַל־כָּל־הָעָם אֲשֶׁר־בּוֹ וַיִּהְיוּ הַמֵּתִים אֲשֶׁר הֵמִית בְּמוֹתוֹ רַבִּים מֵאֲשֶׁר הֵמִית בְּחַיָּיו׃ 31 וַיֵּרְדוּ אֶחָיו וְכָל־בֵּית אָבִיהוּ וַיִּשְׂאוּ אֹתוֹ וַיַּעֲלוּ וַיִּקְבְּרוּ אוֹתוֹ בֵּין צָרְעָה וּבֵין אֶשְׁתָּאֹל בְּקֶבֶר מָנוֹחַ אָבִיו וְהוּא שָׁפַט אֶת־יִשְׂרָאֵל עֶשְׂרִים שָׁנָה׃ פ

יז וַיְהִי־אִישׁ מֵהַר־אֶפְרָיִם וּשְׁמוֹ מִיכָיְהוּ׃ 2 וַיֹּאמֶר לְאִמּוֹ אֶלֶף וּמֵאָה הַכֶּסֶף אֲשֶׁר לֻקַּח־לָךְ וְאַתְּ ק אָלִית וְגַם אָמַרְתְּ בְּאָזְנַי הִנֵּה־הַכֶּסֶף אִתִּי אֲנִי לְקַחְתִּיו וַתֹּאמֶר אִמּוֹ בָּרוּךְ בְּנִי לַיהוָה׃ 3 וַיָּשֶׁב אֶת־אֶלֶף־וּמֵאָה הַכֶּסֶף לְאִמּוֹ וַתֹּאמֶר אִמּוֹ הַקְדֵּשׁ הִקְדַּשְׁתִּי אֶת־הַכֶּסֶף לַיהוָה מִיָּדִי לִבְנִי לַעֲשׂוֹת פֶּסֶל וּמַסֵּכָה וְעַתָּה אֲשִׁיבֶנּוּ לָךְ׃ 4 וַיָּשֶׁב אֶת־הַכֶּסֶף לְאִמּוֹ וַתִּקַּח אִמּוֹ מָאתַיִם כֶּסֶף וַתִּתְּנֵהוּ לַצּוֹרֵף וַיַּעֲשֵׂהוּ פֶּסֶל וּמַסֵּכָה וַיְהִי בְּבֵית מִיכָיְהוּ׃ 5 וְהָאִישׁ מִיכָה לוֹ בֵּית אֱלֹהִים וַיַּעַשׂ אֵפוֹד וּתְרָפִים וַיְמַלֵּא אֶת־יַד אַחַד מִבָּנָיו וַיְהִי־לוֹ לְכֹהֵן׃ 6 בַּיָּמִים הָהֵם אֵין מֶלֶךְ בְּיִשְׂרָאֵל אִישׁ הַיָּשָׁר בְּעֵינָיו יַעֲשֶׂה׃ פ

טו 25 כְּטוֹב, הָאֲסוּרִים 26 וַהֲמִישֵׁנִי
יז 2 וְאַתְּ

7 Now there was a young man from Bethlehem in Judah, of the family of Judah; he *was* a Levite, and was staying there. 8 The man departed from the city of Bethlehem in Judah to stay wherever he could find *a place*. Then he came to the mountains of Ephraim, to the house of Micah, as he journeyed. 9 And Micah said to him, "Where do you come from?"

So he said to him, "I *am* a Levite from Bethlehem in Judah, and I am on my way to find *a place* to stay."

10 Micah said to him, "Dwell with me, and be a father and a priest to me, and I will give you ten *shekels* of silver per year, a suit of clothes, and your sustenance." So the Levite went in. 11 Then the Levite was content to dwell with the man; and the young man became like one of his sons to him. 12 So Micah consecrated the Levite, and the young man became his priest, and lived in the house of Micah. 13 Then Micah said, "Now I know that the LORD will be good to me, since I have a Levite as priest!"

18 In those days *there was* no king in Israel. And in those days the tribe of the Danites was seeking an inheritance for itself to dwell in; for until that day *their* inheritance among the tribes of Israel had not fallen to them. 2 So the children of Dan sent five men of their family from their territory, men of valor from Zorah and Eshtaol, to spy out the land and search it. They said to them, "Go, search the land." So they went to the mountains of Ephraim, to the house of Micah, and lodged there. 3 While they *were* at the house of Micah, they recognized the voice of the young Levite. They turned aside and said to him, "Who brought you here? What are you doing in this *place*? What do you have here?"

4 He said to them, "Thus and so Micah did for me. He has hired me, and I have become his priest."

5 So they said to him, "Please inquire of God, that we may know whether the journey on which we go will be prosperous."

6 And the priest said to them, "Go in peace. The presence of the LORD *be* with you on your way."

7 So the five men departed and went to Laish. They saw the people who *were* there, how they dwelt safely, in the manner of the Sidonians, quiet and secure. *There were* no rulers in the land who might put *them* to shame for anything. They *were* far from the Sidonians, and they had no ties with anyone.

8 Then *the spies* came back to their brethren at Zorah and Eshtaol, and their brethren said to them, "What *is* your *report*?"

7 וַיְהִי־נַעַר מִבֵּית לֶחֶם יְהוּדָה מִמִּשְׁפַּחַת יְהוּדָה וְהוּא לֵוִי וְהוּא גָר־שָׁם: 8 וַיֵּלֶךְ הָאִישׁ מֵהָעִיר מִבֵּית לֶחֶם יְהוּדָה לָגוּר בַּאֲשֶׁר יִמְצָא וַיָּבֹא הַר־ אֶפְרַיִם עַד־בֵּית מִיכָה לַעֲשׂוֹת דַּרְכּוֹ: 9 וַיֹּאמֶר־לוֹ מִיכָה מֵאַיִן תָּבוֹא וַיֹּאמֶר אֵלָיו לֵוִי אָנֹכִי מִבֵּית לֶחֶם יְהוּדָה וְאָנֹכִי הֹלֵךְ לָגוּר בַּאֲשֶׁר אֶמְצָא: 10 וַיֹּאמֶר לוֹ מִיכָה שְׁבָה עִמָּדִי וֶהְיֵה־לִי לְאָב וּלְכֹהֵן וְאָנֹכִי אֶתֶּן־לְךָ עֲשֶׂרֶת כֶּסֶף לַיָּמִים וְעֵרֶךְ בְּגָדִים וּמִחְיָתֶךָ וַיֵּלֶךְ הַלֵּוִי: 11 וַיּוֹאֶל הַלֵּוִי לָשֶׁבֶת אֶת־הָאִישׁ וַיְהִי הַנַּעַר לוֹ כְּאַחַד מִבָּנָיו: 12 וַיְמַלֵּא מִיכָה אֶת־יַד הַלֵּוִי וַיְהִי־לוֹ הַנַּעַר לְכֹהֵן וַיְהִי בְּבֵית מִיכָה: 13 וַיֹּאמֶר מִיכָה עַתָּה יָדַעְתִּי כִּי־יֵיטִיב יְהוָה לִי כִּי הָיָה־לִי הַלֵּוִי לְכֹהֵן:

יח בַּיָּמִים הָהֵם אֵין מֶלֶךְ בְּיִשְׂרָאֵל וּבַיָּמִים הָהֵם שֵׁבֶט הַדָּנִי מְבַקֶּשׁ־לוֹ נַחֲלָה לָשֶׁבֶת כִּי לֹא־נָפְלָה לּוֹ עַד־הַיּוֹם הַהוּא בְּתוֹךְ־שִׁבְטֵי יִשְׂרָאֵל בְּנַחֲלָה: ס 2 וַיִּשְׁלְחוּ בְנֵי־דָן מִמִּשְׁפַּחְתָּם חֲמִשָּׁה אֲנָשִׁים מִקְצוֹתָם אֲנָשִׁים בְּנֵי־ חַיִל מִצָּרְעָה וּמֵאֶשְׁתָּאֹל לְרַגֵּל אֶת־הָאָרֶץ וּלְחָקְרָהּ וַיֹּאמְרוּ אֲלֵהֶם לְכוּ חִקְרוּ אֶת־הָאָרֶץ וַיָּבֹאוּ הַר־ אֶפְרַיִם עַד־בֵּית מִיכָה וַיָּלִינוּ שָׁם: 3 הֵמָּה עִם־בֵּית מִיכָה וְהֵמָּה הִכִּירוּ אֶת־קוֹל הַנַּעַר הַלֵּוִי וַיָּסוּרוּ שָׁם וַיֹּאמְרוּ לוֹ מִי־הֱבִיאֲךָ הֲלֹם וּמָה־אַתָּה עֹשֶׂה בָּזֶה וּמַה־לְּךָ פֹּה: 4 וַיֹּאמֶר אֲלֵהֶם כָּזֹה וְכָזֹה עָשָׂה לִי מִיכָה וַיִּשְׂכְּרֵנִי וָאֱהִי־לוֹ לְכֹהֵן: 5 וַיֹּאמְרוּ לוֹ שְׁאַל־נָא בֵאלֹהִים וְנֵדְעָה הֲתַצְלִיחַ דַּרְכֵּנוּ אֲשֶׁר אֲנַחְנוּ הֹלְכִים עָלֶיהָ: 6 וַיֹּאמֶר לָהֶם הַכֹּהֵן לְכוּ לְשָׁלוֹם נֹכַח יְהוָה דַּרְכְּכֶם אֲשֶׁר תֵּלְכוּ־בָהּ: פ

7 וַיֵּלְכוּ חֲמֵשֶׁת הָאֲנָשִׁים וַיָּבֹאוּ לַיְשָׁה וַיִּרְאוּ אֶת־ הָעָם אֲשֶׁר־בְּקִרְבָּהּ יוֹשֶׁבֶת־לָבֶטַח כְּמִשְׁפַּט צִדֹנִים שֹׁקֵט וּבֹטֵחַ וְאֵין־מַכְלִים דָּבָר בָּאָרֶץ יוֹרֵשׁ עֶצֶר וּרְחֹקִים הֵמָּה מִצִּדֹנִים וְדָבָר אֵין־לָהֶם עִם־ אָדָם: 8 וַיָּבֹאוּ אֶל־אֲחֵיהֶם צָרְעָה וְאֶשְׁתָּאֹל וַיֹּאמְרוּ

9 So they said, "Arise, let us go up against them. For we have seen the land, and indeed it *is* very good. *Would* you *do* nothing? Do not hesitate to go, *and* enter to possess the land. 10 When you go, you will come to a secure people and a large land. For God has given it into your hands, a place where *there is* no lack of anything that *is* on the earth."

11 And six hundred men of the family of the Danites went from there, from Zorah and Eshtaol, armed with weapons of war. 12 Then they went up and encamped in Kirjath Jearim in Judah. (Therefore they call that place Mahaneh Dan to this day. There *it is,* west of Kirjath Jearim.) 13 And they passed from there to the mountains of Ephraim, and came to the house of Micah.

14 Then the five men who had gone to spy out the country of Laish answered and said to their brethren, "Do you know that there are in these houses an ephod, household idols, a carved image, and a molded image? Now therefore, consider what you should do." 15 So they turned aside there, and came to the house of the young Levite man—to the house of Micah—and greeted him. 16 The six hundred men armed with their weapons of war, who *were* of the children of Dan, stood by the entrance of the gate. 17 Then the five men who had gone to spy out the land went up. Entering there, they took the carved image, the ephod, the household idols, and the molded image. The priest stood at the entrance of the gate with the six hundred men *who were* armed with weapons of war.

18 When these went into Micah's house and took the carved image, the ephod, the household idols, and the molded image, the priest said to them, "What are you doing?"

19 And they said to him, "Be quiet, put your hand over your mouth, and come with us; be a father and a priest to us. *Is it* better for you to be a priest to the household of one man, or that you be a priest to a tribe and a family in Israel?" 20 So the priest's heart was glad; and he took the ephod, the household idols, and the carved image, and took his place among the people.

21 Then they turned and departed, and put the little ones, the livestock, and the goods in front of them. 22 When they were a good way from the house of Micah, the men who *were* in the houses near Micah's house gathered together and overtook the children of Dan. 23 And they called out to the children of Dan. So they turned around and said to Micah, "What ails you, that you have gathered such a company?"

לָהֶם אֲחֵיהֶם מָה אַתֶּם: 9 וַיֹּאמְרוּ קוּמָה וְנַעֲלֶה עֲלֵיהֶם כִּי רָאִינוּ אֶת־הָאָרֶץ וְהִנֵּה טוֹבָה מְאֹד וְאַתֶּם מַחְשִׁים אַל־תֵּעָצְלוּ לָלֶכֶת לָבֹא לָרֶשֶׁת אֶת־הָאָרֶץ: 10 כְּבֹאֲכֶם תָּבֹאוּ ׀ אֶל־עַם בֹּטֵחַ וְהָאָרֶץ רַחֲבַת יָדַיִם כִּי־נְתָנָהּ אֱלֹהִים בְּיֶדְכֶם מָקוֹם אֲשֶׁר אֵין־שָׁם מַחְסוֹר כָּל־דָּבָר אֲשֶׁר בָּאָרֶץ: 11 וַיִּסְעוּ מִשָּׁם מִמִּשְׁפַּחַת הַדָּנִי מִצָּרְעָה וּמֵאֶשְׁתָּאֹל שֵׁשׁ־מֵאוֹת אִישׁ חָגוּר כְּלֵי מִלְחָמָה: 12 וַיַּעֲלוּ וַיַּחֲנוּ בְּקִרְיַת יְעָרִים בִּיהוּדָה עַל־כֵּן קָרְאוּ לַמָּקוֹם הַהוּא מַחֲנֵה־דָן עַד הַיּוֹם הַזֶּה הִנֵּה אַחֲרֵי קִרְיַת יְעָרִים: 13 וַיַּעַבְרוּ מִשָּׁם הַר־אֶפְרָיִם וַיָּבֹאוּ עַד־בֵּית מִיכָה:

14 וַיַּעֲנוּ חֲמֵשֶׁת הָאֲנָשִׁים הַהֹלְכִים לְרַגֵּל אֶת־הָאָרֶץ לַיִשׁ וַיֹּאמְרוּ אֶל־אֲחֵיהֶם הַיְדַעְתֶּם כִּי יֵשׁ בַּבָּתִּים הָאֵלֶּה אֵפוֹד וּתְרָפִים וּפֶסֶל וּמַסֵּכָה וְעַתָּה דְּעוּ מַה־תַּעֲשׂוּ: 15 וַיָּסוּרוּ שָׁמָּה וַיָּבֹאוּ אֶל־בֵּית־הַנַּעַר הַלֵּוִי בֵּית מִיכָה וַיִּשְׁאֲלוּ־לוֹ לְשָׁלוֹם: 16 וְשֵׁשׁ־מֵאוֹת אִישׁ חֲגוּרִים כְּלֵי מִלְחַמְתָּם נִצָּבִים פֶּתַח הַשָּׁעַר אֲשֶׁר מִבְּנֵי־דָן: 17 וַיַּעֲלוּ חֲמֵשֶׁת הָאֲנָשִׁים הַהֹלְכִים לְרַגֵּל אֶת־הָאָרֶץ בָּאוּ שָׁמָּה לָקְחוּ אֶת־הַפֶּסֶל וְאֶת־הָאֵפוֹד וְאֶת־הַתְּרָפִים וְאֶת־הַמַּסֵּכָה וְהַכֹּהֵן נִצָּב פֶּתַח הַשַּׁעַר וְשֵׁשׁ־מֵאוֹת הָאִישׁ הֶחָגוּר כְּלֵי הַמִּלְחָמָה: 18 וְאֵלֶּה בָּאוּ בֵּית מִיכָה וַיִּקְחוּ אֶת־פֶּסֶל הָאֵפוֹד וְאֶת־הַתְּרָפִים וְאֶת־הַמַּסֵּכָה וַיֹּאמֶר אֲלֵיהֶם הַכֹּהֵן מָה אַתֶּם עֹשִׂים:

19 וַיֹּאמְרוּ לוֹ הַחֲרֵשׁ שִׂים־יָדְךָ עַל־פִּיךָ וְלֵךְ עִמָּנוּ וֶהְיֵה־לָנוּ לְאָב וּלְכֹהֵן הֲטוֹב ׀ הֱיוֹתְךָ כֹהֵן לְבֵית אִישׁ אֶחָד אוֹ הֱיוֹתְךָ כֹהֵן לְשֵׁבֶט וּלְמִשְׁפָּחָה בְּיִשְׂרָאֵל: 20 וַיִּיטַב לֵב הַכֹּהֵן וַיִּקַּח אֶת־הָאֵפוֹד וְאֶת־הַתְּרָפִים וְאֶת־הַפָּסֶל וַיָּבֹא בְּקֶרֶב הָעָם: 21 וַיִּפְנוּ וַיֵּלֵכוּ וַיָּשִׂימוּ אֶת־הַטַּף וְאֶת־הַמִּקְנֶה וְאֶת־הַכְּבוּדָּה לִפְנֵיהֶם: 22 הֵמָּה הִרְחִיקוּ מִבֵּית מִיכָה וְהָאֲנָשִׁים אֲשֶׁר בַּבָּתִּים אֲשֶׁר עִם־בֵּית מִיכָה נִזְעֲקוּ וַיַּדְבִּיקוּ אֶת־בְּנֵי־דָן: 23 וַיִּקְרְאוּ אֶל־בְּנֵי־דָן וַיַּסֵּבּוּ פְּנֵיהֶם וַיֹּאמְרוּ לְמִיכָה מַה־לְּךָ כִּי נִזְעָקְתָּ:

24 So he said, "You have taken away my gods which I made, and the priest, and you have gone away. Now what more do I have? How can you say to me, 'What ails you?' "

25 And the children of Dan said to him, "Do not let your voice be heard among us, lest angry men fall upon you, and you lose your life, with the lives of your household!" 26 Then the children of Dan went their way. And when Micah saw that they *were* too strong for him, he turned and went back to his house.

27 So they took *the things* Micah had made, and the priest who had belonged to him, and went to Laish, to a people quiet and secure; and they struck them with the edge of the sword and burned the city with fire. 28 *There was* no deliverer, because it *was* far from Sidon, and they had no ties with anyone. It was in the valley that belongs to Beth Rehob. So they rebuilt the city and dwelt there. 29 And they called the name of the city Dan, after the name of Dan their father, who was born to Israel. However, the name of the city formerly *was* Laish.

30 Then the children of Dan set up for themselves the carved image; and Jonathan the son of Gershom, the son of Manasseh, and his sons were priests to the tribe of Dan until the day of the captivity of the land. 31 So they set up for themselves Micah's carved image which he made, all the time that the house of God was in Shiloh.

19 And it came to pass in those days, when *there was* no king in Israel, that there was a certain Levite staying in the remote mountains of Ephraim. He took for himself a concubine from Bethlehem in Judah. 2 But his concubine played the harlot against him, and went away from him to her father's house at Bethlehem in Judah, and was there four whole months. 3 Then her husband arose and went after her, to speak kindly to her *and* bring her back, having his servant and a couple of donkeys with him. So she brought him into her father's house; and when the father of the young woman saw him, he was glad to meet him. 4 Now his father-in-law, the young woman's father, detained him; and he stayed with him three days. So they ate and drank and lodged there.

5 Then it came to pass on the fourth day that they arose early in the morning, and he stood to depart; but the young woman's father said to his son-in-law, "Refresh your heart with a morsel of bread, and afterward go your way."

6 So they sat down, and the two of them ate and drank together. Then the young woman's father said to the man, "Please be content to stay all night,

---

24 וַיֹּאמֶר אֶת־אֱלֹהַי אֲשֶׁר־עָשִׂיתִי לְקַחְתֶּם וְאֶת־הַכֹּהֵן וַתֵּלְכוּ וּמַה־לִּי עוֹד וּמַה־זֶּה תֹּאמְרוּ אֵלַי מַה־לָּךְ: 25 וַיֹּאמְרוּ אֵלָיו בְּנֵי־דָן אַל־תַּשְׁמַע קוֹלְךָ עִמָּנוּ פֶּן־יִפְגְּעוּ בָכֶם אֲנָשִׁים מָרֵי נֶפֶשׁ וְאָסַפְתָּה נַפְשְׁךָ וְנֶפֶשׁ בֵּיתֶךָ: 26 וַיֵּלְכוּ בְנֵי־דָן לְדַרְכָּם וַיַּרְא מִיכָה כִּי־חֲזָקִים הֵמָּה מִמֶּנּוּ וַיִּפֶן וַיָּשָׁב אֶל־בֵּיתוֹ:

27 וְהֵמָּה לָקְחוּ אֵת אֲשֶׁר־עָשָׂה מִיכָה וְאֶת־הַכֹּהֵן אֲשֶׁר הָיָה־לוֹ וַיָּבֹאוּ עַל־לַיִשׁ עַל־עַם שֹׁקֵט וּבֹטֵחַ וַיַּכּוּ אוֹתָם לְפִי־חָרֶב וְאֶת־הָעִיר שָׂרְפוּ בָאֵשׁ:

28 וְאֵין מַצִּיל כִּי רְחוֹקָה־הִיא מִצִּידוֹן וְדָבָר אֵין לָהֶם עִם־אָדָם וְהִיא בָּעֵמֶק אֲשֶׁר לְבֵית־רְחוֹב וַיִּבְנוּ אֶת־הָעִיר וַיֵּשְׁבוּ בָהּ: 29 וַיִּקְרְאוּ שֵׁם־הָעִיר דָּן בְּשֵׁם דָּן אֲבִיהֶם אֲשֶׁר יוּלַּד לְיִשְׂרָאֵל וְאוּלָם לַיִשׁ שֵׁם־הָעִיר לָרִאשֹׁנָה: 30 וַיָּקִימוּ לָהֶם בְּנֵי־דָן אֶת־הַפָּסֶל וִיהוֹנָתָן בֶּן־גֵּרְשֹׁם בֶּן־מְנַשֶּׁה הוּא וּבָנָיו הָיוּ כֹהֲנִים לְשֵׁבֶט הַדָּנִי עַד־יוֹם גְּלוֹת הָאָרֶץ:

31 וַיָּשִׂימוּ לָהֶם אֶת־פֶּסֶל מִיכָה אֲשֶׁר עָשָׂה כָּל־יְמֵי הֱיוֹת בֵּית־הָאֱלֹהִים בְּשִׁלֹה: פ

יט 1 וַיְהִי בַּיָּמִים הָהֵם וּמֶלֶךְ אֵין בְּיִשְׂרָאֵל וַיְהִי אִישׁ לֵוִי גָּר בְּיַרְכְּתֵי הַר־אֶפְרַיִם וַיִּקַּח־לוֹ אִשָּׁה פִילֶגֶשׁ מִבֵּית לֶחֶם יְהוּדָה: 2 וַתִּזְנֶה עָלָיו פִּילַגְשׁוֹ וַתֵּלֶךְ מֵאִתּוֹ אֶל־בֵּית אָבִיהָ אֶל־בֵּית לֶחֶם יְהוּדָה וַתְּהִי־שָׁם יָמִים אַרְבָּעָה חֳדָשִׁים: 3 וַיָּקָם אִישָׁהּ וַיֵּלֶךְ אַחֲרֶיהָ לְדַבֵּר עַל־לִבָּהּ לַהֲשִׁיבוֹ וְנַעֲרוֹ עִמּוֹ וְצֶמֶד חֲמֹרִים וַתְּבִיאֵהוּ בֵּית אָבִיהָ וַיִּרְאֵהוּ אֲבִי הַנַּעֲרָה וַיִּשְׂמַח לִקְרָאתוֹ: 4 וַיֶּחֱזַק־בּוֹ חֹתְנוֹ אֲבִי הַנַּעֲרָה וַיֵּשֶׁב אִתּוֹ שְׁלֹשֶׁת יָמִים וַיֹּאכְלוּ וַיִּשְׁתּוּ וַיָּלִינוּ שָׁם: 5 וַיְהִי בַּיּוֹם הָרְבִיעִי וַיַּשְׁכִּימוּ בַבֹּקֶר וַיָּקָם לָלֶכֶת וַיֹּאמֶר אֲבִי הַנַּעֲרָה אֶל־חֲתָנוֹ סְעָד לִבְּךָ פַּת־לֶחֶם וְאַחַר תֵּלֵכוּ: 6 וַיֵּשְׁבוּ וַיֹּאכְלוּ שְׁנֵיהֶם יַחְדָּו וַיִּשְׁתּוּ וַיֹּאמֶר אֲבִי הַנַּעֲרָה אֶל־הָאִישׁ

and let your heart be merry." [7] And when the man stood to depart, his father-in-law urged him; so he lodged there again. [8] Then he arose early in the morning on the fifth day to depart, but the young woman's father said, "Please refresh your heart." So they delayed until afternoon; and both of them ate.

[9] And when the man stood to depart—he and his concubine and his servant—his father-in-law, the young woman's father, said to him, "Look, the day is now drawing toward evening; please spend the night. See, the day is coming to an end; lodge here, that your heart may be merry. Tomorrow go your way early, so that you may get home."

[10] However, the man was not willing to spend that night; so he rose and departed, and came opposite Jebus (that is, Jerusalem). With him were the two saddled donkeys; his concubine was also with him. [11] They were near Jebus, and the day was far spent; and the servant said to his master, "Come, please, and let us turn aside into this city of the Jebusites and lodge in it."

[12] But his master said to him, "We will not turn aside here into a city of foreigners, who are not of the children of Israel; we will go on to Gibeah." [13] So he said to his servant, "Come, let us draw near to one of these places, and spend the night in Gibeah or in Ramah." [14] And they passed by and went their way; and the sun went down on them near Gibeah, which belongs to Benjamin. [15] They turned aside there to go in to lodge in Gibeah. And when he went in, he sat down in the open square of the city, for no one would take them into his house to spend the night.

[16] Just then an old man came in from his work in the field at evening, who also was from the mountains of Ephraim; he was staying in Gibeah, whereas the men of the place were Benjamites. [17] And when he raised his eyes, he saw the traveler in the open square of the city; and the old man said, "Where are you going, and where do you come from?"

[18] So he said to him, "We are passing from Bethlehem in Judah toward the remote mountains of Ephraim; I am from there. I went to Bethlehem in Judah; now I am going to the house of the LORD. But there is no one who will take me into his house, [19] although we have both straw and fodder for our donkeys, and bread and wine for myself, for your female servant, and for the young man who is with your servant; there is no lack of anything."

[20] And the old man said, "Peace be with you! However, let all your needs be my responsibility; only do not spend the night in the open square."

הוֹאֶל־נָא וְלִין וְיִטַב לְבָבֶךָ: [7] וַיָּקָם הָאִישׁ לָלֶכֶת וַיִּפְצַר־בּוֹ חֹתְנוֹ וַיָּשָׁב וַיָּלֶן שָׁם: [8] וַיַּשְׁכֵּם בַּבֹּקֶר בַּיּוֹם הַחֲמִישִׁי לָלֶכֶת וַיֹּאמֶר | אֲבִי הַנַּעֲרָה סְעָד־נָא לְבָבְךָ וְהִתְמַהְמְהוּ עַד־נְטוֹת הַיּוֹם וַיֹּאכְלוּ שְׁנֵיהֶם: [9] וַיָּקָם הָאִישׁ לָלֶכֶת הוּא וּפִילַגְשׁוֹ וְנַעֲרוֹ וַיֹּאמֶר לוֹ חֹתְנוֹ אֲבִי הַנַּעֲרָה הִנֵּה נָא רָפָה הַיּוֹם לַעֲרֹב לִינוּ־נָא הִנֵּה חֲנוֹת הַיּוֹם לִין פֹּה וְיִיטַב לְבָבֶךָ וְהִשְׁכַּמְתֶּם מָחָר לְדַרְכְּכֶם וְהָלַכְתָּ לְאֹהָלֶךָ: [10] וְלֹא־אָבָה הָאִישׁ לָלוּן וַיָּקָם וַיֵּלֶךְ וַיָּבֹא עַד־נֹכַח יְבוּס הִיא יְרוּשָׁלִַם וְעִמּוֹ צֶמֶד חֲמוֹרִים חֲבוּשִׁים וּפִילַגְשׁוֹ עִמּוֹ: [11] הֵם עִם־יְבוּס וְהַיּוֹם רַד מְאֹד וַיֹּאמֶר הַנַּעַר אֶל־אֲדֹנָיו לְכָה־נָּא וְנָסוּרָה אֶל־עִיר־הַיְבוּסִי הַזֹּאת וְנָלִין בָּהּ: [12] וַיֹּאמֶר אֵלָיו אֲדֹנָיו לֹא נָסוּר אֶל־עִיר נָכְרִי אֲשֶׁר לֹא־מִבְּנֵי יִשְׂרָאֵל הֵנָּה וְעָבַרְנוּ עַד־גִּבְעָה: [13] וַיֹּאמֶר לְנַעֲרוֹ לֵךְ וְנִקְרְבָה בְּאַחַד הַמְּקֹמוֹת וְלַנּוּ בַגִּבְעָה אוֹ בָרָמָה: [14] וַיַּעַבְרוּ וַיֵּלֵכוּ וַתָּבֹא לָהֶם הַשֶּׁמֶשׁ אֵצֶל הַגִּבְעָה אֲשֶׁר לְבִנְיָמִן: [15] וַיָּסֻרוּ שָׁם לָבוֹא לָלוּן בַּגִּבְעָה וַיָּבֹא וַיֵּשֶׁב בִּרְחוֹב הָעִיר וְאֵין אִישׁ מְאַסֵּף־אוֹתָם הַבַּיְתָה לָלוּן: [16] וְהִנֵּה | אִישׁ זָקֵן בָּא מִן־מַעֲשֵׂהוּ מִן־הַשָּׂדֶה בָּעֶרֶב וְהָאִישׁ מֵהַר אֶפְרַיִם וְהוּא־גָר בַּגִּבְעָה וְאַנְשֵׁי הַמָּקוֹם בְּנֵי יְמִינִי: [17] וַיִּשָּׂא עֵינָיו וַיַּרְא אֶת־הָאִישׁ הָאֹרֵחַ בִּרְחֹב הָעִיר וַיֹּאמֶר הָאִישׁ הַזָּקֵן אָנָה תֵלֵךְ וּמֵאַיִן תָּבוֹא: [18] וַיֹּאמֶר אֵלָיו עֹבְרִים אֲנַחְנוּ מִבֵּית־לֶחֶם יְהוּדָה עַד־יַרְכְּתֵי הַר־אֶפְרַיִם מִשָּׁם אָנֹכִי וָאֵלֵךְ עַד־בֵּית לֶחֶם יְהוּדָה וְאֶת־בֵּית יְהֹוָה אֲנִי הֹלֵךְ וְאֵין אִישׁ מְאַסֵּף אוֹתִי הַבָּיְתָה: [19] וְגַם־תֶּבֶן גַּם־מִסְפּוֹא יֵשׁ לַחֲמוֹרֵינוּ וְגַם לֶחֶם וָיַיִן יֶשׁ־לִי וְלַאֲמָתֶךָ וְלַנַּעַר עִם־עֲבָדֶיךָ אֵין מַחְסוֹר כָּל־דָּבָר: [20] וַיֹּאמֶר הָאִישׁ הַזָּקֵן שָׁלוֹם לָךְ רַק כָּל־מַחְסוֹרְךָ עָלָי רַק בָּרְחוֹב אַל־

²¹So he brought him into his house, and gave fodder to the donkeys. And they washed their feet, and ate and drank.

²²As they were enjoying themselves, suddenly certain men of the city, perverted men, surrounded the house *and* beat on the door. They spoke to the master of the house, the old man, saying, "Bring out the man who came to your house, that we may know him *carnally!*"

²³But the man, the master of the house, went out to them and said to them, "No, my brethren! I beg you, do not act *so* wickedly! Seeing this man has come into my house, do not commit this outrage.
²⁴Look, *here is* my virgin daughter and *the man's* concubine; let me bring them out now. Humble them, and do with them as you please; but to this man do not do such a vile thing!" ²⁵But the men would not heed him. So the man took his concubine and brought *her* out to them. And they knew her and abused her all night until morning; and when the day began to break, they let her go.

²⁶Then the woman came as the day was dawning, and fell down at the door of the man's house where her master *was,* till it was light.

²⁷When her master arose in the morning, and opened the doors of the house and went out to go his way, there was his concubine, fallen *at* the door of the house with her hands on the threshold. ²⁸And he said to her, "Get up and let us be going." But there was no answer. So the man lifted her onto the donkey; and the man got up and went to his place.

²⁹When he entered his house he took a knife, laid hold of his concubine, and divided her into twelve pieces, limb by limb, and sent her throughout all the territory of Israel. ³⁰And so it was that all who saw it said, "No such deed has been done or seen from the day that the children of Israel came up from the land of Egypt until this day. Consider it, confer, and speak up!"

20 So all the children of Israel came out, from Dan to Beersheba, as well as from the land of Gilead, and the congregation gathered together as one man before the LORD at Mizpah. ²And the leaders of all the people, all the tribes of Israel, presented themselves in the assembly of the people of God, four hundred thousand foot soldiers who drew the sword. ³(Now the children of Benjamin heard that the children of Israel had gone up to Mizpah.)

Then the children of Israel said, "Tell *us,* how did this wicked deed happen?"

תֵּלֶן: 21 וַיְבִיאֵהוּ לְבֵיתוֹ וַיָּבֹל לַחֲמוֹרִים וַיִּרְחֲצוּ
רַגְלֵיהֶם וַיֹּאכְלוּ וַיִּשְׁתּוּ: 22 הֵמָּה מֵיטִיבִים אֶת־
לִבָּם וְהִנֵּה אַנְשֵׁי הָעִיר אַנְשֵׁי בְנֵי־בְלִיַּעַל נָסַבּוּ
אֶת־הַבַּיִת מִתְדַּפְּקִים עַל־הַדָּלֶת וַיֹּאמְרוּ אֶל־הָאִישׁ
בַּעַל הַבַּיִת הַזָּקֵן לֵאמֹר הוֹצֵא אֶת־הָאִישׁ אֲשֶׁר־
בָּא אֶל־בֵּיתְךָ וְנֵדָעֶנּוּ: 23 וַיֵּצֵא אֲלֵיהֶם הָאִישׁ
בַּעַל הַבַּיִת וַיֹּאמֶר אֲלֵהֶם אַל־אַחַי אַל־תָּרֵעוּ
נָא אַחֲרֵי אֲשֶׁר־בָּא הָאִישׁ הַזֶּה אֶל־בֵּיתִי אַל־
תַּעֲשׂוּ אֶת־הַנְּבָלָה הַזֹּאת: 24 הִנֵּה בִתִּי הַבְּתוּלָה
וּפִילַגְשֵׁהוּ אוֹצִיאָה־נָּא אוֹתָם וְעַנּוּ אוֹתָם וַעֲשׂוּ
לָהֶם הַטּוֹב בְּעֵינֵיכֶם וְלָאִישׁ הַזֶּה לֹא תַעֲשׂוּ
דְּבַר הַנְּבָלָה הַזֹּאת: 25 וְלֹא־אָבוּ הָאֲנָשִׁים לִשְׁמֹעַ
לוֹ וַיַּחֲזֵק הָאִישׁ בְּפִילַגְשׁוֹ וַיֹּצֵא אֲלֵיהֶם הַחוּץ
וַיֵּדְעוּ אוֹתָהּ וַיִּתְעַלְּלוּ־בָהּ כָּל־הַלַּיְלָה עַד־הַבֹּקֶר
וַיְשַׁלְּחוּהָ בַּעֲלוֹת הַשָּׁחַר: 26 וַתָּבֹא הָאִשָּׁה לִפְנוֹת
הַבֹּקֶר וַתִּפֹּל פֶּתַח בֵּית־הָאִישׁ אֲשֶׁר־אֲדוֹנֶיהָ שָּׁם
עַד־הָאוֹר: 27 וַיָּקָם אֲדֹנֶיהָ בַּבֹּקֶר וַיִּפְתַּח דַּלְתוֹת
הַבַּיִת וַיֵּצֵא לָלֶכֶת לְדַרְכּוֹ וְהִנֵּה הָאִשָּׁה פִילַגְשׁוֹ
נֹפֶלֶת פֶּתַח הַבַּיִת וְיָדֶיהָ עַל־הַסַּף: 28 וַיֹּאמֶר אֵלֶיהָ
קוּמִי וְנֵלֵכָה וְאֵין עֹנֶה וַיִּקָּחֶהָ עַל־הַחֲמוֹר וַיָּקָם
הָאִישׁ וַיֵּלֶךְ לִמְקֹמוֹ: 29 וַיָּבֹא אֶל־בֵּיתוֹ וַיִּקַּח אֶת־
הַמַּאֲכֶלֶת וַיַּחֲזֵק בְּפִילַגְשׁוֹ וַיְנַתְּחֶהָ לַעֲצָמֶיהָ לִשְׁנֵים
עָשָׂר נְתָחִים וַיְשַׁלְּחֶהָ בְּכֹל גְּבוּל יִשְׂרָאֵל: 30 וְהָיָה
כָל־הָרֹאֶה וְאָמַר לֹא־נִהְיְתָה וְלֹא־נִרְאֲתָה כָּזֹאת
לְמִיּוֹם עֲלוֹת בְּנֵי־יִשְׂרָאֵל מֵאֶרֶץ מִצְרַיִם עַד הַיּוֹם
הַזֶּה שִׂימוּ־לָכֶם עָלֶיהָ עֻצוּ וְדַבֵּרוּ: פ

כ וַיֵּצְאוּ כָּל־בְּנֵי יִשְׂרָאֵל וַתִּקָּהֵל הָעֵדָה כְּאִישׁ
אֶחָד לְמִדָּן וְעַד־בְּאֵר שֶׁבַע וְאֶרֶץ הַגִּלְעָד אֶל־
יְהוָה הַמִּצְפָּה: 2 וַיִּתְיַצְּבוּ פִּנּוֹת כָּל־הָעָם כֹּל שִׁבְטֵי
יִשְׂרָאֵל בִּקְהַל עַם הָאֱלֹהִים אַרְבַּע מֵאוֹת אֶלֶף
אִישׁ רַגְלִי שֹׁלֵף חָרֶב: פ
3 וַיִּשְׁמְעוּ בְּנֵי בִנְיָמִן כִּי־עָלוּ בְנֵי־יִשְׂרָאֵל הַמִּצְפָּה
וַיֹּאמְרוּ בְּנֵי יִשְׂרָאֵל דַּבְּרוּ אֵיכָה נִהְיְתָה הָרָעָה

⁴ So the Levite, the husband of the woman who was murdered, answered and said, "My concubine and I went into Gibeah, which belongs to Benjamin, to spend the night. ⁵ And the men of Gibeah rose against me, and surrounded the house at night because of me. They intended to kill me, but instead they ravished my concubine so that she died. ⁶ So I took hold of my concubine, cut her in pieces, and sent her throughout all the territory of the inheritance of Israel, because they committed lewdness and outrage in Israel. ⁷ Look! All of you *are* children of Israel; give your advice and counsel here and now!"

⁸ So all the people arose as one man, saying, "None *of us* will go to his tent, nor will any turn back to his house; ⁹ but now this *is* the thing which we will do to Gibeah: *We will go up* against it by lot. ¹⁰ We will take ten men out of *every* hundred throughout all the tribes of Israel, a hundred out of *every* thousand, and a thousand out of *every* ten thousand, to make provisions for the people, that when they come to Gibeah in Benjamin, they may repay all the vileness that they have done in Israel." ¹¹ So all the men of Israel were gathered against the city, united together as one man.

¹² Then the tribes of Israel sent men through all the tribe of Benjamin, saying, "What *is* this wickedness that has occurred among you? ¹³ Now therefore, deliver up the men, the perverted men who *are* in Gibeah, that we may put them to death and remove the evil from Israel!" But the children of Benjamin would not listen to the voice of their brethren, the children of Israel. ¹⁴ Instead, the children of Benjamin gathered together from their cities to Gibeah, to go to battle against the children of Israel. ¹⁵ And from their cities at that time the children of Benjamin numbered twenty-six thousand men who drew the sword, besides the inhabitants of Gibeah, who numbered seven hundred select men. ¹⁶ Among all this people *were* seven hundred select men *who were* left-handed; every one could sling a stone at a hair's *breadth* and not miss. ¹⁷ Now besides Benjamin, the men of Israel numbered four hundred thousand men who drew the sword; all of these *were* men of war.

¹⁸ Then the children of Israel arose and went up to the house of God to inquire of God. They said, "Which of us shall go up first to battle against the children of Benjamin?"

The LORD said, "Judah first!"

¹⁹ So the children of Israel rose in the morning and encamped against Gibeah. ²⁰ And the men of Israel went out to battle against Benjamin, and the men of Israel put themselves in battle array to fight

הַזֹּאת: 4 וַיַּעַן הָאִישׁ הַלֵּוִי אִישׁ הָאִשָּׁה הַנִּרְצָחָה וַיֹּאמַר הַגִּבְעָתָה אֲשֶׁר לְבִנְיָמִן בָּאתִי אֲנִי וּפִילַגְשִׁי לָלוּן: 5 וַיָּקֻמוּ עָלַי בַּעֲלֵי הַגִּבְעָה וַיָּסֹבּוּ עָלַי אֶת־הַבַּיִת לַיְלָה אוֹתִי דִּמּוּ לַהֲרֹג וְאֶת־פִּילַגְשִׁי עִנּוּ וַתָּמֹת: 6 וָאֹחֵז בְּפִילַגְשִׁי וָאֲנַתְּחֶהָ וָאֲשַׁלְּחֶהָ בְּכָל־שְׂדֵה נַחֲלַת יִשְׂרָאֵל כִּי עָשׂוּ זִמָּה וּנְבָלָה בְּיִשְׂרָאֵל: 7 הִנֵּה כֻלְּכֶם בְּנֵי יִשְׂרָאֵל הָבוּ לָכֶם דָּבָר וְעֵצָה הֲלֹם: 8 וַיָּקָם כָּל־הָעָם כְּאִישׁ אֶחָד לֵאמֹר לֹא נֵלֵךְ אִישׁ לְאָהֳלוֹ וְלֹא נָסוּר אִישׁ לְבֵיתוֹ: 9 וְעַתָּה זֶה הַדָּבָר אֲשֶׁר נַעֲשֶׂה לַגִּבְעָה עָלֶיהָ בְּגוֹרָל: 10 וְלָקַחְנוּ עֲשָׂרָה אֲנָשִׁים לַמֵּאָה לְכֹל | שִׁבְטֵי יִשְׂרָאֵל וּמֵאָה לָאֶלֶף וְאֶלֶף לָרְבָבָה לָקַחַת צֵדָה לָעָם לַעֲשׂוֹת לְבוֹאָם לְגֶבַע בִּנְיָמִן כְּכָל־הַנְּבָלָה אֲשֶׁר עָשָׂה בְּיִשְׂרָאֵל: 11 וַיֵּאָסֵף כָּל־אִישׁ יִשְׂרָאֵל אֶל־הָעִיר כְּאִישׁ אֶחָד חֲבֵרִים: פ

12 וַיִּשְׁלְחוּ שִׁבְטֵי יִשְׂרָאֵל אֲנָשִׁים בְּכָל־שִׁבְטֵי בִנְיָמִן לֵאמֹר מָה הָרָעָה הַזֹּאת אֲשֶׁר נִהְיְתָה בָּכֶם: 13 וְעַתָּה תְּנוּ אֶת־הָאֲנָשִׁים בְּנֵי־בְלִיַּעַל אֲשֶׁר בַּגִּבְעָה וּנְמִיתֵם וּנְבַעֲרָה רָעָה מִיִּשְׂרָאֵל וְלֹא אָבוּ בְּנֵי בִּנְיָמִן לִשְׁמֹעַ בְּקוֹל אֲחֵיהֶם בְּנֵי־יִשְׂרָאֵל: 14 וַיֵּאָסְפוּ בְנֵי־בִנְיָמִן מִן־הֶעָרִים הַגִּבְעָתָה לָצֵאת לַמִּלְחָמָה עִם־בְּנֵי יִשְׂרָאֵל: 15 וַיִּתְפָּקְדוּ בְנֵי בִנְיָמִן בַּיּוֹם הַהוּא מֵהֶעָרִים עֶשְׂרִים וְשִׁשָּׁה אֶלֶף אִישׁ שֹׁלֵף חָרֶב לְבַד מִיֹּשְׁבֵי הַגִּבְעָה הִתְפָּקְדוּ שְׁבַע מֵאוֹת אִישׁ בָּחוּר: 16 מִכֹּל | הָעָם הַזֶּה שְׁבַע מֵאוֹת אִישׁ בָּחוּר אִטֵּר יַד־יְמִינוֹ כָּל־זֶה קֹלֵעַ בָּאֶבֶן אֶל־הַשַּׂעֲרָה וְלֹא יַחֲטִא: פ

17 וְאִישׁ יִשְׂרָאֵל הִתְפָּקְדוּ לְבַד מִבִּנְיָמִן אַרְבַּע מֵאוֹת אֶלֶף אִישׁ שֹׁלֵף חָרֶב כָּל־זֶה אִישׁ מִלְחָמָה: 18 וַיָּקֻמוּ וַיַּעֲלוּ בֵית־אֵל וַיִּשְׁאֲלוּ בֵאלֹהִים וַיֹּאמְרוּ בְּנֵי יִשְׂרָאֵל מִי יַעֲלֶה־לָּנוּ בַתְּחִלָּה לַמִּלְחָמָה עִם־בְּנֵי בִנְיָמִן וַיֹּאמֶר יְהוָה יְהוּדָה בַתְּחִלָּה: 19 וַיָּקוּמוּ בְנֵי־יִשְׂרָאֵל בַּבֹּקֶר וַיַּחֲנוּ עַל־הַגִּבְעָה: פ

20 וַיֵּצֵא אִישׁ יִשְׂרָאֵל לַמִּלְחָמָה עִם־בִּנְיָמִן וַיַּעַרְכוּ

against them at Gibeah. ²¹Then the children of
Benjamin came out of Gibeah, and on that day cut
down to the ground twenty-two thousand men of
the Israelites. ²²And the people, that is, the men of
Israel, encouraged themselves and again formed the
battle line at the place where they had put
themselves in array on the first day. ²³Then the
children of Israel went up and wept before the
LORD until evening, and asked counsel of the LORD,
saying, "Shall I again draw near for battle against
the children of my brother Benjamin?"

And the LORD said, "Go up against him."

²⁴So the children of Israel approached the
children of Benjamin on the second day. ²⁵And
Benjamin went out against them from Gibeah on
the second day, and cut down to the ground
eighteen thousand more of the children of Israel;
all these drew the sword.

²⁶Then all the children of Israel, that is, all the
people, went up and came to the house of God and
wept. They sat there before the LORD and fasted
that day until evening; and they offered burnt
offerings and peace offerings before the LORD. ²⁷So
the children of Israel inquired of the LORD (the ark
of the covenant of God *was* there in those days,
²⁸and Phinehas the son of Eleazar, the son of
Aaron, stood before it in those days), saying, "Shall
I yet again go out to battle against the children of
my brother Benjamin, or shall I cease?"

And the LORD said, "Go up, for tomorrow I will
deliver them into your hand."

²⁹Then Israel set men in ambush all around
Gibeah. ³⁰And the children of Israel went up
against the children of Benjamin on the third day,
and put themselves in battle array against Gibeah
as at the other times. ³¹So the children of Benjamin
went out against the people, *and* were drawn away
from the city. They began to strike down *and* kill
some of the people, as at the other times, in the
highways (one of which goes up to Bethel and the
other to Gibeah) and in the field, about thirty men
of Israel. ³²And the children of Benjamin said,
"They *are* defeated before us, as at first."

But the children of Israel said, "Let us flee and
draw them away from the city to the highways."
³³So all the men of Israel rose from their place and
put themselves in battle array at Baal Tamar. Then
Israel's men in ambush burst forth from their
position in the plain of Geba. ³⁴And ten thousand
select men from all Israel came against Gibeah, and
the battle was fierce. But *the Benjamites* did not
know that disaster *was* upon them. ³⁵The LORD

אַתֶּם אִישׁ־יִשְׂרָאֵל מִלְחָמָה אֶל־הַגִּבְעָה: 21 וַיֵּצְאוּ
בְנֵי־בִנְיָמִן מִן־הַגִּבְעָה וַיַּשְׁחִיתוּ בְיִשְׂרָאֵל בַּיּוֹם
הַהוּא שְׁנַיִם וְעֶשְׂרִים אֶלֶף אִישׁ אָרְצָה: 22 וַיִּתְחַזַּק
הָעָם אִישׁ יִשְׂרָאֵל וַיֹּסִפוּ לַעֲרֹךְ מִלְחָמָה בַּמָּקוֹם
אֲשֶׁר־עָרְכוּ שָׁם בַּיּוֹם הָרִאשׁוֹן: 23 וַיַּעֲלוּ בְנֵי־
יִשְׂרָאֵל וַיִּבְכּוּ לִפְנֵי־יְהֹוָה עַד־הָעֶרֶב וַיִּשְׁאֲלוּ בַיהֹוָה
לֵאמֹר הַאוֹסִיף לָגֶשֶׁת לַמִּלְחָמָה עִם־בְּנֵי בִנְיָמִן
אָחִי וַיֹּאמֶר יְהֹוָה עֲלוּ אֵלָיו:
פ

24 וַיִּקְרְבוּ בְנֵי־יִשְׂרָאֵל אֶל־בְּנֵי בִנְיָמִן בַּיּוֹם הַשֵּׁנִי:
25 וַיֵּצֵא בִנְיָמִן | לִקְרָאתָם | מִן־הַגִּבְעָה בַּיּוֹם
הַשֵּׁנִי וַיַּשְׁחִיתוּ בִבְנֵי יִשְׂרָאֵל עוֹד שְׁמֹנַת עָשָׂר אֶלֶף
אִישׁ אָרְצָה כָּל־אֵלֶּה שֹׁלְפֵי חָרֶב: 26 וַיַּעֲלוּ כָל־בְּנֵי
יִשְׂרָאֵל וְכָל־הָעָם וַיָּבֹאוּ בֵית־אֵל וַיִּבְכּוּ וַיֵּשְׁבוּ שָׁם
לִפְנֵי יְהֹוָה וַיָּצוּמוּ בַיּוֹם־הַהוּא עַד־הָעָרֶב וַיַּעֲלוּ
עֹלוֹת וּשְׁלָמִים לִפְנֵי יְהֹוָה: 27 וַיִּשְׁאֲלוּ בְנֵי־יִשְׂרָאֵל
בַּיהֹוָה וְשָׁם אֲרוֹן בְּרִית הָאֱלֹהִים בַּיָּמִים הָהֵם:
28 וּפִינְחָס בֶּן־אֶלְעָזָר בֶּן־אַהֲרֹן עֹמֵד | לְפָנָיו בַּיָּמִים
הָהֵם לֵאמֹר הַאוֹסִף עוֹד לָצֵאת לַמִּלְחָמָה עִם־
בְּנֵי־בִנְיָמִן אָחִי אִם־אֶחְדָּל וַיֹּאמֶר יְהֹוָה עֲלוּ כִּי
מָחָר אֶתְּנֶנּוּ בְיָדֶךָ: 29 וַיָּשֶׂם יִשְׂרָאֵל אֹרְבִים אֶל־
הַגִּבְעָה סָבִיב:
פ

30 וַיַּעֲלוּ בְנֵי־יִשְׂרָאֵל אֶל־בְּנֵי בִנְיָמִן בַּיּוֹם הַשְּׁלִישִׁי
וַיַּעַרְכוּ אֶל־הַגִּבְעָה כְּפַעַם בְּפָעַם: 31 וַיֵּצְאוּ בְנֵי־
בִנְיָמִן לִקְרַאת הָעָם הָנְתְּקוּ מִן־הָעִיר וַיָּחֵלּוּ
לְהַכּוֹת מֵהָעָם חֲלָלִים כְּפַעַם | בְּפַעַם בַּמְסִלּוֹת
אֲשֶׁר אַחַת עֹלָה בֵית־אֵל וְאַחַת גִּבְעָתָה בַּשָּׂדֶה
כִּשְׁלֹשִׁים אִישׁ בְּיִשְׂרָאֵל: 32 וַיֹּאמְרוּ בְּנֵי בִנְיָמִן
נִגָּפִים הֵם לְפָנֵינוּ כְּבָרִאשֹׁנָה וּבְנֵי יִשְׂרָאֵל אָמְרוּ
נָנוּסָה וּנְתַקְּנֻהוּ מִן־הָעִיר אֶל־הַמְסִלּוֹת: 33 וְכֹל |
אִישׁ יִשְׂרָאֵל קָמוּ מִמְּקוֹמוֹ וַיַּעַרְכוּ בְּבַעַל תָּמָר
וְאֹרֵב יִשְׂרָאֵל מֵגִיחַ מִמְּקֹמוֹ מִמַּעֲרֵה־גָבַע: 34 וַיָּבֹאוּ
מִנֶּגֶד לַגִּבְעָה עֲשֶׂרֶת אֲלָפִים אִישׁ בָּחוּר מִכָּל־
יִשְׂרָאֵל וְהַמִּלְחָמָה כָּבֵדָה וְהֵם לֹא יָדְעוּ כִּי־נֹגַעַת
עֲלֵיהֶם הָרָעָה:
פ

35 וַיִּגֹּף יְהֹוָה | אֶת־בִּנְיָמִן | לִפְנֵי יִשְׂרָאֵל וַיַּשְׁחִיתוּ
בְנֵי יִשְׂרָאֵל בְּבִנְיָמִן בַּיּוֹם הַהוּא עֶשְׂרִים וַחֲמִשָּׁה

defeated Benjamin before Israel. And the children
of Israel destroyed that day twenty-five thousand
one hundred Benjamites; all these drew the sword.

³⁶ So the children of Benjamin saw that they were
defeated. The men of Israel had given ground to the
Benjamites, because they relied on the men in
ambush whom they had set against Gibeah. ³⁷ And
the men in ambush quickly rushed upon Gibeah;
the men in ambush spread out and struck the whole
city with the edge of the sword. ³⁸ Now the
appointed signal between the men of Israel and
the men in ambush was that they would make a
great cloud of smoke rise up from the city,
³⁹ whereupon the men of Israel would turn in battle.
Now Benjamin had begun to strike and kill about
thirty of the men of Israel. For they said, "Surely
they are defeated before us, as in the first battle."
⁴⁰ But when the cloud began to rise from the city in
a column of smoke, the Benjamites looked behind
them, and there was the whole city going up in
smoke to heaven. ⁴¹ And when the men of Israel
turned back, the men of Benjamin panicked, for
they saw that disaster had come upon them.
⁴² Therefore they turned their backs before the
men of Israel in the direction of the wilderness;
but the battle overtook them, and whoever came
out of the cities they destroyed in their midst.
⁴³ They surrounded the Benjamites, chased them,
and easily trampled them down as far as the front of
Gibeah toward the east. ⁴⁴ And eighteen thousand
men of Benjamin fell; all these were men of valor.
⁴⁵ Then they turned and fled toward the wilderness
to the rock of Rimmon; and they cut down five
thousand of them on the highways. Then they
pursued them relentlessly up to Gidom, and killed
two thousand of them. ⁴⁶ So all who fell of
Benjamin that day were twenty-five thousand men
who drew the sword; all these were men of valor.

⁴⁷ But six hundred men turned and fled toward
the wilderness to the rock of Rimmon, and they
stayed at the rock of Rimmon for four months.
⁴⁸ And the men of Israel turned back against the
children of Benjamin, and struck them down with
the edge of the sword—from every city, men and
beasts, all who were found. They also set fire to all
the cities they came to.

21 Now the men of Israel had sworn an oath at
Mizpah, saying, "None of us shall give his daughter
to Benjamin as a wife." ² Then the people came to
the house of God, and remained there before God
till evening. They lifted up their voices and wept

אֶ֫לֶף וּמֵאָ֣ה אִ֑ישׁ כָּל־אֵ֖לֶּה שֹׁ֥לֵף חָֽרֶב: 36 וַיִּרְא֤וּ
בְנֵֽי־בִנְיָמִן֙ כִּ֣י נִגָּ֔פוּ וַיִּתְּנ֤וּ אִֽישׁ־יִשְׂרָאֵל֙ מָק֣וֹם לְבִנְיָמִ֔ן
כִּ֤י בָֽטְחוּ֙ אֶל־הָ֣אֹרֵ֔ב אֲשֶׁ֥ר שָׂ֖מוּ אֶל־הַגִּבְעָֽה:
37 וְהָֽאֹרֵ֣ב הֵחִ֔ישׁוּ וַֽיִּפְשְׁט֖וּ אֶל־הַגִּבְעָ֑ה וַיִּמְשֹׁךְ֙
הָ֣אֹרֵ֔ב וַיַּ֥ךְ אֶת־כָּל־הָעִ֖יר לְפִי־חָֽרֶב: 38 וְהַמּוֹעֵ֗ד
הָיָ֛ה לְאִ֥ישׁ יִשְׂרָאֵ֖ל עִם־הָֽאֹרֵ֑ב הֶ֗רֶב לְהַֽעֲלוֹתָ֛ם
מַשְׂאַ֥ת הֶֽעָשָׁ֖ן מִן־הָעִֽיר: 39 וַיַּֽהֲפֹ֤ךְ אִֽישׁ־יִשְׂרָאֵל֙
בַּמִּלְחָמָ֔ה וּבִנְיָמִ֗ן הֵחֵ֤ל לְהַכּ֤וֹת חֲלָלִים֙ בְּאִֽישׁ־
יִשְׂרָאֵ֔ל כִּשְׁלֹשִׁ֖ים אִ֑ישׁ כִּ֣י אָֽמְר֔וּ אַ֣ךְ נָג֤וֹף נִגָּף֙
ה֔וּא לְפָנֵ֖ינוּ כַּמִּלְחָמָ֥ה הָרִֽאשֹׁנָֽה: 40 וְהַמַּשְׂאֵ֗ת
הֵחֵ֛לָּה לַֽעֲל֥וֹת מִן־הָעִ֖יר עַמּ֣וּד עָשָׁ֑ן וַיִּ֤פֶן בִּנְיָמִן֙
אַֽחֲרָ֔יו וְהִנֵּ֛ה עָלָ֥ה כְלִֽיל־הָעִ֖יר הַשָּׁמָֽיְמָה: 41 וְאִ֤ישׁ
יִשְׂרָאֵל֙ הָפַ֔ךְ וַיִּבָּהֵ֖ל אִ֣ישׁ בִּנְיָמִ֑ן כִּ֣י רָאָ֔ה כִּֽי־
נָֽגְעָ֥ה עָלָ֖יו הָֽרָעָֽה: 42 וַיִּפְנ֞וּ לִפְנֵ֣י אִ֣ישׁ יִשְׂרָאֵ֗ל
אֶל־דֶּ֨רֶךְ֙ הַמִּדְבָּ֔ר וְהַמִּלְחָמָ֖ה הִדְבִּיקָ֑תְהוּ וַֽאֲשֶׁר֙
מֵֽהֶֽעָרִ֔ים מַשְׁחִיתִ֥ים אוֹת֖וֹ בְּתוֹכֽוֹ: 43 כִּתְּר֣וּ אֶת־
בִּנְיָמִ֗ן הִרְדִיפֻ֨הוּ֙ מְנוּחָ֣ה הִדְרִיכֻ֔הוּ עַ֛ד נֹ֥כַח הַגִּבְעָ֖ה
מִמִּזְרַח־שָֽׁמֶשׁ: 44 וַיִּפְּלוּ֙ מִבִּנְיָמִ֔ן שְׁמֹנָֽה־עָשָׂ֖ר אֶ֑לֶף
אִ֕ישׁ אֶת־כָּל־אֵ֖לֶּה אַנְשֵׁי־חָֽיִל: 45 וַיִּפְנ֞וּ וַיָּנֻ֣סוּ
הַמִּדְבָּ֗רָה אֶל־סֶ֨לַע֙ הָֽרִמּ֔וֹן וַיְעֹֽלְלֻ֨הוּ֙ בַּֽמְסִלּ֔וֹת
חֲמֵ֥שֶׁת אֲלָפִ֖ים אִ֑ישׁ וַיַּדְבִּ֤יקוּ אַֽחֲרָיו֙ עַד־גִּדְעֹ֔ם וַיַּכּ֥וּ
מִמֶּ֖נּוּ אַלְפַּ֥יִם אִֽישׁ: 46 וַיְהִי֩ כָל־הַנֹּֽפְלִ֨ים מִבִּנְיָמִ֜ן
עֶשְׂרִ֨ים וַֽחֲמִשָּׁ֥ה אֶ֛לֶף אִ֥ישׁ שֹׁ֖לֵף חֶ֑רֶב בַּיּ֣וֹם הַה֔וּא
אֶת־כָּל־אֵ֖לֶּה אַנְשֵׁי־חָֽיִל: 47 וַיִּפְנ֞וּ וַיָּנֻ֣סוּ הַמִּדְבָּ֗רָה
אֶל־סֶ֨לַע֙ הָֽרִמּ֔וֹן שֵׁ֥שׁ מֵא֖וֹת אִ֑ישׁ וַיֵּֽשְׁבוּ֙ בְּסֶ֣לַע
רִמּ֔וֹן אַרְבָּעָ֖ה חֳדָשִֽׁים: 48 וְאִ֨ישׁ יִשְׂרָאֵ֜ל שָׁ֣בוּ אֶל־
בְּנֵ֤י בִנְיָמִן֙ וַיַּכּ֣וּם לְפִי־חֶ֔רֶב מֵעִ֣יר מְתֹ֔ם עַד־בְּהֵמָ֖ה
עַ֣ד כָּל־הַנִּמְצָ֑א גַּ֤ם כָּל־הֶֽעָרִים֙ הַנִּמְצָא֔וֹת שִׁלְּח֥וּ
בָאֵֽשׁ: פ

כא וְאִ֥ישׁ יִשְׂרָאֵ֖ל נִשְׁבַּ֣ע בַּמִּצְפָּ֣ה לֵאמֹ֑ר אִ֣ישׁ
מִמֶּ֔נּוּ לֹֽא־יִתֵּ֥ן בִּתּ֖וֹ לְבִנְיָמִ֥ן לְאִשָּֽׁה: 2 וַיָּבֹ֤א הָעָם֙
בֵּֽית־אֵ֔ל וַיֵּ֤שְׁבוּ שָׁם֙ עַד־הָעֶ֔רֶב לִפְנֵ֖י הָֽאֱלֹהִ֑ים

bitterly, [3] and said, "O LORD God of Israel, why has this come to pass in Israel, that today there should be one tribe *missing* in Israel?"

[4] So it was, on the next morning, that the people rose early and built an altar there, and offered burnt offerings and peace offerings. [5] The children of Israel said, "Who *is there* among all the tribes of Israel who did not come up with the assembly to the LORD?" For they had made a great oath concerning anyone who had not come up to the LORD at Mizpah, saying, "He shall surely be put to death." [6] And the children of Israel grieved for Benjamin their brother, and said, "One tribe is cut off from Israel today. [7] What shall we do for wives for those who remain, seeing we have sworn by the LORD that we will not give them our daughters as wives?"

[8] And they said, "What one *is there* from the tribes of Israel who did not come up to Mizpah to the LORD?" And, in fact, no one had come to the camp from Jabesh Gilead to the assembly. [9] For when the people were counted, indeed, not one of the inhabitants of Jabesh Gilead *was* there. [10] So the congregation sent out there twelve thousand of their most valiant men, and commanded them, saying, "Go and strike the inhabitants of Jabesh Gilead with the edge of the sword, including the women and children. [11] And this *is* the thing that you shall do: You shall utterly destroy every male, and every woman who has known a man intimately." [12] So they found among the inhabitants of Jabesh Gilead four hundred young virgins who had not known a man intimately; and they brought them to the camp at Shiloh, which is in the land of Canaan.

[13] Then the whole congregation sent *word* to the children of Benjamin who *were* at the rock of Rimmon, and announced peace to them. [14] So Benjamin came back at that time, and they gave them the women whom they had saved alive of the women of Jabesh Gilead; and yet they had not found enough for them.

[15] And the people grieved for Benjamin, because the LORD had made a void in the tribes of Israel.

[16] Then the elders of the congregation said, "What shall we do for wives for those who remain, since the women of Benjamin have been destroyed?" [17] And they said, "*There must be* an inheritance for the survivors of Benjamin, that a tribe may not be destroyed from Israel. [18] However, we cannot give them wives from our daughters, for the children of Israel have sworn an oath, saying, 'Cursed *be* the one who gives a wife to Benjamin.' "

[19] Then they said, "In fact, *there is* a yearly feast of

וַיִּשְׂא֣וּ קוֹלָ֔ם וַיִּבְכּ֖וּ בְּכִ֥י גָד֑וֹל: 3 וַיֹּ֣אמְר֔וּ לָמָ֤ה יְהוָה֙ אֱלֹהֵ֣י יִשְׂרָאֵ֔ל הָ֥יְתָה זֹּ֖את בְּיִשְׂרָאֵ֑ל לְהִפָּקֵ֤ד הַיּוֹם֙ מִיִּשְׂרָאֵ֔ל שֵׁ֖בֶט אֶחָֽד: 4 וַיְהִי֙ מִֽמָּחֳרָ֔ת וַיַּשְׁכִּ֣ימוּ הָעָ֔ם וַיִּבְנוּ־שָׁ֖ם מִזְבֵּ֑חַ וַיַּעֲל֥וּ עֹל֖וֹת וּשְׁלָמִֽים: פ

5 וַיֹּֽאמְרוּ֙ בְּנֵ֣י יִשְׂרָאֵ֔ל מִ֣י אֲשֶׁ֧ר לֹא־עָלָ֛ה בַקָּהָ֖ל מִכָּל־שִׁבְטֵ֣י יִשְׂרָאֵל֮ אֶל־יְהוָה֒ כִּי֩ הַשְּׁבוּעָ֨ה הַגְּדוֹלָ֜ה הָיְתָ֗ה לַ֠אֲשֶׁר לֹא־עָלָ֤ה אֶל־יְהוָה֙ הַמִּצְפָּ֣ה לֵאמֹ֔ר מ֥וֹת יוּמָֽת: 6 וַיִּנָּֽחֲמוּ֙ בְּנֵ֣י יִשְׂרָאֵ֔ל אֶל־בִּנְיָמִ֖ן אָחִ֑יו וַיֹּ֣אמְר֔וּ נִגְדַּ֥ע הַיּ֛וֹם שֵׁ֥בֶט אֶחָ֖ד מִיִּשְׂרָאֵֽל: 7 מַה־ נַּעֲשֶׂ֥ה לָהֶ֛ם לַנּוֹתָרִ֖ים לְנָשִׁ֑ים וַאֲנַ֙חְנוּ֙ נִשְׁבַּ֣עְנוּ בַֽיהוָ֔ה לְבִלְתִּ֥י תֵּת־לָהֶ֖ם מִבְּנוֹתֵ֥ינוּ לְנָשִֽׁים: 8 וַיֹּ֣אמְר֔וּ מִ֚י אֶחָד֙ מִשִּׁבְטֵ֣י יִשְׂרָאֵ֔ל אֲשֶׁ֛ר לֹא־עָלָ֥ה אֶל־יְהוָ֖ה הַמִּצְפָּ֑ה וְ֠הִנֵּה לֹ֣א בָא־אִ֥ישׁ אֶל־הַֽמַּחֲנֶ֛ה מִיָּבֵ֥ישׁ גִּלְעָ֖ד אֶל־הַקָּהָֽל: 9 וַיִּתְפָּקֵ֖ד הָעָ֑ם וְהִנֵּ֤ה אֵֽין־שָׁם֙ אִ֔ישׁ מִיּוֹשְׁבֵ֖י יָבֵ֥ישׁ גִּלְעָֽד: 10 וַיִּשְׁלְחוּ־ שָׁ֣ם הָעֵדָ֗ה שְׁנֵים־עָשָׂ֥ר אֶ֛לֶף אִ֖ישׁ מִבְּנֵ֣י הֶחָ֑יִל וַיְצַוּ֨וּ אוֹתָ֜ם לֵאמֹ֗ר לְ֠כוּ וְהִכִּיתֶ֞ם אֶת־יוֹשְׁבֵ֨י יָבֵ֤שׁ גִּלְעָד֙ לְפִי־חֶ֔רֶב וְהַנָּשִׁ֖ים וְהַטָּֽף: 11 וְזֶ֥ה הַדָּבָ֖ר אֲשֶׁ֣ר תַּעֲשׂ֑וּ כָּל־זָכָ֗ר וְכָל־אִשָּׁ֛ה יֹדַ֥עַת מִשְׁכַּב־זָכָ֖ר תַּחֲרִֽימוּ: 12 וַיִּמְצְא֞וּ מִיּוֹשְׁבֵ֣י | יָבֵ֣ישׁ גִּלְעָ֗ד אַרְבַּ֤ע מֵאוֹת֙ נַעֲרָ֣ה בְתוּלָ֔ה אֲשֶׁ֧ר לֹא־יָדְעָ֛ה אִ֖ישׁ לְמִשְׁכַּ֣ב זָכָ֑ר וַיָּבִ֤יאוּ אוֹתָם֙ אֶל־הַֽמַּחֲנֶ֣ה שִׁלֹ֔ה אֲשֶׁ֖ר בְּאֶ֥רֶץ כְּנָֽעַן: ס 13 וַֽיִּשְׁלְחוּ֙ כָּל־הָ֣עֵדָ֔ה וַֽיְדַבְּרוּ֙ אֶל־בְּנֵ֣י בִנְיָמִ֔ן אֲשֶׁ֖ר בְּסֶ֣לַע רִמּ֑וֹן וַיִּקְרְא֥וּ לָהֶ֖ם שָׁלֽוֹם: 14 וַיָּ֤שָׁב בִּנְיָמִן֙ בָּעֵ֣ת הַהִ֔יא וַיִּתְּנ֤וּ לָהֶם֙ הַנָּשִׁ֔ים אֲשֶׁ֣ר חִיּ֔וּ מִנְּשֵׁ֖י יָבֵ֣שׁ גִּלְעָ֑ד וְלֹֽא־מָצְא֥וּ לָהֶ֖ם כֵּֽן: 15 וְהָעָ֥ם נִחָ֖ם לְבִנְיָמִ֑ן כִּֽי־עָשָׂ֧ה יְהוָ֛ה פֶּ֖רֶץ בְּשִׁבְטֵ֥י יִשְׂרָאֵֽל: 16 וַיֹּֽאמְר֨וּ זִקְנֵ֤י הָֽעֵדָה֙ מַה־ נַּעֲשֶׂ֥ה לַנּוֹתָרִ֖ים לְנָשִׁ֑ים כִּֽי־נִשְׁמְדָ֥ה מִבִּנְיָמִ֖ן אִשָּֽׁה: 17 וַיֹּ֣אמְר֔וּ יְרֻשַּׁ֥ת פְּלֵיטָ֖ה לְבִנְיָמִ֑ן וְלֹֽא־יִמָּחֶ֥ה שֵׁ֖בֶט מִיִּשְׂרָאֵֽל: 18 וַאֲנַ֗חְנוּ לֹ֥א נוּכַ֛ל לָתֵת־לָהֶ֥ם נָשִׁ֖ים מִבְּנוֹתֵ֑ינוּ כִּֽי־נִשְׁבְּע֤וּ בְנֵֽי־יִשְׂרָאֵל֙ לֵאמֹ֔ר אָר֕וּר נֹתֵ֥ן אִשָּׁ֖ה לְבִנְיָמִֽן: ס 19 וַיֹּאמְר֡וּ הִנֵּה֩ חַג־ יְהוָ֨ה בְּשִׁל֜וֹ מִיָּמִ֣ים | יָמִ֗ימָה אֲשֶׁ֞ר מִצְּפ֤וֹנָה לְבֵֽית־

the LORD in Shiloh, which *is* north of Bethel, on the east side of the highway that goes up from Bethel to Shechem, and south of Lebonah."

20 Therefore they instructed the children of Benjamin, saying, "Go, lie in wait in the vineyards, 21 and watch; and just when the daughters of Shiloh come out to perform their dances, then come out from the vineyards, and every man catch a wife for himself from the daughters of Shiloh; then go to the land of Benjamin. 22 Then it shall be, when their fathers or their brothers come to us to complain, that we will say to them, 'Be kind to them for our sakes, because we did not take a wife for any of them in the war; for *it is* not *as though* you have given the *women* to them at this time, making yourselves guilty of your oath.'"

23 And the children of Benjamin did so; they took enough wives for their number from those who danced, whom they caught. Then they went and returned to their inheritance, and they rebuilt the cities and dwelt in them. 24 So the children of Israel departed from there at that time, every man to his tribe and family; they went out from there, every man to his inheritance.

25 In those days *there was* no king in Israel; everyone did *what was* right in his own eyes.

אֶל מִזְרְחָה הַשֶּׁמֶשׁ לִמְסִלָּה הָעֹלָה מִבֵּית־אֵל שְׁכֶמָה וּמִנֶּגֶב לִלְבוֹנָה: 20 וַיְצַוּ פ אֶת־בְּנֵי בִנְיָמִן לֵאמֹר לְכוּ וַאֲרַבְתֶּם בַּכְּרָמִים: 21 וּרְאִיתֶם וְהִנֵּה אִם־יֵצְאוּ בְנוֹת־שִׁילוֹ לָחוּל בַּמְּחֹלוֹת וִיצָאתֶם מִן־הַכְּרָמִים וַחֲטַפְתֶּם לָכֶם אִישׁ אִשְׁתּוֹ מִבְּנוֹת שִׁילוֹ וַהֲלַכְתֶּם אֶרֶץ בִּנְיָמִן: 22 וְהָיָה כִּי־יָבֹאוּ אֲבוֹתָם אוֹ אֲחֵיהֶם לָרוּב פ אֵלֵינוּ וְאָמַרְנוּ אֲלֵיהֶם חָנּוּנוּ אוֹתָם כִּי לֹא לָקַחְנוּ אִישׁ אִשְׁתּוֹ בַּמִּלְחָמָה כִּי לֹא אַתֶּם נְתַתֶּם לָהֶם כָּעֵת תֶּאְשָׁמוּ: ס 23 וַיַּעֲשׂוּ־כֵן בְּנֵי בִנְיָמִן וַיִּשְׂאוּ נָשִׁים לְמִסְפָּרָם מִן־הַמְּחֹלְלוֹת אֲשֶׁר גָּזָלוּ וַיֵּלְכוּ וַיָּשׁוּבוּ אֶל־נַחֲלָתָם וַיִּבְנוּ אֶת־הֶעָרִים וַיֵּשְׁבוּ בָּהֶם: 24 וַיִּתְהַלְּכוּ מִשָּׁם בְּנֵי־יִשְׂרָאֵל בָּעֵת הַהִיא אִישׁ לְשִׁבְטוֹ וּלְמִשְׁפַּחְתּוֹ וַיֵּצְאוּ מִשָּׁם אִישׁ לְנַחֲלָתוֹ: 25 בַּיָּמִים הָהֵם אֵין מֶלֶךְ בְּיִשְׂרָאֵל אִישׁ הַיָּשָׁר בְּעֵינָיו יַעֲשֶׂה:

The First Book of
SAMUEL

1 Now there was a certain man of Ramathaim
Zophim, of the mountains of Ephraim, and his
name *was* Elkanah the son of Jeroham, the son of
Elihu, the son of Tohu, the son of Zuph, an
Ephraimite. [2] And he had two wives: the name of
one *was* Hannah, and the name of the other
Peninnah. Peninnah had children, but Hannah
had no children. [3] This man went up from his city
yearly to worship and sacrifice to the LORD of hosts
in Shiloh. Also the two sons of Eli, Hophni and
Phinehas, the priests of the LORD, *were* there. [4] And
whenever the time came for Elkanah to make an
offering, he would give portions to Peninnah his
wife and to all her sons and daughters. [5] But to
Hannah he would give a double portion, for he
loved Hannah, although the LORD had closed her
womb. [6] And her rival also provoked her severely,
to make her miserable, because the LORD had
closed her womb. [7] So it was, year by year, when she
went up to the house of the LORD, that she
provoked her; therefore she wept and did not eat.

[8] Then Elkanah her husband said to her, "Hannah, why do you weep? Why do you not eat? And
why is your heart grieved? *Am* I not better to you
than ten sons?"

[9] So Hannah arose after they had finished eating
and drinking in Shiloh. Now Eli the priest was
sitting on the seat by the doorpost of the tabernacle
of the LORD. [10] And she *was* in bitterness of soul,
and prayed to the LORD and wept in anguish.
[11] Then she made a vow and said, "O LORD of
hosts, if You will indeed look on the affliction of
Your maidservant and remember me, and not
forget Your maidservant, but will give Your
maidservant a male child, then I will give him to
the LORD all the days of his life, and no razor shall
come upon his head."

[12] And it happened, as she continued praying
before the LORD, that Eli watched her mouth.
[13] Now Hannah spoke in her heart; only her lips
moved, but her voice was not heard. Therefore Eli
thought she was drunk. [14] So Eli said to her, "How
long will you be drunk? Put your wine away from
you!"

[15] But Hannah answered and said, "No, my lord,
I *am* a woman of sorrowful spirit. I have drunk
neither wine nor intoxicating drink, but have

שמואל א

א וַיְהִי אִישׁ אֶחָד מִן־הָרָמָתַיִם צוֹפִים מֵהַר
אֶפְרָיִם וּשְׁמוֹ אֶלְקָנָה בֶּן־יְרֹחָם בֶּן־אֱלִיהוּא בֶּן־
תֹּחוּ בֶן־צוּף אֶפְרָתִי: 2 וְלוֹ שְׁתֵּי נָשִׁים שֵׁם אַחַת
חַנָּה וְשֵׁם הַשֵּׁנִית פְּנִנָּה וַיְהִי לִפְנִנָּה יְלָדִים וּלְחַנָּה
אֵין יְלָדִים: 3 וְעָלָה הָאִישׁ הַהוּא מֵעִירוֹ מִיָּמִים |
יָמִימָה לְהִשְׁתַּחֲוֹת וְלִזְבֹּחַ לַיהוָה צְבָאוֹת בְּשִׁלֹה
וְשָׁם שְׁנֵי בְנֵי־עֵלִי חָפְנִי וּפִנְחָס כֹּהֲנִים לַיהוָה:

4 וַיְהִי הַיּוֹם וַיִּזְבַּח אֶלְקָנָה וְנָתַן לִפְנִנָּה אִשְׁתּוֹ
וּלְכָל־בָּנֶיהָ וּבְנוֹתֶיהָ מָנוֹת: 5 וּלְחַנָּה יִתֵּן מָנָה
אַחַת אַפָּיִם כִּי אֶת־חַנָּה אָהֵב וַיהוָה סָגַר רַחְמָהּ:
6 וְכִעֲסַתָּה צָרָתָהּ גַּם־כַּעַס בַּעֲבוּר הַרְּעִמָהּ כִּי־
סָגַר יְהוָה בְּעַד רַחְמָהּ: 7 וְכֵן יַעֲשֶׂה שָׁנָה בְשָׁנָה
מִדֵּי עֲלֹתָהּ בְּבֵית יְהוָה כֵּן תַּכְעִסֶנָּה וַתִּבְכֶּה וְלֹא
תֹאכַל: 8 וַיֹּאמֶר לָהּ אֶלְקָנָה אִישָׁהּ חַנָּה לָמֶה
תִבְכִּי וְלָמֶה לֹא תֹאכְלִי וְלָמֶה יֵרַע לְבָבֵךְ הֲלוֹא
אָנֹכִי טוֹב לָךְ מֵעֲשָׂרָה בָּנִים: 9 וַתָּקָם חַנָּה אַחֲרֵי
אָכְלָה בְשִׁלֹה וְאַחֲרֵי שָׁתֹה וְעֵלִי הַכֹּהֵן יֹשֵׁב עַל־
הַכִּסֵּא עַל־מְזוּזַת הֵיכַל יְהוָה: 10 וְהִיא מָרַת נָפֶשׁ
וַתִּתְפַּלֵּל עַל־יְהוָה וּבָכֹה תִבְכֶּה: 11 וַתִּדֹּר נֶדֶר
וַתֹּאמַר יְהוָה צְבָאוֹת אִם־רָאֹה תִרְאֶה | בָּעֳנִי
אֲמָתֶךָ וּזְכַרְתַּנִי וְלֹא־תִשְׁכַּח אֶת־אֲמָתֶךָ וְנָתַתָּה
לַאֲמָתְךָ זֶרַע אֲנָשִׁים וּנְתַתִּיו לַיהוָה כָּל־יְמֵי חַיָּיו
וּמוֹרָה לֹא־יַעֲלֶה עַל־רֹאשׁוֹ: 12 וְהָיָה כִּי הִרְבְּתָה
לְהִתְפַּלֵּל לִפְנֵי יְהוָה וְעֵלִי שֹׁמֵר אֶת־פִּיהָ: 13 וְחַנָּה
הִיא מְדַבֶּרֶת עַל־לִבָּהּ רַק שְׂפָתֶיהָ נָּעוֹת וְקוֹלָהּ
לֹא יִשָּׁמֵעַ וַיַּחְשְׁבֶהָ עֵלִי לְשִׁכֹּרָה: 14 וַיֹּאמֶר אֵלֶיהָ
עֵלִי עַד־מָתַי תִּשְׁתַּכָּרִין הָסִירִי אֶת־יֵינֵךְ מֵעָלָיִךְ:

15 וַתַּעַן חַנָּה וַתֹּאמֶר לֹא אֲדֹנִי אִשָּׁה קְשַׁת־רוּחַ
אָנֹכִי וְיַיִן וְשֵׁכָר לֹא שָׁתִיתִי וָאֶשְׁפֹּךְ אֶת־נַפְשִׁי

poured out my soul before the LORD. ¹⁶Do not consider your maidservant a wicked woman, for out of the abundance of my complaint and grief I have spoken until now."

¹⁷Then Eli answered and said, "Go in peace, and the God of Israel grant your petition which you have asked of Him."

¹⁸And she said, "Let your maidservant find favor in your sight." So the woman went her way and ate, and her face was no longer *sad*.

¹⁹Then they rose early in the morning and worshiped before the LORD, and returned and came to their house at Ramah. And Elkanah knew Hannah his wife, and the LORD remembered her. ²⁰So it came to pass in the process of time that Hannah conceived and bore a son, and called his name Samuel, *saying,* "Because I have asked for him from the LORD."

²¹Now the man Elkanah and all his house went up to offer to the LORD the yearly sacrifice and his vow. ²²But Hannah did not go up, for she said to her husband, "*Not* until the child is weaned; then I will take him, that he may appear before the LORD and remain there forever."

²³So Elkanah her husband said to her, "Do what seems best to you; wait until you have weaned him. Only let the LORD establish His word." Then the woman stayed and nursed her son until she had weaned him.

²⁴Now when she had weaned him, she took him up with her, with three bulls, one ephah of flour, and a skin of wine, and brought him to the house of the LORD in Shiloh. And the child *was* young. ²⁵Then they slaughtered a bull, and brought the child to Eli. ²⁶And she said, "O my lord! As your soul lives, my lord, I *am* the woman who stood by you here, praying to the LORD. ²⁷For this child I prayed, and the LORD has granted me my petition which I asked of Him. ²⁸Therefore I also have lent him to the LORD; as long as he lives he shall be lent to the LORD." So they worshiped the LORD there.

2 And Hannah prayed and said:

> "My heart rejoices in the LORD;
> My horn is exalted in the LORD.
> I smile at my enemies,
> Because I rejoice in Your salvation.

² "No one is holy like the LORD,
> For *there is* none besides You,
> Nor *is there* any rock like our God.

³ "Talk no more so very proudly;
> Let no arrogance come from your mouth,
> For the LORD *is* the God of knowledge;
> And by Him actions are weighed.

לִפְנֵי יְהֹוָה׃ 16 אַל־תִּתֵּן אֶת־אֲמָתְךָ לִפְנֵי בַּת־בְּלִיָּעַל כִּי־מֵרֹב שִׂיחִי וְכַעְסִי דִּבַּרְתִּי עַד־הֵנָּה׃

17 וַיַּעַן עֵלִי וַיֹּאמֶר לְכִי לְשָׁלוֹם וֵאלֹהֵי יִשְׂרָאֵל יִתֵּן אֶת־שֵׁלָתֵךְ אֲשֶׁר שָׁאַלְתְּ מֵעִמּוֹ׃ 18 וַתֹּאמֶר תִּמְצָא שִׁפְחָתְךָ חֵן בְּעֵינֶיךָ וַתֵּלֶךְ הָאִשָּׁה לְדַרְכָּהּ וַתֹּאכַל וּפָנֶיהָ לֹא־הָיוּ־לָהּ עוֹד׃ 19 וַיַּשְׁכִּמוּ בַבֹּקֶר וַיִּשְׁתַּחֲווּ לִפְנֵי יְהֹוָה וַיָּשֻׁבוּ וַיָּבֹאוּ אֶל־בֵּיתָם הָרָמָתָה וַיֵּדַע אֶלְקָנָה אֶת־חַנָּה אִשְׁתּוֹ וַיִּזְכְּרֶהָ יְהֹוָה׃ 20 וַיְהִי לִתְקֻפוֹת הַיָּמִים וַתַּהַר חַנָּה וַתֵּלֶד בֵּן וַתִּקְרָא אֶת־שְׁמוֹ שְׁמוּאֵל כִּי מֵיְהֹוָה שְׁאִלְתִּיו׃ 21 וַיַּעַל הָאִישׁ אֶלְקָנָה וְכָל־בֵּיתוֹ לִזְבֹּחַ לַיהֹוָה אֶת־זֶבַח הַיָּמִים וְאֶת־נִדְרוֹ׃ 22 וְחַנָּה לֹא עָלָתָה כִּי־אָמְרָה לְאִישָׁהּ עַד יִגָּמֵל הַנַּעַר וַהֲבִאֹתִיו וְנִרְאָה אֶת־פְּנֵי יְהֹוָה וְיָשַׁב שָׁם עַד־עוֹלָם׃ 23 וַיֹּאמֶר לָהּ אֶלְקָנָה אִישָׁהּ עֲשִׂי הַטּוֹב בְּעֵינַיִךְ שְׁבִי עַד־גָּמְלֵךְ אֹתוֹ אַךְ יָקֵם יְהֹוָה אֶת־דְּבָרוֹ וַתֵּשֶׁב הָאִשָּׁה וַתֵּינֶק אֶת־בְּנָהּ עַד־גָּמְלָהּ אֹתוֹ׃ 24 וַתַּעֲלֵהוּ עִמָּהּ כַּאֲשֶׁר גְּמָלַתּוּ בְּפָרִים שְׁלֹשָׁה וְאֵיפָה אַחַת קֶמַח וְנֵבֶל יַיִן וַתְּבִאֵהוּ בֵית־יְהֹוָה שִׁלוֹ וְהַנַּעַר נָעַר׃ 25 וַיִּשְׁחֲטוּ אֶת־הַפָּר וַיָּבִיאוּ אֶת־הַנַּעַר אֶל־עֵלִי׃ 26 וַתֹּאמֶר בִּי אֲדֹנִי חֵי נַפְשְׁךָ אֲדֹנִי אֲנִי הָאִשָּׁה הַנִּצֶּבֶת עִמְּכָה בָּזֶה לְהִתְפַּלֵּל אֶל־יְהֹוָה׃ 27 אֶל־הַנַּעַר הַזֶּה הִתְפַּלָּלְתִּי וַיִּתֵּן יְהֹוָה לִי אֶת־שְׁאֵלָתִי אֲשֶׁר שָׁאַלְתִּי מֵעִמּוֹ׃ 28 וְגַם אָנֹכִי הִשְׁאִלְתִּהוּ לַיהֹוָה כָּל־הַיָּמִים אֲשֶׁר הָיָה הוּא שָׁאוּל לַיהֹוָה וַיִּשְׁתַּחוּ שָׁם לַיהֹוָה׃ פ

ב וַתִּתְפַּלֵּל חַנָּה וַתֹּאמַר עָלַץ לִבִּי בַּיהֹוָה רָמָה קַרְנִי בַּיהֹוָה רָחַב פִּי עַל־אוֹיְבַי כִּי שָׂמַחְתִּי בִּישׁוּעָתֶךָ׃ 2 אֵין־קָדוֹשׁ כַּיהֹוָה כִּי אֵין בִּלְתֶּךָ וְאֵין צוּר כֵּאלֹהֵינוּ׃ 3 אַל־תַּרְבּוּ תְדַבְּרוּ גְּבֹהָה גְבֹהָה יֵצֵא עָתָק מִפִּיכֶם כִּי אֵל דֵּעוֹת יְהֹוָה וְלֹא נִתְכְּנוּ

4 "The bows of the mighty men *are* broken,
   And those who stumbled are girded with
      strength.
5 *Those who were* full have hired themselves out for
      bread,
   And the hungry have ceased *to hunger.*
   Even the barren has borne seven,
   And she who has many children has become
      feeble.
6 "The LORD kills and makes alive;
   He brings down to the grave and brings up.
7 The LORD makes poor and makes rich;
   He brings low and lifts up.
8 He raises the poor from the dust
   And lifts the beggar from the ash heap,
   To set *them* among princes
   And make them inherit the throne of glory.

   "For the pillars of the earth *are* the LORD's,
   And He has set the world upon them.
9 He will guard the feet of His saints,
   But the wicked shall be silent in darkness.

   "For by strength no man shall prevail.
10 The adversaries of the LORD shall be broken in
      pieces;
   From heaven He will thunder against them.
   The LORD will judge the ends of the earth.

   "He will give strength to His king,
   And exalt the horn of His anointed."

11 Then Elkanah went to his house at Ramah. But
the child ministered to the LORD before Eli the
priest.

12 Now the sons of Eli *were* corrupt; they did not
know the LORD. 13 And the priests' custom with the
people *was that* when any man offered a sacrifice,
the priest's servant would come with a three-
pronged fleshhook in his hand while the meat was
boiling. 14 Then he would thrust *it* into the pan, or
kettle, or caldron, or pot; and the priest would take
for himself all that the fleshhook brought up. So
they did in Shiloh to all the Israelites who came
there. 15 Also, before they burned the fat, the
priest's servant would come and say to the man
who sacrificed, "Give meat for roasting to the
priest, for he will not take boiled meat from you,
but raw."

16 And *if* the man said to him, "They should
really burn the fat first; *then* you may take *as much
as your heart desires," he would then answer him,
"No, but you must give *it* now; and if not, I will
take *it* by force."

17 Therefore the sin of the young men was very
great before the LORD, for men abhorred the
offering of the LORD.

18 But Samuel ministered before the LORD, *even
as* a child, wearing a linen ephod. 19 Moreover his
mother used to make him a little robe, and bring *it*

עֲלֹלֽוֹת: 4 קֶ֣שֶׁת גִּבֹּרִ֖ים חַתִּ֑ים וְנִכְשָׁלִ֖ים אָ֥זְרוּ חָֽיִל:
5 שְׂבֵעִ֤ים בַּלֶּ֙חֶם֙ נִשְׂכָּ֔רוּ וּרְעֵבִ֖ים חָדֵ֑לּוּ עַד־עֲקָרָה֙
יָֽלְדָ֣ה שִׁבְעָ֔ה וְרַבַּ֥ת בָּנִ֖ים אֻמְלָֽלָה: 6 יְהוָ֖ה מֵמִ֣ית
וּמְחַיֶּ֑ה מוֹרִ֥יד שְׁא֖וֹל וַיָּֽעַל: 7 יְהוָ֖ה מוֹרִ֣ישׁ וּמַעֲשִׁ֑יר
מַשְׁפִּ֖יל אַף־מְרוֹמֵֽם: 8 מֵקִ֨ים מֵעָפָ֜ר דָּ֗ל מֵֽאַשְׁפֹּת֙
יָרִ֣ים אֶבְי֔וֹן לְהוֹשִׁיב֙ עִם־נְדִיבִ֔ים וְכִסֵּ֥א כָב֖וֹד יַנְחִלֵ֑ם
כִּ֤י לַֽיהוָה֙ מְצֻ֣קֵי אֶ֔רֶץ וַיָּ֥שֶׁת עֲלֵיהֶ֖ם תֵּבֵֽל: 9 רַגְלֵ֤י
חֲסִידָו֙ יִשְׁמֹ֔ר וּרְשָׁעִ֖ים בַּחֹ֣שֶׁךְ יִדָּ֑מּוּ כִּֽי־לֹ֥א בְכֹ֖חַ
יִגְבַּר־אִֽישׁ: 10 יְהוָ֗ה יֵחַ֤תּוּ מְרִיבָו֙ עָלָ֜יו בַּשָּׁמַ֣יִם
יַרְעֵ֗ם יְהוָה֙ יָדִ֣ין אַפְסֵי־אָ֔רֶץ וְיִתֶּן־עֹ֣ז לְמַלְכּ֔וֹ וְיָרֵ֖ם
קֶ֥רֶן מְשִׁיחֽוֹ:   פ

11 וַיֵּ֧לֶךְ אֶלְקָנָ֛ה הָרָמָ֖תָה עַל־בֵּית֑וֹ וְהַנַּ֗עַר הָיָ֤ה
מְשָׁרֵת֙ אֶת־יְהוָ֔ה אֶת־פְּנֵ֖י עֵלִ֥י הַכֹּהֵֽן: 12 וּבְנֵ֥י עֵלִ֖י
בְּנֵ֣י בְלִיָּ֑עַל לֹ֥א יָֽדְע֖וּ אֶת־יְהוָֽה: 13 וּמִשְׁפַּ֣ט הַכֹּהֲנִים֮
אֶת־הָעָם֒ כָּל־אִ֞ישׁ זֹבֵ֣חַ זֶ֗בַח וּבָ֨א נַ֤עַר הַכֹּהֵן֙ כְּבַשֵּׁ֣ל
הַבָּשָׂ֔ר וְהַמַּזְלֵ֛ג שְׁלֹ֥שׁ־הַשִּׁנַּ֖יִם בְּיָדֽוֹ: 14 וְהִכָּ֨ה בַכִּיּ֜וֹר
א֣וֹ בַדּ֗וּד א֤וֹ בַקַּלַּ֙חַת֙ א֣וֹ בַפָּר֔וּר כֹּ֚ל אֲשֶׁ֣ר יַעֲלֶ֣ה
הַמַּזְלֵ֔ג יִקַּ֥ח הַכֹּהֵ֖ן בּ֑וֹ כָּ֚כָה יַעֲשׂ֣וּ לְכָל־יִשְׂרָאֵ֔ל
הַבָּאִ֥ים שָׁ֖ם בְּשִׁלֹֽה: 15 גַּם֮ בְּטֶרֶם֮ יַקְטִר֣וּן אֶת־
הַחֵלֶב֒ וּבָ֣א ׀ נַ֣עַר הַכֹּהֵ֗ן וְאָמַר֙ לָאִ֣ישׁ הַזֹּבֵ֔חַ
תְּנָ֤ה בָשָׂר֙ לִצְל֣וֹת לַכֹּהֵ֔ן וְלֹֽא־יִקַּ֧ח מִמְּךָ֛ בָּשָׂ֥ר
מְבֻשָּׁ֖ל כִּ֥י אִם־חָֽי: 16 וַיֹּ֨אמֶר אֵלָ֜יו הָאִ֗ישׁ קַטֵּ֨ר
יַקְטִיר֤וּן כַּיּוֹם֙ הַחֵ֔לֶב וְקַ֨ח־לְךָ֔ כַּאֲשֶׁ֥ר תְּאַוֶּ֖ה נַפְשֶׁ֑ךָ
וְאָמַ֣ר ׀ לוֹ֩ כִּ֨י עַתָּ֤ה תִתֵּן֙ וְאִם־לֹ֔א לָקַ֖חְתִּי
בְחָזְקָֽה: 17 וַתְּהִ֨י חַטַּ֧את הַנְּעָרִ֛ים גְּדוֹלָ֥ה מְאֹ֖ד
אֶת־פְּנֵ֣י יְהוָ֑ה כִּ֤י נִֽאֲצוּ֙ הָֽאֲנָשִׁ֔ים אֵ֖ת מִנְחַ֥ת יְהוָֽה:

18 וּשְׁמוּאֵ֖ל מְשָׁרֵ֣ת אֶת־פְּנֵ֣י יְהוָ֑ה נַ֕עַר חָג֖וּר אֵפ֥וֹד
בָּֽד: 19 וּמְעִ֤יל קָטֹן֙ תַּעֲשֶׂה־לּ֣וֹ אִמּ֔וֹ וְהַעַלְתָ֥ה

ב 9 חֲסִידָ֖יו   10 מְרִיבָ֖יו, עָלָ֖יו   16 לֹ֖א

to him year by year when she came up with her husband to offer the yearly sacrifice. 20 And Eli would bless Elkanah and his wife, and say, "The LORD give you descendants from this woman for the loan that was given to the LORD." Then they would go to their own home.

21 And the LORD visited Hannah, so that she conceived and bore three sons and two daughters. Meanwhile the child Samuel grew before the LORD.

22 Now Eli was very old; and he heard everything his sons did to all Israel, and how they lay with the women who assembled at the door of the tabernacle of meeting. 23 So he said to them, "Why do you do such things? For I hear of your evil dealings from all the people. 24 No, my sons! For it is not a good report that I hear. You make the LORD's people transgress. 25 If one man sins against another, God will judge him. But if a man sins against the LORD, who will intercede for him?" Nevertheless they did not heed the voice of their father, because the LORD desired to kill them.

26 And the child Samuel grew in stature, and in favor both with the LORD and men.

27 Then a man of God came to Eli and said to him, "Thus says the LORD: 'Did I not clearly reveal Myself to the house of your father when they were in Egypt in Pharaoh's house? 28 Did I not choose him out of all the tribes of Israel to be My priest, to offer upon My altar, to burn incense, and to wear an ephod before Me? And did I not give to the house of your father all the offerings of the children of Israel made by fire? 29 Why do you kick at My sacrifice and My offering which I have commanded in My dwelling place, and honor your sons more than Me, to make yourselves fat with the best of all the offerings of Israel My people?' 30 Therefore the LORD God of Israel says: 'I said indeed that your house and the house of your father would walk before Me forever.' But now the LORD says: 'Far be it from Me; for those who honor Me I will honor, and those who despise Me shall be lightly esteemed. 31 Behold, the days are coming that I will cut off your arm and the arm of your father's house, so that there will not be an old man in your house. 32 And you will see an enemy in My dwelling place, despite all the good which God does for Israel. And there shall not be an old man in your house forever. 33 But any of your men whom I do not cut off from My altar shall consume your eyes and grieve your heart. And all the descendants of your house shall die in the flower of their age. 34 Now this shall be a sign to you that will come upon your two sons, on Hophni and Phinehas: in one day they shall die, both of them. 35 Then I will raise up for Myself a

לוֹ מִיָּמִים | יָמִימָה בַּעֲלוֹתָהּ אֶת־אִישָׁהּ לִזְבֹּחַ אֶת־זֶבַח הַיָּמִים: 20 וּבֵרַךְ עֵלִי אֶת־אֶלְקָנָה וְאֶת־אִשְׁתּוֹ וְאָמַר יָשֵׂם יְהוָה לְךָ זֶרַע מִן־הָאִשָּׁה הַזֹּאת תַּחַת הַשְּׁאֵלָה אֲשֶׁר שָׁאַל לַיהוָה וְהָלְכוּ לִמְקֹמוֹ: 21 כִּי־פָקַד יְהוָה אֶת־חַנָּה וַתַּהַר וַתֵּלֶד שְׁלֹשָׁה־בָנִים וּשְׁתֵּי בָנוֹת וַיִּגְדַּל הַנַּעַר שְׁמוּאֵל עִם־יְהוָה: ס 22 וְעֵלִי זָקֵן מְאֹד וְשָׁמַע אֵת כָּל־אֲשֶׁר יַעֲשׂוּן בָּנָיו לְכָל־יִשְׂרָאֵל וְאֵת אֲשֶׁר־יִשְׁכְּבוּן אֶת־הַנָּשִׁים הַצֹּבְאוֹת פֶּתַח אֹהֶל מוֹעֵד:

23 וַיֹּאמֶר לָהֶם לָמָּה תַעֲשׂוּן כַּדְּבָרִים הָאֵלֶּה אֲשֶׁר אָנֹכִי שֹׁמֵעַ אֶת־דִּבְרֵיכֶם רָעִים מֵאֵת כָּל־הָעָם אֵלֶּה: 24 אַל בָּנָי כִּי לוֹא־טוֹבָה הַשְּׁמֻעָה אֲשֶׁר אָנֹכִי שֹׁמֵעַ מַעֲבִרִים עַם־יְהוָה: 25 אִם־יֶחֱטָא אִישׁ לְאִישׁ וּפִלְלוֹ אֱלֹהִים וְאִם לַיהוָה יֶחֱטָא־אִישׁ מִי יִתְפַּלֶּל־לוֹ וְלֹא יִשְׁמְעוּ לְקוֹל אֲבִיהֶם כִּי־חָפֵץ יְהוָה לַהֲמִיתָם: 26 וְהַנַּעַר שְׁמוּאֵל הֹלֵךְ וְגָדֵל וָטוֹב גַּם עִם־יְהוָה וְגַם עִם־אֲנָשִׁים: ס 27 וַיָּבֹא אִישׁ־אֱלֹהִים אֶל־עֵלִי וַיֹּאמֶר אֵלָיו כֹּה אָמַר יְהוָה הֲנִגְלֹה נִגְלֵיתִי אֶל־בֵּית אָבִיךָ בִּהְיוֹתָם בְּמִצְרַיִם לְבֵית פַּרְעֹה: 28 וּבָחֹר אֹתוֹ מִכָּל־שִׁבְטֵי יִשְׂרָאֵל לִי לְכֹהֵן לַעֲלוֹת עַל־מִזְבְּחִי לְהַקְטִיר קְטֹרֶת לָשֵׂאת אֵפוֹד לְפָנָי וָאֶתְּנָה לְבֵית אָבִיךָ אֶת־כָּל־אִשֵּׁי בְּנֵי יִשְׂרָאֵל: 29 לָמָּה תִבְעֲטוּ בְּזִבְחִי וּבְמִנְחָתִי אֲשֶׁר צִוִּיתִי מָעוֹן וַתְּכַבֵּד אֶת־בָּנֶיךָ מִמֶּנִּי לְהַבְרִיאֲכֶם מֵרֵאשִׁית כָּל־מִנְחַת יִשְׂרָאֵל לְעַמִּי: 30 לָכֵן נְאֻם־יְהוָה אֱלֹהֵי יִשְׂרָאֵל אָמוֹר אָמַרְתִּי בֵּיתְךָ וּבֵית אָבִיךָ יִתְהַלְּכוּ לְפָנַי עַד־עוֹלָם וְעַתָּה נְאֻם־יְהוָה חָלִילָה לִּי כִּי־מְכַבְּדַי אֲכַבֵּד וּבֹזַי יֵקָלּוּ: 31 הִנֵּה יָמִים בָּאִים וְגָדַעְתִּי אֶת־זְרֹעֲךָ וְאֶת־זְרֹעַ בֵּית אָבִיךָ מִהְיוֹת זָקֵן בְּבֵיתֶךָ: 32 וְהִבַּטְתָּ צַר מָעוֹן בְּכֹל אֲשֶׁר־יֵיטִיב אֶת־יִשְׂרָאֵל וְלֹא־יִהְיֶה זָקֵן בְּבֵיתְךָ כָּל־הַיָּמִים: 33 וְאִישׁ לֹא־אַכְרִית לְךָ מֵעִם מִזְבְּחִי לְכַלּוֹת אֶת־עֵינֶיךָ וְלַאֲדִיב אֶת־נַפְשֶׁךָ וְכָל־מַרְבִּית בֵּיתְךָ יָמוּתוּ אֲנָשִׁים: 34 וְזֶה־לְּךָ הָאוֹת אֲשֶׁר יָבֹא אֶל־שְׁנֵי בָנֶיךָ אֶל־חָפְנִי וּפִינְחָס בְּיוֹם אֶחָד יָמוּתוּ שְׁנֵיהֶם: 35 וַהֲקִימֹתִי לִי כֹּהֵן נֶאֱמָן כַּאֲשֶׁר בִּלְבָבִי

faithful priest *who* shall do according to what *is* in My heart and in My mind. I will build him a sure house, and he shall walk before My anointed forever. [36] And it shall come to pass that everyone who is left in your house will come *and* bow down to him for a piece of silver and a morsel of bread, and say, "Please, put me in one of the priestly positions, that I may eat a piece of bread."'"

3 Now the boy Samuel ministered to the LORD before Eli. And the word of the LORD was rare in those days; *there was* no widespread revelation. [2] And it came to pass at that time, while Eli *was* lying down in his place, and when his eyes had begun to grow so dim that he could not see, [3] and before the lamp of God went out in the tabernacle of the LORD where the ark of God *was,* and while Samuel was lying down, [4] that the LORD called Samuel. And he answered, "Here I am!" [5] So he ran to Eli and said, "Here I am, for you called me."

And he said, "I did not call; lie down again." And he went and lay down.

[6] Then the LORD called yet again, "Samuel!"

So Samuel arose and went to Eli, and said, "Here I am, for you called me." He answered, "I did not call, my son; lie down again." [7] (Now Samuel did not yet know the LORD, nor was the word of the LORD yet revealed to him.)

[8] And the LORD called Samuel again the third time. So he arose and went to Eli, and said, "Here I am, for you did call me."

Then Eli perceived that the LORD had called the boy. [9] Therefore Eli said to Samuel, "Go, lie down; and it shall be, if He calls you, that you must say, 'Speak, LORD, for Your servant hears.'" So Samuel went and lay down in his place.

[10] Now the LORD came and stood and called as at other times, "Samuel! Samuel!"

And Samuel answered, "Speak, for Your servant hears."

[11] Then the LORD said to Samuel: "Behold, I will do something in Israel at which both ears of everyone who hears it will tingle. [12] In that day I will perform against Eli all that I have spoken concerning his house, from beginning to end. [13] For I have told him that I will judge his house forever for the iniquity which he knows, because his sons made themselves vile, and he did not restrain them. [14] And therefore I have sworn to the house of Eli that the iniquity of Eli's house shall not be atoned for by sacrifice or offering forever."

וּבְנַפְשִׁי יַעֲשֶׂה וּבָנִיתִי לוֹ בַּיִת נֶאֱמָן וְהִתְהַלֵּךְ לִפְנֵי־מְשִׁיחִי כָּל־הַיָּמִים: 36 וְהָיָה כָּל־הַנּוֹתָר בְּבֵיתְךָ יָבוֹא לְהִשְׁתַּחֲוֺת לוֹ לַאֲגוֹרַת כֶּסֶף וְכִכַּר־לָחֶם וְאָמַר סְפָחֵנִי נָא אֶל־אַחַת הַכְּהֻנּוֹת לֶאֱכֹל פַּת־לָחֶם: ס

ג וְהַנַּעַר שְׁמוּאֵל מְשָׁרֵת אֶת־יְהֹוָה לִפְנֵי עֵלִי וּדְבַר־יְהֹוָה הָיָה יָקָר בַּיָּמִים הָהֵם אֵין חָזוֹן נִפְרָץ: ס 2 וַיְהִי בַּיּוֹם הַהוּא וְעֵלִי שֹׁכֵב בִּמְקֹמוֹ וְעֵינָו הֵחֵלּוּ כֵהוֹת לֹא יוּכַל לִרְאוֹת: 3 וְנֵר אֱלֹהִים טֶרֶם יִכְבֶּה וּשְׁמוּאֵל שֹׁכֵב בְּהֵיכַל יְהֹוָה אֲשֶׁר־שָׁם אֲרוֹן אֱלֹהִים: פ

4 וַיִּקְרָא יְהֹוָה אֶל־שְׁמוּאֵל וַיֹּאמֶר הִנֵּנִי: 5 וַיָּרׇץ אֶל־עֵלִי וַיֹּאמֶר הִנְנִי כִּי־קָרָאתָ לִּי וַיֹּאמֶר לֹא־קָרָאתִי שׁוּב שְׁכָב וַיֵּלֶךְ וַיִּשְׁכָּב: ס 6 וַיֹּסֶף יְהֹוָה קְרֹא עוֹד שְׁמוּאֵל וַיָּקׇם שְׁמוּאֵל וַיֵּלֶךְ אֶל־עֵלִי וַיֹּאמֶר הִנְנִי כִּי קָרָאתָ לִּי וַיֹּאמֶר לֹא־קָרָאתִי בְנִי שׁוּב שְׁכָב: 7 וּשְׁמוּאֵל טֶרֶם יָדַע אֶת־יְהֹוָה וְטֶרֶם יִגָּלֶה אֵלָיו דְּבַר־יְהֹוָה: 8 וַיֹּסֶף יְהֹוָה קְרֹא־שְׁמוּאֵל בַּשְּׁלִשִׁית וַיָּקׇם וַיֵּלֶךְ אֶל־עֵלִי וַיֹּאמֶר הִנְנִי כִּי קָרָאתָ לִּי וַיָּבֶן עֵלִי כִּי יְהֹוָה קֹרֵא לַנָּעַר: 9 וַיֹּאמֶר עֵלִי לִשְׁמוּאֵל לֵךְ שְׁכָב וְהָיָה אִם־יִקְרָא אֵלֶיךָ וְאָמַרְתָּ דַּבֵּר יְהֹוָה כִּי שֹׁמֵעַ עַבְדֶּךָ וַיֵּלֶךְ שְׁמוּאֵל וַיִּשְׁכַּב בִּמְקוֹמוֹ: 10 וַיָּבֹא יְהֹוָה וַיִּתְיַצַּב וַיִּקְרָא כְפַעַם־בְּפַעַם שְׁמוּאֵל ׀ שְׁמוּאֵל וַיֹּאמֶר שְׁמוּאֵל דַּבֵּר כִּי שֹׁמֵעַ עַבְדֶּךָ: פ

11 וַיֹּאמֶר יְהֹוָה אֶל־שְׁמוּאֵל הִנֵּה אָנֹכִי עֹשֶׂה דָבָר בְּיִשְׂרָאֵל אֲשֶׁר כָּל־שֹׁמְעוֹ תְּצִלֶּינָה שְׁתֵּי אָזְנָיו: 12 בַּיּוֹם הַהוּא אָקִים אֶל־עֵלִי אֵת כָּל־אֲשֶׁר דִּבַּרְתִּי אֶל־בֵּיתוֹ הָחֵל וְכַלֵּה: 13 וְהִגַּדְתִּי לוֹ כִּי־שֹׁפֵט אֲנִי אֶת־בֵּיתוֹ עַד־עוֹלָם בַּעֲוֺן אֲשֶׁר־יָדַע כִּי־מְקַלְלִים לָהֶם בָּנָיו וְלֹא כִהָה בָּם: 14 וְלָכֵן נִשְׁבַּעְתִּי לְבֵית עֵלִי אִם־יִתְכַּפֵּר עֲוֺן בֵּית־עֵלִי בְּזֶבַח

15 So Samuel lay down until morning, and opened the doors of the house of the LORD. And Samuel was afraid to tell Eli the vision. 16 Then Eli called Samuel and said, "Samuel, my son!"

He answered, "Here I am."

17 And he said, "What is the word that the LORD spoke to you? Please do not hide it from me. God do so to you, and more also, if you hide anything from me of all the things that He said to you." 18 Then Samuel told him everything, and hid nothing from him. And he said, "It is the LORD. Let Him do what seems good to Him."

19 So Samuel grew, and the LORD was with him and let none of his words fall to the ground. 20 And all Israel from Dan to Beersheba knew that Samuel had been established as a prophet of the LORD. 21 Then the LORD appeared again in Shiloh. For the LORD revealed Himself to Samuel in Shiloh by the word of the LORD.

4 And the word of Samuel came to all Israel.

Now Israel went out to battle against the Philistines, and encamped beside Ebenezer; and the Philistines encamped in Aphek. 2 Then the Philistines put themselves in battle array against Israel. And when they joined battle, Israel was defeated by the Philistines, who killed about four thousand men of the army in the field. 3 And when the people had come into the camp, the elders of Israel said, "Why has the LORD defeated us today before the Philistines? Let us bring the ark of the covenant of the LORD from Shiloh to us, that when it comes among us it may save us from the hand of our enemies." 4 So the people sent to Shiloh, that they might bring from there the ark of the covenant of the LORD of hosts, who dwells between the cherubim. And the two sons of Eli, Hophni and Phinehas, were there with the ark of the covenant of God.

5 And when the ark of the covenant of the LORD came into the camp, all Israel shouted so loudly that the earth shook. 6 Now when the Philistines heard the noise of the shout, they said, "What does the sound of this great shout in the camp of the Hebrews mean?" Then they understood that the ark of the LORD had come into the camp. 7 So the Philistines were afraid, for they said, "God has come into the camp!" And they said, "Woe to us! For such a thing has never happened before. 8 Woe to us! Who will deliver us from the hand of these mighty gods? These are the gods who struck the Egyptians with all the plagues in the wilderness. 9 Be strong and conduct yourselves like men, you

15 וַיִּשְׁכַּב שְׁמוּאֵל עַד־הַבֹּקֶר וַיִּפְתַּח אֶת־דַּלְתוֹת בֵּית־יְהֹוָה וּשְׁמוּאֵל יָרֵא מֵהַגִּיד אֶת־הַמַּרְאָה אֶל־עֵלִי: 16 וַיִּקְרָא עֵלִי אֶת־שְׁמוּאֵל וַיֹּאמֶר שְׁמוּאֵל בְּנִי וַיֹּאמֶר הִנֵּנִי: 17 וַיֹּאמֶר מָה הַדָּבָר אֲשֶׁר דִּבֶּר אֵלֶיךָ אַל־נָא תְכַחֵד מִמֶּנִּי כֹּה יַעֲשֶׂה־לְּךָ אֱלֹהִים וְכֹה יוֹסִיף אִם־תְּכַחֵד מִמֶּנִּי דָּבָר מִכָּל־הַדָּבָר אֲשֶׁר־דִּבֶּר אֵלֶיךָ: 18 וַיַּגֶּד־לוֹ שְׁמוּאֵל אֶת־כָּל־הַדְּבָרִים וְלֹא כִחֵד מִמֶּנּוּ וַיֹּאמַר יְהֹוָה הוּא הַטּוֹב בְּעֵינָו יַעֲשֶׂה: פ

19 וַיִּגְדַּל שְׁמוּאֵל וַיהֹוָה הָיָה עִמּוֹ וְלֹא־הִפִּיל מִכָּל־דְּבָרָיו אָרְצָה: 20 וַיֵּדַע כָּל־יִשְׂרָאֵל מִדָּן וְעַד־בְּאֵר שָׁבַע כִּי נֶאֱמָן שְׁמוּאֵל לְנָבִיא לַיהֹוָה: 21 וַיֹּסֶף יְהֹוָה לְהֵרָאֹה בְשִׁלֹה כִּי־נִגְלָה יְהֹוָה אֶל־שְׁמוּאֵל בְּשִׁלוֹ בִּדְבַר יְהֹוָה: פ

ד וַיְהִי דְבַר־שְׁמוּאֵל לְכָל־יִשְׂרָאֵל וַיֵּצֵא יִשְׂרָאֵל לִקְרַאת פְּלִשְׁתִּים לַמִּלְחָמָה וַיַּחֲנוּ עַל־הָאֶבֶן הָעֵזֶר וּפְלִשְׁתִּים חָנוּ בַאֲפֵק: 2 וַיַּעַרְכוּ פְלִשְׁתִּים לִקְרַאת יִשְׂרָאֵל וַתִּטֹּשׁ הַמִּלְחָמָה וַיִּנָּגֶף יִשְׂרָאֵל לִפְנֵי פְלִשְׁתִּים וַיַּכּוּ בַמַּעֲרָכָה בַּשָּׂדֶה כְּאַרְבַּעַת אֲלָפִים אִישׁ: 3 וַיָּבֹא הָעָם אֶל־הַמַּחֲנֶה וַיֹּאמְרוּ זִקְנֵי יִשְׂרָאֵל לָמָּה נְגָפָנוּ יְהֹוָה הַיּוֹם לִפְנֵי פְלִשְׁתִּים נִקְחָה אֵלֵינוּ מִשִּׁלֹה אֶת־אֲרוֹן בְּרִית יְהֹוָה וְיָבֹא בְקִרְבֵּנוּ וְיֹשִׁעֵנוּ מִכַּף אֹיְבֵינוּ: 4 וַיִּשְׁלַח הָעָם שִׁלֹה וַיִּשְׂאוּ מִשָּׁם אֵת אֲרוֹן בְּרִית־יְהֹוָה צְבָאוֹת יֹשֵׁב הַכְּרֻבִים וְשָׁם שְׁנֵי בְנֵי־עֵלִי עִם־אֲרוֹן בְּרִית הָאֱלֹהִים חָפְנִי וּפִינְחָס: 5 וַיְהִי כְּבוֹא אֲרוֹן בְּרִית־יְהֹוָה אֶל־הַמַּחֲנֶה וַיָּרִעוּ כָל־יִשְׂרָאֵל תְּרוּעָה גְדוֹלָה וַתֵּהֹם הָאָרֶץ: 6 וַיִּשְׁמְעוּ פְלִשְׁתִּים אֶת־קוֹל הַתְּרוּעָה וַיֹּאמְרוּ מֶה קוֹל הַתְּרוּעָה הַגְּדוֹלָה הַזֹּאת בְּמַחֲנֵה הָעִבְרִים וַיֵּדְעוּ כִּי אֲרוֹן יְהֹוָה בָּא אֶל־הַמַּחֲנֶה: 7 וַיִּרְאוּ הַפְּלִשְׁתִּים כִּי אָמְרוּ בָּא אֱלֹהִים אֶל־הַמַּחֲנֶה וַיֹּאמְרוּ אוֹי לָנוּ כִּי לֹא הָיְתָה כָּזֹאת אֶתְמוֹל שִׁלְשֹׁם: 8 אוֹי לָנוּ מִי יַצִּילֵנוּ מִיַּד הָאֱלֹהִים הָאַדִּירִים הָאֵלֶּה אֵלֶּה הֵם הָאֱלֹהִים הַמַּכִּים אֶת־מִצְרַיִם בְּכָל־מַכָּה בַּמִּדְבָּר: 9 הִתְחַזְּקוּ וִהְיוּ לַאֲנָשִׁים פְּלִשְׁתִּים פֶּן תַּעַבְדוּ לָעִבְרִים כַּאֲשֶׁר

Philistines, that you do not become servants of the Hebrews, as they have been to you. Conduct yourselves like men, and fight!"

10 So the Philistines fought, and Israel was defeated, and every man fled to his tent. There was a very great slaughter, and there fell of Israel thirty thousand foot soldiers. 11 Also the ark of God was captured; and the two sons of Eli, Hophni and Phinehas, died.

12 Then a man of Benjamin ran from the battle line the same day, and came to Shiloh with his clothes torn and dirt on his head. 13 Now when he came, there was Eli, sitting on a seat by the wayside watching, for his heart trembled for the ark of God. And when the man came into the city and told *it,* all the city cried out. 14 When Eli heard the noise of the outcry, he said, "What *does* the sound of this tumult *mean?*" And the man came quickly and told Eli. 15 Eli was ninety-eight years old, and his eyes were so dim that he could not see.

16 Then the man said to Eli, "I *am* he who came from the battle. And I fled today from the battle line."

And he said, "What happened, my son?"

17 So the messenger answered and said, "Israel has fled before the Philistines, and there has been a great slaughter among the people. Also your two sons, Hophni and Phinehas, are dead; and the ark of God has been captured."

18 Then it happened, when he made mention of the ark of God, that Eli fell off the seat backward by the side of the gate; and his neck was broken and he died, for the man was old and heavy. And he had judged Israel forty years.

19 Now his daughter-in-law, Phinehas' wife, was with child, *due* to be delivered; and when she heard the news that the ark of God was captured, and that her father-in-law and her husband were dead, she bowed herself and gave birth, for her labor pains came upon her. 20 And about the time of her death the women who stood by her said to her, "Do not fear, for you have borne a son." But she did not answer, nor did she regard *it.* 21 Then she named the child Ichabod, saying, "The glory has departed from Israel!" because the ark of God had been captured and because of her father-in-law and her husband. 22 And she said, "The glory has departed from Israel, for the ark of God has been captured."

5 Then the Philistines took the ark of God and brought it from Ebenezer to Ashdod. 2 When the Philistines took the ark of God, they brought it into the house of Dagon and set it by Dagon. 3 And when the people of Ashdod arose early in the

עָבְדוּ לָכֶם וִהְיִיתֶם לַאֲנָשִׁים וְנִלְחַמְתֶּם: 10 וַיִּלָּחֲמוּ פְלִשְׁתִּים וַיִּנָּגֶף יִשְׂרָאֵל וַיָּנֻסוּ אִישׁ לְאֹהָלָיו וַתְּהִי הַמַּכָּה גְדוֹלָה מְאֹד וַיִּפֹּל מִיִּשְׂרָאֵל שְׁלֹשִׁים אֶלֶף רַגְלִי: 11 וַאֲרוֹן אֱלֹהִים נִלְקָח וּשְׁנֵי בְנֵי־עֵלִי מֵתוּ חָפְנִי וּפִינְחָס: 12 וַיָּרָץ אִישׁ־בִּנְיָמִן מֵהַמַּעֲרָכָה וַיָּבֹא שִׁלֹה בַּיּוֹם הַהוּא וּמַדָּיו קְרֻעִים וַאֲדָמָה עַל־רֹאשׁוֹ: 13 וַיָּבוֹא וְהִנֵּה עֵלִי יֹשֵׁב עַל־הַכִּסֵּא יָ֯ד דֶּרֶךְ מְצַפֶּה כִּי־הָיָה לִבּוֹ חָרֵד עַל אֲרוֹן הָאֱלֹהִים וְהָאִישׁ בָּא לְהַגִּיד בָּעִיר וַתִּזְעַק כָּל־ הָעִיר: 14 וַיִּשְׁמַע עֵלִי אֶת־קוֹל הַצְּעָקָה וַיֹּאמֶר מֶה קוֹל הֶהָמוֹן הַזֶּה וְהָאִישׁ מִהַר וַיָּבֹא וַיַּגֵּד לְעֵלִי: 15 וְעֵלִי בֶּן־תִּשְׁעִים וּשְׁמֹנֶה שָׁנָה וְעֵינָיו קָמָה וְלֹא יָכוֹל לִרְאוֹת: 16 וַיֹּאמֶר הָאִישׁ אֶל־עֵלִי אָנֹכִי הַבָּא מִן־הַמַּעֲרָכָה וַאֲנִי מִן־הַמַּעֲרָכָה נַסְתִּי הַיּוֹם וַיֹּאמֶר מֶה־הָיָה הַדָּבָר בְּנִי: 17 וַיַּעַן הַמְבַשֵּׂר וַיֹּאמֶר נָס יִשְׂרָאֵל לִפְנֵי פְלִשְׁתִּים וְגַם מַגֵּפָה גְדוֹלָה הָיְתָה בָעָם וְגַם־שְׁנֵי בָנֶיךָ מֵתוּ חָפְנִי וּפִינְחָס וַאֲרוֹן הָאֱלֹהִים נִלְקָחָה: פ

18 וַיְהִי כְּהַזְכִּירוֹ ׀ אֶת־אֲרוֹן הָאֱלֹהִים וַיִּפֹּל מֵעַל־ הַכִּסֵּא אֲחֹרַנִּית בְּעַד ׀ יַד הַשַּׁעַר וַתִּשָּׁבֵר מַפְרַקְתּוֹ וַיָּמֹת כִּי־זָקֵן הָאִישׁ וְכָבֵד וְהוּא שָׁפַט אֶת־יִשְׂרָאֵל אַרְבָּעִים שָׁנָה: 19 וְכַלָּתוֹ אֵשֶׁת־פִּינְחָס הָרָה לָלַת וַתִּשְׁמַע אֶת־הַשְּׁמֻעָה אֶל־הִלָּקַח אֲרוֹן הָאֱלֹהִים וּמֵת חָמִיהָ וְאִישָׁהּ וַתִּכְרַע וַתֵּלֶד כִּי־נֶהֶפְכוּ עָלֶיהָ צִרֶיהָ: 20 וּכְעֵת מוּתָהּ וַתְּדַבֵּרְנָה הַנִּצָּבוֹת עָלֶיהָ אַל־תִּירְאִי כִּי בֵן יָלָדְתְּ וְלֹא עָנְתָה וְלֹא־שָׁתָה לִבָּהּ: 21 וַתִּקְרָא לַנַּעַר אִי־כָבוֹד לֵאמֹר גָּלָה כָבוֹד מִיִּשְׂרָאֵל אֶל־הִלָּקַח אֲרוֹן הָאֱלֹהִים וְאֶל־חָמִיהָ וְאִישָׁהּ: 22 וַתֹּאמֶר גָּלָה כָבוֹד מִיִּשְׂרָאֵל כִּי נִלְקַח אֲרוֹן הָאֱלֹהִים: פ

ה וּפְלִשְׁתִּים לָקְחוּ אֵת אֲרוֹן הָאֱלֹהִים וַיְבִאֻהוּ מֵאֶבֶן הָעֵזֶר אַשְׁדּוֹדָה: 2 וַיִּקְחוּ פְלִשְׁתִּים אֶת־אֲרוֹן הָאֱלֹהִים וַיָּבִיאוּ אֹתוֹ בֵּית דָּגוֹן וַיַּצִּיגוּ אֹתוֹ אֵצֶל דָּגוֹן: 3 וַיַּשְׁכִּמוּ אַשְׁדּוֹדִים מִמָּחֳרָת וְהִנֵּה דָגוֹן נֹפֵל

ד 13 דְּ

morning, there was Dagon, fallen on its face to the earth before the ark of the LORD. So they took Dagon and set it in its place again. ⁴And when they arose early the next morning, there was Dagon, fallen on its face to the ground before the ark of the LORD. The head of Dagon and both the palms of its hands *were* broken off on the threshold; only Dagon's torso was left of it. ⁵Therefore neither the priests of Dagon nor any who come into Dagon's house tread on the threshold of Dagon in Ashdod to this day.

⁶But the hand of the LORD was heavy on the people of Ashdod, and He ravaged them and struck them with tumors, *both* Ashdod and its territory. ⁷And when the men of Ashdod saw how *it was,* they said, "The ark of the God of Israel must not remain with us, for His hand is harsh toward us and Dagon our god." ⁸Therefore they sent and gathered to themselves all the lords of the Philistines, and said, "What shall we do with the ark of the God of Israel?"

And they answered, "Let the ark of the God of Israel be carried away to Gath." So they carried the ark of the God of Israel away. ⁹So it was, after they had carried it away, that the hand of the LORD was against the city with a very great destruction; and He struck the men of the city, both small and great, and tumors broke out on them.

¹⁰Therefore they sent the ark of God to Ekron. So it was, as the ark of God came to Ekron, that the Ekronites cried out, saying, "They have brought the ark of the God of Israel to us, to kill us and our people!" ¹¹So they sent and gathered together all the lords of the Philistines, and said, "Send away the ark of the God of Israel, and let it go back to its own place, so that it does not kill us and our people." For there was a deadly destruction throughout all the city; the hand of God was very heavy there. ¹²And the men who did not die were stricken with the tumors, and the cry of the city went up to heaven.

6 Now the ark of the LORD was in the country of the Philistines seven months. ²And the Philistines called for the priests and the diviners, saying, "What shall we do with the ark of the LORD? Tell us how we should send it to its place."

³So they said, "If you send away the ark of the God of Israel, do not send it empty; but by all means return *it* to Him *with* a trespass offering. Then you will be healed, and it will be known to you why His hand is not removed from you."

⁴Then they said, "What *is* the trespass offering which we shall return to Him?"

לְפָנָיו אַ֫רְצָה לִפְנֵי אֲרוֹן יְהֹוָה וַיִּקְח֙וּ אֶת־דָּג֔וֹן וַיָּשִׁ֖בוּ אֹת֣וֹ לִמְקוֹמֽוֹ׃ ⁴וַיַּשְׁכִּ֣מוּ בַבֹּ֗קֶר מִֽמׇּחֳרָת֒ וְהִנֵּ֤ה דָגוֹן֙ נֹפֵ֤ל לְפָנָיו֙ אַ֔רְצָה לִפְנֵ֖י אֲר֣וֹן יְהֹוָ֑ה וְרֹ֨אשׁ דָּג֜וֹן וּשְׁתֵּ֣י ׀ כַּפּ֣וֹת יָדָ֗יו כְּרֻתוֹת֙ אֶל־הַמִּפְתָּ֔ן רַ֥ק דָּג֖וֹן נִשְׁאַ֥ר עָלָֽיו׃ ⁵עַל־כֵּ֡ן לֹֽא־יִדְרְכוּ֩ כֹהֲנֵ֨י דָג֜וֹן וְכׇל־הַבָּאִ֧ים בֵּית־דָּג֛וֹן עַל־מִפְתַּ֥ן דָּג֖וֹן בְּאַשְׁדּ֑וֹד עַ֖ד הַיּ֥וֹם הַזֶּֽה׃ ס ⁶וַתִּכְבַּ֧ד יַד־יְהֹוָ֛ה אֶל־הָאַשְׁדּוֹדִ֖ים וַיְשִׁמֵּ֑ם וַיַּ֤ךְ אֹתָם֙ בעפלים[בַּטְּחֹרִ֔ים]° אֶת־אַשְׁדּ֖וֹד וְאֶת־גְּבוּלֶֽיהָ׃ ⁷וַיִּרְא֥וּ אַנְשֵֽׁי־אַשְׁדּ֖וֹד כִּי־כֵ֑ן וְאָ֣מְר֔וּ לֹא־יֵשֵׁ֞ב אֲר֨וֹן אֱלֹהֵ֤י יִשְׂרָאֵל֙ עִמָּ֔נוּ כִּֽי־קָשְׁתָ֤ה יָדוֹ֙ עָלֵ֔ינוּ וְעַ֖ל דָּג֥וֹן אֱלֹהֵֽינוּ׃ ⁸וַיִּשְׁלְח֡וּ וַיַּאַסְפ֣וּ אֶת־כׇּל־סַרְנֵ֨י פְלִשְׁתִּ֜ים אֲלֵיהֶ֗ם וַיֹּֽאמְרוּ֙ מַֽה־נַּעֲשֶׂ֗ה לַֽאֲרוֹן֙ אֱלֹהֵ֣י יִשְׂרָאֵ֔ל וַיֹּ֣אמְר֔וּ גַּ֣ת יִסֹּ֔ב אֲר֖וֹן אֱלֹהֵ֣י יִשְׂרָאֵ֑ל וַיַּסֵּ֕בּוּ אֶת־אֲר֖וֹן אֱלֹהֵ֥י יִשְׂרָאֵֽל׃ ס ⁹וַיְהִ֞י אַחֲרֵ֣י ׀ הֵסַ֣בּוּ אֹת֗וֹ וַתְּהִ֨י יַד־יְהֹוָ֤ה ׀ בָּעִיר֙ מְהוּמָה֙ גְּדוֹלָ֣ה מְאֹ֔ד וַיַּךְ֙ אֶת־אַנְשֵׁ֣י הָעִ֔יר מִקָּטֹ֖ן וְעַד־גָּד֑וֹל וַיִּשָּׂתְר֥וּ לָהֶ֖ם עפלים[טְּחֹרִֽים]°׃ ¹⁰וַֽיְשַׁלְּח֛וּ אֶת־אֲר֥וֹן הָאֱלֹהִ֖ים עֶקְר֑וֹן וַיְהִ֗י כְּב֨וֹא אֲר֤וֹן הָֽאֱלֹהִים֙ עֶקְר֔וֹן וַיִּזְעֲק֨וּ הָֽעֶקְרֹנִ֜ים לֵאמֹ֗ר הֵסַ֤בּוּ אֵלַי֙ אֶת־אֲרוֹן֙ אֱלֹהֵ֣י יִשְׂרָאֵ֔ל לַהֲמִיתֵ֖נִי וְאֶת־עַמִּֽי׃ ¹¹וַיִּשְׁלְח֡וּ וַיַּאַסְפוּ֩ אֶת־כׇּל־סַרְנֵ֨י פְלִשְׁתִּ֜ים וַיֹּֽאמְרוּ֙ שַׁלְּח֞וּ אֶת־אֲר֨וֹן אֱלֹהֵ֤י יִשְׂרָאֵל֙ וְיָשֹׁ֣ב לִמְקֹמ֔וֹ וְלֹֽא־יָמִ֥ית אֹתִ֖י וְאֶת־עַמִּ֑י כִּֽי־הָיְתָ֤ה מְהֽוּמַת־מָ֙וֶת֙ בְּכׇל־הָעִ֔יר כָּבְדָ֧ה מְאֹ֛ד יַ֥ד הָאֱלֹהִ֖ים שָֽׁם׃ ¹²וְהָֽאֲנָשִׁים֙ אֲשֶׁ֣ר לֹא־מֵ֔תוּ הֻכּ֖וּ בעפלים[בַּטְּחֹרִ֑ים]° וַתַּ֛עַל שַׁוְעַ֥ת הָעִ֖יר הַשָּׁמָֽיִם׃

ו וַיְהִ֧י אֲרֽוֹן־יְהֹוָ֛ה בִּשְׂדֵ֥ה פְלִשְׁתִּ֖ים שִׁבְעָ֥ה חֳדָשִֽׁים׃ ²וַיִּקְרְא֣וּ פְלִשְׁתִּ֗ים לַכֹּהֲנִ֤ים וְלַקֹּֽסְמִים֙ לֵאמֹ֔ר מַֽה־נַּעֲשֶׂ֖ה לַֽאֲר֣וֹן יְהֹוָ֑ה הוֹדִעֻ֕נוּ בַּמֶּ֖ה נְשַׁלְּחֶ֥נּוּ לִמְקוֹמֽוֹ׃ ³וַיֹּֽאמְר֗וּ אִֽם־מְשַׁלְּחִ֞ים אֶת־אֲר֨וֹן אֱלֹהֵ֤י יִשְׂרָאֵל֙ אַל־תְּשַׁלְּח֤וּ אֹתוֹ֙ רֵיקָ֔ם כִּֽי־הָשֵׁ֥ב תָּשִׁ֛יבוּ ל֖וֹ אָשָׁ֑ם אָ֤ז תֵּרָֽפְאוּ֙ וְנוֹדַ֣ע לָכֶ֔ם לָ֛מָּה לֹא־תָס֥וּר יָד֖וֹ מִכֶּֽם׃ ⁴וַיֹּֽאמְר֗וּ מָ֣ה הָאָשָׁם֙

They answered, "Five golden tumors and five golden rats, *according to* the number of the lords of the Philistines. For the same plague *was* on all of you and on your lords. ⁵Therefore you shall make images of your tumors and images of your rats that ravage the land, and you shall give glory to the God of Israel; perhaps He will lighten His hand from you, from your gods, and from your land. ⁶Why then do you harden your hearts as the Egyptians and Pharaoh hardened their hearts? When He did mighty things among them, did they not let the people go, that they might depart? ⁷Now therefore, make a new cart, take two milk cows which have never been yoked, and hitch the cows to the cart; and take their calves home, away from them. ⁸Then take the ark of the LORD and set it on the cart; and put the articles of gold which you are returning to Him *as* a trespass offering in a chest by its side. Then send it away, and let it go. ⁹And watch: if it goes up the road to its own territory, to Beth Shemesh, *then* He has done us this great evil. But if not, then we shall know that *it is* not His hand *that* struck us—it happened to us by chance."

¹⁰Then the men did so; they took two milk cows and hitched them to the cart, and shut up their calves at home. ¹¹And they set the ark of the LORD on the cart, and the chest with the gold rats and the images of their tumors. ¹²Then the cows headed straight for the road to Beth Shemesh, *and* went along the highway, lowing as they went, and did not turn aside to the right hand or the left. And the lords of the Philistines went after them to the border of Beth Shemesh.

¹³Now *the people of* Beth Shemesh *were* reaping their wheat harvest in the valley; and they lifted their eyes and saw the ark, and rejoiced to see *it*. ¹⁴Then the cart came into the field of Joshua of Beth Shemesh, and stood there; a large stone *was* there. So they split the wood of the cart and offered the cows as a burnt offering to the LORD. ¹⁵The Levites took down the ark of the LORD and the chest that *was* with it, in which *were* the articles of gold, and put *them* on the large stone. Then the men of Beth Shemesh offered burnt offerings and made sacrifices the same day to the LORD. ¹⁶So when the five lords of the Philistines had seen *it,* they returned to Ekron the same day.

¹⁷These *are* the golden tumors which the Philistines returned *as* a trespass offering to the LORD: one for Ashdod, one for Gaza, one for Ashkelon, one for Gath, one for Ekron; ¹⁸and the golden rats, *according to* the number of all the cities of the Philistines *belonging* to the five lords, *both* fortified cities and country villages, even as far as

אֲשֶׁר נָשִׁיב לוֹ וַיֹּאמְרוּ מִסְפַּר סַרְנֵי פְלִשְׁתִּים חֲמִשָּׁה עֳפְלֵי° זָהָב וַחֲמִשָּׁה עַכְבְּרֵי זָהָב כִּי־מַגֵּפָה אַחַת לְכֻלָּם וּלְסַרְנֵיכֶם: 5 וַעֲשִׂיתֶם צַלְמֵי עׇפְלֵיכֶם° וְצַלְמֵי עַכְבְּרֵיכֶם הַמַּשְׁחִיתִם אֶת־הָאָרֶץ וּנְתַתֶּם לֵאלֹהֵי יִשְׂרָאֵל כָּבוֹד אוּלַי יָקֵל אֶת־יָדוֹ מֵעֲלֵיכֶם וּמֵעַל אֱלֹהֵיכֶם וּמֵעַל אַרְצְכֶם: 6 וְלָמָּה תְכַבְּדוּ אֶת־לְבַבְכֶם כַּאֲשֶׁר כִּבְּדוּ מִצְרַיִם וּפַרְעֹה אֶת־לִבָּם הֲלוֹא כַּאֲשֶׁר הִתְעַלֵּל בָּהֶם וַיְשַׁלְּחוּם וַיֵּלֵכוּ: 7 וְעַתָּה קְחוּ וַעֲשׂוּ עֲגָלָה חֲדָשָׁה אֶחָת וּשְׁתֵּי פָרוֹת עָלוֹת אֲשֶׁר לֹא־עָלָה עֲלֵיהֶם עֹל וַאֲסַרְתֶּם אֶת־הַפָּרוֹת בָּעֲגָלָה וַהֲשֵׁיבֹתֶם בְּנֵיהֶם מֵאַחֲרֵיהֶם הַבָּיְתָה: 8 וּלְקַחְתֶּם אֶת־אֲרוֹן יְהֹוָה וּנְתַתֶּם אֹתוֹ אֶל־הָעֲגָלָה וְאֵת | כְּלֵי הַזָּהָב אֲשֶׁר הֲשֵׁבֹתֶם לוֹ אָשָׁם תָּשִׂימוּ בָאַרְגַּז מִצִּדּוֹ וְשִׁלַּחְתֶּם אֹתוֹ וְהָלָךְ: 9 וּרְאִיתֶם אִם־דֶּרֶךְ גְּבוּלוֹ יַעֲלֶה בֵּית שֶׁמֶשׁ הוּא עָשָׂה לָנוּ אֶת־הָרָעָה הַגְּדוֹלָה הַזֹּאת וְאִם־לֹא וְיָדַעְנוּ כִּי לֹא יָדוֹ נָגְעָה בָּנוּ מִקְרֶה הוּא הָיָה לָנוּ: 10 וַיַּעֲשׂוּ הָאֲנָשִׁים כֵּן וַיִּקְחוּ שְׁתֵּי פָרוֹת עָלוֹת וַיַּאַסְרוּם בָּעֲגָלָה וְאֶת־בְּנֵיהֶם כָּלוּ בַבָּיִת: 11 וַיָּשִׂמוּ אֶת־אֲרוֹן יְהֹוָה אֶל־הָעֲגָלָה וְאֵת הָאַרְגַּז וְאֵת עַכְבְּרֵי הַזָּהָב וְאֵת צַלְמֵי טְחֹרֵיהֶם: 12 וַיִּשַּׁרְנָה הַפָּרוֹת בַּדֶּרֶךְ עַל־דֶּרֶךְ בֵּית שֶׁמֶשׁ בִּמְסִלָּה אַחַת הָלְכוּ הָלֹךְ וְגָעוֹ וְלֹא־סָרוּ יָמִין וּשְׂמֹאול וְסַרְנֵי פְלִשְׁתִּים הֹלְכִים אַחֲרֵיהֶם עַד־גְּבוּל בֵּית שָׁמֶשׁ: 13 וּבֵית שֶׁמֶשׁ קֹצְרִים קְצִיר־חִטִּים בָּעֵמֶק וַיִּשְׂאוּ אֶת־עֵינֵיהֶם וַיִּרְאוּ אֶת־הָאָרֹון וַיִּשְׂמְחוּ לִרְאוֹת: 14 וְהָעֲגָלָה בָּאָה אֶל־שְׂדֵה יְהוֹשֻׁעַ בֵּית־הַשִּׁמְשִׁי וַתַּעֲמֹד שָׁם וְשָׁם אֶבֶן גְּדוֹלָה וַיְבַקְּעוּ אֶת־עֲצֵי הָעֲגָלָה וְאֶת־הַפָּרוֹת הֶעֱלוּ עֹלָה לַיהֹוָה: 15 וְהַלְוִיִּם הוֹרִידוּ | אֶת־אֲרוֹן יְהֹוָה וְאֶת־הָאַרְגַּז אֲשֶׁר־אִתּוֹ אֲשֶׁר־בּוֹ כְלֵי־זָהָב וַיָּשִׂמוּ אֶל־הָאֶבֶן הַגְּדוֹלָה וְאַנְשֵׁי בֵית־שֶׁמֶשׁ הֶעֱלוּ עֹלוֹת וַיִּזְבְּחוּ זְבָחִים בַּיּוֹם הַהוּא לַיהֹוָה: 16 וַחֲמִשָּׁה סַרְנֵי־פְלִשְׁתִּים רָאוּ וַיָּשֻׁבוּ עֶקְרוֹן בַּיּוֹם הַהוּא: ס 17 וְאֵלֶּה טְחֹרֵי הַזָּהָב אֲשֶׁר הֵשִׁיבוּ פְלִשְׁתִּים

אָשָׁם לַיהֹוָה לְאַשְׁדּוֹד אֶחָד לְעַזָּה אֶחָד לְאַשְׁקְלוֹן אֶחָד לְגַת אֶחָד לְעֶקְרוֹן אֶחָד: ס 18 וְעַכְבְּרֵי הַזָּהָב מִסְפַּר כָּל־עָרֵי פְלִשְׁתִּים לַחֲמֵשֶׁת הַסְּרָנִים מֵעִיר מִבְצָר וְעַד כֹּפֶר הַפְּרָזִי וְעַד אָבֵל הַגְּדוֹלָה אֲשֶׁר הִנִּיחוּ עָלֶיהָ אֵת אֲרוֹן יְהֹוָה עַד הַיּוֹם הַזֶּה בִּשְׂדֵה יְהוֹשֻׁעַ בֵּית־הַשִּׁמְשִׁי:

the large *stone of* Abel on which they set the ark of the LORD, *which stone remains* to this day in the field of Joshua of Beth Shemesh.

¹⁹ Then He struck the men of Beth Shemesh, because they had looked into the ark of the LORD. He struck fifty thousand and seventy men of the people, and the people lamented because the LORD had struck the people with a great slaughter.

²⁰ And the men of Beth Shemesh said, "Who is able to stand before this holy LORD God? And to whom shall it go up from us?" ²¹ So they sent messengers to the inhabitants of Kirjath Jearim, saying, "The Philistines have brought back the ark of the LORD; come down *and* take it up with you."

7 Then the men of Kirjath Jearim came and took the ark of the LORD, and brought it into the house of Abinadab on the hill, and consecrated Eleazar his son to keep the ark of the LORD.

² So it was that the ark remained in Kirjath Jearim a long time; it was there twenty years. And all the house of Israel lamented after the LORD.

³ Then Samuel spoke to all the house of Israel, saying, "If you return to the LORD with all your hearts, *then* put away the foreign gods and the Ashtoreths from among you, and prepare your hearts for the LORD, and serve Him only; and He will deliver you from the hand of the Philistines." ⁴ So the children of Israel put away the Baals and the Ashtoreths, and served the LORD only.

⁵ And Samuel said, "Gather all Israel to Mizpah, and I will pray to the LORD for you." ⁶ So they gathered together at Mizpah, drew water, and poured *it* out before the LORD. And they fasted that day, and said there, "We have sinned against the LORD." And Samuel judged the children of Israel at Mizpah.

⁷ Now when the Philistines heard that the children of Israel had gathered together at Mizpah, the lords of the Philistines went up against Israel. And when the children of Israel heard *of it,* they were afraid of the Philistines. ⁸ So the children of Israel said to Samuel, "Do not cease to cry out to the LORD our God for us, that He may save us from the hand of the Philistines."

⁹ And Samuel took a suckling lamb and offered *it as* a whole burnt offering to the LORD. Then Samuel cried out to the LORD for Israel, and the LORD answered him. ¹⁰ Now as Samuel was offering up the burnt offering, the Philistines drew near to battle against Israel. But the LORD thundered with a loud thunder upon the Philistines that day, and so confused them that they were overcome before Israel. ¹¹ And the men of Israel went out of Mizpah

19 וַיַּ֞ךְ בְּאַנְשֵׁ֣י בֵֽית־שֶׁ֗מֶשׁ כִּ֤י רָאוּ֙ בַּֽאֲר֣וֹן יְהֹוָ֔ה וַיַּ֤ךְ בָּעָם֙ שִׁבְעִ֣ים אִ֔ישׁ חֲמִשִּׁ֥ים אֶ֖לֶף אִ֑ישׁ וַיִּֽתְאַבְּל֣וּ הָעָ֔ם כִּֽי־הִכָּ֧ה יְהֹוָ֛ה בָּעָ֖ם מַכָּ֥ה גְדוֹלָֽה׃ 20 וַיֹּֽאמְרוּ֙ אַנְשֵׁ֣י בֵֽית־שֶׁ֔מֶשׁ מִ֚י יוּכַ֣ל לַֽעֲמֹ֔ד לִפְנֵ֨י יְהֹוָ֧ה הָֽאֱלֹהִ֛ים הַקָּד֖וֹשׁ הַזֶּ֑ה וְאֶל־מִ֖י יַֽעֲלֶ֥ה מֵֽעָלֵֽינוּ׃ ס 21 וַיִּשְׁלְחוּ֙ מַלְאָכִ֔ים אֶל־יֽוֹשְׁבֵ֖י קִרְיַת־יְעָרִ֣ים לֵאמֹ֑ר הֵשִׁ֤בוּ פְלִשְׁתִּים֙ אֶת־אֲר֣וֹן יְהֹוָ֔ה רְד֕וּ הַֽעֲל֥וּ אֹת֖וֹ אֲלֵיכֶֽם׃ ס

ז וַיָּבֹ֜אוּ אַנְשֵׁ֣י ׀ קִרְיַ֣ת יְעָרִ֗ים וַֽיַּעֲלוּ֙ אֶת־אֲר֣וֹן יְהֹוָ֔ה וַיָּבִ֣אוּ אֹת֔וֹ אֶל־בֵּ֥ית אֲבִֽינָדָ֖ב בַּגִּבְעָ֑ה וְאֶת־אֶלְעָזָ֤ר בְּנוֹ֙ קִדְּשׁ֔וּ לִשְׁמֹ֖ר אֶת־אֲר֥וֹן יְהֹוָֽה׃ פ 2 וַיְהִ֗י מִיּ֞וֹם שֶׁ֤בֶת הָֽאָרוֹן֙ בְּקִרְיַ֣ת יְעָרִ֔ים וַיִּרְבּוּ֙ הַיָּמִ֔ים וַיִּֽהְי֖וּ עֶשְׂרִ֣ים שָׁנָ֑ה וַיִּנָּה֛וּ כָּל־בֵּ֥ית יִשְׂרָאֵ֖ל אַֽחֲרֵ֥י יְהֹוָֽה׃ ס 3 וַיֹּ֣אמֶר שְׁמוּאֵ֗ל אֶל־כָּל־בֵּ֣ית יִשְׂרָאֵל֮ לֵאמֹר֒ אִם־בְּכָל־לְבַבְכֶ֗ם אַתֶּ֤ם שָׁבִים֙ אֶל־יְהֹוָ֔ה הָסִ֜ירוּ אֶת־אֱלֹהֵ֧י הַנֵּכָ֛ר מִתּֽוֹכְכֶ֖ם וְהָֽעַשְׁתָּר֑וֹת וְהָכִ֤ינוּ לְבַבְכֶם֙ אֶל־יְהֹוָ֔ה וְעִבְדֻ֣הוּ לְבַדּ֔וֹ וְיַצֵּ֥ל אֶתְכֶ֖ם מִיַּ֥ד פְּלִשְׁתִּֽים׃ 4 וַיָּסִ֨ירוּ֙ בְּנֵ֣י יִשְׂרָאֵ֔ל אֶת־הַבְּעָלִ֖ים וְאֶת־הָֽעַשְׁתָּרֹ֑ת וַיַּֽעַבְד֥וּ אֶת־יְהֹוָ֖ה לְבַדּֽוֹ׃ פ 5 וַיֹּ֣אמֶר שְׁמוּאֵ֔ל קִבְצ֥וּ אֶת־כָּל־יִשְׂרָאֵ֖ל הַמִּצְפָּ֑תָה וְאֶתְפַּלֵּ֥ל בַּֽעַדְכֶ֖ם אֶל־יְהֹוָֽה׃ 6 וַיִּקָּבְצ֣וּ הַ֠מִּצְפָּ֠תָה וַיִּֽשְׁאֲבוּ־מַ֜יִם וַֽיִּשְׁפְּכ֣וּ ׀ לִפְנֵ֣י יְהֹוָ֗ה וַיָּצ֙וּמוּ֙ בַּיּ֣וֹם הַה֔וּא וַיֹּ֣אמְרוּ שָׁ֔ם חָטָ֖אנוּ לַֽיהֹוָ֑ה וַיִּשְׁפֹּ֧ט שְׁמוּאֵ֛ל אֶת־בְּנֵ֥י יִשְׂרָאֵ֖ל בַּמִּצְפָּֽה׃ 7 וַיִּשְׁמְע֣וּ פְלִשְׁתִּ֗ים כִּֽי־הִתְקַבְּצ֤וּ בְנֵֽי־יִשְׂרָאֵל֙ הַמִּצְפָּ֔תָה וַיַּֽעֲל֥וּ סַרְנֵֽי־פְלִשְׁתִּ֖ים אֶל־יִשְׂרָאֵ֑ל וַיִּשְׁמְעוּ֙ בְּנֵ֣י יִשְׂרָאֵ֔ל וַיִּֽרְא֖וּ מִפְּנֵ֥י פְלִשְׁתִּֽים׃ 8 וַיֹּֽאמְר֤וּ בְנֵֽי־יִשְׂרָאֵל֙ אֶל־שְׁמוּאֵ֔ל אַל־תַּֽחֲרֵ֣שׁ מִמֶּ֔נּוּ מִזְּעֹ֖ק אֶל־יְהֹוָ֣ה אֱלֹהֵ֑ינוּ וְיֹֽשִׁעֵ֖נוּ מִיַּ֥ד פְּלִשְׁתִּֽים׃ 9 וַיִּקַּ֣ח שְׁמוּאֵ֗ל טְלֵ֤ה חָלָב֙ אֶחָ֔ד וַיַּֽעֲלֵ֧הוּ עוֹלָ֛ה כָּלִ֖יל לַֽיהֹוָ֑ה וַיִּזְעַ֨ק שְׁמוּאֵ֤ל אֶל־יְהֹוָה֙ בְּעַ֣ד יִשְׂרָאֵ֔ל וַֽיַּעֲנֵ֖הוּ יְהֹוָֽה׃ 10 וַיְהִ֣י שְׁמוּאֵ֗ל מַֽעֲלֶ֣ה הָֽעוֹלָ֔ה וּפְלִשְׁתִּ֣ים נִגְּשׁ֔וּ לַמִּלְחָמָ֖ה בְּיִשְׂרָאֵ֑ל וַיַּרְעֵ֣ם יְהֹוָ֣ה ׀ בְּקוֹל־גָּד֠וֹל בַּיּ֨וֹם הַה֤וּא עַל־פְּלִשְׁתִּים֙ וַיְהֻמֵּ֔ם וַיִּנָּֽגְפ֖וּ לִפְנֵ֥י יִשְׂרָאֵֽל׃ 11 וַיֵּ֥צְא֛וּ אַנְשֵׁ֥י יִשְׂרָאֵ֖ל

and pursued the Philistines, and drove them back as far as below Beth Car. 12 Then Samuel took a stone and set *it* up between Mizpah and Shen, and called its name Ebenezer, saying, "Thus far the LORD has helped us."

13 So the Philistines were subdued, and they did not come anymore into the territory of Israel. And the hand of the LORD was against the Philistines all the days of Samuel. 14 Then the cities which the Philistines had taken from Israel were restored to Israel, from Ekron to Gath; and Israel recovered its territory from the hands of the Philistines. Also there was peace between Israel and the Amorites.

15 And Samuel judged Israel all the days of his life. 16 He went from year to year on a circuit to Bethel, Gilgal, and Mizpah, and judged Israel in all those places. 17 But he always returned to Ramah, for his home *was* there. There he judged Israel, and there he built an altar to the LORD.

8 Now it came to pass when Samuel was old that he made his sons judges over Israel. 2 The name of his firstborn was Joel, and the name of his second, Abijah; *they were* judges in Beersheba. 3 But his sons did not walk in his ways; they turned aside after dishonest gain, took bribes, and perverted justice.

4 Then all the elders of Israel gathered together and came to Samuel at Ramah, 5 and said to him, "Look, you are old, and your sons do not walk in your ways. Now make us a king to judge us like all the nations."

6 But the thing displeased Samuel when they said, "Give us a king to judge us." So Samuel prayed to the LORD. 7 And the LORD said to Samuel, "Heed the voice of the people in all that they say to you; for they have not rejected you, but they have rejected Me, that I should not reign over them. 8 According to all the works which they have done since the day that I brought them up out of Egypt, even to this day—with which they have forsaken Me and served other gods—so they are doing to you also. 9 Now therefore, heed their voice. However, you shall solemnly forewarn them, and show them the behavior of the king who will reign over them."

10 So Samuel told all the words of the LORD to the people who asked him for a king. 11 And he said, "This will be the behavior of the king who will reign over you: He will take your sons and appoint *them* for his own chariots and *to be* his horsemen, and *some* will run before his chariots. 12 He will appoint captains over his thousands and captains over his fifties, *will set some* to plow his ground and reap his

מִן־הַמִּצְפָּה וַיִּרְדְּפוּ אֶת־פְּלִשְׁתִּים וַיַּכּוּם עַד־מִתַּחַת לְבֵית כָּר: 12 וַיִּקַּח שְׁמוּאֵל אֶבֶן אַחַת וַיָּשֶׂם בֵּין־הַמִּצְפָּה וּבֵין הַשֵּׁן וַיִּקְרָא אֶת־שְׁמָהּ אֶבֶן הָעָזֶר וַיֹּאמַר עַד־הֵנָּה עֲזָרָנוּ יְהוָה: 13 וַיִּכָּנְעוּ הַפְּלִשְׁתִּים וְלֹא־יָסְפוּ עוֹד לָבוֹא בִּגְבוּל יִשְׂרָאֵל וַתְּהִי יַד־יְהוָה בַּפְּלִשְׁתִּים כֹּל יְמֵי שְׁמוּאֵל: 14 וַתָּשֹׁבְנָה הֶעָרִים אֲשֶׁר לָקְחוּ־פְלִשְׁתִּים מֵאֵת יִשְׂרָאֵל | לְיִשְׂרָאֵל מֵעֶקְרוֹן וְעַד־גַּת וְאֶת־גְּבוּלָן הִצִּיל יִשְׂרָאֵל מִיַּד פְּלִשְׁתִּים וַיְהִי שָׁלוֹם בֵּין יִשְׂרָאֵל וּבֵין הָאֱמֹרִי: 15 וַיִּשְׁפֹּט שְׁמוּאֵל אֶת־יִשְׂרָאֵל כֹּל יְמֵי חַיָּיו: 16 וְהָלַךְ מִדֵּי שָׁנָה בְּשָׁנָה וְסָבַב בֵּית־אֵל וְהַגִּלְגָּל וְהַמִּצְפָּה וְשָׁפַט אֶת־יִשְׂרָאֵל אֵת כָּל־הַמְּקוֹמוֹת הָאֵלֶּה: 17 וּתְשֻׁבָתוֹ הָרָמָתָה כִּי־שָׁם בֵּיתוֹ וְשָׁם שָׁפַט אֶת־יִשְׂרָאֵל וַיִּבֶן־שָׁם מִזְבֵּחַ לַיהוָה: פ

ח וַיְהִי כַּאֲשֶׁר זָקֵן שְׁמוּאֵל וַיָּשֶׂם אֶת־בָּנָיו שֹׁפְטִים לְיִשְׂרָאֵל: 2 וַיְהִי שֶׁם־בְּנוֹ הַבְּכוֹר יוֹאֵל וְשֵׁם מִשְׁנֵהוּ אֲבִיָּה שֹׁפְטִים בִּבְאֵר שָׁבַע: 3 וְלֹא־הָלְכוּ בָנָיו בִּדְרָכָו וַיִּטּוּ אַחֲרֵי הַבָּצַע וַיִּקְחוּ־שֹׁחַד וַיַּטּוּ מִשְׁפָּט: פ 4 וַיִּתְקַבְּצוּ כֹּל זִקְנֵי יִשְׂרָאֵל וַיָּבֹאוּ אֶל־שְׁמוּאֵל הָרָמָתָה: 5 וַיֹּאמְרוּ אֵלָיו הִנֵּה אַתָּה זָקַנְתָּ וּבָנֶיךָ לֹא הָלְכוּ בִּדְרָכֶךָ עַתָּה שִׂימָה־לָּנוּ מֶלֶךְ לְשָׁפְטֵנוּ כְּכָל־הַגּוֹיִם: 6 וַיֵּרַע הַדָּבָר בְּעֵינֵי שְׁמוּאֵל כַּאֲשֶׁר אָמְרוּ תְּנָה־לָּנוּ מֶלֶךְ לְשָׁפְטֵנוּ וַיִּתְפַּלֵּל שְׁמוּאֵל אֶל־יְהוָה: פ 7 וַיֹּאמֶר יְהוָה אֶל־שְׁמוּאֵל שְׁמַע בְּקוֹל הָעָם לְכֹל אֲשֶׁר־יֹאמְרוּ אֵלֶיךָ כִּי לֹא אֹתְךָ מָאָסוּ כִּי־אֹתִי מָאֲסוּ מִמְּלֹךְ עֲלֵיהֶם: 8 כְּכָל־הַמַּעֲשִׂים אֲשֶׁר־עָשׂוּ מִיּוֹם הַעֲלֹתִי אֹתָם מִמִּצְרַיִם וְעַד־הַיּוֹם הַזֶּה וַיַּעַזְבֻנִי וַיַּעַבְדוּ אֱלֹהִים אֲחֵרִים כֵּן הֵמָּה עֹשִׂים גַּם־לָךְ: 9 וְעַתָּה שְׁמַע בְּקוֹלָם אַךְ כִּי־הָעֵד תָּעִיד בָּהֶם וְהִגַּדְתָּ לָהֶם מִשְׁפַּט הַמֶּלֶךְ אֲשֶׁר יִמְלֹךְ עֲלֵיהֶם: ס 10 וַיֹּאמֶר שְׁמוּאֵל אֵת כָּל־דִּבְרֵי יְהוָה אֶל־הָעָם הַשֹּׁאֲלִים מֵאִתּוֹ מֶלֶךְ: ס 11 וַיֹּאמֶר זֶה יִהְיֶה מִשְׁפַּט הַמֶּלֶךְ אֲשֶׁר יִמְלֹךְ עֲלֵיכֶם אֶת־בְּנֵיכֶם יִקָּח וְשָׂם לוֹ בְּמֶרְכַּבְתּוֹ וּבְפָרָשָׁיו וְרָצוּ לִפְנֵי מֶרְכַּבְתּוֹ: 12 וְלָשׂוּם לוֹ שָׂרֵי אֲלָפִים וְשָׂרֵי חֲמִשִּׁים וְלַחֲרֹשׁ חֲרִישׁוֹ

ח 3 בִּדְרָכָו

harvest, and *some* to make his weapons of war and equipment for his chariots. [13] He will take your daughters *to be* perfumers, cooks, and bakers. [14] And he will take the best of your fields, your vineyards, and your olive groves, and give *them* to his servants. [15] He will take a tenth of your grain and your vintage, and give it to his officers and servants. [16] And he will take your male servants, your female servants, your finest young men, and your donkeys, and put *them* to his work. [17] He will take a tenth of your sheep. And you will be his servants. [18] And you will cry out in that day because of your king whom you have chosen for yourselves, and the LORD will not hear you in that day."

[19] Nevertheless the people refused to obey the voice of Samuel; and they said, "No, but we will have a king over us, [20] that we also may be like all the nations, and that our king may judge us and go out before us and fight our battles."

[21] And Samuel heard all the words of the people, and he repeated them in the hearing of the LORD. [22] So the LORD said to Samuel, "Heed their voice, and make them a king."

And Samuel said to the men of Israel, "Every man go to his city."

9 There was a man of Benjamin whose name *was* Kish the son of Abiel, the son of Zeror, the son of Bechorath, the son of Aphiah, a Benjamite, a mighty man of power. [2] And he had a choice and handsome son whose name *was* Saul. *There was* not a more handsome person than he among the children of Israel. From his shoulders upward *he was* taller than any of the people.

[3] Now the donkeys of Kish, Saul's father, were lost. And Kish said to his son Saul, "Please take one of the servants with you, and arise, go and look for the donkeys." [4] So he passed through the mountains of Ephraim and through the land of Shalisha, but they did not find *them*. Then they passed through the land of Shaalim, and *they were* not *there*. Then he passed through the land of the Benjamites, but they did not find *them*.

[5] When they had come to the land of Zuph, Saul said to his servant who *was* with him, "Come, let us return, lest my father cease *caring* about the donkeys and become worried about us."

[6] And he said to him, "Look now, *there is* in this city a man of God, and *he is* an honorable man; all that he says surely comes to pass. So let us go there; perhaps he can show us the way that we should go."

וְלִקְצֹר קְצִירוֹ וְלַעֲשׂוֹת כְּלֵי־מִלְחַמְתּוֹ וּכְלֵי רִכְבּוֹ׃
13 וְאֶת־בְּנוֹתֵיכֶם יִקָּח לְרַקָּחוֹת וּלְטַבָּחוֹת וּלְאֹפוֹת׃
14 וְאֶת־שְׂדוֹתֵיכֶם וְאֶת־כַּרְמֵיכֶם וְזֵיתֵיכֶם הַטּוֹבִים יִקָּח וְנָתַן לַעֲבָדָיו׃ 15 וְזַרְעֵיכֶם וְכַרְמֵיכֶם יַעְשֹׂר וְנָתַן לְסָרִיסָיו וְלַעֲבָדָיו׃ 16 וְאֶת־עַבְדֵיכֶם וְאֶת־שִׁפְחוֹתֵיכֶם וְאֶת־בַּחוּרֵיכֶם הַטּוֹבִים וְאֶת־חֲמוֹרֵיכֶם יִקָּח וְעָשָׂה לִמְלַאכְתּוֹ׃ 17 צֹאנְכֶם יַעְשֹׂר וְאַתֶּם תִּהְיוּ־לוֹ לַעֲבָדִים׃ 18 וּזְעַקְתֶּם בַּיּוֹם הַהוּא מִלִּפְנֵי מַלְכְּכֶם אֲשֶׁר בְּחַרְתֶּם לָכֶם וְלֹא־יַעֲנֶה יְהֹוָה אֶתְכֶם בַּיּוֹם הַהוּא׃ 19 וַיְמָאֲנוּ הָעָם לִשְׁמֹעַ בְּקוֹל שְׁמוּאֵל וַיֹּאמְרוּ לֹּא כִּי אִם־מֶלֶךְ יִהְיֶה עָלֵינוּ׃ 20 וְהָיִינוּ גַם־אֲנַחְנוּ כְּכָל־הַגּוֹיִם וּשְׁפָטָנוּ מַלְכֵּנוּ וְיָצָא לְפָנֵינוּ וְנִלְחַם אֶת־מִלְחֲמֹתֵנוּ׃ 21 וַיִּשְׁמַע שְׁמוּאֵל אֵת כָּל־דִּבְרֵי הָעָם וַיְדַבְּרֵם בְּאָזְנֵי יְהֹוָה׃ פ
22 וַיֹּאמֶר יְהֹוָה אֶל־שְׁמוּאֵל שְׁמַע בְּקוֹלָם וְהִמְלַכְתָּ לָהֶם מֶלֶךְ וַיֹּאמֶר שְׁמוּאֵל אֶל־אַנְשֵׁי יִשְׂרָאֵל לְכוּ אִישׁ לְעִירוֹ׃ פ

ט וַיְהִי־אִישׁ מִבִּן־יָמִין וּשְׁמוֹ קִישׁ בֶּן־אֲבִיאֵל בֶּן־צְרוֹר בֶּן־בְּכוֹרַת בֶּן־אֲפִיחַ בֶּן־אִישׁ יְמִינִי גִּבּוֹר חָיִל׃ 2 וְלוֹ־הָיָה בֵן וּשְׁמוֹ שָׁאוּל בָּחוּר וָטוֹב וְאֵין אִישׁ מִבְּנֵי יִשְׂרָאֵל טוֹב מִמֶּנּוּ מִשִּׁכְמוֹ וָמַעְלָה גָּבֹהַּ מִכָּל־הָעָם׃ 3 וַתֹּאבַדְנָה הָאֲתֹנוֹת לְקִישׁ אֲבִי שָׁאוּל וַיֹּאמֶר קִישׁ אֶל־שָׁאוּל בְּנוֹ קַח־נָא אִתְּךָ אֶת־אַחַד מֵהַנְּעָרִים וְקוּם לֵךְ בַּקֵּשׁ אֶת־הָאֲתֹנֹת׃ 4 וַיַּעֲבֹר בְּהַר־אֶפְרַיִם וַיַּעֲבֹר בְּאֶרֶץ־שָׁלִשָׁה וְלֹא מָצָאוּ וַיַּעַבְרוּ בְאֶרֶץ־שַׁעֲלִים וָאַיִן וַיַּעֲבֹר בְּאֶרֶץ־יְמִינִי וְלֹא מָצָאוּ׃ 5 הֵמָּה בָּאוּ בְּאֶרֶץ צוּף וְשָׁאוּל אָמַר לְנַעֲרוֹ אֲשֶׁר־עִמּוֹ לְכָה וְנָשׁוּבָה פֶּן־יֶחְדַּל אָבִי מִן־הָאֲתֹנוֹת וְדָאַג לָנוּ׃ 6 וַיֹּאמֶר לוֹ הִנֵּה־נָא אִישׁ־אֱלֹהִים בָּעִיר הַזֹּאת וְהָאִישׁ נִכְבָּד כֹּל אֲשֶׁר־יְדַבֵּר בּוֹא יָבוֹא עַתָּה נֵלְכָה שָּׁם אוּלַי

7 Then Saul said to his servant, "But look, *if we go*, what shall we bring the man? For the bread in our vessels is all gone, and *there is* no present to bring to the man of God. What do we have?"

8 And the servant answered Saul again and said, "Look, I have here at hand one-fourth of a shekel of silver. I will give *that* to the man of God, to tell us our way." 9 (Formerly in Israel, when a man went to inquire of God, he spoke thus: "Come, let us go to the seer"; for *he who is* now *called* a prophet was formerly called a seer.)

10 Then Saul said to his servant, "Well said; come, let us go." So they went to the city where the man of God *was*.

11 As they went up the hill to the city, they met some young women going out to draw water, and said to them, "Is the seer here?"

12 And they answered them and said, "Yes, there he is, just ahead of you. Hurry now; for today he came to this city, because there is a sacrifice of the people today on the high place. 13 As soon as you come into the city, you will surely find him before he goes up to the high place to eat. For the people will not eat until he comes, because he must bless the sacrifice; afterward those who are invited will eat. Now therefore, go up, for about this time you will find him." 14 So they went up to the city. As they were coming into the city, there was Samuel, coming out toward them on his way up to the high place.

15 Now the LORD had told Samuel in his ear the day before Saul came, saying, 16 "Tomorrow about this time I will send you a man from the land of Benjamin, and you shall anoint him commander over My people Israel, that he may save My people from the hand of the Philistines; for I have looked upon My people, because their cry has come to Me."

17 So when Samuel saw Saul, the LORD said to him, "There he is, the man of whom I spoke to you. This one shall reign over My people." 18 Then Saul drew near to Samuel in the gate, and said, "Please tell me, where *is* the seer's house?"

19 Samuel answered Saul and said, "I *am* the seer. Go up before me to the high place, for you shall eat with me today; and tomorrow I will let you go and will tell you all that *is* in your heart. 20 But as for your donkeys that were lost three days ago, do not be anxious about them, for they have been found. And on whom *is* all the desire of Israel? *Is it* not on you and on all your father's house?"

7 וַיֹּאמֶר הַגִּיד לָּנוּ אֶת־דַּרְכֵּנוּ אֲשֶׁר־הָלַכְנוּ עָלֶיהָ: וַיֹּאמֶר שָׁאוּל לְנַעֲרוֹ וְהִנֵּה נֵלֵךְ וּמַה־נָּבִיא לָאִישׁ כִּי הַלֶּחֶם אָזַל מִכֵּלֵינוּ וּתְשׁוּרָה אֵין־לְהָבִיא לְאִישׁ הָאֱלֹהִים מָה אִתָּנוּ: 8 וַיֹּסֶף הַנַּעַר לַעֲנוֹת אֶת־שָׁאוּל וַיֹּאמֶר הִנֵּה נִמְצָא בְיָדִי רֶבַע שֶׁקֶל כָּסֶף וְנָתַתִּי לְאִישׁ הָאֱלֹהִים וְהִגִּיד לָנוּ אֶת־דַּרְכֵּנוּ:

9 לְפָנִים בְּיִשְׂרָאֵל כֹּה־אָמַר הָאִישׁ בְּלֶכְתּוֹ לִדְרוֹשׁ אֱלֹהִים לְכוּ וְנֵלְכָה עַד־הָרֹאֶה כִּי לַנָּבִיא הַיּוֹם יִקָּרֵא לְפָנִים הָרֹאֶה: 10 וַיֹּאמֶר שָׁאוּל לְנַעֲרוֹ טוֹב דְּבָרְךָ לְכָה נֵלֵכָה וַיֵּלְכוּ אֶל־הָעִיר אֲשֶׁר־שָׁם אִישׁ הָאֱלֹהִים: 11 הֵמָּה עֹלִים בְּמַעֲלֵה הָעִיר וְהֵמָּה מָצְאוּ נְעָרוֹת יֹצְאוֹת לִשְׁאֹב מָיִם וַיֹּאמְרוּ לָהֶן הֲיֵשׁ בָּזֶה הָרֹאֶה: 12 וַתַּעֲנֶינָה אוֹתָם וַתֹּאמַרְנָה יֵּשׁ הִנֵּה לְפָנֶיךָ מַהֵר עַתָּה כִּי הַיּוֹם בָּא לָעִיר כִּי זֶבַח הַיּוֹם לָעָם בַּבָּמָה: 13 כְּבֹאֲכֶם הָעִיר כֵּן תִּמְצְאוּן אֹתוֹ בְּטֶרֶם יַעֲלֶה הַבָּמָתָה לֶאֱכֹל כִּי לֹא־יֹאכַל הָעָם עַד־בֹּאוֹ כִּי־הוּא יְבָרֵךְ הַזֶּבַח אַחֲרֵי־כֵן יֹאכְלוּ הַקְּרֻאִים וְעַתָּה עֲלוּ כִּי־אֹתוֹ כְהַיּוֹם תִּמְצְאוּן אֹתוֹ: 14 וַיַּעֲלוּ הָעִיר הֵמָּה בָּאִים בְּתוֹךְ הָעִיר וְהִנֵּה שְׁמוּאֵל יֹצֵא לִקְרָאתָם לַעֲלוֹת הַבָּמָה: ס 15 וַיהֹוָה גָּלָה אֶת־אֹזֶן שְׁמוּאֵל יוֹם אֶחָד לִפְנֵי בוֹא־שָׁאוּל לֵאמֹר:

16 כָּעֵת מָחָר אֶשְׁלַח אֵלֶיךָ אִישׁ מֵאֶרֶץ בִּנְיָמִן וּמְשַׁחְתּוֹ לְנָגִיד עַל־עַמִּי יִשְׂרָאֵל וְהוֹשִׁיעַ אֶת־עַמִּי מִיַּד פְּלִשְׁתִּים כִּי רָאִיתִי אֶת־עַמִּי כִּי בָּאָה צַעֲקָתוֹ אֵלָי: 17 וּשְׁמוּאֵל רָאָה אֶת־שָׁאוּל וַיהֹוָה עָנָהוּ הִנֵּה הָאִישׁ אֲשֶׁר אָמַרְתִּי אֵלֶיךָ זֶה יַעְצֹר בְּעַמִּי: 18 וַיִּגַּשׁ שָׁאוּל אֶת־שְׁמוּאֵל בְּתוֹךְ הַשָּׁעַר וַיֹּאמֶר הַגִּידָה־נָּא לִי אֵי־זֶה בֵּית הָרֹאֶה: 19 וַיַּעַן שְׁמוּאֵל אֶת־שָׁאוּל וַיֹּאמֶר אָנֹכִי הָרֹאֶה עֲלֵה לְפָנַי הַבָּמָה וַאֲכַלְתֶּם עִמִּי הַיּוֹם וְשִׁלַּחְתִּיךָ בַבֹּקֶר וְכֹל אֲשֶׁר בִּלְבָבְךָ אַגִּיד לָךְ: 20 וְלָאֲתֹנוֹת הָאֹבְדוֹת לְךָ הַיּוֹם שְׁלֹשֶׁת הַיָּמִים אַל־תָּשֵׂם אֶת־לִבְּךָ לָהֶם כִּי נִמְצָאוּ וּלְמִי כָּל־חֶמְדַּת יִשְׂרָאֵל הֲלוֹא לְךָ וּלְכֹל

21 And Saul answered and said, "*Am* I not a Benjamite, of the smallest of the tribes of Israel, and my family the least of all the families of the tribe of Benjamin? Why then do you speak like this to me?"

22 Now Samuel took Saul and his servant and brought them into the hall, and had them sit in the place of honor among those who were invited; there *were* about thirty persons. 23 And Samuel said to the cook, "Bring the portion which I gave you, of which I said to you, 'Set it apart.'" 24 So the cook took up the thigh with its upper part and set *it* before Saul. And *Samuel* said, "Here it is, what was kept back. *It* was set apart for you. Eat; for until this time it has been kept for you, since I said I invited the people." So Saul ate with Samuel that day.

25 When they had come down from the high place into the city, *Samuel* spoke with Saul on the top of the house. 26 They arose early; and it was about the dawning of the day that Samuel called to Saul on the top of the house, saying, "Get up, that I may send you on your way." And Saul arose, and both of them went outside, he and Samuel.

27 As they were going down to the outskirts of the city, Samuel said to Saul, "Tell the servant to go on ahead of us." And he went on. "But you stand here awhile, that I may announce to you the word of God."

10 Then Samuel took a flask of oil and poured *it* on his head, and kissed him and said: "*Is it* not because the LORD has anointed you commander over His inheritance? 2 When you have departed from me today, you will find two men by Rachel's tomb in the territory of Benjamin at Zelzah; and they will say to you, 'The donkeys which you went to look for have been found. And now your father has ceased caring about the donkeys and is worrying about you, saying, "What shall I do about my son?"' 3 Then you shall go on forward from there and come to the terebinth tree of Tabor. There three men going up to God at Bethel will meet you, one carrying three young goats, another carrying three loaves of bread, and another carrying a skin of wine. 4 And they will greet you and give you two *loaves* of bread, which you shall receive from their hands. 5 After that you shall come to the hill of God where the Philistine garrison *is*. And it will happen, when you have come there to the city, that you will meet a group of prophets coming down from the high place with a stringed instrument, a tambourine, a flute, and a harp before them; and they will be prophesying. 6 Then the Spirit of the LORD will come upon you, and you will

21 וַיַּעַן שָׁאוּל וַיֹּאמֶר הֲלוֹא בֶן־יְמִינִי אָנֹכִי מִקְּטַנֵּי שִׁבְטֵי יִשְׂרָאֵל וּמִשְׁפַּחְתִּי הַצְּעִרָה מִכָּל־מִשְׁפְּחוֹת שִׁבְטֵי בִנְיָמִן וְלָמָּה דִּבַּרְתָּ אֵלַי כַּדָּבָר הַזֶּה: ס 22 וַיִּקַּח שְׁמוּאֵל אֶת־שָׁאוּל וְאֶת־נַעֲרוֹ וַיְבִיאֵם לִשְׁכָּתָה וַיִּתֵּן לָהֶם מָקוֹם בְּרֹאשׁ הַקְּרוּאִים וְהֵמָּה כִּשְׁלֹשִׁים אִישׁ: 23 וַיֹּאמֶר שְׁמוּאֵל לַטַּבָּח תְּנָה אֶת־הַמָּנָה אֲשֶׁר נָתַתִּי לָךְ אֲשֶׁר אָמַרְתִּי אֵלֶיךָ שִׂים אֹתָהּ עִמָּךְ: 24 וַיָּרֶם הַטַּבָּח אֶת־הַשּׁוֹק וְהֶעָלֶיהָ וַיָּשֶׂם ׀ לִפְנֵי שָׁאוּל וַיֹּאמֶר הִנֵּה הַנִּשְׁאָר שִׂים־לְפָנֶיךָ אֱכֹל כִּי לַמּוֹעֵד שָׁמוּר־לְךָ לֵאמֹר הָעָם ׀ קָרָאתִי וַיֹּאכַל שָׁאוּל עִם־שְׁמוּאֵל בַּיּוֹם הַהוּא: 25 וַיֵּרְדוּ מֵהַבָּמָה הָעִיר וַיְדַבֵּר עִם־שָׁאוּל עַל־הַגָּג: 26 וַיַּשְׁכִּמוּ וַיְהִי כַּעֲלוֹת הַשַּׁחַר וַיִּקְרָא שְׁמוּאֵל אֶל־שָׁאוּל הַגָּגָ֯ה לֵאמֹר קוּמָה וַאֲשַׁלְּחֶךָּ וַיָּקָם שָׁאוּל וַיֵּצְאוּ שְׁנֵיהֶם הוּא וּשְׁמוּאֵל הַחוּצָה: 27 הֵמָּה יוֹרְדִים בִּקְצֵה הָעִיר וּשְׁמוּאֵל אָמַר אֶל־שָׁאוּל אֱמֹר לַנַּעַר וְיַעֲבֹר לְפָנֵינוּ וַיַּעֲבֹר וְאַתָּה עֲמֹד כַּיּוֹם וְאַשְׁמִיעֲךָ אֶת־דְּבַר אֱלֹהִים: פ

י וַיִּקַּח שְׁמוּאֵל אֶת־פַּךְ הַשֶּׁמֶן וַיִּצֹק עַל־רֹאשׁוֹ וַיִּשָּׁקֵהוּ וַיֹּאמֶר הֲלוֹא כִּי־מְשָׁחֲךָ יְהֹוָה עַל־נַחֲלָתוֹ לְנָגִיד: 2 בְּלֶכְתְּךָ הַיּוֹם מֵעִמָּדִי וּמָצָאתָ שְׁנֵי אֲנָשִׁים עִם־קְבֻרַת רָחֵל בִּגְבוּל בִּנְיָמִן בְּצֶלְצַח וְאָמְרוּ אֵלֶיךָ נִמְצְאוּ הָאֲתֹנוֹת אֲשֶׁר הָלַכְתָּ לְבַקֵּשׁ וְהִנֵּה נָטַשׁ אָבִיךָ אֶת־דִּבְרֵי הָאֲתֹנוֹת וְדָאַג לָכֶם לֵאמֹר מָה אֶעֱשֶׂה לִבְנִי: 3 וְחָלַפְתָּ מִשָּׁם וָהָלְאָה וּבָאתָ עַד־אֵלוֹן תָּבוֹר וּמְצָאוּךָ שָׁם שְׁלֹשָׁה אֲנָשִׁים עֹלִים אֶל־הָאֱלֹהִים בֵּית־אֵל אֶחָד נֹשֵׂא ׀ שְׁלֹשָׁה גְדָיִים וְאֶחָד נֹשֵׂא שְׁלֹשֶׁת כִּכְּרוֹת לֶחֶם וְאֶחָד נֹשֵׂא נֵבֶל־יָיִן: 4 וְשָׁאֲלוּ לְךָ לְשָׁלוֹם וְנָתְנוּ לְךָ שְׁתֵּי־לֶחֶם וְלָקַחְתָּ מִיָּדָם: 5 אַחַר כֵּן תָּבוֹא גִּבְעַת הָאֱלֹהִים אֲשֶׁר־שָׁם נְצִבֵי פְלִשְׁתִּים וִיהִי כְבֹאֲךָ שָׁם הָעִיר וּפָגַעְתָּ חֶבֶל נְבִיאִים יֹרְדִים מֵהַבָּמָה וְלִפְנֵיהֶם נֵבֶל וְתֹף וְחָלִיל וְכִנּוֹר וְהֵמָּה מִתְנַבְּאִים: 6 וְצָלְחָה עָלֶיךָ רוּחַ יְהֹוָה וְהִתְנַבִּיתָ עִמָּם וְנֶהְפַּכְתָּ

prophesy with them and be turned into another man. ⁷And let it be, when these signs come to you, *that* you do as the occasion demands; for God *is* with you. ⁸You shall go down before me to Gilgal; and surely I will come down to you to offer burnt offerings *and* make sacrifices of peace offerings. Seven days you shall wait, till I come to you and show you what you should do."

⁹So it was, when he had turned his back to go from Samuel, that God gave him another heart; and all those signs came to pass that day. ¹⁰When they came there to the hill, there was a group of prophets to meet him; then the Spirit of God came upon him, and he prophesied among them. ¹¹And it happened, when all who knew him formerly saw that he indeed prophesied among the prophets, that the people said to one another, "What *is* this *that* has come upon the son of Kish? *Is* Saul also among the prophets?" ¹²Then a man from there answered and said, "But who *is* their father?" Therefore it became a proverb: "*Is* Saul also among the prophets?" ¹³And when he had finished prophesying, he went to the high place.

¹⁴Then Saul's uncle said to him and his servant, "Where did you go?"

So he said, "To look for the donkeys. When we saw that *they were* nowhere *to be found,* we went to Samuel."

¹⁵And Saul's uncle said, "Tell me, please, what Samuel said to you."

¹⁶So Saul said to his uncle, "He told us plainly that the donkeys had been found." But about the matter of the kingdom, he did not tell him what Samuel had said.

¹⁷Then Samuel called the people together to the LORD at Mizpah, ¹⁸and said to the children of Israel, "Thus says the LORD God of Israel: 'I brought up Israel out of Egypt, and delivered you from the hand of the Egyptians *and* from the hand of all kingdoms and from those who oppressed you.' ¹⁹But you have today rejected your God, who Himself saved you from all your adversities and your tribulations; and you have said to Him, 'No, set a king over us!' Now therefore, present yourselves before the LORD by your tribes and by your clans."

²⁰And when Samuel had caused all the tribes of Israel to come near, the tribe of Benjamin was chosen. ²¹When he had caused the tribe of Benjamin to come near by their families, the family of Matri was chosen. And Saul the son of Kish was chosen. But when they sought him, he could not be found. ²²Therefore they inquired of the LORD further, "Has the man come here yet?"

לְאִ֣ישׁ אַחֵ֑ר: ⁷וְהָיָ֞ה כִּ֥י תָבֹ֙אנָה֙ הָאֹת֤וֹת הָאֵ֙לֶּה֙ לָ֔ךְ עֲשֵׂ֥ה לְךָ֖ אֲשֶׁ֣ר תִּמְצָ֣א יָדֶ֑ךָ כִּ֥י הָאֱלֹהִ֖ים עִמָּֽךְ: ⁸וְיָרַדְתָּ֣ לְפָנַי֮ הַגִּלְגָּל֒ וְהִנֵּ֤ה אָֽנֹכִי֙ יֹרֵ֣ד אֵלֶ֔יךָ לְהַעֲל֣וֹת עֹל֔וֹת לִזְבֹּ֖חַ זִבְחֵ֣י שְׁלָמִ֑ים שִׁבְעַ֣ת יָמִ֣ים תּוֹחֵ֗ל עַד־בּוֹאִ֣י אֵלֶ֔יךָ וְהוֹדַעְתִּ֣י לְךָ֔ אֵ֖ת אֲשֶׁ֥ר תַּעֲשֶֽׂה: ⁹וְהָיָ֗ה כְּהַפְנֹת֤וֹ שִׁכְמוֹ֙ לָלֶ֣כֶת מֵעִ֣ם שְׁמוּאֵ֔ל וַיַּהֲפׇךְ־ל֥וֹ אֱלֹהִ֖ים לֵ֣ב אַחֵ֑ר וַיָּבֹ֛אוּ כׇּל־ הָאֹת֥וֹת הָאֵ֖לֶּה בַּיּ֥וֹם הַהֽוּא: ס ¹⁰וַיָּבֹ֙אוּ שָׁ֜ם הַגִּבְעָ֗תָה וְהִנֵּ֤ה חֶֽבֶל־נְבִאִים֙ לִקְרָאת֔וֹ וַתִּצְלַ֤ח עָלָיו֙ ר֣וּחַ אֱלֹהִ֔ים וַיִּתְנַבֵּ֖א בְּתוֹכָֽם: ¹¹וַיְהִ֗י כׇּל־ יֽוֹדְעוֹ֙ מֵֽאִתְּמ֣וֹל שִׁלְשׁ֔וֹם וַיִּרְא֕וּ וְהִנֵּ֥ה עִם־נְבִאִ֖ים נִבָּ֑א וַיֹּ֙אמֶר הָעָ֜ם אִ֣ישׁ אֶל־רֵעֵ֗הוּ מַה־זֶּה֙ הָיָ֣ה לְבֶן־קִ֔ישׁ הֲגַ֥ם שָׁא֖וּל בַּנְּבִיאִֽים: ¹²וַיַּ֨עַן אִ֣ישׁ מִשָּׁם֮ וַיֹּ֙אמֶר֙ וּמִ֣י אֲבִיהֶ֑ם עַל־כֵּן֙ הָיְתָ֣ה לְמָשָׁ֔ל הֲגַ֥ם שָׁא֖וּל בַּנְּבִאִֽים: ¹³וַיְכַל֙ מֵֽהִתְנַבּ֔וֹת וַיָּבֹ֖א הַבָּמָֽה: ¹⁴וַיֹּ֙אמֶר֩ דּ֨וֹד שָׁא֤וּל אֵלָיו֙ וְאֶֽל־נַעֲר֔וֹ אָ֖ן הֲלַכְתֶּ֑ם וַיֹּ֙אמֶר֙ לְבַקֵּ֣שׁ אֶת־הָ֣אֲתֹנ֔וֹת וַנִּרְאֶ֣ה כִי־אַ֔יִן וַנָּב֖וֹא אֶל־שְׁמוּאֵֽל: ¹⁵וַיֹּ֕אמֶר דּ֖וֹד שָׁא֑וּל הַגִּֽידָה־נָּ֣א לִ֔י מָֽה־אָמַ֥ר לָכֶ֖ם שְׁמוּאֵֽל: ¹⁶וַיֹּ֤אמֶר שָׁאוּל֙ אֶל־דּוֹד֔וֹ הַגֵּ֤ד הִגִּיד֙ לָ֔נוּ כִּ֥י נִמְצְא֖וּ הָאֲתֹנ֑וֹת וְאֶת־דְּבַ֤ר הַמְּלוּכָה֙ לֹֽא־הִגִּ֣יד ל֔וֹ אֲשֶׁ֥ר אָמַ֖ר שְׁמוּאֵֽל: פ

¹⁷וַיַּצְעֵ֤ק שְׁמוּאֵל֙ אֶת־הָעָ֔ם אֶל־יְהֹוָ֖ה הַמִּצְפָּֽה: ¹⁸וַיֹּ֣אמֶר ׀ אֶל־בְּנֵ֣י יִשְׂרָאֵ֗ל פ כֹּֽה־אָמַ֤ר יְהֹוָה֙ אֱלֹהֵ֣י יִשְׂרָאֵ֔ל אָנֹכִ֛י הֶעֱלֵ֥יתִי אֶת־יִשְׂרָאֵ֖ל מִמִּצְרָ֑יִם וָאַצִּ֤יל אֶתְכֶם֙ מִיַּ֣ד מִצְרַ֔יִם וּמִיַּד֙ כׇּל־הַמַּמְלָכ֔וֹת הַלֹּחֲצִ֖ים אֶתְכֶֽם: ¹⁹וְאַתֶּ֨ם הַיּ֜וֹם מְאַסְתֶּ֣ם אֶת־אֱלֹֽהֵיכֶ֗ם אֲשֶׁר־ה֣וּא מוֹשִׁ֣יעַ לָכֶ֗ם מִכׇּל־רָעֽוֹתֵיכֶם֙ וְצָ֣רֹתֵיכֶ֔ם וַתֹּ֣אמְרוּ ל֔וֹ כִּי־מֶ֖לֶךְ תָּשִׂ֣ים עָלֵ֑ינוּ וְעַתָּ֗ה הִֽתְיַצְּבוּ֙ לִפְנֵ֣י יְהֹוָ֔ה לְשִׁבְטֵיכֶ֖ם וּלְאַלְפֵיכֶֽם: ²⁰וַיַּקְרֵ֣ב שְׁמוּאֵ֔ל אֵ֖ת כׇּל־שִׁבְטֵ֣י יִשְׂרָאֵ֑ל וַיִּלָּכֵ֖ד שֵׁ֥בֶט בִּנְיָמִֽן:

²¹וַיַּקְרֵ֞ב אֶת־שֵׁ֤בֶט בִּנְיָמִן֙ לְמִשְׁפְּחֹתָ֔ו וַתִּלָּכֵ֖ד מִשְׁפַּ֣חַת הַמַּטְרִ֑י וַיִּלָּכֵד֙ שָׁא֣וּל בֶּן־קִ֔ישׁ וַיְבַקְשֻׁ֖הוּ וְלֹ֣א נִמְצָֽא: ²²וַיִּשְׁאֲלוּ־עוֹד֙ בַּֽיהֹוָ֔ה הֲבָ֥א ע֖וֹד הֲלֹ֣ם אִ֑ישׁ ס וַיֹּ֣אמֶר יְהֹוָ֔ה הִנֵּה־ה֥וּא נֶחְבָּ֖א

⁷ תָּבֹ֑אנָה 21 לְמִשְׁפְּחֹתָֽיו

And the LORD answered, "There he is, hidden among the equipment."

23 So they ran and brought him from there; and when he stood among the people, he was taller than any of the people from his shoulders upward. 24 And Samuel said to all the people, "Do you see him whom the LORD has chosen, that *there is* no one like him among all the people?"

So all the people shouted and said, "Long live the king!"

25 Then Samuel explained to the people the behavior of royalty, and wrote *it* in a book and laid *it* up before the LORD. And Samuel sent all the people away, every man to his house. 26 And Saul also went home to Gibeah; and valiant *men* went with him, whose hearts God had touched. 27 But some rebels said, "How can this man save us?" So they despised him, and brought him no presents. But he held his peace.

11 Then Nahash the Ammonite came up and encamped against Jabesh Gilead; and all the men of Jabesh said to Nahash, "Make a covenant with us, and we will serve you."

2 And Nahash the Ammonite answered them, "On this *condition* I will make *a covenant* with you, that I may put out all your right eyes, and bring reproach on all Israel."

3 Then the elders of Jabesh said to him, "Hold off for seven days, that we may send messengers to all the territory of Israel. And then, if *there is* no one to save us, we will come out to you."

4 So the messengers came to Gibeah of Saul and told the news in the hearing of the people. And all the people lifted up their voices and wept. 5 Now there was Saul, coming behind the herd from the field; and Saul said, "What *troubles* the people, that they weep?" And they told him the words of the men of Jabesh. 6 Then the Spirit of God came upon Saul when he heard this news, and his anger was greatly aroused. 7 So he took a yoke of oxen and cut them in pieces, and sent *them* throughout all the territory of Israel by the hands of messengers, saying, "Whoever does not go out with Saul and Samuel to battle, so it shall be done to his oxen."

And the fear of the LORD fell on the people, and they came out with one consent. 8 When he numbered them in Bezek, the children of Israel were three hundred thousand, and the men of Judah thirty thousand. 9 And they said to the messengers who came, "Thus you shall say to the men of Jabesh Gilead: 'Tomorrow, by *the time* the sun is hot, you shall have help.'" Then the messengers came and reported *it* to the men of

אֶל־הַכֵּלִֽים: 23 וַיָּרֻ֫צוּ֮ וַיִּקָּחֻ֣הוּ מִשָּׁם֒ וַיִּתְיַצֵּ֖ב בְּת֣וֹךְ הָעָ֑ם וַיִּגְבַּהּ֙ מִכָּל־הָעָ֔ם מִשִּׁכְמ֖וֹ וָמָֽעְלָה: 24 וַיֹּ֨אמֶר שְׁמוּאֵ֜ל אֶל־כָּל־הָעָ֗ם הַרְּאִיתֶם֙ אֲשֶׁ֣ר בָּֽחַר־בּ֣וֹ יְהֹוָ֔ה כִּ֛י אֵ֥ין כָּמֹ֖הוּ בְּכָל־הָעָ֑ם וַיָּרִ֤עוּ כָל־הָעָם֙ וַיֹּ֣אמְר֔וּ יְחִ֖י הַמֶּֽלֶךְ: פ

25 וַיְדַבֵּ֣ר שְׁמוּאֵ֣ל אֶל־הָעָ֗ם אֵ֚ת מִשְׁפַּ֣ט הַמְּלֻכָ֔ה וַיִּכְתֹּ֣ב בַּסֵּ֔פֶר וַיַּנַּ֖ח לִפְנֵ֣י יְהֹוָ֑ה וַיְשַׁלַּ֧ח שְׁמוּאֵ֛ל אֶת־כָּל־הָעָ֖ם אִ֥ישׁ לְבֵיתֽוֹ: 26 וְגַ֨ם־שָׁא֔וּל הָלַ֥ךְ לְבֵית֖וֹ גִּבְעָ֑תָה וַיֵּלְכ֣וּ עִמּ֔וֹ הַחַ֕יִל אֲשֶׁר־נָגַ֥ע אֱלֹהִ֖ים בְּלִבָּֽם: 27 וּבְנֵ֧י בְלִיַּ֣עַל אָמְר֗וּ מַה־יֹּשִׁעֵ֙נוּ֙ זֶ֔ה וַיִּבְזֻ֕הוּ וְלֹֽא־הֵבִ֥יאוּ ל֖וֹ מִנְחָ֑ה וַיְהִ֖י כְּמַחֲרִֽישׁ: פ

יא וַיַּ֗עַל נָחָשׁ֙ הָֽעַמּוֹנִ֔י וַיִּ֖חַן עַל־יָבֵ֣שׁ גִּלְעָ֑ד וַיֹּ֨אמְר֜וּ כָּל־אַנְשֵׁ֤י יָבֵישׁ֙ אֶל־נָחָ֔שׁ כְּרָת־לָ֥נוּ בְרִ֖ית וְנַעַבְדֶֽךָ:

2 וַיֹּ֣אמֶר אֲלֵיהֶ֗ם נָחָשׁ֙ הָעַמּוֹנִ֔י בְּזֹאת֙ אֶכְרֹ֣ת לָכֶ֔ם בִּנְק֖וֹר לָכֶ֣ם כָּל־עֵ֣ין יָמִ֑ין וְשַׂמְתִּ֥יהָ חֶרְפָּ֖ה עַל־כָּל־יִשְׂרָאֵֽל: 3 וַיֹּֽאמְר֨וּ אֵלָ֜יו זִקְנֵ֣י יָבֵ֗ישׁ הֶ֤רֶף לָ֙נוּ֙ שִׁבְעַ֣ת יָמִ֔ים וְנִשְׁלְחָה֙ מַלְאָכִ֔ים בְּכֹ֖ל גְּב֣וּל יִשְׂרָאֵ֑ל וְאִם־אֵ֥ין מוֹשִׁ֛יעַ אֹתָ֖נוּ וְיָצָ֥אנוּ אֵלֶֽיךָ: 4 וַיָּבֹ֤אוּ הַמַּלְאָכִים֙ גִּבְעַ֣ת שָׁא֔וּל וַיְדַבְּר֥וּ הַדְּבָרִ֖ים בְּאָזְנֵ֣י הָעָ֑ם וַיִּשְׂא֧וּ כָל־הָעָ֛ם אֶת־קוֹלָ֖ם וַיִּבְכּֽוּ: 5 וְהִנֵּ֣ה שָׁא֗וּל בָּ֣א אַחֲרֵ֤י הַבָּקָר֙ מִן־הַשָּׂדֶ֔ה וַיֹּ֣אמֶר שָׁא֔וּל מַה־לָּעָ֖ם כִּ֣י יִבְכּ֑וּ וַיְסַ֙פְּרוּ־ל֔וֹ אֶת־דִּבְרֵ֖י אַנְשֵׁ֥י יָבֵֽישׁ: 6 וַתִּצְלַ֧ח רֽוּחַ־אֱלֹהִ֛ים עַל־שָׁא֖וּל בְּשָׁמְע֣וֹ‏ אֶת־הַדְּבָרִ֣ים הָאֵ֑לֶּה וַיִּ֥חַר אַפּ֖וֹ מְאֹֽד: 7 וַיִּקַּח֩ צֶ֨מֶד בָּקָ֜ר וַֽיְנַתְּחֵ֗הוּ וַיְשַׁלַּ֞ח בְּכָל־גְּב֤וּל יִשְׂרָאֵל֙ בְּיַ֣ד הַמַּלְאָכִ֣ים ׀ לֵאמֹ֗ר אֲשֶׁ֨ר אֵינֶ֜נּוּ יֹצֵ֣א אַחֲרֵ֤י שָׁאוּל֙ וְאַחַ֣ר שְׁמוּאֵ֔ל כֹּ֥ה יֵעָשֶׂ֖ה לִבְקָר֑וֹ וַיִּפֹּ֤ל פַּֽחַד־יְהֹוָה֙ עַל־הָעָ֔ם וַיֵּצְא֖וּ כְּאִ֥ישׁ אֶחָֽד: 8 וַֽיִּפְקְדֵ֖ם בְּבָ֑זֶק וַיִּהְי֤וּ בְנֵֽי־יִשְׂרָאֵל֙ שְׁלֹ֣שׁ מֵא֣וֹת אֶ֔לֶף וְאִ֥ישׁ יְהוּדָ֖ה שְׁלֹשִׁ֥ים אָֽלֶף: 9 וַיֹּאמְר֣וּ לַמַּלְאָכִ֣ים הַבָּאִ֗ים כֹּ֤ה תֹֽאמְרוּן֙ לְאִישׁ֙ יָבֵ֣ישׁ גִּלְעָ֔ד מָחָ֛ר תִּֽהְיֶה־לָכֶ֥ם תְּשׁוּעָ֖ה כְּחֹ֣ם‏ הַשָּׁ֑מֶשׁ וַיָּבֹ֣אוּ

Jabesh, and they were glad. ¹⁰Therefore the men of Jabesh said, "Tomorrow we will come out to you, and you may do with us whatever seems good to you."

¹¹So it was, on the next day, that Saul put the people in three companies; and they came into the midst of the camp in the morning watch, and killed Ammonites until the heat of the day. And it happened that those who survived were scattered, so that no two of them were left together.

¹²Then the people said to Samuel, "Who is he who said, 'Shall Saul reign over us?' Bring the men, that we may put them to death."

¹³But Saul said, "Not a man shall be put to death this day, for today the LORD has accomplished salvation in Israel."

¹⁴Then Samuel said to the people, "Come, let us go to Gilgal and renew the kingdom there." ¹⁵So all the people went to Gilgal, and there they made Saul king before the LORD in Gilgal. There they made sacrifices of peace offerings before the LORD, and there Saul and all the men of Israel rejoiced greatly.

12 Now Samuel said to all Israel: "Indeed I have heeded your voice in all that you said to me, and have made a king over you. ²And now here is the king, walking before you; and I am old and grayheaded, and look, my sons are with you. I have walked before you from my childhood to this day. ³Here I am. Witness against me before the LORD and before His anointed: Whose ox have I taken, or whose donkey have I taken, or whom have I cheated? Whom have I oppressed, or from whose hand have I received any bribe with which to blind my eyes? I will restore it to you."

⁴And they said, "You have not cheated us or oppressed us, nor have you taken anything from any man's hand."

⁵Then he said to them, "The LORD is witness against you, and His anointed is witness this day, that you have not found anything in my hand."

And they answered, "He is witness."

⁶Then Samuel said to the people, "It is the LORD who raised up Moses and Aaron, and who brought your fathers up from the land of Egypt. ⁷Now therefore, stand still, that I may reason with you before the LORD concerning all the righteous acts of the LORD which He did to you and your fathers: ⁸When Jacob had gone into Egypt, and your fathers cried out to the LORD, then the LORD sent Moses and Aaron, who brought your fathers out of Egypt and made them dwell in this place. ⁹And when they forgot the LORD their God, He sold them into the hand of Sisera, commander of the army of

הַמַּלְאָכִים וַיַּגִּידוּ לְאַנְשֵׁי יָבֵישׁ וַיִּשְׂמָחוּ: 10 וַיֹּאמְרוּ אַנְשֵׁי יָבֵישׁ מָחָר נֵצֵא אֲלֵיכֶם וַעֲשִׂיתֶם לָנוּ כְּכָל־הַטּוֹב בְּעֵינֵיכֶם: ס 11 וַיְהִי מִמָּחֳרָת וַיָּשֶׂם שָׁאוּל אֶת־הָעָם שְׁלֹשָׁה רָאשִׁים וַיָּבֹאוּ בְתוֹךְ־הַמַּחֲנֶה בְּאַשְׁמֹרֶת הַבֹּקֶר וַיַּכּוּ אֶת־עַמּוֹן עַד־חֹם הַיּוֹם וַיְהִי הַנִּשְׁאָרִים וַיָּפֻצוּ וְלֹא נִשְׁאֲרוּ־בָם שְׁנַיִם יָחַד: 12 וַיֹּאמֶר הָעָם אֶל־שְׁמוּאֵל מִי הָאֹמֵר שָׁאוּל יִמְלֹךְ עָלֵינוּ תְּנוּ הָאֲנָשִׁים וּנְמִיתֵם: 13 וַיֹּאמֶר שָׁאוּל לֹא־יוּמַת אִישׁ בַּיּוֹם הַזֶּה כִּי הַיּוֹם עָשָׂה־יְהוָה תְּשׁוּעָה בְּיִשְׂרָאֵל: ס 14 וַיֹּאמֶר שְׁמוּאֵל אֶל־הָעָם לְכוּ וְנֵלְכָה הַגִּלְגָּל וּנְחַדֵּשׁ שָׁם הַמְּלוּכָה: 15 וַיֵּלְכוּ כָל־הָעָם הַגִּלְגָּל וַיַּמְלִכוּ שָׁם אֶת־שָׁאוּל לִפְנֵי יְהוָה בַּגִּלְגָּל וַיִּזְבְּחוּ־שָׁם זְבָחִים שְׁלָמִים לִפְנֵי יְהוָה וַיִּשְׂמַח שָׁם שָׁאוּל וְכָל־אַנְשֵׁי יִשְׂרָאֵל עַד־מְאֹד: פ

יב וַיֹּאמֶר שְׁמוּאֵל אֶל־כָּל־יִשְׂרָאֵל הִנֵּה שָׁמַעְתִּי בְקֹלְכֶם לְכֹל אֲשֶׁר־אֲמַרְתֶּם לִי וָאַמְלִיךְ עֲלֵיכֶם מֶלֶךְ: 2 וְעַתָּה הִנֵּה הַמֶּלֶךְ מִתְהַלֵּךְ לִפְנֵיכֶם וַאֲנִי זָקַנְתִּי וָשַׂבְתִּי וּבָנַי הִנָּם אִתְּכֶם וַאֲנִי הִתְהַלַּכְתִּי לִפְנֵיכֶם מִנְּעֻרַי עַד־הַיּוֹם הַזֶּה: 3 הִנְנִי עֲנוּ בִי נֶגֶד יְהוָה וְנֶגֶד מְשִׁיחוֹ אֶת־שׁוֹר | מִי לָקַחְתִּי וַחֲמוֹר מִי לָקַחְתִּי וְאֶת־מִי עָשַׁקְתִּי אֶת־מִי רַצּוֹתִי וּמִיַּד־מִי לָקַחְתִּי כֹפֶר וְאַעְלִים עֵינַי בּוֹ וְאָשִׁיב לָכֶם: 4 וַיֹּאמְרוּ לֹא עֲשַׁקְתָּנוּ וְלֹא רַצּוֹתָנוּ וְלֹא־לָקַחְתָּ מִיַּד־אִישׁ מְאוּמָה: 5 וַיֹּאמֶר אֲלֵיהֶם עֵד יְהוָה בָּכֶם וְעֵד מְשִׁיחוֹ הַיּוֹם הַזֶּה כִּי לֹא מְצָאתֶם בְּיָדִי מְאוּמָה וַיֹּאמֶר עֵד: פ

6 וַיֹּאמֶר שְׁמוּאֵל אֶל־הָעָם יְהוָה אֲשֶׁר עָשָׂה אֶת־מֹשֶׁה וְאֶת־אַהֲרֹן וַאֲשֶׁר הֶעֱלָה אֶת־אֲבֹתֵיכֶם מֵאֶרֶץ מִצְרָיִם: 7 וְעַתָּה הִתְיַצְּבוּ וְאִשָּׁפְטָה אִתְּכֶם לִפְנֵי יְהוָה אֵת כָּל־צִדְקוֹת יְהוָה אֲשֶׁר־עָשָׂה אִתְּכֶם וְאֶת־אֲבוֹתֵיכֶם: 8 כַּאֲשֶׁר־בָּא יַעֲקֹב מִצְרָיִם וַיִּזְעֲקוּ אֲבוֹתֵיכֶם אֶל־יְהוָה וַיִּשְׁלַח יְהוָה אֶת־מֹשֶׁה וְאֶת־אַהֲרֹן וַיּוֹצִיאוּ אֶת־אֲבֹתֵיכֶם מִמִּצְרַיִם וַיֹּשִׁבוּם בַּמָּקוֹם הַזֶּה: 9 וַיִּשְׁכְּחוּ אֶת־יְהוָה אֱלֹהֵיהֶם וַיִּמְכֹּר אֹתָם בְּיַד סִיסְרָא שַׂר־צְבָא חָצוֹר וּבְיַד־פְּלִשְׁתִּים

Hazor, into the hand of the Philistines, and into the hand of the king of Moab; and they fought against them. 10 Then they cried out to the LORD, and said, 'We have sinned, because we have forsaken the LORD and served the Baals and Ashtoreths; but now deliver us from the hand of our enemies, and we will serve You.' 11 And the LORD sent Jerubbaal, Bedan, Jephthah, and Samuel, and delivered you out of the hand of your enemies on every side; and you dwelt in safety. 12 And when you saw that Nahash king of the Ammonites came against you, you said to me, 'No, but a king shall reign over us,' when the LORD your God *was* your king.

13 "Now therefore, here is the king whom you have chosen *and* whom you have desired. And take note, the LORD has set a king over you. 14 If you fear the LORD and serve Him and obey His voice, and do not rebel against the commandment of the LORD, then both you and the king who reigns over you will continue following the LORD your God. 15 However, if you do not obey the voice of the LORD, but rebel against the commandment of the LORD, then the hand of the LORD will be against you, as *it was* against your fathers.

16 "Now therefore, stand and see this great thing which the LORD will do before your eyes: 17 *Is* today not the wheat harvest? I will call to the LORD, and He will send thunder and rain, that you may perceive and see that your wickedness *is* great, which you have done in the sight of the LORD, in asking a king for yourselves."

18 So Samuel called to the LORD, and the LORD sent thunder and rain that day; and all the people greatly feared the LORD and Samuel.

19 And all the people said to Samuel, "Pray for your servants to the LORD your God, that we may not die; for we have added to all our sins the evil of asking a king for ourselves."

20 Then Samuel said to the people, "Do not fear. You have done all this wickedness; yet do not turn aside from following the LORD, but serve the LORD with all your heart. 21 And do not turn aside; for *then you would go* after empty things which cannot profit or deliver, for they *are* nothing. 22 For the LORD will not forsake His people, for His great name's sake, because it has pleased the LORD to make you His people. 23 Moreover, as for me, far be it from me that I should sin against the LORD in ceasing to pray for you; but I will teach you the good and the right way. 24 Only fear the LORD, and serve Him in truth with all your heart; for consider what great things He has done for you. 25 But if you still do wickedly, you shall be swept away, both you and your king."

וּבְיַד־מֶלֶךְ מוֹאָב וַיִּלָּחֲמוּ בָּם: 10 וַיִּזְעֲקוּ אֶל־
יְהוָה וַיֹּאמֶר חָטָאנוּ כִּי עָזַבְנוּ אֶת־יְהוָה וַנַּעֲבֹד
אֶת־הַבְּעָלִים וְאֶת־הָעַשְׁתָּרוֹת וְעַתָּה הַצִּילֵנוּ מִיַּד
אֹיְבֵינוּ וְנַעַבְדֶךָּ: 11 וַיִּשְׁלַח יְהוָה אֶת־יְרֻבַּעַל וְאֶת־
בְּדָן וְאֶת־יִפְתָּח וְאֶת־שְׁמוּאֵל וַיַּצֵּל אֶתְכֶם מִיַּד
אֹיְבֵיכֶם מִסָּבִיב וַתֵּשְׁבוּ בֶּטַח: 12 וַתִּרְאוּ כִּי־
נָחָשׁ מֶלֶךְ בְּנֵי־עַמּוֹן בָּא עֲלֵיכֶם וַתֹּאמְרוּ לִי לֹא
כִּי־מֶלֶךְ יִמְלֹךְ עָלֵינוּ וַיהוָה אֱלֹהֵיכֶם מַלְכְּכֶם:

13 וְעַתָּה הִנֵּה הַמֶּלֶךְ אֲשֶׁר בְּחַרְתֶּם אֲשֶׁר שְׁאֶלְתֶּם
וְהִנֵּה נָתַן יְהוָה עֲלֵיכֶם מֶלֶךְ: 14 אִם־תִּירְאוּ אֶת־
יְהוָה וַעֲבַדְתֶּם אֹתוֹ וּשְׁמַעְתֶּם בְּקֹלוֹ וְלֹא תַמְרוּ
אֶת־פִּי יְהוָה וִהְיִתֶם גַּם־אַתֶּם וְגַם־הַמֶּלֶךְ אֲשֶׁר
מָלַךְ עֲלֵיכֶם אַחַר יְהוָה אֱלֹהֵיכֶם: 15 וְאִם־לֹא
תִשְׁמְעוּ בְּקוֹל יְהוָה וּמְרִיתֶם אֶת־פִּי יְהוָה וְהָיְתָה
יַד־יְהוָה בָּכֶם וּבַאֲבֹתֵיכֶם: 16 גַּם־עַתָּה הִתְיַצְּבוּ
וּרְאוּ אֶת־הַדָּבָר הַגָּדוֹל הַזֶּה אֲשֶׁר יְהוָה עֹשֶׂה
לְעֵינֵיכֶם: 17 הֲלוֹא קְצִיר־חִטִּים הַיּוֹם אֶקְרָא אֶל־
יְהוָה וְיִתֵּן קֹלוֹת וּמָטָר וּדְעוּ וּרְאוּ כִּי־רָעַתְכֶם
רַבָּה אֲשֶׁר עֲשִׂיתֶם בְּעֵינֵי יְהוָה לִשְׁאוֹל לָכֶם
מֶלֶךְ: ס 18 וַיִּקְרָא שְׁמוּאֵל אֶל־יְהוָה וַיִּתֵּן
יְהוָה קֹלֹת וּמָטָר בַּיּוֹם הַהוּא וַיִּירָא כָל־הָעָם
מְאֹד אֶת־יְהוָה וְאֶת־שְׁמוּאֵל: 19 וַיֹּאמְרוּ כָל־הָעָם
אֶל־שְׁמוּאֵל הִתְפַּלֵּל בְּעַד־עֲבָדֶיךָ אֶל־יְהוָה אֱלֹהֶיךָ
וְאַל־נָמוּת כִּי־יָסַפְנוּ עַל־כָּל־חַטֹּאתֵינוּ רָעָה לִשְׁאֹל
לָנוּ מֶלֶךְ: ס 20 וַיֹּאמֶר שְׁמוּאֵל אֶל־הָעָם
אַל־תִּירָאוּ אַתֶּם עֲשִׂיתֶם אֵת כָּל־הָרָעָה הַזֹּאת אַךְ
אַל־תָּסוּרוּ מֵאַחֲרֵי יְהוָה וַעֲבַדְתֶּם אֶת־יְהוָה בְּכָל־
לְבַבְכֶם: 21 וְלֹא תָּסוּרוּ כִּי אַחֲרֵי הַתֹּהוּ אֲשֶׁר
לֹא־יוֹעִילוּ וְלֹא יַצִּילוּ כִּי־תֹהוּ הֵמָּה: 22 כִּי לֹא־
יִטֹּשׁ יְהוָה אֶת־עַמּוֹ בַּעֲבוּר שְׁמוֹ הַגָּדוֹל כִּי הוֹאִיל
יְהוָה לַעֲשׂוֹת אֶתְכֶם לוֹ לְעָם: 23 גַּם אָנֹכִי חָלִילָה
לִּי מֵחֲטֹא לַיהוָה מֵחֲדֹל לְהִתְפַּלֵּל בַּעַדְכֶם וְהוֹרֵיתִי
אֶתְכֶם בְּדֶרֶךְ הַטּוֹבָה וְהַיְשָׁרָה: 24 אַךְ יְראוּ
אֶת־יְהוָה וַעֲבַדְתֶּם אֹתוֹ בֶּאֱמֶת בְּכָל־לְבַבְכֶם כִּי
רְאוּ אֵת אֲשֶׁר־הִגְדִּל עִמָּכֶם: 25 וְאִם־הָרֵעַ תָּרֵעוּ
גַּם־אַתֶּם גַּם־מַלְכְּכֶם תִּסָּפוּ: פ

13 Saul reigned one year; and when he had reigned two years over Israel, ² Saul chose for himself three thousand *men* of Israel. Two thousand were with Saul in Michmash and in the mountains of Bethel, and a thousand were with Jonathan in Gibeah of Benjamin. The rest of the people he sent away, every man to his tent.

³ And Jonathan attacked the garrison of the Philistines that *was* in Geba, and the Philistines heard *of it.* Then Saul blew the trumpet throughout all the land, saying, "Let the Hebrews hear!" ⁴ Now all Israel heard it said *that* Saul had attacked a garrison of the Philistines, and *that* Israel had also become an abomination to the Philistines. And the people were called together to Saul at Gilgal.

⁵ Then the Philistines gathered together to fight with Israel, thirty thousand chariots and six thousand horsemen, and people as the sand which *is* on the seashore in multitude. And they came up and encamped in Michmash, to the east of Beth Aven. ⁶ When the men of Israel saw that they were in danger (for the people were distressed), then the people hid in caves, in thickets, in rocks, in holes, and in pits. ⁷ And *some of* the Hebrews crossed over the Jordan to the land of Gad and Gilead.

As for Saul, he *was* still in Gilgal, and all the people followed him trembling. ⁸ Then he waited seven days, according to the time set by Samuel. But Samuel did not come to Gilgal; and the people were scattered from him. ⁹ So Saul said, "Bring a burnt offering and peace offerings here to me." And he offered the burnt offering. ¹⁰ Now it happened, as soon as he had finished presenting the burnt offering, that Samuel came; and Saul went out to meet him, that he might greet him.

¹¹ And Samuel said, "What have you done?"

Saul said, "When I saw that the people were scattered from me, and *that* you did not come within the days appointed, and *that* the Philistines gathered together at Michmash, ¹² then I said, 'The Philistines will now come down on me at Gilgal, and I have not made supplication to the LORD.' Therefore I felt compelled, and offered a burnt offering."

¹³ And Samuel said to Saul, "You have done foolishly. You have not kept the commandment of the LORD your God, which He commanded you. For now the LORD would have established your kingdom over Israel forever. ¹⁴ But now your kingdom shall not continue. The LORD has sought for Himself a man after His own heart, and the LORD has commanded him *to be* commander over His people, because you have not kept what the LORD commanded you."

יג בֶּן־שָׁנָה שָׁאוּל בְּמָלְכוֹ וּשְׁתֵּי שָׁנִים מָלַךְ עַל־יִשְׂרָאֵל: 2 וַיִּבְחַר־לוֹ שָׁאוּל שְׁלֹשֶׁת אֲלָפִים מִיִּשְׂרָאֵל וַיִּהְיוּ עִם־שָׁאוּל אַלְפַּיִם בְּמִכְמָשׂ וּבְהַר בֵּית־אֵל וְאֶלֶף הָיוּ עִם־יוֹנָתָן בְּגִבְעַת בִּנְיָמִן וְיֶתֶר הָעָם שִׁלַּח אִישׁ לְאֹהָלָיו: 3 וַיַּךְ יוֹנָתָן אֵת נְצִיב פְּלִשְׁתִּים אֲשֶׁר בְּגֶבַע וַיִּשְׁמְעוּ פְלִשְׁתִּים וְשָׁאוּל תָּקַע בַּשּׁוֹפָר בְּכָל־הָאָרֶץ לֵאמֹר יִשְׁמְעוּ הָעִבְרִים: 4 וְכָל־יִשְׂרָאֵל שָׁמְעוּ לֵאמֹר הִכָּה שָׁאוּל אֶת־נְצִיב פְּלִשְׁתִּים וְגַם־נִבְאַשׁ יִשְׂרָאֵל בַּפְּלִשְׁתִּים וַיִּצָּעֲקוּ הָעָם אַחֲרֵי שָׁאוּל הַגִּלְגָּל: 5 וּפְלִשְׁתִּים נֶאֶסְפוּ לְהִלָּחֵם עִם־יִשְׂרָאֵל שְׁלֹשִׁים אֶלֶף רֶכֶב וְשֵׁשֶׁת אֲלָפִים פָּרָשִׁים וְעָם כַּחוֹל אֲשֶׁר עַל־שְׂפַת־הַיָּם לָרֹב וַיַּעֲלוּ וַיַּחֲנוּ בְמִכְמָשׂ קִדְמַת בֵּית אָוֶן: 6 וְאִישׁ יִשְׂרָאֵל רָאוּ כִּי צַר־לוֹ כִּי נִגַּשׂ הָעָם וַיִּתְחַבְּאוּ הָעָם בַּמְּעָרוֹת וּבַחֲוָחִים וּבַסְּלָעִים וּבַצְּרִחִים וּבַבֹּרוֹת: 7 וְעִבְרִים עָבְרוּ אֶת־הַיַּרְדֵּן אֶרֶץ גָּד וְגִלְעָד וְשָׁאוּל עוֹדֶנּוּ בַגִּלְגָּל וְכָל־הָעָם חָרְדוּ אַחֲרָיו: 8 וַיִּיחֶל ׀ שִׁבְעַת יָמִים לַמּוֹעֵד אֲשֶׁר שְׁמוּאֵל וְלֹא־בָא שְׁמוּאֵל הַגִּלְגָּל וַיָּפֶץ הָעָם מֵעָלָיו: 9 וַיֹּאמֶר שָׁאוּל הַגִּשׁוּ אֵלַי הָעֹלָה וְהַשְּׁלָמִים וַיַּעַל הָעֹלָה: 10 וַיְהִי כְּכַלֹּתוֹ לְהַעֲלוֹת הָעֹלָה וְהִנֵּה שְׁמוּאֵל בָּא וַיֵּצֵא שָׁאוּל לִקְרָאתוֹ לְבָרְכוֹ: 11 וַיֹּאמֶר שְׁמוּאֵל מֶה עָשִׂיתָ וַיֹּאמֶר שָׁאוּל כִּי־רָאִיתִי כִּי־נָפַץ הָעָם מֵעָלַי וְאַתָּה לֹא־בָאתָ לְמוֹעֵד הַיָּמִים וּפְלִשְׁתִּים נֶאֱסָפִים מִכְמָשׂ: 12 וָאֹמַר עַתָּה יֵרְדוּ פְלִשְׁתִּים אֵלַי הַגִּלְגָּל וּפְנֵי יְהֹוָה לֹא חִלִּיתִי וָאֶתְאַפַּק וָאַעֲלֶה הָעֹלָה: 13 וַיֹּאמֶר שְׁמוּאֵל אֶל־שָׁאוּל ס נִסְכָּלְתָּ לֹא שָׁמַרְתָּ אֶת־מִצְוַת יְהֹוָה אֱלֹהֶיךָ אֲשֶׁר צִוָּךְ כִּי עַתָּה הֵכִין יְהֹוָה אֶת־מַמְלַכְתְּךָ אֶל־יִשְׂרָאֵל עַד־עוֹלָם: 14 וְעַתָּה מַמְלַכְתְּךָ לֹא־תָקוּם בִּקֵּשׁ יְהֹוָה לוֹ אִישׁ כִּלְבָבוֹ וַיְצַוֵּהוּ יְהֹוָה לְנָגִיד עַל־עַמּוֹ כִּי לֹא שָׁמַרְתָּ אֵת אֲשֶׁר־צִוְּךָ יְהֹוָה: פ

יג 8 וַיִּיחֶל

15 Then Samuel arose and went up from Gilgal to Gibeah of Benjamin. And Saul numbered the people present with him, about six hundred men.

16 Saul, Jonathan his son, and the people present with them remained in Gibeah of Benjamin. But the Philistines encamped in Michmash. 17 Then raiders came out of the camp of the Philistines in three companies. One company turned onto the road to Ophrah, to the land of Shual, 18 another company turned to the road to Beth Horon, and another company turned to the road of the border that overlooks the Valley of Zeboim toward the wilderness.

19 Now there was no blacksmith to be found throughout all the land of Israel, for the Philistines said, "Lest the Hebrews make swords or spears." 20 But all the Israelites would go down to the Philistines to sharpen each man's plowshare, his mattock, his ax, and his sickle; 21 and the charge for a sharpening was a pim for the plowshares, the mattocks, the forks, and the axes, and to set the points of the goads. 22 So it came about, on the day of battle, that there was neither sword nor spear found in the hand of any of the people who were with Saul and Jonathan. But they were found with Saul and Jonathan his son.

23 And the garrison of the Philistines went out to the pass of Michmash.

14 Now it happened one day that Jonathan the son of Saul said to the young man who bore his armor, "Come, let us go over to the Philistines' garrison that is on the other side." But he did not tell his father. 2 And Saul was sitting in the outskirts of Gibeah under a pomegranate tree which is in Migron. The people who were with him were about six hundred men. 3 Ahijah the son of Ahitub, Ichabod's brother, the son of Phinehas, the son of Eli, the LORD's priest in Shiloh, was wearing an ephod. But the people did not know that Jonathan had gone.

4 Between the passes, by which Jonathan sought to go over to the Philistines' garrison, there was a sharp rock on one side and a sharp rock on the other side. And the name of one was Bozez, and the name of the other Seneh. 5 The front of one faced northward opposite Michmash, and the other southward opposite Gibeah.

6 Then Jonathan said to the young man who bore his armor, "Come, let us go over to the garrison of these uncircumcised; it may be that the LORD will work for us. For nothing restrains the LORD from saving by many or by few."

15 וַיָּקָם שְׁמוּאֵל וַיַּעַל מִן־הַגִּלְגָּל גִּבְעַת בִּנְיָמִן וַיִּפְקֹד שָׁאוּל אֶת־הָעָם הַנִּמְצְאִים עִמּוֹ כְּשֵׁשׁ מֵאוֹת אִישׁ: 16 וְשָׁאוּל וְיוֹנָתָן בְּנוֹ וְהָעָם הַנִּמְצָא עִמָּם יֹשְׁבִים בְּגֶבַע בִּנְיָמִן וּפְלִשְׁתִּים חָנוּ בְמִכְמָשׂ: 17 וַיֵּצֵא הַמַּשְׁחִית מִמַּחֲנֵה פְלִשְׁתִּים שְׁלֹשָׁה רָאשִׁים הָרֹאשׁ אֶחָד יִפְנֶה אֶל־דֶּרֶךְ עָפְרָה אֶל־אֶרֶץ שׁוּעָל: 18 וְהָרֹאשׁ אֶחָד יִפְנֶה דֶּרֶךְ בֵּית חֹרוֹן וְהָרֹאשׁ אֶחָד יִפְנֶה דֶּרֶךְ הַגְּבוּל הַנִּשְׁקָף עַל־גֵּי הַצְּבֹעִים הַמִּדְבָּרָה: ס 19 וְחָרָשׁ לֹא יִמָּצֵא בְּכֹל אֶרֶץ יִשְׂרָאֵל כִּי־אָמַר פְּלִשְׁתִּים פֶּן יַעֲשׂוּ הָעִבְרִים חֶרֶב אוֹ חֲנִית: 20 וַיֵּרְדוּ כָל־יִשְׂרָאֵל הַפְּלִשְׁתִּים לִלְטוֹשׁ אִישׁ אֶת־מַחֲרַשְׁתּוֹ וְאֶת־אֵתוֹ וְאֶת־קַרְדֻּמּוֹ וְאֵת מַחֲרֵשָׁתוֹ: 21 וְהָיְתָה הַפְּצִירָה פִים לַמַּחֲרֵשֹׁת וְלָאֵתִים וְלִשְׁלֹשׁ קִלְּשׁוֹן וּלְהַקַּרְדֻּמִּים וּלְהַצִּיב הַדָּרְבָן: 22 וְהָיָה בְּיוֹם מִלְחֶמֶת וְלֹא נִמְצָא חֶרֶב וַחֲנִית בְּיַד כָּל־הָעָם אֲשֶׁר אֶת־שָׁאוּל וְאֶת־יוֹנָתָן וַתִּמָּצֵא לְשָׁאוּל וּלְיוֹנָתָן בְּנוֹ: 23 וַיֵּצֵא מַצַּב פְּלִשְׁתִּים אֶל־מַעֲבַר מִכְמָשׂ: ס

יד וַיְהִי הַיּוֹם וַיֹּאמֶר יוֹנָתָן בֶּן־שָׁאוּל אֶל־הַנַּעַר נֹשֵׂא כֵלָיו לְכָה וְנַעְבְּרָה אֶל־מַצַּב פְּלִשְׁתִּים אֲשֶׁר מֵעֵבֶר הַלָּז וּלְאָבִיו לֹא הִגִּיד: 2 וְשָׁאוּל יוֹשֵׁב בִּקְצֵה הַגִּבְעָה תַּחַת הָרִמּוֹן אֲשֶׁר בְּמִגְרוֹן וְהָעָם אֲשֶׁר עִמּוֹ כְּשֵׁשׁ מֵאוֹת אִישׁ: 3 וַאֲחִיָּה בֶן־אֲחִטוּב אֲחִי אִיכָבוֹד ׀ בֶּן־פִּינְחָס בֶּן־עֵלִי כֹּהֵן ׀ יְהֹוָה בְּשִׁלוֹ נֹשֵׂא אֵפוֹד וְהָעָם לֹא יָדַע כִּי הָלַךְ יוֹנָתָן: 4 וּבֵין הַמַּעְבְּרוֹת אֲשֶׁר בִּקֵּשׁ יוֹנָתָן לַעֲבֹר עַל־מַצַּב פְּלִשְׁתִּים שֵׁן־הַסֶּלַע מֵהָעֵבֶר מִזֶּה וְשֵׁן־הַסֶּלַע מֵהָעֵבֶר מִזֶּה וְשֵׁם הָאֶחָד בּוֹצֵץ וְשֵׁם הָאֶחָד סֶנֶּה: 5 הַשֵּׁן הָאֶחָד מָצוּק מִצָּפוֹן מוּל מִכְמָשׂ וְהָאֶחָד מִנֶּגֶב מוּל גָּבַע: ס 6 וַיֹּאמֶר יְהוֹנָתָן אֶל־הַנַּעַר ׀ נֹשֵׂא כֵלָיו לְכָה וְנַעְבְּרָה אֶל־מַצַּב הָעֲרֵלִים הָאֵלֶּה אוּלַי יַעֲשֶׂה יְהֹוָה לָנוּ כִּי אֵין לַיהֹוָה

7 So his armorbearer said to him, "Do all that is in your heart. Go then; here I am with you, according to your heart."

8 Then Jonathan said, "Very well, let us cross over to *these* men, and we will show ourselves to them. 9 If they say thus to us, 'Wait until we come to you,' then we will stand still in our place and not go up to them. 10 But if they say thus, 'Come up to us,' then we will go up. For the LORD has delivered them into our hand, and this *will be* a sign to us."

11 So both of them showed themselves to the garrison of the Philistines. And the Philistines said, "Look, the Hebrews are coming out of the holes where they have hidden." 12 Then the men of the garrison called to Jonathan and his armorbearer, and said, "Come up to us, and we will show you something."

Jonathan said to his armorbearer, "Come up after me, for the LORD has delivered them into the hand of Israel." 13 And Jonathan climbed up on his hands and knees with his armorbearer after him; and they fell before Jonathan. And as he came after him, his armorbearer killed them. 14 That first slaughter which Jonathan and his armorbearer made was about twenty men within about half an acre of land.

15 And there was trembling in the camp, in the field, and among all the people. The garrison and the raiders also trembled; and the earth quaked, so that it was a very great trembling. 16 Now the watchmen of Saul in Gibeah of Benjamin looked, and *there* was the multitude, melting away; and they went here and there. 17 Then Saul said to the people who *were* with him, "Now call the roll and see who has gone from us." And when they had called the roll, surprisingly, Jonathan and his armorbearer *were* not *there*. 18 And Saul said to Ahijah, "Bring the ark of God here" (for at that time the ark of God *was* with the children of Israel). 19 Now it happened, while Saul talked to the priest, that the noise which *was* in the camp of the Philistines continued to increase; so Saul said to the priest, "Withdraw your hand." 20 Then Saul and all the people who *were* with him assembled, and they went to the battle; and indeed every man's sword was against his neighbor, *and there was* very great confusion. 21 Moreover the Hebrews *who were* with the Philistines before that time, who went up with them into the camp *from the* surrounding *country,* they also joined the Israelites who *were* with Saul and Jonathan. 22 Likewise all the men of Israel who had hidden in the mountains of Ephraim, *when they*

מַעְצ֔וֹר לְהוֹשִׁ֖יעַ בְּרַ֣ב א֣וֹ בִמְעָֽט׃ 7 וַיֹּ֤אמֶר לוֹ֙ נֹשֵׂ֣א כֵלָ֔יו עֲשֵׂ֖ה כָּל־אֲשֶׁ֣ר בִּלְבָבֶ֑ךָ נְטֵ֣ה לָ֔ךְ הִנְנִ֥י עִמְּךָ֖ כִּלְבָבֶֽךָ׃ ס 8 וַיֹּ֨אמֶר֙ יְה֣וֹנָתָ֔ן הִנֵּ֛ה אֲנַ֥חְנוּ עֹבְרִ֖ים אֶל־הָאֲנָשִׁ֑ים וְנִגְלִ֖ינוּ אֲלֵיהֶֽם׃ 9 אִם־ כֹּ֤ה יֹֽאמְרוּ֙ אֵלֵ֔ינוּ דֹּ֕מּוּ עַד־הַגִּיעֵ֖נוּ אֲלֵיכֶ֑ם וְעָמַ֣דְנוּ תַחְתֵּ֔ינוּ וְלֹ֥א נַעֲלֶ֖ה אֲלֵיהֶֽם׃ 10 וְאִם־כֹּ֨ה יֹאמְר֜וּ עֲלֵ֣ה עָלֵ֗ינוּ וְעָלִ֔ינוּ כִּֽי־נְתָנָ֥ם יְהוָ֖ה בְּיָדֵ֑נוּ וְזֶה־לָּ֖נוּ הָאֽוֹת׃ 11 וַיִּגָּל֣וּ שְׁנֵיהֶ֔ם אֶל־מַצַּ֖ב פְּלִשְׁתִּ֑ים וַיֹּאמְר֣וּ פְלִשְׁתִּ֔ים הִנֵּ֤ה עִבְרִים֙ יֹֽצְאִ֔ים מִן־הַחֹרִ֖ים אֲשֶׁ֥ר הִתְחַבְּאוּ־שָֽׁם׃ 12 וַיַּעֲנוּ֩ אַנְשֵׁ֨י הַמַּצָּבָ֜ה אֶת־יוֹנָתָ֣ן ׀ וְאֶת־נֹשֵׂ֣א כֵלָ֗יו וַיֹּֽאמְרוּ֙ עֲל֣וּ אֵלֵ֔ינוּ וְנוֹדִ֥יעָה אֶתְכֶ֖ם דָּבָ֑ר פ וַיֹּ֨אמֶר יוֹנָתָ֜ן אֶל־נֹשֵׂ֤א כֵלָיו֙ עֲלֵ֣ה אַחֲרַ֔י כִּֽי־נְתָנָ֥ם יְהוָ֖ה בְּיַ֥ד יִשְׂרָאֵֽל׃ 13 וַיַּ֣עַל יוֹנָתָ֗ן עַל־ יָדָיו֙ וְעַל־רַגְלָ֔יו וְנֹשֵׂ֥א כֵלָ֖יו אַחֲרָ֑יו וַֽיִּפְּלוּ֙ לִפְנֵ֣י יוֹנָתָ֔ן וְנֹשֵׂ֥א כֵלָ֖יו מְמוֹתֵ֥ת אַחֲרָֽיו׃ 14 וַתְּהִ֞י הַמַּכָּ֣ה הָרִאשֹׁנָ֗ה אֲשֶׁ֨ר הִכָּ֧ה יוֹנָתָ֛ן וְנֹשֵׂ֥א כֵלָ֖יו כְּעֶשְׂרִ֣ים אִ֑ישׁ כְּבַחֲצִ֥י מַעֲנָ֖ה צֶ֥מֶד שָׂדֶֽה׃ 15 וַתְּהִי֩ חֲרָדָ֨ה בַמַּחֲנֶ֤ה בַשָּׂדֶה֙ וּבְכָל־הָעָ֔ם הַמַּצָּב֙ וְהַמַּשְׁחִ֔ית חָרְד֖וּ גַּם־הֵ֑מָּה וַתִּרְגַּ֣ז הָאָ֔רֶץ וַתְּהִ֖י לְחֶרְדַּ֥ת אֱלֹהִֽים׃ 16 וַיִּרְא֤וּ הַצֹּפִים֙ לְשָׁא֔וּל בְּגִבְעַ֖ת בִּנְיָמִ֑ן וְהִנֵּ֧ה הֶהָמ֛וֹן נָמ֖וֹג וַיֵּ֥לֶךְ וַהֲלֹֽם׃ פ 17 וַיֹּ֣אמֶר שָׁא֗וּל לָעָם֙ אֲשֶׁ֣ר אִתּ֔וֹ פִּקְדוּ־נָ֣א וּרְא֔וּ מִ֥י הָלַ֖ךְ מֵעִמָּ֑נוּ וַֽיִּפְקְד֔וּ וְהִנֵּ֛ה אֵ֥ין יוֹנָתָ֖ן וְנֹשֵׂ֥א כֵלָֽיו׃ 18 וַיֹּ֤אמֶר שָׁאוּל֙ לַֽאֲחִיָּ֔ה הַגִּ֖ישָׁה אֲר֣וֹן הָאֱלֹהִ֑ים כִּֽי־הָיָ֞ה אֲר֧וֹן הָאֱלֹהִ֛ים בַּיּ֥וֹם הַה֖וּא וּבְנֵ֥י יִשְׂרָאֵֽל׃ 19 וַיְהִ֗י עַ֣ד דִּבֶּ֤ר שָׁאוּל֙ אֶל־הַכֹּהֵ֔ן וְהֶהָמ֗וֹן אֲשֶׁר֙ בְּמַחֲנֵ֣ה פְלִשְׁתִּ֔ים וַיֵּ֥לֶךְ הָל֖וֹךְ וָרָ֑ב פ וַיֹּ֧אמֶר שָׁא֛וּל אֶל־הַכֹּהֵ֖ן אֱסֹ֥ף יָדֶֽךָ׃ 20 וַיִּזָּעֵ֣ק שָׁא֗וּל וְכָל־הָעָם֙ אֲשֶׁ֣ר אִתּ֔וֹ וַיָּבֹ֖אוּ עַד־הַמִּלְחָמָ֑ה וְהִנֵּ֨ה הָיְתָ֜ה חֶ֤רֶב אִישׁ֙ בְּרֵעֵ֔הוּ מְהוּמָ֖ה גְּדוֹלָ֥ה מְאֹֽד׃ 21 וְהָעִבְרִ֗ים הָי֤וּ לַפְּלִשְׁתִּים֙ כְּאֶתְמ֣וֹל שִׁלְשׁ֔וֹם אֲשֶׁ֨ר עָל֥וּ עִמָּ֛ם בַּֽמַּחֲנֶ֖ה סָבִ֑יב וְגַם־הֵ֗מָּה לִֽהְיוֹת֙ עִם־יִשְׂרָאֵ֔ל אֲשֶׁ֥ר עִם־שָׁא֖וּל וְיֽוֹנָתָֽן׃ 22 וְכֹל֩ אִ֨ישׁ יִשְׂרָאֵ֜ל הַמִּֽתְחַבְּאִ֤ים בְּהַר־אֶפְרַ֙יִם֙ שָֽׁמְע֔וּ כִּֽי־נָ֖סוּ פְּלִשְׁתִּ֑ים וַֽיַּדְבְּק֥וּ גַם־

heard that the Philistines fled, they also followed
hard after them in the battle. 23 So the LORD saved
Israel that day, and the battle shifted to Beth Aven.

24 And the men of Israel were distressed that day,
for Saul had placed the people under oath, saying,
"Cursed *is* the man who eats *any* food until evening,
before I have taken vengeance on my enemies." So
none of the people tasted food. 25 Now all *the people*
of the land came to a forest; and there was honey
on the ground. 26 And when the people had come into
the woods, there was the honey, dripping; but no
one put his hand to his mouth, for the people feared
the oath. 27 But Jonathan had not heard his father
charge the people with the oath; therefore he
stretched out the end of the rod that *was* in his
hand and dipped it in a honeycomb, and put his
hand to his mouth; and his countenance brightened.
28 Then one of the people said, "Your father strictly
charged the people with an oath, saying, 'Cursed *is*
the man who eats food this day.'" And the people
were faint.

29 But Jonathan said, "My father has troubled
the land. Look now, how my countenance has
brightened because I tasted a little of this honey.
30 How much better if the people had eaten freely
today of the spoil of their enemies which they
found! For now would there not have been a much
greater slaughter among the Philistines?"

31 Now they had driven back the Philistines that
day from Michmash to Aijalon. So the people were
very faint. 32 And the people rushed on the spoil,
and took sheep, oxen, and calves, and slaughtered
them on the ground; and the people ate *them* with
the blood. 33 Then they told Saul, saying, "Look,
the people are sinning against the LORD by eating
with the blood!"

So he said, "You have dealt treacherously; roll a
large stone to me this day." 34 Then Saul said,
"Disperse yourselves among the people, and say to
them, 'Bring me here every man's ox and every
man's sheep, slaughter *them* here, and eat; and do
not sin against the LORD by eating with the
blood.'" So every one of the people brought his
ox with him that night, and slaughtered *it* there.
35 Then Saul built an altar to the LORD. This was
the first altar that he built to the LORD.

36 Now Saul said, "Let us go down after the
Philistines by night, and plunder them until the
morning light; and let us not leave a man of them."

And they said, "Do whatever seems good to
you."

Then the priest said, "Let us draw near to God
here."

23 וַיּ֥וֹשַׁע יְהוָ֖ה בַּיּ֣וֹם
הַה֑וּא אֶת־יִשְׂרָאֵ֑ל וְהַ֨מִּלְחָמָ֔ה עָבְרָ֖ה אֶת־בֵּ֥ית אָֽוֶן׃
24 וְאִֽישׁ־יִשְׂרָאֵ֥ל נִגַּ֖שׂ בַּיּ֣וֹם הַה֑וּא וַיֹּ֣אֶל שָׁא֣וּל
אֶת־הָעָם֮ לֵאמֹר֒ אָר֣וּר הָאִ֗ישׁ אֲשֶׁר־יֹ֨אכַל לֶ֜חֶם
עַד־הָעֶ֗רֶב וְנִקַּמְתִּי֙ מֵאֹ֣יְבַ֔י וְלֹ֥א טָעַ֖ם כָּל־הָעָ֥ם
לָֽחֶם׃ ס 25 וְכָל־הָאָ֖רֶץ בָּ֣אוּ בַיָּ֑עַר וַיְהִ֥י
דְבַ֖שׁ עַל־פְּנֵ֥י הַשָּׂדֶֽה׃ 26 וַיָּבֹ֤א הָעָם֙ אֶל־הַיַּ֔עַר
וְהִנֵּ֖ה הֵ֣לֶךְ דְּבָ֑שׁ וְאֵין־מַשִּׂ֤יג יָדוֹ֙ אֶל־פִּ֔יו כִּֽי־יָרֵ֥א
הָעָ֖ם אֶת־הַשְּׁבֻעָֽה׃ 27 וְיוֹנָתָ֣ן לֹֽא־שָׁמַ֗ע בְּהַשְׁבִּ֣יעַ אֲשֶׁר־
אָבִיו֮ אֶת־הָעָם֒ וַיִּשְׁלַ֗ח אֶת־קְצֵ֤ה הַמַּטֶּה֙ אֲשֶׁר
בְּיָד֔וֹ וַיִּטְבֹּ֥ל אוֹתָ֖הּ בְּיַעְרַ֣ת הַדְּבָ֑שׁ וַיָּ֤שֶׁב יָדוֹ֙ אֶל־
פִּ֔יו וַתָּרֹ֖אנָה עֵינָֽיו׃ 28 וַיַּ֨עַן אִ֤ישׁ מֵהָעָם֙ וַיֹּ֔אמֶר
הַשְׁבֵּ֨עַ הִשְׁבִּ֤יעַ אָבִ֨יךָ֙ אֶת־הָעָם֙ לֵאמֹ֔ר אָר֥וּר הָאִ֖ישׁ
אֲשֶׁר־יֹ֥אכַל לֶ֖חֶם הַיּ֑וֹם וַיָּ֖עַף הָעָֽם׃ 29 וַיֹּ֨אמֶר֙ יֽוֹנָתָ֔ן
עָכַ֥ר אָבִ֖י אֶת־הָאָ֑רֶץ רְאוּ־נָא֙ כִּֽי־אֹ֣רוּ עֵינַ֔י כִּ֣י
טָעַ֔מְתִּי מְעַ֖ט דְּבַ֥שׁ הַזֶּֽה׃ 30 אַ֗ף כִּ֤י לוּא֙ אָכֹ֤ל
אָכַל֙ הַיּ֣וֹם הָעָ֔ם מִשְּׁלַ֥ל אֹיְבָ֖יו אֲשֶׁ֣ר מָצָ֑א כִּ֥י
עַתָּ֛ה לֹֽא־רָבְתָ֥ה מַכָּ֖ה בַּפְּלִשְׁתִּֽים׃ 31 וַיַּכּ֣וּ בַּיּ֤וֹם
הַהוּא֙ בַּפְּלִשְׁתִּ֔ים מִמִּכְמָ֖שׂ אַיָּלֹ֑נָה וַיָּ֥עַף הָעָ֖ם
מְאֹֽד׃ 32 וַיַּ֤עַשׂ הָעָם֙ אֶל־שׁלל וַיִּקְח֨וּ צֹ֤אן וּבָקָר֙
וּבְנֵ֣י בָקָ֔ר וַיִּשְׁחֲטוּ־אָ֑רְצָה וַיֹּ֥אכַל הָעָ֖ם עַל־הַדָּֽם׃
33 וַיַּגִּ֤ידוּ לְשָׁאוּל֙ לֵאמֹ֔ר הִנֵּ֥ה הָעָ֛ם חֹטִ֥אים לַֽיהוָ֖ה
לֶאֱכֹ֣ל עַל־הַדָּ֑ם וַיֹּ֣אמֶר בְּגַדְתֶּ֔ם גֹּֽלּוּ־אֵלַ֥י הַיּ֖וֹם אֶ֥בֶן
גְּדוֹלָֽה׃ 34 וַיֹּ֣אמֶר שָׁא֣וּל פֻּ֣צוּ בָעָ֗ם וַאֲמַרְתֶּ֤ם לָהֶם֙
הַגִּ֣ישׁוּ אֵלַ֗י אִ֤ישׁ שׁוֹרוֹ֙ וְאִ֣ישׁ שְׂיֵ֔הוּ וּשְׁחַטְתֶּ֣ם
בָּזֶ֗ה וַאֲכַלְתֶּ֔ם וְלֹֽא־תֶחֶטְא֥וּ לַֽיהוָ֖ה לֶאֱכֹ֣ל אֶל־הַדָּ֑ם
וַיַּגִּ֣שׁוּ כָל־הָעָ֡ם אִ֣ישׁ שׁוֹרוֹ֩ בְיָד֨וֹ הַלַּ֤יְלָה וַיִּשְׁחֲטוּ־
שָֽׁם׃ 35 וַיִּ֧בֶן שָׁא֛וּל מִזְבֵּ֖חַ לַֽיהוָ֑ה אֹת֣וֹ הֵחֵ֔ל לִבְנ֥וֹת
מִזְבֵּ֖חַ לַֽיהוָֽה׃ פ
36 וַיֹּ֣אמֶר שָׁא֗וּל נֵרְדָ֨ה אַחֲרֵ֤י פְלִשְׁתִּים֙ ׀
לַ֔יְלָה וְנָבֹ֤זָּה בָהֶם֙ ׀ עַד־א֣וֹר הַבֹּ֔קֶר וְלֹֽא־
נַשְׁאֵ֥ר בָּהֶ֖ם אִ֑ישׁ וַיֹּ֣אמְר֔וּ כָּל־הַטּ֥וֹב בְּעֵינֶ֖יךָ
עֲשֵׂ֑ה ס וַיֹּ֨אמֶר֙ הַכֹּהֵ֔ן נִקְרְבָ֥ה הֲלֹ֖ם אֶל־

37 So Saul asked counsel of God, "Shall I go down after the Philistines? Will You deliver them into the hand of Israel?" But He did not answer him that day. 38 And Saul said, "Come over here, all you chiefs of the people, and know and see what this sin was today. 39 For *as* the LORD lives, who saves Israel, though it be in Jonathan my son, he shall surely die." But not a man among all the people answered him. 40 Then he said to all Israel, "You be on one side, and my son Jonathan and I will be on the other side."

And the people said to Saul, "Do what seems good to you."

41 Therefore Saul said to the LORD God of Israel, "Give a perfect *lot*." So Saul and Jonathan were taken, but the people escaped. 42 And Saul said, "Cast *lots* between my son Jonathan and me." So Jonathan was taken. 43 Then Saul said to Jonathan, "Tell me what you have done."

And Jonathan told him, and said, "I only tasted a little honey with the end of the rod that *was* in my hand. So now I must die!"

44 Saul answered, "God do so and more also; for you shall surely die, Jonathan."

45 But the people said to Saul, "Shall Jonathan die, who has accomplished this great deliverance in Israel? Certainly not! *As* the LORD lives, not one hair of his head shall fall to the ground, for he has worked with God this day." So the people rescued Jonathan, and he did not die.

46 Then Saul returned from pursuing the Philistines, and the Philistines went to their own place.

47 So Saul established his sovereignty over Israel, and fought against all his enemies on every side, against Moab, against the people of Ammon, against Edom, against the kings of Zobah, and against the Philistines. Wherever he turned, he harassed *them.* 48 And he gathered an army and attacked the Amalekites, and delivered Israel from the hands of those who plundered them.

49 The sons of Saul were Jonathan, Jishui, and Malchishua. And the names of his two daughters *were these:* the name of the firstborn Merab, and the name of the younger Michal. 50 The name of Saul's wife *was* Ahinoam the daughter of Ahimaaz. And the name of the commander of his army *was* Abner the son of Ner, Saul's uncle. 51 Kish *was* the father of Saul, and Ner the father of Abner *was* the son of Abiel.

52 Now there was fierce war with the Philistines all the days of Saul. And when Saul saw any strong man or any valiant man, he took him for himself.

הָאֱלֹהִים: 37 וַיִּשְׁאַל שָׁאוּל בֵּאלֹהִים הַאֵרֵד אַחֲרֵי פְלִשְׁתִּים הֲתִתְּנֵם בְּיַד יִשְׂרָאֵל וְלֹא עָנָהוּ בַּיּוֹם הַהוּא: 38 וַיֹּאמֶר שָׁאוּל גֹּשׁוּ הֲלֹם כֹּל פִּנּוֹת הָעָם וּדְעוּ וּרְאוּ בַּמָּה הָיְתָה הַחַטָּאת הַזֹּאת הַיּוֹם: 39 כִּי חַי־יְהֹוָה הַמּוֹשִׁיעַ אֶת־יִשְׂרָאֵל כִּי אִם־יֶשְׁנוֹ בְּיוֹנָתָן בְּנִי כִּי מוֹת יָמוּת וְאֵין עֹנֵהוּ מִכָּל־הָעָם: 40 וַיֹּאמֶר אֶל־כָּל־יִשְׂרָאֵל אַתֶּם תִּהְיוּ לְעֵבֶר אֶחָד וַאֲנִי וְיוֹנָתָן בְּנִי נִהְיֶה לְעֵבֶר אֶחָד וַיֹּאמְרוּ הָעָם אֶל־שָׁאוּל הַטּוֹב בְּעֵינֶיךָ עֲשֵׂה: ס 41 וַיֹּאמֶר שָׁאוּל אֶל־יְהֹוָה אֱלֹהֵי יִשְׂרָאֵל הָבָה תָמִים וַיִּלָּכֵד יוֹנָתָן וְשָׁאוּל וְהָעָם יָצָאוּ: 42 וַיֹּאמֶר שָׁאוּל הַפִּילוּ בֵּינִי וּבֵין יוֹנָתָן בְּנִי וַיִּלָּכֵד יוֹנָתָן: 43 וַיֹּאמֶר שָׁאוּל אֶל־יוֹנָתָן הַגִּידָה לִּי מֶה עָשִׂיתָה וַיַּגֶּד־לוֹ יוֹנָתָן וַיֹּאמֶר טָעֹם טָעַמְתִּי בִּקְצֵה הַמַּטֶּה אֲשֶׁר־בְּיָדִי מְעַט דְּבַשׁ הִנְנִי אָמוּת: 44 וַיֹּאמֶר שָׁאוּל כֹּה־יַעֲשֶׂה אֱלֹהִים וְכֹה יוֹסִף כִּי־מוֹת תָּמוּת יוֹנָתָן: 45 וַיֹּאמֶר הָעָם אֶל־שָׁאוּל הֲיוֹנָתָן יָמוּת אֲשֶׁר עָשָׂה הַיְשׁוּעָה הַגְּדוֹלָה הַזֹּאת בְּיִשְׂרָאֵל חָלִילָה חַי־יְהֹוָה אִם־יִפֹּל מִשַּׂעֲרַת רֹאשׁוֹ אַרְצָה כִּי־עִם־אֱלֹהִים עָשָׂה הַיּוֹם הַזֶּה וַיִּפְדּוּ הָעָם אֶת־יוֹנָתָן וְלֹא־מֵת: ס 46 וַיַּעַל שָׁאוּל מֵאַחֲרֵי פְלִשְׁתִּים וּפְלִשְׁתִּים הָלְכוּ לִמְקוֹמָם: 47 וְשָׁאוּל לָכַד הַמְּלוּכָה עַל־יִשְׂרָאֵל וַיִּלָּחֶם סָבִיב בְּכָל־אֹיְבָיו בְּמוֹאָב וּבִבְנֵי־עַמּוֹן וּבֶאֱדוֹם וּבְמַלְכֵי צוֹבָה וּבַפְּלִשְׁתִּים וּבְכֹל אֲשֶׁר־יִפְנֶה יַרְשִׁיעַ: 48 וַיַּעַשׂ חַיִל וַיַּךְ אֶת־עֲמָלֵק וַיַּצֵּל אֶת־יִשְׂרָאֵל מִיַּד שֹׁסֵהוּ: ס 49 וַיִּהְיוּ בְּנֵי שָׁאוּל יוֹנָתָן וְיִשְׁוִי וּמַלְכִּי־שׁוּעַ וְשֵׁם שְׁתֵּי בְנֹתָיו שֵׁם הַבְּכִירָה מֵרַב וְשֵׁם הַקְּטַנָּה מִיכַל: 50 וְשֵׁם אֵשֶׁת שָׁאוּל אֲחִינֹעַם בַּת־אֲחִימָעַץ וְשֵׁם שַׂר־צְבָאוֹ אֲבִינֵר בֶּן־נֵר דּוֹד שָׁאוּל: 51 וְקִישׁ אֲבִי־שָׁאוּל וְנֵר אֲבִי־אַבְנֵר בֶּן־אֲבִיאֵל: 52 וַתְּהִי הַמִּלְחָמָה חֲזָקָה עַל־פְּלִשְׁתִּים כֹּל יְמֵי שָׁאוּל וְרָאָה שָׁאוּל כָּל־אִישׁ גִּבּוֹר וְכָל־בֶּן־חַיִל וַיַּאַסְפֵהוּ אֵלָיו: פ

15 Samuel also said to Saul, "The LORD sent me to anoint you king over His people, over Israel. Now therefore, heed the voice of the words of the LORD. ²Thus says the LORD of hosts: 'I will punish Amalek *for* what he did to Israel, how he ambushed him on the way when he came up from Egypt. ³Now go and attack Amalek, and utterly destroy all that they have, and do not spare them. But kill both man and woman, infant and nursing child, ox and sheep, camel and donkey.' "

⁴So Saul gathered the people together and numbered them in Telaim, two hundred thousand foot soldiers and ten thousand men of Judah. ⁵And Saul came to a city of Amalek, and lay in wait in the valley.

⁶Then Saul said to the Kenites, "Go, depart, get down from among the Amalekites, lest I destroy you with them. For you showed kindness to all the children of Israel when they came up out of Egypt." So the Kenites departed from among the Amalekites. ⁷And Saul attacked the Amalekites, from Havilah all the way to Shur, which is east of Egypt. ⁸He also took Agag king of the Amalekites alive, and utterly destroyed all the people with the edge of the sword. ⁹But Saul and the people spared Agag and the best of the sheep, the oxen, the fatlings, the lambs, and all *that was* good, and were unwilling to utterly destroy them. But everything despised and worthless, that they utterly destroyed.

¹⁰Now the word of the LORD came to Samuel, saying, ¹¹"I greatly regret that I have set up Saul *as* king, for he has turned back from following Me, and has not performed My commandments." And it grieved Samuel, and he cried out to the LORD all night. ¹²So when Samuel rose early in the morning to meet Saul, it was told Samuel, saying, "Saul went to Carmel, and indeed, he set up a monument for himself; and he has gone on around, passed by, and gone down to Gilgal." ¹³Then Samuel went to Saul, and Saul said to him, "Blessed *are* you of the LORD! I have performed the commandment of the LORD."

¹⁴But Samuel said, "What then *is* this bleating of the sheep in my ears, and the lowing of the oxen which I hear?"

¹⁵And Saul said, "They have brought them from the Amalekites; for the people spared the best of the sheep and the oxen, to sacrifice to the LORD your God; and the rest we have utterly destroyed."

¹⁶Then Samuel said to Saul, "Be quiet! And I will tell you what the LORD said to me last night."

And he said to him, "Speak on."

¹⁷So Samuel said, "When you *were* little in your own eyes, *were* you not head of the tribes of Israel? And did not the LORD anoint you king over Israel?

טו וַיֹּ֤אמֶר שְׁמוּאֵל֙ אֶל־שָׁא֔וּל אֹתִ֗י שָׁלַ֤ח יְהוָה֙ לִמְשָׁחֳךָ֣ לְמֶ֔לֶךְ עַל־עַמּ֖וֹ עַל־יִשְׂרָאֵ֑ל וְעַתָּ֣ה שְׁמַ֔ע לְק֖וֹל דִּבְרֵ֥י יְהוָֽה׃ ס 2 כֹּ֤ה אָמַר֙ יְהוָ֣ה צְבָא֔וֹת פָּקַ֕דְתִּי אֵ֛ת אֲשֶׁר־עָשָׂ֥ה עֲמָלֵ֖ק לְיִשְׂרָאֵ֑ל אֲשֶׁר־שָׂ֥ם לוֹ֙ בַּדֶּ֔רֶךְ בַּעֲלֹת֖וֹ מִמִּצְרָֽיִם׃ 3 עַתָּה֩ לֵ֨ךְ וְהִכִּיתָ֜ה אֶת־עֲמָלֵ֗ק וְהַֽחֲרַמְתֶּם֙ אֶת־כָּל־אֲשֶׁר־ל֔וֹ וְלֹ֥א תַחְמֹ֖ל עָלָ֑יו וְהֵמַתָּ֞ה מֵאִ֣ישׁ עַד־אִשָּׁ֗ה מֵֽעֹלֵל֙ וְעַד־יוֹנֵ֔ק מִשּׁ֣וֹר וְעַד־שֶׂ֔ה מִגָּמָ֖ל וְעַד־חֲמֽוֹר׃ ס 4 וַיְשַׁמַּ֤ע שָׁאוּל֙ אֶת־הָעָ֔ם וַֽיִּפְקְדֵם֙ בַּטְּלָאִ֔ים מָאתַ֥יִם אֶ֖לֶף רַגְלִ֑י וַעֲשֶׂ֥רֶת אֲלָפִ֖ים אֶת־אִ֥ישׁ יְהוּדָֽה׃ 5 וַיָּבֹ֥א שָׁא֖וּל עַד־עִ֣יר עֲמָלֵ֑ק וַיָּ֖רֶב בַּנָּֽחַל׃ 6 וַיֹּ֣אמֶר שָׁא֣וּל אֶל־הַקֵּינִ֡י לְכוּ֩ סֻּ֨רוּ רְד֜וּ מִתּ֣וֹךְ עֲמָלֵקִ֗י פֶּן־אֹֽסִפְךָ֙ עִמּ֔וֹ וְאַתָּ֞ה עָשִׂ֤יתָה חֶ֙סֶד֙ עִם־כָּל־בְּנֵ֣י יִשְׂרָאֵ֔ל בַּעֲלוֹתָ֖ם מִמִּצְרָ֑יִם וַיָּ֥סַר קֵינִ֖י מִתּ֥וֹךְ עֲמָלֵֽק׃ 7 וַיַּ֥ךְ שָׁא֖וּל אֶת־עֲמָלֵ֑ק מֵֽחֲוִילָה֙ בּוֹאֲךָ֣ שׁ֔וּר אֲשֶׁ֖ר עַל־פְּנֵ֥י מִצְרָֽיִם׃ 8 וַיִּתְפֹּ֛שׂ אֶת־אֲגַ֥ג מֶֽלֶךְ־עֲמָלֵ֖ק חָ֑י וְאֶת־כָּל־הָעָ֖ם הֶחֱרִ֥ים לְפִי־חָֽרֶב׃ 9 וַיַּחְמֹל֩ שָׁא֨וּל וְהָעָ֜ם עַל־אֲגָ֗ג וְעַל־מֵיטַ֣ב הַצֹּ֣אן וְהַבָּקָ֡ר וְהַמִּשְׁנִים֩ וְעַל־הַכָּרִ֨ים וְעַל־כָּל־הַטּ֜וֹב וְלֹ֤א אָבוּ֙ הַחֲרִימָ֔ם וְכָל־הַמְּלָאכָ֛ה נְמִבְזָ֥ה וְנָמֵ֖ס אֹתָ֥הּ הֶחֱרִֽימוּ׃ פ 10 וַֽיְהִי֙ דְּבַר־יְהוָ֔ה אֶל־שְׁמוּאֵ֖ל לֵאמֹֽר׃ 11 נִחַ֗מְתִּי כִּֽי־הִמְלַ֤כְתִּי אֶת־שָׁאוּל֙ לְמֶ֔לֶךְ כִּֽי־שָׁב֙ מֵאַֽחֲרַ֔י וְאֶת־דְּבָרַ֖י לֹ֣א הֵקִ֑ים וַיִּ֙חַר֙ לִשְׁמוּאֵ֔ל וַיִּזְעַ֥ק אֶל־יְהוָ֖ה כָּל־הַלָּֽיְלָה׃ 12 וַיַּשְׁכֵּ֧ם שְׁמוּאֵ֛ל לִקְרַ֥את שָׁא֖וּל בַּבֹּ֑קֶר וַיֻּגַּ֨ד לִשְׁמוּאֵ֜ל לֵאמֹ֗ר בָּֽא־שָׁא֤וּל הַכַּרְמֶ֙לָה֙ וְהִנֵּ֨ה מַצִּ֥יב לוֹ֙ יָ֔ד וַיִּסֹּב֙ וַֽיַּעֲבֹ֔ר וַיֵּ֖רֶד הַגִּלְגָּֽל׃ 13 וַיָּבֹ֥א שְׁמוּאֵ֖ל אֶל־שָׁא֑וּל וַיֹּ֧אמֶר ל֣וֹ שָׁא֗וּל בָּר֤וּךְ אַתָּה֙ לַֽיהוָ֔ה הֲקִימֹ֖תִי אֶת־דְּבַ֥ר יְהוָֽה׃ 14 וַיֹּ֣אמֶר שְׁמוּאֵ֔ל וּמֶ֛ה קֽוֹל־הַצֹּ֥אן הַזֶּ֖ה בְּאָזְנָ֑י וְק֣וֹל הַבָּקָ֔ר אֲשֶׁ֥ר אָנֹכִ֖י שֹׁמֵֽעַ׃ 15 וַיֹּ֨אמֶר שָׁא֜וּל מֵעֲמָלֵקִ֣י הֱבִיא֗וּם אֲשֶׁ֨ר חָמַ֤ל הָעָם֙ עַל־מֵיטַ֤ב הַצֹּאן֙ וְהַבָּקָ֔ר לְמַ֥עַן זְבֹ֖חַ לַֽיהוָ֣ה אֱלֹהֶ֑יךָ וְאֶת־הַיּוֹתֵ֖ר הֶחֱרַֽמְנוּ׃ ס 16 וַיֹּ֤אמֶר שְׁמוּאֵל֙ אֶל־שָׁא֔וּל הֶ֚רֶף וְאַגִּ֣ידָה לְּךָ֔ אֵת֩ אֲשֶׁ֨ר דִּבֶּ֧ר יְהוָ֛ה אֵלַ֖י הַלָּ֑יְלָה וַיֹּ֥אמְרוּ ל֖וֹ דַּבֵּֽר׃ ס 17 וַיֹּ֣אמֶר שְׁמוּאֵ֔ל הֲל֗וֹא אִם־קָטֹ֤ן אַתָּה֙ בְּעֵינֶ֔יךָ רֹ֛אשׁ שִׁבְטֵ֥י יִשְׂרָאֵ֖ל

¹⁸Now the LORD sent you on a mission, and said, 'Go, and utterly destroy the sinners, the Amalekites, and fight against them until they are consumed.' ¹⁹Why then did you not obey the voice of the LORD? Why did you swoop down on the spoil, and do evil in the sight of the LORD?"

²⁰And Saul said to Samuel, "But I have obeyed the voice of the LORD, and gone on the mission on which the LORD sent me, and brought back Agag king of Amalek; I have utterly destroyed the Amalekites. ²¹But the people took of the plunder, sheep and oxen, the best of the things which should have been utterly destroyed, to sacrifice to the LORD your God in Gilgal."

²²So Samuel said:

"Has the LORD *as great* delight in burnt offerings
  and sacrifices,
As in obeying the voice of the LORD?
Behold, to obey is better than sacrifice,
And to heed than the fat of rams.
²³ For rebellion *is as* the sin of witchcraft,
And stubbornness *is as* iniquity and idolatry.
Because you have rejected the word of the LORD,
He also has rejected you from *being* king."

²⁴Then Saul said to Samuel, "I have sinned, for I have transgressed the commandment of the LORD and your words, because I feared the people and obeyed their voice. ²⁵Now therefore, please pardon my sin, and return with me, that I may worship the LORD."

²⁶But Samuel said to Saul, "I will not return with you, for you have rejected the word of the LORD, and the LORD has rejected you from being king over Israel."

²⁷And as Samuel turned around to go away, *Saul* seized the edge of his robe, and it tore. ²⁸So Samuel said to him, "The LORD has torn the kingdom of Israel from you today, and has given it to a neighbor of yours, *who is* better than you. ²⁹And also the Strength of Israel will not lie nor relent. For He *is* not a man, that He should relent."

³⁰Then he said, "I have sinned; *yet* honor me now, please, before the elders of my people and before Israel, and return with me, that I may worship the LORD your God." ³¹So Samuel turned back after Saul, and Saul worshiped the LORD.

³²Then Samuel said, "Bring Agag king of the Amalekites here to me." So Agag came to him cautiously.

And Agag said, "Surely the bitterness of death is past."

18 וַיִּשְׁלָחֲךָ֥ יְהוָ֖ה בְּדָ֑רֶךְ וַיֹּ֗אמֶר לֵ֣ךְ וְהַחֲרַמְתָּ֞ה אֶת־הַֽחַטָּאִים֙ אֶת־עֲמָלֵ֔ק וְנִלְחַמְתָּ֣ ב֔וֹ עַ֥ד כַּלּוֹתָ֖ם אֹתָֽם: 19 וְלָ֛מָּה לֹא־שָׁמַ֖עְתָּ בְּק֣וֹל יְהוָ֑ה וַתַּ֙עַט֙ אֶל־הַשָּׁלָ֔ל וַתַּ֥עַשׂ הָרַ֖ע בְּעֵינֵ֥י יְהוָֽה: ס 20 וַיֹּ֨אמֶר שָׁא֜וּל אֶל־שְׁמוּאֵ֗ל אֲשֶׁ֤ר שָׁמַ֙עְתִּי֙ בְּק֣וֹל יְהוָ֔ה וָאֵלֵ֕ךְ בַּדֶּ֖רֶךְ אֲשֶׁר־שְׁלָחַ֣נִי יְהוָ֑ה וָאָבִ֗יא אֶת־אֲגַג֙ מֶ֣לֶךְ עֲמָלֵ֔ק וְאֶת־עֲמָלֵ֖ק הֶחֱרַֽמְתִּי: 21 וַיִּקַּ֨ח הָעָ֤ם מֵהַשָּׁלָל֙ צֹ֣אן וּבָקָ֔ר רֵאשִׁ֖ית הַחֵ֑רֶם לִזְבֹּ֛חַ לַיהוָ֥ה אֱלֹהֶ֖יךָ בַּגִּלְגָּֽל: 22 וַיֹּ֣אמֶר שְׁמוּאֵ֗ל הַחֵ֤פֶץ לַֽיהוָה֙ בְּעֹל֣וֹת וּזְבָחִ֔ים כִּשְׁמֹ֖עַ בְּק֣וֹל יְהוָ֑ה הִנֵּ֤ה שְׁמֹ֙עַ֙ מִזֶּ֣בַח ט֔וֹב לְהַקְשִׁ֖יב מֵחֵ֥לֶב אֵילִֽים: 23 כִּ֤י חַטַּאת־קֶ֙סֶם֙ מֶ֔רִי וְאָ֥וֶן וּתְרָפִ֖ים הַפְצַ֑ר יַ֗עַן מָאַ֙סְתָּ֙ אֶת־דְּבַ֣ר יְהוָ֔ה וַיִּמְאָסְךָ֖ מִמֶּֽלֶךְ: ס 24 וַיֹּ֨אמֶר שָׁא֣וּל אֶל־שְׁמוּאֵל֮ חָטָ֒אתִי֒ כִּֽי־עָבַ֧רְתִּי אֶת־פִּֽי־יְהוָ֛ה וְאֶת־דְּבָרֶ֖יךָ כִּ֤י יָרֵ֙אתִי֙ אֶת־הָעָ֔ם וָאֶשְׁמַ֖ע בְּקוֹלָֽם: 25 וְעַתָּ֕ה שָׂ֥א נָ֖א אֶת־חַטָּאתִ֑י וְשׁ֣וּב עִמִּ֔י וְאֶֽשְׁתַּחֲוֶ֖ה לַֽיהוָֽה: 26 וַיֹּ֤אמֶר שְׁמוּאֵל֙ אֶל־שָׁא֔וּל לֹ֥א אָשׁ֖וּב עִמָּ֑ךְ כִּ֤י מָאַ֙סְתָּה֙ אֶת־דְּבַ֣ר יְהוָ֔ה וַיִּמְאָסְךָ֣ יְהוָ֔ה מִהְי֥וֹת מֶ֖לֶךְ עַל־יִשְׂרָאֵֽל: ס 27 וַיִּסֹּ֥ב שְׁמוּאֵ֖ל לָלֶ֑כֶת וַיַּחֲזֵ֥ק בִּכְנַף־מְעִיל֖וֹ וַיִּקָּרַֽע: 28 וַיֹּ֤אמֶר אֵלָיו֙ שְׁמוּאֵ֔ל קָרַ֨ע יְהוָ֜ה אֶת־מַמְלְכ֧וּת יִשְׂרָאֵ֛ל מֵעָלֶ֖יךָ הַיּ֑וֹם וּנְתָנָ֕הּ לְרֵעֲךָ֖ הַטּ֥וֹב מִמֶּֽךָּ: 29 וְגַם֙ נֵ֣צַח יִשְׂרָאֵ֔ל לֹ֥א יְשַׁקֵּ֖ר וְלֹ֣א יִנָּחֵ֑ם כִּ֣י לֹ֥א אָדָ֛ם ה֖וּא לְהִנָּחֵֽם: 30 וַיֹּ֣אמֶר חָטָ֔אתִי עַתָּ֗ה כַּבְּדֵ֥נִי נָ֛א נֶ֥גֶד זִקְנֵֽי־עַמִּ֖י וְנֶ֣גֶד יִשְׂרָאֵ֑ל וְשׁ֣וּב עִמִּ֔י וְהִֽשְׁתַּחֲוֵ֖יתִי לַֽיהוָ֥ה אֱלֹהֶֽיךָ: 31 וַיָּ֥שָׁב שְׁמוּאֵ֖ל אַחֲרֵ֣י שָׁא֑וּל וַיִּשְׁתַּ֥חוּ שָׁא֖וּל לַֽיהוָֽה: 32 וַיֹּ֣אמֶר שְׁמוּאֵ֗ל הַגִּ֤ישׁוּ אֵלַי֙ אֶת־אֲגַג֙ מֶ֣לֶךְ עֲמָלֵ֔ק וַיֵּ֣לֶךְ אֵלָ֖יו אֲגַ֣ג מַעֲדַנֹּ֑ת וַיֹּ֣אמֶר

33 But Samuel said, "As your sword has made women childless, so shall your mother be childless among women." And Samuel hacked Agag in pieces before the LORD in Gilgal.

34 Then Samuel went to Ramah, and Saul went up to his house at Gibeah of Saul. 35 And Samuel went no more to see Saul until·the day of his death. Nevertheless Samuel mourned for Saul, and the LORD regretted that He had made Saul king over Israel.

16 Now the LORD said to Samuel, "How long will you mourn for Saul, seeing I have rejected him from reigning over Israel? Fill your horn with oil, and go; I am sending you to Jesse the Bethlehemite. For I have provided Myself a king among his sons."

2 And Samuel said, "How can I go? If Saul hears it, he will kill me."

But the LORD said, "Take a heifer with you, and say, 'I have come to sacrifice to the LORD.' 3 Then invite Jesse to the sacrifice, and I will show you what you shall do; you shall anoint for Me the one I name to you."

4 So Samuel did what the LORD said, and went to Bethlehem. And the elders of the town trembled at his coming, and said, "Do you come peaceably?"

5 And he said, "Peaceably; I have come to sacrifice to the LORD. Sanctify yourselves, and come with me to the sacrifice." Then he consecrated Jesse and his sons, and invited them to the sacrifice.

6 So it was, when they came, that he looked at Eliab and said, "Surely the LORD's anointed is before Him!"

7 But the LORD said to Samuel, "Do not look at his appearance or at his physical stature, because I have refused him. For the LORD does not see as man sees; for man looks at the outward appearance, but the LORD looks at the heart."

8 So Jesse called Abinadab, and made him pass before Samuel. And he said, "Neither has the LORD chosen this one." 9 Then Jesse made Shammah pass by. And he said, "Neither has the LORD chosen this one." 10 Thus Jesse made seven of his sons pass before Samuel. And Samuel said to Jesse, "The LORD has not chosen these." 11 And Samuel said to Jesse, "Are all the young men here?" Then he said, "There remains yet the youngest, and there he is, keeping the sheep."

And Samuel said to Jesse, "Send and bring him. For we will not sit down till he comes here." 12 So he sent and brought him in. Now he was ruddy, with bright eyes, and good-looking. And the LORD said, "Arise, anoint him; for this is the one!" 13 Then Samuel took the horn of oil and anointed him in the

אֲגַג אָכֵן סָר מַר־הַמָּוֶת: ס 33 וַיֹּאמֶר
שְׁמוּאֵל כַּאֲשֶׁר שִׁכְּלָה נָשִׁים חַרְבֶּךָ כֵּן־תִּשְׁכַּל
מִנָּשִׁים אִמֶּךָ וַיְשַׁסֵּף שְׁמוּאֵל אֶת־אֲגַג לִפְנֵי
יְהוָה בַּגִּלְגָּל: ס 34 וַיֵּלֶךְ שְׁמוּאֵל הָרָמָתָה
וְשָׁאוּל עָלָה אֶל־בֵּיתוֹ גִּבְעַת שָׁאוּל: 35 וְלֹא־יָסַף
שְׁמוּאֵל לִרְאוֹת אֶת־שָׁאוּל עַד־יוֹם מוֹתוֹ כִּי־
הִתְאַבֵּל שְׁמוּאֵל אֶל־שָׁאוּל וַיהוָה נִחָם כִּי־הִמְלִיךְ
אֶת־שָׁאוּל עַל־יִשְׂרָאֵל: פ

טז וַיֹּאמֶר יְהוָה אֶל־שְׁמוּאֵל עַד־מָתַי אַתָּה
מִתְאַבֵּל אֶל־שָׁאוּל וַאֲנִי מְאַסְתִּיו מִמְּלֹךְ עַל־
יִשְׂרָאֵל מַלֵּא קַרְנְךָ שֶׁמֶן וְלֵךְ אֶשְׁלָחֲךָ אֶל־יִשַׁי בֵּית־
הַלַּחְמִי כִּי־רָאִיתִי בְּבָנָיו לִי מֶלֶךְ: 2 וַיֹּאמֶר שְׁמוּאֵל
אֵיךְ אֵלֵךְ וְשָׁמַע שָׁאוּל וַהֲרָגָנִי ס וַיֹּאמֶר
יְהוָה עֶגְלַת בָּקָר תִּקַּח בְּיָדֶךָ וְאָמַרְתָּ לִזְבֹּחַ לַיהוָה
בָּאתִי: 3 וְקָרָאתָ לְיִשַׁי בַּזָּבַח וְאָנֹכִי אוֹדִיעֲךָ אֵת
אֲשֶׁר־תַּעֲשֶׂה וּמָשַׁחְתָּ לִי אֵת אֲשֶׁר־אֹמַר אֵלֶיךָ:
4 וַיַּעַשׂ שְׁמוּאֵל אֵת אֲשֶׁר דִּבֶּר יְהוָה וַיָּבֹא בֵּית
לָחֶם וַיֶּחֶרְדוּ זִקְנֵי הָעִיר לִקְרָאתוֹ וַיֹּאמֶר שָׁלֹם
בּוֹאֶךָ: 5 וַיֹּאמֶר ׀ שָׁלוֹם לִזְבֹּחַ לַיהוָה בָּאתִי
הִתְקַדְּשׁוּ וּבָאתֶם אִתִּי בַּזָּבַח וַיְקַדֵּשׁ אֶת־יִשַׁי וְאֶת־
בָּנָיו וַיִּקְרָא לָהֶם לַזָּבַח: 6 וַיְהִי בְּבוֹאָם וַיַּרְא אֶת־
אֱלִיאָב וַיֹּאמֶר אַךְ נֶגֶד יְהוָה מְשִׁיחוֹ: 7 וַיֹּאמֶר יְהוָה
אֶל־שְׁמוּאֵל אַל־תַּבֵּט אֶל־מַרְאֵהוּ וְאֶל־גְּבֹהַּ קוֹמָתוֹ
כִּי מְאַסְתִּיהוּ כִּי ׀ לֹא אֲשֶׁר יִרְאֶה הָאָדָם כִּי
הָאָדָם יִרְאֶה לַעֵינַיִם וַיהוָה יִרְאֶה לַלֵּבָב: 8 וַיִּקְרָא
יִשַׁי אֶל־אֲבִינָדָב וַיַּעֲבִרֵהוּ לִפְנֵי שְׁמוּאֵל וַיֹּאמֶר
גַּם־בָּזֶה לֹא־בָחַר יְהוָה: 9 וַיַּעֲבֵר יִשַׁי שַׁמָּה וַיֹּאמֶר
גַּם־בָּזֶה לֹא־בָחַר יְהוָה: 10 וַיַּעֲבֵר יִשַׁי שִׁבְעַת בָּנָיו
לִפְנֵי שְׁמוּאֵל וַיֹּאמֶר שְׁמוּאֵל אֶל־יִשַׁי לֹא־בָחַר
יְהוָה בָּאֵלֶּה: 11 וַיֹּאמֶר שְׁמוּאֵל אֶל־יִשַׁי הֲתַמּוּ
הַנְּעָרִים וַיֹּאמֶר עוֹד שָׁאַר הַקָּטָן וְהִנֵּה רֹעֶה בַּצֹּאן
וַיֹּאמֶר שְׁמוּאֵל אֶל־יִשַׁי שִׁלְחָה וְקָחֶנּוּ כִּי לֹא־נָסֹב
עַד־בֹּאוֹ פֹה: 12 וַיִּשְׁלַח וַיְבִיאֵהוּ וְהוּא אַדְמוֹנִי
עִם־יְפֵה עֵינַיִם וְטוֹב רֹאִי פ
וַיֹּאמֶר יְהוָה קוּם מְשָׁחֵהוּ כִּי־זֶה הוּא: 13 וַיִּקַּח
שְׁמוּאֵל אֶת־קֶרֶן הַשֶּׁמֶן וַיִּמְשַׁח אֹתוֹ בְּקֶרֶב אֶחָיו

midst of his brothers; and the Spirit of the LORD came upon David from that day forward. So Samuel arose and went to Ramah.

[14] But the Spirit of the LORD departed from Saul, and a distressing spirit from the LORD troubled him. [15] And Saul's servants said to him, "Surely, a distressing spirit from God is troubling you. [16] Let our master now command your servants, *who are* before you, to seek out a man *who is* a skillful player on the harp. And it shall be that he will play it with his hand when the distressing spirit from God is upon you, and you shall be well."

[17] So Saul said to his servants, "Provide me now a man who can play well, and bring *him* to me."

[18] Then one of the servants answered and said, "Look, I have seen a son of Jesse the Bethlehemite, *who is* skillful in playing, a mighty man of valor, a man of war, prudent in speech, and a handsome person; and the LORD *is* with him."

[19] Therefore Saul sent messengers to Jesse, and said, "Send me your son David, who *is* with the sheep." [20] And Jesse took a donkey *loaded with* bread, a skin of wine, and a young goat, and sent *them* by his son David to Saul. [21] So David came to Saul and stood before him. And he loved him greatly, and he became his armorbearer. [22] Then Saul sent to Jesse, saying, "Please let David stand before me, for he has found favor in my sight." [23] And so it was, whenever the spirit from God was upon Saul, that David would take a harp and play *it* with his hand. Then Saul would become refreshed and well, and the distressing spirit would depart from him.

17 Now the Philistines gathered their armies together to battle, and were gathered at Sochoh, which *belongs* to Judah; they encamped between Sochoh and Azekah, in Ephes Dammim. [2] And Saul and the men of Israel were gathered together, and they encamped in the Valley of Elah, and drew up in battle array against the Philistines. [3] The Philistines stood on a mountain on one side, and Israel stood on a mountain on the other side, with a valley between them.

[4] And a champion went out from the camp of the Philistines, named Goliath, from Gath, whose height *was* six cubits and a span. [5] *He had* a bronze helmet on his head, and he *was* armed with a coat of mail, and the weight of the coat *was* five thousand shekels of bronze. [6] And *he had* bronze armor on his legs and a bronze javelin between his shoulders. [7] Now the staff of his spear *was* like a weaver's beam, and his iron spearhead *weighed* six hundred shekels; and a shield-bearer went before him. [8] Then

וַתִּצְלַח רֽוּחַ־יְהוָה אֶל־דָּוִד מֵהַיּוֹם הַהוּא וָמָעְלָה וַיָּקָם שְׁמוּאֵל וַיֵּלֶךְ הָרָמָֽתָה׃ ס 14 וְרֽוּחַ יְהוָה סָרָה מֵעִם שָׁאוּל וּבִעֲתַתּוּ רֽוּחַ־רָעָה מֵאֵת יְהוָֽה׃ 15 וַיֹּאמְרוּ עַבְדֵֽי־שָׁאוּל אֵלָיו הִנֵּה־נָא רֽוּחַ־אֱלֹהִים רָעָה מְבַעִתֶּֽךָ׃ 16 יֹֽאמַר־נָא אֲדֹנֵנוּ עֲבָדֶיךָ לְפָנֶיךָ יְבַקְשׁוּ אִישׁ יֹדֵעַ מְנַגֵּן בַּכִּנּוֹר וְהָיָה בִּהְיוֹת עָלֶיךָ רֽוּחַ־אֱלֹהִים רָעָה וְנִגֵּן בְּיָדוֹ וְטוֹב לָֽךְ׃ פ

17 וַיֹּאמֶר שָׁאוּל אֶל־עֲבָדָיו רְאוּ־נָא לִי אִישׁ מֵיטִיב לְנַגֵּן וַהֲבִיאוֹתֶם אֵלָֽי׃ 18 וַיַּעַן אֶחָד מֵֽהַנְּעָרִים וַיֹּאמֶר הִנֵּה רָאִיתִי בֵּן לְיִשַׁי בֵּית הַלַּחְמִי יֹדֵעַ נַגֵּן וְגִבּוֹר חַיִל וְאִישׁ מִלְחָמָה וּנְבוֹן דָּבָר וְאִישׁ תֹּאַר וַֽיהוָה עִמּֽוֹ׃ 19 וַיִּשְׁלַח שָׁאוּל מַלְאָכִים אֶל־יִשָׁי וַיֹּאמֶר שִׁלְחָה אֵלַי אֶת־דָּוִד בִּנְךָ אֲשֶׁר בַּצֹּֽאן׃ 20 וַיִּקַּח יִשַׁי חֲמוֹר לֶחֶם וְנֹאד יַיִן וּגְדִי עִזִּים אֶחָד וַיִּשְׁלַח בְּיַד־דָּוִד בְּנוֹ אֶל־שָׁאֽוּל׃ 21 וַיָּבֹא דָוִד אֶל־שָׁאוּל וַיַּעֲמֹד לְפָנָיו וַיֶּאֱהָבֵהוּ מְאֹד וַֽיְהִי־לוֹ נֹשֵׂא כֵלִֽים׃ 22 וַיִּשְׁלַח שָׁאוּל אֶל־יִשַׁי לֵאמֹר יַעֲמָד־נָא דָוִד לְפָנַי כִּֽי־מָצָא חֵן בְּעֵינָֽי׃ 23 וְהָיָה בִּהְיוֹת רֽוּחַ־אֱלֹהִים אֶל־שָׁאוּל וְלָקַח דָּוִד אֶת־הַכִּנּוֹר וְנִגֵּן בְּיָדוֹ וְרָוַח לְשָׁאוּל וְטוֹב לוֹ וְסָרָה מֵעָלָיו רֽוּחַ הָרָעָֽה׃ פ

יז וַיַּאַסְפוּ פְלִשְׁתִּים אֶת־מַֽחֲנֵיהֶם לַמִּלְחָמָה וַיֵּאָֽסְפוּ שֹׂכֹה אֲשֶׁר לִֽיהוּדָה וַֽיַּחֲנוּ בֵּֽין־שׂוֹכֹה וּבֵין־עֲזֵקָה בְּאֶפֶס דַּמִּֽים׃ 2 וְשָׁאוּל וְאִֽישׁ־יִשְׂרָאֵל נֶאֶסְפוּ וַֽיַּחֲנוּ בְּעֵמֶק הָאֵלָה וַיַּעַרְכוּ מִלְחָמָה לִקְרַאת פְּלִשְׁתִּֽים׃ 3 וּפְלִשְׁתִּים עֹמְדִים אֶל־הָהָר מִזֶּה וְיִשְׂרָאֵל עֹמְדִים אֶל־הָהָר מִזֶּה וְהַגַּיְא בֵּינֵיהֶֽם׃ 4 וַיֵּצֵא אִֽישׁ־הַבֵּנַיִם מִמַּֽחֲנוֹת פְּלִשְׁתִּים גָּלְיָת שְׁמוֹ מִגַּת גָּבְהוֹ שֵׁשׁ אַמּוֹת וָזָֽרֶת׃ 5 וְכוֹבַע נְחֹשֶׁת עַל־רֹאשׁוֹ וְשִׁרְיוֹן קַשְׂקַשִּׂים הוּא לָבוּשׁ וּמִשְׁקַל הַשִּׁרְיוֹן חֲמֵֽשֶׁת־אֲלָפִים שְׁקָלִים נְחֹֽשֶׁת׃ 6 וּמִצְחַת נְחֹשֶׁת עַל־רַגְלָיו וְכִידוֹן נְחֹשֶׁת בֵּין כְּתֵפָֽיו׃ 7 וְחֵץ חֲנִיתוֹ כִּמְנוֹר אֹרְגִים וְלַהֶבֶת חֲנִיתוֹ שֵֽׁשׁ־מֵאוֹת שְׁקָלִים בַּרְזֶל וְנֹשֵׂא הַצִּנָּה הֹלֵךְ לְפָנָֽיו׃ 8 וַֽיַּעֲמֹד וַיִּקְרָא אֶל־מַֽעַרְכֹת יִשְׂרָאֵל וַיֹּאמֶר לָהֶם לָמָּה תֵצְאוּ

יז 7 וְעֵץ

he stood and cried out to the armies of Israel, and
said to them, "Why have you come out to line up
for battle? *Am* I not a Philistine, and you the
servants of Saul? Choose a man for yourselves, and
let him come down to me. [9] If he is able to fight with
me and kill me, then we will be your servants. But if
I prevail against him and kill him, then you shall be
our servants and serve us." [10] And the Philistine
said, "I defy the armies of Israel this day; give me a
man, that we may fight together." [11] When Saul and
all Israel heard these words of the Philistine, they
were dismayed and greatly afraid.

[12] Now David *was* the son of that Ephrathite of
Bethlehem Judah, whose name *was* Jesse, and who
had eight sons. And the man was old, advanced *in
years*, in the days of Saul. [13] The three oldest sons of
Jesse had gone to follow Saul to the battle. The
names of his three sons who went to the battle *were*
Eliab the firstborn, next to him Abinadab, and the
third Shammah. [14] David *was* the youngest. And the
three oldest followed Saul. [15] But David occasion-
ally went and returned from Saul to feed his father's
sheep at Bethlehem.

[16] And the Philistine drew near and presented
himself forty days, morning and evening.

[17] Then Jesse said to his son David, "Take now
for your brothers an ephah of this dried *grain* and
these ten loaves, and run to your brothers at the
camp. [18] And carry these ten cheeses to the captain
of *their* thousand, and see how your brothers fare,
and bring back news of them." [19] Now Saul and
they and all the men of Israel *were* in the Valley of
Elah, fighting with the Philistines.

[20] So David rose early in the morning, left the
sheep with a keeper, and took *the things* and went
as Jesse had commanded him. And he came to the
camp as the army was going out to the fight and
shouting for the battle. [21] For Israel and the
Philistines had drawn up in battle array, army
against army. [22] And David left his supplies in the
hand of the supply keeper, ran to the army, and
came and greeted his brothers. [23] Then as he talked
with them, there was the champion, the Philistine of
Gath, Goliath by name, coming up from the armies
of the Philistines; and he spoke according to the
same words. So David heard *them*. [24] And all the
men of Israel, when they saw the man, fled from
him and were dreadfully afraid. [25] So the men of
Israel said, "Have you seen this man who has come
up? Surely he has come up to defy Israel; and it
shall be *that* the man who kills him the king will
enrich with great riches, will give him his daughter,
and give his father's house exemption *from taxes* in
Israel."

לַעֲרֹךְ מִלְחָמָה הֲלוֹא אָנֹכִי הַפְּלִשְׁתִּי וְאַתֶּם
עֲבָדִים לְשָׁאוּל בְּרוּ־לָכֶם אִישׁ וְיֵרֵד אֵלָי׃ 9 אִם־
יוּכַל לְהִלָּחֵם אִתִּי וְהִכָּנִי וְהָיִינוּ לָכֶם לַעֲבָדִים
וְאִם־אֲנִי אוּכַל־לוֹ וְהִכִּיתִיו וִהְיִיתֶם לָנוּ לַעֲבָדִים
וַעֲבַדְתֶּם אֹתָנוּ׃ 10 וַיֹּאמֶר הַפְּלִשְׁתִּי אֲנִי חֵרַפְתִּי
אֶת־מַעַרְכוֹת יִשְׂרָאֵל הַיּוֹם הַזֶּה תְּנוּ־לִי אִישׁ
וְנִלָּחֲמָה יָחַד׃ 11 וַיִּשְׁמַע שָׁאוּל וְכָל־יִשְׂרָאֵל אֶת־
דִּבְרֵי הַפְּלִשְׁתִּי הָאֵלֶּה וַיֵּחַתּוּ וַיִּרְאוּ מְאֹד׃ פ
12 וְדָוִד בֶּן־אִישׁ אֶפְרָתִי הַזֶּה מִבֵּית לֶחֶם
יְהוּדָה וּשְׁמוֹ יִשַׁי וְלוֹ שְׁמֹנָה בָנִים וְהָאִישׁ
בִּימֵי שָׁאוּל זָקֵן בָּא בַאֲנָשִׁים׃ 13 וַיֵּלְכוּ שְׁלֹשֶׁת
בְּנֵי־יִשַׁי הַגְּדֹלִים הָלְכוּ אַחֲרֵי־שָׁאוּל לַמִּלְחָמָה
וְשֵׁם ׀ שְׁלֹשֶׁת בָּנָיו אֲשֶׁר הָלְכוּ בַּמִּלְחָמָה
אֱלִיאָב הַבְּכוֹר וּמִשְׁנֵהוּ אֲבִינָדָב וְהַשְּׁלִשִׁי שַׁמָּה׃
14 וְדָוִד הוּא הַקָּטָן וּשְׁלֹשָׁה הַגְּדֹלִים הָלְכוּ אַחֲרֵי
שָׁאוּל׃ ס 15 וְדָוִד הֹלֵךְ וָשָׁב מֵעַל שָׁאוּל
לִרְעוֹת אֶת־צֹאן אָבִיו בֵּית־לָחֶם׃ 16 וַיִּגַּשׁ הַפְּלִשְׁתִּי
הַשְׁכֵּם וְהַעֲרֵב וַיִּתְיַצֵּב אַרְבָּעִים יוֹם׃ פ
17 וַיֹּאמֶר יִשַׁי לְדָוִד בְּנוֹ קַח־נָא לְאַחֶיךָ אֵיפַת
הַקָּלִיא הַזֶּה וַעֲשָׂרָה לֶחֶם הַזֶּה וְהָרֵץ הַמַּחֲנֶה
לְאַחֶיךָ׃ 18 וְאֵת עֲשֶׂרֶת חֲרִצֵי הֶחָלָב הָאֵלֶּה
תָּבִיא לְשַׂר־הָאָלֶף וְאֶת־אַחֶיךָ תִּפְקֹד לְשָׁלוֹם וְאֶת־
עֲרֻבָּתָם תִּקָּח׃ 19 וְשָׁאוּל וְהֵמָּה וְכָל־אִישׁ יִשְׂרָאֵל
בְּעֵמֶק הָאֵלָה נִלְחָמִים עִם־פְּלִשְׁתִּים׃ 20 וַיַּשְׁכֵּם
דָּוִד בַּבֹּקֶר וַיִּטֹּשׁ אֶת־הַצֹּאן עַל־שֹׁמֵר וַיִּשָּׂא וַיֵּלֶךְ
כַּאֲשֶׁר צִוָּהוּ יִשָׁי וַיָּבֹא הַמַּעְגָּלָה וְהַחַיִל הַיֹּצֵא
אֶל־הַמַּעֲרָכָה וְהֵרֵעוּ בַּמִּלְחָמָה׃ 21 וַתַּעֲרֹךְ יִשְׂרָאֵל
וּפְלִשְׁתִּים מַעֲרָכָה לִקְרַאת מַעֲרָכָה׃ 22 וַיִּטֹּשׁ דָּוִד
אֶת־הַכֵּלִים מֵעָלָיו עַל־יַד שׁוֹמֵר הַכֵּלִים וַיָּרָץ
הַמַּעֲרָכָה וַיָּבֹא וַיִּשְׁאַל לְאֶחָיו לְשָׁלוֹם׃ 23 וְהוּא ׀
מְדַבֵּר עִמָּם וְהִנֵּה אִישׁ הַבֵּנַיִם עוֹלֶה גָּלְיָת
הַפְּלִשְׁתִּי שְׁמוֹ מִגַּת מִמַּעֲרוֹת^פ פְּלִשְׁתִּים וַיְדַבֵּר
כַּדְּבָרִים הָאֵלֶּה וַיִּשְׁמַע דָּוִד׃ 24 וְכֹל אִישׁ יִשְׂרָאֵל
בִּרְאוֹתָם אֶת־הָאִישׁ וַיָּנֻסוּ מִפָּנָיו וַיִּרְאוּ מְאֹד׃
25 וַיֹּאמֶר ׀ אִישׁ יִשְׂרָאֵל הַרְאִיתֶם הָאִישׁ הָעֹלֶה

26 Then David spoke to the men who stood by him, saying, "What shall be done for the man who kills this Philistine and takes away the reproach from Israel? For who *is* this uncircumcised Philistine, that he should defy the armies of the living God?"

27 And the people answered him in this manner, saying, "So shall it be done for the man who kills him."

28 Now Eliab his oldest brother heard when he spoke to the men; and Eliab's anger was aroused against David, and he said, "Why did you come down here? And with whom have you left those few sheep in the wilderness? I know your pride and the insolence of your heart, for you have come down to see the battle."

29 And David said, "What have I done now? *Is* there not a cause?" 30 Then he turned from him toward another and said the same thing; and these people answered him as the first ones *did*.

31 Now when the words which David spoke were heard, they reported *them* to Saul; and he sent for him. 32 Then David said to Saul, "Let no man's heart fail because of him; your servant will go and fight with this Philistine."

33 And Saul said to David, "You are not able to go against this Philistine to fight with him; for you *are* a youth, and he a man of war from his youth."

34 But David said to Saul, "Your servant used to keep his father's sheep, and when a lion or a bear came and took a lamb out of the flock, 35 I went out after it and struck it, and delivered *the lamb* from its mouth; and when it arose against me, I caught *it* by its beard, and struck and killed it. 36 Your servant has killed both lion and bear; and this uncircumcised Philistine will be like one of them, seeing he has defied the armies of the living God." 37 Moreover David said, "The LORD, who delivered me from the paw of the lion and from the paw of the bear, He will deliver me from the hand of this Philistine."

And Saul said to David, "Go, and the LORD be with you!"

38 So Saul clothed David with his armor, and he put a bronze helmet on his head; he also clothed him with a coat of mail. 39 David fastened his sword to his armor and tried to walk, for he had not tested *them*. And David said to Saul, "I cannot walk with these, for I have not tested *them*." So David took them off.

40 Then he took his staff in his hand; and he chose for himself five smooth stones from the brook, and put them in a shepherd's bag, in a pouch which he had, and his sling was in his hand. And he drew

הֶיֶה כִּי־לְחָרֵף אֶת־יִשְׂרָאֵל עָלָה וְהָיָה הָאִישׁ
אֲשֶׁר־יַכֶּנּוּ יַעְשְׁרֶנּוּ הַמֶּלֶךְ עֹשֶׁר גָּדוֹל וְאֶת־בִּתּוֹ
יִתֶּן־לוֹ וְאֵת בֵּית אָבִיו יַעֲשֶׂה חָפְשִׁי בְּיִשְׂרָאֵל:
26 וַיֹּאמֶר דָּוִד אֶל־הָאֲנָשִׁים הָעֹמְדִים עִמּוֹ לֵאמֹר
מַה־יֵּעָשֶׂה לָאִישׁ אֲשֶׁר יַכֶּה אֶת־הַפְּלִשְׁתִּי הַלָּז
וְהֵסִיר חֶרְפָּה מֵעַל יִשְׂרָאֵל כִּי מִי הַפְּלִשְׁתִּי הֶעָרֵל
הַזֶּה כִּי חֵרֵף מַעַרְכוֹת אֱלֹהִים חַיִּים: 27 וַיֹּאמֶר לוֹ
הָעָם כַּדָּבָר הַזֶּה לֵאמֹר כֹּה יֵעָשֶׂה לָאִישׁ אֲשֶׁר
יַכֶּנּוּ: 28 וַיִּשְׁמַע אֱלִיאָב אָחִיו הַגָּדוֹל בְּדַבְּרוֹ אֶל־
הָאֲנָשִׁים וַיִּחַר־אַף אֱלִיאָב בְּדָוִד וַיֹּאמֶר לָמָּה־זֶּה
יָרַדְתָּ וְעַל־מִי נָטַשְׁתָּ מְעַט הַצֹּאן הָהֵנָּה בַּמִּדְבָּר
אֲנִי יָדַעְתִּי אֶת־זְדֹנְךָ וְאֵת רֹעַ לְבָבֶךָ כִּי לְמַעַן
רְאוֹת הַמִּלְחָמָה יָרָדְתָּ: 29 וַיֹּאמֶר דָּוִד מֶה עָשִׂיתִי
עָתָּה הֲלוֹא דָּבָר הוּא: 30 וַיִּסֹּב מֵאֶצְלוֹ אֶל־מוּל
אַחֵר וַיֹּאמֶר כַּדָּבָר הַזֶּה וַיְשִׁבֻהוּ הָעָם דָּבָר כַּדָּבָר
הָרִאשׁוֹן: 31 וַיִּשָּׁמְעוּ הַדְּבָרִים אֲשֶׁר דִּבֶּר דָּוִד וַיַּגִּדוּ
לִפְנֵי־שָׁאוּל וַיִּקָּחֵהוּ: 32 וַיֹּאמֶר דָּוִד אֶל־שָׁאוּל אַל־
יִפֹּל לֵב־אָדָם עָלָיו עַבְדְּךָ יֵלֵךְ וְנִלְחַם עִם־הַפְּלִשְׁתִּי
הַזֶּה: 33 וַיֹּאמֶר שָׁאוּל אֶל־דָּוִד לֹא תוּכַל לָלֶכֶת
אֶל־הַפְּלִשְׁתִּי הַזֶּה לְהִלָּחֵם עִמּוֹ כִּי־נַעַר אַתָּה וְהוּא
אִישׁ מִלְחָמָה מִנְּעֻרָיו: ס 34 וַיֹּאמֶר דָּוִד
אֶל־שָׁאוּל רֹעֶה הָיָה עַבְדְּךָ לְאָבִיו בַּצֹּאן וּבָא הָאֲרִי
וְאֶת־הַדּוֹב וְנָשָׂא שֶׂה מֵהָעֵדֶר: 35 וְיָצָאתִי אַחֲרָיו
וְהִכִּתִיו וְהִצַּלְתִּי מִפִּיו וַיָּקָם עָלַי וְהֶחֱזַקְתִּי בִּזְקָנוֹ
וְהִכִּתִיו וַהֲמִיתִיו: 36 גַּם אֶת־הָאֲרִי גַּם־הַדּוֹב הִכָּה
עַבְדֶּךָ וְהָיָה הַפְּלִשְׁתִּי הֶעָרֵל הַזֶּה כְּאַחַד מֵהֶם כִּי
חֵרֵף מַעַרְכֹת אֱלֹהִים חַיִּים: ס 37 וַיֹּאמֶר
דָּוִד יְהוָה אֲשֶׁר הִצִּלַנִי מִיַּד הָאֲרִי וּמִיַּד הַדֹּב
הוּא יַצִּילֵנִי מִיַּד הַפְּלִשְׁתִּי הַזֶּה ס וַיֹּאמֶר
שָׁאוּל אֶל־דָּוִד לֵךְ וַיהוָה יִהְיֶה עִמָּךְ: 38 וַיַּלְבֵּשׁ
שָׁאוּל אֶת־דָּוִד מַדָּיו וְנָתַן קוֹבַע נְחֹשֶׁת עַל־רֹאשׁוֹ
וַיַּלְבֵּשׁ אֹתוֹ שִׁרְיוֹן: 39 וַיַּחְגֹּר דָּוִד אֶת־חַרְבּוֹ מֵעַל
לְמַדָּיו וַיֹּאֶל לָלֶכֶת כִּי לֹא־נִסָּה וַיֹּאמֶר דָּוִד אֶל־
שָׁאוּל לֹא אוּכַל לָלֶכֶת בָּאֵלֶּה כִּי לֹא נִסִּיתִי
וַיְסִרֵם דָּוִד מֵעָלָיו: 40 וַיִּקַּח מַקְלוֹ בְּיָדוֹ וַיִּבְחַר־
לוֹ חֲמִשָּׁה חַלֻּקֵי־אֲבָנִים מִן־הַנַּחַל וַיָּשֶׂם אֹתָם

near to the Philistine. ⁴¹ So the Philistine came, and began drawing near to David, and the man who bore the shield *went* before him. ⁴² And when the Philistine looked about and saw David, he disdained him; for he was *only* a youth, ruddy and good-looking. ⁴³ So the Philistine said to David, "*Am* I a dog, that you come to me with sticks?" And the Philistine cursed David by his gods. ⁴⁴ And the Philistine said to David, "Come to me, and I will give your flesh to the birds of the air and the beasts of the field!"

⁴⁵ Then David said to the Philistine, "You come to me with a sword, with a spear, and with a javelin. But I come to you in the name of the LORD of hosts, the God of the armies of Israel, whom you have defied. ⁴⁶ This day the LORD will deliver you into my hand, and I will strike you and take your head from you. And this day I will give the carcasses of the camp of the Philistines to the birds of the air and the wild beasts of the earth, that all the earth may know that there is a God in Israel. ⁴⁷ Then all this assembly shall know that the LORD does not save with sword and spear; for the battle *is* the LORD's, and He will give you into our hands."

⁴⁸ So it was, when the Philistine arose and came and drew near to meet David, that David hurried and ran toward the army to meet the Philistine. ⁴⁹ Then David put his hand in his bag and took out a stone; and he slung *it* and struck the Philistine in his forehead, so that the stone sank into his forehead, and he fell on his face to the earth. ⁵⁰ So David prevailed over the Philistine with a sling and a stone, and struck the Philistine and killed him. But *there was* no sword in the hand of David. ⁵¹ Therefore David ran and stood over the Philistine, took his sword and drew it out of its sheath and killed him, and cut off his head with it.

And when the Philistines saw that their champion was dead, they fled. ⁵² Now the men of Israel and Judah arose and shouted, and pursued the Philistines as far as the entrance of the valley and to the gates of Ekron. And the wounded of the Philistines fell along the road to Shaaraim, even as far as Gath and Ekron. ⁵³ Then the children of Israel returned from chasing the Philistines, and they plundered their tents. ⁵⁴ And David took the head of the Philistine and brought it to Jerusalem, but he put his armor in his tent.

⁵⁵ When Saul saw David going out against the Philistine, he said to Abner, the commander of the army, "Abner, whose son *is* this youth?"

And Abner said, "As your soul lives, O king, I do not know."

בִּכְלֵי הָרֹעִים אֲשֶׁר־לוֹ וּבַיַּלְקוּט וְקַלְעוֹ בְיָדוֹ וַיִּגַּשׁ אֶל־הַפְּלִשְׁתִּי: ⁴¹ וַיֵּלֶךְ הַפְּלִשְׁתִּי הֹלֵךְ וְקָרֵב אֶל־דָּוִד וְהָאִישׁ נֹשֵׂא הַצִּנָּה לְפָנָיו: ⁴² וַיַּבֵּט הַפְּלִשְׁתִּי וַיִּרְאֶה אֶת־דָּוִד וַיִּבְזֵהוּ כִּי־הָיָה נַעַר וְאַדְמֹנִי עִם־יְפֵה מַרְאֶה: ⁴³ וַיֹּאמֶר הַפְּלִשְׁתִּי אֶל־דָּוִד הֲכֶלֶב אָנֹכִי כִּי־אַתָּה בָא־אֵלַי בַּמַּקְלוֹת וַיְקַלֵּל הַפְּלִשְׁתִּי אֶת־דָּוִד בֵּאלֹהָיו: ⁴⁴ וַיֹּאמֶר הַפְּלִשְׁתִּי אֶל־דָּוִד לְכָה אֵלַי וְאֶתְּנָה אֶת־בְּשָׂרְךָ לְעוֹף הַשָּׁמַיִם וּלְבֶהֱמַת הַשָּׂדֶה: ס ⁴⁵ וַיֹּאמֶר דָּוִד אֶל־הַפְּלִשְׁתִּי אַתָּה בָּא אֵלַי בְּחֶרֶב וּבַחֲנִית וּבְכִידוֹן וְאָנֹכִי בָא־אֵלֶיךָ בְּשֵׁם יְהֹוָה צְבָאוֹת אֱלֹהֵי מַעַרְכוֹת יִשְׂרָאֵל אֲשֶׁר חֵרַפְתָּ: ⁴⁶ הַיּוֹם הַזֶּה יְסַגֶּרְךָ יְהֹוָה בְּיָדִי וְהִכִּיתִךָ וַהֲסִרֹתִי אֶת־רֹאשְׁךָ מֵעָלֶיךָ וְנָתַתִּי פֶּגֶר מַחֲנֵה פְלִשְׁתִּים הַיּוֹם הַזֶּה לְעוֹף הַשָּׁמַיִם וּלְחַיַּת הָאָרֶץ וְיֵדְעוּ כָּל־הָאָרֶץ כִּי יֵשׁ אֱלֹהִים לְיִשְׂרָאֵל: ⁴⁷ וְיֵדְעוּ כָּל־הַקָּהָל הַזֶּה כִּי־לֹא בְּחֶרֶב וּבַחֲנִית יְהוֹשִׁיעַ יְהֹוָה כִּי לַיהֹוָה הַמִּלְחָמָה וְנָתַן אֶתְכֶם בְּיָדֵנוּ: ⁴⁸ וְהָיָה כִּי־קָם הַפְּלִשְׁתִּי וַיֵּלֶךְ וַיִּקְרַב לִקְרַאת דָּוִד וַיְמַהֵר דָּוִד וַיָּרָץ הַמַּעֲרָכָה לִקְרַאת הַפְּלִשְׁתִּי: ⁴⁹ וַיִּשְׁלַח דָּוִד אֶת־יָדוֹ אֶל־הַכֶּלִי וַיִּקַּח מִשָּׁם אֶבֶן וַיְקַלַּע וַיַּךְ אֶת־הַפְּלִשְׁתִּי אֶל־מִצְחוֹ וַתִּטְבַּע הָאֶבֶן בְּמִצְחוֹ וַיִּפֹּל עַל־פָּנָיו אָרְצָה: ⁵⁰ וַיֶּחֱזַק דָּוִד מִן־הַפְּלִשְׁתִּי בַּקֶּלַע וּבָאֶבֶן וַיַּךְ אֶת־הַפְּלִשְׁתִּי וַיְמִיתֵהוּ וְחֶרֶב אֵין בְּיַד־דָּוִד: ⁵¹ וַיָּרָץ דָּוִד וַיַּעֲמֹד אֶל־הַפְּלִשְׁתִּי וַיִּקַּח אֶת־חַרְבּוֹ וַיִּשְׁלְפָהּ מִתַּעְרָהּ וַיְמֹתְתֵהוּ וַיִּכְרָת־בָּהּ אֶת־רֹאשׁוֹ וַיִּרְאוּ הַפְּלִשְׁתִּים כִּי־מֵת גִּבּוֹרָם וַיָּנֻסוּ: ⁵² וַיָּקֻמוּ אַנְשֵׁי יִשְׂרָאֵל וִיהוּדָה וַיָּרִעוּ וַיִּרְדְּפוּ אֶת־הַפְּלִשְׁתִּים עַד־בּוֹאֲךָ גַיְא וְעַד שַׁעֲרֵי עֶקְרוֹן וַיִּפְּלוּ חַלְלֵי פְלִשְׁתִּים בְּדֶרֶךְ שַׁעֲרַיִם וְעַד־גַּת וְעַד־עֶקְרוֹן: ⁵³ וַיָּשֻׁבוּ בְּנֵי יִשְׂרָאֵל מִדְּלֹק אַחֲרֵי פְלִשְׁתִּים וַיָּשֹׁסּוּ אֶת־מַחֲנֵיהֶם: ⁵⁴ וַיִּקַּח דָּוִד אֶת־רֹאשׁ הַפְּלִשְׁתִּי וַיְבִאֵהוּ יְרוּשָׁלִָם וְאֶת־כֵּלָיו שָׂם בְּאָהֳלוֹ: ס ⁵⁵ וְכִרְאוֹת שָׁאוּל אֶת־דָּוִד יֹצֵא לִקְרַאת הַפְּלִשְׁתִּי אָמַר אֶל־אַבְנֵר שַׂר הַצָּבָא בֶּן־מִי־זֶה הַנַּעַר אַבְנֵר וַיֹּאמֶר אַבְנֵר חֵי־נַפְשְׁךָ

56 So the king said, "Inquire whose son this young man *is*."

57 Then, as David returned from the slaughter of the Philistine, Abner took him and brought him before Saul with the head of the Philistine in his hand. 58 And Saul said to him, "Whose son *are* you, young man?"

So David answered, "*I am* the son of your servant Jesse the Bethlehemite."

18 Now when he had finished speaking to Saul, the soul of Jonathan was knit to the soul of David, and Jonathan loved him as his own soul. 2 Saul took him that day, and would not let him go home to his father's house anymore. 3 Then Jonathan and David made a covenant, because he loved him as his own soul. 4 And Jonathan took off the robe that *was* on him and gave it to David, with his armor, even to his sword and his bow and his belt.

5 So David went out wherever Saul sent him, *and* behaved wisely. And Saul set him over the men of war, and he was accepted in the sight of all the people and also in the sight of Saul's servants. 6 Now it had happened as they were coming *home,* when David was returning from the slaughter of the Philistine, that the women had come out of all the cities of Israel, singing and dancing, to meet King Saul, with tambourines, with joy, and with musical instruments. 7 So the women sang as they danced, and said:

> "Saul has slain his thousands,
> And David his ten thousands."

8 Then Saul was very angry, and the saying displeased him; and he said, "They have ascribed to David ten thousands, and to me they have ascribed *only* thousands. Now *what* more can he have but the kingdom?" 9 So Saul eyed David from that day forward.

10 And it happened on the next day that the distressing spirit from God came upon Saul, and he prophesied inside the house. So David played *music* with his hand, as at other times; but *there was* a spear in Saul's hand. 11 And Saul cast the spear, for he said, "I will pin David to the wall!" But David escaped his presence twice.

12 Now Saul was afraid of David, because the LORD was with him, but had departed from Saul. 13 Therefore Saul removed him from his presence, and made him his captain over a thousand; and he went out and came in before the people. 14 And David behaved wisely in all his ways, and the LORD *was* with him. 15 Therefore, when Saul saw that he

הַמֶּלֶךְ אִם־יָדַעְתִּי: 56 וַיֹּאמֶר הַמֶּלֶךְ שְׁאַל אַתָּה בֶּן־
מִי־זֶה הָעָלֶם: ס 57 וּכְשׁוּב דָּוִד מֵהַכּוֹת
אֶת־הַפְּלִשְׁתִּי וַיִּקַּח אֹתוֹ אַבְנֵר וַיְבִאֵהוּ לִפְנֵי שָׁאוּל
וְרֹאשׁ הַפְּלִשְׁתִּי בְּיָדוֹ: 58 וַיֹּאמֶר אֵלָיו שָׁאוּל בֶּן־
מִי אַתָּה הַנַּעַר וַיֹּאמֶר דָּוִד בֶּן־עַבְדְּךָ יִשַׁי בֵּית
הַלַּחְמִי:

יח וַיְהִי כְּכַלֹּתוֹ לְדַבֵּר אֶל־שָׁאוּל וְנֶפֶשׁ יְהוֹנָתָן
נִקְשְׁרָה בְּנֶפֶשׁ דָּוִד וַיֶּאֱהָבֵהוּ יְהוֹנָתָן כְּנַפְשׁוֹ:
2 וַיִּקָּחֵהוּ שָׁאוּל בַּיּוֹם הַהוּא וְלֹא נְתָנוֹ לָשׁוּב בֵּית
אָבִיו: 3 וַיִּכְרֹת יְהוֹנָתָן וְדָוִד בְּרִית בְּאַהֲבָתוֹ אֹתוֹ
כְּנַפְשׁוֹ: 4 וַיִּתְפַּשֵּׁט יְהוֹנָתָן אֶת־הַמְּעִיל אֲשֶׁר עָלָיו
וַיִּתְּנֵהוּ לְדָוִד וּמַדָּיו וְעַד־חַרְבּוֹ וְעַד־קַשְׁתּוֹ וְעַד־
חֲגֹרוֹ: 5 וַיֵּצֵא דָוִד בְּכֹל אֲשֶׁר יִשְׁלָחֶנּוּ שָׁאוּל יַשְׂכִּיל
וַיְשִׂמֵהוּ שָׁאוּל עַל אַנְשֵׁי הַמִּלְחָמָה וַיִּיטַב בְּעֵינֵי
כָל־הָעָם וְגַם בְּעֵינֵי עַבְדֵי שָׁאוּל:

6 וַיְהִי בְּבוֹאָם בְּשׁוּב דָּוִד מֵהַכּוֹת אֶת־
הַפְּלִשְׁתִּי וַתֵּצֶאנָה הַנָּשִׁים מִכָּל־עָרֵי יִשְׂרָאֵל
לָשִׁיר וְהַמְּחֹלוֹת לִקְרַאת שָׁאוּל הַמֶּלֶךְ בְּתֻפִּים
בְּשִׂמְחָה וּבְשָׁלִשִׁים: 7 וַתַּעֲנֶינָה הַנָּשִׁים הַמְשַׂחֲקוֹת
וַתֹּאמַרְןָ הִכָּה שָׁאוּל בַּאֲלָפָו וְדָוִד בְּרִבְבֹתָיו:
8 וַיִּחַר לְשָׁאוּל מְאֹד וַיֵּרַע בְּעֵינָיו הַדָּבָר הַזֶּה
וַיֹּאמֶר נָתְנוּ לְדָוִד רְבָבוֹת וְלִי נָתְנוּ הָאֲלָפִים וְעוֹד
לוֹ אַךְ הַמְּלוּכָה: 9 וַיְהִי שָׁאוּל עוֹן אֶת־דָּוִד
מֵהַיּוֹם הַהוּא וָהָלְאָה: ס 10 וַיְהִי מִמָּחֳרָת
וַתִּצְלַח רוּחַ אֱלֹהִים רָעָה אֶל־שָׁאוּל וַיִּתְנַבֵּא
בְתוֹךְ־הַבַּיִת וְדָוִד מְנַגֵּן בְּיָדוֹ כְּיוֹם בְּיוֹם וְהַחֲנִית
בְּיַד־שָׁאוּל: 11 וַיָּטֶל שָׁאוּל אֶת־הַחֲנִית וַיֹּאמֶר אַכֶּה
בְדָוִד וּבַקִּיר וַיִּסֹּב דָּוִד מִפָּנָיו פַּעֲמָיִם: 12 וַיִּרָא
שָׁאוּל מִלִּפְנֵי דָוִד כִּי־הָיָה יְהוָה עִמּוֹ וּמֵעִם שָׁאוּל
סָר: 13 וַיְסִרֵהוּ שָׁאוּל מֵעִמּוֹ וַיְשִׂמֵהוּ לוֹ שַׂר־אָלֶף
וַיֵּצֵא וַיָּבֹא לִפְנֵי הָעָם: פ

14 וַיְהִי דָוִד לְכָל־דְּרָכָו מַשְׂכִּיל וַיהוָה עִמּוֹ:
15 וַיַּרְא שָׁאוּל אֲשֶׁר־הוּא מַשְׂכִּיל מְאֹד וַיָּגָר

יח 1 וַיֶּאֱרָבֵהוּ   6 לָשִׁיר   7 בַּאֲלָפָיו   9 עֹיֵן

behaved very wisely, he was afraid of him. ¹⁶But all
Israel and Judah loved David, because he went out
and came in before them.

¹⁷Then Saul said to David, "Here is my older
daughter Merab; I will give her to you as a wife.
Only be valiant for me, and fight the LORD's
battles." For Saul thought, "Let my hand not be
against him, but let the hand of the Philistines be
against him."

¹⁸So David said to Saul, "Who *am* I, and what *is*
my life *or* my father's family in Israel, that I should
be son-in-law to the king?" ¹⁹But it happened at the
time when Merab, Saul's daughter, should have
been given to David, that she was given to Adriel
the Meholathite as a wife.

²⁰Now Michal, Saul's daughter, loved David.
And they told Saul, and the thing pleased him. ²¹So
Saul said, "I will give her to him, that she may be a
snare to him, and that the hand of the Philistines
may be against him." Therefore Saul said to David
a second time, "You shall be my son-in-law today."

²²And Saul commanded his servants, "Communi-
cate with David secretly, and say, 'Look, the king
has delight in you, and all his servants love you.
Now therefore, become the king's son-in-law.'"

²³So Saul's servants spoke those words in the
hearing of David. And David said, "Does it seem to
you *a light thing* to be a king's son-in-law, seeing I
am a poor and lightly esteemed man?" ²⁴And the
servants of Saul told him, saying, "In this manner
David spoke."

²⁵Then Saul said, "Thus you shall say to David:
'The king does not desire any dowry but one
hundred foreskins of the Philistines, to take
vengeance on the king's enemies.'" But Saul
thought to make David fall by the hand of the
Philistines. ²⁶So when his servants told David these
words, it pleased David well to become the king's
son-in-law. Now the days had not expired; ²⁷there-
fore David arose and went, he and his men, and
killed two hundred men of the Philistines. And
David brought their foreskins, and they gave them
in full count to the king, that he might become the
king's son-in-law. Then Saul gave him Michal his
daughter as a wife.

²⁸Thus Saul saw and knew that the LORD *was*
with David, and *that* Michal, Saul's daughter, loved
him; ²⁹and Saul was still more afraid of David. So
Saul became David's enemy continually. ³⁰Then the
princes of the Philistines went out *to war*. And so it
was, whenever they went out, *that* David behaved
more wisely than all the servants of Saul, so that his
name became highly esteemed.

מִפָּנָיו: 16 וְכָל־יִשְׂרָאֵל וִיהוּדָה אֹהֵב אֶת־דָּוִד כִּי־
הוּא יוֹצֵא וָבָא לִפְנֵיהֶם: פ

17 וַיֹּאמֶר שָׁאוּל אֶל־דָּוִד הִנֵּה בִתִּי הַגְּדוֹלָה מֵרַב
אֹתָהּ אֶתֶּן־לְךָ לְאִשָּׁה אַךְ הֱיֵה־לִּי לְבֶן־חַיִל וְהִלָּחֵם
מִלְחֲמוֹת יְהוָה וְשָׁאוּל אָמַר אַל־תְּהִי יָדִי בּוֹ וּתְהִי־
בוֹ יַד־פְּלִשְׁתִּים: ס 18 וַיֹּאמֶר דָּוִד אֶל־
שָׁאוּל מִי אָנֹכִי וּמִי חַיַּי מִשְׁפַּחַת אָבִי בְּיִשְׂרָאֵל
כִּי־אֶהְיֶה חָתָן לַמֶּלֶךְ: 19 וַיְהִי בְּעֵת תֵּת אֶת־מֵרַב
בַּת־שָׁאוּל לְדָוִד וְהִיא נִתְּנָה לְעַדְרִיאֵל הַמְּחֹלָתִי
לְאִשָּׁה: 20 וַתֶּאֱהַב מִיכַל בַּת־שָׁאוּל אֶת־דָּוִד וַיַּגִּדוּ
לְשָׁאוּל וַיִּשַׁר הַדָּבָר בְּעֵינָיו: 21 וַיֹּאמֶר שָׁאוּל
אֶתְּנֶנָּה לּוֹ וּתְהִי־לוֹ לְמוֹקֵשׁ וּתְהִי־בוֹ יַד־פְּלִשְׁתִּים
וַיֹּאמֶר שָׁאוּל אֶל־דָּוִד בִּשְׁתַּיִם תִּתְחַתֵּן בִּי הַיּוֹם:
22 וַיְצַו שָׁאוּל אֶת־עֲבָדָו דַּבְּרוּ אֶל־דָּוִד בַּלָּט לֵאמֹר
הִנֵּה חָפֵץ בְּךָ הַמֶּלֶךְ וְכָל־עֲבָדָיו אֲהֵבוּךָ וְעַתָּה
הִתְחַתֵּן בַּמֶּלֶךְ: 23 וַיְדַבְּרוּ עַבְדֵי שָׁאוּל בְּאָזְנֵי דָוִד
אֶת־הַדְּבָרִים הָאֵלֶּה וַיֹּאמֶר דָּוִד הַנְקַלָּה בְעֵינֵיכֶם
הִתְחַתֵּן בַּמֶּלֶךְ וְאָנֹכִי אִישׁ־רָשׁ וְנִקְלֶה: 24 וַיַּגִּדוּ
עַבְדֵי שָׁאוּל לוֹ לֵאמֹר כַּדְּבָרִים הָאֵלֶּה דִּבֶּר דָּוִד: פ

25 וַיֹּאמֶר שָׁאוּל כֹּה־תֹאמְרוּ לְדָוִד אֵין־חֵפֶץ לַמֶּלֶךְ
בְּמֹהַר כִּי בְּמֵאָה עָרְלוֹת פְּלִשְׁתִּים לְהִנָּקֵם בְּאֹיְבֵי
הַמֶּלֶךְ וְשָׁאוּל חָשַׁב לְהַפִּיל אֶת־דָּוִד בְּיַד־פְּלִשְׁתִּים:
26 וַיַּגִּדוּ עֲבָדָיו לְדָוִד אֶת־הַדְּבָרִים הָאֵלֶּה וַיִּשַׁר
הַדָּבָר בְּעֵינֵי דָוִד לְהִתְחַתֵּן בַּמֶּלֶךְ וְלֹא מָלְאוּ
הַיָּמִים: 27 וַיָּקָם דָּוִד וַיֵּלֶךְ הוּא וַאֲנָשָׁיו וַיַּךְ
בַּפְּלִשְׁתִּים מָאתַיִם אִישׁ וַיָּבֵא דָוִד אֶת־עָרְלֹתֵיהֶם
וַיְמַלְאוּם לַמֶּלֶךְ לְהִתְחַתֵּן בַּמֶּלֶךְ וַיִּתֶּן־לוֹ שָׁאוּל
אֶת־מִיכַל בִּתּוֹ לְאִשָּׁה: ס 28 וַיַּרְא שָׁאוּל
וַיֵּדַע כִּי יְהוָה עִם־דָּוִד וּמִיכַל בַּת־שָׁאוּל אֲהֵבַתְהוּ:
29 וַיֹּאסֶף שָׁאוּל לֵרֹא מִפְּנֵי דָוִד עוֹד וַיְהִי שָׁאוּל
אֹיֵב אֶת־דָּוִד כָּל־הַיָּמִים: ס 30 וַיֵּצְאוּ שָׂרֵי
פְלִשְׁתִּים וַיְהִי מִדֵּי צֵאתָם שָׂכַל דָּוִד מִכֹּל עַבְדֵי
שָׁאוּל וַיִּיקַר שְׁמוֹ מְאֹד: ס

19 Now Saul spoke to Jonathan his son and to all his servants, that they should kill David; but Jonathan, Saul's son, delighted greatly in David. [2] So Jonathan told David, saying, "My father Saul seeks to kill you. Therefore please be on your guard until morning, and stay in a secret *place* and hide. [3] And I will go out and stand beside my father in the field where you *are*, and I will speak with my father about you. Then what I observe, I will tell you."

[4] Thus Jonathan spoke well of David to Saul his father, and said to him, "Let not the king sin against his servant, against David, because he has not sinned against you, and because his works *have been* very good toward you. [5] For he took his life in his hands and killed the Philistine, and the LORD brought about a great deliverance for all Israel. You saw *it* and rejoiced. Why then will you sin against innocent blood, to kill David without a cause?"

[6] So Saul heeded the voice of Jonathan, and Saul swore, "*As* the LORD lives, he shall not be killed." [7] Then Jonathan called David, and Jonathan told him all these things. So Jonathan brought David to Saul, and he was in his presence as in times past.

[8] And there was war again; and David went out and fought with the Philistines, and struck them with a mighty blow, and they fled from him.

[9] Now the distressing spirit from the LORD came upon Saul as he sat in his house with his spear in his hand. And David was playing *music* with *his* hand. [10] Then Saul sought to pin David to the wall with the spear, but he slipped away from Saul's presence; and he drove the spear into the wall. So David fled and escaped that night.

[11] Saul also sent messengers to David's house to watch him and to kill him in the morning. And Michal, David's wife, told him, saying, "If you do not save your life tonight, tomorrow you will be killed." [12] So Michal let David down through a window. And he went and fled and escaped. [13] And Michal took an image and laid *it* in the bed, put a cover of goats' *hair* for his head, and covered *it* with clothes. [14] So when Saul sent messengers to take David, she said, "He *is* sick."

[15] Then Saul sent the messengers *back* to see David, saying, "Bring him up to me in the bed, that I may kill him." [16] And when the messengers had come in, there was the image in the bed, with a cover of goats' *hair* for his head. [17] Then Saul said to Michal, "Why have you deceived me like this, and sent my enemy away, so that he has escaped?"

And Michal answered Saul, "He said to me, 'Let me go! Why should I kill you?'"

יט וַיְדַבֵּ֣ר שָׁא֗וּל אֶל־יוֹנָתָ֤ן בְּנוֹ֙ וְאֶל־כָּל־עֲבָדָ֔יו לְהָמִ֖ית אֶת־דָּוִ֑ד וִיהֽוֹנָתָן֙ בֶּן־שָׁא֔וּל חָפֵ֥ץ בְּדָוִ֖ד מְאֹֽד: 2 וַיַּגֵּ֤ד יְהוֹנָתָן֙ לְדָוִ֣ד לֵאמֹ֔ר מְבַקֵּ֛שׁ שָׁא֥וּל אָבִ֖י לַהֲמִיתֶ֑ךָ וְעַתָּה֙ הִשָּֽׁמֶר־נָ֣א בַבֹּ֔קֶר וְיָשַׁבְתָּ֥ בַסֵּ֖תֶר וְנַחְבֵּֽאתָ: 3 וַאֲנִ֨י אֵצֵ֜א וְעָמַדְתִּ֣י לְיַד־אָבִ֗י בַּשָּׂדֶה֙ אֲשֶׁ֣ר אַתָּ֣ה שָׁ֔ם וַאֲנִ֕י אֲדַבֵּ֥ר בְּךָ֖ אֶל־אָבִ֑י וְרָאִ֥יתִי מָ֖ה וְהִגַּ֥דְתִּי לָֽךְ: ס 4 וַיְדַבֵּ֨ר יְהֽוֹנָתָ֤ן בְּדָוִד֙ ט֔וֹב אֶל־שָׁא֣וּל אָבִ֑יו וַיֹּ֣אמֶר אֵלָ֗יו אַל־יֶחֱטָ֤א הַמֶּ֨לֶךְ֙ בְּעַבְדּ֣וֹ בְדָוִ֔ד כִּ֛י ל֥וֹא חָטָ֖א לָ֑ךְ וְכִ֥י מַעֲשָׂ֖יו טֽוֹב־לְךָ֥ מְאֹֽד: 5 וַיָּשֶׂם֩ אֶת־נַפְשׁ֨וֹ בְכַפּ֜וֹ וַיַּ֣ךְ אֶת־הַפְּלִשְׁתִּ֗י וַיַּ֨עַשׂ יְהוָ֤ה תְּשׁוּעָ֤ה גְדוֹלָה֙ לְכָל־יִשְׂרָאֵ֔ל רָאִ֖יתָ וַתִּשְׂמָ֑ח וְלָ֤מָּה תֶֽחֱטָא֙ בְּדָ֣ם נָקִ֔י לְהָמִ֥ית אֶת־דָּוִ֖ד חִנָּֽם: 6 וַיִּשְׁמַ֥ע שָׁא֖וּל בְּק֣וֹל יְהוֹנָתָ֑ן וַיִּשָּׁבַ֣ע שָׁא֔וּל חַי־יְהוָ֖ה אִם־יוּמָֽת: 7 וַיִּקְרָ֤א יְהוֹנָתָן֙ לְדָוִ֔ד וַיַּגֶּד־לוֹ֙ יְה֣וֹנָתָ֔ן אֵ֥ת כָּל־הַדְּבָרִ֖ים הָאֵ֑לֶּה וַיָּבֵ֨א יְהוֹנָתָ֤ן אֶת־דָּוִד֙ אֶל־שָׁא֔וּל וַיְהִ֥י לְפָנָ֖יו כְּאֶתְמ֥וֹל שִׁלְשֽׁוֹם: ס 8 וַתּ֥וֹסֶף הַמִּלְחָמָ֖ה לִהְי֑וֹת וַיֵּצֵ֨א דָוִ֜ד וַיִּלָּ֣חֶם בַּפְּלִשְׁתִּ֗ים וַיַּ֤ךְ בָּהֶם֙ מַכָּ֣ה גְדוֹלָ֔ה וַיָּנֻ֖סוּ מִפָּנָֽיו: 9 וַתְּהִי֩ ר֨וּחַ יְהוָ֤ה ׀ רָעָה֙ אֶל־שָׁא֔וּל וְה֗וּא בְּבֵית֙וֹ יוֹשֵׁ֔ב וַחֲנִית֖וֹ בְּיָד֑וֹ וְדָוִ֖ד מְנַגֵּ֥ן בְּיָֽד: 10 וַיְבַקֵּ֨שׁ שָׁא֜וּל לְהַכּ֤וֹת בַּחֲנִית֙ בְּדָוִ֣ד וּבַקִּ֔יר וַיִּפְטַ֣ר מִפְּנֵ֣י שָׁא֔וּל וַיַּ֥ךְ אֶת־הַחֲנִ֖ית בַּקִּ֑יר וְדָוִ֣ד נָ֔ס וַיִּמָּלֵ֖ט בַּלַּ֥יְלָה הֽוּא: פ

11 וַיִּשְׁלַח֩ שָׁא֨וּל מַלְאָכִ֜ים אֶל־בֵּ֤ית דָּוִד֙ לְשָׁמְר֔וֹ וְלַהֲמִית֖וֹ בַּבֹּ֑קֶר וַתַּגֵּ֣ד לְדָוִ֗ד מִיכַ֤ל אִשְׁתּוֹ֙ לֵאמֹ֔ר אִם־אֵ֨ינְךָ֜ מְמַלֵּ֤ט אֶֽת־נַפְשְׁךָ֙ הַלַּ֔יְלָה מָחָ֖ר אַתָּ֥ה מוּמָֽת: 12 וַתֹּ֧רֶד מִיכַ֛ל אֶת־דָּוִ֖ד בְּעַ֣ד הַחַלּ֑וֹן וַיֵּ֥לֶךְ וַיִּבְרַ֖ח וַיִּמָּלֵֽט: 13 וַתִּקַּ֨ח מִיכַ֜ל אֶת־הַתְּרָפִ֗ים וַתָּ֨שֶׂם֙ אֶל־הַמִּטָּ֔ה וְאֵת֙ כְּבִ֣יר הָֽעִזִּ֔ים שָׂ֖מָה מְרַֽאֲשֹׁתָ֑יו וַתְּכַ֖ס בַּבָּֽגֶד: ס 14 וַיִּשְׁלַ֤ח שָׁאוּל֙ מַלְאָכִ֔ים לָקַ֖חַת אֶת־דָּוִ֑ד וַתֹּ֖אמֶר חֹלֶ֥ה הֽוּא: פ

15 וַיִּשְׁלַ֤ח שָׁאוּל֙ אֶת־הַמַּלְאָכִ֔ים לִרְא֥וֹת אֶת־דָּוִ֖ד לֵאמֹ֑ר הַעֲל֨וּ אֹת֧וֹ בַמִּטָּ֛ה אֵלַ֖י לַהֲמִתֽוֹ: 16 וַיָּבֹ֨אוּ֙ הַמַּלְאָכִ֔ים וְהִנֵּ֥ה הַתְּרָפִ֖ים אֶל־הַמִּטָּ֑ה וּכְבִ֥יר הָעִזִּ֖ים מְרַאֲשֹׁתָֽיו: 17 וַיֹּ֨אמֶר שָׁא֜וּל אֶל־מִיכַ֗ל לָ֚מָּה כָּ֣כָה

18 So David fled and escaped, and went to Samuel at Ramah, and told him all that Saul had done to him. And he and Samuel went and stayed in Naioth. 19 Now it was told Saul, saying, "Take note, David *is* at Naioth in Ramah!" 20 Then Saul sent messengers to take David. And when they saw the group of prophets prophesying, and Samuel standing *as* leader over them, the Spirit of God came upon the messengers of Saul, and they also prophesied. 21 And when Saul was told, he sent other messengers, and they prophesied likewise. Then Saul sent messengers again the third time, and they prophesied also. 22 Then he also went to Ramah, and came to the great well that *is* at Sechu. So he asked, and said, "Where *are* Samuel and David?"

And *someone* said, "Indeed *they are* at Naioth in Ramah." 23 So he went there to Naioth in Ramah. Then the Spirit of God was upon him also, and he went on and prophesied until he came to Naioth in Ramah. 24 And he also stripped off his clothes and prophesied before Samuel in like manner, and lay down naked all that day and all that night. Therefore they say, "*Is* Saul also among the prophets?"

20 Then David fled from Naioth in Ramah, and went and said to Jonathan, "What have I done? What *is* my iniquity, and what *is* my sin before your father, that he seeks my life?"

2 So Jonathan said to him, "By no means! You shall not die! Indeed, my father will do nothing either great or small without first telling me. And why should my father hide this thing from me? It *is* not *so!*"

3 Then David took an oath again, and said, "Your father certainly knows that I have found favor in your eyes, and he has said, 'Do not let Jonathan know this, lest he be grieved.' But truly, *as* the LORD lives and *as* your soul lives, *there is* but a step between me and death."

4 So Jonathan said to David, "Whatever you yourself desire, I will do *it* for you."

5 And David said to Jonathan, "Indeed tomorrow *is* the New Moon, and I should not fail to sit with the king to eat. But let me go, that I may hide in the field until the third *day* at evening. 6 If your father misses me at all, then say, 'David earnestly asked *permission* of me that he might run over to Bethlehem, his city, for *there is* a yearly sacrifice there for all the family.' 7 If he says thus: '*It is* well,' your servant will be safe. But if he is very angry, be sure that evil is determined by him. 8 Therefore you shall deal kindly with your servant, for you have

רְמִיתַ֔נִי וַתְּשַׁלְּחִ֥י אֶת־אֹיְבִ֖י וַיִּמָּלֵ֑ט וַתֹּ֧אמֶר מִיכַ֣ל
אֶל־שָׁא֗וּל ה֤וּא־אָמַר֙ אֵלַ֔י שַׁלְּחִ֖נִי לָ֥מָה אֲמִיתֵֽךְ: 18 וְדָוִ֨ד בָּרַ֜ח וַיִּמָּלֵ֗ט וַיָּבֹ֤א אֶל־שְׁמוּאֵל֙ הָרָמָ֔תָה וַיַּגֶּד־ל֗וֹ אֵ֚ת כָּל־אֲשֶׁ֣ר עָֽשָׂה־ל֣וֹ שָׁא֔וּל וַיֵּ֥לֶךְ ה֛וּא וּשְׁמוּאֵ֖ל וַיֵּשְׁב֥וּ בְּנָֽיותP: 19 וַיֻּגַּ֥ד לְשָׁא֖וּל לֵאמֹ֑ר הִנֵּ֣ה דָוִ֔ד בְּנָיֹ֖ת P בָּרָמָֽה: 20 וַיִּשְׁלַ֤ח שָׁאוּל֙ מַלְאָכִים֙ לָקַ֣חַת אֶת־דָּוִ֔ד וַיַּ֗רְא אֶֽת־לַהֲקַ֤ת הַנְּבִיאִים֙ נִבְּאִ֔ים וּשְׁמוּאֵ֛ל עֹמֵ֥ד נִצָּ֖ב עֲלֵיהֶ֑ם וַתְּהִ֞י עַֽל־מַלְאֲכֵ֤י שָׁאוּל֙ ר֣וּחַ אֱלֹהִ֔ים וַיִּֽתְנַבְּא֖וּ גַּם־הֵֽמָּה: 21 וַיַּגִּ֣דוּ לְשָׁא֗וּל וַיִּשְׁלַ֞ח מַלְאָכִ֤ים אֲחֵרִים֙ וַיִּֽתְנַבְּא֣וּ גַם־הֵ֔מָּה וַיֹּ֣סֶף שָׁא֗וּל וַיִּשְׁלַ֞ח מַלְאָכִים֙ שְׁלִשִׁ֔ים וַיִּֽתְנַבְּא֖וּ גַּם־הֵֽמָּה: 22 וַיֵּ֨לֶךְ גַּם־ה֜וּא הָרָמָ֗תָה וַיָּבֹא֙ עַד־בּ֣וֹר הַגָּד֔וֹל אֲשֶׁ֣ר בַּשֶּׂ֔כוּ וַיִּשְׁאַ֣ל וַיֹּ֔אמֶר אֵיפֹ֥ה שְׁמוּאֵ֖ל וְדָוִ֑ד וַיֹּ֕אמֶר הִנֵּ֥ה בְּנָיֹ֖ת P בָּרָמָֽה: 23 וַיֵּ֣לֶךְ שָׁ֗ם אֶל־נָיֹ֖ת P בָּרָמָ֑ה וַתְּהִי֩ עָלָ֨יו גַּם־ה֤וּא ר֣וּחַ אֱלֹהִ֔ים וַיֵּ֗לֶךְ הָלוֹךְ֙ וַיִּתְנַבֵּ֔א עַד־בֹּא֖וֹ בְּנָיֹ֖ת P בָּרָמָֽה: 24 וַיִּפְשַׁ֨ט גַּם־ה֜וּא בְּגָדָ֗יו וַיִּתְנַבֵּ֤א גַם־הוּא֙ לִפְנֵ֣י שְׁמוּאֵ֔ל וַיִּפֹּ֣ל עָרֹ֔ם כָּל־הַיּ֥וֹם הַה֖וּא וְכָל־הַלָּ֑יְלָה עַל־כֵּן֙ יֹֽאמְר֔וּ הֲגַ֥ם שָׁא֖וּל בַּנְּבִיאִֽם:
פ

כ וַיִּבְרַ֣ח דָּוִ֔ד מנָוִ֖ת P בָּֽרָמָ֑ה וַיָּבֹ֞א וַיֹּ֣אמֶר ׀ לִפְנֵ֣י יְהוֹנָתָ֗ן מֶ֤ה עָשִׂ֙יתִי֙ מֶֽה־עֲוֹנִ֣י וּמֶֽה־חַטָּאתִ֖י לִפְנֵ֣י אָבִ֑יךָ כִּ֥י מְבַקֵּ֖שׁ אֶת־נַפְשִֽׁי: 2 וַיֹּ֨אמֶר ל֜וֹ חָלִ֗ילָה לֹ֤א תָמ֔וּת הִנֵּ֣ה לֹֽא־יַעֲשֶׂ֨ה אָבִ֜י דָּבָ֣ר גָּד֗וֹל א֣וֹ דָּבָ֣ר קָטֹ֔ן וְלֹ֥א יִגְלֶ֖ה אֶת־אָזְנִ֑י וּמַדּ֩וּעַ יַסְתִּ֨יר אָבִ֥י מִמֶּ֛נִּי אֶת־הַדָּבָ֥ר הַזֶּ֖ה אֵ֥ין זֹֽאת: 3 וַיִּשָּׁבַ֨ע ע֜וֹד דָּוִ֗ד וַיֹּ֙אמֶר֙ יָדֹ֨עַ יָדַ֜ע אָבִ֗יךָ כִּֽי־מָצָ֤אתִי חֵן֙ בְּעֵינֶ֔יךָ וַיֹּ֛אמֶר אַל־יֵֽדַע־זֹ֥את יְהוֹנָתָ֖ן פֶּן־יֵֽעָצֵ֑ב וְאוּלָ֗ם חַי־יְהוָה֙ וְחֵ֣י נַפְשֶׁ֔ךָ כִּ֣י כְפֶ֔שַׂע בֵּינִ֖י וּבֵ֥ין הַמָּֽוֶת: 4 וַיֹּ֥אמֶר יְהוֹנָתָ֖ן אֶל־דָּוִ֑ד מַה־תֹּאמַ֥ר נַפְשְׁךָ֖ וְאֶעֱשֶׂה־לָּֽךְ:
פ

5 וַיֹּ֨אמֶר דָּוִ֜ד אֶל־יְהוֹנָתָ֗ן הִנֵּה־חֹ֙דֶשׁ֙ מָחָ֔ר וְאָֽנֹכִ֛י יָשֹׁב־אֵשֵׁ֥ב עִם־הַמֶּ֖לֶךְ לֶאֱכ֑וֹל וְשִׁלַּחְתַּ֙נִי֙ וְנִסְתַּרְתִּ֣י בַשָּׂדֶ֔ה עַ֖ד הָעֶ֥רֶב הַשְּׁלִשִֽׁית: 6 אִם־פָּקֹ֥ד יִפְקְדֵ֖נִי אָבִ֑יךָ וְאָמַרְתָּ֗ נִשְׁאֹל֩ נִשְׁאַ֨ל מִמֶּ֤נִּי דָוִד֙ לָרוּץ֙ בֵּֽית־לֶ֣חֶם עִיר֔וֹ כִּ֣י זֶ֧בַח הַיָּמִ֛ים שָׁ֖ם לְכָל־הַמִּשְׁפָּחָֽה: 7 אִם־כֹּ֥ה יֹאמַ֛ר ט֖וֹב שָׁל֣וֹם לְעַבְדֶּ֑ךָ וְאִם־חָרֹ֤ה יֶֽחֱרֶה֙ ל֔וֹ דַּ֕ע כִּֽי־כָלְתָ֥ה הָרָעָ֖ה מֵעִמּֽוֹ: 8 וְעָשִׂ֤יתָ

brought your servant into a covenant of the LORD with you. Nevertheless, if there is iniquity in me, kill me yourself, for why should you bring me to your father?"

9 But Jonathan said, "Far be it from you! For if I knew certainly that evil was determined by my father to come upon you, then would I not tell you?"

10 Then David said to Jonathan, "Who will tell me, or what *if* your father answers you roughly?"

11 And Jonathan said to David, "Come, let us go out into the field." So both of them went out into the field. 12 Then Jonathan said to David: "The LORD God of Israel *is witness!* When I have sounded out my father sometime tomorrow, *or* the third *day,* and indeed *there is* good toward David, and I do not send to you and tell you, 13 may the LORD do so and much more to Jonathan. But if it pleases my father *to do* you evil, then I will report it to you and send you away, that you may go in safety. And the LORD be with you as He has been with my father. 14 And you shall not only show me the kindness of the LORD while I still live, that I may not die; 15 but you shall not cut off your kindness from my house forever, no, not when the LORD has cut off every one of the enemies of David from the face of the earth." 16 So Jonathan made *a covenant* with the house of David, *saying,* "Let the LORD require *it* at the hand of David's enemies."

17 Now Jonathan again caused David to vow, because he loved him; for he loved him as he loved his own soul. 18 Then Jonathan said to David, "Tomorrow *is* the New Moon; and you will be missed, because your seat will be empty. 19 And *when* you have stayed three days, go down quickly and come to the place where you hid on the day of the deed; and remain by the stone Ezel. 20 Then I will shoot three arrows to the side, as though I shot at a target; 21 and there I will send a lad, *saying,* 'Go, find the arrows.' If I expressly say to the lad, 'Look, the arrows *are* on this side of you; get them and come'—then, as the LORD lives, *there is* safety for you and no harm. 22 But if I say thus to the young man, 'Look, the arrows *are* beyond you'—go your way, for the LORD has sent you away. 23 And as for the matter which you and I have spoken of, indeed the LORD *be* between you and me forever."

24 Then David hid in the field. And when the New Moon had come, the king sat down to eat the feast. 25 Now the king sat on his seat, as at other times, on a seat by the wall. And Jonathan arose, and Abner sat by Saul's side, but David's place was empty. 26 Nevertheless Saul did not say anything that day, for he thought, "Something has happened to him;

חֶסֶד עַל־עַבְדְּךָ כִּי בִּבְרִית יְהֹוָה הֵבֵאתָ אֶת־עַבְדְּךָ עִמָּךְ וְאִם־יֶשׁ־בִּי עָוֹן הֲמִיתֵנִי אַתָּה וְעַד־אָבִיךָ לָמָּה־זֶּה תְבִיאֵנִי: פ

9 וַיֹּאמֶר יְהוֹנָתָן חָלִילָה לָּךְ כִּי ׀ אִם־יָדֹעַ אֵדַע כִּי־כָלְתָה הָרָעָה מֵעִם אָבִי לָבוֹא עָלֶיךָ וְלֹא אֹתָהּ אַגִּיד לָךְ: ס 10 וַיֹּאמֶר דָּוִד אֶל־יְהוֹנָתָן מִי יַגִּיד לִי אוֹ מַה־יַּעַנְךָ אָבִיךָ קָשָׁה: ס 11 וַיֹּאמֶר יְהוֹנָתָן אֶל־דָּוִד לְכָה וְנֵצֵא הַשָּׂדֶה וַיֵּצְאוּ שְׁנֵיהֶם הַשָּׂדֶה: ס 12 וַיֹּאמֶר יְהוֹנָתָן אֶל־דָּוִד יְהֹוָה אֱלֹהֵי יִשְׂרָאֵל כִּי־אֶחְקֹר אֶת־אָבִי כָּעֵת ׀ מָחָר הַשְּׁלִשִׁית וְהִנֵּה־טוֹב אֶל־דָּוִד וְלֹא־אָז אֶשְׁלַח אֵלֶיךָ וְגָלִיתִי אֶת־אָזְנֶךָ: 13 כֹּה־יַעֲשֶׂה יְהֹוָה לִיהוֹנָתָן וְכֹה יֹסִיף כִּי־יֵיטִב אֶל־אָבִי אֶת־הָרָעָה עָלֶיךָ וְגָלִיתִי אֶת־אָזְנֶךָ וְשִׁלַּחְתִּיךָ וְהָלַכְתָּ לְשָׁלוֹם וִיהִי יְהֹוָה עִמָּךְ כַּאֲשֶׁר הָיָה עִם־אָבִי: 14 וְלֹא אִם־עוֹדֶנִּי חַי וְלֹא־תַעֲשֶׂה עִמָּדִי חֶסֶד יְהֹוָה וְלֹא אָמוּת: 15 וְלֹא־תַכְרִת אֶת־חַסְדְּךָ מֵעִם בֵּיתִי עַד־עוֹלָם וְלֹא בְּהַכְרִת יְהֹוָה אֶת־אֹיְבֵי דָוִד אִישׁ מֵעַל פְּנֵי הָאֲדָמָה: 16 וַיִּכְרֹת יְהוֹנָתָן עִם־בֵּית דָּוִד וּבִקֵּשׁ יְהֹוָה מִיַּד אֹיְבֵי דָוִד: 17 וַיּוֹסֶף יְהוֹנָתָן לְהַשְׁבִּיעַ אֶת־דָּוִד בְּאַהֲבָתוֹ אֹתוֹ כִּי־אַהֲבַת נַפְשׁוֹ אֲהֵבוֹ: 18 וַיֹּאמֶר־לוֹ יְהוֹנָתָן מָחָר חֹדֶשׁ וְנִפְקַדְתָּ כִּי יִפָּקֵד מוֹשָׁבֶךָ: 19 וְשִׁלַּשְׁתָּ תֵּרֵד מְאֹד וּבָאתָ אֶל־הַמָּקוֹם אֲשֶׁר־נִסְתַּרְתָּ שָּׁם בְּיוֹם הַמַּעֲשֶׂה וְיָשַׁבְתָּ אֵצֶל הָאֶבֶן הָאָזֶל: 20 וַאֲנִי שְׁלֹשֶׁת הַחִצִּים צִדָּה אוֹרֶה לְשַׁלַּח־לִי לְמַטָּרָה: 21 וְהִנֵּה אֶשְׁלַח אֶת־הַנַּעַר לֵךְ מְצָא אֶת־הַחִצִּים אִם־אָמֹר אֹמַר לַנַּעַר הִנֵּה הַחִצִּים ׀ מִמְּךָ וָהֵנָּה קָחֶנּוּ ׀ וָבֹאָה כִּי־שָׁלוֹם לְךָ וְאֵין דָּבָר חַי־יְהֹוָה: 22 וְאִם־כֹּה אֹמַר לָעֶלֶם הִנֵּה הַחִצִּים מִמְּךָ וָהָלְאָה לֵךְ כִּי שִׁלַּחֲךָ יְהֹוָה: 23 וְהַדָּבָר אֲשֶׁר דִּבַּרְנוּ אֲנִי וָאָתָּה הִנֵּה יְהֹוָה בֵּינִי וּבֵינְךָ עַד־עוֹלָם: 24 וַיִּסָּתֵר דָּוִד בַּשָּׂדֶה וַיְהִי הַחֹדֶשׁ וַיֵּשֶׁב הַמֶּלֶךְ עַל־הַלֶּחֶם לֶאֱכוֹל: 25 וַיֵּשֶׁב הַמֶּלֶךְ עַל־מוֹשָׁבוֹ כְּפַעַם ׀ בְּפַעַם אֶל־מוֹשַׁב הַקִּיר וַיָּקָם יְהוֹנָתָן וַיֵּשֶׁב אַבְנֵר מִצַּד שָׁאוּל וַיִּפָּקֵד מְקוֹם דָּוִד: 26 וְלֹא־דִבֶּר שָׁאוּל מְאוּמָה

he *is* unclean, surely he *is* unclean." ²⁷And it happened the next day, the second *day* of the month, that David's place was empty. And Saul said to Jonathan his son, "Why has the son of Jesse not come to eat, either yesterday or today?"

²⁸So Jonathan answered Saul, "David earnestly asked *permission* of me *to go* to Bethlehem. ²⁹And he said, 'Please let me go, for our family has a sacrifice in the city, and my brother has commanded me *to be there*. And now, if I have found favor in your eyes, please let me get away and see my brothers.' Therefore he has not come to the king's table."

³⁰Then Saul's anger was aroused against Jonathan, and he said to him, "You son of a perverse, rebellious *woman!* Do I not know that you have chosen the son of Jesse to your own shame and to the shame of your mother's nakedness? ³¹For as long as the son of Jesse lives on the earth, you shall not be established, nor your kingdom. Now therefore, send and bring him to me, for he shall surely die."

³²And Jonathan answered Saul his father, and said to him, "Why should he be killed? What has he done?" ³³Then Saul cast a spear at him to kill him, by which Jonathan knew that it was determined by his father to kill David.

³⁴So Jonathan arose from the table in fierce anger, and ate no food the second day of the month, for he was grieved for David, because his father had treated him shamefully.

³⁵And so it was, in the morning, that Jonathan went out into the field at the time appointed with David, and a little lad *was* with him. ³⁶Then he said to his lad, "Now run, find the arrows which I shoot." As the lad ran, he shot an arrow beyond him. ³⁷When the lad had come to the place where the arrow was which Jonathan had shot, Jonathan cried out after the lad and said, "*Is* not the arrow beyond you?" ³⁸And Jonathan cried out after the lad, "Make haste, hurry, do not delay!" So Jonathan's lad gathered up the arrows and came back to his master. ³⁹But the lad did not know anything. Only Jonathan and David knew of the matter. ⁴⁰Then Jonathan gave his weapons to his lad, and said to him, "Go, carry *them* to the city."

⁴¹As soon as the lad had gone, David arose from *a place* toward the south, fell on his face to the ground, and bowed down three times. And they kissed one another; and they wept together, but David more so. ⁴²Then Jonathan said to David, "Go in peace, since we have both sworn in the name of the LORD, saying, 'May the LORD be between

בַּיּוֹם הַהוּא כִּי אָמַר מִקְרֶה הוּא בִּלְתִּי טָהוֹר הוּא כִּי־לֹא טָהוֹר: ס 27 וַיְהִי מִמָּחֳרַת הַחֹדֶשׁ הַשֵּׁנִי וַיִּפָּקֵד מְקוֹם דָּוִד ס וַיֹּאמֶר שָׁאוּל אֶל־יְהוֹנָתָן בְּנוֹ מַדּוּעַ לֹא־בָא בֶן־יִשַׁי גַּם־תְּמוֹל גַּם־הַיּוֹם אֶל־הַלָּחֶם: 28 וַיַּעַן יְהוֹנָתָן אֶת־שָׁאוּל נִשְׁאֹל נִשְׁאַל דָּוִד מֵעִמָּדִי עַד־בֵּית לָחֶם: 29 וַיֹּאמֶר שַׁלְּחֵנִי נָא כִּי זֶבַח מִשְׁפָּחָה לָנוּ בָּעִיר וְהוּא צִוָּה־לִי אָחִי וְעַתָּה אִם־מָצָאתִי חֵן בְּעֵינֶיךָ אִמָּלְטָה נָּא וְאֶרְאֶה אֶת־אֶחָי עַל־כֵּן לֹא־בָא אֶל־שֻׁלְחַן הַמֶּלֶךְ: ס 30 וַיִּחַר־אַף שָׁאוּל בִּיהוֹנָתָן וַיֹּאמֶר לוֹ בֶּן־נַעֲוַת הַמַּרְדּוּת הֲלוֹא יָדַעְתִּי כִּי־בֹחֵר אַתָּה לְבֶן־יִשַׁי לְבָשְׁתְּךָ וּלְבֹשֶׁת עֶרְוַת אִמֶּךָ: 31 כִּי כָל־הַיָּמִים אֲשֶׁר בֶּן־יִשַׁי חַי עַל־הָאֲדָמָה לֹא תִכּוֹן אַתָּה וּמַלְכוּתֶךָ וְעַתָּה שְׁלַח וְקַח אֹתוֹ אֵלַי כִּי בֶן־מָוֶת הוּא: ס 32 וַיַּעַן יְהוֹנָתָן אֶת־שָׁאוּל אָבִיו וַיֹּאמֶר אֵלָיו לָמָּה יוּמַת מֶה עָשָׂה: 33 וַיָּטֶל שָׁאוּל אֶת־הַחֲנִית עָלָיו לְהַכֹּתוֹ וַיֵּדַע יְהוֹנָתָן כִּי־כָלָה הִיא מֵעִם אָבִיו לְהָמִית אֶת־דָּוִד: ס 34 וַיָּקָם יְהוֹנָתָן מֵעִם הַשֻּׁלְחָן בָּחֳרִי־אָף וְלֹא־אָכַל בְּיוֹם־הַחֹדֶשׁ הַשֵּׁנִי לֶחֶם כִּי נֶעְצַב אֶל־דָּוִד כִּי הִכְלִמוֹ אָבִיו: ס 35 וַיְהִי בַבֹּקֶר וַיֵּצֵא יְהוֹנָתָן הַשָּׂדֶה לְמוֹעֵד דָּוִד וְנַעַר קָטֹן עִמּוֹ: 36 וַיֹּאמֶר לְנַעֲרוֹ רֻץ מְצָא נָא אֶת־הַחִצִּים אֲשֶׁר אָנֹכִי מוֹרֶה הַנַּעַר רָץ וְהוּא־יָרָה הַחֵצִי לְהַעֲבִרוֹ: 37 וַיָּבֹא הַנַּעַר עַד־מְקוֹם הַחֵצִי אֲשֶׁר יָרָה יְהוֹנָתָן וַיִּקְרָא יְהוֹנָתָן אַחֲרֵי הַנַּעַר וַיֹּאמֶר הֲלוֹא הַחֵצִי מִמְּךָ וָהָלְאָה: 38 וַיִּקְרָא יְהוֹנָתָן אַחֲרֵי הַנַּעַר מְהֵרָה חוּשָׁה אַל־תַּעֲמֹד וַיְלַקֵּט נַעַר יְהוֹנָתָן אֶת־הַחִצִּיP וַיָּבֹא אֶל־אֲדֹנָיו: 39 וְהַנַּעַר לֹא־יָדַע מְאוּמָה אַךְ יְהוֹנָתָן וְדָוִד יָדְעוּ אֶת־הַדָּבָר: 40 וַיִּתֵּן יְהוֹנָתָן אֶת־כֵּלָיו אֶל־הַנַּעַר אֲשֶׁר־לוֹ וַיֹּאמֶר לוֹ לֵךְ הָבֵיא הָעִיר: 41 הַנַּעַר בָּא וְדָוִד קָם מֵאֵצֶל הַנֶּגֶב וַיִּפֹּל לְאַפָּיו אַרְצָה וַיִּשְׁתַּחוּ שָׁלֹשׁ פְּעָמִים וַיִּשְּׁקוּ אִישׁ אֶת־רֵעֵהוּ וַיִּבְכּוּ אִישׁ אֶת־רֵעֵהוּ עַד־דָּוִד הִגְדִּיל: 42 וַיֹּאמֶר יְהוֹנָתָן לְדָוִד לֵךְ לְשָׁלוֹם אֲשֶׁר נִשְׁבַּעְנוּ

you and me, and between your descendants and my descendants, forever.'" So he arose and departed, and Jonathan went into the city.

21 Now David came to Nob, to Ahimelech the priest. And Ahimelech was afraid when he met David, and said to him, "Why *are* you alone, and no one is with you?"

2 So David said to Ahimelech the priest, "The king has ordered me on some business, and said to me, 'Do not let anyone know anything about the business on which I send you, or what I have commanded you.' And I have directed *my* young men to such and such a place. 3 Now therefore, what have you on hand? Give *me* five *loaves of* bread in my hand, or whatever can be found."

4 And the priest answered David and said, "*There is* no common bread on hand; but there is holy bread, if the young men have at least kept themselves from women."

5 Then David answered the priest, and said to him, "Truly, women *have been* kept from us about three days since I came out. And the vessels of the young men are holy, and the *bread is* in effect common, even though it was consecrated in the vessel this day."

6 So the priest gave him holy *bread;* for there was no bread there but the showbread which had been taken from before the LORD, in order to put hot bread *in its place* on the day when it was taken away.

7 Now a certain man of the servants of Saul *was* there that day, detained before the LORD. And his name *was* Doeg, an Edomite, the chief of the herdsmen who *belonged* to Saul.

8 And David said to Ahimelech, "Is there not here on hand a spear or a sword? For I have brought neither my sword nor my weapons with me, because the king's business required haste."

9 So the priest said, "The sword of Goliath the Philistine, whom you killed in the Valley of Elah, there it is, wrapped in a cloth behind the ephod. If you will take that, take *it.* For *there is* no other except that one here."

And David said, "*There is* none like it; give it to me."

10 Then David arose and fled that day from before Saul, and went to Achish the king of Gath. 11 And the servants of Achish said to him, "*Is* this not David the king of the land? Did they not sing of him to one another in dances, saying:

'Saul has slain his thousands,
And David his ten thousands'?"

שְׁנֵינוּ אֲנַחְנוּ בְּשֵׁם יְהוָה לֵאמֹר יְהוָה יִהְיֶה ׀ בֵּינִי
וּבֵינֶךָ וּבֵין זַרְעִי וּבֵין זַרְעֲךָ עַד־עוֹלָם׃ פ

כא וַיָּקָם וַיֵּלַךְ וִיהוֹנָתָן בָּא הָעִיר׃ 2 וַיָּבֹא דָוִד
נֹבֶה אֶל־אֲחִימֶלֶךְ הַכֹּהֵן וַיֶּחֱרַד אֲחִימֶלֶךְ לִקְרַאת
דָוִד וַיֹּאמֶר לוֹ מַדּוּעַ אַתָּה לְבַדֶּךָ וְאִישׁ אֵין
אִתָּךְ׃ 3 וַיֹּאמֶר דָּוִד לַאֲחִימֶלֶךְ הַכֹּהֵן הַמֶּלֶךְ צִוַּנִי
דָבָר וַיֹּאמֶר אֵלַי אִישׁ אַל־יֵדַע מְאוּמָה אֶת־
הַדָּבָר אֲשֶׁר־אָנֹכִי שֹׁלֵחֲךָ וַאֲשֶׁר צִוִּיתִךָ וְאֶת־
הַנְּעָרִים יוֹדַעְתִּי אֶל־מְקוֹם פְּלֹנִי אַלְמוֹנִי׃ 4 וְעַתָּה
מַה־יֵּשׁ תַּחַת־יָדְךָ חֲמִשָּׁה־לֶחֶם תְּנָה בְיָדִי אוֹ
הַנִּמְצָא׃ 5 וַיַּעַן הַכֹּהֵן אֶת־דָּוִד וַיֹּאמֶר אֵין־לֶחֶם חֹל
אֶל־תַּחַת יָדִי כִּי־אִם־לֶחֶם קֹדֶשׁ יֵשׁ אִם־נִשְׁמְרוּ
הַנְּעָרִים אַךְ מֵאִשָּׁה׃ פ

6 וַיַּעַן דָּוִד אֶת־הַכֹּהֵן וַיֹּאמֶר לוֹ כִּי אִם־אִשָּׁה
עֲצֻרָה־לָנוּ כִּתְמוֹל שִׁלְשֹׁם בְּצֵאתִי וַיִּהְיוּ כְלֵי־
הַנְּעָרִים קֹדֶשׁ וְהוּא דֶּרֶךְ חֹל וְאַף כִּי הַיּוֹם יִקְדַּשׁ
בַּכֶּלִי׃ 7 וַיִּתֶּן־לוֹ הַכֹּהֵן קֹדֶשׁ כִּי לֹא־הָיָה שָׁם
לֶחֶם כִּי־אִם־לֶחֶם הַפָּנִים הַמּוּסָרִים מִלִּפְנֵי יְהוָה
לָשׂוּם לֶחֶם חֹם בְּיוֹם הִלָּקְחוֹ׃ 8 וְשָׁם אִישׁ מֵעַבְדֵי
שָׁאוּל בַּיּוֹם הַהוּא נֶעְצָר לִפְנֵי יְהוָה וּשְׁמוֹ דֹּאֵג
הָאֲדֹמִי אַבִּיר הָרֹעִים אֲשֶׁר לְשָׁאוּל׃ 9 וַיֹּאמֶר דָּוִד
לַאֲחִימֶלֶךְ וְאִין יֶשׁ־פֹּה תַחַת־יָדְךָ חֲנִית אוֹ־חָרֶב כִּי
גַם־חַרְבִּי וְגַם־כֵּלַי לֹא־לָקַחְתִּי בְיָדִי כִּי־הָיָה דְבַר־
הַמֶּלֶךְ נָחוּץ׃ ס 10 וַיֹּאמֶר הַכֹּהֵן חֶרֶב
גָּלְיָת הַפְּלִשְׁתִּי אֲשֶׁר־הִכִּיתָ ׀ בְּעֵמֶק הָאֵלָה הִנֵּה־
הִיא לוּטָה בַשִּׂמְלָה אַחֲרֵי הָאֵפוֹד אִם־אֹתָהּ תִּקַּח־
לְךָ קָח כִּי אֵין אַחֶרֶת זוּלָתָהּ בָּזֶה וַיֹּאמֶר דָּוִד
אֵין כָּמוֹהָ תְּנֶנָּה לִּי׃ 11 וַיָּקָם דָּוִד וַיִּבְרַח בַּיּוֹם־
הַהוּא מִפְּנֵי שָׁאוּל וַיָּבֹא אֶל־אָכִישׁ מֶלֶךְ גַּת׃

12 Now David took these words to heart, and was very much afraid of Achish the king of Gath. 13 So he changed his behavior before them, pretended madness in their hands, scratched on the doors of the gate, and let his saliva fall down on his beard. 14 Then Achish said to his servants, "Look, you see the man is insane. Why have you brought him to me? 15 Have I need of madmen, that you have brought this *fellow* to play the madman in my presence? Shall this *fellow* come into my house?"

22 David therefore departed from there and escaped to the cave of Adullam. So when his brothers and all his father's house heard *it,* they went down there to him. 2 And everyone *who was* in distress, everyone who *was* in debt, and everyone *who was* discontented gathered to him. So he became captain over them. And there were about four hundred men with him.

3 Then David went from there to Mizpah of Moab; and he said to the king of Moab, "Please let my father and mother come here with you, till I know what God will do for me." 4 So he brought them before the king of Moab, and they dwelt with him all the time that David was in the stronghold.

5 Now the prophet Gad said to David, "Do not stay in the stronghold; depart, and go to the land of Judah." So David departed and went into the forest of Hereth.

6 When Saul heard that David and the men who *were* with him had been discovered—now Saul was staying in Gibeah under a tamarisk tree in Ramah, with his spear in his hand, and all his servants standing about him— 7 then Saul said to his servants who stood about him, "Hear now, you Benjamites! Will the son of Jesse give every one of you fields and vineyards, *and* make you all captains of thousands and captains of hundreds? 8 All of you have conspired against me, and *there is* no one who reveals to me that my son has made a covenant with the son of Jesse; and *there is* not one of you who is sorry for me or reveals to me that my son has stirred up my servant against me, to lie in wait, as *it is* this day."

9 Then answered Doeg the Edomite, who was set over the servants of Saul, and said, "I saw the son of Jesse going to Nob, to Ahimelech the son of Ahitub. 10 And he inquired of the LORD for him, gave him provisions, and gave him the sword of Goliath the Philistine."

11 So the king sent to call Ahimelech the priest, the son of Ahitub, and all his father's house, the priests who *were* in Nob. And they all came to the king. 12 And Saul said, "Hear now, son of Ahitub!"

12 וַיֹּאמְרוּ֩ עַבְדֵ֨י אָכִ֜ישׁ אֵלָ֗יו הֲלוֹא־זֶ֤ה דָוִד֙ מֶ֣לֶךְ הָאָ֔רֶץ הֲל֣וֹא לָזֶ֔ה יַעֲנ֥וּ בַמְּחֹל֖וֹת לֵאמֹ֑ר הִכָּ֤ה שָׁאוּל֙ בַּֽאֲלָפָ֔ו וְדָוִ֖ד בְּרִבְבֹתָֽו׃ 13 וַיָּ֧שֶׂם דָּוִ֛ד אֶת־הַדְּבָרִ֥ים הָאֵ֖לֶּה בִּלְבָב֑וֹ וַיִּרָ֣א מְאֹ֔ד מִפְּנֵ֖י אָכִ֥ישׁ מֶֽלֶךְ־גַּֽת׃ 14 וַיְשַׁנּ֤וֹ אֶת־טַעְמוֹ֙ בְּעֵ֣ינֵיהֶ֔ם וַיִּתְהֹלֵ֖ל בְּיָדָ֑ם וַיְתָו֙ עַל־דַּלְת֣וֹת הַשַּׁ֔עַר וַיּ֥וֹרֶד רִיר֖וֹ אֶל־זְקָנֽוֹ׃ 15 וַיֹּ֤אמֶר אָכִישׁ֙ אֶל־עֲבָדָ֔יו הִנֵּ֥ה תִרְא֖וּ אִ֣ישׁ מִשְׁתַּגֵּ֑עַ לָ֛מָּה תָּבִ֥יאוּ אֹת֖וֹ אֵלָֽי׃ 16 חֲסַ֤ר מְשֻׁגָּעִים֙ אָ֔נִי כִּֽי־הֲבֵאתֶ֣ם אֶת־זֶ֔ה לְהִשְׁתַּגֵּ֖עַ עָלָ֑י הֲזֶ֖ה יָב֥וֹא אֶל־בֵּיתִֽי׃ ס

כב וַיֵּ֤לֶךְ דָּוִד֙ מִשָּׁ֔ם וַיִּמָּלֵ֖ט אֶל־מְעָרַ֣ת עֲדֻלָּ֑ם וַיִּשְׁמְע֤וּ אֶחָיו֙ וְכָל־בֵּ֣ית אָבִ֔יו וַיֵּרְד֥וּ אֵלָ֖יו שָֽׁמָּה׃ 2 וַיִּֽתְקַבְּצ֣וּ אֵ֠לָיו כָּל־אִ֨ישׁ מָצ֜וֹק וְכָל־אִ֨ישׁ אֲשֶׁר־ל֤וֹ נֹשֶׁא֙ וְכָל־אִ֣ישׁ מַר־נֶ֔פֶשׁ וַיְהִ֥י עֲלֵיהֶ֖ם לְשָׂ֑ר וַיִּהְי֣וּ עִמּ֔וֹ כְּאַרְבַּ֥ע מֵא֖וֹת אִֽישׁ׃ 3 וַיֵּ֧לֶךְ דָּוִ֛ד מִשָּׁ֖ם מִצְפֵּ֣ה מוֹאָ֑ב וַיֹּ֣אמֶר ׀ אֶל־מֶ֣לֶךְ מוֹאָ֗ב יֵֽצֵא־נָ֞א אָבִ֤י וְאִמִּי֙ אִתְּכֶ֔ם עַ֚ד אֲשֶׁ֣ר אֵדַ֔ע מַה־יַּֽעֲשֶׂה־לִּ֖י אֱלֹהִֽים׃ 4 וַיַּנְחֵ֕ם אֶת־פְּנֵ֖י מֶ֣לֶךְ מוֹאָ֑ב וַיֵּשְׁב֣וּ עִמּ֔וֹ כָּל־יְמֵ֥י הֱיוֹת־דָּוִ֖ד בַּמְּצוּדָֽה׃ ס 5 וַיֹּאמֶר֩ גָּ֨ד הַנָּבִ֜יא אֶל־דָּוִ֗ד לֹ֤א תֵשֵׁב֙ בַּמְּצוּדָ֔ה לֵ֥ךְ וּבָֽאתָ־לְּךָ֖ אֶ֣רֶץ יְהוּדָ֑ה וַיֵּ֣לֶךְ דָּוִ֔ד וַיָּבֹ֖א יַ֥עַר חָֽרֶת׃ ס 6 וַיִּשְׁמַ֣ע שָׁא֔וּל כִּ֚י נוֹדַ֣ע דָּוִ֔ד וַֽאֲנָשִׁ֖ים אֲשֶׁ֣ר אִתּ֑וֹ וְשָׁאוּל֩ יוֹשֵׁ֨ב בַּגִּבְעָ֜ה תַּֽחַת־הָאֶ֤שֶׁל בָּֽרָמָה֙ וַחֲנִית֣וֹ בְיָד֔וֹ וְכָל־עֲבָדָ֖יו נִצָּבִ֥ים עָלָֽיו׃ 7 וַיֹּ֣אמֶר שָׁא֗וּל לַֽעֲבָדָיו֙ הַנִּצָּבִ֣ים עָלָ֔יו שִׁמְעוּ־נָ֖א בְּנֵ֣י יְמִינִ֑י גַּם־לְכֻלְּכֶ֗ם יִתֵּ֤ן בֶּן־יִשַׁי֙ שָׂד֣וֹת וּכְרָמִ֔ים לְכֻלְּכֶ֣ם יָשִׂ֔ים שָׂרֵ֥י אֲלָפִ֖ים וְשָׂרֵ֥י מֵאֽוֹת׃ 8 כִּ֣י קְשַׁרְתֶּ֣ם כֻּלְּכֶם֮ עָלַי֒ וְאֵין־גֹּלֶ֤ה אֶת־אָזְנִי֙ בִּכְרָת־בְּנִ֣י עִם־בֶּן־יִשַׁ֔י וְאֵין־חֹלֶ֥ה מִכֶּ֛ם עָלַ֖י וְגֹלֶ֣ה אֶת־אָזְנִ֑י כִּ֣י הֵקִים֩ בְּנִ֨י אֶת־עַבְדִּ֥י עָלַ֛י לְאֹרֵ֖ב כַּיּ֥וֹם הַזֶּֽה׃ ס 9 וַיַּ֜עַן דֹּאֵ֣ג הָאֲדֹמִ֗י וְה֛וּא נִצָּ֥ב עַל־עַבְדֵֽי־שָׁא֖וּל וַיֹּאמַ֑ר רָאִ֙יתִי֙ אֶת־בֶּן־יִשַׁ֔י בָּ֣א נֹ֔בֶה אֶל־אֲחִימֶ֖לֶךְ בֶּן־אֲחִטֽוּב׃ 10 וַיִּשְׁאַל־לוֹ֙ בַּֽיהוָ֔ה וְצֵידָ֖ה נָ֣תַן ל֑וֹ וְאֵ֗ת חֶ֛רֶב גָּלְיָ֥ת הַפְּלִשְׁתִּ֖י נָ֥תַן לֽוֹ׃ 11 וַיִּשְׁלַ֣ח הַמֶּ֡לֶךְ לִקְרֹא֩ אֶת־אֲחִימֶ֨לֶךְ בֶּן־אֲחִיט֜וּב הַכֹּהֵ֗ן וְאֵ֨ת כָּל־בֵּ֥ית אָבִ֛יו הַכֹּֽהֲנִ֖ים אֲשֶׁ֣ר בְּנֹ֑ב וַיָּבֹ֥אוּ כֻלָּ֖ם אֶל־הַמֶּֽלֶךְ׃ 12 וַיֹּ֣אמֶר שָׁא֔וּל ס

He answered, "Here I am, my lord."

¹³ Then Saul said to him, "Why have you conspired against me, you and the son of Jesse, in that you have given him bread and a sword, and have inquired of God for him, that he should rise against me, to lie in wait, as it is this day?"

¹⁴ So Ahimelech answered the king and said, "And who among all your servants is as faithful as David, who is the king's son-in-law, who goes at your bidding, and is honorable in your house? ¹⁵ Did I then begin to inquire of God for him? Far be it from me! Let not the king impute anything to his servant, or to any in the house of my father. For your servant knew nothing of all this, little or much."

¹⁶ And the king said, "You shall surely die, Ahimelech, you and all your father's house!" ¹⁷ Then the king said to the guards who stood about him, "Turn and kill the priests of the LORD, because their hand also is with David, and because they knew when he fled and did not tell it to me." But the servants of the king would not lift their hands to strike the priests of the LORD. ¹⁸ And the king said to Doeg, "You turn and kill the priests!" So Doeg the Edomite turned and struck the priests, and killed on that day eighty-five men who wore a linen ephod. ¹⁹ Also Nob, the city of the priests, he struck with the edge of the sword, both men and women, children and nursing infants, oxen and donkeys and sheep—with the edge of the sword.

²⁰ Now one of the sons of Ahimelech the son of Ahitub, named Abiathar, escaped and fled after David. ²¹ And Abiathar told David that Saul had killed the LORD's priests. ²² So David said to Abiathar, "I knew that day, when Doeg the Edomite was there, that he would surely tell Saul. I have caused the death of all the persons of your father's house. ²³ Stay with me; do not fear. For he who seeks my life seeks your life, but with me you shall be safe."

23

Then they told David, saying, "Look, the Philistines are fighting against Keilah, and they are robbing the threshing floors."

² Therefore David inquired of the LORD, saying, "Shall I go and attack these Philistines?"

And the LORD said to David, "Go and attack the Philistines, and save Keilah."

³ But David's men said to him, "Look, we are afraid here in Judah. How much more then if we go to Keilah against the armies of the Philistines?" ⁴ Then David inquired of the LORD once again.

שְׁמַֽע־נָ֖א בֶּן־אֲחִיט֑וּב וַיֹּ֖אמֶר הִנְנִ֥י אֲדֹנִֽי: 13 וַיֹּ֨אמֶר
אֵלָ֜יו שָׁא֗וּל לָ֤מָּה קְשַׁרְתֶּם֙ עָלַ֔י אַתָּ֖ה וּבֶן־יִשָׁ֑י
בְּתִתְּךָ֨ ל֜וֹ לֶ֤חֶם וְחֶ֨רֶב֙ וְשָׁא֥וֹל לוֹ֙ בֵּֽאלֹהִ֔ים לָק֥וּם
אֵלַ֛י לְאֹרֵ֖ב כַּיּ֥וֹם הַזֶּֽה: ס   14 וַיַּ֣עַן אֲחִימֶ֩לֶךְ֩
אֶת־הַמֶּ֨לֶךְ וַיֹּאמַ֜ר וּמִ֣י בְכָל־עֲבָדֶ֗יךָ כְּדָוִד֙ נֶֽאֱמָ֔ן
וַחֲתַ֥ן הַמֶּ֖לֶךְ וְסָ֣ר אֶל־מִשְׁמַעְתֶּ֑ךָ וְנִכְבָּ֖ד בְּבֵיתֶֽךָ:
15 הַיּ֧וֹם הַחִלֹּ֛תִי לִשְׁאָל־ל֥וֹ בֵאלֹהִ֖ים חָלִ֣ילָה לִּ֑י אַל־יָשֵׂם֩ הַמֶּ֨לֶךְ בְּעַבְדּ֜וֹ דָבָ֗ר בְּכָל־
בֵּ֣ית אָבִ֔י כִּ֠י לֹֽא־יָדַ֤ע עַבְדְּךָ֙ בְּכָל־זֹ֔את דָּבָ֥ר קָטֹ֖ן
א֥וֹ גָד֑וֹל: 16 וַיֹּ֣אמֶר הַמֶּ֔לֶךְ מ֥וֹת תָּמ֖וּת אֲחִימֶ֑לֶךְ
אַתָּ֖ה וְכָל־בֵּ֥ית אָבִֽיךָ: 17 וַיֹּ֣אמֶר הַמֶּ֡לֶךְ לָרָצִים֩
הַנִּצָּבִ֨ים עָלָ֜יו סֹ֥בּוּ וְהָמִ֣יתוּ ׀ כֹּהֲנֵ֣י יְהוָ֗ה כִּ֤י גַם־
יָדָם֙ עִם־דָּוִ֔ד וְכִ֤י יָֽדְעוּ֙ כִּֽי־בֹרֵ֣חַ ה֔וּא וְלֹ֥א גָל֖וּ
אֶת־אָזְנִ֑י וְלֹֽא־אָב֞וּ עַבְדֵ֤י הַמֶּ֨לֶךְ֙ לִשְׁלֹ֣חַ אֶת־יָדָ֔ם
לִפְגֹּ֖עַ בְּכֹהֲנֵ֥י יְהוָֽה: ס   18 וַיֹּ֨אמֶר הַמֶּ֜לֶךְ
לְדוֹיֵ֗ג סֹ֤ב אַתָּה֙ וּפְגַ֣ע בַּכֹּהֲנִ֔ים וַיִּסֹּ֞ב דּוֹיֵ֣ג הָאֲדֹמִ֗י
וַיִּפְגַּע־הוּא֙ בַּכֹּ֣הֲנִ֔ים וַיָּ֣מֶת ׀ בַּיּ֣וֹם הַה֗וּא שְׁמֹנִ֤ים
וַחֲמִשָּׁה֙ אִ֔ישׁ נֹשֵׂ֖א אֵפ֥וֹד בָּֽד: 19 וְאֵ֨ת נֹ֤ב עִיר־
הַכֹּֽהֲנִים֙ הִכָּ֣ה לְפִי־חֶ֔רֶב מֵאִישׁ֙ וְעַד־אִשָּׁ֔ה מֵֽעוֹלֵ֖ל
וְעַד־יוֹנֵ֑ק וְשׁ֧וֹר וַחֲמ֛וֹר וָשֶׂ֖ה לְפִי־חָֽרֶב: 20 וַיִּמָּלֵ֣ט
בֵּן־אֶחָ֗ד לַאֲחִימֶ֨לֶךְ֙ בֶּן־אֲחִט֔וּב וּשְׁמ֖וֹ אֶבְיָתָ֑ר וַיִּבְרַ֖ח
אַחֲרֵ֥י דָוִֽד: 21 וַיַּגֵּ֥ד אֶבְיָתָ֖ר לְדָוִ֑ד כִּ֚י הָרַ֣ג שָׁא֔וּל
אֵ֖ת כֹּהֲנֵ֥י יְהוָֽה: 22 וַיֹּ֨אמֶר דָּוִ֜ד לְאֶבְיָתָ֗ר יָדַ֜עְתִּי
בַּיּ֤וֹם הַהוּא֙ כִּֽי־שָׁ֣ם דּוֹיֵ֣ג הָֽאֲדֹמִ֔י כִּֽי־הַגֵּ֥ד יַגִּ֖יד
לְשָׁא֑וּל אָנֹכִ֣י סַבֹּ֗תִי בְּכָל־נֶ֖פֶשׁ בֵּ֥ית אָבִֽיךָ: 23 שְׁבָ֣ה
אִתִּ֗י אַל־תִּירָא֙ כִּ֠י אֲשֶׁר־יְבַקֵּ֤שׁ אֶת־נַפְשִׁי֙ יְבַקֵּ֣שׁ
אֶת־נַפְשֶׁ֔ךָ כִּֽי־מִשְׁמֶ֥רֶת אַתָּ֖ה עִמָּדִֽי:

כג וַיַּגִּ֥דוּ לְדָוִ֖ד לֵאמֹ֑ר הִנֵּ֤ה פְלִשְׁתִּים֙
נִלְחָמִ֣ים בִּקְעִילָ֔ה וְהֵ֖מָּה שֹׁסִ֥ים אֶת־הַגֳּרָנֽוֹת:
2 וַיִּשְׁאַ֨ל דָּוִ֤ד בַּֽיהוָה֙ לֵאמֹ֔ר הַאֵלֵ֣ךְ וְהִכֵּ֔יתִי
בַּפְּלִשְׁתִּ֖ים הָאֵ֑לֶּה   ס   וַיֹּ֨אמֶר יְהוָ֤ה אֶל־
דָּוִד֙ לֵ֣ךְ וְהִכִּ֣יתָ בַפְּלִשְׁתִּ֔ים וְהוֹשַׁעְתָּ֖ אֶת־קְעִילָֽה:
3 וַיֹּ֨אמְר֜וּ אַנְשֵׁ֤י דָוִד֙ אֵלָ֔יו הִנֵּ֛ה אֲנַ֥חְנוּ פֹ֖ה
בִֽיהוּדָ֣ה יְרֵאִ֑ים וְאַ֗ף כִּֽי־נֵלֵךְ֙ קְעִלָ֔ה אֶל־מַֽעַרְכ֖וֹת
פְּלִשְׁתִּֽים: ס   4 וַיּ֨וֹסֶף ע֤וֹד דָּוִד֙ לִשְׁאֹ֣ל

And the LORD answered him and said, "Arise, go down to Keilah. For I will deliver the Philistines into your hand." ⁵And David and his men went to Keilah and fought with the Philistines, struck them with a mighty blow, and took away their livestock. So David saved the inhabitants of Keilah.

⁶Now it happened, when Abiathar the son of Ahimelech fled to David at Keilah, *that* he went down *with* an ephod in his hand.

⁷And Saul was told that David had gone to Keilah. So Saul said, "God has delivered him into my hand, for he has shut himself in by entering a town that has gates and bars." ⁸Then Saul called all the people together for war, to go down to Keilah to besiege David and his men.

⁹When David knew that Saul plotted evil against him, he said to Abiathar the priest, "Bring the ephod here." ¹⁰Then David said, "O LORD God of Israel, Your servant has certainly heard that Saul seeks to come to Keilah to destroy the city for my sake. ¹¹Will the men of Keilah deliver me into his hand? Will Saul come down, as Your servant has heard? O LORD God of Israel, I pray, tell Your servant."

And the LORD said, "He will come down."

¹²Then David said, "Will the men of Keilah deliver me and my men into the hand of Saul?"

And the LORD said, "They will deliver *you*."

¹³So David and his men, about six hundred, arose and departed from Keilah and went wherever they could go. Then it was told Saul that David had escaped from Keilah; so he halted the expedition.

¹⁴And David stayed in strongholds in the wilderness, and remained in the mountains in the Wilderness of Ziph. Saul sought him every day, but God did not deliver him into his hand. ¹⁵So David saw that Saul had come out to seek his life. And David *was* in the Wilderness of Ziph in a forest. ¹⁶Then Jonathan, Saul's son, arose and went to David in the woods and strengthened his hand in God. ¹⁷And he said to him, "Do not fear, for the hand of Saul my father shall not find you. You shall be king over Israel, and I shall be next to you. Even my father Saul knows that." ¹⁸So the two of them made a covenant before the LORD. And David stayed in the woods, and Jonathan went to his own house.

¹⁹Then the Ziphites came up to Saul at Gibeah, saying, "Is David not hiding with us in strongholds in the woods, in the hill of Hachilah, which *is* on the south of Jeshimon? ²⁰Now therefore, O king, come down according to all the desire of your soul to come down; and our part *shall be* to deliver him into the king's hand."

בִּיהוָֹה ס וַיַּעֲנֵהוּ יְהוָֹה וַיֹּאמֶר קוּם רֵד
קְעִילָה כִּי־אֲנִי נֹתֵן אֶת־פְּלִשְׁתִּים בְּיָדֶךָ: 5 וַיֵּלֶךְ
דָּוִד וַאֲנָשָׁיו קְעִילָה וַיִּלָּחֶם בַּפְּלִשְׁתִּים וַיִּנְהַג אֶת־
מִקְנֵיהֶם וַיַּךְ בָּהֶם מַכָּה גְדוֹלָה וַיּשַׁע דָּוִד אֵת
יֹשְׁבֵי קְעִילָה: ס 6 וַיְהִי בִּבְרֹחַ אֶבְיָתָר בֶּן־
אֲחִימֶלֶךְ אֶל־דָּוִד קְעִילָה אֵפוֹד יָרַד בְּיָדוֹ: 7 וַיֻּגַּד
לְשָׁאוּל כִּי־בָא דָוִד קְעִילָה וַיֹּאמֶר שָׁאוּל נִכַּר אֹתוֹ
אֱלֹהִים בְּיָדִי כִּי נִסְגַּר לָבוֹא בְּעִיר דְּלָתַיִם וּבְרִיחַ:
8 וַיְשַׁמַּע שָׁאוּל אֶת־כָּל־הָעָם לַמִּלְחָמָה לָרֶדֶת
קְעִילָה לָצוּר אֶל־דָּוִד וְאֶל־אֲנָשָׁיו: 9 וַיֵּדַע דָּוִד
כִּי עָלָיו שָׁאוּל מַחֲרִישׁ הָרָעָה וַיֹּאמֶר אֶל־אֶבְיָתָר
הַכֹּהֵן הַגִּישָׁה הָאֵפוֹד: ס 10 וַיֹּאמֶר דָּוִד
יְהוָֹה אֱלֹהֵי יִשְׂרָאֵל שָׁמֹעַ שָׁמַע עַבְדְּךָ כִּי־מְבַקֵּשׁ
שָׁאוּל לָבוֹא אֶל־קְעִילָה לְשַׁחֵת לָעִיר בַּעֲבוּרִי:
11 הֲיַסְגִּרֻנִי בַעֲלֵי קְעִילָה בְּיָדוֹ הֲיֵרֵד שָׁאוּל
כַּאֲשֶׁר שָׁמַע עַבְדֶּךָ יְהוָֹה אֱלֹהֵי יִשְׂרָאֵל הַגֶּד־נָא
לְעַבְדֶּךָ ס וַיֹּאמֶר יְהוָֹה יֵרֵד: 12 וַיֹּאמֶר
דָּוִד הֲיַסְגִּרוּ בַּעֲלֵי קְעִילָה אֹתִי וְאֶת־אֲנָשַׁי בְּיַד־
שָׁאוּל וַיֹּאמֶר יְהוָֹה יַסְגִּירוּ: ס 13 וַיָּקָם
דָּוִד וַאֲנָשָׁיו כְּשֵׁשׁ־מֵאוֹת אִישׁ וַיֵּצְאוּ מִקְּעִלָה
וַיִּתְהַלְּכוּ בַּאֲשֶׁר יִתְהַלָּכוּ וּלְשָׁאוּל הֻגַּד כִּי־נִמְלַט
דָּוִד מִקְּעִילָה וַיֶּחְדַּל לָצֵאת: 14 וַיֵּשֶׁב דָּוִד בַּמִּדְבָּר
בַּמְּצָדוֹת וַיֵּשֶׁב בָּהָר בְּמִדְבַּר־זִיף וַיְבַקְשֵׁהוּ שָׁאוּל
כָּל־הַיָּמִים וְלֹא־נְתָנוֹ אֱלֹהִים בְּיָדוֹ: 15 וַיַּרְא דָוִד
כִּי־יָצָא שָׁאוּל לְבַקֵּשׁ אֶת־נַפְשׁוֹ וְדָוִד בְּמִדְבַּר־
זִיף בַּחֹרְשָׁה: ס 16 וַיָּקָם יְהוֹנָתָן בֶּן־שָׁאוּל
וַיֵּלֶךְ אֶל־דָּוִד חֹרְשָׁה וַיְחַזֵּק אֶת־יָדוֹ בֵּאלֹהִים:
17 וַיֹּאמֶר אֵלָיו אַל־תִּירָא כִּי לֹא תִמְצָאֲךָ יַד שָׁאוּל
אָבִי וְאַתָּה תִּמְלֹךְ עַל־יִשְׂרָאֵל וְאָנֹכִי אֶהְיֶה־לְּךָ
לְמִשְׁנֶה וְגַם־שָׁאוּל אָבִי יֹדֵעַ כֵּן: 18 וַיִּכְרְתוּ שְׁנֵיהֶם
בְּרִית לִפְנֵי יְהוָֹה וַיֵּשֶׁב דָּוִד בַּחֹרְשָׁה וִיהוֹנָתָן
הָלַךְ לְבֵיתוֹ: ס 19 וַיַּעֲלוּ זִפִים אֶל־שָׁאוּל
הַגִּבְעָתָה לֵאמֹר הֲלוֹא דָוִד מִסְתַּתֵּר עִמָּנוּ בַמְּצָדוֹת
בַּחֹרְשָׁה בְּגִבְעַת הַחֲכִילָה אֲשֶׁר מִימִין הַיְשִׁימוֹן:
20 וְעַתָּה לְכָל־אַוַּת נַפְשְׁךָ הַמֶּלֶךְ לָרֶדֶת רֵד וְלָנוּ

21 And Saul said, "Blessed *are* you of the LORD, for you have compassion on me. 22 Please go and find out for sure, and see the place where his hideout is, *and* who has seen him there. For I am told he is very crafty. 23 See therefore, and take knowledge of all the lurking places where he hides; and come back to me with certainty, and I will go with you. And it shall be, if he is in the land, that I will search for him throughout all the clans of Judah."

24 So they arose and went to Ziph before Saul. But David and his men *were* in the Wilderness of Maon, in the plain on the south of Jeshimon. 25 When Saul and his men went to seek *him,* they told David. Therefore he went down to the rock, and stayed in the Wilderness of Maon. And when Saul heard *that,* he pursued David in the Wilderness of Maon. 26 Then Saul went on one side of the mountain, and David and his men on the other side of the mountain. So David made haste to get away from Saul, for Saul and his men were encircling David and his men to take them.

27 But a messenger came to Saul, saying, "Hurry and come, for the Philistines have invaded the land!" 28 Therefore Saul returned from pursuing David, and went against the Philistines; so they called that place the Rock of Escape. 29 Then David went up from there and dwelt in strongholds at En Gedi.

24 Now it happened, when Saul had returned from following the Philistines, that it was told him, saying, "Take note! David *is* in the Wilderness of En Gedi." 2 Then Saul took three thousand chosen men from all Israel, and went to seek David and his men on the Rocks of the Wild Goats. 3 So he came to the sheepfolds by the road, where there *was* a cave; and Saul went in to attend to his needs. (David and his men were staying in the recesses of the cave.) 4 Then the men of David said to him, "This is the day of which the LORD said to you, 'Behold, I will deliver your enemy into your hand, that you may do to him as it seems good to you.'" And David arose and secretly cut off a corner of Saul's robe. 5 Now it happened afterward that David's heart troubled him because he had cut Saul's *robe.* 6 And he said to his men, "The LORD forbid that I should do this thing to my master, the LORD's anointed, to stretch out my hand against him, seeing he *is* the anointed of the LORD." 7 So David restrained his servants with *these* words, and did not allow them to rise against Saul. And Saul got up from the cave and went on *his* way.

21 וַיֹּאמֶר שָׁאוּל בְּרֻכִים אַתֶּם הַסְגִּירוּ בְּיַד הַמֶּלֶךְ:
22 לַיהוָה כִּי חֲמַלְתֶּם עָלָי: לְכוּ־נָא הָכִינוּ עוֹד וּדְעוּ וּרְאוּ אֶת־מְקוֹמוֹ אֲשֶׁר תִּהְיֶה רַגְלוֹ מִי רָאָהוּ שָׁם כִּי אָמַר אֵלַי עָרוֹם יַעְרִם הוּא: 23 וּרְאוּ וּדְעוּ מִכֹּל הַמַּחֲבֹאִים אֲשֶׁר יִתְחַבֵּא שָׁם וְשַׁבְתֶּם אֵלַי אֶל־נָכוֹן וְהָלַכְתִּי אִתְּכֶם וְהָיָה אִם־יֶשְׁנוֹ בָאָרֶץ וְחִפַּשְׂתִּי אֹתוֹ בְּכֹל אַלְפֵי יְהוּדָה: 24 וַיָּקוּמוּ וַיֵּלְכוּ זִיפָה לִפְנֵי שָׁאוּל וְדָוִד וַאֲנָשָׁיו בְּמִדְבַּר מָעוֹן בָּעֲרָבָה אֶל יְמִין הַיְשִׁימוֹן: 25 וַיֵּלֶךְ שָׁאוּל וַאֲנָשָׁיו לְבַקֵּשׁ וַיַּגִּדוּ לְדָוִד וַיֵּרֶד הַסֶּלַע וַיֵּשֶׁב בְּמִדְבַּר מָעוֹן וַיִּשְׁמַע שָׁאוּל וַיִּרְדֹּף אַחֲרֵי־דָוִד מִדְבַּר מָעוֹן: 26 וַיֵּלֶךְ שָׁאוּל מִצַּד הָהָר מִזֶּה וְדָוִד וַאֲנָשָׁיו מִצַּד הָהָר מִזֶּה וַיְהִי דָוִד נֶחְפָּז לָלֶכֶת מִפְּנֵי שָׁאוּל וְשָׁאוּל וַאֲנָשָׁיו עֹטְרִים אֶל־דָּוִד וְאֶל־אֲנָשָׁיו לְתָפְשָׂם: 27 וּמַלְאָךְ בָּא אֶל־שָׁאוּל לֵאמֹר מַהֲרָה וְלֵכָה כִּי־פָשְׁטוּ פְלִשְׁתִּים עַל־הָאָרֶץ: 28 וַיָּשָׁב שָׁאוּל מִרְדֹף אַחֲרֵי דָוִד וַיֵּלֶךְ לִקְרַאת פְּלִשְׁתִּים עַל־כֵּן קָרְאוּ לַמָּקוֹם הַהוּא סֶלַע הַמַּחְלְקוֹת: 29 וַיַּעַל דָּוִד מִשָּׁם וַיֵּשֶׁב בִּמְצָדוֹת עֵין גֶּדִי:

כד וַיְהִי כַּאֲשֶׁר שָׁב שָׁאוּל מֵאַחֲרֵי פְּלִשְׁתִּים וַיַּגִּדוּ לוֹ לֵאמֹר הִנֵּה דָוִד בְּמִדְבַּר עֵין גֶּדִי: ס 2 וַיִּקַּח שָׁאוּל שְׁלֹשֶׁת אֲלָפִים אִישׁ בָּחוּר מִכָּל־יִשְׂרָאֵל וַיֵּלֶךְ לְבַקֵּשׁ אֶת־דָּוִד וַאֲנָשָׁיו עַל־פְּנֵי צוּרֵי הַיְּעֵלִים: 3 וַיָּבֹא אֶל־גִּדְרוֹת הַצֹּאן עַל־הַדֶּרֶךְ וְשָׁם מְעָרָה וַיָּבֹא שָׁאוּל לְהָסֵךְ אֶת־רַגְלָיו וְדָוִד וַאֲנָשָׁיו בְּיַרְכְּתֵי הַמְּעָרָה יֹשְׁבִים: 4 וַיֹּאמְרוּ אַנְשֵׁי דָוִד אֵלָיו הִנֵּה הַיּוֹם אֲשֶׁר־אָמַר יְהוָה אֵלֶיךָ הִנֵּה אָנֹכִי נֹתֵן אֶת־אֹיִבְךָ בְּיָדֶךָ וְעָשִׂיתָ לּוֹ כַּאֲשֶׁר יִטַב בְּעֵינֶיךָ וַיָּקָם דָּוִד וַיִּכְרֹת אֶת־כְּנַף־הַמְּעִיל אֲשֶׁר־לְשָׁאוּל בַּלָּט: 5 וַיְהִי אַחֲרֵי־כֵן וַיַּךְ לֵב־דָּוִד אֹתוֹ עַל אֲשֶׁר כָּרַת אֶת־כָּנָף אֲשֶׁר לְשָׁאוּל: ס 6 וַיֹּאמֶר לַאֲנָשָׁיו חָלִילָה לִּי מֵיהוָה אִם־אֶעֱשֶׂה אֶת־הַדָּבָר הַזֶּה לַאדֹנִי לִמְשִׁיחַ יְהוָה לִשְׁלֹחַ יָדִי בּוֹ כִּי־מְשִׁיחַ יְהוָה הוּא: 7 וַיְשַׁסַּע דָּוִד אֶת־אֲנָשָׁיו בַּדְּבָרִים

כד 4 אֹיִבְךָ

8 David also arose afterward, went out of the cave, and called out to Saul, saying, "My lord the king!" And when Saul looked behind him, David stooped with his face to the earth, and bowed down. 9 And David said to Saul: "Why do you listen to the words of men who say, 'Indeed David seeks your harm'? 10 Look, this day your eyes have seen that the LORD delivered you today into my hand in the cave, and *someone* urged *me* to kill you. But *my eye* spared you, and I said, 'I will not stretch out my hand against my lord, for he *is* the LORD's anointed.' 11 Moreover, my father, see! Yes, see the corner of your robe in my hand! For in that I cut off the corner of your robe, and did not kill you, know and see that *there is* neither evil nor rebellion in my hand, and I have not sinned against you. Yet you hunt my life to take it. 12 Let the LORD judge between you and me, and let the LORD avenge me on you. But my hand shall not be against you. 13 As the proverb of the ancients says, 'Wickedness proceeds from the wicked.' But my hand shall not be against you. 14 After whom has the king of Israel come out? Whom do you pursue? A dead dog? A flea? 15 Therefore let the LORD be judge, and judge between you and me, and see and plead my case, and deliver me out of your hand."

16 So it was, when David had finished speaking these words to Saul, that Saul said, "*Is* this your voice, my son David?" And Saul lifted up his voice and wept. 17 Then he said to David: "You *are* more righteous than I; for you have rewarded me with good, whereas I have rewarded you with evil. 18 And you have shown this day how you have dealt well with me; for when the LORD delivered me into your hand, you did not kill me. 19 For if a man finds his enemy, will he let him get away safely? Therefore may the LORD reward you with good for what you have done to me this day. 20 And now I know indeed that you shall surely be king, and that the kingdom of Israel shall be established in your hand. 21 Therefore swear now to me by the LORD that you will not cut off my descendants after me, and that you will not destroy my name from my father's house."

22 So David swore to Saul. And Saul went home, but David and his men went up to the stronghold.

25 Then Samuel died; and the Israelites gathered together and lamented for him, and buried him at his home in Ramah. And David arose and went down to the Wilderness of Paran.

2 Now *there was* a man in Maon whose business *was* in Carmel, and the man *was* very rich. He had three thousand sheep and a thousand goats. And he

וְלֹא נְתָנָם לָקוּם אֶל־שָׁאוּל וְשָׁאוּל קָם מֵהַמְּעָרָה וַיֵּלֶךְ בְּדַרְכּוֹ: ס 8 וַיָּקָם דָּוִד אַחֲרֵי־כֵן וַיֵּצֵא מן־הַמְּעָרָה וַיִּקְרָא אַחֲרֵי־שָׁאוּל לֵאמֹר אֲדֹנִי הַמֶּלֶךְ וַיַּבֵּט שָׁאוּל אַחֲרָיו וַיִּקֹּד דָּוִד אַפַּיִם אַרְצָה וַיִּשְׁתָּחוּ: ס 9 וַיֹּאמֶר דָּוִד לְשָׁאוּל לָמָּה תִשְׁמַע אֶת־דִּבְרֵי אָדָם לֵאמֹר הִנֵּה דָוִד מְבַקֵּשׁ רָעָתֶךָ: 10 הִנֵּה הַיּוֹם הַזֶּה רָאוּ עֵינֶיךָ אֵת אֲשֶׁר־נְתָנְךָ יְהוָה ׀ הַיּוֹם ׀ בְּיָדִי בַּמְּעָרָה וְאָמַר לַהֲרָגֲךָ וַתָּחָס עָלֶיךָ וָאֹמַר לֹא־אֶשְׁלַח יָדִי בַּאדֹנִי כִּי־מְשִׁיחַ יְהוָה הוּא: 11 וְאָבִי רְאֵה גַּם רְאֵה אֶת־כְּנַף מְעִילְךָ בְּיָדִי כִּי בְּכָרְתִי אֶת־כְּנַף מְעִילְךָ וְלֹא הֲרַגְתִּיךָ דַּע וּרְאֵה כִּי אֵין בְּיָדִי רָעָה וָפֶשַׁע וְלֹא־חָטָאתִי לָךְ וְאַתָּה צֹדֶה אֶת־נַפְשִׁי לְקַחְתָּהּ: 12 יִשְׁפֹּט יְהוָה בֵּינִי וּבֵינֶךָ וּנְקָמַנִי יְהוָה מִמֶּךָּ וְיָדִי לֹא תִהְיֶה־בָּךְ: 13 כַּאֲשֶׁר יֹאמַר מְשַׁל הַקַּדְמֹנִי מֵרְשָׁעִים יֵצֵא רֶשַׁע וְיָדִי לֹא תִהְיֶה־בָּךְ: 14 אַחֲרֵי מִי יָצָא מֶלֶךְ יִשְׂרָאֵל אַחֲרֵי מִי אַתָּה רֹדֵף אַחֲרֵי כֶּלֶב מֵת אַחֲרֵי פַּרְעֹשׁ אֶחָד: 15 וְהָיָה יְהוָה לְדַיָּן וְשָׁפַט בֵּינִי וּבֵינֶךָ וְיֵרֶא וְיָרֵב אֶת־רִיבִי וְיִשְׁפְּטֵנִי מִיָּדֶךָ: פ

16 וַיְהִי ׀ כְּכַלּוֹת דָּוִד לְדַבֵּר אֶת־הַדְּבָרִים הָאֵלֶּה אֶל־שָׁאוּל וַיֹּאמֶר שָׁאוּל הֲקֹלְךָ זֶה בְּנִי דָוִד וַיִּשָּׂא שָׁאוּל קֹלוֹ וַיֵּבְךְּ: 17 וַיֹּאמֶר אֶל־דָּוִד צַדִּיק אַתָּה מִמֶּנִּי כִּי אַתָּה גְּמַלְתַּנִי הַטּוֹבָה וַאֲנִי גְּמַלְתִּיךָ הָרָעָה: 18 וְאַתְּ הִגַּדְתָּ הַיּוֹם אֵת אֲשֶׁר־עָשִׂיתָה אִתִּי טוֹבָה אֵת אֲשֶׁר סִגְּרַנִי יְהוָה בְּיָדְךָ וְלֹא הֲרַגְתָּנִי: 19 וְכִי־יִמְצָא אִישׁ אֶת־אֹיְבוֹ וְשִׁלְּחוֹ בְּדֶרֶךְ טוֹבָה וַיהוָה יְשַׁלֶּמְךָ טוֹבָה תַּחַת הַיּוֹם הַזֶּה אֲשֶׁר עָשִׂיתָה לִי: 20 וְעַתָּה הִנֵּה יָדַעְתִּי כִּי מָלֹךְ תִּמְלוֹךְ וְקָמָה בְּיָדְךָ מַמְלֶכֶת יִשְׂרָאֵל: 21 וְעַתָּה הִשָּׁבְעָה לִּי בַּיהוָה אִם־תַּכְרִית אֶת־זַרְעִי אַחֲרָי וְאִם־תַּשְׁמִיד אֶת־שְׁמִי מִבֵּית אָבִי: 22 וַיִּשָּׁבַע דָּוִד לְשָׁאוּל וַיֵּלֶךְ שָׁאוּל אֶל־בֵּיתוֹ וְדָוִד וַאֲנָשָׁיו עָלוּ עַל־הַמְּצוּדָה: פ

כה וַיָּמָת שְׁמוּאֵל וַיִּקָּבְצוּ כָל־יִשְׂרָאֵל וַיִּסְפְּדוּ־לוֹ וַיִּקְבְּרֻהוּ בְּבֵיתוֹ בָּרָמָה וַיָּקָם דָּוִד וַיֵּרֶד אֶל־מִדְבַּר פָּארָן: ס 2 וְאִישׁ בְּמָעוֹן וּמַעֲשֵׂהוּ בַכַּרְמֶל וְהָאִישׁ גָּדוֹל מְאֹד וְלוֹ צֹאן שְׁלֹשֶׁת־אֲלָפִים

was shearing his sheep in Carmel. ³ The name of the man *was* Nabal, and the name of his wife Abigail. And *she was* a woman of good understanding and beautiful appearance; but the man *was* harsh and evil in *his* doings. He *was of the house of* Caleb.

⁴ When David heard in the wilderness that Nabal was shearing his sheep, ⁵ David sent ten young men; and David said to the young men, "Go up to Carmel, go to Nabal, and greet him in my name. ⁶ And thus you shall say to him who lives in *prosperity:* 'Peace *be* to you, peace to your house, and peace to all that you have! ⁷ Now I have heard that you have shearers. Your shepherds were with us, and we did not hurt them, nor was there anything missing from them all the while they were in Carmel. ⁸ Ask your young men, and they will tell you. Therefore let *my* young men find favor in your eyes, for we come on a feast day. Please give whatever comes to your hand to your servants and to your son David.' "

⁹ So when David's young men came, they spoke to Nabal according to all these words in the name of David, and waited.

¹⁰ Then Nabal answered David's servants, and said, "Who *is* David, and who *is* the son of Jesse? There are many servants nowadays who break away each one from his master. ¹¹ Shall I then take my bread and my water and my meat that I have killed for my shearers, and give *it* to men when I do not know where they *are* from?"

¹² So David's young men turned on their heels and went back; and they came and told him all these words. ¹³ Then David said to his men, "Every man gird on his sword." So every man girded on his sword, and David also girded on his sword. And about four hundred men went with David, and two hundred stayed with the supplies.

¹⁴ Now one of the young men told Abigail, Nabal's wife, saying, "Look, David sent messengers from the wilderness to greet our master; and he reviled them. ¹⁵ But the men *were* very good to us, and we were not hurt, nor did we miss anything as long as we accompanied them, when we were in the fields. ¹⁶ They were a wall to us both by night and day, all the time we were with them keeping the sheep. ¹⁷ Now therefore, know and consider what you will do, for harm is determined against our master and against all his household. For he *is such* a scoundrel that *one* cannot speak to him."

¹⁸ Then Abigail made haste and took two hundred *loaves* of bread, two skins of wine, five sheep already dressed, five seahs of roasted *grain,* one hundred clusters of raisins, and two hundred cakes of figs, and loaded *them* on donkeys. ¹⁹ And

3 וְשָׁם אֶלֶף עִזִּים וַיְהִי בִגְזֹז אֶת־צֹאנוֹ בַּכַּרְמֶל: וְשֵׁם הָאִישׁ נָבָל וְשֵׁם אִשְׁתּוֹ אֲבִגָיִל וְהָאִשָּׁה טוֹבַת־שֶׂכֶל וִיפַת תֹּאַר וְהָאִישׁ קָשֶׁה וְרַע מַעֲלָלִים וְהוּא כָלֵבּיᴾ: 4 וַיִּשְׁמַע דָּוִד בַּמִּדְבָּר כִּי־גֹזֵז נָבָל אֶת־צֹאנוֹ: 5 וַיִּשְׁלַח דָּוִד עֲשָׂרָה נְעָרִים וַיֹּאמֶר דָּוִד לַנְּעָרִים עֲלוּ כַרְמֶלָה וּבָאתֶם אֶל־נָבָל וּשְׁאֶלְתֶּם־לוֹ בִשְׁמִי לְשָׁלוֹם: 6 וַאֲמַרְתֶּם כֹּה לֶחָי וְאַתָּה שָׁלוֹם וּבֵיתְךָ שָׁלוֹם וְכֹל אֲשֶׁר־לְךָ שָׁלוֹם: 7 וְעַתָּה שָׁמַעְתִּי כִּי גֹזְזִים לָךְ עַתָּה הָרֹעִים אֲשֶׁר־לְךָ הָיוּ עִמָּנוּ לֹא הֶכְלַמְנוּם וְלֹא־נִפְקַד לָהֶם מְאוּמָה כָּל־יְמֵי הֱיוֹתָם בַּכַּרְמֶל: 8 שְׁאַל אֶת־נְעָרֶיךָ וְיַגִּידוּ לָךְ וְיִמְצְאוּ הַנְּעָרִים חֵן בְּעֵינֶיךָ כִּי־עַל־יוֹם טוֹב בָּנוּᴾ תְּנָה־נָּא אֵת אֲשֶׁר תִּמְצָא יָדְךָ לַעֲבָדֶיךָ וּלְבִנְךָ לְדָוִד: 9 וַיָּבֹאוּ נַעֲרֵי דָוִד וַיְדַבְּרוּ אֶל־נָבָל כְּכָל־הַדְּבָרִים הָאֵלֶּה בְּשֵׁם דָּוִד וַיָּנוּחוּ: 10 וַיַּעַן נָבָל אֶת־עַבְדֵי דָוִד וַיֹּאמֶר מִי דָוִד וּמִי בֶן־יִשַׁי הַיּוֹם רַבּוּ עֲבָדִים הַמִּתְפָּרְצִים אִישׁ מִפְּנֵי אֲדֹנָיו: 11 וְלָקַחְתִּי אֶת־לַחְמִי וְאֶת־מֵימַי וְאֵת טִבְחָתִי אֲשֶׁר טָבַחְתִּי לְגֹזְזָי וְנָתַתִּי לַאֲנָשִׁים אֲשֶׁר לֹא יָדַעְתִּי אֵי מִזֶּה הֵמָּה: 12 וַיַּהַפְכוּ נַעֲרֵי־דָוִד לְדַרְכָּם וַיָּשֻׁבוּ וַיָּבֹאוּ וַיַּגִּדוּ לוֹ כְּכֹל הַדְּבָרִים הָאֵלֶּה: 13 וַיֹּאמֶר דָּוִד לַאֲנָשָׁיו חִגְרוּ ׀ אִישׁ אֶת־חַרְבּוֹ וַיַּחְגְּרוּ אִישׁ אֶת־חַרְבּוֹ וַיַּחְגֹּר גַּם־דָּוִד אֶת־חַרְבּוֹ וַיַּעֲלוּ ׀ אַחֲרֵי דָוִד כְּאַרְבַּע מֵאוֹת אִישׁ וּמָאתַיִם יָשְׁבוּ עַל־הַכֵּלִים: 14 וְלַאֲבִיגַיִל אֵשֶׁת נָבָל הִגִּיד נַעַר־אֶחָד מֵהַנְּעָרִים לֵאמֹר הִנֵּה שָׁלַח דָּוִד מַלְאָכִים ׀ מֵהַמִּדְבָּר לְבָרֵךְ אֶת־אֲדֹנֵינוּ וַיָּעַט בָּהֶם: 15 וְהָאֲנָשִׁים טֹבִים לָנוּ מְאֹד וְלֹא הָכְלַמְנוּ וְלֹא־פָקַדְנוּ מְאוּמָה כָּל־יְמֵי הִתְהַלַּכְנוּ אִתָּם בִּהְיוֹתֵנוּ בַּשָּׂדֶה: 16 חוֹמָה הָיוּ עָלֵינוּ גַּם־לַיְלָה גַּם־יוֹמָם כָּל־יְמֵי הֱיוֹתֵנוּ עִמָּם רֹעִים הַצֹּאן: 17 וְעַתָּה דְּעִי וּרְאִי מַה־תַּעֲשִׂי כִּי־כָלְתָה הָרָעָה אֶל־אֲדֹנֵינוּ וְעַל כָּל־בֵּיתוֹ וְהוּא בֶּן־בְּלִיַּעַל מִדַּבֵּר אֵלָיו: 18 וַתְּמַהֵר אֲבוֹגַיִלᴾ וַתִּקַּח מָאתַיִם לֶחֶם וּשְׁנַיִם נִבְלֵי־יַיִן וְחָמֵשׁ צֹאן עֲשׂוּוֹתᴾ וְחָמֵשׁ סְאִים קָלִי וּמֵאָה צִמֻּקִים וּמָאתַיִם דְּבֵלִים וַתָּשֶׂם עַל־הַחֲמֹרִים: 19 וַתֹּאמֶר

כה 3 כָּלִבּי　8 בָּאנוּ　18 אֲבִיגַיִל, עֲשׂוּוֹת

she said to her servants, "Go on before me; see, I am coming after you." But she did not tell her husband Nabal.

20 So it was, *as* she rode on the donkey, that she went down under cover of the hill; and there were David and his men, coming down toward her, and she met them. 21 Now David had said, "Surely in vain I have protected all that this *fellow* has in the wilderness, so that nothing was missed of all that *belongs* to him. And he has repaid me evil for good. 22 May God do so, and more also, to the enemies of David, if I leave one male of all who *belong* to him by morning light."

23 Now when Abigail saw David, she dismounted quickly from the donkey, fell on her face before David, and bowed down to the ground. 24 So she fell at his feet and said: "On me, my lord, *on me let* this iniquity *be!* And please let your maidservant speak in your ears, and hear the words of your maidservant. 25 Please, let not my lord regard this scoundrel Nabal. For as his name *is,* so *is* he: Nabal *is* his name, and folly *is* with him! But I, your maidservant, did not see the young men of my lord whom you sent. 26 Now therefore, my lord, *as* the LORD lives and *as* your soul lives, since the LORD has held you back from coming to bloodshed and from avenging yourself with your own hand, now then, let your enemies and those who seek harm for my lord be as Nabal. 27 And now this present which your maidservant has brought to my lord, let it be given to the young men who follow my lord. 28 Please forgive the trespass of your maidservant. For the LORD will certainly make for my lord an enduring house, because my lord fights the battles of the LORD, and evil is not found in you throughout your days. 29 Yet a man has risen to pursue you and seek your life, but the life of my lord shall be bound in the bundle of the living with the LORD your God; and the lives of your enemies He shall sling out, *as from* the pocket of a sling. 30 And it shall come to pass, when the LORD has done for my lord according to all the good that He has spoken concerning you, and has appointed you ruler over Israel, 31 that this will be no grief to you, nor offense of heart to my lord, either that you have shed blood without cause, or that my lord has avenged himself. But when the LORD has dealt well with my lord, then remember your maidservant."

32 Then David said to Abigail: "Blessed *is* the LORD God of Israel, who sent you this day to meet me! 33 And blessed *is* your advice and blessed *are* you, because you have kept me this day from coming to bloodshed and from avenging myself with my own hand. 34 For indeed, *as* the LORD God

---

לְנַעֲרֶיהָ עִבְרוּ לְפָנַי הִנְנִי אַחֲרֵיכֶם בָּאָה וּלְאִישָׁהּ
נָבָל לֹא הִגִּידָה: 20 וְהָיָה הִיא רֹכֶבֶת עַל־
הַחֲמוֹר וְיֹרֶדֶת בְּסֵתֶר הָהָר וְהִנֵּה דָוִד וַאֲנָשָׁיו
יֹרְדִים לִקְרָאתָהּ וַתִּפְגֹּשׁ אֹתָם: 21 וְדָוִד אָמַר
אַךְ לַשֶּׁקֶר שָׁמַרְתִּי אֶת־כָּל־אֲשֶׁר לָזֶה בַּמִּדְבָּר
וְלֹא־נִפְקַד מִכָּל־אֲשֶׁר־לוֹ מְאוּמָה וַיָּשֶׁב־לִי רָעָה
תַּחַת טוֹבָה: 22 כֹּה־יַעֲשֶׂה אֱלֹהִים לְאֹיְבֵי דָוִד
וְכֹה יֹסִיף אִם־אַשְׁאִיר מִכָּל־אֲשֶׁר־לוֹ עַד־הַבֹּקֶר
מַשְׁתִּין בְּקִיר: 23 וַתֵּרֶא אֲבִיגַיִל אֶת־דָּוִד וַתְּמַהֵר
וַתֵּרֶד מֵעַל הַחֲמוֹר וַתִּפֹּל לְאַפֵּי דָוִד עַל־פָּנֶיהָ
וַתִּשְׁתַּחוּ אָרֶץ: 24 וַתִּפֹּל עַל־רַגְלָיו וַתֹּאמֶר בִּי־אֲנִי
אֲדֹנִי הֶעָוֹן וּתְדַבֶּר־נָא אֲמָתְךָ בְּאָזְנֶיךָ וּשְׁמַע אֵת
דִּבְרֵי אֲמָתֶךָ: 25 אַל־נָא יָשִׂים אֲדֹנִי אֶת־לִבּוֹ
אֶל־אִישׁ הַבְּלִיַּעַל הַזֶּה עַל־נָבָל כִּי כִשְׁמוֹ כֶּן־הוּא
נָבָל שְׁמוֹ וּנְבָלָה עִמּוֹ וַאֲנִי אֲמָתְךָ לֹא רָאִיתִי אֶת־
נַעֲרֵי אֲדֹנִי אֲשֶׁר שָׁלָחְתָּ: 26 וְעַתָּה אֲדֹנִי חַי־יְהֹוָה
וְחֵי־נַפְשְׁךָ אֲשֶׁר מְנָעֲךָ יְהֹוָה מִבּוֹא בְדָמִים וְהוֹשֵׁעַ
יָדְךָ לָךְ וְעַתָּה יִהְיוּ כְנָבָל אֹיְבֶיךָ וְהַמְבַקְשִׁים
אֶל־אֲדֹנִי רָעָה: 27 וְעַתָּה הַבְּרָכָה הַזֹּאת אֲשֶׁר־
הֵבִיא שִׁפְחָתְךָ לַאדֹנִי וְנִתְּנָה לַנְּעָרִים הַמִּתְהַלְּכִים
בְּרַגְלֵי אֲדֹנִי: 28 שָׂא נָא לְפֶשַׁע אֲמָתֶךָ כִּי עָשֹׂה־
יַעֲשֶׂה יְהֹוָה לַאדֹנִי בַּיִת נֶאֱמָן כִּי־מִלְחֲמוֹת יְהֹוָה
אֲדֹנִי נִלְחָם וְרָעָה לֹא־תִמָּצֵא בְךָ מִיָּמֶיךָ: 29 וַיָּקָם
אָדָם לִרְדָפְךָ וּלְבַקֵּשׁ אֶת־נַפְשֶׁךָ וְהָיְתָה נֶפֶשׁ אֲדֹנִי
צְרוּרָה בִּצְרוֹר הַחַיִּים אֵת יְהֹוָה אֱלֹהֶיךָ וְאֵת
נֶפֶשׁ אֹיְבֶיךָ יְקַלְּעֶנָּה בְּתוֹךְ כַּף הַקָּלַע: 30 וְהָיָה
כִּי־יַעֲשֶׂה יְהֹוָה לַאדֹנִי כְּכֹל אֲשֶׁר־דִּבֶּר אֶת־הַטּוֹבָה
עָלֶיךָ וְצִוְּךָ לְנָגִיד עַל־יִשְׂרָאֵל: 31 וְלֹא תִהְיֶה זֹאת
לְךָ לְפוּקָה וּלְמִכְשׁוֹל לֵב לַאדֹנִי וְלִשְׁפָּךְ־דָּם חִנָּם
וּלְהוֹשִׁיעַ אֲדֹנִי לוֹ וְהֵיטִב יְהֹוָה לַאדֹנִי וְזָכַרְתָּ אֶת־
אֲמָתֶךָ: ס 32 וַיֹּאמֶר דָּוִד לַאֲבִיגַל בָּרוּךְ
יְהֹוָה אֱלֹהֵי יִשְׂרָאֵל אֲשֶׁר שְׁלָחֵךְ הַיּוֹם הַזֶּה
לִקְרָאתִי: 33 וּבָרוּךְ טַעְמֵךְ וּבְרוּכָה אָתְּ אֲשֶׁר
כְּלִתִנִי הַיּוֹם הַזֶּה מִבּוֹא בְדָמִים וְהֹשֵׁעַ יָדִי לִי:
34 וְאוּלָם חַי־יְהֹוָה אֱלֹהֵי יִשְׂרָאֵל אֲשֶׁר מְנָעַנִי
מֵהָרַע אֹתָךְ כִּי לוּלֵי מִהַרְתְּ וַתָּבֹאתִ לִקְרָאתִי

of Israel lives, who has kept me back from hurting you, unless you had hurried and come to meet me, surely by morning light no males would have been left to Nabal!" 35 So David received from her hand what she had brought him, and said to her, "Go up in peace to your house. See, I have heeded your voice and respected your person."

36 Now Abigail went to Nabal, and there he was, holding a feast in his house, like the feast of a king. And Nabal's heart *was* merry within him, for he *was* very drunk; therefore she told him nothing, little or much, until morning light. 37 So it was, in the morning, when the wine had gone from Nabal, and his wife had told him these things, that his heart died within him, and he became *like* a stone. 38 Then it happened, *after* about ten days, that the LORD struck Nabal, and he died.

39 So when David heard that Nabal was dead, he said, "Blessed *be* the LORD, who has pleaded the cause of my reproach from the hand of Nabal, and has kept His servant from evil! For the LORD has returned the wickedness of Nabal on his own head."

And David sent and proposed to Abigail, to take her as his wife. 40 When the servants of David had come to Abigail at Carmel, they spoke to her saying, "David sent us to you, to ask you to become his wife."

41 Then she arose, bowed her face to the earth, and said, "Here is your maidservant, a servant to wash the feet of the servants of my lord." 42 So Abigail rose in haste and rode on a donkey, attended by five of her maidens; and she followed the messengers of David, and became his wife. 43 David also took Ahinoam of Jezreel, and so both of them were his wives.

44 But Saul had given Michal his daughter, David's wife, to Palti the son of Laish, who *was* from Gallim.

26 Now the Ziphites came to Saul at Gibeah, saying, "Is David not hiding in the hill of Hachilah, opposite Jeshimon?" 2 Then Saul arose and went down to the Wilderness of Ziph, having three thousand chosen men of Israel with him, to seek David in the Wilderness of Ziph. 3 And Saul encamped in the hill of Hachilah, which *is* opposite Jeshimon, by the road. But David stayed in the wilderness, and he saw that Saul came after him into the wilderness. 4 David therefore sent out spies, and understood that Saul had indeed come.

5 So David arose and came to the place where Saul had encamped. And David saw the place where Saul lay, and Abner the son of Ner, the

כִּי אִם־נוֹתַר לְנָבָל עַד־אוֹר הַבֹּקֶר מַשְׁתִּין בְּקִיר: 35 וַיִּקַּח דָּוִד מִיָּדָהּ אֵת אֲשֶׁר־הֵבִיאָה לוֹ וְלָהּ אָמַר עֲלִי לְשָׁלוֹם לְבֵיתֵךְ רְאִי שָׁמַעְתִּי בְקוֹלֵךְ וָאֶשָּׂא פָנָיִךְ: 36 וַתָּבֹא אֲבִיגַיִל ׀ אֶל־נָבָל וְהִנֵּה־לוֹ מִשְׁתֶּה בְּבֵיתוֹ כְּמִשְׁתֵּה הַמֶּלֶךְ וְלֵב נָבָל טוֹב עָלָיו וְהוּא שִׁכֹּר עַד־מְאֹד וְלֹא־הִגִּידָה לוֹ דָּבָר קָטֹן וְגָדוֹל עַד־אוֹר הַבֹּקֶר: 37 וַיְהִי בַבֹּקֶר בְּצֵאת הַיַּיִן מִנָּבָל וַתַּגֶּד־לוֹ אִשְׁתּוֹ אֶת־הַדְּבָרִים הָאֵלֶּה וַיָּמָת לִבּוֹ בְּקִרְבּוֹ וְהוּא הָיָה לְאָבֶן: 38 וַיְהִי כַּעֲשֶׂרֶת הַיָּמִים וַיִּגֹּף יְהוָה אֶת־נָבָל וַיָּמֹת: 39 וַיִּשְׁמַע דָּוִד כִּי מֵת נָבָל וַיֹּאמֶר בָּרוּךְ יְהוָה אֲשֶׁר רָב אֶת־רִיב חֶרְפָּתִי מִיַּד נָבָל וְאֶת־עַבְדּוֹ חָשַׂךְ מֵרָעָה וְאֵת רָעַת נָבָל הֵשִׁיב יְהוָה בְּרֹאשׁוֹ וַיִּשְׁלַח דָּוִד וַיְדַבֵּר בַּאֲבִיגַיִל לְקַחְתָּהּ לוֹ לְאִשָּׁה: 40 וַיָּבֹאוּ עַבְדֵי דָוִד אֶל־ אֲבִיגַיִל הַכַּרְמֶלָה וַיְדַבְּרוּ אֵלֶיהָ לֵאמֹר דָּוִד שְׁלָחָנוּ אֵלַיִךְ לְקַחְתֵּךְ לוֹ לְאִשָּׁה: 41 וַתָּקָם וַתִּשְׁתַּחוּ אַפַּיִם אָרְצָה וַתֹּאמֶר הִנֵּה אֲמָתְךָ לְשִׁפְחָה לִרְחֹץ רַגְלֵי עַבְדֵי אֲדֹנִי: 42 וַתְּמַהֵר וַתָּקָם אֲבִיגַיִל וַתִּרְכַּב עַל־ הַחֲמוֹר וְחָמֵשׁ נַעֲרֹתֶיהָ הַהֹלְכוֹת לְרַגְלָהּ וַתֵּלֶךְ אַחֲרֵי מַלְאֲכֵי דָוִד וַתְּהִי־לוֹ לְאִשָּׁה: 43 וְאֶת־ אֲחִינֹעַם לָקַח דָּוִד מִיִּזְרְעֶאל וַתִּהְיֶיןָ גַּם־שְׁתֵּיהֶן לוֹ לְנָשִׁים: 44 וְשָׁאוּל נָתַן אֶת־מִיכַל בִּתּוֹ אֵשֶׁת דָּוִד לְפַלְטִי בֶן־לַיִשׁ אֲשֶׁר מִגַּלִּים:

כו וַיָּבֹאוּ הַזִּפִים אֶל־שָׁאוּל הַגִּבְעָתָה לֵאמֹר הֲלוֹא דָוִד מִסְתַּתֵּר בְּגִבְעַת הַחֲכִילָה עַל פְּנֵי הַיְשִׁימֹן: 2 וַיָּקָם שָׁאוּל וַיֵּרֶד אֶל־מִדְבַּר־זִיף וְאִתּוֹ שְׁלֹשֶׁת־אֲלָפִים אִישׁ בְּחוּרֵי יִשְׂרָאֵל לְבַקֵּשׁ אֶת־ דָּוִד בְּמִדְבַּר־זִיף: 3 וַיִּחַן שָׁאוּל בְּגִבְעַת הַחֲכִילָה אֲשֶׁר עַל־פְּנֵי הַיְשִׁימֹן עַל־הַדָּרֶךְ וְדָוִד יֹשֵׁב בַּמִּדְבָּר וַיַּרְא כִּי בָא שָׁאוּל אַחֲרָיו הַמִּדְבָּרָה: 4 וַיִּשְׁלַח דָּוִד מְרַגְּלִים וַיֵּדַע כִּי־בָא שָׁאוּל אֶל־נָכוֹן: 5 וַיָּקָם דָּוִד וַיָּבֹא אֶל־הַמָּקוֹם אֲשֶׁר חָנָה־שָׁם שָׁאוּל וַיַּרְא דָּוִד אֶת־הַמָּקוֹם אֲשֶׁר שָׁכַב־שָׁם שָׁאוּל וְאַבְנֵר

commander of his army. Now Saul lay within the camp, with the people encamped all around him. [6] Then David answered, and said to Ahimelech the Hittite and to Abishai the son of Zeruiah, brother of Joab, saying, "Who will go down with me to Saul in the camp?"

And Abishai said, "I will go down with you."

[7] So David and Abishai came to the people by night; and there Saul lay sleeping within the camp, with his spear stuck in the ground by his head. And Abner and the people lay all around him. [8] Then Abishai said to David, "God has delivered your enemy into your hand this day. Now therefore, please, let me strike him at once with the spear, right to the earth; and I will not *have to strike* him a second time!"

[9] But David said to Abishai, "Do not destroy him; for who can stretch out his hand against the LORD's anointed, and be guiltless?" [10] David said furthermore, "*As* the LORD lives, the LORD shall strike him, or his day shall come to die, or he shall go out to battle and perish. [11] The LORD forbid that I should stretch out my hand against the LORD's anointed. But please, take now the spear and the jug of water that *are* by his head, and let us go." [12] So David took the spear and the jug of water *by* Saul's head, and they got away; and no man saw or knew *it* or awoke. For they *were* all asleep, because a deep sleep from the LORD had fallen on them.

[13] Now David went over to the other side, and stood on the top of a hill afar off, a great distance *being* between them. [14] And David called out to the people and to Abner the son of Ner, saying, "Do you not answer, Abner?"

Then Abner answered and said, "Who *are* you, calling out to the king?"

[15] So David said to Abner, "*Are* you not a man? And who *is* like you in Israel? Why then have you not guarded your lord the king? For one of the people came in to destroy your lord the king. [16] This thing that you have done *is* not good. *As* the LORD lives, you deserve to die, because you have not guarded your master, the LORD's anointed. And now see where the king's spear *is,* and the jug of water that *was* by his head."

[17] Then Saul knew David's voice, and said, "*Is* that your voice, my son David?"

David said, "*It is* my voice, my lord, O king." [18] And he said, "Why does my lord thus pursue his servant? For what have I done, or what evil *is* in my hand? [19] Now therefore, please, let my lord the king hear the words of his servant: If the LORD has stirred you up against me, let Him accept an offering. But if *it is* the children of men, *may they be*

בֶּן־נֵר שַׂר־צְבָאוֹ וְשָׁאוּל שֹׁכֵב בַּמַּעְגָּל וְהָעָם חֹנִים סְבִיבֹתָו: 6 וַיַּעַן דָּוִד וַיֹּאמֶר ׀ אֶל־אֲחִימֶלֶךְ הַחִתִּי וְאֶל־אֲבִישַׁי בֶּן־צְרוּיָה אֲחִי יוֹאָב לֵאמֹר מִי־יֵרֵד אִתִּי אֶל־שָׁאוּל אֶל־הַמַּחֲנֶה וַיֹּאמֶר אֲבִישַׁי אֲנִי אֵרֵד עִמָּךְ: 7 וַיָּבֹא דָוִד וַאֲבִישַׁי ׀ אֶל־הָעָם לַיְלָה וְהִנֵּה שָׁאוּל שֹׁכֵב יָשֵׁן בַּמַּעְגָּל וַחֲנִיתוֹ מְעוּכָה־בָאָרֶץ מְרַאֲשֹׁתָו וְאַבְנֵר וְהָעָם שֹׁכְבִים סְבִיבֹתָו: 8 וַיֹּאמֶר אֲבִישַׁי אֶל־דָּוִד סִגַּר אֱלֹהִים הַיּוֹם אֶת־אוֹיִבְךָ בְּיָדֶךָ וְעַתָּה אַכֶּנּוּ נָא בַּחֲנִית וּבָאָרֶץ פַּעַם אַחַת וְלֹא אֶשְׁנֶה לוֹ: 9 וַיֹּאמֶר דָּוִד אֶל־אֲבִישַׁי אַל־תַּשְׁחִיתֵהוּ כִּי מִי שָׁלַח יָדוֹ בִּמְשִׁיחַ יְהוָה וְנִקָּה:

10 וַיֹּאמֶר דָּוִד חַי־יְהוָה כִּי אִם־יְהוָה יִגָּפֶנּוּ אוֹ־יוֹמוֹ יָבוֹא וָמֵת אוֹ בַמִּלְחָמָה יֵרֵד וְנִסְפָּה: 11 חָלִילָה לִּי מֵיהוָה מִשְּׁלֹחַ יָדִי בִּמְשִׁיחַ יְהוָה וְעַתָּה קַח־נָא אֶת־הַחֲנִית אֲשֶׁר מְרַאֲשֹׁתָו וְאֶת־צַפַּחַת הַמַּיִם וְנֵלְכָה לָּנוּ: 12 וַיִּקַּח דָּוִד אֶת־הַחֲנִית וְאֶת־צַפַּחַת הַמַּיִם מֵרַאֲשֹׁתֵי שָׁאוּל וַיֵּלְכוּ לָהֶם וְאֵין רֹאֶה וְאֵין יוֹדֵעַ וְאֵין מֵקִיץ כִּי כֻלָּם יְשֵׁנִים כִּי תַּרְדֵּמַת יְהוָה נָפְלָה עֲלֵיהֶם: 13 וַיַּעֲבֹר דָּוִד הָעֵבֶר וַיַּעֲמֹד עַל־רֹאשׁ־הָהָר מֵרָחֹק רַב הַמָּקוֹם בֵּינֵיהֶם: 14 וַיִּקְרָא דָוִד אֶל־הָעָם וְאֶל־אַבְנֵר בֶּן־נֵר לֵאמֹר הֲלוֹא תַעֲנֶה אַבְנֵר וַיַּעַן אַבְנֵר וַיֹּאמֶר מִי אַתָּה קָרָאתָ אֶל־הַמֶּלֶךְ:

15 וַיֹּאמֶר דָּוִד אֶל־אַבְנֵר הֲלוֹא־אִישׁ אַתָּה וּמִי כָמוֹךָ בְּיִשְׂרָאֵל וְלָמָּה לֹא שָׁמַרְתָּ אֶל־אֲדֹנֶיךָ הַמֶּלֶךְ כִּי־בָא אַחַד הָעָם לְהַשְׁחִית אֶת־הַמֶּלֶךְ אֲדֹנֶיךָ: 16 לֹא־טוֹב הַדָּבָר הַזֶּה אֲשֶׁר עָשִׂיתָ חַי־יְהוָה כִּי בְנֵי־מָוֶת אַתֶּם אֲשֶׁר לֹא־שְׁמַרְתֶּם עַל־אֲדֹנֵיכֶם עַל־מְשִׁיחַ יְהוָה וְעַתָּה ׀ רְאֵה אֵי־חֲנִית הַמֶּלֶךְ וְאֶת־צַפַּחַת הַמַּיִם אֲשֶׁר מְרַאֲשֹׁתָו: 17 וַיַּכֵּר שָׁאוּל אֶת־קוֹל דָּוִד וַיֹּאמֶר הֲקוֹלְךָ זֶה בְּנִי דָוִד וַיֹּאמֶר דָּוִד קוֹלִי אֲדֹנִי הַמֶּלֶךְ: 18 וַיֹּאמֶר לָמָּה זֶּה אֲדֹנִי רֹדֵף אַחֲרֵי עַבְדּוֹ כִּי מֶה עָשִׂיתִי וּמַה־בְּיָדִי רָעָה: 19 וְעַתָּה יִשְׁמַע־נָא אֲדֹנִי הַמֶּלֶךְ אֵת דִּבְרֵי עַבְדּוֹ

cursed before the LORD, for they have driven me out this day from sharing in the inheritance of the LORD, saying, 'Go, serve other gods.' 20 So now, do not let my blood fall to the earth before the face of the LORD. For the king of Israel has come out to seek a flea, as when one hunts a partridge in the mountains."

21 Then Saul said, "I have sinned. Return, my son David. For I will harm you no more, because my life was precious in your eyes this day. Indeed I have played the fool and erred exceedingly."

22 And David answered and said, "Here is the king's spear. Let one of the young men come over and get it. 23 May the LORD repay every man *for* his righteousness and his faithfulness; for the LORD delivered you into *my* hand today, but I would not stretch out my hand against the LORD's anointed. 24 And indeed, as your life was valued much this day in my eyes, so let my life be valued much in the eyes of the LORD, and let Him deliver me out of all tribulation."

25 Then Saul said to David, "*May* you *be* blessed, my son David! You shall both do great things and also still prevail."

So David went on his way, and Saul returned to his place.

27 And David said in his heart, "Now I shall perish someday by the hand of Saul. *There is* nothing better for me than that I should speedily escape to the land of the Philistines; and Saul will despair of me, to seek me anymore in any part of Israel. So I shall escape out of his hand." 2 Then David arose and went over with the six hundred men who *were* with him to Achish the son of Maoch, king of Gath. 3 So David dwelt with Achish at Gath, he and his men, each man with his household, *and* David with his two wives, Ahinoam the Jezreelitess, and Abigail the Carmelitess, Nabal's widow. 4 And it was told Saul that David had fled to Gath; so he sought him no more.

5 Then David said to Achish, "If I have now found favor in your eyes, let them give me a place in some town in the country, that I may dwell there. For why should your servant dwell in the royal city with you?" 6 So Achish gave him Ziklag that day. Therefore Ziklag has belonged to the kings of Judah to this day. 7 Now the time that David dwelt in the country of the Philistines was one full year and four months.

8 And David and his men went up and raided the Geshurites, the Girzites, and the Amalekites. For those nations *were* the inhabitants of the land from of old, as you go to Shur, even as far as the land of

אִם־יְהוָה הֱסִיתְךָ בִי יָרַח מִנְחָה וְאִם ׀ בְּנֵי הָאָדָם אֲרוּרִים הֵם לִפְנֵי יְהוָה כִּי־גֵרְשׁוּנִי הַיּוֹם מֵהִסְתַּפֵּחַ בְּנַחֲלַת יְהוָה לֵאמֹר לֵךְ עֲבֹד אֱלֹהִים אֲחֵרִים: 20 וְעַתָּה אַל־יִפֹּל דָּמִי אַרְצָה מִנֶּגֶד פְּנֵי יְהוָה כִּי־יָצָא מֶלֶךְ יִשְׂרָאֵל לְבַקֵּשׁ אֶת־פַּרְעֹשׁ אֶחָד כַּאֲשֶׁר יִרְדֹּף הַקֹּרֵא בֶּהָרִים: 21 וַיֹּאמֶר שָׁאוּל חָטָאתִי שׁוּב בְּנִי־דָוִד כִּי לֹא־אָרַע לְךָ עוֹד תַּחַת אֲשֶׁר יָקְרָה נַפְשִׁי בְּעֵינֶיךָ הַיּוֹם הַזֶּה הִנֵּה הִסְכַּלְתִּי וָאֶשְׁגֶּה הַרְבֵּה מְאֹד: 22 וַיַּעַן דָּוִד וַיֹּאמֶר הִנֵּה הַחֲנִית הַמֶּלֶךְ וְיַעֲבֹר אֶחָד מֵהַנְּעָרִים וְיִקָּחֶהָ: 23 וַיהוָה יָשִׁיב לָאִישׁ אֶת־צִדְקָתוֹ וְאֶת־אֱמֻנָתוֹ אֲשֶׁר נְתָנְךָ יְהוָה ׀ הַיּוֹם בְּיָד וְלֹא אָבִיתִי לִשְׁלֹחַ יָדִי בִּמְשִׁיחַ יְהוָה: 24 וְהִנֵּה כַּאֲשֶׁר גָּדְלָה נַפְשְׁךָ הַיּוֹם הַזֶּה בְּעֵינָי כֵּן תִּגְדַּל נַפְשִׁי בְּעֵינֵי יְהוָה וְיַצִּלֵנִי מִכָּל־צָרָה: פ

25 וַיֹּאמֶר שָׁאוּל אֶל־דָּוִד בָּרוּךְ אַתָּה בְּנִי דָוִד גַּם עָשֹׂה תַעֲשֶׂה וְגַם יָכֹל תּוּכָל וַיֵּלֶךְ דָּוִד לְדַרְכּוֹ וְשָׁאוּל שָׁב לִמְקוֹמוֹ: פ

כז וַיֹּאמֶר דָּוִד אֶל־לִבּוֹ עַתָּה אֶסָּפֶה יוֹם־אֶחָד בְּיַד־שָׁאוּל אֵין־לִי טוֹב כִּי הִמָּלֵט אִמָּלֵט ׀ אֶל־אֶרֶץ פְּלִשְׁתִּים וְנוֹאַשׁ מִמֶּנִּי שָׁאוּל לְבַקְשֵׁנִי עוֹד בְּכָל־גְּבוּל יִשְׂרָאֵל וְנִמְלַטְתִּי מִיָּדוֹ: 2 וַיָּקָם דָּוִד וַיַּעֲבֹר הוּא וְשֵׁשׁ־מֵאוֹת אִישׁ אֲשֶׁר עִמּוֹ אֶל־אָכִישׁ בֶּן־מָעוֹךְ מֶלֶךְ גַּת: 3 וַיֵּשֶׁב דָּוִד עִם־אָכִישׁ בְּגַת הוּא וַאֲנָשָׁיו אִישׁ וּבֵיתוֹ דָּוִד וּשְׁתֵּי נָשָׁיו אֲחִינֹעַם הַיִּזְרְעֵאלִית וַאֲבִיגַיִל אֵשֶׁת־נָבָל הַכַּרְמְלִית: 4 וַיֻּגַּד לְשָׁאוּל כִּי־בָרַח דָּוִד גַּת וְלֹא־יָסַף עוֹד לְבַקְשׁוֹ: ס 5 וַיֹּאמֶר דָּוִד אֶל־אָכִישׁ אִם־נָא מָצָאתִי חֵן בְּעֵינֶיךָ יִתְּנוּ־לִי מָקוֹם בְּאַחַת עָרֵי הַשָּׂדֶה וְאֵשְׁבָה שָּׁם וְלָמָּה יֵשֵׁב עַבְדְּךָ בְּעִיר הַמַּמְלָכָה עִמָּךְ: 6 וַיִּתֶּן־לוֹ אָכִישׁ בַּיּוֹם הַהוּא אֶת־צִקְלָג לָכֵן הָיְתָה צִקְלַג לְמַלְכֵי יְהוּדָה עַד הַיּוֹם הַזֶּה: פ 7 וַיְהִי מִסְפַּר הַיָּמִים אֲשֶׁר־יָשַׁב דָּוִד בִּשְׂדֵה פְלִשְׁתִּים יָמִים וְאַרְבָּעָה חֳדָשִׁים: 8 וַיַּעַל דָּוִד וַאֲנָשָׁיו וַיִּפְשְׁטוּ אֶל־הַגְּשׁוּרִי וְהַגִּרְזִי וְהָעֲמָלֵקִי כִּי

Egypt. ⁹Whenever David attacked the land, he left neither man nor woman alive, but took away the sheep, the oxen, the donkeys, the camels, and the apparel, and returned and came to Achish. ¹⁰Then Achish would say, "Where have you made a raid today?" And David would say, "Against the southern *area* of Judah, or against the southern *area* of the Jerahmeelites, or against the southern *area* of the Kenites." ¹¹David would save neither man nor woman alive, to bring *news* to Gath, saying, "Lest they should inform on us, saying, 'Thus David did.'" And thus *was* his behavior all the time he dwelt in the country of the Philistines. ¹²So Achish believed David, saying, "He has made his people Israel utterly abhor him; therefore he will be my servant forever."

28 Now it happened in those days that the Philistines gathered their armies together for war, to fight with Israel. And Achish said to David, "You assuredly know that you will go out with me to battle, you and your men."

²So David said to Achish, "Surely you know what your servant can do."

And Achish said to David, "Therefore I will make you one of my chief guardians forever."

³Now Samuel had died, and all Israel had lamented for him and buried him in Ramah, in his own city. And Saul had put the mediums and the spiritists out of the land.

⁴Then the Philistines gathered together, and came and encamped at Shunem. So Saul gathered all Israel together, and they encamped at Gilboa. ⁵When Saul saw the army of the Philistines, he was afraid, and his heart trembled greatly. ⁶And when Saul inquired of the LORD, the LORD did not answer him, either by dreams or by Urim or by the prophets.

⁷Then Saul said to his servants, "Find me a woman who is a medium, that I may go to her and inquire of her."

And his servants said to him, "In fact, *there is* a woman who is a medium at En Dor."

⁸So Saul disguised himself and put on other clothes, and he went, and two men with him; and they came to the woman by night. And he said, "Please conduct a séance for me, and bring up for me the one I shall name to you."

⁹Then the woman said to him, "Look, you know what Saul has done, how he has cut off the mediums and the spiritists from the land. Why then do you lay a snare for my life, to cause me to die?"

הִנֵּה יֹשְׁבָת הָאָרֶץ אֲשֶׁר מֵעוֹלָם בּוֹאֲךָ שׁוּרָה וְעַד־אֶרֶץ מִצְרָיִם: ⁹ וְהִכָּה דָוִד אֶת־הָאָרֶץ וְלֹא יְחַיֶּה אִישׁ וְאִשָּׁה וְלָקַח צֹאן וּבָקָר וַחֲמֹרִים וּגְמַלִּים וּבְגָדִים וַיָּשָׁב וַיָּבֹא אֶל־אָכִישׁ: ¹⁰ וַיֹּאמֶר אָכִישׁ אַל־פְּשַׁטְתֶּם הַיּוֹם וַיֹּאמֶר דָּוִד עַל־נֶגֶב יְהוּדָה וְעַל־נֶגֶב הַיְּרַחְמְאֵלִי וְאֶל־נֶגֶב הַקֵּינִי: ¹¹ וְאִישׁ וְאִשָּׁה לֹא־יְחַיֶּה דָוִד לְהָבִיא גַת לֵאמֹר פֶּן־יַגִּדוּ עָלֵינוּ לֵאמֹר כֹּה־עָשָׂה דָוִד וְכֹה מִשְׁפָּטוֹ כָּל־הַיָּמִים אֲשֶׁר יָשַׁב בִּשְׂדֵה פְלִשְׁתִּים: ¹² וַיַּאֲמֵן אָכִישׁ בְּדָוִד לֵאמֹר הַבְאֵשׁ הִבְאִישׁ בְּעַמּוֹ בְיִשְׂרָאֵל וְהָיָה לִי לְעֶבֶד עוֹלָם: פ

כח וַיְהִי בַּיָּמִים הָהֵם וַיִּקְבְּצוּ פְלִשְׁתִּים אֶת־מַחֲנֵיהֶם לַצָּבָא לְהִלָּחֵם בְּיִשְׂרָאֵל וַיֹּאמֶר אָכִישׁ אֶל־דָּוִד יָדֹעַ תֵּדַע כִּי אִתִּי תֵּצֵא בַמַּחֲנֶה אַתָּה וַאֲנָשֶׁיךָ: ² וַיֹּאמֶר דָּוִד אֶל־אָכִישׁ לָכֵן אַתָּה תֵּדַע אֵת אֲשֶׁר־יַעֲשֶׂה עַבְדֶּךָ וַיֹּאמֶר אָכִישׁ אֶל־דָּוִד לָכֵן שֹׁמֵר לְרֹאשִׁי אֲשִׂימְךָ כָּל־הַיָּמִים: פ

³ וּשְׁמוּאֵל מֵת וַיִּסְפְּדוּ־לוֹ כָּל־יִשְׂרָאֵל וַיִּקְבְּרֻהוּ בָרָמָה וּבְעִירוֹ וְשָׁאוּל הֵסִיר הָאֹבוֹת וְאֶת־הַיִּדְּעֹנִים מֵהָאָרֶץ: ⁴ וַיִּקָּבְצוּ פְלִשְׁתִּים וַיָּבֹאוּ וַיַּחֲנוּ בְשׁוּנֵם וַיִּקְבֹּץ שָׁאוּל אֶת־כָּל־יִשְׂרָאֵל וַיַּחֲנוּ בַּגִּלְבֹּעַ: ⁵ וַיַּרְא שָׁאוּל אֶת־מַחֲנֵה פְלִשְׁתִּים וַיִּרָא וַיֶּחֱרַד לִבּוֹ מְאֹד: ⁶ וַיִּשְׁאַל שָׁאוּל בַּיהוָה וְלֹא עָנָהוּ יְהוָה גַּם בַּחֲלֹמוֹת גַּם בָּאוּרִים גַּם בַּנְּבִיאִם: ⁷ וַיֹּאמֶר שָׁאוּל לַעֲבָדָיו בַּקְּשׁוּ־לִי אֵשֶׁת בַּעֲלַת־אוֹב וְאֵלְכָה אֵלֶיהָ וְאֶדְרְשָׁה־בָּהּ וַיֹּאמְרוּ עֲבָדָיו אֵלָיו הִנֵּה אֵשֶׁת בַּעֲלַת־אוֹב בְּעֵין דּוֹר: ⁸ וַיִּתְחַפֵּשׂ שָׁאוּל וַיִּלְבַּשׁ בְּגָדִים אֲחֵרִים וַיֵּלֶךְ הוּא וּשְׁנֵי אֲנָשִׁים עִמּוֹ וַיָּבֹאוּ אֶל־הָאִשָּׁה לָיְלָה וַיֹּאמֶר קָסֳמִי־ק נָא לִי בָּאוֹב וְהַעֲלִי לִי אֵת אֲשֶׁר־אֹמַר אֵלָיִךְ: ⁹ וַתֹּאמֶר הָאִשָּׁה אֵלָיו הִנֵּה אַתָּה יָדַעְתָּ אֵת אֲשֶׁר־עָשָׂה שָׁאוּל אֲשֶׁר הִכְרִית אֶת־הָאֹבוֹת וְאֶת־הַיִּדְּעֹנִי מִן־הָאָרֶץ וְלָמָה אַתָּה מִתְנַקֵּשׁ בְּנַפְשִׁי

¹⁰And Saul swore to her by the LORD, saying, "*As* the LORD lives, no punishment shall come upon you for this thing."

¹¹Then the woman said, "Whom shall I bring up for you?"

And he said, "Bring up Samuel for me."

¹²When the woman saw Samuel, she cried out with a loud voice. And the woman spoke to Saul, saying, "Why have you deceived me? For you *are* Saul!"

¹³And the king said to her, "Do not be afraid. What did you see?"

And the woman said to Saul, "I saw a spirit ascending out of the earth."

¹⁴So he said to her, "What *is* his form?"

And she said, "An old man is coming up, and he *is* covered with a mantle." And Saul perceived that it *was* Samuel, and he stooped with *his* face to the ground and bowed down.

¹⁵Now Samuel said to Saul, "Why have you disturbed me by bringing me up?"

And Saul answered, "I am deeply distressed; for the Philistines make war against me, and God has departed from me and does not answer me anymore, neither by prophets nor by dreams. Therefore I have called you, that you may reveal to me what I should do."

¹⁶Then Samuel said: "So why do you ask me, seeing the LORD has departed from you and has become your enemy? ¹⁷And the LORD has done for Himself as He spoke by me. For the LORD has torn the kingdom out of your hand and given it to your neighbor, David. ¹⁸Because you did not obey the voice of the LORD nor execute His fierce wrath upon Amalek, therefore the LORD has done this thing to you this day. ¹⁹Moreover the LORD will also deliver Israel with you into the hand of the Philistines. And tomorrow you and your sons *will be* with me. The LORD will also deliver the army of Israel into the hand of the Philistines."

²⁰Immediately Saul fell full length on the ground, and was dreadfully afraid because of the words of Samuel. And there was no strength in him, for he had eaten no food all day or all night.

²¹And the woman came to Saul and saw that he was severely troubled, and said to him, "Look, your maidservant has obeyed your voice, and I have put my life in my hands and heeded the words which you spoke to me. ²²Now therefore, please, heed also the voice of your maidservant, and let me set a piece of bread before you; and eat, that you may have strength when you go on *your* way."

²³But he refused and said, "I will not eat."

לַהֲמִיתֵנִי: 10 וַיִּשָּׁבַע לָהּ שָׁאוּל בַּיהוָה לֵאמֹר חַי־יְהוָה אִם־יִקְּרֵךְ עָוֹן בַּדָּבָר הַזֶּה: 11 וַתֹּאמֶר הָאִשָּׁה אֶת־מִי אַעֲלֶה־לָּךְ וַיֹּאמֶר אֶת־שְׁמוּאֵל הַעֲלִי־לִי: 12 וַתֵּרֶא הָאִשָּׁה אֶת־שְׁמוּאֵל וַתִּזְעַק בְּקוֹל גָּדוֹל וַתֹּאמֶר הָאִשָּׁה אֶל־שָׁאוּל לֵאמֹר לָמָּה רִמִּיתָנִי וְאַתָּה שָׁאוּל: 13 וַיֹּאמֶר לָהּ הַמֶּלֶךְ אַל־תִּירְאִי כִּי מָה רָאִית וַתֹּאמֶר הָאִשָּׁה אֶל־שָׁאוּל אֱלֹהִים רָאִיתִי עֹלִים מִן־הָאָרֶץ: 14 וַיֹּאמֶר לָהּ מַה־תָּאֳרוֹ וַתֹּאמֶר אִישׁ זָקֵן עֹלֶה וְהוּא עֹטֶה מְעִיל וַיֵּדַע שָׁאוּל כִּי־שְׁמוּאֵל הוּא וַיִּקֹּד אַפַּיִם אַרְצָה וַיִּשְׁתָּחוּ: ס 15 וַיֹּאמֶר שְׁמוּאֵל אֶל־שָׁאוּל לָמָּה הִרְגַּזְתַּנִי לְהַעֲלוֹת אֹתִי וַיֹּאמֶר שָׁאוּל צַר־לִי מְאֹד וּפְלִשְׁתִּים נִלְחָמִים בִּי וֵאלֹהִים סָר מֵעָלַי וְלֹא־עָנָנִי עוֹד גַּם בְּיַד־ הַנְּבִיאִם גַּם־בַּחֲלֹמוֹת וָאֶקְרָאֶה לְךָ לְהוֹדִיעֵנִי מָה אֶעֱשֶׂה: ס 16 וַיֹּאמֶר שְׁמוּאֵל וְלָמָּה תִּשְׁאָלֵנִי וַיהוָה סָר מֵעָלֶיךָ וַיְהִי עָרֶךָ: 17 וַיַּעַשׂ יְהוָה לוֹ כַּאֲשֶׁר דִּבֶּר בְּיָדִי וַיִּקְרַע יְהוָה אֶת־ הַמַּמְלָכָה מִיָּדֶךָ וַיִּתְּנָהּ לְרֵעֲךָ לְדָוִד: 18 כַּאֲשֶׁר לֹא־ שָׁמַעְתָּ בְּקוֹל יְהוָה וְלֹא־עָשִׂיתָ חֲרוֹן־אַפּוֹ בַּעֲמָלֵק עַל־כֵּן הַדָּבָר הַזֶּה עָשָׂה־לְךָ יְהוָה הַיּוֹם הַזֶּה: 19 וְיִתֵּן יְהוָה גַּם אֶת־יִשְׂרָאֵל עִמְּךָ בְּיַד־פְּלִשְׁתִּים וּמָחָר אַתָּה וּבָנֶיךָ עִמִּי גַּם אֶת־מַחֲנֵה יִשְׂרָאֵל יִתֵּן יְהוָה בְּיַד־פְּלִשְׁתִּים: 20 וַיְמַהֵר שָׁאוּל וַיִּפֹּל מְלֹא־ קוֹמָתוֹ אַרְצָה וַיִּרָא מְאֹד מִדִּבְרֵי שְׁמוּאֵל גַּם־כֹּחַ לֹא־הָיָה בוֹ כִּי לֹא אָכַל לֶחֶם כָּל־הַיּוֹם וְכָל־ הַלָּיְלָה: 21 וַתָּבוֹא הָאִשָּׁה אֶל־שָׁאוּל וַתֵּרֶא כִּי־ נִבְהַל מְאֹד וַתֹּאמֶר אֵלָיו הִנֵּה שָׁמְעָה שִׁפְחָתְךָ בְּקוֹלֶךָ וָאָשִׂים נַפְשִׁי בְּכַפִּי וָאֶשְׁמַע אֶת־דְּבָרֶיךָ אֲשֶׁר דִּבַּרְתָּ אֵלָי: 22 וְעַתָּה שְׁמַע־נָא גַם־אַתָּה בְּקוֹל שִׁפְחָתֶךָ וְאָשִׂמָה לְפָנֶיךָ פַּת־לֶחֶם וֶאֱכוֹל וִיהִי בְךָ כֹּחַ כִּי תֵלֵךְ בַּדָּרֶךְ: 23 וַיְמָאֵן וַיֹּאמֶר לֹא

So his servants, together with the woman, urged him; and he heeded their voice. Then he arose from the ground and sat on the bed. 24 Now the woman had a fatted calf in the house, and she hastened to kill it. And she took flour and kneaded *it,* and baked unleavened bread from it. 25 So she brought *it* before Saul and his servants; and they ate. Then they rose and went away that night.

29 Then the Philistines gathered together all their armies at Aphek, and the Israelites encamped by a fountain which *is* in Jezreel. 2 And the lords of the Philistines passed in review by hundreds and by thousands, but David and his men passed in review at the rear with Achish. 3 Then the princes of the Philistines said, "What *are* these Hebrews *doing here?*"

And Achish said to the princes of the Philistines, "*Is* this not David, the servant of Saul king of Israel, who has been with me these days, or these years? And to this day I have found no fault in him since he defected *to me.*"

4 But the princes of the Philistines were angry with him; so the princes of the Philistines said to him, "Make this fellow return, that he may go back to the place which you have appointed for him, and do not let him go down with us to battle, lest in the battle he become our adversary. For with what could he reconcile himself to his master, if not with the heads of these men? 5 *Is* this not David, of whom they sang to one another in dances, saying:

'Saul has slain his thousands,
And David his ten thousands'?"

6 Then Achish called David and said to him, "Surely, *as* the LORD lives, you have been upright, and your going out and your coming in with me in the army *is* good in my sight. For to this day I have not found evil in you since the day of your coming to me. Nevertheless the lords do not favor you. 7 Therefore return now, and go in peace, that you may not displease the lords of the Philistines."

8 So David said to Achish, "But what have I done? And to this day what have you found in your servant as long as I have been with you, that I may not go and fight against the enemies of my lord the king?"

9 Then Achish answered and said to David, "I know that you *are* as good in my sight as an angel of God; nevertheless the princes of the Philistines have said, 'He shall not go up with us to the battle.' 10 Now therefore, rise early in the morning with

אֹכֵל וַיִּפְרְצוּ־בוֹ עֲבָדָיו וְגַם־הָאִשָּׁה וַיִּשְׁמַע לְקֹלָם וַיָּקָם מֵהָאָרֶץ וַיֵּשֶׁב אֶל־הַמִּטָּה: 24 וְלָאִשָּׁה עֵגֶל־מַרְבֵּק בַּבַּיִת וַתְּמַהֵר וַתִּזְבָּחֵהוּ וַתִּקַּח־קֶמַח וַתָּלָשׁ וַתֹּפֵהוּ מַצּוֹת: 25 וַתַּגֵּשׁ לִפְנֵי־שָׁאוּל וְלִפְנֵי עֲבָדָיו וַיֹּאכֵלוּ וַיָּקֻמוּ וַיֵּלְכוּ בַּלַּיְלָה הַהוּא: פ

כט וַיִּקְבְּצוּ פְלִשְׁתִּים אֶת־כָּל־מַחֲנֵיהֶם אֲפֵקָה וְיִשְׂרָאֵל חֹנִים בַּעַיִן אֲשֶׁר בְּיִזְרְעֶאל: 2 וְסַרְנֵי פְלִשְׁתִּים עֹבְרִים לְמֵאוֹת וְלַאֲלָפִים וְדָוִד וַאֲנָשָׁיו עֹבְרִים בָּאַחֲרֹנָה עִם־אָכִישׁ: 3 וַיֹּאמְרוּ שָׂרֵי פְלִשְׁתִּים מָה הָעִבְרִים הָאֵלֶּה וַיֹּאמֶר אָכִישׁ אֶל־שָׂרֵי פְלִשְׁתִּים הֲלוֹא־זֶה דָוִד עֶבֶד שָׁאוּל מֶלֶךְ־יִשְׂרָאֵל אֲשֶׁר הָיָה אִתִּי זֶה יָמִים אוֹ־זֶה שָׁנִים וְלֹא־מָצָאתִי בוֹ מְאוּמָה מִיּוֹם נָפְלוֹ עַד־הַיּוֹם הַזֶּה: פ 4 וַיִּקְצְפוּ עָלָיו שָׂרֵי פְלִשְׁתִּים וַיֹּאמְרוּ לוֹ שָׂרֵי פְלִשְׁתִּים הָשֵׁב אֶת־הָאִישׁ וְיָשֹׁב אֶל־מְקוֹמוֹ אֲשֶׁר הִפְקַדְתּוֹ שָׁם וְלֹא־יֵרֵד עִמָּנוּ בַּמִּלְחָמָה וְלֹא־יִהְיֶה־לָּנוּ לְשָׂטָן בַּמִּלְחָמָה וּבַמֶּה יִתְרַצֶּה זֶה אֶל־אֲדֹנָיו הֲלוֹא בְּרָאשֵׁי הָאֲנָשִׁים הָהֵם: 5 הֲלוֹא־זֶה דָוִד אֲשֶׁר יַעֲנוּ־לוֹ בַּמְּחֹלוֹת לֵאמֹר הִכָּה שָׁאוּל בַּאֲלָפָיו וְדָוִד בְּרִבְבֹתָו: 6 וַיִּקְרָא אָכִישׁ אֶל־דָּוִד וַיֹּאמֶר אֵלָיו חַי־יְהוָה כִּי־יָשָׁר אַתָּה וְטוֹב בְּעֵינַי צֵאתְךָ וּבֹאֲךָ אִתִּי בַּמַּחֲנֶה כִּי לֹא־מָצָאתִי בְךָ רָעָה מִיּוֹם בֹּאֲךָ אֵלַי עַד־הַיּוֹם הַזֶּה וּבְעֵינֵי הַסְּרָנִים לֹא־טוֹב אָתָּה: 7 וְעַתָּה שׁוּב וְלֵךְ בְּשָׁלוֹם וְלֹא־תַעֲשֶׂה רָע בְּעֵינֵי סַרְנֵי פְלִשְׁתִּים: 8 וַיֹּאמֶר דָּוִד אֶל־אָכִישׁ כִּי מֶה עָשִׂיתִי וּמַה־מָּצָאתָ בְעַבְדְּךָ מִיּוֹם אֲשֶׁר הָיִיתִי לְפָנֶיךָ עַד הַיּוֹם הַזֶּה כִּי לֹא אָבוֹא וְנִלְחַמְתִּי בְּאֹיְבֵי אֲדֹנִי הַמֶּלֶךְ: 9 וַיַּעַן אָכִישׁ וַיֹּאמֶר אֶל־דָּוִד יָדַעְתִּי כִּי טוֹב אַתָּה בְּעֵינַי כְּמַלְאַךְ אֱלֹהִים אַךְ שָׂרֵי פְלִשְׁתִּים אָמְרוּ לֹא־יַעֲלֶה עִמָּנוּ בַּמִּלְחָמָה: 10 וְעַתָּה הַשְׁכֵּם בַּבֹּקֶר וְעַבְדֵי אֲדֹנֶיךָ אֲשֶׁר־בָּאוּ

your master's servants who have come with you.
And as soon as you are up early in the morning and
have light, depart."

11 So David and his men rose early to depart in
the morning, to return to the land of the Philistines.
And the Philistines went up to Jezreel.

30 Now it happened, when David and his men
came to Ziklag, on the third day, that the
Amalekites had invaded the South and Ziklag,
attacked Ziklag and burned it with fire, 2 and had
taken captive the women and those who *were* there,
from small to great; they did not kill anyone, but
carried *them* away and went their way. 3 So David
and his men came to the city, and there it was,
burned with fire; and their wives, their sons, and
their daughters had been taken captive. 4 Then
David and the people who *were* with him lifted up
their voices and wept, until they had no more power
to weep. 5 And David's two wives, Ahinoam the
Jezreelitess, and Abigail the widow of Nabal the
Carmelite, had been taken captive. 6 Now David
was greatly distressed, for the people spoke of
stoning him, because the soul of all the people was
grieved, every man for his sons and his daughters.
But David strengthened himself in the LORD his
God.

7 Then David said to Abiathar the priest, Ahimelech's son, "Please bring the ephod here to me."
And Abiathar brought the ephod to David. 8 So
David inquired of the LORD, saying, "Shall I pursue
this troop? Shall I overtake them?"

And He answered him, "Pursue, for you shall
surely overtake *them* and without fail recover *all*."

9 So David went, he and the six hundred men
who *were* with him, and came to the Brook Besor,
where those stayed who were left behind. 10 But
David pursued, he and four hundred men; for two
hundred stayed *behind*, who were so weary that they
could not cross the Brook Besor.

11 Then they found an Egyptian in the field, and
brought him to David; and they gave him bread
and he ate, and they let him drink water. 12 And
they gave him a piece of a cake of figs and two
clusters of raisins. So when he had eaten, his
strength came back to him; for he had eaten no
bread nor drunk water for three days and three
nights. 13 Then David said to him, "To whom do
you *belong,* and where *are* you from?"

And he said, "I *am* a young man from Egypt,
servant of an Amalekite; and my master left me
behind, because three days ago I fell sick. 14 We
made an invasion of the southern *area* of the

אִתָּךְ וְהִשְׁכַּמְתֶּם בַּבֹּקֶר וְאוֹר לָכֶם וָלֵכוּ: 11 וַיַּשְׁכֵּם
דָּוִד הוּא וַאֲנָשָׁיו לָלֶכֶת בַּבֹּקֶר לָשׁוּב אֶל־אֶרֶץ
פְּלִשְׁתִּים וּפְלִשְׁתִּים עָלוּ יִזְרְעֶאל: ס

ל 1 וַיְהִי בְּבֹא דָוִד וַאֲנָשָׁיו צִקְלַג בַּיּוֹם הַשְּׁלִישִׁי
וַעֲמָלֵקִי פָשְׁטוּ אֶל־נֶגֶב וְאֶל־צִקְלַג וַיַּכּוּ אֶת־צִקְלַג
וַיִּשְׂרְפוּ אֹתָהּ בָּאֵשׁ: 2 וַיִּשְׁבּוּ אֶת־הַנָּשִׁים אֲשֶׁר־
בָּהּ מִקָּטֹן וְעַד־גָּדוֹל לֹא הֵמִיתוּ אִישׁ וַיִּנְהֲגוּ
וַיֵּלְכוּ לְדַרְכָּם: 3 וַיָּבֹא דָוִד וַאֲנָשָׁיו אֶל־הָעִיר וְהִנֵּה
שְׂרוּפָה בָּאֵשׁ וּנְשֵׁיהֶם וּבְנֵיהֶם וּבְנֹתֵיהֶם נִשְׁבּוּ:
4 וַיִּשָּׂא דָוִד וְהָעָם אֲשֶׁר־אִתּוֹ אֶת־קוֹלָם וַיִּבְכּוּ עַד
אֲשֶׁר אֵין־בָּהֶם כֹּחַ לִבְכּוֹת: 5 וּשְׁתֵּי נְשֵׁי־דָוִד נִשְׁבּוּ
אֲחִינֹעַם הַיִּזְרְעֵלִית וַאֲבִיגַיִל אֵשֶׁת נָבָל הַכַּרְמְלִי:
6 וַתֵּצֶר לְדָוִד מְאֹד כִּי־אָמְרוּ הָעָם לְסָקְלוֹ כִּי־מָרָה
נֶפֶשׁ כָּל־הָעָם אִישׁ עַל־בָּנָיו וְעַל־בְּנֹתָיו וַיִּתְחַזֵּק
דָּוִד בַּיהוָה אֱלֹהָיו: ס 7 וַיֹּאמֶר דָּוִד אֶל־
אֶבְיָתָר הַכֹּהֵן בֶּן־אֲחִימֶלֶךְ הַגִּישָׁה־נָּא לִי הָאֵפֹד
וַיַּגֵּשׁ אֶבְיָתָר אֶת־הָאֵפֹד אֶל־דָּוִד: 8 וַיִּשְׁאַל דָּוִד
בַּיהוָה לֵאמֹר אֶרְדֹּף אַחֲרֵי הַגְּדוּד־הַזֶּה הַאַשִּׂגֶנּוּ
וַיֹּאמֶר לוֹ רְדֹף כִּי־הַשֵּׂג תַּשִּׂיג וְהַצֵּל תַּצִּיל: 9 וַיֵּלֶךְ
דָּוִד הוּא וְשֵׁשׁ־מֵאוֹת אִישׁ אֲשֶׁר אִתּוֹ וַיָּבֹאוּ
עַד־נַחַל הַבְּשׂוֹר וְהַנּוֹתָרִים עָמָדוּ: 10 וַיִּרְדֹּף דָּוִד
הוּא וְאַרְבַּע־מֵאוֹת אִישׁ וַיַּעַמְדוּ מָאתַיִם אִישׁ
אֲשֶׁר פִּגְּרוּ מֵעֲבֹר אֶת־נַחַל הַבְּשׂוֹר: 11 וַיִּמְצְאוּ
אִישׁ־מִצְרִי בַּשָּׂדֶה וַיִּקְחוּ אֹתוֹ אֶל־דָּוִד וַיִּתְּנוּ־
לוֹ לֶחֶם וַיֹּאכַל וַיַּשְׁקֻהוּ מָיִם: 12 וַיִּתְּנוּ־לוֹ פֶלַח
דְּבֵלָה וּשְׁנֵי צִמֻּקִים וַיֹּאכַל וַתָּשָׁב רוּחוֹ אֵלָיו
כִּי לֹא־אָכַל לֶחֶם וְלֹא־שָׁתָה מַיִם שְׁלֹשָׁה יָמִים
וּשְׁלֹשָׁה לֵילוֹת: ס 13 וַיֹּאמֶר לוֹ דָוִד לְמִי־
אַתָּה וְאֵי מִזֶּה אָתָּה וַיֹּאמֶר נַעַר מִצְרִי אָנֹכִי
עֶבֶד לְאִישׁ עֲמָלֵקִי וַיַּעַזְבֵנִי אֲדֹנִי כִּי חָלִיתִי
הַיּוֹם שְׁלֹשָׁה: 14 אֲנַחְנוּ פָּשַׁטְנוּ נֶגֶב הַכְּרֵתִי וְעַל־
אֲשֶׁר לִיהוּדָה וְעַל־נֶגֶב כָּלֵב וְאֶת־צִקְלַג שָׂרַפְנוּ

ל 6 בָּנָיו

Cherithites, in the *territory* which *belongs* to Judah, and of the southern *area* of Caleb; and we burned Ziklag with fire."

15 And David said to him, "Can you take me down to this troop?"

So he said, "Swear to me by God that you will neither kill me nor deliver me into the hands of my master, and I will take you down to this troop."

16 And when he had brought him down, there they were, spread out over all the land, eating and drinking and dancing, because of all the great spoil which they had taken from the land of the Philistines and from the land of Judah. 17 Then David attacked them from twilight until the evening of the next day. Not a man of them escaped, except four hundred young men who rode on camels and fled. 18 So David recovered all that the Amalekites had carried away, and David rescued his two wives. 19 And nothing of theirs was lacking, either small or great, sons or daughters, spoil or anything which they had taken from them; David recovered all. 20 Then David took all the flocks and herds they had driven before those *other* livestock, and said, "This *is* David's spoil."

21 Now David came to the two hundred men who had been so weary that they could not follow David, whom they also had made to stay at the Brook Besor. So they went out to meet David and to meet the people who *were* with him. And when David came near the people, he greeted them. 22 Then all the wicked and worthless men of those who went with David answered and said, "Because they did not go with us, we will not give them *any* of the spoil that we have recovered, except for every man's wife and children, that they may lead *them* away and depart."

23 But David said, "My brethren, you shall not do so with what the LORD has given us, who has preserved us and delivered into our hand the troop that came against us. 24 For who will heed you in this matter? But as his part *is* who goes down to the battle, so *shall* his part *be* who stays by the supplies; they shall share alike." 25 So it was, from that day forward; he made it a statute and an ordinance for Israel to this day.

26 Now when David came to Ziklag, he sent *some* of the spoil to the elders of Judah, to his friends, saying, "Here is a present for you from the spoil of the enemies of the LORD"— 27 to *those* who *were* in Bethel, *those* who *were* in Ramoth of the South, *those* who *were* in Jattir, 28 *those* who *were* in Aroer, *those* who *were* in Siphmoth, *those* who *were* in Eshtemoa, 29 *those* who *were* in Rachal, *those* who *were* in the cities of the Jerahmeelites, *those* who

בָּאֵשׁ: 15 וַיֹּאמֶר אֵלָיו דָּוִד הֲתוֹרִדֵנִי אֶל־הַגְּדוּד הַזֶּה וַיֹּאמֶר הִשָּׁבְעָה לִּי בֵאלֹהִים אִם־תְּמִיתֵנִי וְאִם־תַּסְגִּרֵנִי בְּיַד־אֲדֹנִי וְאוֹרִדְךָ אֶל־הַגְּדוּד הַזֶּה:

16 וַיֹּרִדֵהוּ וְהִנֵּה נְטֻשִׁים עַל־פְּנֵי כָל־הָאָרֶץ אֹכְלִים וְשֹׁתִים וְחֹגְגִים בְּכֹל הַשָּׁלָל הַגָּדוֹל אֲשֶׁר לָקְחוּ מֵאֶרֶץ פְּלִשְׁתִּים וּמֵאֶרֶץ יְהוּדָה: 17 וַיַּכֵּם דָּוִד מֵהַנֶּשֶׁף וְעַד־הָעֶרֶב לְמָחֳרָתָם וְלֹא־נִמְלַט מֵהֶם אִישׁ כִּי אִם־אַרְבַּע מֵאוֹת אִישׁ־נַעַר אֲשֶׁר־רָכְבוּ עַל־הַגְּמַלִּים וַיָּנֻסוּ: 18 וַיַּצֵּל דָּוִד אֵת כָּל־אֲשֶׁר לָקְחוּ עֲמָלֵק וְאֶת־שְׁתֵּי נָשָׁיו הִצִּיל דָּוִד: 19 וְלֹא נֶעְדַּר־לָהֶם מִן־הַקָּטֹן וְעַד־הַגָּדוֹל וְעַד־בָּנִים וּבָנוֹת וּמִשָּׁלָל וְעַד כָּל־אֲשֶׁר לָקְחוּ לָהֶם הַכֹּל הֵשִׁיב דָּוִד: 20 וַיִּקַּח דָּוִד אֶת־כָּל־הַצֹּאן וְהַבָּקָר נָהֲגוּ לִפְנֵי הַמִּקְנֶה הַהוּא וַיֹּאמְרוּ זֶה שְׁלַל דָּוִד: 21 וַיָּבֹא דָוִד אֶל־מָאתַיִם הָאֲנָשִׁים אֲשֶׁר־פִּגְּרוּ מִלֶּכֶת אַחֲרֵי דָוִד וַיֹּשִׁיבֻם בְּנַחַל הַבְּשׂוֹר וַיֵּצְאוּ לִקְרַאת דָּוִד וְלִקְרַאת הָעָם אֲשֶׁר־אִתּוֹ וַיִּגַּשׁ דָּוִד אֶת־הָעָם וַיִּשְׁאַל לָהֶם לְשָׁלוֹם: ס 22 וַיַּעַן כָּל־אִישׁ־רָע וּבְלִיַּעַל מֵהָאֲנָשִׁים אֲשֶׁר הָלְכוּ עִם־דָּוִד וַיֹּאמְרוּ יַעַן אֲשֶׁר לֹא־הָלְכוּ עִמִּי לֹא־נִתֵּן לָהֶם מֵהַשָּׁלָל אֲשֶׁר הִצַּלְנוּ כִּי־אִם־אִישׁ אֶת־אִשְׁתּוֹ וְאֶת־בָּנָיו וְיִנְהֲגוּ וְיֵלֵכוּ: ס 23 וַיֹּאמֶר דָּוִד לֹא־תַעֲשׂוּ כֵן אֶחָי אֵת אֲשֶׁר־נָתַן יְהוָה לָנוּ וַיִּשְׁמֹר אֹתָנוּ וַיִּתֵּן אֶת־הַגְּדוּד הַבָּא עָלֵינוּ בְּיָדֵנוּ: 24 וּמִי יִשְׁמַע לָכֶם לַדָּבָר הַזֶּה כִּי כְּחֵלֶק הַיֹּרֵד בַּמִּלְחָמָה וּכְחֵלֶק הַיֹּשֵׁב עַל־הַכֵּלִים יַחְדָּו יַחֲלֹקוּ: ס 25 וַיְהִי מֵהַיּוֹם הַהוּא וָמָעְלָה וַיְשִׂמֶהָ לְחֹק וּלְמִשְׁפָּט לְיִשְׂרָאֵל עַד הַיּוֹם הַזֶּה: פ

26 וַיָּבֹא דָוִד אֶל־צִקְלַג וַיְשַׁלַּח מֵהַשָּׁלָל לְזִקְנֵי יְהוּדָה לְרֵעֵהוּ לֵאמֹר הִנֵּה לָכֶם בְּרָכָה מִשְּׁלַל אֹיְבֵי יְהוָה:

27 לַאֲשֶׁר בְּבֵית־אֵל   וְלַאֲשֶׁר בְּרָמוֹת־נֶגֶב
וְלַאֲשֶׁר בְּיַתִּר:

28 וְלַאֲשֶׁר בַּעֲרֹעֵר   וְלַאֲשֶׁר בְּשִׂפְמוֹת
וְלַאֲשֶׁר בְּאֶשְׁתְּמֹעַ: פ

29 וְלַאֲשֶׁר בְּרָכָל   וְלַאֲשֶׁר בְּעָרֵי הַיְּרַחְמְאֵלִי
וְלַאֲשֶׁר בְּעָרֵי הַקֵּינִי:

were in the cities of the Kenites, ³⁰ *those* who *were* in Hormah, *those* who *were* in Chorashan, *those* who *were* in Athach, ³¹ *those* who *were* in Hebron, and to all the places where David himself and his men were accustomed to rove.

31 Now the Philistines fought against Israel; and the men of Israel fled from before the Philistines, and fell slain on Mount Gilboa. ² Then the Philistines followed hard after Saul and his sons. And the Philistines killed Jonathan, Abinadab, and Malchishua, Saul's sons. ³ The battle became fierce against Saul. The archers hit him, and he was severely wounded by the archers.

⁴ Then Saul said to his armorbearer, "Draw your sword, and thrust me through with it, lest these uncircumcised men come and thrust me through and abuse me."

But his armorbearer would not, for he was greatly afraid. Therefore Saul took a sword and fell on it. ⁵ And when his armorbearer saw that Saul was dead, he also fell on his sword, and died with him. ⁶ So Saul, his three sons, his armorbearer, and all his men died together that same day.

⁷ And when the men of Israel who *were* on the other side of the valley, and *those* who *were* on the other side of the Jordan, saw that the men of Israel had fled and that Saul and his sons were dead, they forsook the cities and fled; and the Philistines came and dwelt in them. ⁸ So it happened the next day, when the Philistines came to strip the slain, that they found Saul and his three sons fallen on Mount Gilboa. ⁹ And they cut off his head and stripped off his armor, and sent *word* throughout the land of the Philistines, to proclaim *it* in the temple of their idols and among the people. ¹⁰ Then they put his armor in the temple of the Ashtoreths, and they fastened his body to the wall of Beth Shan.

¹¹ Now when the inhabitants of Jabesh Gilead heard what the Philistines had done to Saul, ¹² all the valiant men arose and traveled all night, and took the body of Saul and the bodies of his sons from the wall of Beth Shan; and they came to Jabesh and burned them there. ¹³ Then they took their bones and buried *them* under the tamarisk tree at Jabesh, and fasted seven days.

וְלַאֲשֶׁר בְּחָרְמָה֙ וְלַאֲשֶׁ֖ר בְּבֹֽור־עָשָׁ֑ן 30
וְלַאֲשֶׁ֖ר בַּעֲתָֽךְ׃
וְלַאֲשֶׁ֤ר בְּחֶבְרֹון֙ וּֽלְכָל־הַמְּקֹמֹ֔ות 31
אֲשֶֽׁר־הִתְהַלֶּךְ־שָׁ֥ם דָּוִ֖ד ה֥וּא וַאֲנָשָֽׁיו׃ פ

לא וּפְלִשְׁתִּ֖ים נִלְחָמִ֣ים בְּיִשְׂרָאֵ֑ל וַיָּנֻ֜סוּ אַנְשֵׁ֣י
יִשְׂרָאֵ֗ל מִפְּנֵ֤י פְלִשְׁתִּים֙ וַיִּפְּל֣וּ חֲלָלִ֔ים בְּהַ֖ר הַגִּלְבֹּֽעַ׃
וַיַּדְבְּק֣וּ פְלִשְׁתִּ֔ים אֶת־שָׁא֖וּל וְאֶת־בָּנָ֑יו וַיַּכּ֣וּ 2
פְלִשְׁתִּ֗ים אֶת־יְהֹֽונָתָ֤ן וְאֶת־אֲבִֽינָדָב֙ וְאֶת־מַלְכִּֽי־
שׁ֔וּעַ בְּנֵ֖י שָׁאֽוּל׃ 3 וַתִּכְבַּ֤ד הַמִּלְחָמָה֙ אֶל־שָׁא֔וּל
וַיִּמְצָאֻ֥הוּ הַמֹּורִ֖ים אֲנָשִׁ֣ים בַּקָּ֑שֶׁת וַיָּ֥חֶל מְאֹ֖ד
מֵהַמֹּורִֽים׃ 4 וַיֹּ֣אמֶר שָׁא֣וּל לְנֹשֵׂ֣א כֵלָ֡יו שְׁלֹ֣ף
חַרְבְּךָ֣ ׀ וְדָקְרֵ֣נִי בָ֗הּ פֶּן־יָבֹ֜ואוּ הָעֲרֵלִ֤ים הָאֵ֙לֶּה֙
וּדְקָרֻ֔נִי וְהִתְעַלְּלוּ־בִ֔י וְלֹ֤א אָבָה֙ נֹשֵׂ֣א כֵלָ֔יו כִּ֥י יָרֵ֖א
מְאֹ֑ד וַיִּקַּ֤ח שָׁאוּל֙ אֶת־הַחֶ֔רֶב וַיִּפֹּ֖ל עָלֶֽיהָ׃ 5 וַיַּ֥רְא
נֹשֵֽׂא־כֵלָ֖יו כִּ֣י מֵ֣ת שָׁא֑וּל וַיִּפֹּ֥ל גַּם־ה֛וּא עַל־חַרְבֹּ֖ו
וַיָּ֥מָת עִמֹּֽו׃ 6 וַיָּ֣מָת שָׁ֠אוּל וּשְׁלֹ֨שֶׁת בָּנָ֜יו וְנֹשֵׂ֣א
כֵלָ֗יו גַּ֧ם כָּל־אֲנָשָׁ֛יו בַּיֹּ֥ום הַה֖וּא יַחְדָּֽו׃ 7 וַיִּרְא֣וּ
אַנְשֵֽׁי־יִ֠שְׂרָאֵל אֲשֶׁר־בְּעֵ֨בֶר הָעֵ֜מֶק וַאֲשֶׁ֣ר ׀ בְּעֵ֣בֶר
הַיַּרְדֵּ֗ן כִּֽי־נָ֜סוּ אַנְשֵׁ֤י יִשְׂרָאֵל֙ וְכִֽי־מֵ֙תוּ֙ שָׁא֣וּל וּבָנָ֔יו
וַיַּעַזְב֥וּ אֶת־הֶעָרִ֖ים וַיָּנֻ֑סוּ וַיָּבֹ֣אוּ פְלִשְׁתִּ֔ים וַיֵּֽשְׁב֖וּ
בָּהֶֽן׃ ס 8 וַֽיְהִי֙ מִֽמָּחֳרָ֔ת וַיָּבֹ֣אוּ פְלִשְׁתִּ֔ים
לְפַשֵּׁ֖ט אֶת־הַחֲלָלִ֑ים וַיִּמְצְא֤וּ אֶת־שָׁאוּל֙ וְאֶת־
שְׁלֹ֣שֶׁת בָּנָ֔יו נֹפְלִ֖ים בְּהַ֥ר הַגִּלְבֹּֽעַ׃ 9 וַֽיִּכְרְתוּ֙ אֶת־
רֹאשֹׁ֔ו וַיַּפְשִׁ֖יטוּ אֶת־כֵּלָ֑יו וַיְשַׁלְּח֨וּ בְאֶֽרֶץ־פְּלִשְׁתִּ֜ים
סָבִ֗יב לְבַשֵּׂ֛ר בֵּ֥ית עֲצַבֵּיהֶ֖ם וְאֶת־הָעָֽם׃ 10 וַיָּשִׂ֙מוּ֙
אֶת־כֵּלָ֔יו בֵּ֖ית עַשְׁתָּרֹ֑ות וְאֶת־גְּוִיָּתֹו֙ תָּקְע֔וּ בְּחֹומַ֖ת
בֵּ֥ית שָֽׁן׃ 11 וַיִּשְׁמְע֣וּ אֵלָ֗יו יֹשְׁבֵ֛י יָבֵ֖ישׁ גִּלְעָ֑ד אֵ֛ת
אֲשֶׁר־עָשׂ֥וּ פְלִשְׁתִּ֖ים לְשָׁאֽוּל׃ 12 וַיָּק֣וּמוּ כָּל־אִ֣ישׁ
חַ֗יִל וַיֵּלְכ֣וּ כָל־הַלַּ֔יְלָה וַיִּקְח֞וּ אֶת־גְּוִיַּ֣ת שָׁא֗וּל וְאֵ֣ת
גְּוִיֹּ֤ת בָּנָיו֙ מֵחֹומַ֣ת בֵּ֣ית שָׁ֔ן וַיָּבֹ֥אוּ יָבֵ֖שָׁה וַיִּשְׂרְפ֥וּ
אֹתָ֖ם שָֽׁם׃ 13 וַיִּקְחוּ֙ אֶת־עַצְמֹ֣תֵיהֶ֔ם וַיִּקְבְּר֥וּ תַֽחַת־
הָאֶ֖שֶׁל בְּיָבֵ֑שָׁה וַיָּצֻ֖מוּ שִׁבְעַ֥ת יָמִֽים׃ פ

The Second Book of
SAMUEL

שמואל ב

1 Now it came to pass after the death of Saul, when David had returned from the slaughter of the Amalekites, and David had stayed two days in Ziklag, ²on the third day, behold, it happened that a man came from Saul's camp with his clothes torn and dust on his head. So it was, when he came to David, that he fell to the ground and prostrated himself.

³And David said to him, "Where have you come from?"

So he said to him, "I have escaped from the camp of Israel."

⁴Then David said to him, "How did the matter go? Please tell me."

And he answered, "The people have fled from the battle, many of the people are fallen and dead, and Saul and Jonathan his son are dead also."

⁵So David said to the young man who told him, "How do you know that Saul and Jonathan his son are dead?"

⁶Then the young man who told him said, "As I happened by chance to be on Mount Gilboa, there was Saul, leaning on his spear; and indeed the chariots and horsemen followed hard after him. ⁷Now when he looked behind him, he saw me and called to me. And I answered, 'Here I am.' ⁸And he said to me, 'Who are you?' So I answered him, 'I am an Amalekite.' ⁹He said to me again, 'Please stand over me and kill me, for anguish has come upon me, but my life still remains in me.' ¹⁰So I stood over him and killed him, because I was sure that he could not live after he had fallen. And I took the crown that was on his head and the bracelet that was on his arm, and have brought them here to my lord."

¹¹Therefore David took hold of his own clothes and tore them, and so did all the men who were with him. ¹²And they mourned and wept and fasted until evening for Saul and for Jonathan his son, for the people of the LORD and for the house of Israel, because they had fallen by the sword.

¹³Then David said to the young man who told him, "Where are you from?"

And he answered, "I am the son of an alien, an Amalekite."

¹⁴So David said to him, "How was it you were not afraid to put forth your hand to destroy the LORD's anointed?" ¹⁵Then David called one of the

א וַיְהִ֗י אַחֲרֵי֙ מ֣וֹת שָׁא֔וּל וְדָוִ֣ד שָׁ֔ב מֵהַכּ֖וֹת אֶת־
הָעֲמָלֵ֑ק וַיֵּ֧שֶׁב דָּוִ֛ד בְּצִקְלָ֖ג יָמִ֥ים שְׁנָֽיִם׃ ²וַיְהִ֣י ׀
בַּיּ֣וֹם הַשְּׁלִישִׁ֗י וְהִנֵּה֩ אִ֨ישׁ בָּ֤א מִן־הַֽמַּחֲנֶה֙ מֵעִ֣ם
שָׁא֔וּל וּבְגָדָ֣יו קְרֻעִ֔ים וַאֲדָמָ֖ה עַל־רֹאשׁ֑וֹ וַיְהִי֙
בְּבֹא֣וֹ אֶל־דָּוִ֔ד וַיִּפֹּ֥ל אַ֖רְצָה וַיִּשְׁתָּֽחוּ׃ ³וַיֹּ֤אמֶר
ל֣וֹ דָּוִ֔ד אֵ֥י מִזֶּ֖ה תָּב֑וֹא וַיֹּ֣אמֶר אֵלָ֔יו מִמַּחֲנֵ֥ה
יִשְׂרָאֵ֖ל נִמְלָֽטְתִּי׃ ⁴וַיֹּ֨אמֶר אֵלָ֤יו דָּוִד֙ מֶה־הָיָ֣ה
הַדָּבָ֔ר הַגֶּד־נָ֖א לִ֑י וַ֠יֹּאמֶר אֲשֶׁר־נָ֨ס הָעָ֜ם מִן־
הַמִּלְחָמָ֗ה וְגַם־הַרְבֵּ֞ה נָפַ֤ל מִן־הָעָם֙ וַיָּמֻ֔תוּ וְגַ֗ם
שָׁא֛וּל וִיהֽוֹנָתָ֥ן בְּנ֖וֹ מֵֽתוּ׃ ⁵וַיֹּ֣אמֶר דָּוִ֔ד אֶל־הַנַּ֖עַר
הַמַּגִּ֣יד ל֑וֹ אֵ֣יךְ יָדַ֔עְתָּ כִּי־מֵ֥ת שָׁא֖וּל וִיהֽוֹנָתָ֥ן בְּנֽוֹ׃

⁶וַיֹּ֜אמֶר הַנַּ֣עַר ׀ הַמַּגִּ֣יד ל֗וֹ נִקְרֹ֤א נִקְרֵ֙יתִי֙ בְּהַ֣ר
הַגִּלְבֹּ֔עַ וְהִנֵּ֥ה שָׁא֖וּל נִשְׁעָ֣ן עַל־חֲנִית֑וֹ וְהִנֵּ֥ה הָרֶ֛כֶב
וּבַעֲלֵ֥י הַפָּרָשִׁ֖ים הִדְבִּקֻֽהוּ׃ ⁷וַיִּ֥פֶן אַחֲרָ֖יו וַיִּרְאֵ֑נִי
וַיִּקְרָ֣א אֵלָ֔י וָאֹמַ֖ר הִנֵּֽנִי׃ ⁸וַיֹּ֥אמֶר לִ֖י מִי־אָ֑תָּה
וָאֹמַ֣ר אֵלָ֔יו עֲמָלֵקִ֖י אָנֹֽכִי׃ ⁹וַיֹּ֣אמֶר אֵלַ֗י עֲמָד־נָ֤א
עָלַי֙ וּמֹ֣תְתֵ֔נִי כִּ֥י אֲחָזַ֖נִי הַשָּׁבָ֑ץ כִּֽי־כָל־ע֥וֹד נַפְשִׁ֖י
בִּֽי׃ ¹⁰וָאֶעֱמֹ֤ד עָלָיו֙ וַאֲמֹ֣תְתֵ֔הוּ כִּ֣י יָדַ֔עְתִּי כִּ֛י לֹ֥א
יִחְיֶ֖ה אַחֲרֵ֣י נִפְל֑וֹ וָאֶקַּ֞ח הַנֵּ֣זֶר ׀ אֲשֶׁ֣ר עַל־רֹאשׁ֗וֹ
וְאֶצְעָדָה֙ אֲשֶׁ֣ר עַל־זְרֹע֔וֹ וָאֲבִיאֵ֥ם אֶל־אֲדֹנִ֖י הֵֽנָּה׃
¹¹וַיַּחֲזֵ֥ק דָּוִ֛ד בִּבְגָדָ֖ו וַיִּקְרָעֵ֑ם וְגַ֖ם כָּל־הָאֲנָשִׁ֥ים
אֲשֶׁ֥ר אִתּֽוֹ׃ ¹²וַֽיִּסְפְּדוּ֙ וַיִּבְכּ֔וּ וַיָּצֻ֖מוּ עַד־הָעָ֑רֶב עַל־
שָׁא֞וּל וְעַל־יְהוֹנָתָ֣ן בְּנ֗וֹ וְעַל־עַ֤ם יְהֹוָה֙ וְעַל־בֵּ֣ית
יִשְׂרָאֵ֔ל כִּ֥י נָפְל֖וּ בֶּחָֽרֶב׃ ¹³וַיֹּ֣אמֶר דָּוִ֗ד ס
אֶל־הַנַּ֙עַר֙ הַמַּגִּ֣יד ל֔וֹ אֵ֥י מִזֶּ֖ה אָ֑תָּה וַיֹּ֕אמֶר בֶּן־
אִ֛ישׁ גֵּ֥ר עֲמָלֵקִ֖י אָנֹֽכִי׃ ¹⁴וַיֹּ֤אמֶר אֵלָיו֙ דָּוִ֔ד אֵ֖יךְ
לֹ֣א יָרֵ֑אתָ לִשְׁלֹ֙חַ֙ יָ֣דְךָ֔ לְשַׁחֵ֖ת אֶת־מְשִׁ֥יחַ יְהֹוָֽה׃
¹⁵וַיִּקְרָ֣א דָוִ֗ד לְאַחַד֙ מֵֽהַנְּעָרִ֔ים וַיֹּ֖אמֶר גַּ֣שׁ פְּגַֽע־

young men and said, "Go near, *and* execute him!" And he struck him so that he died. [16] So David said to him, "Your blood *is* on your own head, for your own mouth has testified against you, saying, 'I have killed the LORD's anointed.' "

[17] Then David lamented with this lamentation over Saul and over Jonathan his son, [18] and he told *them* to teach the children of Judah *the Song of* the Bow; indeed *it is* written in the Book of Jasher:

[19]   "The beauty of Israel is slain on your high places!
       How the mighty have fallen!
[20]   Tell *it* not in Gath,
       Proclaim *it* not in the streets of Ashkelon—
       Lest the daughters of the Philistines rejoice,
       Lest the daughters of the uncircumcised triumph.

[21]   "O mountains of Gilboa,
       Let there be no dew nor rain upon you,
       Nor fields of offerings.
       For the shield of the mighty is cast away there!
       The shield of Saul, not anointed with oil.
[22]   From the blood of the slain,
       From the fat of the mighty,
       The bow of Jonathan did not turn back,
       And the sword of Saul did not return empty.

[23]   "Saul and Jonathan *were* beloved and pleasant in their lives,
       And in their death they were not divided;
       They were swifter than eagles,
       They were stronger than lions.

[24]   "O daughters of Israel, weep over Saul,
       Who clothed you in scarlet, with luxury;
       Who put ornaments of gold on your apparel.

[25]   "How the mighty have fallen in the midst of the battle!
       Jonathan *was* slain in your high places.
[26]   I am distressed for you, my brother Jonathan;
       You have been very pleasant to me;
       Your love to me was wonderful,
       Surpassing the love of women.

[27]   "How the mighty have fallen,
       And the weapons of war perished!"

2 It happened after this that David inquired of the LORD, saying, "Shall I go up to any of the cities of Judah?"

And the LORD said to him, "Go up."

David said, "Where shall I go up?"

And He said, "To Hebron."

[2] So David went up there, and his two wives also, Ahinoam the Jezreelitess, and Abigail the widow of Nabal the Carmelite. [3] And David brought up the men who *were* with him, every man with his household. So they dwelt in the cities of Hebron.

בּוֹ וַיַּכֵּהוּ וַיָּמֹת: 16 וַיֹּאמֶר אֵלָיו דָּוִד דָּמֶיךָ עַל־רֹאשֶׁךָ כִּי פִיךָ עָנָה בְךָ לֵאמֹר אָנֹכִי מֹתַתִּי אֶת־מְשִׁיחַ יְהֹוָה: ס 17 וַיְקֹנֵן דָּוִד אֶת־הַקִּינָה הַזֹּאת עַל־שָׁאוּל וְעַל־יְהוֹנָתָן בְּנוֹ: 18 וַיֹּאמֶר לְלַמֵּד בְּנֵי־יְהוּדָה קָשֶׁת הִנֵּה כְתוּבָה עַל־סֵפֶר הַיָּשָׁר:

19 הַצְּבִי יִשְׂרָאֵל עַל־בָּמוֹתֶיךָ חָלָל אֵיךְ נָפְלוּ גִבּוֹרִים: 20 אַל־תַּגִּידוּ בְגַת אַל־תְּבַשְּׂרוּ בְּחוּצֹת אַשְׁקְלוֹן פֶּן־תִּשְׂמַחְנָה בְּנוֹת פְּלִשְׁתִּים פֶּן־תַּעֲלֹזְנָה בְּנוֹת הָעֲרֵלִים: 21 הָרֵי בַגִּלְבֹּעַ אַל־טַל וְאַל־מָטָר עֲלֵיכֶם וּשְׂדֵי תְרוּמֹת כִּי שָׁם נִגְעַל מָגֵן גִּבּוֹרִים מָגֵן שָׁאוּל בְּלִי מָשִׁיחַ בַּשָּׁמֶן: 22 מִדַּם חֲלָלִים מֵחֵלֶב גִּבּוֹרִים קֶשֶׁת יְהוֹנָתָן לֹא נָשׂוֹג אָחוֹר וְחֶרֶב שָׁאוּל לֹא תָשׁוּב רֵיקָם: 23 שָׁאוּל וִיהוֹנָתָן הַנֶּאֱהָבִים וְהַנְּעִימִם בְּחַיֵּיהֶם וּבְמוֹתָם לֹא נִפְרָדוּ מִנְּשָׁרִים קַלּוּ מֵאֲרָיוֹת גָּבֵרוּ: 24 בְּנוֹת יִשְׂרָאֵל אֶל־שָׁאוּל בְּכֶינָה הַמַּלְבִּשְׁכֶם שָׁנִי עִם־עֲדָנִים הַמַּעֲלֶה עֲדִי זָהָב עַל לְבוּשְׁכֶן: 25 אֵיךְ נָפְלוּ גִבֹּרִים בְּתוֹךְ הַמִּלְחָמָה יְהוֹנָתָן עַל־בָּמוֹתֶיךָ חָלָל: 26 צַר־לִי עָלֶיךָ אָחִי יְהוֹנָתָן נָעַמְתָּ לִּי מְאֹד נִפְלְאַתָה אַהֲבָתְךָ לִי מֵאַהֲבַת נָשִׁים: 27 אֵיךְ נָפְלוּ גִבּוֹרִים וַיֹּאבְדוּ כְּלֵי מִלְחָמָה: פ

ב 1 וַיְהִי אַחֲרֵי־כֵן וַיִּשְׁאַל דָּוִד בַּיהֹוָה לֵאמֹר הַאֶעֱלֶה בְּאַחַת עָרֵי יְהוּדָה וַיֹּאמֶר יְהֹוָה אֵלָיו עֲלֵה וַיֹּאמֶר דָּוִד אָנָה אֶעֱלֶה וַיֹּאמֶר חֶבְרֹנָה: 2 וַיַּעַל שָׁם דָּוִד וְגַם שְׁתֵּי נָשָׁיו אֲחִינֹעַם הַיִּזְרְעֵלִית וַאֲבִיגַיִל אֵשֶׁת נָבָל הַכַּרְמְלִי: 3 וַאֲנָשָׁיו אֲשֶׁר־עִמּוֹ

⁴ Then the men of Judah came, and there they anointed David king over the house of Judah. And they told David, saying, "The men of Jabesh Gilead *were the ones* who buried Saul." ⁵ So David sent messengers to the men of Jabesh Gilead, and said to them, "You *are* blessed of the LORD, for you have shown this kindness to your lord, to Saul, and have buried him. ⁶ And now may the LORD show kindness and truth to you. I also will repay you this kindness, because you have done this thing. ⁷ Now therefore, let your hands be strengthened, and be valiant; for your master Saul is dead, and also the house of Judah has anointed me king over them."

⁸ But Abner the son of Ner, commander of Saul's army, took Ishbosheth the son of Saul and brought him over to Mahanaim; ⁹ and he made him king over Gilead, over the Ashurites, over Jezreel, over Ephraim, over Benjamin, and over all Israel. ¹⁰ Ishbosheth, Saul's son, *was* forty years old when he began to reign over Israel, and he reigned two years. Only the house of Judah followed David. ¹¹ And the time that David was king in Hebron over the house of Judah was seven years and six months.

¹² Now Abner the son of Ner, and the servants of Ishbosheth the son of Saul, went out from Mahanaim to Gibeon. ¹³ And Joab the son of Zeruiah, and the servants of David, went out and met them by the pool of Gibeon. So they sat down, one on one side of the pool and the other on the other side of the pool. ¹⁴ Then Abner said to Joab, "Let the young men now arise and compete before us."

And Joab said, "Let them arise."

¹⁵ So they arose and went over by number, twelve from Benjamin, *followers* of Ishbosheth the son of Saul, and twelve from the servants of David. ¹⁶ And each one grasped his opponent by the head and *thrust* his sword in his opponent's side; so they fell down together. Therefore that place was called the Field of Sharp Swords, which *is* in Gibeon. ¹⁷ So there was a very fierce battle that day, and Abner and the men of Israel were beaten before the servants of David.

¹⁸ Now the three sons of Zeruiah were there: Joab and Abishai and Asahel. And Asahel *was as* fleet of foot as a wild gazelle. ¹⁹ So Asahel pursued Abner, and in going he did not turn to the right hand or to the left from following Abner.

²⁰ Then Abner looked behind him and said, "*Are* you Asahel?"

He answered, "I *am*."

הֶעֱלָה דָוִד אִישׁ וּבֵיתוֹ וַיֵּשְׁבוּ בְּעָרֵי חֶבְרוֹן: 4 וַיָּבֹאוּ אַנְשֵׁי יְהוּדָה וַיִּמְשְׁחוּ־שָׁם אֶת־דָּוִד לְמֶלֶךְ עַל־בֵּית יְהוּדָה וַיַּגִּדוּ לְדָוִד לֵאמֹר אַנְשֵׁי יָבֵישׁ גִּלְעָד אֲשֶׁר קָבְרוּ אֶת־שָׁאוּל: ס 5 וַיִּשְׁלַח דָּוִד מַלְאָכִים אֶל־אַנְשֵׁי יָבֵישׁ גִּלְעָד וַיֹּאמֶר אֲלֵיהֶם בְּרֻכִים אַתֶּם לַיהוָה אֲשֶׁר עֲשִׂיתֶם הַחֶסֶד הַזֶּה עִם־אֲדֹנֵיכֶם עִם־שָׁאוּל וַתִּקְבְּרוּ אֹתוֹ: 6 וְעַתָּה יַעַשׂ־יְהוָה עִמָּכֶם חֶסֶד וֶאֱמֶת וְגַם אָנֹכִי אֶעֱשֶׂה אִתְּכֶם הַטּוֹבָה הַזֹּאת אֲשֶׁר עֲשִׂיתֶם הַדָּבָר הַזֶּה: 7 וְעַתָּה תֶּחֱזַקְנָה יְדֵיכֶם וִהְיוּ לִבְנֵי־חַיִל כִּי־מֵת אֲדֹנֵיכֶם שָׁאוּל וְגַם־אֹתִי מָשְׁחוּ בֵית־יְהוּדָה לְמֶלֶךְ עֲלֵיהֶם: פ

8 וְאַבְנֵר בֶּן־נֵר שַׂר־צָבָא אֲשֶׁר לְשָׁאוּל לָקַח אֶת־אִישׁ בֹּשֶׁת בֶּן־שָׁאוּל וַיַּעֲבִרֵהוּ מַחֲנָיִם: 9 וַיַּמְלִכֵהוּ אֶל־הַגִּלְעָד וְאֶל־הָאֲשׁוּרִי וְאֶל־יִזְרְעֶאל וְעַל־אֶפְרַיִם וְעַל־בִּנְיָמִן וְעַל־יִשְׂרָאֵל כֻּלֹּה: פ

10 בֶּן־אַרְבָּעִים שָׁנָה אִישׁ־בֹּשֶׁת בֶּן־שָׁאוּל בְּמָלְכוֹ עַל־יִשְׂרָאֵל וּשְׁתַּיִם שָׁנִים מָלָךְ אַךְ בֵּית יְהוּדָה הָיוּ אַחֲרֵי דָוִד: 11 וַיְהִי מִסְפַּר הַיָּמִים אֲשֶׁר הָיָה דָוִד מֶלֶךְ בְּחֶבְרוֹן עַל־בֵּית יְהוּדָה שֶׁבַע שָׁנִים וְשִׁשָּׁה חֳדָשִׁים: ס 12 וַיֵּצֵא אַבְנֵר בֶּן־נֵר וְעַבְדֵי אִישׁ־בֹּשֶׁת בֶּן־שָׁאוּל מִמַּחֲנַיִם גִּבְעוֹנָה: 13 וְיוֹאָב בֶּן־צְרוּיָה וְעַבְדֵי דָוִד יָצְאוּ וַיִּפְגְּשׁוּם עַל־בְּרֵכַת גִּבְעוֹן יַחְדָּו וַיֵּשְׁבוּ אֵלֶּה עַל־הַבְּרֵכָה מִזֶּה וְאֵלֶּה עַל־הַבְּרֵכָה מִזֶּה: 14 וַיֹּאמֶר אַבְנֵר אֶל־יוֹאָב יָקוּמוּ נָא הַנְּעָרִים וִישַׂחֲקוּ לְפָנֵינוּ וַיֹּאמֶר יוֹאָב יָקֻמוּ: 15 וַיָּקֻמוּ וַיַּעַבְרוּ בְמִסְפָּר שְׁנֵים עָשָׂר לְבִנְיָמִן וּלְאִישׁ בֹּשֶׁת בֶּן־שָׁאוּל וּשְׁנֵים עָשָׂר מֵעַבְדֵי דָוִד: 16 וַיַּחֲזִקוּ אִישׁ בְּרֹאשׁ רֵעֵהוּ וְחַרְבּוֹ בְּצַד רֵעֵהוּ וַיִּפְּלוּ יַחְדָּו וַיִּקְרָא לַמָּקוֹם הַהוּא חֶלְקַת הַצֻּרִים אֲשֶׁר בְּגִבְעוֹן: 17 וַתְּהִי הַמִּלְחָמָה קָשָׁה עַד־מְאֹד בַּיּוֹם הַהוּא וַיִּנָּגֶף אַבְנֵר וְאַנְשֵׁי יִשְׂרָאֵל לִפְנֵי עַבְדֵי דָוִד: 18 וַיִּהְיוּ־שָׁם שְׁלֹשָׁה בְּנֵי צְרוּיָה יוֹאָב וַאֲבִישַׁי וַעֲשָׂהאֵל וַעֲשָׂהאֵל קַל בְּרַגְלָיו כְּאַחַד הַצְּבָיִם אֲשֶׁר בַּשָּׂדֶה: 19 וַיִּרְדֹּף עֲשָׂהאֵל אַחֲרֵי אַבְנֵר וְלֹא־נָטָה לָלֶכֶת עַל־הַיָּמִין וְעַל־הַשְּׂמֹאול מֵאַחֲרֵי אַבְנֵר: 20 וַיִּפֶן אַבְנֵר אַחֲרָיו וַיֹּאמֶר הַאַתָּה זֶה עֲשָׂהאֵל

²¹ And Abner said to him, "Turn aside to your right hand or to your left, and lay hold on one of the young men and take his armor for yourself." But Asahel would not turn aside from following him. ²² So Abner said again to Asahel, "Turn aside from following me. Why should I strike you to the ground? How then could I face your brother Joab?" ²³ However, he refused to turn aside. Therefore Abner struck him in the stomach with the blunt end of the spear, so that the spear came out of his back; and he fell down there and died on the spot. So it was *that* as many as came to the place where Asahel fell down and died, stood still.

²⁴ Joab and Abishai also pursued Abner. And the sun was going down when they came to the hill of Ammah, which *is* before Giah by the road to the Wilderness of Gibeon. ²⁵ Now the children of Benjamin gathered together behind Abner and became a unit, and took their stand on top of a hill. ²⁶ Then Abner called to Joab and said, "Shall the sword devour forever? Do you not know that it will be bitter in the latter end? How long will it be then until you tell the people to return from pursuing their brethren?"

²⁷ And Joab said, "*As* God lives, unless you had spoken, surely then by morning all the people would have given up pursuing their brethren." ²⁸ So Joab blew a trumpet; and all the people stood still and did not pursue Israel anymore, nor did they fight anymore. ²⁹ Then Abner and his men went on all that night through the plain, crossed over the Jordan, and went through all Bithron; and they came to Mahanaim.

³⁰ So Joab returned from pursuing Abner. And when he had gathered all the people together, there were missing of David's servants nineteen men and Asahel. ³¹ But the servants of David had struck down, of Benjamin and Abner's men, three hundred and sixty men who died. ³² Then they took up Asahel and buried him in his father's tomb, which *was in* Bethlehem. And Joab and his men went all night, and they came to Hebron at daybreak.

3 Now there was a long war between the house of Saul and the house of David. But David grew stronger and stronger, and the house of Saul grew weaker and weaker.

² Sons were born to David in Hebron: His firstborn was Amnon by Ahinoam the Jezreelitess; ³ his second, Chileab, by Abigail the widow of Nabal the Carmelite; the third, Absalom the son of Maacah, the daughter of Talmai, king of Geshur; ⁴ the fourth, Adonijah the son of Haggith; the fifth,

וַיֹּאמֶר אָנֹכִי: ²¹ וַיֹּאמֶר לוֹ אַבְנֵר נְטֵה לְךָ עַל־יְמִינְךָ אוֹ עַל־שְׂמֹאלֶךָ וֶאֱחֹז לְךָ אֶחָד מֵהַנְּעָרִים וְקַח־לְךָ אֶת־חֲלִצָתוֹ וְלֹא־אָבָה עֲשָׂהאֵל לָסוּר מֵאַחֲרָיו: ²² וַיֹּסֶף עוֹד אַבְנֵר לֵאמֹר אֶל־עֲשָׂהאֵל סוּר לְךָ מֵאַחֲרָי לָמָּה אַכֶּכָּה אַרְצָה וְאֵיךְ אֶשָּׂא פָנַי אֶל־יוֹאָב אָחִיךָ: ²³ וַיְמָאֵן לָסוּר וַיַּכֵּהוּ אַבְנֵר בְּאַחֲרֵי הַחֲנִית אֶל־הַחֹמֶשׁ וַתֵּצֵא הַחֲנִית מֵאַחֲרָיו וַיִּפָּל־שָׁם וַיָּמָת תַּחְתָּו וַיְהִי כָּל־הַבָּא אֶל־הַמָּקוֹם אֲשֶׁר־נָפַל שָׁם עֲשָׂהאֵל וַיָּמֹת וַיַּעֲמֹדוּ: ²⁴ וַיִּרְדְּפוּ יוֹאָב וַאֲבִישַׁי אַחֲרֵי אַבְנֵר וְהַשֶּׁמֶשׁ בָּאָה וְהֵמָּה בָּאוּ עַד־גִּבְעַת אַמָּה אֲשֶׁר עַל־פְּנֵי־גִיחַ דֶּרֶךְ מִדְבַּר גִּבְעוֹן: ²⁵ וַיִּתְקַבְּצוּ בְנֵי־בִנְיָמִן אַחֲרֵי אַבְנֵר וַיִּהְיוּ לַאֲגֻדָּה אֶחָת וַיַּעַמְדוּ עַל רֹאשׁ־גִּבְעָה אֶחָת: ²⁶ וַיִּקְרָא אַבְנֵר אֶל־יוֹאָב וַיֹּאמֶר הֲלָנֶצַח תֹּאכַל חֶרֶב הֲלוֹא יָדַעְתָּה כִּי־מָרָה תִהְיֶה בָּאַחֲרוֹנָה וְעַד־מָתַי לֹא־תֹאמַר לָעָם לָשׁוּב מֵאַחֲרֵי אֲחֵיהֶם: ²⁷ וַיֹּאמֶר יוֹאָב חַי הָאֱלֹהִים כִּי לוּלֵא דִּבַּרְתָּ כִּי אָז מֵהַבֹּקֶר נַעֲלָה הָעָם אִישׁ מֵאַחֲרֵי אָחִיו: ²⁸ וַיִּתְקַע יוֹאָב בַּשּׁוֹפָר וַיַּעַמְדוּ כָּל־הָעָם וְלֹא־יִרְדְּפוּ עוֹד אַחֲרֵי יִשְׂרָאֵל וְלֹא־יָסְפוּ עוֹד לְהִלָּחֵם: ²⁹ וְאַבְנֵר וַאֲנָשָׁיו הָלְכוּ בָּעֲרָבָה כֹּל הַלַּיְלָה הַהוּא וַיַּעַבְרוּ אֶת־הַיַּרְדֵּן וַיֵּלְכוּ כָּל־הַבִּתְרוֹן וַיָּבֹאוּ מַחֲנָיִם: ³⁰ וְיוֹאָב שָׁב מֵאַחֲרֵי אַבְנֵר וַיִּקְבֹּץ אֶת־כָּל־הָעָם וַיִּפָּקְדוּ מֵעַבְדֵי דָוִד תִּשְׁעָה־עָשָׂר אִישׁ וַעֲשָׂהאֵל: ³¹ וְעַבְדֵי דָוִד הִכּוּ מִבִּנְיָמִן וּבְאַנְשֵׁי אַבְנֵר שְׁלֹשׁ־מֵאוֹת וְשִׁשִּׁים אִישׁ מֵתוּ: ³² וַיִּשְׂאוּ אֶת־עֲשָׂהאֵל וַיִּקְבְּרֻהוּ בְּקֶבֶר אָבִיו אֲשֶׁר בֵּית לָחֶם וַיֵּלְכוּ כָל־הַלַּיְלָה יוֹאָב וַאֲנָשָׁיו וַיֵּאֹר לָהֶם בְּחֶבְרוֹן:

ג וַתְּהִי הַמִּלְחָמָה אֲרֻכָּה בֵּין בֵּית שָׁאוּל וּבֵין בֵּית דָּוִד וְדָוִד הֹלֵךְ וְחָזֵק וּבֵית שָׁאוּל הֹלְכִים וְדַלִּים: ס ² וַיִּלְדוּ לְדָוִד בָּנִים בְּחֶבְרוֹן וַיְהִי בְכוֹרוֹ אַמְנוֹן לַאֲחִינֹעַם הַיִּזְרְעֵאלִת: ³ וּמִשְׁנֵהוּ כִלְאָב לַאֲבִיגַיִל אֵשֶׁת נָבָל הַכַּרְמְלִי וְהַשְּׁלִשִׁי אַבְשָׁלוֹם בֶּן־מַעֲכָה בַּת־תַּלְמַי מֶלֶךְ גְּשׁוּר: ⁴ וְהָרְבִיעִי אֲדֹנִיָּה בֶן־חַגִּית וְהַחֲמִישִׁי

ב 23 תַּחְתָּו   ג 2 וַיִּלְדוּ   3 לַאֲבִיגַיִל

Shephatiah the son of Abital; ⁵and the sixth, Ithream, by David's wife Eglah. These were born to David in Hebron.

⁶Now it was so, while there was war between the house of Saul and the house of David, that Abner was strengthening *his hold* on the house of Saul.

⁷And Saul had a concubine, whose name *was* Rizpah, the daughter of Aiah. So *Ishbosheth* said to Abner, "Why have you gone in to my father's concubine?"

⁸Then Abner became very angry at the words of Ishbosheth, and said, "*Am* I a dog's head that belongs to Judah? Today I show loyalty to the house of Saul your father, to his brothers, and to his friends, and have not delivered you into the hand of David; and you charge me today with a fault concerning this woman? ⁹May God do so to Abner, and more also, if I do not do for David as the LORD has sworn to him— ¹⁰to transfer the kingdom from the house of Saul, and set up the throne of David over Israel and over Judah, from Dan to Beersheba." ¹¹And he could not answer Abner another word, because he feared him.

¹²Then Abner sent messengers on his behalf to David, saying, "Whose *is* the land?" saying *also,* "Make your covenant with me, and indeed my hand *shall be* with you to bring all Israel to you."

¹³And *David* said, "Good, I will make a covenant with you. But one thing I require of you: you shall not see my face unless you first bring Michal, Saul's daughter, when you come to see my face." ¹⁴So David sent messengers to Ishbosheth, Saul's son, saying, "Give *me* my wife Michal, whom I betrothed to myself for a hundred foreskins of the Philistines." ¹⁵And Ishbosheth sent and took her from *her* husband, from Paltiel the son of Laish. ¹⁶Then her husband went along with her to Bahurim, weeping behind her. So Abner said to him, "Go, return!" And he returned.

¹⁷Now Abner had communicated with the elders of Israel, saying, "In time past you were seeking for David *to be* king over you. ¹⁸Now then, do *it!* For the LORD has spoken of David, saying, 'By the hand of My servant David, I will save My people Israel from the hand of the Philistines and the hand of all their enemies.'" ¹⁹And Abner also spoke in the hearing of Benjamin. Then Abner also went to speak in the hearing of David in Hebron all that seemed good to Israel and the whole house of Benjamin.

²⁰So Abner and twenty men with him came to David at Hebron. And David made a feast for Abner and the men who *were* with him. ²¹Then Abner said to David, "I will arise and go, and

וְהַשִּׁשִּׁי יִתְרְעָם לְעֶגְלָה אֵשֶׁת 5 דָּוִד אֵלֶּה יֻלְּדוּ לְדָוִד בְּחֶבְרוֹן: פ
6 וַיְהִי בִּהְיוֹת הַמִּלְחָמָה בֵּין בֵּית שָׁאוּל וּבֵין בֵּית דָּוִד וְאַבְנֵר הָיָה מִתְחַזֵּק בְּבֵית שָׁאוּל: 7 וּלְשָׁאוּל פִּלֶגֶשׁ וּשְׁמָהּ רִצְפָּה בַת־אַיָּה וַיֹּאמֶר אֶל־אַבְנֵר מַדּוּעַ בָּאתָה אֶל־פִּילֶגֶשׁ אָבִי: 8 וַיִּחַר לְאַבְנֵר מְאֹד עַל־דִּבְרֵי אִישׁ־בֹּשֶׁת וַיֹּאמֶר הֲרֹאשׁ כֶּלֶב אָנֹכִי אֲשֶׁר לִיהוּדָה הַיּוֹם אֶעֱשֶׂה־חֶסֶד עִם־בֵּית שָׁאוּל אָבִיךָ אֶל־אֶחָיו וְאֶל־מֵרֵעֵהוּ וְלֹא הִמְצִיתְךָ בְּיַד־דָּוִד וַתִּפְקֹד עָלַי עֲוֹן הָאִשָּׁה הַיּוֹם: 9 כֹּה־יַעֲשֶׂה אֱלֹהִים לְאַבְנֵר וְכֹה יֹסִיף לוֹ כִּי כַּאֲשֶׁר נִשְׁבַּע יְהֹוָה לְדָוִד כִּי־כֵן אֶעֱשֶׂה־לּוֹ: 10 לְהַעֲבִיר הַמַּמְלָכָה מִבֵּית שָׁאוּל וּלְהָקִים אֶת־כִּסֵּא דָוִד עַל־יִשְׂרָאֵל וְעַל־יְהוּדָה מִדָּן וְעַד־בְּאֵר שָׁבַע: 11 וְלֹא־יָכֹל עוֹד לְהָשִׁיב אֶת־אַבְנֵר דָּבָר מִיִּרְאָתוֹ אֹתוֹ: ס 12 וַיִּשְׁלַח אַבְנֵר מַלְאָכִים | אֶל־דָּוִד תַּחְתָּו לֵאמֹר לְמִי־אָרֶץ לֵאמֹר כָּרְתָה בְרִיתְךָ אִתִּי וְהִנֵּה יָדִי עִמָּךְ לְהָסֵב אֵלֶיךָ אֶת־כָּל־יִשְׂרָאֵל: 13 וַיֹּאמֶר טוֹב אֲנִי אֶכְרֹת אִתְּךָ בְּרִית אַךְ דָּבָר אֶחָד אָנֹכִי שֹׁאֵל מֵאִתְּךָ לֵאמֹר לֹא־תִרְאֶה אֶת־פָּנַי כִּי | אִם־לִפְנֵי הֱבִיאֲךָ אֵת מִיכַל בַּת־שָׁאוּל בְּבֹאֲךָ לִרְאוֹת אֶת־פָּנָי: ס 14 וַיִּשְׁלַח דָּוִד מַלְאָכִים אֶל־אִישׁ־בֹּשֶׁת בֶּן־שָׁאוּל לֵאמֹר תְּנָה אֶת־אִשְׁתִּי אֶת־מִיכַל אֲשֶׁר אֵרַשְׂתִּי לִי בְּמֵאָה עָרְלוֹת פְּלִשְׁתִּים: 15 וַיִּשְׁלַח אִישׁ בֹּשֶׁת וַיִּקָּחֶהָ מֵעִם אִישׁ מֵעִם פַּלְטִיאֵל בֶּן־לָיִשׁ: 16 וַיֵּלֶךְ אִתָּהּ אִישָׁהּ הָלוֹךְ וּבָכֹה אַחֲרֶיהָ עַד־בַּחֻרִים וַיֹּאמֶר אֵלָיו אַבְנֵר לֵךְ שׁוּב וַיָּשֹׁב: 17 וּדְבַר־אַבְנֵר הָיָה עִם־זִקְנֵי יִשְׂרָאֵל לֵאמֹר גַּם־תְּמוֹל גַּם־שִׁלְשֹׁם הֱיִיתֶם מְבַקְשִׁים אֶת־דָּוִד לְמֶלֶךְ עֲלֵיכֶם: 18 וְעַתָּה עֲשׂוּ כִּי יְהֹוָה אָמַר אֶל־דָּוִד לֵאמֹר בְּיַד | דָּוִד עַבְדִּי הוֹשִׁיעַ אֶת־עַמִּי יִשְׂרָאֵל מִיַּד פְּלִשְׁתִּים וּמִיַּד כָּל־אֹיְבֵיהֶם: 19 וַיְדַבֵּר גַּם־אַבְנֵר בְּאָזְנֵי בִנְיָמִן וַיֵּלֶךְ גַּם־אַבְנֵר לְדַבֵּר בְּאָזְנֵי דָוִד בְּחֶבְרוֹן אֵת כָּל־אֲשֶׁר טוֹב בְּעֵינֵי יִשְׂרָאֵל וּבְעֵינֵי כָּל־בֵּית בִּנְיָמִן: 20 וַיָּבֹא אַבְנֵר אֶל־דָּוִד חֶבְרוֹן וְאִתּוֹ עֶשְׂרִים אֲנָשִׁים וַיַּעַשׂ דָּוִד לְאַבְנֵר וְלָאֲנָשִׁים אֲשֶׁר־אִתּוֹ מִשְׁתֶּה: 21 וַיֹּאמֶר אַבְנֵר אֶל־דָּוִד אָקוּמָה | וְאֵלֵכָה וְאֶקְבְּצָה אֶל־

gather all Israel to my lord the king, that they may make a covenant with you, and that you may reign over all that your heart desires." So David sent Abner away, and he went in peace.

22 At that moment the servants of David and Joab came from a raid and brought much spoil with them. But Abner *was* not with David in Hebron, for he had sent him away, and he had gone in peace. 23 When Joab and all the troops that *were* with him had come, they told Joab, saying, "Abner the son of Ner came to the king, and he sent him away, and he has gone in peace." 24 Then Joab came to the king and said, "What have you done? Look, Abner came to you; why *is* it *that* you sent him away, and he has already gone? 25 Surely you realize that Abner the son of Ner came to deceive you, to know your going out and your coming in, and to know all that you are doing."

26 And when Joab had gone from David's presence, he sent messengers after Abner, who brought him back from the well of Sirah. But David did not know *it*. 27 Now when Abner had returned to Hebron, Joab took him aside in the gate to speak with him privately, and there stabbed him in the stomach, so that he died for the blood of Asahel his brother.

28 Afterward, when David heard *it*, he said, "My kingdom and I *are* guiltless before the LORD forever of the blood of Abner the son of Ner. 29 Let it rest on the head of Joab and on all his father's house; and let there never fail to be in the house of Joab one who has a discharge or is a leper, who leans on a staff or falls by the sword, or who lacks bread." 30 So Joab and Abishai his brother killed Abner, because he had killed their brother Asahel at Gibeon in the battle.

31 Then David said to Joab and to all the people who were with him, "Tear your clothes, gird yourselves with sackcloth, and mourn for Abner." And King David followed the coffin. 32 So they buried Abner in Hebron; and the king lifted up his voice and wept at the grave of Abner, and all the people wept. 33 And the king sang *a lament* over Abner and said:

"Should Abner die as a fool dies?
34 Your hands were not bound
Nor your feet put into fetters;
As a man falls before wicked men, *so* you fell."

Then all the people wept over him again.

35 And when all the people came to persuade David to eat food while it was still day, David took an oath, saying, "God do so to me, and more also, if I taste bread or anything else till the sun goes down!" 36 Now all the people took note *of it*, and it

אֲדֹנִי הַמֶּלֶךְ אֶת־כָּל־יִשְׂרָאֵל וְיִכְרְתוּ אִתְּךָ בְּרִית וּמָלַכְתָּ בְּכֹל אֲשֶׁר־תְּאַוֶּה נַפְשֶׁךָ וַיְשַׁלַּח דָּוִד אֶת־אַבְנֵר וַיֵּלֶךְ בְּשָׁלוֹם: 22 וְהִנֵּה עַבְדֵי דָוִד וְיוֹאָב בָּא מֵהַגְּדוּד וְשָׁלָל רַב עִמָּם הֵבִיאוּ וְאַבְנֵר אֵינֶנּוּ עִם־דָּוִד בְּחֶבְרוֹן כִּי שִׁלְּחוֹ וַיֵּלֶךְ בְּשָׁלוֹם: 23 וְיוֹאָב וְכָל־הַצָּבָא אֲשֶׁר־אִתּוֹ בָּאוּ וַיַּגִּדוּ לְיוֹאָב לֵאמֹר בָּא־אַבְנֵר בֶּן־נֵר אֶל־הַמֶּלֶךְ וַיְשַׁלְּחֵהוּ וַיֵּלֶךְ בְּשָׁלוֹם: 24 וַיָּבֹא יוֹאָב אֶל־הַמֶּלֶךְ וַיֹּאמֶר מֶה עָשִׂיתָה הִנֵּה בָא אַבְנֵר אֵלֶיךָ לָמָּה־זֶּה שִׁלַּחְתּוֹ וַיֵּלֶךְ הָלוֹךְ: 25 יָדַעְתָּ אֶת־אַבְנֵר בֶּן־נֵר כִּי לְפַתֹּתְךָ בָּא וְלָדַעַת אֶת־מוֹצָאֲךָ וְאֶת־מִבוֹאֲךָ וְלָדַעַת אֵת כָּל־אֲשֶׁר אַתָּה עֹשֶׂה: 26 וַיֵּצֵא יוֹאָב מֵעִם דָּוִד וַיִּשְׁלַח מַלְאָכִים אַחֲרֵי אַבְנֵר וַיָּשִׁבוּ אֹתוֹ מִבּוֹר הַסִּרָה וְדָוִד לֹא יָדָע: 27 וַיָּשָׁב אַבְנֵר חֶבְרוֹן וַיַּטֵּהוּ יוֹאָב אֶל־תּוֹךְ הַשַּׁעַר לְדַבֵּר אִתּוֹ בַּשֶּׁלִי וַיַּכֵּהוּ שָׁם הַחֹמֶשׁ וַיָּמָת בְּדַם עֲשָׂה־אֵל אָחִיו: 28 וַיִּשְׁמַע דָּוִד מֵאַחֲרֵי כֵן וַיֹּאמֶר נָקִי אָנֹכִי וּמַמְלַכְתִּי מֵעִם יְהוָה עַד־עוֹלָם מִדְּמֵי אַבְנֵר בֶּן־נֵר: 29 יָחֻלוּ עַל־רֹאשׁ יוֹאָב וְאֶל כָּל־בֵּית אָבִיו וְאַל־יִכָּרֵת מִבֵּית יוֹאָב זָב וּמְצֹרָע וּמַחֲזִיק בַּפֶּלֶךְ וְנֹפֵל בַּחֶרֶב וַחֲסַר־לָחֶם: 30 וְיוֹאָב וַאֲבִישַׁי אָחִיו הָרְגוּ לְאַבְנֵר עַל אֲשֶׁר הֵמִית אֶת־עֲשָׂהאֵל אֲחִיהֶם בְּגִבְעוֹן בַּמִּלְחָמָה: פ 31 וַיֹּאמֶר דָּוִד אֶל־יוֹאָב וְאֶל־כָּל־הָעָם אֲשֶׁר־אִתּוֹ קִרְעוּ בִגְדֵיכֶם וְחִגְרוּ שַׂקִּים וְסִפְדוּ לִפְנֵי אַבְנֵר וְהַמֶּלֶךְ דָּוִד הֹלֵךְ אַחֲרֵי הַמִּטָּה: 32 וַיִּקְבְּרוּ אֶת־אַבְנֵר בְּחֶבְרוֹן וַיִּשָּׂא הַמֶּלֶךְ אֶת־קוֹלוֹ וַיֵּבְךְ אֶל־קֶבֶר אַבְנֵר וַיִּבְכּוּ כָּל־הָעָם: פ 33 וַיְקֹנֵן הַמֶּלֶךְ אֶל־אַבְנֵר וַיֹּאמַר הַכְּמוֹת נָבָל יָמוּת אַבְנֵר: 34 יָדֶךָ לֹא־אֲסֻרוֹת וְרַגְלֶיךָ לֹא־לִנְחֻשְׁתַּיִם הֻגָּשׁוּ כִּנְפוֹל לִפְנֵי בְנֵי־עַוְלָה נָפָלְתָּ וַיֹּסִפוּ כָל־הָעָם לִבְכּוֹת עָלָיו: 35 וַיָּבֹא כָל־הָעָם לְהַבְרוֹת אֶת־דָּוִד לֶחֶם בְּעוֹד הַיּוֹם וַיִּשָּׁבַע דָּוִד לֵאמֹר כֹּה יַעֲשֶׂה־לִּי אֱלֹהִים וְכֹה יֹסִיף כִּי אִם־לִפְנֵי בוֹא־הַשֶּׁמֶשׁ אֶטְעַם־לֶחֶם אוֹ כָל־מְאוּמָה: 36 וְכָל־הָעָם הִכִּירוּ וַיִּיטַב בְּעֵינֵיהֶם כְּכֹל אֲשֶׁר עָשָׂה הַמֶּלֶךְ בְּעֵינֵי כָל־

pleased them, since whatever the king did pleased all the people. [37] For all the people and all Israel understood that day that it had not been the king's *intent* to kill Abner the son of Ner. [38] Then the king said to his servants, "Do you not know that a prince and a great man has fallen this day in Israel? [39] And I *am* weak today, though anointed king; and these men, the sons of Zeruiah, *are* too harsh for me. The LORD shall repay the evildoer according to his wickedness."

4 When Saul's son heard that Abner had died in Hebron, he lost heart, and all Israel was troubled. [2] Now Saul's son *had* two men *who were* captains of troops. The name of one *was* Baanah and the name of the other Rechab, the sons of Rimmon the Beerothite, of the children of Benjamin. (For Beeroth also was *part* of Benjamin, [3] because the Beerothites fled to Gittaim and have been sojourners there until this day.)

[4] Jonathan, Saul's son, had a son *who was* lame in *his* feet. He was five years old when the news about Saul and Jonathan came from Jezreel; and his nurse took him up and fled. And it happened, as she made haste to flee, that he fell and became lame. His name *was* Mephibosheth.

[5] Then the sons of Rimmon the Beerothite, Rechab and Baanah, set out and came at about the heat of the day to the house of Ishbosheth, who was lying on his bed at noon. [6] And they came there, all the way into the house, *as though* to get wheat, and they stabbed him in the stomach. Then Rechab and Baanah his brother escaped. [7] For when they came into the house, he was lying on his bed in his bedroom; then they struck him and killed him, beheaded him and took his head, and were all night escaping through the plain. [8] And they brought the head of Ishbosheth to David at Hebron, and said to the king, "Here is the head of Ishbosheth, the son of Saul your enemy, who sought your life; and the LORD has avenged my lord the king this day of Saul and his descendants."

[9] But David answered Rechab and Baanah his brother, the sons of Rimmon the Beerothite, and said to them, "*As* the LORD lives, who has redeemed my life from all adversity, [10] when someone told me, saying, 'Look, Saul is dead,' thinking to have brought good news, I arrested him and had him executed in Ziklag—the one who *thought* I would give him a reward for *his* news. [11] How much more, when wicked men have killed a righteous person in his own house on his bed? Therefore, shall I not now require his blood at your hand and remove you from the earth?" [12] So David commanded his young

הָעָם טֽוֹב: 37 וַיֵּדְע֤וּ כָל־הָעָם֙ וְכָל־יִשְׂרָאֵל֙ בַּיּ֣וֹם הַה֔וּא כִּ֣י לֹ֤א הָֽיְתָה֙ מֵהַמֶּ֔לֶךְ לְהָמִ֖ית אֶת־אַבְנֵ֥ר בֶּן־נֵֽר: פ

38 וַיֹּ֥אמֶר הַמֶּ֖לֶךְ אֶל־עֲבָדָ֑יו הֲל֣וֹא תֵֽדְע֔וּ כִּי־שַׂ֣ר וְגָד֗וֹל נָפַ֛ל הַיּ֥וֹם הַזֶּ֖ה בְּיִשְׂרָאֵֽל: 39 וְאָנֹכִ֨י הַיּ֤וֹם רַךְ֙ וּמָשׁ֣וּחַ מֶ֔לֶךְ וְהָאֲנָשִׁ֤ים הָאֵ֙לֶּה֙ בְּנֵ֣י צְרוּיָ֔ה קָשִׁ֖ים מִמֶּ֑נִּי יְשַׁלֵּ֧ם יְהֹוָ֛ה לְעֹשֵׂ֥ה הָרָעָ֖ה כְּרָעָתֽוֹ: פ

ד וַיִּשְׁמַ֣ע בֶּן־שָׁא֗וּל כִּ֣י מֵ֤ת אַבְנֵר֙ בְּחֶבְר֔וֹן וַיִּרְפּ֖וּ יָדָ֑יו וְכָל־יִשְׂרָאֵ֖ל נִבְהָֽלוּ: 2 וּשְׁנֵ֣י אֲנָשִׁ֣ים שָׂרֵֽי־גְדוּדִ֣ים הָי֣וּ בֶן־שָׁא֗וּל שֵׁם֩ הָאֶחָ֨ד בַּֽעֲנָ֜ה וְשֵׁ֧ם הַשֵּׁנִ֣י רֵכָ֗ב בְּנֵ֛י רִמּ֥וֹן הַבְּאֵֽרֹתִ֖י מִבְּנֵ֣י בִנְיָמִ֑ן כִּ֚י גַּם־בְּאֵר֔וֹת תֵּֽחָשֵׁ֖ב עַל־בִּנְיָמִֽן: 3 וַיִּבְרְח֥וּ הַבְּאֵֽרֹתִ֖ים גִּתָּ֑יְמָה וַיִּֽהְיוּ־שָׁ֣ם גָּרִ֔ים עַ֖ד הַיּ֥וֹם הַזֶּֽה: ס 4 וְלִיהֽוֹנָתָן֙ בֶּן־שָׁא֔וּל בֵּ֖ן נְכֵ֣ה רַגְלָ֑יִם בֶּן־חָמֵ֣שׁ שָׁנִ֗ים הָיָ֞ה בְּבֹ֨א שְׁמֻעַ֤ת שָׁאוּל֙ וִיהֽוֹנָתָן֙ מִ֣יִּזְרְעֶ֔אל וַתִּשָּׂאֵ֥הוּ אֹֽמַנְתּ֖וֹ וַתָּנֹ֑ס וַיְהִ֞י בְּחׇפְזָ֥הּ לָנ֛וּס וַיִּפֹּ֥ל וַיִּפָּסֵ֖חַ וּשְׁמ֥וֹ מְפִיבֹֽשֶׁת: 5 וַיֵּ֨לְכ֜וּ בְּנֵֽי־רִמּ֤וֹן הַבְּאֵֽרֹתִי֙ רֵכָ֣ב וּבַֽעֲנָ֔ה וַיָּבֹ֙אוּ֙ כְּחֹ֣ם הַיּ֔וֹם אֶל־בֵּ֖ית אִ֣ישׁ בֹּ֑שֶׁת וְה֣וּא שֹׁכֵ֔ב אֵ֖ת מִשְׁכַּ֥ב הַֽצׇּהֳרָֽיִם: 6 וְ֠הֵ֠נָּה בָּ֜אוּ עַד־תּ֤וֹךְ הַבַּ֙יִת֙ לֹקְחֵ֣י חִטִּ֔ים וַיַּכֻּ֖הוּ אֶל־הַחֹ֑מֶשׁ וְרֵכָ֛ב וּבַֽעֲנָ֥ה אָחִ֖יו נִמְלָֽטוּ: 7 וַיָּבֹ֣אוּ הַבַּ֗יִת וְהֽוּא־שֹׁכֵ֤ב עַל־מִטָּתוֹ֙ בַּֽחֲדַ֣ר מִשְׁכָּב֔וֹ וַיַּכֻּ֙הוּ֙ וַיְמִתֻ֔הוּ וַיָּסִ֖ירוּ אֶת־רֹאשׁ֑וֹ וַיִּקְחוּ֙ אֶת־רֹאשׁ֔וֹ וַיֵּֽלְכ֛וּ דֶּ֥רֶךְ הָֽעֲרָבָ֖ה כָּל־הַלָּֽיְלָה: 8 וַ֠יָּבִ֠אוּ אֶת־רֹ֨אשׁ אִֽישׁ־בֹּ֥שֶׁת אֶל־דָּוִד֮ חֶבְרוֹן֒ וַיֹּֽאמְרוּ֙ אֶל־הַמֶּ֔לֶךְ הִנֵּה־רֹ֣אשׁ אִֽישׁ־בֹּ֗שֶׁת בֶּן־שָׁאוּל֙ אֹֽיִבְךָ֔ אֲשֶׁ֥ר בִּקֵּ֖שׁ אֶת־נַפְשֶׁ֑ךָ וַיִּתֵּ֣ן יְ֠הֹוָ֠ה לַֽאדֹנִ֨י הַמֶּ֤לֶךְ נְקָמוֹת֙ הַיּ֣וֹם הַזֶּ֔ה מִשָּׁא֖וּל וּמִזַּרְעֽוֹ: ס 9 וַיַּ֨עַן דָּוִ֜ד אֶת־ רֵכָ֣ב ׀ וְאֶת־בַּֽעֲנָ֣ה אָחִ֗יו בְּנֵ֛י רִמּ֥וֹן הַבְּאֵֽרֹתִ֖י וַיֹּ֣אמֶר לָהֶ֑ם חַי־יְהֹוָ֕ה אֲשֶׁר־פָּדָ֥ה אֶת־נַפְשִׁ֖י מִכָּל־צָרָֽה: 10 כִּ֣י הַמַּגִּיד֩ לִ֨י לֵאמֹ֜ר הִנֵּה־מֵ֣ת שָׁא֗וּל וְהֽוּא־הָיָ֤ה כִמְבַשֵּׂר֙ בְּעֵינָ֔יו וָאֹֽחֲזָ֣ה ב֔וֹ וָאֶהְרְגֵ֖הוּ בְּצִֽקְלָ֑ג אֲשֶׁ֥ר לְתִתִּי־ל֖וֹ בְּשֹׂרָֽה: 11 אַ֞ף כִּֽי־אֲנָשִׁ֣ים רְשָׁעִ֗ים הָֽרְג֧וּ אֶת־אִֽישׁ־צַדִּ֛יק בְּבֵית֖וֹ עַל־מִשְׁכָּב֑וֹ וְעַתָּ֗ה הֲל֨וֹא אֲבַקֵּ֤שׁ אֶת־דָּמוֹ֙ מִיֶּדְכֶ֔ם וּבִֽעַרְתִּ֥י אֶתְכֶ֖ם מִן־הָאָֽרֶץ: 12 וַיְצַ֨ו דָּוִ֜ד אֶת־הַנְּעָרִ֗ים וַיַּֽהַרְג�it֒וּם וַֽיְקַצְּצ֣וּ אֶת־

men, and they executed them, cut off their hands and feet, and hanged *them* by the pool in Hebron. But they took the head of Ishbosheth and buried *it* in the tomb of Abner in Hebron.

5 Then all the tribes of Israel came to David at Hebron and spoke, saying, "Indeed we *are* your bone and your flesh. ² Also, in time past, when Saul was king over us, you were the one who led Israel out and brought them in; and the LORD said to you, 'You shall shepherd My people Israel, and be ruler over Israel.'" ³ Therefore all the elders of Israel came to the king at Hebron, and King David made a covenant with them at Hebron before the LORD. And they anointed David king over Israel. ⁴ David *was* thirty years old when he began to reign, *and* he reigned forty years. ⁵ In Hebron he reigned over Judah seven years and six months, and in Jerusalem he reigned thirty-three years over all Israel and Judah.

⁶ And the king and his men went to Jerusalem against the Jebusites, the inhabitants of the land, who spoke to David, saying, "You shall not come in here; but the blind and the lame will repel you," thinking, "David cannot come in here." ⁷ Nevertheless David took the stronghold of Zion (that *is*, the City of David).

⁸ Now David said on that day, "Whoever climbs up by way of the water shaft and defeats the Jebusites (the lame and the blind, *who are* hated by David's soul), *he shall be chief and captain*." Therefore they say, "The blind and the lame shall not come into the house."

⁹ Then David dwelt in the stronghold, and called it the City of David. And David built all around from the Millo and inward. ¹⁰ So David went on and became great, and the LORD God of hosts *was* with him.

¹¹ Then Hiram king of Tyre sent messengers to David, and cedar trees, and carpenters and masons. And they built David a house. ¹² So David knew that the LORD had established him as king over Israel, and that He had exalted His kingdom for the sake of His people Israel.

¹³ And David took more concubines and wives from Jerusalem, after he had come from Hebron. Also more sons and daughters were born to David. ¹⁴ Now these *are* the names of those who were born to him in Jerusalem: Shammua, Shobab, Nathan, Solomon, ¹⁵ Ibhar, Elishua, Nepheg, Japhia, ¹⁶ Elishama, Eliada, and Eliphelet.

¹⁷ Now when the Philistines heard that they had anointed David king over Israel, all the Philistines went up to search for David. And David heard *of it*

יְדֵיהֶם וְאֶת־רַגְלֵיהֶם וַיִּתְלוּ עַל־הַבְּרֵכָה בְּחֶבְרוֹן וְאֵת רֹאשׁ אִישׁ־בֹּשֶׁת לָקָחוּ וַיִּקְבְּרוּ בְקֶבֶר־אַבְנֵר בְּחֶבְרוֹן: פ

ה וַיָּבֹאוּ כָּל־שִׁבְטֵי יִשְׂרָאֵל אֶל־דָּוִד חֶבְרוֹנָה וַיֹּאמְרוּ לֵאמֹר הִנְנוּ עַצְמְךָ וּבְשָׂרְךָ אֲנָחְנוּ: ² גַּם־אֶתְמוֹל גַּם־שִׁלְשׁוֹם בִּהְיוֹת שָׁאוּל מֶלֶךְ עָלֵינוּ אַתָּה הָיִיתָה ⁺ מוֹצִיא ⁺ וְהַמֵּבִי ⁺ אֶת־יִשְׂרָאֵל וַיֹּאמֶר יְהוָה לְךָ אַתָּה תִרְעֶה אֶת־עַמִּי אֶת־יִשְׂרָאֵל וְאַתָּה תִּהְיֶה לְנָגִיד עַל־יִשְׂרָאֵל: ³ וַיָּבֹאוּ כָּל־זִקְנֵי יִשְׂרָאֵל אֶל־הַמֶּלֶךְ חֶבְרוֹנָה וַיִּכְרֹת לָהֶם הַמֶּלֶךְ דָּוִד בְּרִית בְּחֶבְרוֹן לִפְנֵי יְהוָה וַיִּמְשְׁחוּ אֶת־דָּוִד לְמֶלֶךְ עַל־יִשְׂרָאֵל: פ

⁴ בֶּן־שְׁלֹשִׁים שָׁנָה דָּוִד בְּמָלְכוֹ אַרְבָּעִים שָׁנָה מָלָךְ: ⁵ בְּחֶבְרוֹן מָלַךְ עַל־יְהוּדָה שֶׁבַע שָׁנִים וְשִׁשָּׁה חֳדָשִׁים וּבִירוּשָׁלַ͏ִם מָלַךְ שְׁלֹשִׁים וְשָׁלֹשׁ שָׁנָה עַל כָּל־יִשְׂרָאֵל וִיהוּדָה: ⁶ וַיֵּלֶךְ הַמֶּלֶךְ וַאֲנָשָׁיו יְרוּשָׁלַ͏ִם אֶל־הַיְבֻסִי יוֹשֵׁב הָאָרֶץ וַיֹּאמֶר לְדָוִד לֵאמֹר לֹא־תָבוֹא הֵנָּה כִּי אִם־הֱסִירְךָ הַעִוְרִים וְהַפִּסְחִים לֵאמֹר לֹא־יָבוֹא דָוִד הֵנָּה: ⁷ וַיִּלְכֹּד דָּוִד אֵת מְצֻדַת צִיּוֹן הִיא עִיר דָּוִד: ⁸ וַיֹּאמֶר דָּוִד בַּיּוֹם הַהוּא כָּל־מַכֵּה יְבֻסִי וְיִגַּע בַּצִּנּוֹר וְאֶת־הַפִּסְחִים וְאֶת־הַעִוְרִים שְׂנֻאֵי נֶפֶשׁ דָּוִד עַל־כֵּן יֹאמְרוּ עִוֵּר וּפִסֵּחַ לֹא יָבוֹא אֶל־הַבָּיִת: ⁹ וַיֵּשֶׁב דָּוִד בַּמְּצֻדָה וַיִּקְרָא־לָהּ עִיר דָּוִד וַיִּבֶן דָּוִד סָבִיב מִן־הַמִּלּוֹא וָבָיְתָה: ¹⁰ וַיֵּלֶךְ דָּוִד הָלוֹךְ וְגָדוֹל וַיהוָה אֱלֹהֵי צְבָאוֹת עִמּוֹ: פ

¹¹ וַיִּשְׁלַח חִירָם מֶלֶךְ־צֹר מַלְאָכִים אֶל־דָּוִד וַעֲצֵי אֲרָזִים וְחָרָשֵׁי עֵץ וְחָרָשֵׁי אֶבֶן קִיר וַיִּבְנוּ־בַיִת לְדָוִד: ¹² וַיֵּדַע דָּוִד כִּי־הֱכִינוֹ יְהוָה לְמֶלֶךְ עַל־יִשְׂרָאֵל וְכִי נִשֵּׂא מַמְלַכְתּוֹ בַּעֲבוּר עַמּוֹ יִשְׂרָאֵל: ס ¹³ וַיִּקַּח דָּוִד עוֹד פִּלַגְשִׁים וְנָשִׁים מִירוּשָׁלַ͏ִם אַחֲרֵי בֹאוֹ מֵחֶבְרוֹן וַיִּוָּלְדוּ עוֹד לְדָוִד בָּנִים וּבָנוֹת: ¹⁴ וְאֵלֶּה שְׁמוֹת הַיִּלֹדִים לוֹ בִּירוּשָׁלָ͏ִם שַׁמּוּעַ וְשׁוֹבָב וְנָתָן וּשְׁלֹמֹה: ¹⁵ וְיִבְחָר וֶאֱלִישׁוּעַ וְנֶפֶג וְיָפִיעַ: ¹⁶ וֶאֱלִישָׁמָע וְאֶלְיָדָע וֶאֱלִיפָלֶט: פ

¹⁷ וַיִּשְׁמְעוּ פְלִשְׁתִּים כִּי־מָשְׁחוּ אֶת־דָּוִד לְמֶלֶךְ עַל־יִשְׂרָאֵל וַיַּעֲלוּ כָל־פְּלִשְׁתִּים לְבַקֵּשׁ אֶת־דָּוִד

ה 2 הָיִיתָ, הַמּוֹצִיא, וְהַמֵּבִיא   8 שְׂנֻאֵי

and went down to the stronghold. 18 The Philistines also went and deployed themselves in the Valley of Rephaim. 19 So David inquired of the LORD, saying, "Shall I go up against the Philistines? Will You deliver them into my hand?"

And the LORD said to David, "Go up, for I will doubtless deliver the Philistines into your hand."

20 So David went to Baal Perazim, and David defeated them there; and he said, "The LORD has broken through my enemies before me, like a breakthrough of water." Therefore he called the name of that place Baal Perazim. 21 And they left their images there, and David and his men carried them away.

22 Then the Philistines went up once again and deployed themselves in the Valley of Rephaim. 23 Therefore David inquired of the LORD, and He said, "You shall not go up; circle around behind them, and come upon them in front of the mulberry trees. 24 And it shall be, when you hear the sound of marching in the tops of the mulberry trees, then you shall advance quickly. For then the LORD will go out before you to strike the camp of the Philistines." 25 And David did so, as the LORD commanded him; and he drove back the Philistines from Geba as far as Gezer.

6 Again David gathered all the choice men of Israel, thirty thousand. 2 And David arose and went with all the people who were with him from Baale Judah to bring up from there the ark of God, whose name is called by the Name, the LORD of Hosts, who dwells between the cherubim. 3 So they set the ark of God on a new cart, and brought it out of the house of Abinadab, which was on the hill; and Uzzah and Ahio, the sons of Abinadab, drove the new cart. 4 And they brought it out of the house of Abinadab, which was on the hill, accompanying the ark of God; and Ahio went before the ark. 5 Then David and all the house of Israel played music before the LORD on all kinds of instruments of fir wood, on harps, on stringed instruments, on tambourines, on sistrums, and on cymbals.

6 And when they came to Nachon's threshing floor, Uzzah put out his hand to the ark of God and took hold of it, for the oxen stumbled. 7 Then the anger of the LORD was aroused against Uzzah, and God struck him there for his error; and he died there by the ark of God. 8 And David became angry because of the LORD's outbreak against Uzzah; and he called the name of the place Perez Uzzah to this day.

וַיִּשְׁמַע דָּוִד וַיֵּרֶד אֶל־הַמְּצוּדָה: 18 וּפְלִשְׁתִּים בָּאוּ וַיִּנָּטְשׁוּ בְּעֵמֶק רְפָאִים: 19 וַיִּשְׁאַל דָּוִד בַּיהֹוָה לֵאמֹר הַאֶעֱלֶה אֶל־פְּלִשְׁתִּים הֲתִתְּנֵם בְּיָדִי וַיֹּאמֶר יְהֹוָה אֶל־דָּוִד עֲלֵה כִּי־נָתֹן אֶתֵּן אֶת־הַפְּלִשְׁתִּים בְּיָדֶךָ: 20 וַיָּבֹא דָוִד בְּבַעַל־פְּרָצִים וַיַּכֵּם שָׁם דָּוִד וַיֹּאמֶר פָּרַץ יְהֹוָה אֶת־אֹיְבַי לְפָנַי כְּפֶרֶץ מָיִם עַל־כֵּן קָרָא שֵׁם־הַמָּקוֹם הַהוּא בַּעַל פְּרָצִים: 21 וַיַּעַזְבוּ־ שָׁם אֶת־עֲצַבֵּיהֶם וַיִּשָּׂאֵם דָּוִד וַאֲנָשָׁיו: פ

22 וַיֹּסִפוּ עוֹד פְּלִשְׁתִּים לַעֲלוֹת וַיִּנָּטְשׁוּ בְּעֵמֶק רְפָאִים: 23 וַיִּשְׁאַל דָּוִד בַּיהֹוָה וַיֹּאמֶר לֹא תַעֲלֶה הָסֵב אֶל־אַחֲרֵיהֶם וּבָאתָ לָהֶם מִמּוּל בְּכָאִים:

24 וִיהִי בְּשָׁמְעֲךָ אֶת־קוֹל צְעָדָה בְּרָאשֵׁי הַבְּכָאִים אָז תֶּחֱרָץ כִּי אָז יָצָא יְהֹוָה לְפָנֶיךָ לְהַכּוֹת בְּמַחֲנֵה פְלִשְׁתִּים: 25 וַיַּעַשׂ דָּוִד כֵּן כַּאֲשֶׁר צִוָּהוּ יְהֹוָה וַיַּךְ אֶת־פְּלִשְׁתִּים מִגֶּבַע עַד־בֹּאֲךָ גָזֶר: פ

ו וַיֹּסֶף עוֹד דָּוִד אֶת־כָּל־בָּחוּר בְּיִשְׂרָאֵל שְׁלֹשִׁים אָלֶף: 2 וַיָּקָם וַיֵּלֶךְ דָּוִד וְכָל־הָעָם אֲשֶׁר אִתּוֹ מִבַּעֲלֵי יְהוּדָה לְהַעֲלוֹת מִשָּׁם אֵת אֲרוֹן הָאֱלֹהִים אֲשֶׁר־נִקְרָא שֵׁם שֵׁם יְהֹוָה צְבָאוֹת יֹשֵׁב הַכְּרֻבִים עָלָיו: 3 וַיַּרְכִּבוּ אֶת־אֲרוֹן הָאֱלֹהִים אֶל־עֲגָלָה חֲדָשָׁה וַיִּשָּׂאֻהוּ מִבֵּית אֲבִינָדָב אֲשֶׁר בַּגִּבְעָה וְעֻזָּא וְאַחְיוֹ בְּנֵי אֲבִינָדָב נֹהֲגִים אֶת־הָעֲגָלָה חֲדָשָׁה: 4 וַיִּשָּׂאֻהוּ מִבֵּית אֲבִינָדָב אֲשֶׁר בַּגִּבְעָה עִם אֲרוֹן הָאֱלֹהִים וְאַחְיוֹ הֹלֵךְ לִפְנֵי הָאָרוֹן: 5 וְדָוִד וְכָל־בֵּית יִשְׂרָאֵל מְשַׂחֲקִים לִפְנֵי יְהֹוָה בְּכֹל עֲצֵי בְרוֹשִׁים וּבְכִנֹּרוֹת וּבִנְבָלִים וּבְתֻפִּים וּבִמְנַעַנְעִים וּבְצֶלְצֶלִים: 6 וַיָּבֹאוּ עַד־גֹּרֶן נָכוֹן וַיִּשְׁלַח עֻזָּא אֶל־אֲרוֹן הָאֱלֹהִים וַיֹּאחֶז בּוֹ כִּי שָׁמְטוּ הַבָּקָר: 7 וַיִּחַר אַף יְהֹוָה בְּעֻזָּה וַיַּכֵּהוּ שָׁם הָאֱלֹהִים עַל־הַשַּׁל וַיָּמָת שָׁם עִם אֲרוֹן הָאֱלֹהִים: 8 וַיִּחַר לְדָוִד עַל אֲשֶׁר פָּרַץ יְהֹוָה פֶּרֶץ בְּעֻזָּה וַיִּקְרָא לַמָּקוֹם הַהוּא פֶּרֶץ

ה 24 כְּשָׁמְעֲךָ

9 David was afraid of the LORD that day; and he said, "How can the ark of the LORD come to me?" 10 So David would not move the ark of the LORD with him into the City of David; but David took it aside into the house of Obed-Edom the Gittite. 11 The ark of the LORD remained in the house of Obed-Edom the Gittite three months. And the LORD blessed Obed-Edom and all his household.

12 Now it was told King David, saying, "The LORD has blessed the house of Obed-Edom and all that *belongs* to him, because of the ark of God." So David went and brought up the ark of God from the house of Obed-Edom to the City of David with gladness. 13 And so it was, when those bearing the ark of the LORD had gone six paces, that he sacrificed oxen and fatted sheep. 14 Then David danced before the LORD with all *his* might; and David *was* wearing a linen ephod. 15 So David and all the house of Israel brought up the ark of the LORD with shouting and with the sound of the trumpet.

16 Now as the ark of the LORD came into the City of David, Michal, Saul's daughter, looked through a window and saw King David leaping and whirling before the LORD; and she despised him in her heart. 17 So they brought the ark of the LORD, and set it in its place in the midst of the tabernacle that David had erected for it. Then David offered burnt offerings and peace offerings before the LORD. 18 And when David had finished offering burnt offerings and peace offerings, he blessed the people in the name of the LORD of hosts. 19 Then he distributed among all the people, among the whole multitude of Israel, both the women and the men, to everyone a loaf of bread, a piece *of meat,* and a cake of raisins. So all the people departed, everyone to his house.

20 Then David returned to bless his household. And Michal the daughter of Saul came out to meet David, and said, "How glorious was the king of Israel today, uncovering himself today in the eyes of the maids of his servants, as one of the base fellows shamelessly uncovers himself!"

21 So David said to Michal, "*It was* before the LORD, who chose me instead of your father and all his house, to appoint me ruler over the people of the LORD, over Israel. Therefore I will play *music* before the LORD. 22 And I will be even more undignified than this, and will be humble in my own sight. But as for the maidservants of whom you have spoken, by them I will be held in honor."

23 Therefore Michal the daughter of Saul had no children to the day of her death.

עֻזָּה עַד הַיּוֹם הַזֶּה: 9 וַיִּרָא דָוִד אֶת־יְהוָה בַּיּוֹם הַהוּא וַיֹּאמֶר אֵיךְ יָבוֹא אֵלַי אֲרוֹן יְהוָה: 10 וְלֹא־אָבָה דָוִד לְהָסִיר אֵלָיו אֶת־אֲרוֹן יְהוָה עַל־עִיר דָּוִד וַיַּטֵּהוּ דָוִד בֵּית עֹבֵד־אֱדֹם הַגִּתִּי: 11 וַיֵּשֶׁב אֲרוֹן יְהוָה בֵּית עֹבֵד אֱדֹם הַגִּתִּי שְׁלֹשָׁה חֳדָשִׁים וַיְבָרֶךְ יְהוָה אֶת־עֹבֵד אֱדֹם וְאֶת־כָּל־בֵּיתוֹ: 12 וַיֻּגַּד לַמֶּלֶךְ דָּוִד לֵאמֹר בֵּרַךְ יְהוָה אֶת־בֵּית עֹבֵד אֱדֹם וְאֶת־כָּל־אֲשֶׁר־לוֹ בַּעֲבוּר אֲרוֹן הָאֱלֹהִים וַיֵּלֶךְ דָּוִד וַיַּעַל אֶת־אֲרוֹן הָאֱלֹהִים מִבֵּית עֹבֵד אֱדֹם עִיר דָּוִד בְּשִׂמְחָה: 13 וַיְהִי כִּי צָעֲדוּ נֹשְׂאֵי אֲרוֹן־יְהוָה שִׁשָּׁה צְעָדִים וַיִּזְבַּח שׁוֹר וּמְרִיא: 14 וְדָוִד מְכַרְכֵּר בְּכָל־עֹז לִפְנֵי יְהוָה וְדָוִד חָגוּר אֵפוֹד בָּד: 15 וְדָוִד וְכָל־בֵּית יִשְׂרָאֵל מַעֲלִים אֶת־אֲרוֹן יְהוָה בִּתְרוּעָה וּבְקוֹל שׁוֹפָר: 16 וְהָיָה אֲרוֹן יְהוָה בָּא עִיר דָּוִד וּמִיכַל בַּת־שָׁאוּל נִשְׁקְפָה ׀ בְּעַד הַחַלּוֹן וַתֵּרֶא אֶת־הַמֶּלֶךְ דָּוִד מְפַזֵּז וּמְכַרְכֵּר לִפְנֵי יְהוָה וַתִּבֶז לוֹ בְּלִבָּהּ: 17 וַיָּבִאוּ אֶת־אֲרוֹן יְהוָה וַיַּצִּגוּ אֹתוֹ בִּמְקוֹמוֹ בְּתוֹךְ הָאֹהֶל אֲשֶׁר נָטָה־לוֹ דָוִד וַיַּעַל דָּוִד עֹלוֹת לִפְנֵי יְהוָה וּשְׁלָמִים: 18 וַיְכַל דָּוִד מֵהַעֲלוֹת הָעוֹלָה וְהַשְּׁלָמִים וַיְבָרֶךְ אֶת־הָעָם בְּשֵׁם יְהוָה צְבָאוֹת: 19 וַיְחַלֵּק לְכָל־הָעָם לְכָל־הֲמוֹן יִשְׂרָאֵל לְמֵאִישׁ וְעַד־אִשָּׁה לְאִישׁ חַלַּת לֶחֶם אַחַת וְאֶשְׁפָּר אֶחָד וַאֲשִׁישָׁה אֶחָת וַיֵּלֶךְ כָּל־הָעָם אִישׁ לְבֵיתוֹ: 20 וַיָּשָׁב דָּוִד לְבָרֵךְ אֶת־בֵּיתוֹ וַתֵּצֵא מִיכַל בַּת־שָׁאוּל לִקְרַאת דָּוִד וַתֹּאמֶר מַה־נִּכְבַּד הַיּוֹם מֶלֶךְ יִשְׂרָאֵל אֲשֶׁר נִגְלָה הַיּוֹם לְעֵינֵי אַמְהוֹת עֲבָדָיו כְּהִגָּלוֹת נִגְלוֹת אַחַד הָרֵקִים: 21 וַיֹּאמֶר דָּוִד אֶל־מִיכַל לִפְנֵי יְהוָה אֲשֶׁר בָּחַר־בִּי מֵאָבִיךְ וּמִכָּל־בֵּיתוֹ לְצַוֹּת אֹתִי נָגִיד עַל־עַם יְהוָה עַל־יִשְׂרָאֵל וְשִׂחַקְתִּי לִפְנֵי יְהוָה: 22 וּנְקַלֹּתִי עוֹד מִזֹּאת וְהָיִיתִי שָׁפָל בְּעֵינָי וְעִם־הָאֲמָהוֹת אֲשֶׁר אָמַרְתְּ עִמָּם אִכָּבֵדָה: 23 וּלְמִיכַל בַּת־שָׁאוּל לֹא־הָיָה לָהּ יָלֶד עַד יוֹם מוֹתָהּ:

פ

7 Now it came to pass when the king was dwelling in his house, and the LORD had given him rest from all his enemies all around, ²that the king said to Nathan the prophet, "See now, I dwell in a house of cedar, but the ark of God dwells inside tent curtains."

³Then Nathan said to the king, "Go, do all that *is* in your heart, for the LORD *is* with you."

⁴But it happened that night that the word of the LORD came to Nathan, saying, ⁵"Go and tell My servant David, 'Thus says the LORD: "Would you build a house for Me to dwell in? ⁶For I have not dwelt in a house since the time that I brought the children of Israel up from Egypt, even to this day, but have moved about in a tent and in a tabernacle. ⁷Wherever I have moved about with all the children of Israel, have I ever spoken a word to anyone from the tribes of Israel, whom I commanded to shepherd My people Israel, saying, 'Why have you not built Me a house of cedar?' " ' ⁸Now therefore, thus shall you say to My servant David, 'Thus says the LORD of hosts: "I took you from the sheepfold, from following the sheep, to be ruler over My people, over Israel. ⁹And I have been with you wherever you have gone, and have cut off all your enemies from before you, and have made you a great name, like the name of the great men who *are* on the earth. ¹⁰Moreover I will appoint a place for My people Israel, and will plant them, that they may dwell in a place of their own and move no more; nor shall the sons of wickedness oppress them anymore, as previously, ¹¹since the time that I commanded judges *to be* over My people Israel, and have caused you to rest from all your enemies. Also the LORD tells you that He will make you a house.

¹²"When your days are fulfilled and you rest with your fathers, I will set up your seed after you, who will come from your body, and I will establish his kingdom. ¹³He shall build a house for My name, and I will establish the throne of his kingdom forever. ¹⁴I will be his Father, and he shall be My son. If he commits iniquity, I will chasten him with the rod of men and with the blows of the sons of men. ¹⁵But My mercy shall not depart from him, as I took *it* from Saul, whom I removed from before you. ¹⁶And your house and your kingdom shall be established forever before you. Your throne shall be established forever." ' "

¹⁷According to all these words and according to all this vision, so Nathan spoke to David.

¹⁸Then King David went in and sat before the LORD; and he said: "Who *am* I, O Lord GOD? And what is my house, that You have brought me this far? ¹⁹And yet this was a small thing in Your sight,

ז וַיְהִי כִּי־יָשַׁב הַמֶּלֶךְ בְּבֵיתוֹ וַיהוָה הֵנִיחַ־לוֹ מִסָּבִיב מִכָּל־אֹיְבָיו: 2 וַיֹּאמֶר הַמֶּלֶךְ אֶל־נָתָן הַנָּבִיא רְאֵה נָא אָנֹכִי יוֹשֵׁב בְּבֵית אֲרָזִים וַאֲרוֹן הָאֱלֹהִים יֹשֵׁב בְּתוֹךְ הַיְרִיעָה: 3 וַיֹּאמֶר נָתָן אֶל־הַמֶּלֶךְ כֹּל אֲשֶׁר בִּלְבָבְךָ לֵךְ עֲשֵׂה כִּי יְהוָה עִמָּךְ: ס 4 וַיְהִי בַּלַּיְלָה הַהוּא וַיְהִי דְּבַר־יְהוָה אֶל־נָתָן לֵאמֹר: 5 לֵךְ וְאָמַרְתָּ אֶל־עַבְדִּי אֶל־דָּוִד כֹּה אָמַר יְהוָה הַאַתָּה תִּבְנֶה־לִּי בַיִת לְשִׁבְתִּי: 6 כִּי לֹא יָשַׁבְתִּי בְּבַיִת לְמִיּוֹם הַעֲלֹתִי אֶת־בְּנֵי יִשְׂרָאֵל מִמִּצְרַיִם וְעַד הַיּוֹם הַזֶּה וָאֶהְיֶה מִתְהַלֵּךְ בְּאֹהֶל וּבְמִשְׁכָּן: 7 בְּכֹל אֲשֶׁר־הִתְהַלַּכְתִּי בְּכָל־בְּנֵי יִשְׂרָאֵל הֲדָבָר דִּבַּרְתִּי אֶת־אַחַד שִׁבְטֵי יִשְׂרָאֵל אֲשֶׁר צִוִּיתִי לִרְעוֹת אֶת־עַמִּי אֶת־יִשְׂרָאֵל לֵאמֹר לָמָּה לֹא־בְנִיתֶם לִי בֵּית אֲרָזִים: 8 וְעַתָּה כֹּה־תֹאמַר לְעַבְדִּי לְדָוִד כֹּה אָמַר יְהוָה צְבָאוֹת אֲנִי לְקַחְתִּיךָ מִן־הַנָּוֶה מֵאַחַר הַצֹּאן לִהְיוֹת נָגִיד עַל־עַמִּי עַל־יִשְׂרָאֵל: 9 וָאֶהְיֶה עִמְּךָ בְּכֹל אֲשֶׁר הָלַכְתָּ וָאַכְרִתָה אֶת־כָּל־אֹיְבֶיךָ מִפָּנֶיךָ וְעָשִׂתִי לְךָ שֵׁם גָּדוֹל כְּשֵׁם הַגְּדֹלִים אֲשֶׁר בָּאָרֶץ: 10 וְשַׂמְתִּי מָקוֹם לְעַמִּי לְיִשְׂרָאֵל וּנְטַעְתִּיו וְשָׁכַן תַּחְתָּיו וְלֹא יִרְגַּז עוֹד וְלֹא־יֹסִיפוּ בְנֵי־עַוְלָה לְעַנּוֹתוֹ כַּאֲשֶׁר בָּרִאשׁוֹנָה: 11 וּלְמִן־הַיּוֹם אֲשֶׁר צִוִּיתִי שֹׁפְטִים עַל־עַמִּי יִשְׂרָאֵל וַהֲנִיחֹתִי לְךָ מִכָּל־אֹיְבֶיךָ וְהִגִּיד לְךָ יְהוָה כִּי־בַיִת יַעֲשֶׂה־לְּךָ יְהוָה: 12 כִּי | יִמְלְאוּ יָמֶיךָ וְשָׁכַבְתָּ אֶת־אֲבֹתֶיךָ וַהֲקִימֹתִי אֶת־זַרְעֲךָ אַחֲרֶיךָ אֲשֶׁר יֵצֵא מִמֵּעֶיךָ וַהֲכִינֹתִי אֶת־מַמְלַכְתּוֹ: 13 הוּא יִבְנֶה־בַּיִת לִשְׁמִי וְכֹנַנְתִּי אֶת־כִּסֵּא מַמְלַכְתּוֹ עַד־עוֹלָם: 14 אֲנִי אֶהְיֶה־לּוֹ לְאָב וְהוּא יִהְיֶה־לִּי לְבֵן אֲשֶׁר בְּהַעֲוֹתוֹ וְהֹכַחְתִּיו בְּשֵׁבֶט אֲנָשִׁים וּבְנִגְעֵי בְּנֵי אָדָם: 15 וְחַסְדִּי לֹא־יָסוּר מִמֶּנּוּ כַּאֲשֶׁר הֲסִרֹתִי מֵעִם שָׁאוּל אֲשֶׁר הֲסִרֹתִי מִלְּפָנֶיךָ: 16 וְנֶאְמַן בֵּיתְךָ וּמַמְלַכְתְּךָ עַד־עוֹלָם לְפָנֶיךָ כִּסְאֲךָ יִהְיֶה נָכוֹן עַד־עוֹלָם: 17 כְּכֹל הַדְּבָרִים הָאֵלֶּה וּכְכֹל הַחִזָּיוֹן הַזֶּה כֵּן דִּבֶּר נָתָן אֶל־דָּוִד: ס 18 וַיָּבֹא הַמֶּלֶךְ דָּוִד וַיֵּשֶׁב לִפְנֵי יְהוָה וַיֹּאמֶר מִי אָנֹכִי אֲדֹנָי יְהוִה וּמִי בֵיתִי כִּי הֲבִיאֹתַנִי עַד־הֲלֹם: 19 וַתִּקְטַן עוֹד זֹאת בְּעֵינֶיךָ אֲדֹנָי יְהוִה וַתְּדַבֵּר גַּם אֶל־בֵּית־

O Lord GOD; and You have also spoken of Your
servant's house for a great while to come. *Is* this the
manner of man, O Lord GOD? [20] Now what more
can David say to You? For You, Lord GOD, know
Your servant. [21] For Your word's sake, and
according to Your own heart, You have done all
these great things, to make Your servant know
them. [22] Therefore You are great, O Lord GOD. For
there is none like You, nor *is there any* God besides
You, according to all that we have heard with our
ears. [23] And who *is* like Your people, like Israel, the
one nation on the earth whom God went to redeem
for Himself as a people, to make for Himself a
name—and to do for Yourself great and awesome
deeds for Your land—before Your people whom
You redeemed for Yourself from Egypt, the
nations, and their gods? [24] For You have made
Your people Israel Your very own people forever;
and You, LORD, have become their God.

[25] "Now, O LORD God, the word which You
have spoken concerning Your servant and concerning his house, establish *it* forever and do as You
have said. [26] So let Your name be magnified forever,
saying, 'The LORD of hosts *is* the God over Israel.'
And let the house of Your servant David be
established before You. [27] For You, O LORD of
hosts, God of Israel, have revealed *this* to Your
servant, saying, 'I will build you a house.' Therefore
Your servant has found it in his heart to pray this
prayer to You.

[28] "And now, O Lord GOD, You are God, and
Your words are true, and You have promised this
goodness to Your servant. [29] Now therefore, let it
please You to bless the house of Your servant, that
it may continue before You forever; for You, O
Lord GOD, have spoken *it,* and with Your blessing
let the house of Your servant be blessed forever."

8 After this it came to pass that David attacked the
Philistines and subdued them. And David took
Metheg Ammah from the hand of the Philistines.
[2] Then he defeated Moab. Forcing them down to
the ground, he measured them off with a line. With
two lines he measured off those to be put to death,
and with one full line those to be kept alive. So the
Moabites became David's servants, *and* brought
tribute.
[3] David also defeated Hadadezer the son of
Rehob, king of Zobah, as he went to recover his
territory at the River Euphrates. [4] David took from
him one thousand *chariots,* seven hundred horsemen, and twenty thousand foot soldiers. Also
David hamstrung all the chariot horses, except that
he spared *enough* of them for one hundred chariots.

עַבְדְּךָ לְמֵרָחוֹק וְזֹאת תּוֹרַת הָאָדָם אֲדֹנָי יְהוִה׃
20 וּמַה־יּוֹסִיף דָּוִד עוֹד לְדַבֵּר אֵלֶיךָ וְאַתָּה יָדַעְתָּ
אֶת־עַבְדְּךָ אֲדֹנָי יְהוִה׃ 21 בַּעֲבוּר דְּבָרְךָ וּכְלִבְּךָ
עָשִׂיתָ אֵת כָּל־הַגְּדוּלָּה הַזֹּאת לְהוֹדִיעַ אֶת־עַבְדֶּךָ׃
22 עַל־כֵּן גָּדַלְתָּ אֲדֹנָי יְהוִה כִּי־אֵין כָּמוֹךָ וְאֵין
אֱלֹהִים זוּלָתֶךָ בְּכֹל אֲשֶׁר־שָׁמַעְנוּ בְּאָזְנֵינוּ׃ 23 וּמִי
כְעַמְּךָ כְּיִשְׂרָאֵל גּוֹי אֶחָד בָּאָרֶץ אֲשֶׁר הָלְכוּ־אֱלֹהִים
לִפְדּוֹת־לוֹ לְעָם וְלָשׂוּם לוֹ שֵׁם וְלַעֲשׂוֹת לָכֶם
הַגְּדוּלָּה וְנֹרָאוֹת לְאַרְצֶךָ מִפְּנֵי עַמְּךָ אֲשֶׁר פָּדִיתָ
לְּךָ מִמִּצְרַיִם גּוֹיִם וֵאלֹהָיו׃ 24 וַתְּכוֹנֵן לְךָ אֶת־עַמְּךָ
יִשְׂרָאֵל ׀ לְךָ לְעָם עַד־עוֹלָם וְאַתָּה יְהוָה הָיִיתָ
לָהֶם לֵאלֹהִים׃ ס 25 וְעַתָּה יְהוָה אֱלֹהִים
הַדָּבָר אֲשֶׁר דִּבַּרְתָּ עַל־עַבְדְּךָ וְעַל־בֵּיתוֹ הָקֵם עַד־
עוֹלָם וַעֲשֵׂה כַּאֲשֶׁר דִּבַּרְתָּ׃ 26 וְיִגְדַּל שִׁמְךָ עַד־
עוֹלָם לֵאמֹר יְהוָה צְבָאוֹת אֱלֹהִים עַל־יִשְׂרָאֵל
וּבֵית עַבְדְּךָ דָוִד יִהְיֶה נָכוֹן לְפָנֶיךָ׃ 27 כִּי־אַתָּה
יְהוָה צְבָאוֹת אֱלֹהֵי יִשְׂרָאֵל גָּלִיתָה אֶת־אֹזֶן עַבְדְּךָ
לֵאמֹר בַּיִת אֶבְנֶה־לָּךְ עַל־כֵּן מָצָא עַבְדְּךָ אֶת־לִבּוֹ
לְהִתְפַּלֵּל אֵלֶיךָ אֶת־הַתְּפִלָּה הַזֹּאת׃ 28 וְעַתָּה ׀
אֲדֹנָי יְהוִה אַתָּה־הוּא הָאֱלֹהִים וּדְבָרֶיךָ יִהְיוּ אֱמֶת
וַתְּדַבֵּר אֶל־עַבְדְּךָ אֶת־הַטּוֹבָה הַזֹּאת׃ 29 וְעַתָּה
הוֹאֵל וּבָרֵךְ אֶת־בֵּית עַבְדְּךָ לִהְיוֹת לְעוֹלָם לְפָנֶיךָ
כִּי־אַתָּה אֲדֹנָי יְהוִה דִּבַּרְתָּ וּמִבִּרְכָתְךָ יְבֹרַךְ בֵּית־
עַבְדְּךָ לְעוֹלָם׃ פ

ח וַיְהִי אַחֲרֵי־כֵן וַיַּךְ דָּוִד אֶת־פְּלִשְׁתִּים וַיַּכְנִיעֵם
וַיִּקַּח דָּוִד אֶת־מֶתֶג הָאַמָּה מִיַּד פְּלִשְׁתִּים׃ 2 וַיַּךְ
אֶת־מוֹאָב וַיְמַדְּדֵם בַּחֶבֶל הַשְׁכֵּב אוֹתָם אַרְצָה
וַיְמַדֵּד שְׁנֵי־חֲבָלִים לְהָמִית וּמְלֹא הַחֶבֶל לְהַחֲיוֹת
וַתְּהִי מוֹאָב לְדָוִד לַעֲבָדִים נֹשְׂאֵי מִנְחָה׃ 3 וַיַּךְ דָּוִד
אֶת־הֲדַדְעֶזֶר בֶּן־רְחֹב מֶלֶךְ צוֹבָה בְּלֶכְתּוֹ לְהָשִׁיב
יָדוֹ בִּנְהַר־פְּרָת ק׃ 4 וַיִּלְכֹּד דָּוִד מִמֶּנּוּ אֶלֶף וּשְׁבַע־
מֵאוֹת פָּרָשִׁים וְעֶשְׂרִים אֶלֶף אִישׁ רַגְלִי וַיְעַקֵּר דָּוִד

ח 3 פְּרָת

5 When the Syrians of Damascus came to help Hadadezer king of Zobah, David killed twenty-two thousand of the Syrians. 6 Then David put garrisons in Syria of Damascus; and the Syrians became David's servants, *and* brought tribute. So the LORD preserved David wherever he went. 7 And David took the shields of gold that had belonged to the servants of Hadadezer, and brought them to Jerusalem. 8 Also from Betah and from Berothai, cities of Hadadezer, King David took a large amount of bronze.

9 When Toi king of Hamath heard that David had defeated all the army of Hadadezer, 10 then Toi sent Joram his son to King David, to greet him and bless him, because he had fought against Hadadezer and defeated him (for Hadadezer had been at war with Toi); and *Joram* brought with him articles of silver, articles of gold, and articles of bronze. 11 King David also dedicated these to the LORD, along with the silver and gold that he had dedicated from all the nations which he had subdued— 12 from Syria, from Moab, from the people of Ammon, from the Philistines, from Amalek, and from the spoil of Hadadezer the son of Rehob, king of Zobah.

13 And David made *himself* a name when he returned from killing eighteen thousand Syrians in the Valley of Salt. 14 He also put garrisons in Edom; throughout all Edom he put garrisons, and all the Edomites became David's servants. And the LORD preserved David wherever he went.

15 So David reigned over all Israel; and David administered judgment and justice to all his people. 16 Joab the son of Zeruiah *was* over the army; Jehoshaphat the son of Ahilud *was* recorder; 17 Zadok the son of Ahitub and Ahimelech the son of Abiathar *were* the priests; Seraiah *was* the scribe; 18 Benaiah the son of Jehoiada *was over* both the Cherethites and the Pelethites; and David's sons were chief ministers.

9

Now David said, "Is there still anyone who is left of the house of Saul, that I may show him kindness for Jonathan's sake?"

2 And *there was* a servant of the house of Saul whose name *was* Ziba. So when they had called him to David, the king said to him, "*Are* you Ziba?"

He said, "At your service!"

3 Then the king said, "*Is* there not still someone of the house of Saul, to whom I may show the kindness of God?"

And Ziba said to the king, "There is still a son of Jonathan *who is* lame in *his* feet."

4 So the king said to him, "Where *is* he?"

אֶת־כָּל־הָרֶכֶב וַיּוֹתֵר מִמֶּנּוּ מֵאָה רָכֶב: 5 וַתָּבֹא אֲרַם דַּמֶּשֶׂק לַעְזֹר לַהֲדַדְעֶזֶר מֶלֶךְ צוֹבָה וַיַּךְ דָּוִד בַּאֲרָם עֶשְׂרִים־וּשְׁנַיִם אֶלֶף אִישׁ: 6 וַיָּשֶׂם דָּוִד נְצִבִים בַּאֲרַם דַּמֶּשֶׂק וַתְּהִי אֲרָם לְדָוִד לַעֲבָדִים נוֹשְׂאֵי מִנְחָה וַיֹּשַׁע יְהֹוָה אֶת־דָּוִד בְּכֹל אֲשֶׁר הָלָךְ: 7 וַיִּקַּח דָּוִד אֵת שִׁלְטֵי הַזָּהָב אֲשֶׁר הָיוּ אֶל עַבְדֵי הֲדַדְעֶזֶר וַיְבִיאֵם יְרוּשָׁלָ͏ִם: 8 וּמִבֶּטַח וּמִבֵּרֹתַי עָרֵי הֲדַדְעֶזֶר לָקַח הַמֶּלֶךְ דָּוִד נְחֹשֶׁת הַרְבֵּה מְאֹד: ס

9 וַיִּשְׁמַע תֹּעִי מֶלֶךְ חֲמָת כִּי הִכָּה דָוִד אֵת כָּל־חֵיל הֲדַדְעֶזֶר: 10 וַיִּשְׁלַח תֹּעִי אֶת־יוֹרָם־בְּנוֹ אֶל־הַמֶּלֶךְ־דָּוִד לִשְׁאָל־לוֹ לְשָׁלוֹם וּלְבָרֲכוֹ עַל אֲשֶׁר נִלְחַם בַּהֲדַדְעֶזֶר וַיַּכֵּהוּ כִּי־אִישׁ מִלְחֲמוֹת תֹּעִי הָיָה הֲדַדְעֶזֶר וּבְיָדוֹ הָיוּ כְּלֵי־כֶסֶף וּכְלֵי־זָהָב וּכְלֵי נְחֹשֶׁת: 11 גַּם־אֹתָם הִקְדִּישׁ הַמֶּלֶךְ דָּוִד לַיהֹוָה עִם־הַכֶּסֶף וְהַזָּהָב אֲשֶׁר הִקְדִּישׁ מִכָּל־ הַגּוֹיִם אֲשֶׁר כִּבֵּשׁ: 12 מֵאֲרָם וּמִמּוֹאָב וּמִבְּנֵי עַמּוֹן וּמִפְּלִשְׁתִּים וּמֵעֲמָלֵק וּמִשְּׁלַל הֲדַדְעֶזֶר בֶּן־רְחֹב מֶלֶךְ צוֹבָה: 13 וַיַּעַשׂ דָּוִד שֵׁם בְּשֻׁבוֹ מֵהַכּוֹתוֹ אֶת־אֲרָם בְּגֵיא־מֶלַח שְׁמוֹנָה עָשָׂר אָלֶף: 14 וַיָּשֶׂם בֶּאֱדוֹם נְצִבִים בְּכָל־אֱדוֹם שָׂם נְצִבִים וַיְהִי כָל־ אֱדוֹם עֲבָדִים לְדָוִד וַיּוֹשַׁע יְהֹוָה אֶת־דָּוִד בְּכֹל אֲשֶׁר הָלָךְ: 15 וַיִּמְלֹךְ דָּוִד עַל־כָּל־יִשְׂרָאֵל וַיְהִי דָוִד עֹשֶׂה מִשְׁפָּט וּצְדָקָה לְכָל־עַמּוֹ: 16 וְיוֹאָב בֶּן־צְרוּיָה עַל־הַצָּבָא וִיהוֹשָׁפָט בֶּן־אֲחִילוּד מַזְכִּיר: 17 וְצָדוֹק בֶּן־אֲחִיטוּב וַאֲחִימֶלֶךְ בֶּן־אֶבְיָתָר כֹּהֲנִים וּשְׂרָיָה סוֹפֵר: 18 וּבְנָיָהוּ בֶּן־יְהוֹיָדָע וְהַכְּרֵתִי וְהַפְּלֵתִי וּבְנֵי דָוִד כֹּהֲנִים הָיוּ: פ

ט וַיֹּאמֶר דָּוִד הֲכִי יֶשׁ־עוֹד אֲשֶׁר נוֹתַר לְבֵית שָׁאוּל וְאֶעֱשֶׂה עִמּוֹ חֶסֶד בַּעֲבוּר יְהוֹנָתָן: 2 וּלְבֵית שָׁאוּל עֶבֶד וּשְׁמוֹ צִיבָא וַיִּקְרְאוּ־לוֹ אֶל־דָּוִד וַיֹּאמֶר הַמֶּלֶךְ אֵלָיו הַאַתָּה צִיבָא וַיֹּאמֶר עַבְדֶּךָ: 3 וַיֹּאמֶר הַמֶּלֶךְ הַאֶפֶס עוֹד אִישׁ לְבֵית שָׁאוּל וְאֶעֱשֶׂה עִמּוֹ חֶסֶד אֱלֹהִים וַיֹּאמֶר צִיבָא אֶל־הַמֶּלֶךְ עוֹד בֵּן לִיהוֹנָתָן נְכֵה רַגְלָיִם: 4 וַיֹּאמֶר־לוֹ הַמֶּלֶךְ אֵיפֹה

And Ziba said to the king, "Indeed he *is* in the house of Machir the son of Ammiel, in Lo Debar."

5 Then King David sent and brought him out of the house of Machir the son of Ammiel, from Lo Debar.

6 Now when Mephibosheth the son of Jonathan, the son of Saul, had come to David, he fell on his face and prostrated himself. Then David said, "Mephibosheth?"

And he answered, "Here is your servant!"

7 So David said to him, "Do not fear, for I will surely show you kindness for Jonathan your father's sake, and will restore to you all the land of Saul your grandfather; and you shall eat bread at my table continually."

8 Then he bowed himself, and said, "What *is* your servant, that you should look upon such a dead dog as I?"

9 And the king called to Ziba, Saul's servant, and said to him, "I have given to your master's son all that belonged to Saul and to all his house. 10 You therefore, and your sons and your servants, shall work the land for him, and you shall bring in *the harvest,* that your master's son may have food to eat. But Mephibosheth your master's son shall eat bread at my table always." Now Ziba had fifteen sons and twenty servants.

11 Then Ziba said to the king, "According to all that my lord the king has commanded his servant, so will your servant do."

"As for Mephibosheth," *said the king,* "he shall eat at my table like one of the king's sons." 12 Mephibosheth had a young son whose name *was* Micha. And all who dwelt in the house of Ziba *were* servants of Mephibosheth. 13 So Mephibosheth dwelt in Jerusalem, for he ate continually at the king's table. And he was lame in both his feet.

10 It happened after this that the king of the people of Ammon died, and Hanun his son reigned in his place. 2 Then David said, "I will show kindness to Hanun the son of Nahash, as his father showed kindness to me."

So David sent by the hand of his servants to comfort him concerning his father. And David's servants came into the land of the people of Ammon. 3 And the princes of the people of Ammon said to Hanun their lord, "Do you think that David really honors your father because he has sent comforters to you? Has David not *rather* sent his servants to you to search the city, to spy it out, and to overthrow it?"

הוּא וַיֹּאמֶר צִיבָא אֶל־הַמֶּלֶךְ הִנֵּה־הוּא בֵּית מָכִיר
בֶּן־עַמִּיאֵל בְּלוֹ דְבָר: 5 וַיִּשְׁלַח הַמֶּלֶךְ דָּוִד וַיִּקָּחֵהוּ
מִבֵּית מָכִיר בֶּן־עַמִּיאֵל מִלּוֹ דְבָר: 6 וַיָּבֹא מְפִיבֹשֶׁת
בֶּן־יְהוֹנָתָן בֶּן־שָׁאוּל אֶל־דָּוִד וַיִּפֹּל עַל־פָּנָיו וַיִּשְׁתָּחוּ
וַיֹּאמֶר דָּוִד מְפִיבֹשֶׁת וַיֹּאמֶר הִנֵּה עַבְדֶּךָ: 7 וַיֹּאמֶר
לוֹ דָוִד אַל־תִּירָא כִּי עָשֹׂה אֶעֱשֶׂה עִמְּךָ חֶסֶד
בַּעֲבוּר יְהוֹנָתָן אָבִיךָ וַהֲשִׁבֹתִי לְךָ אֶת־כָּל־שְׂדֵה
שָׁאוּל אָבִיךָ וְאַתָּה תֹּאכַל לֶחֶם עַל־שֻׁלְחָנִי תָּמִיד:

8 וַיִּשְׁתַּחוּ וַיֹּאמֶר מֶה עַבְדֶּךָ כִּי פָנִיתָ אֶל־הַכֶּלֶב
הַמֵּת אֲשֶׁר כָּמוֹנִי: 9 וַיִּקְרָא הַמֶּלֶךְ אֶל־צִיבָא נַעַר
שָׁאוּל וַיֹּאמֶר אֵלָיו כֹּל אֲשֶׁר הָיָה לְשָׁאוּל וּלְכָל־
בֵּיתוֹ נָתַתִּי לְבֶן־אֲדֹנֶיךָ: 10 וְעָבַדְתָּ לּוֹ אֶת־הָאֲדָמָה
אַתָּה וּבָנֶיךָ וַעֲבָדֶיךָ וְהֵבֵאתָ וְהָיָה לְבֶן־אֲדֹנֶיךָ
לֶחֶם וַאֲכָלוֹ וּמְפִיבֹשֶׁת בֶּן־אֲדֹנֶיךָ יֹאכַל תָּמִיד לֶחֶם
עַל־שֻׁלְחָנִי וּלְצִיבָא חֲמִשָּׁה עָשָׂר בָּנִים וְעֶשְׂרִים
עֲבָדִים: 11 וַיֹּאמֶר צִיבָא אֶל־הַמֶּלֶךְ כְּכֹל אֲשֶׁר
יְצַוֶּה אֲדֹנִי הַמֶּלֶךְ אֶת־עַבְדּוֹ כֵּן יַעֲשֶׂה עַבְדֶּךָ
וּמְפִיבֹשֶׁת אֹכֵל עַל־שֻׁלְחָנִי כְּאַחַד מִבְּנֵי הַמֶּלֶךְ:

12 וְלִמְפִיבֹשֶׁת בֶּן־קָטָן וּשְׁמוֹ מִיכָא וְכֹל מוֹשַׁב
בֵּית־צִיבָא עֲבָדִים לִמְפִיבֹשֶׁת: 13 וּמְפִיבֹשֶׁת יֹשֵׁב
בִּירוּשָׁלַםִ כִּי עַל־שֻׁלְחַן הַמֶּלֶךְ תָּמִיד הוּא אֹכֵל
וְהוּא פִּסֵּחַ שְׁתֵּי רַגְלָיו: פ

י וַיְהִי אַחֲרֵי־כֵן וַיָּמָת מֶלֶךְ בְּנֵי עַמּוֹן וַיִּמְלֹךְ
חָנוּן בְּנוֹ תַּחְתָּיו: 2 וַיֹּאמֶר דָּוִד אֶעֱשֶׂה־חֶסֶד |
עִם־חָנוּן בֶּן־נָחָשׁ כַּאֲשֶׁר עָשָׂה אָבִיו עִמָּדִי חֶסֶד
וַיִּשְׁלַח דָּוִד לְנַחֲמוֹ בְּיַד־עֲבָדָיו אֶל־אָבִיו וַיָּבֹאוּ
עַבְדֵי דָוִד אֶרֶץ בְּנֵי עַמּוֹן: 3 וַיֹּאמְרוּ שָׂרֵי בְנֵי־
עַמּוֹן אֶל־חָנוּן אֲדֹנֵיהֶם הַמְכַבֵּד דָּוִד אֶת־אָבִיךָ
בְּעֵינֶיךָ כִּי־שָׁלַח לְךָ מְנַחֲמִים הֲלוֹא בַּעֲבוּר חֲקוֹר
אֶת־הָעִיר וּלְרַגְּלָהּ וּלְהָפְכָהּ שָׁלַח דָּוִד אֶת־עֲבָדָיו

4 Therefore Hanun took David's servants, shaved off half of their beards, cut off their garments in the middle, at their buttocks, and sent them away. 5 When they told David, he sent to meet them, because the men were greatly ashamed. And the king said, "Wait at Jericho until your beards have grown, and *then* return."

6 When the people of Ammon saw that they had made themselves repulsive to David, the people of Ammon sent and hired the Syrians of Beth Rehob and the Syrians of Zoba, twenty thousand foot soldiers; and from the king of Maacah one thousand men, and from Ish-Tob twelve thousand men. 7 Now when David heard *of it,* he sent Joab and all the army of the mighty men. 8 Then the people of Ammon came out and put themselves in battle array at the entrance of the gate. And the Syrians of Zoba, Beth Rehob, Ish-Tob, and Maacah *were* by themselves in the field.

9 When Joab saw that the battle line was against him before and behind, he chose some of Israel's best and put *them* in battle array against the Syrians. 10 And the rest of the people he put under the command of Abishai his brother, that he might set *them* in battle array against the people of Ammon. 11 Then he said, "If the Syrians are too strong for me, then you shall help me; but if the people of Ammon are too strong for you, then I will come and help you. 12 Be of good courage, and let us be strong for our people and for the cities of our God. And may the LORD do *what is* good in His sight."

13 So Joab and the people who *were* with him drew near for the battle against the Syrians, and they fled before him. 14 When the people of Ammon saw that the Syrians were fleeing, they also fled before Abishai, and entered the city. So Joab returned from the people of Ammon and went to Jerusalem.

15 When the Syrians saw that they had been defeated by Israel, they gathered together. 16 Then Hadadezer sent and brought out the Syrians who *were* beyond the River, and they came to Helam. And Shobach the commander of Hadadezer's army *went* before them. 17 When it was told David, he gathered all Israel, crossed over the Jordan, and came to Helam. And the Syrians set themselves in battle array against David and fought with him. 18 Then the Syrians fled before Israel; and David killed seven hundred charioteers and forty thousand horsemen of the Syrians, and struck Shobach the commander of their army, who died there. 19 And when all the kings *who were* servants to Hadadezer saw that they were defeated by Israel,

אֵלֶיךָ: 4 וַיִּקַּח חָנוּן אֶת־עַבְדֵי דָוִד וַיְגַלַּח אֶת־חֲצִי זְקָנָם וַיִּכְרֹת אֶת־מַדְוֵיהֶם בַּחֵצִי עַד שְׁתוֹתֵיהֶם וַיְשַׁלְּחֵם: 5 וַיַּגִּדוּ לְדָוִד וַיִּשְׁלַח לִקְרָאתָם כִּי־הָיוּ הָאֲנָשִׁים נִכְלָמִים מְאֹד וַיֹּאמֶר הַמֶּלֶךְ שְׁבוּ בִירֵחוֹ עַד־יְצַמַּח זְקַנְכֶם וְשַׁבְתֶּם: 6 וַיִּרְאוּ בְּנֵי עַמּוֹן כִּי נִבְאֲשׁוּ בְּדָוִד וַיִּשְׁלְחוּ בְנֵי־עַמּוֹן וַיִּשְׂכְּרוּ אֶת־אֲרַם בֵּית־רְחוֹב וְאֶת־אֲרַם צוֹבָא עֶשְׂרִים אֶלֶף רַגְלִי וְאֶת־מֶלֶךְ מַעֲכָה אֶלֶף אִישׁ וְאִישׁ טוֹב שְׁנֵים־ עָשָׂר אֶלֶף אִישׁ: 7 וַיִּשְׁמַע דָּוִד וַיִּשְׁלַח אֶת־יוֹאָב וְאֵת כָּל־הַצָּבָא הַגִּבֹּרִים: 8 וַיֵּצְאוּ בְּנֵי עַמּוֹן וַיַּעַרְכוּ מִלְחָמָה פֶּתַח הַשָּׁעַר וַאֲרַם צוֹבָא וּרְחוֹב וְאִישׁ־ טוֹב וּמַעֲכָה לְבַדָּם בַּשָּׂדֶה: 9 וַיַּרְא יוֹאָב כִּי־הָיְתָה אֵלָיו פְּנֵי הַמִּלְחָמָה מִפָּנִים וּמֵאָחוֹר וַיִּבְחַר מִכֹּל בְּחוּרֵי בְיִשְׂרָאֵל וַיַּעֲרֹךְ לִקְרַאת אֲרָם: 10 וְאֵת יֶתֶר הָעָם נָתַן בְּיַד אַבְשַׁי אָחִיו וַיַּעֲרֹךְ לִקְרַאת בְּנֵי עַמּוֹן: 11 וַיֹּאמֶר אִם־תֶּחֱזַק אֲרָם מִמֶּנִּי וְהָיִתָה לִּי לִישׁוּעָה וְאִם־בְּנֵי עַמּוֹן יֶחֱזְקוּ מִמְּךָ וְהָלַכְתִּי לְהוֹשִׁיעַ לָךְ: 12 חֲזַק וְנִתְחַזַּק בְּעַד־עַמֵּנוּ וּבְעַד עָרֵי אֱלֹהֵינוּ וַיהֹוָה יַעֲשֶׂה הַטּוֹב בְּעֵינָיו: 13 וַיִּגַּשׁ יוֹאָב וְהָעָם אֲשֶׁר עִמּוֹ לַמִּלְחָמָה בַּאֲרָם וַיָּנֻסוּ מִפָּנָיו: 14 וּבְנֵי עַמּוֹן רָאוּ כִּי־נָס אֲרָם וַיָּנֻסוּ מִפְּנֵי אֲבִישַׁי וַיָּבֹאוּ הָעִיר וַיָּשָׁב יוֹאָב מֵעַל בְּנֵי עַמּוֹן וַיָּבֹא יְרוּשָׁלָםִ: 15 וַיַּרְא אֲרָם כִּי נִגַּף לִפְנֵי יִשְׂרָאֵל וַיֵּאָסְפוּ יָחַד: 16 וַיִּשְׁלַח הֲדַדְעֶזֶר וַיֹּצֵא אֶת־אֲרָם אֲשֶׁר מֵעֵבֶר הַנָּהָר וַיָּבֹאוּ חֵילָם וְשׁוֹבַךְ שַׂר־צְבָא הֲדַדְעֶזֶר לִפְנֵיהֶם: 17 וַיֻּגַּד לְדָוִד ס וַיֶּאֱסֹף אֶת־כָּל־יִשְׂרָאֵל וַיַּעֲבֹר אֶת־הַיַּרְדֵּן וַיָּבֹא חֵלָאמָה וַיַּעַרְכוּ אֲרָם לִקְרַאת דָּוִד וַיִּלָּחֲמוּ עִמּוֹ: 18 וַיָּנָס אֲרָם מִפְּנֵי יִשְׂרָאֵל וַיַּהֲרֹג דָּוִד מֵאֲרָם שְׁבַע מֵאוֹת רֶכֶב וְאַרְבָּעִים אֶלֶף פָּרָשִׁים וְאֵת שׁוֹבַךְ שַׂר־ צְבָאוֹ הִכָּה וַיָּמָת שָׁם: 19 וַיִּרְאוּ כָל־הַמְּלָכִים עַבְדֵי

they made peace with Israel and served them. So the Syrians were afraid to help the people of Ammon anymore.

11 It happened in the spring of the year, at the time when kings go out *to battle,* that David sent Joab and his servants with him, and all Israel; and they destroyed the people of Ammon and besieged Rabbah. But David remained at Jerusalem.

[2] Then it happened one evening that David arose from his bed and walked on the roof of the king's house. And from the roof he saw a woman bathing, and the woman *was* very beautiful to behold. [3] So David sent and inquired about the woman. And *someone* said, "*Is* this not Bathsheba, the daughter of Eliam, the wife of Uriah the Hittite?" [4] Then David sent messengers, and took her; and she came to him, and he lay with her, for she was cleansed from her impurity; and she returned to her house. [5] And the woman conceived; so she sent and told David, and said, "I *am* with child."

[6] Then David sent to Joab, *saying,* "Send me Uriah the Hittite." And Joab sent Uriah to David. [7] When Uriah had come to him, David asked how Joab was doing, and how the people were doing, and how the war prospered. [8] And David said to Uriah, "Go down to your house and wash your feet." So Uriah departed from the king's house, and a gift *of food* from the king followed him. [9] But Uriah slept at the door of the king's house with all the servants of his lord, and did not go down to his house. [10] So when they told David, saying, "Uriah did not go down to his house," David said to Uriah, "Did you not come from a journey? Why did you not go down to your house?"

[11] And Uriah said to David, "The ark and Israel and Judah are dwelling in tents, and my lord Joab and the servants of my lord are encamped in the open fields. Shall I then go to my house to eat and drink, and to lie with my wife? *As* you live, and *as* your soul lives, I will not do this thing."

[12] Then David said to Uriah, "Wait here today also, and tomorrow I will let you depart." So Uriah remained in Jerusalem that day and the next. [13] Now when David called him, he ate and drank before him; and he made him drunk. And at evening he went out to lie on his bed with the servants of his lord, but he did not go down to his house.

[14] In the morning it happened that David wrote a letter to Joab and sent *it* by the hand of Uriah. [15] And he wrote in the letter, saying, "Set Uriah in the forefront of the hottest battle, and retreat from him, that he may be struck down and die." [16] So it

הֲדַדְעֶזֶר כִּי נִגְּפוּ לִפְנֵי יִשְׂרָאֵל וַיַּשְׁלִמוּ אֶת־יִשְׂרָאֵל וַיַּעַבְדוּם וַיִּרְאוּ אֲרָם לְהוֹשִׁיעַ עוֹד אֶת־בְּנֵי עַמּוֹן: פ

יא וַיְהִי לִתְשׁוּבַת הַשָּׁנָה לְעֵת ׀ צֵאת הַמַּלְאָכִים וַיִּשְׁלַח דָּוִד אֶת־יוֹאָב וְאֶת־עֲבָדָיו עִמּוֹ וְאֶת־כָּל־ יִשְׂרָאֵל וַיַּשְׁחִתוּ אֶת־בְּנֵי עַמּוֹן וַיָּצֻרוּ עַל־רַבָּה וְדָוִד יוֹשֵׁב בִּירוּשָׁלָםִ: ס [2] וַיְהִי ׀ לְעֵת הָעֶרֶב וַיָּקָם דָּוִד מֵעַל מִשְׁכָּבוֹ וַיִּתְהַלֵּךְ עַל־גַּג בֵּית־הַמֶּלֶךְ וַיַּרְא אִשָּׁה רֹחֶצֶת מֵעַל הַגָּג וְהָאִשָּׁה טוֹבַת מַרְאֶה מְאֹד: [3] וַיִּשְׁלַח דָּוִד וַיִּדְרֹשׁ לָאִשָּׁה וַיֹּאמֶר הֲלוֹא־ זֹאת בַּת־שֶׁבַע בַּת־אֱלִיעָם אֵשֶׁת אוּרִיָּה הַחִתִּי: [4] וַיִּשְׁלַח דָּוִד מַלְאָכִים וַיִּקָּחֶהָ וַתָּבוֹא אֵלָיו וַיִּשְׁכַּב עִמָּהּ וְהִיא מִתְקַדֶּשֶׁת מִטֻּמְאָתָהּ וַתָּשָׁב אֶל־בֵּיתָהּ: [5] וַתַּהַר הָאִשָּׁה וַתִּשְׁלַח וַתַּגֵּד לְדָוִד וַתֹּאמֶר הָרָה אָנֹכִי: [6] וַיִּשְׁלַח דָּוִד אֶל־יוֹאָב שְׁלַח אֵלַי אֶת־אוּרִיָּה הַחִתִּי וַיִּשְׁלַח יוֹאָב אֶת־אוּרִיָּה אֶל־דָּוִד: [7] וַיָּבֹא אוּרִיָּה אֵלָיו וַיִּשְׁאַל דָּוִד לִשְׁלוֹם יוֹאָב וְלִשְׁלוֹם הָעָם וְלִשְׁלוֹם הַמִּלְחָמָה: [8] וַיֹּאמֶר דָּוִד לְאוּרִיָּה רֵד לְבֵיתְךָ וּרְחַץ רַגְלֶיךָ וַיֵּצֵא אוּרִיָּה מִבֵּית הַמֶּלֶךְ וַתֵּצֵא אַחֲרָיו מַשְׂאַת הַמֶּלֶךְ: [9] וַיִּשְׁכַּב אוּרִיָּה פֶּתַח בֵּית הַמֶּלֶךְ אֵת כָּל־עַבְדֵי אֲדֹנָיו וְלֹא יָרַד אֶל־ בֵּיתוֹ: [10] וַיַּגִּדוּ לְדָוִד לֵאמֹר לֹא־יָרַד אוּרִיָּה אֶל־ בֵּיתוֹ וַיֹּאמֶר דָּוִד אֶל־אוּרִיָּה הֲלוֹא מִדֶּרֶךְ אַתָּה בָא מַדּוּעַ לֹא־יָרַדְתָּ אֶל־בֵּיתֶךָ: [11] וַיֹּאמֶר אוּרִיָּה אֶל־ דָּוִד הָאָרוֹן וְיִשְׂרָאֵל וִיהוּדָה יֹשְׁבִים בַּסֻּכּוֹת וַאדֹנִי יוֹאָב וְעַבְדֵי אֲדֹנִי עַל־פְּנֵי הַשָּׂדֶה חֹנִים וַאֲנִי אָבוֹא אֶל־בֵּיתִי לֶאֱכֹל וְלִשְׁתּוֹת וְלִשְׁכַּב עִם־אִשְׁתִּי חַיֶּךָ וְחֵי נַפְשֶׁךָ אִם־אֶעֱשֶׂה אֶת־הַדָּבָר הַזֶּה: [12] וַיֹּאמֶר דָּוִד אֶל־אוּרִיָּה שֵׁב בָּזֶה גַּם־הַיּוֹם וּמָחָר אֲשַׁלְּחֶךָּ וַיֵּשֶׁב אוּרִיָּה בִירוּשָׁלַםִ בַּיּוֹם הַהוּא וּמִמָּחֳרָת: [13] וַיִּקְרָא־לוֹ דָוִד וַיֹּאכַל לְפָנָיו וַיֵּשְׁתְּ וַיְשַׁכְּרֵהוּ וַיֵּצֵא בָעֶרֶב לִשְׁכַּב בְּמִשְׁכָּבוֹ עִם־עַבְדֵי אֲדֹנָיו וְאֶל־בֵּיתוֹ לֹא יָרָד: [14] וַיְהִי בַבֹּקֶר וַיִּכְתֹּב דָּוִד סֵפֶר אֶל־יוֹאָב וַיִּשְׁלַח בְּיַד אוּרִיָּה: [15] וַיִּכְתֹּב בַּסֵּפֶר לֵאמֹר הָבוּ אֶת־אוּרִיָּה אֶל־מוּל פְּנֵי הַמִּלְחָמָה הַחֲזָקָה וְשַׁבְתֶּם מֵאַחֲרָיו וְנִכָּה וָמֵת: [16] וַיְהִי בִּשְׁמוֹר ס

was, while Joab besieged the city, that he assigned Uriah to a place where he knew there *were* valiant men. ¹⁷ Then the men of the city came out and fought with Joab. And *some* of the people of the servants of David fell; and Uriah the Hittite died also.

¹⁸ Then Joab sent and told David all the things concerning the war, ¹⁹ and charged the messenger, saying, "When you have finished telling the matters of the war to the king, ²⁰ if it happens that the king's wrath rises, and he says to you: 'Why did you approach so near to the city when you fought? Did you not know that they would shoot from the wall? ²¹ Who struck Abimelech the son of Jerubbesheth? Was it not a woman who cast a piece of a millstone on him from the wall, so that he died in Thebez? Why did you go near the wall?'—then you shall say, 'Your servant Uriah the Hittite is dead also.'"

²² So the messenger went, and came and told David all that Joab had sent by him. ²³ And the messenger said to David, "Surely the men prevailed against us and came out to us in the field; then we drove them back as far as the entrance of the gate. ²⁴ The archers shot from the wall at your servants; and *some* of the king's servants are dead, and your servant Uriah the Hittite is dead also."

²⁵ Then David said to the messenger, "Thus you shall say to Joab: 'Do not let this thing displease you, for the sword devours one as well as another. Strengthen your attack against the city, and overthrow it.' So encourage him."

²⁶ When the wife of Uriah heard that Uriah her husband was dead, she mourned for her husband. ²⁷ And when her mourning was over, David sent and brought her to his house, and she became his wife and bore him a son. But the thing that David had done displeased the Lord.

12 Then the Lord sent Nathan to David. And he came to him, and said to him: "There were two men in one city, one rich and the other poor. ² The rich *man* had exceedingly many flocks and herds. ³ But the poor *man* had nothing, except one little ewe lamb which he had bought and nourished; and it grew up together with him and with his children. It ate of his own food and drank from his own cup and lay in his bosom; and it was like a daughter to him. ⁴ And a traveler came to the rich man, who refused to take from his own flock and from his own herd to prepare one for the wayfaring man who had come to him; but he took the poor man's lamb and prepared it for the man who had come to him."

יוֹאָב אֶל־הָעִיר וַיִּתֵּן אֶת־אוּרִיָּה אֶל־הַמָּקוֹם אֲשֶׁר יָדַע כִּי אַנְשֵׁי־חַיִל שָׁם: 17 וַיֵּצְאוּ אַנְשֵׁי הָעִיר וַיִּלָּחֲמוּ אֶת־יוֹאָב וַיִּפֹּל מִן־הָעָם מֵעַבְדֵי דָוִד וַיָּמׇת גַּם אוּרִיָּה הַחִתִּי: 18 וַיִּשְׁלַח יוֹאָב וַיַּגֵּד לְדָוִד אֶת־כׇּל־דִּבְרֵי הַמִּלְחָמָה: 19 וַיְצַו אֶת־הַמַּלְאָךְ לֵאמֹר כְּכַלּוֹתְךָ אֵת כׇּל־דִּבְרֵי הַמִּלְחָמָה לְדַבֵּר אֶל־הַמֶּלֶךְ: 20 וְהָיָה אִם־תַּעֲלֶה חֲמַת הַמֶּלֶךְ וְאָמַר לְךָ מַדּוּעַ נִגַּשְׁתֶּם אֶל־הָעִיר לְהִלָּחֵם הֲלוֹא יְדַעְתֶּם אֵת אֲשֶׁר־יֹרוּ מֵעַל הַחוֹמָה: 21 מִי־הִכָּה אֶת־אֲבִימֶלֶךְ בֶּן־יְרֻבֶּשֶׁת הֲלוֹא־אִשָּׁה הִשְׁלִיכָה עָלָיו פֶּלַח רֶכֶב מֵעַל הַחוֹמָה וַיָּמׇת בְּתֵבֵץ לָמָּה נִגַּשְׁתֶּם אֶל־הַחוֹמָה וְאָמַרְתָּ גַּם עַבְדְּךָ אוּרִיָּה הַחִתִּי מֵת: 22 וַיֵּלֶךְ הַמַּלְאָךְ וַיָּבֹא וַיַּגֵּד לְדָוִד אֵת כׇּל־אֲשֶׁר שְׁלָחוֹ יוֹאָב: 23 וַיֹּאמֶר הַמַּלְאָךְ אֶל־דָּוִד כִּי־גָבְרוּ עָלֵינוּ הָאֲנָשִׁים וַיֵּצְאוּ אֵלֵינוּ הַשָּׂדֶה וַנִּהְיֶה עֲלֵיהֶם עַד־פֶּתַח הַשָּׁעַר: 24 וַיֹּרוּ הַמּוֹרְאִים° אֶל־עֲבָדֶךָ מֵעַל הַחוֹמָה וַיָּמוּתוּ מֵעַבְדֵי הַמֶּלֶךְ וְגַם עַבְדְּךָ אוּרִיָּה הַחִתִּי מֵת: ס 25 וַיֹּאמֶר דָּוִד אֶל־הַמַּלְאָךְ כֹּה־תֹאמַר אֶל־יוֹאָב אַל־יֵרַע בְּעֵינֶיךָ אֶת־הַדָּבָר הַזֶּה כִּי־כָזֹה וְכָזֶה תֹּאכַל הֶחָרֶב הַחֲזֵק מִלְחַמְתְּךָ אֶל־הָעִיר וְהׇרְסָהּ וְחַזְּקֵהוּ: 26 וַתִּשְׁמַע אֵשֶׁת אוּרִיָּה כִּי־מֵת אוּרִיָּה אִישָׁהּ וַתִּסְפֹּד עַל־בַּעְלָהּ: 27 וַיַּעֲבֹר הָאֵבֶל וַיִּשְׁלַח דָּוִד וַיַּאַסְפָהּ אֶל־בֵּיתוֹ וַתְּהִי־לוֹ לְאִשָּׁה וַתֵּלֶד לוֹ בֵּן וַיֵּרַע הַדָּבָר אֲשֶׁר־עָשָׂה דָוִד בְּעֵינֵי יְהֹוָה: פ

יב וַיִּשְׁלַח יְהֹוָה אֶת־נָתָן אֶל־דָּוִד וַיָּבֹא אֵלָיו וַיֹּאמֶר לוֹ שְׁנֵי אֲנָשִׁים הָיוּ בְּעִיר אֶחָת אֶחָד עָשִׁיר וְאֶחָד רָאשׁ: 2 לְעָשִׁיר הָיָה צֹאן וּבָקָר הַרְבֵּה מְאֹד: 3 וְלָרָשׁ אֵין־כֹּל כִּי אִם־כִּבְשָׂה אַחַת קְטַנָּה אֲשֶׁר קָנָה וַיְחַיֶּהָ וַתִּגְדַּל עִמּוֹ וְעִם־בָּנָיו יַחְדָּו מִפִּתּוֹ תֹאכַל וּמִכֹּסוֹ תִשְׁתֶּה וּבְחֵיקוֹ תִשְׁכָּב וַתְּהִי־לוֹ כְּבַת: 4 וַיָּבֹא הֵלֶךְ לְאִישׁ הֶעָשִׁיר וַיַּחְמֹל לָקַחַת מִצֹּאנוֹ וּמִבְּקָרוֹ לַעֲשׂוֹת לָאֹרֵחַ הַבָּא־לוֹ וַיִּקַּח אֶת־כִּבְשַׂת הָאִישׁ הָרָאשׁ וַיַּעֲשֶׂהָ לָאִישׁ הַבָּא אֵלָיו:

5 So David's anger was greatly aroused against the man, and he said to Nathan, "*As* the LORD lives, the man who has done this shall surely die! 6 And he shall restore fourfold for the lamb, because he did this thing and because he had no pity."

7 Then Nathan said to David, "You *are* the man! Thus says the LORD God of Israel: 'I anointed you king over Israel, and I delivered you from the hand of Saul. 8 I gave you your master's house and your master's wives into your keeping, and gave you the house of Israel and Judah. And if *that had been* too little, I also would have given you much more! 9 Why have you despised the commandment of the LORD, to do evil in His sight? You have killed Uriah the Hittite with the sword; you have taken his wife *to be* your wife, and have killed him with the sword of the people of Ammon. 10 Now therefore, the sword shall never depart from your house, because you have despised Me, and have taken the wife of Uriah the Hittite to be your wife.' 11 Thus says the LORD: 'Behold, I will raise up adversity against you from your own house; and I will take your wives before your eyes and give *them* to your neighbor, and he shall lie with your wives in the sight of this sun. 12 For you did *it* secretly, but I will do this thing before all Israel, before the sun.' "

13 So David said to Nathan, "I have sinned against the LORD."

And Nathan said to David, "The LORD also has put away your sin; you shall not die. 14 However, because by this deed you have given great occasion to the enemies of the LORD to blaspheme, the child also *who is* born to you shall surely die." 15 Then Nathan departed to his house.

And the LORD struck the child that Uriah's wife bore to David, and it became ill. 16 David therefore pleaded with God for the child, and David fasted and went in and lay all night on the ground. 17 So the elders of his house arose *and went* to him, to raise him up from the ground. But he would not, nor did he eat food with them. 18 Then on the seventh day it came to pass that the child died. And the servants of David were afraid to tell him that the child was dead. For they said, "Indeed, while the child was alive, we spoke to him, and he would not heed our voice. How can we tell him that the child is dead? He may do some harm!"

19 When David saw that his servants were whispering, David perceived that the child was dead. Therefore David said to his servants, "Is the child dead?"

And they said, "He is dead."

5 וַיִּחַר־אַף דָּוִד בָּאִישׁ מְאֹד וַיֹּאמֶר אֶל־נָתָן חַי־
יְהוָה כִּי בֶן־מָוֶת הָאִישׁ הָעֹשֶׂה זֹאת: 6 וְאֶת־
הַכִּבְשָׂה יְשַׁלֵּם אַרְבַּעְתָּיִם עֵקֶב אֲשֶׁר עָשָׂה אֶת־
הַדָּבָר הַזֶּה וְעַל אֲשֶׁר לֹא־חָמָל: 7 וַיֹּאמֶר נָתָן אֶל־
דָּוִד אַתָּה הָאִישׁ כֹּה־אָמַר יְהוָה אֱלֹהֵי יִשְׂרָאֵל
אָנֹכִי מְשַׁחְתִּיךָ לְמֶלֶךְ עַל־יִשְׂרָאֵל וְאָנֹכִי הִצַּלְתִּיךָ
מִיַּד שָׁאוּל: 8 וָאֶתְּנָה לְךָ אֶת־בֵּית אֲדֹנֶיךָ וְאֶת־
נְשֵׁי אֲדֹנֶיךָ בְּחֵיקֶךָ וָאֶתְּנָה לְךָ אֶת־בֵּית יִשְׂרָאֵל
וִיהוּדָה וְאִם־מְעָט וְאֹסִפָה לְךָ כָּהֵנָּה וְכָהֵנָּה:

9 מַדּוּעַ בָּזִיתָ | אֶת־דְּבַר יְהוָה לַעֲשׂוֹת הָרַע
בְּעֵינַו אֵת אוּרִיָּה הַחִתִּי הִכִּיתָ בַחֶרֶב וְאֶת־
אִשְׁתּוֹ לָקַחְתָּ לְּךָ לְאִשָּׁה וְאֹתוֹ הָרַגְתָּ בְּחֶרֶב בְּנֵי
עַמּוֹן: 10 וְעַתָּה לֹא־תָסוּר חֶרֶב מִבֵּיתְךָ עַד־עוֹלָם
עֵקֶב כִּי בְזִתָנִי וַתִּקַּח אֶת־אֵשֶׁת אוּרִיָּה הַחִתִּי
לִהְיוֹת לְךָ לְאִשָּׁה: ס 11 כֹּה | אָמַר
יְהוָה הִנְנִי מֵקִים עָלֶיךָ רָעָה מִבֵּיתֶךָ וְלָקַחְתִּי
אֶת־נָשֶׁיךָ לְעֵינֶיךָ וְנָתַתִּי לְרֵעֶיךָ וְשָׁכַב עִם־נָשֶׁיךָ
לְעֵינֵי הַשֶּׁמֶשׁ הַזֹּאת: 12 כִּי אַתָּה עָשִׂיתָ בַסָּתֶר
וַאֲנִי אֶעֱשֶׂה אֶת־הַדָּבָר הַזֶּה נֶגֶד כָּל־יִשְׂרָאֵל
וְנֶגֶד הַשָּׁמֶשׁ: ס 13 וַיֹּאמֶר דָּוִד אֶל־נָתָן
חָטָאתִי לַיהוָה ס וַיֹּאמֶר נָתָן אֶל־דָּוִד
גַּם־יְהוָה הֶעֱבִיר חַטָּאתְךָ לֹא תָמוּת: 14 אֶפֶס כִּי־
נִאֵץ נִאַצְתָּ אֶת־אֹיְבֵי יְהוָה בַּדָּבָר הַזֶּה גַּם הַבֵּן
הַיִּלּוֹד לְךָ מוֹת יָמוּת: 15 וַיֵּלֶךְ נָתָן אֶל־בֵּיתוֹ וַיִּגֹּף
יְהוָה אֶת־הַיֶּלֶד אֲשֶׁר יָלְדָה אֵשֶׁת־אוּרִיָּה לְדָוִד
וַיֵּאָנַשׁ: 16 וַיְבַקֵּשׁ דָּוִד אֶת־הָאֱלֹהִים בְּעַד הַנָּעַר
וַיָּצָם דָּוִד צוֹם וּבָא וְלָן וְשָׁכַב אָרְצָה: 17 וַיָּקֻמוּ
זִקְנֵי בֵיתוֹ עָלָיו לַהֲקִימוֹ מִן־הָאָרֶץ וְלֹא אָבָה וְלֹא־
בָרָא אִתָּם לָחֶם: 18 וַיְהִי בַּיּוֹם הַשְּׁבִיעִי וַיָּמָת הַיֶּלֶד
וַיִּרְאוּ עַבְדֵי דָוִד לְהַגִּיד לוֹ | כִּי־מֵת הַיֶּלֶד כִּי
אָמְרוּ הִנֵּה בִהְיוֹת הַיֶּלֶד חַי דִּבַּרְנוּ אֵלָיו וְלֹא־
שָׁמַע בְּקוֹלֵנוּ וְאֵיךְ נֹאמַר אֵלָיו מֵת הַיֶּלֶד וְעָשָׂה
רָעָה: 19 וַיַּרְא דָּוִד כִּי עֲבָדָיו מִתְלַחֲשִׁים וַיָּבֶן דָּוִד
כִּי מֵת הַיָּלֶד וַיֹּאמֶר דָּוִד אֶל־עֲבָדָיו הֲמֵת הַיֶּלֶד

20 So David arose from the ground, washed and anointed himself, and changed his clothes; and he went into the house of the LORD and worshiped. Then he went to his own house; and when he requested, they set food before him, and he ate. 21 Then his servants said to him, "What *is* this that you have done? You fasted and wept for the child *while he was* alive, but when the child died, you arose and ate food."

22 And he said, "While the child was alive, I fasted and wept; for I said, 'Who can tell *whether* the LORD will be gracious to me, that the child may live?' 23 But now he is dead; why should I fast? Can I bring him back again? I shall go to him, but he shall not return to me."

24 Then David comforted Bathsheba his wife, and went in to her and lay with her. So she bore a son, and he called his name Solomon. Now the LORD loved him, 25 and He sent *word* by the hand of Nathan the prophet: So he called his name Jedidiah, because of the LORD.

26 Now Joab fought against Rabbah of the people of Ammon, and took the royal city. 27 And Joab sent messengers to David, and said, "I have fought against Rabbah, and I have taken the city's water *supply*. 28 Now therefore, gather the rest of the people together and encamp against the city and take it, lest I take the city and it be called after my name." 29 So David gathered all the people together and went to Rabbah, fought against it, and took it. 30 Then he took their king's crown from his head. Its weight *was* a talent of gold, with precious stones. And it was *set* on David's head. Also he brought out the spoil of the city in great abundance. 31 And he brought out the people who *were* in it, and put *them to work* with saws and iron picks and iron axes, and made them cross over to the brick works. So he did to all the cities of the people of Ammon. Then David and all the people returned to Jerusalem.

13 After this Absalom the son of David had a lovely sister, whose name *was* Tamar; and Amnon the son of David loved her. 2 Amnon was so distressed over his sister Tamar that he became sick; for she *was* a virgin. And it was improper for Amnon to do anything to her. 3 But Amnon had a friend whose name *was* Jonadab the son of Shimeah, David's brother. Now Jonadab *was* a very crafty man. 4 And he said to him, "Why *are* you, the king's son, becoming thinner day after day? Will you not tell me?"

Amnon said to him, "I love Tamar, my brother Absalom's sister."

20 וַיָּ֣קָם דָּוִד֩ מֵהָאָ֨רֶץ וַיִּרְחַ֜ץ וַיָּ֗סֶךְ וַיְחַלֵּף֙ שִׂמְלֹתָ֔יו וַיָּבֹ֥א בֵית־יְהוָ֖ה וַיִּשְׁתָּ֑חוּ וַיָּבֹא֙ אֶל־בֵּית֔וֹ וַיִּשְׁאַ֕ל וַיָּשִׂ֥ימוּ ל֛וֹ לֶ֖חֶם וַיֹּאכַֽל׃ 21 וַיֹּאמְר֤וּ עֲבָדָיו֙ אֵלָ֔יו מָֽה־הַדָּבָ֥ר הַזֶּ֖ה אֲשֶׁ֣ר עָשִׂ֑יתָה בַּעֲב֞וּר הַיֶּ֤לֶד חַי֙ צַ֣מְתָּ וַתֵּ֔בְךְּ וְכַאֲשֶׁר֙ מֵ֣ת הַיֶּ֔לֶד קַ֖מְתָּ וַתֹּ֥אכַל לָֽחֶם׃ 22 וַיֹּ֕אמֶר בְּעוֹד֙ הַיֶּ֣לֶד חַ֔י צַ֖מְתִּי וָֽאֶבְכֶּ֑ה כִּ֤י אָמַ֙רְתִּי֙ מִ֣י יוֹדֵ֔עַ יְחָנַּ֥נִי יְהוָ֖ה וְחַ֥י הַיָּֽלֶד׃ 23 וְעַתָּ֣ה ׀ מֵ֗ת לָ֤מָּה זֶּה֙ אֲנִ֣י צָ֔ם הַאוּכַ֥ל לַהֲשִׁיב֖וֹ ע֑וֹד אֲנִי֙ הֹלֵ֣ךְ אֵלָ֔יו וְה֖וּא לֹֽא־יָשׁ֥וּב אֵלָֽי׃ 24 וַיְנַחֵ֣ם דָּוִ֗ד אֵ֚ת בַּת־שֶׁ֣בַע אִשְׁתּ֔וֹ וַיָּבֹ֥א אֵלֶ֖יהָ וַיִּשְׁכַּ֣ב עִמָּ֑הּ וַתֵּ֣לֶד בֵּ֗ן וַיִּקְרָ֤א אֶת־שְׁמוֹ֙ שְׁלֹמֹ֔ה וַיהוָ֖ה אֲהֵבֽוֹ׃ 25 וַיִּשְׁלַ֗ח בְּיַד֙ נָתָ֣ן הַנָּבִ֔יא וַיִּקְרָ֥א אֶת־שְׁמ֖וֹ יְדִֽידְיָ֑הּ בַּעֲב֖וּר יְהוָֽה׃ פ

26 וַיִּלָּ֣חֶם יוֹאָ֔ב בְּרַבַּ֖ת בְּנֵ֣י עַמּ֑וֹן וַיִּלְכֹּ֖ד אֶת־עִ֥יר הַמְּלוּכָֽה׃ 27 וַיִּשְׁלַ֤ח יוֹאָב֙ מַלְאָכִ֔ים אֶל־דָּוִ֑ד וַיֹּ֕אמֶר נִלְחַ֣מְתִּי בְרַבָּ֔ה גַּם־לָכַ֖דְתִּי אֶת־עִ֥יר הַמָּֽיִם׃ 28 וְעַתָּ֗ה אֱסֹף֙ אֶת־יֶ֣תֶר הָעָ֔ם וַחֲנֵ֥ה עַל־הָעִ֖יר וְלָכְדָ֑הּ פֶּן־אֶלְכֹּ֤ד אֲנִי֙ אֶת־הָעִ֔יר וְנִקְרָ֥א שְׁמִ֖י עָלֶֽיהָ׃ 29 וַיֶּאֱסֹ֥ף דָּוִ֛ד אֶת־כָּל־הָעָ֖ם וַיֵּ֣לֶךְ רַבָּ֑תָה וַיִּלָּ֥חֶם בָּ֖הּ וַֽיִּלְכְּדָֽהּ׃ 30 וַיִּקַּ֣ח אֶת־עֲטֶֽרֶת־מַלְכָּם֩ מֵעַ֨ל רֹאשׁ֜וֹ וּמִשְׁקָלָ֨הּ כִּכַּ֤ר זָהָב֙ וְאֶ֣בֶן יְקָרָ֔ה וַתְּהִ֖י עַל־רֹ֣אשׁ דָּוִ֑ד וּשְׁלַ֥ל הָעִ֛יר הוֹצִ֖יא הַרְבֵּ֥ה מְאֹֽד׃ 31 וְאֶת־הָעָ֨ם אֲשֶׁר־בָּ֜הּ הוֹצִ֗יא וַיָּ֣שֶׂם בַּ֠מְּגֵרָה וּבַחֲרִצֵ֨י הַבַּרְזֶ֜ל וּֽבְמַגְזְרֹ֣ת הַבַּרְזֶ֗ל וְהֶעֱבִ֤יר אוֹתָם֙ בַּמַּלְבֵּ֔ן וְכֵ֣ן יַעֲשֶׂ֔ה לְכֹ֖ל עָרֵ֣י בְנֵֽי־עַמּ֑וֹן וַיָּ֧שָׁב דָּוִ֛ד וְכָל־הָעָ֖ם יְרוּשָׁלָֽ͏ִם׃ פ

יג וַיְהִ֣י אַֽחֲרֵי־כֵ֗ן וּלְאַבְשָׁל֧וֹם בֶּן־דָּוִ֛ד אָח֥וֹת יָפָ֖ה וּשְׁמָ֣הּ תָּמָ֑ר וַיֶּאֱהָבֶ֖הָ אַמְנ֥וֹן בֶּן־דָּוִֽד׃ 2 וַיֵּ֨צֶר לְאַמְנ֜וֹן לְהִתְחַלּ֗וֹת בַּֽעֲבוּר֙ תָּמָ֣ר אֲחֹת֔וֹ כִּ֥י בְתוּלָ֖ה הִ֑יא וַיִּפָּלֵא֙ בְּעֵינֵ֣י אַמְנ֔וֹן לַעֲשׂ֥וֹת לָ֖הּ מְאֽוּמָה׃ 3 וּלְאַמְנ֣וֹן רֵ֗עַ וּשְׁמוֹ֙ יֽוֹנָדָ֔ב בֶּן־שִׁמְעָ֖ה אֲחִ֣י דָוִ֑ד וְי֣וֹנָדָ֔ב אִ֥ישׁ חָכָ֖ם מְאֹֽד׃ 4 וַיֹּ֣אמֶר ל֗וֹ מַדּ֣וּעַ אַ֠תָּה כָּ֣כָה דַּ֤ל בֶּן־הַמֶּ֙לֶךְ֙ בַּבֹּ֣קֶר בַּבֹּ֔קֶר הֲל֖וֹא תַּגִּ֣יד לִ֑י וַיֹּ֤אמֶר לוֹ֙ אַמְנ֔וֹן אֶת־תָּמָ֗ר אֲח֛וֹת אַבְשָׁלֹ֥ם אָחִ֖י אֲנִ֥י אֹהֵֽב׃

יג 20 שְׂמַלֹתָיו 22 וַחֲנַנִי 24 וַתִּקְרָא 31 בַּמַּלְבֵּן

⁵So Jonadab said to him, "Lie down on your bed and pretend to be ill. And when your father comes to see you, say to him, 'Please let my sister Tamar come and give me food, and prepare the food in my sight, that I may see *it* and eat it from her hand.'" ⁶Then Amnon lay down and pretended to be ill; and when the king came to see him, Amnon said to the king, "Please let Tamar my sister come and make a couple of cakes for me in my sight, that I may eat from her hand."

⁷And David sent home to Tamar, saying, "Now go to your brother Amnon's house, and prepare food for him." ⁸So Tamar went to her brother Amnon's house; and he was lying down. Then she took flour and kneaded *it,* made cakes in his sight, and baked the cakes. ⁹And she took the pan and placed *them* out before him, but he refused to eat. Then Amnon said, "Have everyone go out from me." And they all went out from him. ¹⁰Then Amnon said to Tamar, "Bring the food into the bedroom, that I may eat from your hand." And Tamar took the cakes which she had made, and brought *them* to Amnon her brother in the bedroom. ¹¹Now when she had brought *them* to him to eat, he took hold of her and said to her, "Come, lie with me, my sister."

¹²But she answered him, "No, my brother, do not force me, for no such thing should be done in Israel. Do not do this disgraceful thing! ¹³And I, where could I take my shame? And as for you, you would be like one of the fools in Israel. Now therefore, please speak to the king; for he will not withhold me from you." ¹⁴However, he would not heed her voice; and being stronger than she, he forced her and lay with her.

¹⁵Then Amnon hated her exceedingly, so that the hatred with which he hated her *was* greater than the love with which he had loved her. And Amnon said to her, "Arise, be gone!"

¹⁶So she said to him, "No, indeed! This evil of sending me away *is* worse than the other that you did to me."

But he would not listen to her. ¹⁷Then he called his servant who attended him, and said, "Here! Put this *woman* out, away from me, and bolt the door behind her." ¹⁸Now she had on a robe of many colors, for the king's virgin daughters wore such apparel. And his servant put her out and bolted the door behind her.

¹⁹Then Tamar put ashes on her head, and tore her robe of many colors that *was* on her, and laid her hand on her head and went away crying bitterly. ²⁰And Absalom her brother said to her, "Has Amnon your brother been with you? But now

5 וַיֹּ֤אמֶר לוֹ֙ יְה֣וֹנָדָ֔ב שְׁכַ֥ב עַֽל־מִשְׁכָּבְךָ֖ וְהִתְחָ֑ל
וּבָ֤א אָבִ֙יךָ֙ לִרְאוֹתֶ֔ךָ וְאָמַרְתָּ֣ אֵלָ֗יו תָּ֣בֹא נָ֞א תָמָ֤ר
אֲחוֹתִי֙ וְתַבְרֵ֣נִי לֶ֔חֶם וְעָשְׂתָ֤ה לְעֵינַי֙ אֶת־הַבִּרְיָ֔ה
לְמַ֙עַן֙ אֲשֶׁ֣ר אֶרְאֶ֔ה וְאָכַלְתִּ֖י מִיָּדָֽהּ׃ 6 וַיִּשְׁכַּ֖ב אַמְנ֑וֹן
וַיִּתְחָ֑ל וַיָּבֹ֨א הַמֶּ֜לֶךְ לִרְאֹת֗וֹ וַיֹּ֨אמֶר אַמְנ֤וֹן אֶל־
הַמֶּ֙לֶךְ֙ תָּֽבוֹא־נָ֞א תָּמָ֣ר אֲחֹתִ֗י וּתְלַבֵּ֤ב לְעֵינַי֙ שְׁתֵּ֣י
לְבִב֔וֹת וְאֶבְרֶ֖ה מִיָּדָֽהּ׃ 7 וַיִּשְׁלַ֥ח דָּוִ֛ד אֶל־תָּמָ֖ר
הַבַּ֣יְתָה לֵאמֹ֑ר לְכִ֣י נָ֗א בֵּ֚ית אַמְנ֣וֹן אָחִ֔יךְ וַעֲשִׂי־ל֖וֹ
הַבִּרְיָֽה׃ 8 וַתֵּ֣לֶךְ תָּמָ֗ר בֵּ֛ית אַמְנ֥וֹן אָחִ֖יהָ וְה֣וּא שֹׁכֵ֑ב
וַתִּקַּ֣ח אֶת־הַבָּצֵ֡ק וַתָּ֩לָשׁ֩ וַתְּלַבֵּ֨ב לְעֵינָ֜יו וַתְּבַשֵּׁ֖ל
אֶת־הַלְּבִבֽוֹת׃ 9 וַתִּקַּ֤ח אֶת־הַמַּשְׂרֵת֙ וַתִּצֹ֣ק לְפָנָ֔יו
וַיְמָאֵ֖ן לֶאֱכ֑וֹל וַיֹּ֣אמֶר אַמְנ֗וֹן הוֹצִ֤יאוּ כָל־אִישׁ֙ מֵֽעָלַ֔י
וַיֵּצְא֖וּ כָל־אִ֥ישׁ מֵעָלָֽיו׃ 10 וַיֹּ֨אמֶר אַמְנ֜וֹן אֶל־תָּמָ֗ר
הָבִ֤יאִי הַבִּרְיָה֙ הַחֶ֔דֶר וְאֶבְרֶ֖ה מִיָּדֵ֑ךְ וַתִּקַּ֣ח תָּמָ֗ר
אֶת־הַלְּבִבוֹת֙ אֲשֶׁ֣ר עָשָׂ֔תָה וַתָּבֵ֛א לְאַמְנ֥וֹן אָחִ֖יהָ
הֶחָֽדְרָה׃ 11 וַתַּגֵּ֥שׁ אֵלָ֖יו לֶאֱכֹ֑ל וַיַּֽחֲזֶק־בָּהּ֙ וַיֹּ֣אמֶר
לָ֔הּ בּ֛וֹאִי שִׁכְבִ֥י עִמִּ֖י אֲחוֹתִֽי׃ 12 וַתֹּ֣אמֶר ל֗וֹ אַל־אָחִי֙
אַל־תְּעַנֵּ֔נִי כִּ֛י לֹא־יֵעָשֶׂ֥ה כֵ֖ן בְּיִשְׂרָאֵ֑ל אַֽל־תַּעֲשֵׂ֖ה
אֶת־הַנְּבָלָ֥ה הַזֹּֽאת׃ 13 וַאֲנִ֗י אָ֤נָה אוֹלִיךְ֙ אֶת־חֶרְפָּתִ֔י
וְאַתָּ֗ה תִּהְיֶ֛ה כְּאַחַ֥ד הַנְּבָלִ֖ים בְּיִשְׂרָאֵ֑ל וְעַתָּה֙ דַּבֶּר־
נָ֣א אֶל־הַמֶּ֔לֶךְ כִּ֛י לֹ֥א יִמְנָעֵ֖נִי מִמֶּֽךָּ׃ 14 וְלֹ֤א אָבָה֙
לִשְׁמֹ֣עַ בְּקוֹלָ֔הּ וַיֶּחֱזַ֤ק מִמֶּ֙נָּה֙ וַיְעַנֶּ֔הָ וַיִּשְׁכַּ֖ב אֹתָֽהּ׃
15 וַיִּשְׂנָאֶ֣הָ אַמְנ֗וֹן שִׂנְאָה֙ גְּדוֹלָ֣ה מְאֹ֔ד כִּ֣י גְדוֹלָ֗ה
הַשִּׂנְאָה֙ אֲשֶׁ֣ר שְׂנֵאָ֔הּ מֵאַהֲבָ֖ה אֲשֶׁ֣ר אֲהֵבָ֑הּ וַיֹּֽאמֶר־
לָ֥הּ אַמְנ֖וֹן ק֥וּמִי לֵֽכִי׃ 16 וַתֹּ֣אמֶר ל֗וֹ אַל־אוֹדֹ֞ת
הָרָעָ֤ה הַגְּדוֹלָה֙ הַזֹּ֔את מֵאַחֶ֛רֶת אֲשֶׁר־עָשִׂ֥יתָ עִמִּ֖י
לְשַׁלְּחֵ֑נִי וְלֹ֥א אָבָ֖ה לִשְׁמֹ֥עַֽ לָֽהּ׃ 17 וַיִּקְרָ֗א אֶת־
נַעֲרוֹ֙ מְשָׁ֣רְת֔וֹ וַיֹּ֕אמֶר שִׁלְחוּ־נָ֥א אֶת־זֹ֛את מֵעָלַ֖י
הַח֑וּצָה וּנְעֹ֥ל הַדֶּ֖לֶת אַחֲרֶֽיהָ׃ 18 וְעָלֶ֙יהָ֙ כְּתֹ֣נֶת
פַּסִּ֔ים כִּי֩ כֵ֨ן תִּלְבַּ֧שְׁןָ בְנוֹת־הַמֶּ֛לֶךְ הַבְּתוּלֹ֖ת מְעִילִ֑ים
וַיֹּצֵ֨א אוֹתָ֤הּ מְשָֽׁרְתוֹ֙ הַח֔וּץ וְנָעַ֥ל הַדֶּ֖לֶת אַחֲרֶֽיהָ׃
19 וַתִּקַּ֨ח תָּמָ֥ר אֵ֙פֶר֙ עַל־רֹאשָׁ֔הּ וּכְתֹ֧נֶת הַפַּסִּ֛ים
אֲשֶׁ֥ר עָלֶ֖יהָ קָרָ֑עָה וַתָּ֤שֶׂם יָדָהּ֙ עַל־רֹאשָׁ֔הּ וַתֵּ֥לֶךְ
הָל֖וֹךְ וְזָעָֽקָה׃ 20 וַיֹּ֨אמֶר אֵלֶ֜יהָ אַבְשָׁל֣וֹם אָחִ֗יהָ
הַאֲמִינ֤וֹן אָחִיךְ֙ הָיָ֣ה עִמָּ֔ךְ וְעַתָּ֤ה אֲחוֹתִי֙ הַחֲרִ֔ישִׁי

hold your peace, my sister. He *is* your brother; do not take this thing to heart." So Tamar remained desolate in her brother Absalom's house.

²¹ But when King David heard of all these things, he was very angry. ²² And Absalom spoke to his brother Amnon neither good nor bad. For Absalom hated Amnon, because he had forced his sister Tamar.

²³ And it came to pass, after two full years, that Absalom had sheepshearers in Baal Hazor, which *is* near Ephraim; so Absalom invited all the king's sons. ²⁴ Then Absalom came to the king and said, "Kindly note, your servant has sheepshearers; please, let the king and his servants go with your servant."

²⁵ But the king said to Absalom, "No, my son, let us not all go now, lest we be a burden to you." Then he urged him, but he would not go; and he blessed him.

²⁶ Then Absalom said, "If not, please let my brother Amnon go with us."

And the king said to him, "Why should he go with you?" ²⁷ But Absalom urged him; so he let Amnon and all the king's sons go with him.

²⁸ Now Absalom had commanded his servants, saying, "Watch now, when Amnon's heart is merry with wine, and when I say to you, 'Strike Amnon!' then kill him. Do not be afraid. Have I not commanded you? Be courageous and valiant." ²⁹ So the servants of Absalom did to Amnon as Absalom had commanded. Then all the king's sons arose, and each one got on his mule and fled.

³⁰ And it came to pass, while they were on the way, that news came to David, saying, "Absalom has killed all the king's sons, and not one of them is left!" ³¹ So the king arose and tore his garments and lay on the ground, and all his servants stood by with their clothes torn. ³² Then Jonadab the son of Shimeah, David's brother, answered and said, "Let not my lord suppose they have killed all the young men, the king's sons, for only Amnon is dead. For by the command of Absalom this has been determined from the day that he forced his sister Tamar. ³³ Now therefore, let not my lord the king take the thing to his heart, to think that all the king's sons are dead. For only Amnon is dead."

³⁴ Then Absalom fled. And the young man who was keeping watch lifted his eyes and looked, and there, many people were coming from the road on the hillside behind him. ³⁵ And Jonadab said to the king, "Look, the king's sons are coming; as your servant said, so it is." ³⁶ So it was, as soon as he had

אָחִיךְ הוּא אַל־תָּשִׁיתִי אֶת־לִבֵּךְ לַדָּבָר הַזֶּה וַתֵּשֶׁב תָּמָר וְשֹׁמֵמָה בֵּית אַבְשָׁלוֹם אָחִיהָ: 21 וְהַמֶּלֶךְ דָּוִד שָׁמַע אֵת כָּל־הַדְּבָרִים הָאֵלֶּה וַיִּחַר לוֹ מְאֹד: 22 וְלֹא־דִבֶּר אַבְשָׁלוֹם עִם־אַמְנוֹן לְמֵרָע וְעַד־טוֹב כִּי־שָׂנֵא אַבְשָׁלוֹם אֶת־אַמְנוֹן עַל־דְּבַר אֲשֶׁר עִנָּה אֵת תָּמָר אֲחֹתוֹ: פ

23 וַיְהִי לִשְׁנָתַיִם יָמִים וַיִּהְיוּ גֹזְזִים לְאַבְשָׁלוֹם בְּבַעַל חָצוֹר אֲשֶׁר עִם־אֶפְרָיִם וַיִּקְרָא אַבְשָׁלוֹם לְכָל־בְּנֵי הַמֶּלֶךְ: 24 וַיָּבֹא אַבְשָׁלוֹם אֶל־הַמֶּלֶךְ וַיֹּאמֶר הִנֵּה־ נָא גֹזְזִים לְעַבְדֶּךָ יֵלֶךְ־נָא הַמֶּלֶךְ וַעֲבָדָיו עִם־עַבְדֶּךָ: 25 וַיֹּאמֶר הַמֶּלֶךְ אֶל־אַבְשָׁלוֹם אַל־בְּנִי אַל־נָא נֵלֵךְ כֻּלָּנוּ וְלֹא נִכְבַּד עָלֶיךָ וַיִּפְרָץ־בּוֹ וְלֹא־אָבָה לָלֶכֶת וַיְבָרֲכֵהוּ: 26 וַיֹּאמֶר אַבְשָׁלוֹם וָלֹא יֵלֶךְ־נָא אִתָּנוּ אַמְנוֹן אָחִי וַיֹּאמֶר לוֹ הַמֶּלֶךְ לָמָּה יֵלֵךְ עִמָּךְ: 27 וַיִּפְרָץ־בּוֹ אַבְשָׁלוֹם וַיִּשְׁלַח אִתּוֹ אֶת־אַמְנוֹן וְאֵת כָּל־בְּנֵי הַמֶּלֶךְ: ס 28 וַיְצַו אַבְשָׁלוֹם אֶת־ נְעָרָיו לֵאמֹר רְאוּ נָא כְּטוֹב לֵב־אַמְנוֹן בַּיַּיִן וְאָמַרְתִּי אֲלֵיכֶם הַכּוּ אֶת־אַמְנוֹן וַהֲמִתֶּם אֹתוֹ אַל־תִּירָאוּ הֲלוֹא כִּי אָנֹכִי צִוִּיתִי אֶתְכֶם חִזְקוּ וִהְיוּ לִבְנֵי־ חָיִל: 29 וַיַּעֲשׂוּ נַעֲרֵי אַבְשָׁלוֹם לְאַמְנוֹן כַּאֲשֶׁר צִוָּה אַבְשָׁלוֹם וַיָּקֻמוּ | כָּל־בְּנֵי הַמֶּלֶךְ וַיִּרְכְּבוּ אִישׁ עַל־פִּרְדּוֹ וַיָּנֻסוּ: 30 וַיְהִי הֵמָּה בַדֶּרֶךְ וְהַשְּׁמֻעָה בָאָה אֶל־דָּוִד לֵאמֹר הִכָּה אַבְשָׁלוֹם אֶת־כָּל־בְּנֵי הַמֶּלֶךְ וְלֹא־נוֹתַר מֵהֶם אֶחָד: ס 31 וַיָּקָם הַמֶּלֶךְ וַיִּקְרַע אֶת־בְּגָדָיו וַיִּשְׁכַּב אָרְצָה וְכָל־עֲבָדָיו נִצָּבִים קְרֻעֵי בְגָדִים: ס 32 וַיַּעַן יוֹנָדָב | בֶּן־שִׁמְעָה אֲחִי־דָוִד וַיֹּאמֶר אַל־יֹאמַר אֲדֹנִי אֵת כָּל־הַנְּעָרִים בְּנֵי־הַמֶּלֶךְ הֵמִיתוּ כִּי־אַמְנוֹן לְבַדּוֹ מֵת כִּי־עַל־פִּי אַבְשָׁלוֹם הָיְתָה שׂוּמָה מִיּוֹם עַנֹּתוֹ אֵת תָּמָר אֲחֹתוֹ: 33 וְעַתָּה אַל־יָשֵׂם אֲדֹנִי הַמֶּלֶךְ אֶל־ לִבּוֹ דָּבָר לֵאמֹר כָּל־בְּנֵי הַמֶּלֶךְ מֵתוּ כִּי־אִם־ אַמְנוֹן לְבַדּוֹ מֵת: פ

34 וַיִּבְרַח אַבְשָׁלוֹם וַיִּשָּׂא הַנַּעַר הַצֹּפֶה אֶת־ עֵינָו וַיַּרְא וְהִנֵּה עַם־רַב הֹלְכִים מִדֶּרֶךְ אַחֲרָיו מִצַּד הָהָר: 35 וַיֹּאמֶר יוֹנָדָב אֶל־הַמֶּלֶךְ הִנֵּה בְנֵי־ הַמֶּלֶךְ בָּאוּ כִּדְבַר עַבְדְּךָ כֵּן הָיָה: 36 וַיְהִי | כְּכַלֹּתוֹ לְדַבֵּר וְהִנֵּה בְנֵי־הַמֶּלֶךְ בָּאוּ וַיִּשְׂאוּ קוֹלָם

finished speaking, that the king's sons indeed came, and they lifted up their voice and wept. Also the king and all his servants wept very bitterly.

37 But Absalom fled and went to Talmai the son of Ammihud, king of Geshur. And *David* mourned for his son every day. 38 So Absalom fled and went to Geshur, and was there three years. 39 And King David longed to go to Absalom. For he had been comforted concerning Amnon, because he was dead.

14 So Joab the son of Zeruiah perceived that the king's heart *was* concerned about Absalom. 2 And Joab sent to Tekoa and brought from there a wise woman, and said to her, "Please pretend to be a mourner, and put on mourning apparel; do not anoint yourself with oil, but act like a woman who has been mourning a long time for the dead. 3 Go to the king and speak to him in this manner." So Joab put the words in her mouth.

4 And when the woman of Tekoa spoke to the king, she fell on her face to the ground and prostrated herself, and said, "Help, O king!"

5 Then the king said to her, "What troubles you?"

And she answered, "Indeed I *am* a widow, my husband is dead. 6 Now your maidservant had two sons; and the two fought with each other in the field, and *there was* no one to part them, but the one struck the other and killed him. 7 And now the whole family has risen up against your maidservant, and they said, 'Deliver him who struck his brother, that we may execute him for the life of his brother whom he killed; and we will destroy the heir also.' So they would extinguish my ember that is left, and leave to my husband *neither* name nor remnant on the earth."

8 Then the king said to the woman, "Go to your house, and I will give orders concerning you."

9 And the woman of Tekoa said to the king, "My lord, O king, *let* the iniquity *be* on me and on my father's house, and the king and his throne *be* guiltless."

10 So the king said, "Whoever says *anything* to you, bring him to me, and he shall not touch you anymore."

11 Then she said, "Please let the king remember the LORD your God, and do not permit the avenger of blood to destroy anymore, lest they destroy my son."

And he said, "*As* the LORD lives, not one hair of your son shall fall to the ground."

12 Therefore the woman said, "Please, let your maidservant speak *another* word to my lord the king."

וַיְכֻלּ וְגַם־הַמֶּלֶךְ וְכָל־עֲבָדָיו בָּכוּ בְּכִי גָּדוֹל
מְאֹד: 37 וְאַבְשָׁלוֹם בָּרַח וַיֵּלֶךְ אֶל־תַּלְמַי בֶּן־
עַמִּיחוּר מֶלֶךְ גְּשׁוּר וַיִּתְאַבֵּל עַל־בְּנוֹ כָּל־הַיָּמִים:
38 וְאַבְשָׁלוֹם בָּרַח וַיֵּלֶךְ גְּשׁוּר וַיְהִי־שָׁם שָׁלֹשׁ
שָׁנִים: 39 וַתְּכַל דָּוִד הַמֶּלֶךְ לָצֵאת אֶל־אַבְשָׁלוֹם
כִּי־נִחַם עַל־אַמְנוֹן כִּי־מֵת: פ

יד וַיֵּדַע יוֹאָב בֶּן־צְרֻיָה כִּי־לֵב הַמֶּלֶךְ עַל־
אַבְשָׁלוֹם: 2 וַיִּשְׁלַח יוֹאָב תְּקוֹעָה וַיִּקַּח מִשָּׁם
אִשָּׁה חֲכָמָה וַיֹּאמֶר אֵלֶיהָ הִתְאַבְּלִי־נָא וְלִבְשִׁי־
נָא בִגְדֵי־אֵבֶל וְאַל־תָּסוּכִי שֶׁמֶן וְהָיִית כְּאִשָּׁה
זֶה יָמִים רַבִּים מִתְאַבֶּלֶת עַל־מֵת: 3 וּבָאת אֶל־
הַמֶּלֶךְ וְדִבַּרְתְּ אֵלָיו כַּדָּבָר הַזֶּה וַיָּשֶׂם יוֹאָב אֶת־
הַדְּבָרִים בְּפִיהָ: 4 וַתֹּאמֶר הָאִשָּׁה הַתְּקֹעִית אֶל־
הַמֶּלֶךְ וַתִּפֹּל עַל־אַפֶּיהָ אַרְצָה וַתִּשְׁתָּחוּ וַתֹּאמֶר
הוֹשִׁעָה הַמֶּלֶךְ: ס 5 וַיֹּאמֶר לָהּ הַמֶּלֶךְ
מַה־לָּךְ וַתֹּאמֶר אֲבָל אִשָּׁה־אַלְמָנָה אָנִי וַיָּמָת
אִישִׁי: 6 וּלְשִׁפְחָתְךָ שְׁנֵי בָנִים וַיִּנָּצוּ שְׁנֵיהֶם בַּשָּׂדֶה
וְאֵין מַצִּיל בֵּינֵיהֶם וַיַּכּוֹ הָאֶחָד אֶת־הָאֶחָד וַיָּמֶת
אֹתוֹ: 7 וְהִנֵּה קָמָה כָל־הַמִּשְׁפָּחָה עַל־שִׁפְחָתְךָ
וַיֹּאמְרוּ תְּנִי ׀ אֶת־מַכֵּה אָחִיו וּנְמִתֵהוּ בְּנֶפֶשׁ אָחִיו
אֲשֶׁר הָרָג וְנַשְׁמִידָה גַּם אֶת־הַיּוֹרֵשׁ וְכִבּוּ אֶת־
גַּחַלְתִּי אֲשֶׁר נִשְׁאָרָה לְבִלְתִּי שׂוּם־לְאִישִׁי
שֵׁם וּשְׁאֵרִית עַל־פְּנֵי הָאֲדָמָה: פ

8 וַיֹּאמֶר הַמֶּלֶךְ אֶל־הָאִשָּׁה לְכִי לְבֵיתֵךְ וַאֲנִי אֲצַוֶּה
עָלָיִךְ: 9 וַתֹּאמֶר הָאִשָּׁה הַתְּקוֹעִית אֶל־הַמֶּלֶךְ עָלַי
אֲדֹנִי הַמֶּלֶךְ הֶעָוֹן וְעַל־בֵּית אָבִי וְהַמֶּלֶךְ וְכִסְאוֹ
נָקִי: ס 10 וַיֹּאמֶר הַמֶּלֶךְ הַמְדַבֵּר אֵלַיִךְ
וַהֲבֵאתוֹ אֵלַי וְלֹא־יֹסִיף עוֹד לָגַעַת בָּךְ: 11 וַתֹּאמֶר
יִזְכָּר־נָא הַמֶּלֶךְ אֶת־יְהוָה אֱלֹהֶיךָ מֵהַרְבִּית גֹּאֵל
הַדָּם לְשַׁחֵת וְלֹא יַשְׁמִידוּ אֶת־בְּנִי וַיֹּאמֶר חַי־
יְהוָה אִם־יִפֹּל מִשַּׂעֲרַת בְּנֵךְ אָרְצָה: 12 וַתֹּאמֶר
הָאִשָּׁה תְּדַבֶּר־נָא שִׁפְחָתְךָ אֶל־אֲדֹנִי הַמֶּלֶךְ דָּבָר

And he said, "Say on."

13 So the woman said: "Why then have you schemed such a thing against the people of God? For the king speaks this thing as one who is guilty, *in that* the king does not bring his banished one home again. 14 For we will surely die and *become* like water spilled on the ground, which cannot be gathered up again. Yet God does not take away a life; but He devises means, so that His banished ones are not expelled from Him. 15 Now therefore, I have come to speak of this thing to my lord the king because the people have made me afraid. And your maidservant said, 'I will now speak to the king; it may be that the king will perform the request of his maidservant. 16 For the king will hear and deliver his maidservant from the hand of the man *who would* destroy me and my son together from the inheritance of God.' 17 Your maidservant said, 'The word of my lord the king will now be comforting; for as the angel of God, so *is* my lord the king in discerning good and evil. And may the LORD your God be with you.'"

18 Then the king answered and said to the woman, "Please do not hide from me anything that I ask you."

And the woman said, "Please, let my lord the king speak."

19 So the king said, "*Is* the hand of Joab with you in all this?" And the woman answered and said, "*As* you live, my lord the king, no one can turn to the right hand or to the left from anything that my lord the king has spoken. For your servant Joab commanded me, and he put all these words in the mouth of your maidservant. 20 To bring about this change of affairs your servant Joab has done this thing; but my lord *is* wise, according to the wisdom of the angel of God, to know everything that *is* in the earth."

21 And the king said to Joab, "All right, I have granted this thing. Go therefore, bring back the young man Absalom."

22 Then Joab fell to the ground on his face and bowed himself, and thanked the king. And Joab said, "Today your servant knows that I have found favor in your sight, my lord, O king, in that the king has fulfilled the request of his servant." 23 So Joab arose and went to Geshur, and brought Absalom to Jerusalem. 24 And the king said, "Let him return to his own house, but do not let him see my face." So Absalom returned to his own house, but did not see the king's face.

25 Now in all Israel there was no one who was praised as much as Absalom for his good looks. From the sole of his foot to the crown of his head

---

וַיֹּאמֶר דַּבֵּרִי: ס 13 וַתֹּאמֶר הָאִשָּׁה וְלָמָה חָשַׁבְתָּה כָּזֹאת עַל־עַם אֱלֹהִים וּמִדַּבֵּר הַמֶּלֶךְ הַדָּבָר הַזֶּה כְּאָשֵׁם לְבִלְתִּי הָשִׁיב הַמֶּלֶךְ אֶת־נִדְּחוֹ: 14 כִּי־מוֹת נָמוּת וְכַמַּיִם הַנִּגָּרִים אַרְצָה אֲשֶׁר לֹא יֵאָסֵפוּ וְלֹא־יִשָּׂא אֱלֹהִים נֶפֶשׁ וְחָשַׁב מַחֲשָׁבוֹת לְבִלְתִּי יִדַּח מִמֶּנּוּ נִדָּח: 15 וְעַתָּה אֲשֶׁר־בָּאתִי לְדַבֵּר אֶל־הַמֶּלֶךְ אֲדֹנִי אֶת־הַדָּבָר הַזֶּה כִּי יֵרְאֻנִי הָעָם וַתֹּאמֶר שִׁפְחָתְךָ אֲדַבְּרָה־נָּא אֶל־הַמֶּלֶךְ אוּלַי יַעֲשֶׂה הַמֶּלֶךְ אֶת־דְּבַר אֲמָתוֹ: 16 כִּי יִשְׁמַע הַמֶּלֶךְ לְהַצִּיל אֶת־אֲמָתוֹ מִכַּף הָאִישׁ לְהַשְׁמִיד אֹתִי וְאֶת־בְּנִי יַחַד מִנַּחֲלַת אֱלֹהִים: 17 וַתֹּאמֶר שִׁפְחָתְךָ יִהְיֶה־נָּא דְּבַר־אֲדֹנִי הַמֶּלֶךְ לִמְנֻחָה כִּי כְּמַלְאַךְ הָאֱלֹהִים כֵּן אֲדֹנִי הַמֶּלֶךְ לִשְׁמֹעַ הַטּוֹב וְהָרָע וַיהוָה אֱלֹהֶיךָ יְהִי עִמָּךְ: פ

18 וַיַּעַן הַמֶּלֶךְ וַיֹּאמֶר אֶל־הָאִשָּׁה אַל־נָא תְכַחֲדִי מִמֶּנִּי דָּבָר אֲשֶׁר אָנֹכִי שֹׁאֵל אֹתָךְ וַתֹּאמֶר הָאִשָּׁה יְדַבֶּר־נָא אֲדֹנִי הַמֶּלֶךְ: 19 וַיֹּאמֶר הַמֶּלֶךְ הֲיַד יוֹאָב אִתָּךְ בְּכָל־זֹאת וַתַּעַן הָאִשָּׁה וַתֹּאמֶר חֵי־ נַפְשְׁךָ אֲדֹנִי הַמֶּלֶךְ אִם־אִשׁ ׀ לְהֵמִין וּלְהַשְׂמִיל מִכֹּל אֲשֶׁר־דִּבֶּר אֲדֹנִי הַמֶּלֶךְ כִּי־עַבְדְּךָ יוֹאָב הוּא צִוָּנִי וְהוּא שָׂם בְּפִי שִׁפְחָתְךָ אֵת כָּל־ הַדְּבָרִים הָאֵלֶּה: 20 לְבַעֲבוּר סַבֵּב אֶת־פְּנֵי הַדָּבָר עָשָׂה עַבְדְּךָ יוֹאָב אֶת־הַדָּבָר הַזֶּה וַאדֹנִי חָכָם כְּחָכְמַת מַלְאַךְ הָאֱלֹהִים לָדַעַת אֶת־כָּל־אֲשֶׁר בָּאָרֶץ: ס 21 וַיֹּאמֶר הַמֶּלֶךְ אֶל־יוֹאָב הִנֵּה־נָא עָשִׂיתִי אֶת־הַדָּבָר הַזֶּה וְלֵךְ הָשֵׁב אֶת־ הַנַּעַר אֶת־אַבְשָׁלוֹם: 22 וַיִּפֹּל יוֹאָב אֶל־פָּנָיו אַרְצָה וַיִּשְׁתַּחוּ וַיְבָרֶךְ אֶת־הַמֶּלֶךְ וַיֹּאמֶר יוֹאָב הַיּוֹם יָדַע עַבְדְּךָ כִּי־מָצָאתִי חֵן בְּעֵינֶיךָ אֲדֹנִי הַמֶּלֶךְ אֲשֶׁר־ עָשָׂה הַמֶּלֶךְ אֶת־דְּבַר עַבְדּוֹᵖ: 23 וַיָּקָם יוֹאָב וַיֵּלֶךְ גְּשׁוּרָה וַיָּבֵא אֶת־אַבְשָׁלוֹם יְרוּשָׁלָ͏ִם: פ

24 וַיֹּאמֶר הַמֶּלֶךְ יִסֹּב אֶל־בֵּיתוֹ וּפָנַי לֹא יִרְאֶה וַיִּסֹּב אַבְשָׁלוֹם אֶל־בֵּיתוֹ וּפְנֵי הַמֶּלֶךְ לֹא רָאָה: ס 25 וּכְאַבְשָׁלוֹם לֹא־הָיָה אִישׁ יָפֶה בְּכָל־יִשְׂרָאֵל לְהַלֵּל מְאֹד מִכַּף רַגְלוֹ וְעַד

there was no blemish in him. 26 And when he cut the hair of his head—at the end of every year he cut *it* because it was heavy on him—when he cut it, he weighed the hair of his head at two hundred shekels according to the king's standard. 27 To Absalom were born three sons, and one daughter whose name *was* Tamar. She was a woman of beautiful appearance.

28 And Absalom dwelt two full years in Jerusalem, but did not see the king's face. 29 Therefore Absalom sent for Joab, to send him to the king, but he would not come to him. And when he sent again the second time, he would not come. 30 So he said to his servants, "See, Joab's field is near mine, and he has barley there; go and set it on fire." And Absalom's servants set the field on fire.

31 Then Joab arose and came to Absalom's house, and said to him, "Why have your servants set my field on fire?"

32 And Absalom answered Joab, "Look, I sent to you, saying, 'Come here, so that I may send you to the king, to say, "Why have I come from Geshur? *It would be* better for me *to be* there still."' Now therefore, let me see the king's face; but if there is iniquity in me, let him execute me."

33 So Joab went to the king and told him. And when he had called for Absalom, he came to the king and bowed himself on his face to the ground before the king. Then the king kissed Absalom.

15 After this it happened that Absalom provided himself with chariots and horses, and fifty men to run before him. 2 Now Absalom would rise early and stand beside the way to the gate. *So* it was, whenever anyone who had a lawsuit came to the king for a decision, that Absalom would call to him and say, "What city *are* you from?" And he would say, "Your servant *is* from such and such a tribe of Israel." 3 Then Absalom would say to him, "Look, your case *is* good and right; but *there is* no deputy of the king to hear you." 4 Moreover Absalom would say, "Oh, that I were made judge in the land, and everyone who has any suit or cause would come to me; then I would give him justice." 5 And *so* it was, whenever anyone came near to bow down to him, that he would put out his hand and take him and kiss him. 6 In this manner Absalom acted toward all Israel who came to the king for judgment. So Absalom stole the hearts of the men of Israel.

7 Now it came to pass after forty years that Absalom said to the king, "Please, let me go to Hebron and pay the vow which I made to the LORD. 8 For your servant took a vow while I dwelt

---

קׇדְקֳדוֹ לֹא־הָיָה בוֹ מוּם: 26 וּבְגַלְּחוֹ אֶת־רֹאשׁוֹ וְהָיָה מִקֵּץ יָמִים | לַיָּמִים אֲשֶׁר יְגַלֵּחַ כִּי־כָבֵד עָלָיו וְגִלְּחוֹ וְשָׁקַל אֶת־שְׂעַר רֹאשׁוֹ מָאתַיִם שְׁקָלִים בְּאֶבֶן הַמֶּלֶךְ: 27 וַיִּוָּלְדוּ לְאַבְשָׁלוֹם שְׁלוֹשָׁה בָנִים וּבַת אַחַת וּשְׁמָהּ תָּמָר הִיא הָיְתָה אִשָּׁה יְפַת מַרְאֶה: פ

28 וַיֵּשֶׁב אַבְשָׁלוֹם בִּירוּשָׁלַ͏ִם שְׁנָתַיִם יָמִים וּפְנֵי הַמֶּלֶךְ לֹא רָאָה: 29 וַיִּשְׁלַח אַבְשָׁלוֹם אֶל־יוֹאָב לִשְׁלֹחַ אֹתוֹ אֶל־הַמֶּלֶךְ וְלֹא אָבָה לָבוֹא אֵלָיו וַיִּשְׁלַח עוֹד שֵׁנִית וְלֹא אָבָה לָבוֹא: 30 וַיֹּאמֶר אֶל־עֲבָדָיו רְאוּ חֶלְקַת יוֹאָב אֶל־יָדִי וְלוֹ־שָׁם שְׂעֹרִים לְכוּ וְהַוצִּתֻהָ בָאֵשׁ וַיַּצִּתוּ עַבְדֵי אַבְשָׁלוֹם אֶת־הַחֶלְקָה בָּאֵשׁ: פ

31 וַיָּקׇם יוֹאָב וַיָּבֹא אֶל־אַבְשָׁלוֹם הַבָּיְתָה וַיֹּאמֶר אֵלָיו לָמָּה הִצִּיתוּ עֲבָדֶךָ אֶת־הַחֶלְקָה אֲשֶׁר־לִי בָּאֵשׁ: 32 וַיֹּאמֶר אַבְשָׁלוֹם אֶל־יוֹאָב הִנֵּה שָׁלַחְתִּי אֵלֶיךָ | לֵאמֹר בֹּא הֵנָּה וְאֶשְׁלְחָה אֹתְךָ אֶל־הַמֶּלֶךְ לֵאמֹר לָמָּה בָּאתִי מִגְּשׁוּר טוֹב לִי עֹד אֲנִי־שָׁם וְעַתָּה אֶרְאֶה פְּנֵי הַמֶּלֶךְ וְאִם־יֶשׁ־בִּי עָוֹן וֶהֱמִתָנִי: 33 וַיָּבֹא יוֹאָב אֶל־הַמֶּלֶךְ וַיַּגֶּד־לוֹ וַיִּקְרָא אֶל־אַבְשָׁלוֹם וַיָּבֹא אֶל־הַמֶּלֶךְ וַיִּשְׁתַּחוּ לוֹ עַל־אַפָּיו אַרְצָה לִפְנֵי הַמֶּלֶךְ וַיִּשַּׁק הַמֶּלֶךְ לְאַבְשָׁלוֹם: פ

טו וַיְהִי מֵאַחֲרֵי כֵן וַיַּעַשׂ לוֹ אַבְשָׁלוֹם מֶרְכָּבָה וְסֻסִים וַחֲמִשִּׁים אִישׁ רָצִים לְפָנָיו: 2 וְהִשְׁכִּים אַבְשָׁלוֹם וְעָמַד עַל־יַד דֶּרֶךְ הַשָּׁעַר וַיְהִי כׇּל־הָאִישׁ אֲשֶׁר־יִהְיֶה־לּוֹ־רִיב לָבוֹא אֶל־הַמֶּלֶךְ לַמִּשְׁפָּט וַיִּקְרָא אַבְשָׁלוֹם אֵלָיו וַיֹּאמֶר אֵי־מִזֶּה עִיר אַתָּה וַיֹּאמֶר מֵאַחַד שִׁבְטֵי־יִשְׂרָאֵל עַבְדֶּךָ: 3 וַיֹּאמֶר אֵלָיו אַבְשָׁלוֹם רְאֵה דְבָרֶךָ טוֹבִים וּנְכֹחִים וְשֹׁמֵעַ אֵין־לְךָ מֵאֵת הַמֶּלֶךְ: 4 וַיֹּאמֶר אַבְשָׁלוֹם מִי־יְשִׂמֵנִי שֹׁפֵט בָּאָרֶץ וְעָלַי יָבוֹא כׇּל־אִישׁ אֲשֶׁר־יִהְיֶה־לּוֹ־רִיב וּמִשְׁפָּט וְהִצְדַּקְתִּיו: 5 וְהָיָה בִּקְרׇב־אִישׁ לְהִשְׁתַּחֲוֺת לוֹ וְשָׁלַח אֶת־יָדוֹ וְהֶחֱזִיק לוֹ וְנָשַׁק לוֹ: 6 וַיַּעַשׂ אַבְשָׁלוֹם כַּדָּבָר הַזֶּה לְכׇל־יִשְׂרָאֵל אֲשֶׁר־יָבֹאוּ לַמִּשְׁפָּט אֶל־הַמֶּלֶךְ וַיְגַנֵּב אַבְשָׁלוֹם אֶת־לֵב אַנְשֵׁי יִשְׂרָאֵל: פ

7 וַיְהִי מִקֵּץ אַרְבָּעִים שָׁנָה וַיֹּאמֶר אַבְשָׁלוֹם אֶל־הַמֶּלֶךְ אֵלְכָה נָּא וַאֲשַׁלֵּם אֶת־נִדְרִי אֲשֶׁר־נָדַרְתִּי לַיהֹוָה בְּחֶבְרוֹן: 8 כִּי־נֵדֶר נָדַר עַבְדְּךָ בְּשִׁבְתִּי

at Geshur in Syria, saying, 'If the LORD indeed
brings me back to Jerusalem, then I will serve the
LORD.' "

9 And the king said to him, "Go in peace." So he
arose and went to Hebron.

10 Then Absalom sent spies throughout all the
tribes of Israel, saying, "As soon as you hear the
sound of the trumpet, then you shall say, 'Absalom
reigns in Hebron!' " 11 And with Absalom went two
hundred men invited from Jerusalem, and they went
along innocently and did not know anything.
12 Then Absalom sent for Ahithophel the Gilonite,
David's counselor, from his city—from Giloh—
while he offered sacrifices. And the conspiracy grew
strong, for the people with Absalom continually
increased in number.

13 Now a messenger came to David, saying, "The
hearts of the men of Israel are with Absalom."

14 So David said to all his servants who were with
him at Jerusalem, "Arise, and let us flee, or we shall
not escape from Absalom. Make haste to depart,
lest he overtake us suddenly and bring disaster
upon us, and strike the city with the edge of the
sword."

15 And the king's servants said to the king, "We
are your servants, ready to do whatever my lord the
king commands." 16 Then the king went out with all
his household after him. But the king left ten
women, concubines, to keep the house. 17 And the
king went out with all the people after him, and
stopped at the outskirts. 18 Then all his servants
passed before him; and all the Cherethites, all the
Pelethites, and all the Gittites, six hundred men who
had followed him from Gath, passed before the
king.

19 Then the king said to Ittai the Gittite, "Why
are you also going with us? Return and remain with
the king. For you are a foreigner and also an exile
from your own place. 20 In fact, you came only
yesterday. Should I make you wander up and down
with us today, since I go I know not where? Return,
and take your brethren back. Mercy and truth be
with you."

21 But Ittai answered the king and said, "As the
LORD lives, and as my lord the king lives, surely in
whatever place my lord the king shall be, whether in
death or life, even there also your servant will be."

22 So David said to Ittai, "Go, and cross over."
Then Ittai the Gittite and all his men and all the
little ones who were with him crossed over. 23 And
all the country wept with a loud voice, and all the
people crossed over. The king himself also crossed
over the Brook Kidron, and all the people crossed
over toward the way of the wilderness.

בִּגְשׁוּר בַּאֲרָם לֵאמֹר אִם־יָשִׁיב [P] יְשִׁיבֵנִי יְהֹוָה
יְרוּשָׁלִַם וְעָבַדְתִּי אֶת־יְהֹוָה: 9 וַיֹּאמֶר־לוֹ הַמֶּלֶךְ לֵךְ
בְּשָׁלוֹם וַיָּקָם וַיֵּלֶךְ חֶבְרוֹנָה: [פ]

10 וַיִּשְׁלַח אַבְשָׁלוֹם מְרַגְּלִים בְּכָל־שִׁבְטֵי יִשְׂרָאֵל
לֵאמֹר כְּשָׁמְעֲכֶם אֶת־קוֹל הַשֹּׁפָר וַאֲמַרְתֶּם מָלַךְ
אַבְשָׁלוֹם בְּחֶבְרוֹן: 11 וְאֶת־אַבְשָׁלוֹם הָלְכוּ מָאתַיִם
אִישׁ מִירוּשָׁלִַם קְרֻאִים וְהֹלְכִים לְתֻמָּם וְלֹא יָדְעוּ
כָּל־דָּבָר: 12 וַיִּשְׁלַח אַבְשָׁלוֹם אֶת־אֲחִיתֹפֶל הַגִּילֹנִי
יוֹעֵץ דָּוִד מֵעִירוֹ מִגִּלֹה בְּזָבְחוֹ אֶת־הַזְּבָחִים וַיְהִי
הַקֶּשֶׁר אַמִּץ וְהָעָם הוֹלֵךְ וָרָב אֶת־אַבְשָׁלוֹם:
13 וַיָּבֹא הַמַּגִּיד אֶל־דָּוִד לֵאמֹר הָיָה לֶב־אִישׁ
יִשְׂרָאֵל אַחֲרֵי אַבְשָׁלוֹם: 14 וַיֹּאמֶר דָּוִד לְכָל־עֲבָדָיו
אֲשֶׁר־אִתּוֹ בִירוּשָׁלִַם קוּמוּ וְנִבְרָחָה כִּי לֹא־תִהְיֶה
לָּנוּ פְלֵיטָה מִפְּנֵי אַבְשָׁלוֹם מַהֲרוּ לָלֶכֶת פֶּן־יְמַהֵר
וְהִשִּׂגָנוּ וְהִדִּיחַ עָלֵינוּ אֶת־הָרָעָה וְהִכָּה הָעִיר
לְפִי־חָרֶב: 15 וַיֹּאמְרוּ עַבְדֵי־הַמֶּלֶךְ אֶל־הַמֶּלֶךְ כְּכֹל
אֲשֶׁר־יִבְחַר אֲדֹנִי הַמֶּלֶךְ הִנֵּה עֲבָדֶיךָ: 16 וַיֵּצֵא
הַמֶּלֶךְ וְכָל־בֵּיתוֹ בְּרַגְלָיו וַיַּעֲזֹב הַמֶּלֶךְ אֵת עֶשֶׂר
נָשִׁים פִּלַגְשִׁים לִשְׁמֹר הַבָּיִת: 17 וַיֵּצֵא הַמֶּלֶךְ
וְכָל־הָעָם בְּרַגְלָיו וַיַּעַמְדוּ בֵּית הַמֶּרְחָק: 18 וְכָל־
עֲבָדָיו עֹבְרִים עַל־יָדוֹ וְכָל־הַכְּרֵתִי וְכָל־הַפְּלֵתִי
וְכָל־הַגִּתִּים שֵׁשׁ־מֵאוֹת אִישׁ אֲשֶׁר־בָּאוּ בְרַגְלוֹ
מִגַּת עֹבְרִים עַל־פְּנֵי הַמֶּלֶךְ: 19 וַיֹּאמֶר הַמֶּלֶךְ אֶל־
אִתַּי הַגִּתִּי לָמָּה תֵלֵךְ גַּם־אַתָּה אִתָּנוּ שׁוּב וְשֵׁב
עִם־הַמֶּלֶךְ כִּי־נָכְרִי אַתָּה וְגַם־גֹּלֶה אַתָּה לִמְקוֹמֶךָ:
20 תְּמוֹל | בּוֹאֶךָ וְהַיּוֹם אֲנֹועֲךָ [P] עִמָּנוּ לָלֶכֶת וַאֲנִי
הוֹלֵךְ עַל אֲשֶׁר־אֲנִי הוֹלֵךְ שׁוּב וְהָשֵׁב אֶת־אַחֶיךָ
עִמָּךְ חֶסֶד וֶאֱמֶת: 21 וַיַּעַן אִתַּי אֶת־הַמֶּלֶךְ וַיֹּאמַר
חַי־יְהֹוָה וְחֵי אֲדֹנִי הַמֶּלֶךְ כִּי אִם [P] בִּמְקוֹם אֲשֶׁר
יִהְיֶה־שָּׁם | אֲדֹנִי הַמֶּלֶךְ אִם־לְמָוֶת אִם־לְחַיִּים
כִּי־שָׁם יִהְיֶה עַבְדֶּךָ: 22 וַיֹּאמֶר דָּוִד אֶל־אִתַּי לֵךְ
וַעֲבֹר וַיַּעֲבֹר אִתַּי הַגִּתִּי וְכָל־אֲנָשָׁיו וְכָל־הַטַּף אֲשֶׁר
אִתּוֹ: 23 וְכָל־הָאָרֶץ בּוֹכִים קוֹל גָּדוֹל וְכָל־הָעָם
עֹבְרִים וְהַמֶּלֶךְ עֹבֵר בְּנַחַל קִדְרוֹן וְכָל־הָעָם עֹבְרִים

טו 8 יָשׁוֹב   20 אֲנֹועֲךָ   21 כתיב ולא קרי

24 There was Zadok also, and all the Levites with him, bearing the ark of the covenant of God. And they set down the ark of God, and Abiathar went up until all the people had finished crossing over from the city. 25 Then the king said to Zadok, "Carry the ark of God back into the city. If I find favor in the eyes of the LORD, He will bring me back and show me *both* it and His dwelling place. 26 But if He says thus: 'I have no delight in you,' here I am, let Him do to me as seems good to Him." 27 The king also said to Zadok the priest, "*Are you not* a seer? Return to the city in peace, and your two sons with you, Ahimaaz your son, and Jonathan the son of Abiathar. 28 See, I will wait in the plains of the wilderness until word comes from you to inform me." 29 Therefore Zadok and Abiathar carried the ark of God back to Jerusalem. And they remained there.

30 So David went up by the Ascent of the *Mount of* Olives, and wept as he went up; and he had his head covered and went barefoot. And all the people who *were* with him covered their heads and went up, weeping as they went up. 31 Then *someone* told David, saying, "Ahithophel *is* among the conspirators with Absalom." And David said, "O LORD, I pray, turn the counsel of Ahithophel into foolishness!"

32 Now it happened when David had come to the top *of the mountain,* where he worshiped God— there was Hushai the Archite coming to meet him with his robe torn and dust on his head. 33 David said to him, "If you go on with me, then you will become a burden to me. 34 But if you return to the city, and say to Absalom, 'I will be your servant, O king; *as* I *was* your father's servant previously, so I *will* now also *be* your servant,' then you may defeat the counsel of Ahithophel for me. 35 And *do* you not *have* Zadok and Abiathar the priests with you there? Therefore it will be *that* whatever you hear from the king's house, you shall tell to Zadok and Abiathar the priests. 36 Indeed *they have* there with them their two sons, Ahimaaz, Zadok's *son,* and Jonathan, Abiathar's *son;* and by them you shall send me everything you hear."

37 So Hushai, David's friend, went into the city. And Absalom came into Jerusalem.

16

When David was a little past the top *of the mountain,* there was Ziba the servant of Mephibosheth, who met him with a couple of saddled donkeys, and on them two hundred *loaves* of bread, one hundred clusters of raisins, one hundred

עַל־פְּנֵי־דֶרֶךְ אֶת־הַמִּדְבָּר׃ 24 וְהִנֵּה גַם־צָדוֹק וְכָל־ הַלְוִיִּם אִתּוֹ נֹשְׂאִים אֶת־אֲרוֹן בְּרִית הָאֱלֹהִים וַיַּצִּקוּ אֶת־אֲרוֹן הָאֱלֹהִים וַיַּעַל אֶבְיָתָר עַד־תֹּם כָּל־הָעָם לַעֲבוֹר מִן־הָעִיר׃ 25 וַיֹּאמֶר הַמֶּלֶךְ לְצָדוֹק הָשֵׁב אֶת־אֲרוֹן הָאֱלֹהִים הָעִיר אִם־אֶמְצָא חֵן בְּעֵינֵי יְהוָה וֶהֱשִׁבַנִי וְהִרְאַנִי אֹתוֹ וְאֶת־נָוֵהוּ׃ 26 וְאִם כֹּה יֹאמַר לֹא חָפַצְתִּי בָּךְ הִנְנִי יַעֲשֶׂה־לִּי כַּאֲשֶׁר טוֹב בְּעֵינָיו׃ ס 27 וַיֹּאמֶר הַמֶּלֶךְ אֶל־צָדוֹק הַכֹּהֵן הֲרוֹאֶה אַתָּה שֻׁבָה הָעִיר בְּשָׁלוֹם וַאֲחִימַעַץ בִּנְךָ וִיהוֹנָתָן בֶּן־אֶבְיָתָר שְׁנֵי בְנֵיכֶם אִתְּכֶם׃ 28 רְאוּ אָנֹכִי מִתְמַהְמֵהַּ בְּעַבְרוֹת הַמִּדְבָּר עַד בּוֹא דָבָר מֵעִמָּכֶם לְהַגִּיד לִי׃ 29 וַיָּשֶׁב צָדוֹק וְאֶבְיָתָר אֶת־ אֲרוֹן הָאֱלֹהִים יְרוּשָׁלִָם וַיֵּשְׁבוּ שָׁם׃ 30 וְדָוִד עֹלֶה בְמַעֲלֵה הַזֵּיתִים עֹלֶה וּבוֹכֶה וְרֹאשׁ לוֹ חָפוּי וְהוּא הֹלֵךְ יָחֵף וְכָל־הָעָם אֲשֶׁר־אִתּוֹ חָפוּ אִישׁ רֹאשׁוֹ וְעָלוּ עָלֹה וּבָכֹה׃ 31 וְדָוִד הִגִּיד לֵאמֹר אֲחִיתֹפֶל בַּקֹּשְׁרִים עִם־אַבְשָׁלוֹם וַיֹּאמֶר דָּוִד סַכֶּל־ נָא אֶת־עֲצַת אֲחִיתֹפֶל יְהוָה׃ 32 וַיְהִי דָוִד בָּא עַד־ הָרֹאשׁ אֲשֶׁר־יִשְׁתַּחֲוֶה שָׁם לֵאלֹהִים וְהִנֵּה לִקְרָאתוֹ חוּשַׁי הָאַרְכִּי קָרוּעַ כֻּתָּנְתּוֹ וַאֲדָמָה עַל־רֹאשׁוֹ׃

33 וַיֹּאמֶר לוֹ דָּוִד אִם עָבַרְתָּ אִתִּי וְהָיִתָ עָלַי לְמַשָּׂא׃ 34 וְאִם־הָעִיר תָּשׁוּב וְאָמַרְתָּ לְאַבְשָׁלוֹם עַבְדְּךָ אֲנִי הַמֶּלֶךְ אֶהְיֶה עֶבֶד אָבִיךָ וַאֲנִי מֵאָז וְעַתָּה וַאֲנִי עַבְדֶּךָ וְהֵפַרְתָּה לִי אֵת עֲצַת אֲחִיתֹפֶל׃ 35 וַהֲלוֹא עִמְּךָ שָׁם צָדוֹק וְאֶבְיָתָר הַכֹּהֲנִים וְהָיָה כָּל־הַדָּבָר אֲשֶׁר תִּשְׁמַע מִבֵּית הַמֶּלֶךְ תַּגִּיד לְצָדוֹק וּלְאֶבְיָתָר הַכֹּהֲנִים׃ 36 הִנֵּה־שָׁם עִמָּם שְׁנֵי בְנֵיהֶם אֲחִימַעַץ לְצָדוֹק וִיהוֹנָתָן לְאֶבְיָתָר וּשְׁלַחְתֶּם בְּיָדָם אֵלַי כָּל־דָּבָר אֲשֶׁר תִּשְׁמָעוּ׃ 37 וַיָּבֹא חוּשַׁי רֵעֶה דָוִד הָעִיר וְאַבְשָׁלֹם יָבֹא יְרוּשָׁלָםִ׃

טז וְדָוִד עָבַר מְעַט מֵהָרֹאשׁ וְהִנֵּה צִיבָא נַעַר מְפִי־בֹשֶׁת לִקְרָאתוֹ וְצֶמֶד חֲמֹרִים חֲבֻשִׁים וַעֲלֵיהֶם מָאתַיִם לֶחֶם וּמֵאָה צִמּוּקִים וּמֵאָה קַיִץ

טז 28 בְּעַרְבוֹת

summer fruits, and a skin of wine. ²And the king said to Ziba, "What do you mean to do with these?"

So Ziba said, "The donkeys *are* for the king's household to ride on, the bread and summer fruit for the young men to eat, and the wine for those who are faint in the wilderness to drink."

³Then the king said, "And where *is* your master's son?"

And Ziba said to the king, "Indeed he is staying in Jerusalem, for he said, 'Today the house of Israel will restore the kingdom of my father to me.'"

⁴So the king said to Ziba, "Here, all that *belongs* to Mephibosheth *is* yours."

And Ziba said, "I humbly bow before you, *that* I may find favor in your sight, my lord, O king!"

⁵Now when King David came to Bahurim, there was a man from the family of the house of Saul, whose name *was* Shimei the son of Gera, coming from there. He came out, cursing continuously as he came. ⁶And he threw stones at David and at all the servants of King David. And all the people and all the mighty men *were* on his right hand and on his left. ⁷Also Shimei said thus when he cursed: "Come out! Come out! You bloodthirsty man, you rogue! ⁸The LORD has brought upon you all the blood of the house of Saul, in whose place you have reigned; and the LORD has delivered the kingdom into the hand of Absalom your son. So now you *are caught* in your own evil, because you are a bloodthirsty man!"

⁹Then Abishai the son of Zeruiah said to the king, "Why should this dead dog curse my lord the king? Please, let me go over and take off his head!"

¹⁰But the king said, "What have I to do with you, you sons of Zeruiah? So let him curse, because the LORD has said to him, 'Curse David.' Who then shall say, 'Why have you done so?'"

¹¹And David said to Abishai and all his servants, "See how my son who came from my own body seeks my life. How much more now *may this* Benjamite? Let him alone, and let him curse; for so the LORD has ordered him. ¹²It may be that the LORD will look on my affliction, and that the LORD will repay me with good for his cursing this day."

¹³And as David and his men went along the road, Shimei went along the hillside opposite him and cursed as he went, threw stones at him and kicked up dust. ¹⁴Now the king and all the people who *were* with him became weary; so they refreshed themselves there.

¹⁵Meanwhile Absalom and all the people, the men of Israel, came to Jerusalem; and Ahithophel *was* with him. ¹⁶And so it was, when Hushai the

וְנֵבֶל יָיִן: 2 וַיֹּאמֶר הַמֶּלֶךְ אֶל־צִיבָא מָה־אֵלֶּה
לָּךְ וַיֹּאמֶר צִיבָא הַחֲמוֹרִים לְבֵית־הַמֶּלֶךְ לִרְכֹּב
וְלַלֶּחֶםᴾ וְהַקַּיִץ לֶאֱכוֹל הַנְּעָרִים וְהַיַּיִן לִשְׁתּוֹת
הַיָּעֵף בַּמִּדְבָּר: 3 וַיֹּאמֶר הַמֶּלֶךְ וְאַיֵּה בֶּן־אֲדֹנֶיךָ
וַיֹּאמֶר צִיבָא אֶל־הַמֶּלֶךְ הִנֵּה יוֹשֵׁב בִּירוּשָׁלִַם כִּי
אָמַר הַיּוֹם יָשִׁיבוּ לִי בֵּית יִשְׂרָאֵל אֵת מַמְלְכוּת
אָבִי: 4 וַיֹּאמֶר הַמֶּלֶךְ לְצִבָא הִנֵּה לְךָ כֹּל אֲשֶׁר
לִמְפִי־בֹשֶׁת וַיֹּאמֶר צִיבָא הִשְׁתַּחֲוֵיתִי אֶמְצָא־חֵן
בְּעֵינֶיךָ אֲדֹנִי הַמֶּלֶךְ: 5 וּבָא הַמֶּלֶךְ דָּוִד עַד־בַּחוּרִים
וְהִנֵּה מִשָּׁם אִישׁ יוֹצֵא מִמִּשְׁפַּחַת בֵּית־שָׁאוּל
וּשְׁמוֹ שִׁמְעִי בֶן־גֵּרָא יֹצֵא יָצוֹא וּמְקַלֵּל: 6 וַיְסַקֵּל
בָּאֲבָנִים אֶת־דָּוִד וְאֶת־כָּל־עַבְדֵי הַמֶּלֶךְ דָּוִד וְכָל־
הָעָם וְכָל־הַגִּבֹּרִים מִימִינוֹ וּמִשְּׂמֹאלוֹ: 7 וְכֹה־אָמַר
שִׁמְעִי בְּקַלְלוֹ צֵא צֵא אִישׁ הַדָּמִים וְאִישׁ הַבְּלִיָּעַל:
8 הֵשִׁיב עָלֶיךָ יְהוָה כֹּל ׀ דְּמֵי בֵית־שָׁאוּל אֲשֶׁר
מָלַכְתָּ תַּחְתָּוᴾ וַיִּתֵּן יְהוָה אֶת־הַמְּלוּכָה בְּיַד
אַבְשָׁלוֹם בְּנֶךָ וְהִנְּךָ בְּרָעָתֶךָ כִּי אִישׁ דָּמִים אָתָּה:
9 וַיֹּאמֶר אֲבִישַׁי בֶּן־צְרוּיָה אֶל־הַמֶּלֶךְ לָמָּה יְקַלֵּל
הַכֶּלֶב הַמֵּת הַזֶּה אֶת־אֲדֹנִי הַמֶּלֶךְ אֶעְבְּרָה־נָּא
וְאָסִירָה אֶת־רֹאשׁוֹ: ס 10 וַיֹּאמֶר הַמֶּלֶךְ
מַה־לִּי וְלָכֶם בְּנֵי צְרֻיָה כִּיᴾ יְקַלֵּל וְכִיᴾ יְהוָה
אָמַר לוֹ קַלֵּל אֶת־דָּוִד וּמִי יֹאמַר מַדּוּעַ עָשִׂיתָה
כֵּן: ס 11 וַיֹּאמֶר דָּוִד אֶל־אֲבִישַׁי וְאֶל־
כָּל־עֲבָדָיו הִנֵּה בְנִי אֲשֶׁר־יָצָא מִמֵּעַי מְבַקֵּשׁ אֶת־
נַפְשִׁי וְאַף כִּי־עַתָּה בֶּן־הַיְמִינִי הַנִּחוּ לוֹ וִיקַלֵּל כִּי
אָמַר־לוֹ יְהוָה: 12 אוּלַי יִרְאֶה יְהוָה בְּעֵינִיᴾ וְהֵשִׁיב
יְהוָה לִי טוֹבָה תַּחַת קִלְלָתוֹ הַיּוֹם הַזֶּה: 13 וַיֵּלֶךְ
דָּוִד וַאֲנָשָׁיו בַּדָּרֶךְ ס וְשִׁמְעִי הֹלֵךְ בְּצֵלַע
הָהָר לְעֻמָּתוֹ הָלוֹךְ וַיְקַלֵּל וַיְסַקֵּל בָּאֲבָנִים לְעֻמָּתוֹ
וְעִפַּר בֶּעָפָר:
פ
14 וַיָּבֹא הַמֶּלֶךְ וְכָל־הָעָם אֲשֶׁר־אִתּוֹ עֲיֵפִים וַיִּנָּפֵשׁ
שָׁם: 15 וְאַבְשָׁלוֹם וְכָל־הָעָם אִישׁ יִשְׂרָאֵל בָּאוּ
יְרוּשָׁלִָם וַאֲחִיתֹפֶל אִתּוֹ: 16 וַיְהִי כַּאֲשֶׁר־בָּא חוּשַׁי
הָאַרְכִּי רֵעֶה דָוִד אֶל־אַבְשָׁלוֹם וַיֹּאמֶר חוּשַׁי אֶל־

טז 2 וְלַלֶּחֶם 8 תַּחְתָּיו 10 כֹּה, כִּי 12 בְּעֵינִי

Archite, David's friend, came to Absalom, that Hushai said to Absalom, "Long live the king! Long live the king!"

17 So Absalom said to Hushai, "Is this your loyalty to your friend? Why did you not go with your friend?"

18 And Hushai said to Absalom, "No, but whom the LORD and this people and all the men of Israel choose, his I will be, and with him I will remain. 19 "Furthermore, whom should I serve? Should I not serve in the presence of his son? As I have served in your father's presence, so will I be in your presence."

20 Then Absalom said to Ahithophel, "Give advice as to what we should do."

21 And Ahithophel said to Absalom, "Go in to your father's concubines, whom he has left to keep the house; and all Israel will hear that you are abhorred by your father. Then the hands of all who are with you will be strong." 22 So they pitched a tent for Absalom on the top of the house, and Absalom went in to his father's concubines in the sight of all Israel.

23 Now the advice of Ahithophel, which he gave in those days, was as if one had inquired at the oracle of God. So was all the advice of Ahithophel both with David and with Absalom.

17 Moreover Ahithophel said to Absalom, "Now let me choose twelve thousand men, and I will arise and pursue David tonight. 2 I will come upon him while he is weary and weak, and make him afraid. And all the people who are with him will flee, and I will strike only the king. 3 Then I will bring back all the people to you. When all return except the man whom you seek, all the people will be at peace." 4 And the saying pleased Absalom and all the elders of Israel.

5 Then Absalom said, "Now call Hushai the Archite also, and let us hear what he says too." 6 And when Hushai came to Absalom, Absalom spoke to him, saying, "Ahithophel has spoken in this manner. Shall we do as he says? If not, speak up."

7 So Hushai said to Absalom: "The advice that Ahithophel has given is not good at this time. 8 For," said Hushai, "you know your father and his men, that they are mighty men, and they are enraged in their minds, like a bear robbed of her cubs in the field; and your father is a man of war, and will not camp with the people. 9 Surely by now he is hidden in some pit, or in some other place. And it will be, when some of them are overthrown at the first, that whoever hears it will say, 'There is a

אַבְשָׁלֹם יְחִי הַמֶּלֶךְ יְחִי הַמֶּלֶךְ: 17 וַיֹּאמֶר אַבְשָׁלֹם אֶל־חוּשַׁי זֶה חַסְדְּךָ אֶת־רֵעֶךָ לָמָּה לֹא־הָלַכְתָּ אֶת־רֵעֶךָ: 18 וַיֹּאמֶר חוּשַׁי אֶל־אַבְשָׁלֹם לֹא כִּי אֲשֶׁר בָּחַר יְהוָה וְהָעָם הַזֶּה וְכָל־אִישׁ יִשְׂרָאֵל לֹא פ אֶהְיֶה וְאִתּוֹ אֵשֵׁב: 19 וְהַשֵּׁנִית לְמִי אֲנִי אֶעֱבֹד הֲלוֹא לִפְנֵי בְנוֹ כַּאֲשֶׁר עָבַדְתִּי לִפְנֵי אָבִיךָ כֵּן אֶהְיֶה לְפָנֶיךָ: פ

20 וַיֹּאמֶר אַבְשָׁלֹם אֶל־אֲחִיתֹפֶל הָבוּ לָכֶם עֵצָה מַה־נַּעֲשֶׂה: 21 וַיֹּאמֶר אֲחִיתֹפֶל אֶל־אַבְשָׁלֹם בּוֹא אֶל־פִּלַגְשֵׁי אָבִיךָ אֲשֶׁר הִנִּיחַ לִשְׁמוֹר הַבַּיִת וְשָׁמַע כָּל־יִשְׂרָאֵל כִּי־נִבְאַשְׁתָּ אֶת־אָבִיךָ וְחָזְקוּ יְדֵי כָּל־ אֲשֶׁר אִתָּךְ: 22 וַיַּטּוּ לְאַבְשָׁלֹם הָאֹהֶל עַל־הַגָּג וַיָּבֹא אַבְשָׁלֹם אֶל־פִּלַגְשֵׁי אָבִיו לְעֵינֵי כָּל־יִשְׂרָאֵל: 23 וַעֲצַת אֲחִיתֹפֶל אֲשֶׁר יָעַץ בַּיָּמִים הָהֵם כַּאֲשֶׁר יִשְׁאַל־ p בִּדְבַר הָאֱלֹהִים כֵּן כָּל־עֲצַת אֲחִיתֹפֶל גַּם־לְדָוִד גַּם לְאַבְשָׁלֹם: ס

יז וַיֹּאמֶר אֲחִיתֹפֶל אֶל־אַבְשָׁלֹם אֶבְחֲרָה נָּא שְׁנֵים־ עָשָׂר אֶלֶף אִישׁ וְאָקוּמָה וְאֶרְדְּפָה אַחֲרֵי־דָוִד הַלָּיְלָה: 2 וְאָבוֹא עָלָיו וְהוּא יָגֵעַ וּרְפֵה יָדַיִם וְהַחֲרַדְתִּי אֹתוֹ וְנָס כָּל־הָעָם אֲשֶׁר־אִתּוֹ וְהִכֵּיתִי אֶת־הַמֶּלֶךְ לְבַדּוֹ: 3 וְאָשִׁיבָה כָל־הָעָם אֵלֶיךָ כְּשׁוּב הַכֹּל הָאִישׁ אֲשֶׁר אַתָּה מְבַקֵּשׁ כָּל־הָעָם יִהְיֶה שָׁלוֹם: 4 וַיִּישַׁר הַדָּבָר בְּעֵינֵי אַבְשָׁלֹם וּבְעֵינֵי כָּל־ זִקְנֵי יִשְׂרָאֵל: ס 5 וַיֹּאמֶר אַבְשָׁלֹם קְרָא נָא גַם לְחוּשַׁי הָאַרְכִּי וְנִשְׁמְעָה מַה־בְּפִיו גַּם־ הוּא: 6 וַיָּבֹא חוּשַׁי אֶל־אַבְשָׁלֹם וַיֹּאמֶר אַבְשָׁלֹם אֵלָיו לֵאמֹר כַּדָּבָר הַזֶּה דִּבֶּר אֲחִיתֹפֶל הֲנַעֲשֶׂה אֶת־דְּבָרוֹ אִם־אַיִן אַתָּה דַבֵּר: ס 7 וַיֹּאמֶר חוּשַׁי אֶל־אַבְשָׁלֹם לֹא־טוֹבָה הָעֵצָה אֲשֶׁר־יָעַץ אֲחִיתֹפֶל בַּפַּעַם הַזֹּאת: 8 וַיֹּאמֶר חוּשַׁי אַתָּה יָדַעְתָּ אֶת־אָבִיךָ וְאֶת־אֲנָשָׁיו כִּי גִבֹּרִים הֵמָּה וּמָרֵי נֶפֶשׁ הֵמָּה כְּדֹב שַׁכּוּל בַּשָּׂדֶה וְאָבִיךָ אִישׁ מִלְחָמָה וְלֹא יָלִין אֶת־הָעָם: 9 הִנֵּה עַתָּה הוּא־נֶחְבָּא בְּאַחַת הַפְּחָתִים אוֹ בְּאַחַד הַמְּקוֹמֹת וְהָיָה כִּנְפֹל בָּהֶם בַּתְּחִלָּה וְשָׁמַע הַשֹּׁמֵעַ וְאָמַר הָיְתָה מַגֵּפָה בָּעָם

slaughter among the people who follow Absalom.'
¹⁰ And even he *who is* valiant, whose heart *is* like the
heart of a lion, will melt completely. For all Israel
knows that your father *is* a mighty man, and *those*
who *are* with him *are* valiant men. ¹¹ Therefore I
advise that all Israel be fully gathered to you, from
Dan to Beersheba, like the sand that *is* by the sea
for multitude, and that you go to battle in person.
¹² So we will come upon him in some place where he
may be found, and we will fall on him as the dew
falls on the ground. And of him and all the men
who *are* with him there shall not be left so much as
one. ¹³ Moreover, if he has withdrawn into a city,
then all Israel shall bring ropes to that city; and we
will pull it into the river, until there is not one small
stone found there."

¹⁴ So Absalom and all the men of Israel said,
"The advice of Hushai the Archite *is* better than the
advice of Ahithophel." For the LORD had purposed
to defeat the good advice of Ahithophel, to the
intent that the LORD might bring disaster on
Absalom.

¹⁵ Then Hushai said to Zadok and Abiathar the
priests, "Thus and so Ahithophel advised Absalom
and the elders of Israel, and thus and so I have
advised. ¹⁶ Now therefore, send quickly and tell
David, saying, 'Do not spend this night in the plains
of the wilderness, but speedily cross over, lest the
king and all the people who *are* with him be
swallowed up.'" ¹⁷ Now Jonathan and Ahimaaz
stayed at En Rogel, for they dared not be seen
coming into the city; so a female servant would
come and tell them, and they would go and tell
King David. ¹⁸ Nevertheless a lad saw them, and
told Absalom. But both of them went away quickly
and came to a man's house in Bahurim, who had a
well in his court; and they went down into it.
¹⁹ Then the woman took and spread a covering over
the well's mouth, and spread ground grain on it;
and the thing was not known. ²⁰ And when
Absalom's servants came to the woman at the
house, they said, "Where *are* Ahimaaz and
Jonathan?"

So the woman said to them, "They have gone
over the water brook."

And when they had searched and could not find
them, they returned to Jerusalem. ²¹ Now it came to
pass, after they had departed, that they came up out
of the well and went and told King David, and said
to David, "Arise and cross over the water quickly.
For thus has Ahithophel advised against you." ²² So
David and all the people who *were* with him arose

אֲשֶׁר אַחֲרֵי אַבְשָׁלֽוֹם: 10 וְהוּא גַם־בֶּן־חַ֫יִל אֲשֶׁר
לִבּוֹ כְּלֵב הָאַרְיֵ֖ה הִמֵּ֣ס יִמָּ֑ס כִּי־יֹדֵ֙עַ֙ כָּל־יִשְׂרָאֵ֔ל
כִּי־גִבּ֣וֹר אָבִ֔יךָ וּבְנֵי־חַ֖יִל אֲשֶׁ֥ר אִתּֽוֹ: 11 כִּ֣י יָעַ֡צְתִּי
הֵ֠אָסֹף יֵאָסֵ֙ף עָלֶ֤יךָ כָל־יִשְׂרָאֵל֙ מִדָּן֙ וְעַד־בְּאֵ֣ר שֶׁ֔בַע
כַּח֛וֹל אֲשֶׁר־עַל־הַיָּ֖ם לָרֹ֑ב וּפָנֶ֥יךָ הֹלְכִ֖ים בַּקְרָֽב:
12 וּבָ֣אנוּ אֵלָ֗יו בְּאַחַ֤ת הַמְּקוֹמֹת֙ אֲשֶׁ֣ר נִמְצָ֣א שָׁ֔ם
וְנַ֣חְנוּ עָלָ֔יו כַּאֲשֶׁ֛ר יִפֹּ֥ל הַטַּ֖ל עַל־הָאֲדָמָ֑ה וְלֹֽא־נ֤וֹתַר
בּוֹ֙ וּבְכָל־הָאֲנָשִׁ֣ים אֲשֶׁר־אִתּ֔וֹ גַּם־אֶחָֽד: 13 וְאִם־
אֶל־עִ֣יר יֵֽאָסֵ֔ף וְהִשִּׂ֧יאוּ כָל־יִשְׂרָאֵ֛ל אֶל־הָעִ֥יר הַהִ֖יא
חֲבָלִ֑ים וְסָחַ֤בְנוּ אֹתוֹ֙ עַד־הַנַּ֔חַל עַ֛ד אֲשֶׁר־לֹֽא־נִמְצָ֥א
שָׁ֖ם גַּם־צְרֽוֹר: ף

14 וַיֹּ֤אמֶר אַבְשָׁלוֹם֙ וְכָל־אִ֣ישׁ יִשְׂרָאֵ֔ל טוֹבָ֗ה עֲצַ֤ת
חוּשַׁ֣י הָאַרְכִּ֔י מֵעֲצַ֖ת אֲחִיתֹ֑פֶל וַיהֹוָ֣ה צִוָּ֗ה לְהָפֵ֞ר
אֶת־עֲצַ֤ת אֲחִיתֹ֙פֶל֙ הַטּוֹבָ֔ה לְבַֽעֲב֗וּר הָבִ֤יא יְהֹוָה֙
אֶל־אַבְשָׁל֔וֹם אֶת־הָרָעָֽה: ס 15 וַיֹּ֣אמֶר
חוּשַׁ֗י אֶל־צָד֤וֹק וְאֶל־אֶבְיָתָר֙ הַכֹּ֣הֲנִ֔ים כָּזֹ֤את וְכָזֹאת֙
יָעַ֣ץ אֲחִיתֹ֔פֶל אֶת־אַבְשָׁלֹ֖ם וְאֵ֣ת זִקְנֵ֣י יִשְׂרָאֵ֑ל
וְכָזֹ֥את וְכָזֹ֖את יָעַ֥צְתִּי אָֽנִי: 16 וְעַתָּ֡ה שִׁלְח֣וּ מְהֵרָה֩
וְהַגִּ֨ידוּ לְדָוִ֜ד לֵאמֹ֗ר אַל־תָּ֤לֶן הַלַּ֙יְלָה֙ בְּעַֽרְב֣וֹת
הַמִּדְבָּ֔ר וְגַ֖ם עָב֣וֹר תַּעֲב֑וֹר פֶּ֚ן יְבֻלַּ֣ע לַמֶּ֔לֶךְ
וּלְכָל־הָעָ֖ם אֲשֶׁ֥ר אִתּֽוֹ: 17 וִיהוֹנָתָ֨ן וַאֲחִימַ֜עַץ
עֹמְדִ֣ים בְּעֵין־רֹגֵ֗ל וְהָלְכָ֤ה הַשִּׁפְחָה֙ וְהִגִּ֣ידָה לָהֶ֔ם
וְהֵם֙ יֵֽלְכ֔וּ וְהִגִּ֖ידוּ לַמֶּ֣לֶךְ דָּוִ֑ד כִּ֣י לֹ֤א יֽוּכְלוּ֙
לְהֵרָא֔וֹת לָב֖וֹא הָעִֽירָה: 18 וַיַּ֤רְא אֹתָם֙ נַ֔עַר
וַיַּגֵּ֖ד לְאַבְשָׁלֹ֑ם וַיֵּלְכוּ֩ שְׁנֵיהֶ֨ם מְהֵרָ֜ה וַיָּבֹ֣אוּ ׀
אֶל־בֵּֽית־אִ֣ישׁ בְּבַֽחוּרִ֗ים וְל֥וֹ בְאֵ֛ר בַּחֲצֵר֖וֹ וַיֵּ֥רְדוּ
שָֽׁם: 19 וַתִּקַּ֣ח הָֽאִשָּׁ֗ה וַתִּפְרֹ֤שׂ אֶת־הַמָּסָךְ֙ עַל־
פְּנֵ֣י הַבְּאֵ֔ר וַתִּשְׁטַ֥ח עָלָ֖יו הָֽרִפ֑וֹת וְלֹ֥א נוֹדַ֖ע
דָּבָֽר: 20 וַיָּבֹ֣אוּ עַבְדֵ֣י אַבְשָׁל֩וֹם אֶל־הָאִשָּׁ֨ה הַבַּ֜יְתָה
וַיֹּֽאמְר֗וּ אַיֵּ֤ה אֲחִימַ֙עַץ֙ וִיה֣וֹנָתָ֔ן וַתֹּ֤אמֶר לָהֶם֙ הָֽאִשָּׁ֔ה
עָבְר֖וּ מִיכַ֣ל הַמָּ֑יִם וַיְבַקְשׁוּ֙ וְלֹ֣א מָצָ֔אוּ וַיָּשֻׁ֖בוּ
יְרוּשָׁלָֽ͏ִם: ס 21 וַיְהִ֣י ׀ אַחֲרֵ֣י לֶכְתָּ֗ם וַֽיַּעֲלוּ֙
מֵֽהַבְּאֵ֔ר וַיֵּֽלְכ֗וּ וַיַּגִּ֙דוּ֙ לַמֶּ֣לֶךְ דָּוִ֔ד וַיֹּֽאמְר֣וּ אֶל־
דָּוִ֔ד ק֣וּמוּ וְעִבְר֤וּ מְהֵרָה֙ אֶת־הַמַּ֔יִם כִּי־כָ֛כָה יָעַ֥ץ
עֲלֵיכֶ֖ם אֲחִיתֹֽפֶל: 22 וַיָּ֣קָם דָּוִ֗ד וְכָל־הָעָם֙ אֲשֶׁ֣ר

and crossed over the Jordan. By morning light not one of them was left who had not gone over the Jordan.

23 Now when Ahithophel saw that his advice was not followed, he saddled a donkey, and arose and went home to his house, to his city. Then he put his household in order, and hanged himself, and died; and he was buried in his father's tomb.

24 Then David went to Mahanaim. And Absalom crossed over the Jordan, he and all the men of Israel with him. 25 And Absalom made Amasa captain of the army instead of Joab. This Amasa was the son of a man whose name was Jithra, an Israelite, who had gone in to Abigail the daughter of Nahash, sister of Zeruiah, Joab's mother. 26 So Israel and Absalom encamped in the land of Gilead.

27 Now it happened, when David had come to Mahanaim, that Shobi the son of Nahash from Rabbah of the people of Ammon, Machir the son of Ammiel from Lo Debar, and Barzillai the Gileadite from Rogelim, 28 brought beds and basins, earthen vessels and wheat, barley and flour, parched *grain* and beans, lentils and parched *seeds*, 29 honey and curds, sheep and cheese of the herd, for David and the people who *were* with him to eat. For they said, "The people are hungry and weary and thirsty in the wilderness."

18 And David numbered the people who *were* with him, and set captains of thousands and captains of hundreds over them. 2 Then David sent out one third of the people under the hand of Joab, one third under the hand of Abishai the son of Zeruiah, Joab's brother, and one third under the hand of Ittai the Gittite. And the king said to the people, "I also will surely go out with you myself."

3 But the people answered, "You shall not go out! For if we flee away, they will not care about us; nor if half of us die, will they care about us. But *you are* worth ten thousand of us now. For you are now more help to us in the city."

4 Then the king said to them, "Whatever seems best to you I will do." So the king stood beside the gate, and all the people went out by hundreds and by thousands. 5 Now the king had commanded Joab, Abishai, and Ittai, saying, "*Deal* gently for my sake with the young man Absalom." And all the people heard when the king gave all the captains orders concerning Absalom.

6 So the people went out into the field of battle against Israel. And the battle was in the woods of Ephraim. 7 The people of Israel were overthrown there before the servants of David, and a great slaughter of twenty thousand took place there that

אֹתֹו וַיַּעַבְרוּ אֶת־הַיַּרְדֵּן עַד־אֹור הַבֹּקֶר עַד־אַחַד לֹא נֶעְדָּר אֲשֶׁר לֹא־עָבַר אֶת־הַיַּרְדֵּן: 23 וַאֲחִיתֹפֶל רָאָה כִּי לֹא נֶעֶשְׂתָה עֲצָתֹו וַיַּחֲבֹשׁ אֶת־הַחֲמֹור וַיָּקָם וַיֵּלֶךְ אֶל־בֵּיתֹו אֶל־עִירֹו וַיְצַו אֶל־בֵּיתֹו וַיֵּחָנַק וַיָּמָת וַיִּקָּבֵר בְּקֶבֶר אָבִיו: ס 24 וְדָוִד בָּא מַחֲנָיְמָה וְאַבְשָׁלֹם עָבַר אֶת־הַיַּרְדֵּן הוּא וְכָל־אִישׁ יִשְׂרָאֵל עִמֹּו: 25 וְאֶת־עֲמָשָׂא שָׂם אַבְשָׁלֹם תַּחַת יֹואָב עַל־הַצָּבָא וַעֲמָשָׂא בֶן־אִישׁ וּשְׁמֹו יִתְרָא הַיִּשְׂרְאֵלִי אֲשֶׁר־בָּא אֶל־אֲבִיגַל בַּת־נָחָשׁ אֲחֹות צְרוּיָה אֵם יֹואָב: 26 וַיִּחַן יִשְׂרָאֵל וְאַבְשָׁלֹם אֶרֶץ הַגִּלְעָד: ס 27 וַיְהִי כְּבֹוא דָוִד מַחֲנָיְמָה וְשֹׁבִי בֶן־נָחָשׁ מֵרַבַּת בְּנֵי־עַמֹּון וּמָכִיר בֶּן־עַמִּיאֵל מִלֹּא דְבָר וּבַרְזִלַּי הַגִּלְעָדִי מֵרֹגְלִים: 28 מִשְׁכָּב וְסַפֹּות וּכְלִי יֹוצֵר וְחִטִּים וּשְׂעֹרִים וְקֶמַח וְקָלִי וּפֹול וַעֲדָשִׁים וְקָלִי: 29 וּדְבַשׁ וְחֶמְאָה וְצֹאן וּשְׁפֹות בָּקָר הִגִּישׁוּ לְדָוִד וְלָעָם אֲשֶׁר־אִתֹּו לֶאֱכֹול כִּי אָמְרוּ הָעָם רָעֵב וְעָיֵף וְצָמֵא בַּמִּדְבָּר:

יח וַיִּפְקֹד דָּוִד אֶת־הָעָם אֲשֶׁר אִתֹּו וַיָּשֶׂם עֲלֵיהֶם שָׂרֵי אֲלָפִים וְשָׂרֵי מֵאֹות: 2 וַיְשַׁלַּח דָּוִד אֶת־הָעָם הַשְּׁלִשִׁית בְּיַד־יֹואָב וְהַשְּׁלִשִׁית בְּיַד אֲבִישַׁי בֶּן־צְרוּיָה אֲחִי יֹואָב וְהַשְּׁלִשִׁת בְּיַד אִתַּי הַגִּתִּי ס וַיֹּאמֶר הַמֶּלֶךְ אֶל־הָעָם יָצֹא אֵצֵא גַם־אֲנִי עִמָּכֶם: 3 וַיֹּאמֶר הָעָם לֹא תֵצֵא כִּי אִם־נֹס נָנוּס לֹא־יָשִׂימוּ אֵלֵינוּ לֵב וְאִם־ יָמֻתוּ חֶצְיֵנוּ לֹא־יָשִׂימוּ אֵלֵינוּ לֵב כִּי־עַתָּה כָמֹנוּ עֲשָׂרָה אֲלָפִים וְעַתָּה טֹוב כִּי־תִהְיֶה־לָּנוּ מֵעִיר לַעְזֹור: ס 4 וַיֹּאמֶר אֲלֵיהֶם הַמֶּלֶךְ אֲשֶׁר־יִיטַב בְּעֵינֵיכֶם אֶעֱשֶׂה וַיַּעֲמֹד הַמֶּלֶךְ אֶל־יַד הַשַּׁעַר וְכָל־ הָעָם יָצְאוּ לְמֵאֹות וְלַאֲלָפִים: 5 וַיְצַו הַמֶּלֶךְ אֶת־ יֹואָב וְאֶת־אֲבִישַׁי וְאֶת־אִתַּי לֵאמֹר לְאַט־לִי לַנַּעַר לְאַבְשָׁלֹום וְכָל־הָעָם שָׁמְעוּ בְּצַוֹּת הַמֶּלֶךְ אֶת־כָּל־ הַשָּׂרִים עַל־דְּבַר אַבְשָׁלֹום: 6 וַיֵּצֵא הָעָם הַשָּׂדֶה לִקְרַאת יִשְׂרָאֵל וַתְּהִי הַמִּלְחָמָה בְּיַעַר אֶפְרָיִם: 7 וַיִּנָּגְפוּ שָׁם עַם יִשְׂרָאֵל לִפְנֵי עַבְדֵי דָוִד וַתְּהִי

day. ⁸ For the battle there was scattered over the face of the whole countryside, and the woods devoured more people that day than the sword devoured.

⁹ Then Absalom met the servants of David. Absalom rode on a mule. The mule went under the thick boughs of a great terebinth tree, and his head caught in the terebinth; so he was left hanging between heaven and earth. And the mule which *was* under him went on. ¹⁰ Now a certain man saw *it* and told Joab, and said, "I just saw Absalom hanging in a terebinth tree!"

¹¹ So Joab said to the man who told him, "You just saw *him!* And why did you not strike him there to the ground? I would have given you ten *shekels* of silver and a belt."

¹² But the man said to Joab, "Though I were to receive a thousand *shekels* of silver in my hand, I would not raise my hand against the king's son. For in our hearing the king commanded you and Abishai and Ittai, saying, 'Beware lest anyone *touch* the young man Absalom!' ¹³ Otherwise I would have dealt falsely against my own life. For there is nothing hidden from the king, and you yourself would have set yourself against *me.*"

¹⁴ Then Joab said, "I cannot linger with you." And he took three spears in his hand and thrust them through Absalom's heart, while he was *still* alive in the midst of the terebinth tree. ¹⁵ And ten young men who bore Joab's armor surrounded Absalom, and struck and killed him.

¹⁶ So Joab blew the trumpet, and the people returned from pursuing Israel. For Joab held back the people. ¹⁷ And they took Absalom and cast him into a large pit in the woods, and laid a very large heap of stones over him. Then all Israel fled, everyone to his tent.

¹⁸ Now Absalom in his lifetime had taken and set up a pillar for himself, which *is* in the King's Valley. For he said, "I have no son to keep my name in remembrance." He called the pillar after his own name. And to this day it is called Absalom's Monument.

¹⁹ Then Ahimaaz the son of Zadok said, "Let me run now and take the news to the king, how the LORD has avenged him of his enemies."

²⁰ And Joab said to him, "You shall not take the news this day, for you shall take the news another day. But today you shall take no news, because the king's son is dead." ²¹ Then Joab said to the Cushite, "Go, tell the king what you have seen." So the Cushite bowed himself to Joab and ran.

שָׁם הַמַּגֵּפָה גְדוֹלָה בַּיּוֹם הַהוּא עֶשְׂרִים אָלֶף: 8 וַתְּהִי־שָׁם הַמִּלְחָמָה נָפֹצֵית ᴾ עַל־פְּנֵי כָל־הָאָרֶץ וַיֶּרֶב הַיַּעַר לֶאֱכֹל בָּעָם מֵאֲשֶׁר אָכְלָה הַחֶרֶב בַּיּוֹם הַהוּא: 9 וַיִּקָּרֵא אַבְשָׁלוֹם לִפְנֵי עַבְדֵי דָוִד וְאַבְשָׁלוֹם רֹכֵב עַל־הַפֶּרֶד וַיָּבֹא הַפֶּרֶד תַּחַת שׂוֹבֶךְ הָאֵלָה הַגְּדוֹלָה וַיֶּחֱזַק רֹאשׁוֹ בָאֵלָה וַיֻּתַּן בֵּין הַשָּׁמַיִם וּבֵין הָאָרֶץ וְהַפֶּרֶד אֲשֶׁר־תַּחְתָּיו עָבָר: 10 וַיַּרְא אִישׁ אֶחָד וַיַּגֵּד לְיוֹאָב וַיֹּאמֶר הִנֵּה רָאִיתִי אֶת־אַבְשָׁלִם תָּלוּי בָּאֵלָה: 11 וַיֹּאמֶר יוֹאָב לָאִישׁ הַמַּגִּיד לוֹ וְהִנֵּה רָאִיתָ וּמַדּוּעַ לֹא־הִכִּיתוֹ שָׁם אָרְצָה וְעָלַי לָתֶת לְךָ עֲשָׂרָה כֶסֶף וַחֲגֹרָה אֶחָת: 12 וַיֹּאמֶר הָאִישׁ אֶל־יוֹאָב וְלֹא ᴾ אָנֹכִי שֹׁקֵל עַל־כַּפִּי אֶלֶף כֶּסֶף לֹא־אֶשְׁלַח יָדִי אֶל־בֶּן־הַמֶּלֶךְ כִּי בְאָזְנֵינוּ צִוָּה הַמֶּלֶךְ אֹתְךָ וְאֶת־אֲבִישַׁי וְאֶת־אִתַּי לֵאמֹר שִׁמְרוּ־מִי בַּנַּעַר בְּאַבְשָׁלוֹם: 13 אוֹ־עָשִׂיתִי בְנַפְשׁוֹ ᴾ שֶׁקֶר וְכָל־דָּבָר לֹא־יִכָּחֵד מִן־הַמֶּלֶךְ וְאַתָּה תִּתְיַצֵּב מִנֶּגֶד: 14 וַיֹּאמֶר יוֹאָב לֹא־כֵן אֹחִילָה לְפָנֶיךָ וַיִּקַּח שְׁלֹשָׁה שְׁבָטִים בְּכַפּוֹ וַיִּתְקָעֵם בְּלֵב אַבְשָׁלוֹם עוֹדֶנּוּ חַי בְּלֵב הָאֵלָה: 15 וַיָּסֹבּוּ עֲשָׂרָה נְעָרִים נֹשְׂאֵי כְּלֵי יוֹאָב וַיַּכּוּ אֶת־אַבְשָׁלוֹם וַיְמִיתֻהוּ: 16 וַיִּתְקַע יוֹאָב בַּשֹּׁפָר וַיָּשָׁב הָעָם מִרְדֹף אַחֲרֵי יִשְׂרָאֵל כִּי־חָשַׂךְ יוֹאָב אֶת־הָעָם: 17 וַיִּקְחוּ אֶת־אַבְשָׁלוֹם וַיַּשְׁלִיכוּ אֹתוֹ בַיַּעַר אֶל־הַפַּחַת הַגָּדוֹל וַיַּצִּבוּ עָלָיו גַּל־אֲבָנִים גָּדוֹל מְאֹד וְכָל־יִשְׂרָאֵל נָסוּ אִישׁ לְאֹהָלָו ᴾ: ס 18 וְאַבְשָׁלֹם לָקַח וַיַּצֶּב־לוֹ בְחַיָּו ᴾ אֶת־מַצֶּבֶת אֲשֶׁר בְּעֵמֶק־הַמֶּלֶךְ כִּי אָמַר אֵין־לִי בֵן בַּעֲבוּר הַזְכִּיר שְׁמִי וַיִּקְרָא לַמַּצֶּבֶת עַל־שְׁמוֹ וַיִּקָּרֵא לָהּ יַד אַבְשָׁלֹם עַד הַיּוֹם הַזֶּה: ס 19 וַאֲחִימַעַץ בֶּן־צָדוֹק אָמַר אָרוּצָה נָּא וַאֲבַשְּׂרָה אֶת־הַמֶּלֶךְ כִּי־שְׁפָטוֹ יְהוָה מִיַּד אֹיְבָיו: 20 וַיֹּאמֶר לוֹ יוֹאָב לֹא אִישׁ בְּשֹׂרָה אַתָּה הַיּוֹם הַזֶּה וּבִשַּׂרְתָּ בְּיוֹם אַחֵר וְהַיּוֹם הַזֶּה לֹא תְבַשֵּׂר כִּי־עַל ᴾ בֶּן־הַמֶּלֶךְ מֵת: 21 וַיֹּאמֶר יוֹאָב לַכּוּשִׁי לֵךְ הַגֵּד לַמֶּלֶךְ אֲשֶׁר רָאִיתָה וַיִּשְׁתַּחוּ

יח 8 נָפֹצֶת 12 וְלֹא 13 בְנַפְשִׁי 17 לְאֹהָלָיו
18 בְּחַיָּיו 20 כֵּן

22 And Ahimaaz the son of Zadok said again to
Joab, "But whatever happens, please let me also
run after the Cushite."

So Joab said, "Why will you run, my son, since
you have no news ready?"

23 "But whatever happens," *he said,* "let me run."

So he said to him, "Run." Then Ahimaaz ran by
way of the plain, and outran the Cushite.

24 Now David was sitting between the two gates.
And the watchman went up to the roof over the
gate, to the wall, lifted his eyes and looked, and
there was a man, running alone. 25 Then the
watchman cried out and told the king. And the
king said, "If he *is* alone, *there is* news in his
mouth." And he came rapidly and drew near.

26 Then the watchman saw *another* man running,
and the watchman called to the gatekeeper and
said, "There is *another* man, running alone!"

And the king said, "He also brings news."

27 So the watchman said, "I think the running of
the first is like the running of Ahimaaz the son of
Zadok."

And the king said, "He *is* a good man, and comes
with good news."

28 So Ahimaaz called out and said to the king,
"All is well!" Then he bowed down with his face to
the earth before the king, and said, "Blessed *be* the
LORD your God, who has delivered up the men who
raised their hand against my lord the king!"

29 The king said, "Is the young man Absalom
safe?"

Ahimaaz answered, "When Joab sent the king's
servant and *me* your servant, I saw a great tumult,
but I did not know what *it was about.*"

30 And the king said, "Turn aside *and* stand
here." So he turned aside and stood still.

31 Just then the Cushite came, and the Cushite
said, "There is good news, my lord the king! For the
LORD has avenged you this day of all those who
rose against you."

32 And the king said to the Cushite, "Is the young
man Absalom safe?"

So the Cushite answered, "May the enemies of
my lord the king, and all who rise against you to do
harm, be like *that* young man!"

33 Then the king was deeply moved, and went up
to the chamber over the gate, and wept. And as he
went, he said thus: "O my son Absalom—my son,
my son Absalom—if only I had died in your place!
O Absalom my son, my son!"

19

And Joab was told, "Behold, the king is
weeping and mourning for Absalom." 2 So the
victory that day was *turned* into mourning for all

כּוּשִׁי לְיוֹאָב וַיָּרֹץ: 22 וַיֹּסֶף עוֹד אֲחִימַעַץ בֶּן־צָדוֹק
וַיֹּאמֶר אֶל־יוֹאָב וִיהִי מָה אָרֻצָה־נָּא גַם־אָנִי אַחֲרֵי
הַכּוּשִׁי וַיֹּאמֶר יוֹאָב לָמָה־זֶּה אַתָּה רָץ בְּנִי וּלְכָה
אֵין־בְּשׂוֹרָה מֹצֵאת: 23 וִיהִי־מָה אָרוּץ וַיֹּאמֶר לוֹ
רוּץ וַיָּרָץ אֲחִימַעַץ דֶּרֶךְ הַכִּכָּר וַיַּעֲבֹר אֶת־הַכּוּשִׁי:
24 וְדָוִד יוֹשֵׁב בֵּין־שְׁנֵי הַשְּׁעָרִים וַיֵּלֶךְ הַצֹּפֶה אֶל־
גַּג הַשַּׁעַר אֶל־הַחוֹמָה וַיִּשָּׂא אֶת־עֵינָיו וַיַּרְא וְהִנֵּה־
אִישׁ רָץ לְבַדּוֹ: 25 וַיִּקְרָא הַצֹּפֶה וַיַּגֵּד לַמֶּלֶךְ
וַיֹּאמֶר הַמֶּלֶךְ אִם־לְבַדּוֹ בְּשׂוֹרָה בְּפִיו וַיֵּלֶךְ הָלוֹךְ
וְקָרֵב: 26 וַיַּרְא הַצֹּפֶה אִישׁ־אַחֵר רָץ וַיִּקְרָא הַצֹּפֶה
אֶל־הַשֹּׁעֵר וַיֹּאמֶר הִנֵּה־אִישׁ רָץ לְבַדּוֹ וַיֹּאמֶר
הַמֶּלֶךְ גַּם־זֶה מְבַשֵּׂר: 27 וַיֹּאמֶר הַצֹּפֶה אֲנִי רֹאֶה
אֶת־מְרוּצַת הָרִאשׁוֹן כִּמְרֻצַת אֲחִימַעַץ בֶּן־צָדוֹק
וַיֹּאמֶר הַמֶּלֶךְ אִישׁ־טוֹב זֶה וְאֶל־בְּשׂוֹרָה טוֹבָה
יָבוֹא: 28 וַיִּקְרָא אֲחִימַעַץ וַיֹּאמֶר אֶל־הַמֶּלֶךְ שָׁלוֹם
וַיִּשְׁתַּחוּ לַמֶּלֶךְ לְאַפָּיו אָרְצָה ס וַיֹּאמֶר
בָּרוּךְ יְהוָה אֱלֹהֶיךָ אֲשֶׁר סִגַּר אֶת־הָאֲנָשִׁים אֲשֶׁר־
נָשְׂאוּ אֶת־יָדָם בַּאדֹנִי הַמֶּלֶךְ: 29 וַיֹּאמֶר הַמֶּלֶךְ
שָׁלוֹם לַנַּעַר לְאַבְשָׁלוֹם וַיֹּאמֶר אֲחִימַעַץ רָאִיתִי
הֶהָמוֹן הַגָּדוֹל לִשְׁלֹחַ אֶת־עֶבֶד הַמֶּלֶךְ יוֹאָב וְאֶת־
עַבְדֶּךָ וְלֹא יָדַעְתִּי מָה: 30 וַיֹּאמֶר הַמֶּלֶךְ סֹב
הִתְיַצֵּב כֹּה וַיִּסֹּב וַיַּעֲמֹד: 31 וְהִנֵּה הַכּוּשִׁי בָּא
וַיֹּאמֶר הַכּוּשִׁי יִתְבַּשֵּׂר אֲדֹנִי הַמֶּלֶךְ כִּי־שְׁפָטְךָ יְהוָה
הַיּוֹם מִיַּד כָּל־הַקָּמִים עָלֶיךָ: ס 32 וַיֹּאמֶר
הַמֶּלֶךְ אֶל־הַכּוּשִׁי הֲשָׁלוֹם לַנַּעַר לְאַבְשָׁלוֹם וַיֹּאמֶר
הַכּוּשִׁי יִהְיוּ כַנַּעַר אֹיְבֵי אֲדֹנִי הַמֶּלֶךְ וְכֹל אֲשֶׁר־
קָמוּ עָלֶיךָ לְרָעָה: ס

יט וַיֻּרְגַּז הַמֶּלֶךְ וַיַּעַל עַל־עֲלִיַּת הַשַּׁעַר וַיֵּבְךְּ
וְכֹה ׀ אָמַר בְּלֶכְתּוֹ בְּנִי אַבְשָׁלוֹם בְּנִי בְנִי אַבְשָׁלוֹם
מִי־יִתֵּן מוּתִי אֲנִי תַחְתֶּיךָ אַבְשָׁלוֹם בְּנִי בְנִי: 2 וַיֻּגַּד
לְיוֹאָב הִנֵּה הַמֶּלֶךְ בֹּכֶה וַיִּתְאַבֵּל עַל־אַבְשָׁלוֹם:
3 וַתְּהִי הַתְּשֻׁעָה בַּיּוֹם הַהוּא לְאֵבֶל לְכָל־הָעָם
כִּי־שָׁמַע הָעָם בַּיּוֹם הַהוּא לֵאמֹר נֶעֱצַב הַמֶּלֶךְ

the people. For the people heard it said that day,
"The king is grieved for his son." ³And the people
stole back into the city that day, as people who are
ashamed steal away when they flee in battle. ⁴But
the king covered his face, and the king cried out
with a loud voice, "O my son Absalom! O
Absalom, my son, my son!"

⁵Then Joab came into the house to the king, and
said, "Today you have disgraced all your servants
who today have saved your life, the lives of your
sons and daughters, the lives of your wives and the
lives of your concubines, ⁶in that you love your
enemies and hate your friends. For you have
declared today that you regard neither princes nor
servants; for today I perceive that if Absalom had
lived and all of us had died today, then it would
have pleased you well. ⁷Now therefore, arise, go
out and speak comfort to your servants. For I
swear by the LORD, if you do not go out, not one
will stay with you this night. And that will be worse
for you than all the evil that has befallen you from
your youth until now." ⁸Then the king arose and
sat in the gate. And they told all the people, saying,
"There is the king, sitting in the gate." So all the
people came before the king.

For everyone of Israel had fled to his tent.

⁹Now all the people were in a dispute throughout
all the tribes of Israel, saying, "The king saved us
from the hand of our enemies, he delivered us from
the hand of the Philistines, and now he has fled
from the land because of Absalom. ¹⁰But Absalom,
whom we anointed over us, has died in battle. Now
therefore, why do you say nothing about bringing
back the king?"

¹¹So King David sent to Zadok and Abiathar the
priests, saying, "Speak to the elders of Judah,
saying, 'Why are you the last to bring the king back
to his house, since the words of all Israel have come
to the king, to his *very* house? ¹²You *are* my
brethren, you *are* my bone and my flesh. Why then
are you the last to bring back the king?' ¹³And say
to Amasa, '*Are* you not my bone and my flesh? God
do so to me, and more also, if you are not
commander of the army before me continually in
place of Joab.'" ¹⁴So he swayed the hearts of all the
men of Judah, just as *the heart of* one man, so that
they sent *this word* to the king: "Return, you and all
your servants!"

¹⁵Then the king returned and came to the
Jordan. And Judah came to Gilgal, to go to meet
the king, to escort the king across the Jordan.
¹⁶And Shimei the son of Gera, a Benjamite, who
was from Bahurim, hurried and came down with
the men of Judah to meet King David. ¹⁷*There were*

עַל־בְּנֽוֹ׃ 4 וַיִּתְגַּנֵּב הָעָם בַּיּוֹם הַהוּא לָבוֹא הָעִיר
כַּאֲשֶׁר יִתְגַּנֵּב הָעָם הַנִּכְלָמִים בְּנוּסָם בַּמִּלְחָמָֽה׃
5 וְהַמֶּלֶךְ לָאַט אֶת־פָּנָיו וַיִּזְעַק הַמֶּלֶךְ קוֹל גָּדוֹל בְּנִי
אַבְשָׁלוֹם אַבְשָׁלוֹם בְּנִי בְנִֽי׃ ס 6 וַיָּבֹא
יוֹאָב אֶל־הַמֶּלֶךְ הַבָּיִת וַיֹּאמֶר הֹבַשְׁתָּ הַיּוֹם אֶת־
פְּנֵי כָל־עֲבָדֶיךָ הַֽמְמַלְּטִים אֶת־נַפְשְׁךָ הַיּוֹם וְאֵת
נֶפֶשׁ בָּנֶיךָ וּבְנֹתֶיךָ וְנֶפֶשׁ נָשֶׁיךָ וְנֶפֶשׁ פִּלַגְשֶֽׁיךָ׃
7 לְאַהֲבָה אֶת־שֹׂנְאֶיךָ וְלִשְׂנֹא אֶת־אֹהֲבֶיךָ כִּי ׀
הִגַּדְתָּ הַיּוֹם כִּי אֵין לְךָ שָׂרִים וַעֲבָדִים כִּי ׀
יָדַעְתִּי הַיּוֹם כִּי לֹא ⁵אַבְשָׁלוֹם חַי וְכֻלָּנוּ הַיּוֹם
מֵתִים כִּי־אָז יָשָׁר בְּעֵינֶֽיךָ׃ 8 וְעַתָּה קוּם צֵא
וְדַבֵּר עַל־לֵב עֲבָדֶיךָ כִּי בַיהֹוָה נִשְׁבַּעְתִּי כִּי־
אֵינְךָ יוֹצֵא אִם־יָלִין אִישׁ אִתְּךָ הַלַּיְלָה וְרָעָה
לְךָ זֹאת מִכָּל־הָרָעָה אֲשֶׁר־בָּאָה עָלֶיךָ מִנְּעֻרֶיךָ
עַד־עָֽתָּה׃ ס 9 וַיָּקָם הַמֶּלֶךְ וַיֵּשֶׁב בַּשָּׁעַר
וּֽלְכָל־הָעָם הִגִּידוּ לֵאמֹר הִנֵּה הַמֶּלֶךְ יוֹשֵׁב בַּשַּׁעַר
וַיָּבֹא כָל־הָעָם לִפְנֵי הַמֶּלֶךְ וְיִשְׂרָאֵל נָס אִישׁ
לְאֹהָלָֽיו׃ ס 10 וַיְהִי כָל־הָעָם נָדוֹן בְּכָל־
שִׁבְטֵי יִשְׂרָאֵל לֵאמֹר הַמֶּלֶךְ הִצִּילָנוּ ׀ מִכַּף אֹיְבֵינוּ
וְהוּא מִלְּטָנוּ מִכַּף פְּלִשְׁתִּים וְעַתָּה בָּרַח מִן־הָאָרֶץ
מֵעַל אַבְשָׁלֽוֹם׃ 11 וְאַבְשָׁלוֹם אֲשֶׁר מָשַׁחְנוּ עָלֵינוּ
מֵת בַּמִּלְחָמָה וְעַתָּה לָמָה אַתֶּם מַחֲרִשִׁים לְהָשִׁיב
אֶת־הַמֶּֽלֶךְ׃ ס 12 וְהַמֶּלֶךְ דָּוִד שָׁלַח אֶל־
צָדוֹק וְאֶל־אֶבְיָתָר הַכֹּהֲנִים לֵאמֹר דַּבְּרוּ אֶל־זִקְנֵי
יְהוּדָה לֵאמֹר לָמָּה תִהְיוּ אַחֲרֹנִים לְהָשִׁיב אֶת־
הַמֶּלֶךְ אֶל־בֵּיתוֹ וּדְבַר כָּל־יִשְׂרָאֵל בָּא אֶל־הַמֶּלֶךְ
אֶל־בֵּיתֽוֹ׃ 13 אַחַי אַתֶּם עַצְמִי וּבְשָׂרִי אַתֶּם וְלָמָּה
תִהְיוּ אַחֲרֹנִים לְהָשִׁיב אֶת־הַמֶּֽלֶךְ׃ 14 וְלַעֲמָשָׂא
תֹּמְרוּ הֲלוֹא עַצְמִי וּבְשָׂרִי אָתָּה כֹּה יַעֲשֶׂה־
לִּי אֱלֹהִים וְכֹה יֹסִיף אִם־לֹא שַׂר־צָבָא תִּהְיֶה
לְפָנַי כָּל־הַיָּמִים תַּחַת יוֹאָֽב׃ 15 וַיַּט אֶת־לְבַב
כָּל־אִישׁ־יְהוּדָה כְּאִישׁ אֶחָד וַיִּשְׁלְחוּ אֶל־הַמֶּלֶךְ
שׁוּב אַתָּה וְכָל־עֲבָדֶֽיךָ׃ 16 וַיָּשָׁב הַמֶּלֶךְ וַיָּבֹא עַד־
הַיַּרְדֵּן וִיהוּדָה בָּא הַגִּלְגָּלָה לָלֶכֶת לִקְרַאת הַמֶּלֶךְ
לְהַעֲבִיר אֶת־הַמֶּלֶךְ אֶת־הַיַּרְדֵּֽן׃ 17 וַיְמַהֵר שִׁמְעִי
בֶן־גֵּרָא בֶּן־הַיְמִינִי אֲשֶׁר מִבַּחוּרִים וַיֵּרֶד עִם־אִישׁ
יְהוּדָה לִקְרַאת הַמֶּלֶךְ דָּוִֽד׃ 18 וְאֶלֶף אִישׁ עִמּוֹ

יט 7 לֹו

a thousand men of Benjamin with him, and Ziba the servant of the house of Saul, and his fifteen sons and his twenty servants with him; and they went over the Jordan before the king. 18 Then a ferryboat went across to carry over the king's household, and to do what he thought good.

Now Shimei the son of Gera fell down before the king when he had crossed the Jordan. 19 Then he said to the king, "Do not let my lord impute iniquity to me, or remember what wrong your servant did on the day that my lord the king left Jerusalem, that the king should take it to heart. 20 For I, your servant, know that I have sinned. Therefore here I am, the first to come today of all the house of Joseph to go down to meet my lord the king."

21 But Abishai the son of Zeruiah answered and said, "Shall not Shimei be put to death for this, because he cursed the LORD's anointed?"

22 And David said, "What have I to do with you, you sons of Zeruiah, that you should be adversaries to me today? Shall any man be put to death today in Israel? For do I not know that today I am king over Israel?" 23 Therefore the king said to Shimei, "You shall not die." And the king swore to him.

24 Now Mephibosheth the son of Saul came down to meet the king. And he had not cared for his feet, nor trimmed his mustache, nor washed his clothes, from the day the king departed until the day he returned in peace. 25 So it was, when he had come to Jerusalem to meet the king, that the king said to him, "Why did you not go with me, Mephibosheth?"

26 And he answered, "My lord, O king, my servant deceived me. For your servant said, 'I will saddle a donkey for myself, that I may ride on it and go to the king,' because your servant is lame. 27 And he has slandered your servant to my lord the king, but my lord the king is like the angel of God. Therefore do what is good in your eyes. 28 For all my father's house were but dead men before my lord the king. Yet you set your servant among those who eat at your own table. Therefore what right have I still to cry out anymore to the king?"

29 So the king said to him, "Why do you speak anymore of your matters? I have said, 'You and Ziba divide the land.'"

30 Then Mephibosheth said to the king, "Rather, let him take it all, inasmuch as my lord the king has come back in peace to his own house."

31 And Barzillai the Gileadite came down from Rogelim and went across the Jordan with the king, to escort him across the Jordan. 32 Now Barzillai was a very aged man, eighty years old. And he had

מִבִּנְיָמִן וְצִיבָא נַעַר בֵּית שָׁאוּל וַחֲמֵשֶׁת עָשָׂר בָּנָיו
וְעֶשְׂרִים עֲבָדָיו אִתּוֹ וְצָלְחוּ הַיַּרְדֵּן לִפְנֵי הַמֶּלֶךְ: 19 וְעָבְרָה הָעֲבָרָה לַעֲבִיר אֶת־בֵּית הַמֶּלֶךְ וְלַעֲשׂוֹת הַטּוֹב בְּעֵינָיו וְשִׁמְעִי בֶן־גֵּרָא נָפַל לִפְנֵי הַמֶּלֶךְ בְּעָבְרוֹ בַּיַּרְדֵּן: 20 וַיֹּאמֶר אֶל־הַמֶּלֶךְ אַל־יַחֲשָׁב־לִי אֲדֹנִי עָוֹן וְאַל־תִּזְכֹּר אֵת אֲשֶׁר הֶעֱוָה עַבְדְּךָ בַּיּוֹם אֲשֶׁר־יָצָא אֲדֹנִי־הַמֶּלֶךְ מִירוּשָׁלִָם לָשׂוּם הַמֶּלֶךְ אֶל־לִבּוֹ: 21 כִּי יָדַע עַבְדְּךָ כִּי אֲנִי חָטָאתִי וְהִנֵּה־בָאתִי הַיּוֹם רִאשׁוֹן לְכָל־בֵּית יוֹסֵף לָרֶדֶת לִקְרַאת אֲדֹנִי הַמֶּלֶךְ: ס 22 וַיַּעַן אֲבִישַׁי בֶּן־צְרוּיָה וַיֹּאמֶר הֲתַחַת זֹאת לֹא יוּמַת שִׁמְעִי כִּי קִלֵּל אֶת־מְשִׁיחַ יְהוָה: 23 וַיֹּאמֶר דָּוִד מַה־לִּי וְלָכֶם בְּנֵי צְרוּיָה כִּי־תִהְיוּ־לִי הַיּוֹם לְשָׂטָן הַיּוֹם יוּמַת אִישׁ בְּיִשְׂרָאֵל כִּי הֲלוֹא יָדַעְתִּי כִּי הַיּוֹם אֲנִי־מֶלֶךְ עַל־יִשְׂרָאֵל: 24 וַיֹּאמֶר הַמֶּלֶךְ אֶל־שִׁמְעִי לֹא תָמוּת וַיִּשָּׁבַע לוֹ הַמֶּלֶךְ: ס 25 וּמְפִבֹשֶׁת בֶּן־שָׁאוּל יָרַד לִקְרַאת הַמֶּלֶךְ וְלֹא־עָשָׂה רַגְלָיו וְלֹא־עָשָׂה שְׂפָמוֹ וְאֶת־בְּגָדָיו לֹא כִבֵּס לְמִן־הַיּוֹם לֶכֶת הַמֶּלֶךְ עַד־הַיּוֹם אֲשֶׁר־בָּא בְשָׁלוֹם: 26 וַיְהִי כִּי־בָא יְרוּשָׁלִַם לִקְרַאת הַמֶּלֶךְ וַיֹּאמֶר לוֹ הַמֶּלֶךְ לָמָּה לֹא־הָלַכְתָּ עִמִּי מְפִיבֹשֶׁת: 27 וַיֹּאמַר אֲדֹנִי הַמֶּלֶךְ עַבְדִּי רִמָּנִי כִּי־אָמַר עַבְדְּךָ אֶחְבְּשָׁה־לִּי הַחֲמוֹר וְאֶרְכַּב עָלֶיהָ וְאֵלֵךְ אֶת־הַמֶּלֶךְ כִּי פִסֵּחַ עַבְדֶּךָ: 28 וַיְרַגֵּל בְּעַבְדְּךָ אֶל־אֲדֹנִי הַמֶּלֶךְ וַאדֹנִי הַמֶּלֶךְ כְּמַלְאַךְ הָאֱלֹהִים וַעֲשֵׂה הַטּוֹב בְּעֵינֶיךָ: 29 כִּי לֹא הָיָה כָּל־בֵּית אָבִי כִּי אִם־אַנְשֵׁי־מָוֶת לַאדֹנִי הַמֶּלֶךְ וַתָּשֶׁת אֶת־עַבְדְּךָ בְּאֹכְלֵי שֻׁלְחָנֶךָ וּמַה־יֶּשׁ־לִי עוֹד צְדָקָה וְלִזְעֹק עוֹד אֶל־הַמֶּלֶךְ: פ 30 וַיֹּאמֶר לוֹ הַמֶּלֶךְ לָמָּה תְּדַבֵּר עוֹד דְּבָרֶיךָ אָמַרְתִּי אַתָּה וְצִיבָא תַּחְלְקוּ אֶת־הַשָּׂדֶה: 31 וַיֹּאמֶר מְפִיבֹשֶׁת אֶל־הַמֶּלֶךְ גַּם אֶת־הַכֹּל יִקָּח אַחֲרֵי אֲשֶׁר־בָּא אֲדֹנִי הַמֶּלֶךְ בְּשָׁלוֹם אֶל־בֵּיתוֹ: ס 32 וּבַרְזִלַּי הַגִּלְעָדִי יָרַד מֵרֹגְלִים וַיַּעֲבֹר אֶת־הַמֶּלֶךְ הַיַּרְדֵּן לְשַׁלְּחוֹ אֶת־בַּיַּרְדֵּן: 33 וּבַרְזִלַּי זָקֵן מְאֹד בֶּן־שְׁמֹנִים שָׁנָה וְהוּא־כִלְכַּל

provided the king with supplies while he stayed at Mahanaim, for he *was* a very rich man. 33 And the king said to Barzillai, "Come across with me, and I will provide for you while you are with me in Jerusalem."

34 But Barzillai said to the king, "How long have I to live, that I should go up with the king to Jerusalem? 35 I *am* today eighty years old. Can I discern between the good and bad? Can your servant taste what I eat or what I drink? Can I hear any longer the voice of singing men and singing women? Why then should your servant be a further burden to my lord the king? 36 Your servant will go a little way across the Jordan with the king. And why should the king repay me *with* such a reward? 37 Please let your servant turn back again, that I may die in my own city, near the grave of my father and mother. But here is your servant Chimham; let him cross over with my lord the king, and do for him what seems good to you."

38 And the king answered, "Chimham shall cross over with me, and I will do for him what seems good to you. Now whatever you request of me, I will do for you." 39 Then all the people went over the Jordan. And when the king had crossed over, the king kissed Barzillai and blessed him, and he returned to his own place.

40 Now the king went on to Gilgal, and Chimham went on with him. And all the people of Judah escorted the king, and also half the people of Israel.

41 Just then all the men of Israel came to the king, and said to the king, "Why have our brethren, the men of Judah, stolen you away and brought the king, his household, and all David's men with him across the Jordan?"

42 So all the men of Judah answered the men of Israel, "Because the king *is* a close relative of ours. Why then are you angry over this matter? Have we ever eaten at the king's *expense?* Or has he given us any gift?"

43 And the men of Israel answered the men of Judah, and said, "We have ten shares in the king; therefore we also have more *right* to David than you. Why then do you despise us—were we not the first to advise bringing back our king?"

Yet the words of the men of Judah were fiercer than the words of the men of Israel.

20 And there happened to be there a rebel, whose name *was* Sheba the son of Bichri, a Benjamite. And he blew a trumpet, and said:

"We have no share in David,
    Nor do we have inheritance in the son of Jesse;
    Every man to his tents, O Israel!"

אֶת־הַמֶּ֨לֶךְ֙ בְּשִׁיבָת֣וֹ בְמַחֲנַ֔יִם כִּי־אִ֛ישׁ גָּד֥וֹל ה֖וּא מְאֹֽד: 34 וַיֹּ֥אמֶר הַמֶּ֖לֶךְ אֶל־בַּרְזִלָּ֑י אַתָּה֙ עֲבֹ֣ר אִתִּ֔י וְכִלְכַּלְתִּ֥י אֹתְךָ֛ עִמָּדִ֖י בִּירוּשָׁלָ͏ִם: 35 וַיֹּ֥אמֶר בַּרְזִלַּ֖י אֶל־הַמֶּ֑לֶךְ כַּמָּ֗ה יְמֵי֙ שְׁנֵ֣י חַיַּ֔י כִּי־אֶעֱלֶ֥ה אֶת־הַמֶּ֖לֶךְ יְרוּשָׁלָ͏ִם: 36 בֶּן־שְׁמֹנִ֣ים שָׁנָה֮ אָנֹכִי֒ הַיּ֗וֹם הַאֵדַ֤ע ׀ בֵּין־ט֣וֹב לְרָ֔ע אִם־יִטְעַ֤ם עַבְדְּךָ֙ אֶת־אֲשֶׁ֤ר אֹכַל֙ וְאֶת־אֲשֶׁ֣ר אֶשְׁתֶּ֔ה אִם־אֶשְׁמַ֣ע ע֗וֹד בְּק֛וֹל שָׁרִ֖ים וְשָׁר֑וֹת וְלָ֩מָּה֩ יִֽהְיֶ֨ה עַבְדְּךָ֥ ע֛וֹד לְמַשָּׂ֖א אֶל־אֲדֹנִ֥י הַמֶּֽלֶךְ: 37 כִּמְעַ֞ט יַעֲבֹ֧ר עַבְדְּךָ֛ אֶת־הַיַּרְדֵּ֖ן אֶת־הַמֶּ֑לֶךְ וְלָ֙מָּה֙ יִגְמְלֵ֣נִי הַמֶּ֔לֶךְ הַגְּמוּלָ֖ה הַזֹּֽאת: 38 יָֽשׇׁב־נָ֤א עַבְדְּךָ֙ וְאָמֻ֣ת בְּעִירִ֔י עִ֛ם קֶ֥בֶר אָבִ֖י וְאִמִּ֑י וְהִנֵּ֣ה ׀ עַבְדְּךָ֣ כִמְהָ֗ם יַֽעֲבֹר֙ עִם־אֲדֹנִ֣י הַמֶּ֔לֶךְ וַעֲשֵׂה־ל֕וֹ אֵ֥ת אֲשֶׁר־ט֖וֹב בְּעֵינֶֽיךָ: ס 39 וַיֹּ֣אמֶר הַמֶּ֗לֶךְ אִתִּי֙ יַעֲבֹ֣ר כִּמְהָ֔ם וַאֲנִי֙ אֶעֱשֶׂה־לּ֔וֹ אֶת־הַטּ֖וֹב בְּעֵינֶ֑יךָ וְכֹ֧ל אֲשֶׁר־תִּבְחַ֛ר עָלַ֖י אֶֽעֱשֶׂה־לָּֽךְ: 40 וַיַּעֲבֹ֧ר כׇּל־הָעָ֛ם אֶת־הַיַּרְדֵּ֖ן וְהַמֶּ֣לֶךְ עָבָ֑ר וַיִּשַּׁ֨ק הַמֶּ֤לֶךְ לְבַרְזִלַּי֙ וַיְבָ֣רְכֵ֔הוּ וַיָּ֖שׇׁב לִמְקֹמֽוֹ: ס 41 וַיַּעֲבֹ֤ר הַמֶּ֙לֶךְ֙ הַגִּלְגָּ֔לָה וְכִמְהָ֖ן עָבַ֣ר עִמּ֑וֹ וְכׇל־עַ֤ם יְהוּדָה֙ וַיַּעֲבִ֣רוּ אֶת־הַמֶּ֔לֶךְ וְגַ֕ם חֲצִ֖י עַ֥ם יִשְׂרָאֵֽל: 42 וְהִנֵּ֛ה כׇּל־אִ֥ישׁ יִשְׂרָאֵ֖ל בָּאִ֣ים אֶל־הַמֶּ֑לֶךְ וַיֹּאמְר֣וּ אֶל־הַמֶּ֡לֶךְ מַדּ֩וּעַ֩ גְּנָב֨וּךָ אַחֵ֜ינוּ אִ֣ישׁ יְהוּדָ֗ה וַיַּעֲבִ֨רוּ אֶת־הַמֶּ֤לֶךְ וְאֶת־בֵּיתוֹ֙ אֶת־הַיַּרְדֵּ֔ן וְכׇל־אַנְשֵׁ֥י דָוִ֖ד עִמּֽוֹ: ס 43 וַיַּ֣עַן כׇּל־אִ֣ישׁ יְהוּדָה֮ עַל־אִ֣ישׁ יִשְׂרָאֵל֒ כִּֽי־קָר֤וֹב הַמֶּ֙לֶךְ֙ אֵלַ֔י וְלָ֤מָּה זֶּה֙ חָ֣רָה לְךָ֔ עַל־הַדָּבָ֖ר הַזֶּ֑ה הֶאָכ֤וֹל אָכַ֙לְנוּ֙ מִן־הַמֶּ֔לֶךְ אִם־נִשֵּׂ֖את נִשָּׂ֥א לָֽנוּ: ס 44 וַיַּ֨עַן אִֽישׁ־יִשְׂרָאֵ֜ל אֶת־אִ֣ישׁ יְהוּדָ֗ה וַיֹּ֙אמֶר֙ עֶ֣שֶׂר יָד֥וֹת לִ֣י בַמֶּ֘לֶךְ֮ וְגַם־בְּדָוִד֮ אֲנִ֣י מִמְּךָ֒ וּמַדּ֙וּעַ֙ הֱקִלֹּתַ֔נִי וְלֹא־הָיָ֨ה דְבָרִ֥י רִאשׁ֛וֹן לִ֖י לְהָשִׁ֣יב אֶת־מַלְכִּ֑י וַיִּ֙קֶשׁ֙ דְּבַר־אִ֣ישׁ יְהוּדָ֔ה מִדְּבַ֖ר אִ֥ישׁ יִשְׂרָאֵֽל: ס

כ וְשָׁ֙ם נִקְרָ֜א אִ֣ישׁ בְּלִיַּ֗עַל וּשְׁמ֛וֹ שֶׁ֥בַע בֶּן־בִּכְרִ֖י אִ֣ישׁ יְמִינִ֑י וַיִּתְקַ֣ע בַּשֹּׁפָ֗ר וַיֹּ֙אמֶר֙ אֵֽין־לָ֜נוּ חֵ֣לֶק בְּדָוִ֗ד וְלֹ֤א נַחֲלָה־לָ֙נוּ֙ בְּבֶן־יִשַׁ֔י אִ֥ישׁ לְאֹהָלָ֖יו

² So every man of Israel deserted David, *and* followed Sheba the son of Bichri. But the men of Judah, from the Jordan as far as Jerusalem, remained loyal to their king.

³ Now David came to his house at Jerusalem. And the king took the ten women, his concubines whom he had left to keep the house, and put them in seclusion and supported them, but did not go in to them. So they were shut up to the day of their death, living in widowhood.

⁴ And the king said to Amasa, "Assemble the men of Judah for me within three days, and be present here yourself." ⁵ So Amasa went to assemble *the men of* Judah. But he delayed longer than the set time which David had appointed him. ⁶ And David said to Abishai, "Now Sheba the son of Bichri will do us more harm than Absalom. Take your lord's servants and pursue him, lest he find for himself fortified cities, and escape us." ⁷ So Joab's men, with the Cherethites, the Pelethites, and all the mighty men, went out after him. And they went out of Jerusalem to pursue Sheba the son of Bichri. ⁸ When they *were* at the large stone which *is* in Gibeon, Amasa came before them. Now Joab was dressed in battle armor; on it was a belt *with* a sword fastened in its sheath at his hips; and as he was going forward, it fell out. ⁹ Then Joab said to Amasa, "*Are* you in health, my brother?" And Joab took Amasa by the beard with his right hand to kiss him. ¹⁰ But Amasa did not notice the sword that *was* in Joab's hand. And he struck him with it in the stomach, and his entrails poured out on the ground; and he did not *strike* him again. Thus he died.

Then Joab and Abishai his brother pursued Sheba the son of Bichri. ¹¹ Meanwhile one of Joab's men stood near Amasa, and said, "Whoever favors Joab and whoever *is* for David—follow Joab!" ¹² But Amasa wallowed in *his* blood in the middle of the highway. And when the man saw that all the people stood still, he moved Amasa from the highway to the field and threw a garment over him, when he saw that everyone who came upon him halted. ¹³ When he was removed from the highway, all the people went on after Joab to pursue Sheba the son of Bichri.

¹⁴ And he went through all the tribes of Israel to Abel and Beth Maachah and all the Berites. So they were gathered together and also went after *Sheba.* ¹⁵ Then they came and besieged him in Abel of Beth Maachah; and they cast up a siege mound against the city, and it stood by the rampart. And all the people who *were* with Joab battered the wall to throw it down.

ישראל: 2 וַיַּעַל כָּל־אִישׁ יִשְׂרָאֵל מֵאַחֲרֵי דָוִד אַחֲרֵי שֶׁבַע בֶּן־בִּכְרִי וְאִישׁ יְהוּדָה דָּבְקוּ בְמַלְכָּם מִן־הַיַּרְדֵּן וְעַד־יְרוּשָׁלִָם: 3 וַיָּבֹא דָוִד אֶל־בֵּיתוֹ יְרוּשָׁלַם וַיִּקַּח הַמֶּלֶךְ אֵת עֶשֶׂר־נָשִׁים פִּלַגְשִׁים אֲשֶׁר הִנִּיחַ לִשְׁמֹר הַבַּיִת וַיִּתְּנֵם בֵּית־מִשְׁמֶרֶת וַיְכַלְכְּלֵם וַאֲלֵיהֶם לֹא־בָא וַתִּהְיֶינָה צְרֻרוֹת עַד־יוֹם מֻתָן אַלְמְנוּת חַיּוּת: ס 4 וַיֹּאמֶר הַמֶּלֶךְ אֶל־עֲמָשָׂא הַזְעֶק־לִי אֶת־אִישׁ־יְהוּדָה שְׁלֹשֶׁת יָמִים וְאַתָּה פֹּה עֲמֹד: 5 וַיֵּלֶךְ עֲמָשָׂא לְהַזְעִיק אֶת־יְהוּדָה וַיִּיחַר מִן־הַמּוֹעֵד אֲשֶׁר יְעָדוֹ: ס 6 וַיֹּאמֶר דָּוִד אֶל־אֲבִישַׁי עַתָּה יֵרַע לָנוּ שֶׁבַע בֶּן־בִּכְרִי מִן־אַבְשָׁלוֹם אַתָּה קַח אֶת־עַבְדֵי אֲדֹנֶיךָ וּרְדֹף אַחֲרָיו פֶּן־מָצָא לוֹ עָרִים בְּצֻרוֹת וְהִצִּיל עֵינֵנוּ: 7 וַיֵּצְאוּ אַחֲרָיו אַנְשֵׁי יוֹאָב וְהַכְּרֵתִי וְהַפְּלֵתִי וְכָל־הַגִּבֹּרִים וַיֵּצְאוּ מִירוּשָׁלַם לִרְדֹף אַחֲרֵי שֶׁבַע בֶּן־בִּכְרִי: 8 הֵם עִם־הָאֶבֶן הַגְּדוֹלָה אֲשֶׁר בְּגִבְעוֹן וַעֲמָשָׂא בָּא לִפְנֵיהֶם וְיוֹאָב חָגוּר מִדּוֹ לְבֻשׁוּ וְעָלָו חֲגוֹר חֶרֶב מְצֻמֶּדֶת עַל־מָתְנָיו בְּתַעְרָהּ וְהוּא יָצָא וַתִּפֹּל: ס 9 וַיֹּאמֶר יוֹאָב לַעֲמָשָׂא הֲשָׁלוֹם אַתָּה אָחִי וַתֹּחֶז יַד־יְמִין יוֹאָב בִּזְקַן עֲמָשָׂא לִנְשָׁק־לוֹ: 10 וַעֲמָשָׂא לֹא־נִשְׁמַר בַּחֶרֶב אֲשֶׁר בְּיַד־יוֹאָב וַיַּכֵּהוּ בָהּ אֶל־הַחֹמֶשׁ וַיִּשְׁפֹּךְ מֵעָיו אַרְצָה וְלֹא־שָׁנָה לוֹ וַיָּמֹת ס וְיוֹאָב וַאֲבִישַׁי אָחִיו רָדַף אַחֲרֵי שֶׁבַע בֶּן־בִּכְרִי: 11 וְאִישׁ עָמַד עָלָיו מִנַּעֲרֵי יוֹאָב וַיֹּאמֶר מִי אֲשֶׁר חָפֵץ בְּיוֹאָב וּמִי אֲשֶׁר־לְדָוִד אַחֲרֵי יוֹאָב: 12 וַעֲמָשָׂא מִתְגֹּלֵל בַּדָּם בְּתוֹךְ הַמְּסִלָּה וַיַּרְא הָאִישׁ כִּי־עָמַד כָּל־הָעָם וַיַּסֵּב אֶת־עֲמָשָׂא מִן־הַמְּסִלָּה הַשָּׂדֶה וַיַּשְׁלֵךְ עָלָיו בֶּגֶד כַּאֲשֶׁר רָאָה כָּל־הַבָּא עָלָיו וְעָמָד: 13 כַּאֲשֶׁר הֹגָה מִן־הַמְּסִלָּה עָבַר כָּל־אִישׁ אַחֲרֵי יוֹאָב לִרְדֹף אַחֲרֵי שֶׁבַע בֶּן־בִּכְרִי: 14 וַיַּעֲבֹר בְּכָל־שִׁבְטֵי יִשְׂרָאֵל אָבֵלָה וּבֵית מַעֲכָה וְכָל־הַבֵּרִים ס וַיִּקָּלֻהוּ וַיָּבֹאוּ אַף־אַחֲרָיו: 15 וַיָּבֹאוּ וַיָּצֻרוּ עָלָיו בְּאָבֵלָה בֵּית הַמַּעֲכָה וַיִּשְׁפְּכוּ סֹלְלָה אֶל־הָעִיר וַתַּעֲמֹד בַּחֵל וְכָל־הָעָם אֲשֶׁר אֶת־יוֹאָב

כ 5 וַיִּיחַר   8 וְעָלָו   14 וַיִּקָּהֲלוּ

¹⁶Then a wise woman cried out from the city, "Hear, hear! Please say to Joab, 'Come nearby, that I may speak with you.' " ¹⁷When he had come near to her, the woman said, "*Are* you Joab?"

He answered, "I *am*."

Then she said to him, "Hear the words of your maidservant."

And he answered, "I am listening."

¹⁸So she spoke, saying, "They used to talk in former times, saying, 'They shall surely seek *guidance* at Abel,' and so they would end *disputes*. ¹⁹I *am* among the peaceable *and* faithful in Israel. You seek to destroy a city and a mother in Israel. Why would you swallow up the inheritance of the Lord?"

²⁰And Joab answered and said, "Far be it, far be it from me, that I should swallow up or destroy! ²¹That *is* not so. But a man from the mountains of Ephraim, Sheba the son of Bichri by name, has raised his hand against the king, against David. Deliver him only, and I will depart from the city."

So the woman said to Joab, "Watch, his head will be thrown to you over the wall." ²²Then the woman in her wisdom went to all the people. And they cut off the head of Sheba the son of Bichri, and threw *it* out to Joab. Then he blew a trumpet, and they withdrew from the city, every man to his tent. So Joab returned to the king at Jerusalem.

²³And Joab *was* over all the army of Israel; Benaiah the son of Jehoiada *was* over the Cherethites and the Pelethites; ²⁴Adoram *was* in charge of revenue; Jehoshaphat the son of Ahilud *was* recorder; ²⁵Sheva *was* scribe; Zadok and Abiathar *were* the priests; ²⁶and Ira the Jairite was a chief minister under David.

21 Now there was a famine in the days of David for three years, year after year; and David inquired of the Lord. And the Lord answered, "*It is* because of Saul and *his* bloodthirsty house, because he killed the Gibeonites." ²So the king called the Gibeonites and spoke to them. Now the Gibeonites *were* not of the children of Israel, but of the remnant of the Amorites; the children of Israel had sworn protection to them, but Saul had sought to kill them in his zeal for the children of Israel and Judah.

³Therefore David said to the Gibeonites, "What shall I do for you? And with what shall I make atonement, that you may bless the inheritance of the Lord?"

⁴And the Gibeonites said to him, "We will have no silver or gold from Saul or from his house, nor shall you kill any man in Israel for us."

16 וַתִּקְרָא אִשָּׁה חֲכָמָה מַשְׁחִיתֶם לְהַפִּיל הַחוֹמָה: מִן־הָעִיר שִׁמְעוּ שִׁמְעוּ אִמְרוּ־נָא אֶל־יוֹאָב קְרַב עַד־הֵנָּה וַאֲדַבְּרָה אֵלֶיךָ: 17 וַיִּקְרַב אֵלֶיהָ וַתֹּאמֶר הָאִשָּׁה הַאַתָּה יוֹאָב וַיֹּאמֶר אָנִי וַתֹּאמֶר לוֹ שְׁמַע דִּבְרֵי אֲמָתֶךָ וַיֹּאמֶר שֹׁמֵעַ אָנֹכִי: 18 וַתֹּאמֶר לֵאמֹר דַּבֵּר יְדַבְּרוּ בָרִאשֹׁנָה לֵאמֹר שָׁאֹל יְשָׁאֲלוּ בְּאָבֵל וְכֵן הֵתַמּוּ: 19 אָנֹכִי שְׁלֻמֵי אֱמוּנֵי יִשְׂרָאֵל אַתָּה מְבַקֵּשׁ לְהָמִית עִיר וְאֵם בְּיִשְׂרָאֵל לָמָּה תְבַלַּע נַחֲלַת יְהֹוָה: פ

20 וַיַּעַן יוֹאָב וַיֹּאמַר חָלִילָה חָלִילָה לִּי אִם־אֲבַלַּע וְאִם־אַשְׁחִית: 21 לֹא־כֵן הַדָּבָר כִּי אִישׁ מֵהַר אֶפְרַיִם שֶׁבַע בֶּן־בִּכְרִי שְׁמוֹ נָשָׂא יָדוֹ בַּמֶּלֶךְ בְּדָוִד תְּנוּ־אֹתוֹ לְבַדּוֹ וְאֵלְכָה מֵעַל הָעִיר וַתֹּאמֶר הָאִשָּׁה אֶל־יוֹאָב הִנֵּה רֹאשׁוֹ מֻשְׁלָךְ אֵלֶיךָ בְּעַד הַחוֹמָה: 22 וַתָּבוֹא הָאִשָּׁה אֶל־כָּל־הָעָם בְּחָכְמָתָהּ וַיִּכְרְתוּ אֶת־רֹאשׁ שֶׁבַע בֶּן־בִּכְרִי וַיַּשְׁלִכוּ אֶל־יוֹאָב וַיִּתְקַע בַּשּׁוֹפָר וַיָּפֻצוּ מֵעַל־הָעִיר אִישׁ לְאֹהָלָיו וְיוֹאָב שָׁב יְרוּשָׁלִַם אֶל־הַמֶּלֶךְ: ס 23 וְיוֹאָב אֶל כָּל־ הַצָּבָא יִשְׂרָאֵל וּבְנָיָה בֶּן־יְהוֹיָדָע עַל־הַכְּרֵי וְעַל־ הַפְּלֵתִי: 24 וַאֲדֹרָם עַל־הַמַּס וִיהוֹשָׁפָט בֶּן־אֲחִילוּד הַמַּזְכִּיר: 25 וּשְׁיָא^p סֹפֵר וְצָדוֹק וְאֶבְיָתָר כֹּהֲנִים: 26 וְגַם עִירָא הַיָּאִרִי הָיָה כֹהֵן לְדָוִד: ס

כא וַיְהִי רָעָב בִּימֵי דָוִד שָׁלֹשׁ שָׁנִים שָׁנָה אַחֲרֵי שָׁנָה וַיְבַקֵּשׁ דָּוִד אֶת־פְּנֵי יְהֹוָה ס וַיֹּאמֶר יְהֹוָה אֶל־שָׁאוּל וְאֶל־בֵּית הַדָּמִים עַל־אֲשֶׁר־הֵמִית אֶת־הַגִּבְעֹנִים: 2 וַיִּקְרָא הַמֶּלֶךְ לַגִּבְעֹנִים וַיֹּאמֶר אֲלֵיהֶם וְהַגִּבְעֹנִים לֹא מִבְּנֵי יִשְׂרָאֵל הֵמָּה כִּי אִם־ מִיֶּתֶר הָאֱמֹרִי וּבְנֵי יִשְׂרָאֵל נִשְׁבְּעוּ לָהֶם וַיְבַקֵּשׁ שָׁאוּל לְהַכֹּתָם בְּקַנֹּאתוֹ לִבְנֵי־יִשְׂרָאֵל וִיהוּדָה: 3 וַיֹּאמֶר דָּוִד אֶל־הַגִּבְעֹנִים מָה אֶעֱשֶׂה לָכֶם וּבַמָּה אֲכַפֵּר וּבָרְכוּ אֶת־נַחֲלַת יְהֹוָה: 4 וַיֹּאמְרוּ לוֹ הַגִּבְעֹנִים אֵין־לָי^p כֶּסֶף וְזָהָב עִם־שָׁאוּל וְעִם־ בֵּיתוֹ וְאֵין־לָנוּ אִישׁ לְהָמִית בְּיִשְׂרָאֵל וַיֹּאמֶר

So he said, "Whatever you say, I will do for you."

5 Then they answered the king, "As for the man who consumed us and plotted against us, *that* we should be destroyed from remaining in any of the territories of Israel, 6 let seven men of his descendants be delivered to us, and we will hang them before the LORD in Gibeah of Saul, *whom* the LORD chose."

And the king said, "I will give *them*."

7 But the king spared Mephibosheth the son of Jonathan, the son of Saul, because of the LORD's oath that *was* between them, between David and Jonathan the son of Saul. 8 So the king took Armoni and Mephibosheth, the two sons of Rizpah the daughter of Aiah, whom she bore to Saul, and the five sons of Michal the daughter of Saul, whom she brought up for Adriel the son of Barzillai the Meholathite; 9 and he delivered them into the hands of the Gibeonites, and they hanged them on the hill before the LORD. So they fell, *all* seven together, and were put to death in the days of harvest, in the first *days,* in the beginning of barley harvest.

10 Now Rizpah the daughter of Aiah took sackcloth and spread it for herself on the rock, from the beginning of harvest until the late rains poured on them from heaven. And she did not allow the birds of the air to rest on them by day nor the beasts of the field by night.

11 And David was told what Rizpah the daughter of Aiah, the concubine of Saul, had done. 12 Then David went and took the bones of Saul and the bones of Jonathan his son, from the men of Jabesh Gilead who had stolen them from the street of Beth Shan, where the Philistines had hung them up, after the Philistines had struck down Saul in Gilboa. 13 So he brought up the bones of Saul and the bones of Jonathan his son from there; and they gathered the bones of those who had been hanged. 14 They buried the bones of Saul and Jonathan his son in the country of Benjamin in Zelah, in the tomb of Kish his father. So they performed all that the king commanded. And after that God heeded the prayer for the land.

15 When the Philistines were at war again with Israel, David and his servants with him went down and fought against the Philistines; and David grew faint. 16 Then Ishbi-Benob, who *was* one of the sons of the giant, the weight of whose bronze spear *was* three hundred *shekels,* who was bearing a new *sword,* thought he could kill David. 17 But Abishai the son of Zeruiah came to his aid, and struck the Philistine and killed him. Then the men of David

מַה־אַתֶּם אֹמְרִים אֶעֱשֶׂה לָכֶם: 5 וַיֹּאמְרוּ אֶל־
הַמֶּלֶךְ הָאִישׁ אֲשֶׁר כִּלָּנוּ וַאֲשֶׁר דִּמָּה־לָנוּ נִשְׁמַדְנוּ
מֵהִתְיַצֵּב בְּכָל־גְּבֻל יִשְׂרָאֵל: 6 יֻנְתַּן־פ לָנוּ שִׁבְעָה
אֲנָשִׁים מִבָּנָיו וְהוֹקַעֲנוּם לַיהוָה בְּגִבְעַת שָׁאוּל
בְּחִיר יְהוָה ס וַיֹּאמֶר הַמֶּלֶךְ אֲנִי אֶתֵּן:
7 וַיַּחְמֹל הַמֶּלֶךְ עַל־מְפִי־בֹשֶׁת בֶּן־יְהוֹנָתָן בֶּן־שָׁאוּל
עַל־שְׁבֻעַת יְהוָה אֲשֶׁר בֵּינֹתָם בֵּין דָּוִד וּבֵין
יְהוֹנָתָן בֶּן־שָׁאוּל: 8 וַיִּקַּח הַמֶּלֶךְ אֶת־שְׁנֵי בְּנֵי
רִצְפָּה בַת־אַיָּה אֲשֶׁר יָלְדָה לְשָׁאוּל אֶת־אַרְמֹנִי
וְאֶת־מְפִבֹשֶׁת וְאֶת־חֲמֵשֶׁת בְּנֵי מִיכַל בַּת־שָׁאוּל
אֲשֶׁר יָלְדָה לְעַדְרִיאֵל בֶּן־בַּרְזִלַּי הַמְּחֹלָתִי: 9 וַיִּתְּנֵם
בְּיַד הַגִּבְעֹנִים וַיֹּקִיעֻם בָּהָר לִפְנֵי יְהוָה וַיִּפְּלוּ
שְׁבַעְתָּם פ יָחַד וְהֵם פ הֻמְתוּ בִּימֵי קָצִיר בָּרִאשֹׁנִים
תְּחִלַּת פ קְצִיר שְׂעֹרִים: 10 וַתִּקַּח רִצְפָּה בַת־אַיָּה
אֶת־הַשַּׂק וַתַּטֵּהוּ לָהּ אֶל־הַצּוּר מִתְּחִלַּת קָצִיר
עַד נִתַּךְ־מַיִם עֲלֵיהֶם מִן־הַשָּׁמָיִם וְלֹא־נָתְנָה עוֹף
הַשָּׁמַיִם לָנוּחַ עֲלֵיהֶם יוֹמָם וְאֶת־חַיַּת הַשָּׂדֶה
לָיְלָה: 11 וַיֻּגַּד לְדָוִד אֵת אֲשֶׁר־עָשְׂתָה רִצְפָּה
בַת־אַיָּה פִּלֶגֶשׁ שָׁאוּל: 12 וַיֵּלֶךְ דָּוִד וַיִּקַּח אֶת־
עַצְמוֹת שָׁאוּל וְאֶת־עַצְמוֹת יְהוֹנָתָן בְּנוֹ מֵאֵת
בַּעֲלֵי יָבֵישׁ גִּלְעָד אֲשֶׁר גָּנְבוּ אֹתָם מֵרְחֹב בֵּית־
שַׁן אֲשֶׁר תְּלָאוּם פ שָׁם פ הַפְּלִשְׁתִּים פ בְּיוֹם הַכּוֹת
פְּלִשְׁתִּים אֶת־שָׁאוּל בַּגִּלְבֹּעַ: 13 וַיַּעַל מִשָּׁם אֶת־
עַצְמוֹת שָׁאוּל וְאֶת־עַצְמוֹת יְהוֹנָתָן בְּנוֹ וַיַּאַסְפוּ
אֶת־עַצְמוֹת הַמּוּקָעִים: 14 וַיִּקְבְּרוּ אֶת־עַצְמוֹת־
שָׁאוּל וִיהוֹנָתָן־בְּנוֹ בְּאֶרֶץ בִּנְיָמִן בְּצֵלָע בְּקֶבֶר קִישׁ
אָבִיו וַיַּעֲשׂוּ כֹּל אֲשֶׁר־צִוָּה הַמֶּלֶךְ וַיֵּעָתֵר אֱלֹהִים
לָאָרֶץ אַחֲרֵי־כֵן:
פ
15 וַתְּהִי־עוֹד מִלְחָמָה לַפְּלִשְׁתִּים אֶת־יִשְׂרָאֵל וַיֵּרֶד
דָּוִד וַעֲבָדָיו עִמּוֹ וַיִּלָּחֲמוּ אֶת־פְּלִשְׁתִּים וַיָּעַף דָּוִד:
16 וישבו בְּנֹב אֲשֶׁר | בִּילִידֵי הָרָפָה וּמִשְׁקַל קֵינוֹ
שְׁלֹשׁ מֵאוֹת מִשְׁקַל נְחֹשֶׁת וְהוּא חָגוּר חֲדָשָׁה
וַיֹּאמֶר לְהַכּוֹת אֶת־דָּוִד: 17 וַיַּעֲזָר־לוֹ אֲבִישַׁי בֶּן־
צְרוּיָה וַיַּךְ אֶת־הַפְּלִשְׁתִּי וַיְמִיתֵהוּ אָז נִשְׁבְּעוּ

swore to him, saying, "You shall go out no more with us to battle, lest you quench the lamp of Israel."

18 Now it happened afterward that there was again a battle with the Philistines at Gob. Then Sibbechai the Hushathite killed Saph, who *was* one of the sons of the giant. 19 Again there was war at Gob with the Philistines, where Elhanan the son of Jaare-Oregim the Bethlehemite killed *the brother of* Goliath the Gittite, the shaft of whose spear *was* like a weaver's beam.

20 Yet again there was war at Gath, where there was a man of *great* stature, who had six fingers on each hand and six toes on each foot, twenty-four in number; and he also was born to the giant. 21 So when he defied Israel, Jonathan the son of Shimea, David's brother, killed him.

22 These four were born to the giant in Gath, and fell by the hand of David and by the hand of his servants.

22 Then David spoke to the LORD the words of this song, on the day when the LORD had delivered him from the hand of all his enemies, and from the hand of Saul. 2 And he said:

"The LORD *is* my rock and my fortress and my deliverer;

3 The God of my strength, in whom I will trust;
My shield and the horn of my salvation,
My stronghold and my refuge;
My Savior, You save me from violence.

4 I will call upon the LORD, *who is worthy* to be praised;
So shall I be saved from my enemies.

5 "When the waves of death surrounded me,
The floods of ungodliness made me afraid.

6 The sorrows of Sheol surrounded me;
The snares of death confronted me.

7 In my distress I called upon the LORD,
And cried out to my God;
He heard my voice from His temple,
And my cry *entered* His ears.

8 "Then the earth shook and trembled;
The foundations of heaven quaked and were shaken,
Because He was angry.

9 Smoke went up from His nostrils,
And devouring fire from His mouth;
Coals were kindled by it.

10 He bowed the heavens also, and came down
With darkness under His feet.

אַנְשֵׁי־דָוִד לוֹ לֵאמֹר לֹא־תֵצֵא עוֹד אִתָּנוּ לַמִּלְחָמָה
וְלֹא תְכַבֶּה אֶת־נֵר יִשְׂרָאֵל: פ

18 וַיְהִי אַחֲרֵי־כֵן וַתְּהִי־עוֹד הַמִּלְחָמָה בְּגוֹב עִם־
פְּלִשְׁתִּים אָז הִכָּה סִבְּכַי הַחֻשָׁתִי אֶת־סַף אֲשֶׁר
בִּילִדֵי הָרָפָה: פ

19 וַתְּהִי־עוֹד הַמִּלְחָמָה בְּגוֹב עִם־פְּלִשְׁתִּים וַיַּךְ
אֶלְחָנָן בֶּן־יַעְרֵי אֹרְגִים בֵּית הַלַּחְמִי אֵת גָּלְיָת הַגִּתִּי
וְעֵץ חֲנִיתוֹ כִּמְנוֹר אֹרְגִים: ס   20 וַתְּהִי־
עוֹד מִלְחָמָה בְּגַת וַיְהִי ׀ אִישׁ מָדִין וְאֶצְבְּעֹת יָדָיו
וְאֶצְבְּעֹת רַגְלָיו שֵׁשׁ וָשֵׁשׁ עֶשְׂרִים וְאַרְבַּע מִסְפָּר
וְגַם־הוּא יֻלַּד לְהָרָפָה: 21 וַיְחָרֵף אֶת־יִשְׂרָאֵל וַיַּכֵּהוּ
יְהוֹנָתָן בֶּן־שִׁמְעִי אֲחִי דָוִד: 22 אֶת־אַרְבַּעַת אֵלֶּה
יֻלְּדוּ לְהָרָפָה בְּגַת וַיִּפְּלוּ בְיַד־דָּוִד וּבְיַד עֲבָדָיו: פ

כב וַיְדַבֵּר דָּוִד לַיהֹוָה אֶת־דִּבְרֵי הַשִּׁירָה
הַזֹּאת בְּיוֹם הִצִּיל יְהֹוָה אֹתוֹ מִכַּף
כָּל־אֹיְבָיו וּמִכַּף שָׁאוּל:
2 וַיֹּאמַר יְהֹוָה סַלְעִי וּמְצֻדָתִי וּמְפַלְטִי־לִי:
3 אֱלֹהֵי צוּרִי אֶחֱסֶה־בּוֹ
מָגִנִּי וְקֶרֶן יִשְׁעִי
מִשְׂגַּבִּי וּמְנוּסִי
מֹשִׁעִי מֵחָמָס תֹּשִׁעֵנִי:
4 מְהֻלָּל אֶקְרָא יְהֹוָה
וּמֵאֹיְבַי אִוָּשֵׁעַ:
5 כִּי אֲפָפֻנִי מִשְׁבְּרֵי־מָוֶת
נַחֲלֵי בְלִיַּעַל יְבַעֲתֻנִי:
6 חֶבְלֵי שְׁאוֹל סַבֻּנִי
קִדְּמֻנִי מֹקְשֵׁי־מָוֶת:
7 בַּצַּר־לִי אֶקְרָא יְהֹוָה
וְאֶל־אֱלֹהַי אֶקְרָא
וַיִּשְׁמַע מֵהֵיכָלוֹ קוֹלִי
וְשַׁוְעָתִי בְּאָזְנָיו:
8 וַתִּגְעַשׁ וַתִּרְעַשׁ הָאָרֶץ
מוֹסְדוֹת הַשָּׁמַיִם יִרְגָּזוּ
וַיִּתְגָּעֲשׁוּ כִּי־חָרָה לוֹ:
9 עָלָה עָשָׁן בְּאַפּוֹ
וְאֵשׁ מִפִּיו תֹּאכֵל
גֶּחָלִים בָּעֲרוּ מִמֶּנּוּ:
10 וַיֵּט שָׁמַיִם וַיֵּרַד
וַעֲרָפֶל תַּחַת רַגְלָיו:

כא 20 מָדוֹן   21 שְׁמַעָה כב   8 וַיִּתְגָּעֵשׁ

11 He rode upon a cherub, and flew;
   And He was seen upon the wings of the
   wind.
12 He made darkness canopies around Him,
   Dark waters *and* thick clouds of the skies.
13 From the brightness before Him
   Coals of fire were kindled.
14 "The Lord thundered from heaven,
   And the Most High uttered His voice.
15 He sent out arrows and scattered them;
   Lightning bolts, and He vanquished them.
16 Then the channels of the sea were seen,
   The foundations of the world were uncov-
     ered,
   At the rebuke of the Lord,
   At the blast of the breath of His nostrils.

17 "He sent from above, He took me,
   He drew me out of many waters.
18 He delivered me from my strong enemy,
   From those who hated me;
   For they were too strong for me.
19 They confronted me in the day of my
     calamity,
   But the Lord was my support.
20 He also brought me out into a broad place;
   He delivered me because He delighted in me.
21 "The Lord rewarded me according to my
     righteousness;
   According to the cleanness of my hands
   He has recompensed me.
22 For I have kept the ways of the Lord,
   And have not wickedly departed from my
     God.
23 For all His judgments *were* before me;
   And *as for* His statutes, I did not depart from
     them.
24 I was also blameless before Him,
   And I kept myself from my iniquity.
25 Therefore the Lord has recompensed me
     according to my righteousness,
   According to my cleanness in His eyes.
26 "With the merciful You will show Yourself
     merciful;
   With a blameless man You will show
     Yourself blameless;
27 With the pure You will show Yourself pure;
   And with the devious You will show
     Yourself shrewd.
28 You will save the humble people;
   But Your eyes *are* on the haughty, *that* You
     may bring *them* down.

29 "For You *are* my lamp, O Lord;

וַיִּרְכַּב עַל־כְּרוּב וַיָּעֹף 11
וַיֵּרָא עַל־כַּנְפֵי־רֽוּחַ׃

וַיָּשֶׁת חֹשֶׁךְ סְבִיבֹתָיו סֻכּוֹת 12
חַֽשְׁרַת־מַיִם עָבֵי שְׁחָקִֽים׃

מִנֹּגַהּ נֶגְדּוֹ בָּעֲרוּ גַּחֲלֵי־אֵֽשׁ׃ 13

יַרְעֵם מִן־שָׁמַיִם יְהוָה 14
וְעֶלְיוֹן יִתֵּן קוֹלֽוֹ׃

וַיִּשְׁלַח חִצִּים וַיְפִיצֵם 15
בָּרָק וַיָּהֹֽם׃

וַיֵּֽרָאוּ אֲפִקֵי יָם 16
יִגָּלוּ מֹסְדוֹת תֵּבֵל
בְּגַעֲרַת יְהוָה
מִנִּשְׁמַת רוּחַ אַפּֽוֹ׃

יִשְׁלַח מִמָּרוֹם יִקָּחֵנִי 17
יַֽמְשֵׁנִי מִמַּיִם רַבִּֽים׃

יַצִּילֵנִי מֵאֹיְבִי עָז 18
מִשֹּׂנְאַי כִּי אָמְצוּ מִמֶּֽנִּי׃

יְקַדְּמֻנִי בְּיוֹם אֵידִי 19
וַיְהִי יְהוָה מִשְׁעָן לִֽי׃

וַיֹּצֵא לַמֶּרְחָב אֹתִי 20
יְחַלְּצֵנִי כִּי־חָפֵֽץ בִּֽי׃

יִגְמְלֵנִי יְהוָה כְּצִדְקָתִי 21
כְּבֹר יָדַי יָשִׁיב לִֽי׃

כִּי שָׁמַרְתִּי דַּרְכֵי יְהוָה 22
וְלֹא רָשַׁעְתִּי מֵאֱלֹהָֽי׃

כִּי כָל־מִשְׁפָּטוֹ לְנֶגְדִּי 23
וְחֻקֹּתָיו לֹא־אָסוּר מִמֶּֽנָּה׃

וָאֶהְיֶה תָמִים לוֹ 24
וָאֶשְׁתַּמְּרָה מֵעֲוֺנִֽי׃

וַיָּשֶׁב יְהוָה לִי כְּצִדְקָתִי 25
כְּבֹרִי לְנֶגֶד עֵינָֽיו׃

עִם־חָסִיד תִּתְחַסָּד 26
עִם־גִּבּוֹר תָּמִים תִּתַּמָּֽם׃

עִם־נָבָר תִּתָּבָר 27
וְעִם־עִקֵּשׁ תִּתַּפָּֽל׃

וְאֶת־עַם עָנִי תּוֹשִׁיעַ 28
וְעֵינֶיךָ עַל־רָמִים תַּשְׁפִּֽיל׃

כִּי־אַתָּה נֵירִי יְהוָה 29

כב 15 וַיָּהֹם   23 מִשְׁפָּטָיו

The LORD shall enlighten my darkness.

30 For by You I can run against a troop;
By my God I can leap over a wall.

31 *As for God, His way is* perfect;
The word of the LORD *is* proven;
He *is* a shield to all who trust in Him.

32 "For who *is* God, except the LORD?
And who *is* a rock, except our God?

33 God *is* my strength *and* power,
And He makes my way perfect.

34 He makes my feet like the *feet* of deer,
And sets me on my high places.

35 He teaches my hands to make war,
So that my arms can bend a bow of bronze.

36 "You have also given me the shield of Your
salvation;
Your gentleness has made me great.

37 You enlarged my path under me;
So my feet did not slip.

38 "I have pursued my enemies and destroyed
them;
Neither did I turn back again till they were
destroyed.

39 And I have destroyed them and wounded
them,
So that they could not rise;
They have fallen under my feet.

40 For You have armed me with strength for
the battle;
You have subdued under me those who rose
against me.

41 You have also given me the necks of my
enemies,
So that I destroyed those who hated me.

42 They looked, but *there was* none to save;
Even to the LORD, but He did not answer
them.

43 Then I beat them as fine as the dust of the
earth;
I trod them like dirt in the streets,
And I spread them out.

44 "You have also delivered me from the
strivings of my people;
You have kept me as the head of the nations.
A people I have not known shall serve me.

45 The foreigners submit to me;
As soon as they hear, they obey me.

46 The foreigners fade away,
And come frightened from their hideouts.

47 "The LORD lives!
Blessed *be* my Rock!
Let God be exalted,

וַיהֹוָה יַגִּיהַּ חָשְׁכִּי׃

30 כִּי בְכָה אָרוּץ גְּדוּד
בֵּאלֹהַי אֲדַלֶּג־שׁוּר׃

31 הָאֵל תָּמִים דַּרְכּוֹ
אִמְרַת יְהֹוָה צְרוּפָה
מָגֵן הוּא לְכֹל הַחֹסִים בּוֹ׃

32 כִּי מִי־אֵל מִבַּלְעֲדֵי יְהֹוָה
וּמִי צוּר מִבַּלְעֲדֵי אֱלֹהֵינוּ׃

33 הָאֵל מָעוּזִּי חָיִל
וַיַּתֵּר תָּמִים דַּרְכִּוֹ׃

34 מְשַׁוֶּה רַגְלַיוֹ כָּאַיָּלוֹת
וְעַל בָּמוֹתַי יַעֲמִדֵנִי׃

35 מְלַמֵּד יָדַי לַמִּלְחָמָה
וְנִחַת קֶשֶׁת־נְחוּשָׁה זְרֹעֹתָי׃

36 וַתִּתֶּן־לִי מָגֵן יִשְׁעֶךָ
וַעֲנֹתְךָ תַּרְבֵּנִי׃

37 תַּרְחִיב צַעֲדִי תַּחְתֵּנִי
וְלֹא מָעֲדוּ קַרְסֻלָּי׃

38 אֶרְדְּפָה אֹיְבַי וָאַשְׁמִידֵם
וְלֹא אָשׁוּב עַד־כַּלּוֹתָם׃

39 וָאֲכַלֵּם וָאֶמְחָצֵם וְלֹא יְקוּמוּן
וַיִּפְּלוּ תַּחַת רַגְלָי׃

40 וַתַּזְרֵנִי חַיִל לַמִּלְחָמָה
תַּכְרִיעַ קָמַי תַּחְתֵּנִי׃

41 וְאֹיְבַי תַּתָּה לִּי עֹרֶף
מְשַׂנְאַי וָאַצְמִיתֵם׃

42 יִשְׁעוּ וְאֵין מֹשִׁעַ
אֶל־יְהֹוָה וְלֹא עָנָם׃

43 וְאֶשְׁחָקֵם כַּעֲפַר־אָרֶץ
כְּטִיט־חוּצוֹת אֲדִקֵּם אֶרְקָעֵם׃

44 וַתְּפַלְּטֵנִי מֵרִיבֵי עַמִּי
תִּשְׁמְרֵנִי לְרֹאשׁ גּוֹיִם
עַם לֹא־יָדַעְתִּי יַעַבְדֻנִי׃

45 בְּנֵי נֵכָר יִתְכַּחֲשׁוּ־לִי
לִשְׁמוֹעַ אֹזֶן יִשָּׁמְעוּ לִי׃

46 בְּנֵי נֵכָר יִבֹּלוּ
וְיַחְגְּרוּ מִמִּסְגְּרוֹתָם׃

47 חַי־יְהֹוָה וּבָרוּךְ צוּרִי

The Rock of my salvation!

48 *It is* God who avenges me,
And subdues the peoples under me;

49 He delivers me from my enemies.
You also lift me up above those who rise
against me;
You have delivered me from the violent man.

50 Therefore I will give thanks to You, O LORD,
among the Gentiles,
And sing praises to Your name.

51 *He is* the tower of salvation to His king,
And shows mercy to His anointed,
To David and his descendants forevermore."

23

Now these *are* the last words of David.

Thus says David the son of Jesse;
Thus says the man raised up on high,
The anointed of the God of Jacob,
And the sweet psalmist of Israel:

2 "The Spirit of the LORD spoke by me,
And His word *was* on my tongue.

3 The God of Israel said,
The Rock of Israel spoke to me:
'He who rules over men *must be* just,
Ruling in the fear of God.

4 And *he shall be* like the light of the morning
when the sun rises,
A morning without clouds,
Like the tender grass *springing* out of the earth,
By clear shining after rain.'

5 "Although my house *is* not so with God,
Yet He has made with me an
everlasting covenant,
Ordered in all *things* and secure.
For *this is* all my salvation and all *my* desire;
Will He not make *it* increase?

6 But *the sons* of rebellion *shall* all *be* as
thorns thrust away,
Because they cannot be taken with hands.

7 But the man *who* touches them
Must be armed with iron and the shaft of a spear,
And they shall be utterly burned with fire in *their*
place."

8 These *are* the names of the mighty men whom
David had: Josheb-Basshebeth the Tachmonite,
chief among the captains. He was called Adino
the Eznite, because he had killed eight hundred men
at one time. 9 And after him *was* Eleazar the son of
Dodo, the Ahohite, *one* of the three mighty men
with David when they defied the Philistines *who*
were gathered there for battle, and the men of Israel
had retreated. 10 He arose and attacked the Philistines until his hand was weary, and his hand stuck
to the sword. The LORD brought about a great

וַיָּרֶם אֱלֹהֵי צוּר יִשְׁעִי׃

48 הָאֵל הַנֹּתֵן נְקָמֹת לִי
וּמוֹרִיד עַמִּים תַּחְתֵּנִי׃

49 וּמוֹצִיאִי מֵאֹיְבָי
וּמִקָּמַי תְּרוֹמְמֵנִי
מֵאִישׁ חֲמָסִים תַּצִּילֵנִי׃

50 עַל־כֵּן אוֹדְךָ יְהוָה בַּגּוֹיִם
וּלְשִׁמְךָ אֲזַמֵּר׃

51 מִגְדִּיל[P] יְשׁוּעוֹת מַלְכּוֹ
וְעֹשֶׂה־חֶסֶד לִמְשִׁיחוֹ
לְדָוִד וּלְזַרְעוֹ עַד־עוֹלָם׃ פ

כג וְאֵלֶּה דִּבְרֵי דָוִד הָאַחֲרֹנִים נְאֻם דָּוִד בֶּן־יִשַׁי
וּנְאֻם הַגֶּבֶר הֻקַם עָל מְשִׁיחַ אֱלֹהֵי יַעֲקֹב וּנְעִים
זְמִרוֹת יִשְׂרָאֵל׃ 2 רוּחַ יְהוָה דִּבֶּר־בִּי וּמִלָּתוֹ עַל־
לְשׁוֹנִי׃ 3 אָמַר אֱלֹהֵי יִשְׂרָאֵל לִי דִבֶּר צוּר יִשְׂרָאֵל
מוֹשֵׁל בָּאָדָם צַדִּיק מוֹשֵׁל יִרְאַת אֱלֹהִים׃ 4 וּכְאוֹר
בֹּקֶר יִזְרַח־שָׁמֶשׁ בֹּקֶר לֹא עָבוֹת מִנֹּגַהּ מִמָּטָר דֶּשֶׁא
מֵאָרֶץ׃ 5 כִּי־לֹא־כֵן בֵּיתִי עִם־אֵל כִּי בְרִית עוֹלָם
שָׂם לִי עֲרוּכָה בַכֹּל וּשְׁמֻרָה כִּי־כָל־יִשְׁעִי וְכָל־
חֵפֶץ כִּי־לֹא יַצְמִיחַ׃ 6 וּבְלִיַּעַל כְּקוֹץ מֻנָד כֻּלָּהַם
כִּי־לֹא בְיָד יִקָּחוּ׃ 7 וְאִישׁ יִגַּע בָּהֶם יִמָּלֵא בַרְזֶל
וְעֵץ חֲנִית וּבָאֵשׁ שָׂרוֹף יִשָּׂרְפוּ בַּשָּׁבֶת׃ פ

8 אֵלֶּה שְׁמוֹת הַגִּבֹּרִים אֲשֶׁר לְדָוִד יֹשֵׁב
בַּשֶּׁבֶת תַּחְכְּמֹנִי ׀ רֹאשׁ הַשָּׁלִשִׁי הוּא עֲדִינוֹ
הָעֶצְנוֹ[P] עַל־שְׁמֹנֶה מֵאוֹת חָלָל בְּפַעַם אֶחָד׃

9 וְאַחֲרוֹ[P] אֶלְעָזָר בֶּן־דֹּדִי[P] בֶּן־אֲחֹחִי ס
בִּשְׁלֹשָׁה גִבֹּרִים[P] עִם־דָּוִד בְּחָרְפָם בַּפְּלִשְׁתִּים
נֶאֶסְפוּ־שָׁם לַמִּלְחָמָה וַיַּעֲלוּ אִישׁ יִשְׂרָאֵל׃ 10 הוּא
קָם וַיַּךְ בַּפְּלִשְׁתִּים עַד ׀ כִּי־יָגְעָה יָדוֹ וַתִּדְבַּק
יָדוֹ אֶל־הַחֶרֶב וַיַּעַשׂ יְהוָה תְּשׁוּעָה גְדוֹלָה
בַּיּוֹם הַהוּא וְהָעָם יָשֻׁבוּ אַחֲרָיו אַךְ־

כב 51 מִגְדּוֹל

כג 8 הָעֶצְנִי אָחָת 9 וְאַחֲרָיו דֹּו הַגִּבֹּרִים

victory that day; and the people returned after him only to plunder. 11 And after him *was* Shammah the son of Agee the Hararite. The Philistines had gathered together into a troop where there was a piece of ground full of lentils. So the people fled from the Philistines. 12 But he stationed himself in the middle of the field, defended it, and killed the Philistines. So the LORD brought about a great victory.

13 Then three of the thirty chief men went down at harvest time and came to David at the cave of Adullam. And the troop of Philistines encamped in the Valley of Rephaim. 14 David *was* then in the stronghold, and the garrison of the Philistines *was* then *in* Bethlehem. 15 And David said with longing, "Oh, that someone would give me a drink of the water from the well of Bethlehem, which *is* by the gate!" 16 So the three mighty men broke through the camp of the Philistines, drew water from the well of Bethlehem that *was* by the gate, and took *it* and brought *it* to David. Nevertheless he would not drink it, but poured it out to the LORD. 17 And he said, "Far be it from me, O LORD, that I should do this! Is *this not* the blood of the men who went in *jeopardy of* their lives?" Therefore he would not drink it.

These things were done by the three mighty men.

18 Now Abishai the brother of Joab, the son of Zeruiah, was chief of *another* three. He lifted his spear against three hundred *men,* killed *them,* and won a name among *these* three. 19 Was he not the most honored of three? Therefore he became their captain. However, he did not attain to the *first* three.

20 Benaiah *was* the son of Jehoiada, the son of a valiant man from Kabzeel, who had done many deeds. He had killed two lion-like heroes of Moab. He also had gone down and killed a lion in the midst of a pit on a snowy day. 21 And he killed an Egyptian, a spectacular man. The Egyptian *had* a spear in his hand; so he went down to him with a staff, wrested the spear out of the Egyptian's hand, and killed him with his own spear. 22 These *things* Benaiah the son of Jehoiada did, and won a name among three mighty men. 23 He was more honored than the thirty, but he did not attain to the *first* three. And David appointed him over his guard.

24 Asahel the brother of Joab *was* one of the thirty; Elhanan the son of Dodo of Bethlehem, 25 Shammah the Harodite, Elika the Harodite, 26 Helez the Paltite, Ira the son of Ikkesh the Tekoite, 27 Abiezer the Anathothite, Mebunnai the Hushathite, 28 Zalmon the Ahohite, Maharai the Netophathite, 29 Heleb the son of Baanah (the

---

לְפָשֵׁט: ס 11 וְאַחֲרָיו שַׁמָּא בֶן־אָגֵא
הָרָרִי וַיֵּאָסְפוּ פְלִשְׁתִּים לַחַיָּה וַתְּהִי־שָׁם חֶלְקַת
הַשָּׂדֶה מְלֵאָה עֲדָשִׁים וְהָעָם נָס מִפְּנֵי פְלִשְׁתִּים:
12 וַיִּתְיַצֵּב בְּתוֹךְ־הַחֶלְקָה וַיַּצִּילֶהָ וַיַּךְ אֶת־פְּלִשְׁתִּים
וַיַּעַשׂ יְהוָה תְּשׁוּעָה גְדוֹלָה: ס 13 וַיֵּרְדוּ
שְׁלֹשִׁים מֵהַשְּׁלֹשִׁים רֹאשׁ וַיָּבֹאוּ אֶל־קָצִיר אֶל־
דָּוִד אֶל־מְעָרַת עֲדֻלָּם וְחַיַּת פְּלִשְׁתִּים חֹנָה בְּעֵמֶק
רְפָאִים: 14 וְדָוִד אָז בַּמְצוּדָה וּמַצַּב פְּלִשְׁתִּים
אָז בֵּית לָחֶם: 15 וַיִּתְאַוֶּה דָוִד וַיֹּאמֶר מִי יַשְׁקֵנִי
מַיִם מִבְּאֹר בֵּית־לֶחֶם אֲשֶׁר בַּשָּׁעַר: 16 וַיִּבְקְעוּ
שְׁלֹשֶׁת הַגִּבֹּרִים בְּמַחֲנֵה פְלִשְׁתִּים וַיִּשְׁאֲבוּ־מַיִם
מִבֹּאר בֵּית־לֶחֶם אֲשֶׁר בַּשַּׁעַר וַיִּשְׂאוּ וַיָּבִאוּ אֶל־
דָּוִד וְלֹא אָבָה לִשְׁתּוֹתָם וַיַּסֵּךְ אֹתָם לַיהוָה:
17 וַיֹּאמֶר חָלִילָה לִּי יְהוָה מֵעֲשׂתִי זֹאת הֲדַם
הָאֲנָשִׁים הַהֹלְכִים בְּנַפְשׁוֹתָם וְלֹא אָבָה לִשְׁתּוֹתָם
אֵלֶּה עָשׂוּ שְׁלֹשֶׁת הַגִּבֹּרִים: ס 18 וַאֲבִישַׁי
אֲחִי יוֹאָב בֶּן־צְרוּיָה הוּא רֹאשׁ הַשְּׁלֹשִׁי וְהוּא
עוֹרֵר אֶת־חֲנִיתוֹ עַל־שְׁלֹשׁ מֵאוֹת חָלָל וְלוֹ־שֵׁם
בַּשְּׁלֹשָׁה: 19 מִן־הַשְּׁלֹשָׁה הֲכִי נִכְבָּד וַיְהִי לָהֶם
לְשָׂר וְעַד־הַשְּׁלֹשָׁה לֹא־בָא: ס 20 וּבְנָיָהוּ
בֶן־יְהוֹיָדָע בֶּן־אִישׁ־חַי רַב־פְּעָלִים מִקַּבְצְאֵל הוּא
הִכָּה אֵת שְׁנֵי אֲרִאֵל מוֹאָב וְהוּא יָרַד וְהִכָּה
אֶת־הָאֲרִיה בְּתוֹךְ הַבֹּאר בְּיוֹם הַשָּׁלֶג: 21 וְהוּא־
הִכָּה אֶת־אִישׁ מִצְרִי אֲשֶׁר מַרְאֶה וּבְיַד הַמִּצְרִי
חֲנִית וַיֵּרֶד אֵלָיו בַּשָּׁבֶט וַיִּגְזֹל אֶת־הַחֲנִית מִיַּד
הַמִּצְרִי וַיַּהַרְגֵהוּ בַּחֲנִיתוֹ: 22 אֵלֶּה עָשָׂה בְּנָיָהוּ
בֶּן־יְהוֹיָדָע וְלוֹ־שֵׁם בִּשְׁלֹשָׁה הַגִּבֹּרִים: 23 מִן־
הַשְּׁלֹשִׁים נִכְבָּד וְאֶל־הַשְּׁלֹשָׁה לֹא־בָא וַיְשִׂמֵהוּ דָוִד
אֶל־מִשְׁמַעְתּוֹ: ס 24 עֲשָׂה־אֵל אֲחִי־יוֹאָב
בַּשְּׁלֹשִׁים אֶלְחָנָן בֶּן־דֹּדוֹ בֵּית לָחֶם:
25 שַׁמָּה הַחֲרֹדִי   אֱלִיקָא הַחֲרֹדִי:
26 חֶלֶץ הַפַּלְטִי   עִירָא בֶן־עִקֵּשׁ הַתְּקוֹעִי:
27 אֲבִיעֶזֶר הָעַנְּתֹתִי   מְבֻנַּי הַחֻשָׁתִי:
28 צַלְמוֹן הָאֲחֹחִי   מַהְרַי הַנְּטֹפָתִי:
29 חֵלֶב בֶּן־בַּעֲנָה הַנְּטֹפָתִי
אִתַּי בֶּן־רִיבַי מִגִּבְעַת בְּנֵי בִנְיָמִן:

כג 13 שְׁלֹשָׁה   18 הַשְּׁלֹשָׁה   20 חַיִל הָאֲרִי   21 אִישׁ

Netophathite), Ittai the son of Ribai from Gibeah of the children of Benjamin, ³⁰ Benaiah a Pirathonite, Hiddai from the brooks of Gaash, ³¹ Abi-Albon the Arbathite, Azmaveth the Barhumite, ³² Eliahba the Shaalbonite (of the sons of Jashen), Jonathan, ³³ Shammah the Hararite, Ahiam the son of Sharar the Hararite, ³⁴ Eliphelet the son of Ahasbai, the son of the Maachathite, Eliam the son of Ahithophel the Gilonite, ³⁵ Hezrai the Carmelite, Paarai the Arbite, ³⁶ Igal the son of Nathan of Zobah, Bani the Gadite, ³⁷ Zelek the Ammonite, Naharai the Beerothite (armorbearer of Joab the son of Zeruiah), ³⁸ Ira the Ithrite, Gareb the Ithrite, ³⁹ and Uriah the Hittite: thirty-seven in all.

24

Again the anger of the LORD was aroused against Israel, and He moved David against them to say, "Go, number Israel and Judah."

² So the king said to Joab the commander of the army who *was* with him, "Now go throughout all the tribes of Israel, from Dan to Beersheba, and count the people, that I may know the number of the people."

³ And Joab said to the king, "Now may the LORD your God add to the people a hundred times more than there are, and may the eyes of my lord the king see *it*. But why does my lord the king desire this thing?" ⁴ Nevertheless the king's word prevailed against Joab and against the captains of the army. Therefore Joab and the captains of the army went out from the presence of the king to count the people of Israel.

⁵ And they crossed over the Jordan and camped in Aroer, on the right side of the town which *is* in the midst of the ravine of Gad, and toward Jazer. ⁶ Then they came to Gilead and to the land of Tahtim Hodshi; they came to Dan Jaan and around to Sidon; ⁷ and they came to the stronghold of Tyre and to all the cities of the Hivites and the Canaanites. Then they went out to South Judah as far as Beersheba. ⁸ So when they had gone through all the land, they came to Jerusalem at the end of nine months and twenty days. ⁹ Then Joab gave the sum of the number of the people to the king. And there were in Israel eight hundred thousand valiant men who drew the sword, and the men of Judah were five hundred thousand men.

¹⁰ And David's heart condemned him after he had numbered the people. So David said to the LORD, "I have sinned greatly in what I have done; but now, I pray, O LORD, take away the iniquity of Your servant, for I have done very foolishly."

30 הִדַּי מִנַּחֲלֵי גָעַשׁ: בְּנָיָהוּ פִּרְעָתֹנִי

31 אֲבִי־עַלְבוֹן הָעַרְבָתִי עַזְמָוֶת הַבַּרְחֻמִי

32 אֶלְיַחְבָּא הַשַּׁעַלְבֹנִי בְּנֵי יָשֵׁן יְהוֹנָתָן:

33 שַׁמָּה הַהֲרָרִי אֲחִיאָם בֶּן־שָׁרָר הָאֲרָרִי:

34 אֱלִיפֶלֶט בֶּן־אֲחַסְבַּי בֶּן־הַמַּעֲכָתִי אֱלִיעָם בֶּן־אֲחִיתֹפֶל הַגִּלֹנִי:

35 חֶצְרוֹ הַכַּרְמְלִי פַּעֲרַי הָאַרְבִּי:

36 יִגְאָל בֶּן־נָתָן מִצֹּבָה בָּנִי הַגָּדִי:

37 צֶלֶק הָעַמֹּנִי נַחְרַי הַבְּאֵרֹתִי נֹשְׂאֵי כְּלֵי יוֹאָב בֶּן־צְרֻיָה:

38 עִירָא הַיִּתְרִי גָּרֵב הַיִּתְרִי:

39 אוּרִיָּה הַחִתִּי כֹּל שְׁלֹשִׁים וְשִׁבְעָה: פ

כד וַיֹּסֶף אַף־יְהוָֹה לַחֲרוֹת בְּיִשְׂרָאֵל וַיָּסֶת אֶת־דָּוִד בָּהֶם לֵאמֹר לֵךְ מְנֵה אֶת־יִשְׂרָאֵל וְאֶת־יְהוּדָה: 2 וַיֹּאמֶר הַמֶּלֶךְ אֶל־יוֹאָב שַׂר־הַחַיִל אֲשֶׁר־אִתּוֹ שׁוּט־נָא בְּכָל־שִׁבְטֵי יִשְׂרָאֵל מִדָּן וְעַד־בְּאֵר שֶׁבַע וּפִקְדוּ אֶת־הָעָם וְיָדַעְתִּי אֵת מִסְפַּר הָעָם: ס 3 וַיֹּאמֶר יוֹאָב אֶל־הַמֶּלֶךְ וְיוֹסֵף יְהוָֹה אֱלֹהֶיךָ אֶל־הָעָם כָּהֶם וְכָהֶם מֵאָה פְעָמִים וְעֵינֵי אֲדֹנִי־הַמֶּלֶךְ רֹאוֹת וַאדֹנִי הַמֶּלֶךְ לָמָּה חָפֵץ בַּדָּבָר הַזֶּה: 4 וַיֶּחֱזַק דְּבַר־הַמֶּלֶךְ אֶל־יוֹאָב וְעַל שָׂרֵי הֶחָיִל וַיֵּצֵא יוֹאָב וְשָׂרֵי הַחַיִל לִפְנֵי הַמֶּלֶךְ לִפְקֹד אֶת־הָעָם אֶת־יִשְׂרָאֵל: 5 וַיַּעַבְרוּ אֶת־הַיַּרְדֵּן וַיַּחֲנוּ בַעֲרוֹעֵר יְמִין הָעִיר אֲשֶׁר בְּתוֹךְ־הַנַּחַל הַגָּד וְאֶל־יַעְזֵר: 6 וַיָּבֹאוּ הַגִּלְעָדָה וְאֶל־אֶרֶץ תַּחְתִּים חָדְשִׁי וַיָּבֹאוּ דָּנָה יַּעַן וְסָבִיב אֶל־צִידוֹן: 7 וַיָּבֹאוּ מִבְצַר־צֹר וְכָל־עָרֵי הַחִוִּי וְהַכְּנַעֲנִי וַיֵּצְאוּ אֶל־נֶגֶב יְהוּדָה בְּאֵר שָׁבַע: 8 וַיָּשֻׁטוּ בְּכָל־הָאָרֶץ וַיָּבֹאוּ מִקְצֵה תִשְׁעָה חֳדָשִׁים וְעֶשְׂרִים יוֹם יְרוּשָׁלָ‍ִם: 9 וַיִּתֵּן יוֹאָב אֶת־מִסְפַּר מִפְקַד־הָעָם אֶל־הַמֶּלֶךְ וַתְּהִי יִשְׂרָאֵל שְׁמֹנֶה מֵאוֹת אֶלֶף אִישׁ־חַיִל שֹׁלֵף חֶרֶב וְאִישׁ יְהוּדָה חֲמֵשׁ־מֵאוֹת אֶלֶף אִישׁ: 10 וַיַּךְ לֵב־דָּוִד אֹתוֹ אַחֲרֵי־כֵן סָפַר אֶת־הָעָם ס וַיֹּאמֶר דָּוִד אֶל־יְהוָֹה חָטָאתִי מְאֹד אֲשֶׁר עָשִׂיתִי וְעַתָּה יְהוָֹה הַעֲבֶר־נָא אֶת־

11 Now when David arose in the morning, the word of the LORD came to the prophet Gad, David's seer, saying, 12 "Go and tell David, 'Thus says the LORD: "I offer you three *things;* choose one of them for yourself, that I may do *it* to you." ' " 13 So Gad came to David and told him; and he said to him, "Shall seven years of famine come to you in your land? Or shall you flee three months before your enemies, while they pursue you? Or shall there be three days' plague in your land? Now consider and see what answer I should take back to Him who sent me."

14 And David said to Gad, "I am in great distress. Please let us fall into the hand of the LORD, for His mercies *are* great; but do not let me fall into the hand of man."

15 So the LORD sent a plague upon Israel from the morning till the appointed time. From Dan to Beersheba seventy thousand men of the people died. 16 And when the angel stretched out His hand over Jerusalem to destroy it, the LORD relented from the destruction, and said to the angel who was destroying the people, "It is enough; now restrain your hand." And the angel of the LORD was by the threshing floor of Araunah the Jebusite.

17 Then David spoke to the LORD when he saw the angel who was striking the people, and said, "Surely I have sinned, and I have done wickedly; but these sheep, what have they done? Let Your hand, I pray, be against me and against my father's house."

18 And Gad came that day to David and said to him, "Go up, erect an altar to the LORD on the threshing floor of Araunah the Jebusite." 19 So David, according to the word of Gad, went up as the LORD commanded. 20 Now Araunah looked, and saw the king and his servants coming toward him. So Araunah went out and bowed before the king with his face to the ground.

21 Then Araunah said, "Why has my lord the king come to his servant?"

And David said, "To buy the threshing floor from you, to build an altar to the LORD, that the plague may be withdrawn from the people."

22 Now Araunah said to David, "Let my lord the king take and offer up whatever *seems* good to him. Look, *here are* oxen for burnt sacrifice, and threshing implements and the yokes of the oxen for wood. 23 All these, O king, Araunah has given to the king."

And Araunah said to the king, "May the LORD your God accept you."

עֲוֹן עַבְדְּךָ כִּי־נִסְכַּלְתִּי מְאֹד: 11 וַיָּקָם דָּוִד בַּבֹּקֶר
וּדְבַר־יְהוָה הָיָה אֶל־גָּד הַנָּבִיא חֹזֵה דָוִד פ
לֵאמֹר: 12 הָלוֹךְ וְדִבַּרְתָּ אֶל־דָּוִד כֹּה אָמַר יְהוָה
שָׁלֹשׁ אָנֹכִי נוֹטֵל עָלֶיךָ בְּחַר־לְךָ אַחַת־מֵהֶם
וְאֶעֱשֶׂה־לָּךְ: 13 וַיָּבֹא־גָד אֶל־דָּוִד וַיַּגֶּד־לוֹ וַיֹּאמֶר
לוֹ הֲתָבוֹא לְךָ שֶׁבַע שָׁנִים ׀ רָעָב ׀ בְּאַרְצֶךָ
אִם־שְׁלֹשָׁה חֳדָשִׁים נֻסְךָ לִפְנֵי־צָרֶיךָ וְהוּא רֹדְפֶךָ
וְאִם־הֱיוֹת שְׁלֹשֶׁת יָמִים דֶּבֶר בְּאַרְצֶךָ עַתָּה דַּע
וּרְאֵה מָה־אָשִׁיב שֹׁלְחִי דָּבָר: ס 14 וַיֹּאמֶר
דָּוִד אֶל־גָּד צַר־לִי מְאֹד נִפְּלָה־נָּא בְיַד־יְהוָה כִּי־
רַבִּים רַחֲמוֹ וּבְיַד־אָדָם אַל־אֶפֹּלָה: 15 וַיִּתֵּן יְהוָה
דֶּבֶר בְּיִשְׂרָאֵל מֵהַבֹּקֶר וְעַד־עֵת מוֹעֵד וַיָּמָת מִן־
הָעָם מִדָּן וְעַד־בְּאֵר שֶׁבַע שִׁבְעִים אֶלֶף אִישׁ:
16 וַיִּשְׁלַח יָדוֹ הַמַּלְאָךְ ׀ יְרוּשָׁלַםִ לְשַׁחֲתָהּ וַיִּנָּחֶם
יְהוָה אֶל־הָרָעָה וַיֹּאמֶר לַמַּלְאָךְ הַמַּשְׁחִית בָּעָם
רַב עַתָּה הֶרֶף יָדֶךָ וּמַלְאַךְ יְהוָה הָיָה עִם־גֹּרֶן
הָאֲרַוְנָה הַיְבֻסִי: ס 17 וַיֹּאמֶר דָּוִד אֶל־
יְהוָה בִּרְאֹתוֹ ׀ אֶת־הַמַּלְאָךְ ׀ הַמַּכֶּה בָעָם וַיֹּאמֶר
הִנֵּה אָנֹכִי חָטָאתִי וְאָנֹכִי הֶעֱוֵיתִי וְאֵלֶּה הַצֹּאן מֶה
עָשׂוּ תְּהִי נָא יָדְךָ בִּי וּבְבֵית אָבִי: פ
18 וַיָּבֹא־גָד אֶל־דָּוִד בַּיּוֹם הַהוּא וַיֹּאמֶר לוֹ עֲלֵה
הָקֵם לַיהוָה מִזְבֵּחַ בְּגֹרֶן אֲרַוְנָה הַיְבֻסִי: 19 וַיַּעַל
דָּוִד כִּדְבַר־גָּד כַּאֲשֶׁר צִוָּה יְהוָה: 20 וַיַּשְׁקֵף אֲרַוְנָה
וַיַּרְא אֶת־הַמֶּלֶךְ וְאֶת־עֲבָדָיו עֹבְרִים עָלָיו וַיֵּצֵא
אֲרַוְנָה וַיִּשְׁתַּחוּ לַמֶּלֶךְ אַפָּיו אָרְצָה: 21 וַיֹּאמֶר
אֲרַוְנָה מַדּוּעַ בָּא אֲדֹנִי־הַמֶּלֶךְ אֶל־עַבְדּוֹ וַיֹּאמֶר
דָּוִד לִקְנוֹת מֵעִמְּךָ אֶת־הַגֹּרֶן לִבְנוֹת מִזְבֵּחַ לַיהוָה
וְתֵעָצַר הַמַּגֵּפָה מֵעַל הָעָם: 22 וַיֹּאמֶר אֲרַוְנָה אֶל־
דָּוִד יִקַּח וְיַעַל אֲדֹנִי הַמֶּלֶךְ הַטּוֹב בְּעֵינָו רְאֵה
הַבָּקָר לָעֹלָה וְהַמֹּרִגִּים וּכְלֵי הַבָּקָר לָעֵצִים: 23 הַכֹּל
נָתַן אֲרַוְנָה הַמֶּלֶךְ לַמֶּלֶךְ ס וַיֹּאמֶר אֲרַוְנָה

כד 14 רַחֲמָיו 16 הָאֲרַוְנָה 18 אֲרַוְנָה 22 בְּעֵינָיו

24 Then the king said to Araunah, "No, but I will
surely buy *it* from you for a price; nor will I offer
burnt offerings to the LORD my God with that
which costs me nothing." So David bought the
threshing floor and the oxen for fifty shekels of
silver. 25 And David built there an altar to the
LORD, and offered burnt offerings and peace
offerings. So the LORD heeded the prayers for the
land, and the plague was withdrawn from Israel.

אֶל־הַמֶּלֶךְ יְהוָה אֱלֹהֶיךָ יִרְצֶךָ: 24 וַיֹּאמֶר הַמֶּלֶךְ
אֶל־אֲרַוְנָה לֹא כִּי־קָנוֹ אֶקְנֶה מֵאוֹתְךָ בִּמְחִיר וְלֹא
אַעֲלֶה לַיהוָה אֱלֹהַי עֹלוֹת חִנָּם וַיִּקֶן דָּוִד אֶת־
הַגֹּרֶן וְאֶת־הַבָּקָר בְּכֶסֶף שְׁקָלִים חֲמִשִּׁים: 25 וַיִּבֶן
שָׁם דָּוִד מִזְבֵּחַ לַיהוָה וַיַּעַל עֹלוֹת וּשְׁלָמִים וַיֵּעָתֵר
יְהוָה לָאָרֶץ וַתֵּעָצַר הַמַּגֵּפָה מֵעַל יִשְׂרָאֵל:

KINGS

1 Now King David was old, advanced in years; and they put covers on him, but he could not get warm. ²Therefore his servants said to him, "Let a young woman, a virgin, be sought for our lord the king, and let her stand before the king, and let her care for him; and let her lie in your bosom, that our lord the king may be warm." ³So they sought for a lovely young woman throughout all the territory of Israel, and found Abishag the Shunammite, and brought her to the king. ⁴The young woman *was* very lovely; and she cared for the king, and served him; but the king did not know her.

⁵Then Adonijah the son of Haggith exalted himself, saying, "I will be king"; and he prepared for himself chariots and horsemen, and fifty men to run before him. ⁶(And his father had not rebuked him at any time by saying, "Why have you done so?" He *was* also very good-looking. *His mother* had borne him after Absalom.) ⁷Then he conferred with Joab the son of Zeruiah and with Abiathar the priest, and they followed and helped Adonijah. ⁸But Zadok the priest, Benaiah the son of Jehoiada, Nathan the prophet, Shimei, Rei, and the mighty men who *belonged* to David were not with Adonijah.

⁹And Adonijah sacrificed sheep and oxen and fattened cattle by the stone of Zoheleth, which *is* by En Rogel; he also invited all his brothers, the king's sons, and all the men of Judah, the king's servants. ¹⁰But he did not invite Nathan the prophet, Benaiah, the mighty men, or Solomon his brother.

¹¹So Nathan spoke to Bathsheba the mother of Solomon, saying, "Have you not heard that Adonijah the son of Haggith has become king, and David our lord does not know *it?* ¹²Come, please, let me now give you advice, that you may save your own life and the life of your son Solomon. ¹³Go immediately to King David and say to him, 'Did you not, my lord, O king, swear to your maidservant, saying, "Assuredly your son Solomon shall reign after me, and he shall sit on my throne"? Why then has Adonijah become king?' ¹⁴Then, while you are still talking there with the king, I also will come in after you and confirm your words."

א וְהַמֶּלֶךְ דָּוִד זָקֵן בָּא בַּיָּמִים וַיְכַסֻּהוּ בַּבְּגָדִים
וְלֹא יִחַם לוֹ: ² וַיֹּאמְרוּ לוֹ עֲבָדָיו יְבַקְשׁוּ לַאדֹנִי
הַמֶּלֶךְ נַעֲרָה בְתוּלָה וְעָמְדָה לִפְנֵי הַמֶּלֶךְ וּתְהִי־לוֹ
סֹכֶנֶת וְשָׁכְבָה בְחֵיקֶךָ וְחַם לַאדֹנִי הַמֶּלֶךְ: ³ וַיְבַקְשׁוּ
נַעֲרָה יָפָה בְּכֹל גְּבוּל יִשְׂרָאֵל וַיִּמְצְאוּ אֶת־אֲבִישַׁג
הַשּׁוּנַמִּית וַיָּבִאוּ אֹתָהּ לַמֶּלֶךְ: ⁴ וְהַנַּעֲרָה יָפָה עַד־
מְאֹד וַתְּהִי לַמֶּלֶךְ סֹכֶנֶת וַתְּשָׁרְתֵהוּ וְהַמֶּלֶךְ לֹא
יְדָעָהּ: ⁵ וַאֲדֹנִיָּה בֶן־חַגִּית מִתְנַשֵּׂא לֵאמֹר אֲנִי
אֶמְלֹךְ וַיַּעַשׂ לוֹ רֶכֶב וּפָרָשִׁים וַחֲמִשִּׁים אִישׁ
רָצִים לְפָנָיו: ⁶ וְלֹא־עֲצָבוֹ אָבִיו מִיָּמָיו לֵאמֹר מַדּוּעַ
כָּכָה עָשִׂיתָ וְגַם־הוּא טוֹב־תֹּאַר מְאֹד וְאֹתוֹ יָלְדָה
אַחֲרֵי אַבְשָׁלוֹם: ⁷ וַיִּהְיוּ דְבָרָיו עִם יוֹאָב בֶּן־
צְרוּיָה וְעִם אֶבְיָתָר הַכֹּהֵן וַיַּעְזְרוּ אַחֲרֵי אֲדֹנִיָּה:
⁸ וְצָדוֹק הַכֹּהֵן וּבְנָיָהוּ בֶן־יְהוֹיָדָע וְנָתָן הַנָּבִיא
וְשִׁמְעִי וְרֵעִי וְהַגִּבּוֹרִים אֲשֶׁר לְדָוִד לֹא הָיוּ עִם־
אֲדֹנִיָּהוּ: ⁹ וַיִּזְבַּח אֲדֹנִיָּהוּ צֹאן וּבָקָר וּמְרִיא עִם
אֶבֶן הַזֹּחֶלֶת אֲשֶׁר־אֵצֶל עֵין רֹגֵל וַיִּקְרָא אֶת־כָּל־
אֶחָיו בְּנֵי הַמֶּלֶךְ וּלְכָל־אַנְשֵׁי יְהוּדָה עַבְדֵי הַמֶּלֶךְ:
¹⁰ וְאֶת־נָתָן הַנָּבִיא וּבְנָיָהוּ וְאֶת־הַגִּבּוֹרִים וְאֶת־
שְׁלֹמֹה אָחִיו לֹא קָרָא: ¹¹ וַיֹּאמֶר נָתָן אֶל־בַּת־
שֶׁבַע אֵם־שְׁלֹמֹה לֵאמֹר הֲלוֹא שָׁמַעַתְּ כִּי מָלַךְ
אֲדֹנִיָּהוּ בֶן־חַגִּית וַאֲדֹנֵינוּ דָוִד לֹא יָדָע: ¹² וְעַתָּה
לְכִי אִיעָצֵךְ נָא עֵצָה וּמַלְּטִי אֶת־נַפְשֵׁךְ וְאֶת־נֶפֶשׁ
בְּנֵךְ שְׁלֹמֹה: ¹³ לְכִי וּבֹאִי | אֶל־הַמֶּלֶךְ דָּוִד וְאָמַרְתְּ
אֵלָיו הֲלֹא־אַתָּה אֲדֹנִי הַמֶּלֶךְ נִשְׁבַּעְתָּ לַאֲמָתְךָ
לֵאמֹר כִּי־שְׁלֹמֹה בְנֵךְ יִמְלֹךְ אַחֲרַי וְהוּא יֵשֵׁב עַל־
כִּסְאִי וּמַדּוּעַ מָלַךְ אֲדֹנִיָּהוּ: ¹⁴ הִנֵּה עוֹדָךְ מְדַבֶּרֶת
שָׁם עִם־הַמֶּלֶךְ וַאֲנִי אָבוֹא אַחֲרַיִךְ וּמִלֵּאתִי אֶת־

¹⁵So Bathsheba went into the chamber to the king. (Now the king was very old, and Abishag the Shunammite was serving the king.) ¹⁶And Bathsheba bowed and did homage to the king. Then the king said, "What is your wish?"

¹⁷Then she said to him, "My lord, you swore by the LORD your God to your maidservant, *saying,* 'Assuredly Solomon your son shall reign after me, and he shall sit on my throne.' ¹⁸So now, look! Adonijah has become king; and now, my lord the king, you do not know about *it.* ¹⁹He has sacrificed oxen and fattened cattle and sheep in abundance, and has invited all the sons of the king, Abiathar the priest, and Joab the commander of the army; but Solomon your servant he has not invited. ²⁰And as for you, my lord, O king, the eyes of all Israel *are* on you, that you should tell them who will sit on the throne of my lord the king after him. ²¹Otherwise it will happen, when my lord the king rests with his fathers, that I and my son Solomon will be counted as offenders."

²²And just then, while she was still talking with the king, Nathan the prophet also came in. ²³So they told the king, saying, "Here is Nathan the prophet." And when he came in before the king, he bowed down before the king with his face to the ground. ²⁴And Nathan said, "My lord, O king, have you said, 'Adonijah shall reign after me, and he shall sit on my throne'? ²⁵For he has gone down today, and has sacrificed oxen and fattened cattle and sheep in abundance, and has invited all the king's sons, and the commanders of the army, and Abiathar the priest; and look! They are eating and drinking before him; and they say, '*Long* live King Adonijah!' ²⁶But he has not invited me—me your servant—nor Zadok the priest, nor Benaiah the son of Jehoiada, nor your servant Solomon. ²⁷Has this thing been done by my lord the king, and you have not told your servant who should sit on the throne of my lord the king after him?"

²⁸Then King David answered and said, "Call Bathsheba to me." So she came into the king's presence and stood before the king. ²⁹And the king took an oath and said, "*As* the LORD lives, who has redeemed my life from every distress, ³⁰just as I swore to you by the LORD God of Israel, saying, 'Assuredly Solomon your son shall be king after me, and he shall sit on my throne in my place,' so I certainly will do this day."

³¹Then Bathsheba bowed with *her* face to the earth, and paid homage to the king, and said, "Let my lord King David live forever!"

דִּבְרֵיךְ: 15 וַתָּבֹא בַת־שֶׁבַע אֶל־הַמֶּלֶךְ הַחַדְרָה וְהַמֶּלֶךְ זָקֵן מְאֹד וַאֲבִישַׁג הַשּׁוּנַמִּית מְשָׁרַת אֶת־הַמֶּלֶךְ: 16 וַתִּקֹּד בַּת־שֶׁבַע וַתִּשְׁתַּחוּ לַמֶּלֶךְ וַיֹּאמֶר הַמֶּלֶךְ מַה־לָּךְ: 17 וַתֹּאמֶר לוֹ אֲדֹנִי אַתָּה נִשְׁבַּעְתָּ בַּיהוָה אֱלֹהֶיךָ לַאֲמָתֶךָ כִּי־שְׁלֹמֹה בְנֵךְ יִמְלֹךְ אַחֲרָי וְהוּא יֵשֵׁב עַל־כִּסְאִי: 18 וְעַתָּה הִנֵּה אֲדֹנִיָּה מָלָךְ וְעַתָּה אֲדֹנִי הַמֶּלֶךְ לֹא יָדָעְתָּ: 19 וַיִּזְבַּח שׁוֹר וּמְרִיא־וְצֹאן לָרֹב וַיִּקְרָא לְכָל־בְּנֵי הַמֶּלֶךְ וּלְאֶבְיָתָר הַכֹּהֵן וּלְיֹאָב שַׂר הַצָּבָא וְלִשְׁלֹמֹה עַבְדְּךָ לֹא קָרָא: 20 וְאַתָּה אֲדֹנִי הַמֶּלֶךְ עֵינֵי כָל־יִשְׂרָאֵל עָלֶיךָ לְהַגִּיד לָהֶם מִי יֵשֵׁב עַל־כִּסֵּא אֲדֹנִי־הַמֶּלֶךְ אַחֲרָיו: 21 וְהָיָה כִּשְׁכַב אֲדֹנִי־הַמֶּלֶךְ עִם־אֲבֹתָיו וְהָיִיתִי אֲנִי וּבְנִי שְׁלֹמֹה חַטָּאִים: 22 וְהִנֵּה עוֹדֶנָּה מְדַבֶּרֶת עִם־הַמֶּלֶךְ וְנָתָן הַנָּבִיא בָּא: 23 וַיַּגִּידוּ לַמֶּלֶךְ לֵאמֹר הִנֵּה נָתָן הַנָּבִיא וַיָּבֹא לִפְנֵי הַמֶּלֶךְ וַיִּשְׁתַּחוּ לַמֶּלֶךְ עַל־אַפָּיו אָרְצָה: 24 וַיֹּאמֶר נָתָן אֲדֹנִי הַמֶּלֶךְ אַתָּה אָמַרְתָּ אֲדֹנִיָּהוּ יִמְלֹךְ אַחֲרָי וְהוּא יֵשֵׁב עַל־כִּסְאִי: 25 כִּי יָרַד הַיּוֹם וַיִּזְבַּח שׁוֹר וּמְרִיא־וְצֹאן לָרֹב וַיִּקְרָא לְכָל־בְּנֵי הַמֶּלֶךְ וּלְשָׂרֵי הַצָּבָא וּלְאֶבְיָתָר הַכֹּהֵן וְהִנָּם אֹכְלִים וְשֹׁתִים לְפָנָיו וַיֹּאמְרוּ יְחִי הַמֶּלֶךְ אֲדֹנִיָּהוּ: 26 וְלִי אֲנִי־עַבְדֶּךָ וּלְצָדֹק הַכֹּהֵן וְלִבְנָיָהוּ בֶן־יְהוֹיָדָע וְלִשְׁלֹמֹה עַבְדְּךָ לֹא קָרָא: 27 אִם מֵאֵת אֲדֹנִי הַמֶּלֶךְ נִהְיָה הַדָּבָר הַזֶּה וְלֹא הוֹדַעְתָּ אֶת־עַבְדְּיךָ מִי יֵשֵׁב עַל־כִּסֵּא אֲדֹנִי־הַמֶּלֶךְ אַחֲרָיו: ס 28 וַיַּעַן הַמֶּלֶךְ דָּוִד וַיֹּאמֶר קִרְאוּ־לִי לְבַת־שָׁבַע וַתָּבֹא לִפְנֵי הַמֶּלֶךְ וַתַּעֲמֹד לִפְנֵי הַמֶּלֶךְ: 29 וַיִּשָּׁבַע הַמֶּלֶךְ וַיֹּאמֶר חַי־יְהוָה אֲשֶׁר־פָּדָה אֶת־נַפְשִׁי מִכָּל־צָרָה: 30 כִּי כַּאֲשֶׁר נִשְׁבַּעְתִּי לָךְ בַּיהוָה אֱלֹהֵי יִשְׂרָאֵל לֵאמֹר כִּי־שְׁלֹמֹה בְנֵךְ יִמְלֹךְ אַחֲרַי וְהוּא יֵשֵׁב עַל־כִּסְאִי תַּחְתָּי כִּי כֵּן אֶעֱשֶׂה הַיּוֹם הַזֶּה: 31 וַתִּקֹּד בַּת־שֶׁבַע אַפַּיִם אֶרֶץ וַתִּשְׁתַּחוּ לַמֶּלֶךְ וַתֹּאמֶר יְחִי אֲדֹנִי הַמֶּלֶךְ דָּוִד לְעֹלָם: פ

³² And King David said, "Call to me Zadok the priest, Nathan the prophet, and Benaiah the son of Jehoiada." So they came before the king. ³³ The king also said to them, "Take with you the servants of your lord, and have Solomon my son ride on my own mule, and take him down to Gihon. ³⁴ There let Zadok the priest and Nathan the prophet anoint him king over Israel; and blow the horn, and say, '*Long* live King Solomon!' ³⁵ Then you shall come up after him, and he shall come and sit on my throne, and he shall be king in my place. For I have appointed him to be ruler over Israel and Judah."

³⁶ Benaiah the son of Jehoiada answered the king and said, "Amen! May the LORD God of my lord the king say so *too*. ³⁷ As the LORD has been with my lord the king, even so may He be with Solomon, and make his throne greater than the throne of my lord King David."

³⁸ So Zadok the priest, Nathan the prophet, Benaiah the son of Jehoiada, the Cherethites, and the Pelethites went down and had Solomon ride on King David's mule, and took him down to Gihon. ³⁹ Then Zadok the priest took a horn of oil from the tabernacle and anointed Solomon. And they blew the horn, and all the people said, *"Long* live King Solomon!" ⁴⁰ And all the people went up after him; and the people played the flutes and rejoiced with great joy, so that the earth *seemed to* split with their sound.

⁴¹ Now Adonijah and all the guests who *were* with him heard *it* as they finished eating. And when Joab heard the sound of the horn, he said, "Why *is* the city in such a noisy uproar?" ⁴² While he was still speaking, there came Jonathan, the son of Abiathar the priest. And Adonijah said to him, "Come in, for you *are* a prominent man, and bring good news."

⁴³ Then Jonathan answered and said to Adonijah, "No! Our lord King David has made Solomon king. ⁴⁴ The king has sent with him Zadok the priest, Nathan the prophet, Benaiah the son of Jehoiada, the Cherethites, and the Pelethites; and they have made him ride on the king's mule. ⁴⁵ So Zadok the priest and Nathan the prophet have anointed him king at Gihon; and they have gone up from there rejoicing, so that the city is in an uproar. This *is* the noise that you have heard. ⁴⁶ Also Solomon sits on the throne of the kingdom. ⁴⁷ And moreover the king's servants have gone to bless our lord King David, saying, 'May God make the name of Solomon better than your name, and may He make his throne greater than your throne.' Then the king bowed himself on the bed. ⁴⁸ Also the king said

32 וַיֹּאמֶר הַמֶּלֶךְ דָּוִד קִרְאוּ־לִי לְצָדוֹק הַכֹּהֵן וּלְנָתָן הַנָּבִיא וְלִבְנָיָהוּ בֶּן־יְהוֹיָדָע וַיָּבֹאוּ לִפְנֵי הַמֶּלֶךְ: 33 וַיֹּאמֶר הַמֶּלֶךְ לָהֶם קְחוּ עִמָּכֶם אֶת־עַבְדֵי אֲדֹנֵיכֶם וְהִרְכַּבְתֶּם אֶת־שְׁלֹמֹה בְנִי עַל־הַפִּרְדָּה אֲשֶׁר־לִי וְהוֹרַדְתֶּם אֹתוֹ אֶל־גִּחוֹן: 34 וּמָשַׁח אֹתוֹ שָׁם צָדוֹק הַכֹּהֵן וְנָתָן הַנָּבִיא לְמֶלֶךְ עַל־יִשְׂרָאֵל וּתְקַעְתֶּם בַּשּׁוֹפָר וַאֲמַרְתֶּם יְחִי הַמֶּלֶךְ שְׁלֹמֹה: 35 וַעֲלִיתֶם אַחֲרָיו וּבָא וְיָשַׁב עַל־כִּסְאִי וְהוּא יִמְלֹךְ תַּחְתָּי וְאֹתוֹ צִוִּיתִי לִהְיוֹת נָגִיד עַל־יִשְׂרָאֵל וְעַל־יְהוּדָה: 36 וַיַּעַן בְּנָיָהוּ בֶן־יְהוֹיָדָע אֶת־הַמֶּלֶךְ וַיֹּאמֶר אָמֵן כֵּן יֹאמַר יְהוָה אֱלֹהֵי אֲדֹנִי הַמֶּלֶךְ: 37 כַּאֲשֶׁר הָיָה יְהוָה עִם־אֲדֹנִי הַמֶּלֶךְ כֵּן יִהְיֶה עִם־שְׁלֹמֹה וִיגַדֵּל אֶת־כִּסְאוֹ מִכִּסֵּא אֲדֹנִי הַמֶּלֶךְ דָּוִד: 38 וַיֵּרֶד צָדוֹק הַכֹּהֵן וְנָתָן הַנָּבִיא וּבְנָיָהוּ בֶן־יְהוֹיָדָע וְהַכְּרֵתִי וְהַפְּלֵתִי וַיַּרְכִּבוּ אֶת־שְׁלֹמֹה עַל־פִּרְדַּת הַמֶּלֶךְ דָּוִד וַיֹּלִכוּ אֹתוֹ עַל־גִּחוֹן: 39 וַיִּקַּח צָדוֹק הַכֹּהֵן אֶת־קֶרֶן הַשֶּׁמֶן מִן־הָאֹהֶל וַיִּמְשַׁח אֶת־שְׁלֹמֹה וַיִּתְקְעוּ בַּשּׁוֹפָר וַיֹּאמְרוּ כָּל־הָעָם יְחִי הַמֶּלֶךְ שְׁלֹמֹה: 40 וַיַּעֲלוּ כָל־הָעָם אַחֲרָיו וְהָעָם מְחַלְּלִים בַּחֲלִלִים וּשְׂמֵחִים שִׂמְחָה גְדוֹלָה וַתִּבָּקַע הָאָרֶץ בְּקוֹלָם: 41 וַיִּשְׁמַע אֲדֹנִיָּהוּ וְכָל־הַקְּרֻאִים אֲשֶׁר אִתּוֹ וְהֵם כִּלּוּ לֶאֱכֹל וַיִּשְׁמַע יוֹאָב אֶת־קוֹל הַשּׁוֹפָר וַיֹּאמֶר מַדּוּעַ קוֹל־הַקִּרְיָה הוֹמָה: 42 עוֹדֶנּוּ מְדַבֵּר וְהִנֵּה יוֹנָתָן בֶּן־אֶבְיָתָר הַכֹּהֵן בָּא וַיֹּאמֶר אֲדֹנִיָּהוּ בֹּא כִּי אִישׁ חַיִל אַתָּה וְטוֹב תְּבַשֵּׂר: 43 וַיַּעַן יוֹנָתָן וַיֹּאמֶר לַאֲדֹנִיָּהוּ אֲבָל אֲדֹנֵינוּ הַמֶּלֶךְ־דָּוִד הִמְלִיךְ אֶת־שְׁלֹמֹה: 44 וַיִּשְׁלַח אִתּוֹ־הַמֶּלֶךְ אֶת־צָדוֹק הַכֹּהֵן וְאֶת־נָתָן הַנָּבִיא וּבְנָיָהוּ בֶּן־יְהוֹיָדָע וְהַכְּרֵתִי וְהַפְּלֵתִי וַיַּרְכִּבוּ אֹתוֹ עַל פִּרְדַּת הַמֶּלֶךְ: 45 וַיִּמְשְׁחוּ אֹתוֹ צָדוֹק הַכֹּהֵן וְנָתָן הַנָּבִיא לְמֶלֶךְ בְּגִחוֹן וַיַּעֲלוּ מִשָּׁם שְׂמֵחִים וַתֵּהֹם הַקִּרְיָה הוּא הַקּוֹל אֲשֶׁר שְׁמַעְתֶּם: 46 וְגַם יָשַׁב שְׁלֹמֹה עַל כִּסֵּא הַמְּלוּכָה: 47 וְגַם־בָּאוּ עַבְדֵי הַמֶּלֶךְ לְבָרֵךְ אֶת־אֲדֹנֵינוּ הַמֶּלֶךְ דָּוִד לֵאמֹר יֵיטֵב אֱלֹהֶיךָ אֶת־שֵׁם שְׁלֹמֹה מִשְּׁמֶךָ וִיגַדֵּל אֶת־כִּסְאוֹ מִכִּסְאֶךָ וַיִּשְׁתַּחוּ הַמֶּלֶךְ עַל־הַמִּשְׁכָּב: 48 וְגַם־כָּכָה אָמַר הַמֶּלֶךְ בָּרוּךְ

thus, 'Blessed *be* the LORD God of Israel, who has given *one* to sit on my throne this day, while my eyes see *it!*' "

⁴⁹ So all the guests who were with Adonijah were afraid, and arose, and each one went his way.

⁵⁰ Now Adonijah was afraid of Solomon; so he arose, and went and took hold of the horns of the altar. ⁵¹ And it was told Solomon, saying, "Indeed Adonijah is afraid of King Solomon; for look, he has taken hold of the horns of the altar, saying, 'Let King Solomon swear to me today that he will not put his servant to death with the sword.' "

⁵² Then Solomon said, "If he proves himself a worthy man, not one hair of him shall fall to the earth; but if wickedness is found in him, he shall die." ⁵³ So King Solomon sent them to bring him down from the altar. And he came and fell down before King Solomon; and Solomon said to him, "Go to your house."

2 Now the days of David drew near that he should die, and he charged Solomon his son, saying: ² "I go the way of all the earth; be strong, therefore, and prove yourself a man. ³ And keep the charge of the LORD your God: to walk in His ways, to keep His statutes, His commandments, His judgments, and His testimonies, as it is written in the Law of Moses, that you may prosper in all that you do and wherever you turn; ⁴ that the LORD may fulfill His word which He spoke concerning me, saying, 'If your sons take heed to their way, to walk before Me in truth with all their heart and with all their soul,' He said, 'you shall not lack a man on the throne of Israel.'

⁵ "Moreover you know also what Joab the son of Zeruiah did to me, *and* what he did to the two commanders of the armies of Israel, to Abner the son of Ner and Amasa the son of Jether, whom he killed. And he shed the blood of war in peacetime, and put the blood of war on his belt that *was* around his waist, and on his sandals that *were* on his feet. ⁶ Therefore do according to your wisdom, and do not let his gray hair go down to the grave in peace.

⁷ "But show kindness to the sons of Barzillai the Gileadite, and let them be among those who eat at your table, for so they came to me when I fled from Absalom your brother.

⁸ "And see, *you have* with you Shimei the son of Gera, a Benjamite from Bahurim, who cursed me with a malicious curse in the day when I went to Mahanaim. But he came down to meet me at the Jordan, and I swore to him by the LORD, saying, 'I will not put you to death with the sword.' ⁹ Now

יְהֹוָה אֱלֹהֵי יִשְׂרָאֵל אֲשֶׁר נָתַן הַיּוֹם יֹשֵׁב עַל־כִּסְאִי וְעֵינַי רֹאוֹת: ⁴⁹ וַיֶּחֶרְדוּ וַיָּקֻמוּ כָּל־הַקְּרֻאִים אֲשֶׁר לַאֲדֹנִיָּהוּ וַיֵּלְכוּ אִישׁ לְדַרְכּוֹ: ⁵⁰ וַאֲדֹנִיָּהוּ יָרֵא מִפְּנֵי שְׁלֹמֹה וַיָּקָם וַיֵּלֶךְ וַיַּחֲזֵק בְּקַרְנוֹת הַמִּזְבֵּחַ:

⁵¹ וַיֻּגַּד לִשְׁלֹמֹה לֵאמֹר הִנֵּה אֲדֹנִיָּהוּ יָרֵא אֶת־הַמֶּלֶךְ שְׁלֹמֹה וְהִנֵּה אָחַז בְּקַרְנוֹת הַמִּזְבֵּחַ לֵאמֹר יִשָּׁבַע־לִי כַיּוֹם הַמֶּלֶךְ שְׁלֹמֹה אִם־יָמִית אֶת־עַבְדּוֹ בֶּחָרֶב: ⁵² וַיֹּאמֶר שְׁלֹמֹה אִם יִהְיֶה לְבֶן־חַיִל לֹא־יִפֹּל מִשַּׂעֲרָתוֹ אָרְצָה וְאִם־רָעָה תִמָּצֵא־בוֹ וָמֵת: ⁵³ וַיִּשְׁלַח הַמֶּלֶךְ שְׁלֹמֹה וַיֹּרִדֻהוּ מֵעַל הַמִּזְבֵּחַ וַיָּבֹא וַיִּשְׁתַּחוּ לַמֶּלֶךְ שְׁלֹמֹה וַיֹּאמֶר־לוֹ שְׁלֹמֹה לֵךְ לְבֵיתֶךָ: פ

ב וַיִּקְרְבוּ יְמֵי־דָוִד לָמוּת וַיְצַו אֶת־שְׁלֹמֹה בְנוֹ לֵאמֹר: ² אָנֹכִי הֹלֵךְ בְּדֶרֶךְ כָּל־הָאָרֶץ וְחָזַקְתָּ וְהָיִיתָ לְאִישׁ: ³ וְשָׁמַרְתָּ אֶת־מִשְׁמֶרֶת | יְהֹוָה אֱלֹהֶיךָ לָלֶכֶת בִּדְרָכָיו לִשְׁמֹר חֻקֹּתָיו מִצְוֹתָיו וּמִשְׁפָּטָיו וְעֵדְוֹתָיו כַּכָּתוּב בְּתוֹרַת מֹשֶׁה לְמַעַן תַּשְׂכִּיל אֵת כָּל־אֲשֶׁר תַּעֲשֶׂה וְאֵת כָּל־אֲשֶׁר תִּפְנֶה שָׁם:

⁴ לְמַעַן יָקִים יְהֹוָה אֶת־דְּבָרוֹ אֲשֶׁר דִּבֶּר עָלַי לֵאמֹר אִם־יִשְׁמְרוּ בָנֶיךָ אֶת־דַּרְכָּם לָלֶכֶת לְפָנַי בֶּאֱמֶת בְּכָל־לְבָבָם וּבְכָל־נַפְשָׁם לֵאמֹר לֹא־יִכָּרֵת לְךָ אִישׁ מֵעַל כִּסֵּא יִשְׂרָאֵל: ⁵ וְגַם אַתָּה יָדַעְתָּ אֵת אֲשֶׁר־עָשָׂה לִי יוֹאָב בֶּן־צְרוּיָה אֲשֶׁר עָשָׂה לִשְׁנֵי־שָׂרֵי צִבְאוֹת יִשְׂרָאֵל לְאַבְנֵר בֶּן־נֵר וְלַעֲמָשָׂא בֶן־יֶתֶר וַיַּהַרְגֵם וַיָּשֶׂם דְּמֵי־מִלְחָמָה בְּשָׁלֹם וַיִּתֵּן דְּמֵי מִלְחָמָה בַּחֲגֹרָתוֹ אֲשֶׁר בְּמָתְנָיו וּבְנַעֲלוֹ אֲשֶׁר בְּרַגְלָיו: ⁶ וְעָשִׂיתָ כְּחָכְמָתֶךָ וְלֹא־תוֹרֵד שֵׂיבָתוֹ בְּשָׁלֹם שְׁאֹל: ס ⁷ וְלִבְנֵי בַרְזִלַּי הַגִּלְעָדִי תַּעֲשֶׂה־חֶסֶד וְהָיוּ בְּאֹכְלֵי שֻׁלְחָנֶךָ כִּי־כֵן קָרְבוּ אֵלַי בְּבָרְחִי מִפְּנֵי אַבְשָׁלוֹם אָחִיךָ: ⁸ וְהִנֵּה עִמְּךָ שִׁמְעִי בֶן־גֵּרָא בֶן־הַיְמִינִי מִבַּחֻרִים וְהוּא קִלְלַנִי קְלָלָה נִמְרֶצֶת בְּיוֹם לֶכְתִּי מַחֲנָיִם וְהוּא־יָרַד לִקְרָאתִי הַיַּרְדֵּן וָאֶשָּׁבַע לוֹ בַיהֹוָה לֵאמֹר אִם־אֲמִיתְךָ בֶּחָרֶב: ⁹ וְעַתָּה אַל־תְּנַקֵּהוּ כִּי אִישׁ חָכָם אָתָּה

therefore, do not hold him guiltless, for you *are* a wise man and know what you ought to do to him; but bring his gray hair down to the grave with blood."

10 So David rested with his fathers, and was buried in the City of David. 11 The period that David reigned over Israel *was* forty years; seven years he reigned in Hebron, and in Jerusalem he reigned thirty-three years. 12 Then Solomon sat on the throne of his father David; and his kingdom was firmly established.

13 Now Adonijah the son of Haggith came to Bathsheba the mother of Solomon. So she said, "Do you come peaceably?"

And he said, "Peaceably." 14 Moreover he said, "I have something *to say* to you."

And she said, "Say it."

15 Then he said, "You know that the kingdom was mine, and all Israel had set their expectations on me, that I should reign. However, the kingdom has been turned over, and has become my brother's; for it was his from the LORD. 16 Now I ask one petition of you; do not deny me."

And she said to him, "Say it."

17 Then he said, "Please speak to King Solomon, for he will not refuse you, that he may give me Abishag the Shunammite as wife."

18 So Bathsheba said, "Very well, I will speak for you to the king."

19 Bathsheba therefore went to King Solomon, to speak to him for Adonijah. And the king rose up to meet her and bowed down to her, and sat down on his throne and had a throne set for the king's mother; so she sat at his right hand. 20 Then she said, "I desire one small petition of you; do not refuse me."

And the king said to her, "Ask it, my mother, for I will not refuse you."

21 So she said, "Let Abishag the Shunammite be given to Adonijah your brother as wife."

22 And King Solomon answered and said to his mother, "Now why do you ask Abishag the Shunammite for Adonijah? Ask for him the kingdom also—for he *is* my older brother—for him, and for Abiathar the priest, and for Joab the son of Zeruiah." 23 Then King Solomon swore by the LORD, saying, "May God do so to me, and more also, if Adonijah has not spoken this word against his own life! 24 Now therefore, *as* the LORD lives, who has confirmed me and set me on the throne of David my father, and who has established a house for me, as He promised, Adonijah shall be put to death today!"

וְיָדַעְתָּ אֵת אֲשֶׁר תַּעֲשֶׂה־לּוֹ וְהוֹרַדְתָּ אֶת־שֵׂיבָתוֹ בְּדָם שְׁאוֹל׃ 10 וַיִּשְׁכַּב דָּוִד עִם־אֲבֹתָיו וַיִּקָּבֵר בְּעִיר דָּוִד׃ פ

11 וְהַיָּמִים אֲשֶׁר מָלַךְ דָּוִד עַל־יִשְׂרָאֵל אַרְבָּעִים שָׁנָה בְּחֶבְרוֹן מָלַךְ שֶׁבַע שָׁנִים וּבִירוּשָׁלַ͏ִם מָלַךְ שְׁלֹשִׁים וְשָׁלֹשׁ שָׁנִים׃ 12 וּשְׁלֹמֹה יָשַׁב עַל־כִּסֵּא דָּוִד אָבִיו וַתִּכֹּן מַלְכֻתוֹ מְאֹד׃ 13 וַיָּבֹא אֲדֹנִיָּהוּ בֶן־חַגֵּית אֶל־בַּת־שֶׁבַע אֵם־שְׁלֹמֹה וַתֹּאמֶר הֲשָׁלוֹם בֹּאֶךָ וַיֹּאמֶר שָׁלוֹם׃ 14 וַיֹּאמֶר דָּבָר לִי אֵלַיִךְ וַתֹּאמֶר דַּבֵּר׃ 15 וַיֹּאמֶר אַתְּ יָדַעַתְּ כִּי־לִי הָיְתָה הַמְּלוּכָה וְעָלַי שָׂמוּ כָל־יִשְׂרָאֵל פְּנֵיהֶם לִמְלֹךְ וַתִּסֹּב הַמְּלוּכָה וַתְּהִי לְאָחִי כִּי מֵיהֹוָה הָיְתָה לּוֹ׃ 16 וְעַתָּה שְׁאֵלָה אַחַת אָנֹכִי שֹׁאֵל מֵאִתָּךְ אַל־ תָּשִׁבִי אֶת־פָּנָי וַתֹּאמֶר אֵלָיו דַּבֵּר׃ 17 וַיֹּאמֶר אִמְרִי־ נָא לִשְׁלֹמֹה הַמֶּלֶךְ כִּי לֹא־יָשִׁיב אֶת־פָּנָיִךְ וְיִתֶּן־ לִי אֶת־אֲבִישַׁג הַשּׁוּנַמִּית לְאִשָּׁה׃ 18 וַתֹּאמֶר בַּת־ שֶׁבַע טוֹב אָנֹכִי אֲדַבֵּר עָלֶיךָ אֶל־הַמֶּלֶךְ׃ 19 וַתָּבֹא בַת־שֶׁבַע אֶל־הַמֶּלֶךְ שְׁלֹמֹה לְדַבֶּר־לוֹ עַל־אֲדֹנִיָּהוּ וַיָּקָם הַמֶּלֶךְ לִקְרָאתָהּ וַיִּשְׁתַּחוּ לָהּ וַיֵּשֶׁב עַל־כִּסְאוֹ וַיָּשֶׂם כִּסֵּא לְאֵם הַמֶּלֶךְ וַתֵּשֶׁב לִימִינוֹ׃ 20 וַתֹּאמֶר שְׁאֵלָה אַחַת קְטַנָּה אָנֹכִי שֹׁאֶלֶת מֵאִתָּךְ אַל־ תָּשֵׁב אֶת־פָּנָי וַיֹּאמֶר־לָהּ הַמֶּלֶךְ שַׁאֲלִי אִמִּי כִּי לֹא־אָשִׁיב אֶת־פָּנָיִךְ׃ 21 וַתֹּאמֶר יֻתַּן אֶת־אֲבִישַׁג הַשֻּׁנַמִּית לַאֲדֹנִיָּהוּ אָחִיךָ לְאִשָּׁה׃ 22 וַיַּעַן הַמֶּלֶךְ שְׁלֹמֹה וַיֹּאמֶר לְאִמּוֹ וְלָמָה אַתְּ שֹׁאֶלֶת אֶת־אֲבִישַׁג הַשֻּׁנַמִּית לַאֲדֹנִיָּהוּ וְשַׁאֲלִי־לוֹ אֶת־הַמְּלוּכָה כִּי הוּא אָחִי הַגָּדוֹל מִמֶּנִּי וְלוֹ וּלְאֶבְיָתָר הַכֹּהֵן וּלְיוֹאָב בֶּן־ צְרוּיָה׃ פ

23 וַיִּשָּׁבַע הַמֶּלֶךְ שְׁלֹמֹה בַּיהֹוָה לֵאמֹר כֹּה יַעֲשֶׂה־ לִּי אֱלֹהִים וְכֹה יוֹסִיף כִּי בְנַפְשׁוֹ דִּבֶּר אֲדֹנִיָּהוּ אֶת־הַדָּבָר הַזֶּה׃ 24 וְעַתָּה חַי־יְהֹוָה אֲשֶׁר הֱכִינַנִי וַיּוֹשִׁיבַנִי עַל־כִּסֵּא דָּוִד אָבִי וַאֲשֶׁר עָשָׂה־לִי בַּיִת

ב 24 וַיֹּשִׁיבֵנִי

²⁵ So King Solomon sent by the hand of Benaiah the son of Jehoiada; and he struck him down, and he died.

²⁶ And to Abiathar the priest the king said, "Go to Anathoth, to your own fields, for you *are* deserving of death; but I will not put you to death at this time, because you carried the ark of the Lord GOD before my father David, and because you were afflicted every time my father was afflicted." ²⁷ So Solomon removed Abiathar from being priest to the LORD, that he might fulfill the word of the LORD which He spoke concerning the house of Eli at Shiloh.

²⁸ Then news came to Joab, for Joab had defected to Adonijah, though he had not defected to Absalom. So Joab fled to the tabernacle of the LORD, and took hold of the horns of the altar. ²⁹ And King Solomon was told, "Joab has fled to the tabernacle of the LORD; there *he is,* by the altar." Then Solomon sent Benaiah the son of Jehoiada, saying, "Go, strike him down." ³⁰ So Benaiah went to the tabernacle of the LORD, and said to him, "Thus says the king, 'Come out!'"

And he said, "No, but I will die here." And Benaiah brought back word to the king, saying, "Thus said Joab, and thus he answered me."

³¹ Then the king said to him, "Do as he has said, and strike him down and bury him, that you may take away from me and from the house of my father the innocent blood which Joab shed. ³² So the LORD will return his blood on his head, because he struck down two men more righteous and better than he, and killed them with the sword—Abner the son of Ner, the commander of the army of Israel, and Amasa the son of Jether, the commander of the army of Judah—though my father David did not know *it.* ³³ Their blood shall therefore return upon the head of Joab and upon the head of his descendants forever. But upon David and his descendants, upon his house and his throne, there shall be peace forever from the LORD."

³⁴ So Benaiah the son of Jehoiada went up and struck and killed him; and he was buried in his own house in the wilderness. ³⁵ The king put Benaiah the son of Jehoiada in his place over the army, and the king put Zadok the priest in the place of Abiathar.

³⁶ Then the king sent and called for Shimei, and said to him, "Build yourself a house in Jerusalem and dwell there, and do not go out from there anywhere. ³⁷ For it shall be, on the day you go out and cross the Brook Kidron, know for certain you shall surely die; your blood shall be on your own head."

²⁵ וַיִּשְׁלַ֞ח כַּאֲשֶׁ֤ר דִּבֶּר֙ כִּ֣י הַיּ֔וֹם יֻמַּ֖ת אֲדֹנִיָּֽהוּ׃ הַמֶּ֣לֶךְ שְׁלֹמֹ֗ה בְּיַד֙ בְּנָיָ֣הוּ בֶן־יְהוֹיָדָ֔ע וַיִּפְגַּע־בּ֖וֹ וַיָּמֹֽת׃ ס ²⁶ וּלְאֶבְיָתָ֨ר הַכֹּהֵ֜ן אָמַ֣ר הַמֶּ֗לֶךְ עֲנָתֹת֙ לֵ֣ךְ עַל־שָׂדֶ֔יךָ כִּ֛י אִ֥ישׁ מָ֖וֶת אָ֑תָּה וּבַיּ֨וֹם הַזֶּ֜ה לֹ֣א אֲמִיתֶ֗ךָ כִּֽי־נָשָׂ֜אתָ אֶת־אֲר֨וֹן אֲדֹנָ֤י יְהוִֹה֙ לִפְנֵי֙ דָּוִ֣ד אָבִ֔י וְכִ֥י הִתְעַנִּ֖יתָ בְּכֹ֥ל אֲשֶׁר־הִתְעַנָּ֖ה אָבִֽי׃ ²⁷ וַיְגָ֤רֶשׁ שְׁלֹמֹה֙ אֶת־אֶבְיָתָ֔ר מִהְי֥וֹת כֹּהֵ֖ן לַֽיהוָ֑ה לְמַלֵּא֙ אֶת־דְּבַ֣ר יְהוָ֔ה אֲשֶׁ֥ר דִּבֶּ֛ר עַל־בֵּ֥ית עֵלִ֖י בְּשִׁלֹֽה׃ פ

²⁸ וְהַשְּׁמֻעָה֙ בָּ֣אָה עַד־יוֹאָ֔ב כִּ֣י יוֹאָ֗ב נָטָ֞ה אַחֲרֵ֤י אֲדֹנִיָּ֔ה וְאַחֲרֵ֥י אַבְשָׁל֖וֹם לֹ֣א נָטָ֑ה וַיָּ֤נָס יוֹאָב֙ אֶל־אֹ֣הֶל יְהוָ֔ה וַֽיַּחֲזֵ֖ק בְּקַרְנ֥וֹת הַמִּזְבֵּֽחַ׃ ²⁹ וַיֻּגַּ֞ד לַמֶּ֣לֶךְ שְׁלֹמֹ֗ה כִּ֤י נָס֙ יוֹאָב֙ אֶל־אֹ֣הֶל יְהוָ֔ה וְהִנֵּ֖ה אֵ֣צֶל הַמִּזְבֵּ֑חַ וַיִּשְׁלַ֨ח שְׁלֹמֹ֜ה אֶת־בְּנָיָ֧הוּ בֶן־יְהוֹיָדָ֛ע לֵאמֹ֖ר לֵ֥ךְ פְּגַע־בּֽוֹ׃ ³⁰ וַיָּבֹ֨א בְנָיָ֜הוּ אֶל־אֹ֣הֶל יְהוָ֗ה וַיֹּ֤אמֶר אֵלָיו֙ כֹּֽה־אָמַ֤ר הַמֶּ֙לֶךְ֙ צֵ֔א וַיֹּ֥אמֶר ׀ לֹ֖א כִּ֣י פֹ֣ה אָמ֑וּת וַיָּ֨שֶׁב בְּנָיָ֤הוּ אֶת־הַמֶּ֙לֶךְ֙ דָּבָ֣ר לֵאמֹ֔ר כֹּֽה־דִבֶּ֥ר יוֹאָ֖ב וְכֹ֥ה עָנָֽנִי׃ ³¹ וַיֹּ֧אמֶר ל֣וֹ הַמֶּ֗לֶךְ עֲשֵׂה֙ כַּאֲשֶׁ֣ר דִּבֶּ֔ר וּפְגַע־בּ֖וֹ וּקְבַרְתּ֑וֹ וַהֲסִירֹ֣תָ ׀ דְּמֵ֣י חִנָּ֗ם אֲשֶׁ֤ר שָׁפַ֣ךְ יוֹאָ֔ב מֵעָלַ֖י וּמֵעַ֥ל בֵּ֥ית אָבִֽי׃ ³² וְהֵשִׁיב֩ יְהוָ֨ה אֶת־דָּמ֜וֹ עַל־רֹאשׁ֗וֹ אֲשֶׁ֣ר פָּגַ֣ע בִּשְׁנֵֽי־אֲ֠נָשִׁים צַדִּקִ֨ים וְטֹבִ֤ים מִמֶּ֙נּוּ֙ וַיַּהַרְגֵ֣ם בַּחֶ֔רֶב וְאָבִ֥י דָוִ֖ד לֹ֣א יָדָ֑ע אֶת־אַבְנֵ֤ר בֶּן־נֵר֙ שַׂר־צְבָ֣א יִשְׂרָאֵ֔ל וְאֶת־עֲמָשָׂ֥א בֶן־יֶ֖תֶר שַׂר־צְבָ֥א יְהוּדָֽה׃ ³³ וְשָׁ֤בוּ דְמֵיהֶם֙ בְּרֹ֣אשׁ יוֹאָ֔ב וּבְרֹ֥אשׁ זַרְע֖וֹ לְעֹלָ֑ם וּלְדָוִ֣ד וּ֠לְזַרְעוֹ וּלְבֵית֨וֹ וּלְכִסְא֜וֹ יִהְיֶ֥ה שָׁל֛וֹם עַד־עוֹלָ֖ם מֵעִ֥ם יְהוָֽה׃ ³⁴ וַיַּ֗עַל בְּנָיָ֙הוּ֙ בֶּן־יְה֣וֹיָדָ֔ע וַיִּפְגַּע־בּ֖וֹ וַיְמִתֵ֑הוּ וַיִּקָּבֵ֥ר בְּבֵית֖וֹ בַּמִּדְבָּֽר׃ ³⁵ וַיִּתֵּ֨ן הַמֶּ֜לֶךְ אֶת־בְּנָיָ֧הוּ בֶן־יְהוֹיָדָ֛ע תַּחְתָּ֖יו עַל־הַצָּבָ֑א וְאֶת־צָד֤וֹק הַכֹּהֵן֙ נָתַ֣ן הַמֶּ֔לֶךְ תַּ֖חַת אֶבְיָתָֽר׃ ³⁶ וַיִּשְׁלַ֤ח הַמֶּ֙לֶךְ֙ וַיִּקְרָ֣א לְשִׁמְעִ֔י וַיֹּ֤אמֶר לוֹ֙ בְּֽנֵה־לְךָ֥ בַ֙יִת֙ בִּיר֣וּשָׁלַ֔͏ִם וְיָשַׁבְתָּ֖ שָׁ֑ם וְלֹא־תֵצֵ֥א מִשָּׁ֖ם אָ֥נֶה וָאָֽנָה׃ ³⁷ וְהָיָ֣ה ׀ בְּי֣וֹם צֵאתְךָ֗ וְעָֽבַרְתָּ֙ אֶת־נַ֣חַל קִדְר֔וֹן יָדֹ֥עַ תֵּדַ֖ע כִּ֣י מ֣וֹת תָּמ֑וּת דָּמְךָ֖ יִהְיֶ֥ה

³⁸ And Shimei said to the king, "The saying *is* good. As my lord the king has said, so your servant will do." So Shimei dwelt in Jerusalem many days.

³⁹ Now it happened at the end of three years, that two slaves of Shimei ran away to Achish the son of Maachah, king of Gath. And they told Shimei, saying, "Look, your slaves *are* in Gath!" ⁴⁰ So Shimei arose, saddled his donkey, and went to Achish at Gath to seek his slaves. And Shimei went and brought his slaves from Gath. ⁴¹ And Solomon was told that Shimei had gone from Jerusalem to Gath and had come back. ⁴² Then the king sent and called for Shimei, and said to him, "Did I not make you swear by the LORD, and warn you, saying, 'Know for certain that on the day you go out and travel anywhere, you shall surely die'? And you said to me, 'The word I have heard *is* good.' ⁴³ Why then have you not kept the oath of the LORD and the commandment that I gave you?" ⁴⁴ The king said moreover to Shimei, "You know, as your heart acknowledges, all the wickedness that you did to my father David; therefore the LORD will return your wickedness on your own head. ⁴⁵ But King Solomon *shall be* blessed, and the throne of David shall be established before the LORD forever."

⁴⁶ So the king commanded Benaiah the son of Jehoiada; and he went out and struck him down, and he died. Thus the kingdom was established in the hand of Solomon.

3 Now Solomon made a treaty with Pharaoh king of Egypt, and married Pharaoh's daughter; then he brought her to the City of David until he had finished building his own house, and the house of the LORD, and the wall all around Jerusalem. ² Meanwhile the people sacrificed at the high places, because there was no house built for the name of the LORD until those days. ³ And Solomon loved the LORD, walking in the statutes of his father David, except that he sacrificed and burned incense at the high places.

⁴ Now the king went to Gibeon to sacrifice there, for that *was* the great high place: Solomon offered a thousand burnt offerings on that altar. ⁵ At Gibeon the LORD appeared to Solomon in a dream by night; and God said, "Ask! What shall I give you?"

⁶ And Solomon said: "You have shown great mercy to Your servant David my father, because he walked before You in truth, in righteousness, and in uprightness of heart with You; You have continued this great kindness for him, and You have given him a son to sit on his throne, as *it is* this day. ⁷ Now, O LORD my God, You have made Your servant king instead of my father David, but I *am* a

בְּרֹאשֶׁךָ: 38 וַיֹּאמֶר שִׁמְעִי לַמֶּלֶךְ טוֹב הַדָּבָר כַּאֲשֶׁר דִּבֶּר אֲדֹנִי הַמֶּלֶךְ כֵּן יַעֲשֶׂה עַבְדֶּךָ וַיֵּשֶׁב שִׁמְעִי בִּירוּשָׁלִַם יָמִים רַבִּים: ס 39 וַיְהִי מִקֵּץ שָׁלֹשׁ שָׁנִים וַיִּבְרְחוּ שְׁנֵי־עֲבָדִים לְשִׁמְעִי אֶל־אָכִישׁ בֶּן־מַעֲכָה מֶלֶךְ גַּת וַיַּגִּידוּ לְשִׁמְעִי לֵאמֹר הִנֵּה עֲבָדֶיךָ בְּגַת: 40 וַיָּקָם שִׁמְעִי וַיַּחֲבֹשׁ אֶת־חֲמֹרוֹ וַיֵּלֶךְ גַּתָה אֶל־אָכִישׁ לְבַקֵּשׁ אֶת־עֲבָדָיו וַיֵּלֶךְ שִׁמְעִי וַיָּבֵא אֶת־עֲבָדָיו מִגַּת: 41 וַיֻּגַּד לִשְׁלֹמֹה כִּי־הָלַךְ שִׁמְעִי מִירוּשָׁלִַם גַּת וַיָּשֹׁב: 42 וַיִּשְׁלַח הַמֶּלֶךְ וַיִּקְרָא לְשִׁמְעִי וַיֹּאמֶר אֵלָיו הֲלוֹא הִשְׁבַּעְתִּיךָ בַיהוָה וָאָעִד בְּךָ לֵאמֹר בְּיוֹם צֵאתְךָ וְהָלַכְתָּ אָנֶה וָאָנָה יָדֹעַ תֵּדַע כִּי מוֹת תָּמוּת וַתֹּאמֶר אֵלַי טוֹב הַדָּבָר שָׁמָעְתִּי: 43 וּמַדּוּעַ לֹא שָׁמַרְתָּ אֵת שְׁבֻעַת יְהוָה וְאֶת־הַמִּצְוָה אֲשֶׁר־צִוִּיתִי עָלֶיךָ: 44 וַיֹּאמֶר הַמֶּלֶךְ אֶל־שִׁמְעִי אַתָּה יָדַעְתָּ אֵת כָּל־הָרָעָה אֲשֶׁר יָדַע לְבָבְךָ אֲשֶׁר עָשִׂיתָ לְדָוִד אָבִי וְהֵשִׁיב יְהוָה אֶת־רָעָתְךָ בְּרֹאשֶׁךָ: 45 וְהַמֶּלֶךְ שְׁלֹמֹה בָּרוּךְ וְכִסֵּא דָוִד יִהְיֶה נָכוֹן לִפְנֵי יְהוָה עַד־עוֹלָם: 46 וַיְצַו הַמֶּלֶךְ אֶת־בְּנָיָהוּ בֶּן־יְהוֹיָדָע וַיֵּצֵא וַיִּפְגַּע־בּוֹ וַיָּמֹת וְהַמַּמְלָכָה נָכוֹנָה בְּיַד־שְׁלֹמֹה:

ג וַיִּתְחַתֵּן שְׁלֹמֹה אֶת־פַּרְעֹה מֶלֶךְ מִצְרָיִם וַיִּקַּח אֶת־בַּת־פַּרְעֹה וַיְבִיאֶהָ אֶל־עִיר דָּוִד עַד כַּלֹּתוֹ לִבְנוֹת אֶת־בֵּיתוֹ וְאֶת־בֵּית יְהוָה וְאֶת־חוֹמַת יְרוּשָׁלִַם סָבִיב: 2 רַק הָעָם מְזַבְּחִים בַּבָּמוֹת כִּי לֹא־נִבְנָה בַיִת לְשֵׁם יְהוָה עַד הַיָּמִים הָהֵם: פ 3 וַיֶּאֱהַב שְׁלֹמֹה אֶת־יְהוָה לָלֶכֶת בְּחֻקּוֹת דָּוִד אָבִיו רַק בַּבָּמוֹת הוּא מְזַבֵּחַ וּמַקְטִיר: 4 וַיֵּלֶךְ הַמֶּלֶךְ גִּבְעֹנָה לִזְבֹּחַ שָׁם כִּי הִיא הַבָּמָה הַגְּדוֹלָה אֶלֶף עֹלוֹת יַעֲלֶה שְׁלֹמֹה עַל הַמִּזְבֵּחַ הַהוּא: 5 בְּגִבְעוֹן נִרְאָה יְהוָה אֶל־שְׁלֹמֹה בַּחֲלוֹם הַלָּיְלָה וַיֹּאמֶר אֱלֹהִים שְׁאַל מָה אֶתֶּן־לָךְ: 6 וַיֹּאמֶר שְׁלֹמֹה אַתָּה עָשִׂיתָ עִם־עַבְדְּךָ דָוִד אָבִי חֶסֶד גָּדוֹל כַּאֲשֶׁר הָלַךְ לְפָנֶיךָ בֶּאֱמֶת וּבִצְדָקָה וּבְיִשְׁרַת לֵבָב עִמָּךְ וַתִּשְׁמָר־לוֹ אֶת־הַחֶסֶד הַגָּדוֹל הַזֶּה וַתִּתֶּן־לוֹ בֵן יֹשֵׁב עַל־כִּסְאוֹ כַּיּוֹם הַזֶּה: 7 וְעַתָּה יְהוָה אֱלֹהָי אַתָּה הִמְלַכְתָּ אֶת־עַבְדְּךָ תַּחַת דָּוִד אָבִי וְאָנֹכִי

little child; I do not know *how* to go out or come in.
⁸ And Your servant *is* in the midst of Your people
whom You have chosen, a great people, too
numerous to be numbered or counted. ⁹ Therefore
give to Your servant an understanding heart to
judge Your people, that I may discern between
good and evil. For who is able to judge this great
people of Yours?"

¹⁰ The speech pleased the LORD, that Solomon
had asked this thing. ¹¹ Then God said to him:
"Because you have asked this thing, and have not
asked long life for yourself, nor have asked riches
for yourself, nor have asked the life of your
enemies, but have asked for yourself understanding
to discern justice, ¹² behold, I have done according
to your words; see, I have given you a wise and
understanding heart, so that there has not been
anyone like you before you, nor shall any like you
arise after you. ¹³ And I have also given you what
you have not asked: both riches and honor, so that
there shall not be anyone like you among the kings
all your days. ¹⁴ So if you walk in My ways, to keep
My statutes and My commandments, as your father
David walked, then I will lengthen your days."

¹⁵ Then Solomon awoke; and indeed it had been a
dream. And he came to Jerusalem and stood before
the ark of the covenant of the LORD, offered up
burnt offerings, offered peace offerings, and made a
feast for all his servants.

¹⁶ Now two women *who were* harlots came to the
king, and stood before him. ¹⁷ And one woman
said, "O my lord, this woman and I dwell in the
same house; and I gave birth while she *was* in the
house. ¹⁸ Then it happened, the third day after I had
given birth, that this woman also gave birth. And
we *were* together; no one *was* with us in the house,
except the two of us in the house. ¹⁹ And this
woman's son died in the night, because she lay on
him. ²⁰ So she arose in the middle of the night and
took my son from my side, while your maidservant
slept, and laid him in her bosom, and laid her dead
child in my bosom. ²¹ And when I rose in the
morning to nurse my son, there he was, dead. But
when I had examined him in the morning, indeed,
he was not my son whom I had borne."

²² Then the other woman said, "No! But the
living one *is* my son, and the dead one *is* your son."

And the first woman said, "No! But the dead one
is your son, and the living one *is* my son."

Thus they spoke before the king.

²³ And the king said, "The one says, 'This *is* my
son, who lives, and your son *is* the dead one'; and
the other says, 'No! But your son *is* the dead one,
and my son *is* the living one.'" ²⁴ Then the king

נַעַר קָטֹן לֹא אֵדַע צֵאת וָבֹא: 8 וְעַבְדְּךָ בְּתוֹךְ
עַמְּךָ אֲשֶׁר בָּחָרְתָּ עַם־רָב אֲשֶׁר לֹא־יִמָּנֶה וְלֹא
יִסָּפֵר מֵרֹב: 9 וְנָתַתָּ לְעַבְדְּךָ לֵב שֹׁמֵעַ לִשְׁפֹּט אֶת־
עַמְּךָ לְהָבִין בֵּין־טוֹב לְרָע כִּי מִי יוּכַל לִשְׁפֹּט אֶת־
עַמְּךָ הַכָּבֵד הַזֶּה: 10 וַיִּיטַב הַדָּבָר בְּעֵינֵי אֲדֹנָי כִּי
שָׁאַל שְׁלֹמֹה אֶת־הַדָּבָר הַזֶּה: 11 וַיֹּאמֶר אֱלֹהִים
אֵלָיו יַעַן אֲשֶׁר שָׁאַלְתָּ אֶת־הַדָּבָר הַזֶּה וְלֹא־שָׁאַלְתָּ
לְּךָ יָמִים רַבִּים וְלֹא־שָׁאַלְתָּ לְּךָ עֹשֶׁר וְלֹא שָׁאַלְתָּ
נֶפֶשׁ אֹיְבֶיךָ וְשָׁאַלְתָּ לְּךָ הָבִין לִשְׁמֹעַ מִשְׁפָּט:
12 הִנֵּה עָשִׂיתִי כִּדְבָרֶיךָ הִנֵּה | נָתַתִּי לְךָ לֵב
חָכָם וְנָבוֹן אֲשֶׁר כָּמוֹךָ לֹא־הָיָה לְפָנֶיךָ וְאַחֲרֶיךָ
לֹא־יָקוּם כָּמוֹךָ: 13 וְגַם אֲשֶׁר לֹא־שָׁאַלְתָּ נָתַתִּי
לָךְ גַּם־עֹשֶׁר גַּם־כָּבוֹד אֲשֶׁר לֹא־הָיָה כָמוֹךָ אִישׁ
בַּמְּלָכִים כָּל־יָמֶיךָ: 14 וְאִם | תֵּלֵךְ בִּדְרָכַי לִשְׁמֹר
חֻקַּי וּמִצְוֹתַי כַּאֲשֶׁר הָלַךְ דָּוִיד אָבִיךָ וְהַאֲרַכְתִּי
אֶת־יָמֶיךָ: ס 15 וַיִּקַץ שְׁלֹמֹה וְהִנֵּה חֲלוֹם
וַיָּבוֹא יְרוּשָׁלַ͏ִם וַיַּעֲמֹד | לִפְנֵי | אֲרוֹן בְּרִית־אֲדֹנָי
וַיַּעַל עֹלוֹת וַיַּעַשׂ שְׁלָמִים וַיַּעַשׂ מִשְׁתֶּה לְכָל־
עֲבָדָיו:
פ

16 אָז תָּבֹאנָה שְׁתַּיִם נָשִׁים זֹנוֹת אֶל־הַמֶּלֶךְ
וַתַּעֲמֹדְנָה לְפָנָיו: 17 וַתֹּאמֶר הָאִשָּׁה הָאַחַת בִּי
אֲדֹנִי אֲנִי וְהָאִשָּׁה הַזֹּאת יֹשְׁבֹת בְּבַיִת אֶחָד
וָאֵלֵד עִמָּהּ בַּבָּיִת: 18 וַיְהִי בַּיּוֹם הַשְּׁלִישִׁי לְלִדְתִּי
וַתֵּלֶד גַּם־הָאִשָּׁה הַזֹּאת וַאֲנַחְנוּ יַחְדָּו אֵין־זָר אִתָּנוּ
בַּבַּיִת זוּלָתִי שְׁתַּיִם־אֲנַחְנוּ בַּבָּיִת: 19 וַיָּמָת בֶּן־
הָאִשָּׁה הַזֹּאת לָיְלָה אֲשֶׁר שָׁכְבָה עָלָיו: 20 וַתָּקָם
בְּתוֹךְ הַלַּיְלָה וַתִּקַּח אֶת־בְּנִי מֵאֶצְלִי וַאֲמָתְךָ
יְשֵׁנָה וַתַּשְׁכִּיבֵהוּ בְּחֵיקָהּ וְאֶת־בְּנָהּ הַמֵּת הִשְׁכִּיבָה
בְחֵיקִי: 21 וָאָקֻם בַּבֹּקֶר לְהֵינִיק אֶת־בְּנִי וְהִנֵּה־מֵת
וָאֶתְבּוֹנֵן אֵלָיו בַּבֹּקֶר וְהִנֵּה לֹא־הָיָה בְנִי אֲשֶׁר
יָלָדְתִּי: 22 וַתֹּאמֶר הָאִשָּׁה הָאַחֶרֶת לֹא כִי בְּנִי
הַחַי וּבְנֵךְ הַמֵּת וְזֹאת אֹמֶרֶת לֹא כִי בְּנֵךְ הַמֵּת
וּבְנִי הֶחָי וַתְּדַבֵּרְנָה לִפְנֵי הַמֶּלֶךְ: 23 וַיֹּאמֶר הַמֶּלֶךְ
זֹאת אֹמֶרֶת זֶה־בְּנִי הַחַי וּבְנֵךְ הַמֵּת וְזֹאת אֹמֶרֶת
לֹא כִי בְּנֵךְ הַמֵּת וּבְנִי הֶחָי:
פ
24 וַיֹּאמֶר הַמֶּלֶךְ קְחוּ לִי־חָרֶב וַיָּבִאוּ הַחֶרֶב לִפְנֵי

said, "Bring me a sword." So they brought a sword before the king. 25 And the king said, "Divide the living child in two, and give half to one, and half to the other."

26 Then the woman whose son *was* living spoke to the king, for she yearned with compassion for her son; and she said, "O my lord, give her the living child, and by no means kill him!"

But the other said, "Let him be neither mine nor yours, *but divide him.*"

27 So the king answered and said, "Give the first woman the living child, and by no means kill him; she *is* his mother."

28 And all Israel heard of the judgment which the king had rendered; and they feared the king, for they saw that the wisdom of God *was* in him to administer justice.

4 So King Solomon was king over all Israel. 2 And these *were* his officials: Azariah the son of Zadok, the priest; 3 Elihoreph and Ahijah, the sons of Shisha, scribes; Jehoshaphat the son of Ahilud, the recorder; 4 Benaiah the son of Jehoiada, over the army; Zadok and Abiathar, the priests; 5 Azariah the son of Nathan, over the officers; Zabud the son of Nathan, a priest *and* the king's friend; 6 Ahishar, over the household; and Adoniram the son of Abda, over the labor force.

7 And Solomon had twelve governors over all Israel, who provided food for the king and his household; each one made provision for one month of the year. 8 These *are* their names: Ben-Hur, in the mountains of Ephraim; 9 Ben-Deker, in Makaz, Shaalbim, Beth Shemesh, and Elon Beth Hanan; 10 Ben-Hesed, in Arubboth; to him *belonged* Sochoh and all the land of Hepher; 11 Ben-Abinadab, *in* all the regions of Dor; he had Taphath the daughter of Solomon as wife; 12 Baana the son of Ahilud, *in* Taanach, Megiddo, and all Beth Shean, which *is* beside Zaretan below Jezreel, from Beth Shean to Abel Meholah, as far as the other side of Jokneam; 13 Ben-Geber, in Ramoth Gilead; to him *belonged* the towns of Jair the son of Manasseh, in Gilead; to him *also belonged* the region of Argob in Bashan— sixty large cities with walls and bronze gate-bars; 14 Ahinadab the son of Iddo, *in* Mahanaim; 15 Ahimaaz, in Naphtali; he also took Basemath the daughter of Solomon as wife; 16 Baanah the son of Hushai, in Asher and Aloth; 17 Jehoshaphat the son of Paruah, in Issachar; 18 Shimei the son of Elah, in Benjamin; 19 Geber the son of Uri, in the land of Gilead, *in* the country of Sihon king of the Amorites, and of Og king of Bashan. *He was* the only governor who *was* in the land.

הַמֶּלֶךְ: 25 וַיֹּאמֶר הַמֶּלֶךְ גִּזְרוּ אֶת־הַיֶּלֶד הַחַי לִשְׁנָיִם וּתְנוּ אֶת־הַחֲצִי לְאַחַת וְאֶת־הַחֲצִי לְאֶחָת: 26 וַתֹּאמֶר הָאִשָּׁה אֲשֶׁר־בְּנָהּ הַחַי אֶל־הַמֶּלֶךְ כִּי־נִכְמְרוּ רַחֲמֶיהָ עַל־בְּנָהּ וַתֹּאמֶר ׀ בִּי אֲדֹנִי תְּנוּ־לָהּ אֶת־הַיָּלוּד הַחַי וְהָמֵת אַל־תְּמִיתֻהוּ וְזֹאת אֹמֶרֶת גַּם־לִי גַם־לָךְ לֹא יִהְיֶה גְּזֹרוּ: 27 וַיַּעַן הַמֶּלֶךְ וַיֹּאמֶר תְּנוּ־לָהּ אֶת־הַיָּלוּד הַחַי וְהָמֵת לֹא תְמִיתֻהוּ הִיא אִמּוֹ: 28 וַיִּשְׁמְעוּ כָל־יִשְׂרָאֵל אֶת־הַמִּשְׁפָּט אֲשֶׁר שָׁפַט הַמֶּלֶךְ וַיִּרְאוּ מִפְּנֵי הַמֶּלֶךְ כִּי רָאוּ כִּי־חָכְמַת אֱלֹהִים בְּקִרְבּוֹ לַעֲשׂוֹת מִשְׁפָּט: ס

ד וַיְהִי הַמֶּלֶךְ שְׁלֹמֹה מֶלֶךְ עַל־כָּל־יִשְׂרָאֵל: ס 2 וְאֵלֶּה הַשָּׂרִים אֲשֶׁר־לוֹ עֲזַרְיָהוּ בֶן־צָדוֹק הַכֹּהֵן: ס 3 אֱלִיחֹרֶף וַאֲחִיָּה בְּנֵי שִׁישָׁא סֹפְרִים יְהוֹשָׁפָט בֶּן־אֲחִילוּד הַמַּזְכִּיר: 4 וּבְנָיָהוּ בֶן־יְהוֹיָדָע עַל־הַצָּבָא וְצָדוֹק וְאֶבְיָתָר כֹּהֲנִים: ס 5 וַעֲזַרְיָהוּ בֶן־נָתָן עַל־הַנִּצָּבִים וְזָבוּד בֶּן־נָתָן כֹּהֵן רֵעֶה הַמֶּלֶךְ: 6 וַאֲחִישָׁר עַל־הַבָּיִת וַאֲדֹנִירָם בֶּן־עַבְדָּא עַל־הַמַּס: ס 7 וְלִשְׁלֹמֹה שְׁנֵים־עָשָׂר נִצָּבִים עַל־כָּל־יִשְׂרָאֵל וְכִלְכְּלוּ אֶת־הַמֶּלֶךְ וְאֶת־בֵּיתוֹ חֹדֶשׁ בַּשָּׁנָה יִהְיֶה עַל־אֶחָד לְכַלְכֵּל: ס 8 וְאֵלֶּה שְׁמוֹתָם בֶּן־חוּר בְּהַר אֶפְרָיִם: ס 9 בֶּן־דֶּקֶר בְּמָקַץ וּבְשַׁעַלְבִים וּבֵית שֶׁמֶשׁ וְאֵילוֹן בֵּית חָנָן: ס 10 בֶּן־חֶסֶד בָּאֲרֻבּוֹת לוֹ שֹׂכֹה וְכָל־אֶרֶץ חֵפֶר: ס 11 בֶּן־אֲבִינָדָב כָּל־נָפַת דֹּאר טָפַת בַּת־שְׁלֹמֹה הָיְתָה לּוֹ לְאִשָּׁה: ס 12 בַּעֲנָא בֶּן־אֲחִילוּד תַּעְנַךְ וּמְגִדּוֹ וְכָל־בֵּית שְׁאָן אֲשֶׁר אֵצֶל צָרְתַנָה מִתַּחַת לְיִזְרְעֶאל מִבֵּית שְׁאָן עַד אָבֵל מְחוֹלָה עַד מֵעֵבֶר לְיָקְמְעָם: ס 13 בֶּן־גֶּבֶר בְּרָמֹת גִּלְעָד לוֹ חַוֹּת יָאִיר בֶּן־מְנַשֶּׁה אֲשֶׁר בַּגִּלְעָד לוֹ חֶבֶל אַרְגֹּב אֲשֶׁר בַּבָּשָׁן שִׁשִּׁים עָרִים גְּדֹלוֹת חוֹמָה וּבְרִיחַ נְחֹשֶׁת: 14 אֲחִינָדָב בֶּן־עִדֹּא מַחֲנָיְמָה: ס 15 אֲחִימַעַץ בְּנַפְתָּלִי גַּם־הוּא לָקַח אֶת־בָּשְׂמַת בַּת־שְׁלֹמֹה לְאִשָּׁה: 16 בַּעֲנָא בֶן־חוּשַׁי בְּאָשֵׁר וּבְעָלוֹת: ס 17 יְהוֹשָׁפָט בֶּן־פָּרוּחַ בְּיִשָּׂשכָר: ס 18 שִׁמְעִי בֶן־אֵלָא בְּבִנְיָמִן: ס 19 גֶּבֶר בֶּן־אֻרִי בְּאֶרֶץ גִּלְעָד אֶרֶץ סִיחוֹן ׀ מֶלֶךְ הָאֱמֹרִי וְעֹג מֶלֶךְ הַבָּשָׁן וּנְצִיב

ד 7 הָאֶחָד

²⁰ Judah and Israel *were* as numerous as the sand by the sea in multitude, eating and drinking and rejoicing. ²¹ So Solomon reigned over all kingdoms from the River *to* the land of the Philistines, as far as the border of Egypt. *They* brought tribute and served Solomon all the days of his life.

²² Now Solomon's provision for one day was thirty kors of fine flour, sixty kors of meal, ²³ ten fatted oxen, twenty oxen from the pastures, and one hundred sheep, besides deer, gazelles, roebucks, and fatted fowl.

²⁴ For he had dominion over all *the region* on this side of the River from Tiphsah even to Gaza, namely over all the kings on this side of the River; and he had peace on every side all around him. ²⁵ And Judah and Israel dwelt safely, each man under his vine and his fig tree, from Dan as far as Beersheba, all the days of Solomon.

²⁶ Solomon had forty thousand stalls of horses for his chariots, and twelve thousand horsemen. ²⁷ And these governors, each man in his month, provided food for King Solomon and for all who came to King Solomon's table. There was no lack in their supply. ²⁸ They also brought barley and straw to the proper place, for the horses and steeds, each man according to his charge.

²⁹ And God gave Solomon wisdom and exceedingly great understanding, and largeness of heart like the sand on the seashore. ³⁰ Thus Solomon's wisdom excelled the wisdom of all the men of the East and all the wisdom of Egypt. ³¹ For he was wiser than all men—than Ethan the Ezrahite, and Heman, Chalcol, and Darda, the sons of Mahol; and his fame was in all the surrounding nations. ³² He spoke three thousand proverbs, and his songs were one thousand and five. ³³ Also he spoke of trees, from the cedar tree of Lebanon even to the hyssop that springs out of the wall; he spoke also of animals, of birds, of creeping things, and of fish. ³⁴ And men of all nations, from all the kings of the earth who had heard of his wisdom, came to hear the wisdom of Solomon.

5

Now Hiram king of Tyre sent his servants to Solomon, because he heard that they had anointed him king in place of his father, for Hiram had always loved David. ² Then Solomon sent to Hiram, saying:

³ You know how my father David could not build a house for the name of the LORD his God because of the wars which were fought against him on every side, until the LORD put *his foes* under the soles of his feet.

אֶחָד אֲשֶׁר בָּאָרֶץ: 20 יְהוּדָה וְיִשְׂרָאֵל רַבִּים כַּחוֹל אֲשֶׁר־עַל־הַיָּם לָרֹב אֹכְלִים וְשֹׁתִים וּשְׂמֵחִים:

ה וּשְׁלֹמֹה הָיָה מוֹשֵׁל בְּכָל־הַמַּמְלָכוֹת מִן־הַנָּהָר אֶרֶץ פְּלִשְׁתִּים וְעַד גְּבוּל מִצְרָיִם מַגִּשִׁים מִנְחָה וְעֹבְדִים אֶת־שְׁלֹמֹה כָּל־יְמֵי חַיָּיו: פ 2 וַיְהִי לֶחֶם־שְׁלֹמֹה לְיוֹם אֶחָד שְׁלֹשִׁים כֹּר סֹלֶת וְשִׁשִּׁים כֹּר קָמַח: 3 עֲשָׂרָה בָקָר בְּרִאִים וְעֶשְׂרִים בָּקָר רְעִי וּמֵאָה צֹאן לְבַד מֵאַיָּל וּצְבִי וְיַחְמוּר וּבַרְבֻּרִים אֲבוּסִים: 4 כִּי־הוּא רֹדֶה בְּכָל־עֵבֶר הַנָּהָר מִתִּפְסַח וְעַד־עַזָּה בְּכָל־מַלְכֵי עֵבֶר הַנָּהָר וְשָׁלוֹם הָיָה לוֹ מִכָּל־עֲבָרָיו מִסָּבִיב: 5 וַיֵּשֶׁב יְהוּדָה וְיִשְׂרָאֵל לָבֶטַח אִישׁ תַּחַת גַּפְנוֹ וְתַחַת תְּאֵנָתוֹ מִדָּן וְעַד־בְּאֵר שָׁבַע כֹּל יְמֵי שְׁלֹמֹה: ס 6 וַיְהִי לִשְׁלֹמֹה אַרְבָּעִים אֶלֶף אֻרְוֹת סוּסִים לְמֶרְכָּבוֹ וּשְׁנֵים־עָשָׂר אֶלֶף פָּרָשִׁים: 7 וְכִלְכְּלוּ הַנִּצָּבִים הָאֵלֶּה אֶת־הַמֶּלֶךְ שְׁלֹמֹה וְאֵת כָּל־הַקָּרֵב אֶל־שֻׁלְחַן הַמֶּלֶךְ־שְׁלֹמֹה אִישׁ חָדְשׁוֹ לֹא יְעַדְּרוּ דָּבָר: 8 וְהַשְּׂעֹרִים וְהַתֶּבֶן לַסּוּסִים וְלָרֶכֶשׁ יָבִאוּ אֶל־הַמָּקוֹם אֲשֶׁר יִהְיֶה־שָּׁם אִישׁ כְּמִשְׁפָּטוֹ: ס 9 וַיִּתֵּן אֱלֹהִים חָכְמָה לִשְׁלֹמֹה וּתְבוּנָה הַרְבֵּה מְאֹד וְרֹחַב לֵב כַּחוֹל אֲשֶׁר עַל־שְׂפַת הַיָּם: 10 וַתֵּרֶב חָכְמַת שְׁלֹמֹה מֵחָכְמַת כָּל־בְּנֵי־קֶדֶם וּמִכֹּל חָכְמַת מִצְרָיִם: 11 וַיֶּחְכַּם מִכָּל־הָאָדָם מֵאֵיתָן הָאֶזְרָחִי וְהֵימָן וְכַלְכֹּל וְדַרְדַּע בְּנֵי מָחוֹל וַיְהִי־שְׁמוֹ בְכָל־הַגּוֹיִם סָבִיב: 12 וַיְדַבֵּר שְׁלֹשֶׁת אֲלָפִים מָשָׁל וַיְהִי שִׁירוֹ חֲמִשָּׁה וָאָלֶף: 13 וַיְדַבֵּר עַל־הָעֵצִים מִן־הָאֶרֶז אֲשֶׁר בַּלְּבָנוֹן וְעַד הָאֵזוֹב אֲשֶׁר יֹצֵא בַּקִּיר וַיְדַבֵּר עַל־הַבְּהֵמָה וְעַל־הָעוֹף וְעַל־הָרֶמֶשׂ וְעַל־הַדָּגִים: 14 וַיָּבֹאוּ מִכָּל־הָעַמִּים לִשְׁמֹעַ אֵת חָכְמַת שְׁלֹמֹה מֵאֵת כָּל־מַלְכֵי הָאָרֶץ אֲשֶׁר שָׁמְעוּ אֶת־חָכְמָתוֹ: ס 15 וַיִּשְׁלַח חִירָם מֶלֶךְ־צוֹר אֶת־עֲבָדָיו אֶל־שְׁלֹמֹה כִּי שָׁמַע כִּי אֹתוֹ מָשְׁחוּ לְמֶלֶךְ תַּחַת אָבִיהוּ כִּי אֹהֵב הָיָה חִירָם לְדָוִד כָּל־הַיָּמִים: ס 16 וַיִּשְׁלַח שְׁלֹמֹה אֶל־חִירָם לֵאמֹר: 17 אַתָּה יָדַעְתָּ אֶת־דָּוִד אָבִי כִּי לֹא יָכֹל לִבְנוֹת בַּיִת לְשֵׁם יְהוָה אֱלֹהָיו מִפְּנֵי הַמִּלְחָמָה

4 But now the LORD my God has given me rest on every side; *there is* neither adversary nor evil occurrence.

5 And behold, I propose to build a house for the name of the LORD my God, as the LORD spoke to my father David, saying, "Your son, whom I will set on your throne in your place, he shall build the house for My name."

6 Now therefore, command that they cut down cedars for me from Lebanon; and my servants will be with your servants, and I will pay you wages for your servants according to whatever you say. For you know *there is* none among us who has skill to cut timber like the Sidonians.

7 So it was, when Hiram heard the words of Solomon, that he rejoiced greatly and said,

Blessed *be* the LORD this day, for He has given David a wise son over this great people!

8 Then Hiram sent to Solomon, saying:

I have considered *the message* which you sent me, *and* I will do all you desire concerning the cedar and cypress logs.

9 My servants shall bring *them* down from Lebanon to the sea; I will float them in rafts by sea to the place you indicate to me, and will have them broken apart there; then you can take *them* away. And you shall fulfill my desire by giving food for my household.

10 Then Hiram gave Solomon cedar and cypress logs *according to* all his desire. 11 And Solomon gave Hiram twenty thousand kors of wheat *as* food for his household, and twenty kors of pressed oil. Thus Solomon gave to Hiram year by year.

12 So the LORD gave Solomon wisdom, as He had promised him; and there was peace between Hiram and Solomon, and the two of them made a treaty together.

13 Then King Solomon raised up a labor force out of all Israel; and the labor force was thirty thousand men. 14 And he sent them to Lebanon, ten thousand a month in shifts: they were one month in Lebanon *and* two months at home; Adoniram *was* in charge of the labor force. 15 Solomon had seventy thousand who carried burdens, and eighty thousand who quarried *stone* in the mountains, 16 besides three thousand three hundred from the chiefs of Solomon's deputies, who supervised the people who labored in the work. 17 And the king commanded them to quarry large stones, costly stones, *and* hewn stones, to lay the foundation of the temple. 18 So Solomon's builders, Hiram's builders, and the Gebalites quarried *them;* and they prepared timber and stones to build the temple.

אֲשֶׁר סְבָבֻהוּ עַד תֵּת־יְהֹוָה אֹתָם תַּחַת כַּפּוֹת רַגְלָיׄ: 18 וְעַתָּה הֵנִיחַ יְהֹוָה אֱלֹהַי לִי מִסָּבִיב אֵין שָׂטָן וְאֵין פֶּגַע רָע: 19 וְהִנְנִי אֹמֵר לִבְנוֹת בַּיִת לְשֵׁם יְהֹוָה אֱלֹהָי כַּאֲשֶׁר ׀ דִּבֶּר יְהֹוָה אֶל־דָּוִד אָבִי לֵאמֹר בִּנְךָ אֲשֶׁר אֶתֵּן תַּחְתֶּיךָ עַל־כִּסְאֶךָ הוּא־ יִבְנֶה הַבַּיִת לִשְׁמִי: 20 וְעַתָּה צַוֵּה וְיִכְרְתוּ־לִי אֲרָזִים מִן־הַלְּבָנוֹן וַעֲבָדַי יִהְיוּ עִם־עֲבָדֶיךָ וּשְׂכַר עֲבָדֶיךָ אֶתֵּן לְךָ כְּכֹל אֲשֶׁר תֹּאמֵר כִּי ׀ אַתָּה יָדַעְתָּ כִּי אֵין בָּנוּ אִישׁ יֹדֵעַ לִכְרָת־עֵצִים כַּצִּדֹנִים: 21 וַיְהִי כִּשְׁמֹעַ חִירָם אֶת־דִּבְרֵי שְׁלֹמֹה וַיִּשְׂמַח מְאֹד וַיֹּאמֶר בָּרוּךְ יְהֹוָה הַיּוֹם אֲשֶׁר נָתַן לְדָוִד בֵּן חָכָם עַל־הָעָם הָרָב הַזֶּה: 22 וַיִּשְׁלַח חִירָם אֶל־שְׁלֹמֹה לֵאמֹר שָׁמַעְתִּי אֵת אֲשֶׁר־שָׁלַחְתָּ אֵלָי אֲנִי אֶעֱשֶׂה אֶת־כָּל־חֶפְצְךָ בַּעֲצֵי אֲרָזִים וּבַעֲצֵי בְרוֹשִׁים: 23 עֲבָדַי יֹרִדוּ מִן־ הַלְּבָנוֹן יָמָּה וַאֲנִי אֲשִׂימֵם דֹּבְרוֹת בַּיָּם עַד־הַמָּקוֹם אֲשֶׁר־תִּשְׁלַח אֵלַי וְנִפַּצְתִּים שָׁם וְאַתָּה תִשָּׂא וְאַתָּה תַּעֲשֶׂה אֶת־חֶפְצִי לָתֵת לֶחֶם בֵּיתִי: 24 וַיְהִי חִירוֹם נֹתֵן לִשְׁלֹמֹה עֲצֵי אֲרָזִים וַעֲצֵי בְרוֹשִׁים כָּל־חֶפְצוֹ: 25 וּשְׁלֹמֹה נָתַן לְחִירָם עֶשְׂרִים אֶלֶף כֹּר חִטִּים מַכֹּלֶת לְבֵיתוֹ וְעֶשְׂרִים כֹּר שֶׁמֶן כָּתִית כֹּה־יִתֵּן שְׁלֹמֹה לְחִירָם שָׁנָה בְשָׁנָה: פ 26 וַיהֹוָה נָתַן חָכְמָה לִשְׁלֹמֹה כַּאֲשֶׁר דִּבֶּר־ לוֹ וַיְהִי שָׁלֹם בֵּין חִירָם וּבֵין שְׁלֹמֹה וַיִּכְרְתוּ בְרִית שְׁנֵיהֶם: 27 וַיַּעַל הַמֶּלֶךְ שְׁלֹמֹה מַס מִכָּל־ יִשְׂרָאֵל וַיְהִי הַמַּס שְׁלֹשִׁים אֶלֶף אִישׁ: 28 וַיִּשְׁלָחֵם לְבָנוֹנָה עֲשֶׂרֶת אֲלָפִים בַּחֹדֶשׁ חֲלִיפוֹת חֹדֶשׁ יִהְיוּ בַלְּבָנוֹן שְׁנַיִם חֳדָשִׁים בְּבֵיתוֹ וַאֲדֹנִירָם עַל־ הַמַּס: ס 29 וַיְהִי לִשְׁלֹמֹה שִׁבְעִים אֶלֶף נֹשֵׂא סַבָּל וּשְׁמֹנִים אֶלֶף חֹצֵב בָּהָר: 30 לְבַד מִשָּׂרֵי הַנִּצָּבִים לִשְׁלֹמֹה אֲשֶׁר עַל־הַמְּלָאכָה שְׁלֹשֶׁת אֲלָפִים וּשְׁלֹשׁ מֵאוֹת הָרֹדִים בָּעָם הָעֹשִׂים בַּמְּלָאכָה: 31 וַיְצַו הַמֶּלֶךְ וַיַּסִּעוּ אֲבָנִים גְּדֹלוֹת אֲבָנִים יְקָרוֹת לְיַסֵּד הַבָּיִת אַבְנֵי גָזִית: 32 וַיִּפְסְלוּ בֹּנֵי שְׁלֹמֹה וּבֹנֵי חִירוֹם וְהַגִּבְלִים וַיָּכִינוּ הָעֵצִים וְהָאֲבָנִים לִבְנוֹת הַבָּיִת: פ

6 And it came to pass in the four hundred and eightieth year after the children of Israel had come out of the land of Egypt, in the fourth year of Solomon's reign over Israel, in the month of Ziv, which *is* the second month, that he began to build the house of the LORD. 2 Now the house which King Solomon built for the LORD, its length was sixty cubits, its width twenty, and its height thirty cubits. 3 The vestibule in front of the sanctuary of the house *was* twenty cubits long across the width of the house, *and* the width of *the vestibule extended* ten cubits from the front of the house. 4 And he made for the house windows with beveled frames.

5 Against the wall of the temple he built chambers all around, *against* the walls of the temple, all around the sanctuary and the inner sanctuary. Thus he made side chambers all around it. 6 The lowest chamber *was* five cubits wide, the middle *was* six cubits wide, and the third *was* seven cubits wide; for he made narrow ledges around the outside of the temple, so that *the support beams* would not be fastened into the walls of the temple. 7 And the temple, when it was being built, was built with stone finished at the quarry, so that no hammer or chisel *or* any iron tool was heard in the temple while it was being built. 8 The doorway for the middle story *was* on the right side of the temple. They went up by stairs to the middle *story*, and from the middle to the third.

9 So he built the temple and finished it, and he paneled the temple with beams and boards of cedar. 10 And he built side chambers against the entire temple, each five cubits high; they were attached to the temple with cedar beams.

11 Then the word of the LORD came to Solomon, saying: 12 "*Concerning* this temple which you are building, if you walk in My statutes, execute My judgments, keep all My commandments, and walk in them, then I will perform My word with you, which I spoke to your father David. 13 And I will dwell among the children of Israel, and will not forsake My people Israel."

14 So Solomon built the temple and finished it. 15 And he built the inside walls of the temple with cedar boards; from the floor of the temple to the ceiling he paneled the inside with wood; and he covered the floor of the temple with planks of cypress. 16 Then he built the twenty-cubit room at the rear of the temple, from floor to ceiling, with cedar boards; he built *it* inside as the inner sanctuary, as the Most Holy *Place*. 17 And in front of it the temple sanctuary was forty cubits *long*.

וַיְהִי בִשְׁמוֹנִים שָׁנָה וְאַרְבַּע מֵאוֹת שָׁנָה לְצֵאת **ו** בְּנֵי־יִשְׂרָאֵל מֵאֶרֶץ־מִצְרַיִם בַּשָּׁנָה הָרְבִיעִית בְּחֹדֶשׁ זִו הוּא הַחֹדֶשׁ הַשֵּׁנִי לִמְלֹךְ שְׁלֹמֹה עַל־יִשְׂרָאֵל וַיִּבֶן הַבַּיִת לַיהוָה: 2 וְהַבַּיִת אֲשֶׁר בָּנָה הַמֶּלֶךְ שְׁלֹמֹה לַיהוָה שִׁשִּׁים־אַמָּה אָרְכּוֹ וְעֶשְׂרִים רָחְבּוֹ וּשְׁלֹשִׁים אַמָּה קוֹמָתוֹ: 3 וְהָאוּלָם עַל־פְּנֵי הֵיכַל הַבַּיִת עֶשְׂרִים אַמָּה אָרְכּוֹ עַל־פְּנֵי רֹחַב הַבָּיִת עֶשֶׂר בָּאַמָּה רָחְבּוֹ עַל־פְּנֵי הַבָּיִת: 4 וַיַּעַשׂ לַבַּיִת חַלּוֹנֵי שְׁקֻפִים אֲטֻמִים: 5 וַיִּבֶן עַל־קִיר הַבַּיִת יָצוּעַ֩ סָבִיב אֶת־קִירוֹת הַבַּיִת סָבִיב לַהֵיכָל וְלַדְּבִיר וַיַּעַשׂ צְלָעוֹת סָבִיב: 6 הַיָּצוּעַ֩ הַתַּחְתֹּנָה חָמֵשׁ בָּאַמָּה רָחְבָּהּ וְהַתִּיכֹנָה שֵׁשׁ בָּאַמָּה רָחְבָּהּ וְהַשְּׁלִישִׁית שֶׁבַע בָּאַמָּה רָחְבָּהּ כִּי מִגְרָעוֹת נָתַן לַבַּיִת סָבִיב חוּצָה לְבִלְתִּי אֲחֹז בְּקִירוֹת־ הַבָּיִת: 7 וְהַבַּיִת בְּהִבָּנֹתוֹ אֶבֶן־שְׁלֵמָה מַסָּע נִבְנָה וּמַקָּבוֹת וְהַגַּרְזֶן כָּל־כְּלִי בַרְזֶל לֹא־נִשְׁמַע בַּבַּיִת בְּהִבָּנֹתוֹ: 8 פֶּתַח הַצֵּלָע הַתִּיכֹנָה אֶל־כֶּתֶף הַבַּיִת הַיְמָנִית וּבְלוּלִּים יַעֲלוּ עַל־הַתִּיכֹנָה וּמִן־הַתִּיכֹנָה אֶל־הַשְּׁלִשִׁים: 9 וַיִּבֶן אֶת־הַבַּיִת וַיְכַלֵּהוּ וַיִּסְפֹּן אֶת־הַבַּיִת גֵּבִים וּשְׂדֵרֹת בָּאֲרָזִים: 10 וַיִּבֶן אֶת־ הַיָּצוּעַ֩ עַל־כָּל־הַבַּיִת חָמֵשׁ אַמּוֹת קוֹמָתוֹ וַיֶּאֱחֹז אֶת־הַבַּיִת בַּעֲצֵי אֲרָזִים:

ס

11 וַיְהִי דְּבַר־יְהוָה אֶל־שְׁלֹמֹה לֵאמֹר: 12 הַבַּיִת הַזֶּה אֲשֶׁר־אַתָּה בֹנֶה אִם־תֵּלֵךְ בְּחֻקֹּתַי וְאֶת־ מִשְׁפָּטַי תַּעֲשֶׂה וְשָׁמַרְתָּ אֶת־כָּל־מִצְוֹתַי לָלֶכֶת בָּהֶם וַהֲקִמֹתִי אֶת־דְּבָרִי אִתָּךְ אֲשֶׁר דִּבַּרְתִּי אֶל־דָּוִד אָבִיךָ: 13 וְשָׁכַנְתִּי בְּתוֹךְ בְּנֵי יִשְׂרָאֵל וְלֹא אֶעֱזֹב אֶת־עַמִּי יִשְׂרָאֵל: ס 14 וַיִּבֶן שְׁלֹמֹה אֶת־הַבַּיִת וַיְכַלֵּהוּ: 15 וַיִּבֶן אֶת־קִירוֹת הַבַּיִת מִבַּיְתָה בְּצַלְעוֹת אֲרָזִים מִקַּרְקַע הַבַּיִת עַד־ קִירוֹת הַסִּפֻּן צִפָּה עֵץ מִבַּיִת וַיְצַף אֶת־קַרְקַע הַבַּיִת בְּצַלְעוֹת בְּרוֹשִׁים: 16 וַיִּבֶן אֶת־עֶשְׂרִים אַמָּה מִיַּרְכְּתֵי הַבַּיִת בְּצַלְעוֹת אֲרָזִים מִן־הַקַּרְקַע עַד־ הַקִּירוֹת וַיִּבֶן לוֹ מִבַּיִת לִדְבִיר לְקֹדֶשׁ הַקֳּדָשִׁים: 17 וְאַרְבָּעִים בָּאַמָּה הָיָה הַבָּיִת הוּא הַהֵיכָל לִפְנָי:

¹⁸The inside of the temple was cedar, carved with ornamental buds and open flowers. All *was* cedar; there was no stone *to be seen.*

¹⁹And he prepared the inner sanctuary inside the temple, to set the ark of the covenant of the LORD there. ²⁰The inner sanctuary *was* twenty cubits long, twenty cubits wide, and twenty cubits high. He overlaid it with pure gold, and overlaid the altar of cedar. ²¹So Solomon overlaid the inside of the temple with pure gold. He stretched gold chains across the front of the inner sanctuary, and overlaid it with gold. ²²The whole temple he overlaid with gold, until he had finished all the temple; also he overlaid with gold the entire altar that *was* by the inner sanctuary.

²³Inside the inner sanctuary he made two cherubim *of* olive wood, *each* ten cubits high. ²⁴One wing of the cherub *was* five cubits, and the other wing of the cherub five cubits: ten cubits from the tip of one wing to the tip of the other. ²⁵And the other cherub *was* ten cubits; both cherubim *were* of the same size and shape. ²⁶The height of one cherub *was* ten cubits, and so *was* the other cherub. ²⁷Then he set the cherubim inside the inner room; and they stretched out the wings of the cherubim so that the wing of the one touched *one* wall, and the wing of the other cherub touched the other wall. And their wings touched each other in the middle of the room. ²⁸Also he overlaid the cherubim with gold.

²⁹Then he carved all the walls of the temple all around, both the inner and outer *sanctuaries,* with carved figures of cherubim, palm trees, and open flowers. ³⁰And the floor of the temple he overlaid with gold, both the inner and outer *sanctuaries.*

³¹For the entrance of the inner sanctuary he made doors *of* olive wood; the lintel *and* doorposts *were* one-fifth *of the wall.* ³²The two doors *were* of olive wood; and he carved on them figures of cherubim, palm trees, and open flowers, and overlaid *them* with gold; and he spread gold on the cherubim and on the palm trees. ³³So for the door of the sanctuary he also made doorposts *of* olive wood, one-fourth *of the wall.* ³⁴And the two doors *were* of cypress wood; two panels *comprised* one folding door, and two panels *comprised* the other folding door. ³⁵Then he carved cherubim, palm trees, and open flowers *on them,* and overlaid *them* with gold applied evenly on the carved work.

³⁶And he built the inner court with three rows of hewn stone and a row of cedar beams.

³⁷In the fourth year the foundation of the house of the LORD was laid, in the month of Ziv. ³⁸And in the eleventh year, in the month of Bul, which is the

18 וְאֶ֨רֶז אֶל־הַבַּ֜יִת פְּנִ֗ימָה מִקְלַ֨עַת פְּקָעִ֜ים וּפְטוּרֵ֣י צִצִּ֔ים הַכֹּ֣ל אֶ֔רֶז אֵ֥ין אֶ֖בֶן נִרְאָֽה׃ 19 וּדְבִ֧יר בְּתוֹךְ־הַבַּ֛יִת מִפְּנִ֖ימָה הֵכִ֑ין לְתִתֵּ֣ן שָׁ֔ם אֶת־אֲר֖וֹן בְּרִ֥ית יְהוָֽה׃ 20 וְלִפְנֵ֣י הַדְּבִ֗יר עֶשְׂרִ֨ים אַמָּ֥ה אֹ֜רֶךְ וְעֶשְׂרִ֧ים אַמָּ֣ה רֹ֗חַב וְעֶשְׂרִ֤ים אַמָּה֙ קֽוֹמָת֔וֹ וַיְצַפֵּ֖הוּ זָהָ֣ב סָג֑וּר וַיְצַ֥ף מִזְבֵּ֖חַ אָֽרֶז׃ 21 וַיְצַ֨ף שְׁלֹמֹ֧ה אֶת־הַבַּ֛יִת מִפְּנִ֖ימָה זָהָ֣ב סָג֑וּר וַיְעַבֵּ֞ר בְּרַתֻּק֤וֹת זָהָב֙ לִפְנֵ֣י הַדְּבִ֔יר וַיְצַפֵּ֖הוּ זָהָֽב׃ 22 וְאֶת־כָּל־הַבַּ֛יִת צִפָּ֥ה זָהָ֖ב עַד־תֹּ֣ם כָּל־הַבָּ֑יִת וְכָל־הַמִּזְבֵּ֛חַ אֲשֶׁר־לַדְּבִ֖יר צִפָּ֥ה זָהָֽב׃ 23 וַיַּ֣עַשׂ בַּדְּבִ֔יר שְׁנֵ֥י כְרוּבִ֖ים עֲצֵי־שָׁ֑מֶן עֶ֥שֶׂר אַמּ֖וֹת קֽוֹמָתֽוֹ׃ 24 וְחָמֵ֣שׁ אַמּ֗וֹת כְּנַ֤ף הַכְּרוּב֙ הָֽאֶחָ֔ת וְחָמֵ֣שׁ אַמּ֔וֹת כְּנַ֥ף הַכְּר֖וּב הַשֵּׁנִ֑ית עֶ֣שֶׂר אַמּ֔וֹת מִקְצ֥וֹת כְּנָפָ֖יו וְעַד־קְצ֥וֹת כְּנָפָֽיו׃ 25 וְעֶ֙שֶׂר֙ בָּֽאַמָּ֔ה הַכְּר֖וּב הַשֵּׁנִ֑י מִדָּ֥ה אַחַ֛ת וְקֶ֥צֶב אֶחָ֖ד לִשְׁנֵ֥י הַכְּרֻבִֽים׃ 26 קוֹמַת֙ הַכְּר֣וּב הָֽאֶחָ֔ד עֶ֖שֶׂר בָּֽאַמָּ֑ה וְכֵ֖ן הַכְּר֥וּב הַשֵּׁנִֽי׃ 27 וַיִּתֵּ֨ן אֶת־הַכְּרוּבִ֜ים בְּת֣וֹךְ ׀ הַבַּ֣יִת הַפְּנִימִ֗י וַֽיִּפְרְשׂוּ֮ אֶת־כַּנְפֵ֣י הַכְּרֻבִים֒ וַתִּגַּ֤ע כְּנַף־הָֽאֶחָד֙ בַּקִּ֔יר וּכְנַ֤ף הַכְּרוּב֙ הַשֵּׁנִ֔י נֹגַ֖עַת בַּקִּ֣יר הַשֵּׁנִ֑י וְכַנְפֵיהֶ֗ם אֶל־תּ֤וֹךְ הַבַּ֙יִת֙ נֹגְעֹ֣ת כָּנָ֖ף אֶל־כָּנָֽף׃ 28 וַיְצַ֥ף אֶת־הַכְּרוּבִ֖ים זָהָֽב׃ 29 וְאֵת֩ כָּל־קִיר֨וֹת הַבַּ֤יִת מֵסַב֙ קָלַ֣ע פִּתּוּחֵ֔י ׀ מִקְלְעוֹת֙ כְּרוּבִ֣ים וְתִֽמֹרֹ֔ת וּפְטוּרֵ֖י צִצִּ֑ים מִלִּפְנִ֖ים וְלַחִיצֽוֹן׃ 30 וְאֶת־קַרְקַ֥ע הַבַּ֖יִת צִפָּ֣ה זָהָ֑ב לִפְנִ֖ימָה וְלַחִיצֽוֹן׃ 31 וְאֵת֙ פֶּ֣תַח הַדְּבִ֔יר עָשָׂ֖ה דַּלְת֣וֹת עֲצֵי־שָׁ֑מֶן הָאַ֥יִל מְזוּז֖וֹת חֲמִשִֽׁית׃ 32 וּשְׁתֵּי֮ דַּלְתוֹת֮ עֲצֵי־שֶׁמֶן֒ וְקָלַ֣ע עֲלֵיהֶ֗ם מִקְלְעוֹת֩ כְּרוּבִ֨ים וְתִמֹר֜וֹת וּפְטוּרֵ֣י צִצִּ֗ים וְצִפָּ֣ה זָהָ֑ב וַיָּ֛רֶד עַל־הַכְּרוּבִ֥ים וְעַל־הַתִּמֹר֖וֹת אֶת־הַזָּהָֽב׃ 33 וְכֵן֙ עָשָׂ֔ה לְפֶ֖תַח הַֽהֵיכָ֑ל מְזוּז֥וֹת עֲצֵי־שֶׁ֖מֶן מֵאֵ֥ת רְבִעִֽית׃ 34 וּשְׁתֵּ֥י דַלְת֖וֹת עֲצֵ֣י בְרוֹשִׁ֑ים שְׁנֵ֤י צְלָעִים֙ הַדֶּ֣לֶת הָֽאַחַ֔ת גְּלִילִ֔ים וּשְׁנֵ֥י קְלָעִ֖ים הַדֶּ֥לֶת הַשֵּׁנִ֖ית גְּלִילִֽים׃ 35 וְקָלַ֤ע כְּרוּבִים֙ וְתִ֣מֹר֔וֹת וּפְטֻרֵ֖י צִצִּ֑ים וְצִפָּ֣ה זָהָ֔ב מְיֻשָּׁ֖ר עַל־הַמְּחֻקֶּֽה׃ 36 וַיִּ֙בֶן֙ אֶת־הֶֽחָצֵ֣ר הַפְּנִימִ֔ית שְׁלֹשָׁ֖ה טוּרֵ֣י גָזִ֑ית וְט֖וּר כְּרֻתֹ֥ת אֲרָזִֽים׃ 37 בַּשָּׁנָה֙ הָֽרְבִיעִ֔ית יֻסַּ֖ד בֵּ֣ית יְהוָ֑ה בְּיֶ֖רַח זִֽו׃ 38 וּבַשָּׁנָה֩ הָאַחַ֨ת עֶשְׂרֵ֜ה בְּיֶ֣רַח בּ֗וּל ה֛וּא

eighth month, the house was finished in all its details and according to all its plans. So he was seven years in building it.

7 But Solomon took thirteen years to build his own house; so he finished all his house.

²He also built the House of the Forest of Lebanon; its length *was* one hundred cubits, its width fifty cubits, and its height thirty cubits, with four rows of cedar pillars, and cedar beams on the pillars. ³And *it was* paneled with cedar above the beams that *were* on forty-five pillars, fifteen *to a* row. ⁴ *There were* windows *with beveled frames in* three rows, and window *was* opposite window *in* three tiers. ⁵And all the doorways and doorposts *had* rectangular frames; and window *was* opposite window *in* three tiers.

⁶He also made the Hall of Pillars: its length *was* fifty cubits, and its width thirty cubits; and in front of them *was* a portico with pillars, and a canopy *was* in front of them.

⁷Then he made a hall for the throne, the Hall of Judgment, where he might judge; and *it was* paneled with cedar from floor to ceiling.

⁸And the house where he dwelt *had* another court inside the hall, of like workmanship. Solomon also made a house like this hall for Pharaoh's daughter, whom he had taken *as wife.*

⁹All these *were* of costly stones cut to size, trimmed with saws, inside and out, from the foundation to the eaves, and also on the outside to the great court. ¹⁰The foundation *was of* costly stones, large stones, some ten cubits and some eight cubits. ¹¹And above *were* costly stones, hewn to size, and cedar wood. ¹²The great court *was* enclosed with three rows of hewn stones and a row of cedar beams. So were the inner court of the house of the LORD and the vestibule of the temple.

¹³Now King Solomon sent and brought Huram from Tyre. ¹⁴He *was* the son of a widow from the tribe of Naphtali, and his father *was* a man of Tyre, a bronze worker; he was filled with wisdom and understanding and skill in working with all kinds of bronze work. So he came to King Solomon and did all his work.

¹⁵And he cast two pillars of bronze, each one eighteen cubits high, and a line of twelve cubits measured the circumference of each. ¹⁶Then he made two capitals *of* cast bronze, to set on the tops of the pillars. The height of one capital *was* five cubits, and the height of the other capital *was* five cubits. ¹⁷He made a lattice network, with wreaths of chainwork, for the capitals which *were* on top of the pillars: seven chains for one capital and seven for

הֶחָדֶשׁ הַשְּׁמִינִי כָּלָה הַבַּיִת לְכָל־דְּבָרָיו וּלְכָל־
מִשְׁפָּטָו וַיִּבְנֵהוּ שֶׁבַע שָׁנִים:

ז וְאֶת־בֵּיתוֹ בָּנָה שְׁלֹמֹה שְׁלֹשׁ עֶשְׂרֵה שָׁנָה וַיְכַל
אֶת־כָּל־בֵּיתוֹ: ² וַיִּבֶן אֶת־בֵּית ׀ יַעַר הַלְּבָנוֹן מֵאָה
אַמָּה אָרְכּוֹ וַחֲמִשִּׁים אַמָּה רָחְבּוֹ וּשְׁלֹשִׁים אַמָּה
קוֹמָתוֹ עַל אַרְבָּעָה טוּרֵי עַמּוּדֵי אֲרָזִים וּכְרֻתוֹת
אֲרָזִים עַל־הָעַמּוּדִים: ³ וְסָפֻן בָּאֶרֶז מִמַּעַל עַל־
הַצְּלָעֹת אֲשֶׁר עַל־הָעַמּוּדִים אַרְבָּעִים וַחֲמִשָּׁה
חֲמִשָּׁה עָשָׂר הַטּוּר: ⁴ וּשְׁקֻפִים שְׁלֹשָׁה טוּרִים
וּמֶחֱזָה אֶל־מֶחֱזָה שָׁלֹשׁ פְּעָמִים: ⁵ וְכָל־הַפְּתָחִים
וְהַמְּזוּזוֹת רְבֻעִים שָׁקֶף וּמוּל מֶחֱזָה אֶל־מֶחֱזָה שָׁלֹשׁ
פְּעָמִים: ⁶ וְאֵת אוּלָם הָעַמּוּדִים עָשָׂה חֲמִשִּׁים
אַמָּה אָרְכּוֹ וּשְׁלֹשִׁים אַמָּה רָחְבּוֹ וְאוּלָם עַל־
פְּנֵיהֶם וְעַמֻּדִים וְעָב עַל־פְּנֵיהֶם: ⁷ וְאוּלָם הַכִּסֵּא
אֲשֶׁר יִשְׁפָּט־שָׁם אֻלָם הַמִּשְׁפָּט עָשָׂה וְסָפוּן
בָּאֶרֶז מֵהַקַּרְקַע עַד־הַקַּרְקָע: ⁸ וּבֵיתוֹ אֲשֶׁר־יֵשֵׁב
שָׁם חָצֵר הָאַחֶרֶת מִבֵּית לָאוּלָם כַּמַּעֲשֶׂה הַזֶּה
הָיָה וּבַיִת יַעֲשֶׂה לְבַת־פַּרְעֹה אֲשֶׁר לָקַח שְׁלֹמֹה
כָּאוּלָם הַזֶּה: ⁹ כָּל־אֵלֶּה אֲבָנִים יְקָרֹת כְּמִדֹּת
גָּזִית מְגֹרָרוֹת בַּמְּגֵרָה מִבַּיִת וּמִחוּץ וּמִמַּסָּד עַד־
הַטְּפָחוֹת וּמִחוּץ עַד־הֶחָצֵר הַגְּדוֹלָה: ¹⁰ וּמְיֻסָּד
אֲבָנִים יְקָרוֹת אֲבָנִים גְּדֹלוֹת אַבְנֵי עֶשֶׂר אַמּוֹת
וְאַבְנֵי שְׁמֹנֶה אַמּוֹת: ¹¹ וּמִלְמַעְלָה אֲבָנִים יְקָרוֹת
כְּמִדּוֹת גָּזִית וָאָרֶז: ¹² וְחָצֵר הַגְּדוֹלָה סָבִיב שְׁלֹשָׁה
טוּרִים גָּזִית וְטוּר כְּרֻתֹת אֲרָזִים וְלַחֲצַר בֵּית־יְהוָה
הַפְּנִימִית וּלְאֻלָם הַבָּיִת: פ
¹³ וַיִּשְׁלַח הַמֶּלֶךְ שְׁלֹמֹה וַיִּקַּח אֶת־חִירָם מִצֹּר:
¹⁴ בֶּן־אִשָּׁה אַלְמָנָה הוּא מִמַּטֵּה נַפְתָּלִי וְאָבִיו
אִישׁ־צֹרִי חֹרֵשׁ נְחֹשֶׁת וַיִּמָּלֵא אֶת־הַחָכְמָה וְאֶת־
הַתְּבוּנָה וְאֶת־הַדַּעַת לַעֲשׂוֹת כָּל־מְלָאכָה בַּנְּחֹשֶׁת
וַיָּבוֹא אֶל־הַמֶּלֶךְ שְׁלֹמֹה וַיַּעַשׂ אֶת־כָּל־מְלַאכְתּוֹ:
¹⁵ וַיָּצַר אֶת־שְׁנֵי הָעַמּוּדִים נְחֹשֶׁת שְׁמֹנֶה עֶשְׂרֵה
אַמָּה קוֹמַת הָעַמּוּד הָאֶחָד וְחוּט שְׁתֵּים־עֶשְׂרֵה
אַמָּה יָסֹב אֶת־הָעַמּוּד הַשֵּׁנִי: ¹⁶ וּשְׁתֵּי כֹתָרֹת
עָשָׂה לָתֵת עַל־רָאשֵׁי הָעַמּוּדִים מֻצַק נְחֹשֶׁת
חָמֵשׁ אַמּוֹת קוֹמַת הַכֹּתֶרֶת הָאֶחָת וְחָמֵשׁ אַמּוֹת
קוֹמַת הַכֹּתֶרֶת הַשֵּׁנִית: ¹⁷ שְׂבָכִים מַעֲשֵׂה שְׂבָכָה
גְּדִלִים מַעֲשֵׂה שַׁרְשְׁרוֹת לַכֹּתָרֹת אֲשֶׁר עַל־
רֹאשׁ הָעַמּוּדִים שִׁבְעָה לַכֹּתֶרֶת הָאֶחָת וְשִׁבְעָה

the other capital. 18 So he made the pillars, and two rows of pomegranates above the network all around to cover the capitals that *were* on top; and thus he did for the other capital.

19 The capitals which *were* on top of the pillars in the hall *were* in the shape of lilies, four cubits. 20 The capitals on the two pillars also *had pomegranates* above, by the convex surface which *was* next to the network; and there *were* two hundred such pomegranates in rows on each of the capitals all around.

21 Then he set up the pillars by the vestibule of the temple; he set up the pillar on the right and called its name Jachin, and he set up the pillar on the left and called its name Boaz. 22 The tops of the pillars were in the shape of lilies. So the work of the pillars was finished.

23 And he made the Sea of cast bronze, ten cubits from one brim to the other; *it was* completely round. Its height *was* five cubits, and a line of thirty cubits measured its circumference.

24 Below its brim *were* ornamental buds encircling it all around, ten to a cubit, all the way around the Sea. The ornamental buds *were* cast in two rows when it was cast. 25 It stood on twelve oxen: three looking toward the north, three looking toward the west, three looking toward the south, and three looking toward the east; the Sea *was set* upon them, and all their back parts *pointed* inward. 26 It *was* a handbreadth thick; and its brim was shaped like the brim of a cup, *like* a lily blossom. It contained two thousand baths.

27 He also made ten carts of bronze; four cubits *was* the length of each cart, four cubits its width, and three cubits its height. 28 And this *was* the design of the carts: They had panels, and the panels *were* between frames; 29 on the panels that *were* between the frames *were* lions, oxen, and cherubim. And on the frames *was* a pedestal on top. Below the lions and oxen *were* wreaths of plaited work. 30 Every cart had four bronze wheels and axles of bronze, and its four feet had supports. Under the laver *were* supports of cast *bronze* beside each wreath. 31 Its opening inside the crown at the top *was* one cubit in diameter; and the opening *was* round, shaped *like* a pedestal, one and a half cubits in outside diameter; and also on the opening *were* engravings, but the panels were square, not round. 32 Under the panels *were* the four wheels, and the axles of the wheels *were joined* to the cart. The height of a wheel *was* one and a half cubits. 33 The workmanship of the wheels *was* like the workmanship of a chariot wheel; their axle pins, their rims, their spokes, and their hubs *were* all of cast *bronze*. 34 And *there were* four supports at the four corners

לְכֹתֶרֶת הַשֵּׁנִית: 18 וַיַּעַשׂ אֶת־הָעַמּוּדִים וּשְׁנֵי טוּרִים סָבִיב עַל־הַשְּׂבָכָה הָאֶחָת לְכַסּוֹת אֶת־הַכֹּתָרֹת אֲשֶׁר עַל־רֹאשׁ הָרִמֹּנִים וְכֵן עָשָׂה לַכֹּתֶרֶת הַשֵּׁנִית: 19 וְכֹתָרֹת אֲשֶׁר עַל־רֹאשׁ הָעַמּוּדִים מַעֲשֵׂה שׁוּשַׁן בָּאוּלָם אַרְבַּע אַמּוֹת: 20 וְכֹתָרֹת עַל־שְׁנֵי הָעַמּוּדִים גַּם־מִמַּעַל מִלְעֻמַּת הַבֶּטֶן אֲשֶׁר לְעֵבֶר הַשְּׂבָכָה וְהָרִמּוֹנִים מָאתַיִם טֻרִים סָבִיב עַל הַכֹּתֶרֶת הַשֵּׁנִית: 21 וַיָּקֶם אֶת־הָעַמֻּדִים לְאֻלָם הַהֵיכָל וַיָּקֶם אֶת־הָעַמּוּד הַיְמָנִי וַיִּקְרָא אֶת־שְׁמוֹ יָכִין וַיָּקֶם אֶת־הָעַמּוּד הַשְּׂמָאלִי וַיִּקְרָא אֶת־שְׁמוֹ בֹּעַז: 22 וְעַל רֹאשׁ הָעַמּוּדִים מַעֲשֵׂה שׁוֹשָׁן וַתִּתֹּם מְלֶאכֶת הָעַמּוּדִים: 23 וַיַּעַשׂ אֶת־הַיָּם מוּצָק עֶשֶׂר בָּאַמָּה מִשְּׂפָתוֹ עַד־שְׂפָתוֹ עָגֹל סָבִיב וְחָמֵשׁ בָּאַמָּה קוֹמָתוֹ וְקָו שְׁלֹשִׁים בָּאַמָּה יָסֹב אֹתוֹ סָבִיב: 24 וּפְקָעִים מִתַּחַת לִשְׂפָתוֹ סָבִיב סֹבְבִים אֹתוֹ עֶשֶׂר בָּאַמָּה מַקִּפִים אֶת־הַיָּם סָבִיב שְׁנֵי טוּרִים הַפְּקָעִים יְצֻקִים בִּיצֻקָתוֹ: 25 עֹמֵד עַל־שְׁנֵי עָשָׂר בָּקָר שְׁלֹשָׁה פֹנִים צָפוֹנָה וּשְׁלֹשָׁה פֹנִים יָמָּה וּשְׁלֹשָׁה פֹּנִים נֶגְבָּה וּשְׁלֹשָׁה פֹנִים מִזְרָחָה וְהַיָּם עֲלֵיהֶם מִלְמָעְלָה וְכָל־אֲחֹרֵיהֶם בָּיְתָה: 26 וְעָבְיוֹ טֶפַח וּשְׂפָתוֹ כְּמַעֲשֵׂה שְׂפַת־כּוֹס פֶּרַח שׁוֹשָׁן אַלְפַּיִם בַּת יָכִיל: פ
27 וַיַּעַשׂ אֶת־הַמְּכֹנוֹת עֶשֶׂר נְחֹשֶׁת אַרְבַּע בָּאַמָּה אֹרֶךְ הַמְּכוֹנָה הָאֶחָת וְאַרְבַּע בָּאַמָּה רָחְבָּהּ וְשָׁלֹשׁ בָּאַמָּה קוֹמָתָהּ: 28 וְזֶה מַעֲשֵׂה הַמְּכוֹנָה מִסְגְּרֹת לָהֶם וּמִסְגְּרֹת בֵּין הַשְׁלַבִּים: 29 וְעַל־הַמִּסְגְּרוֹת אֲשֶׁר בֵּין הַשְׁלַבִּים אֲרָיוֹת בָּקָר וּכְרוּבִים וְעַל־הַשְׁלַבִּים כֵּן מִמָּעַל וּמִתַּחַת לַאֲרָיוֹת וְלַבָּקָר לֹיוֹת מַעֲשֵׂה מוֹרָד: 30 וְאַרְבָּעָה אוֹפַנֵּי נְחֹשֶׁת לַמְּכוֹנָה הָאַחַת וְסַרְנֵי נְחֹשֶׁת וְאַרְבָּעָה פַעֲמֹתָיו כְּתֵפֹת לָהֶם מִתַּחַת לַכִּיֹּר הַכְּתֵפֹת יְצֻקוֹת מֵעֵבֶר אִישׁ לֹיוֹת: 31 וּפִיהוּ מִבֵּית לַכֹּתֶרֶת וָמַעְלָה בָּאַמָּה וּפִיהָ עָגֹל מַעֲשֵׂה־כֵן אַמָּה וַחֲצִי הָאַמָּה וְגַם־עַל־פִּיהָ מִקְלָעוֹת וּמִסְגְּרֹתֵיהֶם מְרֻבָּעוֹת לֹא עֲגֻלּוֹת: 32 וְאַרְבַּעַת הָאוֹפַנִּים לְמִתַּחַת לַמִּסְגְּרוֹת וִידוֹת הָאוֹפַנִּים בַּמְּכוֹנָה וְקוֹמַת הָאוֹפַן הָאֶחָד אַמָּה וַחֲצִי הָאַמָּה: 33 וּמַעֲשֵׂה הָאוֹפַנִּים כְּמַעֲשֵׂה אוֹפַן הַמֶּרְכָּבָה יְדוֹתָם וְגַבֵּיהֶם וְחִשֻּׁקֵיהֶם וְחִשֻּׁרֵיהֶם הַכֹּל מוּצָק: 34 וְאַרְבַּע כְּתֵפוֹת אֶל אַרְבַּע פִּנּוֹת

of each cart; its supports *were* part of the cart itself.
35 On the top of the cart, at the height of half a
cubit, *it was* perfectly round. And on the top of the
cart, its flanges and its panels *were* of the same
casting. 36 On the plates of its flanges and on its
panels he engraved cherubim, lions, and palm trees,
wherever there was a clear space on each, with
wreaths all around. 37 Thus he made the ten carts.
All of them were of the same mold, one measure,
and one shape.

38 Then he made ten lavers of bronze; each laver
contained forty baths, *and* each laver *was* four
cubits. On each of the ten carts *was* a laver. 39 And
he put five carts on the right side of the house, and
five on the left side of the house. He set the Sea on
the right side of the house, toward the southeast.

40 Huram made the lavers and the shovels and the
bowls. So Huram finished doing all the work that
he was to do for King Solomon *for* the house of the
LORD: 41 the two pillars, the *two* bowl-shaped
capitals that *were* on top of the two pillars; the
two networks covering the two bowl-shaped capitals which *were* on top of the pillars; 42 four hundred
pomegranates for the two networks (two rows of
pomegranates for each network, to cover the two
bowl-shaped capitals that *were* on top of the
pillars); 43 the ten carts, and ten lavers on the carts;
44 one Sea, and twelve oxen under the Sea; 45 the
pots, the shovels, and the bowls.

All these articles which Huram made for King
Solomon *for* the house of the LORD *were of*
burnished bronze. 46 In the plain of Jordan the king
had them cast in clay molds, between Succoth and
Zaretan. 47 And Solomon did not weigh all the
articles, because *there were* so many; the weight of
the bronze was not determined.

48 Thus Solomon had all the furnishings made for
the house of the LORD: the altar of gold, and the
table of gold on which *was* the showbread; 49 the
lampstands of pure gold, five on the right *side* and
five on the left in front of the inner sanctuary, with
the flowers and the lamps and the wick-trimmers of
gold; 50 the basins, the trimmers, the bowls, the
ladles, and the censers of pure gold; and the hinges
of gold, *both* for the doors of the inner room (the
Most Holy *Place*) *and* for the doors of the main hall
of the temple.

51 So all the work that King Solomon had done
for the house of the LORD was finished; and
Solomon brought in the things which his father
David had dedicated: the silver and the gold and the
furnishings. He put them in the treasuries of the
house of the LORD.

הַמְּכֹנָה הָאַחַת מִן־הַמְּכֹנָה כְּתֻפֶּיהָ: 35 וּבְרֹאשׁ
הַמְּכוֹנָה חֲצִי הָאַמָּה קוֹמָה עָגֹל | סָבִיב וְעַל
רֹאשׁ הַמְּכֹנָה יְדֹתֶיהָ וּמִסְגְּרֹתֶיהָ מִמֶּנָּה: 36 וַיְפַתַּח
עַל־הַלֻּחֹת יְדֹתֶיהָ וְעַל וּמִסְגְּרֹתֶיהָ כְּרוּבִים אֲרָיוֹת
וְתִמֹרֹת כְּמַעַר־אִישׁ וְלֹיוֹת סָבִיב: 37 כָּזֹאת עָשָׂה
אֵת עֶשֶׂר הַמְּכֹנוֹת מוּצָק אֶחָד מִדָּה אַחַת
קֶצֶב אֶחָד לְכֻלָּהְנָה: ס 38 וַיַּעַשׂ עֲשָׂרָה
כִיֹּרוֹת נְחֹשֶׁת אַרְבָּעִים בַּת יָכִיל | הַכִּיּוֹר הָאֶחָד
אַרְבַּע בָּאַמָּה הַכִּיּוֹר הָאֶחָד כִּיּוֹר אֶחָד עַל־
הַמְּכוֹנָה הָאַחַת לַעֲשֶׂר הַמְּכֹנוֹת: 39 וַיִּתֵּן אֶת־
הַמְּכֹנוֹת חָמֵשׁ עַל־כֶּתֶף הַבַּיִת מִיָּמִין וְחָמֵשׁ עַל־
כֶּתֶף הַבַּיִת מִשְּׂמֹאלוֹ וְאֶת־הַיָּם נָתַן מִכֶּתֶף הַבַּיִת
הַיְמָנִית קֵדְמָה מִמּוּל נֶגֶב: ס 40 וַיַּעַשׂ
חִירוֹם אֶת־הַכִּיֹּרוֹת וְאֶת־הַיָּעִים וְאֶת־הַמִּזְרָקוֹת
וַיְכַל חִירָם לַעֲשׂוֹת אֶת־כָּל־הַמְּלָאכָה אֲשֶׁר עָשָׂה
לַמֶּלֶךְ שְׁלֹמֹה בֵּית יְהוָה: 41 עַמֻּדִים שְׁנַיִם וְגֻלֹּת
הַכֹּתָרֹת אֲשֶׁר־עַל־רֹאשׁ הָעַמֻּדִים שְׁתָּיִם וְהַשְּׂבָכוֹת
שְׁתַּיִם לְכַסּוֹת אֶת־שְׁתֵּי גֻּלֹּת הַכֹּתָרֹת אֲשֶׁר עַל־
רֹאשׁ הָעַמּוּדִים: 42 וְאֶת־הָרִמֹּנִים אַרְבַּע מֵאוֹת
לִשְׁתֵּי הַשְּׂבָכוֹת שְׁנֵי־טוּרִים רִמֹּנִים לַשְּׂבָכָה
הָאֶחָת לְכַסּוֹת אֶת־שְׁתֵּי גֻּלֹּת הַכֹּתָרֹת אֲשֶׁר
עַל־פְּנֵי הָעַמּוּדִים: 43 וְאֶת־הַמְּכֹנוֹת עֶשֶׂר וְאֶת־
הַכִּיֹּרֹת עֲשָׂרָה עַל־הַמְּכֹנוֹת: 44 וְאֶת־הַיָּם הָאֶחָד
וְאֶת־הַבָּקָר שְׁנֵים־עָשָׂר תַּחַת הַיָּם: 45 וְאֶת־
הַסִּירוֹת וְאֶת־הַיָּעִים וְאֶת־הַמִּזְרָקוֹת וְאֵת כָּל־
הַכֵּלִים הָאֹהֶל אֲשֶׁר עָשָׂה חִירָם לַמֶּלֶךְ שְׁלֹמֹה
בֵּית יְהוָה נְחֹשֶׁת מְמֹרָט: 46 בְּכִכַּר הַיַּרְדֵּן יְצָקָם
הַמֶּלֶךְ בְּמַעֲבֵה הָאֲדָמָה בֵּין סֻכּוֹת וּבֵין צָרְתָן:
47 וַיַּנַּח שְׁלֹמֹה אֶת־כָּל־הַכֵּלִים מֵרֹב מְאֹד מְאֹד
לֹא נֶחְקַר מִשְׁקַל הַנְּחֹשֶׁת: 48 וַיַּעַשׂ שְׁלֹמֹה אֵת
כָּל־הַכֵּלִים אֲשֶׁר בֵּית יְהוָה אֵת מִזְבַּח הַזָּהָב וְאֶת־
הַשֻּׁלְחָן אֲשֶׁר עָלָיו לֶחֶם הַפָּנִים זָהָב: 49 וְאֶת־
הַמְּנֹרוֹת חָמֵשׁ מִיָּמִין וְחָמֵשׁ מִשְּׂמֹאול לִפְנֵי
הַדְּבִיר זָהָב סָגוּר וְהַפֶּרַח וְהַנֵּרֹת וְהַמֶּלְקַחַיִם
זָהָב: 50 וְהַסִּפּוֹת וְהַמְזַמְּרוֹת וְהַמִּזְרָקוֹת וְהַכַּפּוֹת
וְהַמַּחְתּוֹת זָהָב סָגוּר וְהַפֹּתוֹת לְדַלְתוֹת הַבַּיִת
הַפְּנִימִי לְקֹדֶשׁ הַקֳּדָשִׁים לְדַלְתֵי הַבַּיִת לַהֵיכָל
זָהָב: פ
51 וַתִּשְׁלַם כָּל־הַמְּלָאכָה אֲשֶׁר עָשָׂה הַמֶּלֶךְ שְׁלֹמֹה
בֵּית יְהוָה וַיָּבֵא שְׁלֹמֹה אֶת־קָדְשֵׁי | דָּוִד אָבִיו
אֶת־הַכֶּסֶף וְאֶת־הַזָּהָב וְאֶת־הַכֵּלִים נָתַן בְּאֹצְרוֹת
בֵּית יְהוָה: פ

8 Now Solomon assembled the elders of Israel and all the heads of the tribes, the chief fathers of the children of Israel, to King Solomon in Jerusalem, that they might bring up the ark of the covenant of the LORD from the City of David, which *is* Zion. [2]Therefore all the men of Israel assembled with King Solomon at the feast in the month of Ethanim, which *is* the seventh month. [3]So all the elders of Israel came, and the priests took up the ark. [4]Then they brought up the ark of the LORD, the tabernacle of meeting, and all the holy furnishings that *were* in the tabernacle. The priests and the Levites brought them up. [5]Also King Solomon, and all the congregation of Israel who were assembled with him, *were* with him before the ark, sacrificing sheep and oxen that could not be counted or numbered for multitude. [6]Then the priests brought in the ark of the covenant of the LORD to its place, into the inner sanctuary of the temple, to the Most Holy *Place*, under the wings of the cherubim. [7]For the cherubim spread *their* two wings over the place of the ark, and the cherubim overshadowed the ark and its poles. [8]The poles extended so that the ends of the poles could be seen from the holy *place*, in front of the inner sanctuary; but they could not be seen from outside. And they are there to this day. [9]Nothing *was* in the ark except the two tablets of stone which Moses put there at Horeb, when the LORD made *a covenant* with the children of Israel, when they came out of the land of Egypt.

[10]And it came to pass, when the priests came out of the holy *place*, that the cloud filled the house of the LORD, [11]so that the priests could not continue ministering because of the cloud; for the glory of the LORD filled the house of the LORD.

[12]Then Solomon spoke:

"The LORD said He would dwell in the dark cloud.
[13]   I have surely built You an exalted house,
And a place for You to dwell in forever."

[14]Then the king turned around and blessed the whole assembly of Israel, while all the assembly of Israel was standing. [15]And he said: "Blessed *be* the LORD God of Israel, who spoke with His mouth to my father David, and with His hand has fulfilled *it*, saying, [16]'Since the day that I brought My people Israel out of Egypt, I have chosen no city from any tribe of Israel *in which* to build a house, that My name might be there; but I chose David to be over My people Israel.' [17]Now it was in the heart of my father David to build a temple for the name of the LORD God of Israel. [18]But the LORD said to my father David, 'Whereas it was in your heart to build a temple for My name, you did well that it was in

ח אָז יַקְהֵל שְׁלֹמֹה אֶת־זִקְנֵי יִשְׂרָאֵל אֶת־כָּל־
רָאשֵׁי הַמַּטּוֹת נְשִׂיאֵי הָאָבוֹת לִבְנֵי יִשְׂרָאֵל אֶל־
הַמֶּלֶךְ שְׁלֹמֹה יְרוּשָׁלָ͏ִם לְהַעֲלוֹת אֶת־אֲרוֹן בְּרִית־
יְהוָה מֵעִיר דָּוִד הִיא צִיּוֹן: 2 וַיִּקָּהֲלוּ אֶל־הַמֶּלֶךְ
שְׁלֹמֹה כָּל־אִישׁ יִשְׂרָאֵל בְּיֶרַח הָאֵתָנִים בֶּחָג הוּא
הַחֹדֶשׁ הַשְּׁבִיעִי: 3 וַיָּבֹאוּ כֹּל זִקְנֵי יִשְׂרָאֵל וַיִּשְׂאוּ
הַכֹּהֲנִים אֶת־הָאָרוֹן: 4 וַיַּעֲלוּ אֶת־אֲרוֹן יְהוָה וְאֶת־
אֹהֶל מוֹעֵד וְאֶת־כָּל־כְּלֵי הַקֹּדֶשׁ אֲשֶׁר בָּאֹהֶל וַיַּעֲלוּ
אֹתָם הַכֹּהֲנִים וְהַלְוִיִּם: 5 וְהַמֶּלֶךְ שְׁלֹמֹה וְכָל־עֲדַת
יִשְׂרָאֵל הַנּוֹעָדִים עָלָיו אִתּוֹ לִפְנֵי הָאָרוֹן מְזַבְּחִים
צֹאן וּבָקָר אֲשֶׁר לֹא־יִסָּפְרוּ וְלֹא יִמָּנוּ מֵרֹב: 6 וַיָּבִאוּ
הַכֹּהֲנִים אֶת־אֲרוֹן בְּרִית־יְהוָה אֶל־מְקוֹמוֹ אֶל־
דְּבִיר הַבַּיִת אֶל־קֹדֶשׁ הַקֳּדָשִׁים אֶל־תַּחַת כַּנְפֵי
הַכְּרוּבִים: 7 כִּי הַכְּרוּבִים פֹּרְשִׂים כְּנָפַיִם אֶל־
מְקוֹם הָאָרוֹן וַיָּסֹכּוּ הַכְּרֻבִים עַל־הָאָרוֹן וְעַל־בַּדָּיו
מִלְמָעְלָה: 8 וַיַּאֲרִכוּ הַבַּדִּים וַיֵּרָאוּ רָאשֵׁי הַבַּדִּים
מִן־הַקֹּדֶשׁ עַל־פְּנֵי הַדְּבִיר וְלֹא יֵרָאוּ הַחוּצָה וַיִּהְיוּ
שָׁם עַד הַיּוֹם הַזֶּה: 9 אֵין בָּאָרוֹן רַק שְׁנֵי לֻחוֹת
הָאֲבָנִים אֲשֶׁר הִנִּחַ שָׁם מֹשֶׁה בְּחֹרֵב אֲשֶׁר כָּרַת
יְהוָה עִם־בְּנֵי יִשְׂרָאֵל בְּצֵאתָם מֵאֶרֶץ מִצְרָיִם:

10 וַיְהִי בְּצֵאת הַכֹּהֲנִים מִן־הַקֹּדֶשׁ וְהֶעָנָן מָלֵא
אֶת־בֵּית יְהוָה: 11 וְלֹא־יָכְלוּ הַכֹּהֲנִים לַעֲמֹד לְשָׁרֵת
מִפְּנֵי הֶעָנָן כִּי־מָלֵא כְבוֹד־יְהוָה אֶת־בֵּית יְהוָה: פ

12 אָז אָמַר שְׁלֹמֹה יְהוָה אָמַר לִשְׁכֹּן בָּעֲרָפֶל:
13 בָּנֹה בָנִיתִי בֵּית זְבֻל לָךְ מָכוֹן לְשִׁבְתְּךָ עוֹלָמִים:

14 וַיַּסֵּב הַמֶּלֶךְ אֶת־פָּנָיו וַיְבָרֶךְ אֵת כָּל־קְהַל
יִשְׂרָאֵל וְכָל־קְהַל יִשְׂרָאֵל עֹמֵד: 15 וַיֹּאמֶר בָּרוּךְ
יְהוָה אֱלֹהֵי יִשְׂרָאֵל אֲשֶׁר דִּבֶּר בְּפִיו אֵת דָּוִד
אָבִי וּבְיָדוֹ מִלֵּא לֵאמֹר: 16 מִן־הַיּוֹם אֲשֶׁר הוֹצֵאתִי
אֶת־עַמִּי אֶת־יִשְׂרָאֵל מִמִּצְרַיִם לֹא־בָחַרְתִּי בְעִיר
מִכֹּל שִׁבְטֵי יִשְׂרָאֵל לִבְנוֹת בַּיִת לִהְיוֹת שְׁמִי שָׁם
וָאֶבְחַר בְּדָוִד לִהְיוֹת עַל־עַמִּי יִשְׂרָאֵל: 17 וַיְהִי עִם־
לְבַב דָּוִד אָבִי לִבְנוֹת בַּיִת לְשֵׁם יְהוָה אֱלֹהֵי
יִשְׂרָאֵל: 18 וַיֹּאמֶר יְהוָה אֶל־דָּוִד אָבִי יַעַן אֲשֶׁר
הָיָה עִם־לְבָבְךָ לִבְנוֹת בַּיִת לִשְׁמִי הֱטִיבֹתָ כִּי

your heart. ¹⁹Nevertheless you shall not build the temple, but your son who will come from your body, he shall build the temple for My name.' ²⁰So the LORD has fulfilled His word which He spoke; and I have filled the position of my father David, and sit on the throne of Israel, as the LORD promised; and I have built a temple for the name of the LORD God of Israel. ²¹And there I have made a place for the ark, in which is the covenant of the LORD which He made with our fathers, when He brought them out of the land of Egypt."

²²Then Solomon stood before the altar of the LORD in the presence of all the assembly of Israel, and spread out his hands toward heaven; ²³and he said: "LORD God of Israel, there is no God in heaven above or on earth below like You, who keep Your covenant and mercy with Your servants who walk before You with all their hearts. ²⁴You have kept what You promised Your servant David my father; You have both spoken with Your mouth and fulfilled it with Your hand, as it is this day. ²⁵Therefore, LORD God of Israel, now keep what You promised Your servant David my father, saying, 'You shall not fail to have a man sit before Me on the throne of Israel, only if your sons take heed to their way, that they walk before Me as you have walked before Me.' ²⁶And now I pray, O God of Israel, let Your word come true, which You have spoken to Your servant David my father.

²⁷"But will God indeed dwell on the earth? Behold, heaven and the heaven of heavens cannot contain You: How much less this temple which I have built! ²⁸Yet regard the prayer of Your servant and his supplication, O LORD my God, and listen to the cry and the prayer which Your servant is praying before You today: ²⁹that Your eyes may be open toward this temple night and day, toward the place of which You said, 'My name shall be there,' that You may hear the prayer which Your servant makes toward this place. ³⁰And may You hear the supplication of Your servant and of Your people Israel, when they pray toward this place. Hear in heaven Your dwelling place; and when You hear, forgive.

³¹"When anyone sins against his neighbor, and is forced to take an oath, and comes and takes an oath before Your altar in this temple, ³²then hear in heaven, and act, and judge Your servants, condemning the wicked, bringing his way on his head, and justifying the righteous by giving him according to his righteousness.

³³"When Your people Israel are defeated before an enemy because they have sinned against You, and when they turn back to You and confess Your

הָיָה עִם־לְבָבֶךָ: ¹⁹ רַק אַתָּה לֹא תִבְנֶה הַבָּיִת כִּי אִם־בִּנְךָ הַיֹּצֵא מֵחֲלָצֶיךָ הוּא־יִבְנֶה הַבַּיִת לִשְׁמִי: ²⁰ וַיָּקֶם יְהֹוָה אֶת־דְּבָרוֹ אֲשֶׁר דִּבֵּר וָאָקֻם תַּחַת דָּוִד אָבִי וָאֵשֵׁב עַל־כִּסֵּא יִשְׂרָאֵל כַּאֲשֶׁר דִּבֶּר יְהֹוָה וָאֶבְנֶה הַבַּיִת לְשֵׁם יְהֹוָה אֱלֹהֵי יִשְׂרָאֵל: ²¹ וָאָשִׂם שָׁם מָקוֹם לָאָרוֹן אֲשֶׁר־שָׁם בְּרִית יְהֹוָה אֲשֶׁר כָּרַת עִם־אֲבֹתֵינוּ בְּהוֹצִיאוֹ אֹתָם מֵאֶרֶץ מִצְרָיִם: ס ²² וַיַּעֲמֹד שְׁלֹמֹה לִפְנֵי מִזְבַּח יְהֹוָה נֶגֶד כָּל־קְהַל יִשְׂרָאֵל וַיִּפְרֹשׂ כַּפָּיו הַשָּׁמָיִם: ²³ וַיֹּאמַר יְהֹוָה אֱלֹהֵי יִשְׂרָאֵל אֵין־כָּמוֹךָ אֱלֹהִים בַּשָּׁמַיִם מִמַּעַל וְעַל־הָאָרֶץ מִתָּחַת שֹׁמֵר הַבְּרִית וְהַחֶסֶד לַעֲבָדֶיךָ הַהֹלְכִים לְפָנֶיךָ בְּכָל־ לִבָּם: ²⁴ אֲשֶׁר שָׁמַרְתָּ לְעַבְדְּךָ דָּוִד אָבִי אֵת אֲשֶׁר־ דִּבַּרְתָּ לוֹ וַתְּדַבֵּר בְּפִיךָ וּבְיָדְךָ מִלֵּאתָ כַּיּוֹם הַזֶּה: ²⁵ וְעַתָּה יְהֹוָה ׀ אֱלֹהֵי יִשְׂרָאֵל שְׁמֹר לְעַבְדְּךָ דָוִד אָבִי אֵת אֲשֶׁר דִּבַּרְתָּ לּוֹ לֵאמֹר לֹא־יִכָּרֵת לְךָ אִישׁ מִלְּפָנַי יֹשֵׁב עַל־כִּסֵּא יִשְׂרָאֵל רַק אִם־יִשְׁמְרוּ בָנֶיךָ אֶת־דַּרְכָּם לָלֶכֶת לְפָנַי כַּאֲשֶׁר הָלַכְתָּ לְפָנָי: ²⁶ וְעַתָּה אֱלֹהֵי יִשְׂרָאֵל יֵאָמֶן נָא דְבָרֶיךָ אֲשֶׁר דִּבַּרְתָּ לְעַבְדְּךָ דָּוִד אָבִי: ²⁷ כִּי הַאֻמְנָם יֵשֵׁב אֱלֹהִים עַל־הָאָרֶץ הִנֵּה הַשָּׁמַיִם וּשְׁמֵי הַשָּׁמַיִם לֹא יְכַלְכְּלוּךָ אַף כִּי־הַבַּיִת הַזֶּה אֲשֶׁר בָּנִיתִי: ²⁸ וּפָנִיתָ אֶל־תְּפִלַּת עַבְדְּךָ וְאֶל־תְּחִנָּתוֹ יְהֹוָה אֱלֹהָי לִשְׁמֹעַ אֶל־הָרִנָּה וְאֶל־הַתְּפִלָּה אֲשֶׁר עַבְדְּךָ מִתְפַּלֵּל לְפָנֶיךָ הַיּוֹם: ²⁹ לִהְיוֹת עֵינֶךָ פְתֻחוֹת אֶל־הַבַּיִת הַזֶּה לַיְלָה וָיוֹם אֶל־הַמָּקוֹם אֲשֶׁר אָמַרְתָּ יִהְיֶה שְׁמִי שָׁם לִשְׁמֹעַ אֶל־הַתְּפִלָּה אֲשֶׁר יִתְפַּלֵּל עַבְדְּךָ אֶל־ הַמָּקוֹם הַזֶּה: ³⁰ וְשָׁמַעְתָּ אֶל־תְּחִנַּת עַבְדְּךָ וְעַמְּךָ יִשְׂרָאֵל אֲשֶׁר יִתְפַּלְלוּ אֶל־הַמָּקוֹם הַזֶּה וְאַתָּה תִּשְׁמַע אֶל־מְקוֹם שִׁבְתְּךָ אֶל־הַשָּׁמַיִם וְשָׁמַעְתָּ וְסָלָחְתָּ: ³¹ אֵת אֲשֶׁר יֶחֱטָא אִישׁ לְרֵעֵהוּ וְנָשָׁא־בוֹ אָלָה לְהַאֲלֹתוֹ וּבָא אָלָה לִפְנֵי מִזְבַּחֲךָ בַּבַּיִת הַזֶּה: ³² וְאַתָּה ׀ תִּשְׁמַע הַשָּׁמַיִם וְעָשִׂיתָ וְשָׁפַטְתָּ אֶת־ עֲבָדֶיךָ לְהַרְשִׁיעַ רָשָׁע לָתֵת דַּרְכּוֹ בְּרֹאשׁוֹ וּלְהַצְדִּיק צַדִּיק לָתֶת לוֹ כְּצִדְקָתוֹ: ס ³³ בְּהִנָּגֵף

name, and pray and make supplication to You in this temple, ³⁴then hear in heaven, and forgive the sin of Your people Israel, and bring them back to the land which You gave to their fathers.

³⁵"When the heavens are shut up and there is no rain because they have sinned against You, when they pray toward this place and confess Your name, and turn from their sin because You afflict them, ³⁶then hear in heaven, and forgive the sin of Your servants, Your people Israel, that You may teach them the good way in which they should walk; and send rain on Your land which You have given to Your people as an inheritance.

³⁷"When there is famine in the land, pestilence *or* blight *or* mildew, locusts *or* grasshoppers; when their enemy besieges them in the land of their cities; whatever plague or whatever sickness *there is;* ³⁸whatever prayer, whatever supplication is made by anyone, *or* by all Your people Israel, when each one knows the plague of his own heart, and spreads out his hands toward this temple: ³⁹then hear in heaven Your dwelling place, and forgive, and act, and give to everyone according to all his ways, whose heart You know (for You alone know the hearts of all the sons of men), ⁴⁰that they may fear You all the days that they live in the land which You gave to our fathers.

⁴¹"Moreover, concerning a foreigner, who *is* not of Your people Israel, but has come from a far country for Your name's sake ⁴²(for they will hear of Your great name and Your strong hand and Your outstretched arm), when he comes and prays toward this temple, ⁴³hear in heaven Your dwelling place, and do according to all for which the foreigner calls to You, that all peoples of the earth may know Your name and fear You, as *do* Your people Israel, and that they may know that this temple which I have built is called by Your name.

⁴⁴"When Your people go out to battle against their enemy, wherever You send them, and when they pray to the LORD toward the city which You have chosen and the temple which I have built for Your name, ⁴⁵then hear in heaven their prayer and their supplication, and maintain their cause.

⁴⁶"When they sin against You (for *there is* no one who does not sin), and You become angry with them and deliver them to the enemy, and they take them captive to the land of the enemy, far or near; ⁴⁷yet when they come to themselves in the land where they were carried captive, and repent, and make supplication to You in the land of those who took them captive, saying, 'We have sinned and done wrong, we have committed wickedness'; ⁴⁸and *when* they return to You with all their heart and

עַמְּךָ יִשְׂרָאֵל לִפְנֵי אוֹיֵב אֲשֶׁר יֶחֶטְאוּ־לָךְ וְשָׁבוּ אֵלֶיךָ וְהוֹדוּ אֶת־שְׁמֶךָ וְהִתְפַּלְלוּ וְהִתְחַנְּנוּ אֵלֶיךָ בַּבַּיִת הַזֶּה: 34 וְאַתָּה תִּשְׁמַע הַשָּׁמַיִם וְסָלַחְתָּ לְחַטַּאת עַמְּךָ יִשְׂרָאֵל וַהֲשֵׁבֹתָם אֶל־הָאֲדָמָה אֲשֶׁר נָתַתָּ לַאֲבוֹתָם: ס 35 בְּהֵעָצֵר שָׁמַיִם וְלֹא־ יִהְיֶה מָטָר כִּי יֶחֶטְאוּ־לָךְ וְהִתְפַּלְלוּ אֶל־הַמָּקוֹם הַזֶּה וְהוֹדוּ אֶת־שְׁמֶךָ וּמֵחַטָּאתָם יְשׁוּבוּן כִּי תַעֲנֵם: 36 וְאַתָּה | תִּשְׁמַע הַשָּׁמַיִם וְסָלַחְתָּ לְחַטַּאת עֲבָדֶיךָ וְעַמְּךָ יִשְׂרָאֵל כִּי תוֹרֵם אֶת־הַדֶּרֶךְ הַטּוֹבָה אֲשֶׁר יֵלְכוּ־בָהּ וְנָתַתָּה מָטָר עַל־אַרְצְךָ אֲשֶׁר־ נָתַתָּה לְעַמְּךָ לְנַחֲלָה: ס 37 רָעָב כִּי־ יִהְיֶה בָאָרֶץ דֶּבֶר כִּי־יִהְיֶה שִׁדָּפוֹן יֵרָקוֹן אַרְבֶּה חָסִיל כִּי יִהְיֶה כִּי יָצַר־לוֹ אֹיְבוֹ בְּאֶרֶץ שְׁעָרָיו כָּל־נֶגַע כָּל־מַחֲלָה: 38 כָּל־תְּפִלָּה כָל־תְּחִנָּה אֲשֶׁר תִּהְיֶה לְכָל־הָאָדָם לְכֹל עַמְּךָ יִשְׂרָאֵל אֲשֶׁר יֵדְעוּן אִישׁ נֶגַע לְבָבוֹ וּפָרַשׂ כַּפָּיו אֶל־הַבַּיִת הַזֶּה: 39 וְאַתָּה תִּשְׁמַע הַשָּׁמַיִם מְכוֹן שִׁבְתֶּךָ וְסָלַחְתָּ וְעָשִׂיתָ וְנָתַתָּ לָאִישׁ כְּכָל־דְּרָכָיו אֲשֶׁר תֵּדַע אֶת־ לְבָבוֹ כִּי־אַתָּה יָדַעְתָּ לְבַדְּךָ אֶת־לְבַב כָּל־בְּנֵי הָאָדָם: 40 לְמַעַן יִרָאוּךָ כָּל־הַיָּמִים אֲשֶׁר־הֵם חַיִּים עַל־פְּנֵי הָאֲדָמָה אֲשֶׁר נָתַתָּה לַאֲבֹתֵינוּ: 41 וְגַם אֶל־הַנָּכְרִי אֲשֶׁר לֹא־מֵעַמְּךָ יִשְׂרָאֵל הוּא וּבָא מֵאֶרֶץ רְחוֹקָה לְמַעַן שְׁמֶךָ: 42 כִּי יִשְׁמְעוּן אֶת־ שִׁמְךָ הַגָּדוֹל וְאֶת־יָדְךָ הַחֲזָקָה וּזְרֹעֲךָ הַנְּטוּיָה וּבָא וְהִתְפַּלֵּל אֶל־הַבַּיִת הַזֶּה: 43 אַתָּה תִּשְׁמַע הַשָּׁמַיִם מְכוֹן שִׁבְתֶּךָ וְעָשִׂיתָ כְּכֹל אֲשֶׁר־יִקְרָא אֵלֶיךָ הַנָּכְרִי לְמַעַן יֵדְעוּן כָּל־עַמֵּי הָאָרֶץ אֶת־ שְׁמֶךָ לְיִרְאָה אֹתְךָ כְּעַמְּךָ יִשְׂרָאֵל וְלָדַעַת כִּי־ שִׁמְךָ נִקְרָא עַל־הַבַּיִת הַזֶּה אֲשֶׁר בָּנִיתִי: 44 כִּי־ יֵצֵא עַמְּךָ לַמִּלְחָמָה עַל־אֹיְבוֹ בַּדֶּרֶךְ אֲשֶׁר תִּשְׁלָחֵם וְהִתְפַּלְלוּ אֶל־יְהוָה דֶּרֶךְ הָעִיר אֲשֶׁר בָּחַרְתָּ בָּהּ וְהַבַּיִת אֲשֶׁר־בָּנִתִי לִשְׁמֶךָ: 45 וְשָׁמַעְתָּ הַשָּׁמַיִם אֶת־תְּפִלָּתָם וְאֶת־תְּחִנָּתָם וְעָשִׂיתָ מִשְׁפָּטָם: 46 כִּי יֶחֶטְאוּ־לָךְ כִּי אֵין אָדָם אֲשֶׁר לֹא־יֶחֱטָא וְאָנַפְתָּ בָם וּנְתַתָּם לִפְנֵי אוֹיֵב וְשָׁבוּם שֹׁבֵיהֶם אֶל־אֶרֶץ הָאוֹיֵב רְחוֹקָה אוֹ קְרוֹבָה: 47 וְהֵשִׁיבוּ אֶל־לִבָּם בָּאָרֶץ אֲשֶׁר נִשְׁבּוּ־שָׁם וְשָׁבוּ | וְהִתְחַנְּנוּ אֵלֶיךָ בְּאֶרֶץ שֹׁבֵיהֶם לֵאמֹר חָטָאנוּ וְהֶעֱוִינוּ רָשָׁעְנוּ: 48 וְשָׁבוּ אֵלֶיךָ בְּכָל־לְבָבָם וּבְכָל־נַפְשָׁם בְּאֶרֶץ אֹיְבֵיהֶם אֲשֶׁר־שָׁבוּ אֹתָם וְהִתְפַּלְלוּ אֵלֶיךָ דֶּרֶךְ

with all their soul in the land of their enemies who led them away captive, and pray to You toward their land which You gave to their fathers, the city which You have chosen and the temple which I have built for Your name: [49] then hear in heaven Your dwelling place their prayer and their supplication, and maintain their cause, [50] and forgive Your people who have sinned against You, and all their transgressions which they have transgressed against You; and grant them compassion before those who took them captive, that they may have compassion on them [51] (for they *are* Your people and Your inheritance, whom You brought out of Egypt, out of the iron furnace), [52] that Your eyes may be open to the supplication of Your servant and the supplication of Your people Israel, to listen to them whenever they call to You. [53] For You separated them from among all the peoples of the earth *to be* Your inheritance, as You spoke by Your servant Moses, when You brought our fathers out of Egypt, O Lord GOD."

[54] And so it was, when Solomon had finished praying all this prayer and supplication to the LORD, that he arose from before the altar of the LORD, from kneeling on his knees with his hands spread up to heaven. [55] Then he stood and blessed all the assembly of Israel with a loud voice, saying: [56] "Blessed *be* the LORD, who has given rest to His people Israel, according to all that He promised. There has not failed one word of all His good promise, which He promised through His servant Moses. [57] May the LORD our God be with us, as He was with our fathers. May He not leave us nor forsake us, [58] that He may incline our hearts to Himself, to walk in all His ways, and to keep His commandments and His statutes and His judgments, which He commanded our fathers. [59] And may these words of mine, with which I have made supplication before the LORD, be near the LORD our God day and night, that He may maintain the cause of His servant and the cause of His people Israel, as each day may require, [60] that all the peoples of the earth may know that the LORD *is* God; *there is* no other. [61] Let your heart therefore be loyal to the LORD our God, to walk in His statutes and keep His commandments, as at this day."

[62] Then the king and all Israel with him offered sacrifices before the LORD. [63] And Solomon offered a sacrifice of peace offerings, which he offered to the LORD, twenty-two thousand bulls and one hundred and twenty thousand sheep. So the king and all the children of Israel dedicated the house of the LORD. [64] On the same day the king consecrated the middle of the court that *was* in front of the

אַרְצָם אֲשֶׁר־נָתַתָּה לַאֲבוֹתָם הָעִיר אֲשֶׁר בָּחַרְתָּ
וְהַבַּיִת אֲשֶׁר־בָּנִיתִֽ לִשְׁמֶֽךָ׃ 49 וְשָׁמַעְתָּ הַשָּׁמַיִם
מְכוֹן שִׁבְתְּךָ אֶת־תְּפִלָּתָם וְאֶת־תְּחִנָּתָם וְעָשִׂיתָ
מִשְׁפָּטָֽם׃ 50 וְסָלַחְתָּ לְעַמְּךָ אֲשֶׁר חָטְאוּ־לָךְ וּלְכָל־
פִּשְׁעֵיהֶם אֲשֶׁר פָּשְׁעוּ־בָךְ וּנְתַתָּם לְרַחֲמִים לִפְנֵי
שֹׁבֵיהֶם וְרִֽחֲמֽוּם׃ 51 כִּֽי־עַמְּךָ וְנַחֲלָתְךָ הֵם אֲשֶׁר
הוֹצֵאתָ מִמִּצְרַיִם מִתּוֹךְ כּוּר הַבַּרְזֶֽל׃ 52 לִהְיוֹת
עֵינֶיךָ פְתֻחוֹת אֶל־תְּחִנַּת עַבְדְּךָ וְאֶל־תְּחִנַּת עַמְּךָ
יִשְׂרָאֵל לִשְׁמֹעַ אֲלֵיהֶם בְּכֹל קָרְאָם אֵלֶֽיךָ׃ 53 כִּֽי־
אַתָּה הִבְדַּלְתָּם לְךָ לְנַחֲלָה מִכֹּל עַמֵּי הָאָרֶץ כַּאֲשֶׁר
דִּבַּרְתָּ בְּיַד ׀ מֹשֶׁה עַבְדֶּךָ בְּהוֹצִיאֲךָ אֶת־אֲבֹתֵינוּ
מִמִּצְרַיִם אֲדֹנָי יֱהֹוִֽה׃ פ

54 וַיְהִי ׀ כְּכַלּוֹת שְׁלֹמֹה לְהִתְפַּלֵּל אֶל־יְהֹוָה אֵת
כָּל־הַתְּפִלָּה וְהַתְּחִנָּה הַזֹּאת קָם מִלִּפְנֵי מִזְבַּח יְהֹוָה
מִכְּרֹעַ עַל־בִּרְכָּיו וְכַפָּיו פְּרֻשׂוֹת הַשָּׁמָֽיִם׃ 55 וַֽיַּעֲמֹד
וַיְבָרֶךְ אֵת כָּל־קְהַל יִשְׂרָאֵל קוֹל גָּדוֹל לֵאמֹֽר׃
56 בָּרוּךְ יְהֹוָה אֲשֶׁר נָתַן מְנוּחָה לְעַמּוֹ יִשְׂרָאֵל
כְּכֹל אֲשֶׁר דִּבֵּר לֹא־נָפַל דָּבָר אֶחָד מִכֹּל דְּבָרוֹ
הַטּוֹב אֲשֶׁר דִּבֶּר בְּיַד מֹשֶׁה עַבְדּֽוֹ׃ 57 יְהִי יְהֹוָה
אֱלֹהֵינוּ עִמָּנוּ כַּאֲשֶׁר הָיָה עִם־אֲבֹתֵינוּ אַל־יַֽעַזְבֵנוּ
וְאַֽל־יִטְּשֵֽׁנוּ׃ 58 לְהַטּוֹת לְבָבֵנוּ אֵלָיו לָלֶכֶת בְּכָל־
דְּרָכָיו וְלִשְׁמֹר מִצְוֺתָיו וְחֻקָּיו וּמִשְׁפָּטָיו אֲשֶׁר צִוָּה
אֶת־אֲבֹתֵֽינוּ׃ 59 וְיִֽהְיוּ דְבָרַי אֵלֶּה אֲשֶׁר הִתְחַנַּנְתִּי
לִפְנֵי יְהֹוָה קְרֹבִים אֶל־יְהֹוָה אֱלֹהֵינוּ יוֹמָם וָלָֽיְלָה
לַעֲשׂוֹת ׀ מִשְׁפַּט עַבְדּוֹ וּמִשְׁפַּט עַמּוֹ יִשְׂרָאֵל דְּבַר־
יוֹם בְּיוֹמֽוֹ׃ 60 לְמַעַן דַּעַת כָּל־עַמֵּי הָאָרֶץ כִּי יְהֹוָה
הוּא הָאֱלֹהִים אֵין עֽוֹד׃ 61 וְהָיָה לְבַבְכֶם שָׁלֵם
עִם יְהֹוָה אֱלֹהֵינוּ לָלֶכֶת בְּחֻקָּיו וְלִשְׁמֹר מִצְוֺתָיו
כַּיּוֹם הַזֶּֽה׃ 62 וְהַמֶּלֶךְ וְכָל־יִשְׂרָאֵל עִמּוֹ זֹבְחִים זֶבַח
לִפְנֵי יְהֹוָֽה׃ 63 וַיִּזְבַּח שְׁלֹמֹה אֵת זֶבַח הַשְּׁלָמִים
אֲשֶׁר זָבַח לַֽיהֹוָה בָּקָר עֶשְׂרִים וּשְׁנַיִם אֶלֶף וְצֹאן
מֵאָה וְעֶשְׂרִים אָלֶף וַֽיַּחְנְכוּ אֶת־בֵּית יְהֹוָה הַמֶּלֶךְ
וְכָל־בְּנֵי יִשְׂרָאֵֽל׃ 64 בַּיּוֹם הַהוּא קִדַּשׁ הַמֶּלֶךְ אֶת־
תּוֹךְ הֶחָצֵר אֲשֶׁר לִפְנֵי בֵית־יְהֹוָה כִּֽי־עָשָׂה שָׁם
אֶת־הָעֹלָה וְאֶת־הַמִּנְחָה וְאֵת חֶלְבֵי הַשְּׁלָמִים כִּֽי־

house of the LORD; for there he offered burnt offerings, grain offerings, and the fat of the peace offerings, because the bronze altar that *was* before the LORD *was* too small to receive the burnt offerings, the grain offerings, and the fat of the peace offerings.

65 At that time Solomon held a feast, and all Israel with him, a great assembly from the entrance of Hamath to the Brook of Egypt, before the LORD our God, seven days and seven *more* days— fourteen days. 66 On the eighth day he sent the people away; and they blessed the king, and went to their tents joyful and glad of heart for all the good that the LORD had done for His servant David, and for Israel His people.

9 And it came to pass, when Solomon had finished building the house of the LORD and the king's house, and all Solomon's desire which he wanted to do, 2 that the LORD appeared to Solomon the second time, as He had appeared to him at Gibeon. 3 And the LORD said to him: "I have heard your prayer and your supplication that you have made before Me; I have consecrated this house which you have built to put My name there forever, and My eyes and My heart will be there perpetually. 4 Now if you walk before Me as your father David walked, in integrity of heart and in uprightness, to do according to all that I have commanded you, *and* if you keep My statutes and My judgments, 5 then I will establish the throne of your kingdom over Israel forever, as I promised David your father, saying, 'You shall not fail to have a man on the throne of Israel.' 6 *But* if you or your sons at all turn from following Me, and do not keep My commandments *and* My statutes which I have set before you, but go and serve other gods and worship them, 7 then I will cut off Israel from the land which I have given them; and this house which I have consecrated for My name I will cast out of My sight. Israel will be a proverb and a byword among all peoples. 8 And *as for* this house, *which* is exalted, everyone who passes by it will be astonished and will hiss, and say, 'Why has the LORD done thus to this land and to this house?' 9 Then they will answer, 'Because they forsook the LORD their God, who brought their fathers out of the land of Egypt, and have embraced other gods, and worshiped them and served them; therefore the LORD has brought all this calamity on them.' "

10 Now it happened at the end of twenty years, when Solomon had built the two houses, the house of the LORD and the king's house 11 (Hiram the king of Tyre had supplied Solomon with cedar and

מִזְבַּח הַנְּחֹשֶׁת אֲשֶׁר לִפְנֵי יְהוָה קָטֹן מֵהָכִיל אֶת־הָעֹלָה וְאֶת־הַמִּנְחָה וְאֵת חֶלְבֵי הַשְּׁלָמִים: 65 וַיַּעַשׂ שְׁלֹמֹה בָעֵת־הַהִיא ׀ אֶת־הֶחָג וְכָל־יִשְׂרָאֵל עִמּוֹ קָהָל גָּדוֹל מִלְּבוֹא חֲמָת ׀ עַד־נַחַל מִצְרַיִם לִפְנֵי יְהוָה אֱלֹהֵינוּ שִׁבְעַת יָמִים וְשִׁבְעַת יָמִים אַרְבָּעָה עָשָׂר יוֹם: 66 בַּיּוֹם הַשְּׁמִינִי שִׁלַּח אֶת־הָעָם וַיְבָרֲכוּ אֶת־הַמֶּלֶךְ וַיֵּלְכוּ לְאָהֳלֵיהֶם שְׂמֵחִים וְטוֹבֵי לֵב עַל כָּל־הַטּוֹבָה אֲשֶׁר עָשָׂה יְהוָה לְדָוִד עַבְדּוֹ וּלְיִשְׂרָאֵל עַמּוֹ:

ט וַיְהִי כְּכַלּוֹת שְׁלֹמֹה לִבְנוֹת אֶת־בֵּית־יְהוָה וְאֶת־בֵּית הַמֶּלֶךְ וְאֵת כָּל־חֵשֶׁק שְׁלֹמֹה אֲשֶׁר חָפֵץ לַעֲשׂוֹת: פ 2 וַיֵּרָא יְהוָה אֶל־שְׁלֹמֹה שֵׁנִית כַּאֲשֶׁר נִרְאָה אֵלָיו בְּגִבְעוֹן: 3 וַיֹּאמֶר יְהוָה אֵלָיו שָׁמַעְתִּי אֶת־תְּפִלָּתְךָ וְאֶת־תְּחִנָּתְךָ אֲשֶׁר הִתְחַנַּנְתָּה לְפָנַי הִקְדַּשְׁתִּי אֶת־הַבַּיִת הַזֶּה אֲשֶׁר בָּנִתָה לָשׂוּם־שְׁמִי שָׁם עַד־עוֹלָם וְהָיוּ עֵינַי וְלִבִּי שָׁם כָּל־הַיָּמִים: 4 וְאַתָּה אִם־תֵּלֵךְ לְפָנַי כַּאֲשֶׁר הָלַךְ דָּוִד אָבִיךָ בְּתָם־לֵבָב וּבְיֹשֶׁר לַעֲשׂוֹת כְּכֹל אֲשֶׁר צִוִּיתִיךָ חֻקַּי וּמִשְׁפָּטַי תִּשְׁמֹר: 5 וַהֲקִמֹתִי אֶת־כִּסֵּא מַמְלַכְתְּךָ עַל־יִשְׂרָאֵל לְעֹלָם כַּאֲשֶׁר דִּבַּרְתִּי עַל־דָּוִד אָבִיךָ לֵאמֹר לֹא־יִכָּרֵת לְךָ אִישׁ מֵעַל כִּסֵּא יִשְׂרָאֵל: 6 אִם־שׁוֹב תְּשֻׁבוּן אַתֶּם וּבְנֵיכֶם מֵאַחֲרַי וְלֹא תִשְׁמְרוּ מִצְו‍ֹתַי חֻקֹּתַי אֲשֶׁר נָתַתִּי לִפְנֵיכֶם וַהֲלַכְתֶּם וַעֲבַדְתֶּם אֱלֹהִים אֲחֵרִים וְהִשְׁתַּחֲוִיתֶם לָהֶם: 7 וְהִכְרַתִּי אֶת־יִשְׂרָאֵל מֵעַל פְּנֵי הָאֲדָמָה אֲשֶׁר נָתַתִּי לָהֶם וְאֶת־הַבַּיִת אֲשֶׁר הִקְדַּשְׁתִּי לִשְׁמִי אֲשַׁלַּח מֵעַל פָּנָי וְהָיָה יִשְׂרָאֵל לְמָשָׁל וְלִשְׁנִינָה בְּכָל־הָעַמִּים: 8 וְהַבַּיִת הַזֶּה יִהְיֶה עֶלְיוֹן כָּל־עֹבֵר עָלָיו יִשֹּׁם וְשָׁרָק וְאָמְרוּ עַל־מֶה עָשָׂה יְהוָה כָּכָה לָאָרֶץ הַזֹּאת וְלַבַּיִת הַזֶּה: 9 וְאָמְרוּ עַל אֲשֶׁר עָזְבוּ אֶת־יְהוָה אֱלֹהֵיהֶם אֲשֶׁר הוֹצִיא אֶת־אֲבֹתָם מֵאֶרֶץ מִצְרַיִם וַיַּחֲזִקוּ בֵּאלֹהִים אֲחֵרִים וַיִּשְׁתַּחֲווּ לָהֶם וַיַּעַבְדֻם עַל־כֵּן הֵבִיא יְהוָה עֲלֵיהֶם אֵת כָּל־הָרָעָה הַזֹּאת: פ 10 וַיְהִי מִקְצֵה עֶשְׂרִים שָׁנָה אֲשֶׁר־בָּנָה שְׁלֹמֹה אֶת־שְׁנֵי הַבָּתִּים אֶת־בֵּית יְהוָה וְאֶת־בֵּית הַמֶּלֶךְ: 11 חִירָם מֶלֶךְ־צֹר נִשָּׂא אֶת־שְׁלֹמֹה בַּעֲצֵי אֲרָזִים

cypress and gold, as much as he desired), *that* King Solomon then gave Hiram twenty cities in the land of Galilee. 12 Then Hiram went from Tyre to see the cities which Solomon had given him, but they did not please him. 13 So he said, "What *kind of* cities *are* these which you have given me, my brother?" And he called them the land of Cabul, as they are to this day. 14 Then Hiram sent the king one hundred and twenty talents of gold.

15 And this *is* the reason for the labor force which King Solomon raised: to build the house of the LORD, his own house, the Millo, the wall of Jerusalem, Hazor, Megiddo, and Gezer. 16 (Pharaoh king of Egypt had gone up and taken Gezer and burned it with fire, had killed the Canaanites who dwelt in the city, and had given it *as* a dowry to his daughter, Solomon's wife.) 17 And Solomon built Gezer, Lower Beth Horon, 18 Baalath, and Tadmor in the wilderness, in the land *of Judah,* 19 all the storage cities that Solomon had, cities for his chariots and cities for his cavalry, and whatever Solomon desired to build in Jerusalem, in Lebanon, and in all the land of his dominion.

20 All the people *who were* left of the Amorites, Hittites, Perizzites, Hivites, and Jebusites, who *were* not of the children of Israel— 21 that is, their descendants who were left in the land after them, whom the children of Israel had not been able to destroy completely—from these Solomon raised forced labor, as it is to this day. 22 But of the children of Israel Solomon made no forced laborers, because they *were* men of war and his servants: his officers, his captains, commanders of his chariots, and his cavalry.

23 Others *were* chiefs of the officials who *were* over Solomon's work: five hundred and fifty, who ruled over the people who did the work.

24 But Pharaoh's daughter came up from the City of David to her house which *Solomon* had built for her. Then he built the Millo.

25 Now three times a year Solomon offered burnt offerings and peace offerings on the altar which he had built for the LORD, and he burned incense with them *on the altar* that *was* before the LORD. So he finished the temple.

26 King Solomon also built a fleet of ships at Ezion Geber, which *is* near Elath on the shore of the Red Sea, in the land of Edom. 27 Then Hiram sent his servants with the fleet, seamen who knew the sea, to work with the servants of Solomon. 28 And they went to Ophir, and acquired four hundred and twenty talents of gold from there, and brought *it* to King Solomon.

וּבַעֲצֵי בְרוֹשִׁים וּבַזָּהָב לְכָל־חֶפְצוֹ אָז יִתֵּן הַמֶּלֶךְ 12 שְׁלֹמֹה לְחִירָם עֶשְׂרִים עִיר בְּאֶרֶץ הַגָּלִיל: וַיֵּצֵא חִירָם מִצֹּר לִרְאוֹת אֶת־הֶעָרִים אֲשֶׁר נָתַן־לוֹ שְׁלֹמֹה וְלֹא יָשְׁרוּ בְּעֵינָיו: 13 וַיֹּאמֶר מָה הֶעָרִים הָאֵלֶּה אֲשֶׁר־נָתַתָּה לִּי אָחִי וַיִּקְרָא לָהֶם אֶרֶץ כָּבוּל עַד הַיּוֹם הַזֶּה: פ

14 וַיִּשְׁלַח חִירָם לַמֶּלֶךְ מֵאָה וְעֶשְׂרִים כִּכַּר זָהָב: 15 וְזֶה דְבַר־הַמַּס אֲשֶׁר־הֶעֱלָה הַמֶּלֶךְ שְׁלֹמֹה לִבְנוֹת אֶת־בֵּית יְהֹוָה וְאֶת־בֵּיתוֹ וְאֶת־הַמִּלּוֹא וְאֵת חוֹמַת יְרוּשָׁלָ‍ִם וְאֶת־חָצֹר וְאֶת־מְגִדּוֹ וְאֶת־גָּזֶר: 16 פַּרְעֹה מֶלֶךְ־מִצְרַיִם עָלָה וַיִּלְכֹּד אֶת־גֶּזֶר וַיִּשְׂרְפָהּ בָּאֵשׁ וְאֶת־הַכְּנַעֲנִי הַיֹּשֵׁב בָּעִיר הָרָג וַיִּתְּנָהּ שִׁלֻּחִים לְבִתּוֹ אֵשֶׁת שְׁלֹמֹה: 17 וַיִּבֶן שְׁלֹמֹה אֶת־גָּזֶר וְאֶת־בֵּית חֹרֹן תַּחְתּוֹן: 18 וְאֶת־ בַּעֲלָת וְאֶת־תַּמֹר בַּמִּדְבָּר בָּאָרֶץ: 19 וְאֵת כָּל־עָרֵי הַמִּסְכְּנוֹת אֲשֶׁר הָיוּ לִשְׁלֹמֹה וְאֵת עָרֵי הָרֶכֶב וְאֵת עָרֵי הַפָּרָשִׁים וְאֵת חֵשֶׁק שְׁלֹמֹה אֲשֶׁר חָשַׁק לִבְנוֹת בִּירוּשָׁלַ‍ִם וּבַלְּבָנוֹן וּבְכֹל אֶרֶץ מֶמְשַׁלְתּוֹ: 20 כָּל־הָעָם הַנּוֹתָר מִן־הָאֱמֹרִי הַחִתִּי הַפְּרִזִּי הַחִוִּי וְהַיְבוּסִי אֲשֶׁר לֹא־מִבְּנֵי יִשְׂרָאֵל הֵמָּה: 21 בְּנֵיהֶם אֲשֶׁר נֹתְרוּ אַחֲרֵיהֶם בָּאָרֶץ אֲשֶׁר לֹא־יָכְלוּ בְּנֵי יִשְׂרָאֵל לְהַחֲרִימָם וַיַּעֲלֵם שְׁלֹמֹה לְמַס־עֹבֵד עַד הַיּוֹם הַזֶּה: 22 וּמִבְּנֵי יִשְׂרָאֵל לֹא־נָתַן שְׁלֹמֹה עָבֶד כִּי־הֵם אַנְשֵׁי הַמִּלְחָמָה וַעֲבָדָיו וְשָׂרָיו וְשָׁלִשָׁיו וְשָׂרֵי רִכְבּוֹ וּפָרָשָׁיו: ס 23 אֵלֶּה שָׂרֵי הַנִּצָּבִים אֲשֶׁר עַל־הַמְּלָאכָה לִשְׁלֹמֹה חֲמִשִּׁים וַחֲמֵשׁ מֵאוֹת הָרֹדִים בָּעָם הָעֹשִׂים בַּמְּלָאכָה: 24 אַךְ בַּת־פַּרְעֹה עָלְתָה מֵעִיר דָּוִד אֶל־בֵּיתָהּ אֲשֶׁר בָּנָה־לָהּ אָז בָּנָה אֶת־הַמִּלּוֹא: 25 וְהֶעֱלָה שְׁלֹמֹה שָׁלֹשׁ פְּעָמִים בַּשָּׁנָה עֹלוֹת וּשְׁלָמִים עַל־ הַמִּזְבֵּחַ אֲשֶׁר בָּנָה לַיהֹוָה וְהַקְטֵיר אִתּוֹ אֲשֶׁר לִפְנֵי יְהֹוָה וְשִׁלַּם אֶת־הַבָּיִת: 26 וָאֳנִי עָשָׂה הַמֶּלֶךְ שְׁלֹמֹה בְּעֶצְיוֹן־גֶּבֶר אֲשֶׁר אֶת־אֵלוֹת עַל־שְׂפַת יַם־ סוּף בְּאֶרֶץ אֱדוֹם: 27 וַיִּשְׁלַח חִירָם בָּאֳנִי אֶת־ עֲבָדָיו אַנְשֵׁי אֳנִיּוֹת יֹדְעֵי הַיָּם עִם עַבְדֵי שְׁלֹמֹה: 28 וַיָּבֹאוּ אוֹפִירָה וַיִּקְחוּ מִשָּׁם זָהָב אַרְבַּע־מֵאוֹת וְעֶשְׂרִים כִּכָּר וַיָּבִאוּ אֶל־הַמֶּלֶךְ שְׁלֹמֹה: פ

10 Now when the queen of Sheba heard of the fame of Solomon concerning the name of the LORD, she came to test him with hard questions. [2] She came to Jerusalem with a very great retinue, with camels that bore spices, very much gold, and precious stones; and when she came to Solomon, she spoke with him about all that was in her heart. [3] So Solomon answered all her questions; there was nothing so difficult for the king that he could not explain *it* to her. [4] And when the queen of Sheba had seen all the wisdom of Solomon, the house that he had built, [5] the food on his table, the seating of his servants, the service of his waiters and their apparel, his cupbearers, and his entryway by which he went up to the house of the LORD, there was no more spirit in her. [6] Then she said to the king: "It was a true report which I heard in my own land about your words and your wisdom. [7] However I did not believe the words until I came and saw with my own eyes; and indeed the half was not told me. Your wisdom and prosperity exceed the fame of which I heard. [8] Happy *are* your men and happy *are* these your servants, who stand continually before you *and* hear your wisdom! [9] Blessed be the LORD your God, who delighted in you, setting you on the throne of Israel! Because the LORD has loved Israel forever, therefore He made you king, to do justice and righteousness."

[10] Then she gave the king one hundred and twenty talents of gold, spices in great quantity, and precious stones. There never again came such abundance of spices as the queen of Sheba gave to King Solomon. [11] Also, the ships of Hiram, which brought gold from Ophir, brought great *quantities* of almug wood and precious stones from Ophir. [12] And the king made steps of the almug wood for the house of the LORD and for the king's house, also harps and stringed instruments for singers. There never again came such almug wood, nor has the like been seen to this day.

[13] Now King Solomon gave the queen of Sheba all she desired, whatever she asked, besides what Solomon had given her according to the royal generosity. So she turned and went to her own country, she and her servants.

[14] The weight of gold that came to Solomon yearly was six hundred and sixty-six talents of gold, [15] besides *that* from the traveling merchants, from the income of traders, from all the kings of Arabia, and from the governors of the country.

[16] And King Solomon made two hundred large shields *of* hammered gold; six hundred *shekels* of gold went into each shield. [17] He also *made* three

י וּמַלְכַּת־שְׁבָא שֹׁמַעַת אֶת־שֵׁמַע שְׁלֹמֹה לְשֵׁם יְהוָה וַתָּבֹא לְנַסֹּתוֹ בְּחִידוֹת: ² וַתָּבֹא יְרוּשָׁלְַמָה בְּחַיִל כָּבֵד מְאֹד גְּמַלִּים נֹשְׂאִים בְּשָׂמִים וְזָהָב רַב־מְאֹד וְאֶבֶן יְקָרָה וַתָּבֹא אֶל־שְׁלֹמֹה וַתְּדַבֵּר אֵלָיו אֵת כָּל־אֲשֶׁר הָיָה עִם־לְבָבָהּ: ³ וַיַּגֶּד־לָהּ שְׁלֹמֹה אֶת־כָּל־דְּבָרֶיהָ לֹא־הָיָה דָּבָר נֶעְלָם מִן־הַמֶּלֶךְ אֲשֶׁר לֹא הִגִּיד לָהּ: ⁴ וַתֵּרֶא מַלְכַּת־שְׁבָא אֵת כָּל־חָכְמַת שְׁלֹמֹה וְהַבַּיִת אֲשֶׁר בָּנָה: ⁵ וּמַאֲכַל שֻׁלְחָנוֹ וּמוֹשַׁב עֲבָדָיו וּמַעֲמַד מְשָׁרְתָו וּמַלְבֻּשֵׁיהֶם וּמַשְׁקָיו וְעֹלָתוֹ אֲשֶׁר יַעֲלֶה בֵּית יְהוָה וְלֹא־הָיָה בָהּ עוֹד רוּחַ: ⁶ וַתֹּאמֶר אֶל־הַמֶּלֶךְ אֱמֶת הָיָה הַדָּבָר אֲשֶׁר שָׁמַעְתִּי בְּאַרְצִי עַל־דְּבָרֶיךָ וְעַל־חָכְמָתֶךָ: ⁷ וְלֹא־הֶאֱמַנְתִּי לַדְּבָרִים עַד אֲשֶׁר־בָּאתִי וַתִּרְאֶינָה עֵינַי וְהִנֵּה לֹא־הֻגַּד־לִי הַחֵצִי הוֹסַפְתָּ חָכְמָה וָטוֹב אֶל־הַשְּׁמוּעָה אֲשֶׁר שָׁמָעְתִּי: ⁸ אַשְׁרֵי אֲנָשֶׁיךָ אַשְׁרֵי עֲבָדֶיךָ אֵלֶּה הָעֹמְדִים לְפָנֶיךָ תָּמִיד הַשֹּׁמְעִים אֶת־חָכְמָתֶךָ: ⁹ יְהִי יְהוָה אֱלֹהֶיךָ בָּרוּךְ אֲשֶׁר חָפֵץ בְּךָ לְתִתְּךָ עַל־כִּסֵּא יִשְׂרָאֵל בְּאַהֲבַת יְהוָה אֶת־יִשְׂרָאֵל לְעֹלָם וַיְשִׂימְךָ לְמֶלֶךְ לַעֲשׂוֹת מִשְׁפָּט וּצְדָקָה: ¹⁰ וַתִּתֵּן לַמֶּלֶךְ מֵאָה וְעֶשְׂרִים ׀ כִּכַּר זָהָב וּבְשָׂמִים הַרְבֵּה מְאֹד וְאֶבֶן יְקָרָה לֹא־בָא כַבֹּשֶׂם הַהוּא עוֹד לָרֹב אֲשֶׁר־נָתְנָה מַלְכַּת־שְׁבָא לַמֶּלֶךְ שְׁלֹמֹה: ¹¹ וְגַם אֳנִי חִירָם אֲשֶׁר־נָשָׂא זָהָב מֵאוֹפִיר הֵבִיא מֵאֹפִיר עֲצֵי אַלְמֻגִּים הַרְבֵּה מְאֹד וְאֶבֶן יְקָרָה: ¹² וַיַּעַשׂ הַמֶּלֶךְ אֶת־עֲצֵי הָאַלְמֻגִּים מִסְעָד לְבֵית־יְהוָה וּלְבֵית הַמֶּלֶךְ וְכִנֹּרוֹת וּנְבָלִים לַשָּׁרִים לֹא בָא־כֵן עֲצֵי אַלְמֻגִּים ׀ וְלֹא נִרְאָה עַד הַיּוֹם הַזֶּה: ¹³ וְהַמֶּלֶךְ שְׁלֹמֹה נָתַן לְמַלְכַּת־שְׁבָא אֶת־כָּל־חֶפְצָהּ אֲשֶׁר שָׁאָלָה מִלְּבַד אֲשֶׁר נָתַן־לָהּ כְּיַד הַמֶּלֶךְ שְׁלֹמֹה וַתֵּפֶן וַתֵּלֶךְ לְאַרְצָהּ הִיא וַעֲבָדֶיהָ: ס ¹⁴ וַיְהִי מִשְׁקַל הַזָּהָב אֲשֶׁר בָּא לִשְׁלֹמֹה בְּשָׁנָה אֶחָת שֵׁשׁ מֵאוֹת שִׁשִּׁים וָשֵׁשׁ כִּכַּר זָהָב: ¹⁵ לְבַד מֵאַנְשֵׁי הַתָּרִים וּמִסְחַר הָרֹכְלִים וְכָל־מַלְכֵי הָעֶרֶב וּפַחוֹת הָאָרֶץ: ¹⁶ וַיַּעַשׂ הַמֶּלֶךְ שְׁלֹמֹה מָאתַיִם צִנָּה זָהָב שָׁחוּט שֵׁשׁ־מֵאוֹת זָהָב יַעֲלֶה עַל־הַצִּנָּה הָאֶחָת: ¹⁷ וּשְׁלֹשׁ־מֵאוֹת מָגִנִּים

hundred shields *of* hammered gold; three minas of gold went into each shield. The king put them in the House of the Forest of Lebanon.

¹⁸ Moreover the king made a great throne of ivory, and overlaid it with pure gold. ¹⁹ The throne had six steps, and the top of the throne *was* round at the back; *there were* armrests on either side of the place of the seat, and two lions stood beside the armrests. ²⁰ Twelve lions stood there, one on each side of the six steps; nothing like *this* had been made for any *other* kingdom.

²¹ All King Solomon's drinking vessels *were* gold, and all the vessels of the House of the Forest of Lebanon *were* pure gold. Not *one was* silver, for this was accounted as nothing in the days of Solomon. ²² For the king had merchant ships at sea with the fleet of Hiram. Once every three years the merchant ships came bringing gold, silver, ivory, apes, and monkeys. ²³ So King Solomon surpassed all the kings of the earth in riches and wisdom.

²⁴ Now all the earth sought the presence of Solomon to hear his wisdom, which God had put in his heart. ²⁵ Each man brought his present: articles of silver and gold, garments, armor, spices, horses, and mules, at a set rate year by year.

²⁶ And Solomon gathered chariots and horsemen; he had one thousand four hundred chariots and twelve thousand horsemen, whom he stationed in the chariot cities and with the king at Jerusalem. ²⁷ The king made silver *as common* in Jerusalem as stones, and he made cedar trees as abundant as the sycamores which *are* in the lowland.

²⁸ Also Solomon had horses imported from Egypt and Keveh; the king's merchants bought them in Keveh at the *current* price. ²⁹ Now a chariot that was imported from Egypt cost six hundred *shekels* of silver, and a horse one hundred and fifty; and thus, through their agents, they exported *them* to all the kings of the Hittites and the kings of Syria.

11 But King Solomon loved many foreign women, as well as the daughter of Pharaoh: women of the Moabites, Ammonites, Edomites, Sidonians, *and* Hittites— ² from the nations of whom the LORD had said to the children of Israel, "You shall not intermarry with them, nor they with you. Surely they will turn away your hearts after their gods." Solomon clung to these in love. ³ And he had seven hundred wives, princesses, and three hundred concubines; and his wives turned away his heart. ⁴ For it was so, when Solomon was old, that his wives turned his heart after other gods; and his heart was not loyal to the LORD his God, as *was* the

זָהָב שָׁחוּט שְׁלֹשֶׁת מָנִים זָהָב יַעֲלֶה עַל־הַמָּגֵן
הָאֶחָת וַיִּתְּנֵם הַמֶּלֶךְ בֵּית יַעַר הַלְּבָנוֹן: פ
18 וַיַּעַשׂ הַמֶּלֶךְ כִּסֵּא־שֵׁן גָּדוֹל וַיְצַפֵּהוּ זָהָב מוּפָז:
19 שֵׁשׁ מַעֲלוֹת לַכִּסֵּה וְרֹאשׁ־עָגֹל לַכִּסֵּה מֵאַחֲרָיו
וְיָדֹת מִזֶּה וּמִזֶּה אֶל־מְקוֹם הַשָּׁבֶת וּשְׁנַיִם אֲרָיוֹת
עֹמְדִים אֵצֶל הַיָּדוֹת: 20 וּשְׁנֵים עָשָׂר אֲרָיִים
עֹמְדִים שָׁם עַל־שֵׁשׁ הַמַּעֲלוֹת מִזֶּה וּמִזֶּה לֹא־
נַעֲשָׂה כֵן לְכָל־מַמְלָכוֹת: 21 וְכֹל כְּלֵי מַשְׁקֵה
הַמֶּלֶךְ שְׁלֹמֹה זָהָב וְכֹל כְּלֵי בֵּית־יַעַר הַלְּבָנוֹן
זָהָב סָגוּר אֵין כֶּסֶף לֹא נֶחְשָׁב בִּימֵי שְׁלֹמֹה
לִמְאוּמָה: 22 כִּי אֳנִי תַרְשִׁישׁ לַמֶּלֶךְ בַּיָּם עִם
אֳנִי חִירָם אַחַת לְשָׁלֹשׁ שָׁנִים תָּבוֹא | אֳנִי
תַרְשִׁישׁ נֹשְׂאֵת זָהָב וָכֶסֶף שֶׁנְהַבִּים וְקֹפִים וְתֻכִּיִּים:
23 וַיִּגְדַּל הַמֶּלֶךְ שְׁלֹמֹה מִכֹּל מַלְכֵי הָאָרֶץ לְעֹשֶׁר
וּלְחָכְמָה: 24 וְכָל־הָאָרֶץ מְבַקְשִׁים אֶת־פְּנֵי שְׁלֹמֹה
לִשְׁמֹעַ אֶת־חָכְמָתוֹ אֲשֶׁר־נָתַן אֱלֹהִים בְּלִבּוֹ:
25 וְהֵמָּה מְבִאִים אִישׁ מִנְחָתוֹ כְּלֵי כֶסֶף וּכְלֵי
זָהָב וּשְׂלָמוֹת וְנֶשֶׁק וּבְשָׂמִים סוּסִים וּפְרָדִים דְּבַר־
שָׁנָה בְּשָׁנָה: ס 26 וַיֶּאֱסֹף שְׁלֹמֹה רֶכֶב
וּפָרָשִׁים וַיְהִי־לוֹ אֶלֶף וְאַרְבַּע־מֵאוֹת רֶכֶב וּשְׁנֵים־
עָשָׂר אֶלֶף פָּרָשִׁים וַיַּנְחֵם בְּעָרֵי הָרֶכֶב וְעִם־הַמֶּלֶךְ
בִּירוּשָׁלִָם: 27 וַיִּתֵּן הַמֶּלֶךְ אֶת־הַכֶּסֶף בִּירוּשָׁלִַם
כָּאֲבָנִים וְאֵת הָאֲרָזִים נָתַן כַּשִּׁקְמִים אֲשֶׁר־בַּשְּׁפֵלָה
לָרֹב: 28 וּמוֹצָא הַסּוּסִים אֲשֶׁר לִשְׁלֹמֹה מִמִּצְרָיִם
וּמִקְוֵה סֹחֲרֵי הַמֶּלֶךְ יִקְחוּ מִקְוֵה בִּמְחִיר: 29 וַתַּעֲלֶה
וַתֵּצֵא מֶרְכָּבָה מִמִּצְרַיִם בְּשֵׁשׁ מֵאוֹת כֶּסֶף וְסוּס
בַּחֲמִשִּׁים וּמֵאָה וְכֵן לְכָל־מַלְכֵי הַחִתִּים וּלְמַלְכֵי
אֲרָם בְּיָדָם יֹצִאוּ: פ

יא וְהַמֶּלֶךְ שְׁלֹמֹה אָהַב נָשִׁים נָכְרִיּוֹת רַבּוֹת
וְאֶת־בַּת־פַּרְעֹה מוֹאֲבִיּוֹת עַמֳּנִיּוֹת אֲדֹמִית צִדְנִית
חִתִּית: 2 מִן־הַגּוֹיִם אֲשֶׁר אָמַר־יְהוָֹה אֶל־בְּנֵי
יִשְׂרָאֵל לֹא־תָבֹאוּ בָהֶם וְהֵם לֹא־יָבֹאוּ בָכֶם אָכֵן
יַטּוּ אֶת־לְבַבְכֶם אַחֲרֵי אֱלֹהֵיהֶם בָּהֶם דָּבַק שְׁלֹמֹה
לְאַהֲבָה: 3 וַיְהִי־לוֹ נָשִׁים שָׂרוֹת שְׁבַע מֵאוֹת
וּפִלַגְשִׁים שְׁלֹשׁ מֵאוֹת וַיַּטּוּ נָשָׁיו אֶת־לִבּוֹ: 4 וַיְהִי
לְעֵת זִקְנַת שְׁלֹמֹה נָשָׁיו הִטּוּ אֶת־לְבָבוֹ אַחֲרֵי

heart of his father David. ⁵For Solomon went after Ashtoreth the goddess of the Sidonians, and after Milcom the abomination of the Ammonites. ⁶Solomon did evil in the sight of the LORD, and did not fully follow the LORD, as *did* his father David. ⁷Then Solomon built a high place for Chemosh the abomination of Moab, on the hill that *is* east of Jerusalem, and for Molech the abomination of the people of Ammon. ⁸And he did likewise for all his foreign wives, who burned incense and sacrificed to their gods.

⁹So the LORD became angry with Solomon, because his heart had turned from the LORD God of Israel, who had appeared to him twice, ¹⁰and had commanded him concerning this thing, that he should not go after other gods; but he did not keep what the LORD had commanded. ¹¹Therefore the LORD said to Solomon, "Because you have done this, and have not kept My covenant and My statutes, which I have commanded you, I will surely tear the kingdom away from you and give it to your servant. ¹²Nevertheless I will not do it in your days, for the sake of your father David; I will tear it out of the hand of your son. ¹³However I will not tear away the whole kingdom; I will give one tribe to your son for the sake of my servant David, and for the sake of Jerusalem which I have chosen."

¹⁴Now the LORD raised up an adversary against Solomon, Hadad the Edomite; he *was* a descendant of the king in Edom. ¹⁵For it happened, when David was in Edom, and Joab the commander of the army had gone up to bury the slain, after he had killed every male in Edom ¹⁶(because for six months Joab remained there with all Israel, until he had cut down every male in Edom), ¹⁷that Hadad fled to go to Egypt, he and certain Edomites of his father's servants with him. Hadad *was* still a little child. ¹⁸Then they arose from Midian and came to Paran; and they took men with them from Paran and came to Egypt, to Pharaoh king of Egypt, who gave him a house, apportioned food for him, and gave him land. ¹⁹And Hadad found great favor in the sight of Pharaoh, so that he gave him as wife the sister of his own wife, that is, the sister of Queen Tahpenes. ²⁰Then the sister of Tahpenes bore him Genubath his son, whom Tahpenes weaned in Pharaoh's house. And Genubath was in Pharaoh's household among the sons of Pharaoh.

²¹So when Hadad heard in Egypt that David rested with his fathers, and that Joab the commander of the army was dead, Hadad said to Pharaoh, "Let me depart, that I may go to my own country."

אֱלֹהִים אֲחֵרִים וְלֹא־הָיָה לְבָבוֹ שָׁלֵם עִם־יְהוָה אֱלֹהָיו כִּלְבַב דָּוִיד אָבִיו: 5 וַיֵּלֶךְ שְׁלֹמֹה אַחֲרֵי עַשְׁתֹּרֶת אֱלֹהֵי צִדֹנִים וְאַחֲרֵי מִלְכֹּם שִׁקֻּץ עַמֹּנִים:

6 וַיַּעַשׂ שְׁלֹמֹה הָרַע בְּעֵינֵי יְהוָה וְלֹא מִלֵּא אַחֲרֵי יְהוָה כְּדָוִד אָבִיו: ס 7 אָז יִבְנֶה שְׁלֹמֹה בָּמָה לִכְמוֹשׁ שִׁקֻּץ מוֹאָב בָּהָר אֲשֶׁר עַל־פְּנֵי יְרוּשָׁלִָם וּלְמֹלֶךְ שִׁקֻּץ בְּנֵי עַמּוֹן: 8 וְכֵן עָשָׂה לְכָל־נָשָׁיו הַנָּכְרִיּוֹת מַקְטִירוֹת וּמְזַבְּחוֹת לֵאלֹהֵיהֶן:

9 וַיִּתְאַנַּף יְהוָה בִּשְׁלֹמֹה כִּי־נָטָה לְבָבוֹ מֵעִם יְהוָה אֱלֹהֵי יִשְׂרָאֵל הַנִּרְאָה אֵלָיו פַּעֲמָיִם: 10 וְצִוָּה אֵלָיו עַל־הַדָּבָר הַזֶּה לְבִלְתִּי־לֶכֶת אַחֲרֵי אֱלֹהִים אֲחֵרִים וְלֹא שָׁמַר אֵת אֲשֶׁר־צִוָּה יְהוָה: פ

11 וַיֹּאמֶר יְהוָה לִשְׁלֹמֹה יַעַן אֲשֶׁר הָיְתָה־זֹּאת עִמָּךְ וְלֹא שָׁמַרְתָּ בְּרִיתִי וְחֻקֹּתַי אֲשֶׁר צִוִּיתִי עָלֶיךָ קָרֹעַ אֶקְרַע אֶת־הַמַּמְלָכָה מֵעָלֶיךָ וּנְתַתִּיהָ לְעַבְדֶּךָ: 12 אַךְ־בְּיָמֶיךָ לֹא אֶעֱשֶׂנָּה לְמַעַן דָּוִד אָבִיךָ מִיַּד בִּנְךָ אֶקְרָעֶנָּה: 13 רַק אֶת־כָּל־הַמַּמְלָכָה לֹא אֶקְרָע שֵׁבֶט אֶחָד אֶתֵּן לִבְנֶךָ לְמַעַן דָּוִד עַבְדִּי וּלְמַעַן יְרוּשָׁלִַם אֲשֶׁר בָּחָרְתִּי: 14 וַיָּקֶם יְהוָה שָׂטָן לִשְׁלֹמֹה אֵת הֲדַד הָאֲדֹמִי מִזֶּרַע הַמֶּלֶךְ הוּא בֶּאֱדוֹם: 15 וַיְהִי בִּהְיוֹת דָּוִד אֶת־אֱדוֹם בַּעֲלוֹת יוֹאָב שַׂר הַצָּבָא לְקַבֵּר אֶת־הַחֲלָלִים וַיַּךְ כָּל־זָכָר בֶּאֱדוֹם: 16 כִּי שֵׁשֶׁת חֳדָשִׁים יָשַׁב־שָׁם יוֹאָב וְכָל־יִשְׂרָאֵל עַד־הִכְרִית כָּל־זָכָר בֶּאֱדוֹם: 17 וַיִּבְרַח אֲדַד הוּא וַאֲנָשִׁים אֲדֹמִיִּים מֵעַבְדֵי אָבִיו אִתּוֹ לָבוֹא מִצְרָיִם וַהֲדַד נַעַר קָטָן: 18 וַיָּקֻמוּ מִמִּדְיָן וַיָּבֹאוּ פָּארָן וַיִּקְחוּ אֲנָשִׁים עִמָּם מִפָּארָן וַיָּבֹאוּ מִצְרַיִם אֶל־פַּרְעֹה מֶלֶךְ־מִצְרַיִם וַיִּתֶּן־לוֹ בַיִת וְלֶחֶם אָמַר לוֹ וְאֶרֶץ נָתַן לוֹ: 19 וַיִּמְצָא הֲדַד חֵן בְּעֵינֵי פַרְעֹה מְאֹד וַיִּתֶּן־לוֹ אִשָּׁה אֶת־אֲחוֹת אִשְׁתּוֹ אֲחוֹת תַּחְפְּנֵיס הַגְּבִירָה: 20 וַתֵּלֶד לוֹ אֲחוֹת תַּחְפְּנֵיס אֵת גְּנֻבַת בְּנוֹ וַתִּגְמְלֵהוּ תַחְפְּנֵס בְּתוֹךְ בֵּית פַּרְעֹה וַיְהִי גְנֻבַת בֵּית פַּרְעֹה בְּתוֹךְ בְּנֵי פַרְעֹה: 21 וַהֲדַד שָׁמַע בְּמִצְרַיִם כִּי־שָׁכַב דָּוִד עִם־אֲבֹתָיו וְכִי־מֵת יוֹאָב שַׂר־הַצָּבָא וַיֹּאמֶר הֲדַד אֶל־פַּרְעֹה שַׁלְּחֵנִי וְאֵלֵךְ

22 Then Pharaoh said to him, "But what have you lacked with me, that suddenly you seek to go to your own country?"

So he answered, "Nothing, but do let me go anyway."

23 And God raised up *another* adversary against him, Rezon the son of Eliadah, who had fled from his lord, Hadadezer king of Zobah. 24 So he gathered men to him and became captain over a band *of raiders,* when David killed those *of Zobah.* And they went to Damascus and dwelt there, and reigned in Damascus. 25 He was an adversary of Israel all the days of Solomon (besides the trouble that Hadad *caused*); and he abhorred Israel, and reigned over Syria.

26 Then Solomon's servant, Jeroboam the son of Nebat, an Ephraimite from Zereda, whose mother's name *was* Zeruah, a widow, also rebelled against the king.

27 And this *is* what caused him to rebel against the king: Solomon had built the Millo *and* repaired the damages to the City of David his father. 28 The man Jeroboam *was* a mighty man of valor; and Solomon, seeing that the young man was industrious, made him the officer over all the labor force of the house of Joseph.

29 Now it happened at that time, when Jeroboam went out of Jerusalem, that the prophet Ahijah the Shilonite met him on the way; and he had clothed himself with a new garment, and the two *were* alone in the field. 30 Then Ahijah took hold of the new garment that *was* on him, and tore it *into* twelve pieces. 31 And he said to Jeroboam, "Take for yourself ten pieces, for thus says the LORD, the God of Israel: 'Behold, I will tear the kingdom out of the hand of Solomon and will give ten tribes to you 32 (but he shall have one tribe for the sake of My servant David, and for the sake of Jerusalem, the city which I have chosen out of all the tribes of Israel), 33 because they have forsaken Me, and worshiped Ashtoreth the goddess of the Sidonians, Chemosh the god of the Moabites, and Milcom the god of the people of Ammon, and have not walked in My ways to do *what is* right in My eyes and *keep* My statutes and My judgments, as *did* his father David. 34 However I will not take the whole kingdom out of his hand, because I have made him ruler all the days of his life for the sake of My servant David, whom I chose because he kept My commandments and My statutes. 35 But I will take the kingdom out of his son's hand and give it to you—ten tribes. 36 And to his son I will give one tribe, that My servant David may always have a lamp before Me in Jerusalem, the city which I have

אֶל־אַרְצֶךָ: 22 וַיֹּאמֶר לוֹ פַרְעֹה כִּי מַה־אַתָּה חָסֵר עִמִּי וְהִנְּךָ מְבַקֵּשׁ לָלֶכֶת אֶל־אַרְצֶךָ וַיֹּאמֶר ׀ לֹא כִּי שַׁלֵּחַ תְּשַׁלְּחֵנִי: 23 וַיָּקֶם אֱלֹהִים לוֹ שָׂטָן אֶת־רְזוֹן בֶּן־אֶלְיָדָע אֲשֶׁר בָּרַח מֵאֵת הֲדַדְעֶזֶר מֶלֶךְ־צוֹבָה אֲדֹנָיו: 24 וַיִּקְבֹּץ עָלָיו אֲנָשִׁים וַיְהִי שַׂר־גְּדוּד בַּהֲרֹג דָּוִד אֹתָם וַיֵּלְכוּ דַמֶּשֶׂק וַיֵּשְׁבוּ בָהּ וַיִּמְלְכוּ בְּדַמָּשֶׂק: 25 וַיְהִי שָׂטָן לְיִשְׂרָאֵל כָּל־יְמֵי שְׁלֹמֹה וְאֶת־הָרָעָה אֲשֶׁר הֲדָד וַיָּקָץ בְּיִשְׂרָאֵל וַיִּמְלֹךְ עַל־אֲרָם: פ

26 וְיָרָבְעָם בֶּן־נְבָט אֶפְרָתִי מִן־הַצְּרֵדָה וְשֵׁם אִמּוֹ צְרוּעָה אִשָּׁה אַלְמָנָה עֶבֶד לִשְׁלֹמֹה וַיָּרֶם יָד בַּמֶּלֶךְ: 27 וְזֶה הַדָּבָר אֲשֶׁר־הֵרִים יָד בַּמֶּלֶךְ שְׁלֹמֹה בָּנָה אֶת־הַמִּלּוֹא סָגַר אֶת־פֶּרֶץ עִיר דָּוִד אָבִיו: 28 וְהָאִישׁ יָרָבְעָם גִּבּוֹר חָיִל וַיַּרְא שְׁלֹמֹה אֶת־הַנַּעַר כִּי־עֹשֵׂה מְלָאכָה הוּא וַיַּפְקֵד אֹתוֹ לְכָל־סֵבֶל בֵּית יוֹסֵף: ס 29 וַיְהִי בָּעֵת הַהִיא וְיָרָבְעָם יָצָא מִירוּשָׁלִַם וַיִּמְצָא אֹתוֹ אֲחִיָּה הַשִּׁילֹנִי הַנָּבִיא בַּדֶּרֶךְ וְהוּא מִתְכַּסֶּה בְּשַׂלְמָה חֲדָשָׁה וּשְׁנֵיהֶם לְבַדָּם בַּשָּׂדֶה: 30 וַיִּתְפֹּשׂ אֲחִיָּה בַּשַּׂלְמָה הַחֲדָשָׁה אֲשֶׁר עָלָיו וַיִּקְרָעֶהָ שְׁנֵים עָשָׂר קְרָעִים: 31 וַיֹּאמֶר לְיָרָבְעָם קַח־לְךָ עֲשָׂרָה קְרָעִים כִּי כֹה אָמַר יְהוָה אֱלֹהֵי יִשְׂרָאֵל הִנְנִי קֹרֵעַ אֶת־הַמַּמְלָכָה מִיַּד שְׁלֹמֹה וְנָתַתִּי לְךָ אֵת עֲשָׂרָה הַשְּׁבָטִים: 32 וְהַשֵּׁבֶט הָאֶחָד יִהְיֶה־לּוֹ לְמַעַן ׀ עַבְדִּי דָוִד וּלְמַעַן יְרוּשָׁלִַם הָעִיר אֲשֶׁר בָּחַרְתִּי בָהּ מִכֹּל שִׁבְטֵי יִשְׂרָאֵל: 33 יַעַן ׀ אֲשֶׁר עֲזָבוּנִי וַיִּשְׁתַּחֲווּ לְעַשְׁתֹּרֶת אֱלֹהֵי צִדֹנִין לִכְמוֹשׁ אֱלֹהֵי מוֹאָב וּלְמִלְכֹּם אֱלֹהֵי בְנֵי־עַמּוֹן וְלֹא־הָלְכוּ בִדְרָכַי לַעֲשׂוֹת הַיָּשָׁר בְּעֵינַי וְחֻקֹּתַי וּמִשְׁפָּטַי כְּדָוִד אָבִיו: 34 וְלֹא־אֶקַּח אֶת־כָּל־הַמַּמְלָכָה מִיָּדוֹ כִּי ׀ נָשִׂיא אֲשִׁתֶנּוּ כֹּל יְמֵי חַיָּיו לְמַעַן דָּוִד עַבְדִּי אֲשֶׁר בָּחַרְתִּי אֹתוֹ אֲשֶׁר שָׁמַר מִצְוֹתַי וְחֻקֹּתָי: 35 וְלָקַחְתִּי הַמְּלוּכָה מִיַּד בְּנוֹ וּנְתַתִּיהָ לְּךָ אֵת עֲשֶׂרֶת הַשְּׁבָטִים: 36 וְלִבְנוֹ אֶתֵּן שֵׁבֶט־אֶחָד לְמַעַן הֱיוֹת־נִיר לְדָוִיד־עַבְדִּי כָּל־הַיָּמִים ׀ לְפָנַי בִּירוּשָׁלִַם

chosen for Myself, to put My name there. ³⁷So I will take you, and you shall reign over all your heart desires, and you shall be king over Israel. ³⁸Then it shall be, if you heed all that I command you, walk in My ways, and do *what is* right in My sight, to keep My statutes and My commandments, as My servant David did, then I will be with you and build for you an enduring house, as I built for David, and will give Israel to you. ³⁹And I will afflict the descendants of David because of this, but not forever.'"

⁴⁰Solomon therefore sought to kill Jeroboam. But Jeroboam arose and fled to Egypt, to Shishak king of Egypt, and was in Egypt until the death of Solomon.

⁴¹Now the rest of the acts of Solomon, all that he did, and his wisdom, *are* they not written in the book of the acts of Solomon? ⁴²And the period that Solomon reigned in Jerusalem over all Israel *was* forty years. ⁴³Then Solomon rested with his fathers, and was buried in the City of David his father. And Rehoboam his son reigned in his place.

12 And Rehoboam went to Shechem, for all Israel had gone to Shechem to make him king. ²So it happened, when Jeroboam the son of Nebat heard *it* (he was still in Egypt, for he had fled from the presence of King Solomon and had been dwelling in Egypt), ³that they sent and called him. Then Jeroboam and the whole assembly of Israel came and spoke to Rehoboam, saying, ⁴"Your father made our yoke heavy; now therefore, lighten the burdensome service of your father, and his heavy yoke which he put on us, and we will serve you."

⁵So he said to them, "Depart *for* three days, then come back to me." And the people departed.

⁶Then King Rehoboam consulted the elders who stood before his father Solomon while he still lived, and he said, "How do you advise *me* to answer these people?"

⁷And they spoke to him, saying, "If you will be a servant to these people today, and serve them, and answer them, and speak good words to them, then they will be your servants forever."

⁸But he rejected the advice which the elders had given him, and consulted the young men who had grown up with him, who stood before him. ⁹And he said to them, "What advice do you give? How should we answer this people who have spoken to me, saying, 'Lighten the yoke which your father put on us'?"

הָעִ֔יר אֲשֶׁ֣ר בָּחַ֧רְתִּי לִ֛י לָשׂ֥וּם שְׁמִ֖י שָֽׁם׃ 37 וְאֹֽתְךָ֣ אֶקַּ֔ח וּמָ֣לַכְתָּ֔ בְּכֹ֥ל אֲשֶׁר־תְּאַוֶּ֖ה נַפְשֶׁ֑ךָ וְהָיִ֥יתָ מֶּ֖לֶךְ עַל־יִשְׂרָאֵֽל׃ 38 וְהָיָ֗ה אִם־תִּשְׁמַע֙ אֶת־כָּל־אֲשֶׁ֣ר אֲצַוֶּ֔ךָ וְהָלַכְתָּ֣ בִדְרָכַ֗י וְעָשִׂ֨יתָ הַיָּשָׁ֤ר בְּעֵינַי֙ לִשְׁמ֣וֹר חֻקּוֹתַ֣י וּמִצְוֺתַ֔י כַּאֲשֶׁ֥ר עָשָׂ֖ה דָּוִ֣ד עַבְדִּ֑י וְהָיִ֣יתִי עִמָּ֗ךְ וּבָנִ֨יתִי לְךָ֤ בַֽיִת־נֶֽאֱמָן֙ כַּאֲשֶׁ֣ר בָּנִ֣יתִי לְדָוִ֔ד וְנָתַתִּ֥י לְךָ֖ אֶת־יִשְׂרָאֵֽל׃ 39 וַֽאֲעַנֶּ֛ה אֶת־זֶ֥רַע דָּוִ֖ד לְמַ֣עַן זֹ֑את אַ֖ךְ לֹ֥א כָל־הַיָּמִֽים׃ ס 40 וַיְבַקֵּ֤שׁ שְׁלֹמֹה֙ לְהָמִ֣ית אֶת־יָֽרָבְעָ֔ם וַיָּ֥קָם יָֽרָבְעָ֖ם וַיִּבְרַ֣ח מִצְרַ֔יִם אֶל־שִׁישַׁ֥ק מֶֽלֶךְ־מִצְרַ֖יִם וַיְהִ֣י בְמִצְרַ֔יִם עַד־ מ֖וֹת שְׁלֹמֹֽה׃ 41 וְיֶ֨תֶר דִּבְרֵ֤י שְׁלֹמֹה֙ וְכָל־אֲשֶׁ֣ר עָשָׂ֔ה וְחָכְמָת֑וֹ הֲלֽוֹא־הֵ֣ם כְּתֻבִ֗ים עַל־סֵ֖פֶר דִּבְרֵ֥י שְׁלֹמֹֽה׃ 42 וְהַיָּמִ֗ים אֲשֶׁר֩ מָלַ֨ךְ שְׁלֹמֹ֤ה בִירֽוּשָׁלַ֙͏ִם֙ עַל־כָּל־יִשְׂרָאֵ֔ל אַרְבָּעִ֖ים שָׁנָֽה׃ 43 וַיִּשְׁכַּ֤ב שְׁלֹמֹה֙ עִם־אֲבֹתָ֔יו וַיִּקָּבֵר֙ בְּעִ֣יר דָּוִ֣ד אָבִ֔יו וַיִּמְלֹ֛ךְ רְחַבְעָ֥ם בְּנ֖וֹ תַּחְתָּֽיו׃ ס

יב וַיֵּ֥לֶךְ רְחַבְעָ֖ם שְׁכֶ֑ם כִּ֥י שְׁכֶ֛ם בָּ֥א כָל־ יִשְׂרָאֵ֖ל לְהַמְלִ֥יךְ אֹתֽוֹ׃ 2 וַיְהִ֞י כִּשְׁמֹ֣עַ ׀ יָֽרָבְעָ֣ם בֶּן־נְבָ֗ט וְהוּא֙ עוֹדֶ֣נּוּ בְמִצְרַ֔יִם אֲשֶׁ֣ר בָּרַ֔ח מִפְּנֵ֖י הַמֶּ֣לֶךְ שְׁלֹמֹ֑ה וַיֵּ֥שֶׁב יָֽרָבְעָ֖ם בְּמִצְרָֽיִם׃ 3 וַיִּשְׁלְחוּ֙ וַיִּקְרְאוּ־ל֔וֹ וַיָּבֹ֨אוּ֙ יָֽרָבְעָ֔ם וְכָל־קְהַ֖ל יִשְׂרָאֵ֑ל וַיְדַבְּר֔וּ אֶל־רְחַבְעָ֖ם לֵאמֹֽר׃ 4 אָבִ֖יךָ הִקְשָׁ֣ה אֶת־עֻלֵּ֑נוּ וְאַתָּ֡ה עַתָּה֩ הָקֵ֨ל מֵעֲבֹדַ֧ת אָבִ֛יךָ הַקָּשָׁ֖ה וּמֵעֻלּ֥וֹ הַכָּבֵ֛ד אֲשֶׁר־נָתַ֥ן עָלֵ֖ינוּ וְנַעַבְדֶֽךָּ׃ 5 וַיֹּ֣אמֶר אֲלֵיהֶ֗ם לְכ֥וּ עֹ֛ד שְׁלֹשָׁ֥ה יָמִ֖ים וְשׁ֣וּבוּ אֵלָ֑י וַיֵּֽלְכ֖וּ הָעָֽם׃ 6 וַיִּוָּעַ֞ץ הַמֶּ֣לֶךְ רְחַבְעָ֗ם אֶת־הַזְּקֵנִים֙ אֲשֶׁר־הָי֣וּ עֹמְדִ֗ים אֶת־פְּנֵי֙ שְׁלֹמֹ֣ה אָבִ֔יו בִּֽהְיֹת֖וֹ חַ֣י לֵאמֹ֑ר אֵ֚יךְ אַתֶּ֣ם נֽוֹעָצִ֔ים לְהָשִׁ֥יב אֶת־הָֽעָם־הַזֶּ֖ה דָּבָֽר׃ 7 וַיְדַבֵּ֨ר אֵלָ֜יו לֵאמֹ֗ר אִם־הַיּ֜וֹם תִּֽהְיֶה־עֶ֤בֶד לָעָ֣ם הַזֶּה֙ וַֽעֲבַדְתָּ֔ם וַעֲנִיתָ֕ם וְדִבַּרְתָּ֥ אֲלֵיהֶ֖ם דְּבָרִ֣ים טוֹבִ֑ים וְהָי֥וּ לְךָ֛ עֲבָדִ֖ים כָּל־הַיָּמִֽים׃ 8 וַֽיַּעֲזֹ֛ב אֶת־ עֲצַ֥ת הַזְּקֵנִ֖ים אֲשֶׁ֣ר יְעָצֻ֑הוּ וַיִּוָּעַ֗ץ אֶת־הַיְלָדִים֙ אֲשֶׁ֣ר גָּדְל֣וּ אִתּ֔וֹ אֲשֶׁ֥ר הָעֹמְדִ֖ים לְפָנָֽיו׃ 9 וַיֹּ֣אמֶר אֲלֵיהֶ֗ם מָ֤ה אַתֶּם֙ נֽוֹעָצִ֔ים וְנָשִׁ֥יב דָּבָ֖ר אֶת־הָעָ֣ם הַזֶּ֑ה אֲשֶׁ֨ר דִּבְּר֤וּ אֵלַי֙ לֵאמֹ֔ר הָקֵל֙ מִן־הָעֹ֔ל אֲשֶׁר־נָתַ֥ן

¹⁰ Then the young men who had grown up with him spoke to him, saying, "Thus you should speak to this people who have spoken to you, saying, 'Your father made our yoke heavy, but you make it lighter on us'—thus you shall say to them: 'My little finger shall be thicker than my father's waist! ¹¹ And now, whereas my father put a heavy yoke on you, I will add to your yoke; my father chastised you with whips, but I will chastise you with scourges!' "

¹² So Jeroboam and all the people came to Rehoboam the third day, as the king had directed, saying, "Come back to me the third day." ¹³ Then the king answered the people roughly, and rejected the advice which the elders had given him; ¹⁴ and he spoke to them according to the advice of the young men, saying, "My father made your yoke heavy, but I will add to your yoke; my father chastised you with whips, but I will chastise you with scourges!" ¹⁵ So the king did not listen to the people; for the turn of events was from the LORD, that He might fulfill His word, which the LORD had spoken by Ahijah the Shilonite to Jeroboam the son of Nebat.

¹⁶ Now when all Israel saw that the king did not listen to them, the people answered the king, saying:

"What share have we in David?
We have no inheritance in the son of Jesse.
To your tents, O Israel!
Now, see to your own house, O David!"

So Israel departed to their tents. ¹⁷ But Rehoboam reigned over the children of Israel who dwelt in the cities of Judah.

¹⁸ Then King Rehoboam sent Adoram, who was in charge of the revenue; but all Israel stoned him with stones, and he died. Therefore King Rehoboam mounted his chariot in haste to flee to Jerusalem. ¹⁹ So Israel has been in rebellion against the house of David to this day.

²⁰ Now it came to pass when all Israel heard that Jeroboam had come back, they sent for him and called him to the congregation, and made him king over all Israel. There was none who followed the house of David, but the tribe of Judah only.

²¹ And when Rehoboam came to Jerusalem, he assembled all the house of Judah with the tribe of Benjamin, one hundred and eighty thousand chosen men who were warriors, to fight against the house of Israel, that he might restore the kingdom to Rehoboam the son of Solomon. ²² But the word of God came to Shemaiah the man of God, saying, ²³ "Speak to Rehoboam the son of Solomon, king of Judah, to all the house of Judah and Benjamin, and to the rest of the people, saying, ²⁴ 'Thus says the LORD: "You shall not go up nor fight against your brethren the children of Israel. Let every man

אָבִיךָ עָלֵינוּ: ¹⁰ וַיְדַבְּרוּ אֵלָיו הַיְלָדִים אֲשֶׁר גָּדְלוּ אִתּוֹ לֵאמֹר כֹּה־תֹאמַר לָעָם הַזֶּה אֲשֶׁר דִּבְּרוּ אֵלֶיךָ לֵאמֹר אָבִיךָ הִכְבִּיד אֶת־עֻלֵּנוּ וְאַתָּה הָקֵל מֵעָלֵינוּ כֹּה תְּדַבֵּר אֲלֵיהֶם קָטָנִּי עָבָה מִמָּתְנֵי אָבִי: ¹¹ וְעַתָּה אָבִי הֶעְמִיס עֲלֵיכֶם עֹל כָּבֵד וַאֲנִי אוֹסִיף עַל־עֻלְּכֶם אָבִי יִסַּר אֶתְכֶם בַּשּׁוֹטִים וַאֲנִי אֲיַסֵּר אֶתְכֶם בָּעַקְרַבִּים: ¹² וַיָּבוֹ יָרָבְעָם וְכָל־הָעָם אֶל־רְחַבְעָם בַּיּוֹם הַשְּׁלִישִׁי כַּאֲשֶׁר דִּבֶּר הַמֶּלֶךְ לֵאמֹר שׁוּבוּ אֵלַי בַּיּוֹם הַשְּׁלִישִׁי: ¹³ וַיַּעַן הַמֶּלֶךְ אֶת־הָעָם קָשָׁה וַיַּעֲזֹב אֶת־עֲצַת הַזְּקֵנִים אֲשֶׁר יְעָצֻהוּ: ¹⁴ וַיְדַבֵּר אֲלֵיהֶם כַּעֲצַת הַיְלָדִים לֵאמֹר אָבִי הִכְבִּיד אֶת־עֻלְּכֶם וַאֲנִי אֹסִיף עַל־עֻלְּכֶם אָבִי יִסַּר אֶתְכֶם בַּשּׁוֹטִים וַאֲנִי אֲיַסֵּר אֶתְכֶם בָּעַקְרַבִּים: ¹⁵ וְלֹא־שָׁמַע הַמֶּלֶךְ אֶל־הָעָם כִּי־הָיְתָה סִבָּה מֵעִם יְהֹוָה לְמַעַן הָקִים אֶת־דְּבָרוֹ אֲשֶׁר דִּבֶּר יְהֹוָה בְּיַד אֲחִיָּה הַשִּׁילֹנִי אֶל־יָרָבְעָם בֶּן־נְבָט: ¹⁶ וַיַּרְא כָּל־יִשְׂרָאֵל כִּי לֹא־שָׁמַע הַמֶּלֶךְ אֲלֵיהֶם וַיָּשִׁבוּ הָעָם אֶת־הַמֶּלֶךְ דָּבָר לֵאמֹר מַה־לָּנוּ חֵלֶק בְּדָוִד וְלֹא־נַחֲלָה בְּבֶן־יִשַׁי לְאֹהָלֶיךָ יִשְׂרָאֵל עַתָּה רְאֵה בֵיתְךָ דָּוִד וַיֵּלֶךְ יִשְׂרָאֵל לְאֹהָלָיו: ¹⁷ וּבְנֵי יִשְׂרָאֵל הַיֹּשְׁבִים בְּעָרֵי יְהוּדָה וַיִּמְלֹךְ עֲלֵיהֶם רְחַבְעָם: פ

¹⁸ וַיִּשְׁלַח הַמֶּלֶךְ רְחַבְעָם אֶת־אֲדֹרָם אֲשֶׁר עַל־הַמַּס וַיִּרְגְּמוּ כָל־יִשְׂרָאֵל בּוֹ אֶבֶן וַיָּמֹת וְהַמֶּלֶךְ רְחַבְעָם הִתְאַמֵּץ לַעֲלוֹת בַּמֶּרְכָּבָה לָנוּס יְרוּשָׁלָ͏ִם: ¹⁹ וַיִּפְשְׁעוּ יִשְׂרָאֵל בְּבֵית דָּוִד עַד הַיּוֹם הַזֶּה: ס ²⁰ וַיְהִי כִּשְׁמֹעַ כָּל־יִשְׂרָאֵל כִּי־שָׁב יָרָבְעָם וַיִּשְׁלְחוּ וַיִּקְרְאוּ אֹתוֹ אֶל־הָעֵדָה וַיַּמְלִיכוּ אֹתוֹ עַל־כָּל־יִשְׂרָאֵל לֹא הָיָה אַחֲרֵי בֵית־דָּוִד זוּלָתִי שֵׁבֶט־יְהוּדָה לְבַדּוֹ: ²¹ וַיָּבֹא רְחַבְעָם יְרוּשָׁלַ͏ִם וַיַּקְהֵל אֶת־כָּל־בֵּית יְהוּדָה וְאֶת־שֵׁבֶט בִּנְיָמִן מֵאָה וּשְׁמֹנִים אֶלֶף בָּחוּר עֹשֵׂה מִלְחָמָה לְהִלָּחֵם עִם־בֵּית יִשְׂרָאֵל לְהָשִׁיב אֶת־הַמְּלוּכָה לִרְחַבְעָם בֶּן־שְׁלֹמֹה: פ

²² וַיְהִי דְּבַר הָאֱלֹהִים אֶל־שְׁמַעְיָה אִישׁ־הָאֱלֹהִים לֵאמֹר: ²³ אֱמֹר אֶל־רְחַבְעָם בֶּן־שְׁלֹמֹה מֶלֶךְ יְהוּדָה וְאֶל־כָּל־בֵּית יְהוּדָה וּבִנְיָמִין וְיֶתֶר הָעָם לֵאמֹר: ²⁴ כֹּה אָמַר יְהֹוָה לֹא־תַעֲלוּ וְלֹא־תִלָּחֲמוּן עִם־אֲחֵיכֶם בְּנֵי־יִשְׂרָאֵל שׁוּבוּ אִישׁ לְבֵיתוֹ כִּי מֵאִתִּי

return to his house, for this thing is from Me.'"' Therefore they obeyed the word of the LORD, and turned back, according to the word of the LORD.

25 Then Jeroboam built Shechem in the mountains of Ephraim, and dwelt there. Also he went out from there and built Penuel. 26 And Jeroboam said in his heart, "Now the kingdom may return to the house of David: 27 If these people go up to offer sacrifices in the house of the LORD at Jerusalem, then the heart of this people will turn back to their lord, Rehoboam king of Judah, and they will kill me and go back to Rehoboam king of Judah."

28 Therefore the king asked advice, made two calves of gold, and said to the people, "It is too much for you to go up to Jerusalem. Here are your gods, O Israel, which brought you up from the land of Egypt!" 29 And he set up one in Bethel, and the other he put in Dan. 30 Now this thing became a sin, for the people went to *worship* before the one as far as Dan. 31 He made shrines on the high places, and made priests from every class of people, who were not of the sons of Levi.

32 Jeroboam ordained a feast on the fifteenth day of the eighth month, like the feast that *was* in Judah, and offered sacrifices on the altar. So he did at Bethel, sacrificing to the calves that he had made. And at Bethel he installed the priests of the high places which he had made. 33 So he made offerings on the altar which he had made at Bethel on the fifteenth day of the eighth month, in the month which he had devised in his own heart. And he ordained a feast for the children of Israel, and offered sacrifices on the altar and burned incense.

13 And behold, a man of God went from Judah to Bethel by the word of the LORD, and Jeroboam stood by the altar to burn incense. 2 Then he cried out against the altar by the word of the LORD, and said, "O altar, altar! Thus says the LORD: 'Behold, a child, Josiah by name, shall be born to the house of David; and on you he shall sacrifice the priests of the high places who burn incense on you, and men's bones shall be burned on you.'" 3 And he gave a sign the same day, saying, "This *is* the sign which the LORD has spoken: Surely the altar shall split apart, and the ashes on it shall be poured out."

4 So it came to pass when King Jeroboam heard the saying of the man of God, who cried out against the altar in Bethel, that he stretched out his hand from the altar, saying, "Arrest him!" Then his hand, which he stretched out toward him, withered, so that he could not pull it back to himself. 5 The altar also was split apart, and the ashes poured out from the altar, according to the sign which the man

נִהְיָה הַדָּבָר הַזֶּה וַיִּשְׁמְעוּ אֶת־דְּבַר יְהוָה וַיָּשֻׁבוּ לָלֶכֶת כִּדְבַר יְהוָה: ס 25 וַיִּבֶן יָרָבְעָם אֶת־שְׁכֶם בְּהַר אֶפְרַיִם וַיֵּשֶׁב בָּהּ וַיֵּצֵא מִשָּׁם וַיִּבֶן אֶת־פְּנוּאֵל: 26 וַיֹּאמֶר יָרָבְעָם בְּלִבּוֹ עַתָּה תָּשׁוּב הַמַּמְלָכָה לְבֵית דָּוִד: 27 אִם־יַעֲלֶה ׀ הָעָם הַזֶּה לַעֲשׂוֹת זְבָחִים בְּבֵית־יְהוָה בִּירוּשָׁלִַם וְשָׁב לֵב הָעָם הַזֶּה אֶל־אֲדֹנֵיהֶם אֶל־רְחַבְעָם מֶלֶךְ יְהוּדָה וַהֲרָגֻנִי וְשָׁבוּ אֶל־רְחַבְעָם מֶלֶךְ־יְהוּדָה: 28 וַיִּוָּעַץ הַמֶּלֶךְ וַיַּעַשׂ שְׁנֵי עֶגְלֵי זָהָב וַיֹּאמֶר אֲלֵהֶם רַב־לָכֶם מֵעֲלוֹת יְרוּשָׁלִַם הִנֵּה אֱלֹהֶיךָ יִשְׂרָאֵל אֲשֶׁר הֶעֱלוּךָ מֵאֶרֶץ מִצְרָיִם: 29 וַיָּשֶׂם אֶת־הָאֶחָד בְּבֵית־אֵל וְאֶת־הָאֶחָד נָתַן בְּדָן: 30 וַיְהִי הַדָּבָר הַזֶּה לְחַטָּאת וַיֵּלְכוּ הָעָם לִפְנֵי הָאֶחָד עַד־דָּן: 31 וַיַּעַשׂ אֶת־בֵּית בָּמוֹת וַיַּעַשׂ כֹּהֲנִים מִקְצוֹת הָעָם אֲשֶׁר לֹא־הָיוּ מִבְּנֵי לֵוִי: 32 וַיַּעַשׂ יָרָבְעָם ׀ חָג בַּחֹדֶשׁ הַשְּׁמִינִי בַּחֲמִשָּׁה־עָשָׂר יוֹם ׀ לַחֹדֶשׁ כֶּחָג ׀ אֲשֶׁר בִּיהוּדָה וַיַּעַל עַל־הַמִּזְבֵּחַ כֵּן עָשָׂה בְּבֵית־אֵל לְזַבֵּחַ לָעֲגָלִים אֲשֶׁר־עָשָׂה וְהֶעֱמִיד בְּבֵית אֵל אֶת־כֹּהֲנֵי הַבָּמוֹת אֲשֶׁר עָשָׂה: 33 וַיַּעַל עַל־הַמִּזְבֵּחַ ׀ אֲשֶׁר־עָשָׂה בְּבֵית־אֵל בַּחֲמִשָּׁה עָשָׂר יוֹם בַּחֹדֶשׁ הַשְּׁמִינִי בַּחֹדֶשׁ אֲשֶׁר־בָּדָא מִלִּבַּד ׀ וַיַּעַשׂ חָג לִבְנֵי יִשְׂרָאֵל וַיַּעַל עַל־הַמִּזְבֵּחַ לְהַקְטִיר: פ

יג וְהִנֵּה ׀ אִישׁ אֱלֹהִים בָּא מִיהוּדָה בִּדְבַר יְהוָה אֶל־בֵּית־אֵל וְיָרָבְעָם עֹמֵד עַל־הַמִּזְבֵּחַ לְהַקְטִיר: 2 וַיִּקְרָא עַל־הַמִּזְבֵּחַ בִּדְבַר יְהוָה וַיֹּאמֶר מִזְבֵּחַ מִזְבֵּחַ כֹּה אָמַר יְהוָה הִנֵּה־בֵן נוֹלָד לְבֵית־דָּוִד יֹאשִׁיָּהוּ שְׁמוֹ וְזָבַח עָלֶיךָ אֶת־כֹּהֲנֵי הַבָּמוֹת הַמַּקְטִרִים עָלֶיךָ וְעַצְמוֹת אָדָם יִשְׂרְפוּ עָלֶיךָ: 3 וְנָתַן בַּיּוֹם הַהוּא מוֹפֵת לֵאמֹר זֶה הַמּוֹפֵת אֲשֶׁר דִּבֶּר יְהוָה הִנֵּה הַמִּזְבֵּחַ נִקְרָע וְנִשְׁפַּךְ הַדֶּשֶׁן אֲשֶׁר־עָלָיו: 4 וַיְהִי כִשְׁמֹעַ הַמֶּלֶךְ אֶת־דְּבַר אִישׁ־הָאֱלֹהִים אֲשֶׁר קָרָא עַל־הַמִּזְבֵּחַ בְּבֵית־אֵל וַיִּשְׁלַח יָרָבְעָם אֶת־יָדוֹ מֵעַל הַמִּזְבֵּחַ לֵאמֹר ׀ תִּפְשֻׂהוּ וַתִּיבַשׁ יָדוֹ אֲשֶׁר שָׁלַח עָלָיו וְלֹא יָכֹל לַהֲשִׁיבָהּ אֵלָיו: 5 וְהַמִּזְבֵּחַ נִקְרָע וַיִּשָּׁפֵךְ הַדֶּשֶׁן מִן־הַמִּזְבֵּחַ

of God had given by the word of the LORD. ⁶ Then the king answered and said to the man of God, "Please entreat the favor of the LORD your God, and pray for me, that my hand may be restored to me."

So the man of God entreated the LORD, and the king's hand was restored to him, and became as before. ⁷ Then the king said to the man of God, "Come home with me and refresh yourself, and I will give you a reward."

⁸ But the man of God said to the king, "If you were to give me half your house, I would not go in with you; nor would I eat bread nor drink water in this place. ⁹ For so it was commanded me by the word of the LORD, saying, 'You shall not eat bread, nor drink water, nor return by the same way you came.'" ¹⁰ So he went another way and did not return by the way he came to Bethel.

¹¹ Now an old prophet dwelt in Bethel, and his sons came and told him all the works that the man of God had done that day in Bethel; they also told their father the words which he had spoken to the king. ¹² And their father said to them, "Which way did he go?" For his sons had seen which way the man of God went who came from Judah. ¹³ Then he said to his sons, "Saddle the donkey for me." So they saddled the donkey for him; and he rode on it, ¹⁴ and went after the man of God, and found him sitting under an oak. Then he said to him, "*Are* you the man of God who came from Judah?"

And he said, "I *am*."

¹⁵ Then he said to him, "Come home with me and eat bread."

¹⁶ And he said, "I cannot return with you nor go in with you; neither can I eat bread nor drink water with you in this place. ¹⁷ For I have been told by the word of the LORD, 'You shall not eat bread nor drink water there, nor return by going the way you came.'"

¹⁸ He said to him, "I too *am* a prophet as you *are,* and an angel spoke to me by the word of the LORD, saying, 'Bring him back with you to your house, that he may eat bread and drink water.'" (He was lying to him.)

¹⁹ So he went back with him, and ate bread in his house, and drank water.

²⁰ Now it happened, as they sat at the table, that the word of the LORD came to the prophet who had brought him back; ²¹ and he cried out to the man of God who came from Judah, saying, "Thus says the LORD: 'Because you have disobeyed the word of the LORD, and have not kept the commandment which the LORD your God commanded you, ²² but you came back, ate bread, and drank water in the place

כְּמוֹפֵת אֲשֶׁר נָתַן אִישׁ הָאֱלֹהִים בִּדְבַר יְהֹוָה:
6 וַיַּעַן הַמֶּלֶךְ וַיֹּאמֶר ׀ אֶל־אִישׁ הָאֱלֹהִים חַל־נָא
אֶת־פְּנֵי יְהֹוָה אֱלֹהֶיךָ וְהִתְפַּלֵּל בַּעֲדִי וְתָשֹׁב יָדִי
אֵלָי וַיְחַל אִישׁ־הָאֱלֹהִים אֶת־פְּנֵי יְהֹוָה וַתָּשָׁב יַד־
הַמֶּלֶךְ אֵלָיו וַתְּהִי כְּבָרִאשֹׁנָה: 7 וַיְדַבֵּר הַמֶּלֶךְ אֶל־
אִישׁ הָאֱלֹהִים בֹּאָה־אִתִּי הַבַּיְתָה וּסְעָדָה וְאֶתְּנָה
לְךָ מַתָּת: 8 וַיֹּאמֶר אִישׁ־הָאֱלֹהִים אֶל־הַמֶּלֶךְ אִם־
תִּתֶּן־לִי אֶת־חֲצִי בֵיתֶךָ לֹא אָבֹא עִמָּךְ וְלֹא־אֹכַל
לֶחֶם וְלֹא אֶשְׁתֶּה־מַּיִם בַּמָּקוֹם הַזֶּה: 9 כִּי־כֵן ׀
צִוָּה אֹתִי בִּדְבַר יְהֹוָה לֵאמֹר לֹא־תֹאכַל לֶחֶם
וְלֹא תִשְׁתֶּה־מָּיִם וְלֹא תָשׁוּב בַּדֶּרֶךְ אֲשֶׁר הָלָכְתָּ:
10 וַיֵּלֶךְ בְּדֶרֶךְ אַחֵר וְלֹא־שָׁב בַּדֶּרֶךְ אֲשֶׁר בָּא בָהּ
אֶל־בֵּית־אֵל:
פ
11 וְנָבִיא אֶחָד זָקֵן יֹשֵׁב בְּבֵית־אֵל וַיָּבוֹא בְנוֹ וַיְסַפֶּר־
לוֹ אֶת־כָּל־הַמַּעֲשֶׂה אֲשֶׁר־עָשָׂה אִישׁ־הָאֱלֹהִים
הַיּוֹם בְּבֵית־אֵל אֶת־הַדְּבָרִים אֲשֶׁר דִּבֶּר אֶל־הַמֶּלֶךְ
וַיְסַפְּרוּם לַאֲבִיהֶם: 12 וַיְדַבֵּר אֲלֵהֶם אֲבִיהֶם אֵי־זֶה
הַדֶּרֶךְ הָלָךְ וַיִּרְאוּ בָנָיו אֶת־הַדֶּרֶךְ אֲשֶׁר הָלַךְ אִישׁ
הָאֱלֹהִים אֲשֶׁר־בָּא מִיהוּדָה: 13 וַיֹּאמֶר אֶל־בָּנָיו
חִבְשׁוּ־לִי הַחֲמוֹר וַיַּחְבְּשׁוּ־לוֹ הַחֲמוֹר וַיִּרְכַּב עָלָיו:
14 וַיֵּלֶךְ אַחֲרֵי אִישׁ הָאֱלֹהִים וַיִּמְצָאֵהוּ יֹשֵׁב תַּחַת
הָאֵלָה וַיֹּאמֶר אֵלָיו הַאַתָּה אִישׁ־הָאֱלֹהִים אֲשֶׁר־
בָּאתָ מִיהוּדָה וַיֹּאמֶר אָנִי: 15 וַיֹּאמֶר אֵלָיו לֵךְ אִתִּי
הַבָּיְתָה וֶאֱכֹל לָחֶם: 16 וַיֹּאמֶר לֹא אוּכַל לָשׁוּב
אִתָּךְ וְלָבוֹא אִתָּךְ וְלֹא־אֹכַל לֶחֶם וְלֹא־אֶשְׁתֶּה
אִתְּךָ מַיִם בַּמָּקוֹם הַזֶּה: 17 כִּי־דָבָר אֵלַי בִּדְבַר
יְהֹוָה לֹא־תֹאכַל לֶחֶם וְלֹא־תִשְׁתֶּה שָׁם מָיִם לֹא־
תָשׁוּב לָלֶכֶת בַּדֶּרֶךְ אֲשֶׁר־הָלַכְתָּ בָּהּ: 18 וַיֹּאמֶר לוֹ
גַּם־אֲנִי נָבִיא כָּמוֹךָ וּמַלְאָךְ דִּבֶּר אֵלַי בִּדְבַר יְהֹוָה
לֵאמֹר הֲשִׁבֵהוּ אִתְּךָ אֶל־בֵּיתֶךָ וְיֹאכַל לֶחֶם וְיֵשְׁתְּ
מָיִם כִּחֵשׁ לוֹ: 19 וַיָּשָׁב אִתּוֹ וַיֹּאכַל לֶחֶם בְּבֵיתוֹ
וַיֵּשְׁתְּ מָיִם: 20 וַיְהִי הֵם יֹשְׁבִים אֶל־הַשֻּׁלְחָן
פ
וַיְהִי דְּבַר־יְהֹוָה אֶל־הַנָּבִיא אֲשֶׁר הֱשִׁיבוֹ: 21 וַיִּקְרָא
אֶל־אִישׁ הָאֱלֹהִים אֲשֶׁר־בָּא מִיהוּדָה לֵאמֹר כֹּה
אָמַר יְהֹוָה יַעַן כִּי מָרִיתָ פִּי יְהֹוָה וְלֹא שָׁמַרְתָּ
אֶת־הַמִּצְוָה אֲשֶׁר צִוְּךָ יְהֹוָה אֱלֹהֶיךָ: 22 וַתָּשָׁב
וַתֹּאכַל לֶחֶם וַתֵּשְׁתְּ מַיִם בַּמָּקוֹם אֲשֶׁר דִּבֶּר
אֵלֶיךָ אַל־תֹּאכַל לֶחֶם וְאַל־תֵּשְׁתְּ מַיִם לֹא־תָבוֹא

of which *the* LORD said to you, "Eat no bread and drink no water," your corpse shall not come to the tomb of your fathers.' "

²³ So it was, after he had eaten bread and after he had drunk, that he saddled the donkey for him, the prophet whom he had brought back. ²⁴ When he was gone, a lion met him on the road and killed him. And his corpse was thrown on the road, and the donkey stood by it. The lion also stood by the corpse. ²⁵ And there, men passed by and saw the corpse thrown on the road, and the lion standing by the corpse. Then they went and told *it* in the city where the old prophet dwelt.

²⁶ Now when the prophet who had brought him back from the way heard *it,* he said, "It *is* the man of God who was disobedient to the word of the LORD. Therefore the LORD has delivered him to the lion, which has torn him and killed him, according to the word of the LORD which He spoke to him." ²⁷ And he spoke to his sons, saying, "Saddle the donkey for me." So they saddled *it.* ²⁸ Then he went and found his corpse thrown on the road, and the donkey and the lion standing by the corpse. The lion had not eaten the corpse nor torn the donkey. ²⁹ And the prophet took up the corpse of the man of God, laid it on the donkey, and brought it back. So the old prophet came to the city to mourn, and to bury him. ³⁰ Then he laid the corpse in his own tomb; and they mourned over him, *saying,* "Alas, my brother!" ³¹ So it was, after he had buried him, that he spoke to his sons, saying, "When I am dead, then bury me in the tomb where the man of God *is* buried; lay my bones beside his bones. ³² For the saying which he cried out by the word of the LORD against the altar in Bethel, and against all the shrines on the high places which *are* in the cities of Samaria, will surely come to pass."

³³ After this event Jeroboam did not turn from his evil way, but again he made priests from every class of people for the high places; whoever wished, he consecrated him, and he became *one* of the priests of the high places. ³⁴ And this thing was the sin of the house of Jeroboam, so as to exterminate and destroy *it* from the face of the earth.

14 At that time Abijah the son of Jeroboam became sick. ² And Jeroboam said to his wife, "Please arise, and disguise yourself, that they may not recognize you as the wife of Jeroboam, and go to Shiloh. Indeed, Ahijah the prophet *is* there, who told me that I *would be* king over this people. ³ Also take with you ten loaves, *some* cakes, and a jar of honey, and go to him; he will tell you what will become of the child." ⁴ And Jeroboam's wife did so;

23 וַיְהִי אַחֲרֵי אָכְלוֹ לֶחֶם נִבְלָתְךָ אֶל־קֶבֶר אֲבֹתֶיךָ: וְאַחֲרֵי שְׁתוֹתוֹ וַיַּחֲבָשׁ־לוֹ הַחֲמוֹר לַנָּבִיא אֲשֶׁר הֱשִׁיבוֹ: 24 וַיֵּלֶךְ וַיִּמְצָאֵהוּ אַרְיֵה בַּדֶּרֶךְ וַיְמִיתֵהוּ וַתְּהִי נִבְלָתוֹ מֻשְׁלֶכֶת בַּדֶּרֶךְ וְהַחֲמוֹר עֹמֵד אֶצְלָהּ וְהָאַרְיֵה עֹמֵד אֵצֶל הַנְּבֵלָה: 25 וְהִנֵּה אֲנָשִׁים עֹבְרִים וַיִּרְאוּ אֶת־הַנְּבֵלָה מֻשְׁלֶכֶת בַּדֶּרֶךְ וְאֶת־הָאַרְיֵה עֹמֵד אֵצֶל הַנְּבֵלָה וַיָּבֹאוּ וַיְדַבְּרוּ בָעִיר אֲשֶׁר הַנָּבִיא הַזָּקֵן יֹשֵׁב בָּהּ: 26 וַיִּשְׁמַע הַנָּבִיא אֲשֶׁר הֱשִׁיבוֹ מִן־הַדֶּרֶךְ וַיֹּאמֶר אִישׁ הָאֱלֹהִים הוּא אֲשֶׁר מָרָה אֶת־פִּי יְהֹוָה וַיִּתְּנֵהוּ יְהֹוָה לָאַרְיֵה וַיִּשְׁבְּרֵהוּ וַיְמִתֵהוּ כִּדְבַר יְהֹוָה אֲשֶׁר דִּבֶּר־לוֹ: 27 וַיְדַבֵּר אֶל־בָּנָיו לֵאמֹר חִבְשׁוּ־לִי אֶת־הַחֲמוֹר וַיַּחֲבֹשׁוּ: 28 וַיֵּלֶךְ וַיִּמְצָא אֶת־נִבְלָתוֹ מֻשְׁלֶכֶת בַּדֶּרֶךְ וַחֲמוֹר וְהָאַרְיֵה עֹמְדִים אֵצֶל הַנְּבֵלָה לֹא־אָכַל הָאַרְיֵה אֶת־הַנְּבֵלָה וְלֹא שָׁבַר אֶת־הַחֲמוֹר: 29 וַיִּשָּׂא הַנָּבִיא אֶת־נִבְלַת אִישׁ־הָאֱלֹהִים וַיַּנִּחֵהוּ אֶל־הַחֲמוֹר וַיְשִׁיבֵהוּ וַיָּבֹא אֶל־עִיר הַנָּבִיא הַזָּקֵן לִסְפֹּד וּלְקָבְרוֹ: 30 וַיַּנַּח אֶת־נִבְלָתוֹ בְּקִבְרוֹ וַיִּסְפְּדוּ עָלָיו הוֹי אָחִי: 31 וַיְהִי אַחֲרֵי קָבְרוֹ אֹתוֹ וַיֹּאמֶר אֶל־בָּנָיו לֵאמֹר בְּמוֹתִי וּקְבַרְתֶּם אֹתִי בַּקֶּבֶר אֲשֶׁר אִישׁ הָאֱלֹהִים קָבוּר בּוֹ אֵצֶל עַצְמֹתָיו הַנִּיחוּ אֶת־עַצְמֹתָי: 32 כִּי הָיֹה יִהְיֶה הַדָּבָר אֲשֶׁר קָרָא בִּדְבַר יְהֹוָה עַל־הַמִּזְבֵּחַ אֲשֶׁר בְּבֵית־אֵל וְעַל כָּל־בָּתֵּי הַבָּמוֹת אֲשֶׁר בְּעָרֵי שֹׁמְרוֹן: פ

33 אַחַר הַדָּבָר הַזֶּה לֹא־שָׁב יָרָבְעָם מִדַּרְכּוֹ הָרָעָה וַיָּשָׁב וַיַּעַשׂ מִקְצוֹת הָעָם כֹּהֲנֵי בָמוֹת הֶחָפֵץ יְמַלֵּא אֶת־יָדוֹ וִיהִי כֹּהֲנֵי בָמוֹת: 34 וַיְהִי בַּדָּבָר הַזֶּה לְחַטַּאת בֵּית יָרָבְעָם וּלְהַכְחִיד וּלְהַשְׁמִיד מֵעַל פְּנֵי הָאֲדָמָה: פ

יד בָּעֵת הַהִיא חָלָה אֲבִיָּה בֶן־יָרָבְעָם: 2 וַיֹּאמֶר יָרָבְעָם לְאִשְׁתּוֹ קוּמִי נָא וְהִשְׁתַּנִּית וְלֹא יֵדְעוּ כִּי־אַתְּי אֵשֶׁת יָרָבְעָם וְהָלַכְתְּ שִׁלֹה הִנֵּה־שָׁם אֲחִיָּה הַנָּבִיא הוּא־דִבֶּר עָלַי לְמֶלֶךְ עַל־הָעָם הַזֶּה: 3 וְלָקַחַתְּ בְּיָדֵךְ עֲשָׂרָה לֶחֶם וְנִקֻּדִים וּבַקְבֻּק דְּבַשׁ וּבָאת אֵלָיו הוּא יַגִּיד לָךְ מַה־יִּהְיֶה לַנָּעַר: 4 וַתַּעַשׂ

she arose and went to Shiloh, and came to the house of Ahijah. But Ahijah could not see, for his eyes were glazed by reason of his age.

5 Now the LORD had said to Ahijah, "Here is the wife of Jeroboam, coming to ask you something about her son, for he *is* sick. Thus and thus you shall say to her; for it will be, when she comes in, that she will pretend *to be* another *woman*."

6 And so it was, when Ahijah heard the sound of her footsteps as she came through the door, he said, "Come in, wife of Jeroboam. Why do you pretend *to be* another *person?* For I *have been* sent to you *with* bad *news.* 7 Go, tell Jeroboam, 'Thus says the LORD God of Israel: "Because I exalted you from among the people, and made you ruler over My people Israel, 8 and tore the kingdom away from the house of David, and gave it to you; and *yet* you have not been as My servant David, who kept My commandments and who followed Me with all his heart, to do only *what was* right in My eyes; 9 but you have done more evil than all who were before you, for you have gone and made for yourself other gods and molded images to provoke Me to anger, and have cast Me behind your back— 10 therefore behold! I will bring disaster on the house of Jeroboam, and will cut off from Jeroboam every male in Israel, bond and free; I will take away the remnant of the house of Jeroboam, as one takes away refuse until it is all gone. 11 The dogs shall eat whoever belongs to Jeroboam and dies in the city, and the birds of the air shall eat whoever dies in the field; for the LORD has spoken!" ' 12 Arise therefore, go to your own house. When your feet enter the city, the child shall die. 13 And all Israel shall mourn for him and bury him, for he is the only one of Jeroboam who shall come to the grave, because in him there is found something good toward the LORD God of Israel in the house of Jeroboam.

14 "Moreover the LORD will raise up for Himself a king over Israel who shall cut off the house of Jeroboam; this is the day. What? Even now! 15 For the LORD will strike Israel, as a reed is shaken in the water. He will uproot Israel from this good land which He gave to their fathers, and will scatter them beyond the River, because they have made their wooden images, provoking the LORD to anger. 16 And He will give Israel up because of the sins of Jeroboam, who sinned and who made Israel sin."

17 Then Jeroboam's wife arose and departed, and came to Tirzah. When she came to the threshold of the house, the child died. 18 And they buried him; and all Israel mourned for him, according to the word of the LORD which He spoke through His servant Ahijah the prophet.

כֵּן אֵשֶׁת יָרָבְעָם וַתָּקָם וַתֵּלֶךְ שִׁלֹה וַתָּבֹא בֵּית אֲחִיָּה וַאֲחִיָּהוּ לֹא־יָכֹל לִרְאוֹת כִּי קָמוּ עֵינָיו מִשֵּׂיבוֹ: ס 5 וַיהֹוָה אָמַר אֶל־אֲחִיָּהוּ הִנֵּה אֵשֶׁת יָרָבְעָם בָּאָה לִדְרֹשׁ דָּבָר מֵעִמְּךָ אֶל־בְּנָהּ כִּי־חֹלֶה הוּא כָּזֹה וְכָזֶה תְּדַבֵּר אֵלֶיהָ וִיהִי כְבֹאָהּ וְהִיא מִתְנַכֵּרָה: 6 וַיְהִי כִשְׁמֹעַ אֲחִיָּהוּ אֶת־קוֹל רַגְלֶיהָ בָּאָה בַפֶּתַח וַיֹּאמֶר בֹּאִי אֵשֶׁת יָרָבְעָם לָמָּה זֶּה אַתְּ מִתְנַכֵּרָה וְאָנֹכִי שָׁלוּחַ אֵלַיִךְ קָשָׁה: 7 לְכִי אִמְרִי לְיָרָבְעָם כֹּה־אָמַר יְהֹוָה אֱלֹהֵי יִשְׂרָאֵל יַעַן אֲשֶׁר הֲרִימֹתִיךָ מִתּוֹךְ הָעָם וָאֶתֶּנְךָ נָגִיד עַל עַמִּי יִשְׂרָאֵל: 8 וָאֶקְרַע אֶת־הַמַּמְלָכָה מִבֵּית דָּוִד וָאֶתְּנֶהָ לָךְ וְלֹא־הָיִיתָ כְּעַבְדִּי דָוִד אֲשֶׁר שָׁמַר מִצְוֹתַי וַאֲשֶׁר־הָלַךְ אַחֲרַי בְּכָל־לְבָבוֹ לַעֲשׂוֹת רַק הַיָּשָׁר בְּעֵינָי: 9 וַתָּרַע לַעֲשׂוֹת מִכֹּל אֲשֶׁר־הָיוּ לְפָנֶיךָ וַתֵּלֶךְ וַתַּעֲשֶׂה־לְּךָ אֱלֹהִים אֲחֵרִים וּמַסֵּכוֹת לְהַכְעִיסֵנִי וְאֹתִי הִשְׁלַכְתָּ אַחֲרֵי גַוֶּךָ: ס 10 לָכֵן הִנְנִי מֵבִיא רָעָה אֶל־בֵּית יָרָבְעָם וְהִכְרַתִּי לְיָרָבְעָם מַשְׁתִּין בְּקִיר עָצוּר וְעָזוּב בְּיִשְׂרָאֵל וּבִעַרְתִּי אַחֲרֵי בֵית־יָרָבְעָם כַּאֲשֶׁר יְבַעֵר הַגָּלָל עַד־תֻּמּוֹ: 11 הַמֵּת לְיָרָבְעָם בָּעִיר יֹאכְלוּ הַכְּלָבִים וְהַמֵּת בַּשָּׂדֶה יֹאכְלוּ עוֹף הַשָּׁמָיִם כִּי יְהֹוָה דִּבֵּר: 12 וְאַתְּ קוּמִי לְכִי לְבֵיתֵךְ בְּבֹאָה רַגְלַיִךְ הָעִירָה וּמֵת הַיָּלֶד:

13 וְסָפְדוּ־לוֹ כָל־יִשְׂרָאֵל וְקָבְרוּ אֹתוֹ כִּי־זֶה לְבַדּוֹ יָבֹא לְיָרָבְעָם אֶל־קָבֶר יַעַן נִמְצָא־בוֹ דָּבָר טוֹב אֶל־יְהֹוָה אֱלֹהֵי יִשְׂרָאֵל בְּבֵית יָרָבְעָם: 14 וְהֵקִים יְהֹוָה לוֹ מֶלֶךְ עַל־יִשְׂרָאֵל אֲשֶׁר יַכְרִית אֶת־בֵּית יָרָבְעָם זֶה הַיּוֹם וּמֶה גַּם־עָתָּה: 15 וְהִכָּה יְהֹוָה אֶת־יִשְׂרָאֵל כַּאֲשֶׁר יָנוּד הַקָּנֶה בַּמַּיִם וְנָתַשׁ אֶת־יִשְׂרָאֵל מֵעַל הָאֲדָמָה הַטּוֹבָה הַזֹּאת אֲשֶׁר נָתַן לַאֲבוֹתֵיהֶם וְזֵרָם מֵעֵבֶר לַנָּהָר יַעַן אֲשֶׁר עָשׂוּ אֶת־אֲשֵׁרֵיהֶם מַכְעִיסִים אֶת־יְהֹוָה: 16 וְיִתֵּן אֶת־יִשְׂרָאֵל בִּגְלַל חַטֹּאות יָרָבְעָם אֲשֶׁר חָטָא וַאֲשֶׁר הֶחֱטִיא אֶת־יִשְׂרָאֵל: 17 וַתָּקָם אֵשֶׁת יָרָבְעָם וַתֵּלֶךְ וַתָּבֹא תִרְצָתָה הִיא בָּאָה בְסַף־הַבַּיִת וְהַנַּעַר מֵת: 18 וַיִּקְבְּרוּ אֹתוֹ וַיִּסְפְּדוּ־לוֹ כָּל־יִשְׂרָאֵל כִּדְבַר יְהֹוָה

19 Now the rest of the acts of Jeroboam, how he made war and how he reigned, indeed they *are* written in the book of the chronicles of the kings of Israel. 20 The period that Jeroboam reigned *was* twenty-two years. So he rested with his fathers. Then Nadab his son reigned in his place.

21 And Rehoboam the son of Solomon reigned in Judah. Rehoboam *was* forty-one years old when he became king. He reigned seventeen years in Jerusalem, the city which the LORD had chosen out of all the tribes of Israel, to put His name there. His mother's name *was* Naamah, an Ammonitess. 22 Now Judah did evil in the sight of the LORD, and they provoked Him to jealousy with their sins which they committed, more than all that their fathers had done. 23 For they also built for themselves high places, *sacred* pillars, and wooden images on every high hill and under every green tree. 24 And there were also perverted persons in the land. They did according to all the abominations of the nations which the LORD had cast out before the children of Israel.

25 It happened in the fifth year of King Rehoboam *that* Shishak king of Egypt came up against Jerusalem. 26 And he took away the treasures of the house of the LORD and the treasures of the king's house; he took away everything. He also took away all the gold shields which Solomon had made. 27 Then King Rehoboam made bronze shields in their place, and committed *them* to the hands of the captains of the guard, who guarded the doorway of the king's house. 28 And whenever the king entered the house of the LORD, the guards carried them, then brought them back into the guardroom.

29 Now the rest of the acts of Rehoboam, and all that he did, *are* they not written in the book of the chronicles of the kings of Judah? 30 And there was war between Rehoboam and Jeroboam all *their* days. 31 So Rehoboam rested with his fathers, and was buried with his fathers in the City of David. His mother's name *was* Naamah, an Ammonitess. Then Abijam his son reigned in his place.

15 In the eighteenth year of King Jeroboam the son of Nebat, Abijam became king over Judah. 2 He reigned three years in Jerusalem. His mother's name *was* Maachah the granddaughter of Abishalom. 3 And he walked in all the sins of his father, which he had done before him; his heart was not loyal to the LORD his God, as was the heart of his father David. 4 Nevertheless for David's sake the LORD his God gave him a lamp in Jerusalem, by setting up his son after him and by establishing Jerusalem; 5 because David did *what was* right in the eyes of

19 וְיֶ֣תֶר דִּבְרֵ֤י אֲשֶׁ֣ר דִּבֶּ֔ר בְּיַ֥ד־עֲבָדּ֖וֹ אֲחִיָּ֣הוּ הַנָּבִ֑יא: יָרׇבְעָ֡ם אֲשֶׁ֣ר נִלְחַם֩ וַאֲשֶׁ֨ר מָלָ֜ךְ הִנָּ֣ם כְּתוּבִ֗ים עַל־סֵ֛פֶר דִּבְרֵ֥י הַיָּמִ֖ים לְמַלְכֵ֥י יִשְׂרָאֵֽל׃ 20 וְהַיָּמִים֙ אֲשֶׁ֣ר מָלַ֣ךְ יָרׇבְעָ֔ם עֶשְׂרִ֥ים וּשְׁתַּ֖יִם שָׁנָ֑ה וַיִּשְׁכַּ֣ב עִם־אֲבֹתָ֔יו וַיִּמְלֹ֛ךְ נָדָ֥ב בְּנ֖וֹ תַּחְתָּֽיו׃ פ

21 וּרְחַבְעָ֣ם בֶּן־שְׁלֹמֹ֔ה מָלַ֖ךְ בִּֽיהוּדָ֑ה בֶּן־אַרְבָּעִ֣ים וְאַחַ֣ת שָׁנָ֩ה רְחַבְעָ֨ם בְּמׇלְכ֜וֹ וּֽשְׁבַ֥ע עֶשְׂרֵ֣ה שָׁנָ֣ה ׀ מָלַ֣ךְ בִּירֽוּשָׁלַ֗͏ִם הָעִ֞יר אֲשֶׁר־בָּחַ֤ר יְהֹוָה֙ לָשׂ֣וּם אֶת־ שְׁמ֥וֹ שָׁם֙ מִכֹּל֙ שִׁבְטֵ֣י יִשְׂרָאֵ֔ל וְשֵׁ֣ם אִמּ֔וֹ נַעֲמָ֖ה הָעַמֹּנִֽית׃ 22 וַיַּ֧עַשׂ יְהוּדָ֛ה הָרַ֖ע בְּעֵינֵ֣י יְהֹוָ֑ה וַיְקַנְא֣וּ אֹת֗וֹ מִכֹּל֙ אֲשֶׁ֣ר עָשׂ֣וּ אֲבֹתָ֔ם בְּחַטֹּאתָ֖ם אֲשֶׁ֥ר חָטָֽאוּ׃ 23 וַיִּבְנ֨וּ גַם־הֵ֧מָּה לָהֶ֛ם בָּמ֖וֹת וּמַצֵּב֑וֹת וַאֲשֵׁרִ֔ים עַ֚ל כׇּל־גִּבְעָ֣ה גְבֹהָ֔ה וְתַ֖חַת כׇּל־עֵ֥ץ רַעֲנָֽן׃ 24 וְגַם־קָדֵ֖שׁ הָיָ֣ה בָאָ֑רֶץ עָשׂ֗וּ כְּכֹל֙ הַתּוֹעֲבֹ֣ת הַגּוֹיִ֔ם אֲשֶׁר֙ הוֹרִ֣ישׁ יְהֹוָ֔ה מִפְּנֵ֖י בְּנֵ֥י יִשְׂרָאֵֽל׃ פ

25 וַיְהִ֞י בַּשָּׁנָ֤ה הַחֲמִישִׁית֙ לַמֶּ֣לֶךְ רְחַבְעָ֔ם עָלָ֛ה שׁוּשַׁ֥ק מֶֽלֶךְ־מִצְרַ֖יִם עַל־יְרוּשָׁלָֽ͏ִם׃ 26 וַיִּקַּ֞ח אֶת־ אֹצְר֣וֹת בֵּית־יְהֹוָ֗ה וְאֶת־אֽוֹצְרוֹת֙ בֵּ֣ית הַמֶּ֔לֶךְ וְאֶת־ הַכֹּ֖ל לָקָ֑ח וַיִּקַּח֙ אֶת־כׇּל־מָגִנֵּ֣י הַזָּהָ֔ב אֲשֶׁ֥ר עָשָׂ֖ה שְׁלֹמֹֽה׃ 27 וַיַּ֨עַשׂ הַמֶּ֤לֶךְ רְחַבְעָם֙ תַּחְתָּ֔ם מָגִנֵּ֖י נְחֹ֑שֶׁת וְהִפְקִ֗יד עַל־יַד֙ שָׂרֵ֣י הָרָצִ֔ים הַשֹּׁמְרִ֕ים פֶּ֖תַח בֵּ֥ית הַמֶּֽלֶךְ׃ 28 וַיְהִ֛י מִדֵּי־בֹ֥א הַמֶּ֖לֶךְ בֵּ֣ית יְהֹוָ֑ה יִשָּׂאוּם֙ הָֽרָצִ֔ים וֶהֱשִׁיב֖וּם אֶל־תָּ֥א הָרָצִֽים׃ 29 וְיֶ֨תֶר דִּבְרֵ֤י רְחַבְעָם֙ וְכׇל־אֲשֶׁ֣ר עָשָׂ֔ה הֲלֹא־הֵ֣מָּה כְתוּבִ֗ים עַל־סֵ֛פֶר דִּבְרֵ֥י הַיָּמִ֖ים לְמַלְכֵ֥י יְהוּדָֽה׃ 30 וּמִלְחָמָ֨ה הָיְתָ֧ה בֵין־רְחַבְעָ֛ם וּבֵ֥ין יָרׇבְעָ֖ם כׇּל־ הַיָּמִֽים׃ 31 וַיִּשְׁכַּ֤ב רְחַבְעָם֙ עִם־אֲבֹתָ֔יו וַיִּקָּבֵ֥ר עִם־ אֲבֹתָ֖יו בְּעִ֣יר דָּוִ֑ד וְשֵׁ֣ם אִמּ֗וֹ נַעֲמָה֙ הָעַמֹּנִ֔ית וַיִּמְלֹ֛ךְ אֲבִיָּ֥ם בְּנ֖וֹ תַּחְתָּֽיו׃ פ

טו וּבִשְׁנַ֨ת שְׁמֹנֶ֤ה עֶשְׂרֵה֙ לַמֶּ֣לֶךְ יָרׇבְעָ֣ם בֶּן־ נְבָ֑ט מָלַ֥ךְ אֲבִיָּ֖ם עַל־יְהוּדָֽה׃ 2 שָׁלֹ֣שׁ שָׁנִ֔ים מָלַ֖ךְ בִּירוּשָׁלָ֑͏ִם וְשֵׁ֣ם אִמּ֔וֹ מַעֲכָ֖ה בַּת־אֲבִישָׁלֽוֹם׃ 3 וַיֵּ֕לֶךְ בְּכׇל־חַטֹּא֥ות אָבִ֖יו אֲשֶׁר־עָשָׂ֣ה לְפָנָ֑יו וְלֹא־הָיָ֨ה לְבָב֤וֹ שָׁלֵם֙ עִם־יְהֹוָ֣ה אֱלֹהָ֔יו כִּלְבַ֖ב דָּוִ֥ד אָבִֽיו׃ 4 כִּ֚י לְמַ֣עַן דָּוִ֔ד נָתַן֩ יְהֹוָ֨ה אֱלֹהָ֥יו ל֛וֹ נִ֖יר בִּירֽוּשָׁלָ֑͏ִם לְהָקִ֤ים אֶת־בְּנוֹ֙ אַחֲרָ֔יו וּֽלְהַעֲמִ֖יד אֶת־יְרֽוּשָׁלָֽ͏ִם׃ 5 אֲשֶׁ֨ר עָשָׂ֥ה דָוִ֛ד אֶת־הַיָּשָׁ֖ר בְּעֵינֵ֣י יְהֹוָ֑ה וְלֹא־סָ֞ר

the LORD, and had not turned aside from anything that He commanded him all the days of his life, except in the matter of Uriah the Hittite. 6 And there was war between Rehoboam and Jeroboam all the days of his life. 7 Now the rest of the acts of Abijam, and all that he did, *are* they not written in the book of the chronicles of the kings of Judah? And there was war between Abijam and Jeroboam.

8 So Abijam rested with his fathers, and they buried him in the City of David. Then Asa his son reigned in his place.

9 In the twentieth year of Jeroboam king of Israel, Asa became king over Judah. 10 And he reigned forty-one years in Jerusalem. His grandmother's name *was* Maachah the granddaughter of Abishalom. 11 Asa did *what was* right in the eyes of the LORD, as *did* his father David. 12 And he banished the perverted persons from the land, and removed all the idols that his fathers had made. 13 Also he removed Maachah his grandmother from *being* queen mother, because she had made an obscene image of Asherah. And Asa cut down her obscene image and burned *it* by the Brook Kidron. 14 But the high places were not removed. Nevertheless Asa's heart was loyal to the LORD all his days. 15 He also brought into the house of the LORD the things which his father had dedicated, and the things which he himself had dedicated: silver and gold and utensils.

16 Now there was war between Asa and Baasha king of Israel all their days. 17 And Baasha king of Israel came up against Judah, and built Ramah, that he might let none go out or come in to Asa king of Judah. 18 Then Asa took all the silver and gold *that was* left in the treasuries of the house of the LORD and the treasuries of the king's house, and delivered them into the hand of his servants. And King Asa sent them to Ben-Hadad the son of Tabrimmon, the son of Hezion, king of Syria, who dwelt in Damascus, saying, 19 "*Let there be* a treaty between you and me, as there was between my father and your father. See, I have sent you a present of silver and gold. Come and break your treaty with Baasha king of Israel, so that he will withdraw from me."

20 So Ben-Hadad heeded King Asa, and sent the captains of his armies against the cities of Israel. He attacked Ijon, Dan, Abel Beth Maachah, and all Chinneroth, with all the land of Naphtali. 21 Now it happened, when Baasha heard *it,* that he stopped building Ramah, and remained in Tirzah.

מִכֹּל אֲשֶׁר־צִוָּהוּ כֹּל יְמֵי חַיָּיו רַק בִּדְבַר אוּרִיָּה
הַחִתִּי: 6 וּמִלְחָמָה הָיְתָה בֵין־רְחַבְעָם וּבֵין יָרָבְעָם
כָּל־יְמֵי חַיָּיו: 7 וְיֶתֶר דִּבְרֵי אֲבִיָּם וְכָל־אֲשֶׁר עָשָׂה
הֲלוֹא־הֵם כְּתוּבִים עַל־סֵפֶר דִּבְרֵי הַיָּמִים לְמַלְכֵי
יְהוּדָה וּמִלְחָמָה הָיְתָה בֵּין אֲבִיָּם וּבֵין יָרָבְעָם:

8 וַיִּשְׁכַּב אֲבִיָּם עִם־אֲבֹתָיו וַיִּקְבְּרוּ אֹתוֹ בְּעִיר דָּוִד
וַיִּמְלֹךְ אָסָא בְנוֹ תַּחְתָּיו: פ

9 וּבִשְׁנַת עֶשְׂרִים לְיָרָבְעָם מֶלֶךְ יִשְׂרָאֵל מָלַךְ
אָסָא מֶלֶךְ יְהוּדָה: 10 וְאַרְבָּעִים וְאַחַת שָׁנָה
מָלַךְ בִּירוּשָׁלָ͏ִם וְשֵׁם אִמּוֹ מַעֲכָה בַּת־אֲבִישָׁלוֹם:
11 וַיַּעַשׂ אָסָא הַיָּשָׁר בְּעֵינֵי יְהוָה כְּדָוִד אָבִיו:
12 וַיַּעֲבֵר הַקְּדֵשִׁים מִן־הָאָרֶץ וַיָּסַר אֶת־כָּל־הַגִּלֻּלִים
אֲשֶׁר עָשׂוּ אֲבֹתָיו: 13 וְגַם אֶת־מַעֲכָה אִמּוֹ
וַיְסִרֶהָ מִגְּבִירָה אֲשֶׁר־עָשְׂתָה מִפְלֶצֶת לָאֲשֵׁרָה
וַיִּכְרֹת אָסָא אֶת־מִפְלַצְתָּהּ וַיִּשְׂרֹף בְּנַחַל קִדְרוֹן:
14 וְהַבָּמוֹת לֹא־סָרוּ רַק לְבַב־אָסָא הָיָה שָׁלֵם
עִם־יְהוָה כָּל־יָמָיו: 15 וַיָּבֵא אֶת־קָדְשֵׁי אָבִיו
וְקָדְשׁוֹ[ק] בֵּית יְהוָה כֶּסֶף וְזָהָב וְכֵלִים: 16 וּמִלְחָמָה
הָיְתָה בֵּין אָסָא וּבֵין בַּעְשָׁא מֶלֶךְ־יִשְׂרָאֵל כָּל־
יְמֵיהֶם: 17 וַיַּעַל בַּעְשָׁא מֶלֶךְ־יִשְׂרָאֵל עַל־יְהוּדָה
וַיִּבֶן אֶת־הָרָמָה לְבִלְתִּי תֵּת יֹצֵא וָבָא לְאָסָא
מֶלֶךְ יְהוּדָה: 18 וַיִּקַּח אָסָא אֶת־כָּל־הַכֶּסֶף וְהַזָּהָב
הַנּוֹתָרִים בְּאוֹצְרוֹת בֵּית־יְהוָה וְאֶת־אוֹצְרוֹת
בֵּית מֶלֶךְ[ק] וַיִּתְּנֵם בְּיַד־עֲבָדָיו וַיִּשְׁלָחֵם הַמֶּלֶךְ
אָסָא אֶל־בֶּן־הֲדַד בֶּן־טַבְרִמֹּן בֶּן־חֶזְיוֹן מֶלֶךְ אֲרָם
הַיֹּשֵׁב בְּדַמֶּשֶׂק לֵאמֹר: 19 בְּרִית בֵּינִי וּבֵינֶךָ בֵּין
אָבִי וּבֵין אָבִיךָ הִנֵּה שָׁלַחְתִּי לְךָ שֹׁחַד כֶּסֶף וְזָהָב
לֵךְ הָפֵרָה אֶת־בְּרִיתְךָ אֶת־בַּעְשָׁא מֶלֶךְ־יִשְׂרָאֵל
וְיַעֲלֶה מֵעָלָי: 20 וַיִּשְׁמַע בֶּן־הֲדַד אֶל־הַמֶּלֶךְ אָסָא
וַיִּשְׁלַח אֶת־שָׂרֵי הַחֲיָלִים אֲשֶׁר־לוֹ עַל־עָרֵי יִשְׂרָאֵל
וַיַּךְ אֶת־עִיּוֹן וְאֶת־דָּן וְאֵת אָבֵל בֵּית־מַעֲכָה וְאֵת
כָּל־כִּנְרוֹת עַל כָּל־אֶרֶץ נַפְתָּלִי: 21 וַיְהִי כִּשְׁמֹעַ
בַּעְשָׁא וַיֶּחְדַּל מִבְּנוֹת אֶת־הָרָמָה וַיֵּשֶׁב בְּתִרְצָה:

22 Then King Asa made a proclamation through-out all Judah; none *was* exempted. And they took away the stones and timber of Ramah, which Baasha had used for building; and with them King Asa built Geba of Benjamin, and Mizpah.

23 The rest of all the acts of Asa, all his might, all that he did, and the cities which he built, *are they* not written in the book of the chronicles of the kings of Judah? But in the time of his old age he was diseased in his feet. 24 So Asa rested with his fathers, and was buried with his fathers in the City of David his father. Then Jehoshaphat his son reigned in his place.

25 Now Nadab the son of Jeroboam became king over Israel in the second year of Asa king of Judah, and he reigned over Israel two years. 26 And he did evil in the sight of the LORD, and walked in the way of his father, and in his sin by which he had made Israel sin.

27 Then Baasha the son of Ahijah, of the house of Issachar, conspired against him. And Baasha killed him at Gibbethon, which *belonged* to the Philistines, while Nadab and all Israel laid siege to Gibbethon. 28 Baasha killed him in the third year of Asa king of Judah, and reigned in his place. 29 And it was so, when he became king, *that* he killed all the house of Jeroboam. He did not leave to Jeroboam anyone that breathed, until he had destroyed him, according to the word of the LORD which He had spoken by His servant Ahijah the Shilonite, 30 because of the sins of Jeroboam, which he had sinned and by which he had made Israel sin, because of his provocation with which he had provoked the LORD God of Israel to anger.

31 Now the rest of the acts of Nadab, and all that he did, *are they* not written in the book of the chronicles of the kings of Israel? 32 And there was war between Asa and Baasha king of Israel all their days.

33 In the third year of Asa king of Judah, Baasha the son of Ahijah became king over all Israel in Tirzah, and *reigned* twenty-four years. 34 He did evil in the sight of the LORD, and walked in the way of Jeroboam, and in his sin by which he had made Israel sin.

16 Then the word of the LORD came to Jehu the son of Hanani, against Baasha, saying: 2 "Inasmuch as I lifted you out of the dust and made you ruler over My people Israel, and you have walked in the way of Jeroboam, and have made My people Israel sin, to provoke Me to anger with their sins, 3 surely I will take away the posterity of Baasha and the posterity of his house, and I will make your house

22 וְהַמֶּלֶךְ אָסָא הִשְׁמִיעַ אֶת־כָּל־יְהוּדָה אֵין נָקִי
וַיִּשְׂאוּ אֶת־אַבְנֵי הָרָמָה וְאֶת־עֵצֶיהָ אֲשֶׁר בָּנָה
בַּעְשָׁא וַיִּבֶן בָּם הַמֶּלֶךְ אָסָא אֶת־גֶּבַע בִּנְיָמִן וְאֶת־
הַמִּצְפָּה: 23 וְיֶתֶר כָּל־דִּבְרֵי־אָסָא וְכָל־גְּבוּרָתוֹ וְכָל־
אֲשֶׁר עָשָׂה וְהֶעָרִים אֲשֶׁר בָּנָה הֲלֹא־הֵמָּה כְתוּבִים
עַל־סֵפֶר דִּבְרֵי הַיָּמִים לְמַלְכֵי יְהוּדָה רַק לְעֵת
זִקְנָתוֹ חָלָה אֶת־רַגְלָיו: 24 וַיִּשְׁכַּב אָסָא עִם־אֲבֹתָיו
וַיִּקָּבֵר עִם־אֲבֹתָיו בְּעִיר דָּוִד אָבִיו וַיִּמְלֹךְ יְהוֹשָׁפָט
בְּנוֹ תַּחְתָּיו: פ

25 וְנָדָב בֶּן־יָרָבְעָם מָלַךְ עַל־יִשְׂרָאֵל בִּשְׁנַת שְׁתַּיִם
לְאָסָא מֶלֶךְ יְהוּדָה וַיִּמְלֹךְ עַל־יִשְׂרָאֵל שְׁנָתָיִם:
26 וַיַּעַשׂ הָרַע בְּעֵינֵי יְהוָה וַיֵּלֶךְ בְּדֶרֶךְ אָבִיו
וּבְחַטָּאתוֹ אֲשֶׁר הֶחֱטִיא אֶת־יִשְׂרָאֵל: 27 וַיִּקְשֹׁר
עָלָיו בַּעְשָׁא בֶן־אֲחִיָּה לְבֵית יִשָּׂשכָר וַיַּכֵּהוּ
בַעְשָׁא בְּגִבְּתוֹן אֲשֶׁר לַפְּלִשְׁתִּים וְנָדָב וְכָל־יִשְׂרָאֵל
צָרִים עַל־גִּבְּתוֹן: 28 וַיְמִתֵהוּ בַעְשָׁא בִּשְׁנַת שָׁלֹשׁ
לְאָסָא מֶלֶךְ יְהוּדָה וַיִּמְלֹךְ תַּחְתָּיו: 29 וַיְהִי כְמָלְכוֹ
הִכָּה אֶת־כָּל־בֵּית יָרָבְעָם לֹא־הִשְׁאִיר כָּל־נְשָׁמָה
לְיָרָבְעָם עַד־הִשְׁמִדוֹ כִּדְבַר יְהוָה אֲשֶׁר דִּבֶּר בְּיַד־
עַבְדּוֹ אֲחִיָּה הַשִּׁילֹנִי: 30 עַל־חַטֹּאות יָרָבְעָם אֲשֶׁר
חָטָא וַאֲשֶׁר הֶחֱטִיא אֶת־יִשְׂרָאֵל בְּכַעְסוֹ אֲשֶׁר
הִכְעִיס אֶת־יְהוָה אֱלֹהֵי יִשְׂרָאֵל: 31 וְיֶתֶר דִּבְרֵי
נָדָב וְכָל־אֲשֶׁר עָשָׂה הֲלֹא־הֵם כְּתוּבִים עַל־סֵפֶר
דִּבְרֵי הַיָּמִים לְמַלְכֵי יִשְׂרָאֵל: 32 וּמִלְחָמָה הָיְתָה
בֵּין אָסָא וּבֵין בַּעְשָׁא מֶלֶךְ־יִשְׂרָאֵל כָּל־יְמֵיהֶם: פ

33 בִּשְׁנַת שָׁלֹשׁ לְאָסָא מֶלֶךְ יְהוּדָה מָלַךְ בַּעְשָׁא
בֶן־אֲחִיָּה עַל־כָּל־יִשְׂרָאֵל בְּתִרְצָה עֶשְׂרִים וְאַרְבַּע
שָׁנָה: 34 וַיַּעַשׂ הָרַע בְּעֵינֵי יְהוָה וַיֵּלֶךְ בְּדֶרֶךְ יָרָבְעָם
וּבְחַטָּאתוֹ אֲשֶׁר הֶחֱטִיא אֶת־יִשְׂרָאֵל: ס

טז וַיְהִי דְבַר־יְהוָה אֶל־יֵהוּא בֶן־חֲנָנִי עַל־בַּעְשָׁא
לֵאמֹר: 2 יַעַן אֲשֶׁר הֲרִימֹתִיךָ מִן־הֶעָפָר וָאֶתֶּנְךָ
נָגִיד עַל עַמִּי יִשְׂרָאֵל וַתֵּלֶךְ ׀ בְּדֶרֶךְ יָרָבְעָם
וַתַּחֲטִא אֶת־עַמִּי יִשְׂרָאֵל לְהַכְעִיסֵנִי בְּחַטֹּאתָם:
3 הִנְנִי מַבְעִיר אַחֲרֵי בַעְשָׁא וְאַחֲרֵי בֵיתוֹ וְנָתַתִּי

like the house of Jeroboam the son of Nebat. ⁴The
dogs shall eat whoever belongs to Baasha and dies
in the city, and the birds of the air shall eat whoever
dies in the fields."

⁵Now the rest of the acts of Baasha, what he did,
and his might, *are* they not written in the book of
the chronicles of the kings of Israel? ⁶So Baasha
rested with his fathers and was buried in Tirzah.
Then Elah his son reigned in his place.

⁷And also the word of the LORD came by the
prophet Jehu the son of Hanani against Baasha and
his house, because of all the evil that he did in the
sight of the LORD in provoking Him to anger with
the work of his hands, in being like the house of
Jeroboam, and because he killed them.

⁸In the twenty-sixth year of Asa king of Judah,
Elah the son of Baasha became king over Israel, *and
reigned* two years in Tirzah. ⁹Now his servant
Zimri, commander of half *his* chariots, conspired
against him as he was in Tirzah drinking himself
drunk in the house of Arza, steward of *his* house in
Tirzah. ¹⁰And Zimri went in and struck him and
killed him in the twenty-seventh year of Asa king of
Judah, and reigned in his place.

¹¹Then it came to pass, when he began to reign,
as soon as he was seated on his throne, *that* he
killed all the household of Baasha; he did not leave
him one male, neither of his relatives nor of his
friends. ¹²Thus Zimri destroyed all the household
of Baasha, according to the word of the LORD,
which He spoke against Baasha by Jehu the
prophet, ¹³for all the sins of Baasha and the sins
of Elah his son, by which they had sinned and by
which they had made Israel sin, in provoking the
LORD God of Israel to anger with their idols.

¹⁴Now the rest of the acts of Elah, and all that he
did, *are* they not written in the book of the
chronicles of the kings of Israel?

¹⁵In the twenty-seventh year of Asa king of
Judah, Zimri had reigned in Tirzah seven days. And
the people *were* encamped against Gibbethon,
which *belonged* to the Philistines. ¹⁶Now the people
who were encamped heard it said, "Zimri has
conspired and also has killed the king." So all
Israel made Omri, the commander of the army, king
over Israel that day in the camp. ¹⁷Then Omri and
all Israel with him went up from Gibbethon, and
they besieged Tirzah. ¹⁸And it happened, when
Zimri saw that the city was taken, that he went into
the citadel of the king's house and burned the king's
house down upon himself with fire, and died,
¹⁹because of the sins which he had committed in

אֶת־בֵּיתְךָ כְּבֵית יָרָבְעָם בֶּן־נְבָט: ⁴ הַמֵּת לְבַעְשָׁא
בָּעִיר יֹאכְלוּ הַכְּלָבִים וְהַמֵּת לוֹ בַּשָּׂדֶה יֹאכְלוּ
עוֹף הַשָּׁמָיִם: ⁵ וְיֶתֶר דִּבְרֵי בַעְשָׁא וַאֲשֶׁר עָשָׂה
וּגְבוּרָתוֹ הֲלֹא־הֵם כְּתוּבִים עַל־סֵפֶר דִּבְרֵי הַיָּמִים
לְמַלְכֵי יִשְׂרָאֵל: ⁶ וַיִּשְׁכַּב בַּעְשָׁא עִם־אֲבֹתָיו וַיִּקָּבֵר
בְּתִרְצָה וַיִּמְלֹךְ אֵלָה בְנוֹ תַּחְתָּיו: ⁷ וְגַם בְּיַד־יֵהוּא
בֶן־חֲנָנִי הַנָּבִיא דְּבַר־יְהוָה הָיָה אֶל־בַּעְשָׁא וְאֶל־
בֵּיתוֹ וְעַל כָּל־הָרָעָה ׀ אֲשֶׁר־עָשָׂה ׀ בְּעֵינֵי יְהוָה
לְהַכְעִיסוֹ בְּמַעֲשֵׂה יָדָיו לִהְיוֹת כְּבֵית יָרָבְעָם וְעַל
אֲשֶׁר־הִכָּה אֹתוֹ: פ

⁸ בִּשְׁנַת עֶשְׂרִים וָשֵׁשׁ שָׁנָה לְאָסָא מֶלֶךְ יְהוּדָה
מָלַךְ אֵלָה בֶן־בַּעְשָׁא עַל־יִשְׂרָאֵל בְּתִרְצָה שְׁנָתָיִם:
⁹ וַיִּקְשֹׁר עָלָיו עַבְדּוֹ זִמְרִי שַׂר מַחֲצִית הָרָכֶב וְהוּא
בְתִרְצָה שֹׁתֶה שִׁכּוֹר בֵּית אַרְצָא אֲשֶׁר עַל־הַבַּיִת
בְּתִרְצָה: ¹⁰ וַיָּבֹא זִמְרִי וַיַּכֵּהוּ וַיְמִיתֵהוּ בִּשְׁנַת
עֶשְׂרִים וָשֶׁבַע לְאָסָא מֶלֶךְ יְהוּדָה וַיִּמְלֹךְ תַּחְתָּיו:
¹¹ וַיְהִי בְמָלְכוֹ כְּשִׁבְתּוֹ עַל־כִּסְאוֹ הִכָּה אֶת־כָּל־
בֵּית בַּעְשָׁא לֹא־הִשְׁאִיר לוֹ מַשְׁתִּין בְּקִיר וְגֹאֲלָיו
וְרֵעֵהוּ: ¹² וַיַּשְׁמֵד זִמְרִי אֵת כָּל־בֵּית בַּעְשָׁא כִּדְבַר
יְהוָה אֲשֶׁר דִּבֶּר אֶל־בַּעְשָׁא בְּיַד יֵהוּא הַנָּבִיא:
¹³ אֶל כָּל־חַטֹּאות בַּעְשָׁא וְחַטֹּאות אֵלָה בְנוֹ אֲשֶׁר
חָטְאוּ וַאֲשֶׁר הֶחֱטִיאוּ אֶת־יִשְׂרָאֵל לְהַכְעִיס אֶת־
יְהוָה אֱלֹהֵי יִשְׂרָאֵל בְּהַבְלֵיהֶם: ¹⁴ וְיֶתֶר דִּבְרֵי אֵלָה
וְכָל־אֲשֶׁר עָשָׂה הֲלוֹא־הֵם כְּתוּבִים עַל־סֵפֶר דִּבְרֵי
הַיָּמִים לְמַלְכֵי יִשְׂרָאֵל: פ

¹⁵ בִּשְׁנַת עֶשְׂרִים וָשֶׁבַע שָׁנָה לְאָסָא מֶלֶךְ יְהוּדָה
מָלַךְ זִמְרִי שִׁבְעַת יָמִים בְּתִרְצָה וְהָעָם חֹנִים עַל־
גִּבְּתוֹן אֲשֶׁר לַפְּלִשְׁתִּים: ¹⁶ וַיִּשְׁמַע הָעָם הַחֹנִים
לֵאמֹר קָשַׁר זִמְרִי וְגַם הִכָּה אֶת־הַמֶּלֶךְ וַיַּמְלִכוּ
כָל־יִשְׂרָאֵל אֶת־עָמְרִי שַׂר־צָבָא עַל־יִשְׂרָאֵל בַּיּוֹם
הַהוּא בַּמַּחֲנֶה: ¹⁷ וַיַּעֲלֶה עָמְרִי וְכָל־יִשְׂרָאֵל עִמּוֹ
מִגִּבְּתוֹן וַיָּצֻרוּ עַל־תִּרְצָה: ¹⁸ וַיְהִי כִּרְאוֹת זִמְרִי
כִּי־נִלְכְּדָה הָעִיר וַיָּבֹא אֶל־אַרְמוֹן בֵּית־הַמֶּלֶךְ
וַיִּשְׂרֹף עָלָיו אֶת־בֵּית־מֶלֶךְ בָּאֵשׁ וַיָּמֹת: ¹⁹ עַל־
חַטֹּאתָיוᵖ אֲשֶׁר חָטָא לַעֲשׂוֹת הָרַע בְּעֵינֵי יְהוָה

חטאתיו 19 טז

doing evil in the sight of the LORD, in walking in the way of Jeroboam, and in his sin which he had committed to make Israel sin. ²⁰ Now the rest of the acts of Zimri, and the treason he committed, *are* they not written in the book of the chronicles of the kings of Israel?

²¹ Then the people of Israel were divided into two parts: half of the people followed Tibni the son of Ginath, to make him king, and half followed Omri. ²² But the people who followed Omri prevailed over the people who followed Tibni the son of Ginath. So Tibni died and Omri reigned. ²³ In the thirty-first year of Asa king of Judah, Omri became king over Israel, *and reigned* twelve years. Six years he reigned in Tirzah. ²⁴ And he bought the hill of Samaria from Shemer for two talents of silver; then he built on the hill, and called the name of the city which he built, Samaria, after the name of Shemer, owner of the hill. ²⁵ Omri did evil in the eyes of the LORD, and did worse than all who *were* before him. ²⁶ For he walked in all the ways of Jeroboam the son of Nebat, and in his sin by which he had made Israel sin, provoking the LORD God of Israel to anger with their idols.

²⁷ Now the rest of the acts of Omri which he did, and the might that he showed, *are* they not written in the book of the chronicles of the kings of Israel? ²⁸ So Omri rested with his fathers and was buried in Samaria. Then Ahab his son reigned in his place.

²⁹ In the thirty-eighth year of Asa king of Judah, Ahab the son of Omri became king over Israel; and Ahab the son of Omri reigned over Israel in Samaria twenty-two years. ³⁰ Now Ahab the son of Omri did evil in the sight of the LORD, more than all who *were* before him. ³¹ And it came to pass, as though it had been a trivial thing for him to walk in the sins of Jeroboam the son of Nebat, that he took as wife Jezebel the daughter of Ethbaal, king of the Sidonians; and he went and served Baal and worshiped him. ³² Then he set up an altar for Baal in the temple of Baal, which he had built in Samaria. ³³ And Ahab made a wooden image. Ahab did more to provoke the LORD God of Israel to anger than all the kings of Israel who were before him. ³⁴ In his days Hiel of Bethel built Jericho. He laid its foundation with Abiram his firstborn, and with his youngest *son* Segub he set up its gates, according to the word of the LORD, which He had spoken through Joshua the son of Nun.

17 And Elijah the Tishbite, of the inhabitants of Gilead, said to Ahab, "*As* the LORD God of Israel lives, before whom I stand, there shall not be dew nor rain these years, except at my word."

לָלֶכֶת בְּדֶרֶךְ יָרָבְעָם וּבְחַטָּאתוֹ אֲשֶׁר עָשָׂה
לְהַחֲטִיא אֶת־יִשְׂרָאֵל: 20 וְיֶתֶר דִּבְרֵי זִמְרִי וְקִשְׁרוֹ
אֲשֶׁר קָשָׁר הֲלֹא־הֵם כְּתוּבִים עַל־סֵפֶר דִּבְרֵי
הַיָּמִים לְמַלְכֵי יִשְׂרָאֵל: פ

21 אָז יֵחָלֵק הָעָם יִשְׂרָאֵל לַחֵצִי חֲצִי הָעָם הָיָה
אַחֲרֵי תִבְנִי בֶן־גִּינַת לְהַמְלִיכוֹ וְהַחֲצִי אַחֲרֵי עָמְרִי:
22 וַיֶּחֱזַק הָעָם אֲשֶׁר אַחֲרֵי עָמְרִי אֶת־הָעָם אֲשֶׁר
אַחֲרֵי תִבְנִי בֶן־גִּינַת וַיָּמָת תִּבְנִי וַיִּמְלֹךְ עָמְרִי: פ
23 בִּשְׁנַת שְׁלֹשִׁים וְאַחַת שָׁנָה לְאָסָא מֶלֶךְ יְהוּדָה
מָלַךְ עָמְרִי עַל־יִשְׂרָאֵל שְׁתֵּים עֶשְׂרֵה שָׁנָה בְּתִרְצָה
מָלַךְ שֵׁשׁ־שָׁנִים: 24 וַיִּקֶן אֶת־הָהָר שֹׁמְרוֹן מֵאֵת
שֶׁמֶר בְּכִכְּרַיִם כָּסֶף וַיִּבֶן אֶת־הָהָר וַיִּקְרָא אֶת־שֵׁם
הָעִיר אֲשֶׁר בָּנָה עַל שֶׁם־שֶׁמֶר אֲדֹנֵי הָהָר שֹׁמְרוֹן:
25 וַיַּעֲשֶׂה עָמְרִי הָרַע בְּעֵינֵי יְהוָה וַיָּרַע מִכֹּל
אֲשֶׁר לְפָנָיו: 26 וַיֵּלֶךְ בְּכָל־דֶּרֶךְ יָרָבְעָם בֶּן־נְבָט
וּבְחַטֹּאתָיו אֲשֶׁר הֶחֱטִיא אֶת־יִשְׂרָאֵל לְהַכְעִיס
אֶת־יְהוָה אֱלֹהֵי יִשְׂרָאֵל בְּהַבְלֵיהֶם: 27 וְיֶתֶר דִּבְרֵי
עָמְרִי אֲשֶׁר עָשָׂה וּגְבוּרָתוֹ אֲשֶׁר עָשָׂה הֲלֹא־הֵם
כְּתוּבִים עַל־סֵפֶר דִּבְרֵי הַיָּמִים לְמַלְכֵי יִשְׂרָאֵל:
28 וַיִּשְׁכַּב עָמְרִי עִם־אֲבֹתָיו וַיִּקָּבֵר בְּשֹׁמְרוֹן וַיִּמְלֹךְ
אַחְאָב בְּנוֹ תַּחְתָּיו: פ

29 וְאַחְאָב בֶּן־עָמְרִי מָלַךְ עַל־יִשְׂרָאֵל בִּשְׁנַת
שְׁלֹשִׁים וּשְׁמֹנֶה שָׁנָה לְאָסָא מֶלֶךְ יְהוּדָה וַיִּמְלֹךְ
אַחְאָב בֶּן־עָמְרִי עַל־יִשְׂרָאֵל בְּשֹׁמְרוֹן עֶשְׂרִים
וּשְׁתַּיִם שָׁנָה: 30 וַיַּעַשׂ אַחְאָב בֶּן־עָמְרִי הָרַע בְּעֵינֵי
יְהוָה מִכֹּל אֲשֶׁר לְפָנָיו: 31 וַיְהִי הֲנָקֵל לֶכְתּוֹ
בְּחַטֹּאות יָרָבְעָם בֶּן־נְבָט וַיִּקַּח אִשָּׁה אֶת־אִיזֶבֶל
בַּת־אֶתְבַּעַל מֶלֶךְ צִידֹנִים וַיֵּלֶךְ וַיַּעֲבֹד אֶת־הַבַּעַל
וַיִּשְׁתַּחוּ לוֹ: 32 וַיָּקֶם מִזְבֵּחַ לַבָּעַל בֵּית הַבַּעַל אֲשֶׁר
בָּנָה בְּשֹׁמְרוֹן: 33 וַיַּעַשׂ אַחְאָב אֶת־הָאֲשֵׁרָה וַיּוֹסֶף
אַחְאָב לַעֲשׂוֹת לְהַכְעִיס אֶת־יְהֹוָה אֱלֹהֵי יִשְׂרָאֵל
מִכֹּל מַלְכֵי יִשְׂרָאֵל אֲשֶׁר הָיוּ לְפָנָיו: 34 בְּיָמָיו בָּנָה
חִיאֵל בֵּית הָאֱלִי אֶת־יְרִיחֹה בַּאֲבִירָם בְּכֹרוֹ יִסְּדָהּ
וּבִשְׂגוּב צְעִירוֹ הִצִּיב דְּלָתֶיהָ כִּדְבַר יְהוָה אֲשֶׁר
דִּבֶּר בְּיַד יְהוֹשֻׁעַ בֶּן־נוּן: ס

יז וַיֹּאמֶר אֵלִיָּהוּ הַתִּשְׁבִּי מִתֹּשָׁבֵי גִלְעָד אֶל־
אַחְאָב חַי־יְהֹוָה אֱלֹהֵי יִשְׂרָאֵל אֲשֶׁר עָמַדְתִּי לְפָנָיו
אִם־יִהְיֶה הַשָּׁנִים הָאֵלֶּה טַל וּמָטָר כִּי אִם־לְפִי

² Then the word of the LORD came to him, saying, ³ "Get away from here and turn eastward, and hide by the Brook Cherith, which flows into the Jordan. ⁴ And it will be *that* you shall drink from the brook, and I have commanded the ravens to feed you there."

⁵ So he went and did according to the word of the LORD, for he went and stayed by the Brook Cherith, which flows into the Jordan. ⁶ The ravens brought him bread and meat in the morning, and bread and meat in the evening; and he drank from the brook. ⁷ And it happened after a while that the brook dried up, because there had been no rain in the land.

⁸ Then the word of the LORD came to him, saying, ⁹ "Arise, go to Zarephath, which *belongs* to Sidon, and dwell there. See, I have commanded a widow there to provide for you." ¹⁰ So he arose and went to Zarephath. And when he came to the gate of the city, indeed a widow *was* there gathering sticks. And he called to her and said, "Please bring me a little water in a cup, that I may drink." ¹¹ And as she was going to get *it*, he called to her and said, "Please bring me a morsel of bread in your hand."

¹² So she said, "As the LORD your God lives, I do not have bread, only a handful of flour in a bin, and a little oil in a jar; and see, I *am* gathering a couple of sticks that I may go in and prepare it for myself and my son, that we may eat it, and die."

¹³ And Elijah said to her, "Do not fear; go *and* do as you have said, but make me a small cake from it first, and bring *it* to me; and afterward make *some* for yourself and your son. ¹⁴ For thus says the LORD God of Israel: 'The bin of flour shall not be used up, nor shall the jar of oil run dry, until the day the LORD sends rain on the earth.'"

¹⁵ So she went away and did according to the word of Elijah; and she and he and her household ate for *many* days. ¹⁶ The bin of flour was not used up, nor did the jar of oil run dry, according to the word of the LORD which He spoke by Elijah.

¹⁷ Now it happened after these things *that* the son of the woman who owned the house became sick. And his sickness was so serious that there was no breath left in him. ¹⁸ So she said to Elijah, "What have I to do with you, O man of God? Have you come to me to bring my sin to remembrance, and to kill my son?"

¹⁹ And he said to her, "Give me your son." So he took him out of her arms and carried him to the upper room where he was staying, and laid him on his own bed. ²⁰ Then he cried out to the LORD and said, "O LORD my God, have You also brought tragedy on the widow with whom I lodge, by killing

דְּבָרָי: ס ² וַיְהִי דְבַר־יְהוָה אֵלָיו לֵאמֹר:
³ לֵךְ מִזֶּה וּפָנִיתָ לְּךָ קֵדְמָה וְנִסְתַּרְתָּ בְּנַחַל כְּרִית
אֲשֶׁר עַל־פְּנֵי הַיַּרְדֵּן: ⁴ וְהָיָה מֵהַנַּחַל תִּשְׁתֶּה
וְאֶת־הָעֹרְבִים צִוִּיתִי לְכַלְכֶּלְךָ שָׁם: ⁵ וַיֵּלֶךְ וַיַּעַשׂ
כִּדְבַר יְהוָה וַיֵּלֶךְ וַיֵּשֶׁב בְּנַחַל כְּרִית אֲשֶׁר עַל־
פְּנֵי הַיַּרְדֵּן: ⁶ וְהָעֹרְבִים מְבִיאִים לוֹ לֶחֶם וּבָשָׂר
בַּבֹּקֶר וְלֶחֶם וּבָשָׂר בָּעָרֶב וּמִן־הַנַּחַל יִשְׁתֶּה:
⁷ וַיְהִי מִקֵּץ יָמִים וַיִּיבַשׁ הַנָּחַל כִּי לֹא־הָיָה גֶשֶׁם
בָּאָרֶץ: ס ⁸ וַיְהִי דְבַר־יְהוָה אֵלָיו לֵאמֹר:
⁹ קוּם לֵךְ צָרְפַתָה אֲשֶׁר לְצִידוֹן וְיָשַׁבְתָּ שָׁם הִנֵּה
צִוִּיתִי שָׁם אִשָּׁה אַלְמָנָה לְכַלְכְּלֶךָ | ¹⁰ וַיָּקָם
וַיֵּלֶךְ צָרְפַתָה וַיָּבֹא אֶל־פֶּתַח הָעִיר וְהִנֵּה־שָׁם
אִשָּׁה אַלְמָנָה מְקֹשֶׁשֶׁת עֵצִים וַיִּקְרָא אֵלֶיהָ וַיֹּאמַר
קְחִי־נָא לִי מְעַט־מַיִם בַּכְּלִי וְאֶשְׁתֶּה: ¹¹ וַתֵּלֶךְ
לָקַחַת וַיִּקְרָא אֵלֶיהָ וַיֹּאמַר לִקְחִי־נָא לִי פַּת־לֶחֶם
בְּיָדֵךְ: ¹² וַתֹּאמֶר חַי־יְהוָה אֱלֹהֶיךָ אִם־יֶשׁ־לִי מָעוֹג
כִּי אִם־מְלֹא כַף־קֶמַח בַּכַּד וּמְעַט־שֶׁמֶן בַּצַּפָּחַת
וְהִנְנִי מְקֹשֶׁשֶׁת שְׁנַיִם עֵצִים וּבָאתִי וַעֲשִׂיתִיהוּ לִי
וְלִבְנִי וַאֲכַלְנֻהוּ וָמָתְנוּ: ¹³ וַיֹּאמֶר אֵלֶיהָ אֵלִיָּהוּ
אַל־תִּירְאִי בֹּאִי עֲשִׂי כִדְבָרֵךְ אַךְ עֲשִׂי־לִי מִשָּׁם
עֻגָה קְטַנָּה בָרִאשֹׁנָה וְהוֹצֵאת לִי וְלָךְ וְלִבְנֵךְ
תַּעֲשִׂי בָּאַחֲרֹנָה: ס ¹⁴ כִּי כֹה אָמַר יְהוָה
אֱלֹהֵי יִשְׂרָאֵל כַּד הַקֶּמַח לֹא תִכְלָה וְצַפַּחַת הַשֶּׁמֶן
לֹא תֶחְסָר עַד יוֹם תֵּתֵּן^ק יְהוָה גֶּשֶׁם עַל־פְּנֵי
הָאֲדָמָה: ¹⁵ וַתֵּלֶךְ וַתַּעֲשֶׂה כִּדְבַר אֵלִיָּהוּ וַתֹּאכַל
הוּא^ק הִיא^ק וּבֵיתָה יָמִים: ¹⁶ כַּד הַקֶּמַח לֹא
כָלָתָה וְצַפַּחַת הַשֶּׁמֶן לֹא חָסֵר כִּדְבַר יְהוָה אֲשֶׁר
דִּבֶּר בְּיַד אֵלִיָּהוּ:
פ
¹⁷ וַיְהִי אַחַר הַדְּבָרִים הָאֵלֶּה חָלָה בֶּן־הָאִשָּׁה
בַּעֲלַת הַבָּיִת וַיְהִי חָלְיוֹ חָזָק מְאֹד עַד אֲשֶׁר לֹא־
נוֹתְרָה־בּוֹ נְשָׁמָה: ¹⁸ וַתֹּאמֶר אֶל־אֵלִיָּהוּ מַה־לִּי
וָלָךְ אִישׁ הָאֱלֹהִים בָּאתָ אֵלַי לְהַזְכִּיר אֶת־עֲוֹנִי
וּלְהָמִית אֶת־בְּנִי: ¹⁹ וַיֹּאמֶר אֵלֶיהָ תְּנִי־לִי אֶת־
בְּנֵךְ וַיִּקָּחֵהוּ מֵחֵיקָהּ וַיַּעֲלֵהוּ אֶל־הָעֲלִיָּה אֲשֶׁר
הוּא יֹשֵׁב שָׁם וַיַּשְׁכִּבֵהוּ עַל־מִטָּתוֹ: ²⁰ וַיִּקְרָא

her son?" 21 And he stretched himself out on the child three times, and cried out to the Lord and said, "O Lord my God, I pray, let this child's soul come back to him." 22 Then the Lord heard the voice of Elijah; and the soul of the child came back to him, and he revived.

23 And Elijah took the child and brought him down from the upper room into the house, and gave him to his mother. And Elijah said, "See, your son lives!"

24 Then the woman said to Elijah, "Now by this I know that you *are* a man of God, *and* that the word of the Lord in your mouth *is* the truth."

18 And it came to pass *after* many days that the word of the Lord came to Elijah, in the third year, saying, "Go, present yourself to Ahab, and I will send rain on the earth."

2 So Elijah went to present himself to Ahab; and *there was* a severe famine in Samaria. 3 And Ahab had called Obadiah, who *was* in charge of *his* house. (Now Obadiah feared the Lord greatly. 4 For so it was, while Jezebel massacred the prophets of the Lord, that Obadiah had taken one hundred prophets and hidden them, fifty to a cave, and had fed them with bread and water.) 5 And Ahab had said to Obadiah, "Go into the land to all the springs of water and to all the brooks; perhaps we may find grass to keep the horses and mules alive, so that we will not have to kill any livestock." 6 So they divided the land between them to explore it; Ahab went one way by himself, and Obadiah went another way by himself.

7 Now as Obadiah was on his way, suddenly Elijah met him; and he recognized him, and fell on his face, and said, "*Is* that you, my lord Elijah?"

8 And he answered him, "*It is* I. Go, tell your master, 'Elijah *is here*.' "

9 So he said, "How have I sinned, that you are delivering your servant into the hand of Ahab, to kill me? 10 As the Lord your God lives, there is no nation or kingdom where my master has not sent someone to hunt for you; and when they said, '*He is not here*,' he took an oath from the kingdom or nation that they could not find you. 11 And now you say, 'Go, tell your master, "Elijah *is here*" '! 12 And it shall come to pass, *as soon as* I am gone from you, that the Spirit of the Lord will carry you to a place I do not know; so when I go and tell Ahab, and he cannot find you, he will kill me. But I your servant have feared the Lord from my youth. 13 Was it not reported to my lord what I did when Jezebel killed the prophets of the Lord, how I hid one hundred men of the Lord's prophets, fifty to a cave, and fed

אֶל־יְהֹוָה וַיֹּאמַר יְהֹוָה אֱלֹהָי הֲגַם עַל־הָאַלְמָנָה
אֲשֶׁר־אֲנִי מִתְגּוֹרֵר עִמָּהּ הֲרֵעוֹתָ לְהָמִית אֶת־בְּנָהּ:
21 וַיִּתְמֹדֵד עַל־הַיֶּלֶד שָׁלֹשׁ פְּעָמִים וַיִּקְרָא אֶל־
יְהֹוָה וַיֹּאמַר יְהֹוָה אֱלֹהָי תָּשָׁב נָא נֶפֶשׁ־הַיֶּלֶד הַזֶּה
עַל־קִרְבּוֹ: 22 וַיִּשְׁמַע יְהֹוָה בְּקוֹל אֵלִיָּהוּ וַתָּשָׁב
נֶפֶשׁ־הַיֶּלֶד עַל־קִרְבּוֹ וַיֶּחִי: 23 וַיִּקַּח אֵלִיָּהוּ אֶת־
הַיֶּלֶד וַיֹּרִדֵהוּ מִן־הָעֲלִיָּה הַבַּיְתָה וַיִּתְּנֵהוּ לְאִמּוֹ
וַיֹּאמֶר אֵלִיָּהוּ רְאִי חַי בְּנֵךְ: 24 וַתֹּאמֶר הָאִשָּׁה
אֶל־אֵלִיָּהוּ עַתָּה זֶה יָדַעְתִּי כִּי אִישׁ אֱלֹהִים אָתָּה
וּדְבַר־יְהֹוָה בְּפִיךָ אֱמֶת: פ

יח וַיְהִי יָמִים רַבִּים וּדְבַר־יְהֹוָה הָיָה אֶל־אֵלִיָּהוּ
בַּשָּׁנָה הַשְּׁלִישִׁית לֵאמֹר לֵךְ הֵרָאֵה אֶל־אַחְאָב
וְאֶתְּנָה מָטָר עַל־פְּנֵי הָאֲדָמָה: 2 וַיֵּלֶךְ אֵלִיָּהוּ
לְהֵרָאוֹת אֶל־אַחְאָב וְהָרָעָב חָזָק בְּשֹׁמְרוֹן: 3 וַיִּקְרָא
אַחְאָב אֶל־עֹבַדְיָהוּ אֲשֶׁר עַל־הַבָּיִת וְעֹבַדְיָהוּ הָיָה
יָרֵא אֶת־יְהֹוָה מְאֹד: 4 וַיְהִי בְּהַכְרִית אִיזֶבֶל אֵת
נְבִיאֵי יְהֹוָה וַיִּקַּח עֹבַדְיָהוּ מֵאָה נְבִאִים וַיַּחְבִּיאֵם
חֲמִשִּׁים אִישׁ בַּמְּעָרָה וְכִלְכְּלָם לֶחֶם וָמָיִם: 5 וַיֹּאמֶר
אַחְאָב אֶל־עֹבַדְיָהוּ לֵךְ בָּאָרֶץ אֶל־כָּל־מַעְיְנֵי הַמַּיִם
וְאֶל כָּל־הַנְּחָלִים אוּלַי | נִמְצָא חָצִיר וּנְחַיֶּה סוּס
וָפֶרֶד וְלוֹא נַכְרִית מֵהַבְּהֵמָה: 6 וַיְחַלְּקוּ לָהֶם אֶת־
הָאָרֶץ לַעֲבָר־בָּהּ אַחְאָב הָלַךְ בְּדֶרֶךְ אֶחָד לְבַדּוֹ
וְעֹבַדְיָהוּ הָלַךְ בְּדֶרֶךְ־אֶחָד לְבַדּוֹ: 7 וַיְהִי עֹבַדְיָהוּ
בַּדֶּרֶךְ וְהִנֵּה אֵלִיָּהוּ לִקְרָאתוֹ וַיַּכִּרֵהוּ וַיִּפֹּל עַל־פָּנָיו
וַיֹּאמֶר הַאַתָּה זֶה אֲדֹנִי אֵלִיָּהוּ: 8 וַיֹּאמֶר לוֹ אָנִי לֵךְ
אֱמֹר לַאדֹנֶיךָ הִנֵּה אֵלִיָּהוּ: 9 וַיֹּאמֶר מֶה חָטָאתִי
כִּי־אַתָּה נֹתֵן אֶת־עַבְדְּךָ בְּיַד־אַחְאָב לַהֲמִיתֵנִי:
10 חַי | יְהֹוָה אֱלֹהֶיךָ אִם־יֶשׁ־גּוֹי וּמַמְלָכָה אֲשֶׁר
לֹא־שָׁלַח אֲדֹנִי שָׁם לְבַקֶּשְׁךָ וְאָמְרוּ אָיִן וְהִשְׁבִּיעַ
אֶת־הַמַּמְלָכָה וְאֶת־הַגּוֹי כִּי לֹא יִמְצָאֶכָּה: 11 וְעַתָּה
אַתָּה אֹמֵר לֵךְ אֱמֹר לַאדֹנֶיךָ הִנֵּה אֵלִיָּהוּ: 12 וְהָיָה
אֲנִי | אֵלֵךְ מֵאִתָּךְ וְרוּחַ יְהֹוָה | יִשָּׂאֲךָ עַל
אֲשֶׁר לֹא־אֵדָע וּבָאתִי לְהַגִּיד לְאַחְאָב וְלֹא יִמְצָאֲךָ
וַהֲרָגָנִי וְעַבְדְּךָ יָרֵא אֶת־יְהֹוָה מִנְּעֻרָי: 13 הֲלֹא־
הֻגַּד לַאדֹנִי אֵת אֲשֶׁר־עָשִׂיתִי בַּהֲרֹג אִיזֶבֶל אֵת

them with bread and water? ¹⁴ And now you say,
'Go, tell your master, "Elijah *is here*."' He will kill
me!"

¹⁵ Then Elijah said, "*As* the LORD of hosts lives,
before whom I stand, I will surely present myself to
him today."

¹⁶ So Obadiah went to meet Ahab, and told him;
and Ahab went to meet Elijah.

¹⁷ Then it happened, when Ahab saw Elijah, that
Ahab said to him, "*Is that* you, O troubler of
Israel?"

¹⁸ And he answered, "I have not troubled Israel,
but you and your father's house *have,* in that you
have forsaken the commandments of the LORD and
have followed the Baals. ¹⁹ Now therefore, send *and*
gather all Israel to me on Mount Carmel, the four
hundred and fifty prophets of Baal, and the four
hundred prophets of Asherah, who eat at Jezebel's
table."

²⁰ So Ahab sent for all the children of Israel, and
gathered the prophets together on Mount Carmel.
²¹ And Elijah came to all the people, and said,
"How long will you falter between two opinions? If
the LORD *is* God, follow Him; but if Baal, follow
him." But the people answered him not a word.
²² Then Elijah said to the people, "I alone am left a
prophet of the LORD; but Baal's prophets *are* four
hundred and fifty men. ²³ Therefore let them give us
two bulls; and let them choose one bull for
themselves, cut it in pieces, and lay *it* on the wood,
but put no fire *under it;* and I will prepare the other
bull, and lay *it* on the wood, but put no fire *under it.*
²⁴ Then you call on the name of your gods, and I
will call on the name of the LORD; and the God who
answers by fire, He is God."

So all the people answered and said, "It is well
spoken."

²⁵ Now Elijah said to the prophets of Baal,
"Choose one bull for yourselves and prepare *it*
first, for you *are* many; and call on the name of
your god, but put no fire *under it.*"

²⁶ So they took the bull which was given them,
and they prepared *it,* and called on the name of
Baal from morning even till noon, saying, "O Baal,
hear us!" But *there was* no voice; no one answered.
Then they leaped about the altar which they had
made.

²⁷ And so it was, at noon, that Elijah mocked
them and said, "Cry aloud, for he *is* a god; either he
is meditating, or he is busy, or he is on a journey, *or*
perhaps he is sleeping and must be awakened." ²⁸ So
they cried aloud, and cut themselves, as was their
custom, with knives and lances, until the blood
gushed out on them. ²⁹ And when midday was past,

נְבִיאֵי יְהֹוָה וָאַחְבִּא מִנְּבִיאֵי יְהֹוָה מֵאָה אִישׁ
חֲמִשִּׁים חֲמִשִּׁים אִישׁ בַּמְּעָרָה וָאֲכַלְכְּלֵם לֶחֶם
וָמָיִם: 14 וְעַתָּה אַתָּה אֹמֵר לֵךְ אֱמֹר לַאדֹנֶיךָ
הִנֵּה אֵלִיָּהוּ וַהֲרָגָנִי: 15 ס וַיֹּאמֶר אֵלִיָּהוּ
חַי יְהֹוָה צְבָאוֹת אֲשֶׁר עָמַדְתִּי לְפָנָיו כִּי הַיּוֹם
אֵרָאֶה אֵלָיו: 16 וַיֵּלֶךְ עֹבַדְיָהוּ לִקְרַאת אַחְאָב וַיַּגֶּד־
לוֹ וַיֵּלֶךְ אַחְאָב לִקְרַאת אֵלִיָּהוּ: 17 וַיְהִי כִּרְאוֹת
אַחְאָב אֶת־אֵלִיָּהוּ וַיֹּאמֶר אַחְאָב אֵלָיו הַאַתָּה זֶה
עֹכֵר יִשְׂרָאֵל: 18 וַיֹּאמֶר לֹא עָכַרְתִּי אֶת־יִשְׂרָאֵל כִּי
אִם־אַתָּה וּבֵית אָבִיךָ בַּעֲזָבְכֶם אֶת־מִצְוֹת יְהֹוָה
וַתֵּלֶךְ אַחֲרֵי הַבְּעָלִים: 19 וְעַתָּה שְׁלַח קְבֹץ אֵלַי
אֶת־כָּל־יִשְׂרָאֵל אֶל־הַר הַכַּרְמֶל וְאֶת־נְבִיאֵי הַבַּעַל
אַרְבַּע מֵאוֹת וַחֲמִשִּׁים וּנְבִיאֵי הָאֲשֵׁרָה אַרְבַּע
מֵאוֹת אֹכְלֵי שֻׁלְחַן אִיזָבֶל: 20 וַיִּשְׁלַח אַחְאָב בְּכָל־
בְּנֵי יִשְׂרָאֵל וַיִּקְבֹּץ אֶת־הַנְּבִיאִים אֶל־הַר הַכַּרְמֶל:
21 וַיִּגַּשׁ אֵלִיָּהוּ אֶל־כָּל־הָעָם וַיֹּאמֶר עַד־מָתַי אַתֶּם
פֹּסְחִים עַל־שְׁתֵּי הַסְּעִפִּים אִם־יְהֹוָה הָאֱלֹהִים לְכוּ
אַחֲרָיו וְאִם־הַבַּעַל לְכוּ אַחֲרָיו וְלֹא־עָנוּ הָעָם אֹתוֹ
דָּבָר: 22 וַיֹּאמֶר אֵלִיָּהוּ אֶל־הָעָם אֲנִי נוֹתַרְתִּי נָבִיא
לַיהֹוָה לְבַדִּי וּנְבִיאֵי הַבַּעַל אַרְבַּע־מֵאוֹת וַחֲמִשִּׁים
אִישׁ: 23 וְיִתְּנוּ־לָנוּ שְׁנַיִם פָּרִים וְיִבְחֲרוּ לָהֶם הַפָּר
הָאֶחָד וִינַתְּחֻהוּ וְיָשִׂימוּ עַל־הָעֵצִים וְאֵשׁ לֹא יָשִׂימוּ
וַאֲנִי אֶעֱשֶׂה אֶת־הַפָּר הָאֶחָד וְנָתַתִּי עַל־הָעֵצִים
וְאֵשׁ לֹא אָשִׂים: 24 וּקְרָאתֶם בְּשֵׁם אֱלֹהֵיכֶם וַאֲנִי
אֶקְרָא בְשֵׁם־יְהֹוָה וְהָיָה הָאֱלֹהִים אֲשֶׁר־יַעֲנֶה בָאֵשׁ
הוּא הָאֱלֹהִים וַיַּעַן כָּל־הָעָם וַיֹּאמְרוּ טוֹב הַדָּבָר:
25 וַיֹּאמֶר אֵלִיָּהוּ לִנְבִיאֵי הַבַּעַל בַּחֲרוּ לָכֶם הַפָּר
הָאֶחָד וַעֲשׂוּ רִאשֹׁנָה כִּי אַתֶּם הָרַבִּים וְקִרְאוּ
בְּשֵׁם אֱלֹהֵיכֶם וְאֵשׁ לֹא תָשִׂימוּ: 26 וַיִּקְחוּ אֶת־
הַפָּר אֲשֶׁר־נָתַן לָהֶם וַיַּעֲשׂוּ וַיִּקְרְאוּ בְשֵׁם־הַבַּעַל
מֵהַבֹּקֶר וְעַד־הַצָּהֳרַיִם לֵאמֹר הַבַּעַל עֲנֵנוּ וְאֵין קוֹל
וְאֵין עֹנֶה וַיְפַסְּחוּ עַל־הַמִּזְבֵּחַ אֲשֶׁר עָשָׂה: 27 וַיְהִי
בַצָּהֳרַיִם וַיְהַתֵּל בָּהֶם אֵלִיָּהוּ וַיֹּאמֶר קִרְאוּ בְקוֹל־
גָּדוֹל כִּי־אֱלֹהִים הוּא כִּי שִׂיחַ וְכִי־שִׂיג לוֹ וְכִי־דֶרֶךְ
לוֹ אוּלַי יָשֵׁן הוּא וְיִקָץ: 28 וַיִּקְרְאוּ בְּקוֹל גָּדוֹל
וַיִּתְגֹּדְדוּ כְּמִשְׁפָּטָם בַּחֲרָבוֹת וּבָרְמָחִים עַד־שְׁפָךְ־
דָּם עֲלֵיהֶם: 29 וַיְהִי כַּעֲבֹר הַצָּהֳרַיִם וַיִּתְנַבְּאוּ עַד

they prophesied until the *time* of the offering of the *evening* sacrifice. But *there was* no voice; no one answered, no one paid attention.

³⁰ Then Elijah said to all the people, "Come near to me." So all the people came near to him. And he repaired the altar of the LORD *that was* broken down. ³¹ And Elijah took twelve stones, according to the number of the tribes of the sons of Jacob, to whom the word of the LORD had come, saying, "Israel shall be your name." ³² Then with the stones he built an altar in the name of the LORD; and he made a trench around the altar large enough to hold two seahs of seed. ³³ And he put the wood in order, cut the bull in pieces, and laid *it* on the wood, and said, "Fill four waterpots with water, and pour *it* on the burnt sacrifice and on the wood." ³⁴ Then he said, "Do *it* a second time," and they did *it* a second time; and he said, "Do *it* a third time," and they did *it* a third time. ³⁵ So the water ran all around the altar; and he also filled the trench with water.

³⁶ And it came to pass, at *the time of* the offering of the *evening* sacrifice, that Elijah the prophet came near and said, "LORD God of Abraham, Isaac, and Israel, let it be known this day that You *are* God in Israel and I *am* Your servant, and *that* I have done all these things at Your word. ³⁷ Hear me, O LORD, hear me, that this people may know that You *are* the LORD God, and *that* You have turned their hearts back *to You* again."

³⁸ Then the fire of the LORD fell and consumed the burnt sacrifice, and the wood and the stones and the dust, and it licked up the water that *was* in the trench. ³⁹ Now when all the people saw *it,* they fell on their faces; and they said, "The LORD, He *is* God! The LORD, He *is* God!"

⁴⁰ And Elijah said to them, "Seize the prophets of Baal! Do not let one of them escape!" So they seized them; and Elijah brought them down to the Brook Kishon and executed them there.

⁴¹ Then Elijah said to Ahab, "Go up, eat and drink; for *there is* the sound of abundance of rain." ⁴² So Ahab went up to eat and drink. And Elijah went up to the top of Carmel; then he bowed down on the ground, and put his face between his knees, ⁴³ and said to his servant, "Go up now, look toward the sea."

So he went up and looked, and said, "*There is* nothing." And seven times he said, "Go again."

⁴⁴ Then it came to pass the seventh *time,* that he said, "There is a cloud, as small as a man's hand, rising out of the sea!" So he said, "Go up, say to Ahab, 'Prepare *your chariot,* and go down before the rain stops you.'"

לַעֲלוֹת הַמִּנְחָה וְאֵין־קוֹל וְאֵין־עֹנֶה וְאֵין קָשֶׁב: 30 וַיֹּאמֶר אֵלִיָּהוּ לְכָל־הָעָם גְּשׁוּ אֵלַי וַיִּגְּשׁוּ כָל־הָעָם אֵלָיו וַיְרַפֵּא אֶת־מִזְבַּח יְהוָה הֶהָרוּס: 31 וַיִּקַּח אֵלִיָּהוּ שְׁתֵּים עֶשְׂרֵה אֲבָנִים כְּמִסְפַּר שִׁבְטֵי בְנֵי־יַעֲקֹב אֲשֶׁר הָיָה דְבַר־יְהוָה אֵלָיו לֵאמֹר יִשְׂרָאֵל יִהְיֶה שְׁמֶךָ: 32 וַיִּבְנֶה אֶת־הָאֲבָנִים מִזְבֵּחַ בְּשֵׁם יְהוָה וַיַּעַשׂ תְּעָלָה כְּבֵית סָאתַיִם זֶרַע סָבִיב לַמִּזְבֵּחַ: 33 וַיַּעֲרֹךְ אֶת־הָעֵצִים וַיְנַתַּח אֶת־הַפָּר וַיָּשֶׂם עַל־הָעֵצִים: 34 וַיֹּאמֶר מִלְאוּ אַרְבָּעָה כַדִּים מַיִם וְיִצְקוּ עַל־הָעֹלָה וְעַל־הָעֵצִים וַיֹּאמֶר שְׁנוּ וַיִּשְׁנוּ וַיֹּאמֶר שַׁלֵּשׁוּ וַיְשַׁלֵּשׁוּ: 35 וַיֵּלְכוּ הַמַּיִם סָבִיב לַמִּזְבֵּחַ וְגַם אֶת־הַתְּעָלָה מִלֵּא־מָיִם: 36 וַיְהִי בַּעֲלוֹת הַמִּנְחָה וַיִּגַּשׁ אֵלִיָּהוּ הַנָּבִיא וַיֹּאמַר יְהוָה אֱלֹהֵי אַבְרָהָם יִצְחָק וְיִשְׂרָאֵל הַיּוֹם יִוָּדַע כִּי־אַתָּה אֱלֹהִים בְּיִשְׂרָאֵל וַאֲנִי עַבְדֶּךָ וּבִדְבָרְךָ עָשִׂיתִי אֵת כָּל־הַדְּבָרִים הָאֵלֶּה: 37 עֲנֵנִי יְהוָה עֲנֵנִי וְיֵדְעוּ הָעָם הַזֶּה כִּי־אַתָּה יְהוָה הָאֱלֹהִים וְאַתָּה הֲסִבֹּתָ אֶת־לִבָּם אֲחֹרַנִּית: 38 וַתִּפֹּל אֵשׁ־יְהוָה וַתֹּאכַל אֶת־הָעֹלָה וְאֶת־הָעֵצִים וְאֶת־הָאֲבָנִים וְאֶת־הֶעָפָר וְאֶת־הַמַּיִם אֲשֶׁר־בַּתְּעָלָה לִחֵכָה: 39 וַיַּרְא כָּל־הָעָם וַיִּפְּלוּ עַל־פְּנֵיהֶם וַיֹּאמְרוּ יְהוָה הוּא הָאֱלֹהִים יְהוָה הוּא הָאֱלֹהִים: 40 וַיֹּאמֶר אֵלִיָּהוּ לָהֶם תִּפְשׂוּ אֶת־נְבִיאֵי הַבַּעַל אִישׁ אַל־יִמָּלֵט מֵהֶם וַיִּתְפְּשׂוּם וַיּוֹרִדֵם אֵלִיָּהוּ אֶל־נַחַל קִישׁוֹן וַיִּשְׁחָטֵם שָׁם:

41 וַיֹּאמֶר אֵלִיָּהוּ לְאַחְאָב עֲלֵה אֱכֹל וּשְׁתֵה כִּי־קוֹל הֲמוֹן הַגָּשֶׁם: 42 וַיַּעֲלֶה אַחְאָב לֶאֱכֹל וְלִשְׁתּוֹת וְאֵלִיָּהוּ עָלָה אֶל־רֹאשׁ הַכַּרְמֶל וַיִּגְהַר אַרְצָה וַיָּשֶׂם פָּנָיו בֵּין בִּרְכָּו: 43 וַיֹּאמֶר אֶל־נַעֲרוֹ עֲלֵה־נָא הַבֵּט דֶּרֶךְ־יָם וַיַּעַל וַיַּבֵּט וַיֹּאמֶר אֵין מְאוּמָה וַיֹּאמֶר שֻׁב שֶׁבַע פְּעָמִים: 44 וַיְהִי בַּשְּׁבִעִית וַיֹּאמֶר הִנֵּה־עָב קְטַנָּה כְּכַף־אִישׁ עֹלָה מִיָּם וַיֹּאמֶר עֲלֵה אֱמֹר אֶל־

45 Now it happened in the meantime that the sky became black with clouds and wind, and there was a heavy rain. So Ahab rode away and went to Jezreel. 46 Then the hand of the LORD came upon Elijah; and he girded up his loins and ran ahead of Ahab to the entrance of Jezreel.

19 And Ahab told Jezebel all that Elijah had done, also how he had executed all the prophets with the sword. 2 Then Jezebel sent a messenger to Elijah, saying, "So let the gods do *to me,* and more also, if I do not make your life as the life of one of them by tomorrow about this time." 3 And when he saw *that,* he arose and ran for his life, and went to Beersheba, which *belongs* to Judah, and left his servant there.

4 But he himself went a day's journey into the wilderness, and came and sat down under a broom tree. And he prayed that he might die, and said, "It is enough! Now, LORD, take my life, for I *am* no better than my fathers!"

5 Then as he lay and slept under a broom tree, suddenly an angel touched him, and said to him, "Arise *and* eat." 6 Then he looked, and there by his head *was* a cake baked on coals, and a jar of water. So he ate and drank, and lay down again. 7 And the angel of the LORD came back the second time, and touched him, and said, "Arise *and* eat, because the journey *is* too great for you." 8 So he arose, and ate and drank; and he went in the strength of that food forty days and forty nights as far as Horeb, the mountain of God.

9 And there he went into a cave, and spent the night in that place; and behold, the word of the LORD *came* to him, and He said to him, "What are you doing here, Elijah?"

10 So he said, "I have been very zealous for the LORD God of hosts; for the children of Israel have forsaken Your covenant, torn down Your altars, and killed Your prophets with the sword. I alone am left; and they seek to take my life."

11 Then He said, "Go out, and stand on the mountain before the LORD." And behold, the LORD passed by, and a great and strong wind tore into the mountains and broke the rocks in pieces before the LORD, *but* the LORD *was* not in the wind; and after the wind an earthquake, *but* the LORD *was* not in the earthquake; 12 and after the earthquake a fire, *but* the LORD *was* not in the fire; and after the fire a still small voice.

אַחְאָב אֱסֹר וָרֵד וְלֹא יַעַצָרְכָה הַגָּשֶׁם: 45 וַיְהִי ׀ עַד־כֹּה וְעַד־כֹּה וְהַשָּׁמַ֫יִם הִתְקַדְּרוּ עָבִים וְר֫וּחַ וַיְהִי גֶּשֶׁם גָּדוֹל וַיִּרְכַּב אַחְאָב וַיֵּלֶךְ יִזְרְעֶאלָה: 46 וְיַד־יְהוָה הָיְתָה אֶל־אֵלִיָּהוּ וַיְשַׁנֵּס מָתְנָיו וַיָּרָץ לִפְנֵי אַחְאָב עַד־בֹּאֲכָה יִזְרְעֶאלָה:

יט וַיַּגֵּד אַחְאָב לְאִיזֶבֶל אֵת כָּל־אֲשֶׁר עָשָׂה אֵלִיָּהוּ וְאֵת כָּל־אֲשֶׁר הָרַג אֶת־כָּל־הַנְּבִיאִים בֶּחָרֶב: 2 וַתִּשְׁלַח אִיזֶבֶל מַלְאָךְ אֶל־אֵלִיָּהוּ לֵאמֹר כֹּה־יַעֲשׂוּן אֱלֹהִים וְכֹה יוֹסִפוּן כִּי־כָעֵת מָחָר אָשִׂים אֶת־נַפְשְׁךָ כְּנֶפֶשׁ אַחַד מֵהֶם: 3 וַיַּרְא וַיָּקָם וַיֵּלֶךְ אֶל־נַפְשׁוֹ וַיָּבֹא בְּאֵר שֶׁבַע אֲשֶׁר לִיהוּדָה וַיַּנַּח אֶת־נַעֲרוֹ שָׁם: 4 וְהוּא־הָלַךְ בַּמִּדְבָּר דֶּרֶךְ יוֹם וַיָּבֹא וַיֵּשֶׁב תַּחַת רֹתֶם אֶחָד[ס] וַיִּשְׁאַל אֶת־נַפְשׁוֹ לָמוּת וַיֹּאמֶר ׀ רַב עַתָּה יְהוָה קַח נַפְשִׁי כִּי־לֹא־טוֹב אָנֹכִי מֵאֲבֹתָי: 5 וַיִּשְׁכַּב וַיִּישַׁן תַּחַת רֹתֶם אֶחָד וְהִנֵּה־זֶה מַלְאָךְ נֹגֵעַ בּוֹ וַיֹּאמֶר לוֹ קוּם אֱכוֹל: 6 וַיַּבֵּט וְהִנֵּה מְרַאֲשֹׁתָיו עֻגַת רְצָפִים וְצַפַּחַת מָיִם וַיֹּאכַל וַיֵּשְׁתְּ וַיָּשָׁב וַיִּשְׁכָּב: 7 וַיָּשָׁב מַלְאַךְ יְהוָה ׀ שֵׁנִית וַיִּגַּע־בּוֹ וַיֹּאמֶר קוּם אֱכֹל כִּי רַב מִמְּךָ הַדָּרֶךְ: 8 וַיָּקָם וַיֹּאכַל וַיִּשְׁתֶּה וַיֵּלֶךְ בְּכֹחַ ׀ הָאֲכִילָה הַהִיא אַרְבָּעִים יוֹם וְאַרְבָּעִים לַיְלָה עַד הַר הָאֱלֹהִים חֹרֵב: 9 וַיָּבֹא־שָׁם אֶל־הַמְּעָרָה וַיָּלֶן שָׁם וְהִנֵּה דְבַר־יְהוָה אֵלָיו וַיֹּאמֶר לוֹ מַה־לְּךָ פֹה אֵלִיָּהוּ: 10 וַיֹּאמֶר קַנֹּא קִנֵּאתִי לַיהוָה ׀ אֱלֹהֵי צְבָאוֹת כִּי־עָזְבוּ בְרִיתְךָ בְּנֵי יִשְׂרָאֵל אֶת־מִזְבְּחֹתֶיךָ הָרָסוּ וְאֶת־נְבִיאֶיךָ הָרְגוּ בֶחָרֶב וָאִוָּתֵר אֲנִי לְבַדִּי וַיְבַקְשׁוּ אֶת־נַפְשִׁי לְקַחְתָּהּ: 11 וַיֹּאמֶר צֵא וְעָמַדְתָּ בָהָר לִפְנֵי יְהוָה וְהִנֵּה יְהוָה עֹבֵר וְר֫וּחַ גְּדוֹלָה וְחָזָק מְפָרֵק הָרִים וּמְשַׁבֵּר סְלָעִים לִפְנֵי יְהוָה לֹא בָר֫וּחַ יְהוָה וְאַחַר הָר֫וּחַ רַעַשׁ לֹא בָרַעַשׁ יְהוָה: 12 וְאַחַר הָרַעַשׁ אֵשׁ לֹא בָאֵשׁ

יט 4 אֶחָד

13 So it was, when Elijah heard *it,* that he wrapped his face in his mantle and went out and stood in the entrance of the cave. Suddenly a voice *came* to him, and said, "What are you doing here, Elijah?"

14 And he said, "I have been very zealous for the LORD God of hosts; because the children of Israel have forsaken Your covenant, · torn down Your altars, and killed Your prophets with the sword. I alone am left; and they seek to take my life."

15 Then the LORD said to him: "Go, return on your way to the Wilderness of Damascus; and when you arrive, anoint Hazael *as* king over Syria. 16 Also you shall anoint Jehu the son of Nimshi *as* king over Israel. And Elisha the son of Shaphat of Abel Meholah you shall anoint *as* prophet in your place. 17 It shall be *that* whoever escapes the sword of Hazael, Jehu will kill; and whoever escapes the sword of Jehu, Elisha will kill. 18 Yet I have reserved seven thousand in Israel, all whose knees have not bowed to Baal, and every mouth that has not kissed him."

19 So he departed from there, and found Elisha the son of Shaphat, who *was* plowing *with* twelve yoke *of oxen* before him, and he was with the twelfth. Then Elijah passed by him and threw his mantle on him. 20 And he left the oxen and ran after Elijah, and said, "Please let me kiss my father and my mother, and *then* I will follow you."

And he said to him, "Go back again, for what have I done to you?"

21 So *Elisha* turned back from him, and took a yoke of oxen and slaughtered them and boiled their flesh, using the oxen's equipment, and gave it to the people, and they ate. Then he arose and followed Elijah, and became his servant.

20 Now Ben-Hadad the king of Syria gathered all his forces together; thirty-two kings *were* with him, with horses and chariots. And he went up and besieged Samaria, and made war against it. 2 Then he sent messengers into the city to Ahab king of Israel, and said to him, "Thus says Ben-Hadad: 3 'Your silver and your gold *are* mine; your loveliest wives and children are mine.'"

4 And the king of Israel answered and said, "My lord, O king, just as you say, I and all that I have *are* yours."

5 Then the messengers came back and said, "Thus speaks Ben-Hadad, saying, 'Indeed I have sent to you, saying, "You shall deliver to me your silver and your gold, your wives and your children"; 6 but I will send my servants to you tomorrow about this time, and they shall search your house and the

13 וַיְהִי דְּמָמָה דַקָּה: וְאַחַר הָאֵשׁ קוֹל יְהוָה וַיְהִי כִּשְׁמֹעַ אֵלִיָּהוּ וַיָּלֶט פָּנָיו בְּאַדַּרְתּוֹ וַיֵּצֵא וַיַּעֲמֹד פֶּתַח הַמְּעָרָה וְהִנֵּה אֵלָיו קוֹל וַיֹּאמֶר מַה־לְּךָ פֹה אֵלִיָּהוּ: 14 וַיֹּאמֶר קַנֹּא קִנֵּאתִי לַיהוָה | אֱלֹהֵי צְבָאוֹת כִּי־עָזְבוּ בְרִיתְךָ בְּנֵי יִשְׂרָאֵל אֶת־מִזְבְּחֹתֶיךָ הָרָסוּ וְאֶת־נְבִיאֶיךָ הָרְגוּ בֶחָרֶב וָאִוָּתֵר אֲנִי לְבַדִּי וַיְבַקְשׁוּ אֶת־נַפְשִׁי לְקַחְתָּהּ: ס 15 וַיֹּאמֶר יְהוָה אֵלָיו לֵךְ שׁוּב לְדַרְכְּךָ מִדְבַּרָה דַמָּשֶׂק וּבָאתָ וּמָשַׁחְתָּ אֶת־חֲזָאֵל לְמֶלֶךְ עַל־אֲרָם: 16 וְאֵת יֵהוּא בֶן־נִמְשִׁי תִּמְשַׁח לְמֶלֶךְ עַל־יִשְׂרָאֵל וְאֶת־ אֱלִישָׁע בֶּן־שָׁפָט מֵאָבֵל מְחוֹלָה תִּמְשַׁח לְנָבִיא תַּחְתֶּיךָ: 17 וְהָיָה הַנִּמְלָט מֵחֶרֶב חֲזָאֵל יָמִית יֵהוּא וְהַנִּמְלָט מֵחֶרֶב יֵהוּא יָמִית אֱלִישָׁע: 18 וְהִשְׁאַרְתִּי בְיִשְׂרָאֵל שִׁבְעַת אֲלָפִים כָּל־הַבִּרְכַּיִם אֲשֶׁר לֹא־ כָרְעוּ לַבַּעַל וְכָל־הַפֶּה אֲשֶׁר לֹא־נָשַׁק לוֹ: 19 וַיֵּלֶךְ מִשָּׁם וַיִּמְצָא אֶת־אֱלִישָׁע בֶּן־שָׁפָט וְהוּא חֹרֵשׁ שְׁנֵים־עָשָׂר צְמָדִים לְפָנָיו וְהוּא בִּשְׁנֵים הֶעָשָׂר וַיַּעֲבֹר אֵלִיָּהוּ אֵלָיו וַיַּשְׁלֵךְ אַדַּרְתּוֹ אֵלָיו: 20 וַיַּעֲזֹב אֶת־הַבָּקָר וַיָּרָץ אַחֲרֵי אֵלִיָּהוּ וַיֹּאמֶר אֶשְּׁקָה־נָּא לְאָבִי וּלְאִמִּי וְאֵלְכָה אַחֲרֶיךָ וַיֹּאמֶר לוֹ לֵךְ שׁוּב כִּי מֶה־עָשִׂיתִי לָךְ: 21 וַיָּשָׁב מֵאַחֲרָיו וַיִּקַּח אֶת־צֶמֶד הַבָּקָר וַיִּזְבָּחֵהוּ וּבִכְלִי הַבָּקָר בִּשְּׁלָם הַבָּשָׂר וַיִּתֵּן לָעָם וַיֹּאכֵלוּ וַיָּקָם וַיֵּלֶךְ אַחֲרֵי אֵלִיָּהוּ וַיְשָׁרְתֵהוּ: פ

כ וּבֶן־הֲדַד מֶלֶךְ־אֲרָם קָבַץ אֶת־כָּל־חֵילוֹ וּשְׁלֹשִׁים וּשְׁנַיִם מֶלֶךְ אִתּוֹ וְסוּס וָרָכֶב וַיַּעַל וַיָּצַר עַל־ שֹׁמְרוֹן וַיִּלָּחֶם בָּהּ: 2 וַיִּשְׁלַח מַלְאָכִים אֶל־אַחְאָב מֶלֶךְ־יִשְׂרָאֵל הָעִירָה: 3 וַיֹּאמֶר לוֹ כֹּה אָמַר בֶּן־ הֲדַד כַּסְפְּךָ וּזְהָבְךָ לִי־הוּא וְנָשֶׁיךָ וּבָנֶיךָ הַטּוֹבִים לִי־הֵם: 4 וַיַּעַן מֶלֶךְ־יִשְׂרָאֵל וַיֹּאמֶר כִּדְבָרְךָ אֲדֹנִי הַמֶּלֶךְ לְךָ אֲנִי וְכָל־אֲשֶׁר־לִי: 5 וַיָּשֻׁבוּ הַמַּלְאָכִים וַיֹּאמְרוּ כֹּה־אָמַר בֶּן־הֲדַד לֵאמֹר כִּי־שָׁלַחְתִּי אֵלֶיךָ לֵאמֹר כַּסְפְּךָ וּזְהָבְךָ וְנָשֶׁיךָ וּבָנֶיךָ לִי תִתֵּן: 6 כִּי אִם־כָּעֵת מָחָר אֶשְׁלַח אֶת־עֲבָדַי אֵלֶיךָ וְחִפְּשׂוּ אֶת־בֵּיתְךָ וְאֵת בָּתֵּי עֲבָדֶיךָ וְהָיָה כָּל־מַחְמַד עֵינֶיךָ

houses of your servants. And it shall be, *that* whatever is pleasant in your eyes, they will put *it* in their hands and take *it*.'"

7 So the king of Israel called all the elders of the land, and said, "Notice, please, and see how this *man* seeks trouble, for he sent to me for my wives, my children, my silver, and my gold; and I did not deny him."

8 And all the elders and all the people said to him, "Do not listen or consent."

9 Therefore he said to the messengers of Ben-Hadad, "Tell my lord the king, 'All that you sent for to your servant the first time I will do, but this thing I cannot do.'"

And the messengers departed and brought back word to him.

10 Then Ben-Hadad sent to him and said, "The gods do so to me, and more also, if enough dust is left of Samaria for a handful for each of the people who follow me."

11 So the king of Israel answered and said, "Tell *him,* 'Let not the one who puts on *his* armor boast like the one who takes *it off.*'"

12 And it happened when *Ben-Hadad* heard this message, as he and the kings *were* drinking at the command post, that he said to his servants, "Get ready." And they got ready to attack the city.

13 Suddenly a prophet approached Ahab king of Israel, saying, "Thus says the LORD: 'Have you seen all this great multitude? Behold, I will deliver it into your hand today, and you shall know that I *am* the LORD.'"

14 So Ahab said, "By whom?"

And he said, "Thus says the LORD: 'By the young leaders of the provinces.'"

Then he said, "Who will set the battle in order?" And he answered, "You."

15 Then he mustered the young leaders of the provinces, and there were two hundred and thirty-two; and after them he mustered all the people, all the children of Israel—seven thousand.

16 So they went out at noon. Meanwhile Ben-Hadad and the thirty-two kings helping him were getting drunk at the command post. 17 The young leaders of the provinces went out first. And Ben-Hadad sent out *a patrol,* and they told him, saying, "Men are coming out of Samaria!" 18 So he said, "If they have come out for peace, take them alive; and if they have come out for war, take them alive."

19 Then these young leaders of the provinces went out of the city with the army which followed them. 20 And each one killed his man; so the Syrians fled, and Israel pursued them; and Ben-Hadad the king of Syria escaped on a horse with the cavalry.

7 וַיִּקְרָא מֶלֶךְ־יִשְׂרָאֵל לְכָל־זִקְנֵי הָאָרֶץ וַיֹּאמֶר דְּעוּ־נָא וּרְאוּ כִּי רָעָה זֶה מְבַקֵּשׁ כִּי־שָׁלַח אֵלַי לְנָשַׁי וּלְבָנַי וּלְכַסְפִּי וְלִזְהָבִי וְלֹא מָנַעְתִּי מִמֶּנּוּ: 8 וַיֹּאמְרוּ אֵלָיו כָּל־הַזְּקֵנִים וְכָל־הָעָם אַל־תִּשְׁמַע וְלוֹא תֹאבֶה: 9 וַיֹּאמֶר לְמַלְאֲכֵי בֶן־הֲדַד אִמְרוּ לַאדֹנִי הַמֶּלֶךְ כֹּל אֲשֶׁר־שָׁלַחְתָּ אֶל־עַבְדְּךָ בָרִאשֹׁנָה אֶעֱשֶׂה וְהַדָּבָר הַזֶּה לֹא אוּכַל לַעֲשׂוֹת וַיֵּלְכוּ הַמַּלְאָכִים וַיְשִׁבֻהוּ דָּבָר: 10 וַיִּשְׁלַח אֵלָיו בֶּן־הֲדַד וַיֹּאמֶר כֹּה־יַעֲשׂוּן לִי אֱלֹהִים וְכֹה יוֹסִפוּ אִם־יִשְׂפֹּק עֲפַר שֹׁמְרוֹן לִשְׁעָלִים לְכָל־הָעָם אֲשֶׁר בְּרַגְלָי: 11 וַיַּעַן מֶלֶךְ־יִשְׂרָאֵל וַיֹּאמֶר דַּבְּרוּ אַל־יִתְהַלֵּל חֹגֵר כִּמְפַתֵּחַ: 12 וַיְהִי כִּשְׁמֹעַ אֶת־הַדָּבָר הַזֶּה וְהוּא שֹׁתֶה הוּא וְהַמְּלָכִים בַּסֻּכּוֹת וַיֹּאמֶר אֶל־עֲבָדָיו שִׂימוּ וַיָּשִׂימוּ עַל־הָעִיר: 13 וְהִנֵּה נָבִיא אֶחָד נִגַּשׁ אֶל־אַחְאָב מֶלֶךְ־יִשְׂרָאֵל וַיֹּאמֶר כֹּה אָמַר יְהֹוָה הֲרָאִיתָ אֵת כָּל־הֶהָמוֹן הַגָּדוֹל הַזֶּה הִנְנִי נֹתְנוֹ בְיָדְךָ הַיּוֹם וְיָדַעְתָּ כִּי־אֲנִי יְהֹוָה: 14 וַיֹּאמֶר אַחְאָב בְּמִי וַיֹּאמֶר כֹּה־אָמַר יְהֹוָה בְּנַעֲרֵי שָׂרֵי הַמְּדִינוֹת וַיֹּאמֶר מִי־יֶאְסֹר הַמִּלְחָמָה וַיֹּאמֶר אָתָּה: 15 וַיִּפְקֹד אֶת־נַעֲרֵי שָׂרֵי הַמְּדִינוֹת וַיִּהְיוּ מָאתַיִם שְׁנַיִם וּשְׁלֹשִׁים וְאַחֲרֵיהֶם פָּקַד אֶת־כָּל־הָעָם כָּל־בְּנֵי יִשְׂרָאֵל שִׁבְעַת אֲלָפִים: 16 וַיֵּצְאוּ בַּצָּהֳרָיִם וּבֶן־הֲדַד שֹׁתֶה שִׁכּוֹר בַּסֻּכּוֹת הוּא וְהַמְּלָכִים שְׁלֹשִׁים־וּשְׁנַיִם מֶלֶךְ עֹזֵר אֹתוֹ: 17 וַיֵּצְאוּ נַעֲרֵי שָׂרֵי הַמְּדִינוֹת בָּרִאשֹׁנָה וַיִּשְׁלַח בֶּן־הֲדַד וַיַּגִּידוּ לוֹ לֵאמֹר אֲנָשִׁים יָצְאוּ מִשֹּׁמְרוֹן: 18 וַיֹּאמֶר אִם־לְשָׁלוֹם יָצָאוּ תִּפְשׂוּם חַיִּים וְאִם לְמִלְחָמָה יָצָאוּ חַיִּים תִּפְשׂוּם: 19 וְאֵלֶּה יָצְאוּ מִן־הָעִיר נַעֲרֵי שָׂרֵי הַמְּדִינוֹת וְהַחַיִל אֲשֶׁר אַחֲרֵיהֶם: 20 וַיַּכּוּ אִישׁ אִישׁוֹ וַיָּנֻסוּ אֲרָם וַיִּרְדְּפֵם יִשְׂרָאֵל וַיִּמָּלֵט בֶּן־הֲדַד מֶלֶךְ אֲרָם עַל־

21 Then the king of Israel went out and attacked the horses and chariots, and killed the Syrians with a great slaughter.

22 And the prophet came to the king of Israel and said to him, "Go, strengthen yourself; take note, and see what you should do, for in the spring of the year the king of Syria will come up against you."

23 Then the servants of the king of Syria said to him, "Their gods *are* gods of the hills. Therefore they were stronger than we; but if we fight against them in the plain, surely we will be stronger than they. 24 So do this thing: Dismiss the kings, each from his position, and put captains in their places; 25 and you shall muster an army like the army that you have lost, horse for horse and chariot for chariot. Then we will fight against them in the plain; surely we will be stronger than they."

And he listened to their voice and did so.

26 So it was, in the spring of the year, that Ben-Hadad mustered the Syrians and went up to Aphek to fight against Israel. 27 And the children of Israel were mustered and given provisions, and they went against them. Now the children of Israel encamped before them like two little flocks of goats, while the Syrians filled the countryside.

28 Then a man of God came and spoke to the king of Israel, and said, "Thus says the LORD: 'Because the Syrians have said, "The LORD *is* God of the hills, but He *is* not God of the valleys," therefore I will deliver all this great multitude into your hand, and you shall know that I *am* the LORD.'" 29 And they encamped opposite each other for seven days. So it was that on the seventh day the battle was joined; and the children of Israel killed one hundred thousand foot soldiers *of* the Syrians in one day. 30 But the rest fled to Aphek, into the city; then a wall fell on twenty-seven thousand of the men *who were* left.

And Ben-Hadad fled and went into the city, into an inner chamber.

31 Then his servants said to him, "Look now, we have heard that the kings of the house of Israel *are* merciful kings. Please, let us put sackcloth around our waists and ropes around our heads, and go out to the king of Israel; perhaps he will spare your life." 32 So they wore sackcloth around their waists and *put* ropes around their heads, and came to the king of Israel and said, "Your servant Ben-Hadad says, 'Please let me live.'"

And he said, "*Is* he still alive? He *is* my brother."

33 Now the men were watching closely to see whether *any sign of mercy would come* from him; and they quickly grasped *at this word* and said, "Your brother Ben-Hadad."

21 וַיֵּצֵא מֶלֶךְ יִשְׂרָאֵל וַיַּךְ אֶת־הַסּוּס וְאֶת־הָרָכֶב וְהִכָּה בַאֲרָם מַכָּה גְדוֹלָה: 22 וַיִּגַּשׁ הַנָּבִיא אֶל־מֶלֶךְ יִשְׂרָאֵל וַיֹּאמֶר לוֹ לֵךְ הִתְחַזַּק וְדַע וּרְאֵה אֵת אֲשֶׁר־תַּעֲשֶׂה כִּי לִתְשׁוּבַת הַשָּׁנָה מֶלֶךְ אֲרָם עֹלֶה עָלֶיךָ: 23 וְעַבְדֵי מֶלֶךְ־אֲרָם אָמְרוּ אֵלָיו אֱלֹהֵי הָרִים אֱלֹהֵיהֶם עַל־כֵּן חָזְקוּ מִמֶּנּוּ וְאוּלָם נִלָּחֵם אִתָּם בַּמִּישׁוֹר אִם־לֹא נֶחֱזַק מֵהֶם: 24 וְאֶת־הַדָּבָר הַזֶּה עֲשֵׂה הָסֵר הַמְּלָכִים אִישׁ מִמְּקֹמוֹ וְשִׂים פַּחוֹת תַּחְתֵּיהֶם: 25 וְאַתָּה תִמְנֶה־לְךָ חַיִל כַּחַיִל הַנֹּפֵל מֵאוֹתָךְ וְסוּס כַּסּוּס וְרֶכֶב כָּרֶכֶב וְנִלָּחֲמָה אוֹתָם בַּמִּישׁוֹר אִם־לֹא נֶחֱזַק מֵהֶם וַיִּשְׁמַע לְקֹלָם וַיַּעַשׂ כֵּן: פ

26 וַיְהִי לִתְשׁוּבַת הַשָּׁנָה וַיִּפְקֹד בֶּן־הֲדַד אֶת־אֲרָם וַיַּעַל אֲפֵקָה לַמִּלְחָמָה עִם־יִשְׂרָאֵל: 27 וּבְנֵי יִשְׂרָאֵל הָתְפָּקְדוּ וְכָלְכְּלוּ וַיֵּלְכוּ לִקְרָאתָם וַיַּחֲנוּ בְנֵי־יִשְׂרָאֵל נֶגְדָּם כִּשְׁנֵי חֲשִׂפֵי עִזִּים וַאֲרָם מִלְאוּ אֶת־הָאָרֶץ: 28 וַיִּגַּשׁ אִישׁ הָאֱלֹהִים וַיֹּאמֶר אֶל־מֶלֶךְ יִשְׂרָאֵל וַיֹּאמֶר כֹּה־אָמַר יְהֹוָה יַעַן אֲשֶׁר אָמְרוּ אֲרָם אֱלֹהֵי הָרִים יְהֹוָה וְלֹא־אֱלֹהֵי עֲמָקִים הוּא וְנָתַתִּי אֶת־כָּל־הֶהָמוֹן הַגָּדוֹל הַזֶּה בְּיָדֶךָ וִידַעְתֶּם כִּי־אֲנִי יְהֹוָה: 29 וַיַּחֲנוּ אֵלֶּה נֹכַח אֵלֶּה שִׁבְעַת יָמִים וַיְהִי בַּיּוֹם הַשְּׁבִיעִי וַתִּקְרַב הַמִּלְחָמָה וַיַּכּוּ בְנֵי־יִשְׂרָאֵל אֶת־אֲרָם מֵאָה־אֶלֶף רַגְלִי בְּיוֹם אֶחָד: 30 וַיָּנֻסוּ הַנּוֹתָרִים אֲפֵקָה אֶל־הָעִיר וַתִּפֹּל הַחוֹמָה עַל־עֶשְׂרִים וְשִׁבְעָה אֶלֶף אִישׁ הַנּוֹתָרִים וּבֶן־הֲדַד נָס וַיָּבֹא אֶל־הָעִיר חֶדֶר בְּחָדֶר: ס 31 וַיֹּאמְרוּ אֵלָיו עֲבָדָיו הִנֵּה־נָא שָׁמַעְנוּ כִּי מַלְכֵי בֵּית יִשְׂרָאֵל כִּי־מַלְכֵי חֶסֶד הֵם נָשִׂימָה נָּא שַׂקִּים בְּמָתְנֵינוּ וַחֲבָלִים בְּרֹאשֵׁנוּ וְנֵצֵא אֶל־מֶלֶךְ יִשְׂרָאֵל אוּלַי יְחַיֶּה אֶת־נַפְשֶׁךָ: 32 וַיַּחְגְּרוּ שַׂקִּים בְּמָתְנֵיהֶם וַחֲבָלִים בְּרָאשֵׁיהֶם וַיָּבֹאוּ אֶל־מֶלֶךְ יִשְׂרָאֵל וַיֹּאמְרוּ עַבְדְּךָ בֶן־הֲדַד אָמַר תְּחִי־נָא נַפְשִׁי וַיֹּאמֶר הַעוֹדֶנּוּ חַי אָחִי הוּא: 33 וְהָאֲנָשִׁים יְנַחֲשׁוּ וַיְמַהֲרוּ וַיַּחְלְטוּ הֲמִמֶּנּוּ וַיֹּאמְרוּ אָחִיךָ בֶן־הֲדַד וַיֹּאמֶר בֹּאוּ קָחֻהוּ וַיֵּצֵא אֵלָיו בֶּן־הֲדַד וַיַּעֲלֵהוּ

So he said, "Go, bring him." Then Ben-Hadad came out to him; and he had him come up into the chariot.

34 So *Ben-Hadad* said to him, "The cities which my father took from your father I will restore; and you may set up marketplaces for yourself in Damascus, as my father did in Samaria."

Then *Ahab said,* "I will send you away with this treaty." So he made a treaty with him and sent him away.

35 Now a certain man of the sons of the prophets said to his neighbor by the word of the LORD, "Strike me, please." And the man refused to strike him. 36 Then he said to him, "Because you have not obeyed the voice of the LORD, surely, as soon as you depart from me, a lion shall kill you." And as soon as he left him, a lion found him and killed him.

37 And he found another man, and said, "Strike me, please." So the man struck him, inflicting a wound. 38 Then the prophet departed and waited for the king by the road, and disguised himself with a bandage over his eyes. 39 Now as the king passed by, he cried out to the king and said, "Your servant went out into the midst of the battle; and there, a man came over and brought a man to me, and said, 'Guard this man; if by any means he is missing, your life shall be for his life, or else you shall pay a talent of silver.' 40 While your servant was busy here and there, he was gone."

Then the king of Israel said to him, "So *shall* your judgment *be; you* yourself have decided *it.*"

41 And he hastened to take the bandage away from his eyes; and the king of Israel recognized him as one of the prophets. 42 Then he said to him, "Thus says the LORD: 'Because you have let slip out of *your* hand a man whom I appointed to utter destruction, therefore your life shall go for his life, and your people for his people.' "

43 So the king of Israel went to his house sullen and displeased, and came to Samaria.

21 And it came to pass after these things *that* Naboth the Jezreelite had a vineyard which *was* in Jezreel, next to the palace of Ahab king of Samaria. 2 So Ahab spoke to Naboth, saying, "Give me your vineyard, that I may have it for a vegetable garden, because it *is* near, next to my house; and for it I will give you a vineyard better than it. *Or,* if it seems good to you, I will give you its worth in money."

3 But Naboth said to Ahab, "The LORD forbid that I should give the inheritance of my fathers to you!"

עַל־הַמֶּרְכָּבָה: 34 וַיֹּאמֶר אֵלָיו הֶעָרִים אֲשֶׁר־לָקַח־
אָבִי מֵאֵת אָבִיךָ אָשִׁיב וְחֻצוֹת תָּשִׂים לְךָ בְדַמֶּשֶׂק
כַּאֲשֶׁר־שָׂם אָבִי בְּשֹׁמְרוֹן וַאֲנִי בַּבְּרִית אֲשַׁלְּחֶךָּ
וַיִּכְרָת־לוֹ בְרִית וַיְשַׁלְּחֵהוּ: ס 35 וְאִישׁ
אֶחָד מִבְּנֵי הַנְּבִיאִים אָמַר אֶל־רֵעֵהוּ בִּדְבַר יְהֹוָה
הַכֵּינִי נָא וַיְמָאֵן הָאִישׁ לְהַכֹּתוֹ: 36 וַיֹּאמֶר לוֹ
יַעַן אֲשֶׁר לֹא־שָׁמַעְתָּ בְּקוֹל יְהֹוָה הִנְּךָ הוֹלֵךְ
מֵאִתִּי וְהִכְּךָ הָאַרְיֵה וַיֵּלֶךְ מֵאֶצְלוֹ וַיִּמְצָאֵהוּ הָאַרְיֵה
וַיַּכֵּהוּ: 37 וַיִּמְצָא אִישׁ אַחֵר וַיֹּאמֶר הַכֵּינִי נָא
וַיַּכֵּהוּ הָאִישׁ הַכֵּה וּפָצֹעַ: 38 וַיֵּלֶךְ הַנָּבִיא וַיַּעֲמֹד
לַמֶּלֶךְ עַל־הַדָּרֶךְ וַיִּתְחַפֵּשׂ בָּאֲפֵר עַל־עֵינָיו: 39 וַיְהִי
הַמֶּלֶךְ עֹבֵר וְהוּא צָעַק אֶל־הַמֶּלֶךְ וַיֹּאמֶר עַבְדְּךָ |
יָצָא בְקֶרֶב־הַמִּלְחָמָה וְהִנֵּה־אִישׁ סָר וַיָּבֵא אֵלַי
אִישׁ וַיֹּאמֶר שְׁמֹר אֶת־הָאִישׁ הַזֶּה אִם־הִפָּקֵד
יִפָּקֵד וְהָיְתָה נַפְשְׁךָ תַּחַת נַפְשׁוֹ אוֹ כִכַּר־כֶּסֶף
תִּשְׁקוֹל: 40 וַיְהִי עַבְדְּךָ עֹשֶׂה הֵנָּה וָהֵנָּה וְהוּא
אֵינֶנּוּ וַיֹּאמֶר אֵלָיו מֶלֶךְ־יִשְׂרָאֵל כֵּן מִשְׁפָּטֶךָ אַתָּה
חָרָצְתָּ: 41 וַיְמַהֵר וַיָּסַר אֶת־הָאֲפֵר מֵעֲלֵי עֵינָיו וַיַּכֵּר
אֹתוֹ מֶלֶךְ יִשְׂרָאֵל כִּי מֵהַנְּבִאִים הוּא: 42 וַיֹּאמֶר
אֵלָיו כֹּה אָמַר יְהֹוָה יַעַן שִׁלַּחְתָּ אֶת־אִישׁ־חֶרְמִי
מִיָּד וְהָיְתָה נַפְשְׁךָ תַּחַת נַפְשׁוֹ וְעַמְּךָ תַּחַת עַמּוֹ:
43 וַיֵּלֶךְ מֶלֶךְ־יִשְׂרָאֵל עַל־בֵּיתוֹ סַר וְזָעֵף וַיָּבֹא
שֹׁמְרוֹנָה:
פ

כא וַיְהִי אַחַר הַדְּבָרִים הָאֵלֶּה כֶּרֶם הָיָה לְנָבוֹת
הַיִּזְרְעֵאלִי אֲשֶׁר בְּיִזְרְעֶאל אֵצֶל הֵיכַל אַחְאָב מֶלֶךְ
שֹׁמְרוֹן: 2 וַיְדַבֵּר אַחְאָב אֶל־נָבוֹת | לֵאמֹר |
תְּנָה־לִּי אֶת־כַּרְמְךָ וִיהִי־לִי לְגַן־יָרָק כִּי הוּא קָרוֹב
אֵצֶל בֵּיתִי וְאֶתְּנָה לְךָ תַּחְתָּיו כֶּרֶם טוֹב מִמֶּנּוּ אִם
טוֹב בְּעֵינֶיךָ אֶתְּנָה־לְךָ כֶסֶף מְחִיר זֶה: 3 וַיֹּאמֶר
נָבוֹת אֶל־אַחְאָב חָלִילָה לִּי מֵיהֹוָה מִתִּתִּי אֶת־
כ 41 מַעֲלֵי

⁴So Ahab went into his house sullen and displeased because of the word which Naboth the Jezreelite had spoken to him; for he had said, "I will not give you the inheritance of my fathers." And he lay down on his bed, and turned away his face, and would eat no food. ⁵But Jezebel his wife came to him, and said to him, "Why is your spirit so sullen that you eat no food?"

⁶He said to her, "Because I spoke to Naboth the Jezreelite, and said to him, 'Give me your vineyard for money; or else, if it pleases you, I will give you *another* vineyard for it.' And he answered, 'I will not give you my vineyard.'"

⁷Then Jezebel his wife said to him, "You now exercise authority over Israel! Arise, eat food, and let your heart be cheerful; I will give you the vineyard of Naboth the Jezreelite."

⁸And she wrote letters in Ahab's name, sealed *them* with his seal, and sent the letters to the elders and the nobles who *were* dwelling in the city with Naboth. ⁹She wrote in the letters, saying,

> Proclaim a fast, and seat Naboth with high honor among the people; ¹⁰and seat two men, scoundrels, before him to bear witness against him, saying, "You have blasphemed God and the king." *Then* take him out, and stone him, that he may die.

¹¹So the men of his city, the elders and nobles who were inhabitants of his city, did as Jezebel had sent to them, as it *was* written in the letters which she had sent to them. ¹²They proclaimed a fast, and seated Naboth with high honor among the people. ¹³And two men, scoundrels, came in and sat before him; and the scoundrels witnessed against him, against Naboth, in the presence of the people, saying, "Naboth has blasphemed God and the king!" Then they took him outside the city and stoned him with stones, so that he died. ¹⁴Then they sent to Jezebel, saying, "Naboth has been stoned and is dead."

¹⁵And it came to pass, when Jezebel heard that Naboth had been stoned and was dead, that Jezebel said to Ahab, "Arise, take possession of the vineyard of Naboth the Jezreelite, which he refused to give you for money; for Naboth is not alive, but dead." ¹⁶So it was, when Ahab heard that Naboth was dead, that Ahab got up and went down to take possession of the vineyard of Naboth the Jezreelite.

¹⁷Then the word of the LORD came to Elijah the Tishbite, saying, ¹⁸"Arise, go down to meet Ahab king of Israel, who *lives* in Samaria. There he is, in the vineyard of Naboth, where he has gone down to take possession of it. ¹⁹You shall speak to him, saying, 'Thus says the LORD: "Have you murdered

נַחֲלַת אֲבֹתָי לָךְ: 4 וַיָּבֹא אַחְאָב אֶל־בֵּיתוֹ סַר וְזָעֵף
עַל־הַדָּבָר אֲשֶׁר־דִּבֶּר אֵלָיו נָבוֹת הַיִּזְרְעֵאלִי וַיֹּאמֶר
לֹא־אֶתֵּן לְךָ אֶת־נַחֲלַת אֲבוֹתָי וַיִּשְׁכַּב עַל־מִטָּתוֹ
וַיַּסֵּב אֶת־פָּנָיו וְלֹא־אָכַל לָחֶם: 5 וַתָּבֹא אֵלָיו אִיזֶבֶל
אִשְׁתּוֹ וַתְּדַבֵּר אֵלָיו מַה־זֶּה רוּחֲךָ סָרָה וְאֵינְךָ
אֹכֵל לָחֶם: 6 וַיְדַבֵּר אֵלֶיהָ כִּי־אֲדַבֵּר אֶל־נָבוֹת
הַיִּזְרְעֵאלִי וָאֹמַר לוֹ תְּנָה־לִּי אֶת־כַּרְמְךָ בְּכֶסֶף
אוֹ אִם־חָפֵץ אַתָּה אֶתְּנָה־לְךָ כֶרֶם תַּחְתָּיו וַיֹּאמֶר
לֹא־אֶתֵּן לְךָ אֶת־כַּרְמִי: 7 וַתֹּאמֶר אֵלָיו אִיזֶבֶל
אִשְׁתּוֹ אַתָּה עַתָּה תַּעֲשֶׂה מְלוּכָה עַל־יִשְׂרָאֵל
קוּם אֱכָל־לֶחֶם וְיִטַב לִבֶּךָ אֲנִי אֶתֵּן לְךָ אֶת־כֶּרֶם
נָבוֹת הַיִּזְרְעֵאלִי: 8 וַתִּכְתֹּב סְפָרִים בְּשֵׁם אַחְאָב
וַתַּחְתֹּם בְּחֹתָמוֹ וַתִּשְׁלַח הַסְּפָרִים ᵖ אֶל־הַזְּקֵנִים
וְאֶל־הַחֹרִים אֲשֶׁר בְּעִירוֹ הַיֹּשְׁבִים אֶת־נָבוֹת:
9 וַתִּכְתֹּב בַּסְּפָרִים לֵאמֹר קִרְאוּ־צוֹם וְהוֹשִׁיבוּ אֶת־
נָבוֹת בְּרֹאשׁ הָעָם: 10 וְהוֹשִׁיבוּ שְׁנַיִם אֲנָשִׁים בְּנֵי־
בְלִיַּעַל נֶגְדּוֹ וִיעִדֻהוּ לֵאמֹר בֵּרַכְתָּ אֱלֹהִים וָמֶלֶךְ
וְהוֹצִיאֻהוּ וְסִקְלֻהוּ וְיָמֹת: 11 וַיַּעֲשׂוּ אַנְשֵׁי עִירוֹ
הַזְּקֵנִים וְהַחֹרִים אֲשֶׁר הַיֹּשְׁבִים בְּעִירוֹ כַּאֲשֶׁר
שָׁלְחָה אֲלֵיהֶם אִיזָבֶל כַּאֲשֶׁר כָּתוּב בַּסְּפָרִים אֲשֶׁר
שָׁלְחָה אֲלֵיהֶם: 12 קָרְאוּ צוֹם וְהֹשִׁיבוּ אֶת־נָבוֹת
בְּרֹאשׁ הָעָם: 13 וַיָּבֹאוּ שְׁנֵי הָאֲנָשִׁים בְּנֵי־בְלִיַּעַל
וַיֵּשְׁבוּ נֶגְדּוֹ וַיְעִדֻהוּ אַנְשֵׁי הַבְּלִיַּעַל אֶת־נָבוֹת נֶגֶד
הָעָם לֵאמֹר בֵּרַךְ נָבוֹת אֱלֹהִים וָמֶלֶךְ וַיֹּצִאֻהוּ
מִחוּץ לָעִיר וַיִּסְקְלֻהוּ בָאֲבָנִים וַיָּמֹת: 14 וַיִּשְׁלְחוּ
אֶל־אִיזֶבֶל לֵאמֹר סֻקַּל נָבוֹת וַיָּמֹת: 15 וַיְהִי כִּשְׁמֹעַ
אִיזֶבֶל כִּי־סֻקַּל נָבוֹת וַיָּמֹת וַתֹּאמֶר אִיזֶבֶל אֶל־
אַחְאָב קוּם רֵשׁ אֶת־כֶּרֶם | נָבוֹת הַיִּזְרְעֵאלִי
אֲשֶׁר מֵאֵן לָתֶת־לְךָ בְכֶסֶף כִּי אֵין נָבוֹת חַי
כִּי־מֵת: 16 וַיְהִי כִּשְׁמֹעַ אַחְאָב כִּי מֵת נָבוֹת
וַיָּקָם אַחְאָב לָרֶדֶת אֶל־כֶּרֶם נָבוֹת הַיִּזְרְעֵאלִי
לְרִשְׁתּוֹ: ס 17 וַיְהִי דְּבַר־יְהֹוָה אֶל־אֵלִיָּהוּ
הַתִּשְׁבִּי לֵאמֹר: 18 קוּם רֵד לִקְרַאת אַחְאָב מֶלֶךְ
יִשְׂרָאֵל אֲשֶׁר בְּשֹׁמְרוֹן הִנֵּה בְּכֶרֶם נָבוֹת אֲשֶׁר
יָרַד שָׁם לְרִשְׁתּוֹ: 19 וְדִבַּרְתָּ אֵלָיו לֵאמֹר כֹּה אָמַר

and also taken possession?" ' And you shall speak to him, saying, 'Thus says the LORD: "In the place where dogs licked the blood of Naboth, dogs shall lick your blood, even yours." ' "

20 So Ahab said to Elijah, "Have you found me, O my enemy?"

And he answered, "I have found *you,* because you have sold yourself to do evil in the sight of the LORD: 21 'Behold, I will bring calamity on you. I will take away your posterity, and will cut off from Ahab every male in Israel, both bond and free. 22 I will make your house like the house of Jeroboam the son of Nebat, and like the house of Baasha the son of Ahijah, because of the provocation with which you have provoked *Me* to anger, and made Israel sin.' 23 And concerning Jezebel the LORD also spoke, saying, 'The dogs shall eat Jezebel by the wall of Jezreel.' 24 The dogs shall eat whoever belongs to Ahab and dies in the city, and the birds of the air shall eat whoever dies in the field."

25 But there was no one like Ahab who sold himself to do wickedness in the sight of the LORD, because Jezebel his wife stirred him up. 26 And he behaved very abominably in following idols, according to all *that* the Amorites had done, whom the LORD had cast out before the children of Israel.

27 So it was, when Ahab heard those words, that he tore his clothes and put sackcloth on his body, and fasted and lay in sackcloth, and went about mourning.

28 And the word of the LORD came to Elijah the Tishbite, saying, 29 "See how Ahab has humbled himself before Me? Because he has humbled himself before Me, I will not bring the calamity in his days. In the days of his son I will bring the calamity on his house."

22 Now three years passed without war between Syria and Israel. 2 Then it came to pass, in the third year, that Jehoshaphat the king of Judah went down to *visit* the king of Israel.

3 And the king of Israel said to his servants, "Do you know that Ramoth in Gilead *is* ours, but we hesitate to take it out of the hand of the king of Syria?" 4 So he said to Jehoshaphat, "Will you go with me to fight at Ramoth Gilead?"

Jehoshaphat said to the king of Israel, "I *am* as you *are,* my people as your people, my horses as your horses." 5 Also Jehoshaphat said to the king of Israel, "Please inquire for the word of the LORD today."

יְהוָה הַרָצַחְתָּ וְגַם־יָרָשְׁתָּ וְדִבַּרְתָּ אֵלָיו לֵאמֹר כֹּה אָמַר יְהוָה בִּמְקוֹם אֲשֶׁר לָקְקוּ הַכְּלָבִים אֶת־דַּם נָבוֹת יָלֹקּוּ הַכְּלָבִים אֶת־דָּמְךָ גַּם־אָתָּה: 20 וַיֹּאמֶר אַחְאָב אֶל־אֵלִיָּהוּ הַמְצָאתַנִי אֹיְבִי וַיֹּאמֶר מָצָאתִי יַעַן הִתְמַכֶּרְךָ לַעֲשׂוֹת הָרַע בְּעֵינֵי יְהוָה: 21 הִנְנִי מֵבִיא אֵלֶיךָ רָעָה וּבִעַרְתִּי אַחֲרֶיךָ וְהִכְרַתִּי לְאַחְאָב מַשְׁתִּין בְּקִיר וְעָצוּר וְעָזוּב בְּיִשְׂרָאֵל: 22 וְנָתַתִּי אֶת־בֵּיתְךָ כְּבֵית יָרָבְעָם בֶּן־נְבָט וּכְבֵית בַּעְשָׁא בֶן־אֲחִיָּה אֶל־הַכַּעַס אֲשֶׁר הִכְעַסְתָּ וַתַּחֲטִא אֶת־יִשְׂרָאֵל: 23 וְגַם־לְאִיזֶבֶל דִּבֶּר יְהוָה לֵאמֹר הַכְּלָבִים יֹאכְלוּ אֶת־אִיזֶבֶל בְּחֵל יִזְרְעֶאל: 24 הַמֵּת לְאַחְאָב בָּעִיר יֹאכְלוּ הַכְּלָבִים וְהַמֵּת בַּשָּׂדֶה יֹאכְלוּ עוֹף הַשָּׁמָיִם: 25 רַק לֹא־הָיָה כְאַחְאָב אֲשֶׁר הִתְמַכֵּר לַעֲשׂוֹת הָרַע בְּעֵינֵי יְהוָה אֲשֶׁר־הֵסַתָּה אֹתוֹ אִיזֶבֶל אִשְׁתּוֹ: 26 וַיַּתְעֵב מְאֹד לָלֶכֶת אַחֲרֵי הַגִּלֻּלִים כְּכֹל אֲשֶׁר עָשׂוּ הָאֱמֹרִי אֲשֶׁר הוֹרִישׁ יְהוָה מִפְּנֵי בְּנֵי יִשְׂרָאֵל: ס 27 וַיְהִי כִּשְׁמֹעַ אַחְאָב אֶת־הַדְּבָרִים הָאֵלֶּה וַיִּקְרַע בְּגָדָיו וַיָּשֶׂם־שַׂק עַל־בְּשָׂרוֹ וַיָּצוֹם וַיִּשְׁכַּב בַּשָּׂק וַיְהַלֵּךְ אַט: ס 28 וַיְהִי דְּבַר־יְהוָה אֶל־אֵלִיָּהוּ הַתִּשְׁבִּי לֵאמֹר: 29 הֲרָאִיתָ כִּי־נִכְנַע אַחְאָב מִלְּפָנָי יַעַן כִּי־נִכְנַע מִפָּנַי לֹא־אָבִיא הָרָעָה בְּיָמָיו בִּימֵי בְנוֹ אָבִיא הָרָעָה עַל־בֵּיתוֹ:

כב וַיֵּשְׁבוּ שָׁלֹשׁ שָׁנִים אֵין מִלְחָמָה בֵּין אֲרָם וּבֵין יִשְׂרָאֵל: פ 2 וַיְהִי בַּשָּׁנָה הַשְּׁלִישִׁית וַיֵּרֶד יְהוֹשָׁפָט מֶלֶךְ־יְהוּדָה אֶל־מֶלֶךְ יִשְׂרָאֵל: 3 וַיֹּאמֶר מֶלֶךְ־יִשְׂרָאֵל אֶל־עֲבָדָיו הַיְדַעְתֶּם כִּי־לָנוּ רָמֹת גִּלְעָד וַאֲנַחְנוּ מַחְשִׁים מִקַּחַת אֹתָהּ מִיַּד מֶלֶךְ אֲרָם: 4 וַיֹּאמֶר אֶל־יְהוֹשָׁפָט הֲתֵלֵךְ אִתִּי לַמִּלְחָמָה רָמֹת גִּלְעָד וַיֹּאמֶר יְהוֹשָׁפָט אֶל־מֶלֶךְ יִשְׂרָאֵל כָּמוֹנִי כָמוֹךָ כְּעַמִּי כְעַמֶּךָ כְּסוּסַי כְּסוּסֶיךָ: 5 וַיֹּאמֶר יְהוֹשָׁפָט אֶל־מֶלֶךְ יִשְׂרָאֵל דְּרָשׁ־

⁶Then the king of Israel gathered the prophets together, about four hundred men, and said to them, "Shall I go against Ramoth Gilead to fight, or shall I refrain?"

So they said, "Go up, for the Lord will deliver *it* into the hand of the king."

⁷And Jehoshaphat said, "*Is there* not still a prophet of the LORD here, that we may inquire of Him?"

⁸So the king of Israel said to Jehoshaphat, "*There is* still one man, Micaiah the son of Imlah, by whom we may inquire of the LORD; but I hate him, because he does not prophesy good concerning me, but evil."

And Jehoshaphat said, "Let not the king say such things!"

⁹Then the king of Israel called an officer and said, "Bring Micaiah the son of Imlah quickly!"

¹⁰The king of Israel and Jehoshaphat the king of Judah, having put on *their* robes, sat each on his throne, at a threshing floor at the entrance of the gate of Samaria; and all the prophets prophesied before them. ¹¹Now Zedekiah the son of Chenaanah had made horns of iron for himself; and he said, "Thus says the LORD: 'With these you shall gore the Syrians until they are destroyed.'" ¹²And all the prophets prophesied so, saying, "Go up to Ramoth Gilead and prosper, for the LORD will deliver *it* into the king's hand."

¹³Then the messenger who had gone to call Micaiah spoke to him, saying, "Now listen, the words of the prophets with one accord encourage the king. Please, let your word be like the word of one of them, and speak encouragement."

¹⁴And Micaiah said, "*As* the LORD lives, whatever the LORD says to me, that I will speak."

¹⁵Then he came to the king; and the king said to him, "Micaiah, shall we go to war against Ramoth Gilead, or shall we refrain?"

And he answered him, "Go and prosper, for the LORD will deliver *it* into the hand of the king!"

¹⁶So the king said to him, "How many times shall I make you swear that you tell me nothing but the truth in the name of the LORD?"

¹⁷Then he said, "I saw all Israel scattered on the mountains, as sheep that have no shepherd. And the LORD said, 'These have no master. Let each return to his house in peace.'"

¹⁸And the king of Israel said to Jehoshaphat, "Did I not tell you he would not prophesy good concerning me, but evil?"

¹⁹Then *Micaiah* said, "Therefore hear the word of the LORD: I saw the LORD sitting on His throne, and all the host of heaven standing by, on His right

---

נָא כַיּוֹם אֶת־דְּבַר יְהֹוָה: 6 וַיִּקְבֹּץ מֶלֶךְ־יִשְׂרָאֵל אֶת־הַנְּבִיאִים כְּאַרְבַּע מֵאוֹת אִישׁ וַיֹּאמֶר אֲלֵהֶם הַאֵלֵךְ עַל־רָמֹת גִּלְעָד לַמִּלְחָמָה אִם־אֶחְדָּל וַיֹּאמְרוּ עֲלֵה וְיִתֵּן אֲדֹנָי בְּיַד הַמֶּלֶךְ: 7 וַיֹּאמֶר יְהוֹשָׁפָט הַאֵין פֹּה נָבִיא לַיהֹוָה עוֹד וְנִדְרְשָׁה מֵאוֹתוֹ: 8 וַיֹּאמֶר מֶלֶךְ־יִשְׂרָאֵל ׀ אֶל־יְהוֹשָׁפָט עוֹד אִישׁ־אֶחָד לִדְרֹשׁ אֶת־יְהֹוָה מֵאֹתוֹ וַאֲנִי שְׂנֵאתִיו כִּי לֹא־יִתְנַבֵּא עָלַי טוֹב כִּי אִם־רָע מִיכָיְהוּ בֶּן־יִמְלָה וַיֹּאמֶר יְהוֹשָׁפָט אַל־יֹאמַר הַמֶּלֶךְ כֵּן: 9 וַיִּקְרָא מֶלֶךְ יִשְׂרָאֵל אֶל־סָרִיס אֶחָד וַיֹּאמֶר מַהֲרָה מִיכָיְהוּ בֶן־יִמְלָה:

10 וּמֶלֶךְ יִשְׂרָאֵל וִיהוֹשָׁפָט מֶלֶךְ־יְהוּדָה יֹשְׁבִים אִישׁ עַל־כִּסְאוֹ מְלֻבָּשִׁים בְּגָדִים בְּגֹרֶן פֶּתַח שַׁעַר שֹׁמְרוֹן וְכָל־הַנְּבִיאִים מִתְנַבְּאִים לִפְנֵיהֶם: 11 וַיַּעַשׂ לוֹ צִדְקִיָּה בֶן־כְּנַעֲנָה קַרְנֵי בַרְזֶל וַיֹּאמֶר כֹּה־אָמַר יְהֹוָה בְּאֵלֶּה תְּנַגַּח אֶת־אֲרָם עַד־כַּלֹּתָם: 12 וְכָל־הַנְּבִאִים נִבְּאִים כֵּן לֵאמֹר עֲלֵה רָמֹת גִּלְעָד וְהַצְלַח וְנָתַן יְהֹוָה בְּיַד הַמֶּלֶךְ: 13 וְהַמַּלְאָךְ אֲשֶׁר־הָלַךְ ׀ לִקְרֹא מִיכָיְהוּ דִּבֶּר אֵלָיו לֵאמֹר הִנֵּה־נָא דִּבְרֵי הַנְּבִיאִים פֶּה־אֶחָד טוֹב אֶל־הַמֶּלֶךְ יְהִי־נָא דְבָרְךָֿ כִּדְבַר אַחַד מֵהֶם וְדִבַּרְתָּ טּוֹב: 14 וַיֹּאמֶר מִיכָיְהוּ חַי־יְהֹוָה כִּי אֶת־אֲשֶׁר יֹאמַר יְהֹוָה אֵלַי אֹתוֹ אֲדַבֵּר:

15 וַיָּבוֹא אֶל־הַמֶּלֶךְ וַיֹּאמֶר הַמֶּלֶךְ אֵלָיו מִיכָיְהוּ הֲנֵלֵךְ אֶל־רָמֹת גִּלְעָד לַמִּלְחָמָה אִם־נֶחְדָּל וַיֹּאמֶר אֵלָיו עֲלֵה וְהַצְלַח וְנָתַן יְהֹוָה בְּיַד הַמֶּלֶךְ: 16 וַיֹּאמֶר אֵלָיו הַמֶּלֶךְ עַד־כַּמֶּה פְעָמִים אֲנִי מַשְׁבִּעֶךָ אֲשֶׁר לֹא־תְדַבֵּר אֵלַי רַק־אֱמֶת בְּשֵׁם יְהֹוָה: 17 וַיֹּאמֶר רָאִיתִי אֶת־כָּל־יִשְׂרָאֵל נְפֹצִים אֶל־הֶהָרִים כַּצֹּאן אֲשֶׁר אֵין־לָהֶם רֹעֶה וַיֹּאמֶר יְהֹוָה לֹא־אֲדֹנִים לָאֵלֶּה יָשׁוּבוּ אִישׁ־לְבֵיתוֹ בְּשָׁלוֹם: 18 וַיֹּאמֶר מֶלֶךְ־יִשְׂרָאֵל אֶל־יְהוֹשָׁפָט הֲלוֹא אָמַרְתִּי אֵלֶיךָ לוֹא־יִתְנַבֵּא עָלַי טוֹב כִּי אִם־רָע: 19 וַיֹּאמֶר לָכֵן שְׁמַע דְּבַר־יְהֹוָה רָאִיתִי אֶת־יְהֹוָה יֹשֵׁב עַל־כִּסְאוֹ וְכָל־צְבָא הַשָּׁמַיִם

hand and on His left. 20 And the LORD said, 'Who will persuade Ahab to go up, that he may fall at Ramoth Gilead?' So one spoke in this manner, and another spoke in that manner. 21 Then a spirit came forward and stood before the LORD, and said, 'I will persuade him.' 22 The LORD said to him, 'In what way?' So he said, 'I will go out and be a lying spirit in the mouth of all his prophets.' And the LORD said, 'You shall persuade *him*, and also prevail. Go out and do so.' 23 Therefore look! The LORD has put a lying spirit in the mouth of all these prophets of yours, and the LORD has declared disaster against you."

24 Now Zedekiah the son of Chenaanah went near and struck Micaiah on the cheek, and said, "Which way did the spirit from the LORD go from me to speak to you?"

25 And Micaiah said, "Indeed, you shall see on that day when you go into an inner chamber to hide!"

26 So the king of Israel said, "Take Micaiah, and return him to Amon the governor of the city and to Joash the king's son; 27 and say, 'Thus says the king: "Put this *fellow* in prison, and feed him with bread of affliction and water of affliction, until I come in peace." ' "

28 But Micaiah said, "If you ever return in peace, the LORD has not spoken by me." And he said, "Take heed, all you people!"

29 So the king of Israel and Jehoshaphat the king of Judah went up to Ramoth Gilead. 30 And the king of Israel said to Jehoshaphat, "I will disguise myself and go into battle; but you put on your robes." So the king of Israel disguised himself and went into battle.

31 Now the king of Syria had commanded the thirty-two captains of his chariots, saying, "Fight with no one small or great, but only with the king of Israel." 32 So it was, when the captains of the chariots saw Jehoshaphat, that they said, "Surely it *is* the king of Israel!" Therefore they turned aside to fight against him, and Jehoshaphat cried out. 33 And it happened, when the captains of the chariots saw that it *was* not the king of Israel, that they turned back from pursuing him. 34 Now a *certain* man drew a bow at random, and struck the king of Israel between the joints of his armor. So he said to the driver of his chariot, "Turn around and take me out of the battle, for I am wounded."

35 The battle increased that day; and the king was propped up in his chariot, facing the Syrians, and died at evening. The blood ran out from the wound onto the floor of the chariot. 36 Then, as the sun was

20 וַיֹּאמֶר יְהוָה מִי יְפַתֶּה אֶת־אַחְאָב וְיַעַל וְיִפֹּל בְּרָמֹת גִּלְעָד וַיֹּאמֶר זֶה בְּכֹה וְזֶה אֹמֵר בְּכֹה: 21 וַיֵּצֵא הָרוּחַ וַיַּעֲמֹד לִפְנֵי יְהוָה וַיֹּאמֶר אֲנִי אֲפַתֶּנּוּ וַיֹּאמֶר יְהוָה אֵלָיו בַּמָּה: 22 וַיֹּאמֶר אֵצֵא וְהָיִיתִי רוּחַ שֶׁקֶר בְּפִי כָּל־נְבִיאָיו וַיֹּאמֶר תְּפַתֶּה וְגַם־תּוּכָל צֵא וַעֲשֵׂה־כֵן: 23 וְעַתָּה הִנֵּה נָתַן יְהוָה רוּחַ שֶׁקֶר בְּפִי כָּל־נְבִיאֶיךָ אֵלֶּה וַיהוָה דִּבֶּר עָלֶיךָ רָעָה: 24 וַיִּגַּשׁ צִדְקִיָּהוּ בֶן־כְּנַעֲנָה וַיַּכֶּה אֶת־מִיכָיְהוּ עַל־הַלֶּחִי וַיֹּאמֶר אֵי־זֶה עָבַר רוּחַ־יְהוָה מֵאִתִּי לְדַבֵּר אוֹתָךְ: 25 וַיֹּאמֶר מִיכָיְהוּ הִנְּךָ רֹאֶה בַּיּוֹם הַהוּא אֲשֶׁר תָּבֹא חֶדֶר בְּחֶדֶר לְהֵחָבֵה: 26 וַיֹּאמֶר מֶלֶךְ יִשְׂרָאֵל קַח אֶת־מִיכָיְהוּ וַהֲשִׁיבֵהוּ אֶל־אָמֹן שַׂר־הָעִיר וְאֶל־יוֹאָשׁ בֶּן־הַמֶּלֶךְ: 27 וְאָמַרְתָּ כֹּה אָמַר הַמֶּלֶךְ שִׂימוּ אֶת־זֶה בֵּית הַכֶּלֶא וְהַאֲכִילֻהוּ לֶחֶם לַחַץ וּמַיִם לַחַץ עַד בֹּאִי בְשָׁלוֹם: 28 וַיֹּאמֶר מִיכָיְהוּ אִם־שׁוֹב תָּשׁוּב בְּשָׁלוֹם לֹא־דִבֶּר יְהוָה בִּי וַיֹּאמֶר שִׁמְעוּ עַמִּים כֻּלָּם: 29 וַיַּעַל מֶלֶךְ־יִשְׂרָאֵל וִיהוֹשָׁפָט מֶלֶךְ־יְהוּדָה רָמֹת גִּלְעָד: 30 וַיֹּאמֶר מֶלֶךְ יִשְׂרָאֵל אֶל־יְהוֹשָׁפָט הִתְחַפֵּשׂ וָבֹא בַמִּלְחָמָה וְאַתָּה לְבַשׁ בְּגָדֶיךָ וַיִּתְחַפֵּשׂ מֶלֶךְ יִשְׂרָאֵל וַיָּבוֹא בַּמִּלְחָמָה: 31 וּמֶלֶךְ אֲרָם צִוָּה אֶת־שָׂרֵי הָרֶכֶב אֲשֶׁר־לוֹ שְׁלֹשִׁים וּשְׁנַיִם לֵאמֹר לֹא תִּלָּחֲמוּ אֶת־קָטֹן וְאֶת־גָּדוֹל כִּי אִם־אֶת־מֶלֶךְ יִשְׂרָאֵל לְבַדּוֹ: 32 וַיְהִי כִּרְאוֹת שָׂרֵי הָרֶכֶב אֶת־יְהוֹשָׁפָט וְהֵמָּה אָמְרוּ אַךְ מֶלֶךְ־יִשְׂרָאֵל הוּא וַיָּסֻרוּ עָלָיו לְהִלָּחֵם וַיִּזְעַק יְהוֹשָׁפָט: 33 וַיְהִי כִּרְאוֹת שָׂרֵי הָרֶכֶב כִּי־לֹא מֶלֶךְ יִשְׂרָאֵל הוּא וַיָּשׁוּבוּ מֵאַחֲרָיו: 34 וְאִישׁ מָשַׁךְ בַּקֶּשֶׁת לְתֻמּוֹ וַיַּכֶּה אֶת־מֶלֶךְ יִשְׂרָאֵל בֵּין הַדְּבָקִים וּבֵין הַשִּׁרְיָן וַיֹּאמֶר לְרַכָּבוֹ הֲפֹךְ יָדְךָ וְהוֹצִיאֵנִי מִן־הַמַּחֲנֶה כִּי הָחֳלֵיתִי: 35 וַתַּעֲלֶה הַמִּלְחָמָה בַּיּוֹם הַהוּא וְהַמֶּלֶךְ הָיָה מָעֳמָד בַּמֶּרְכָּבָה נֹכַח אֲרָם וַיָּמָת בָּעֶרֶב וַיִּצֶק דַּם־הַמַּכָּה אֶל־חֵיק הָרָכֶב: 36 וַיַּעֲבֹר הָרִנָּה בַּמַּחֲנֶה כְּבֹא הַשֶּׁמֶשׁ לֵאמֹר אִישׁ

going down, a shout went throughout the army, saying, "Every man to his city, and every man to his own country!"

37 So the king died, and was brought to Samaria. And they buried the king in Samaria. 38 Then *someone* washed the chariot at a pool in Samaria, and the dogs licked up his blood while the harlots bathed, according to the word of the LORD which He had spoken.

39 Now the rest of the acts of Ahab, and all that he did, the ivory house which he built and all the cities that he built, *are* they not written in the book of the chronicles of the kings of Israel? 40 So Ahab rested with his fathers. Then Ahaziah his son reigned in his place.

41 Jehoshaphat the son of Asa had become king over Judah in the fourth year of Ahab king of Israel. 42 Jehoshaphat *was* thirty-five years old when he became king, and he reigned twenty-five years in Jerusalem. His mother's name *was* Azubah the daughter of Shilhi. 43 And he walked in all the ways of his father Asa. He did not turn aside from them, doing *what was* right in the eyes of the LORD. Nevertheless the high places were not taken away, *for* the people offered sacrifices and burned incense on the high places. 44 Also Jehoshaphat made peace with the king of Israel.

45 Now the rest of the acts of Jehoshaphat, the might that he showed, and how he made war, *are* they not written in the book of the chronicles of the kings of Judah? 46 And the rest of the perverted persons, who remained in the days of his father Asa, he banished from the land. 47 *There was* then no king in Edom, only a deputy of the king.

48 Jehoshaphat made merchant ships to go to Ophir for gold; but they never sailed, for the ships were wrecked at Ezion Geber. 49 Then Ahaziah the son of Ahab said to Jehoshaphat, "Let my servants go with your servants in the ships." But Jehoshaphat would not.

50 And Jehoshaphat rested with his fathers, and was buried with his fathers in the City of David his father. Then Jehoram his son reigned in his place.

51 Ahaziah the son of Ahab became king over Israel in Samaria in the seventeenth year of Jehoshaphat king of Judah, and reigned two years over Israel. 52 He did evil in the sight of the LORD, and walked in the way of his father and in the way of his mother and in the way of Jeroboam the son of Nebat, who had made Israel sin; 53 for he served Baal and worshiped him, and provoked the LORD God of Israel to anger, according to all that his father had done.

37 וַיָּ֤מָת הַמֶּ֙לֶךְ֙ וַיָּב֣וֹא אֶל־עֵיר֔וֹ וְאִ֖ישׁ אֶל־אַרְצֽוֹ׃ שֹׁמְר֔וֹן וַיִּקְבְּר֥וּ אֶת־הַמֶּ֖לֶךְ בְּשֹׁמְרֽוֹן׃ 38 וַיִּשְׁטֹ֨ף אֶת־ הָרֶ֜כֶב עַ֣ל ׀ בְּרֵכַ֣ת שֹׁמְר֗וֹן וַיָּלֹ֤קּוּ הַכְּלָבִים֙ אֶת־ דָּמ֔וֹ וְהַזֹּנ֖וֹת רָחָ֑צוּ כִּדְבַ֥ר יְהֹוָ֖ה אֲשֶׁ֥ר דִּבֵּֽר׃ 39 וְיֶ֨תֶר דִּבְרֵ֤י אַחְאָב֙ וְכָל־אֲשֶׁ֣ר עָשָׂ֔ה וּבֵ֥ית הַשֵּׁ֖ן אֲשֶׁ֣ר בָּנָ֑ה וְכָל־הֶעָרִ֖ים אֲשֶׁ֣ר בָּנָ֑ה הֲלֽוֹא־הֵ֣ם כְּתוּבִ֗ים עַל־סֵ֛פֶר דִּבְרֵ֥י הַיָּמִ֖ים לְמַלְכֵ֥י יִשְׂרָאֵֽל׃ 40 וַיִּשְׁכַּ֤ב אַחְאָב֙ עִם־אֲבֹתָ֔יו וַיִּמְלֹ֛ךְ אֲחַזְיָ֥הוּ בְנ֖וֹ תַּחְתָּֽיו׃ פ

41 וִיהֽוֹשָׁפָט֙ בֶּן־אָסָ֔א מָלַ֖ךְ עַל־יְהוּדָ֑ה בִּשְׁנַ֣ת אַרְבַּ֔ע לְאַחְאָ֖ב מֶ֥לֶךְ יִשְׂרָאֵֽל׃ 42 יְהֽוֹשָׁפָ֡ט בֶּן־ שְׁלֹשִׁים֩ וְחָמֵ֨שׁ שָׁנָ֜ה בְּמָלְכ֗וֹ וְעֶשְׂרִ֤ים וְחָמֵשׁ֙ שָׁנָ֔ה מָלַ֖ךְ בִּירֽוּשָׁלָ֑͏ִם וְשֵׁ֣ם אִמּ֔וֹ עֲזוּבָ֖ה בַּת־ שִׁלְחִֽי׃ 43 וַיֵּ֗לֶךְ בְּכָל־דֶּ֛רֶךְ אָסָ֥א אָבִ֖יו לֹֽא־סָ֣ר מִמֶּ֑נּוּ לַעֲשׂ֥וֹת הַיָּשָׁ֖ר בְּעֵינֵ֥י יְהֹוָֽה׃ 44 אַ֥ךְ הַבָּמ֖וֹת לֹא־סָ֑רוּ ע֤וֹד הָעָם֙ מְזַבְּחִ֣ים וּֽמְקַטְּרִ֖ים בַּבָּמֽוֹת׃

45 וַיַּשְׁלֵ֥ם יְהוֹשָׁפָ֖ט עִם־מֶ֥לֶךְ יִשְׂרָאֵֽל׃ 46 וְיֶ֨תֶר דִּבְרֵ֤י יְהֽוֹשָׁפָט֙ וּגְבֽוּרָת֣וֹ אֲשֶׁר־עָשָׂ֔ה וַאֲשֶׁ֖ר נִלְחָ֑ם הֲלֹֽא־הֵ֣ם כְּתוּבִ֗ים עַל־סֵ֛פֶר דִּבְרֵ֥י הַיָּמִ֖ים לְמַלְכֵ֥י יְהוּדָֽה׃ 47 וְיֶ֙תֶר֙ הַקָּדֵ֔שׁ אֲשֶׁ֣ר נִשְׁאַ֔ר בִּימֵ֖י אָסָ֣א אָבִ֑יו בִּעֵ֖ר מִן־הָאָֽרֶץ׃ 48 וּמֶ֥לֶךְ אֵ֛ין בֶּאֱד֖וֹם נִצָּ֥ב מֶֽלֶךְ׃ 49 יְהוֹשָׁפָ֡ט עָשָׂה֩ אֳנִיּ֨וֹת תַּרְשִׁ֜ישׁ לָלֶ֧כֶת אוֹפִ֛ירָה לַזָּהָ֖ב וְלֹ֣א הָלָ֑ךְ כִּֽי־נִשְׁבְּר֥וּ אֳנִיּ֖וֹת בְּעֶצְי֥וֹן גָּֽבֶר׃ 50 אָ֣ז אָמַ֗ר אֲחַזְיָ֤הוּ בֶן־אַחְאָב֙ אֶל־ יְהוֹשָׁפָ֔ט יֵלְכ֧וּ עֲבָדַ֛י עִם־עֲבָדֶ֖יךָ בָּאֳנִיּ֑וֹת וְלֹ֥א אָבָ֖ה יְהוֹשָׁפָֽט׃ 51 וַיִּשְׁכַּ֤ב יְהֽוֹשָׁפָט֙ עִם־אֲבֹתָ֔יו וַיִּקָּבֵר֙ עִם־אֲבֹתָ֔יו בְּעִ֖יר דָּוִ֣ד אָבִ֑יו וַיִּמְלֹ֛ךְ יְהוֹרָ֥ם בְּנ֖וֹ תַּחְתָּֽיו׃ ס

52 אֲחַזְיָ֙הוּ֙ בֶן־אַחְאָ֔ב מָלַ֤ךְ עַל־יִשְׂרָאֵל֙ בְּשֹׁ֣מְר֔וֹן בִּשְׁנַת֙ שְׁבַ֣ע עֶשְׂרֵ֔ה לִיהֽוֹשָׁפָ֖ט מֶ֣לֶךְ יְהוּדָ֑ה וַיִּמְלֹ֥ךְ עַל־יִשְׂרָאֵ֖ל שְׁנָתָֽיִם׃ 53 וַיַּ֙עַשׂ֙ הָרַ֔ע בְּעֵינֵ֖י יְהֹוָ֑ה וַיֵּ֗לֶךְ בְּדֶ֤רֶךְ אָבִיו֙ וּבְדֶ֣רֶךְ אִמּ֔וֹ וּבְדֶ֙רֶךְ֙ יָרׇבְעָ֣ם בֶּן־נְבָ֔ט אֲשֶׁ֥ר הֶחֱטִ֖יא אֶת־יִשְׂרָאֵֽל׃ 54 וַֽיַּעֲבֹד֙ אֶת־הַבַּ֔עַל וַיִּשְׁתַּ֖חֲוֶ֣ה ל֑וֹ וַיַּכְעֵ֗ס אֶת־יְהֹוָ֞ה אֱלֹהֵ֣י יִשְׂרָאֵ֔ל כְּכֹ֥ל אֲשֶׁר־עָשָׂ֖ה אָבִֽיו׃

The Second Book of the

KINGS

1 Moab rebelled against Israel after the death of Ahab.

2 Now Ahaziah fell through the lattice of his upper room in Samaria, and was injured; so he sent messengers and said to them, "Go, inquire of Baal-Zebub, the god of Ekron, whether I shall recover from this injury." 3 But the angel of the LORD said to Elijah the Tishbite, "Arise, go up to meet the messengers of the king of Samaria, and say to them, '*Is it* because *there is* no God in Israel *that* you are going to inquire of Baal-Zebub, the god of Ekron?' 4 Now therefore, thus says the LORD: 'You shall not come down from the bed to which you have gone up, but you shall surely die.' " So Elijah departed.

5 And when the messengers returned to him, he said to them, "Why have you come back?"

6 So they said to him, "A man came up to meet us, and said to us, 'Go, return to the king who sent you, and say to him, "Thus says the LORD: '*Is it* because *there is* no God in Israel *that* you are sending to inquire of Baal-Zebub, the god of Ekron? Therefore you shall not come down from the bed to which you have gone up, but you shall surely die.' " ' "

7 Then he said to them, "What kind of man *was it* who came up to meet you and told you these words?"

8 So they answered him, "A hairy man wearing a leather belt around his waist."

And he said, "It *is* Elijah the Tishbite."

9 Then the king sent to him a captain of fifty with his fifty men. So he went up to him; and there he was, sitting on the top of a hill. And he spoke to him: "Man of God, the king has said, 'Come down!' "

10 So Elijah answered and said to the captain of fifty, "If I *am* a man of God, then let fire come down from heaven and consume you and your fifty men." And fire came down from heaven and consumed him and his fifty. 11 Then he sent to him another captain of fifty with his fifty men.

And he answered and said to him: "Man of God, thus has the king said, 'Come down quickly!' "

מלכים ב

א וַיִּפְשַׁע מוֹאָב בְּיִשְׂרָאֵל אַחֲרֵי מוֹת אַחְאָב: 2 וַיִּפֹּל אֲחַזְיָה בְּעַד הַשְּׂבָכָה בַּעֲלִיָּתוֹ אֲשֶׁר בְּשֹׁמְרוֹן וַיָּחַל וַיִּשְׁלַח מַלְאָכִים וַיֹּאמֶר אֲלֵהֶם לְכוּ דִרְשׁוּ בְּבַעַל זְבוּב אֱלֹהֵי עֶקְרוֹן אִם־אֶחְיֶה מֵחֳלִי זֶה: ס 3 וּמַלְאַךְ יְהוָה דִּבֶּר אֶל־אֵלִיָּה הַתִּשְׁבִּי קוּם עֲלֵה לִקְרַאת מַלְאֲכֵי מֶלֶךְ־שֹׁמְרוֹן וְדַבֵּר אֲלֵהֶם הַמִבְּלִי אֵין־אֱלֹהִים בְּיִשְׂרָאֵל אַתֶּם הֹלְכִים לִדְרֹשׁ בְּבַעַל זְבוּב אֱלֹהֵי עֶקְרוֹן: 4 וְלָכֵן כֹּה־אָמַר יְהוָה הַמִּטָּה אֲשֶׁר־עָלִיתָ שָּׁם לֹא־תֵרֵד מִמֶּנָּה כִּי מוֹת תָּמוּת וַיֵּלֶךְ אֵלִיָּה:

5 וַיָּשׁוּבוּ הַמַּלְאָכִים אֵלָיו וַיֹּאמֶר אֲלֵהֶם מַה־זֶּה שַׁבְתֶּם: 6 וַיֹּאמְרוּ אֵלָיו אִישׁ ׀ עָלָה לִקְרָאתֵנוּ וַיֹּאמֶר אֵלֵינוּ לְכוּ שׁוּבוּ אֶל־הַמֶּלֶךְ אֲשֶׁר־שָׁלַח אֶתְכֶם וְדִבַּרְתֶּם אֵלָיו כֹּה אָמַר יְהוָה הַמִבְּלִי אֵין־אֱלֹהִים בְּיִשְׂרָאֵל אַתָּה שֹׁלֵחַ לִדְרֹשׁ בְּבַעַל זְבוּב אֱלֹהֵי עֶקְרוֹן לָכֵן הַמִּטָּה אֲשֶׁר־עָלִיתָ שָּׁם לֹא־תֵרֵד מִמֶּנָּה כִּי־מוֹת תָּמוּת: 7 וַיְדַבֵּר אֲלֵהֶם מֶה מִשְׁפַּט הָאִישׁ אֲשֶׁר עָלָה לִקְרַאתְכֶם וַיְדַבֵּר אֲלֵיכֶם אֶת־הַדְּבָרִים הָאֵלֶּה: 8 וַיֹּאמְרוּ אֵלָיו אִישׁ בַּעַל שֵׂעָר וְאֵזוֹר עוֹר אָזוּר בְּמָתְנָיו וַיֹּאמַר אֵלִיָּה הַתִּשְׁבִּי הוּא: 9 וַיִּשְׁלַח אֵלָיו שַׂר־חֲמִשִּׁים וַחֲמִשָּׁיו וַיַּעַל אֵלָיו וְהִנֵּה יֹשֵׁב עַל־רֹאשׁ הָהָר וַיְדַבֵּר אֵלָיו אִישׁ הָאֱלֹהִים הַמֶּלֶךְ דִּבֶּר רֵדָה: 10 וַיַּעֲנֶה אֵלִיָּהוּ וַיְדַבֵּר אֶל־שַׂר הַחֲמִשִּׁים וְאִם־אִישׁ אֱלֹהִים אָנִי תֵּרֶד אֵשׁ מִן־הַשָּׁמַיִם וְתֹאכַל אֹתְךָ וְאֶת־חֲמִשֶּׁיךָ וַתֵּרֶד אֵשׁ מִן־הַשָּׁמַיִם וַתֹּאכַל אֹתוֹ וְאֶת־חֲמִשָּׁיו: 11 וַיָּשָׁב וַיִּשְׁלַח אֵלָיו שַׂר־חֲמִשִּׁים אַחֵר וַחֲמִשָּׁיו וַיַּעַן וַיְדַבֵּר אֵלָיו אִישׁ הָאֱלֹהִים כֹּה־אָמַר הַמֶּלֶךְ

12 So Elijah answered and said to them, "If I *am* a man of God, let fire come down from heaven and consume you and your fifty men." And the fire of God came down from heaven and consumed him and his fifty.

13 Again, he sent a third captain of fifty with his fifty men. And the third captain of fifty went up, and came and fell on his knees before Elijah, and pleaded with him, and said to him: "Man of God, please let my life and the life of these fifty servants of yours be precious in your sight. 14 Look, fire has come down from heaven and burned up the first two captains of fifties with their fifties. But let my life now be precious in your sight."

15 And the angel of the LORD said to Elijah, "Go down with him; do not be afraid of him." So he arose and went down with him to the king. 16 Then he said to him, "Thus says the LORD: 'Because you have sent messengers to inquire of Baal-Zebub, the god of Ekron, *is it* because *there is* no God in Israel to inquire of His word? Therefore you shall not come down from the bed to which you have gone up, but you shall surely die.'"

17 So *Ahaziah* died according to the word of the LORD which Elijah had spoken. Because he had no son, Jehoram became king in his place, in the second year of Jehoram the son of Jehoshaphat, king of Judah.

18 Now the rest of the acts of Ahaziah which he did, *are* they not written in the book of the chronicles of the kings of Israel?

2 And it came to pass, when the LORD was about to take up Elijah into heaven by a whirlwind, that Elijah went with Elisha from Gilgal. 2 Then Elijah said to Elisha, "Stay here, please, for the LORD has sent me on to Bethel."

But Elisha said, "*As* the LORD lives, and *as* your soul lives, I will not leave you!" So they went down to Bethel.

3 Now the sons of the prophets who *were* at Bethel came out to Elisha, and said to him, "Do you know that the LORD will take away your master from over you today?"

And he said, "Yes, I know; keep silent!"

4 Then Elijah said to him, "Elisha, stay here, please, for the LORD has sent me on to Jericho."

But he said, "*As* the LORD lives, and *as* your soul lives, I will not leave you!" So they came to Jericho.

5 Now the sons of the prophets who *were* at Jericho came to Elisha and said to him, "Do you know that the LORD will take away your master from over you today?"

So he answered, "Yes, I know; keep silent!"

מְהֵרָה רֶדָה: 12 וַיַּ֫עַן אֵלִיָּ֗ה וַיְדַבֵּר֙ אֲלֵיהֶם֙ אִם־
אִישׁ הָאֱלֹהִים֙ אָ֔נִי תֵּ֤רֶד אֵשׁ֙ מִן־הַשָּׁמַ֔יִם וְתֹאכַ֥ל
אֹֽתְךָ֖ וְאֶת־חֲמִשֶּׁ֑יךָ וַתֵּ֤רֶד אֵשׁ־אֱלֹהִים֙ מִן־הַשָּׁמַ֔יִם
וַתֹּ֥אכַל אֹת֖וֹ וְאֶת־חֲמִשָּֽׁיו: 13 וַיָּ֗שָׁב וַיִּשְׁלַ֛ח שַׂר־
חֲמִשִּׁ֥ים שְׁלֹשִׁ֖ים וַחֲמִשָּׁ֑יו וַיַּ֡עַל וַיָּבֹא֩ שַׂר־הַחֲמִשִּׁ֨ים
הַשְּׁלִישִׁ֜י וַיִּכְרַ֥ע עַל־בִּרְכָּ֣יו ׀ לְנֶ֣גֶד אֵלִיָּ֗הוּ וַיִּתְחַנֵּ֤ן
אֵלָיו֙ וַיְדַבֵּ֣ר אֵלָ֔יו אִ֚ישׁ הָ֣אֱלֹהִ֔ים תִּֽיקַר־נָ֣א נַפְשִׁ֗י
וְנֶ֨פֶשׁ עֲבָדֶ֥יךָ אֵ֛לֶּה חֲמִשִּׁ֖ים בְּעֵינֶֽיךָ: 14 הִ֠נֵּה
יָ֤רְדָה אֵשׁ֙ מִן־הַשָּׁמַ֔יִם וַ֠תֹּאכַל אֶת־שְׁנֵ֞י שָׂרֵ֧י
הַחֲמִשִּׁ֛ים הָרִאשֹׁנִ֖ים וְאֶת־חֲמִשֵּׁיהֶ֑ם וְעַתָּ֕ה תִּיקַ֥ר
נַפְשִׁ֖י בְּעֵינֶֽיךָ: ס   15 וַיְדַבֵּ֤ר מַלְאַ֨ךְ יְהֹוָה֙
אֶל־אֵ֣לִיָּ֔הוּ רֵ֥ד אוֹת֖וֹ אַל־תִּירָ֣א מִפָּנָ֑יו וַיָּ֣קָם וַיֵּ֧רֶד
אוֹת֖וֹ אֶל־הַמֶּֽלֶךְ: 16 וַיְדַבֵּ֨ר אֵלָ֜יו כֹּֽה־אָמַ֣ר יְהֹוָ֗ה
יַ֜עַן אֲשֶׁר־שָׁלַ֣חְתָּ מַלְאָכִים֮ לִדְרֹשׁ֮ בְּבַ֣עַל זְב֣וּב אֱלֹהֵ֣י
עֶקְרוֹן֒ הֲֽמִבְּלִ֤י אֵין־אֱלֹהִים֙ בְּיִשְׂרָאֵ֔ל לִדְרֹ֖שׁ בִּדְבָר֑וֹ
לָ֠כֵן הַמִּטָּ֞ה אֲשֶׁר־עָלִ֥יתָ שָּׁ֛ם לֹֽא־תֵרֵ֥ד מִמֶּ֖נָּה כִּֽי־
מ֥וֹת תָּמֽוּת: 17 וַיָּ֜מׇת כִּדְבַ֣ר יְהֹוָ֣ה ׀ אֲשֶׁר־דִּבֶּ֣ר
אֵלִיָּ֗הוּ וַיִּמְלֹ֤ךְ יְהוֹרָם֙ תַּחְתָּ֔יו פ בִּשְׁנַ֣ת שְׁתַּ֔יִם
לִיהוֹרָ֥ם בֶּן־יְהוֹשָׁפָ֖ט מֶ֣לֶךְ יְהוּדָ֑ה כִּ֥י לֹֽא־הָ֖יָה לֽוֹ
בֵּֽן: 18 וְיֶ֛תֶר דִּבְרֵ֥י אֲחַזְיָ֖הוּ אֲשֶׁ֣ר עָשָׂ֑ה הֲלוֹא־הֵ֣מָּה
כְתוּבִ֗ים עַל־סֵ֛פֶר דִּבְרֵ֥י הַיָּמִ֖ים לְמַלְכֵ֥י יִשְׂרָאֵֽל: פ

ב וַיְהִ֗י בְּהַעֲל֤וֹת יְהֹוָה֙ אֶת־אֵ֣לִיָּ֔הוּ בַּסְּעָרָ֖ה הַשָּׁמָ֑יִם
וַיֵּ֧לֶךְ אֵלִיָּ֛הוּ וֶאֱלִישָׁ֖ע מִן־הַגִּלְגָּֽל: 2 וַיֹּ֩אמֶר֩ אֵלִיָּ֨הוּ
אֶל־אֱלִישָׁ֜ע שֵֽׁב־נָ֣א פֹ֗ה כִּ֤י יְהֹוָה֙ שְׁלָחַ֣נִי עַד־בֵּֽית־
אֵ֔ל וַיֹּ֣אמֶר אֱלִישָׁ֗ע חַי־יְהֹוָ֤ה וְחֵֽי־נַפְשְׁךָ֙ אִם־אֶעֶזְבֶ֔ךָּ
וַיֵּרְד֖וּ בֵּֽית־אֵֽל: 3 וַיֵּצְא֨וּ בְנֵֽי־הַנְּבִיאִ֥ים אֲשֶׁר־בֵּֽית־
אֵל֮ אֶל־אֱלִישָׁע֒ וַיֹּאמְר֣וּ אֵלָ֗יו הֲיָדַ֙עְתָּ֙ כִּ֣י הַיּ֔וֹם
יְהֹוָ֛ה לֹקֵ֥חַ אֶת־אֲדֹנֶ֖יךָ מֵעַ֣ל רֹאשֶׁ֑ךָ וַיֹּ֛אמֶר גַּם־אֲנִ֥י
יָדַ֖עְתִּי הֶחֱשֽׁוּ: 4 וַיֹּ֩אמֶר֩ ל֨וֹ אֵלִיָּ֜הוּ אֱלִישָׁ֣ע ׀ שֵֽׁב־
נָ֣א פֹ֗ה כִּ֤י יְהֹוָה֙ שְׁלָחַ֣נִי יְרִיח֔וֹ וַיֹּ֕אמֶר חַי־יְהֹוָ֛ה
וְחֵֽי־נַפְשְׁךָ֖ אִם־אֶעֶזְבֶ֑ךָּ וַיָּבֹ֖אוּ יְרִיחֽוֹ: 5 וַיִּגְּשׁ֨וּ בְנֵֽי־
הַנְּבִיאִ֥ים אֲשֶׁר־בִּֽירִיחוֹ֮ אֶל־אֱלִישָׁע֒ וַיֹּאמְר֣וּ אֵלָ֗יו
הֲיָדַ֙עְתָּ֙ כִּ֣י הַיּ֔וֹם יְהֹוָ֛ה לֹקֵ֥חַ אֶת־אֲדֹנֶ֖יךָ מֵעַ֣ל

6 Then Elijah said to him, "Stay here, please, for the LORD has sent me on to the Jordan."

But he said, "*As the LORD lives, and as your soul lives, I will not leave you!*" So the two of them went on. 7 And fifty men of the sons of the prophets went and stood facing *them* at a distance, while the two of them stood by the Jordan. 8 Now Elijah took his mantle, rolled *it* up, and struck the water; and it was divided this way and that, so that the two of them crossed over on dry ground.

9 And so it was, when they had crossed over, that Elijah said to Elisha, "Ask! What may I do for you, before I am taken away from you?"

Elisha said, "Please let a double portion of your spirit be upon me."

10 So he said, "You have asked a hard thing. *Nevertheless,* if you see me *when I am* taken from you, it shall be so for you; but if not, it shall not be *so.*" 11 Then it happened, as they continued on and talked, that suddenly a chariot of fire *appeared* with horses of fire, and separated the two of them; and Elijah went up by a whirlwind into heaven.

12 And Elisha saw *it,* and he cried out, "My father, my father, the chariot of Israel and its horsemen!" So he saw him no more. And he took hold of his own clothes and tore them into two pieces. 13 He also took up the mantle of Elijah that had fallen from him, and went back and stood by the bank of the Jordan. 14 Then he took the mantle of Elijah that had fallen from him, and struck the water, and said, "Where *is* the LORD God of Elijah?" And when he also had struck the water, it was divided this way and that; and Elisha crossed over.

15 Now when the sons of the prophets who *were* from Jericho saw him, they said, "The spirit of Elijah rests on Elisha." And they came to meet him, and bowed to the ground before him. 16 Then they said to him, "Look now, there are fifty strong men with your servants. Please let them go and search for your master, lest perhaps the Spirit of the LORD has taken him up and cast him upon some mountain or into some valley."

And he said, "You shall not send anyone."

17 But when they urged him till he was ashamed, he said, "Send *them!*" Therefore they sent fifty men, and they searched for three days but did not find him. 18 And when they came back to him, for he had stayed in Jericho, he said to them, "Did I not say to you, 'Do not go'?"

19 Then the men of the city said to Elisha, "Please notice, the situation of this city *is* pleasant, as my lord sees; but the water *is* bad, and the ground barren."

6 וַיֹּ֤אמֶר לוֹ֙ רֵאשֹׁ֔ךְ וַיֹּ֗אמֶר גַּם־אֲנִ֤י יָדַ֙עְתִּי֙ הֶחֱשׁ֔וּ אֵלִיָּ֜הוּ שֵֽׁב־נָ֣א פֹ֗ה כִּ֤י יְהוָה֙ שְׁלָחַ֣נִי הַיַּרְדֵּ֔נָה וַיֹּ֗אמֶר חַי־יְהוָ֤ה וְחֵֽי־נַפְשְׁךָ֙ אִם־אֶעֶזְבֶ֔ךָּ וַיֵּלְכ֖וּ שְׁנֵיהֶֽם׃ 7 וַחֲמִשִּׁ֣ים אִ֗ישׁ מִבְּנֵ֤י הַנְּבִיאִים֙ הָֽלְכ֔וּ וַיַּעַמְד֥וּ מִנֶּ֖גֶד מֵרָח֑וֹק וּשְׁנֵיהֶ֖ם עָמְד֥וּ עַל־הַיַּרְדֵּֽן׃ 8 וַיִּקַּח֩ אֵלִיָּ֨הוּ אֶת־אַדַּרְתּ֤וֹ וַיִּגְלֹם֙ וַיַּכֶּ֣ה אֶת־הַמַּ֔יִם וַיֵּֽחָצ֖וּ הֵ֣נָּה וָהֵ֑נָּה וַיַּעַבְר֥וּ שְׁנֵיהֶ֖ם בֶּחָרָבָֽה׃ 9 וַיְהִ֣י כְעָבְרָ֗ם וְאֵ֨לִיָּ֜הוּ אָמַ֣ר אֶל־אֱלִישָׁ֗ע שְׁאַל֙ מָ֣ה אֶֽעֱשֶׂה־לָּ֔ךְ בְּטֶ֖רֶם אֶלָּקַ֣ח מֵעִמָּ֑ךְ וַיֹּ֣אמֶר אֱלִישָׁ֔ע וִֽיהִי־נָ֛א פִּֽי־שְׁנַ֥יִם בְּרוּחֲךָ֖ אֵלָֽי׃ 10 וַיֹּ֖אמֶר הִקְשִׁ֣יתָ לִשְׁא֑וֹל אִם־תִּרְאֶ֨ה אֹתִ֜י לֻקָּ֤ח מֵֽאִתָּךְ֙ יְהִֽי־לְךָ֣ כֵ֔ן וְאִם־אַ֖יִן לֹ֥א יִהְיֶֽה׃ 11 וַיְהִ֗י הֵ֣מָּה הֹלְכִ֤ים הָלוֹךְ֙ וְדַבֵּ֔ר וְהִנֵּ֤ה רֶֽכֶב־אֵשׁ֙ וְס֣וּסֵי אֵ֔שׁ וַיַּפְרִ֖דוּ בֵּ֣ין שְׁנֵיהֶ֑ם וַיַּ֚עַל אֵ֣לִיָּ֔הוּ בַּֽסְּעָרָ֖ה הַשָּׁמָֽיִם׃ 12 וֶאֱלִישָׁ֣ע רֹאֶ֗ה וְה֤וּא מְצַעֵק֙ אָבִ֣י ׀ אָבִ֗י רֶ֤כֶב יִשְׂרָאֵל֙ וּפָ֣רָשָׁ֔יו וְלֹ֥א רָאָ֖הוּ ע֑וֹד וַֽיַּחֲזֵק֙ בִּבְגָדָ֔יו וַיִּקְרָעֵ֖ם לִשְׁנַ֥יִם קְרָעִֽים׃ 13 וַיָּ֙רֶם֙ אֶת־אַדֶּ֣רֶת אֵלִיָּ֔הוּ אֲשֶׁ֥ר נָפְלָ֖ה מֵֽעָלָ֑יו וַיָּ֥שָׁב וַֽיַּעֲמֹ֖ד עַל־שְׂפַ֥ת הַיַּרְדֵּֽן׃ 14 וַיִּקַּח֩ אֶת־אַדֶּ֨רֶת אֵלִיָּ֜הוּ אֲשֶׁר־נָפְלָ֤ה מֵֽעָלָיו֙ וַיַּכֶּ֣ה אֶת־הַמַּ֔יִם וַיֹּ֕אמֶר אַיֵּ֕ה יְהוָ֖ה אֱלֹהֵ֣י אֵֽלִיָּ֑הוּ אַף־ה֣וּא ׀ וַיַּכֶּ֣ה אֶת־הַמַּ֗יִם וַיֵּחָצוּ֙ הֵ֣נָּה וָהֵ֔נָּה וַֽיַּעֲבֹ֖ר אֱלִישָֽׁע׃ 15 וַיִּרְאֻ֨הוּ בְנֵֽי־הַנְּבִיאִ֤ים אֲשֶׁר־בִּֽירִיחוֹ֙ מִנֶּ֔גֶד וַיֹּ֣אמְר֔וּ נָ֛חָה ר֥וּחַ אֵלִיָּ֖הוּ עַל־אֱלִישָׁ֑ע וַיָּבֹ֙אוּ֙ לִקְרָאת֔וֹ וַיִּשְׁתַּחֲווּ־ל֖וֹ אָֽרְצָה׃ 16 וַיֹּאמְר֣וּ אֵלָ֡יו הִנֵּה־נָ֣א יֵֽשׁ־אֶת־עֲבָדֶ֩יךָ֩ חֲמִשִּׁ֨ים אֲנָשִׁ֜ים בְּנֵֽי־חַ֗יִל יֵ֤לְכוּ נָא֙ וִיבַקְשׁ֣וּ אֶת־אֲדֹנֶ֔יךָ פֶּן־נְשָׂאוֹ֙ ר֣וּחַ יְהוָ֔ה וַיַּשְׁלִכֵ֙הוּ֙ בְּאַחַ֣ד הֶהָרִ֔ים א֖וֹ בְּאַחַ֣ת הַגֵּיאוֹת׃ וַיֹּ֖אמֶר לֹ֥א תִשְׁלָֽחוּ׃ 17 וַיִּפְצְרוּ־ב֥וֹ עַד־בֹּ֖שׁ וַיֹּ֣אמֶר שְׁלָ֑חוּ וַֽיִּשְׁלְחוּ֙ חֲמִשִּׁ֣ים אִ֔ישׁ וַיְבַקְשׁ֥וּ שְׁלֹשָֽׁה־יָמִ֖ים וְלֹ֥א מְצָאֻֽהוּ׃ 18 וַיָּשֻׁ֣בוּ אֵלָ֔יו וְה֖וּא יֹשֵׁ֣ב בִּֽירִיח֑וֹ וַיֹּ֣אמֶר אֲלֵהֶ֔ם הֲלֽוֹא־אָמַ֥רְתִּי אֲלֵיכֶ֖ם אַל־תֵּלֵֽכוּ׃ 19 וַיֹּ֨אמְר֜וּ אַנְשֵׁ֤י הָעִיר֙ אֶל־אֱלִישָׁ֔ע הִנֵּה־נָ֞א מוֹשַׁ֤ב הָעִיר֙ ט֔וֹב כַּאֲשֶׁ֖ר אֲדֹנִ֣י

ב 16 הַגֵּאָיֽוֹת

²⁰ And he said, "Bring me a new bowl, and put salt in it." So they brought *it* to him. ²¹ Then he went out to the source of the water, and cast in the salt there, and said, "Thus says the LORD: 'I have healed this water; from it there shall be no more death or barrenness.'" ²² So the water remains healed to this day, according to the word of Elisha which he spoke.

²³ Then he went up from there to Bethel; and as he was going up the road, some youths came from the city and mocked him, and said to him, "Go up, you baldhead! Go up, you baldhead!"

²⁴ So he turned around and looked at them, and pronounced a curse on them in the name of the LORD. And two female bears came out of the woods and mauled forty-two of the youths.

²⁵ Then he went from there to Mount Carmel, and from there he returned to Samaria.

3 Now Jehoram the son of Ahab became king over Israel at Samaria in the eighteenth year of Jehoshaphat king of Judah, and reigned twelve years. ² And he did evil in the sight of the LORD, but not like his father and mother; for he put away the *sacred* pillar of Baal that his father had made. ³ Nevertheless he persisted in the sins of Jeroboam the son of Nebat, who had made Israel sin; he did not depart from them.

⁴ Now Mesha king of Moab was a sheepbreeder, and he regularly paid the king of Israel one hundred thousand lambs and the wool of one hundred thousand rams. ⁵ But it happened, when Ahab died, that the king of Moab rebelled against the king of Israel.

⁶ So King Jehoram went out of Samaria at that time and mustered all Israel. ⁷ Then he went and sent to Jehoshaphat king of Judah, saying, "The king of Moab has rebelled against me. Will you go with me to fight against Moab?"

And he said, "I will go up; I *am* as you *are*, my people as your people, my horses as your horses." ⁸ Then he said, "Which way shall we go up?"

And he answered, "By way of the Wilderness of Edom."

⁹ So the king of Israel went with the king of Judah and the king of Edom, and they marched on that roundabout route seven days; and there was no water for the army, nor for the animals that followed them. ¹⁰ And the king of Israel said, "Alas! For the LORD has called these three kings together to deliver them into the hand of Moab."

¹¹ But Jehoshaphat said, "*Is there* no prophet of the LORD here, that we may inquire of the LORD by him?"

רְאֵה וְהַמַּיִם רָעִים וְהָאָרֶץ מְשַׁכָּלֶת: 20 וַיֹּאמֶר
קְחוּ־לִי צְלֹחִית חֲדָשָׁה וְשִׂימוּ שָׁם מֶלַח וַיִּקְחוּ
אֵלָיו: 21 וַיֵּצֵא אֶל־מוֹצָא הַמַּיִם וַיַּשְׁלֶךְ־שָׁם מֶלַח
וַיֹּאמֶר כֹּה־אָמַר יְהֹוָה רִפִּאתִי לַמַּיִם הָאֵלֶּה לֹא־
יִהְיֶה מִשָּׁם עוֹד מָוֶת וּמְשַׁכָּלֶת: 22 וַיֵּרָפוּ הַמַּיִם
עַד הַיּוֹם הַזֶּה כִּדְבַר אֱלִישָׁע אֲשֶׁר דִּבֵּר: פ

23 וַיַּעַל מִשָּׁם בֵּית־אֵל וְהוּא ׀ עֹלֶה בַדֶּרֶךְ וּנְעָרִים
קְטַנִּים יָצְאוּ מִן־הָעִיר וַיִּתְקַלְּסוּ־בוֹ וַיֹּאמְרוּ לוֹ
עֲלֵה קֵרֵחַ עֲלֵה קֵרֵחַ: 24 וַיִּפֶן אַחֲרָיו וַיִּרְאֵם
וַיְקַלְלֵם בְּשֵׁם יְהֹוָה וַתֵּצֶאנָה שְׁתַּיִם דֻּבִּים מִן־הַיַּעַר
וַתְּבַקַּעְנָה מֵהֶם אַרְבָּעִים וּשְׁנֵי יְלָדִים: 25 וַיֵּלֶךְ
מִשָּׁם אֶל־הַר הַכַּרְמֶל וּמִשָּׁם שָׁב שֹׁמְרוֹן: פ

ג וִיהוֹרָם בֶּן־אַחְאָב מָלַךְ עַל־יִשְׂרָאֵל בְּשֹׁמְרוֹן
בִּשְׁנַת שְׁמֹנֶה עֶשְׂרֵה לִיהוֹשָׁפָט מֶלֶךְ יְהוּדָה
וַיִּמְלֹךְ שְׁתֵּים־עֶשְׂרֵה שָׁנָה: 2 וַיַּעֲשֶׂה הָרַע בְּעֵינֵי
יְהֹוָה רַק לֹא כְאָבִיו וּכְאִמּוֹ וַיָּסַר אֶת־מַצְּבַת
הַבַּעַל אֲשֶׁר עָשָׂה אָבִיו: 3 רַק בְּחַטֹּאות יָרָבְעָם
בֶּן־נְבָט אֲשֶׁר־הֶחֱטִיא אֶת־יִשְׂרָאֵל דָּבֵק לֹא־סָר
מִמֶּנָּה: ס 4 וּמֵישַׁע מֶלֶךְ־מוֹאָב הָיָה נֹקֵד
וְהֵשִׁיב לְמֶלֶךְ־יִשְׂרָאֵל מֵאָה־אֶלֶף כָּרִים וּמֵאָה אֶלֶף
אֵילִים צָמֶר: 5 וַיְהִי כְּמוֹת אַחְאָב וַיִּפְשַׁע מֶלֶךְ־
מוֹאָב בְּמֶלֶךְ יִשְׂרָאֵל: 6 וַיֵּצֵא הַמֶּלֶךְ יְהוֹרָם בַּיּוֹם
הַהוּא מִשֹּׁמְרוֹן וַיִּפְקֹד אֶת־כָּל־יִשְׂרָאֵל: 7 וַיֵּלֶךְ
וַיִּשְׁלַח אֶל־יְהוֹשָׁפָט מֶלֶךְ־יְהוּדָה לֵאמֹר מֶלֶךְ מוֹאָב
פָּשַׁע בִּי הֲתֵלֵךְ אִתִּי אֶל־מוֹאָב לַמִּלְחָמָה וַיֹּאמֶר
אֶעֱלֶה כָּמוֹנִי כָמוֹךָ כְּעַמִּי כְעַמֶּךָ כְּסוּסַי כְּסוּסֶיךָ:

8 וַיֹּאמֶר אֵי־זֶה הַדֶּרֶךְ נַעֲלֶה וַיֹּאמֶר דֶּרֶךְ מִדְבַּר
אֱדוֹם: 9 וַיֵּלֶךְ מֶלֶךְ יִשְׂרָאֵל וּמֶלֶךְ־יְהוּדָה וּמֶלֶךְ
אֱדוֹם וַיָּסֹבּוּ דֶּרֶךְ שִׁבְעַת יָמִים וְלֹא־הָיָה מַיִם
לַמַּחֲנֶה וְלַבְּהֵמָה אֲשֶׁר בְּרַגְלֵיהֶם: 10 וַיֹּאמֶר מֶלֶךְ
יִשְׂרָאֵל אֲהָהּ כִּי־קָרָא יְהֹוָה לִשְׁלֹשֶׁת הַמְּלָכִים
הָאֵלֶּה לָתֵת אוֹתָם בְּיַד־מוֹאָב: 11 וַיֹּאמֶר יְהוֹשָׁפָט
הַאֵין פֹּה נָבִיא לַיהֹוָה וְנִדְרְשָׁה אֶת־יְהֹוָה מֵאוֹתוֹ
וַיַּעַן אֶחָד מֵעַבְדֵי מֶלֶךְ־יִשְׂרָאֵל וַיֹּאמֶר פֹּה אֱלִישָׁע

So one of the servants of the king of Israel answered and said, "Elisha the son of Shaphat *is* here, who poured water on the hands of Elijah."

12 And Jehoshaphat said, "The word of the LORD is with him." So the king of Israel and Jehoshaphat and the king of Edom went down to him.

13 Then Elisha said to the king of Israel, "What have I to do with you? Go to the prophets of your father and the prophets of your mother."

But the king of Israel said to him, "No, for the LORD has called these three kings *together* to deliver them into the hand of Moab."

14 And Elisha said, "*As* the LORD of hosts lives, before whom I stand, surely were it not that I regard the presence of Jehoshaphat king of Judah, I would not look at you, nor see you. 15 But now bring me a musician."

Then it happened, when the musician played, that the hand of the LORD came upon him. 16 And he said, "Thus says the LORD: 'Make this valley full of ditches.' 17 For thus says the LORD: 'You shall not see wind, nor shall you see rain; yet that valley shall be filled with water, so that you, your cattle, and your animals may drink.' 18 And this is a simple matter in the sight of the LORD; He will also deliver the Moabites into your hand. 19 Also you shall attack every fortified city and every choice city, and shall cut down every good tree, and stop up every spring of water, and ruin every good piece of land with stones.'"

20 Now it happened in the morning, when the grain offering was offered, that suddenly water came by way of Edom, and the land was filled with water.

21 And when all the Moabites heard that the kings had come up to fight against them, all who were able to bear arms and older were gathered; and they stood at the border. 22 Then they rose up early in the morning, and the sun was shining on the water; and the Moabites saw the water on the other side *as* red as blood. 23 And they said, "This is blood; the kings have surely struck swords and have killed one another; now therefore, Moab, to the spoil!"

24 So when they came to the camp of Israel, Israel rose up and attacked the Moabites, so that they fled before them; and they entered *their* land, killing the Moabites. 25 Then they destroyed the cities, and each man threw a stone on every good piece of land and filled it; and they stopped up all the springs of water and cut down all the good trees. But they left the stones of Kir Haraseth *intact*. However the slingers surrounded and attacked it.

בֶּן־שָׁפָט אֲשֶׁר־יָצַק מַיִם עַל־יְדֵי אֵלִיָּהוּ: 12 וַיֹּאמֶר יְהוֹשָׁפָט יֵשׁ אוֹתוֹ דְּבַר־יְהֹוָה וַיֵּרְדוּ אֵלָיו מֶלֶךְ יִשְׂרָאֵל וִיהוֹשָׁפָט וּמֶלֶךְ אֱדוֹם: 13 וַיֹּאמֶר אֱלִישָׁע אֶל־מֶלֶךְ יִשְׂרָאֵל מַה־לִּי וָלָךְ לֵךְ אֶל־נְבִיאֵי אָבִיךָ וְאֶל־נְבִיאֵי אִמֶּךָ וַיֹּאמֶר לוֹ מֶלֶךְ יִשְׂרָאֵל אַל כִּי־ קָרָא יְהֹוָה לִשְׁלֹשֶׁת הַמְּלָכִים הָאֵלֶּה לָתֵת אוֹתָם בְּיַד־מוֹאָב: 14 וַיֹּאמֶר אֱלִישָׁע חַי־יְהֹוָה צְבָאוֹת אֲשֶׁר עָמַדְתִּי לְפָנָיו כִּי לוּלֵי פְּנֵי יְהוֹשָׁפָט מֶלֶךְ־ יְהוּדָה אֲנִי נֹשֵׂא אִם־אַבִּיט אֵלֶיךָ וְאִם־אֶרְאֶךָּ: 15 וְעַתָּה קְחוּ־לִי מְנַגֵּן וְהָיָה כְּנַגֵּן הַמְנַגֵּן וַתְּהִי עָלָיו יַד־יְהֹוָה: 16 וַיֹּאמֶר כֹּה אָמַר יְהֹוָה עָשֹׂה הַנַּחַל הַזֶּה גֵּבִים | גֵּבִים: 17 כִּי־כֹה | אָמַר יְהֹוָה לֹא־תִרְאוּ רוּחַ וְלֹא־תִרְאוּ גֶשֶׁם וְהַנַּחַל הַהוּא יִמָּלֵא מָיִם וּשְׁתִיתֶם אַתֶּם וּמִקְנֵיכֶם וּבְהֶמְתְּכֶם: 18 וְנָקַל זֹאת בְּעֵינֵי יְהֹוָה וְנָתַן אֶת־מוֹאָב בְּיֶדְכֶם: 19 וְהִכִּיתֶם כָּל־עִיר מִבְצָר וְכָל־עִיר מִבְחוֹר וְכָל־ עֵץ טוֹב תַּפִּילוּ וְכָל־מַעְיְנֵי־מַיִם תִּסְתֹּמוּ וְכָל הַחֶלְקָה הַטּוֹבָה תַּכְאִבוּ בָּאֲבָנִים: 20 וַיְהִי בַבֹּקֶר כַּעֲלוֹת הַמִּנְחָה וְהִנֵּה־מַיִם בָּאִים מִדֶּרֶךְ אֱדוֹם וַתִּמָּלֵא הָאָרֶץ אֶת־הַמָּיִם: 21 וְכָל־מוֹאָב שָׁמְעוּ כִּי־עָלוּ הַמְּלָכִים לְהִלָּחֶם בָּם וַיִּצָּעֲקוּ מִכֹּל חֹגֵר חֲגֹרָה וָמַעְלָה וַיַּעַמְדוּ עַל־הַגְּבוּל: 22 וַיַּשְׁכִּימוּ בַבֹּקֶר וְהַשֶּׁמֶשׁ זָרְחָה עַל־הַמָּיִם וַיִּרְאוּ מוֹאָב מִנֶּגֶד אֶת־הַמַּיִם אֲדֻמִּים כַּדָּם: 23 וַיֹּאמְרוּ דָּם זֶה הָחֳרֵב נֶחֶרְבוּ הַמְּלָכִים וַיַּכּוּ אִישׁ אֶת־רֵעֵהוּ וְעַתָּה לַשָּׁלָל מוֹאָב: 24 וַיָּבֹאוּ אֶל־מַחֲנֵה יִשְׂרָאֵל וַיָּקֻמוּ יִשְׂרָאֵל וַיַּכּוּ אֶת־מוֹאָב וַיָּנֻסוּ מִפְּנֵיהֶם וַיַּבּוּ־בָהּ וְהַכּוֹת אֶת־מוֹאָב: 25 וְהֶעָרִים יַהֲרֹסוּ וְכָל־חֶלְקָה טוֹבָה יַשְׁלִיכוּ אִישׁ־אַבְנוֹ וּמִלְאוּהָ וְכָל־מַעְיַן־מַיִם יִסְתֹּמוּ וְכָל־עֵץ־טוֹב יַפִּילוּ עַד־הִשְׁאִיר אֲבָנֶיהָ

26 And when the king of Moab saw that the battle was too fierce for him, he took with him seven hundred men who drew swords, to break through to the king of Edom, but they could not. 27 Then he took his eldest son who would have reigned in his place, and offered him *as* a burnt offering upon the wall; and there was great indignation against Israel. So they departed from him and returned to *their own* land.

4 A certain woman of the wives of the sons of the prophets cried out to Elisha, saying, "Your servant my husband is dead, and you know that your servant feared the LORD. And the creditor is coming to take my two sons to be his slaves."

2 So Elisha said to her, "What shall I do for you? Tell me, what do you have in the house?" And she said, "Your maidservant has nothing in the house but a jar of oil."

3 Then he said, "Go, borrow vessels from everywhere, from all your neighbors—empty vessels; do not gather just a few. 4 And when you have come in, you shall shut the door behind you and your sons; then pour it into all those vessels, and set aside the full ones."

5 So she went from him and shut the door behind her and her sons, who brought *the vessels* to her; and she poured *it* out. 6 Now it came to pass, when the vessels were full, that she said to her son, "Bring me another vessel."

And he said to her, "*There is* not another vessel." So the oil ceased. 7 Then she came and told the man of God. And he said, "Go, sell the oil and pay your debt; and you *and* your sons live on the rest."

8 Now it happened one day that Elisha went to Shunem, where there *was* a notable woman, and she persuaded him to eat some food. So it was, as often as he passed by, he would turn in there to eat some food. 9 And she said to her husband, "Look now, I know that this *is* a holy man of God, who passes by us regularly. 10 Please, let us make a small upper room on the wall; and let us put a bed for him there, and a table and a chair and a lampstand; so it will be, whenever he comes to us, he can turn in there."

11 And it happened one day that he came there, and he turned in to the upper room and lay down there. 12 Then he said to Gehazi his servant, "Call this Shunammite woman." When he had called her, she stood before him. 13 And he said to him, "Say now to her, 'Look, you have been concerned for us with all this care. What *can* I do for you? Do you want me to speak on your behalf to the king or to the commander of the army?'"

She answered, "I dwell among my own people."

בְּקִיר חֲרָשֶׂת וַיָּסֹבּוּ הַקְּלָעִים וַיַּכּוּהוּ: 26 וַיַּרְא מֶלֶךְ
מוֹאָב כִּי־חָזַק מִמֶּנּוּ הַמִּלְחָמָה וַיִּקַּח אוֹתוֹ שְׁבַע־
מֵאוֹת אִישׁ שֹׁלֵף חֶרֶב לְהַבְקִיעַ אֶל־מֶלֶךְ אֱדוֹם
וְלֹא יָכֹלוּ: 27 וַיִּקַּח אֶת־בְּנוֹ הַבְּכוֹר אֲשֶׁר־יִמְלֹךְ
תַּחְתָּיו וַיַּעֲלֵהוּ עֹלָה עַל־הַחֹמָה וַיְהִי קֶצֶף־גָּדוֹל
עַל־יִשְׂרָאֵל וַיִּסְעוּ מֵעָלָיו וַיָּשֻׁבוּ לָאָרֶץ: פ

ד וְאִשָּׁה אַחַת מִנְּשֵׁי בְנֵי־הַנְּבִיאִים צָעֲקָה אֶל־
אֱלִישָׁע לֵאמֹר עַבְדְּךָ אִישִׁי מֵת וְאַתָּה יָדַעְתָּ כִּי
עַבְדְּךָ הָיָה יָרֵא אֶת־יְהֹוָה וְהַנֹּשֶׁה בָּא לָקַחַת אֶת־
שְׁנֵי יְלָדַי לוֹ לַעֲבָדִים: 2 וַיֹּאמֶר אֵלֶיהָ אֱלִישָׁע מָה
אֶעֱשֶׂה־לָּךְ הַגִּידִי לִי מַה־יֶּשׁ־לָכִי בַּבָּיִת וַתֹּאמֶר
אֵין לְשִׁפְחָתְךָ כֹל בַּבַּיִת כִּי אִם־אָסוּךְ שָׁמֶן: 3 וַיֹּאמֶר
לְכִי שַׁאֲלִי־לָךְ כֵּלִים מִן־הַחוּץ מֵאֵת כָּל־
שְׁכֵנָכִי כֵּלִים רֵקִים אַל־תַּמְעִיטִי: 4 וּבָאת וְסָגַרְתְּ
הַדֶּלֶת בַּעֲדֵךְ וּבְעַד־בָּנַיִךְ וְיָצַקְתְּ עַל כָּל־הַכֵּלִים
הָאֵלֶּה וְהַמָּלֵא תַּסִּיעִי: 5 וַתֵּלֶךְ מֵאִתּוֹ וַתִּסְגֹּר
הַדֶּלֶת בַּעֲדָהּ וּבְעַד בָּנֶיהָ הֵם מַגִּשִׁים אֵלֶיהָ וְהִיא
מיצקת (מוֹצָקֶת): 6 וַיְהִי כִּמְלֹאת הַכֵּלִים וַתֹּאמֶר אֶל־
בְּנָהּ הַגִּישָׁה אֵלַי עוֹד כֶּלִי וַיֹּאמֶר אֵלֶיהָ אֵין
עוֹד כֶּלִי וַיַּעֲמֹד הַשָּׁמֶן: 7 וַתָּבֹא וַתַּגֵּד לְאִישׁ
הָאֱלֹהִים וַיֹּאמֶר לְכִי מִכְרִי אֶת־הַשֶּׁמֶן וְשַׁלְּמִי אֶת־
נשיכי (נִשְׁיֵךְ) וְאַתְּ בניכי (וּבָנַיִךְ) תִחְיִי בַּנּוֹתָר: פ

8 וַיְהִי הַיּוֹם וַיַּעֲבֹר אֱלִישָׁע אֶל־שׁוּנֵם וְשָׁם אִשָּׁה
גְדוֹלָה וַתַּחֲזֶק־בּוֹ לֶאֱכָל־לָחֶם וַיְהִי מִדֵּי עָבְרוֹ יָסֻר
שָׁמָּה לֶאֱכָל־לָחֶם: 9 וַתֹּאמֶר אֶל־אִישָׁהּ הִנֵּה־נָא
יָדַעְתִּי כִּי אִישׁ אֱלֹהִים קָדוֹשׁ הוּא עֹבֵר עָלֵינוּ
תָּמִיד: 10 נַעֲשֶׂה־נָּא עֲלִיַּת־קִיר קְטַנָּה וְנָשִׂים לוֹ
שָׁם מִטָּה וְשֻׁלְחָן וְכִסֵּא וּמְנוֹרָה וְהָיָה בְּבֹאוֹ
אֵלֵינוּ יָסוּר שָׁמָּה: 11 וַיְהִי הַיּוֹם וַיָּבֹא שָׁמָּה וַיָּסַר
אֶל־הָעֲלִיָּה וַיִּשְׁכַּב־שָׁמָּה: 12 וַיֹּאמֶר אֶל־גֵּחֲזִי נַעֲרוֹ
קְרָא לַשּׁוּנַמִּית הַזֹּאת וַיִּקְרָא־לָהּ וַתַּעֲמֹד לְפָנָיו:
13 וַיֹּאמֶר לוֹ אֱמָר־נָא אֵלֶיהָ הִנֵּה חָרַדְתְּ אֵלֵינוּ
אֶת־כָּל־הַחֲרָדָה הַזֹּאת מֶה לַעֲשׂוֹת לָךְ הֲיֵשׁ
לְדַבֶּר־לָךְ אֶל־הַמֶּלֶךְ אוֹ אֶל־שַׂר הַצָּבָא וַתֹּאמֶר

14 So he said, "What then *is* to be done for her?"

And Gehazi answered, "Actually, she has no son, and her husband is old."

15 So he said, "Call her." When he had called her, she stood in the doorway. 16 Then he said, "About this time next year you shall embrace a son."

And she said, "No, my lord. Man of God, do not lie to your maidservant!"

17 But the woman conceived, and bore a son when the appointed time had come, of which Elisha had told her.

18 And the child grew. Now it happened one day that he went out to his father, to the reapers. 19 And he said to his father, "My head, my head!"

So he said to a servant, "Carry him to his mother." 20 When he had taken him and brought him to his mother, he sat on her knees till noon, and *then* died. 21 And she went up and laid him on the bed of the man of God, shut *the door* upon him, and went out. 22 Then she called to her husband, and said, "Please send me one of the young men and one of the donkeys, that I may run to the man of God and come back."

23 So he said, "Why are you going to him today? *It is* neither the New Moon nor the Sabbath."

And she said, "*It is* well." 24 Then she saddled a donkey, and said to her servant, "Drive, and go forward; do not slacken the pace for me unless I tell you." 25 And so she departed, and went to the man of God at Mount Carmel.

So it was, when the man of God saw her afar off, that he said to his servant Gehazi, "Look, the Shunammite woman! 26 Please run now to meet her, and say to her, 'Is it well with you? Is it well with your husband? Is it well with the child?'"

And she answered, "*It is* well." 27 Now when she came to the man of God at the hill, she caught him by the feet, but Gehazi came near to push her away. But the man of God said, "Let her alone; for her soul *is* in deep distress, and the LORD has hidden *it* from me, and has not told me."

28 So she said, "Did I ask a son of my lord? Did I not say, 'Do not deceive me'?"

29 Then he said to Gehazi, "Get yourself ready, and take my staff in your hand, and be on your way. If you meet anyone, do not greet him; and if anyone greets you, do not answer him; but lay my staff on the face of the child."

30 And the mother of the child said, "*As the* LORD lives, and *as* your soul lives, I will not leave you." So he arose and followed her. 31 Now Gehazi went on ahead of them, and laid the staff on the

בְּתוֹךְ עַמִּי אָנֹכִי יֹשָׁבֶת׃ 14 וַיֹּאמֶר וּמֶה לַעֲשׂוֹת
לָהּ וַיֹּאמֶר גֵּיחֲזִי אֲבָל בֵּן אֵין־לָהּ וְאִישָׁהּ זָקֵן׃
15 וַיֹּאמֶר קְרָא־לָהּ וַיִּקְרָא־לָהּ וַתַּעֲמֹד בַּפָּתַח׃
16 וַיֹּאמֶר לַמּוֹעֵד הַזֶּה כָּעֵת חַיָּה אַתִּ חֹבֶקֶת
בֵּן וַתֹּאמֶר אַל־אֲדֹנִי אִישׁ הָאֱלֹהִים אַל־תְּכַזֵּב
בְּשִׁפְחָתֶךָ׃ 17 וַתַּהַר הָאִשָּׁה וַתֵּלֶד בֵּן לַמּוֹעֵד הַזֶּה
כָּעֵת חַיָּה אֲשֶׁר־דִּבֶּר אֵלֶיהָ אֱלִישָׁע׃ 18 וַיִּגְדַּל
הַיָּלֶד וַיְהִי הַיּוֹם וַיֵּצֵא אֶל־אָבִיו אֶל־הַקֹּצְרִים׃
19 וַיֹּאמֶר אֶל־אָבִיו רֹאשִׁי ׀ רֹאשִׁי וַיֹּאמֶר אֶל־
הַנַּעַר שָׂאֵהוּ אֶל־אִמּוֹ׃ 20 וַיִּשָּׂאֵהוּ וַיְבִיאֵהוּ אֶל־
אִמּוֹ וַיֵּשֶׁב עַל־בִּרְכֶּיהָ עַד־הַצָּהֳרַיִם וַיָּמֹת׃ 21 וַתַּעַל
וַתַּשְׁכִּבֵהוּ עַל־מִטַּת אִישׁ הָאֱלֹהִים וַתִּסְגֹּר בַּעֲדוֹ
וַתֵּצֵא׃ 22 וַתִּקְרָא אֶל־אִישָׁהּ וַתֹּאמֶר שִׁלְחָה נָא
לִי אֶחָד מִן־הַנְּעָרִים וְאַחַת הָאֲתֹנוֹת וְאָרוּצָה
עַד־אִישׁ הָאֱלֹהִים וְאָשׁוּבָה׃ 23 וַיֹּאמֶר מַדּוּעַ
אַתִּי הֹלֶכֶתי אֵלָיו הַיּוֹם לֹא־חֹדֶשׁ וְלֹא שַׁבָּת
וַתֹּאמֶר שָׁלוֹם׃ 24 וַתַּחֲבֹשׁ הָאָתוֹן וַתֹּאמֶר אֶל־
נַעֲרָהּ נְהַג וָלֵךְ אַל־תַּעֲצָר־לִי לִרְכֹּב כִּי אִם־אָמַרְתִּי
לָךְ׃ 25 וַתֵּלֶךְ וַתָּבוֹא אֶל־אִישׁ הָאֱלֹהִים אֶל־הַר
הַכַּרְמֶל וַיְהִי כִּרְאוֹת אִישׁ־הָאֱלֹהִים אֹתָהּ מִנֶּגֶד
וַיֹּאמֶר אֶל־גֵּיחֲזִי נַעֲרוֹ הִנֵּה הַשּׁוּנַמִּית הַלָּז׃ 26 עַתָּה
רוּץ־נָא לִקְרָאתָהּ וֶאֱמָר־לָהּ הֲשָׁלוֹם לָךְ הֲשָׁלוֹם
לְאִישֵׁךְ הֲשָׁלוֹם לַיָּלֶד וַתֹּאמֶר שָׁלוֹם׃ 27 וַתָּבֹא
אֶל־אִישׁ הָאֱלֹהִים אֶל־הָהָר וַתַּחֲזֵק בְּרַגְלָיו וַיִּגַּשׁ
גֵּיחֲזִי לְהָדְפָהּ וַיֹּאמֶר אִישׁ הָאֱלֹהִים הַרְפֵּה־לָהּ כִּי־
נַפְשָׁהּ מָרָה־לָהּ וַיהוָה הֶעְלִים מִמֶּנִּי וְלֹא הִגִּיד לִי׃
28 וַתֹּאמֶר הֲשָׁאַלְתִּי בֵן מֵאֵת אֲדֹנִי הֲלֹא אָמַרְתִּי
לֹא תַשְׁלֶה אֹתִי׃ 29 וַיֹּאמֶר לְגֵיחֲזִי חֲגֹר מָתְנֶיךָ וְקַח
מִשְׁעַנְתִּי בְיָדְךָ וָלֵךְ כִּי־תִמְצָא אִישׁ לֹא תְבָרְכֶנּוּ
וְכִי־יְבָרֶכְךָ אִישׁ לֹא תַעֲנֶנּוּ וְשַׂמְתָּ מִשְׁעַנְתִּי עַל־
פְּנֵי הַנָּעַר׃ 30 וַתֹּאמֶר אֵם הַנַּעַר חַי־יְהוָה וְחֵי־
נַפְשְׁךָ אִם־אֶעֶזְבֶךָּ וַיָּקָם וַיֵּלֶךְ אַחֲרֶיהָ׃ 31 וְגֵיחֲזִי
עָבַר לִפְנֵיהֶם וַיָּשֶׂם אֶת־הַמִּשְׁעֶנֶת עַל־פְּנֵי הַנַּעַר
וְאֵין קוֹל וְאֵין קָשֶׁב וַיָּשָׁב לִקְרָאתוֹ וַיַּגֶּד־לוֹ לֵאמֹר

face of the child; but *there was* neither voice nor hearing. Therefore he went back to meet him, and told him, saying, "The child has not awakened."

32 When Elisha came into the house, there was the child, lying dead on his bed. 33 He went in therefore, shut the door behind the two of them, and prayed to the LORD. 34 And he went up and lay on the child, and put his mouth on his mouth, his eyes on his eyes, and his hands on his hands; and he stretched himself out on the child, and the flesh of the child became warm. 35 He returned and walked back and forth in the house, and again went up and stretched himself out on him; then the child sneezed seven times, and the child opened his eyes. 36 And he called Gehazi and said, "Call this Shunammite woman." So he called her. And when she came in to him, he said, "Pick up your son." 37 So she went in, fell at his feet, and bowed to the ground; then she picked up her son and went out.

38 And Elisha returned to Gilgal, and *there was* a famine in the land. Now the sons of the prophets *were* sitting before him; and he said to his servant, "Put on the large pot, and boil stew for the sons of the prophets." 39 So one went out into the field to gather herbs, and found a wild vine, and gathered from it a lapful of wild gourds, and came and sliced *them* into the pot of stew, though they did not know *what they were.* 40 Then they served it to the men to eat. Now it happened, as they were eating the stew, that they cried out and said, "Man of God, *there is* death in the pot!" And they could not eat *it.*

41 So he said, "Then bring some flour." And he put *it* into the pot, and said, "Serve *it* to the people, that they may eat." And there was nothing harmful in the pot.

42 Then a man came from Baal Shalisha, and brought the man of God bread of the firstfruits, twenty loaves of barley bread, and newly ripened grain in his knapsack. And he said, "Give *it* to the people, that they may eat."

43 But his servant said, "What? Shall I set this before one hundred men?"

He said again, "Give it to the people, that they may eat; for thus says the LORD: 'They shall eat and have *some* left over.'" 44 So he set *it* before them; and they ate and had *some* left over, according to the word of the LORD.

5 Now Naaman, commander of the army of the king of Syria, was a great and honorable man in the eyes of his master, because by him the LORD had given victory to Syria. He was also a mighty man of valor, *but* a leper. 2 And the Syrians had gone out on raids, and had brought back captive a young girl

לֹא הֵקִיץ הַנָּעַר: 32 וַיָּבֹא אֱלִישָׁע הַבַּיְתָה וְהִנֵּה הַנַּעַר מֵת מֻשְׁכָּב עַל־מִטָּתוֹ: 33 וַיָּבֹא וַיִּסְגֹּר הַדֶּלֶת בְּעַד שְׁנֵיהֶם וַיִּתְפַּלֵּל אֶל־יְהוָה: 34 וַיַּעַל וַיִּשְׁכַּב עַל־הַיֶּלֶד וַיָּשֶׂם פִּיו עַל־פִּיו וְעֵינָיו עַל־עֵינָיו וְכַפָּיו עַל־כַּפָּו וַיִּגְהַר עָלָיו וַיָּחָם בְּשַׂר הַיָּלֶד: 35 וַיָּשָׁב וַיֵּלֶךְ בַּבַּיִת אַחַת הֵנָּה וְאַחַת הֵנָּה וַיַּעַל וַיִּגְהַר עָלָיו וַיְזוֹרֵר הַנַּעַר עַד־שֶׁבַע פְּעָמִים וַיִּפְקַח הַנַּעַר אֶת־עֵינָיו: 36 וַיִּקְרָא אֶל־גֵּיחֲזִי וַיֹּאמֶר קְרָא אֶל־הַשֻּׁנַמִּית הַזֹּאת וַיִּקְרָאֶהָ וַתָּבוֹא אֵלָיו וַיֹּאמֶר שְׂאִי בְנֵךְ: 37 וַתָּבֹא וַתִּפֹּל עַל־רַגְלָיו וַתִּשְׁתַּחוּ אָרְצָה וַתִּשָּׂא אֶת־בְּנָהּ וַתֵּצֵא: פ

38 וֶאֱלִישָׁע שָׁב הַגִּלְגָּלָה וְהָרָעָב בָּאָרֶץ וּבְנֵי הַנְּבִיאִים יֹשְׁבִים לְפָנָיו וַיֹּאמֶר לְנַעֲרוֹ שְׁפֹת הַסִּיר הַגְּדוֹלָה וּבַשֵּׁל נָזִיד לִבְנֵי הַנְּבִיאִים: 39 וַיֵּצֵא אֶחָד אֶל־הַשָּׂדֶה לְלַקֵּט אֹרֹת וַיִּמְצָא גֶּפֶן שָׂדֶה וַיְלַקֵּט מִמֶּנּוּ פַּקֻּעֹת שָׂדֶה מְלֹא בִגְדוֹ וַיָּבֹא וַיְפַלַּח אֶל־סִיר הַנָּזִיד כִּי־לֹא יָדָעוּ: 40 וַיִּצְקוּ לַאֲנָשִׁים לֶאֱכוֹל וַיְהִי כְּאָכְלָם מֵהַנָּזִיד וְהֵמָּה צָעָקוּ וַיֹּאמְרוּ מָוֶת בַּסִּיר אִישׁ הָאֱלֹהִים וְלֹא יָכְלוּ לֶאֱכֹל: 41 וַיֹּאמֶר וּקְחוּ־קֶמַח וַיַּשְׁלֵךְ אֶל־הַסִּיר וַיֹּאמֶר צַק לָעָם וְיֹאכֵלוּ וְלֹא הָיָה דָּבָר רָע בַּסִּיר: ס 42 וְאִישׁ בָּא מִבַּעַל שָׁלִשָׁה וַיָּבֵא לְאִישׁ הָאֱלֹהִים לֶחֶם בִּכּוּרִים עֶשְׂרִים־לֶחֶם שְׂעֹרִים וְכַרְמֶל בְּצִקְלֹנוֹ וַיֹּאמֶר תֵּן לָעָם וְיֹאכֵלוּ: 43 וַיֹּאמֶר מְשָׁרְתוֹ מָה אֶתֵּן זֶה לִפְנֵי מֵאָה אִישׁ וַיֹּאמֶר תֵּן לָעָם וְיֹאכֵלוּ כִּי כֹה אָמַר יְהוָה אָכֹל וְהוֹתֵר: 44 וַיִּתֵּן לִפְנֵיהֶם וַיֹּאכְלוּ וַיּוֹתִרוּ כִּדְבַר יְהוָה: פ

ה וְנַעֲמָן שַׂר־צְבָא מֶלֶךְ־אֲרָם הָיָה אִישׁ גָּדוֹל לִפְנֵי אֲדֹנָיו וּנְשֻׂא פָנִים כִּי־בוֹ נָתַן־יְהוָה תְּשׁוּעָה לַאֲרָם וְהָאִישׁ הָיָה גִּבּוֹר חַיִל מְצֹרָע: 2 וַאֲרָם יָצְאוּ גְדוּדִים וַיִּשְׁבּוּ מֵאֶרֶץ יִשְׂרָאֵל נַעֲרָה קְטַנָּה וַתְּהִי

from the land of Israel. She waited on Naaman's wife. ³ Then she said to her mistress, "If only my master *were* with the prophet who *is* in Samaria! For he would heal him of his leprosy." ⁴ And *Naaman* went in and told his master, saying, "Thus and thus said the girl who *is* from the land of Israel."

⁵ Then the king of Syria said, "Go now, and I will send a letter to the king of Israel."

So he departed and took with him ten talents of silver, six thousand *shekels* of gold, and ten changes of clothing. ⁶ Then he brought the letter to the king of Israel, which said,

Now be advised, when this letter comes to you, that I have sent Naaman my servant to you, that you may heal him of his leprosy.

⁷ And it happened, when the king of Israel read the letter, that he tore his clothes and said, "*Am* I God, to kill and make alive, that this man sends a man to me to heal him of his leprosy? Therefore please consider, and see how he seeks a quarrel with me."

⁸ So it was, when Elisha the man of God heard that the king of Israel had torn his clothes, that he sent to the king, saying, "Why have you torn your clothes? Please let him come to me, and he shall know that there is a prophet in Israel."

⁹ Then Naaman went with his horses and chariot, and he stood at the door of Elisha's house. ¹⁰ And Elisha sent a messenger to him, saying, "Go and wash in the Jordan seven times, and your flesh shall be restored to you, and *you shall* be clean." ¹¹ But Naaman became furious, and went away and said, "Indeed, I said to myself, 'He will surely come out *to me,* and stand and call on the name of the LORD his God, and wave his hand over the place, and heal the leprosy.' ¹² *Are* not the Abanah and the Pharpar, the rivers of Damascus, better than all the waters of Israel? Could I not wash in them and be clean?" So he turned and went away in a rage. ¹³ And his servants came near and spoke to him, and said, "My father, *if* the prophet had told you *to do* something great, would you not have done *it?* How much more then, when he says to you, 'Wash, and be clean'?" ¹⁴ So he went down and dipped seven times in the Jordan, according to the saying of the man of God; and his flesh was restored like the flesh of a little child, and he was clean.

¹⁵ And he returned to the man of God, he and all his aides, and came and stood before him; and he said, "Indeed, now I know that *there is* no God in all the earth, except in Israel; now therefore, please take a gift from your servant."

לִפְנֵי אֵשֶׁת נַעֲמָן: ³ וַתֹּאמֶר אֶל־גְּבִרְתָּהּ אַחֲלֵי אֲדֹנִי לִפְנֵי הַנָּבִיא אֲשֶׁר בְּשֹׁמְרוֹן אָז יֶאֱסֹף אֹתוֹ מִצָּרַעְתּוֹ: ⁴ וַיָּבֹא וַיַּגֵּד לַאדֹנָיו לֵאמֹר כָּזֹאת וְכָזֹאת דִּבְּרָה הַנַּעֲרָה אֲשֶׁר מֵאֶרֶץ יִשְׂרָאֵל: ⁵ וַיֹּאמֶר מֶלֶךְ־אֲרָם לֶךְ־בֹּא וְאֶשְׁלְחָה סֵפֶר אֶל־מֶלֶךְ יִשְׂרָאֵל וַיֵּלֶךְ וַיִּקַּח בְּיָדוֹ עֶשֶׂר כִּכְּרֵי־כֶסֶף וְשֵׁשֶׁת אֲלָפִים זָהָב וְעֶשֶׂר חֲלִיפוֹת בְּגָדִים: ⁶ וַיָּבֵא הַסֵּפֶר אֶל־מֶלֶךְ יִשְׂרָאֵל לֵאמֹר וְעַתָּה כְּבוֹא הַסֵּפֶר הַזֶּה אֵלֶיךָ הִנֵּה שָׁלַחְתִּי אֵלֶיךָ אֶת־נַעֲמָן עַבְדִּי וַאֲסַפְתּוֹ מִצָּרַעְתּוֹ:

⁷ וַיְהִי כִּקְרֹא מֶלֶךְ־יִשְׂרָאֵל אֶת־הַסֵּפֶר וַיִּקְרַע בְּגָדָיו וַיֹּאמֶר הַאֱלֹהִים אָנִי לְהָמִית וּלְהַחֲיוֹת כִּי־זֶה שֹׁלֵחַ אֵלַי לֶאֱסֹף אִישׁ מִצָּרַעְתּוֹ כִּי אַךְ־דְּעוּ־נָא וּרְאוּ כִּי־מִתְאַנֶּה הוּא לִי: ⁸ וַיְהִי כִּשְׁמֹעַ אֱלִישָׁע אִישׁ־הָאֱלֹהִים כִּי־קָרַע מֶלֶךְ־יִשְׂרָאֵל אֶת־בְּגָדָיו וַיִּשְׁלַח אֶל־הַמֶּלֶךְ לֵאמֹר לָמָּה קָרַעְתָּ בְּגָדֶיךָ יָבֹא־נָא אֵלַי וְיֵדַע כִּי יֵשׁ נָבִיא בְּיִשְׂרָאֵל: ⁹ וַיָּבֹא נַעֲמָן בְּסוּסָוֹ וּבְרִכְבּוֹ וַיַּעֲמֹד פֶּתַח־הַבַּיִת לֶאֱלִישָׁע: ¹⁰ וַיִּשְׁלַח אֵלָיו אֱלִישָׁע מַלְאָךְ לֵאמֹר הָלוֹךְ וְרָחַצְתָּ שֶׁבַע־פְּעָמִים בַּיַּרְדֵּן וְיָשֹׁב בְּשָׂרְךָ לְךָ וּטְהָר: ¹¹ וַיִּקְצֹף נַעֲמָן וַיֵּלַךְ וַיֹּאמֶר הִנֵּה אָמַרְתִּי אֵלַי יֵצֵא יָצוֹא וְעָמַד וְקָרָא בְּשֵׁם־יְהוָה אֱלֹהָיו וְהֵנִיף יָדוֹ אֶל־הַמָּקוֹם וְאָסַף הַמְּצֹרָע: ¹² הֲלֹא טוֹב אֲבָנָה וּפַרְפַּר נַהֲרוֹת דַּמֶּשֶׂק מִכֹּל מֵימֵי יִשְׂרָאֵל הֲלֹא־אֶרְחַץ בָּהֶם וְטָהָרְתִּי וַיִּפֶן וַיֵּלֶךְ בְּחֵמָה: ¹³ וַיִּגְּשׁוּ עֲבָדָיו וַיְדַבְּרוּ אֵלָיו וַיֹּאמְרוּ אָבִי דָּבָר גָּדוֹל הַנָּבִיא דִּבֶּר אֵלֶיךָ הֲלוֹא תַעֲשֶׂה וְאַף כִּי־אָמַר אֵלֶיךָ רְחַץ וּטְהָר: ¹⁴ וַיֵּרֶד וַיִּטְבֹּל בַּיַּרְדֵּן שֶׁבַע פְּעָמִים כִּדְבַר אִישׁ הָאֱלֹהִים וַיָּשָׁב בְּשָׂרוֹ כִּבְשַׂר נַעַר קָטֹן וַיִּטְהָר: ¹⁵ וַיָּשָׁב אֶל־אִישׁ הָאֱלֹהִים הוּא וְכָל־מַחֲנֵהוּ וַיָּבֹא וַיַּעֲמֹד לְפָנָיו וַיֹּאמֶר הִנֵּה־נָא יָדַעְתִּי כִּי אֵין אֱלֹהִים בְּכָל־הָאָרֶץ כִּי אִם־בְּיִשְׂרָאֵל

ה 9 בְּסוּסָיו 12 אֲמָנָה

¹⁶But he said, "*As* the LORD lives, before whom I stand, I will receive nothing." And he urged him to take *it,* but he refused.

¹⁷So Naaman said, "Then, if not, please let your servant be given two mule-loads of earth; for your servant will no longer offer either burnt offering or sacrifice to other gods, but to the LORD. ¹⁸Yet in this thing may the LORD pardon your servant: when my master goes into the temple of Rimmon to worship there, and he leans on my hand, and I bow down in the temple of Rimmon—when I bow down in the temple of Rimmon, may the LORD please pardon your servant in this thing."

¹⁹Then he said to him, "Go in peace." So he departed from him a short distance.

²⁰But Gehazi, the servant of Elisha the man of God, said, "Look, my master has spared Naaman this Syrian, while not receiving from his hands what he brought; but *as* the LORD lives, I will run after him and take something from him." ²¹So Gehazi pursued Naaman. When Naaman saw *him* running after him, he got down from the chariot to meet him, and said, "*Is* all well?"

²²And he said, "All *is* well. My master has sent me, saying, 'Indeed, just now two young men of the sons of the prophets have come to me from the mountains of Ephraim. Please give them a talent of silver and two changes of garments.'"

²³So Naaman said, "Please, take two talents." And he urged him, and bound two talents of silver in two bags, with two changes of garments, and handed *them* to two of his servants; and they carried *them* on ahead of him. ²⁴When he came to the citadel, he took *them* from their hand, and stored *them* away in the house; then he let the men go, and they departed. ²⁵Now he went in and stood before his master. Elisha said to him, "Where *did you go,* Gehazi?"

And he said, "Your servant did not go anywhere."

²⁶Then he said to him, "Did not my heart go *with you* when the man turned back from his chariot to meet you? *Is it* time to receive money and to receive clothing, olive groves and vineyards, sheep and oxen, male and female servants? ²⁷Therefore the leprosy of Naaman shall cling to you and your descendants forever." And he went out from his presence leprous, *as white* as snow.

6 And the sons of the prophets said to Elisha, "See now, the place where we dwell with you is too small for us. ²Please, let us go to the Jordan, and let every man take a beam from there, and let us make there a place where we may dwell."

16 וְעַתָּ֕ה קַח־נָ֥א בְרָכָ֖ה מֵאֵ֣ת עַבְדֶּֽךָ׃ וַיֹּ֕אמֶר חַי־יְהֹוָ֞ה אֲשֶׁר־עָמַ֧דְתִּי לְפָנָ֛יו אִם־אֶקָּ֖ח וַיִּפְצַר־בּ֥וֹ לָקַ֖חַת וַיְמָאֵֽן׃ 17 וַיֹּאמֶר֮ נַעֲמָן֒ וָלֹ֕א יֻתַּן־נָ֣א לְעַבְדְּךָ֔ מַשָּׂ֥א צֶֽמֶד־פְּרָדִ֖ים אֲדָמָ֑ה כִּ֣י לֽוֹא־יַעֲשֶׂ֩ה ע֨וֹד עַבְדְּךָ֜ עֹלָ֤ה וָזֶ֙בַח֙ לֵאלֹהִ֣ים אֲחֵרִ֔ים כִּ֖י אִם־לַיהֹוָֽה׃ 18 לַדָּבָ֣ר הַזֶּ֔ה יִסְלַ֥ח יְהֹוָ֖ה לְעַבְדֶּ֑ךָ בְּב֣וֹא אֲדֹנִ֣י בֵית־רִמּוֹן֩ לְהִשְׁתַּחֲוֺ֨ת שָׁ֜מָּה וְה֣וּא ׀ נִשְׁעָ֣ן עַל־יָדִ֗י וְהִֽשְׁתַּחֲוֵ֙יתִי֙ בֵּ֣ית רִמֹּ֔ן בְּהִשְׁתַּחֲוָיָ֙תִי֙ בֵּ֣ית רִמֹּ֔ן יִסְלַֽח־נָ֧א P יְהֹוָ֛ה לְעַבְדְּךָ֖ בַּדָּבָ֥ר הַזֶּֽה׃ 19 וַיֹּ֥אמֶר ל֖וֹ לֵ֣ךְ לְשָׁל֑וֹם וַיֵּ֥לֶךְ מֵאִתּ֖וֹ כִּבְרַת־אָֽרֶץ׃ ס 20 וַיֹּ֣אמֶר גֵּיחֲזִ֗י נַ֙עַר֙ אֱלִישָׁ֣ע אִישׁ־הָאֱלֹהִים֮ הִנֵּ֣ה ׀ חָשַׂ֣ךְ אֲדֹנִי֮ אֶֽת־נַעֲמָ֣ן הָאֲרַמִּ֣י הַזֶּ֔ה מִקַּ֥חַת מִיָּד֖וֹ אֵ֣ת אֲשֶׁר־הֵבִ֑יא חַי־יְהֹוָה֙ כִּֽי־אִם־רַ֣צְתִּי אַחֲרָ֔יו וְלָקַחְתִּ֥י מֵאִתּ֖וֹ מְאֽוּמָה׃ 21 וַיִּרְדֹּ֥ף גֵּיחֲזִ֖י אַחֲרֵ֣י נַֽעֲמָ֑ן וַיִּרְאֶ֤ה נַֽעֲמָן֙ רָ֣ץ אַחֲרָ֔יו וַיִּפֹּ֞ל מֵעַ֧ל הַמֶּרְכָּבָ֛ה לִקְרָאת֖וֹ וַיֹּ֥אמֶר הֲשָׁלֽוֹם׃ 22 וַיֹּ֣אמֶר ׀ שָׁל֗וֹם אֲדֹנִי֮ שְׁלָחַ֣נִי לֵאמֹר֒ הִנֵּ֣ה עַתָּ֡ה זֶ֣ה בָ֣אוּ אֵלַ֡י שְׁנֵֽי־נְעָרִ֞ים מֵהַ֤ר אֶפְרַ֙יִם֙ מִבְּנֵ֣י הַנְּבִיאִ֔ים תְּנָה־נָּ֤א לָהֶם֙ כִּכַּר־כֶּ֔סֶף וּשְׁתֵּ֖י חֲלִפ֥וֹת בְּגָדִֽים׃ 23 וַיֹּ֣אמֶר נַעֲמָ֔ן הוֹאֵ֖ל קַ֣ח כִּכָּרָ֑יִם וַיִּפְרׇץ־בּ֗וֹ וַיָּצַר֩ כִּכְּרַ֨יִם כֶּ֜סֶף בִּשְׁנֵ֣י חֲרִטִ֗ים וּשְׁתֵּי֙ חֲלִפ֣וֹת בְּגָדִ֔ים וַיִּתֵּן֙ אֶל־שְׁנֵ֣י נְעָרָ֔יו וַיִּשְׂא֖וּ לְפָנָֽיו׃ 24 וַיָּבֹא֙ אֶל־הָעֹ֔פֶל וַיִּקַּ֥ח מִיָּדָ֖ם וַיִּפְקֹ֣ד בַּבָּ֑יִת וַיְשַׁלַּ֥ח אֶת־הָאֲנָשִׁ֖ים וַיֵּלֵֽכוּ׃ 25 וְהוּא־בָא֙ וַיַּעֲמֹ֣ד אֶל־אֲדֹנָ֔יו וַיֹּ֤אמֶר אֵלָיו֙ אֱלִישָׁ֔ע מֵאַ֖ן P גֵּחֲזִ֑י וַיֹּ֕אמֶר לֹֽא־הָלַ֥ךְ עַבְדְּךָ֖ אָ֥נֶה וָאָֽנָה׃ 26 וַיֹּ֤אמֶר אֵלָיו֙ לֹא־לִבִּ֣י הָלַ֔ךְ כַּאֲשֶׁ֧ר הָֽפַךְ־אִ֛ישׁ מֵעַ֥ל מֶרְכַּבְתּ֖וֹ לִקְרָאתֶ֑ךָ הַעֵ֞ת לָקַ֤חַת אֶת־הַכֶּ֙סֶף֙ וְלָקַ֣חַת בְּגָדִ֔ים וְזֵיתִ֥ים וּכְרָמִ֖ים וְצֹ֣אן וּבָקָ֑ר וַעֲבָדִ֖ים וּשְׁפָחֽוֹת׃ 27 וְצָרַ֤עַת נַֽעֲמָן֙ תִּֽדְבַּק־בְּךָ֔ וּֽבְזַרְעֲךָ֖ לְעוֹלָ֑ם וַיֵּצֵ֥א מִלְּפָנָ֖יו מְצֹרָ֥ע כַּשָּֽׁלֶג׃ ס

ו וַיֹּאמְר֥וּ בְנֵֽי־הַנְּבִיאִ֖ים אֶל־אֱלִישָׁ֑ע הִנֵּֽה־נָ֣א הַמָּק֗וֹם אֲשֶׁ֨ר אֲנַ֜חְנוּ יֹשְׁבִ֥ים שָׁ֛ם לְפָנֶ֖יךָ צַ֥ר מִמֶּֽנּוּ׃ 2 נֵֽלְכָה־נָּ֣א עַד־הַיַּרְדֵּ֗ן וְנִקְחָ֤ה מִשָּׁם֙ אִ֣ישׁ קוֹרָ֣ה

ה 25 מֵאָן

So he answered, "Go."

3 Then one said, "Please consent to go with your servants."

And he answered, "I will go." 4 So he went with them. And when they came to the Jordan, they cut down trees. 5 But as one was cutting down a tree, the iron ax head fell into the water; and he cried out and said, "Alas, master! For it was borrowed."

6 So the man of God said, "Where did it fall?" And he showed him the place. So he cut off a stick, and threw it in there; and he made the iron float. 7 Therefore he said, "Pick it up for yourself." So he reached out his hand and took it.

8 Now the king of Syria was making war against Israel; and he consulted with his servants, saying, "My camp will be in such and such a place." 9 And the man of God sent to the king of Israel, saying, "Beware that you do not pass this place, for the Syrians are coming down there." 10 Then the king of Israel sent someone to the place of which the man of God had told him. Thus he warned him, and he was watchful there, not just once or twice.

11 Therefore the heart of the king of Syria was greatly troubled by this thing; and he called his servants and said to them, "Will you not show me which of us is for the king of Israel?"

12 And one of his servants said, "None, my lord, O king; but Elisha, the prophet who is in Israel, tells the king of Israel the words that you speak in your bedroom."

13 So he said, "Go and see where he is, that I may send and get him."

And it was told him, saying, "Surely he is in Dothan."

14 Therefore he sent horses and chariots and a great army there, and they came by night and surrounded the city. 15 And when the servant of the man of God arose early and went out, there was an army, surrounding the city with horses and chariots. And his servant said to him, "Alas, my master! What shall we do?"

16 So he answered, "Do not fear, for those who are with us are more than those who are with them." 17 And Elisha prayed, and said, "LORD, I pray, open his eyes that he may see." Then the LORD opened the eyes of the young man, and he saw. And behold, the mountain was full of horses and chariots of fire all around Elisha. 18 So when the Syrians came down to him, Elisha prayed to the LORD, and said, "Strike this people, I pray, with blindness." And He struck them with blindness according to the word of Elisha.

אַחַת וְנַעֲשֶׂה־לָּנוּ שָׁם מָקוֹם לָשֶׁבֶת שָׁם וַיֹּאמֶר
לֵכוּ: 3 וַיֹּאמֶר הָאֶחָד הוֹאֶל נָא וְלֵךְ אֶת־עֲבָדֶיךָ
וַיֹּאמֶר אֲנִי אֵלֵךְ: 4 וַיֵּלֶךְ אִתָּם וַיָּבֹאוּ הַיַּרְדֵּנָה וַיִּגְזְרוּ
הָעֵצִים: 5 וַיְהִי הָאֶחָד מַפִּיל הַקּוֹרָה וְאֶת־הַבַּרְזֶל
נָפַל אֶל־הַמָּיִם וַיִּצְעַק וַיֹּאמֶר אֲהָהּ אֲדֹנִי וְהוּא
שָׁאוּל: 6 וַיֹּאמֶר אִישׁ־הָאֱלֹהִים אָנָה נָפָל וַיַּרְאֵהוּ
אֶת־הַמָּקוֹם וַיִּקְצָב־עֵץ וַיַּשְׁלֶךְ־שָׁמָּה וַיָּצֶף הַבַּרְזֶל:
7 וַיֹּאמֶר הָרֶם לָךְ וַיִּשְׁלַח יָדוֹ וַיִּקָּחֵהוּ: פ

8 וּמֶלֶךְ אֲרָם הָיָה נִלְחָם בְּיִשְׂרָאֵל וַיִּוָּעַץ אֶל־
עֲבָדָיו לֵאמֹר אֶל־מְקוֹם פְּלֹנִי אַלְמֹנִי תַּחֲנֹתִי:
9 וַיִּשְׁלַח אִישׁ הָאֱלֹהִים אֶל־מֶלֶךְ יִשְׂרָאֵל לֵאמֹר
הִשָּׁמֶר מֵעֲבֹר הַמָּקוֹם הַזֶּה כִּי־שָׁם אֲרָם נְחִתִּים:
10 וַיִּשְׁלַח מֶלֶךְ יִשְׂרָאֵל אֶל־הַמָּקוֹם אֲשֶׁר אָמַר־לוֹ
אִישׁ־הָאֱלֹהִים וְהִזְהִירֹהּ וְנִשְׁמַר שָׁם לֹא אַחַת
וְלֹא שְׁתָּיִם: 11 וַיִּסָּעֵר לֵב מֶלֶךְ־אֲרָם עַל־הַדָּבָר
הַזֶּה וַיִּקְרָא אֶל־עֲבָדָיו וַיֹּאמֶר אֲלֵיהֶם הֲלוֹא תַּגִּידוּ
לִי מִי מִשֶּׁלָּנוּ אֶל־מֶלֶךְ יִשְׂרָאֵל: 12 וַיֹּאמֶר אַחַד
מֵעֲבָדָיו לוֹא אֲדֹנִי הַמֶּלֶךְ כִּי־אֱלִישָׁע הַנָּבִיא אֲשֶׁר
בְּיִשְׂרָאֵל יַגִּיד לְמֶלֶךְ יִשְׂרָאֵל אֶת־הַדְּבָרִים אֲשֶׁר
תְּדַבֵּר בַּחֲדַר מִשְׁכָּבֶךָ: 13 וַיֹּאמֶר לְכוּ וּרְאוּ אֵיכֹה
הוּא וְאֶשְׁלַח וְאֶקָּחֵהוּ וַיֻּגַּד־לוֹ לֵאמֹר הִנֵּה בְדֹתָן:
14 וַיִּשְׁלַח־שָׁמָּה סוּסִים וְרֶכֶב וְחַיִל כָּבֵד וַיָּבֹאוּ
לַיְלָה וַיַּקִּפוּ עַל־הָעִיר: 15 וַיַּשְׁכֵּם מְשָׁרֵת אִישׁ
הָאֱלֹהִים לָקוּם וַיֵּצֵא וְהִנֵּה־חַיִל סוֹבֵב אֶת־הָעִיר
וְסוּס וָרָכֶב וַיֹּאמֶר נַעֲרוֹ אֵלָיו אֲהָהּ אֲדֹנִי אֵיכָה
נַעֲשֶׂה: 16 וַיֹּאמֶר אַל־תִּירָא כִּי רַבִּים אֲשֶׁר אִתָּנוּ
מֵאֲשֶׁר אוֹתָם: 17 וַיִּתְפַּלֵּל אֱלִישָׁע וַיֹּאמַר יְהוָה
פְּקַח־נָא אֶת־עֵינָיו וְיִרְאֶה וַיִּפְקַח יְהוָה אֶת־עֵינֵי
הַנַּעַר וַיַּרְא וְהִנֵּה הָהָר מָלֵא סוּסִים וְרֶכֶב אֵשׁ
סְבִיבֹת אֱלִישָׁע: 18 וַיֵּרְדוּ אֵלָיו וַיִּתְפַּלֵּל אֱלִישָׁע
אֶל־יְהוָה וַיֹּאמַר הַךְ־נָא אֶת־הַגּוֹי־הַזֶּה בַּסַּנְוֵרִים

¹⁹ Now Elisha said to them, "This *is* not the way, nor *is* this the city. Follow me, and I will bring you to the man whom you seek." But he led them to Samaria.

²⁰ So it was, when they had come to Samaria, that Elisha said, "LORD, open the eyes of these *men*, that they may see." And the LORD opened their eyes, and they saw; and there *they were*, inside Samaria!

²¹ Now when the king of Israel saw them, he said to Elisha, "My father, shall I kill *them*? Shall I kill *them*?"

²² But he answered, "You shall not kill *them*. Would you kill those whom you have taken captive with your sword and your bow? Set food and water before them, that they may eat and drink and go to their master." ²³ Then he prepared a great feast for them; and after they ate and drank, he sent them away and they went to their master. So the bands of Syrian *raiders* came no more into the land of Israel.

²⁴ And it happened after this that Ben-Hadad king of Syria gathered all his army, and went up and besieged Samaria. ²⁵ And there was a great famine in Samaria; and indeed they besieged it until a donkey's head was *sold* for eighty *shekels* of silver, and one-fourth of a kab of dove droppings for five *shekels* of silver.

²⁶ Then, as the king of Israel was passing by on the wall, a woman cried out to him, saying, "Help, my lord, O king!"

²⁷ And he said, "If the LORD does not help you, where can I find help for you? From the threshing floor or from the winepress?" ²⁸ Then the king said to her, "What is troubling you?"

And she answered, "This woman said to me, 'Give your son, that we may eat him today, and we will eat my son tomorrow.' ²⁹ So we boiled my son, and ate him. And I said to her on the next day, 'Give your son, that we may eat him'; but she has hidden her son."

³⁰ Now it happened, when the king heard the words of the woman, that he tore his clothes; and as he passed by on the wall, the people looked, and there underneath *he had* sackcloth on his body. ³¹ Then he said, "God do so to me and more also, if the head of Elisha the son of Shaphat remains on him today!"

³² But Elisha was sitting in his house, and the elders were sitting with him. And *the king* sent a man ahead of him, but before the messenger came to him, he said to the elders, "Do you see how this son of a murderer has sent someone to take away my head? Look, when the messenger comes, shut the door, and hold him fast at the door. *Is* not the sound of his master's feet behind him?" ³³ And

19 וַיֹּאמֶר אֲלֵהֶם אֱלִישָׁע לֹא זֶה הַדֶּרֶךְ וְלֹא זֹה הָעִיר לְכוּ אַחֲרַי וְאוֹלִיכָה אֶתְכֶם אֶל־הָאִישׁ אֲשֶׁר תְּבַקֵּשׁוּן וַיֹּלֶךְ אוֹתָם שֹׁמְרוֹנָה: 20 וַיְהִי כְּבֹאָם שֹׁמְרוֹן וַיֹּאמֶר אֱלִישָׁע יְהֹוָה פְּקַח אֶת־עֵינֵי־אֵלֶּה וְיִרְאוּ וַיִּפְקַח יְהֹוָה אֶת־עֵינֵיהֶם וַיִּרְאוּ וְהִנֵּה בְּתוֹךְ שֹׁמְרוֹן: 21 וַיֹּאמֶר מֶלֶךְ־יִשְׂרָאֵל אֶל־אֱלִישָׁע כִּרְאֹתוֹ אוֹתָם הַאַכֶּה אַכֶּה אָבִי: 22 וַיֹּאמֶר לֹא תַכֶּה הַאֲשֶׁר שָׁבִיתָ בְּחַרְבְּךָ וּבְקַשְׁתְּךָ אַתָּה מַכֶּה שִׂים לֶחֶם וָמַיִם לִפְנֵיהֶם וְיֹאכְלוּ וְיִשְׁתּוּ וְיֵלְכוּ אֶל־אֲדֹנֵיהֶם: 23 וַיִּכְרֶה לָהֶם כֵּרָה גְדוֹלָה וַיֹּאכְלוּ וַיִּשְׁתּוּ וַיְשַׁלְּחֵם וַיֵּלְכוּ אֶל־אֲדֹנֵיהֶם וְלֹא־יָסְפוּ עוֹד גְּדוּדֵי אֲרָם לָבוֹא בְּאֶרֶץ יִשְׂרָאֵל: פ

24 וַיְהִי אַחֲרֵי־כֵן וַיִּקְבֹּץ בֶּן־הֲדַד מֶלֶךְ־אֲרָם אֶת־כָּל־מַחֲנֵהוּ וַיַּעַל וַיָּצַר עַל־שֹׁמְרוֹן: 25 וַיְהִי רָעָב גָּדוֹל בְּשֹׁמְרוֹן וְהִנֵּה צָרִים עָלֶיהָ עַד הֱיוֹת רֹאשׁ־חֲמוֹר בִּשְׁמֹנִים כֶּסֶף וְרֹבַע הַקַּב חֲרֵייוֹנִים בַּחֲמִשָּׁה־כָסֶף: 26 וַיְהִי מֶלֶךְ יִשְׂרָאֵל עֹבֵר עַל־הַחֹמָה וְאִשָּׁה צָעֲקָה אֵלָיו לֵאמֹר הוֹשִׁיעָה אֲדֹנִי הַמֶּלֶךְ: 27 וַיֹּאמֶר אַל־יוֹשִׁעֵךְ יְהֹוָה מֵאַיִן אוֹשִׁיעֵךְ הֲמִן־הַגֹּרֶן אוֹ מִן־הַיָּקֶב: 28 וַיֹּאמֶר־לָהּ הַמֶּלֶךְ מַה־לָּךְ וַתֹּאמֶר הָאִשָּׁה הַזֹּאת אָמְרָה אֵלַי תְּנִי אֶת־בְּנֵךְ וְנֹאכְלֶנּוּ הַיּוֹם וְאֶת־בְּנִי נֹאכַל מָחָר: 29 וַנְּבַשֵּׁל אֶת־בְּנִי וַנֹּאכְלֵהוּ וָאֹמַר אֵלֶיהָ בַּיּוֹם הָאַחֵר תְּנִי אֶת־בְּנֵךְ וְנֹאכְלֶנּוּ וַתַּחְבִּא אֶת־בְּנָהּ: 30 וַיְהִי כִשְׁמֹעַ הַמֶּלֶךְ אֶת־דִּבְרֵי הָאִשָּׁה וַיִּקְרַע אֶת־בְּגָדָיו וְהוּא עֹבֵר עַל־הַחֹמָה וַיַּרְא הָעָם וְהִנֵּה הַשַּׂק עַל־בְּשָׂרוֹ מִבָּיִת: 31 וַיֹּאמֶר כֹּה־יַעֲשֶׂה־לִּי אֱלֹהִים וְכֹה יוֹסִף אִם־יַעֲמֹד רֹאשׁ אֱלִישָׁע בֶּן־שָׁפָט עָלָיו הַיּוֹם: 32 וֶאֱלִישָׁע יֹשֵׁב בְּבֵיתוֹ וְהַזְּקֵנִים יֹשְׁבִים אִתּוֹ וַיִּשְׁלַח אִישׁ מִלְּפָנָיו בְּטֶרֶם יָבֹא הַמַּלְאָךְ אֵלָיו וְהוּא אָמַר אֶל־הַזְּקֵנִים הַרְאִיתֶם כִּי־שָׁלַח בֶּן־הַמְרַצֵּחַ הַזֶּה לְהָסִיר אֶת־רֹאשִׁי רְאוּ כְּבֹא הַמַּלְאָךְ סִגְרוּ הַדֶּלֶת וּלְחַצְתֶּם אֹתוֹ בַּדֶּלֶת הֲלוֹא קוֹל רַגְלֵי אֲדֹנָיו אַחֲרָיו: 33 עוֹדֶנּוּ מְדַבֵּר עִמָּם וְהִנֵּה הַמַּלְאָךְ יֹרֵד אֵלָיו

ו 25 דִּבְיוֹנִים

while he was still talking with them, there was the messenger, coming down to him; and then *the king* said, "Surely this calamity *is* from the LORD; why should I wait for the LORD any longer?"

7 Then Elisha said, "Hear the word of the LORD. Thus says the LORD: 'Tomorrow about this time a seah of fine flour *shall be sold* for a shekel, and two seahs of barley for a shekel, at the gate of Samaria.'"

² So an officer on whose hand the king leaned answered the man of God and said, "Look, *if the* LORD would make windows in heaven, could this thing be?"

And he said, "In fact, you shall see *it* with your eyes, but you shall not eat of it."

³ Now there were four leprous men at the entrance of the gate; and they said to one another, "Why are we sitting here until we die? ⁴ If we say, 'We will enter the city,' the famine *is* in the city, and we shall die there. And if we sit here, we die also. Now therefore, come, let us surrender to the army of the Syrians. If they keep us alive, we shall live; and if they kill us, we shall only die." ⁵ And they rose at twilight to go to the camp of the Syrians; and when they had come to the outskirts of the Syrian camp, to their surprise no one *was* there. ⁶ For the LORD had caused the army of the Syrians to hear the noise of chariots and the noise of horses—the noise of a great army; so they said to one another, "Look, the king of Israel has hired against us the kings of the Hittites and the kings of the Egyptians to attack us!" ⁷ Therefore they arose and fled at twilight, and left the camp intact—their tents, their horses, and their donkeys—and they fled for their lives. ⁸ And when these lepers came to the outskirts of the camp, they went into one tent and ate and drank, and carried from it silver and gold and clothing, and went and hid *them;* then they came back and entered another tent, and carried *some* from there *also,* and went and hid *it.*

⁹ Then they said to one another, "We are not doing right. This day *is* a day of good news, and we remain silent. If we wait until morning light, some punishment will come upon us. Now therefore, come, let us go and tell the king's household." ¹⁰ So they went and called to the gatekeepers of the city, and told them, saying, "We went to the Syrian camp, and surprisingly no one *was* there, not a human sound—only horses and donkeys tied, and the tents intact." ¹¹ And the gatekeepers called out, and they told *it* to the king's household inside.

וַיֹּאמֶר הִנֵּה־זֹאת הָרָעָה מֵאֵת יְהֹוָה מָה־אוֹחִיל לַיהֹוָה עוֹד: ס

ז וַיֹּאמֶר אֱלִישָׁע שִׁמְעוּ דְּבַר־יְהֹוָה כֹּה אָמַר יְהֹוָה כָּעֵת | מָחָר סְאָה־סֹלֶת בְּשֶׁקֶל וְסָאתַיִם שְׂעֹרִים בְּשֶׁקֶל בְּשַׁעַר שֹׁמְרוֹן: ² וַיַּעַן הַשָּׁלִישׁ אֲשֶׁר־לַמֶּלֶךְ נִשְׁעָן עַל־יָדוֹ אֶת־אִישׁ הָאֱלֹהִים וַיֹּאמַר הִנֵּה יְהֹוָה עֹשֶׂה אֲרֻבּוֹת בַּשָּׁמַיִם הֲיִהְיֶה הַדָּבָר הַזֶּה וַיֹּאמֶר הִנְּכָה רֹאֶה בְּעֵינֶיךָ וּמִשָּׁם לֹא תֹאכֵל: ס ³ וְאַרְבָּעָה אֲנָשִׁים הָיוּ מְצֹרָעִים פֶּתַח הַשָּׁעַר וַיֹּאמְרוּ אִישׁ אֶל־רֵעֵהוּ מָה אֲנַחְנוּ יֹשְׁבִים פֹּה עַד־מָתְנוּ: ⁴ אִם־אָמַרְנוּ נָבוֹא הָעִיר וְהָרָעָב בָּעִיר וָמַתְנוּ שָׁם וְאִם־יָשַׁבְנוּ פֹה וָמָתְנוּ וְעַתָּה לְכוּ וְנִפְּלָה אֶל־מַחֲנֵה אֲרָם אִם־יְחַיֻּנוּ נִחְיֶה וְאִם־יְמִיתֻנוּ וָמָתְנוּ: ⁵ וַיָּקוּמוּ בַנֶּשֶׁף לָבוֹא אֶל־מַחֲנֵה אֲרָם וַיָּבֹאוּ עַד־קְצֵה מַחֲנֵה אֲרָם וְהִנֵּה אֵין־שָׁם אִישׁ: ⁶ וַאדֹנָי הִשְׁמִיעַ | אֶת־מַחֲנֵה אֲרָם קוֹל רֶכֶב קוֹל סוּס קוֹל חַיִל גָּדוֹל וַיֹּאמְרוּ אִישׁ אֶל־אָחִיו הִנֵּה שָׂכַר־עָלֵינוּ מֶלֶךְ יִשְׂרָאֵל אֶת־מַלְכֵי הַחִתִּים וְאֶת־מַלְכֵי מִצְרַיִם לָבוֹא עָלֵינוּ: ⁷ וַיָּקוּמוּ וַיָּנוּסוּ בַנֶּשֶׁף וַיַּעַזְבוּ אֶת־אָהֳלֵיהֶם וְאֶת־סוּסֵיהֶם וְאֶת־חֲמֹרֵיהֶם הַמַּחֲנֶה כַּאֲשֶׁר־הִיא וַיָּנֻסוּ אֶל־נַפְשָׁם: ⁸ וַיָּבֹאוּ הַמְצֹרָעִים הָאֵלֶּה עַד־קְצֵה הַמַּחֲנֶה וַיָּבֹאוּ אֶל־אֹהֶל אֶחָד וַיֹּאכְלוּ וַיִּשְׁתּוּ וַיִּשְׂאוּ מִשָּׁם כֶּסֶף וְזָהָב וּבְגָדִים וַיֵּלְכוּ וַיַּטְמִנוּ וַיָּשֻׁבוּ וַיָּבֹאוּ אֶל־אֹהֶל אַחֵר וַיִּשְׂאוּ מִשָּׁם וַיֵּלְכוּ וַיַּטְמִנוּ: ⁹ וַיֹּאמְרוּ אִישׁ אֶל־רֵעֵהוּ לֹא־כֵן | אֲנַחְנוּ עֹשִׂים הַיּוֹם הַזֶּה יוֹם־בְּשֹׂרָה הוּא וַאֲנַחְנוּ מַחְשִׁים וְחִכִּינוּ עַד־אוֹר הַבֹּקֶר וּמְצָאָנוּ עָווֹן וְעַתָּה לְכוּ וְנָבֹאָה וְנַגִּידָה בֵּית הַמֶּלֶךְ: ¹⁰ וַיָּבֹאוּ וַיִּקְרְאוּ אֶל־שֹׁעֵר הָעִיר וַיַּגִּידוּ לָהֶם לֵאמֹר בָּאנוּ אֶל־מַחֲנֵה אֲרָם וְהִנֵּה אֵין־שָׁם אִישׁ וְקוֹל אָדָם כִּי אִם־הַסּוּס אָסוּר וְהַחֲמוֹר אָסוּר וְאֹהָלִים כַּאֲשֶׁר־הֵמָּה: ¹¹ וַיִּקְרָא הַשֹּׁעֲרִים וַיַּגִּידוּ בֵּית הַמֶּלֶךְ פְּנִימָה:

¹²So the king arose in the night and said to his servants, "Let me now tell you what the Syrians have done to us. They know that we *are* hungry; therefore they have gone out of the camp to hide themselves in the field, saying, 'When they come out of the city, we shall catch them alive, and get into the city.'"

¹³And one of his servants answered and said, "Please, let several *men* take five of the remaining horses which are left in the city. Look, they *may either become* like all the multitude of Israel that are left in it; or indeed, *I say,* they *may become* like all the multitude of Israel left from those who are consumed; so let us send them and see." ¹⁴Therefore they took two chariots with horses; and the king sent them in the direction of the Syrian army, saying, "Go and see." ¹⁵And they went after them to the Jordan; and indeed all the road *was* full of garments and weapons which the Syrians had thrown away in their haste. So the messengers returned and told the king. ¹⁶Then the people went out and plundered the tents of the Syrians. So a seah of fine flour was *sold* for a shekel, and two seahs of barley for a shekel, according to the word of the LORD.

¹⁷Now the king had appointed the officer on whose hand he leaned to have charge of the gate. But the people trampled him in the gate, and he died, just as the man of God had said, who spoke when the king came down to him. ¹⁸So it happened just as the man of God had spoken to the king, saying, "Two seahs of barley for a shekel, and a seah of fine flour for a shekel, shall be *sold* tomorrow about this time in the gate of Samaria."

¹⁹Then that officer had answered the man of God, and said, "Now look, *if* the LORD would make windows in heaven, could such a thing be?"

And he had said, "In fact, you shall see *it* with your eyes, but you shall not eat of it." ²⁰And so it happened to him, for the people trampled him in the gate, and he died.

8 Then Elisha spoke to the woman whose son he had restored to life, saying, "Arise and go, you and your household, and stay wherever you can; for the LORD has called for a famine, and furthermore, it will come upon the land for seven years." ²So the woman arose and did according to the saying of the man of God, and she went with her household and dwelt in the land of the Philistines seven years.

³It came to pass, at the end of seven years, that the woman returned from the land of the Philistines; and she went to make an appeal to the king for her house and for her land. ⁴Then the king

12 וַיָּ֨קָם הַמֶּ֜לֶךְ לַ֗יְלָה וַיֹּ֨אמֶר֙ אֶל־עֲבָדָ֔יו אַגִּֽידָה־נָּ֣א לָכֶ֔ם אֵ֛ת אֲשֶׁר־עָ֥שׂוּ לָ֖נוּ אֲרָ֑ם יָדְע֞וּ כִּֽי־רְעֵבִ֣ים אֲנַ֗חְנוּ וַיֵּצְא֤וּ מִן־הַֽמַּחֲנֶה֙ לְהֵחָבֵ֣ה בַהשָּׂדֶ֣הʰ לֵאמֹ֔ר כִּֽי־יֵצְא֤וּ מִן־הָעִיר֙ וְנִתְפְּשֵׂ֣ם חַיִּ֔ים וְאֶל־הָעִ֖יר נָבֹֽא׃

13 וַיַּ֩עַן֩ אֶחָ֨ד מֵעֲבָדָ֜יו וַיֹּ֗אמֶר וְיִקְחוּ־נָ֞א חֲמִשָּׁ֣ה מִן־הַסּוּסִים֮ הַנִּשְׁאָרִים֮ אֲשֶׁ֣ר נִשְׁאֲרוּ־בָהּ֒ הִנָּ֗ם כְּכָל־הֲההָמ֨וֹןʰ יִשְׂרָאֵל֙ אֲשֶׁ֣ר נִשְׁאֲרוּ־בָ֔הּ הִנָּ֕ם כְּכָל־הֲמ֥וֹן יִשְׂרָאֵ֖ל אֲשֶׁר־תָּ֑מּוּ וְנִשְׁלְחָ֖ה וְנִרְאֶֽה׃ 14 וַיִּקְח֗וּ שְׁנֵ֛י רֶ֥כֶב סוּסִ֖ים וַיִּשְׁלַ֣ח הַמֶּ֑לֶךְ אַחֲרֵ֥י מַֽחֲנֵה־אֲרָ֖ם לֵאמֹ֥ר לְכ֥וּ וּרְאֽוּ׃ 15 וַיֵּלְכ֣וּ אַחֲרֵיהֶם֮ עַד־הַיַּרְדֵּן֒ וְהִנֵּ֣ה כָל־הַדֶּ֗רֶךְ מְלֵאָ֤ה בְגָדִים֙ וְכֵלִ֔ים אֲשֶׁר־הִשְׁלִ֥יכוּ אֲרָ֖ם בְּהֵֽחָפְזָ֑םʰ וַיָּשֻׁ֨בוּ֙ הַמַּלְאָכִ֔ים וַיַּגִּ֖דוּ לַמֶּֽלֶךְ׃ 16 וַיֵּצֵ֣א הָעָ֔ם וַיָּבֹ֕זּוּ אֵ֖ת מַחֲנֵ֣ה אֲרָ֑ם וַֽיְהִ֨י סְאָֽה־סֹ֜לֶת בְּשֶׁ֗קֶל וְסָאתַ֧יִם שְׂעֹרִ֛ים בְּשֶׁ֖קֶל כִּדְבַ֥ר יְהוָֽה׃ 17 וְהַמֶּ֩לֶךְ֩ הִפְקִ֨יד אֶת־הַשָּׁלִ֜ישׁ אֲשֶׁר־נִשְׁעָ֤ן עַל־יָדוֹ֙ עַל־הַשַּׁ֔עַר וַיִּרְמְסֻ֧הוּ הָעָ֛ם בַּשַּׁ֖עַר וַיָּמֹ֑ת כַּֽאֲשֶׁ֤ר דִּבֶּר֙ אִ֣ישׁ הָאֱלֹהִ֔ים אֲשֶׁ֣ר דִּבֶּ֔ר בְּרֶ֥דֶת הַמֶּ֖לֶךְ אֵלָֽיו׃ 18 וַיְהִ֗י כְּדַבֵּר֙ אִ֣ישׁ הָאֱלֹהִ֔ים אֶל־הַמֶּ֖לֶךְ לֵאמֹ֑ר סָאתַ֨יִם שְׂעֹרִ֜ים בְּשֶׁ֗קֶל וּֽסְאָֽה־סֹ֨לֶת֙ בְּשֶׁ֔קֶל יִהְיֶה֙ כָּעֵ֣ת מָחָ֔ר בְּשַׁ֖עַר שֹׁמְרֽוֹן׃ 19 וַיַּ֨עַן הַשָּׁלִ֜ישׁ אֶת־אִ֣ישׁ הָאֱלֹהִים֮ וַיֹּאמַר֒ וְהִנֵּ֣ה יְהוָ֗ה עֹשֶׂ֤ה אֲרֻבּוֹת֙ בַּשָּׁמַ֔יִם הֲיִהְיֶ֖ה כַּדָּבָ֣ר הַזֶּ֑ה וַיֹּ֗אמֶר הִנְּךָ֤ רֹאֶה֙ בְּעֵינֶ֔יךָ וּמִשָּׁ֖ם לֹ֥א תֹאכֵֽל׃ 20 וַיְהִי־ל֣וֹ כֵּ֔ן וַיִּרְמְס֨וּ אֹת֥וֹ הָעָ֛ם בַּשַּׁ֖עַר וַיָּמֹֽת׃ ס

ח וֶאֱלִישָׁ֡ע דִּבֶּ֣ר אֶל־הָאִשָּׁה֩ אֲשֶׁר־הֶחֱיָ֨ה אֶת־בְּנָ֜הּ לֵאמֹ֗ר ק֤וּמִי וּלְכִי֙ *אתי*ʰ וּבֵיתֵ֔ךְ וְג֖וּרִי בַּאֲשֶׁ֣ר תָּג֑וּרִי כִּֽי־קָרָ֤א יְהוָה֙ לָֽרָעָ֔ב וְגַם־בָּ֥א אֶל־הָאָ֖רֶץ שֶׁ֥בַע שָׁנִֽים׃ 2 וַתָּ֣קָם הָֽאִשָּׁ֗ה וַתַּ֛עַשׂ כִּדְבַ֥ר אִ֣ישׁ הָאֱלֹהִ֑ים וַתֵּ֤לֶךְ הִיא֙ וּבֵיתָ֔הּ וַתָּ֥גָר בְּאֶֽרֶץ־פְּלִשְׁתִּ֖ים שֶׁ֥בַע שָׁנִֽים׃ 3 וַיְהִ֗י מִקְצֵה֙ שֶׁ֣בַע שָׁנִ֔ים וַתָּ֥שָׁב הָאִשָּׁ֖ה מֵאֶ֣רֶץ פְּלִשְׁתִּ֑ים וַתֵּצֵ֗א לִצְעֹ֤ק אֶל־הַמֶּ֨לֶךְ֙ אֶל־בֵּיתָ֖הּ וְאֶל־שָׂדָֽהּ׃ 4 וְהַמֶּ֣לֶךְ מְדַבֵּ֔ר אֶל־גֵּחֲזִ֗י

talked with Gehazi, the servant of the man of God, saying, "Tell me, please, all the great things Elisha has done." ⁵Now it happened, as he was telling the king how he had restored the dead to life, that there was the woman whose son he had restored to life, appealing to the king for her house and for her land. And Gehazi said, "My lord, O king, this *is* the woman, and this *is* her son whom Elisha restored to life." ⁶And when the king asked the woman, she told him.

So the king appointed a certain officer for her, saying, "Restore all that *was* hers, and all the proceeds of the field from the day that she left the land until now."

⁷Then Elisha went to Damascus, and Ben-Hadad king of Syria was sick; and it was told him, saying, "The man of God has come here." ⁸And the king said to Hazael, "Take a present in your hand, and go to meet the man of God, and inquire of the LORD by him, saying, 'Shall I recover from this disease?'" ⁹So Hazael went to meet him and took a present with him, of every good thing of Damascus, forty camel-loads; and he came and stood before him, and said, "Your son Ben-Hadad king of Syria has sent me to you, saying, 'Shall I recover from this disease?'"

¹⁰And Elisha said to him, "Go, say to him, 'You shall certainly recover.' However the LORD has shown me that he will really die." ¹¹Then he set his countenance in a stare until he was ashamed; and the man of God wept. ¹²And Hazael said, "Why is my lord weeping?"

He answered, "Because I know the evil that you will do to the children of Israel: Their strongholds you will set on fire, and their young men you will kill with the sword; and you will dash their children, and rip open their women with child."

¹³So Hazael said, "But what *is* your servant—a dog, that he should do this gross thing?"

And Elisha answered, "The LORD has shown me that you *will become* king over Syria."

¹⁴Then he departed from Elisha, and came to his master, who said to him, "What did Elisha say to you?" And he answered, "He told me you would surely recover." ¹⁵But it happened on the next day that he took a thick cloth and dipped *it* in water, and spread *it* over his face so that he died; and Hazael reigned in his place.

¹⁶Now in the fifth year of Joram the son of Ahab, king of Israel, Jehoshaphat *having been* king of Judah, Jehoram the son of Jehoshaphat began to reign as king of Judah. ¹⁷He was thirty-two years old when he became king, and he reigned eight years in Jerusalem. ¹⁸And he walked in the way of

נַעַר אִישׁ־הָאֱלֹהִים לֵאמֹר סַפְּרָה־נָּא לִי אֵת כָּל־הַגְּדֹלוֹת אֲשֶׁר־עָשָׂה אֱלִישָׁע: 5 וַיְהִי הוּא מְסַפֵּר לַמֶּלֶךְ אֵת אֲשֶׁר־הֶחֱיָה אֶת־הַמֵּת וְהִנֵּה הָאִשָּׁה אֲשֶׁר־הֶחֱיָה אֶת־בְּנָהּ צֹעֶקֶת אֶל־הַמֶּלֶךְ עַל־בֵּיתָהּ וְעַל־שָׂדָהּ וַיֹּאמֶר גֵּחֲזִי אֲדֹנִי הַמֶּלֶךְ זֹאת הָאִשָּׁה וְזֶה־בְּנָהּ אֲשֶׁר־הֶחֱיָה אֱלִישָׁע: 6 וַיִּשְׁאַל הַמֶּלֶךְ לָאִשָּׁה וַתְּסַפֶּר־לוֹ וַיִּתֶּן־לָהּ הַמֶּלֶךְ סָרִיס אֶחָד לֵאמֹר הָשֵׁיב אֶת־כָּל־אֲשֶׁר־לָהּ וְאֵת כָּל־תְּבוּאֹת הַשָּׂדֶה מִיּוֹם עָזְבָה אֶת־הָאָרֶץ וְעַד־עָתָּה: פ

7 וַיָּבֹא אֱלִישָׁע דַּמֶּשֶׂק וּבֶן־הֲדַד מֶלֶךְ־אֲרָם חֹלֶה וַיֻּגַּד־לוֹ לֵאמֹר בָּא אִישׁ הָאֱלֹהִים עַד־הֵנָּה: 8 וַיֹּאמֶר הַמֶּלֶךְ אֶל־חֲזָהאֵל קַח בְּיָדְךָ מִנְחָה וְלֵךְ לִקְרַאת אִישׁ הָאֱלֹהִים וְדָרַשְׁתָּ אֶת־יְהוָה מֵאוֹתוֹ לֵאמֹר הַאֶחְיֶה מֵחֳלִי זֶה: 9 וַיֵּלֶךְ חֲזָהאֵל לִקְרָאתוֹ וַיִּקַּח מִנְחָה בְיָדוֹ וְכָל־טוּב דַּמֶּשֶׂק מַשָּׂא אַרְבָּעִים גָּמָל וַיָּבֹא וַיַּעֲמֹד לְפָנָיו וַיֹּאמֶר בִּנְךָ בֶן־הֲדַד מֶלֶךְ־אֲרָם שְׁלָחַנִי אֵלֶיךָ לֵאמֹר הַאֶחְיֶה מֵחֳלִי זֶה: 10 וַיֹּאמֶר אֵלָיו אֱלִישָׁע לֵךְ אֱמָר־לֹא חָיֹה תִחְיֶה וְהִרְאַנִי יְהוָה כִּי־מוֹת יָמוּת: 11 וַיַּעֲמֵד אֶת־פָּנָיו וַיָּשֶׂם עַד־בֹּשׁ וַיֵּבְךְּ אִישׁ הָאֱלֹהִים: 12 וַיֹּאמֶר חֲזָהאֵל מַדּוּעַ אֲדֹנִי בֹכֶה וַיֹּאמֶר כִּי־יָדַעְתִּי אֵת אֲשֶׁר־תַּעֲשֶׂה לִבְנֵי יִשְׂרָאֵל רָעָה מִבְצְרֵיהֶם תְּשַׁלַּח בָּאֵשׁ וּבַחֻרֵיהֶם בַּחֶרֶב תַּהֲרֹג וְעֹלְלֵיהֶם תְּרַטֵּשׁ וְהָרֹתֵיהֶם תְּבַקֵּעַ: 13 וַיֹּאמֶר חֲזָהאֵל כִּי מָה עַבְדְּךָ הַכֶּלֶב כִּי יַעֲשֶׂה הַדָּבָר הַגָּדוֹל הַזֶּה וַיֹּאמֶר אֱלִישָׁע הִרְאַנִי יְהוָה אֹתְךָ מֶלֶךְ עַל־אֲרָם: 14 וַיֵּלֶךְ מֵאֵת אֱלִישָׁע וַיָּבֹא אֶל־אֲדֹנָיו וַיֹּאמֶר לוֹ מָה־אָמַר לְךָ אֱלִישָׁע וַיֹּאמֶר אָמַר לִי חָיֹה תִחְיֶה: 15 וַיְהִי מִמָּחֳרָת וַיִּקַּח הַמַּכְבֵּר וַיִּטְבֹּל בַּמַּיִם וַיִּפְרֹשׂ עַל־פָּנָיו וַיָּמֹת וַיִּמְלֹךְ חֲזָהאֵל תַּחְתָּיו: פ

16 וּבִשְׁנַת חָמֵשׁ לְיוֹרָם בֶּן־אַחְאָב מֶלֶךְ יִשְׂרָאֵל וִיהוֹשָׁפָט מֶלֶךְ יְהוּדָה מָלַךְ יְהוֹרָם בֶּן־יְהוֹשָׁפָט מֶלֶךְ יְהוּדָה: 17 בֶּן־שְׁלֹשִׁים וּשְׁתַּיִם שָׁנָה הָיָה בְמָלְכוֹ וּשְׁמֹנֶה שָׁנָה מָלַךְ בִּירוּשָׁלָםִ: 18 וַיֵּלֶךְ בְּדֶרֶךְ מַלְכֵי יִשְׂרָאֵל כַּאֲשֶׁר עָשׂוּ בֵּית אַחְאָב

ח 10 לוֹ 17 שָׁנִים

the kings of Israel, just as the house of Ahab had done, for the daughter of Ahab was his wife; and he did evil in the sight of the LORD. 19 Yet the LORD would not destroy Judah, for the sake of his servant David, as He promised him to give a lamp to him *and his sons forever.

20 In his days Edom revolted against Judah's authority, and made a king over themselves. 21 So Joram went to Zair, and all his chariots with him. Then he rose by night and attacked the Edomites who had surrounded him and the captains of the chariots; and the troops fled to their tents. 22 Thus Edom has been in revolt against Judah's authority to this day. And Libnah revolted at that time.

23 Now the rest of the acts of Joram, and all that he did, *are they not written in the book of the chronicles of the kings of Judah? 24 So Joram rested with his fathers, and was buried with his fathers in the City of David. Then Ahaziah his son reigned in his place.

25 In the twelfth year of Joram the son of Ahab, king of Israel, Ahaziah the son of Jehoram, king of Judah, began to reign. 26 Ahaziah *was twenty-two years old when he became king, and he reigned one year in Jerusalem. His mother's name *was Athaliah the granddaughter of Omri, king of Israel. 27 And he walked in the way of the house of Ahab, and did evil in the sight of the LORD, like the house of Ahab, for he *was the son-in-law of the house of Ahab.

28 Now he went with Joram the son of Ahab to war against Hazael king of Syria at Ramoth Gilead; and the Syrians wounded Joram. 29 Then King Joram went back to Jezreel to recover from the wounds which the Syrians had inflicted on him at Ramah, when he fought against Hazael king of Syria. And Ahaziah the son of Jehoram, king of Judah, went down to see Joram the son of Ahab in Jezreel, because he was sick.

9 And Elisha the prophet called one of the sons of the prophets, and said to him, "Get yourself ready, take this flask of oil in your hand, and go to Ramoth Gilead. 2 Now when you arrive at that place, look there for Jehu the son of Jehoshaphat, the son of Nimshi, and go in and make him rise up from among his associates, and take him to an inner room. 3 Then take the flask of oil, and pour *it on his head, and say, 'Thus says the LORD: "I have anointed you king over Israel."' Then open the door and flee, and do not delay."

כִּי בַת־אַחְאָב הָיְתָה־לּוֹ לְאִשָּׁה וַיַּעַשׂ הָרַע בְּעֵינֵי יְהוָה: 19 וְלֹא־אָבָה יְהוָה לְהַשְׁחִית אֶת־יְהוּדָה לְמַעַן דָּוִד עַבְדּוֹ כַּאֲשֶׁר אָמַר־לוֹ לָתֵת לוֹ נִיר לְבָנָיו כָּל־הַיָּמִים: 20 בְּיָמָיו פָּשַׁע אֱדוֹם מִתַּחַת יַד־יְהוּדָה וַיַּמְלִכוּ עֲלֵיהֶם מֶלֶךְ: 21 וַיַּעֲבֹר יוֹרָם צָעִירָה וְכָל־הָרֶכֶב עִמּוֹ וַיְהִי־הוּא קָם לַיְלָה וַיַּכֶּה אֶת־אֱדוֹם הַסֹּבֵיב אֵלָיו וְאֵת שָׂרֵי הָרֶכֶב וַיָּנָס הָעָם לְאֹהָלָיו:

22 וַיִּפְשַׁע אֱדוֹם מִתַּחַת יַד־יְהוּדָה עַד הַיּוֹם הַזֶּה אָז תִּפְשַׁע לִבְנָה בָּעֵת הַהִיא: 23 וְיֶתֶר דִּבְרֵי יוֹרָם וְכָל־אֲשֶׁר עָשָׂה הֲלוֹא־הֵם כְּתוּבִים עַל־סֵפֶר דִּבְרֵי הַיָּמִים לְמַלְכֵי יְהוּדָה: 24 וַיִּשְׁכַּב יוֹרָם עִם־אֲבֹתָיו וַיִּקָּבֵר עִם־אֲבֹתָיו בְּעִיר דָּוִד וַיִּמְלֹךְ אֲחַזְיָהוּ בְנוֹ תַּחְתָּיו: פ

25 בִּשְׁנַת שְׁתֵּים־עֶשְׂרֵה שָׁנָה לְיוֹרָם בֶּן־אַחְאָב מֶלֶךְ יִשְׂרָאֵל מָלַךְ אֲחַזְיָהוּ בֶן־יְהוֹרָם מֶלֶךְ יְהוּדָה: 26 בֶּן־עֶשְׂרִים וּשְׁתַּיִם שָׁנָה אֲחַזְיָהוּ בְמָלְכוֹ וְשָׁנָה אַחַת מָלַךְ בִּירוּשָׁלַ͏ִם וְשֵׁם אִמּוֹ עֲתַלְיָהוּ בַּת־עָמְרִי מֶלֶךְ יִשְׂרָאֵל: 27 וַיֵּלֶךְ בְּדֶרֶךְ בֵּית אַחְאָב וַיַּעַשׂ הָרַע בְּעֵינֵי יְהוָה כְּבֵית אַחְאָב כִּי חֲתַן בֵּית־אַחְאָב הוּא: 28 וַיֵּלֶךְ אֶת־יוֹרָם בֶּן־אַחְאָב לַמִּלְחָמָה עִם־חֲזָהאֵל מֶלֶךְ־אֲרָם בְּרָמֹת גִּלְעָד וַיַּכּוּ אֲרַמִּים אֶת־יוֹרָם: 29 וַיָּשָׁב יוֹרָם הַמֶּלֶךְ לְהִתְרַפֵּא בְיִזְרְעֶאל מִן־הַמַּכִּים אֲשֶׁר יַכֻּהוּ אֲרַמִּים בָּרָמָה בְּהִלָּחֲמוֹ אֶת־חֲזָהאֵל מֶלֶךְ אֲרָם וַאֲחַזְיָהוּ בֶן־יְהוֹרָם מֶלֶךְ יְהוּדָה יָרַד לִרְאוֹת אֶת־יוֹרָם בֶּן־אַחְאָב בְּיִזְרְעֶאל כִּי־חֹלֶה הוּא: פ

ט וֶאֱלִישָׁע הַנָּבִיא קָרָא לְאַחַד מִבְּנֵי הַנְּבִיאִים וַיֹּאמֶר לוֹ חֲגֹר מָתְנֶיךָ וְקַח פַּךְ הַשֶּׁמֶן הַזֶּה בְּיָדֶךָ וְלֵךְ רָמֹת גִּלְעָד: 2 וּבָאתָ שָׁמָּה וּרְאֵה־שָׁם יֵהוּא בֶן־יְהוֹשָׁפָט בֶּן־נִמְשִׁי וּבָאתָ וַהֲקֵמֹתוֹ מִתּוֹךְ אֶחָיו וְהֵבֵיאתָ אֹתוֹ חֶדֶר בְּחָדֶר: 3 וְלָקַחְתָּ פַךְ־הַשֶּׁמֶן וְיָצַקְתָּ עַל־רֹאשׁוֹ וְאָמַרְתָּ כֹּה־אָמַר יְהוָה מְשַׁחְתִּיךָ לְמֶלֶךְ אֶל־יִשְׂרָאֵל וּפָתַחְתָּ הַדֶּלֶת וְנַסְתָּה וְלֹא

⁴So the young man, the servant of the prophet, went to Ramoth Gilead. ⁵And when he arrived, there *were* the captains of the army sitting; and he said, "I have a message for you, Commander."

Jehu said, "For which *one* of us?"

And he said, "For you, Commander." ⁶Then he arose and went into the house. And he poured the oil on his head, and said to him, "Thus says the LORD God of Israel: 'I have anointed you king over the people of the LORD, over Israel. ⁷You shall strike down the house of Ahab your master, that I may avenge the blood of My servants the prophets, and the blood of all the servants of the LORD, at the hand of Jezebel. ⁸For the whole house of Ahab shall perish; and I will cut off from Ahab all the males in Israel, both bond and free. ⁹So I will make the house of Ahab like the house of Jeroboam the son of Nebat, and like the house of Baasha the son of Ahijah. ¹⁰The dogs shall eat Jezebel on the plot *of ground* at Jezreel, and *there shall be* none to bury her.'" And he opened the door and fled.

¹¹Then Jehu came out to the servants of his master, and *one* said to him, "*Is* all well? Why did this madman come to you?"

And he said to them, "You know the man and his babble."

¹²And they said, "A lie! Tell us now."

So he said, "Thus and thus he spoke to me, saying, 'Thus says the LORD: "I have anointed you king over Israel."'"

¹³Then each man hastened to take his garment and put *it* under him on the top of the steps; and they blew trumpets, saying, "Jehu is king!"

¹⁴So Jehu the son of Jehoshaphat, the son of Nimshi, conspired against Joram. (Now Joram had been defending Ramoth Gilead, he and all Israel, against Hazael king of Syria. ¹⁵But King Joram had returned to Jezreel to recover from the wounds which the Syrians had inflicted on him when he fought with Hazael king of Syria.) And Jehu said, "If you are so minded, let no one leave *or* escape from the city to go and tell *it* in Jezreel." ¹⁶So Jehu rode in a chariot and went to Jezreel, for Joram was laid up there; and Ahaziah king of Judah had come down to see Joram.

¹⁷Now a watchman stood on the tower in Jezreel, and he saw the company of Jehu as he came, and said, "I see a company of men."

And Joram said, "Get a horseman and send him to meet them, and let him say, '*Is* it peace?'"

¹⁸So the horseman went to meet him, and said, "Thus says the king: '*Is* it peace?'"

And Jehu said, "What have you to do with peace? Turn around and follow me."

תְּחֶה: ⁴ וַיֵּלֶךְ הַנַּעַר הַנַּעַר הַנָּבִיא רָמֹת גִּלְעָד:
⁵ וַיָּבֹא וְהִנֵּה שָׂרֵי הַחַיִל יֹשְׁבִים וַיֹּאמֶר דָּבָר לִי
אֵלֶיךָ הַשָּׂר וַיֹּאמֶר יֵהוּא אֶל־מִי מִכֻּלָּנוּ וַיֹּאמֶר אֵלֶיךָ
הַשָּׂר: ⁶ וַיָּקָם וַיָּבֹא הַבַּיְתָה וַיִּצֹק הַשֶּׁמֶן אֶל־רֹאשׁוֹ
וַיֹּאמֶר לוֹ כֹּה־אָמַר יְהוָה אֱלֹהֵי יִשְׂרָאֵל מְשַׁחְתִּיךָ
לְמֶלֶךְ אֶל־עַם יְהוָה אֶל־יִשְׂרָאֵל: ⁷ וְהִכִּיתָה אֶת־
בֵּית אַחְאָב אֲדֹנֶיךָ וְנִקַּמְתִּי דְּמֵי | עֲבָדַי הַנְּבִיאִים
וּדְמֵי כָּל־עַבְדֵי יְהוָה מִיַּד אִיזָבֶל: ⁸ וְאָבַד כָּל־
בֵּית אַחְאָב וְהִכְרַתִּי לְאַחְאָב מַשְׁתִּין בְּקִיר וְעָצוּר
וְעָזוּב בְּיִשְׂרָאֵל: ⁹ וְנָתַתִּי אֶת־בֵּית אַחְאָב כְּבֵית
יָרָבְעָם בֶּן־נְבָט וּכְבֵית בַּעְשָׁא בֶן־אֲחִיָּה: ¹⁰ וְאֶת־
אִיזֶבֶל יֹאכְלוּ הַכְּלָבִים בְּחֵלֶק יִזְרְעֶאל וְאֵין קֹבֵר
וַיִּפְתַּח הַדֶּלֶת וַיָּנֹס: ¹¹ וְיֵהוּא יָצָא אֶל־עַבְדֵי אֲדֹנָיו
וַיֹּאמֶר לוֹ הֲשָׁלוֹם מַדּוּעַ בָּא־הַמְשֻׁגָּע הַזֶּה אֵלֶיךָ
וַיֹּאמֶר אֲלֵיהֶם אַתֶּם יְדַעְתֶּם אֶת־הָאִישׁ וְאֶת־
שִׂיחוֹ: ¹² וַיֹּאמְרוּ שֶׁקֶר הַגֶּד־נָא לָנוּ וַיֹּאמֶר כָּזֹאת
וְכָזֹאת אָמַר אֵלַי לֵאמֹר כֹּה אָמַר יְהוָה מְשַׁחְתִּיךָ
לְמֶלֶךְ אֶל־יִשְׂרָאֵל: ¹³ וַיְמַהֲרוּ וַיִּקְחוּ אִישׁ בִּגְדוֹ
וַיָּשִׂימוּ תַחְתָּיו אֶל־גֶּרֶם הַמַּעֲלוֹת וַיִּתְקְעוּ בַּשּׁוֹפָר
וַיֹּאמְרוּ מָלַךְ יֵהוּא: ¹⁴ וַיִּתְקַשֵּׁר יֵהוּא בֶּן־יְהוֹשָׁפָט
בֶּן־נִמְשִׁי אֶל־יוֹרָם וְיוֹרָם הָיָה שֹׁמֵר בְּרָמֹת גִּלְעָד
הוּא וְכָל־יִשְׂרָאֵל מִפְּנֵי חֲזָאֵל מֶלֶךְ־אֲרָם: ¹⁵ וַיָּשָׁב
יְהוֹרָם הַמֶּלֶךְ לְהִתְרַפֵּא בְיִזְרְעֶאל מִן־הַמַּכִּים אֲשֶׁר
יַכֻּהוּ אֲרַמִּים בְּהִלָּחֲמוֹ אֶת־חֲזָאֵל מֶלֶךְ אֲרָם
וַיֹּאמֶר יֵהוּא אִם־יֵשׁ נַפְשְׁכֶם אַל־יֵצֵא פָלִיט מִן־
הָעִיר לָלֶכֶת לַגִּיד בְּיִזְרְעֶאל: ¹⁶ וַיִּרְכַּב יֵהוּא וַיֵּלֶךְ
יִזְרְעֶאלָה כִּי יוֹרָם שֹׁכֵב שָׁמָּה וַאֲחַזְיָה מֶלֶךְ יְהוּדָה
יָרַד לִרְאוֹת אֶת־יוֹרָם: ¹⁷ וְהַצֹּפֶה עֹמֵד עַל־הַמִּגְדָּל
בְּיִזְרְעֶאל וַיַּרְא אֶת־שִׁפְעַת יֵהוּא בְּבֹאוֹ וַיֹּאמֶר
שִׁפְעַת אֲנִי רֹאֶה וַיֹּאמֶר יְהוֹרָם קַח רַכָּב וּשְׁלַח
לִקְרָאתָם וַיֹּאמֶר הֲשָׁלוֹם: ¹⁸ וַיֵּלֶךְ רֹכֵב הַסּוּס
לִקְרָאתוֹ וַיֹּאמֶר כֹּה־אָמַר הַמֶּלֶךְ הֲשָׁלוֹם וַיֹּאמֶר
יֵהוּא מַה־לְּךָ וּלְשָׁלוֹם סֹב אֶל־אַחֲרָי וַיַּגֵּד הַצֹּפֶה

So the watchman reported, saying, "The messenger went to them, but is not coming back."

19 Then he sent out a second horseman who came to them, and said, "Thus says the king: 'Is it peace?' "

And Jehu answered, "What have you to do with peace? Turn around and follow me."

20 So the watchman reported, saying, "He went up to them and is not coming back; and the driving is like the driving of Jehu the son of Nimshi, for he drives furiously!"

21 Then Joram said, "Make ready." And his chariot was made ready. Then Joram king of Israel and Ahaziah king of Judah went out, each in his chariot; and they went out to meet Jehu, and met him on the property of Naboth the Jezreelite. 22 Now it happened, when Joram saw Jehu, that he said, "Is it peace, Jehu?"

So he answered, "What peace, as long as the harlotries of your mother Jezebel and her witchcraft are so many?"

23 Then Joram turned around and fled, and said to Ahaziah, "Treachery, Ahaziah!" 24 Now Jehu drew his bow with full strength and shot Jehoram between his arms; and the arrow came out at his heart, and he sank down in his chariot. 25 Then Jehu said to Bidkar his captain, "Pick him up, and throw him into the tract of the field of Naboth the Jezreelite; for remember, when you and I were riding together behind Ahab his father, that the LORD laid this burden upon him: 26 'Surely I saw yesterday the blood of Naboth and the blood of his sons,' says the LORD, 'and I will repay you in this plot,' says the LORD. Now therefore, take and throw him on the plot of ground, according to the word of the LORD."

27 But when Ahaziah king of Judah saw this, he fled by the road to Beth Haggan. So Jehu pursued him, and said, "Shoot him also in the chariot." And they shot him at the Ascent of Gur, which is by Ibleam. Then he fled to Megiddo, and died there. 28 And his servants carried him in the chariot to Jerusalem, and buried him in his tomb with his fathers in the City of David. 29 In the eleventh year of Joram the son of Ahab, Ahaziah had become king over Judah.

30 Now when Jehu had come to Jezreel, Jezebel heard of it; and she put paint on her eyes and adorned her head, and looked through a window. 31 Then, as Jehu entered at the gate, she said, "Is it peace, Zimri, murderer of your master?"

32 And he looked up at the window, and said, "Who is on my side? Who?" So two or three eunuchs looked out at him. 33 Then he said, "Throw

19 וַיִּשְׁלַח לֵאמֹר בָּא־הַמַּלְאָךְ עַד־הֶם וְלֹא־שָׁב רֹכֵב סוּס שֵׁנִי וַיָּבֹא אֲלֵהֶם וַיֹּאמֶר כֹּה־אָמַר הַמֶּלֶךְ שָׁלוֹם וַיֹּאמֶר יֵהוּא מַה־לְּךָ וּלְשָׁלוֹם סֹב אֶל־אַחֲרָי: 20 וַיַּגֵּד הַצֹּפֶה לֵאמֹר בָּא עַד־אֲלֵיהֶם וְלֹא־שָׁב וְהַמִּנְהָג כְּמִנְהַג יֵהוּא בֶן־נִמְשִׁי כִּי בְשִׁגָּעוֹן יִנְהָג: 21 וַיֹּאמֶר יְהוֹרָם אֱסֹר וַיֶּאְסֹר רִכְבּוֹ וַיֵּצֵא יְהוֹרָם מֶלֶךְ־יִשְׂרָאֵל וַאֲחַזְיָהוּ מֶלֶךְ־יְהוּדָה אִישׁ בְּרִכְבּוֹ וַיֵּצְאוּ לִקְרַאת יֵהוּא וַיִּמְצָאֻהוּ בְּחֶלְקַת נָבוֹת הַיִּזְרְעֵאלִי: 22 וַיְהִי כִּרְאוֹת יְהוֹרָם אֶת־יֵהוּא וַיֹּאמֶר הֲשָׁלוֹם יֵהוּא וַיֹּאמֶר מָה הַשָּׁלוֹם עַד־זְנוּנֵי אִיזֶבֶל אִמְּךָ וּכְשָׁפֶיהָ הָרַבִּים: 23 וַיַּהֲפֹךְ יְהוֹרָם יָדָיו וַיָּנֹס וַיֹּאמֶר אֶל־אֲחַזְיָהוּ מִרְמָה אֲחַזְיָה:

24 וְיֵהוּא מִלֵּא יָדוֹ בַקֶּשֶׁת וַיַּךְ אֶת־יְהוֹרָם בֵּין זְרֹעָיו וַיֵּצֵא הַחֵצִי מִלִּבּוֹ וַיִּכְרַע בְּרִכְבּוֹ: 25 וַיֹּאמֶר אֶל־בִּדְקַר שָׁלִשֹׁה שָׂא הַשְׁלִכֵהוּ בְּחֶלְקַת שְׂדֵה נָבוֹת הַיִּזְרְעֵאלִי כִּי־זְכֹר אֲנִי וָאַתָּה אֵת רֹכְבִים צְמָדִים אַחֲרֵי אַחְאָב אָבִיו וַיהֹוָה נָשָׂא עָלָיו אֶת־הַמַּשָּׂא הַזֶּה: 26 אִם־לֹא אֶת־דְּמֵי נָבוֹת וְאֶת־דְּמֵי בָנָיו רָאִיתִי אֶמֶשׁ נְאֻם־יְהֹוָה וְשִׁלַּמְתִּי לְךָ בַּחֶלְקָה הַזֹּאת נְאֻם־יְהֹוָה וְעַתָּה שָׂא הַשְׁלִכֵהוּ בַּחֶלְקָה כִּדְבַר יְהֹוָה: 27 וַאֲחַזְיָה מֶלֶךְ־יְהוּדָה רָאָה וַיָּנָס דֶּרֶךְ בֵּית הַגָּן וַיִּרְדֹּף אַחֲרָיו יֵהוּא וַיֹּאמֶר גַּם־אֹתוֹ הַכֻּהוּ אֶל־הַמֶּרְכָּבָה בְּמַעֲלֵה־גוּר אֲשֶׁר אֶת־יִבְלְעָם וַיָּנָס מְגִדּוֹ וַיָּמָת שָׁם: 28 וַיַּרְכִּבוּ אֹתוֹ עֲבָדָיו יְרוּשָׁלְָמָה וַיִּקְבְּרוּ אֹתוֹ בִקְבֻרָתוֹ עִם־אֲבֹתָיו בְּעִיר דָּוִד: פ

29 וּבִשְׁנַת אַחַת עֶשְׂרֵה שָׁנָה לְיוֹרָם בֶּן־אַחְאָב מָלַךְ אֲחַזְיָה עַל־יְהוּדָה: 30 וַיָּבוֹא יֵהוּא יִזְרְעֶאלָה וְאִיזֶבֶל שָׁמְעָה וַתָּשֶׂם בַּפּוּךְ עֵינֶיהָ וַתֵּיטֶב אֶת־רֹאשָׁהּ וַתַּשְׁקֵף בְּעַד הַחַלּוֹן: 31 וְיֵהוּא בָּא בַשָּׁעַר וַתֹּאמֶר הֲשָׁלוֹם זִמְרִי הֹרֵג אֲדֹנָיו: 32 וַיִּשָּׂא פָנָיו אֶל־הַחַלּוֹן וַיֹּאמֶר מִי אִתִּי מִי וַיַּשְׁקִיפוּ אֵלָיו שְׁנַיִם שְׁלֹשָׁה סָרִיסִים: 33 וַיֹּאמֶר שִׁמְטֻהוּ וַיִּשְׁמְטוּהָ וַיִּז מִדָּמָהּ

her down." So they threw her down, and *some* of her blood spattered on the wall and on the horses; and he trampled her underfoot. ³⁴ And when he had gone in, he ate and drank. Then he said, "Go now, see to this accursed *woman*, and bury her, for she was a king's daughter." ³⁵ So they went to bury her, but they found no more of her than the skull and the feet and the palms of *her* hands. ³⁶ Therefore they came back and told him. And he said, "This *is* the word of the LORD, which He spoke by His servant Elijah the Tishbite, saying, 'On the plot *of ground* at Jezreel dogs shall eat the flesh of Jezebel; ³⁷ and the corpse of Jezebel shall be as refuse on the surface of the field, in the plot at Jezreel, so that they shall not say, "Here *lies* Jezebel."'"

10 Now Ahab had seventy sons in Samaria. And Jehu wrote and sent letters to Samaria, to the rulers of Jezreel, to the elders, and to those who reared Ahab's *sons,* saying:

2   Now as soon as this letter comes to you, since your master's sons *are* with you, and you have chariots and horses, a fortified city also, and weapons, ³ choose the best qualified of your master's sons, set *him* on his father's throne, and fight for your master's house.

⁴ But they were exceedingly afraid, and said, "Look, two kings could not stand up to him; how then can we stand?" ⁵ And he who *was* in charge of the house, and he who *was* in charge of the city, the elders also, and those who reared *the* sons, sent to Jehu, saying, "We *are* your servants, we will do all you tell us; but we will not make anyone king. Do *what is* good in your sight." ⁶ Then he wrote a second letter to them, saying:

If you *are* for me and will obey my voice, take the heads of the men, your master's sons, and come to me at Jezreel by this time tomorrow.

Now the king's sons, seventy persons, *were* with the great men of the city, *who* were rearing them. ⁷ So it was, when the letter came to them, that they took the king's sons and slaughtered seventy persons, put their heads in baskets and sent *them* to him at Jezreel.

⁸ Then a messenger came and told him, saying, "They have brought the heads of the king's sons."

And he said, "Lay them in two heaps at the entrance of the gate until morning."

⁹ So it was, in the morning, that he went out and stood, and said to all the people, "You *are* righteous. Indeed I conspired against my master and killed him; but who killed all these? ¹⁰ Know now that nothing shall fall to the earth of the word

אֶל־הַקִּיר וְאֶל־הַסּוּסִים וַיִּרְמְסֶנָּה: 34 וַיָּבֹא וַיֹּאכַל וַיֵּשְׁתְּ וַיֹּאמֶר פִּקְדוּ־נָא אֶת־הָאֲרוּרָה הַזֹּאת וְקִבְרוּהָ כִּי בַת־מֶלֶךְ הִיא: 35 וַיֵּלְכוּ לְקָבְרָהּ וְלֹא־מָצְאוּ בָהּ כִּי אִם־הַגֻּלְגֹּלֶת וְהָרַגְלַיִם וְכַפּוֹת הַיָּדָיִם: 36 וַיָּשֻׁבוּ וַיַּגִּידוּ לוֹ וַיֹּאמֶר דְּבַר־יְהֹוָה הוּא אֲשֶׁר דִּבֶּר בְּיַד־עַבְדּוֹ אֵלִיָּהוּ הַתִּשְׁבִּי לֵאמֹר בְּחֵלֶק יִזְרְעֶאל יֹאכְלוּ הַכְּלָבִים אֶת־בְּשַׂר אִיזָבֶל: 37 וְהָיְתָ֞ נִבְלַת אִיזֶבֶל כְּדֹמֶן עַל־פְּנֵי הַשָּׂדֶה בְּחֵלֶק יִזְרְעֶאל אֲשֶׁר לֹא־יֹאמְרוּ זֹאת אִיזָבֶל: פ

י וּלְאַחְאָב שִׁבְעִים בָּנִים בְּשֹׁמְרוֹן וַיִּכְתֹּב יֵהוּא סְפָרִים וַיִּשְׁלַח שֹׁמְרוֹן אֶל־שָׂרֵי יִזְרְעֶאל הַזְּקֵנִים וְאֶל־הָאֹמְנִים אַחְאָב לֵאמֹר: 2 וְעַתָּה כְּבֹא הַסֵּפֶר הַזֶּה אֲלֵיכֶם וְאִתְּכֶם בְּנֵי אֲדֹנֵיכֶם וְאִתְּכֶם הָרֶכֶב וְהַסּוּסִים וְעִיר מִבְצָר וְהַנָּשֶׁק: 3 וּרְאִיתֶם הַטּוֹב וְהַיָּשָׁר מִבְּנֵי אֲדֹנֵיכֶם וְשַׂמְתֶּם עַל־כִּסֵּא אָבִיו וְהִלָּחֲמוּ עַל־בֵּית אֲדֹנֵיכֶם: 4 וַיִּרְאוּ מְאֹד מְאֹד וַיֹּאמְרוּ הִנֵּה שְׁנֵי הַמְּלָכִים לֹא עָמְדוּ לְפָנָיו וְאֵיךְ נַעֲמֹד אֲנָחְנוּ: 5 וַיִּשְׁלַח אֲשֶׁר־עַל־הַבַּיִת וַאֲשֶׁר עַל־הָעִיר וְהַזְּקֵנִים וְהָאֹמְנִים אֶל־יֵהוּא לֵאמֹר עֲבָדֶיךָ אֲנַחְנוּ וְכֹל אֲשֶׁר־תֹּאמַר אֵלֵינוּ נַעֲשֶׂה לֹא־נַמְלִיךְ אִישׁ הַטּוֹב בְּעֵינֶיךָ עֲשֵׂה: 6 וַיִּכְתֹּב אֲלֵיהֶם סֵפֶר שֵׁנִית לֵאמֹר אִם־לִי אַתֶּם וּלְקֹלִי אַתֶּם שֹׁמְעִים קְחוּ אֶת־רָאשֵׁי אַנְשֵׁי בְנֵי־אֲדֹנֵיכֶם וּבֹאוּ אֵלַי כָּעֵת מָחָר יִזְרְעֶאלָה וּבְנֵי הַמֶּלֶךְ שִׁבְעִים אִישׁ אֶת־גְּדֹלֵי הָעִיר מְגַדְּלִים אוֹתָם: 7 וַיְהִי כְּבֹא הַסֵּפֶר אֲלֵיהֶם וַיִּקְחוּ אֶת־בְּנֵי הַמֶּלֶךְ וַיִּשְׁחֲטוּ שִׁבְעִים אִישׁ וַיָּשִׂימוּ אֶת־רָאשֵׁיהֶם בַּדּוּדִים וַיִּשְׁלְחוּ אֵלָיו יִזְרְעֶאלָה: 8 וַיָּבֹא הַמַּלְאָךְ וַיַּגֶּד־לוֹ לֵאמֹר הֵבִיאוּ רָאשֵׁי בְנֵי־הַמֶּלֶךְ וַיֹּאמֶר שִׂימוּ אֹתָם שְׁנֵי צִבֻּרִים פֶּתַח הַשַּׁעַר עַד־הַבֹּקֶר: 9 וַיְהִי בַבֹּקֶר וַיֵּצֵא וַיַּעֲמֹד וַיֹּאמֶר אֶל־כָּל־הָעָם צַדִּקִים אַתֶּם הִנֵּה אֲנִי קָשַׁרְתִּי עַל־אֲדֹנִי וָאֶהְרְגֵהוּ וּמִי הִכָּה אֶת־כָּל־אֵלֶּה: 10 דְּעוּ אֵפוֹא כִּי לֹא יִפֹּל מִדְּבַר יְהֹוָה אַרְצָה אֲשֶׁר־דִּבֶּר יְהֹוָה עַל־

of the LORD which the LORD spoke concerning the house of Ahab; for the LORD has done what He spoke by His servant Elijah." ¹¹So Jehu killed all who remained of the house of Ahab in Jezreel, and all his great men and his close acquaintances and his priests, until he left him none remaining.

¹²And he arose and departed and went to Samaria. On the way, at Beth Eked of the Shepherds, ¹³Jehu met with the brothers of Ahaziah king of Judah, and said, "Who *are* you?"

So they answered, "We *are* the brothers of Ahaziah; we have come down to greet the sons of the king and the sons of the queen mother."

¹⁴And he said, "Take them alive!" So they took them alive, and killed them at the well of Beth Eked, forty-two men; and he left none of them.

¹⁵Now when he departed from there, he met Jehonadab the son of Rechab, *coming* to meet him; and he greeted him and said to him, "Is your heart right, as my heart *is* toward your heart?"

And Jehonadab answered, "It is."

Jehu said, "If it is, give *me* your hand." So he gave *him* his hand, and he took him up to him into the chariot. ¹⁶Then he said, "Come with me, and see my zeal for the LORD." So they had him ride in his chariot. ¹⁷And when he came to Samaria, he killed all who remained to Ahab in Samaria, till he had destroyed them, according to the word of the LORD which He spoke to Elijah.

¹⁸Then Jehu gathered all the people together, and said to them, "Ahab served Baal a little, Jehu will serve him much. ¹⁹Now therefore, call to me all the prophets of Baal, all his servants, and all his priests. Let no one be missing, for I have a great sacrifice for Baal. Whoever is missing shall not live." But Jehu acted deceptively, with the intent of destroying the worshipers of Baal. ²⁰And Jehu said, "Proclaim a solemn assembly for Baal." So they proclaimed *it*. ²¹Then Jehu sent throughout all Israel; and all the worshipers of Baal came, so that there was not a man left who did not come. So they came into the temple of Baal, and the temple of Baal was full from one end to the other. ²²And he said to the one in charge of the wardrobe, "Bring out vestments for all the worshipers of Baal." So he brought out vestments for them. ²³Then Jehu and Jehonadab the son of Rechab went into the temple of Baal, and said to the worshipers of Baal, "Search and see that no servants of the LORD are here with you, but only the worshipers of Baal." ²⁴So they went in to offer sacrifices and burnt offerings. Now Jehu had appointed for himself eighty men on the outside, and had said, "*If* any of the men whom I

בֵּית אַחְאָב וַיהֹוָה עָשָׂה אֵת אֲשֶׁר דִּבֶּר בְּיַד עֲבָדֽוֹ אֵלִיָּֽהוּ: 11 וַיַּ֣ךְ יֵהוּא אֵת כָּל־הַנִּשְׁאָרִים לְבֵית־אַחְאָב בְּיִזְרְעֶאל וְכָל־גְּדֹלָיו וּמְיֻדָּעָיו וְכֹהֲנָיו עַד־בִּלְתִּי הִשְׁאִֽיר־לוֹ שָׂרִֽיד: 12 וַיָּ֙קָם֙ וַיָּבֹא וַיֵּ֖לֶךְ שֹׁמְר֑וֹן הוּא בֵּֽית־עֵ֥קֶד הָרֹעִ֖ים בַּדָּֽרֶךְ: 13 וְיֵהוּא מָצָא אֶת־אֲחֵ֙י אֲחַזְיָ֜הוּ מֶֽלֶךְ־יְהוּדָ֗ה וַיֹּ֙אמֶר֙ מִ֣י אַתֶּ֔ם וַיֹּ֣אמְר֔וּ אֲחֵ֤י אֲחַזְיָ֙הוּ֙ אֲנַ֔חְנוּ וַנֵּ֕רֶד לִשְׁל֖וֹם בְּנֵֽי־הַמֶּ֥לֶךְ וּבְנֵ֥י הַגְּבִירָֽה: 14 וַיֹּ֙אמֶר֙ תִּפְשׂ֣וּם חַיִּ֔ים וַֽיִּתְפְּשׂ֖וּם חַיִּ֑ים וַֽיִּשְׁחָט֣וּם אֶל־בּ֣וֹר בֵּֽית־עֵ֗קֶד אַרְבָּעִ֤ים וּשְׁנַ֙יִם֙ אִ֔ישׁ וְלֹֽא־הִשְׁאִ֥יר אִ֖ישׁ מֵהֶֽם: ס 15 וַיֵּ֣לֶךְ מִשָּׁ֡ם וַיִּמְצָ֣א אֶת־יְהֽוֹנָדָב֩ בֶּן־רֵכָ֙ב לִקְרָאת֜וֹ וַֽיְבָרְכֵ֗הוּ וַיֹּ֙אמֶר אֵלָ֜יו הֲיֵ֧שׁ אֶת־לְבָבְךָ֣ יָשָׁ֗ר כַּאֲשֶׁ֤ר לְבָבִי֙ עִם־לְבָבֶ֔ךָ וַיֹּ֙אמֶר יְהוֹנָדָ֥ב יֵ֖שׁ וָיֵ֑שׁ תְּנָ֣ה אֶת־יָדֶ֔ךָ וַיִּתֵּ֣ן יָד֔וֹ וַיַּעֲלֵ֥הוּ אֵלָ֖יו אֶל־הַמֶּרְכָּבָֽה: 16 וַיֹּ֙אמֶר֙ לְכָ֣ה אִתִּ֔י וּרְאֵ֖ה בְּקִנְאָתִ֣י לַֽיהֹוָ֑ה וַיַּרְכִּ֥בוּ אֹת֖וֹ בְּרִכְבּֽוֹ: 17 וַיָּבֹ֣א שֹׁמְר֗וֹן וַ֠יַּ֠ךְ אֶת־כָּל־הַנִּשְׁאָרִ֤ים לְאַחְאָב֙ בְּשֹׁ֣מְר֔וֹן עַד־הִשְׁמִיד֑וֹ כִּדְבַ֣ר יְהֹוָ֔ה אֲשֶׁ֥ר דִּבֶּ֖ר אֶל־אֵלִיָּֽהוּ: פ

18 וַיִּקְבֹּ֤ץ יֵהוּא֙ אֶת־כָּל־הָעָ֔ם וַיֹּ֣אמֶר אֲלֵהֶ֔ם אַחְאָ֕ב עָבַ֥ד אֶת־הַבַּ֖עַל מְעָ֑ט יֵה֖וּא יַעַבְדֶ֥נּוּ הַרְבֵּֽה: 19 וְעַתָּ֣ה כָל־נְבִיאֵ֣י הַבַּ֡עַל כָּל־עֹבְדָ֣יו וְכָל־כֹּֽהֲנָיו֩ קִרְא֨וּ אֵלַ֜י אִ֣ישׁ אַל־יִפָּקֵ֗ד כִּי֩ זֶ֙בַח גָּד֥וֹל לִי֙ לַבַּ֔עַל כֹּ֥ל אֲשֶׁר־יִפָּקֵ֖ד לֹ֣א יִֽחְיֶ֑ה וְיֵהוּא֙ עָשָׂ֣ה בְעָקְבָּ֔ה לְמַ֖עַן הַאֲבִ֥יד אֶת־עֹבְדֵ֥י הַבָּֽעַל: 20 וַיֹּ֣אמֶר יֵה֗וּא קַדְּשׁ֧וּ עֲצָרָ֛ה לַבַּ֖עַל וַיִּקְרָֽאוּ: 21 וַיִּשְׁלַ֤ח יֵהוּא֙ בְּכָל־יִשְׂרָאֵ֔ל וַיָּבֹ֙אוּ֙ כָּל־עֹבְדֵ֣י הַבַּ֔עַל וְלֹֽא־נִשְׁאַ֥ר אִ֖ישׁ אֲשֶׁ֣ר לֹֽא־בָ֑א וַיָּבֹ֙אוּ֙ בֵּ֣ית הַבַּ֔עַל וַיִּמָּלֵ֧א בֵית־הַבַּ֛עַל פֶּ֥ה לָפֶֽה: 22 וַיֹּ֗אמֶר לַֽאֲשֶׁר֙ עַל־הַמֶּלְתָּחָ֔ה הוֹצֵ֣א לְב֔וּשׁ לְכֹ֖ל עֹבְדֵ֣י הַבָּ֑עַל וַיֹּצֵ֥א לָהֶ֖ם הַמַּלְבּֽוּשׁ: 23 וַיָּבֹ֧א יֵה֛וּא וִיהוֹנָדָ֥ב בֶּן־רֵכָ֖ב בֵּ֣ית הַבָּ֑עַל וַיֹּ֜אמֶר לְעֹבְדֵ֤י הַבַּ֙עַל֙ חַפְּשׂ֣וּ וּרְא֔וּ פֶּן־יֶשׁ־פֹּ֣ה עִמָּכֶ֗ם מֵעַבְדֵ֤י יְהֹוָה֙ כִּ֣י אִם־עֹבְדֵ֥י הַבַּ֖עַל לְבַדָּֽם: 24 וַיָּבֹ֕אוּ לַעֲשׂ֖וֹת זְבָחִ֣ים וְעֹל֑וֹת וְיֵה֞וּא שָֽׂם־ל֤וֹ בַחוּץ֙ שְׁמֹנִ֣ים אִ֔ישׁ וַיֹּ֙אמֶר֙ הָאִ֗ישׁ אֲשֶׁר־יִמָּלֵ֤ט מִן־הָֽאֲנָשִׁים֙ אֲשֶׁ֣ר אֲנִ֔י מֵבִ֖יא עַל־יְדֵיכֶ֑ם נַפְשׁ֖וֹ תַּ֥חַת

have brought into your hands escapes, *whoever lets him escape, it shall be* his life for the life of the other."

²⁵ Now it happened, as soon as he had made an end of offering the burnt offering, that Jehu said to the guard and to the captains, "Go in *and* kill them; let no one come out!" And they killed them with the edge of the sword; then the guards and the officers threw *them* out, and went into the inner room of the temple of Baal. ²⁶ And they brought the *sacred* pillars out of the temple of Baal and burned them. ²⁷ Then they broke down the *sacred* pillar of Baal, and tore down the temple of Baal and made it a refuse dump to this day. ²⁸ Thus Jehu destroyed Baal from Israel.

²⁹ However Jehu did not turn away from the sins of Jeroboam the son of Nebat, who had made Israel sin, *that is,* from the golden calves that *were* at Bethel and Dan. ³⁰ And the LORD said to Jehu, "Because you have done well in doing *what is right* in My sight, *and* have done to the house of Ahab all that *was* in My heart, your sons shall sit on the throne of Israel to the fourth *generation.*" ³¹ But Jehu took no heed to walk in the law of the LORD God of Israel with all his heart; for he did not depart from the sins of Jeroboam, who had made Israel sin.

³² In those days the LORD began to cut off *parts* of Israel; and Hazael conquered them in all the territory of Israel ³³ from the Jordan eastward: all the land of Gilead—Gad, Reuben, and Manasseh—from Aroer, which *is* by the River Arnon, including Gilead and Bashan.

³⁴ Now the rest of the acts of Jehu, all that he did, and all his might, *are* they not written in the book of the chronicles of the kings of Israel? ³⁵ So Jehu rested with his fathers, and they buried him in Samaria. Then Jehoahaz his son reigned in his place. ³⁶ And the period that Jehu reigned over Israel in Samaria *was* twenty-eight years.

11 When Athaliah the mother of Ahaziah saw that her son was dead, she arose and destroyed all the royal heirs. ² But Jehosheba, the daughter of King Joram, sister of Ahaziah, took Joash the son of Ahaziah, and stole him away from among the king's sons *who were* being murdered; and they hid him and his nurse in the bedroom, from Athaliah, so that he was not killed. ³ So he was hidden with her in the house of the LORD for six years, while Athaliah reigned over the land.

⁴ In the seventh year Jehoiada sent and brought the captains of hundreds—of the bodyguards and the escorts—and brought them into the house of the

נַפְשׁוֹ: 25 וַיְהִי כְּכַלֹּתוֹ | לַעֲשׂוֹת הָעֹלָה וַיֹּאמֶר
יֵהוּא לָרָצִים וְלַשָּׁלִשִׁים בֹּאוּ הַכּוּם אִישׁ אַל־
יֵצֵא וַיַּכּוּם לְפִי־חָרֶב וַיַּשְׁלִכוּ הָרָצִים וְהַשָּׁלִשִׁים
וַיֵּלְכוּ עַד־עִיר בֵּית־הַבָּעַל: 26 וַיֹּצִאוּ אֶת־מַצְּבוֹת
בֵּית־הַבַּעַל וַיִּשְׂרְפוּהָ: 27 וַיִּתְּצוּ אֵת מַצְּבַת הַבָּעַל
וַיִּתְּצוּ אֶת־בֵּית הַבַּעַל וַיְשִׂמֻהוּ לְמוֹחֲרָאוֹת עַד־
הַיּוֹם: 28 וַיַּשְׁמֵד יֵהוּא אֶת־הַבַּעַל מִיִּשְׂרָאֵל: 29 רַק
חֲטָאֵי יָרָבְעָם בֶּן־נְבָט אֲשֶׁר הֶחֱטִיא אֶת־יִשְׂרָאֵל
לֹא־סָר יֵהוּא מֵאַחֲרֵיהֶם עֶגְלֵי הַזָּהָב אֲשֶׁר בֵּית־
אֵל וַאֲשֶׁר בְּדָן: ס 30 וַיֹּאמֶר יְהֹוָה אֶל־
יֵהוּא יַעַן אֲשֶׁר־הֱטִיבֹתָ לַעֲשׂוֹת הַיָּשָׁר בְּעֵינַי
כְּכֹל אֲשֶׁר בִּלְבָבִי עָשִׂיתָ לְבֵית אַחְאָב בְּנֵי
רְבֵעִים יֵשְׁבוּ לְךָ עַל־כִּסֵּא יִשְׂרָאֵל: 31 וְיֵהוּא לֹא
שָׁמַר לָלֶכֶת בְּתוֹרַת־יְהֹוָה אֱלֹהֵי־יִשְׂרָאֵל בְּכָל־
לְבָבוֹ לֹא סָר מֵעַל חַטֹּאות יָרָבְעָם אֲשֶׁר הֶחֱטִיא
אֶת־יִשְׂרָאֵל: 32 בַּיָּמִים הָהֵם הֵחֵל יְהֹוָה לְקַצּוֹת
בְּיִשְׂרָאֵל וַיַּכֵּם חֲזָאֵל בְּכָל־גְּבוּל יִשְׂרָאֵל: 33 מִן־
הַיַּרְדֵּן מִזְרַח הַשֶּׁמֶשׁ אֵת כָּל־אֶרֶץ הַגִּלְעָד הַגָּדִי
וְהָראוּבֵנִי וְהַמְנַשִּׁי מֵעֲרֹעֵר אֲשֶׁר עַל־נַחַל אַרְנֹן
וְהַגִּלְעָד וְהַבָּשָׁן: 34 וְיֶתֶר דִּבְרֵי יֵהוּא וְכָל־אֲשֶׁר
עָשָׂה וְכָל־גְּבוּרָתוֹ הֲלוֹא־הֵם כְּתוּבִים עַל־סֵפֶר
דִּבְרֵי הַיָּמִים לְמַלְכֵי יִשְׂרָאֵל: 35 וַיִּשְׁכַּב יֵהוּא עִם־
אֲבֹתָיו וַיִּקְבְּרוּ אֹתוֹ בְּשֹׁמְרוֹן וַיִּמְלֹךְ יְהוֹאָחָז בְּנוֹ
תַּחְתָּיו: 36 וְהַיָּמִים אֲשֶׁר מָלַךְ יֵהוּא עַל־יִשְׂרָאֵל
עֶשְׂרִים וּשְׁמֹנֶה־שָׁנָה בְּשֹׁמְרוֹן:
פ

יא וַעֲתַלְיָה אֵם אֲחַזְיָהוּ וְרָאֲתָה כִּי מֵת בְּנָהּ
וַתָּקָם וַתְּאַבֵּד אֵת כָּל־זֶרַע הַמַּמְלָכָה: 2 וַתִּקַּח
יְהוֹשֶׁבַע בַּת־הַמֶּלֶךְ־יוֹרָם אֲחוֹת אֲחַזְיָהוּ אֶת־
יוֹאָשׁ בֶּן־אֲחַזְיָה וַתִּגְנֹב אֹתוֹ מִתּוֹךְ בְּנֵי־הַמֶּלֶךְ
הַמּוּמָתִים אֹתוֹ וְאֶת־מֵינִקְתּוֹ בַּחֲדַר הַמִּטּוֹת
וַיַּסְתִּרוּ אֹתוֹ מִפְּנֵי עֲתַלְיָהוּ וְלֹא הוּמָת: 3 וַיְהִי
אִתָּהּ בֵּית יְהֹוָה מִתְחַבֵּא שֵׁשׁ שָׁנִים וַעֲתַלְיָה
מֹלֶכֶת עַל־הָאָרֶץ:
פ
4 וּבַשָּׁנָה הַשְּׁבִיעִית שָׁלַח יְהוֹיָדָע וַיִּקַּח | אֶת־

׳ 27 לִמְצָאוֹת

יא 1 רָאֲתָה 2 הַמּוּמָתִים

LORD to him. And he made a covenant with them and took an oath from them in the house of the LORD, and showed them the king's son. [5]Then he commanded them, saying, "This *is* what you shall do: One-third of you who come on duty on the Sabbath shall be keeping watch over the king's house, [6]one-third *shall be* at the gate of Sur, and one-third at the gate behind the escorts. You shall keep the watch of the house, lest it be broken down. [7]The two contingents of you who go off duty on the Sabbath shall keep the watch of the house of the LORD for the king. [8]But you shall surround the king on all sides, every man with his weapons in his hand; and whoever comes within range, let him be put to death. You are to be with the king as he goes out and as he comes in."

[9]So the captains of the hundreds did according to all that Jehoiada the priest commanded. Each of them took his men who were to be on duty on the Sabbath, with those who were going off duty on the Sabbath, and came to Jehoiada the priest. [10]And the priest gave the captains of hundreds the spears and shields which *had belonged* to King David, that were in the temple of the LORD. [11]Then the escorts stood, every man with his weapons in his hand, all around the king, from the right side of the temple to the left side of the temple, by the altar and the house. [12]And he brought out the king's son, put the crown on him, and *gave him* the Testimony; they made him king and anointed him, and they clapped their hands and said, "Long live the king!"

[13]Now when Athaliah heard the noise of the escorts *and* the people, she came to the people *in* the temple of the LORD. [14]When she looked, there was the king standing by a pillar according to custom; and the leaders and the trumpeters were by the king. All the people of the land were rejoicing and blowing trumpets. So Athaliah tore her clothes and cried out, "Treason! Treason!"

[15]And Jehoiada the priest commanded the captains of the hundreds, the officers of the army, and said to them, "Take her outside under guard, and slay with the sword whoever follows her." For the priest had said, "Do not let her be killed in the house of the LORD." [16]So they seized her; and she went by way of the horses' entrance *into* the king's house, and there she was killed.

[17]Then Jehoiada made a covenant between the LORD, the king, and the people, that they should be the LORD's people, and *also* between the king and the people. [18]And all the people of the land went to the temple of Baal, and tore it down. They thoroughly broke in pieces its altars and images, and killed Mattan the priest of Baal before the

שָׂרֵי הַמֵּאוֹת לַכָּרִי וְלָרָצִים וַיָּבֵא אֹתָם אֵלָיו בֵּית יְהוָה וַיִּכְרֹת לָהֶם בְּרִית וַיַּשְׁבַּע אֹתָם בְּבֵית יְהוָה וַיַּרְא אֹתָם אֶת־בֶּן־הַמֶּלֶךְ: 5 וַיְצַוֵּם לֵאמֹר זֶה הַדָּבָר אֲשֶׁר תַּעֲשׂוּן הַשְּׁלִשִׁית מִכֶּם בָּאֵי הַשַּׁבָּת וְשֹׁמְרֵי מִשְׁמֶרֶת בֵּית הַמֶּלֶךְ: 6 וְהַשְּׁלִשִׁית בְּשַׁעַר סוּר וְהַשְּׁלִשִׁית בַּשַּׁעַר אַחַר הָרָצִים וּשְׁמַרְתֶּם אֶת־מִשְׁמֶרֶת הַבַּיִת מַסָּח: 7 וּשְׁתֵּי הַיָּדוֹת בָּכֶם כֹּל יֹצְאֵי הַשַּׁבָּת וְשָׁמְרוּ אֶת־מִשְׁמֶרֶת בֵּית־יְהוָה אֶל־הַמֶּלֶךְ: 8 וְהִקַּפְתֶּם עַל־הַמֶּלֶךְ סָבִיב אִישׁ וְכֵלָיו בְּיָדוֹ וְהַבָּא אֶל־הַשְּׂדֵרוֹת יוּמָת וִהְיוּ אֶת־הַמֶּלֶךְ בְּצֵאתוֹ וּבְבֹאוֹ: 9 וַיַּעֲשׂוּ שָׂרֵי הַמֵּאוֹת כְּכֹל אֲשֶׁר־צִוָּה יְהוֹיָדָע הַכֹּהֵן וַיִּקְחוּ אִישׁ אֶת־אֲנָשָׁיו בָּאֵי הַשַּׁבָּת עִם יֹצְאֵי הַשַּׁבָּת וַיָּבֹאוּ אֶל־יְהוֹיָדָע הַכֹּהֵן: 10 וַיִּתֵּן הַכֹּהֵן לְשָׂרֵי הַמֵּאוֹת אֶת־הַחֲנִית וְאֶת־הַשְּׁלָטִים אֲשֶׁר לַמֶּלֶךְ דָּוִד אֲשֶׁר בְּבֵית יְהוָה: 11 וַיַּעַמְדוּ הָרָצִים אִישׁ וְכֵלָיו בְּיָדוֹ מִכֶּתֶף הַבַּיִת הַיְמָנִית עַד־כֶּתֶף הַבַּיִת הַשְּׂמָאלִית לַמִּזְבֵּחַ וְלַבָּיִת עַל־הַמֶּלֶךְ סָבִיב: 12 וַיּוֹצִא אֶת־בֶּן־הַמֶּלֶךְ וַיִּתֵּן עָלָיו אֶת־הַנֵּזֶר וְאֶת־הָעֵדוּת וַיַּמְלִכוּ אֹתוֹ וַיִּמְשָׁחֻהוּ וַיַּכּוּ־כָף וַיֹּאמְרוּ יְחִי הַמֶּלֶךְ: ס 13 וַתִּשְׁמַע עֲתַלְיָה אֶת־קוֹל הָרָצִין הָעָם וַתָּבֹא אֶל־הָעָם בֵּית יְהוָה: 14 וַתֵּרֶא וְהִנֵּה הַמֶּלֶךְ עֹמֵד עַל־הָעַמּוּד כַּמִּשְׁפָּט וְהַשָּׂרִים וְהַחֲצֹצְרוֹת אֶל־הַמֶּלֶךְ וְכָל־עַם הָאָרֶץ שָׂמֵחַ וְתֹקֵעַ בַּחֲצֹצְרוֹת וַתִּקְרַע עֲתַלְיָה אֶת־בְּגָדֶיהָ וַתִּקְרָא קֶשֶׁר קָשֶׁר: ס 15 וַיְצַו יְהוֹיָדָע הַכֹּהֵן אֶת־שָׂרֵי הַמֵּאוֹת פְּקֻדֵי הַחַיִל וַיֹּאמֶר אֲלֵיהֶם הוֹצִיאוּ אֹתָהּ אֶל־מִבֵּית לַשְּׂדֵרֹת וְהַבָּא אַחֲרֶיהָ הָמֵת בֶּחָרֶב כִּי אָמַר הַכֹּהֵן אַל־תּוּמַת בֵּית יְהוָה: 16 וַיָּשִׂמוּ לָהּ יָדַיִם וַתָּבוֹא דֶּרֶךְ־מְבוֹא הַסּוּסִים בֵּית הַמֶּלֶךְ וַתּוּמַת שָׁם: ס 17 וַיִּכְרֹת יְהוֹיָדָע אֶת־הַבְּרִית בֵּין יְהוָה וּבֵין הַמֶּלֶךְ וּבֵין הָעָם לִהְיוֹת לְעָם לַיהוָה וּבֵין הַמֶּלֶךְ וּבֵין הָעָם: 18 וַיָּבֹאוּ כָל־עַם הָאָרֶץ בֵּית־הַבַּעַל וַיִּתְּצֻהוּ אֶת־מִזְבְּחֹתָו וְאֶת־צְלָמָיו שִׁבְּרוּ הֵיטֵב וְאֵת מַתָּן כֹּהֵן

altars. And the priest appointed officers over the house of the LORD. ¹⁹ Then he took the captains of hundreds, the bodyguards, the escorts, and all the people of the land; and they brought the king down from the house of the LORD, and went by way of the gate of the escorts to the king's house. Then he sat on the throne of the kings. ²⁰ So all the people of the land rejoiced; and the city was quiet, for they had slain Athaliah with the sword *in* the king's house. ²¹ Jehoash *was* seven years old when he became king.

12 In the seventh year of Jehu, Jehoash became king, and he reigned forty years in Jerusalem. His mother's name *was* Zibiah of Beersheba. ² Jehoash did *what was* right in the sight of the LORD all the days in which Jehoiada the priest instructed him. ³ But the high places were not taken away; the people still sacrificed and burned incense on the high places.

⁴ And Jehoash said to the priests, "All the money of the dedicated gifts that are brought into the house of the LORD—each man's census money, each man's assessment money—*and* all the money that a man purposes in his heart to bring into the house of the LORD, ⁵ let the priests take *it* themselves, each from his constituency; and let them repair the damages of the temple, wherever any dilapidation is found."

⁶ Now it was so, by the twenty-third year of King Jehoash, *that* the priests had not repaired the damages of the temple. ⁷ So King Jehoash called Jehoiada the priest and the *other* priests, and said to them, "Why have you not repaired the damages of the temple? Now therefore, do not take *more* money from your constituency, but deliver it for repairing the damages of the temple." ⁸ And the priests agreed that they would neither receive *more* money from the people, nor repair the damages of the temple.

⁹ Then Jehoiada the priest took a chest, bored a hole in its lid, and set it beside the altar, on the right side as one comes into the house of the LORD; and the priests who kept the door put there all the money brought into the house of the LORD. ¹⁰ So it was, whenever they saw that *there was* much money in the chest, that the king's scribe and the high priest came up and put it in bags, and counted the money that was found in the house of the LORD. ¹¹ Then they gave the money, which had been apportioned, into the hands of those who did the work, who had the oversight of the house of the LORD; and they paid it out to the carpenters and builders who worked on the house of the LORD, ¹² and to masons and stonecutters, and for buying

הַבַּעַל הָרְגוּ לִפְנֵי הַמִּזְבְּחוֹת וַיָּשֶׂם הַכֹּהֵן פְּקֻדּוֹת עַל־בֵּית יְהוָה: 19 וַיִּקַּח אֶת־שָׂרֵי הַמֵּאוֹת וְאֶת־הַכָּרִי וְאֶת־הָרָצִים וְאֵת | כָּל־עַם הָאָרֶץ וַיֹּרִידוּ אֶת־הַמֶּלֶךְ מִבֵּית יְהוָה וַיָּבוֹאוּ דֶּרֶךְ־שַׁעַר הָרָצִים בֵּית הַמֶּלֶךְ וַיֵּשֶׁב עַל־כִּסֵּא הַמְּלָכִים: 20 וַיִּשְׂמַח כָּל־עַם־הָאָרֶץ וְהָעִיר שָׁקָטָה וְאֶת־עֲתַלְיָהוּ הֵמִיתוּ בַחֶרֶב בֵּית מֶלֶךְ: ס

יב בֶּן־שֶׁבַע שָׁנִים יְהוֹאָשׁ בְּמָלְכוֹ: פ 2 בִּשְׁנַת־שֶׁבַע לְיֵהוּא מָלַךְ יְהוֹאָשׁ וְאַרְבָּעִים שָׁנָה מָלַךְ בִּירוּשָׁלִָם וְשֵׁם אִמּוֹ צִבְיָה מִבְּאֵר שָׁבַע: 3 וַיַּעַשׂ יְהוֹאָשׁ הַיָּשָׁר בְּעֵינֵי יְהוָה כָּל־יָמָיו אֲשֶׁר הוֹרָהוּ יְהוֹיָדָע הַכֹּהֵן: 4 רַק הַבָּמוֹת לֹא־סָרוּ עוֹד הָעָם מְזַבְּחִים וּמְקַטְּרִים בַּבָּמוֹת: 5 וַיֹּאמֶר יְהוֹאָשׁ אֶל־הַכֹּהֲנִים כֹּל כֶּסֶף הַקֳּדָשִׁים אֲשֶׁר־יוּבָא בֵית־ יְהוָה כֶּסֶף עוֹבֵר אִישׁ כֶּסֶף נַפְשׁוֹת עֶרְכּוֹ כָּל־כֶּסֶף אֲשֶׁר יַעֲלֶה עַל לֶב־אִישׁ לְהָבִיא בֵּית יְהוָה: 6 יִקְחוּ לָהֶם הַכֹּהֲנִים אִישׁ מֵאֵת מַכָּרוֹ וְהֵם יְחַזְּקוּ אֶת־ בֶּדֶק הַבַּיִת לְכֹל אֲשֶׁר־יִמָּצֵא שָׁם בָּדֶק: פ 7 וַיְהִי בִּשְׁנַת עֶשְׂרִים וְשָׁלֹשׁ שָׁנָה לַמֶּלֶךְ יְהוֹאָשׁ לֹא־חִזְּקוּ הַכֹּהֲנִים אֶת־בֶּדֶק הַבָּיִת: 8 וַיִּקְרָא הַמֶּלֶךְ יְהוֹאָשׁ לִיהוֹיָדָע הַכֹּהֵן וְלַכֹּהֲנִים וַיֹּאמֶר אֲלֵהֶם מַדּוּעַ אֵינְכֶם מְחַזְּקִים אֶת־בֶּדֶק הַבָּיִת וְעַתָּה אַל־ תִּקְחוּ־כֶסֶף מֵאֵת מַכָּרֵיכֶם כִּי־לְבֶדֶק הַבַּיִת תִּתְּנֻהוּ: 9 וַיֵּאֹתוּ הַכֹּהֲנִים לְבִלְתִּי קְחַת־כֶּסֶף מֵאֵת הָעָם וּלְבִלְתִּי חַזֵּק אֶת־בֶּדֶק הַבָּיִת: 10 וַיִּקַּח יְהוֹיָדָע הַכֹּהֵן אֲרוֹן אֶחָד וַיִּקֹּב חֹר בְּדַלְתּוֹ וַיִּתֵּן אֹתוֹ אֵצֶל הַמִּזְבֵּחַ בַּיָּמִין בְּבוֹא־אִישׁ בֵּית יְהוָה וְנָתְנוּ־ שָׁמָּה הַכֹּהֲנִים שֹׁמְרֵי הַסַּף אֶת־כָּל־הַכֶּסֶף הַמּוּבָא בֵית־יְהוָה: 11 וַיְהִי כִּרְאוֹתָם כִּי־רַב הַכֶּסֶף בָּאָרוֹן וַיַּעַל סֹפֵר הַמֶּלֶךְ וְהַכֹּהֵן הַגָּדוֹל וַיָּצֻרוּ וַיִּמְנוּ אֶת־ הַכֶּסֶף הַנִּמְצָא בֵית־יְהוָה: 12 וְנָתְנוּ אֶת־הַכֶּסֶף הַמְתֻכָּן עַל־יְדֵ עֹשֵׂי הַמְּלָאכָה הַפְּקֻדִים בֵּית יְהוָה וַיּוֹצִיאֻהוּ לְחָרָשֵׁי הָעֵץ וְלַבֹּנִים הָעֹשִׂים בֵּית

---

timber and hewn stone, to repair the damage of the house of the LORD, and for all that was paid out to repair the temple. ¹³However there were not made for the house of the LORD basins of silver, trimmers, sprinkling-bowls, trumpets, any articles of gold or articles of silver, from the money brought into the house of the LORD. ¹⁴But they gave that to the workmen, and they repaired the house of the LORD with it. ¹⁵Moreover they did not require an account from the men into whose hand they delivered the money to be paid to workmen, for they dealt faithfully. ¹⁶The money from the trespass offerings and the money from the sin offerings was not brought into the house of the LORD. It belonged to the priests.

¹⁷Hazael king of Syria went up and fought against Gath, and took it; then Hazael set his face to go up to Jerusalem. ¹⁸And Jehoash king of Judah took all the sacred things that his fathers, Jehoshaphat and Jehoram and Ahaziah, kings of Judah, had dedicated, and his own sacred things, and all the gold found in the treasuries of the house of the LORD and in the king's house, and sent *them* to Hazael king of Syria. Then he went away from Jerusalem.

¹⁹Now the rest of the acts of Joash, and all that he did, *are* they not written in the book of the chronicles of the kings of Judah? ²⁰And his servants arose and formed a conspiracy, and killed Joash in the house of the Millo, which goes down to Silla. ²¹For Jozachar the son of Shimeath and Jehozabad the son of Shomer, his servants, struck him. So he died, and they buried him with his fathers in the City of David. Then Amaziah his son reigned in his place.

13 In the twenty-third year of Joash the son of Ahaziah, king of Judah, Jehoahaz the son of Jehu became king over Israel in Samaria, *and reigned* seventeen years. ²And he did evil in the sight of the LORD, and followed the sins of Jeroboam the son of Nebat, who had made Israel sin. He did not depart from them.

³Then the anger of the LORD was aroused against Israel, and He delivered them into the hand of Hazael king of Syria, and into the hand of Ben-Hadad the son of Hazael, all *their* days. ⁴So Jehoahaz pleaded with the LORD, and the LORD listened to him; for He saw the oppression of Israel, because the king of Syria oppressed them. ⁵Then the LORD gave Israel a deliverer, so that they escaped from under the hand of the Syrians; and the children of Israel dwelt in their tents as before. ⁶Nevertheless they did not depart from the sins of

יְהוָֽה: 13 וְלַגֹּֽדְרִים֙ וּלְחֹצְבֵ֣י הָאֶ֔בֶן וְלִקְנֹ֖ות עֵצִ֑ים וְאַבְנֵ֣י מַחְצֵ֔ב לְחַזֵּ֖ק אֶת־בֶּ֣דֶק בֵּית־יְהוָ֑ה וּלְכֹ֛ל אֲשֶׁר־יֵצֵ֥א עַל־הַבַּ֖יִת לְחָזְקָֽה: 14 אַ֣ךְ לֹ֣א יֵעָשֶׂ֣ה בֵּ֣ית יְהוָ֗ה סִפֹּ֥ות כֶּ֨סֶף֙ מְזַמְּרֹ֤ות מִזְרָקֹות֙ חֲצֹ֣צְרֹ֔ות כָּל־כְּלִ֥י זָהָ֖ב וּכְלִי־כָ֑סֶף מִן־הַכֶּ֖סֶף הַמּוּבָ֥א בֵּית־יְהוָֽה: 15 כִּֽי־לְעֹשֵׂ֥י הַמְּלָאכָ֖ה יִתְּנֻ֑הוּ וְחִזְּקוּ־בֹ֖ו אֶת־בֵּ֥ית יְהוָֽה: 16 וְלֹ֧א יְחַשְּׁב֣וּ אֶת־הָאֲנָשִׁ֗ים אֲשֶׁ֨ר יִתְּנ֤וּ אֶת־הַכֶּ֨סֶף֙ עַל־יָדָ֔ם לָתֵ֖ת לְעֹשֵׂ֣י הַמְּלָאכָ֑ה כִּ֥י בֶאֱמֻנָ֖ה הֵ֥ם עֹשִֽׂים: 17 כֶּ֤סֶף אָשָׁם֙ וְכֶ֣סֶף חַטָּאֹ֔ות לֹ֥א יוּבָ֖א בֵּ֣ית יְהוָ֑ה לַכֹּהֲנִ֖ים יִהְיֽוּ: פ

18 אָ֣ז יַעֲלֶ֗ה חֲזָאֵל֙ מֶ֣לֶךְ אֲרָ֔ם וַיִּלָּ֖חֶם עַל־גַּ֑ת וַֽיִּלְכְּדָ֑הּ וַיָּ֤שֶׂם חֲזָאֵל֙ פָּנָ֔יו לַעֲלֹ֖ות עַל־יְרוּשָׁלָֽ͏ִם: 19 וַיִּקַּ֞ח יְהֹואָ֣שׁ מֶֽלֶךְ־יְהוּדָ֗ה אֵ֣ת כָּל־הַקֳּדָשִׁ֡ים אֲשֶׁר־הִקְדִּ֣ישׁוּ יְהֹושָׁפָ֣ט וִיהֹורָם֩ וַאֲחַזְיָ֨הוּ אֲבֹתָ֜יו מַלְכֵ֤י יְהוּדָה֙ וְאֶת־קֳדָשָׁ֔יו וְאֵ֣ת כָּל־הַזָּהָ֗ב הַנִּמְצָ֛א בְּאֹצְרֹ֥ות בֵּית־יְהוָ֖ה וּבֵ֣ית הַמֶּ֑לֶךְ וַיִּשְׁלַ֖ח לַחֲזָאֵ֣ל מֶ֣לֶךְ אֲרָ֑ם וַיַּ֖עַל מֵעַ֥ל יְרוּשָׁלָֽ͏ִם: 20 וְיֶ֨תֶר֙ דִּבְרֵ֣י יֹואָ֔שׁ וְכָל־אֲשֶׁ֖ר עָשָׂ֑ה הֲלֹוא־הֵ֣ם כְּתוּבִ֗ים עַל־סֵ֛פֶר דִּבְרֵ֥י הַיָּמִ֖ים לְמַלְכֵ֥י יְהוּדָֽה: 21 וַיָּקֻ֥מוּ עֲבָדָ֖יו וַיִּקְשְׁרוּ־קָ֑שֶׁר וַיַּכּוּ֙ אֶת־יֹואָ֔שׁ בֵּ֥ית מִלֹּ֖א הַיֹּורֵ֥ד סִלָּֽא: 22 וְיֹוזָבָ֣ד בֶּן־שִׁמְעָ֡ת וִיהֹוזָבָ֣ד בֶּן־שֹׁמֵ֣ר ׀ עֲבָדָ֡יו הִכֻּ֣הוּ וַיָּמֹ֑ת וַיִּקְבְּר֥וּ אֹתֹ֛ו עִם־אֲבֹתָ֖יו בְּעִ֣יר דָּוִ֑ד וַיִּמְלֹ֛ךְ אֲמַצְיָ֥ה בְנֹ֖ו תַּחְתָּֽיו: פ

יג בִּשְׁנַ֨ת עֶשְׂרִ֤ים וְשָׁלֹשׁ֙ שָׁנָ֔ה לְיֹואָ֥שׁ בֶּן־אֲחַזְיָ֖הוּ מֶ֣לֶךְ יְהוּדָ֑ה מָ֠לַךְ יְהֹואָחָ֨ז בֶּן־יֵה֤וּא עַל־יִשְׂרָאֵל֙ בְּשֹׁ֣מְרֹ֔ון שְׁבַ֥ע עֶשְׂרֵ֖ה שָׁנָֽה: 2 וַיַּ֥עַשׂ הָרַ֖ע בְּעֵינֵ֣י יְהוָ֑ה וַ֠יֵּלֶךְ אַחַ֨ר חַטֹּ֜את יָרָבְעָ֧ם בֶּן־נְבָ֛ט אֲשֶׁר־הֶחֱטִ֥יא אֶת־יִשְׂרָאֵ֖ל לֹא־סָ֥ר מִמֶּֽנָּה: 3 וַיִּֽחַר־אַ֤ף יְהוָה֙ בְּיִשְׂרָאֵ֔ל וַֽיִּתְּנֵ֞ם בְּיַ֣ד ׀ חֲזָאֵ֣ל מֶֽלֶךְ־אֲרָ֗ם וּבְיַ֛ד בֶּן־הֲדַ֥ד בֶּן־חֲזָאֵ֖ל כָּל־הַיָּמִֽים: 4 וַיְחַ֥ל יְהֹואָחָ֖ז אֶת־פְּנֵ֣י יְהוָ֑ה וַיִּשְׁמַ֤ע אֵלָיו֙ יְהוָ֔ה כִּ֣י רָאָ֔ה אֶת־לַ֖חַץ יִשְׂרָאֵ֑ל כִּֽי־לָחַ֥ץ אֹתָ֖ם מֶ֥לֶךְ אֲרָֽם: 5 וַיִּתֵּ֨ן יְהוָ֤ה לְיִשְׂרָאֵל֙ מֹושִׁ֔יעַ וַיֵּ֣צְא֔וּ מִתַּ֖חַת יַד־אֲרָ֑ם וַיֵּשְׁב֧וּ בְנֵֽי־יִשְׂרָאֵ֛ל בְּאָהֳלֵיהֶ֖ם כִּתְמֹ֥ול שִׁלְשֹֽׁום: 6 אַ֠ךְ לֹֽא־סָ֜רוּ מֵחַטֹּ֧אות בֵּֽית־יָרָבְעָ֛ם אֲשֶׁר־הֶחֱטִ֥יא אֶת־יִשְׂרָאֵ֖ל

the house of Jeroboam, who had made Israel sin, *but* walked in them; and the wooden image also remained in Samaria. ⁷For He left of the army of Jehoahaz only fifty horsemen, ten chariots, and ten thousand foot soldiers; for the king of Syria had destroyed them and made them like the dust at threshing.

⁸Now the rest of the acts of Jehoahaz, all that he did, and his might, *are* they not written in the book of the chronicles of the kings of Israel? ⁹So Jehoahaz rested with his fathers, and they buried him in Samaria. Then Joash his son reigned in his place.

¹⁰In the thirty-seventh year of Joash king of Judah, Jehoash the son of Jehoahaz became king over Israel in Samaria, *and reigned* sixteen years. ¹¹And he did evil in the sight of the LORD. He did not depart from all the sins of Jeroboam the son of Nebat, who made Israel sin, *but* walked in them.

¹²Now the rest of the acts of Joash, all that he did, and his might with which he fought against Amaziah king of Judah, *are* they not written in the book of the chronicles of the kings of Israel? ¹³So Joash rested with his fathers. Then Jeroboam sat on his throne. And Joash was buried in Samaria with the kings of Israel.

¹⁴Elisha had become sick with the illness of which he would die. Then Joash the king of Israel came down to him, and wept over his face, and said, "O my father, my father, the chariots of Israel and their horsemen!"

¹⁵And Elisha said to him, "Take a bow and some arrows." So he took himself a bow and some arrows. ¹⁶Then he said to the king of Israel, "Put your hand on the bow." So he put his hand *on it,* and Elisha put his hands on the king's hands. ¹⁷And he said, "Open the east window"; and he opened *it.* Then Elisha said, "Shoot"; and he shot. And he said, "The arrow of the LORD's deliverance and the arrow of deliverance from Syria; for you must strike the Syrians at Aphek till you have destroyed *them.*" ¹⁸Then he said, "Take the arrows"; so he took *them.* And he said to the king of Israel, "Strike the ground"; so he struck three times, and stopped. ¹⁹And the man of God was angry with him, and said, "You should have struck five or six times; then you would have struck Syria till you had destroyed *it!* But now you will strike Syria *only* three times."

²⁰Then Elisha died, and they buried him. And the *raiding* bands from Moab invaded the land in the spring of the year. ²¹So it was, as they were burying a man, that suddenly they spied a band of

בָּהּ הָלָךְ וְגַם הָאֲשֵׁרָה עָמְדָה בְּשֹׁמְרוֹן: ⁷ כִּי לֹא הִשְׁאִיר לִיהוֹאָחָז עָם כִּי אִם־חֲמִשִּׁים פָּרָשִׁים וַעֲשָׂרָה רֶכֶב וַעֲשֶׂרֶת אֲלָפִים רַגְלִי כִּי אִבְּדָם מֶלֶךְ אֲרָם וַיְשִׂמֵם כֶּעָפָר לָדֻשׁ: ⁸ וְיֶתֶר דִּבְרֵי יְהוֹאָחָז וְכָל־אֲשֶׁר עָשָׂה וּגְבוּרָתוֹ הֲלוֹא־הֵם כְּתוּבִים עַל־ סֵפֶר דִּבְרֵי הַיָּמִים לְמַלְכֵי יִשְׂרָאֵל: ⁹ וַיִּשְׁכַּב יְהוֹאָחָז עִם־אֲבֹתָיו וַיִּקְבְּרֻהוּ בְּשֹׁמְרוֹן וַיִּמְלֹךְ יוֹאָשׁ בְּנוֹ תַּחְתָּיו:

¹⁰ בִּשְׁנַת שְׁלֹשִׁים וָשֶׁבַע שָׁנָה לְיוֹאָשׁ מֶלֶךְ יְהוּדָה מָלַךְ יְהוֹאָשׁ בֶּן־יְהוֹאָחָז עַל־יִשְׂרָאֵל בְּשֹׁמְרוֹן שֵׁשׁ עֶשְׂרֵה שָׁנָה: ¹¹ וַיַּעֲשֶׂה הָרַע בְּעֵינֵי יְהֹוָה לֹא סָר מִכָּל־חַטֹּאות יָרָבְעָם בֶּן־נְבָט אֲשֶׁר־הֶחֱטִיא אֶת־יִשְׂרָאֵל בָּהּ הָלָךְ: ¹² וְיֶתֶר דִּבְרֵי יוֹאָשׁ וְכָל־ אֲשֶׁר עָשָׂה וּגְבוּרָתוֹ אֲשֶׁר נִלְחַם עִם אֲמַצְיָה מֶלֶךְ־יְהוּדָה הֲלוֹא־הֵם כְּתוּבִים עַל־סֵפֶר דִּבְרֵי הַיָּמִים לְמַלְכֵי יִשְׂרָאֵל: ¹³ וַיִּשְׁכַּב יוֹאָשׁ עִם־אֲבֹתָיו וְיָרָבְעָם יָשַׁב עַל־כִּסְאוֹ וַיִּקָּבֵר יוֹאָשׁ בְּשֹׁמְרוֹן עִם מַלְכֵי יִשְׂרָאֵל:

¹⁴ וֶאֱלִישָׁע חָלָה אֶת־חָלְיוֹ אֲשֶׁר יָמוּת בּוֹ וַיֵּרֶד אֵלָיו יוֹאָשׁ מֶלֶךְ־יִשְׂרָאֵל וַיֵּבְךְּ עַל־פָּנָיו וַיֹּאמַר אָבִי | אָבִי רֶכֶב יִשְׂרָאֵל וּפָרָשָׁיו: ¹⁵ וַיֹּאמֶר לוֹ אֱלִישָׁע קַח קֶשֶׁת וְחִצִּים וַיִּקַּח אֵלָיו קֶשֶׁת וְחִצִּים: ¹⁶ וַיֹּאמֶר | לְמֶלֶךְ יִשְׂרָאֵל הַרְכֵּב יָדְךָ עַל־הַקֶּשֶׁת וַיַּרְכֵּב יָדוֹ וַיָּשֶׂם אֱלִישָׁע יָדָיו עַל־יְדֵי הַמֶּלֶךְ: ¹⁷ וַיֹּאמֶר פְּתַח הַחַלּוֹן קֵדְמָה וַיִּפְתָּח וַיֹּאמֶר אֱלִישָׁע יְרֵה וַיּוֹר וַיֹּאמֶר חֵץ־תְּשׁוּעָה לַיהֹוָה וְחֵץ תְּשׁוּעָה בַאֲרָם וְהִכִּיתָ אֶת־אֲרָם בַּאֲפֵק עַד־כַּלֵּה: ¹⁸ וַיֹּאמֶר קַח הַחִצִּים וַיִּקָּח וַיֹּאמֶר לְמֶלֶךְ־יִשְׂרָאֵל הַךְ־אַרְצָה וַיַּךְ שָׁלֹשׁ־פְּעָמִים וַיַּעֲמֹד: ¹⁹ וַיִּקְצֹף עָלָיו אִישׁ הָאֱלֹהִים וַיֹּאמֶר לְהַכּוֹת חָמֵשׁ אוֹ־שֵׁשׁ פְּעָמִים אָז הִכִּיתָ אֶת־אֲרָם עַד־כַּלֵּה וְעַתָּה שָׁלֹשׁ פְּעָמִים תַּכֶּה אֶת־אֲרָם: ²⁰ וַיָּמָת אֱלִישָׁע וַיִּקְבְּרֻהוּ וּגְדוּדֵי מוֹאָב יָבֹאוּ בָאָרֶץ בָּא שָׁנָה: ²¹ וַיְהִי הֵם | קֹבְרִים אִישׁ וְהִנֵּה רָאוּ אֶת־הַגְּדוּד וַיַּשְׁלִיכוּ אֶת־ הָאִישׁ בְּקֶבֶר אֱלִישָׁע וַיֵּלֶךְ וַיִּגַּע הָאִישׁ בְּעַצְמוֹת

raiders; and they put the man in the tomb of Elisha; and when the man was let down and touched the bones of Elisha, he revived and stood on his feet.

22 And Hazael king of Syria oppressed Israel all the days of Jehoahaz. 23 But the LORD was gracious to them, had compassion on them, and regarded them, because of His covenant with Abraham, Isaac, and Jacob, and would not yet destroy them or cast them from His presence.

24 Now Hazael king of Syria died. Then Ben-Hadad his son reigned in his place. 25 And Jehoash the son of Jehoahaz recaptured from the hand of Ben-Hadad, the son of Hazael, the cities which he had taken out of the hand of Jehoahaz his father by war. Three times Joash defeated him and recaptured the cities of Israel.

14 In the second year of Joash the son of Jehoahaz, king of Israel, Amaziah the son of Joash, king of Judah, became king. 2 He was twenty-five years old when he became king, and he reigned twenty-nine years in Jerusalem. His mother's name was Jehoaddan of Jerusalem. 3 And he did *what was* right in the sight of the LORD, yet not like his father David; he did everything as his father Joash had done. 4 However the high places were not taken away, and the people still sacrificed and burned incense on the high places.

5 Now it happened, as soon as the kingdom was established in his hand, that he executed his servants who had murdered his father the king. 6 But the children of the murderers he did not execute, according to what is written in the Book of the Law of Moses, in which the LORD commanded, saying, "Fathers shall not be put to death for their children, nor shall children be put to death for their fathers; but a person shall be put to death for his own sin."

7 He killed ten thousand Edomites in the Valley of Salt, and took Sela by war, and called its name Joktheel to this day.

8 Then Amaziah sent messengers to Jehoash the son of Jehoahaz, the son of Jehu, king of Israel, saying, "Come, let us face one another *in battle.*" 9 And Jehoash king of Israel sent to Amaziah king of Judah, saying, "The thistle that *was* in Lebanon sent to the cedar that *was* in Lebanon, saying, 'Give your daughter to my son as wife'; and a wild beast that *was* in Lebanon passed by and trampled the thistle. 10 You have indeed defeated Edom, and your heart has lifted you up. Glory *in that,* and stay at home; for why should you meddle with trouble so that you fall—you and Judah with you?"

אֱלִישָׁע וַיְחִי וַיָּקָם עַל־רַגְלָיו: פ

22 וַחֲזָאֵל מֶלֶךְ אֲרָם לָחַץ אֶת־יִשְׂרָאֵל כֹּל יְמֵי יְהוֹאָחָז: 23 וַיָּחָן יְהוָה אֹתָם וַיְרַחֲמֵם וַיִּפֶן אֲלֵיהֶם לְמַעַן בְּרִיתוֹ אֶת־אַבְרָהָם יִצְחָק וְיַעֲקֹב וְלֹא אָבָה הַשְׁחִיתָם וְלֹא־הִשְׁלִיכָם מֵעַל־פָּנָיו עַד־עָתָּה: 24 וַיָּמָת חֲזָאֵל מֶלֶךְ־אֲרָם וַיִּמְלֹךְ בֶּן־הֲדַד בְּנוֹ תַּחְתָּיו: 25 וַיָּשָׁב יְהוֹאָשׁ בֶּן־יְהוֹאָחָז וַיִּקַּח אֶת־הֶעָרִים מִיַּד בֶּן־הֲדַד בֶּן־חֲזָאֵל אֲשֶׁר לָקַח מִיַּד יְהוֹאָחָז אָבִיו בַּמִּלְחָמָה שָׁלֹשׁ פְּעָמִים הִכָּהוּ יוֹאָשׁ וַיָּשֶׁב אֶת־עָרֵי יִשְׂרָאֵל: פ

יד בִּשְׁנַת שְׁתַּיִם לְיוֹאָשׁ בֶּן־יוֹאָחָז מֶלֶךְ יִשְׂרָאֵל מָלַךְ אֲמַצְיָהוּ בֶן־יוֹאָשׁ מֶלֶךְ יְהוּדָה: 2 בֶּן־עֶשְׂרִים וְחָמֵשׁ שָׁנָה הָיָה בְמָלְכוֹ וְעֶשְׂרִים וָתֵשַׁע שָׁנָה מָלַךְ בִּירוּשָׁלִָם וְשֵׁם אִמּוֹ יְהוֹעַדָּןᴾ מִן־יְרוּשָׁלָ͏ִם: 3 וַיַּעַשׂ הַיָּשָׁר בְּעֵינֵי יְהוָה רַק לֹא כְּדָוִד אָבִיו כְּכֹל אֲשֶׁר־עָשָׂה יוֹאָשׁ אָבִיו עָשָׂה: 4 רַק הַבָּמוֹת לֹא־סָרוּ עוֹד הָעָם מְזַבְּחִים וּמְקַטְּרִים בַּבָּמוֹת: 5 וַיְהִי כַּאֲשֶׁר חָזְקָה הַמַּמְלָכָה בְּיָדוֹ וַיַּךְ אֶת־עֲבָדָיו הַמַּכִּים אֶת־הַמֶּלֶךְ אָבִיו: 6 וְאֶת־בְּנֵי הַמַּכִּים לֹא הֵמִית כַּכָּתוּב בְּסֵפֶר תּוֹרַת־מֹשֶׁה אֲשֶׁר־צִוָּה יְהוָה לֵאמֹר לֹא־יוּמְתוּ אָבוֹת עַל־בָּנִים וּבָנִים לֹא־יוּמְתוּ עַל־אָבוֹת כִּי אִם־אִישׁ בְּחֶטְאוֹ יָמֻתᴾ: 7 הוּא־הִכָּה אֶת־אֱדוֹם בְּגֵיא־הַמֶּלַחᴾ עֲשֶׂרֶת אֲלָפִים וְתָפַשׂ אֶת־הַסֶּלַע בַּמִּלְחָמָה וַיִּקְרָא אֶת־שְׁמָהּ יָקְתְאֵל עַד הַיּוֹם הַזֶּה: פ

8 אָז שָׁלַח אֲמַצְיָה מַלְאָכִים אֶל־יְהוֹאָשׁ בֶּן־יְהוֹאָחָז בֶּן־יֵהוּא מֶלֶךְ יִשְׂרָאֵל לֵאמֹר לְכָה נִתְרָאֶה פָנִים: 9 וַיִּשְׁלַח יְהוֹאָשׁ מֶלֶךְ־יִשְׂרָאֵל אֶל־אֲמַצְיָהוּ מֶלֶךְ־יְהוּדָה לֵאמֹר הַחוֹחַ אֲשֶׁר בַּלְּבָנוֹן שָׁלַח אֶל־הָאֶרֶז אֲשֶׁר בַּלְּבָנוֹן לֵאמֹר תְּנָה־אֶת־בִּתְּךָ לִבְנִי לְאִשָּׁה וַתַּעֲבֹר חַיַּת הַשָּׂדֶה אֲשֶׁר בַּלְּבָנוֹן וַתִּרְמֹס אֶת־הַחוֹחַ: 10 הַכֵּה הִכִּיתָ אֶת־אֱדוֹם וּנְשָׂאֲךָ לִבֶּךָ הִכָּבֵד וְשֵׁב בְּבֵיתֶךָ וְלָמָּה תִתְגָּרֶה בְּרָעָה וְנָפַלְתָּה

11 But Amaziah would not heed. Therefore Jehoash king of Israel went out; so he and Amaziah king of Judah faced one another at Beth Shemesh, which *belongs* to Judah. 12 And Judah was defeated by Israel, and every man fled to his tent. 13 Then Jehoash king of Israel captured Amaziah king of Judah, the son of Jehoash, the son of Ahaziah, at Beth Shemesh; and he went to Jerusalem, and broke down the wall of Jerusalem from the Gate of Ephraim to the Corner Gate—four hundred cubits. 14 And he took all the gold and silver, all the articles that were found in the house of the LORD and in the treasuries of the king's house, and hostages, and returned to Samaria.

15 Now the rest of the acts of Jehoash which he did—his might, and how he fought with Amaziah king of Judah—*are* they not written in the book of the chronicles of the kings of Israel? 16 So Jehoash rested with his fathers, and was buried in Samaria with the kings of Israel. Then Jeroboam his son reigned in his place.

17 Amaziah the son of Joash, king of Judah, lived fifteen years after the death of Jehoash the son of Jehoahaz, king of Israel. 18 Now the rest of the acts of Amaziah, *are* they not written in the book of the chronicles of the kings of Judah? 19 And they formed a conspiracy against him in Jerusalem, and he fled to Lachish; but they sent after him to Lachish and killed him there. 20 Then they brought him on horses, and he was buried at Jerusalem with his fathers in the City of David.

21 And all the people of Judah took Azariah, who *was* sixteen years old, and made him king instead of his father Amaziah. 22 He built Elath and restored it to Judah, after the king rested with his fathers.

23 In the fifteenth year of Amaziah the son of Joash, king of Judah, Jeroboam the son of Joash, king of Israel, became king in Samaria, *and reigned* forty-one years. 24 And he did evil in the sight of the LORD; he did not depart from all the sins of Jeroboam the son of Nebat, who had made Israel sin. 25 He restored the territory of Israel from the entrance of Hamath to the Sea of the Arabah, according to the word of the LORD God of Israel, which He had spoken through His servant Jonah the son of Amittai, the prophet who *was* from Gath Hepher. 26 For the LORD saw *that* the affliction of Israel *was* very bitter; and whether bond or free, there was no helper for Israel. 27 And the LORD did not say that He would blot out the name of Israel from under heaven; but He saved them by the hand of Jeroboam the son of Joash.

אַתָּה וִיהוּדָה עִמָּךְ: 11 וְלֹא־שָׁמַע אֲמַצְיָהוּ וַיַּעַל יְהוֹאָשׁ מֶלֶךְ־יִשְׂרָאֵל וַיִּתְרָאוּ פָנִים הוּא וַאֲמַצְיָהוּ מֶלֶךְ־יְהוּדָה בְּבֵית שֶׁמֶשׁ אֲשֶׁר לִיהוּדָה: 12 וַיִּנָּגֶף יְהוּדָה לִפְנֵי יִשְׂרָאֵל וַיָּנֻסוּ אִישׁ לְאֹהָלָיו P 13 וְאֵת אֲמַצְיָהוּ מֶלֶךְ־יְהוּדָה בֶּן־יְהוֹאָשׁ בֶּן־אֲחַזְיָהוּ תָּפַשׂ יְהוֹאָשׁ מֶלֶךְ־יִשְׂרָאֵל בְּבֵית שָׁמֶשׁ וַיָּבֹאוּ P יְרוּשָׁלַ͏ִם וַיִּפְרֹץ בְּחוֹמַת יְרוּשָׁלַ͏ִם בְּשַׁעַר אֶפְרַיִם עַד־שַׁעַר הַפִּנָּה אַרְבַּע מֵאוֹת אַמָּה: 14 וְלָקַח אֶת־כָּל־ הַזָּהָב־וְהַכֶּסֶף וְאֵת כָּל־הַכֵּלִים הַנִּמְצְאִים בֵּית־ יְהוָה וּבְאֹצְרוֹת בֵּית הַמֶּלֶךְ וְאֵת בְּנֵי הַתַּעֲרֻבוֹת וַיָּשָׁב שֹׁמְרוֹנָה: 15 וְיֶתֶר דִּבְרֵי יְהוֹאָשׁ אֲשֶׁר עָשָׂה וּגְבוּרָתוֹ וַאֲשֶׁר נִלְחַם עִם אֲמַצְיָהוּ מֶלֶךְ־ יְהוּדָה הֲלֹא־הֵם כְּתוּבִים עַל־סֵפֶר דִּבְרֵי הַיָּמִים לְמַלְכֵי יִשְׂרָאֵל: 16 וַיִּשְׁכַּב יְהוֹאָשׁ עִם־אֲבֹתָיו וַיִּקָּבֵר בְּשֹׁמְרוֹן עִם מַלְכֵי יִשְׂרָאֵל וַיִּמְלֹךְ יָרָבְעָם בְּנוֹ תַּחְתָּיו: פ

17 וַיְחִי אֲמַצְיָהוּ בֶן־יוֹאָשׁ מֶלֶךְ יְהוּדָה אַחֲרֵי מוֹת יְהוֹאָשׁ בֶּן־יְהוֹאָחָז מֶלֶךְ יִשְׂרָאֵל חֲמֵשׁ עֶשְׂרֵה שָׁנָה: 18 וְיֶתֶר דִּבְרֵי אֲמַצְיָהוּ הֲלֹא־הֵם כְּתוּבִים עַל־סֵפֶר דִּבְרֵי הַיָּמִים לְמַלְכֵי יְהוּדָה: 19 וַיִּקְשְׁרוּ עָלָיו קֶשֶׁר בִּירוּשָׁלַ͏ִם וַיָּנָס לָכִישָׁה וַיִּשְׁלְחוּ אַחֲרָיו לָכִישָׁה וַיְמִתֻהוּ שָׁם: 20 וַיִּשְׂאוּ אֹתוֹ עַל־הַסּוּסִים וַיִּקָּבֵר בִּירוּשָׁלַ͏ִם עִם־אֲבֹתָיו בְּעִיר דָּוִד: 21 וַיִּקְחוּ כָּל־ עַם יְהוּדָה אֶת־עֲזַרְיָה וְהוּא בֶּן־שֵׁשׁ עֶשְׂרֵה שָׁנָה וַיַּמְלִכוּ אֹתוֹ תַּחַת אָבִיו אֲמַצְיָהוּ: 22 הוּא בָּנָה אֶת־אֵילַת וַיְשִׁבֶהָ לִיהוּדָה אַחֲרֵי שְׁכַב־הַמֶּלֶךְ עִם־ אֲבֹתָיו: פ

23 בִּשְׁנַת חֲמֵשׁ־עֶשְׂרֵה שָׁנָה לַאֲמַצְיָהוּ בֶן־יוֹאָשׁ מֶלֶךְ יְהוּדָה מָלַךְ יָרָבְעָם בֶּן־יוֹאָשׁ מֶלֶךְ־יִשְׂרָאֵל בְּשֹׁמְרוֹן אַרְבָּעִים וְאַחַת שָׁנָה: 24 וַיַּעַשׂ הָרַע בְּעֵינֵי יְהוָה לֹא סָר מִכָּל־חַטֹּאות יָרָבְעָם בֶּן־נְבָט אֲשֶׁר הֶחֱטִיא אֶת־יִשְׂרָאֵל: 25 הוּא הֵשִׁיב אֶת־ גְּבוּל יִשְׂרָאֵל מִלְּבוֹא חֲמָת עַד־יָם הָעֲרָבָה כִּדְבַר יְהוָה אֱלֹהֵי יִשְׂרָאֵל אֲשֶׁר דִּבֶּר בְּיַד־עַבְדּוֹ יוֹנָה בֶן־אֲמִתַּי הַנָּבִיא אֲשֶׁר מִגַּת הַחֵפֶר: 26 כִּי־רָאָה יְהוָה אֶת־עֳנִי יִשְׂרָאֵל מֹרֶה מְאֹד וְאֶפֶס עָצוּר וְאֶפֶס עָזוּב וְאֵין עֹזֵר לְיִשְׂרָאֵל: 27 וְלֹא־דִבֶּר יְהוָה לִמְחוֹת אֶת־שֵׁם יִשְׂרָאֵל מִתַּחַת הַשָּׁמָיִם וַיּוֹשִׁיעֵם

יד 12 לְאֹהָלָיו 13 וַיָּבֹא

28 Now the rest of the acts of Jeroboam, and all that he did—his might, how he made war, and how he recaptured for Israel, from Damascus and Hamath, *what had belonged* to Judah—*are* they not written in the book of the chronicles of the kings of Israel? 29 So Jeroboam rested with his fathers, the kings of Israel. Then Zechariah his son reigned in his place.

15 In the twenty-seventh year of Jeroboam king of Israel, Azariah the son of Amaziah, king of Judah, became king. 2 He was sixteen years old when he became king, and he reigned fifty-two years in Jerusalem. His mother's name *was* Jecholiah of Jerusalem. 3 And he did *what was* right in the sight of the LORD, according to all that his father Amaziah had done, 4 except that the high places were not removed; the people still sacrificed and burned incense on the high places. 5 Then the LORD struck the king, so that he was a leper until the day of his death; so he dwelt in an isolated house. And Jotham the king's son *was* over the *royal* house, judging the people of the land.

6 Now the rest of the acts of Azariah, and all that he did, *are* they not written in the book of the chronicles of the kings of Judah? 7 So Azariah rested with his fathers, and they buried him with his fathers in the City of David. Then Jotham his son reigned in his place.

8 In the thirty-eighth year of Azariah king of Judah, Zechariah the son of Jeroboam reigned over Israel in Samaria six months. 9 And he did evil in the sight of the LORD, as his fathers had done; he did not depart from the sins of Jeroboam the son of Nebat, who had made Israel sin. 10 Then Shallum the son of Jabesh conspired against him, and struck and killed him in front of the people; and he reigned in his place.

11 Now the rest of the acts of Zechariah, indeed they *are* written in the book of the chronicles of the kings of Israel.

12 This *was* the word of the LORD which He spoke to Jehu, saying, "Your sons shall sit on the throne of Israel to the fourth *generation*." And so it was.

13 Shallum the son of Jabesh became king in the thirty-ninth year of Uzziah king of Judah; and he reigned a full month in Samaria. 14 For Menahem the son of Gadi went up from Tirzah, came to Samaria, and struck Shallum the son of Jabesh in Samaria and killed him; and he reigned in his place.

15 Now the rest of the acts of Shallum, and the conspiracy which he led, indeed they *are* written in the book of the chronicles of the kings of Israel.

16 Then from Tirzah, Menahem attacked Tiphsah,

28 וְיֶ֤תֶר דִּבְרֵ֤י יָרׇבְעָם֙ וְכׇל־ אֲשֶׁ֣ר עָשָׂ֔ה וּגְבֽוּרָת֖וֹ אֲשֶׁר־נִלְחָ֑ם וַאֲשֶׁ֣ר הֵשִׁ֞יב אֶת־דַּמֶּ֧שֶׂק וְאֶת־חֲמָ֛ת לִיהוּדָ֖ה בְּיִשְׂרָאֵ֑ל הֲלֹא־הֵ֣ם כְּתוּבִ֗ים עַל־סֵ֛פֶר דִּבְרֵ֥י הַיָּמִ֖ים לְמַלְכֵ֥י יִשְׂרָאֵֽל׃ 29 וַיִּשְׁכַּ֤ב יָרׇבְעָם֙ עִם־אֲבֹתָ֔יו עִ֖ם מַלְכֵ֣י יִשְׂרָאֵ֑ל וַיִּמְלֹ֛ךְ זְכַרְיָ֥ה בְנ֖וֹ תַּחְתָּֽיו׃ פ

טו בִּשְׁנַ֨ת עֶשְׂרִ֤ים וָשֶׁ֙בַע֙ שָׁנָ֔ה לְיָרׇבְעָ֖ם מֶ֣לֶךְ יִשְׂרָאֵ֑ל מָלַ֛ךְ עֲזַרְיָ֥ה בֶן־אֲמַצְיָ֖ה מֶ֥לֶךְ יְהוּדָֽה׃ 2 בֶּן־ שֵׁ֨שׁ עֶשְׂרֵ֤ה שָׁנָה֙ הָיָ֣ה בְמׇלְכ֔וֹ וַחֲמִשִּׁ֤ים וּשְׁתַּ֙יִם֙ שָׁנָ֔ה מָלַ֖ךְ בִּירֽוּשָׁלִָ֑ם וְשֵׁ֣ם אִמּ֔וֹ יְכׇלְיָ֖הוּ מִירֽוּשָׁלָֽ͏ִם׃ 3 וַיַּ֥עַשׂ הַיָּשָׁ֖ר בְּעֵינֵ֣י יְהֹוָ֑ה כְּכֹ֥ל אֲשֶׁר־עָשָׂ֖ה אֲמַצְיָ֥הוּ אָבִֽיו׃ 4 רַ֥ק הַבָּמ֖וֹת לֹא־סָ֑רוּ ע֥וֹד הָעָ֛ם מְזַבְּחִ֥ים וּֽמְקַטְּרִ֖ים בַּבָּמֽוֹת׃ 5 וַיְנַגַּ֨ע יְהֹוָ֜ה אֶת־הַמֶּ֗לֶךְ וַיְהִ֤י מְצֹרָע֙ עַד־י֣וֹם מֹת֔וֹ וַיֵּ֖שֶׁב בְּבֵ֣ית הַחׇפְשִׁ֑ית וְיוֹתָ֤ם בֶּן־הַמֶּ֙לֶךְ֙ עַל־הַבַּ֔יִת שֹׁפֵ֖ט אֶת־עַ֥ם הָאָֽרֶץ׃ 6 וְיֶ֛תֶר דִּבְרֵ֥י עֲזַרְיָ֖הוּ וְכׇל־אֲשֶׁ֣ר עָשָׂ֑ה הֲלֹא־הֵ֣ם כְּתוּבִ֗ים עַל־סֵ֛פֶר דִּבְרֵ֥י הַיָּמִ֖ים לְמַלְכֵ֥י יְהוּדָֽה׃ 7 וַיִּשְׁכַּ֤ב עֲזַרְיָה֙ עִם־אֲבֹתָ֔יו וַיִּקְבְּר֥וּ אֹת֛וֹ עִם־אֲבֹתָ֖יו בְּעִ֣יר דָּוִ֑ד וַיִּמְלֹ֛ךְ יוֹתָ֥ם בְּנ֖וֹ תַּחְתָּֽיו׃ פ

8 בִּשְׁנַ֨ת שְׁלֹשִׁ֤ים וּשְׁמֹנֶה֙ שָׁנָ֔ה לַעֲזַרְיָ֖הוּ מֶ֣לֶךְ יְהוּדָ֑ה מָ֠לַ֠ךְ זְכַרְיָ֨הוּ בֶן־יָרׇבְעָ֧ם עַל־יִשְׂרָאֵ֛ל בְּשֹׁמְר֖וֹן שִׁשָּׁ֥ה חֳדָשִֽׁים׃ 9 וַיַּ֤עַשׂ הָרַע֙ בְּעֵינֵ֣י יְהֹוָ֔ה כַּאֲשֶׁ֥ר עָשׂ֖וּ אֲבֹתָ֑יו לֹ֣א סָ֗ר מֵֽחַטֹּאות֙ יָרׇבְעָ֣ם בֶּן־נְבָ֔ט אֲשֶׁ֥ר הֶחֱטִ֖יא אֶת־יִשְׂרָאֵֽל׃ 10 וַיִּקְשֹׁ֤ר עָלָיו֙ שַׁלֻּ֣ם בֶּן־יָבֵ֔שׁ וַיַּכֵּ֥הוּ קׇבׇלְעָ֖ם וַיְמִתֵ֑הוּ וַיִּמְלֹ֖ךְ תַּחְתָּֽיו׃ 11 וְיֶ֛תֶר דִּבְרֵ֥י זְכַרְיָ֖ה הִנָּ֣ם כְּתוּבִ֑ים עַל־סֵ֛פֶר דִּבְרֵ֥י הַיָּמִ֖ים לְמַלְכֵ֥י יִשְׂרָאֵֽל׃ 12 ה֣וּא דְבַר־יְהֹוָ֗ה אֲשֶׁ֨ר דִּבֶּ֤ר אֶל־יֵהוּא֙ לֵאמֹ֔ר בְּנֵ֣י רְבִיעִ֔ים יֵשְׁב֥וּ לְךָ֖ עַל־כִּסֵּ֣א יִשְׂרָאֵ֑ל וַֽיְהִי־כֵֽן׃ פ

13 שַׁלּ֤וּם בֶּן־יָבֵישׁ֙ מָלַ֔ךְ בִּשְׁנַ֛ת שְׁלֹשִׁ֥ים וָתֵ֖שַׁע שָׁנָ֑ה לְעֻזִּיָּ֖ה מֶ֣לֶךְ יְהוּדָ֑ה וַיִּמְלֹ֥ךְ יֶֽרַח־יָמִ֖ים בְּשֹׁמְרֽוֹן׃ 14 וַיַּֽעַל֩ מְנַחֵ֨ם בֶּן־גָּדִ֜י מִתִּרְצָ֗ה וַיָּבֹא֙ שֹׁמְר֔וֹן וַיַּ֛ךְ אֶת־שַׁלּ֥וּם בֶּן־יָבֵ֖ישׁ בְּשֹׁמְר֑וֹן וַיְמִיתֵ֖הוּ וַיִּמְלֹ֥ךְ תַּחְתָּֽיו׃ 15 וְיֶ֤תֶר דִּבְרֵ֤י שַׁלּוּם֙ וְקִשְׁר֣וֹ אֲשֶׁ֣ר קָשָׁ֔ר הִנָּ֣ם כְּתֻבִ֗ים עַל־סֵ֛פֶר דִּבְרֵ֥י הַיָּמִ֖ים לְמַלְכֵ֥י יִשְׂרָאֵֽל׃ ס 16 אָ֣ז יַכֶּה־מְנַחֵ֞ם אֶת־תִּפְסַ֣ח

all who *were* there, and its territory. Because they did not surrender, therefore he attacked *it*. All the women there who were with child he ripped open.

17 In the thirty-ninth year of Azariah king of Judah, Menahem the son of Gadi became king over Israel, *and reigned* ten years in Samaria. 18 And he did evil in the sight of the LORD; he did not depart all his days from the sins of Jeroboam the son of Nebat, who had made Israel sin. 19 Pul king of Assyria came against the land; and Menahem gave Pul a thousand talents of silver, that his hand might be with him to strengthen the kingdom under his control. 20 And Menahem exacted the money from Israel, from all the very wealthy, from each man fifty shekels of silver, to give to the king of Assyria. So the king of Assyria turned back, and did not stay there in the land.

21 Now the rest of the acts of Menahem, and all that he did, *are* they not written in the book of the chronicles of the kings of Israel? 22 So Menahem rested with his fathers. Then Pekahiah his son reigned in his place.

23 In the fiftieth year of Azariah king of Judah, Pekahiah the son of Menahem became king over Israel in Samaria, *and reigned* two years. 24 And he did evil in the sight of the LORD; he did not depart from the sins of Jeroboam the son of Nebat, who had made Israel sin. 25 Then Pekah the son of Remaliah, an officer of his, conspired against him and killed him in Samaria, in the citadel of the king's house, along with Argob and Arieh; and with him were fifty men of Gilead. He killed him and reigned in his place.

26 Now the rest of the acts of Pekahiah, and all that he did, indeed they *are* written in the book of the chronicles of the kings of Israel.

27 In the fifty-second year of Azariah king of Judah, Pekah the son of Remaliah became king over Israel in Samaria, *and reigned* twenty years. 28 And he did evil in the sight of the LORD; he did not depart from the sins of Jeroboam the son of Nebat, who had made Israel sin. 29 In the days of Pekah king of Israel, Tiglath-Pileser king of Assyria came and took Ijon, Abel Beth Maachah, Janoah, Kedesh, Hazor, Gilead, and Galilee, all the land of Naphtali; and he carried them captive to Assyria. 30 Then Hoshea the son of Elah led a conspiracy against Pekah the son of Remaliah, and struck and killed him; so he reigned in his place in the twentieth year of Jotham the son of Uzziah.

31 Now the rest of the acts of Pekah, and all that he did, indeed they *are* written in the book of the chronicles of the kings of Israel.

וְאֶת־כָּל־אֲשֶׁר־בָּהּ וְאֶת־גְּבוּלֶיהָ מִתִּרְצָה כִּי לֹא
פָתַח וַיָּךְ אֵת כָּל־הֶהָרוֹתֶיהָ בִּקֵּעַ: פ

17 בִּשְׁנַת שְׁלֹשִׁים וָתֵשַׁע שָׁנָה לַעֲזַרְיָה מֶלֶךְ
יְהוּדָה מָלַךְ מְנַחֵם בֶּן־גָּדִי עַל־יִשְׂרָאֵל עֶשֶׂר שָׁנִים
בְּשֹׁמְרוֹן: 18 וַיַּעַשׂ הָרַע בְּעֵינֵי יְהֹוָה לֹא סָר מֵעַל
חַטֹּאות יָרָבְעָם בֶּן־נְבָט אֲשֶׁר־הֶחֱטִיא אֶת־יִשְׂרָאֵל
כָּל־יָמָיו: 19 בָּא פוּל מֶלֶךְ־אַשּׁוּר עַל־הָאָרֶץ וַיִּתֵּן
מְנַחֵם לְפוּל אֶלֶף כִּכַּר־כָּסֶף לִהְיוֹת יָדָיו אִתּוֹ
לְהַחֲזִיק הַמַּמְלָכָה בְּיָדוֹ: 20 וַיֹּצֵא מְנַחֵם אֶת־הַכֶּסֶף
עַל־יִשְׂרָאֵל עַל כָּל־גִּבּוֹרֵי הַחַיִל לָתֵת לְמֶלֶךְ אַשּׁוּר
חֲמִשִּׁים שְׁקָלִים כֶּסֶף לְאִישׁ אֶחָד וַיָּשָׁב מֶלֶךְ
אַשּׁוּר וְלֹא־עָמַד שָׁם בָּאָרֶץ: 21 וְיֶתֶר דִּבְרֵי מְנַחֵם
וְכָל־אֲשֶׁר עָשָׂה הֲלוֹא־הֵם כְּתוּבִים עַל־סֵפֶר דִּבְרֵי
הַיָּמִים לְמַלְכֵי יִשְׂרָאֵל: 22 וַיִּשְׁכַּב מְנַחֵם עִם־אֲבֹתָיו
וַיִּמְלֹךְ פְּקַחְיָה בְנוֹ תַּחְתָּיו:
פ

23 בִּשְׁנַת חֲמִשִּׁים שָׁנָה לַעֲזַרְיָה מֶלֶךְ יְהוּדָה מָלַךְ
פְּקַחְיָה בֶן־מְנַחֵם עַל־יִשְׂרָאֵל בְּשֹׁמְרוֹן שְׁנָתָיִם:
24 וַיַּעַשׂ הָרַע בְּעֵינֵי יְהֹוָה לֹא סָר מֵחַטֹּאות יָרָבְעָם
בֶּן־נְבָט אֲשֶׁר הֶחֱטִיא אֶת־יִשְׂרָאֵל: 25 וַיִּקְשֹׁר עָלָיו
פֶּקַח בֶּן־רְמַלְיָהוּ שָׁלִישׁוֹ וַיַּכֵּהוּ בְשֹׁמְרוֹן בְּאַרְמוֹן
בֵּית־ מֶלֶךְ אֶת־אַרְגֹּב וְאֶת־הָאַרְיֵה וְעִמּוֹ חֲמִשִּׁים
אִישׁ מִבְּנֵי גִלְעָדִים וַיְמִיתֵהוּ וַיִּמְלֹךְ תַּחְתָּיו: 26 וְיֶתֶר
דִּבְרֵי פְקַחְיָה וְכָל־אֲשֶׁר עָשָׂה הִנָּם כְּתוּבִים עַל־
סֵפֶר דִּבְרֵי הַיָּמִים לְמַלְכֵי יִשְׂרָאֵל:
פ

27 בִּשְׁנַת חֲמִשִּׁים וּשְׁתַּיִם שָׁנָה לַעֲזַרְיָה מֶלֶךְ יְהוּדָה
מָלַךְ פֶּקַח בֶּן־רְמַלְיָהוּ עַל־יִשְׂרָאֵל בְּשֹׁמְרוֹן עֶשְׂרִים
שָׁנָה: 28 וַיַּעַשׂ הָרַע בְּעֵינֵי יְהֹוָה לֹא סָר מִן־חַטֹּאות
יָרָבְעָם בֶּן־נְבָט אֲשֶׁר הֶחֱטִיא אֶת־יִשְׂרָאֵל: 29 בִּימֵי
פֶּקַח מֶלֶךְ־יִשְׂרָאֵל בָּא תִּגְלַת פִּלְאֶסֶר מֶלֶךְ אַשּׁוּר
וַיִּקַּח אֶת־עִיּוֹן וְאֶת־אָבֵל בֵּית־מַעֲכָה וְאֶת־יָנוֹחַ
וְאֶת־קֶדֶשׁ וְאֶת־חָצוֹר וְאֶת־הַגִּלְעָד וְאֶת־הַגָּלִילָה
כֹּל אֶרֶץ נַפְתָּלִי וַיַּגְלֵם אַשּׁוּרָה: 30 וַיִּקְשָׁר־קֶשֶׁר
הוֹשֵׁעַ בֶּן־אֵלָה עַל־פֶּקַח בֶּן־רְמַלְיָהוּ וַיַּכֵּהוּ וַיְמִיתֵהוּ
וַיִּמְלֹךְ תַּחְתָּיו בִּשְׁנַת עֶשְׂרִים לְיוֹתָם בֶּן־עֻזִּיָּה:
31 וְיֶתֶר דִּבְרֵי־פֶקַח וְכָל־אֲשֶׁר עָשָׂה הִנָּם כְּתוּבִים
עַל־סֵפֶר דִּבְרֵי הַיָּמִים לְמַלְכֵי יִשְׂרָאֵל:
פ

טו 25 הַמֶּלֶךְ

32 In the second year of Pekah the son of Remaliah, king of Israel, Jotham the son of Uzziah, king of Judah, began to reign. 33 He was twenty-five years old when he became king, and he reigned sixteen years in Jerusalem. His mother's name *was* Jerusha the daughter of Zadok. 34 And he did *what was* right in the sight of the LORD; he did according to all that his father Uzziah had done. 35 However the high places were not removed; the people still sacrificed and burned incense on the high places. He built the Upper Gate of the house of the LORD.

36 Now the rest of the acts of Jotham, and all that he did, *are* they not written in the book of the chronicles of the kings of Judah? 37 In those days the LORD began to send Rezin king of Syria and Pekah the son of Remaliah against Judah. 38 So Jotham rested with his fathers, and was buried with his fathers in the City of David his father. Then Ahaz his son reigned in his place.

16 In the seventeenth year of Pekah the son of Remaliah, Ahaz the son of Jotham, king of Judah, began to reign. 2 Ahaz *was* twenty years old when he became king, and he reigned sixteen years in Jerusalem; and he did not do *what was* right in the sight of the LORD his God, as his father David *had done*. 3 But he walked in the way of the kings of Israel; indeed he made his son pass through the fire, according to the abominations of the nations whom the LORD had cast out from before the children of Israel. 4 And he sacrificed and burned incense on the high places, on the hills, and under every green tree.

5 Then Rezin king of Syria and Pekah the son of Remaliah, king of Israel, came up to Jerusalem to *make* war; and they besieged Ahaz but could not overcome *him*. 6 At that time Rezin king of Syria captured Elath for Syria, and drove the men of Judah from Elath. Then the Edomites went to Elath, and dwell there to this day.

7 So Ahaz sent messengers to Tiglath-Pileser king of Assyria, saying, "I *am* your servant and your son. Come up and save me from the hand of the king of Syria and from the hand of the king of Israel, who rise up against me." 8 And Ahaz took the silver and gold that *was* found in the house of the LORD, and in the treasuries of the king's house, and sent *it as* a present to the king of Assyria. 9 So the king of Assyria heeded him; for the king of Assyria went up against Damascus and took it, carried *its people* captive to Kir, and killed Rezin.

10 Now King Ahaz went to Damascus to meet Tiglath-Pileser king of Assyria, and saw an altar that *was* at Damascus; and King Ahaz sent to

32 בִּשְׁנַת שְׁתַּיִם לְפֶקַח בֶּן־רְמַלְיָהוּ מֶלֶךְ יִשְׂרָאֵל מָלַךְ יוֹתָם בֶּן־עֻזִּיָּהוּ מֶלֶךְ יְהוּדָה: 33 בֶּן־עֶשְׂרִים וְחָמֵשׁ שָׁנָה הָיָה בְמָלְכוֹ וְשֵׁשׁ־עֶשְׂרֵה שָׁנָה מָלַךְ בִּירוּשָׁלִָם וְשֵׁם אִמּוֹ יְרוּשָׁא בַּת־צָדוֹק: 34 וַיַּעַשׂ הַיָּשָׁר בְּעֵינֵי יְהוָה כְּכֹל אֲשֶׁר־עָשָׂה עֻזִּיָּהוּ אָבִיו עָשָׂה: 35 רַק הַבָּמוֹת לֹא סָרוּ עוֹד הָעָם מְזַבְּחִים וּמְקַטְּרִים בַּבָּמוֹת הוּא בָּנָה אֶת־שַׁעַר בֵּית־יְהוָה הָעֶלְיוֹן: 36 וְיֶתֶר דִּבְרֵי יוֹתָם אֲשֶׁר עָשָׂה הֲלֹא־הֵם כְּתוּבִים עַל־סֵפֶר דִּבְרֵי הַיָּמִים לְמַלְכֵי יְהוּדָה: 37 בַּיָּמִים הָהֵם הֵחֵל יְהוָה לְהַשְׁלִיחַ בִּיהוּדָה רְצִין מֶלֶךְ אֲרָם וְאֵת פֶּקַח בֶּן־רְמַלְיָהוּ: 38 וַיִּשְׁכַּב יוֹתָם עִם־אֲבֹתָיו וַיִּקָּבֵר עִם־אֲבֹתָיו בְּעִיר דָּוִד אָבִיו וַיִּמְלֹךְ אָחָז בְּנוֹ תַּחְתָּיו: פ

טז בִּשְׁנַת שְׁבַע־עֶשְׂרֵה שָׁנָה לְפֶקַח בֶּן־רְמַלְיָהוּ מָלַךְ אָחָז בֶּן־יוֹתָם מֶלֶךְ יְהוּדָה: 2 בֶּן־עֶשְׂרִים שָׁנָה אָחָז בְּמָלְכוֹ וְשֵׁשׁ־עֶשְׂרֵה שָׁנָה מָלַךְ בִּירוּשָׁלִָם וְלֹא־עָשָׂה הַיָּשָׁר בְּעֵינֵי יְהוָה אֱלֹהָיו כְּדָוִד אָבִיו: 3 וַיֵּלֶךְ בְּדֶרֶךְ מַלְכֵי יִשְׂרָאֵל וְגַם אֶת־בְּנוֹ הֶעֱבִיר בָּאֵשׁ כְּתֹעֲבוֹת הַגּוֹיִם אֲשֶׁר הוֹרִישׁ יְהוָה אֹתָם מִפְּנֵי בְּנֵי יִשְׂרָאֵל: 4 וַיְזַבֵּחַ וַיְקַטֵּר בַּבָּמוֹת וְעַל־הַגְּבָעוֹת וְתַחַת כָּל־עֵץ רַעֲנָן: 5 אָז יַעֲלֶה רְצִין מֶלֶךְ־אֲרָם וּפֶקַח בֶּן־רְמַלְיָהוּ מֶלֶךְ־יִשְׂרָאֵל יְרוּשָׁלִַם לַמִּלְחָמָה וַיָּצֻרוּ עַל־אָחָז וְלֹא יָכְלוּ לְהִלָּחֵם: 6 בָּעֵת הַהִיא הֵשִׁיב רְצִין מֶלֶךְ־אֲרָם אֶת־אֵילַת לַאֲרָם וַיְנַשֵּׁל אֶת־הַיְהוּדִים מֵאֵילוֹת וַאֲרַמִּים בָּאוּ אֵילַת וַיֵּשְׁבוּ שָׁם עַד הַיּוֹם הַזֶּה: פ 7 וַיִּשְׁלַח אָחָז מַלְאָכִים אֶל־תִּגְלַת פְּלֶסֶר מֶלֶךְ־אַשּׁוּר לֵאמֹר עַבְדְּךָ וּבִנְךָ אָנִי עֲלֵה וְהוֹשִׁעֵנִי מִכַּף מֶלֶךְ־אֲרָם וּמִכַּף מֶלֶךְ יִשְׂרָאֵל הַקּוֹמִים עָלָי: 8 וַיִּקַּח אָחָז אֶת־הַכֶּסֶף וְאֶת־הַזָּהָב הַנִּמְצָא בֵּית יְהוָה וּבְאֹצְרוֹת בֵּית הַמֶּלֶךְ וַיִּשְׁלַח לְמֶלֶךְ־אַשּׁוּר שֹׁחַד: 9 וַיִּשְׁמַע אֵלָיו מֶלֶךְ אַשּׁוּר וַיַּעַל מֶלֶךְ אַשּׁוּר אֶל־דַּמֶּשֶׂק וַיִּתְפְּשֶׂהָ וַיַּגְלֶהָ קִירָה וְאֶת־רְצִין הֵמִית: 10 וַיֵּלֶךְ הַמֶּלֶךְ אָחָז לִקְרַאת תִּגְלַת פִּלְאֶסֶר מֶלֶךְ־אַשּׁוּר דּוּמֶּשֶׂק וַיַּרְא אֶת־הַמִּזְבֵּחַ אֲשֶׁר בְּדַמָּשֶׂק

Urijah the priest the design of the altar and its pattern, according to all its workmanship. ¹¹Then Urijah the priest built an altar according to all that King Ahaz had sent from Damascus. So Urijah the priest made *it* before King Ahaz came back from Damascus. ¹²And when the king came back from Damascus, the king saw the altar; and the king approached the altar and made offerings on it. ¹³So he burned his burnt offering and his grain offering; and he poured his drink offering and sprinkled the blood of his peace offerings on the altar. ¹⁴He also brought the bronze altar which *was* before the LORD, from the front of the temple—from between the *new* altar and the house of the LORD—and put it on the north side of the *new* altar. ¹⁵Then King Ahaz commanded Urijah the priest, saying, "On the great *new* altar burn the morning burnt offering, the evening grain offering, the king's burnt sacrifice, and his grain offering, with the burnt offering of all the people of the land, their grain offering, and their drink offerings; and sprinkle on it all the blood of the burnt offering and all the blood of the sacrifice. And the bronze altar shall be for me to inquire *by*." ¹⁶Thus did Urijah the priest, according to all that King Ahaz commanded.

¹⁷And King Ahaz cut off the panels of the carts, and removed the lavers from them; and he took down the Sea from the bronze oxen that *were* under it, and put it on a pavement of stones. ¹⁸Also he removed the Sabbath pavilion which they had built in the temple, and he removed the king's outer entrance from the house of the LORD, on account of the king of Assyria.

¹⁹Now the rest of the acts of Ahaz which he did, *are* they not written in the book of the chronicles of the kings of Judah? ²⁰So Ahaz rested with his fathers, and was buried with his fathers in the City of David. Then Hezekiah his son reigned in his place.

17 In the twelfth year of Ahaz king of Judah, Hoshea the son of Elah became king of Israel in Samaria, *and he reigned* nine years. ²And he did evil in the sight of the LORD, but not as the kings of Israel who were before him. ³Shalmaneser king of Assyria came up against him; and Hoshea became his vassal, and paid him tribute money. ⁴And the king of Assyria uncovered a conspiracy by Hoshea; for he had sent messengers to So, king of Egypt, and brought no tribute to the king of Assyria, as *he had done* year by year. Therefore the king of Assyria shut him up, and bound him in prison.

וַיִּשְׁלַח הַמֶּלֶךְ אָחָז אֶל־אוּרִיָּה הַכֹּהֵן אֶת־דְּמוּת הַמִּזְבֵּחַ וְאֶת־תַּבְנִיתוֹ לְכָל־מַעֲשֵׂהוּ: 11 וַיִּבֶן אוּרִיָּה הַכֹּהֵן אֶת־הַמִּזְבֵּחַ כְּכֹל אֲשֶׁר־שָׁלַח הַמֶּלֶךְ אָחָז מִדַּמֶּשֶׂק כֵּן עָשָׂה אוּרִיָּה הַכֹּהֵן עַד־בּוֹא הַמֶּלֶךְ־אָחָז מִדַּמָּשֶׂק: 12 וַיָּבֹא הַמֶּלֶךְ מִדַּמֶּשֶׂק וַיַּרְא הַמֶּלֶךְ אֶת־הַמִּזְבֵּחַ וַיִּקְרַב הַמֶּלֶךְ עַל־הַמִּזְבֵּחַ וַיַּעַל עָלָיו: 13 וַיַּקְטֵר אֶת־עֹלָתוֹ וְאֶת־מִנְחָתוֹ וַיַּסֵּךְ אֶת־נִסְכּוֹ וַיִּזְרֹק אֶת־דַּם־הַשְּׁלָמִים אֲשֶׁר־לוֹ עַל־הַמִּזְבֵּחַ:

14 וְאֵת הַמִּזְבֵּחַ הַנְּחֹשֶׁת אֲשֶׁר לִפְנֵי יְהוָה וַיַּקְרֵב מֵאֵת פְּנֵי הַבַּיִת מִבֵּין הַמִּזְבֵּחַ וּמִבֵּין בֵּית יְהוָה וַיִּתֵּן אֹתוֹ עַל־יֶרֶךְ הַמִּזְבֵּחַ צָפוֹנָה: 15 וַיְצַוֵּהוּ הַמֶּלֶךְ־אָחָז אֶת־אוּרִיָּה הַכֹּהֵן לֵאמֹר עַל הַמִּזְבֵּחַ הַגָּדוֹל הַקְטֵר אֶת־עֹלַת־הַבֹּקֶר וְאֶת־מִנְחַת הָעֶרֶב וְאֶת־עֹלַת הַמֶּלֶךְ וְאֶת־מִנְחָתוֹ וְאֵת עֹלַת כָּל־עַם הָאָרֶץ וּמִנְחָתָם וְנִסְכֵּיהֶם וְכָל־דַּם עֹלָה וְכָל־דַּם־זֶבַח עָלָיו תִּזְרֹק וּמִזְבַּח הַנְּחֹשֶׁת יִהְיֶה־לִּי לְבַקֵּר: 16 וַיַּעַשׂ אוּרִיָּה הַכֹּהֵן כְּכֹל אֲשֶׁר־צִוָּה הַמֶּלֶךְ אָחָז: 17 וַיְקַצֵּץ הַמֶּלֶךְ אָחָז אֶת־הַמִּסְגְּרוֹת הַמְּכֹנוֹת וַיָּסַר מֵעֲלֵיהֶם וְאֶת־הַכִּיֹּר וְאֶת־הַיָּם הוֹרִד מֵעַל הַבָּקָר הַנְּחֹשֶׁת אֲשֶׁר תַּחְתֶּיהָ וַיִּתֵּן אֹתוֹ עַל מַרְצֶפֶת אֲבָנִים: 18 וְאֶת־מִיסַךְ הַשַּׁבָּת אֲשֶׁר־בָּנוּ בַבַּיִת וְאֶת־מְבוֹא הַמֶּלֶךְ הַחִיצוֹנָה הֵסֵב בֵּית יְהוָה מִפְּנֵי מֶלֶךְ אַשּׁוּר: 19 וְיֶתֶר דִּבְרֵי אָחָז אֲשֶׁר עָשָׂה הֲלֹא־הֵם כְּתוּבִים עַל־סֵפֶר דִּבְרֵי הַיָּמִים לְמַלְכֵי יְהוּדָה: 20 וַיִּשְׁכַּב אָחָז עִם־אֲבֹתָיו וַיִּקָּבֵר עִם־אֲבֹתָיו בְּעִיר דָּוִד וַיִּמְלֹךְ חִזְקִיָּהוּ בְנוֹ תַּחְתָּיו: פ

יז בִּשְׁנַת שְׁתֵּים עֶשְׂרֵה לְאָחָז מֶלֶךְ יְהוּדָה מָלַךְ הוֹשֵׁעַ בֶּן־אֵלָה בְשֹׁמְרוֹן עַל־יִשְׂרָאֵל תֵּשַׁע שָׁנִים: 2 וַיַּעַשׂ הָרַע בְּעֵינֵי יְהוָה רַק לֹא כְּמַלְכֵי יִשְׂרָאֵל אֲשֶׁר הָיוּ לְפָנָיו: 3 עָלָיו עָלָה שַׁלְמַנְאֶסֶר מֶלֶךְ אַשּׁוּר וַיְהִי־לוֹ הוֹשֵׁעַ עֶבֶד וַיָּשֶׁב לוֹ מִנְחָה: 4 וַיִּמְצָא מֶלֶךְ־אַשּׁוּר בְּהוֹשֵׁעַ קֶשֶׁר אֲשֶׁר שָׁלַח מַלְאָכִים אֶל־סוֹא מֶלֶךְ־מִצְרַיִם וְלֹא־הֶעֱלָה מִנְחָה

טז 15 וְצִוָּהוּ   18 מוּסַךְ

⁵ Now the king of Assyria went throughout all the land, and went up to Samaria and besieged it for three years. ⁶ In the ninth year of Hoshea, the king of Assyria took Samaria and carried Israel away to Assyria, and placed them in Halah and by the Habor, the River of Gozan, and in the cities of the Medes.

⁷ For so it was that the children of Israel had sinned against the LORD their God, who had brought them up out of the land of Egypt, from under the hand of Pharaoh king of Egypt; and they had feared other gods, ⁸ and had walked in the statutes of the nations whom the LORD had cast out from before the children of Israel, and of the kings of Israel, which they had made. ⁹ Also the children of Israel secretly did against the LORD their God things that *were* not right, and they built for themselves high places in all their cities, from watchtower to fortified city. ¹⁰ They set up for themselves *sacred* pillars and wooden images on every high hill and under every green tree. ¹¹ There they burned incense on all the high places, like the nations whom the LORD had carried away before them; and they did wicked things to provoke the LORD to anger, ¹² for they served idols, of which the LORD had said to them, "You shall not do this thing."

¹³ Yet the LORD testified against Israel and against Judah, by all of His prophets, every seer, saying, "Turn from your evil ways, and keep My commandments *and* My statutes, according to all the law which I commanded your fathers, and which I sent to you by My servants the prophets." ¹⁴ Nevertheless they would not hear, but stiffened their necks, like the necks of their fathers, who did not believe in the LORD their God. ¹⁵ And they rejected His statutes and His covenant that He had made with their fathers, and His testimonies which He had testified against them; they followed idols, became idolaters, and *went* after the nations who *were* all around them, *concerning* whom the LORD had charged them that they should not do like them. ¹⁶ So they left all the commandments of the LORD their God, made for themselves a molded image *and* two calves, made a wooden image and worshiped all the host of heaven, and served Baal. ¹⁷ And they caused their sons and daughters to pass through the fire, practiced witchcraft and soothsaying, and sold themselves to do evil in the sight of the LORD, to provoke Him to anger. ¹⁸ Therefore the LORD was very angry with Israel, and removed them from His sight; there was none left but the tribe of Judah alone.

לְמֶ֣לֶךְ אַשּׁ֔וּר כְּשָׁנָ֥ה בְשָׁנָ֖ה וַיַּעַצְרֵ֑הוּ מֶ֣לֶךְ אַשּׁ֔וּר וַיַּאַסְרֵ֖הוּ בֵּ֣ית כֶּֽלֶא: ⁵ וַיַּ֤עַל מֶֽלֶךְ־אַשּׁוּר֙ בְּכָל־הָאָ֔רֶץ וַיַּ֥עַל שֹׁמְר֖וֹן וַיָּ֥צַר עָלֶ֖יהָ שָׁלֹ֥שׁ שָׁנִֽים: ⁶ בִּשְׁנַ֨ת הַתְּשִׁיעִ֜ית לְהוֹשֵׁ֗עַ לָכַ֤ד מֶֽלֶךְ־אַשּׁוּר֙ אֶת־שֹׁ֣מְר֔וֹן וַיֶּ֥גֶל אֶת־יִשְׂרָאֵ֖ל אַשּׁ֑וּרָה וַיֹּ֨שֶׁב אֹתָ֤ם בַּחְלַח֙ וּבְחָב֔וֹר נְהַ֣ר גּוֹזָ֔ן וְעָרֵ֖י מָדָֽי: פ

⁷ וַיְהִ֗י כִּי־חָטְא֤וּ בְנֵֽי־יִשְׂרָאֵל֙ לַיהֹוָ֣ה אֱלֹֽהֵיהֶ֔ם הַמַּעֲלֶ֤ה אֹתָם֙ מֵאֶ֣רֶץ מִצְרַ֔יִם מִתַּ֕חַת יַ֖ד פַּרְעֹ֣ה מֶֽלֶךְ־מִצְרָ֑יִם וַיִּֽירְא֖וּ אֱלֹהִ֥ים אֲחֵרִֽים: ⁸ וַיֵּֽלְכוּ֙ בְּחֻקּ֣וֹת הַגּוֹיִ֔ם אֲשֶׁ֨ר הוֹרִ֤ישׁ יְהֹוָה֙ מִפְּנֵ֣י בְּנֵ֣י יִשְׂרָאֵ֔ל וּמַלְכֵ֥י יִשְׂרָאֵ֖ל אֲשֶׁ֥ר עָשֽׂוּ: ⁹ וַיְחַפְּא֣וּ בְנֵֽי־יִשְׂרָאֵ֗ל דְּבָרִים֙ אֲשֶׁ֣ר לֹא־כֵ֔ן עַל־יְהֹוָ֖ה אֱלֹֽהֵיהֶ֑ם וַיִּבְנ֨וּ לָהֶ֤ם בָּמוֹת֙ בְּכָל־עָ֣רֵיהֶ֔ם מִמִּגְדַּ֥ל נוֹצְרִ֖ים עַד־עִ֥יר מִבְצָֽר: ¹⁰ וַיַּצִּ֧בוּ לָהֶ֛ם מַצֵּב֖וֹת וַאֲשֵׁרִ֑ים עַ֚ל כָּל־גִּבְעָ֣ה גְבֹהָ֔ה וְתַ֖חַת כָּל־עֵ֥ץ רַעֲנָֽן: ¹¹ וַיְקַטְּרוּ־שָׁם֙ בְּכָל־בָּמ֔וֹת כַּגּוֹיִ֕ם אֲשֶׁר־הֶגְלָ֥ה יְהֹוָ֖ה מִפְּנֵיהֶ֑ם וַיַּֽעֲשׂוּ֙ דְּבָרִ֣ים רָעִ֔ים לְהַכְעִ֖יס אֶת־יְהֹוָֽה: ¹² וַיַּֽעַבְד֖וּ הַגִּלֻּלִ֑ים אֲשֶׁ֨ר אָמַ֤ר יְהֹוָה֙ לָהֶ֔ם לֹ֥א תַעֲשׂ֖וּ אֶת־הַדָּבָ֥ר הַזֶּֽה: ¹³ וַיָּ֣עַד יְהֹוָ֡ה בְּיִשְׂרָאֵ֣ל וּבִֽיהוּדָ֡ה בְּיַד֩ כָּל־נְבִיא֨וֹ כָל־חֹזֶ֜ה לֵאמֹ֗ר שֻׁ֤בוּ מִדַּרְכֵיכֶ֤ם הָֽרָעִים֙ וְשִׁמְרוּ֙ מִצְוֺתַ֣י חֻקּוֹתַ֔י כְּכָל־הַ֨תּוֹרָ֔ה אֲשֶׁ֥ר צִוִּ֖יתִי אֶת־אֲבֹֽתֵיכֶ֑ם וַֽאֲשֶׁר֙ שָׁלַ֣חְתִּי אֲלֵיכֶ֔ם בְּיַ֖ד עֲבָדַ֥י הַנְּבִיאִֽים: ¹⁴ וְלֹ֖א שָׁמֵ֑עוּ וַיַּקְשׁ֤וּ אֶת־עָרְפָּם֙ כְּעֹ֣רֶף אֲבוֹתָ֔ם אֲשֶׁר֙ לֹ֣א הֶאֱמִ֔ינוּ בַּיהֹוָ֖ה אֱלֹֽהֵיהֶֽם: ¹⁵ וַיִּמְאֲס֣וּ אֶת־חֻקָּ֗יו וְאֶת־בְּרִיתוֹ֙ אֲשֶׁ֣ר כָּרַ֣ת אֶת־אֲבוֹתָ֔ם וְאֵת֙ עֵֽדְוֺתָ֔יו אֲשֶׁ֥ר הֵעִ֖יד בָּ֑ם וַיֵּ֨לְכ֜וּ אַחֲרֵ֤י הַהֶ֨בֶל֙ וַיֶּהְבָּ֔לוּ וְאַֽחֲרֵ֤י הַגּוֹיִם֙ אֲשֶׁ֣ר סְבִֽיבֹתָ֔ם אֲשֶׁ֨ר צִוָּ֤ה יְהֹוָה֙ אֹתָ֔ם לְבִלְתִּ֖י עֲשׂ֥וֹת כָּהֶֽם: ¹⁶ וַיַּֽעַזְב֗וּ אֶת־כָּל־מִצְוֺת֙ יְהֹוָ֣ה אֱלֹֽהֵיהֶ֔ם וַיַּעֲשׂ֥וּ לָהֶ֛ם מַסֵּכָ֖ה שְׁנַ֣יִם עֲגָלִ֑ים וַיַּעֲשׂ֣וּ אֲשֵׁרָ֗ה וַיִּֽשְׁתַּֽחֲווּ֙ לְכָל־צְבָ֣א הַשָּׁמַ֔יִם וַיַּֽעַבְד֖וּ אֶת־הַבָּֽעַל: ¹⁷ וַֽ֠יַּעֲבִ֠ירוּ אֶת־בְּנֵיהֶ֤ם וְאֶת־בְּנֽוֹתֵיהֶם֙ בָּאֵ֔שׁ וַיִּקְסְמ֥וּ קְסָמִ֖ים וַיְנַחֵ֑שׁוּ וַיִּֽתְמַכְּר֗וּ לַעֲשׂ֥וֹת הָרַ֛ע בְּעֵינֵ֥י יְהֹוָ֖ה לְהַכְעִיסֽוֹ: ¹⁸ וַיִּתְאַנַּ֨ף יְהֹוָ֤ה מְאֹד֙ בְּיִשְׂרָאֵ֔ל וַיְסִרֵ֖ם מֵעַ֣ל פָּנָ֑יו

¹⁹ Also Judah did not keep the commandments of the LORD their God, but walked in the statutes of Israel which they made. ²⁰ And the LORD rejected all the descendants of Israel, afflicted them, and delivered them into the hand of plunderers, until He had cast them from His sight. ²¹ For He tore Israel from the house of David, and they made Jeroboam the son of Nebat king. Then Jeroboam drove Israel from following the LORD, and made them commit a great sin. ²² For the children of Israel walked in all the sins of Jeroboam which he did; they did not depart from them, ²³ until the LORD removed Israel out of His sight, as He had said by all His servants the prophets. So Israel was carried away from their own land to Assyria, *as it is* to this day.

²⁴ Then the king of Assyria brought *people* from Babylon, Cuthah, Ava, Hamath, and from Sepharvaim, and placed *them* in the cities of Samaria instead of the children of Israel; and they took possession of Samaria and dwelt in its cities. ²⁵ And it was so, at the beginning of their dwelling there, *that* they did not fear the LORD; therefore the LORD sent lions among them, which killed *some* of them. ²⁶ So they spoke to the king of Assyria, saying, "The nations whom you have removed and placed in the cities of Samaria do not know the rituals of the God of the land; therefore He has sent lions among them, and indeed, they are killing them because they do not know the rituals of the God of the land." ²⁷ Then the king of Assyria commanded, saying, "Send there one of the priests whom you brought from there; let him go and dwell there, and let him teach them the rituals of the God of the land." ²⁸ Then one of the priests whom they had carried away from Samaria came and dwelt in Bethel, and taught them how they should fear the LORD.

²⁹ However every nation continued to make gods of its own, and put *them* in the shrines on the high places which the Samaritans had made, *every* nation in the cities where they dwelt. ³⁰ The men of Babylon made Succoth Benoth, the men of Cuth made Nergal, the men of Hamath made Ashima, ³¹ and the Avites made Nibhaz and Tartak; and the Sepharvites burned their children in fire to Adrammelech and Anammelech, the gods of Sepharvaim. ³² So they feared the LORD, and from every class they appointed for themselves priests of the high places, who sacrificed for them in the shrines of the high places. ³³ They feared the LORD, yet served their own gods—according to the rituals of the nations from among whom they were carried away.

לֹא נִשְׁאַר רַק שֵׁבֶט יְהוּדָה לְבַדּֽוֹ: ¹⁹ גַּם־יְהוּדָ֔ה לֹא שָׁמַ֔ר אֶת־מִצְוֺ֖ת יְהֹוָ֣ה אֱלֹֽהֵיהֶ֑ם וַיֵּ֣לְכ֔וּ בְּחֻקּ֖וֹת יִשְׂרָאֵ֖ל אֲשֶׁ֥ר עָשֽׂוּ: ²⁰ וַיִּמְאַ֨ס יְהֹוָ֜ה בְּכׇל־זֶ֣רַע יִשְׂרָאֵ֗ל וַיְעַנֵּ֛ם וַֽיִּתְּנֵ֖ם בְּיַד־שֹׁסִ֑ים עַ֛ד אֲשֶׁ֥ר הִשְׁלִיכָ֖ם מִפָּנָֽיו: ²¹ כִּֽי־קָרַ֣ע יִשְׂרָאֵ֗ל מֵעַל֙ בֵּ֣ית דָּוִ֔ד וַיַּמְלִ֖יכוּ אֶת־יָרׇבְעָ֣ם בֶּן־נְבָ֑ט וַיַּדֵּ֣אᴾ יָרׇבְעָ֤ם אֶת־יִשְׂרָאֵל֙ מֵאַחֲרֵ֣י יְהֹוָ֔ה וְהֶחֱטֵיאָ֖ם חֲטָאָ֥ה גְדוֹלָֽה: ²² וַיֵּֽלְכוּ֙ בְּנֵ֣י יִשְׂרָאֵ֔ל בְּכׇל־חַטֹּ֥אות יָרׇבְעָ֖ם אֲשֶׁ֣ר עָשָׂ֑ה לֹא־סָ֖רוּ מִמֶּֽנָּה: ²³ עַ֠ד אֲשֶׁר־הֵסִ֨יר יְהֹוָ֤ה אֶת־יִשְׂרָאֵל֙ מֵעַ֣ל פָּנָ֔יו כַּאֲשֶׁ֣ר דִּבֶּ֔ר בְּיַ֖ד כׇּל־עֲבָדָ֣יו הַנְּבִיאִ֑ים וַיִּ֧גֶל יִשְׂרָאֵ֛ל מֵעַ֥ל אַדְמָת֖וֹ אַשּׁ֑וּרָה עַ֖ד הַיּ֥וֹם הַזֶּֽה: פ

²⁴ וַיָּבֵ֣א מֶֽלֶךְ־אַשּׁ֡וּר מִבָּבֶ֡ל וּ֠מִכּ֠וּתָה וּמֵעַוָּ֤א וּמֵֽחֲמָת֙ וּסְפַרְוַ֔יִם וַיֹּ֙שֶׁב֙ בְּעָרֵ֣י שֹֽׁמְר֔וֹן תַּ֖חַת בְּנֵ֣י יִשְׂרָאֵ֑ל וַיִּֽרְשׁוּ֙ אֶת־שֹׁ֣מְר֔וֹן וַיֵּֽשְׁב֖וּ בְּעָרֶֽיהָ: ²⁵ וַיְהִ֗י בִּתְחִלַּ֤ת שִׁבְתָּם֙ שָׁ֔ם לֹ֥א יָֽרְא֖וּ אֶת־יְהֹוָ֑ה וַיְשַׁלַּ֨ח יְהֹוָ֤ה בָּהֶם֙ אֶת־הָ֣אֲרָי֔וֹת וַיִּֽהְי֥וּ הֹרְגִ֖ים בָּהֶֽם: ²⁶ וַיֹּאמְר֣וּ לְמֶ֣לֶךְ אַשּׁוּר֘ לֵאמֹר֒ הַגּוֹיִ֗ם אֲשֶׁ֤ר הִגְלִ֙יתָ֙ וַתּ֣וֹשֶׁב בְּעָרֵ֣י שֹֽׁמְר֔וֹן לֹ֣א יָֽדְע֔וּ אֶת־מִשְׁפַּ֖ט אֱלֹהֵ֣י הָאָ֑רֶץ וַיְשַׁלַּח־בָּ֣ם אֶת־הָֽאֲרָי֗וֹת וְהִנָּם֙ מְמִיתִ֣ים אוֹתָ֔ם כַּֽאֲשֶׁר֙ אֵינָ֣ם יֹֽדְעִ֔ים אֶת־מִשְׁפַּ֖ט אֱלֹהֵ֥י הָאָֽרֶץ: ²⁷ וַיְצַ֨ו מֶֽלֶךְ־אַשּׁ֜וּר לֵאמֹ֗ר הֹלִ֤יכוּ שָׁ֙מָּה֙ אֶחָ֤ד מֵהַכֹּֽהֲנִים֙ אֲשֶׁ֣ר הִגְלִיתֶ֣ם מִשָּׁ֔ם וְיֵלְכ֖וּ וְיֵ֣שְׁבוּ שָׁ֑ם וְיֹרֵ֕ם אֶת־מִשְׁפַּ֖ט אֱלֹהֵ֥י הָאָֽרֶץ: ²⁸ וַיָּבֹ֞א אֶחָ֣ד מֵהַכֹּהֲנִ֗ים אֲשֶׁ֤ר הִגְלוּ֙ מִשֹּׁ֣מְר֔וֹן וַיֵּ֖שֶׁב בְּבֵֽית־אֵ֑ל וַֽיְהִי֙ מוֹרֶ֣ה אֹתָ֔ם אֵ֖יךְ יִֽירְא֥וּ אֶת־יְהֹוָֽה: ²⁹ וַיִּֽהְי֣וּ עֹשִׂ֔ים גּ֥וֹי גּ֖וֹי אֱלֹהָ֑יו וַיַּנִּ֣יחוּ ׀ בְּבֵ֣ית הַבָּמ֗וֹת אֲשֶׁ֤ר עָשׂוּ֙ הַשֹּׁ֣מְרֹנִ֔ים גּ֥וֹי גּ֛וֹי בְּעָ֣רֵיהֶ֔ם אֲשֶׁ֛ר הֵ֥ם יֹֽשְׁבִ֖ים שָֽׁם: ³⁰ וְאַנְשֵׁ֣י בָבֶ֗ל עָשׂוּ֙ אֶת־סֻכּ֣וֹת בְּנ֔וֹת וְאַנְשֵׁי־כ֔וּת עָשׂ֖וּ אֶת־נֵֽרְגַ֑ל וְאַנְשֵׁ֥י חֲמָ֖ת עָשׂ֥וּ אֶת־אֲשִׁימָֽא: ³¹ וְהָעַוִּ֛ים עָשׂ֥וּ נִבְחַ֖ז וְאֶת־תַּרְתָּ֑ק וְהַסְפַרְוִ֗ים שֹׂרְפִ֤ים אֶת־בְּנֵיהֶם֙ בָּאֵ֔שׁ לְאַדְרַמֶּ֥לֶךְ וַֽעֲנַמֶּ֖לֶךְ אֱלֹהֵ֥[יᴾ] סְפַרְוָֽיִם: ³² וַיִּֽהְי֖וּ יְרֵאִ֣ים אֶת־יְהֹוָ֑ה וַיַּֽעֲשׂ֨וּ לָהֶ֤ם מִקְצוֹתָם֙ כֹּהֲנֵ֣י בָמ֔וֹת וַיִּֽהְי֤וּ עֹשִׂים֙ לָהֶ֔ם בְּבֵ֖ית הַבָּמֽוֹת: ³³ אֶת־יְהֹוָ֖ה הָי֣וּ יְרֵאִ֑ים וְאֶת־אֱלֹֽהֵיהֶם֙ הָי֣וּ עֹֽבְדִ֔ים כְּמִשְׁפַּט֙ הַגּוֹיִ֔ם

כא יוּ ‏ ‏ וידה 31 אֱלֹהֵי סְפַרְוַיִם

34 To this day they continue practicing the former rituals; they do not fear the LORD, nor do they follow their statutes or their ordinances, or the law and commandment which the LORD had commanded the children of Jacob, whom He named Israel, 35 with whom the LORD had made a covenant and charged them, saying: "You shall not fear other gods, nor bow down to them nor serve them nor sacrifice to them; 36 but the LORD, who brought you up from the land of Egypt with great power and an outstretched arm, Him you shall fear, Him you shall worship, and to Him you shall offer sacrifice. 37 And the statutes, the ordinances, the law, and the commandment which He wrote for you, you shall be careful to observe forever; you shall not fear other gods. 38 And the covenant that I have made with you, you shall not forget, nor shall you fear other gods. 39 But the LORD your God you shall fear; and He will deliver you from the hand of all your enemies." 40 However they did not obey, but they followed their former rituals. 41 So these nations feared the LORD, yet served their carved images; also their children and their children's children have continued doing as their fathers did, even to this day.

18 Now it came to pass in the third year of Hoshea the son of Elah, king of Israel, *that* Hezekiah the son of Ahaz, king of Judah, began to reign. 2 He was twenty-five years old when he became king, and he reigned twenty-nine years in Jerusalem. His mother's name *was* Abi the daughter of Zechariah. 3 And he did *what was* right in the sight of the LORD, according to all that his father David had done.

4 He removed the high places and broke the *sacred* pillars, cut down the wooden image and broke in pieces the bronze serpent that Moses had made; for until those days the children of Israel burned incense to it, and called it Nehushtan. 5 He trusted in the LORD God of Israel, so that after him was none like him among all the kings of Judah, nor who were before him. 6 For he held fast to the LORD; he did not depart from following Him, but kept His commandments, which the LORD had commanded Moses. 7 The LORD was with him; he prospered wherever he went. And he rebelled against the king of Assyria and did not serve him. 8 He subdued the Philistines, as far as Gaza and its territory, from watchtower to fortified city.

9 Now it came to pass in the fourth year of King Hezekiah, which *was* the seventh year of Hoshea the son of Elah, king of Israel, *that* Shalmaneser king of Assyria came up against Samaria and

34 עַד הַיּוֹם הַזֶּה הֵם עֹשִׂים כַּמִּשְׁפָּטִים הָרִאשֹׁנִים אֵינָם יְרֵאִים אֶת־יְהֹוָה וְאֵינָם עֹשִׂים כְּחֻקֹּתָם וּכְמִשְׁפָּטָם וְכַתּוֹרָה וְכַמִּצְוָה אֲשֶׁר צִוָּה יְהֹוָה אֶת־בְּנֵי יַעֲקֹב אֲשֶׁר־שָׂם שְׁמוֹ יִשְׂרָאֵל: 35 וַיִּכְרֹת יְהֹוָה אִתָּם בְּרִית וַיְצַוֵּם לֵאמֹר לֹא תִירְאוּ אֱלֹהִים אֲחֵרִים וְלֹא־תִשְׁתַּחֲווּ לָהֶם וְלֹא תַעַבְדוּם וְלֹא תִזְבְּחוּ לָהֶם: 36 כִּי אִם־אֶת־יְהֹוָה אֲשֶׁר הֶעֱלָה אֶתְכֶם מֵאֶרֶץ מִצְרַיִם בְּכֹחַ גָּדוֹל וּבִזְרוֹעַ נְטוּיָה אֹתוֹ תִירָאוּ וְלוֹ תִשְׁתַּחֲווּ וְלוֹ תִזְבָּחוּ: 37 וְאֶת־הַחֻקִּים וְאֶת־הַמִּשְׁפָּטִים וְהַתּוֹרָה וְהַמִּצְוָה אֲשֶׁר כָּתַב לָכֶם תִּשְׁמְרוּן לַעֲשׂוֹת כָּל־הַיָּמִים וְלֹא תִירְאוּ אֱלֹהִים אֲחֵרִים: 38 וְהַבְּרִית אֲשֶׁר־כָּרַתִּי אִתְּכֶם לֹא תִשְׁכָּחוּ וְלֹא תִירְאוּ אֱלֹהִים אֲחֵרִים: 39 כִּי אִם־אֶת־יְהֹוָה אֱלֹהֵיכֶם תִּירָאוּ וְהוּא יַצִּיל אֶתְכֶם מִיַּד כָּל־אֹיְבֵיכֶם: 40 וְלֹא שָׁמֵעוּ כִּי אִם־כְּמִשְׁפָּטָם הָרִאשׁוֹן הֵם עֹשִׂים: 41 וַיִּהְיוּ ׀ הַגּוֹיִם הָאֵלֶּה יְרֵאִים אֶת־יְהֹוָה וְאֶת־פְּסִילֵיהֶם הָיוּ עֹבְדִים גַּם־בְּנֵיהֶם ׀ וּבְנֵי בְנֵיהֶם כַּאֲשֶׁר עָשׂוּ אֲבֹתָם הֵם עֹשִׂים עַד הַיּוֹם הַזֶּה: פ

יח וַיְהִי בִּשְׁנַת שָׁלֹשׁ לְהוֹשֵׁעַ בֶּן־אֵלָה מֶלֶךְ יִשְׂרָאֵל מָלַךְ חִזְקִיָּה בֶן־אָחָז מֶלֶךְ יְהוּדָה: 2 בֶּן־עֶשְׂרִים וְחָמֵשׁ שָׁנָה הָיָה בְמָלְכוֹ וְעֶשְׂרִים וָתֵשַׁע שָׁנָה מָלַךְ בִּירוּשָׁלָ‍ִם וְשֵׁם אִמּוֹ אֲבִי בַּת־זְכַרְיָה: 3 וַיַּעַשׂ הַיָּשָׁר בְּעֵינֵי יְהֹוָה כְּכֹל אֲשֶׁר־עָשָׂה דָּוִד אָבִיו: 4 הוּא ׀ הֵסִיר אֶת־הַבָּמוֹת וְשִׁבַּר אֶת־הַמַּצֵּבֹת וְכָרַת אֶת־הָאֲשֵׁרָה וְכִתַּת נְחַשׁ הַנְּחֹשֶׁת אֲשֶׁר־עָשָׂה מֹשֶׁה כִּי עַד־הַיָּמִים הָהֵמָּה הָיוּ בְנֵי־יִשְׂרָאֵל מְקַטְּרִים לוֹ וַיִּקְרָא־לוֹ נְחֻשְׁתָּן: 5 בַּיהֹוָה אֱלֹהֵי־יִשְׂרָאֵל בָּטָח וְאַחֲרָיו לֹא־הָיָה כָמֹהוּ בְּכֹל מַלְכֵי יְהוּדָה וַאֲשֶׁר הָיוּ לְפָנָיו: 6 וַיִּדְבַּק בַּיהֹוָה לֹא־סָר מֵאַחֲרָיו וַיִּשְׁמֹר מִצְוֹתָיו אֲשֶׁר־צִוָּה יְהֹוָה אֶת־מֹשֶׁה: 7 וְהָיָה יְהֹוָה עִמּוֹ בְּכֹל אֲשֶׁר־יֵצֵא יַשְׂכִּיל וַיִּמְרֹד בְּמֶלֶךְ־אַשּׁוּר וְלֹא עֲבָדוֹ: 8 הוּא־הִכָּה אֶת־פְּלִשְׁתִּים עַד־עַזָּה וְאֶת־גְּבוּלֶיהָ מִמִּגְדַּל נוֹצְרִים עַד־עִיר מִבְצָר: פ

9 וַיְהִי בַּשָּׁנָה הָרְבִיעִית לַמֶּלֶךְ חִזְקִיָּהוּ הִיא הַשָּׁנָה הַשְּׁבִיעִית לְהוֹשֵׁעַ בֶּן־אֵלָה מֶלֶךְ יִשְׂרָאֵל עָלָה שַׁלְמַנְאֶסֶר מֶלֶךְ־אַשּׁוּר עַל־שֹׁמְרוֹן וַיָּצַר עָלֶיהָ:

besieged it. ¹⁰And at the end of three years they took it. In the sixth year of Hezekiah, that *is,* the ninth year of Hoshea king of Israel, Samaria was taken. ¹¹Then the king of Assyria carried Israel away captive to Assyria, and put them in Halah and by the Habor, the River of Gozan, and in the cities of the Medes, ¹²because they did not obey the voice of the LORD their God, but transgressed His covenant *and* all that Moses the servant of the LORD had commanded; and they would neither hear nor do *them.*

¹³And in the fourteenth year of King Hezekiah, Sennacherib king of Assyria came up against all the fortified cities of Judah and took them. ¹⁴Then Hezekiah king of Judah sent to the king of Assyria at Lachish, saying, "I have done wrong; turn away from me; whatever you impose on me I will pay." And the king of Assyria assessed Hezekiah king of Judah three hundred talents of silver and thirty talents of gold. ¹⁵So Hezekiah gave *him* all the silver that was found in the house of the LORD and in the treasuries of the king's house. ¹⁶At that time Hezekiah stripped *the gold from* the doors of the temple of the LORD, and *from* the pillars which Hezekiah king of Judah had overlaid, and gave it to the king of Assyria.

¹⁷Then the king of Assyria sent *the* Tartan, *the* Rabsaris, *and the* Rabshakeh from Lachish, with a great army against Jerusalem, to King Hezekiah. And they went up and came to Jerusalem. When they had come up, they went and stood by the aqueduct from the upper pool, which *was* on the highway to the Fuller's Field. ¹⁸And when they had called to the king, Eliakim the son of Hilkiah, who *was* over the household, Shebna the scribe, and Joah the son of Asaph, the recorder, came out to them. ¹⁹Then *the* Rabshakeh said to them, "Say now to Hezekiah, 'Thus says the great king, the king of Assyria: "What confidence *is* this in which you trust? ²⁰You speak of *having* plans and power for war; but *they are* mere words. And in whom do you trust, that you rebel against me? ²¹Now look! You are trusting in the staff of this broken reed, Egypt, on which if a man leans, it will go into his hand and pierce it. So *is* Pharaoh king of Egypt to all who trust in him. ²²But if you say to me, 'We trust in the LORD our God,' *is* it not He whose high places and whose altars Hezekiah has taken away, and said to Judah and Jerusalem, 'You shall worship before this altar in Jerusalem'?" ' ²³Now therefore, I urge you, give a pledge to my master the king of Assyria, and I will give you two thousand horses—if you are able on your part to put riders on them! ²⁴How then will you repel one captain of

10 וַיִּלְכְּדֻהָ מִקְצֵה שָׁלֹשׁ שָׁנִים בִּשְׁנַת־שֵׁשׁ לְחִזְקִיָּה הִיא שְׁנַת־תֵּשַׁע לְהוֹשֵׁעַ מֶלֶךְ יִשְׂרָאֵל נִלְכְּדָה שֹׁמְרוֹן: 11 וַיֶּגֶל מֶלֶךְ־אַשּׁוּר אֶת־יִשְׂרָאֵל אַשּׁוּרָה וַיַּנְחֵם בַּחְלַח וּבְחָבוֹר נְהַר גּוֹזָן וְעָרֵי מָדָי: 12 עַל | אֲשֶׁר לֹא־שָׁמְעוּ בְּקוֹל יְהוָה אֱלֹהֵיהֶם וַיַּעַבְרוּ אֶת־ בְּרִיתוֹ אֵת כָּל־אֲשֶׁר צִוָּה מֹשֶׁה עֶבֶד יְהוָה וְלֹא שָׁמְעוּ וְלֹא עָשׂוּ: פ

13 וּבְאַרְבַּע עֶשְׂרֵה שָׁנָה לַמֶּלֶךְ חִזְקִיָּה עָלָה סַנְחֵרִיב מֶלֶךְ־אַשּׁוּר עַל כָּל־עָרֵי יְהוּדָה הַבְּצֻרוֹת וַיִּתְפְּשֵׂם: 14 וַיִּשְׁלַח חִזְקִיָּה מֶלֶךְ־יְהוּדָה אֶל־מֶלֶךְ־ אַשּׁוּר | לָכִישָׁה | לֵאמֹר | חָטָאתִי שׁוּב מֵעָלַי אֵת אֲשֶׁר־תִּתֵּן עָלַי אֶשָּׂא וַיָּשֶׂם מֶלֶךְ־אַשּׁוּר עַל־חִזְקִיָּה מֶלֶךְ־יְהוּדָה שְׁלֹשׁ מֵאוֹת כִּכַּר־כֶּסֶף וּשְׁלֹשִׁים כִּכַּר זָהָב: 15 וַיִּתֵּן חִזְקִיָּה אֶת־כָּל־הַכֶּסֶף הַנִּמְצָא בֵית־יְהוָה וּבְאֹצְרוֹת בֵּית הַמֶּלֶךְ: 16 בָּעֵת הַהִיא קִצַּץ חִזְקִיָּה אֶת־דַּלְתוֹת הֵיכַל יְהוָה וְאֶת־ הָאֹמְנוֹת אֲשֶׁר צִפָּה חִזְקִיָּה מֶלֶךְ יְהוּדָה וַיִּתְּנֵם לְמֶלֶךְ אַשּׁוּר: פ

17 וַיִּשְׁלַח מֶלֶךְ־אַשּׁוּר אֶת־תַּרְתָּן וְאֶת־רַב־סָרִיס | וְאֶת־רַב־שָׁקֵה מִן־לָכִישׁ אֶל־הַמֶּלֶךְ חִזְקִיָּהוּ בְּחֵיל כָּבֵד יְרוּשָׁלִָם וַיַּעֲלוּ וַיָּבֹאוּ יְרוּשָׁלִַם וַיַּעֲלוּ וַיָּבֹאוּ וַיַּעַמְדוּ בִּתְעָלַת הַבְּרֵכָה הָעֶלְיוֹנָה אֲשֶׁר בִּמְסִלַּת שְׂדֵה כוֹבֵס: 18 וַיִּקְרְאוּ אֶל־הַמֶּלֶךְ וַיֵּצֵא אֲלֵהֶם אֶלְיָקִים בֶּן־חִלְקִיָּהוּ אֲשֶׁר עַל־הַבָּיִת וְשֶׁבְנָה הַסֹּפֵר וְיוֹאָח בֶּן־אָסָף הַמַּזְכִּיר: 19 וַיֹּאמֶר אֲלֵהֶם רַב־שָׁקֵה אִמְרוּ־נָא אֶל־חִזְקִיָּהוּ כֹּה־אָמַר הַמֶּלֶךְ הַגָּדוֹל מֶלֶךְ אַשּׁוּר מָה הַבִּטָּחוֹן הַזֶּה אֲשֶׁר בָּטָחְתָּ: 20 אָמַרְתָּ אַךְ־דְּבַר־שְׂפָתַיִם עֵצָה וּגְבוּרָה לַמִּלְחָמָה עַתָּה עַל־מִי בָטַחְתָּ כִּי מָרַדְתָּ בִּי: 21 עַתָּה הִנֵּה בָטַחְתָּ לְּךָ עַל־מִשְׁעֶנֶת הַקָּנֶה הָרָצוּץ הַזֶּה עַל־מִצְרַיִם אֲשֶׁר יִסָּמֵךְ אִישׁ עָלָיו וּבָא בְכַפּוֹ וּנְקָבָהּ כֵּן פַּרְעֹה מֶלֶךְ־מִצְרַיִם לְכָל־הַבֹּטְחִים עָלָיו: 22 וְכִי־תֹאמְרוּן אֵלַי אֶל־יְהוָה אֱלֹהֵינוּ בָּטָחְנוּ הֲלוֹא־הוּא אֲשֶׁר הֵסִיר חִזְקִיָּהוּ אֶת־בָּמֹתָיו וְאֶת־מִזְבְּחֹתָיו וַיֹּאמֶר לִיהוּדָה וְלִירוּשָׁלִַם לִפְנֵי הַמִּזְבֵּחַ הַזֶּה תִּשְׁתַּחֲווּ בִּירוּשָׁלִָם: 23 וְעַתָּה הִתְעָרֶב נָא אֶת־אֲדֹנִי אֶת־ מֶלֶךְ אַשּׁוּר וְאֶתְּנָה לְךָ אַלְפַּיִם סוּסִים אִם־תּוּכַל לָתֶת לְךָ רֹכְבִים עֲלֵיהֶם: 24 וְאֵיךְ תָּשִׁיב אֵת

the least of my master's servants, and put your trust in Egypt for chariots and horsemen? 25 Have I now come up without the LORD against this place to destroy it? The LORD said to me, 'Go up against this land, and destroy it.' "

26 Then Eliakim the son of Hilkiah, Shebna, and Joah said to *the* Rabshakeh, "Please speak to your servants in Aramaic, for we understand *it;* and do not speak to us in Hebrew in the hearing of the people who *are* on the wall."

27 But *the* Rabshakeh said to them, "Has my master sent me to your master and to you to speak these words, and not to the men who sit on the wall, who will eat and drink their own waste with you?"

28 Then *the* Rabshakeh stood and called out with a loud voice in Hebrew, and spoke, saying, "Hear the word of the great king, the king of Assyria! 29 Thus says the king: 'Do not let Hezekiah deceive you, for he shall not be able to deliver you from his hand; 30 nor let Hezekiah make you trust in the LORD, saying, "The LORD will surely deliver us; this city shall not be given into the hand of the king of Assyria."' 31 Do not listen to Hezekiah; for thus says the king of Assyria: 'Make *peace* with me by a present and come out to me; and every one of you eat from his own vine and every one from his own fig tree, and every one of you drink the waters of his own cistern; 32 until I come and take you away to a land like your own land, a land of grain and new wine, a land of bread and vineyards, a land of olive groves and honey, that you may live and not die. But do not listen to Hezekiah, lest he persuade you, saying, "The LORD will deliver us." 33 Has any of the gods of the nations at all delivered its land from the hand of the king of Assyria? 34 Where *are* the gods of Hamath and Arpad? Where *are* the gods of Sepharvaim and Hena and Ivah? Indeed, have they delivered Samaria from my hand? 35 Who among all the gods of the lands have delivered their countries from my hand, that the LORD should deliver Jerusalem from my hand?' "

36 But the people held their peace and answered him not a word; for the king's commandment was, "Do not answer him." 37 Then Eliakim the son of Hilkiah, who *was* over the household, Shebna the scribe, and Joah the son of Asaph, the recorder, came to Hezekiah with *their* clothes torn, and told him the words of *the* Rabshakeh.

19 And so it was, when King Hezekiah heard *it,* that he tore his clothes, covered himself with sackcloth, and went into the house of the LORD. 2 Then he sent Eliakim, who *was* over the household, Shebna the scribe, and the elders of the

פְּנֵי פַחַת אַחַד עַבְדֵי אֲדֹנִי הַקְּטַנִּים וַתִּבְטַח לְךָ עַל־מִצְרַיִם לְרֶכֶב וּלְפָרָשִׁים: 25 עַתָּה הֲמִבַּלְעֲדֵי יְהֹוָה עָלִיתִי עַל־הַמָּקוֹם הַזֶּה לְהַשְׁחִתוֹ יְהֹוָה אָמַר אֵלַי עֲלֵה עַל־הָאָרֶץ הַזֹּאת וְהַשְׁחִיתָהּ: 26 וַיֹּאמֶר אֶלְיָקִים בֶּן־חִלְקִיָּהוּ וְשֶׁבְנָה וְיוֹאָח אֶל־רַב־שָׁקֵה דַּבֶּר־נָא אֶל־עֲבָדֶיךָ אֲרָמִית כִּי שֹׁמְעִים אֲנָחְנוּ וְאַל־תְּדַבֵּר עִמָּנוּ יְהוּדִית בְּאָזְנֵי הָעָם אֲשֶׁר עַל־הַחֹמָה: 27 וַיֹּאמֶר אֲלֵיהֶם רַב־שָׁקֵה הַעַל אֲדֹנֶיךָ וְאֵלֶיךָ שְׁלָחַנִי אֲדֹנִי לְדַבֵּר אֶת־הַדְּבָרִים הָאֵלֶּה הֲלֹא עַל־הָאֲנָשִׁים הַיֹּשְׁבִים עַל־הַחֹמָה לֶאֱכֹל אֶת־חֲרֵיהֶם‪°‬ וְלִשְׁתּוֹת אֶת־שֵׁינֵיהֶם‪°‬ עִמָּכֶם: 28 וַיַּעֲמֹד רַב־שָׁקֵה וַיִּקְרָא בְקוֹל־גָּדוֹל יְהוּדִית וַיְדַבֵּר וַיֹּאמֶר שִׁמְעוּ דְּבַר־הַמֶּלֶךְ הַגָּדוֹל מֶלֶךְ אַשּׁוּר: 29 כֹּה אָמַר הַמֶּלֶךְ אַל־יַשִּׁיא לָכֶם חִזְקִיָּהוּ כִּי־לֹא יוּכַל לְהַצִּיל אֶתְכֶם מִיָּדוֹ: 30 וְאַל־יַבְטַח אֶתְכֶם חִזְקִיָּהוּ אֶל־יְהֹוָה לֵאמֹר הַצֵּל יַצִּילֵנוּ יְהֹוָה וְלֹא תִנָּתֵן אֶת־הָעִיר הַזֹּאת בְּיַד מֶלֶךְ אַשּׁוּר: 31 אַל־תִּשְׁמְעוּ אֶל־חִזְקִיָּהוּ כִּי כֹה אָמַר מֶלֶךְ אַשּׁוּר עֲשׂוּ־אִתִּי בְרָכָה וּצְאוּ אֵלַי וְאִכְלוּ אִישׁ־גַּפְנוֹ וְאִישׁ תְּאֵנָתוֹ וּשְׁתוּ אִישׁ מֵי־בוֹרוֹ: 32 עַד־בֹּאִי וְלָקַחְתִּי אֶתְכֶם אֶל־אֶרֶץ כְּאַרְצְכֶם אֶרֶץ דָּגָן וְתִירוֹשׁ אֶרֶץ לֶחֶם וּכְרָמִים אֶרֶץ זֵית יִצְהָר וּדְבַשׁ וִחְיוּ וְלֹא תָמֻתוּ וְאַל־תִּשְׁמְעוּ אֶל־חִזְקִיָּהוּ כִּי־יַסִּית אֶתְכֶם לֵאמֹר יְהֹוָה יַצִּילֵנוּ: 33 הַהַצֵּל הִצִּילוּ אֱלֹהֵי הַגּוֹיִם אִישׁ אֶת־אַרְצוֹ מִיַּד מֶלֶךְ אַשּׁוּר: 34 אַיֵּה אֱלֹהֵי חֲמָת וְאַרְפָּד אַיֵּה אֱלֹהֵי סְפַרְוַיִם הֵנַע וְעִוָּה כִּי־הִצִּילוּ אֶת־שֹׁמְרוֹן מִיָּדִי: 35 מִי בְּכָל־אֱלֹהֵי הָאֲרָצוֹת אֲשֶׁר־הִצִּילוּ אֶת־אַרְצָם מִיָּדִי כִּי־יַצִּיל יְהֹוָה אֶת־יְרוּשָׁלִַם מִיָּדִי: 36 וְהֶחֱרִישׁוּ הָעָם וְלֹא־עָנוּ אֹתוֹ דָּבָר כִּי־מִצְוַת הַמֶּלֶךְ הִיא לֵאמֹר לֹא תַעֲנֻהוּ: 37 וַיָּבֹא אֶלְיָקִים בֶּן־חִלְקִיָּה אֲשֶׁר־עַל־הַבַּיִת וְשֶׁבְנָא הַסֹּפֵר וְיוֹאָח בֶּן־אָסָף הַמַּזְכִּיר אֶל־חִזְקִיָּהוּ קְרוּעֵי בְגָדִים וַיַּגִּדוּ לוֹ דִּבְרֵי רַב־שָׁקֵה:

יט וַיְהִי כִּשְׁמֹעַ הַמֶּלֶךְ חִזְקִיָּהוּ וַיִּקְרַע אֶת־בְּגָדָיו וַיִּתְכַּס בַּשָּׂק וַיָּבֹא בֵּית יְהֹוָה: 2 וַיִּשְׁלַח אֶת־אֶלְיָקִים

priests, covered with sackcloth, to Isaiah the prophet, the son of Amoz. [3] And they said to him, "Thus says Hezekiah: 'This day *is* a day of trouble, and rebuke, and blasphemy; for the children have come to birth, but *there is* no strength to bring them forth. [4] It may be that the LORD your God will hear all the words of *the* Rabshakeh, whom his master the king of Assyria has sent to reproach the living God, and will rebuke the words which the LORD your God has heard. Therefore lift up *your* prayer for the remnant that is left.'"

[5] So the servants of King Hezekiah came to Isaiah. [6] And Isaiah said to them, "Thus you shall say to your master, 'Thus says the LORD: "Do not be afraid of the words which you have heard, with which the servants of the king of Assyria have blasphemed Me. [7] Surely I will send a spirit upon him, and he shall hear a rumor and return to his own land; and I will cause him to fall by the sword in his own land."'"

[8] Then *the* Rabshakeh returned and found the king of Assyria warring against Libnah, for he heard that he had departed from Lachish. [9] And the king heard concerning Tirhakah king of Ethiopia, "Look, he has come out to make war with you." So he again sent messengers to Hezekiah, saying, [10] "Thus you shall speak to Hezekiah king of Judah, saying: 'Do not let your God in whom you trust deceive you, saying, "Jerusalem shall not be given into the hand of the king of Assyria." [11] Look! You have heard what the kings of Assyria have done to all lands by utterly destroying them; and shall you be delivered? [12] Have the gods of the nations delivered those whom my fathers have destroyed, Gozan and Haran and Rezeph, and the people of Eden who *were* in Telassar? [13] Where *is* the king of Hamath, the king of Arpad, and the king of the city of Sepharvaim, Hena, and Ivah?'"

[14] And Hezekiah received the letter from the hand of the messengers, and read it; and Hezekiah went up to the house of the LORD, and spread it before the LORD. [15] Then Hezekiah prayed before the LORD, and said: "O LORD God of Israel, *the One* who dwells *between* the cherubim, You are God, You alone, of all the kingdoms of the earth. You have made heaven and earth. [16] Incline Your ear, O LORD, and hear; open Your eyes, O LORD, and see; and hear the words of Sennacherib, which he has sent to reproach the living God. [17] Truly, LORD, the kings of Assyria have laid waste the nations and their lands, [18] and have cast their gods into the fire; for they *were* not gods, but the work of men's hands—wood and stone. Therefore they destroyed them. [19] Now therefore, O LORD our

אֲשֶׁר־עַל־הַבַּ֫יִת וְשֶׁבְנָא הַסֹּפֵר וְאֵת זִקְנֵי הַכֹּהֲנִים מִתְכַּסִּים בַּשַּׂקִּים אֶל־יְשַׁעְיָהוּ הַנָּבִיא בֶן־אָמֽוֹץ׃ 3 וַיֹּאמְרוּ אֵלָיו כֹּה אָמַר חִזְקִיָּהוּ יוֹם־צָרָה וְתוֹכֵחָה וּנְאָצָה הַיּוֹם הַזֶּה כִּי בָאוּ בָנִים עַד־מַשְׁבֵּר וְכֹחַ אַיִן לְלֵדָֽה׃ 4 אוּלַי יִשְׁמַע יְהוָה אֱלֹהֶיךָ אֵת ׀ כָּל־דִּבְרֵי רַב־שָׁקֵה אֲשֶׁר שְׁלָחוֹ מֶלֶךְ־אַשּׁוּר ׀ אֲדֹנָיו לְחָרֵף אֱלֹהִים חַי וְהוֹכִיחַ בַּדְּבָרִים אֲשֶׁר שָׁמַע יְהוָה אֱלֹהֶיךָ וְנָשָׂאתָ תְפִלָּה בְּעַד הַשְּׁאֵרִית הַנִּמְצָאָֽה׃ 5 וַיָּבֹאוּ עַבְדֵי הַמֶּלֶךְ חִזְקִיָּהוּ אֶל־יְשַׁעְיָֽהוּ׃ 6 וַיֹּאמֶר לָהֶם יְשַׁעְיָהוּ כֹּה תֹאמְרוּן אֶל־אֲדֹנֵיכֶם כֹּה ׀ אָמַר יְהוָה אַל־תִּירָא מִפְּנֵי הַדְּבָרִים אֲשֶׁר שָׁמַעְתָּ אֲשֶׁר גִּדְּפוּ נַעֲרֵי מֶֽלֶךְ־אַשּׁוּר אֹתִֽי׃ 7 הִנְנִי נֹתֵן בּוֹ רוּחַ וְשָׁמַע שְׁמוּעָה וְשָׁב לְאַרְצוֹ וְהִפַּלְתִּיו בַּחֶרֶב בְּאַרְצֽוֹ׃ 8 וַיָּשָׁב רַב־שָׁקֵה וַיִּמְצָא אֶת־מֶלֶךְ אַשּׁוּר נִלְחָם עַל־לִבְנָה כִּי שָׁמַע כִּי נָסַע מִלָּכִֽישׁ׃ 9 וַיִּשְׁמַע אֶל־תִּרְהָקָה מֶֽלֶךְ־כּוּשׁ לֵאמֹר הִנֵּה יָצָא לְהִלָּחֵם אִתָּךְ וַיָּשָׁב וַיִּשְׁלַח מַלְאָכִים אֶל־חִזְקִיָּהוּ לֵאמֹֽר׃ 10 כֹּה תֹאמְרוּן אֶל־חִזְקִיָּהוּ מֶֽלֶךְ־יְהוּדָה לֵאמֹר אַל־יַשִּׁאֲךָ אֱלֹהֶיךָ אֲשֶׁר אַתָּה בֹּטֵחַ בּוֹ לֵאמֹר לֹא תִנָּתֵן יְרוּשָׁלִַם בְּיַד מֶלֶךְ אַשּֽׁוּר׃ 11 הִנֵּה ׀ אַתָּה שָׁמַעְתָּ אֵת אֲשֶׁר עָשׂוּ מַלְכֵי אַשּׁוּר לְכָל־הָאֲרָצוֹת לְהַחֲרִימָם וְאַתָּה תִּנָּצֵֽל׃ 12 הַהִצִּילוּ אֹתָם אֱלֹהֵי הַגּוֹיִם אֲשֶׁר שִׁחֲתוּ אֲבוֹתַי אֶת־גּוֹזָן וְאֶת־חָרָן וְרֶצֶף וּבְנֵי־עֶדֶן אֲשֶׁר בִּתְלַאשָּֽׂר׃ 13 אַיּוֹ מֶֽלֶךְ־חֲמָת וּמֶלֶךְ אַרְפָּד וּמֶלֶךְ לָעִיר סְפַרְוָיִם הֵנַע וְעִוָּֽה׃ 14 וַיִּקַּח חִזְקִיָּהוּ אֶת־הַסְּפָרִים מִיַּד הַמַּלְאָכִים וַיִּקְרָאֵם וַיַּעַל בֵּית יְהוָה וַיִּפְרְשֵׂהוּ חִזְקִיָּהוּ לִפְנֵי יְהוָֽה׃ פ
15 וַיִּתְפַּלֵּל חִזְקִיָּהוּ לִפְנֵי יְהוָה וַיֹּאמַר יְהוָה אֱלֹהֵי יִשְׂרָאֵל יֹשֵׁב הַכְּרֻבִים אַתָּה־הוּא הָאֱלֹהִים לְבַדְּךָ לְכֹל מַמְלְכוֹת הָאָרֶץ אַתָּה עָשִׂיתָ אֶת־הַשָּׁמַיִם וְאֶת־הָאָֽרֶץ׃ 16 הַטֵּה יְהוָה ׀ אָזְנְךָ וּֽשְׁמָע פְּקַח יְהוָה עֵינֶיךָ וּרְאֵה וּשְׁמַע אֵת דִּבְרֵי סַנְחֵרִיב אֲשֶׁר שְׁלָחוֹ לְחָרֵף אֱלֹהִים חָֽי׃ 17 אָמְנָם יְהוָה הֶחֱרִיבוּ מַלְכֵי אַשּׁוּר אֶת־הַגּוֹיִם וְאֶת־אַרְצָֽם׃ 18 וְנָתְנוּ אֶת־אֱלֹהֵיהֶם בָּאֵשׁ כִּי לֹא אֱלֹהִים הֵמָּה כִּי אִם־מַעֲשֵׂה יְדֵֽי־אָדָם עֵץ וָאֶבֶן וַֽיְאַבְּדֽוּם׃ 19 וְעַתָּה יְהוָה אֱלֹהֵינוּ הוֹשִׁיעֵנוּ נָא

God, I pray, save us from his hand, that all the kingdoms of the earth may know that You *are* the LORD God, You alone."

20 Then Isaiah the son of Amoz sent to Hezekiah, saying, "Thus says the LORD God of Israel: 'Because you have prayed to Me against Sennacherib king of Assyria, I have heard.' 21 This *is* the word which the LORD has spoken concerning him:

'The virgin, the daughter of Zion,
Has despised you, laughed you to scorn;
The daughter of Jerusalem
Has shaken *her* head behind your back!

22 'Whom have you reproached and blasphemed?
Against whom have you raised *your* voice,
And lifted up your eyes on high?
Against the Holy *One* of Israel.
23 By your messengers you have reproached the Lord,
And said: "By the multitude of my chariots
I have come up to the height of the mountains,
To the limits of Lebanon;
I will cut down its tall cedars
And its choice cypress trees;
I will enter the extremity of its borders,
To its fruitful forest.
24 I have dug and drunk strange water,
And with the soles of my feet I have dried up
All the brooks of defense."

25 'Did you not hear long ago
How I made it,
From ancient times that I formed it?
Now I have brought it to pass,
That you should be
For crushing fortified cities *into* heaps of ruins.
26 Therefore their inhabitants had little power;
They were dismayed and confounded;
They were *as* the grass of the field
And the green herb,
As the grass on the housetops
And *grain* blighted before it is grown.
27 'But I know your dwelling place,
Your going out and your coming in,
And your rage against Me.
28 Because your rage against Me and your tumult
Have come up to My ears,
Therefore I will put My hook in your nose
And My bridle in your lips,
And I will turn you back
By the way which you came.

29 'This *shall be* a sign to you:
You shall eat this year such as grows of itself,
And in the second year what springs from the same;
Also in the third year sow and reap,
Plant vineyards and eat the fruit of them.
30 And the remnant who have escaped of the house of Judah
Shall again take root downward,
And bear fruit upward.

מִדָּן וְיֵדְעוּ כָּל־מַמְלְכוֹת הָאָרֶץ כִּי אַתָּה יְהֹוָה
אֱלֹהִים לְבַדֶּךָ: ס 20 וַיִּשְׁלַח יְשַׁעְיָהוּ בֶן־
אָמוֹץ אֶל־חִזְקִיָּהוּ לֵאמֹר כֹּה־אָמַר יְהֹוָה אֱלֹהֵי
יִשְׂרָאֵל אֲשֶׁר הִתְפַּלַּלְתָּ אֵלַי אֶל־סַנְחֵרִב מֶלֶךְ־
אַשּׁוּר שָׁמָעְתִּי: 21 זֶה הַדָּבָר אֲשֶׁר־דִּבֶּר יְהֹוָה עָלָיו
בָּזָה לְךָ לָעֲגָה לְךָ בְּתוּלַת בַּת־צִיּוֹן אַחֲרֶיךָ רֹאשׁ
הֵנִיעָה בַּת יְרוּשָׁלָ͏ִם: 22 אֶת־מִי חֵרַפְתָּ וְגִדַּפְתָּ וְעַל־
מִי הֲרִימוֹתָ קּוֹל וַתִּשָּׂא מָרוֹם עֵינֶיךָ עַל־קְדוֹשׁ
יִשְׂרָאֵל: 23 בְּיַד מַלְאָכֶיךָ חֵרַפְתָּ ׀ אֲדֹנָי וַתֹּאמֶר
בְּרֶכֶב רִכְבִּי אֲנִי עָלִיתִי מְרוֹם הָרִים יַרְכְּתֵי לְבָנוֹן
וְאֶכְרֹת קוֹמַת אֲרָזָיו מִבְחוֹר בְּרֹשָׁיו וְאָבוֹאָה מְלוֹן
קִצֹּה יַעַר כַּרְמִלּוֹ: 24 אֲנִי קַרְתִּי וְשָׁתִיתִי מַיִם זָרִים
וְאַחְרִב בְּכַף־פְּעָמַי כֹּל יְאֹרֵי מָצוֹר: 25 הֲלֹא־שָׁמַעְתָּ
לְמֵרָחוֹק אֹתָהּ עָשִׂיתִי לְמִימֵי קֶדֶם וִיצַרְתִּיהָ
עַתָּה הֲבֵיאתִיהָ וּתְהִי לַהְשׁוֹת גַּלִּים נִצִּים עָרִים
בְּצֻרוֹת: 26 וְיֹשְׁבֵיהֶן קִצְרֵי־יָד חַתּוּ וַיֵּבֹשׁוּ הָיוּ עֵשֶׂב
שָׂדֶה וִירַק דֶּשֶׁא חֲצִיר גַּגּוֹת וּשְׁדֵפָה לִפְנֵי קָמָה:
27 וְשִׁבְתְּךָ וְצֵאתְךָ וּבֹאֲךָ יָדָעְתִּי וְאֵת הִתְרַגֶּזְךָ אֵלָי:
28 יַעַן הִתְרַגֶּזְךָ אֵלַי וְשַׁאֲנַנְךָ עָלָה בְאָזְנָי וְשַׂמְתִּי
חַחִי בְּאַפֶּךָ וּמִתְגִּי בִּשְׂפָתֶיךָ וַהֲשִׁבֹתִיךָ בַּדֶּרֶךְ
אֲשֶׁר־בָּאתָ בָּהּ: 29 וְזֶה־לְּךָ הָאוֹת אָכוֹל הַשָּׁנָה
סָפִיחַ וּבַשָּׁנָה הַשֵּׁנִית סָחִישׁ וּבַשָּׁנָה הַשְּׁלִישִׁית
זִרְעוּ וְקִצְרוּ וְנִטְעוּ כְרָמִים וְאִכְלוּ פִרְיָם: 30 וְיָסְפָה
פְּלֵיטַת בֵּית־יְהוּדָה הַנִּשְׁאָרָה שֹׁרֶשׁ

³¹ For out of Jerusalem shall go a remnant,
And those who escape from Mount Zion.
The zeal of the LORD of hosts will do this.'

³²"Therefore thus says the LORD concerning the king of Assyria:

'He shall not come into this city,
Nor shoot an arrow there,
Nor come before it with shield,
Nor build a siege mound against it.
³³ By the way that he came,
By the same shall he return;
And he shall not come into this city,'
Says the LORD.
³⁴ 'For I will defend this city, to save it
For My own sake and for My servant
David's sake.'"

³⁵And it came to pass on a certain night that the angel of the LORD went out, and killed in the camp of the Assyrians one hundred and eighty-five thousand; and when *people* arose early in the morning, there were the corpses—all dead. ³⁶So Sennacherib king of Assyria departed and went away, returned *home,* and remained at Nineveh. ³⁷Now it came to pass, as he was worshiping in the temple of Nisroch his god, that his sons Adrammelech and Sharezer struck him down with the sword; and they escaped into the land of Ararat. Then Esarhaddon his son reigned in his place.

20 In those days Hezekiah was sick and near death. And Isaiah the prophet, the son of Amoz, went to him and said to him, "Thus says the LORD: 'Set your house in order, for you shall die, and not live.'"

²Then he turned his face toward the wall, and prayed to the LORD, saying, ³"Remember now, O LORD, I pray, how I have walked before You in truth and with a loyal heart, and have done *what was* good in Your sight." And Hezekiah wept bitterly.

⁴And it happened, before Isaiah had gone out into the middle court, that the word of the LORD came to him, saying, ⁵"Return and tell Hezekiah the leader of My people, 'Thus says the LORD, the God of David your father: "I have heard your prayer, I have seen your tears; surely I will heal you. On the third day you shall go up to the house of the LORD. ⁶And I will add to your days fifteen years. I will deliver you and this city from the hand of the king of Assyria; and I will defend this city for My own sake, and for the sake of My servant David."'"

⁷Then Isaiah said, "Take a lump of figs." So they took and laid *it* on the boil, and he recovered.

לְמַטָּה וְעָשָׂה פְּרִי לְמָעְלָה׃ ³¹ כִּי מִירוּשָׁלַ֙͏ִם תֵּצֵא
שְׁאֵרִית וּפְלֵיטָה מֵהַר צִיּוֹן קִנְאַת יְהוָ֔ה תַּעֲשֶׂה־
זֹּאת׃ ס ³² לָכֵן כֹּה־אָמַר יְהוָה אֶל־מֶלֶךְ
אַשּׁוּר לֹא יָבֹא אֶל־הָעִיר הַזֹּאת וְלֹא־יוֹרֶה שָׁם
חֵץ וְלֹא־יְקַדְּמֶנָּה מָגֵן וְלֹא־יִשְׁפֹּךְ עָלֶיהָ סֹלְלָה׃
³³ בַּדֶּרֶךְ אֲשֶׁר־יָבֹא בָּהּ יָשׁוּב וְאֶל־הָעִיר הַזֹּאת
לֹא יָבֹא נְאֻם־יְהוָה׃ ³⁴ וְגַנּוֹתִי אֶל־הָעִיר הַזֹּאת
לְהוֹשִׁיעָהּ לְמַעֲנִי וּלְמַעַן דָּוִד עַבְדִּי׃ ³⁵ וַיְהִי בַּלַּיְלָה
הַהוּא וַיֵּצֵא ׀ מַלְאַךְ יְהוָה וַיַּךְ בְּמַחֲנֵה אַשּׁוּר
מֵאָה שְׁמוֹנִים וַחֲמִשָּׁה אָלֶף וַיַּשְׁכִּימוּ בַבֹּקֶר וְהִנֵּה
כֻלָּם פְּגָרִים מֵתִים׃ ³⁶ וַיִּסַּע וַיֵּלֶךְ וַיָּשָׁב סַנְחֵרִיב
מֶלֶךְ־אַשּׁוּר וַיֵּשֶׁב בְּנִינְוֵה׃ ³⁷ וַיְהִי הוּא מִשְׁתַּחֲוֶה
בֵּית ׀ נִסְרֹךְ אֱלֹהָיו וְאַדְרַמֶּלֶךְ וְשַׂרְאֶצֶר הִכֻּהוּ
בַחֶרֶב וְהֵמָּה נִמְלְטוּ אֶרֶץ אֲרָרָט וַיִּמְלֹךְ אֵסַר־חַדֹּן
בְּנוֹ תַּחְתָּיו׃ פ

כ בַּיָּמִים הָהֵם חָלָה חִזְקִיָּהוּ לָמוּת וַיָּבֹא אֵלָיו
יְשַׁעְיָהוּ בֶן־אָמוֹץ הַנָּבִיא וַיֹּאמֶר אֵלָיו כֹּה־אָמַר
יְהוָה צַו לְבֵיתֶךָ כִּי מֵת אַתָּה וְלֹא תִחְיֶה׃ ² וַיַּסֵּב
אֶת־פָּנָיו אֶל־הַקִּיר וַיִּתְפַּלֵּל אֶל־יְהוָה לֵאמֹר׃ ³ אָנָּה
יְהוָה זְכָר־נָא אֵת אֲשֶׁר הִתְהַלַּכְתִּי לְפָנֶיךָ בֶּאֱמֶת
וּבְלֵבָב שָׁלֵם וְהַטּוֹב בְּעֵינֶיךָ עָשִׂיתִי וַיֵּבְךְּ חִזְקִיָּהוּ
בְּכִי גָדוֹל׃ ס ⁴ וַיְהִי יְשַׁעְיָהוּ לֹא יָצָא
הָעִיר הַתִּיכֹנָה וּדְבַר־יְהוָה הָיָה אֵלָיו לֵאמֹר׃
⁵ שׁוּב וְאָמַרְתָּ אֶל־חִזְקִיָּהוּ נְגִיד־עַמִּי כֹּה־אָמַר
יְהוָה אֱלֹהֵי דָּוִד אָבִיךָ שָׁמַעְתִּי אֶת־תְּפִלָּתֶךָ רָאִיתִי
אֶת־דִּמְעָתֶךָ הִנְנִי רֹפֶא לָךְ בַּיּוֹם הַשְּׁלִישִׁי תַּעֲלֶה
בֵּית יְהוָה׃ ⁶ וְהֹסַפְתִּי עַל־יָמֶיךָ חֲמֵשׁ עֶשְׂרֵה שָׁנָה
וּמִכַּף מֶלֶךְ־אַשּׁוּר אַצִּילְךָ וְאֵת הָעִיר הַזֹּאת וְגַנּוֹתִי
עַל־הָעִיר הַזֹּאת לְמַעֲנִי וּלְמַעַן דָּוִד עַבְדִּי׃ ⁷ וַיֹּאמֶר
יְשַׁעְיָהוּ קְחוּ דְּבֶלֶת תְּאֵנִים וַיִּקְחוּ וַיָּשִׂימוּ עַל־

יט ³¹ צְבָאוֹת   ³⁷ בָּנָיו
כ ⁴ חָצֵר

8 And Hezekiah said to Isaiah, "What *is* the sign that the LORD will heal me, and that I shall go up to the house of the LORD the third day?"

9 Then Isaiah said, "This is the sign to you from the LORD, that the LORD will do the thing which He has spoken: *shall* the shadow go forward ten degrees or go backward ten degrees?"

10 And Hezekiah answered, "It is an easy thing for the shadow to go down ten degrees; no, but let the shadow go backward ten degrees."

11 So Isaiah the prophet cried out to the LORD, and He brought the shadow ten degrees backward, by which it had gone down on the sundial of Ahaz.

12 At that time Berodach-Baladan the son of Baladan, king of Babylon, sent letters and a present to Hezekiah, for he heard that Hezekiah had been sick. 13 And Hezekiah was attentive to them, and showed them all the house of his treasures—the silver and gold, the spices and precious ointment, and all his armory—all that was found among his treasures. There was nothing in his house or in all his dominion that Hezekiah did not show them.

14 Then Isaiah the prophet went to King Hezekiah, and said to him, "What did these men say, and from where did they come to you?"

So Hezekiah said, "They came from a far country, from Babylon."

15 And he said, "What have they seen in your house?"

So Hezekiah answered, "They have seen all that *is* in my house; there is nothing among my treasures that I have not shown them."

16 Then Isaiah said to Hezekiah, "Hear the word of the LORD: 17 'Behold, the days are coming when all that *is* in your house, and what your fathers have accumulated until this day, shall be carried to Babylon; nothing shall be left,' says the LORD. 18 'And they shall take away some of your sons who will descend from you, whom you will beget; and they shall be eunuchs in the palace of the king of Babylon.'"

19 So Hezekiah said to Isaiah, "The word of the LORD which you have spoken *is* good!" For he said, "Will there not be peace and truth at least in my days?"

20 Now the rest of the acts of Hezekiah—all his might, and how he made a pool and a tunnel and brought water into the city—*are* they not written in the book of the chronicles of the kings of Judah? 21 So Hezekiah rested with his fathers. Then Manasseh his son reigned in his place.

הַשָּׁחִין וַיֶּחִי: 8 וַיֹּאמֶר חִזְקִיָּהוּ אֶל־יְשַׁעְיָהוּ מָה אוֹת כִּי־יִרְפָּא יְהוָה לִי וְעָלִיתִי בַּיּוֹם הַשְּׁלִישִׁי בֵּית יְהוָה: 9 וַיֹּאמֶר יְשַׁעְיָהוּ זֶה־לְּךָ הָאוֹת מֵאֵת יְהוָה כִּי יַעֲשֶׂה יְהוָה אֶת־הַדָּבָר אֲשֶׁר דִּבֵּר הָלַךְ הַצֵּל עֶשֶׂר מַעֲלוֹת אִם־יָשׁוּב עֶשֶׂר מַעֲלוֹת: 10 וַיֹּאמֶר יְחִזְקִיָּהוּ נָקֵל לַצֵּל לִנְטוֹת עֶשֶׂר מַעֲלוֹת לֹא כִי יָשׁוּב הַצֵּל אֲחֹרַנִּית עֶשֶׂר מַעֲלוֹת: 11 וַיִּקְרָא יְשַׁעְיָהוּ הַנָּבִיא אֶל־יְהוָה וַיָּשֶׁב אֶת־הַצֵּל בַּמַּעֲלוֹת אֲשֶׁר יָרְדָה בְּמַעֲלוֹת אָחָז אֲחֹרַנִּית עֶשֶׂר מַעֲלוֹת: פ

12 בָּעֵת הַהִיא שָׁלַח בְּראֹדַךְ בַּלְאֲדָן בֶּן־בַּלְאֲדָן מֶלֶךְ־בָּבֶל סְפָרִים וּמִנְחָה אֶל־חִזְקִיָּהוּ כִּי שָׁמַע כִּי חָלָה חִזְקִיָּהוּ: 13 וַיִּשְׁמַע עֲלֵיהֶם חִזְקִיָּהוּ וַיַּרְאֵם אֶת־כָּל־בֵּית נְכֹתֹה אֶת־הַכֶּסֶף וְאֶת־הַזָּהָב וְאֶת־הַבְּשָׂמִים וְאֵת שֶׁמֶן הַטּוֹב וְאֵת בֵּית כֵּלָיו וְאֵת כָּל־אֲשֶׁר נִמְצָא בְּאוֹצְרֹתָיו לֹא־הָיָה דָבָר אֲשֶׁר לֹא־הֶרְאָם חִזְקִיָּהוּ בְּבֵיתוֹ וּבְכָל־מֶמְשַׁלְתּוֹ: 14 וַיָּבֹא יְשַׁעְיָהוּ הַנָּבִיא אֶל־הַמֶּלֶךְ חִזְקִיָּהוּ וַיֹּאמֶר אֵלָיו מָה אָמְרוּ | הָאֲנָשִׁים הָאֵלֶּה וּמֵאַיִן יָבֹאוּ אֵלֶיךָ וַיֹּאמֶר חִזְקִיָּהוּ מֵאֶרֶץ רְחוֹקָה בָּאוּ מִבָּבֶל: 15 וַיֹּאמֶר מָה רָאוּ בְּבֵיתֶךָ וַיֹּאמֶר חִזְקִיָּהוּ אֶת כָּל־אֲשֶׁר בְּבֵיתִי רָאוּ לֹא־הָיָה דָבָר אֲשֶׁר לֹא־הִרְאִיתִם בְּאוֹצְרֹתָי: 16 וַיֹּאמֶר יְשַׁעְיָהוּ אֶל־חִזְקִיָּהוּ שְׁמַע דְּבַר־יְהוָה: 17 הִנֵּה יָמִים בָּאִים וְנִשָּׂא | כָּל־אֲשֶׁר בְּבֵיתֶךָ וַאֲשֶׁר אָצְרוּ אֲבֹתֶיךָ עַד־הַיּוֹם הַזֶּה בָּבֶלָה לֹא־יִוָּתֵר דָּבָר אָמַר יְהוָה: 18 וּמִבָּנֶיךָ אֲשֶׁר יֵצְאוּ מִמְּךָ אֲשֶׁר תּוֹלִיד יִקָּח וְהָיוּ סָרִיסִים בְּהֵיכַל מֶלֶךְ בָּבֶל: 19 וַיֹּאמֶר חִזְקִיָּהוּ אֶל־יְשַׁעְיָהוּ טוֹב דְּבַר־יְהוָה אֲשֶׁר דִּבַּרְתָּ וַיֹּאמֶר הֲלוֹא אִם־שָׁלוֹם וֶאֱמֶת יִהְיֶה בְיָמָי:

20 וְיֶתֶר דִּבְרֵי חִזְקִיָּהוּ וְכָל־גְּבוּרָתוֹ וַאֲשֶׁר עָשָׂה אֶת־הַבְּרֵכָה וְאֶת־הַתְּעָלָה וַיָּבֵא אֶת־הַמַּיִם הָעִירָה הֲלֹא־הֵם כְּתוּבִים עַל־סֵפֶר דִּבְרֵי הַיָּמִים לְמַלְכֵי יְהוּדָה: 21 וַיִּשְׁכַּב חִזְקִיָּהוּ עִם־אֲבֹתָיו וַיִּמְלֹךְ מְנַשֶּׁה בְנוֹ תַּחְתָּיו: פ

21 Manasseh *was* twelve years old when he became king, and he reigned fifty-five years in Jerusalem. His mother's name *was* Hephzibah. ²And he did evil in the sight of the LORD, according to the abominations of the nations whom the LORD had cast out before the children of Israel. ³For he rebuilt the high places which Hezekiah his father had destroyed; he raised up altars for Baal, and made a wooden image, as Ahab king of Israel had done; and he worshiped all the host of heaven and served them. ⁴He also built altars in the house of the LORD, of which the LORD had said, "In Jerusalem I will put My name." ⁵And he built altars for all the host of heaven in the two courts of the house of the LORD. ⁶Also he made his son pass through the fire, practiced soothsaying, used witchcraft, and consulted spiritists and mediums. He did much evil in the sight of the LORD, to provoke *Him* to anger. ⁷He even set a carved image of Asherah that he had made, in the house of which the LORD had said to David and to Solomon his son, "In this house and in Jerusalem, which I have chosen out of all the tribes of Israel, I will put My name forever; ⁸and I will not make the feet of Israel wander anymore from the land which I gave their fathers— only if they are careful to do according to all that I have commanded them, and according to all the law that My servant Moses commanded them." ⁹But they paid no attention, and Manasseh seduced them to do more evil than the nations whom the LORD had destroyed before the children of Israel.

¹⁰And the LORD spoke by His servants the prophets, saying, ¹¹"Because Manasseh king of Judah has done these abominations (he has acted more wickedly than all the Amorites who *were* before him, and has also made Judah sin with his idols), ¹²therefore thus says the LORD God of Israel: 'Behold, *I* am bringing *such* calamity upon Jerusalem and Judah, that whoever hears of it, both his ears will tingle. ¹³And I will stretch over Jerusalem the measuring line of Samaria and the plummet of the house of Ahab; I will wipe Jerusalem as *one* wipes a dish, wiping *it* and turning *it* upside down. ¹⁴So I will forsake the remnant of My inheritance and deliver them into the hand of their enemies; and they shall become victims of plunder to all their enemies, ¹⁵because they have done evil in My sight, and have provoked Me to anger since the day their fathers came out of Egypt, even to this day.'"

¹⁶Moreover Manasseh shed very much innocent blood, till he had filled Jerusalem from one end to another, besides his sin by which he made Judah sin, in doing evil in the sight of the LORD.

כא בֶּן־שְׁתֵּים עֶשְׂרֵה שָׁנָה מְנַשֶּׁה בְמָלְכוֹ
וַחֲמִשִּׁים וְחָמֵשׁ שָׁנָה מָלַךְ בִּירוּשָׁלִָם וְשֵׁם אִמּוֹ
חֶפְצִי־בָהּ: 2 וַיַּעַשׂ הָרַע בְּעֵינֵי יְהוָה כְּתוֹעֲבֹת
הַגּוֹיִם אֲשֶׁר הוֹרִישׁ יְהוָה מִפְּנֵי בְּנֵי יִשְׂרָאֵל: 3 וַיָּשָׁב
וַיִּבֶן אֶת־הַבָּמוֹת אֲשֶׁר אִבַּד חִזְקִיָּהוּ אָבִיו וַיָּקֶם
מִזְבְּחֹת לַבַּעַל וַיַּעַשׂ אֲשֵׁרָה כַּאֲשֶׁר עָשָׂה אַחְאָב
מֶלֶךְ יִשְׂרָאֵל וַיִּשְׁתַּחוּ לְכָל־צְבָא הַשָּׁמַיִם וַיַּעֲבֹד
אֹתָם: 4 וּבָנָה מִזְבְּחֹת בְּבֵית יְהוָה אֲשֶׁר אָמַר
יְהוָה בִּירוּשָׁלִַם אָשִׂים אֶת־שְׁמִי: 5 וַיִּבֶן מִזְבְּחוֹת
לְכָל־צְבָא הַשָּׁמָיִם בִּשְׁתֵּי חַצְרוֹת בֵּית־יְהוָה:
6 וְהֶעֱבִיר אֶת־בְּנוֹ בָּאֵשׁ וְעוֹנֵן וְנִחֵשׁ וְעָשָׂה אוֹב
וְיִדְּעֹנִים הִרְבָּה לַעֲשׂוֹת הָרַע בְּעֵינֵי יְהוָה לְהַכְעִיס:
7 וַיָּשֶׂם אֶת־פֶּסֶל הָאֲשֵׁרָה אֲשֶׁר עָשָׂה בַּבַּיִת אֲשֶׁר
אָמַר יְהוָה אֶל־דָּוִד וְאֶל־שְׁלֹמֹה בְנוֹ בַּבַּיִת הַזֶּה
וּבִירוּשָׁלִַם אֲשֶׁר בָּחַרְתִּי מִכֹּל שִׁבְטֵי יִשְׂרָאֵל אָשִׂים
אֶת־שְׁמִי לְעוֹלָם: 8 וְלֹא אֹסִיף לְהָנִיד רֶגֶל יִשְׂרָאֵל
מִן־הָאֲדָמָה אֲשֶׁר נָתַתִּי לַאֲבוֹתָם רַק אִם־
יִשְׁמְרוּ לַעֲשׂוֹת כְּכֹל אֲשֶׁר צִוִּיתִים וּלְכָל־הַתּוֹרָה
אֲשֶׁר־צִוָּה אֹתָם עַבְדִּי מֹשֶׁה: 9 וְלֹא שָׁמֵעוּ וַיַּתְעֵם
מְנַשֶּׁה לַעֲשׂוֹת אֶת־הָרָע מִן־הַגּוֹיִם אֲשֶׁר הִשְׁמִיד
יְהוָה מִפְּנֵי בְּנֵי יִשְׂרָאֵל: 10 וַיְדַבֵּר יְהוָה בְּיַד־
עֲבָדָיו הַנְּבִיאִים לֵאמֹר: 11 יַעַן אֲשֶׁר עָשָׂה מְנַשֶּׁה
מֶלֶךְ־יְהוּדָה הַתֹּעֵבוֹת הָאֵלֶּה הֵרַע מִכֹּל אֲשֶׁר
עָשׂוּ הָאֱמֹרִי אֲשֶׁר לְפָנָיו וַיַּחֲטִא גַם־אֶת־יְהוּדָה
בְּגִלּוּלָיו:
פ
12 לָכֵן כֹּה־אָמַר יְהוָה אֱלֹהֵי יִשְׂרָאֵל הִנְנִי
מֵבִיא רָעָה עַל־יְרוּשָׁלִַם וִיהוּדָה אֲשֶׁר כָּל־
שֹׁמְעָיו תְּצַלֶּנָה שְׁתֵּי אָזְנָיו: 13 וְנָטִיתִי עַל־
יְרוּשָׁלִַם אֵת קָו שֹׁמְרוֹן וְאֶת־מִשְׁקֹלֶת בֵּית אַחְאָב
וּמָחִיתִי אֶת־יְרוּשָׁלִַם כַּאֲשֶׁר־יִמְחֶה אֶת־הַצַּלַּחַת
מָחָה וְהָפַךְ עַל־פָּנֶיהָ: 14 וְנָטַשְׁתִּי אֵת שְׁאֵרִית
נַחֲלָתִי וּנְתַתִּים בְּיַד אֹיְבֵיהֶם וְהָיוּ לְבַז וְלִמְשִׁסָּה
לְכָל־אֹיְבֵיהֶם: 15 יַעַן אֲשֶׁר עָשׂוּ אֶת־הָרַע בְּעֵינַי
וַיִּהְיוּ מַכְעִסִים אֹתִי מִן־הַיּוֹם אֲשֶׁר יָצְאוּ אֲבוֹתָם
מִמִּצְרַיִם וְעַד הַיּוֹם הַזֶּה: 16 וְגַם דָּם נָקִי שָׁפַךְ
מְנַשֶּׁה הַרְבֵּה מְאֹד עַד אֲשֶׁר־מִלֵּא אֶת־יְרוּשָׁלִַם

כא 12 שֹׁמְעָה

17 Now the rest of the acts of Manasseh—all that he did, and the sin that he committed—*are* they not written in the book of the chronicles of the kings of Judah? 18 So Manasseh rested with his fathers, and was buried in the garden of his own house, in the garden of Uzza. Then his son Amon reigned in his place.

19 Amon *was* twenty-two years old when he became king, and he reigned two years in Jerusalem. His mother's name *was* Meshullemeth the daughter of Haruz of Jotbah. 20 And he did evil in the sight of the LORD, as his father Manasseh had done. 21 So he walked in all the ways that his father had walked; and he served the idols that his father had served, and worshiped them. 22 He forsook the LORD God of his fathers, and did not walk in the way of the LORD.

23 Then the servants of Amon conspired against him, and killed the king in his own house. 24 But the people of the land executed all those who had conspired against King Amon. Then the people of the land made his son Josiah king in his place.

25 Now the rest of the acts of Amon which he did, *are* they not written in the book of the chronicles of the kings of Judah? 26 And he was buried in his tomb in the garden of Uzza. Then Josiah his son reigned in his place.

22 Josiah *was* eight years old when he became king, and he reigned thirty-one years in Jerusalem. His mother's name *was* Jedidah the daughter of Adaiah of Bozkath. 2 And he did *what was* right in the sight of the LORD, and walked in all the ways of his father David; he did not turn aside to the right hand or to the left.

3 Now it came to pass, in the eighteenth year of King Josiah, *that* the king sent Shaphan the scribe, the son of Azaliah, the son of Meshullam, to the house of the LORD, saying: 4 "Go up to Hilkiah the high priest, that he may count the money which has been brought into the house of the LORD, which the doorkeepers have gathered from the people. 5 And let them deliver it into the hand of those doing the work, who are the overseers in the house of the LORD; let them give it to those who *are* in the house of the LORD doing the work, to repair the damages of the house— 6 to carpenters and builders and masons—and to buy timber and hewn stone to repair the house. 7 However there need be no accounting made with them of the money delivered into their hand, because they deal faithfully."

8 Then Hilkiah the high priest said to Shaphan the scribe, "I have found the Book of the Law in the house of the LORD." And Hilkiah gave the book to

פֹּה לָפֹה לְבַד מֵחַטָּאתוֹ אֲשֶׁר הֶחֱטִיא אֶת־יְהוּדָה לַעֲשׂוֹת הָרַע בְּעֵינֵי יְהוָה: 17 וְיֶתֶר דִּבְרֵי מְנַשֶּׁה וְכָל־אֲשֶׁר עָשָׂה וְחַטָּאתוֹ אֲשֶׁר חָטָא הֲלֹא־הֵם כְּתוּבִים עַל־סֵפֶר דִּבְרֵי הַיָּמִים לְמַלְכֵי יְהוּדָה: 18 וַיִּשְׁכַּב מְנַשֶּׁה עִם־אֲבֹתָיו וַיִּקָּבֵר בְּגַן־בֵּיתוֹ בְּגַן עֻזָּא וַיִּמְלֹךְ אָמוֹן בְּנוֹ תַּחְתָּיו: פ

19 בֶּן־עֶשְׂרִים וּשְׁתַּיִם שָׁנָה אָמוֹן בְּמָלְכוֹ וּשְׁתַּיִם שָׁנִים מָלַךְ בִּירוּשָׁלִָם וְשֵׁם אִמּוֹ מְשֻׁלֶּמֶת בַּת־חָרוּץ מִן־יָטְבָה: 20 וַיַּעַשׂ הָרַע בְּעֵינֵי יְהוָה כַּאֲשֶׁר עָשָׂה מְנַשֶּׁה אָבִיו: 21 וַיֵּלֶךְ בְּכָל־הַדֶּרֶךְ אֲשֶׁר־הָלַךְ אָבִיו וַיַּעֲבֹד אֶת־הַגִּלֻּלִים אֲשֶׁר עָבַד אָבִיו וַיִּשְׁתַּחוּ לָהֶם: 22 וַיַּעֲזֹב אֶת־יְהוָה אֱלֹהֵי אֲבֹתָיו וְלֹא הָלַךְ בְּדֶרֶךְ יְהוָה: 23 וַיִּקְשְׁרוּ עַבְדֵי־אָמוֹן עָלָיו וַיָּמִיתוּ אֶת־הַמֶּלֶךְ בְּבֵיתוֹ: 24 וַיַּךְ עַם־הָאָרֶץ אֵת כָּל־הַקֹּשְׁרִים עַל־הַמֶּלֶךְ אָמוֹן וַיַּמְלִיכוּ עַם־הָאָרֶץ אֶת־יֹאשִׁיָּהוּ בְנוֹ תַּחְתָּיו: 25 וְיֶתֶר דִּבְרֵי אָמוֹן אֲשֶׁר עָשָׂה הֲלֹא־הֵם כְּתוּבִים עַל־סֵפֶר דִּבְרֵי הַיָּמִים לְמַלְכֵי יְהוּדָה: 26 וַיִּקְבֹּר אֹתוֹ בִּקְבֻרָתוֹ בְּגַן־עֻזָּא וַיִּמְלֹךְ יֹאשִׁיָּהוּ בְנוֹ תַּחְתָּיו: פ

כב בֶּן־שְׁמֹנֶה שָׁנָה יֹאשִׁיָּהוּ בְמָלְכוֹ וּשְׁלֹשִׁים וְאַחַת שָׁנָה מָלַךְ בִּירוּשָׁלִָם וְשֵׁם אִמּוֹ יְדִידָה בַת־עֲדָיָה מִבָּצְקַת: 2 וַיַּעַשׂ הַיָּשָׁר בְּעֵינֵי יְהוָה וַיֵּלֶךְ בְּכָל־דֶּרֶךְ דָּוִד אָבִיו וְלֹא־סָר יָמִין וּשְׂמֹאול: פ

3 וַיְהִי בִּשְׁמֹנֶה עֶשְׂרֵה שָׁנָה לַמֶּלֶךְ יֹאשִׁיָּהוּ שָׁלַח הַמֶּלֶךְ אֶת־שָׁפָן בֶּן־אֲצַלְיָהוּ בֶן־מְשֻׁלָּם הַסֹּפֵר בֵּית יְהוָה לֵאמֹר: 4 עֲלֵה אֶל־חִלְקִיָּהוּ הַכֹּהֵן הַגָּדוֹל וְיַתֵּם אֶת־הַכֶּסֶף הַמּוּבָא בֵּית יְהוָה אֲשֶׁר אָסְפוּ שֹׁמְרֵי הַסַּף מֵאֵת הָעָם: 5 וְיִתְּנֻהוּ עַל־יַד עֹשֵׂי הַמְּלָאכָה הַמֻּפְקָדִים בְּבֵית יְהוָה וְיִתְּנוּ אֹתוֹ לְעֹשֵׂי הַמְּלָאכָה אֲשֶׁר בְּבֵית יְהוָה לְחַזֵּק בֶּדֶק הַבָּיִת: 6 לֶחָרָשִׁים וְלַבֹּנִים וְלַגֹּדְרִים וְלִקְנוֹת עֵצִים וְאַבְנֵי מַחְצֵב לְחַזֵּק אֶת־הַבָּיִת: 7 אַךְ לֹא־יֵחָשֵׁב אִתָּם הַכֶּסֶף הַנִּתָּן עַל־יָדָם כִּי בֶאֱמוּנָה הֵם עֹשִׂים: 8 וַיֹּאמֶר חִלְקִיָּהוּ הַכֹּהֵן הַגָּדוֹל עַל־שָׁפָן הַסֹּפֵר סֵפֶר הַתּוֹרָה מָצָאתִי בְּבֵית יְהוָה וַיִּתֵּן חִלְקִיָּה

Shaphan, and he read it. ⁹ So Shaphan the scribe went to the king, bringing the king word, saying, "Your servants have gathered the money that was found in the house, and have delivered it into the hand of those who do the work, who oversee the house of the LORD." ¹⁰ Then Shaphan the scribe showed the king, saying, "Hilkiah the priest has given me a book." And Shaphan read it before the king.

¹¹ Now it happened, when the king heard the words of the Book of the Law, that he tore his clothes. ¹² Then the king commanded Hilkiah the priest, Ahikam the son of Shaphan, Achbor the son of Michaiah, Shaphan the scribe, and Asaiah a servant of the king, saying, ¹³ "Go, inquire of the LORD for me, for the people and for all Judah, concerning the words of this book that has been found; for great is the wrath of the LORD that is aroused against us, because our fathers have not obeyed the words of this book, to do according to all that is written concerning us."

¹⁴ So Hilkiah the priest, Ahikam, Achbor, Shaphan, and Asaiah went to Huldah the prophetess, the wife of Shallum the son of Tikvah, the son of Harhas, keeper of the wardrobe. (She dwelt in Jerusalem in the Second Quarter.) And they spoke with her. ¹⁵ Then she said to them, "Thus says the LORD God of Israel, 'Tell the man who sent you to Me,' ¹⁶ "Thus says the LORD: 'Behold, I will bring calamity on this place and on its inhabitants—all the words of the book which the king of Judah has read— ¹⁷ because they have forsaken Me and burned incense to other gods, that they might provoke Me to anger with all the works of their hands. Therefore My wrath shall be aroused against this place and shall not be quenched.' " ' ¹⁸ But as for the king of Judah, who sent you to inquire of the LORD, in this manner you shall speak to him, 'Thus says the LORD God of Israel: "Concerning the words which you have heard— ¹⁹ because your heart was tender, and you humbled yourself before the LORD when you heard what I spoke against this place and against its inhabitants, that they would become a desolation and a curse, and you tore your clothes and wept before Me, I also have heard you," says the LORD. ²⁰ Surely, therefore, I will gather you to your fathers, and you shall be gathered to your grave in peace; and your eyes shall not see all the calamity which I will bring on this place." ' " So they brought back word to the king.

23 Now the king sent them to gather all the elders of Judah and Jerusalem to him. ² The king went up to the house of the LORD with all the men of Judah,

אֶת־הַסֵּפֶר וַיִּקְרָאֵהוּ: ⁹ וַיָּבֹא שָׁפָן הַסֹּפֵר אֶל־הַמֶּלֶךְ וַיָּשֶׁב אֶת־הַמֶּלֶךְ דָּבָר וַיֹּאמֶר הִתִּיכוּ עֲבָדֶיךָ אֶת־הַכֶּסֶף הַנִּמְצָא בַבַּיִת וַיִּתְּנֻהוּ עַל־יַד עֹשֵׂי הַמְּלָאכָה הַמֻּפְקָדִים בֵּית יְהוָה: ¹⁰ וַיַּגֵּד שָׁפָן הַסֹּפֵר לַמֶּלֶךְ לֵאמֹר סֵפֶר נָתַן לִי חִלְקִיָּה הַכֹּהֵן וַיִּקְרָאֵהוּ שָׁפָן לִפְנֵי הַמֶּלֶךְ: ¹¹ וַיְהִי כִּשְׁמֹעַ הַמֶּלֶךְ אֶת־דִּבְרֵי סֵפֶר הַתּוֹרָה וַיִּקְרַע אֶת־בְּגָדָיו: ¹² וַיְצַו הַמֶּלֶךְ אֶת־חִלְקִיָּה הַכֹּהֵן וְאֶת־אֲחִיקָם בֶּן־שָׁפָן וְאֶת־עַכְבּוֹר בֶּן־מִיכָיָה וְאֵת | שָׁפָן הַסֹּפֵר וְאֵת עֲשָׂיָה עֶבֶד־הַמֶּלֶךְ לֵאמֹר: ¹³ לְכוּ דִרְשׁוּ אֶת־יְהוָה בַּעֲדִי וּבְעַד־הָעָם וּבְעַד כָּל־יְהוּדָה עַל־דִּבְרֵי הַסֵּפֶר הַנִּמְצָא הַזֶּה כִּי־גְדוֹלָה חֲמַת יְהוָה אֲשֶׁר־הִיא נִצְּתָה בָנוּ עַל אֲשֶׁר לֹא־שָׁמְעוּ אֲבֹתֵינוּ עַל־דִּבְרֵי הַסֵּפֶר הַזֶּה לַעֲשׂוֹת כְּכָל־הַכָּתוּב עָלֵינוּ: ¹⁴ וַיֵּלֶךְ חִלְקִיָּהוּ הַכֹּהֵן וַאֲחִיקָם וְעַכְבּוֹר וְשָׁפָן וַעֲשָׂיָה אֶל־חֻלְדָּה הַנְּבִיאָה אֵשֶׁת | שַׁלֻּם בֶּן־תִּקְוָה בֶּן־חַרְחַס שֹׁמֵר הַבְּגָדִים וְהִיא יֹשֶׁבֶת בִּירוּשָׁלַ͏ִם בַּמִּשְׁנֶה וַיְדַבְּרוּ אֵלֶיהָ: ¹⁵ וַתֹּאמֶר אֲלֵיהֶם כֹּה־אָמַר יְהוָה אֱלֹהֵי יִשְׂרָאֵל אִמְרוּ לָאִישׁ אֲשֶׁר־שָׁלַח אֶתְכֶם אֵלָי:

¹⁶ כֹּה אָמַר יְהוָה הִנְנִי מֵבִיא רָעָה אֶל־הַמָּקוֹם הַזֶּה וְעַל־יֹשְׁבָיו אֵת כָּל־דִּבְרֵי הַסֵּפֶר אֲשֶׁר קָרָא מֶלֶךְ יְהוּדָה: ¹⁷ תַּחַת | אֲשֶׁר עֲזָבוּנִי וַיְקַטְּרוּ לֵאלֹהִים אֲחֵרִים לְמַעַן הַכְעִיסֵנִי בְּכֹל מַעֲשֵׂה יְדֵיהֶם וְנִצְּתָה חֲמָתִי בַּמָּקוֹם הַזֶּה וְלֹא תִכְבֶּה: ¹⁸ וְאֶל־מֶלֶךְ יְהוּדָה הַשֹּׁלֵחַ אֶתְכֶם לִדְרֹשׁ אֶת־יְהוָה כֹּה תֹאמְרוּ אֵלָיו כֹּה־אָמַר יְהוָה אֱלֹהֵי יִשְׂרָאֵל הַדְּבָרִים אֲשֶׁר שָׁמָעְתָּ: ¹⁹ יַעַן רַךְ־לְבָבְךָ וַתִּכָּנַע | מִפְּנֵי יְהוָה בְּשָׁמְעֲךָ אֲשֶׁר דִּבַּרְתִּי עַל־הַמָּקוֹם הַזֶּה וְעַל־יֹשְׁבָיו לִהְיוֹת לְשַׁמָּה וְלִקְלָלָה וַתִּקְרַע אֶת־בְּגָדֶיךָ וַתִּבְכֶּה לְפָנַי וְגַם אָנֹכִי שָׁמַעְתִּי נְאֻם־יְהוָה: ²⁰ לָכֵן הִנְנִי אֹסִפְךָ עַל־אֲבֹתֶיךָ וְנֶאֱסַפְתָּ אֶל־קִבְרֹתֶיךָ בְּשָׁלוֹם וְלֹא־תִרְאֶינָה עֵינֶיךָ בְּכֹל הָרָעָה אֲשֶׁר־אֲנִי מֵבִיא עַל־הַמָּקוֹם הַזֶּה וַיָּשִׁיבוּ אֶת־הַמֶּלֶךְ דָּבָר:

כג וַיִּשְׁלַח הַמֶּלֶךְ וַיַּאַסְפוּ אֵלָיו כָּל־זִקְנֵי יְהוּדָה וִירוּשָׁלָ͏ִם: ² וַיַּעַל הַמֶּלֶךְ בֵּית־יְהוָה וְכָל־אִישׁ

and with him all the inhabitants of Jerusalem—the priests and the prophets and all the people, both small and great. And he read in their hearing all the words of the Book of the Covenant which had been found in the house of the LORD.

³ Then the king stood by a pillar and made a covenant before the LORD, to follow the LORD and to keep His commandments and His testimonies and His statutes, with all *his* heart and all *his* soul, to perform the words of this covenant that were written in this book. And all the people took a stand for the covenant. ⁴ And the king commanded Hilkiah the high priest, the priests of the second order, and the doorkeepers, to bring out of the temple of the LORD all the articles that were made for Baal, for Asherah, and for all the host of heaven; and he burned them outside Jerusalem in the fields of Kidron, and carried their ashes to Bethel. ⁵ Then he removed the idolatrous priests whom the kings of Judah had ordained to burn incense on the high places in the cities of Judah and in the places all around Jerusalem, and those who burned incense to Baal, to the sun, to the moon, to the constellations, and to all the host of heaven. ⁶ And he brought out the wooden image from the house of the LORD, to the Brook Kidron outside Jerusalem, burned it at the Brook Kidron and ground *it* to ashes, and threw its ashes on the graves of the common people. ⁷ Then he tore down the *ritual* booths of the perverted persons that *were* in the house of the LORD, where the women wove hangings for the wooden image. ⁸ And he brought all the priests from the cities of Judah, and defiled the high places where the priests had burned incense, from Geba to Beersheba; also he broke down the high places at the gates which *were* at the entrance of the Gate of Joshua the governor of the city, which *were* to the left of the city gate. ⁹ Nevertheless the priests of the high places did not come up to the altar of the LORD in Jerusalem, but they ate unleavened bread among their brethren.

¹⁰ And he defiled Topheth, which *is* in the Valley of the Son of Hinnom, that no man might make his son or his daughter pass through the fire to Molech. ¹¹ Then he removed the horses that the kings of Judah had dedicated to the sun, at the entrance to the house of the LORD, by the chamber of Nathan-Melech, the officer who *was* in the court; and he burned the chariots of the sun with fire. ¹² The altars that *were* on the roof, the upper chamber of Ahaz, which the kings of Judah had made, and the altars which Manasseh had made in the two courts of the house of the LORD, the king broke down and pulverized there, and threw their dust into the

יְהוּדָה וְכָל־יֹשְׁבֵי יְרוּשָׁלַ͏ִם אִתּוֹ וְהַכֹּהֲנִים וְהַנְּבִיאִים
וְכָל־הָעָם לְמִקָּטֹן וְעַד־גָּדוֹל וַיִּקְרָא בְאָזְנֵיהֶם אֶת־
כָּל־דִּבְרֵי סֵפֶר הַבְּרִית הַנִּמְצָא בְּבֵית יְהוָה:
3 וַיַּעֲמֹד הַמֶּלֶךְ עַל־הָעַמּוּד וַיִּכְרֹת אֶת־הַבְּרִית |
לִפְנֵי יְהוָה לָלֶכֶת אַחַר יְהוָה וְלִשְׁמֹר מִצְוֺתָיו וְאֶת־
עֵדְוֺתָיו וְאֶת־חֻקֹּתָיו בְּכָל־לֵב וּבְכָל־נֶפֶשׁ לְהָקִים
אֶת־דִּבְרֵי הַבְּרִית הַזֹּאת הַכְּתֻבִים עַל־הַסֵּפֶר הַזֶּה
וַיַּעֲמֹד כָּל־הָעָם בַּבְּרִית: 4 וַיְצַו הַמֶּלֶךְ אֶת־חִלְקִיָּהוּ
הַכֹּהֵן הַגָּדוֹל וְאֶת־כֹּהֲנֵי הַמִּשְׁנֶה וְאֶת־שֹׁמְרֵי הַסַּף
לְהוֹצִיא מֵהֵיכַל יְהוָה אֵת כָּל־הַכֵּלִים הָעֲשׂוּיִם
לַבַּעַל וְלָאֲשֵׁרָה וּלְכֹל צְבָא הַשָּׁמָיִם וַיִּשְׂרְפֵם
מִחוּץ לִירוּשָׁלַ͏ִם בְּשַׁדְמוֹת קִדְרוֹן וְנָשָׂא אֶת־
עֲפָרָם בֵּית־אֵל: 5 וְהִשְׁבִּית אֶת־הַכְּמָרִים אֲשֶׁר
נָתְנוּ מַלְכֵי יְהוּדָה וַיְקַטֵּר בַּבָּמוֹת בְּעָרֵי יְהוּדָה
וּמְסִבֵּי יְרוּשָׁלָ͏ִם וְאֶת־הַמְקַטְּרִים לַבַּעַל לַשֶּׁמֶשׁ
וְלַיָּרֵחַ וְלַמַּזָּלוֹת וּלְכֹל צְבָא הַשָּׁמָיִם: 6 וַיֹּצֵא אֶת־
הָאֲשֵׁרָה מִבֵּית יְהוָה מִחוּץ לִירוּשָׁלַ͏ִם אֶל־נַחַל
קִדְרוֹן וַיִּשְׂרֹף אֹתָהּ בְּנַחַל קִדְרוֹן וַיָּדֶק לְעָפָר
וַיַּשְׁלֵךְ אֶת־עֲפָרָהּ עַל־קֶבֶר בְּנֵי הָעָם: 7 וַיִּתֹּץ אֶת־
בָּתֵּי הַקְּדֵשִׁים אֲשֶׁר בְּבֵית יְהוָה אֲשֶׁר הַנָּשִׁים
אֹרְגוֹת שָׁם בָּתִּים לָאֲשֵׁרָה: 8 וַיָּבֵא אֶת־כָּל־
הַכֹּהֲנִים מֵעָרֵי יְהוּדָה וַיְטַמֵּא אֶת־הַבָּמוֹת אֲשֶׁר
קִטְּרוּ־שָׁמָּה הַכֹּהֲנִים מִגֶּבַע עַד־בְּאֵר שָׁבַע וְנָתַץ
אֶת־בָּמוֹת הַשְּׁעָרִים אֲשֶׁר־פֶּתַח שַׁעַר יְהוֹשֻׁעַ
שַׂר־הָעִיר אֲשֶׁר־עַל־שְׂמֹאול אִישׁ בְּשַׁעַר הָעִיר:
9 אַךְ לֹא יַעֲלוּ כֹּהֲנֵי הַבָּמוֹת אֶל־מִזְבַּח יְהוָה
בִּירוּשָׁלָ͏ִם כִּי אִם־אָכְלוּ מַצּוֹת בְּתוֹךְ אֲחֵיהֶם:
10 וְטִמֵּא אֶת־הַתֹּפֶת אֲשֶׁר בְּגֵי בֶן־הִנֹּם לְבִלְתִּי
לְהַעֲבִיר אִישׁ אֶת־בְּנוֹ וְאֶת־בִּתּוֹ בָּאֵשׁ לַמֹּלֶךְ:
11 וַיַּשְׁבֵּת אֶת־הַסּוּסִים אֲשֶׁר נָתְנוּ מַלְכֵי יְהוּדָה
לַשֶּׁמֶשׁ מִבֹּא בֵית־יְהוָה אֶל־לִשְׁכַּת נְתַן־מֶלֶךְ
הַסָּרִיס אֲשֶׁר בַּפַּרְוָרִים וְאֶת־מַרְכְּבוֹת הַשֶּׁמֶשׁ
שָׂרַף בָּאֵשׁ: 12 וְאֶת־הַמִּזְבְּחוֹת אֲשֶׁר עַל־הַגָּג
עֲלִיַּת אָחָז אֲשֶׁר־עָשׂוּ | מַלְכֵי יְהוּדָה וְאֶת־
הַמִּזְבְּחוֹת אֲשֶׁר־עָשָׂה מְנַשֶּׁה בִּשְׁתֵּי חַצְרוֹת בֵּית־
יְהוָה נָתַץ הַמֶּלֶךְ וַיָּרָץ מִשָּׁם וְהִשְׁלִיךְ אֶת־עֲפָרָם

Brook Kidron. ¹³Then the king defiled the high places that *were* east of Jerusalem, which *were* on the south of the Mount of Corruption, which Solomon king of Israel had built for Ashtoreth the abomination of the Sidonians, for Chemosh the abomination of the Moabites, and for Milcom the abomination of the people of Ammon. ¹⁴And he broke in pieces the *sacred* pillars and cut down the wooden images, and filled their places with the bones of men.

¹⁵Moreover the altar that *was* at Bethel, *and* the high place which Jeroboam the son of Nebat, who made Israel sin, had made, both that altar and the high place he broke down; and he burned the high place *and* crushed *it* to powder, and burned the wooden image. ¹⁶As Josiah turned, he saw the tombs that *were* there on the mountain. And he sent and took the bones out of the tombs and burned *them* on the altar, and defiled it according to the word of the LORD which the man of God proclaimed, who proclaimed these words. ¹⁷Then he said, "What gravestone *is* this that I see?"

So the men of the city told him, "*It is* the tomb of the man of God who came from Judah and proclaimed these things which you have done against the altar of Bethel."

¹⁸And he said, "Let him alone; let no one move his bones." So they let his bones alone, with the bones of the prophet who came from Samaria.

¹⁹Now Josiah also took away all the shrines of the high places that *were* in the cities of Samaria, which the kings of Israel had made to provoke the LORD to anger; and he did to them according to all the deeds he had done in Bethel. ²⁰He executed all the priests of the high places who *were* there, on the altars, and burned men's bones on them; and he returned to Jerusalem.

²¹Then the king commanded all the people, saying, "Keep the Passover to the LORD your God, as *it is* written in this Book of the Covenant." ²²Such a Passover surely had never been held since the days of the judges who judged Israel, nor in all the days of the kings of Israel and the kings of Judah. ²³But in the eighteenth year of King Josiah this Passover was held before the LORD in Jerusalem. ²⁴Moreover Josiah put away those who consulted mediums and spiritists, the household gods and idols, all the abominations that were seen in the land of Judah and in Jerusalem, that he might perform the words of the law which were written in the book that Hilkiah the priest found in the house of the LORD. ²⁵Now before him there was no king like him, who turned to the LORD with all

אֶל־נַ֣חַל קִדְר֑וֹן: 13 וְאֶת־הַבָּמ֣וֹת אֲשֶׁ֣ר ׀ עַל־פְּנֵ֣י יְרוּשָׁלִַ֗ם אֲשֶׁר֮ מִימִ֣ין לְהַר־הַמַּשְׁחִית֒ אֲשֶׁ֣ר בָּנָ֗ה שְׁלֹמֹ֣ה מֶֽלֶךְ־יִשְׂרָאֵ֡ל לְעַשְׁתֹּ֣רֶת ׀ שִׁקֻּ֣ץ צִֽידֹנִ֗ים וְלִכְמוֹשׁ֙ שִׁקֻּ֣ץ מוֹאָ֔ב וּלְמִלְכֹּ֖ם תּוֹעֲבַ֣ת בְּנֵֽי־עַמּ֑וֹן טִמֵּ֖א הַמֶּֽלֶךְ: 14 וְשִׁבַּר֙ אֶת־הַמַּצֵּב֔וֹת וַיִּכְרֹ֖ת אֶת־ הָאֲשֵׁרִ֑ים וַיְמַלֵּ֥א אֶת־מְקוֹמָ֖ם עַצְמ֥וֹת אָדָֽם: 15 וְגַ֨ם אֶת־הַמִּזְבֵּ֜חַ אֲשֶׁ֣ר בְּבֵֽית־אֵ֗ל הַבָּמָה֙ אֲשֶׁ֣ר עָשָׂ֞ה יָרָבְעָ֤ם בֶּן־נְבָט֙ אֲשֶׁ֣ר הֶחֱטִ֣יא אֶת־יִשְׂרָאֵ֔ל גַּ֣ם אֶת־ הַמִּזְבֵּ֧חַ הַה֛וּא וְאֶת־הַבָּמָ֖ה נָתָ֑ץ וַיִּשְׂרֹ֧ף אֶת־הַבָּמָ֛ה הֵדַ֥ק לְעָפָ֖ר וְשָׂרַ֥ף אֲשֵׁרָֽה: 16 וַיִּ֣פֶן יֹֽאשִׁיָּ֗הוּ וַיַּ֞רְא אֶת־הַקְּבָרִ֤ים אֲשֶׁר־שָׁם֙ בָּהָ֔ר וַיִּשְׁלַ֗ח וַיִּקַּ֤ח אֶת־ הָֽעֲצָמוֹת֙ מִן־הַקְּבָרִ֔ים וַיִּשְׂרֹ֥ף עַל־הַמִּזְבֵּ֖חַ וַֽיְטַמְּאֵ֑הוּ כִּדְבַ֣ר יְהוָ֗ה אֲשֶׁ֤ר קָרָא֙ אִ֣ישׁ הָֽאֱלֹהִ֔ים אֲשֶׁ֣ר קָרָ֔א אֶת־הַדְּבָרִ֖ים הָאֵֽלֶּה: 17 וַיֹּ֕אמֶר מָ֚ה הַצִּיּ֣וּן הַלָּ֔ז אֲשֶׁ֖ר אֲנִ֣י רֹאֶ֑ה וַיֹּאמְר֨וּ אֵלָ֜יו אַנְשֵׁ֣י הָעִ֗יר הַקֶּ֤בֶר אִישׁ־הָֽאֱלֹהִים֙ אֲשֶׁר־בָּ֣א מִֽיהוּדָ֔ה וַיִּקְרָ֗א אֶת־הַדְּבָרִ֤ים הָאֵ֨לֶּה֙ אֲשֶׁ֣ר עָשִׂ֔יתָ עַ֖ל הַמִּזְבַּ֥ח בֵּֽית־ אֵֽל: 18 וַיֹּ֨אמֶר֙ הַנִּ֣יחוּ ל֔וֹ אִ֖ישׁ אַל־יָנַ֣ע עַצְמֹתָ֑יו וַֽיְמַלְּטוּ֙ עַצְמֹתָ֔יו אֵ֚ת עַצְמ֣וֹת הַנָּבִ֔יא אֲשֶׁר־בָּ֖א מִשֹּׁמְרֽוֹן: 19 וְגַם֩ אֶת־כָּל־בָּתֵּ֨י הַבָּמ֜וֹת אֲשֶׁ֣ר ׀ בְּעָרֵ֣י שֹׁמְר֗וֹן אֲשֶׁ֤ר עָשׂוּ֙ מַלְכֵ֣י יִשְׂרָאֵ֔ל לְהַכְעִ֖יס הֵסִ֣יר יֹֽאשִׁיָּ֑הוּ וַיַּ֣עַשׂ לָהֶ֔ם כְּכָל־הַֽמַּעֲשִׂ֔ים אֲשֶׁ֥ר עָשָׂ֖ה בְּבֵֽית־אֵֽל: 20 וַ֠יִּזְבַּח אֶת־כָּל־כֹּהֲנֵ֨י הַבָּמ֤וֹת אֲשֶׁר־שָׁם֙ עַל־הַֽמִּזְבְּח֔וֹת וַיִּשְׂרֹ֛ף אֶת־עַצְמ֥וֹת אָדָ֖ם עֲלֵיהֶ֑ם וַיָּ֖שָׁב יְרוּשָׁלִָֽם: 21 וַיְצַ֤ו הַמֶּ֨לֶךְ֙ אֶת־כָּל־הָעָ֣ם לֵאמֹ֔ר עֲשׂ֣וּ פֶ֔סַח לַֽיהוָ֖ה אֱלֹֽהֵיכֶ֑ם כַּכָּת֕וּב עַ֕ל סֵ֖פֶר הַבְּרִ֥ית הַזֶּֽה: 22 כִּ֣י לֹ֤א נַֽעֲשָׂה֙ כַּפֶּ֣סַח הַזֶּ֔ה מִימֵי֙ הַשֹּׁ֣פְטִ֔ים אֲשֶׁ֥ר שָׁפְט֖וּ אֶת־יִשְׂרָאֵ֑ל וְכֹ֗ל יְמֵ֛י מַלְכֵ֥י יִשְׂרָאֵ֖ל וּמַלְכֵ֥י יְהוּדָֽה: 23 כִּ֗י אִם־בִּשְׁמֹנֶ֤ה עֶשְׂרֵה֙ שָׁנָ֔ה לַמֶּ֖לֶךְ יֹֽאשִׁיָּ֑הוּ נַעֲשָׂ֞ה הַפֶּ֧סַח הַזֶּ֛ה לַֽיהוָ֖ה בִּירוּשָׁלִָֽם: 24 וְגַ֣ם אֶת־הָאֹב֣וֹת וְאֶת־הַ֠יִּדְּעֹנִ֤ים וְאֶת־ הַתְּרָפִ֨ים וְאֶת־הַגִּלֻּלִ֜ים וְאֵ֣ת כָּל־הַשִּׁקֻּצִ֗ים אֲשֶׁ֤ר נִרְאוּ֙ בְּאֶ֤רֶץ יְהוּדָה֙ וּבִיר֣וּשָׁלִַ֔ם בִּעֵ֖ר יֹֽאשִׁיָּ֑הוּ לְמַ֗עַן הָקִ֞ים אֶת־דִּבְרֵ֤י הַתּוֹרָה֙ הַכְּתֻבִ֣ים עַל־הַסֵּ֔פֶר אֲשֶׁ֥ר מָצָ֛א חִלְקִיָּ֥הוּ הַכֹּהֵ֖ן בֵּ֣ית יְהוָֽה: 25 וְכָמֹהוּ֩ לֹֽא־ הָיָ֨ה לְפָנָ֜יו מֶ֗לֶךְ אֲשֶׁר־שָׁ֤ב אֶל־יְהוָה֙ בְּכָל־לְבָבוֹ֩

his heart, with all his soul, and with all his might, according to all the Law of Moses; nor after him did *any* arise like him.

26 Nevertheless the LORD did not turn from the fierceness of His great wrath, with which His anger was aroused against Judah, because of all the provocations with which Manasseh had provoked Him. 27 And the LORD said, "I will also remove Judah from My sight, as I have removed Israel, and will cast off this city Jerusalem which I have chosen, and the house of which I said, 'My name shall be there.'"

28 Now the rest of the acts of Josiah, and all that he did, *are* they not written in the book of the chronicles of the kings of Judah? 29 In his days Pharaoh Necho king of Egypt went to the aid of the king of Assyria, to the River Euphrates; and King Josiah went against him. And *Pharaoh Necho* killed him at Megiddo when he confronted him. 30 Then his servants moved his body in a chariot from Megiddo, brought him to Jerusalem, and buried him in his own tomb. And the people of the land took Jehoahaz the son of Josiah, anointed him, and made him king in his father's place.

31 Jehoahaz *was* twenty-three years old when he became king, and he reigned three months in Jerusalem. His mother's name *was* Hamutal the daughter of Jeremiah of Libnah. 32 And he did evil in the sight of the LORD, according to all that his fathers had done. 33 Now Pharaoh Necho put him in prison at Riblah in the land of Hamath, that he might not reign in Jerusalem; and he imposed on the land a tribute of one hundred talents of silver and a talent of gold. 34 Then Pharaoh Necho made Eliakim the son of Josiah king in place of his father Josiah, and changed his name to Jehoiakim. And *Pharaoh* took Jehoahaz and went to Egypt, and he died there.

35 So Jehoiakim gave the silver and gold to Pharaoh; but he taxed the land to give money according to the command of Pharaoh; he exacted the silver and gold from the people of the land, from every one according to his assessment, to give *it* to Pharaoh Necho. 36 Jehoiakim *was* twenty-five years old when he became king, and he reigned eleven years in Jerusalem. His mother's name *was* Zebudah the daughter of Pedaiah of Rumah. 37 And he did evil in the sight of the LORD, according to all that his fathers had done.

24 In his days Nebuchadnezzar king of Babylon came up, and Jehoiakim became his vassal *for* three years. Then he turned and rebelled against him. 2 And the LORD sent against him *raiding* bands of

וּבְכָל־נַפְשׁוֹ וּבְכָל־מְאֹדוֹ כְּכֹל תּוֹרַת מֹשֶׁה וְאַחֲרָיו לֹא־קָם כָּמֹהוּ: 26 אַךְ ׀ לֹא־שָׁב יְהוָה מֵחֲרוֹן אַפּוֹ הַגָּדוֹל אֲשֶׁר־חָרָה אַפּוֹ בִּיהוּדָה עַל כָּל־ הַכְּעָסִים אֲשֶׁר הִכְעִיסוֹ מְנַשֶּׁה: 27 וַיֹּאמֶר יְהוָה גַּם אֶת־יְהוּדָה אָסִיר מֵעַל פָּנַי כַּאֲשֶׁר הֲסִרֹתִי אֶת־ יִשְׂרָאֵל וּמָאַסְתִּי אֶת־הָעִיר הַזֹּאת אֲשֶׁר־בָּחַרְתִּי אֶת־יְרוּשָׁלַ͏ִם וְאֶת־הַבַּיִת אֲשֶׁר אָמַרְתִּי יִהְיֶה שְׁמִי שָׁם: 28 וְיֶתֶר דִּבְרֵי יֹאשִׁיָּהוּ וְכָל־אֲשֶׁר עָשָׂה הֲלֹא־ הֵם כְּתוּבִים עַל־סֵפֶר דִּבְרֵי הַיָּמִים לְמַלְכֵי יְהוּדָה: 29 בְּיָמָיו עָלָה פַרְעֹה נְכֹה מֶלֶךְ־מִצְרַיִם עַל־מֶלֶךְ אַשּׁוּר עַל־נְהַר־פְּרָת וַיֵּלֶךְ הַמֶּלֶךְ יֹאשִׁיָּהוּ לִקְרָאתוֹ וַיְמִיתֵהוּ בִּמְגִדּוֹ כִּרְאֹתוֹ אֹתוֹ: 30 וַיַּרְכִּבֻהוּ עֲבָדָיו מֵת מִמְּגִדּוֹ וַיְבִאֻהוּ יְרוּשָׁלַ͏ִם וַיִּקְבְּרֻהוּ בִּקְבֻרָתוֹ וַיִּקַּח עַם־הָאָרֶץ אֶת־יְהוֹאָחָז בֶּן־יֹאשִׁיָּהוּ וַיִּמְשְׁחוּ אֹתוֹ וַיַּמְלִיכוּ אֹתוֹ תַּחַת אָבִיו: פ

31 בֶּן־עֶשְׂרִים וְשָׁלֹשׁ שָׁנָה יְהוֹאָחָז בְּמָלְכוֹ וּשְׁלֹשָׁה חֳדָשִׁים מָלַךְ בִּירוּשָׁלָ͏ִם וְשֵׁם אִמּוֹ חֲמוּטַל בַּת־ יִרְמְיָהוּ מִלִּבְנָה: 32 וַיַּעַשׂ הָרַע בְּעֵינֵי יְהוָה כְּכֹל אֲשֶׁר־עָשׂוּ אֲבֹתָיו: 33 וַיַּאַסְרֵהוּ פַרְעֹה נְכֹה בְרִבְלָה בְּאֶרֶץ חֲמָת בִּמְלֹךְ בִּירוּשָׁלָ͏ִם וַיִּתֶּן־ עֹנֶשׁ עַל־הָאָרֶץ מֵאָה כִכַּר־כֶּסֶף וְכִכַּר זָהָב: 34 וַיַּמְלֵךְ פַּרְעֹה נְכֹה אֶת־אֶלְיָקִים בֶּן־יֹאשִׁיָּהוּ תַּחַת יֹאשִׁיָּהוּ אָבִיו וַיַּסֵּב אֶת־שְׁמוֹ יְהוֹיָקִים וְאֶת־ יְהוֹאָחָז לָקָח וַיָּבֹא מִצְרַיִם וַיָּמָת שָׁם: 35 וְהַכֶּסֶף וְהַזָּהָב נָתַן יְהוֹיָקִים לְפַרְעֹה אַךְ הֶעֱרִיךְ אֶת־ הָאָרֶץ לָתֵת אֶת־הַכֶּסֶף עַל־פִּי פַרְעֹה אִישׁ כְּעֶרְכּוֹ נָגַשׂ אֶת־הַכֶּסֶף וְאֶת־הַזָּהָב אֶת־עַם הָאָרֶץ לָתֵת לְפַרְעֹה נְכֹה: ס 36 בֶּן־עֶשְׂרִים וְחָמֵשׁ שָׁנָה יְהוֹיָקִים בְּמָלְכוֹ וְאַחַת עֶשְׂרֵה שָׁנָה מָלַךְ בִּירוּשָׁלָ͏ִם וְשֵׁם אִמּוֹ זְבִידָהׁ בַת־פְּדָיָהׁ מִן־רוּמָה: 37 וַיַּעַשׂ הָרַע בְּעֵינֵי יְהוָה כְּכֹל אֲשֶׁר־עָשׂוּ אֲבֹתָיו:

כד בְּיָמָיו עָלָה נְבֻכַדְנֶאצַּר מֶלֶךְ בָּבֶל וַיְהִי־ לוֹ יְהוֹיָקִים עֶבֶד שָׁלֹשׁ שָׁנִים וַיָּשָׁב וַיִּמְרָד־בּוֹ: 2 וַיְשַׁלַּח יְהוָה ׀ בּוֹ אֶת־גְּדוּדֵי כַשְׂדִּים וְאֶת־

Chaldeans, bands of Syrians, bands of Moabites, and bands of the people of Ammon; He sent them against Judah to destroy it, according to the word of the LORD which He had spoken by His servants the prophets. ³ Surely at the commandment of the LORD *this* came upon Judah, to remove *them* from His sight because of the sins of Manasseh, according to all that he had done, ⁴ and also because of the innocent blood that he had shed; for he had filled Jerusalem with innocent blood, which the LORD would not pardon.

⁵ Now the rest of the acts of Jehoiakim, and all that he did, *are* they not written in the book of the chronicles of the kings of Judah? ⁶ So Jehoiakim rested with his fathers. Then Jehoiachin his son reigned in his place.

⁷ And the king of Egypt did not come out of his land anymore, for the king of Babylon had taken all that belonged to the king of Egypt from the Brook of Egypt to the River Euphrates.

⁸ Jehoiachin *was* eighteen years old when he became king, and he reigned in Jerusalem three months. His mother's name *was* Nehushta the daughter of Elnathan of Jerusalem. ⁹ And he did evil in the sight of the LORD, according to all that his father had done.

¹⁰ At that time the servants of Nebuchadnezzar king of Babylon came up against Jerusalem, and the city was besieged. ¹¹ And Nebuchadnezzar king of Babylon came against the city, as his servants were besieging it. ¹² Then Jehoiachin king of Judah, his mother, his servants, his princes, and his officers went out to the king of Babylon; and the king of Babylon, in the eighth year of his reign, took him prisoner.

¹³ And he carried out from there all the treasures of the house of the LORD and the treasures of the king's house, and he cut in pieces all the articles of gold which Solomon king of Israel had made in the temple of the LORD, as the LORD had said. ¹⁴ Also he carried into captivity all Jerusalem: all the captains and all the mighty men of valor, ten thousand captives, and all the craftsmen and smiths. None remained except the poorest people of the land. ¹⁵ And he carried Jehoiachin captive to Babylon. The king's mother, the king's wives, his officers, and the mighty of the land he carried into captivity from Jerusalem to Babylon. ¹⁶ All the valiant men, seven thousand, and craftsmen and smiths, one thousand, all *who were* strong *and* fit for war, these the king of Babylon brought captive to Babylon.

גְּדוּדֵי אֲרָם וְאֵת | גְּדוּדֵי מוֹאָב וְאֵת גְּדוּדֵי
בְנֵי־עַמּוֹן וַיְשַׁלְּחֵם בִּיהוּדָה לְהַאֲבִידוֹ כִּדְבַר יְהֹוָה
אֲשֶׁר דִּבֶּר בְּיַד עֲבָדָיו הַנְּבִיאִים: 3 אַךְ | עַל־פִּי
יְהֹוָה הָיְתָה בִּיהוּדָה לְהָסִיר מֵעַל פָּנָיו בְּחַטֹּאת
מְנַשֶּׁה כְּכֹל אֲשֶׁר עָשָׂה: 4 וְגַם דַּם־הַנָּקִי אֲשֶׁר
שָׁפָךְ וַיְמַלֵּא אֶת־יְרוּשָׁלִַם דָּם נָקִי וְלֹא־אָבָה יְהֹוָה
לִסְלֹחַ: 5 וְיֶתֶר דִּבְרֵי יְהוֹיָקִים וְכָל־אֲשֶׁר עָשָׂה
הֲלֹא־הֵם כְּתוּבִים עַל־סֵפֶר דִּבְרֵי הַיָּמִים לְמַלְכֵי
יְהוּדָה: 6 וַיִּשְׁכַּב יְהוֹיָקִים עִם־אֲבֹתָיו וַיִּמְלֹךְ יְהוֹיָכִין
בְּנוֹ תַּחְתָּיו: 7 וְלֹא־הֹסִיף עוֹד מֶלֶךְ מִצְרַיִם לָצֵאת
מֵאַרְצוֹ כִּי־לָקַח מֶלֶךְ בָּבֶל מִנַּחַל מִצְרַיִם עַד־נְהַר־
פְּרָת כֹּל אֲשֶׁר הָיְתָה לְמֶלֶךְ מִצְרָיִם: פ

8 בֶּן־שְׁמֹנֶה עֶשְׂרֵה שָׁנָה יְהוֹיָכִין בְּמָלְכוֹ וּשְׁלֹשָׁה
חֳדָשִׁים מָלַךְ בִּירוּשָׁלִָם וְשֵׁם אִמּוֹ נְחֻשְׁתָּא בַת־
אֶלְנָתָן מִירוּשָׁלִָם: 9 וַיַּעַשׂ הָרַע בְּעֵינֵי יְהֹוָה כְּכֹל
אֲשֶׁר־עָשָׂה אָבִיו: 10 בָּעֵת הַהִיא עָלָה עַבְדֵי
נְבֻכַדְנֶאצַּר מֶלֶךְ־בָּבֶל יְרוּשָׁלִָם וַתָּבֹא הָעִיר בַּמָּצוֹר:
11 וַיָּבֹא נְבוּכַדְנֶאצַּר מֶלֶךְ־בָּבֶל עַל־הָעִיר וַעֲבָדָיו
צָרִים עָלֶיהָ: 12 וַיֵּצֵא יְהוֹיָכִין מֶלֶךְ־יְהוּדָה עַל־מֶלֶךְ
בָּבֶל הוּא וְאִמּוֹ וַעֲבָדָיו וְשָׂרָיו וְסָרִיסָיו וַיִּקַּח אֹתוֹ
מֶלֶךְ בָּבֶל בִּשְׁנַת שְׁמֹנֶה לְמָלְכוֹ: 13 וַיּוֹצֵא מִשָּׁם
אֶת־כָּל־אוֹצְרוֹת בֵּית יְהֹוָה וְאוֹצְרוֹת בֵּית הַמֶּלֶךְ
וַיְקַצֵּץ אֶת־כָּל־כְּלֵי הַזָּהָב אֲשֶׁר עָשָׂה שְׁלֹמֹה מֶלֶךְ־
יִשְׂרָאֵל בְּהֵיכַל יְהֹוָה כַּאֲשֶׁר דִּבֶּר יְהֹוָה: 14 וְהִגְלָה
אֶת־כָּל־יְרוּשָׁלִַם וְאֶת־כָּל־הַשָּׂרִים וְאֵת | כָּל־גִּבּוֹרֵי
הַחַיִל עֲשָׂרָה אֲלָפִים גּוֹלֶה וְכָל־הֶחָרָשׁ וְהַמַּסְגֵּר
לֹא נִשְׁאַר זוּלַת דַּלַּת עַם־הָאָרֶץ: 15 וַיֶּגֶל אֶת־
יְהוֹיָכִין בָּבֶלָה וְאֶת־אֵם הַמֶּלֶךְ וְאֶת־נְשֵׁי הַמֶּלֶךְ
וְאֶת־סָרִיסָיו וְאֵת אוּלֵי הָאָרֶץ הוֹלִיךְ גּוֹלָה
מִירוּשָׁלִַם בָּבֶלָה: 16 וְאֵת כָּל־אַנְשֵׁי הַחַיִל שִׁבְעַת
אֲלָפִים וְהֶחָרָשׁ וְהַמַּסְגֵּר אֶלֶף הַכֹּל גִּבּוֹרִים עֹשֵׂי
מִלְחָמָה וַיְבִיאֵם מֶלֶךְ־בָּבֶל גּוֹלָה בָּבֶלָה: 17 וַיַּמְלֵךְ
מֶלֶךְ־בָּבֶל אֶת־מַתַּנְיָה דֹדוֹ תַּחְתָּיו וַיַּסֵּב אֶת־שְׁמוֹ
צִדְקִיָּהוּ:
פ

כד 10 עָלוּ   14 עֲשֶׂרֶת   15 אֵילֵי

17 Then the king of Babylon made Mattaniah, *Jehoiachin's* uncle, king in his place, and changed his name to Zedekiah.

18 Zedekiah *was* twenty-one years old when he became king, and he reigned eleven years in Jerusalem. His mother's name *was* Hamutal the daughter of Jeremiah of Libnah. 19 He also did evil in the sight of the LORD, according to all that Jehoiakim had done. 20 For because of the anger of the LORD *this* happened in Jerusalem and Judah, that He finally cast them out from His presence. Then Zedekiah rebelled against the king of Babylon.

25 Now it came to pass in the ninth year of his reign, in the tenth month, on the tenth *day* of the month, *that* Nebuchadnezzar king of Babylon and all his army came against Jerusalem and encamped against it; and they built a siege wall against it all around. 2 So the city was besieged until the eleventh year of King Zedekiah. 3 By the ninth *day* of the *fourth* month the famine had become so severe in the city that there was no food for the people of the land.

4 Then the city wall was broken through, and all the men of war *fled* at night by way of the gate between two walls, which was by the king's garden, even though the Chaldeans *were* still encamped all around against the city. And *the king* went by way of the plain. 5 But the army of the Chaldeans pursued the king, and they overtook him in the plains of Jericho. All his army was scattered from him. 6 So they took the king and brought him up to the king of Babylon at Riblah, and they pronounced judgment on him. 7 Then they killed the sons of Zedekiah before his eyes, put out the eyes of Zedekiah, bound him with bronze fetters, and took him to Babylon.

8 And in the fifth month, on the seventh *day* of the month (which *was* the nineteenth year of King Nebuchadnezzar king of Babylon), Nebuzaradan the captain of the guard, a servant of the king of Babylon, came to Jerusalem. 9 He burned the house of the LORD and the king's house; all the houses of Jerusalem, that is, all the houses of the great, he burned with fire. 10 And all the army of the Chaldeans who *were with* the captain of the guard broke down the walls of Jerusalem all around.

11 Then Nebuzaradan the captain of the guard carried away captive the rest of the people *who* remained in the city and the defectors who had deserted to the king of Babylon, with the rest of the multitude. 12 But the captain of the guard left *some* of the poor of the land as vinedressers and farmers.

18 בֶּן־עֶשְׂרִים וְאַחַת שָׁנָה צִדְקִיָּהוּ בְמָלְכֹו וְאַחַת עֶשְׂרֵה שָׁנָה מָלַךְ בִּירוּשָׁלִָם וְשֵׁם אִמֹּו חֲמִיטַל בַּת־יִרְמְיָהוּ מִלִּבְנָה: 19 וַיַּעַשׂ הָרַע בְּעֵינֵי יְהֹוָה כְּכֹל אֲשֶׁר־עָשָׂה יְהֹויָקִים: 20 כִּי | עַל־אַף יְהֹוָה הָיְתָה בִּירוּשָׁלִַם וּבִיהוּדָה עַד־הִשְׁלִכֹו אֹתָם מֵעַל פָּנָיו וַיִּמְרֹד צִדְקִיָּהוּ בְּמֶלֶךְ בָּבֶל: ס

כה וַיְהִי בִשְׁנַת הַתְּשִׁיעִית לְמָלְכֹו בַּחֹדֶשׁ הָעֲשִׂירִי בֶּעָשֹׂור לַחֹדֶשׁ בָּא נְבֻכַדְנֶאצַּר מֶלֶךְ־ בָּבֶל הוּא וְכָל־חֵילֹו עַל־יְרוּשָׁלִַם וַיִּחַן עָלֶיהָ וַיִּבְנוּ עָלֶיהָ דָּיֵק סָבִיב: 2 וַתָּבֹא הָעִיר בַּמָּצֹור עַד עַשְׁתֵּי עֶשְׂרֵה שָׁנָה לַמֶּלֶךְ צִדְקִיָּהוּ: 3 בְּתִשְׁעָה לַחֹדֶשׁ וַיֶּחֱזַק הָרָעָב בָּעִיר וְלֹא־הָיָה לֶחֶם לְעַם הָאָרֶץ: 4 וַתִּבָּקַע הָעִיר וְכָל־אַנְשֵׁי הַמִּלְחָמָה | הַלַּיְלָה דֶּרֶךְ שַׁעַר | בֵּין הַחֹמֹתַיִם אֲשֶׁר עַל־ גַּן הַמֶּלֶךְ וְכַשְׂדִּים עַל־הָעִיר סָבִיב וַיֵּלֶךְ דֶּרֶךְ הָעֲרָבָה: 5 וַיִּרְדְּפוּ חֵיל־כַּשְׂדִּים אַחַר הַמֶּלֶךְ וַיַּשִּׂגוּ אֹתֹו בְּעַרְבֹות יְרֵחֹו וְכָל־חֵילֹו נָפֹצוּ מֵעָלָיו: 6 וַיִּתְפְּשׂוּ אֶת־הַמֶּלֶךְ וַיַּעֲלוּ אֹתֹו אֶל־מֶלֶךְ בָּבֶל רִבְלָתָה וַיְדַבְּרוּ אִתֹּו מִשְׁפָּט: 7 וְאֶת־בְּנֵי צִדְקִיָּהוּ שָׁחֲטוּ לְעֵינָיו וְאֶת־עֵינֵי צִדְקִיָּהוּ עִוֵּר וַיַּאַסְרֵהוּ בַנְחֻשְׁתַּיִם וַיְבִאֵהוּ בָּבֶל: ס 8 וּבַחֹדֶשׁ הַחֲמִישִׁי בְּשִׁבְעָה לַחֹדֶשׁ הִיא שְׁנַת תְּשַׁע־עֶשְׂרֵה שָׁנָה לַמֶּלֶךְ נְבֻכַדְנֶאצַּר מֶלֶךְ־בָּבֶל בָּא נְבוּזַרְאֲדָן רַב־טַבָּחִים עֶבֶד מֶלֶךְ־בָּבֶל יְרוּשָׁלִָם: 9 וַיִּשְׂרֹף אֶת־ בֵּית־יְהֹוָה וְאֶת־בֵּית הַמֶּלֶךְ וְאֵת כָּל־בָּתֵּי יְרוּשָׁלִַם וְאֶת־כָּל־בֵּית גָּדֹול שָׂרַף בָּאֵשׁ: 10 וְאֶת־חֹומֹת יְרוּשָׁלִַם סָבִיב נָתְצוּ כָּל־חֵיל כַּשְׂדִּים אֲשֶׁר רַב־ טַבָּחִים: 11 וְאֵת יֶתֶר הָעָם הַנִּשְׁאָרִים בָּעִיר וְאֶת־ הַנֹּפְלִים אֲשֶׁר נָפְלוּ עַל־הַמֶּלֶךְ בָּבֶל וְאֵת יֶתֶר הֶהָמֹון הֶגְלָה נְבוּזַרְאֲדָן רַב־טַבָּחִים: 12 וּמִדַּלַּת הָאָרֶץ הִשְׁאִיר רַב־טַבָּחִים לְכֹרְמִים וּלְיֹגְבִים:

כד 18 חֲמוּטַל

13 The bronze pillars that *were* in the house of the
LORD, and the carts and the bronze Sea that *were* in
the house of the LORD, the Chaldeans broke in
pieces, and carried their bronze to Babylon. 14 They
also took away the pots, the shovels, the trimmers,
the spoons, and all the bronze utensils with which
the priests ministered. 15 The firepans and the
basins, the things of solid gold and solid silver,
the captain of the guard took away. 16 The two
pillars, one Sea, and the carts, which Solomon had
made for the house of the LORD, the bronze of all
these articles was beyond measure. 17 The height of
one pillar *was* eighteen cubits, and the capital on it
was of bronze. The height of the capital was three
cubits, and the network and pomegranates all
around the capital were all of bronze. The second
pillar was the same, with a network.

18 And the captain of the guard took Seraiah the
chief priest, Zephaniah the second priest, and the
three doorkeepers. 19 He also took out of the city an
officer who had charge of the men of war, five men
of the king's close associates who were found in the
city, the chief recruiting officer of the army, who
mustered the people of the land, and sixty men of
the people of the land *who were* found in the city.
20 So Nebuzaradan, captain of the guard, took these
and brought them to the king of Babylon at Riblah.
21 Then the king of Babylon struck them and put
them to death at Riblah in the land of Hamath.
Thus Judah was carried away captive from its own
land.

22 Then he made Gedaliah the son of Ahikam, the
son of Shaphan, governor over the people who
remained in the land of Judah, whom Nebuchadnezzar king of Babylon had left. 23 Now when all
the captains of the armies, they and *their* men,
heard that the king of Babylon had made Gedaliah
governor, they came to Gedaliah at Mizpah—
Ishmael the son of Nethaniah, Johanan the son of
Careah, Seraiah the son of Tanhumeth the Netophathite, and Jaazaniah the son of a Maachathite,
they and their men. 24 And Gedaliah took an oath
before them and their men, and said to them, "Do
not be afraid of the servants of the Chaldeans.
Dwell in the land and serve the king of Babylon,
and it shall be well with you."

25 But it happened in the seventh month that
Ishmael the son of Nethaniah, the son of Elishama,
of the royal family, came with ten men and struck
and killed Gedaliah, the Jews, as well as the
Chaldeans who were with him at Mizpah. 26 And
all the people, small and great, and the captains of
the armies, arose and went to Egypt; for they were
afraid of the Chaldeans.

13 וְאֶת־עַמּוּדֵי הַנְּחֹשֶׁת אֲשֶׁר בֵּית־יְהוָה וְאֶת־
הַמְּכֹנוֹת וְאֶת־יָם הַנְּחֹשֶׁת אֲשֶׁר בְּבֵית־יְהוָה שִׁבְּרוּ
כַשְׂדִּים וַיִּשְׂאוּ אֶת־נְחֻשְׁתָּם בָּבֶלָה: 14 וְאֶת־הַסִּירֹת
וְאֶת־הַיָּעִים וְאֶת־הַמְזַמְּרוֹת וְאֶת־הַכַּפּוֹת וְאֵת כָּל־
כְּלֵי הַנְּחֹשֶׁת אֲשֶׁר יְשָׁרְתוּ־בָם לָקָחוּ: 15 וְאֶת־
הַמַּחְתּוֹת וְאֶת־הַמִּזְרָקוֹת אֲשֶׁר זָהָב זָהָב וַאֲשֶׁר־
כֶּסֶף כָּסֶף לָקַח רַב־טַבָּחִים: 16 הָעַמּוּדִים | שְׁנַיִם
הַיָּם הָאֶחָד וְהַמְּכֹנוֹת אֲשֶׁר־עָשָׂה שְׁלֹמֹה לְבֵית
יְהוָה לֹא־הָיָה מִשְׁקָל לִנְחֹשֶׁת כָּל־הַכֵּלִים הָאֵלֶּה:
17 שְׁמֹנֶה עֶשְׂרֵה אַמָּה קוֹמַת | הָעַמּוּד הָאֶחָד
וְכֹתֶרֶת עָלָיו | נְחֹשֶׁת וְקוֹמַת הַכֹּתֶרֶת שָׁלֹשׁ
אַמָּה[ק] וּשְׂבָכָה וְרִמֹּנִים עַל־הַכֹּתֶרֶת סָבִיב הַכֹּל
נְחֹשֶׁת וְכָאֵלֶּה לָעַמּוּד הַשֵּׁנִי עַל־הַשְּׂבָכָה: 18 וַיִּקַּח
רַב־טַבָּחִים אֶת־שְׂרָיָה כֹּהֵן הָרֹאשׁ וְאֶת־צְפַנְיָהוּ
כֹּהֵן מִשְׁנֶה וְאֶת־שְׁלֹשֶׁת שֹׁמְרֵי הַסַּף: 19 וּמִן־הָעִיר
לָקַח סָרִיס אֶחָד אֲשֶׁר־הוּא פָקִיד | עַל־אַנְשֵׁי
הַמִּלְחָמָה וַחֲמִשָּׁה אֲנָשִׁים מֵרֹאֵי פְנֵי־הַמֶּלֶךְ אֲשֶׁר
נִמְצְאוּ בָעִיר וְאֵת הַסֹּפֵר שַׂר הַצָּבָא הַמַּצְבִּא אֶת־
עַם הָאָרֶץ וְשִׁשִּׁים אִישׁ מֵעַם הָאָרֶץ הַנִּמְצְאִים
בָּעִיר: 20 וַיִּקַּח אֹתָם נְבוּזַרְאֲדָן רַב־טַבָּחִים וַיֹּלֶךְ
אֹתָם עַל־מֶלֶךְ בָּבֶל רִבְלָתָה: 21 וַיַּךְ אֹתָם מֶלֶךְ
בָּבֶל וַיְמִיתֵם בְּרִבְלָה בְּאֶרֶץ חֲמָת וַיִּגֶל יְהוּדָה מֵעַל
אַדְמָתוֹ: 22 וְהָעָם הַנִּשְׁאָר בְּאֶרֶץ יְהוּדָה אֲשֶׁר
הִשְׁאִיר נְבוּכַדְנֶאצַּר מֶלֶךְ בָּבֶל וַיַּפְקֵד עֲלֵיהֶם אֶת־
גְּדַלְיָהוּ בֶּן־אֲחִיקָם בֶּן־שָׁפָן: פ

23 וַיִּשְׁמְעוּ כָל־שָׂרֵי הַחֲיָלִים הֵמָּה וְהָאֲנָשִׁים
כִּי־הִפְקִיד מֶלֶךְ־בָּבֶל אֶת־גְּדַלְיָהוּ וַיָּבֹאוּ אֶל־
גְּדַלְיָהוּ הַמִּצְפָּה וְיִשְׁמָעֵאל בֶּן־נְתַנְיָה וְיוֹחָנָן
בֶּן־קָרֵחַ וּשְׂרָיָה בֶן־תַּנְחֻמֶת הַנְּטֹפָתִי וְיַאֲזַנְיָהוּ
בֶּן־הַמַּעֲכָתִי הֵמָּה וְאַנְשֵׁיהֶם: 24 וַיִּשָּׁבַע לָהֶם
גְּדַלְיָהוּ וּלְאַנְשֵׁיהֶם וַיֹּאמֶר לָהֶם אַל־תִּירְאוּ מֵעַבְדֵי
הַכַּשְׂדִּים שְׁבוּ בָאָרֶץ וְעִבְדוּ אֶת־מֶלֶךְ בָּבֶל וְיִטַב
לָכֶם: ס 25 וַיְהִי | בַּחֹדֶשׁ הַשְּׁבִיעִי בָּא
יִשְׁמָעֵאל בֶּן־נְתַנְיָה בֶּן־אֱלִישָׁמָע מִזֶּרַע הַמְּלוּכָה
וַעֲשָׂרָה אֲנָשִׁים אִתּוֹ וַיַּכּוּ אֶת־גְּדַלְיָהוּ וַיָּמֹת וְאֶת־
הַיְּהוּדִים וְאֶת־הַכַּשְׂדִּים אֲשֶׁר־הָיוּ אִתּוֹ בַּמִּצְפָּה:
26 וַיָּקֻמוּ כָל־הָעָם מִקָּטֹן וְעַד־גָּדוֹל וְשָׂרֵי הַחֲיָלִים
וַיָּבֹאוּ מִצְרָיִם כִּי יָרְאוּ מִפְּנֵי כַשְׂדִּים: פ

כה 17 אמות

27 Now it came to pass in the thirty-seventh year of the captivity of Jehoiachin king of Judah, in the twelfth month, on the twenty-seventh *day* of the month, *that* Evil-Merodach king of Babylon, in the year that he began to reign, released Jehoiachin king of Judah from prison. 28 He spoke kindly to him, and gave him a more prominent seat than those of the kings who *were* with him in Babylon. 29 So Jehoiachin changed from his prison garments, and he ate bread regularly before the king all the days of his life. 30 And as for his provisions, *there was* a regular ration given him by the king, a portion for each day, all the days of his life.

27 וַיְהִי בִשְׁלֹשִׁים וָשֶׁבַע שָׁנָה לְגָלוּת יְהוֹיָכִין מֶלֶךְ־
יְהוּדָה בִּשְׁנֵים עָשָׂר חֹדֶשׁ בְּעֶשְׂרִים וְשִׁבְעָה לַחֹדֶשׁ
נָשָׂא אֱוִיל מְרֹדַךְ מֶלֶךְ בָּבֶל בִּשְׁנַת מָלְכוֹ אֶת־
רֹאשׁ יְהוֹיָכִין מֶלֶךְ־יְהוּדָה מִבֵּית כֶּלֶא: 28 וַיְדַבֵּר
אִתּוֹ טֹבוֹת וַיִּתֵּן אֶת־כִּסְאוֹ מֵעַל כִּסֵּא הַמְּלָכִים
אֲשֶׁר אִתּוֹ בְּבָבֶל: 29 וְשִׁנָּא אֵת בִּגְדֵי כִלְאוֹ וְאָכַל
לֶחֶם תָּמִיד לְפָנָיו כָּל־יְמֵי חַיָּו: 30 וַאֲרֻחָתוֹ אֲרֻחַת
תָּמִיד נִתְּנָה־לּוֹ מֵאֵת הַמֶּלֶךְ דְּבַר־יוֹם בְּיוֹמוֹ כֹּל
יְמֵי חַיָּו:

The Book of

ISAIAH

1 The vision of Isaiah the son of Amoz, which he saw concerning Judah and Jerusalem in the days of Uzziah, Jotham, Ahaz, *and* Hezekiah, kings of Judah.

2 Hear, O heavens, and give ear, O earth!
For the LORD has spoken:
"I have nourished and brought up children,
And they have rebelled against Me;

3 The ox knows its owner
And the donkey its master's crib;
But Israel does not know,
My people do not consider."

4 Alas, sinful nation,
A people laden with iniquity,
A brood of evildoers,
Children who are corrupters!
They have forsaken the LORD,
They have provoked to anger
The Holy One of Israel,
They have turned away backward.

5 Why should you be stricken again?
You will revolt more and more.
The whole head is sick,
And the whole heart faints.

6 From the sole of the foot even to the head,
There is no soundness in it,
But wounds and bruises and putrefying
sores;
They have not been closed or bound up,
Or soothed with ointment.

7 Your country *is* desolate,
Your cities *are* burned with fire;
Strangers devour your land in your presence;
And *it is* desolate, as overthrown by stran-
gers.

8 So the daughter of Zion is left as a booth in a
vineyard,
As a hut in a garden of cucumbers,
As a besieged city.

9 Unless the LORD of hosts
Had left to us a very small remnant,
We would have become like Sodom,
We would have been made like Gomorrah.

ישעיהו

א חֲזוֹן יְשַׁעְיָהוּ בֶן־אָמוֹץ אֲשֶׁר חָזָה עַל־יְהוּדָה
וִירוּשָׁלָ͏ִם בִּימֵי עֻזִּיָּהוּ יוֹתָם אָחָז יְחִזְקִיָּהוּ מַלְכֵי
יְהוּדָה:

2 שִׁמְעוּ שָׁמַיִם וְהַאֲזִינִי אֶרֶץ
כִּי יְהֹוָה דִּבֵּר
בָּנִים גִּדַּלְתִּי וְרוֹמַמְתִּי
וְהֵם פָּשְׁעוּ בִי:

3 יָדַע שׁוֹר קֹנֵהוּ וַחֲמוֹר אֵבוּס בְּעָלָיו
יִשְׂרָאֵל לֹא יָדַע עַמִּי לֹא הִתְבּוֹנָן:

4 הוֹי ׀ גּוֹי חֹטֵא עַם כֶּבֶד עָוֹן
זֶרַע מְרֵעִים בָּנִים מַשְׁחִיתִים
עָזְבוּ אֶת־יְהֹוָה נִאֲצוּ אֶת־קְדוֹשׁ יִשְׂרָאֵל
נָזֹרוּ אָחוֹר:

5 עַל מֶה תֻכּוּ עוֹד תּוֹסִיפוּ סָרָה
כָּל־רֹאשׁ לָחֳלִי וְכָל־לֵבָב דַּוָּי:

6 מִכַּף־רֶגֶל וְעַד־רֹאשׁ
אֵין־בּוֹ מְתֹם
פֶּצַע וְחַבּוּרָה וּמַכָּה טְרִיָּה
לֹא־זֹרוּ וְלֹא חֻבָּשׁוּ
וְלֹא רֻכְּכָה בַּשָּׁמֶן:

7 אַרְצְכֶם שְׁמָמָה עָרֵיכֶם שְׂרֻפוֹת אֵשׁ
אַדְמַתְכֶם לְנֶגְדְּכֶם זָרִים
אֹכְלִים אֹתָהּ
וּשְׁמָמָה כְּמַהְפֵּכַת זָרִים:

8 וְנוֹתְרָה בַת־צִיּוֹן כְּסֻכָּה בְכָרֶם
כִּמְלוּנָה בְמִקְשָׁה כְּעִיר נְצוּרָה:

9 לוּלֵי יְהֹוָה צְבָאוֹת
הוֹתִיר לָנוּ שָׂרִיד כִּמְעָט
כִּסְדֹם הָיִינוּ לַעֲמֹרָה דָּמִינוּ: ס

10 Hear the word of the Lord,
You rulers of Sodom;
Give ear to the law of our God,
You people of Gomorrah:

11 "To what purpose *is* the multitude of your
sacrifices to Me?"
Says the Lord.
"I have had enough of burnt offerings of rams
And the fat of fed cattle;
I do not delight in the blood of bulls,
Or of lambs or goats.

12 "When you come to appear before Me,
Who has required this from your hand,
To trample My courts?

13 Bring no more futile sacrifices;
Incense is an abomination to Me.
The New Moons, the Sabbaths, and the
calling of assemblies—
I cannot endure iniquity and the sacred
meeting.

14 Your New Moons and your appointed feasts
My soul hates;
They are a trouble to Me,
I am weary of bearing *them*.

15 When you spread out your hands,
I will hide My eyes from you;
Even though you make many prayers,
I will not hear.
Your hands are full of blood.

16 "Wash yourselves, make yourselves clean;
Put away the evil of your doings from before
My eyes.
Cease to do evil,

17 Learn to do good;
Seek justice,
Rebuke the oppressor;
Defend the fatherless,
Plead for the widow.

18 "Come now, and let us reason together,"
Says the Lord,
"Though your sins are like scarlet,
They shall be as white as snow;
Though they are red like crimson,
They shall be as wool.

19 If you are willing and obedient,
You shall eat the good of the land;

20 But if you refuse and rebel,
You shall be devoured by the sword";
For the mouth of the Lord has spoken.

21 How the faithful city has become a harlot!
It was full of justice;
Righteousness lodged in it,

10 שִׁמְע֤וּ דְבַר־יְהוָה֙ קְצִינֵ֣י סְדֹ֔ם
הַאֲזִ֛ינוּ תּוֹרַ֥ת אֱלֹהֵ֖ינוּ
עַ֥ם עֲמֹרָֽה׃

11 לָמָּה־לִּ֤י רֹב־זִבְחֵיכֶם֙
יֹאמַ֣ר יְהוָ֔ה
שָׂבַ֛עְתִּי עֹל֥וֹת אֵילִ֖ים
וְחֵ֣לֶב מְרִיאִ֑ים
וְדַ֨ם פָּרִ֧ים וּכְבָשִׂ֛ים
וְעַתּוּדִ֖ים לֹ֥א חָפָֽצְתִּי׃

12 כִּ֣י תָבֹ֔אוּ לֵרָא֖וֹת פָּנָ֑י
מִי־בִקֵּ֥שׁ זֹ֛את מִיֶּדְכֶ֖ם רְמֹ֥ס חֲצֵרָֽי׃

13 לֹ֣א תוֹסִ֗יפוּ הָבִיא֙ מִנְחַת־שָׁ֔וְא
קְטֹ֧רֶת תּוֹעֵבָ֛ה הִ֖יא לִ֑י
חֹ֤דֶשׁ וְשַׁבָּת֙ קְרֹ֣א מִקְרָ֔א
לֹא־אוּכַ֥ל אָ֖וֶן וַעֲצָרָֽה׃

14 חָדְשֵׁיכֶ֤ם וּמוֹעֲדֵיכֶם֙ שָׂנְאָ֣ה נַפְשִׁ֔י
הָי֥וּ עָלַ֖י לָטֹ֑רַח נִלְאֵ֖יתִי נְשֹֽׂא׃

15 וּבְפָרִשְׂכֶ֣ם כַּפֵּיכֶ֗ם
אַעְלִ֤ים עֵינַי֙ מִכֶּ֔ם
גַּ֛ם כִּֽי־תַרְבּ֥וּ תְפִלָּ֖ה אֵינֶ֣נִּי שֹׁמֵ֑עַ
יְדֵיכֶ֖ם דָּמִ֥ים מָלֵֽאוּ׃

16 רַחֲצוּ֙ הִזַּכּ֔וּ
הָסִ֛ירוּ רֹ֥עַ מַעַלְלֵיכֶ֖ם
מִנֶּ֣גֶד עֵינָ֑י חִדְל֖וּ הָרֵֽעַ׃

17 לִמְד֥וּ הֵיטֵ֖ב
דִּרְשׁ֣וּ מִשְׁפָּ֔ט אַשְּׁר֖וּ חָמ֑וֹץ
שִׁפְט֣וּ יָת֔וֹם רִ֖יבוּ אַלְמָנָֽה׃ ס

18 לְכוּ־נָ֛א וְנִוָּֽכְחָ֖ה
יֹאמַ֣ר יְהוָ֑ה
אִם־יִהְי֨וּ חֲטָאֵיכֶ֤ם כַּשָּׁנִים֙
כַּשֶּׁ֣לֶג יַלְבִּ֔ינוּ
אִם־יַאְדִּ֥ימוּ כַתּוֹלָ֖ע
כַּצֶּ֥מֶר יִהְיֽוּ׃

19 אִם־תֹּאב֖וּ וּשְׁמַעְתֶּ֑ם
ט֥וּב הָאָ֖רֶץ תֹּאכֵֽלוּ׃

20 וְאִם־תְּמָאֲנ֖וּ וּמְרִיתֶ֑ם
חֶ֖רֶב תְּאֻכְּל֑וּ
כִּ֛י פִּ֥י יְהוָ֖ה דִּבֵּֽר׃ ס

21 אֵיכָה֙ הָיְתָ֣ה לְזוֹנָ֔ה
קִרְיָ֖ה נֶאֱמָנָ֑ה מְלֵאֲתִ֣י מִשְׁפָּ֔ט
צֶ֛דֶק יָלִ֥ין בָּ֖הּ
וְעַתָּ֥ה מְרַצְּחִֽים׃

But now murderers.

22 Your silver has become dross,
Your wine mixed with water.

23 Your princes *are* rebellious,
And companions of thieves;
Everyone loves bribes,
And follows after rewards.
They do not defend the fatherless,
Nor does the cause of the widow come before
them.

24 Therefore the Lord says,
The LORD of hosts, the Mighty One of Israel,
"Ah, I will rid Myself of My adversaries,
And take vengeance on My enemies.

25 I will turn My hand against you,
And thoroughly purge away your dross,
And take away all your alloy.

26 I will restore your judges as at the first,
And your counselors as at the beginning.
Afterward you shall be called the city of
righteousness, the faithful city."

27 Zion shall be redeemed with justice,
And her penitents with righteousness.

28 The destruction of transgressors and of
sinners *shall be* together,
And those who forsake the LORD shall be
consumed.

29 For they shall be ashamed of the terebinth
trees
Which you have desired;
And you shall be embarrassed because of the
gardens
Which you have chosen.

30 For you shall be as a terebinth whose leaf
fades,
And as a garden that has no water.

31 The strong shall be as tinder,
And the work of it as a spark;
Both will burn together,
And no one shall quench *them.*

2 The word that Isaiah the son of Amoz saw
concerning Judah and Jerusalem.

2 Now it shall come to pass in the latter days
That the mountain of the LORD's house
Shall be established on the top of the
mountains,
And shall be exalted above the hills;
And all nations shall flow to it.

3 Many people shall come and say,
"Come, and let us go up to the mountain of
the LORD,

כִּסְפֵּךְ הָיָה לְסִיגִים 22
סׇבְאֵךְ מָהוּל בַּמָּיִם:

שָׂרַיִךְ סוֹרְרִים 23
וְחַבְרֵי גַּנָּבִים
כֻּלּוֹ אֹהֵב שֹׁחַד
וְרֹדֵף שַׁלְמֹנִים
יָתוֹם לֹא יִשְׁפֹּטוּ
וְרִיב אַלְמָנָה לֹא־יָבוֹא אֲלֵיהֶם: פ

לָכֵן נְאֻם הָאָדוֹן יְהֹוָה צְבָאוֹת 24
אֲבִיר יִשְׂרָאֵל
הוֹי אֶנָּחֵם מִצָּרַי
וְאִנָּקְמָה מֵאוֹיְבָי:

וְאָשִׁיבָה יָדִי עָלַיִךְ 25
וְאֶצְרֹף כַּבֹּר סִיגָיִךְ
וְאָסִירָה כָּל־בְּדִילָיִךְ:

וְאָשִׁיבָה שֹׁפְטַיִךְ כְּבָרִאשֹׁנָה 26
וְיֹעֲצַיִךְ כְּבַתְּחִלָּה
אַחֲרֵי־כֵן יִקָּרֵא לָךְ עִיר הַצֶּדֶק
קִרְיָה נֶאֱמָנָה:

צִיּוֹן בְּמִשְׁפָּט תִּפָּדֶה 27
וְשָׁבֶיהָ בִּצְדָקָה:

וְשֶׁבֶר פֹּשְׁעִים וְחַטָּאִים יַחְדָּו 28
וְעֹזְבֵי יְהֹוָה יִכְלוּ:

כִּי יֵבֹשׁוּ מֵאֵילִים אֲשֶׁר חֲמַדְתֶּם 29
וְתַחְפְּרוּ מֵהַגַּנּוֹת אֲשֶׁר בְּחַרְתֶּם:

כִּי תִהְיוּ כְּאֵלָה נֹבֶלֶת עָלֶהָ 30
וּכְגַנָּה אֲשֶׁר־מַיִם אֵין לָהּ:

וְהָיָה הֶחָסֹן לִנְעֹרֶת 31
וּפֹעֲלוֹ לְנִיצוֹץ
וּבָעֲרוּ שְׁנֵיהֶם יַחְדָּו
וְאֵין מְכַבֶּה: ס

ב הַדָּבָר אֲשֶׁר חָזָה יְשַׁעְיָהוּ בֶּן־אָמוֹץ
עַל־יְהוּדָה וִירוּשָׁלָ͏ִם:

וְהָיָה ׀ בְּאַחֲרִית הַיָּמִים 2
נָכוֹן יִהְיֶה הַר בֵּית־יְהֹוָה
בְּרֹאשׁ הֶהָרִים
וְנִשָּׂא מִגְּבָעוֹת
וְנָהֲרוּ אֵלָיו כָּל־הַגּוֹיִם:

וְהָלְכוּ עַמִּים רַבִּים וְאָמְרוּ 3

To the house of the God of Jacob;
He will teach us His ways,
And we shall walk in His paths."
For out of Zion shall go forth the law,
And the word of the LORD from Jerusalem.

4 He shall judge between the nations,
And rebuke many people;
They shall beat their swords into plowshares,
And their spears into pruning hooks;
Nation shall not lift up sword against nation,
Neither shall they learn war anymore.

5 O house of Jacob, come and let us walk
In the light of the LORD.

6 For You have forsaken Your people, the
house of Jacob,
Because they are filled with eastern ways;
They *are* soothsayers like the Philistines,
And they are pleased with the children of
foreigners.

7 Their land is also full of silver and gold,
And there is no end to their treasures;
Their land is also full of horses,
And there is no end to their chariots.

8 Their land is also full of idols;
They worship the work of their own hands,
That which their own fingers have made.

9 People bow down,
And each man humbles himself;
Therefore do not forgive them.

10 Enter into the rock, and hide in the dust,
From the terror of the LORD
And the glory of His majesty.

11 The lofty looks of man shall be humbled,
The haughtiness of men shall be bowed
down,
And the LORD alone shall be exalted in that
day.

12 For the day of the LORD of hosts
Shall come upon everything proud and lofty,
Upon everything lifted up—
And it shall be brought low—

13 Upon all the cedars of Lebanon *that are* high
and lifted up,
And upon all the oaks of Bashan;

14 Upon all the high mountains,
And upon all the hills *that are* lifted up;

15 Upon every high tower,
And upon every fortified wall;

16 Upon all the ships of Tarshish,
And upon all the beautiful sloops.

17 The loftiness of man shall be bowed down,

לְכוּ | וְנַעֲלֶה אֶל־הַר־יְהֹוָה
אֶל־בֵּית אֱלֹהֵי יַעֲקֹב וְיֹרֵנוּ מִדְּרָכָיו
וְנֵלְכָה בְּאֹרְחֹתָיו
כִּי מִצִּיּוֹן תֵּצֵא תוֹרָה
וּדְבַר־יְהֹוָה מִירוּשָׁלָ͏ִם:

4 וְשָׁפַט בֵּין הַגּוֹיִם
וְהוֹכִיחַ לְעַמִּים רַבִּים
וְכִתְּתוּ חַרְבוֹתָם לְאִתִּים
וַחֲנִיתוֹתֵיהֶם לְמַזְמֵרוֹת
לֹא־יִשָּׂא גוֹי אֶל־גּוֹי חֶרֶב
וְלֹא־יִלְמְדוּ עוֹד מִלְחָמָה: פ

5 בֵּית יַעֲקֹב לְכוּ וְנֵלְכָה בְּאוֹר יְהֹוָה:

6 כִּי נָטַשְׁתָּה עַמְּךָ בֵּית יַעֲקֹב
כִּי מָלְאוּ מִקֶּדֶם וְעֹנְנִים כַּפְּלִשְׁתִּים
וּבְיַלְדֵי נָכְרִים יַשְׂפִּיקוּ:

7 וַתִּמָּלֵא אַרְצוֹ כֶּסֶף וְזָהָב
וְאֵין קֵצֶה לְאֹצְרֹתָיו
וַתִּמָּלֵא אַרְצוֹ סוּסִים
וְאֵין קֵצֶה לְמַרְכְּבֹתָיו:

8 וַתִּמָּלֵא אַרְצוֹ אֱלִילִים
לְמַעֲשֵׂה יָדָיו יִשְׁתַּחֲווּ
לַאֲשֶׁר עָשׂוּ אֶצְבְּעֹתָיו:

9 וַיִּשַּׁח אָדָם וַיִּשְׁפַּל־אִישׁ
וְאַל־תִּשָּׂא לָהֶם:

10 בּוֹא בַצּוּר וְהִטָּמֵן בֶּעָפָר
מִפְּנֵי פַּחַד יְהֹוָה וּמֵהֲדַר גְּאֹנוֹ:

11 עֵינֵי גַּבְהוּת אָדָם שָׁפֵל
וְשַׁח רוּם אֲנָשִׁים
וְנִשְׂגַּב יְהֹוָה לְבַדּוֹ בַּיּוֹם הַהוּא: ס

12 כִּי יוֹם לַיהֹוָה צְבָאוֹת
עַל כָּל־גֵּאֶה וָרָם
וְעַל כָּל־נִשָּׂא וְשָׁפֵל:

13 וְעַל כָּל־אַרְזֵי הַלְּבָנוֹן
הָרָמִים וְהַנִּשָּׂאִים
וְעַל כָּל־אַלּוֹנֵי הַבָּשָׁן:

14 וְעַל כָּל־הֶהָרִים הָרָמִים
וְעַל כָּל־הַגְּבָעוֹת הַנִּשָּׂאוֹת:

15 וְעַל כָּל־מִגְדָּל גָּבֹהַ
וְעַל כָּל־חוֹמָה בְצוּרָה:

16 וְעַל כָּל־אֳנִיּוֹת תַּרְשִׁישׁ
וְעַל כָּל־שְׂכִיּוֹת הַחֶמְדָּה:

17 וְשַׁח גַּבְהוּת הָאָדָם

And the haughtiness of men shall be brought
    low;
The LORD alone will be exalted in that day,

18 But the idols He shall utterly abolish.

19 They shall go into the holes of the rocks,
And into the caves of the earth,
From the terror of the LORD
And the glory of His majesty,
When He arises to shake the earth mightily.

20 In that day a man will cast away his idols of
        silver
And his idols of gold,
Which they made, *each* for himself to wor-
        ship,
To the moles and bats,

21 To go into the clefts of the rocks,
And into the crags of the rugged rocks,
From the terror of the LORD
And the glory of His majesty,
When He arises to shake the earth mightily.

22 Sever yourselves from such a man,
Whose breath *is* in his nostrils;
For of what account is he?

3   For behold, the Lord, the LORD of hosts,
Takes away from Jerusalem and from Judah
The stock and the store,
The whole supply of bread and the whole
        supply of water;

2   The mighty man and the man of war,
The judge and the prophet,
And the diviner and the elder;

3   The captain of fifty and the honorable man,
The counselor and the skillful artisan,
And the expert enchanter.

4   "I will give children *to be* their princes,
And babes shall rule over them.

5   The people will be oppressed,
Every one by another and every one by his
        neighbor;
The child will be insolent toward the elder,
And the base toward the honorable."

6   When a man takes hold of his brother
In the house of his father, *saying,*
"You have clothing;
You be our ruler,
And *let* these ruins *be* under your power,"

7   In that day he will protest, saying,
"I cannot cure *your* ills,
For in my house *is* neither food nor clothing;
Do not make me a ruler of the people."

וְשָׁפֵל רוּם אֲנָשִׁים
וְנִשְׂגַּב יְהוָה לְבַדּוֹ בַּיּוֹם הַהוּא׃
18 וְהָאֱלִילִים כָּלִיל יַחֲלֹף׃
19 וּבָאוּ בִּמְעָרוֹת צֻרִים
וּבִמְחִלּוֹת עָפָר
מִפְּנֵי פַּחַד יְהוָה
וּמֵהֲדַר גְּאוֹנוֹ
בְּקוּמוֹ לַעֲרֹץ הָאָרֶץ׃
20 בַּיּוֹם הַהוּא יַשְׁלִיךְ הָאָדָם
אֵת אֱלִילֵי כַסְפּוֹ וְאֵת אֱלִילֵי זְהָבוֹ
אֲשֶׁר עָשׂוּ־לוֹ לְהִשְׁתַּחֲוֹת
לַחְפֹּר פֵּרוֹת וְלָעֲטַלֵּפִים׃
21 לָבוֹא בְּנִקְרוֹת הַצֻּרִים
וּבִסְעִפֵי הַסְּלָעִים
מִפְּנֵי פַּחַד יְהוָה
וּמֵהֲדַר גְּאוֹנוֹ
בְּקוּמוֹ לַעֲרֹץ הָאָרֶץ׃
22 חִדְלוּ לָכֶם מִן־הָאָדָם
אֲשֶׁר נְשָׁמָה בְּאַפּוֹ
כִּי־בַמֶּה נֶחְשָׁב הוּא׃   פ

ג   כִּי הִנֵּה הָאָדוֹן יְהוָה צְבָאוֹת
מֵסִיר מִירוּשָׁלַ͏ִם וּמִיהוּדָה
מַשְׁעֵן וּמַשְׁעֵנָה
כֹּל מִשְׁעַן־לֶחֶם וְכֹל מִשְׁעַן־מָיִם׃
2   גִּבּוֹר וְאִישׁ מִלְחָמָה
שׁוֹפֵט וְנָבִיא וְקֹסֵם וְזָקֵן׃
3   שַׂר־חֲמִשִּׁים וּנְשׂוּא פָנִים
וְיוֹעֵץ וַחֲכַם חֲרָשִׁים וּנְבוֹן לָחַשׁ׃
4   וְנָתַתִּי נְעָרִים שָׂרֵיהֶם
וְתַעֲלוּלִים יִמְשְׁלוּ־בָם׃
5   וְנִגַּשׂ הָעָם אִישׁ בְּאִישׁ
וְאִישׁ בְּרֵעֵהוּ
יִרְהֲבוּ הַנַּעַר בַּזָּקֵן
וְהַנִּקְלֶה בַּנִּכְבָּד׃
6   כִּי־יִתְפֹּשׂ אִישׁ בְּאָחִיו בֵּית אָבִיו
שִׂמְלָה לְכָה קָצִין תִּהְיֶה־לָּנוּ
וְהַמַּכְשֵׁלָה הַזֹּאת תַּחַת יָדֶךָ׃
7   יִשָּׂא בַיּוֹם הַהוּא ׀ לֵאמֹר
לֹא־אֶהְיֶה חֹבֵשׁ
וּבְבֵיתִי אֵין לֶחֶם וְאֵין שִׂמְלָה
לֹא תְשִׂימֻנִי קְצִין עָם׃

8 For Jerusalem stumbled,
And Judah is fallen,
Because their tongue and their doings
Are against the LORD,
To provoke the eyes of His glory.
9 The look on their countenance witnesses
against them,
And they declare their sin as Sodom;
They do not hide *it*.
Woe to their soul!
For they have brought evil upon themselves.
10 "Say to the righteous that *it shall be* well *with
them,*
For they shall eat the fruit of their doings.
11 Woe to the wicked! *It shall be* ill *with him,*
For the reward of his hands shall be given
him.
12 *As for* My people, children *are* their oppres-
sors,
And women rule over them.
O My people! Those who lead you cause *you*
to err,
And destroy the way of your paths."
13 The LORD stands up to plead,
And stands to judge the people.
14 The LORD will enter into judgment
With the elders of His people
And His princes:
"For you have eaten up the vineyard;
The plunder of the poor *is* in your houses.
15 What do you mean by crushing My people
And grinding the faces of the poor?"
Says the Lord GOD of hosts.

16 Moreover the LORD says:

"Because the daughters of Zion are haughty,
And walk with outstretched necks
And wanton eyes,
Walking and mincing *as* they go,
Making a jingling with their feet,
17 Therefore the Lord will strike with a scab
The crown of the head of the daughters of
Zion,
And the LORD will uncover their secret
parts."
18 In that day the Lord will take away the finery:
The jingling anklets, the scarves, and the cres-
cents;
19 The pendants, the bracelets, and the veils;
20 The headdresses, the leg ornaments, and the
headbands;
The perfume boxes, the charms,
21 and the rings;
The nose jewels,

8 כִּי כָשְׁלָה יְרוּשָׁלַ͏ִם וִיהוּדָה נָפָל
כִּי־לְשׁוֹנָם וּמַעַלְלֵיהֶם אֶל־יְהֹוָה
לַמְרוֹת עֵנֵי כְבוֹדוֹ:
9 הַכָּרַת פְּנֵיהֶם עָנְתָה בָּם
וְחַטָּאתָם כִּסְדֹם הִגִּידוּ לֹא כִחֵדוּ
אוֹי לְנַפְשָׁם כִּי־גָמְלוּ לָהֶם רָעָה:
10 אִמְרוּ צַדִּיק כִּי־טוֹב
כִּי־פְרִי מַעַלְלֵיהֶם יֹאכֵלוּ:
11 אוֹי לְרָשָׁע רָע
כִּי־גְמוּל יָדָיו יֵעָשֶׂה לּוֹ:
12 עַמִּי נֹגְשָׂיו מְעוֹלֵל
וְנָשִׁים מָשְׁלוּ בוֹ
עַמִּי מְאַשְּׁרֶיךָ מַתְעִים
וְדֶרֶךְ אֹרְחֹתֶיךָ בִּלֵּעוּ:　ס
13 נִצָּב לָרִיב יְהֹוָה
וְעֹמֵד לָדִין עַמִּים:
14 יְהֹוָה בְּמִשְׁפָּט יָבוֹא
עִם־זִקְנֵי עַמּוֹ וְשָׂרָיו
וְאַתֶּם בִּעַרְתֶּם הַכֶּרֶם
גְּזֵלַת הֶעָנִי בְּבָתֵּיכֶם:
15 מַלָּכֶם תְּדַכְּאוּ עַמִּי
וּפְנֵי עֲנִיִּים תִּטְחָנוּ
נְאֻם־אֲדֹנָי יְהֹוִה צְבָאוֹת:　ס
16 וַיֹּאמֶר יְהֹוָה
יַעַן כִּי גָבְהוּ בְּנוֹת צִיּוֹן
וַתֵּלַכְנָה נְטוּוֹת גָּרוֹן
וּמְשַׂקְּרוֹת עֵינָיִם
הָלוֹךְ וְטָפֹף תֵּלַכְנָה
וּבְרַגְלֵיהֶם תְּעַכַּסְנָה:
17 וְשִׂפַּח אֲדֹנָי קָדְקֹד בְּנוֹת צִיּוֹן
וַיהֹוָה פָּתְהֵן יְעָרֶה:　ס
18 בַּיּוֹם הַהוּא יָסִיר אֲדֹנָי אֵת תִּפְאֶרֶת הָעֲכָסִים
וְהַשְּׁבִיסִים וְהַשַּׂהֲרֹנִים: 19 הַנְּטִיפוֹת וְהַשֵּׁירוֹת
וְהָרְעָלוֹת: 20 הַפְּאֵרִים וְהַצְּעָדוֹת וְהַקִּשֻּׁרִים וּבָתֵּי
הַנֶּפֶשׁ וְהַלְּחָשִׁים: 21 הַטַּבָּעוֹת וְנִזְמֵי הָאָף:

ג 15 מַה לָּכֶם　16 נְטוּיוֹת

22 the festal apparel, and the mantles;
The outer garments, the purses,
23   and the mirrors;
The fine linen, the turbans, and the robes.

24 And so it shall be:

Instead of a sweet smell there will be a
  stench;
Instead of a sash, a rope;
Instead of well-set hair, baldness;
Instead of a rich robe, a girding of sackcloth;
And branding instead of beauty.
25 Your men shall fall by the sword,
And your mighty in the war.

26 Her gates shall lament and mourn,
And she *being* desolate shall sit on the
  ground.

4 And in that day seven women shall take hold
of one man, saying,
"We will eat our own food and wear our own
  apparel;
Only let us be called by your name,
To take away our reproach."

2   In that day the Branch of the LORD shall be
  beautiful and glorious;
And the fruit of the earth *shall be* excellent
  and appealing
For those of Israel who have escaped.

3 And it shall come to pass that *he who is* left in
Zion and remains in Jerusalem will be called holy—
everyone who is recorded among the living in
Jerusalem. 4 When the Lord has washed away the
filth of the daughters of Zion, and purged the blood
of Jerusalem from her midst, by the spirit of
judgment and by the spirit of burning, 5 then the
LORD will create above every dwelling place of
Mount Zion, and above her assemblies, a cloud and
smoke by day and the shining of a flaming fire by
night. For over all the glory *there will be* a covering.
6 And there will be a tabernacle for shade in the
daytime from the heat, for a place of refuge, and for
a shelter from storm and rain.

5 Now let me sing to my Well-beloved
A song of my Beloved regarding His
  vineyard:

My Well-beloved has a vineyard
On a very fruitful hill.
2   He dug it up and cleared out its stones,
And planted it with the choicest vine.
He built a tower in its midst,

22 הַמַּחֲלָצוֹת וְהַמַּעֲטָפוֹת וְהַמִּטְפָּחוֹת וְהָחֲרִיטִים:
23 וְהַגִּלְיֹנִים וְהַסְּדִינִים וְהַצְּנִיפוֹת וְהָרְדִידִים:
24 וְהָיָה תַחַת בֹּשֶׂם מַק יִהְיֶה
וְתַחַת חֲגוֹרָה נִקְפָּה
וְתַחַת מַעֲשֶׂה מִקְשֶׁה קָרְחָה
וְתַחַת פְּתִיגִיל מַחֲגֹרֶת שָׂק
כִּי־תַחַת יֹפִי:
25 מְתַיִךְ בַּחֶרֶב יִפֹּלוּ
וּגְבוּרָתֵךְ בַּמִּלְחָמָה:
26 וְאָנוּ וְאָבְלוּ פְּתָחֶיהָ
וְנִקָּתָה לָאָרֶץ תֵּשֵׁב:

ד וְהֶחֱזִיקוּ שֶׁבַע נָשִׁים בְּאִישׁ אֶחָד בַּיּוֹם הַהוּא
לֵאמֹר לַחְמֵנוּ נֹאכֵל וְשִׂמְלָתֵנוּ נִלְבָּשׁ רַק יִקָּרֵא
שִׁמְךָ עָלֵינוּ אֱסֹף חֶרְפָּתֵנוּ: ס
2 בַּיּוֹם הַהוּא יִהְיֶה צֶמַח יְהֹוָה
לִצְבִי וּלְכָבוֹד
וּפְרִי הָאָרֶץ לְגָאוֹן וּלְתִפְאֶרֶת
לִפְלֵיטַת יִשְׂרָאֵל:
3 וְהָיָה הַנִּשְׁאָר בְּצִיּוֹן וְהַנּוֹתָר בִּירוּשָׁלַ͏ִם קָדוֹשׁ
יֵאָמֶר לוֹ כָּל־הַכָּתוּב לַחַיִּים בִּירוּשָׁלָ͏ִם: 4 אִם |
רָחַץ אֲדֹנָי אֵת צֹאַת בְּנוֹת־צִיּוֹן וְאֶת־דְּמֵי יְרוּשָׁלַ͏ִם
יָדִיחַ מִקִּרְבָּהּ בְּרוּחַ מִשְׁפָּט וּבְרוּחַ בָּעֵר: 5 וּבָרָא
יְהֹוָה עַל כָּל־מְכוֹן הַר־צִיּוֹן וְעַל־מִקְרָאֶהָ עָנָן |
יוֹמָם וְעָשָׁן וְנֹגַהּ אֵשׁ לֶהָבָה לָיְלָה כִּי עַל־כָּל־כָּבוֹד
חֻפָּה: 6 וְסֻכָּה תִּהְיֶה לְצֵל־יוֹמָם מֵחֹרֶב וּלְמַחְסֶה
וּלְמִסְתּוֹר מִזֶּרֶם וּמִמָּטָר: פ

ה אָשִׁירָה נָּא לִידִידִי
שִׁירַת דּוֹדִי לְכַרְמוֹ
כֶּרֶם הָיָה לִידִידִי
בְּקֶרֶן בֶּן־שָׁמֶן:
2 וַיְעַזְּקֵהוּ וַיְסַקְּלֵהוּ
וַיִּטָּעֵהוּ שֹׂרֵק

And also made a winepress in it;
So He expected *it* to bring forth *good* grapes,
But it brought forth wild grapes.

3 "And now, O inhabitants of Jerusalem and
   men of Judah,
   Judge, please, between Me and My vineyard.
4 What more could have been done to My
   vineyard
   That I have not done in it?
   Why then, when I expected *it* to bring forth
     good grapes,
   Did it bring forth wild grapes?
5 And now, please let Me tell you what I will
   do to My vineyard:
   I will take away its hedge, and it shall be
     burned;
   And break down its wall, and it shall be
     trampled down.
6 I will lay it waste;
   It shall not be pruned or dug,
   But there shall come up briers and thorns.
   I will also command the clouds
   That they rain no rain on it."

7 For the vineyard of the LORD of hosts *is* the
   house of Israel,
   And the men of Judah are His pleasant plant.
   He looked for justice, but behold, oppres-
     sion;
   For righteousness, but behold, a cry *for help*.

8 Woe to those who join house to house;
   They add field to field,
   Till *there is* no place
   Where they may dwell alone in the midst of
     the land!
9 In my hearing the LORD of hosts *said*,
   "Truly, many houses shall be desolate,
   Great and beautiful ones, without inhabi-
     tant.
10 For ten acres of vineyard shall yield one
     bath,
   And a homer of seed shall yield one ephah."

11 Woe to those who rise early in the morning,
   That they may follow intoxicating drink;
   Who continue until night, *till* wine inflames
     them!
12 The harp and the strings,
   The tambourine and flute,
   And wine are in their feasts;
   But they do not regard the work of the
     LORD,
   Nor consider the operation of His hands.

וַיִּבֶן מִגְדָּל בְּתוֹכוֹ
וְגַם־יֶקֶב חָצֵב בּוֹ
וַיְקַו לַעֲשׂוֹת עֲנָבִים
וַיַּעַשׂ בְּאֻשִׁים:

3 וְעַתָּה יוֹשֵׁב יְרוּשָׁלַ͏ִם וְאִישׁ יְהוּדָה
שִׁפְטוּ־נָא בֵּינִי וּבֵין כַּרְמִי:

4 מַה־לַּעֲשׂוֹת עוֹד לְכַרְמִי
וְלֹא עָשִׂיתִי בּוֹ
מַדּוּעַ קִוֵּיתִי לַעֲשׂוֹת עֲנָבִים
וַיַּעַשׂ בְּאֻשִׁים:

5 וְעַתָּה אוֹדִיעָה־נָּא אֶתְכֶם
אֵת אֲשֶׁר־אֲנִי עֹשֶׂה לְכַרְמִי
הָסֵר מְשׂוּכָּתוֹ
וְהָיָה לְבָעֵר
פָּרֹץ גְּדֵרוֹ
וְהָיָה לְמִרְמָס:

6 וַאֲשִׁיתֵהוּ בָתָה
לֹא יִזָּמֵר וְלֹא יֵעָדֵר
וְעָלָה שָׁמִיר וָשָׁיִת
וְעַל הֶעָבִים אֲצַוֶּה
מֵהַמְטִיר עָלָיו מָטָר:

7 כִּי כֶרֶם יְהֹוָה צְבָאוֹת בֵּית יִשְׂרָאֵל
וְאִישׁ יְהוּדָה נְטַע שַׁעֲשׁוּעָיו
וַיְקַו לְמִשְׁפָּט וְהִנֵּה מִשְׂפָּח
לִצְדָקָה וְהִנֵּה צְעָקָה: ס

8 הוֹי מַגִּיעֵי בַיִת בְּבַיִת
שָׂדֶה בְשָׂדֶה יַקְרִיבוּ
עַד אֶפֶס מָקוֹם וְהוּשַׁבְתֶּם
לְבַדְּכֶם בְּקֶרֶב הָאָרֶץ:

9 בְּאׇזְנָי יְהֹוָה צְבָאוֹת
אִם־לֹא בָּתִּים רַבִּים לְשַׁמָּה יִהְיוּ
גְּדֹלִים וְטוֹבִים מֵאֵין יוֹשֵׁב:

10 כִּי עֲשֶׂרֶת צִמְדֵּי־כֶרֶם
יַעֲשׂוּ בַּת אֶחָת
וְזֶרַע חֹמֶר יַעֲשֶׂה אֵיפָה:

פ

11 הוֹי מַשְׁכִּימֵי בַבֹּקֶר שֵׁכָר יִרְדֹּפוּ
מְאַחֲרֵי בַנֶּשֶׁף יַיִן יַדְלִיקֵם:

12 וְהָיָה כִנּוֹר וָנֶבֶל תֹּף וְחָלִיל
וָיַיִן מִשְׁתֵּיהֶם
וְאֵת פֹּעַל יְהֹוָה לֹא יַבִּיטוּ
וּמַעֲשֵׂה יָדָיו לֹא רָאוּ:

13 Therefore my people have gone into captivity,
Because *they have* no knowledge;
Their honorable men *are* famished,
And their multitude dried up with thirst.

14 Therefore Sheol has enlarged itself
And opened its mouth beyond measure;
Their glory and their multitude and their pomp,
And he who is jubilant, shall descend into it.

15 People shall be brought down,
Each man shall be humbled,
And the eyes of the lofty shall be humbled.

16 But the LORD of hosts shall be exalted in judgment,
And God who is holy shall be hallowed in righteousness.

17 Then the lambs shall feed in their pasture,
And in the waste places of the fat ones strangers shall eat.

18 Woe to those who draw iniquity with cords of vanity,
And sin as if with a cart rope;

19 That say, "Let Him make speed *and* hasten His work,
That we may see *it;*
And let the counsel of the Holy One of Israel draw near and come,
That we may know *it.*"

20 Woe to those who call evil good, and good evil;
Who put darkness for light, and light for darkness;
Who put bitter for sweet, and sweet for bitter!

21 Woe to *those who are* wise in their own eyes,
And prudent in their own sight!

22 Woe to men mighty at drinking wine,
Woe to men valiant for mixing intoxicating drink,

23 Who justify the wicked for a bribe,
And take away justice from the righteous man!

24 Therefore, as the fire devours the stubble,
And the flame consumes the chaff,
So their root will be as rottenness,
And their blossom will ascend like dust;
Because they have rejected the law of the LORD of hosts,
And despised the word of the Holy One of Israel.

לָכֵן גָּלָה עַמִּי מִבְּלִי־דָעַת 13
וּכְבוֹדוֹ מְתֵי רָעָב
וַהֲמוֹנוֹ צִחֵה צָמָא:

לָכֵן הִרְחִיבָה שְּׁאוֹל נַפְשָׁהּ 14
וּפָעֲרָה פִיהָ לִבְלִי־חֹק
וְיָרַד הֲדָרָהּ וַהֲמוֹנָהּ
וּשְׁאוֹנָהּ וְעָלֵז בָּהּ:

וַיִּשַּׁח אָדָם וַיִּשְׁפַּל־אִישׁ 15
וְעֵינֵי גְבֹהִים תִּשְׁפַּלְנָה:

וַיִּגְבַּהּ יְהֹוָה צְבָאוֹת בַּמִּשְׁפָּט 16
וְהָאֵל הַקָּדוֹשׁ נִקְדָּשׁ בִּצְדָקָה:

וְרָעוּ כְבָשִׂים כְּדָבְרָם 17
וְחָרְבוֹת מֵחִים גָּרִים יֹאכֵלוּ:

הוֹי מֹשְׁכֵי הֶעָוֹן בְּחַבְלֵי הַשָּׁוְא 18
וְכַעֲבוֹת הָעֲגָלָה חַטָּאָה:

הָאֹמְרִים יְמַהֵר ׀ יָחִישָׁה מַעֲשֵׂהוּ 19
לְמַעַן נִרְאֶה
וְתִקְרַב וְתָבוֹאָה עֲצַת
קְדוֹשׁ יִשְׂרָאֵל וְנֵדָעָה: ס

הוֹי הָאֹמְרִים לָרַע טוֹב וְלַטּוֹב רָע 20
שָׂמִים חֹשֶׁךְ לְאוֹר
וְאוֹר לְחֹשֶׁךְ
שָׂמִים מַר לְמָתוֹק
וּמָתוֹק לְמָר: ס

הוֹי חֲכָמִים בְּעֵינֵיהֶם 21
וְנֶגֶד פְּנֵיהֶם נְבֹנִים:

הוֹי גִּבּוֹרִים לִשְׁתּוֹת יָיִן 22
וְאַנְשֵׁי־חַיִל לִמְסֹךְ שֵׁכָר:

מַצְדִּיקֵי רָשָׁע עֵקֶב שֹׁחַד 23
וְצִדְקַת צַדִּיקִים יָסִירוּ מִמֶּנּוּ: ס

לָכֵן כֶּאֱכֹל קַשׁ לְשׁוֹן אֵשׁ 24
וַחֲשַׁשׁ לֶהָבָה יִרְפֶּה
שָׁרְשָׁם כַּמָּק יִהְיֶה
וּפִרְחָם כָּאָבָק יַעֲלֶה
כִּי מָאֲסוּ אֵת תּוֹרַת יְהֹוָה צְבָאוֹת
וְאֵת אִמְרַת קְדוֹשׁ־יִשְׂרָאֵל נִאֵצוּ:

25 Therefore the anger of the LORD is aroused
   against His people;
   He has stretched out His hand against them
   And stricken them,
   And the hills trembled.
   Their carcasses *were* as refuse in the midst of
     the streets.

   For all this His anger is not turned away,
   But His hand *is* stretched out still.

26 He will lift up a banner to the nations from
     afar,
   And will whistle to them from the end of the
     earth;
   Surely they shall come with speed, swiftly.

27 No one will be weary or stumble among
     them,
   No one will slumber or sleep;
   Nor will the belt on their loins be loosed,
   Nor the strap of their sandals be broken;

28 Whose arrows *are* sharp,
   And all their bows bent;
   Their horses' hooves will seem like flint,
   And their wheels like a whirlwind.

29 Their roaring *will be* like a lion,
   They will roar like young lions;
   Yes, they will roar
   And lay hold of the prey;
   They will carry *it* away safely,
   And no one will deliver.

30 In that day they will roar against them
   Like the roaring of the sea.
   And if *one* looks to the land,
   Behold, darkness *and* sorrow;
   And the light is darkened by the clouds.

6 In the year that King Uzziah died, I saw the
Lord sitting on a throne, high and lifted up, and the
train of His *robe* filled the temple. ² Above it stood
seraphim; each one had six wings: with two he
covered his face, with two he covered his feet, and
with two he flew. ³ And one cried to another and
said:

   "Holy, holy, holy *is* the LORD of hosts;
   The whole earth *is* full of His glory!"

⁴ And the posts of the door were shaken by the
voice of him who cried out, and the house was filled
with smoke.
⁵ So I said:

   "Woe *is* me, for I am undone!
   Because I *am* a man of unclean lips,
   And I dwell in the midst of a people of
     unclean lips;

25 עַל־כֵּ֣ן חָרָ֤ה אַף־יְהֹוָה֙ בְּעַמּ֔וֹ
וַיֵּ֨ט יָד֤וֹ עָלָיו֙ וַיַּכֵּ֔הוּ וַֽיִּרְגְּז֖וּ הֶֽהָרִ֑ים
וַתְּהִ֤י נִבְלָתָם֙ כַּסּוּחָ֔ה בְּקֶ֖רֶב חוּצ֑וֹת
בְּכָל־זֹאת֙ לֹא־שָׁ֣ב אַפּ֔וֹ
וְע֖וֹד יָד֥וֹ נְטוּיָֽה׃

26 וְנָֽשָׂא־נֵ֤ס לַגּוֹיִם֙ מֵֽרָח֔וֹק
וְשָׁ֥רַק ל֖וֹ מִקְצֵ֣ה הָאָ֑רֶץ
וְהִנֵּ֥ה מְהֵרָ֖ה קַ֥ל יָבֽוֹא׃

27 אֵין־עָיֵ֤ף וְאֵין־כּוֹשֵׁל֙ בּ֔וֹ
לֹ֥א יָנ֖וּם וְלֹ֣א יִישָׁ֑ן
וְלֹ֤א נִפְתַּח֙ אֵז֣וֹר חֲלָצָ֔יו
וְלֹ֥א נִתַּ֖ק שְׂר֥וֹךְ נְעָלָֽיו׃

28 אֲשֶׁ֤ר חִצָּיו֙ שְׁנוּנִ֔ים
וְכָל־קַשְּׁתֹתָ֖יו דְּרֻכ֑וֹת
פַּרְס֤וֹת סוּסָיו֙ כַּצַּ֣ר נֶחְשָׁ֔בוּ
וְגַלְגִּלָּ֖יו כַּסּוּפָֽה׃

29 שְׁאָגָ֥ה ל֖וֹ כַּלָּבִ֑יא
וְשָׁאַ֛ג כַּכְּפִירִ֥ים וְיִנְהֹ֖ם
וְיֹאחֵ֣ז טֶ֔רֶף וְיַפְלִ֖יט וְאֵ֥ין מַצִּֽיל׃

30 וְיִנְהֹ֤ם עָלָיו֙ בַּיּ֣וֹם הַה֔וּא
כְּנַֽהֲמַת־יָ֑ם וְנִבַּ֤ט לָאָ֨רֶץ֙
וְהִנֵּה־חֹ֔שֶׁךְ
צַ֣ר וָא֔וֹר חָשַׁ֖ךְ בַּעֲרִיפֶֽיהָ׃   פ

1 בִּשְׁנַת־מוֹת֙ הַמֶּ֣לֶךְ עֻזִּיָּ֔הוּ וָאֶרְאֶ֥ה אֶת־אֲדֹנָ֖י יֹשֵׁ֥ב
עַל־כִּסֵּ֖א רָ֣ם וְנִשָּׂ֑א וְשׁוּלָ֖יו מְלֵאִ֥ים אֶת־הַהֵיכָֽל׃
2 שְׂרָפִ֨ים עֹמְדִ֤ים ׀ מִמַּ֙עַל֙ ל֔וֹ שֵׁ֧שׁ כְּנָפַ֛יִם שֵׁ֥שׁ
כְּנָפַ֖יִם לְאֶחָ֑ד בִּשְׁתַּ֣יִם ׀ יְכַסֶּ֣ה פָנָ֗יו וּבִשְׁתַּ֛יִם יְכַסֶּ֥ה
רַגְלָ֖יו וּבִשְׁתַּ֥יִם יְעוֹפֵֽף׃ 3 וְקָרָ֨א זֶ֤ה אֶל־זֶה֙ וְאָמַ֔ר
קָד֧וֹשׁ ׀ קָד֛וֹשׁ קָד֖וֹשׁ יְהֹוָ֣ה צְבָא֑וֹת
מְלֹ֥א כָל־הָאָ֖רֶץ כְּבוֹדֽוֹ׃
4 וַיָּנֻ֙עוּ֙ אַמּ֣וֹת הַסִּפִּ֔ים מִקּ֖וֹל הַקּוֹרֵ֑א
וְהַבַּ֖יִת יִמָּלֵ֥א עָשָֽׁן׃
5 וָאֹמַ֞ר
אֽוֹי־לִ֣י כִֽי־נִדְמֵ֗יתִי
כִּ֣י אִ֤ישׁ טְמֵֽא־שְׂפָתַ֙יִם֙ אָנֹ֔כִי

For my eyes have seen the King,
The LORD of hosts."

6 Then one of the seraphim flew to me, having in his hand a live coal *which* he had taken with the tongs from the altar. 7 And he touched my mouth *with it,* and said:

"Behold, this has touched your lips;
Your iniquity is taken away,
And your sin purged."

8 Also I heard the voice of the Lord, saying:

"Whom shall I send,
And who will go for Us?"

Then I said, "Here *am* I! Send me."
9 And He said, "Go, and tell this people:

'Keep on hearing, but do not understand;
Keep on seeing, but do not perceive.'

10 "Make the heart of this people dull,
And their ears heavy,
And shut their eyes;
Lest they see with their eyes,
And hear with their ears,
And understand with their heart,
And return and be healed."

11 Then I said, "Lord, how long?"
And He answered:

"Until the cities are laid waste and without
  inhabitant,
The houses are without a man,
The land is utterly desolate,
12 The LORD has removed men far away,
And the forsaken places *are* many in the
  midst of the land.
13 But yet a tenth *will be* in it,
And will return and be for consuming,
As a terebinth tree or as an oak,
Whose stump *remains* when it is cut down.
So the holy seed *shall be* its stump."

7 Now it came to pass in the days of Ahaz the son of Jotham, the son of Uzziah, king of Judah, *that* Rezin king of Syria and Pekah the son of Remaliah, king of Israel, went up to Jerusalem to *make* war against it, but could not prevail against it. 2 And it was told to the house of David, saying, "Syria's forces are deployed in Ephraim." So his heart and the heart of his people were moved as the trees of the woods are moved with the wind.

3 Then the LORD said to Isaiah, "Go out now to meet Ahaz, you and Shear-Jashub your son, at the end of the aqueduct from the upper pool, on the

וּבְתוֹךְ עַם־טְמֵא שְׂפָתַיִם אָנֹכִי יוֹשֵׁב
כִּי אֶת־הַמֶּלֶךְ
יְהוָה צְבָאוֹת רָאוּ עֵינָי:

6 וַיָּעָף אֵלַי אֶחָד מִן־הַשְּׂרָפִים וּבְיָדוֹ רִצְפָּה
בְּמֶלְקַחַיִם לָקַח מֵעַל הַמִּזְבֵּחַ:

7 וַיַּגַּע עַל־פִּי וַיֹּאמֶר
הִנֵּה נָגַע זֶה עַל־שְׂפָתֶיךָ
וְסָר עֲוֹנֶךָ וְחַטָּאתְךָ תְּכֻפָּר:

8 וָאֶשְׁמַע אֶת־קוֹל אֲדֹנָי אֹמֵר
אֶת־מִי אֶשְׁלַח וּמִי יֵלֶךְ־לָנוּ
וָאֹמַר הִנְנִי שְׁלָחֵנִי:

9 וַיֹּאמֶר לֵךְ וְאָמַרְתָּ לָעָם הַזֶּה
שִׁמְעוּ שָׁמוֹעַ וְאַל־תָּבִינוּ
וּרְאוּ רָאוֹ וְאַל־תֵּדָעוּ:

10 הַשְׁמֵן לֵב־הָעָם הַזֶּה
וְאָזְנָיו הַכְבֵּד וְעֵינָיו הָשַׁע
פֶּן־יִרְאֶה בְעֵינָיו וּבְאָזְנָיו יִשְׁמָע
וּלְבָבוֹ יָבִין וָשָׁב וְרָפָא לוֹ:

11 וָאֹמַר עַד־מָתַי אֲדֹנָי וַיֹּאמֶר
עַד אֲשֶׁר אִם־שָׁאוּ עָרִים מֵאֵין יוֹשֵׁב
וּבָתִּים מֵאֵין אָדָם
וְהָאֲדָמָה תִּשָּׁאֶה שְׁמָמָה:

12 וְרִחַק יְהוָה אֶת־הָאָדָם
וְרַבָּה הָעֲזוּבָה בְּקֶרֶב הָאָרֶץ:

13 וְעוֹד בָּהּ עֲשִׂרִיָּה וְשָׁבָה וְהָיְתָה לְבָעֵר
כָּאֵלָה וְכָאַלּוֹן אֲשֶׁר בְּשַׁלֶּכֶת מַצֶּבֶת בָּם זֶרַע
קֹדֶשׁ מַצַּבְתָּהּ:
פ

7 וַיְהִי בִּימֵי אָחָז בֶּן־יוֹתָם בֶּן־עֻזִּיָּהוּ מֶלֶךְ יְהוּדָה
עָלָה רְצִין מֶלֶךְ־אֲרָם וּפֶקַח בֶּן־רְמַלְיָהוּ מֶלֶךְ־
יִשְׂרָאֵל יְרוּשָׁלַ͏ִם לַמִּלְחָמָה עָלֶיהָ וְלֹא יָכֹל לְהִלָּחֵם
עָלֶיהָ: 2 וַיֻּגַּד לְבֵית דָּוִד לֵאמֹר נָחָה אֲרָם עַל־
אֶפְרָיִם וַיָּנַע לְבָבוֹ וּלְבַב עַמּוֹ כְּנוֹעַ עֲצֵי־יַעַר
מִפְּנֵי־רוּחַ: 3 וַיֹּאמֶר יְהוָה אֶל־יְשַׁעְיָהוּ צֵא־נָא
לִקְרַאת אָחָז אַתָּה וּשְׁאָר יָשׁוּב בְּנֶךָ אֶל־קְצֵה
תְּעָלַת הַבְּרֵכָה הָעֶלְיוֹנָה אֶל־מְסִלַּת שְׂדֵה כוֹבֵס:

highway to the Fuller's Field, ⁴and say to him: 'Take heed, and be quiet; do not fear or be fainthearted for these two stubs of smoking firebrands, for the fierce anger of Rezin and Syria, and the son of Remaliah. ⁵Because Syria, Ephraim, and the son of Remaliah have plotted evil against you, saying, ⁶"Let us go up against Judah and trouble it, and let us make a gap in its wall for ourselves, and set a king over them, the son of Tabel"— ⁷thus says the Lord GOD:

"It shall not stand,
   Nor shall it come to pass.
⁸ For the head of Syria is Damascus,
   And the head of Damascus is Rezin.
   Within sixty-five years Ephraim will be
      broken,
   So that it will not be a people.
⁹ The head of Ephraim is Samaria,
   And the head of Samaria is Remaliah's son.
   If you will not believe,
   Surely you shall not be established." ' "

¹⁰Moreover the LORD spoke again to Ahaz, saying, ¹¹"Ask a sign for yourself from the LORD your God; ask it either in the depth or in the height above."

¹²But Ahaz said, "I will not ask, nor will I test the LORD!"

¹³Then he said, "Hear now, O house of David! Is it a small thing for you to weary men, but will you weary my God also? ¹⁴Therefore the Lord Himself will give you a sign: Behold, the virgin shall conceive and bear a Son, and shall call His name Immanuel. ¹⁵Curds and honey He shall eat, that He may know to refuse the evil and choose the good. ¹⁶For before the Child shall know to refuse the evil and choose the good, the land that you dread will be forsaken by both her kings. ¹⁷The LORD will bring the king of Assyria upon you and your people and your father's house—days that have not come since the day that Ephraim departed from Judah."

¹⁸ And it shall come to pass in that day
   That the LORD will whistle for the fly
   That is in the farthest part of the rivers of
      Egypt,
   And for the bee that is in the land of Assyria.
¹⁹ They will come, and all of them will rest
   In the desolate valleys and in the clefts of the
      rocks,
   And on all thorns and in all pastures.
²⁰ In the same day the Lord will shave with a hired
      razor,
   With those from beyond the River, with the king
      of Assyria,

4 וְאָמַרְתָּ אֵלָיו הִשָּׁמֵר וְהַשְׁקֵט אַל־תִּירָא וּלְבָבְךָ
אַל־יֵרַךְ מִשְּׁנֵי זַנְבוֹת הָאוּדִים הָעֲשֵׁנִים הָאֵלֶּה
בָּחֳרִי־אַף רְצִין וַאֲרָם וּבֶן־רְמַלְיָהוּ: 5 יַעַן כִּי־יָעַץ
עָלֶיךָ אֲרָם רָעָה אֶפְרַיִם וּבֶן־רְמַלְיָהוּ לֵאמֹר:
6 נַעֲלֶה בִיהוּדָה וּנְקִיצֶנָּה וְנַבְקִעֶנָּה אֵלֵינוּ וְנַמְלִיךְ
מֶלֶךְ בְּתוֹכָהּ אֵת בֶּן־טָבְאַל: ס

7 כֹּה אָמַר אֲדֹנָי יְהוִה
לֹא תָקוּם וְלֹא תִהְיֶה:
8 כִּי רֹאשׁ אֲרָם דַּמֶּשֶׂק
וְרֹאשׁ דַּמֶּשֶׂק רְצִין
וּבְעוֹד שִׁשִּׁים וְחָמֵשׁ שָׁנָה
יֵחַת אֶפְרַיִם מֵעָם:
9 וְרֹאשׁ אֶפְרַיִם שֹׁמְרוֹן
וְרֹאשׁ שֹׁמְרוֹן בֶּן־רְמַלְיָהוּ
אִם לֹא תַאֲמִינוּ כִּי לֹא תֵאָמֵנוּ: ס

10 וַיּוֹסֶף יְהוָה דַּבֵּר אֶל־אָחָז לֵאמֹר: 11 שְׁאַל־לְךָ
אוֹת מֵעִם יְהוָה אֱלֹהֶיךָ הַעְמֵק שְׁאָלָה אוֹ הַגְבֵּהַּ
לְמָעְלָה: 12 וַיֹּאמֶר אָחָז לֹא־אֶשְׁאַל וְלֹא־אֲנַסֶּה
אֶת־יְהוָה: 13 וַיֹּאמֶר שִׁמְעוּ־נָא בֵּית דָּוִד הַמְעַט
מִכֶּם הַלְאוֹת אֲנָשִׁים כִּי תַלְאוּ גַּם אֶת־אֱלֹהָי:
14 לָכֵן יִתֵּן אֲדֹנָי הוּא לָכֶם אוֹת הִנֵּה הָעַלְמָה
הָרָה וְיֹלֶדֶת בֵּן וְקָרָאת שְׁמוֹ עִמָּנוּ אֵל: 15 חֶמְאָה
וּדְבַשׁ יֹאכֵל לְדַעְתּוֹ מָאוֹס בָּרָע וּבָחוֹר בַּטּוֹב:
16 כִּי בְּטֶרֶם יֵדַע הַנַּעַר מָאֹס בָּרָע וּבָחֹר בַּטּוֹב
תֵּעָזֵב הָאֲדָמָה אֲשֶׁר אַתָּה קָץ מִפְּנֵי שְׁנֵי מְלָכֶיהָ:
17 יָבִיא יְהוָה עָלֶיךָ וְעַל־עַמְּךָ וְעַל־בֵּית אָבִיךָ יָמִים
אֲשֶׁר לֹא־בָאוּ לְמִיּוֹם סוּר־אֶפְרַיִם מֵעַל יְהוּדָה אֵת
מֶלֶךְ אַשּׁוּר: פ

18 וְהָיָה | בַּיּוֹם הַהוּא יִשְׁרֹק יְהוָה לַזְּבוּב
אֲשֶׁר בִּקְצֵה יְאֹרֵי מִצְרָיִם
וְלַדְּבוֹרָה אֲשֶׁר בְּאֶרֶץ אַשּׁוּר:
19 וּבָאוּ וְנָחוּ כֻלָּם
בְּנַחֲלֵי הַבַּתּוֹת וּבִנְקִיקֵי הַסְּלָעִים
וּבְכֹל הַנַּעֲצוּצִים וּבְכֹל הַנַּהֲלֹלִים:
20 בַּיּוֹם הַהוּא יְגַלַּח אֲדֹנָי בְּתַעַר הַשְּׂכִירָה בְּעֶבְרֵי
נָהָר בְּמֶלֶךְ אַשּׁוּר אֶת־הָרֹאשׁ וְשַׂעַר הָרַגְלָיִם וְגַם

The head and the hair of the legs,
And will also remove the beard.

21 It shall be in that day
That a man will keep alive a young cow and two
sheep;

22 So it shall be, from the abundance of milk they
give,
That he will eat curds;
For curds and honey everyone will eat who is left
in the land.

23 It shall happen in that day,
That wherever there could be a thousand vines
Worth a thousand *shekels* of silver,
It will be for briers and thorns.

24 With arrows and bows men will come there,
Because all the land will become briers and
thorns.

25 And to any hill which could be dug with the hoe,
You will not go there for fear of briers and
thorns;
But it will become a range for oxen
And a place for sheep to roam.

8 Moreover the LORD said to me, "Take a large
scroll, and write on it with a man's pen concerning
Maher-Shalal-Hash-Baz. ²And I will take for
Myself faithful witnesses to record, Uriah the priest
and Zechariah the son of Jeberechiah."

³Then I went to the prophetess, and she
conceived and bore a son. Then the LORD said to
me, "Call his name Maher-Shalal-Hash-Baz; ⁴for
before the child shall have knowledge to cry 'My
father' and 'My mother,' the riches of Damascus
and the spoil of Samaria will be taken away before
the king of Assyria."

⁵The LORD also spoke to me again, saying:

6 "Inasmuch as these people refused
The waters of Shiloah that flow softly,
And rejoice in Rezin and in Remaliah's son;

7 Now therefore, behold, the Lord brings up
over them
The waters of the River, strong and
mighty—
The king of Assyria and all his glory;
He will go up over all his channels
And go over all his banks.

8 He will pass through Judah,
He will overflow and pass over,
He will reach up to the neck;
And the stretching out of his wings
Will fill the breadth of Your land, O
Immanuel.

9 "Be shattered, O you peoples, and be broken
in pieces!
Give ear, all you from far countries.

אֶת־הַזָּקָן תִּסְפֶּה: ס 21 וְהָיָה בַּיּוֹם הַהוּא
יְחַיֶּה־אִישׁ עֶגְלַת בָּקָר וּשְׁתֵּי־צֹאן: 22 וְהָיָה מֵרֹב
עֲשׂוֹת חָלָב יֹאכַל חֶמְאָה כִּי־חֶמְאָה וּדְבַשׁ יֹאכֵל
כָּל־הַנּוֹתָר בְּקֶרֶב הָאָרֶץ: 23 וְהָיָה בַּיּוֹם הַהוּא
יִהְיֶה כָל־מָקוֹם אֲשֶׁר יִהְיֶה־שָׁם אֶלֶף גֶּפֶן בְּאֶלֶף
כָּסֶף לַשָּׁמִיר וְלַשַּׁיִת יִהְיֶה: 24 בַּחִצִּים וּבַקֶּשֶׁת יָבוֹא
שָׁמָּה כִּי־שָׁמִיר וָשַׁיִת תִּהְיֶה כָל־הָאָרֶץ: 25 וְכֹל
הֶהָרִים אֲשֶׁר בַּמַּעְדֵּר יֵעָדֵרוּן לֹא־תָבוֹא שָׁמָּה
יִרְאַת שָׁמִיר וָשָׁיִת וְהָיָה לְמִשְׁלַח שׁוֹר וּלְמִרְמַס
שֶׂה:
פ

ח וַיֹּאמֶר יְהֹוָה אֵלַי קַח־לְךָ גִּלָּיוֹן גָּדוֹל וּכְתֹב
עָלָיו בְּחֶרֶט אֱנוֹשׁ לְמַהֵר שָׁלָל חָשׁ בַּז: 2 וְאָעִידָה
לִּי עֵדִים נֶאֱמָנִים אֵת אוּרִיָּה הַכֹּהֵן וְאֶת־זְכַרְיָהוּ
בֶּן יְבֶרֶכְיָהוּ: 3 וָאֶקְרַב אֶל־הַנְּבִיאָה וַתַּהַר וַתֵּלֶד
בֵּן וַיֹּאמֶר יְהֹוָה אֵלַי קְרָא שְׁמוֹ מַהֵר שָׁלָל חָשׁ
בַּז: 4 כִּי בְּטֶרֶם יֵדַע הַנַּעַר קְרֹא אָבִי וְאִמִּי יִשָּׂא
אֶת־חֵיל דַּמֶּשֶׂק וְאֵת שְׁלַל שֹׁמְרוֹן לִפְנֵי מֶלֶךְ
אַשּׁוּר: ס 5 וַיֹּסֶף יְהֹוָה דַּבֵּר אֵלַי עוֹד
לֵאמֹר:

6 יַעַן כִּי מָאַס הָעָם הַזֶּה
אֵת מֵי הַשִּׁלֹחַ הַהֹלְכִים לְאַט
וּמְשׂוֹשׂ אֶת־רְצִין וּבֶן־רְמַלְיָהוּ:

7 וְלָכֵן הִנֵּה אֲדֹנָי מַעֲלֶה עֲלֵיהֶם
אֶת־מֵי הַנָּהָר הָעֲצוּמִים וְהָרַבִּים
אֶת־מֶלֶךְ אַשּׁוּר וְאֶת־כָּל־כְּבוֹדוֹ
וְעָלָה עַל־כָּל־אֲפִיקָיו
וְהָלַךְ עַל־כָּל־גְּדוֹתָיו:

8 וְחָלַף בִּיהוּדָה
שָׁטַף וְעָבַר
עַד־צַוָּאר יַגִּיעַ
וְהָיָה מֻטּוֹת כְּנָפָיו
מְלֹא רֹחַב־אַרְצְךָ עִמָּנוּ אֵל: ס

9 רֹעוּ עַמִּים וָחֹתּוּ
וְהַאֲזִינוּ כֹּל מֶרְחַקֵּי־אָרֶץ

Gird yourselves, but be broken in pieces;
Gird yourselves, but be broken in pieces.
10 Take counsel together, but it will come to nothing;
Speak the word, but it will not stand,
For God *is* with us."

11 For the LORD spoke thus to me with a strong hand, and instructed me that I should not walk in the way of this people, saying:

12 "Do not say, 'A conspiracy,'
Concerning all that this people call a conspiracy,
Nor be afraid of their threats, nor be troubled.
13 The LORD of hosts, Him you shall hallow;
Let Him *be* your fear,
And *let* Him *be* your dread.
14 He will be as a sanctuary,
But a stone of stumbling and a rock of offense
To both the houses of Israel,
As a trap and a snare to the inhabitants of Jerusalem.
15 And many among them shall stumble;
They shall fall and be broken,
Be snared and taken."

16 Bind up the testimony,
Seal the law among my disciples.
17 And I will wait on the LORD,
Who hides His face from the house of Jacob;
And I will hope in Him.
18 Here am I and the children whom the LORD has given me!
We are for signs and wonders in Israel
From the LORD of hosts,
Who dwells in Mount Zion.

19 And when they say to you, "Seek those who are mediums and wizards, who whisper and mutter," should not a people seek their God? *Should they seek* the dead on behalf of the living? 20 To the law and to the testimony! If they do not speak according to this word, *it is* because *there is* no light in them.

21 They will pass through it hard-pressed and hungry; and it shall happen, when they are hungry, that they will be enraged and curse their king and their God, and look upward. 22 Then they will look to the earth, and see trouble and darkness, gloom of anguish; and *they will be* driven into darkness.

9 Nevertheless the gloom *will* not *be* upon her who *is* distressed,
As when at first He lightly esteemed
The land of Zebulun and the land of Naphtali,
And afterward more heavily oppressed *her*,
By the way of the sea, beyond the Jordan,
In Galilee of the Gentiles.

הִתְאַזְּרוּ וָחֹתּוּ
הִתְאַזְּרוּ וָחֹתּוּ:
10 עֻצוּ עֵצָה וְתֻפָר
דַּבְּרוּ דָבָר וְלֹא יָקוּם
כִּי עִמָּנוּ אֵל: ס

11 כִּי כֹה אָמַר יְהוָֹה אֵלַי כְּחֶזְקַת הַיָּד וְיִסְּרֵנִי
מִלֶּכֶת בְּדֶרֶךְ הָעָם־הַזֶּה לֵאמֹר: 12 לֹא־תֹאמְרוּן
קֶשֶׁר לְכֹל אֲשֶׁר־יֹאמַר הָעָם הַזֶּה קָשֶׁר וְאֶת־
מוֹרָאוֹ לֹא־תִירְאוּ וְלֹא תַעֲרִיצוּ: 13 אֶת־יְהוָֹה
צְבָאוֹת אֹתוֹ תַקְדִּישׁוּ וְהוּא מוֹרַאֲכֶם וְהוּא
מַעֲרִצְכֶם: 14 וְהָיָה לְמִקְדָּשׁ וּלְאֶבֶן נֶגֶף וּלְצוּר
מִכְשׁוֹל לִשְׁנֵי בָתֵּי יִשְׂרָאֵל לְפַח וּלְמוֹקֵשׁ לְיוֹשֵׁב
יְרוּשָׁלָםִ: 15 וְכָשְׁלוּ בָם רַבִּים וְנָפְלוּ וְנִשְׁבָּרוּ וְנוֹקְשׁוּ
וְנִלְכָּדוּ: ס 16 צוֹר תְּעוּדָה חֲתוֹם תּוֹרָה
בְּלִמֻּדָי: 17 וְחִכִּיתִי לַיהוָֹה הַמַּסְתִּיר פָּנָיו מִבֵּית
יַעֲקֹב וְקִוֵּיתִי־לוֹ: 18 הִנֵּה אָנֹכִי וְהַיְלָדִים אֲשֶׁר
נָתַן־לִי יְהוָֹה לְאֹתוֹת וּלְמוֹפְתִים בְּיִשְׂרָאֵל מֵעִם
יְהוָֹה צְבָאוֹת הַשֹּׁכֵן בְּהַר צִיּוֹן: ס 19 וְכִי־
יֹאמְרוּ אֲלֵיכֶם דִּרְשׁוּ אֶל־הָאֹבוֹת וְאֶל־הַיִּדְּעֹנִים
הַמְצַפְצְפִים וְהַמַּהְגִּים הֲלוֹא־עַם אֶל־אֱלֹהָיו יִדְרֹשׁ
בְּעַד הַחַיִּים אֶל־הַמֵּתִים: 20 לְתוֹרָה וְלִתְעוּדָה אִם־
לֹא יֹאמְרוּ כַּדָּבָר הַזֶּה אֲשֶׁר אֵין־לוֹ שָׁחַר: 21 וְעָבַר
בָּהּ נִקְשֶׁה וְרָעֵב וְהָיָה כִי־יִרְעַב וְהִתְקַצַּף וְקִלֵּל
בְּמַלְכּוֹ וּבֵאלֹהָיו וּפָנָה לְמָעְלָה: 22 וְאֶל־אֶרֶץ יַבִּיט
וְהִנֵּה צָרָה וַחֲשֵׁכָה מְעוּף צוּקָה וַאֲפֵלָה מְנֻדָּח:
23 כִּי לֹא מוּעָף לַאֲשֶׁר מוּצָק לָהּ כָּעֵת הָרִאשׁוֹן
הֵקַל אַרְצָה זְבֻלוּן וְאַרְצָה נַפְתָּלִי וְהָאַחֲרוֹן הִכְבִּיד
דֶּרֶךְ הַיָּם עֵבֶר הַיַּרְדֵּן גְּלִיל הַגּוֹיִם:

ט הָעָם הַהֹלְכִים בַּחֹשֶׁךְ
רָאוּ אוֹר גָּדוֹל
יֹשְׁבֵי בְּאֶרֶץ צַלְמָוֶת
אוֹר נָגַהּ עֲלֵיהֶם:

2 The people who walked in darkness
Have seen a great light;
Those who dwelt in the land of the shadow
   of death,
Upon them a light has shined.

3 You have multiplied the nation
And increased its joy;
They rejoice before You
According to the joy of harvest,
As *men* rejoice when they divide the spoil.

4 For You have broken the yoke of his burden
And the staff of his shoulder,
The rod of his oppressor,
As in the day of Midian.

5 For every warrior's sandal from the noisy
   battle,
And garments rolled in blood,
Will be used for burning *and* fuel of fire.

6 For unto us a Child is born,
Unto us a Son is given;
And the government will be upon His
   shoulder.
And His name will be called
Wonderful, Counselor, Mighty God,
Everlasting Father, Prince of Peace.

7 Of the increase of *His* government and peace
There will be no end,
Upon the throne of David and over His
   kingdom,
To order it and establish it with judgment
   and justice
From that time forward, even forever.
The zeal of the Lord of hosts will perform
   this.

8 The LORD sent a word against Jacob,
And it has fallen on Israel.
9 All the people will know—
Ephraim and the inhabitant of Samaria—
Who say in pride and arrogance of heart:
10 "The bricks have fallen down,
But we will rebuild with hewn stones;
The sycamores are cut down,
But we will replace *them* with cedars."
11 Therefore the LORD shall set up
The adversaries of Rezin against him,
And spur his enemies on,
12 The Syrians before and the Philistines
   behind;
And they shall devour Israel with an open
   mouth.

For all this His anger is not turned away,
But His hand *is* stretched out still.

הִרְבִּיתָ הַגּוֹי לֹא הִגְדַּלְתָּ הַשִּׂמְחָה 2
שָׂמְחוּ לְפָנֶיךָ כְּשִׂמְחַת בַּקָּצִיר
כַּאֲשֶׁר יָגִילוּ בְּחַלְּקָם שָׁלָל:

כִּי אֶת־עֹל סֻבֳּלוֹ 3
וְאֵת מַטֵּה שִׁכְמוֹ
שֵׁבֶט הַנֹּגֵשׂ בּוֹ
הַחִתֹּתָ כְּיוֹם מִדְיָן:

כִּי כָל־סְאוֹן סֹאֵן בְּרַעַשׁ 4
וְשִׂמְלָה מְגוֹלָלָה בְדָמִים
וְהָיְתָה לִשְׂרֵפָה מַאֲכֹלֶת אֵשׁ:

כִּי־יֶלֶד יֻלַּד־לָנוּ   בֵּן נִתַּן־לָנוּ 5
וַתְּהִי הַמִּשְׂרָה עַל־שִׁכְמוֹ
וַיִּקְרָא שְׁמוֹ
פֶּלֶא יוֹעֵץ אֵל גִּבּוֹר
אֲבִי־עַד שַׂר־שָׁלוֹם:

לְמַרְבֵּה הַמִּשְׂרָה 6
וּלְשָׁלוֹם אֵין־קֵץ
עַל־כִּסֵּא דָוִד וְעַל־מַמְלַכְתּוֹ
לְהָכִין אֹתָהּ וּלְסַעֲדָהּ
בְּמִשְׁפָּט וּבִצְדָקָה
מֵעַתָּה וְעַד־עוֹלָם
קִנְאַת יְהוָה צְבָאוֹת תַּעֲשֶׂה־זֹּאת: ס

דָּבָר שָׁלַח אֲדֹנָי בְּיַעֲקֹב 7
וְנָפַל בְּיִשְׂרָאֵל:

וְיָדְעוּ הָעָם כֻּלּוֹ 8
אֶפְרַיִם וְיוֹשֵׁב שֹׁמְרוֹן
בְּגַאֲוָה וּבְגֹדֶל לֵבָב לֵאמֹר:

לְבֵנִים נָפָלוּ וְגָזִית נִבְנֶה 9
שִׁקְמִים גֻּדָּעוּ וַאֲרָזִים נַחֲלִיף:

וַיְשַׂגֵּב יְהוָה אֶת־צָרֵי רְצִין עָלָיו 10
וְאֶת־אֹיְבָיו יְסַכְסֵךְ:

אֲרָם מִקֶּדֶם וּפְלִשְׁתִּים מֵאָחוֹר 11
וַיֹּאכְלוּ אֶת־יִשְׂרָאֵל בְּכָל־פֶּה
בְּכָל־זֹאת לֹא־שָׁב אַפּוֹ
וְעוֹד יָדוֹ נְטוּיָה:

13 For the people do not turn to Him who
    strikes them,
    Nor do they seek the LORD of hosts.

14 Therefore the LORD will cut off head and tail
    from Israel,
    Palm branch and bulrush in one day.

15 The elder and honorable, he *is* the head;
    The prophet who teaches lies, he *is* the tail.

16 For the leaders of this people cause *them* to
    err,
    And *those who are* led by them are destroyed.

17 Therefore the Lord will have no joy in their
    young men,
    Nor have mercy on their fatherless and
    widows;
    For everyone *is* a hypocrite and an evildoer,
    And every mouth speaks folly.

    For all this His anger is not turned away,
    But His hand *is* stretched out still.

18 For wickedness burns as the fire;
    It shall devour the briers and thorns,
    And kindle in the thickets of the forest;
    They shall mount up *like* rising smoke.

19 Through the wrath of the LORD of hosts
    The land is burned up,
    And the people shall be as fuel for the fire;
    No man shall spare his brother.

20 And he shall snatch on the right hand
    And be hungry;
    He shall devour on the left hand
    And not be satisfied;
    Every man shall eat the flesh of his own arm.

21 Manasseh *shall devour* Ephraim, and
    Ephraim Manasseh;
    Together they *shall be* against Judah.

    For all this His anger is not turned away,
    But His hand *is* stretched out still.

10

    "Woe to those who decree unrighteous
    decrees,
    Who write misfortune,
    Which they have prescribed

2 To rob the needy of justice,
    And to take what is right from the poor of
    My people,
    That widows may be their prey,
    And *that* they may rob the fatherless.

3 What will you do in the day of punishment,
    And in the desolation *which* will come from
    afar?
    To whom will you flee for help?
    And where will you leave your glory?

12 וְהָעָם לֹא־שָׁב עַד־הַמַּכֵּהוּ
  וְאֶת־יְהוָה צְבָאוֹת לֹא דָרָשׁוּ: ס

13 וַיַּכְרֵת יְהוָה מִיִּשְׂרָאֵל רֹאשׁ וְזָנָב
  כִּפָּה וְאַגְמוֹן יוֹם אֶחָד:

14 זָקֵן וּנְשׂוּא־פָנִים הוּא הָרֹאשׁ
  וְנָבִיא מוֹרֶה־שֶּׁקֶר הוּא הַזָּנָב:

15 וַיִּהְיוּ מְאַשְּׁרֵי הָעָם־הַזֶּה מַתְעִים
  וּמְאֻשָּׁרָיו מְבֻלָּעִים:

16 עַל־כֵּן עַל־בַּחוּרָיו
  לֹא־יִשְׂמַח ׀ אֲדֹנָי
  וְאֶת־יְתֹמָיו וְאֶת־אַלְמְנֹתָיו לֹא יְרַחֵם
  כִּי כֻלּוֹ חָנֵף וּמֵרַע
  וְכָל־פֶּה דֹּבֵר נְבָלָה
  בְּכָל־זֹאת לֹא־שָׁב אַפּוֹ
  וְעוֹד יָדוֹ נְטוּיָה:

17 כִּי־בָעֲרָה כָאֵשׁ רִשְׁעָה
  שָׁמִיר וָשַׁיִת תֹּאכֵל
  וַתִּצַּת בְּסִבְכֵי הַיַּעַר
  וַיִּתְאַבְּכוּ גֵּאוּת עָשָׁן:

18 בְּעֶבְרַת יְהוָה צְבָאוֹת נֶעְתַּם אָרֶץ
  וַיְהִי הָעָם כְּמַאֲכֹלֶת אֵשׁ
  אִישׁ אֶל־אָחִיו לֹא יַחְמֹלוּ:

19 וַיִּגְזֹר עַל־יָמִין וְרָעֵב
  וַיֹּאכַל עַל־שְׂמֹאול וְלֹא שָׂבֵעוּ
  אִישׁ בְּשַׂר־זְרֹעוֹ יֹאכֵלוּ:

20 מְנַשֶּׁה אֶת־אֶפְרַיִם
  וְאֶפְרַיִם אֶת־מְנַשֶּׁה
  יַחְדָּו הֵמָּה עַל־יְהוּדָה
  בְּכָל־זֹאת לֹא־שָׁב אַפּוֹ
  וְעוֹד יָדוֹ נְטוּיָה: ס

י
  הוֹי הַחֹקְקִים חִקְקֵי־אָוֶן
  וּמְכַתְּבִים עָמָל כִּתֵּבוּ:

2 לְהַטּוֹת מִדִּין דַּלִּים
  וְלִגְזֹל מִשְׁפַּט עֲנִיֵּי עַמִּי
  לִהְיוֹת אַלְמָנוֹת שְׁלָלָם
  וְאֶת־יְתוֹמִים יָבֹזּוּ:

3 וּמַה־תַּעֲשׂוּ לְיוֹם פְּקֻדָּה
  וּלְשׁוֹאָה מִמֶּרְחָק תָּבוֹא
  עַל־מִי תָּנוּסוּ לְעֶזְרָה
  וְאָנָה תַעַזְבוּ כְּבוֹדְכֶם:

⁴ Without Me they shall bow down among the
      prisoners,
    And they shall fall among the slain."

    For all this His anger is not turned away,
    But His hand is stretched out still.

⁵ "Woe to Assyria, the rod of My anger
    And the staff in whose hand is My indigna-
      tion.
⁶ I will send him against an ungodly nation,
    And against the people of My wrath
    I will give him charge,
    To seize the spoil, to take the prey,
    And to tread them down like the mire of the
      streets.
⁷ Yet he does not mean so,
    Nor does his heart think so;
    But it is in his heart to destroy,
    And cut off not a few nations.
⁸ For he says,
    'Are not my princes altogether kings?
⁹ Is not Calno like Carchemish?
    Is not Hamath like Arpad?
    Is not Samaria like Damascus?
¹⁰ As my hand has found the kingdoms of the
      idols,
    Whose carved images excelled those of
      Jerusalem and Samaria,
¹¹ As I have done to Samaria and her idols,
    Shall I not do also to Jerusalem and her
      idols?' "

¹² Therefore it shall come to pass, when the Lord
has performed all His work on Mount Zion and on
Jerusalem, that He will say, "I will punish the fruit
of the arrogant heart of the king of Assyria, and the
glory of his haughty looks."
¹³ For he says:

    "By the strength of my hand I have done it,
    And by my wisdom, for I am prudent;
    Also I have removed the boundaries of the
      people,
    And have robbed their treasuries;
    So I have put down the inhabitants like a
      valiant man.
¹⁴ My hand has found like a nest the riches of
      the people,
    And as one gathers eggs that are left,
    I have gathered all the earth;
    And there was no one who moved his wing,
    Nor opened his mouth with even a peep."

¹⁵ Shall the ax boast itself against him who
      chops with it?

בִּלְתִּי כָרַע תַּחַת אַסִּיר ⁴
וְתַחַת הֲרוּגִים יִפֹּלוּ
בְּכָל־זֹאת לֹא־שָׁב אַפּוֹ
וְעוֹד יָדוֹ נְטוּיָה: ס

הוֹי אַשּׁוּר שֵׁבֶט אַפִּי ⁵
וּמַטֶּה־הוּא בְיָדָם זַעְמִי:
בְּגוֹי חָנֵף אֲשַׁלְּחֶנּוּ ⁶
וְעַל־עַם עֶבְרָתִי אֲצַוֶּנּוּ
לִשְׁלֹל שָׁלָל וְלָבֹז בַּז
וּלְשִׂימוֹ מִרְמָס כְּחֹמֶר חוּצוֹת:
וְהוּא לֹא־כֵן יְדַמֶּה ⁷
וּלְבָבוֹ לֹא־כֵן יַחְשֹׁב
כִּי לְהַשְׁמִיד בִּלְבָבוֹ
וּלְהַכְרִית גּוֹיִם לֹא מְעָט:
כִּי יֹאמַר ⁸
הֲלֹא שָׂרַי יַחְדָּו מְלָכִים:
הֲלֹא כְּכַרְכְּמִישׁ כַּלְנוֹ ⁹
אִם־לֹא כְאַרְפַּד חֲמָת
אִם־לֹא כְדַמֶּשֶׂק שֹׁמְרוֹן:
כַּאֲשֶׁר מָצְאָה יָדִי לְמַמְלְכֹת הָאֱלִיל ¹⁰
וּפְסִילֵיהֶם מִירוּשָׁלַ͏ִם וּמִשֹּׁמְרוֹן:
הֲלֹא כַּאֲשֶׁר עָשִׂיתִי ¹¹
לְשֹׁמְרוֹן וְלֶאֱלִילֶיהָ
כֵּן אֶעֱשֶׂה לִירוּשָׁלַ͏ִם וְלַעֲצַבֶּיהָ: ס

וְהָיָה כִּי־יְבַצַּע אֲדֹנָי אֶת־כָּל־מַעֲשֵׂהוּ בְּהַר צִיּוֹן ¹²
וּבִירוּשָׁלָ͏ִם אֶפְקֹד עַל־פְּרִי־גֹדֶל לְבַב מֶלֶךְ־אַשּׁוּר
וְעַל־תִּפְאֶרֶת רוּם עֵינָיו:
כִּי אָמַר ¹³
בְּכֹחַ יָדִי עָשִׂיתִי
וּבְחָכְמָתִי כִּי נְבֻנוֹתִי
וְאָסִיר ׀ גְּבוּלֹת עַמִּים
וַעֲתִידֹתֵיהֶם שׁוֹשֵׂתִי
וְאוֹרִיד כַּאבִּיר יוֹשְׁבִים:
וַתִּמְצָא כַקֵּן ׀ יָדִי לְחֵיל הָעַמִּים ¹⁴
וְכֶאֱסֹף בֵּיצִים עֲזֻבוֹת
כָּל־הָאָרֶץ אֲנִי אָסָפְתִּי
וְלֹא הָיָה נֹדֵד כָּנָף
וּפֹצֶה פֶה וּמְצַפְצֵף:
הֲיִתְפָּאֵר הַגַּרְזֶן עַל הַחֹצֵב בּוֹ ¹⁵
אִם־יִתְגַּדֵּל הַמַּשּׂוֹר עַל־מְנִיפוֹ

י ⁶   וּלְשׂוּמוֹ   13   וַעֲתוּדוֹתֵיהֶם   כְּבִיר

Or shall the saw exalt itself against him who
  saws with it?
As if a rod could wield *itself* against those
  who lift it up,
Or as if a staff could lift up, *as if it were* not
  wood!

16 Therefore the Lord, the Lord of hosts,
  Will send leanness among his fat ones;
  And under his glory
  He will kindle a burning
  Like the burning of a fire.

17 So the Light of Israel will be for a fire,
  And his Holy One for a flame;
  It will burn and devour
  His thorns and his briers in one day.

18 And it will consume the glory of his forest
  and of his fruitful field,
  Both soul and body;
  And they will be as when a sick man wastes
  away.

19 Then the rest of the trees of his forest
  Will be so few in number
  That a child may write them.

20 And it shall come to pass in that day
  That the remnant of Israel,
  And such as have escaped of the house of
    Jacob,
  Will never again depend on him who
    defeated them,
  But will depend on the LORD, the Holy One
    of Israel, in truth.

21 The remnant will return, the remnant of
    Jacob,
  To the Mighty God.

22 For though your people, O Israel, be as the
    sand of the sea,
  A remnant of them will return;
  The destruction decreed shall overflow with
    righteousness.

23 For the Lord GOD of hosts
  Will make a determined end
  In the midst of all the land.

24 Therefore thus says the Lord GOD of hosts: "O
My people, who dwell in Zion, do not be afraid of
the Assyrian. He shall strike you with a rod and lift
up his staff against you, in the manner of Egypt.
25 For yet a very little while and the indignation will
cease, as will My anger in their destruction." 26 And
the LORD of hosts will stir up a scourge for him like
the slaughter of Midian at the rock of Oreb; *as* His
rod was on the sea, so will He lift it up in the
manner of Egypt.

27 It shall come to pass in that day

כְּהָנִיף שֵׁבֶט וְאֶת־מְרִימָיו
כְּהָרִים מַטֶּה לֹא־עֵץ:
16 לָכֵן יְשַׁלַּח הָאָדוֹן
יְהוָה צְבָאוֹת בְּמִשְׁמַנָּיו רָזוֹן
וְתַחַת כְּבֹדוֹ
יֵקַד יְקֹד כִּיקוֹד אֵשׁ:
17 וְהָיָה אוֹר־יִשְׂרָאֵל לְאֵשׁ
וּקְדוֹשׁוֹ לְלֶהָבָה
וּבָעֲרָה וְאָכְלָה
שִׁיתוֹ וּשְׁמִירוֹ בְּיוֹם אֶחָד:
18 וּכְבוֹד יַעְרוֹ וְכַרְמִלּוֹ
מִנֶּפֶשׁ וְעַד־בָּשָׂר יְכַלֶּה
וְהָיָה כִּמְסֹס נֹסֵס:
19 וּשְׁאָר עֵץ יַעְרוֹ מִסְפָּר יִהְיוּ
וְנַעַר יִכְתְּבֵם:
פ
20 וְהָיָה ׀ בַּיּוֹם הַהוּא
לֹא־יוֹסִיף עוֹד
שְׁאָר יִשְׂרָאֵל
וּפְלֵיטַת בֵּית־יַעֲקֹב
לְהִשָּׁעֵן עַל־מַכֵּהוּ
וְנִשְׁעַן עַל־יְהוָה
קְדוֹשׁ יִשְׂרָאֵל בֶּאֱמֶת:
21 שְׁאָר יָשׁוּב שְׁאָר יַעֲקֹב
אֶל־אֵל גִּבּוֹר:
22 כִּי אִם־יִהְיֶה
עַמְּךָ יִשְׂרָאֵל כְּחוֹל הַיָּם
שְׁאָר יָשׁוּב בּוֹ
כִּלָּיוֹן חָרוּץ שׁוֹטֵף צְדָקָה:
23 כִּי כָלָה וְנֶחֱרָצָה
אֲדֹנָי יְהֹוִה צְבָאוֹת
עֹשֶׂה בְּקֶרֶב כָּל־הָאָרֶץ:
ס
24 לָכֵן כֹּה־אָמַר אֲדֹנָי יְהוָה צְבָאוֹת אַל־תִּירָא עַמִּי
יֹשֵׁב צִיּוֹן מֵאַשּׁוּר בַּשֵּׁבֶט יַכֶּכָּה וּמַטֵּהוּ יִשָּׂא־עָלֶיךָ
בְּדֶרֶךְ מִצְרָיִם: 25 כִּי־עוֹד מְעַט מִזְעָר וְכָלָה זַעַם
וְאַפִּי עַל־תַּבְלִיתָם: 26 וְעוֹרֵר עָלָיו יְהוָה צְבָאוֹת
שׁוֹט כְּמַכַּת מִדְיָן בְּצוּר עוֹרֵב וּמַטֵּהוּ עַל־הַיָּם
וּנְשָׂאוֹ בְּדֶרֶךְ מִצְרָיִם:
27 וְהָיָה ׀ בַּיּוֹם הַהוּא

That his burden will be taken away from
    your shoulder,
And his yoke from your neck,
And the yoke will be destroyed because of
    the anointing oil.

28 He has come to Aiath,
    He has passed Migron;
    At Michmash he has attended to his equip-
    ment.

29 They have gone along the ridge,
    They have taken up lodging at Geba.
    Ramah is afraid,
    Gibeah of Saul has fled.

30 Lift up your voice,
    O daughter of Gallim!
    Cause it to be heard as far as Laish—
    O poor Anathoth!

31 Madmenah has fled,
    The inhabitants of Gebim seek refuge.

32 As yet he will remain at Nob that day;
    He will shake his fist at the mount of the
    daughter of Zion,
    The hill of Jerusalem.

33 Behold, the Lord,
    The LORD of hosts,
    Will lop off the bough with terror;
    Those of high stature *will be* hewn down,
    And the haughty will be humbled.

34 He will cut down the thickets of the forest
    with iron,
    And Lebanon will fall by the Mighty One.

11 There shall come forth a Rod from the stem
    of Jesse,
    And a Branch shall grow out of his roots.

2 The Spirit of the LORD shall rest upon Him,
    The Spirit of wisdom and understanding,
    The Spirit of counsel and might,
    The Spirit of knowledge and of the fear of
    the LORD.

3 His delight *is* in the fear of the LORD,
    And He shall not judge by the sight of His
    eyes,
    Nor decide by the hearing of His ears;

4 But with righteousness He shall judge the
    poor,
    And decide with equity for the meek of the
    earth;
    He shall strike the earth with the rod of His
    mouth,
    And with the breath of His lips He shall slay
    the wicked.

יָסוּר סֻבֳּלוֹ מֵעַל שִׁכְמֶךָ
וְעֻלּוֹ מֵעַל צַוָּארֶךָ
וְחֻבַּל עֹל מִפְּנֵי־שָׁמֶן:

28 בָּא עַל־עַיַּת עָבַר בְּמִגְרוֹן
לְמִכְמָשׂ יַפְקִיד כֵּלָיו:

29 עָבְרוּ מַעְבָּרָה
גֶּבַע מָלוֹן לָנוּ
חָרְדָה הָרָמָה
גִּבְעַת שָׁאוּל נָסָה:

30 צַהֲלִי קוֹלֵךְ בַּת־גַּלִּים
הַקְשִׁיבִי לַיְשָׁה עֲנִיָּה עֲנָתוֹת:

31 נָדְדָה מַדְמֵנָה
יֹשְׁבֵי הַגֵּבִים הֵעִיזוּ:

32 עוֹד הַיּוֹם בְּנֹב לַעֲמֹד
יְנֹפֵף יָדוֹ הַר בֵּית־ק צִיּוֹן
גִּבְעַת יְרוּשָׁלָ͏ִם: ס

33 הִנֵּה הָאָדוֹן יְהֹוָה צְבָאוֹת
מְסָעֵף פֻּארָה בְּמַעֲרָצָה
וְרָמֵי הַקּוֹמָה גְּדוּעִים
וְהַגְּבֹהִים יִשְׁפָּלוּ:

34 וְנִקַּף סִבְכֵי הַיַּעַר בַּבַּרְזֶל
וְהַלְּבָנוֹן בְּאַדִּיר יִפּוֹל: ס

יא וְיָצָא חֹטֶר מִגֵּזַע יִשָׁי
וְנֵצֶר מִשָּׁרָשָׁיו יִפְרֶה:

2 וְנָחָה עָלָיו רוּחַ יְהֹוָה
רוּחַ חָכְמָה וּבִינָה
רוּחַ עֵצָה וּגְבוּרָה
רוּחַ דַּעַת וְיִרְאַת יְהֹוָה:

3 וַהֲרִיחוֹ בְּיִרְאַת יְהֹוָה
וְלֹא־לְמַרְאֵה עֵינָיו יִשְׁפּוֹט
וְלֹא־לְמִשְׁמַע אָזְנָיו יוֹכִיחַ:

4 וְשָׁפַט בְּצֶדֶק דַּלִּים
וְהוֹכִיחַ בְּמִישׁוֹר לְעַנְוֵי־אָרֶץ
וְהִכָּה־אֶרֶץ בְּשֵׁבֶט פִּיו
וּבְרוּחַ שְׂפָתָיו יָמִית רָשָׁע:

32 ' בֵּת־

5 Righteousness shall be the belt of His loins,
And faithfulness the belt of His waist.

6 "The wolf also shall dwell with the lamb,
The leopard shall lie down with the young goat,
The calf and the young lion and the fatling together;
And a little child shall lead them.

7 The cow and the bear shall graze;
Their young ones shall lie down together;
And the lion shall eat straw like the ox.

8 The nursing child shall play by the cobra's hole,
And the weaned child shall put his hand in the viper's den.

9 They shall not hurt nor destroy in all My holy mountain,
For the earth shall be full of the knowledge of the LORD
As the waters cover the sea.

10 "And in that day there shall be a Root of Jesse,
Who shall stand as a banner to the people;
For the Gentiles shall seek Him,
And His resting place shall be glorious."

11 It shall come to pass in that day
That the Lord shall set His hand again the second time
To recover the remnant of His people who are left,
From Assyria and Egypt,
From Pathros and Cush,
From Elam and Shinar,
From Hamath and the islands of the sea.

12 He will set up a banner for the nations,
And will assemble the outcasts of Israel,
And gather together the dispersed of Judah
From the four corners of the earth.

13 Also the envy of Ephraim shall depart,
And the adversaries of Judah shall be cut off;
Ephraim shall not envy Judah,
And Judah shall not harass Ephraim.

14 But they shall fly down upon the shoulder of the Philistines toward the west;
Together they shall plunder the people of the East;
They shall lay their hand on Edom and Moab;
And the people of Ammon shall obey them.

15 The LORD will utterly destroy the tongue of the Sea of Egypt;

וְהָיָה צֶדֶק אֵזוֹר מָתְנָיו 5
וְהָאֱמוּנָה אֵזוֹר חֲלָצָיו:

וְגָר זְאֵב עִם־כֶּבֶשׂ 6
וְנָמֵר עִם־גְּדִי יִרְבָּץ
וְעֵגֶל וּכְפִיר וּמְרִיא יַחְדָּו
וְנַעַר קָטֹן נֹהֵג בָּם:

וּפָרָה וָדֹב תִּרְעֶינָה 7
יַחְדָּו יִרְבְּצוּ יַלְדֵיהֶן
וְאַרְיֵה כַּבָּקָר יֹאכַל־תֶּבֶן:

וְשִׁעֲשַׁע יוֹנֵק עַל־חֻר פָּתֶן 8
וְעַל מְאוּרַת צִפְעוֹנִי גָּמוּל יָדוֹ הָדָה:

לֹא־יָרֵעוּ וְלֹא־יַשְׁחִיתוּ 9
בְּכָל־הַר קָדְשִׁי
כִּי־מָלְאָה הָאָרֶץ דֵּעָה אֶת־יְהֹוָה
כַּמַּיִם לַיָּם מְכַסִּים: פ

וְהָיָה בַּיּוֹם הַהוּא 10
שֹׁרֶשׁ יִשַׁי אֲשֶׁר עֹמֵד לְנֵס עַמִּים
אֵלָיו גּוֹיִם יִדְרֹשׁוּ
וְהָיְתָה מְנֻחָתוֹ כָּבוֹד: פ

וְהָיָה בַּיּוֹם הַהוּא 11
יוֹסִיף אֲדֹנָי שֵׁנִית יָדוֹ
לִקְנוֹת אֶת־שְׁאָר עַמּוֹ
אֲשֶׁר יִשָּׁאֵר מֵאַשּׁוּר וּמִמִּצְרַיִם
וּמִפַּתְרוֹס וּמִכּוּשׁ וּמֵעֵילָם
וּמִשִּׁנְעָר וּמֵחֲמָת וּמֵאִיֵּי הַיָּם:

וְנָשָׂא נֵס לַגּוֹיִם 12
וְאָסַף נִדְחֵי יִשְׂרָאֵל
וּנְפֻצוֹת יְהוּדָה יְקַבֵּץ
מֵאַרְבַּע כַּנְפוֹת הָאָרֶץ:

וְסָרָה קִנְאַת אֶפְרַיִם 13
וְצֹרְרֵי יְהוּדָה יִכָּרֵתוּ
אֶפְרַיִם לֹא־יְקַנֵּא אֶת־יְהוּדָה
וִיהוּדָה לֹא־יָצֹר אֶת־אֶפְרָיִם:

וְעָפוּ בְכָתֵף פְּלִשְׁתִּים יָמָה 14
יַחְדָּו יָבֹזּוּ אֶת־בְּנֵי־קֶדֶם
אֱדוֹם וּמוֹאָב מִשְׁלוֹחַ יָדָם
וּבְנֵי עַמּוֹן מִשְׁמַעְתָּם:

וְהֶחֱרִים יְהֹוָה אֵת לְשׁוֹן יָם־מִצְרַיִם 15

With His mighty wind He will shake His fist
    over the River,
And strike it in the seven streams,
And make *men* cross over dryshod.

16 There will be a highway for the remnant of
    His people
Who will be left from Assyria,
As it was for Israel
In the day that he came up from the land of
    Egypt.

12 And in that day you will say:

"O LORD, I will praise You;
Though You were angry with me,
Your anger is turned away, and You comfort
    me.

2 Behold, God *is* my salvation,
I will trust and not be afraid;
'For YAH, the LORD, *is* my strength and song;
He also has become my salvation.'"

3 Therefore with joy you will draw water
From the wells of salvation.

4 And in that day you will say:

"Praise the LORD, call upon His name;
Declare His deeds among the peoples,
Make mention that His name is exalted.

5 Sing to the LORD,
For He has done excellent things;
This *is* known in all the earth.

6 Cry out and shout, O inhabitant of Zion,
For great *is* the Holy One of Israel in your
    midst!"

13 The burden against Babylon which Isaiah the
son of Amoz saw.

2 "Lift up a banner on the high mountain,
Raise your voice to them;
Wave your hand, that they may enter the
    gates of the nobles.

3 I have commanded My sanctified ones;
I have also called My mighty ones for My
    anger—
Those who rejoice in My exaltation."

4 The noise of a multitude in the mountains,
Like that of many people!
A tumultuous noise of the kingdoms of
    nations gathered together!
The LORD of hosts musters
The army for battle.

5 They come from a far country,
From the end of heaven—

וְהֵנִיף יָדוֹ עַל־הַנָּהָר בַּעְיָם רוּחוֹ
וְהִכָּהוּ לְשִׁבְעָה נְחָלִים
וְהִדְרִיךְ בַּנְּעָלִים:

16 וְהָיְתָה מְסִלָּה לִשְׁאָר עַמּוֹ
אֲשֶׁר יִשָּׁאֵר מֵאַשּׁוּר
כַּאֲשֶׁר הָיְתָה לְיִשְׂרָאֵל
בְּיוֹם עֲלֹתוֹ מֵאֶרֶץ מִצְרָיִם:

יב וְאָמַרְתָּ בַּיּוֹם הַהוּא
אוֹדְךָ יְהוָה כִּי אָנַפְתָּ בִּי
יָשֹׁב אַפְּךָ וּתְנַחֲמֵנִי:
2 הִנֵּה אֵל יְשׁוּעָתִי
אֶבְטַח וְלֹא אֶפְחָד
כִּי־עָזִּי וְזִמְרָת יָהּ יְהוָה
וַיְהִי־לִי לִישׁוּעָה:
3 וּשְׁאַבְתֶּם־מַיִם בְּשָׂשׂוֹן
מִמַּעַיְנֵי הַיְשׁוּעָה:
4 וַאֲמַרְתֶּם בַּיּוֹם הַהוּא
הוֹדוּ לַיהוָה קִרְאוּ בִשְׁמוֹ
הוֹדִיעוּ בָעַמִּים עֲלִילֹתָיו
הַזְכִּירוּ כִּי נִשְׂגָּב שְׁמוֹ:
5 זַמְּרוּ יְהוָה כִּי גֵאוּת עָשָׂה
מֵידַעַת זֹאת בְּכָל־הָאָרֶץ:
6 צַהֲלִי וָרֹנִּי יוֹשֶׁבֶת צִיּוֹן
כִּי־גָדוֹל בְּקִרְבֵּךְ קְדוֹשׁ יִשְׂרָאֵל:

יג מַשָּׂא בָּבֶל אֲשֶׁר חָזָה יְשַׁעְיָהוּ בֶּן־אָמוֹץ:
2 עַל הַר־נִשְׁפֶּה שְׂאוּ־נֵס
הָרִימוּ קוֹל לָהֶם
הָנִיפוּ יָד וְיָבֹאוּ פִּתְחֵי נְדִיבִים:
3 אֲנִי צִוֵּיתִי לִמְקֻדָּשָׁי
גַּם קָרָאתִי גִבּוֹרַי לְאַפִּי
עַלִּיזֵי גַּאֲוָתִי:
4 קוֹל הָמוֹן בֶּהָרִים
דְּמוּת עַם־רָב
קוֹל שְׁאוֹן מַמְלְכוֹת גּוֹיִם נֶאֱסָפִים
יְהוָה צְבָאוֹת מְפַקֵּד
צְבָא מִלְחָמָה:
5 בָּאִים מֵאֶרֶץ מֶרְחָק
מִקְצֵה הַשָּׁמָיִם

The LORD and His weapons of indignation,
To destroy the whole land.

יְהֹוָה וּכְלֵי זַעְמֹו
לְחַבֵּל כָּל־הָאָֽרֶץ׃

6 Wail, for the day of the LORD *is* at hand!
It will come as destruction from the Almighty.

6 הֵילִ֕ילוּ כִּ֥י קָרֹ֖וב יֹ֣ום יְהֹוָ֑ה
כְּשֹׁ֖ד מִשַּׁדַּ֥י יָבֹֽוא׃

7 Therefore all hands will be limp,
Every man's heart will melt,

7 עַל־כֵּ֖ן כָּל־יָדַ֣יִם תִּרְפֶּ֑ינָה
וְכָל־לְבַ֥ב אֱנֹ֖ושׁ יִמָּֽס׃

8 And they will be afraid.
Pangs and sorrows will take hold of *them;*
They will be in pain as a woman in
childbirth;
They will be amazed at one another;
Their faces *will be like* flames.

8 וְֽנִבְהָ֓לוּ ׀ צִירִ֤ים וַֽחֲבָלִים֙ יֹֽאחֵז֔וּן
כַּיֹּֽולֵדָ֖ה יְחִיל֑וּן
אִ֤ישׁ אֶל־רֵעֵ֨הוּ֙ יִתְמָ֔הוּ
פְּנֵ֥י לְהָבִ֖ים פְּנֵיהֶֽם׃

9 Behold, the day of the LORD comes,
Cruel, with both wrath and fierce anger,
To lay the land desolate;
And He will destroy its sinners from it.

9 הִנֵּ֤ה יֹום־יְהֹוָה֙ בָּ֔א
אַכְזָרִ֥י וְעֶבְרָ֖ה וַחֲרֹ֣ון אָ֑ף
לָשׂ֤וּם הָאָ֨רֶץ֙ לְשַׁמָּ֔ה
וְחַטָּאֶ֖יהָ יַשְׁמִ֥יד מִמֶּֽנָּה׃

10 For the stars of heaven and their constella-
tions
Will not give their light;
The sun will be darkened in its going forth,
And the moon will not cause its light to
shine.

10 כִּֽי־כֹוכְבֵ֤י הַשָּׁמַ֨יִם֙ וּכְסִ֣ילֵיהֶ֔ם
לֹ֥א יָהֵ֖לּוּ אֹורָ֑ם
חָשַׁ֤ךְ הַשֶּׁ֨מֶשׁ֙ בְּצֵאתֹ֔ו
וְיָרֵ֖חַ לֹא־יַגִּ֥יהַ אֹורֹֽו׃

11 "I will punish the world for *its* evil,
And the wicked for their iniquity;
I will halt the arrogance of the proud,
And will lay low the haughtiness of the
terrible.

11 וּפָקַדְתִּ֤י עַל־תֵּבֵל֙ רָעָ֔ה
וְעַל־רְשָׁעִ֖ים עֲוֹנָ֑ם
וְהִשְׁבַּתִּי֙ גְּאֹ֣ון זֵדִ֔ים
וְגַאֲוַ֥ת עָרִיצִ֖ים אַשְׁפִּֽיל׃

12 I will make a mortal more rare than fine
gold,
A man more than the golden wedge of Ophir.

12 אֹוקִ֥יר אֱנֹ֖ושׁ מִפָּ֑ז
וְאָדָ֖ם מִכֶּ֥תֶם אֹופִֽיר׃

13 Therefore I will shake the heavens,
And the earth will move out of her place,
In the wrath of the LORD of hosts
And in the day of His fierce anger.

13 עַל־כֵּן֙ שָׁמַ֣יִם אַרְגִּ֔יז
וְתִרְעַ֥שׁ הָאָ֖רֶץ מִמְּקֹומָ֑הּ
בְּעֶבְרַת֙ יְהֹוָ֣ה צְבָאֹ֔ות
וּבְיֹ֖ום חֲרֹ֥ון אַפֹּֽו׃

14 It shall be as the hunted gazelle,
And as a sheep that no man takes up;
Every man will turn to his own people,
And everyone will flee to his own land.

14 וְהָיָה֙ כִּצְבִ֣י מֻדָּ֔ח
וּכְצֹ֖אן וְאֵ֣ין מְקַבֵּ֑ץ
אִ֤ישׁ אֶל־עַמֹּו֙ יִפְנ֔וּ
וְאִ֥ישׁ אֶל־אַרְצֹ֖ו יָנֽוּסוּ׃

15 Everyone who is found will be thrust
through,
And everyone who is captured will fall by the
sword.

15 כָּל־הַנִּמְצָ֖א יִדָּקֵ֑ר
וְכָל־הַנִּסְפֶּ֖ה יִפֹּ֥ול בֶּחָֽרֶב׃

16 Their children also will be dashed to pieces
before their eyes;
Their houses will be plundered
And their wives ravished.

16 וְעֹלְלֵיהֶ֥ם יְרֻטְּשׁ֖וּ לְעֵֽינֵיהֶ֑ם
יִשַּׁ֨סּוּ֙ בָּ֣תֵּיהֶ֔ם
וּנְשֵׁיהֶ֖ם תשגלנה תִּשָּׁכַֽבְנָה׃

17 "Behold, I will stir up the Medes against them,
Who will not regard silver;
And *as for* gold, they will not delight in it.

17 הִנְנִ֛י מֵעִ֥יר עֲלֵיהֶ֖ם אֶת־מָדָ֑י
אֲשֶׁר־כֶּ֨סֶף֙ לֹ֣א יַחְשֹׁ֔בוּ
וְזָהָ֖ב לֹ֥א יַחְפְּצוּ־בֹֽו׃

18 Also *their* bows will dash the young men to
pieces,

18 וּקְשָׁתֹ֖ות נְעָרִ֣ים תְּרַטַּשְׁ֑נָה

And they will have no pity on the fruit of the
  womb;
  Their eye will not spare children.
19 And Babylon, the glory of kingdoms,
  The beauty of the Chaldeans' pride,
  Will be as when God overthrew Sodom and
  Gomorrah.
20 It will never be inhabited,
  Nor will it be settled from generation to
  generation;
  Nor will the Arabian pitch tents there,
  Nor will the shepherds make their sheepfolds
  there.
21 But wild beasts of the desert will lie there,
  And their houses will be full of owls;
  Ostriches will dwell there,
  And wild goats will caper there.
22 The hyenas will howl in their citadels,
  And jackals in their pleasant palaces.
  Her time *is* near to come,
  And her days will not be prolonged."

14 For the LORD will have mercy on Jacob, and
will still choose Israel, and settle them in their own
land. The strangers will be joined with them, and
they will cling to the house of Jacob. 2 Then people
will take them and bring them to their place, and
the house of Israel will possess them for servants
and maids in the land of the LORD; they will take
them captive whose captives they were, and rule
over their oppressors.

3 It shall come to pass in the day the LORD gives
you rest from your sorrow, and from your fear and
the hard bondage in which you were made to serve,
4 that you will take up this proverb against the king
of Babylon, and say:

"How the oppressor has ceased,
  The golden city ceased!
5 The LORD has broken the staff of the wicked,
  The scepter of the rulers;
6 He who struck the people in wrath with a
  continual stroke,
  He who ruled the nations in anger,
  Is persecuted *and* no one hinders.
7 The whole earth is at rest *and* quiet;
  They break forth into singing.
8 Indeed the cypress trees rejoice over you,
  And the cedars of Lebanon,
  Saying, 'Since you were cut down,
  No woodsman has come up against us.'
9 "Hell from beneath is excited about you,
  To meet *you* at your coming;
  It stirs up the dead for you,

וּפְרִי־בֶטֶן לֹא יְרַחֵמוּ
עַל־בָּנִים לֹא־תָחוּס עֵינָם:
19 וְהָיְתָה בָבֶל צְבִי מַמְלָכוֹת
תִּפְאֶרֶת גְּאוֹן כַּשְׂדִּים
כְּמַהְפֵּכַת אֱלֹהִים
אֶת־סְדֹם וְאֶת־עֲמֹרָה:
20 לֹא־תֵשֵׁב לָנֶצַח
וְלֹא תִשְׁכֹּן עַד־דּוֹר וָדוֹר
וְלֹא־יַהֵל שָׁם עֲרָבִי
וְרֹעִים לֹא־יַרְבִּצוּ שָׁם:
21 וְרָבְצוּ־שָׁם צִיִּים
וּמָלְאוּ בָתֵּיהֶם אֹחִים
וְשָׁכְנוּ שָׁם בְּנוֹת יַעֲנָה
וּשְׂעִירִים יְרַקְּדוּ־שָׁם:
22 וְעָנָה אִיִּים בְּאַלְמְנוֹתָיו
וְתַנִּים בְּהֵיכְלֵי עֹנֶג
וְקָרוֹב לָבוֹא עִתָּהּ
וְיָמֶיהָ לֹא יִמָּשֵׁכוּ:

יד כִּי יְרַחֵם יְהוָה אֶת־יַעֲקֹב וּבָחַר עוֹד בְּיִשְׂרָאֵל
וְהִנִּיחָם עַל־אַדְמָתָם וְנִלְוָה הַגֵּר עֲלֵיהֶם וְנִסְפְּחוּ
עַל־בֵּית יַעֲקֹב: 2 וּלְקָחוּם עַמִּים וֶהֱבִיאוּם אֶל־
מְקוֹמָם וְהִתְנַחֲלוּם בֵּית־יִשְׂרָאֵל עַל אַדְמַת יְהוָה
לַעֲבָדִים וְלִשְׁפָחוֹת וְהָיוּ שֹׁבִים לְשֹׁבֵיהֶם וְרָדוּ
בְּנֹגְשֵׂיהֶם: ס 3 וְהָיָה בְּיוֹם הָנִיחַ יְהוָה לְךָ
מֵעָצְבְּךָ וּמֵרָגְזֶךָ וּמִן־הָעֲבֹדָה הַקָּשָׁה אֲשֶׁר עֻבַּד־
בָּךְ: 4 וְנָשָׂאתָ הַמָּשָׁל הַזֶּה עַל־מֶלֶךְ בָּבֶל וְאָמָרְתָּ
אֵיךְ שָׁבַת נֹגֵשׂ שָׁבְתָה מַדְהֵבָה:
5 שָׁבַר יְהוָה מַטֵּה רְשָׁעִים
שֵׁבֶט מֹשְׁלִים:
6 מַכֶּה עַמִּים בְּעֶבְרָה
מַכַּת בִּלְתִּי סָרָה
רֹדֶה בָאַף גּוֹיִם
מֻרְדָּף בְּלִי חָשָׂךְ:
7 נָחָה שָׁקְטָה כָּל־הָאָרֶץ
פָּצְחוּ רִנָּה:
8 גַּם־בְּרוֹשִׁים שָׂמְחוּ לְךָ
אַרְזֵי לְבָנוֹן
מֵאָז שָׁכַבְתָּ
לֹא־יַעֲלֶה הַכֹּרֵת עָלֵינוּ:
9 שְׁאוֹל מִתַּחַת רָגְזָה לְךָ
לִקְרַאת בּוֹאֶךָ
עוֹרֵר לְךָ רְפָאִים

All the chief ones of the earth;
It has raised up from their thrones
All the kings of the nations.

כָּל־עַתּוּדֵי אָרֶץ
הֵקִים מִכִּסְאוֹתָם
כֹּל מַלְכֵי גוֹיִם׃

10 They all shall speak and say to you:
'Have you also become as weak as we?
Have you become like us?

10 כֻּלָּם יַעֲנוּ וְיֹאמְרוּ אֵלֶיךָ
גַּם־אַתָּה חֻלֵּיתָ כָמוֹנוּ

11 Your pomp is brought down to Sheol,
And the sound of your stringed instruments;
The maggot is spread under you,
And worms cover you.'

אֵלֵינוּ נִמְשָׁלְתָּ׃
11 הוּרַד שְׁאוֹל גְּאוֹנֶךָ
הֶמְיַת נְבָלֶיךָ תַּחְתֶּיךָ יֻצַּע רִמָּה
וּמְכַסֶּיךָ תּוֹלֵעָה׃

12 "How you are fallen from heaven,
O Lucifer, son of the morning!
How you are cut down to the ground,
You who weakened the nations!

12 אֵיךְ נָפַלְתָּ מִשָּׁמַיִם
הֵילֵל בֶּן־שָׁחַר
נִגְדַּעְתָּ לָאָרֶץ חוֹלֵשׁ עַל־גּוֹיִם׃

13 For you have said in your heart:
'I will ascend into heaven,
I will exalt my throne above the stars of God;
I will also sit on the mount of the congregation
On the farthest sides of the north;

13 וְאַתָּה אָמַרְתָּ בִלְבָבְךָ
הַשָּׁמַיִם אֶעֱלֶה
מִמַּעַל לְכוֹכְבֵי־אֵל
אָרִים כִּסְאִי וְאֵשֵׁב בְּהַר־מוֹעֵד
בְּיַרְכְּתֵי צָפוֹן׃

14 I will ascend above the heights of the clouds,
I will be like the Most High.'

14 אֶעֱלֶה עַל־בָּמֳתֵי עָב
אֶדַּמֶּה לְעֶלְיוֹן׃

15 Yet you shall be brought down to Sheol,
To the lowest depths of the Pit.

15 אַךְ אֶל־שְׁאוֹל
תּוּרָד אֶל־יַרְכְּתֵי־בוֹר׃

16 "Those who see you will gaze at you,
And consider you, saying:
'Is this the man who made the earth tremble,
Who shook kingdoms,

16 רֹאֶיךָ אֵלֶיךָ יַשְׁגִּיחוּ
אֵלֶיךָ יִתְבּוֹנָנוּ
הֲזֶה הָאִישׁ מַרְגִּיז הָאָרֶץ
מַרְעִישׁ מַמְלָכוֹת׃

17 Who made the world as a wilderness
And destroyed its cities,
Who did not open the house of his prisoners?"

17 שָׂם תֵּבֵל כַּמִּדְבָּר וְעָרָיו הָרָס
אֲסִירָיו לֹא־פָתַח בָּיְתָה׃

18 "All the kings of the nations,
All of them, sleep in glory,
Everyone in his own house;

18 כָּל־מַלְכֵי גוֹיִם כֻּלָּם
שָׁכְבוּ בְכָבוֹד
אִישׁ בְּבֵיתוֹ׃

19 But you are cast out of your grave
Like an abominable branch,
Like the garment of those who are slain,
Thrust through with a sword,
Who go down to the stones of the pit,
Like a corpse trodden underfoot.

19 וְאַתָּה הָשְׁלַכְתָּ מִקִּבְרְךָ
כְּנֵצֶר נִתְעָב
לְבֻשׁ הֲרֻגִים מְטֹעֲנֵי חֶרֶב
יוֹרְדֵי אֶל־אַבְנֵי־בוֹר כְּפֶגֶר מוּבָס׃

20 You will not be joined with them in burial,
Because you have destroyed your land
And slain your people.
The brood of evildoers shall never be named.

20 לֹא־תֵחַד אִתָּם בִּקְבוּרָה
כִּי־אַרְצְךָ שִׁחַתָּ
עַמְּךָ הָרָגְתָּ
לֹא־יִקָּרֵא לְעוֹלָם זֶרַע מְרֵעִים׃

21 Prepare slaughter for his children
Because of the iniquity of their fathers,
Lest they rise up and possess the land,
And fill the face of the world with cities."

21 הָכִינוּ לְבָנָיו מַטְבֵּחַ בַּעֲוֺן אֲבוֹתָם
בַּל־יָקֻמוּ וְיָרְשׁוּ אָרֶץ
וּמָלְאוּ פְנֵי־תֵבֵל עָרִים׃

22 "For I will rise up against them," says the LORD of hosts,
"And cut off from Babylon the name and remnant,

22 וְקַמְתִּי עֲלֵיהֶם נְאֻם יְהוָה צְבָאוֹת וְהִכְרַתִּי

And offspring and posterity," says the LORD.

23 "I will also make it a possession for the porcupine,
And marshes of muddy water;
I will sweep it with the broom of destruction,"
says the LORD of hosts.

24 The LORD of hosts has sworn, saying,
"Surely, as I have thought, so it shall come to pass,
And as I have purposed, *so* it shall stand:

25 That I will break the Assyrian in My land,
And on My mountains tread him underfoot.
Then his yoke shall be removed from them,
And his burden removed from their shoulders.

26 This *is* the purpose that is purposed against the whole earth,
And this *is* the hand that is stretched out over all the nations.

27 For the LORD of hosts has purposed,
And who will annul *it?*
His hand *is* stretched out,
And who will turn it back?"

28 This is the burden which came in the year that King Ahaz died.

29 "Do not rejoice, all you of Philistia,
Because the rod that struck you is broken;
For out of the serpent's roots will come forth a viper,
And its offspring *will be* a fiery flying serpent.

30 The firstborn of the poor will feed,
And the needy will lie down in safety;
I will kill your roots with famine,
And it will slay your remnant.

31 Wail, O gate! Cry, O city!
All you of Philistia *are* dissolved;
For smoke will come from the north,
And no one *will be* alone in his appointed times."

32 What will they answer the messengers of the nation?
That the LORD has founded Zion,
And the poor of His people shall take refuge in it.

15 The burden against Moab.

Because in the night Ar of Moab is laid waste
And destroyed,
Because in the night Kir of Moab is laid waste
And destroyed,

2 He has gone up to the temple and Dibon,

לְבֶכֶל שֵׁם וּשְׁאָר וְנִין וָנֶכֶד נְאֻם־יְהֹוָה: 23 וְשַׂמְתִּיהָ
לְמוֹרַשׁ קִפֹּד וְאַגְמֵי־מָיִם וְטֵאטֵאתִיהָ בְּמַטְאֲטֵא
הַשְׁמֵד נְאֻם יְהֹוָה צְבָאוֹת: פ

24 נִשְׁבַּע יְהֹוָה צְבָאוֹת לֵאמֹר
אִם־לֹא כַּאֲשֶׁר דִּמִּיתִי כֵּן הָיָתָה
וְכַאֲשֶׁר יָעַצְתִּי הִיא תָקוּם:

25 לִשְׁבֹּר אַשּׁוּר בְּאַרְצִי
וְעַל־הָרַי אֲבוּסֶנּוּ
וְסָר מֵעֲלֵיהֶם עֻלּוֹ
וְסֻבֳּלוֹ מֵעַל שִׁכְמוֹ יָסוּר:

26 זֹאת הָעֵצָה הַיְּעוּצָה
עַל־כָּל־הָאָרֶץ
וְזֹאת הַיָּד הַנְּטוּיָה עַל־כָּל־הַגּוֹיִם:

27 כִּי־יְהֹוָה צְבָאוֹת
יָעָץ וּמִי יָפֵר
וְיָדוֹ הַנְּטוּיָה
וּמִי יְשִׁיבֶנָּה: פ

28 בִּשְׁנַת־מוֹת הַמֶּלֶךְ אָחָז הָיָה הַמַּשָּׂא הַזֶּה:

29 אַל־תִּשְׂמְחִי פְלֶשֶׁת כֻּלֵּךְ
כִּי נִשְׁבַּר שֵׁבֶט מַכֵּךְ
כִּי־מִשֹּׁרֶשׁ נָחָשׁ יֵצֵא צֶפַע
וּפִרְיוֹ שָׂרָף מְעוֹפֵף:

30 וְרָעוּ בְּכוֹרֵי דַלִּים
וְאֶבְיוֹנִים לָבֶטַח יִרְבָּצוּ
וְהֵמַתִּי בָרָעָב שָׁרְשֵׁךְ
וּשְׁאֵרִיתֵךְ יַהֲרֹג:

31 הֵילִילִי שַׁעַר זַעֲקִי־עִיר
נָמוֹג פְּלֶשֶׁת כֻּלֵּךְ
כִּי מִצָּפוֹן עָשָׁן בָּא
וְאֵין בּוֹדֵד בְּמוֹעָדָיו:

32 וּמַה־יַּעֲנֶה מַלְאֲכֵי־גוֹי
כִּי יְהֹוָה יִסַּד צִיּוֹן
וּבָהּ יֶחֱסוּ עֲנִיֵּי עַמּוֹ: ס

טו מַשָּׂא מוֹאָב כִּי בְּלֵיל
שֻׁדַּד עָר מוֹאָב נִדְמָה כִּי בְּלֵיל
שֻׁדַּד קִיר־מוֹאָב נִדְמָה:

2 עָלָה הַבַּיִת וְדִיבֹן הַבָּמוֹת לְבֶכִי
עַל־נְבוֹ וְעַל מֵידְבָא מוֹאָב יְיֵלִיל

To the high places to weep.
Moab will wail over Nebo and over Medeba;
On all their heads *will be* baldness,
And every beard cut off.

3 In their streets they will clothe themselves
  with sackcloth;
On the tops of their houses
And in their streets
Everyone will wail, weeping bitterly.

4 Heshbon and Elealeh will cry out,
Their voice shall be heard as far as Jahaz;
Therefore the armed soldiers of Moab will
  cry out;
His life will be burdensome to him.

5 "My heart will cry out for Moab;
His fugitives *shall flee* to Zoar,
Like a three-year-old heifer.
For by the Ascent of Luhith
They will go up with weeping;
For in the way of Horonaim
They will raise up a cry of destruction.

6 For the waters of Nimrim will be desolate,
For the green grass has withered away;
The grass fails, there is nothing green.

7 Therefore the abundance they have gained,
And what they have laid up,
They will carry away to the Brook of the
  Willows.

8 For the cry has gone all around the borders
  of Moab,
Its wailing to Eglaim
And its wailing to Beer Elim.

9 For the waters of Dimon will be full of
  blood;
Because I will bring more upon Dimon,
Lions upon him who escapes from Moab,
And on the remnant of the land."

16 Send the lamb to the ruler of the land,
From Sela to the wilderness,
To the mount of the daughter of Zion.

2 For it shall be as a wandering bird thrown
  out of the nest;
So shall be the daughters of Moab at the
  fords of the Arnon.

3 "Take counsel, execute judgment;
Make your shadow like the night in the
  middle of the day;
Hide the outcasts,
Do not betray him who escapes.

4 Let My outcasts dwell with you, O Moab;
Be a shelter to them from the face of the
  spoiler.

בְּכָל־רֹאשָׁיו קָרְחָה
כָּל־זָקָן גְּרוּעָה:

3 בְּחוּצֹתָיו חָגְרוּ שָׂק
עַל גַּגּוֹתֶיהָ וּבִרְחֹבֹתֶיהָ
כֻּלֹּה יְיֵלִיל יֹרֵד בַּבֶּכִי:

4 וַתִּזְעַק חֶשְׁבּוֹן וְאֶלְעָלֵה
עַד־יַהַץ נִשְׁמַע קוֹלָם
עַל־כֵּן חֲלֻצֵי מוֹאָב יָרִיעוּ
נַפְשׁוֹ יָרְעָה לּוֹ:

5 לִבִּי לְמוֹאָב יִזְעָק
בְּרִיחֶהָ עַד־צֹעַר
עֶגְלַת שְׁלִשִׁיָּה
כִּי | מַעֲלֵה הַלּוּחִית
בִּבְכִי יַעֲלֶה־בּוֹ
כִּי דֶּרֶךְ חוֹרֹנַיִם
זַעֲקַת־שֶׁבֶר יְעֹעֵרוּ:

6 כִּי־מֵי נִמְרִים מְשַׁמּוֹת יִהְיוּ
כִּי־יָבֵשׁ חָצִיר כָּלָה דֶשֶׁא
יֶרֶק לֹא הָיָה:

7 עַל־כֵּן יִתְרָה עָשָׂה
וּפְקֻדָּתָם
עַל נַחַל הָעֲרָבִים יִשָּׂאוּם:

8 כִּי־הִקִּיפָה הַזְּעָקָה
אֶת־גְּבוּל מוֹאָב
עַד־אֶגְלַיִם יִלְלָתָהּ
וּבְאֵר אֵילִים יִלְלָתָהּ:

9 כִּי מֵי דִימוֹן מָלְאוּ דָם
כִּי־אָשִׁית עַל־דִּימוֹן נוֹסָפוֹת
לִפְלֵיטַת מוֹאָב אַרְיֵה
וְלִשְׁאֵרִית אֲדָמָה:

טז שִׁלְחוּ־כַר מֹשֵׁל־אֶרֶץ
מִסֶּלַע מִדְבָּרָה
אֶל־הַר בַּת־צִיּוֹן:

2 וְהָיָה כְעוֹף־נוֹדֵד קֵן מְשֻׁלָּח
תִּהְיֶינָה בְּנוֹת מוֹאָב
מַעְבָּרֹת לְאַרְנוֹן:

3 הָבִיאוּ עֵצָה עֲשׂוּ פְלִילָה
שִׁיתִי כַלַּיִל צִלֵּךְ בְּתוֹךְ צָהֳרַיִם
סַתְּרִי נִדָּחִים נֹדֵד אַל־תְּגַלִּי:

4 יָגוּרוּ בָךְ נִדָּחַי
מוֹאָב הֱוִי־סֵתֶר לָמוֹ מִפְּנֵי שׁוֹדֵד

טז 3 הָבִיאִי

For the extortioner is at an end,
Devastation ceases,
The oppressors are consumed out of the
    land.

כִּי־אָפֵס הַמֵּץ כָּלָה שֹׁד
תַּמּוּ רֹמֵס מִן־הָאָרֶץ׃
וְהוּכַן בַּחֶסֶד כִּסֵּא

5 In mercy the throne will be established;
And One will sit on it in truth, in the
    tabernacle of David,
Judging and seeking justice and hastening
    righteousness."

וְיָשַׁב עָלָיו בֶּאֱמֶת בְּאֹהֶל דָּוִד
שֹׁפֵט וְדֹרֵשׁ מִשְׁפָּט וּמְהִר צֶדֶק׃

6 We have heard of the pride of Moab—
He is very proud—
Of his haughtiness and his pride and his
    wrath;
But his lies *shall* not *be* so.

שָׁמַעְנוּ גְאוֹן־מוֹאָב
גֵּא מְאֹד
גַּאֲוָתוֹ וּגְאוֹנוֹ וְעֶבְרָתוֹ
לֹא־כֵן בַּדָּיו׃

7 Therefore Moab shall wail for Moab;
Everyone shall wail.
For the foundations of Kir Hareseth you
    shall mourn;
Surely *they are* stricken.

לָכֵן יְיֵלִיל מוֹאָב לְמוֹאָב
כֻּלֹּה יְיֵלִיל
לַאֲשִׁישֵׁי קִיר־חֲרֶשֶׂת תֶּהְגּוּ
אַךְ־נְכָאִים׃

8 For the fields of Heshbon languish,
And the vine of Sibmah;
The lords of the nations have broken down
    its choice plants,
Which have reached to Jazer
And wandered through the wilderness.
Her branches are stretched out,
They are gone over the sea.

כִּי שַׁדְמוֹת חֶשְׁבּוֹן אֻמְלָל
גֶּפֶן שִׂבְמָה
בַּעֲלֵי גוֹיִם
הָלְמוּ שְׂרוּקֶּיהָ
עַד־יַעְזֵר נָגָעוּ
תָּעוּ מִדְבָּר
שְׁלֻחוֹתֶיהָ נִטְּשׁוּ
עָבְרוּ יָם׃

9 Therefore I will bewail the vine of Sibmah,
With the weeping of Jazer;
I will drench you with my tears,
O Heshbon and Elealeh;
For battle cries have fallen
Over your summer fruits and your harvest.

עַל־כֵּן אֶבְכֶּה בִּבְכִי יַעְזֵר
גֶּפֶן שִׂבְמָה
אֲרַיָּוֶךְ דִּמְעָתִי
חֶשְׁבּוֹן וְאֶלְעָלֵה
כִּי עַל־קֵיצֵךְ וְעַל־קְצִירֵךְ
הֵידָד נָפָל׃

10 Gladness is taken away,
And joy from the plentiful field;
In the vineyards there will be no singing,
Nor will there be shouting;
No treaders will tread out wine in the
    presses;
I have made their shouting cease.

וְנֶאֱסַף שִׂמְחָה וָגִיל
מִן־הַכַּרְמֶל
וּבַכְּרָמִים לֹא־יְרֻנָּן
לֹא יְרֹעָע
יַיִן בַּיְקָבִים לֹא־יִדְרֹךְ הַדֹּרֵךְ
הֵידָד הִשְׁבַּתִּי׃

11 Therefore my heart shall resound like a harp
    for Moab,
And my inner being for Kir Heres.

עַל־כֵּן מֵעַי לְמוֹאָב
כַּכִּנּוֹר יֶהֱמוּ
וְקִרְבִּי לְקִיר חָרֶשׂ׃

12 And it shall come to pass,
When it is seen that Moab is weary on the high
    place,
That he will come to his sanctuary to pray;
But he will not prevail.

וְהָיָה כִי־נִרְאָה כִּי־נִלְאָה מוֹאָב עַל־הַבָּמָה וּבָא
אֶל־מִקְדָּשׁוֹ לְהִתְפַּלֵּל וְלֹא יוּכָל׃
זֶה הַדָּבָר אֲשֶׁר
דִּבֶּר יְהוָה אֶל־מוֹאָב מֵאָז׃
וְעַתָּה דִּבֶּר יְהוָה
לֵאמֹר בְּשָׁלֹשׁ שָׁנִים כִּשְׁנֵי שָׂכִיר וְנִקְלָה כְּבוֹד

13 This *is* the word which the LORD has spoken concerning Moab since that time. 14 But now the LORD has spoken, saying, "Within three years, as

the years of a hired man, the glory of Moab will be despised with all that great multitude, and the remnant *will be* very small *and* feeble."

מוֹאָב בְּכֹל הֶהָמוֹן הָרָב וּשְׁאָר מְעַט מִזְעָר לֹוא כַּבִּיר: ס

17 The burden against Damascus.

יז מַשָּׂא דַּמֶּשֶׂק

"Behold, Damascus will cease from *being* a
  city,
  And it will be a ruinous heap.

הִנֵּה דַמֶּשֶׂק מוּסָר מֵעִיר
וְהָיְתָה מְעִי מַפָּלָה:

2 The cities of Aroer *are* forsaken;
  They will be for flocks
  Which lie down, and no one will make *them*
  afraid.

2 עֲזֻבוֹת עָרֵי עֲרֹעֵר
לַעֲדָרִים תִּהְיֶינָה
וְרָבְצוּ וְאֵין מַחֲרִיד:

3 The fortress also will cease from Ephraim,
  The kingdom from Damascus,
  And the remnant of Syria;
  They will be as the glory of the children of
  Israel,"
  Says the LORD of hosts.

3 וְנִשְׁבַּת מִבְצָר מֵאֶפְרַיִם
וּמַמְלָכָה מִדַּמֶּשֶׂק וּשְׁאָר אֲרָם
כִּכְבוֹד בְּנֵי־יִשְׂרָאֵל יִהְיוּ
נְאֻם יְהוָה צְבָאוֹת: ס

4 "In that day it shall come to pass
  That the glory of Jacob will wane,
  And the fatness of his flesh grow lean.

4 וְהָיָה בַּיּוֹם הַהוּא
יִדַּל כְּבוֹד יַעֲקֹב
וּמִשְׁמַן בְּשָׂרוֹ יֵרָזֶה:

5 It shall be as when the harvester gathers the
  grain,
  And reaps the heads with his arm;
  It shall be as he who gathers heads of grain
  In the Valley of Rephaim.

5 וְהָיָה כֶּאֱסֹף קָצִיר קָמָה
וּזְרֹעוֹ שִׁבֳּלִים יִקְצוֹר
וְהָיָה כִּמְלַקֵּט שִׁבֳּלִים
בְּעֵמֶק רְפָאִים:

6 Yet gleaning grapes will be left in it,
  Like the shaking of an olive tree,
  Two *or* three olives at the top of the
  uppermost bough,
  Four *or* five in its most fruitful branches,"
  Says the LORD God of Israel.

6 וְנִשְׁאַר־בּוֹ עוֹלֵלֹת
כְּנֹקֶף זַיִת
שְׁנַיִם שְׁלֹשָׁה גַּרְגְּרִים
בְּרֹאשׁ אָמִיר
אַרְבָּעָה חֲמִשָּׁה בִּסְעִפֶיהָ פֹּרִיָּה
נְאֻם־יְהוָה אֱלֹהֵי יִשְׂרָאֵל: ס

7 In that day a man will look to his Maker,
  And his eyes will have respect for the Holy
  One of Israel.

7 בַּיּוֹם הַהוּא יִשְׁעֶה הָאָדָם עַל־עֹשֵׂהוּ
וְעֵינָיו אֶל־קְדוֹשׁ יִשְׂרָאֵל תִּרְאֶינָה:

8 He will not look to the altars,
  The work of his hands;
  He will not respect what his fingers have
  made,
  Nor the wooden images nor the incense
  altars.

8 וְלֹא יִשְׁעֶה אֶל־הַמִּזְבְּחוֹת
מַעֲשֵׂה יָדָיו
וַאֲשֶׁר עָשׂוּ אֶצְבְּעֹתָיו לֹא יִרְאֶה
וְהָאֲשֵׁרִים וְהָחַמָּנִים:

9 In that day his strong cities will be as a forsaken
  bough
  And an uppermost branch,
  Which they left because of the children of Israel;
  And there will be desolation.

9 בַּיּוֹם הַהוּא יִהְיוּ | עָרֵי מָעֻזּוֹ כַּעֲזוּבַת הַחֹרֶשׁ
וְהָאָמִיר אֲשֶׁר עָזְבוּ מִפְּנֵי בְּנֵי יִשְׂרָאֵל וְהָיְתָה
שְׁמָמָה:

10 Because you have forgotten the God of your
  salvation,
  And have not been mindful of the Rock of
  your stronghold,
  Therefore you will plant pleasant plants
  And set out foreign seedlings;

10 כִּי שָׁכַחַתְּ אֱלֹהֵי יִשְׁעֵךְ
וְצוּר מָעֻזֵּךְ לֹא זָכָרְתְּ

11 In the day you will make your plant to grow,
And in the morning you will make your seed
  to flourish;
But the harvest *will be* a heap of ruins
In the day of grief and desperate sorrow.

12 Woe to the multitude of many people
Who make a noise like the roar of the seas,
And to the rushing of nations
That make a rushing like the rushing of
  mighty waters!

13 The nations will rush like the rushing of
  many waters;
But *God* will rebuke them and they will flee
  far away,
And be chased like the chaff of the mountains before the wind,
Like a rolling thing before the whirlwind.

14 Then behold, at eventide, trouble!
And before the morning, he *is* no more.
This *is* the portion of those who plunder us,
And the lot of those who rob us.

18 Woe to the land shadowed with buzzing
  wings,
Which *is* beyond the rivers of Ethiopia,

2 Which sends ambassadors by sea,
Even in vessels of reed on the waters, *saying,*
"Go, swift messengers, to a nation tall and
  smooth *of skin,*
To a people terrible from their beginning
  onward,
A nation powerful and treading down,
Whose land the rivers divide."

3 All inhabitants of the world and dwellers on
  the earth:
When he lifts up a banner on the mountains,
  you see *it;*
And when he blows a trumpet, you hear *it.*

4 For so the LORD said to me,
"I will take My rest,
And I will look from My dwelling place
Like clear heat in sunshine,
Like a cloud of dew in the heat of harvest."

5 For before the harvest, when the bud is
  perfect
And the sour grape is ripening in the flower,
He will both cut off the sprigs with pruning
  hooks
And take away *and* cut down the branches.

6 They will be left together for the mountain
  birds of prey
And for the beasts of the earth;
The birds of prey will summer on them,

עַל־כֵּ֤ן תִּטְּעִי֙ נִטְעֵ֣י נַעֲמָנִ֔ים
וּזְמֹרַ֥ת זָ֖ר תִּזְרָעֶֽנּוּ׃

11 בְּי֤וֹם נִטְעֵךְ֙ תְּשַׂגְשֵׂ֔גִי
וּבַבֹּ֖קֶר זַרְעֵ֣ךְ תַּפְרִ֑יחִי
נֵ֥ד קָצִ֛יר בְּי֥וֹם נַחֲלָ֖ה וּכְאֵ֥ב אָנֽוּשׁ׃   ס

12 ה֗וֹי הֲמוֹן֙ עַמִּ֣ים רַבִּ֔ים
כַּהֲמ֥וֹת יַמִּ֖ים יֶהֱמָי֑וּן
וּשְׁא֣וֹן לְאֻמִּ֔ים כִּשְׁא֛וֹן
מַ֥יִם כַּבִּירִ֖ים יִשָּׁאֽוּן׃

13 לְאֻמִּ֗ים כִּשְׁא֞וֹן מַ֤יִם רַבִּים֙ יִשָּׁא֔וּן
וְגָ֥עַר בּ֖וֹ וְנָ֣ס מִמֶּרְחָ֑ק
וְרֻדַּ֗ף כְּמֹ֤ץ הָרִים֙ לִפְנֵי־ר֔וּחַ
וּכְגַלְגַּ֖ל לִפְנֵ֥י סוּפָֽה׃

14 לְעֵ֣ת עֶ֔רֶב וְהִנֵּ֣ה בַלָּהָ֔ה
בְּטֶ֥רֶם בֹּ֖קֶר אֵינֶ֑נּוּ
זֶ֚ה חֵ֣לֶק שׁוֹסֵ֔ינוּ וְגוֹרָ֖ל לְבֹזְזֵֽינוּ׃   ס

יח ה֣וֹי אֶ֔רֶץ צִלְצַ֖ל כְּנָפָ֑יִם
אֲשֶׁ֥ר מֵעֵ֖בֶר לְנַהֲרֵי־כֽוּשׁ׃

2 הַשֹּׁלֵ֨חַ בַּיָּ֜ם צִירִ֗ים
וּבִכְלֵי־גֹמֶא֮ עַל־פְּנֵי־מַיִם֒
לְכ֣וּ ׀ מַלְאָכִ֣ים קַלִּ֗ים
אֶל־גּוֹי֙ מְמֻשָּׁ֣ךְ וּמוֹרָ֔ט
אֶל־עַ֥ם נוֹרָ֖א מִן־ה֣וּא וָהָ֑לְאָה
גּ֚וֹי קַו־קָ֣ו וּמְבוּסָ֔ה
אֲשֶׁר־בָּזְא֥וּ נְהָרִ֖ים אַרְצֽוֹ׃

3 כָּל־יֹשְׁבֵ֥י תֵבֵ֖ל וְשֹׁ֣כְנֵי אָ֑רֶץ
כִּנְשֹׂא־נֵ֤ס הָרִים֙ תִּרְא֔וּ
וְכִתְקֹ֥עַ שׁוֹפָ֖ר תִּשְׁמָֽעוּ׃   ס

4 כִּי֩ כֹ֨ה אָמַ֤ר יְהוָה֙ אֵלַ֔י
אֶשְׁק֣וֹטָהP וְאַבִּ֖יטָה בִמְכוֹנִ֑י
כְּחֹ֥ם צַ֖ח עֲלֵי־א֑וֹר
כְּעָ֥ב טַ֖ל בְּחֹ֥ם קָצִֽיר׃

5 כִּֽי־לִפְנֵ֤י קָצִיר֙ כְּתָם־פֶּ֔רַח
וּבֹ֥סֶר גֹּמֵ֖ל יִֽהְיֶ֣ה נִצָּ֑ה
וְכָרַ֤ת הַזַּלְזַלִּים֙ בַּמַּזְמֵר֔וֹת
וְאֶת־הַנְּטִישׁ֖וֹת הֵסִ֥יר הֵתַֽז׃

6 יֵעָזְב֤וּ יַחְדָּו֙ לְעֵ֣יט הָרִ֔ים

And all the beasts of the earth will winter on
   them.

7 In that time a present will be brought to the LORD
   of hosts
   From a people tall and smooth *of skin,*
   And from a people terrible from their beginning
     onward,
   A nation powerful and treading down,
   Whose land the rivers divide—
   To the place of the name of the LORD of hosts,
   To Mount Zion.

19 The burden against Egypt.

Behold, the LORD rides on a swift cloud,
And will come into Egypt;
The idols of Egypt will totter at His presence,
And the heart of Egypt will melt in its midst.

2 "I will set Egyptians against Egyptians;
   Everyone will fight against his brother,
   And everyone against his neighbor,
   City against city, kingdom against kingdom.
3 The spirit of Egypt will fail in its midst;
   I will destroy their counsel,
   And they will consult the idols and the
     charmers,
   The mediums and the sorcerers.
4 And the Egyptians I will give
   Into the hand of a cruel master,
   And a fierce king will rule over them,"
   Says the Lord, the LORD of hosts.

5 The waters will fail from the sea,
   And the river will be wasted and dried up.
6 The rivers will turn foul;
   The brooks of defense will be emptied and
     dried up;
   The reeds and rushes will wither.
7 The papyrus reeds by the River, by the
     mouth of the River,
   And everything sown by the River,
   Will wither, be driven away, and be no more.
8 The fishermen also will mourn;
   All those will lament who cast hooks into the
     River,
   And they will languish who spread nets on
     the waters.
9 Moreover those who work in fine flax
   And those who weave fine fabric will be
     ashamed;
10 And its foundations will be broken.
   All who make wages *will be* troubled of soul.
11 Surely the princes of Zoan *are* fools;
   Pharaoh's wise counselors give foolish
     counsel.

וּלְבֶהֱמַת הָאָרֶץ
וְקָץ עָלָיו הָעַיִט
וְכָל־בֶּהֱמַת הָאָרֶץ עָלָיו תֶּחֱרָף׃

7 בָּעֵת הַהִיא יוּבַל־שַׁי לַיהוָה צְבָאוֹת עַם מְמֻשָּׁךְ
וּמוֹרָט וּמֵעַם נוֹרָא מִן־הוּא וָהָלְאָה גּוֹי ׀ קַו־קָו
וּמְבוּסָה אֲשֶׁר בָּזְאוּ נְהָרִים אַרְצוֹ אֶל־מְקוֹם שֵׁם־
יְהוָה צְבָאוֹת הַר־צִיּוֹן׃ ס

יט מַשָּׂא מִצְרָיִם
הִנֵּה יְהוָה רֹכֵב עַל־עָב קַל
וּבָא מִצְרַיִם
וְנָעוּ אֱלִילֵי מִצְרַיִם מִפָּנָיו
וּלְבַב מִצְרַיִם יִמַּס בְּקִרְבּוֹ׃

2 וְסִכְסַכְתִּי מִצְרַיִם בְּמִצְרַיִם
וְנִלְחֲמוּ אִישׁ־בְּאָחִיו וְאִישׁ בְּרֵעֵהוּ
עִיר בְּעִיר מַמְלָכָה בְּמַמְלָכָה׃
3 וְנָבְקָה רוּחַ־מִצְרַיִם בְּקִרְבּוֹ
וַעֲצָתוֹ אֲבַלֵּעַ
וְדָרְשׁוּ אֶל־הָאֱלִילִים וְאֶל־הָאִטִּים
וְאֶל־הָאֹבוֹת וְאֶל־הַיִּדְּעֹנִים׃
4 וְסִכַּרְתִּי אֶת־מִצְרַיִם
בְּיַד אֲדֹנִים קָשֶׁה
וּמֶלֶךְ עַז יִמְשָׁל־בָּם
נְאֻם הָאָדוֹן יְהוָה צְבָאוֹת׃

5 וְנִשְּׁתוּ־מַיִם מֵהַיָּם
וְנָהָר יֶחֱרַב וְיָבֵשׁ׃
6 וְהֶאֶזְנִיחוּ נְהָרוֹת
דָּלְלוּ וְחָרְבוּ יְאֹרֵי מָצוֹר
קָנֶה וָסוּף קָמֵלוּ׃
7 עָרוֹת עַל־יְאוֹר עַל־פִּי יְאוֹר
וְכֹל מִזְרַע יְאוֹר
יִיבַשׁ נִדַּף וְאֵינֶנּוּ׃
8 וְאָנוּ הַדַּיָּגִים
וְאָבְלוּ כָּל־מַשְׁלִיכֵי בַיְאוֹר חַכָּה
וּפֹרְשֵׂי מִכְמֹרֶת עַל־פְּנֵי־מַיִם אֻמְלָלוּ׃
9 וּבֹשׁוּ עֹבְדֵי פִשְׁתִּים שְׂרִיקוֹת
וְאֹרְגִים חוֹרָי׃
10 וְהָיוּ שָׁתֹתֶיהָ מְדֻכָּאִים
כָּל־עֹשֵׂי שֶׂכֶר אַגְמֵי־נָפֶשׁ׃
11 אַךְ־אֱוִלִים שָׂרֵי צֹעַן

How do you say to Pharaoh, "I *am* the son
   of the wise,
The son of ancient kings?"
12 Where *are* they?
   Where *are* your wise men?
   Let them tell you now,
   And let them know what the LORD of hosts
     has purposed against Egypt.
13 The princes of Zoan have become fools;
   The princes of Noph are deceived;
   They have also deluded Egypt,
   Those who are the mainstay of its tribes.
14 The LORD has mingled a perverse spirit in
    her midst;
   And they have caused Egypt to err in all her
    work,
   As a drunken man staggers in his vomit.
15 Neither will there be *any* work for Egypt,
   Which the head or tail,
   Palm branch or bulrush, may do.

16 In that day Egypt will be like women, and will
be afraid and fear because of the waving of the
hand of the LORD of hosts, which He waves over it.
17 And the land of Judah will be a terror to Egypt;
everyone who makes mention of it will be afraid in
himself, because of the counsel of the LORD of hosts
which He has determined against it.

18 In that day five cities in the land of Egypt will
speak the language of Canaan and swear by the
LORD of hosts; one will be called the City of
Destruction.

19 In that day there will be an altar to the LORD in
the midst of the land of Egypt, and a pillar to the
LORD at its border. 20 And it will be for a sign and
for a witness to the LORD of hosts in the land of
Egypt; for they will cry to the LORD because of the
oppressors, and He will send them a Savior and a
Mighty One, and He will deliver them. 21 Then the
LORD will be known to Egypt, and the Egyptians
will know the LORD in that day, and will make
sacrifice and offering; yes, they will make a vow to
the LORD and perform *it*. 22 And the LORD will
strike Egypt, He will strike and heal *it;* they will
return to the LORD, and He will be entreated by
them and heal them.

23 In that day there will be a highway from Egypt
to Assyria, and the Assyrian will come into Egypt
and the Egyptian into Assyria, and the Egyptians
will serve with the Assyrians.

חַכְמֵי יֹעֲצֵי פַרְעֹה עֵצָה נִבְעָרָה
אֵיךְ תֹּאמְרוּ אֶל־פַּרְעֹה
בֶּן־חֲכָמִים אֲנִי בֶּן־מַלְכֵי־קֶדֶם׃

12 אַיָּם אֵפוֹא חֲכָמֶיךָ
וְיַגִּידוּ נָא לָךְ
וְיֵדְעוּ מַה־יָּעַץ
יְהוָה צְבָאוֹת עַל־מִצְרָיִם׃

13 נוֹאֲלוּ שָׂרֵי צֹעַן
נִשְּׁאוּ שָׂרֵי נֹף
הִתְעוּ אֶת־מִצְרַיִם
פִּנַּת שְׁבָטֶיהָ׃

14 יְהוָה מָסַךְ בְּקִרְבָּהּ רוּחַ עִוְעִים
וְהִתְעוּ אֶת־מִצְרַיִם בְּכָל־מַעֲשֵׂהוּ
כְּהִתָּעוֹת שִׁכּוֹר בְּקִיאוֹ׃

15 וְלֹא־יִהְיֶה לְמִצְרַיִם מַעֲשֶׂה
אֲשֶׁר יַעֲשֶׂה רֹאשׁ וְזָנָב כִּפָּה וְאַגְמוֹן׃ ס

16 בַּיּוֹם הַהוּא יִהְיֶה מִצְרַיִם כַּנָּשִׁים וְחָרַד ׀ וּפָחַד
מִפְּנֵי תְּנוּפַת יַד־יְהוָה צְבָאוֹת אֲשֶׁר־הוּא מֵנִיף
עָלָיו׃ 17 וְהָיְתָה אַדְמַת יְהוּדָה לְמִצְרַיִם לְחָגָּא
כֹּל אֲשֶׁר יַזְכִּיר אֹתָהּ אֵלָיו יִפְחָד מִפְּנֵי עֲצַת
יְהוָה צְבָאוֹת אֲשֶׁר־הוּא יוֹעֵץ עָלָיו׃ ס 18 בַּיּוֹם
הַהוּא יִהְיוּ חָמֵשׁ עָרִים בְּאֶרֶץ מִצְרַיִם מְדַבְּרוֹת
שְׂפַת כְּנַעַן וְנִשְׁבָּעוֹת לַיהוָה צְבָאוֹת עִיר הַהֶרֶס
יֵאָמֵר לְאֶחָת׃ ס 19 בַּיּוֹם הַהוּא יִהְיֶה מִזְבֵּחַ
לַיהוָה בְּתוֹךְ אֶרֶץ מִצְרָיִם וּמַצֵּבָה אֵצֶל־גְּבוּלָהּ
לַיהוָה׃ 20 וְהָיָה לְאוֹת וּלְעֵד לַיהוָה צְבָאוֹת בְּאֶרֶץ
מִצְרַיִם כִּי־יִצְעֲקוּ אֶל־יְהוָה מִפְּנֵי לֹחֲצִים וְיִשְׁלַח
לָהֶם מוֹשִׁיעַ וָרָב וְהִצִּילָם׃ 21 וְנוֹדַע יְהוָה לְמִצְרַיִם
וְיָדְעוּ מִצְרַיִם אֶת־יְהוָה בַּיּוֹם הַהוּא וְעָבְדוּ זֶבַח
וּמִנְחָה וְנָדְרוּ־נֵדֶר לַיהוָה וְשִׁלֵּמוּ׃ 22 וְנָגַף יְהוָה
אֶת־מִצְרַיִם נָגֹף וְרָפוֹא וְשָׁבוּ עַד־יְהוָה וְנֶעְתַּר לָהֶם
וּרְפָאָם׃ 23 בַּיּוֹם הַהוּא תִּהְיֶה מְסִלָּה מִמִּצְרַיִם
אַשּׁוּרָה וּבָא־אַשּׁוּר בְּמִצְרַיִם וּמִצְרַיִם בְּאַשּׁוּר

²⁴In that day Israel will be one of three with Egypt and Assyria—a blessing in the midst of the land, ²⁵whom the LORD of hosts shall bless, saying, "Blessed *is* Egypt My people, and Assyria the work of My hands, and Israel My inheritance."

20 In the year that Tartan came to Ashdod, when Sargon the king of Assyria sent him, and he fought against Ashdod and took it, ²at the same time the LORD spoke by Isaiah the son of Amoz, saying, "Go, and remove the sackcloth from your body, and take your sandals off your feet." And he did so, walking naked and barefoot.

³Then the LORD said, "Just as My servant Isaiah has walked naked and barefoot three years *for* a sign and a wonder against Egypt and Ethiopia, ⁴so shall the king of Assyria lead away the Egyptians as prisoners and the Ethiopians as captives, young and old, naked and barefoot, with their buttocks uncovered, to the shame of Egypt. ⁵Then they shall be afraid and ashamed of Ethiopia their expectation and Egypt their glory. ⁶And the inhabitant of this territory will say in that day, 'Surely such *is* our expectation, wherever we flee for help to be delivered from the king of Assyria; and how shall we escape?'"

21 The burden against the Wilderness of the Sea.

As whirlwinds in the South pass through,
So it comes from the desert, from a terrible land.

² A distressing vision is declared to me;
The treacherous dealer deals treacherously,
And the plunderer plunders.
Go up, O Elam!
Besiege, O Media!
All its sighing I have made to cease.

³ Therefore my loins are filled with pain;
Pangs have taken hold of me, like the pangs of a woman in labor.
I was distressed when *I* heard *it;*
I was dismayed when *I* saw *it.*

⁴ My heart wavered, fearfulness frightened me;
The night for which I longed He turned into fear for me.

⁵ Prepare the table,
Set a watchman in the tower,
Eat and drink.
Arise, you princes,
Anoint the shield!

⁶ For thus has the Lord said to me:
"Go, set a watchman,

24 בַּיּוֹם הַהוּא ס וְעָבְדוּ מִצְרַיִם אֶת־אַשּׁוּר:
יִהְיֶה יִשְׂרָאֵל שְׁלִישִׁיָּה לְמִצְרַיִם וּלְאַשּׁוּר בְּרָכָה
בְּקֶרֶב הָאָרֶץ: 25 אֲשֶׁר בֵּרֲכוֹ יְהוָה צְבָאוֹת לֵאמֹר
בָּרוּךְ עַמִּי מִצְרַיִם וּמַעֲשֵׂה יָדַי אַשּׁוּר וְנַחֲלָתִי
יִשְׂרָאֵל: ס

כ בִּשְׁנַת בֹּא תַרְתָּן אַשְׁדּוֹדָה בִּשְׁלֹחַ אֹתוֹ סַרְגוֹן
מֶלֶךְ אַשּׁוּר וַיִּלָּחֶם בְּאַשְׁדּוֹד וַיִּלְכְּדָהּ: 2 בָּעֵת הַהִיא
דִּבֶּר יְהוָה בְּיַד יְשַׁעְיָהוּ בֶן־אָמוֹץ לֵאמֹר לֵךְ וּפִתַּחְתָּ
הַשַּׂק מֵעַל מָתְנֶיךָ וְנַעַלְךָ תַחֲלֹץ מֵעַל רַגְלֶיךָ וַיַּעַשׂ
כֵּן הָלֹךְ עָרוֹם וְיָחֵף: ס 3 וַיֹּאמֶר יְהוָה
כַּאֲשֶׁר הָלַךְ עַבְדִּי יְשַׁעְיָהוּ עָרוֹם וְיָחֵף שָׁלֹשׁ שָׁנִים
אוֹת וּמוֹפֵת עַל־מִצְרַיִם וְעַל־כּוּשׁ: 4 כֵּן יִנְהַג מֶלֶךְ־
אַשּׁוּר אֶת־שְׁבִי מִצְרַיִם וְאֶת־גָּלוּת כּוּשׁ נְעָרִים
וּזְקֵנִים עָרוֹם וְיָחֵף וַחֲשׂוּפַי שֵׁת עֶרְוַת מִצְרָיִם:
5 וְחַתּוּ וָבֹשׁוּ מִכּוּשׁ מַבָּטָם וּמִן־מִצְרַיִם תִּפְאַרְתָּם:
6 וְאָמַר יֹשֵׁב הָאִי הַזֶּה בַּיּוֹם הַהוּא הִנֵּה־כֹה מַבָּטֵנוּ
אֲשֶׁר־נַסְנוּ שָׁם לְעֶזְרָה לְהִנָּצֵל מִפְּנֵי מֶלֶךְ אַשּׁוּר
וְאֵיךְ נִמָּלֵט אֲנָחְנוּ: ס

כא מַשָּׂא מִדְבַּר־יָם
כְּסוּפוֹת בַּנֶּגֶב לַחֲלֹף
מִמִּדְבָּר בָּא מֵאֶרֶץ נוֹרָאָה:
2 חָזוּת קָשָׁה הֻגַּד־לִי
הַבּוֹגֵד | בּוֹגֵד וְהַשּׁוֹדֵד | שׁוֹדֵד
עֲלִי עֵילָם צוּרִי מָדַי
כָּל־אַנְחָתָה הִשְׁבַּתִּי:
3 עַל־כֵּן מָלְאוּ מָתְנַי חַלְחָלָה
צִירִים אֲחָזוּנִי כְּצִירֵי יוֹלֵדָה
נַעֲוֵיתִי מִשְּׁמֹעַ נִבְהַלְתִּי מֵרְאוֹת:
4 תָּעָה לְבָבִי פַּלָּצוּת בִּעֲתָתְנִי
אֵת נֶשֶׁף חִשְׁקִי שָׂם לִי לַחֲרָדָה:
5 עָרֹךְ הַשֻּׁלְחָן
צָפֹה הַצָּפִית אָכוֹל שָׁתֹה
קוּמוּ הַשָּׂרִים מִשְׁחוּ מָגֵן: פ
6 כִּי כֹה אָמַר אֵלַי אֲדֹנָי
לֵךְ הַעֲמֵד הַמְצַפֶּה

English	Hebrew
Let him declare what he sees."	אֲשֶׁר יִרְאֶה יַגִּיד:
7 And he saw a chariot *with* a pair of horse-men,	7 וְרָאָה רֶכֶב צֶמֶד פָּרָשִׁים
A chariot of donkeys, *and* a chariot of camels,	רֶכֶב חֲמוֹר רֶכֶב גָּמָל
And he listened earnestly with great care.	וְהִקְשִׁיב קֶשֶׁב רַב־קָשֶׁב:
8 Then he cried, "A lion, my Lord!	8 וַיִּקְרָא אַרְיֵה עַל־מִצְפֶּה ׀ אֲדֹנָי
I stand continually on the watchtower in the daytime;	אָנֹכִי עֹמֵד תָּמִיד יוֹמָם
	וְעַל־מִשְׁמַרְתִּי
I have sat at my post every night.	אָנֹכִי נִצָּב כָּל־הַלֵּילוֹת:
9 And look, here comes a chariot of men *with* a pair of horsemen!"	9 וְהִנֵּה־זֶה בָא רֶכֶב אִישׁ
	צֶמֶד פָּרָשִׁים
Then he answered and said,	וַיַּעַן וַיֹּאמֶר
"Babylon is fallen, is fallen!	נָפְלָה נָפְלָה בָּבֶל
And all the carved images of her gods He has broken to the ground."	וְכָל־פְּסִילֵי אֱלֹהֶיהָ שִׁבַּר לָאָרֶץ:
10 Oh, my threshing and the grain of my floor!	10 מְדֻשָׁתִי וּבֶן־גָּרְנִי
That which I have heard from the LORD of hosts,	אֲשֶׁר שָׁמַעְתִּי מֵאֵת יְהוָה צְבָאוֹת
The God of Israel, I have declared to you.	אֱלֹהֵי יִשְׂרָאֵל הִגַּדְתִּי לָכֶם: ס
11 The burden against Dumah.	11 מַשָּׂא דּוּמָה
He calls to me out of Seir,	אֵלַי קֹרֵא מִשֵּׂעִיר
"Watchman, what of the night?	שֹׁמֵר מַה־מִּלַּיְלָה
Watchman, what of the night?"	שֹׁמֵר מַה־מִּלֵּיל:
12 The watchman said,	12 אָמַר שֹׁמֵר
"The morning comes, and also the night.	אָתָה בֹקֶר וְגַם־לַיְלָה
If you will inquire, inquire; Return! Come back!"	אִם־תִּבְעָיוּן בְּעָיוּ שֻׁבוּ אֵתָיוּ: ס
13 The burden against Arabia.	13 מַשָּׂא בַּעְרָב
In the forest in Arabia you will lodge, O you traveling companies of Dedanites.	בַּיַּעַר בַּעְרַב תָּלִינוּ אֹרְחוֹת דְּדָנִים:
14 O inhabitants of the land of Tema,	14 לִקְרַאת צָמֵא הֵתָיוּ מָיִם
Bring water to him who is thirsty; With their bread they met him who fled.	יֹשְׁבֵי אֶרֶץ תֵּימָא בְּלַחְמוֹ קִדְּמוּ נֹדֵד:
15 For they fled from the swords, from the drawn sword,	15 כִּי־מִפְּנֵי חֲרָבוֹת נָדָדוּ
	מִפְּנֵי ׀ חֶרֶב נְטוּשָׁה
From the bent bow, and from the distress of war.	וּמִפְּנֵי קֶשֶׁת דְּרוּכָה
	וּמִפְּנֵי כֹּבֶד מִלְחָמָה: ס
16 For thus the LORD has said to me: "Within a year, according to the year of a hired man, all the glory of Kedar will fail; 17 and the remainder of the number of archers, the mighty men of the people of Kedar, will be diminished; for the LORD God of Israel has spoken *it*."	16 כִּי־כֹה אָמַר אֲדֹנָי אֵלָי בְּעוֹד שָׁנָה כִּשְׁנֵי שָׂכִיר וְכָלָה כָּל־כְּבוֹד קֵדָר: 17 וּשְׁאָר מִסְפַּר־קֶשֶׁת גִּבּוֹרֵי בְנֵי־קֵדָר יִמְעָטוּ כִּי יְהוָה אֱלֹהֵי־יִשְׂרָאֵל דִּבֵּר: ס
22 The burden against the Valley of Vision.	כב מַשָּׂא גֵּיא חִזָּיוֹן
What ails you now, that you have all gone up to the housetops,	מַה־לָּךְ אֵפוֹא
	כִּי־עָלִית כֻּלָּךְ לַגַּגּוֹת:
2 You who are full of noise, A tumultuous city, a joyous city?	2 תְּשֻׁאוֹת ׀ מְלֵאָה עִיר הוֹמִיָּה

Your slain *men are* not slain with the sword,
Nor dead in battle.

3 All your rulers have fled together;
They are captured by the archers.
All who are found in you are bound
together;
They have fled from afar.

4 Therefore I said, "Look away from me,
I will weep bitterly;
Do not labor to comfort me
Because of the plundering of the daughter of
my people."

5 For *it is* a day of trouble and treading down
and perplexity
By the Lord GOD of hosts
In the Valley of Vision—
Breaking down the walls
And of crying to the mountain.

6 Elam bore the quiver
With chariots of men *and* horsemen,
And Kir uncovered the shield.

7 It shall come to pass *that* your choicest
valleys
Shall be full of chariots,
And the horsemen shall set themselves in
array at the gate.

8 He removed the protection of Judah.
You looked in that day to the armor of the
House of the Forest;

9 You also saw the damage to the city of David,
That it was great;
And you gathered together the waters of the
lower pool.

10 You numbered the houses of Jerusalem,
And the houses you broke down
To fortify the wall.

11 You also made a reservoir between the two
walls
For the water of the old pool.
But you did not look to its Maker,
Nor did you have respect for Him who
fashioned it long ago.

12 And in that day the Lord GOD of hosts
Called for weeping and for mourning,
For baldness and for girding with sackcloth.

13 But instead, joy and gladness,
Slaying oxen and killing sheep,
Eating meat and drinking wine:
"Let us eat and drink, for tomorrow we die!"

14 Then it was revealed in my hearing by the
LORD of hosts,
"Surely for this iniquity there will be no
atonement for you,

קְרֻיָה עָלָיְזָה

חֲלָלַיִךְ לֹא חַלְלֵי־חֶרֶב

וְלֹא מֵתֵי מִלְחָמָה:

3 כָּל־קְצִינַיִךְ נָדְדוּ־יַחַד

מִקֶּשֶׁת אֻסָּרוּ

כָּל־נִמְצָאַיִךְ אֻסְּרוּ יַחְדָּו

מֵרָחוֹק בָּרָחוּ:

4 עַל־כֵּן אָמַרְתִּי

שְׁעוּ מִנִּי אֲמָרֵר בַּבֶּכִי

אַל־תָּאִיצוּ לְנַחֲמֵנִי

עַל־שֹׁד בַּת־עַמִּי:

5 כִּי יוֹם מְהוּמָה וּמְבוּסָה וּמְבוּכָה

לַאדֹנָי יְהוִה צְבָאוֹת בְּגֵיא חִזָּיוֹן

מְקַרְקַר קִר וְשׁוֹעַ אֶל־הָהָר:

6 וְעֵילָם נָשָׂא אַשְׁפָּה

בְּרֶכֶב אָדָם פָּרָשִׁים

וְקִיר עֵרָה מָגֵן:

7 וַיְהִי מִבְחַר־עֲמָקַיִךְ מָלְאוּ רָכֶב

וְהַפָּרָשִׁים שֹׁת שָׁתוּ הַשָּׁעְרָה:

8 וַיְגַל אֵת מָסַךְ יְהוּדָה וַתַּבֵּט בַּיּוֹם הַהוּא אֶל־נֶשֶׁק

בֵּית הַיָּעַר: 9 וְאֵת בְּקִיעֵי עִיר־דָּוִד רְאִיתֶם כִּי־רָבּוּ

וַתְּקַבְּצוּ אֶת־מֵי הַבְּרֵכָה הַתַּחְתּוֹנָה: 10 וְאֶת־בָּתֵּי

יְרוּשָׁלַם סְפַרְתֶּם וַתִּתְצוּ הַבָּתִּים לְבַצֵּר הַחוֹמָה:

11 וּמִקְוָה ׀ עֲשִׂיתֶם בֵּין הַחֹמֹתַיִם לְמֵי הַבְּרֵכָה

הַיְשָׁנָה וְלֹא הִבַּטְתֶּם אֶל־עֹשֶׂיהָ וְיֹצְרָהּ מֵרָחוֹק לֹא

רְאִיתֶם:

12 וַיִּקְרָא אֲדֹנָי יְהוִה

צְבָאוֹת בַּיּוֹם הַהוּא

לִבְכִי וּלְמִסְפֵּד

וּלְקָרְחָה וְלַחֲגֹר שָׂק:

13 וְהִנֵּה ׀ שָׂשׂוֹן וְשִׂמְחָה

הָרֹג ׀ בָּקָר וְשָׁחֹט צֹאן

אָכֹל בָּשָׂר וְשָׁתוֹת יַיִן

אָכוֹל וְשָׁתוֹ כִּי מָחָר נָמוּת:

14 וְנִגְלָה בְאָזְנָי יְהוָה צְבָאוֹת

אִם־יְכֻפַּר הֶעָוֹן

Even to your death," says the Lord GOD of
hosts.

15 Thus says the Lord GOD of hosts:

"Go, proceed to this steward,
To Shebna, who *is* over the house, *and say:*
16 'What have you here, and whom have you
here,
That you have hewn a sepulcher here,
As he who hews himself a sepulcher on high,
Who carves a tomb for himself in a rock?
17 Indeed, the LORD will throw you away
violently,
O mighty man,
And will surely seize you.
18 He will surely turn violently and toss you like
a ball
Into a large country;
There you shall die, and there your glorious
chariots
Shall be the shame of your master's house.
19 So I will drive you out of your office,
And from your position he will pull you
down.
20 'Then it shall be in that day,
That I will call My servant Eliakim the son
of Hilkiah;
21 I will clothe him with your robe
And strengthen him with your belt;
I will commit your responsibility into his
hand.
He shall be a father to the inhabitants of
Jerusalem
And to the house of Judah.
22 The key of the house of David
I will lay on his shoulder;
So he shall open, and no one shall shut;
And he shall shut, and no one shall open.
23 I will fasten him *as* a peg in a secure place,
And he will become a glorious throne to his
father's house.

24 'They will hang on him all the glory of his
father's house, the offspring and the posterity, all
vessels of small quantity, from the cups to all the
pitchers. 25 In that day,' says the LORD of hosts, 'the
peg that is fastened in the secure place will be
removed and be cut down and fall, and the burden
that *was* on it will be cut off; for the LORD has
spoken.'"

23 The burden against Tyre.

Wail, you ships of Tarshish!
For it is laid waste,

הֹוֶה לָכֶם עַד־תְּמֻתוּן
אָמַר אֲדֹנָי יְהוִה צְבָאֽוֹת: פ

15 כֹּה אָמַר אֲדֹנָי יְהוִה צְבָאוֹת
לֶךְ־בֹּא אֶל־הַסֹּכֵן הַזֶּה
עַל־שֶׁבְנָא אֲשֶׁר עַל־הַבָּֽיִת:
16 מַה־לְּךָ פֹה וּמִי לְךָ פֹה
כִּי־חָצַבְתָּ לְּךָ פֹּה קָבֶר
חֹצְבִי מָרוֹם קִבְרוֹ
חֹקְקִי בַסֶּלַע מִשְׁכָּן לֽוֹ:
17 הִנֵּה יְהוָה מְטַלְטֶלְךָ טַלְטֵלָה גָּבֶר
וְעֹטְךָ עָטֹֽה:
18 צָנֹוף יִצְנָפְךָ צְנֵפָה
כַּדּוּר אֶל־אֶרֶץ רַחֲבַת יָדָיִם
שָׁמָּה תָמוּת וְשָׁמָּה מַרְכְּבוֹת כְּבוֹדֶךָ
קְלוֹן בֵּית אֲדֹנֶֽיךָ:
19 וַהֲדַפְתִּיךָ מִמַּצָּבֶךָ
וּמִמַּעֲמָדְךָ יֶהֶרְסֶֽךָ:
20 וְהָיָה בַּיּוֹם הַהוּא
וְקָרָאתִי לְעַבְדִּי
לְאֶלְיָקִים בֶּן־חִלְקִיָּֽהוּ:
21 וְהִלְבַּשְׁתִּיו כֻּתָּנְתֶּךָ
וְאַבְנֵטְךָ אֲחַזְּקֶנּוּ
וּמֶמְשַׁלְתְּךָ אֶתֵּן בְּיָדוֹ
וְהָיָה לְאָב לְיוֹשֵׁב יְרוּשָׁלַ͏ִם וּלְבֵית יְהוּדָֽה:
22 וְנָתַתִּי מַפְתֵּחַ בֵּית־דָּוִד עַל־שִׁכְמוֹ
וּפָתַח וְאֵין סֹגֵר וְסָגַר וְאֵין פֹּתֵֽחַ:
23 וּתְקַעְתִּיו יָתֵד בְּמָקוֹם נֶאֱמָן
וְהָיָה לְכִסֵּא כָבוֹד לְבֵית אָבִֽיו:
24 וְתָלוּ עָלָיו כֹּל ׀ כְּבוֹד בֵּית־אָבִיו הַצֶּאֱצָאִים
וְהַצְּפִעוֹת כֹּל כְּלֵי הַקָּטָן מִכְּלֵי הָאַגָּנוֹת וְעַד כָּל־
כְּלֵי הַנְּבָלִֽים: 25 בַּיּוֹם הַהוּא נְאֻם יְהוָה צְבָאוֹת
תָּמוּשׁ הַיָּתֵד הַתְּקוּעָה בְּמָקוֹם נֶאֱמָן וְנִגְדְּעָה
וְנָפְלָה וְנִכְרַת הַמַּשָּׂא אֲשֶׁר־עָלֶיהָ כִּי יְהוָה דִּבֵּֽר: ס

כג מַשָּׂא צֹר
הֵילִילוּ ׀ אֳנִיּוֹת תַּרְשִׁישׁ

So that there is no house, no harbor;
From the land of Cyprus it is revealed to
them.

2 Be still, you inhabitants of the coastland,
You merchants of Sidon,
Whom those who cross the sea have filled.
3 And on great waters the grain of Shihor,
The harvest of the River, *is* her revenue;
And she is a marketplace for the nations.
4 Be ashamed, O Sidon;
For the sea has spoken,
The strength of the sea, saying,
"I do not labor, nor bring forth children;
Neither do I rear young men,
Nor bring up virgins."
5 When the report *reaches* Egypt,
They also will be in agony at the report of
Tyre.
6 Cross over to Tarshish;
Wail, you inhabitants of the coastland!
7 *Is* this your joyous *city,*
Whose antiquity *is* from ancient days,
Whose feet carried her far off to dwell?
8 Who has taken this counsel against Tyre, the
crowning *city,*
Whose merchants *are* princes,
Whose traders *are* the honorable of the
earth?
9 The LORD of hosts has purposed it,
To bring to dishonor the pride of all glory,
To bring into contempt all the honorable of
the earth.
10 Overflow through your land like the River,
O daughter of Tarshish;
There is no more strength.
11 He stretched out His hand over the sea,
He shook the kingdoms;
The LORD has given a commandment against
Canaan
To destroy its strongholds.
12 And He said, "You will rejoice no more,
O you oppressed virgin daughter of Sidon.
Arise, cross over to Cyprus;
There also you will have no rest."
13 Behold, the land of the Chaldeans,
This people *which* was not;
Assyria founded it for wild beasts of the desert.
They set up its towers,
They raised up its palaces,
And brought it to ruin.
14 Wail, you ships of Tarshish!
For your strength is laid waste.

כִּי־שֻׁדַּד מִבַּיִת מִבּוֹא
מֵאֶרֶץ כִּתִּים נִגְלָה־לָמוֹ׃
2 דֹּמּוּ יֹשְׁבֵי אִי
סֹחֵר צִידוֹן עֹבֵר יָם מִלְאוּךְ׃
3 וּבְמַיִם רַבִּים זֶרַע שִׁחֹר
קְצִיר יְאוֹר תְּבוּאָתָהּ
וַתְּהִי סְחַר גּוֹיִם׃
4 בּוֹשִׁי צִידוֹן כִּי־אָמַר יָם
מָעוֹז הַיָּם לֵאמֹר
לֹא־חַלְתִּי וְלֹא־יָלַדְתִּי
וְלֹא גִדַּלְתִּי בַּחוּרִים
רוֹמַמְתִּי בְתוּלוֹת׃
5 כַּאֲשֶׁר־שֵׁמַע לְמִצְרָיִם
יָחִילוּ כְּשֵׁמַע צֹר׃
6 עִבְרוּ תַּרְשִׁישָׁה
הֵילִילוּ יֹשְׁבֵי אִי׃
7 הֲזֹאת לָכֶם עַלִּיזָה
מִימֵי־קֶדֶם קַדְמָתָהּ
יֹבִלוּהָ רַגְלֶיהָ
מֵרָחוֹק לָגוּר׃
8 מִי יָעַץ זֹאת עַל־צֹר הַמַּעֲטִירָה
אֲשֶׁר סֹחֲרֶיהָ שָׂרִים
כִּנְעָנֶיהָ נִכְבַּדֵּי־אָרֶץ׃
9 יְהוָה צְבָאוֹת יְעָצָהּ
לְחַלֵּל גְּאוֹן כָּל־צְבִי
לְהָקֵל כָּל־נִכְבַּדֵּי־אָרֶץ׃
10 עִבְרִי אַרְצֵךְ כַּיְאֹר
בַּת־תַּרְשִׁישׁ אֵין מֵזַח עוֹד׃
11 יָדוֹ נָטָה עַל־הַיָּם
הִרְגִּיז מַמְלָכוֹת
יְהוָה צִוָּה אֶל־כְּנַעַן
לַשְׁמִד מָעֻזְנֶיהָ׃
12 וַיֹּאמֶר לֹא־תוֹסִיפִי עוֹד לַעְלוֹז
הַמְעֻשָּׁקָה בְּתוּלַת בַּת־צִידוֹן
כִּתִּים ᴾ קוּמִי עֲבֹרִי
גַּם־שָׁם לֹא־יָנוּחַ לָךְ׃
13 הֵן ׀ אֶרֶץ כַּשְׂדִּים זֶה הָעָם לֹא הָיָה אַשּׁוּר
יְסָדָהּ לְצִיִּים הֵקִימוּ בַחִינָיו ᴾ עֹרְרוּ ᴾ אַרְמְנוֹתֶיהָ שָׂמָהּ
לְמַפֵּלָה׃
14 הֵילִילוּ אֳנִיּוֹת תַּרְשִׁישׁ
כִּי שֻׁדַּד מָעֻזְּכֶן׃ ס

15 Now it shall come to pass in that day that Tyre will be forgotten seventy years, according to the days of one king. At the end of seventy years it will happen to Tyre as *in* the song of the harlot:

16 "Take a harp, go about the city,
  You forgotten harlot;
  Make sweet melody, sing many songs,
  That you may be remembered."

17 And it shall be, at the end of seventy years, that the LORD will deal with Tyre. She will return to her hire, and commit fornication with all the kingdoms of the world on the face of the earth. 18 Her gain and her pay will be set apart for the LORD; it will not be treasured nor laid up, for her gain will be for those who dwell before the LORD, to eat sufficiently, and for fine clothing.

24 Behold, the LORD makes the earth empty and makes it waste,
  Distorts its surface
  And scatters abroad its inhabitants.
2 And it shall be:
  As with the people, so with the priest;
  As with the servant, so with his master;
  As with the maid, so with her mistress;
  As with the buyer, so with the seller;
  As with the lender, so with the borrower;
  As with the creditor, so with the debtor.
3 The land shall be entirely emptied and utterly plundered,
  For the LORD has spoken this word.

4 The earth mourns *and* fades away,
  The world languishes *and* fades away;
  The haughty people of the earth languish.
5 The earth is also defiled under its inhabitants,
  Because they have transgressed the laws,
  Changed the ordinance,
  Broken the everlasting covenant.
6 Therefore the curse has devoured the earth,
  And those who dwell in it are desolate.
  Therefore the inhabitants of the earth are burned,
  And few men *are* left.

7 The new wine fails, the vine languishes,
  All the merry-hearted sigh.
8 The mirth of the tambourine ceases,
  The noise of the jubilant ends,
  The joy of the harp ceases.
9 They shall not drink wine with a song;
  Strong drink is bitter to those who drink it.
10 The city of confusion is broken down;

15 וְהָיָה בַּיּוֹם הַהוּא וְנִשְׁכַּחַת צֹר שִׁבְעִים שָׁנָה
כִּימֵי מֶלֶךְ אֶחָד מִקֵּץ שִׁבְעִים שָׁנָה יִהְיֶה לְצֹר
כְּשִׁירַת הַזּוֹנָה:
16 קְחִי כִנּוֹר   סֹבִּי עִיר
זוֹנָה נִשְׁכָּחָה
הֵיטִיבִי נַגֵּן
הַרְבִּי־שִׁיר לְמַעַן תִּזָּכֵרִי:
17 וְהָיָה מִקֵּץ | שִׁבְעִים שָׁנָה יִפְקֹד יְהוָה אֶת־
צֹר וְשָׁבָה לְאֶתְנַנָּה וְזָנְתָה אֶת־כָּל־מַמְלְכוֹת הָאָרֶץ
עַל־פְּנֵי הָאֲדָמָה: 18 וְהָיָה סַחְרָהּ וְאֶתְנַנָּהּ קֹדֶשׁ
לַיהוָה לֹא יֵאָצֵר וְלֹא יֵחָסֵן כִּי לַיֹּשְׁבִים לִפְנֵי יְהוָה
יִהְיֶה סַחְרָהּ לֶאֱכֹל לְשָׂבְעָה וְלִמְכַסֶּה עָתִיק: פ
כד הִנֵּה יְהוָה בּוֹקֵק הָאָרֶץ וּבוֹלְקָהּ
וְעִוָּה פָנֶיהָ וְהֵפִיץ יֹשְׁבֶיהָ:
2 וְהָיָה כָעָם כַּכֹּהֵן
כַּעֶבֶד כַּאדֹנָיו
כַּשִּׁפְחָה כַּגְבִרְתָּהּ
כַּקּוֹנֶה כַּמּוֹכֵר
כַּמַּלְוֶה כַּלֹּוֶה
כַּנֹּשֶׁה כַּאֲשֶׁר נֹשֶׁא בוֹ:
3 הִבּוֹק | תִּבּוֹק הָאָרֶץ וְהִבּוֹז | תִּבּוֹז
כִּי יְהוָה דִּבֶּר אֶת־הַדָּבָר הַזֶּה:
4 אָבְלָה נָבְלָה הָאָרֶץ
אֻמְלְלָה נָבְלָה תֵּבֵל
אֻמְלְלוּ מְרוֹם עַם־הָאָרֶץ:
5 וְהָאָרֶץ חָנְפָה תַּחַת יֹשְׁבֶיהָ
כִּי־עָבְרוּ תוֹרֹת חָלְפוּ חֹק
הֵפֵרוּ בְּרִית עוֹלָם:
6 עַל־כֵּן אָלָה אָכְלָה אֶרֶץ
וַיֶּאְשְׁמוּ יֹשְׁבֵי בָהּ
עַל־כֵּן חָרוּ יֹשְׁבֵי אֶרֶץ
וְנִשְׁאַר אֱנוֹשׁ מִזְעָר:
7 אָבַל תִּירוֹשׁ אֻמְלְלָה־גָפֶן
נֶאֶנְחוּ כָּל־שִׂמְחֵי־לֵב:
8 שָׁבַת מְשׂוֹשׂ תֻּפִּים
חָדַל שְׁאוֹן עַלִּיזִים
שָׁבַת מְשׂוֹשׂ כִּנּוֹר:
9 בַּשִּׁיר לֹא יִשְׁתּוּ־יָיִן
יֵמַר שֵׁכָר לְשֹׁתָיו:
10 נִשְׁבְּרָה קִרְיַת־תֹּהוּ

Every house is shut up, so that none may go in.

11 *There is* a cry for wine in the streets,
All joy is darkened,
The mirth of the land is gone.

12 In the city desolation is left,
And the gate is stricken with destruction.

13 When it shall be thus in the midst of the land among the people,
It shall be like the shaking of an olive tree,
Like the gleaning of grapes when the vintage is done.

14 They shall lift up their voice, they shall sing;
For the majesty of the LORD
They shall cry aloud from the sea.

15 Therefore glorify the LORD in the dawning light,
The name of the LORD God of Israel in the coastlands of the sea.

16 From the ends of the earth we have heard songs:
"Glory to the righteous!"
But I said, "I am ruined, ruined!
Woe to me!
The treacherous dealers have dealt treacherously,
Indeed, the treacherous dealers have dealt very treacherously."

17 Fear and the pit and the snare
Are upon you, O inhabitant of the earth.

18 And it shall be
That he who flees from the noise of the fear
Shall fall into the pit,
And he who comes up from the midst of the pit
Shall be caught in the snare;
For the windows from on high are open,
And the foundations of the earth are shaken.

19 The earth is violently broken,
The earth is split open,
The earth is shaken exceedingly.

20 The earth shall reel to and fro like a drunkard,
And shall totter like a hut;
Its transgression shall be heavy upon it,
And it will fall, and not rise again.

21 It shall come to pass in that day
That the LORD will punish on high the host of exalted ones,
And on the earth the kings of the earth.

22 They will be gathered together,
As prisoners are gathered in the pit,

סֻגַּר כָּל־בַּיִת מִבּוֹא:

11 צְוָחָה עַל־הַיַּיִן בַּחוּצוֹת
עָרְבָה כָּל־שִׂמְחָה
גָּלָה מְשׂוֹשׂ הָאָרֶץ:

12 נִשְׁאַר בָּעִיר שַׁמָּה
וּשְׁאִיָּה יֻכַּת־שָׁעַר:

13 כִּי כֹה יִהְיֶה
בְּקֶרֶב הָאָרֶץ בְּתוֹךְ הָעַמִּים
כְּנֹקֶף זַיִת
כְּעוֹלֵלֹת אִם־כָּלָה בָצִיר:

14 הֵמָּה יִשְׂאוּ קוֹלָם יָרֹנּוּ
בִּגְאוֹן יְהוָה צָהֲלוּ מִיָּם:

15 עַל־כֵּן בָּאֻרִים כַּבְּדוּ יְהוָה
בְּאִיֵּי הַיָּם שֵׁם יְהוָה אֱלֹהֵי יִשְׂרָאֵל: ס

16 מִכְּנַף הָאָרֶץ
זְמִרֹת שָׁמַעְנוּ צְבִי לַצַּדִּיק
וָאֹמַר רָזִי־לִי רָזִי־לִי אוֹי לִי
בֹּגְדִים בָּגָדוּ וּבֶגֶד בּוֹגְדִים בָּגָדוּ:

17 פַּחַד וָפַחַת וָפָח
עָלֶיךָ יוֹשֵׁב הָאָרֶץ:

18 וְהָיָה הַנָּס מִקּוֹל הַפַּחַד
יִפֹּל אֶל־הַפַּחַת
וְהָעוֹלֶה מִתּוֹךְ הַפַּחַת יִלָּכֵד בַּפָּח
כִּי־אֲרֻבּוֹת מִמָּרוֹם נִפְתָּחוּ
וַיִּרְעֲשׁוּ מוֹסְדֵי אָרֶץ:

19 רֹעָה הִתְרֹעֲעָה הָאָרֶץ
פּוֹר הִתְפּוֹרְרָה אָרֶץ
מוֹט הִתְמוֹטְטָה אָרֶץ:

20 נוֹעַ תָּנוּעַ אֶרֶץ כַּשִּׁכּוֹר
וְהִתְנוֹדְדָה כַּמְּלוּנָה
וְכָבַד עָלֶיהָ פִּשְׁעָהּ
וְנָפְלָה וְלֹא־תֹסִיף קוּם: ס

21 וְהָיָה בַּיּוֹם הַהוּא יִפְקֹד יְהוָה
עַל־צְבָא הַמָּרוֹם בַּמָּרוֹם
וְעַל־מַלְכֵי הָאֲדָמָה עַל־הָאֲדָמָה:

22 וְאֻסְּפוּ אֲסֵפָה אַסִּיר עַל־בּוֹר

And will be shut up in the prison;
After many days they will be punished.

23 Then the moon will be disgraced
And the sun ashamed;
For the LORD of hosts will reign
On Mount Zion and in Jerusalem
And before His elders, gloriously.

25

O LORD, You *are* my God.
I will exalt You,
I will praise Your name,
For You have done wonderful *things;*
Your counsels of old *are* faithfulness *and*
    truth.

2 For You have made a city a ruin,
A fortified city a ruin,
A palace of foreigners to be a city no more;
It will never be rebuilt.

3 Therefore the strong people will glorify You;
The city of the terrible nations will fear You.

4 For You have been a strength to the poor,
A strength to the needy in his distress,
A refuge from the storm,
A shade from the heat;
For the blast of the terrible ones *is* as a storm
    against the wall.

5 You will reduce the noise of aliens,
As heat in a dry place;
As heat in the shadow of a cloud,
The song of the terrible ones will be
    diminished.

6 And in this mountain
The LORD of hosts will make for all people
A feast of choice pieces,
A feast of wines on the lees,
Of fat things full of marrow,
Of well-refined wines on the lees.

7 And He will destroy on this mountain
The surface of the covering cast over all
    people,
And the veil that is spread over all nations.

8 He will swallow up death forever,
And the Lord GOD will wipe away tears from
    all faces;
The rebuke of His people
He will take away from all the earth;
For the LORD has spoken.

9 And it will be said in that day:
"Behold, this *is* our God;
We have waited for Him, and He will save
    us.
This *is* the LORD;
We have waited for Him;

וְסֻגְּרוּ עַל־מַסְגֵּר
וּמֵרֹב יָמִים יִפָּקֵדוּ:
23 וְחָפְרָה הַלְּבָנָה וּבוֹשָׁה הַחַמָּה
כִּי־מָלַךְ יְהוָה צְבָאוֹת
בְּהַר צִיּוֹן וּבִירוּשָׁלַםִ
וְנֶגֶד זְקֵנָיו כָּבוֹד:

כה יְהוָה אֱלֹהַי אַתָּה
אֲרוֹמִמְךָ אוֹדֶה שִׁמְךָ
כִּי עָשִׂיתָ פֶּלֶא
עֵצוֹת מֵרָחוֹק אֱמוּנָה אֹמֶן:
2 כִּי שַׂמְתָּ מֵעִיר לַגָּל
קִרְיָה בְצוּרָה לְמַפֵּלָה
אַרְמוֹן זָרִים מֵעִיר
לְעוֹלָם לֹא יִבָּנֶה:
3 עַל־כֵּן יְכַבְּדוּךָ עַם־עָז
קִרְיַת גּוֹיִם עָרִיצִים יִירָאוּךָ:
4 כִּי־הָיִיתָ מָעוֹז לַדָּל
מָעוֹז לָאֶבְיוֹן בַּצַּר־לוֹ
מַחְסֶה מִזֶּרֶם צֵל מֵחֹרֶב
כִּי רוּחַ עָרִיצִים כְּזֶרֶם קִיר:
5 כְּחֹרֶב בְּצָיוֹן שְׁאוֹן זָרִים תַּכְנִיעַ
חֹרֶב בְּצֵל עָב זְמִיר עָרִיצִים יַעֲנֶה:

6 וְעָשָׂה יְהוָה צְבָאוֹת
לְכָל־הָעַמִּים בָּהָר הַזֶּה
מִשְׁתֵּה שְׁמָנִים מִשְׁתֵּה שְׁמָרִים
שְׁמָנִים מְמֻחָיִם שְׁמָרִים מְזֻקָּקִים:
7 וּבִלַּע בָּהָר הַזֶּה
פְּנֵי־הַלּוֹט ׀ הַלּוֹט
עַל־כָּל־הָעַמִּים
וְהַמַּסֵּכָה הַנְּסוּכָה עַל־כָּל־הַגּוֹיִם:
8 בִּלַּע הַמָּוֶת לָנֶצַח
וּמָחָה אֲדֹנָי יְהוִה
דִּמְעָה מֵעַל כָּל־פָּנִים
וְחֶרְפַּת עַמּוֹ יָסִיר מֵעַל כָּל־הָאָרֶץ
כִּי יְהוָה דִּבֵּר:

9 וְאָמַר בַּיּוֹם הַהוּא
הִנֵּה אֱלֹהֵינוּ זֶה
קִוִּינוּ לוֹ וְיוֹשִׁיעֵנוּ

We will be glad and rejoice in His salvation."

זֶה יְהֹוָה קִוִּינוּ לוֹ

10 For on this mountain the hand of the LORD
will rest,
And Moab shall be trampled down under
Him,
As straw is trampled down for the refuse
heap.

נָגִילָה וְנִשְׂמְחָה בִּישׁוּעָתוֹ:

10 כִּי־תָנוּחַ יַד־יְהֹוָה בָּהָר הַזֶּה
וְנָדוֹשׁ מוֹאָב תַּחְתָּיו
כְּהִדּוּשׁ מַתְבֵּן בְּמֵי מַדְמֵנָה:

11 And He will spread out His hands in their
midst
As a swimmer reaches out to swim,
And He will bring down their pride
Together with the trickery of their hands.

11 וּפֵרַשׂ יָדָיו בְּקִרְבּוֹ
כַּאֲשֶׁר יְפָרֵשׂ הַשֹּׂחֶה לִשְׂחוֹת
וְהִשְׁפִּיל גַּאֲוָתוֹ עִם אָרְבּוֹת יָדָיו:

12 The fortress of the high fort of your walls
He will bring down, lay low,
And bring to the ground, down to the dust.

12 וּמִבְצַר מִשְׂגַּב חוֹמֹתֶיךָ הֵשַׁח הִשְׁפִּיל
הִגִּיעַ לָאָרֶץ עַד־עָפָר: ס

26 In that day this song will be sung in the land of
Judah:

כו בַּיּוֹם הַהוּא
יוּשַׁר הַשִּׁיר־הַזֶּה בְּאֶרֶץ יְהוּדָה

"We have a strong city;
God will appoint salvation for walls and
bulwarks.

עִיר עָז־לָנוּ
יְשׁוּעָה יָשִׁית חוֹמוֹת וָחֵל:

2 Open the gates,
That the righteous nation which keeps the
truth may enter in.

2 פִּתְחוּ שְׁעָרִים
וְיָבֹא גוֹי־צַדִּיק שֹׁמֵר אֱמֻנִים:

3 You will keep him in perfect peace,
Whose mind is stayed on You,
Because he trusts in You.

3 יֵצֶר סָמוּךְ תִּצֹּר שָׁלוֹם ׀ שָׁלוֹם
כִּי בְךָ בָּטוּחַ:

4 Trust in the LORD forever,
For in YAH, the LORD, is everlasting
strength.

4 בִּטְחוּ בַיהֹוָה עֲדֵי־עַד
כִּי בְּיָהּ יְהֹוָה צוּר עוֹלָמִים:

5 For He brings down those who dwell on
high,
The lofty city;
He lays it low,
He lays it low to the ground,
He brings it down to the dust.

5 כִּי הֵשַׁח יֹשְׁבֵי מָרוֹם
קִרְיָה נִשְׂגָּבָה
יַשְׁפִּילֶנָּה יַשְׁפִּילָהּ עַד־אֶרֶץ
יַגִּיעֶנָּה עַד־עָפָר:

6 The foot shall tread it down—
The feet of the poor
And the steps of the needy."

6 תִּרְמְסֶנָּה רָגֶל
רַגְלֵי עָנִי פַּעֲמֵי דַלִּים:

7 The way of the just is uprightness;
O Most Upright,
You weigh the path of the just.

7 אֹרַח לַצַּדִּיק מֵישָׁרִים
יָשָׁר מַעְגַּל צַדִּיק תְּפַלֵּס:

8 Yes, in the way of Your judgments,
O LORD, we have waited for You;
The desire of our soul is for Your name
And for the remembrance of You.

8 אַף אֹרַח מִשְׁפָּטֶיךָ
יְהֹוָה קִוִּינוּךָ
לְשִׁמְךָ וּלְזִכְרְךָ תַּאֲוַת־נָפֶשׁ:

9 With my soul I have desired You in the
night,
Yes, by my spirit within me I will seek You
early;
For when Your judgments are in the earth,

9 נַפְשִׁי אִוִּיתִיךָ בַּלַּיְלָה
אַף־רוּחִי בְקִרְבִּי אֲשַׁחֲרֶךָּ

כה 10 כְּמוֹ

The inhabitants of the world will learn
righteousness.

10 Let grace be shown to the wicked,
Yet he will not learn righteousness;
In the land of uprightness he will deal
unjustly,
And will not behold the majesty of the LORD.

11 LORD, *when* Your hand is lifted up, they will
not see.
But they will see and be ashamed
For *their* envy of people;
Yes, the fire of Your enemies shall devour
them.

12 LORD, You will establish peace for us,
For You have also done all our works in us.

13 O LORD our God, masters besides You
Have had dominion over us;
But by You only we make mention of Your
name.

14 *They are* dead, they will not live;
They are deceased, they will not rise.
Therefore You have punished and destroyed
them,
And made all their memory to perish.

15 You have increased the nation, O LORD,
You have increased the nation;
You are glorified;
You have expanded all the borders of the
land.

16 LORD, in trouble they have visited You,
They poured out a prayer *when* Your
chastening *was* upon them.

17 As a woman with child
Is in pain and cries out in her pangs,
When she draws near the time of her delivery,
So have we been in Your sight, O LORD.

18 We have been with child, we have been in
pain;
We have, as it were, brought forth wind;
We have not accomplished any deliverance
in the earth,
Nor have the inhabitants of the world fallen.

19 Your dead shall live;
Together with my dead body they shall arise.
Awake and sing, you who dwell in dust;
For your dew *is like* the dew of herbs,
And the earth shall cast out the dead.

20 Come, my people, enter your chambers,
And shut your doors behind you;
Hide yourself, as it were, for a little moment,
Until the indignation is past.

21 For behold, the LORD comes out of His place

כִּי כַאֲשֶׁר מִשְׁפָּטֶיךָ לָאָרֶץ
צֶדֶק לָמְדוּ יֹשְׁבֵי תֵבֵל:
10 יֻחַן רָשָׁע בַּל־לָמַד צֶדֶק
בְּאֶרֶץ נְכֹחוֹת יְעַוֵּל
וּבַל־יִרְאֶה גֵּאוּת יְהוָה: ס
11 יְהוָה רָמָה יָדְךָ בַּל־יֶחֱזָיוּן
יֶחֱזוּ וְיֵבֹשׁוּ קִנְאַת־עָם
אַף־אֵשׁ צָרֶיךָ תֹאכְלֵם: ס
12 יְהוָה תִּשְׁפֹּת שָׁלוֹם לָנוּ
כִּי גַּם כָּל־מַעֲשֵׂינוּ פָּעַלְתָּ לָּנוּ:
13 יְהוָה אֱלֹהֵינוּ בְּעָלוּנוּ אֲדֹנִים זוּלָתֶךָ
לְבַד־בְּךָ נַזְכִּיר שְׁמֶךָ:
14 מֵתִים בַּל־יִחְיוּ רְפָאִים בַּל־יָקֻמוּ
לָכֵן פָּקַדְתָּ וַתַּשְׁמִידֵם
וַתְּאַבֵּד כָּל־זֵכֶר לָמוֹ:
15 יָסַפְתָּ לַגּוֹי יְהוָה
יָסַפְתָּ לַגּוֹי נִכְבָּדְתָּ
רִחַקְתָּ כָּל־קַצְוֵי־אָרֶץ:
16 יְהוָה בַּצַּר פְּקָדוּךָ
צָקוּן לַחַשׁ מוּסָרְךָ לָמוֹ:
17 כְּמוֹ הָרָה תַּקְרִיב לָלֶדֶת
תָּחִיל תִּזְעַק בַּחֲבָלֶיהָ
כֵּן הָיִינוּ מִפָּנֶיךָ יְהוָה:
18 הָרִינוּ חַלְנוּ כְּמוֹ יָלַדְנוּ רוּחַ
יְשׁוּעֹת בַּל־נַעֲשֶׂה אֶרֶץ
וּבַל־יִפְּלוּ יֹשְׁבֵי תֵבֵל:
19 יִחְיוּ מֵתֶיךָ נְבֵלָתִי יְקוּמוּן
הָקִיצוּ וְרַנְּנוּ שֹׁכְנֵי עָפָר
כִּי טַל אוֹרֹת טַלֶּךָ
וָאָרֶץ רְפָאִים תַּפִּיל: ס
20 לֵךְ עַמִּי בֹּא בַחֲדָרֶיךָ
וּסְגֹר דְּלָתְךָ° בַּעֲדֶךָ
חֲבִי כִמְעַט־רֶגַע
עַד־יַעֲבָור־° עָבָר־זָעַם:
21 כִּי־הִנֵּה יְהוָה יֹצֵא מִמְּקוֹמוֹ

כו 20 דְּלָתֶךָ

To punish the inhabitants of the earth for
　　their iniquity;
The earth will also disclose her blood,
And will no more cover her slain.

לִפְקֹד עֲוֺן יֹשֵׁב־הָאָרֶץ עָלָיו

וְגִלְּתָה הָאָרֶץ אֶת־דָּמֶיהָ

וְלֹא־תְכַסֶּה עוֹד עַל־הֲרוּגֶיהָ׃ ס

27　In that day the LORD with His severe sword, great
　　　　and strong,
　　　Will punish Leviathan the fleeing serpent,
　　　Leviathan that twisted serpent;
　　　And He will slay the reptile that *is* in the sea.

כז בַּיּוֹם הַהוּא יִפְקֹד יְהֹוָה בְּחַרְבּוֹ הַקָּשָׁה

וְהַגְּדוֹלָה וְהַחֲזָקָה עַל לִוְיָתָן נָחָשׁ בָּרִחַ וְעַל לִוְיָתָן

נָחָשׁ עֲקַלָּתוֹן וְהָרַג אֶת־הַתַּנִּין אֲשֶׁר בַּיָּם׃ ס

2　In that day sing to her,
　"A vineyard of red wine!

בַּיּוֹם הַהוּא　2

כֶּרֶם חֶמֶד עַנּוּ־לָהּ׃

3　I, the LORD, keep it,
　I water it every moment;
　Lest any hurt it,
　I keep it night and day.

אֲנִי יְהֹוָה נֹצְרָהּ　3

לִרְגָעִים אַשְׁקֶנָּה

פֶּן יִפְקֹד עָלֶיהָ

לַיְלָה וָיוֹם אֶצֳּרֶנָּה׃

4　Fury *is* not in Me.
　Who would set briers *and* thorns
　Against Me in battle?
　I would go through them,
　I would burn them together.

חֵמָה אֵין לִי　4

מִי־יִתְּנֵנִי שָׁמִיר שַׁיִת בַּמִּלְחָמָה

אֶפְשְׂעָה בָהּ אֲצִיתֶנָּה יָּחַד׃

5　Or let him take hold of My strength,
　That he may make peace with Me;
　And he shall make peace with Me."

אוֹ יַחֲזֵק בְּמָעוּזִּי　5

יַעֲשֶׂה שָׁלוֹם לִי

שָׁלוֹם יַעֲשֶׂה־לִּי׃

6　Those who come He shall cause to take root
　　in Jacob;
　Israel shall blossom and bud,
　And fill the face of the world with fruit.

הַבָּאִים יַשְׁרֵשׁ יַעֲקֹב　6

יָצִיץ וּפָרַח יִשְׂרָאֵל

וּמָלְאוּ פְנֵי־תֵבֵל תְּנוּבָה׃ ס

7　Has He struck Israel as He struck those who
　　struck him?
　Or has He been slain according to the
　　slaughter of those who were slain by
　　Him?

הַכְּמַכַּת מַכֵּהוּ הִכָּהוּ　7

אִם־כְּהֶרֶג הֲרֻגָיו הֹרָג׃

8　In measure, by sending it away,
　You contended with it.
　He removes *it* by His rough wind
　In the day of the east wind.

בְּסַאסְּאָה בְּשַׁלְּחָהּ תְּרִיבֶנָּה　8

הָגָה בְּרוּחוֹ הַקָּשָׁה בְּיוֹם קָדִים׃

9　Therefore by this the iniquity of Jacob will be
　　covered;
　And this *is* all the fruit of taking away his sin:
　When he makes all the stones of the altar
　Like chalkstones that are beaten to dust,
　Wooden images and incense altars shall not
　　stand.

לָכֵן בְּזֹאת יְכֻפַּר עֲוֺן־יַעֲקֹב　9

וְזֶה כָּל־פְּרִי הָסֵר חַטָּאתוֹ

בְּשׂוּמוֹ ׀ כָּל־אַבְנֵי מִזְבֵּחַ

כְּאַבְנֵי־גִר מְנֻפָּצוֹת

לֹא־יָקֻמוּ אֲשֵׁרִים וְחַמָּנִים׃

10　Yet the fortified city *will be* desolate,
　　The habitation forsaken and left like a
　　　wilderness;
　There the calf will feed, and there it will lie
　　down
　And consume its branches.

כִּי עִיר בְּצוּרָה בָּדָד　10

נָוֶה מְשֻׁלָּח וְנֶעֱזָב כַּמִּדְבָּר

שָׁם יִרְעֶה עֵגֶל וְשָׁם יִרְבָּץ

וְכִלָּה סְעִפֶיהָ׃

11　When its boughs are withered, they will be
　　broken off;
　The women come *and* set them on fire.

בִּיבֹשׁ קְצִירָהּ תִּשָּׁבַרְנָה　11

נָשִׁים בָּאוֹת מְאִירוֹת אוֹתָהּ

For it *is* a people of no understanding;
Therefore He who made them will not have mercy on them,
And He who formed them will show them no favor.

12 And it shall come to pass in that day
That the LORD will thresh,
From the channel of the River to the Brook of Egypt;
And you will be gathered one by one,
O you children of Israel.

13 So it shall be in that day:
The great trumpet will be blown;
They will come, who are about to perish in the land of Assyria,
And they who are outcasts in the land of Egypt,
And shall worship the LORD in the holy mount at Jerusalem.

28 Woe to the crown of pride, to the drunkards of Ephraim,
Whose glorious beauty *is* a fading flower
Which *is* at the head of the verdant valleys,
To those who are overcome with wine!

2 Behold, the Lord has a mighty and strong one,
Like a tempest of hail and a destroying storm,
Like a flood of mighty waters overflowing,
Who will bring *them* down to the earth with *His* hand.

3 The crown of pride, the drunkards of Ephraim,
Will be trampled underfoot;

4 And the glorious beauty is a fading flower
Which *is* at the head of the verdant valley,
Like the first fruit before the summer,
Which an observer sees;
He eats it up while it is still in his hand.

5 In that day the LORD of hosts will be
For a crown of glory and a diadem of beauty
To the remnant of His people,

6 For a spirit of justice to him who sits in judgment,
And for strength to those who turn back the battle at the gate.

7 But they also have erred through wine,
And through intoxicating drink are out of the way;
The priest and the prophet have erred through intoxicating drink,

כִּי לֹא עַם־בִּינוֹת הוּא
עַל־כֵּן לֹא־יְרַחֲמֶנּוּ עֹשֵׂהוּ
וְיֹצְרוֹ לֹא יְחֻנֶּנּוּ׃ ס

12 וְהָיָה בַּיּוֹם הַהוּא
יַחְבֹּט יְהוָה
מִשִּׁבֹּלֶת הַנָּהָר עַד־נַחַל מִצְרָיִם
וְאַתֶּם תְּלֻקְּטוּ
לְאַחַד אֶחָד בְּנֵי יִשְׂרָאֵל׃ ס

13 וְהָיָה ׀ בַּיּוֹם הַהוּא
יִתָּקַע בְּשׁוֹפָר גָּדוֹל
וּבָאוּ הָאֹבְדִים בְּאֶרֶץ אַשּׁוּר
וְהַנִּדָּחִים בְּאֶרֶץ מִצְרָיִם
וְהִשְׁתַּחֲווּ לַיהוָה
בְּהַר הַקֹּדֶשׁ בִּירוּשָׁלָ͏ִם׃

כח הוֹי עֲטֶרֶת גֵּאוּת שִׁכֹּרֵי אֶפְרַיִם
וְצִיץ נֹבֵל צְבִי תִפְאַרְתּוֹ
אֲשֶׁר עַל־רֹאשׁ גֵּיא־שְׁמָנִים
הֲלוּמֵי יָיִן׃

2 הִנֵּה חָזָק וְאַמִּץ לַאדֹנָי
כְּזֶרֶם בָּרָד שַׂעַר קָטֶב
כְּזֶרֶם מַיִם כַּבִּירִים שֹׁטְפִים
הִנִּיחַ לָאָרֶץ בְּיָד׃

3 בְּרַגְלַיִם תֵּרָמַסְנָה
עֲטֶרֶת גֵּאוּת שִׁכּוֹרֵי אֶפְרָיִם׃

4 וְהָיְתָה צִיצַת נֹבֵל צְבִי תִפְאַרְתּוֹ
אֲשֶׁר עַל־רֹאשׁ גֵּיא שְׁמָנִים
כְּבִכּוּרָהּ בְּטֶרֶם קַיִץ
אֲשֶׁר יִרְאֶה הָרֹאֶה אוֹתָהּ
בְּעוֹדָהּ בְּכַפּוֹ יִבְלָעֶנָּה׃ ס

5 בַּיּוֹם הַהוּא יִהְיֶה יְהוָה צְבָאוֹת
לַעֲטֶרֶת צְבִי וְלִצְפִירַת תִּפְאָרָה
לִשְׁאָר עַמּוֹ׃

6 וּלְרוּחַ מִשְׁפָּט לַיּוֹשֵׁב עַל־הַמִּשְׁפָּט
וְלִגְבוּרָה מְשִׁיבֵי מִלְחָמָה שָׁעְרָה׃ ס

7 וְגַם־אֵלֶּה בַּיַּיִן שָׁגוּ
וּבַשֵּׁכָר תָּעוּ

They are swallowed up by wine,
They are out of the way through intoxicating
    drink;
They err in vision, they stumble *in* judgment.
8 For all tables are full of vomit *and* filth;
    No place *is* clean.

9 "Whom will he teach knowledge?
    And whom will he make to understand the
      message?
    Those *just* weaned from milk?
    Those *just* drawn from the breasts?
10 For precept *must be* upon precept, precept
      upon precept,
    Line upon line, line upon line,
    Here a little, there a little."

11 For with stammering lips and another
      tongue
    He will speak to this people,
12 To whom He said, "This *is* the rest *with*
      which
    You may cause the weary to rest,"
    And, "This *is* the refreshing";
    Yet they would not hear.
13 But the word of the LORD was to them,
    "Precept upon precept, precept upon precept,
    Line upon line, line upon line,
    Here a little, there a little,"
    That they might go and fall backward, and
      be broken
    And snared and caught.

14 Therefore hear the word of the LORD, you
      scornful men,
    Who rule this people who *are* in Jerusalem,
15 Because you have said, "We have made a
      covenant with death,
    And with Sheol we are in agreement.
    When the overflowing scourge passes
      through,
    It will not come to us,
    For we have made lies our refuge,
    And under falsehood we have hidden our-
      selves."

16 Therefore thus says the Lord GOD:

    "Behold, I lay in Zion a stone for a founda-
      tion,
    A tried stone, a precious cornerstone, a sure
      foundation;
    Whoever believes will not act hastily.
17 Also I will make justice the measuring line,
    And righteousness the plummet;
    The hail will sweep away the refuge of lies,

כֹּהֵן וְנָבִיא שָׁגוּ בַשֵּׁכָר
נִבְלְעוּ מִן־הַיַּיִן
תָּעוּ מִן־הַשֵּׁכָר
שָׁגוּ בָּרֹאֶה פָּקוּ פְּלִילִיָּה:

8 כִּי כָּל־שֻׁלְחָנוֹת מָלְאוּ קִיא צֹאָה
בְּלִי מָקוֹם: ס

9 אֶת־מִי יוֹרֶה דֵעָה
וְאֶת־מִי יָבִין שְׁמוּעָה
גְּמוּלֵי מֵחָלָב
עַתִּיקֵי מִשָּׁדָיִם:

10 כִּי צַו לָצָו צַו לָצָו
קַו לָקָו קַו לָקָו
זְעֵיר שָׁם זְעֵיר שָׁם:

11 כִּי בְּלַעֲגֵי שָׂפָה וּבְלָשׁוֹן אַחֶרֶת
יְדַבֵּר אֶל־הָעָם הַזֶּה:

12 אֲשֶׁר | אָמַר אֲלֵיהֶם זֹאת הַמְּנוּחָה
הָנִיחוּ לֶעָיֵף
וְזֹאת הַמַּרְגֵּעָה
וְלֹא אָבוּא שְׁמוֹעַ:

13 וְהָיָה לָהֶם דְּבַר־יְהוָה
צַו לָצָו צַו לָצָו
קַו לָקָו קַו לָקָו
זְעֵיר שָׁם זְעֵיר שָׁם
לְמַעַן יֵלְכוּ וְכָשְׁלוּ אָחוֹר וְנִשְׁבָּרוּ
וְנוֹקְשׁוּ וְנִלְכָּדוּ: פ

14 לָכֵן שִׁמְעוּ דְבַר־יְהוָה אַנְשֵׁי לָצוֹן
מֹשְׁלֵי הָעָם הַזֶּה אֲשֶׁר בִּירוּשָׁלָ͏ִם:

15 כִּי אֲמַרְתֶּם כָּרַתְנוּ בְרִית אֶת־מָוֶת
וְעִם־שְׁאוֹל עָשִׂינוּ חֹזֶה
שֹׁיט שׁוֹטֵף כִּי־ עָבַר
לֹא יְבוֹאֵנוּ
כִּי שַׂמְנוּ כָזָב מַחְסֵנוּ
וּבַשֶּׁקֶר נִסְתָּרְנוּ: ס

16 לָכֵן כֹּה אָמַר אֲדֹנָי יְהוִה
הִנְנִי יִסַּד בְּצִיּוֹן אָבֶן
אֶבֶן בֹּחַן פִּנַּת יִקְרַת מוּסָד מוּסָּד
הַמַּאֲמִין לֹא יָחִישׁ:

17 וְשַׂמְתִּי מִשְׁפָּט לְקָו
וּצְדָקָה לְמִשְׁקָלֶת

כח 15 שׁוֹט יָעֲבֹר

And the waters will overflow the hiding
   place.

18 Your covenant with death will be annulled,
   And your agreement with Sheol will not
      stand;
   When the overflowing scourge passes
      through,
   Then you will be trampled down by it.

19 As often as it goes out it will take you;
   For morning by morning it will pass over,
   And by day and by night;
   It will be a terror just to understand the
      report."

20 For the bed is too short to stretch out *on,*
   And the covering so narrow that one cannot
      wrap himself *in it.*

21 For the LORD will rise up as *at* Mount
      Perazim,
   He will be angry as in the Valley of Gibeon—
   That He may do His work, His awesome
      work,
   And bring to pass His act, His unusual act.

22 Now therefore, do not be mockers,
   Lest your bonds be made strong;
   For I have heard from the Lord GOD of
      hosts,
   A destruction determined even upon the
      whole earth.

23 Give ear and hear my voice,
   Listen and hear my speech.

24 Does the plowman keep plowing all day to
      sow?
   Does he keep turning his soil and breaking
      the clods?

25 When he has leveled its surface,
   Does he not sow the black cummin
   And scatter the cummin,
   Plant the wheat in rows,
   The barley in the appointed place,
   And the spelt in its place?

26 For He instructs him in right judgment,
   His God teaches him.

27 For the black cummin is not threshed with a
      threshing sledge,
   Nor is a cartwheel rolled over the cummin;
   But the black cummin is beaten out with a
      stick,
   And the cummin with a rod.

28 Bread *flour* must be ground;
   Therefore he does not thresh it forever,
   Break *it* with his cartwheel,
   Or crush *it* with his horsemen.

29 This also comes from the LORD of hosts,

וְיָעָה בָרָד מַחְסֵה כָזָב
וְסֵתֶר מַיִם יִשְׁטֹפוּ:

18 וְכֻפַּר בְּרִיתְכֶם אֶת־מָוֶת
וְחָזוּתְכֶם אֶת־שְׁאוֹל לֹא תָקוּם
שׁוֹט שׁוֹטֵף כִּי יַעֲבֹר
וִהְיִיתֶם לוֹ לְמִרְמָס:

19 מִדֵּי עָבְרוֹ יִקַּח אֶתְכֶם
כִּי־בַבֹּקֶר בַּבֹּקֶר יַעֲבֹר
בַּיּוֹם וּבַלָּיְלָה
וְהָיָה רַק־זְוָעָה הָבִין שְׁמוּעָה:

20 כִּי־קָצַר הַמַּצָּע מֵהִשְׂתָּרֵעַ
וְהַמַּסֵּכָה צָרָה כְּהִתְכַּנֵּס:

21 כִּי כְהַר־פְּרָצִים יָקוּם יְהֹוָה
כְּעֵמֶק בְּגִבְעוֹן יִרְגָּז
לַעֲשׂוֹת מַעֲשֵׂהוּ זָר מַעֲשֵׂהוּ
וְלַעֲבֹד עֲבֹדָתוֹ נָכְרִיָּה עֲבֹדָתוֹ:

22 וְעַתָּה אַל־תִּתְלוֹצָצוּ
פֶּן־יֶחְזְקוּ מוֹסְרֵיכֶם
כִּי־כָלָה וְנֶחֱרָצָה שָׁמַעְתִּי
מֵאֵת אֲדֹנָי יְהֹוִה צְבָאוֹת
עַל־כָּל־הָאָרֶץ:

23 הַאֲזִינוּ וְשִׁמְעוּ קוֹלִי
הַקְשִׁיבוּ וְשִׁמְעוּ אִמְרָתִי:

24 הֲכֹל הַיּוֹם יַחֲרֹשׁ הַחֹרֵשׁ לִזְרֹעַ
יְפַתַּח וִישַׂדֵּד אַדְמָתוֹ:

25 הֲלוֹא אִם־שִׁוָּה פָנֶיהָ
וְהֵפִיץ קֶצַח וְכַמֹּן יִזְרֹק
וְשָׂם חִטָּה שׂוֹרָה וּשְׂעֹרָה נִסְמָן
וְכֻסֶּמֶת גְּבֻלָתוֹ:

26 וְיִסְּרוֹ לַמִּשְׁפָּט
אֱלֹהָיו יוֹרֶנּוּ:

27 כִּי לֹא בֶחָרוּץ יוּדַשׁ קֶצַח
וְאוֹפַן עֲגָלָה עַל־כַּמֹּן יוּסָּב
כִּי בַמַּטֶּה יֵחָבֶט קֶצַח
וְכַמֹּן בַּשָּׁבֶט:

28 לֶחֶם יוּדָק
כִּי לֹא לָנֶצַח אָדוֹשׁ יְדוּשֶׁנּוּ
וְהָמַם גִּלְגַּל עֶגְלָתוֹ וּפָרָשָׁיו
לֹא־יְדֻקֶּנּוּ:

29 גַּם־זֹאת מֵעִם יְהֹוָה צְבָאוֹת יָצָאָה

Who is wonderful in counsel *and* excellent in guidance.

הַפְלִיא עֵצָה הִגְדִּיל תּוּשִׁיָּה: ס

29 "Woe to Ariel, to Ariel, the city *where* David dwelt!
Add year to year;
Let feasts come around.

כט הוֹי אֲרִיאֵל אֲרִיאֵל קִרְיַת חָנָה דָוִד
סְפוּ שָׁנָה עַל־שָׁנָה חַגִּים יִנְקֹפוּ:

2 Yet I will distress Ariel;
There shall be heaviness and sorrow,
And it shall be to Me as Ariel.

2 וַהֲצִיקוֹתִי לַאֲרִיאֵל
וְהָיְתָה תַאֲנִיָּה וַאֲנִיָּה
וְהָיְתָה לִּי כַּאֲרִיאֵל:

3 I will encamp against you all around,
I will lay siege against you with a mound,
And I will raise siegeworks against you.

3 וְחָנִיתִי כַדּוּר עָלָיִךְ
וְצַרְתִּי עָלַיִךְ מֻצָּב
וַהֲקִימֹתִי עָלַיִךְ מְצֻרֹת:

4 You shall be brought down,
You shall speak out of the ground;
Your speech shall be low, out of the dust;
Your voice shall be like a medium's, out of the ground;
And your speech shall whisper out of the dust.

4 וְשָׁפַלְתְּ מֵאֶרֶץ תְּדַבֵּרִי
וּמֵעָפָר תִּשַּׁח אִמְרָתֵךְ
וְהָיָה כְּאוֹב מֵאֶרֶץ קוֹלֵךְ
וּמֵעָפָר אִמְרָתֵךְ תְּצַפְצֵף:

5 "Moreover the multitude of your foes
Shall be like fine dust,
And the multitude of the terrible ones
Like chaff that passes away;
Yes, it shall be in an instant, suddenly.

5 וְהָיָה כְּאָבָק דַּק הֲמוֹן זָרָיִךְ
וּכְמֹץ עֹבֵר הֲמוֹן עָרִיצִים
וְהָיָה לְפֶתַע פִּתְאֹם:

6 You will be punished by the LORD of hosts
With thunder and earthquake and great noise,
With storm and tempest
And the flame of devouring fire.

6 מֵעִם יְהוָה צְבָאוֹת תִּפָּקֵד
בְּרַעַם וּבְרַעַשׁ וְקוֹל גָּדוֹל
סוּפָה וּסְעָרָה וְלַהַב אֵשׁ אוֹכֵלָה:

7 The multitude of all the nations who fight against Ariel,
Even all who fight against her and her fortress,
And distress her,
Shall be as a dream of a night vision.

7 וְהָיָה כַּחֲלוֹם חֲזוֹן לַיְלָה
הֲמוֹן כָּל־הַגּוֹיִם
הַצֹּבְאִים עַל־אֲרִיאֵל
וְכָל־צֹבֶיהָ וּמְצֹדָתָהּ
וְהַמְּצִיקִים לָהּ:

8 It shall even be as when a hungry man dreams,
And look—he eats;
But he awakes, and his soul is still empty;
Or as when a thirsty man dreams,
And look—he drinks;
But he awakes, and indeed *he is* faint,
And his soul still craves:
So the multitude of all the nations shall be,
Who fight against Mount Zion."

8 וְהָיָה כַּאֲשֶׁר יַחֲלֹם הָרָעֵב
וְהִנֵּה אוֹכֵל
וְהֵקִיץ וְרֵיקָה נַפְשׁוֹ
וְכַאֲשֶׁר יַחֲלֹם הַצָּמֵא וְהִנֵּה שֹׁתֶה
וְהֵקִיץ וְהִנֵּה עָיֵף וְנַפְשׁוֹ שׁוֹקֵקָה
כֵּן יִהְיֶה הֲמוֹן כָּל־הַגּוֹיִם
הַצֹּבְאִים עַל־הַר צִיּוֹן: ס

9 Pause and wonder!
Blind yourselves and be blind!
They are drunk, but not with wine;
They stagger, but not with intoxicating drink.

9 הִתְמַהְמְהוּ וּתְמָהוּ
הִשְׁתַּעַשְׁעוּ וָשֹׁעוּ
שָׁכְרוּ וְלֹא־יַיִן
נָעוּ וְלֹא שֵׁכָר:

10 For the LORD has poured out on you
The spirit of deep sleep,

10 כִּי־נָסַךְ עֲלֵיכֶם יְהוָה רוּחַ תַּרְדֵּמָה
וַיְעַצֵּם אֶת־עֵינֵיכֶם

And has closed your eyes, namely, the
    prophets;
And He has covered your heads, *namely*, the
    seers.

11 The whole vision has become to you like the
words of a book that is sealed, which *men* deliver to
one who is literate, saying, "Read this, please."
    And he says, "I cannot, for it *is* sealed."
12 Then the book is delivered to one who is
illiterate, saying, "Read this, please."
    And he says, "I am not literate."
13 Therefore the Lord said:

"Inasmuch as these people draw near with
    their mouths
And honor Me with their lips,
But have removed their hearts far from Me,
And their fear toward Me is taught by the
    commandment of men,
14 Therefore, behold, I will again do a marve-
    lous work
Among this people,
A marvelous work and a wonder;
For the wisdom of their wise *men* shall
    perish,
And the understanding of their prudent *men*
    shall be hidden."
15 Woe to those who seek deep to hide their
    counsel far from the LORD,
And their works are in the dark;
They say, "Who sees us?" and, "Who knows
    us?"
16 Surely you have things turned around!
Shall the potter be esteemed as the clay;
For shall the thing made say of him who
    made it,
"He did not make me"?
Or shall the thing formed say of him who
    formed it,
"He has no understanding"?
17 *Is* it not yet a very little while
Till Lebanon shall be turned into a fruitful
    field,
And the fruitful field be esteemed as a forest?
18 In that day the deaf shall hear the words of
    the book,
And the eyes of the blind shall see out of
    obscurity and out of darkness.
19 The humble also shall increase *their* joy in the
    LORD,
And the poor among men shall rejoice
    In the Holy One of Israel.
20 For the terrible one is brought to nothing,
The scornful one is consumed,

אֶת־הַנְּבִיאִים וְאֶת־רָאשֵׁיכֶם
הַחֹזִים כִּסָּה׃

11 וַתְּהִי לָכֶם חָזוּת הַכֹּל כְּדִבְרֵי הַסֵּפֶר הֶחָתוּם
אֲשֶׁר־יִתְּנוּ אֹתוֹ אֶל־יוֹדֵעַ הַסֵּפֶר לֵאמֹר קְרָא נָא־
זֶה וְאָמַר לֹא אוּכַל כִּי חָתוּם הוּא׃ 12 וְנִתַּן הַסֵּפֶר
עַל אֲשֶׁר לֹא־יָדַע סֵפֶר לֵאמֹר קְרָא נָא־זֶה וְאָמַר
לֹא יָדַעְתִּי סֵפֶר׃ ס

13 וַיֹּאמֶר אֲדֹנָי יַעַן כִּי נִגַּשׁ הָעָם הַזֶּה
בְּפִיו וּבִשְׂפָתָיו כִּבְּדוּנִי
וְלִבּוֹ רִחַק מִמֶּנִּי
וַתְּהִי יִרְאָתָם אֹתִי
מִצְוַת אֲנָשִׁים מְלֻמָּדָה׃
14 לָכֵן הִנְנִי יוֹסִף
לְהַפְלִיא אֶת־הָעָם־הַזֶּה
הַפְלֵא וָפֶלֶא
וְאָבְדָה חָכְמַת חֲכָמָיו
וּבִינַת נְבֹנָיו תִּסְתַּתָּר׃ ס
15 הוֹי הַמַּעֲמִיקִים מֵיהֹוָה לַסְתִּר עֵצָה
וְהָיָה בְמַחְשָׁךְ מַעֲשֵׂיהֶם
וַיֹּאמְרוּ מִי רֹאֵנוּ וּמִי יֹדְעֵנוּ׃
16 הַפְכְּכֶם
אִם־כְּחֹמֶר הַיֹּצֵר יֵחָשֵׁב
כִּי־יֹאמַר מַעֲשֶׂה לְעֹשֵׂהוּ לֹא עָשָׂנִי
וְיֵצֶר אָמַר לְיוֹצְרוֹ לֹא הֵבִין׃
17 הֲלוֹא־עוֹד מְעַט מִזְעָר
וְשָׁב לְבָנוֹן לַכַּרְמֶל
וְהַכַּרְמֶל לַיַּעַר יֵחָשֵׁב׃
18 וְשָׁמְעוּ בַיּוֹם־הַהוּא
הַחֵרְשִׁים דִּבְרֵי־סֵפֶר
וּמֵאֹפֶל וּמֵחֹשֶׁךְ עֵינֵי עִוְרִים תִּרְאֶינָה׃
19 וְיָסְפוּ עֲנָוִים בַּיהֹוָה שִׂמְחָה
וְאֶבְיוֹנֵי אָדָם בִּקְדוֹשׁ יִשְׂרָאֵל יָגִילוּ׃
20 כִּי־אָפֵס עָרִיץ
וְכָלָה לֵץ

And all who watch for iniquity are cut off—
21 Who make a man an offender by a word,
And lay a snare for him who reproves in the
gate,
And turn aside the just by empty words.

22 Therefore thus says the LORD, who redeemed
Abraham, concerning the house of Jacob:

"Jacob shall not now be ashamed,
Nor shall his face now grow pale;
23 But when he sees his children,
The work of My hands, in his midst,
They will hallow My name,
And hallow the Holy One of Jacob,
And fear the God of Israel.
24 These also who erred in spirit will come to
understanding,
And those who complained will learn doc-
trine."

30 "Woe to the rebellious children," says the
LORD,
"Who take counsel, but not of Me,
And who devise plans, but not of My Spirit,
That they may add sin to sin;
2 Who walk to go down to Egypt,
And have not asked My advice,
To strengthen themselves in the strength of
Pharaoh,
And to trust in the shadow of Egypt!
3 Therefore the strength of Pharaoh
Shall be your shame,
And trust in the shadow of Egypt
Shall be *your* humiliation.
4 For his princes were at Zoan,
And his ambassadors came to Hanes.
5 They were all ashamed of a people *who* could
not benefit them,
Or be help or benefit,
But a shame and also a reproach."

6 The burden against the beasts of the South.

Through a land of trouble and anguish,
From which *came* the lioness and lion,
The viper and fiery flying serpent,
They will carry their riches on the backs of
young donkeys,
And their treasures on the humps of camels,
To a people *who* shall not profit;
7 For the Egyptians shall help in vain and to
no purpose.
Therefore I have called her
Rahab-Hem-Shebeth.

8 Now go, write it before them on a tablet,

וְנִכְרְתוּ כָּל־שֹׁקְדֵי אָֽוֶן׃
21 מַחֲטִיאֵי אָדָם בְּדָבָר
וְלַמּוֹכִיחַ בַּשַּׁעַר יְקֹשׁוּן
וַיַּטּוּ בַתֹּהוּ צַדִּֽיק׃ ס
22 לָכֵן כֹּֽה־אָמַר יְהֹוָה אֶל־בֵּית יַעֲקֹב
אֲשֶׁר פָּדָה אֶת־אַבְרָהָם
לֹא־עַתָּה יֵבוֹשׁ יַעֲקֹב
וְלֹא עַתָּה פָּנָיו יֶחֱוָֽרוּ׃
23 כִּי בִרְאֹתוֹ יְלָדָיו מַעֲשֵׂה יָדַי בְּקִרְבּוֹ
יַקְדִּישׁוּ שְׁמִי
וְהִקְדִּישׁוּ אֶת־קְדוֹשׁ יַעֲקֹב
וְאֶת־אֱלֹהֵי יִשְׂרָאֵל יַעֲרִֽיצוּ׃
24 וְיָדְעוּ תֹֽעֵי־רוּחַ בִּינָה
וְרוֹגְנִים יִלְמְדוּ־לֶֽקַח׃

ל הוֹי בָּנִים סֽוֹרְרִים נְאֻם־יְהֹוָה
לַעֲשׂוֹת עֵצָה וְלֹא מִנִּי
וְלִנְסֹךְ מַסֵּכָה וְלֹא רוּחִי
לְמַעַן סְפוֹת חַטָּאת עַל־חַטָּֽאת׃
2 הַהֹלְכִים לָרֶדֶת מִצְרַיִם
וּפִי לֹא שָׁאָלוּ
לָעוֹז בְּמָעוֹז פַּרְעֹה
וְלַחְסוֹת בְּצֵל מִצְרָֽיִם׃
3 וְהָיָה לָכֶם מָעוֹז פַּרְעֹה לְבֹשֶׁת
וְהֶחָסוּת בְּצֵל־מִצְרַיִם לִכְלִמָּֽה׃
4 כִּי־הָיוּ בְצֹעַן שָׂרָיו
וּמַלְאָכָיו חָנֵס יַגִּֽיעוּ׃
5 כֹּל הֹבִאישׁ עַל־עַם לֹא־יוֹעִילוּ לָמוֹ
לֹא לְעֵזֶר וְלֹא לְהוֹעִיל
כִּי לְבֹשֶׁת וְגַם־לְחֶרְפָּֽה׃ ס
6 מַשָּׂא בַּהֲמוֹת נֶגֶב
בְּאֶרֶץ צָרָה וְצוּקָה
לָבִיא וָלַיִשׁ מֵהֶם
אֶפְעֶה וְשָׂרָף מְעוֹפֵף
יִשְׂאוּ עַל־כֶּתֶף עֲיָרִים חֵֽילֵהֶם
וְעַל־דַּבֶּשֶׁת גְּמַלִּים אוֹצְרֹתָם
עַל־עַם לֹא יוֹעִֽילוּ׃
7 וּמִצְרַיִם הֶבֶל וָרִיק יַעְזֹרוּ
לָכֵן קָרָאתִי לָזֹאת
רַהַב הֵם שָֽׁבֶת׃
8 עַתָּה בּוֹא כָתְבָהּ עַל־לוּחַ

And note it on a scroll,
That it may be for time to come,
Forever and ever:

9   That this *is* a rebellious people,
Lying children,
Children *who* will not hear the law of the
    LORD;

10   Who say to the seers, "Do not see,"
And to the prophets, "Do not prophesy to us
    right things;
Speak to us smooth things, prophesy deceits.

11   Get out of the way,
Turn aside from the path,
Cause the Holy One of Israel
To cease from before us."

12 Therefore thus says the Holy One of Israel:

"Because you despise this word,
And trust in oppression and perversity,
And rely on them,

13   Therefore this iniquity shall be to you
Like a breach ready to fall,
A bulge in a high wall,
Whose breaking comes suddenly, in an
    instant.

14   And He shall break it like the breaking of the
    potter's vessel,
Which is broken in pieces;
He shall not spare.
So there shall not be found among its
    fragments
A shard to take fire from the hearth,
Or to take water from the cistern."

15 For thus says the Lord GOD, the Holy One of
Israel:

"In returning and rest you shall be saved;
In quietness and confidence shall be your
    strength."
But you would not,

16   And you said, "No, for we will flee on
    horses"—
Therefore you shall flee!
And, "We will ride on swift *horses*"—
Therefore those who pursue you shall be
    swift!

17   One thousand *shall flee* at the threat of one,
At the threat of five you shall flee,
Till you are left as a pole on top of a
    mountain
And as a banner on a hill.

18   Therefore the LORD will wait, that He may
    be gracious to you;

אַתָּה וְעַל־סֵפֶר חֻקָּהּ
וּתְהִי לְיוֹם אַחֲרוֹן
לָעַד עַד־עוֹלָם:

9 כִּי עַם מְרִי הוּא
בָּנִים כֶּחָשִׁים
בָּנִים לֹא־אָבוּ שְׁמוֹעַ תּוֹרַת יְהֹוָה:

10 אֲשֶׁר אָמְרוּ לָרֹאִים לֹא תִרְאוּ
וְלַחֹזִים לֹא תֶחֱזוּ־לָנוּ נְכֹחוֹת
דַּבְּרוּ־לָנוּ חֲלָקוֹת חֲזוּ מַהֲתַלּוֹת:

11 סוּרוּ מִנֵּי־דֶרֶךְ
הַטּוּ מִנֵּי־אֹרַח
הַשְׁבִּיתוּ מִפָּנֵינוּ
אֶת־קְדוֹשׁ יִשְׂרָאֵל: ס

12 לָכֵן כֹּה אָמַר קְדוֹשׁ יִשְׂרָאֵל
יַעַן מָאָסְכֶם בַּדָּבָר הַזֶּה
וַתִּבְטְחוּ בְּעֹשֶׁק וְנָלוֹז
וַתִּשָּׁעֲנוּ עָלָיו:

13 לָכֵן יִהְיֶה לָכֶם הֶעָו‍ֹן הַזֶּה
כְּפֶרֶץ נֹפֵל נִבְעֶה בְּחוֹמָה נִשְׂגָּבָה
אֲשֶׁר־פִּתְאֹם לְפֶתַע יָבוֹא שִׁבְרָהּ:

14 וּשְׁבָרָהּ כְּשֵׁבֶר נֵבֶל יוֹצְרִים
כָּתוּת לֹא יַחְמֹל
וְלֹא־יִמָּצֵא בִמְכִתָּתוֹ חֶרֶשׂ
לַחְתּוֹת אֵשׁ מִיָּקוּד
וְלַחְשֹׂף מַיִם מִגֶּבֶא: פ

15 כִּי כֹה־אָמַר אֲדֹנָי יְהֹוִה
קְדוֹשׁ יִשְׂרָאֵל
בְּשׁוּבָה וָנַחַת תִּוָּשֵׁעוּן
בְּהַשְׁקֵט וּבְבִטְחָה תִּהְיֶה גְּבוּרַתְכֶם
וְלֹא אֲבִיתֶם:

16 וַתֹּאמְרוּ לֹא־כִי עַל־סוּס נָנוּס
עַל־כֵּן תְּנוּסוּן
וְעַל־קַל נִרְכָּב
עַל־כֵּן יִקַּלּוּ רֹדְפֵיכֶם:

17 אֶלֶף אֶחָד מִפְּנֵי גַּעֲרַת אֶחָד
מִפְּנֵי גַּעֲרַת חֲמִשָּׁה תָּנֻסוּ
עַד אִם־נוֹתַרְתֶּם
כַּתֹּרֶן עַל־רֹאשׁ הָהָר
וְכַנֵּס עַל־הַגִּבְעָה:

18 וְלָכֵן יְחַכֶּה יְהֹוָה לַחֲנַנְכֶם
וְלָכֵן יָרוּם לְרַחֶמְכֶם

And therefore He will be exalted, that He
    may have mercy on you.
For the LORD *is* a God of justice;
Blessed *are* all those who wait for Him.

19 For the people shall dwell in Zion at
    Jerusalem;
You shall weep no more.
He will be very gracious to you at the sound
    of your cry;
When He hears it, He will answer you.

20 And *though* the Lord gives you
The bread of adversity and the water of
    affliction,
Yet your teachers will not be moved into a
    corner anymore,
But your eyes shall see your teachers.

21 Your ears shall hear a word behind you,
    saying,
"This *is* the way, walk in it,"
Whenever you turn to the right hand
Or whenever you turn to the left.

22 You will also defile the covering of your
    images of silver,
And the ornament of your molded images of
    gold.
You will throw them away as an unclean
    thing;
You will say to them, "Get away!"

23 Then He will give the rain for your seed
With which you sow the ground,
And bread of the increase of the earth;
It will be fat and plentiful.
In that day your cattle will feed
In large pastures.

24 Likewise the oxen and the young donkeys
    that work the ground
Will eat cured fodder,
Which has been winnowed with the shovel
    and fan.

25 There will be on every high mountain
And on every high hill
Rivers *and* streams of waters,
In the day of the great slaughter,
When the towers fall.

26 Moreover the light of the moon will be as the
    light of the sun,
And the light of the sun will be sevenfold,
As the light of seven days,
In the day that the LORD binds up the bruise
    of His people
And heals the stroke of their wound.

27 Behold, the name of the LORD comes from
    afar,

כִּי־אֱלֹהֵי מִשְׁפָּט יְהֹוָה
אַשְׁרֵי כָּל־חוֹכֵי לֽוֹ׃ ס

19 כִּי־עַם בְּצִיּוֹן יֵשֵׁב בִּירֽוּשָׁלִָם
בָּכוֹ לֹֽא־תִבְכֶּה
חָנוֹן יָחְנְךָ לְקוֹל זַעֲקֶךָ
כְּשָׁמְעָתוֹ עָנָֽךְ׃

20 וְנָתַן לָכֶם אֲדֹנָי לֶחֶם צָר וּמַיִם לָחַץ
וְלֹֽא־יִכָּנֵף עוֹד מוֹרֶיךָ
וְהָיוּ עֵינֶיךָ רֹאוֹת אֶת־מוֹרֶֽיךָ׃

21 וְאָזְנֶיךָ תִּשְׁמַעְנָה דָבָר
מֵאַחֲרֶיךָ לֵאמֹר
זֶה הַדֶּרֶךְ לְכוּ בוֹ
כִּי תַאֲמִינוּ וְכִי תַשְׂמְאִֽילוּ׃

22 וְטִמֵּאתֶם אֶת־צִפּוּי פְּסִילֵי כַסְפֶּךָ
וְאֶת־אֲפֻדַּת מַסֵּכַת זְהָבֶךָ
תִּזְרֵם כְּמוֹ דָוָה
צֵא תֹּאמַר לֽוֹ׃

23 וְנָתַן מְטַר זַרְעֲךָ
אֲשֶׁר־תִּזְרַע אֶת־הָֽאֲדָמָה
וְלֶחֶם תְּבוּאַת הָֽאֲדָמָה
וְהָיָה דָשֵׁן וְשָׁמֵן
יִרְעֶה מִקְנֶיךָ בַּיּוֹם הַהוּא כַּר נִרְחָֽב׃

24 וְהָֽאֲלָפִים וְהָעֲיָרִים עֹבְדֵי הָֽאֲדָמָה
בְּלִיל חָמִיץ יֹאכֵלוּ
אֲשֶׁר־זֹרֶה בָרַחַת וּבַמִּזְרֶֽה׃

25 וְהָיָה ׀ עַל־כָּל־הַר גָּבֹהַּ
וְעַל כָּל־גִּבְעָה נִשָּׂאָה
פְּלָגִים יִבְלֵי־מָיִם
בְּיוֹם הֶרֶג רָב בִּנְפֹל מִגְדָּלִֽים׃

26 וְהָיָה אֽוֹר־הַלְּבָנָה כְּאוֹר הַֽחַמָּה
וְאוֹר הַחַמָּה יִהְיֶה שִׁבְעָתַיִם
כְּאוֹר שִׁבְעַת הַיָּמִים
בְּיוֹם חֲבֹשׁ יְהֹוָה אֶת־שֶׁבֶר עַמּוֹ
וּמַחַץ מַכָּתוֹ יִרְפָּֽא׃ ס

27 הִנֵּה שֵׁם־יְהֹוָה בָּא מִמֶּרְחָק
בֹּעֵר אַפּוֹ וְכֹבֶד מַשָּׂאָה

Burning *with* His anger,
And *His* burden *is* heavy;
His lips are full of indignation,
And His tongue like a devouring fire.

28 His breath is like an overflowing stream,
Which reaches up to the neck,
To sift the nations with the sieve of futility;
And *there shall be* a bridle in the jaws of the
    people,
Causing *them* to err.

29 You shall have a song
As in the night *when* a holy festival is kept,
And gladness of heart as when one goes with
    a flute,
To come into the mountain of the LORD,
To the Mighty One of Israel.

30 The LORD will cause His glorious voice to be
    heard,
And show the descent of His arm,
With the indignation of *His* anger
And the flame of a devouring fire,
With scattering, tempest, and hailstones.

31 For through the voice of the LORD
Assyria will be beaten down,
As He strikes with the rod.

32 And *in* every place where the staff of
    punishment passes,
Which the LORD lays on him,
It will be with tambourines and harps;
And in battles of brandishing He will fight
    with it.

33 For Tophet *was* established of old,
Yes, for the king it is prepared.
He has made *it* deep and large;
Its pyre *is* fire with much wood;
The breath of the LORD, like a stream of
    brimstone,
Kindles it.

31 Woe to those who go down to Egypt for help,
And rely on horses,
Who trust in chariots because *they are* many,
And in horsemen because they are very
    strong,
But who do not look to the Holy One of
    Israel,
Nor seek the LORD!

2 Yet He also *is* wise and will bring disaster,
And will not call back His words,
But will arise against the house of evildoers,
And against the help of those who work
    iniquity.

3 Now the Egyptians *are* men, and not God;

שְׂפָתָיו מָלְאוּ זַעַם
וּלְשׁוֹנוֹ כְּאֵשׁ אֹכָלֶת:
28 וְרוּחוֹ כְּנַחַל שׁוֹטֵף
עַד־צַוָּאר יֶחֱצֶה
לַהֲנָפָה גוֹיִם בְּנָפַת שָׁוְא
וְרֶסֶן מַתְעֶה עַל לְחָיֵי עַמִּים:
29 הַשִּׁיר יִהְיֶה לָכֶם
כְּלֵיל הִתְקַדֶּשׁ־חָג
וְשִׂמְחַת לֵבָב כַּהוֹלֵךְ בֶּחָלִיל
לָבוֹא בְהַר־יְהוָה אֶל־צוּר יִשְׂרָאֵל:
30 וְהִשְׁמִיעַ יְהוָה אֶת־הוֹד קוֹלוֹ
וְנַחַת זְרוֹעוֹ יַרְאֶה
בְּזַעַף אַף וְלַהַב אֵשׁ אוֹכֵלָה
נֶפֶץ וָזֶרֶם וְאֶבֶן בָּרָד:
31 כִּי־מִקּוֹל יְהוָה יֵחַת אַשּׁוּר
בַּשֵּׁבֶט יַכֶּה:
32 וְהָיָה כֹּל מַעֲבַר מַטֵּה מוּסָדָה
אֲשֶׁר יָנִיחַ יְהוָה עָלָיו
בְּתֻפִּים וּבְכִנֹּרוֹת
וּבְמִלְחֲמוֹת תְּנוּפָה נִלְחַם־בָּהּ:
33 כִּי־עָרוּךְ מֵאֶתְמוּל תָּפְתֶּה
גַּם־הוּא לַמֶּלֶךְ הוּכָן
הֶעְמִיק הִרְחִב
מְדֻרָתָהּ אֵשׁ וְעֵצִים הַרְבֵּה
נִשְׁמַת יְהוָה כְּנַחַל גָּפְרִית בֹּעֲרָה בָּהּ: ס

לא הוֹי הַיֹּרְדִים מִצְרַיִם לְעֶזְרָה
עַל־סוּסִים יִשָּׁעֵנוּ
וַיִּבְטְחוּ עַל־רֶכֶב כִּי רָב
וְעַל פָּרָשִׁים כִּי־עָצְמוּ מְאֹד
וְלֹא שָׁעוּ עַל־קְדוֹשׁ יִשְׂרָאֵל
וְאֶת־יְהוָה לֹא דָרָשׁוּ:
2 וְגַם־הוּא חָכָם וַיָּבֵא רָע
וְאֶת־דְּבָרָיו לֹא הֵסִיר וְקָם עַל־בֵּית מְרֵעִים
וְעַל־עֶזְרַת פֹּעֲלֵי אָוֶן:
3 וּמִצְרַיִם אָדָם וְלֹא־אֵל

ל 32 בָּם 33 הִיא

And their horses are flesh, and not spirit.
When the LORD stretches out His hand,
Both he who helps will fall,
And he who is helped will fall down;
They all will perish together.

וְסוּסֵיהֶם בָּשָׂר וְלֹא־רוּחַ
וַיהוָה יַטֶּה יָדוֹ
וְכָשַׁל עוֹזֵר וְנָפַל עָזֻר
וְיַחְדָּו כֻּלָּם יִכְלָיוּן: ס

4 For thus the LORD has spoken to me:

4 כִּי כֹה אָמַר־יְהוָה ׀ אֵלַי

"As a lion roars,
And a young lion over his prey
(When a multitude of shepherds is sum-
    moned against him,
He will not be afraid of their voice
Nor be disturbed by their noise),
So the LORD of hosts will come down
To fight for Mount Zion and for its hill.

כַּאֲשֶׁר יֶהְגֶּה הָאַרְיֵה וְהַכְּפִיר
עַל־טַרְפּוֹ
אֲשֶׁר יִקָּרֵא עָלָיו מְלֹא רֹעִים
מִקּוֹלָם לֹא יֵחָת
וּמֵהֲמוֹנָם לֹא יַעֲנֶה
כֵּן יֵרֵד יְהוָה צְבָאוֹת
לִצְבֹּא עַל־הַר־צִיּוֹן וְעַל־גִּבְעָתָהּ:

5 Like birds flying about,
So will the LORD of hosts defend Jerusalem.
Defending, He will also deliver *it;*
Passing over, He will preserve *it.*"

5 כְּצִפֳּרִים עָפוֹת
כֵּן יָגֵן יְהוָה צְבָאוֹת עַל־יְרוּשָׁלַ͏ִם
גָּנוֹן וְהִצִּיל
פָּסֹחַ וְהִמְלִיט:

6 Return *to Him* against whom the children of
Israel have deeply revolted. 7 For in that day every
man shall throw away his idols of silver and his
idols of gold—sin, which your own hands have
made for yourselves.

6 שׁוּבוּ
לַאֲשֶׁר הֶעְמִיקוּ סָרָה בְּנֵי יִשְׂרָאֵל:
7 כִּי בַּיּוֹם הַהוּא יִמְאָסוּן
אִישׁ אֱלִילֵי כַסְפּוֹ וֶאֱלִילֵי זְהָבוֹ
אֲשֶׁר עָשׂוּ לָכֶם יְדֵיכֶם חֵטְא:

8 "Then Assyria shall fall by a sword not of
    man,
And a sword not of mankind shall devour
    him.
But he shall flee from the sword,
And his young men shall become forced
    labor.

8 וְנָפַל אַשּׁוּר בְּחֶרֶב לֹא־אִישׁ
וְחֶרֶב לֹא־אָדָם תֹּאכְלֶנּוּ
וְנָס לוֹ מִפְּנֵי־חֶרֶב
וּבַחוּרָיו לָמַס יִהְיוּ:

9 He shall cross over to his stronghold for fear,
And his princes shall be afraid of the
    banner,"
Says the LORD,
Whose fire *is* in Zion
And whose furnace *is* in Jerusalem.

9 וְסַלְעוֹ מִמָּגוֹר יַעֲבוֹר
וְחַתּוּ מִנֵּס שָׂרָיו
נְאֻם־יְהוָה אֲשֶׁר־אוּר לוֹ בְּצִיּוֹן
וְתַנּוּר לוֹ בִּירוּשָׁלָ͏ִם: ס

32 Behold, a king will reign in righteousness,
And princes will rule with justice.

לב הֵן לְצֶדֶק יִמְלָךְ־מֶלֶךְ
וּלְשָׂרִים לְמִשְׁפָּט יָשֹׂרוּ:

2 A man will be as a hiding place from the
    wind,
And a cover from the tempest,
As rivers of water in a dry place,
As the shadow of a great rock in a weary
    land.

2 וְהָיָה־אִישׁ כְּמַחֲבֵא־רוּחַ
וְסֵתֶר זָרֶם
כְּפַלְגֵי־מַיִם בְּצָיוֹן
כְּצֵל סֶלַע־כָּבֵד בְּאֶרֶץ עֲיֵפָה:

3 The eyes of those who see will not be dim,
And the ears of those who hear will listen.

3 וְלֹא תִשְׁעֶינָה עֵינֵי רֹאִים
וְאָזְנֵי שֹׁמְעִים תִּקְשַׁבְנָה:

4 Also the heart of the rash will understand
    knowledge,
And the tongue of the stammerers will be
    ready to speak plainly.

4 וּלְבַב נִמְהָרִים יָבִין לָדַעַת
וּלְשׁוֹן עִלְּגִים תְּמַהֵר לְדַבֵּר צָחוֹת:

5 The foolish person will no longer be called
  generous,
  Nor the miser said *to be* bountiful;
6 For the foolish person will speak foolishness,
  And his heart will work iniquity:
  To practice ungodliness,
  To utter error against the LORD,
  To keep the hungry unsatisfied,
  And he will cause the drink of the thirsty to
  fail.
7 Also the schemes of the schemer *are* evil;
  He devises wicked plans
  To destroy the poor with lying words,
  Even when the needy speaks justice.
8 But a generous man devises generous things,
  And by generosity he shall stand.

9 Rise up, you women who are at ease,
  Hear my voice;
  You complacent daughters,
  Give ear to my speech.
10 In a year and *some* days
  You will be troubled, you complacent
  women;
  For the vintage will fail,
  The gathering will not come.
11 Tremble, you *women* who are at ease;
  Be troubled, you complacent ones;
  Strip yourselves, make yourselves bare,
  And gird *sackcloth* on *your* waists.

12 People shall mourn upon their breasts
  For the pleasant fields, for the fruitful vine.
13 On the land of my people will come up
  thorns *and* briers,
  Yes, on all the happy homes *in* the joyous
  city;
14 Because the palaces will be forsaken,
  The bustling city will be deserted.
  The forts and towers will become lairs
  forever,
  A joy of wild donkeys, a pasture of flocks—
15 Until the Spirit is poured upon us from on
  high,
  And the wilderness becomes a fruitful field,
  And the fruitful field is counted as a forest.

16 Then justice will dwell in the wilderness,
  And righteousness remain in the fruitful
  field.
17 The work of righteousness will be peace,
  And the effect of righteousness, quietness
  and assurance forever.
18 My people will dwell in a peaceful habitation,

לֹא־יִקָּרֵא עוֹד לְנָבָל נָדִיב 5
וּלְכִילַי לֹא יֵאָמֵר שׁוֹעַ:
כִּי נָבָל נְבָלָה יְדַבֵּר 6
וְלִבּוֹ יַעֲשֶׂה־אָוֶן לַעֲשׂוֹת חֹנֶף
וּלְדַבֵּר אֶל־יְהֹוָה תּוֹעָה
לְהָרִיק נֶפֶשׁ רָעֵב
וּמַשְׁקֶה צָמֵא יַחְסִיר:
וְכֵלַי כֵּלָיו רָעִים 7
הוּא זִמּוֹת יָעָץ
לְחַבֵּל עֲנָוִים בְּאִמְרֵי־שֶׁקֶר
וּבְדַבֵּר אֶבְיוֹן מִשְׁפָּט:
וְנָדִיב נְדִיבוֹת יָעָץ 8
וְהוּא עַל־נְדִיבוֹת יָקוּם: פ
נָשִׁים שַׁאֲנַנּוֹת קֹמְנָה שְׁמַעְנָה קוֹלִי 9
בָּנוֹת בֹּטְחוֹת הַאְזֵנָּה אִמְרָתִי:
יָמִים עַל־שָׁנָה תִּרְגַּזְנָה בֹּטְחוֹת 10
כִּי כָּלָה בָצִיר אֹסֶף בְּלִי יָבוֹא:
חִרְדוּ שַׁאֲנַנּוֹת רְגָזָה בֹּטְחוֹת 11
פְּשֹׁטָה וְעֹרָה וַחֲגוֹרָה עַל־חֲלָצָיִם:
עַל־שָׁדַיִם סֹפְדִים 12
עַל־שְׂדֵי־חֶמֶד
עַל־גֶּפֶן פֹּרִיָּה:
עַל אַדְמַת עַמִּי 13
קוֹץ שָׁמִיר תַּעֲלֶה
כִּי עַל־כָּל־בָּתֵּי מָשׂוֹשׂ
קִרְיָה עַלִּיזָה:
כִּי־אַרְמוֹן נֻטָּשׁ 14
הֲמוֹן עִיר עֻזָּב
עֹפֶל וָבַחַן
הָיָה בְעַד מְעָרוֹת עַד־עוֹלָם
מְשׂוֹשׂ פְּרָאִים מִרְעֵה עֲדָרִים:
עַד־יֵעָרֶה עָלֵינוּ רוּחַ מִמָּרוֹם 15
וְהָיָה מִדְבָּר לַכַּרְמֶל
וְכַרְמֶל לַיַּעַר יֵחָשֵׁב:
וְשָׁכַן בַּמִּדְבָּר מִשְׁפָּט 16
וּצְדָקָה בַּכַּרְמֶל תֵּשֵׁב:
וְהָיָה מַעֲשֵׂה הַצְּדָקָה שָׁלוֹם 17
וַעֲבֹדַת הַצְּדָקָה
הַשְׁקֵט וָבֶטַח עַד־עוֹלָם:
וְיָשַׁב עַמִּי בִּנְוֵה שָׁלוֹם 18
וּבְמִשְׁכְּנוֹת מִבְטַחִים

לב 7 עֲנִיִּים   15 וְהַכַּרְמֶל

In secure dwellings, and in quiet resting places,

19 Though hail comes down on the forest,
And the city is brought low in humiliation.

וּבְמִשְׁכְּנוֹת מִבְטַחִים וּבִמְנוּחֹת שַׁאֲנַנּוֹת:

19 וּבָרַד בְּרֶדֶת הַיָּעַר

וּבַשִּׁפְלָה תִּשְׁפַּל הָעִיר:

20 Blessed *are* you who sow beside all waters,
Who send out freely the feet of the ox and the donkey.

20 אַשְׁרֵיכֶם זֹרְעֵי עַל־כָּל־מָיִם

מְשַׁלְּחֵי רֶגֶל־הַשּׁוֹר וְהַחֲמוֹר: ס

33 Woe to you who plunder, though you *have* not *been* plundered;
And you who deal treacherously, though they have not dealt treacherously with you!
When you cease plundering,
You will be plundered;
When you make an end of dealing treacherously,
They will deal treacherously with you.

לג הוֹי שׁוֹדֵד וְאַתָּה לֹא שָׁדוּד

וּבוֹגֵד וְלֹא־בָגְדוּ בוֹ

כַּהֲתִמְךָ שׁוֹדֵד תּוּשַּׁד

כַּנְּלֹתְךָ לִבְגֹּד יִבְגְּדוּ־בָךְ: ס

2 O LORD, be gracious to us;
We have waited for You.
Be their arm every morning,
Our salvation also in the time of trouble.

2 יְהוָה חָנֵּנוּ

לְךָ קִוִּינוּ

הֱיֵה זְרֹעָם לַבְּקָרִים

אַף־יְשׁוּעָתֵנוּ בְּעֵת צָרָה:

3 At the noise of the tumult the people shall flee;
When You lift Yourself up, the nations shall be scattered;

3 מִקּוֹל הָמוֹן נָדְדוּ עַמִּים

מֵרוֹמְמֻתֶךָ נָפְצוּ גּוֹיִם:

4 And Your plunder shall be gathered
Like the gathering of the caterpillar;
As the running to and fro of locusts,
He shall run upon them.

4 וְאֻסַּף שְׁלַלְכֶם אֹסֶף הֶחָסִיל

כְּמַשַּׁק גֵּבִים שׁוֹקֵק בּוֹ:

5 The LORD is exalted, for He dwells on high;
He has filled Zion with justice and righteousness.

5 נִשְׂגָּב יְהוָה כִּי שֹׁכֵן מָרוֹם

מִלֵּא צִיּוֹן מִשְׁפָּט וּצְדָקָה:

6 Wisdom and knowledge will be the stability of your times,
And the strength of salvation;
The fear of the LORD *is* His treasure.

6 וְהָיָה אֱמוּנַת עִתֶּיךָ

חֹסֶן יְשׁוּעֹת חָכְמַת וָדַעַת

יִרְאַת יְהוָה הִיא אוֹצָרוֹ: ס

7 Surely their valiant ones shall cry outside,
The ambassadors of peace shall weep bitterly.

7 הֵן אֶרְאֶלָּם צָעֲקוּ חֻצָה

מַלְאֲכֵי שָׁלוֹם מַר יִבְכָּיוּן:

8 The highways lie waste,
The traveling man ceases.
He has broken the covenant,
He has despised the cities,
He regards no man.

8 נָשַׁמּוּ מְסִלּוֹת

שָׁבַת עֹבֵר אֹרַח

הֵפֵר בְּרִית

מָאַס עָרִים

לֹא חָשַׁב אֱנוֹשׁ:

9 The earth mourns *and* languishes,
Lebanon is shamed *and* shriveled;
Sharon is like a wilderness,
And Bashan and Carmel shake off *their* fruits.

9 אָבַל אֻמְלְלָה אָרֶץ

הֶחְפִּיר לְבָנוֹן קָמַל

הָיָה הַשָּׁרוֹן כָּעֲרָבָה

וְנֹעֵר בָּשָׁן וְכַרְמֶל:

10 "Now I will rise," says the LORD;
"Now I will be exalted,

10 עַתָּה אָקוּם יֹאמַר יְהוָה

עַתָּה אֵרוֹמָם

Now I will lift Myself up.

11 You shall conceive chaff,
You shall bring forth stubble;
Your breath, *as* fire, shall devour you.

12 And the people shall be *like* the burnings of
lime;
Like thorns cut up they shall be burned in the
fire.

13 Hear, you *who are* afar off, what I have done;
And you *who are* near, acknowledge My
might."

14 The sinners in Zion are afraid;
Fearfulness has seized the hypocrites:
"Who among us shall dwell with the devour-
ing fire?
Who among us shall dwell with everlasting
burnings?"

15 He who walks righteously and speaks up-
rightly,
He who despises the gain of oppressions,
Who gestures with his hands, refusing bribes,
Who stops his ears from hearing of
bloodshed,
And shuts his eyes from seeing evil:

16 He will dwell on high;
His place of defense *will be* the fortress of
rocks;
Bread will be given him,
His water *will be* sure.

17 Your eyes will see the King in His beauty;
They will see the land that is very far off.

18 Your heart will meditate on terror:
"Where *is* the scribe?
Where *is* he who weighs?
Where *is* he who counts the towers?"

19 You will not see a fierce people,
A people of obscure speech, beyond percep-
tion,
Of a stammering tongue *that you* cannot
understand.

20 Look upon Zion, the city of our appointed
feasts;
Your eyes will see Jerusalem, a quiet home,
A tabernacle *that* will not be taken down;
Not one of its stakes will ever be removed,
Nor will any of its cords be broken.

21 But there the majestic LORD *will be* for us
A place of broad rivers *and* streams,
In which no galley with oars will sail,
Nor majestic ships pass by

22 (For the LORD *is* our Judge,
The LORD *is* our Lawgiver,
The LORD *is* our King;

עַתָּה אֶנָּשֵׂא׃

11 תַּהֲרוּ חֲשַׁשׁ תֵּלְדוּ קַשׁ
רוּחֲכֶם אֵשׁ תֹּאכַלְכֶם׃

12 וְהָיוּ עַמִּים מִשְׂרְפוֹת שִׂיד
קוֹצִים כְּסוּחִים בָּאֵשׁ יִצַּתּוּ׃ ס

13 שִׁמְעוּ רְחוֹקִים אֲשֶׁר עָשִׂיתִי
וּדְעוּ קְרוֹבִים גְּבֻרָתִי׃

14 פָּחֲדוּ בְצִיּוֹן חַטָּאִים
אָחֲזָה רְעָדָה חֲנֵפִים
מִי ׀ יָגוּר לָנוּ אֵשׁ אוֹכֵלָה
מִי־יָגוּר לָנוּ מוֹקְדֵי עוֹלָם׃

15 הֹלֵךְ צְדָקוֹת וְדֹבֵר מֵישָׁרִים
מֹאֵס בְּבֶצַע מַעֲשַׁקּוֹת
נֹעֵר כַּפָּיו מִתְּמֹךְ בַּשֹּׁחַד
אֹטֵם אָזְנוֹ מִשְּׁמֹעַ דָּמִים
וְעֹצֵם עֵינָיו מֵרְאוֹת בְּרָע׃

16 הוּא מְרוֹמִים יִשְׁכֹּן
מְצָדוֹת סְלָעִים מִשְׂגַּבּוֹ
לַחְמוֹ נִתָּן מֵימָיו נֶאֱמָנִים׃

17 מֶלֶךְ בְּיָפְיוֹ תֶּחֱזֶינָה עֵינֶיךָ
תִּרְאֶינָה אֶרֶץ מַרְחַקִּים׃

18 לִבְּךָ יֶהְגֶּה אֵימָה
אַיֵּה סֹפֵר אַיֵּה שֹׁקֵל
אַיֵּה סֹפֵר אֶת־הַמִּגְדָּלִים׃

19 אֶת־עַם נוֹעָז לֹא תִרְאֶה
עַם עִמְקֵי שָׂפָה מִשְּׁמוֹעַ
נִלְעַג לָשׁוֹן אֵין בִּינָה׃

20 חֲזֵה צִיּוֹן קִרְיַת מוֹעֲדֵנוּ
עֵינֶיךָ תִרְאֶינָה יְרוּשָׁלִַם נָוֶה שַׁאֲנָן
אֹהֶל בַּל־יִצְעָן
בַּל־יִסַּע יְתֵדֹתָיו לָנֶצַח
וְכָל־חֲבָלָיו בַּל־יִנָּתֵקוּ׃

21 כִּי אִם־שָׁם אַדִּיר יְהוָה לָנוּ
מְקוֹם־נְהָרִים יְאֹרִים רַחֲבֵי יָדָיִם
בַּל־תֵּלֶךְ בּוֹ אֳנִי־שַׁיִט
וְצִי אַדִּיר לֹא יַעַבְרֶנּוּ׃

22 כִּי יְהוָה שֹׁפְטֵנוּ
יְהוָה מְחֹקְקֵנוּ

He will save us);
23 Your tackle is loosed,
 They could not strengthen their mast,
 They could not spread the sail.

Then the prey of great plunder is divided;
 The lame take the prey.
24 And the inhabitant will not say, "I am sick";
 The people who dwell in it *will be* forgiven
  their iniquity.

34 Come near, you nations, to hear;
 And heed, you people!
 Let the earth hear, and all that is in it,
 The world and all things that come forth
  from it.
2 For the indignation of the LORD *is* against all
  nations,
 And *His* fury against all their armies;
 He has utterly destroyed them,
 He has given them over to the slaughter.
3 Also their slain shall be thrown out;
 Their stench shall rise from their corpses,
 And the mountains shall be melted with their
  blood.
4 All the host of heaven shall be dissolved,
 And the heavens shall be rolled up like a
  scroll;
 All their host shall fall down
 As the leaf falls from the vine,
 And as *fruit* falling from a fig tree.

5 "For My sword shall be bathed in heaven;
 Indeed it shall come down on Edom,
 And on the people of My curse, for
  judgment.
6 The sword of the LORD is filled with blood,
 It is made overflowing with fatness,
 With the blood of lambs and goats,
 With the fat of the kidneys of rams.
 For the LORD has a sacrifice in Bozrah,
 And a great slaughter in the land of Edom.
7 The wild oxen shall come down with them,
 And the young bulls with the mighty bulls;
 Their land shall be soaked with blood,
 And their dust saturated with fatness."

8 For *it is* the day of the LORD's vengeance,
 The year of recompense for the cause of
  Zion.
9 Its streams shall be turned into pitch,
 And its dust into brimstone;
 Its land shall become burning pitch.
10 It shall not be quenched night or day;
 Its smoke shall ascend forever.

יְהֹוָה מַלְכֵּנוּ הוּא יוֹשִׁיעֵנוּ:

23 נִטְּשׁוּ חֲבָלָיִךְ
בַּל־יְחַזְּקוּ כֵן־תָּרְנָם בַּל־פָּרְשׂוּ נֵס
אָז חֻלַּק עַד־שָׁלָל מַרְבֶּה
פִּסְחִים בָּזְזוּ בַז:

24 וּבַל־יֹאמַר שָׁכֵן חָלִיתִי
הָעָם הַיֹּשֵׁב בָּהּ נְשֻׂא עָוֹן:

לד קִרְבוּ גוֹיִם לִשְׁמֹעַ
וּלְאֻמִּים הַקְשִׁיבוּ
תִּשְׁמַע הָאָרֶץ וּמְלֹאָהּ
תֵּבֵל וְכָל־צֶאֱצָאֶיהָ:

2 כִּי קֶצֶף לַיהֹוָה עַל־כָּל־הַגּוֹיִם
וְחֵמָה עַל־כָּל־צְבָאָם
הֶחֱרִימָם נְתָנָם לַטָּבַח:

3 וְחַלְלֵיהֶם יֻשְׁלָכוּ
וּפִגְרֵיהֶם יַעֲלֶה בָאְשָׁם
וְנָמַסּוּ הָרִים מִדָּמָם:

4 וְנָמַקּוּ כָּל־צְבָא הַשָּׁמַיִם
וְנָגֹלּוּ כַסֵּפֶר הַשָּׁמָיִם
וְכָל־צְבָאָם יִבּוֹל
כִּנְבֹל עָלֶה מִגֶּפֶן
וּכְנֹבֶלֶת מִתְּאֵנָה:

5 כִּי־רִוְּתָה בַשָּׁמַיִם חַרְבִּי
הִנֵּה עַל־אֱדוֹם תֵּרֵד
וְעַל־עַם חֶרְמִי לְמִשְׁפָּט:

6 חֶרֶב לַיהֹוָה מָלְאָה דָם הֻדַּשְׁנָה מֵחֵלֶב
מִדַּם כָּרִים וְעַתּוּדִים
מֵחֵלֶב כִּלְיוֹת אֵילִים
כִּי זֶבַח לַיהֹוָה בְּבָצְרָה
וְטֶבַח גָּדוֹל בְּאֶרֶץ אֱדוֹם:

7 וְיָרְדוּ רְאֵמִים עִמָּם
וּפָרִים עִם־אַבִּירִים
וְרִוְּתָה אַרְצָם מִדָּם
וַעֲפָרָם מֵחֵלֶב יְדֻשָּׁן:

8 כִּי יוֹם נָקָם לַיהֹוָה
שְׁנַת שִׁלּוּמִים לְרִיב צִיּוֹן:

9 וְנֶהֶפְכוּ נְחָלֶיהָ לְזֶפֶת
וַעֲפָרָהּ לְגָפְרִית
וְהָיְתָה אַרְצָהּ לְזֶפֶת בֹּעֵרָה:

10 לַיְלָה וְיוֹמָם לֹא תִכְבֶּה
לְעוֹלָם יַעֲלֶה עֲשָׁנָהּ

From generation to generation it shall lie
　　waste;
No one shall pass through it forever and
　　ever.

11　But the pelican and the porcupine shall
　　possess it,
Also the owl and the raven shall dwell in it.
And He shall stretch out over it
The line of confusion and the stones of
　　emptiness.

12　They shall call its nobles to the kingdom,
But none *shall be* there, and all its princes
　　shall be nothing.

13　And thorns shall come up in its palaces,
Nettles and brambles in its fortresses;
It shall be a habitation of jackals,
A courtyard for ostriches.

14　The wild beasts of the desert shall also meet
　　with the jackals,
And the wild goat shall bleat to its compa-
　　nion;
Also the night creature shall rest there,
And find for herself a place of rest.

15　There the arrow snake shall make her nest
　　and lay *eggs*
And hatch, and gather *them* under her
　　shadow;
There also shall the hawks be gathered,
Every one with her mate.

16　"Search from the book of the LORD, and read:
Not one of these shall fail;
Not one shall lack her mate.
For My mouth has commanded it, and His
　　Spirit has gathered them.

17　He has cast the lot for them,
And His hand has divided it among them
　　with a measuring line.
They shall possess it forever;
From generation to generation they shall
　　dwell in it."

35

The wilderness and the wasteland shall be
　　glad for them,
And the desert shall rejoice and blossom as
　　the rose;

2　It shall blossom abundantly and rejoice,
Even with joy and singing.
The glory of Lebanon shall be given to it,
The excellence of Carmel and Sharon.
They shall see the glory of the LORD,
The excellency of our God.

3　Strengthen the weak hands,
And make firm the feeble knees.

מָדוֹר לָדוֹר תֶּחֱרָב
לְנֵצַח נְצָחִים אֵין עֹבֵר בָּהּ׃

11　וִירֵשׁוּהָ קָאַת וְקִפּוֹד
וְיַנְשׁוֹף וְעֹרֵב יִשְׁכְּנוּ־בָהּ
וְנָטָה עָלֶיהָ
קַו־תֹהוּ וְאַבְנֵי־בֹהוּ׃

12　חֹרֶיהָ וְאֵין־שָׁם מְלוּכָה יִקְרָאוּ
וְכָל־שָׂרֶיהָ יִהְיוּ אָפֶס׃

13　וְעָלְתָה אַרְמְנֹתֶיהָ סִירִים
קִמּוֹשׂ וָחוֹחַ בְּמִבְצָרֶיהָ
וְהָיְתָה נְוֵה תַנִּים
חָצִיר לִבְנוֹת יַעֲנָה׃

14　וּפָגְשׁוּ צִיִּים אֶת־אִיִּים
וְשָׂעִיר עַל־רֵעֵהוּ יִקְרָא
אַךְ־שָׁם הִרְגִּיעָה לִּילִית
וּמָצְאָה לָהּ מָנוֹחַ׃

15　שָׁמָּה קִנְּנָה קִפּוֹז וַתְּמַלֵּט
וּבָקְעָה וְדָגְרָה בְצִלָּהּ
אַךְ־שָׁם נִקְבְּצוּ דַיּוֹת
אִשָּׁה רְעוּתָהּ׃

16　דִּרְשׁוּ מֵעַל־סֵפֶר יְהוָה וּקְרָאוּ
אַחַת מֵהֵנָּה לֹא נֶעְדָּרָה
אִשָּׁה רְעוּתָהּ לֹא פָקָדוּ
כִּי־פִי הוּא צִוָּה
וְרוּחוֹ הוּא קִבְּצָן׃

17　וְהוּא־הִפִּיל לָהֶן גּוֹרָל
וְיָדוֹ חִלְּקַתָּה לָהֶם בַּקָּו
עַד־עוֹלָם יִירָשׁוּהָ
לְדוֹר וָדוֹר יִשְׁכְּנוּ־בָהּ׃　ס

לה　יְשֻׂשׂוּם מִדְבָּר וְצִיָּה
וְתָגֵל עֲרָבָה וְתִפְרַח כַּחֲבַצָּלֶת׃

2　פָּרֹחַ תִּפְרַח וְתָגֵל
אַף גִּילַת וְרַנֵּן
כְּבוֹד הַלְּבָנוֹן נִתַּן־לָהּ
הֲדַר הַכַּרְמֶל וְהַשָּׁרוֹן
הֵמָּה יִרְאוּ כְבוֹד־יְהוָה
הֲדַר אֱלֹהֵינוּ׃　ס

3　חַזְּקוּ יָדַיִם רָפוֹת
וּבִרְכַּיִם כֹּשְׁלוֹת אַמֵּצוּ׃

4 Say to those *who are* fearful-hearted,
    "Be strong, do not fear!
    Behold, your God will come *with* vengeance,
    With the recompense of God;
    He will come and save you."

5 Then the eyes of the blind shall be opened,
    And the ears of the deaf shall be unstopped.

6 Then the lame shall leap like a deer,
    And the tongue of the dumb sing.
    For waters shall burst forth in the wilderness,
    And streams in the desert.

7 The parched ground shall become a pool,
    And the thirsty land springs of water;
    In the habitation of jackals, where each lay,
    There shall be grass with reeds and rushes.

8 A highway shall be there, and a road,
    And it shall be called the Highway of
        Holiness.
    The unclean shall not pass over it,
    But it *shall be* for others.
    Whoever walks the road, although a fool,
    Shall not go astray.

9 No lion shall be there,
    Nor shall *any* ravenous beast go up on it;
    It shall not be found there.
    But the redeemed shall walk *there,*

10 And the ransomed of the LORD shall return,
    And come to Zion with singing,
    With everlasting joy on their heads.
    They shall obtain joy and gladness,
    And sorrow and sighing shall flee away.

36 Now it came to pass in the fourteenth year of King Hezekiah *that* Sennacherib king of Assyria came up against all the fortified cities of Judah and took them. 2 Then the king of Assyria sent *the* Rabshakeh with a great army from Lachish to King Hezekiah at Jerusalem. And he stood by the aqueduct from the upper pool, on the highway to the Fuller's Field. 3 And Eliakim the son of Hilkiah, who was over the household, Shebna the scribe, and Joah the son of Asaph, the recorder, came out to him.

4 Then *the* Rabshakeh said to them, "Say now to Hezekiah, 'Thus says the great king, the king of Assyria: "What confidence is this in which you trust? 5 I say you speak of having plans and power for war; but *they are* mere words. Now in whom do you trust, that you rebel against me? 6 Look! You are trusting in the staff of this broken reed, Egypt, on which if a man leans, it will go into his hand and pierce it. So *is* Pharaoh king of Egypt to all who trust in him.

4 אִמְרוּ לְנִמְהֲרֵי־לֵב חִזְקוּ אַל־תִּירָאוּ
הִנֵּה אֱלֹהֵיכֶם נָקָם יָבוֹא
גְּמוּל אֱלֹהִים הוּא יָבוֹא וְיֹשַׁעֲכֶם:

5 אָז תִּפָּקַחְנָה עֵינֵי עִוְרִים
וְאָזְנֵי חֵרְשִׁים תִּפָּתַחְנָה:

6 אָז יְדַלֵּג כָּאַיָּל פִּסֵּחַ וְתָרֹן לְשׁוֹן אִלֵּם
כִּי־נִבְקְעוּ בַמִּדְבָּר מַיִם
וּנְחָלִים בָּעֲרָבָה:

7 וְהָיָה הַשָּׁרָב לַאֲגַם
וְצִמָּאוֹן לְמַבּוּעֵי מָיִם
בִּנְוֵה תַנִּים רִבְצָהּ
חָצִיר לְקָנֶה וָגֹמֶא:

8 וְהָיָה־שָׁם מַסְלוּל וָדֶרֶךְ
וְדֶרֶךְ הַקֹּדֶשׁ יִקָּרֵא לָהּ
לֹא־יַעַבְרֶנּוּ טָמֵא וְהוּא־לָמוֹ
הֹלֵךְ דֶּרֶךְ וֶאֱוִילִים לֹא יִתְעוּ:

9 לֹא־יִהְיֶה שָׁם אַרְיֵה
וּפְרִיץ חַיּוֹת בַּל־יַעֲלֶנָּה
לֹא תִמָּצֵא שָׁם
וְהָלְכוּ גְּאוּלִים:

10 וּפְדוּיֵי יְהוָה יְשֻׁבוּן
וּבָאוּ צִיּוֹן בְּרִנָּה
וְשִׂמְחַת עוֹלָם עַל־רֹאשָׁם
שָׂשׂוֹן וְשִׂמְחָה יַשִּׂיגוּ
וְנָסוּ יָגוֹן וַאֲנָחָה:
 פ

לו וַיְהִי בְּאַרְבַּע עֶשְׂרֵה שָׁנָה לַמֶּלֶךְ חִזְקִיָּהוּ עָלָה סַנְחֵרִיב מֶלֶךְ־אַשּׁוּר עַל כָּל־עָרֵי יְהוּדָה הַבְּצֻרוֹת וַיִּתְפְּשֵׂם: 2 וַיִּשְׁלַח מֶלֶךְ־אַשּׁוּר | אֶת־רַב־שָׁקֵה מִלָּכִישׁ יְרוּשָׁלְַמָה אֶל־הַמֶּלֶךְ חִזְקִיָּהוּ בְּחֵיל כָּבֵד וַיַּעֲמֹד בִּתְעָלַת הַבְּרֵכָה הָעֶלְיוֹנָה בִּמְסִלַּת שְׂדֵה כוֹבֵס: 3 וַיֵּצֵא אֵלָיו אֶלְיָקִים בֶּן־חִלְקִיָּהוּ אֲשֶׁר עַל־הַבָּיִת וְשֶׁבְנָא הַסֹּפֵר וְיוֹאָח בֶּן־אָסָף הַמַּזְכִּיר: 4 וַיֹּאמֶר אֲלֵיהֶם רַב־שָׁקֵה אִמְרוּ־נָא אֶל־חִזְקִיָּהוּ כֹּה־אָמַר הַמֶּלֶךְ הַגָּדוֹל מֶלֶךְ אַשּׁוּר מָה הַבִּטָּחוֹן הַזֶּה אֲשֶׁר בָּטָחְתָּ: 5 אָמַרְתִּי אַךְ־דְּבַר־שְׂפָתַיִם עֵצָה וּגְבוּרָה לַמִּלְחָמָה עַתָּה עַל־מִי בָטַחְתָּ כִּי מָרַדְתָּ בִּי: 6 הִנֵּה בָטַחְתָּ עַל־מִשְׁעֶנֶת הַקָּנֶה הָרָצוּץ הַזֶּה עַל־מִצְרַיִם אֲשֶׁר יִסָּמֵךְ אִישׁ עָלָיו וּבָא בְכַפּוֹ וּנְקָבָהּ כֵּן פַּרְעֹה מֶלֶךְ־מִצְרַיִם לְכָל־הַבֹּטְחִים

7 "But if you say to me, 'We trust in the LORD our God,' *is it* not He whose high places and whose altars Hezekiah has taken away, and said to Judah and Jerusalem, 'You shall worship before this altar'?" ' 8 Now therefore, I urge you, give a pledge to my master the king of Assyria, and I will give you two thousand horses—if you are able on your part to put riders on them! 9 How then will you repel one captain of the least of my master's servants, and put your trust in Egypt for chariots and horsemen? 10 Have I now come up without the LORD against this land to destroy it? The LORD said to me, 'Go up against this land, and destroy it.' "

11 Then Eliakim, Shebna, and Joah said to *the* Rabshakeh, "Please speak to your servants in Aramaic, for we understand *it;* and do not speak to us in Hebrew in the hearing of the people who *are* on the wall."

12 But *the* Rabshakeh said, "Has my master sent me to your master and to you to speak these words, and not to the men who sit on the wall, who will eat and drink their own waste with you?"

13 Then *the* Rabshakeh stood and called out with a loud voice in Hebrew, and said, "Hear the words of the great king, the king of Assyria! 14 Thus says the king: 'Do not let Hezekiah deceive you, for he will not be able to deliver you; 15 nor let Hezekiah make you trust in the LORD, saying, "The LORD will surely deliver us; this city will not be given into the hand of the king of Assyria." ' 16 Do not listen to Hezekiah; for thus says the king of Assyria: 'Make *peace* with me *by a* present and come out to me; and every one of you eat from his own vine and every one from his own fig tree, and every one of you drink the waters of his own cistern; 17 until I come and take you away to a land like your own land, a land of grain and new wine, a land of bread and vineyards. 18 *Beware* lest Hezekiah persuade you, saying, "The LORD will deliver us." Has any one of the gods of the nations delivered its land from the hand of the king of Assyria? 19 Where *are* the gods of Hamath and Arpad? Where *are* the gods of Sepharvaim? Indeed, have they delivered Samaria from my hand? 20 Who among all the gods of these lands have delivered their countries from my hand, that the LORD should deliver Jerusalem from my hand?' "

21 But they held their peace and answered him not a word; for the king's commandment was, "Do not answer him." 22 Then Eliakim the son of Hilkiah, who *was* over the household, Shebna the scribe, and Joah the son of Asaph, the recorder, came to Hezekiah with *their* clothes torn, and told him the words of *the* Rabshakeh.

עָלָיו: 7 וְכִי־תֹאמַר אֵלַי אֶל־יְהוָה אֱלֹהֵינוּ בָּטָחְנוּ הֲלוֹא־הוּא אֲשֶׁר הֵסִיר חִזְקִיָּהוּ אֶת־בָּמֹתָיו וְאֶת־מִזְבְּחֹתָיו וַיֹּאמֶר לִיהוּדָה וְלִירוּשָׁלַ͏ִם לִפְנֵי הַמִּזְבֵּחַ הַזֶּה תִּשְׁתַּחֲווּ: 8 וְעַתָּה הִתְעָרֶב נָא אֶת־אֲדֹנִי הַמֶּלֶךְ אַשּׁוּר וְאֶתְּנָה לְךָ אַלְפַּיִם סוּסִים אִם־תּוּכַל לָתֶת לְךָ רֹכְבִים עֲלֵיהֶם: 9 וְאֵיךְ תָּשִׁיב אֵת פְּנֵי פַחַת אַחַד עַבְדֵי אֲדֹנִי הַקְּטַנִּים וַתִּבְטַח לְךָ עַל־מִצְרַיִם לְרֶכֶב וּלְפָרָשִׁים: 10 וְעַתָּה הֲמִבַּלְעֲדֵי יְהוָה עָלִיתִי עַל־הָאָרֶץ הַזֹּאת לְהַשְׁחִיתָהּ יְהוָה אָמַר אֵלַי עֲלֵה אֶל־הָאָרֶץ הַזֹּאת וְהַשְׁחִיתָהּ: 11 וַיֹּאמֶר אֶלְיָקִים וְשֶׁבְנָא וְיוֹאָח אֶל־רַב־שָׁקֵה דַּבֶּר־נָא אֶל־עֲבָדֶיךָ אֲרָמִית כִּי שֹׁמְעִים אֲנָחְנוּ וְאַל־תְּדַבֵּר אֵלֵינוּ יְהוּדִית בְּאָזְנֵי הָעָם אֲשֶׁר עַל־הַחוֹמָה: 12 וַיֹּאמֶר רַב־שָׁקֵה הַאֶל אֲדֹנֶיךָ וְאֵלֶיךָ שְׁלָחַנִי אֲדֹנִי לְדַבֵּר אֶת־הַדְּבָרִים הָאֵלֶּה הֲלֹא עַל־הָאֲנָשִׁים הַיֹּשְׁבִים עַל־הַחוֹמָה לֶאֱכֹל אֶת־חראיהם[צֹאָתָם] וְלִשְׁתּוֹת אֶת־שֵׁינֵיהֶם[מֵימֵי רַגְלֵיהֶם] עִמָּכֶם: 13 וַיַּעֲמֹד רַב־שָׁקֵה וַיִּקְרָא בְקוֹל־גָּדוֹל יְהוּדִית וַיֹּאמֶר שִׁמְעוּ אֶת־דִּבְרֵי הַמֶּלֶךְ הַגָּדוֹל מֶלֶךְ אַשּׁוּר: 14 כֹּה אָמַר הַמֶּלֶךְ אַל־יַשִּׁא לָכֶם חִזְקִיָּהוּ כִּי לֹא־יוּכַל לְהַצִּיל אֶתְכֶם: 15 וְאַל־יַבְטַח אֶתְכֶם חִזְקִיָּהוּ אֶל־יְהוָה לֵאמֹר הַצֵּל יַצִּילֵנוּ יְהוָה לֹא תִנָּתֵן הָעִיר הַזֹּאת בְּיַד מֶלֶךְ אַשּׁוּר: 16 אַל־תִּשְׁמְעוּ אֶל־חִזְקִיָּהוּ ס כִּי כֹה אָמַר הַמֶּלֶךְ אַשּׁוּר עֲשׂוּ־אִתִּי בְרָכָה וּצְאוּ אֵלַי וְאִכְלוּ אִישׁ־גַּפְנוֹ וְאִישׁ תְּאֵנָתוֹ וּשְׁתוּ אִישׁ מֵי־בוֹרוֹ: 17 עַד־בֹּאִי וְלָקַחְתִּי אֶתְכֶם אֶל־אֶרֶץ כְּאַרְצְכֶם אֶרֶץ דָּגָן וְתִירוֹשׁ אֶרֶץ לֶחֶם וּכְרָמִים: 18 פֶּן־יַסִּית אֶתְכֶם חִזְקִיָּהוּ לֵאמֹר יְהוָה יַצִּילֵנוּ הַהִצִּילוּ אֱלֹהֵי הַגּוֹיִם אִישׁ אֶת־אַרְצוֹ מִיַּד מֶלֶךְ אַשּׁוּר: 19 אַיֵּה אֱלֹהֵי חֲמָת וְאַרְפָּד אַיֵּה אֱלֹהֵי סְפַרְוָיִם וְכִי־הִצִּילוּ אֶת־שֹׁמְרוֹן מִיָּדִי: 20 מִי בְּכָל־אֱלֹהֵי הָאֲרָצוֹת הָאֵלֶּה אֲשֶׁר־הִצִּילוּ אֶת־אַרְצָם מִיָּדִי כִּי־יַצִּיל יְהוָה אֶת־יְרוּשָׁלַ͏ִם מִיָּדִי: 21 וַיַּחֲרִישׁוּ וְלֹא־עָנוּ אֹתוֹ דָּבָר כִּי־מִצְוַת הַמֶּלֶךְ הִיא לֵאמֹר לֹא תַעֲנֻהוּ: 22 וַיָּבֹא אֶלְיָקִים בֶּן־חִלְקִיָּהוּ אֲשֶׁר־עַל־הַבַּיִת וְשֶׁבְנָא הַסּוֹפֵר וְיוֹאָח בֶּן־אָסָף הַמַּזְכִּיר אֶל־חִזְקִיָּהוּ קְרוּעֵי בְגָדִים וַיַּגִּידוּ לוֹ אֵת דִּבְרֵי רַב־שָׁקֵה: ס

לו 12 צוֹאָתָם מֵימֵי רַגְלֵיהֶם

37 And so it was, when King Hezekiah heard *it,* that he tore his clothes, covered himself with sackcloth, and went into the house of the LORD. ²Then he sent Eliakim, who *was* over the household, Shebna the scribe, and the elders of the priests, covered with sackcloth, to Isaiah the prophet, the son of Amoz. ³And they said to him, "Thus says Hezekiah: 'This day *is* a day of trouble and rebuke and blasphemy; for the children have come to birth, but *there is* no strength to bring them forth. ⁴It may be that the LORD your God will hear the words of *the* Rabshakeh, whom his master the king of Assyria has sent to reproach the living God, and will rebuke the words which the LORD your God has heard. Therefore lift up *your* prayer for the remnant that is left.' "

⁵So the servants of King Hezekiah came to Isaiah. ⁶And Isaiah said to them, "Thus you shall say to your master, 'Thus says the LORD: "Do not be afraid of the words which you have heard, with which the servants of the king of Assyria have blasphemed Me. ⁷Surely I will send a spirit upon him, and he shall hear a rumor and return to his own land; and I will cause him to fall by the sword in his own land." ' "

⁸Then *the* Rabshakeh returned, and found the king of Assyria warring against Libnah, for he heard that he had departed from Lachish. ⁹And the king heard concerning Tirhakah king of Ethiopia, "He has come out to make war with you." So when he heard *it,* he sent messengers to Hezekiah, saying, ¹⁰"Thus you shall speak to Hezekiah king of Judah, saying: 'Do not let your God in whom you trust deceive you, saying, "Jerusalem shall not be given into the hand of the king of Assyria." ¹¹Look! You have heard what the kings of Assyria have done to all lands by utterly destroying them; and shall you be delivered? ¹²Have the gods of the nations delivered those whom my fathers have destroyed, Gozan and Haran and Rezeph, and the people of Eden who *were* in Telassar? ¹³Where *is* the king of Hamath, the king of Arpad, and the king of the city of Sepharvaim, Hena, and Ivah?' "

¹⁴And Hezekiah received the letter from the hand of the messengers, and read it; and Hezekiah went up to the house of the LORD, and spread it before the LORD. ¹⁵Then Hezekiah prayed to the LORD, saying: ¹⁶"O LORD of hosts, God of Israel, *the One* who dwells *between* the cherubim, You *are* God, You alone, of all the kingdoms of the earth. You have made heaven and earth. ¹⁷Incline Your ear, O LORD, and hear; open Your eyes, O LORD, and see; and hear all the words of Sennacherib, which he has sent to reproach the living God.

לז וַיְהִי כִּשְׁמֹעַ הַמֶּלֶךְ חִזְקִיָּהוּ וַיִּקְרַע אֶת־בְּגָדָיו וַיִּתְכַּס בַּשָּׂק וַיָּבֹא בֵּית יְהֹוָה: 2 וַיִּשְׁלַח אֶת־אֶלְיָקִים אֲשֶׁר־עַל־הַבַּיִת וְאֵת ׀ שֶׁבְנָא הַסּוֹפֵר וְאֵת זִקְנֵי הַכֹּהֲנִים מִתְכַּסִּים בַּשַּׂקִּים אֶל־יְשַׁעְיָהוּ בֶן־אָמוֹץ הַנָּבִיא: 3 וַיֹּאמְרוּ אֵלָיו כֹּה אָמַר חִזְקִיָּהוּ יוֹם־צָרָה וְתוֹכֵחָה וּנְאָצָה הַיּוֹם הַזֶּה כִּי בָאוּ בָנִים עַד־מַשְׁבֵּר וְכֹחַ אַיִן לְלֵדָה: 4 אוּלַי יִשְׁמַע יְהֹוָה אֱלֹהֶיךָ אֵת ׀ דִּבְרֵי רַב־שָׁקֵה אֲשֶׁר שְׁלָחוֹ מֶלֶךְ־אַשּׁוּר ׀ אֲדֹנָיו לְחָרֵף אֱלֹהִים חַי וְהוֹכִיחַ בַּדְּבָרִים אֲשֶׁר שָׁמַע יְהֹוָה אֱלֹהֶיךָ וְנָשָׂאתָ תְפִלָּה בְּעַד הַשְּׁאֵרִית הַנִּמְצָאָה: 5 וַיָּבֹאוּ עַבְדֵי הַמֶּלֶךְ חִזְקִיָּהוּ אֶל־יְשַׁעְיָהוּ: 6 וַיֹּאמֶר אֲלֵיהֶם יְשַׁעְיָהוּ כֹּה תֹאמְרוּן אֶל־אֲדֹנֵיכֶם כֹּה ׀ אָמַר יְהֹוָה אַל־תִּירָא מִפְּנֵי הַדְּבָרִים אֲשֶׁר שָׁמַעְתָּ אֲשֶׁר גִּדְּפוּ נַעֲרֵי מֶלֶךְ־אַשּׁוּר אוֹתִי: 7 הִנְנִי נוֹתֵן בּוֹ רוּחַ וְשָׁמַע שְׁמוּעָה וְשָׁב אֶל־אַרְצוֹ וְהִפַּלְתִּיו בַּחֶרֶב בְּאַרְצוֹ: 8 וַיָּשָׁב רַב־שָׁקֵה וַיִּמְצָא אֶת־מֶלֶךְ אַשּׁוּר נִלְחָם עַל־לִבְנָה כִּי שָׁמַע כִּי נָסַע מִלָּכִישׁ: 9 וַיִּשְׁמַע עַל־תִּרְהָקָה מֶלֶךְ־כּוּשׁ לֵאמֹר יָצָא לְהִלָּחֵם אִתָּךְ וַיִּשְׁמַע וַיִּשְׁלַח מַלְאָכִים אֶל־חִזְקִיָּהוּ לֵאמֹר: 10 כֹּה תֹאמְרוּן אֶל־חִזְקִיָּהוּ מֶלֶךְ־יְהוּדָה לֵאמֹר אַל־יַשִּׁאֲךָ אֱלֹהֶיךָ אֲשֶׁר אַתָּה בּוֹטֵחַ בּוֹ לֵאמֹר לֹא תִנָּתֵן יְרוּשָׁלַם בְּיַד מֶלֶךְ אַשּׁוּר: 11 הִנֵּה ׀ אַתָּה שָׁמַעְתָּ אֲשֶׁר עָשׂוּ מַלְכֵי אַשּׁוּר לְכָל־הָאֲרָצוֹת לְהַחֲרִימָם וְאַתָּה תִּנָּצֵל:

12 הַהִצִּילוּ אוֹתָם אֱלֹהֵי הַגּוֹיִם אֲשֶׁר הִשְׁחִיתוּ אֲבוֹתַי אֶת־גּוֹזָן וְאֶת־חָרָן וְרֶצֶף וּבְנֵי־עֶדֶן אֲשֶׁר בִּתְלַשָּׂר: 13 אַיֵּה מֶלֶךְ־חֲמָת וּמֶלֶךְ אַרְפָּד וּמֶלֶךְ לָעִיר סְפַרְוָיִם הֵנַע וְעִוָּה: 14 וַיִּקַּח חִזְקִיָּהוּ אֶת־הַסְּפָרִים מִיַּד הַמַּלְאָכִים וַיִּקְרָאֵהוּ וַיַּעַל בֵּית יְהֹוָה וַיִּפְרְשֵׂהוּ חִזְקִיָּהוּ לִפְנֵי יְהֹוָה: 15 וַיִּתְפַּלֵּל חִזְקִיָּהוּ אֶל־יְהֹוָה לֵאמֹר: 16 יְהֹוָה צְבָאוֹת אֱלֹהֵי יִשְׂרָאֵל יֹשֵׁב הַכְּרֻבִים אַתָּה־הוּא הָאֱלֹהִים לְבַדְּךָ לְכֹל מַמְלְכוֹת הָאָרֶץ אַתָּה עָשִׂיתָ אֶת־הַשָּׁמַיִם וְאֶת־הָאָרֶץ: 17 הַטֵּה יְהֹוָה ׀ אָזְנְךָ וּשֲׁמָע פְּקַח יְהֹוָה עֵינֶךָ וּרְאֵה וּשְׁמַע אֵת כָּל־דִּבְרֵי סַנְחֵרִיב אֲשֶׁר

18 Truly, LORD, the kings of Assyria have laid waste all the nations and their lands, 19 and have cast their gods into the fire; for they *were* not gods, but the work of men's hands—wood and stone. Therefore they destroyed them. 20 Now therefore, O LORD our God, save us from his hand, that all the kingdoms of the earth may know that You *are* the LORD, You alone."

21 Then Isaiah the son of Amoz sent to Hezekiah, saying, "Thus says the LORD God of Israel, 'Because you have prayed to Me against Sennacherib king of Assyria, 22 this *is* the word which the LORD has spoken concerning him:

"The virgin, the daughter of Zion,
    Has despised you, laughed you to scorn;
The daughter of Jerusalem
    Has shaken *her* head behind your back!

23 "Whom have you reproached and blasphemed?
    Against whom have you raised *your* voice,
And lifted up your eyes on high?
    Against the Holy One of Israel.
24 By your servants you have reproached the Lord,
    And said, 'By the multitude of my chariots
I have come up to the height of the mountains,
    To the limits of Lebanon;
I will cut down its tall cedars
    And its choice cypress trees;
I will enter its farthest height,
    To its fruitful forest.
25 I have dug and drunk water,
    And with the soles of my feet I have dried up
All the brooks of defense.'

26 "Did you not hear long ago
    How I made it,
From ancient times that I formed it?
    Now I have brought it to pass,
That you should be
    For crushing fortified cities *into* heaps of ruins.
27 Therefore their inhabitants *had* little power;
    They were dismayed and confounded;
They were *as* the grass of the field
    And the green herb,
As the grass on the housetops
    And grain blighted before it is grown.

28 "But I know your dwelling place,
    Your going out and your coming in,
And your rage against Me.

שָׁלֹחַ לְחָרֵף אֱלֹהִים חָי: 18 אָמְנָם יְהוָה הֶחֱרִיבוּ מַלְכֵי אַשּׁוּר אֶת־כָּל־הָאֲרָצוֹת וְאֶת־אַרְצָם: 19 וְנָתֹן אֶת־אֱלֹהֵיהֶם בָּאֵשׁ כִּי לֹא אֱלֹהִים הֵמָּה כִּי אִם־ מַעֲשֵׂה יְדֵי־אָדָם עֵץ וָאָבֶן וַיְאַבְּדוּם: 20 וְעַתָּה יְהוָה אֱלֹהֵינוּ הוֹשִׁיעֵנוּ מִיָּדוֹ וְיֵדְעוּ כָּל־מַמְלְכוֹת הָאָרֶץ כִּי־אַתָּה יְהוָה לְבַדֶּךָ: 21 וַיִּשְׁלַח יְשַׁעְיָהוּ בֶן־אָמוֹץ אֶל־חִזְקִיָּהוּ לֵאמֹר כֹּה־אָמַר יְהוָה אֱלֹהֵי יִשְׂרָאֵל אֲשֶׁר הִתְפַּלַּלְתָּ אֵלַי אֶל־סַנְחֵרִיב מֶלֶךְ אַשּׁוּר:

22 זֶה הַדָּבָר אֲשֶׁר־דִּבֶּר יְהוָה עָלָיו
בָּזָה לְךָ לָעֲגָה לְךָ
בְּתוּלַת בַּת־צִיּוֹן
אַחֲרֶיךָ רֹאשׁ הֵנִיעָה
בַּת יְרוּשָׁלָ‍ִם:
23 אֶת־מִי חֵרַפְתָּ וְגִדַּפְתָּ
וְעַל־מִי הֲרִימוֹתָה קּוֹל
וַתִּשָּׂא מָרוֹם עֵינֶיךָ
אֶל־קְדוֹשׁ יִשְׂרָאֵל:
24 בְּיַד עֲבָדֶיךָ חֵרַפְתָּ | אֲדֹנָי
וַתֹּאמֶר בְּרֹב רִכְבִּי
אֲנִי עָלִיתִי מְרוֹם הָרִים
יַרְכְּתֵי לְבָנוֹן
וְאֶכְרֹת קוֹמַת אֲרָזָיו
מִבְחַר בְּרֹשָׁיו
וְאָבוֹא מְרוֹם קִצּוֹ
יַעַר כַּרְמִלּוֹ:
25 אֲנִי קַרְתִּי וְשָׁתִיתִי מָיִם
וְאַחְרִב בְּכַף־פְּעָמַי
כֹּל יְאֹרֵי מָצוֹר:
26 הֲלוֹא־שָׁמַעְתָּ לְמֵרָחוֹק אוֹתָהּ עָשִׂיתִי
מִימֵי קֶדֶם וִיצַרְתִּיהָ
עַתָּה הֲבֵאתִיהָ
וּתְהִי לְהַשְׁאוֹת
גַּלִּים נִצִּים עָרִים בְּצֻרוֹת:
27 וְיֹשְׁבֵיהֶן קִצְרֵי־יָד
חַתּוּ וָבֹשׁוּ
הָיוּ עֵשֶׂב שָׂדֶה וִירַק דֶּשֶׁא
חֲצִיר גַּגּוֹת וּשְׁדֵמָה לִפְנֵי קָמָה:
28 וְשִׁבְתְּךָ וְצֵאתְךָ וּבוֹאֲךָ יָדָעְתִּי
וְאֵת הִתְרַגֶּזְךָ אֵלָי:

29 Because your rage against Me and your
     tumult
     Have come up to My ears,
     Therefore I will put My hook in your nose
     And My bridle in your lips,
     And I will turn you back
     By the way which you came." '

30 "This *shall be* a sign to you:

     You shall eat this year such as grows of itself,
     And the second year what springs from the same;
     Also in the third year sow and reap,
     Plant vineyards and eat the fruit of them.
31   And the remnant who have escaped of the house
     of Judah
     Shall again take root downward,
     And bear fruit upward.
32   For out of Jerusalem shall go a remnant,
     And those who escape from Mount Zion.
     The zeal of the LORD of hosts will do this.

33 "Therefore thus says the LORD concerning the
king of Assyria:

     'He shall not come into this city,
     Nor shoot an arrow there,
     Nor come before it with shield,
     Nor build a siege mound against it.
34   By the way that he came,
     By the same shall he return;
     And he shall not come into this city,'
     Says the LORD.
35   'For I will defend this city, to save it
     For My own sake and for My servant David's
     sake.' "

36 Then the angel of the LORD went out, and
killed in the camp of the Assyrians one hundred and
eighty-five thousand; and when *people* arose early
in the morning, there were the corpses—all dead.
37 So Sennacherib king of Assyria departed and
went away, returned *home,* and remained at
Nineveh. 38 Now it came to pass, as he was
worshiping in the house of Nisroch his god, that
his sons Adrammelech and Sharezer struck him
down with the sword; and they escaped into the
land of Ararat. Then Esarhaddon his son reigned in
his place.

38 In those days Hezekiah was sick and near
death. And Isaiah the prophet, the son of Amoz,
went to him and said to him, "Thus says the LORD:
'Set your house in order, for you shall die and not
live.' "

2 Then Hezekiah turned his face toward the wall,
and prayed to the LORD, 3 and said, "Remember
now, O LORD, I pray, how I have walked before

29 יַעַן הִתְרַגֶּזְךָ אֵלָי
וְשַׁאֲנַנְךָ עָלָה בְאָזְנָי
וְשַׂמְתִּי חַחִי בְּאַפֶּךָ
וּמִתְגִּי בִּשְׂפָתֶיךָ
וַהֲשִׁבֹתִיךָ בַּדֶּרֶךְ
אֲשֶׁר־בָּאתָ בָּהּ:

30 וְזֶה־לְּךָ הָאוֹת אָכוֹל הַשָּׁנָה סָפִיחַ וּבַשָּׁנָה
הַשֵּׁנִית שָׁחִים וּבַשָּׁנָה הַשְּׁלִישִׁית זִרְעוּ וְקִצְרוּ
וְנִטְעוּ כְרָמִים וְאִכְלוֹ פִרְיָם: 31 וְיָסְפָה פְּלֵיטַת
בֵּית־יְהוּדָה הַנִּשְׁאָרָה שֹׁרֶשׁ לְמָטָּה וְעָשָׂה
פְרִי לְמָעְלָה: 32 כִּי מִירוּשָׁלַ͏ִם תֵּצֵא שְׁאֵרִית
וּפְלֵיטָה מֵהַר צִיּוֹן קִנְאַת יְהוָה צְבָאוֹת תַּעֲשֶׂה־
זֹּאת: ס 33 לָכֵן כֹּה־אָמַר יְהוָה אֶל־
מֶלֶךְ אַשּׁוּר לֹא יָבוֹא אֶל־הָעִיר הַזֹּאת וְלֹא־
יוֹרֶה שָׁם חֵץ וְלֹא־יְקַדְּמֶנָּה מָגֵן וְלֹא־יִשְׁפֹּךְ
עָלֶיהָ סֹלְלָה: 34 בַּדֶּרֶךְ אֲשֶׁר־בָּא בָּהּ יָשׁוּב וְאֶל־
הָעִיר הַזֹּאת לֹא יָבוֹא נְאֻם־יְהוָה: 35 וְגַנּוֹתִי
עַל־הָעִיר הַזֹּאת לְהוֹשִׁיעָהּ לְמַעֲנִי וּלְמַעַן דָּוִד
עַבְדִּי: ס 36 וַיֵּצֵא | מַלְאַךְ יְהוָה וַיַּכֶּה
בְּמַחֲנֵה אַשּׁוּר מֵאָה וּשְׁמֹנִים וַחֲמִשָּׁה אָלֶף
וַיַּשְׁכִּימוּ בַבֹּקֶר וְהִנֵּה כֻלָּם פְּגָרִים מֵתִים:
37 וַיִּסַּע וַיֵּלֶךְ וַיָּשָׁב סַנְחֵרִיב מֶלֶךְ־אַשּׁוּר וַיֵּשֶׁב
בְּנִינְוֵה: 38 וַיְהִי הוּא מִשְׁתַּחֲוֶה בֵּית | נִסְרֹךְ
אֱלֹהָיו וְאַדְרַמֶּלֶךְ וְשַׂרְאֶצֶר בָּנָיו הִכֻּהוּ בַחֶרֶב
וְהֵמָּה נִמְלְטוּ אֶרֶץ אֲרָרָט וַיִּמְלֹךְ אֵסַר־חַדֹּן בְּנוֹ
תַּחְתָּיו: ס

לח בַּיָּמִים הָהֵם חָלָה חִזְקִיָּהוּ לָמוּת וַיָּבוֹא אֵלָיו
יְשַׁעְיָהוּ בֶן־אָמוֹץ הַנָּבִיא וַיֹּאמֶר אֵלָיו כֹּה־אָמַר
יְהוָה צַו לְבֵיתֶךָ כִּי מֵת אַתָּה וְלֹא תִחְיֶה: 2 וַיַּסֵּב
חִזְקִיָּהוּ פָּנָיו אֶל־הַקִּיר וַיִּתְפַּלֵּל אֶל־יְהוָה: 3 וַיֹּאמַר

You in truth and with a loyal heart, and have done *what is* good in Your sight." And Hezekiah wept bitterly.

⁴And the word of the LORD came to Isaiah, saying, ⁵"Go and tell Hezekiah, 'Thus says the LORD, the God of David your father: "I have heard your prayer, I have seen your tears; surely I will add to your days fifteen years. ⁶I will deliver you and this city from the hand of the king of Assyria, and I will defend this city." ' ⁷And this *is* the sign to you from the LORD, that the LORD will do this thing which He has spoken: ⁸Behold, I will bring the shadow on the sundial, which has gone down with the sun on the sundial of Ahaz, ten degrees backward." So the sun returned ten degrees on the dial by which it had gone down.

⁹This is the writing of Hezekiah king of Judah, when he had been sick and had recovered from his sickness:

10   I said,
    "In the prime of my life
    I shall go to the gates of Sheol;
    I am deprived of the remainder of my years."

11   I said,
    "I shall not see YAH,
    The LORD in the land of the living;
    I shall observe man no more among the
      inhabitants of the world.

12   My life span is gone,
    Taken from me like a shepherd's tent;
    I have cut off my life like a weaver.
    He cuts me off from the loom;
    From day until night You make an end of
      me.

13   I have considered until morning—
    Like a lion,
    So He breaks all my bones;
    From day until night You make an end of
      me.

14   Like a crane *or* a swallow, so I chattered;
    I mourned like a dove;
    My eyes fail *from looking* upward.
    O LORD, I am oppressed;
    Undertake for me!

15   "What shall I say?
    He has both spoken to me,
    And He Himself has done *it*.
    I shall walk carefully all my years
    In the bitterness of my soul.

16   O Lord, by these *things* men live;
    And in all these *things is* the life of my spirit;
    So You will restore me and make me live.

17   Indeed *it was* for *my own* peace

אָנָּה יְהוָה זְכָר־נָא אֵת אֲשֶׁר הִתְהַלַּכְתִּי לְפָנֶיךָ
בֶּאֱמֶת וּבְלֵב שָׁלֵם וְהַטּוֹב בְּעֵינֶיךָ עָשִׂיתִי וַיֵּבְךְּ
חִזְקִיָּהוּ בְּכִי גָדוֹל׃ ס ⁴ וַיְהִי דְּבַר־יְהוָה
אֶל־יְשַׁעְיָהוּ לֵאמֹר׃ ⁵ הָלוֹךְ וְאָמַרְתָּ אֶל־חִזְקִיָּהוּ
כֹּה־אָמַר יְהוָה אֱלֹהֵי דָּוִד אָבִיךָ שָׁמַעְתִּי אֶת־
תְּפִלָּתֶךָ רָאִיתִי אֶת־דִּמְעָתֶךָ הִנְנִי יוֹסִף עַל־יָמֶיךָ
חֲמֵשׁ עֶשְׂרֵה שָׁנָה׃ ⁶ וּמִכַּף מֶלֶךְ־אַשּׁוּר אַצִּילְךָ
וְאֵת הָעִיר הַזֹּאת וְגַנּוֹתִי עַל־הָעִיר הַזֹּאת׃ ⁷ וְזֶה־
לְּךָ הָאוֹת מֵאֵת יְהוָה אֲשֶׁר יַעֲשֶׂה יְהוָה אֶת־הַדָּבָר
הַזֶּה אֲשֶׁר דִּבֵּר׃ ⁸ הִנְנִי מֵשִׁיב אֶת־צֵל הַמַּעֲלוֹת
אֲשֶׁר יָרְדָה בְמַעֲלוֹת אָחָז בַּשֶּׁמֶשׁ אֲחֹרַנִּית עֶשֶׂר
מַעֲלוֹת וַתָּשָׁב הַשֶּׁמֶשׁ עֶשֶׂר מַעֲלוֹת בַּמַּעֲלוֹת אֲשֶׁר
יָרָדָה׃ ס

9 מִכְתָּב לְחִזְקִיָּהוּ מֶלֶךְ־יְהוּדָה
   בַּחֲלֹתוֹ וַיְחִי מֵחָלְיוֹ׃

10 אֲנִי אָמַרְתִּי בִּדְמִי יָמַי אֵלֵכָה
   בְּשַׁעֲרֵי שְׁאוֹל
   פֻּקַּדְתִּי יֶתֶר שְׁנוֹתָי׃

11 אָמַרְתִּי לֹא־אֶרְאֶה יָּהּ
   יָהּ בְּאֶרֶץ הַחַיִּים
   לֹא־אַבִּיט אָדָם
   עוֹד עִם־יוֹשְׁבֵי חָדֶל׃

12 דּוֹרִי נִסַּע וְנִגְלָה מִנִּי
   כְּאֹהֶל רֹעִי
   קִפַּדְתִּי כָאֹרֵג חַיַּי
   מִדַּלָּה יְבַצְּעֵנִי
   מִיּוֹם עַד־לַיְלָה תַּשְׁלִימֵנִי׃

13 שִׁוִּיתִי עַד־בֹּקֶר כָּאֲרִי
   כֵּן יְשַׁבֵּר כָּל־עַצְמוֹתָי
   מִיּוֹם עַד־לַיְלָה תַּשְׁלִימֵנִי׃

14 כְּסוּס עָגוּר כֵּן אֲצַפְצֵף
   אֶהְגֶּה כַּיּוֹנָה
   דַּלּוּ עֵינַי לַמָּרוֹם
   אֲדֹנָי עָשְׁקָה־לִּי עָרְבֵנִי׃

15 מָה־אֲדַבֵּר וְאָמַר־לִי
   וְהוּא עָשָׂה
   אֶדַּדֶּה כָל־שְׁנוֹתַי עַל־מַר נַפְשִׁי׃

16 אֲדֹנָי עֲלֵיהֶם יִחְיוּ
   וּלְכָל־בָּהֵן חַיֵּי רוּחִי
   וְתַחֲלִימֵנִי וְהַחֲיֵנִי׃

17 הִנֵּה לְשָׁלוֹם מַר־לִי מָר

That I had great bitterness;
But You have lovingly *delivered* my soul from the pit of corruption,
For You have cast all my sins behind Your back.
18 For Sheol cannot thank You, Death cannot praise You;
Those who go down to the pit cannot hope for Your truth.
19 The living, the living man, he shall praise You,
As I *do* this day;
The father shall make known Your truth to the children.
20 "The LORD *was ready* to save me;
Therefore we will sing my songs with stringed instruments
All the days of our life, in the house of the LORD."

21 Now Isaiah had said, "Let them take a lump of figs, and apply *it* as a poultice on the boil, and he shall recover."
22 And Hezekiah had said, "What *is* the sign that I shall go up to the house of the LORD?"

39

At that time Merodach-Baladan the son of Baladan, king of Babylon, sent letters and a present to Hezekiah, for he heard that he had been sick and had recovered. 2 And Hezekiah was pleased with them, and showed them the house of his treasures— the silver and gold, the spices and precious ointment, and all his armory—all that was found among his treasures. There was nothing in his house or in all his dominion that Hezekiah did not show them.

3 Then Isaiah the prophet went to King Hezekiah, and said to him, "What did these men say, and from where did they come to you?"

So Hezekiah said, "They came to me from a far country, from Babylon."

4 And he said, "What have they seen in your house?"

So Hezekiah answered, "They have seen all that *is* in my house; there is nothing among my treasures that I have not shown them."

5 Then Isaiah said to Hezekiah, "Hear the word of the LORD of hosts: 6 'Behold, the days are coming when all that *is* in your house, and what your fathers have accumulated until this day, shall be carried to Babylon; nothing shall be left,' says the LORD. 7 'And they shall take away *some* of your

וְאַתָּה חָשַׁקְתָּ נַפְשִׁי
מִשַּׁחַת בְּלִי
כִּי הִשְׁלַכְתָּ אַחֲרֵי גֵוְךָ כָּל־חֲטָאָי:
18 כִּי לֹא שְׁאוֹל תּוֹדֶךָּ
מָוֶת יְהַלְלֶךָּ
לֹא־יְשַׂבְּרוּ יוֹרְדֵי־בוֹר
אֶל־אֲמִתֶּךָ:
19 חַי חַי הוּא יוֹדֶךָ
כָּמוֹנִי הַיּוֹם
אָב לְבָנִים יוֹדִיעַ אֶל־אֲמִתֶּךָ:
20 יְהוָה לְהוֹשִׁיעֵנִי
וּנְגִינוֹתַי נְנַגֵּן
כָּל־יְמֵי חַיֵּינוּ עַל־בֵּית יְהוָה:
21 וַיֹּאמֶר יְשַׁעְיָהוּ יִשְׂאוּ דְּבֶלֶת תְּאֵנִים וְיִמְרְחוּ עַל־
הַשְּׁחִין וְיֶחִי: 22 וַיֹּאמֶר חִזְקִיָּהוּ מָה אוֹת כִּי אֶעֱלֶה
בֵּית יְהוָה: ס

לט בָּעֵת הַהִוא שָׁלַח מְרֹדַךְ בַּלְאֲדָן בֶּן־בַּלְאֲדָן
מֶלֶךְ־בָּבֶל סְפָרִים וּמִנְחָה אֶל־חִזְקִיָּהוּ וַיִּשְׁמַע כִּי
חָלָה וַיֶּחֱזָק: 2 וַיִּשְׂמַח עֲלֵיהֶם חִזְקִיָּהוּ וַיַּרְאֵם
אֶת־בֵּית נְכֹתֹה אֶת־הַכֶּסֶף וְאֶת־הַזָּהָב וְאֶת־
הַבְּשָׂמִים וְאֵת הַשֶּׁמֶן הַטּוֹב וְאֵת כָּל־בֵּית
כֵּלָיו וְאֵת כָּל־אֲשֶׁר נִמְצָא בְּאֹצְרֹתָיו לֹא־הָיָה דָבָר
אֲשֶׁר לֹא־הֶרְאָם חִזְקִיָּהוּ בְּבֵיתוֹ וּבְכָל־מֶמְשַׁלְתּוֹ:
3 וַיָּבֹא יְשַׁעְיָהוּ הַנָּבִיא אֶל־הַמֶּלֶךְ חִזְקִיָּהוּ וַיֹּאמֶר
אֵלָיו מָה אָמְרוּ הָאֲנָשִׁים הָאֵלֶּה וּמֵאַיִן יָבֹאוּ
אֵלֶיךָ וַיֹּאמֶר חִזְקִיָּהוּ מֵאֶרֶץ רְחוֹקָה בָּאוּ אֵלַי
מִבָּבֶל: 4 וַיֹּאמֶר מָה רָאוּ בְּבֵיתֶךָ וַיֹּאמֶר חִזְקִיָּהוּ
אֵת כָּל־אֲשֶׁר בְּבֵיתִי רָאוּ לֹא־הָיָה דָבָר אֲשֶׁר
לֹא־הִרְאִיתִים בְּאוֹצְרֹתָי: 5 וַיֹּאמֶר יְשַׁעְיָהוּ אֶל־
חִזְקִיָּהוּ שְׁמַע דְּבַר־יְהוָה צְבָאוֹת: 6 הִנֵּה יָמִים
בָּאִים וְנִשָּׂא כָּל־אֲשֶׁר בְּבֵיתֶךָ וַאֲשֶׁר אָצְרוּ
אֲבֹתֶיךָ עַד־הַיּוֹם הַזֶּה בָּבֶל לֹא־יִוָּתֵר דָּבָר אָמַר
יְהוָה: 7 וּמִבָּנֶיךָ אֲשֶׁר יֵצְאוּ מִמְּךָ אֲשֶׁר תּוֹלִיד

sons who will descend from you, whom you will beget; and they shall be eunuchs in the palace of the king of Babylon.'"

[8] So Hezekiah said to Isaiah, "The word of the LORD which you have spoken *is* good!" For he said, "At least there will be peace and truth in my days."

40

"Comfort, yes, comfort My people!"
Says your God.

2 "Speak comfort to Jerusalem, and cry out to her,
That her warfare is ended,
That her iniquity is pardoned;
For she has received from the LORD's hand
Double for all her sins."

3 The voice of one crying in the wilderness:
"Prepare the way of the LORD;
Make straight in the desert
A highway for our God.

4 Every valley shall be exalted
And every mountain and hill brought low;
The crooked places shall be made straight
And the rough places smooth;

5 The glory of the LORD shall be revealed,
And all flesh shall see *it* together;
For the mouth of the LORD has spoken."

6 The voice said, "Cry out!"
And he said, "What shall I cry?"

"All flesh *is* grass,
And all its loveliness *is* like the flower of the field.

7 The grass withers, the flower fades,
Because the breath of the LORD blows upon it;
Surely the people *are* grass.

8 The grass withers, the flower fades,
But the word of our God stands forever."

9 O Zion,
You who bring good tidings,
Get up into the high mountain;
O Jerusalem,
You who bring good tidings,
Lift up your voice with strength,
Lift *it* up, be not afraid;
Say to the cities of Judah, "Behold your God!"

10 Behold, the Lord GOD shall come with a strong *hand,*
And His arm shall rule for Him;
Behold, His reward *is* with Him,
And His work before Him.

11 He will feed His flock like a shepherd;

וְהָיוּ סָרִיסִים בְּהֵיכַל מֶלֶךְ בָּבֶל: 8 וַיֹּאמֶר
חִזְקִיָּהוּ אֶל־יְשַׁעְיָהוּ טוֹב דְּבַר־יְהוָה אֲשֶׁר דִּבַּרְתָּ
וַיֹּאמֶר כִּי יִהְיֶה שָׁלוֹם וֶאֱמֶת בְּיָמָי: פ

מ נַחֲמוּ נַחֲמוּ עַמִּי
יֹאמַר אֱלֹהֵיכֶם:

2 דַּבְּרוּ עַל־לֵב יְרוּשָׁלִַם
וְקִרְאוּ אֵלֶיהָ
כִּי מָלְאָה צְבָאָהּ
כִּי נִרְצָה עֲוֺנָהּ
כִּי לָקְחָה מִיַּד יְהוָה
כִּפְלַיִם בְּכָל־חַטֹּאתֶיהָ: ס

3 קוֹל קוֹרֵא בַּמִּדְבָּר פַּנּוּ דֶּרֶךְ יְהוָה
יַשְּׁרוּ בָּעֲרָבָה
מְסִלָּה לֵאלֹהֵינוּ:

4 כָּל־גֶּיא יִנָּשֵׂא וְכָל־הַר וְגִבְעָה יִשְׁפָּלוּ
וְהָיָה הֶעָקֹב לְמִישׁוֹר
וְהָרְכָסִים לְבִקְעָה:

5 וְנִגְלָה כְּבוֹד יְהוָה
וְרָאוּ כָל־בָּשָׂר יַחְדָּו
כִּי פִּי יְהוָה דִּבֵּר: ס

6 קוֹל אֹמֵר קְרָא
וְאָמַר מָה אֶקְרָא
כָּל־הַבָּשָׂר חָצִיר
וְכָל־חַסְדּוֹ כְּצִיץ הַשָּׂדֶה:

7 יָבֵשׁ חָצִיר נָבֵל צִיץ
כִּי רוּחַ יְהוָה נָשְׁבָה בּוֹ
אָכֵן חָצִיר הָעָם:

8 יָבֵשׁ חָצִיר נָבֵל צִיץ
וּדְבַר־אֱלֹהֵינוּ יָקוּם לְעוֹלָם: ס

9 עַל הַר־גָּבֹהַ עֲלִי־לָךְ
מְבַשֶּׂרֶת צִיּוֹן
הָרִימִי בַכֹּחַ קוֹלֵךְ
מְבַשֶּׂרֶת יְרוּשָׁלִָם
הָרִימִי אַל־תִּירָאִי
אִמְרִי לְעָרֵי יְהוּדָה
הִנֵּה אֱלֹהֵיכֶם:

10 הִנֵּה אֲדֹנָי יְהוִה בְּחָזָק יָבוֹא
וּזְרֹעוֹ מֹשְׁלָה לוֹ
הִנֵּה שְׂכָרוֹ אִתּוֹ וּפְעֻלָּתוֹ לְפָנָיו:

11 כְּרֹעֶה עֶדְרוֹ יִרְעֶה

He will gather the lambs with His arm,
And carry *them* in His bosom,
And gently lead those who are with young.

בִּזְרֹעוֹ יְקַבֵּץ טְלָאִים
וּבְחֵיקוֹ יִשָּׂא
עָלוֹת יְנַהֵל׃ ס

12 Who has measured the waters in the hollow
of His hand,
Measured heaven with a span
And calculated the dust of the earth in a
measure?
Weighed the mountains in scales
And the hills in a balance?

12 מִי־מָדַד בְּשָׁעֳלוֹ מַיִם
וְשָׁמַיִם בַּזֶּרֶת תִּכֵּן
וְכָל בַּשָּׁלִשׁ עֲפַר הָאָרֶץ
וְשָׁקַל בַּפֶּלֶס הָרִים
וּגְבָעוֹת בְּמֹאזְנָיִם׃

13 Who has directed the Spirit of the LORD,
Or *as* His counselor has taught Him?

13 מִי־תִכֵּן אֶת־רוּחַ יְהוָה
וְאִישׁ עֲצָתוֹ יוֹדִיעֶנּוּ׃

14 With whom did He take counsel, and *who*
instructed Him,
And taught Him in the path of justice?
Who taught Him knowledge,
And showed Him the way of understanding?

14 אֶת־מִי נוֹעָץ וַיְבִינֵהוּ
וַיְלַמְּדֵהוּ בְּאֹרַח מִשְׁפָּט
וַיְלַמְּדֵהוּ דַעַת
וְדֶרֶךְ תְּבוּנוֹת יוֹדִיעֶנּוּ׃

15 Behold, the nations *are* as a drop in a bucket,
And are counted as the small dust on the
scales;
Look, He lifts up the isles as a very little
thing.

15 הֵן גּוֹיִם כְּמַר מִדְּלִי
וּכְשַׁחַק מֹאזְנַיִם נֶחְשָׁבוּ
הֵן אִיִּים כַּדַּק יִטּוֹל׃

16 And Lebanon *is* not sufficient to burn,
Nor its beasts sufficient for a burnt offering.

16 וּלְבָנוֹן אֵין דֵּי בָּעֵר
וְחַיָּתוֹ אֵין דֵּי עוֹלָה׃ ס

17 All nations before Him *are* as nothing,
And they are counted by Him less than
nothing and worthless.

17 כָּל־הַגּוֹיִם כְּאַיִן נֶגְדּוֹ
מֵאֶפֶס וָתֹהוּ נֶחְשְׁבוּ־לוֹ׃

18 To whom then will you liken God?
Or what likeness will you compare to Him?

18 וְאֶל־מִי תְּדַמְּיוּן אֵל
וּמַה־דְּמוּת תַּעַרְכוּ לוֹ׃

19 The workman molds an image,
The goldsmith overspreads it with gold,
And the silversmith casts silver chains.

19 הַפֶּסֶל נָסַךְ חָרָשׁ
וְצֹרֵף בַּזָּהָב יְרַקְּעֶנּוּ
וּרְתֻקוֹת כֶּסֶף צוֹרֵף׃

20 Whoever *is* too impoverished for *such* a
contribution
Chooses a tree *that* will not rot;
He seeks for himself a skillful workman
To prepare a carved image *that* will not
totter.

20 הַמְסֻכָּן תְּרוּמָה
עֵץ לֹא־יִרְקַב יִבְחָר
חָרָשׁ חָכָם יְבַקֶּשׁ־לוֹ
לְהָכִין פֶּסֶל לֹא יִמּוֹט׃

21 Have you not known?
Have you not heard?
Has it not been told you from the beginning?
Have you not understood from the founda-
tions of the earth?

21 הֲלוֹא תֵדְעוּ הֲלוֹא תִשְׁמָעוּ
הֲלוֹא הֻגַּד מֵרֹאשׁ לָכֶם
הֲלוֹא הֲבִינֹתֶם מוֹסְדוֹת הָאָרֶץ׃

22 *It is* He who sits above the circle of the earth,
And its inhabitants *are* like grasshoppers,
Who stretches out the heavens like a curtain,
And spreads them out like a tent to dwell in.

22 הַיֹּשֵׁב עַל־חוּג הָאָרֶץ
וְיֹשְׁבֶיהָ כַּחֲגָבִים
הַנּוֹטֶה כַדֹּק שָׁמַיִם
וַיִּמְתָּחֵם כָּאֹהֶל לָשָׁבֶת׃

23 He brings the princes to nothing;
He makes the judges of the earth useless.

23 הַנּוֹתֵן רוֹזְנִים לְאָיִן
שֹׁפְטֵי אֶרֶץ כַּתֹּהוּ עָשָׂה׃

24 Scarcely shall they be planted,
Scarcely shall they be sown,

24 אַף בַּל־נִטָּעוּ
אַף בַּל־זֹרָעוּ

Scarcely shall their stock take root in the
 earth,
When He will also blow on them,
And they will wither,
And the whirlwind will take them away like
 stubble.

25 "To whom then will you liken Me,
 Or *to whom* shall I be equal?" says the Holy
  One.

26 Lift up your eyes on high,
 And see who has created these *things,*
 Who brings out their host by number;
 He calls them all by name,
 By the greatness of His might
 And the strength of *His* power;
 Not one is missing.

27 Why do you say, O Jacob,
 And speak, O Israel:
 "My way is hidden from the LORD,
 And my just claim is passed over by my
  God"?

28 Have you not known?
 Have you not heard?
 The everlasting God, the LORD,
 The Creator of the ends of the earth,
 Neither faints nor is weary.
 His understanding is unsearchable.

29 He gives power to the weak,
 And to *those who have* no might He increases
  strength.

30 Even the youths shall faint and be weary,
 And the young men shall utterly fall,

31 But those who wait on the LORD
 Shall renew *their* strength;
 They shall mount up with wings like eagles,
 They shall run and not be weary,
 They shall walk and not faint.

41 "Keep silence before Me, O coastlands,
 And let the people renew *their* strength!
 Let them come near, then let them speak;
 Let us come near together for judgment.

2 "Who raised up one from the east?
 Who in righteousness called him to His feet?
 Who gave the nations before him,
 And made *him* rule over kings?
 Who gave *them* as the dust *to* his sword,
 As driven stubble to his bow?

3 Who pursued them, *and* passed safely
 By the way *that* he had not gone with his
  feet?

4 Who has performed and done *it,*

אַף בַּל־שֹׁרֵשׁ בָּאָרֶץ גִּזְעָם
וְגַם־נָשַׁף בָּהֶם וַיִּבָשׁוּ
וּסְעָרָה כַּקַּשׁ תִּשָּׂאֵם: ס

25 וְאֶל־מִי תְדַמְּיוּנִי וְאֶשְׁוֶה
יֹאמַר קָדוֹשׁ:

26 שְׂאוּ־מָרוֹם עֵינֵיכֶם
וּרְאוּ מִי־בָרָא אֵלֶּה
הַמּוֹצִיא בְמִסְפָּר צְבָאָם
לְכֻלָּם בְּשֵׁם יִקְרָא
מֵרֹב אוֹנִים וְאַמִּיץ כֹּחַ
אִישׁ לֹא נֶעְדָּר: ס

27 לָמָה תֹאמַר יַעֲקֹב
וּתְדַבֵּר יִשְׂרָאֵל
נִסְתְּרָה דַרְכִּי מֵיהוָה
וּמֵאֱלֹהַי מִשְׁפָּטִי יַעֲבוֹר:

28 הֲלוֹא יָדַעְתָּ אִם־לֹא שָׁמַעְתָּ
אֱלֹהֵי עוֹלָם ׀ יְהוָה
בּוֹרֵא קְצוֹת הָאָרֶץ
לֹא יִיעַף וְלֹא יִיגָע
אֵין חֵקֶר לִתְבוּנָתוֹ:

29 נֹתֵן לַיָּעֵף כֹּחַ
וּלְאֵין אוֹנִים עָצְמָה יַרְבֶּה:

30 וְיִעֲפוּ נְעָרִים וְיִגָעוּ
וּבַחוּרִים כָּשׁוֹל יִכָּשֵׁלוּ:

31 וְקוֹיֵ יְהוָה יַחֲלִיפוּ כֹחַ
יַעֲלוּ אֵבֶר כַּנְּשָׁרִים
יָרוּצוּ וְלֹא יִיגָעוּ
יֵלְכוּ וְלֹא יִיעָפוּ: פ

מא הַחֲרִישׁוּ אֵלַי אִיִּים
וּלְאֻמִּים יַחֲלִיפוּ כֹחַ
יִגְּשׁוּ אָז יְדַבֵּרוּ
יַחְדָּו לַמִּשְׁפָּט נִקְרָבָה:

2 מִי הֵעִיר מִמִּזְרָח
צֶדֶק יִקְרָאֵהוּ לְרַגְלוֹ
יִתֵּן לְפָנָיו גּוֹיִם
וּמְלָכִים יַרְדְּ
יִתֵּן כֶּעָפָר חַרְבּוֹ
כְּקַשׁ נִדָּף קַשְׁתּוֹ:

3 יִרְדְּפֵם יַעֲבוֹר שָׁלוֹם
אֹרַח בְּרַגְלָיו לֹא יָבוֹא:

4 מִי־פָעַל וְעָשָׂה

Calling the generations from the beginning?
'I, the LORD, am the first;
And with the last I *am* He.' "

קֹרֵא הַדֹּרוֹת מֵרֹאשׁ
אֲנִי יְהֹוָה רִאשׁוֹן
וְאֶת־אַחֲרֹנִים אֲנִי־הֽוּא׃

5 The coastlands saw *it* and feared,
The ends of the earth were afraid;
They drew near and came.

5 רָאוּ אִיִּים וְיִירָאוּ
קְצוֹת הָאָרֶץ יֶחֱרָדוּ
קָרְבוּ וַיֶּאֱתָיֽוּן׃

6 Everyone helped his neighbor,
And said to his brother,
"Be of good courage!"

6 אִישׁ אֶת־רֵעֵהוּ יַעְזֹרוּ
וּלְאָחִיו יֹאמַר חֲזָֽק׃

7 So the craftsman encouraged the goldsmith;
He who smooths *with* the hammer *inspired*
    him who strikes the anvil,
Saying, "It *is* ready for the soldering";
Then he fastened it with pegs,
That it might not totter.

7 וַיְחַזֵּק חָרָשׁ אֶת־צֹרֵף
מַחֲלִיק פַּטִּישׁ אֶת־הוֹלֶם פָּעַם
אֹמֵר לַדֶּבֶק טוֹב הוּא
ס וַיְחַזְּקֵהוּ בְמַסְמְרִים לֹא יִמּֽוֹט׃

8 "But you, Israel, *are* My servant,
Jacob whom I have chosen,
The descendants of Abraham My friend.

8 וְאַתָּה יִשְׂרָאֵל עַבְדִּי
יַעֲקֹב אֲשֶׁר בְּחַרְתִּיךָ
זֶרַע אַבְרָהָם אֹהֲבִֽי׃

9 *You* whom I have taken from the ends of the
    earth,
And called from its farthest regions,
And said to you,
'You *are* My servant,
I have chosen you and have not cast you
    away:

9 אֲשֶׁר הֶחֱזַקְתִּיךָ מִקְצוֹת הָאָרֶץ
וּמֵאֲצִילֶיהָ קְרָאתִיךָ
וָאֹמַר לְךָ עַבְדִּי־אַתָּה
בְּחַרְתִּיךָ וְלֹא מְאַסְתִּֽיךָ׃

10 Fear not, for I *am* with you;
Be not dismayed, for I *am* your God.
I will strengthen you,
Yes, I will help you,
I will uphold you with My righteous right
    hand.'

10 אַל־תִּירָא כִּי עִמְּךָ־אָנִי
אַל־תִּשְׁתָּע כִּי־אֲנִי אֱלֹהֶיךָ
אִמַּצְתִּיךָ אַף־עֲזַרְתִּיךָ
אַף־תְּמַכְתִּיךָ בִּימִין צִדְקִֽי׃

11 "Behold, all those who were incensed against
    you
Shall be ashamed and disgraced;
They shall be as nothing,
And those who strive with you shall perish.

11 הֵן יֵבֹשׁוּ וְיִכָּלְמוּ
כֹּל הַנֶּחֱרִים בָּךְ
יִהְיוּ כְאַיִן וְיֹאבְדוּ
אַנְשֵׁי רִיבֶֽךָ׃

12 You shall seek them and not find them—
Those who contended with you.
Those who war against you
Shall be as nothing,
As a nonexistent thing.

12 תְּבַקְשֵׁם וְלֹא תִמְצָאֵם
אַנְשֵׁי מַצֻּתֶךָ
יִהְיוּ כְאַיִן וּכְאֶפֶס
אַנְשֵׁי מִלְחַמְתֶּֽךָ׃

13 For I, the LORD your God, will hold your
    right hand,
Saying to you, 'Fear not, I will help you.'

13 כִּי אֲנִי יְהֹוָה אֱלֹהֶיךָ
מַחֲזִיק יְמִינֶךָ
הָאֹמֵר לְךָ אַל־תִּירָא
ס אֲנִי עֲזַרְתִּֽיךָ׃

14 "Fear not, you worm Jacob,
You men of Israel!
I will help you," says the LORD
And your Redeemer, the Holy One of Israel.

14 אַל־תִּירְאִי תּוֹלַעַת יַעֲקֹב
מְתֵי יִשְׂרָאֵל
אֲנִי עֲזַרְתִּיךְ נְאֻם־יְהֹוָה
וְגֹאֲלֵךְ קְדוֹשׁ יִשְׂרָאֵֽל׃

15 "Behold, I will make you into a new threshing
    sledge with sharp teeth;
You shall thresh the mountains and beat
    them small,

15 הִנֵּה שַׂמְתִּיךְ לְמוֹרַג חָרוּץ חָדָשׁ
בַּעַל פִּיפִיּוֹת

And make the hills like chaff.

16 You shall winnow them, the wind shall carry
        them away,
     And the whirlwind shall scatter them;
     You shall rejoice in the LORD,
     And glory in the Holy One of Israel.

17 "The poor and needy seek water, but *there is*
        none,
     Their tongues fail for thirst.
     I, the LORD, will hear them;
     I, the God of Israel, will not forsake them.

18 I will open rivers in desolate heights,
     And fountains in the midst of the valleys;
     I will make the wilderness a pool of water,
     And the dry land springs of water.

19 I will plant in the wilderness the cedar and
        the acacia tree,
     The myrtle and the oil tree;
     I will set in the desert the cypress tree *and* the
        pine
     And the box tree together,

20 That they may see and know,
     And consider and understand together,
     That the hand of the LORD has done this,
     And the Holy One of Israel has created it.

21 "Present your case," says the LORD.
     "Bring forth your strong *reasons*," says the
        King of Jacob.

22 "Let them bring forth and show us what will
        happen;
     Let them show the former things, what they
        were,
     That we may consider them,
     And know the latter end of them;
     Or declare to us things to come.

23 Show the things that are to come hereafter,
     That we may know that you *are* gods;
     Yes, do good or do evil,
     That we may be dismayed and see *it*
        together.

24 Indeed you *are* nothing,
     And your work *is* nothing;
     He who chooses you *is* an abomination.

25 "I have raised up one from the north,
     And he shall come;
     From the rising of the sun he shall call on
        My name;
     And he shall come against princes as *though*
        mortar,
     As the potter treads clay.

26 Who has declared from the beginning, that
     we may know?

תָּדוּשׁ הָרִים וְתָדֹק
וּגְבָעוֹת כַּמֹּץ תָּשִׂים:

16 תִּזְרֵם וְרוּחַ תִּשָּׂאֵם
וּסְעָרָה תָּפִיץ אוֹתָם
וְאַתָּה תָּגִיל בַּיהוָה
בִּקְדוֹשׁ יִשְׂרָאֵל תִּתְהַלָּל: פ

17 הָעֲנִיִּים וְהָאֶבְיוֹנִים
מְבַקְשִׁים מַיִם וָאַיִן
לְשׁוֹנָם בַּצָּמָא נָשָׁתָּה
אֲנִי יְהוָה אֶעֱנֵם
אֱלֹהֵי יִשְׂרָאֵל לֹא אֶעֶזְבֵם:

18 אֶפְתַּח עַל־שְׁפָיִים נְהָרוֹת
וּבְתוֹךְ בְּקָעוֹת מַעְיָנוֹת
אָשִׂים מִדְבָּר לַאֲגַם־מַיִם
וְאֶרֶץ צִיָּה לְמוֹצָאֵי מָיִם:

19 אֶתֵּן בַּמִּדְבָּר אֶרֶז שִׁטָּה
וַהֲדַס וְעֵץ שָׁמֶן
אָשִׂים בָּעֲרָבָה
בְּרוֹשׁ תִּדְהָר וּתְאַשּׁוּר יַחְדָּו:

20 לְמַעַן יִרְאוּ וְיֵדְעוּ
וְיָשִׂימוּ וְיַשְׂכִּילוּ יַחְדָּו
כִּי יַד־יְהוָה עָשְׂתָה זֹּאת
וּקְדוֹשׁ יִשְׂרָאֵל בְּרָאָהּ: פ

21 קָרְבוּ רִיבְכֶם יֹאמַר יְהוָה
הַגִּישׁוּ עֲצֻמוֹתֵיכֶם
יֹאמַר מֶלֶךְ יַעֲקֹב:

22 יַגִּישׁוּ וְיַגִּידוּ לָנוּ אֵת אֲשֶׁר תִּקְרֶינָה
הָרִאשֹׁנוֹת מָה הֵנָּה
הַגִּידוּ וְנָשִׂימָה לִבֵּנוּ
וְנֵדְעָה אַחֲרִיתָן אוֹ הַבָּאוֹת הַשְׁמִיעֻנוּ:

23 הַגִּידוּ הָאֹתִיּוֹת לְאָחוֹר
וְנֵדְעָה כִּי אֱלֹהִים אַתֶּם
אַף־תֵּיטִיבוּ וְתָרֵעוּ
וְנִשְׁתָּעֶה וְנֵרֶאᵖ יַחְדָּו:

24 הֵן־אַתֶּם מֵאַיִן וּפָעָלְכֶם מֵאָפַע
תּוֹעֵבָה יִבְחַר בָּכֶם:

25 הַעִירוֹתִי מִצָּפוֹן וַיַּאת
מִמִּזְרַח־שֶׁמֶשׁ יִקְרָא בִשְׁמִי
וְיָבֹא סְגָנִים כְּמוֹ־חֹמֶר
וּכְמוֹ יוֹצֵר יִרְמָס־טִיט:

26 מִי־הִגִּיד מֵרֹאשׁ וְנֵדְעָה

מא 23 וְנִרְאֶה

And former times, that we may say, 'He is
  righteous'?
Surely *there is* no one who shows,
Surely *there is* no one who declares,
Surely *there is* no one who hears your words.

27 The first time *I said* to Zion,
  'Look, there they are!'
  And I will give to Jerusalem one who brings
    good tidings.

28 For I looked, and *there was* no man;
  I looked among them, but *there was* no
    counselor,
  Who, when I asked of them, could answer a
    word.

29 Indeed they *are* all worthless;
  Their works *are* nothing;
  Their molded images *are* wind and confu-
    sion.

וּמִלְּפָנִים וְנֹאמַר צַדִּיק

אַף אֵין־מַגִּיד

אַף אֵין מַשְׁמִיעַ

אַף אֵין־שֹׁמֵעַ אִמְרֵיכֶם:

27 רִאשׁוֹן לְצִיּוֹן הִנֵּה הִנָּם

וְלִירוּשָׁלַ͏ִם מְבַשֵּׂר אֶתֵּן:

28 וְאֵרֶא וְאֵין אִישׁ

וּמֵאֵלֶּה וְאֵין יוֹעֵץ

וְאֶשְׁאָלֵם וְיָשִׁיבוּ דָבָר:

29 הֵן כֻּלָּם

אָוֶן אֶפֶס מַעֲשֵׂיהֶם

רוּחַ וָתֹהוּ נִסְכֵּיהֶם: פ

42 "Behold! My Servant whom I uphold,
  My Elect One *in whom* My soul delights!
  I have put My Spirit upon Him;
  He will bring forth justice to the Gentiles.

2 He will not cry out, nor raise *His voice*,
  Nor cause His voice to be heard in the street.

3 A bruised reed He will not break,
  And smoking flax He will not quench;
  He will bring forth justice for truth.

4 He will not fail nor be discouraged,
  Till He has established justice in the earth;
  And the coastlands shall wait for His law."

5 Thus says God the LORD,
  Who created the heavens and stretched them
    out,
  Who spread forth the earth and that which
    comes from it,
  Who gives breath to the people on it,
  And spirit to those who walk on it:

6 "I, the LORD, have called You in righteous-
    ness,
  And will hold Your hand;
  I will keep You and give You as a covenant
    to the people,
  As a light to the Gentiles,

7 To open blind eyes,
  To bring out prisoners from the prison,
  Those who sit in darkness from the prison
    house.

8 I *am* the LORD, that *is* My name;
  And My glory I will not give to another,
  Nor My praise to carved images.

9 Behold, the former things have come to pass,
  And new things I declare;

מב הֵן עַבְדִּי אֶתְמָךְ־בּוֹ

בְּחִירִי רָצְתָה נַפְשִׁי

נָתַתִּי רוּחִי עָלָיו

מִשְׁפָּט לַגּוֹיִם יוֹצִיא:

2 לֹא יִצְעַק וְלֹא יִשָּׂא

וְלֹא־יַשְׁמִיעַ בַּחוּץ קוֹלוֹ:

3 קָנֶה רָצוּץ לֹא יִשְׁבּוֹר

וּפִשְׁתָּה כֵהָה לֹא יְכַבֶּנָּה

לֶאֱמֶת יוֹצִיא מִשְׁפָּט:

4 לֹא יִכְהֶה וְלֹא יָרוּץ

עַד־יָשִׂים בָּאָרֶץ מִשְׁפָּט

וּלְתוֹרָתוֹ אִיִּים יְיַחֵלוּ: פ

5 כֹּה־אָמַר הָאֵל יְהֹוָה

בּוֹרֵא הַשָּׁמַיִם וְנוֹטֵיהֶם

רֹקַע הָאָרֶץ וְצֶאֱצָאֶיהָ

נֹתֵן נְשָׁמָה לָעָם עָלֶיהָ וְרוּחַ לַהֹלְכִים בָּהּ:

6 אֲנִי יְהֹוָה קְרָאתִיךָ בְצֶדֶק

וְאַחְזֵק בְּיָדֶךָ

וְאֶצָּרְךָ וְאֶתֶּנְךָ לִבְרִית עָם

לְאוֹר גּוֹיִם:

7 לִפְקֹחַ עֵינַיִם עִוְרוֹת

לְהוֹצִיא מִמַּסְגֵּר אַסִּיר

מִבֵּית כֶּלֶא יֹשְׁבֵי חֹשֶׁךְ:

8 אֲנִי יְהֹוָה הוּא שְׁמִי

וּכְבוֹדִי לְאַחֵר לֹא־אֶתֵּן

וּתְהִלָּתִי לַפְּסִילִים:

9 הָרִאשֹׁנוֹת הִנֵּה־בָאוּ

Before they spring forth I tell you of them."

10 Sing to the LORD a new song,
   And His praise from the ends of the earth,
   You who go down to the sea, and all that is
      in it,
   You coastlands and you inhabitants of them!

11 Let the wilderness and its cities lift up *their*
      voice,
   The villages *that* Kedar inhabits.
   Let the inhabitants of Sela sing,
   Let them shout from the top of the
      mountains.

12 Let them give glory to the LORD,
   And declare His praise in the coastlands.

13 The LORD shall go forth like a mighty man;
   He shall stir up *His* zeal like a man of war.
   He shall cry out, yes, shout aloud;
   He shall prevail against His enemies.

14 "I have held My peace a long time,
   I have been still and restrained Myself.
   Now I will cry like a woman in labor,
   I will pant and gasp at once.

15 I will lay waste the mountains and hills,
   And dry up all their vegetation;
   I will make the rivers coastlands,
   And I will dry up the pools.

16 I will bring the blind by a way they did not
      know;
   I will lead them in paths they have not
      known.
   I will make darkness light before them,
   And crooked places straight.
   These things I will do for them,
   And not forsake them.

17 They shall be turned back,
   They shall be greatly ashamed,
   Who trust in carved images,
   Who say to the molded images,
   'You *are* our gods.'

18 "Hear, you deaf;
   And look, you blind, that you may see.

19 Who *is* blind but My servant,
   Or deaf as My messenger *whom* I send?
   Who *is* blind as he who is perfect,
   And blind as the LORD's servant?

20 Seeing many things, but you do not observe;
   Opening the ears, but he does not hear."

21 The LORD is well pleased for His right-
      eousness' sake;
   He will exalt the law and make *it* honorable.

22 But this *is* a people robbed and plundered;
   All of them are snared in holes,

וַחֲדָשׁוֹת אֲנִי מַגִּיד
בְּטֶרֶם תִּצְמַחְנָה אַשְׁמִיע אֶתְכֶם: פ
10 שִׁירוּ לַיהוָה שִׁיר חָדָשׁ
תְּהִלָּתוֹ מִקְצֵה הָאָרֶץ
יוֹרְדֵי הַיָּם וּמְלֹאוֹ אִיִּים וְיֹשְׁבֵיהֶם:
11 יִשְׂאוּ מִדְבָּר וְעָרָיו חֲצֵרִים תֵּשֵׁב קֵדָר
יָרֹנּוּ יֹשְׁבֵי סֶלַע מֵרֹאשׁ הָרִים יִצְוָחוּ:
12 יָשִׂימוּ לַיהוָה כָּבוֹד
וּתְהִלָּתוֹ בָּאִיִּים יַגִּידוּ:
13 יְהוָה כַּגִּבּוֹר יֵצֵא
כְּאִישׁ מִלְחָמוֹת יָעִיר קִנְאָה
יָרִיעַ אַף־יַצְרִיחַ
עַל־אֹיְבָיו יִתְגַּבָּר: ס
14 הֶחֱשֵׁיתִי מֵעוֹלָם אַחֲרִישׁ אֶתְאַפָּק
כַּיּוֹלֵדָה אֶפְעֶה אֶשֹּׁם וְאֶשְׁאַף יָחַד:
15 אַחֲרִיב הָרִים וּגְבָעוֹת
וְכָל־עֶשְׂבָּם אוֹבִישׁ
וְשַׂמְתִּי נְהָרוֹת לָאִיִּים
וַאֲגַמִּים אוֹבִישׁ:
16 וְהוֹלַכְתִּי עִוְרִים בְּדֶרֶךְ לֹא יָדָעוּ
בִּנְתִיבוֹת לֹא־יָדְעוּ אַדְרִיכֵם
אָשִׂים מַחְשָׁךְ לִפְנֵיהֶם לָאוֹר
וּמַעֲקַשִּׁים לְמִישׁוֹר
אֵלֶּה הַדְּבָרִים עֲשִׂיתִם
וְלֹא עֲזַבְתִּים:
17 נָסֹגוּ אָחוֹר יֵבֹשׁוּ בֹשֶׁת
הַבֹּטְחִים בַּפָּסֶל
הָאֹמְרִים לְמַסֵּכָה
אַתֶּם אֱלֹהֵינוּ:   ס
18 הַחֵרְשִׁים שְׁמָעוּ
וְהַעִוְרִים הַבִּיטוּ לִרְאוֹת:
19 מִי עִוֵּר כִּי אִם־עַבְדִּי
וְחֵרֵשׁ כְּמַלְאָכִי אֶשְׁלָח
מִי עִוֵּר כִּמְשֻׁלָּם
וְעִוֵּר כְּעֶבֶד יְהוָה:
20 רָאִיתָ רַבּוֹת וְלֹא תִשְׁמֹר
פָּקוֹחַ אָזְנַיִם וְלֹא יִשְׁמָע:
21 יְהוָה חָפֵץ לְמַעַן צִדְקוֹ
יַגְדִּיל תּוֹרָה וְיַאְדִּיר:
22 וְהוּא עַם־בָּזוּז וְשָׁסוּי
הָפֵחַ בַּחוּרִים כֻּלָּם

מב 20 רָאוֹת

And they are hidden in prison houses;
They are for prey, and no one delivers;
For plunder, and no one says, "Restore!"

23 Who among you will give ear to this?
Who will listen and hear for the time to
    come?

24 Who gave Jacob for plunder, and Israel to
    the robbers?
Was it not the LORD,
He against whom we have sinned?
For they would not walk in His ways,
Nor were they obedient to His law.

25 Therefore He has poured on him the fury of
    His anger
And the strength of battle;
It has set him on fire all around,
Yet he did not know;
And it burned him,
Yet he did not take *it* to heart.

43 But now, thus says the LORD, who created
    you, O Jacob,
And He who formed you, O Israel:
"Fear not, for I have redeemed you;
I have called *you* by your name;
You *are* Mine.

2 When you pass through the waters, I *will be*
    with you;
And through the rivers, they shall not
    overflow you.
When you walk through the fire, you shall
    not be burned,
Nor shall the flame scorch you.

3 For I *am* the LORD your God,
The Holy One of Israel, your Savior;
I gave Egypt for your ransom,
Ethiopia and Seba in your place.

4 Since you were precious in My sight,
You have been honored,
And I have loved you;
Therefore I will give men for you,
And people for your life.

5 Fear not, for I *am* with you;
I will bring your descendants from the east,
And gather you from the west;

6 I will say to the north, 'Give them up!'
And to the south, 'Do not keep them back!'
Bring My sons from afar,
And My daughters from the ends of the
    earth—

7 Everyone who is called by My name,
Whom I have created for My glory;
I have formed him, yes, I have made him."

וּכְבָתֵּי כְלָאִים הָחְבָּאוּ
הָיוּ לָבַז וְאֵין מַצִּיל
מְשִׁסָּה וְאֵין־אֹמֵר הָשַׁב:

23 מִי בָכֶם יַאֲזִין זֹאת
יַקְשֵׁב וְיִשְׁמַע לְאָחוֹר:

24 מִי־נָתַן לִמְשׁוּסָה יַעֲקֹב
וְיִשְׂרָאֵל לְבֹזְזִים
הֲלוֹא יְהֹוָה
זוּ חָטָאנוּ לוֹ
וְלֹא־אָבוּ בִדְרָכָיו הָלוֹךְ
וְלֹא שָׁמְעוּ בְּתוֹרָתוֹ:

25 וַיִּשְׁפֹּךְ עָלָיו חֵמָה אַפּוֹ
וֶעֱזוּז מִלְחָמָה
וַתְּלַהֲטֵהוּ מִסָּבִיב וְלֹא יָדָע
וַתִּבְעַר־בּוֹ וְלֹא־יָשִׂים עַל־לֵב: פ

מג וְעַתָּה כֹּה־אָמַר יְהֹוָה בֹּרַאֲךָ יַעֲקֹב
וְיֹצֶרְךָ יִשְׂרָאֵל
אַל־תִּירָא כִּי גְאַלְתִּיךָ
קָרָאתִי בְשִׁמְךָ לִי־אָתָּה:

2 כִּי־תַעֲבֹר בַּמַּיִם אִתְּךָ־אָנִי
וּבַנְּהָרוֹת לֹא יִשְׁטְפוּךָ
כִּי־תֵלֵךְ בְּמוֹ־אֵשׁ לֹא תִכָּוֶה
וְלֶהָבָה לֹא תִבְעַר־בָּךְ:

3 כִּי אֲנִי יְהֹוָה אֱלֹהֶיךָ
קְדוֹשׁ יִשְׂרָאֵל מוֹשִׁיעֶךָ
נָתַתִּי כָפְרְךָ מִצְרַיִם
כּוּשׁ וּסְבָא תַּחְתֶּיךָ:

4 מֵאֲשֶׁר יָקַרְתָּ בְעֵינַי נִכְבַּדְתָּ
וַאֲנִי אֲהַבְתִּיךָ וְאֶתֵּן אָדָם תַּחְתֶּיךָ
וּלְאֻמִּים תַּחַת נַפְשֶׁךָ:

5 אַל־תִּירָא כִּי אִתְּךָ־אָנִי
מִמִּזְרָח אָבִיא זַרְעֶךָ
וּמִמַּעֲרָב אֲקַבְּצֶךָּ:

6 אֹמַר לַצָּפוֹן תֵּנִי
וּלְתֵימָן אַל־תִּכְלָאִי
הָבִיאִי בָנַי מֵרָחוֹק
וּבְנוֹתַי מִקְצֵה הָאָרֶץ:

7 כֹּל הַנִּקְרָא בִשְׁמִי

8 Bring out the blind people who have eyes,
   And the deaf who have ears.
9 Let all the nations be gathered together,
   And let the people be assembled.
   Who among them can declare this,
   And show us former things?
   Let them bring out their witnesses, that they
        may be justified;
   Or let them hear and say, "*It is* truth."
10 "You *are* My witnesses," says the LORD,
   "And My servant whom I have chosen,
   That you may know and believe Me,
   And understand that I *am* He.
   Before Me there was no God formed,
   Nor shall there be after Me.
11 I, *even* I, *am* the LORD,
   And besides Me *there is* no savior.
12 I have declared and saved,
   I have proclaimed,
   And *there was* no foreign *god* among you;
   Therefore you *are* My witnesses,"
   Says the LORD, "that I *am* God.
13 Indeed before the day *was,* I *am* He;
   And *there is* no one who can deliver out of
        My hand;
   I work, and who will reverse it?"

14 Thus says the LORD, your Redeemer,
   The Holy One of Israel:
   "For your sake I will send to Babylon,
   And bring them all down as fugitives—
   The Chaldeans, who rejoice in their ships.
15 I *am* the LORD, your Holy One,
   The Creator of Israel, your King."

16 Thus says the LORD, who makes a way in the
        sea
   And a path through the mighty waters,
17 Who brings forth the chariot and horse,
   The army and the power
   (They shall lie down together, they shall not
        rise;
   They are extinguished, they are quenched
        like a wick):
18 "Do not remember the former things,
   Nor consider the things of old.
19 Behold, I will do a new thing,
   Now it shall spring forth;
   Shall you not know it?
   I will even make a road in the wilderness
   And rivers in the desert.
20 The beast of the field will honor Me,
   The jackals and the ostriches,
   Because I give waters in the wilderness
   And rivers in the desert,

וְלִכְבוֹדִי בְּרָאתִיו
יְצַרְתִּיו אַף־עֲשִׂיתִיו׃

8 הוֹצִיא עַם־עִוֵּר וְעֵינַיִם יֵשׁ
   וְחֵרְשִׁים וְאָזְנַיִם לָמוֹ׃
9 כָּל־הַגּוֹיִם נִקְבְּצוּ יַחְדָּו
   וְיֵאָסְפוּ לְאֻמִּים
   מִי בָהֶם יַגִּיד זֹאת
   וְרִאשֹׁנוֹת יַשְׁמִיעֻנוּ
   יִתְּנוּ עֵדֵיהֶם וְיִצְדָּקוּ
   וְיִשְׁמְעוּ וְיֹאמְרוּ אֱמֶת׃
10 אַתֶּם עֵדַי נְאֻם־יְהֹוָה
   וְעַבְדִּי אֲשֶׁר בָּחָרְתִּי
   לְמַעַן תֵּדְעוּ וְתַאֲמִינוּ לִי וְתָבִינוּ
   כִּי־אֲנִי הוּא לְפָנַי לֹא־נוֹצַר אֵל
   וְאַחֲרַי לֹא יִהְיֶה׃   ס
11 אָנֹכִי אָנֹכִי יְהֹוָה
   וְאֵין מִבַּלְעָדַי מוֹשִׁיעַ׃
12 אָנֹכִי הִגַּדְתִּי וְהוֹשַׁעְתִּי
   וְהִשְׁמַעְתִּי וְאֵין בָּכֶם זָר
   וְאַתֶּם עֵדַי נְאֻם־יְהֹוָה וַאֲנִי־אֵל׃
13 גַּם־מִיּוֹם אֲנִי הוּא וְאֵין מִיָּדִי מַצִּיל
   אֶפְעַל וּמִי יְשִׁיבֶנָּה׃   ס
14 כֹּה־אָמַר יְהֹוָה
   גֹּאַלְכֶם קְדוֹשׁ יִשְׂרָאֵל
   לְמַעַנְכֶם שִׁלַּחְתִּי בָבֶלָה
   וְהוֹרַדְתִּי בָרִיחִים כֻּלָּם
   וְכַשְׂדִּים בָּאֳנִיּוֹת רִנָּתָם׃
15 אֲנִי יְהֹוָה קְדוֹשְׁכֶם
   בּוֹרֵא יִשְׂרָאֵל מַלְכְּכֶם׃   ס
16 כֹּה אָמַר יְהֹוָה הַנּוֹתֵן בַּיָּם דָּרֶךְ
   וּבְמַיִם עַזִּים נְתִיבָה׃
17 הַמּוֹצִיא רֶכֶב־וָסוּס חַיִל וְעִזּוּז
   יַחְדָּו יִשְׁכְּבוּ בַּל־יָקוּמוּ
   דָּעֲכוּ כַּפִּשְׁתָּה כָבוּ׃
18 אַל־תִּזְכְּרוּ רִאשֹׁנוֹת
   וְקַדְמֹנִיּוֹת אַל־תִּתְבֹּנָנוּ׃
19 הִנְנִי עֹשֶׂה חֲדָשָׁה
   עַתָּה תִצְמָח הֲלוֹא תֵדָעוּהָ
   אַף אָשִׂים בַּמִּדְבָּר דֶּרֶךְ
   בִּישִׁמוֹן נְהָרוֹת׃
20 תְּכַבְּדֵנִי חַיַּת הַשָּׂדֶה
   תַּנִּים וּבְנוֹת יַעֲנָה

To give drink to My people, My chosen.
21 This people I have formed for Myself;
They shall declare My praise.

22 "But you have not called upon Me, O Jacob;
And you have been weary of Me, O Israel.
23 You have not brought Me the sheep for your
burnt offerings,
Nor have you honored Me with your
sacrifices.
I have not caused you to serve with grain
offerings,
Nor wearied you with incense.
24 You have bought Me no sweet cane with
money,
Nor have you satisfied Me with the fat of
your sacrifices;
But you have burdened Me with your sins,
You have wearied Me with your iniquities.

25 "I, *even* I, *am* He who blots out your
transgressions for My own sake;
And I will not remember your sins.
26 Put Me in remembrance;
Let us contend together;
State your *case,* that you may be acquitted.
27 Your first father sinned,
And your mediators have transgressed
against Me.
28 Therefore I will profane the princes of the
sanctuary;
I will give Jacob to the curse,
And Israel to reproaches.

44 "Yet hear me now, O Jacob My servant,
And Israel whom I have chosen.
2 Thus says the LORD who made you
And formed you from the womb, *who* will
help you:
'Fear not, O Jacob My servant;
And you, Jeshurun, whom I have chosen.
3 For I will pour water on him who is thirsty,
And floods on the dry ground;
I will pour My Spirit on your descendants,
And My blessing on your offspring;
4 They will spring up among the grass
Like willows by the watercourses.'
5 One will say, 'I *am* the LORD's';
Another will call *himself* by the name of
Jacob;
Another will write *with* his hand, 'The
LORD's,'
And name *himself* by the name of Israel.

6 "Thus says the LORD, the King of Israel,

כִּי־נָתַתִּי בַמִּדְבָּר מַיִם
נְהָרוֹת בִּישִׁימֹן לְהַשְׁקוֹת עַמִּי בְחִירִי:
21 עַם־זוּ יָצַרְתִּי לִי תְּהִלָּתִי יְסַפֵּרוּ: ס
22 וְלֹא־אֹתִי קָרָאתָ יַעֲקֹב
כִּי־יָגַעְתָּ בִּי יִשְׂרָאֵל:
23 לֹא־הֵבֵיאתָ לִּי שֵׂה עֹלֹתֶיךָ
וּזְבָחֶיךָ לֹא כִבַּדְתָּנִי
לֹא הֶעֱבַדְתִּיךָ בְּמִנְחָה
וְלֹא הוֹגַעְתִּיךָ בִּלְבוֹנָה:
24 לֹא־קָנִיתָ לִּי בַכֶּסֶף קָנֶה
וְחֵלֶב זְבָחֶיךָ לֹא הִרְוִיתָנִי
אַךְ הֶעֱבַדְתַּנִי בְּחַטֹּאותֶיךָ
הוֹגַעְתַּנִי בַּעֲוֹנֹתֶיךָ: ס
25 אָנֹכִי אָנֹכִי הוּא מֹחֶה פְשָׁעֶיךָ לְמַעֲנִי
וְחַטֹּאתֶיךָ לֹא אֶזְכֹּר:
26 הַזְכִּירֵנִי נִשָּׁפְטָה יָחַד
סַפֵּר אַתָּה לְמַעַן תִּצְדָּק:
27 אָבִיךָ הָרִאשׁוֹן חָטָא
וּמְלִיצֶיךָ פָּשְׁעוּ בִי:
28 וַאֲחַלֵּל שָׂרֵי קֹדֶשׁ
וְאֶתְּנָה לַחֵרֶם יַעֲקֹב
וְיִשְׂרָאֵל לְגִדּוּפִים: ס

מד וְעַתָּה שְׁמַע יַעֲקֹב עַבְדִּי
וְיִשְׂרָאֵל בָּחַרְתִּי בוֹ:
2 כֹּה־אָמַר יְהֹוָה עֹשֶׂךָ
וְיֹצֶרְךָ מִבֶּטֶן יַעְזְרֶךָ
אַל־תִּירָא עַבְדִּי יַעֲקֹב
וִישֻׁרוּן בָּחַרְתִּי בוֹ:
3 כִּי אֶצָּק־מַיִם עַל־צָמֵא
וְנֹזְלִים עַל־יַבָּשָׁה
אֶצֹּק רוּחִי עַל־זַרְעֶךָ
וּבִרְכָתִי עַל־צֶאֱצָאֶיךָ:
4 וְצָמְחוּ בְּבֵין חָצִיר
כַּעֲרָבִים עַל־יִבְלֵי־מָיִם:
5 זֶה יֹאמַר לַיהֹוָה אָנִי
וְזֶה יִקְרָא בְשֵׁם־יַעֲקֹב
וְזֶה יִכְתֹּב יָדוֹ לַיהֹוָה
וּבְשֵׁם יִשְׂרָאֵל יְכַנֶּה: פ
6 כֹּה־אָמַר יְהֹוָה מֶלֶךְ־יִשְׂרָאֵל
וְגֹאֲלוֹ יְהֹוָה צְבָאוֹת

And his Redeemer, the LORD of hosts:
'I *am* the First and I *am* the Last;
Besides Me *there is* no God.

7 And who can proclaim as I do?
   Then let him declare it and set it in order for
      Me,
   Since I appointed the ancient people.
   And the things that are coming and shall
      come,
   Let them show these to them.

8 Do not fear, nor be afraid;
   Have I not told you from that time, and
      declared *it?*
   You *are* My witnesses.
   Is there a God besides Me?
   Indeed *there is* no other Rock;
   I know not *one.*' "

9 Those who make an image, all of them *are*
      useless,
   And their precious things shall not profit;
   They *are* their own witnesses;
   They neither see nor know, that they may be
      ashamed.

10 Who would form a god or mold an image
   That profits him nothing?

11 Surely all his companions would be ashamed;
   And the workmen, they *are* mere men.
   Let them all be gathered together,
   Let them stand up;
   Yet they shall fear,
   They shall be ashamed together.

12 The blacksmith with the tongs works one in
      the coals,
   Fashions it with hammers,
   And works it with the strength of his arms.
   Even so, he is hungry, and his strength fails;
   He drinks no water and is faint.

13 The craftsman stretches out *his* rule,
   He marks one out with chalk;
   He fashions it with a plane,
   He marks it out with the compass,
   And makes it like the figure of a man,
   According to the beauty of a man, that it
      may remain in the house.

14 He cuts down cedars for himself,
   And takes the cypress and the oak;
   He secures *it* for himself among the trees of
      the forest.
   He plants a pine, and the rain nourishes *it.*

15 Then it shall be for a man to burn,
   For he will take some of it and warm himself;
   Yes, he kindles *it* and bakes bread;

אֲנִי רִאשׁוֹן וַאֲנִי אַחֲרוֹן
וּמִבַּלְעָדַי אֵין אֱלֹהִים׃
7 וּמִי־כָמוֹנִי יִקְרָא
וְיַגִּידֶהָ וְיַעְרְכֶהָ לִי
מִשּׂוּמִי עַם־עוֹלָם
וְאֹתִיּוֹת וַאֲשֶׁר תָּבֹאנָה יַגִּידוּ לָמוֹ׃
8 אַל־תִּפְחֲדוּ וְאַל־תִּרְהוּ
הֲלֹא מֵאָז הִשְׁמַעְתִּיךָ וְהִגַּדְתִּי
וְאַתֶּם עֵדָי
הֲיֵשׁ אֱלוֹהַּ מִבַּלְעָדַי
וְאֵין צוּר בַּל־יָדָעְתִּי׃
9 יֹצְרֵי־פֶסֶל כֻּלָּם תֹּהוּ
וַחֲמוּדֵיהֶם בַּל־יוֹעִילוּ
וְעֵדֵיהֶם הֵמָּה בַּל־יִרְאוּ וּבַל־יֵדְעוּ
לְמַעַן יֵבֹשׁוּ׃
10 מִי־יָצַר אֵל וּפֶסֶל נָסָךְ
לְבִלְתִּי הוֹעִיל׃
11 הֵן כָּל־חֲבֵרָיו יֵבֹשׁוּ
וְחָרָשִׁים הֵמָּה מֵאָדָם
יִתְקַבְּצוּ כֻלָּם יַעֲמֹדוּ
יִפְחֲדוּ יֵבֹשׁוּ יָחַד׃
12 חָרָשׁ בַּרְזֶל מַעֲצָד
וּפָעַל בַּפֶּחָם וּבַמַּקָּבוֹת יִצְּרֵהוּ
וַיִּפְעָלֵהוּ בִּזְרוֹעַ כֹּחוֹ
גַּם־רָעֵב וְאֵין כֹּחַ
לֹא־שָׁתָה מַיִם וַיִּיעָף׃
13 חָרַשׁ עֵצִים נָטָה קָו
יְתָאֲרֵהוּ בַשֶּׂרֶד
יַעֲשֵׂהוּ בַּמַּקְצֻעוֹת
וּבַמְּחוּגָה יְתָאֳרֵהוּ
וַיַּעֲשֵׂהוּ כְּתַבְנִית אִישׁ
כְּתִפְאֶרֶת אָדָם לָשֶׁבֶת בָּיִת׃
14 לִכְרָת־לוֹ אֲרָזִים
וַיִּקַּח תִּרְזָה וְאַלּוֹן
וַיְאַמֶּץ־לוֹ בַּעֲצֵי־יָעַר
נָטַע אֹרֶן וְגֶשֶׁם יְגַדֵּל׃
15 וְהָיָה לְאָדָם לְבָעֵר
וַיִּקַּח מֵהֶם וַיָּחָם
אַף־יַשִּׂיק וְאָפָה לָחֶם

Indeed he makes a god and worships *it;*
He makes it a carved image, and falls down
    to it.

אַף־יִפְעַל־אֵל וַיִּשְׁתָּחוּ
עָשָׂהוּ פֶסֶל וַיִּסְגָּד־לָמוֹ:

16 He burns half of it in the fire;
With this half he eats meat;
He roasts a roast, and is satisfied.
He even warms *himself* and says,
    "Ah! I am warm,
    I have seen the fire."

16 חֶצְיוֹ שָׂרַף בְּמוֹ־אֵשׁ
עַל־חֶצְיוֹ בָּשָׂר יֹאכֵל
יִצְלֶה צָלִי וְיִשְׂבָּע
אַף־יָחֹם וְיֹאמַר הֶאָח
חַמּוֹתִי רָאִיתִי אוּר:

17 And the rest of it he makes into a god,
    His carved image.
He falls down before it and worships *it,*
Prays to it and says,
    "Deliver me, for you *are* my god!"

17 וּשְׁאֵרִיתוֹ לְאֵל עָשָׂה לְפִסְלוֹ
יִסְגָּד־ק לוֹ וְיִשְׁתַּחוּ וְיִתְפַּלֵּל אֵלָיו
וְיֹאמַר הַצִּילֵנִי כִּי אֵלִי אָתָּה:

18 They do not know nor understand;
For He has shut their eyes, so that they
    cannot see,
And their hearts, so that they cannot under-
    stand.

18 לֹא יָדְעוּ וְלֹא יָבִינוּ
כִּי טַח מֵרְאוֹת עֵינֵיהֶם
מֵהַשְׂכִּיל לִבֹּתָם:

19 And no one considers in his heart,
Nor *is there* knowledge nor understanding to
    say,
"I have burned half of it in the fire,
Yes, I have also baked bread on its coals;
I have roasted meat and eaten *it;*
And shall I make the rest of it an abomina-
    tion?
Shall I fall down before a block of wood?"

19 וְלֹא־יָשִׁיב אֶל־לִבּוֹ
וְלֹא דַעַת וְלֹא־תְבוּנָה לֵאמֹר
חֶצְיוֹ שָׂרַפְתִּי בְמוֹ־אֵשׁ
וְאַף אָפִיתִי עַל־גֶּחָלָיו לֶחֶם
אֶצְלֶה בָשָׂר וְאֹכֵל
וְיִתְרוֹ לְתוֹעֵבָה אֶעֱשֶׂה
לְבוּל עֵץ אֶסְגּוֹד:

20 He feeds on ashes;
A deceived heart has turned him aside;
And he cannot deliver his soul,
Nor say, "*Is there* not a lie in my right
    hand?"

20 רֹעֶה אֵפֶר לֵב הוּתַל הִטָּהוּ
וְלֹא־יַצִּיל אֶת־נַפְשׁוֹ וְלֹא יֹאמַר
הֲלוֹא שֶׁקֶר בִּימִינִי: ס

21 "Remember these, O Jacob,
And Israel, for you *are* My servant;
I have formed you, you *are* My servant;
O Israel, you will not be forgotten by Me!

21 זְכָר־אֵלֶּה יַעֲקֹב
וְיִשְׂרָאֵל כִּי עַבְדִּי־אָתָּה
יְצַרְתִּיךָ עֶבֶד־לִי אַתָּה
יִשְׂרָאֵל לֹא תִנָּשֵׁנִי:

22 I have blotted out, like a thick cloud, your
    transgressions,
And like a cloud, your sins.
Return to Me, for I have redeemed you."

22 מָחִיתִי כָעָב פְּשָׁעֶיךָ
וְכֶעָנָן חַטֹּאותֶיךָ
שׁוּבָה אֵלַי כִּי גְאַלְתִּיךָ:

23 Sing, O heavens, for the Lord has done *it!*
Shout, you lower parts of the earth;
Break forth into singing, you mountains,
O forest, and every tree in it!
For the Lord has redeemed Jacob,
And glorified Himself in Israel.

23 רָנּוּ שָׁמַיִם כִּי־עָשָׂה יְהוָה
הָרִיעוּ תַּחְתִּיּוֹת אָרֶץ
פִּצְחוּ הָרִים רִנָּה
יַעַר וְכָל־עֵץ בּוֹ
כִּי־גָאַל יְהוָה יַעֲקֹב
וּבְיִשְׂרָאֵל יִתְפָּאָר:

24 Thus says the Lord, your Redeemer,
And He who formed you from the womb:
"I *am* the Lord, who makes all *things,*
Who stretches out the heavens all alone,
Who spreads abroad the earth by Myself;

24 כֹּה־אָמַר יְהוָה גֹּאַלְךָ
וְיֹצֶרְךָ מִבָּטֶן
אָנֹכִי יְהוָה עֹשֶׂה כֹּל
נֹטֶה שָׁמַיִם לְבַדִּי
רֹקַע הָאָרֶץ מי אתיק:

מד 17 יִסְגָּד־   24 מֵאִתִּי

25 Who frustrates the signs of the babblers,
And drives diviners mad;
Who turns wise men backward,
And makes their knowledge foolishness;

26 Who confirms the word of His servant,
And performs the counsel of His messengers;
Who says to Jerusalem, 'You shall be
    inhabited,'
To the cities of Judah, 'You shall be built,'
And I will raise up her waste places;

27 Who says to the deep, 'Be dry!
And I will dry up your rivers';

28 Who says of Cyrus, '*He is* My shepherd,
And he shall perform all My pleasure,
Saying to Jerusalem, "You shall be built,"
And to the temple, "Your foundation shall
    be laid."'

45 "Thus says the LORD to His anointed,
To Cyrus, whose right hand I have held—
To subdue nations before him
And loose the armor of kings,
To open before him the double doors,
So that the gates will not be shut:

2 'I will go before you
And make the crooked places straight;
I will break in pieces the gates of bronze
And cut the bars of iron.

3 I will give you the treasures of darkness
And hidden riches of secret places,
That you may know that I, the LORD,
Who call *you* by your name,
Am the God of Israel.

4 For Jacob My servant's sake,
And Israel My elect,
I have even called you by your name;
I have named you, though you have not
    known Me.

5 I *am* the LORD, and *there is* no other;
There is no God besides Me.
I will gird you, though you have not known
    Me,

6 That they may know from the rising of the
    sun to its setting
That *there is* none besides Me.
I *am* the LORD, and *there is* no other;

7 I form the light and create darkness,
I make peace and create calamity;
I, the LORD, do all these *things*.'

8 "Rain down, you heavens, from above,
And let the skies pour down righteousness;
Let the earth open, let them bring forth
    salvation,

25 מֵפֵר אֹתֹות בַּדִּים וְקֹסְמִים יְהֹולֵל
מֵשִׁיב חֲכָמִים אָחֹור וְדַעְתָּם יְשַׂכֵּל׃

26 מֵקִים דְּבַר עַבְדֹּו וַעֲצַת מַלְאָכָיו יַשְׁלִים
הָאֹמֵר לִירוּשָׁלִַם תּוּשָׁב
וּלְעָרֵי יְהוּדָה תִּבָּנֶינָה
וְחָרְבֹותֶיהָ אֲקֹומֵם׃

27 הָאֹמֵר לַצּוּלָה חֳרָבִי
וְנַהֲרֹתַיִךְ אֹובִישׁ׃

28 הָאֹמֵר לְכֹורֶשׁ רֹעִי וְכָל־חֶפְצִי יַשְׁלִם
וְלֵאמֹר לִירוּשָׁלִַם תִּבָּנֶה וְהֵיכָל תִּוָּסֵד׃ ס

מה כֹּה־אָמַר יְהוָה לִמְשִׁיחֹו
לְכֹורֶשׁ אֲשֶׁר־הֶחֱזַקְתִּי בִימִינֹו
לְרַד־לְפָנָיו גֹּויִם
וּמָתְנֵי מְלָכִים אֲפַתֵּחַ
לִפְתֹּחַ לְפָנָיו דְּלָתַיִם
וּשְׁעָרִים לֹא יִסָּגֵרוּ׃

2 אֲנִי לְפָנֶיךָ אֵלֵךְ וַהֲדוּרִים אושר
דְּלָתֹות נְחוּשָׁה אֲשַׁבֵּר
וּבְרִיחֵי בַרְזֶל אֲגַדֵּעַ׃

3 וְנָתַתִּי לְךָ אֹוצְרֹות חֹשֶׁךְ
וּמַטְמֻנֵי מִסְתָּרִים
לְמַעַן תֵּדַע כִּי־אֲנִי יְהוָה
הַקֹּורֵא בְשִׁמְךָ אֱלֹהֵי יִשְׂרָאֵל׃

4 לְמַעַן עַבְדִּי יַעֲקֹב
וְיִשְׂרָאֵל בְּחִירִי
וָאֶקְרָא לְךָ בִּשְׁמֶךָ
אֲכַנְּךָ וְלֹא יְדַעְתָּנִי׃

5 אֲנִי יְהוָה וְאֵין עֹוד
זוּלָתִי אֵין אֱלֹהִים
אֲאַזֶּרְךָ וְלֹא יְדַעְתָּנִי׃

6 לְמַעַן יֵדְעוּ מִמִּזְרַח־שֶׁמֶשׁ וּמִמַּעֲרָבָה
כִּי־אֶפֶס בִּלְעָדָי
אֲנִי יְהוָה וְאֵין עֹוד׃

7 יֹוצֵר אֹור וּבֹורֵא חֹשֶׁךְ
עֹשֶׂה שָׁלֹום וּבֹורֵא רָע
אֲנִי יְהוָה עֹשֶׂה כָל־אֵלֶּה׃ ס

8 הַרְעִיפוּ שָׁמַיִם מִמַּעַל
וּשְׁחָקִים יִזְּלוּ־צֶדֶק
תִּפְתַּח־אֶרֶץ וְיִפְרוּ־יֶשַׁע

מה 2 אושר

And let righteousness spring up together.
I, the LORD, have created it.

וּצְדָקָה תַצְמִיחַ יַחַד
אֲנִי יְהוָה בְּרָאתִיו: ס

9 "Woe to him who strives with his Maker!
   Let the potsherd *strive* with the potsherds of
     the earth!
   Shall the clay say to him who forms it, 'What
     are you making?'
   Or shall your handiwork *say,* 'He has no
     hands'?

9 הוֹי רָב אֶת־יֹצְרוֹ
חֶרֶשׂ אֶת־חַרְשֵׂי אֲדָמָה
הֲיֹאמַר חֹמֶר לְיֹצְרוֹ מַה־תַּעֲשֶׂה
וּפָעָלְךָ אֵין־יָדַיִם לוֹ: ס

10 Woe to him who says to *his* father, 'What are
     you begetting?'
   Or to the woman, 'What have you brought
     forth?' "

10 הוֹי אֹמֵר לְאָב מַה־תּוֹלִיד
וּלְאִשָּׁה מַה־תְּחִילִין: ס

11 Thus says the LORD,
   The Holy One of Israel, and his Maker:
   "Ask Me of things to come concerning My
     sons;
   And concerning the work of My hands, you
     command Me.

11 כֹּה־אָמַר יְהוָה
קְדוֹשׁ יִשְׂרָאֵל וְיֹצְרוֹ
הָאֹתִיּוֹת שְׁאָלוּנִי
עַל־בָּנַי וְעַל־פֹּעַל יָדַי תְּצַוֻּנִי:

12 I have made the earth,
   And created man on it.
   I—My hands—stretched out the heavens,
   And all their host I have commanded.

12 אָנֹכִי עָשִׂיתִי אֶרֶץ
וְאָדָם עָלֶיהָ בָרָאתִי
אֲנִי יָדַי נָטוּ שָׁמַיִם
וְכָל־צְבָאָם צִוֵּיתִי:

13 I have raised him up in righteousness,
   And I will direct all his ways;
   He shall build My city
   And let My exiles go free,
   Not for price nor reward,"
   Says the LORD of hosts.

13 אָנֹכִי הַעִירֹתִהוּ בְצֶדֶק
וְכָל־דְּרָכָיו אֲיַשֵּׁר
הוּא־יִבְנֶה עִירִי
וְגָלוּתִי יְשַׁלֵּחַ
לֹא בִמְחִיר וְלֹא בְשֹׁחַד
אָמַר יְהוָה צְבָאוֹת: פ

14 Thus says the LORD:
   "The labor of Egypt and merchandise of Cush
   And of the Sabeans, men of stature,
   Shall come over to you, and they shall be
     yours;
   They shall walk behind you,
   They shall come over in chains;
   And they shall bow down to you.
   They will make supplication to you, *saying,*
   'Surely God *is* in you,
   And *there is* no other;
   There is no other God.' "

14 כֹּה | אָמַר יְהוָה
יְגִיעַ מִצְרַיִם וּסְחַר־כּוּשׁ
וּסְבָאִים אַנְשֵׁי מִדָּה
עָלַיִךְ יַעֲבֹרוּ וְלָךְ יִהְיוּ
אַחֲרַיִךְ יֵלֵכוּ בַּזִּקִּים יַעֲבֹרוּ
וְאֵלַיִךְ יִשְׁתַּחֲווּ
אֵלַיִךְ יִתְפַּלָּלוּ
אַךְ בָּךְ אֵל וְאֵין עוֹד
אֶפֶס אֱלֹהִים:

15 Truly You *are* God, who hide Yourself,
   O God of Israel, the Savior!

15 אָכֵן אַתָּה אֵל מִסְתַּתֵּר
אֱלֹהֵי יִשְׂרָאֵל מוֹשִׁיעַ:

16 They shall be ashamed
   And also disgraced, all of them;
   They shall go in confusion together,
   Who are makers of idols.

16 בּוֹשׁוּ וְגַם־נִכְלְמוּ כֻּלָּם
יַחְדָּו הָלְכוּ בַכְּלִמָּה חָרָשֵׁי צִירִים:

17 *But* Israel shall be saved by the LORD
   With an everlasting salvation;
   You shall not be ashamed or disgraced
   Forever and ever.

17 יִשְׂרָאֵל נוֹשַׁע בַּיהוָה תְּשׁוּעַת עוֹלָמִים
לֹא־תֵבֹשׁוּ וְלֹא־תִכָּלְמוּ
עַד־עוֹלְמֵי עַד: פ

¹⁸ For thus says the LORD,
Who created the heavens,
Who is God,
Who formed the earth and made it,
Who has established it,
Who did not create it in vain,
Who formed it to be inhabited:
"I *am* the LORD, and *there is* no other.

¹⁹ I have not spoken in secret,
In a dark place of the earth;
I did not say to the seed of Jacob,
'Seek Me in vain';
I, the LORD, speak righteousness,
I declare things that are right.

²⁰ "Assemble yourselves and come;
Draw near together,
You *who have* escaped from the nations.
They have no knowledge,
Who carry the wood of their carved image,
And pray to a god *that* cannot save.

²¹ Tell and bring forth *your case;*
Yes, let them take counsel together.
Who has declared this from ancient time?
Who has told it from that time?
Have not I, the LORD?
And *there is* no other God besides Me,
A just God and a Savior;
There is none besides Me.

²² "Look to Me, and be saved,
All you ends of the earth!
For I *am* God, and *there is* no other.

²³ I have sworn by Myself;
The word has gone out of My mouth *in*
righteousness,
And shall not return,
That to Me every knee shall bow,
Every tongue shall take an oath.

²⁴ He shall say,
'Surely in the LORD I have righteousness and
strength.
To Him *men* shall come,
And all shall be ashamed
Who are incensed against Him.

²⁵ In the LORD all the descendants of Israel
Shall be justified, and shall glory.'"

46

¹ Bel bows down, Nebo stoops;
Their idols were on the beasts and on the
cattle.
Your carriages *were* heavily loaded,
A burden to the weary *beast.*

² They stoop, they bow down together;
They could not deliver the burden,

¹⁸ כִּי כֹה אָמַר־יְהוָה בּוֹרֵא הַשָּׁמַיִם
הוּא הָאֱלֹהִים
יֹצֵר הָאָרֶץ וְעֹשָׂהּ
הוּא כוֹנְנָהּ
לֹא־תֹהוּ בְרָאָהּ לָשֶׁבֶת יְצָרָהּ
אֲנִי יְהוָה וְאֵין עוֹד׃

¹⁹ לֹא בַסֵּתֶר דִּבַּרְתִּי
בִּמְקוֹם אֶרֶץ חֹשֶׁךְ
לֹא אָמַרְתִּי לְזֶרַע יַעֲקֹב
תֹּהוּ בַקְּשׁוּנִי
אֲנִי יְהוָה דֹּבֵר צֶדֶק
מַגִּיד מֵישָׁרִים׃

²⁰ הִקָּבְצוּ וָבֹאוּ הִתְנַגְּשׁוּ יַחְדָּו
פְּלִיטֵי הַגּוֹיִם
לֹא יָדְעוּ הַנֹּשְׂאִים אֶת־עֵץ פִּסְלָם
וּמִתְפַּלְלִים אֶל־אֵל לֹא יוֹשִׁיעַ׃

²¹ הַגִּידוּ וְהַגִּישׁוּ אַף יִוָּעֲצוּ יַחְדָּו
מִי הִשְׁמִיעַ זֹאת מִקֶּדֶם מֵאָז הִגִּידָהּ
הֲלוֹא אֲנִי יְהוָה וְאֵין־עוֹד אֱלֹהִים מִבַּלְעָדַי
אֵל־צַדִּיק וּמוֹשִׁיעַ אַיִן זוּלָתִי׃

²² פְּנוּ־אֵלַי וְהִוָּשְׁעוּ
כָּל־אַפְסֵי־אָרֶץ
כִּי אֲנִי־אֵל וְאֵין עוֹד׃

²³ בִּי נִשְׁבַּעְתִּי
יָצָא מִפִּי צְדָקָה דָּבָר
וְלֹא יָשׁוּב
כִּי־לִי תִּכְרַע כָּל־בֶּרֶךְ
תִּשָּׁבַע כָּל־לָשׁוֹן׃

²⁴ אַךְ בַּיהוָה לִי אָמַר צְדָקוֹת וָעֹז
עָדָיו יָבוֹא וְיֵבֹשׁוּ
כֹּל הַנֶּחֱרִים בּוֹ׃

²⁵ בַּיהוָה יִצְדְּקוּ וְיִתְהַלְלוּ
כָּל־זֶרַע יִשְׂרָאֵל׃

מו
כָּרַע בֵּל קֹרֵס נְבוֹ
הָיוּ עֲצַבֵּיהֶם לַחַיָּה וְלַבְּהֵמָה
נְשֻׂאֹתֵיכֶם עֲמוּסוֹת
מַשָּׂא לַעֲיֵפָה׃

² קָרְסוּ כָרְעוּ יַחְדָּו

But have themselves gone into captivity.

3 "Listen to Me, O house of Jacob,
And all the remnant of the house of Israel,
Who have been upheld *by Me* from birth,
Who have been carried from the womb:

4 Even to *your* old age, I *am* He,
And *even* to gray hairs I will carry *you!*
I have made, and I will bear;
Even I will carry, and will deliver *you.*

5 "To whom will you liken Me, and make *Me* equal
And compare Me, that we should be alike?

6 They lavish gold out of the bag,
And weigh silver on the scales;
They hire a goldsmith, and he makes it a god;
They prostrate themselves, yes, they worship.

7 They bear it on the shoulder, they carry it
And set it in its place, and it stands;
From its place it shall not move.
Though *one* cries out to it, yet it cannot answer
Nor save him out of his trouble.

8 "Remember this, and show yourselves men;
Recall to mind, O you transgressors.

9 Remember the former things of old,
For I *am* God, and *there is* no other;
I *am* God, and *there is* none like Me,

10 Declaring the end from the beginning,
And from ancient times *things* that are not yet done,
Saying, 'My counsel shall stand,
And I will do all My pleasure,'

11 Calling a bird of prey from the east,
The man who executes My counsel, from a far country.
Indeed I have spoken *it;*
I will also bring it to pass.
I have purposed *it;*
I will also do it.

12 "Listen to Me, you stubborn-hearted,
Who *are* far from righteousness:

13 I bring My righteousness near, it shall not be far off;
My salvation shall not linger.
And I will place salvation in Zion,
For Israel My glory.

47 "Come down and sit in the dust,
O virgin daughter of Babylon;
Sit on the ground without a throne,
O daughter of the Chaldeans!

לֹא יָכְלוּ מַלֵּט מַשָּׂא
וְנַפְשָׁם בַּשְּׁבִי הָלָכָה: ס

3 שִׁמְעוּ אֵלַי בֵּית יַעֲקֹב
וְכָל־שְׁאֵרִית בֵּית יִשְׂרָאֵל
הַעֲמֻסִים מִנִּי־בֶטֶן
הַנְּשֻׂאִים מִנִּי־רָחַם:

4 וְעַד־זִקְנָה אֲנִי הוּא וְעַד־שֵׂיבָה אֲנִי אֶסְבֹּל
אֲנִי עָשִׂיתִי וַאֲנִי אֶשָּׂא וַאֲנִי אֶסְבֹּל וַאֲמַלֵּט:

5 לְמִי תְדַמְּיוּנִי וְתַשְׁווּ
וְתַמְשִׁלוּנִי וְנִדְמֶה:

6 הַזָּלִים זָהָב מִכִּיס
וְכֶסֶף בַּקָּנֶה יִשְׁקֹלוּ
יִשְׂכְּרוּ צוֹרֵף וְיַעֲשֵׂהוּ אֵל
יִסְגְּדוּ אַף־יִשְׁתַּחֲווּ:

7 יִשָּׂאֻהוּ עַל־כָּתֵף יִסְבְּלֻהוּ
וְיַנִּיחֻהוּ תַחְתָּיו וְיַעֲמֹד
מִמְּקוֹמוֹ לֹא יָמִישׁ
אַף־יִצְעַק אֵלָיו וְלֹא יַעֲנֶה
מִצָּרָתוֹ לֹא יוֹשִׁיעֶנּוּ: ס

8 זִכְרוּ־זֹאת וְהִתְאֹשָׁשׁוּ
הָשִׁיבוּ פוֹשְׁעִים עַל־לֵב:

9 זִכְרוּ רִאשֹׁנוֹת מֵעוֹלָם
כִּי אָנֹכִי אֵל וְאֵין עוֹד
אֱלֹהִים וְאֶפֶס כָּמוֹנִי:

10 מַגִּיד מֵרֵאשִׁית אַחֲרִית
וּמִקֶּדֶם אֲשֶׁר לֹא־נַעֲשׂוּ
אֹמֵר עֲצָתִי תָקוּם
וְכָל־חֶפְצִי אֶעֱשֶׂה:

11 קֹרֵא מִמִּזְרָח עַיִט
מֵאֶרֶץ מֶרְחָק אִישׁ עֲצָתוֹ
אַף־דִּבַּרְתִּי אַף־אֲבִיאֶנָּה
יָצַרְתִּי אַף־אֶעֱשֶׂנָּה: ס

12 שִׁמְעוּ אֵלַי אַבִּירֵי לֵב
הָרְחוֹקִים מִצְּדָקָה:

13 קֵרַבְתִּי צִדְקָתִי לֹא תִרְחָק
וּתְשׁוּעָתִי לֹא תְאַחֵר
וְנָתַתִּי בְצִיּוֹן תְּשׁוּעָה
לְיִשְׂרָאֵל תִּפְאַרְתִּי: ס

מז רְדִי ׀ וּשְׁבִי עַל־עָפָר
בְּתוּלַת בַּת־בָּבֶל

מו 11 עֲצָתִי

For you shall no more be called
Tender and delicate.

2 Take the millstones and grind meal.
Remove your veil,
Take off the skirt,
Uncover the thigh,
Pass through the rivers.

3 Your nakedness shall be uncovered,
Yes, your shame will be seen;
I will take vengeance,
And I will not arbitrate with a man."

4 *As for our Redeemer, the* LORD *of hosts is*
His name,
The Holy One of Israel.

5 "Sit in silence, and go into darkness,
O daughter of the Chaldeans;
For you shall no longer be called
The Lady of Kingdoms.

6 I was angry with My people;
I have profaned My inheritance,
And given them into your hand.
You showed them no mercy;
On the elderly you laid your yoke very
heavily.

7 And you said, 'I shall be a lady forever,'
So that you did not take these *things* to heart,
Nor remember the latter end of them.

8 "Therefore hear this now, *you who are* given
to pleasures,
Who dwell securely,
Who say in your heart, 'I *am,* and *there is* no
one else besides me;
I shall not sit *as* a widow,
Nor shall I know the loss of children';

9 But these two *things* shall come to you
In a moment, in one day:
The loss of children, and widowhood.
They shall come upon you in their fullness
Because of the multitude of your sorceries,
For the great abundance of your
enchantments.

10 "For you have trusted in your wickedness;
You have said, 'No one sees me';
Your wisdom and your knowledge have
warped you;
And you have said in your heart,
'I *am,* and *there is* no one else besides me.'

11 Therefore evil shall come upon you;
You shall not know from where it arises.
And trouble shall fall upon you;
You will not be able to put it off.

שְׁבִי־לָאָרֶץ אֵין־כִּסֵּא
בַּת־כַּשְׂדִּים
כִּי לֹא תוֹסִיפִי יִקְרְאוּ־לָךְ
רַכָּה וַעֲנֻגָּה׃

2 קְחִי רֵחַיִם וְטַחֲנִי קָמַח
גַּלִּי צַמָּתֵךְ חֶשְׂפִּי־שֹׁבֶל גַּלִּי־שׁוֹק
עִבְרִי נְהָרוֹת׃

3 תִּגָּל עֶרְוָתֵךְ גַּם תֵּרָאֶה חֶרְפָּתֵךְ
נָקָם אֶקָּח וְלֹא אֶפְגַּע אָדָם׃ ס

4 גֹּאֲלֵנוּ יְהוָה צְבָאוֹת שְׁמוֹ
קְדוֹשׁ יִשְׂרָאֵל׃

5 שְׁבִי דוּמָם וּבֹאִי בַחֹשֶׁךְ
בַּת־כַּשְׂדִּים
כִּי לֹא תוֹסִיפִי יִקְרְאוּ־לָךְ
גְּבֶרֶת מַמְלָכוֹת׃

6 קָצַפְתִּי עַל־עַמִּי חִלַּלְתִּי נַחֲלָתִי
וָאֶתְּנֵם בְּיָדֵךְ לֹא־שַׂמְתְּ לָהֶם רַחֲמִים
עַל־זָקֵן הִכְבַּדְתְּ עֻלֵּךְ מְאֹד׃

7 וַתֹּאמְרִי
לְעוֹלָם אֶהְיֶה גְבָרֶת
עַד לֹא־שַׂמְתְּ אֵלֶּה עַל־לִבֵּךְ
לֹא זָכַרְתְּ אַחֲרִיתָהּ׃ ס

8 וְעַתָּה שִׁמְעִי־זֹאת עֲדִינָה
הַיּוֹשֶׁבֶת לָבֶטַח
הָאֹמְרָה בִּלְבָבָהּ
אֲנִי וְאַפְסִי עוֹד
לֹא אֵשֵׁב אַלְמָנָה וְלֹא אֵדַע שְׁכוֹל׃

9 וְתָבֹאנָה לָּךְ שְׁתֵּי־אֵלֶּה רֶגַע
בְּיוֹם אֶחָד
שְׁכוֹל וְאַלְמֹן
כְּתֻמָּם בָּאוּ עָלַיִךְ
בְּרֹב כְּשָׁפַיִךְ
בְּעָצְמַת חֲבָרַיִךְ מְאֹד׃

10 וַתִּבְטְחִי בְרָעָתֵךְ
אָמַרְתְּ אֵין רֹאָנִי
חָכְמָתֵךְ וְדַעְתֵּךְ הִיא שׁוֹבְבָתֶךְ
וַתֹּאמְרִי בְלִבֵּךְ
אֲנִי וְאַפְסִי עוֹד׃

11 וּבָא עָלַיִךְ רָעָה
לֹא תֵדְעִי שַׁחְרָהּ
וְתִפֹּל עָלַיִךְ הֹוָה

And desolation shall come upon you suddenly,
  Which you shall not know.

12 "Stand now with your enchantments
  And the multitude of your sorceries,
  In which you have labored from your
    youth—
  Perhaps you will be able to profit,
  Perhaps you will prevail.
13 You are wearied in the multitude of your
  counsels;
  Let now the astrologers, the stargazers,
  And the monthly prognosticators
  Stand up and save you
  From what shall come upon you.
14 Behold, they shall be as stubble,
  The fire shall burn them;
  They shall not deliver themselves
  From the power of the flame;
  It shall not *be* a coal to be warmed by,
  Nor a fire to sit before!
15 Thus shall they be to you
  With whom you have labored,
  Your merchants from your youth;
  They shall wander each one to his quarter.
  No one shall save you.

48 "Hear this, O house of Jacob,
  Who are called by the name of Israel,
  And have come forth from the wellsprings of
    Judah;
  Who swear by the name of the LORD,
  And make mention of the God of Israel,
  But not in truth or in righteousness;
2 For they call themselves after the holy city,
  And lean on the God of Israel;
  The LORD of hosts *is* His name:

3 "I have declared the former things from the
  beginning;
  They went forth from My mouth, and I
    caused them to hear it.
  Suddenly I did *them,* and they came to pass.
4 Because I knew that you *were* obstinate,
  And your neck *was* an iron sinew,
  And your brow bronze,
5 Even from the beginning I have declared *it* to
  you;
  Before it came to pass I proclaimed *it* to you,
  Lest you should say, 'My idol has done them,
  And my carved image and my molded image
  Have commanded them.'

6 "You have heard;

לֹא תוּכְלִי כַּפְּרָהּ
וְתָבֹא עָלַיִךְ פִּתְאֹם
שׁוֹאָה לֹא תֵדָעִי:

12 עִמְדִי־נָא בַחֲבָרַיִךְ וּבְרֹב כְּשָׁפַיִךְ
בַּאֲשֶׁר יָגַעַתְּ מִנְּעוּרָיִךְ
אוּלַי תוּכְלִי הוֹעִיל אוּלַי תַּעֲרוֹצִי:

13 נִלְאֵית בְּרֹב עֲצָתָיִךְ
יַעַמְדוּ־נָא וְיוֹשִׁיעֻךְ
הֹבְרוּ שָׁמַיִם הַחֹזִים בַּכּוֹכָבִים
מוֹדִעִים לֶחֳדָשִׁים
מֵאֲשֶׁר יָבֹאוּ עָלָיִךְ:

14 הִנֵּה הָיוּ כְקַשׁ אֵשׁ שְׂרָפָתַם
לֹא־יַצִּילוּ אֶת־נַפְשָׁם
מִיַּד לֶהָבָה
אֵין־גַּחֶלֶת לַחְמָם אוּר לָשֶׁבֶת נֶגְדּוֹ:

15 כֵּן הָיוּ־לָךְ אֲשֶׁר יָגָעַתְּ
סֹחֲרַיִךְ מִנְּעוּרַיִךְ
אִישׁ לְעֶבְרוֹ תָּעוּ
אֵין מוֹשִׁיעֵךְ: ס

מח שִׁמְעוּ־זֹאת בֵּית־יַעֲקֹב
הַנִּקְרָאִים בְּשֵׁם יִשְׂרָאֵל
וּמִמֵּי יְהוּדָה יָצָאוּ
הַנִּשְׁבָּעִים | בְּשֵׁם יְהוָה
וּבֵאלֹהֵי יִשְׂרָאֵל יַזְכִּירוּ
לֹא בֶאֱמֶת וְלֹא בִצְדָקָה:

2 כִּי־מֵעִיר הַקֹּדֶשׁ נִקְרָאוּ
וְעַל־אֱלֹהֵי יִשְׂרָאֵל נִסְמָכוּ
יְהוָה צְבָאוֹת שְׁמוֹ: ס

3 הָרִאשֹׁנוֹת מֵאָז הִגַּדְתִּי
וּמִפִּי יָצְאוּ וְאַשְׁמִיעֵם
פִּתְאֹם עָשִׂיתִי וַתָּבֹאנָה:

4 מִדַּעְתִּי כִּי קָשֶׁה אָתָּה
וְגִיד בַּרְזֶל עָרְפֶּךָ
וּמִצְחֲךָ נְחוּשָׁה:

5 וָאַגִּיד לְךָ מֵאָז
בְּטֶרֶם תָּבוֹא הִשְׁמַעְתִּיךָ
פֶּן־תֹּאמַר עָצְבִּי עָשָׂם
וּפִסְלִי וְנִסְכִּי צִוָּם:

6 שָׁמַעְתָּ חֲזֵה כֻלָּהּ
וְאַתֶּם הֲלוֹא תַגִּידוּ

See all this.
And will you not declare *it*?
I have made you hear new things from this
  time,
Even hidden things, and you did not know
  them.
7 They are created now and not from the
    beginning;
  And before this day you have not heard
    them,
  Lest you should say, 'Of course I knew
    them.'
8 Surely you did not hear,
  Surely you did not know;
  Surely from long ago your ear was not
    opened.
  For I knew that you would deal very
    treacherously,
  And were called a transgressor from the
    womb.

9 "For My name's sake I will defer My anger,
  And *for* My praise I will restrain it from you,
  So that I do not cut you off.
10 Behold, I have refined you, but not as silver;
  I have tested you in the furnace of affliction.
11 For My own sake, for My own sake, I will do
    it;
  For how should *My name* be profaned?
  And I will not give My glory to another.

12 "Listen to Me, O Jacob,
  And Israel, My called:
  I *am* He, I *am* the First,
  I *am* also the Last.
13 Indeed My hand has laid the foundation of
    the earth,
  And My right hand has stretched out the
    heavens;
  When I call to them,
  They stand up together.

14 "All of you, assemble yourselves, and hear!
  Who among them has declared these *things?*
  The LORD loves him;
  He shall do His pleasure on Babylon,
  And His arm *shall be against* the Chaldeans.
15 I, *even* I, have spoken;
  Yes, I have called him,
  I have brought him, and his way will prosper.

16 "Come near to Me, hear this:
  I have not spoken in secret from the
    beginning;
  From the time that it was, I *was* there.
  And now the Lord GOD and His Spirit

הֲשְׁמַעְתִּיךָ חֲדָשׁוֹת מֵעַתָּה
וּנְצֻרוֹת וְלֹא יְדַעְתָּם׃
7 עַתָּה נִבְרְאוּ וְלֹא מֵאָז
וְלִפְנֵי־יוֹם וְלֹא שְׁמַעְתָּם
פֶּן־תֹּאמַר הִנֵּה יְדַעְתִּין׃
8 גַּם לֹא־שָׁמַעְתָּ
גַּם לֹא יָדַעְתָּ
גַּם מֵאָז לֹא־פִתְּחָה אָזְנֶךָ
כִּי יָדַעְתִּי בָּגוֹד תִּבְגּוֹד
וּפֹשֵׁעַ מִבֶּטֶן קֹרָא לָךְ׃
9 לְמַעַן שְׁמִי אַאֲרִיךְ אַפִּי
וּתְהִלָּתִי אֶחֱטָם־לָךְ
לְבִלְתִּי הַכְרִיתֶךָ׃
10 הִנֵּה צְרַפְתִּיךָ וְלֹא בְכָסֶף
בְּחַרְתִּיךָ בְּכוּר עֹנִי׃
11 לְמַעֲנִי לְמַעֲנִי אֶעֱשֶׂה
כִּי אֵיךְ יֵחָל
וּכְבוֹדִי לְאַחֵר לֹא־אֶתֵּן׃ ס
12 שְׁמַע אֵלַי יַעֲקֹב
וְיִשְׂרָאֵל מְקֹרָאִי
אֲנִי־הוּא אֲנִי רִאשׁוֹן
אַף אֲנִי אַחֲרוֹן׃
13 אַף־יָדִי יָסְדָה אֶרֶץ
וִימִינִי טִפְּחָה שָׁמָיִם
קֹרֵא אֲנִי אֲלֵיהֶם
יַעַמְדוּ יַחְדָּו׃
14 הִקָּבְצוּ כֻלְּכֶם וּשֲׁמָעוּ
מִי בָהֶם הִגִּיד אֶת־אֵלֶּה
יְהוָה אֲהֵבוֹ יַעֲשֶׂה חֶפְצוֹ בְּבָבֶל
וּזְרֹעוֹ כַּשְׂדִּים׃
15 אֲנִי אֲנִי דִּבַּרְתִּי אַף־קְרָאתִיו
הֲבִיאֹתִיו וְהִצְלִיחַ דַּרְכּוֹ׃
16 קִרְבוּ אֵלַי שִׁמְעוּ־זֹאת
לֹא מֵרֹאשׁ בַּסֵּתֶר דִּבַּרְתִּי
מֵעֵת הֱיוֹתָהּ שָׁם אָנִי
וְעַתָּה אֲדֹנָי יְהוִה שְׁלָחַנִי וְרוּחוֹ׃ פ

Have sent Me."

17 Thus says the Lord, your Redeemer,
   The Holy One of Israel:
   "I am the Lord your God,
   Who teaches you to profit,
   Who leads you by the way you should go.
18 Oh, that you had heeded My command-
   ments!
   Then your peace would have been like a
   river,
   And your righteousness like the waves of the
   sea.
19 Your descendants also would have been like
   the sand,
   And the offspring of your body like the
   grains of sand;
   His name would not have been cut off
   Nor destroyed from before Me."

20 Go forth from Babylon!
   Flee from the Chaldeans!
   With a voice of singing,
   Declare, proclaim this,
   Utter it to the end of the earth;
   Say, "The Lord has redeemed
   His servant Jacob!"
21 And they did not thirst
   When He led them through the deserts;
   He caused the waters to flow from the rock
   for them;
   He also split the rock, and the waters gushed
   out.
22 "There is no peace," says the Lord, "for the
   wicked."

49 "Listen, O coastlands, to Me,
   And take heed, you peoples from afar!
   The Lord has called Me from the womb;
   From the matrix of My mother He has made
   mention of My name.
2 And He has made My mouth like a sharp
   sword;
   In the shadow of His hand He has hidden
   Me,
   And made Me a polished shaft;
   In His quiver He has hidden Me."
3 "And He said to me,
   'You are My servant, O Israel,
   In whom I will be glorified.'
4 Then I said, 'I have labored in vain,
   I have spent my strength for nothing and in
   vain;
   Yet surely my just reward is with the Lord,

17 כֹּה־אָמַ֞ר יְהֹוָ֤ה גֹּאֲלֵ֙ךָ֙
קְד֣וֹשׁ יִשְׂרָאֵ֔ל
אֲנִ֧י יְהֹוָ֛ה אֱלֹהֶ֖יךָ
מְלַמֶּדְךָ֣ לְהוֹעִ֑יל
מַדְרִֽיכְךָ֖ בְּדֶ֥רֶךְ תֵּלֵֽךְ׃
18 ל֥וּא הִקְשַׁ֖בְתָּ לְמִצְוֺתָ֑י
וַיְהִ֤י כַנָּהָר֙ שְׁלוֹמֶ֔ךָ
וְצִדְקָתְךָ֖ כְּגַלֵּ֥י הַיָּֽם׃
19 וַיְהִ֤י כַחוֹל֙ זַרְעֶ֔ךָ
וְצֶאֱצָאֵ֥י מֵעֶ֖יךָ כִּמְעֹתָ֑יו
לֹֽא־יִכָּרֵ֥ת וְֽלֹא־יִשָּׁמֵ֖ד
שְׁמ֥וֹ מִלְּפָנָֽי׃
20 צְא֣וּ מִבָּבֶ֗ל
בִּרְח֣וּ מִכַּשְׂדִּים֮
בְּק֣וֹל רִנָּ�al֒
הַגִּ֤ידוּ הַשְׁמִ֙יעוּ֙ זֹ֔את
הוֹצִיא֖וּהָ עַד־קְצֵ֣ה הָאָ֑רֶץ
אִמְר֕וּ גָּאַ֥ל יְהֹוָ֖ה
עַבְדּ֥וֹ יַֽעֲקֹֽב׃
21 וְלֹ֣א צָֽמְא֗וּ בׇּחֳרָבוֹת֙ הֽוֹלִיכָ֔ם
מַ֥יִם מִצּ֖וּר הִזִּ֣יל לָ֑מוֹ
וַיִּ֨בְקַע־צ֔וּר וַיָּזֻ֖בוּ מָֽיִם׃
22 אֵ֣ין שָׁל֔וֹם אָמַ֥ר יְהֹוָ֖ה לָרְשָׁעִֽים׃   ס

מט שִׁמְע֤וּ אִיִּים֙ אֵלַ֔י
וְהַקְשִׁ֥יבוּ לְאֻמִּ֖ים מֵרָח֑וֹק
יְהֹוָה֙ מִבֶּ֣טֶן קְרָאָ֔נִי
מִמְּעֵ֥י אִמִּ֖י הִזְכִּ֥יר שְׁמִֽי׃
2 וַיָּ֤שֶׂם פִּי֙ כְּחֶ֣רֶב חַדָּ֔ה
בְּצֵ֥ל יָד֖וֹ הֶחְבִּיאָ֑נִי
וַיְשִׂימֵ֙נִי֙ לְחֵ֣ץ בָּר֔וּר
בְּאַשְׁפָּת֖וֹ הִסְתִּירָֽנִי׃
3 וַיֹּ֥אמֶר לִ֖י עַבְדִּי־אָ֑תָּה
יִשְׂרָאֵ֕ל אֲשֶׁר־בְּךָ֖ אֶתְפָּאָֽר׃
4 וַאֲנִ֤י אָמַ֙רְתִּי֙ לְרִ֣יק יָגַ֔עְתִּי
לְתֹ֥הוּ וְהֶ֖בֶל כֹּחִ֣י כִלֵּ֑יתִי

And my work with my God.'"

5 "And now the LORD says,
   Who formed Me from the womb *to be* His
       Servant,
   To bring Jacob back to Him,
   So that Israel is gathered to Him
   (For I shall be glorious in the eyes of the
       LORD,
   And My God shall be My strength),

6 Indeed He says,
   'It is too small a thing that You should be My
       Servant
   To raise up the tribes of Jacob,
   And to restore the preserved ones of Israel;
   I will also give You as a light to the Gentiles,
   That You should be My salvation to the ends
       of the earth.'"

7 Thus says the LORD,
   The Redeemer of Israel, their Holy One,
   To Him whom man despises,
   To Him whom the nation abhors,
   To the Servant of rulers:

   "Kings shall see and arise,
   Princes also shall worship,
   Because of the LORD who is faithful,
   The Holy One of Israel;
   And He has chosen You."

8 Thus says the LORD:

   "In an acceptable time I have heard You,
   And in the day of salvation I have helped
       You;
   I will preserve You and give You
   As a covenant to the people,
   To restore the earth,
   To cause them to inherit the desolate
       heritages;

9 That You may say to the prisoners, 'Go
       forth,'
   To those who *are* in darkness, 'Show
       yourselves.'

   "They shall feed along the roads,
   And their pastures *shall be* on all desolate
       heights.

10 They shall neither hunger nor thirst,
   Neither heat nor sun shall strike them;
   For He who has mercy on them will lead
       them,
   Even by the springs of water He will guide
       them.

11 I will make each of My mountains a road,
   And My highways shall be elevated.

אָכֵן מִשְׁפָּטִי אֶת־יְהֹוָה

וּפְעֻלָּתִי אֶת־אֱלֹהָי׃

5 וְעַתָּה ׀ אָמַר יְהֹוָה

יֹצְרִי מִבֶּטֶן לְעֶבֶד לוֹ

לְשׁוֹבֵב יַעֲקֹב אֵלָיו

וְיִשְׂרָאֵל לֹא יֵאָסֵף

וְאֶכָּבֵד בְּעֵינֵי יְהֹוָה

וֵאלֹהַי הָיָה עֻזִּי׃

6 וַיֹּאמֶר נָקֵל מִהְיוֹתְךָ לִי עֶבֶד

לְהָקִים אֶת־שִׁבְטֵי יַעֲקֹב

וּנְצִירֵי יִשְׂרָאֵל לְהָשִׁיב

וּנְתַתִּיךָ לְאוֹר גּוֹיִם

ס   לִהְיוֹת יְשׁוּעָתִי עַד־קְצֵה הָאָרֶץ׃

7 כֹּה אָמַר־יְהֹוָה

גֹּאֵל יִשְׂרָאֵל קְדוֹשׁוֹ

לִבְזֹה־נֶפֶשׁ

לִמְתָעֵב גּוֹי

לְעֶבֶד מֹשְׁלִים

מְלָכִים יִרְאוּ וָקָמוּ

שָׂרִים וְיִשְׁתַּחֲווּ

לְמַעַן יְהֹוָה אֲשֶׁר נֶאֱמָן

קְדֹשׁ יִשְׂרָאֵל וַיִּבְחָרֶךָ׃

8 כֹּה ׀ אָמַר יְהֹוָה

בְּעֵת רָצוֹן עֲנִיתִיךָ

וּבְיוֹם יְשׁוּעָה עֲזַרְתִּיךָ

וְאֶצָּרְךָ וְאֶתֶּנְךָ

לִבְרִית עָם

לְהָקִים אֶרֶץ

לְהַנְחִיל נְחָלוֹת שֹׁמֵמוֹת׃

9 לֵאמֹר לַאֲסוּרִים צֵאוּ

לַאֲשֶׁר בַּחֹשֶׁךְ הִגָּלוּ

עַל־דְּרָכִים יִרְעוּ

וּבְכָל־שְׁפָיִים מַרְעִיתָם׃

10 לֹא יִרְעָבוּ וְלֹא יִצְמָאוּ

וְלֹא־יַכֵּם שָׁרָב וָשָׁמֶשׁ

כִּי־מְרַחֲמָם יְנַהֲגֵם

וְעַל־מַבּוּעֵי מַיִם יְנַהֲלֵם׃

11 וְשַׂמְתִּי כָל־הָרַי לַדָּרֶךְ

וּמְסִלֹּתַי יְרֻמוּן׃

¹² Surely these shall come from afar;
Look! Those from the north and the west,
And these from the land of Sinim.''

¹³ Sing, O heavens!
Be joyful, O earth!
And break out in singing, O mountains!
For the LORD has comforted His people,
And will have mercy on His afflicted.

¹⁴ But Zion said, "The LORD has forsaken me,
And my Lord has forgotten me.''

¹⁵ "Can a woman forget her nursing child,
And not have compassion on the son of her womb?
Surely they may forget,
Yet I will not forget you.

¹⁶ See, I have inscribed you on the palms *of My hands;*
Your walls *are* continually before Me.

¹⁷ Your sons shall make haste;
Your destroyers and those who laid you waste
Shall go away from you.

¹⁸ Lift up your eyes, look around and see;
All these gather together *and* come to you.
As I live,'' says the LORD,
"You shall surely clothe yourselves with them all as an ornament,
And bind them *on you* as a bride *does.*

¹⁹ "For your waste and desolate places,
And the land of your destruction,
Will even now be too small for the inhabitants;
And those who swallowed you up will be far away.

²⁰ The children you will have,
After you have lost the others,
Will say again in your ears,
'The place *is* too small for me;
Give me a place where I may dwell.'

²¹ Then you will say in your heart,
'Who has begotten these for me,
Since I have lost my children and am desolate,
A captive, and wandering to and fro?
And who has brought these up?
There I was, left alone;
But these, where *were* they?' ''

²² Thus says the Lord GOD:

"Behold, I will lift My hand in an oath to the nations,
And set up My standard for the peoples;

הִנֵּה־אֵלֶּה מֵרָחוֹק יָבֹאוּ 12
וְהִנֵּה־אֵלֶּה מִצָּפוֹן וּמִיָּם
וְאֵלֶּה מֵאֶרֶץ סִינִים:
רָנּוּ שָׁמַיִם וְגִילִי אָרֶץ 13
יִפְצְחוּ הָרִים רִנָּה
כִּי־נִחַם יְהֹוָה עַמּוֹ
וַעֲנִיָּו יְרַחֵם: ס
וַתֹּאמֶר צִיּוֹן עֲזָבַנִי יְהֹוָה 14
וַאדֹנָי שְׁכֵחָנִי:
הֲתִשְׁכַּח אִשָּׁה עוּלָהּ 15
מֵרַחֵם בֶּן־בִּטְנָהּ
גַּם־אֵלֶּה תִשְׁכַּחְנָה
וְאָנֹכִי לֹא אֶשְׁכָּחֵךְ:
הֵן עַל־כַּפַּיִם חַקֹּתִיךְ 16
חוֹמֹתַיִךְ נֶגְדִּי תָּמִיד:
מִהֲרוּ בָּנָיִךְ 17
מְהָרְסַיִךְ וּמַחֲרִבַיִךְ מִמֵּךְ יֵצֵאוּ:
שְׂאִי־סָבִיב עֵינַיִךְ וּרְאִי 18
כֻּלָּם נִקְבְּצוּ בָאוּ־לָךְ
חַי־אָנִי נְאֻם־יְהֹוָה
כִּי כֻלָּם כָּעֲדִי תִלְבָּשִׁי
וּתְקַשְּׁרִים כַּכַּלָּה:
כִּי חָרְבֹתַיִךְ וְשֹׁמְמֹתַיִךְ 19
וְאֶרֶץ הֲרִסֻתֵיךְ
כִּי עַתָּה תֵּצְרִי מִיּוֹשֵׁב
וְרָחֲקוּ מְבַלְּעָיִךְ:
עוֹד יֹאמְרוּ בְאָזְנַיִךְ 20
בְּנֵי שִׁכֻּלָיִךְ
צַר־לִי הַמָּקוֹם
גְּשָׁה־לִּי וְאֵשֵׁבָה:
וְאָמַרְתְּ בִּלְבָבֵךְ 21
מִי יָלַד־לִי אֶת־אֵלֶּה
וַאֲנִי שְׁכוּלָה וְגַלְמוּדָה
גֹּלָה | וְסוּרָה
וְאֵלֶּה מִי גִדֵּל
הֵן אֲנִי נִשְׁאַרְתִּי לְבַדִּי
אֵלֶּה אֵיפֹה הֵם: פ
כֹּה־אָמַר אֲדֹנָי יְהֹוָה 22
הִנֵּה אֶשָּׂא אֶל־גּוֹיִם יָדִי

מט 13 וּפִצְחוּ

They shall bring your sons in *their* arms,
And your daughters shall be carried on *their* shoulders;

23 Kings shall be your foster fathers,
And their queens your nursing mothers;
They shall bow down to you with *their* faces to the earth,
And lick up the dust of your feet.
Then you will know that I *am* the LORD,
For they shall not be ashamed who wait for Me."

24 Shall the prey be taken from the mighty,
Or the captives of the righteous be delivered?

25 But thus says the LORD:

"Even the captives of the mighty shall be taken away,
And the prey of the terrible be delivered;
For I will contend with him who contends with you,
And I will save your children.

26 I will feed those who oppress you with their own flesh,
And they shall be drunk with their own blood as with sweet wine.
All flesh shall know
That I, the LORD, *am* your Savior,
And your Redeemer, the Mighty One of Jacob."

50 Thus says the LORD:

"Where *is* the certificate of your mother's divorce,
Whom I have put away?
Or which of My creditors *is it* to whom I have sold you?
For your iniquities you have sold yourselves,
And for your transgressions your mother has been put away.

2 Why, when I came, *was there* no man?
Why, when I called, *was there* none to answer?
Is My hand shortened at all that it cannot redeem?
Or have I no power to deliver?
Indeed with My rebuke I dry up the sea,
I make the rivers a wilderness;
Their fish stink because *there is* no water,
And die of thirst.

3 I clothe the heavens with blackness,
And I make sackcloth their covering."

4 "The Lord GOD has given Me
The tongue of the learned,

וְאֶל־עַמִּים אָרִים נִסִּי
וְהֵבִיאוּ בָנַיִךְ בְּחֹצֶן
וּבְנֹתַיִךְ עַל־כָּתֵף תִּנָּשֶׂאנָה:

23 וְהָיוּ מְלָכִים אֹמְנַיִךְ
וְשָׂרוֹתֵיהֶם מֵינִיקֹתַיִךְ
אַפַּיִם אֶרֶץ יִשְׁתַּחֲווּ לָךְ
וַעֲפַר רַגְלַיִךְ יְלַחֵכוּ
וְיָדַעַתְּ כִּי־אֲנִי יְהוָֹה
אֲשֶׁר לֹא־יֵבֹשׁוּ קֹוָי: ס

24 הֲיֻקַּח מִגִּבּוֹר מַלְקוֹחַ
וְאִם־שְׁבִי צַדִּיק יִמָּלֵט:

25 כִּי־כֹה | אָמַר יְהוָֹה
גַּם־שְׁבִי גִבּוֹר יֻקָּח
וּמַלְקוֹחַ עָרִיץ יִמָּלֵט
וְאֶת־יְרִיבֵךְ אָנֹכִי אָרִיב
וְאֶת־בָּנַיִךְ אָנֹכִי אוֹשִׁיעַ:

26 וְהַאֲכַלְתִּי אֶת־מוֹנַיִךְ אֶת־בְּשָׂרָם
וְכֶעָסִיס דָּמָם יִשְׁכָּרוּן
וְיָדְעוּ כָל־בָּשָׂר כִּי אֲנִי יְהוָֹה מוֹשִׁיעֵךְ
וְגֹאֲלֵךְ אֲבִיר יַעֲקֹב: ס

נ כֹּה | אָמַר יְהוָֹה
אֵי זֶה סֵפֶר כְּרִיתוּת אִמְּכֶם
אֲשֶׁר שִׁלַּחְתִּיהָ
אוֹ מִי מִנּוֹשַׁי
אֲשֶׁר־מָכַרְתִּי אֶתְכֶם לוֹ
הֵן בַּעֲוֹנֹתֵיכֶם נִמְכַּרְתֶּם
וּבְפִשְׁעֵיכֶם שֻׁלְּחָה אִמְּכֶם:

2 מַדּוּעַ בָּאתִי וְאֵין אִישׁ
קָרָאתִי וְאֵין עוֹנֶה
הֲקָצוֹר קָצְרָה יָדִי מִפְּדוּת
וְאִם־אֵין־בִּי כֹחַ לְהַצִּיל
הֵן בְּגַעֲרָתִי אַחֲרִיב יָם
אָשִׂים נְהָרוֹת מִדְבָּר
תִּבְאַשׁ דְּגָתָם מֵאֵין מַיִם
וְתָמֹת בַּצָּמָא:

3 אַלְבִּישׁ שָׁמַיִם קַדְרוּת
וְשַׂק אָשִׂים כְּסוּתָם: ס

4 אֲדֹנָי יְהוִֹה נָתַן לִי
לְשׁוֹן לִמּוּדִים
לָדַעַת לָעוּת אֶת־יָעֵף דָּבָר

That I should know how to speak　　　　　　　　יָעִיר | בַּבֹּקֶר בַּבֹּקֶר
A word in season to *him who is* weary.　　　　יָעִיר לִי אֹזֶן
He awakens Me morning by morning,　　　　　　לִשְׁמֹעַ כַּלִּמּוּדִים:
He awakens My ear
To hear as the learned.　　　　　　　　　5　אֲדֹנָי יְהֹוִה פָּתַח־לִי אֹזֶן
5　The Lord GOD has opened My ear;　　　　　　וְאָנֹכִי לֹא מָרִיתִי
And I was not rebellious,　　　　　　　　　אָחוֹר לֹא נְסוּגֹתִי:
Nor did I turn away.
6　I gave My back to those who struck *Me,*　　6　גֵּוִי נָתַתִּי לְמַכִּים
And My cheeks to those who plucked out the　　וּלְחָיַי לְמֹרְטִים
beard;　　　　　　　　　　　　　　　פָּנַי לֹא הִסְתַּרְתִּי מִכְּלִמּוֹת וָרֹק:
I did not hide My face from shame and
spitting.　　　　　　　　　　　　　7　וַאדֹנָי יְהֹוִה יַעֲזָר־לִי
7　"For the Lord GOD will help Me;　　　　　　עַל־כֵּן לֹא נִכְלָמְתִּי
Therefore I will not be disgraced;　　　　　עַל־כֵּן שַׂמְתִּי פָנַי כַּחַלָּמִישׁ
Therefore I have set My face like a flint,　　וָאֵדַע כִּי־לֹא אֵבוֹשׁ:
And I know that I will not be ashamed.
8　*He is* near who justifies Me;　　　　　8　קָרוֹב מַצְדִּיקִי
Who will contend with Me?　　　　　　　מִי־יָרִיב אִתִּי נַעַמְדָה יָּחַד
Let us stand together.　　　　　　　　מִי־בַעַל מִשְׁפָּטִי יִגַּשׁ אֵלָי:
Who *is* My adversary?
Let him come near Me.　　　　　　　　9　הֵן אֲדֹנָי יְהֹוִה יַעֲזָר־לִי
9　Surely the Lord GOD will help Me;　　　　מִי־הוּא יַרְשִׁיעֵנִי
Who *is* he *who* will condemn Me?　　　הֵן כֻּלָּם כַּבֶּגֶד יִבְלוּ
Indeed they will all grow old like a garment;　עָשׁ יֹאכְלֵם:
The moth will eat them up.
　　　　　　　　　　　　　　　10　מִי בָכֶם יְרֵא יְהֹוָה
10　"Who among you fears the LORD?　　　　שֹׁמֵעַ בְּקוֹל עַבְדּוֹ
Who obeys the voice of His Servant?　　　אֲשֶׁר | הָלַךְ חֲשֵׁכִים
Who walks in darkness　　　　　　　　וְאֵין נֹגַהּ לוֹ
And has no light?　　　　　　　　　　יִבְטַח בְּשֵׁם יְהֹוָה
Let him trust in the name of the LORD　　וְיִשָּׁעֵן בֵּאלֹהָיו:
And rely upon his God.
11　Look, all you who kindle a fire,　　　　11　הֵן כֻּלְּכֶם קֹדְחֵי אֵשׁ
Who encircle *yourselves* with sparks:　　מְאַזְּרֵי זִיקוֹת
Walk in the light of your fire and in the　　לְכוּ | בְּאוֹר אֶשְׁכֶם וּבְזִיקוֹת בִּעַרְתֶּם
sparks you have kindled—　　　　　　מִיָּדִי הָיְתָה־זֹּאת לָכֶם
This you shall have from My hand:　　　　לְמַעֲצֵבָה תִּשְׁכָּבוּן: פ
You shall lie down in torment.

51　"Listen to Me, you who follow after right-　　נא שִׁמְעוּ אֵלַי רֹדְפֵי צֶדֶק
eousness,　　　　　　　　　　　　מְבַקְשֵׁי יְהֹוָה
You who seek the LORD:　　　　　　　הַבִּיטוּ אֶל־צוּר חֻצַּבְתֶּם
Look to the rock *from which* you were hewn,　וְאֶל־מַקֶּבֶת בּוֹר נֻקַּרְתֶּם:
And to the hole of the pit *from which* you
were dug.　　　　　　　　　　　2　הַבִּיטוּ אֶל־אַבְרָהָם אֲבִיכֶם
2　Look to Abraham your father,　　　　　וְאֶל־שָׂרָה תְּחוֹלֶלְכֶם
And to Sarah *who* bore you;　　　　　כִּי־אֶחָד קְרָאתִיו
For I called him alone,　　　　　　　וַאֲבָרְכֵהוּ וְאַרְבֵּהוּ: ס
And blessed him and increased him."
3　For the LORD will comfort Zion,　　　　3　כִּי־נִחַם יְהֹוָה צִיּוֹן
He will comfort all her waste places;
He will make her wilderness like Eden,

And her desert like the garden of the LORD;
Joy and gladness will be found in it,
Thanksgiving and the voice of melody.

4 "Listen to Me, My people;
And give ear to Me, O My nation:
For law will proceed from Me,
And I will make My justice rest
As a light of the peoples.

5 My righteousness *is* near,
My salvation has gone forth,
And My arms will judge the peoples;
The coastlands will wait upon Me,
And on My arm they will trust.

6 Lift up your eyes to the heavens,
And look on the earth beneath.
For the heavens will vanish away like smoke,
The earth will grow old like a garment,
And those who dwell in it will die in like
　　manner;
But My salvation will be forever,
And My righteousness will not be abolished.

7 "Listen to Me, you who know righteousness,
You people in whose heart *is* My law:
Do not fear the reproach of men,
Nor be afraid of their insults.

8 For the moth will eat them up like a garment,
And the worm will eat them like wool;
But My righteousness will be forever,
And My salvation from generation to
　　generation."

9 Awake, awake, put on strength,
O arm of the LORD!
Awake as in the ancient days,
In the generations of old.
Are You not *the arm* that cut Rahab apart,
And wounded the serpent?

10 *Are* You not *the One* who dried up the sea,
The waters of the great deep;
That made the depths of the sea a road
For the redeemed to cross over?

11 So the ransomed of the LORD shall return,
And come to Zion with singing,
With everlasting joy on their heads.
They shall obtain joy and gladness;
Sorrow and sighing shall flee away.

12 "I, *even* I, *am* He who comforts you.
Who *are* you that you should be afraid
Of a man *who* will die,
And of the son of a man *who* will be made
　　like grass?

13 And you forget the LORD your Maker,
Who stretched out the heavens

נָחַם כָּל־חָרְבֹתֶיהָ
וַיָּשֶׂם מִדְבָּרָהּ כְּעֵדֶן
וְעַרְבָתָהּ כְּגַן־יְהוָה
שָׂשׂוֹן וְשִׂמְחָה יִמָּצֵא בָהּ
תּוֹדָה וְקוֹל זִמְרָה׃　ס

4 הַקְשִׁיבוּ אֵלַי עַמִּי
וּלְאוּמִּי אֵלַי הַאֲזִינוּ
כִּי תוֹרָה מֵאִתִּי תֵצֵא
וּמִשְׁפָּטִי לְאוֹר עַמִּים אַרְגִּיעַ׃

5 קָרוֹב צִדְקִי יָצָא יִשְׁעִי
וּזְרֹעַי עַמִּים יִשְׁפֹּטוּ
אֵלַי אִיִּים יְקַוּוּ וְאֶל־זְרֹעִי יְיַחֵלוּן׃

6 שְׂאוּ לַשָּׁמַיִם עֵינֵיכֶם
וְהַבִּיטוּ אֶל־הָאָרֶץ מִתַּחַת
כִּי־שָׁמַיִם כֶּעָשָׁן נִמְלָחוּ
וְהָאָרֶץ כַּבֶּגֶד תִּבְלֶה
וְיֹשְׁבֶיהָ כְּמוֹ־כֵן יְמוּתוּן
וִישׁוּעָתִי לְעוֹלָם תִּהְיֶה
וְצִדְקָתִי לֹא תֵחָת׃　ס

7 שִׁמְעוּ אֵלַי יֹדְעֵי צֶדֶק
עַם תּוֹרָתִי בְלִבָּם
אַל־תִּירְאוּ חֶרְפַּת אֱנוֹשׁ
וּמִגִּדֻּפֹתָם אַל־תֵּחָתּוּ׃

8 כִּי כַבֶּגֶד יֹאכְלֵם עָשׁ
וְכַצֶּמֶר יֹאכְלֵם סָס
וְצִדְקָתִי לְעוֹלָם תִּהְיֶה
וִישׁוּעָתִי לְדוֹר דּוֹרִים׃　ס

9 עוּרִי עוּרִי לִבְשִׁי־עֹז זְרוֹעַ יְהוָה
עוּרִי כִּימֵי קֶדֶם דֹּרוֹת עוֹלָמִים
הֲלוֹא אַתְּ־הִיא הַמַּחְצֶבֶת רַהַב מְחוֹלֶלֶת תַּנִּין׃

10 הֲלוֹא אַתְּ־הִיא הַמַּחֲרֶבֶת יָם
מֵי תְּהוֹם רַבָּה
הַשָּׂמָה מַעֲמַקֵּי־יָם
דֶּרֶךְ לַעֲבֹר גְּאוּלִים׃

11 וּפְדוּיֵי יְהוָה יְשׁוּבוּן וּבָאוּ צִיּוֹן בְּרִנָּה
וְשִׂמְחַת עוֹלָם עַל־רֹאשָׁם
שָׂשׂוֹן וְשִׂמְחָה יַשִּׂיגוּן נָסוּ יָגוֹן וַאֲנָחָה׃　ס

12 אָנֹכִי אָנֹכִי הוּא מְנַחֶמְכֶם
מִי־אַתְּ וַתִּירְאִי מֵאֱנוֹשׁ יָמוּת
וּמִבֶּן־אָדָם חָצִיר יִנָּתֵן׃

13 וַתִּשְׁכַּח יְהוָה עֹשֶׂךָ
נוֹטֶה שָׁמַיִם וְיֹסֵד אָרֶץ

And laid the foundations of the earth;
You have feared continually every day
Because of the fury of the oppressor,
When *he has* prepared to destroy.
And where *is* the fury of the oppressor?
14 The captive exile hastens, that he may be
    loosed,
That he should not die in the pit,
And that his bread should not fail.
15 But I *am* the LORD your God,
Who divided the sea whose waves roared—
The LORD of hosts *is* His name.
16 And I have put My words in your mouth;
I have covered you with the shadow of My
    hand,
That I may plant the heavens,
Lay the foundations of the earth,
And say to Zion, 'You *are* My people.'"

17 Awake, awake!
Stand up, O Jerusalem,
You who have drunk at the hand of the
    LORD
The cup of His fury;
You have drunk the dregs of the cup of
    trembling,
And drained *it* out.
18 *There is* no one to guide her
Among all the sons she has brought forth;
Nor *is there any* who takes her by the hand
Among all the sons she has brought up.
19 These two *things* have come to you;
Who will be sorry for you?—
Desolation and destruction, famine and
    sword—
By whom will I comfort you?
20 Your sons have fainted,
They lie at the head of all the streets,
Like an antelope in a net;
They are full of the fury of the LORD,
The rebuke of your God.
21 Therefore please hear this, you afflicted,
And drunk but not with wine.
22 Thus says your Lord,
The LORD and your God,
Who pleads the cause of His people:
"See, I have taken out of your hand
The cup of trembling,
The dregs of the cup of My fury;
You shall no longer drink it.
23 But I will put it into the hand of those who
    afflict you,
Who have said to you,
'Lie down, that we may walk over you.'

וַתְּפַחֵד תָּמִיד כָּל־הַיּוֹם
מִפְּנֵי חֲמַת הַמֵּצִיק
כַּאֲשֶׁר כּוֹנֵן לְהַשְׁחִית
וְאַיֵּה חֲמַת הַמֵּצִיק׃
14 מִהַר צֹעֶה לְהִפָּתֵחַ
וְלֹא־יָמוּת לַשַּׁחַת
וְלֹא יֶחְסַר לַחְמוֹ׃
15 וְאָנֹכִי יְהוָה אֱלֹהֶיךָ
רֹגַע הַיָּם וַיֶּהֱמוּ גַּלָּיו
יְהוָה צְבָאוֹת שְׁמוֹ׃
16 וָאָשִׂים דְּבָרַי בְּפִיךָ
וּבְצֵל יָדִי כִּסִּיתִיךָ
לִנְטֹעַ שָׁמַיִם
וְלִיסֹד אָרֶץ
וְלֵאמֹר לְצִיּוֹן עַמִּי־אָתָּה׃ ס

17 הִתְעוֹרְרִי הִתְעוֹרְרִי
קוּמִי יְרוּשָׁלִַם
אֲשֶׁר שָׁתִית
מִיַּד יְהוָה אֶת־כּוֹס חֲמָתוֹ
אֶת־קֻבַּעַת כּוֹס הַתַּרְעֵלָה
שָׁתִית מָצִית׃
18 אֵין־מְנַהֵל לָהּ
מִכָּל־בָּנִים יָלָדָה
וְאֵין מַחֲזִיק בְּיָדָהּ
מִכָּל־בָּנִים גִּדֵּלָה׃
19 שְׁתַּיִם הֵנָּה קֹרְאֹתַיִךְ
מִי יָנוּד לָךְ הַשֹּׁד וְהַשֶּׁבֶר
וְהָרָעָב וְהַחֶרֶב מִי אֲנַחֲמֵךְ׃
20 בָּנַיִךְ עֻלְּפוּ שָׁכְבוּ
בְּרֹאשׁ כָּל־חוּצוֹת כְּתוֹא מִכְמָר
הַמְלֵאִים חֲמַת־יְהוָה
גַּעֲרַת אֱלֹהָיִךְ׃
21 לָכֵן שִׁמְעִי־נָא זֹאת עֲנִיָּה
וּשְׁכֻרַת וְלֹא מִיָּיִן׃ ס
22 כֹּה־אָמַר אֲדֹנַיִךְ יְהוָה
וֵאלֹהַיִךְ יָרִיב עַמּוֹ הִנֵּה לָקַחְתִּי
מִיָּדֵךְ אֶת־כּוֹס הַתַּרְעֵלָה
אֶת־קֻבַּעַת כּוֹס חֲמָתִי
לֹא־תוֹסִיפִי לִשְׁתּוֹתָהּ עוֹד׃
23 וְשַׂמְתִּיהָ בְּיַד־מוֹגַיִךְ

And you have laid your body like the
    ground,
And as the street, for those who walk over."

אֲשֶׁר־אָמְרוּ לְנַפְשֵׁךְ
שְׁחִי וְנַעֲבֹרָה וַתָּשִׂימִי כָאָרֶץ גֵּוֵךְ
וְכַחוּץ לַעֹבְרִים: ס

52 Awake, awake!
    Put on your strength, O Zion;
    Put on your beautiful garments,
    O Jerusalem, the holy city!
    For the uncircumcised and the unclean
    Shall no longer come to you.

נב עוּרִי עוּרִי

2 Shake yourself from the dust, arise;
    Sit down, O Jerusalem!
    Loose yourself from the bonds of your neck,
    O captive daughter of Zion!

לִבְשִׁי עֻזֵּךְ צִיּוֹן
לִבְשִׁי | בִּגְדֵי תִפְאַרְתֵּךְ
יְרוּשָׁלַםִ עִיר הַקֹּדֶשׁ
כִּי לֹא יוֹסִיף
יָבֹא־בָךְ עוֹד עָרֵל וְטָמֵא:

3 For thus says the LORD:

    "You have sold yourselves for nothing,
    And you shall be redeemed without money."

2 הִתְנַעֲרִי מֵעָפָר
קוּמִי שְּׁבִי יְרוּשָׁלָםִ
הִתְפַּתְּחִי מוֹסְרֵי צַוָּארֵךְ
שְׁבִיָּה בַּת־צִיּוֹן: ס

4 For thus says the Lord GOD:

    "My people went down at first
    Into Egypt to dwell there;
    Then the Assyrian oppressed them without
      cause.

3 כִּי־כֹה אָמַר יְהוָה
חִנָּם נִמְכַּרְתֶּם
וְלֹא בְכֶסֶף תִּגָּאֵלוּ:

5 Now therefore, what have I here," says the
      LORD,
    "That My people are taken away for nothing?
    Those who rule over them
    Make them wail," says the LORD,

4 כִּי כֹה אָמַר אֲדֹנָי יְהוִה
מִצְרַיִם יָרַד־עַמִּי בָרִאשֹׁנָה לָגוּר שָׁם
וְאַשּׁוּר בְּאֶפֶס עֲשָׁקוֹ:

    "And My name is blasphemed continually
      every day.

5 וְעַתָּה מַי־לִי־פֹה נְאֻם־יְהוָה
כִּי־לֻקַּח עַמִּי חִנָּם
מֹשְׁלָו יְהֵילִילוּ נְאֻם־יְהוָה
וְתָמִיד כָּל־הַיּוֹם שְׁמִי מִנֹּאָץ:

6 Therefore My people shall know My name;
    Therefore they shall know in that day
    That I am He who speaks:
    'Behold, it is I.'"

6 לָכֵן יֵדַע עַמִּי שְׁמִי
לָכֵן בַּיּוֹם הַהוּא
כִּי־אֲנִי־הוּא הַמְדַבֵּר הִנֵּנִי:

7 How beautiful upon the mountains
    Are the feet of him who brings good news,
    Who proclaims peace,
    Who brings glad tidings of good things,
    Who proclaims salvation,
    Who says to Zion,
    "Your God reigns!"

7 מַה־נָּאווּ עַל־הֶהָרִים
רַגְלֵי מְבַשֵּׂר
מַשְׁמִיעַ שָׁלוֹם
מְבַשֵּׂר טוֹב מַשְׁמִיעַ יְשׁוּעָה
אֹמֵר לְצִיּוֹן
מָלַךְ אֱלֹהָיִךְ:

8 Your watchmen shall lift up their voices,
    With their voices they shall sing together;
    For they shall see eye to eye
    When the LORD brings back Zion.

8 קוֹל צֹפַיִךְ נָשְׂאוּ קוֹל
יַחְדָּו יְרַנֵּנוּ
כִּי עַיִן בְּעַיִן יִרְאוּ
בְּשׁוּב יְהוָה צִיּוֹן:

9 Break forth into joy, sing together,
    You waste places of Jerusalem!
    For the LORD has comforted His people,
    He has redeemed Jerusalem.

9 פִּצְחוּ רַנְּנוּ יַחְדָּו חָרְבוֹת יְרוּשָׁלָםִ
כִּי־נִחַם יְהוָה עַמּוֹ גָּאַל יְרוּשָׁלָםִ:

10 The LORD has made bare His holy arm
    In the eyes of all the nations;
    And all the ends of the earth shall see

10 חָשַׂף יְהוָה אֶת־זְרוֹעַ קָדְשׁוֹ
לְעֵינֵי כָּל־הַגּוֹיִם

נב 2 הִתְפַּתְּחִי   5 מֹשְׁלָו

The salvation of our God.

11 Depart! Depart! Go out from there,
Touch no unclean *thing;*
Go out from the midst of her,
Be clean,
You who bear the vessels of the LORD.

12 For you shall not go out with haste,
Nor go by flight;
For the LORD will go before you,
And the God of Israel *will be* your rear
guard.

13 Behold, My Servant shall deal prudently;
He shall be exalted and extolled and be very
high.

14 Just as many were astonished at you,
So His visage was marred more than any
man,
And His form more than the sons of men;

15 So shall He sprinkle many nations.
Kings shall shut their mouths at Him;
For what had not been told them they shall
see,
And what they had not heard they shall
consider.

53 Who has believed our report?
And to whom has the arm of the LORD been
revealed?

2 For He shall grow up before Him as a tender
plant,
And as a root out of dry ground.
He has no form or comeliness;
And when we see Him,
There is no beauty that we should desire
Him.

3 He is despised and rejected by men,
A Man of sorrows and acquainted with grief.
And we hid, as it were, *our* faces from Him;
He was despised, and we did not esteem
Him.

4 Surely He has borne our griefs
And carried our sorrows;
Yet we esteemed Him stricken,
Smitten by God, and afflicted.

5 But He *was* wounded for our transgressions,
He was bruised for our iniquities;
The chastisement for our peace *was* upon
Him,
And by His stripes we are healed.

6 All we like sheep have gone astray;
We have turned, every one, to his own way;

וְרָאוּ כָּל־אַפְסֵי־אָרֶץ
אֵת יְשׁוּעַת אֱלֹהֵינוּ: ס

11 סוּרוּ סוּרוּ צְאוּ מִשָּׁם
טָמֵא אַל־תִּגָּעוּ
צְאוּ מִתּוֹכָהּ הִבָּרוּ
נֹשְׂאֵי כְּלֵי יְהֹוָה:

12 כִּי לֹא בְחִפָּזוֹן תֵּצֵאוּ
וּבִמְנוּסָה לֹא תֵלֵכוּן
כִּי־הֹלֵךְ לִפְנֵיכֶם יְהֹוָה
וּמְאַסִּפְכֶם אֱלֹהֵי יִשְׂרָאֵל: ס

13 הִנֵּה יַשְׂכִּיל עַבְדִּי
יָרוּם וְנִשָּׂא וְגָבַהּ מְאֹד:

14 כַּאֲשֶׁר שָׁמְמוּ עָלֶיךָ רַבִּים
כֵּן־מִשְׁחַת מֵאִישׁ מַרְאֵהוּ
וְתֹאֲרוֹ מִבְּנֵי אָדָם:

15 כֵּן יַזֶּה גּוֹיִם רַבִּים
עָלָיו יִקְפְּצוּ מְלָכִים פִּיהֶם
כִּי אֲשֶׁר לֹא־סֻפַּר לָהֶם רָאוּ
וַאֲשֶׁר לֹא־שָׁמְעוּ הִתְבּוֹנָנוּ:

נג מִי הֶאֱמִין לִשְׁמֻעָתֵנוּ
וּזְרוֹעַ יְהֹוָה עַל־מִי נִגְלָתָה:

2 וַיַּעַל כַּיּוֹנֵק לְפָנָיו
וְכַשֹּׁרֶשׁ מֵאֶרֶץ צִיָּה
לֹא־תֹאַר לוֹ וְלֹא הָדָר
וְנִרְאֵהוּ וְלֹא־מַרְאֶה וְנֶחְמְדֵהוּ:

3 נִבְזֶה וַחֲדַל אִישִׁים
אִישׁ מַכְאֹבוֹת וִידוּעַ חֹלִי
וּכְמַסְתֵּר פָּנִים מִמֶּנּוּ
נִבְזֶה וְלֹא חֲשַׁבְנֻהוּ:

4 אָכֵן חֳלָיֵנוּ הוּא נָשָׂא
וּמַכְאֹבֵינוּ סְבָלָם
וַאֲנַחְנוּ חֲשַׁבְנֻהוּ נָגוּעַ
מֻכֵּה אֱלֹהִים וּמְעֻנֶּה:

5 וְהוּא מְחֹלָל מִפְּשָׁעֵנוּ
מְדֻכָּא מֵעֲוֺנֹתֵינוּ
מוּסַר שְׁלוֹמֵנוּ עָלָיו
וּבַחֲבֻרָתוֹ נִרְפָּא־לָנוּ:

6 כֻּלָּנוּ כַּצֹּאן תָּעִינוּ
אִישׁ לְדַרְכּוֹ פָּנִינוּ

And the LORD has laid on Him the iniquity
   of us all.

וַיהוָה הִפְגִּיעַ בּוֹ
אֵת עֲוֹן כֻּלָּנוּ׃

7 He was oppressed and He was afflicted,
   Yet He opened not His mouth;
   He was led as a lamb to the slaughter,
   And as a sheep before its shearers is silent,
   So He opened not His mouth.

7 נִגַּשׂ וְהוּא נַעֲנֶה
וְלֹא יִפְתַּח־פִּיו
כַּשֶּׂה לַטֶּבַח יוּבָל
וּכְרָחֵל לִפְנֵי גֹזְזֶיהָ נֶאֱלָמָה
וְלֹא יִפְתַּח פִּיו׃

8 He was taken from prison and from judg-
   ment,
   And who will declare His generation?
   For He was cut off from the land of the
     living;
   For the transgressions of My people He was
     stricken.

8 מֵעֹצֶר וּמִמִּשְׁפָּט לֻקָּח
וְאֶת־דּוֹרוֹ מִי יְשׂוֹחֵחַ
כִּי נִגְזַר מֵאֶרֶץ חַיִּים
מִפֶּשַׁע עַמִּי נֶגַע לָמוֹ׃

9 And they made His grave with the wicked—
   But with the rich at His death,
   Because He had done no violence,
   Nor *was any* deceit in His mouth.

9 וַיִּתֵּן אֶת־רְשָׁעִים קִבְרוֹ
וְאֶת־עָשִׁיר בְּמֹתָיו
עַל לֹא־חָמָס עָשָׂה
וְלֹא מִרְמָה בְּפִיו׃

10 Yet it pleased the LORD to bruise Him;
   He has put *Him* to grief.
   When You make His soul an offering for sin,
   He shall see *His* seed, He shall prolong *His*
     days,
   And the pleasure of the LORD shall prosper
     in His hand.

10 וַיהוָה חָפֵץ דַּכְּאוֹ הֶחֱלִי
אִם־תָּשִׂים אָשָׁם נַפְשׁוֹ
יִרְאֶה זֶרַע יַאֲרִיךְ יָמִים
וְחֵפֶץ יְהוָה בְּיָדוֹ יִצְלָח׃

11 He shall see the labor of His soul, *and* be
   satisfied.
   By His knowledge My righteous Servant
     shall justify many,
   For He shall bear their iniquities.

11 מֵעֲמַל נַפְשׁוֹ יִרְאֶה יִשְׂבָּע
בְּדַעְתּוֹ יַצְדִּיק צַדִּיק עַבְדִּי לָרַבִּים
וַעֲוֹנֹתָם הוּא יִסְבֹּל׃

12 Therefore I will divide Him a portion with
     the great,
   And He shall divide the spoil with the strong,
   Because He poured out His soul unto death,
   And He was numbered with the transgres-
   sors,
   And He bore the sin of many,
   And made intercession for the transgressors.

12 לָכֵן אֲחַלֶּק־לוֹ בָרַבִּים
וְאֶת־עֲצוּמִים יְחַלֵּק שָׁלָל
תַּחַת אֲשֶׁר הֶעֱרָה לַמָּוֶת נַפְשׁוֹ
וְאֶת־פֹּשְׁעִים נִמְנָה
וְהוּא חֵטְא־רַבִּים נָשָׂא
וְלַפֹּשְׁעִים יַפְגִּיעַ׃ ס

54 "Sing, O barren,
   You *who* have not borne!
   Break forth into singing, and cry aloud,
   You *who* have not labored with child!
   For more *are* the children of the desolate
   Than the children of the married woman,"
     says the LORD.

נד רָנִּי עֲקָרָה לֹא יָלָדָה
פִּצְחִי רִנָּה וְצַהֲלִי לֹא־חָלָה
כִּי־רַבִּים בְּנֵי־שׁוֹמֵמָה
מִבְּנֵי בְעוּלָה אָמַר יְהוָה׃

2 "Enlarge the place of your tent,
   And let them stretch out the curtains of your
     dwellings;
   Do not spare;
   Lengthen your cords,
   And strengthen your stakes.

2 הַרְחִיבִי ׀ מְקוֹם אָהֳלֵךְ
וִירִיעוֹת מִשְׁכְּנוֹתַיִךְ יַטּוּ אַל־תַּחְשֹׂכִי
הַאֲרִיכִי מֵיתָרַיִךְ וִיתֵדֹתַיִךְ חַזֵּקִי׃

3 For you shall expand to the right and to the
   left,
   And your descendants will inherit the na-
     tions,
   And make the desolate cities inhabited.

4 "Do not fear, for you will not be ashamed;
   Neither be disgraced, for you will not be put
     to shame;
   For you will forget the shame of your youth,
   And will not remember the reproach of your
     widowhood anymore.
5 For your Maker is your husband,
   The LORD of hosts is His name;
   And your Redeemer is the Holy One of
     Israel;
   He is called the God of the whole earth.
6 For the LORD has called you
   Like a woman forsaken and grieved in spirit,
   Like a youthful wife when you were refused,"
   Says your God.
7 "For a mere moment I have forsaken you,
   But with great mercies I will gather you.
8 With a little wrath I hid My face from you
     for a moment;
   But with everlasting kindness I will have
     mercy on you,"
   Says the LORD, your Redeemer.

9 "For this is like the waters of Noah to Me;
   For as I have sworn
   That the waters of Noah would no longer
     cover the earth,
   So have I sworn
   That I would not be angry with you, nor
     rebuke you.
10 For the mountains shall depart
   And the hills be removed,
   But My kindness shall not depart from you,
   Nor shall My covenant of peace be re-
     moved,"
   Says the LORD, who has mercy on you.

11 "O you afflicted one,
   Tossed with tempest, and not comforted,
   Behold, I will lay your stones with colorful
     gems,
   And lay your foundations with sapphires.
12 I will make your pinnacles of rubies,
   Your gates of crystal,
   And all your walls of precious stones.
13 All your children shall be taught by the
     LORD,
   And great shall be the peace of your children.
14 In righteousness you shall be established;

3 כִּי־יָמִין וּשְׂמֹאול תִּפְרֹצִי
וְזַרְעֵךְ גּוֹיִם יִירָשׁ
וְעָרִים נְשַׁמּוֹת יוֹשִׁיבוּ:
4 אַל־תִּירְאִי כִּי־לֹא תֵבוֹשִׁי
וְאַל־תִּכָּלְמִי כִּי לֹא תַחְפִּירִי
כִּי בֹשֶׁת עֲלוּמַיִךְ תִּשְׁכָּחִי
וְחֶרְפַּת אַלְמְנוּתַיִךְ לֹא תִזְכְּרִי־עוֹד:
5 כִּי בֹעֲלַיִךְ עֹשַׂיִךְ
יְהֹוָה צְבָאוֹת שְׁמוֹ
וְגֹאֲלֵךְ קְדוֹשׁ יִשְׂרָאֵל
אֱלֹהֵי כָל־הָאָרֶץ יִקָּרֵא:
6 כִּי־כְאִשָּׁה עֲזוּבָה
וַעֲצוּבַת רוּחַ קְרָאָךְ יְהֹוָה
וְאֵשֶׁת נְעוּרִים
כִּי תִמָּאֵס אָמַר אֱלֹהָיִךְ:
7 בְּרֶגַע קָטֹן עֲזַבְתִּיךְ
וּבְרַחֲמִים גְּדֹלִים אֲקַבְּצֵךְ:
8 בְּשֶׁצֶף קֶצֶף הִסְתַּרְתִּי פָנַי רֶגַע מִמֵּךְ
וּבְחֶסֶד עוֹלָם רִחַמְתִּיךְ
אָמַר גֹּאֲלֵךְ יְהֹוָה: ס
9 כִּי־מֵי נֹחַ זֹאת לִי
אֲשֶׁר נִשְׁבַּעְתִּי מֵעֲבֹר מֵי־נֹחַ
עוֹד עַל־הָאָרֶץ
כֵּן נִשְׁבַּעְתִּי
מִקְּצֹף עָלַיִךְ וּמִגְּעָר־בָּךְ:
10 כִּי הֶהָרִים יָמוּשׁוּ
וְהַגְּבָעוֹת תְּמוּטֶנָה
וְחַסְדִּי מֵאִתֵּךְ לֹא־יָמוּשׁ
וּבְרִית שְׁלוֹמִי לֹא תָמוּט
אָמַר מְרַחֲמֵךְ יְהֹוָה: ס
11 עֲנִיָּה סֹעֲרָה
לֹא נֻחָמָה
הִנֵּה אָנֹכִי מַרְבִּיץ בַּפּוּךְ אֲבָנַיִךְ
וִיסַדְתִּיךְ בַּסַּפִּירִים:
12 וְשַׂמְתִּי כַּדְכֹד שִׁמְשֹׁתַיִךְ
וּשְׁעָרַיִךְ לְאַבְנֵי אֶקְדָּח
וְכָל־גְּבוּלֵךְ לְאַבְנֵי־חֵפֶץ:
13 וְכָל־בָּנַיִךְ לִמּוּדֵי יְהֹוָה
וְרַב שְׁלוֹם בָּנָיִךְ:
14 בִּצְדָקָה תִּכּוֹנָנִי

You shall be far from oppression, for you
shall not fear;
And from terror, for it shall not come near
you.
15 Indeed they shall surely assemble, *but* not
because of Me.
Whoever assembles against you shall fall for
your sake.

16 "Behold, I have created the blacksmith
Who blows the coals in the fire,
Who brings forth an instrument for his work;
And I have created the spoiler to destroy.

17 No weapon formed against you shall pros-
per,
And every tongue *which* rises against you in
judgment
You shall condemn.
This *is* the heritage of the servants of the
LORD,
And their righteousness *is* from Me,"
Says the LORD.

55 "Ho! Everyone who thirsts,
Come to the waters;
And you who have no money,
Come, buy and eat.
Yes, come, buy wine and milk
Without money and without price.

2 Why do you spend money for *what is* not
bread,
And your wages for *what* does not satisfy?
Listen carefully to Me, and eat *what is* good,
And let your soul delight itself in abundance.

3 Incline your ear, and come to Me.
Hear, and your soul shall live;
And I will make an everlasting covenant with
you—
The sure mercies of David.

4 Indeed I have given him *as* a witness to the
people,
A leader and commander for the people.

5 Surely you shall call a nation you do not
know,
And nations *who* do not know you shall run
to you,
Because of the LORD your God,
And the Holy One of Israel;
For He has glorified you."

6 Seek the LORD while He may be found,
Call upon Him while He is near.

7 Let the wicked forsake his way,
And the unrighteous man his thoughts;
Let him return to the LORD,

רָחֲקִי מֵעֹשֶׁק כִּי־לֹא תִירָאִי
וּמִמְּחִתָּה כִּי לֹא־תִקְרַב אֵלָיִךְ׃

15 הֵן גּוֹר יָגוּר אֶפֶס מֵאוֹתִי
מִי־גָר אִתָּךְ עָלַיִךְ יִפּוֹל׃

16 הִנֵּה אָנֹכִי בָּרָאתִי חָרָשׁ
נֹפֵחַ בְּאֵשׁ פֶּחָם
וּמוֹצִיא כְלִי לְמַעֲשֵׂהוּ
וְאָנֹכִי בָּרָאתִי מַשְׁחִית לְחַבֵּל׃

17 כָּל־כְּלִי יוּצַר עָלַיִךְ לֹא יִצְלָח
וְכָל־לָשׁוֹן
תָּקוּם־אִתָּךְ לַמִּשְׁפָּט תַּרְשִׁיעִי
זֹאת נַחֲלַת עַבְדֵי יְהֹוָה
וְצִדְקָתָם מֵאִתִּי נְאֻם־יְהֹוָה׃ ס

נה הוֹי כָּל־צָמֵא לְכוּ לַמַּיִם
וַאֲשֶׁר אֵין־לוֹ כָּסֶף
לְכוּ שִׁבְרוּ וֶאֱכֹלוּ
וּלְכוּ שִׁבְרוּ בְּלוֹא־כֶסֶף
וּבְלוֹא מְחִיר יַיִן וְחָלָב׃

2 לָמָּה תִשְׁקְלוּ־כֶסֶף בְּלוֹא־לֶחֶם
וִיגִיעֲכֶם בְּלוֹא לְשָׂבְעָה
שִׁמְעוּ שָׁמוֹעַ אֵלַי וְאִכְלוּ־טוֹב
וְתִתְעַנַּג בַּדֶּשֶׁן נַפְשְׁכֶם׃

3 הַטּוּ אָזְנְכֶם וּלְכוּ אֵלַי
שִׁמְעוּ וּתְחִי נַפְשְׁכֶם
וְאֶכְרְתָה לָכֶם בְּרִית עוֹלָם
חַסְדֵי דָוִד הַנֶּאֱמָנִים׃

4 הֵן עֵד לְאוּמִּים נְתַתִּיו
נָגִיד וּמְצַוֵּה לְאֻמִּים׃

5 הֵן גּוֹי לֹא־תֵדַע תִּקְרָא
וְגוֹי לֹא־יְדָעוּךָ אֵלֶיךָ יָרוּצוּ
לְמַעַן יְהֹוָה אֱלֹהֶיךָ
וְלִקְדוֹשׁ יִשְׂרָאֵל כִּי פֵאֲרָךְ׃ ס

6 דִּרְשׁוּ יְהֹוָה בְּהִמָּצְאוֹ
קְרָאֻהוּ בִּהְיוֹתוֹ קָרוֹב׃

7 יַעֲזֹב רָשָׁע דַּרְכּוֹ
וְאִישׁ אָוֶן מַחְשְׁבֹתָיו

And He will have mercy on him;
And to our God,
For He will abundantly pardon.

8 "For My thoughts *are* not your thoughts,
Nor *are* your ways My ways," says the
LORD.
9 "For *as* the heavens are higher than the earth,
So are My ways higher than your ways,
And My thoughts than your thoughts.
10 "For as the rain comes down, and the snow
from heaven,
And do not return there,
But water the earth,
And make it bring forth and bud,
That it may give seed to the sower
And bread to the eater,
11 So shall My word be that goes forth from My
mouth;
It shall not return to Me void,
But it shall accomplish what I please,
And it shall prosper *in the thing* for which I
sent it.

12 "For you shall go out with joy,
And be led out with peace;
The mountains and the hills
Shall break forth into singing before you,
And all the trees of the field shall clap *their*
hands.
13 Instead of the thorn shall come up the
cypress tree,
And instead of the brier shall come up the
myrtle tree;
And it shall be to the LORD for a name,
For an everlasting sign *that* shall not be cut
off."

56 Thus says the LORD:

"Keep justice, and do righteousness,
For My salvation *is* about to come,
And My righteousness to be revealed.
2 Blessed *is* the man *who* does this,
And the son of man *who* lays hold on it;
Who keeps from defiling the Sabbath,
And keeps his hand from doing any evil."

3 Do not let the son of the foreigner
Who has joined himself to the LORD
Speak, saying,
"The LORD has utterly separated me from His
people";
Nor let the eunuch say,
"Here I am, a dry tree."
4 For thus says the LORD:

וְיָשֹׁב אֶל־יְהוָה וִירַחֲמֵהוּ
וְאֶל־אֱלֹהֵינוּ כִּי־יַרְבֶּה לִסְלוֹחַ:
8 כִּי לֹא מַחְשְׁבוֹתַי מַחְשְׁבוֹתֵיכֶם
וְלֹא דַרְכֵיכֶם דְּרָכָי נְאֻם יְהוָה:
9 כִּי־גָבְהוּ שָׁמַיִם מֵאָרֶץ
כֵּן גָּבְהוּ דְרָכַי מִדַּרְכֵיכֶם
וּמַחְשְׁבֹתַי מִמַּחְשְׁבֹתֵיכֶם:
10 כִּי כַּאֲשֶׁר יֵרֵד הַגֶּשֶׁם וְהַשֶּׁלֶג
מִן־הַשָּׁמַיִם
וְשָׁמָּה לֹא יָשׁוּב
כִּי אִם־הִרְוָה אֶת־הָאָרֶץ
וְהוֹלִידָהּ וְהִצְמִיחָהּ
וְנָתַן זֶרַע לַזֹּרֵעַ וְלֶחֶם לָאֹכֵל:
11 כֵּן יִהְיֶה דְבָרִי אֲשֶׁר יֵצֵא מִפִּי
לֹא־יָשׁוּב אֵלַי רֵיקָם
כִּי אִם־עָשָׂה אֶת־אֲשֶׁר חָפַצְתִּי
וְהִצְלִיחַ אֲשֶׁר שְׁלַחְתִּיו:
12 כִּי־בְשִׂמְחָה תֵצֵאוּ
וּבְשָׁלוֹם תּוּבָלוּן
הֶהָרִים וְהַגְּבָעוֹת
יִפְצְחוּ לִפְנֵיכֶם רִנָּה
וְכָל־עֲצֵי הַשָּׂדֶה יִמְחֲאוּ־כָף:
13 תַּחַת הַנַּעֲצוּץ יַעֲלֶה בְרוֹשׁ
תַּחַת הַסִּרְפַּד יַעֲלֶה הֲדַס
וְהָיָה לַיהוָה לְשֵׁם
לְאוֹת עוֹלָם לֹא יִכָּרֵת: ס

נו כֹּה אָמַר יְהוָה
שִׁמְרוּ מִשְׁפָּט וַעֲשׂוּ צְדָקָה
כִּי־קְרוֹבָה יְשׁוּעָתִי לָבוֹא
וְצִדְקָתִי לְהִגָּלוֹת:
2 אַשְׁרֵי אֱנוֹשׁ יַעֲשֶׂה־זֹּאת
וּבֶן־אָדָם יַחֲזִיק בָּהּ
שֹׁמֵר שַׁבָּת מֵחַלְּלוֹ
וְשֹׁמֵר יָדוֹ מֵעֲשׂוֹת כָּל־רָע: ס
3 וְאַל־יֹאמַר בֶּן־הַנֵּכָר
הַנִּלְוָה אֶל־יְהוָה לֵאמֹר
הַבְדֵּל יַבְדִּילַנִי יְהוָה מֵעַל עַמּוֹ
וְאַל־יֹאמַר הַסָּרִיס
הֵן אֲנִי עֵץ יָבֵשׁ: ס
4 כִּי־כֹה ׀ אָמַר יְהוָה

"To the eunuchs who keep My Sabbaths,
And choose what pleases Me,
And hold fast My covenant,

5 Even to them I will give in My house
And within My walls a place and a name
Better than that of sons and daughters;
I will give them an everlasting name
That shall not be cut off.

6 "Also the sons of the foreigner
Who join themselves to the LORD, to serve
    Him,
And to love the name of the LORD, to be His
    servants—
Everyone who keeps from defiling the
    Sabbath,
And holds fast My covenant—

7 Even them I will bring to My holy mountain,
And make them joyful in My house of
    prayer.
Their burnt offerings and their sacrifices
Will be accepted on My altar;
For My house shall be called a house of
    prayer for all nations."

8 The Lord GOD, who gathers the outcasts of
    Israel, says,
"Yet I will gather to him
Others besides those who are gathered to
    him."

9 All you beasts of the field, come to devour,
All you beasts in the forest.

10 His watchmen *are* blind,
They are all ignorant;
They *are* all dumb dogs,
They cannot bark;
Sleeping, lying down, loving to slumber.

11 Yes, *they are* greedy dogs
Which never have enough.
And they *are* shepherds
Who cannot understand;
They all look to their own way,
Every one for his own gain,
From his *own* territory.

12 "Come," *one says,* "I will bring wine,
And we will fill ourselves with intoxicating
    drink;
Tomorrow will be as today,
And much more abundant."

57

The righteous perishes,
And no man takes *it* to heart;
Merciful men *are* taken away,
While no one considers
That the righteous is taken away from evil.

לַסָּרִיסִים אֲשֶׁר יִשְׁמְרוּ אֶת־שַׁבְּתוֹתַי
וּבָחֲרוּ בַּאֲשֶׁר חָפָצְתִּי
וּמַחֲזִיקִים בִּבְרִיתִי:

5 וְנָתַתִּי לָהֶם בְּבֵיתִי וּבְחוֹמֹתַי יָד וָשֵׁם
טוֹב מִבָּנִים וּמִבָּנוֹת
שֵׁם עוֹלָם אֶתֶּן־לוֹ
אֲשֶׁר לֹא יִכָּרֵת: ס

6 וּבְנֵי הַנֵּכָר הַנִּלְוִים עַל־יְהֹוָה לְשָׁרְתוֹ
וּלְאַהֲבָה אֶת־שֵׁם יְהֹוָה
לִהְיוֹת לוֹ לַעֲבָדִים
כָּל־שֹׁמֵר שַׁבָּת מֵחַלְּלוֹ
וּמַחֲזִיקִים בִּבְרִיתִי:

7 וַהֲבִיאוֹתִים אֶל־הַר קָדְשִׁי
וְשִׂמַּחְתִּים בְּבֵית תְּפִלָּתִי
עוֹלֹתֵיהֶם וְזִבְחֵיהֶם
לְרָצוֹן עַל־מִזְבְּחִי
כִּי בֵיתִי בֵּית־תְּפִלָּה יִקָּרֵא לְכָל־הָעַמִּים:

8 נְאֻם אֲדֹנָי יְהֹוִה מְקַבֵּץ נִדְחֵי יִשְׂרָאֵל
עוֹד אֲקַבֵּץ עָלָיו לְנִקְבָּצָיו:

9 כֹּל חַיְתוֹ שָׂדָי
אֵתָיוּ לֶאֱכֹל כָּל־חַיְתוֹ בַּיָּעַר: ס

10 צֹפָו עִוְרִים כֻּלָּם לֹא יָדָעוּ
כֻּלָּם כְּלָבִים אִלְּמִים לֹא יוּכְלוּ לִנְבֹּחַ
הֹזִים שֹׁכְבִים אֹהֲבֵי לָנוּם:

11 וְהַכְּלָבִים עַזֵּי־נֶפֶשׁ
לֹא יָדְעוּ שָׂבְעָה
וְהֵמָּה רֹעִים
לֹא יָדְעוּ הָבִין
כֻּלָּם לְדַרְכָּם פָּנוּ
אִישׁ לְבִצְעוֹ מִקָּצֵהוּ:

12 אֵתָיוּ אֶקְחָה־יַיִן
וְנִסְבְּאָה שֵׁכָר
וְהָיָה כָזֶה יוֹם מָחָר
גָּדוֹל יֶתֶר מְאֹד:

נז הַצַּדִּיק אָבָד
וְאֵין אִישׁ שָׂם עַל־לֵב
וְאַנְשֵׁי־חֶסֶד נֶאֱסָפִים
בְּאֵין מֵבִין
כִּי־מִפְּנֵי הָרָעָה נֶאֱסַף הַצַּדִּיק:

נז 10 צֹפָו

<table>
<tr><td>

2 He shall enter into peace;
  They shall rest in their beds,
  Each one walking *in* his uprightness.

3 "But come here,
  You sons of the sorceress,
  You offspring of the adulterer and the
  harlot!

4 Whom do you ridicule?
  Against whom do you make a wide mouth
  And stick out the tongue?
  Are you not children of transgression,
  Offspring of falsehood,

5 Inflaming yourselves with gods under every
  green tree,
  Slaying the children in the valleys,
  Under the clefts of the rocks?

6 Among the smooth *stones* of the stream
  Is your portion;
  They, they, *are* your lot!
  Even to them you have poured a drink
  offering,
  You have offered a grain offering.
  Should I receive comfort in these?

7 "On a lofty and high mountain
  You have set your bed;
  Even there you went up
  To offer sacrifice.

8 Also behind the doors and their posts
  You have set up your remembrance;
  For you have uncovered yourself *to those
  other* than Me,
  And have gone up to them;
  You have enlarged your bed
  And made *a covenant* with them;
  You have loved their bed,
  Where you saw *their* nudity.

9 You went to the king with ointment,
  And increased your perfumes;
  You sent your messengers far off,
  And *even* descended to Sheol.

10 You are wearied in the length of your way;
  Yet you did not say, 'There is no hope.'
  You have found the life of your hand;
  Therefore you were not grieved.

11 "And of whom have you been afraid, or
  feared,
  That you have lied
  And not remembered Me,
  Nor taken *it* to your heart?
  Is it not because I have held My peace from
  of old
  That you do not fear Me?

12 I will declare your righteousness

</td><td dir="rtl">

2 יָבוֹא שָׁלוֹם
  יָנוּחוּ עַל־מִשְׁכְּבוֹתָם
  הֹלֵךְ נְכֹחוֹ:

3 וְאַתֶּם קִרְבוּ־הֵנָּה בְּנֵי עֹנְנָה
  זֶרַע מְנָאֵף וַתִּזְנֶה:

4 עַל־מִי תִּתְעַנָּגוּ
  עַל־מִי תַּרְחִיבוּ פֶה
  תַּאֲרִיכוּ לָשׁוֹן
  הֲלוֹא־אַתֶּם יִלְדֵי־פֶשַׁע
  זֶרַע שָׁקֶר:

5 הַנֵּחָמִים בָּאֵלִים תַּחַת כָּל־עֵץ רַעֲנָן
  שֹׁחֲטֵי הַיְלָדִים בַּנְּחָלִים
  תַּחַת סְעִפֵי הַסְּלָעִים:

6 בְּחַלְּקֵי־נַחַל חֶלְקֵךְ
  הֵם הֵם גּוֹרָלֵךְ
  גַּם־לָהֶם שָׁפַכְתְּ נֶסֶךְ
  הֶעֱלִית מִנְחָה
  הַעַל אֵלֶּה אֶנָּחֵם:

7 עַל הַר־גָּבֹהַּ וְנִשָּׂא
  שַׂמְתְּ מִשְׁכָּבֵךְ
  גַּם־שָׁם עָלִית לִזְבֹּחַ זָבַח:

8 וְאַחַר הַדֶּלֶת וְהַמְּזוּזָה
  שַׂמְתְּ זִכְרוֹנֵךְ
  כִּי מֵאִתִּי גִּלִּית וַתַּעֲלִי
  הִרְחַבְתְּ מִשְׁכָּבֵךְ
  וַתִּכְרָת־לָךְ מֵהֶם
  אָהַבְתְּ מִשְׁכָּבָם יָד חָזִית:

9 וַתָּשֻׁרִי לַמֶּלֶךְ בַּשֶּׁמֶן
  וַתַּרְבִּי רִקֻּחָיִךְ
  וַתְּשַׁלְּחִי צִירַיִךְ עַד־מֵרָחֹק
  וַתַּשְׁפִּילִי עַד־שְׁאוֹל:

10 בְּרֹב דַּרְכֵּךְ יָגַעַתְּ
  לֹא אָמַרְתְּ נוֹאָשׁ
  חַיַּת יָדֵךְ מָצָאת
  עַל־כֵּן לֹא חָלִית:

11 וְאֶת־מִי דָּאַגְתְּ וַתִּירְאִי
  כִּי תְכַזֵּבִי
  וְאוֹתִי לֹא זָכַרְתְּ
  לֹא־שַׂמְתְּ עַל־לִבֵּךְ
  הֲלֹא אֲנִי מַחְשֶׁה וּמֵעֹלָם
  וְאוֹתִי לֹא תִירָאִי:

12 אֲנִי אַגִּיד צִדְקָתֵךְ

</td></tr>
</table>

And your works,
For they will not profit you.

13 When you cry out,
Let your collection *of idols* deliver you.
But the wind will carry them all away,
A breath will take *them*.
But he who puts his trust in Me shall possess
　　the land,
And shall inherit My holy mountain."

14 And one shall say,
"Heap it up! Heap it up!
Prepare the way,
Take the stumbling block out of the way of
　　My people."

15 For thus says the High and Lofty One
Who inhabits eternity, whose name *is* Holy:
"I dwell in the high and holy *place,*
With him *who* has a contrite and humble
　　spirit,
To revive the spirit of the humble,
And to revive the heart of the contrite ones.

16 For I will not contend forever,
Nor will I always be angry;
For the spirit would fail before Me,
And the souls *which* I have made.

17 For the iniquity of his covetousness
I was angry and struck him;
I hid and was angry,
And he went on backsliding in the way of his
　　heart.

18 I have seen his ways, and will heal him;
I will also lead him,
And restore comforts to him
And to his mourners.

19 "I create the fruit of the lips:
Peace, peace to *him who is* far off and to *him
　　who is* near,"
Says the LORD,
"And I will heal him."

20 But the wicked *are* like the troubled sea,
When it cannot rest,
Whose waters cast up mire and dirt.

21 "*There is* no peace,"
Says my God, "for the wicked."

58 "Cry aloud, spare not;
Lift up your voice like a trumpet;
Tell My people their transgression,
And the house of Jacob their sins.

2 Yet they seek Me daily,
And delight to know My ways,
As a nation that did righteousness,

וְאֶת־מַעֲשַׂיִךְ וְלֹא יוֹעִילוּךְ׃

13 בְּזַעֲקֵךְ יַצִּילֻךְ קִבּוּצַיִךְ
וְאֶת־כֻּלָּם יִשָּׂא־רוּחַ יִקַּח־הָבֶל
וְהַחוֹסֶה בִי יִנְחַל־אֶרֶץ
וְיִירַשׁ הַר־קָדְשִׁי׃

14 וְאָמַר סֹלּוּ־סֹלּוּ פַּנּוּ־דָרֶךְ
הָרִימוּ מִכְשׁוֹל מִדֶּרֶךְ עַמִּי׃ ס

15 כִּי כֹה אָמַר רָם וְנִשָּׂא
שֹׁכֵן עַד וְקָדוֹשׁ שְׁמוֹ
מָרוֹם וְקָדוֹשׁ אֶשְׁכּוֹן
וְאֶת־דַּכָּא וּשְׁפַל־רוּחַ
לְהַחֲיוֹת רוּחַ שְׁפָלִים
וּלְהַחֲיוֹת לֵב נִדְכָּאִים׃

16 כִּי לֹא לְעוֹלָם אָרִיב
וְלֹא לָנֶצַח אֶקְצוֹף
כִּי־רוּחַ מִלְּפָנַי יַעֲטוֹף
וּנְשָׁמוֹת אֲנִי עָשִׂיתִי׃

17 בַּעֲוֹן בִּצְעוֹ
קָצַפְתִּי וְאַכֵּהוּ הַסְתֵּר וְאֶקְצֹף
וַיֵּלֶךְ שׁוֹבָב בְּדֶרֶךְ לִבּוֹ׃

18 דְּרָכָיו רָאִיתִי וְאֶרְפָּאֵהוּ
וְאַנְחֵהוּ וַאֲשַׁלֵּם נִחֻמִים לוֹ וְלַאֲבֵלָיו׃

19 בּוֹרֵא נוב שְׂפָתָיִם
שָׁלוֹם ׀ שָׁלוֹם לָרָחוֹק וְלַקָּרוֹב
אָמַר יְהֹוָה וּרְפָאתִיו׃

20 וְהָרְשָׁעִים כַּיָּם נִגְרָשׁ
כִּי הַשְׁקֵט לֹא יוּכָל
וַיִּגְרְשׁוּ מֵימָיו רֶפֶשׁ וָטִיט׃

21 אֵין שָׁלוֹם
אָמַר אֱלֹהַי לָרְשָׁעִים׃ ס

נח קְרָא בְגָרוֹן אַל־תַּחְשֹׂךְ
כַּשּׁוֹפָר הָרֵם קוֹלֶךָ
וְהַגֵּד לְעַמִּי פִּשְׁעָם
וּלְבֵית יַעֲקֹב חַטֹּאתָם׃

2 וְאוֹתִי יוֹם יוֹם יִדְרֹשׁוּן
וְדַעַת דְּרָכַי יֶחְפָּצוּן
כְּגוֹי אֲשֶׁר־צְדָקָה עָשָׂה

And did not forsake the ordinance of their
  God.
They ask of Me the ordinances of justice;
They take delight in approaching God.
3 'Why have we fasted,' *they say,* 'and You
  have not seen?
Why have we afflicted our souls, and You
  take no notice?'

"In fact, in the day of your fast you find
  pleasure,
And exploit all your laborers.
4 Indeed you fast for strife and debate,
And to strike with the fist of wickedness.
You will not fast as *you do* this day,
To make your voice heard on high.
5 Is it a fast that I have chosen,
A day for a man to afflict his soul?
Is it to bow down his head like a bulrush,
And to spread out sackcloth and ashes?
Would you call this a fast,
And an acceptable day to the LORD?

6 "*Is* this not the fast that I have chosen:
To loose the bonds of wickedness,
To undo the heavy burdens,
To let the oppressed go free,
And that you break every yoke?
7 *Is it* not to share your bread with the hungry,
And that you bring to your house the poor
  who are cast out;
When you see the naked, that you cover him,
And not hide yourself from your own flesh?
8 Then your light shall break forth like the
  morning,
Your healing shall spring forth speedily,
And your righteousness shall go before you;
The glory of the LORD shall be your rear
  guard.
9 Then you shall call, and the LORD will
  answer;
You shall cry, and He will say, 'Here I *am.*'

"If you take away the yoke from your midst,
The pointing of the finger, and speaking
  wickedness,
10 *If* you extend your soul to the hungry
And satisfy the afflicted soul,
Then your light shall dawn in the darkness,
And your darkness shall *be* as the noonday.
11 The LORD will guide you continually,
And satisfy your soul in drought,
And strengthen your bones;
You shall be like a watered garden,
And like a spring of water, whose waters do
  not fail.

וּמִשְׁפַּט אֱלֹהָיו לֹא עָזָב
יִשְׁאָלוּנִי מִשְׁפְּטֵי־צֶדֶק
קִרְבַת אֱלֹהִים יֶחְפָּצוּן:
3 לָמָּה צַּמְנוּ וְלֹא רָאִיתָ
עִנִּינוּ נַפְשֵׁנוּ וְלֹא תֵדָע
הֵן בְּיוֹם צֹמְכֶם תִּמְצְאוּ־חֵפֶץ
וְכָל־עַצְּבֵיכֶם תִּנְגֹּשׂוּ:
4 הֵן לְרִיב וּמַצָּה תָּצוּמוּ
וּלְהַכּוֹת בְּאֶגְרֹף רֶשַׁע
לֹא־תָצוּמוּ כַיּוֹם
לְהַשְׁמִיעַ בַּמָּרוֹם קוֹלְכֶם:
5 הֲכָזֶה יִהְיֶה צוֹם אֶבְחָרֵהוּ
יוֹם עַנּוֹת אָדָם נַפְשׁוֹ
הֲלָכֹף כְּאַגְמֹן רֹאשׁוֹ וְשַׂק וָאֵפֶר יַצִּיעַ
הֲלָזֶה תִּקְרָא־צוֹם
וְיוֹם רָצוֹן לַיהֹוָה:
6 הֲלוֹא זֶה צוֹם אֶבְחָרֵהוּ
פַּתֵּחַ חַרְצֻבּוֹת רֶשַׁע
הַתֵּר אֲגֻדּוֹת מוֹטָה
וְשַׁלַּח רְצוּצִים חָפְשִׁים
וְכָל־מוֹטָה תְּנַתֵּקוּ:
7 הֲלוֹא פָרֹס לָרָעֵב לַחְמֶךָ
וַעֲנִיִּים מְרוּדִים תָּבִיא בָיִת
כִּי־תִרְאֶה עָרֹם וְכִסִּיתוֹ
וּמִבְּשָׂרְךָ לֹא תִתְעַלָּם:
8 אָז יִבָּקַע כַּשַּׁחַר אוֹרֶךָ
וַאֲרֻכָתְךָ מְהֵרָה תִצְמָח
וְהָלַךְ לְפָנֶיךָ צִדְקֶךָ
כְּבוֹד יְהֹוָה יַאַסְפֶךָ:
9 אָז תִּקְרָא וַיהֹוָה יַעֲנֶה
תְּשַׁוַּע וְיֹאמַר הִנֵּנִי
אִם־תָּסִיר מִתּוֹכְךָ מוֹטָה
שְׁלַח אֶצְבַּע וְדַבֶּר־אָוֶן:
10 וְתָפֵק לָרָעֵב נַפְשֶׁךָ
וְנֶפֶשׁ נַעֲנָה תַּשְׂבִּיעַ
וְזָרַח בַּחֹשֶׁךְ אוֹרֶךָ
וַאֲפֵלָתְךָ כַּצָּהֳרָיִם:
11 וְנָחֲךָ יְהֹוָה תָּמִיד
וְהִשְׂבִּיעַ בְּצַחְצָחוֹת נַפְשֶׁךָ
וְעַצְמֹתֶיךָ יַחֲלִיץ
וְהָיִיתָ כְּגַן רָוֶה
וּכְמוֹצָא מַיִם אֲשֶׁר לֹא־יְכַזְּבוּ מֵימָיו:

12 Those from among you
Shall build the old waste places;
You shall raise up the foundations of many
generations;
And you shall be called the Repairer of the
Breach,
The Restorer of Streets to Dwell In.

13 "If you turn away your foot from the
Sabbath,
From doing your pleasure on My holy day,
And call the Sabbath a delight,
The holy *day* of the LORD honorable,
And shall honor Him, not doing your own
ways,
Nor finding your own pleasure,
Nor speaking *your own* words,

14 Then you shall delight yourself in the LORD;
And I will cause you to ride on the high hills
of the earth,
And feed you with the heritage of Jacob your
father.
The mouth of the LORD has spoken."

59 Behold, the LORD's hand is not shortened,
That it cannot save;
Nor His ear heavy,
That it cannot hear.

2 But your iniquities have separated you from
your God;
And your sins have hidden *His* face from
you,
So that He will not hear.

3 For your hands are defiled with blood,
And your fingers with iniquity;
Your lips have spoken lies,
Your tongue has muttered perversity.

4 No one calls for justice,
Nor does *any* plead for truth.
They trust in empty words and speak lies;
They conceive evil and bring forth iniquity.

5 They hatch vipers' eggs and weave the
spider's web;
He who eats of their eggs dies,
And *from* that which is crushed a viper
breaks out.

6 Their webs will not become garments,
Nor will they cover themselves with their
works;
Their works *are* works of iniquity,
And the act of violence *is* in their hands.

7 Their feet run to evil,
And they make haste to shed innocent blood;

וּבָנ֤וּ מִמְּךָ֙ חָרְב֣וֹת עוֹלָ֔ם 12
מוֹסְדֵ֥י דוֹר־וָד֖וֹר תְּקוֹמֵ֑ם
וְקֹרָ֤א לְךָ֙ גֹּדֵ֣ר פֶּ֔רֶץ
מְשֹׁבֵ֥ב נְתִיב֖וֹת לָשָֽׁבֶת׃
אִם־תָּשִׁ֤יב מִשַּׁבָּת֙ רַגְלֶ֔ךָ 13
עֲשׂ֥וֹת חֲפָצֶ֖ךָ בְּי֣וֹם קָדְשִׁ֑י
וְקָרָ֨אתָ לַשַּׁבָּ֜ת עֹ֗נֶג
לִקְד֤וֹשׁ יְהֹוָה֙ מְכֻבָּ֔ד
וְכִבַּדְתּוֹ֙ מֵעֲשׂ֣וֹת דְּרָכֶ֔יךָ
מִמְּצ֥וֹא חֶפְצְךָ֖ וְדַבֵּ֥ר דָּבָֽר׃
אָ֗ז תִּתְעַנַּג֙ עַל־יְהֹוָ֔ה 14
וְהִרְכַּבְתִּ֖יךָ עַל־בָּ֣מֳותֵ֥יʳ אָ֑רֶץ
וְהַאֲכַלְתִּ֗יךָ נַחֲלַת֙ יַעֲקֹ֣ב אָבִ֔יךָ
כִּ֛י פִּ֥י יְהֹוָ֖ה דִּבֵּֽר׃ ס

נט הֵ֤ן לֹֽא־קָצְרָה֙ יַד־יְהֹוָ֔ה מֵהוֹשִׁ֑יעַ
וְלֹא־כָבְדָ֥ה אָזְנ֖וֹ מִשְּׁמֽוֹעַ׃
כִּ֤י אִם־עֲוֺנֹֽתֵיכֶם֙ הָי֣וּ מַבְדִּלִ֔ים 2
בֵּינֵכֶ֕ם לְבֵ֖ין אֱלֹֽהֵיכֶ֑ם
וְחַטֹּֽאותֵיכֶ֗ם הִסְתִּ֧ירוּ פָנִ֛ים
מִכֶּ֖ם מִשְּׁמֽוֹעַ׃
כִּ֤י כַפֵּיכֶם֙ נְגֹאֲל֣וּ בַדָּ֔ם 3
וְאֶצְבְּעֽוֹתֵיכֶ֖ם בֶּֽעָוֺ֑ן שִׂפְתֽוֹתֵיכֶם֙ דִּבְּרוּ־שֶׁ֔קֶר
לְשֽׁוֹנְכֶ֖ם עַוְלָ֥ה תֶהְגֶּֽה׃
אֵין־קֹרֵ֣א בְצֶ֔דֶק 4
וְאֵ֥ין נִשְׁפָּ֖ט בֶּאֱמוּנָ֑ה
בָּט֤וֹחַ עַל־תֹּ֙הוּ֙ וְדַבֶּר־שָׁ֔וְא
הָר֥וֹ עָמָ֖ל וְהוֹלֵ֥יד אָֽוֶן׃
בֵּיצֵ֤י צִפְעוֹנִי֙ בִּקֵּ֔עוּ 5
וְקוּרֵ֥י עַכָּבִ֖ישׁ יֶאֱרֹ֑גוּ
הָאֹכֵ֤ל מִבֵּֽיצֵיהֶם֙ יָמ֔וּת
וְהַזּוּרֶ֖ה תִּבָּקַ֥ע אֶפְעֶֽה׃
קֽוּרֵיהֶם֙ לֹא־יִהְי֣וּ לְבֶ֔גֶד 6
וְלֹ֥א יִתְכַּסּ֖וּ בְּמַֽעֲשֵׂיהֶ֑ם
מַֽעֲשֵׂיהֶם֙ מַֽעֲשֵׂי־אָ֔וֶן
וּפֹ֥עַל חָמָ֖ס בְּכַפֵּיהֶֽם׃
רַגְלֵיהֶם֙ לָרַ֣ע יָרֻ֔צוּ 7
וִֽימַהֲר֔וּ לִשְׁפֹּ֖ךְ דָּ֣ם נָקִ֑י

Their thoughts *are* thoughts of iniquity;
Wasting and destruction *are* in their paths.
8 The way of peace they have not known,
And *there is* no justice in their ways;
They have made themselves crooked paths;
Whoever takes that way shall not know
    peace.

9 Therefore justice is far from us,
Nor does righteousness overtake us;
We look for light, but there is darkness!
For brightness, *but* we walk in blackness!
10 We grope for the wall like the blind,
And we grope as if *we had* no eyes;
We stumble at noonday as at twilight;
We are as dead *men* in desolate places.
11 We all growl like bears,
And moan sadly like doves;
We look for justice, but *there is* none;
For salvation, *but* it is far from us.
12 For our transgressions are multiplied before
    You,
And our sins testify against us;
For our transgressions *are* with us,
And *as for* our iniquities, we know them:
13 In transgressing and lying against the LORD,
And departing from our God,
Speaking oppression and revolt,
Conceiving and uttering from the heart
    words of falsehood.
14 Justice is turned back,
And righteousness stands afar off;
For truth is fallen in the street,
And equity cannot enter.
15 So truth fails,
And he *who* departs from evil makes himself
    a prey.

Then the LORD saw *it*, and it displeased Him
That *there was* no justice.
16 He saw that *there was* no man,
And wondered that *there was* no intercessor;
Therefore His own arm brought salvation for
    Him;
And His own righteousness, it sustained
    Him.
17 For He put on righteousness as a breastplate,
And a helmet of salvation on His head;
He put on the garments of vengeance for
    clothing,
And was clad with zeal as a cloak.
18 According to *their* deeds, accordingly He will
    repay,
Fury to His adversaries,
Recompense to His enemies;

מַחְשְׁבוֹתֵיהֶם מַחְשְׁבוֹת אָוֶן
שֹׁד וָשֶׁבֶר בִּמְסִלּוֹתָם׃
8 דֶּרֶךְ שָׁלוֹם לֹא יָדָעוּ
וְאֵין מִשְׁפָּט בְּמַעְגְּלוֹתָם
נְתִיבוֹתֵיהֶם עִקְּשׁוּ לָהֶם
כֹּל דֹּרֵךְ בָּהּ לֹא יָדַע שָׁלוֹם׃
9 עַל־כֵּן רָחַק מִשְׁפָּט מִמֶּנּוּ
וְלֹא תַשִּׂיגֵנוּ צְדָקָה
נְקַוֶּה לָאוֹר וְהִנֵּה־חֹשֶׁךְ
לִנְגֹהוֹת בָּאֲפֵלוֹת נְהַלֵּךְ׃
10 נְגַשְׁשָׁה כַעִוְרִים קִיר
וּכְאֵין עֵינַיִם נְגַשֵּׁשָׁה
כָּשַׁלְנוּ בַצָּהֳרַיִם כַּנֶּשֶׁף
בָּאַשְׁמַנִּים כַּמֵּתִים׃
11 נֶהֱמֶה כַדֻּבִּים כֻּלָּנוּ
וְכַיּוֹנִים הָגֹה נֶהְגֶּה
נְקַוֶּה לַמִּשְׁפָּט וָאַיִן
לִישׁוּעָה רָחֲקָה מִמֶּנּוּ׃
12 כִּי־רַבּוּ פְשָׁעֵינוּ נֶגְדֶּךָ
וְחַטֹּאותֵינוּ עָנְתָה בָּנוּ
כִּי־פְשָׁעֵינוּ אִתָּנוּ וַעֲוֹנֹתֵינוּ יְדַעֲנוּם׃
13 פָּשֹׁעַ וְכַחֵשׁ בַּיהֹוָה
וְנָסוֹג מֵאַחַר אֱלֹהֵינוּ
דַּבֶּר־עֹשֶׁק וְסָרָה
הֹרוֹ וְהֹגוֹ מִלֵּב דִּבְרֵי־שָׁקֶר׃
14 וְהֻסַּג אָחוֹר מִשְׁפָּט
וּצְדָקָה מֵרָחוֹק תַּעֲמֹד
כִּי־כָשְׁלָה בָרְחוֹב אֱמֶת
וּנְכֹחָה לֹא־תוּכַל לָבוֹא׃
15 וַתְּהִי הָאֱמֶת נֶעְדֶּרֶת
וְסָר מֵרָע מִשְׁתּוֹלֵל
וַיַּרְא יְהֹוָה וַיֵּרַע בְּעֵינָיו כִּי־אֵין מִשְׁפָּט׃
16 וַיַּרְא כִּי־אֵין אִישׁ
וַיִּשְׁתּוֹמֵם כִּי אֵין מַפְגִּיעַ
וַתּוֹשַׁע לוֹ זְרֹעוֹ וְצִדְקָתוֹ הִיא סְמָכָתְהוּ׃
17 וַיִּלְבַּשׁ צְדָקָה כַּשִּׁרְיָן
וְכוֹבַע יְשׁוּעָה בְּרֹאשׁוֹ
וַיִּלְבַּשׁ בִּגְדֵי נָקָם תִּלְבֹּשֶׁת
וַיַּעַט כַּמְעִיל קִנְאָה׃
18 כְּעַל גְּמֻלוֹת כְּעַל יְשַׁלֵּם
חֵמָה לְצָרָיו גְּמוּל לְאֹיְבָיו
לָאִיִּים גְּמוּל יְשַׁלֵּם׃

The coastlands He will fully repay.

19 So shall they fear
The name of the LORD from the west,
And His glory from the rising of the sun;
When the enemy comes in like a flood,
The Spirit of the LORD will lift up a standard
against him.

20 "The Redeemer will come to Zion,
And to those who turn from transgression in
Jacob,"
Says the LORD.

21 "As for Me," says the LORD, "this *is* My
covenant with them: My Spirit who *is* upon you,
and My words which I have put in your mouth,
shall not depart from your mouth, nor from the
mouth of your descendants, nor from the mouth of
your descendants' descendants," says the LORD,
"from this time and forevermore."

60 Arise, shine;
For your light has come!
And the glory of the LORD is risen upon you.

2 For behold, the darkness shall cover the
earth,
And deep darkness the people;
But the LORD will arise over you,
And His glory will be seen upon you.

3 The Gentiles shall come to your light,
And kings to the brightness of your rising.

4 "Lift up your eyes all around, and see:
They all gather together, they come to you;
Your sons shall come from afar,
And your daughters shall be nursed at *your*
side.

5 Then you shall see and become radiant,
And your heart shall swell with joy;
Because the abundance of the sea shall be
turned to you,
The wealth of the Gentiles shall come to you.

6 The multitude of camels shall cover your
land,
The dromedaries of Midian and Ephah;
All those from Sheba shall come;
They shall bring gold and incense,
And they shall proclaim the praises of the
LORD.

7 All the flocks of Kedar shall be gathered
together to you,
The rams of Nebaioth shall minister to you;
They shall ascend with acceptance on My
altar,
And I will glorify the house of My glory.

19 וְיִֽירְא֤וּ מִֽמַּעֲרָב֙ אֶת־שֵׁ֣ם יְהוָ֔ה
וּמִמִּזְרַח־שֶׁ֖מֶשׁ אֶת־כְּבוֹד֑וֹ
כִּֽי־יָב֤וֹא כַנָּהָר֙ צָ֔ר
ר֥וּחַ יְהוָ֖ה נֹ֥סְסָה בֽוֹ׃

20 וּבָ֤א לְצִיּוֹן֙ גּוֹאֵ֔ל וּלְשָׁבֵ֥י פֶ֖שַׁע בְּיַעֲקֹ֑ב
נְאֻ֖ם יְהוָֽה׃

21 וַאֲנִ֗י זֹ֣את בְּרִיתִ֤י אוֹתָם֙ אָמַ֣ר יְהוָ֔ה
רוּחִי֙ אֲשֶׁ֣ר עָלֶ֔יךָ וּדְבָרַ֖י אֲשֶׁר־שַׂ֣מְתִּי בְּפִ֑יךָ לֹֽא־
יָמ֡וּשׁוּ מִפִּ֩יךָ֩ וּמִפִּ֨י זַרְעֲךָ֜ וּמִפִּ֨י זֶ֤רַע זַרְעֲךָ֙ אָמַ֣ר
יְהוָ֔ה מֵעַתָּ֖ה וְעַד־עוֹלָֽם׃ ס

ס 1 ק֥וּמִי א֖וֹרִי כִּ֣י בָ֣א אוֹרֵ֑ךְ
וּכְב֥וֹד יְהוָ֖ה עָלַ֥יִךְ זָרָֽח׃

2 כִּֽי־הִנֵּ֤ה הַחֹ֙שֶׁךְ֙ יְכַסֶּה־אֶ֔רֶץ
וַעֲרָפֶ֖ל לְאֻמִּ֑ים
וְעָלַ֙יִךְ֙ יִזְרַ֣ח יְהוָ֔ה
וּכְבוֹד֖וֹ עָלַ֥יִךְ יֵרָאֶֽה׃

3 וְהָלְכ֥וּ גוֹיִ֖ם לְאוֹרֵ֑ךְ
וּמְלָכִ֖ים לְנֹ֥גַהּ זַרְחֵֽךְ׃

4 שְׂאִֽי־סָבִ֤יב עֵינַ֙יִךְ֙ וּרְאִ֔י
כֻּלָּ֖ם נִקְבְּצ֣וּ בָֽאוּ־לָ֑ךְ
בָּנַ֙יִךְ֙ מֵרָח֣וֹק יָבֹ֔אוּ
וּבְנֹתַ֖יִךְ עַל־צַ֥ד תֵּאָמַֽנָה׃

5 אָ֤ז תִּרְאִי֙ וְנָהַ֔רְתְּ
וּפָחַ֥ד וְרָחַ֖ב לְבָבֵ֑ךְ
כִּֽי־יֵהָפֵ֤ךְ עָלַ֙יִךְ֙ הֲמ֣וֹן יָ֔ם
חֵ֥יל גּוֹיִ֖ם יָבֹ֥אוּ לָֽךְ׃

6 שִֽׁפְעַ֨ת גְּמַלִּ֜ים תְּכַסֵּ֗ךְ
בִּכְרֵ֤י מִדְיָן֙ וְעֵיפָ֔ה
כֻּלָּ֖ם מִשְּׁבָ֣א יָבֹ֑אוּ
זָהָ֤ב וּלְבוֹנָה֙ יִשָּׂ֔אוּ
וּתְהִלֹּ֥ת יְהוָ֖ה יְבַשֵּֽׂרוּ׃

7 כָּל־צֹ֤אן קֵדָר֙ יִקָּ֣בְצוּ לָ֔ךְ
אֵילֵ֥י נְבָי֖וֹת יְשָׁרְת֑וּנֶךְ
יַעֲל֤וּ עַל־רָצוֹן֙ מִזְבְּחִ֔י
וּבֵ֥ית תִּפְאַרְתִּ֖י אֲפָאֵֽר׃

8 "Who *are* these *who* fly like a cloud,
  And like doves to their roosts?
9 Surely the coastlands shall wait for Me;
  And the ships of Tarshish *will come* first,
  To bring your sons from afar,
  Their silver and their gold with them,
  To the name of the LORD your God,
  And to the Holy One of Israel,
  Because He has glorified you.

10 "The sons of foreigners shall build up your
     walls,
  And their kings shall minister to you;
  For in My wrath I struck you,
  But in My favor I have had mercy on you.
11 Therefore your gates shall be open continu-
     ally;
  They shall not be shut day or night,
  That *men* may bring to you the wealth of the
     Gentiles,
  And their kings in procession.
12 For the nation and kingdom which will not
     serve you shall perish,
  And *those* nations shall be utterly ruined.

13 "The glory of Lebanon shall come to you,
  The cypress, the pine, and the box tree
     together,
  To beautify the place of My sanctuary;
  And I will make the place of My feet
     glorious.
14 Also the sons of those who afflicted you
  Shall come bowing to you,
  And all those who despised you shall fall
     prostrate at the soles of your feet;
  And they shall call you The City of the
     LORD,
  Zion of the Holy One of Israel.

15 "Whereas you have been forsaken and hated,
  So that no one went through *you,*
  I will make you an eternal excellence,
  A joy of many generations.
16 You shall drink the milk of the Gentiles,
  And milk the breast of kings;
  You shall know that I, the LORD, *am* your
     Savior
  And your Redeemer, the Mighty One of
     Jacob.

17 "Instead of bronze I will bring gold,
  Instead of iron I will bring silver,
  Instead of wood, bronze,
  And instead of stones, iron.
  I will also make your officers peace,
  And your magistrates righteousness.

8 מִי־אֵ֖לֶּה כָּעָ֣ב תְּעוּפֶ֑ינָה
וְכַיּוֹנִ֖ים אֶל־אֲרֻבֹּתֵיהֶֽם׃
9 כִּֽי־לִ֣י ׀ אִיִּ֣ים יְקַוּ֗וּ
וׇאֳנִיּ֤וֹת תַּרְשִׁישׁ֙ בָּרִ֣אשֹׁנָ֔ה
לְהָבִ֤יא בָנַ֨יִךְ֙ מֵֽרָח֔וֹק
כַּסְפָּ֥ם וּזְהָבָ֖ם אִתָּ֑ם
לְשֵׁם֙ יְהֹוָ֣ה אֱלֹהַ֔יִךְ
וְלִקְד֥וֹשׁ יִשְׂרָאֵ֖ל כִּ֥י פֵֽאֲרָֽךְ׃
10 וּבָנ֤וּ בְנֵֽי־נֵכָר֙ חֹמֹתַ֔יִךְ
וּמַלְכֵיהֶ֖ם יְשָׁרְת֑וּנֶךְ
כִּ֤י בְקִצְפִּי֙ הִכִּיתִ֔יךְ
וּבִרְצוֹנִ֖י רִֽחַמְתִּֽיךְ׃
11 וּפִתְּח֨וּ שְׁעָרַ֜יִךְ תָּמִ֗יד
יוֹמָ֧ם וָלַ֛יְלָה לֹ֥א יִסָּגֵ֖רוּ
לְהָבִ֤יא אֵלַ֨יִךְ֙ חֵ֣יל גּוֹיִ֔ם
וּמַלְכֵיהֶ֖ם נְהוּגִֽים׃
12 כִּֽי־הַגּ֧וֹי וְהַמַּמְלָכָ֛ה
אֲשֶׁ֥ר לֹא־יַעַבְד֖וּךְ יֹאבֵ֑דוּ
וְהַגּוֹיִ֖ם חָרֹ֥ב יֶחֱרָֽבוּ׃
13 כְּב֤וֹד הַלְּבָנוֹן֙ אֵלַ֣יִךְ יָב֔וֹא
בְּר֛וֹשׁ תִּדְהָ֥ר וּתְאַשּׁ֖וּר יַחְדָּ֑ו
לְפָאֵר֙ מְק֣וֹם מִקְדָּשִׁ֔י
וּמְק֥וֹם רַגְלַ֖י אֲכַבֵּֽד׃
14 וְהָלְכ֨וּ אֵלַ֤יִךְ שְׁח֨וֹחַ֙ בְּנֵ֣י מְעַנַּ֔יִךְ
וְהִֽשְׁתַּחֲו֛וּ
עַל־כַּפּ֥וֹת רַגְלַ֖יִךְ כׇּל־מְנַֽאֲצָ֑יִךְ
וְקָ֤רְאוּ לָךְ֙ עִ֣יר יְהֹוָ֔ה
צִיּ֖וֹן קְד֥וֹשׁ יִשְׂרָאֵֽל׃
15 תַּ֧חַת הֱיוֹתֵ֣ךְ
עֲזוּבָ֣ה וּשְׂנוּאָ֗ה וְאֵ֣ין עוֹבֵ֔ר
וְשַׂמְתִּיךְ֙ לִגְא֣וֹן עוֹלָ֔ם
מְשׂ֖וֹשׂ דּ֥וֹר וָדֽוֹר׃
16 וְיָנַקְתְּ֙ חֲלֵ֣ב גּוֹיִ֔ם
וְשֹׁ֥ד מְלָכִ֖ים תִּינָ֑קִי
וְיָדַ֗עַתְּ כִּ֣י אֲנִ֤י יְהֹוָה֙ מֽוֹשִׁיעֵ֔ךְ
וְגֹאֲלֵ֖ךְ אֲבִ֥יר יַעֲקֹֽב׃
17 תַּ֣חַת הַנְּחֹ֜שֶׁת אָבִ֣יא זָהָ֗ב
וְתַ֤חַת הַבַּרְזֶל֙ אָבִ֣יא כֶ֔סֶף
וְתַ֤חַת הָֽעֵצִים֙ נְחֹ֔שֶׁת
וְתַ֖חַת הָאֲבָנִ֣ים בַּרְזֶ֑ל
וְשַׂמְתִּ֤י פְקֻדָּתֵךְ֙ שָׁל֔וֹם
וְנֹגְשַׂ֖יִךְ צְדָקָֽה׃

18 Violence shall no longer be heard in your
    land,
Neither wasting nor destruction within your
    borders;
But you shall call your walls Salvation,
And your gates Praise.

19 "The sun shall no longer be your light by day,
Nor for brightness shall the moon give light
    to you;
But the LORD will be to you an everlasting
    light,
And your God your glory.

20 Your sun shall no longer go down,
Nor shall your moon withdraw itself;
For the LORD will be your everlasting light,
And the days of your mourning shall be
    ended.

21 Also your people *shall* all *be* righteous;
They shall inherit the land forever,
The branch of My planting,
The work of My hands,
That I may be glorified.

22 A little one shall become a thousand,
And a small one a strong nation.
I, the LORD, will hasten it in its time."

61 "The Spirit of the Lord GOD *is* upon Me,
Because the LORD has anointed Me
To preach good tidings to the poor;
He has sent Me to heal the brokenhearted,
To proclaim liberty to the captives,
And the opening of the prison to *those who
    are* bound;

2 To proclaim the acceptable year of the LORD,
And the day of vengeance of our God;
To comfort all who mourn,

3 To console those who mourn in Zion,
To give them beauty for ashes,
The oil of joy for mourning,
The garment of praise for the spirit of
    heaviness;
That they may be called trees of right-
    eousness,
The planting of the LORD, that He may be
    glorified."

4 And they shall rebuild the old ruins,
They shall raise up the former desolations,
And they shall repair the ruined cities,
The desolations of many generations.

5 Strangers shall stand and feed your flocks,
And the sons of the foreigner
Shall be your plowmen and your vinedres-
    sers.

18 לֹא־יִשָּׁמַע עוֹד חָמָס בְּאַרְצֵךְ
שֹׁד וָשֶׁבֶר בִּגְבוּלָיִךְ
וְקָרָאת יְשׁוּעָה חוֹמֹתַיִךְ
וּשְׁעָרַיִךְ תְּהִלָּה:
19 לֹא־יִהְיֶה־לָּךְ
עוֹד הַשֶּׁמֶשׁ לְאוֹר יוֹמָם
וּלְנֹגַהּ הַיָּרֵחַ לֹא־יָאִיר לָךְ
וְהָיָה־לָךְ יְהוָה לְאוֹר עוֹלָם
וֵאלֹהַיִךְ לְתִפְאַרְתֵּךְ:
20 לֹא־יָבוֹא עוֹד שִׁמְשֵׁךְ
וִירֵחֵךְ לֹא יֵאָסֵף
כִּי יְהוָה יִהְיֶה־לָּךְ לְאוֹר עוֹלָם
וְשָׁלְמוּ יְמֵי אֶבְלֵךְ:
21 וְעַמֵּךְ כֻּלָּם צַדִּיקִים
לְעוֹלָם יִירְשׁוּ אָרֶץ
נֵצֶר מַטָּעַו‬
מַעֲשֵׂה יָדַי לְהִתְפָּאֵר:
22 הַקָּטֹן יִהְיֶה לָאֶלֶף
וְהַצָּעִיר לְגוֹי עָצוּם
אֲנִי יְהוָה בְּעִתָּהּ אֲחִישֶׁנָּה: ס

61 רוּחַ אֲדֹנָי יְהוִה עָלָי
יַעַן מָשַׁח יְהוָה אֹתִי
לְבַשֵּׂר עֲנָוִים
שְׁלָחַנִי לַחֲבֹשׁ לְנִשְׁבְּרֵי־לֵב
לִקְרֹא לִשְׁבוּיִם דְּרוֹר
וְלַאֲסוּרִים פְּקַח־קוֹחַ:
2 לִקְרֹא שְׁנַת־רָצוֹן לַיהוָה
וְיוֹם נָקָם לֵאלֹהֵינוּ
לְנַחֵם כָּל־אֲבֵלִים:
3 לָשׂוּם | לַאֲבֵלֵי צִיּוֹן
לָתֵת לָהֶם פְּאֵר תַּחַת אֵפֶר
שֶׁמֶן שָׂשׂוֹן תַּחַת אֵבֶל
מַעֲטֵה תְהִלָּה תַּחַת רוּחַ כֵּהָה
וְקֹרָא לָהֶם אֵילֵי הַצֶּדֶק
מַטַּע יְהוָה לְהִתְפָּאֵר:
4 וּבָנוּ חָרְבוֹת עוֹלָם
שֹׁמְמוֹת רִאשֹׁנִים יְקוֹמֵמוּ
וְחִדְּשׁוּ עָרֵי חֹרֶב
שֹׁמְמוֹת דּוֹר וָדוֹר:
5 וְעָמְדוּ זָרִים וְרָעוּ צֹאנְכֶם
וּבְנֵי נֵכָר אִכָּרֵיכֶם וְכֹרְמֵיכֶם:

ס 21 מַטָּעַי

⁶ But you shall be named the priests of the
    LORD,
    They shall call you the servants of our God.
    You shall eat the riches of the Gentiles,
    And in their glory you shall boast.
⁷ Instead of your shame *you shall have* double
    honor,
    And *instead of* confusion they shall rejoice in
    their portion.
    Therefore in their land they shall possess
    double;
    Everlasting joy shall be theirs.

⁸ "For I, the LORD, love justice;
    I hate robbery for burnt offering;
    I will direct their work in truth,
    And will make with them an everlasting
    covenant.
⁹ Their descendants shall be known among the
    Gentiles,
    And their offspring among the people.
    All who see them shall acknowledge them,
    That they *are* the posterity *whom* the LORD
    has blessed."

¹⁰ I will greatly rejoice in the LORD,
    My soul shall be joyful in my God;
    For He has clothed me with the garments of
    salvation,
    He has covered me with the robe of
    righteousness,
    As a bridegroom decks *himself* with
    ornaments,
    And as a bride adorns *herself* with her jewels.
¹¹ For as the earth brings forth its bud,
    As the garden causes the things that are sown
    in it to spring forth,
    So the Lord GOD will cause righteousness
    and praise to spring forth before all the
    nations.

62 For Zion's sake I will not hold My peace,
    And for Jerusalem's sake I will not rest,
    Until her righteousness goes forth as bright-
    ness,
    And her salvation as a lamp *that* burns.
² The Gentiles shall see your righteousness,
    And all kings your glory.
    You shall be called by a new name,
    Which the mouth of the LORD will name.
³ You shall also be a crown of glory
    In the hand of the LORD,
    And a royal diadem
    In the hand of your God.
⁴ You shall no longer be termed Forsaken,

וְאַתֶּם כֹּהֲנֵי יְהוָה תִּקָּרֵאוּ   6
מְשָׁרְתֵי אֱלֹהֵינוּ יֵאָמֵר לָכֶם
חֵיל גּוֹיִם תֹּאכֵלוּ
וּבִכְבוֹדָם תִּתְיַמָּרוּ:
תַּחַת בָּשְׁתְּכֶם מִשְׁנֶה   7
וּכְלִמָּה יָרֹנּוּ חֶלְקָם
לָכֵן בְּאַרְצָם מִשְׁנֶה יִירָשׁוּ
שִׂמְחַת עוֹלָם תִּהְיֶה לָהֶם:
כִּי אֲנִי יְהוָה אֹהֵב מִשְׁפָּט   8
שֹׂנֵא גָזֵל בְּעוֹלָה
וְנָתַתִּי פְעֻלָּתָם בֶּאֱמֶת
וּבְרִית עוֹלָם אֶכְרוֹת לָהֶם:
וְנוֹדַע בַּגּוֹיִם זַרְעָם   9
וְצֶאֱצָאֵיהֶם בְּתוֹךְ הָעַמִּים
כָּל־רֹאֵיהֶם יַכִּירוּם
כִּי הֵם זֶרַע בֵּרַךְ יְהוָה: ס
שׂוֹשׂ אָשִׂישׂ בַּיהוָה   10
תָּגֵל נַפְשִׁי בֵּאלֹהַי
כִּי הִלְבִּישַׁנִי בִּגְדֵי־יֶשַׁע
מְעִיל צְדָקָה יְעָטָנִי
כֶּחָתָן יְכַהֵן פְּאֵר
וְכַכַּלָּה תַּעְדֶּה כֵלֶיהָ:
כִּי כָאָרֶץ תּוֹצִיא צִמְחָהּ   11
וּכְגַנָּה זֵרוּעֶיהָ תַצְמִיחַ
כֵּן | אֲדֹנָי יְהוִה
יַצְמִיחַ צְדָקָה וּתְהִלָּה
נֶגֶד כָּל־הַגּוֹיִם:

לְמַעַן צִיּוֹן לֹא אֶחֱשֶׁה   **סב**
וּלְמַעַן יְרוּשָׁלַםִ לֹא אֶשְׁקוֹט
עַד־יֵצֵא כַנֹּגַהּ צִדְקָהּ
וִישׁוּעָתָהּ כְּלַפִּיד יִבְעָר:
וְרָאוּ גוֹיִם צִדְקֵךְ   2
וְכָל־מְלָכִים כְּבוֹדֵךְ
וְקֹרָא לָךְ שֵׁם חָדָשׁ
אֲשֶׁר פִּי יְהוָה יִקֳּבֶנּוּ:
וְהָיִית עֲטֶרֶת תִּפְאֶרֶת בְּיַד־יְהוָה   3
וּצְנִיף^ק מְלוּכָה בְּכַף־אֱלֹהָיִךְ:
לֹא־יֵאָמֵר לָךְ עוֹד עֲזוּבָה   4

Nor shall your land any more be termed
　　Desolate;
But you shall be called Hephzibah, and your
　　land Beulah;
For the LORD delights in you,
And your land shall be married.

5　For *as* a young man marries a virgin,
　　So shall your sons marry you;
　And *as* the bridegroom rejoices over the
　　bride,
　So shall your God rejoice over you.

6　I have set watchmen on your walls, O
　　Jerusalem;
　They shall never hold their peace day or
　　night.
　You who make mention of the LORD, do not
　　keep silent,

7　And give Him no rest till He establishes
　And till He makes Jerusalem a praise in the
　　earth.

8　The LORD has sworn by His right hand
　And by the arm of His strength:
　"Surely I will no longer give your grain
　　As food for your enemies;
　And the sons of the foreigner shall not drink
　　your new wine,
　For which you have labored.

9　But those who have gathered it shall eat it,
　　And praise the LORD;
　Those who have brought it together shall
　　drink it in My holy courts."

10　Go through,
　Go through the gates!
　Prepare the way for the people;
　Build up,
　Build up the highway!
　Take out the stones,
　Lift up a banner for the peoples!

11　Indeed the LORD has proclaimed
　To the end of the world:
　"Say to the daughter of Zion,
　　'Surely your salvation is coming;
　Behold, His reward *is* with Him,
　And His work before Him.'"

12　And they shall call them The Holy People,
　　The Redeemed of the LORD;
　And you shall be called Sought Out,
　A City Not Forsaken.

63　Who *is* this who comes from Edom,
　With dyed garments from Bozrah,
　This *One who is* glorious in His apparel,

וּלְאַרְצֵךְ לֹא־יֵאָמֵר עוֹד שְׁמָמָה
כִּי לָךְ יִקָּרֵא חֶפְצִי־בָהּ
וּלְאַרְצֵךְ בְּעוּלָה
כִּי־חָפֵץ יְהוָה בָּךְ
וְאַרְצֵךְ תִּבָּעֵל׃

5　כִּי־יִבְעַל בָּחוּר בְּתוּלָה
יִבְעָלוּךְ בָּנָיִךְ
וּמְשׂוֹשׂ חָתָן עַל־כַּלָּה
יָשִׂישׂ עָלַיִךְ אֱלֹהָיִךְ׃

6　עַל־חוֹמֹתַיִךְ יְרוּשָׁלַ͏ִם
הִפְקַדְתִּי שֹׁמְרִים
כָּל־הַיּוֹם וְכָל־הַלַּיְלָה
תָּמִיד לֹא יֶחֱשׁוּ
הַמַּזְכִּרִים אֶת־יְהוָה
אַל־דֳּמִי לָכֶם׃

7　וְאַל־תִּתְּנוּ דֳמִי לוֹ עַד־יְכוֹנֵן
וְעַד־יָשִׂים אֶת־יְרוּשָׁלַ͏ִם
תְּהִלָּה בָּאָרֶץ׃

8　נִשְׁבַּע יְהוָה בִּימִינוֹ וּבִזְרוֹעַ עֻזּוֹ
אִם־אֶתֵּן אֶת־דְּגָנֵךְ
עוֹד מַאֲכָל לְאֹיְבַיִךְ
וְאִם־יִשְׁתּוּ בְנֵי־נֵכָר תִּירוֹשֵׁךְ
אֲשֶׁר יָגַעַתְּ בּוֹ׃

9　כִּי מְאַסְפָיו יֹאכְלֻהוּ
וְהִלְלוּ אֶת־יְהוָה
ס　וּמְקַבְּצָיו יִשְׁתֻּהוּ בְּחַצְרוֹת קָדְשִׁי׃

10　עִבְרוּ עִבְרוּ בַּשְּׁעָרִים
פַּנּוּ דֶּרֶךְ הָעָם
סֹלּוּ סֹלּוּ הַמְסִלָּה סַקְּלוּ מֵאֶבֶן
הָרִימוּ נֵס עַל־הָעַמִּים׃

11　הִנֵּה יְהוָה הִשְׁמִיעַ אֶל־קְצֵה הָאָרֶץ
אִמְרוּ לְבַת־צִיּוֹן
הִנֵּה יִשְׁעֵךְ בָּא
הִנֵּה שְׂכָרוֹ אִתּוֹ וּפְעֻלָּתוֹ לְפָנָיו׃

12　וְקָרְאוּ לָהֶם עַם־הַקֹּדֶשׁ
גְּאוּלֵי יְהוָה
וְלָךְ יִקָּרֵא דְרוּשָׁה
ס　עִיר לֹא נֶעֱזָבָה׃

סג　מִי־זֶה ׀ בָּא מֵאֱדוֹם
חֲמוּץ בְּגָדִים מִבָּצְרָה
זֶה הָדוּר בִּלְבוּשׁוֹ

Traveling in the greatness of His strength?—

"I who speak in righteousness, mighty to
save."

צֹעֶה בְּרֹב כֹּחוֹ

אֲנִי מְדַבֵּר בִּצְדָקָה

רַב לְהוֹשִׁיעַ:

2 Why *is* Your apparel red,
And Your garments like one who treads in
the winepress?

מַדּוּעַ אָדֹם לִלְבוּשֶׁךָ 2

וּבְגָדֶיךָ כְּדֹרֵךְ בְּגַת:

3 "I have trodden the winepress alone,
And from the peoples no one *was* with Me.
For I have trodden them in My anger,
And trampled them in My fury;
Their blood is sprinkled upon My garments,
And I have stained all My robes.

פּוּרָה | דָּרַכְתִּי לְבַדִּי 3

וּמֵעַמִּים אֵין־אִישׁ אִתִּי

וְאֶדְרְכֵם בְּאַפִּי

וְאֶרְמְסֵם בַּחֲמָתִי

וְיֵז נִצְחָם עַל־בְּגָדַי

וְכָל־מַלְבּוּשַׁי אֶגְאָלְתִּי:

4 For the day of vengeance *is* in My heart,
And the year of My redeemed has come.

כִּי יוֹם נָקָם בְּלִבִּי 4

וּשְׁנַת גְּאוּלַי בָּאָה:

5 I looked, but *there was* no one to help,
And I wondered
That *there was* no one to uphold;
Therefore My own arm brought salvation for
Me;
And My own fury, it sustained Me.

וְאַבִּיט וְאֵין עֹזֵר 5

וְאֶשְׁתּוֹמֵם וְאֵין סוֹמֵךְ

וַתּוֹשַׁע לִי זְרֹעִי

וַחֲמָתִי הִיא סְמָכָתְנִי:

6 I have trodden down the peoples in My
anger,
Made them drunk in My fury,
And brought down their strength to the
earth."

וְאָבוּס עַמִּים בְּאַפִּי 6

וַאֲשַׁכְּרֵם בַּחֲמָתִי

וְאוֹרִיד לָאָרֶץ נִצְחָם: ס

7 I will mention the lovingkindnesses of the
LORD
And the praises of the LORD,
According to all that the LORD has bestowed
on us,
And the great goodness toward the house of
Israel,
Which He has bestowed on them according
to His mercies,
According to the multitude of His
lovingkindnesses.

חַסְדֵי יְהוָה | אַזְכִּיר 7

תְּהִלֹּת יְהוָה

כְּעַל כֹּל אֲשֶׁר־גְּמָלָנוּ יְהוָה

וְרַב־טוּב לְבֵית יִשְׂרָאֵל

אֲשֶׁר־גְּמָלָם כְּרַחֲמָיו

וּכְרֹב חֲסָדָיו:

8 For He said, "Surely they *are* My people,
Children *who* will not lie."
So He became their Savior.

וַיֹּאמֶר אַךְ־עַמִּי הֵמָּה 8

בָּנִים לֹא יְשַׁקֵּרוּ

וַיְהִי לָהֶם לְמוֹשִׁיעַ:

9 In all their affliction He was afflicted,
And the Angel of His Presence saved them;
In His love and in His pity He redeemed
them;
And He bore them and carried them
All the days of old.

בְּכָל־צָרָתָם | לֹא* צָר 9

וּמַלְאַךְ פָּנָיו הוֹשִׁיעָם

בְּאַהֲבָתוֹ וּבְחֶמְלָתוֹ הוּא גְאָלָם

וַיְנַטְּלֵם וַיְנַשְּׂאֵם כָּל־יְמֵי עוֹלָם:

10 But they rebelled and grieved His Holy
Spirit;
So He turned Himself against them as an
enemy,
And He fought against them.

וְהֵמָּה מָרוּ וְעִצְּבוּ אֶת־רוּחַ קָדְשׁוֹ 10

וַיֵּהָפֵךְ לָהֶם

לְאוֹיֵב הוּא נִלְחַם־בָּם:

11 Then he remembered the days of old,
Moses *and* his people, *saying:*

וַיִּזְכֹּר יְמֵי־עוֹלָם מֹשֶׁה עַמּוֹ 11

אַיֵּה | הַמַּעֲלֵם מִיָּם

סג 9 לו

"Where *is* He who brought them up out of the
  sea
With the shepherd of His flock?
Where *is* He who put His Holy Spirit within
  them,

אֵת רֹעֵי צֹאנוֹ
אַיֵּה הַשָּׂם בְּקִרְבּוֹ
אֶת־רוּחַ קׇדְשׁוֹ:

12 Who led *them* by the right hand of Moses,
   With His glorious arm,
   Dividing the water before them
   To make for Himself an everlasting name,

12 מוֹלִיךְ לִימִין מֹשֶׁה
זְרוֹעַ תִּפְאַרְתּוֹ
בּוֹקֵעַ מַיִם מִפְּנֵיהֶם
לַעֲשׂוֹת לוֹ שֵׁם עוֹלָם:

13 Who led them through the deep,
   As a horse in the wilderness,
   That they might not stumble?"

13 מוֹלִיכָם בַּתְּהֹמוֹת
כַּסּוּס בַּמִּדְבָּר לֹא יִכָּשֵׁלוּ:

14 As a beast goes down into the valley,
   And the Spirit of the LORD causes him to
     rest,
   So You lead Your people,
   To make Yourself a glorious name.

14 כַּבְּהֵמָה בַּבִּקְעָה תֵרֵד
רוּחַ יְהֹוָה תְּנִיחֶנּוּ
כֵּן נִהַגְתָּ עַמְּךָ
לַעֲשׂוֹת לְךָ שֵׁם תִּפְאָרֶת:

15 Look down from heaven,
   And see from Your habitation, holy and
     glorious.
   Where *are* Your zeal and Your strength,
   The yearning of Your heart and Your
     mercies toward me?
   Are they restrained?

15 הַבֵּט מִשָּׁמַיִם וּרְאֵה
מִזְּבֻל קׇדְשְׁךָ וְתִפְאַרְתֶּךָ
אַיֵּה קִנְאָתְךָ וּגְבוּרֹתֶךָ
הֲמוֹן מֵעֶיךָ
וְרַחֲמֶיךָ אֵלַי הִתְאַפָּקוּ:

16 Doubtless You *are* our Father,
   Though Abraham was ignorant of us,
   And Israel does not acknowledge us.
   You, O LORD, *are* our Father;
   Our Redeemer from Everlasting *is* Your
     name.

16 כִּי־אַתָּה אָבִינוּ
כִּי אַבְרָהָם לֹא יְדָעָנוּ
וְיִשְׂרָאֵל לֹא יַכִּירָנוּ
אַתָּה יְהֹוָה אָבִינוּ
גֹּאֲלֵנוּ מֵעוֹלָם שְׁמֶךָ:

17 O LORD, why have You made us stray from
     Your ways,
   And hardened our heart from Your fear?
   Return for Your servants' sake,
   The tribes of Your inheritance.

17 לָמָּה תַתְעֵנוּ יְהֹוָה מִדְּרָכֶיךָ
תַּקְשִׁיחַ לִבֵּנוּ מִיִּרְאָתֶךָ
שׁוּב לְמַעַן עֲבָדֶיךָ
שִׁבְטֵי נַחֲלָתֶךָ:

18 Your holy people have possessed *it* but a
     little while;
   Our adversaries have trodden down Your
     sanctuary.

18 לַמִּצְעָר יָרְשׁוּ עַם־קׇדְשֶׁךָ
צָרֵינוּ בּוֹסְסוּ מִקְדָּשֶׁךָ:

19 We have become *like* those of old, over
     whom You never ruled,
   Those who were never called by Your name.

19 הָיִינוּ מֵעוֹלָם לֹא־מָשַׁלְתָּ בָּם
לֹא־נִקְרָא שִׁמְךָ עֲלֵיהֶם
לוּא־קָרַעְתָּ שָׁמַיִם יָרַדְתָּ
מִפָּנֶיךָ הָרִים נָזֹלּוּ:

64 Oh, that You would rend the heavens!
   That You would come down!
   That the mountains might shake at Your
     presence—

סד כִּקְדֹחַ אֵשׁ הֲמָסִים
מַיִם תִּבְעֶה־אֵשׁ
לְהוֹדִיעַ שִׁמְךָ לְצָרֶיךָ
מִפָּנֶיךָ גּוֹיִם יִרְגָּזוּ:

2 As fire burns brushwood,
  As fire causes water to boil—
  To make Your name known to Your
    adversaries,
  That the nations may tremble at Your
    presence!

2 בַּעֲשׂוֹתְךָ נוֹרָאוֹת
לֹא נְקַוֶּה
יָרַדְתָּ מִפָּנֶיךָ הָרִים נָזֹלּוּ:

3 When You did awesome things *for which* we
    did not look,
  You came down,
  The mountains shook at Your presence.
4 For since the beginning of the world
  Men have not heard nor perceived by the ear,
  Nor has the eye seen any God besides You,
  Who acts for the one who waits for Him.
5 You meet him who rejoices and does
    righteousness,
  Who remembers You in Your ways.
  You are indeed angry, for we have sinned—
  In these ways we continue;
  And we need to be saved.
6 But we are all like an unclean *thing,*
  And all our righteousnesses *are* like filthy
    rags;
  We all fade as a leaf,
  And our iniquities, like the wind,
  Have taken us away.
7 And *there is* no one who calls on Your name,
  Who stirs himself up to take hold of You;
  For You have hidden Your face from us,
  And have consumed us because of our
    iniquities.
8 But now, O LORD,
  You *are* our Father;
  We *are* the clay, and You our potter;
  And all we *are* the work of Your hand.
9 Do not be furious, O LORD,
  Nor remember iniquity forever;
  Indeed, please look—we all *are* Your people!
10 Your holy cities are a wilderness,
  Zion is a wilderness,
  Jerusalem a desolation.
11 Our holy and beautiful temple,
  Where our fathers praised You,
  Is burned up with fire;
  And all our pleasant things are laid waste.
12 Will You restrain Yourself because of these
    things, O LORD?
  Will You hold Your peace, and afflict us
    very severely?

65 "I was sought by *those who* did not ask *for*
    Me;
  I was found by *those who* did not seek Me.
  I said, 'Here I am, here I am,'
  To a nation *that* was not called by My name.
2 I have stretched out My hands all day long to
    a rebellious people,
  Who walk in a way *that is* not good,
  According to their own thoughts;

3 וּמֵעוֹלָם לֹא־שָׁמְעוּ לֹא הֶאֱזִינוּ
  עַיִן לֹא־רָאָתָה אֱלֹהִים זוּלָתְךָ
  יַעֲשֶׂה לִמְחַכֵּה־לוֹ:
4 פָּגַעְתָּ אֶת־שָׂשׂ וְעֹשֵׂה צֶדֶק
  בִּדְרָכֶיךָ יִזְכְּרוּךָ
  הֵן־אַתָּה קָצַפְתָּ וַנֶּחֱטָא
  בָּהֶם עוֹלָם וְנִוָּשֵׁעַ:
5 וַנְּהִי כַטָּמֵא כֻּלָּנוּ
  וּכְבֶגֶד עִדִּים כָּל־צִדְקֹתֵינוּ
  וַנָּבֶל כֶּעָלֶה כֻּלָּנוּ
  וַעֲוֹנֵנוּ כָּרוּחַ יִשָּׂאֻנוּ:
6 וְאֵין־קוֹרֵא בְשִׁמְךָ
  מִתְעוֹרֵר לְהַחֲזִיק בָּךְ
  כִּי־הִסְתַּרְתָּ פָנֶיךָ מִמֶּנּוּ
  וַתְּמוּגֵנוּ בְּיַד־עֲוֹנֵנוּ:
7 וְעַתָּה יְהֹוָה אָבִינוּ אָתָּה
  אֲנַחְנוּ הַחֹמֶר וְאַתָּה יֹצְרֵנוּ
  וּמַעֲשֵׂה יָדְךָ כֻּלָּנוּ:
8 אַל־תִּקְצֹף יְהֹוָה עַד־מְאֹד
  וְאַל־לָעַד תִּזְכֹּר עָוֹן
  הֵן הַבֶּט־נָא עַמְּךָ כֻלָּנוּ:
9 עָרֵי קָדְשְׁךָ הָיוּ מִדְבָּר
  צִיּוֹן מִדְבָּר הָיָתָה
  יְרוּשָׁלַ͏ִם שְׁמָמָה:
10 בֵּית קָדְשֵׁנוּ וְתִפְאַרְתֵּנוּ
  אֲשֶׁר הִלְלוּךָ אֲבֹתֵינוּ
  הָיָה לִשְׂרֵפַת אֵשׁ
  וְכָל־מַחֲמַדֵּינוּ הָיָה לְחָרְבָּה:
11 הַעַל־אֵלֶּה תִתְאַפַּק יְהֹוָה
  תֶּחֱשֶׁה וּתְעַנֵּנוּ עַד־מְאֹד: ס

סה נִדְרַשְׁתִּי לְלוֹא שָׁאָלוּ
  נִמְצֵאתִי לְלֹא בִקְשֻׁנִי
  אָמַרְתִּי הִנֵּנִי הִנֵּנִי
  אֶל־גּוֹי לֹא־קֹרָא בִשְׁמִי:
2 פֵּרַשְׂתִּי יָדַי
  כָּל־הַיּוֹם אֶל־עַם סוֹרֵר

³ A people who provoke Me to anger con-
   tinually to My face;
Who sacrifice in gardens,
And burn incense on altars of brick;
⁴ Who sit among the graves,
And spend the night in the tombs;
Who eat swine's flesh,
And the broth of abominable things is *in*
   their vessels;
⁵ Who say, 'Keep to yourself,
Do not come near me,
For I am holier than you!'
These *are* smoke in My nostrils,
A fire that burns all the day.

⁶ "Behold, *it is* written before Me:
I will not keep silence, but will repay—
Even repay into their bosom—
⁷ Your iniquities and the iniquities of your
   fathers together,"
Says the LORD,
"Who have burned incense on the mountains
And blasphemed Me on the hills;
Therefore I will measure their former work
   into their bosom."

⁸ Thus says the LORD:

"As the new wine is found in the cluster,
And *one* says, 'Do not destroy it,
For a blessing *is* in it,'
So will I do for My servants' sake,
That I may not destroy them all.
⁹ I will bring forth descendants from Jacob,
And from Judah an heir of My mountains;
My elect shall inherit it,
And My servants shall dwell there.
¹⁰ Sharon shall be a fold of flocks,
And the Valley of Achor a place for herds to
   lie down,
For My people who have sought Me.

¹¹ "But you *are* those who forsake the LORD,
Who forget My holy mountain,
Who prepare a table for Gad,
And who furnish a drink offering for Meni.
¹² Therefore I will number you for the sword,
And you shall all bow down to the slaughter;
Because, when I called, you did not answer;
When I spoke, you did not hear,
But did evil before My eyes,
And chose *that* in which I do not delight."

¹³ Therefore thus says the Lord GOD:

"Behold, My servants shall eat,
But you shall be hungry;

הַהֹלְכִים הַדֶּרֶךְ לֹא־טוֹב
אַחַר מַחְשְׁבֹתֵיהֶם׃
הָעָם הַמַּכְעִיסִים אוֹתִי   3
עַל־פָּנַי תָּמִיד זֹבְחִים בַּגַּנּוֹת
וּמְקַטְּרִים עַל־הַלְּבֵנִים׃
הַיֹּשְׁבִים בַּקְּבָרִים וּבַנְּצוּרִים יָלִינוּ   4
הָאֹכְלִים בְּשַׂר הַחֲזִיר
וּפְרַק פִּגֻּלִים כְּלֵיהֶם׃
הָאֹמְרִים קְרַב אֵלֶיךָ   5
אַל־תִּגַּשׁ־בִּי כִּי קְדַשְׁתִּיךָ
אֵלֶּה עָשָׁן בְּאַפִּי
אֵשׁ יֹקֶדֶת כָּל־הַיּוֹם׃
הִנֵּה כְתוּבָה לְפָנָי   6
לֹא אֶחֱשֶׂה כִּי אִם־שִׁלַּמְתִּי
וְשִׁלַּמְתִּי עַל־חֵיקָם׃
עֲוֹנֹתֵיכֶם וַעֲוֹנֹת אֲבוֹתֵיכֶם יַחְדָּו   7
אָמַר יְהֹוָה אֲשֶׁר קִטְּרוּ עַל־הֶהָרִים
וְעַל־הַגְּבָעוֹת חֵרְפוּנִי
וּמַדֹּתִי פְעֻלָּתָם רִאשֹׁנָה עַל־חֵיקָם׃ ס
כֹּה ׀ אָמַר יְהֹוָה   8
כַּאֲשֶׁר יִמָּצֵא הַתִּירוֹשׁ בָּאֶשְׁכּוֹל
וְאָמַר אַל־תַּשְׁחִיתֵהוּ כִּי בְרָכָה בּוֹ
כֵּן אֶעֱשֶׂה לְמַעַן עֲבָדַי
לְבִלְתִּי הַשְׁחִית הַכֹּל׃
וְהוֹצֵאתִי מִיַּעֲקֹב זֶרַע וּמִיהוּדָה יוֹרֵשׁ הָרָי   9
וִירֵשׁוּהָ בְחִירַי וַעֲבָדַי יִשְׁכְּנוּ־שָׁמָּה׃
וְהָיָה הַשָּׁרוֹן לִנְוֵה־צֹאן   10
וְעֵמֶק עָכוֹר לְרֵבֶץ בָּקָר
לְעַמִּי אֲשֶׁר דְּרָשׁוּנִי׃
וְאַתֶּם עֹזְבֵי יְהֹוָה   11
הַשְּׁכֵחִים אֶת־הַר קָדְשִׁי
הַעֹרְכִים לַגַּד שֻׁלְחָן
וְהַמְמַלְאִים לַמְנִי מִמְסָךְ׃
וּמָנִיתִי אֶתְכֶם לַחֶרֶב   12
וְכֻלְּכֶם לַטֶּבַח תִּכְרָעוּ
יַעַן קָרָאתִי וְלֹא עֲנִיתֶם
דִּבַּרְתִּי וְלֹא שְׁמַעְתֶּם
וַתַּעֲשׂוּ הָרַע בְּעֵינַי
וּבַאֲשֶׁר לֹא־חָפַצְתִּי בְּחַרְתֶּם׃
לָכֵן כֹּה־אָמַר ׀ אֲדֹנָי יְהֹוִה   13
הִנֵּה עֲבָדַי ׀ יֹאכֵלוּ וְאַתֶּם תִּרְעָבוּ

ס

פ

Behold, My servants shall drink,
But you shall be thirsty;
Behold, My servants shall rejoice,
But you shall be ashamed;

14 Behold, My servants shall sing for joy of
heart,
But you shall cry for sorrow of heart,
And wail for grief of spirit.

15 You shall leave your name as a curse to My
chosen;
For the Lord GOD will slay you,
And call His servants by another name;

16 So that he who blesses himself in the earth
Shall bless himself in the God of truth;
And he who swears in the earth
Shall swear by the God of truth;
Because the former troubles are forgotten,
And because they are hidden from My eyes.

17 "For behold, I create new heavens and a new
earth;
And the former shall not be remembered or
come to mind.

18 But be glad and rejoice forever in what I
create;
For behold, I create Jerusalem *as* a rejoicing,
And her people a joy.

19 I will rejoice in Jerusalem,
And joy in My people;
The voice of weeping shall no longer be
heard in her,
Nor the voice of crying.

20 "No more shall an infant from there *live but a
few* days,
Nor an old man who has not fulfilled his
days;
For the child shall die one hundred years old,
But the sinner *being* one hundred years old
shall be accursed.

21 They shall build houses and inhabit *them;*
They shall plant vineyards and eat their fruit.

22 They shall not build and another inhabit;
They shall not plant and another eat;
For as the days of a tree, *so shall be* the days
of My people,
And My elect shall long enjoy the work of
their hands.

23 They shall not labor in vain,
Nor bring forth children for trouble;
For they *shall be* the descendants of the
blessed of the LORD,
And their offspring with them.

24 "It shall come to pass
That before they call, I will answer;

הִנֵּה עֲבָדַי יִשְׁתּוּ
וְאַתֶּם תִּצְמָאוּ
הִנֵּה עֲבָדַי יִשְׂמָחוּ וְאַתֶּם תֵּבֹשׁוּ׃

14 הִנֵּה עֲבָדַי יָרֹנּוּ מִטּוּב לֵב
וְאַתֶּם תִּצְעֲקוּ מִכְּאֵב לֵב
וּמִשֵּׁבֶר רוּחַ תְּיֵלִילוּ׃

15 וְהִנַּחְתֶּם שִׁמְכֶם לִשְׁבוּעָה לִבְחִירַי
וֶהֱמִיתְךָ אֲדֹנָי יְהוִה
וְלַעֲבָדָיו יִקְרָא שֵׁם אַחֵר׃

16 אֲשֶׁר הַמִּתְבָּרֵךְ בָּאָרֶץ
יִתְבָּרֵךְ בֵּאלֹהֵי אָמֵן
וְהַנִּשְׁבָּע בָּאָרֶץ
יִשָּׁבַע בֵּאלֹהֵי אָמֵן
כִּי נִשְׁכְּחוּ הַצָּרוֹת הָרִאשֹׁנוֹת
וְכִי נִסְתְּרוּ מֵעֵינָי׃

17 כִּי־הִנְנִי בוֹרֵא שָׁמַיִם חֲדָשִׁים
וָאָרֶץ חֲדָשָׁה
וְלֹא תִזָּכַרְנָה הָרִאשֹׁנוֹת
וְלֹא תַעֲלֶינָה עַל־לֵב׃

18 כִּי־אִם־שִׂישׂוּ וְגִילוּ עֲדֵי־עַד
אֲשֶׁר אֲנִי בוֹרֵא
כִּי הִנְנִי בוֹרֵא אֶת־יְרוּשָׁלַ͏ִם
גִּילָה וְעַמָּהּ מָשׂוֹשׂ׃

19 וְגַלְתִּי בִירוּשָׁלַ͏ִם וְשַׂשְׂתִּי בְעַמִּי
וְלֹא־יִשָּׁמַע בָּהּ עוֹד
קוֹל בְּכִי וְקוֹל זְעָקָה׃

20 לֹא־יִהְיֶה מִשָּׁם עוֹד עוּל יָמִים וְזָקֵן
אֲשֶׁר לֹא־יְמַלֵּא אֶת־יָמָיו
כִּי הַנַּעַר בֶּן־מֵאָה שָׁנָה יָמוּת
וְהַחוֹטֶא בֶּן־מֵאָה שָׁנָה יְקֻלָּל׃

21 וּבָנוּ בָתִּים וְיָשָׁבוּ
וְנָטְעוּ כְרָמִים וְאָכְלוּ פִּרְיָם׃

22 לֹא יִבְנוּ וְאַחֵר יֵשֵׁב
לֹא יִטְּעוּ וְאַחֵר יֹאכֵל
כִּי־כִימֵי הָעֵץ יְמֵי עַמִּי
וּמַעֲשֵׂה יְדֵיהֶם יְבַלּוּ בְחִירָי׃

23 לֹא יִיגְעוּ לָרִיק וְלֹא יֵלְדוּ לַבֶּהָלָה
כִּי זֶרַע בְּרוּכֵי יְהוָה הֵמָּה
וְצֶאֱצָאֵיהֶם אִתָּם׃

24 וְהָיָה טֶרֶם־יִקְרָאוּ וַאֲנִי אֶעֱנֶה
עוֹד הֵם מְדַבְּרִים וַאֲנִי אֶשְׁמָע׃

And while they are still speaking, I will hear.
25 The wolf and the lamb shall feed together,
The lion shall eat straw like the ox,
And dust *shall be* the serpent's food.
They shall not hurt nor destroy in all My
    holy mountain,"
Says the LORD.

66 Thus says the LORD:

"Heaven *is* My throne,
And earth *is* My footstool.
Where *is* the house that you will build Me?
And where *is* the place of My rest?
2 For all those *things* My hand has made,
And all those *things* exist,"
Says the LORD.
"But on this *one* will I look:
On *him who is* poor and of a contrite spirit,
And who trembles at My word.

3 "He who kills a bull *is as if* he slays a man;
He who sacrifices a lamb, *as if* he breaks a
    dog's neck;
He who offers a grain offering, *as if he offers*
    swine's blood;
He who burns incense, *as if* he blesses an
    idol.
Just as they have chosen their own ways,
And their soul delights in their abomina-
    tions,
4 So will I choose their delusions,
And bring their fears on them;
Because, when I called, no one answered,
When I spoke they did not hear;
But they did evil before My eyes,
And chose *that* in which I do not delight."

5 Hear the word of the LORD,
You who tremble at His word:
"Your brethren who hated you,
Who cast you out for My name's sake, said,
'Let the LORD be glorified,
That we may see your joy.'
But they shall be ashamed."

6 The sound of noise from the city!
A voice from the temple!
The voice of the LORD,
Who fully repays His enemies!

7 "Before she was in labor, she gave birth;
Before her pain came,
She delivered a male child.
8 Who has heard such a thing?
Who has seen such things?

זְאֵב וְטָלֶה יִרְעוּ כְאֶחָד 25
וְאַרְיֵה כַּבָּקָר יֹאכַל־תֶּבֶן
וְנָחָשׁ עָפָר לַחְמוֹ
לֹא־יָרֵעוּ וְלֹא־יַשְׁחִיתוּ
בְּכָל־הַר קָדְשִׁי אָמַר יְהוָה: ס

‫ס‬ כֹּה אָמַר יְהוָה
הַשָּׁמַיִם כִּסְאִי
וְהָאָרֶץ הֲדֹם רַגְלָי
אֵי־זֶה בַיִת אֲשֶׁר תִּבְנוּ־לִי
וְאֵי־זֶה מָקוֹם מְנוּחָתִי:
וְאֶת־כָּל־אֵלֶּה יָדִי עָשָׂתָה 2
וַיִּהְיוּ כָל־אֵלֶּה נְאֻם־יְהוָה
וְאֶל־זֶה אַבִּיט
אֶל־עָנִי וּנְכֵה־רוּחַ
וְחָרֵד עַל־דְּבָרִי:
שׁוֹחֵט הַשּׁוֹר מַכֵּה־אִישׁ 3
זוֹבֵחַ הַשֶּׂה עֹרֵף כֶּלֶב
מַעֲלֵה מִנְחָה דַּם־חֲזִיר
מַזְכִּיר לְבֹנָה מְבָרֵךְ אָוֶן
גַּם־הֵמָּה בָּחֲרוּ בְּדַרְכֵיהֶם
וּבְשִׁקּוּצֵיהֶם נַפְשָׁם חָפֵצָה:
גַּם־אֲנִי אֶבְחַר בְּתַעֲלֻלֵיהֶם 4
וּמְגוּרֹתָם אָבִיא לָהֶם
יַעַן קָרָאתִי וְאֵין עוֹנֶה
דִּבַּרְתִּי וְלֹא שָׁמֵעוּ
וַיַּעֲשׂוּ הָרַע בְּעֵינַי
וּבַאֲשֶׁר לֹא־חָפַצְתִּי בָּחָרוּ: ס
שִׁמְעוּ דְּבַר־יְהוָה 5
הַחֲרֵדִים אֶל־דְּבָרוֹ
אָמְרוּ אֲחֵיכֶם שֹׂנְאֵיכֶם מְנַדֵּיכֶם
לְמַעַן שְׁמִי יִכְבַּד יְהוָה
וְנִרְאֶה בְשִׂמְחַתְכֶם וְהֵם יֵבֹשׁוּ:
קוֹל שָׁאוֹן מֵעִיר 6
קוֹל מֵהֵיכָל
קוֹל יְהוָה מְשַׁלֵּם גְּמוּל לְאֹיְבָיו:
בְּטֶרֶם תָּחִיל יָלָדָה 7
בְּטֶרֶם יָבוֹא חֵבֶל לָהּ
וְהִמְלִיטָה זָכָר:
מִי־שָׁמַע כָּזֹאת 8
מִי רָאָה כָּאֵלֶּה

Shall the earth be made to give birth in one
day?
Or shall a nation be born at once?
For as soon as Zion was in labor,
She gave birth to her children.

9 Shall I bring to the time of birth, and not
cause delivery?" says the LORD.
"Shall I who cause delivery shut up *the
womb?*" says your God.

10 "Rejoice with Jerusalem,
And be glad with her, all you who love her;
Rejoice for joy with her, all you who mourn
for her;

11 That you may feed and be satisfied
With the consolation of her bosom,
That you may drink deeply and be delighted
With the abundance of her glory."

12 For thus says the LORD:

"Behold, I will extend peace to her like a river,
And the glory of the Gentiles like a flowing
stream.
Then you shall feed;
On *her* sides shall you be carried,
And be dandled on *her* knees.

13 As one whom his mother comforts,
So I will comfort you;
And you shall be comforted in Jerusalem."

14 When you see *this,* your heart shall rejoice,
And your bones shall flourish like grass;
The hand of the LORD shall be known to His
servants,
And *His* indignation to His enemies.

15 For behold, the LORD will come with fire
And with His chariots, like a whirlwind,
To render His anger with fury,
And His rebuke with flames of fire.

16 For by fire and by His sword
The LORD will judge all flesh;
And the slain of the LORD shall be many.

17 "Those who sanctify themselves and purify
themselves,
To go to the gardens
After an *idol* in the midst,
Eating swine's flesh and the abomination
and the mouse,
Shall be consumed together," says the LORD.

18 "For I *know* their works and their thoughts. It
shall be that I will gather all nations and tongues;
and they shall come and see My glory. 19 I will set a
sign among them; and those among them who
escape I will send to the nations: *to* Tarshish and
Pul and Lud, who draw the bow, and Tubal and

הֲיוּחַל אֶ֫רֶץ בְּיוֹם אֶחָ֔ד
אִם־יִוָּ֥לֵד גּ֖וֹי פַּ֣עַם אֶחָ֑ת
כִּֽי־חָ֨לָה גַּם־יָלְדָ֥ה צִיּ֖וֹן אֶת־בָּנֶֽיהָ׃
9 הַאֲנִ֥י אַשְׁבִּ֛יר וְלֹ֥א אוֹלִ֖יד יֹאמַ֣ר יְהוָ֑ה
אִם־אֲנִ֧י הַמּוֹלִ֛יד וְעָצַ֖רְתִּי אָמַ֥ר אֱלֹהָֽיִךְ׃ ס
10 שִׂמְח֣וּ אֶת־יְרוּשָׁלַ֗͏ִם
וְגִ֤ילוּ בָהּ֙ כָּל־אֹהֲבֶ֔יהָ
שִׂ֤ישׂוּ אִתָּהּ֙ מָשׂ֔וֹשׂ
כָּל־הַמִּֽתְאַבְּלִ֖ים עָלֶֽיהָ׃
11 לְמַ֤עַן תִּֽינְקוּ֙ וּשְׂבַעְתֶּ֔ם
מִשֹּׁ֖ד תַּנְחֻמֶ֑יהָ לְמַ֤עַן תָּמֹ֙צּוּ֙
וְהִתְעַנַּגְתֶּ֖ם מִזִּ֥יז כְּבוֹדָֽהּ׃ ס
12 כִּֽי־כֹ֣ה ׀ אָמַ֣ר יְהוָ֗ה
הִנְנִ֣י נֹטֶֽה־אֵ֠לֶ֠יהָ כְּנָהָ֨ר שָׁל֜וֹם
וּכְנַ֧חַל שׁוֹטֵ֛ף כְּב֥וֹד גּוֹיִ֖ם וִֽינַקְתֶּ֑ם
עַל־צַד֙ תִּנָּשֵׂ֔אוּ
וְעַל־בִּרְכַּ֖יִם תְּשָׁעֳשָֽׁעוּ׃
13 כְּאִ֕ישׁ אֲשֶׁ֥ר אִמּ֖וֹ תְּנַחֲמֶ֑נּוּ
כֵּ֤ן אָֽנֹכִי֙ אֲנַ֣חֶמְכֶ֔ם
וּבִירֽוּשָׁלַ֖͏ִם תְּנֻחָֽמוּ׃
14 וּרְאִיתֶם֙ וְשָׂ֣שׂ לִבְּכֶ֔ם
וְעַצְמוֹתֵיכֶ֖ם כַּדֶּ֣שֶׁא תִפְרַ֑חְנָה
וְנוֹדְעָ֤ה יַד־יְהוָה֙ אֶת־עֲבָדָ֔יו
וְזָעַ֖ם אֶת־אֹיְבָֽיו׃
15 כִּֽי־הִנֵּ֤ה יְהוָה֙ בָּאֵ֣שׁ יָב֔וֹא
וְכַסּוּפָ֖ה מַרְכְּבֹתָ֑יו
לְהָשִׁ֤יב בְּחֵמָה֙ אַפּ֔וֹ
וְגַעֲרָת֖וֹ בְּלַהֲבֵי־אֵֽשׁ׃
16 כִּ֤י בָאֵשׁ֙ יְהוָ֣ה נִשְׁפָּ֔ט
וּבְחַרְבּ֖וֹ אֶת־כָּל־בָּשָׂ֑ר
וְרַבּ֖וּ חַֽלְלֵ֥י יְהוָֽה׃
17 הַמִּתְקַדְּשִׁ֨ים וְהַמִּֽטַּהֲרִ֜ים
אֶל־הַגַּנּ֗וֹת
אַחַ֤ר אַחַד֙ בַּתָּ֔וֶךְ
אֹֽכְלֵי֙ בְּשַׂ֣ר הַחֲזִ֔יר וְהַשֶּׁ֖קֶץ וְהָעַכְבָּ֑ר
יַחְדָּ֥ו יָסֻ֖פוּ נְאֻם־יְהוָֽה׃
18 וְאָנֹכִ֗י מַעֲשֵׂיהֶם֙ וּמַחְשְׁבֹ֣תֵיהֶ֔ם בָּ֕אָה לְקַבֵּ֖ץ
אֶת־כָּל־הַגּוֹיִ֣ם וְהַלְּשֹׁנ֑וֹת וּבָ֖אוּ וְרָא֥וּ אֶת־כְּבוֹדִֽי׃
19 וְשַׂמְתִּ֨י בָהֶ֜ם א֗וֹת וְשִׁלַּחְתִּ֣י מֵהֶ֣ם ׀ פְּלֵיטִ֡ים
אֶל־הַגּוֹיִ֣ם תַּרְשִׁ֣ישׁ פּ֣וּל וְל֣וּד מֹ֣שְׁכֵי קֶ֗שֶׁת תֻּבַ֣ל

Javan, *to* the coastlands afar off who have not heard My fame nor seen My glory. And they shall declare My glory among the Gentiles. 20 Then they shall bring all your brethren for an offering to the LORD out of all nations, on horses and in chariots and in litters, on mules and on camels, to My holy mountain Jerusalem," says the LORD, "as the children of Israel bring an offering in a clean vessel into the house of the LORD. 21 And I will also take some of them for priests *and* Levites," says the LORD.

22 "For as the new heavens and the new earth
  Which I will make shall remain before Me," says
    the LORD,
  "So shall your descendants and your name remain.
23 And it shall come to pass
  That from one New Moon to another,
  And from one Sabbath to another,
  All flesh shall come to worship before Me,"
    says the LORD.
24 "And they shall go forth and look
  Upon the corpses of the men
  Who have transgressed against Me.
  For their worm does not die,
  And their fire is not quenched.
  They shall be an abhorrence to all flesh."

וְיֵין הָאִיִּים הָרְחֹקִים אֲשֶׁר לֹא־שָׁמְעוּ אֶת־
שִׁמְעִי וְלֹא־רָאוּ אֶת־כְּבוֹדִי וְהִגִּידוּ אֶת־כְּבוֹדִי
בַּגּוֹיִם: 20 וְהֵבִיאוּ אֶת־כָּל־אֲחֵיכֶם מִכָּל־הַגּוֹיִם |
מִנְחָה | לַיהוָה בַּסּוּסִים וּבָרֶכֶב וּבַצַּבִּים וּבַפְּרָדִים
וּבַכִּרְכָּרוֹת עַל הַר קָדְשִׁי יְרוּשָׁלַ͏ִם אָמַר יְהוָה
כַּאֲשֶׁר יָבִיאוּ בְנֵי יִשְׂרָאֵל אֶת־הַמִּנְחָה בִּכְלִי טָהוֹר
בֵּית יְהוָה: 21 וְגַם־מֵהֶם אֶקַּח לַכֹּהֲנִים לַלְוִיִּם אָמַר
יְהוָה: 22 כִּי כַאֲשֶׁר הַשָּׁמַיִם הַחֳדָשִׁים וְהָאָרֶץ
הַחֳדָשָׁה אֲשֶׁר אֲנִי עֹשֶׂה עֹמְדִים לְפָנַי נְאֻם־יְהוָה
כֵּן יַעֲמֹד זַרְעֲכֶם וְשִׁמְכֶם:

23 וְהָיָה
מִדֵּי־חֹדֶשׁ בְּחָדְשׁוֹ
וּמִדֵּי שַׁבָּת בְּשַׁבַּתּוֹ
יָבוֹא כָל־בָּשָׂר
לְהִשְׁתַּחֲוֹת לְפָנַי אָמַר יְהוָה:
24 וְיָצְאוּ וְרָאוּ
בְּפִגְרֵי הָאֲנָשִׁים הַפֹּשְׁעִים בִּי
כִּי תוֹלַעְתָּם לֹא תָמוּת
וְאִשָּׁם לֹא תִכְבֶּה
וְהָיוּ דֵרָאוֹן לְכָל־בָּשָׂר:

The Book of
JEREMIAH

1 The words of Jeremiah the son of Hilkiah, of the priests who *were* in Anathoth in the land of Benjamin, ²to whom the word of the LORD came in the days of Josiah the son of Amon, king of Judah, in the thirteenth year of his reign. ³It came also in the days of Jehoiakim the son of Josiah, king of Judah, until the end of the eleventh year of Zedekiah the son of Josiah, king of Judah, until the carrying away of Jerusalem captive in the fifth month.

⁴Then the word of the LORD came to me, saying:

5 "Before I formed you in the womb I knew you;
Before you were born I sanctified you;
I ordained you a prophet to the nations."

⁶Then said I:

"Ah, Lord GOD!
Behold, I cannot speak, for I *am* a youth."

⁷But the LORD said to me:

"Do not say, 'I *am* a youth,'
For you shall go to all to whom I send you,
And whatever I command you, you shall speak.
8 Do not be afraid of their faces,
For I *am* with you to deliver you," says the LORD.

⁹Then the LORD put forth His hand and touched my mouth, and the LORD said to me:

"Behold, I have put My words in your mouth.
10 See, I have this day set you over the nations and
over the kingdoms,
To root out and to pull down,
To destroy and to throw down,
To build and to plant."

¹¹Moreover the word of the LORD came to me, saying, "Jeremiah, what do you see?"

And I said, "I see a branch of an almond tree."

¹²Then the LORD said to me, "You have seen well, for I am ready to perform My word."

¹³And the word of the LORD came to me the second time, saying, "What do you see?"

And I said, "I see a boiling pot, and it is facing away from the north."

¹⁴Then the LORD said to me:

"Out of the north calamity shall break forth
On all the inhabitants of the land.
15 For behold, I am calling
All the families of the kingdoms of the north,"
says the LORD;
"They shall come and each one set his throne

א דִּבְרֵי יִרְמְיָהוּ בֶּן־חִלְקִיָּהוּ מִן־הַכֹּהֲנִים אֲשֶׁר
בַּעֲנָתוֹת בְּאֶרֶץ בִּנְיָמִן: ² אֲשֶׁר הָיָה דְבַר־יְהֹוָה אֵלָיו
בִּימֵי יֹאשִׁיָּהוּ בֶן־אָמוֹן מֶלֶךְ יְהוּדָה בִּשְׁלֹשׁ־עֶשְׂרֵה
שָׁנָה לְמָלְכוֹ: ³ וַיְהִי בִּימֵי יְהוֹיָקִים בֶּן־יֹאשִׁיָּהוּ מֶלֶךְ
יְהוּדָה עַד־תֹּם עַשְׁתֵּי עֶשְׂרֵה שָׁנָה לְצִדְקִיָּהוּ בֶן־
יֹאשִׁיָּהוּ מֶלֶךְ יְהוּדָה עַד־גְּלוֹת יְרוּשָׁלִַם בַּחֹדֶשׁ
הַחֲמִישִׁי: ס ⁴ וַיְהִי דְבַר־יְהֹוָה אֵלַי לֵאמֹר: ⁵ בְּטֶרֶם
אֶצֳּרְךָ בַבֶּטֶן יְדַעְתִּיךָ וּבְטֶרֶם תֵּצֵא מֵרֶחֶם
הִקְדַּשְׁתִּיךָ נָבִיא לַגּוֹיִם נְתַתִּיךָ: ⁶ וָאֹמַר אֲהָהּ אֲדֹנָי
יְהֹוִה הִנֵּה לֹא־יָדַעְתִּי דַּבֵּר כִּי־נַעַר אָנֹכִי:
פ

⁷ וַיֹּאמֶר יְהֹוָה אֵלַי אַל־תֹּאמַר נַעַר אָנֹכִי כִּי
עַל־כָּל־אֲשֶׁר אֶשְׁלָחֲךָ תֵּלֵךְ וְאֵת כָּל־אֲשֶׁר אֲצַוְּךָ
תְּדַבֵּר: ⁸ אַל־תִּירָא מִפְּנֵיהֶם כִּי־אִתְּךָ אֲנִי לְהַצִּלֶךָ
נְאֻם־יְהֹוָה: ⁹ וַיִּשְׁלַח יְהֹוָה אֶת־יָדוֹ וַיַּגַּע עַל־
פִּי וַיֹּאמֶר יְהֹוָה אֵלַי הִנֵּה נָתַתִּי דְבָרַי בְּפִיךָ:
¹⁰ רְאֵה הִפְקַדְתִּיךָ ׀ הַיּוֹם הַזֶּה עַל־הַגּוֹיִם וְעַל־
הַמַּמְלָכוֹת לִנְתוֹשׁ וְלִנְתוֹץ וּלְהַאֲבִיד וְלַהֲרוֹס
לִבְנוֹת וְלִנְטוֹעַ:
פ

¹¹ וַיְהִי דְבַר־יְהֹוָה אֵלַי לֵאמֹר מָה־אַתָּה רֹאֶה
יִרְמְיָהוּ וָאֹמַר מַקֵּל שָׁקֵד אֲנִי רֹאֶה: ¹² וַיֹּאמֶר
יְהֹוָה אֵלַי הֵיטַבְתָּ לִרְאוֹת כִּי־שֹׁקֵד אֲנִי עַל־דְּבָרִי
לַעֲשֹׂתוֹ:
פ

¹³ וַיְהִי דְבַר־יְהֹוָה ׀ אֵלַי שֵׁנִית לֵאמֹר מָה אַתָּה
רֹאֶה וָאֹמַר סִיר נָפוּחַ אֲנִי רֹאֶה וּפָנָיו מִפְּנֵי צָפוֹנָה:
¹⁴ וַיֹּאמֶר יְהֹוָה אֵלַי מִצָּפוֹן תִּפָּתַח הָרָעָה עַל כָּל־
יֹשְׁבֵי הָאָרֶץ: ¹⁵ כִּי ׀ הִנְנִי קֹרֵא לְכָל־מִשְׁפְּחוֹת
מַמְלְכוֹת צָפוֹנָה נְאֻם־יְהֹוָה וּבָאוּ וְנָתְנוּ אִישׁ כִּסְאוֹ

At the entrance of the gates of Jerusalem,
Against all its walls all around,
And against all the cities of Judah.
16 I will utter My judgments
Against them concerning all their wickedness,
Because they have forsaken Me,
Burned incense to other gods,
And worshiped the works of their own hands.
17 "Therefore prepare yourself and arise,
And speak to them all that I command you.
Do not be dismayed before their faces,
Lest I dismay you before them.
18 For behold, I have made you this day
A fortified city and an iron pillar,
And bronze walls against the whole land—
Against the kings of Judah,
Against its princes,
Against its priests,
And against the people of the land.
19 They will fight against you,
But they shall not prevail against you.
For I *am* with you," says the LORD, "to deliver
you."

2 Moreover the word of the LORD came to me,
saying, 2 "Go and cry in the hearing of Jerusalem,
saying, 'Thus says the LORD:

"I remember you,
The kindness of your youth,
The love of your betrothal,
When you went after Me in the wilderness,
In a land not sown.
3 Israel *was* holiness to the LORD,
The firstfruits of His increase.
All that devour him will offend;
Disaster will come upon them," says the LORD.' "

4 Hear the word of the LORD, O house of Jacob
and all the families of the house of Israel. 5 Thus
says the LORD:

"What injustice have your fathers found in Me,
That they have gone far from Me,
Have followed idols,
And have become idolaters?
6 Neither did they say, 'Where *is* the LORD,
Who brought us up out of the land of Egypt,
Who led us through the wilderness,
Through a land of deserts and pits,
Through a land of drought and the shadow of
death,
Through a land that no one crossed
And where no one dwelt?'
7 I brought you into a bountiful country,
To eat its fruit and its goodness.
But when you entered, you defiled My land
And made My heritage an abomination.
8 The priests did not say, 'Where *is* the LORD?'
And those who handle the law did not know Me;
The rulers also transgressed against Me;
The prophets prophesied by Baal,

פֶּ֫תַח ׀ שַׁעֲרֵ֣י יְרוּשָׁלַ֔͏ִם וְעַ֥ל כָּל־חוֹמֹתֶ֖יהָ סָבִ֑יב
וְעַ֖ל כָּל־עָרֵ֥י יְהוּדָֽה: 16 וְדִבַּרְתִּ֤י מִשְׁפָּטַי֙ אוֹתָ֔ם
עַ֖ל כָּל־רָעָתָ֑ם אֲשֶׁ֣ר עֲזָב֗וּנִי וַֽיְקַטְּרוּ֙ לֵאלֹהִ֣ים
אֲחֵרִ֔ים וַיִּֽשְׁתַּחֲו֖וּ לְמַעֲשֵׂ֥י יְדֵיהֶֽם: 17 וְאַתָּה֙ תֶּאְזֹ֣ר
מָתְנֶ֔יךָ וְקַמְתָּ֙ וְדִבַּרְתָּ֣ אֲלֵיהֶ֔ם אֵ֛ת כָּל־אֲשֶׁ֥ר אָנֹכִ֖י
אֲצַוֶּ֑ךָּ אַל־תֵּחַת֙ מִפְּנֵיהֶ֔ם פֶּֽן־אֲחִתְּךָ֖ לִפְנֵיהֶֽם:
18 וַאֲנִ֞י הִנֵּ֧ה נְתַתִּ֣יךָ הַיּ֗וֹם לְעִ֣יר מִבְצָר֮ וּלְעַמּ֣וּד
בַּרְזֶ֒ל֒ וּלְחֹמ֣וֹת נְחֹ֑שֶׁת עַל־כָּל־הָאָ֑רֶץ לְמַלְכֵ֤י יְהוּדָה֙
לְשָׂרֶ֔יהָ לְכֹהֲנֶ֖יהָ וּלְעַ֥ם הָאָֽרֶץ: 19 וְנִלְחֲמ֥וּ אֵלֶ֖יךָ
וְלֹא־י֣וּכְלוּ לָ֑ךְ כִּֽי־אִתְּךָ֥ אֲנִ֛י נְאֻם־יְהוָ֖ה לְהַצִּילֶֽךָ: פ

ב וַיְהִ֥י דְבַר־יְהוָ֖ה אֵלַ֥י לֵאמֹֽר: 2 הָלֹ֡ךְ וְקָֽרָאתָ֩
בְאָזְנֵי֩ יְרוּשָׁלַ֨͏ִם לֵאמֹ֜ר כֹּ֣ה אָמַ֣ר יְהוָ֗ה זָכַ֤רְתִּי לָךְ֙
חֶ֣סֶד נְעוּרַ֔יִךְ אַהֲבַ֖ת כְּלוּלֹתָ֑יִךְ לֶכְתֵּ֤ךְ אַחֲרַי֙ בַּמִּדְבָּ֔ר
בְּאֶ֖רֶץ לֹ֥א זְרוּעָֽה: 3 קֹ֤דֶשׁ יִשְׂרָאֵל֙ לַֽיהוָ֔ה רֵאשִׁ֖ית
תְּבוּאָתֹ֑ה כָּל־אֹכְלָ֣יו יֶאְשָׁ֔מוּ רָעָ֛ה תָּבֹ֥א אֲלֵיהֶ֖ם
נְאֻם־יְהוָֽה: פ

4 שִׁמְע֥וּ דְבַר־יְהוָ֖ה בֵּ֣ית יַעֲקֹ֑ב וְכָֽל־מִשְׁפְּח֖וֹת בֵּ֥ית
יִשְׂרָאֵֽל: 5 כֹּ֣ה ׀ אָמַ֣ר יְהוָ֗ה מַה־מָּצְא֨וּ אֲבוֹתֵיכֶ֥ם
בִּי֙ עָ֔וֶל כִּ֥י רָחֲק֖וּ מֵעָלָ֑י וַיֵּֽלְכ֛וּ אַחֲרֵ֥י הַהֶ֖בֶל וַיֶּהְבָּֽלוּ:
6 וְלֹ֣א אָמְר֔וּ אַיֵּ֣ה יְהוָ֔ה הַמַּעֲלֶ֥ה אֹתָ֖נוּ מֵאֶ֣רֶץ
מִצְרָ֑יִם הַמּוֹלִ֨יךְ אֹתָ֜נוּ בַּמִּדְבָּ֗ר בְּאֶ֤רֶץ עֲרָבָה֙ וְשׁוּחָ֔ה
בְּאֶ֙רֶץ֙ צִיָּ֣ה וְצַלְמָ֔וֶת בְּאֶ֕רֶץ לֹֽא־עָ֥בַר בָּהּ֙ אִ֔ישׁ וְלֹֽא־
יָשַׁ֥ב אָדָ֖ם שָֽׁם: 7 וָאָבִ֤יא אֶתְכֶם֙ אֶל־אֶ֣רֶץ הַכַּרְמֶ֔ל
לֶאֱכֹ֥ל פִּרְיָ֖הּ וְטוּבָ֑הּ וַתָּבֹ֙אוּ֙ וַתְּטַמְּא֣וּ אֶת־אַרְצִ֔י
וְנַחֲלָתִ֥י שַׂמְתֶּ֖ם לְתוֹעֵבָֽה: 8 הַכֹּהֲנִ֗ים לֹ֤א אָֽמְרוּ֙
אַיֵּ֣ה יְהוָ֔ה וְתֹפְשֵׂ֤י הַתּוֹרָה֙ לֹ֣א יְדָע֔וּנִי וְהָרֹעִ֖ים
פָּ֣שְׁעוּ בִ֑י וְהַנְּבִיאִים֙ נִבְּא֣וּ בַבַּ֔עַל וְאַחֲרֵ֥י לֹֽא־יוֹעִ֖לוּ

And walked after *things that* do not profit.

9 "Therefore I will yet bring charges against you,"
   says the LORD,
   "And against your children's children I will bring
   charges.

10 For pass beyond the coasts of Cyprus and see,
   Send to Kedar and consider diligently,
   And see if there has been such *a thing*.

11 Has a nation changed *its* gods,
   Which *are* not gods?
   But My people have changed their Glory
   For *what* does not profit.

12 Be astonished, O heavens, at this,
   And be horribly afraid;
   Be very desolate," says the LORD.

13 "For My people have committed two evils:
   They have forsaken Me, the fountain of living
      waters,
   And hewn themselves cisterns—broken cisterns
      that can hold no water.

14 "*Is* Israel a servant?
   Is he a homeborn *slave*?
   Why is he plundered?

15 The young lions roared at him, *and* growled;
   They made his land waste;
   His cities are burned, without inhabitant.

16 Also the people of Noph and Tahpanhes
   Have broken the crown of your head.

17 Have you not brought this on yourself,
   In that you have forsaken the LORD your God
   When He led you in the way?

18 And now why take the road to Egypt,
   To drink the waters of Sihor?
   Or why take the road to Assyria,
   To drink the waters of the River?

19 Your own wickedness will correct you,
   And your backslidings will rebuke you.
   Know therefore and see that *it is* an evil and
      bitter *thing*
   That you have forsaken the LORD your God,
   And the fear of Me *is* not in you,"
   Says the Lord GOD of hosts.

20 "For of old I have broken your yoke *and* burst
      your bonds;
   And you said, 'I will not transgress,'
   When on every high hill and under every green
      tree
   You lay down, playing the harlot.

21 Yet I had planted you a noble vine, a seed of
      highest quality.
   How then have you turned before Me
   Into the degenerate plant of an alien vine?

22 For though you wash yourself with lye, and use
      much soap,
   Yet your iniquity is marked before Me," says the
      Lord GOD.

23 "How can you say, 'I am not polluted,
   I have not gone after the Baals'?
   See your way in the valley;
   Know what you have done:

הָלָכוּ: 9 לָכֵן עֹד אָרִיב אִתְּכֶם נְאֻם־יְהֹוָה וְאֶת־
בְּנֵי בְנֵיכֶם אָרִיב: 10 כִּי עִבְרוּ אִיֵּי כִתִּיִּים וּרְאוּ
וְקֵדָר שִׁלְחוּ וְהִתְבּוֹנְנוּ מְאֹד וּרְאוּ הֵן הָיְתָה כָּזֹאת:
11 הַהֵימִיר גּוֹי אֱלֹהִים וְהֵמָּה לֹא אֱלֹהִים וְעַמִּי
הֵמִיר כְּבוֹדוֹ בְּלוֹא יוֹעִיל: 12 שֹׁמּוּ שָׁמַיִם עַל־זֹאת
וְשַׂעֲרוּ חָרְבוּ מְאֹד נְאֻם־יְהֹוָה: 13 כִּי־שְׁתַּיִם רָעוֹת
עָשָׂה עַמִּי אֹתִי עָזְבוּ מְקוֹר | מַיִם חַיִּים לַחְצֹב
לָהֶם בֹּארוֹת בֹּארֹת נִשְׁבָּרִים אֲשֶׁר לֹא־יָכִלוּ הַמָּיִם:
14 הַעֶבֶד יִשְׂרָאֵל אִם־יְלִיד בַּיִת הוּא מַדּוּעַ הָיָה
לָבַז: 15 עָלָיו יִשְׁאֲגוּ כְפִרִים נָתְנוּ קוֹלָם וַיָּשִׁיתוּ
אַרְצוֹ לְשַׁמָּה עָרָיו נִצְּתָהP מִבְּלִי יֹשֵׁב: 16 גַּם־בְּנֵי־
נֹף וְתַחְפַּנְחֵסP יִרְעוּךְ קָדְקֹד: 17 הֲלוֹא־זֹאת תַּעֲשֶׂה־
לָּךְ עָזְבֵךְ אֶת־יְהֹוָה אֱלֹהַיִךְ בְּעֵת מוֹלִיכֵךְ בַּדָּרֶךְ:
18 וְעַתָּה מַה־לָּךְ לְדֶרֶךְ מִצְרַיִם לִשְׁתּוֹת מֵי שִׁחוֹר
וּמַה־לָּךְ לְדֶרֶךְ אַשּׁוּר לִשְׁתּוֹת מֵי נָהָר: 19 תְּיַסְּרֵךְ
רָעָתֵךְ וּמְשֻׁבוֹתַיִךְ תּוֹכִחֻךְ וּדְעִי וּרְאִי כִּי־רַע וָמָר
עָזְבֵךְ אֶת־יְהֹוָה אֱלֹהָיִךְ וְלֹא פַחְדָּתִי אֵלַיִךְ נְאֻם־
אֲדֹנָי יְהֹוִה צְבָאוֹת: 20 כִּי מֵעוֹלָם שָׁבַרְתִּי עֻלֵּךְ
נִתַּקְתִּי מוֹסְרֹתַיִךְ וַתֹּאמְרִי לֹא אֶעֱבוֹרP כִּי עַל־
כָּל־גִּבְעָה גְּבֹהָה וְתַחַת כָּל־עֵץ רַעֲנָן אַתְּ צֹעָה
זֹנָה: 21 וְאָנֹכִי נְטַעְתִּיךְ שֹׂרֵק כֻּלֹּה זֶרַע אֱמֶת וְאֵיךְ
נֶהְפַּכְתְּ לִי סוּרֵי הַגֶּפֶן נָכְרִיָּה: 22 כִּי אִם־תְּכַבְּסִי
בַּנֶּתֶר וְתַרְבִּי־לָךְ בֹּרִית נִכְתָּם עֲוֹנֵךְ לְפָנַי נְאֻם אֲדֹנָי
יְהֹוִה: 23 אֵיךְ תֹּאמְרִי לֹא נִטְמֵאתִי אַחֲרֵי הַבְּעָלִים
לֹא הָלַכְתִּי רְאִי דַרְכֵּךְ בַּגַּיְא דְּעִי מֶה עָשִׂית בִּכְרָה

You are a swift dromedary breaking loose in her
ways,

24 A wild donkey used to the wilderness,
That sniffs at the wind in her desire;
In her time of mating, who can turn her away?
All those who seek her will not weary themselves;
In her month they will find her.

25 Withhold your foot from being unshod, and your
throat from thirst.
But you said, 'There is no hope.
No! For I have loved aliens, and after them I will
go.'

26 "As the thief is ashamed when he is found out,
So is the house of Israel ashamed;
They and their kings and their princes, and their
priests and their prophets,

27 Saying to a tree, 'You *are* my father,'
And to a stone, 'You gave birth to me.'
For they have turned *their* back to Me, and not
their face.
But in the time of their trouble
They will say, 'Arise and save us.'

28 But where *are* your gods that you have made for
yourselves?
Let them arise,
If they can save you in the time of your trouble;
For *according to* the number of your cities
Are your gods, O Judah.

29 "Why will you plead with Me?
You all have transgressed against Me," says the
LORD.

30 "In vain I have chastened your children;
They received no correction.
Your sword has devoured your prophets
Like a destroying lion.

31 "O generation, see the word of the LORD!
Have I been a wilderness to Israel,
Or a land of darkness?
Why do My people say, 'We are lords;
We will come no more to You'?

32 Can a virgin forget her ornaments,
Or a bride her attire?
Yet My people have forgotten Me days without
number.

33 "Why do you beautify your way to seek love?
Therefore you have also taught
The wicked women your ways.

34 Also on your skirts is found
The blood of the lives of the poor innocents.
I have not found it by secret search,
But plainly on all these things.

35 Yet you say, 'Because I am innocent,
Surely His anger shall turn from me.'
Behold, I will plead My case against you,
Because you say, 'I have not sinned.'

36 Why do you gad about so much to change your
way?
Also you shall be ashamed of Egypt as you were
ashamed of Assyria.

37 Indeed you will go forth from him
With your hands on your head;

קַלָּה מְשָׂרֶכֶת דְּרָכֶיהָ: 24 פֶּרֶה ׀ לִמֻּד מִדְבָּר
בְּאַוַּת נַפְשׁוֹ שָׁאֲפָה רוּחַ תַּאֲנָתָהּ מִי יְשִׁיבֶנָּה כָּל־
מְבַקְשֶׁיהָ לֹא יִיעָפוּ בְּחָדְשָׁהּ יִמְצָאוּנְהָ: 25 מִנְעִי
רַגְלֵךְ מִיָּחֵף וּגְרוֹנֵךְ מִצִּמְאָה וַתֹּאמְרִי נוֹאָשׁ לוֹא
כִּי־אָהַבְתִּי זָרִים וְאַחֲרֵיהֶם אֵלֵךְ: 26 כְּבֹשֶׁת גַּנָּב
כִּי יִמָּצֵא כֵּן הֹבִישׁוּ בֵּית יִשְׂרָאֵל הֵמָּה מַלְכֵיהֶם
שָׂרֵיהֶם וְכֹהֲנֵיהֶם וּנְבִיאֵיהֶם: 27 אֹמְרִים לָעֵץ אָבִי
אַתָּה וְלָאֶבֶן אַתְּ יְלִדְתָּנִי כִּי־פָנוּ אֵלַי עֹרֶף
וְלֹא פָנִים וּבְעֵת רָעָתָם יֹאמְרוּ קוּמָה וְהוֹשִׁיעֵנוּ:
28 וְאַיֵּה אֱלֹהֶיךָ אֲשֶׁר עָשִׂיתָ לָּךְ יָקוּמוּ אִם־
יוֹשִׁיעוּךָ בְּעֵת רָעָתֶךָ כִּי מִסְפַּר עָרֶיךָ הָיוּ אֱלֹהֶיךָ
יְהוּדָה: ס   29 לָמָּה תָרִיבוּ אֵלַי כֻּלְּכֶם
פְּשַׁעְתֶּם בִּי נְאֻם־יְהוָה: 30 לַשָּׁוְא הִכֵּיתִי אֶת־
בְּנֵיכֶם מוּסָר לֹא לָקָחוּ אָכְלָה חַרְבְּכֶם נְבִיאֵיכֶם
כְּאַרְיֵה מַשְׁחִית: 31 הַדּוֹר אַתֶּם רְאוּ דְבַר־יְהוָה
הֲמִדְבָּר הָיִיתִי לְיִשְׂרָאֵל אִם אֶרֶץ מַאְפֵּלְיָה מַדּוּעַ
אָמְרוּ עַמִּי רַדְנוּ לוֹא־נָבוֹא עוֹד אֵלֶיךָ: 32 הֲתִשְׁכַּח
בְּתוּלָה עֶדְיָהּ כַּלָּה קִשֻּׁרֶיהָ וְעַמִּי שְׁכֵחוּנִי יָמִים אֵין
מִסְפָּר: 33 מַה־תֵּיטִבִי דַּרְכֵּךְ לְבַקֵּשׁ אַהֲבָה לָכֵן גַּם
אֶת־הָרָעוֹת לִמַּדְתִּי אֶת־דְּרָכָיִךְ: 34 גַּם בִּכְנָפַיִךְ
נִמְצְאוּ דַּם נַפְשׁוֹת אֶבְיוֹנִים נְקִיִּים לֹא־בַמַּחְתֶּרֶת
מְצָאתִים כִּי עַל־כָּל־אֵלֶּה: 35 וַתֹּאמְרִי כִּי נִקֵּיתִי
אַךְ שָׁב אַפּוֹ מִמֶּנִּי הִנְנִי נִשְׁפָּט אוֹתָךְ עַל־אָמְרֵךְ
לֹא חָטָאתִי: 36 מַה־תֵּזְלִי מְאֹד לְשַׁנּוֹת אֶת־דַּרְכֵּךְ
גַּם מִמִּצְרַיִם תֵּבוֹשִׁי כַּאֲשֶׁר־בֹּשְׁתְּ מֵאַשּׁוּר: 37 גַּם
מֵאֵת זֶה תֵּצְאִי וְיָדַיִךְ עַל־רֹאשֵׁךְ כִּי־מָאַס יְהוָה
בְּמִבְטַחַיִךְ וְלֹא תַצְלִיחִי לָהֶם:

ב 24 נַפְשָׁהּ   25 וּגְרוֹנֵךְ   27 יְלִדְתָּנוּ   33 לִמַּדְתְּ

For the LORD has rejected your trusted allies,
And you will not prosper by them.

3 "They say, 'If a man divorces his wife,
And she goes from him
And becomes another man's,
May he return to her again?'
Would not that land be greatly polluted?
But you have played the harlot with many lovers;
Yet return to Me," says the LORD.

2 "Lift up your eyes to the desolate heights and see:
Where have you not lain *with men*?
By the road you have sat for them
Like an Arabian in the wilderness;
And you have polluted the land
With your harlotries and your wickedness.

3 Therefore the showers have been withheld,
And there has been no latter rain.
You have had a harlot's forehead;
You refuse to be ashamed.

4 Will you not from this time cry to Me,
'My Father, You *are* the guide of my youth?

5 Will He remain angry forever?
Will He keep it to the end?'
Behold, you have spoken and done evil things,
As you were able."

6 The LORD said also to me in the days of Josiah
the king: "Have you seen what backsliding Israel
has done? She has gone up on every high mountain
and under every green tree, and there played the
harlot. 7 And I said, after she had done all these
things, 'Return to Me.' But she did not return. And
her treacherous sister Judah saw it. 8 Then I saw
that for all the causes for which backsliding Israel
had committed adultery, I had put her away and
given her a certificate of divorce; yet her treacherous sister Judah did not fear, but went and played
the harlot also. 9 So it came to pass, through her
casual harlotry, that she defiled the land and
committed adultery with stones and trees. 10 And
yet for all this her treacherous sister Judah has not
turned to Me with her whole heart, but in
pretense," says the LORD.

11 Then the LORD said to me, "Backsliding Israel
has shown herself more righteous than treacherous
Judah. 12 Go and proclaim these words toward the
north, and say:

'Return, backsliding Israel,' says the LORD;
'I will not cause My anger to fall on you.
For I *am* merciful,' says the LORD;
'I will not remain angry forever.

13 Only acknowledge your iniquity,
That you have transgressed against the LORD
your God,
And have scattered your charms
To alien deities under every green tree,

מֵאֵת זֶה תֵּצְאִי וְיָדַיִךְ עַל־רֹאשֵׁךְ כִּי־מָאַס יְהוָה
בְּמִבְטַחַיִךְ וְלֹא תַצְלִיחִי לָהֶם:

ג לֵאמֹר הֵן יְשַׁלַּח אִישׁ אֶת־אִשְׁתּוֹ וְהָלְכָה
מֵאִתּוֹ וְהָיְתָה לְאִישׁ־אַחֵר הֲיָשׁוּב אֵלֶיהָ עוֹד הֲלוֹא
חָנוֹף תֶּחֱנַף הָאָרֶץ הַהִיא וְאַתְּ זָנִית רֵעִים רַבִּים
וְשׁוֹב אֵלַי נְאֻם־יְהוָה: 2 שְׂאִי־עֵינַיִךְ עַל־שְׁפָיִם וּרְאִי
אֵיפֹה לֹא שֻׁגַּלְתְּ עַל־דְּרָכִים יָשַׁבְתְּ לָהֶם כַּעֲרָבִי
בַּמִּדְבָּר וַתַּחֲנִיפִי אֶרֶץ בִּזְנוּתַיִךְ וּבְרָעָתֵךְ: 3 וַיִּמָּנְעוּ
רְבִבִים וּמַלְקוֹשׁ לוֹא הָיָה וּמֵצַח אִשָּׁה זוֹנָה הָיָה
לָךְ מֵאַנְתְּ הִכָּלֵם: 4 הֲלוֹא מֵעַתָּה קָרָאתי לִי
אָבִי אַלּוּף נְעֻרַי אָתָּה: 5 הֲיִנְטֹר לְעוֹלָם אִם־יִשְׁמֹר
לָנֶצַח הִנֵּה דִבַּרְתִּ וַתַּעֲשִׂי הָרָעוֹת וַתּוּכָל: פ

6 וַיֹּאמֶר יְהוָה אֵלַי בִּימֵי יֹאשִׁיָּהוּ הַמֶּלֶךְ הֲרָאִיתָ
אֲשֶׁר עָשְׂתָה מְשֻׁבָה יִשְׂרָאֵל הֹלְכָה הִיא עַל־
כָּל־הַר גָּבֹהַּ וְאֶל־תַּחַת כָּל־עֵץ רַעֲנָן וַתִּזְנִי־שָׁם:
7 וָאֹמַר אַחֲרֵי עֲשׂוֹתָהּ אֶת־כָּל־אֵלֶּה אֵלַי תָּשׁוּב
וְלֹא־שָׁבָה וַתֵּרֶאה בָּגוֹדָה אֲחוֹתָהּ יְהוּדָה: 8 וָאֵרֶא
כִּי עַל־כָּל־אֹדוֹת אֲשֶׁר נִאֲפָה מְשֻׁבָה יִשְׂרָאֵל
שִׁלַּחְתִּיהָ וָאֶתֵּן אֶת־סֵפֶר כְּרִיתֻתֶיהָ אֵלֶיהָ וְלֹא
יָרְאָה בֹּגֵדָה יְהוּדָה אֲחוֹתָהּ וַתֵּלֶךְ וַתִּזֶן גַּם־הִיא:
9 וְהָיָה מִקֹּל זְנוּתָהּ וַתֶּחֱנַף אֶת־הָאָרֶץ וַתִּנְאַף אֶת־
הָאֶבֶן וְאֶת־הָעֵץ: 10 וְגַם־בְּכָל־זֹאת לֹא־שָׁבָה אֵלַי
בָּגוֹדָה אֲחוֹתָהּ יְהוּדָה בְּכָל־לִבָּהּ כִּי אִם־בְּשֶׁקֶר
נְאֻם־יְהוָה: פ

11 וַיֹּאמֶר יְהוָה אֵלַי צִדְּקָה נַפְשָׁהּ מְשֻׁבָה יִשְׂרָאֵל
מִבֹּגֵדָה יְהוּדָה: 12 הָלֹךְ וְקָרָאתָ אֶת־הַדְּבָרִים
הָאֵלֶּה צָפוֹנָה וְאָמַרְתָּ שׁוּבָה מְשֻׁבָה יִשְׂרָאֵל נְאֻם־
יְהוָה לוֹא־אַפִּיל פָּנַי בָּכֶם כִּי־חָסִיד אֲנִי נְאֻם־
יְהוָה לֹא אֶטּוֹר לְעוֹלָם: 13 אַךְ דְּעִי עֲוֹנֵךְ כִּי
בַּיהוָה אֱלֹהַיִךְ פָּשָׁעַתְּ וַתְּפַזְּרִי אֶת־דְּרָכַיִךְ לַזָּרִים

And you have not obeyed My voice,' says the
LORD.

14 "Return, O backsliding children," says the
LORD; "for I am married to you. I will take you,
one from a city and two from a family, and I will
bring you to Zion. 15 And I will give you shepherds
according to My heart, who will feed you with
knowledge and understanding.

16 "Then it shall come to pass, when you are
multiplied and increased in the land in those days,"
says the LORD, "that they will say no more, 'The
ark of the covenant of the LORD.' It shall not come
to mind, nor shall they remember it, nor shall they
visit it, nor shall it be made anymore.

17 "At that time Jerusalem shall be called The
Throne of the LORD, and all the nations shall be
gathered to it, to the name of the LORD, to
Jerusalem. No more shall they follow the dictates
of their evil hearts.

18 "In those days the house of Judah shall walk
with the house of Israel, and they shall come
together out of the land of the north to the land that
I have given as an inheritance to your fathers.

19 "But I said:

'How can I put you among the children
And give you a pleasant land,
A beautiful heritage of the hosts of nations?'

"And I said:

'You shall call Me, "My Father,"
And not turn away from Me.'

20   Surely, as a wife treacherously departs from her
     husband,
So have you dealt treacherously with Me,
O house of Israel," says the LORD.

21   A voice was heard on the desolate heights,
Weeping and supplications of the children of
     Israel.
For they have perverted their way;
They have forgotten the LORD their God.

22   "Return, you backsliding children,
And I will heal your backslidings."

"Indeed we do come to You,
For You are the LORD our God.

23   Truly, in vain is salvation hoped for from the hills,
And from the multitude of mountains;
Truly, in the LORD our God
Is the salvation of Israel.

24   For shame has devoured
The labor of our fathers from our youth—
Their flocks and their herds,
Their sons and their daughters.

25   We lie down in our shame,
And our reproach covers us.
For we have sinned against the LORD our God,
We and our fathers,
From our youth even to this day,

תַּחַת כָּל־עֵץ רַעֲנָן וּבְקוֹלִי לֹא־שְׁמַעְתֶּם נְאֻם־
יְהֹוָה: 14 שׁוּבוּ בָנִים שׁוֹבָבִים נְאֻם־יְהֹוָה כִּי אָנֹכִי
בָּעַלְתִּי בָכֶם וְלָקַחְתִּי אֶתְכֶם אֶחָד מֵעִיר וּשְׁנַיִם
מִמִּשְׁפָּחָה וְהֵבֵאתִי אֶתְכֶם צִיּוֹן: 15 וְנָתַתִּי לָכֶם
רֹעִים כְּלִבִּי וְרָעוּ אֶתְכֶם דֵּעָה וְהַשְׂכֵּיל: 16 וְהָיָה
כִּי תִרְבּוּ וּפְרִיתֶם בָּאָרֶץ בַּיָּמִים הָהֵמָּה נְאֻם־יְהֹוָה
לֹא־יֹאמְרוּ עוֹד אֲרוֹן בְּרִית־יְהֹוָה וְלֹא יַעֲלֶה עַל־לֵב
וְלֹא יִזְכְּרוּ־בוֹ וְלֹא יִפְקֹדוּ וְלֹא יֵעָשֶׂה עוֹד: 17 בָּעֵת
הַהִיא יִקְרְאוּ לִירוּשָׁלַםִ כִּסֵּא יְהֹוָה וְנִקְוּוּ אֵלֶיהָ
כָל־הַגּוֹיִם לְשֵׁם יְהֹוָה לִירוּשָׁלָםִ וְלֹא־יֵלְכוּ עוֹד
אַחֲרֵי שְׁרִרוּת לִבָּם הָרָע: ס 18 בַּיָּמִים
הָהֵמָּה יֵלְכוּ בֵית־יְהוּדָה עַל־בֵּית יִשְׂרָאֵל וְיָבֹאוּ
יַחְדָּו מֵאֶרֶץ צָפוֹן עַל־הָאָרֶץ אֲשֶׁר הִנְחַלְתִּי אֶת־
אֲבוֹתֵיכֶם: 19 וְאָנֹכִי אָמַרְתִּי אֵיךְ אֲשִׁיתֵךְ בַּבָּנִים
וְאֶתֶּן־לָךְ אֶרֶץ חֶמְדָּה נַחֲלַת צְבִי צִבְאוֹת גּוֹיִם
וָאֹמַר אָבִי תִּקְרְאוּ־לִי וּמֵאַחֲרַי לֹא
תָשׁוּבוּ: 20 אָכֵן בָּגְדָה אִשָּׁה מֵרֵעָהּ כֵּן בְּגַדְתֶּם בִּי
בֵּית יִשְׂרָאֵל נְאֻם־יְהֹוָה: 21 קוֹל עַל־שְׁפָיִים נִשְׁמָע
בְּכִי תַחֲנוּנֵי בְּנֵי יִשְׂרָאֵל כִּי הֶעֱווּ אֶת־דַּרְכָּם שָׁכְחוּ
אֶת־יְהֹוָה אֱלֹהֵיהֶם: 22 שׁוּבוּ בָּנִים שׁוֹבָבִים אֶרְפָּה
מְשׁוּבֹתֵיכֶם הִנְנוּ אָתָנוּ לָךְ כִּי אַתָּה יְהֹוָה אֱלֹהֵינוּ:
23 אָכֵן לַשֶּׁקֶר מִגְּבָעוֹת הָמוֹן הָרִים אָכֵן בַּיהֹוָה
אֱלֹהֵינוּ תְּשׁוּעַת יִשְׂרָאֵל: 24 וְהַבֹּשֶׁת אָכְלָה אֶת־
יְגִיעַ אֲבוֹתֵינוּ מִנְּעוּרֵינוּ אֶת־צֹאנָם וְאֶת־בְּקָרָם אֶת־
בְּנֵיהֶם וְאֶת־בְּנוֹתֵיהֶם: 25 נִשְׁכְּבָה בְּבָשְׁתֵּנוּ וּתְכַסֵּנוּ
כְּלִמָּתֵנוּ כִּי לַיהֹוָה אֱלֹהֵינוּ חָטָאנוּ אֲנַחְנוּ וַאֲבוֹתֵינוּ

And have not obeyed the voice of the LORD our God."

מְנַעוּרֵינוּ וְעַד־הַיּוֹם הַזֶּה וְלֹא שָׁמַעְנוּ בְּקוֹל יְהוָה
אֱלֹהֵינוּ: ס

4 "If you will return, O Israel," says the LORD,
"Return to Me;
And if you will put away your abominations out
of My sight,
Then you shall not be moved.
2 And you shall swear, 'The LORD lives,'
In truth, in judgment, and in righteousness;
The nations shall bless themselves in Him,
And in Him they shall glory."

אִם־תָּשׁוּב יִשְׂרָאֵל | נְאֻם־יְהוָה אֵלַי תָּשׁוּב
וְאִם־תָּסִיר שִׁקּוּצֶיךָ מִפָּנַי וְלֹא תָנוּד: 2 וְנִשְׁבַּעְתָּ
חַי־יְהוָה בֶּאֱמֶת בְּמִשְׁפָּט וּבִצְדָקָה וְהִתְבָּרְכוּ בוֹ
גּוֹיִם וּבוֹ יִתְהַלָּלוּ: ס

3 For thus says the LORD to the men of Judah and Jerusalem:

"Break up your fallow ground,
And do not sow among thorns.
4 Circumcise yourselves to the LORD,
And take away the foreskins of your hearts,
You men of Judah and inhabitants of Jerusalem,
Lest My fury come forth like fire,
And burn so that no one can quench it,
Because of the evil of your doings."

3 כִּי־כֹה | אָמַר
יְהוָה לְאִישׁ יְהוּדָה וְלִירוּשָׁלִַם נִירוּ לָכֶם נִיר
וְאַל־תִּזְרְעוּ אֶל־קוֹצִים: 4 הִמֹּלוּ לַיהוָה וְהָסִרוּ
עָרְלוֹת לְבַבְכֶם אִישׁ יְהוּדָה וְיֹשְׁבֵי יְרוּשָׁלִָם פֶּן־
תֵּצֵא כָאֵשׁ חֲמָתִי וּבָעֲרָה וְאֵין מְכַבֶּה מִפְּנֵי רֹעַ
מַעַלְלֵיכֶם:

5 Declare in Judah and proclaim in Jerusalem, and say:

"Blow the trumpet in the land;
Cry, 'Gather together,'
And say, 'Assemble yourselves,
And let us go into the fortified cities.'
6 Set up the standard toward Zion.
Take refuge! Do not delay!
For I will bring disaster from the north,
And great destruction."

5 הַגִּידוּ בִיהוּדָה וּבִירוּשָׁלִַם הַשְׁמִיעוּ
וְאִמְרוּ וְתִקְעוּ שׁוֹפָר בָּאָרֶץ קִרְאוּ מַלְאוּ וְאִמְרוּ
הֵאָסְפוּ וְנָבוֹאָה אֶל־עָרֵי הַמִּבְצָר: 6 שְׂאוּ־נֵס צִיּוֹנָה
הָעִיזוּ אַל־תַּעֲמֹדוּ כִּי רָעָה אָנֹכִי מֵבִיא מִצָּפוֹן
וְשֶׁבֶר גָּדוֹל:

7 The lion has come up from his thicket,
And the destroyer of nations is on his way.
He has gone forth from his place
To make your land desolate.
Your cities will be laid waste,
Without inhabitant.
8 For this, clothe yourself with sackcloth,
Lament and wail.
For the fierce anger of the LORD
Has not turned back from us.

7 עָלָה אַרְיֵה מִסֻּבְּכוֹ וּמַשְׁחִית גּוֹיִם
נָסַע יָצָא מִמְּקֹמוֹ לָשׂוּם אַרְצֵךְ לְשַׁמָּה עָרַיִךְ תִּצֶּינָה
מֵאֵין יוֹשֵׁב: 8 עַל־זֹאת חִגְרוּ שַׂקִּים סִפְדוּ וְהֵילִילוּ
כִּי לֹא־שָׁב חֲרוֹן אַף־יְהוָה מִמֶּנּוּ: פ

9 "And it shall come to pass in that day," says the LORD,
"That the heart of the king shall perish,
And the heart of the princes;
The priests shall be astonished,
And the prophets shall wonder."

9 וְהָיָה בַיּוֹם־הַהוּא נְאֻם־יְהוָה יֹאבַד לֵב־הַמֶּלֶךְ
וְלֵב הַשָּׂרִים וְנָשַׁמּוּ הַכֹּהֲנִים וְהַנְּבִיאִים יִתְמָהוּ:

10 Then I said, "Ah, Lord GOD!
Surely You have greatly deceived this people and Jerusalem,
Saying, 'You shall have peace,'
Whereas the sword reaches to the heart."

10 וָאֹמַר אֲהָהּ | אֲדֹנָי יְהוִה אָכֵן הַשֵּׁא הִשֵּׁאתָ
לָעָם הַזֶּה וְלִירוּשָׁלִַם לֵאמֹר שָׁלוֹם יִהְיֶה לָכֶם
וְנָגְעָה חֶרֶב עַד־הַנָּפֶשׁ:

11 At that time it will be said
To this people and to Jerusalem,
"A dry wind of the desolate heights blows in the wilderness
Toward the daughter of My people—

11 בָּעֵת הַהִיא יֵאָמֵר לָעָם־
הַזֶּה וְלִירוּשָׁלִַם רוּחַ צַח שְׁפָיִם בַּמִּדְבָּר דֶּרֶךְ בַּת־

Not to fan or to cleanse—
12 A wind too strong for these will come for Me;
   Now I will also speak judgment against them."

13 "Behold, he shall come up like clouds,
   And his chariots like a whirlwind.
   His horses are swifter than eagles.
   Woe to us, for we are plundered!"

14 O Jerusalem, wash your heart from wickedness,
   That you may be saved.
   How long shall your evil thoughts lodge within
      you?

15 For a voice declares from Dan
   And proclaims affliction from Mount Ephraim:

16 "Make mention to the nations,
   Yes, proclaim against Jerusalem,
   That watchers come from a far country
   And raise their voice against the cities of Judah.

17 Like keepers of a field they are against her all
      around,
   Because she has been rebellious against Me," says
      the LORD.

18 "Your ways and your doings
   Have procured these *things* for you.
   This *is* your wickedness,
   Because it is bitter,
   Because it reaches to your heart."

19 O my soul, my soul!
   I am pained in my very heart!
   My heart makes a noise in me;
   I cannot hold my peace,
   Because you have heard, O my soul,
   The sound of the trumpet,
   The alarm of war.

20 Destruction upon destruction is cried,
   For the whole land is plundered.
   Suddenly my tents are plundered,
   And my curtains in a moment.

21 How long will I see the standard,
   And hear the sound of the trumpet?

22 "For My people *are* foolish,
   They have not known Me.
   They *are* silly children,
   And they have no understanding.
   They *are* wise to do evil,
   But to do good they have no knowledge."

23 I beheld the earth, and indeed *it was* without
      form, and void;
   And the heavens, they *had* no light.

24 I beheld the mountains, and indeed they
      trembled,
   And all the hills moved back and forth.

25 I beheld, and indeed *there was* no man,
   And all the birds of the heavens had fled.

26 I beheld, and indeed the fruitful land *was* a
      wilderness,
   And all its cities were broken down
   At the presence of the LORD,
   By His fierce anger.

27 For thus says the LORD:

   "The whole land shall be desolate;

עַמִּי לֹוא לִזְרֹות וְלֹוא לְהָבַר: 12 רוּחַ מָלֵא מֵאֵלֶּה
יָבֹוא לִי עַתָּה גַּם־אֲנִי אֲדַבֵּר מִשְׁפָּטִים אֹותָם:
13 הִנֵּה | כַּעֲנָנִים יַעֲלֶה וְכַסּוּפָה מַרְכְּבֹותָיו קַלּוּ
מִנְּשָׁרִים סוּסָיו אֹוי לָנוּ כִּי שֻׁדָּדְנוּ: 14 כַּבְּסִי מֵרָעָה
לִבֵּךְ יְרוּשָׁלַ͏ִם לְמַעַן תִּוָּשֵׁעִי עַד־מָתַי תָּלִין בְּקִרְבֵּךְ
מַחְשְׁבֹות אֹונֵךְ: 15 כִּי קֹול מַגִּיד מִדָּן וּמַשְׁמִיעַ אָוֶן
מֵהַר אֶפְרָיִם: 16 הַזְכִּירוּ לַגֹּויִם הִנֵּה הַשְׁמִיעוּ עַל־
יְרוּשָׁלַ͏ִם נֹצְרִים בָּאִים מֵאֶרֶץ הַמֶּרְחָק וַיִּתְּנוּ עַל־עָרֵי
יְהוּדָה קֹולָם: 17 כְּשֹׁמְרֵי שָׂדַי הָיוּ עָלֶיהָ מִסָּבִיב
כִּי־אֹתִי מָרָתָה נְאֻם־יְהֹוָה: 18 דַּרְכֵּךְ וּמַעֲלָלַיִךְ
עָשֹׂו אֵלֶּה לָךְ זֹאת רָעָתֵךְ כִּי מָר כִּי נָגַע עַד־
לִבֵּךְ: ס   19 מֵעַי | מֵעַי | אֹחֹולָהP קִירֹות
לִבִּי הֹמֶה־לִּי לִבִּי לֹא אַחֲרִישׁ כִּי קֹול שֹׁופָר
שָׁמַעַתְּP נַפְשִׁי תְּרוּעַת מִלְחָמָה: 20 שֶׁבֶר עַל־
שֶׁבֶר נִקְרָא כִּי שֻׁדְּדָה כָּל־הָאָרֶץ פִּתְאֹם שֻׁדְּדוּ
אֹהָלַי רֶגַע יְרִיעֹתָי: 21 עַד־מָתַי אֶרְאֶה־נֵּס אֶשְׁמְעָה
קֹול שֹׁופָר: ס   22 כִּי | אֱוִיל עַמִּי אֹותִי
לֹא יָדָעוּ בָּנִים סְכָלִים הֵמָּה וְלֹא נְבֹונִים הֵמָּה
חֲכָמִים הֵמָּה לְהָרַע וּלְהֵיטִיב לֹא יָדָעוּ: 23 רָאִיתִי
אֶת־הָאָרֶץ וְהִנֵּה־תֹהוּ וָבֹהוּ וְאֶל־הַשָּׁמַיִם וְאֵין
אֹורָם: 24 רָאִיתִי הֶהָרִים וְהִנֵּה רֹעֲשִׁים וְכָל־
הַגְּבָעֹות הִתְקַלְקָלוּ: 25 רָאִיתִי וְהִנֵּה אֵין הָאָדָם
וְכָל־עֹוף הַשָּׁמַיִם נָדָדוּ: 26 רָאִיתִי וְהִנֵּה הַכַּרְמֶל
הַמִּדְבָּר וְכָל־עָרָיו נִתְּצוּ מִפְּנֵי יְהֹוָה מִפְּנֵי חֲרֹון
אַפֹּו: ס   27 כִּי־כֹה אָמַר יְהֹוָה שְׁמָמָה

ד 19 אֹוחִילָה שָׁמַעְתִּי

Yet I will not make a full end.

28 For this shall the earth mourn,
And the heavens above be black,
Because I have spoken.
I have purposed and will not relent,
Nor will I turn back from it.

29 The whole city shall flee from the noise of the
    horsemen and bowmen.
They shall go into thickets and climb up on the
    rocks.
Every city *shall be* forsaken,
And not a man shall dwell in it.

30 "And *when* you *are* plundered,
What will you do?
Though you clothe yourself with crimson,
Though you adorn *yourself* with ornaments of
    gold,
Though you enlarge your eyes with paint,
In vain you will make yourself fair;
Your lovers will despise you;
They will seek your life.

31 "For I have heard a voice as of a woman in labor,
The anguish as of her who brings forth her first
    child,
The voice of the daughter of Zion bewailing
    herself;
She spreads her hands, *saying,*
'Woe *is* me now, for my soul is weary
Because of murderers!'

5 "Run to and fro through the streets of Jerusalem;
See now and know;
And seek in her open places
If you can find a man,
If there is *anyone* who executes judgment,
Who seeks the truth,
And I will pardon her.

2 Though they say, 'As the LORD lives,'
Surely they swear falsely."

3 O LORD, *are* not Your eyes on the truth?
You have stricken them,
But they have not grieved;
You have consumed them,
But they have refused to receive correction.
They have made their faces harder than rock;
They have refused to return.

4 Therefore I said, "Surely these *are* poor.
They are foolish;
For they do not know the way of the LORD,
The judgment of their God.

5 I will go to the great men and speak to them,
For they have known the way of the LORD,
The judgment of their God."

But these have altogether broken the yoke
And burst the bonds.

6 Therefore a lion from the forest shall slay them,
A wolf of the deserts shall destroy them;
A leopard will watch over their cities.
Everyone who goes out from there shall be torn
    in pieces,

תִּהְיֶה כָל־הָאָרֶץ וְכָלָה לֹא אֶעֱשֶׂה: 28 עַל־זֹאת
תֶּאֱבַל הָאָרֶץ וְקָדְרוּ הַשָּׁמַיִם מִמָּעַל עַל כִּי־דִבַּרְתִּי
זַמֹּתִי וְלֹא נִחַמְתִּי וְלֹא־אָשׁוּב מִמֶּנָּה: 29 מִקּוֹל
פָּרָשׁ וְרֹמֵה קֶשֶׁת בֹּרַחַת כָּל־הָעִיר בָּאוּ בֶּעָבִים
וּבַכֵּפִים עָלוּ כָּל־הָעִיר עֲזוּבָה וְאֵין־יוֹשֵׁב בָּהֵן
אִישׁ: 30 וְאַתִּי שָׁדוּד מַה־תַּעֲשִׂי כִּי־תִלְבְּשִׁי שָׁנִי
כִּי־תַעְדִּי עֲדִי־זָהָב כִּי־תִקְרְעִי בַפּוּךְ עֵינַיִךְ לַשָּׁוְא
תִּתְיַפִּי מָאֲסוּ־בָךְ עֹגְבִים נַפְשֵׁךְ יְבַקֵּשׁוּ: 31 כִּי
קוֹל כְּחוֹלָה שָׁמַעְתִּי צָרָה כְּמַבְכִּירָה קוֹל בַּת־צִיּוֹן
תִּתְיַפֵּחַ תְּפָרֵשׂ כַּפֶּיהָ אוֹי־נָא לִי כִּי־עָיְפָה נַפְשִׁי
לְהֹרְגִים: פ

ה שׁוֹטְטוּ בְּחוּצוֹת יְרוּשָׁלִַם וּרְאוּ־נָא וּדְעוּ וּבַקְשׁוּ
בִרְחוֹבוֹתֶיהָ אִם־תִּמְצְאוּ אִישׁ אִם־יֵשׁ עֹשֶׂה מִשְׁפָּט
מְבַקֵּשׁ אֱמוּנָה וְאֶסְלַח לָהּ: 2 וְאִם חַי־יְהֹוָה יֹאמֵרוּ
לָכֵן לַשֶּׁקֶר יִשָּׁבֵעוּ: 3 יְהֹוָה עֵינֶיךָ הֲלוֹא לֶאֱמוּנָה
הִכִּיתָה אֹתָם וְלֹא־חָלוּ כִּלִּיתָם מֵאֲנוּ קַחַת מוּסָר
חִזְּקוּ פְנֵיהֶם מִסֶּלַע מֵאֲנוּ לָשׁוּב: 4 וַאֲנִי אָמַרְתִּי
אַךְ־דַּלִּים הֵם נוֹאֲלוּ כִּי לֹא יָדְעוּ דֶּרֶךְ יְהֹוָה
מִשְׁפַּט אֱלֹהֵיהֶם: 5 אֵלְכָה־לִּי אֶל־הַגְּדֹלִים וַאֲדַבְּרָה
אוֹתָם כִּי הֵמָּה יָדְעוּ דֶּרֶךְ יְהֹוָה מִשְׁפַּט אֱלֹהֵיהֶם
אַךְ הֵמָּה יַחְדָּו שָׁבְרוּ עֹל נִתְּקוּ מוֹסֵרוֹת: 6 עַל־
כֵּן הִכָּם אַרְיֵה מִיַּעַר זְאֵב עֲרָבוֹת יְשָׁדְדֵם נָמֵר
שֹׁקֵד עַל־עָרֵיהֶם כָּל־הַיּוֹצֵא מֵהֵנָּה יִטָּרֵף כִּי

Because their transgressions are many;
Their backslidings have increased.

7 "How shall I pardon you for this?
Your children have forsaken Me
And sworn by *those that are* not gods.
When I had fed them to the full,
Then they committed adultery
And assembled themselves by troops in the
harlots' houses.
8 They were *like* well-fed lusty stallions;
Every one neighed after his neighbor's wife.
9 Shall I not punish *them* for these *things?*" says the
LORD.
"And shall I not avenge Myself on such a nation as
this?

10 "Go up on her walls and destroy,
But do not make a complete end.
Take away her branches,
For they *are* not the LORD's.
11 For the house of Israel and the house of Judah
Have dealt very treacherously with Me," says the
LORD.

12 They have lied about the LORD,
And said, "*It is* not He.
Neither will evil come upon us,
Nor shall we see sword or famine.
13 And the prophets become wind,
For the word *is* not in them.
Thus shall it be done to them."

14 Therefore thus says the LORD God of hosts:

"Because you speak this word,
Behold, I will make My words in your mouth fire,
And this people wood,
And it shall devour them.
15 Behold, I will bring a nation against you from
afar,
O house of Israel," says the LORD.
"It *is* a mighty nation,
It *is* an ancient nation,
A nation whose language you do not know,
Nor can you understand what they say.
16 Their quiver *is* like an open tomb;
They *are* all mighty men.
17 And they shall eat up your harvest and your
bread,
Which your sons and daughters should eat.
They shall eat up your flocks and your herds;
They shall eat up your vines and your fig trees;
They shall destroy your fortified cities,
In which you trust, with the sword.

18 "Nevertheless in those days," says the LORD,
"I will not make a complete end of you. 19 And it
will be when you say, 'Why does the LORD our God
do all these *things* to us?' then you shall answer
them, 'Just as you have forsaken Me and served
foreign gods in your land, so you shall serve aliens
in a land *that is* not yours.'

20 "Declare this in the house of Jacob

רַבּוּ פִּשְׁעֵיהֶם עָצְמוּ מְשֻׁבוֹתֵיהֶם׃ 7 אֵי לָזֹאת
אֶסְלוֹחַ־לָךְ בָּנַיִךְ עֲזָבוּנִי וַיִּשָּׁבְעוּ בְּלֹא אֱלֹהִים
וָאַשְׂבִּעַ אוֹתָם וַיִּנְאָפוּ וּבֵית זוֹנָה יִתְגֹּדָדוּ׃ 8 סוּסִים
מְיֻזָּנִים מַשְׁכִּים הָיוּ אִישׁ אֶל־אֵשֶׁת רֵעֵהוּ יִצְהָלוּ׃
9 הַעַל־אֵלֶּה לוֹא־אֶפְקֹד נְאֻם־יְהֹוָה וְאִם בְּגוֹי
אֲשֶׁר־כָּזֶה לֹא תִתְנַקֵּם נַפְשִׁי׃ ס 10 עֲלוּ
בְשָׁרוֹתֶיהָ וְשַׁחֵתוּ וְכָלָה אַל־תַּעֲשׂוּ הָסִירוּ
נְטִישׁוֹתֶיהָ כִּי לוֹא לַיהֹוָה הֵמָּה׃ 11 כִּי בָגוֹד
בָּגְדוּ בִּי בֵּית יִשְׂרָאֵל וּבֵית יְהוּדָה נְאֻם־
יְהֹוָה׃ 12 כִּחֲשׁוּ בַּיהֹוָה וַיֹּאמְרוּ לֹא־הוּא וְלֹא־
תָבוֹא עָלֵינוּ רָעָה וְחֶרֶב וְרָעָב לוֹא נִרְאֶה׃
13 וְהַנְּבִיאִים יִהְיוּ לְרוּחַ וְהַדִּבֵּר אֵין בָּהֶם כֹּה
יֵעָשֶׂה לָהֶם׃ ס 14 לָכֵן כֹּה־אָמַר יְהֹוָה
אֱלֹהֵי צְבָאוֹת יַעַן דַּבֶּרְכֶם אֶת־הַדָּבָר הַזֶּה הִנְנִי
נֹתֵן דְּבָרַי בְּפִיךָ לְאֵשׁ וְהָעָם הַזֶּה עֵצִים וַאֲכָלָתַם׃
15 הִנְנִי מֵבִיא עֲלֵיכֶם גּוֹי מִמֶּרְחָק בֵּית יִשְׂרָאֵל
נְאֻם־יְהֹוָה גּוֹי אֵיתָן הוּא גּוֹי מֵעוֹלָם הוּא גּוֹי
לֹא־תֵדַע לְשֹׁנוֹ וְלֹא תִשְׁמַע מַה־יְדַבֵּר׃ 16 אַשְׁפָּתוֹ
כְּקֶבֶר פָּתוּחַ כֻּלָּם גִּבּוֹרִים׃ 17 וְאָכַל קְצִירְךָ וְלַחְמֶךָ
יֹאכְלוּ בָּנֶיךָ וּבְנוֹתֶיךָ יֹאכַל צֹאנְךָ וּבְקָרֶךָ יֹאכַל
גַּפְנְךָ וּתְאֵנָתֶךָ יְרֹשֵׁשׁ עָרֵי מִבְצָרֶיךָ אֲשֶׁר אַתָּה
בּוֹטֵחַ בָּהֵנָּה בֶּחָרֶב׃ 18 וְגַם בַּיָּמִים הָהֵמָּה נְאֻם־
יְהֹוָה לֹא־אֶעֱשֶׂה אִתְּכֶם כָּלָה׃ 19 וְהָיָה כִּי תֹאמְרוּ
תַּחַת מֶה עָשָׂה יְהֹוָה אֱלֹהֵינוּ לָנוּ אֶת־כָּל־אֵלֶּה
וְאָמַרְתָּ אֲלֵהֶם כַּאֲשֶׁר עֲזַבְתֶּם אוֹתִי וַתַּעַבְדוּ
אֱלֹהֵי נֵכָר בְּאַרְצְכֶם כֵּן תַּעַבְדוּ זָרִים בְּאֶרֶץ
לֹא לָכֶם׃ ס 20 הַגִּידוּ זֹאת בְּבֵית יַעֲקֹב

And proclaim it in Judah, saying,

21 'Hear this now, O foolish people,
Without understanding,
Who have eyes and see not,
And who have ears and hear not:

22 Do you not fear Me?' says the LORD.
'Will you not tremble at My presence,
Who have placed the sand as the bound of the
sea,
By a perpetual decree, that it cannot pass beyond
it?
And though its waves toss to and fro,
Yet they cannot prevail;
Though they roar, yet they cannot pass over it.

23 But this people has a defiant and rebellious heart;
They have revolted and departed.

24 They do not say in their heart,

"Let us now fear the LORD our God,
Who gives rain, both the former and the latter, in
its season.
He reserves for us the appointed weeks of the
harvest."

25 Your iniquities have turned these *things* away,
And your sins have withheld good from you.

26 'For among My people are found wicked *men;*
They lie in wait as one who sets snares;
They set a trap;
They catch men.

27 As a cage is full of birds,
So their houses *are* full of deceit.
Therefore they have become great and grown
rich.

28 They have grown fat, they are sleek;
Yes, they surpass the deeds of the wicked;
They do not plead the cause,
The cause of the fatherless;
Yet they prosper,
And the right of the needy they do not defend.

29 Shall I not punish *them* for these *things?*' says the
LORD.
'Shall I not avenge Myself on such a nation as
this?'

30 "An astonishing and horrible thing
Has been committed in the land:

31 The prophets prophesy falsely,
And the priests rule by their *own* power;
And My people love *to have it* so.
But what will you do in the end?

6 "O you children of Benjamin,
Gather yourselves to flee from the midst of
Jerusalem!
Blow the trumpet in Tekoa,
And set up a signal-fire in Beth Haccerem;
For disaster appears out of the north,
And great destruction.

2 I have likened the daughter of Zion
To a lovely and delicate woman.

3 The shepherds with their flocks shall come to her.
They shall pitch *their* tents against her all around.
Each one shall pasture in his own place."

וְהַשְׁמִיעוּהָ בִיהוּדָה לֵאמֹר: 21 שִׁמְעוּ־נָא זֹאת עַם

סָכָל וְאֵין לֵב עֵינַיִם לָהֶם וְלֹא יִרְאוּ אָזְנַיִם לָהֶם

וְלֹא יִשְׁמָעוּ: 22 הַאוֹתִי לֹא־תִירָאוּ נְאֻם־יְהֹוָה אִם

מִפָּנַי לֹא תָחִילוּ אֲשֶׁר־שַׂמְתִּי חוֹל גְּבוּל לַיָּם חָק־

עוֹלָם וְלֹא יַעַבְרֶנְהוּ וַיִּתְגָּעֲשׁוּ וְלֹא יוּכָלוּ וְהָמוּ גַלָּיו

וְלֹא יַעַבְרֻנְהוּ: 23 וְלָעָם הַזֶּה הָיָה לֵב סוֹרֵר וּמוֹרֶה

סָרוּ וַיֵּלֵכוּ: 24 וְלֹא־אָמְרוּ בִלְבָבָם נִירָא נָא אֶת־

יְהֹוָה אֱלֹהֵינוּ הַנֹּתֵן גֶּשֶׁם וירה וּמַלְקוֹשׁ בְּעִתּוֹ

שְׁבֻעוֹת חֻקּוֹת קָצִיר יִשְׁמָר־לָנוּ: 25 עֲוֺנוֹתֵיכֶם הִטּוּ־

אֵלֶּה וְחַטֹּאותֵיכֶם מָנְעוּ הַטּוֹב מִכֶּם: 26 כִּי־נִמְצְאוּ

בְעַמִּי רְשָׁעִים יָשׁוּר כְּשַׁךְ יְקוּשִׁים הִצִּיבוּ מַשְׁחִית

אֲנָשִׁים יִלְכֹּדוּ: 27 כִּכְלוּב מָלֵא עוֹף כֵּן בָּתֵּיהֶם

מְלֵאִים מִרְמָה עַל־כֵּן גָּדְלוּ וַיַּעֲשִׁירוּ: 28 שָׁמְנוּ

עָשְׁתוּ גַּם עָבְרוּ דִבְרֵי־רָע דִּין לֹא־דָנוּ דִּין יָתוֹם

וְיַצְלִיחוּ וּמִשְׁפַּט אֶבְיוֹנִים לֹא שָׁפָטוּ: 29 הַעַל־

אֵלֶּה לֹא־אֶפְקֹד נְאֻם־יְהֹוָה אִם בְּגוֹי אֲשֶׁר־כָּזֶה

לֹא תִתְנַקֵּם נַפְשִׁי: ס 30 שַׁמָּה וְשַׁעֲרוּרָה

נִהְיְתָה בָּאָרֶץ: 31 הַנְּבִיאִים נִבְּאוּ־בַשֶּׁקֶר וְהַכֹּהֲנִים

יִרְדּוּ עַל־יְדֵיהֶם וְעַמִּי אָהֲבוּ כֵן וּמַה־תַּעֲשׂוּ

לְאַחֲרִיתָהּ:

ו הָעִזוּ ׀ בְּנֵי בִנְיָמִן מִקֶּרֶב יְרוּשָׁלַ‍ִם וּבִתְקוֹעַ

תִּקְעוּ שׁוֹפָר וְעַל־בֵּית הַכֶּרֶם שְׂאוּ מַשְׂאֵת כִּי

רָעָה נִשְׁקְפָה מִצָּפוֹן וְשֶׁבֶר גָּדוֹל: 2 הַנָּוָה וְהַמְּעֻנָּגָה

דָּמִיתִי בַּת־צִיּוֹן: 3 אֵלֶיהָ יָבֹאוּ רֹעִים וְעֶדְרֵיהֶם

תָּקְעוּ עָלֶיהָ אֹהָלִים סָבִיב רָעוּ אִישׁ

4 "Prepare war against her;
  Arise, and let us go up at noon.
  Woe to us, for the day goes away,
  For the shadows of the evening are lengthening.
5 Arise, and let us go by night,
  And let us destroy her palaces."

6 For thus has the LORD of hosts said:

  "Cut down trees,
  And build a mound against Jerusalem.
  This *is* the city to be punished.
  She *is* full of oppression in her midst.
7 As a fountain wells up with water,
  So she wells up with her wickedness.
  Violence and plundering are heard in her.
  Before Me continually *are* grief and wounds.
8 Be instructed, O Jerusalem,
  Lest My soul depart from you;
  Lest I make you desolate,
  A land not inhabited."

9 Thus says the LORD of hosts:

  "They shall thoroughly glean as a vine the
      remnant of Israel;
  As a grape-gatherer, put your hand back into the
      branches."

10 To whom shall I speak and give warning,
   That they may hear?
   Indeed their ear *is* uncircumcised,
   And they cannot give heed.
   Behold, the word of the LORD is a reproach to
       them;
   They have no delight in it.
11 Therefore I am full of the fury of the LORD.
   I am weary of holding *it* in.
   "I will pour it out on the children outside,
   And on the assembly of young men together;
   For even the husband shall be taken with the
       wife,
   The aged with *him who is* full of days.
12 And their houses shall be turned over to others,
   Fields and wives together;
   For I will stretch out My hand
   Against the inhabitants of the land," says the
       LORD.
13 "Because from the least of them even to the
       greatest of them,
   Everyone *is* given to covetousness;
   And from the prophet even to the priest,
   Everyone deals falsely.
14 They have also healed the hurt of My people
       slightly,
   Saying, 'Peace, peace!'
   When *there is* no peace.
15 Were they ashamed when they had committed
       abomination?
   No! They were not at all ashamed;
   Nor did they know how to blush.
   Therefore they shall fall among those who fall;
   At the time I punish them,
   They shall be cast down," says the LORD.

16 Thus says the LORD:

אֶת־יָדְוֹ: 4 קַדְּשׁוּ עָלֶיהָ מִלְחָמָה קוּמוּ וְנַעֲלֶה
בַצָּהֳרָיִם אֽוֹי לָנוּ כִּי־פָנָה הַיּוֹם כִּי יִנָּטוּ
צִלְלֵי־עָרֶב: 5 קוּמוּ וְנַעֲלֶה בַלָּיְלָה וְנַשְׁחִיתָה
אַרְמְנוֹתֶֽיהָ: ס 6 כִּי כֹה אָמַר יְהוָה
צְבָאוֹת כִּרְתוּ עֵצָה וְשִׁפְכוּ עַל־יְרוּשָׁלִַם סֹלְלָה
הִיא הָעִיר הָפְקַד כֻּלָּהּ עֹשֶׁק בְּקִרְבָּהּ: 7 כְּהָקִיר
בַּוֹר מֵימֶיהָ כֵּן הֵקֵרָה רָעָתָהּ חָמָס וָשֹׁד יִשָּׁמַע
בָּהּ עַל־פָּנַי תָּמִיד חֳלִי וּמַכָּה: 8 הִוָּסְרִי יְרוּשָׁלִַם
פֶּן־תֵּקַע נַפְשִׁי מִמֵּךְ פֶּן־אֲשִׂימֵךְ שְׁמָמָה אֶרֶץ לוֹא
נוֹשָֽׁבָה:
פ

9 כֹּה אָמַר יְהוָה צְבָאוֹת עוֹלֵל יְעוֹלְלוּ כַגֶּפֶן שְׁאֵרִית
יִשְׂרָאֵל הָשֵׁב יָדְךָ כְּבוֹצֵר עַל־סַלְסִלּֽוֹת: 10 עַל־
מִי אֲדַבְּרָה וְאָעִידָה וְיִשְׁמָעוּ הִנֵּה עֲרֵלָה אָזְנָם
וְלֹא יוּכְלוּ לְהַקְשִׁיב הִנֵּה דְבַר־יְהוָה הָיָה לָהֶם
לְחֶרְפָּה לֹא יַחְפְּצוּ־בֽוֹ: 11 וְאֵת חֲמַת יְהוָה
מָלֵאתִי נִלְאֵיתִי הָכִיל שְׁפֹךְ עַל־עוֹלָל בַּחוּץ וְעַל
סוֹד בַּחוּרִים יַחְדָּו כִּי־גַם־אִישׁ עִם־אִשָּׁה יִלָּכֵדוּ
זָקֵן עִם־מְלֵא יָמִים: 12 וְנָסַבּוּ בָתֵּיהֶם לַאֲחֵרִים
שָׂדוֹת וְנָשִׁים יַחְדָּו כִּי־אַטֶּה אֶת־יָדִי עַל־יֹשְׁבֵי
הָאָרֶץ נְאֻם־יְהוָֽה: 13 כִּי מִקְּטַנָּם וְעַד־גְּדוֹלָם כֻּלּוֹ
בּוֹצֵעַ בָּצַע וּמִנָּבִיא וְעַד־כֹּהֵן כֻּלּוֹ עֹשֶׂה שָּֽׁקֶר:
14 וַיְרַפְּאוּ אֶת־שֶׁבֶר עַמִּי עַל־נְקַלָּה לֵאמֹר שָׁלוֹם
שָׁלוֹם וְאֵין שָׁלֽוֹם: 15 הֹבִישׁוּ כִּי תוֹעֵבָה עָשׂוּ גַּם־
בּוֹשׁ לֹא־יֵבוֹשׁוּ גַּם־הַכְלִים לֹא יָדָעוּ לָכֵן יִפְּלוּ
בַנֹּפְלִים בְּעֵת־פְּקַדְתִּים יִכָּשְׁלוּ אָמַר
יְהוָֽה: ס 16 כֹּה אָמַר יְהוָה עִמְדוּ עַל־דְּרָכִים

7 ו בֹּר

"Stand in the ways and see,
And ask for the old paths, where the good way *is,*
And walk in it;
Then you will find rest for your souls.
But they said, 'We will not walk *in it.*'

17 Also, I set watchmen over you, *saying,*
'Listen to the sound of the trumpet!'
But they said, 'We will not listen.'

18 Therefore hear, you nations,
And know, O congregation, what *is* among them.

19 Hear, O earth!
Behold, I will certainly bring calamity on this
      people—
The fruit of their thoughts,
Because they have not heeded My words
Nor My law, but rejected it.

20 For what purpose to Me
Comes frankincense from Sheba,
And sweet cane from a far country?
Your burnt offerings *are* not acceptable,
Nor your sacrifices sweet to Me."

21 Therefore thus says the LORD:

"Behold, I will lay stumbling blocks before this
      people,
And the fathers and the sons together shall fall on
      them.
The neighbor and his friend shall perish."

22 Thus says the LORD:

"Behold, a people comes from the north country,
And a great nation will be raised from the
      farthest parts of the earth.

23 They will lay hold on bow and spear;
They *are* cruel and have no mercy;
Their voice roars like the sea;
And they ride on horses,
As men of war set in array against you, O
      daughter of Zion."

24 We have heard the report of it;
Our hands grow feeble.
Anguish has taken hold of us,
Pain as of a woman in labor.

25 Do not go out into the field,
Nor walk by the way.
Because of the sword of the enemy,
Fear *is* on every side.

26 O daughter of my people,
  Dress in sackcloth
And roll about in ashes!
Make mourning *as for* an only son, most bitter
      lamentation;
For the plunderer will suddenly come upon us.

27 "I have set you *as* an assayer *and* a fortress among
      My people,
That you may know and test their way.

28 They *are* all stubborn rebels, walking as slan-
      derers.
They are bronze and iron,
They *are* all corrupters;

29 The bellows blow fiercely,
The lead is consumed by the fire;

וּרְאוּ וְשַׁאֲלוּ ׀ לִנְתִבוֹת עוֹלָם אֵי־זֶה דֶרֶךְ הַטּוֹב
וּלְכוּ־בָהּ וּמִצְאוּ מַרְגּוֹעַ לְנַפְשְׁכֶם וַיֹּאמְרוּ לֹא נֵלֵךְ:
17 וַהֲקִמֹתִי עֲלֵיכֶם צֹפִים הַקְשִׁיבוּ לְקוֹל שׁוֹפָר
וַיֹּאמְרוּ לֹא נַקְשִׁיב: 18 לָכֵן שִׁמְעוּ הַגּוֹיִם וּדְעִי
עֵדָה אֶת־אֲשֶׁר־בָּם: 19 שִׁמְעִי הָאָרֶץ הִנֵּה אָנֹכִי
מֵבִיא רָעָה אֶל־הָעָם הַזֶּה פְּרִי מַחְשְׁבוֹתָם כִּי עַל־
דְּבָרַי לֹא הִקְשִׁיבוּ וְתוֹרָתִי וַיִּמְאֲסוּ־בָהּ: 20 לָמָּה־
זֶּה לִי לְבוֹנָה מִשְּׁבָא תָבוֹא וְקָנֶה הַטּוֹב מֵאֶרֶץ
מֶרְחָק עֹלוֹתֵיכֶם לֹא לְרָצוֹן וְזִבְחֵיכֶם לֹא־עָרְבוּ
לִי: ס   21 לָכֵן כֹּה אָמַר יְהוָֹה הִנְנִי נֹתֵן
אֶל־הָעָם הַזֶּה מִכְשֹׁלִים וְכָשְׁלוּ בָם אָבוֹת וּבָנִים
יַחְדָּו שָׁכֵן וְרֵעוֹ יאֹבֵדוּᵖ: פ
22 כֹּה אָמַר יְהוָֹה הִנֵּה עַם בָּא מֵאֶרֶץ צָפוֹן
וְגוֹי גָּדוֹל יֵעוֹר מִיַּרְכְּתֵי־אָרֶץ: 23 קֶשֶׁת וְכִידוֹן
יַחֲזִיקוּ אַכְזָרִי הוּא וְלֹא יְרַחֵמוּ קוֹלָם כַּיָּם יֶהֱמֶה
וְעַל־סוּסִים יִרְכָּבוּ עָרוּךְ כְּאִישׁ לַמִּלְחָמָה עָלַיִךְ
בַּת־צִיּוֹן: 24 שָׁמַעְנוּ אֶת־שָׁמְעוֹ רָפוּ יָדֵינוּ צָרָה
הֶחֱזִיקַתְנוּ חִיל כַּיּוֹלֵדָה: 25 אַל־תֵּצְאִיᵖ הַשָּׂדֶה
וּבַדֶּרֶךְ אַל־תֵּלֵכִיᵖ כִּי חֶרֶב לְאֹיֵב מָגוֹר מִסָּבִיב:
26 בַּת־עַמִּי חִגְרִי־שָׂק וְהִתְפַּלְּשִׁי בָאֵפֶר אֵבֶל יָחִיד
עֲשִׂי לָךְ מִסְפַּד תַּמְרוּרִים כִּי פִתְאֹם יָבֹא הַשֹּׁדֵד
עָלֵינוּ: 27 בָּחוֹן נְתַתִּיךָ בְעַמִּי מִבְצָר וְתֵדַע וּבָחַנְתָּ
אֶת־דַּרְכָּם: 28 כֻּלָּם סָרֵי סוֹרְרִים הֹלְכֵי רָכִיל
נְחֹשֶׁת וּבַרְזֶל כֻּלָּם מַשְׁחִיתִים הֵמָּה: 29 נָחַר מִפֻּחַ

ו 21 וְאָבָדוּ 25 תֵּצְאִי תֵּלֵכִי

The smelter refines in vain,
For the wicked are not drawn off.
30 *People* will call them rejected silver,
Because the LORD has rejected them."

7 The word that came to Jeremiah from the LORD, saying, ² "Stand in the gate of the LORD's house, and proclaim there this word, and say, 'Hear the word of the LORD, all *you of* Judah who enter in at these gates to worship the LORD!'" ³ Thus says the LORD of hosts, the God of Israel: "Amend your ways and your doings, and I will cause you to dwell in this place. ⁴ Do not trust in these lying words, saying, 'The temple of the LORD, the temple of the LORD, the temple of the LORD *are* these.'

⁵ "For if you thoroughly amend your ways and your doings, if you thoroughly execute judgment between a man and his neighbor, ⁶ *if* you do not oppress the stranger, the fatherless, and the widow, and do not shed innocent blood in this place, or walk after other gods to your hurt, ⁷ then I will cause you to dwell in this place, in the land that I gave to your fathers forever and ever.

⁸ "Behold, you trust in lying words that cannot profit. ⁹ Will you steal, murder, commit adultery, swear falsely, burn incense to Baal, and walk after other gods whom you do not know, ¹⁰ and *then* come and stand before Me in this house which is called by My name, and say, 'We are delivered to do all these abominations'? ¹¹ Has this house, which is called by My name, become a den of thieves in your eyes? Behold, I, even I, have seen *it*," says the LORD.

¹² "But go now to My place which *was* in Shiloh, where I set My name at the first, and see what I did to it because of the wickedness of My people Israel. ¹³ And now, because you have done all these works," says the LORD, "and I spoke to you, rising up early and speaking, but you did not hear, and I called you, but you did not answer, ¹⁴ therefore I will do to the house which is called by My name, in which you trust, and to this place which I gave to you and your fathers, as I have done to Shiloh. ¹⁵ And I will cast you out of My sight, as I have cast out all your brethren—the whole posterity of Ephraim.

¹⁶ "Therefore do not pray for this people, nor lift up a cry or prayer for them, nor make intercession to Me; for I will not hear you. ¹⁷ Do you not see what they do in the cities of Judah and in the streets of Jerusalem? ¹⁸ The children gather wood, the fathers kindle the fire, and the women knead dough, to make cakes for the queen of heaven; and *they* pour out drink offerings to other gods,

מְאָסְתָּ֖ם עֹפֶ֥רֶת לַשָּׁ֑וְא צָרַ֣ף צָר֔וֹף וְרָעִ֖ים לֹ֥א
נִתָּֽקוּ: ³⁰ כֶּ֣סֶף נִמְאָ֗ס קָרְא֣וּ לָהֶ֔ם כִּֽי־מָאַ֥ס יְהוָ֖ה
בָּהֶֽם: פ

7 הַדָּבָר֙ אֲשֶׁ֣ר הָיָ֣ה אֶֽל־יִרְמְיָ֔הוּ מֵאֵ֥ת יְהוָ֖ה
לֵאמֹֽר: ² עֲמֹ֗ד בְּשַׁ֨עַר֙ בֵּ֣ית יְהוָ֔ה וְקָרָ֣אתָ שָּׁ֗ם
אֶת־הַדָּבָ֥ר הַזֶּ֖ה וְאָמַרְתָּ֑ שִׁמְע֣וּ דְבַר־יְהוָ֗ה כָּל־
יְהוּדָ֔ה הַבָּאִים֙ בַּשְּׁעָרִ֣ים הָאֵ֔לֶּה לְהִשְׁתַּחֲוֺ֖ת
לַֽיהוָֽה: ס ³ כֹּֽה־אָמַ֞ר יְהוָ֤ה צְבָאוֹת֙ אֱלֹהֵ֣י
יִשְׂרָאֵ֔ל הֵיטִ֥יבוּ דַרְכֵיכֶ֖ם וּמַֽעַלְלֵיכֶ֑ם וַאֲשַׁכְּנָ֣ה
אֶתְכֶ֔ם בַּמָּק֖וֹם הַזֶּֽה: ⁴ אַל־תִּבְטְח֣וּ לָכֶ֔ם אֶל־דִּבְרֵ֥י
הַשֶּׁ֖קֶר לֵאמֹ֑ר הֵיכַ֤ל יְהוָה֙ הֵיכַ֣ל יְהוָ֔ה הֵיכַ֥ל יְהוָ֖ה
הֵֽמָּה: ⁵ כִּ֤י אִם־הֵיטֵ֣יב תֵּיטִ֔יבוּ אֶת־דַּרְכֵיכֶ֖ם וְאֶֽת־
מַֽעַלְלֵיכֶ֑ם אִם־עָשׂ֤וֹ תַֽעֲשׂוּ֙ מִשְׁפָּ֔ט בֵּ֥ין אִ֖ישׁ וּבֵ֥ין
רֵעֵֽהוּ: ⁶ גֵּ֣ר יָת֤וֹם וְאַלְמָנָה֙ לֹ֣א תַֽעֲשֹׁ֔קוּ וְדָ֣ם נָקִ֔י
אַל־תִּשְׁפְּכ֖וּ בַּמָּק֣וֹם הַזֶּ֑ה וְאַחֲרֵ֨י אֱלֹהִ֧ים אֲחֵרִ֛ים
לֹ֥א תֵֽלְכ֖וּ לְרַ֥ע לָכֶֽם: ⁷ וְשִׁכַּנְתִּ֤י אֶתְכֶם֙ בַּמָּק֣וֹם הַזֶּ֔ה
בָּאָ֕רֶץ אֲשֶׁ֥ר נָתַ֖תִּי לַאֲבֽוֹתֵיכֶ֑ם לְמִן־עוֹלָ֖ם וְעַד־
עוֹלָֽם: ⁸ הִנֵּ֤ה אַתֶּם֙ בֹּטְחִ֣ים לָכֶ֔ם עַל־דִּבְרֵ֥י הַשָּׁ֖קֶר
לְבִלְתִּ֥י הוֹעִֽיל: ⁹ הֲגָנֹ֤ב ׀ רָצֹ֨חַ֙ וְֽנָאֹ֔ף וְהִשָּׁבֵ֥עַ לַשֶּׁ֖קֶר
וְקַטֵּ֣ר לַבָּ֑עַל וְהָלֹ֗ךְ אַחֲרֵ֛י אֱלֹהִ֥ים אֲחֵרִ֖ים אֲשֶׁ֥ר
לֹֽא־יְדַעְתֶּֽם: ¹⁰ וּבָאתֶ֞ם וַעֲמַדְתֶּ֣ם לְפָנַ֗י בַּבַּ֤יִת הַזֶּה֙
אֲשֶׁ֣ר נִקְרָא־שְׁמִ֣י עָלָ֔יו וַאֲמַרְתֶּ֖ם נִצַּ֑לְנוּ לְמַ֣עַן עֲשׂ֔וֹת
אֵ֥ת כָּל־הַתּוֹעֵב֖וֹת הָאֵֽלֶּה: ¹¹ הַמְעָרַ֣ת פָּרִצִ֗ים הָיָ֨ה
הַבַּ֤יִת הַזֶּה֙ אֲשֶׁר־נִקְרָא־שְׁמִ֥י עָלָ֖יו בְּעֵֽינֵיכֶ֑ם גַּ֣ם
אָנֹכִ֗י הִנֵּ֥ה רָאִ֖יתִי נְאֻם־יְהוָֽה: ס ¹² כִּ֣י
לְכוּ־נָ֗א אֶל־מְקוֹמִי֙ אֲשֶׁ֣ר בְּשִׁיל֔וֹ אֲשֶׁ֨ר שִׁכַּ֧נְתִּי שְׁמִ֛י
שָׁ֖ם בָּרִֽאשׁוֹנָ֑ה וּרְאוּ֙ אֵ֣ת אֲשֶׁר־עָשִׂ֣יתִי ל֔וֹ מִפְּנֵ֖י
רָעַ֥ת עַמִּ֖י יִשְׂרָאֵֽל: ¹³ וְעַתָּ֗ה יַ֚עַן עֲשֽׂוֹתְכֶם֙ אֶת־
כָּל־הַמַּֽעֲשִׂ֣ים הָאֵ֔לֶּה נְאֻם־יְהוָ֑ה וָאֲדַבֵּ֨ר אֲלֵיכֶ֜ם
הַשְׁכֵּ֤ם וְדַבֵּר֙ וְלֹ֣א שְׁמַעְתֶּ֔ם וָאֶקְרָ֥א אֶתְכֶ֖ם וְלֹ֥א
עֲנִיתֶֽם: ¹⁴ וְעָשִׂ֣יתִי לַבַּ֣יִת ׀ אֲשֶׁ֣ר נִקְרָא־שְׁמִ֣י עָלָ֗יו
אֲשֶׁ֤ר אַתֶּם֙ בֹּטְחִ֣ים בּ֔וֹ וְלַמָּק֕וֹם אֲשֶׁר־נָתַ֥תִּי לָכֶ֖ם
וְלַאֲבֽוֹתֵיכֶ֑ם כַּאֲשֶׁ֥ר עָשִׂ֖יתִי לְשִׁלֽוֹ: ¹⁵ וְהִשְׁלַכְתִּ֤י
אֶתְכֶם֙ מֵעַ֣ל פָּנָ֔י כַּאֲשֶׁ֥ר הִשְׁלַ֖כְתִּי אֶת־כָּל־אֲחֵיכֶ֑ם
אֵ֖ת כָּל־זֶ֥רַע אֶפְרָֽיִם: ס ¹⁶ וְאַתָּ֣ה אַל־
תִּתְפַּלֵּ֣ל ׀ בְּעַד־הָעָ֣ם הַזֶּ֗ה וְאַל־תִּשָּׂ֧א בַעֲדָ֛ם
רִנָּ֥ה וּתְפִלָּ֖ה וְאַל־תִּפְגַּע־בִּ֑י כִּֽי־אֵינֶ֥נִּי שֹׁמֵ֖עַ אֹתָֽךְ: ¹⁷ הַֽאֵינְךָ֣ רֹאֶ֔ה מָ֛ה הֵ֥מָּה עֹשִׂ֖ים בְּעָרֵ֣י יְהוּדָ֑ה
וּבְחֻצ֖וֹת יְרֽוּשָׁלָֽ͏ִם: ¹⁸ הַבָּנִ֞ים מְלַקְּטִ֣ים עֵצִ֗ים
וְהָאָבוֹת֙ מְבַעֲרִ֣ים אֶת־הָאֵ֔שׁ וְהַנָּשִׁ֖ים לָשׁ֣וֹת בָּצֵ֑ק
לַעֲשׂ֨וֹת כַּוָּנִ֜ים לִמְלֶ֣כֶת הַשָּׁמַ֗יִם וְהַסֵּ֤ךְ נְסָכִים֙

¹ ו 29 מאש תם

that they may provoke Me to anger. ¹⁹Do they provoke Me to anger?" says the LORD. "*Do they not provoke* themselves, to the shame of their own faces?"

²⁰Therefore thus says the Lord GOD: "Behold, My anger and My fury will be poured out on this place—on man and on beast, on the trees of the field and on the fruit of the ground. And it will burn and not be quenched."

²¹Thus says the LORD of hosts, the God of Israel: "Add your burnt offerings to your sacrifices and eat meat. ²²For I did not speak to your fathers, or command them in the day that I brought them out of the land of Egypt, concerning burnt offerings or sacrifices. ²³But this is what I commanded them, saying, 'Obey My voice, and I will be your God, and you shall be My people. And walk in all the ways that I have commanded you, that it may be well with you.' ²⁴Yet they did not obey or incline their ear, but followed the counsels *and* the dictates of their evil hearts, and went backward and not forward. ²⁵Since the day that your fathers came out of the land of Egypt until this day, I have even sent to you all My servants the prophets, daily rising up early and sending *them*. ²⁶Yet they did not obey Me or incline their ear, but stiffened their neck. They did worse than their fathers.

²⁷"Therefore you shall speak all these words to them, but they will not obey you. You shall also call to them, but they will not answer you.

²⁸"So you shall say to them, 'This *is* a nation that does not obey the voice of the LORD their God nor receive correction. Truth has perished and has been cut off from their mouth. ²⁹Cut off your hair and cast *it* away, and take up a lamentation on the desolate heights; for the LORD has rejected and forsaken the generation of His wrath.' ³⁰For the children of Judah have done evil in My sight," says the LORD. "They have set their abominations in the house which is called by My name, to pollute it. ³¹And they have built the high places of Tophet, which *is* in the Valley of the Son of Hinnom, to burn their sons and their daughters in the fire, which I did not command, nor did it come into My heart.

³²"Therefore behold, the days are coming," says the LORD, "when it will no more be called Tophet, or the Valley of the Son of Hinnom, but the Valley of Slaughter; for they will bury in Tophet until there is no room. ³³The corpses of this people will be food for the birds of the heaven and for the beasts of the earth. And no one will frighten *them away*. ³⁴Then I will cause to cease from the cities of Judah and from the streets of Jerusalem the voice of mirth

לֵאלֹהִים אֲחֵרִים לְמַעַן הַכְעִסֵנִי: ¹⁹הַאֹתִי הֵם מַכְעִסִים נְאֻם־יְהֹוָה הֲלוֹא אֹתָם לְמַעַן בֹּשֶׁת פְּנֵיהֶם: ס ²⁰לָכֵן כֹּה־אָמַר ׀ אֲדֹנָי יְהֹוִה הִנֵּה אַפִּי וַחֲמָתִי נִתֶּכֶת אֶל־הַמָּקוֹם הַזֶּה עַל־הָאָדָם וְעַל־הַבְּהֵמָה וְעַל־עֵץ הַשָּׂדֶה וְעַל־פְּרִי הָאֲדָמָה וּבָעֲרָה וְלֹא תִכְבֶּה: ס ²¹כֹּה אָמַר יְהֹוָה צְבָאוֹת אֱלֹהֵי יִשְׂרָאֵל עֹלוֹתֵיכֶם סְפוּ עַל־זִבְחֵיכֶם וְאִכְלוּ בָשָׂר: ²²כִּי לֹא־דִבַּרְתִּי אֶת־אֲבוֹתֵיכֶם וְלֹא צִוִּיתִים בְּיוֹם הוֹצִיאִי אוֹתָם מֵאֶרֶץ מִצְרָיִם עַל־דִּבְרֵי עוֹלָה וָזָבַח: ²³כִּי אִם־אֶת־הַדָּבָר הַזֶּה צִוִּיתִי אוֹתָם לֵאמֹר שִׁמְעוּ בְקוֹלִי וְהָיִיתִי לָכֶם לֵאלֹהִים וְאַתֶּם תִּהְיוּ־לִי לְעָם וַהֲלַכְתֶּם בְּכָל־הַדֶּרֶךְ אֲשֶׁר אֲצַוֶּה אֶתְכֶם לְמַעַן יִיטַב לָכֶם: ²⁴וְלֹא שָׁמְעוּ וְלֹא־הִטּוּ אֶת־אָזְנָם וַיֵּלְכוּ בְּמֹעֵצוֹת בִּשְׁרִרוּת לִבָּם הָרָע וַיִּהְיוּ לְאָחוֹר וְלֹא לְפָנִים: ²⁵לְמִן־הַיּוֹם אֲשֶׁר יָצְאוּ אֲבוֹתֵיכֶם מֵאֶרֶץ מִצְרַיִם עַד הַיּוֹם הַזֶּה וָאֶשְׁלַח אֲלֵיכֶם אֶת־כָּל־עֲבָדַי הַנְּבִיאִים יוֹם הַשְׁכֵּם וְשָׁלֹחַ: ²⁶וְלוֹא שָׁמְעוּ אֵלַי וְלֹא הִטּוּ אֶת־אָזְנָם וַיַּקְשׁוּ אֶת־עָרְפָּם הֵרֵעוּ מֵאֲבוֹתָם: ²⁷וְדִבַּרְתָּ אֲלֵיהֶם אֶת־כָּל־הַדְּבָרִים הָאֵלֶּה וְלֹא יִשְׁמְעוּ אֵלֶיךָ וְקָרָאתָ אֲלֵיהֶם וְלֹא יַעֲנוּכָה: ²⁸וְאָמַרְתָּ אֲלֵיהֶם זֶה הַגּוֹי אֲשֶׁר לוֹא־שָׁמְעוּ בְּקוֹל יְהֹוָה אֱלֹהָיו וְלֹא לָקְחוּ מוּסָר אָבְדָה הָאֱמוּנָה וְנִכְרְתָה מִפִּיהֶם: ס ²⁹גָּזִּי נִזְרֵךְ וְהַשְׁלִיכִי וּשְׂאִי עַל־שְׁפָיִם קִינָה כִּי מָאַס יְהֹוָה וַיִּטֹּשׁ אֶת־דּוֹר עֶבְרָתוֹ: ³⁰כִּי־עָשׂוּ בְנֵי־יְהוּדָה הָרַע בְּעֵינַי נְאֻם־יְהֹוָה שָׂמוּ שִׁקּוּצֵיהֶם בַּבַּיִת אֲשֶׁר־נִקְרָא־שְׁמִי עָלָיו לְטַמְּאוֹ: ³¹וּבָנוּ בָּמוֹת הַתֹּפֶת אֲשֶׁר בְּגֵיא בֶן־הִנֹּם לִשְׂרֹף אֶת־בְּנֵיהֶם וְאֶת־בְּנֹתֵיהֶם בָּאֵשׁ אֲשֶׁר לֹא צִוִּיתִי וְלֹא עָלְתָה עַל־לִבִּי: ³²לָכֵן הִנֵּה־יָמִים בָּאִים נְאֻם־יְהֹוָה וְלֹא־יֵאָמֵר עוֹד הַתֹּפֶת וְגֵיא בֶן־הִנֹּם כִּי אִם־גֵּיא הַהֲרֵגָה וְקָבְרוּ בְתֹפֶת מֵאֵין מָקוֹם: ³³וְהָיְתָה נִבְלַת הָעָם הַזֶּה לְמַאֲכָל לְעוֹף הַשָּׁמַיִם וּלְבֶהֱמַת הָאָרֶץ וְאֵין מַחֲרִיד: ³⁴וְהִשְׁבַּתִּי ׀ מֵעָרֵי יְהוּדָה וּמֵחֻצוֹת יְרוּשָׁלַ͏ִם קוֹל

and the voice of gladness, the voice of the bride-groom and the voice of the bride. For the land shall be desolate.

8 "At that time," says the LORD, "they shall bring out the bones of the kings of Judah, and the bones of its princes, and the bones of the priests, and the bones of the prophets, and the bones of the inhabitants of Jerusalem, out of their graves. ²They shall spread them before the sun and the moon and all the host of heaven, which they have loved and which they have served and after which they have walked, which they have sought and which they have worshiped. They shall not be gathered nor buried; they shall be like refuse on the face of the earth. ³Then death shall be chosen rather than life by all the residue of those who remain of this evil family, who remain in all the places where I have driven them," says the LORD of hosts.

⁴"Moreover you shall say to them, 'Thus says the LORD:

"Will they fall and not rise?
Will one turn away and not return?
⁵ Why has this people slidden back,
Jerusalem, in a perpetual backsliding?
They hold fast to deceit,
They refuse to return.
⁶ I listened and heard,
But they do not speak aright.
No man repented of his wickedness,
Saying, 'What have I done?'
Everyone turned to his own course,
As the horse rushes into the battle.
⁷ "Even the stork in the heavens
Knows her appointed times;
And the turtledove, the swift, and the swallow
Observe the time of their coming.
But My people do not know the judgment of the
LORD.
⁸ "How can you say, 'We *are* wise,
And the law of the LORD *is* with us'?
Look, the false pen of the scribe certainly works
falsehood.
⁹ The wise men are ashamed,
They are dismayed and taken.
Behold, they have rejected the word of the LORD;
So what wisdom do they have?
¹⁰ Therefore I will give their wives to others,
And their fields to those who will inherit *them;*
Because from the least even to the greatest
Everyone is given to covetousness;
From the prophet even to the priest
Everyone deals falsely.
¹¹ For they have healed the hurt of the daughter of
My people slightly,
Saying, 'Peace, peace!'
When *there is* no peace.

שָׂשׂוֹן וְקוֹל שִׂמְחָה קוֹל חָתָן וְקוֹל כַּלָּה כִּי לְחָרְבָּה
תִהְיֶה הָאָרֶץ׃

ח בָּעֵת הַהִיא נְאֻם־יְהֹוָה וְיֹצִיאֽוּ אֶת־
עַצְמוֹת מַלְכֵי־יְהוּדָה וְאֶת־עַצְמוֹת־שָׂרָיו וְאֶת־
עַצְמוֹת הַכֹּהֲנִים וְאֵת ׀ עַצְמוֹת הַנְּבִיאִים וְאֵת
עַצְמוֹת יוֹשְׁבֵי־יְרוּשָׁלָ͏ִם מִקִּבְרֵיהֶם׃ ²וּשְׁטָחוּם
לַשֶּׁמֶשׁ וְלַיָּרֵחַ וּלְכֹל ׀ צְבָא הַשָּׁמַיִם אֲשֶׁר אֲהֵבוּם
וַאֲשֶׁר עֲבָדוּם וַאֲשֶׁר הָלְכוּ אַחֲרֵיהֶם וַאֲשֶׁר דְּרָשׁוּם
וַאֲשֶׁר הִשְׁתַּחֲווּ לָהֶם לֹא יֵאָסְפוּ וְלֹא יִקָּבֵרוּ
לְדֹמֶן עַל־פְּנֵי הָאֲדָמָה יִהְיוּ׃ ³וְנִבְחַר מָוֶת מֵחַיִּים
לְכֹל הַשְּׁאֵרִית הַנִּשְׁאָרִים מִן־הַמִּשְׁפָּחָה הָרָעָה
הַזֹּאת בְּכׇל־הַמְּקֹמוֹת הַנִּשְׁאָרִים אֲשֶׁר הִדַּחְתִּים
שָׁם נְאֻם יְהֹוָה צְבָאֽוֹת׃ ס ⁴וְאָמַרְתָּ
אֲלֵיהֶם כֹּה אָמַר יְהֹוָה הֲיִפְּלוּ וְלֹא יָקוּמוּ אִם־
יָשׁוּב וְלֹא יָשֽׁוּב׃ ⁵מַדּוּעַ שׁוֹבְבָה הָעָם הַזֶּה
יְרוּשָׁלַ͏ִם מְשֻׁבָה נִצַּחַת הֶחֱזִיקוּ בַּתַּרְמִית מֵאֲנוּ
לָשֽׁוּב׃ ⁶הִקְשַׁבְתִּי וָאֶשְׁמָע לוֹא־כֵן יְדַבֵּרוּ אֵין
אִישׁ נִחָם עַל־רָעָתוֹ לֵאמֹר מֶה עָשִׂיתִי כֻּלֹּה
שָׁב בִּמְרֻצוֹתָם כְּסוּס שׁוֹטֵף בַּמִּלְחָמָה׃ ⁷גַּם־
חֲסִידָה בַשָּׁמַיִם יָדְעָה מוֹעֲדֶיהָ וְתֹר וְסוּס ׀ וְעָגוּר
שָׁמְרוּ אֶת־עֵת בֹּאָנָה וְעַמִּי לֹא יָדְעוּ אֵת מִשְׁפַּט
יְהֹוָה׃ ⁸אֵיכָה תֹאמְרוּ חֲכָמִים אֲנַחְנוּ וְתוֹרַת יְהֹוָה
אִתָּנוּ אָכֵן הִנֵּה לַשֶּׁקֶר עָשָׂה עֵט שֶׁקֶר סֹפְרִים׃
⁹הֹבִישׁוּ חֲכָמִים חַתּוּ וַיִּלָּכֵדוּ הִנֵּה בִדְבַר־יְהֹוָה
מָאָסוּ וְחׇכְמַת־מֶה לָהֶם׃ ס ¹⁰לָכֵן אֶתֵּן
אֶת־נְשֵׁיהֶם לַאֲחֵרִים שְׂדוֹתֵיהֶם לְיוֹרְשִׁים כִּי מִקָּטֹן
וְעַד־גָּדוֹל כֻּלֹּה בֹּצֵעַ בָּצַע מִנָּבִיא וְעַד־כֹּהֵן כֻּלֹּה
עֹשֶׂה שָּׁקֶר׃ ¹¹וַיְרַפּוּ אֶת־שֶׁבֶר בַּת־עַמִּי עַל־נְקַלָּה

12 לֵאמֹר שָׁל֣וֹם ׀ שָׁל֑וֹם וְאֵ֖ין שָׁל֑וֹם: 12 הֹבִ֗שׁוּ כִּ֤י

תוֹעֵבָ֣ה עָשׂ֔וּ גַּם־בּ֖וֹשׁ לֹֽא־יֵב֑שׁוּ וְהִכָּלֵ֖ם לֹ֣א יָדָ֑עוּ

לָכֵ֞ן יִפְּל֣וּ בַנֹּפְלִ֗ים בְּעֵ֧ת פְּקֻדָּתָ֛ם יִכָּשְׁל֖וּ אָמַ֥ר

13 יְהוָֽה: ס 13 אָסֹ֥ף אֲסִיפֵ֖ם נְאֻם־יְהֹוָ֑ה אֵֽין

עֲנָבִ֣ים בַּגֶּ֗פֶן וְאֵ֤ין תְּאֵנִים֙ בַּתְּאֵנָ֔ה וְהֶעָלֶ֖ה נָבֵ֑ל

וָאֶתֵּ֥ן לָהֶ֖ם יַעַבְרֽוּם: 14 עַל־מָה֙ אֲנַ֣חְנוּ יֹֽשְׁבִ֔ים

הֵאָ֣סְפ֗וּ וְנָב֛וֹא אֶל־עָרֵ֥י הַמִּבְצָ֖ר וְנִדְּמָה־שָּׁ֑ם כִּי֩

יְהֹוָ֨ה אֱלֹהֵ֜ינוּ הֲדִמָּ֗נוּ וַיַּשְׁקֵ֣נוּ מֵי־רֹ֔אשׁ כִּ֥י חָטָ֖אנוּ

15 לַיהֹוָֽה: 15 קַוֵּ֥ה לְשָׁל֖וֹם וְאֵ֣ין ט֑וֹב לְעֵ֥ת מַרְפֵּ֖ה וְהִנֵּ֥ה

16 בְעָתָֽה: 16 מִדָּ֞ן נִשְׁמַ֣ע נַחְרַ֣ת סוּסָ֗יו מִקּוֹל֙ מִצְהֲל֣וֹת

אַבִּירָ֔יו רָעֲשָׁ֖ה כָּל־הָאָ֑רֶץ וַיָּב֗וֹאוּ וַיֹּֽאכְלוּ֙ אֶ֔רֶץ

17 וּמְלוֹאָ֔הּ עִ֖יר וְיֹ֥שְׁבֵי בָֽהּ: ס 17 כִּ֣י הִנְנִ֞י

מְשַׁלֵּ֤חַ בָּכֶם֙ נְחָשִׁ֣ים צִפְעֹנִ֔ים אֲשֶׁ֥ר אֵין־לָהֶ֖ם לָ֑חַשׁ

18 וְנִשְּׁכ֥וּ אֶתְכֶ֖ם נְאֻם־יְהֹוָֽה: ס 18 מַבְלִ֥יגִיתִ֖י

עֲלֵ֣י יָג֑וֹן עָלַ֖י לִבִּ֥י דַוָּֽי: 19 הִנֵּה־ק֞וֹל שַׁוְעַ֣ת בַּת־עַמִּ֗י

מֵאֶ֙רֶץ֙ מַרְחַקִּ֔ים הַֽיהוָה֙ אֵ֣ין בְּצִיּ֔וֹן אִם־מַלְכָּ֖הּ אֵ֣ין

בָּ֑הּ מַדּ֗וּעַ הִכְעִס֙וּנִי֙ בִּפְסִלֵיהֶ֔ם בְּהַבְלֵ֖י נֵכָֽר: 20 עָבַ֥ר

21 קָצִ֖יר כָּ֣לָה קָ֑יִץ וַאֲנַ֖חְנוּ ל֥וֹא נוֹשָֽׁעְנוּ: 21 עַל־שֶׁ֥בֶר

בַּת־עַמִּ֖י הָשְׁבָּ֑רְתִּי קָדַ֕רְתִּי שַׁמָּ֖ה הֶחֱזִקָֽתְנִי: 22 הַצֳרִי֙

אֵ֣ין בְּגִלְעָ֔ד אִם־רֹפֵ֖א אֵ֣ין שָׁ֑ם כִּ֗י מַדּ֙וּעַ֙ לֹ֣א עָֽלְתָ֔ה

23 אֲרֻכַ֖ת בַּת־עַמִּֽי: 23 מִֽי־יִתֵּ֤ן רֹאשִׁי֙ מַ֔יִם וְעֵינִ֖י מְק֣וֹר

דִּמְעָ֑ה וְאֶבְכֶּ֤ה יוֹמָם֙ וָלַ֔יְלָה אֵ֖ת חַֽלְלֵ֥י בַת־עַמִּֽי:

ט מִֽי־יִתְּנֵ֣נִי בַמִּדְבָּ֗ר מְלוֹן֙ אֹֽרְחִ֔ים וְאֶֽעֶזְבָה֙ אֶת־

עַמִּ֔י וְאֵלְכָ֖ה מֵֽאִתָּ֑ם כִּ֤י כֻלָּם֙ מְנָ֣אֲפִ֔ים עֲצֶ֖רֶת

12 Were they ashamed when they had committed
   abomination?
  No! They were not at all ashamed,
  Nor did they know how to blush.
  Therefore they shall fall among those who fall;
  In the time of their punishment
  They shall be cast down," says the LORD.

13 "I will surely consume them," says the LORD.
  "No grapes *shall be* on the vine,
  Nor figs on the fig tree,
  And the leaf shall fade;
  And *the things* I have given them shall pass away
    from them." ' "

14 "Why do we sit still?
  Assemble yourselves,
  And let us enter the fortified cities,
  And let us be silent there.
  For the LORD our God has put us to silence
  And given us water of gall to drink,
  Because we have sinned against the LORD.

15 *We* looked for peace, but no good *came*;
  And for a time of health, and there was trouble!
16 The snorting of His horses was heard from Dan.
  The whole land trembled at the sound of the
    neighing of His strong ones;
  For they have come and devoured the land and
    all that is in it,
  The city and those who dwell in it."

17 "For behold, I will send serpents among you,
  Vipers which cannot be charmed,
  And they shall bite you," says the LORD.

18 I would comfort myself in sorrow;
  My heart *is* faint in me.
19 Listen! The voice,
  The cry of the daughter of my people
  From a far country:
  "Is not the LORD in Zion?
  Is not her King in her?"

  "Why have they provoked Me to anger
  With their carved images—
  With foreign idols?"

20 "The harvest is past,
  The summer is ended,
  And we are not saved!"

21 For the hurt of the daughter of my people I am
   hurt.
  I am mourning;
  Astonishment has taken hold of me.

22 *Is there* no balm in Gilead,
  Is there no physician there?
  Why then is there no recovery
  For the health of the daughter of my people?

9

  Oh, that my head were waters,
  And my eyes a fountain of tears,
  That I might weep day and night
  For the slain of the daughter of my people!
2   Oh, that I had in the wilderness

A lodging place for travelers;
That I might leave my people,
And go from them!
For they *are* all adulterers,
An assembly of treacherous men.

3 "And *like* their bow they have bent their tongues
   for lies.
They are not valiant for the truth on the earth.
For they proceed from evil to evil,
And they do not know Me," says the LORD.

4 "Everyone take heed to his neighbor,
And do not trust any brother;
For every brother will utterly supplant,
And every neighbor will walk with slanderers.

5 Everyone will deceive his neighbor,
And will not speak the truth;
They have taught their tongue to speak lies;
They weary themselves to commit iniquity.

6 Your dwelling place *is* in the midst of deceit;
Through deceit they refuse to know Me," says the
   LORD.

7 Therefore thus says the LORD of hosts:

"Behold, I will refine them and try them;
For how shall I deal with the daughter of My
   people?

8 Their tongue *is* an arrow shot out;
It speaks deceit;
One speaks peaceably to his neighbor with his
   mouth,
But in his heart he lies in wait.

9 Shall I not punish them for these *things?*" says the
   LORD.
"Shall I not avenge Myself on such a nation as
   this?"

10 I will take up a weeping and wailing for the
   mountains,
And for the dwelling places of the wilderness a
   lamentation,
Because they are burned up,
So that no one can pass through;
Nor can *men* hear the voice of the cattle.
Both the birds of the heavens and the beasts have
   fled;
They are gone.

11 "I will make Jerusalem a heap of ruins, a den of
   jackals.
I will make the cities of Judah desolate, without
   an inhabitant."

12 Who *is* the wise man who may understand this?
And *who is he* to whom the mouth of the LORD has
spoken, that he may declare it? Why does the land
perish *and* burn up like a wilderness, so that no one
can pass through?

13 And the LORD said, "Because they have
forsaken My law which I set before them, and have
not obeyed My voice, nor walked according to it,
14 but they have walked according to the dictates of
their own hearts and after the Baals, which their

בְּגָדִים: ² וַיַּדְרְכוּ אֶת־לְשׁוֹנָם קַשְׁתָּם שֶׁקֶר וְלֹא
לֶאֱמוּנָה גָּבְרוּ בָאָרֶץ כִּי מֵרָעָה אֶל־רָעָה ׀
יָצָאוּ וְאֹתִי לֹא־יָדָעוּ נְאֻם־יְהֹוָה: ס ³ אִישׁ
מֵרֵעֵהוּ הִשָּׁמֵרוּ וְעַל־כָּל־אָח אַל־תִּבְטָחוּ כִּי כָל־
אָח עָקוֹב יַעְקֹב וְכָל־רֵעַ רָכִיל יַהֲלֹךְ: ⁴ וְאִישׁ
בְּרֵעֵהוּ יְהָתֵלּוּ וֶאֱמֶת לֹא יְדַבֵּרוּ לִמְּדוּ לְשׁוֹנָם דַּבֶּר־
שֶׁקֶר הַעֲוֵה נִלְאוּ: ⁵ שִׁבְתְּךָ בְּתוֹךְ מִרְמָה בְּמִרְמָה
מֵאֲנוּ דַעַת־אוֹתִי נְאֻם־יְהֹוָה: ס ⁶ לָכֵן כֹּה
אָמַר יְהֹוָה צְבָאוֹת הִנְנִי צוֹרְפָם וּבְחַנְתִּים כִּי־
אֵיךְ אֶעֱשֶׂה מִפְּנֵי בַּת־עַמִּי: ⁷ חֵץ שֹׁוחֵטP לְשׁוֹנָם
מִרְמָה דִבֵּר בְּפִיו שָׁלוֹם אֶת־רֵעֵהוּ יְדַבֵּר
וּבְקִרְבּוֹ יָשִׂים אָרְבּוֹ: ⁸ הַעַל־אֵלֶּה לֹא־אֶפְקָד
בָּם נְאֻם־יְהֹוָה אִם בְּגוֹי אֲשֶׁר־כָּזֶה לֹא תִתְנַקֵּם
נַפְשִׁי: ס ⁹ עַל־הֶהָרִים אֶשָּׂא בְכִי וָנֶהִי
וְעַל־נְאוֹת מִדְבָּר קִינָה כִּי נִצְּתוּ מִבְּלִי־אִישׁ
עֹבֵר וְלֹא שָׁמְעוּ קוֹל מִקְנֶה מֵעוֹף הַשָּׁמַיִם
וְעַד־בְּהֵמָה נָדְדוּ הָלָכוּ: ¹⁰ וְנָתַתִּי אֶת־יְרוּשָׁלַ͏ִם
לְגַלִּים מְעוֹן תַּנִּים וְאֶת־עָרֵי יְהוּדָה אֶתֵּן שְׁמָמָה
מִבְּלִי יוֹשֵׁב: ס ¹¹ מִי־הָאִישׁ הֶחָכָם
וְיָבֵן אֶת־זֹאת וַאֲשֶׁר דִּבֶּר פִּי־יְהֹוָה אֵלָיו וְיַגִּדָהּ
עַל־מָה אָבְדָה הָאָרֶץ נִצְּתָה כַמִּדְבָּר מִבְּלִי
עֹבֵר: ס ¹² וַיֹּאמֶר יְהֹוָה עַל־עָזְבָם אֶת־
תּוֹרָתִי אֲשֶׁר נָתַתִּי לִפְנֵיהֶם וְלֹא־שָׁמְעוּ בְקוֹלִי
וְלֹא־הָלְכוּ בָהּ: ¹³ וַיֵּלְכוּ אַחֲרֵי שְׁרִרוּת לִבָּם וְאַחֲרֵי

fathers taught them," ¹⁵ therefore thus says the LORD of hosts, the God of Israel: "Behold, I will feed them, this people, with wormwood, and give them water of gall to drink. ¹⁶ I will scatter them also among the Gentiles, whom neither they nor their fathers have known. And I will send a sword after them until I have consumed them."

¹⁷ Thus says the LORD of hosts:

"Consider and call for the mourning women,
   That they may come,
And send for skillful wailing women,
   That they may come.
¹⁸ Let them make haste
   And take up a wailing for us,
That our eyes may run with tears,
   And our eyelids gush with water.
¹⁹ For a voice of wailing is heard from Zion:
   'How we are plundered!
We are greatly ashamed,
   Because we have forsaken the land,
Because we have been cast out of our
     dwellings.' "

²⁰ Yet hear the word of the LORD, O women,
   And let your ear receive the word of His mouth;
Teach your daughters wailing,
   And everyone her neighbor a lamentation.
²¹ For death has come through our windows,
   Has entered our palaces,
To kill off the children—*no longer to be* outside!
   And the young men—*no longer* on the streets!

²² Speak, "Thus says the LORD:

'Even the carcasses of men shall fall as refuse on
     the open field,
Like cuttings after the harvester,
   And no one shall gather *them*.' "

²³ Thus says the LORD:

"Let not the wise *man* glory in his wisdom,
Let not the mighty *man* glory in his might,
   Nor let the rich *man* glory in his riches;
²⁴ But let him who glories glory in this,
   That he understands and knows Me,
That I *am* the LORD, exercising lovingkindness,
   judgment, and righteousness in the earth.
For in these I delight," says the LORD.

²⁵ "Behold, the days are coming," says the LORD, "that I will punish all *who are* circumcised with the uncircumcised— ²⁶ Egypt, Judah, Edom, the people of Ammon, Moab, and all *who are* in the farthest corners, who dwell in the wilderness. For all *these* nations *are* uncircumcised, and all the house of Israel *are* uncircumcised in the heart."

10

Hear the word which the LORD speaks to you, O house of Israel.

² Thus says the LORD:

הַבְּעָלִים אֲשֶׁר לִמְּדוּם אֲבוֹתָם: ס 14 לָכֵן

כֹּה־אָמַר יְהֹוָה צְבָאוֹת אֱלֹהֵי יִשְׂרָאֵל הִנְנִי

מַאֲכִילָם אֶת־הָעָם הַזֶּה לַעֲנָה וְהִשְׁקִיתִים מֵי־

רֹאשׁ: 15 וַהֲפִצוֹתִים בַּגּוֹיִם אֲשֶׁר לֹא יָדְעוּ הֵמָּה

וַאֲבוֹתָם וְשִׁלַּחְתִּי אַחֲרֵיהֶם אֶת־הַחֶרֶב עַד כַּלּוֹתִי

אוֹתָם: פ

16 כֹּה אָמַר יְהֹוָה צְבָאוֹת הִתְבּוֹנְנוּ וְקִרְאוּ

לַמְקוֹנְנוֹת וּתְבוֹאֶינָה וְאֶל־הַחֲכָמוֹת שִׁלְחוּ

וְתָבוֹאנָה: 17 וּתְמַהֵרְנָה וְתִשֶּׂנָה עָלֵינוּ נֶהִי וְתֵרַדְנָה

עֵינֵינוּ דִּמְעָה וְעַפְעַפֵּינוּ יִזְּלוּ־מָיִם: 18 כִּי קוֹל נְהִי

נִשְׁמַע מִצִּיּוֹן אֵיךְ שֻׁדָּדְנוּ בֹּשְׁנוּ מְאֹד כִּי־עָזַבְנוּ

אָרֶץ כִּי הִשְׁלִיכוּ מִשְׁכְּנוֹתֵינוּ: ס 19 כִּי־

שְׁמַעְנָה נָשִׁים דְּבַר־יְהֹוָה וְתִקַּח אָזְנְכֶם דְּבַר־פִּיו

וְלַמֵּדְנָה בְנוֹתֵיכֶם נֶהִי וְאִשָּׁה רְעוּתָהּ קִינָה: 20 כִּי־

עָלָה מָוֶת בְּחַלּוֹנֵינוּ בָּא בְּאַרְמְנוֹתֵינוּ לְהַכְרִית עוֹלָל

מִחוּץ בַּחוּרִים מֵרְחֹבוֹת: 21 דַּבֵּר כֹּה נְאֻם־יְהֹוָה

וְנָפְלָה נִבְלַת הָאָדָם כְּדֹמֶן עַל־פְּנֵי הַשָּׂדֶה וּכְעָמִיר

מֵאַחֲרֵי הַקֹּצֵר וְאֵין מְאַסֵּף: ס 22 כֹּה |

אָמַר יְהֹוָה אַל־יִתְהַלֵּל חָכָם בְּחָכְמָתוֹ וְאַל־יִתְהַלֵּל

הַגִּבּוֹר בִּגְבוּרָתוֹ אַל־יִתְהַלֵּל עָשִׁיר בְּעָשְׁרוֹ: 23 כִּי

אִם־בְּזֹאת יִתְהַלֵּל הַמִּתְהַלֵּל הַשְׂכֵּל וְיָדֹעַ אוֹתִי

כִּי אֲנִי יְהֹוָה עֹשֶׂה חֶסֶד מִשְׁפָּט וּצְדָקָה בָּאָרֶץ

כִּי־בְאֵלֶּה חָפַצְתִּי נְאֻם־יְהֹוָה: ס 24 הִנֵּה

יָמִים בָּאִים נְאֻם־יְהֹוָה וּפָקַדְתִּי עַל־כָּל־מוּל

בְּעָרְלָה: 25 עַל־מִצְרַיִם וְעַל־יְהוּדָה וְעַל־אֱדוֹם

וְעַל־בְּנֵי עַמּוֹן וְעַל־מוֹאָב וְעַל כָּל־קְצוּצֵי פֵאָה

הַיֹּשְׁבִים בַּמִּדְבָּר כִּי כָל־הַגּוֹיִם עֲרֵלִים וְכָל־בֵּית

יִשְׂרָאֵל עַרְלֵי־לֵב: ס

י שִׁמְעוּ אֶת־הַדָּבָר אֲשֶׁר דִּבֶּר יְהֹוָה עֲלֵיכֶם

בֵּית יִשְׂרָאֵל: 2 כֹּה | אָמַר יְהֹוָה אֶל־דֶּרֶךְ הַגּוֹיִם

"Do not learn the way of the Gentiles;
Do not be dismayed at the signs of heaven,
For the Gentiles are dismayed at them.
3 For the customs of the peoples *are* futile;
For *one* cuts a tree from the forest,
The work of the hands of the workman, with the
ax.
4 They decorate it with silver and gold;
They fasten it with nails and hammers
So that it will not topple.
5 They *are* upright, like a palm tree,
And they cannot speak;
They must be carried,
Because they cannot go *by themselves.*
Do not be afraid of them,
For they cannot do evil,
Nor can they do any good."

6 Inasmuch as *there is* none like You, O LORD
(You *are* great, and Your name *is* great in might),
7 Who would not fear You, O King of the nations?
For this is Your rightful due.
For among all the wise *men* of the nations,
And in all their kingdoms,
There is none like You.
8 But they are altogether dull-hearted and foolish;
A wooden idol *is* a worthless doctrine.
9 Silver is beaten into plates;
It is brought from Tarshish,
And gold from Uphaz,
The work of the craftsman
And of the hands of the metalsmith;
Blue and purple *are* their clothing;
They *are* all the work of skillful *men.*
10 But the LORD *is* the true God;
He *is* the living God and the everlasting King.
At His wrath the earth will tremble,
And the nations will not be able to endure His
indignation.

11 Thus you shall say to them: "The gods that
have not made the heavens and the earth shall
perish from the earth and from under these
heavens."

12 He has made the earth by His power,
He has established the world by His wisdom,
And has stretched out the heavens at His
discretion.
13 When He utters His voice,
There is a multitude of waters in the heavens:
"And He causes the vapors to ascend from the
ends of the earth.
He makes lightning for the rain,
He brings the wind out of His treasuries."
14 Everyone is dull-hearted, without knowledge;
Every metalsmith is put to shame by an image;
For his molded image *is* falsehood,
And *there is* no breath in them.
15 They *are* futile, a work of errors;
In the time of their punishment they shall perish.
16 The Portion of Jacob *is* not like them,
For He *is* the Maker of all *things,*
And Israel *is* the tribe of His inheritance;

אַל־תִּלְמָדוּ וּמֵאֹתוֹת הַשָּׁמַיִם אַל־תֵּחָתּוּ כִּי־יֵחַתּוּ
הַגּוֹיִם מֵהֵמָּה׃ 3 כִּי־חֻקּוֹת הָעַמִּים הֶבֶל הוּא כִּי־
עֵץ מִיַּעַר כְּרָתוֹ מַעֲשֵׂה יְדֵי־חָרָשׁ בַּמַּעֲצָד׃ 4 בְּכֶסֶף
וּבְזָהָב יְיַפֵּהוּ בְּמַסְמְרוֹת וּבְמַקָּבוֹת יְחַזְּקוּם וְלוֹא
יָפִיק׃ 5 כְּתֹמֶר מִקְשָׁה הֵמָּה וְלֹא יְדַבֵּרוּ נָשׂוֹא
יִנָּשׂוּא כִּי לֹא יִצְעָדוּ אַל־תִּירְאוּ מֵהֶם כִּי־לֹא
יָרֵעוּ וְגַם־הֵיטֵיב אֵין אוֹתָם׃ ס 6 מֵאֵין
כָּמוֹךָ יְהוָה גָּדוֹל אַתָּה וְגָדוֹל שִׁמְךָ בִּגְבוּרָה׃
7 מִי לֹא יִרָאֲךָ מֶלֶךְ הַגּוֹיִם כִּי לְךָ יָאָתָה כִּי
בְכָל־חַכְמֵי הַגּוֹיִם וּבְכָל־מַלְכוּתָם מֵאֵין כָּמוֹךָ׃
8 וּבְאַחַת יִבְעֲרוּ וְיִכְסָלוּ מוּסַר הֲבָלִים עֵץ הוּא׃
9 כֶּסֶף מְרֻקָּע מִתַּרְשִׁישׁ יוּבָא וְזָהָב מֵאוּפָז מַעֲשֵׂה
חָרָשׁ וִידֵי צוֹרֵף תְּכֵלֶת וְאַרְגָּמָן לְבוּשָׁם מַעֲשֵׂה
חֲכָמִים כֻּלָּם׃ 10 וַיהוָה אֱלֹהִים אֱמֶת הוּא־אֱלֹהִים
חַיִּים וּמֶלֶךְ עוֹלָם מִקִּצְפּוֹ תִּרְעַשׁ הָאָרֶץ וְלֹא־יָכִלוּ
גוֹיִם זַעְמוֹ׃ ס 11 כִּדְנָה תֵּאמְרוּן לְהוֹם
אֱלָהַיָּא דִּי־שְׁמַיָּא וְאַרְקָא לָא עֲבַדוּ יֵאבַדוּ מֵאַרְעָא
וּמִן־תְּחוֹת שְׁמַיָּא אֵלֶּה׃ ס 12 עֹשֵׂה אֶרֶץ
בְּכֹחוֹ מֵכִין תֵּבֵל בְּחָכְמָתוֹ וּבִתְבוּנָתוֹ נָטָה שָׁמָיִם׃
13 לְקוֹל תִּתּוֹ הֲמוֹן מַיִם בַּשָּׁמַיִם וַיַּעֲלֶה נְשִׂאִים
מִקְצֵה ,אָרֶץ בְּרָקִים לַמָּטָר עָשָׂה וַיּוֹצֵא רוּחַ
מֵאֹצְרֹתָיו׃ 14 נִבְעַר כָּל־אָדָם מִדַּעַת הֹבִישׁ כָּל־
צוֹרֵף מִפָּסֶל כִּי שֶׁקֶר נִסְכּוֹ וְלֹא־רוּחַ בָּם׃ 15 הֶבֶל
הֵמָּה מַעֲשֵׂה תַּעְתֻּעִים בְּעֵת פְּקֻדָּתָם יֹאבֵדוּ׃
16 לֹא־כְאֵלֶּה חֵלֶק יַעֲקֹב כִּי־

The LORD of hosts *is* His name.

17 Gather up your wares from the land,
O inhabitant of the fortress!

18 For thus says the LORD:

"Behold, I will throw out at this time
The inhabitants of the land,
And will distress them,
That they may find *it so*."

19 Woe is me for my hurt!
My wound is severe.
But I say, "Truly this *is* an infirmity,
And I must bear it."

20 My tent is plundered,
And all my cords are broken;
My children have gone from me,
And they *are* no more.
There is no one to pitch my tent anymore,
Or set up my curtains.

21 For the shepherds have become dull-hearted,
And have not sought the LORD;
Therefore they shall not prosper,
And all their flocks shall be scattered.

22 Behold, the noise of the report has come,
And a great commotion out of the north country,
To make the cities of Judah desolate, a den of jackals.

23 O LORD, I know the way of man *is* not in himself;
It is not in man who walks to direct his own steps.

24 O LORD, correct me, but with justice;
Not in Your anger, lest You bring me to nothing.

25 Pour out Your fury on the Gentiles, who do not know You,
And on the families who do not call on Your name;
For they have eaten up Jacob,
Devoured him and consumed him,
And made his dwelling place desolate.

11 The word that came to Jeremiah from the LORD, saying, 2 "Hear the words of this covenant, and speak to the men of Judah and to the inhabitants of Jerusalem; 3 and say to them, 'Thus says the LORD God of Israel: "Cursed *is* the man who does not obey the words of this covenant 4 which I commanded your fathers in the day I brought them out of the land of Egypt, from the iron furnace, saying, 'Obey My voice, and do according to all that I command you; so shall you be My people, and I will be your God,' 5 that I may establish the oath which I have sworn to your fathers, to give them 'a land flowing with milk and honey,' as *it is* this day." ' "

And I answered and said, "So be it, LORD."

6 Then the LORD said to me, "Proclaim all these words in the cities of Judah and in the streets of Jerusalem, saying: 'Hear the words of this covenant and do them. 7 For I earnestly exhorted your fathers in the day I brought them up out of the land of

יוֹצֵר הַכֹּל הוּא וְיִשְׂרָאֵל שֵׁבֶט נַחֲלָתוֹ יְהוָה
צְבָאוֹת שְׁמוֹ: ס 17 אִסְפִּי מֵאֶרֶץ כִּנְעָתֵךְ
יֹשֶׁבֶת בַּמָּצוֹר: ס 18 כִּי־כֹה אָמַר יְהוָה
הִנְנִי קוֹלֵעַ אֶת־יוֹשְׁבֵי הָאָרֶץ בַּפַּעַם הַזֹּאת
וַהֲצֵרוֹתִי לָהֶם לְמַעַן יִמְצָאוּ: ס 19 אוֹי
לִי עַל־שִׁבְרִי נַחְלָה מַכָּתִי וַאֲנִי אָמַרְתִּי אַךְ זֶה
חֳלִי וְאֶשָּׂאֶנּוּ: 20 אָהֳלִי שֻׁדָּד וְכָל־מֵיתָרַי נִתָּקוּ
בָּנַי יְצָאֻנִי וְאֵינָם אֵין־נֹטֶה עוֹד אָהֳלִי וּמֵקִים
יְרִיעוֹתָי: 21 כִּי נִבְעֲרוּ הָרֹעִים וְאֶת־יְהוָה לֹא
דָרָשׁוּ עַל־כֵּן לֹא הִשְׂכִּילוּ וְכָל־מַרְעִיתָם נָפוֹצָה:
22 קוֹל שְׁמוּעָה הִנֵּה בָאָה וְרַעַשׁ גָּדוֹל ס
מֵאֶרֶץ צָפוֹן לָשׂוּם אֶת־עָרֵי יְהוּדָה שְׁמָמָה מְעוֹן
תַּנִּים: ס 23 יָדַעְתִּי יְהוָה כִּי לֹא לָאָדָם
דַּרְכּוֹ לֹא־לְאִישׁ הֹלֵךְ וְהָכִין אֶת־צַעֲדוֹ: 24 יַסְּרֵנִי
יְהוָה אַךְ־בְּמִשְׁפָּט אַל־בְּאַפְּךָ פֶּן־תַּמְעִטֵנִי: 25 שְׁפֹךְ
חֲמָתְךָ עַל־הַגּוֹיִם אֲשֶׁר לֹא־יְדָעוּךָ וְעַל מִשְׁפָּחוֹת
אֲשֶׁר בְּשִׁמְךָ לֹא קָרָאוּ כִּי־אָכְלוּ אֶת־יַעֲקֹב וַאֲכָלֻהוּ
וַיְכַלֻּהוּ וְאֶת־נָוֵהוּ הֵשַׁמּוּ: פ

יא הַדָּבָר אֲשֶׁר הָיָה אֶל־יִרְמְיָהוּ מֵאֵת יְהוָה
לֵאמֹר: 2 שִׁמְעוּ אֶת־דִּבְרֵי הַבְּרִית הַזֹּאת וְדִבַּרְתָּם
אֶל־אִישׁ יְהוּדָה וְעַל־יֹשְׁבֵי יְרוּשָׁלִָם: 3 וְאָמַרְתָּ
אֲלֵיהֶם כֹּה־אָמַר יְהוָה אֱלֹהֵי יִשְׂרָאֵל אָרוּר
הָאִישׁ אֲשֶׁר לֹא יִשְׁמַע אֶת־דִּבְרֵי הַבְּרִית הַזֹּאת:
4 אֲשֶׁר צִוִּיתִי אֶת־אֲבוֹתֵיכֶם בְּיוֹם הוֹצִיאִי־אוֹתָם
מֵאֶרֶץ־מִצְרַיִם מִכּוּר הַבַּרְזֶל לֵאמֹר שִׁמְעוּ בְקוֹלִי
וַעֲשִׂיתֶם אוֹתָם כְּכֹל אֲשֶׁר־אֲצַוֶּה אֶתְכֶם וִהְיִיתֶם
לִי לְעָם וְאָנֹכִי אֶהְיֶה לָכֶם לֵאלֹהִים: 5 לְמַעַן
הָקִים אֶת־הַשְּׁבוּעָה אֲשֶׁר־נִשְׁבַּעְתִּי לַאֲבוֹתֵיכֶם
לָתֵת לָהֶם אֶרֶץ זָבַת חָלָב וּדְבַשׁ כַּיּוֹם הַזֶּה
וָאַעַן וָאֹמַר אָמֵן ׀ יְהוָה: ס 6 וַיֹּאמֶר
יְהוָה אֵלַי קְרָא אֶת־כָּל־הַדְּבָרִים הָאֵלֶּה בְּעָרֵי
יְהוּדָה וּבְחֻצוֹת יְרוּשָׁלִַם לֵאמֹר שִׁמְעוּ אֶת־
דִּבְרֵי הַבְּרִית הַזֹּאת וַעֲשִׂיתֶם אוֹתָם: 7 כִּי הָעֵד

Egypt, until this day, rising early and exhorting, saying, "Obey My voice." 8 Yet they did not obey or incline their ear, but everyone followed the dictates of his evil heart; therefore I will bring upon them all the words of this covenant, which I commanded *them* to do, but *which* they have not done.' "

9 And the LORD said to me, "A conspiracy has been found among the men of Judah and among the inhabitants of Jerusalem. 10 They have turned back to the iniquities of their forefathers who refused to hear My words, and they have gone after other gods to serve them; the house of Israel and the house of Judah have broken My covenant which I made with their fathers."

11 Therefore thus says the LORD: "Behold, I will surely bring calamity on them which they will not be able to escape; and though they cry out to Me, I will not listen to them. 12 Then the cities of Judah and the inhabitants of Jerusalem will go and cry out to the gods to whom they offer incense, but they will not save them at all in the time of their trouble. 13 For *according to* the number of your cities were your gods, O Judah; and *according to* the number of the streets of Jerusalem you have set up altars to *that* shameful thing, altars to burn incense to Baal.

14 "So do not pray for this people, or lift up a cry or prayer for them; for I will not hear *them* in the time that they cry out to Me because of their trouble.

15 "What has My beloved to do in My house,
    Having done lewd deeds with many?
    And the holy flesh has passed from you.
    When you do evil, then you rejoice.
16   The LORD called your name,
    Green Olive Tree, Lovely *and* of Good Fruit.
    With the noise of a great tumult
    He has kindled fire on it,
    And its branches are broken.

17 "For the LORD of hosts, who planted you, has pronounced doom against you for the evil of the house of Israel and of the house of Judah, which they have done against themselves to provoke Me to anger in offering incense to Baal."

18 Now the LORD gave me knowledge *of it*, and I know *it*; for You showed me their doings. 19 But I *was* like a docile lamb brought to the slaughter; and I did not know that they had devised schemes against me, *saying*, "Let us destroy the tree with its fruit, and let us cut him off from the land of the living, that his name may be remembered no more."

20   But, O LORD of hosts,
    You who judge righteously,
    Testing the mind and the heart,
    Let me see Your vengeance on them,

הַעִדֹתִי בַּאֲבוֹתֵיכֶם בְּיוֹם הַעֲלוֹתִי אוֹתָם מֵאֶרֶץ מִצְרַיִם וְעַד־הַיּוֹם הַזֶּה הַשְׁכֵּם וְהָעֵד לֵאמֹר שִׁמְעוּ בְּקוֹלִי: 8 וְלֹא שָׁמְעוּ וְלֹא־הִטּוּ אֶת־אָזְנָם וַיֵּלְכוּ אִישׁ בִּשְׁרִירוּת לִבָּם הָרָע וָאָבִיא עֲלֵיהֶם אֶת־ כָּל־דִּבְרֵי הַבְּרִית־הַזֹּאת אֲשֶׁר־צִוִּיתִי לַעֲשׂוֹת וְלֹא עָשׂוּ: ס 9 וַיֹּאמֶר יְהוָה אֵלָי נִמְצָא־קֶשֶׁר בְּאִישׁ יְהוּדָה וּבְיֹשְׁבֵי יְרוּשָׁלִָם: 10 שָׁבוּ עַל־עֲוֹנֹת אֲבוֹתָם הָרִאשֹׁנִים אֲשֶׁר מֵאֲנוּ לִשְׁמוֹעַ אֶת־דְּבָרַי וְהֵמָּה הָלְכוּ אַחֲרֵי אֱלֹהִים אֲחֵרִים לְעָבְדָם הֵפֵרוּ בֵית־יִשְׂרָאֵל וּבֵית יְהוּדָה אֶת־בְּרִיתִי אֲשֶׁר כָּרַתִּי אֶת־אֲבוֹתָם: ס 11 לָכֵן כֹּה אָמַר יְהוָה הִנְנִי מֵבִיא אֲלֵיהֶם רָעָה אֲשֶׁר לֹא־יוּכְלוּ לָצֵאת מִמֶּנָּה וְזָעֲקוּ אֵלַי וְלֹא אֶשְׁמַע אֲלֵיהֶם: 12 וְהָלְכוּ עָרֵי יְהוּדָה וְיֹשְׁבֵי יְרוּשָׁלִַם וְזָעֲקוּ אֶל־הָאֱלֹהִים אֲשֶׁר הֵם מְקַטְּרִים לָהֶם וְהוֹשֵׁעַ לֹא־יוֹשִׁיעוּ לָהֶם בְּעֵת רָעָתָם: 13 כִּי מִסְפַּר עָרֶיךָ הָיוּ אֱלֹהֶיךָ יְהוּדָה וּמִסְפַּר חֻצוֹת יְרוּשָׁלִַם שַׂמְתֶּם מִזְבְּחוֹת לַבֹּשֶׁת מִזְבְּחוֹת לְקַטֵּר לַבָּעַל: ס 14 וְאַתָּה אַל־ תִּתְפַּלֵּל בְּעַד־הָעָם הַזֶּה וְאַל־תִּשָּׂא בַעֲדָם רִנָּה וּתְפִלָּה כִּי אֵינֶנִּי שֹׁמֵעַ בְּעֵת קָרְאָם אֵלַי בְּעַד רָעָתָם: ס 15 מֶה לִידִידִי בְּבֵיתִי עֲשׂוֹתָהּ הַמְזִמָּתָה הָרַבִּים וּבְשַׂר־קֹדֶשׁ יַעַבְרוּ מֵעָלָיִךְ כִּי רָעָתֵכִי אָז תַּעֲלֹזִי: 16 זַיִת רַעֲנָן יְפֵה פְרִי־תֹאַר קָרָא יְהוָה שְׁמֵךְ לְקוֹל | הֲמוּלָּה גְדֹלָה הִצִּית אֵשׁ עָלֶיהָ וְרָעוּ דָּלִיּוֹתָיו: 17 וַיהוָה צְבָאוֹת הַנּוֹטֵעַ אוֹתָךְ דִּבֶּר עָלַיִךְ רָעָה בִּגְלַל רָעַת בֵּית־יִשְׂרָאֵל וּבֵית יְהוּדָה אֲשֶׁר עָשׂוּ לָהֶם לְהַכְעִסֵנִי לְקַטֵּר לַבָּעַל: ס 18 וַיהוָה הוֹדִיעַנִי וָאֵדָעָה אָז הִרְאִיתַנִי מַעַלְלֵיהֶם: 19 וַאֲנִי כְּכֶבֶשׂ אַלּוּף יוּבַל לִטְבוֹחַ וְלֹא־יָדַעְתִּי כִּי־עָלַי | חָשְׁבוּ מַחֲשָׁבוֹת נַשְׁחִיתָה עֵץ בְּלַחְמוֹ וְנִכְרְתֶנּוּ מֵאֶרֶץ חַיִּים וּשְׁמוֹ לֹא־יִזָּכֵר עוֹד: 20 וַיהוָה צְבָאוֹת שֹׁפֵט צֶדֶק בֹּחֵן כְּלָיוֹת וָלֵב אֶרְאֶה נִקְמָתְךָ מֵהֶם כִּי

For to You I have revealed my cause.

21 "Therefore thus says the LORD concerning the men of Anathoth who seek your life, saying, 'Do not prophesy in the name of the LORD, lest you die by our hand'— 22 therefore thus says the LORD of hosts: 'Behold, I will punish them. The young men shall die by the sword, their sons and their daughters shall die by famine; 23 and there shall be no remnant of them, for I will bring catastrophe on the men of Anathoth, *even* the year of their punishment.'"

12 Righteous *are* You, O LORD, when I plead with You;
   Yet let me talk with You about *Your* judgments.
   Why does the way of the wicked prosper?
   Why are those happy who deal so treacherously?
2 You have planted them, yes, they have taken root;
   They grow, yes, they bear fruit.
   You *are* near in their mouth
   But far from their mind.

3 But You, O LORD, know me;
   You have seen me,
   And You have tested my heart toward You.
   Pull them out like sheep for the slaughter,
   And prepare them for the day of slaughter.
4 How long will the land mourn,
   And the herbs of every field wither?
   The beasts and birds are consumed,
   For the wickedness of those who dwell there,
   Because they said, "He will not see our final end."

5 "If you have run with the footmen, and they have wearied you,
   Then how can you contend with horses?
   And *if* in the land of peace,
   In which you trusted, *they wearied you,*
   Then how will you do in the floodplain of the Jordan?
6 For even your brothers, the house of your father,
   Even they have dealt treacherously with you;
   Yes, they have called a multitude after you.
   Do not believe them,
   Even though they speak smooth words to you.

7 "I have forsaken My house, I have left My heritage;
   I have given the dearly beloved of My soul into the hand of her enemies.
8 My heritage is to Me like a lion in the forest;
   It cries out against Me;
   Therefore I have hated it.
9 My heritage *is* to Me *like* a speckled vulture;
   The vultures all around *are* against her.
   Come, assemble all the beasts of the field,
   Bring them to devour!

10 "Many rulers have destroyed My vineyard,
   They have trodden My portion underfoot;

‫21 לָכֵן כֹּה־‬ ס ‫אֵלֶיךָ גִּלִּיתִי אֶת־רִיבִי:‬
‫אָמַר יְהוָה עַל־אַנְשֵׁי עֲנָתוֹת הַמְבַקְשִׁים אֶת־‬
‫נַפְשְׁךָ לֵאמֹר לֹא תִנָּבֵא בְּשֵׁם יְהוָה וְלֹא תָמוּת‬
‫בְּיָדֵנוּ:‬ ס ‫22 לָכֵן כֹּה אָמַר יְהוָה צְבָאוֹת‬
‫הִנְנִי פֹקֵד עֲלֵיהֶם הַבַּחוּרִים יָמֻתוּ בַחֶרֶב בְּנֵיהֶם‬
‫וּבְנוֹתֵיהֶם יָמֻתוּ בָּרָעָב: 23 וּשְׁאֵרִית לֹא תִהְיֶה‬
‫לָהֶם כִּי־אָבִיא רָעָה אֶל־אַנְשֵׁי עֲנָתוֹת שְׁנַת‬
‫פְּקֻדָּתָם:‬ ס

‫יב צַדִּיק אַתָּה יְהוָה כִּי אָרִיב אֵלֶיךָ אַךְ מִשְׁפָּטִים‬
‫אֲדַבֵּר אוֹתָךְ מַדּוּעַ דֶּרֶךְ רְשָׁעִים צָלֵחָה שָׁלוּ כָּל־‬
‫בֹּגְדֵי בָגֶד: 2 נְטַעְתָּם גַּם־שֹׁרָשׁוּ יֵלְכוּ גַּם־עָשׂוּ פֶרִי‬
‫קָרוֹב אַתָּה בְּפִיהֶם וְרָחוֹק מִכִּלְיוֹתֵיהֶם: 3 וְאַתָּה‬
‫יְהוָה יְדַעְתָּנִי תִּרְאֵנִי וּבָחַנְתָּ לִבִּי אִתָּךְ הַתִּקֵם כְּצֹאן‬
‫לְטִבְחָה וְהַקְדִּשֵׁם לְיוֹם הֲרֵגָה:‬ ס ‫4 עַד־‬
‫מָתַי תֶּאֱבַל הָאָרֶץ וְעֵשֶׂב כָּל־הַשָּׂדֶה יִיבָשׁ מֵרָעַת‬
‫יֹשְׁבֵי־בָהּ סָפְתָה בְהֵמוֹת וָעוֹף כִּי אָמְרוּ לֹא‬
‫יִרְאֶה אֶת־אַחֲרִיתֵנוּ: 5 כִּי אֶת־רַגְלִים ׀ רַצְתָּה‬
‫וַיַּלְאוּךָ וְאֵיךְ תְּתַחֲרֶה אֶת־הַסּוּסִים וּבְאֶרֶץ שָׁלוֹם‬
‫אַתָּה בוֹטֵחַ וְאֵיךְ תַּעֲשֶׂה בִּגְאוֹן הַיַּרְדֵּן: 6 כִּי‬
‫גַם־אַחֶיךָ וּבֵית־אָבִיךָ גַּם־הֵמָּה בָּגְדוּ בָךְ גַּם־‬
‫הֵמָּה קָרְאוּ אַחֲרֶיךָ מָלֵא אַל־תַּאֲמֵן בָּם כִּי־‬
‫יְדַבְּרוּ אֵלֶיךָ טוֹבוֹת:‬ ס ‫7 עָזַבְתִּי אֶת־‬
‫בֵּיתִי נָטַשְׁתִּי אֶת־נַחֲלָתִי נָתַתִּי אֶת־יְדִדוּת נַפְשִׁי‬
‫בְּכַף אֹיְבֶיהָ: 8 הָיְתָה־לִּי נַחֲלָתִי כְּאַרְיֵה בַיָּעַר‬
‫נָתְנָה עָלַי בְּקוֹלָהּ עַל־כֵּן שְׂנֵאתִיהָ: 9 הַעַיִט צָבוּעַ‬
‫נַחֲלָתִי לִי הַעַיִט סָבִיב עָלֶיהָ לְכוּ אִסְפוּ כָּל־חַיַּת‬
‫הַשָּׂדֶה הֵתָיוּ לְאָכְלָה: 10 רֹעִים רַבִּים שִׁחֲתוּ כַרְמִי‬
‫בֹּסְסוּ אֶת־חֶלְקָתִי נָתְנוּ אֶת־חֶלְקַת חֶמְדָּתִי לְמִדְבַּר‬

They have made My pleasant portion a desolate
    wilderness.
11 They have made it desolate;
    Desolate, it mourns to Me;
    The whole land is made desolate,
    Because no one takes *it* to heart.
12 The plunderers have come
    On all the desolate heights in the wilderness,
    For the sword of the LORD shall devour
    From *one* end of the land to the *other* end of the
    land;
    No flesh shall have peace.
13 They have sown wheat but reaped thorns;
    They have put themselves to pain *but* do not
    profit.
    But be ashamed of your harvest
    Because of the fierce anger of the LORD."

14 Thus says the LORD: "Against all My evil
neighbors who touch the inheritance which I have
caused My people Israel to inherit—behold, I will
pluck them out of their land and pluck out the
house of Judah from among them. 15 Then it shall
be, after I have plucked them out, that I will return
and have compassion on them and bring them
back, everyone to his heritage and everyone to his
land. 16 And it shall be, if they will learn carefully
the ways of My people, to swear by My name, 'As
the LORD lives,' as they taught My people to swear
by Baal, then they shall be established in the midst
of My people. 17 But if they do not obey, I will
utterly pluck up and destroy that nation," says the
LORD.

13 Thus the LORD said to me: "Go and get
yourself a linen sash, and put it around your waist,
but do not put it in water." 2 So I got a sash
according to the word of the LORD, and put *it*
around my waist.

3 And the word of the LORD came to me the
second time, saying, 4 "Take the sash that you
acquired, which *is* around your waist, and arise, go
to the Euphrates, and hide it there in a hole in the
rock." 5 So I went and hid it by the Euphrates, as
the LORD commanded me.

6 Now it came to pass after many days that the
LORD said to me, "Arise, go to the Euphrates, and
take from there the sash which I commanded you to
hide there." 7 Then I went to the Euphrates and
dug, and I took the sash from the place where I had
hidden it; and there was the sash, ruined. It was
profitable for nothing.

8 Then the word of the LORD came to me, saying,
9 "Thus says the LORD: 'In this manner I will ruin
the pride of Judah and the great pride of Jerusalem.
10 This evil people, who refuse to hear My words,
who follow the dictates of their hearts, and walk

שְׁמֵמָה: 11 שָׁמָהּ לִשְׁמָמָה אָבְלָה עָלַי שְׁמֵמָה
נָשַׁמָּה כָּל־הָאָרֶץ כִּי אֵין אִישׁ שָׂם עַל־לֵב: 12 עַל־
כָּל־שְׁפָיִם בַּמִּדְבָּר בָּאוּ שֹׁדְדִים כִּי חֶרֶב לַיהֹוָה
אֹכְלָה מִקְצֵה־אֶרֶץ וְעַד־קְצֵה הָאָרֶץ אֵין שָׁלוֹם
לְכָל־בָּשָׂר: ס 13 זָרְעוּ חִטִּים וְקֹצִים קָצָרוּ
נֶחְלוּ לֹא יוֹעִלוּ וּבֹשׁוּ מִתְּבוּאֹתֵיכֶם מֵחֲרוֹן אַף־
יְהֹוָה: ס 14 כֹּה | אָמַר יְהֹוָה עַל־כָּל־
שְׁכֵנַי הָרָעִים הַנֹּגְעִים בַּנַּחֲלָה אֲשֶׁר־הִנְחַלְתִּי אֶת־
עַמִּי אֶת־יִשְׂרָאֵל הִנְנִי נֹתְשָׁם מֵעַל אַדְמָתָם וְאֶת־
בֵּית יְהוּדָה אֶתּוֹשׁ מִתּוֹכָם: 15 וְהָיָה אַחֲרֵי נָתְשִׁי
אוֹתָם אָשׁוּב וְרִחַמְתִּים וַהֲשִׁבֹתִים אִישׁ לְנַחֲלָתוֹ
וְאִישׁ לְאַרְצוֹ: 16 וְהָיָה אִם־לָמֹד יִלְמְדוּ אֶת־דַּרְכֵי
עַמִּי לְהִשָּׁבֵעַ בִּשְׁמִי חַי־יְהֹוָה כַּאֲשֶׁר לִמְּדוּ אֶת־
עַמִּי לְהִשָּׁבֵעַ בַּבָּעַל וְנִבְנוּ בְּתוֹךְ עַמִּי: 17 וְאִם
לֹא יִשְׁמָעוּ וְנָתַשְׁתִּי אֶת־הַגּוֹי הַהוּא נָתוֹשׁ וְאַבֵּד
נְאֻם־יְהֹוָה: ס

יג כֹּה־אָמַר יְהֹוָה אֵלַי הָלוֹךְ וְקָנִיתָ לְּךָ אֵזוֹר
פִּשְׁתִּים וְשַׂמְתּוֹ עַל־מָתְנֶיךָ וּבַמַּיִם לֹא תְבִאֵהוּ:
2 וָאֶקְנֶה אֶת־הָאֵזוֹר כִּדְבַר יְהֹוָה וָאָשִׂם עַל־
מָתְנָי: ס 3 וַיְהִי דְבַר־יְהֹוָה אֵלַי שֵׁנִית
לֵאמֹר: 4 קַח אֶת־הָאֵזוֹר אֲשֶׁר קָנִיתָ אֲשֶׁר עַל־
מָתְנֶיךָ וְקוּם לֵךְ פְּרָתָה וְטָמְנֵהוּ שָׁם בִּנְקִיק הַסָּלַע:
5 וָאֵלֵךְ וָאֶטְמְנֵהוּ בִּפְרָת כַּאֲשֶׁר צִוָּה יְהֹוָה אוֹתִי:
6 וַיְהִי מִקֵּץ יָמִים רַבִּים וַיֹּאמֶר יְהֹוָה אֵלַי קוּם לֵךְ
פְּרָתָה וְקַח מִשָּׁם אֶת־הָאֵזוֹר אֲשֶׁר צִוִּיתִיךָ לְטָמְנוֹ־
שָׁם: 7 וָאֵלֵךְ פְּרָתָה וָאֶחְפֹּר וָאֶקַּח אֶת־הָאֵזוֹר מִן־
הַמָּקוֹם אֲשֶׁר־טְמַנְתִּיו שָׁמָּה וְהִנֵּה נִשְׁחַת הָאֵזוֹר
לֹא יִצְלַח לַכֹּל: פ

8 וַיְהִי דְבַר־יְהֹוָה אֵלַי לֵאמֹר: 9 כֹּה אָמַר
יְהֹוָה כָּכָה אַשְׁחִית אֶת־גְּאוֹן יְהוּדָה וְאֶת־גְּאוֹן
יְרוּשָׁלִַם הָרָב: 10 הָעָם הַזֶּה הָרָע הַמֵּאֲנִים |

after other gods to serve them and worship them, shall be just like this sash which is profitable for nothing. [11] For as the sash clings to the waist of a man, so I have caused the whole house of Israel and the whole house of Judah to cling to Me,' says the LORD, 'that they may become My people, for renown, for praise, and for glory; but they would not hear.'

[12] "Therefore you shall speak to them this word: 'Thus says the LORD God of Israel: "Every bottle shall be filled with wine."'

"And they will say to you, 'Do we not certainly know that every bottle will be filled with wine?'

[13] "Then you shall say to them, 'Thus says the LORD: "Behold, I will fill all the inhabitants of this land—even the kings who sit on David's throne, the priests, the prophets, and all the inhabitants of Jerusalem—with drunkenness! [14] And I will dash them one against another, even the fathers and the sons together," says the LORD. "I will not pity nor spare nor have mercy, but will destroy them."'"

[15] Hear and give ear:
Do not be proud,
For the LORD has spoken.
[16] Give glory to the LORD your God
Before He causes darkness,
And before your feet stumble
On the dark mountains,
And while you are looking for light,
He turns it into the shadow of death
And makes it dense darkness.
[17] But if you will not hear it,
My soul will weep in secret for your pride;
My eyes will weep bitterly
And run down with tears,
Because the LORD's flock has been taken captive.

[18] Say to the king and to the queen mother,

"Humble yourselves;
Sit down,
For your rule shall collapse, the crown of your glory."
[19] The cities of the South shall be shut up,
And no one shall open them;
Judah shall be carried away captive, all of it;
It shall be wholly carried away captive.

[20] Lift up your eyes and see
Those who come from the north.
Where is the flock that was given to you,
Your beautiful sheep?
[21] What will you say when He punishes you?
For you have taught them
To be chieftains, to be head over you.
Will not pangs seize you,
Like a woman in labor?
[22] And if you say in your heart,
"Why have these things come upon me?"
For the greatness of your iniquity

לִשְׁמֹעַ אֶת־דְּבָרַי הַהֹלְכִים בִּשְׁרִרוּת לִבָּם וַיֵּלְכוּ
אַחֲרֵי אֱלֹהִים אֲחֵרִים לְעָבְדָם וּלְהִשְׁתַּחֲוֺת לָהֶם
וִיהִי כָּאֵזוֹר הַזֶּה אֲשֶׁר לֹא־יִצְלַח לַכֹּל: 11 כִּי
כַּאֲשֶׁר יִדְבַּק הָאֵזוֹר אֶל־מָתְנֵי־אִישׁ כֵּן הִדְבַּקְתִּי
אֵלַי אֶת־כָּל־בֵּית יִשְׂרָאֵל וְאֶת־כָּל־בֵּית יְהוּדָה
נְאֻם־יְהֹוָה לִהְיוֹת לִי לְעָם וּלְשֵׁם וְלִתְהִלָּה
וּלְתִפְאָרֶת וְלֹא שָׁמֵעוּ: 12 וְאָמַרְתָּ אֲלֵיהֶם אֶת־
הַדָּבָר הַזֶּה ס כֹּה־אָמַר יְהֹוָה אֱלֹהֵי
יִשְׂרָאֵל כָּל־נֵבֶל יִמָּלֵא יָיִן וְאָמְרוּ אֵלֶיךָ הֲיָדֹעַ לֹא
נֵדַע כִּי כָל־נֵבֶל יִמָּלֵא יָיִן: 13 וְאָמַרְתָּ אֲלֵיהֶם כֹּה־
אָמַר יְהֹוָה הִנְנִי מְמַלֵּא אֶת־כָּל־יֹשְׁבֵי הָאָרֶץ הַזֹּאת
וְאֶת־הַמְּלָכִים הַיֹּשְׁבִים לְדָוִד עַל־כִּסְאוֹ וְאֶת־
הַכֹּהֲנִים וְאֶת־הַנְּבִיאִים וְאֵת כָּל־יֹשְׁבֵי יְרוּשָׁלַ͏ִם
שִׁכָּרוֹן: 14 וְנִפַּצְתִּים אִישׁ אֶל־אָחִיו וְהָאָבוֹת
וְהַבָּנִים יַחְדָּו נְאֻם־יְהֹוָה לֹא־אֶחְמוֹל וְלֹא־אָחוּס
וְלֹא אֲרַחֵם מֵהַשְׁחִיתָם: ס 15 שִׁמְעוּ
וְהַאֲזִינוּ אַל־תִּגְבָּהוּ כִּי יְהֹוָה דִּבֵּר: 16 תְּנוּ
לַיהֹוָה אֱלֹהֵיכֶם כָּבוֹד בְּטֶרֶם יַחְשִׁךְ וּבְטֶרֶם
יִתְנַגְּפוּ רַגְלֵיכֶם עַל־הָרֵי נָשֶׁף וְקִוִּיתֶם לְאוֹר
וְשָׂמָהּ לְצַלְמָוֶת יָשִׁית לַעֲרָפֶל: 17 וְאִם לֹא
תִשְׁמָעוּהָ בְּמִסְתָּרִים תִּבְכֶּה־נַפְשִׁי מִפְּנֵי גֵוָה
וְדָמֹעַ תִּדְמַע וְתֵרַד עֵינִי דִּמְעָה כִּי נִשְׁבָּה עֵדֶר
יְהֹוָה: ס 18 אֱמֹר לַמֶּלֶךְ וְלַגְּבִירָה הַשְׁפִּילוּ
שֵׁבוּ כִּי יָרַד מַרְאֲשׁוֹתֵיכֶם עֲטֶרֶת תִּפְאַרְתְּכֶם:
19 עָרֵי הַנֶּגֶב סֻגְּרוּ וְאֵין פֹּתֵחַ הָגְלָת יְהוּדָה
כֻּלָּהּ הָגְלָת שְׁלוֹמִים: ס 20 שְׂאִי עֵינֵיכֶם
וּרְאִי הַבָּאִים מִצָּפוֹן אַיֵּה הָעֵדֶר נִתַּן־לָךְ צֹאן
תִּפְאַרְתֵּךְ: 21 מַה־תֹּאמְרִי כִּי־יִפְקֹד עָלַיִךְ וְאַתְּ
לִמַּדְתְּ אֹתָם עָלַיִךְ אַלֻּפִים לְרֹאשׁ הֲלוֹא חֲבָלִים
יֹאחֱזוּךְ כְּמוֹ אֵשֶׁת לֵדָה: 22 וְכִי תֹאמְרִי בִּלְבָבֵךְ
מַדּוּעַ קְרָאֻנִי אֵלֶּה בְּרֹב עֲוֺנֵךְ נִגְלוּ שׁוּלַיִךְ נֶחְמְסוּ

Your skirts have been uncovered,
Your heels made bare.
23 Can the Ethiopian change his skin or the leopard
its spots?
Then may you also do good who are accustomed
to do evil.

24 "Therefore I will scatter them like stubble
That passes away by the wind of the wilderness.
25 This is your lot,
The portion of your measures from Me," says the
LORD,
"Because you have forgotten Me
And trusted in falsehood.
26 Therefore I will uncover your skirts over your
face,
That your shame may appear.
27 I have seen your adulteries
And your *lustful* neighings,
The lewdness of your harlotry,
Your abominations on the hills in the fields.
Woe to you, O Jerusalem!
Will you still not be made clean?"

14 The word of the LORD that came to Jeremiah
concerning the droughts.

2 "Judah mourns,
And her gates languish;
They mourn for the land,
And the cry of Jerusalem has gone up.
3 Their nobles have sent their lads for water;
They went to the cisterns *and* found no water.
They returned with their vessels empty;
They were ashamed and confounded
And covered their heads.
4 Because the ground is parched,
For there was no rain in the land,
The plowmen were ashamed;
They covered their heads.
5 Yes, the deer also gave birth in the field,
But left because there was no grass.
6 And the wild donkeys stood in the desolate
heights;
They sniffed at the wind like jackals;
Their eyes failed because *there was* no grass."

7 O LORD, though our iniquities testify against us,
Do it for Your name's sake;
For our backslidings are many,
We have sinned against You.
8 O the Hope of Israel, his Savior in time of
trouble,
Why should You be like a stranger in the land,
And like a traveler *who* turns aside to tarry for a
night?
9 Why should You be like a man astonished,
Like a mighty one *who* cannot save?
Yet You, O LORD, *are* in our midst,
And we are called by Your name;
Do not leave us!

10 Thus says the LORD to this people:

"Thus they have loved to wander;

עֲקֵבָֽיִךְ: 23 הֲיַהֲפֹךְ כּוּשִׁי עוֹרוֹ וְנָמֵר חֲבַרְבֻּרֹתָיו
גַּם־אַתֶּם תּוּכְלוּ לְהֵיטִיב לִמֻּדֵי הָרֵעַ: 24 וַאֲפִיצֵם
כְּקַשׁ־עוֹבֵר לְרוּחַ מִדְבָּר: 25 זֶה גוֹרָלֵךְ מְנָת־מִדַּיִךְ
מֵאִתִּי נְאֻם־יְהוָה אֲשֶׁר שָׁכַחַתְּ אוֹתִי וַתִּבְטְחִי
בַּשָּׁקֶר: 26 וְגַם־אֲנִי חָשַׂפְתִּי שׁוּלַיִךְ עַל־פָּנָיִךְ וְנִרְאָה
קְלוֹנֵךְ: 27 נִאֻפַיִךְ וּמִצְהֲלוֹתַיִךְ זִמַּת זְנוּתֵךְ עַל־
גְּבָעוֹת בַּשָּׂדֶה רָאִיתִי שִׁקּוּצָיִךְ אוֹי לָךְ יְרוּשָׁלִַם
לֹא תִטְהֲרִי אַחֲרֵי מָתַי עֹד: פ

יד אֲשֶׁר הָיָה דְבַר־יְהוָה אֶל־יִרְמְיָהוּ עַל־דִּבְרֵי
הַבַּצָּרוֹת: 2 אָבְלָה יְהוּדָה וּשְׁעָרֶיהָ אֻמְלְלוּ קָדְרוּ
לָאָרֶץ וְצִוְחַת יְרוּשָׁלִַם עָלָתָה: 3 וְאַדִּרֵיהֶם שָׁלְחוּ
צְעוֹרֵיהֶם לַמָּיִם בָּאוּ עַל־גֵּבִים לֹא־מָצְאוּ מַיִם
שָׁבוּ כְלֵיהֶם רֵיקָם בֹּשׁוּ וְהָכְלְמוּ וְחָפוּ רֹאשָׁם:
4 בַּעֲבוּר הָאֲדָמָה חַתָּה כִּי לֹא־הָיָה גֶשֶׁם בָּאָרֶץ
בֹּשׁוּ אִכָּרִים חָפוּ רֹאשָׁם: 5 כִּי גַם־אַיֶּלֶת בַּשָּׂדֶה
יָלְדָה וְעָזוֹב כִּי לֹא־הָיָה דֶּשֶׁא: 6 וּפְרָאִים עָמְדוּ
עַל־שְׁפָיִם שָׁאֲפוּ רוּחַ כַּתַּנִּים כָּלוּ עֵינֵיהֶם כִּי־אֵין
עֵשֶׂב: 7 אִם־עֲוֹנֵינוּ עָנוּ בָנוּ יְהוָה עֲשֵׂה לְמַעַן שְׁמֶךָ
כִּי־רַבּוּ מְשׁוּבֹתֵינוּ לְךָ חָטָאנוּ: 8 מִקְוֵה יִשְׂרָאֵל
מוֹשִׁיעוֹ בְּעֵת צָרָה לָמָּה תִהְיֶה כְּגֵר בָּאָרֶץ וּכְאֹרֵחַ
נָטָה לָלוּן: 9 לָמָּה תִהְיֶה כְּאִישׁ נִדְהָם כְּגִבּוֹר לֹא־
יוּכַל לְהוֹשִׁיעַ וְאַתָּה בְקִרְבֵּנוּ יְהוָה וְשִׁמְךָ עָלֵינוּ
נִקְרָא אַל־תַּנִּחֵנוּ: ס 10 כֹּה־אָמַר יְהוָה
לָעָם הַזֶּה כֵּן אָהֲבוּ לָנוּעַ רַגְלֵיהֶם

They have not restrained their feet.
Therefore the LORD does not accept them;
He will remember their iniquity now,
And punish their sins."

11 Then the LORD said to me, "Do not pray for this people, for *their* good. 12 When they fast, I will not hear their cry; and when they offer burnt offering and grain offering, I will not accept them. But I will consume them by the sword, by the famine, and by the pestilence."

13 Then I said, "Ah, Lord GOD! Behold, the prophets say to them, 'You shall not see the sword, nor shall you have famine, but I will give you assured peace in this place.'"

14 And the LORD said to me, "The prophets prophesy lies in My name. I have not sent them, commanded them, nor spoken to them; they prophesy to you a false vision, divination, a worthless thing, and the deceit of their heart. 15 Therefore thus says the LORD concerning the prophets who prophesy in My name, whom I did not send, and who say, 'Sword and famine shall not be in this land'—'By sword and famine those prophets shall be consumed! 16 And the people to whom they prophesy shall be cast out in the streets of Jerusalem because of the famine and the sword; they will have no one to bury them—them nor their wives, their sons nor their daughters—for I will pour their wickedness on them.'

17 "Therefore you shall say this word to them:

'Let my eyes flow with tears night and day,
And let them not cease;
For the virgin daughter of my people
Has been broken with a mighty stroke, with a
very severe blow.

18   If I go out to the field,
Then behold, those slain with the sword!
And if I enter the city,
Then behold, those sick from famine!
Yes, both prophet and priest go about in a land
they do not know.'"

19   Have You utterly rejected Judah?
Has Your soul loathed Zion?
Why have You stricken us so that *there is* no
healing for us?
We looked for peace, but *there was* no good;
And for the time of healing, and there was
trouble.

20   We acknowledge, O LORD, our wickedness
And the iniquity of our fathers,
For we have sinned against You.

21   Do not abhor *us*, for Your name's sake;
Do not disgrace the throne of Your glory.
Remember, do not break Your covenant with us.

22   Are there any among the idols of the nations that
can cause rain?
Or can the heavens give showers?

לֹא חָשָׂכוּ וַיהֹוָה לֹא רָצָם עַתָּה יִזְכֹּר עֲוֺנָם
וְיִפְקֹד חַטֹּאתָם: ס 11 וַיֹּאמֶר יְהֹוָה אֵלַי
אַל־תִּתְפַּלֵּל בְּעַד־הָעָם הַזֶּה לְטוֹבָה: 12 כִּי יָצֻמוּ
אֵינֶנִּי שֹׁמֵעַ אֶל־רִנָּתָם וְכִי יַעֲלוּ עֹלָה וּמִנְחָה
אֵינֶנִּי רֹצָם כִּי בַּחֶרֶב וּבָרָעָב וּבַדֶּבֶר אָנֹכִי
מְכַלֶּה אוֹתָם: ס 13 וָאֹמַר אֲהָהּ אֲדֹנָי
יְהֹוִה הִנֵּה הַנְּבִאִים אֹמְרִים לָהֶם לֹא־תִרְאוּ
חֶרֶב וְרָעָב לֹא־יִהְיֶה לָכֶם כִּי־שְׁלוֹם אֱמֶת אֶתֵּן
לָכֶם בַּמָּקוֹם הַזֶּה: ס 14 וַיֹּאמֶר יְהֹוָה
אֵלַי שֶׁקֶר הַנְּבִאִים נִבְּאִים בִּשְׁמִי לֹא שְׁלַחְתִּים
וְלֹא צִוִּיתִים וְלֹא דִבַּרְתִּי אֲלֵיהֶם חֲזוֹן שֶׁקֶר
וְקֶסֶם וֶאֱלִיל וְתַרְמוּת לִבָּם הֵמָּה מִתְנַבְּאִים
לָכֶם: ס 15 לָכֵן כֹּה־אָמַר יְהֹוָה עַל־
הַנְּבִאִים הַנִּבְּאִים בִּשְׁמִי וַאֲנִי לֹא־שְׁלַחְתִּים וְהֵמָּה
אֹמְרִים חֶרֶב וְרָעָב לֹא יִהְיֶה בָּאָרֶץ הַזֹּאת בַּחֶרֶב
וּבָרָעָב יִתַּמּוּ הַנְּבִאִים הָהֵמָּה: 16 וְהָעָם אֲשֶׁר־הֵמָּה
נִבְּאִים לָהֶם יִהְיוּ מֻשְׁלָכִים בְּחֻצוֹת יְרוּשָׁלַ͏ִם מִפְּנֵי ׀
הָרָעָב וְהַחֶרֶב וְאֵין מְקַבֵּר לָהֵמָּה הֵמָּה נְשֵׁיהֶם
וּבְנֵיהֶם וּבְנֹתֵיהֶם וְשָׁפַכְתִּי עֲלֵיהֶם אֶת־רָעָתָם:
17 וְאָמַרְתָּ אֲלֵיהֶם אֶת־הַדָּבָר הַזֶּה תֵּרַדְנָה עֵינַי
דִּמְעָה לַיְלָה וְיוֹמָם וְאַל־תִּדְמֶינָה כִּי שֶׁבֶר גָּדוֹל
נִשְׁבְּרָה בְּתוּלַת בַּת־עַמִּי מַכָּה נַחְלָה מְאֹד: 18 אִם־
יָצָאתִי הַשָּׂדֶה וְהִנֵּה חַלְלֵי־חֶרֶב וְאִם בָּאתִי הָעִיר
וְהִנֵּה תַּחֲלוּאֵי רָעָב כִּי־גַם־נָבִיא גַם־כֹּהֵן סָחֲרוּ
אֶל־אֶרֶץ וְלֹא יָדָעוּ: ס 19 הֲמָאֹס מָאַסְתָּ
אֶת־יְהוּדָה אִם־בְּצִיּוֹן גָּעֲלָה נַפְשֶׁךָ מַדּוּעַ הִכִּיתָנוּ
וְאֵין לָנוּ מַרְפֵּא קַוֵּה לְשָׁלוֹם וְאֵין טוֹב וּלְעֵת מַרְפֵּא
וְהִנֵּה בְעָתָה: 20 יָדַעְנוּ יְהֹוָה רִשְׁעֵנוּ עֲוֺן אֲבוֹתֵינוּ
כִּי חָטָאנוּ לָךְ: 21 אַל־תִּנְאַץ לְמַעַן שִׁמְךָ אַל־תְּנַבֵּל
כִּסֵּא כְבוֹדֶךָ זְכֹר אַל־תָּפֵר בְּרִיתְךָ אִתָּנוּ: 22 הֲיֵשׁ
בְּהַבְלֵי הַגּוֹיִם מַגְשִׁמִים וְאִם־הַשָּׁמַיִם יִתְּנוּ רְבִבִים

יד 14 וֶאֱלִיל וְתַרְמִית

Are You not He, O LORD our God?
Therefore we will wait for You,
Since You have made all these.

הֲלֹא אַתָּה־הוּא יְהוָה אֱלֹהֵינוּ וּנְקַוֶּה־לָּךְ כִּי־אַתָּה
עָשִׂיתָ אֶת־כָּל־אֵלֶּה: פ

15 Then the LORD said to me, "*Even* if Moses and Samuel stood before Me, My mind *would* not *be* favorable toward this people. Cast *them* out of My sight, and let them go forth. ² And it shall be, if they say to you, 'Where should we go?' then you shall tell them, 'Thus says the LORD:

טו וַיֹּאמֶר יְהוָה אֵלַי אִם־יַעֲמֹד מֹשֶׁה וּשְׁמוּאֵל
לְפָנַי אֵין נַפְשִׁי אֶל־הָעָם הַזֶּה שַׁלַּח מֵעַל־פָּנַי
וְיֵצֵאוּ: ² וְהָיָה כִּי־יֹאמְרוּ אֵלֶיךָ אָנָה נֵצֵא וְאָמַרְתָּ

"Such as *are* for death, to death;
And such as *are* for the sword, to the sword;
And such as *are* for the famine, to the famine;
And such as *are* for the captivity, to the captivity.'"

אֲלֵיהֶם כֹּה־אָמַר יְהוָה אֲשֶׁר לַמָּוֶת לַמָּוֶת וַאֲשֶׁר
לַחֶרֶב לַחֶרֶב וַאֲשֶׁר לָרָעָב לָרָעָב וַאֲשֶׁר לַשְּׁבִי
לַשֶּׁבִי:

³ "And I will appoint over them four forms *of destruction*," says the LORD: "the sword to slay, the dogs to drag, the birds of the heavens and the beasts of the earth to devour and destroy. ⁴ I will hand them over to trouble, to all kingdoms of the earth, because of Manasseh the son of Hezekiah, king of Judah, for what he did in Jerusalem.

³ וּפָקַדְתִּי עֲלֵיהֶם אַרְבַּע מִשְׁפָּחוֹת נְאֻם־
יְהוָה אֶת־הַחֶרֶב לַהֲרֹג וְאֶת־הַכְּלָבִים לִסְחֹב וְאֶת־
עוֹף הַשָּׁמַיִם וְאֶת־בֶּהֱמַת הָאָרֶץ לֶאֱכֹל וּלְהַשְׁחִית:
⁴ וּנְתַתִּים לְזַעֲוָה לְכֹל מַמְלְכוֹת הָאָרֶץ בִּגְלַל
מְנַשֶּׁה בֶן־יְחִזְקִיָּהוּ מֶלֶךְ יְהוּדָה עַל אֲשֶׁר־עָשָׂה
בִּירוּשָׁלָ͏ִם:

⁵ "For who will have pity on you, O Jerusalem?
Or who will bemoan you?
Or who will turn aside to ask how you are doing?
⁶ You have forsaken Me," says the LORD,
"You have gone backward.
Therefore I will stretch out My hand against you
and destroy you;
I am weary of relenting!
⁷ And I will winnow them with a winnowing fan in
the gates of the land;
I will bereave *them* of children;
I will destroy My people,
Since they do not return from their ways.
⁸ Their widows will be increased to Me more than
the sand of the seas;
I will bring against them,
Against the mother of the young men,
A plunderer at noonday;
I will cause anguish and terror to fall on them
suddenly.
⁹ "She languishes who has borne seven;
She has breathed her last;
Her sun has gone down
While *it was* yet day;
She has been ashamed and confounded.
And the remnant of them I will deliver to the
sword
Before their enemies," says the LORD.
¹⁰ Woe is me, my mother,
That you have borne me,
A man of strife and a man of contention to the
whole earth!
I have neither lent for interest,
Nor have men lent to me for interest.
Every one of them curses me.

⁵ כִּי מִי־יַחְמֹל עָלַיִךְ יְרוּשָׁלַ͏ִם וּמִי יָנוּד
לָךְ וּמִי יָסוּר לִשְׁאֹל לְשָׁלֹם לָךְ: ⁶ אַתְּ נָטַשְׁתְּ
אֹתִי נְאֻם־יְהוָה אָחוֹר תֵּלֵכִי וָאַט אֶת־יָדִי עָלַיִךְ
וָאַשְׁחִיתֵךְ נִלְאֵיתִי הִנָּחֵם: ⁷ וָאֶזְרֵם בְּמִזְרֶה בְּשַׁעֲרֵי
הָאָרֶץ שִׁכַּלְתִּי אִבַּדְתִּי אֶת־עַמִּי מִדַּרְכֵיהֶם לוֹא־
שָׁבוּ: ⁸ עָצְמוּ־לִי אַלְמְנֹתָו מֵחוֹל יַמִּים הֵבֵאתִי
לָהֶם עַל־אֵם בָּחוּר שֹׁדֵד בַּצָּהֳרָיִם הִפַּלְתִּי עָלֶיהָ
פִּתְאֹם עִיר וּבֶהָלוֹת: ⁹ אֻמְלְלָה יֹלֶדֶת הַשִּׁבְעָה
נָפְחָה נַפְשָׁהּ בָּאָה שִׁמְשָׁהּ בְּעֹד יוֹמָם בּוֹשָׁה
וְחָפֵרָה וּשְׁאֵרִיתָם לַחֶרֶב אֶתֵּן לִפְנֵי אֹיְבֵיהֶם נְאֻם־
יְהוָה: ס ¹⁰ אוֹי־לִי אִמִּי כִּי יְלִדְתִּנִי אִישׁ
רִיב וְאִישׁ מָדוֹן לְכָל־הָאָרֶץ לֹא־נָשִׁיתִי וְלֹא־נָשׁוּ־

טו ⁴ לִזְוָעָה ⁹ בָּא

11 אָמַר יְהֹוָה אִם־ ס ‏ בִּי כֻּלֹּה מְקַלְלַוֹנִי:

לֹא שֵׁרוֹתִךְ לְטוֹב אִם־לוֹא | הִפְגַּעְתִּי בְךָ בְּעֵת־

רָעָה וּבְעֵת צָרָה אֶת־הָאֹיֵב: 12 הֲיָרֹעַ בַּרְזֶל |

בַּרְזֶל מִצָּפוֹן וּנְחֹשֶׁת: 13 חֵילְךָ וְאוֹצְרוֹתֶיךָ לָבַז

אֶתֵּן לֹא בִמְחִיר וּבְכָל־חַטֹּאותֶיךָ וּבְכָל־גְּבוּלֶיךָ:

14 וְהַעֲבַרְתִּי אֶת־אֹיְבֶיךָ בְּאֶרֶץ לֹא יָדָעְתָּ כִּי־אֵשׁ

קָדְחָה בְאַפִּי עֲלֵיכֶם תּוּקָד: ס ‏ 15 אַתָּה

יָדַעְתָּ יְהֹוָה זָכְרֵנִי וּפָקְדֵנִי וְהִנָּקֶם לִי מֵרֹדְפַי אַל־

לְאֶרֶךְ אַפְּךָ תִּקָּחֵנִי דַּע שְׂאֵתִי עָלֶיךָ חֶרְפָּה:

16 נִמְצְאוּ דְבָרֶיךָ וָאֹכְלֵם וַיְהִי דְבָרֶיךָ לִי לְשָׂשׂוֹן

וּלְשִׂמְחַת לְבָבִי כִּי־נִקְרָא שִׁמְךָ עָלַי יְהֹוָה

אֱלֹהֵי צְבָאוֹת: ס ‏ 17 לֹא־יָשַׁבְתִּי בְסוֹד־

מְשַׂחֲקִים וָאֶעְלֹז מִפְּנֵי יָדְךָ בָּדָד יָשַׁבְתִּי כִּי־זַעַם

מִלֵּאתָנִי: ס ‏ 18 לָמָּה הָיָה כְאֵבִי נֶצַח

וּמַכָּתִי אֲנוּשָׁה מֵאֲנָה הֵרָפֵא הָיוֹ תִהְיֶה לִי כְּמוֹ

אַכְזָב מַיִם לֹא נֶאֱמָנוּ: ס ‏ 19 לָכֵן כֹּה־

אָמַר יְהֹוָה אִם־תָּשׁוּב וַאֲשִׁיבְךָ לְפָנַי תַּעֲמֹד וְאִם־

תּוֹצִיא יָקָר מִזּוֹלֵל כְּפִי תִהְיֶה יָשֻׁבוּ הֵמָּה אֵלֶיךָ

וְאַתָּה לֹא־תָשׁוּב אֲלֵיהֶם: 20 וּנְתַתִּיךָ לָעָם הַזֶּה

לְחוֹמַת נְחֹשֶׁת בְּצוּרָה וְנִלְחֲמוּ אֵלֶיךָ וְלֹא־יוּכְלוּ

לָךְ כִּי־אִתְּךָ אֲנִי לְהוֹשִׁיעֲךָ וּלְהַצִּילֶךָ נְאֻם־יְהֹוָה:

21 וְהִצַּלְתִּיךָ מִיַּד רָעִים וּפְדִתִיךָ מִכַּף עָרִצִים: פ

טז וַיְהִי דְבַר־יְהֹוָה אֵלַי לֵאמֹר: 2 לֹא־תִקַּח

לְךָ אִשָּׁה וְלֹא־יִהְיוּ לְךָ בָּנִים וּבָנוֹת בַּמָּקוֹם

הַזֶּה: 3 כִּי־כֹה | אָמַר יְהֹוָה עַל־הַבָּנִים וְעַל־

טו 11 שֵׁרִיתִךָ 16 דְּבָרְךָ

11 The LORD said:

"Surely it will be well with your remnant;
Surely I will cause the enemy to intercede with you
In the time of adversity and in the time of affliction.
12 Can anyone break iron,
The northern iron and the bronze?
13 Your wealth and your treasures
I will give as plunder without price,
Because of all your sins,
Throughout your territories.
14 And I will make *you* cross over with your enemies
Into a land *which* you do not know;
For a fire is kindled in My anger,
Which shall burn upon you."

15 O LORD, You know;
Remember me and visit me,
And take vengeance for me on my persecutors.
In Your enduring patience, do not take me away.
Know that for Your sake I have suffered rebuke.
16 Your words were found, and I ate them,
And Your word was to me the joy and rejoicing of my heart;
For I am called by Your name,
O LORD God of hosts.
17 I did not sit in the assembly of the mockers,
Nor did I rejoice;
I sat alone because of Your hand,
For You have filled me with indignation.
18 Why is my pain perpetual
And my wound incurable,
Which refuses to be healed?
Will You surely be to me like an unreliable stream,
As waters *that* fail?

19 Therefore thus says the LORD:

"If you return,
Then I will bring you back;
You shall stand before Me;
If you take out the precious from the vile,
You shall be as My mouth.
Let them return to you,
But you must not return to them.
20 And I will make you to this people a fortified bronze wall;
And they will fight against you,
But they shall not prevail against you;
For I *am* with you to save you
And deliver you," says the LORD.
21 "I will deliver you from the hand of the wicked,
And I will redeem you from the grip of the terrible."

16 The word of the LORD also came to me, saying, 2 "You shall not take a wife, nor shall you have sons or daughters in this place." 3 For thus says the LORD concerning the sons and daughters who are born in this place, and concerning their mothers who bore them and their fathers who begot them in this land: 4"They shall die gruesome deaths; they shall not be lamented nor shall they be buried, *but* they shall be like refuse on the face of the earth. They shall be consumed by the sword and by famine, and their corpses shall be meat for the birds of heaven and for the beasts of the earth."

5For thus says the LORD: "Do not enter the house of mourning, nor go to lament or bemoan them; for I have taken away My peace from this people," says the LORD, "lovingkindness and mercies. 6Both the great and the small shall die in this land. They shall not be buried; neither shall men lament for them, cut themselves, nor make themselves bald for them. 7Nor shall *men* break *bread* in mourning for them, to comfort them for the dead; nor shall *men* give them the cup of consolation to drink for their father or their mother. 8Also you shall not go into the house of feasting to sit with them, to eat and drink."

9For thus says the LORD of hosts, the God of Israel: "Behold, I will cause to cease from this place, before your eyes and in your days, the voice of mirth and the voice of gladness, the voice of the bridegroom and the voice of the bride.

10"And it shall be, when you show this people all these words, and they say to you, 'Why has the LORD pronounced all this great disaster against us? Or what *is* our iniquity? Or what *is* our sin that we have committed against the LORD our God?' 11then you shall say to them, 'Because your fathers have forsaken Me,' says the LORD; 'they have walked after other gods and have served them and worshiped them, and have forsaken Me and not kept My law. 12And you have done worse than your fathers, for behold, each one follows the dictates of his own evil heart, so that no one listens to Me. 13Therefore I will cast you out of this land into a land that you do not know, neither you nor your fathers; and there you shall serve other gods day and night, where I will not show you favor.'

14"Therefore behold, the days are coming," says the LORD, "that it shall no more be said, 'The LORD lives who brought up the children of Israel from the land of Egypt,' 15but, 'The LORD lives who brought up the children of Israel from the land of the north and from all the lands where He had driven them.' For I will bring them back into their land which I gave to their fathers.

16"Behold, I will send for many fishermen," says the LORD, "and they shall fish them; and afterward I will send for many hunters, and they shall hunt them from every mountain and every hill, and out of the holes of the rocks. 17For My eyes *are* on all

הַבָּנוֹת הַיִּלּוֹדִים בַּמָּקוֹם הַזֶּה וְעַל־אִמֹּתָם הַיֹּלְדוֹת
אוֹתָם וְעַל־אֲבוֹתָם הַמּוֹלְדִים אוֹתָם בָּאָרֶץ הַזֹּאת:
4 מְמוֹתֵי תַחֲלֻאִים יָמֻתוּ לֹא יִסָּפְדוּ וְלֹא יִקָּבֵרוּ
לְדֹמֶן עַל־פְּנֵי הָאֲדָמָה יִהְיוּ וּבַחֶרֶב וּבָרָעָב יִכְלוּ
וְהָיְתָה נִבְלָתָם לְמַאֲכָל לְעוֹף הַשָּׁמַיִם וּלְבֶהֱמַת
הָאָרֶץ: ס 5 כִּי־כֹה ׀ אָמַר יְהוָה אַל־
תָּבוֹא בֵּית מַרְזֵחַ וְאַל־תֵּלֵךְ לִסְפּוֹד וְאַל־תָּנֹד
לָהֶם כִּי־אָסַפְתִּי אֶת־שְׁלוֹמִי מֵאֵת הָעָם־הַזֶּה נְאֻם־
יְהוָה אֶת־הַחֶסֶד וְאֶת־הָרַחֲמִים: 6 וּמֵתוּ גְדֹלִים
וּקְטַנִּים בָּאָרֶץ הַזֹּאת לֹא יִקָּבֵרוּ וְלֹא־יִסְפְּדוּ
לָהֶם וְלֹא יִתְגֹּדַד וְלֹא יִקָּרֵחַ לָהֶם: 7 וְלֹא־
יִפְרְסוּ לָהֶם עַל־אֵבֶל לְנַחֲמוֹ עַל־מֵת וְלֹא־
יַשְׁקוּ אוֹתָם כּוֹס תַּנְחוּמִים עַל־אָבִיו וְעַל־אִמּוֹ:
8 וּבֵית־מִשְׁתֶּה לֹא־תָבוֹא לָשֶׁבֶת אוֹתָם לֶאֱכֹל
וְלִשְׁתּוֹת: ס 9 כִּי כֹה אָמַר יְהוָה צְבָאוֹת
אֱלֹהֵי יִשְׂרָאֵל הִנְנִי מַשְׁבִּית מִן־הַמָּקוֹם הַזֶּה
לְעֵינֵיכֶם וּבִימֵיכֶם קוֹל שָׂשׂוֹן וְקוֹל שִׂמְחָה קוֹל
חָתָן וְקוֹל כַּלָּה: 10 וְהָיָה כִּי תַגִּיד לָעָם הַזֶּה אֵת
כָּל־הַדְּבָרִים הָאֵלֶּה וְאָמְרוּ אֵלֶיךָ עַל־מֶה דִבֶּר
יְהוָה עָלֵינוּ אֵת כָּל־הָרָעָה הַגְּדוֹלָה הַזֹּאת וּמֶה
עֲוֹנֵנוּ וּמֶה חַטָּאתֵנוּ אֲשֶׁר חָטָאנוּ לַיהוָה אֱלֹהֵינוּ:
11 וְאָמַרְתָּ אֲלֵיהֶם עַל אֲשֶׁר־עָזְבוּ אֲבוֹתֵיכֶם אוֹתִי
נְאֻם־יְהוָה וַיֵּלְכוּ אַחֲרֵי אֱלֹהִים אֲחֵרִים וַיַּעַבְדוּם
וַיִּשְׁתַּחֲווּ לָהֶם וְאֹתִי עָזָבוּ וְאֶת־תּוֹרָתִי לֹא שָׁמָרוּ:
12 וְאַתֶּם הֲרֵעֹתֶם לַעֲשׂוֹת מֵאֲבוֹתֵיכֶם וְהִנְּכֶם
הֹלְכִים אִישׁ אַחֲרֵי שְׁרִרוּת לִבּוֹ־הָרָע לְבִלְתִּי
שְׁמֹעַ אֵלָי: 13 וְהֵטַלְתִּי אֶתְכֶם מֵעַל הָאָרֶץ הַזֹּאת
עַל־הָאָרֶץ אֲשֶׁר לֹא יְדַעְתֶּם אַתֶּם וַאֲבוֹתֵיכֶם
וַעֲבַדְתֶּם־שָׁם אֶת־אֱלֹהִים אֲחֵרִים יוֹמָם וָלַיְלָה
אֲשֶׁר לֹא־אֶתֵּן לָכֶם חֲנִינָה: ס 14 לָכֵן
הִנֵּה־יָמִים בָּאִים נְאֻם־יְהוָה וְלֹא־יֵאָמֵר עוֹד חַי־
יְהוָה אֲשֶׁר הֶעֱלָה אֶת־בְּנֵי יִשְׂרָאֵל מֵאֶרֶץ
מִצְרָיִם: 15 כִּי אִם־חַי־יְהוָה אֲשֶׁר הֶעֱלָה אֶת־
בְּנֵי יִשְׂרָאֵל מֵאֶרֶץ צָפוֹן וּמִכֹּל הָאֲרָצוֹת אֲשֶׁר
הִדִּיחָם שָׁמָּה וַהֲשִׁבֹתִים עַל־אַדְמָתָם אֲשֶׁר נָתַתִּי
לַאֲבוֹתָם: ס 16 הִנְנִי שֹׁלֵחַ לְדַוָּגִים רַבִּים
נְאֻם־יְהוָה וְדִיגוּם וְאַחֲרֵי־כֵן אֶשְׁלַח לְרַבִּים צַיָּדִים
וְצָדוּם מֵעַל כָּל־הַר וּמֵעַל כָּל־גִּבְעָה וּמִנְּקִיקֵי
הַסְּלָעִים: 17 כִּי עֵינַי עַל־כָּל־דַּרְכֵיהֶם לֹא נִסְתְּרוּ

their ways; they are not hidden from My face, nor is their iniquity hidden from My eyes. ¹⁸And first I will repay double for their iniquity and their sin, because they have defiled My land; they have filled My inheritance with the carcasses of their detestable and abominable idols."

¹⁹ O LORD, my strength and my fortress,
My refuge in the day of affliction,
The Gentiles shall come to You
From the ends of the earth and say,
"Surely our fathers have inherited lies,
Worthlessness and unprofitable *things*."
²⁰ Will a man make gods for himself,
Which *are* not gods?
²¹ "Therefore behold, I will this once cause them to know,
I will cause them to know
My hand and My might;
And they shall know that My name *is* the LORD.

17 "The sin of Judah *is* written with a pen of iron;
With the point of a diamond *it is* engraved
On the tablet of their heart,
And on the horns of your altars,
² While their children remember
Their altars and their wooden images
By the green trees on the high hills.
³ O My mountain in the field,
I will give as plunder your wealth, all your treasures,
And your high places of sin within all your borders.
⁴ And you, even yourself,
Shall let go of your heritage which I gave you;
And I will cause you to serve your enemies
In the land which you do not know;
For you have kindled a fire in My anger *which* shall burn forever."

⁵Thus says the LORD:

"Cursed *is* the man who trusts in man
And makes flesh his strength,
Whose heart departs from the LORD.
⁶ For he shall be like a shrub in the desert,
And shall not see when good comes,
But shall inhabit the parched places in the wilderness,
In a salt land *which is* not inhabited.
⁷ "Blessed *is* the man who trusts in the LORD,
And whose hope is the LORD.
⁸ For he shall be like a tree planted by the waters,
Which spreads out its roots by the river,
And will not fear when heat comes;
But its leaf will be green,
And will not be anxious in the year of drought,
Nor will cease from yielding fruit.
⁹ "The heart *is* deceitful above all *things,*
And desperately wicked;
Who can know it?

מִלְּפָנָי וְלֹא־נִצְפַּן עֲוֺנָם מִנֶּגֶד עֵינָי: ¹⁸ וְשִׁלַּמְתִּי רִאשׁוֺנָה מִשְׁנֵה עֲוֺנָם וְחַטָּאתָם עַל חַלְּלָם אֶת־אַרְצִי בְּנִבְלַת שִׁקּוּצֵיהֶם וְתוֺעֲבוֺתֵיהֶם מָלְאוּ אֶת־נַחֲלָתִי: ס ¹⁹ יְהוָה עֻזִּי וּמָעֻזִּי וּמְנוּסִי בְּיוֺם צָרָה אֵלֶיךָ גּוֺיִם יָבֹאוּ מֵאַפְסֵי־אָרֶץ וְיֹאמְרוּ אַךְ־שֶׁקֶר נָחֲלוּ אֲבוֺתֵינוּ הֶבֶל וְאֵין־בָּם מוֺעִיל: ²⁰ הֲיַעֲשֶׂה־לּוֺ אָדָם אֱלֹהִים וְהֵמָּה לֹא אֱלֹהִים: ²¹ לָכֵן הִנְנִי מוֺדִיעָם בַּפַּעַם הַזֹּאת אוֺדִיעֵם אֶת־יָדִי וְאֶת־גְּבוּרָתִי וְיָדְעוּ כִּי־שְׁמִי יְהוָה: ס

¹⁷ חַטַּאת יְהוּדָה כְּתוּבָה בְּעֵט בַּרְזֶל בְּצִפֹּרֶן שָׁמִיר חֲרוּשָׁה עַל־לוּחַ לִבָּם וּלְקַרְנוֺת מִזְבְּחוֺתֵיכֶם: ² כִּזְכֹּר בְּנֵיהֶם מִזְבְּחוֺתָם וַאֲשֵׁרֵיהֶם עַל־עֵץ רַעֲנָן עַל גְּבָעוֺת הַגְּבֹהוֺת: ³ הֲרָרִי בַּשָּׂדֶה חֵילְךָ כָל־אוֺצְרוֺתֶיךָ לָבַז אֶתֵּן בָּמֹתֶיךָ בְּחַטָּאת בְּכָל־גְּבוּלֶיךָ: ⁴ וְשָׁמַטְתָּה וּבְךָ מִנַּחֲלָתְךָ אֲשֶׁר נָתַתִּי לָךְ וְהַעֲבַדְתִּיךָ אֶת־אֹיְבֶיךָ בָּאָרֶץ אֲשֶׁר לֹא־יָדָעְתָּ כִּי־אֵשׁ קְדַחְתֶּם בְּאַפִּי עַד־עוֺלָם תּוּקָד: ס ⁵ כֹּה ׀ אָמַר יְהֹוָה אָרוּר הַגֶּבֶר אֲשֶׁר יִבְטַח בָּאָדָם וְשָׂם בָּשָׂר זְרֹעוֺ וּמִן־יְהוָה יָסוּר לִבּוֺ: ⁶ וְהָיָה כְּעַרְעָר בָּעֲרָבָה וְלֹא יִרְאֶה כִּי־יָבוֺא טוֺב וְשָׁכַן חֲרֵרִים בַּמִּדְבָּר אֶרֶץ מְלֵחָה וְלֹא תֵשֵׁב: ס ⁷ בָּרוּךְ הַגֶּבֶר אֲשֶׁר יִבְטַח בַּיהוָה וְהָיָה יְהוָה מִבְטַחוֺ: ⁸ וְהָיָה כְּעֵץ ׀ שָׁתוּל עַל־מַיִם וְעַל־יוּבַל יְשַׁלַּח שָׁרָשָׁיו וְלֹא יִרְאֶ^P כִּי־יָבֹא חֹם וְהָיָה עָלֵהוּ רַעֲנָן וּבִשְׁנַת בַּצֹּרֶת לֹא יִדְאָג וְלֹא יָמִישׁ מֵעֲשׂוֺת פֶּרִי: ⁹ עָקֹב הַלֵּב מִכֹּל וְאָנֻשׁ הוּא

10 I, the LORD, search the heart,
   I test the mind,
   Even to give every man according to his ways,
   According to the fruit of his doings.

11 "*As* a partridge that broods but does not hatch,
   So is he who gets riches, but not by right;
   It will leave him in the midst of his days,
   And at his end he will be a fool."

12 A glorious high throne from the beginning
   Is the place of our sanctuary.

13 O LORD, the hope of Israel,
   All who forsake You shall be ashamed.

   "Those who depart from Me
   Shall be written in the earth,
   Because they have forsaken the LORD,
   The fountain of living waters."

14 Heal me, O LORD, and I shall be healed;
   Save me, and I shall be saved,
   For You *are* my praise.

15 Indeed they say to me,
   "Where *is* the word of the LORD?
   Let it come now!"

16 As for me, I have not hurried away from *being* a
       shepherd *who* follows You,
   Nor have I desired the woeful day;
   You know what came out of my lips;
   It was right there before You.

17 Do not be a terror to me;
   You *are* my hope in the day of doom.

18 Let them be ashamed who persecute me,
   But do not let me be put to shame;
   Let them be dismayed,
   But do not let me be dismayed.
   Bring on them the day of doom,
   And destroy them with double destruction!

19 Thus the LORD said to me: "Go and stand in the gate of the children of the people, by which the kings of Judah come in and by which they go out, and in all the gates of Jerusalem; 20 and say to them, 'Hear the word of the LORD, you kings of Judah, and all Judah, and all the inhabitants of Jerusalem, who enter by these gates. 21 Thus says the LORD: "Take heed to yourselves, and bear no burden on the Sabbath day, nor bring *it* in by the gates of Jerusalem; 22 nor carry a burden out of your houses on the Sabbath day, nor do any work, but hallow the Sabbath day, as I commanded your fathers. 23 But they did not obey nor incline their ear, but made their neck stiff, that they might not hear nor receive instruction.

24 "And it shall be, if you heed Me carefully," says the LORD, "to bring no burden through the gates of this city on the Sabbath day, but hallow the Sabbath day, to do no work in it, 25 then shall enter the gates of this city kings and princes sitting on the throne of David, riding in chariots and on horses, they and their princes, accompanied by the men of

מִי יְדָעֶנּוּ: 10 אֲנִי יְהוָה חֹקֵר לֵב בֹּחֵן כְּלָיוֹת וְלָתֵת
לְאִישׁ כִּדְרָכָו כִּפְרִי מַעֲלָלָיו: ס 11 קֹרֵא
דָגַר וְלֹא יָלָד עֹשֶׂה עֹשֶׁר וְלֹא בְמִשְׁפָּט בַּחֲצִי
יָמָו יַעַזְבֶנּוּ וּבְאַחֲרִיתוֹ יִהְיֶה נָבָל: 12 כִּסֵּא כָבוֹד
מָרוֹם מֵרִאשׁוֹן מְקוֹם מִקְדָּשֵׁנוּ: 13 מִקְוֵה יִשְׂרָאֵל
יְהוָה כָּל־עֹזְבֶיךָ יֵבֹשׁוּ יְסוּרַי בָּאָרֶץ יִכָּתֵבוּ כִּי עָזְבוּ
מְקוֹר מַיִם־חַיִּים אֶת־יְהוָה: ס 14 רְפָאֵנִי
יְהוָה וְאֵרָפֵא הוֹשִׁיעֵנִי וְאִוָּשֵׁעָה כִּי תְהִלָּתִי אָתָּה:
15 הִנֵּה־הֵמָּה אֹמְרִים אֵלָי אַיֵּה דְבַר־יְהוָה יָבוֹא
נָא: 16 וַאֲנִי לֹא־אַצְתִּי מֵרֹעֶה אַחֲרֶיךָ וְיוֹם
אָנוּשׁ לֹא הִתְאַוֵּיתִי אַתָּה יָדָעְתָּ מוֹצָא שְׂפָתַי נֹכַח
פָּנֶיךָ הָיָה: 17 אַל־תִּהְיֵה־לִי לִמְחִתָּה מַחֲסִי־אַתָּה
בְּיוֹם רָעָה: 18 יֵבֹשׁוּ רֹדְפַי וְאַל־אֵבֹשָׁה אָנִי יֵחַתּוּ
הֵמָּה וְאַל־אֵחַתָּה אָנִי הָבִיא עֲלֵיהֶם יוֹם רָעָה
וּמִשְׁנֶה שִׁבָּרוֹן שָׁבְרֵם: ס 19 כֹּה־אָמַר
יְהוָה אֵלַי הָלֹךְ וְעָמַדְתָּ בְּשַׁעַר בְּנֵי־ הָעָם אֲשֶׁר
יָבֹאוּ בוֹ מַלְכֵי יְהוּדָה וַאֲשֶׁר יֵצְאוּ בוֹ וּבְכֹל
שַׁעֲרֵי יְרוּשָׁלָ͏ִם: 20 וְאָמַרְתָּ אֲלֵיהֶם שִׁמְעוּ דְבַר־
יְהוָה מַלְכֵי יְהוּדָה וְכָל־יְהוּדָה וְכֹל יֹשְׁבֵי יְרוּשָׁלָ͏ִם
הַבָּאִים בַּשְּׁעָרִים הָאֵלֶּה: ס 21 כֹּה אָמַר
יְהוָה הִשָּׁמְרוּ בְּנַפְשׁוֹתֵיכֶם וְאַל־תִּשְׂאוּ מַשָּׂא בְּיוֹם
הַשַּׁבָּת וַהֲבֵאתֶם בְּשַׁעֲרֵי יְרוּשָׁלָ͏ִם: 22 וְלֹא־תוֹצִיאוּ
מַשָּׂא מִבָּתֵּיכֶם בְּיוֹם הַשַּׁבָּת וְכָל־מְלָאכָה לֹא
תַעֲשׂוּ וְקִדַּשְׁתֶּם אֶת־יוֹם הַשַּׁבָּת כַּאֲשֶׁר צִוִּיתִי
אֶת־אֲבוֹתֵיכֶם: 23 וְלֹא שָׁמְעוּ וְלֹא הִטּוּ אֶת־
אָזְנָם וַיַּקְשׁוּ אֶת־עָרְפָּם לְבִלְתִּי שׁוֹמֵעַ וּלְבִלְתִּי
קַחַת מוּסָר: 24 וְהָיָה אִם־שָׁמֹעַ תִּשְׁמְעוּן אֵלַי
נְאֻם־יְהוָה לְבִלְתִּי הָבִיא מַשָּׂא בְּשַׁעֲרֵי הָעִיר
הַזֹּאת בְּיוֹם הַשַּׁבָּת וּלְקַדֵּשׁ אֶת־יוֹם הַשַּׁבָּת לְבִלְתִּי
עֲשׂוֹת־בֹּה כָּל־מְלָאכָה: 25 וּבָאוּ בְשַׁעֲרֵי הָעִיר
הַזֹּאת מְלָכִים וְשָׂרִים יֹשְׁבִים עַל־כִּסֵּא דָוִד

Judah and the inhabitants of Jerusalem; and this city shall remain forever. 26 And they shall come from the cities of Judah and from the places around Jerusalem, from the land of Benjamin and from the lowland, from the mountains and from the South, bringing burnt offerings and sacrifices, grain offerings and incense, bringing sacrifices of praise to the house of the LORD.

27 "But if you will not heed Me to hallow the Sabbath day, such as not carrying a burden when entering the gates of Jerusalem on the Sabbath day, then I will kindle a fire in its gates, and it shall devour the palaces of Jerusalem, and it shall not be quenched." ' "

18 The word which came to Jeremiah from the LORD, saying: 2 "Arise and go down to the potter's house, and there I will cause you to hear My words." 3 Then I went down to the potter's house, and there he was, making something at the wheel. 4 And the vessel that he made of clay was marred in the hand of the potter; so he made it again into another vessel, as it seemed good to the potter to make.

5 Then the word of the LORD came to me, saying: 6 "O house of Israel, can I not do with you as this potter?" says the LORD. "Look, as the clay is in the potter's hand, so are you in My hand, O house of Israel! 7 The instant I speak concerning a nation and concerning a kingdom, to pluck up, to pull down, and to destroy it, 8 if that nation against whom I have spoken turns from its evil, I will relent of the disaster that I thought to bring upon it. 9 And the instant I speak concerning a nation and concerning a kingdom, to build and to plant it, 10 if it does evil in My sight so that it does not obey My voice, then I will relent concerning the good with which I said I would benefit it.

11 "Now therefore, speak to the men of Judah and to the inhabitants of Jerusalem, saying, 'Thus says the LORD: "Behold, I am fashioning a disaster and devising a plan against you. Return now every one from his evil way, and make your ways and your doings good." ' "

12 And they said, "That is hopeless! So we will walk according to our own plans, and we will every one obey the dictates of his evil heart."

13 Therefore thus says the LORD:

"Ask now among the Gentiles,
Who has heard such things?
The virgin of Israel has done a very horrible thing.
14 Will a man leave the snow water of Lebanon,
Which comes from the rock of the field?

רֹכְבִ֤ים ׀ בָּרֶ֙כֶב֙ וּבַסּוּסִ֔ים הֵ֥מָּה וְשָׂרֵיהֶ֖ם אִ֑ישׁ יְהוּדָ֖ה וְיֹשְׁבֵ֣י יְרוּשָׁלִָ֑ם וְיָשְׁבָ֥ה הָעִֽיר־הַזֹּ֖את לְעוֹלָֽם: 26 וּבָ֣אוּ מֵעָרֵֽי־יְ֠הוּדָה וּמִסְּבִיב֨וֹת יְרוּשָׁלִַ֜ם וּמֵאֶ֧רֶץ בִּנְיָמִ֣ן וּמִן־הַשְּׁפֵלָ֗ה וּמִן־הָהָר֙ וּמִן־הַנֶּ֔גֶב מְבִאִ֛ים עוֹלָ֥ה וְזֶ֖בַח וּמִנְחָ֣ה וּלְבוֹנָ֑ה וּמְבִאֵ֥י תוֹדָ֖ה בֵּ֥ית יְהוָֽה: 27 וְאִם־לֹ֨א תִשְׁמְע֜וּ אֵלַ֗י לְקַדֵּשׁ֙ אֶת־י֣וֹם הַשַּׁבָּ֔ת וּלְבִלְתִּ֣י ׀ שְׂאֵ֣ת מַשָּׂ֗א וּבֹ֛א בְּשַׁעֲרֵ֥י יְרוּשָׁלִַ֖ם בְּי֣וֹם הַשַּׁבָּ֑ת וְהִצַּ֧תִּי אֵ֣שׁ בִּשְׁעָרֶ֗יהָ וְאָֽכְלָ֛ה אַרְמְנ֥וֹת יְרוּשָׁלִַ֖ם וְלֹ֥א תִכְבֶּֽה: פ

יח הַדָּבָר֙ אֲשֶׁ֣ר הָיָ֣ה אֶֽל־יִרְמְיָ֔הוּ מֵאֵ֥ת יְהוָ֖ה לֵאמֹֽר: 2 ק֥וּם וְיָרַדְתָּ֖ בֵּ֣ית הַיּוֹצֵ֑ר וְשָׁ֖מָּה אַשְׁמִֽיעֲךָ֖ אֶת־דְּבָרָֽי: 3 וָאֵרֵ֖ד בֵּ֣ית הַיּוֹצֵ֑ר וְהִנֵּה־ה֛וּא עֹשֶׂ֥ה מְלָאכָ֖ה עַל־הָאָבְנָֽיִם: 4 וְנִשְׁחַ֣ת הַכְּלִ֗י אֲשֶׁ֨ר ה֤וּא עֹשֶׂה֙ בַּחֹ֣מֶר בְּיַ֣ד הַיּוֹצֵ֑ר וְשָׁ֗ב וַֽיַּעֲשֵׂ֙הוּ֙ כְּלִ֣י אַחֵ֔ר כַּאֲשֶׁ֥ר יָשַׁ֛ר בְּעֵינֵ֥י הַיּוֹצֵ֖ר לַעֲשֽׂוֹת: פ

5 וַיְהִ֥י דְבַר־יְהוָ֖ה אֵלַ֥י לֵאמֽוֹר: 6 הֲכַיּוֹצֵ֤ר הַזֶּה֙ לֹא־אוּכַ֤ל לַעֲשׂוֹת֙ לָכֶ֔ם בֵּ֥ית יִשְׂרָאֵ֖ל נְאֻם־יְהוָ֑ה הִנֵּ֤ה כַחֹ֙מֶר֙ בְּיַ֣ד הַיּוֹצֵ֔ר כֵּן־אַתֶּ֥ם בְּיָדִ֖י בֵּ֥ית יִשְׂרָאֵֽל: ס 7 רֶ֣גַע אֲדַבֵּ֗ר עַל־גּ֤וֹי וְעַל־מַמְלָכָ֔ה לִנְת֥וֹשׁ וְלִנְת֖וֹץ וּֽלְהַאֲבִֽיד: 8 וְשָׁב֙ הַגּ֣וֹי הַה֔וּא מֵרָ֣עָת֔וֹ אֲשֶׁ֥ר דִּבַּ֖רְתִּי עָלָ֑יו וְנִֽחַמְתִּי֙ עַל־הָ֣רָעָ֔ה אֲשֶׁ֥ר חָשַׁ֖בְתִּי לַעֲשׂ֥וֹת לֽוֹ: ס 9 וְרֶ֣גַע אֲדַבֵּ֗ר עַל־גּ֤וֹי וְעַל־מַמְלָכָ֖ה לִבְנֹ֥ת וְלִנְטֹֽעַ: 10 וְעָשָׂ֤ה הָרָעָה֙ בְּעֵינַ֔י לְבִלְתִּ֖י שְׁמֹ֣עַ בְּקוֹלִ֑י וְנִֽחַמְתִּי֙ עַל־הַטּוֹבָ֔ה אֲשֶׁ֥ר אָמַ֖רְתִּי לְהֵיטִ֥יב אוֹתֽוֹ: ס 11 וְעַתָּ֡ה אֱמָר־נָ֣א אֶל־אִישׁ־יְהוּדָה֩ וְעַל־יוֹשְׁבֵ֨י יְרוּשָׁלִַ֜ם לֵאמֹ֗ר כֹּ֚ה אָמַ֣ר יְהוָ֔ה הִנֵּ֨ה אָנֹכִ֜י יוֹצֵ֤ר עֲלֵיכֶם֙ רָעָ֔ה וְחֹשֵׁ֥ב עֲלֵיכֶ֖ם מַֽחֲשָׁבָ֑ה שׁ֣וּבוּ נָ֗א אִ֚ישׁ מִדַּרְכּ֣וֹ הָֽרָעָ֔ה וְהֵיטִ֥יבוּ דַרְכֵיכֶ֖ם וּמַֽעַלְלֵיכֶֽם: 12 וְאָמְר֖וּ נוֹאָ֑שׁ כִּֽי־אַחֲרֵ֤י מַחְשְׁבוֹתֵ֙ינוּ֙ נֵלֵ֔ךְ וְאִ֕ישׁ שְׁרִר֥וּת לִבּֽוֹ־הָרָ֖ע נַעֲשֶֽׂה: ס 13 לָכֵ֗ן כֹּ֚ה אָמַ֣ר יְהוָ֔ה שַׁאֲלוּ־נָא֙ בַּגּוֹיִ֔ם מִ֥י שָׁמַ֖ע כָּאֵ֑לֶּה שַׁעֲרֻרִ֖ת עָשְׂתָ֥ה מְאֹ֔ד בְּתוּלַ֖ת יִשְׂרָאֵֽל: 14 הֲיַעֲזֹ֥ב מִצּ֛וּר שָׂדַ֖י שֶׁ֣לֶג

Will the cold flowing waters be forsaken for
    strange waters?
15 "Because My people have forgotten Me,
    They have burned incense to worthless idols.
    And they have caused themselves to stumble in
        their ways,
    From the ancient paths,
    To walk in pathways and not on a highway,
16 To make their land desolate *and* a perpetual
        hissing;
    Everyone who passes by it will be astonished
    And shake his head.
17 I will scatter them as with an east wind before the
        enemy;
    I will show them the back and not the face
    In the day of their calamity."

18 Then they said, "Come and let us devise plans
against Jeremiah; for the law shall not perish from
the priest, nor counsel from the wise, nor the word
from the prophet. Come and let us attack him with
the tongue, and let us not give heed to any of his
words."

19   Give heed to me, O LORD,
    And listen to the voice of those who contend with
        me!
20   Shall evil be repaid for good?
    For they have dug a pit for my life.
    Remember that I stood before You
    To speak good for them,
    To turn away Your wrath from them.
21   Therefore deliver up their children to the famine,
    And pour out their *blood*
    By the force of the sword;
    Let their wives *become* widows
    And bereaved of their children.
    Let their men be put to death,
    Their young men *be* slain
    By the sword in battle.
22   Let a cry be heard from their houses,
    When You bring a troop suddenly upon them;
    For they have dug a pit to take me,
    And hidden snares for my feet.
23   Yet, LORD, You know all their counsel
    Which is against me, to slay *me*.
    Provide no atonement for their iniquity,
    Nor blot out their sin from Your sight;
    But let them be overthrown before You.
    Deal *thus* with them
    In the time of Your anger.

19 Thus says the LORD: "Go and get a potter's
earthen flask, and *take* some of the elders of the
people and some of the elders of the priests. 2 And
go out to the Valley of the Son of Hinnom, which *is*
by the entry of the Potsherd Gate; and proclaim
there the words that I will tell you, 3 and say, 'Hear
the word of the LORD, O kings of Judah and
inhabitants of Jerusalem. Thus says the LORD of

לִבְנֹון אִם־יִנָּתְשׁוּ מַיִם קָרִים זָרִים נֹוזְלִים: 15 כִּי־
שְׁכֵחֻנִי עַמִּי לַשָּׁוְא יְקַטֵּרוּ וַיַּכְשִׁלוּם בְּדַרְכֵיהֶם
שְׁבִילֵי עֹולָם לָלֶכֶת נְתִיבֹות דֶּרֶךְ לֹא סְלוּלָה:
16 לָשׂוּם אַרְצָם לְשַׁמָּה שְׁרוּקֹתP עֹולָם כֹּל
עֹובֵר עָלֶיהָ יִשֹּׁם וְיָנִיד בְּרֹאשֹׁו: 17 כְּרוּחַ־קָדִים
אֲפִיצֵם לִפְנֵי אֹויֵב עֹרֶף וְלֹא־פָנִים אֶרְאֵם בְּיֹום
אֵידָם: ס   18 וַיֹּאמְרוּ לְכוּ וְנַחְשְׁבָה עַל־
יִרְמְיָהוּ מַחֲשָׁבֹות כִּי לֹא־תֹאבַד תֹּורָה מִכֹּהֵן וְעֵצָה
מֵחָכָם וְדָבָר מִנָּבִיא לְכוּ וְנַכֵּהוּ בַלָּשֹׁון וְאַל־
נַקְשִׁיבָה אֶל־כָּל־דְּבָרָיו: 19 הַקְשִׁיבָה יְהוָה אֵלַי
וּשְׁמַע לְקֹול יְרִיבָי: 20 הַיְשֻׁלַּם תַּחַת־טֹובָה רָעָה
כִּי־כָרוּ שׁוּחָה לְנַפְשִׁי זְכֹר | עָמְדִי לְפָנֶיךָ לְדַבֵּר
עֲלֵיהֶם טֹובָה לְהָשִׁיב אֶת־חֲמָתְךָ מֵהֶם: 21 לָכֵן
תֵּן אֶת־בְּנֵיהֶם לָרָעָב וְהַגִּרֵם עַל־יְדֵי־חֶרֶב וְתִהְיֶנָה
נְשֵׁיהֶם שַׁכֻּלֹות וְאַלְמָנֹות וְאַנְשֵׁיהֶם יִהְיוּ הֲרֻגֵי מָוֶת
בַּחוּרֵיהֶם מֻכֵּי־חֶרֶב בַּמִּלְחָמָה: 22 תִּשָּׁמַע זְעָקָה
מִבָּתֵּיהֶם כִּי־תָבִיא עֲלֵיהֶם גְּדוּד פִּתְאֹם כִּי־כָרוּ
שׁוּחָהP לְלָכְדֵנִי וּפַחִים טָמְנוּ לְרַגְלָי: 23 וְאַתָּה יְהוָה
יָדַעְתָּ אֶת־כָּל־עֲצָתָם עָלַי לַמָּוֶת אַל־תְּכַפֵּר עַל־
עֲוֹנָם וְחַטָּאתָם מִלְּפָנֶיךָ אַל־תֶּמְחִי וְהָיוּP מֻכְשָׁלִים
לְפָנֶיךָ בְּעֵת אַפְּךָ עֲשֵׂה בָהֶם: ס

יט כֹּה אָמַר יְהוָה הָלֹוךְ וְקָנִיתָ בַקְבֻּק יֹוצֵר
חָרֶשׂ וּמִזִּקְנֵי הָעָם וּמִזִּקְנֵי הַכֹּהֲנִים: 2 וְיָצָאתָ אֶל־
גֵּיא בֶן־הִנֹּם אֲשֶׁר פֶּתַח שַׁעַר הַחַרְסוּתP וְקָרֵאתָ
שָׁם אֶת־הַדְּבָרִים אֲשֶׁר־אֲדַבֵּר אֵלֶיךָ: 3 וְאָמַרְתָּ

יח 16 שְׁרוּקֹות   22 שׁוּחָה   23 וְיִהְיוּ
יט 2 הַחַרְסִית

hosts, the God of Israel: "Behold, I will bring such a catastrophe on this place, that whoever hears of it, his ears will tingle.

4 "Because they have forsaken Me and made this an alien place, because they have burned incense in it to other gods whom neither they, their fathers, nor the kings of Judah have known, and have filled this place with the blood of the innocents 5(they have also built the high places of Baal, to burn their sons with fire *for* burnt offerings to Baal, which I did not command or speak, nor did it come into My mind), 6 therefore behold, the days are coming," says the LORD, "that this place shall no more be called Tophet or the Valley of the Son of Hinnom, but the Valley of Slaughter. 7 And I will make void the counsel of Judah and Jerusalem in this place, and I will cause them to fall by the sword before their enemies and by the hands of those who seek their lives; their corpses I will give as meat for the birds of the heaven and for the beasts of the earth. 8 I will make this city desolate and a hissing; everyone who passes by it will be astonished and hiss because of all its plagues. 9 And I will cause them to eat the flesh of their sons and the flesh of their daughters, and everyone shall eat the flesh of his friend in the siege and in the desperation with which their enemies and those who seek their lives shall drive them to despair."'

10 "Then you shall break the flask in the sight of the men who go with you, 11 and say to them, 'Thus says the LORD of hosts: "Even so I will break this people and this city, as *one* breaks a potter's vessel, which cannot be made whole again; and they shall bury *them* in Tophet till *there is* no place to bury. 12 Thus I will do to this place," says the LORD, "and to its inhabitants, and make this city like Tophet. 13 And the houses of Jerusalem and the houses of the kings of Judah shall be defiled like the place of Tophet, because of all the houses on whose roofs they have burned incense to all the host of heaven, and poured out drink offerings to other gods."'"

14 Then Jeremiah came from Tophet, where the LORD had sent him to prophesy; and he stood in the court of the Lord's house and said to all the people, 15 "Thus says the LORD of hosts, the God of Israel: 'Behold, I will bring on this city and on all her towns all the doom that I have pronounced against it, because they have stiffened their necks that they might not hear My words.'"

20 Now Pashhur the son of Immer, the priest who *was* also chief governor in the house of the LORD, heard that Jeremiah prophesied these things.

שִׁמְעוּ דְבַר־יְהֹוָה מַלְכֵי יְהוּדָה וְיֹשְׁבֵי יְרוּשָׁלָ͏ִם
כֹּה־אָמַר יְהֹוָה צְבָאוֹת אֱלֹהֵי יִשְׂרָאֵל הִנְנִי מֵבִיא
רָעָה עַל־הַמָּקוֹם הַזֶּה אֲשֶׁר כָּל־שֹׁמְעָהּ תִּצַּלְנָה
אָזְנָיו: 4 יַעַן ׀ אֲשֶׁר עֲזָבֻנִי וַיְנַכְּרוּ אֶת־הַמָּקוֹם הַזֶּה
וַיְקַטְּרוּ־בוֹ לֵאלֹהִים אֲחֵרִים אֲשֶׁר לֹא־יְדָעוּם הֵמָּה
וַאֲבֽוֹתֵיהֶם וּמַלְכֵי יְהוּדָה וּמָלְאוּ אֶת־הַמָּקוֹם הַזֶּה
דַּם נְקִיִּֽם: 5 וּבָנוּ אֶת־בָּמוֹת הַבַּעַל לִשְׂרֹף אֶת־
בְּנֵיהֶם בָּאֵשׁ עֹלוֹת לַבָּעַל אֲשֶׁר לֹֽא־צִוִּיתִי וְלֹא
דִבַּרְתִּי וְלֹא עָלְתָה עַל־לִבִּֽי׃ פ

6 לָכֵן הִנֵּֽה־יָמִים בָּאִים נְאֻם־יְהֹוָה וְלֹא־יִקָּרֵא
לַמָּקוֹם הַזֶּה עוֹד הַתֹּפֶת וְגֵיא בֶן־הִנֹּם כִּי אִם־
גֵּיא הַהֲרֵגָֽה׃ 7 וּבַקֹּתִי אֶת־עֲצַת יְהוּדָה וִירוּשָׁלַ͏ִם
בַּמָּקוֹם הַזֶּה וְהִפַּלְתִּים בַּחֶרֶב לִפְנֵי אֹֽיְבֵיהֶם
וּבְיַד מְבַקְשֵׁי נַפְשָׁם וְנָתַתִּי אֶת־נִבְלָתָם לְמַאֲכָל
לְעוֹף הַשָּׁמַיִם וּלְבֶהֱמַת הָאָֽרֶץ׃ 8 וְשַׂמְתִּי אֶת־
הָעִיר הַזֹּאת לְשַׁמָּה וְלִשְׁרֵקָה כֹּל עֹבֵר עָלֶיהָ
יִשֹּׁם וְיִשְׁרֹק עַל־כָּל־מַכֹּתֶֽהָ׃ 9 וְהַאֲכַלְתִּים אֶת־
בְּשַׂר בְּנֵיהֶם וְאֵת בְּשַׂר בְּנֹתֵיהֶם וְאִישׁ בְּשַׂר־
רֵעֵהוּ יֹאכֵלוּ בְּמָצוֹר וּבְמָצוֹק אֲשֶׁר יָצִיקוּ לָהֶם
אֹֽיְבֵיהֶם וּמְבַקְשֵׁי נַפְשָֽׁם׃ 10 וְשָׁבַרְתָּ הַבַּקְבֻּק לְעֵינֵי
הָאֲנָשִׁים הַהֹלְכִים אוֹתָֽךְ׃ 11 וְאָמַרְתָּ אֲלֵיהֶם כֹּה־
אָמַר ׀ יְהֹוָה צְבָאוֹת כָּכָה אֶשְׁבֹּר אֶת־הָעָם הַזֶּה
וְאֶת־הָעִיר הַזֹּאת כַּאֲשֶׁר יִשְׁבֹּר אֶת־כְּלִי הַיּוֹצֵר
אֲשֶׁר לֹֽא־יוּכַל לְהֵרָפֵה עוֹד וּבְתֹפֶת יִקְבְּרוּ מֵאֵין
מָקוֹם לִקְבּֽוֹר׃ 12 כֵּֽן־אֶעֱשֶׂה לַמָּקוֹם הַזֶּה נְאֻם־
יְהֹוָה וּלְיוֹשְׁבָיו וְלָתֵת אֶת־הָעִיר הַזֹּאת כְּתֹֽפֶת׃
13 וְהָיוּ בָּתֵּי יְרוּשָׁלַ͏ִם וּבָתֵּי מַלְכֵי יְהוּדָה כִּמְקוֹם
הַתֹּפֶת הַטְּמֵאִים לְכֹל הַבָּתִּים אֲשֶׁר קִטְּרוּ עַל־
גַּגֹּתֵיהֶם לְכֹל צְבָא הַשָּׁמַיִם וְהַסֵּךְ נְסָכִים לֵאלֹהִים
אֲחֵרִֽים׃ פ

14 וַיָּבֹא יִרְמְיָהוּ מֵהַתֹּפֶת אֲשֶׁר שְׁלָחוֹ יְהֹוָה שָׁם
לְהִנָּבֵא וַיַּעֲמֹד בַּחֲצַר בֵּית־יְהֹוָה וַיֹּאמֶר אֶל־כָּל־
הָעָֽם׃ ס 15 כֹּה־אָמַר יְהֹוָה צְבָאוֹת אֱלֹהֵי
יִשְׂרָאֵל הִנְנִי מֵבִי אֶל־הָעִיר הַזֹּאת וְעַל־כָּל־עָרֶיהָ
אֵת כָּל־הָרָעָה אֲשֶׁר דִּבַּרְתִּי עָלֶיהָ כִּי הִקְשׁוּ אֶת־
עָרְפָּם לְבִלְתִּי שְׁמוֹעַ אֶת־דְּבָרָֽי׃

כ וַיִּשְׁמַע פַּשְׁחוּר בֶּן־אִמֵּר הַכֹּהֵן וְהֽוּא־פָקִיד נָגִיד
בְּבֵית יְהֹוָה אֶת־יִרְמְיָהוּ נִבָּא אֶת־הַדְּבָרִים הָאֵֽלֶּה׃

²Then Pashhur struck Jeremiah the prophet, and put him in the stocks that *were* in the high gate of Benjamin, which *was* by the house of the LORD.

³And it happened on the next day that Pashhur brought Jeremiah out of the stocks. Then Jeremiah said to him, "The LORD has not called your name Pashhur, but Magor-Missabib. ⁴For thus says the LORD: 'Behold, I will make you a terror to yourself and to all your friends; and they shall fall by the sword of their enemies, and your eyes shall see *it*. I will give all Judah into the hand of the king of Babylon, and he shall carry them captive to Babylon and slay them with the sword. ⁵Moreover I will deliver all the wealth of this city, all its produce, and all its precious things; all the treasures of the kings of Judah I will give into the hand of their enemies, who will plunder them, seize them, and carry them to Babylon. ⁶And you, Pashhur, and all who dwell in your house, shall go into captivity. You shall go to Babylon, and there you shall die, and be buried there, you and all your friends, to whom you have prophesied lies.'"

⁷ O LORD, You induced me, and I was persuaded;
      You are stronger than I, and have prevailed.
      I am in derision daily;
      Everyone mocks me.
⁸ For when I spoke, I cried out;
      I shouted, "Violence and plunder!"
      Because the word of the LORD was made to me
      A reproach and a derision daily.
⁹ Then I said, "I will not make mention of Him,
      Nor speak anymore in His name."
      But *His* word was in my heart like a burning fire
      Shut up in my bones;
      I was weary of holding *it* back,
      And I could not.
¹⁰ For I heard many mocking:
      "Fear on every side!"
      "Report," *they say*, "and we will report it!"
      All my acquaintances watched for my stumbling,
      saying,
      "Perhaps he can be induced;
      Then we will prevail against him,
      And we will take our revenge on him."
¹¹ But the LORD *is* with me as a mighty, awesome One.
      Therefore my persecutors will stumble, and will not prevail.
      They will be greatly ashamed, for they will not prosper.
      Their everlasting confusion will never be forgotten.
¹² But, O LORD of hosts,
      You who test the righteous,
      And see the mind and heart,
      Let me see Your vengeance on them;
      For I have pleaded my cause before You.
¹³ Sing to the LORD! Praise the LORD!

2 וַיַּכֶּה פַשְׁחוּר אֶת יִרְמְיָהוּ הַנָּבִיא וַיִּתֵּן אֹתוֹ עַל־
הַמַּהְפֶּכֶת אֲשֶׁר בְּשַׁעַר בִּנְיָמִן הָעֶלְיוֹן אֲשֶׁר בְּבֵית
יְהוָה: 3 וַיְהִי מִמָּחֳרָת וַיֹּצֵא פַשְׁחוּר אֶת־יִרְמְיָהוּ
מִן־הַמַּהְפָּכֶת וַיֹּאמֶר אֵלָיו יִרְמְיָהוּ לֹא פַשְׁחוּר קָרָא
יְהוָה שְׁמֶךָ כִּי אִם־מָגוֹר מִסָּבִיב: פ

4 כִּי כֹה אָמַר יְהוָה הִנְנִי נֹתֶנְךָ לְמָגוֹר לְךָ וּלְכָל־
אֹהֲבֶיךָ וְנָפְלוּ בְּחֶרֶב אֹיְבֵיהֶם וְעֵינֶיךָ רֹאוֹת וְאֶת־
כָּל־יְהוּדָה אֶתֵּן בְּיַד מֶלֶךְ־בָּבֶל וְהִגְלָם בָּבֶלָה
וְהִכָּם בֶּחָרֶב: 5 וְנָתַתִּי אֶת־כָּל־חֹסֶן הָעִיר הַזֹּאת
וְאֶת־כָּל־יְגִיעָהּ וְאֶת־כָּל־יְקָרָהּ וְאֵת כָּל־אוֹצְרוֹת
מַלְכֵי יְהוּדָה אֶתֵּן בְּיַד אֹיְבֵיהֶם וּבְזָזוּם וּלְקָחוּם
וֶהֱבִיאוּם בָּבֶלָה: 6 וְאַתָּה פַשְׁחוּר וְכֹל יֹשְׁבֵי
בֵיתֶךָ תֵּלְכוּ בַּשֶּׁבִי וּבָבֶל תָּבוֹא וְשָׁם תָּמוּת
וְשָׁם תִּקָּבֵר אַתָּה וְכָל־אֹהֲבֶיךָ אֲשֶׁר־נִבֵּאתָ לָהֶם
בַּשָּׁקֶר: ס 7 פִּתִּיתַנִי יְהוָה וָאֶפָּת חֲזַקְתַּנִי
וַתּוּכָל הָיִיתִי לִשְׂחוֹק כָּל־הַיּוֹם כֻּלֹּה לֹעֵג לִי:
8 כִּי־מִדֵּי אֲדַבֵּר אֶזְעָק חָמָס וָשֹׁד אֶקְרָא כִּי־
הָיָה דְבַר־יְהוָה לִי לְחֶרְפָּה וּלְקֶלֶס כָּל־הַיּוֹם:
9 וְאָמַרְתִּי לֹא־אֶזְכְּרֶנּוּ וְלֹא־אֲדַבֵּר עוֹד בִּשְׁמוֹ וְהָיָה
בְלִבִּי כְּאֵשׁ בֹּעֶרֶת עָצֻר בְּעַצְמֹתָי וְנִלְאֵיתִי כַּלְכֵל
וְלֹא אוּכָל: 10 כִּי שָׁמַעְתִּי דִּבַּת רַבִּים מָגוֹר
מִסָּבִיב הַגִּידוּ וְנַגִּידֶנּוּ כֹּל אֱנוֹשׁ שְׁלוֹמִי שֹׁמְרֵי
צַלְעִי אוּלַי יְפֻתֶּה וְנוּכְלָה לוֹ וְנִקְחָה נִקְמָתֵנוּ
מִמֶּנּוּ: 11 וַיהוָה אוֹתִי כְּגִבּוֹר עָרִיץ עַל־כֵּן רֹדְפַי
יִכָּשְׁלוּ וְלֹא יֻכָלוּ בֹּשׁוּ מְאֹד כִּי־לֹא הִשְׂכִּילוּ
כְּלִמַּת עוֹלָם לֹא תִשָּׁכֵחַ: 12 וַיהוָה צְבָאוֹת בֹּחֵן
צַדִּיק רֹאֶה כְלָיוֹת וָלֵב אֶרְאֶה נִקְמָתְךָ מֵהֶם כִּי
אֵלֶיךָ גִּלִּיתִי אֶת־רִיבִי: ס 13 שִׁירוּ לַיהוָה

For He has delivered the life of the poor
From the hand of evildoers.

14 Cursed *be* the day in which I was born!
Let the day not be blessed in which my mother
bore me!

15 Let the man *be* cursed
Who brought news to my father, saying,
"A male child has been born to you!"
Making him very glad.

16 And let that man be like the cities
Which the LORD overthrew, and did not relent;
Let him hear the cry in the morning
And the shouting at noon,

17 Because he did not kill me from the womb,
That my mother might have been my grave,
And her womb always enlarged *with me*.

18 Why did I come forth from the womb to see labor
and sorrow,
That my days should be consumed with shame?

21 The word which came to Jeremiah from the
LORD when King Zedekiah sent to him Pashhur the
son of Melchiah, and Zephaniah the son of
Maaseiah, the priest, saying, 2 "Please inquire of
the LORD for us, for Nebuchadnezzar king of
Babylon makes war against us. Perhaps the LORD
will deal with us according to all His wonderful
works, that *the king* may go away from us."

3 Then Jeremiah said to them, "Thus you shall
say to Zedekiah, 4 'Thus says the LORD God of
Israel: "Behold, I will turn back the weapons of war
that *are* in your hands, with which you fight against
the king of Babylon and the Chaldeans who besiege
you outside the walls; and I will assemble them in
the midst of this city. 5 I Myself will fight against
you with an outstretched hand and with a strong
arm, even in anger and fury and great wrath. 6 I will
strike the inhabitants of this city, both man and
beast; they shall die of a great pestilence. 7 And
afterward," says the LORD, "I will deliver Zedekiah
king of Judah, his servants and the people, and such
as are left in this city from the pestilence and the
sword and the famine, into the hand of Nebuchadnezzar king of Babylon, into the hand of their
enemies, and into the hand of those who seek their
life; and he shall strike them with the edge of the
sword. He shall not spare them, or have pity or
mercy." '

8 "Now you shall say to this people, 'Thus says
the LORD: "Behold, I set before you the way of life
and the way of death. 9 He who remains in this city
shall die by the sword, by famine, and by pestilence;
but he who goes out and defects to the Chaldeans
who besiege you, he shall live, and his life shall be as
a prize to him. 10 For I have set My face against this

הַלְלוּ אֶת־יְהֹוָה כִּי הִצִּיל אֶת־נֶפֶשׁ אֶבְיוֹן מִיַּד
מְרֵעִים: ס 14 אָרוּר הַיּוֹם אֲשֶׁר יֻלַּדְתִּי
בּוֹ יוֹם אֲשֶׁר־יְלָדַתְנִי אִמִּי אַל־יְהִי בָרוּךְ: 15 אָרוּר
הָאִישׁ אֲשֶׁר בִּשַּׂר אֶת־אָבִי לֵאמֹר יֻלַּד־לְךָ בֵּן
זָכָר שַׂמֵּחַ שִׂמֳחָהוּ: 16 וְהָיָה הָאִישׁ הַהוּא כֶּעָרִים
אֲשֶׁר־הָפַךְ יְהֹוָה וְלֹא נִחָם וְשָׁמַע זְעָקָה בַּבֹּקֶר
וּתְרוּעָה בְּעֵת צָהֳרָיִם: 17 אֲשֶׁר לֹא־מוֹתְתַנִי מֵרָחֶם
וַתְּהִי־לִי אִמִּי קִבְרִי וְרַחְמָה הֲרַת עוֹלָם: 18 לָמָּה
זֶּה מֵרֶחֶם יָצָאתִי לִרְאוֹת עָמָל וְיָגוֹן וַיִּכְלוּ בְּבֹשֶׁת
יָמָי: פ

כא הַדָּבָר אֲשֶׁר־הָיָה אֶל־יִרְמְיָהוּ מֵאֵת יְהֹוָה
בִּשְׁלֹחַ אֵלָיו הַמֶּלֶךְ צִדְקִיָּהוּ אֶת־פַּשְׁחוּר בֶּן־
מַלְכִּיָּה וְאֶת־צְפַנְיָה בֶן־מַעֲשֵׂיָה הַכֹּהֵן לֵאמֹר:
2 דְּרָשׁ־נָא בַעֲדֵנוּ אֶת־יְהֹוָה כִּי נְבוּכַדְרֶאצַּר מֶלֶךְ־
בָּבֶל נִלְחָם עָלֵינוּ אוּלַי יַעֲשֶׂה יְהֹוָה אוֹתָנוּ
כְּכָל־נִפְלְאֹתָיו וְיַעֲלֶה מֵעָלֵינוּ: ס 3 וַיֹּאמֶר
יִרְמְיָהוּ אֲלֵיהֶם כֹּה תֹאמְרֻן אֶל־צִדְקִיָּהוּ: 4 כֹּה־
אָמַר יְהֹוָה אֱלֹהֵי יִשְׂרָאֵל הִנְנִי מֵסֵב אֶת־כְּלֵי
הַמִּלְחָמָה אֲשֶׁר בְּיֶדְכֶם אֲשֶׁר אַתֶּם נִלְחָמִים
בָּם אֶת־מֶלֶךְ בָּבֶל וְאֶת־הַכַּשְׂדִּים הַצָּרִים עֲלֵיכֶם
מִחוּץ לַחוֹמָה וְאָסַפְתִּי אוֹתָם אֶל־תּוֹךְ הָעִיר
הַזֹּאת: 5 וְנִלְחַמְתִּי אֲנִי אִתְּכֶם בְּיָד נְטוּיָה וּבִזְרוֹעַ
חֲזָקָה וּבְאַף וּבְחֵמָה וּבְקֶצֶף גָּדוֹל: 6 וְהִכֵּיתִי אֶת־
יוֹשְׁבֵי הָעִיר הַזֹּאת וְאֶת־הָאָדָם וְאֶת־הַבְּהֵמָה
בְּדֶבֶר גָּדוֹל יָמֻתוּ: 7 וְאַחֲרֵי־כֵן נְאֻם־יְהֹוָה אֶתֵּן
אֶת־צִדְקִיָּהוּ מֶלֶךְ־יְהוּדָה וְאֶת־עֲבָדָיו וְאֶת־
הָעָם וְאֶת־הַנִּשְׁאָרִים בָּעִיר הַזֹּאת מִן־הַדֶּבֶר
מִן־הַחֶרֶב וּמִן־הָרָעָב בְּיַד נְבוּכַדְרֶאצַּר מֶלֶךְ־בָּבֶל
וּבְיַד אֹיְבֵיהֶם וּבְיַד מְבַקְשֵׁי נַפְשָׁם וְהִכָּם לְפִי־
חֶרֶב לֹא־יָחוּס עֲלֵיהֶם וְלֹא יַחְמֹל וְלֹא יְרַחֵם:
8 וְאֶל־הָעָם הַזֶּה תֹּאמַר כֹּה אָמַר יְהֹוָה הִנְנִי נֹתֵן
לִפְנֵיכֶם אֶת־דֶּרֶךְ הַחַיִּים וְאֶת־דֶּרֶךְ הַמָּוֶת: 9 הַיֹּשֵׁב
בָּעִיר הַזֹּאת יָמוּת בַּחֶרֶב וּבָרָעָב וּבַדָּבֶר וְהַיּוֹצֵא
וְנָפַל עַל־הַכַּשְׂדִּים הַצָּרִים עֲלֵיכֶם יִחְיֶהﬡ וְהָיְתָה־
לּוֹ נַפְשׁוֹ לְשָׁלָל: 10 כִּי שַׂמְתִּי פָנַי בָּעִיר הַזֹּאת

city for adversity and not for good," says the LORD. "It shall be given into the hand of the king of Babylon, and he shall burn it with fire."'

11 "And concerning the house of the king of Judah, say, 'Hear the word of the LORD, 12 O house of David! Thus says the LORD:

> "Execute judgment in the morning;
> And deliver *him who is* plundered
> Out of the hand of the oppressor,
> Lest My fury go forth like fire
> And burn so that no one can quench *it,*
> Because of the evil of your doings.

13 "Behold, I *am* against you, O inhabitant of the valley,
> *And* rock of the plain," says the LORD,
> "Who say, 'Who shall come down against us?
> Or who shall enter our dwellings?'

14 But I will punish you according to the fruit of your doings," says the LORD;
> "I will kindle a fire in its forest,
> And it shall devour all things around it."'"

22 Thus says the LORD: "Go down to the house of the king of Judah, and there speak this word, 2 and say, 'Hear the word of the LORD, O king of Judah, you who sit on the throne of David, you and your servants and your people who enter these gates! 3 Thus says the LORD: "Execute judgment and righteousness, and deliver the plundered out of the hand of the oppressor. Do no wrong and do no violence to the stranger, the fatherless, or the widow, nor shed innocent blood in this place. 4 For if you indeed do this thing, then shall enter the gates of this house, riding on horses and in chariots, accompanied by servants and people, kings who sit on the throne of David. 5 But if you will not hear these words, I swear by Myself," says the LORD, "that this house shall become a desolation."'"

6 For thus says the LORD to the house of the king of Judah:

> "You *are* Gilead to Me,
> The head of Lebanon;
> *Yet* I surely will make you a wilderness,
> Cities *which* are not inhabited.

7 I will prepare destroyers against you,
> Everyone with his weapons;
> They shall cut down your choice cedars
> And cast *them* into the fire.

8 And many nations will pass by this city; and everyone will say to his neighbor, 'Why has the LORD done so to this great city?' 9 Then they will answer, 'Because they have forsaken the covenant of the LORD their God, and worshiped other gods and served them.'"

10 Weep not for the dead, nor bemoan him;

לְרָעָה וְלֹא לְטוֹבָה נְאֻם־יְהֹוָה בְּיַד־מֶלֶךְ בָּבֶל תִּתְּנֶנָּה וּשְׂרָפָהּ בָּאֵשׁ׃ ס 11 וּלְבֵית מֶלֶךְ יְהוּדָה שְׁמְעוּ דְּבַר־יְהֹוָה׃ 12 בֵּית דָּוִד כֹּה אָמַר יְהֹוָה דִּינוּ לַבֹּקֶר מִשְׁפָּט וְהַצִּילוּ גָזוּל מִיַּד עוֹשֵׁק פֶּן־תֵּצֵא כָאֵשׁ חֲמָתִי וּבָעֲרָה וְאֵין מְכַבֶּה מִפְּנֵי רֹעַ מַעַלְלֵיהֶםᵖ׃ 13 הִנְנִי אֵלַיִךְ יֹשֶׁבֶת הָעֵמֶק צוּר הַמִּישֹׁר נְאֻם־יְהֹוָה הָאֹמְרִים מִי־יֵחַת עָלֵינוּ וּמִי יָבוֹא בִּמְעוֹנוֹתֵינוּ׃ 14 וּפָקַדְתִּי עֲלֵיכֶם כִּפְרִי מַעַלְלֵיכֶם נְאֻם־יְהֹוָה וְהִצַּתִּי אֵשׁ בְּיַעְרָהּ וְאָכְלָה כָּל־סְבִיבֶיהָ׃ ס

כב כֹּה אָמַר יְהֹוָה רֵד בֵּית־מֶלֶךְ יְהוּדָה וְדִבַּרְתָּ שָׁם אֶת־הַדָּבָר הַזֶּה׃ 2 וְאָמַרְתָּ שְׁמַע דְּבַר־יְהֹוָה מֶלֶךְ יְהוּדָה הַיֹּשֵׁב עַל־כִּסֵּא דָוִד אַתָּה וַעֲבָדֶיךָ וְעַמְּךָ הַבָּאִים בַּשְּׁעָרִים הָאֵלֶּה׃ ס 3 כֹּה ׀ אָמַר יְהֹוָה עֲשׂוּ מִשְׁפָּט וּצְדָקָה וְהַצִּילוּ גָזוּל מִיַּד עָשׁוֹק וְגֵר יָתוֹם וְאַלְמָנָה אַל־תֹּנוּ אַל־תַּחְמֹסוּ וְדָם נָקִי אַל־תִּשְׁפְּכוּ בַּמָּקוֹם הַזֶּה׃ 4 כִּי אִם־עָשׂוֹ תַּעֲשׂוּ אֶת־הַדָּבָר הַזֶּה וּבָאוּ בְשַׁעֲרֵי הַבַּיִת הַזֶּה מְלָכִים יֹשְׁבִים לְדָוִד עַל־כִּסְאוֹ רֹכְבִים בָּרֶכֶב וּבַסּוּסִים הוּא וַעֲבָדָוᵖ וְעַמּוֹ׃ 5 וְאִם לֹא תִשְׁמְעוּ אֶת־הַדְּבָרִים הָאֵלֶּה בִּי נִשְׁבַּעְתִּי נְאֻם־יְהֹוָה כִּי־לְחָרְבָּה יִהְיֶה הַבַּיִת הַזֶּה׃ ס 6 כִּי־כֹה ׀ אָמַר יְהֹוָה עַל־בֵּית מֶלֶךְ יְהוּדָה גִּלְעָד אַתָּה לִי רֹאשׁ הַלְּבָנוֹן אִם־לֹא אֲשִׁיתְךָ מִדְבָּר עָרִים לֹא נוֹשָׁבֶהᵖ׃ 7 וְקִדַּשְׁתִּי עָלֶיךָ מַשְׁחִתִים אִישׁ וְכֵלָיו וְכָרְתוּ מִבְחַר אֲרָזֶיךָ וְהִפִּילוּ עַל־הָאֵשׁ׃ 8 וְעָבְרוּ גּוֹיִם רַבִּים עַל הָעִיר הַזֹּאת וְאָמְרוּ אִישׁ אֶל־רֵעֵהוּ עַל־מֶה עָשָׂה יְהֹוָה כָּכָה לָעִיר הַגְּדוֹלָה הַזֹּאת׃ 9 וְאָמְרוּ עַל אֲשֶׁר עָזְבוּ אֶת־בְּרִית יְהֹוָה אֱלֹהֵיהֶם וַיִּשְׁתַּחֲווּ לֵאלֹהִים אֲחֵרִים וַיַּעַבְדוּם׃ ס 10 אַל־תִּבְכּוּ לְמֵת

כא 12 מַעַלְלֵיכֶם
כב 4 וַעֲבָדָיו 6 נוֹשָׁבוּ

Weep bitterly for him who goes away,
For he shall return no more,
Nor see his native country.

11 For thus says the LORD concerning Shallum the son of Josiah, king of Judah, who reigned instead of Josiah his father, who went from this place: "He shall not return here anymore, 12 but he shall die in the place where they have led him captive, and shall see this land no more.

13 "Woe to him who builds his house by unright-
    eousness
And his chambers by injustice,
Who uses his neighbor's service without wages
And gives him nothing for his work,
14 Who says, 'I will build myself a wide house with
    spacious chambers,
And cut out windows for it,
Paneling *it* with cedar
And painting *it* with vermilion.'

15 "Shall you reign because you enclose *yourself* in
    cedar?
Did not your father eat and drink,
And do justice and righteousness?
Then *it was* well with him.
16 He judged the cause of the poor and needy;
Then *it was* well.
Was not this knowing Me?" says the LORD.
17 "Yet your eyes and your heart *are* for nothing but
    your covetousness,
For shedding innocent blood,
And practicing oppression and violence."

18 Therefore thus says the LORD concerning Jehoiakim the son of Josiah, king of Judah:

"They shall not lament for him,
Saying, 'Alas, my brother!' or 'Alas, my sister!'
They shall not lament for him,
Saying, 'Alas, master!' or 'Alas, his glory!'
19 He shall be buried with the burial of a donkey,
Dragged and cast out beyond the gates of
    Jerusalem.
20 "Go up to Lebanon, and cry out,
And lift up your voice in Bashan;
Cry from Abarim,
For all your lovers are destroyed.
21 I spoke to you in your prosperity,
But you said, 'I will not hear.'
This *has been* your manner from your youth,
That you did not obey My voice.
22 The wind shall eat up all your rulers,
And your lovers shall go into captivity;
Surely then you will be ashamed and humiliated
For all your wickedness.
23 O inhabitant of Lebanon,
Making your nest in the cedars,
How gracious will you be when pangs come upon
    you,
Like the pain of a woman in labor?

וְאַל־תָּנֻ֣דוּ ל֑וֹ בְּכ֤וּ בָכוֹ֙ לַֽהֹלֵ֔ךְ כִּ֣י לֹ֤א יָשׁ֣וּב
ע֔וֹד וְרָאָ֖ה אֶת־אֶ֥רֶץ מוֹלַדְתּֽוֹ׃ ס 11 כִּ֣י
כֹּֽה־אָמַ֣ר יְהוָ֗ה אֶל־שַׁלֻּ֤ם בֶּן־יֹֽאשִׁיָּ֙הוּ֙ מֶ֣לֶךְ יְהוּדָ֔ה
הַמֹּלֵ֖ךְ תַּ֣חַת יֹֽאשִׁיָּ֣הוּ אָבִ֑יו אֲשֶׁ֥ר יָצָ֖א מִן־הַמָּק֣וֹם
הַזֶּ֑ה לֹֽא־יָשׁ֥וּב שָׁ֖ם עֽוֹד׃ 12 כִּ֣י בִּמְק֤וֹם אֲשֶׁר־
הִגְל֤וּ אֹתוֹ֙ שָׁ֣ם יָמ֔וּת וְאֶת־הָאָ֥רֶץ הַזֹּ֖את לֹֽא־
יִרְאֶ֥ה עֽוֹד׃ ס 13 ה֣וֹי בֹּנֶ֤ה בֵיתוֹ֙ בְּלֹא־
צֶ֔דֶק וַֽעֲלִיּוֹתָ֖יו בְּלֹ֣א מִשְׁפָּ֑ט בְּרֵעֵ֙הוּ֙ יַֽעֲבֹ֣ד חִנָּ֔ם
וּפֹֽעֲל֖וֹ לֹ֥א יִתֶּן־לֽוֹ׃ 14 הָֽאֹמֵ֗ר אֶבְנֶה־לִּי֙ בֵּ֣ית מִדּ֔וֹת
וַֽעֲלִיּ֖וֹת מְרֻוָּחִ֑ים וְקָ֤רַֽע לוֹ֙ חַלּוֹנָ֔י וְסָפ֖וּן בָּאָ֔רֶז
וּמָשׁ֖וֹחַ בַּשָּׁשַֽׁר׃ 15 הֲתִֽמְלֹ֔ךְ כִּ֥י אַתָּ֖ה מְתַֽחֲרֶ֣ה בָאָ֑רֶז
אָבִ֙יךָ֙ הֲל֣וֹא אָכַ֣ל וְשָׁתָ֔ה וְעָשָׂ֥ה מִשְׁפָּ֛ט וּצְדָקָ֖ה אָ֣ז
ט֣וֹב לֽוֹ׃ 16 דָּ֛ן דִּֽין־עָנִ֥י וְאֶבְי֖וֹן אָ֣ז ט֑וֹב הֲלוֹא־הִ֥יא
הַדַּ֛עַת אֹתִ֖י נְאֻם־יְהוָֽה׃ 17 כִּ֣י אֵ֤ין עֵינֶ֙יךָ֙ וְלִבְּךָ֔
כִּ֣י אִם־עַל־בִּצְעֶ֑ךָ וְעַ֤ל דַּֽם־הַנָּקִי֙ לִשְׁפּ֔וֹךְ וְעַל־
הָעֹ֥שֶׁק וְעַל־הַמְּרוּצָ֖ה לַֽעֲשֽׂוֹת׃ ס 18 לָכֵ֞ן
כֹּֽה־אָמַ֣ר יְהוָ֗ה אֶל־יְהֽוֹיָקִ֤ים בֶּן־יֹֽאשִׁיָּ֙הוּ֙ מֶ֣לֶךְ
יְהוּדָ֔ה לֹא־יִסְפְּד֣וּ ל֔וֹ ה֥וֹי אָחִ֖י וְה֣וֹי אָח֑וֹת
לֹֽא־יִסְפְּד֣וּ ל֔וֹ ה֥וֹי אָד֖וֹן וְה֥וֹי הֹדֹֽה׃ 19 קְבוּרַ֣ת
חֲמ֖וֹר יִקָּבֵ֑ר סָח֣וֹב וְהַשְׁלֵ֔ךְ מֵהָ֖לְאָה לְשַֽׁעֲרֵ֥י
יְרֽוּשָׁלָֽ͏ִם׃ ס 20 עֲלִ֤י הַלְּבָנוֹן֙ וּצְעָ֔קִי וּבַבָּשָׁ֖ן
תְּנִ֣י קוֹלֵ֑ךְ וְצַֽעֲקִי֙ מֵֽעֲבָרִ֔ים כִּ֥י נִשְׁבְּר֖וּ כָּל־מְאַֽהֲבָֽיִךְ׃
21 דִּבַּ֤רְתִּי אֵלַ֙יִךְ֙ בְּשַׁלְוֺתַ֔יִךְ אָמַ֖רְתְּ לֹ֣א אֶשְׁמָ֑ע
זֶ֤ה דַרְכֵּךְ֙ מִנְּעוּרַ֔יִךְ כִּ֥י לֹֽא־שָׁמַ֖עַתְּ בְּקוֹלִֽי׃ 22 כָּל־
רֹעַ֙יִךְ֙ תִּרְעֶה־ר֔וּחַ וּמְאַֽהֲבַ֖יִךְ בַּשְּׁבִ֣י יֵלֵ֑כוּ כִּ֣י אָ֤ז
תֵּבֹ֙שִׁי֙ וְנִכְלַ֔מְתְּ מִכֹּ֖ל רָֽעָתֵֽךְ׃ 23 ישַׁבְתְּ֙ בַּלְּבָנ֔וֹן
מְקֻנַּנְתְּ בָּֽאֲרָזִ֑ים מַה־נֵּחַנְתְּ֙ בְּבֹא־לָ֣ךְ חֲבָלִ֔ים חִ֖יל

24 "*As* I live," says the LORD, "though Coniah the son of Jehoiakim, king of Judah, were the signet on My right hand, yet I would pluck you off; 25 and I will give you into the hand of those who seek your life, and into the hand *of those* whose face you fear—the hand of Nebuchadnezzar king of Babylon and the hand of the Chaldeans. 26 So I will cast you out, and your mother who bore you, into another country where you were not born; and there you shall die. 27 But to the land to which they desire to return, there they shall not return.

28 "Is this man Coniah a despised, broken idol—
A vessel in which *is* no pleasure?
Why are they cast out, he and his descendants,
And cast into a land which they do not know?

29 O earth, earth, earth,
Hear the word of the LORD!

30 Thus says the LORD:
'Write this man down as childless,
A man *who* shall not prosper in his days;
For none of his descendants shall prosper,
Sitting on the throne of David,
And ruling anymore in Judah.'"

23 "Woe to the shepherds who destroy and scatter the sheep of My pasture!" says the LORD. 2 Therefore thus says the LORD God of Israel against the shepherds who feed My people: "You have scattered My flock, driven them away, and not attended to them. Behold, I will attend to you for the evil of your doings," says the LORD. 3 "But I will gather the remnant of My flock out of all countries where I have driven them, and bring them back to their folds; and they shall be fruitful and increase. 4 I will set up shepherds over them who will feed them; and they shall fear no more, nor be dismayed, nor shall they be lacking," says the LORD.

5 "Behold, *the* days are coming," says the LORD,
"That I will raise to David a Branch of right-
eousness;
A King shall reign and prosper,
And execute judgment and righteousness in the
earth.

6 In His days Judah will be saved,
And Israel will dwell safely;
Now this *is* His name by which He will be called:

THE LORD OUR RIGHTEOUSNESS.

7 "Therefore, behold, *the* days are coming," says the LORD, "that they shall no longer say, 'As the LORD lives who brought up the children of Israel from the land of Egypt,' 8 but, 'As the LORD lives who brought up and led the descendants of the house of Israel from the north country and from all the countries where I had driven them.' And they shall dwell in their own land."

כְּיֹלַדָה: 24 חַי־אָנִי נְאֻם־יְהֹוָה כִּי אִם־יִהְיֶה כָּנְיָהוּ בֶן־יְהוֹיָקִים מֶלֶךְ יְהוּדָה חוֹתָם עַל־יַד יְמִינִי כִּי מִשָּׁם אֶתְּקֶנְךָ: 25 וּנְתַתִּיךָ בְּיַד מְבַקְשֵׁי נַפְשֶׁךָ וּבְיַד אֲשֶׁר־אַתָּה יָגוֹר מִפְּנֵיהֶם וּבְיַד נְבוּכַדְרֶאצַּר מֶלֶךְ־בָּבֶל וּבְיַד הַכַּשְׂדִּים: 26 וְהֵטַלְתִּי אֹתְךָ וְאֶת־אִמְּךָ אֲשֶׁר יְלָדַתְךָ עַל הָאָרֶץ אַחֶרֶת אֲשֶׁר לֹא־יֻלַּדְתֶּם שָׁם וְשָׁם תָּמוּתוּ: 27 וְעַל־הָאָרֶץ אֲשֶׁר־הֵם מְנַשְּׂאִים אֶת־נַפְשָׁם לָשׁוּב שָׁם שָׁמָּה לֹא יָשׁוּבוּ: ס 28 הַעֶצֶב נִבְזֶה נָפוּץ הָאִישׁ הַזֶּה כָּנְיָהוּ אִם־כְּלִי אֵין חֵפֶץ בּוֹ מַדּוּעַ הוּטֲלוּ הוּא וְזַרְעוֹ וְהֻשְׁלְכוּ עַל־הָאָרֶץ אֲשֶׁר לֹא־יָדָעוּ: 29 אֶרֶץ אֶרֶץ אָרֶץ שִׁמְעִי דְּבַר־יְהֹוָה: ס 30 כֹּה אָמַר יְהֹוָה כִּתְבוּ אֶת־הָאִישׁ הַזֶּה עֲרִירִי גֶּבֶר לֹא־יִצְלַח בְּיָמָיו כִּי לֹא יִצְלַח מִזַּרְעוֹ אִישׁ יֹשֵׁב עַל־כִּסֵּא דָוִד וּמֹשֵׁל עוֹד בִּיהוּדָה:

כג הוֹי רֹעִים מְאַבְּדִים וּמְפִצִים אֶת־צֹאן מַרְעִיתִי נְאֻם־יְהֹוָה: 2 לָכֵן כֹּה־אָמַר יְהֹוָה אֱלֹהֵי יִשְׂרָאֵל עַל־הָרֹעִים הָרֹעִים אֶת־עַמִּי אַתֶּם הֲפִצֹתֶם אֶת־צֹאנִי וַתַּדִּחוּם וְלֹא פְקַדְתֶּם אֹתָם הִנְנִי פֹקֵד עֲלֵיכֶם אֶת־רֹעַ מַעַלְלֵיכֶם נְאֻם־יְהֹוָה: 3 וַאֲנִי אֲקַבֵּץ אֶת־שְׁאֵרִית צֹאנִי מִכֹּל הָאֲרָצוֹת אֲשֶׁר־הִדַּחְתִּי אֹתָם שָׁם וַהֲשִׁבֹתִי אֶתְהֶן עַל־נְוֵהֶן וּפָרוּ וְרָבוּ: 4 וַהֲקִמֹתִי עֲלֵיהֶם רֹעִים וְרָעוּם וְלֹא־יִירְאוּ עוֹד וְלֹא־יֵחַתּוּ וְלֹא יִפָּקֵדוּ נְאֻם־יְהֹוָה: ס 5 הִנֵּה יָמִים בָּאִים נְאֻם־יְהֹוָה וַהֲקִמֹתִי לְדָוִד צֶמַח צַדִּיק וּמָלַךְ מֶלֶךְ וְהִשְׂכִּיל וְעָשָׂה מִשְׁפָּט וּצְדָקָה בָּאָרֶץ: 6 בְּיָמָיו תִּוָּשַׁע יְהוּדָה וְיִשְׂרָאֵל יִשְׁכֹּן לָבֶטַח וְזֶה־שְּׁמוֹ אֲשֶׁר־יִקְרְאוֹ יְהֹוָה צִדְקֵנוּ: ס 7 לָכֵן הִנֵּה־יָמִים בָּאִים נְאֻם־יְהֹוָה וְלֹא־יֹאמְרוּ עוֹד חַי־יְהֹוָה אֲשֶׁר הֶעֱלָה אֶת־בְּנֵי יִשְׂרָאֵל מֵאֶרֶץ מִצְרָיִם: 8 כִּי אִם־חַי־יְהֹוָה אֲשֶׁר הֶעֱלָה וַאֲשֶׁר הֵבִיא אֶת־זֶרַע בֵּית יִשְׂרָאֵל מֵאֶרֶץ צָפוֹנָה וּמִכֹּל הָאֲרָצוֹת אֲשֶׁר הִדַּחְתִּים שָׁם

ירמיה כג

9 My heart within me is broken
  Because of the prophets;
  All my bones shake.
  I am like a drunken man,
  And like a man whom wine has overcome,
  Because of the LORD,
  And because of His holy words.
10 For the land is full of adulterers;
  For because of a curse the land mourns.
  The pleasant places of the wilderness are dried
    up.
  Their course of life is evil,
  And their might *is* not right.

11 "For both prophet and priest are profane;
  Yes, in My house I have found their wickedness,"
    says the LORD.
12 "Therefore their way shall be to them
  Like slippery *ways*;
  In the darkness they shall be driven on
  And fall in them;
  For I will bring disaster on them,
  The year of their punishment," says the LORD.
13 "And I have seen folly in the prophets of Samaria:
  They prophesied by Baal
  And caused My people Israel to err.
14 Also I have seen a horrible thing in the prophets
    of Jerusalem:
  They commit adultery and walk in lies;
  They also strengthen the hands of evildoers,
  So that no one turns back from his wickedness.
  All of them are like Sodom to Me,
  And her inhabitants like Gomorrah.

15 "Therefore thus says the LORD of hosts
concerning the prophets:

  'Behold, I will feed them with wormwood,
  And make them drink the water of gall;
  For from the prophets of Jerusalem
  Profaneness has gone out into all the land.'"

16 Thus says the LORD of hosts:

  "Do not listen to the words of the prophets who
    prophesy to you.
  They make you worthless;
  They speak a vision of their own heart,
  Not from the mouth of the LORD.
17 They continually say to those who despise Me,
  'The LORD has said, "You shall have peace"';
  And *to* everyone who walks according to the
    dictates of his own heart, they say,
  'No evil shall come upon you.'"

18 For who has stood in the counsel of the LORD,
  And has perceived and heard His word?
  Who has marked His word and heard *it*?
19 Behold, a whirlwind of the LORD has gone forth
    in fury—
  A violent whirlwind!
  It will fall violently on the head of the wicked.
20 The anger of the LORD will not turn back
  Until He has executed and performed the
    thoughts of His heart.

וְיָשְׁבוּ עַל־אַדְמָתָם: ס 9 לַנְּבִאִים נִשְׁבַּר
לִבִּי בְקִרְבִּי רָחֲפוּ כָּל־עַצְמוֹתַי הָיִיתִי כְּאִישׁ שִׁכּוֹר
וּכְגֶבֶר עֲבָרוֹ יָיִן מִפְּנֵי יְהֹוָה וּמִפְּנֵי דִּבְרֵי קָדְשׁוֹ:
10 כִּי מְנָאֲפִים מָלְאָה הָאָרֶץ כִּי־מִפְּנֵי אָלָה אָבְלָה
הָאָרֶץ יָבְשׁוּ נְאוֹת מִדְבָּר וַתְּהִי מְרוּצָתָם רָעָה
וּגְבוּרָתָם לֹא־כֵן: 11 כִּי־גַם־נָבִיא גַם־כֹּהֵן חָנֵפוּ
גַּם־בְּבֵיתִי מָצָאתִי רָעָתָם נְאֻם־יְהֹוָה: 12 לָכֵן יִהְיֶה
דַרְכָּם לָהֶם כַּחֲלַקְלַקּוֹת בָּאֲפֵלָה יִדַּחוּ וְנָפְלוּ בָהּ
כִּי־אָבִיא עֲלֵיהֶם רָעָה שְׁנַת פְּקֻדָּתָם נְאֻם־יְהֹוָה:
13 וּבִנְבִיאֵי שֹׁמְרוֹן רָאִיתִי תִפְלָה הִנַּבְּאוּ בַבַּעַל
וַיַּתְעוּ אֶת־עַמִּי אֶת־יִשְׂרָאֵל: ס 14 וּבִנְבִאֵי
יְרוּשָׁלִַם רָאִיתִי שַׁעֲרוּרָה נָאוֹף וְהָלֹךְ בַּשֶּׁקֶר וְחִזְּקוּ
יְדֵי מְרֵעִים לְבִלְתִּי־שָׁבוּ אִישׁ מֵרָעָתוֹ הָיוּ־לִי כֻלָּם
כִּסְדֹם וְיֹשְׁבֶיהָ כַּעֲמֹרָה: ס 15 לָכֵן כֹּה־
אָמַר יְהֹוָה צְבָאוֹת עַל־הַנְּבִאִים הִנְנִי מַאֲכִיל אוֹתָם
לַעֲנָה וְהִשְׁקִתִים מֵי־רֹאשׁ כִּי מֵאֵת נְבִיאֵי יְרוּשָׁלִַם
יָצְאָה חֲנֻפָּה לְכָל־הָאָרֶץ: פ
16 כֹּה־אָמַר יְהֹוָה צְבָאוֹת אַל־תִּשְׁמְעוּ עַל־דִּבְרֵי
הַנְּבִאִים הַנִּבְּאִים לָכֶם מַהְבִּלִים הֵמָּה אֶתְכֶם
חֲזוֹן לִבָּם יְדַבֵּרוּ לֹא מִפִּי יְהֹוָה: 17 אֹמְרִים אָמוֹר
לִמְנַאֲצַי דִּבֶּר יְהֹוָה שָׁלוֹם יִהְיֶה לָכֶם וְכֹל הֹלֵךְ
בִּשְׁרִרוּת לִבּוֹ אָמְרוּ לֹא־תָבוֹא עֲלֵיכֶם רָעָה: 18 כִּי
מִי עָמַד בְּסוֹד יְהֹוָה וְיֵרֶא וְיִשְׁמַע אֶת־דְּבָרוֹ
מִי־הִקְשִׁיב דְּבָרוֹ וַיִּשְׁמָע: ס 19 הִנֵּה |
סַעֲרַת יְהֹוָה חֵמָה יָצְאָה וְסַעַר מִתְחוֹלֵל עַל רֹאשׁ
רְשָׁעִים יָחוּל: 20 לֹא יָשׁוּב אַף־יְהֹוָה עַד־עֲשֹׂתוֹ
וְעַד־הֲקִימוֹ מְזִמּוֹת לִבּוֹ בְּאַחֲרִית הַיָּמִים תִּתְבּוֹנְנוּ

כג 18 דְּבָרוֹ

In the latter days you will understand it perfectly.

21 "I have not sent these prophets, yet they ran.
I have not spoken to them, yet they prophesied.
22 But if they had stood in My counsel,
And had caused My people to hear My words,
Then they would have turned them from their
    evil way
And from the evil of their doings.

23 "*Am* I a God near at hand," says the LORD,
"And not a God afar off?
24 Can anyone hide himself in secret places,
So I shall not see him?" says the LORD;
"Do I not fill heaven and earth?" says the LORD.

25 "I have heard what the prophets have said who
prophesy lies in My name, saying, 'I have dreamed,
I have dreamed!' 26 How long will *this* be in the
heart of the prophets who prophesy lies? Indeed
they are prophets of the deceit of their own heart,
27 who try to make My people forget My name by
their dreams which everyone tells his neighbor, as
their fathers forgot My name for Baal.

28 "The prophet who has a dream, let him tell a
    dream;
And he who has My word, let him speak My
    word faithfully.
What *is* the chaff to the wheat?" says the LORD.
29 "*Is* not My word like a fire?" says the LORD,
"And like a hammer *that* breaks the rock in pieces?"

30 "Therefore behold, I *am* against the prophets,"
says the LORD, "who steal My words every one
from his neighbor. 31 Behold, I *am* against the
prophets," says the LORD, "who use their tongues
and say, 'He says.' 32 Behold, I *am* against those
who prophesy false dreams," says the LORD, "and
tell them, and cause My people to err by their lies
and by their recklessness. Yet I did not send them
or command them; therefore they shall not profit
this people at all," says the LORD.

33 "So when these people or the prophet or the
priest ask you, saying, 'What is the oracle of the
LORD?' you shall then say to them, 'What oracle?' I
will even forsake you," says the LORD. 34 "And *as
for* the prophet and the priest and the people who
say, 'The oracle of the LORD!' I will even punish
that man and his house. 35 Thus every one of you
shall say to his neighbor, and every one to his
brother, 'What has the LORD answered?' and,
'What has the LORD spoken?' 36 And the oracle of
the LORD you shall mention no more. For every
man's word will be his oracle, for you have
perverted the words of the living God, the LORD
of hosts, our God. 37 Thus you shall say to the
prophet, 'What has the LORD answered you?' and,
'What has the LORD spoken?' 38 But since you say,
'The oracle of the LORD!' therefore thus says the

בָּה בִּינָה: 21 לֹא־שָׁלַחְתִּי אֶת־הַנְּבִאִים וְהֵם רָצוּ
לֹא־דִבַּרְתִּי אֲלֵיהֶם וְהֵם נִבָּאוּ: 22 וְאִם־עָמְדוּ
בְּסוֹדִי וְיַשְׁמִעוּ דְבָרַי אֶת־עַמִּי וִישִׁבוּם מִדַּרְכָּם
הָרָע וּמֵרֹעַ מַעַלְלֵיהֶם: ס 23 הַאֱלֹהֵי
מִקָּרֹב אָנִי נְאֻם־יְהוָה וְלֹא אֱלֹהֵי מֵרָחֹק: 24 אִם־
יִסָּתֵר אִישׁ בַּמִּסְתָּרִים וַאֲנִי לֹא־אֶרְאֶנּוּ נְאֻם־
יְהוָה הֲלוֹא אֶת־הַשָּׁמַיִם וְאֶת־הָאָרֶץ אֲנִי מָלֵא
נְאֻם־יְהוָה: 25 שָׁמַעְתִּי אֵת אֲשֶׁר־אָמְרוּ הַנְּבִאִים
הַנִּבְּאִים בִּשְׁמִי שֶׁקֶר לֵאמֹר חָלַמְתִּי חָלָמְתִּי:
26 עַד־מָתַי הֲיֵשׁ בְּלֵב הַנְּבִאִים נִבְּאֵי הַשָּׁקֶר
וּנְבִיאֵי תַּרְמִת לִבָּם: 27 הַחֹשְׁבִים לְהַשְׁכִּיחַ אֶת־
עַמִּי שְׁמִי בַּחֲלוֹמֹתָם אֲשֶׁר יְסַפְּרוּ אִישׁ לְרֵעֵהוּ
כַּאֲשֶׁר שָׁכְחוּ אֲבוֹתָם אֶת־שְׁמִי בַּבָּעַל: 28 הַנָּבִיא
אֲשֶׁר־אִתּוֹ חֲלוֹם יְסַפֵּר חֲלוֹם וַאֲשֶׁר דְּבָרִי אִתּוֹ
יְדַבֵּר דְּבָרִי אֱמֶת מַה־לַתֶּבֶן אֶת־הַבָּר נְאֻם־יְהוָה:
29 הֲלוֹא כֹה דְבָרִי כָּאֵשׁ נְאֻם־יְהוָה וּכְפַטִּישׁ יְפֹצֵץ
סָלַע: ס 30 לָכֵן הִנְנִי עַל־הַנְּבִאִים נְאֻם־
יְהוָה מְגַנְּבֵי דְבָרַי אִישׁ מֵאֵת רֵעֵהוּ: 31 הִנְנִי עַל־
הַנְּבִיאִם נְאֻם־יְהוָה הַלֹּקְחִים לְשׁוֹנָם וַיִּנְאֲמוּ נְאֻם:
32 הִנְנִי עַל־נִבְּאֵי חֲלֹמוֹת שֶׁקֶר נְאֻם־יְהוָה וַיְסַפְּרוּם
וַיַּתְעוּ אֶת־עַמִּי בְּשִׁקְרֵיהֶם וּבְפַחֲזוּתָם וְאָנֹכִי לֹא־
שְׁלַחְתִּים וְלֹא צִוִּיתִים וְהוֹעֵיל לֹא־יוֹעִילוּ לָעָם־
הַזֶּה נְאֻם־יְהוָה: 33 וְכִי־יִשְׁאָלְךָ הָעָם הַזֶּה אוֹ־
הַנָּבִיא אוֹ־כֹהֵן לֵאמֹר מַה־מַשָּׂא יְהוָה וְאָמַרְתָּ
אֲלֵיהֶם אֶת־מַה־מַשָּׂא וְנָטַשְׁתִּי אֶתְכֶם נְאֻם־יְהוָה:
34 וְהַנָּבִיא וְהַכֹּהֵן וְהָעָם אֲשֶׁר יֹאמַר מַשָּׂא יְהוָה
וּפָקַדְתִּי עַל־הָאִישׁ הַהוּא וְעַל־בֵּיתוֹ: 35 כֹּה תֹאמְרוּ
אִישׁ עַל־רֵעֵהוּ וְאִישׁ אֶל־אָחִיו מֶה־עָנָה יְהוָה
וּמַה־דִּבֶּר יְהוָה: 36 וּמַשָּׂא יְהוָה לֹא תִזְכְּרוּ־עוֹד
כִּי הַמַּשָּׂא יִהְיֶה לְאִישׁ דְּבָרוֹ וַהֲפַכְתֶּם אֶת־
דִּבְרֵי אֱלֹהִים חַיִּים יְהוָה צְבָאוֹת אֱלֹהֵינוּ: 37 כֹּה
תֹאמַר אֶל־הַנָּבִיא מֶה־עָנָךְ יְהוָה וּמַה־דִּבֶּר יְהוָה:
38 וְאִם־מַשָּׂא יְהוָה תֹּאמֵרוּ לָכֵן כֹּה אָמַר יְהוָה
יַעַן אֲמָרְכֶם אֶת־הַדָּבָר הַזֶּה מַשָּׂא יְהוָה וָאֶשְׁלַח

LORD: 'Because you say this word, "The oracle of the LORD!" and I have sent to you, saying, "Do not say, 'The oracle of the LORD!' " ³⁹ therefore behold, I, even I, will utterly forget you and forsake you, and the city that I gave you and your fathers, and *will cast you* out of My presence. ⁴⁰ And I will bring an everlasting reproach upon you, and a perpetual shame, which shall not be forgotten.' "

24 The LORD showed me, and there were two baskets of figs set before the temple of the LORD, after Nebuchadnezzar king of Babylon had carried away captive Jeconiah the son of Jehoiakim, king of Judah, and the princes of Judah with the craftsmen and smiths, from Jerusalem, and had brought them to Babylon. ² One basket *had* very good figs, like the figs *that are* first ripe; and the other basket *had* very bad figs which could not be eaten, they were so bad. ³ Then the LORD said to me, "What do you see, Jeremiah?"

And I said, "Figs, the good figs, very good; and the bad, very bad, which cannot be eaten, they are so bad."

⁴ Again the word of the LORD came to me, saying, ⁵ "Thus says the LORD, the God of Israel: 'Like these good figs, so will I acknowledge those who are carried away captive from Judah, whom I have sent out of this place for *their own* good, into the land of the Chaldeans. ⁶ For I will set My eyes on them for good, and I will bring them back to this land; I will build them and not pull *them* down, and I will plant them and not pluck *them* up. ⁷ Then I will give them a heart to know Me, that I *am* the LORD; and they shall be My people, and I will be their God, for they shall return to Me with their whole heart.

⁸ 'And as the bad figs which cannot be eaten, they are so bad'—surely thus says the LORD—'so will I give up Zedekiah the king of Judah, his princes, the residue of Jerusalem who remain in this land, and those who dwell in the land of Egypt. ⁹ I will deliver them to trouble into all the kingdoms of the earth, for *their* harm, *to be* a reproach and a byword, a taunt and a curse, in all places where I shall drive them. ¹⁰ And I will send the sword, the famine, and the pestilence among them, till they are consumed from the land that I gave to them and their fathers.' "

25 The word that came to Jeremiah concerning all the people of Judah, in the fourth year of Jehoiakim the son of Josiah, king of Judah (which *was* the first year of Nebuchadnezzar king of

אֲלֵיכֶם לֵאמֹר לֹא תֹאמְרוּ מַשָּׂא יְהֹוָה: ³⁹ לָכֵן הִנְנִי וְנָשִׁיתִי אֶתְכֶם נָשֹׁא וְנָטַשְׁתִּי אֶתְכֶם וְאֶת־ הָעִיר אֲשֶׁר נָתַתִּי לָכֶם וְלַאֲבוֹתֵיכֶם מֵעַל פָּנָי: ⁴⁰ וְנָתַתִּי עֲלֵיכֶם חֶרְפַּת עוֹלָם וּכְלִמּוּת עוֹלָם אֲשֶׁר לֹא תִשָּׁכֵחַ: ס

כד הִרְאַנִי יְהֹוָה וְהִנֵּה שְׁנֵי דּוּדָאֵי תְאֵנִים מוּעָדִים לִפְנֵי הֵיכַל יְהֹוָה אַחֲרֵי הַגְלוֹת נְבוּכַדְרֶאצַּר מֶלֶךְ־בָּבֶל אֶת־יְכׇנְיָהוּ בֶן־יְהוֹיָקִים מֶלֶךְ־יְהוּדָה וְאֶת־שָׂרֵי יְהוּדָה וְאֶת־הֶחָרָשׁ וְאֶת־ הַמַּסְגֵּר מִירוּשָׁלַ͏ִם וַיְבִאֵם בָּבֶל: ² הַדּוּד אֶחָד תְּאֵנִים טֹבוֹת מְאֹד כִּתְאֵנֵי הַבַּכֻּרוֹת וְהַדּוּד אֶחָד תְּאֵנִים רָעוֹת מְאֹד אֲשֶׁר לֹא־תֵאָכַלְנָה מֵרֹעַ: ס ³ וַיֹּאמֶר יְהֹוָה אֵלַי מָה־אַתָּה רֹאֶה יִרְמְיָהוּ וָאֹמַר תְּאֵנִים הַתְּאֵנִים הַטֹּבוֹת טֹבוֹת מְאֹד וְהָרָעוֹת רָעוֹת מְאֹד אֲשֶׁר לֹא־תֵאָכַלְנָה מֵרֹעַ: פ

⁴ וַיְהִי דְבַר־יְהֹוָה אֵלַי לֵאמֹר: ⁵ כֹּה־אָמַר יְהֹוָה אֱלֹהֵי יִשְׂרָאֵל כַּתְּאֵנִים הַטֹּבוֹת הָאֵלֶּה כֵּן־אַכִּיר אֶת־גָּלוּת יְהוּדָה אֲשֶׁר שִׁלַּחְתִּי מִן־הַמָּקוֹם הַזֶּה אֶרֶץ כַּשְׂדִּים לְטוֹבָה: ⁶ וְשַׂמְתִּי עֵינִי עֲלֵיהֶם לְטוֹבָה וַהֲשִׁבֹתִים עַל־הָאָרֶץ הַזֹּאת וּבְנִיתִים וְלֹא אֶהֱרֹס וּנְטַעְתִּים וְלֹא אֶתּוֹשׁ: ⁷ וְנָתַתִּי לָהֶם לֵב לָדַעַת אֹתִי כִּי אֲנִי יְהֹוָה וְהָיוּ־לִי לְעָם וְאָנֹכִי אֶהְיֶה לָהֶם לֵאלֹהִים כִּי־יָשֻׁבוּ אֵלַי בְּכׇל־ לִבָּם: ס ⁸ וְכַתְּאֵנִים הָרָעוֹת אֲשֶׁר לֹא־ תֵאָכַלְנָה מֵרֹעַ כִּי־כֹה ׀ אָמַר יְהֹוָה כֵּן אֶתֵּן אֶת־ צִדְקִיָּהוּ מֶלֶךְ־יְהוּדָה וְאֶת־שָׂרָיו וְאֶת ׀ שְׁאֵרִית יְרוּשָׁלַ͏ִם הַנִּשְׁאָרִים בָּאָרֶץ הַזֹּאת וְהַיֹּשְׁבִים בְּאֶרֶץ מִצְרָיִם: ⁹ וּנְתַתִּים לְזַעֲוָה לְרָעָה לְכֹל מַמְלְכוֹת הָאָרֶץ לְחֶרְפָּה וּלְמָשָׁל לִשְׁנִינָה וְלִקְלָלָה בְּכׇל־ הַמְּקֹמוֹת אֲשֶׁר־אַדִּיחֵם שָׁם: ¹⁰ וְשִׁלַּחְתִּי בָם אֶת־ הַחֶרֶב אֶת־הָרָעָב וְאֶת־הַדָּבֶר עַד־תֻּמָּם מֵעַל הָאֲדָמָה אֲשֶׁר־נָתַתִּי לָהֶם וְלַאֲבוֹתֵיהֶם: פ

כה הַדָּבָר אֲשֶׁר־הָיָה עַל־יִרְמְיָהוּ עַל־כׇּל־עַם יְהוּדָה בַּשָּׁנָה הָרְבִעִית לִיהוֹיָקִים בֶּן־יֹאשִׁיָּהוּ מֶלֶךְ יְהוּדָה הִיא הַשָּׁנָה הָרִאשֹׁנִית לִנְבוּכַדְרֶאצַּר מֶלֶךְ

Babylon), ²which Jeremiah the prophet spoke to all the people of Judah and to all the inhabitants of Jerusalem, saying: ³"From the thirteenth year of Josiah the son of Amon, king of Judah, even to this day, this *is* the twenty-third year in which the word of the LORD has come to me; and I have spoken to you, rising early and speaking, but you have not listened. ⁴And the LORD has sent to you all His servants the prophets, rising early and sending *them*, but you have not listened nor inclined your ear to hear. ⁵They said, 'Repent now everyone of his evil way and his evil doings, and dwell in the land that the LORD has given to you and your fathers forever and ever. ⁶Do not go after other gods to serve them and worship them, and do not provoke Me to anger with the works of your hands; and I will not harm you.' ⁷Yet you have not listened to Me," says the LORD, "that you might provoke Me to anger with the works of your hands to your own hurt.

⁸"Therefore thus says the LORD of hosts: 'Because you have not heard My words, ⁹behold, I will send and take all the families of the north,' says the LORD, 'and Nebuchadnezzar the king of Babylon, My servant, and will bring them against this land, against its inhabitants, and against these nations all around, and will utterly destroy them, and make them an astonishment, a hissing, and perpetual desolations. ¹⁰Moreover I will take from them the voice of mirth and the voice of gladness, the voice of the bridegroom and the voice of the bride, the sound of the millstones and the light of the lamp. ¹¹And this whole land shall be a desolation *and* an astonishment, and these nations shall serve the king of Babylon seventy years.

¹²'Then it will come to pass, when seventy years are completed, *that* I will punish the king of Babylon and that nation, the land of the Chaldeans, for their iniquity,' says the LORD; 'and I will make it a perpetual desolation. ¹³So I will bring on that land all My words which I have pronounced against it, all that is written in this book, which Jeremiah has prophesied concerning all the nations. ¹⁴(For many nations and great kings shall be served by them also; and I will repay them according to their deeds and according to the works of their own hands.)' "

¹⁵For thus says the LORD God of Israel to me: "Take this wine cup of fury from My hand, and cause all the nations, to whom I send you, to drink it. ¹⁶And they will drink and stagger and go mad because of the sword that I will send among them."

בְּבֶל: ² אֲשֶׁר דִּבֶּר יִרְמְיָהוּ הַנָּבִיא עַל־כָּל־עַם יְהוּדָה וְאֶל כָּל־יֹשְׁבֵי יְרוּשָׁלָ‍ִם לֵאמֹר: ³ מִן־שְׁלֹשׁ עֶשְׂרֵה שָׁנָה לְיֹאשִׁיָּהוּ בֶן־אָמוֹן מֶלֶךְ יְהוּדָה וְעַד | הַיּוֹם הַזֶּה זֶה שָׁלֹשׁ וְעֶשְׂרִים שָׁנָה הָיָה דְבַר־ יְהוָה אֵלָי וָאֲדַבֵּר אֲלֵיכֶם אַשְׁכֵּים וְדַבֵּר וְלֹא שְׁמַעְתֶּם: ⁴ וְשָׁלַח יְהוָה אֲלֵיכֶם אֶת־כָּל־עֲבָדָיו הַנְּבִאִים הַשְׁכֵּם וְשָׁלֹחַ וְלֹא שְׁמַעְתֶּם וְלֹא־הִטִּיתֶם אֶת־אָזְנְכֶם לִשְׁמֹעַ: ⁵ לֵאמֹר שׁוּבוּ־נָא אִישׁ מִדַּרְכּוֹ הָרָעָה וּמֵרֹעַ מַעַלְלֵיכֶם וּשְׁבוּ עַל־הָאֲדָמָה אֲשֶׁר נָתַן יְהוָה לָכֶם וְלַאֲבוֹתֵיכֶם לְמִן־עוֹלָם וְעַד־ עוֹלָם: ⁶ וְאַל־תֵּלְכוּ אַחֲרֵי אֱלֹהִים אֲחֵרִים לְעָבְדָם וּלְהִשְׁתַּחֲוֹת לָהֶם וְלֹא־תַכְעִיסוּ אוֹתִי בְּמַעֲשֵׂה יְדֵיכֶם וְלֹא אָרַע לָכֶם: ⁷ וְלֹא־שְׁמַעְתֶּם אֵלַי נְאֻם־יְהוָה לְמַעַן הַכְעִסוֹנִי בְּמַעֲשֵׂה יְדֵיכֶם לְרַע לָכֶם: ס ⁸ לָכֵן כֹּה אָמַר יְהוָה צְבָאוֹת יַעַן אֲשֶׁר לֹא־שְׁמַעְתֶּם אֶת־דְּבָרָי: ⁹ הִנְנִי שֹׁלֵחַ וְלָקַחְתִּי אֶת־כָּל־מִשְׁפְּחוֹת צָפוֹן נְאֻם־יְהוָה וְאֶל־ נְבוּכַדְרֶאצַּר מֶלֶךְ־בָּבֶל עַבְדִּי וַהֲבִאֹתִים עַל־הָאָרֶץ הַזֹּאת וְעַל־יֹשְׁבֶיהָ וְעַל כָּל־הַגּוֹיִם הָאֵלֶּה סָבִיב וְהַחֲרַמְתִּים וְשַׂמְתִּים לְשַׁמָּה וְלִשְׁרֵקָה וּלְחָרְבוֹת עוֹלָם: ¹⁰ וְהַאֲבַדְתִּי מֵהֶם קוֹל שָׂשׂוֹן וְקוֹל שִׂמְחָה קוֹל חָתָן וְקוֹל כַּלָּה קוֹל רֵחַיִם וְאוֹר נֵר: ¹¹ וְהָיְתָה כָּל־הָאָרֶץ הַזֹּאת לְחָרְבָּה לְשַׁמָּה וְעָבְדוּ הַגּוֹיִם הָאֵלֶּה אֶת־מֶלֶךְ בָּבֶל שִׁבְעִים שָׁנָה: ¹² וְהָיָה כִמְלֹאות שִׁבְעִים שָׁנָה אֶפְקֹד עַל־מֶלֶךְ־בָּבֶל וְעַל־ הַגּוֹי הַהוּא נְאֻם־יְהוָה אֶת־עֲוֹנָם וְעַל־אֶרֶץ כַּשְׂדִּים וְשַׂמְתִּי אֹתוֹ לְשִׁמְמוֹת עוֹלָם: ¹³ וְהֵבֵאתִי עַל־ הָאָרֶץ הַהִיא אֶת־כָּל־דְּבָרַי אֲשֶׁר־דִּבַּרְתִּי עָלֶיהָ אֵת כָּל־הַכָּתוּב בַּסֵּפֶר הַזֶּה אֲשֶׁר־נִבָּא יִרְמְיָהוּ עַל־ כָּל־הַגּוֹיִם: ¹⁴ כִּי עָבְדוּ־בָם גַּם־הֵמָּה גּוֹיִם רַבִּים וּמְלָכִים גְּדוֹלִים וְשִׁלַּמְתִּי לָהֶם כְּפָעֳלָם וּכְמַעֲשֵׂה יְדֵיהֶם: ס ¹⁵ כִּי כֹה אָמַר יְהוָה אֱלֹהֵי יִשְׂרָאֵל אֵלַי קַח אֶת־כּוֹס הַיַּיִן הַחֵמָה הַזֹּאת מִיָּדִי וְהִשְׁקִיתָה אֹתוֹ אֶת־כָּל־הַגּוֹיִם אֲשֶׁר אָנֹכִי שֹׁלֵחַ אוֹתְךָ אֲלֵיהֶם: ¹⁶ וְשָׁתוּ וְהִתְגֹּעֲשׁוּ וְהִתְהֹלָלוּ מִפְּנֵי

כה 7 הַכְעִסֵנִי   13 וְהֵבֵאתִי

¹⁷Then I took the cup from the LORD's hand, and made all the nations drink, to whom the LORD had sent me: ¹⁸Jerusalem and the cities of Judah, its kings and its princes, to make them a desolation, an astonishment, a hissing, and a curse, as *it is* this day; ¹⁹Pharaoh king of Egypt, his servants, his princes, and all his people; ²⁰all the mixed multitude, all the kings of the land of Uz, all the kings of the land of the Philistines (namely, Ashkelon, Gaza, Ekron, and the remnant of Ashdod); ²¹Edom, Moab, and the people of Ammon; ²²all the kings of Tyre, all the kings of Sidon, and the kings of the coastlands which *are* across the sea; ²³Dedan, Tema, Buz, and all *who are* in the farthest corners; ²⁴all the kings of Arabia and all the kings of the mixed multitude who dwell in the desert; ²⁵all the kings of Zimri, all the kings of Elam, and all the kings of the Medes; ²⁶all the kings of the north, far and near, one with another; and all the kingdoms of the world which *are* on the face of the earth. Also the king of Sheshach shall drink after them.

²⁷"Therefore you shall say to them, 'Thus says the LORD of hosts, the God of Israel: "Drink, be drunk, and vomit! Fall and rise no more, because of the sword which I will send among you."' ²⁸And it shall be, if they refuse to take the cup from your hand to drink, then you shall say to them, 'Thus says the LORD of hosts: "You shall certainly drink! ²⁹For behold, I begin to bring calamity on the city which is called by My name, and should you be utterly unpunished? You shall not be unpunished, for I will call for a sword on all the inhabitants of the earth," says the LORD of hosts.'

³⁰"Therefore prophesy against them all these words, and say to them:

'The LORD will roar from on high,
And utter His voice from His holy habitation;
He will roar mightily against His fold.
He will give a shout, as those who tread *the grapes,*
Against all the inhabitants of the earth.
³¹ A noise will come to the ends of the earth—
For the LORD has a controversy with the nations;
He will plead His case with all flesh.
He will give those *who are* wicked to the sword,'
says the LORD."

³²Thus says the LORD of hosts:

"Behold, disaster shall go forth
From nation to nation,
And a great whirlwind shall be raised up
From the farthest parts of the earth.

הַחֶ֗רֶב אֲשֶׁ֨ר אָנֹכִ֜י שֹׁלֵ֤חַ בֵּֽינֹתָם֙: 17 וָאֶקַּ֥ח אֶת־
הַכּ֖וֹס מִיַּ֣ד יְהֹוָ֑ה וָאַשְׁקֶה֙ אֶת־כׇּל־הַגּוֹיִ֔ם אֲשֶׁ֨ר
שְׁלָחַ֧נִי יְהֹוָ֛ה אֲלֵיהֶֽם: 18 אֶת־יְרוּשָׁלַ֙͏ִם֙ וְאֶת־עָרֵ֣י
יְהוּדָ֔ה וְאֶת־מְלָכֶ֖יהָ אֶת־שָׂרֶ֑יהָ לָתֵ֨ת אֹתָ֤ם לְחׇרְבָּה֙
לְשַׁמָּ֔ה לִשְׁרֵקָ֖ה וְלִקְלָלָ֑ה כַּיּ֖וֹם הַזֶּֽה: 19 אֶת־פַּרְעֹ֧ה
מֶֽלֶךְ־מִצְרַ֛יִם וְאֶת־עֲבָדָ֥יו וְאֶת־שָׂרָ֖יו וְאֶת־כׇּל־עַמּֽוֹ:
20 וְאֵת֙ כׇּל־הָעֶ֔רֶב וְאֵ֕ת כׇּל־מַלְכֵ֖י אֶ֣רֶץ הָע֑וּץ וְאֵת֙
כׇּל־מַלְכֵ֣י אֶ֣רֶץ פְּלִשְׁתִּ֔ים וְאֶת־אַשְׁקְל֥וֹן וְאֶת־עַזָּ֖ה
וְאֶת־עֶקְר֑וֹן וְאֵ֖ת שְׁאֵרִ֥ית אַשְׁדּֽוֹד: 21 אֶת־אֱד֣וֹם
וְאֶת־מוֹאָ֔ב וְאֶת־בְּנֵ֖י עַמּֽוֹן: 22 וְאֵת֙ כׇּל־מַלְכֵי־צֹ֔ר
וְאֵ֖ת כׇּל־מַלְכֵ֣י צִיד֑וֹן וְאֵת֙ מַלְכֵ֣י הָאִ֔י אֲשֶׁ֖ר בְּעֵ֥בֶר
הַיָּֽם: 23 וְאֶת־דְּדָ֤ן וְאֶת־תֵּימָא֙ וְאֶת־בּ֔וּז וְאֵ֖ת כׇּל־
קְצוּצֵ֥י פֵאָֽה: 24 וְאֵ֖ת כׇּל־מַלְכֵ֣י עֲרָ֑ב וְאֵ֕ת כׇּל־
מַלְכֵ֥י הָעֶ֖רֶב הַשֹּׁכְנִ֥ים בַּמִּדְבָּֽר: 25 וְאֵ֣ת ׀ כׇּל־מַלְכֵ֣י
זִמְרִ֗י וְאֵת֙ כׇּל־מַלְכֵ֣י עֵילָ֔ם וְאֵ֖ת כׇּל־מַלְכֵ֥י מָדָֽי:
26 וְאֵ֣ת ׀ כׇּל־מַלְכֵ֣י הַצָּפ֗וֹן הַקְּרֹבִ֤ים וְהָֽרְחֹקִים֙ אִ֣ישׁ
אֶל־אָחִ֔יו וְאֵת֙ כׇּל־הַמַּמְלְכ֣וֹת הָאָ֔רֶץ אֲשֶׁ֖ר עַל־פְּנֵ֣י
הָאֲדָמָ֑ה וּמֶ֥לֶךְ שֵׁשַׁ֖ךְ יִשְׁתֶּ֥ה אַחֲרֵיהֶֽם: 27 וְאָמַרְתָּ֣
אֲלֵיהֶ֗ם ס כֹּֽה־אָמַ֞ר יְהֹוָ֤ה צְבָאוֹת֙ אֱלֹהֵ֣י
יִשְׂרָאֵ֔ל שְׁת֤וּ וְשִׁכְרוּ֙ וּקְי֔וּ וְנִפְל֖וּ וְלֹ֣א תָק֑וּמוּ מִפְּנֵ֣י
הַחֶ֔רֶב אֲשֶׁ֛ר אָנֹכִ֥י שֹׁלֵ֖חַ בֵּינֵיכֶֽם: 28 וְהָיָ֗ה כִּ֤י יְמָֽאֲנוּ֙
לָקַֽחַת־הַכּ֤וֹס מִיָּֽדְךָ֙ לִשְׁתּ֔וֹת וְאָמַרְתָּ֣ אֲלֵיהֶ֔ם כֹּ֥ה
אָמַ֖ר יְהֹוָ֣ה צְבָא֑וֹת שָׁת֖וֹ תִשְׁתּֽוּ: 29 כִּי֩ הִנֵּ֨ה בָעִ֜יר
אֲשֶׁ֧ר נִקְרָֽא־שְׁמִ֣י עָלֶ֗יהָ אָֽנֹכִי֙ מֵחֵ֣ל לְהָרַ֔ע וְאַתֶּ֖ם
הִנָּקֵ֣ה תִנָּק֑וּ לֹ֣א תִנָּק֔וּ כִּ֣י חֶ֗רֶב אֲנִ֤י קֹרֵא֙ עַל־כׇּל־
יֹשְׁבֵ֣י הָאָ֔רֶץ נְאֻ֖ם יְהֹוָ֥ה צְבָאֽוֹת: 30 וְאַתָּה֙ תִּנָּבֵ֣א
אֲלֵיהֶ֔ם אֵ֥ת כׇּל־הַדְּבָרִ֖ים הָאֵ֑לֶּה וְאָמַרְתָּ֣ אֲלֵיהֶ֔ם
יְהֹוָ֞ה מִמָּר֤וֹם יִשְׁאָג֙ וּמִמְּע֤וֹן קׇדְשׁוֹ֙ יִתֵּ֣ן קוֹל֔וֹ שָׁאֹ֥ג
יִשְׁאַ֖ג עַל־נָוֵ֑הוּ הֵידָ֞ד כְּדֹרְכִ֣ים יַֽעֲנֶ֔ה אֶ֥ל כׇּל־יֹשְׁבֵ֖י
הָאָֽרֶץ: 31 בָּ֤א שָׁאוֹן֙ עַד־קְצֵ֣ה הָאָ֔רֶץ כִּ֣י רִ֤יב לַֽיהֹוָה֙
בַּגּוֹיִ֔ם נִשְׁפָּ֥ט ה֖וּא לְכׇל־בָּשָׂ֑ר הָרְשָׁעִ֛ים נְתָנָ֥ם לַחֶ֖רֶב
נְאֻם־יְהֹוָֽה: ס 32 כֹּ֤ה אָמַר֙ יְהֹוָ֣ה צְבָא֔וֹת
הִנֵּ֥ה רָעָ֛ה יֹצֵ֖את מִגּ֣וֹי אֶל־גּ֑וֹי וְסַ֣עַר גָּד֔וֹל יֵע֖וֹר

33 "And at that day the slain of the LORD shall be from *one* end of the earth even to the *other* end of the earth. They shall not be lamented, or gathered, or buried; they shall become refuse on the ground.

34 "Wail, shepherds, and cry!
　　Roll about *in the ashes*,
　　You leaders of the flock!
　　For the days of your slaughter and your
　　　　dispersions are fulfilled;
　　You shall fall like a precious vessel.
35 And the shepherds will have no way to flee,
　　Nor the leaders of the flock to escape.
36 A voice of the cry of the shepherds,
　　And a wailing of the leaders to the flock *will be
　　　　heard*.
　　For the LORD has plundered their pasture,
37 And the peaceful dwellings are cut down
　　Because of the fierce anger of the LORD.
38 He has left His lair like the lion;
　　For their land is desolate
　　Because of the fierceness of the Oppressor,
　　And because of His fierce anger."

26 In the beginning of the reign of Jehoiakim the son of Josiah, king of Judah, this word came from the LORD, saying, 2 "Thus says the LORD: 'Stand in the court of the LORD's house, and speak to all the cities of Judah, which come to worship *in* the LORD's house, all the words that I command you to speak to them. Do not diminish a word. 3 Perhaps everyone will listen and turn from his evil way, that I may relent concerning the calamity which I purpose to bring on them because of the evil of their doings.' 4 And you shall say to them, 'Thus says the LORD: "If you will not listen to Me, to walk in My law which I have set before you, 5 to heed the words of My servants the prophets whom I sent to you, both rising up early and sending *them* (but you have not heeded), 6 then I will make this house like Shiloh, and will make this city a curse to all the nations of the earth." ' "

7 So the priests and the prophets and all the people heard Jeremiah speaking these words in the house of the LORD. 8 Now it happened, when Jeremiah had made an end of speaking all that the LORD had commanded *him* to speak to all the people, that the priests and the prophets and all the people seized him, saying, "You will surely die! 9 Why have you prophesied in the name of the LORD, saying, 'This house shall be like Shiloh, and this city shall be desolate, without an inhabitant'?" And all the people were gathered against Jeremiah in the house of the LORD.

10 When the princes of Judah heard these things, they came up from the king's house to the house of the LORD and sat down in the entry of the New

מִיַּרְכְּתֵי־אָרֶץ: 33 וְהָיוּ חַלְלֵי יְהֹוָה בַּיּוֹם הַהוּא
מִקְצֵה הָאָרֶץ וְעַד־קְצֵה הָאָרֶץ לֹא יִסָּפְדוּ וְלֹא
יֵאָסְפוּ וְלֹא יִקָּבֵרוּ לְדֹמֶן עַל־פְּנֵי הָאֲדָמָה יִהְיוּ:
34 הֵילִילוּ הָרֹעִים וְזַעֲקוּ וְהִתְפַּלְּשׁוּ אַדִּירֵי הַצֹּאן
כִּי־מָלְאוּ יְמֵיכֶם לִטְבוֹחַ וּתְפוֹצוֹתִיכֶם וּנְפַלְתֶּם
כִּכְלִי חֶמְדָּה: 35 וְאָבַד מָנוֹס מִן־הָרֹעִים וּפְלֵיטָה
מֵאַדִּירֵי הַצֹּאן: 36 קוֹל צַעֲקַת הָרֹעִים וִילְלַת אַדִּירֵי
הַצֹּאן כִּי־שֹׁדֵד יְהֹוָה אֶת־מַרְעִיתָם: 37 וְנָדַמּוּ נְאוֹת
הַשָּׁלוֹם מִפְּנֵי חֲרוֹן אַף־יְהֹוָה: 38 עָזַב כַּכְּפִיר סֻכּוֹ
כִּי־הָיְתָה אַרְצָם לְשַׁמָּה מִפְּנֵי חֲרוֹן הַיּוֹנָה וּמִפְּנֵי
חֲרוֹן אַפּוֹ: פ

כו בְּרֵאשִׁית מַמְלְכוּת יְהוֹיָקִים בֶּן־יֹאשִׁיָּהוּ מֶלֶךְ
יְהוּדָה הָיָה הַדָּבָר הַזֶּה מֵאֵת יְהֹוָה לֵאמֹר: 2 כֹּה |
אָמַר יְהֹוָה עֲמֹד בַּחֲצַר בֵּית־יְהֹוָה וְדִבַּרְתָּ עַל־כָּל־
עָרֵי יְהוּדָה הַבָּאִים לְהִשְׁתַּחֲוֹת בֵּית־יְהֹוָה אֵת כָּל־
הַדְּבָרִים אֲשֶׁר צִוִּיתִיךָ לְדַבֵּר אֲלֵיהֶם אַל־תִּגְרַע
דָּבָר: 3 אוּלַי יִשְׁמְעוּ וְיָשֻׁבוּ אִישׁ מִדַּרְכּוֹ הָרָעָה
וְנִחַמְתִּי אֶל־הָרָעָה אֲשֶׁר אָנֹכִי חֹשֵׁב לַעֲשׂוֹת
לָהֶם מִפְּנֵי רֹעַ מַעַלְלֵיהֶם: 4 וְאָמַרְתָּ אֲלֵיהֶם
כֹּה אָמַר יְהֹוָה אִם־לֹא תִשְׁמְעוּ אֵלַי לָלֶכֶת
בְּתוֹרָתִי אֲשֶׁר נָתַתִּי לִפְנֵיכֶם: 5 לִשְׁמֹעַ עַל־דִּבְרֵי
עֲבָדַי הַנְּבִאִים אֲשֶׁר אָנֹכִי שֹׁלֵחַ אֲלֵיכֶם וְהַשְׁכֵּם
וְשָׁלֹחַ וְלֹא שְׁמַעְתֶּם: 6 וְנָתַתִּי אֶת־הַבַּיִת הַזֶּה
כְּשִׁלֹה וְאֶת־הָעִיר הַזֹּאתה אֶתֵּן לִקְלָלָה לְכֹל גּוֹיֵי
הָאָרֶץ: ס 7 וַיִּשְׁמְעוּ הַכֹּהֲנִים וְהַנְּבִאִים
וְכָל־הָעָם אֶת־יִרְמְיָהוּ מְדַבֵּר אֶת־הַדְּבָרִים הָאֵלֶּה
בְּבֵית יְהֹוָה: 8 וַיְהִי | כְּכַלּוֹת יִרְמְיָהוּ לְדַבֵּר אֵת
כָּל־אֲשֶׁר־צִוָּה יְהֹוָה לְדַבֵּר אֶל־כָּל־הָעָם וַיִּתְפְּשׂוּ
אֹתוֹ הַכֹּהֲנִים וְהַנְּבִאִים וְכָל־הָעָם לֵאמֹר מוֹת
תָּמוּת: 9 מַדּוּעַ נִבֵּיתָ בְשֵׁם־יְהֹוָה לֵאמֹר כְּשִׁלוֹ
יִהְיֶה הַבַּיִת הַזֶּה וְהָעִיר הַזֹּאת תֶּחֱרַב מֵאֵין
יוֹשֵׁב וַיִּקָּהֵל כָּל־הָעָם אֶל־יִרְמְיָהוּ בְּבֵית יְהֹוָה:
10 וַיִּשְׁמְעוּ | שָׂרֵי יְהוּדָה אֵת הַדְּבָרִים הָאֵלֶּה
וַיַּעֲלוּ מִבֵּית־הַמֶּלֶךְ בֵּית יְהֹוָה וַיֵּשְׁבוּ בְּפֶתַח

Gate of the LORD's *house.* ¹¹ And the priests and the prophets spoke to the princes and all the people, saying, "This man deserves to die! For he has prophesied against this city, as you have heard with your ears."

¹² Then Jeremiah spoke to all the princes and all the people, saying: "The LORD sent me to prophesy against this house and against this city with all the words that you have heard. ¹³ Now therefore, amend your ways and your doings, and obey the voice of the LORD your God; then the LORD will relent concerning the doom that He has pronounced against you. ¹⁴ As for me, here I am, in your hand; do with me as seems good and proper to you. ¹⁵ But know for certain that if you put me to death, you will surely bring innocent blood on yourselves, on this city, and on its inhabitants; for truly the LORD has sent me to you to speak all these words in your hearing."

¹⁶ So the princes and all the people said to the priests and the prophets, "This man does not deserve to die. For he has spoken to us in the name of the LORD our God."

¹⁷ Then certain of the elders of the land rose up and spoke to all the assembly of the people, saying: ¹⁸ "Micah of Moresheth prophesied in the days of Hezekiah king of Judah, and spoke to all the people of Judah, saying, 'Thus says the LORD of hosts:

"Zion shall be plowed *like* a field,
Jerusalem shall become heaps of ruins,
And the mountain of the temple
Like the bare hills of the forest." '

¹⁹ Did Hezekiah king of Judah and all Judah ever put him to death? Did he not fear the LORD and seek the LORD's favor? And the LORD relented concerning the doom which He had pronounced against them. But we are doing great evil against ourselves."

²⁰ Now there was also a man who prophesied in the name of the LORD, Urijah the son of Shemaiah of Kirjath Jearim, who prophesied against this city and against this land according to all the words of Jeremiah. ²¹ And when Jehoiakim the king, with all his mighty men and all the princes, heard his words, the king sought to put him to death; but when Urijah heard *it,* he was afraid and fled, and went to Egypt. ²² Then Jehoiakim the king sent men to Egypt: Elnathan the son of Achbor, and *other* men *who went* with him to Egypt. ²³ And they brought Urijah from Egypt and brought him to Jehoiakim the king, who killed him with the sword and cast his dead body into the graves of the common people.

שַׁעַר־יְהֹוָה הֶחָדָשׁ: ס ‏11 וַיֹּאמְר֤וּ הַכֹּהֲנִ֨ים
וְהַנְּבִאִים֙ אֶל־הַשָּׂרִ֔ים וְאֶל־כָּל־הָעָ֖ם לֵאמֹ֑ר מִשְׁפַּט־
מָ֙וֶת֙ לָאִ֣ישׁ הַזֶּ֔ה כִּ֣י נִבָּ֔א אֶל־הָעִ֖יר הַזֹּ֑את
כַּאֲשֶׁ֥ר שְׁמַעְתֶּ֖ם בְּאָזְנֵיכֶֽם: ‏12 וַיֹּ֤אמֶר יִרְמְיָ֙הוּ֙ אֶל־
כָּל־הַשָּׂרִ֔ים וְאֶל־כָּל־הָעָ֖ם לֵאמֹ֑ר יְהֹוָ֣ה שְׁלָחַ֗נִי
לְהִנָּבֵ֞א אֶל־הַבַּ֤יִת הַזֶּה֙ וְאֶל־הָעִ֣יר הַזֹּ֔את אֵ֖ת כָּל־
הַדְּבָרִ֖ים אֲשֶׁ֥ר שְׁמַעְתֶּֽם: ‏13 וְעַתָּ֗ה הֵיטִ֤יבוּ דַרְכֵיכֶם֙
וּמַ֣עַלְלֵיכֶ֔ם וְשִׁמְע֕וּ בְּק֖וֹל יְהֹוָ֣ה אֱלֹהֵיכֶ֑ם וְיִנָּחֵ֣ם
יְהֹוָ֔ה אֶל־הָ֣רָעָ֔ה אֲשֶׁ֥ר דִּבֶּ֖ר עֲלֵיכֶֽם: ‏14 וַאֲנִ֗י הִנְנִ֣י
בְיֶדְכֶ֑ם עֲשׂוּ־לִ֛י כַּטּ֥וֹב וְכַיָּשָׁ֖ר בְּעֵינֵיכֶֽם: ‏15 אַ֣ךְ ׀
יָדֹ֣עַ תֵּֽדְע֗וּ כִּ֣י אִם־מְמִתִ֣ים אַתֶּם֮ אֹתִי֒ כִּי־דָ֣ם נָקִ֗י
אַתֶּ֤ם נֹֽתְנִים֙ עֲלֵיכֶ֔ם וְאֶל־הָעִ֥יר הַזֹּ֖את וְאֶל־יֹֽשְׁבֶ֑יהָ
כִּ֣י בֶֽאֱמֶ֗ת שְׁלָחַ֤נִי יְהֹוָה֙ עֲלֵיכֶ֔ם לְדַבֵּר֙ בְּאָזְנֵיכֶ֔ם
אֵ֥ת כָּל־הַדְּבָרִ֖ים הָאֵֽלֶּה: ס ‏16 וַיֹּֽאמְר֤וּ
הַשָּׂרִים֙ וְכָל־הָעָ֔ם אֶל־הַכֹּהֲנִ֖ים וְאֶל־הַנְּבִיאִ֑ים אֵין־
לָאִ֤ישׁ הַזֶּה֙ מִשְׁפַּט־מָ֔וֶת כִּ֗י בְּשֵׁ֛ם יְהֹוָ֥ה אֱלֹהֵ֖ינוּ
דִּבֶּ֥ר אֵלֵֽינוּ: ‏17 וַיָּקֻ֣מוּ אֲנָשִׁ֔ים מִזִּקְנֵ֖י הָאָ֑רֶץ וַיֹּ֣אמְר֔וּ
אֶל־כָּל־קְהַ֥ל הָעָ֖ם לֵאמֹֽר: ‏18 מִיכָה֙ הַמּ֣וֹרַשְׁתִּ֔י
הָיָ֣ה נִבָּ֔א בִּימֵ֖י חִזְקִיָּ֣הֽוּ מֶֽלֶךְ־יְהוּדָ֑ה וַיֹּ֣אמֶר אֶל־
כָּל־עַ֣ם יְהוּדָה֮ לֵאמֹר֒ כֹּֽה־אָמַ֣ר ׀ יְהֹוָ֣ה צְבָא֗וֹת
צִיּ֞וֹן שָׂדֶ֤ה תֵֽחָרֵשׁ֙ וִירוּשָׁלַ֙יִם֙ עִיִּ֣ים תִּֽהְיֶ֔ה וְהַ֥ר
הַבַּ֖יִת לְבָמ֥וֹת יָֽעַר: ‏19 הֶֽהָמֵ֣ת הֱ֠מִתֻ֠הוּ חִזְקִיָּ֤הוּ
מֶֽלֶךְ־יְהוּדָה֙ וְכָל־יְהוּדָ֔ה הֲלֹא֙ יָרֵ֣א אֶת־יְהֹוָ֔ה וַיְחַל֙
אֶת־פְּנֵ֣י יְהֹוָ֔ה וַיִּנָּ֣חֶם יְהֹוָ֔ה אֶל־הָרָעָ֖ה אֲשֶׁר־דִּבֶּ֣ר
עֲלֵיהֶ֑ם וַאֲנַ֗חְנוּ עֹשִׂ֛ים רָעָ֥ה גְדוֹלָ֖ה עַל־נַפְשׁוֹתֵֽינוּ:

‏20 וְגַם־אִ֗ישׁ הָיָ֤ה מִתְנַבֵּא֙ בְּשֵׁ֣ם יְהֹוָ֔ה אוּרִיָּ֙הוּ֙ בֶּֽן־
שְׁמַעְיָ֔הוּ מִקִּרְיַ֖ת הַיְּעָרִ֑ים וַיִּנָּבֵ֞א עַל־הָעִ֤יר הַזֹּאת֙
וְעַל־הָאָ֣רֶץ הַזֹּ֔את כְּכֹ֖ל דִּבְרֵ֥י יִרְמְיָֽהוּ: ‏21 וַיִּשְׁמַ֣ע
הַמֶּֽלֶךְ־יְ֠הוֹיָקִ֠ים וְכָל־גִּבּוֹרָ֤יו וְכָל־הַשָּׂרִים֙ אֶת־דְּבָרָ֔יו
וַיְבַקֵּ֥שׁ הַמֶּ֖לֶךְ הֲמִית֑וֹ וַיִּשְׁמַ֤ע אוּרִיָּ֙הוּ֙ וַיִּרָ֔א וַיִּבְרַ֖ח
וַיָּבֹ֥א מִצְרָֽיִם: ‏22 וַיִּשְׁלַ֞ח הַמֶּ֧לֶךְ יְהוֹיָקִ֛ים אֲנָשִׁ֖ים
מִצְרָ֑יִם אֵ֣ת אֶלְנָתָ֧ן בֶּן־עַכְבּ֛וֹר וַאֲנָשִׁ֥ים אִתּ֖וֹ אֶל־
מִצְרָֽיִם: ‏23 וַיּוֹצִ֤יאוּ אֶת־אוּרִיָּ֙הוּ֙ מִמִּצְרַ֔יִם וַיְבִאֻ֖הוּ
אֶל־הַמֶּ֣לֶךְ יְהוֹיָקִ֔ים וַיַּכֵּ֖הוּ בֶּחָ֑רֶב וַיַּשְׁלֵךְ֙ אֶת־נִבְלָת֔וֹ

כו ‏18 מיכה

24 Nevertheless the hand of Ahikam the son of Shaphan was with Jeremiah, so that they should not give him into the hand of the people to put him to death.

27 In the beginning of the reign of Jehoiakim the son of Josiah, king of Judah, this word came to Jeremiah from the LORD, saying, 2 "Thus says the LORD to me: 'Make for yourselves bonds and yokes, and put them on your neck, 3 and send them to the king of Edom, the king of Moab, the king of the Ammonites, the king of Tyre, and the king of Sidon, by the hand of the messengers who come to Jerusalem to Zedekiah king of Judah. 4 And command them to say to their masters, "Thus says the LORD of hosts, the God of Israel—thus you shall say to your masters: 5 'I have made the earth, the man and the beast that *are* on the ground, by My great power and by My outstretched arm, and have given it to whom it seemed proper to Me. 6 And now I have given all these lands into the hand of Nebuchadnezzar the king of Babylon, My servant; and the beasts of the field I have also given him to serve him. 7 So all nations shall serve him and his son and his son's son, until the time of his land comes; and then many nations and great kings shall make him serve them. 8 And it shall be, *that* the nation and kingdom which will not serve Nebuchadnezzar the king of Babylon, and which will not put its neck under the yoke of the king of Babylon, that nation I will punish,' says the LORD, 'with the sword, the famine, and the pestilence, until I have consumed them by his hand. 9 Therefore do not listen to your prophets, your diviners, your dreamers, your soothsayers, or your sorcerers, who speak to you, saying, "You shall not serve the king of Babylon." 10 For they prophesy a lie to you, to remove you far from your land; and I will drive you out, and you will perish. 11 But the nations that bring their necks under the yoke of the king of Babylon and serve him, I will let them remain in their own land,' says the LORD, 'and they shall till it and dwell in it.'"'"

12 I also spoke to Zedekiah king of Judah according to all these words, saying, "Bring your necks under the yoke of the king of Babylon, and serve him and his people, and live! 13 Why will you die, you and your people, by the sword, by the famine, and by the pestilence, as the LORD has spoken against the nation that will not serve the king of Babylon? 14 Therefore do not listen to the words of the prophets who speak to you, saying, 'You shall not serve the king of Babylon,' for they prophesy a lie to you; 15 for I have not sent them,"

אֶל־קִבְרֵי בְּנֵי הָעָם: 24 אַךְ יַד אֲחִיקָם בֶּן־שָׁפָּן הָיְתָה אֶת־יִרְמְיָהוּ לְבִלְתִּי תֵּת־אֹתוֹ בְיַד־הָעָם לַהֲמִיתוֹ: פ

כז בְּרֵאשִׁית מַמְלֶכֶת יְהוֹיָקִם בֶּן־יֹאושִׁיָּהוּ מֶלֶךְ יְהוּדָה הָיָה הַדָּבָר הַזֶּה אֶל־יִרְמְיָה מֵאֵת יְהֹוָה לֵאמֹר: 2 כֹּה־אָמַר יְהֹוָה אֵלַי עֲשֵׂה לְךָ מוֹסֵרוֹת וּמֹטוֹת וּנְתַתָּם עַל־צַוָּארֶךָ: 3 וְשִׁלַּחְתָּם אֶל־מֶלֶךְ אֱדוֹם וְאֶל־מֶלֶךְ מוֹאָב וְאֶל־מֶלֶךְ בְּנֵי עַמּוֹן וְאֶל־מֶלֶךְ צֹר וְאֶל־מֶלֶךְ צִידוֹן בְּיַד מַלְאָכִים הַבָּאִים יְרוּשָׁלַ͏ִם אֶל־צִדְקִיָּהוּ מֶלֶךְ יְהוּדָה: 4 וְצִוִּיתָ אֹתָם אֶל־אֲדֹנֵיהֶם לֵאמֹר כֹּה־אָמַר יְהֹוָה צְבָאוֹת אֱלֹהֵי יִשְׂרָאֵל כֹּה תֹאמְרוּ אֶל־אֲדֹנֵיכֶם: 5 אָנֹכִי עָשִׂיתִי אֶת־הָאָרֶץ אֶת־הָאָדָם וְאֶת־הַבְּהֵמָה אֲשֶׁר עַל־פְּנֵי הָאָרֶץ בְּכֹחִי הַגָּדוֹל וּבִזְרוֹעִי הַנְּטוּיָה וּנְתַתִּיהָ לַאֲשֶׁר יָשַׁר בְּעֵינָי: 6 וְעַתָּה אָנֹכִי נָתַתִּי אֶת־כָּל־הָאֲרָצוֹת הָאֵלֶּה בְּיַד נְבוּכַדְנֶאצַּר מֶלֶךְ־בָּבֶל עַבְדִּי וְגַם אֶת־חַיַּת הַשָּׂדֶה נָתַתִּי לוֹ לְעָבְדוֹ: 7 וְעָבְדוּ אֹתוֹ כָּל־הַגּוֹיִם וְאֶת־בְּנוֹ וְאֶת־בֶּן־בְּנוֹ עַד בֹּא־עֵת אַרְצוֹ גַּם־הוּא וְעָבְדוּ בוֹ גּוֹיִם רַבִּים וּמְלָכִים גְּדֹלִים: 8 וְהָיָה הַגּוֹי וְהַמַּמְלָכָה אֲשֶׁר לֹא־יַעַבְדוּ אֹתוֹ אֶת־נְבוּכַדְנֶאצַּר מֶלֶךְ־בָּבֶל וְאֵת אֲשֶׁר לֹא־יִתֵּן אֶת־צַוָּארוֹ בְּעֹל מֶלֶךְ בָּבֶל בַּחֶרֶב וּבָרָעָב וּבַדֶּבֶר אֶפְקֹד עַל־הַגּוֹי הַהוּא נְאֻם־יְהֹוָה עַד־תֻּמִּי אֹתָם בְּיָדוֹ: 9 וְאַתֶּם אַל־תִּשְׁמְעוּ אֶל־נְבִיאֵיכֶם וְאֶל־קֹסְמֵיכֶם וְאֶל חֲלֹמֹתֵיכֶם וְאֶל־עֹנְנֵיכֶם וְאֶל־כַּשָּׁפֵיכֶם אֲשֶׁר־הֵם אֹמְרִים אֲלֵיכֶם לֵאמֹר לֹא תַעַבְדוּ אֶת־מֶלֶךְ בָּבֶל: 10 כִּי שֶׁקֶר הֵם נִבְּאִים לָכֶם לְמַעַן הַרְחִיק אֶתְכֶם מֵעַל אַדְמַתְכֶם וְהִדַּחְתִּי אֶתְכֶם וַאֲבַדְתֶּם: 11 וְהַגּוֹי אֲשֶׁר יָבִיא אֶת־צַוָּארוֹ בְּעֹל מֶלֶךְ־בָּבֶל וַעֲבָדוֹ וְהִנַּחְתִּיו עַל־אַדְמָתוֹ נְאֻם־יְהֹוָה וַעֲבָדָהּ וְיָשַׁב בָּהּ: 12 וְאֶל־צִדְקִיָּה מֶלֶךְ־יְהוּדָה דִּבַּרְתִּי כְּכָל־הַדְּבָרִים הָאֵלֶּה לֵאמֹר הָבִיאוּ אֶת־צַוְּארֵיכֶם בְּעֹל מֶלֶךְ־בָּבֶל וְעִבְדוּ אֹתוֹ וְעַמּוֹ וִחְיוּ: 13 לָמָּה תָמוּתוּ אַתָּה וְעַמֶּךָ בַּחֶרֶב בָּרָעָב וּבַדֶּבֶר כַּאֲשֶׁר דִּבֶּר יְהֹוָה אֶל־הַגּוֹי אֲשֶׁר לֹא־יַעֲבֹד אֶת־מֶלֶךְ בָּבֶל: 14 וְאַל־תִּשְׁמְעוּ אֶל־דִּבְרֵי הַנְּבִאִים הָאֹמְרִים אֲלֵיכֶם לֵאמֹר לֹא תַעַבְדוּ אֶת־מֶלֶךְ בָּבֶל כִּי שֶׁקֶר הֵם נִבְּאִים לָכֶם: 15 כִּי לֹא שְׁלַחְתִּים

says the LORD, "yet they prophesy a lie in My name, that I may drive you out, and that you may perish, you and the prophets who prophesy to you."

16 Also I spoke to the priests and to all this people, saying, "Thus says the LORD: 'Do not listen to the words of your prophets who prophesy to you, saying, "Behold, the vessels of the LORD's house will now shortly be brought back from Babylon"; for they prophesy a lie to you. 17 Do not listen to them; serve the king of Babylon, and live! Why should this city be laid waste? 18 But if they *are* prophets, and if the word of the LORD is with them, let them now make intercession to the LORD of hosts, that the vessels which are left in the house of the LORD, *in* the house of the king of Judah, and at Jerusalem, do not go to Babylon.'

19 "For thus says the LORD of hosts concerning the pillars, concerning the Sea, concerning the carts, and concerning the remainder of the vessels that remain in this city, 20 which Nebuchadnezzar king of Babylon did not take, when he carried away captive Jeconiah the son of Jehoiakim, king of Judah, from Jerusalem to Babylon, and all the nobles of Judah and Jerusalem— 21 yes, thus says the LORD of hosts, the God of Israel, concerning the vessels that remain in the house of the LORD, and in the house of the king of Judah and of Jerusalem: 22 'They shall be carried to Babylon, and there they shall be until the day that I visit them,' says the LORD. 'Then I will bring them up and restore them to this place.' "

28 And it happened in the same year, at the beginning of the reign of Zedekiah king of Judah, in the fourth year *and* in the fifth month, *that* Hananiah the son of Azur the prophet, who *was* from Gibeon, spoke to me in the house of the LORD in the presence of the priests and of all the people, saying, 2 "Thus speaks the LORD of hosts, the God of Israel, saying: 'I have broken the yoke of the king of Babylon. 3 Within two full years I will bring back to this place all the vessels of the LORD's house, that Nebuchadnezzar king of Babylon took away from this place and carried to Babylon. 4 And I will bring back to this place Jeconiah the son of Jehoiakim, king of Judah, with all the captives of Judah who went to Babylon,' says the LORD, 'for I will break the yoke of the king of Babylon.' "

5 Then the prophet Jeremiah spoke to the prophet Hananiah in the presence of the priests and in the presence of all the people who stood in the house of the LORD, 6 and the prophet Jeremiah said, "Amen! The LORD do so; the LORD perform your words which you have prophesied, to bring back the

וְהֵם נִבְּאִים בִּשְׁמִי לַשֶּׁקֶר לְמַעַן הַדִּיחִי
אֶתְכֶם וַאֲבַדְתֶּם אַתֶּם וְהַנְּבִאִים הַנִּבְּאִים לָכֶם:
וְאֶל־הַכֹּהֲנִים וְאֶל־כָּל־הָעָם הַזֶּה דִּבַּרְתִּי לֵאמֹר
כֹּה אָמַר יְהוָה אַל־תִּשְׁמְעוּ אֶל־דִּבְרֵי נְבִיאֵיכֶם
הַנִּבְּאִים לָכֶם לֵאמֹר הִנֵּה כְלֵי בֵית־יְהוָה מוּשָׁבִים
מִבָּבֶלָה עַתָּה מְהֵרָה כִּי שֶׁקֶר הֵמָּה נִבְּאִים לָכֶם:
17 אַל־תִּשְׁמְעוּ אֲלֵיהֶם עִבְדוּ אֶת־מֶלֶךְ־בָּבֶל וִחְיוּ
לָמָּה תִהְיֶה הָעִיר הַזֹּאת חָרְבָּה: 18 וְאִם־נְבִאִים
הֵם וְאִם־יֵשׁ דְּבַר־יְהוָה אִתָּם יִפְגְּעוּ־נָא בַּיהוָה
צְבָאוֹת לְבִלְתִּי־בֹאוּ הַכֵּלִים ׀ הַנּוֹתָרִים בְּבֵית־
יְהוָה וּבֵית מֶלֶךְ יְהוּדָה וִירוּשָׁלִַם בָּבֶלָה: פ
19 כִּי כֹה אָמַר יְהוָה צְבָאוֹת אֶל־הָעַמֻּדִים וְעַל־
הַיָּם וְעַל־הַמְּכֹנוֹת וְעַל יֶתֶר הַכֵּלִים הַנּוֹתָרִים
בָּעִיר הַזֹּאת: 20 אֲשֶׁר לֹא־לְקָחָם נְבוּכַדְנֶאצַּר
מֶלֶךְ בָּבֶל בַּגְלוֹתוֹ אֶת־יְכָנְיָה בֶן־יְהוֹיָקִים מֶלֶךְ־
יְהוּדָה מִירוּשָׁלִַם בָּבֶלָה וְאֵת כָּל־חֹרֵי יְהוּדָה
וִירוּשָׁלִָם: ס 21 כִּי כֹה אָמַר יְהוָה צְבָאוֹת
אֱלֹהֵי יִשְׂרָאֵל עַל־הַכֵּלִים הַנּוֹתָרִים בֵּית יְהוָה
וּבֵית מֶלֶךְ־יְהוּדָה וִירוּשָׁלִָם: 22 בָּבֶלָה יוּבָאוּ וְשָׁמָּה
יִהְיוּ עַד יוֹם פָּקְדִי אֹתָם נְאֻם־יְהוָה וְהַעֲלִיתִים
וַהֲשִׁיבֹתִים אֶל־הַמָּקוֹם הַזֶּה: פ

כח וַיְהִי ׀ בַּשָּׁנָה הַהִיא בְּרֵאשִׁית מַמְלֶכֶת
צִדְקִיָּה מֶלֶךְ־יְהוּדָה בַּשָּׁנָה הָרְבִעִית בַּחֹדֶשׁ
הַחֲמִישִׁי אָמַר אֵלַי חֲנַנְיָה בֶן־עַזּוּר הַנָּבִיא אֲשֶׁר
מִגִּבְעוֹן בְּבֵית יְהוָה לְעֵינֵי הַכֹּהֲנִים וְכָל־הָעָם
לֵאמֹר: 2 כֹּה־אָמַר יְהוָה צְבָאוֹת אֱלֹהֵי יִשְׂרָאֵל
לֵאמֹר שָׁבַרְתִּי אֶת־עֹל מֶלֶךְ בָּבֶל: 3 בְּעוֹד ׀
שְׁנָתַיִם יָמִים אֲנִי מֵשִׁיב אֶל־הַמָּקוֹם הַזֶּה אֶת־כָּל־
כְּלֵי בֵּית יְהוָה אֲשֶׁר לָקַח נְבוּכַדְנֶאצַּר מֶלֶךְ־בָּבֶל
מִן־הַמָּקוֹם הַזֶּה וַיְבִיאֵם בָּבֶל: 4 וְאֶת־יְכָנְיָה בֶן־
יְהוֹיָקִים מֶלֶךְ־יְהוּדָה וְאֶת־כָּל־גָּלוּת יְהוּדָה הַבָּאִים
בָּבֶלָה אֲנִי מֵשִׁיב אֶל־הַמָּקוֹם הַזֶּה נְאֻם־יְהוָה
כִּי אֶשְׁבֹּר אֶת־עֹל מֶלֶךְ בָּבֶל: 5 וַיֹּאמֶר יִרְמְיָה
הַנָּבִיא אֶל־חֲנַנְיָה הַנָּבִיא לְעֵינֵי הַכֹּהֲנִים וּלְעֵינֵי
כָל־הָעָם הָעֹמְדִים בְּבֵית יְהוָה: 6 וַיֹּאמֶר יִרְמְיָה

כז 20 יְכָנְיָה
כח 1 בַּשָּׁנָה

vessels of the LORD's house and all who were carried away captive, from Babylon to this place. ⁷Nevertheless hear now this word that I speak in your hearing and in the hearing of all the people: ⁸The prophets who have been before me and before you of old prophesied against many countries and great kingdoms—of war and disaster and pestilence. ⁹As for the prophet who prophesies of peace, when the word of the prophet comes to pass, the prophet will be known *as* one whom the LORD has truly sent."

¹⁰Then Hananiah the prophet took the yoke off the prophet Jeremiah's neck and broke it. ¹¹And Hananiah spoke in the presence of all the people, saying, "Thus says the LORD: 'Even so I will break the yoke of Nebuchadnezzar king of Babylon from the neck of all nations within the space of two full years.'" And the prophet Jeremiah went his way.

¹²Now the word of the LORD came to Jeremiah, after Hananiah the prophet had broken the yoke from the neck of the prophet Jeremiah, saying, ¹³"Go and tell Hananiah, saying, 'Thus says the LORD: "You have broken the yokes of wood, but you have made in their place yokes of iron." ¹⁴For thus says the LORD of hosts, the God of Israel: "I have put a yoke of iron on the neck of all these nations, that they may serve Nebuchadnezzar king of Babylon; and they shall serve him. I have given him the beasts of the field also."'"

¹⁵Then the prophet Jeremiah said to Hananiah the prophet, "Hear now, Hananiah, the LORD has not sent you, but you make this people trust in a lie. ¹⁶Therefore thus says the LORD: 'Behold, I will cast you from the face of the earth. This year you shall die, because you have taught rebellion against the LORD.'"

¹⁷So Hananiah the prophet died the same year in the seventh month.

29

Now these *are* the words of the letter that Jeremiah the prophet sent from Jerusalem to the remainder of the elders who were carried away captive—to the priests, the prophets, and all the people whom Nebuchadnezzar had carried away captive from Jerusalem to Babylon. ²(This happened after Jeconiah the king, the queen mother, the eunuchs, the princes of Judah and Jerusalem, the craftsmen, and the smiths had departed from Jerusalem.) ³*The letter was sent* by the hand of Elasah the son of Shaphan, and Gemariah the son of Hilkiah, whom Zedekiah king of Judah sent to Babylon, to Nebuchadnezzar king of Babylon, saying,

הַנָּבִיא אָמֵן כֵּן יַעֲשֶׂה יְהֹוָה יָקֵם יְהֹוָה אֶת־ דְּבָרֶיךָ אֲשֶׁר נִבֵּאתָ לְהָשִׁיב כְּלֵי בֵית־יְהֹוָה וְכָל־ הַגּוֹלָה מִבָּבֶל אֶל־הַמָּקוֹם הַזֶּה: 7 אַךְ־שְׁמַע־נָא הַדָּבָר הַזֶּה אֲשֶׁר אָנֹכִי דֹּבֵר בְּאָזְנֶיךָ וּבְאָזְנֵי כָּל־ הָעָם: 8 הַנְּבִיאִים אֲשֶׁר הָיוּ לְפָנַי וּלְפָנֶיךָ מִן־ הָעוֹלָם וַיִּנָּבְאוּ אֶל־אֲרָצוֹת רַבּוֹת וְעַל־מַמְלָכוֹת גְּדֹלוֹת לְמִלְחָמָה וּלְרָעָה וּלְדָבֶר: 9 הַנָּבִיא אֲשֶׁר יִנָּבֵא לְשָׁלוֹם בְּבֹא דְּבַר הַנָּבִיא יִוָּדַע הַנָּבִיא אֲשֶׁר־שְׁלָחוֹ יְהֹוָה בֶּאֱמֶת: 10 וַיִּקַּח חֲנַנְיָה הַנָּבִיא אֶת־הַמּוֹטָה מֵעַל צַוַּאר יִרְמְיָה הַנָּבִיא וַיִּשְׁבְּרֵהוּ: 11 וַיֹּאמֶר חֲנַנְיָה לְעֵינֵי כָל־הָעָם לֵאמֹר כֹּה אָמַר יְהֹוָה כָּכָה אֶשְׁבֹּר אֶת־עֹל | נְבֻכַדְנֶאצַּר מֶלֶךְ־בָּבֶל בְּעוֹד שְׁנָתַיִם יָמִים מֵעַל־צַוַּאר כָּל־הַגּוֹיִם וַיֵּלֶךְ יִרְמְיָה הַנָּבִיא לְדַרְכּוֹ: פ

12 וַיְהִי דְבַר־יְהֹוָה אֶל־יִרְמְיָה אַחֲרֵי שְׁבוֹר חֲנַנְיָה הַנָּבִיא אֶת־הַמּוֹטָה מֵעַל צַוַּאר יִרְמְיָה הַנָּבִיא לֵאמֹר: 13 הָלוֹךְ וְאָמַרְתָּ אֶל־חֲנַנְיָה לֵאמֹר כֹּה אָמַר יְהֹוָה מוֹטֹת עֵץ שָׁבָרְתָּ וְעָשִׂיתָ תַחְתֵּיהֶן מֹטוֹת בַּרְזֶל: 14 כִּי כֹה־אָמַר יְהֹוָה צְבָאוֹת אֱלֹהֵי יִשְׂרָאֵל עֹל בַּרְזֶל נָתַתִּי עַל־צַוַּאר | כָּל־הַגּוֹיִם הָאֵלֶּה לַעֲבֹד אֶת־נְבֻכַדְנֶאצַּר מֶלֶךְ־בָּבֶל וַעֲבָדֻהוּ וְגַם אֶת־חַיַּת הַשָּׂדֶה נָתַתִּי לוֹ: 15 וַיֹּאמֶר יִרְמְיָה הַנָּבִיא אֶל־חֲנַנְיָה הַנָּבִיא שְׁמַע־נָא חֲנַנְיָה לֹא־ שְׁלָחֲךָ יְהֹוָה וְאַתָּה הִבְטַחְתָּ אֶת־הָעָם הַזֶּה עַל־ שָׁקֶר: 16 לָכֵן כֹּה אָמַר יְהֹוָה הִנְנִי מְשַׁלֵּחֲךָ מֵעַל פְּנֵי הָאֲדָמָה הַשָּׁנָה אַתָּה מֵת כִּי־סָרָה דִבַּרְתָּ אֶל־ יְהֹוָה: 17 וַיָּמָת חֲנַנְיָה הַנָּבִיא בַּשָּׁנָה הַהִיא בַּחֹדֶשׁ הַשְּׁבִיעִי: פ

כט וְאֵלֶּה דִּבְרֵי הַסֵּפֶר אֲשֶׁר שָׁלַח יִרְמְיָה הַנָּבִיא מִירוּשָׁלִָם אֶל־יֶתֶר זִקְנֵי הַגּוֹלָה וְאֶל־ הַכֹּהֲנִים וְאֶל־הַנְּבִיאִים וְאֶל־כָּל־הָעָם אֲשֶׁר הֶגְלָה נְבוּכַדְנֶאצַּר מִירוּשָׁלִַם בָּבֶלָה: 2 אַחֲרֵי צֵאת יְכָנְיָה־ הַמֶּלֶךְ וְהַגְּבִירָה וְהַסָּרִיסִים שָׂרֵי יְהוּדָה וִירוּשָׁלִַם וְהֶחָרָשׁ וְהַמַּסְגֵּר מִירוּשָׁלִָם: 3 בְּיַד אֶלְעָשָׂה בֶן־ שָׁפָן וּגְמַרְיָה בֶּן־חִלְקִיָּה אֲשֶׁר שָׁלַח צִדְקִיָּה מֶלֶךְ־יְהוּדָה אֶל־נְבוּכַדְנֶאצַּר מֶלֶךְ בָּבֶל בָּבֶלָה

⁴ Thus says the LORD of hosts, the God of Israel, to all who were carried away captive, whom I have caused to be carried away from Jerusalem to Babylon:

⁵ Build houses and dwell *in them;* plant gardens and eat their fruit. ⁶ Take wives and beget sons and daughters; and take wives for your sons and give your daughters to husbands, so that they may bear sons and daughters—that you may be increased there, and not diminished. ⁷ And seek the peace of the city where I have caused you to be carried away captive, and pray to the LORD for it; for in its peace you will have peace. ⁸ For thus says the LORD of hosts, the God of Israel: Do not let your prophets and your diviners who are in your midst deceive you, nor listen to your dreams which you cause to be dreamed. ⁹ For they prophesy falsely to you in My name; I have not sent them, says the LORD.

¹⁰ For thus says the LORD: After seventy years are completed at Babylon, I will visit you and perform My good word toward you, and cause you to return to this place. ¹¹ For I know the thoughts that I think toward you, says the LORD, thoughts of peace and not of evil, to give you a future and a hope. ¹² Then you will call upon Me and go and pray to Me, and I will listen to you. ¹³ And you will seek Me and find *Me,* when you search for Me with all your heart. ¹⁴ I will be found by you, says the LORD, and I will bring you back from your captivity; I will gather you from all the nations and from all the places where I have driven you, says the LORD, and I will bring you to the place from which I cause you to be carried away captive.

¹⁵ Because you have said, "The LORD has raised up prophets for us in Babylon"— ¹⁶ therefore thus says the LORD concerning the king who sits on the throne of David, concerning all the people who dwell in this city, and concerning your brethren who have not gone out with you into captivity— ¹⁷ thus says the LORD of hosts: Behold, I will send on them the sword, the famine, and the pestilence, and will make them like rotten figs that cannot be eaten, they are so bad. ¹⁸ And I will pursue them with the sword, with famine, and with pestilence; and I will deliver them to trouble among all the kingdoms of the earth—to be a curse, an astonishment, a hissing, and a reproach among all the nations where I have driven them, ¹⁹ because they have not heeded My words, says the LORD, which I sent to them by My servants the prophets, rising up early and sending *them;* neither would you heed, says the LORD. ²⁰ Therefore hear the word of the LORD, all you of the captivity, whom I have sent from Jerusalem to Babylon:

²¹ Thus says the LORD of hosts, the God of Israel, concerning Ahab the son of Kolaiah, and Zedekiah the son of Maaseiah, who prophesy a lie to you in My name: Behold, I will deliver them

לֵאמֹר: ס ‏4 כֹּה אָמַר יְהוָה צְבָאוֹת אֱלֹהֵי יִשְׂרָאֵל לְכָל־הַגּוֹלָה אֲשֶׁר־הִגְלֵיתִי מִירוּשָׁלַ͏ִם בָּבֶלָה: ‏5 בְּנוּ בָתִּים וְשֵׁבוּ וְנִטְעוּ גַנּוֹת וְאִכְלוּ אֶת־פִּרְיָן: ‏6 קְחוּ נָשִׁים וְהוֹלִידוּ בָּנִים וּבָנוֹת וּקְחוּ לִבְנֵיכֶם נָשִׁים וְאֶת־בְּנוֹתֵיכֶם תְּנוּ לַאֲנָשִׁים וְתֵלַדְנָה בָּנִים וּבָנוֹת וּרְבוּ־שָׁם וְאַל־תִּמְעָטוּ: ‏7 וְדִרְשׁוּ אֶת־שְׁלוֹם הָעִיר אֲשֶׁר הִגְלֵיתִי אֶתְכֶם שָׁמָּה וְהִתְפַּלְלוּ בַעֲדָהּ אֶל־יְהוָה כִּי בִשְׁלוֹמָהּ יִהְיֶה לָכֶם שָׁלוֹם: פ ‏8 כִּי כֹה אָמַר יְהוָה צְבָאוֹת אֱלֹהֵי יִשְׂרָאֵל אַל־יַשִּׁיאוּ לָכֶם נְבִיאֵיכֶם אֲשֶׁר־בְּקִרְבְּכֶם וְקֹסְמֵיכֶם וְאַל־תִּשְׁמְעוּ אֶל־חֲלֹמֹתֵיכֶם אֲשֶׁר אַתֶּם מַחְלְמִים: ‏9 כִּי בְשֶׁקֶר הֵם נִבְּאִים לָכֶם בִּשְׁמִי לֹא שְׁלַחְתִּים נְאֻם־יְהוָה: ס ‏10 כִּי־כֹה אָמַר יְהוָה כִּי לְפִי מְלֹאת לְבָבֶל שִׁבְעִים שָׁנָה אֶפְקֹד אֶתְכֶם וַהֲקִמֹתִי עֲלֵיכֶם אֶת־דְּבָרִי הַטּוֹב לְהָשִׁיב אֶתְכֶם אֶל־הַמָּקוֹם הַזֶּה: ‏11 כִּי אָנֹכִי יָדַעְתִּי אֶת־הַמַּחֲשָׁבֹת אֲשֶׁר אָנֹכִי חֹשֵׁב עֲלֵיכֶם נְאֻם־יְהוָה מַחְשְׁבוֹת שָׁלוֹם וְלֹא לְרָעָה לָתֵת לָכֶם אַחֲרִית וְתִקְוָה: ‏12 וּקְרָאתֶם אֹתִי וַהֲלַכְתֶּם וְהִתְפַּלַּלְתֶּם אֵלָי וְשָׁמַעְתִּי אֲלֵיכֶם: ‏13 וּבִקַּשְׁתֶּם אֹתִי וּמְצָאתֶם כִּי תִדְרְשֻׁנִי בְּכָל־לְבַבְכֶם: ‏14 וְנִמְצֵאתִי לָכֶם נְאֻם־יְהוָה וְשַׁבְתִּי אֶת־שְׁבִיתְכֶם‏ְ וְקִבַּצְתִּי אֶתְכֶם מִכָּל־הַגּוֹיִם וּמִכָּל־הַמְּקוֹמוֹת אֲשֶׁר הִדַּחְתִּי אֶתְכֶם שָׁם נְאֻם־יְהוָה וַהֲשִׁבֹתִי אֶתְכֶם אֶל־הַמָּקוֹם אֲשֶׁר־הִגְלֵיתִי אֶתְכֶם מִשָּׁם: ‏15 כִּי אֲמַרְתֶּם הֵקִים לָנוּ יְהוָה נְבִאִים בָּבֶלָה: ס ‏16 כִּי כֹה אָמַר | יְהוָה אֶל־הַמֶּלֶךְ הַיּוֹשֵׁב אֶל־כִּסֵּא דָוִד וְאֶל־כָּל־הָעָם הַיּוֹשֵׁב בָּעִיר הַזֹּאת אֲחֵיכֶם אֲשֶׁר לֹא־יָצְאוּ אִתְּכֶם בַּגּוֹלָה: ‏17 כֹּה אָמַר יְהוָה צְבָאוֹת הִנְנִי מְשַׁלֵּחַ בָּם אֶת־הַחֶרֶב אֶת־הָרָעָב וְאֶת־הַדָּבֶר וְנָתַתִּי אוֹתָם כַּתְּאֵנִים הַשֹּׁעָרִים אֲשֶׁר לֹא־תֵאָכַלְנָה מֵרֹעַ: ‏18 וְרָדַפְתִּי אַחֲרֵיהֶם בַּחֶרֶב בָּרָעָב וּבַדָּבֶר וּנְתַתִּים לְזַעֲוָה‏ְ לְכֹל | מַמְלְכוֹת הָאָרֶץ לְאָלָה וּלְשַׁמָּה וְלִשְׁרֵקָה וּלְחֶרְפָּה בְּכָל־הַגּוֹיִם אֲשֶׁר־הִדַּחְתִּים שָׁם: ‏19 תַּחַת אֲשֶׁר־לֹא־שָׁמְעוּ אֶל־דְּבָרַי נְאֻם־יְהוָה אֲשֶׁר שָׁלַחְתִּי אֲלֵיהֶם אֶת־עֲבָדַי הַנְּבִאִים הַשְׁכֵּם וְשָׁלֹחַ וְלֹא שְׁמַעְתֶּם נְאֻם־יְהוָה: ‏20 וְאַתֶּם שִׁמְעוּ דְבַר־יְהוָה כָּל־הַגּוֹלָה אֲשֶׁר־שִׁלַּחְתִּי מִירוּשָׁלַ͏ִם בָּבֶלָה: ס ‏21 כֹּה־אָמַר יְהוָה צְבָאוֹת אֱלֹהֵי יִשְׂרָאֵל אֶל־אַחְאָב בֶּן־קוֹלָיָה

into the hand of Nebuchadnezzar king of Babylon, and he shall slay them before your eyes. ²²And because of them a curse shall be taken up by all the captivity of Judah who *are* in Babylon, saying, "The LORD make you like Zedekiah and Ahab, whom the king of Babylon roasted in the fire"; ²³because they have done disgraceful things in Israel, have committed adultery with their neighbors' wives, and have spoken lying words in My name, which I have not commanded them. Indeed I know, and *am* a witness, says the LORD.

24 You shall also speak to Shemaiah the Nehelamite, saying, ²⁵Thus speaks the LORD of hosts, the God of Israel, saying: You have sent letters in your name to all the people who *are* at Jerusalem, to Zephaniah the son of Maaseiah the priest, and to all the priests, saying, ²⁶"The LORD has made you priest instead of Jehoiada the priest, so that there should be officers *in* the house of the LORD over every man *who* is demented and considers himself a prophet, that you should put him in prison and in the stocks. ²⁷Now therefore, why have you not rebuked Jeremiah of Anathoth who makes himself a prophet to you? ²⁸For he has sent to us *in* Babylon, saying, 'This *captivity is* long; build houses and dwell *in them*, and plant gardens and eat their fruit.'"

29 Now Zephaniah the priest read this letter in the hearing of Jeremiah the prophet. ³⁰Then the word of the LORD came to Jeremiah, saying: ³¹Send to all those in captivity, saying, Thus says the LORD concerning Shemaiah the Nehelamite: Because Shemaiah has prophesied to you, and I have not sent him, and he has caused you to trust in a lie— ³²therefore thus says the LORD: Behold, I will punish Shemaiah the Nehelamite and his family: he shall not have anyone to dwell among this people, nor shall he see the good that I will do for My people, says the LORD, because he has taught rebellion against the LORD.

30

The word that came to Jeremiah from the LORD, saying, ²"Thus speaks the LORD God of Israel, saying: 'Write in a book for yourself all the words that I have spoken to you. ³For behold, the days are coming,' says the LORD, 'that I will bring back from captivity My people Israel and Judah,' says the LORD. 'And I will cause them to return to the land that I gave to their fathers, and they shall possess it.'"

⁴Now these *are* the words that the LORD spoke concerning Israel and Judah.

⁵"For thus says the LORD:

'We have heard a voice of trembling,
Of fear, and not of peace.
⁶ Ask now, and see,
Whether a man is ever in labor with child?

וְאֶל־צִדְקִיָּ֣הוּ בֶן־מַֽעֲשֵׂיָ֗ה הַנִּבְּאִ֥ים לָכֶ֛ם בִּשְׁמִ֖י שָׁ֑קֶר הִנְנִ֣י ׀ נֹתֵ֣ן אֹתָ֗ם בְּיַ֤ד נְבֽוּכַדְרֶאצַּר֙ מֶֽלֶךְ־בָּבֶ֔ל וְהִכָּ֖ם לְעֵינֵיכֶֽם: ²² וְלֻקַּ֨ח מֵהֶ֤ם קְלָלָה֙ לְכֹל֙ גָּל֣וּת יְהוּדָ֔ה אֲשֶׁ֣ר בְּבָבֶ֖ל לֵאמֹ֑ר יְשִֽׂמְךָ֤ יְהֹוָה֙ כְּצִדְקִיָּ֣הוּ וּכְאֶחָ֔ב אֲשֶׁר־קָלָ֥ם מֶֽלֶךְ־בָּבֶ֖ל בָּאֵֽשׁ: ²³ יַ֣עַן אֲשֶׁ֣ר עָשׂ֣וּ נְבָלָ֣ה בְּיִשְׂרָאֵ֗ל וַיְנַֽאֲפוּ֙ אֶת־נְשֵׁ֣י רֵֽעֵיהֶ֔ם וַיְדַבְּר֨וּ דָבָ֤ר בִּשְׁמִי֙ שֶׁ֔קֶר אֲשֶׁ֖ר ל֣וֹא צִוִּיתִ֑ם וְאָנֹכִ֛י הוּיֹודֵ֥עַ וָעֵ֖ד נְאֻם־יְהֹוָֽה: ס ²⁴ וְאֶל־שְׁמַֽעְיָ֥הוּ הַנֶּחֱלָמִ֖י תֹּאמַ֥ר לֵאמֹֽר: ²⁵ כֹּה־אָמַ֞ר יְהֹוָ֧ה צְבָא֛וֹת אֱלֹהֵ֥י יִשְׂרָאֵ֖ל לֵאמֹ֑ר יַ֣עַן אֲשֶׁ֣ר אַתָּ֡ה שָׁלַ֣חְתָּ בְשִׁמְכָ֣ה סְפָרִ֡ים אֶל־כָּל־הָעָ֣ם אֲשֶׁ֪ר בִּירֽוּשָׁלִַ֟ם וְאֶל־צְפַנְיָ֨ה בֶן־מַֽעֲשֵׂיָ֤ה הַכֹּהֵן֙ וְאֶ֥ל כָּל־הַכֹּֽהֲנִ֖ים לֵאמֹֽר: ²⁶ יְהֹוָ֞ה נְתָנְךָ֣ כֹהֵ֗ן תַּ֚חַת יְהֽוֹיָדָ֣ע הַכֹּהֵ֔ן לִֽהְי֤וֹת פְּקִדִים֙ בֵּ֣ית יְהֹוָ֔ה לְכָל־אִ֥ישׁ מְשֻׁגָּ֖ע וּמִתְנַבֵּ֑א וְנָֽתַתָּ֤ה אֹתוֹ֙ אֶל־הַמַּהְפֶּ֔כֶת וְאֶל־הַצִּינֹֽק: ²⁷ וְעַתָּ֕ה לָ֧מָּה לֹ֣א גָעַ֗רְתָּ בְּיִרְמְיָ֖הוּ הָֽעֲנְּתֹתִ֑י הַמִּתְנַבֵּ֖א לָכֶֽם: ²⁸ כִּ֣י עַל־כֵּ֞ן שָׁלַ֥ח אֵלֵ֛ינוּ בָּבֶ֖ל לֵאמֹ֑ר אֲרֻכָּ֣ה הִ֔יא בְּנ֥וּ בָתִּ֖ים וְשֵׁ֔בוּ וְנִטְע֣וּ גַנּ֔וֹת וְאִכְל֖וּ אֶת־פְּרִיהֶֽן: ²⁹ וַיִּקְרָ֞א צְפַנְיָ֤ה הַכֹּהֵן֙ אֶת־הַסֵּ֣פֶר הַזֶּ֔ה בְּאָזְנֵ֖י יִרְמְיָ֥הוּ הַנָּבִֽיא: פ ³⁰ וַֽיְהִי֙ דְּבַר־יְהֹוָ֔ה אֶֽל־יִרְמְיָ֖הוּ לֵאמֹֽר: ³¹ שְׁלַ֣ח עַל־כָּל־הַגּוֹלָה֮ לֵאמֹר֒ כֹּ֣ה אָמַ֣ר יְהֹוָ֗ה אֶל־שְׁמַֽעְיָ֣ה הַנֶּֽחֱלָמִ֑י יַ֡עַן אֲשֶׁר֩ נִבָּ֨א לָכֶ֜ם שְׁמַֽעְיָ֗ה וַֽאֲנִי֙ לֹ֣א שְׁלַחְתִּ֔יו וַיַּבְטַ֥ח אֶתְכֶ֖ם עַל־שָֽׁקֶר: ³² לָכֵ֞ן כֹּֽה־אָמַ֣ר יְהֹוָ֗ה הִנְנִ֨י פֹקֵ֜ד עַל־שְׁמַֽעְיָ֤ה הַנֶּֽחֱלָמִי֙ וְעַל־זַרְע֔וֹ לֹֽא־יִהְיֶ֥ה ל֣וֹ אִ֣ישׁ ׀ יֹושֵׁ֣ב ׀ בְּתֽוֹךְ־הָעָ֣ם הַזֶּ֗ה וְלֹֽא־יִרְאֶ֥ה בַטּ֛וֹב אֲשֶׁר־אֲנִ֥י עֹשֶֽׂה־לְעַמִּ֖י נְאֻם־יְהֹוָ֑ה כִּֽי־סָרָ֥ה דִבֶּ֖ר עַל־יְהֹוָֽה: ס

ל הַדָּבָר֙ אֲשֶׁ֣ר הָיָ֣ה אֶֽל־יִרְמְיָ֔הוּ מֵאֵ֥ת יְהֹוָ֖ה לֵאמֹֽר: ² כֹּֽה־אָמַ֧ר יְהֹוָ֛ה אֱלֹהֵ֥י יִשְׂרָאֵ֖ל לֵאמֹ֑ר כְּתָב־לְךָ֗ אֵ֧ת כָּל־הַדְּבָרִ֛ים אֲשֶׁר־דִּבַּ֥רְתִּי אֵלֶ֖יךָ אֶל־סֵֽפֶר: ³ כִּ֠י הִנֵּ֨ה יָמִ֤ים בָּאִים֙ נְאֻם־יְהֹוָ֔ה וְשַׁבְתִּ֗י אֶת־שְׁב֛וּת עַמִּ֥י יִשְׂרָאֵ֖ל וִֽיהוּדָה֙ אָמַ֣ר יְהֹוָ֔ה וַהֲשִֽׁבֹתִ֗ים אֶל־הָאָ֛רֶץ אֲשֶׁר־נָתַ֥תִּי לַֽאֲבוֹתָ֖ם וִירֵשֽׁוּהָ: פ ⁴ וְאֵ֣לֶּה הַדְּבָרִ֗ים אֲשֶׁ֨ר דִּבֶּ֧ר יְהֹוָ֛ה אֶל־יִשְׂרָאֵ֖ל וְאֶל־יְהוּדָֽה: ⁵ כִּי־כֹה֙ אָמַ֣ר יְהֹוָ֔ה ק֥וֹל חֲרָדָ֖ה שָׁמָ֑עְנוּ פַּ֖חַד וְאֵ֥ין שָׁלֽוֹם: ⁶ שַֽׁאֲלוּ־נָ֣א וּרְא֔וּ אִם־יֹלֵ֖ד זָכָ֑ר מַדּוּעַ֩ רָאִ֨יתִי כָל־גֶּ֜בֶר יָדָ֤יו עַל־חֲלָצָיו֙

So why do I see every man *with* his hands on his loins
Like a woman in labor,
And all faces turned pale?

7 Alas! For that day *is* great,
So that none *is* like it;
And it *is* the time of Jacob's trouble,
But he shall be saved out of it.

8 'For it shall come to pass in that day,'
Says the LORD of hosts,
'*That* I will break his yoke from your neck,
And will burst your bonds;
Foreigners shall no more enslave them.

9 But they shall serve the LORD their God,
And David their king,
Whom I will raise up for them.

10 'Therefore do not fear, O My servant Jacob,' says the LORD,
'Nor be dismayed, O Israel;
For behold, I will save you from afar,
And your seed from the land of their captivity.
Jacob shall return, have rest and be quiet,
And no one shall make *him* afraid.

11 For I *am* with you,' says the LORD, 'to save you;
Though I make a full end of all nations where I have scattered you,
Yet I will not make a complete end of you.
But I will correct you in justice,
And will not let you go altogether unpunished.'

12 "For thus says the LORD:

'Your affliction *is* incurable,
Your wound *is* severe.

13 *There is* no one to plead your cause,
That you may be bound up;
You have no healing medicines.

14 All your lovers have forgotten you;
They do not seek you;
For I have wounded you with the wound of an enemy,
With the chastisement of a cruel one,
For the multitude of your iniquities,
Because your sins have increased.

15 Why do you cry about your affliction?
Your sorrow *is* incurable.
Because of the multitude of your iniquities,
Because your sins have increased,
I have done these things to you.

16 'Therefore all those who devour you shall be devoured;
And all your adversaries, every one of them, shall go into captivity;
Those who plunder you shall become plunder,
And all who prey upon you I will make a prey.

17 For I will restore health to you
And heal you of your wounds,' says the LORD,
'Because they called you an outcast *saying:*
"This *is* Zion;
No one seeks her." '

18 "Thus says the LORD:

כְּיוֹלֵדָה וְנֶהֶפְכוּ כָל־פָּנִים לְיֵרָקוֹן: 7 הוֹי כִּי גָדוֹל
הַיּוֹם הַהוּא מֵאַיִן כָּמֹהוּ וְעֵת־צָרָה הִיא לְיַעֲקֹב
וּמִמֶּנָּה יִוָּשֵׁעַ: 8 וְהָיָה בַיּוֹם הַהוּא נְאֻם | יְהוָה
צְבָאוֹת אֶשְׁבֹּר עֻלּוֹ מֵעַל צַוָּארֶךָ וּמוֹסְרוֹתֶיךָ
אֲנַתֵּק וְלֹא־יַעַבְדוּ־בוֹ עוֹד זָרִים: 9 וְעָבְדוּ אֶת
יְהוָה אֱלֹהֵיהֶם וְאֵת דָּוִד מַלְכָּם אֲשֶׁר אָקִים
לָהֶם: ס 10 וְאַתָּה אַל־תִּירָא עַבְדִּי יַעֲקֹב
נְאֻם־יְהוָה וְאַל־תֵּחַת יִשְׂרָאֵל כִּי הִנְנִי מוֹשִׁיעֲךָ
מֵרָחוֹק וְאֶת־זַרְעֲךָ מֵאֶרֶץ שִׁבְיָם וְשָׁב יַעֲקֹב וְשָׁקַט
וְשַׁאֲנַן וְאֵין מַחֲרִיד: 11 כִּי־אִתְּךָ אֲנִי נְאֻם־יְהוָה
לְהוֹשִׁיעֶךָ כִּי אֶעֱשֶׂה כָלָה בְּכָל־הַגּוֹיִם | אֲשֶׁר
הֲפִצוֹתִיךָ שָּׁם אַךְ אֹתְךָ לֹא־אֶעֱשֶׂה כָלָה וְיִסַּרְתִּיךָ
לַמִּשְׁפָּט וְנַקֵּה לֹא אֲנַקֶּךָ: פ

12 כִּי כֹה אָמַר יְהוָה אָנוּשׁ לְשִׁבְרֵךְ נַחְלָה מַכָּתֵךְ:
13 אֵין־דָּן דִּינֵךְ לְמָזוֹר רְפֻאוֹת תְּעָלָה אֵין לָךְ:
14 כָּל־מְאַהֲבַיִךְ שְׁכֵחוּךְ אוֹתָךְ לֹא יִדְרֹשׁוּ כִּי מַכַּת
אוֹיֵב הִכִּיתִיךְ מוּסַר אַכְזָרִי עַל רֹב עֲוֹנֵךְ עָצְמוּ
חַטֹּאתָיִךְ: 15 מַה־תִּזְעַק עַל־שִׁבְרֵךְ אָנוּשׁ מַכְאֹבֵךְ
עַל | רֹב עֲוֹנֵךְ עָצְמוּ חַטֹּאתַיִךְ עָשִׂיתִי אֵלֶּה לָךְ:
16 לָכֵן כָּל־אֹכְלַיִךְ יֵאָכֵלוּ וְכָל־צָרַיִךְ כֻּלָּם בַּשְּׁבִי
יֵלֵכוּ וְהָיוּ שֹׁאסַיִךְ לִמְשִׁסָּה וְכָל־בֹּזְזַיִךְ אֶתֵּן לָבַז:
17 כִּי אַעֲלֶה אֲרֻכָה לָךְ וּמִמַּכּוֹתַיִךְ אֶרְפָּאֵךְ נְאֻם־
יְהוָה כִּי נִדָּחָה קָרְאוּ לָךְ צִיּוֹן הִיא דֹּרֵשׁ אֵין
לָהּ: ס 18 כֹּה | אָמַר יְהוָה הִנְנִי־שָׁב

'Behold, I will bring back the captivity of Jacob's tents,
And have mercy on his dwelling places;
The city shall be built upon its own mound,
And the palace shall remain according to its own plan.

19 Then out of them shall proceed thanksgiving
And the voice of those who make merry;
I will multiply them, and they shall not diminish;
I will also glorify them, and they shall not be small.

20 Their children also shall be as before,
And their congregation shall be established before Me;
And I will punish all who oppress them.

21 Their nobles shall be from among them,
And their governor shall come from their midst;
Then I will cause him to draw near,
And he shall approach Me;
For who is this who pledged his heart to approach Me?' says the LORD.

22 'You shall be My people,
And I will be your God.' "

23 Behold, the whirlwind of the LORD
Goes forth with fury,
A continuing whirlwind;
It will fall violently on the head of the wicked.

24 The fierce anger of the LORD will not return until He has done it,
And until He has performed the intents of His heart.
In the latter days you will consider it.

31 "At the same time," says the LORD, "I will be the God of all the families of Israel, and they shall be My people."

2 Thus says the LORD:

"The people who survived the sword
Found grace in the wilderness—
Israel, when I went to give him rest."

3 The LORD has appeared of old to me, *saying:*

"Yes, I have loved you with an everlasting love;
Therefore with lovingkindness I have drawn you.

4 Again I will build you, and you shall be rebuilt,
O virgin of Israel!
You shall again be adorned with your tambourines,
And shall go forth in the dances of those who rejoice.

5 You shall yet plant vines on the mountains of Samaria;
The planters shall plant and eat *them* as ordinary food.

6 For there shall be a day
When the watchmen will cry on Mount Ephraim,
'Arise, and let us go up *to* Zion,
To the LORD our God.' "

7 For thus says the LORD:

"Sing with gladness for Jacob,

שְׁבוּת֩ אָהֳלֵ֨י יַעֲק֜וֹב וּמִשְׁכְּנֹתָ֣יו אֲרַחֵ֗ם וְנִבְנְתָ֥ה
עִיר֙ עַל־תִּלָּ֔הּ וְאַרְמ֖וֹן עַל־מִשְׁפָּט֥וֹ יֵשֵֽׁב׃ 19 וְיָצָ֨א
מֵהֶ֤ם תּוֹדָה֙ וְק֣וֹל מְשַׂחֲקִ֔ים וְהִרְבִּתִ֖ים וְלֹ֣א יִמְעָ֑טוּ
וְהִכְבַּדְתִּ֖ים וְלֹ֥א יִצְעָֽרוּ׃ 20 וְהָי֤וּ בָנָיו֙ כְּקֶ֔דֶם וַעֲדָת֖וֹ
לְפָנַ֣י תִּכּ֑וֹן וּפָ֣קַדְתִּ֔י עַ֖ל כָּל־לֹחֲצָֽיו׃ 21 וְהָיָ֨ה אַדִּיר֜וֹ
מִמֶּ֗נּוּ וּמֹֽשְׁלוֹ֙ מִקִּרְבּ֣וֹ יֵצֵ֔א וְהִקְרַבְתִּ֖יו וְנִגַּ֣שׁ אֵלָ֑י
כִּי֩ מִ֨י הוּא־זֶ֜ה עָרַ֧ב אֶת־לִבּ֛וֹ לָגֶ֥שֶׁת אֵלַ֖י נְאֻם־
יְהוָֽה׃ 22 וִהְיִ֥יתֶם לִ֖י לְעָ֑ם וְאָ֣נֹכִ֔י אֶהְיֶ֥ה לָכֶ֖ם
לֵאלֹהִֽים׃ ס 23 הִנֵּ֣ה ׀ סַעֲרַ֣ת יְהוָ֗ה חֵמָה֙
יָֽצְאָ֔ה סַ֖עַר מִתְגּוֹרֵ֑ר עַ֛ל רֹ֥אשׁ רְשָׁעִ֖ים יָחֽוּל׃ 24 לֹ֣א
יָשׁ֗וּב חֲרוֹן֙ אַף־יְהוָ֔ה עַד־עֲשֹׂת֥וֹ וְעַד־הֲקִימ֖וֹ מְזִמּ֣וֹת
לִבּ֑וֹ בְּאַחֲרִ֥ית הַיָּמִ֖ים תִּתְבּ֥וֹנְנוּ בָֽהּ׃ 25 בָּעֵ֤ת הַהִיא֙
נְאֻם־יְהוָ֔ה אֶֽהְיֶה֙ לֵֽאלֹהִ֔ים לְכֹ֖ל מִשְׁפְּח֣וֹת יִשְׂרָאֵ֑ל
וְהֵ֖מָּה יִֽהְיוּ־לִ֥י לְעָֽם׃ ס

לא כֹּ֚ה אָמַ֣ר יְהוָ֔ה מָצָ֥א חֵן֙ בַּמִּדְבָּ֔ר עַ֖ם שְׂרִ֣ידֵי
חָ֑רֶב הָל֥וֹךְ לְהַרְגִּיע֖וֹ יִשְׂרָאֵֽל׃ 2 מֵרָח֕וֹק יְהוָ֖ה נִרְאָ֣ה
לִ֑י וְאַהֲבַ֤ת עוֹלָם֙ אֲהַבְתִּ֔יךְ עַל־כֵּ֖ן מְשַׁכְתִּ֥יךְ חָֽסֶד׃
3 ע֤וֹד אֶבְנֵךְ֙ וְֽנִבְנֵ֔ית בְּתוּלַ֖ת יִשְׂרָאֵ֑ל ע֚וֹד תַּעְדִּ֣י
תֻפַּ֔יִךְ וְיָצָ֖את בִּמְח֥וֹל מְשַׂחֲקִֽים׃ 4 ע֚וֹד תִּטְּעִ֣י
כְרָמִ֔ים בְּהָרֵ֖י שֹֽׁמְר֑וֹן נָטְע֥וּ נֹטְעִ֖ים וְחִלֵּֽלוּ׃ 5 כִּ֣י
יֶשׁ־י֔וֹם קָרְא֥וּ נֹצְרִ֖ים בְּהַ֣ר אֶפְרָ֑יִם ק֚וּמוּ וְנַעֲלֶ֣ה
צִיּ֔וֹן אֶל־יְהוָ֖ה אֱלֹהֵֽינוּ׃ פ
6 כִּי־כֹ֣ה ׀ אָמַ֣ר יְהוָ֗ה רָנּ֤וּ לְיַֽעֲקֹב֙ שִׂמְחָ֔ה וְצַהֲל֖וּ
בְּרֹ֣אשׁ הַגּוֹיִ֑ם הַשְׁמִ֤יעוּ הַֽלְלוּ֙ וְאִמְר֔וּ הוֹשַׁ֤ע יְהוָה֙
אֶֽת־עַמְּךָ֔ אֵ֖ת שְׁאֵרִ֣ית יִשְׂרָאֵֽל׃ 7 הִנְנִי֩ מֵבִ֨יא אוֹתָ֜ם
מֵאֶ֣רֶץ צָפ֗וֹן וְקִבַּצְתִּים֮ מִיַּרְכְּתֵי־אָרֶץ֒ בָּ֚ם עִוֵּ֣ר וּפִסֵּ֔חַ
הָרָ֥ה וְיֹלֶ֖דֶת יַחְדָּ֑ו קָהָ֥ל גָּד֖וֹל יָשׁ֥וּבוּ הֵֽנָּה׃ 8 בִּבְכִ֣י
יָבֹ֗אוּ וּֽבְתַחֲנוּנִים֮ אֽוֹבִילֵם֒ אֽוֹלִיכֵם֙ אֶל־נַ֣חֲלֵי מַ֔יִם
בְּדֶ֣רֶךְ יָשָׁ֔ר לֹ֥א יִכָּשְׁל֖וּ בָּ֑הּ כִּֽי־הָיִ֤יתִי לְיִשְׂרָאֵל֙

And shout among the chief of the nations;
Proclaim, give praise, and say,
'O LORD, save Your people,
The remnant of Israel!'
8 Behold, I will bring them from the north country,
And gather them from the ends of the earth,
Among them the blind and the lame,
The woman with child
And the one who labors with child, together;
A great throng shall return there.
9 They shall come with weeping,
And with supplications I will lead them.
I will cause them to walk by the rivers of waters,
In a straight way in which they shall not stumble;
For I am a Father to Israel,
And Ephraim *is* My firstborn.

10 "Hear the word of the LORD, O nations,
And declare *it* in the isles afar off, and say,
'He who scattered Israel will gather him,
And keep him as a shepherd *does* his flock.'
11 For the LORD has redeemed Jacob,
And ransomed him from the hand of one
stronger than he.
12 Therefore they shall come and sing in the height
of Zion,
Streaming to the goodness of the LORD—
For wheat and new wine and oil,
For the young of the flock and the herd;
Their souls shall be like a well-watered garden,
And they shall sorrow no more at all.
13 "Then shall the virgin rejoice in the dance,
And the young men and the old, together;
For I will turn their mourning to joy,
Will comfort them,
And make them rejoice rather than sorrow.
14 I will satiate the soul of the priests with
abundance,
And My people shall be satisfied with My
goodness, says the LORD."

15 Thus says the LORD:

"A voice was heard in Ramah,
Lamentation *and* bitter weeping,
Rachel weeping for her children,
Refusing to be comforted for her children,
Because they *are* no more."

16 Thus says the LORD:

"Refrain your voice from weeping,
And your eyes from tears;
For your work shall be rewarded, says the LORD,
And they shall come back from the land of the
enemy.
17 There is hope in your future, says the LORD,
That *your* children shall come back to their own
border.
18 "I have surely heard Ephraim bemoaning himself:
'You have chastised me, and I was chastised,
Like an untrained bull;
Restore me, and I will return,
For You *are* the LORD my God.

לְאָב וְאֶפְרַיִם בְּכֹרִי הוּא׃ ס 9 שִׁמְעוּ

דְבַר־יְהֹוָה גּוֹיִם וְהַגִּידוּ בָאִיִּים מִמֶּרְחָק וְאִמְרוּ

מְזָרֵה יִשְׂרָאֵל יְקַבְּצֶנּוּ וּשְׁמָרוֹ כְּרֹעֶה עֶדְרוֹ׃ 10 כִּי־

פָדָה יְהֹוָה אֶת־יַעֲקֹב וּגְאָלוֹ מִיַּד חָזָק מִמֶּנּוּ׃

11 וּבָאוּ וְרִנְּנוּ בִמְרוֹם־צִיּוֹן וְנָהֲרוּ אֶל־טוּב יְהֹוָה

עַל־דָּגָן וְעַל־תִּירֹשׁ וְעַל־יִצְהָר וְעַל־בְּנֵי־צֹאן וּבָקָר

וְהָיְתָה נַפְשָׁם כְּגַן רָוֶה וְלֹא־יוֹסִיפוּ לְדַאֲבָה עוֹד׃

12 אָז תִּשְׂמַח בְּתוּלָה בְּמָחוֹל וּבַחֻרִים וּזְקֵנִים

יַחְדָּו וְהָפַכְתִּי אֶבְלָם לְשָׂשׂוֹן וְנִחַמְתִּים וְשִׂמַּחְתִּים

מִיגוֹנָם׃ 13 וְרִוֵּיתִי נֶפֶשׁ הַכֹּהֲנִים דֶּשֶׁן וְעַמִּי אֶת־

טוּבִי יִשְׂבָּעוּ נְאֻם־יְהֹוָה׃ ס 14 כֹּה |

אָמַר יְהֹוָה קוֹל בְּרָמָה נִשְׁמָע נְהִי בְּכִי תַמְרוּרִים

רָחֵל מְבַכָּה עַל־בָּנֶיהָ מֵאֲנָה לְהִנָּחֵם עַל־בָּנֶיהָ

כִּי אֵינֶנּוּ׃ ס 15 כֹּה | אָמַר יְהֹוָה

מִנְעִי קוֹלֵךְ מִבֶּכִי וְעֵינַיִךְ מִדִּמְעָה כִּי יֵשׁ

שָׂכָר לִפְעֻלָּתֵךְ נְאֻם־יְהֹוָה וְשָׁבוּ מֵאֶרֶץ אוֹיֵב׃

16 וְיֵשׁ־תִּקְוָה לְאַחֲרִיתֵךְ נְאֻם־יְהֹוָה וְשָׁבוּ בָנִים

לִגְבוּלָם׃ ס 17 שָׁמוֹעַ שָׁמַעְתִּי אֶפְרַיִם

מִתְנוֹדֵד יִסַּרְתַּנִי וָאִוָּסֵר כְּעֵגֶל לֹא לֻמָּד הֲשִׁיבֵנִי

19 Surely, after my turning, I repented;
And after I was instructed, I struck myself on the thigh;
I was ashamed, yes, even humiliated,
Because I bore the reproach of my youth.'
20 Is Ephraim My dear son?
Is he a pleasant child?
For though I spoke against him,
I earnestly remember him still;
Therefore My heart yearns for him;
I will surely have mercy on him, says the LORD.

21 "Set up signposts,
Make landmarks;
Set your heart toward the highway,
The way in which you went.
Turn back, O virgin of Israel,
Turn back to these your cities.
22 How long will you gad about,
O you backsliding daughter?
For the LORD has created a new thing in the earth—
A woman shall encompass a man."

23 Thus says the LORD of hosts, the God of Israel: "They shall again use this speech in the land of Judah and in its cities, when I bring back their captivity: 'The LORD bless you, O home of justice, and mountain of holiness!' 24 And there shall dwell in Judah itself, and in all its cities together, farmers and those going out with flocks. 25 For I have satiated the weary soul, and I have replenished every sorrowful soul."

26 After this I awoke and looked around, and my sleep was sweet to me.

27 "Behold, the days are coming, says the LORD, that I will sow the house of Israel and the house of Judah with the seed of man and the seed of beast. 28 And it shall come to pass, that as I have watched over them to pluck up, to break down, to throw down, to destroy, and to afflict, so I will watch over them to build and to plant, says the LORD. 29 In those days they shall say no more:

'The fathers have eaten sour grapes,
And the children's teeth are set on edge.'

30 But every one shall die for his own iniquity; every man who eats the sour grapes, his teeth shall be set on edge.

31 "Behold, the days are coming, says the LORD, when I will make a new covenant with the house of Israel and with the house of Judah— 32 not according to the covenant that I made with their fathers in the day that I took them by the hand to lead them out of the land of Egypt, My covenant which they broke, though I was a husband to them, says the LORD. 33 But this is the covenant that I will make with the house of Israel after those days, says the LORD: I will put My law in their minds, and

וְאָשׁוּבָה כִּי אַתָּה יְהוָה אֱלֹהָי: 18 כִּי־אַחֲרֵי שׁוּבִי נִחַמְתִּי וְאַחֲרֵי הִוָּדְעִי סָפַקְתִּי עַל־יָרֵךְ בֹּשְׁתִּי וְגַם־נִכְלַמְתִּי כִּי נָשָׂאתִי חֶרְפַּת נְעוּרָי: 19 הֲבֵן יַקִּיר לִי אֶפְרַיִם אִם יֶלֶד שַׁעֲשֻׁעִים כִּי־מִדֵּי דַבְּרִי בּוֹ זָכֹר אֶזְכְּרֶנּוּ עוֹד עַל־כֵּן הָמוּ מֵעַי לוֹ רַחֵם אֲרַחֲמֶנּוּ נְאֻם־יְהוָה: ס 20 הַצִּיבִי לָךְ צִיֻּנִים שִׂמִי לָךְ תַּמְרוּרִים שִׁתִי לִבֵּךְ לַמְסִלָּה דֶּרֶךְ הָלָכְתְּ שׁוּבִי בְּתוּלַת יִשְׂרָאֵל שֻׁבִי אֶל־עָרַיִךְ אֵלֶּה: 21 עַד־מָתַי תִּתְחַמָּקִין הַבַּת הַשּׁוֹבֵבָה כִּי־בָרָא יְהוָה חֲדָשָׁה בָּאָרֶץ נְקֵבָה תְּסוֹבֵב גָּבֶר: ס 22 כֹּה־אָמַר יְהוָה צְבָאוֹת אֱלֹהֵי יִשְׂרָאֵל עוֹד יֹאמְרוּ אֶת־הַדָּבָר הַזֶּה בְּאֶרֶץ יְהוּדָה וּבְעָרָיו בְּשׁוּבִי אֶת־שְׁבוּתָם יְבָרֶכְךָ יְהוָה נְוֵה־צֶדֶק הַר הַקֹּדֶשׁ: 23 וְיָשְׁבוּ בָהּ יְהוּדָה וְכָל־עָרָיו יַחְדָּו אִכָּרִים וְנָסְעוּ בַּעֵדֶר: 24 כִּי הִרְוֵיתִי נֶפֶשׁ עֲיֵפָה וְכָל־נֶפֶשׁ דָּאֲבָה מִלֵּאתִי: 25 עַל־זֹאת הֱקִיצֹתִי וָאֶרְאֶה וּשְׁנָתִי עָרְבָה לִּי: ס 26 הִנֵּה יָמִים בָּאִים נְאֻם־יְהוָה וְזָרַעְתִּי אֶת־בֵּית יִשְׂרָאֵל וְאֶת־בֵּית יְהוּדָה זֶרַע אָדָם וְזֶרַע בְּהֵמָה: 27 וְהָיָה כַּאֲשֶׁר שָׁקַדְתִּי עֲלֵיהֶם לִנְתוֹשׁ וְלִנְתוֹץ וְלַהֲרֹס וּלְהַאֲבִיד וּלְהָרֵעַ כֵּן אֶשְׁקֹד עֲלֵיהֶם לִבְנוֹת וְלִנְטוֹעַ נְאֻם־יְהוָה: 28 בַּיָּמִים הָהֵם לֹא־יֹאמְרוּ עוֹד אָבוֹת אָכְלוּ בֹסֶר וְשִׁנֵּי בָנִים תִּקְהֶינָה: 29 כִּי אִם־אִישׁ בַּעֲוֹנוֹ יָמוּת כָּל־הָאָדָם הָאֹכֵל הַבֹּסֶר תִּקְהֶינָה שִׁנָּיו: ס 30 הִנֵּה יָמִים בָּאִים נְאֻם־יְהוָה וְכָרַתִּי אֶת־בֵּית יִשְׂרָאֵל וְאֶת־בֵּית יְהוּדָה בְּרִית חֲדָשָׁה: 31 לֹא כַבְּרִית אֲשֶׁר כָּרַתִּי אֶת־אֲבוֹתָם בְּיוֹם הֶחֱזִיקִי בְיָדָם לְהוֹצִיאָם מֵאֶרֶץ מִצְרָיִם אֲשֶׁר־הֵמָּה הֵפֵרוּ אֶת־בְּרִיתִי וְאָנֹכִי בָּעַלְתִּי בָם נְאֻם־יְהוָה: 32 כִּי זֹאת הַבְּרִית אֲשֶׁר אֶכְרֹת אֶת־בֵּית יִשְׂרָאֵל אַחֲרֵי הַיָּמִים הָהֵם נְאֻם־יְהוָה נָתַתִּי אֶת־תּוֹרָתִי בְּקִרְבָּם וְעַל־לִבָּם אֶכְתֲּבֶנָּה וְהָיִיתִי לָהֶם

לא 20 הֲלֹכְתְּ

write it on their hearts; and I will be their God, and
they shall be My people. 34 No more shall every
man teach his neighbor, and every man his brother,
saying, 'Know the LORD,' for they all shall know
Me, from the least of them to the greatest of them,
says the LORD. For I will forgive their iniquity, and
their sin I will remember no more."

35　Thus says the LORD,
　　Who gives the sun for a light by day,
　　The ordinances of the moon and the stars for a
　　　　light by night,
　　Who disturbs the sea,
　　And its waves roar
　　(The LORD of hosts is His name):

36　"If those ordinances depart
　　From before Me, says the LORD,
　　Then the seed of Israel shall also cease
　　From being a nation before Me forever."

37 Thus says the LORD:

　　"If heaven above can be measured,
　　And the foundations of the earth searched out
　　　　beneath,
　　I will also cast off all the seed of Israel
　　For all that they have done, says the LORD.

38 "Behold, the days are coming, says the LORD,
that the city shall be built for the LORD from the
Tower of Hananel to the Corner Gate. 39 The
surveyor's line shall again extend straight forward
over the hill Gareb; then it shall turn toward Goath.
40 And the whole valley of the dead bodies and of
the ashes, and all the fields as far as the Brook
Kidron, to the corner of the Horse Gate toward the
east, shall be holy to the LORD. It shall not be
plucked up or thrown down anymore forever."

32　The word that came to Jeremiah from the
LORD in the tenth year of Zedekiah king of Judah,
which was the eighteenth year of Nebuchadnezzar.
2 For then the king of Babylon's army besieged
Jerusalem, and Jeremiah the prophet was shut up in
the court of the prison, which was in the king of
Judah's house. 3 For Zedekiah king of Judah had
shut him up, saying, "Why do you prophesy and
say, 'Thus says the LORD: "Behold, I will give this
city into the hand of the king of Babylon, and he
shall take it; 4 and Zedekiah king of Judah shall not
escape from the hand of the Chaldeans, but shall
surely be delivered into the hand of the king of
Babylon, and shall speak with him face to face, and
see him eye to eye; 5 then he shall lead Zedekiah to
Babylon, and there he shall be until I visit him,"
says the LORD; "though you fight with the
Chaldeans, you shall not succeed" '?"

לֵאלֹהִ֔ים וְהֵ֖מָּה יִֽהְיוּ־לִ֥י לְעָֽם׃ 33 וְלֹ֣א יְלַמְּד֣וּ
ע֗וֹד אִ֣ישׁ אֶת־רֵעֵ֜הוּ וְאִ֤ישׁ אֶת־אָחִיו֙ לֵאמֹ֔ר דְּע֖וּ
אֶת־יְהֹוָ֑ה כִּֽי־כוּלָּם֩ יֵדְע֨וּ אוֹתִ֜י לְמִקְּטַנָּ֤ם וְעַד־
גְּדוֹלָם֙ נְאֻם־יְהֹוָ֔ה כִּ֤י אֶסְלַח֙ לַֽעֲוֹנָ֔ם וּלְחַטָּאתָ֖ם
לֹ֥א אֶזְכׇּר־עֽוֹד׃ ס 34 כֹּ֣ה ׀ אָמַ֣ר יְהֹוָ֗ה
נֹתֵ֥ן שֶׁ֙מֶשׁ֙ לְא֣וֹר יוֹמָ֔ם חֻקֹּ֛ת יָרֵ֥חַ וְכֽוֹכָבִ֖ים לְא֣וֹר
לָ֑יְלָה רֹגַ֤ע הַיָּם֙ וַיֶּֽהֱמ֣וּ גַלָּ֔יו יְהֹוָ֥ה צְבָא֖וֹת שְׁמֽוֹ׃
35 אִם־יָמֻ֜שׁוּ הַֽחֻקִּ֤ים הָאֵ֙לֶּה֙ מִלְּפָנַ֔י נְאֻם־יְהֹוָ֑ה
גַּם֩ זֶ֨רַע יִשְׂרָאֵ֜ל יִשְׁבְּת֗וּ מִֽהְי֥וֹת גּ֛וֹי לְפָנַ֖י כׇּל־
הַיָּמִֽים׃ ס 36 כֹּ֣ה ׀ אָמַ֣ר יְהֹוָ֗ה אִם־יִמַּ֤דּוּ
שָׁמַ֙יִם֙ מִלְמַ֔עְלָה וְיֵחָקְר֥וּ מֽוֹסְדֵי־אֶ֖רֶץ לְמָ֑טָּה גַּם־
אֲנִ֞י אֶמְאַ֨ס בְּכׇל־זֶ֧רַע יִשְׂרָאֵ֛ל עַֽל־כׇּל־אֲשֶׁ֥ר עָשׂ֖וּ
נְאֻם־יְהֹוָֽה׃ ס 37 הִנֵּ֛ה יָמִ֥ים נָאֻם־
יְהֹוָ֑ה וְנִבְנְתָ֤ה הָעִיר֙ לַֽיהֹוָ֔ה מִמִּגְדַּ֥ל חֲנַנְאֵ֖ל שַׁ֥עַר
הַפִּנָּֽה׃ 38 וְיָצָ֨א ע֜וֹד *קָוֵ֤ה* הַמִּדָּה֙ נֶגְדּ֔וֹ עַ֖ל גִּבְעַ֣ת
גָּרֵ֑ב וְנָסַ֖ב גֹּֽעָֽתָה׃ 39 וְכׇל־הָעֵ֣מֶק הַפְּגָרִ֣ים ׀ וְהַדֶּ֗שֶׁן
וְכׇל־*הַשְּׁרֵמוֹת֙* עַד־נַ֣חַל קִדְר֗וֹן עַד־פִּנַּ֞ת שַׁ֤עַר
הַסּוּסִים֙ מִזְרָ֔חָה קֹ֖דֶשׁ לַֽיהֹוָ֑ה לֹֽא־יִנָּתֵ֧שׁ וְלֹֽא־יֵהָרֵ֛ס
ע֖וֹד לְעוֹלָֽם׃ ס

לב הַדָּבָ֞ר אֲשֶׁר־הָיָ֤ה אֶֽל־יִרְמְיָ֙הוּ֙ מֵאֵ֣ת יְהֹוָ֔ה
בַּשָּׁנַת֙ הָֽעֲשִׂרִ֔ת לְצִדְקִיָּ֖הוּ מֶ֣לֶךְ יְהוּדָ֑ה הִ֧יא
הַשָּׁנָ֛ה שְׁמֹנֶֽה־עֶשְׂרֵ֥ה שָׁנָ֖ה לִנְבֽוּכַדְרֶאצַּֽר׃ 2 וְאָ֗ז
חֵ֚יל מֶ֣לֶךְ בָּבֶ֔ל צָרִ֖ים עַל־יְרֽוּשָׁלָ֑͏ִם וְיִרְמְיָ֙הוּ֙ הַנָּבִ֔יא
הָיָ֣ה כָל֔וּא בַּֽחֲצַ֖ר הַמַּטָּרָ֑ה אֲשֶׁ֖ר בֵּֽית־מֶ֥לֶךְ יְהוּדָֽה׃
3 אֲשֶׁ֣ר כְּלָא֔וֹ צִדְקִיָּ֥הוּ מֶֽלֶךְ־יְהוּדָ֖ה לֵאמֹ֑ר מַדּ֩וּעַ֩
אַתָּ֨ה נִבָּ֜א לֵאמֹ֗ר כֹּ֚ה אָמַ֣ר יְהֹוָ֔ה הִנְנִ֨י נֹתֵ֜ן אֶת־
הָעִ֥יר הַזֹּ֛את בְּיַ֥ד מֶֽלֶךְ־בָּבֶ֖ל וּלְכָדָֽהּ׃ 4 וְצִדְקִיָּ֣הוּ
מֶ֣לֶךְ יְהוּדָ֗ה לֹ֤א יִמָּלֵט֙ מִיַּ֣ד הַכַּשְׂדִּ֔ים כִּ֣י הִנָּתֹ֤ן
יִנָּתֵן֙ בְּיַ֣ד מֶֽלֶךְ־בָּבֶ֔ל וְדִבֶּר־פִּ֖יו עִם־פִּ֑יו וְעֵינָ֖יו אֶת־
עֵינָו֥ תִּרְאֶֽינָה׃ 5 וּבָבֶ֞ל יוֹלִ֤ךְ אֶת־צִדְקִיָּ֙הוּ֙ וְשָׁ֣ם
יִֽהְיֶ֔ה עַד־פׇּקְדִ֥י אֹת֖וֹ נְאֻם־יְהֹוָ֑ה כִּ֧י תִלָּֽחֲמ֛וּ אֶת־
הַכַּשְׂדִּ֖ים לֹ֥א תַצְלִֽיחוּ׃ פ

6 And Jeremiah said, "The word of the LORD came to me, saying, 7 'Behold, Hanamel the son of Shallum your uncle will come to you, saying, "Buy my field which *is* in Anathoth, for the right of redemption *is* yours to buy *it*." ' 8 Then Hanamel my uncle's son came to me in the court of the prison according to the word of the LORD, and said to me, 'Please buy my field that *is* in Anathoth, which *is* in the country of Benjamin; for the right of inheritance *is* yours, and the redemption yours; buy *it* for yourself.' Then I knew that this was the word of the LORD. 9 So I bought the field from Hanamel, the son of my uncle who *was* in Anathoth, and weighed *out* to him the money—seventeen shekels of silver. 10 And I signed the deed and sealed *it,* took witnesses, and weighed the money on the scales. 11 So I took the purchase deed, *both* that which was sealed *according* to the law and custom, and that which was open; 12 and I gave the purchase deed to Baruch the son of Neriah, son of Mahseiah, in the presence of Hanamel my uncle's *son,* and in the presence of the witnesses who signed the purchase deed, before all the Jews who sat in the court of the prison.

13 "Then I charged Baruch before them, saying, 14 'Thus says the LORD of hosts, the God of Israel: "Take these deeds, both this purchase deed which is sealed and this deed which is open, and put them in an earthen vessel, that they may last many days." 15 For thus says the LORD of hosts, the God of Israel: "Houses and fields and vineyards shall be possessed again in this land." '

16 "Now when I had delivered the purchase deed to Baruch the son of Neriah, I prayed to the LORD, saying: 17 'Ah, Lord GOD! Behold, You have made the heavens and the earth by Your great power and outstretched arm. There is nothing too hard for You. 18 *You* show lovingkindness to thousands, and repay the iniquity of the fathers into the bosom of their children after them—the Great, the Mighty God, whose name *is* the LORD of hosts. 19 *You are* great in counsel and mighty in work, for your eyes *are* open to all the ways of the sons of men, to give everyone according to his ways and according to the fruit of his doings. 20 You have set signs and wonders in the land of Egypt, to this day, and in Israel and among *other* men; and You have made Yourself a name, as it is this day. 21 You have brought Your people Israel out of the land of Egypt with signs and wonders, with a strong hand and an outstretched arm, and with great terror; 22 You have given them this land, of which You swore to their fathers to give them—"a land flowing with milk and honey." 23 And they came in and took

6 וַיֹּאמֶר יִרְמְיָהוּ הָיָה דְבַר־יְהֹוָה אֵלַי לֵאמֹר׃ 7 הִנֵּה חֲנַמְאֵל בֶּן־שַׁלֻּם דֹּדְךָ בָּא אֵלֶיךָ לֵאמֹר קְנֵה לְךָ אֶת־שָׂדִי אֲשֶׁר בַּעֲנָתוֹת כִּי לְךָ מִשְׁפַּט הַגְּאֻלָּה לִקְנוֹת׃ 8 וַיָּבֹא אֵלַי חֲנַמְאֵל בֶּן־דֹּדִי כִּדְבַר יְהֹוָה אֶל־חֲצַר הַמַּטָּרָה וַיֹּאמֶר אֵלַי קְנֵה נָא אֶת־שָׂדִי אֲשֶׁר־בַּעֲנָתוֹת אֲשֶׁר ׀ בְּאֶרֶץ בִּנְיָמִין כִּי־לְךָ מִשְׁפַּט הַיְרֻשָּׁה וּלְךָ הַגְּאֻלָּה קְנֵה־לָךְ וָאֵדַע כִּי דְבַר־יְהֹוָה הוּא׃ 9 וָאֶקְנֶה אֶת־הַשָּׂדֶה מֵאֵת חֲנַמְאֵל בֶּן־דֹּדִי אֲשֶׁר בַּעֲנָתוֹת וָאֶשְׁקֲלָה־לּוֹ אֶת־הַכֶּסֶף שִׁבְעָה שְׁקָלִים וַעֲשָׂרָה הַכָּסֶף׃ 10 וָאֶכְתֹּב בַּסֵּפֶר וָאֶחְתֹּם וָאָעֵד עֵדִים וָאֶשְׁקֹל הַכֶּסֶף בְּמֹאזְנָיִם׃ 11 וָאֶקַּח אֶת־סֵפֶר הַמִּקְנָה אֶת־הֶחָתוּם הַמִּצְוָה וְהַחֻקִּים וְאֶת־הַגָּלוּי׃ 12 וָאֶתֵּן אֶת־הַסֵּפֶר הַמִּקְנָה אֶל־בָּרוּךְ בֶּן־נֵרִיָּה בֶּן־מַחְסֵיָה לְעֵינֵי חֲנַמְאֵל דֹּדִי וּלְעֵינֵי הָעֵדִים הַכֹּתְבִים בְּסֵפֶר הַמִּקְנָה לְעֵינֵי כָּל־הַיְּהוּדִים הַיֹּשְׁבִים בַּחֲצַר הַמַּטָּרָה׃ 13 וָאֲצַוֶּה אֶת־בָּרוּךְ לְעֵינֵיהֶם לֵאמֹר׃ 14 כֹּה־אָמַר יְהֹוָה צְבָאוֹת אֱלֹהֵי יִשְׂרָאֵל לָקוֹחַ אֶת־הַסְּפָרִים הָאֵלֶּה אֵת סֵפֶר הַמִּקְנָה הַזֶּה וְאֵת הֶחָתוּם וְאֵת סֵפֶר הַגָּלוּי הַזֶּה וּנְתַתָּם בִּכְלִי־חָרֶשׂ לְמַעַן יַעַמְדוּ יָמִים רַבִּים׃ ס 15 כִּי כֹה אָמַר יְהֹוָה צְבָאוֹת אֱלֹהֵי יִשְׂרָאֵל עוֹד יִקָּנוּ בָתִּים וְשָׂדוֹת וּכְרָמִים בָּאָרֶץ הַזֹּאת׃ פ

16 וָאֶתְפַּלֵּל אֶל־יְהֹוָה אַחֲרֵי תִתִּי אֶת־סֵפֶר הַמִּקְנָה אֶל־בָּרוּךְ בֶּן־נֵרִיָּה לֵאמֹר׃ 17 אֲהָהּ אֲדֹנָי יְהֹוִה הִנֵּה ׀ אַתָּה עָשִׂיתָ אֶת־הַשָּׁמַיִם וְאֶת־הָאָרֶץ בְּכֹחֲךָ הַגָּדוֹל וּבִזְרֹעֲךָ הַנְּטוּיָה לֹא־יִפָּלֵא מִמְּךָ כָּל־דָּבָר׃ 18 עֹשֶׂה חֶסֶד לַאֲלָפִים וּמְשַׁלֵּם עֲוֹן אָבוֹת אֶל־חֵיק בְּנֵיהֶם אַחֲרֵיהֶם הָאֵל הַגָּדוֹל הַגִּבּוֹר יְהֹוָה צְבָאוֹת שְׁמוֹ׃ 19 גְּדֹל הָעֵצָה וְרַב הָעֲלִילִיָּה אֲשֶׁר־עֵינֶיךָ פְקֻחוֹת עַל־כָּל־דַּרְכֵי בְּנֵי אָדָם לָתֵת לְאִישׁ כִּדְרָכָיו וְכִפְרִי מַעֲלָלָיו׃ 20 אֲשֶׁר־שַׂמְתָּ אֹתוֹת וּמֹפְתִים בְּאֶרֶץ־מִצְרַיִם עַד־הַיּוֹם הַזֶּה וּבְיִשְׂרָאֵל וּבָאָדָם וַתַּעֲשֶׂה־לְּךָ שֵׁם כַּיּוֹם הַזֶּה׃ 21 וַתֹּצֵא אֶת־עַמְּךָ אֶת־יִשְׂרָאֵל מֵאֶרֶץ מִצְרַיִם בְּאֹתוֹת וּבְמוֹפְתִים וּבְיָד חֲזָקָה וּבְאֶזְרוֹעַ נְטוּיָה וּבְמוֹרָא גָּדוֹל׃ 22 וַתִּתֵּן לָהֶם אֶת־הָאָרֶץ הַזֹּאת אֲשֶׁר־נִשְׁבַּעְתָּ לַאֲבוֹתָם לָתֵת לָהֶם אֶרֶץ זָבַת חָלָב וּדְבָשׁ׃ 23 וַיָּבֹאוּ וַיִּרְשׁוּ אֹתָהּ וְלֹא־שָׁמְעוּ בְקוֹלֶךָ וּבְתוֹרֹתְךָ לֹא־הָלָכוּ אֵת

possession of it, but they have not obeyed Your voice or walked in Your law. They have done nothing of all that You commanded them to do; therefore You have caused all this calamity to come upon them.

24 'Look, the siege mounds! They have come to the city to take it; and the city has been given into the hand of the Chaldeans who fight against it, because of the sword and famine and pestilence. What You have spoken has happened; there You see it! 25 And You have said to me, O Lord GOD, "Buy the field for money, and take witnesses"!—yet the city has been given into the hand of the Chaldeans.' "

26 Then the word of the LORD came to Jeremiah, saying, 27 "Behold, I am the LORD, the God of all flesh. Is there anything too hard for Me? 28 Therefore thus says the LORD: 'Behold, I will give this city into the hand of the Chaldeans, into the hand of Nebuchadnezzar king of Babylon, and he shall take it. 29 And the Chaldeans who fight against this city shall come and set fire to this city and burn it, with the houses on whose roofs they have offered incense to Baal and poured out drink offerings to other gods, to provoke Me to anger; 30 because the children of Israel and the children of Judah have done only evil before Me from their youth. For the children of Israel have provoked Me only to anger with the work of their hands,' says the LORD. 31 'For this city has been to Me a provocation of My anger and My fury from the day that they built it, even to this day; so I will remove it from before My face 32 because of all the evil of the children of Israel and the children of Judah, which they have done to provoke Me to anger—they, their kings, their princes, their priests, their prophets, the men of Judah, and the inhabitants of Jerusalem. 33 And they have turned to Me the back, and not the face; though I taught them, rising up early and teaching them, yet they have not listened to receive instruction. 34 But they set their abominations in the house which is called by My name, to defile it. 35 And they built the high places of Baal which are in the Valley of the Son of Hinnom, to cause their sons and their daughters to pass through the fire to Molech, which I did not command them, nor did it come into My mind that they should do this abomination, to cause Judah to sin.'

36 "Now therefore, thus says the LORD, the God of Israel, concerning this city of which you say, 'It shall be delivered into the hand of the king of Babylon by the sword, by the famine, and by the pestilence: 37 Behold, I will gather them out of all countries where I have driven them in My anger, in

כָּל־אֲשֶׁר צִוִּיתָה לָהֶם לַעֲשׂוֹת לֹא עָשׂוּ וַתִּקְרָא אֹתָם אֵת כָּל־הָרָעָה הַזֹּאת: 24 הִנֵּה הַסֹּלְלוֹת בָּאוּ הָעִיר לְלָכְדָהּ וְהָעִיר נִתְּנָה בְּיַד הַכַּשְׂדִּים הַנִּלְחָמִים עָלֶיהָ מִפְּנֵי הַחֶרֶב וְהָרָעָב וְהַדָּבֶר וַאֲשֶׁר דִּבַּרְתָּ הָיָה וְהִנְּךָ רֹאֶה: 25 וְאַתָּה אָמַרְתָּ אֵלַי אֲדֹנָי יְהוִה קְנֵה־לְךָ הַשָּׂדֶה בַּכֶּסֶף וְהָעֵד עֵדִים וְהָעִיר נִתְּנָה בְּיַד הַכַּשְׂדִּים: 26 וַיְהִי דְּבַר־יְהֹוָה אֶל־יִרְמְיָהוּ לֵאמֹר: 27 הִנֵּה אֲנִי יְהוָה אֱלֹהֵי כָּל־בָּשָׂר הֲמִמֶּנִּי יִפָּלֵא כָּל־דָּבָר: 28 לָכֵן כֹּה אָמַר יְהֹוָה הִנְנִי נֹתֵן אֶת־הָעִיר הַזֹּאת בְּיַד הַכַּשְׂדִּים וּבְיַד נְבוּכַדְרֶאצַּר מֶלֶךְ־בָּבֶל וּלְכָדָהּ: 29 וּבָאוּ הַכַּשְׂדִּים הַנִּלְחָמִים עַל־הָעִיר הַזֹּאת וְהִצִּיתוּ אֶת־הָעִיר הַזֹּאת בָּאֵשׁ וּשְׂרָפוּהָ וְאֵת הַבָּתִּים אֲשֶׁר קִטְּרוּ עַל־גַּגּוֹתֵיהֶם לַבַּעַל וְהִסִּכוּ נְסָכִים לֵאלֹהִים אֲחֵרִים לְמַעַן הַכְעִסֵנִי: 30 כִּי־הָיוּ בְנֵי־יִשְׂרָאֵל וּבְנֵי יְהוּדָה אַךְ עֹשִׂים הָרַע בְּעֵינַי מִנְּעֻרֹתֵיהֶם כִּי בְנֵי־ יִשְׂרָאֵל אַךְ מַכְעִסִים אֹתִי בְּמַעֲשֵׂה יְדֵיהֶם נְאֻם־ יְהֹוָה: 31 כִּי עַל־אַפִּי וְעַל־חֲמָתִי הָיְתָה לִּי הָעִיר הַזֹּאת לְמִן־הַיּוֹם אֲשֶׁר בָּנוּ אוֹתָהּ וְעַד הַיּוֹם הַזֶּה לַהֲסִירָהּ מֵעַל פָּנָי: 32 עַל כָּל־רָעַת בְּנֵי־ יִשְׂרָאֵל וּבְנֵי יְהוּדָה אֲשֶׁר עָשׂוּ לְהַכְעִסֵנִי הֵמָּה מַלְכֵיהֶם שָׂרֵיהֶם כֹּהֲנֵיהֶם וּנְבִיאֵיהֶם וְאִישׁ יְהוּדָה וְיֹשְׁבֵי יְרוּשָׁלִָם: 33 וַיִּפְנוּ אֵלַי עֹרֶף וְלֹא פָנִים וְלַמֵּד אֹתָם הַשְׁכֵּם וְלַמֵּד וְאֵינָם שֹׁמְעִים לָקַחַת מוּסָר: 34 וַיָּשִׂימוּ שִׁקּוּצֵיהֶם בַּבַּיִת אֲשֶׁר־נִקְרָא־ שְׁמִי עָלָיו לְטַמְּאוֹ: 35 וַיִּבְנוּ אֶת־בָּמוֹת הַבַּעַל אֲשֶׁר | בְּגֵיא בֶן־הִנֹּם לְהַעֲבִיר אֶת־בְּנֵיהֶם וְאֶת־ בְּנוֹתֵיהֶם לַמֹּלֶךְ אֲשֶׁר לֹא־צִוִּיתִים וְלֹא עָלְתָה עַל־ לִבִּי לַעֲשׂוֹת הַתּוֹעֵבָה הַזֹּאת לְמַעַן הַחֲטִיᵃ אֶת־ יְהוּדָה: ס 36 וְעַתָּה לָכֵן כֹּה־אָמַר יְהֹוָה אֱלֹהֵי יִשְׂרָאֵל אֶל־הָעִיר הַזֹּאת אֲשֶׁר | אַתֶּם אֹמְרִים נִתְּנָה בְּיַד מֶלֶךְ־בָּבֶל בַּחֶרֶב וּבָרָעָב וּבַדָּבֶר: 37 הִנְנִי מְקַבְּצָם מִכָּל־הָאֲרָצוֹת אֲשֶׁר הִדַּחְתִּים שָׁם בְּאַפִּי וּבַחֲמָתִי וּבְקֶצֶף גָּדוֹל וַהֲשִׁבֹתִים אֶל־הַמָּקוֹם

My fury, and in great wrath; I will bring them back to this place, and I will cause them to dwell safely. [38] They shall be My people, and I will be their God; [39] then I will give them one heart and one way, that they may fear Me forever, for the good of them and their children after them. [40] And I will make an everlasting covenant with them, that I will not turn away from doing them good; but I will put My fear in their hearts so that they will not depart from Me. [41] Yes, I will rejoice over them to do them good, and I will assuredly plant them in this land, with all My heart and with all My soul.'

[42] "For thus says the LORD: 'Just as I have brought all this great calamity on this people, so I will bring on them all the good that I have promised them. [43] And fields will be bought in this land of which you say, "*It is* desolate, without man or beast; it has been given into the hand of the Chaldeans." [44] Men will buy fields for money, sign deeds and seal *them,* and take witnesses, in the land of Benjamin, in the places around Jerusalem, in the cities of Judah, in the cities of the mountains, in the cities of the lowland, and in the cities of the South; for I will cause their captives to return,' says the LORD."

33 Moreover the word of the LORD came to Jeremiah a second time, while he was still shut up in the court of the prison, saying, [2] "Thus says the LORD who made it, the LORD who formed it to establish it (the LORD *is* His name): [3] 'Call to Me, and I will answer you, and show you great and mighty things, which you do not know.'

[4] "For thus says the LORD, the God of Israel, concerning the houses of this city and the houses of the kings of Judah, which have been pulled down *to fortify* against the siege mounds and the sword: [5] 'They come to fight with the Chaldeans, but *only* to fill their places with the dead bodies of men whom I will slay in My anger and My fury, all for whose wickedness I have hidden My face from this city. [6] Behold, I will bring it health and healing; I will heal them and reveal to them the abundance of peace and truth. [7] And I will cause the captives of Judah and the captives of Israel to return, and will rebuild those places as at the first. [8] I will cleanse them from all their iniquity by which they have sinned against Me, and I will pardon all their iniquities by which they have sinned and by which they have transgressed against Me. [9] Then it shall be to Me a name of joy, a praise, and an honor before all nations of the earth, who shall hear all the good

הֹוֶה וְהִשְׁבַּתִּ֖ים לָבֶ֑טַח: 38 וְהָ֥יוּ לִ֖י לְעָ֑ם וַאֲנִ֕י אֶהְיֶ֥ה לָהֶ֖ם לֵאלֹהִֽים: 39 וְנָתַתִּ֨י לָהֶ֜ם לֵ֤ב אֶחָד֙ וְדֶ֣רֶךְ אֶחָ֔ד לְיִרְאָ֥ה אֹותִ֖י כָּל־הַיָּמִ֑ים לְטֹ֣וב לָהֶ֔ם וְלִבְנֵיהֶ֖ם אַחֲרֵיהֶֽם: 40 וְכָרַתִּ֤י לָהֶם֙ בְּרִ֣ית עֹולָ֔ם אֲשֶׁ֤ר לֹֽא־אָשׁוּב֙ מֵאַ֣חֲרֵיהֶ֔ם לְהֵיטִיבִ֖י אֹותָ֑ם וְאֶת־יִרְאָתִי֙ אֶתֵּ֣ן בִּלְבָבָ֔ם לְבִלְתִּ֖י ס֥וּר מֵעָלָֽי: 41 וְשַׂשְׂתִּ֥י עֲלֵיהֶ֖ם לְהֵטִ֣יב אֹותָ֑ם וּנְטַעְתִּ֞ים בָּאָ֤רֶץ הַזֹּאת֙ בֶּאֱמֶ֔ת בְּכָל־לִבִּ֖י וּבְכָל־נַפְשִֽׁי: ס 42 כִּי־

כֹ֖ה אָמַ֣ר יְהֹוָ֑ה כַּאֲשֶׁ֨ר הֵבֵ֜אתִי אֶל־הָעָ֤ם הַזֶּה֙ אֵ֚ת כָּל־הָרָעָ֣ה הַגְּדֹולָ֔ה הַזֹּ֑את כֵּ֣ן אָנֹכִ֞י מֵבִ֤יא עֲלֵיהֶם֙ אֶת־כָּל־הַטֹּובָ֔ה אֲשֶׁ֥ר אָנֹכִ֖י דֹּבֵ֥ר עֲלֵיהֶֽם: 43 וְנִקְנָ֥ה הַשָּׂדֶ֖ה בָּאָ֣רֶץ הַזֹּ֑את אֲשֶׁ֣ר ׀ אַתֶּ֣ם אֹמְרִ֗ים שְׁמָמָ֥ה הִיא֙ מֵאֵ֤ין אָדָם֙ וּבְהֵמָ֔ה נִתְּנָ֖ה בְּיַ֥ד הַכַּשְׂדִּֽים: 44 שָׂדֹ֞ות בַּכֶּ֣סֶף יִקְנ֗וּ וְכָתֹ֣וב בַּסֵּ֣פֶר ׀ וְחָתֹום֮ וְהָעֵ֣ד עֵדִים֒ בְּאֶ֣רֶץ בִּנְיָמִ֗ן וּבִסְבִיבֵ֤י יְרוּשָׁלִַ֙ם֙ וּבְעָרֵ֣י יְהוּדָ֔ה וּבְעָרֵ֤י הָהָר֙ וּבְעָרֵ֣י הַשְּׁפֵלָ֔ה וּבְעָרֵ֖י הַנֶּ֑גֶב כִּֽי־אָשִׁ֥יב אֶת־שְׁבוּתָ֖ם נְאֻם־יְהֹוָֽה: פ

לג וַיְהִ֧י דְבַר־יְהֹוָ֛ה אֶֽל־יִרְמְיָ֖הוּ שֵׁנִ֑ית וְהוּא֙ עֹודֶ֣נּוּ עָצ֔וּר בַּחֲצַ֥ר הַמַּטָּרָ֖ה לֵאמֹֽר: 2 כֹּֽה־אָמַ֤ר יְהֹוָה֙ עֹשָׂ֔הּ יְהֹוָ֛ה יֹוצֵ֥ר אֹותָ֖הּ לַהֲכִינָ֑הּ יְהֹוָ֖ה שְׁמֹֽו: 3 קְרָ֥א אֵלַ֖י וְאֶֽעֱנֶ֑ךָּ וְאַגִּ֧ידָה לְּךָ֛ גְּדֹלֹ֥ות וּבְצֻרֹ֖ות לֹ֥א יְדַעְתָּֽם: ס 4 כִּ֣י כֹ֥ה אָמַ֛ר יְהֹוָ֖ה אֱלֹהֵ֣י יִשְׂרָאֵ֔ל עַל־בָּתֵּי֙ הָעִ֣יר הַזֹּ֔את וְעַל־בָּתֵּ֖י מַלְכֵ֣י יְהוּדָ֑ה הַנְּתֻצִ֕ים אֶל־הַסֹּלְלֹ֖ות וְאֶל־הֶחָֽרֶב: 5 בָּאִ֗ים לְהִלָּחֵם֙ אֶת־הַכַּשְׂדִּ֔ים וּלְמַלְאָם֙ אֶת־פִּגְרֵ֣י הָאָדָ֔ם אֲשֶׁר־הִכֵּ֥יתִי בְאַפִּ֖י וּבַחֲמָתִ֑י וַאֲשֶׁ֨ר הִסְתַּ֧רְתִּי פָנַ֛י מֵהָעִ֥יר הַזֹּ֖את עַ֥ל כָּל־רָעָתָֽם: 6 הִנְנִ֧י מַעֲלֶה־לָּ֛הּ אֲרֻכָ֥ה וּמַרְפֵּ֖א וּרְפָאתִ֑ים וְגִלֵּיתִ֣י לָהֶ֔ם עֲתֶ֥רֶת שָׁלֹ֖ום וֶאֱמֶֽת: 7 וַהֲשִׁבֹתִי֙ אֶת־שְׁב֣וּת יְהוּדָ֔ה וְאֵ֖ת שְׁב֣וּת יִשְׂרָאֵ֑ל וּבְנִתִ֖ים כְּבָרִֽאשֹׁנָֽה: 8 וְטִ֣הַרְתִּ֔ים מִכָּל־עֲוֹנָ֖ם אֲשֶׁ֣ר חָֽטְאוּ־לִ֑י וְסָלַחְתִּ֗י לְכֹל־ עֲוֹנֹֽותֵיהֶם֙ אֲשֶׁ֣ר חָֽטְאוּ־לִ֔י וַאֲשֶׁ֖ר פָּ֥שְׁעוּ בִֽי: 9 וְהָ֣יְתָה לִּ֗י לְשֵׁ֤ם שָׂשֹׂון֙ לִתְהִלָּ֣ה וּלְתִפְאֶ֔רֶת לְכֹ֖ל גֹּויֵ֣י הָאָ֑רֶץ אֲשֶׁ֣ר יִשְׁמְע֗וּ אֶת־כָּל־הַטֹּובָה֙ אֲשֶׁ֣ר אָנֹכִי֙ עֹשֶׂ֣ה אֹתָ֔ם וּפָחֲד֣וּ וְרָֽגְז֗וּ עַ֤ל כָּל־הַטֹּובָה֙ וְעַ֣ל כָּל־הַשָּׁלֹ֔ום אֲשֶׁ֥ר

that I do to them; they shall fear and tremble for all the goodness and all the prosperity that I provide for it.'

10 "Thus says the LORD: 'Again there shall be heard in this place—of which you say, "It is desolate, without man and without beast"—in the cities of Judah, in the streets of Jerusalem that are desolate, without man and without inhabitant and without beast, 11 the voice of joy and the voice of gladness, the voice of the bridegroom and the voice of the bride, the voice of those who will say:

"Praise the LORD of hosts,
  For the LORD is good,
  For His mercy endures forever"—

and of those who will bring the sacrifice of praise into the house of the LORD. For I will cause the captives of the land to return as at the first,' says the LORD.

12 "Thus says the LORD of hosts: 'In this place which is desolate, without man and without beast, and in all its cities, there shall again be a dwelling place of shepherds causing their flocks to lie down. 13 In the cities of the mountains, in the cities of the lowland, in the cities of the South, in the land of Benjamin, in the places around Jerusalem, and in the cities of Judah, the flocks shall again pass under the hands of him who counts them,' says the LORD.

14 'Behold, the days are coming,' says the LORD, 'that I will perform that good thing which I have promised to the house of Israel and to the house of Judah:

15 'In those days and at that time
  I will cause to grow up to David
  A Branch of righteousness;
  He shall execute judgment and righteousness in
    the earth.
16 In those days Judah will be saved,
  And Jerusalem will dwell safely.
  And this is the name by which she will be called:

THE LORD OUR RIGHTEOUSNESS.'

17 "For thus says the LORD: 'David shall never lack a man to sit on the throne of the house of Israel; 18 nor shall the priests, the Levites, lack a man to offer burnt offerings before Me, to kindle grain offerings, and to sacrifice continually.' "

19 And the word of the LORD came to Jeremiah, saying, 20 "Thus says the LORD: 'If you can break My covenant with the day and My covenant with the night, so that there will not be day and night in their season, 21 then My covenant may also be broken with David My servant, so that he shall not have a son to reign on his throne, and with the Levites, the priests, My ministers. 22 As the host of

10 ס   כֹּה ׀ אָמַר יְהֹוָה עוֹד
יִשָּׁמַע בַּמָּקוֹם־הַזֶּה אֲשֶׁר אַתֶּם אֹמְרִים חָרֵב הוּא
מֵאֵין אָדָם וּמֵאֵין בְּהֵמָה בְּעָרֵי יְהוּדָה וּבְחֻצוֹת
יְרוּשָׁלַ͏ִם הַנְשַׁמּוֹת מֵאֵין אָדָם וּמֵאֵין יוֹשֵׁב וּמֵאֵין
בְּהֵמָה: 11 קוֹל שָׂשׂוֹן וְקוֹל שִׂמְחָה קוֹל חָתָן
וְקוֹל כַּלָּה קוֹל אֹמְרִים הוֹדוּ אֶת־יְהֹוָה צְבָאוֹת
כִּי־טוֹב יְהֹוָה כִּי־לְעוֹלָם חַסְדּוֹ מְבִאִים תּוֹדָה
בֵּית יְהֹוָה כִּי־אָשִׁיב אֶת־שְׁבוּת־הָאָרֶץ כְּבָרִאשֹׁנָה
אָמַר יְהֹוָה: ס   12 כֹּה־אָמַר יְהֹוָה צְבָאוֹת עוֹד
יִהְיֶה ׀ בַּמָּקוֹם הַזֶּה הֶחָרֵב מֵאֵין־אָדָם וְעַד־בְּהֵמָה
וּבְכָל־עָרָיו נְוֵה רֹעִים מַרְבִּצִים צֹאן: 13 בְּעָרֵי
הָהָר בְּעָרֵי הַשְּׁפֵלָה וּבְעָרֵי הַנֶּגֶב וּבְאֶרֶץ בִּנְיָמִן
וּבִסְבִיבֵי יְרוּשָׁלַ͏ִם וּבְעָרֵי יְהוּדָה עֹד תַּעֲבֹרְנָה
הַצֹּאן עַל־יְדֵי מוֹנֶה אָמַר יְהֹוָה: ס   14 הִנֵּה
יָמִים בָּאִים נְאֻם־יְהֹוָה וַהֲקִמֹתִי אֶת־הַדָּבָר הַטּוֹב
אֲשֶׁר דִּבַּרְתִּי אֶל־בֵּית יִשְׂרָאֵל וְעַל־בֵּית יְהוּדָה:
15 בַּיָּמִים הָהֵם וּבָעֵת הַהִיא אַצְמִיחַ לְדָוִד צֶמַח
צְדָקָה וְעָשָׂה מִשְׁפָּט וּצְדָקָה בָּאָרֶץ: 16 בַּיָּמִים
הָהֵם תִּוָּשַׁע יְהוּדָה וִירוּשָׁלַ͏ִם תִּשְׁכּוֹן לָבֶטַח וְזֶה
אֲשֶׁר־יִקְרָא־לָהּ יְהֹוָה ׀ צִדְקֵנוּ: ס   17 כִּי־כֹה
אָמַר יְהֹוָה לֹא־יִכָּרֵת לְדָוִד אִישׁ יֹשֵׁב עַל־כִּסֵּא
בֵית־יִשְׂרָאֵל: 18 וְלַכֹּהֲנִים הַלְוִיִּם לֹא־יִכָּרֵת אִישׁ
מִלְּפָנָי מַעֲלֶה עוֹלָה וּמַקְטִיר מִנְחָה וְעֹשֶׂה־זֶּבַח
כָּל־הַיָּמִים: ס   19 וַיְהִי דְּבַר־יְהֹוָה אֶל־יִרְמְיָהוּ
לֵאמוֹר: 20 כֹּה אָמַר יְהֹוָה אִם־תָּפֵרוּ אֶת־בְּרִיתִי
הַיּוֹם וְאֶת־בְּרִיתִי הַלַּיְלָה וּלְבִלְתִּי הֱיוֹת יוֹמָם־
וָלַיְלָה בְּעִתָּם: 21 גַּם־בְּרִיתִי תֻפַר אֶת־דָּוִד עַבְדִּי
מִהְיוֹת־לוֹ בֵן מֹלֵךְ עַל־כִּסְאוֹ וְאֶת־הַלְוִיִּם הַכֹּהֲנִים
מְשָׁרְתָי: 22 אֲשֶׁר לֹא־יִסָּפֵר צְבָא הַשָּׁמַיִם וְלֹא

heaven cannot be numbered, nor the sand of the sea measured, so will I multiply the descendants of David My servant and the Levites who minister to Me.' "

23 Moreover the word of the LORD came to Jeremiah, saying, 24 "Have you not considered what these people have spoken, saying, 'The two families which the LORD has chosen, He has also cast them off'? Thus they have despised My people, as if they should no more be a nation before them.

25 "Thus says the LORD: 'If My covenant is not with day and night, and if I have not appointed the ordinances of heaven and earth, 26 then I will cast away the descendants of Jacob and David My servant, so that I will not take any of his descendants to be rulers over the descendants of Abraham, Isaac, and Jacob. For I will cause their captives to return, and will have mercy on them.' "

34

The word which came to Jeremiah from the LORD, when Nebuchadnezzar king of Babylon and all his army, all the kingdoms of the earth under his dominion, and all the people, fought against Jerusalem and all its cities, saying, 2 "Thus says the LORD, the God of Israel: 'Go and speak to Zedekiah king of Judah and tell him, "Thus says the LORD: 'Behold, I will give this city into the hand of the king of Babylon, and he shall burn it with fire. 3 And you shall not escape from his hand, but shall surely be taken and delivered into his hand; your eyes shall see the eyes of the king of Babylon, he shall speak with you face to face, and you shall go to Babylon.' " ' 4 Yet hear the word of the LORD, O Zedekiah king of Judah! Thus says the LORD concerning you: 'You shall not die by the sword. 5 You shall die in peace; as in the ceremonies of your fathers, the former kings who were before you, so they shall burn incense for you and lament for you, saying, "Alas, lord!" For I have pronounced the word, says the LORD.' "

6 Then Jeremiah the prophet spoke all these words to Zedekiah king of Judah in Jerusalem, 7 when the king of Babylon's army fought against Jerusalem and all the cities of Judah that were left, against Lachish and Azekah; for only these fortified cities remained of the cities of Judah.

8 This is the word that came to Jeremiah from the LORD, after King Zedekiah had made a covenant with all the people who were at Jerusalem to proclaim liberty to them: 9 that every man should set free his male and female slave—a Hebrew man or woman—that no one should keep a Jewish brother in bondage. 10 Now when all the princes and all the people, who had entered into the

יִמַּד֙ ח֣וֹל הַיָּ֔ם כֵּ֣ן אַרְבֶּ֗ה אֶת־זֶ֙רַע֙ דָּוִ֣ד עַבְדִּ֔י וְאֶת־הַלְוִיִּ֖ם מְשָׁרְתֵ֥י אֹתִֽי׃ ס 23 וַיְהִי֙ דְּבַר־ יְהֹוָ֔ה אֶֽל־יִרְמְיָ֖הוּ לֵאמֹֽר׃ 24 הֲל֣וֹא רָאִ֗יתָ מָֽה־ הָעָ֤ם הַזֶּה֙ דִּבְּר֣וּ לֵאמֹ֔ר שְׁתֵּ֣י הַמִּשְׁפָּח֗וֹת אֲשֶׁ֨ר בָּחַ֤ר יְהֹוָה֙ בָּהֶ֔ם וַיִּמְאָסֵ֑ם וְאֶת־עַמִּי֙ יִנְאָצ֔וּן מִֽהְי֥וֹת ע֖וֹד גּ֥וֹי לִפְנֵיהֶֽם׃ ס 25 כֹּ֚ה אָמַ֣ר יְהֹוָ֔ה אִם־ לֹ֥א בְרִיתִ֖י יוֹמָ֣ם וָלָ֑יְלָה חֻקּ֛וֹת שָׁמַ֥יִם וָאָ֖רֶץ לֹא־ שָֽׂמְתִּי׃ 26 גַּם־זֶ֣רַע יַעֲקוֹב֩ וְדָוִ֨ד עַבְדִּ֜י אֶמְאַ֗ס מִקַּ֤חַת מִזַּרְעוֹ֙ מֹֽשְׁלִ֔ים אֶל־זֶ֥רַע אַבְרָהָ֖ם יִשְׂחָ֣ק וְיַעֲקֹ֑ב כִּֽי־אָשׁוּב֙ אֶת־שְׁבוּתָ֖ם וְרִחַמְתִּֽים׃ ס

לד הַדָּבָ֞ר אֲשֶׁר־הָיָ֤ה אֶֽל־יִרְמְיָ֙הוּ֙ מֵאֵ֣ת יְהֹוָ֔ה וּנְבֽוּכַדְרֶאצַּ֣ר מֶֽלֶךְ־בָּבֶ֣ל ׀ וְכָל־חֵיל֡וֹ וְכָל־מַמְלְכ֣וֹת אֶ֗רֶץ מֶמְשֶׁ֤לֶת יָדוֹ֙ וְכָל־הָ֣עַמִּ֔ים נִלְחָמִ֣ים עַל־ יְרוּשָׁלִַ֖ם וְעַל־כָּל־עָרֶ֑יהָ לֵאמֹֽר׃ 2 כֹּֽה־אָמַ֤ר יְהֹוָה֙ אֱלֹהֵ֣י יִשְׂרָאֵ֔ל הָלֹ֤ךְ וְאָֽמַרְתָּ֙ אֶל־צִדְקִיָּ֣הוּ מֶ֣לֶךְ יְהוּדָ֔ה וְאָמַרְתָּ֣ אֵלָ֔יו כֹּ֚ה אָמַ֣ר יְהֹוָ֔ה הִנְנִ֣י נֹתֵ֞ן אֶת־הָעִ֤יר הַזֹּאת֙ בְּיַ֣ד מֶֽלֶךְ־בָּבֶ֔ל וּשְׂרָפָ֖הּ בָּאֵֽשׁ׃ 3 וְאַתָּ֗ה לֹ֤א תִמָּלֵט֙ מִיָּד֔וֹ כִּ֚י תָּפֹ֣שׂ תִּתָּפֵ֔שׂ וּבְיָד֖וֹ תִּנָּתֵ֑ן וְֽעֵינֶ֞יךָ אֶת־עֵינֵ֤י מֶֽלֶךְ־בָּבֶל֙ תִּרְאֶ֔ינָה וּפִ֖יהוּ אֶת־פִּ֣יךָ יְדַבֵּ֑ר וּבָבֶ֖ל תָּבֽוֹא׃ 4 אַ֚ךְ שְׁמַ֣ע דְּבַר־יְהֹוָ֔ה צִדְקִיָּ֖הוּ מֶ֣לֶךְ יְהוּדָ֑ה כֹּֽה־אָמַ֤ר יְהֹוָה֙ עָלֶ֔יךָ לֹ֥א תָמ֖וּת בֶּחָֽרֶב׃ 5 בְּשָׁל֣וֹם תָּמ֗וּת וּֽכְמִשְׂרְפ֣וֹת אֲבוֹתֶ֡יךָ הַמְּלָכִ֣ים הָרִֽאשֹׁנִ֡ים אֲשֶׁר־הָיוּ֩ לְפָנֶ֨יךָ כֵּ֣ן יִשְׂרְפוּ־לָ֗ךְ וְה֤וֹי אָדוֹן֙ יִסְפְּדוּ־לָ֔ךְ כִּֽי־דָבָ֥ר אֲנִֽי־דִבַּ֖רְתִּי נְאֻם־ יְהֹוָֽה׃ ס 6 וַיְדַבֵּר֙ יִרְמְיָ֣הוּ הַנָּבִ֔יא אֶל־ צִדְקִיָּ֖הוּ מֶ֣לֶךְ יְהוּדָ֑ה אֵ֛ת כָּל־הַדְּבָרִ֥ים הָאֵ֖לֶּה בִּירֽוּשָׁלִָֽם׃ 7 וְחֵ֣יל מֶֽלֶךְ־בָּבֶ֗ל נִלְחָמִים֙ עַל־יְר֣וּשָׁלִַ֔ם וְעַ֛ל כָּל־עָרֵ֥י יְהוּדָ֖ה הַנּֽוֹתָר֑וֹת אֶל־לָכִ֣ישׁ וְאֶל־עֲזֵקָ֔ה כִּ֣י הֵ֗נָּה נִשְׁאֲר֛וּ בְּעָרֵ֥י יְהוּדָ֖ה עָרֵ֥י מִבְצָֽר׃ פ 8 הַדָּבָ֞ר אֲשֶׁר־הָיָ֤ה אֶֽל־יִרְמְיָ֙הוּ֙ מֵאֵ֣ת יְהֹוָ֔ה אַֽחֲרֵ֡י כְּרֹת֩ הַמֶּ֨לֶךְ צִדְקִיָּ֜הוּ בְּרִ֗ית אֶת־כָּל־ הָעָם֙ אֲשֶׁ֣ר בִּירֽוּשָׁלִַ֔ם לִקְרֹ֥א לָהֶ֖ם דְּרֽוֹר׃ 9 לְ֠שַׁלַּ֠ח אִ֣ישׁ אֶת־עַבְדּ֞וֹ וְאִ֧ישׁ אֶת־שִׁפְחָת֛וֹ הָעִבְרִ֥י וְהָעִבְרִיָּ֖ה חׇפְשִׁ֑ים לְבִלְתִּ֧י עֲבָד־בָּ֛ם בִּיהוּדִ֥י אָחִ֖יהוּ אִֽישׁ׃ 10 וַיִּשְׁמְע֣וּ כָל־הַשָּׂרִ֗ים וְכָל־הָעָם֙ אֲשֶׁר־בָּ֣אוּ

לג 26 אָשִׁיב

covenant, heard that everyone should set free his male and female slaves, that no one should keep them in bondage anymore, they obeyed and let *them* go. 11 But afterward they changed their minds and made the male and female slaves return, whom they had set free, and brought them into subjection as male and female slaves.

12 Therefore the word of the LORD came to Jeremiah from the LORD, saying, 13 "Thus says the LORD, the God of Israel: 'I made a covenant with your fathers in the day that I brought them out of the land of Egypt, out of the house of bondage, saying, 14 "At the end of seven years let every man set free his Hebrew brother, who has been sold to him; and when he has served you six years, you shall let him go free from you." But your fathers did not obey Me nor incline their ear. 15 Then you recently turned and did what was right in My sight—every man proclaiming liberty to his neighbor; and you made a covenant before Me in the house which is called by My name. 16 Then you turned around and profaned My name, and every one of you brought back his male and female slaves, whom he had set at liberty, at their pleasure, and brought them back into subjection, to be your male and female slaves.'

17 "Therefore thus says the LORD: 'You have not obeyed Me in proclaiming liberty, every one to his brother and every one to his neighbor. Behold, I proclaim liberty to you,' says the LORD—'to the sword, to pestilence, and to famine! And I will deliver you to trouble among all the kingdoms of the earth. 18 And I will give the men who have transgressed My covenant, who have not performed the words of the covenant which they made before Me, when they cut the calf in two and passed between the parts of it— 19 the princes of Judah, the princes of Jerusalem, the eunuchs, the priests, and all the people of the land who passed between the parts of the calf— 20 I will give them into the hand of their enemies and into the hand of those who seek their life. Their dead bodies shall be for meat for the birds of the heaven and the beasts of the earth. 21 And I will give Zedekiah king of Judah and his princes into the hand of their enemies, into the hand of those who seek their life, and into the hand of the king of Babylon's army which has gone back from you. 22 Behold, I will command,' says the LORD, 'and cause them to return to this city. They will fight against it and take it and burn it with fire; and I will make the cities of Judah a desolation without inhabitant.'"

בְּרִית לְשַׁלַּח אִישׁ אֶת־עַבְדּוֹ וְאִישׁ אֶת־שִׁפְחָתוֹ חׇפְשִׁים לְבִלְתִּי עֲבׇד־בָּם עוֹד וַיִּשְׁמְעוּ וַיְשַׁלֵּחוּ׃

11 וַיָּשׁוּבוּ אַחֲרֵי־כֵן וַיָּשִׁבוּ אֶת־הָעֲבָדִים וְאֶת־הַשְּׁפָחוֹת אֲשֶׁר שִׁלְּחוּ חׇפְשִׁים וַיִּכְבְּשׁוּם לַעֲבָדִים וְלִשְׁפָחוֹת׃ ס 12 וַיְהִי דְבַר־יְהֹוָה אֶל־יִרְמְיָהוּ מֵאֵת יְהֹוָה לֵאמֹר׃ 13 כֹּה־אָמַר יְהֹוָה אֱלֹהֵי יִשְׂרָאֵל אָנֹכִי כָּרַתִּי בְרִית אֶת־אֲבֽוֹתֵיכֶם בְּיוֹם הוֹצִאִי אוֹתָם מֵאֶרֶץ מִצְרַיִם מִבֵּית עֲבָדִים לֵאמֹר׃ 14 מִקֵּץ שֶׁבַע שָׁנִים תְּשַׁלְּחוּ אִישׁ אֶת־אָחִיו הָעִבְרִי אֲשֶׁר־יִמָּכֵר לְךָ וַעֲבָדְךָ שֵׁשׁ שָׁנִים וְשִׁלַּחְתּוֹ חׇפְשִׁי מֵעִמָּךְ וְלֹא־שָׁמְעוּ אֲבֽוֹתֵיכֶם אֵלַי וְלֹא הִטּוּ אֶת־אׇזְנָם׃ 15 וַתָּשֻׁבוּ אַתֶּם הַיּוֹם וַתַּעֲשׂוּ אֶת־הַיָּשָׁר בְּעֵינַי לִקְרֹא דְרוֹר אִישׁ לְרֵעֵהוּ וַתִּכְרְתוּ בְרִית לְפָנַי בַּבַּיִת אֲשֶׁר־נִקְרָא שְׁמִי עָלָיו׃

16 וַתָּשֻׁבוּ וַתְּחַלְּלוּ אֶת־שְׁמִי וַתָּשִׁבוּ אִישׁ אֶת־עַבְדּוֹ וְאִישׁ אֶת־שִׁפְחָתוֹ אֲשֶׁר־שִׁלַּחְתֶּם חׇפְשִׁים לְנַפְשָׁם וַתִּכְבְּשׁוּ אֹתָם לִהְיוֹת לָכֶם לַעֲבָדִים וְלִשְׁפָחוֹת׃ ס 17 לָכֵן כֹּה־אָמַר יְהֹוָה אַתֶּם לֹא־שְׁמַעְתֶּם אֵלַי לִקְרֹא דְרוֹר אִישׁ לְאָחִיו וְאִישׁ לְרֵעֵהוּ הִנְנִי קֹרֵא לָכֶם דְּרוֹר נְאֻם־יְהֹוָה אֶל־הַחֶרֶב אֶל־הַדֶּבֶר וְאֶל־הָרָעָב וְנָתַתִּי אֶתְכֶם לזועה לְכֹל מַמְלְכוֹת הָאָרֶץ׃ 18 וְנָתַתִּי אֶת־הָאֲנָשִׁים הָעֹבְרִים אֶת־בְּרִתִי אֲשֶׁר לֹא־הֵקִימוּ אֶת־דִּבְרֵי הַבְּרִית אֲשֶׁר כָּרְתוּ לְפָנָי הָעֵגֶל אֲשֶׁר כָּרְתוּ לִשְׁנַיִם וַיַּעַבְרוּ בֵּין בְּתָרָיו׃ 19 שָׂרֵי יְהוּדָה וְשָׂרֵי יְרוּשָׁלַ͏ִם הַסָּרִסִים וְהַכֹּהֲנִים וְכֹל עַם הָאָרֶץ הָעֹבְרִים בֵּין בִּתְרֵי הָעֵגֶל׃ 20 וְנָתַתִּי אוֹתָם בְּיַד אֹיְבֵיהֶם וּבְיַד מְבַקְשֵׁי נַפְשָׁם וְהָיְתָה נִבְלָתָם לְמַאֲכָל לְעוֹף הַשָּׁמַיִם וּלְבֶהֱמַת הָאָרֶץ׃ 21 וְאֶת־צִדְקִיָּהוּ מֶלֶךְ־יְהוּדָה וְאֶת־שָׂרָיו אֶתֵּן בְּיַד אֹיְבֵיהֶם וּבְיַד מְבַקְשֵׁי נַפְשָׁם וּבְיַד חֵיל מֶלֶךְ בָּבֶל הָעֹלִים מֵעֲלֵיכֶם׃ 22 הִנְנִי מְצַוֶּה נְאֻם־יְהֹוָה וַהֲשִׁבֹתִים אֶל־הָעִיר הַזֹּאת וְנִלְחֲמוּ עָלֶיהָ וּלְכָדוּהָ וּשְׂרָפֻהָ בָאֵשׁ וְאֶת־עָרֵי יְהוּדָה אֶתֵּן שְׁמָמָה מֵאֵין יֹשֵׁב׃ פ

לד 11 וַיִּכְבְּשׁוּם   17 לְזַעֲוָה

35 The word which came to Jeremiah from the LORD in the days of Jehoiakim the son of Josiah, king of Judah, saying, 2 "Go to the house of the Rechabites, speak to them, and bring them into the house of the LORD, into one of the chambers, and give them wine to drink."

3 Then I took Jaazaniah the son of Jeremiah, the son of Habazziniah, his brothers and all his sons, and the whole house of the Rechabites, 4 and I brought them into the house of the LORD, into the chamber of the sons of Hanan the son of Igdaliah, a man of God, which *was* by the chamber of the princes, above the chamber of Maaseiah the son of Shallum, the keeper of the door. 5 Then I set before the sons of the house of the Rechabites bowls full of wine, and cups; and I said to them, "Drink wine."

6 But they said, "We will drink no wine, for Jonadab the son of Rechab, our father, commanded us, saying, 'You shall drink no wine, you nor your sons, forever. 7 You shall not build a house, sow seed, plant a vineyard, nor have *any of these;* but all your days you shall dwell in tents, that you may live many days in the land where you are sojourners.' 8 Thus we have obeyed the voice of Jonadab the son of Rechab, our father, in all that he charged us, to drink no wine all our days, we, our wives, our sons, or our daughters, 9 nor to build ourselves houses to dwell in; nor do we have vineyard, field, or seed. 10 But we have dwelt in tents, and have obeyed and done according to all that Jonadab our father commanded us. 11 But it came to pass, when Nebuchadnezzar king of Babylon came up into the land, that we said, 'Come, let us go to Jerusalem for fear of the army of the Chaldeans and for fear of the army of the Syrians.' So we dwell at Jerusalem."

12 Then came the word of the LORD to Jeremiah, saying, 13 "Thus says the LORD of hosts, the God of Israel: 'Go and tell the men of Judah and the inhabitants of Jerusalem, "Will you not receive instruction to obey My words?" says the LORD. 14 "The words of Jonadab the son of Rechab, which he commanded his sons, not to drink wine, are performed; for to this day they drink none, and obey their father's commandment. But although I have spoken to you, rising early and speaking, you did not obey Me. 15 I have also sent to you all My servants the prophets, rising up early and sending *them,* saying, 'Turn now everyone from his evil way, amend your doings, and do not go after other gods to serve them; then you will dwell in the land which I have given you and your fathers.' But you have not inclined your ear, nor obeyed Me. 16 Surely the sons of Jonadab the son of Rechab have performed

לה הַדָּבָר אֲשֶׁר־הָיָה אֶל־יִרְמְיָהוּ מֵאֵת יְהֹוָה בִּימֵי יְהוֹיָקִים בֶּן־יֹאשִׁיָּהוּ מֶלֶךְ יְהוּדָה לֵאמֹר: 2 הָלוֹךְ אֶל־בֵּית הָרֵכָבִים וְדִבַּרְתָּ אוֹתָם וַהֲבִאוֹתָם בֵּית יְהֹוָה אֶל־אַחַת הַלְּשָׁכוֹת וְהִשְׁקִיתָ אוֹתָם יָיִן: 3 וָאֶקַּח אֶת־יַאֲזַנְיָה בֶן־יִרְמְיָהוּ בֶּן־חֲבַצִּנְיָה וְאֶת־ אֶחָיו וְאֶת־כָּל־בָּנָיו וְאֵת כָּל־בֵּית הָרֵכָבִים: 4 וָאָבִא אֹתָם בֵּית יְהֹוָה אֶל־לִשְׁכַּת בְּנֵי חָנָן בֶּן־יִגְדַּלְיָהוּ אִישׁ הָאֱלֹהִים אֲשֶׁר־אֵצֶל לִשְׁכַּת הַשָּׂרִים אֲשֶׁר מִמַּעַל לְלִשְׁכַּת מַעֲשֵׂיָהוּ בֶן־שַׁלֻּם שֹׁמֵר הַסַּף: 5 וָאֶתֵּן לִפְנֵי | בְּנֵי בֵית־הָרֵכָבִים גְּבִעִים מְלֵאִים יַיִן וְכֹסוֹת וָאֹמַר אֲלֵיהֶם שְׁתוּ־יָיִן: 6 וַיֹּאמְרוּ לֹא נִשְׁתֶּה־יָּיִן כִּי יוֹנָדָב בֶּן־רֵכָב אָבִינוּ צִוָּה עָלֵינוּ לֵאמֹר לֹא תִשְׁתּוּ־יַיִן אַתֶּם וּבְנֵיכֶם עַד־עוֹלָם: 7 וּבַיִת לֹא־תִבְנוּ וְזֶרַע לֹא־תִזְרָעוּ וְכֶרֶם לֹא־תִטָּעוּ וְלֹא יִהְיֶה לָכֶם כִּי בָּאֳהָלִים תֵּשְׁבוּ כָּל־יְמֵיכֶם לְמַעַן תִּחְיוּ יָמִים רַבִּים עַל־פְּנֵי הָאֲדָמָה אֲשֶׁר אַתֶּם גָּרִים שָׁם: 8 וַנִּשְׁמַע בְּקוֹל יְהוֹנָדָב בֶּן־רֵכָב אָבִינוּ לְכֹל אֲשֶׁר צִוָּנוּ לְבִלְתִּי שְׁתוֹת־יַיִן כָּל־יָמֵינוּ אֲנַחְנוּ נָשֵׁינוּ בָּנֵינוּ וּבְנֹתֵינוּ: 9 וּלְבִלְתִּי בְּנוֹת בָּתִּים לְשִׁבְתֵּנוּ וְכֶרֶם וְשָׂדֶה וָזֶרַע לֹא יִהְיֶה־לָּנוּ: 10 וַנֵּשֶׁב בָּאֳהָלִים וַנִּשְׁמַע וַנַּעַשׂ כְּכֹל אֲשֶׁר־צִוָּנוּ יוֹנָדָב אָבִינוּ: 11 וַיְהִי בַּעֲלוֹת נְבוּכַדְרֶאצַּר מֶלֶךְ־בָּבֶל אֶל־הָאָרֶץ וַנֹּאמֶר בֹּאוּ וְנָבוֹא יְרוּשָׁלִַם מִפְּנֵי חֵיל הַכַּשְׂדִּים וּמִפְּנֵי חֵיל אֲרָם וַנֵּשֶׁב בִּירוּשָׁלָ͏ִם: פ

12 וַיְהִי דְּבַר־יְהֹוָה אֶל־יִרְמְיָהוּ לֵאמֹר: 13 כֹּה־אָמַר יְהֹוָה צְבָאוֹת אֱלֹהֵי יִשְׂרָאֵל הָלֹךְ וְאָמַרְתָּ לְאִישׁ יְהוּדָה וּלְיוֹשְׁבֵי יְרוּשָׁלָ͏ִם הֲלוֹא תִקְחוּ מוּסָר לִשְׁמֹעַ אֶל־דְּבָרַי נְאֻם־יְהֹוָה: 14 הוּקַם אֶת־דִּבְרֵי יְהוֹנָדָב בֶּן־רֵכָב אֲשֶׁר־צִוָּה אֶת־בָּנָיו לְבִלְתִּי שְׁתוֹת־יַיִן וְלֹא שָׁתוּ עַד־הַיּוֹם הַזֶּה כִּי שָׁמְעוּ אֵת מִצְוַת אֲבִיהֶם וְאָנֹכִי דִּבַּרְתִּי אֲלֵיכֶם הַשְׁכֵּם וְדַבֵּר וְלֹא שְׁמַעְתֶּם אֵלָי: 15 וָאֶשְׁלַח אֲלֵיכֶם אֶת־כָּל־עֲבָדַי הַנְּבִאִים | הַשְׁכֵּים וְשָׁלֹחַ | לֵאמֹר שֻׁבוּ־נָא אִישׁ מִדַּרְכּוֹ הָרָעָה וְהֵיטִיבוּ מַעַלְלֵיכֶם וְאַל־תֵּלְכוּ אַחֲרֵי אֱלֹהִים אֲחֵרִים לְעָבְדָם וּשְׁבוּ אֶל־הָאֲדָמָה אֲשֶׁר־נָתַתִּי לָכֶם וְלַאֲבֹתֵיכֶם וְלֹא הִטִּיתֶם אֶת־אָזְנְכֶם וְלֹא שְׁמַעְתֶּם אֵלָי: 16 כִּי הֵקִימוּ בְּנֵי יְהוֹנָדָב בֶּן־רֵכָב

the commandment of their father, which he commanded them, but this people has not obeyed Me."'

17 "Therefore thus says the LORD God of hosts, the God of Israel: 'Behold, I will bring on Judah and on all the inhabitants of Jerusalem all the doom that I have pronounced against them; because I have spoken to them but they have not heard, and I have called to them but they have not answered.'"

18 And Jeremiah said to the house of the Rechabites, "Thus says the LORD of hosts, the God of Israel: 'Because you have obeyed the commandment of Jonadab your father, and kept all his precepts and done according to all that he commanded you, 19 therefore thus says the LORD of hosts, the God of Israel: "Jonadab the son of Rechab shall not lack a man to stand before Me forever."'"

36 Now it came to pass in the fourth year of Jehoiakim the son of Josiah, king of Judah, *that* this word came to Jeremiah from the LORD, saying: 2 "Take a scroll of a book and write on it all the words that I have spoken to you against Israel, against Judah, and against all the nations, from the day I spoke to you, from the days of Josiah even to this day. 3 It may be that the house of Judah will hear all the adversities which I purpose to bring upon them, that everyone may turn from his evil way, that I may forgive their iniquity and their sin."

4 Then Jeremiah called Baruch the son of Neriah; and Baruch wrote on a scroll of a book, at the instruction of Jeremiah, all the words of the LORD which He had spoken to him. 5 And Jeremiah commanded Baruch, saying, "I *am* confined, I cannot go into the house of the LORD. 6 You go, therefore, and read from the scroll which you have written at my instruction, the words of the LORD, in the hearing of the people in the LORD's house on the day of fasting. And you shall also read them in the hearing of all Judah who come from their cities. 7 It may be that they will present their supplication before the LORD, and everyone will turn from his evil way. For great *is* the anger and the fury that the LORD has pronounced against this people." 8 And Baruch the son of Neriah did according to all that Jeremiah the prophet commanded him, reading from the book the words of the LORD in the LORD's house.

9 Now it came to pass in the fifth year of Jehoiakim the son of Josiah, king of Judah, in the ninth month, *that* they proclaimed a fast before the LORD to all the people in Jerusalem, and to all the people who came from the cities of Judah to

אֶת־מִצְוֹת אֲבִיהֶם אֲשֶׁר צִוָּם וְהָעָם הַזֶּה לֹא שָׁמְעוּ אֵלָי: ס 17 לָכֵן כֹּה־אָמַר יְהֹוָה אֱלֹהֵי צְבָאוֹת אֱלֹהֵי יִשְׂרָאֵל הִנְנִי מֵבִיא אֶל־יְהוּדָה וְאֶל כָּל־יוֹשְׁבֵי יְרוּשָׁלַ͏ִם אֵת כָּל־הָרָעָה אֲשֶׁר דִּבַּרְתִּי עֲלֵיהֶם יַעַן דִּבַּרְתִּי אֲלֵיהֶם וְלֹא שָׁמֵעוּ וָאֶקְרָא לָהֶם וְלֹא עָנוּ: 18 וּלְבֵית הָרֵכָבִים אָמַר יִרְמְיָהוּ כֹּה־אָמַר יְהֹוָה צְבָאוֹת אֱלֹהֵי יִשְׂרָאֵל יַעַן אֲשֶׁר שְׁמַעְתֶּם עַל־מִצְוַת יְהוֹנָדָב אֲבִיכֶם וַתִּשְׁמְרוּ אֶת־כָּל־מִצְוֹתָיו וַתַּעֲשׂוּ כְּכֹל אֲשֶׁר־צִוָּה אֶתְכֶם: ס 19 לָכֵן כֹּה אָמַר יְהֹוָה צְבָאוֹת אֱלֹהֵי יִשְׂרָאֵל לֹא־יִכָּרֵת אִישׁ לְיוֹנָדָב בֶּן־רֵכָב עֹמֵד לְפָנַי כָּל־הַיָּמִים: פ

לו וַיְהִי בַּשָּׁנָה הָרְבִיעִת לִיהוֹיָקִים בֶּן־יֹאשִׁיָּהוּ מֶלֶךְ יְהוּדָה הָיָה הַדָּבָר הַזֶּה אֶל־יִרְמְיָהוּ מֵאֵת יְהֹוָה לֵאמֹר: 2 קַח־לְךָ מְגִלַּת־סֵפֶר וְכָתַבְתָּ אֵלֶיהָ אֵת כָּל־הַדְּבָרִים אֲשֶׁר־דִּבַּרְתִּי אֵלֶיךָ עַל־יִשְׂרָאֵל וְעַל־יְהוּדָה וְעַל־כָּל־הַגּוֹיִם מִיּוֹם דִּבַּרְתִּי אֵלֶיךָ מִימֵי יֹאשִׁיָּהוּ וְעַד הַיּוֹם הַזֶּה: 3 אוּלַי יִשְׁמְעוּ בֵּית יְהוּדָה אֵת כָּל־הָרָעָה אֲשֶׁר אָנֹכִי חֹשֵׁב לַעֲשׂוֹת לָהֶם לְמַעַן יָשׁוּבוּ אִישׁ מִדַּרְכּוֹ הָרָעָה וְסָלַחְתִּי לַעֲוֹנָם וּלְחַטָּאתָם: ס 4 וַיִּקְרָא יִרְמְיָהוּ אֶת־בָּרוּךְ בֶּן־נֵרִיָּה וַיִּכְתֹּב בָּרוּךְ מִפִּי יִרְמְיָהוּ אֵת כָּל־דִּבְרֵי יְהֹוָה אֲשֶׁר־דִּבֶּר אֵלָיו עַל־מְגִלַּת־סֵפֶר:

5 וַיְצַוֶּה יִרְמְיָהוּ אֶת־בָּרוּךְ לֵאמֹר אֲנִי עָצוּר לֹא אוּכַל לָבוֹא בֵּית יְהֹוָה: 6 וּבָאתָ אַתָּה וְקָרָאתָ בַמְּגִלָּה אֲשֶׁר־כָּתַבְתָּ־מִפִּי אֶת־דִּבְרֵי יְהֹוָה בְּאָזְנֵי הָעָם בֵּית יְהֹוָה בְּיוֹם צוֹם וְגַם בְּאָזְנֵי כָל־יְהוּדָה הַבָּאִים מֵעָרֵיהֶם תִּקְרָאֵם: 7 אוּלַי תִּפֹּל תְּחִנָּתָם לִפְנֵי יְהֹוָה וְיָשֻׁבוּ אִישׁ מִדַּרְכּוֹ הָרָעָה כִּי־גָדוֹל הָאַף וְהַחֵמָה אֲשֶׁר־דִּבֶּר יְהֹוָה אֶל־הָעָם הַזֶּה: 8 וַיַּעַשׂ בָּרוּךְ בֶּן־נֵרִיָּה כְּכֹל אֲשֶׁר־צִוָּהוּ יִרְמְיָהוּ הַנָּבִיא לִקְרֹא בַסֵּפֶר דִּבְרֵי יְהֹוָה בֵּית יְהֹוָה: ס 9 וַיְהִי בַשָּׁנָה הַחֲמִשִׁית לִיהוֹיָקִים בֶּן־יֹאשִׁיָּהוּ מֶלֶךְ־יְהוּדָה בַּחֹדֶשׁ הַתְּשִׁעִי קָרְאוּ צוֹם לִפְנֵי יְהֹוָה כָּל־הָעָם בִּירוּשָׁלָ͏ִם וְכָל־

Jerusalem. ¹⁰Then Baruch read from the book the words of Jeremiah in the house of the LORD, in the chamber of Gemariah the son of Shaphan the scribe, in the upper court at the entry of the New Gate of the LORD's house, in the hearing of all the people.

¹¹When Michaiah the son of Gemariah, the son of Shaphan, heard all the words of the LORD from the book, ¹²he then went down to the king's house, into the scribe's chamber; and there all the princes were sitting—Elishama the scribe, Delaiah the son of Shemaiah, Elnathan the son of Achbor, Gemariah the son of Shaphan, Zedekiah the son of Hananiah, and all the princes. ¹³Then Michaiah declared to them all the words that he had heard when Baruch read the book in the hearing of the people. ¹⁴Therefore all the princes sent Jehudi the son of Nethaniah, the son of Shelemiah, the son of Cushi, to Baruch, saying, "Take in your hand the scroll from which you have read in the hearing of the people, and come." So Baruch the son of Neriah took the scroll in his hand and came to them. ¹⁵And they said to him, "Sit down now, and read it in our hearing." So Baruch read it in their hearing.

¹⁶Now it happened, when they had heard all the words, that they looked in fear from one to another, and said to Baruch, "We will surely tell the king of all these words." ¹⁷And they asked Baruch, saying, "Tell us now, how did you write all these words—at his instruction?"

¹⁸So Baruch answered them, "He proclaimed with his mouth all these words to me, and I wrote *them* with ink in the book."

¹⁹Then the princes said to Baruch, "Go and hide, you and Jeremiah; and let no one know where you are."

²⁰And they went to the king, into the court; but they stored the scroll in the chamber of Elishama the scribe, and told all the words in the hearing of the king. ²¹So the king sent Jehudi to bring the scroll, and he took it from Elishama the scribe's chamber. And Jehudi read it in the hearing of the king and in the hearing of all the princes who stood beside the king. ²²Now the king was sitting in the winter house in the ninth month, with *a fire* burning on the hearth before him. ²³And it happened, when Jehudi had read three or four columns, *that the king* cut it with the scribe's knife and cast *it* into the fire that *was* on the hearth, until all the scroll was consumed in the fire that *was* on the hearth. ²⁴Yet they were not afraid, nor did they tear their garments, the king nor any of his servants who heard all these words. ²⁵Nevertheless Elnathan, Delaiah, and Gemariah implored the king not to

הָעָם הַבָּאִים מֵעָרֵי יְהוּדָה בִּירוּשָׁלָֽ͏ִם: 10 וַיִּקְרָא בָרוּךְ בַּסֵּפֶר אֶת־דִּבְרֵי יִרְמְיָהוּ בֵּית יְהֹוָה בְּלִשְׁכַּת גְּמַרְיָהוּ בֶן־שָׁפָן הַסֹּפֵר בֶּחָצֵר הָעֶלְיוֹן פֶּתַח שַׁעַר בֵּית־יְהֹוָה הֶחָדָשׁ בְּאָזְנֵי כָּל־הָעָם: 11 וַיִּשְׁמַע מִכָיְהוּ בֶן־גְּמַרְיָהוּ בֶן־שָׁפָן אֶת־כָּל־דִּבְרֵי יְהֹוָה מֵעַל הַסֵּפֶר: 12 וַיֵּרֶד בֵּית־הַמֶּלֶךְ עַל־לִשְׁכַּת הַסֹּפֵר וְהִנֵּה־שָׁם כָּל־הַשָּׂרִים יוֹשְׁבִים אֱלִישָׁמָע הַסֹּפֵר וּדְלָיָהוּ בֶן־שְׁמַעְיָהוּ וְאֶלְנָתָן בֶּן־עַכְבּוֹר וּגְמַרְיָהוּ בֶן־שָׁפָן וְצִדְקִיָּהוּ בֶן־חֲנַנְיָהוּ וְכָל־הַשָּׂרִים: 13 וַיַּגֵּד לָהֶם מִכָיְהוּ אֵת כָּל־הַדְּבָרִים אֲשֶׁר שָׁמֵעַ בִּקְרֹא בָרוּךְ בַּסֵּפֶר בְּאָזְנֵי הָעָם: 14 וַיִּשְׁלְחוּ כָל־הַשָּׂרִים אֶל־בָּרוּךְ אֶת־יְהוּדִי בֶּן־נְתַנְיָהוּ בֶּן־שֶׁלֶמְיָהוּ בֶּן־כּוּשִׁי לֵאמֹר הַמְּגִלָּה אֲשֶׁר קָרָאתָ בָּהּ בְּאָזְנֵי הָעָם קָחֶנָּה בְיָדְךָ וָלֵךְ וַיִּקַּח בָּרוּךְ בֶּן־נֵרִיָּהוּ אֶת־הַמְּגִלָּה בְּיָדוֹ וַיָּבֹא אֲלֵיהֶם: 15 וַיֹּאמְרוּ אֵלָיו שֵׁב נָא וּקְרָאֶנָּה בְּאָזְנֵינוּ וַיִּקְרָא בָרוּךְ בְּאָזְנֵיהֶם: 16 וַיְהִי כְּשָׁמְעָם אֶת־כָּל־הַדְּבָרִים פָּחֲדוּ אִישׁ אֶל־רֵעֵהוּ וַיֹּאמְרוּ אֶל־בָּרוּךְ הַגֵּיד נַגִּיד לַמֶּלֶךְ אֵת כָּל־הַדְּבָרִים הָאֵלֶּה: 17 וְאֶת־בָּרוּךְ שָׁאֲלוּ לֵאמֹר הַגֶּד־נָא לָנוּ אֵיךְ כָּתַבְתָּ אֶת־כָּל־הַדְּבָרִים הָאֵלֶּה מִפִּיו: 18 וַיֹּאמֶר לָהֶם בָּרוּךְ מִפִּיו יִקְרָא אֵלַי אֵת כָּל־הַדְּבָרִים הָאֵלֶּה וַאֲנִי כֹּתֵב עַל־הַסֵּפֶר בַּדְּיוֹ: פ 19 וַיֹּאמְרוּ הַשָּׂרִים אֶל־בָּרוּךְ לֵךְ הִסָּתֵר אַתָּה וְיִרְמְיָהוּ וְאִישׁ אַל־יֵדַע אֵיפֹה אַתֶּם: 20 וַיָּבֹאוּ אֶל־הַמֶּלֶךְ חָצֵרָה וְאֶת־הַמְּגִלָּה הִפְקִדוּ בְּלִשְׁכַּת אֱלִישָׁמָע הַסֹּפֵר וַיַּגִּידוּ בְּאָזְנֵי הַמֶּלֶךְ אֵת כָּל־הַדְּבָרִים: 21 וַיִּשְׁלַח הַמֶּלֶךְ אֶת־יְהוּדִי לָקַחַת אֶת־הַמְּגִלָּה וַיִּקָּחֶהָ מִלִּשְׁכַּת אֱלִישָׁמָע הַסֹּפֵר וַיִּקְרָאֶהָ יְהוּדִי בְּאָזְנֵי הַמֶּלֶךְ וּבְאָזְנֵי כָּל־הַשָּׂרִים הָעֹמְדִים מֵעַל הַמֶּלֶךְ: 22 וְהַמֶּלֶךְ יוֹשֵׁב בֵּית הַחֹרֶף בַּחֹדֶשׁ הַתְּשִׁיעִי וְאֶת־הָאָח לְפָנָיו מְבֹעָרֶת | 23 וַיְהִי כִּקְרוֹא יְהוּדִי שָׁלֹשׁ דְּלָתוֹת וְאַרְבָּעָה יִקְרָעֶהָ בְּתַעַר הַסֹּפֵר וְהַשְׁלֵךְ אֶל־הָאֵשׁ אֲשֶׁר אֶל־הָאָח עַד־תֹּם כָּל־הַמְּגִלָּה עַל־הָאֵשׁ אֲשֶׁר עַל־הָאָח: 24 וְלֹא פָחֲדוּ וְלֹא קָרְעוּ אֶת־בִּגְדֵיהֶם הַמֶּלֶךְ וְכָל־עֲבָדָיו הַשֹּׁמְעִים אֵת כָּל־הַדְּבָרִים הָאֵלֶּה: 25 וְגַם אֶלְנָתָן

burn the scroll; but he would not listen to them.
26 And the king commanded Jerahmeel the king's son, Seraiah the son of Azriel, and Shelemiah the son of Abdeel, to seize Baruch the scribe and Jeremiah the prophet, but the LORD hid them.

27 Now after the king had burned the scroll with the words which Baruch had written at the instruction of Jeremiah, the word of the LORD came to Jeremiah, saying: 28 "Take yet another scroll, and write on it all the former words that were in the first scroll which Jehoiakim the king of Judah has burned. 29 And you shall say to Jehoiakim king of Judah, 'Thus says the LORD: "You have burned this scroll, saying, 'Why have you written in it that the king of Babylon will certainly come and destroy this land, and cause man and beast to cease from here?' " 30 Therefore thus says the LORD concerning Jehoiakim king of Judah: "He shall have no one to sit on the throne of David, and his dead body shall be cast out to the heat of the day and the frost of the night. 31 I will punish him, his family, and his servants for their iniquity; and I will bring on them, on the inhabitants of Jerusalem, and on the men of Judah all the doom that I have pronounced against them; but they did not heed." ' "

32 Then Jeremiah took another scroll and gave it to Baruch the scribe, the son of Neriah, who wrote on it at the instruction of Jeremiah all the words of the book which Jehoiakim king of Judah had burned in the fire. And besides, there were added to them many similar words.

37 Now King Zedekiah the son of Josiah reigned instead of Coniah the son of Jehoiakim, whom Nebuchadnezzar king of Babylon made king in the land of Judah. 2 But neither he nor his servants nor the people of the land gave heed to the words of the LORD which He spoke by the prophet Jeremiah.

3 And Zedekiah the king sent Jehucal the son of Shelemiah, and Zephaniah the son of Maaseiah, the priest, to the prophet Jeremiah, saying, "Pray now to the LORD our God for us." 4 Now Jeremiah was coming and going among the people, for they had not yet put him in prison. 5 Then Pharaoh's army came up from Egypt; and when the Chaldeans who were besieging Jerusalem heard news of them, they departed from Jerusalem.

6 Then the word of the LORD came to the prophet Jeremiah, saying, 7 "Thus says the LORD, the God of Israel, 'Thus you shall say to the king of Judah, who sent you to Me to inquire of Me: "Behold, Pharaoh's army which has come up to help you will return to Egypt, to their own land. 8 And the Chaldeans shall come back and fight against this

וְדֵלָיָהוּ וּגְמַרְיָהוּ הִפְגִּעוּ בַמֶּלֶךְ לְבִלְתִּי שְׂרֹף אֶת־
הַמְּגִלָּה וְלֹא שָׁמַע אֲלֵיהֶם: 26 וַיְצַוֶּה הַמֶּלֶךְ אֶת־
יְרַחְמְאֵל בֶּן־הַמֶּלֶךְ וְאֶת־שְׂרָיָהוּ בֶן־עַזְרִיאֵל וְאֶת־
שֶׁלֶמְיָהוּ בֶּן־עַבְדְּאֵל לָקַחַת אֶת־בָּרוּךְ הַסֹּפֵר וְאֵת
יִרְמְיָהוּ הַנָּבִיא וַיַּסְתִּרֵם יְהוָה: ס 27 וַיְהִי
דְבַר־יְהוָה אֶל־יִרְמְיָהוּ אַחֲרֵי | שְׂרֹף הַמֶּלֶךְ אֶת־
הַמְּגִלָּה וְאֶת־הַדְּבָרִים אֲשֶׁר כָּתַב בָּרוּךְ מִפִּי
יִרְמְיָהוּ לֵאמֹר: 28 שׁוּב קַח־לְךָ מְגִלָּה אַחֶרֶת
וּכְתֹב עָלֶיהָ אֵת כָּל־הַדְּבָרִים הָרִאשֹׁנִים אֲשֶׁר הָיוּ
עַל־הַמְּגִלָּה הָרִאשֹׁנָה אֲשֶׁר שָׂרַף יְהוֹיָקִים מֶלֶךְ־
יְהוּדָה: 29 וְעַל־יְהוֹיָקִים מֶלֶךְ־יְהוּדָה תֹאמַר כֹּה
אָמַר יְהוָה אַתָּה שָׂרַפְתָּ אֶת־הַמְּגִלָּה הַזֹּאת לֵאמֹר
מַדּוּעַ כָּתַבְתָּ עָלֶיהָ לֵאמֹר בֹּא־יָבוֹא מֶלֶךְ־בָּבֶל
וְהִשְׁחִית אֶת־הָאָרֶץ הַזֹּאת וְהִשְׁבִּית מִמֶּנָּה אָדָם
וּבְהֵמָה: 30 לָכֵן כֹּה־אָמַר יְהוָה עַל־
יְהוֹיָקִים מֶלֶךְ יְהוּדָה לֹא־יִהְיֶה־לּוֹ יוֹשֵׁב עַל־כִּסֵּא
דָוִד וְנִבְלָתוֹ תִּהְיֶה מֻשְׁלֶכֶת לַחֹרֶב בַּיּוֹם וְלַקֶּרַח
בַּלָּיְלָה: 31 וּפָקַדְתִּי עָלָיו וְעַל־זַרְעוֹ וְעַל־עֲבָדָיו אֶת־
עֲוֹנָם וְהֵבֵאתִי עֲלֵיהֶם וְעַל־יֹשְׁבֵי יְרוּשָׁלַםִ וְאֶל־
אִישׁ יְהוּדָה אֵת כָּל־הָרָעָה אֲשֶׁר־דִּבַּרְתִּי אֲלֵיהֶם
וְלֹא שָׁמֵעוּ: ס 32 וְיִרְמְיָהוּ לָקַח | מְגִלָּה
אַחֶרֶת וַיִּתְּנָהּ אֶל־בָּרוּךְ בֶּן־נֵרִיָּהוּ הַסֹּפֵר וַיִּכְתֹּב
עָלֶיהָ מִפִּי יִרְמְיָהוּ אֵת כָּל־דִּבְרֵי הַסֵּפֶר אֲשֶׁר שָׂרַף
יְהוֹיָקִים מֶלֶךְ־יְהוּדָה בָּאֵשׁ וְעוֹד נוֹסַף עֲלֵיהֶם
דְּבָרִים רַבִּים כָּהֵמָּה: ס

לז וַיִּמְלָךְ־מֶלֶךְ צִדְקִיָּהוּ בֶּן־יֹאשִׁיָּהוּ תַּחַת כָּנְיָהוּ
בֶּן־יְהוֹיָקִים אֲשֶׁר הִמְלִיךְ נְבוּכַדְרֶאצַּר מֶלֶךְ־בָּבֶל
בְּאֶרֶץ יְהוּדָה: 2 וְלֹא שָׁמַע הוּא וַעֲבָדָיו וְעַם
הָאָרֶץ אֶל־דִּבְרֵי יְהוָה אֲשֶׁר דִּבֶּר בְּיַד יִרְמְיָהוּ
הַנָּבִיא: 3 וַיִּשְׁלַח הַמֶּלֶךְ צִדְקִיָּהוּ אֶת־יְהוּכַל בֶּן־
שֶׁלֶמְיָה וְאֶת־צְפַנְיָהוּ בֶן־מַעֲשֵׂיָה הַכֹּהֵן אֶל־יִרְמְיָהוּ
הַנָּבִיא לֵאמֹר הִתְפַּלֶּל־נָא בַעֲדֵנוּ אֶל־יְהוָה אֱלֹהֵינוּ:
4 וְיִרְמְיָהוּ בָּא וְיֹצֵא בְּתוֹךְ הָעָם וְלֹא־נָתְנוּ אֹתוֹ
בֵּית הַכְּלִיא: 5 וְחֵיל פַּרְעֹה יָצָא מִמִּצְרָיִם וַיִּשְׁמְעוּ
הַכַּשְׂדִּים הַצָּרִים עַל־יְרוּשָׁלַםִ אֶת־שִׁמְעָם וַיֵּעָלוּ
מֵעַל יְרוּשָׁלָםִ: פ
6 וַיְהִי דְּבַר־יְהוָה אֶל־יִרְמְיָהוּ הַנָּבִיא לֵאמֹר: 7 כֹּה־
אָמַר יְהוָה אֱלֹהֵי יִשְׂרָאֵל כֹּה תֹאמְרוּ אֶל־מֶלֶךְ
יְהוּדָה הַשֹּׁלֵחַ אֶתְכֶם אֵלַי לְדָרְשֵׁנִי הִנֵּה | חֵיל
פַּרְעֹה הַיֹּצֵא לָכֶם לְעֶזְרָה שָׁב לְאַרְצוֹ מִצְרָיִם:
8 וְשָׁבוּ הַכַּשְׂדִּים וְנִלְחֲמוּ עַל־הָעִיר הַזֹּאת וּלְכָדֻהָ

city, and take it and burn it with fire."' 9 Thus says
the LORD: 'Do not deceive yourselves, saying, "The
Chaldeans will surely depart from us," for they will
not depart. 10 For though you had defeated the
whole army of the Chaldeans who fight against you,
and there remained *only* wounded men among
them, they would rise up, every man in his tent, and
burn the city with fire.'"

11 And it happened, when the army of the
Chaldeans left *the siege* of Jerusalem for fear of
Pharaoh's army, 12 that Jeremiah went out of
Jerusalem to go into the land of Benjamin to claim
his property there among the people. 13 And when
he was in the Gate of Benjamin, a captain of the
guard *was* there whose name *was* Irijah the son of
Shelemiah, the son of Hananiah; and he seized
Jeremiah the prophet, saying, "You are defecting to
the Chaldeans!"

14 Then Jeremiah said, "False! I am not defecting
to the Chaldeans." But he did not listen to him.

So Irijah seized Jeremiah and brought him to the
princes. 15 Therefore the princes were angry with
Jeremiah, and they struck him and put him in
prison in the house of Jonathan the scribe. For they
had made that the prison.

16 When Jeremiah entered the dungeon and the
cells, and Jeremiah had remained there many days,
17 then Zedekiah the king sent and took him *out*.
The king asked him secretly in his house, and said,
"Is there *any* word from the LORD?"

And Jeremiah said, "There is." Then he said,
"You shall be delivered into the hand of the king of
Babylon!"

18 Moreover Jeremiah said to King Zedekiah,
"What offense have I committed against you,
against your servants, or against this people, that
you have put me in prison? 19 Where now *are* your
prophets who prophesied to you, saying, 'The king
of Babylon will not come against you or against this
land?' 20 Therefore please hear now, O my lord the
king. Please, let my petition be accepted before you,
and do not make me return to the house of
Jonathan the scribe, lest I die there."

21 Then Zedekiah the king commanded that they
should commit Jeremiah to the court of the prison,
and that they should give him daily a piece of bread
from the bakers' street, until all the bread in the city
was gone. Thus Jeremiah remained in the court of
the prison.

38

Now Shephatiah the son of Mattan, Gedaliah
the son of Pashhur, Jucal the son of Shelemiah, and
Pashhur the son of Malchiah heard the words that
Jeremiah had spoken to all the people, saying,

וְשָׂרְפָהּ בָּאֵשׁ: ס 9 כֹּה ׀ אָמַר יְהֹוָה
אַל־תַּשִּׁאוּ נַפְשֹׁתֵיכֶם לֵאמֹר הָלֹךְ יֵלְכוּ מֵעָלֵינוּ
הַכַּשְׂדִּים כִּי־לֹא יֵלֵכוּ: 10 כִּי אִם־הִכִּיתֶם כָּל־חֵיל
כַּשְׂדִּים הַנִּלְחָמִים אִתְּכֶם וְנִשְׁאֲרוּ בָם אֲנָשִׁים
מְדֻקָּרִים אִישׁ בְּאָהֳלוֹ יָקוּמוּ וְשָׂרְפוּ אֶת־הָעִיר
הַזֹּאת בָּאֵשׁ: 11 וְהָיָה בְּהֵעָלוֹת חֵיל הַכַּשְׂדִּים מֵעַל
יְרוּשָׁלָ͏ִם מִפְּנֵי חֵיל פַּרְעֹה: ס 12 וַיֵּצֵא
יִרְמְיָהוּ מִירוּשָׁלַ͏ִם לָלֶכֶת אֶרֶץ בִּנְיָמִן לַחֲלִק מִשָּׁם
בְּתוֹךְ הָעָם: 13 וַיְהִי־הוּא בְּשַׁעַר בִּנְיָמִן וְשָׁם בַּעַל
פְּקִדֻת וּשְׁמוֹ יִרְאִיָּיה בֶּן־שֶׁלֶמְיָה בֶּן־חֲנַנְיָה וַיִּתְפֹּשׂ
אֶת־יִרְמְיָהוּ הַנָּבִיא לֵאמֹר אֶל־הַכַּשְׂדִּים אַתָּה נֹפֵל:
14 וַיֹּאמֶר יִרְמְיָהוּ שֶׁקֶר אֵינֶנִּי נֹפֵל עַל־הַכַּשְׂדִּים
וְלֹא שָׁמַע אֵלָיו וַיִּתְפֹּשׂ יִרְאִיָּיה בְּיִרְמְיָהוּ וַיְבִאֵהוּ
אֶל־הַשָּׂרִים: 15 וַיִּקְצְפוּ הַשָּׂרִים עַל־יִרְמְיָהוּ וְהִכּוּ
אֹתוֹ וְנָתְנוּ אוֹתוֹ בֵּית הָאֵסוּר בֵּית יְהוֹנָתָן הַסֹּפֵר
כִּי־אֹתוֹ עָשׂוּ לְבֵית הַכֶּלֶא: 16 כִּי בָא יִרְמְיָהוּ אֶל־
בֵּית הַבּוֹר וְאֶל־הַחֲנֻיוֹת וַיֵּשֶׁב־שָׁם יִרְמְיָהוּ יָמִים
רַבִּים:
פ

17 וַיִּשְׁלַח הַמֶּלֶךְ צִדְקִיָּהוּ וַיִּקָּחֵהוּ וַיִּשְׁאָלֵהוּ
הַמֶּלֶךְ בְּבֵיתוֹ בַּסֵּתֶר וַיֹּאמֶר הֲיֵשׁ דָּבָר מֵאֵת
יְהֹוָה וַיֹּאמֶר יִרְמְיָהוּ יֵשׁ וַיֹּאמֶר בְּיַד מֶלֶךְ־בָּבֶל
תִּנָּתֵן: ס 18 וַיֹּאמֶר יִרְמְיָהוּ אֶל־הַמֶּלֶךְ
צִדְקִיָּהוּ מֶה חָטָאתִי לְךָ וְלַעֲבָדֶיךָ וְלָעָם הַזֶּה כִּי־
נְתַתֶּם אוֹתִי אֶל־בֵּית הַכֶּלֶא: 19 וְאַיֵּה נְבִיאֵיכֶם
אֲשֶׁר־נִבְּאוּ לָכֶם לֵאמֹר לֹא־יָבֹא מֶלֶךְ־בָּבֶל עֲלֵיכֶם
וְעַל הָאָרֶץ הַזֹּאת: 20 וְעַתָּה שְׁמַע־נָא אֲדֹנִי הַמֶּלֶךְ
תִּפָּל־נָא תְחִנָּתִי לְפָנֶיךָ וְאַל־תְּשִׁבֵנִי בֵּית יְהוֹנָתָן
הַסֹּפֵר וְלֹא אָמוּת שָׁם: 21 וַיְצַוֶּה הַמֶּלֶךְ צִדְקִיָּהוּ
וַיַּפְקִדוּ אֶת־יִרְמְיָהוּ בַּחֲצַר הַמַּטָּרָה וְנָתֹן לוֹ כִכַּר־
לֶחֶם לַיּוֹם מִחוּץ הָאֹפִים עַד־תֹּם כָּל־הַלֶּחֶם מִן־
הָעִיר וַיֵּשֶׁב יִרְמְיָהוּ בַּחֲצַר הַמַּטָּרָה:

לח וַיִּשְׁמַע שְׁפַטְיָה בֶן־מַתָּן וּגְדַלְיָהוּ בֶּן־
פַּשְׁחוּר וְיוּכַל בֶּן־שֶׁלֶמְיָהוּ וּפַשְׁחוּר בֶּן־מַלְכִּיָּה
אֶת־הַדְּבָרִים אֲשֶׁר יִרְמְיָהוּ מְדַבֵּר אֶל־כָּל־הָעָם

לח 19 וְאַיֵּה

2 "Thus says the LORD: 'He who remains in this city shall die by the sword, by famine, and by pestilence; but he who goes over to the Chaldeans shall live; his life shall be as a prize to him, and he shall live.'
3 Thus says the LORD: 'This city shall surely be given into the hand of the king of Babylon's army, which shall take it.'"

4 Therefore the princes said to the king, "Please, let this man be put to death, for thus he weakens the hands of the men of war who remain in this city, and the hands of all the people, by speaking such words to them. For this man does not seek the welfare of this people, but their harm."

5 Then Zedekiah the king said, "Look, he is in your hand. For the king can do nothing against you." 6 So they took Jeremiah and cast him into the dungeon of Malchiah the king's son, which was in the court of the prison, and they let Jeremiah down with ropes. And in the dungeon there was no water, but mire. So Jeremiah sank in the mire.

7 Now Ebed-Melech the Ethiopian, one of the eunuchs, who was in the king's house, heard that they had put Jeremiah in the dungeon. When the king was sitting at the Gate of Benjamin, 8 Ebed-Melech went out of the king's house and spoke to the king, saying: 9 "My lord the king, these men have done evil in all that they have done to Jeremiah the prophet, whom they have cast into the dungeon, and he is likely to die from hunger in the place where he is. For there is no more bread in the city." 10 Then the king commanded Ebed-Melech the Ethiopian, saying, "Take from here thirty men with you, and lift Jeremiah the prophet out of the dungeon before he dies." 11 So Ebed-Melech took the men with him and went into the house of the king under the treasury, and took from there old clothes and old rags, and let them down by ropes into the dungeon to Jeremiah. 12 Then Ebed-Melech the Ethiopian said to Jeremiah, "Please put these old clothes and rags under your armpits, under the ropes." And Jeremiah did so. 13 So they pulled Jeremiah up with ropes and lifted him out of the dungeon. And Jeremiah remained in the court of the prison.

14 Then Zedekiah the king sent and had Jeremiah the prophet brought to him at the third entrance of the house of the LORD. And the king said to Jeremiah, "I will ask you something. Hide nothing from me."

15 Jeremiah said to Zedekiah, "If I declare it to you, will you not surely put me to death? And if I give you advice, you will not listen to me."

16 So Zedekiah the king swore secretly to Jeremiah, saying, "*As* the LORD lives, who made our very souls, I will not put you to death, nor will I give you into the hand of these men who seek your life."

17 Then Jeremiah said to Zedekiah, "Thus says the LORD, the God of hosts, the God of Israel: 'If you surely surrender to the king of Babylon's princes, then your soul shall live; this city shall not be burned with fire, and you and your house shall live. 18 But if you do not surrender to the king of Babylon's princes, then this city shall be given into the hand of the Chaldeans; they shall burn it with fire, and you shall not escape from their hand.' "

19 And Zedekiah the king said to Jeremiah, "I am afraid of the Jews who have defected to the Chaldeans, lest they deliver me into their hand, and they abuse me."

20 But Jeremiah said, "They shall not deliver *you.* Please, obey the voice of the LORD which I speak to you. So it shall be well with you, and your soul shall live. 21 But if you refuse to surrender, this *is* the word that the LORD has shown me: 22 'Now behold, all the women who are left in the king of Judah's house *shall be* surrendered to the king of Babylon's princes, and those *women* shall say:

"Your close friends have set upon you
And prevailed against you;
Your feet have sunk in the mire,
And they have turned away again."

23 'So they shall surrender all your wives and children to the Chaldeans. You shall not escape from their hand, but shall be taken by the hand of the king of Babylon. And you shall cause this city to be burned with fire.' "

24 Then Zedekiah said to Jeremiah, "Let no one know of these words, and you shall not die. 25 But if the princes hear that I have talked with you, and they come to you and say to you, 'Declare to us now what you have said to the king, and also what the king said to you; do not hide *it* from us, and we will not put you to death,' 26 then you shall say to them, 'I presented my request before the king, that he would not make me return to Jonathan's house to die there.' "

27 Then all the princes came to Jeremiah and asked him. And he told them according to all these words that the king had commanded. So they stopped speaking with him, for the conversation had not been heard. 28 Now Jeremiah remained in the court of the prison until the day that Jerusalem was taken. And he was *there* when Jerusalem was taken.

16 וַיִּשָּׁבַ֞ע הַמֶּ֧לֶךְ צִדְקִיָּ֛הוּ אֶֽל־יִרְמְיָ֖הוּ בַּסֵּ֣תֶר לֵאמֹ֑ר חַי־יְהוָ֗ה אֲשֶׁ֨ר עָשָׂה־לָ֜נוּ אֶת־הַנֶּ֤פֶשׁ הַזֹּאת֙ אִם־אֲמִיתֶ֔ךָ וְאִם־אֶתֶּנְךָ֗ בְּיַד֙ הָאֲנָשִׁ֣ים הָאֵ֔לֶּה אֲשֶׁ֥ר מְבַקְשִׁ֖ים אֶת־נַפְשֶֽׁךָ׃ ס 17 וַיֹּ֤אמֶר יִרְמְיָ֙הוּ֙ אֶל־צִדְקִיָּ֔הוּ כֹּֽה־אָמַ֞ר יְהוָ֤ה אֱלֹהֵ֣י צְבָא֔וֹת אֱלֹהֵ֖י יִשְׂרָאֵ֑ל אִם־יָצֹ֣א תֵצֵ֗א אֶל־שָׂרֵ֤י מֶֽלֶךְ־בָּבֶל֙ וְחָיְתָ֣ה נַפְשֶׁ֔ךָ וְהָעִ֣יר הַזֹּ֔את לֹ֥א תִשָּׂרֵ֖ף בָּאֵ֑שׁ וְחָיִ֖תָה אַתָּ֥ה וּבֵיתֶֽךָ׃ 18 וְאִ֣ם לֹֽא־תֵצֵ֗א אֶל־שָׂרֵי֙ מֶ֣לֶךְ בָּבֶ֔ל וְנִתְּנָ֞ה הָעִ֤יר הַזֹּאת֙ בְּיַ֣ד הַכַּשְׂדִּ֔ים וּשְׂרָפ֖וּהָ בָּאֵ֑שׁ וְאַתָּ֖ה לֹֽא־תִמָּלֵ֥ט מִיָּדָֽם׃ ס 19 וַיֹּ֛אמֶר הַמֶּ֥לֶךְ צִדְקִיָּ֖הוּ אֶֽל־יִרְמְיָ֑הוּ אֲנִ֧י דֹאֵ֣ג אֶת־הַיְּהוּדִ֗ים אֲשֶׁ֤ר נָֽפְלוּ֙ אֶל־הַכַּשְׂדִּ֔ים פֶּֽן־יִתְּנ֥וּ אֹתִ֛י בְּיָדָ֖ם וְהִתְעַלְּלוּ־בִֽי׃ 20 וַיֹּ֥אמֶר יִרְמְיָ֖הוּ לֹ֣א יִתֵּ֑נוּ שְֽׁמַע־נָ֣א ׀ בְּק֣וֹל יְהוָ֗ה לַאֲשֶׁ֤ר אֲנִי֙ דֹּבֵ֣ר אֵלֶ֔יךָ וְיִ֥יטַב לְךָ֖ וּתְחִ֥י נַפְשֶֽׁךָ׃ 21 וְאִם־מָאֵ֥ן אַתָּ֖ה לָצֵ֑את זֶ֣ה הַדָּבָ֔ר אֲשֶׁ֥ר הִרְאַ֖נִי יְהוָֽה׃ 22 וְהִנֵּ֣ה כָל־הַנָּשִׁ֗ים אֲשֶׁ֤ר נִשְׁאֲרוּ֙ בְּבֵ֣ית מֶֽלֶךְ־יְהוּדָ֔ה מֽוּצָא֕וֹת אֶל־שָׂרֵ֖י מֶ֣לֶךְ בָּבֶ֑ל וְהֵ֣נָּה אֹמְר֗וֹת הִסִּית֜וּךָ וְיָכְל֤וּ לְךָ֙ אַנְשֵׁ֣י שְׁלֹמֶ֔ךָ הָטְבְּע֥וּ בַבֹּ֛ץ רַגְלֶ֖ךָ נָסֹ֥גוּ אָחֽוֹר׃ 23 וְאֶת־כָּל־נָשֶׁ֣יךָ וְאֶת־בָּנֶ֗יךָ מֽוֹצִאִים֙ אֶל־הַכַּשְׂדִּ֔ים וְאַתָּ֖ה לֹא־תִמָּלֵ֣ט מִיָּדָ֑ם כִּ֣י בְיַ֤ד מֶֽלֶךְ־בָּבֶל֙ תִּתָּפֵ֔שׂ וְאֶת־הָעִ֥יר הַזֹּ֖את תִּשְׂרֹ֥ף בָּאֵֽשׁ׃ פ 24 וַיֹּ֨אמֶר צִדְקִיָּ֜הוּ אֶל־יִרְמְיָ֗הוּ אִ֥ישׁ אַל־יֵדַ֛ע בַּדְּבָרִֽים־הָאֵ֖לֶּה וְלֹ֥א תָמֽוּת׃ 25 וְכִֽי־יִשְׁמְע֣וּ הַשָּׂרִים֮ כִּֽי־דִבַּ֣רְתִּי אִתָּךְ֒ וּבָ֣אוּ אֵלֶ֣יךָ וְאָמְר֣וּ אֵלֶ֡יךָ הַגִּֽידָה־נָּ֣א לָנוּ֩ מַה־דִּבַּ֨רְתָּ אֶל־הַמֶּ֜לֶךְ אַל־תְּכַחֵ֤ד מִמֶּ֙נּוּ֙ וְלֹ֣א נְמִיתֶ֔ךָ וּמַה־דִּבֶּ֥ר אֵלֶ֖יךָ הַמֶּֽלֶךְ׃ 26 וְאָמַרְתָּ֣ אֲלֵיהֶ֔ם מַפִּיל־אֲנִ֥י תְחִנָּתִ֖י לִפְנֵ֣י הַמֶּ֑לֶךְ לְבִלְתִּ֧י הֲשִׁיבֵ֛נִי בֵּ֥ית יְהוֹנָתָ֖ן לָמ֥וּת שָֽׁם׃ פ 27 וַיָּבֹ֨אוּ כָל־הַשָּׂרִ֤ים אֶֽל־יִרְמְיָ֙הוּ֙ וַיִּשְׁאֲל֣וּ אֹת֔וֹ וַיַּגֵּ֤ד לָהֶם֙ כְּכָל־הַדְּבָרִ֣ים הָאֵ֔לֶּה אֲשֶׁ֥ר צִוָּ֖ה הַמֶּ֑לֶךְ וַיַּחֲרִ֣שׁוּ מִמֶּ֔נּוּ כִּ֥י לֹֽא־נִשְׁמַ֖ע הַדָּבָֽר׃ פ 28 וַיֵּ֤שֶׁב יִרְמְיָ֙הוּ֙ בַּחֲצַ֣ר הַמַּטָּרָ֔ה עַד־י֖וֹם אֲשֶׁר־נִלְכְּדָ֣ה יְרוּשָׁלָ֑͏ִם ס וְהָיָ֕ה כַּאֲשֶׁ֥ר נִלְכְּדָ֖ה יְרוּשָׁלָֽ͏ִם׃ פ

16 כתיב ולא קרי

39 In the ninth year of Zedekiah king of Judah, in the tenth month, Nebuchadnezzar king of Babylon and all his army came against Jerusalem, and besieged it. [2] In the eleventh year of Zedekiah, in the fourth month, on the ninth *day* of the month, the city was penetrated.

[3] Then all the princes of the king of Babylon came in and sat in the Middle Gate: Nergal-Sharezer, Samgar-Nebo, Sarsechim, Rabsaris, Nergal-Sarezer, Rabmag, with the rest of the princes of the king of Babylon.

[4] So it was, when Zedekiah the king of Judah and all the men of war saw them, that they fled and went out of the city by night, by way of the king's garden, by the gate between the two walls. And he went out by way of the plain. [5] But the Chaldean army pursued them and overtook Zedekiah in the plains of Jericho. And when they had captured him, they brought him up to Nebuchadnezzar king of Babylon, to Riblah in the land of Hamath, where he pronounced judgment on him. [6] Then the king of Babylon killed the sons of Zedekiah before his eyes in Riblah; the king of Babylon also killed all the nobles of Judah. [7] Moreover he put out Zedekiah's eyes, and bound him with bronze fetters to carry him off to Babylon. [8] And the Chaldeans burned the king's house and the houses of the people with fire, and broke down the walls of Jerusalem. [9] Then Nebuzaradan the captain of the guard carried away captive to Babylon the remnant of the people who remained in the city and those who defected to him, with the rest of the people who remained. [10] But Nebuzaradan the captain of the guard left in the land of Judah the poor people, who had nothing, and gave them vineyards and fields at the same time.

[11] Now Nebuchadnezzar king of Babylon gave charge concerning Jeremiah to Nebuzaradan the captain of the guard, saying, [12] "Take him and look after him, and do him no harm; but do to him just as he says to you." [13] So Nebuzaradan the captain of the guard sent Nebushasban, Rabsaris, Nergal-Sharezer, Rabmag, and all the king of Babylon's chief officers; [14] then they sent *someone* to take Jeremiah from the court of the prison, and committed him to Gedaliah the son of Ahikam, the son of Shaphan, that he should take him home. So he dwelt among the people.

[15] Meanwhile the word of the LORD had come to Jeremiah while he was shut up in the court of the prison, saying, [16] "Go and speak to Ebed-Melech the Ethiopian, saying, 'Thus says the LORD of hosts, the God of Israel: "Behold, I will bring My words upon this city for adversity and not for good,

לט בַּשָּׁנָה הַתְּשִׁעִית לְצִדְקִיָּהוּ מֶלֶךְ־יְהוּדָה בַּחֹדֶשׁ הָעֲשִׂרִי בָּא נְבוּכַדְרֶאצַּר מֶלֶךְ־בָּבֶל וְכָל־חֵילוֹ אֶל־יְרוּשָׁלַ͏ִם וַיָּצֻרוּ עָלֶיהָ: ס 2 בְּעַשְׁתֵּי־עֶשְׂרֵה שָׁנָה לְצִדְקִיָּהוּ בַּחֹדֶשׁ הָרְבִיעִי בְּתִשְׁעָה לַחֹדֶשׁ הָבְקְעָה הָעִיר: 3 וַיָּבֹאוּ כֹּל שָׂרֵי מֶלֶךְ־בָּבֶל וַיֵּשְׁבוּ בְּשַׁעַר הַתָּוֶךְ נֵרְגַל שַׂר־אֶצֶר סַמְגַּר־נְבוֹ שַׂר־סְכִים רַב־סָרִיס נֵרְגַל שַׂר־אֶצֶר רַב־מָג וְכָל־שְׁאֵרִית שָׂרֵי מֶלֶךְ בָּבֶל: 4 וַיְהִי כַּאֲשֶׁר רָאָם צִדְקִיָּהוּ מֶלֶךְ־יְהוּדָה וְכֹל ׀ אַנְשֵׁי הַמִּלְחָמָה וַיִּבְרְחוּ וַיֵּצְאוּ לַיְלָה מִן־הָעִיר דֶּרֶךְ גַּן הַמֶּלֶךְ בְּשַׁעַר בֵּין הַחֹמֹתָיִם וַיֵּצֵא דֶּרֶךְ הָעֲרָבָה: 5 וַיִּרְדְּפוּ חֵיל־כַּשְׂדִּים אַחֲרֵיהֶם וַיַּשִּׂגוּ אֶת־צִדְקִיָּהוּ בְּעַרְבוֹת יְרֵחוֹ וַיִּקְחוּ אֹתוֹ וַיַּעֲלֻהוּ אֶל־נְבוּכַדְרֶאצַּר מֶלֶךְ־בָּבֶל רִבְלָתָה בְּאֶרֶץ חֲמָת וַיְדַבֵּר אִתּוֹ מִשְׁפָּטִים: 6 וַיִּשְׁחַט מֶלֶךְ בָּבֶל אֶת־בְּנֵי צִדְקִיָּהוּ בְּרִבְלָה לְעֵינָיו וְאֵת כָּל־חֹרֵי יְהוּדָה שָׁחַט מֶלֶךְ בָּבֶל: 7 וְאֶת־עֵינֵי צִדְקִיָּהוּ עִוֵּר וַיַּאַסְרֵהוּ בַּנְחֻשְׁתַּיִם לָבִיא אֹתוֹ בָּבֶלָה: 8 וְאֶת־בֵּית הַמֶּלֶךְ וְאֶת־בֵּית הָעָם שָׂרְפוּ הַכַּשְׂדִּים בָּאֵשׁ וְאֶת־חֹמוֹת יְרוּשָׁלַ͏ִם נָתָצוּ: 9 וְאֵת יֶתֶר הָעָם הַנִּשְׁאָרִים בָּעִיר וְאֶת־הַנֹּפְלִים אֲשֶׁר נָפְלוּ עָלָיו וְאֵת יֶתֶר הָעָם הַנִּשְׁאָרִים הֶגְלָה נְבוּזַרְאֲדָן רַב־טַבָּחִים בָּבֶל: 10 וּמִן־הָעָם הַדַּלִּים אֲשֶׁר אֵין־לָהֶם מְאוּמָה הִשְׁאִיר נְבוּזַרְאֲדָן רַב־טַבָּחִים בְּאֶרֶץ יְהוּדָה וַיִּתֵּן לָהֶם כְּרָמִים וִיגֵבִים בַּיּוֹם הַהוּא: 11 וַיְצַו נְבוּכַדְרֶאצַּר מֶלֶךְ־בָּבֶל עַל־יִרְמְיָהוּ בְּיַד נְבוּזַרְאֲדָן רַב־טַבָּחִים לֵאמֹר: 12 קָחֶנּוּ וְעֵינֶיךָ שִׂים עָלָיו וְאַל־תַּעַשׂ לוֹ מְאוּמָה רָע כִּי אִם כַּאֲשֶׁר יְדַבֵּר אֵלֶיךָ כֵּן עֲשֵׂה עִמּוֹ: 13 וַיִּשְׁלַח נְבוּזַרְאֲדָן רַב־טַבָּחִים וּנְבוּשַׁזְבָּן רַב־סָרִיס וְנֵרְגַל שַׂר־אֶצֶר רַב־מָג וְכֹל רַבֵּי מֶלֶךְ־בָּבֶל: 14 וַיִּשְׁלְחוּ וַיִּקְחוּ אֶת־יִרְמְיָהוּ מֵחֲצַר הַמַּטָּרָה וַיִּתְּנוּ אֹתוֹ אֶל־גְּדַלְיָהוּ בֶּן־אֲחִיקָם בֶּן־שָׁפָן לְהוֹצִאֵהוּ אֶל־הַבָּיִת וַיֵּשֶׁב בְּתוֹךְ הָעָם: ס 15 וְאֶל־יִרְמְיָהוּ הָיָה דְבַר־יְהוָה בִּהְיֹתוֹ עָצוּר בַּחֲצַר הַמַּטָּרָה לֵאמֹר: 16 הָלוֹךְ וְאָמַרְתָּ לְעֶבֶד־מֶלֶךְ הַכּוּשִׁי לֵאמֹר כֹּה־אָמַר יְהוָה צְבָאוֹת אֱלֹהֵי יִשְׂרָאֵל הִנְנִי מֵבִי אֶת־דְּבָרַי אֶל־

and they shall be *performed* in that day before you.
17 But I will deliver you in that day," says the LORD,
"and you shall not be given into the hand of the
men of whom you *are* afraid. 18 For I will surely
deliver you, and you shall not fall by the sword; but
your life shall be as a prize to you, because you have
put your trust in Me," says the LORD.' "

40 The word that came to Jeremiah from the
LORD after Nebuzaradan the captain of the guard
had let him go from Ramah, when he had taken
him bound in chains among all who were carried
away captive from Jerusalem and Judah, who were
carried away captive to Babylon.

2 And the captain of the guard took Jeremiah and
said to him: "The LORD your God has pronounced
this doom on this place. 3 Now the LORD has
brought *it,* and has done just as He said. Because
you *people* have sinned against the LORD, and not
obeyed His voice, therefore this thing has come
upon you. 4 And now look, I free you this day from
the chains that *were* on your hand. If it seems good
to you to come with me to Babylon, come, and I
will look after you. But if it seems wrong for you to
come with me to Babylon, remain here. See, all the
land *is* before you; wherever it seems good and
convenient for you to go, go there."

5 Now while Jeremiah had not yet gone back,
Nebuzaradan said, "Go back to Gedaliah the son of
Ahikam, the son of Shaphan, whom the king of
Babylon has made governor over the cities of
Judah, and dwell with him among the people. Or go
wherever it seems convenient for you to go." So the
captain of the guard gave him rations and a gift and
let him go. 6 Then Jeremiah went to Gedaliah the
son of Ahikam, to Mizpah, and dwelt with him
among the people who were left in the land.

7 And when all the captains of the armies who
were in the fields, they and their men, heard that the
king of Babylon had made Gedaliah the son of
Ahikam governor in the land, and had committed
to him men, women, children, and the poorest of
the land who had not been carried away captive to
Babylon, 8 then they came to Gedaliah at Mizpah—
Ishmael the son of Nethaniah, Johanan and
Jonathan the sons of Kareah, Seraiah the son of
Tanhumeth, the sons of Ephai the Netophathite,
and Jezaniah the son of a Maachathite, they and
their men. 9 And Gedaliah the son of Ahikam, the
son of Shaphan, took an oath before them and their
men, saying, "Do not be afraid to serve the
Chaldeans. Dwell in the land and serve the king
of Babylon, and it shall be well with you. 10 As for
me, I will indeed dwell at Mizpah and serve the

הָעִיר הַזֹּאת לְרָעָה וְלֹא לְטוֹבָה וְהָיוּ לְפָנֶיךָ בַּיּוֹם
הַהוּא: 17 וְהִצַּלְתִּיךָ בַיּוֹם־הַהוּא נְאֻם־יְהֹוָה וְלֹא
תִנָּתֵן בְּיַד הָאֲנָשִׁים אֲשֶׁר־אַתָּה יָגוֹר מִפְּנֵיהֶם:
18 כִּי מַלֵּט אֲמַלֶּטְךָ וּבַחֶרֶב לֹא תִפֹּל וְהָיְתָה לְךָ
נַפְשְׁךָ לְשָׁלָל כִּי־בָטַחְתָּ בִּי נְאֻם־יְהֹוָה: ס

מ הַדָּבָר אֲשֶׁר־הָיָה אֶל־יִרְמְיָהוּ מֵאֵת יְהֹוָה
אַחַר ׀ שַׁלַּח אֹתוֹ נְבוּזַרְאֲדָן רַב־טַבָּחִים מִן־
הָרָמָה בְּקַחְתּוֹ אֹתוֹ וְהוּא־אָסוּר בָּאזִקִּים בְּתוֹךְ
כָּל־גָּלוּת יְרוּשָׁלַ͏ִם וִיהוּדָה הַמֻּגְלִים בָּבֶלָה: 2 וַיִּקַּח
רַב־טַבָּחִים לְיִרְמְיָהוּ וַיֹּאמֶר אֵלָיו יְהֹוָה אֱלֹהֶיךָ
דִּבֶּר אֶת־הָרָעָה הַזֹּאת אֶל־הַמָּקוֹם הַזֶּה: 3 וַיָּבֵא
וַיַּעַשׂ יְהֹוָה כַּאֲשֶׁר דִּבֵּר כִּי־חֲטָאתֶם לַיהֹוָה וְלֹא־
שְׁמַעְתֶּם בְּקוֹלוֹ וְהָיָה לָכֶם דָּבָר הַזֶּה: 4 וְעַתָּה
הִנֵּה פִתַּחְתִּיךָ הַיּוֹם מִן־הָאזִקִּים אֲשֶׁר עַל־יָדֶךָ
אִם־טוֹב בְּעֵינֶיךָ לָבוֹא אִתִּי בָבֶל בֹּא וְאָשִׂים
אֶת־עֵינִי עָלֶיךָ וְאִם־רַע בְּעֵינֶיךָ לָבוֹא־אִתִּי בָבֶל
חֲדָל רְאֵה כָּל־הָאָרֶץ לְפָנֶיךָ אֶל־טוֹב וְאֶל־הַיָּשָׁר
בְּעֵינֶיךָ לָלֶכֶת שָׁמָּה לֵךְ: 5 וְעוֹדֶנּוּ לֹא־יָשׁוּב וְשֻׁבָה
אֶל־גְּדַלְיָה בֶן־אֲחִיקָם בֶּן־שָׁפָן אֲשֶׁר הִפְקִיד מֶלֶךְ־
בָּבֶל בְּעָרֵי יְהוּדָה וְשֵׁב אִתּוֹ בְּתוֹךְ הָעָם אוֹ אֶל־
כָּל־הַיָּשָׁר בְּעֵינֶיךָ לָלֶכֶת לֵךְ וַיִּתֶּן־לוֹ רַב־טַבָּחִים
אֲרֻחָה וּמַשְׂאֵת וַיְשַׁלְּחֵהוּ: 6 וַיָּבֹא יִרְמְיָהוּ אֶל־
גְּדַלְיָה בֶן־אֲחִיקָם הַמִּצְפָּתָה וַיֵּשֶׁב אִתּוֹ בְּתוֹךְ
הָעָם הַנִּשְׁאָרִים בָּאָרֶץ: ס 7 וַיִּשְׁמְעוּ כָל־
שָׂרֵי הַחֲיָלִים אֲשֶׁר בַּשָּׂדֶה הֵמָּה וְאַנְשֵׁיהֶם כִּי־
הִפְקִיד מֶלֶךְ־בָּבֶל אֶת־גְּדַלְיָהוּ בֶן־אֲחִיקָם בָּאָרֶץ
וְכִי ׀ הִפְקִיד אִתּוֹ אֲנָשִׁים וְנָשִׁים וָטָף וּמִדַּלַּת
הָאָרֶץ מֵאֲשֶׁר לֹא־הָגְלוּ בָּבֶלָה: 8 וַיָּבֹאוּ אֶל־גְּדַלְיָה
הַמִּצְפָּתָה וְיִשְׁמָעֵאל בֶּן־נְתַנְיָהוּ וְיוֹחָנָן וְיוֹנָתָן בְּנֵי־
קָרֵחַ וּשְׂרָיָה בֶן־תַּנְחֻמֶת וּבְנֵי ׀ עֵיפַי הַנְּטֹפָתִי
וִיזַנְיָהוּ בֶּן־הַמַּעֲכָתִי הֵמָּה וְאַנְשֵׁיהֶם: 9 וַיִּשָּׁבַע
לָהֶם גְּדַלְיָהוּ בֶן־אֲחִיקָם בֶּן־שָׁפָן וּלְאַנְשֵׁיהֶם לֵאמֹר
אַל־תִּירְאוּ מֵעֲבוֹד הַכַּשְׂדִּים שְׁבוּ בָאָרֶץ וְעִבְדוּ
אֶת־מֶלֶךְ בָּבֶל וְיִטַב לָכֶם: 10 וַאֲנִי הִנְנִי יֹשֵׁב
בַּמִּצְפָּה לַעֲמֹד לִפְנֵי הַכַּשְׂדִּים אֲשֶׁר יָבֹאוּ אֵלֵינוּ

מ 3 הַדָּבָר 8 עֵיפַי

Chaldeans who come to us. But you, gather wine and summer fruit and oil, put *them* in your vessels, and dwell in your cities that you have taken." [11] Likewise, when all the Jews who *were* in Moab, among the Ammonites, in Edom, and who *were* in all the countries, heard that the king of Babylon had left a remnant of Judah, and that he had set over them Gedaliah the son of Ahikam, the son of Shaphan, [12] then all the Jews returned out of all places where they had been driven, and came to the land of Judah, to Gedaliah at Mizpah, and gathered wine and summer fruit in abundance.

[13] Moreover Johanan the son of Kareah and all the captains of the forces that *were* in the fields came to Gedaliah at Mizpah, [14] and said to him, "Do you certainly know that Baalis the king of the Ammonites has sent Ishmael the son of Nethaniah to murder you?" But Gedaliah the son of Ahikam did not believe them.

[15] Then Johanan the son of Kareah spoke secretly to Gedaliah in Mizpah, saying, "Let me go, please, and I will kill Ishmael the son of Nethaniah, and no one will know *it*. Why should he murder you, so that all the Jews who are gathered to you would be scattered, and the remnant in Judah perish?"

[16] But Gedaliah the son of Ahikam said to Johanan the son of Kareah, "You shall not do this thing, for you speak falsely concerning Ishmael."

41 Now it came to pass in the seventh month *that* Ishmael the son of Nethaniah, the son of Elishama, of the royal family and of the officers of the king, came with ten men to Gedaliah the son of Ahikam, at Mizpah. And there they ate bread together in Mizpah. [2] Then Ishmael the son of Nethaniah, and the ten men who were with him, arose and struck Gedaliah the son of Ahikam, the son of Shaphan, with the sword, and killed him whom the king of Babylon had made governor over the land. [3] Ishmael also struck down all the Jews who were with him, *that is,* with Gedaliah at Mizpah, and the Chaldeans who were found there, the men of war.

[4] And it happened, on the second day after he had killed Gedaliah, when as yet no one knew *it,* [5] that certain men came from Shechem, from Shiloh, and from Samaria, eighty men with their beards shaved and their clothes torn, having cut themselves, with offerings and incense in their hand, to bring *them* to the house of the LORD. [6] Now Ishmael the son of Nethaniah went out from Mizpah to meet them, weeping as he went along; and it happened as he met them that he said to them, "Come to Gedaliah the son of Ahikam!" [7] So it was, when they came into the midst of the city,

וְאַתֶּם אִסְפוּ יַיִן וָקַיִץ וְשֶׁמֶן וְשִׂמוּ בִּכְלֵיכֶם וּשְׁבוּ בְּעָרֵיכֶם אֲשֶׁר־תְּפַשְׂתֶּם: 11 וְגַם כָּל־הַיְּהוּדִים אֲשֶׁר־בְּמוֹאָב ׀ וּבִבְנֵי־עַמּוֹן וּבֶאֱדוֹם וַאֲשֶׁר בְּכָל־הָאֲרָצוֹת שָׁמְעוּ כִּי־נָתַן מֶלֶךְ־בָּבֶל שְׁאֵרִית לִיהוּדָה וְכִי הִפְקִיד עֲלֵיהֶם אֶת־גְּדַלְיָהוּ בֶּן־אֲחִיקָם בֶּן־שָׁפָן: 12 וַיָּשֻׁבוּ כָל־הַיְּהוּדִים מִכָּל־הַמְּקֹמוֹת אֲשֶׁר נִדְּחוּ־שָׁם וַיָּבֹאוּ אֶרֶץ־יְהוּדָה אֶל־גְּדַלְיָהוּ הַמִּצְפָּתָה וַיַּאַסְפוּ יַיִן וָקַיִץ הַרְבֵּה מְאֹד: פ

13 וְיוֹחָנָן בֶּן־קָרֵחַ וְכָל־שָׂרֵי הַחֲיָלִים אֲשֶׁר בַּשָּׂדֶה בָּאוּ אֶל־גְּדַלְיָהוּ הַמִּצְפָּתָה: 14 וַיֹּאמְרוּ אֵלָיו הֲיָדֹעַ תֵּדַע כִּי בַּעֲלִיס ׀ מֶלֶךְ בְּנֵי־עַמּוֹן שָׁלַח אֶת־יִשְׁמָעֵאל בֶּן־נְתַנְיָה לְהַכֹּתְךָ נָפֶשׁ וְלֹא־הֶאֱמִין לָהֶם גְּדַלְיָהוּ בֶּן־אֲחִיקָם: 15 וְיוֹחָנָן בֶּן־קָרֵחַ אָמַר אֶל־גְּדַלְיָהוּ בַסֵּתֶר בַּמִּצְפָּה לֵאמֹר אֵלְכָה נָּא וְאַכֶּה אֶת־יִשְׁמָעֵאל בֶּן־נְתַנְיָה וְאִישׁ לֹא יֵדָע לָמָּה יַכֶּכָּה נֶּפֶשׁ וְנָפֹצוּ כָּל־יְהוּדָה הַנִּקְבָּצִים אֵלֶיךָ וְאָבְדָה שְׁאֵרִית יְהוּדָה: 16 וַיֹּאמֶר גְּדַלְיָהוּ בֶן־אֲחִיקָם אֶל־יוֹחָנָן בֶּן־קָרֵחַ אַל־תַּעַשׂ אֶת־הַדָּבָר הַזֶּה כִּי־שֶׁקֶר אַתָּה דֹבֵר אֶל־יִשְׁמָעֵאל: ס

מא וַיְהִי ׀ בַּחֹדֶשׁ הַשְּׁבִיעִי בָּא יִשְׁמָעֵאל בֶּן־נְתַנְיָה בֶן־אֱלִישָׁמָע מִזֶּרַע הַמְּלוּכָה וְרַבֵּי הַמֶּלֶךְ וַעֲשָׂרָה אֲנָשִׁים אִתּוֹ אֶל־גְּדַלְיָהוּ בֶן־אֲחִיקָם הַמִּצְפָּתָה וַיֹּאכְלוּ שָׁם לֶחֶם יַחְדָּו בַּמִּצְפָּה: 2 וַיָּקָם יִשְׁמָעֵאל בֶּן־נְתַנְיָה וַעֲשֶׂרֶת הָאֲנָשִׁים ׀ אֲשֶׁר־הָיוּ אִתּוֹ וַיַּכּוּ אֶת־גְּדַלְיָהוּ בֶן־אֲחִיקָם בֶּן־שָׁפָן בַּחֶרֶב וַיָּמֶת אֹתוֹ אֲשֶׁר־הִפְקִיד מֶלֶךְ־בָּבֶל בָּאָרֶץ: 3 וְאֵת כָּל־הַיְּהוּדִים אֲשֶׁר־הָיוּ אִתּוֹ אֶת־גְּדַלְיָהוּ בַּמִּצְפָּה וְאֶת־הַכַּשְׂדִּים אֲשֶׁר נִמְצְאוּ־שָׁם אֵת אַנְשֵׁי הַמִּלְחָמָה הִכָּה יִשְׁמָעֵאל: 4 וַיְהִי בַּיּוֹם הַשֵּׁנִי לְהָמִית אֶת־גְּדַלְיָהוּ וְאִישׁ לֹא יָדָע: 5 וַיָּבֹאוּ אֲנָשִׁים מִשְּׁכֶם מִשִּׁלוֹ וּמִשֹּׁמְרוֹן שְׁמֹנִים אִישׁ מְגֻלְּחֵי זָקָן וּקְרֻעֵי בְגָדִים וּמִתְגֹּדְדִים וּמִנְחָה וּלְבוֹנָה בְּיָדָם לְהָבִיא בֵּית יְהוָה: 6 וַיֵּצֵא יִשְׁמָעֵאל בֶּן־נְתַנְיָה לִקְרָאתָם מִן־הַמִּצְפָּה הֹלֵךְ הָלֹךְ וּבֹכֶה וַיְהִי כִּפְגֹשׁ אֹתָם וַיֹּאמֶר אֲלֵיהֶם בֹּאוּ אֶל־גְּדַלְיָהוּ בֶן־אֲחִיקָם: ס 7 וַיְהִי כְּבוֹאָם אֶל־תּוֹךְ הָעִיר וַיִּשְׁחָטֵם יִשְׁמָעֵאל בֶּן־נְתַנְיָה אֶל־

that Ishmael the son of Nethaniah killed them *and cast them* into the midst of a pit, he and the men who were with him. [8] But ten men were found among them who said to Ishmael, "Do not kill us, for we have treasures of wheat, barley, oil, and honey in the field." So he desisted and did not kill them among their brethren. [9] Now the pit into which Ishmael had cast all the dead bodies of the men whom he had slain, because of Gedaliah, *was* the same one Asa the king had made for fear of Baasha king of Israel. Ishmael the son of Nethaniah filled it with *the* slain. [10] Then Ishmael carried away captive all the rest of the people who *were* in Mizpah, the king's daughters and all the people who remained in Mizpah, whom Nebuzaradan the captain of the guard had committed to Gedaliah the son of Ahikam. And Ishmael the son of Nethaniah carried them away captive and departed to go over to the Ammonites.

[11] But when Johanan the son of Kareah and all the captains of the forces that *were* with him heard of all the evil that Ishmael the son of Nethaniah had done, [12] they took all the men and went to fight with Ishmael the son of Nethaniah; and they found him by the great pool that *is* in Gibeon. [13] So it was, when all the people who *were* with Ishmael saw Johanan the son of Kareah, and all the captains of the forces who *were* with him, that they were glad. [14] Then all the people whom Ishmael had carried away captive from Mizpah turned around and came back, and went to Johanan the son of Kareah. [15] But Ishmael the son of Nethaniah escaped from Johanan with eight men and went to the Ammonites.

[16] Then Johanan the son of Kareah, and all the captains of the forces that were with him, took from Mizpah all the rest of the people whom he had recovered from Ishmael the son of Nethaniah after he had murdered Gedaliah the son of Ahikam—the mighty men of war and the women and the children and the eunuchs, whom he had brought back from Gibeon. [17] And they departed and dwelt in the habitation of Chimham, which is near Bethlehem, as they went on their way to Egypt, [18] because of the Chaldeans; for they were afraid of them, because Ishmael the son of Nethaniah had murdered Gedaliah the son of Ahikam, whom the king of Babylon had made governor in the land.

42 Now all the captains of the forces, Johanan the son of Kareah, Jezaniah the son of Hoshaiah, and all the people, from the least to the greatest, came near [2] and said to Jeremiah the prophet, "Please, let our petition be acceptable to you, and

תּוֹךְ הַבּוֹר הוּא וְהָאֲנָשִׁים אֲשֶׁר־אִתּוֹ: 8 וַעֲשָׂרָה אֲנָשִׁים נִמְצְאוּ־בָם וַיֹּאמְרוּ אֶל־יִשְׁמָעֵאל אַל־תְּמִתֵנוּ כִּי־יֶשׁ־לָנוּ מַטְמֹנִים בַּשָּׂדֶה חִטִּים וּשְׂעֹרִים וְשֶׁמֶן וּדְבָשׁ וַיֶּחְדַּל וְלֹא הֱמִיתָם בְּתוֹךְ אֲחֵיהֶם: 9 וְהַבּוֹר אֲשֶׁר הִשְׁלִיךְ שָׁם יִשְׁמָעֵאל אֵת | כָּל־פִּגְרֵי הָאֲנָשִׁים אֲשֶׁר הִכָּה בְּיַד־גְּדַלְיָהוּ הוּא אֲשֶׁר עָשָׂה הַמֶּלֶךְ אָסָא מִפְּנֵי בַּעְשָׁא מֶלֶךְ־יִשְׂרָאֵל אֹתוֹ מִלֵּא יִשְׁמָעֵאל בֶּן־נְתַנְיָהוּ חֲלָלִים: 10 וַיִּשְׁבְּ | יִשְׁמָעֵאל אֶת־כָּל־שְׁאֵרִית הָעָם אֲשֶׁר בַּמִּצְפָּה אֶת־בְּנוֹת הַמֶּלֶךְ וְאֶת־כָּל־הָעָם הַנִּשְׁאָרִים בַּמִּצְפָּה אֲשֶׁר הִפְקִיד נְבוּזַרְאֲדָן רַב־טַבָּחִים אֶת־גְּדַלְיָהוּ בֶּן־אֲחִיקָם וַיִּשְׁבֵּם יִשְׁמָעֵאל בֶּן־נְתַנְיָה וַיֵּלֶךְ לַעֲבֹר אֶל־בְּנֵי עַמּוֹן: ס 11 וַיִּשְׁמַע יוֹחָנָן בֶּן־קָרֵחַ וְכָל־שָׂרֵי הַחֲיָלִים אֲשֶׁר אִתּוֹ אֵת כָּל־הָרָעָה אֲשֶׁר עָשָׂה יִשְׁמָעֵאל בֶּן־נְתַנְיָה: 12 וַיִּקְחוּ אֶת־כָּל־הָאֲנָשִׁים וַיֵּלְכוּ לְהִלָּחֵם עִם־יִשְׁמָעֵאל בֶּן־נְתַנְיָה וַיִּמְצְאוּ אֹתוֹ אֶל־מַיִם רַבִּים אֲשֶׁר בְּגִבְעוֹן: 13 וַיְהִי כִּרְאוֹת כָּל־הָעָם אֲשֶׁר אֶת־יִשְׁמָעֵאל אֶת־יוֹחָנָן בֶּן־קָרֵחַ וְאֵת כָּל־שָׂרֵי הַחֲיָלִים אֲשֶׁר אִתּוֹ וַיִּשְׂמָחוּ: 14 וַיָּסֹבּוּ כָּל־הָעָם אֲשֶׁר־שָׁבָה יִשְׁמָעֵאל מִן־הַמִּצְפָּה וַיָּשֻׁבוּ וַיֵּלְכוּ אֶל־יוֹחָנָן בֶּן־קָרֵחַ: 15 וְיִשְׁמָעֵאל בֶּן־נְתַנְיָה נִמְלַט בִּשְׁמֹנָה אֲנָשִׁים מִפְּנֵי יוֹחָנָן וַיֵּלֶךְ אֶל־בְּנֵי עַמּוֹן: ס 16 וַיִּקַּח יוֹחָנָן בֶּן־קָרֵחַ וְכָל־שָׂרֵי הַחֲיָלִים אֲשֶׁר־אִתּוֹ אֵת כָּל־שְׁאֵרִית הָעָם אֲשֶׁר הֵשִׁיב מֵאֵת יִשְׁמָעֵאל בֶּן־נְתַנְיָה מִן־הַמִּצְפָּה אַחַר הִכָּה אֶת־גְּדַלְיָה בֶּן־אֲחִיקָם גְּבָרִים אַנְשֵׁי הַמִּלְחָמָה וְנָשִׁים וְטַף וְסָרִסִים אֲשֶׁר הֵשִׁיב מִגִּבְעוֹן: 17 וַיֵּלְכוּ וַיֵּשְׁבוּ בְּגֵרוּת כְּמוֹהֶם אֲשֶׁר־אֵצֶל בֵּית לָחֶם לָלֶכֶת לָבוֹא מִצְרָיִם: 18 מִפְּנֵי הַכַּשְׂדִּים כִּי יָרְאוּ מִפְּנֵיהֶם כִּי־הִכָּה יִשְׁמָעֵאל בֶּן־נְתַנְיָה אֶת־גְּדַלְיָהוּ בֶּן־אֲחִיקָם אֲשֶׁר־הִפְקִיד מֶלֶךְ־בָּבֶל בָּאָרֶץ: ס

מב וַיִּגְּשׁוּ כָּל־שָׂרֵי הַחֲיָלִים וְיוֹחָנָן בֶּן־קָרֵחַ וִיזַנְיָה בֶּן־הוֹשַׁעְיָה וְכָל־הָעָם מִקָּטֹן וְעַד־גָּדוֹל: 2 וַיֹּאמְרוּ אֶל־יִרְמְיָהוּ הַנָּבִיא תִּפָּל־נָא תְחִנָּתֵנוּ

מא 17 כְּמוֹהָם

pray for us to the LORD your God, for all this remnant (since we are left *but* a few of many, as you can see), ³that the LORD your God may show us the way in which we should walk and the thing we should do."

⁴Then Jeremiah the prophet said to them, "I have heard. Indeed, I will pray to the LORD your God according to your words, and it shall be, *that* whatever the LORD answers you, I will declare *it* to you. I will keep nothing back from you."

⁵So they said to Jeremiah, "Let the LORD be a true and faithful witness between us, if we do not do according to everything which the LORD your God sends us by you. ⁶Whether *it is* pleasing or displeasing, we will obey the voice of the LORD our God to whom we send you, that it may be well with us when we obey the voice of the LORD our God."

⁷And it happened after ten days that the word of the LORD came to Jeremiah. ⁸Then he called Johanan the son of Kareah, all the captains of the forces which *were* with him, and all the people from the least even to the greatest, ⁹and said to them, "Thus says the LORD, the God of Israel, to whom you sent me to present your petition before Him: ¹⁰'If you will still remain in this land, then I will build you and not pull *you* down, and I will plant you and not pluck *you* up. For I relent concerning the disaster that I have brought upon you. ¹¹Do not be afraid of the king of Babylon, of whom you are afraid; do not be afraid of him,' says the LORD, 'for I *am* with you, to save you and deliver you from his hand. ¹²And I will show you mercy, that he may have mercy on you and cause you to return to your own land.'

¹³"But if you say, 'We will not dwell in this land,' disobeying the voice of the LORD your God, ¹⁴saying, 'No, but we will go to the land of Egypt where we shall see no war, nor hear the sound of the trumpet, nor be hungry for bread, and there we will dwell'— ¹⁵Then hear now the word of the LORD, O remnant of Judah! Thus says the LORD of hosts, the God of Israel: 'If you wholly set your faces to enter Egypt, and go to dwell there, ¹⁶then it shall be *that* the sword which you feared shall overtake you there in the land of Egypt; the famine of which you were afraid shall follow close after you there *in* Egypt; and there you shall die. ¹⁷So shall it be with all the men who set their faces to go to Egypt to dwell there. They shall die by the sword, by famine, and by pestilence. And none of them shall remain or escape from the disaster that I will bring upon them.'

לְפָנֶיךָ וְהִתְפַּלֵּל בַּעֲדֵנוּ אֶל־יְהֹוָה אֱלֹהֶיךָ בְּעַד כָּל־הַשְּׁאֵרִית הַזֹּאת כִּי־נִשְׁאַרְנוּ מְעַט מֵהַרְבֵּה כַּאֲשֶׁר עֵינֶיךָ רֹאוֹת אֹתָנוּ: 3 וַיַּגֶּד־לָנוּ יְהֹוָה אֱלֹהֶיךָ אֶת־הַדֶּרֶךְ אֲשֶׁר נֵלֶךְ־בָּהּ וְאֶת־הַדָּבָר אֲשֶׁר נַעֲשֶׂה: 4 וַיֹּאמֶר אֲלֵיהֶם יִרְמְיָהוּ הַנָּבִיא שָׁמַעְתִּי הִנְנִי מִתְפַּלֵּל אֶל־יְהֹוָה אֱלֹהֵיכֶם כְּדִבְרֵיכֶם וְהָיָה כָּל־הַדָּבָר אֲשֶׁר־יַעֲנֶה יְהֹוָה אֶתְכֶם אַגִּיד לָכֶם לֹא־אֶמְנַע מִכֶּם דָּבָר: 5 וְהֵמָּה אָמְרוּ אֶל־יִרְמְיָהוּ יְהִי יְהֹוָה בָּנוּ לְעֵד אֱמֶת וְנֶאֱמָן אִם־לֹא כְּכָל־הַדָּבָר אֲשֶׁר יִשְׁלָחֲךָ יְהֹוָה אֱלֹהֶיךָ אֵלֵינוּ כֵּן נַעֲשֶׂה: 6 אִם־טוֹב וְאִם־רָע בְּקוֹל | יְהֹוָה אֱלֹהֵינוּ אֲשֶׁר אֲנוּ שֹׁלְחִים אֹתְךָ אֵלָיו נִשְׁמָע לְמַעַן אֲשֶׁר יִיטַב־לָנוּ כִּי נִשְׁמַע בְּקוֹל יְהֹוָה אֱלֹהֵינוּ: ס 7 וַיְהִי מִקֵּץ עֲשֶׂרֶת יָמִים וַיְהִי דְבַר־יְהֹוָה אֶל־יִרְמְיָהוּ: 8 וַיִּקְרָא אֶל־יוֹחָנָן בֶּן־קָרֵחַ וְאֶל כָּל־שָׂרֵי הַחֲיָלִים אֲשֶׁר אִתּוֹ וּלְכָל־הָעָם לְמִקָּטֹן וְעַד־גָּדוֹל: 9 וַיֹּאמֶר אֲלֵיהֶם כֹּה־אָמַר יְהֹוָה אֱלֹהֵי יִשְׂרָאֵל אֲשֶׁר שְׁלַחְתֶּם אֹתִי אֵלָיו לְהַפִּיל תְּחִנַּתְכֶם לְפָנָיו: 10 אִם־שׁוֹב תֵּשְׁבוּ בָּאָרֶץ הַזֹּאת וּבָנִיתִי אֶתְכֶם וְלֹא אֶהֱרֹס וְנָטַעְתִּי אֶתְכֶם וְלֹא אֶתּוֹשׁ כִּי נִחַמְתִּי אֶל־הָרָעָה אֲשֶׁר עָשִׂיתִי לָכֶם: 11 אַל־תִּירְאוּ מִפְּנֵי מֶלֶךְ בָּבֶל אֲשֶׁר־אַתֶּם יְרֵאִים מִפָּנָיו אַל־תִּירְאוּ מִמֶּנּוּ נְאֻם־יְהֹוָה כִּי־אִתְּכֶם אָנִי לְהוֹשִׁיעַ אֶתְכֶם וּלְהַצִּיל אֶתְכֶם מִיָּדוֹ: 12 וְאֶתֵּן לָכֶם רַחֲמִים וְרִחַם אֶתְכֶם וְהֵשִׁיב אֶתְכֶם אֶל־אַדְמַתְכֶם: 13 וְאִם־אֹמְרִים אַתֶּם לֹא נֵשֵׁב בָּאָרֶץ הַזֹּאת לְבִלְתִּי שְׁמֹעַ בְּקוֹל יְהֹוָה אֱלֹהֵיכֶם: 14 לֵאמֹר לֹא כִּי אֶרֶץ מִצְרַיִם נָבוֹא אֲשֶׁר לֹא־נִרְאֶה מִלְחָמָה וְקוֹל שׁוֹפָר לֹא נִשְׁמָע וְלַלֶּחֶם לֹא־נִרְעָב וְשָׁם נֵשֵׁב: 15 וְעַתָּה לָכֵן שִׁמְעוּ דְבַר־יְהֹוָה שְׁאֵרִית יְהוּדָה כֹּה־אָמַר יְהֹוָה צְבָאוֹת אֱלֹהֵי יִשְׂרָאֵל אִם־אַתֶּם שׂוֹם תְּשִׂמוּן פְּנֵיכֶם לָבֹא מִצְרַיִם וּבָאתֶם לָגוּר שָׁם: 16 וְהָיְתָה הַחֶרֶב אֲשֶׁר אַתֶּם יְרֵאִים מִמֶּנָּה שָׁם תַּשִּׂיג אֶתְכֶם בְּאֶרֶץ מִצְרָיִם וְהָרָעָב אֲשֶׁר־אַתֶּם | דֹּאֲגִים מִמֶּנּוּ שָׁם יִדְבַּק אַחֲרֵיכֶם מִצְרַיִם וְשָׁם תָּמֻתוּ: 17 וְיִהְיוּ כָל־הָאֲנָשִׁים אֲשֶׁר־שָׂמוּ אֶת־פְּנֵיהֶם לָבוֹא מִצְרַיִם לָגוּר שָׁם יָמוּתוּ בַּחֶרֶב בָּרָעָב וּבַדָּבֶר וְלֹא־יִהְיֶה לָהֶם שָׂרִיד וּפָלִיט מִפְּנֵי הָרָעָה

18 "For thus says the LORD of hosts, the God of Israel: 'As My anger and My fury have been poured out on the inhabitants of Jerusalem, so will My fury be poured out on you when you enter Egypt. And you shall be an oath, an astonishment, a curse, and a reproach; and you shall see this place no more.'

19 "The LORD has said concerning you, O remnant of Judah, 'Do not go to Egypt!' Know certainly that I have admonished you this day. 20 For you were hypocrites in your hearts when you sent me to the LORD your God, saying, 'Pray for us to the LORD our God, and according to all that the LORD your God says, so declare to us and we will do it.' 21 And I have this day declared it to you, but you have not obeyed the voice of the LORD your God, or anything which He has sent you by me. 22 Now therefore, know certainly that you shall die by the sword, by famine, and by pestilence in the place where you desire to go to dwell."

43 Now it happened, when Jeremiah had stopped speaking to all the people all the words of the LORD their God, for which the LORD their God had sent him to them, all these words, 2 that Azariah the son of Hoshaiah, Johanan the son of Kareah, and all the proud men spoke, saying to Jeremiah, "You speak falsely! The LORD our God has not sent you to say, 'Do not go to Egypt to dwell there.' 3 But Baruch the son of Neriah has set you against us, to deliver us into the hand of the Chaldeans, that they may put us to death or carry us away captive to Babylon." 4 So Johanan the son of Kareah, all the captains of the forces, and all the people would not obey the voice of the LORD, to remain in the land of Judah. 5 But Johanan the son of Kareah and all the captains of the forces took all the remnant of Judah who had returned to dwell in the land of Judah, from all nations where they had been driven— 6 men, women, children, the king's daughters, and every person whom Nebuzaradan the captain of the guard had left with Gedaliah the son of Ahikam, the son of Shaphan, and Jeremiah the prophet and Baruch the son of Neriah. 7 So they went to the land of Egypt, for they did not obey the voice of the LORD. And they went as far as Tahpanhes.

8 Then the word of the LORD came to Jeremiah in Tahpanhes, saying, 9 "Take large stones in your hand, and hide them in the sight of the men of Judah, in the clay in the brick courtyard which is at the entrance to Pharaoh's house in Tahpanhes; 10 and say to them, 'Thus says the LORD of hosts, the God of Israel: "Behold, I will send and bring Nebuchadnezzar the king of Babylon, My servant, and will set his throne above these stones that I

18 כִּי כֹה ס אֲשֶׁר אֲנִי מֵבִיא עֲלֵיהֶם:
אָמַר יְהֹוָה צְבָאוֹת אֱלֹהֵי יִשְׂרָאֵל כַּאֲשֶׁר נִתַּךְ
אַפִּי וַחֲמָתִי עַל־יֹשְׁבֵי יְרוּשָׁלַ͏ִם כֵּן תִּתַּךְ חֲמָתִי
עֲלֵיכֶם בְּבֹאֲכֶם מִצְרָיִם וִהְיִיתֶם לְאָלָה וּלְשַׁמָּה
וְלִקְלָלָה וּלְחֶרְפָּה וְלֹא־תִרְאוּ עוֹד אֶת־הַמָּקוֹם
הַזֶּה: 19 דִּבֶּר יְהֹוָה עֲלֵיכֶם שְׁאֵרִית יְהוּדָה אַל־
תָּבֹאוּ מִצְרָיִם יָדֹעַ תֵּדְעוּ כִּי־הַעִידֹתִי בָכֶם הַיּוֹם:
20 כִּי הִתְעֵתֶם בְּנַפְשׁוֹתֵיכֶם כִּי־אַתֶּם שְׁלַחְתֶּם
אֹתִי אֶל־יְהֹוָה אֱלֹהֵיכֶם לֵאמֹר הִתְפַּלֵּל בַּעֲדֵנוּ אֶל־
יְהֹוָה אֱלֹהֵינוּ וּכְכֹל אֲשֶׁר יֹאמַר יְהֹוָה אֱלֹהֵינוּ כֵּן
הַגֶּד־לָנוּ וְעָשִׂינוּ: 21 וָאַגִּד לָכֶם הַיּוֹם וְלֹא שְׁמַעְתֶּם
בְּקוֹל יְהֹוָה אֱלֹהֵיכֶם וּלְכֹל אֲשֶׁר־שְׁלָחַנִי אֲלֵיכֶם:
22 וְעַתָּה יָדֹעַ תֵּדְעוּ כִּי בַּחֶרֶב בָּרָעָב וּבַדֶּבֶר תָּמוּתוּ
בַּמָּקוֹם אֲשֶׁר חֲפַצְתֶּם לָבוֹא לָגוּר שָׁם: ס

מג וַיְהִי כְּכַלּוֹת יִרְמְיָהוּ לְדַבֵּר אֶל־כָּל־
הָעָם אֶת־כָּל־דִּבְרֵי יְהֹוָה אֱלֹהֵיהֶם אֲשֶׁר
שְׁלָחוֹ יְהֹוָה אֱלֹהֵיהֶם אֲלֵיהֶם אֵת כָּל־הַדְּבָרִים
הָאֵלֶּה: ס 2 וַיֹּאמֶר עֲזַרְיָה בֶן־הוֹשַׁעְיָה
וְיוֹחָנָן בֶּן־קָרֵחַ וְכָל־הָאֲנָשִׁים הַזֵּדִים אֹמְרִים אֶל־
יִרְמְיָהוּ שֶׁקֶר אַתָּה מְדַבֵּר לֹא שְׁלָחֲךָ יְהֹוָה אֱלֹהֵינוּ
לֵאמֹר לֹא־תָבֹאוּ מִצְרַיִם לָגוּר שָׁם: 3 כִּי בָּרוּךְ
בֶּן־נֵרִיָּה מַסִּית אֹתְךָ בָּנוּ לְמַעַן תֵּת אֹתָנוּ בְיַד־
הַכַּשְׂדִּים לְהָמִית אֹתָנוּ וּלְהַגְלוֹת אֹתָנוּ בָּבֶל:
4 וְלֹא־שָׁמַע יוֹחָנָן בֶּן־קָרֵחַ וְכָל־שָׂרֵי הַחֲיָלִים וְכָל־
הָעָם בְּקוֹל יְהֹוָה לָשֶׁבֶת בְּאֶרֶץ יְהוּדָה: 5 וַיִּקַּח
יוֹחָנָן בֶּן־קָרֵחַ וְכָל־שָׂרֵי הַחֲיָלִים אֵת כָּל־שְׁאֵרִית
יְהוּדָה אֲשֶׁר־שָׁבוּ מִכָּל־הַגּוֹיִם אֲשֶׁר נִדְּחוּ־שָׁם לָגוּר
בְּאֶרֶץ יְהוּדָה: 6 אֶת־הַגְּבָרִים וְאֶת־הַנָּשִׁים וְאֶת־
הַטַּף וְאֶת־בְּנוֹת הַמֶּלֶךְ וְאֵת כָּל־הַנֶּפֶשׁ אֲשֶׁר הִנִּיחַ
נְבוּזַרְאֲדָן רַב־טַבָּחִים אֶת־גְּדַלְיָהוּ בֶּן־אֲחִיקָם בֶּן־
שָׁפָן וְאֵת יִרְמְיָהוּ הַנָּבִיא וְאֶת־בָּרוּךְ בֶּן־נֵרִיָּהוּ:
7 וַיָּבֹאוּ אֶרֶץ מִצְרַיִם כִּי לֹא שָׁמְעוּ בְּקוֹל יְהֹוָה
וַיָּבֹאוּ עַד־תַּחְפַּנְחֵס: ס 8 וַיְהִי דְבַר־יְהֹוָה
אֶל־יִרְמְיָהוּ בְּתַחְפַּנְחֵס לֵאמֹר: 9 קַח בְּיָדְךָ אֲבָנִים
גְּדֹלוֹת וּטְמַנְתָּם בַּמֶּלֶט בַּמַּלְבֵּן אֲשֶׁר בְּפֶתַח בֵּית־
פַּרְעֹה בְּתַחְפַּנְחֵס לְעֵינֵי אֲנָשִׁים יְהוּדִים: 10 וְאָמַרְתָּ
אֲלֵיהֶם כֹּה־אָמַר יְהֹוָה צְבָאוֹת אֱלֹהֵי יִשְׂרָאֵל הִנְנִי
שֹׁלֵחַ וְלָקַחְתִּי אֶת־נְבוּכַדְרֶאצַּר מֶלֶךְ־בָּבֶל עַבְדִּי
וְשַׂמְתִּי כִסְאוֹ מִמַּעַל לָאֲבָנִים הָאֵלֶּה אֲשֶׁר טָמָנְתִּי

מב 20 התעיתם

have hidden. And he will spread his royal pavilion over them. [11] When he comes, he shall strike the land of Egypt *and deliver* to death *those appointed* for death, and to captivity *those appointed* for captivity, and to the sword *those appointed* for the sword. [12] I will kindle a fire in the houses of the gods of Egypt, and he shall burn them and carry them away captive. And he shall array himself with the land of Egypt, as a shepherd puts on his garment, and he shall go out from there in peace. [13] He shall also break the sacred pillars of Beth Shemesh that *are* in the land of Egypt; and the houses of the gods of the Egyptians he shall burn with fire." ' "

44 The word that came to Jeremiah concerning all the Jews who dwell in the land of Egypt, who dwell at Migdol, at Tahpanhes, at Noph, and in the country of Pathros, saying, [2] "Thus says the LORD of hosts, the God of Israel: 'You have seen all the calamity that I have brought on Jerusalem and on all the cities of Judah; and behold, this day they *are* a desolation, and no one dwells in them, [3] because of their wickedness which they have committed to provoke Me to anger, in that they went to burn incense *and* to serve other gods whom they did not know, they nor you nor your fathers. [4] However I have sent to you all My servants the prophets, rising early and sending *them,* saying, "Oh, do not do this abominable thing that I hate!" [5] But they did not listen or incline their ear to turn from their wickedness, to burn no incense to other gods. [6] So My fury and My anger were poured out and kindled in the cities of Judah and in the streets of Jerusalem; and they are wasted *and* desolate, as it is this day.'

[7] "Now therefore, thus says the LORD, the God of hosts, the God of Israel: 'Why do you commit *this* great evil against yourselves, to cut off from you man and woman, child and infant, out of Judah, leaving none to remain, [8] in that you provoke Me to wrath with the works of your hands, burning incense to other gods in the land of Egypt where you have gone to dwell, that you may cut yourselves off and be a curse and a reproach among all the nations of the earth? [9] Have you forgotten the wickedness of your fathers, the wickedness of the kings of Judah, the wickedness of their wives, your own wickedness, and the wickedness of your wives, which they committed in the land of Judah and in the streets of Jerusalem? [10] They have not been humbled, to this day, nor have they feared; they have not walked in My law or in My statutes that I set before you and your fathers.'

וְנָטָה אֶת־שַׁפְרִירוֹ עֲלֵיהֶם: 11 וּבָאה וְהִכָּה אֶת־
אֶרֶץ מִצְרַיִם אֲשֶׁר לַמָּוֶת לַמָּוֶת וַאֲשֶׁר לַשְּׁבִי
לַשֶּׁבִי וַאֲשֶׁר לַחֶרֶב לֶחָרֶב: 12 וְהִצַּתִּי אֵשׁ בְּבָתֵּי
אֱלֹהֵי מִצְרַיִם וּשְׂרָפָם וְשָׁבָם וְעָטָה אֶת־אֶרֶץ
מִצְרַיִם כַּאֲשֶׁר־יַעְטֶה הָרֹעֶה אֶת־בִּגְדוֹ וְיָצָא מִשָּׁם
בְּשָׁלוֹם: 13 וְשִׁבַּר אֶת־מַצְּבוֹת בֵּית שֶׁמֶשׁ אֲשֶׁר
בְּאֶרֶץ מִצְרָיִם וְאֶת־בָּתֵּי אֱלֹהֵי־מִצְרַיִם יִשְׂרֹף
בָּאֵשׁ: ס

מד הַדָּבָר אֲשֶׁר הָיָה אֶל־יִרְמְיָהוּ אֶל כָּל־
הַיְּהוּדִים הַיֹּשְׁבִים בְּאֶרֶץ מִצְרַיִם הַיֹּשְׁבִים
בְּמִגְדֹּל וּבְתַחְפַּנְחֵס וּבְנֹף וּבְאֶרֶץ פַּתְרוֹס
לֵאמֹר: ס 2 כֹּה־אָמַר יְהוָה צְבָאוֹת אֱלֹהֵי
יִשְׂרָאֵל אַתֶּם רְאִיתֶם אֵת כָּל־הָרָעָה אֲשֶׁר הֵבֵאתִי
עַל־יְרוּשָׁלַ͏ִם וְעַל כָּל־עָרֵי יְהוּדָה וְהִנָּם חָרְבָּה
הַיּוֹם הַזֶּה וְאֵין בָּהֶם יוֹשֵׁב: 3 מִפְּנֵי רָעָתָם אֲשֶׁר
עָשׂוּ לְהַכְעִסֵנִי לָלֶכֶת לְקַטֵּר לַעֲבֹד לֵאלֹהִים
אֲחֵרִים אֲשֶׁר לֹא יְדָעוּם הֵמָּה אַתֶּם וַאֲבֹתֵיכֶם:
4 וָאֶשְׁלַח אֲלֵיכֶם אֶת־כָּל־עֲבָדַי הַנְּבִיאִים הַשְׁכֵּים
וְשָׁלֹחַ לֵאמֹר אַל־נָא תַעֲשׂוּ אֵת דְּבַר־הַתֹּעֵבָה
הַזֹּאת אֲשֶׁר שָׂנֵאתִי: 5 וְלֹא שָׁמְעוּ וְלֹא־הִטּוּ
אֶת־אָזְנָם לָשׁוּב מֵרָעָתָם לְבִלְתִּי קַטֵּר לֵאלֹהִים
אֲחֵרִים: 6 וַתִּתַּךְ חֲמָתִי וְאַפִּי וַתִּבְעַר בְּעָרֵי
יְהוּדָה וּבְחֻצוֹת יְרוּשָׁלָ͏ִם וַתִּהְיֶינָה לְחָרְבָּה לִשְׁמָמָה
כַּיּוֹם הַזֶּה: ס 7 וְעַתָּה כֹּה־אָמַר יְהוָה
אֱלֹהֵי צְבָאוֹת אֱלֹהֵי יִשְׂרָאֵל לָמָה אַתֶּם עֹשִׂים
רָעָה גְדוֹלָה אֶל־נַפְשֹׁתֵכֶם לְהַכְרִית לָכֶם אִישׁ־
וְאִשָּׁה עוֹלֵל וְיוֹנֵק מִתּוֹךְ יְהוּדָה לְבִלְתִּי הוֹתִיר
לָכֶם שְׁאֵרִית: 8 לְהַכְעִסֵנִי בְּמַעֲשֵׂי יְדֵיכֶם לְקַטֵּר
לֵאלֹהִים אֲחֵרִים בְּאֶרֶץ מִצְרַיִם אֲשֶׁר־אַתֶּם בָּאִים
לָגוּר שָׁם לְמַעַן הַכְרִית לָכֶם וּלְמַעַן הֱיוֹתְכֶם
לִקְלָלָה וּלְחֶרְפָּה בְּכֹל גּוֹיֵי הָאָרֶץ: 9 הַשְׁכַחְתֶּם
אֶת־רָעוֹת אֲבוֹתֵיכֶם וְאֶת־רָעוֹת מַלְכֵי יְהוּדָה
וְאֵת רָעוֹת נָשָׁיו וְאֵת רָעֹתֵכֶם וְאֵת רָעֹת נְשֵׁיכֶם
אֲשֶׁר עָשׂוּ בְּאֶרֶץ יְהוּדָה וּבְחֻצוֹת יְרוּשָׁלָ͏ִם:
10 לֹא דֻכְּאוּ עַד הַיּוֹם הַזֶּה וְלֹא יָרְאוּ וְלֹא־

11 "Therefore thus says the LORD of hosts, the God of Israel: 'Behold, I will set My face against you for catastrophe and for cutting off all Judah. 12 And I will take the remnant of Judah who have set their faces to go into the land of Egypt to dwell there, and they shall all be consumed *and* fall in the land of Egypt. They shall be consumed by the sword *and* by famine. They shall die, from the least to the greatest, by the sword and by famine; and they shall be an oath, an astonishment, a curse and a reproach! 13 For I will punish those who dwell in the land of Egypt, as I have punished Jerusalem, by the sword, by famine, and by pestilence, 14 so that none of the remnant of Judah who have gone into the land of Egypt to dwell there shall escape or survive, lest they return to the land of Judah, to which they desire to return and dwell. For none shall return except those who escape.' "

15 Then all the men who knew that their wives had burned incense to other gods, with all the women who stood by, a great multitude, and all the people who dwelt in the land of Egypt, in Pathros, answered Jeremiah, saying: 16 "*As for* the word that you have spoken to us in the name of the LORD, we will not listen to you! 17 But we will certainly do whatever has gone out of our own mouth, to burn incense to the queen of heaven and pour out drink offerings to her, as we have done, we and our fathers, our kings and our princes, in the cities of Judah and in the streets of Jerusalem. For *then* we had plenty of food, were well-off, and saw no trouble. 18 But since we stopped burning incense to the queen of heaven and pouring out drink offerings to her, we have lacked everything and have been consumed by the sword and by famine."

19 *The women also said,* "And when we burned incense to the queen of heaven and poured out drink offerings to her, did we make cakes for her, to worship her, and pour out drink offerings to her without our husbands' *permission?*"

20 Then Jeremiah spoke to all the people—the men, the women, and all the people who had given him *that* answer—saying: 21 "The incense that you burned in the cities of Judah and in the streets of Jerusalem, you and your fathers, your kings and your princes, and the people of the land, did not the LORD remember them, and did it *not* come into His mind? 22 So the LORD could no longer bear *it,* because of the evil of your doings *and* because of the abominations which you committed. Therefore your land is a desolation, an astonishment, a curse, and without an inhabitant, as *it is* this day. 23 Because you have burned incense and because you have sinned against the LORD, and have not

הָלַכְתֶּם בְּתוֹרָתִי וּבְחֻקֹּתַי אֲשֶׁר־נָתַתִּי לִפְנֵיכֶם וְלִפְנֵי אֲבוֹתֵיכֶם: ס 11 לָכֵן כֹּה־אָמַר יְהוָה צְבָאוֹת אֱלֹהֵי יִשְׂרָאֵל הִנְנִי שָׂם פָּנַי בָּכֶם לְרָעָה וּלְהַכְרִית אֶת־כָּל־יְהוּדָה: 12 וְלָקַחְתִּי אֶת־שְׁאֵרִית יְהוּדָה אֲשֶׁר־שָׂמוּ פְנֵיהֶם לָבוֹא אֶרֶץ־מִצְרַיִם לָגוּר שָׁם וְתַמּוּ כֹל בְּאֶרֶץ מִצְרַיִם יִפֹּלוּ בַּחֶרֶב בָּרָעָב יִתַּמּוּ מִקָּטֹן וְעַד־גָּדוֹל בַּחֶרֶב וּבָרָעָב יָמֻתוּ וְהָיוּ לְאָלָה לְשַׁמָּה וְלִקְלָלָה וּלְחֶרְפָּה: 13 וּפָקַדְתִּי עַל הַיּוֹשְׁבִים בְּאֶרֶץ מִצְרַיִם כַּאֲשֶׁר פָּקַדְתִּי עַל־יְרוּשָׁלָ͏ִם בַּחֶרֶב בָּרָעָב וּבַדָּבֶר: 14 וְלֹא יִהְיֶה פָּלִיט וְשָׂרִיד לִשְׁאֵרִית יְהוּדָה הַבָּאִים לָגוּר־שָׁם בְּאֶרֶץ מִצְרָיִם וְלָשׁוּב אֶרֶץ יְהוּדָה אֲשֶׁר־הֵמָּה מְנַשְּׂאִים אֶת־נַפְשָׁם לָשׁוּב לָשֶׁבֶת שָׁם כִּי לֹא־יָשׁוּבוּ כִּי אִם־פְּלֵטִים: ס 15 וַיַּעֲנוּ אֶת־יִרְמְיָהוּ כָּל־ הָאֲנָשִׁים הַיֹּדְעִים כִּי־מְקַטְּרוֹת נְשֵׁיהֶם לֵאלֹהִים אֲחֵרִים וְכָל־הַנָּשִׁים הָעֹמְדוֹת קָהָל גָּדוֹל וְכָל־ הָעָם הַיֹּשְׁבִים בְּאֶרֶץ־מִצְרַיִם בְּפַתְרוֹס לֵאמֹר: 16 הַדָּבָר אֲשֶׁר־דִּבַּרְתָּ אֵלֵינוּ בְּשֵׁם יְהוָה אֵינֶנּוּ שֹׁמְעִים אֵלֶיךָ: 17 כִּי עָשֹׂה נַעֲשֶׂה אֶת־כָּל־הַדָּבָר אֲשֶׁר־יָצָא מִפִּינוּ לְקַטֵּר לִמְלֶכֶת הַשָּׁמַיִם וְהַסֵּךְ־ לָהּ נְסָכִים כַּאֲשֶׁר עָשִׂינוּ אֲנַחְנוּ וַאֲבֹתֵינוּ מְלָכֵינוּ וְשָׂרֵינוּ בְּעָרֵי יְהוּדָה וּבְחֻצוֹת יְרוּשָׁלָ͏ִם וַנִּשְׂבַּע־לֶחֶם וַנִּהְיֶה טוֹבִים וְרָעָה לֹא רָאִינוּ: 18 וּמִן־אָז חָדַלְנוּ לְקַטֵּר לִמְלֶכֶת הַשָּׁמַיִם וְהַסֵּךְ־לָהּ נְסָכִים חָסַרְנוּ כֹל וּבַחֶרֶב וּבָרָעָב תָּמְנוּ: 19 וְכִי־אֲנַחְנוּ מְקַטְּרִים לִמְלֶכֶת הַשָּׁמַיִם וּלְהַסֵּךְ לָהּ נְסָכִים הֲמִבַּלְעֲדֵי אֲנָשֵׁינוּ עָשִׂינוּ לָהּ כַּוָּנִים לְהַעֲצִבָה וְהַסֵּךְ לָהּ נְסָכִים: פ

20 וַיֹּאמֶר יִרְמְיָהוּ אֶל־כָּל־הָעָם עַל־הַגְּבָרִים וְעַל־ הַנָּשִׁים וְעַל־כָּל־הָעָם הָעֹנִים אֹתוֹ דָּבָר לֵאמֹר: 21 הֲלוֹא אֶת־הַקִּטֵּר אֲשֶׁר קִטַּרְתֶּם בְּעָרֵי יְהוּדָה וּבְחֻצוֹת יְרוּשָׁלַ͏ִם אַתֶּם וַאֲבוֹתֵיכֶם מַלְכֵיכֶם וְשָׂרֵיכֶם וְעַם הָאָרֶץ אֹתָם זָכַר יְהוָה וַתַּעֲלֶה עַל־לִבּוֹ: 22 וְלֹא־יוּכַל יְהוָה עוֹד לָשֵׂאת מִפְּנֵי רֹעַ מַעַלְלֵיכֶם מִפְּנֵי הַתּוֹעֵבֹת אֲשֶׁר עֲשִׂיתֶם וַתְּהִי אַרְצְכֶם לְחָרְבָּה וּלְשַׁמָּה וְלִקְלָלָה מֵאֵין יוֹשֵׁב כְּהַיּוֹם הַזֶּה: 23 מִפְּנֵי אֲשֶׁר קִטַּרְתֶּם וַאֲשֶׁר חֲטָאתֶם לַיהוָה וְלֹא שְׁמַעְתֶּם בְּקוֹל

obeyed the voice of the LORD or walked in His law, in His statutes or in His testimonies, therefore this calamity has happened to you, as *at this day*."

24 Moreover Jeremiah said to all the people and to all the women, "Hear the word of the LORD, all Judah who *are* in the land of Egypt! 25 Thus says the LORD of hosts, the God of Israel, saying: 'You and your wives have spoken with your mouths and fulfilled with your hands, saying, "We will surely keep our vows that we have made, to burn incense to the queen of heaven and pour out drink offerings to her." You will surely keep your vows and perform your vows!' 26 Therefore hear the word of the LORD, all Judah who dwell in the land of Egypt: 'Behold, I have sworn by My great name,' says the LORD, 'that My name shall no more be named in the mouth of any man of Judah in all the land of Egypt, saying, "The Lord GOD lives." 27 Behold, I will watch over them for adversity and not for good. And all the men of Judah who *are* in the land of Egypt shall be consumed by the sword and by famine, until there is an end to them. 28 Yet a small number who escape the sword shall return from the land of Egypt to the land of Judah; and all the remnant of Judah, who have gone to the land of Egypt to dwell there, shall know whose words will stand, Mine or theirs. 29 And this *shall be* a sign to you,' says the LORD, 'that I will punish you in this place, that you may know that My words will surely stand against you for adversity.'

30 "Thus says the LORD: 'Behold, I will give Pharaoh Hophra king of Egypt into the hand of his enemies and into the hand of those who seek his life, as I gave Zedekiah king of Judah into the hand of Nebuchadnezzar king of Babylon, his enemy who sought his life.' "

45 The word that Jeremiah the prophet spoke to Baruch the son of Neriah, when he had written these words in a book at the instruction of Jeremiah, in the fourth year of Jehoiakim the son of Josiah, king of Judah, saying, 2 "Thus says the LORD, the God of Israel, to you, O Baruch: 3 'You said, "Woe is me now! For the LORD has added grief to my sorrow. I fainted in my sighing, and I find no rest." '

4 "Thus you shall say to him, 'Thus says the LORD: "Behold, what I have built I will break down, and what I have planted I will pluck up, that is, this whole land. 5 And do you seek great things for yourself? Do not seek *them;* for behold, I will bring adversity on all flesh," says the LORD. "But I will give your life to you as a prize in all places, wherever you go." ' "

יְהֹוָה וּבְחֻקֹּתָיו וּבְעֵדְוֹתָיו לֹא הֲלַכְתֶּם עַל־כֵּן קָרֵאת אֶתְכֶם הָרָעָה הַזֹּאת כַּיּוֹם הַזֶּה: ס 24 וַיֹּאמֶר יִרְמְיָהוּ אֶל־כָּל־הָעָם וְאֶל־כָּל־הַנָּשִׁים שִׁמְעוּ דְּבַר־יְהֹוָה כָּל־יְהוּדָה אֲשֶׁר בְּאֶרֶץ מִצְרָיִם: ס 25 כֹּה־אָמַר יְהֹוָה־ צְבָאוֹת אֱלֹהֵי יִשְׂרָאֵל לֵאמֹר אַתֶּם וּנְשֵׁיכֶם וַתְּדַבֵּרְנָה בְּפִיכֶם וּבִידֵיכֶם מִלֵּאתֶם | לֵאמֹר עָשֹׂה נַעֲשֶׂה אֶת־נְדָרֵינוּ אֲשֶׁר נָדַרְנוּ לְקַטֵּר לִמְלֶכֶת הַשָּׁמַיִם וּלְהַסֵּךְ לָהּ נְסָכִים הָקֵים תָּקִימְנָה אֶת־ נִדְרֵיכֶם וְעָשֹׂה תַעֲשֶׂינָה אֶת־נִדְרֵיכֶם: פ

26 לָכֵן שִׁמְעוּ דְבַר־יְהֹוָה כָּל־יְהוּדָה הַיֹּשְׁבִים בְּאֶרֶץ מִצְרָיִם הִנְנִי נִשְׁבַּעְתִּי בִּשְׁמִי הַגָּדוֹל אָמַר יְהֹוָה אִם־יִהְיֶה עוֹד שְׁמִי נִקְרָא | בְּפִי | כָּל־אִישׁ יְהוּדָה אֹמֵר חַי־אֲדֹנָי יֱהֹוִה בְּכָל־אֶרֶץ מִצְרָיִם: 27 הִנְנִי שֹׁקֵד עֲלֵיהֶם לְרָעָה וְלֹא לְטוֹבָה וְתַמּוּ כָל־אִישׁ יְהוּדָה אֲשֶׁר בְּאֶרֶץ־מִצְרַיִם בַּחֶרֶב וּבָרָעָב עַד־כְּלוֹתָם: 28 וּפְלִיטֵי חֶרֶב יְשֻׁבוּן מִן־אֶרֶץ מִצְרַיִם אֶרֶץ יְהוּדָה מְתֵי מִסְפָּר וְיָדְעוּ כָּל־שְׁאֵרִית יְהוּדָה הַבָּאִים לְאֶרֶץ־מִצְרַיִם לָגוּר שָׁם דְּבַר־מִי יָקוּם מִמֶּנִּי וּמֵהֶם: 29 וְזֹאת־לָכֶם הָאוֹת נְאֻם־יְהֹוָה כִּי־ פֹקֵד אֲנִי עֲלֵיכֶם בַּמָּקוֹם הַזֶּה לְמַעַן תֵּדְעוּ כִּי קוֹם יָקוּמוּ דְבָרַי עֲלֵיכֶם לְרָעָה: ס 30 כֹּה |

אָמַר יְהֹוָה הִנְנִי נֹתֵן אֶת־פַּרְעֹה חָפְרַע מֶלֶךְ־מִצְרַיִם בְּיַד אֹיְבָיו וּבְיַד מְבַקְשֵׁי נַפְשׁוֹ כַּאֲשֶׁר נָתַתִּי אֶת־ צִדְקִיָּהוּ מֶלֶךְ־יְהוּדָה בְּיַד נְבוּכַדְרֶאצַּר מֶלֶךְ־בָּבֶל אֹיְבוֹ וּמְבַקֵּשׁ נַפְשׁוֹ: ס

מה הַדָּבָר אֲשֶׁר דִּבֶּר יִרְמְיָהוּ הַנָּבִיא אֶל־בָּרוּךְ בֶּן־נֵרִיָּה בְּכָתְבוֹ אֶת־הַדְּבָרִים הָאֵלֶּה עַל־סֵפֶר מִפִּי יִרְמְיָהוּ בַּשָּׁנָה הָרְבִעִית לִיהוֹיָקִים בֶּן־יֹאשִׁיָּהוּ מֶלֶךְ יְהוּדָה לֵאמֹר: ס 2 כֹּה־אָמַר יְהֹוָה אֱלֹהֵי יִשְׂרָאֵל עָלֶיךָ בָּרוּךְ: 3 אָמַרְתָּ אוֹי־נָא לִי כִּי־יָסַף יְהֹוָה יָגוֹן עַל־מַכְאֹבִי יָגַעְתִּי בְּאַנְחָתִי וּמְנוּחָה לֹא מָצָאתִי: 4 כֹּה | תֹּאמַר אֵלָיו כֹּה אָמַר יְהֹוָה הִנֵּה אֲשֶׁר־בָּנִיתִי אֲנִי הֹרֵס וְאֵת אֲשֶׁר־נָטַעְתִּי אֲנִי נֹתֵשׁ וְאֶת־כָּל־הָאָרֶץ הִיא: 5 וְאַתָּה תְּבַקֶּשׁ־לְךָ גְדֹלוֹת אַל־תְּבַקֵּשׁ כִּי הִנְנִי מֵבִיא רָעָה עַל־כָּל־ בָּשָׂר נְאֻם־יְהֹוָה וְנָתַתִּי לְךָ אֶת־נַפְשְׁךָ לְשָׁלָל עַל כָּל־הַמְּקֹמוֹת אֲשֶׁר תֵּלֶךְ־שָׁם: ס

46

The word of the LORD which came to Jeremiah the prophet against the nations. ² Against Egypt.

Concerning the army of Pharaoh Necho, king of Egypt, which was by the River Euphrates in Carchemish, and which Nebuchadnezzar king of Babylon defeated in the fourth year of Jehoiakim the son of Josiah, king of Judah:

³ "Order the buckler and shield,
    And draw near to battle!
⁴ Harness the horses,
    And mount up, you horsemen!
    Stand forth with *your* helmets,
    Polish the spears,
    Put on the armor!
⁵ Why have I seen them dismayed *and* turned back?
    Their mighty ones are beaten down;
    They have speedily fled,
    And did not look back,
    For fear *was* all around," says the LORD.
⁶ "Do not let the swift flee away,
    Nor the mighty man escape;
    They will stumble and fall
    Toward the north, by the River Euphrates.

⁷ "Who *is* this coming up like a flood,
    Whose waters move like the rivers?
⁸ Egypt rises up like a flood,
    And *its* waters move like the rivers;
    And he says, 'I will go up *and* cover the earth,
    I will destroy the city and its inhabitants.'
⁹ Come up, O horses, and rage, O chariots!
    And let the mighty men come forth:
    The Ethiopians and the Libyans who handle the shield,
    And the Lydians who handle *and* bend the bow.
¹⁰ For this *is* the day of the Lord GOD of hosts,
    A day of vengeance,
    That He may avenge Himself on His adversaries.
    The sword shall devour;
    It shall be satiated and made drunk with their blood;
    For the Lord GOD of hosts has a sacrifice
    In the north country by the River Euphrates.

¹¹ "Go up to Gilead and take balm,
    O virgin, the daughter of Egypt;
    In vain you will use many medicines;
    You shall not be cured.
¹² The nations have heard of your shame,
    And your cry has filled the land;
    For the mighty man has stumbled against the mighty;
    They both have fallen together."

¹³ The word that the LORD spoke to Jeremiah the prophet, how Nebuchadnezzar king of Babylon would come *and* strike the land of Egypt.

¹⁴ "Declare in Egypt, and proclaim in Migdol;
    Proclaim in Noph and in Tahpanhes;
    Say, 'Stand fast and prepare yourselves,
    For the sword devours all around you.'

מו אֲשֶׁר הָיָה דְבַר־יְהוָה אֶל־יִרְמְיָהוּ הַנָּבִיא
עַל־הַגּוֹיִם: 2 לְמִצְרַיִם עַל־חֵיל פַּרְעֹה נְכוֹ מֶלֶךְ
מִצְרַיִם אֲשֶׁר־הָיָה עַל־נְהַר־פְּרָת בְּכַרְכְּמִשׁ אֲשֶׁר
הִכָּה נְבוּכַדְרֶאצַּר מֶלֶךְ בָּבֶל בִּשְׁנַת הָרְבִיעִית
לִיהוֹיָקִים בֶּן־יֹאשִׁיָּהוּ מֶלֶךְ יְהוּדָה: 3 עִרְכוּ מָגֵן
וְצִנָּה וּגְשׁוּ לַמִּלְחָמָה: 4 אִסְרוּ הַסּוּסִים וַעֲלוּ
הַפָּרָשִׁים וְהִתְיַצְּבוּ בְּכוֹבָעִים מִרְקוּ הָרְמָחִים לִבְשׁוּ
הַסִּרְיֹנֹת: 5 מַדּוּעַ רָאִיתִי הֵמָּה חַתִּים נְסֹגִים אָחוֹר
וְגִבּוֹרֵיהֶם יֻכַּתּוּ וּמָנוֹס נָסוּ וְלֹא הִפְנוּ מָגוֹר מִסָּבִיב
נְאֻם־יְהוָה: 6 אַל־יָנוּס הַקַּל וְאַל־יִמָּלֵט הַגִּבּוֹר
צָפוֹנָה עַל־יַד נְהַר־פְּרָת כָּשְׁלוּ וְנָפָלוּ: 7 מִי־זֶה
כַּיְאֹר יַעֲלֶה כַּנְּהָרוֹת יִתְגָּעֲשׁוּ מֵימָיו: 8 מִצְרַיִם
כַּיְאֹר יַעֲלֶה וְכַנְּהָרוֹת יִתְגֹּעֲשׁוּ מָיִם וַיֹּאמֶר אַעֲלֶה
אֲכַסֶּה־אֶרֶץ אֹבִידָה עִיר וְיֹשְׁבֵי בָהּ: 9 עֲלוּ הַסּוּסִים
וְהִתְהֹלְלוּ הָרֶכֶב וְיֵצְאוּ הַגִּבּוֹרִים כּוּשׁ וּפוּט תֹּפְשֵׂי
מָגֵן וְלוּדִים תֹּפְשֵׂי דֹּרְכֵי קָשֶׁת: 10 וְהַיּוֹם הַהוּא
לַאדֹנָי יְהוִה צְבָאוֹת יוֹם נְקָמָה לְהִנָּקֵם מִצָּרָיו
וְאָכְלָה חֶרֶב וְשָׂבְעָה וְרָוְתָה מִדָּמָם כִּי זֶבַח
לַאדֹנָי יְהוִה צְבָאוֹת בְּאֶרֶץ צָפוֹן אֶל־נְהַר־פְּרָת:
11 עֲלִי גִלְעָד וּקְחִי צֳרִי בְּתוּלַת בַּת־מִצְרָיִם לַשָּׁוְא
הִרְבֵּיתִי רְפֻאוֹת תְּעָלָה אֵין לָךְ: 12 שָׁמְעוּ גוֹיִם
קְלוֹנֵךְ וְצִוְחָתֵךְ מָלְאָה הָאָרֶץ כִּי־גִבּוֹר בְּגִבּוֹר כָּשָׁלוּ
יַחְדָּו נָפְלוּ שְׁנֵיהֶם: פ

13 הַדָּבָר אֲשֶׁר דִּבֶּר יְהוָה אֶל־יִרְמְיָהוּ הַנָּבִיא לָבוֹא
נְבוּכַדְרֶאצַּר מֶלֶךְ בָּבֶל לְהַכּוֹת אֶת־אֶרֶץ מִצְרָיִם:
14 הַגִּידוּ בְמִצְרַיִם וְהַשְׁמִיעוּ בְמִגְדּוֹל וְהַשְׁמִיעוּ בְנֹף
וּבְתַחְפַּנְחֵס אִמְרוּ הִתְיַצֵּב וְהָכֵן לָךְ כִּי־אָכְלָה חֶרֶב

מו 11 הִרְבֵּית

15 Why are your valiant *men* swept away?
   They did not stand
   Because the LORD drove them away.
16 He made many fall;
   Yes, one fell upon another.
   And they said, 'Arise!
   Let us go back to our own people
   And to the land of our nativity
   From the oppressing sword.'
17 They cried there,
   'Pharaoh, king of Egypt, *is but* a noise.
   He has passed by the appointed time!'

18 "*As* I live," says the King,
   Whose name *is* the LORD of hosts,

   "Surely as Tabor *is* among the mountains
   And as Carmel by the sea, *so* he shall come.
19 O you daughter dwelling in Egypt,
   Prepare yourself to go into captivity!
   For Noph shall be waste and desolate, without
     inhabitant.
20 "Egypt *is* a very pretty heifer,
   But destruction comes, it comes from the north.
21 Also her mercenaries are in her midst like fat
     bulls,
   For they also are turned back,
   They have fled away together.
   They did not stand,
   For the day of their calamity had come upon
     them,
   The time of their punishment.
22 Her noise shall go like a serpent,
   For they shall march with an army
   And come against her with axes,
   Like those who chop wood.
23 "They shall cut down her forest," says the LORD,
   "Though it cannot be searched,
   Because they *are* innumerable,
   And more numerous than grasshoppers.
24 The daughter of Egypt shall be ashamed;
   She shall be delivered into the hand
   Of the people of the north."

25 The LORD of hosts, the God of Israel, says: "Behold, I will bring punishment on Amon of No, and Pharaoh and Egypt, with their gods and their kings—Pharaoh and those who trust in him. 26 And I will deliver them into the hand of those who seek their lives, into the hand of Nebuchadnezzar king of Babylon and the hand of his servants. Afterward it shall be inhabited as in the days of old," says the LORD.

27 "But do not fear, O My servant Jacob,
   And do not be dismayed, O Israel!
   For behold, I will save you from afar,
   And your offspring from the land of their
     captivity;
   Jacob shall return, have rest and be at ease;
   No one shall make *him* afraid.
28 Do not fear, O Jacob My servant," says the
     LORD,

סְבִיבֶיךָ: 15 מַדּוּעַ נִסְחַף אַבִּירֶיךָ לֹא עָמַד כִּי

יְהוָה הֲדָפוֹ: 16 הִרְבָּה כּוֹשֵׁל גַּם־נָפַל אִישׁ אֶל־

רֵעֵהוּ וַיֹּאמְרוּ ׀ קוּמָה וְנָשֻׁבָה אֶל־עַמֵּנוּ וְאֶל־

אֶרֶץ מוֹלַדְתֵּנוּ מִפְּנֵי חֶרֶב הַיּוֹנָה: 17 קָרְאוּ שָׁם

פַּרְעֹה מֶלֶךְ־מִצְרַיִם שָׁאוֹן הֶעֱבִיר הַמּוֹעֵד: 18 חַי־

אָנִי נְאֻם־הַמֶּלֶךְ יְהוָה צְבָאוֹת שְׁמוֹ כִּי כְּתָבוֹר

בֶּהָרִים וּכְכַרְמֶל בַּיָּם יָבוֹא: 19 כְּלֵי גוֹלָה עֲשִׂי לָךְ

יוֹשֶׁבֶת בַּת־מִצְרָיִם כִּי־נֹף לְשַׁמָּה תִהְיֶה וְנִצְּתָה

מֵאֵין יוֹשֵׁב: ס 20 עֶגְלָה יְפֵה־פִיָּה מִצְרָיִם קֶרֶץ

מִצָּפוֹן בָּא בָא: 21 גַּם־שְׂכִרֶיהָ בְקִרְבָּהּ כְּעֶגְלֵי

מַרְבֵּק כִּי־גַם־הֵמָּה הִפְנוּ נָסוּ יַחְדָּיו לֹא עָמָדוּ כִּי

יוֹם אֵידָם בָּא עֲלֵיהֶם עֵת פְּקֻדָּתָם: 22 קוֹלָהּ כַּנָּחָשׁ

יֵלֵךְ כִּי־בְחַיִל יֵלֵכוּ וּבְקַרְדֻּמּוֹת בָּאוּ לָהּ כְּחֹטְבֵי

עֵצִים: 23 כָּרְתוּ יַעְרָהּ נְאֻם־יְהוָה כִּי לֹא יֵחָקֵר כִּי

רַבּוּ מֵאַרְבֶּה וְאֵין לָהֶם מִסְפָּר: 24 הֹבִישָׁה בַּת־

מִצְרָיִם נִתְּנָה בְּיַד עַם־צָפוֹן: 25 אָמַר יְהוָה צְבָאוֹת

אֱלֹהֵי יִשְׂרָאֵל הִנְנִי פוֹקֵד אֶל־אָמוֹן מִנֹּא וְעַל־פַּרְעֹה

וְעַל־מִצְרַיִם וְעַל־אֱלֹהֶיהָ וְעַל־מְלָכֶיהָ וְעַל־פַּרְעֹה

וְעַל הַבֹּטְחִים בּוֹ: 26 וּנְתַתִּים בְּיַד מְבַקְשֵׁי נַפְשָׁם

וּבְיַד נְבוּכַדְרֶאצַּר מֶלֶךְ־בָּבֶל וּבְיַד־עֲבָדָיו וְאַחֲרֵי־

כֵן תִּשְׁכֹּן כִּימֵי־קֶדֶם נְאֻם־יְהוָה: ס 27 וְאַתָּה

אַל־תִּירָא עַבְדִּי יַעֲקֹב וְאַל־תֵּחַת יִשְׂרָאֵל כִּי הִנְנִי

מוֹשִׁעֲךָ מֵרָחוֹק וְאֶת־זַרְעֲךָ מֵאֶרֶץ שִׁבְיָם וְשָׁב

יַעֲקוֹב וְשָׁקַט וְשַׁאֲנַן וְאֵין מַחֲרִיד: ס 28 אַתָּה

אַל־תִּירָא עַבְדִּי יַעֲקֹב נְאֻם־יְהוָה כִּי אִתְּךָ אָנִי כִּי

"For I *am* with you;
For I will make a complete end of all the nations
To which I have driven you,
But I will not make a complete end of you.
I will rightly correct you,
For I will not leave you wholly unpunished."

47 The word of the LORD that came to Jeremiah the prophet against the Philistines, before Pharaoh attacked Gaza.

2 Thus says the LORD:

"Behold, waters rise out of the north,
And shall be an overflowing flood;
They shall overflow the land and all that is in it,
The city and those who dwell within;
Then the men shall cry,
And all the inhabitants of the land shall wail.

3 At the noise of the stamping hooves of his strong
    horses,
At the rushing of his chariots,
At the rumbling of his wheels,
The fathers will not look back for *their* children,
Lacking courage,

4 Because of the day that comes to plunder all the
    Philistines,
To cut off from Tyre and Sidon every helper who
    remains;
For the LORD shall plunder the Philistines,
The remnant of the country of Caphtor.

5 Baldness has come upon Gaza,
Ashkelon is cut off
With the remnant of their valley.
How long will you cut yourself?

6 "O you sword of the LORD,
How long until you are quiet?
Put yourself up into your scabbard,
Rest and be still!

7 How can it be quiet,
Seeing the LORD has given it a charge
Against Ashkelon and against the seashore?
There He has appointed it."

48 Against Moab.

Thus says the LORD of hosts, the God of Israel:

"Woe to Nebo!
For it is plundered,
Kirjathaim is shamed *and* taken;
The high stronghold is shamed and dismayed—

2 No more praise of Moab.
In Heshbon they have devised evil against her:
'Come, and let us cut her off as a nation.'
You also shall be cut down, O Madmen!
The sword shall pursue you;

3 A voice of crying *shall be* from Horonaim:
'Plundering and great destruction!'

4 "Moab is destroyed;
Her little ones have caused a cry to be heard;

5 For in the Ascent of Luhith they ascend with
    continual weeping;

אֶעֱשֶׂה כָלָה בְּכָל־הַגּוֹיִם ׀ אֲשֶׁר הֲדַחְתִּיךָ שָׁמָּה
וְאֹתְךָ לֹא־אֶעֱשֶׂה כָלָה וְיִסַּרְתִּיךָ לַמִּשְׁפָּט וְנַקֵּה
לֹא אֲנַקֶּךָּ: ס

מז אֲשֶׁר הָיָה דְבַר־יְהוָה אֶל־יִרְמְיָהוּ
הַנָּבִיא אֶל־פְּלִשְׁתִּים בְּטֶרֶם יַכֶּה פַרְעֹה אֶת־
עַזָּה: ס 2 כֹּה ׀ אָמַר יְהוָה הִנֵּה־מַיִם
עֹלִים מִצָּפוֹן וְהָיוּ לְנַחַל שׁוֹטֵף וְיִשְׁטְפוּ אֶרֶץ
וּמְלוֹאָהּ עִיר וְיֹשְׁבֵי בָהּ וְזָעֲקוּ הָאָדָם וְהֵילִל
כֹּל יוֹשֵׁב הָאָרֶץ: 3 מִקּוֹל שַׁעֲטַת פַּרְסוֹת אַבִּירָיו
מֵרַעַשׁ לְרִכְבּוֹ הֲמוֹן גַּלְגִּלָּיו לֹא־הִפְנוּ אָבוֹת אֶל־
בָּנִים מֵרִפְיוֹן יָדָיִם: 4 עַל־הַיּוֹם הַבָּא לִשְׁדוֹד אֶת־
כָּל־פְּלִשְׁתִּים לְהַכְרִית לְצֹר וּלְצִידוֹן כֹּל שָׂרִיד עֹזֵר
כִּי־שֹׁדֵד יְהוָה אֶת־פְּלִשְׁתִּים שְׁאֵרִית אִי כַפְתּוֹר:
5 בָּאָה קָרְחָה אֶל־עַזָּה נִדְמְתָה אַשְׁקְלוֹן שְׁאֵרִית
עִמְקָם עַד־מָתַי תִּתְגּוֹדָדִי: ס 6 הוֹי חֶרֶב
לַיהוָה עַד־אָנָה לֹא תִשְׁקֹטִי הֵאָסְפִי אַל־תַּעְרֵךְ
הֵרָגְעִי וָדֹמִּי: 7 אֵיךְ תִּשְׁקֹטִי וַיהוָה צִוָּה־לָהּ אֶל־
אַשְׁקְלוֹן וְאֶל־חוֹף הַיָּם שָׁם יְעָדָהּ: ס

מח לְמוֹאָב כֹּה־אָמַר יְהוָה צְבָאוֹת אֱלֹהֵי
יִשְׂרָאֵל הוֹי אֶל־נְבוֹ כִּי שֻׁדָּדָה הֹבִישָׁה נִלְכְּדָה
קִרְיָתָיִם הֹבִישָׁה הַמִּשְׂגָּב וָחָתָּה: 2 אֵין עוֹד
תְּהִלַּת מוֹאָב בְּחֶשְׁבּוֹן חָשְׁבוּ עָלֶיהָ רָעָה לְכוּ
וְנַכְרִיתֶנָּה מִגּוֹי גַּם־מַדְמֵן תִּדֹּמִּי אַחֲרַיִךְ תֵּלֶךְ
חָרֶב: 3 קוֹל צְעָקָה מֵחֹרוֹנָיִם שֹׁד וָשֶׁבֶר גָּדוֹל:
4 נִשְׁבְּרָה מוֹאָב הִשְׁמִיעוּ זְעָקָה צְעוֹרֶיהָ[P]: 5 כִּי
מַעֲלֵה הַלֻּחוֹת[P] בִּבְכִי יַעֲלֶה־בֶּכִי כִּי בְּמוֹרַד

מח 4 צְעִירֶיהָ   5 הַלֻּחִית

For in the descent of Horonaim the enemies have
  heard a cry of destruction.

6 "Flee, save your lives!
  And be like the juniper in the wilderness.

7 For because you have trusted in your works and
    your treasures,
  You also shall be taken.
  And Chemosh shall go forth into captivity,
  His priests and his princes together.

8 And the plunderer shall come against every city;
  No one shall escape.
  The valley also shall perish,
  And the plain shall be destroyed,
  As the LORD has spoken.

9 "Give wings to Moab,
  That she may flee and get away;
  For her cities shall be desolate,
  Without any to dwell in them.

10 Cursed *is* he who does the work of the LORD
  deceitfully,
  And cursed *is* he who keeps back his sword from
  blood.

11 "Moab has been at ease from his youth;
  He has settled on his dregs,
  And has not been emptied from vessel to vessel,
  Nor has he gone into captivity.
  Therefore his taste remained in him,
  And his scent has not changed.

12 "Therefore behold, the days are coming," says the
  LORD,
  "That I shall send him wine-workers
  Who will tip him over
  And empty his vessels
  And break the bottles.

13 Moab shall be ashamed of Chemosh,
  As the house of Israel was ashamed of Bethel,
  their confidence.

14 "How can you say, 'We *are* mighty
  And strong men for the war'?

15 Moab is plundered and gone up *from* her cities;
  Her chosen young men have gone down to the
    slaughter," says the King,
  Whose name *is* the LORD of hosts.

16 "The calamity of Moab *is* near at hand,
  And his affliction comes quickly.

17 Bemoan him, all you who are around him;
  And all you who know his name,
  Say, 'How the strong staff is broken,
  The beautiful rod!'

18 "O daughter inhabiting Dibon,
  Come down from *your* glory,
  And sit in thirst;
  For the plunderer of Moab has come against you,
  He has destroyed your strongholds.

19 O inhabitant of Aroer,
  Stand by the way and watch;
  Ask him who flees
  And her who escapes;
  Say, 'What has happened?'

חוֹרֹנַ֔יִם צָרֵ֥י צַעֲקַת־שֶׁ֖בֶר שָׁמֵֽעוּ׃ 6 נֻ֖סוּ מַלְּט֣וּ

נַפְשְׁכֶ֑ם וְתִֽהְיֶ֕ינָה כַּעֲרוֹעֵ֖ר בַּמִּדְבָּֽר׃ 7 כִּ֣י יַ֤עַן

בִּטְחֵךְ֙ בְּמַעֲשַׂ֣יִךְ וּבְאֽוֹצְרוֹתַ֔יִךְ גַּם־אַ֖תְּ תִּלָּכֵ֑דִי

וְיָצָ֤א כְמִישׁ֙ בַּגּוֹלָ֔ה כֹּהֲנָ֥יו וְשָׂרָ֖יו יַחְדָּֽיו׃ 8 וְיָבֹ֨א

שֹׁדֵ֜ד אֶל־כָּל־עִ֗יר וְעִיר֙ לֹ֣א תִמָּלֵ֔ט וְאָבַ֥ד הָעֵ֖מֶק

וְנִשְׁמַ֣ד הַמִּישֹׁ֑ר אֲשֶׁ֖ר אָמַ֥ר יְהוָֽה׃ 9 תְּנוּ־צִ֣יץ

לְמוֹאָ֔ב כִּ֥י נָצֹ֖א תֵּצֵ֑א וְעָרֶ֨יהָ֙ לְשַׁמָּ֣ה תִֽהְיֶ֔ינָה מֵאֵ֥ין

יוֹשֵׁ֖ב בָּהֵֽן׃ 10 אָר֗וּר עֹשֶׂ֛ה מְלֶ֥אכֶת יְהוָ֖ה רְמִיָּ֑ה

וְאָר֕וּר מֹנֵ֥עַ חַרְבּ֖וֹ מִדָּֽם׃ 11 שַׁאֲנַ֨ן מוֹאָ֜ב מִנְּעוּרָ֗יו

וְשֹׁקֵ֥ט הוּא֙ אֶל־שְׁמָרָ֔יו וְלֹֽא־הוּרַ֤ק מִכְּלִי֙ אֶל־כֶּ֔לִי

וּבַגּוֹלָ֖ה לֹ֣א הָלָ֑ךְ עַל־כֵּ֗ן עָמַ֤ד טַעְמוֹ֙ בּ֔וֹ וְרֵיח֖וֹ

לֹ֥א נָמָֽר׃ ס 12 לָכֵ֞ן הִנֵּֽה־יָמִ֤ים בָּאִים֙

נְאֻם־יְהוָ֔ה וְשִׁלַּחְתִּי־ל֥וֹ צֹעִ֖ים וְצֵעֻ֑הוּ וְכֵלָ֣יו יָרִ֔יקוּ

וְנִבְלֵיהֶ֖ם יְנַפֵּֽצוּ׃ 13 וּבֹ֤שׁ מוֹאָב֙ מִכְּמ֔וֹשׁ כַּאֲשֶׁר־בֹּ֙שׁוּ֙

בֵּ֣ית יִשְׂרָאֵ֔ל מִבֵּ֖ית אֵ֥ל מִבְטֶחָֽם׃ 14 אֵ֚יךְ תֹּֽאמְר֔וּ

גִּבּוֹרִ֖ים אֲנָ֑חְנוּ וְאַנְשֵׁי־חַ֖יִל לַמִּלְחָמָֽה׃ 15 שֻׁדַּ֤ד

מוֹאָב֙ וְעָרֶ֣יהָ עָלָ֔ה וּמִבְחַ֥ר בַּחוּרָ֖יו יָרְד֣וּ לַטָּ֑בַח

נְאֻם־הַמֶּ֔לֶךְ יְהוָ֥ה צְבָא֖וֹת שְׁמֽוֹ׃ 16 קָר֥וֹב אֵיד־

מוֹאָ֖ב לָב֑וֹא וְרָ֣עָת֔וֹ מִהֲרָ֖ה מְאֹֽד׃ 17 נֻ֤דוּ לוֹ֙ כָּל־

סְבִיבָ֔יו וְכֹ֖ל יֹדְעֵ֣י שְׁמ֑וֹ אִמְר֗וּ אֵיכָ֤ה נִשְׁבַּר֙ מַטֵּה־עֹ֔ז

מַקֵּ֖ל תִּפְאָרָֽה׃ 18 רְדִ֤י מִכָּבוֹד֙ ישְׁבִ֣י בַצָּמָ֔א יֹשֶׁ֖בֶת

בַּת־דִּיבֹ֑ון כִּֽי־שֹׁדֵ֤ד מוֹאָב֙ עָ֣לָה בָ֔ךְ שִׁחֵ֖ת מִבְצָרָֽיִךְ׃

19 אֶל־דֶּ֣רֶךְ עִמְדִ֣י וְצַפִּ֔י יוֹשֶׁ֖בֶת עֲרוֹעֵ֑ר שַׁאֲלִי־נָ֣ס

מח 7 כְּמוֹשׁ   יַחְדָּֽיו   18 שְׁבִֽי

20 Moab is shamed, for he is broken down.
    Wail and cry!
    Tell it in Arnon, that Moab is plundered.

21 "And judgment has come on the plain country:
    On Holon and Jahzah and Mephaath,
22 On Dibon and Nebo and Beth Diblathaim,
23 On Kirjathaim and Beth Gamul and Beth Meon,
24 On Kerioth and Bozrah,
    On all the cities of the land of Moab,
    Far or near.
25 The horn of Moab is cut off,
    And his arm is broken," says the LORD.

26 "Make him drunk,
    Because he exalted *himself* against the LORD.
    Moab shall wallow in his vomit,
    And he shall also be in derision.
27 For was not Israel a derision to you?
    Was he found among thieves?
    For whenever you speak of him,
    You shake *your head in scorn*.
28 You who dwell in Moab,
    Leave the cities and dwell in the rock,
    And be like the dove *which* makes her nest
    In the sides of the cave's mouth.

29 "We have heard the pride of Moab
    (He *is* exceedingly proud),
    Of his loftiness and arrogance and pride, ·
    And of the haughtiness of his heart."
30 "I know his wrath," says the LORD,
    "But *it is* not right;
    His lies have made nothing right.
31 Therefore I will wail for Moab,
    And I will cry out for all Moab;
    I will mourn for the men of Kir Heres.
32 O vine of Sibmah! I will weep for you with the
        weeping of Jazer.
    Your plants have gone over the sea,
    They reach to the sea of Jazer.
    The plunderer has fallen on your summer fruit
        and your vintage.
33 Joy and gladness are taken
    From the plentiful field
    And from the land of Moab;
    I have caused wine to fail from the winepresses;
    No one will tread with joyous shouting—
    Not joyous shouting!

34 "From the cry of Heshbon to Elealeh and to Jahaz
    They have uttered their voice,
    From Zoar to Horonaim,
    Like a three-year-old heifer;
    For the waters of Nimrim also shall be desolate.

35 "Moreover," says the LORD,
    "I will cause to cease in Moab
    The one who offers *sacrifices* in the high places
    And burns incense to his gods.
36 Therefore My heart shall wail like flutes for
        Moab,
    And like flutes My heart shall wail
    For the men of Kir Heres.

וְנִמְלְטָה אִמְרֵי מַה־נֶּהְיָתָה: 20 הֹבִישׁ מוֹאָב כִּי־
חַתָּה הֵילִילוּ P ׀ וּֽזְעָקוּ P הַגִּידוּ בְאַרְנוֹן כִּי שֻׁדַּד
מוֹאָב: 21 וּמִשְׁפָּט בָּא אֶל־אֶרֶץ הַמִּישֹׁר אֶל־חֹלוֹן
וְאֶל־יַהְצָה וְעַל־מֵופָעַת P: 22 וְעַל־דִּיבוֹן וְעַל־נְבוֹ
וְעַל־בֵּית דִּבְלָתָיִם: 23 וְעַל קִרְיָתַיִם וְעַל־בֵּית גָּמוּל
וְעַל־בֵּית מְעוֹן: 24 וְעַל־קְרִיּוֹת וְעַל־בָּצְרָה וְעַל כָּל־
עָרֵי אֶרֶץ מוֹאָב הָרְחֹקוֹת וְהַקְּרֹבוֹת: 25 נִגְדְּעָה
קֶרֶן מוֹאָב וּזְרֹעוֹ נִשְׁבָּרָה נְאֻם יְהֹוָה: 26 הַשְׁכִּירֻהוּ
כִּי עַל־יְהֹוָה הִגְדִּיל וְסָפַק מוֹאָב בְּקִיאוֹ וְהָיָה
לִשְׂחֹק גַּם־הוּא: 27 וְאִם ׀ לוֹא הַשְּׂחֹק הָיָה לְךָ
יִשְׂרָאֵל אִם־בְּגַנָּבִים נִמְצָאָה P כִּי־מִדֵּי דְבָרֶיךָ בּוֹ
תִּתְנוֹדָד: 28 עִזְבוּ עָרִים וְשִׁכְנוּ בַּסֶּלַע יֹשְׁבֵי מוֹאָב
וִהְיוּ כְיוֹנָה תְּקַנֵּן בְּעֶבְרֵי פִי־פָחַת: 29 שָׁמַעְנוּ גְאוֹן־
מוֹאָב גֵּאֶה מְאֹד גָּבְהוֹ וּגְאוֹנוֹ וְגַאֲוָתוֹ וְרֻם לִבּוֹ:
30 אֲנִי יָדַעְתִּי נְאֻם־יְהֹוָה עֶבְרָתוֹ וְלֹא־כֵן בַּדָּיו לֹא־
כֵן עָשׂוּ: 31 עַל־כֵּן עַל־מוֹאָב אֲיֵלִיל וּלְמוֹאָב כֻּלֹּה
אֶזְעָק אֶל־אַנְשֵׁי קִיר־חֶרֶשׂ יֶהְגֶּה: 32 מִבְּכִי יַעְזֵר
אֶבְכֶּה־לָּךְ הַגֶּפֶן שִׂבְמָה נְטִישֹׁתַיִךְ עָבְרוּ יָם עַד
יָם יַעְזֵר נָגָעוּ עַל־קֵיצֵךְ וְעַל־בְּצִירֵךְ שֹׁדֵד נָפָל:
33 וְנֶאֶסְפָה שִׂמְחָה וָגִיל מִכַּרְמֶל וּמֵאֶרֶץ מוֹאָב
וְיַיִן מִיקָבִים הִשְׁבַּתִּי לֹא־יִדְרֹךְ הֵידָד הֵידָד לֹא
הֵידָד: 34 מִזַּעֲקַת חֶשְׁבּוֹן עַד־אֶלְעָלֵה עַד־יַהַץ נָתְנוּ
קוֹלָם מִצֹּעַר עַד־חֹרֹנַיִם עֶגְלַת שְׁלִשִׁיָּה כִּי גַּם־
מֵי נִמְרִים לִמְשַׁמּוֹת יִהְיוּ: 35 וְהִשְׁבַּתִּי לְמוֹאָב
נְאֻם־יְהֹוָה מַעֲלֶה בָמָה וּמַקְטִיר לֵאלֹהָיו: 36 עַל־
כֵּן לִבִּי לְמוֹאָב כַּחֲלִילִים יֶהֱמֶה וְלִבִּי אֶל־אַנְשֵׁי
קִיר־חֶרֶשׂ כַּחֲלִילִים יֶהֱמֶה עַל־כֵּן יִתְרַת עָשָׂה

מח 20 הֵילִילוּ ׀ וּֽזְעָקוּ 21 מֵופָעַת 27 נִמְצָא

Therefore the riches they have acquired have
 perished.

37 "For every head *shall be* bald, and every beard
 clipped;
On all the hands *shall be* cuts, and on the loins
 sackcloth—

38 A general lamentation
On all the housetops of Moab,
And in its streets;
For I have broken Moab like a vessel in which *is*
 no pleasure," says the LORD.

39 "They shall wail;
'How she is broken down!
How Moab has turned her back with shame!'
So Moab shall be a derision
And a dismay to all those about her."

40 For thus says the LORD:

"Behold, one shall fly like an eagle,
And spread his wings over Moab.
41 Kerioth is taken,
And the strongholds are surprised;
The mighty men's hearts in Moab on that day
 shall be
Like the heart of a woman in birth pangs.
42 And Moab shall be destroyed as a people,
Because he exalted *himself* against the LORD.
43 Fear and the pit and the snare *shall be* upon you,
O inhabitant of Moab," says the LORD.
44 "He who flees from the fear shall fall into the pit,
And he who gets out of the pit shall be caught in
 the snare.
For upon Moab, upon it I will bring
The year of their punishment," says the LORD.

45 "Those who fled stood under the shadow of
 Heshbon
Because of exhaustion.
But a fire shall come out of Heshbon,
A flame from the midst of Sihon,
And shall devour the brow of Moab,
The crown of the head of the sons of tumult.
46 Woe to you, O Moab!
The people of Chemosh perish;
For your sons have been taken captive,
And your daughters captive.

47 "Yet I will bring back the captives of Moab
In the latter days," says the LORD.

Thus far *is* the judgment of Moab.

49 Against the Ammonites.

Thus says the LORD:

"Has Israel no sons?
Has he no heir?
Why *then* does Milcom inherit Gad,
And his people dwell in its cities?
2 Therefore behold, the days are coming," says the
 LORD,
"That I will cause to be heard an alarm of war
In Rabbah of the Ammonites;

אֹבֵד: 37 כִּי כָל־רֹאשׁ קָרְחָה וְכָל־זָקָן גְּרֻעָה עַל
כָּל־יָדַיִם גְּדֻדֹת וְעַל־מָתְנַיִם שָׂק: 38 עַל כָּל־גַּגּוֹת
מוֹאָב וּבִרְחֹבֹתֶיהָ כֻּלֹּה מִסְפֵּד כִּי־שָׁבַרְתִּי אֶת־
מוֹאָב כִּכְלִי אֵין־חֵפֶץ בּוֹ נְאֻם־יְהֹוָה: 39 אֵיךְ חַתָּה
הֵילִילוּ אֵיךְ הִפְנָה־עֹרֶף מוֹאָב בּוֹשׁ וְהָיָה מוֹאָב
לִשְׂחֹק וְלִמְחִתָּה לְכָל־סְבִיבָיו: ס   40 כִּי־

כֹה אָמַר יְהֹוָה הִנֵּה כַנֶּשֶׁר יִדְאֶה וּפָרַשׂ כְּנָפָיו
אֶל־מוֹאָב: 41 נִלְכְּדָה הַקְּרִיּוֹת וְהַמְּצָדוֹת נִתְפָּשָׂה
וְהָיָה לֵב גִּבּוֹרֵי מוֹאָב בַּיּוֹם הַהוּא כְּלֵב אִשָּׁה
מְצֵרָה: 42 וְנִשְׁמַד מוֹאָב מֵעָם כִּי עַל־יְהֹוָה הִגְדִּיל:
43 פַּחַד וָפַחַת וָפָח עָלֶיךָ יוֹשֵׁב מוֹאָב נְאֻם־יְהֹוָה:
44 הַנִּ֯יס מִפְּנֵי הַפַּחַד יִפֹּל אֶל־הַפַּחַת וְהָעֹלֶה מִן־
הַפַּחַת יִלָּכֵד בַּפָּח כִּי־אָבִיא אֵלֶיהָ אֶל־מוֹאָב שְׁנַת
פְּקֻדָּתָם נְאֻם־יְהֹוָה: 45 בְּצֵל חֶשְׁבּוֹן עָמְדוּ מִכֹּחַ
נָסִים כִּי־אֵשׁ יָצָא מֵחֶשְׁבּוֹן וְלֶהָבָה מִבֵּין סִיחוֹן
וַתֹּאכַל פְּאַת מוֹאָב וְקָדְקֹד בְּנֵי שָׁאוֹן: 46 אוֹי־לְךָ
מוֹאָב אָבַד עַם־כְּמוֹשׁ כִּי־לֻקְּחוּ בָנֶיךָ בַּשֶּׁבִי וּבְנֹתֶיךָ
בַּשִּׁבְיָה: 47 וְשַׁבְתִּי שְׁבוּת־מוֹאָב בְּאַחֲרִית הַיָּמִים
נְאֻם־יְהֹוָה עַד־הֵנָּה מִשְׁפַּט מוֹאָב: ס

מט לִבְנֵי עַמּוֹן כֹּה אָמַר יְהֹוָה הֲבָנִים אֵין
לְיִשְׂרָאֵל אִם־יוֹרֵשׁ אֵין לוֹ מַדּוּעַ יָרַשׁ מַלְכָּם
אֶת־גָּד וְעַמּוֹ בְּעָרָיו יָשָׁב: 2 לָכֵן הִנֵּה יָמִים
בָּאִים נְאֻם־יְהֹוָה וְהִשְׁמַעְתִּי אֶל־רַבַּת בְּנֵי־עַמּוֹן
תְּרוּעַת מִלְחָמָה וְהָיְתָה לְתֵל שְׁמָמָה וּבְנֹתֶיהָ
בָּאֵשׁ תִּצַּתְנָה וְיָרַשׁ יִשְׂרָאֵל אֶת־יֹרְשָׁיו אָמַר

It shall be a desolate mound,
And her villages shall be burned with fire.
Then Israel shall take possession of his inheritance," says the LORD.

3 "Wail, O Heshbon, for Ai is plundered!
Cry, you daughters of Rabbah,
Gird yourselves with sackcloth!
Lament and run to and fro by the walls;
For Milcom shall go into captivity
With his priests and his princes together.

4 Why do you boast in the valleys,
Your flowing valley, O backsliding daughter?
Who trusted in her treasures, *saying,*
'Who will come against me?'

5 Behold, I will bring fear upon you,"
Says the Lord GOD of hosts,
"From all those who are around you;
You shall be driven out, everyone headlong,
And no one will gather those who wander off.

6 But afterward I will bring back
The captives of the people of Ammon," says the
LORD.

7 Against Edom.

Thus says the LORD of hosts:

"*Is* wisdom no more in Teman?
Has counsel perished from the prudent?
Has their wisdom vanished?

8 Flee, turn back, dwell in the depths, O inhabitants of Dedan!
For I will bring the calamity of Esau upon him,
The time *that* I will punish him.

9 If grape-gatherers came to you,
Would they not leave *some* gleaning grapes?
If thieves by night,
Would they not destroy until they have enough?

10 But I have made Esau bare;
I have uncovered his secret places,
And he shall not be able to hide himself.
His descendants are plundered,
His brethren and his neighbors,
And he *is* no more.

11 Leave your fatherless children,
I will preserve *them* alive;
And let your widows trust in Me."

12 For thus says the LORD: "Behold, those whose
judgment *was* not to drink of the cup have
assuredly drunk. And *are* you the one who will
altogether go unpunished? You shall not go
unpunished, but you shall surely drink *of it.* 13 For
I have sworn by Myself," says the LORD, "that
Bozrah shall become a desolation, a reproach, a
waste, and a curse. And all its cities shall be
perpetual wastes."

14 I have heard a message from the LORD,
And an ambassador has been sent to the nations:
"Gather together, come against her,
And rise up to battle!

15 "For indeed, I will make you small among nations,

יְהֹוָה: 3 הֵילִילִי חֶשְׁבּוֹן כִּי שֻׁדְּדָה־עַי צְעַקְנָה
בְּנוֹת רַבָּה חֲגֹרְנָה שַׂקִּים סְפֹדְנָה וְהִתְשׁוֹטַטְנָה
בַּגְּדֵרוֹת כִּי מַלְכָּם בַּגּוֹלָה יֵלֵךְ כֹּהֲנָיו וְשָׂרָיו
יַחְדָּיו: 4 מַה־תִּתְהַלְלִי בָּעֲמָקִים זָב עִמְקֵךְ הַבַּת
הַשּׁוֹבֵבָה הַבֹּטְחָה בְּאֹצְרֹתֶיהָ מִי יָבוֹא אֵלָי: 5 הִנְנִי
מֵבִיא עָלַיִךְ פַּחַד נְאֻם־אֲדֹנָי יְהֹוִה צְבָאוֹת מִכָּל־
סְבִיבָיִךְ וְנִדַּחְתֶּם אִישׁ לְפָנָיו וְאֵין מְקַבֵּץ לַנֹּדֵד:
6 וְאַחֲרֵי־כֵן אָשִׁיב אֶת־שְׁבוּת בְּנֵי־עַמּוֹן נְאֻם־
יְהֹוָה: ס 7 לֶאֱדוֹם כֹּה אָמַר יְהֹוָה צְבָאוֹת
הַאֵין עוֹד חָכְמָה בְּתֵימָן אָבְדָה עֵצָה מִבָּנִים
נִסְרְחָה חָכְמָתָם: 8 נֻסוּ הָפְנוּ הֶעְמִיקוּ לָשֶׁבֶת יֹשְׁבֵי
דְדָן כִּי אֵיד עֵשָׂו הֵבֵאתִי עָלָיו עֵת פְּקַדְתִּיו: 9 אִם־
בֹּצְרִים בָּאוּ לָךְ לֹא יַשְׁאִרוּ עוֹלֵלוֹת אִם־גַּנָּבִים
בַּלַּיְלָה הִשְׁחִיתוּ דַיָּם: 10 כִּי־אֲנִי חָשַׂפְתִּי אֶת־עֵשָׂו
גִּלֵּיתִי אֶת־מִסְתָּרָיו וְנֶחְבָּה לֹא יוּכָל שֻׁדַּד זַרְעוֹ
וְאֶחָיו וּשְׁכֵנָיו וְאֵינֶנּוּ: 11 עָזְבָה יְתֹמֶיךָ אֲנִי אֲחַיֶּה
וְאַלְמְנֹתֶיךָ עָלַי תִּבְטָחוּ: ס 12 כִּי־כֹה |
אָמַר יְהֹוָה הִנֵּה אֲשֶׁר־אֵין מִשְׁפָּטָם לִשְׁתּוֹת הַכּוֹס
שָׁתוֹ יִשְׁתּוּ וְאַתָּה הוּא נָקֹה תִּנָּקֶה לֹא תִנָּקֶה כִּי
שָׁתֹה תִשְׁתֶּה: 13 כִּי בִי נִשְׁבַּעְתִּי נְאֻם־יְהֹוָה כִּי־
לְשַׁמָּה לְחֶרְפָּה לְחֹרֶב וְלִקְלָלָה תִּהְיֶה בָצְרָה וְכָל־
עָרֶיהָ תִהְיֶינָה לְחָרְבוֹת עוֹלָם: 14 שְׁמוּעָה שָׁמַעְתִּי
מֵאֵת יְהֹוָה וְצִיר בַּגּוֹיִם שָׁלוּחַ הִתְקַבְּצוּ וּבֹאוּ עָלֶיהָ
וְקוּמוּ לַמִּלְחָמָה: 15 כִּי־הִנֵּה קָטֹן נְתַתִּיךָ בַּגּוֹיִם

Despised among men.

16 Your fierceness has deceived you,
The pride of your heart,
O you who dwell in the clefts of the rock,
Who hold the height of the hill!
Though you make your nest as high as the eagle,
I will bring you down from there," says the LORD.

17 "Edom also shall be an astonishment;
Everyone who goes by it will be astonished
And will hiss at all its plagues.

18 As in the overthrow of Sodom and Gomorrah
And their neighbors," says the LORD,
"No one shall remain there,
Nor shall a son of man dwell in it.

19 "Behold, he shall come up like a lion from the
floodplain of the Jordan
Against the dwelling place of the strong;
But I will suddenly make him run away from her.
And who is a chosen man that I may appoint over
her?
For who is like Me?
Who will arraign Me?
And who is that shepherd
Who will withstand Me?"

20 Therefore hear the counsel of the LORD that He
has taken against Edom,
And His purposes that He has proposed against
the inhabitants of Teman:
Surely the least of the flock shall draw them out;
Surely He shall make their dwelling places
desolate with them.

21 The earth shakes at the noise of their fall;
At the cry its noise is heard at the Red Sea.

22 Behold, He shall come up and fly like the eagle,
And spread His wings over Bozrah;
The heart of the mighty men of Edom in that day
shall be
Like the heart of a woman in birth pangs.

23 Against Damascus.

"Hamath and Arpad are shamed,
For they have heard bad news.
They are fainthearted;
There is trouble on the sea;
It cannot be quiet.

24 Damascus has grown feeble;
She turns to flee,
And fear has seized her.
Anguish and sorrows have taken her like a
woman in labor.

25 Why is the city of praise not deserted, the city of
My joy?

26 Therefore her young men shall fall in her streets,
And all the men of war shall be cut off in that
day," says the LORD of hosts.

27 "I will kindle a fire in the wall of Damascus,
And it shall consume the palaces of Ben-Hadad."

28 Against Kedar and against the kingdoms of
Hazor, which Nebuchadnezzar king of Babylon
shall strike.

בְּזוּי בָּאָדָם: 16 תִּפְלַצְתְּךָ הִשִּׁיא אֹתָךְ זְדוֹן לִבֶּךָ
שֹׁכְנִי בְּחַגְוֵי הַסֶּלַע תֹּפְשִׂי מְרוֹם גִּבְעָה כִּי־תַגְבִּיהַ
כַּנֶּשֶׁר קִנֶּךָ מִשָּׁם אוֹרִידְךָ נְאֻם־יְהוָה: 17 וְהָיְתָה
אֱדוֹם לְשַׁמָּה כֹּל עֹבֵר עָלֶיהָ יִשֹּׁם וְיִשְׁרֹק עַל־כָּל־
מַכּוֹתֶהָ: 18 כְּמַהְפֵּכַת סְדֹם וַעֲמֹרָה וּשְׁכֵנֶיהָ אָמַר
יְהוָה לֹא־יֵשֵׁב שָׁם אִישׁ וְלֹא־יָגוּר בָּהּ בֶּן־אָדָם:
19 הִנֵּה כְּאַרְיֵה יַעֲלֶה מִגְּאוֹן הַיַּרְדֵּן אֶל־נְוֵה אֵיתָן
כִּי־אַרְגִּיעָה אֲרִיצֶנּוּ מֵעָלֶיהָ וּמִי בָחוּר אֵלֶיהָ אֶפְקֹד
כִּי מִי כָמוֹנִי וּמִי יֹעִידֶנִּי וּמִי־זֶה רֹעֶה אֲשֶׁר יַעֲמֹד
לְפָנָי: ס 20 לָכֵן שִׁמְעוּ עֲצַת־יְהוָה אֲשֶׁר
יָעַץ אֶל־אֱדוֹם וּמַחְשְׁבוֹתָיו אֲשֶׁר חָשַׁב אֶל־יֹשְׁבֵי
תֵימָן אִם־לֹא יִסְחָבוּם צְעִירֵי הַצֹּאן אִם־לֹא יַשִּׁים
עֲלֵיהֶם נְוֵהֶם: 21 מִקּוֹל נִפְלָם רָעֲשָׁה הָאָרֶץ צְעָקָה
בְּיַם־סוּף נִשְׁמַע קוֹלָהּ: 22 הִנֵּה כַנֶּשֶׁר יַעֲלֶה וְיִדְאֶה
וְיִפְרֹשׂ כְּנָפָיו עַל־בָּצְרָה וְהָיָה לֵב גִּבּוֹרֵי אֱדוֹם בַּיּוֹם
הַהוּא כְּלֵב אִשָּׁה מְצֵרָה: ס 23 לְדַמֶּשֶׂק
בּוֹשָׁה חֲמָת וְאַרְפָּד כִּי־שְׁמֻעָה רָעָה שָׁמְעוּ
נָמֹגוּ בַּיָּם דְּאָגָה הַשְׁקֵט לֹא יוּכָל: 24 רָפְתָה
דַמֶּשֶׂק הִפְנְתָה לָנוּס וְרֶטֶט | הֶחֱזִיקָה צָרָה
וַחֲבָלִים אֲחָזַתָּה כַּיּוֹלֵדָה: 25 אֵיךְ לֹא־עֻזְּבָה עִיר
תְּהִלָּהᵖ קִרְיַת מְשׂוֹשִׂי: 26 לָכֵן יִפְּלוּ בַחוּרֶיהָ
בִּרְחֹבֹתֶיהָ וְכָל־אַנְשֵׁי הַמִּלְחָמָה יִדַּמּוּ בַּיּוֹם הַהוּא
נְאֻם יְהוָה צְבָאוֹת: 27 וְהִצַּתִּי אֵשׁ בְּחוֹמַת דַּמָּשֶׂק
וְאָכְלָה אַרְמְנוֹת בֶּן־הֲדָד: ס 28 לְקֵדָר |
וּלְמַמְלְכוֹת חָצוֹר אֲשֶׁר הִכָּה נְבוּכַדְרֶאצּוֹרᵖ מֶלֶךְ־
בָּבֶל כֹּה אָמַר יְהוָה קוּמוּ עֲלוּ אֶל־קֵדָר וְשָׁדְדוּ

Thus says the LORD:

"Arise, go up to Kedar,
  And devastate the men of the East!
29 Their tents and their flocks they shall take away.
  They shall take for themselves their curtains,
  All their vessels and their camels;
  And they shall cry out to them,
  'Fear is on every side!'
30 "Flee, get far away! Dwell in the depths,
  O inhabitants of Hazor!" says the LORD.

"For Nebuchadnezzar king of Babylon has taken
  counsel against you,
  And has conceived a plan against you.

31 "Arise, go up to the wealthy nation that dwells
  securely," says the LORD,
"Which has neither gates nor bars,
  Dwelling alone.
32 Their camels shall be for booty,
  And the multitude of their cattle for plunder.
  I will scatter to all winds those in the farthest
    corners,
  And I will bring their calamity from all its sides,"
    says the LORD.
33 "Hazor shall be a dwelling for jackals, a desolation
    forever;
  No one shall reside there,
  Nor son of man dwell in it."

34 The word of the LORD that came to Jeremiah
the prophet against Elam, in the beginning of the
reign of Zedekiah king of Judah, saying, 35 "Thus
says the LORD of hosts:

'Behold, I will break the bow of Elam,
  The foremost of their might.
36 Against Elam I will bring the four winds
  From the four quarters of heaven,
  And scatter them toward all those winds;
  There shall be no nations where the outcasts of
    Elam will not go.
37 For I will cause Elam to be dismayed before their
    enemies
  And before those who seek their life.
  I will bring disaster upon them,
  My fierce anger,' says the LORD;
  'And I will send the sword after them
  Until I have consumed them.
38 I will set My throne in Elam,
  And will destroy from there the king and the
    princes,' says the LORD.
39 'But it shall come to pass in the latter days:
  I will bring back the captives of Elam,' says the
    LORD."

50 The word that the LORD spoke against
Babylon and against the land of the Chaldeans by
Jeremiah the prophet.
2 "Declare among the nations,
  Proclaim, and set up a standard;
  Proclaim—do not conceal it—
  Say, 'Babylon is taken, Bel is shamed.

אֶת־בְּנֵי־קֶדֶם: 29 אָהֳלֵיהֶם וְצֹאנָם יִקָּחוּ יְרִיעוֹתֵיהֶם
וְכָל־כְּלֵיהֶם וּגְמַלֵּיהֶם יִשְׂאוּ לָהֶם וְקָרְאוּ עֲלֵיהֶם
מָגוֹר מִסָּבִיב: 30 נֻסוּ נֻּדוּ מְאֹד הֶעְמִיקוּ לָשֶׁבֶת
יֹשְׁבֵי חָצוֹר נְאֻם־יְהֹוָה כִּי־יָעַץ עֲלֵיכֶם נְבוּכַדְרֶאצַּר
מֶלֶךְ־בָּבֶל עֵצָה וְחָשַׁב עֲלֵיהֶם מַחֲשָׁבָה: 31 קוּמוּ
עֲלוּ אֶל־גּוֹי שְׁלֵיו יוֹשֵׁב לָבֶטַח נְאֻם־יְהֹוָה לֹא־
דְלָתַיִם וְלֹא־בְרִיחַ לוֹ בָּדָד יִשְׁכֹּנוּ: 32 וְהָיוּ גְמַלֵּיהֶם
לָבַז וַהֲמוֹן מִקְנֵיהֶם לְשָׁלָל וְזֵרִתִים לְכָל־רוּחַ
קְצוּצֵי פֵאָה וּמִכָּל־עֲבָרָיו אָבִיא אֶת־אֵידָם נְאֻם־
יְהֹוָה: 33 וְהָיְתָה חָצוֹר לִמְעוֹן תַּנִּים שְׁמָמָה עַד־
עוֹלָם לֹא־יֵשֵׁב שָׁם אִישׁ וְלֹא־יָגוּר בָּהּ בֶּן־
אָדָם: ס 34 אֲשֶׁר הָיָה דְבַר־יְהֹוָה אֶל־
יִרְמְיָהוּ הַנָּבִיא אֶל־עֵילָם בְּרֵאשִׁית מַלְכוּת צִדְקִיָּה
מֶלֶךְ־יְהוּדָה לֵאמֹר: 35 כֹּה אָמַר יְהֹוָה צְבָאוֹת הִנְנִי
שֹׁבֵר אֶת־קֶשֶׁת עֵילָם רֵאשִׁית גְּבוּרָתָם: 36 וְהֵבֵאתִי
אֶל־עֵילָם אַרְבַּע רוּחוֹת מֵאַרְבַּע קְצוֹת הַשָּׁמַיִם
וְזֵרִתִים לְכֹל הָרֻחוֹת הָאֵלֶּה וְלֹא־יִהְיֶה הַגּוֹי אֲשֶׁר
לֹא־יָבוֹא שָׁם נִדְּחֵי עֵילָם: 37 וְהַחְתַּתִּי אֶת־עֵילָם
לִפְנֵי אֹיְבֵיהֶם וְלִפְנֵי מְבַקְשֵׁי נַפְשָׁם וְהֵבֵאתִי
עֲלֵיהֶם רָעָה אֶת־חֲרוֹן אַפִּי נְאֻם־יְהֹוָה וְשִׁלַּחְתִּי
אַחֲרֵיהֶם אֶת־הַחֶרֶב עַד כַּלּוֹתִי אוֹתָם: 38 וְשַׂמְתִּי
כִסְאִי בְּעֵילָם וְהַאֲבַדְתִּי מִשָּׁם מֶלֶךְ וְשָׂרִים נְאֻם־
יְהֹוָה: 39 וְהָיָה בְּאַחֲרִית הַיָּמִים אָשִׁיב אֶת־
שְׁבִית עֵילָם נְאֻם־יְהֹוָה: ס

נ הַדָּבָר אֲשֶׁר דִּבֶּר יְהֹוָה אֶל־בָּבֶל אֶל־אֶרֶץ
כַּשְׂדִּים בְּיַד יִרְמְיָהוּ הַנָּבִיא: 2 הַגִּידוּ בַגּוֹיִם
וְהַשְׁמִיעוּ וּשְׂאוּ־נֵס הַשְׁמִיעוּ אַל־תְּכַחֵדוּ אִמְרוּ
נִלְכְּדָה בָבֶל הֹבִישׁ בֵּל חַת מְרֹדָךְ הֹבִישׁוּ עֲצַבֶּיהָ

Merodach is broken in pieces; Her idols are humiliated, Her images are broken in pieces.' 3 For out of the north a nation comes up against her, Which shall make her land desolate, And no one shall dwell therein. They shall move, they shall depart, Both man and beast.	חַתּוּ גִלּוּלֶיהָ: 3 כִּי עָלָה עָלֶיהָ גּוֹי מִצָּפוֹן הוּא־יָשִׁית אֶת־אַרְצָהּ לְשַׁמָּה וְלֹא־יִהְיֶה יוֹשֵׁב בָּהּ מֵאָדָם וְעַד־ בְּהֵמָה נָדוּ הָלָכוּ: 4 בַּיָּמִים הָהֵמָּה וּבָעֵת הַהִיא
4 "In those days and in that time," says the LORD, "The children of Israel shall come, They and the children of Judah together; With continual weeping they shall come, And seek the LORD their God. 5 They shall ask the way to Zion, With their faces toward it, *saying,* 'Come and let us join ourselves to the LORD *In* a perpetual covenant *That* will not be forgotten.'	נְאֻם־יְהֹוָה יָבֹאוּ בְנֵי־יִשְׂרָאֵל הֵמָּה וּבְנֵי־יְהוּדָה יַחְדָּו הָלוֹךְ וּבָכֹה יֵלֵכוּ וְאֶת־יְהֹוָה אֱלֹהֵיהֶם יְבַקֵּשׁוּ: 5 צִיּוֹן יִשְׁאָלוּ דֶּרֶךְ הֵנָּה פְנֵיהֶם בֹּאוּ וְנִלְווּ אֶל־ יְהֹוָה בְּרִית עוֹלָם לֹא תִשָּׁכֵחַ: ס 6 צֹאן
6 "My people have been lost sheep. Their shepherds have led them astray; They have turned them away *on* the mountains. They have gone from mountain to hill; They have forgotten their resting place. 7 All who found them have devoured them; And their adversaries said, 'We have not offended, Because they have sinned against the LORD, the habitation of justice, The LORD, the hope of their fathers.'	אֹבְדוֹת הָיָהᴾ עַמִּי רֹעֵיהֶם הִתְעוּם הָרִים שׁוֹבְבִיםᴾ מֵהַר אֶל־גִּבְעָה הָלָכוּ שָׁכְחוּ רִבְצָם: 7 כָּל־מוֹצְאֵיהֶם אֲכָלוּם וְצָרֵיהֶם אָמְרוּ לֹא נֶאְשָׁם תַּחַת אֲשֶׁר חָטְאוּ לַיהֹוָה נְוֵה־צֶדֶק וּמִקְוֵה אֲבוֹתֵיהֶם יְהֹוָה: ס 8 נֻדוּ מִתּוֹךְ בָּבֶל
8 "Move from the midst of Babylon, Go out of the land of the Chaldeans; And be like the rams before the flocks. 9 For behold, I will raise and cause to come up against Babylon An assembly of great nations from the north country, And they shall array themselves against her; From there she shall be captured. Their arrows *shall be* like *those* of an expert warrior; None shall return in vain.	וּמֵאֶרֶץ כַּשְׂדִּים יֵצֵאוᴾ וִהְיוּ כְּעַתּוּדִים לִפְנֵי־ צֹאן: 9 כִּי הִנֵּה אָנֹכִי מֵעִיר וּמַעֲלֶה עַל־בָּבֶל קְהַל־גּוֹיִם גְּדֹלִים מֵאֶרֶץ צָפוֹן וְעָרְכוּ לָהּ מִשָּׁם תִּלָּכֵד חִצָּיו כְּגִבּוֹר מַשְׁכִּיל לֹא יָשׁוּב רֵיקָם:
10 And Chaldea shall become plunder; All who plunder her shall be satisfied," says the LORD.	10 וְהָיְתָה כַשְׂדִּים לְשָׁלָל כָּל־שֹׁלְלֶיהָ יִשְׂבָּעוּ נְאֻם־
11 "Because you were glad, because you rejoiced, You destroyers of My heritage, Because you have grown fat like a heifer threshing grain, And you bellow like bulls, 12 Your mother shall be deeply ashamed; She who bore you shall be ashamed. Behold, the least of the nations *shall be* a wilderness, A dry land and a desert.	יְהֹוָה: 11 כִּי תִשְׂמְחִיᴾ כִּי תַעַלְזוּᴾ שֹׁסֵי נַחֲלָתִי כִּי תָפוּשִׁיᴾ כְּעֶגְלָה דָשָׁה וְתִצְהֲלִיᴾ כָּאַבִּרִים: 12 בּוֹשָׁה אִמְּכֶם מְאֹד חָפְרָה יוֹלַדְתְּכֶם הִנֵּה אַחֲרִית גּוֹיִם מִדְבָּר צִיָּה וַעֲרָבָה: 13 מִקֶּצֶף יְהֹוָה לֹא תֵשֵׁב
13 Because of the wrath of the LORD She shall not be inhabited, But she shall be wholly desolate. Everyone who goes by Babylon shall be horrified And hiss at all her plagues.	וְהָיְתָה שְׁמָמָה כֻּלָּהּ כֹּל עֹבֵר עַל־בָּבֶל יִשֹּׁם

נ 6 הָיוּ שׁוֹבְבִים 8 צֵאוּ
11 תִּשְׂמְחוּ תַּעַלְזוּ תָּפוֹשׁוּ וְתִצְהֲלוּ

14 "Put yourselves in array against Babylon all
　　around,
　　All you who bend the bow;
　　Shoot at her, spare no arrows,
　　For she has sinned against the LORD.
15 Shout against her all around;
　　She has given her hand,
　　Her foundations have fallen,
　　Her walls are thrown down;
　　For it is the vengeance of the LORD.
　　Take vengeance on her.
　　As she has done, so do to her.
16 Cut off the sower from Babylon,
　　And him who handles the sickle at harvest time.
　　For fear of the oppressing sword
　　Everyone shall turn to his own people,
　　And everyone shall flee to his own land.

17 "Israel is like scattered sheep;
　　The lions have driven him away.
　　First the king of Assyria devoured him;
　　Now at last this Nebuchadnezzar king of
　　　Babylon has broken his bones."

18 Therefore thus says the LORD of hosts, the God
of Israel:

　　"Behold, I will punish the king of Babylon and his
　　　land,
　　As I have punished the king of Assyria.
19 But I will bring back Israel to his home,
　　And he shall feed on Carmel and Bashan;
　　His soul shall be satisfied on Mount Ephraim and
　　　Gilead.
20 In those days and in that time," says the LORD,
　　"The iniquity of Israel shall be sought, but there
　　　shall be none;
　　And the sins of Judah, but they shall not be
　　　found;
　　For I will pardon those whom I preserve.

21 "Go up against the land of Merathaim, against it,
　　And against the inhabitants of Pekod.
　　Waste and utterly destroy them," says the LORD,
　　"And do according to all that I have commanded
　　　you.
22 A sound of battle is in the land,
　　And of great destruction.
23 How the hammer of the whole earth has been cut
　　　apart and broken!
　　How Babylon has become a desolation among
　　　the nations!
　　I have laid a snare for you;
24 You have indeed been trapped, O Babylon,
　　And you were not aware;
　　You have been found and also caught,
　　Because you have contended against the LORD.
25 The LORD has opened His armory,
　　And has brought out the weapons of His
　　　indignation;
　　For this is the work of the Lord GOD of hosts
　　In the land of the Chaldeans.
26 Come against her from the farthest border;
　　Open her storehouses;
　　Cast her up as heaps of ruins,

וְיִשְׂרָק עַל־כָּל־מַכּוֹתֶיהָ: 14 עִרְכוּ עַל־בָּבֶל ׀ סָבִיב
כָּל־דֹּרְכֵי קֶשֶׁת יְדוּ אֵלֶיהָ אַל־תַּחְמְלוּ אֶל־חֵץ
כִּי לַיהֹוָה חָטָאָה: 15 הָרִיעוּ עָלֶיהָ סָבִיב נָתְנָה
יָדָהּ נָפְלוּ אֲשְׁוִיּוֹתֶיהָ נֶהֶרְסוּ חוֹמוֹתֶיהָ כִּי נִקְמַת
יְהֹוָה הִיא הִנָּקְמוּ בָהּ כַּאֲשֶׁר עָשְׂתָה עֲשׂוּ־לָהּ:
16 כִּרְתוּ זוֹרֵעַ מִבָּבֶל וְתֹפֵשׂ מַגָּל בְּעֵת קָצִיר מִפְּנֵי
חֶרֶב הַיּוֹנָה אִישׁ אֶל־עַמּוֹ יִפְנוּ וְאִישׁ לְאַרְצוֹ
יָנֻסוּ: ס 17 שֶׂה פְזוּרָה יִשְׂרָאֵל אֲרָיוֹת
הִדִּיחוּ הָרִאשׁוֹן אֲכָלוֹ מֶלֶךְ אַשּׁוּר וְזֶה הָאַחֲרוֹן
עִצְּמוֹ נְבוּכַדְרֶאצַּר מֶלֶךְ בָּבֶל: ס 18 לָכֵן
כֹּה־אָמַר יְהֹוָה צְבָאוֹת אֱלֹהֵי יִשְׂרָאֵל הִנְנִי פֹקֵד
אֶל־מֶלֶךְ בָּבֶל וְאֶל־אַרְצוֹ כַּאֲשֶׁר פָּקַדְתִּי אֶל־מֶלֶךְ
אַשּׁוּר: 19 וְשֹׁבַבְתִּי אֶת־יִשְׂרָאֵל אֶל־נָוֵהוּ וְרָעָה
הַכַּרְמֶל וְהַבָּשָׁן וּבְהַר אֶפְרַיִם וְהַגִּלְעָד תִּשְׂבַּע
נַפְשׁוֹ: 20 בַּיָּמִים הָהֵם וּבָעֵת הַהִיא נְאֻם־יְהֹוָה
יְבֻקַּשׁ אֶת־עֲוֹן יִשְׂרָאֵל וְאֵינֶנּוּ וְאֶת־חַטֹּאת יְהוּדָה
וְלֹא תִמָּצֶאינָה כִּי אֶסְלַח לַאֲשֶׁר אַשְׁאִיר: 21 עַל־
הָאָרֶץ מְרָתַיִם עֲלֵה עָלֶיהָ וְאֶל־יוֹשְׁבֵי פְּקוֹד חֲרֹב
וְהַחֲרֵם אַחֲרֵיהֶם נְאֻם־יְהֹוָה וַעֲשֵׂה כְּכֹל אֲשֶׁר
צִוִּיתִךָ: ס 22 קוֹל מִלְחָמָה בָּאָרֶץ וְשֶׁבֶר
גָּדוֹל: 23 אֵיךְ נִגְדַּע וַיִּשָּׁבֵר פַּטִּישׁ כָּל־הָאָרֶץ אֵיךְ
הָיְתָה לְשַׁמָּה בָּבֶל בַּגּוֹיִם: 24 יָקֹשְׁתִּי לָךְ וְגַם־
נִלְכַּדְתְּ בָּבֶל וְאַתְּ לֹא יָדָעַתְּ נִמְצֵאת וְגַם־נִתְפַּשְׂתְּ
כִּי בַיהֹוָה הִתְגָּרִית: 25 פָּתַח יְהֹוָה אֶת־אוֹצָרוֹ
וַיּוֹצֵא אֶת־כְּלֵי זַעְמוֹ כִּי־מְלָאכָה הִיא לַאדֹנָי יְהֹוִה
צְבָאוֹת בְּאֶרֶץ כַּשְׂדִּים: 26 בֹּאוּ־לָהּ מִקֵּץ פִּתְחוּ
מַאֲבֻסֶיהָ סָלּוּהָ כְמוֹ־עֲרֵמִים

And destroy her utterly;
Let nothing of her be left.
27 Slay all her bulls,
Let them go down to the slaughter.
Woe to them!
For their day has come, the time of their
punishment.
28 The voice of those who flee and escape from the
land of Babylon
Declares in Zion the vengeance of the LORD our
God,
The vengeance of His temple.
29 "Call together the archers against Babylon.
All you who bend the bow, encamp against it all
around;
Let none of them escape.
Repay her according to her work;
According to all she has done, do to her;
For she has been proud against the LORD,
Against the Holy One of Israel.
30 Therefore her young men shall fall in the streets,
And all her men of war shall be cut off in that
day," says the LORD.
31 "Behold, I am against you,
O most haughty one!" says the Lord GOD of
hosts;
"For your day has come,
The time that I will punish you.
32 The most proud shall stumble and fall,
And no one will raise him up;
I will kindle a fire in his cities,
And it will devour all around him."

33 Thus says the LORD of hosts:

"The children of Israel were oppressed,
Along with the children of Judah;
All who took them captive have held them fast;
They have refused to let them go.
34 Their Redeemer is strong;
The LORD of hosts is His name.
He will thoroughly plead their case,
That He may give rest to the land,
And disquiet the inhabitants of Babylon.
35 "A sword is against the Chaldeans," says the
LORD,
"Against the inhabitants of Babylon,
And against her princes and her wise men.
36 A sword is against the soothsayers, and they will
be fools.
A sword is against her mighty men, and they will
be dismayed.
37 A sword is against their horses,
Against their chariots,
And against all the mixed peoples who are in her
midst;
And they will become like women.
A sword is against her treasures, and they will be
robbed.
38 A drought is against her waters, and they will be
dried up.
For it is the land of carved images,
And they are insane with their idols.

וְהַחֲרִימוּ אַל־תְּהִי־לָהּ שְׁאֵרִית: 27 חִרְבוּ כָּל־
פָּרֶיהָ יֵרְדוּ לַטָּבַח הוֹי עֲלֵיהֶם כִּי־בָא יוֹמָם עֵת
פְּקֻדָּתָם: ס 28 קוֹל נָסִים וּפְלֵטִים מֵאֶרֶץ
בָּבֶל לְהַגִּיד בְּצִיּוֹן אֶת־נִקְמַת יְהוָה אֱלֹהֵינוּ נִקְמַת
הֵיכָלוֹ: 29 הַשְׁמִיעוּ אֶל־בָּבֶל ׀ רַבִּים כָּל־דֹּרְכֵי
קֶשֶׁת חֲנוּ עָלֶיהָ סָבִיב אַל־יְהִי־ קׁ פְּלֵטָה שַׁלְּמוּ־
לָהּ כְּפָעֳלָהּ כְּכֹל אֲשֶׁר עָשְׂתָה עֲשׂוּ־לָהּ כִּי אֶל־
יְהוָה זָדָה אֶל־קְדוֹשׁ יִשְׂרָאֵל: 30 לָכֵן יִפְּלוּ בַחוּרֶיהָ
בִּרְחֹבֹתֶיהָ וְכָל־אַנְשֵׁי מִלְחַמְתָּהּ יִדַּמּוּ בַּיּוֹם הַהוּא
נְאֻם־יְהוָה: ס 31 הִנְנִי אֵלֶיךָ זָדוֹן נְאֻם־
אֲדֹנָי יְהוִה צְבָאוֹת כִּי בָּא יוֹמְךָ עֵת פְּקַדְתִּיךָ:
32 וְכָשַׁל זָדוֹן וְנָפַל וְאֵין לוֹ מֵקִים וְהִצַּתִּי אֵשׁ
בְּעָרָיו וְאָכְלָה כָּל־סְבִיבֹתָיו: ס 33 כֹּה
אָמַר יְהוָה צְבָאוֹת עֲשׁוּקִים בְּנֵי־יִשְׂרָאֵל וּבְנֵי־
יְהוּדָה יַחְדָּו וְכָל־שֹׁבֵיהֶם הֶחֱזִיקוּ בָם מֵאֲנוּ
שַׁלְּחָם: 34 גֹּאֲלָם ׀ חָזָק יְהוָה צְבָאוֹת שְׁמוֹ רִיב
יָרִיב אֶת־רִיבָם לְמַעַן הִרְגִּיעַ אֶת־הָאָרֶץ וְהִרְגִּיז
לְיֹשְׁבֵי בָבֶל: 35 חֶרֶב עַל־כַּשְׂדִּים נְאֻם־יְהוָה וְאֶל־
יֹשְׁבֵי בָבֶל וְאֶל־שָׂרֶיהָ וְאֶל־חֲכָמֶיהָ: 36 חֶרֶב אֶל־
הַבַּדִּים וְנֹאָלוּ חֶרֶב אֶל־גִּבּוֹרֶיהָ וָחָתּוּ: 37 חֶרֶב
אֶל־סוּסָיו וְאֶל־רִכְבּוֹ וְאֶל־כָּל־הָעֶרֶב אֲשֶׁר בְּתוֹכָהּ
וְהָיוּ לְנָשִׁים חֶרֶב אֶל־אוֹצְרֹתֶיהָ וּבֻזָּזוּ: 38 חֹרֶב
אֶל־מֵימֶיהָ וְיָבֵשׁוּ כִּי אֶרֶץ פְּסִלִים הִיא וּבָאֵימִים

39 "Therefore the wild desert beasts shall dwell *there*
    with the jackals,
  And the ostriches shall dwell in it.
  It shall be inhabited no more forever,
  Nor shall it be dwelt in from generation to
    generation.
40 As God overthrew Sodom and Gomorrah
  And their neighbors," says the LORD,

  "*So* no one shall reside there,
  Nor son of man dwell in it.

41 "Behold, a people shall come from the north,
  And a great nation and many kings
  Shall be raised up from the ends of the earth.
42 They shall hold the bow and the lance;
  They *are* cruel and shall not show mercy.
  Their voice shall roar like the sea;
  They shall ride on horses,
  Set in array, like a man for the battle,
  Against you, O daughter of Babylon.

43 "The king of Babylon has heard the report about
    them,
  And his hands grow feeble;
  Anguish has taken hold of him,
  Pangs as of a woman in childbirth.

44 "Behold, he shall come up like a lion from the
    floodplain of the Jordan
  Against the dwelling place of the strong; .
  But I will make them suddenly run away from
    her.
  And who *is* a chosen *man that* I may appoint over
    her?
  For who *is* like Me?
  Who will arraign Me?
  And who *is* that shepherd
  Who will withstand Me?"

45 Therefore hear the counsel of the LORD that He
    has taken against Babylon,
  And His purposes that He has proposed against
    the land of the Chaldeans:
  Surely the least of the flock shall draw them out;
  Surely He will make their dwelling place desolate
    with them.
46 At the noise of the taking of Babylon
  The earth trembles,
  And the cry is heard among the nations.

51 Thus says the LORD:

  "Behold, I will raise up against Babylon,
  Against those who dwell in Leb Kamai,
  A destroying wind.
2 And I will send winnowers to Babylon,
  Who shall winnow her and empty her land.
  For in the day of doom
  They shall be against her all around.
3 Against *her* let the archer bend his bow,
  And lift himself up against *her* in his armor.
  Do not spare her young men;
  Utterly destroy all her army.

יִתְהַלָּלוּ: 39 לָכֵן יֵשְׁבוּ צִיִּים אֶת־אִיִּים וְיָשְׁבוּ בָהּ

בְּנוֹת יַעֲנָה וְלֹא־תֵשֵׁב עוֹד לָנֶצַח וְלֹא תִשְׁכּוֹן עַד־

דּוֹר וָדוֹר: 40 כְּמַהְפֵּכַת אֱלֹהִים אֶת־סְדֹם וְאֶת־

עֲמֹרָה וְאֶת־שְׁכֵנֶיהָ נְאֻם־יְהוָה לֹא־יֵשֵׁב שָׁם אִישׁ

וְלֹא־יָגוּר בָּהּ בֶּן־אָדָם: 41 הִנֵּה עַם בָּא מִצָּפוֹן וְגוֹי

גָּדוֹל וּמְלָכִים רַבִּים יֵעֹרוּ מִיַּרְכְּתֵי־אָרֶץ: 42 קֶשֶׁת

וְכִידֹן יַחֲזִיקוּ אַכְזָרִי הֵמָּה וְלֹא יְרַחֵמוּ קוֹלָם כַּיָּם

יֶהֱמֶה וְעַל־סוּסִים יִרְכָּבוּ עָרוּךְ כְּאִישׁ לַמִּלְחָמָה

עָלַיִךְ בַּת־בָּבֶל: 43 שָׁמַע מֶלֶךְ־בָּבֶל אֶת־שִׁמְעָם

וְרָפוּ יָדָיו צָרָה הֶחֱזִיקַתְהוּ חִיל כַּיּוֹלֵדָה: 44 הִנֵּה

כְּאַרְיֵה יַעֲלֶה מִגְּאוֹן הַיַּרְדֵּן אֶל־נְוֵה אֵיתָן כִּי־

אַרְגִּעָה אֲרִיצֵם° מֵעָלֶיהָ וּמִי בָחוּר אֵלֶיהָ אֶפְקֹד

כִּי מִי כָמוֹנִי וּמִי יוֹעִדֶנִּי וּמִי־זֶה רֹעֶה אֲשֶׁר יַעֲמֹד

לְפָנָי: 45 לָכֵן שִׁמְעוּ עֲצַת־יְהוָה אֲשֶׁר יָעַץ אֶל־בָּבֶל

וּמַחְשְׁבוֹתָיו אֲשֶׁר חָשַׁב אֶל־אֶרֶץ כַּשְׂדִּים אִם־לֹא

יִסְחָבוּם צְעִירֵי הַצֹּאן אִם־לֹא יַשִּׁים עֲלֵיהֶם נָוֶה:

46 מִקּוֹל נִתְפְּשָׂה בָבֶל נִרְעֲשָׁה הָאָרֶץ וּזְעָקָה בַּגּוֹיִם

נִשְׁמָע: ס

נא כֹּה אָמַר יְהוָה הִנְנִי מֵעִיר עַל־בָּבֶל וְאֶל־
יֹשְׁבֵי לֵב קָמָי רוּחַ מַשְׁחִית: 2 וְשִׁלַּחְתִּי לְבָבֶל
זָרִים וְזֵרוּהָ וִיבֹקְקוּ אֶת־אַרְצָהּ כִּי־הָיוּ עָלֶיהָ מִסָּבִיב
בְּיוֹם רָעָה: 3 אֶל־יִדְרֹךְ° יִדְרֹךְ° הַדֹּרֵךְ קַשְׁתּוֹ וְאֶל־
יִתְעַל בְּסִרְיֹנוֹ וְאַל־תַּחְמְלוּ אֶל־בַּחֻרֶיהָ הַחֲרִימוּ כָּל־

4 Thus the slain shall fall in the land of the
      Chaldeans,
  And *those* thrust through in her streets.
5 For Israel is not forsaken, nor Judah,
  By his God, the LORD of hosts,
  Though their land was filled with sin against the
      Holy One of Israel."

6 Flee from the midst of Babylon,
  And every one save his life!
  Do not be cut off in her iniquity,
  For this *is* the time of the LORD's vengeance;
  He shall recompense her.
7 Babylon *was* a golden cup in the LORD's hand,
  That made all the earth drunk.
  The nations drank her wine;
  Therefore the nations are deranged.
8 Babylon has suddenly fallen and been destroyed.
  Wail for her!
  Take balm for her pain;
  Perhaps she may be healed.

9 We would have healed Babylon,
  But she is not healed.
  Forsake her, and let us go everyone to his own
      country;
  For her judgment reaches to heaven and is lifted
      up to the skies.
10 The LORD has revealed our righteousness.
  Come and let us declare in Zion the work of the
      LORD our God.

11 Make the arrows bright!
  Gather the shields!
  The LORD has raised up the spirit of the kings of
      the Medes.
  For His plan *is* against Babylon to destroy it,
  Because it *is* the vengeance of the LORD,
  The vengeance for His temple.
12 Set up the standard on the walls of Babylon;
  Make the guard strong,
  Set up the watchmen,
  Prepare the ambushes.
  For the LORD has both devised and done
  What He spoke against the inhabitants of
      Babylon.
13 O you who dwell by many waters,
  Abundant in treasures,
  Your end has come,
  The measure of your covetousness.
14 The LORD of hosts has sworn by Himself:
  "Surely I will fill you with men, as with locusts,
  And they shall lift up a shout against you."

15 He has made the earth by His power;
  He has established the world by His wisdom,
  And stretched out the heaven by His under-
      standing.
16 When He utters *His* voice—
  There is a multitude of waters in the heavens:

  "He causes the vapors to ascend from the ends of
      the earth;
  He makes lightnings for the rain;
  He brings the wind out of His treasuries."

צְבָאָה: 4 וְנָפְלוּ חֲלָלִים בְּאֶרֶץ כַּשְׂדִּים וּמְדֻקָּרִים

בְּחוּצוֹתֶיהָ: 5 כִּי לֹא־אַלְמָן יִשְׂרָאֵל וִיהוּדָה מֵאֱלֹהָיו

מֵיהֹוָה צְבָאוֹת כִּי אַרְצָם מָלְאָה אָשָׁם מִקְּדוֹשׁ

יִשְׂרָאֵל: 6 נֻסוּ ׀ מִתּוֹךְ בָּבֶל וּמַלְּטוּ אִישׁ נַפְשׁוֹ

אַל־תִּדַּמּוּ בַּעֲוֹנָהּ כִּי עֵת נְקָמָה הִיא לַיהֹוָה

גְּמוּל הוּא מְשַׁלֵּם לָהּ: 7 כּוֹס־זָהָב בָּבֶל בְּיַד־

יְהֹוָה מְשַׁכֶּרֶת כָּל־הָאָרֶץ מִיֵּינָהּ שָׁתוּ גוֹיִם עַל־

כֵּן יִתְהֹלְלוּ גוֹיִם: 8 פִּתְאֹם נָפְלָה בָבֶל וַתִּשָּׁבֵר

הֵילִילוּ עָלֶיהָ קְחוּ צֳרִי לְמַכְאוֹבָהּ אוּלַי תֵּרָפֵא:

9 רִפִּאנוּ אֶת־בָּבֶל וְלֹא נִרְפָּתָה עִזְבוּהָ וְנֵלֵךְ

אִישׁ לְאַרְצוֹ כִּי־נָגַע אֶל־הַשָּׁמַיִם מִשְׁפָּטָהּ וְנִשָּׂא

עַד־שְׁחָקִים: 10 הוֹצִיא יְהֹוָה אֶת־צִדְקֹתֵינוּ בֹּאוּ

וּנְסַפְּרָה בְצִיּוֹן אֶת־מַעֲשֵׂה יְהֹוָה אֱלֹהֵינוּ: 11 הָבֵרוּ

הַחִצִּים מִלְאוּ הַשְּׁלָטִים הֵעִיר יְהֹוָה אֶת־רוּחַ

מַלְכֵי מָדַי כִּי־עַל־בָּבֶל מְזִמָּתוֹ לְהַשְׁחִיתָהּ כִּי־

נִקְמַת יְהֹוָה הִיא נִקְמַת הֵיכָלוֹ: 12 אֶל־חוֹמֹת בָּבֶל

שְׂאוּ־נֵס הַחֲזִיקוּ הַמִּשְׁמָר הָקִימוּ שֹׁמְרִים הָכִינוּ

הָאֹרְבִים כִּי גַּם־זָמַם יְהֹוָה גַּם־עָשָׂה אֵת אֲשֶׁר

דִּבֶּר אֶל־יֹשְׁבֵי בָבֶל: 13 שֹׁכַנְתִּי עַל־מַיִם רַבִּים

רַבַּת אוֹצָרֹת בָּא קִצֵּךְ אַמַּת בִּצְעֵךְ: 14 נִשְׁבַּע

יְהֹוָה צְבָאוֹת בְּנַפְשׁוֹ כִּי אִם־מִלֵּאתִיךְ אָדָם כַּיֶּלֶק

וְעָנוּ עָלַיִךְ הֵידָד: ס 15 עֹשֵׂה אֶרֶץ בְּכֹחוֹ מֵכִין

תֵּבֵל בְּחָכְמָתוֹ וּבִתְבוּנָתוֹ נָטָה שָׁמָיִם: 16 לְקוֹל

תִּתּוֹ הֲמוֹן מַיִם בַּשָּׁמַיִם וַיַּעַל נְשִׂאִים מִקְצֵה־אָרֶץ

17 Everyone is dull-hearted, without knowledge;
Every metalsmith is put to shame by the carved image;
For his molded image *is* falsehood,
And *there is* no breath in them.

18 They *are* futile, a work of errors;
In the time of their punishment they shall perish.

19 The Portion of Jacob *is* not like them,
For He *is* the Maker of all things;
And *Israel is* the tribe of His inheritance.
The LORD of hosts *is* His name.

20 "You *are* My battle-ax *and* weapons of war:
For with you I will break the nation in pieces;
With you I will destroy kingdoms;

21 With you I will break in pieces the horse and its rider;
With you I will break in pieces the chariot and its rider;

22 With you also I will break in pieces man and woman;
With you I will break in pieces old and young;
With you I will break in pieces the young man and the maiden;

23 With you also I will break in pieces the shepherd and his flock;
With you I will break in pieces the farmer and his yoke of oxen;
And with you I will break in pieces governors and rulers.

24 "And I will repay Babylon
And all the inhabitants of Chaldea
For all the evil they have done
In Zion in your sight," says the LORD.

25 "Behold, I *am* against you, O destroying mountain,
Who destroys all the earth," says the LORD.
"And I will stretch out My hand against you,
Roll you down from the rocks,
And make you a burnt mountain.

26 They shall not take from you a stone for a corner
Nor a stone for a foundation,
But you shall be desolate forever," says the LORD.

27 Set up a banner in the land,
Blow the trumpet among the nations!
Prepare the nations against her,
Call the kingdoms together against her:
Ararat, Minni, and Ashkenaz.
Appoint a general against her;
Cause the horses to come up like the bristling locusts.

28 Prepare against her the nations,
With the kings of the Medes,
Its governors and all its rulers,
All the land of his dominion.

29 And the land will tremble and sorrow;
For every purpose of the LORD shall be performed against Babylon,
To make the land of Babylon a desolation without inhabitant.

30 The mighty men of Babylon have ceased fighting,
They have remained in their strongholds;

בְּרָקִים לַמָּטָר עָשָׂה וַיּוֹצֵא רוּחַ מֵאֹצְרֹתָיו: 17 נִבְעַר
כָּל־אָדָם מִדַּעַת הֹבִישׁ כָּל־צֹרֵף מִפָּסֶל כִּי שֶׁקֶר
נִסְכּוֹ וְלֹא־רוּחַ בָּם: 18 הֶבֶל הֵמָּה מַעֲשֵׂה תַּעְתֻּעִים
בְּעֵת פְּקֻדָּתָם יֹאבֵדוּ: 19 לֹא־כְאֵלֶּה חֵלֶק יַעֲקוֹב
כִּי־יוֹצֵר הַכֹּל הוּא וְשֵׁבֶט נַחֲלָתוֹ יְהוָה צְבָאוֹת
שְׁמוֹ: ס 20 מַפֵּץ־אַתָּה לִי כְּלֵי מִלְחָמָה וְנִפַּצְתִּי
בְךָ גּוֹיִם וְהִשְׁחַתִּי בְךָ מַמְלָכוֹת: 21 וְנִפַּצְתִּי בְךָ
סוּס וְרֹכְבוֹ וְנִפַּצְתִּי בְךָ רֶכֶב וְרֹכְבוֹ: 22 וְנִפַּצְתִּי בְךָ
אִישׁ וְאִשָּׁה וְנִפַּצְתִּי בְךָ זָקֵן וָנָעַר וְנִפַּצְתִּי בְךָ בָּחוּר
וּבְתוּלָה: 23 וְנִפַּצְתִּי בְךָ רֹעֶה וְעֶדְרוֹ וְנִפַּצְתִּי בְךָ
אִכָּר וְצִמְדּוֹ וְנִפַּצְתִּי בְךָ פַּחוֹת וּסְגָנִים: 24 וְשִׁלַּמְתִּי
לְבָבֶל וּלְכֹל | יוֹשְׁבֵי כַשְׂדִּים אֵת כָּל־רָעָתָם אֲשֶׁר־
עָשׂוּ בְצִיּוֹן לְעֵינֵיכֶם נְאֻם יְהוָה: ס 25 הִנְנִי
אֵלֶיךָ הַר הַמַּשְׁחִית נְאֻם־יְהוָה הַמַּשְׁחִית אֶת־
כָּל־הָאָרֶץ וְנָטִיתִי אֶת־יָדִי עָלֶיךָ וְגִלְגַּלְתִּיךָ מִן־
הַסְּלָעִים וּנְתַתִּיךָ לְהַר שְׂרֵפָה: 26 וְלֹא־יִקְחוּ מִמְּךָ
אֶבֶן לְפִנָּה וְאֶבֶן לְמוֹסָדוֹת כִּי־שִׁמְמוֹת עוֹלָם
תִּהְיֶה נְאֻם־יְהוָה: 27 שְׂאוּ־נֵס בָּאָרֶץ תִּקְעוּ שׁוֹפָר
בַּגּוֹיִם קַדְּשׁוּ עָלֶיהָ גּוֹיִם הַשְׁמִיעוּ עָלֶיהָ מַמְלְכוֹת
אֲרָרַט מִנִּי וְאַשְׁכְּנַז פִּקְדוּ עָלֶיהָ טִפְסָר הַעֲלוּ־
סוּס כְּיֶלֶק סָמָר: 28 קַדְּשׁוּ עָלֶיהָ גוֹיִם אֶת־מַלְכֵי
מָדַי אֶת־פַּחוֹתֶיהָ וְאֶת־כָּל־סְגָנֶיהָ וְאֵת כָּל־אֶרֶץ
מֶמְשַׁלְתּוֹ: 29 וַתִּרְעַשׁ הָאָרֶץ וַתָּחֹל כִּי קָמָה עַל־
בָּבֶל מַחְשְׁבוֹת יְהוָה לָשׂוּם אֶת־אֶרֶץ בָּבֶל לְשַׁמָּה
מֵאֵין יוֹשֵׁב: 30 חָדְלוּ גִבּוֹרֵי בָבֶל לְהִלָּחֵם יָשְׁבוּ
בַּמְּצָדוֹת נָשְׁתָה גְבוּרָתָם הָיוּ לְנָשִׁים הִצִּיתוּ

Their might has failed,
They became *like* women;
They have burned her dwelling places,
The bars of her *gate* are broken.
31 One runner will run to meet another,
And one messenger to meet another,
To show the king of Babylon that his city is taken
on *all* sides;
32 The passages are blocked,
The reeds they have burned with fire,
And the men of war are terrified.

33 For thus says the LORD of hosts, the God of
Israel:

"The daughter of Babylon *is* like a threshing floor
When it is time to thresh her;
Yet a little while
And the time of her harvest will come."

34 "Nebuchadnezzar the king of Babylon
Has devoured me, he has crushed me;
He has made me an empty vessel,
He has swallowed me up like a monster;
He has filled his stomach with my delicacies,
He has spit me out.
35 Let the violence *done* to me and my flesh *be* upon
Babylon,"
The inhabitant of Zion will say;
"And my blood be upon the inhabitants of
Chaldea!"
Jerusalem will say.

36 Therefore thus says the LORD:

"Behold, I will plead your case and take vengeance
for you.
I will dry up her sea and make her springs dry.
37 Babylon shall become a heap,
A dwelling place for jackals,
An astonishment and a hissing,
Without an inhabitant.
38 They shall roar together like lions,
They shall growl like lions' whelps.
39 In their excitement I will prepare their feasts;
I will make them drunk,
That they may rejoice,
And sleep a perpetual sleep
And not awake," says the LORD.
40 "I will bring them down
Like lambs to the slaughter,
Like rams with male goats.

41 "Oh, how Sheshach is taken!
Oh, how the praise of the whole earth is seized!
How Babylon has become desolate among the
nations!
42 The sea has come up over Babylon;
She is covered with the multitude of its waves.
43 Her cities are a desolation,
A dry land and a wilderness,
A land where no one dwells,
Through which no son of man passes.
44 I will punish Bel in Babylon,

מִשְׁכְּנֹתֶיהָ נִשְׁבְּרוּ בְרִיחֶיהָ: 31 רָץ לִקְרַאת־רָץ יָרוּץ
וּמַגִּיד לִקְרַאת מַגִּיד לְהַגִּיד לְמֶלֶךְ בָּבֶל כִּי־נִלְכְּדָה
עִירוֹ מִקָּצֶה: 32 וְהַמַּעְבָּרוֹת נִתְפָּשׂוּ וְאֶת־הָאֲגַמִּים
שָׂרְפוּ בָאֵשׁ וְאַנְשֵׁי הַמִּלְחָמָה נִבְהָלוּ: ס 33 כִּי
כֹה אָמַר יְהוָה צְבָאוֹת אֱלֹהֵי יִשְׂרָאֵל בַּת־
בָּבֶל כְּגֹרֶן עֵת הִדְרִיכָהּ עוֹד מְעַט וּבָאָה עֵת־
הַקָּצִיר לָהּ: 34 אֲכָלַנוּ הֲמָמַנוּ נְבוּכַדְרֶאצַּר מֶלֶךְ
בָּבֶל הִצִּיגַנוּ כְּלִי רִיק בְּלָעַנוּ כַּתַּנִּין מִלָּא
כְרֵשׂוֹ מֵעֲדָנָי הֱדִיחָנוּ: 35 חֲמָסִי וּשְׁאֵרִי עַל־בָּבֶל
תֹּאמַר יֹשֶׁבֶת צִיּוֹן וְדָמִי אֶל־יֹשְׁבֵי כַשְׂדִּים תֹּאמַר
יְרוּשָׁלִָם: ס 36 לָכֵן כֹּה אָמַר יְהוָה הִנְנִי־רָב
אֶת־רִיבֵךְ וְנִקַּמְתִּי אֶת־נִקְמָתֵךְ וְהַחֲרַבְתִּי אֶת־יַמָּהּ
וְהֹבַשְׁתִּי אֶת־מְקוֹרָהּ: 37 וְהָיְתָה בָבֶל ׀ לְגַלִּים
מְעוֹן־תַּנִּים שַׁמָּה וּשְׁרֵקָה מֵאֵין יוֹשֵׁב: 38 יַחְדָּו
כַּכְּפִרִים יִשְׁאָגוּ נָעֲרוּ כְּגוֹרֵי אֲרָיוֹת: 39 בְּחֻמָּם
אָשִׁית אֶת־מִשְׁתֵּיהֶם וְהִשְׁכַּרְתִּים לְמַעַן יַעֲלֹזוּ
וְיָשְׁנוּ שְׁנַת־עוֹלָם וְלֹא יָקִיצוּ נְאֻם יְהוָה: 40 אוֹרִידֵם
כְּכָרִים לִטְבוֹחַ כְּאֵילִים עִם־עַתּוּדִים: 41 אֵיךְ
נִלְכְּדָה שֵׁשַׁךְ וַתִּתָּפֵשׂ תְּהִלַּת כָּל־הָאָרֶץ אֵיךְ
הָיְתָה לְשַׁמָּה בָּבֶל בַּגּוֹיִם: 42 עָלָה עַל־בָּבֶל הַיָּם
בַּהֲמוֹן גַּלָּיו נִכְסָתָה: 43 הָיוּ עָרֶיהָ לְשַׁמָּה אֶרֶץ צִיָּה
וַעֲרָבָה אֶרֶץ לֹא־יֵשֵׁב בָּהֵן כָּל־אִישׁ וְלֹא־יַעֲבֹר בָּהֵן
בֶּן־אָדָם: 44 וּפָקַדְתִּי עַל־בֵּל בְּבָבֶל וְהֹצֵאתִי אֶת־
בִּלְעוֹ מִפִּיו וְלֹא־יִנְהֲרוּ אֵלָיו עוֹד גּוֹיִם גַּם־חוֹמַת

And I will bring out of his mouth what he has swallowed;
And the nations shall not stream to him any-more.
Yes, the wall of Babylon shall fall.

45 "My people, go out of the midst of her!
And let everyone deliver himself from the fierce anger of the LORD.
46 And lest your heart faint,
And you fear for the rumor that *will be* heard in the land
(A rumor will come *one* year,
And after that, in *another* year
A rumor *will come,*
And violence in the land,
Ruler against ruler),
47 Therefore behold, the days are coming
That I will bring judgment on the carved images of Babylon;
Her whole land shall be ashamed,
And all her slain shall fall in her midst.
48 Then the heavens and the earth and all that *is* in them
Shall sing joyously over Babylon;
For the plunderers shall come to her from the north," says the LORD.

49 As Babylon *has caused* the slain of Israel to fall,
So at Babylon the slain of all the earth shall fall.
50 You who have escaped the sword,
Get away! Do not stand still!
Remember the LORD afar off,
And let Jerusalem come to your mind.

51 We are ashamed because we have heard re-proach.
Shame has covered our faces,
For strangers have come into the sanctuaries of the LORD's house.

52 "Therefore behold, the days are coming," says the LORD,
"That I will bring judgment on her carved images,
And throughout all her land the wounded shall groan.
53 Though Babylon were to mount up to heaven,
And though she were to fortify the height of her strength,
Yet from Me plunderers would come to her," says the LORD.

54 The sound of a cry *comes* from Babylon,
And great destruction from the land of the Chaldeans,
55 Because the LORD is plundering Babylon
And silencing her loud voice,
Though her waves roar like great waters,
And the noise of their voice is uttered,
56 Because the plunderer comes against her, against Babylon,
And her mighty men are taken.
Every one of their bows is broken;
For the LORD *is* the God of recompense,
He will surely repay.

בְּבֶל נָפֵלָה: 45 צְאוּ מִתּוֹכָהּ עַמִּי וּמַלְּטוּ אִישׁ אֶת־
נַפְשׁוֹ מֵחֲרוֹן אַף־יְהוָה: 46 וּפֶן־יֵרַךְ לְבַבְכֶם וְתִירְאוּ
בַּשְּׁמוּעָה הַנִּשְׁמַעַת בָּאָרֶץ וּבָא בַשָּׁנָה הַשְּׁמוּעָה
וְאַחֲרָיו בַּשָּׁנָה הַשְּׁמוּעָה וְחָמָס בָּאָרֶץ וּמֹשֵׁל עַל־
מֹשֵׁל: 47 לָכֵן הִנֵּה יָמִים בָּאִים וּפָקַדְתִּי עַל־פְּסִילֵי
בָבֶל וְכָל־אַרְצָהּ תֵּבוֹשׁ וְכָל־חֲלָלֶיהָ יִפְּלוּ בְתוֹכָהּ:
48 וְרִנְּנוּ עַל־בָּבֶל שָׁמַיִם וָאָרֶץ וְכֹל אֲשֶׁר בָּהֶם
כִּי מִצָּפוֹן יָבוֹא־לָהּ הַשּׁוֹדְדִים נְאֻם־יְהוָה: 49 גַּם־
בָּבֶל לִנְפֹּל חַלְלֵי יִשְׂרָאֵל גַּם־לְבָבֶל נָפְלוּ חַלְלֵי כָל־
הָאָרֶץ: 50 פְּלֵטִים מֵחֶרֶב הִלְכוּ אַל־תַּעֲמֹדוּ זִכְרוּ
מֵרָחוֹק אֶת־יְהוָה וִירוּשָׁלַ͏ִם תַּעֲלֶה עַל־לְבַבְכֶם:
51 בֹּשְׁנוּ כִּי־שָׁמַעְנוּ חֶרְפָּה כִּסְּתָה כְלִמָּה פָּנֵינוּ כִּי
בָּאוּ זָרִים עַל־מִקְדְּשֵׁי בֵּית יְהוָה: ס 52 לָכֵן
הִנֵּה־יָמִים בָּאִים נְאֻם־יְהוָה וּפָקַדְתִּי עַל־פְּסִילֶיהָ
וּבְכָל־אַרְצָהּ יֶאֱנֹק חָלָל: 53 כִּי־תַעֲלֶה בָבֶל הַשָּׁמַיִם
וְכִי תְבַצֵּר מְרוֹם עֻזָּהּ מֵאִתִּי יָבֹאוּ שֹׁדְדִים לָהּ
נְאֻם־יְהוָה: ס 54 קוֹל זְעָקָה מִבָּבֶל וְשֶׁבֶר גָּדוֹל
מֵאֶרֶץ כַּשְׂדִּים: 55 כִּי־שֹׁדֵד יְהוָה אֶת־בָּבֶל וְאִבַּד
מִמֶּנָּה קוֹל גָּדוֹל וְהָמוּ גַלֵּיהֶם כְּמַיִם רַבִּים נִתַּן
שְׁאוֹן קוֹלָם: 56 כִּי בָא עָלֶיהָ עַל־בָּבֶל שׁוֹדֵד
וְנִלְכְּדוּ גִּבּוֹרֶיהָ חִתְּתָה קַשְּׁתוֹתָם

57 "And I will make drunk
    Her princes and wise men,
    Her governors, her deputies, and her mighty men.
    And they shall sleep a perpetual sleep
    And not awake," says the King,
    Whose name is the LORD of hosts.

58 Thus says the LORD of hosts:

    "The broad walls of Babylon shall be utterly
        broken,
    And her high gates shall be burned with fire;
    The people will labor in vain,
    And the nations, because of the fire;
    And they shall be weary."

59 The word which Jeremiah the prophet commanded Seraiah the son of Neriah, the son of
Mahseiah, when he went with Zedekiah the king of
Judah to Babylon in the fourth year of his reign.
And Seraiah was the quartermaster. 60 So Jeremiah
wrote in a book all the evil that would come upon
Babylon, all these words that are written against
Babylon. 61 And Jeremiah said to Seraiah, "When
you arrive in Babylon and see it, and read all these
words, 62 then you shall say, 'O LORD, You have
spoken against this place to cut it off, so that none
shall remain in it, neither man nor beast, but it shall
be desolate forever.' 63 Now it shall be, when you
have finished reading this book, that you shall tie a
stone to it and throw it out into the Euphrates.
64 Then you shall say, 'Thus Babylon shall sink and
not rise from the catastrophe that I will bring upon
her. And they shall be weary.'"

Thus far are the words of Jeremiah.

52 Zedekiah was twenty-one years old when he
became king, and he reigned eleven years in
Jerusalem. His mother's name was Hamutal the
daughter of Jeremiah of Libnah. 2 He also did evil
in the sight of the LORD, according to all that
Jehoiakim had done. 3 For because of the anger of
the LORD this happened in Jerusalem and Judah, till
He finally cast them out from His presence. Then
Zedekiah rebelled against the king of Babylon.

4 Now it came to pass in the ninth year of his
reign, in the tenth month, on the tenth day of the
month, that Nebuchadnezzar king of Babylon and
all his army came against Jerusalem and encamped
against it; and they built a siege wall against it all
around. 5 So the city was besieged until the eleventh
year of King Zedekiah. 6 By the fourth month, on
the ninth day of the month, the famine had become
so severe in the city that there was no food for the
people of the land. 7 Then the city wall was broken
through, and all the men of war fled and went out
of the city at night by way of the gate between the

כִּי אֶל גְּמֻלוֹת יְהוָה שַׁלֵּם יְשַׁלֵּם: 57 וְהִשְׁכַּרְתִּי
שָׂרֶיהָ וַחֲכָמֶיהָ פַּחוֹתֶיהָ וּסְגָנֶיהָ וְגִבּוֹרֶיהָ וְיָשְׁנוּ
שְׁנַת־עוֹלָם וְלֹא יָקִיצוּ נְאֻם־הַמֶּלֶךְ יְהוָה צְבָאוֹת
שְׁמוֹ: ס 58 כֹּה־אָמַר יְהוָה צְבָאוֹת חֹמוֹת
בָּבֶל הָרְחָבָה עַרְעֵר תִּתְעַרְעָר וּשְׁעָרֶיהָ הַגְּבֹהִים
בָּאֵשׁ יִצַּתּוּ וְיִגְעוּ עַמִּים בְּדֵי־רִיק וּלְאֻמִּים בְּדֵי־
אֵשׁ וְיָעֵפוּ: ס 59 הַדָּבָר אֲשֶׁר־צִוָּה | יִרְמְיָהוּ
הַנָּבִיא אֶת־שְׂרָיָה בֶן־נֵרִיָּה בֶּן־מַחְסֵיָה בְּלֶכְתּוֹ
אֶת־צִדְקִיָּהוּ מֶלֶךְ־יְהוּדָה בָּבֶל בִּשְׁנַת הָרְבִעִית
לְמָלְכוֹ וּשְׂרָיָה שַׂר מְנוּחָה: 60 וַיִּכְתֹּב יִרְמְיָהוּ
אֵת כָּל־הָרָעָה אֲשֶׁר־תָּבוֹא אֶל־בָּבֶל אֶל־סֵפֶר
אֶחָד אֵת כָּל־הַדְּבָרִים הָאֵלֶּה הַכְּתֻבִים אֶל־בָּבֶל:
61 וַיֹּאמֶר יִרְמְיָהוּ אֶל־שְׂרָיָה כְּבֹאֲךָ בָבֶל וְרָאִיתָ
וְקָרָאתָ אֵת כָּל־הַדְּבָרִים הָאֵלֶּה: 62 וְאָמַרְתָּ יְהוָה
אַתָּה דִבַּרְתָּ אֶל־הַמָּקוֹם הַזֶּה לְהַכְרִיתוֹ לְבִלְתִּי
הֱיוֹת־בּוֹ יוֹשֵׁב לְמֵאָדָם וְעַד־בְּהֵמָה כִּי־שִׁמְמוֹת
עוֹלָם תִּהְיֶה: 63 וְהָיָה כְּכַלֹּתְךָ לִקְרֹא אֶת־הַסֵּפֶר
הַזֶּה תִּקְשֹׁר עָלָיו אֶבֶן וְהִשְׁלַכְתּוֹ אֶל־תּוֹךְ פְּרָת:
64 וְאָמַרְתָּ כָּכָה תִּשְׁקַע בָּבֶל וְלֹא־תָקוּם מִפְּנֵי
הָרָעָה אֲשֶׁר אָנֹכִי מֵבִיא עָלֶיהָ וְיָעֵפוּ עַד־הֵנָּה
דִּבְרֵי יִרְמְיָהוּ: ס

נב בֶּן־עֶשְׂרִים וְאַחַת שָׁנָה צִדְקִיָּהוּ בְמָלְכוֹ
וְאַחַת עֶשְׂרֵה שָׁנָה מָלַךְ בִּירוּשָׁלָ͏ִם וְשֵׁם אִמּוֹ
חֲמִיטַלᵏ בַּת־יִרְמְיָהוּ מִלִּבְנָה: 2 וַיַּעַשׂ הָרַע בְּעֵינֵי
יְהוָה כְּכֹל אֲשֶׁר־עָשָׂה יְהוֹיָקִים: 3 כִּי | עַל־
אַף יְהוָה הָיְתָה בִּירוּשָׁלַ͏ִם וִיהוּדָה עַד־הִשְׁלִיכוֹ
אוֹתָם מֵעַל פָּנָיו וַיִּמְרֹד צִדְקִיָּהוּ בְּמֶלֶךְ בָּבֶל:
4 וַיְהִי בַשָּׁנָה הַתְּשִׁעִית לְמָלְכוֹ בַּחֹדֶשׁ הָעֲשִׂירִי
בֶּעָשׂוֹר לַחֹדֶשׁ בָּא נְבוּכַדְרֶאצַּר מֶלֶךְ־בָּבֶל הוּא
וְכָל־חֵילוֹ עַל־יְרוּשָׁלַ͏ִם וַיַּחֲנוּ עָלֶיהָ וַיִּבְנוּ עָלֶיהָ
דָּיֵק סָבִיב: 5 וַתָּבֹא הָעִיר בַּמָּצוֹר עַד עַשְׁתֵּי
עֶשְׂרֵה שָׁנָה לַמֶּלֶךְ צִדְקִיָּהוּ: 6 בַּחֹדֶשׁ הָרְבִיעִי
בְּתִשְׁעָה לַחֹדֶשׁ וַיֶּחֱזַק הָרָעָב בָּעִיר וְלֹא־הָיָה לֶחֶם
לְעַם הָאָרֶץ: 7 וַתִּבָּקַע הָעִיר וְכָל־אַנְשֵׁי הַמִּלְחָמָה

נב 1 חֲמוּטַל

two walls, which *was* by the king's garden, even though the Chaldeans *were* near the city all around. And they went by way of the plain.

8 But the army of the Chaldeans pursued the king, and they overtook Zedekiah in the plains of Jericho. All his army was scattered from him. 9 So they took the king and brought him up to the king of Babylon at Riblah in the land of Hamath, and he pronounced judgment on him. 10 Then the king of Babylon killed the sons of Zedekiah before his eyes. And he killed all the princes of Judah in Riblah. 11 He also put out the eyes of Zedekiah; and the king of Babylon bound him in bronze fetters, took him to Babylon, and put him in prison till the day of his death.

12 Now in the fifth month, on the tenth *day* of the month (which *was* the nineteenth year of King Nebuchadnezzar king of Babylon), Nebuzaradan, the captain of the guard, *who* served the king of Babylon, came to Jerusalem. 13 He burned the house of the LORD and the king's house; all the houses of Jerusalem, that is, all the houses of the great, he burned with fire. 14 And all the army of the Chaldeans who *were* with the captain of the guard broke down all the walls of Jerusalem all around. 15 Then Nebuzaradan the captain of the guard carried away captive *some* of the poor people, the rest of the people who remained in the city, the defectors who had deserted to the king of Babylon, and the rest of the craftsmen. 16 But Nebuzaradan the captain of the guard left *some* of the poor of the land as vinedressers and farmers.

17 The bronze pillars that *were* in the house of the LORD, and the carts and the bronze Sea that *were* in the house of the LORD, the Chaldeans broke in pieces, and carried all their bronze to Babylon. 18 They also took away the pots, the shovels, the trimmers, the bowls, the spoons, and all the bronze utensils with which the priests ministered. 19 The basins, the firepans, the bowls, the pots, the lampstands, the spoons, and the cups, whatever *was* solid gold and whatever *was* solid silver, the captain of the guard took away. 20 The two pillars, one Sea, the twelve bronze bulls which *were* under *it, and* the carts, which King Solomon had made for the house of the LORD—the bronze of all these articles was beyond measure. 21 Now *concerning* the pillars: the height of one pillar *was* eighteen cubits, a measuring line of twelve cubits could measure its circumference, and its thickness *was* four fingers; *it was* hollow. 22 A capital of bronze *was* on it; and the height of one capital *was* five cubits, with a network and pomegranates all around the capital, all of bronze. The second pillar, with pomegranates was

יִבְרְחוּ וַיֵּצְאוּ מֵהָעִיר לַיְלָה דֶּרֶךְ שַׁעַר בֵּין־הַחֹמֹתַיִם אֲשֶׁר עַל־גַּן הַמֶּלֶךְ וְכַשְׂדִּים עַל־הָעִיר סָבִיב וַיֵּלְכוּ דֶּרֶךְ הָעֲרָבָה: 8 וַיִּרְדְּפוּ חֵיל־כַּשְׂדִּים אַחֲרֵי הַמֶּלֶךְ וַיַּשִּׂיגוּ אֶת־צִדְקִיָּהוּ בְּעַרְבֹת יְרֵחוֹ וְכָל־חֵילוֹ נָפֹצוּ מֵעָלָיו: 9 וַיִּתְפְּשׂוּ אֶת־הַמֶּלֶךְ וַיַּעֲלוּ אֹתוֹ אֶל־מֶלֶךְ בָּבֶל רִבְלָתָה בְּאֶרֶץ חֲמָת וַיְדַבֵּר אִתּוֹ מִשְׁפָּטִים: 10 וַיִּשְׁחַט מֶלֶךְ־בָּבֶל אֶת־בְּנֵי צִדְקִיָּהוּ לְעֵינָיו וְגַם אֶת־כָּל־שָׂרֵי יְהוּדָה שָׁחַט בְּרִבְלָתָה: 11 וְאֶת־עֵינֵי צִדְקִיָּהוּ עִוֵּר וַיַּאַסְרֵהוּ בַנְחֻשְׁתַּיִם וַיְבִאֵהוּ מֶלֶךְ־בָּבֶל בָּבֶלָה וַיִּתְּנֵהוּ בְבֵית־ הַפְּקֻדֹּת עַד־יוֹם מוֹתוֹ: 12 וּבַחֹדֶשׁ הַחֲמִישִׁי בֶּעָשׂוֹר לַחֹדֶשׁ הִיא שְׁנַת תְּשַׁע־עֶשְׂרֵה שָׁנָה לַמֶּלֶךְ נְבוּכַדְרֶאצַּר מֶלֶךְ־ בָּבֶל בָּא נְבוּזַרְאֲדָן רַב־טַבָּחִים עָמַד לִפְנֵי מֶלֶךְ־ בָּבֶל בִּירוּשָׁלִָם: 13 וַיִּשְׂרֹף אֶת־בֵּית־יְהוָה וְאֶת־בֵּית הַמֶּלֶךְ וְאֵת כָּל־בָּתֵּי יְרוּשָׁלִַם וְאֶת־כָּל־בֵּית הַגָּדוֹל שָׂרַף בָּאֵשׁ: 14 וְאֶת־כָּל־חֹמוֹת יְרוּשָׁלִַם סָבִיב נָתְצוּ כָּל־חֵיל כַּשְׂדִּים אֲשֶׁר אֶת־רַב־טַבָּחִים: 15 וּמִדַּלּוֹת הָעָם וְאֶת־יֶתֶר הָעָם ׀ הַנִּשְׁאָרִים בָּעִיר וְאֶת־ הַנֹּפְלִים אֲשֶׁר נָפְלוּ אֶל־מֶלֶךְ בָּבֶל וְאֵת יֶתֶר הָאָמוֹן הֶגְלָה נְבוּזַרְאֲדָן רַב־טַבָּחִים: 16 וּמִדַּלּוֹת הָאָרֶץ הִשְׁאִיר נְבוּזַרְאֲדָן רַב־טַבָּחִים לְכֹרְמִים וּלְיֹגְבִים: 17 וְאֶת־עַמּוּדֵי הַנְּחֹשֶׁת אֲשֶׁר לְבֵית־יְהוָה וְאֶת־הַמְּכֹנוֹת וְאֶת־יָם הַנְּחֹשֶׁת אֲשֶׁר בְּבֵית־יְהוָה שִׁבְּרוּ כַשְׂדִּים וַיִּשְׂאוּ אֶת־כָּל־נְחֻשְׁתָּם בָּבֶלָה: 18 וְאֶת־הַסִּרוֹת וְאֶת־הַיָּעִים וְאֶת־הַמְזַמְּרוֹת וְאֶת־ הַמִּזְרָקֹת וְאֶת־הַכַּפּוֹת וְאֵת כָּל־כְּלֵי הַנְּחֹשֶׁת אֲשֶׁר־ יְשָׁרְתוּ בָהֶם לָקָחוּ: 19 וְאֶת־הַסִּפִּים וְאֶת־הַמַּחְתּוֹת וְאֶת־הַמִּזְרָקוֹת וְאֶת־הַסִּירוֹת וְאֶת־הַמְּנֹרוֹת וְאֶת־ הַכַּפּוֹת וְאֶת־הַמְּנַקִיּוֹת אֲשֶׁר זָהָב זָהָב וַאֲשֶׁר־ כֶּסֶף כָּסֶף לָקַח רַב־טַבָּחִים: 20 הָעַמּוּדִים ׀ שְׁנַיִם הַיָּם אֶחָד וְהַבָּקָר שְׁנֵים־עָשָׂר נְחֹשֶׁת אֲשֶׁר־תַּחַת הַמְּכֹנוֹת אֲשֶׁר עָשָׂה הַמֶּלֶךְ שְׁלֹמֹה לְבֵית יְהוָה לֹא־הָיָה מִשְׁקָל לִנְחֻשְׁתָּם כָּל־הַכֵּלִים הָאֵלֶּה: 21 וְהָעַמּוּדִים שְׁמֹנֶה עֶשְׂרֵה אַמָּה קוֹמָה הָעַמֻּד הָאֶחָד וְחוּט שְׁתֵּים־עֶשְׂרֵה אַמָּה יְסֻבֶּנּוּ וְעָבְיוֹ אַרְבַּע אַצְבָּעוֹת נָבוּב: 22 וְכֹתֶרֶת עָלָיו נְחֹשֶׁת

the same. ²³ There were ninety-six pomegranates on the sides; all the pomegranates, all around on the network, *were* one hundred.

²⁴ The captain of the guard took Seraiah the chief priest, Zephaniah the second priest, and the three doorkeepers. ²⁵ He also took out of the city an officer who had charge of the men of war, seven men of the king's close associates who were found in the city, the principal scribe of the army who mustered the people of the land, and sixty men of the people of the land who were found in the midst of the city. ²⁶ And Nebuzaradan the captain of the guard took these and brought them to the king of Babylon at Riblah. ²⁷ Then the king of Babylon struck them and put them to death at Riblah in the land of Hamath. Thus Judah was carried away captive from its own land.

²⁸ These *are* the people whom Nebuchadnezzar carried away captive: in the seventh year, three thousand and twenty-three Jews; ²⁹ in the eighteenth year of Nebuchadnezzar he carried away captive from Jerusalem eight hundred and thirty-two persons; ³⁰ in the twenty-third year of Nebuchadnezzar, Nebuzaradan the captain of the guard carried away captive of the Jews seven hundred and forty-five persons. All the persons *were* four thousand six hundred.

³¹ Now it came to pass in the thirty-seventh year of the captivity of Jehoiachin king of Judah, in the twelfth month, on the twenty-fifth *day* of the month, *that* Evil-Merodach king of Babylon, in the first *year* of his reign, lifted up the head of Jehoiachin king of Judah and brought him out of prison. ³² And he spoke kindly to him and gave him a more prominent seat than those of the kings who *were* with him in Babylon. ³³ So Jehoiachin changed from his prison garments, and he ate bread regularly before the king all the days of his life. ³⁴ And as for his provisions, there was a regular ration given him by the king of Babylon, a portion for each day until the day of his death, all the days of his life.

וְקוֹמַת֩ הַכֹּתֶ֨רֶת הָאַחַ֜ת חָמֵ֣שׁ אַמּוֹת֮ וּשְׂבָכָ֒ה וְרִמּוֹנִ֣ים עַל־הַכּוֹתֶ֣רֶת סָבִ֗יב הַכֹּ֛ל נְחֹ֖שֶׁת וְכָאֵ֥לֶּה לָעַמּ֖וּד הַשֵּׁנִ֥י וְרִמּוֹנִֽים: ²³ וַיִּֽהְיוּ֙ הָרִמֹּנִ֔ים תִּשְׁעִ֥ים וְשִׁשָּׁ֖ה ר֑וּחָה כָּל־הָרִמּוֹנִ֥ים מֵאָ֛ה עַל־הַשְּׂבָכָ֖ה סָבִֽיב: ²⁴ וַיִּקַּ֣ח רַב־טַבָּחִ֗ים אֶת־שְׂרָיָה֙ כֹּהֵ֣ן הָרֹ֔אשׁ וְאֶת־צְפַנְיָ֖ה כֹּהֵ֣ן הַמִּשְׁנֶ֑ה וְאֶת־שְׁלֹ֖שֶׁת שֹׁמְרֵ֥י הַסַּֽף: ²⁵ וּמִן־הָעִ֡יר לָקַח֩ סָרִ֨יס אֶחָ֜ד אֲֽשֶׁר־הָיָ֥ה פָקִ֣יד ׀ עַל־אַנְשֵׁ֣י הַמִּלְחָמָ֗ה וְשִׁבְעָ֨ה אֲנָשִׁ֜ים מֵרֹאֵ֤י פְנֵֽי־הַמֶּ֙לֶךְ֙ אֲשֶׁ֣ר נִמְצְא֣וּ בָעִ֔יר וְאֵ֗ת סֹפֵר֙ שַׂ֣ר הַצָּבָ֔א הַמַּצְבִּ֖א אֶת־עַ֣ם הָאָ֑רֶץ וְשִׁשִּׁ֥ים אִישׁ֙ מֵעַ֣ם הָאָ֔רֶץ הַֽנִּמְצְאִ֖ים בְּת֥וֹךְ הָעִֽיר: ²⁶ וַיִּקַּ֣ח אוֹתָ֔ם נְבֽוּזַרְאֲדָ֖ן רַב־טַבָּחִ֑ים וַיֹּ֧לֶךְ אוֹתָ֛ם אֶל־מֶ֥לֶךְ בָּבֶ֖ל רִבְלָֽתָה: ²⁷ וַיַּכֶּ֣ה אוֹתָם֩ מֶ֨לֶךְ בָּבֶ֤ל וַיְמִתֵם֙ בְּרִבְלָ֔ה בְּאֶ֖רֶץ חֲמָ֑ת וַיִּ֥גֶל יְהוּדָ֖ה מֵעַ֥ל אַדְמָתֽוֹ: ²⁸ זֶ֣ה הָעָ֔ם אֲשֶׁ֥ר הֶגְלָ֖ה נְבֽוּכַדְרֶאצַּ֑ר בִּשְׁנַת־שֶׁ֕בַע יְהוּדִ֕ים שְׁלֹ֥שֶׁת אֲלָפִ֖ים וְעֶשְׂרִ֥ים וּשְׁלֹשָֽׁה: ²⁹ בִּשְׁנַ֣ת שְׁמוֹנֶ֣ה עֶשְׂרֵ֔ה לִנְבֽוּכַדְרֶאצַּ֑ר מִיר֣וּשָׁלַ֔͏ִם נֶ֕פֶשׁ שְׁמֹנֶ֥ה מֵא֖וֹת שְׁלֹשִׁ֥ים וּשְׁנָֽיִם: ³⁰ בִּשְׁנַ֨ת שָׁלֹ֣שׁ וְעֶשְׂרִים֮ לִנְבֽוּכַדְרֶאצַּר֒ הֶגְלָ֞ה נְבֽוּזַרְאֲדָ֣ן רַב־טַבָּחִ֗ים יְהוּדִ֕ים נֶ֕פֶשׁ שְׁבַ֥ע מֵא֖וֹת אַרְבָּעִ֣ים וַחֲמִשָּׁ֑ה כָּל־נֶ֕פֶשׁ אַרְבַּ֥עַת אֲלָפִ֖ים וְשֵׁ֥שׁ מֵאֽוֹת: פ

³¹ וַיְהִי֩ בִשְׁלֹשִׁ֨ים וָשֶׁ֜בַע שָׁנָ֗ה לְגָלוּת֙ יְהוֹיָכִ֣ין מֶֽלֶךְ־יְהוּדָ֔ה בִּשְׁנֵ֤ים עָשָׂר֙ חֹ֔דֶשׁ בְּעֶשְׂרִ֥ים וַחֲמִשָּׁ֖ה לַחֹ֑דֶשׁ נָשָׂ֡א אֱוִ֣יל מְרֹדַךְ֩ מֶ֨לֶךְ בָּבֶ֜ל בִּשְׁנַ֣ת מַלְכֻת֗וֹ אֶת־רֹאשׁ֙ יְהוֹיָכִ֣ין מֶֽלֶךְ־יְהוּדָ֔ה וַיֹּצֵ֥א אֹת֖וֹ מִבֵּ֥ית הַכְּלֻֽיא^ק: ³² וַיְדַבֵּ֥ר אִתּ֖וֹ טֹב֑וֹת וַיִּתֵּן֙ אֶת־כִּסְא֔וֹ מִמַּ֗עַל לְכִסֵּ֧א מְלָכִים^ק אֲשֶׁ֥ר אִתּ֖וֹ בְּבָבֶֽל: ³³ וְשִׁנָּ֕ה אֵ֖ת בִּגְדֵ֣י כִלְא֑וֹ וְאָכַ֨ל לֶ֧חֶם לְפָנָ֛יו תָּמִ֖יד כָּל־יְמֵ֥י חַיָּֽו: ³⁴ וַאֲרֻחָת֗וֹ אֲרֻחַת֩ תָּמִ֨יד נִתְּנָה־לּ֤וֹ מֵאֵ֤ת מֶֽלֶךְ־בָּבֶל֙ דְּבַר־י֣וֹם בְּיוֹמ֔וֹ עַד־י֖וֹם מוֹת֑וֹ כֹּ֖ל יְמֵ֥י חַיָּֽו:

The Book of

EZEKIEL

1 Now it came to pass in the thirtieth year, in the fourth *month,* on the fifth *day* of the month, as I *was* among the captives by the River Chebar, *that* the heavens were opened and I saw visions of God. ² On the fifth *day* of the month, which *was* in the fifth year of King Jehoiachin's captivity, ³ the word of the LORD came expressly to Ezekiel the priest, the son of Buzi, in the land of the Chaldeans by the River Chebar; and the hand of the LORD was upon him there.

⁴ Then I looked, and behold, a whirlwind was coming out of the north, a great cloud with raging fire engulfing itself; and brightness *was* all around it and radiating out of its midst like the color of amber, out of the midst of the fire. ⁵ Also from within it *came* the likeness of four living creatures. And this *was* their appearance: they had the likeness of a man. ⁶ Each one had four faces, and each one had four wings. ⁷ Their legs *were* straight, and the soles of their feet *were* like the soles of calves' feet. They sparkled like the color of burnished bronze. ⁸ The hands of a man *were* under their wings on their four sides; and each of the four had faces and wings. ⁹ Their wings touched one another. *The creatures* did not turn when they went, but each one went straight forward.

¹⁰ As for the likeness of their faces, *each* had the face of a man; each of the four had the face of a lion on the right side, each of the four had the face of an ox on the left side, and each of the four had the face of an eagle. ¹¹ Thus *were* their faces. Their wings stretched upward; two *wings* of each one touched one another, and two covered their bodies. ¹² And each one went straight forward; they went wherever the spirit wanted to go, and they did not turn when they went.

¹³ As for the likeness of the living creatures, their appearance *was* like burning coals of fire, like the appearance of torches going back and forth among the living creatures. The fire was bright, and out of the fire went lightning. ¹⁴ And the living creatures ran back and forth, in appearance like a flash of lightning.

¹⁵ Now as I looked at the living creatures, behold, a wheel *was* on the earth beside each living creature with its four faces. ¹⁶ The appearance of the wheels and their workings *was* like the color of beryl, and

א וַיְהִי | בִּשְׁלֹשִׁים שָׁנָה בָּרְבִיעִי בַּחֲמִשָּׁה לַחֹדֶשׁ וַאֲנִי בְתוֹךְ־הַגּוֹלָה עַל־נְהַר־כְּבָר נִפְתְּחוּ הַשָּׁמַיִם וָאֶרְאֶה מַרְאוֹת אֱלֹהִים: ² בַּחֲמִשָּׁה לַחֹדֶשׁ הִיא הַשָּׁנָה הַחֲמִישִׁית לְגָלוּת הַמֶּלֶךְ יוֹיָכִין: ³ הָיֹה הָיָה דְבַר־יְהֹוָה אֶל־יְחֶזְקֵאל בֶּן־בּוּזִי הַכֹּהֵן בְּאֶרֶץ כַּשְׂדִּים עַל־נְהַר־כְּבָר וַתְּהִי עָלָיו שָׁם יַד־יְהֹוָה:

⁴ וָאֵרֶא וְהִנֵּה רוּחַ סְעָרָה בָּאָה מִן־הַצָּפוֹן עָנָן גָּדוֹל וְאֵשׁ מִתְלַקַּחַת וְנֹגַהּ לוֹ סָבִיב וּמִתּוֹכָהּ כְּעֵין הַחַשְׁמַל מִתּוֹךְ הָאֵשׁ: ⁵ וּמִתּוֹכָהּ דְּמוּת אַרְבַּע חַיּוֹת וְזֶה מַרְאֵיהֶן דְּמוּת אָדָם לָהֵנָּה: ⁶ וְאַרְבָּעָה פָנִים לְאֶחָת וְאַרְבַּע כְּנָפַיִם לְאַחַת לָהֶם: ⁷ וְרַגְלֵיהֶם רֶגֶל יְשָׁרָה וְכַף רַגְלֵיהֶם כְּכַף רֶגֶל עֵגֶל וְנֹצְצִים כְּעֵין נְחֹשֶׁת קָלָל: ⁸ וְיָדוֹ אָדָם מִתַּחַת כַּנְפֵיהֶם עַל אַרְבַּעַת רִבְעֵיהֶם וּפְנֵיהֶם וְכַנְפֵיהֶם לְאַרְבַּעְתָּם: ⁹ חֹבְרֹת אִשָּׁה אֶל־אֲחוֹתָהּ כַּנְפֵיהֶם לֹא־יִסַּבּוּ בְלֶכְתָּן אִישׁ אֶל־עֵבֶר פָּנָיו יֵלֵכוּ: ¹⁰ וּדְמוּת פְּנֵיהֶם פְּנֵי אָדָם וּפְנֵי אַרְיֵה אֶל־הַיָּמִין לְאַרְבַּעְתָּם וּפְנֵי־שׁוֹר מֵהַשְּׂמֹאול לְאַרְבַּעְתָּן וּפְנֵי־נֶשֶׁר לְאַרְבַּעְתָּן: ¹¹ וּפְנֵיהֶם וְכַנְפֵיהֶם פְּרֻדוֹת מִלְמָעְלָה לְאִישׁ שְׁתַּיִם חֹבְרוֹת אִישׁ וּשְׁתַּיִם מְכַסּוֹת אֵת גְּוִיֹתֵיהֶנָה: ¹² וְאִישׁ אֶל־עֵבֶר פָּנָיו יֵלֵכוּ אֶל אֲשֶׁר יִהְיֶה־שָּׁמָּה הָרוּחַ לָלֶכֶת יֵלֵכוּ לֹא יִסַּבּוּ בְּלֶכְתָּן: ¹³ וּדְמוּת הַחַיּוֹת מַרְאֵיהֶם כְּגַחֲלֵי־אֵשׁ בֹּעֲרוֹת כְּמַרְאֵה הַלַּפִּדִים הִיא מִתְהַלֶּכֶת בֵּין הַחַיּוֹת וְנֹגַהּ לָאֵשׁ וּמִן־הָאֵשׁ יוֹצֵא בָרָק: ¹⁴ וְהַחַיּוֹת רָצוֹא וָשׁוֹב כְּמַרְאֵה הַבָּזָק: ¹⁵ וָאֵרֶא הַחַיּוֹת וְהִנֵּה אוֹפַן אֶחָד בָּאָרֶץ אֵצֶל הַחַיּוֹת לְאַרְבַּעַת פָּנָיו: ¹⁶ מַרְאֵה הָאוֹפַנִּים וּמַעֲשֵׂיהֶם כְּעֵין תַּרְשִׁישׁ וּדְמוּת אֶחָד לְאַרְבַּעְתָּן וּמַרְאֵיהֶם וּמַעֲשֵׂיהֶם כַּאֲשֶׁר יִהְיֶה הָאוֹפַן

all four had the same likeness. The appearance of
their workings *was,* as it were, a wheel in the middle
of a wheel. 17 When they moved, they went toward
any one of four directions; they did not turn aside
when they went. 18 As for their rims, they were so
high they were awesome; and their rims *were* full of
eyes, all around the four of them. 19 When the living
creatures went, the wheels went beside them; and
when the living creatures were lifted up from the
earth, the wheels were lifted up. 20 Wherever the
spirit wanted to go, they went, *because* there the
spirit went; and the wheels were lifted together with
them, for the spirit of the living creatures *was* in the
wheels. 21 When those went, *these* went; when those
stood, *these* stood; and when those were lifted up
from the earth, the wheels were lifted up together
with them, for the spirit of the living creatures *was*
in the wheels.

22 The likeness of the firmament above the heads
of the living creatures *was* like the color of an
awesome crystal, stretched out over their heads.
23 And under the firmament their wings *spread out*
straight, one toward another. Each one had two
which covered one side, and each one had two
which covered the other side of the body. 24 When
they went, I heard the noise of their wings, like the
noise of many waters, like the voice of the
Almighty, a tumult like the noise of an army; and
when they stood still, they let down their wings. 25 A
voice came from above the firmament that *was* over
their heads; whenever they stood, they let down
their wings.

26 And above the firmament over their heads *was*
the likeness of a throne, in appearance like a
sapphire stone; on the likeness of the throne *was* a
likeness with the appearance of a man high above it.
27 Also from the appearance of His waist and
upward I saw, as it were, the color of amber with
the appearance of fire all around within it; and from
the appearance of His waist and downward I saw,
as it were, the appearance of fire with brightness all
around. 28 Like the appearance of a rainbow in a
cloud on a rainy day, so *was* the appearance of the
brightness all around it. This *was* the appearance of
the likeness of the glory of the LORD.

So when I saw *it,* I fell on my face, and I heard a
voice of One speaking.

2 And He said to me, "Son of man, stand on your
feet, and I will speak to you." 2 Then the Spirit
entered me when He spoke to me, and set me on my
feet; and I heard Him who spoke to me. 3 And He
said to me: "Son of man, I am sending you to the
children of Israel, to a rebellious nation that has

בְּתוֹךְ הָאוֹפָן: 17 עַל־אַרְבַּעַת רִבְעֵיהֶן בְּלֶכְתָּם יֵלֵכוּ
לֹא יִסַּבּוּ בְּלֶכְתָּן: 18 וְגַבֵּיהֶן וְגֹבַהּ לָהֶם וְיִרְאָה לָהֶם
וְגַבֹּתָם מְלֵאֹת עֵינַיִם סָבִיב לְאַרְבַּעְתָּן: 19 וּבְלֶכֶת
הַחַיּוֹת יֵלְכוּ הָאוֹפַנִּים אֶצְלָם וּבְהִנָּשֵׂא הַחַיּוֹת מֵעַל
הָאָרֶץ יִנָּשְׂאוּ הָאוֹפַנִּים: 20 עַל אֲשֶׁר יִהְיֶה־שָּׁם
הָרוּחַ לָלֶכֶת יֵלֵכוּ שָׁמָּה הָרוּחַ לָלֶכֶת וְהָאוֹפַנִּים
יִנָּשְׂאוּ לְעֻמָּתָם כִּי רוּחַ הַחַיָּה בָּאוֹפַנִּים: 21 בְּלֶכְתָּם
יֵלֵכוּ וּבְעָמְדָם יַעֲמֹדוּ וּבְהִנָּשְׂאָם מֵעַל הָאָרֶץ
יִנָּשְׂאוּ הָאוֹפַנִּים לְעֻמָּתָם כִּי רוּחַ הַחַיָּה בָּאוֹפַנִּים:

22 וּדְמוּת עַל־רָאשֵׁי הַחַיָּה רָקִיעַ כְּעֵין הַקֶּרַח
הַנּוֹרָא נָטוּי עַל־רָאשֵׁיהֶם מִלְמָעְלָה: 23 וְתַחַת
הָרָקִיעַ כַּנְפֵיהֶם יְשָׁרוֹת אִשָּׁה אֶל־אֲחוֹתָהּ לְאִישׁ
שְׁתַּיִם מְכַסּוֹת לָהֵנָּה וּלְאִישׁ שְׁתַּיִם מְכַסּוֹת לָהֵנָּה
אֵת גְּוִיֹּתֵיהֶם: 24 וָאֶשְׁמַע אֶת־קוֹל כַּנְפֵיהֶם כְּקוֹל
מַיִם רַבִּים כְּקוֹל־שַׁדַּי בְּלֶכְתָּם קוֹל הֲמֻלָּה כְּקוֹל
מַחֲנֶה בְּעָמְדָם תְּרַפֶּינָה כַנְפֵיהֶן: 25 וַיְהִי־קוֹל מֵעַל
לָרָקִיעַ אֲשֶׁר עַל־רֹאשָׁם בְּעָמְדָם תְּרַפֶּינָה כַנְפֵיהֶן:

26 וּמִמַּעַל לָרָקִיעַ אֲשֶׁר עַל־רֹאשָׁם כְּמַרְאֵה אֶבֶן
סַפִּיר דְּמוּת כִּסֵּא וְעַל דְּמוּת הַכִּסֵּא דְּמוּת
כְּמַרְאֵה אָדָם עָלָיו מִלְמָעְלָה: 27 וָאֵרֶא | כְּעֵין
חַשְׁמַל כְּמַרְאֵה־אֵשׁ בֵּית־לָהּ סָבִיב מִמַּרְאֵה מָתְנָיו
וּלְמָעְלָה וּמִמַּרְאֵה מָתְנָיו וּלְמַטָּה רָאִיתִי כְּמַרְאֵה־
אֵשׁ וְנֹגַהּ לוֹ סָבִיב: 28 כְּמַרְאֵה הַקֶּשֶׁת אֲשֶׁר יִהְיֶה
בֶעָנָן בְּיוֹם הַגֶּשֶׁם כֵּן מַרְאֵה הַנֹּגַהּ סָבִיב הוּא
מַרְאֵה דְּמוּת כְּבוֹד־יהוה וָאֶרְאֶה וָאֶפֹּל עַל־פָּנַי
וָאֶשְׁמַע קוֹל מְדַבֵּר: ס

ב וַיֹּאמֶר אֵלַי בֶּן־אָדָם עֲמֹד עַל־רַגְלֶיךָ וַאֲדַבֵּר
אֹתָךְ: 2 וַתָּבֹא בִי רוּחַ כַּאֲשֶׁר דִּבֶּר אֵלַי וַתַּעֲמִדֵנִי
עַל־רַגְלָי וָאֶשְׁמַע אֵת מִדַּבֵּר אֵלָי: פ
3 וַיֹּאמֶר אֵלַי בֶּן־אָדָם שׁוֹלֵחַ אֲנִי אוֹתְךָ אֶל־בְּנֵי

rebelled against Me; they and their fathers have transgressed against Me to this very day. ⁴ For *they are* impudent and stubborn children. I am sending you to them, and you shall say to them, 'Thus says the Lord GOD.' ⁵ As for them, whether they hear or whether they refuse—for they *are* a rebellious house—yet they will know that a prophet has been among them.

⁶ "And you, son of man, do not be afraid of them nor be afraid of their words, though briers and thorns *are* with you and you dwell among scorpions; do not be afraid of their words or dismayed by their looks, though they *are* a rebellious house. ⁷ You shall speak My words to them, whether they hear or whether they refuse, for they *are* rebellious. ⁸ But you, son of man, hear what I say to you. Do not be rebellious like that rebellious house; open your mouth and eat what I give you."

⁹ Now when I looked, there was a hand stretched out to me; and behold, a scroll of a book *was* in it. ¹⁰ Then He spread it before me; and *there was* writing on the inside and on the outside, and written on it *were* lamentations and mourning and woe.

3 Moreover He said to me, "Son of man, eat what you find; eat this scroll, and go, speak to the house of Israel." ² So I opened my mouth, and He caused me to eat that scroll.

³ And He said to me, "Son of man, feed your belly, and fill your stomach with this scroll that I give you." So I ate, and it was in my mouth like honey in sweetness.

⁴ Then He said to me: "Son of man, go to the house of Israel and speak with My words to them. ⁵ For you *are* not sent to a people of unfamiliar speech and of hard language, *but* to the house of Israel, ⁶ not to many people of unfamiliar speech and of hard language, whose words you cannot understand. Surely, had I sent you to them, they would have listened to you. ⁷ But the house of Israel will not listen to you, because they will not listen to Me; for all the house of Israel *are* impudent and hard-hearted. ⁸ Behold, I have made your face strong against their faces, and your forehead strong against their foreheads. ⁹ Like adamant stone, harder than flint, I have made your forehead; do not be afraid of them, nor be dismayed at their looks, though they *are* a rebellious house."

¹⁰ Moreover He said to me: "Son of man, receive into your heart all My words that I speak to you, and hear with your ears. ¹¹ And go, get to the

יִשְׂרָאֵל אֶל־גּוֹיִם הַמּוֹרְדִים אֲשֶׁר מָרְדוּ־בִי הֵמָּה וַאֲבוֹתָם פָּשְׁעוּ בִי עַד־עֶצֶם הַיּוֹם הַזֶּה: 4 וְהַבָּנִים קְשֵׁי פָנִים וְחִזְקֵי־לֵב אֲנִי שׁוֹלֵחַ אוֹתְךָ אֲלֵיהֶם וְאָמַרְתָּ אֲלֵיהֶם כֹּה אָמַר אֲדֹנָי יְהוִֹה: 5 וְהֵמָּה אִם־יִשְׁמְעוּ וְאִם־יֶחְדָּלוּ כִּי בֵּית מְרִי הֵמָּה וְיָדְעוּ כִּי נָבִיא הָיָה בְתוֹכָם:
פ

6 וְאַתָּה בֶן־אָדָם אַל־תִּירָא מֵהֶם וּמִדִּבְרֵיהֶם אַל־תִּירָא כִּי סָרָבִים וְסַלּוֹנִים אוֹתָךְ וְאֶל־עַקְרַבִּים אַתָּה יוֹשֵׁב מִדִּבְרֵיהֶם אַל־תִּירָא וּמִפְּנֵיהֶם אַל־תֵּחָת כִּי בֵּית מְרִי הֵמָּה: 7 וְדִבַּרְתָּ אֶת־דְּבָרַי אֲלֵיהֶם אִם־יִשְׁמְעוּ וְאִם־יֶחְדָּלוּ כִּי מְרִי הֵמָּה: פ

8 וְאַתָּה בֶן־אָדָם שְׁמַע אֵת אֲשֶׁר־אֲנִי מְדַבֵּר אֵלֶיךָ אַל־תְּהִי־מֶרִי כְּבֵית הַמֶּרִי פְּצֵה פִיךָ וֶאֱכֹל אֵת אֲשֶׁר־אֲנִי נֹתֵן אֵלֶיךָ: 9 וָאֶרְאֶה וְהִנֵּה־יָד שְׁלוּחָה אֵלָי וְהִנֵּה־בוֹ מְגִלַּת־סֵפֶר: 10 וַיִּפְרֹשׂ אוֹתָהּ לְפָנַי וְהִיא כְתוּבָה פָּנִים וְאָחוֹר וְכָתוּב אֵלֶיהָ קִנִים וָהֶגֶה וָהִי: ס

ג וַיֹּאמֶר אֵלַי בֶּן־אָדָם אֵת אֲשֶׁר־תִּמְצָא אֱכוֹל אֱכוֹל אֶת־הַמְּגִלָּה הַזֹּאת וְלֵךְ דַּבֵּר אֶל־בֵּית יִשְׂרָאֵל: 2 וָאֶפְתַּח אֶת־פִּי וַיַּאֲכִלֵנִי אֵת הַמְּגִלָּה הַזֹּאת: 3 וַיֹּאמֶר אֵלַי בֶּן־אָדָם בִּטְנְךָ תַאֲכֵל וּמֵעֶיךָ תְמַלֵּא אֵת הַמְּגִלָּה הַזֹּאת אֲשֶׁר אֲנִי נֹתֵן אֵלֶיךָ וָאֹכְלָה וַתְּהִי בְּפִי כִּדְבַשׁ לְמָתוֹק: פ

4 וַיֹּאמֶר אֵלַי בֶּן־אָדָם לֶךְ־בֹּא אֶל־בֵּית יִשְׂרָאֵל וְדִבַּרְתָּ בִדְבָרַי אֲלֵיהֶם: 5 כִּי לֹא אֶל־עַם עִמְקֵי שָׂפָה וְכִבְדֵי לָשׁוֹן אַתָּה שָׁלוּחַ אֶל־בֵּית יִשְׂרָאֵל: 6 לֹא ׀ אֶל־עַמִּים רַבִּים עִמְקֵי שָׂפָה וְכִבְדֵי לָשׁוֹן אֲשֶׁר לֹא־תִשְׁמַע דִּבְרֵיהֶם אִם־לֹא אֲלֵיהֶם שְׁלַחְתִּיךָ הֵמָּה יִשְׁמְעוּ אֵלֶיךָ: 7 וּבֵית יִשְׂרָאֵל לֹא יֹאבוּ לִשְׁמֹעַ אֵלֶיךָ כִּי־אֵינָם אֹבִים לִשְׁמֹעַ אֵלָי כִּי כָּל־בֵּית יִשְׂרָאֵל חִזְקֵי־מֵצַח וּקְשֵׁי־לֵב הֵמָּה: 8 הִנֵּה נָתַתִּי אֶת־פָּנֶיךָ חֲזָקִים לְעֻמַּת פְּנֵיהֶם וְאֶת־מִצְחֲךָ חָזָק לְעֻמַּת מִצְחָם: 9 כְּשָׁמִיר חָזָק מִצֹּר נָתַתִּי מִצְחֶךָ לֹא־תִירָא אוֹתָם וְלֹא־תֵחַת מִפְּנֵיהֶם כִּי בֵּית־מְרִי הֵמָּה: פ

10 וַיֹּאמֶר אֵלַי בֶּן־אָדָם אֶת־כָּל־דְּבָרַי אֲשֶׁר אֲדַבֵּר

captives, to the children of your people, and speak to them and tell them, 'Thus says the Lord GOD,' whether they hear, or whether they refuse."

12 Then the Spirit lifted me up, and I heard behind me a great thunderous voice: "Blessed *is* the glory of the LORD from His place!" 13 *I* also *heard* the noise of the wings of the living creatures that touched one another, and the noise of the wheels beside them, and a great thunderous noise. 14 So the Spirit lifted me up and took me away, and I went in bitterness, in the heat of my spirit; but the hand of the LORD was strong upon me. 15 Then I came to the captives at Tel Abib, who dwelt by the River Chebar; and I sat where they sat, and remained there astonished among them seven days.

16 Now it came to pass at the end of seven days that the word of the LORD came to me, saying, 17 "Son of man, I have made you a watchman for the house of Israel; therefore hear a word from My mouth, and give them warning from Me: 18 When I say to the wicked, 'You shall surely die,' and you give him no warning, nor speak to warn the wicked from his wicked way, to save his life, that same wicked *man* shall die in his iniquity; but his blood I will require at your hand. 19 Yet, if you warn the wicked, and he does not turn from his wickedness, nor from his wicked way, he shall die in his iniquity; but you have delivered your soul.

20 "Again, when a righteous *man* turns from his righteousness and commits iniquity, and I lay a stumbling block before him, he shall die; because you did not give him warning, he shall die in his sin, and his righteousness which he has done shall not be remembered; but his blood I will require at your hand. 21 Nevertheless if you warn the righteous *man* that the righteous should not sin, and he does not sin, he shall surely live because he took warning; also you will have delivered your soul."

22 Then the hand of the LORD was upon me there, and He said to me, "Arise, go out into the plain, and there I shall talk with you."

23 So I arose and went out into the plain, and behold, the glory of the LORD stood there, like the glory which I saw by the River Chebar; and I fell on my face. 24 Then the Spirit entered me and set me on my feet, and spoke with me and said to me: "Go, shut yourself inside your house. 25 And you, O son of man, surely they will put ropes on you and bind you with them, so that you cannot go out among them. 26 I will make your tongue cling to the roof of your mouth, so that you shall be mute and not be one to rebuke them, for they *are* a rebellious house. 27 But when I speak with you, I will open your mouth, and you shall say to them, 'Thus says the

אֵלֶ֔יךָ קַ֣ח בִּלְבָבְךָ֔ וּבְאָזְנֶ֖יךָ שְׁמָ֑ע: 11 וְלֵ֨ךְ בֹּ֜א אֶל־הַגּוֹלָ֗ה אֶל־בְּנֵ֤י עַמֶּ֙ךָ֙ וְדִבַּרְתָּ֤ אֲלֵיהֶם֙ וְאָמַרְתָּ֣ אֲלֵיהֶ֔ם כֹּ֤ה אָמַר֙ אֲדֹנָ֣י יְהֹוִ֔ה אִֽם־יִשְׁמְע֖וּ וְאִם־ יֶחְדָּֽלוּ: 12 וַתִּשָּׂאֵ֣נִי ר֔וּחַ וָאֶשְׁמַ֣ע אַחֲרַ֔י ק֖וֹל רַ֣עַשׁ גָּד֑וֹל בָּר֥וּךְ כְּבוֹד־יְהֹוָ֖ה מִמְּקוֹמֽוֹ: 13 וְק֣וֹל | כַּנְפֵ֣י הַחַיּ֗וֹת מַשִּׁיק֙וֹת֙ אִשָּׁ֣ה אֶל־אֲחוֹתָ֔הּ וְק֥וֹל הָאוֹפַנִּ֖ים לְעֻמָּתָ֑ם וְק֖וֹל רַ֥עַשׁ גָּדֽוֹל: 14 וְר֙וּחַ֙ נְשָׂאַ֣תְנִי וַתִּקָּחֵ֑נִי וָאֵלֵ֥ךְ מַ֖ר בַּחֲמַ֣ת רוּחִ֑י וְיַד־יְהֹוָ֖ה עָלַ֥י חָזָֽקָה: 15 וָאָב֨וֹא אֶל־הַגּוֹלָ֜ה תֵּ֣ל אָבִ֗יב הַיֹּשְׁבִים֙ אֶל־נְהַר־ כְּבָ֔ר וָאֵשֵׁר הֵ֣מָּה יֽוֹשְׁבִ֣ים שָׁ֔ם וָאֵשֵׁ֥ב שָׁ֛ם שִׁבְעַ֥ת יָמִ֖ים מַשְׁמִ֥ים בְּתוֹכָֽם: 16 וַיְהִ֕י מִקְצֵ֖ה שִׁבְעַ֣ת יָמִ֑ים פ וַיְהִ֥י דְבַר־יְהֹוָ֖ה אֵלַ֥י לֵאמֹֽר: 17 בֶּן־אָדָ֕ם צֹפֶ֥ה נְתַתִּ֖יךָ לְבֵ֣ית יִשְׂרָאֵ֑ל וְשָׁמַעְתָּ֤ מִפִּי֙ דָּבָ֔ר וְהִזְהַרְתָּ֥ אוֹתָ֖ם מִמֶּֽנִּי: 18 בְּאׇמְרִ֤י לָֽרָשָׁע֙ מ֣וֹת תָּמ֔וּת וְלֹ֣א הִזְהַרְתּ֗וֹ וְלֹ֤א דִבַּ֙רְתָּ֙ לְהַזְהִ֤יר רָשָׁע֙ מִדַּרְכּ֣וֹ הָרְשָׁעָ֔ה לְחַיֹּת֑וֹ ה֤וּא רָשָׁע֙ בַּעֲוֺנ֣וֹ יָמ֔וּת וְדָמ֖וֹ מִיָּדְךָ֥ אֲבַקֵּֽשׁ: 19 וְאַתָּה֙ כִּֽי־הִזְהַ֣רְתָּ רָשָׁ֔ע וְלֹא־ שָׁ֤ב מֵֽרִשְׁעוֹ֙ וּמִדַּרְכּ֣וֹ הָרְשָׁעָ֔ה ה֛וּא בַּעֲוֺנ֖וֹ יָמ֑וּת וְאַתָּ֖ה אֶת־נַפְשְׁךָ֥ הִצַּֽלְתָּ: ס 20 וּבְשׁ֣וּב צַדִּ֤יק מִצִּדְקוֹ֙ וְעָ֣שָׂה עָ֔וֶל וְנָתַתִּ֥י מִכְשׁ֖וֹל לְפָנָ֑יו ה֣וּא יָמ֔וּת כִּ֣י לֹ֤א הִזְהַרְתּוֹ֙ בְּחַטָּאת֣וֹ יָמ֔וּת וְלֹ֣א תִזָּכַ֗רְןָ צִדְקֹתָו֙ אֲשֶׁ֣ר עָשָׂ֔ה וְדָמ֖וֹ מִיָּדְךָ֥ אֲבַקֵּֽשׁ: 21 וְאַתָּ֞ה כִּ֧י הִזְהַרְתּ֣וֹ צַדִּ֗יק לְבִלְתִּ֤י חֲטֹא֙ צַדִּ֔יק וְה֖וּא לֹא־חָטָ֑א חָי֤וֹ יִֽחְיֶה֙ כִּ֣י נִזְהָ֔ר וְאַתָּ֖ה אֶת־ נַפְשְׁךָ֥ הִצַּֽלְתָּ: ס 22 וַתְּהִ֥י עָלַ֛י שָׁ֖ם יַד־ יְהֹוָ֑ה וַיֹּ֣אמֶר אֵלַ֗י ק֥וּם צֵא֙ אֶל־הַבִּקְעָ֔ה וְשָׁ֖ם אֲדַבֵּ֥ר אוֹתָֽךְ: 23 וָאָק֜וּם וָאֵצֵ֣א אֶל־הַבִּקְעָ֗ה וְהִנֵּה־שָׁ֤ם כְּבוֹד־יְהֹוָה֙ עֹמֵ֔ד כַּכָּב֕וֹד אֲשֶׁ֥ר רָאִ֖יתִי עַל־נְהַר־ כְּבָ֑ר וָאֶפֹּ֖ל עַל־פָּנָֽי: 24 וַתָּבֹא־בִ֣י ר֗וּחַ וַתַּֽעֲמִדֵ֙נִי֙ עַל־רַגְלָ֔י וַיְדַבֵּ֤ר אֹתִי֙ וַיֹּ֣אמֶר אֵלַ֔י בֹּ֥א הִסָּגֵ֖ר בְּת֥וֹךְ בֵּיתֶֽךָ: 25 וְאַתָּ֣ה בֶן־אָדָ֗ם הִנֵּ֨ה נָתְנ֤וּ עָלֶ֙יךָ֙ עֲבוֹתִ֔ים וַאֲסָר֖וּךָ בָּהֶ֑ם וְלֹ֥א תֵצֵ֖א בְּתוֹכָֽם: 26 וּלְשֽׁוֹנְךָ֙ אַדְבִּ֣יק אֶל־חִכֶּ֔ךָ וְנֶ֣אֱלַ֔מְתָּ וְלֹא־תִֽהְיֶ֥ה לָהֶ֖ם לְאִ֣ישׁ מוֹכִ֑יחַ כִּ֛י בֵּ֥ית מְרִ֖י הֵֽמָּה: 27 וּֽבְדַבְּרִ֤י אֽוֹתְךָ֙ אֶפְתַּ֣ח אֶת־פִּ֔יךָ וְאָמַרְתָּ֣ אֲלֵיהֶ֔ם כֹּ֥ה אָמַ֖ר אֲדֹנָ֥י יְהֹוִ֑ה

Lord GOD.' He who hears, let him hear; and he who refuses, let him refuse; for they *are* a rebellious house.

4 "You also, son of man, take a clay tablet and lay it before you, and portray on it a city, Jerusalem. 2 Lay siege against it, build a siege wall against it, and heap up a mound against it; set camps against it also, and place battering rams against it all around. 3 Moreover take for yourself an iron plate, and set it *as* an iron wall between you and the city. Set your face against it, and it shall be besieged, and you shall lay siege against it. This *will be* a sign to the house of Israel.

4 "Lie also on your left side, and lay the iniquity of the house of Israel upon it. *According* to the number of the days that you lie on it, you shall bear their iniquity. 5 For I have laid on you the years of their iniquity, according to the number of the days, three hundred and ninety days; so you shall bear the iniquity of the house of Israel. 6 And when you have completed them, lie again on your right side; then you shall bear the iniquity of the house of Judah forty days. I have laid on you a day for each year.

7 "Therefore you shall set your face toward the siege of Jerusalem; your arm *shall be* uncovered, and you shall prophesy against it. 8 And surely I will restrain you so that you cannot turn from one side to another till you have ended the days of your siege.

9 "Also take for yourself wheat, barley, beans, lentils, millet, and spelt; put them into one vessel, and make bread of them for yourself. *During* the number of days that you lie on your side, three hundred and ninety days, you shall eat it. 10 And your food which you eat *shall be* by weight, twenty shekels a day; from time to time you shall eat it. 11 You shall also drink water by measure, one-sixth of a hin; from time to time you shall drink. 12 And you shall eat it *as* barley cakes; and bake it using fuel of human waste in their sight."

13 Then the LORD said, "So shall the children of Israel eat their defiled bread among the Gentiles, where I will drive them."

14 So I said, "Ah, Lord GOD! Indeed I have never defiled myself from my youth till now; I have never eaten what died of itself or was torn by beasts, nor has abominable flesh ever come into my mouth."

15 Then He said to me, "See, I am giving you cow dung instead of human waste, and you shall prepare your bread over it."

16 Moreover He said to me, "Son of man, surely I will cut off the supply of bread in Jerusalem; they shall eat bread by weight and with anxiety, and

הַשֹּׁמֵעַ ׀ יִשְׁמָע ׀ וְהֶחָדֵל ׀ יֶחְדָּל כִּי בֵּית מְרִי
הֵמָּה: ס

ד וְאַתָּה בֶן־אָדָם קַח־לְךָ לְבֵנָה וְנָתַתָּה אוֹתָהּ
לְפָנֶיךָ וְחַקּוֹתָ עָלֶיהָ עִיר אֶת־יְרוּשָׁלִָם: 2 וְנָתַתָּה
עָלֶיהָ מָצוֹר וּבָנִיתָ עָלֶיהָ דָּיֵק וְשָׁפַכְתָּ עָלֶיהָ
סֹלְלָה וְנָתַתָּה עָלֶיהָ מַחֲנוֹת וְשִׂים־עָלֶיהָ כָּרִים
סָבִיב: 3 וְאַתָּה קַח־לְךָ מַחֲבַת בַּרְזֶל וְנָתַתָּה
אוֹתָהּ קִיר בַּרְזֶל בֵּינְךָ וּבֵין הָעִיר וַהֲכִינֹתָה אֶת־
פָּנֶיךָ אֵלֶיהָ וְהָיְתָה בַמָּצוֹר וְצַרְתָּ עָלֶיהָ אוֹת
הִיא לְבֵית יִשְׂרָאֵל: ס 4 וְאַתָּה שְׁכַב עַל־
צִדְּךָ הַשְּׂמָאלִי וְשַׂמְתָּ אֶת־עֲוֺן בֵּית־יִשְׂרָאֵל עָלָיו
מִסְפַּר הַיָּמִים אֲשֶׁר תִּשְׁכַּב עָלָיו תִּשָּׂא אֶת־
עֲוֺנָם: 5 וַאֲנִי נָתַתִּי לְךָ אֶת־שְׁנֵי עֲוֺנָם לְמִסְפַּר
יָמִים שְׁלֹשׁ־מֵאוֹת וְתִשְׁעִים יוֹם וְנָשָׂאתָ עֲוֺן
בֵּית־יִשְׂרָאֵל: 6 וְכִלִּיתָ אֶת־אֵלֶּה וְשָׁכַבְתָּ עַל־
צִדְּךָ הַיְמִינִי שֵׁנִית וְנָשָׂאתָ אֶת־עֲוֺן בֵּית־יְהוּדָה
אַרְבָּעִים יוֹם יוֹם לַשָּׁנָה יוֹם לַשָּׁנָה נְתַתִּיו לָךְ:
7 וְאֶל־מְצוֹר יְרוּשָׁלִַם תָּכִין פָּנֶיךָ וּזְרֹעֲךָ חֲשׂוּפָה
וְנִבֵּאתָ עָלֶיהָ: 8 וְהִנֵּה נָתַתִּי עָלֶיךָ עֲבוֹתִים וְלֹא־
תֵהָפֵךְ מִצִּדְּךָ אֶל־צִדֶּךָ עַד־כַּלּוֹתְךָ יְמֵי מְצוּרֶךָ:
9 וְאַתָּה קַח־לְךָ חִטִּין וּשְׂעֹרִים וּפוֹל וַעֲדָשִׁים
וְדֹחַן וְכֻסְּמִים וְנָתַתָּה אוֹתָם בִּכְלִי אֶחָד וְעָשִׂיתָ
אוֹתָם לְךָ לְלֶחֶם מִסְפַּר הַיָּמִים אֲשֶׁר־אַתָּה ׀
שׁוֹכֵב עַל־צִדְּךָ שְׁלֹשׁ־מֵאוֹת וְתִשְׁעִים יוֹם תֹּאכֲלֶנּוּ:
10 וּמַאֲכָלְךָ אֲשֶׁר תֹּאכֲלֶנּוּ בְּמִשְׁקוֹל עֶשְׂרִים שֶׁקֶל
לַיּוֹם מֵעֵת עַד־עֵת תֹּאכֲלֶנּוּ: 11 וּמַיִם בִּמְשׂוּרָה
תִשְׁתֶּה שִׁשִּׁית הַהִין מֵעֵת עַד־עֵת תִּשְׁתֶּה:
12 וְעֻגַת שְׂעֹרִים תֹּאכֲלֶנָּה וְהִיא בְּגֶלְלֵי צֵאַת
הָאָדָם תְּעֻגֶנָה לְעֵינֵיהֶם: ס 13 וַיֹּאמֶר
יְהוָה כָּכָה יֹאכְלוּ בְנֵי־יִשְׂרָאֵל אֶת־לַחְמָם טָמֵא
בַּגּוֹיִם אֲשֶׁר אַדִּיחֵם שָׁם: 14 וָאֹמַר אֲהָהּ אֲדֹנָי
יְהוִה הִנֵּה נַפְשִׁי לֹא מְטֻמָּאָה וּנְבֵלָה וּטְרֵפָה
לֹא־אָכַלְתִּי מִנְּעוּרַי וְעַד־עַתָּה וְלֹא־בָא בְּפִי בְּשַׂר
פִּגּוּל: ס 15 וַיֹּאמֶר אֵלַי רְאֵה נָתַתִּי לְךָ
אֶת־צפועי הַבָּקָר תַּחַת גֶּלְלֵי הָאָדָם וְעָשִׂיתָ
אֶת־לַחְמְךָ עֲלֵיהֶם: ס 16 וַיֹּאמֶר אֵלַי בֶּן־
אָדָם הִנְנִי שֹׁבֵר מַטֵּה־לֶחֶם בִּירוּשָׁלִַם וְאָכְלוּ־לֶחֶם

ד 6 הַיְמָנִי   15 צְפִיעֵי

shall drink water by measure and with dread, 17 that they may lack bread and water, and be dismayed with one another, and waste away because of their iniquity.

5 "And you, son of man, take a sharp sword, take it as a barber's razor, and pass *it* over your head and your beard; then take scales to weigh and divide the hair. 2 You shall burn with fire one-third in the midst of the city, when the days of the siege are finished; then you shall take one-third and strike around *it* with the sword, and one-third you shall scatter in the wind: I will draw out a sword after them. 3 You shall also take a small number of them and bind them in the edge of your *garment.* 4 Then take some of them again and throw them into the midst of the fire, and burn them in the fire. From there a fire will go out into all the house of Israel.

5 "Thus says the Lord GOD: 'This *is* Jerusalem; I have set her in the midst of the nations and the countries all around her. 6 She has rebelled against My judgments by doing wickedness more than the nations, and against My statutes more than the countries that *are* all around her; for they have refused My judgments, and they have not walked in My statutes.' 7 Therefore thus says the Lord GOD: 'Because you have multiplied *disobedience* more than the nations that *are* all around you, have not walked in My statutes nor kept My judgments, nor even done according to the judgments of the nations that *are* all around you'— 8 therefore thus says the Lord GOD: 'Indeed I, even I, *am* against you and will execute judgments in your midst in the sight of the nations. 9 And I will do among you what I have never done, and the like of which I will never do again, because of all your abominations. 10 Therefore fathers shall eat *their* sons in your midst, and sons shall eat their fathers; and I will execute judgments among you, and all of you who remain I will scatter to all the winds.

11 'Therefore, *as* I live,' says the Lord GOD, 'surely, because you have defiled My sanctuary with all your detestable things and with all your abominations, therefore I will also diminish *you;* My eye will not spare, nor will I have any pity. 12 One-third of you shall die of the pestilence, and be consumed with famine in your midst; and one-third shall fall by the sword all around you; and I will scatter another third to all the winds, and I will draw out a sword after them.

13 'Thus shall My anger be spent, and I will cause My fury to rest upon them, and I will be avenged; and they shall know that I, the LORD, have spoken

בְּמִשְׁקָל וּבְדְאָגָה וּמַיִם בִּמְשׂוּרָה וּבְשִׁמָּמוֹן יִשְׁתּוּ: 17 לְמַעַן יַחְסְרוּ לֶחֶם וָמָיִם וְנָשַׁמּוּ אִישׁ וְאָחִיו וְנָמַקּוּ בַּעֲוֹנָם: פ

ה וְאַתָּה בֶן־אָדָם קַח־לְךָ ׀ חֶרֶב חַדָּה תַּעַר הַגַּלָּבִים תִּקָּחֶנָּה לָּךְ וְהַעֲבַרְתָּ עַל־רֹאשְׁךָ וְעַל־זְקָנֶךָ וְלָקַחְתָּ לְךָ מֹאזְנֵי מִשְׁקָל וְחִלַּקְתָּם: 2 שְׁלִשִׁית בָּאוּר תַּבְעִיר בְּתוֹךְ הָעִיר כִּמְלֹאת יְמֵי הַמָּצוֹר וְלָקַחְתָּ אֶת־הַשְּׁלִשִׁית תַּכֶּה בַחֶרֶב סְבִיבוֹתֶיהָ וְהַשְּׁלִשִׁית תִּזְרֶה לָרוּחַ וְחֶרֶב אָרִיק אַחֲרֵיהֶם: 3 וְלָקַחְתָּ מִשָּׁם מְעַט בְּמִסְפָּר וְצַרְתָּ אוֹתָם בִּכְנָפֶיךָ: 4 וּמֵהֶם עוֹד תִּקָּח וְהִשְׁלַכְתָּ אוֹתָם אֶל־תּוֹךְ הָאֵשׁ וְשָׂרַפְתָּ אֹתָם בָּאֵשׁ מִמֶּנּוּ תֵצֵא־אֵשׁ אֶל־כָּל־בֵּית יִשְׂרָאֵל: פ

5 כֹּה אָמַר אֲדֹנָי יְהוִֹה זֹאת יְרוּשָׁלַם בְּתוֹךְ הַגּוֹיִם שַׂמְתִּיהָ וּסְבִיבוֹתֶיהָ אֲרָצוֹת: 6 וַתֶּמֶר אֶת־מִשְׁפָּטַי לְרִשְׁעָה מִן־הַגּוֹיִם וְאֶת־חֻקּוֹתַי מִן־הָאֲרָצוֹת אֲשֶׁר סְבִיבוֹתֶיהָ כִּי בְמִשְׁפָּטַי מָאָסוּ וְחֻקּוֹתַי לֹא־הָלְכוּ בָהֶם: ס 7 לָכֵן כֹּה־אָמַר ׀ אֲדֹנָי יְהוִֹה יַעַן הֲמָנְכֶם מִן־הַגּוֹיִם אֲשֶׁר סְבִיבוֹתֵיכֶם בְּחֻקּוֹתַי לֹא הֲלַכְתֶּם וְאֶת־מִשְׁפָּטַי לֹא עֲשִׂיתֶם וּכְמִשְׁפְּטֵי הַגּוֹיִם אֲשֶׁר סְבִיבוֹתֵיכֶם לֹא עֲשִׂיתֶם: ס 8 לָכֵן כֹּה אָמַר אֲדֹנָי יְהוִֹה הִנְנִי עָלַיִךְ גַּם־אָנִי וְעָשִׂיתִי בְתוֹכֵךְ מִשְׁפָּטִים לְעֵינֵי הַגּוֹיִם: 9 וְעָשִׂיתִי בָךְ אֵת אֲשֶׁר לֹא־עָשִׂיתִי וְאֵת אֲשֶׁר־לֹא־אֶעֱשֶׂה כָמֹהוּ עוֹד יַעַן כָּל־תּוֹעֲבֹתָיִךְ: ס 10 לָכֵן אָבוֹת יֹאכְלוּ בָנִים בְּתוֹכֵךְ וּבָנִים יֹאכְלוּ אֲבוֹתָם וְעָשִׂיתִי בָךְ שְׁפָטִים וְזֵרִיתִי אֶת־כָּל־שְׁאֵרִיתֵךְ לְכָל־רוּחַ: פ

11 לָכֵן חַי־אָנִי נְאֻם אֲדֹנָי יְהוִֹה אִם־לֹא יַעַן אֶת־מִקְדָּשִׁי טִמֵּאת בְּכָל־שִׁקּוּצַיִךְ וּבְכָל־תּוֹעֲבֹתָיִךְ וְגַם־אֲנִי אֶגְרַע וְלֹא־תָחוֹס עֵינִי וְגַם־אֲנִי לֹא אֶחְמוֹל: 12 שְׁלִשִׁתֵךְ בַּדֶּבֶר יָמוּתוּ וּבָרָעָב יִכְלוּ בְתוֹכֵךְ וְהַשְּׁלִשִׁית בַּחֶרֶב יִפְּלוּ סְבִיבוֹתָיִךְ וְהַשְּׁלִישִׁית לְכָל־רוּחַ אֱזָרֶה וְחֶרֶב אָרִיק אַחֲרֵיהֶם: 13 וְכָלָה אַפִּי וַהֲנִחוֹתִי חֲמָתִי בָּם וְהִנֶּחָמְתִּי וְיָדְעוּ כִּי־אֲנִי יְהוָֹה

it in My zeal, when I have spent My fury upon them. ¹⁴Moreover I will make you a waste and a reproach among the nations that *are* all around you, in the sight of all who pass by.

¹⁵'So it shall be a reproach, a taunt, a lesson, and an astonishment to the nations that *are* all around you, when I execute judgments among you in anger and in fury and in furious rebukes. I, the LORD, have spoken. ¹⁶When I send against them the terrible arrows of famine which shall be for destruction, which I will send to destroy you, I will increase the famine upon you and cut off your supply of bread. ¹⁷So I will send against you famine and wild beasts, and they will bereave you. Pestilence and blood shall pass through you, and I will bring the sword against you. I, the LORD, have spoken.'"

6 Now the word of the LORD came to me, saying: ²"Son of man, set your face toward the mountains of Israel, and prophesy against them, ³and say, 'O mountains of Israel, hear the word of the Lord GOD! Thus says the Lord GOD to the mountains, to the hills, to the ravines, and to the valleys: "Indeed I, *even* I, will bring a sword against you, and I will destroy your high places. ⁴Then your altars shall be desolate, your incense altars shall be broken, and I will cast down your slain *men* before your idols. ⁵And I will lay the corpses of the children of Israel before their idols, and I will scatter your bones all around your altars. ⁶In all your dwelling places the cities shall be laid waste, and the high places shall be desolate, so that your altars may be laid waste and made desolate, your idols may be broken and made to cease, your incense altars may be cut down, and your works may be abolished. ⁷The slain shall fall in your midst, and you shall know that I *am* the LORD.

⁸"Yet I will leave a remnant, so that you may have *some* who escape the sword among the nations, when you are scattered through the countries. ⁹Then those of you who escape will remember Me among the nations where they are carried captive, because I was crushed by their adulterous heart which has departed from Me, and by their eyes which play the harlot after their idols; they will loathe themselves for the evils which they committed in all their abominations. ¹⁰And they shall know that I *am* the LORD; I have not said in vain that I would bring this calamity upon them."

¹¹'Thus says the Lord GOD: "Pound your fists and stamp your feet, and say, 'Alas, for all the evil abominations of the house of Israel! For they shall fall by the sword, by famine, and by pestilence.

דִּבַּ֖רְתִּי בְּקִנְאָתִ֑י בְּכַלּוֹתִ֥י חֲמָתִ֖י בָּֽם: ¹⁴וְאֶתֵּ֨ן אֹתָ֜ךְ לְחָרְבָּ֣ה וּלְחֶרְפָּ֗ה בַּגּוֹיִם֙ אֲשֶׁ֣ר סְבִיבוֹתָ֔יִךְ לְעֵינֵ֖י כָּל־עוֹבֵֽר: ¹⁵וְהָ֨יְתָ֜ה חֶרְפָּ֣ה וּגְדוּפָ֗ה מוּסָ֣ר וּמְשַׁמָּ֔ה לַגּוֹיִ֖ם אֲשֶׁ֣ר סְבִיבוֹתָ֑יִךְ בַּעֲשׂוֹתִי֩ בָ֨ךְ שְׁפָטִ֜ים בְּאַ֤ף וּבְחֵמָה֙ וּבְתֹכְח֣וֹת חֵמָ֔ה אֲנִ֥י יְהֹוָ֖ה דִּבַּֽרְתִּי: ¹⁶בְּשַׁלְּחִ֣י אֶת־חִצֵּ֣י הָרָעָ֣ב הָרָעִ֡ים בָּהֶם֩ אֲשֶׁ֨ר הָי֜וּ לְמַשְׁחִ֗ית אֲשֶׁר־אֲשַׁלַּ֤ח אוֹתָם֙ לְשַֽׁחֶתְכֶ֔ם וְרָעָ֕ב אֹסֵ֖ף עֲלֵיכֶ֑ם וְשָׁבַרְתִּ֥י לָכֶ֖ם מַטֵּה־לָֽחֶם: ¹⁷וְשִׁלַּחְתִּ֣י עֲלֵיכֶ֡ם רָעָ֣ב וְחַיָּ֣ה רָעָה֩ וְשִׁכְּלֻ֨ךְ וְדֶ֤בֶר וָדָם֙ יַ֣עֲבָר־בָּ֔ךְ וְחֶ֖רֶב אָבִ֣יא עָלָ֑יִךְ אֲנִ֥י יְהֹוָ֖ה דִּבַּֽרְתִּי: פ

ו וַיְהִ֥י דְבַר־יְהֹוָ֖ה אֵלַ֥י לֵאמֹֽר: ²בֶּן־אָדָ֕ם שִׂ֥ים פָּנֶ֖יךָ אֶל־הָרֵ֣י יִשְׂרָאֵ֑ל וְהִנָּבֵ֖א אֲלֵיהֶֽם: ³וְאָ֣מַרְתָּ֔ הָרֵי֙ יִשְׂרָאֵ֔ל שִׁמְע֖וּ דְּבַר־אֲדֹנָ֣י יְהֹוִ֑ה כֹּה־אָמַ֣ר אֲדֹנָ֣י יְהֹוִ֡ה לֶהָרִ֣ים וְלַגְּבָעוֹת֩ לָאֲפִיקִ֨ים וְלַגֵּֽאָיֹ֜ת הִנְנִ֨י אֲנִ֜י מֵבִ֤יא עֲלֵיכֶם֙ חֶ֔רֶב וְאִבַּדְתִּ֖י בָּמוֹתֵיכֶֽם: ⁴וְנָשַׁ֙מּוּ֙ מִזְבְּחוֹתֵיכֶ֔ם וְנִשְׁבְּר֖וּ חַמָּֽנֵיכֶ֑ם וְהִפַּלְתִּי֙ חַלְלֵיכֶ֔ם לִפְנֵ֖י גִּלּֽוּלֵיכֶֽם: ⁵וְנָתַתִּ֗י אֶת־פִּגְרֵי֙ בְּנֵ֣י יִשְׂרָאֵ֔ל לִפְנֵ֖י גִּלּֽוּלֵיהֶ֑ם וְזֵרִיתִי֙ אֶת־עַצְמ֣וֹתֵיכֶ֔ם סְבִיב֖וֹת מִזְבְּחוֹתֵיכֶֽם: ⁶בְּכֹל֙ מוֹשְׁבֽוֹתֵיכֶ֔ם הֶעָרִ֣ים תֶּחֱרַ֔בְנָה וְהַבָּמ֖וֹת תִּישָׁ֑מְנָה לְמַ֨עַן יֶחֶרְב֜וּ וְיֶאְשְׁמ֣וּ מִזְבְּחֽוֹתֵיכֶ֗ם וְנִשְׁבְּר֤וּ וְנִשְׁבְּתוּ֙ גִּלּ֣וּלֵיכֶ֔ם וְנִגְדְּעוּ֙ חַמָּ֣נֵיכֶ֔ם וְנִמְח֖וּ מַעֲשֵׂיכֶֽם: ⁷וְנָפַ֥ל חָלָ֖ל בְּתֽוֹכְכֶ֑ם וִידַעְתֶּ֖ם כִּֽי־אֲנִ֥י יְהֹוָֽה: ⁸וְהוֹתַרְתִּ֗י בִּהְי֥וֹת לָכֶ֛ם פְּלִ֥יטֵי חֶ֖רֶב בַּגּוֹיִ֑ם בְּהִזָּרֽוֹתֵיכֶ֖ם בָּאֲרָצֽוֹת: ⁹וְזָכְר֨וּ פְלִֽיטֵיכֶ֜ם אוֹתִ֗י בַּגּוֹיִם֙ אֲשֶׁ֣ר נִשְׁבּוּ־שָׁ֔ם אֲשֶׁ֣ר נִשְׁבַּ֗רְתִּי אֶת־לִבָּ֤ם הַזּוֹנֶה֙ אֲשֶׁר־סָ֣ר מֵֽעָלַ֔י וְאֵת֙ עֵֽינֵיהֶ֔ם הַזֹּנ֕וֹת אַחֲרֵ֖י גִּלּֽוּלֵיהֶ֑ם וְנָקֹ֨טּוּ֙ בִּפְנֵיהֶ֔ם אֶל־הָֽרָעוֹת֙ אֲשֶׁ֣ר עָשׂ֔וּ לְכֹ֖ל תּוֹעֲבֹֽתֵיהֶֽם: ¹⁰וְיָדְע֖וּ כִּֽי־אֲנִ֣י יְהֹוָ֑ה לֹ֤א אֶל־חִנָּם֙ דִּבַּ֔רְתִּי לַעֲשׂ֥וֹת לָהֶ֖ם הָרָעָ֥ה הַזֹּֽאת: פ

¹¹כֹּֽה־אָמַ֞ר אֲדֹנָ֣י יְהֹוִ֗ה הַכֵּ֤ה בְכַפְּךָ֙ וּרְקַ֣ע בְּרַגְלְךָ֔ וֶאֱמָר־אָ֕ח אֶ֛ל כָּל־תּוֹעֲב֥וֹת רָע֖וֹת בֵּ֥ית יִשְׂרָאֵ֑ל

¹²He who is far off shall die by the pestilence, he who is near shall fall by the sword, and he who remains and is besieged shall die by the famine. Thus will I spend My fury upon them. ¹³Then you shall know that I *am* the LORD, when their slain are among their idols all around their altars, on every high hill, on all the mountaintops, under every green tree, and under every thick oak, wherever they offered sweet incense to all their idols. ¹⁴So I will stretch out My hand against them and make the land desolate, yes, more desolate than the wilderness toward Diblah, in all their dwelling places. Then they shall know that I *am* the LORD.' " "

7 Moreover the word of the LORD came to me, saying, ²"And you, son of man, thus says the Lord GOD to the land of Israel:

'An end! The end has come upon the four corners of the land.
³ Now the end *has come* upon you,
   And I will send My anger against you;
   I will judge you according to your ways,
   And I will repay you for all your abominations.
⁴ My eye will not spare you,
   Nor will I have pity;
   But I will repay your ways,
   And your abominations will be in your midst;
   Then you shall know that I *am* the LORD!'

⁵"Thus says the Lord GOD:

'A disaster, a singular disaster;
   Behold, it has come!
⁶ An end has come,
   The end has come;
   It has dawned for you;
   Behold, it has come!
⁷ Doom has come to you, you who dwell in the land;
   The time has come,
   A day of trouble *is* near,
   And not of rejoicing in the mountains.
⁸ Now upon you I will soon pour out My fury,
   And spend My anger upon you;
   I will judge you according to your ways,
   And I will repay you for all your abominations.
⁹ 'My eye will not spare,
   Nor will I have pity;
   I will repay you according to your ways,
   And your abominations will be in your midst.
   Then you shall know that I *am* the LORD who strikes.
¹⁰ 'Behold, the day!
   Behold, it has come!
   Doom has gone out;
   The rod has blossomed,
   Pride has budded.
¹¹ Violence has risen up into a rod of wickedness;
   None of them *shall remain*,

אֲשֶׁר בַּחֶרֶב בָּרָעָב וּבַדֶּבֶר יִפֹּלוּ: 12 הָרָחוֹק בַּדֶּבֶר יָמוּת וְהַקָּרוֹב בַּחֶרֶב יִפּוֹל וְהַנִּשְׁאָר וְהַנָּצוּר בָּרָעָב יָמוּת וְכִלֵּיתִי חֲמָתִי בָּם: 13 וִידַעְתֶּם כִּי־אֲנִי יְהוָה בִּהְיוֹת חַלְלֵיהֶם בְּתוֹךְ גִּלּוּלֵיהֶם סְבִיבוֹת מִזְבְּחוֹתֵיהֶם אֶל כָּל־גִּבְעָה רָמָה בְּכֹל ׀ רָאשֵׁי הֶהָרִים וְתַחַת כָּל־עֵץ רַעֲנָן וְתַחַת כָּל־אֵלָה עֲבֻתָּה מְקוֹם אֲשֶׁר נָתְנוּ־שָׁם רֵיחַ נִיחֹחַ לְכֹל גִּלּוּלֵיהֶם: 14 וְנָטִיתִי אֶת־יָדִי עֲלֵיהֶם וְנָתַתִּי אֶת־הָאָרֶץ שְׁמָמָה וּמְשַׁמָּה מִמִּדְבַּר דִּבְלָתָה בְּכֹל מוֹשְׁבוֹתֵיהֶם וְיָדְעוּ כִּי־אֲנִי יְהוָה: פ

ז וַיְהִי דְבַר־יְהוָה אֵלַי לֵאמֹר: 2 וְאַתָּה בֶן־אָדָם כֹּה־אָמַר אֲדֹנָי יְהוִה לְאַדְמַת יִשְׂרָאֵל קֵץ בָּא הַקֵּץ עַל־אַרְבַּעת כַּנְפוֹת הָאָרֶץ: 3 עַתָּה הַקֵּץ עָלַיִךְ וְשִׁלַּחְתִּי אַפִּי בָּךְ וּשְׁפַטְתִּיךְ כִּדְרָכָיִךְ וְנָתַתִּי עָלַיִךְ אֵת כָּל־תּוֹעֲבֹתָיִךְ: 4 וְלֹא־תָחוֹס עֵינִי עָלַיִךְ וְלֹא אֶחְמוֹל כִּי דְרָכַיִךְ עָלַיִךְ אֶתֵּן וְתוֹעֲבוֹתַיִךְ בְּתוֹכֵךְ תִּהְיֶיןָ וִידַעְתֶּם כִּי־אֲנִי יְהוָה: פ

5 כֹּה אָמַר אֲדֹנָי יְהוִה רָעָה אַחַת רָעָה הִנֵּה בָאָה: 6 קֵץ בָּא בָּא הַקֵּץ הֵקִיץ אֵלָיִךְ הִנֵּה בָּאָה: 7 בָּאָה הַצְּפִירָה אֵלַיִךְ יוֹשֵׁב הָאָרֶץ בָּא הָעֵת קָרוֹב הַיּוֹם מְהוּמָה וְלֹא־הֵד הָרִים: 8 עַתָּה מִקָּרוֹב אֶשְׁפּוֹךְ חֲמָתִי עָלַיִךְ וְכִלֵּיתִי אַפִּי בָּךְ וּשְׁפַטְתִּיךְ כִּדְרָכָיִךְ וְנָתַתִּי עָלַיִךְ אֵת כָּל־תּוֹעֲבוֹתָיִךְ: 9 וְלֹא־תָחוֹס עֵינִי וְלֹא אֶחְמוֹל כִּדְרָכַיִךְ עָלַיִךְ אֶתֵּן וְתוֹעֲבוֹתַיִךְ בְּתוֹכֵךְ תִּהְיֶיןָ וִידַעְתֶּם כִּי אֲנִי יְהוָה מַכֶּה: 10 הִנֵּה הַיּוֹם הִנֵּה בָאָה יָצְאָה הַצְּפִרָה צָץ הַמַּטֶּה פָּרַח הַזָּדוֹן: 11 הֶחָמָס ׀ קָם לְמַטֵּה־

None of their multitude,
None of them;
Nor *shall there be* wailing for them.
12 The time has come,
The day draws near.

'Let not the buyer rejoice,
Nor the seller mourn,
For wrath *is* on their whole multitude.
13 For the seller shall not return to what has been
sold,
Though he may still be alive;
For the vision concerns the whole multitude,
And it shall not turn back;
No one will strengthen himself
Who lives in iniquity.

14 'They have blown the trumpet and made everyone
ready,
But no one goes to battle;
For My wrath *is* on all their multitude.
15 The sword *is* outside,
And the pestilence and famine within.
Whoever *is* in the field
Will die by the sword;
And whoever *is* in the city,
Famine and pestilence will devour him.
16 'Those who survive will escape and be on the
mountains
Like doves of the valleys,
All of them mourning,
Each for his iniquity.
17 Every hand will be feeble,
And every knee will be *as* weak *as* water.
18 They will also be girded with sackcloth;
Horror will cover them;
Shame *will be* on every face,
Baldness on all their heads.

19 'They will throw their silver into the streets,
And their gold will be like refuse;
Their silver and their gold will not be able to
deliver them
In the day of the wrath of the LORD;
They will not satisfy their souls,
Nor fill their stomachs,
Because it became their stumbling block of
iniquity.

20 'As for the beauty of his ornaments,
He set it in majesty;
But they made from it
The images of their abominations—
Their detestable things;
Therefore I have made it
Like refuse to them.
21 I will give it as plunder
Into the hands of strangers,
And to the wicked of the earth as spoil;
And they shall defile it.
22 I will turn My face from them,
And they will defile My secret place;
For robbers shall enter it and defile it.

23 'Make a chain,

רֶשַׁע לֹא־מֵהֶם וְלֹא מֵהֲמוֹנָם וְלֹא מֶהֱמֵהֶם וְלֹא־נֹהַּ
בָּהֶם: 12 בָּא הָעֵת הִגִּיעַ הַיּוֹם הַקּוֹנֶה אַל־יִשְׂמָח
וְהַמּוֹכֵר אַל־יִתְאַבָּל כִּי חָרוֹן אֶל־כָּל־הֲמוֹנָהּ: 13 כִּי
הַמּוֹכֵר אֶל־הַמִּמְכָּר לֹא יָשׁוּב וְעוֹד בַּחַיִּים חַיָּתָם
כִּי־חָזוֹן אֶל־כָּל־הֲמוֹנָהּ לֹא יָשׁוּב וְאִישׁ בַּעֲוֹנוֹ חַיָּתוֹ
לֹא יִתְחַזָּקוּ: 14 תָּקְעוּ בַתָּקוֹעַ וְהָכִין הַכֹּל וְאֵין
הֹלֵךְ לַמִּלְחָמָה כִּי חֲרוֹנִי אֶל־כָּל־הֲמוֹנָהּ: 15 הַחֶרֶב
בַּחוּץ וְהַדֶּבֶר וְהָרָעָב מִבָּיִת אֲשֶׁר בַּשָּׂדֶה בַּחֶרֶב
יָמוּת וַאֲשֶׁר בָּעִיר רָעָב וָדֶבֶר יֹאכֲלֶנּוּ: 16 וּפָלְטוּ
פְּלִיטֵיהֶם וְהָיוּ אֶל־הֶהָרִים כְּיוֹנֵי הַגֵּאָיוֹת כֻּלָּם
הֹמוֹת אִישׁ בַּעֲוֹנוֹ: 17 כָּל־הַיָּדַיִם תִּרְפֶּינָה וְכָל־
בִּרְכַּיִם תֵּלַכְנָה מָּיִם: 18 וְחָגְרוּ שַׂקִּים וְכִסְּתָה
אוֹתָם פַּלָּצוּת וְאֶל כָּל־פָּנִים בּוּשָׁה וּבְכָל־רָאשֵׁיהֶם
קָרְחָה: 19 כַּסְפָּם בַּחוּצוֹת יַשְׁלִיכוּ וּזְהָבָם לְנִדָּה
יִהְיֶה כַּסְפָּם וּזְהָבָם לֹא־יוּכַל לְהַצִּילָם בְּיוֹם עֶבְרַת
יְהֹוָה נַפְשָׁם לֹא יְשַׂבֵּעוּ וּמֵעֵיהֶם לֹא יְמַלֵּאוּ כִּי־
מִכְשׁוֹל עֲוֹנָם הָיָה: 20 וּצְבִי עֶדְיוֹ לְגָאוֹן שָׂמָהוּ
וְצַלְמֵי תוֹעֲבֹתָם שִׁקּוּצֵיהֶם עָשׂוּ בוֹ עַל־כֵּן נְתַתִּיו
לָהֶם לְנִדָּה: 21 וּנְתַתִּיו בְּיַד־הַזָּרִים לָבַז וּלְרִשְׁעֵי
הָאָרֶץ לְשָׁלָל וְחִלְּלֻהוּ: 22 וַהֲסִבּוֹתִי פָנַי מֵהֶם
וְחִלְּלוּ אֶת־צְפוּנִי וּבָאוּ־בָהּ פָּרִיצִים וְחִלְּלוּהָ: פ

23 עֲשֵׂה הָרַתּוֹק כִּי הָאָרֶץ מָלְאָה מִשְׁפַּט דָּמִים

For the land is filled with crimes of blood,
And the city is full of violence.
24 Therefore I will bring the worst of the Gentiles,
And they will possess their houses;
I will cause the pomp of the strong to cease,
And their holy places shall be defiled.
25 Destruction comes;
They will seek peace, but *there shall be* none.
26 Disaster will come upon disaster,
And rumor will be upon rumor.
Then they will seek a vision from a prophet;
But the law will perish from the priest,
And counsel from the elders.
27 'The king will mourn,
The prince will be clothed with desolation,
And the hands of the common people will
tremble.
I will do to them according to their way,
And according to what they deserve I will judge
them;
Then they shall know that I *am* the LORD!' "

8 And it came to pass in the sixth year, in the sixth
month, on the fifth *day* of the month, as I sat in my
house with the elders of Judah sitting before me,
that the hand of the Lord GOD fell upon me there.
2 Then I looked, and there was a likeness, like the
appearance of fire—from the appearance of His
waist and downward, fire; and from His waist and
upward, like the appearance of brightness, like the
color of amber. 3 He stretched out the form of a
hand, and took me by a lock of my hair; and the
Spirit lifted me up between earth and heaven, and
brought me in visions of God to Jerusalem, to the
door of the north gate of the inner court, where the
seat of the image of jealousy *was,* which provokes to
jealousy. 4 And behold, the glory of the God of
Israel *was* there, like the vision that I saw in the
plain.

5 Then He said to me, "Son of man, lift your eyes
now toward the north." So I lifted my eyes toward
the north, and there, north of the altar gate, was
this image of jealousy in the entrance.

6 Furthermore He said to me, "Son of man, do
you see what they are doing, the great abominations
that the house of Israel commits here, to make Me
go far away from My sanctuary? Now turn again,
you will see greater abominations." 7 So He brought
me to the door of the court; and when I looked,
there was a hole in the wall. 8 Then He said to me,
"Son of man, dig into the wall"; and when I dug
into the wall, there was a door.

9 And He said to me, "Go in, and see the wicked
abominations which they are doing there." 10 So I
went in and saw, and there—every sort of creeping
thing, abominable beasts, and all the idols of the

וְהָעִיר מָלְאָה חָמָס: 24 וְהֵבֵאתִי רָעֵי גוֹיִם

וְיָרְשׁוּ אֶת־בָּתֵּיהֶם וְהִשְׁבַּתִּי גְּאוֹן עַזִּים וְנִחֲלוּ

מִקְדְּשֵׁיהֶם: 25 קְפָדָה־בָא וּבִקְשׁוּ שָׁלוֹם וָאָיִן:

26 הֹוָה עַל־הֹוָה תָּבוֹא וּשְׁמֻעָה אֶל־שְׁמוּעָה תִהְיֶה

וּבִקְשׁוּ חָזוֹן מִנָּבִיא וְתוֹרָה תֹּאבַד מִכֹּהֵן וְעֵצָה

מִזְּקֵנִים: 27 הַמֶּלֶךְ יִתְאַבָּל וְנָשִׂיא יִלְבַּשׁ שְׁמָמָה

וִידֵי עַם־הָאָרֶץ תִּבָּהַלְנָה מִדַּרְכָּם אֶעֱשֶׂה אוֹתָם

וּבְמִשְׁפְּטֵיהֶם אֶשְׁפְּטֵם וְיָדְעוּ כִּי־אֲנִי יְהוָה: פ

ח וַיְהִי ׀ בַּשָּׁנָה הַשִּׁשִּׁית בַּשִּׁשִּׁי בַּחֲמִשָּׁה לַחֹדֶשׁ

אֲנִי יוֹשֵׁב בְּבֵיתִי וְזִקְנֵי יְהוּדָה יוֹשְׁבִים לְפָנָי

וַתִּפֹּל עָלַי שָׁם יַד אֲדֹנָי יְהוִה: 2 וָאֶרְאֶה וְהִנֵּה

דְמוּת כְּמַרְאֵה־אֵשׁ מִמַּרְאֵה מָתְנָיו וּלְמַטָּה אֵשׁ

וּמִמָּתְנָיו וּלְמַעְלָה כְּמַרְאֵה־זֹהַר כְּעֵין הַחַשְׁמַלָה:

3 וַיִּשְׁלַח תַּבְנִית יָד וַיִּקָּחֵנִי בְּצִיצִת רֹאשִׁי וַתִּשָּׂא

אֹתִי רוּחַ ׀ בֵּין־הָאָרֶץ וּבֵין הַשָּׁמַיִם וַתָּבֵא

אֹתִי יְרוּשָׁלַמָה בְּמַרְאוֹת אֱלֹהִים אֶל־פֶּתַח שַׁעַר

הַפְּנִימִית הַפּוֹנָה צָפוֹנָה אֲשֶׁר־שָׁם מוֹשַׁב סֵמֶל

הַקִּנְאָה הַמַּקְנֶה: 4 וְהִנֵּה־שָׁם כְּבוֹד אֱלֹהֵי יִשְׂרָאֵל

כַּמַּרְאֶה אֲשֶׁר רָאִיתִי בַּבִּקְעָה: 5 וַיֹּאמֶר אֵלַי בֶּן־

אָדָם שָׂא־נָא עֵינֶיךָ דֶּרֶךְ צָפוֹנָה וָאֶשָּׂא עֵינַי דֶּרֶךְ

צָפוֹנָה וְהִנֵּה מִצָּפוֹן לְשַׁעַר הַמִּזְבֵּחַ סֵמֶל הַקִּנְאָה

הַזֶּה בַּבִּאָה: 6 וַיֹּאמֶר אֵלַי בֶּן־אָדָם הֲרֹאֶה אַתָּה

מֶהֶם p תּוֹעֵבוֹת גְּדֹלוֹת אֲשֶׁר בֵּית־יִשְׂרָאֵל ׀ עֹשִׂים

פֹּה לְרָחֳקָה מֵעַל מִקְדָּשִׁי וְעוֹד תָּשׁוּב תִּרְאֶה

תּוֹעֵבוֹת גְּדֹלוֹת: ס 7 וַיָּבֵא אֹתִי אֶל־פֶּתַח

הֶחָצֵר וָאֶרְאֶה וְהִנֵּה חֹר־אֶחָד בַּקִּיר: 8 וַיֹּאמֶר

אֵלַי בֶּן־אָדָם חֲתָר־נָא בַקִּיר וָאֶחְתֹּר בַּקִּיר וְהִנֵּה

פֶּתַח אֶחָד: 9 וַיֹּאמֶר אֵלַי בֹּא וּרְאֵה אֶת־הַתּוֹעֵבוֹת

הָרָעוֹת אֲשֶׁר הֵם עֹשִׂים פֹּה: 10 וָאָבוֹא וָאֶרְאֶה

וְהִנֵּה כָל־תַּבְנִית רֶמֶשׂ וּבְהֵמָה שֶׁקֶץ וְכָל־גִּלּוּלֵי

ח 6 מֶה הֵם עֹשִׂים

house of Israel, portrayed all around on the walls. ¹¹ And there stood before them seventy men of the elders of the house of Israel, and in their midst stood Jaazaniah the son of Shaphan. Each man had a censer in his hand, and a thick cloud of incense went up. ¹² Then He said to me, "Son of man, have you seen what the elders of the house of Israel do in the dark, every man in the room of his idols? For they say, 'The LORD does not see us, the LORD has forsaken the land.' "

¹³ And He said to me, "Turn again, *and* you will see greater abominations that they are doing." ¹⁴ So He brought me to the door of the north gate of the LORD's house; and to my dismay, women were sitting there weeping for Tammuz.

¹⁵ Then He said to me, "Have you seen *this,* O son of man? Turn again, you will see greater abominations than these." ¹⁶ So He brought me into the inner court of the LORD's house; and there, at the door of the temple of the LORD, between the porch and the altar, *were* about twenty-five men with their backs toward the temple of the LORD and their faces toward the east, and they were worshiping the sun toward the east.

¹⁷ And He said to me, "Have you seen *this,* O son of man? Is it a trivial thing to the house of Judah to commit the abominations which they commit here? For they have filled the land with violence; then they have returned to provoke Me to anger. Indeed they put the branch to their nose. ¹⁸ Therefore I also will act in fury. My eye will not spare nor will I have pity; and though they cry in My ears with a loud voice, I will not hear them."

9 Then He called out in my hearing with a loud voice, saying, "Let those who have charge over the city draw near, each *with* a deadly weapon in his hand." ² And suddenly six men came from the direction of the upper gate, which faces north, each with his battle-ax in his hand. One man among them *was* clothed with linen and had a writer's inkhorn at his side. They went in and stood beside the bronze altar.

³ Now the glory of the God of Israel had gone up from the cherub, where it had been, to the threshold of the temple. And He called to the man clothed with linen, who *had* the writer's inkhorn at his side; ⁴ and the LORD said to him, "Go through the midst of the city, through the midst of Jerusalem, and put a mark on the foreheads of the men who sigh and cry over all the abominations that are done within it."

בֵּית יִשְׂרָאֵל מְחֻקֶּה עַל־הַקִּיר סָבִיב ׀ סָבִיב: 11 וְשִׁבְעִים אִישׁ מִזִּקְנֵי בֵית־יִשְׂרָאֵל וְיַאֲזַנְיָהוּ בֶן־שָׁפָן עֹמֵד בְּתוֹכָם עֹמְדִים לִפְנֵיהֶם וְאִישׁ מִקְטַרְתּוֹ בְּיָדוֹ וַעֲתַר עֲנַן־הַקְּטֹרֶת עֹלֶה: 12 וַיֹּאמֶר אֵלַי הֲרָאִיתָ בֶן־אָדָם אֲשֶׁר זִקְנֵי בֵית־יִשְׂרָאֵל עֹשִׂים בַּחֹשֶׁךְ אִישׁ בְּחַדְרֵי מַשְׂכִּיתוֹ כִּי אֹמְרִים אֵין יְהוָֹה רֹאֶה אֹתָנוּ עָזַב יְהוָֹה אֶת־הָאָרֶץ: 13 וַיֹּאמֶר אֵלַי עוֹד תָּשׁוּב תִּרְאֶה תּוֹעֵבוֹת גְּדֹלוֹת אֲשֶׁר־הֵמָּה עֹשִׂים: 14 וַיָּבֵא אֹתִי אֶל־פֶּתַח שַׁעַר בֵּית־יְהוָֹה אֲשֶׁר אֶל־הַצָּפוֹנָה וְהִנֵּה־שָׁם הַנָּשִׁים יֹשְׁבוֹת מְבַכּוֹת אֶת־הַתַּמּוּז: ס 15 וַיֹּאמֶר אֵלַי הֲרָאִיתָ בֶן־אָדָם עוֹד תָּשׁוּב תִּרְאֶה תּוֹעֵבוֹת גְּדֹלוֹת מֵאֵלֶּה: 16 וַיָּבֵא אֹתִי אֶל־חֲצַר בֵּית־יְהוָֹה הַפְּנִימִית וְהִנֵּה־פֶתַח הֵיכַל יְהוָֹה בֵּין הָאוּלָם וּבֵין הַמִּזְבֵּחַ כְּעֶשְׂרִים וַחֲמִשָּׁה אִישׁ אֲחֹרֵיהֶם אֶל־הֵיכַל יְהוָֹה וּפְנֵיהֶם קֵדְמָה וְהֵמָּה מִשְׁתַּחֲוִיתֶם קֵדְמָה לַשָּׁמֶשׁ: 17 וַיֹּאמֶר אֵלַי הֲרָאִיתָ בֶן־אָדָם הֲנָקֵל לְבֵית יְהוּדָה מֵעֲשׂוֹת אֶת־הַתּוֹעֵבוֹת אֲשֶׁר עָשׂוּ־פֹה כִּי־מָלְאוּ אֶת־הָאָרֶץ חָמָס וַיָּשֻׁבוּ לְהַכְעִיסֵנִי וְהִנָּם שֹׁלְחִים אֶת־הַזְּמוֹרָה אֶל־אַפָּם: 18 וְגַם־אֲנִי אֶעֱשֶׂה בְחֵמָה לֹא־תָחוֹס עֵינִי וְלֹא אֶחְמֹל וְקָרְאוּ בְאָזְנַי קוֹל גָּדוֹל וְלֹא אֶשְׁמַע אוֹתָם:

ט וַיִּקְרָא בְאָזְנַי קוֹל גָּדוֹל לֵאמֹר קָרְבוּ פְּקֻדּוֹת הָעִיר וְאִישׁ כְּלִי מַשְׁחֵתוֹ בְּיָדוֹ: 2 וְהִנֵּה שִׁשָּׁה אֲנָשִׁים בָּאִים ׀ מִדֶּרֶךְ־שַׁעַר הָעֶלְיוֹן אֲשֶׁר ׀ מָפְנֶה צָפוֹנָה וְאִישׁ כְּלִי מַפָּצוֹ בְּיָדוֹ וְאִישׁ־אֶחָד בְּתוֹכָם לָבֻשׁ בַּדִּים וְקֶסֶת הַסֹּפֵר בְּמָתְנָיו וַיָּבֹאוּ וַיַּעַמְדוּ אֵצֶל מִזְבַּח הַנְּחֹשֶׁת: 3 וּכְבוֹד ׀ אֱלֹהֵי יִשְׂרָאֵל נַעֲלָה מֵעַל הַכְּרוּב אֲשֶׁר הָיָה עָלָיו אֶל מִפְתַּן הַבָּיִת וַיִּקְרָא אֶל־הָאִישׁ הַלָּבֻשׁ הַבַּדִּים אֲשֶׁר קֶסֶת הַסֹּפֵר בְּמָתְנָיו: ס 4 וַיֹּאמֶר יְהוָֹה אֵלָו עֲבֹר בְּתוֹךְ הָעִיר בְּתוֹךְ יְרוּשָׁלִָם וְהִתְוִיתָ תָּו עַל־מִצְחוֹת הָאֲנָשִׁים הַנֶּאֱנָחִים וְהַנֶּאֱנָקִים עַל

⁵To the others He said in my hearing, "Go after him through the city and kill; do not let your eye spare, nor have any pity. ⁶Utterly slay old *and* young men, maidens and little children and women; but do not come near anyone on whom *is* the mark; and begin at My sanctuary." So they began with the elders who *were* before the temple. ⁷Then He said to them, "Defile the temple, and fill the courts with the slain. Go out!" And they went out and killed in the city.

⁸So it was, that while they were killing them, I was left *alone;* and I fell on my face and cried out, and said, "Ah, Lord GOD! Will You destroy all the remnant of Israel in pouring out Your fury on Jerusalem?"

⁹Then He said to me, "The iniquity of the house of Israel and Judah *is* exceedingly great, and the land is full of bloodshed, and the city full of perversity; for they say, 'The LORD has forsaken the land, and the LORD does not see!' ¹⁰And as for Me also, My eye will neither spare, nor will I have pity, *but* I will recompense their deeds on their own head."

¹¹Just then, the man clothed with linen, who *had* the inkhorn at his side, reported back and said, "I have done as You commanded me."

10 And I looked, and there in the firmament that was above the head of the cherubim, there appeared something like a sapphire stone, having the appearance of the likeness of a throne. ²Then He spoke to the man clothed with a linen, and said, "Go in among the wheels, under the cherub, fill your hands with coals of fire from among the cherubim, and scatter *them* over the city." And he went in as I watched.

³Now the cherubim were standing on the south side of the temple when the man went in, and the cloud filled the inner court. ⁴Then the glory of the LORD went up from the cherub, *and paused* over the threshold of the temple; and the house was filled with the cloud, and the court was full of the brightness of the LORD's glory. ⁵And the sound of the wings of the cherubim was heard *even* in the outer court, like the voice of Almighty God when He speaks.

⁶Then it happened, when He commanded the man clothed in linen, saying, "Take fire from among the wheels, from among the cherubim," that he went in and stood beside the wheels. ⁷And the cherub stretched out his hand from among the cherubim to the fire that *was* among the cherubim, and took *some of it* and put *it* into the hands of the

כָּל־הַתּוֹעֵבוֹת הַנַּעֲשׂוֹת בְּתוֹכָהּ: 5 וּלְאֵ֙לֶּה֙ אָמַר בְּאָזְנַי עִבְר֤וּ בָעִיר֙ אַחֲרָ֔יו וְהַכּ֖וּ עַל־פ אַל־תָּחֹ֥ס עֵינְכֶם וְאַל־תַּחְמֹֽלוּ: 6 זָקֵ֡ן בָּחוּר֩ וּבְתוּלָ֨ה וְטַ֤ף וְנָשִׁים֙ תַּהַרְג֣וּ לְמַשְׁחִ֔ית וְעַל־כָּל־אִ֞ישׁ אֲשֶׁר־עָלָ֣יו הַתָּ֗ו אַל־תִּגַּ֙שׁוּ֙ וּמִמִּקְדָּשִׁ֣י תָּחֵ֔לּוּ וַיָּחֵ֙לּוּ֙ בָּאֲנָשִׁ֣ים הַזְּקֵנִ֔ים אֲשֶׁ֖ר לִפְנֵ֥י הַבָּֽיִת: 7 וַיֹּ֣אמֶר אֲלֵיהֶ֗ם טַמְּא֣וּ אֶת־הַבַּ֙יִת֙ וּמַלְא֧וּ אֶת־הַחֲצֵר֛וֹת חֲלָלִ֖ים צֵ֑אוּ וְיָצְא֖וּ וְהִכּ֥וּ בָעִֽיר: 8 וַֽיְהִי֙ כְּהַכּוֹתָ֔ם וְנֵֽאשֲׁאַ֖ר אָ֑נִי וָאֶפְּלָ֨ה עַל־פָּנַ֜י וָאֶזְעַ֗ק וָאֹמַר֙ אֲהָ֙הּ֙ אֲדֹנָ֣י יְהֹוִ֔ה הֲמַשְׁחִ֣ית אַתָּ֗ה אֵ֚ת כָּל־שְׁאֵרִ֣ית יִשְׂרָאֵ֔ל בְּשָׁפְכְּךָ֥ אֶת־חֲמָתְךָ֖ עַל־יְרוּשָׁלָֽ͏ִם: 9 וַיֹּ֣אמֶר אֵלַ֔י עֲוֺ֞ן בֵּֽית־יִשְׂרָאֵ֤ל וִֽיהוּדָה֙ גָּד֣וֹל בִּמְאֹ֣ד מְאֹ֔ד וַתִּמָּלֵ֤א הָאָ֙רֶץ֙ דָּמִ֔ים וְהָעִ֖יר מָלְאָ֣ה מֻטֶּ֑ה כִּ֣י אָמְר֗וּ עָזַ֤ב יְהֹוָה֙ אֶת־הָאָ֔רֶץ וְאֵ֥ין יְהֹוָ֖ה רֹאֶֽה: 10 וְגַם־אֲנִ֗י לֹֽא־תָח֥וֹס עֵינִ֖י וְלֹ֣א אֶחְמֹ֑ל דַּרְכָּ֖ם בְּרֹאשָׁ֥ם נָתָֽתִּי: 11 וְהִנֵּ֣ה הָאִ֣ישׁ ׀ לְבֻ֣שׁ הַבַּדִּ֗ים אֲשֶׁ֤ר הַקֶּ֙סֶת֙ בְּמָתְנָ֔יו מֵשִׁ֥יב דָּבָ֖ר לֵאמֹ֑ר עָשִׂ֕יתִי כַּאֲשֶׁ֖ר צִוִּיתָֽנִי: ס

י וָאֶרְאֶ֗ה וְהִנֵּ֤ה אֶל־הָרָקִ֙יעַ֙ אֲשֶׁר֙ עַל־רֹ֣אשׁ הַכְּרֻבִ֔ים כְּאֶ֣בֶן סַפִּ֔יר כְּמַרְאֵ֖ה דְּמ֣וּת כִּסֵּ֑א נִרְאָ֖ה עֲלֵיהֶֽם: 2 וַיֹּ֜אמֶר אֶל־הָאִ֣ישׁ ׀ לְבֻ֣שׁ הַבַּדִּ֗ים וַיֹּ֡אמֶר בֹּא֩ אֶל־בֵּינ֙וֹת לַגַּלְגַּ֤ל אֶל־תַּ֙חַת֙ לַכְּר֔וּב וּמַלֵּ֨א חָפְנֶ֤יךָ גַֽחֲלֵי־אֵשׁ֙ מִבֵּינ֣וֹת לַכְּרֻבִ֔ים וּזְרֹ֖ק עַל־הָעִ֑יר וַיָּבֹ֖א לְעֵינָֽי: 3 וְהַכְּרֻבִ֗ים עֹֽמְדִ֛ים מִימִ֥ין לַבַּ֖יִת בְּבֹא֣וֹ הָאִ֑ישׁ וְהֶעָנָ֣ן מָלֵ֔א אֶת־הֶחָצֵ֖ר הַפְּנִימִֽית: 4 וַיָּ֤רׇם כְּבוֹד־יְהֹוָה֙ מֵעַ֣ל הַכְּר֔וּב עַ֖ל מִפְתַּ֣ן הַבָּ֑יִת וַיִּמָּלֵ֤א הַבַּ֙יִת֙ אֶת־הֶ֣עָנָ֔ן וְהֶ֣חָצֵ֔ר מָלְאָ֖ה אֶת־נֹ֥גַהּ כְּב֥וֹד יְהֹוָֽה: 5 וְק֙וֹל֙ כַּנְפֵ֣י הַכְּרוּבִ֔ים נִשְׁמַ֖ע עַד־הֶחָצֵ֣ר הַחִיצֹנָ֑ה כְּק֥וֹל אֵל־שַׁדַּ֖י בְּדַבְּרֽוֹ: 6 וַיְהִ֗י בְּצַוֺּת֞וֹ אֶת־הָאִ֣ישׁ לְבֻֽשׁ־הַבַּדִּים֮ לֵאמֹר֒ קַ֣ח אֵ֗שׁ מִבֵּינ֙וֹת֙ לַגַּלְגַּ֔ל מִבֵּינ֖וֹת לַכְּרוּבִ֑ים וַיָּבֹא֙ וַֽיַּעֲמֹ֔ד אֵ֖צֶל הָאוֹפָֽן: 7 וַיִּשְׁלַח֩ הַכְּר֨וּב אֶת־יָד֜וֹ מִבֵּינ֣וֹת לַכְּרוּבִ֗ים אֶל־הָאֵשׁ֙ אֲשֶׁר֙ בֵּינ֣וֹת הַכְּרֻבִ֔ים וַיִּשָּׂא֙

man clothed with linen, who took *it* and went out.
⁸ The cherubim appeared to have the form of a man's hand under their wings.

⁹ And when I looked, there were four wheels by the cherubim, one wheel by one cherub and another wheel by each other cherub; the wheels appeared *to* have the color of a beryl stone. ¹⁰ As *for their* appearance, all four looked alike—as it were, a wheel in the middle of a wheel. ¹¹ When they went, they went toward *any of* their four directions; they did not turn aside when they went, but followed in the direction the head was facing. They did not turn aside when they went. ¹² And their whole body, with their back, their hands, their wings, and the wheels that the four had, *were* full of eyes all around. ¹³ As for the wheels, they were called in my hearing, "Wheel."

¹⁴ Each one had four faces: the first face *was* the face of a cherub, the second face the face of a man, the third the face of a lion, and the fourth the face of an eagle. ¹⁵ And the cherubim were lifted up. This *was* the living creature I saw by the River Chebar. ¹⁶ When the cherubim went, the wheels went beside them; and when the cherubim lifted their wings to mount up from the earth, the same wheels also did not turn from beside them. ¹⁷ When *the cherubim* stood still, *the wheels* stood still, and when *one* was lifted up, *the other* lifted itself up, for the spirit of the living creature *was* in them.

¹⁸ Then the glory of the LORD departed from the threshold of the temple and stood over the cherubim. ¹⁹ And the cherubim lifted their wings and mounted up from the earth in my sight. When they went out, the wheels *were* beside them; and they stood at the door of the east gate of the LORD's house, and the glory of the God of Israel *was* above them.

²⁰ This *is* the living creature I saw under the God of Israel by the River Chebar, and I knew they *were* cherubim. ²¹ Each one had four faces and each one four wings, and the likeness of the hands of a man *was* under their wings. ²² And the likeness of their faces *was* the same *as* the faces which I had seen by the River Chebar, their appearance and their persons. They each went straight forward.

11 Then the Spirit lifted me up and brought me to the East Gate of the LORD's house, which faces eastward; and there at the door of the gate were twenty-five men, among whom I saw Jaazaniah the son of Azzur, and Pelatiah the son of Benaiah, princes of the people. ² And He said to me: "Son of man, these *are* the men who devise iniquity and give wicked counsel in this city, ³ who say, '*The time is*

וַיִּתֵּן אֶל־חָפְנֵי לְבֻשׁ הַבַּדִּים וַיִּקַּח וַיֵּצֵא: ⁸ וַיֵּרָא לַכְּרֻבִים תַּבְנִית יַד־אָדָם תַּחַת כַּנְפֵיהֶם: ⁹ וָאֶרְאֶה וְהִנֵּה אַרְבָּעָה אוֹפַנִּים אֵצֶל הַכְּרוּבִים אוֹפַן אֶחָד אֵצֶל הַכְּרוּב אֶחָד וְאוֹפַן אֶחָד אֵצֶל הַכְּרוּב אֶחָד וּמַרְאֵה הָאוֹפַנִּים כְּעֵין אֶבֶן תַּרְשִׁישׁ: ¹⁰ וּמַרְאֵיהֶם דְּמוּת אֶחָד לְאַרְבַּעְתָּם כַּאֲשֶׁר יִהְיֶה הָאוֹפַן בְּתוֹךְ הָאוֹפָן: ¹¹ בְּלֶכְתָּם אֶל־אַרְבַּעַת רִבְעֵיהֶם יֵלֵכוּ לֹא יִסַּבּוּ בְּלֶכְתָּן כִּי הַמָּקוֹם אֲשֶׁר־יִפְנֶה הָרֹאשׁ אַחֲרָיו יֵלֵכוּ לֹא יִסַּבּוּ בְּלֶכְתָּם: ¹² וְכָל־בְּשָׂרָם וְגַבֵּהֶם וִידֵיהֶם וְכַנְפֵיהֶם וְהָאוֹפַנִּים מְלֵאִים עֵינַיִם סָבִיב לְאַרְבַּעְתָּם אוֹפַנֵּיהֶם: ¹³ לָאוֹפַנִּים לָהֶם קוֹרָא הַגַּלְגַּל בְּאָזְנָי: ¹⁴ וְאַרְבָּעָה פָנִים לְאֶחָד פְּנֵי הָאֶחָד פְּנֵי הַכְּרוּב וּפְנֵי הַשֵּׁנִי פְּנֵי אָדָם וְהַשְּׁלִישִׁי פְּנֵי אַרְיֵה וְהָרְבִיעִי פְּנֵי־נָשֶׁר: ¹⁵ וַיֵּרֹמּוּ הַכְּרוּבִים הִיא הַחַיָּה אֲשֶׁר רָאִיתִי בִּנְהַר־כְּבָר: ¹⁶ וּבְלֶכֶת הַכְּרוּבִים יֵלְכוּ הָאוֹפַנִּים אֶצְלָם וּבִשְׂאֵת הַכְּרוּבִים אֶת־כַּנְפֵיהֶם לָרוּם מֵעַל הָאָרֶץ לֹא־יִסַּבּוּ הָאוֹפַנִּים גַּם־הֵם מֵאֶצְלָם: ¹⁷ בְּעָמְדָם יַעֲמֹדוּ וּבְרוֹמָם יֵרוֹמּוּ אוֹתָם כִּי רוּחַ הַחַיָּה בָּהֶם: ¹⁸ וַיֵּצֵא כְּבוֹד יְהוָה מֵעַל מִפְתַּן הַבַּיִת וַיַּעֲמֹד עַל־הַכְּרוּבִים: ¹⁹ וַיִּשְׂאוּ הַכְּרוּבִים אֶת־כַּנְפֵיהֶם וַיֵּרוֹמּוּ מִן־הָאָרֶץ לְעֵינַי בְּצֵאתָם וְהָאוֹפַנִּים לְעֻמָּתָם וַיַּעֲמֹד פֶּתַח שַׁעַר בֵּית־יְהוָה הַקַּדְמוֹנִי וּכְבוֹד אֱלֹהֵי־יִשְׂרָאֵל עֲלֵיהֶם מִלְמָעְלָה: ²⁰ הִיא הַחַיָּה אֲשֶׁר רָאִיתִי תַּחַת אֱלֹהֵי־יִשְׂרָאֵל בִּנְהַר־כְּבָר וָאֵדַע כִּי כְרוּבִים הֵמָּה:

²¹ אַרְבָּעָה אַרְבָּעָה פָנִים לְאֶחָד וְאַרְבַּע כְּנָפַיִם לְאֶחָד וּדְמוּת יְדֵי אָדָם תַּחַת כַּנְפֵיהֶם: ²² וּדְמוּת פְּנֵיהֶם הֵמָּה הַפָּנִים אֲשֶׁר רָאִיתִי עַל־נְהַר־כְּבָר מַרְאֵיהֶם וְאוֹתָם אִישׁ אֶל־עֵבֶר פָּנָיו יֵלֵכוּ:

יא וַתִּשָּׂא אֹתִי רוּחַ וַתָּבֵא אֹתִי אֶל־שַׁעַר בֵּית־יְהוָה הַקַּדְמוֹנִי הַפּוֹנֶה קָדִימָה וְהִנֵּה בְּפֶתַח הַשַּׁעַר עֶשְׂרִים וַחֲמִשָּׁה אִישׁ וָאֶרְאֶה בְתוֹכָם אֶת־יַאֲזַנְיָה בֶן־עַזֻּר וְאֶת־פְּלַטְיָהוּ בֶן־בְּנָיָהוּ שָׂרֵי הָעָם: פ ² וַיֹּאמֶר אֵלַי בֶּן־אָדָם אֵלֶּה הָאֲנָשִׁים הַחֹשְׁבִים אָוֶן וְהַיֹּעֲצִים עֲצַת־רָע בָּעִיר הַזֹּאת: ³ הָאֹמְרִים לֹא

not near to build houses; this *city is* the caldron, and we *are* the meat.' ⁴ Therefore prophesy against them, prophesy, O son of man!"

⁵ Then the Spirit of the LORD fell upon me, and said to me, "Speak! 'Thus says the LORD: "Thus you have said, O house of Israel; for I know the things that come into your mind. ⁶ You have multiplied your slain in this city, and you have filled its streets with the slain." ⁷ Therefore thus says the Lord GOD: "Your slain whom you have laid in its midst, they *are* the meat, and this *city is* the caldron; but I shall bring you out of the midst of it. ⁸ You have feared the sword; and I will bring a sword upon you," says the Lord GOD. ⁹ "And I will bring you out of its midst, and deliver you into the hands of strangers, and execute judgments on you. ¹⁰ You shall fall by the sword. I will judge you at the border of Israel. Then you shall know that I *am* the LORD. ¹¹ This *city* shall not be your caldron, nor shall you be the meat in its midst. I will judge you at the border of Israel. ¹² And you shall know that I *am* the LORD; for you have not walked in My statutes nor executed My judgments, but have done according to the customs of the Gentiles which *are* all around you."' "

¹³ Now it happened, while I was prophesying, that Pelatiah the son of Benaiah died. Then I fell on my face and cried with a loud voice, and said, "Ah, Lord GOD! Will You make a complete end of the remnant of Israel?"

¹⁴ Again the word of the LORD came to me, saying, ¹⁵ "Son of man, your brethren, your relatives, your countrymen, and all the house of Israel in its entirety, *are* those about whom the inhabitants of Jerusalem have said, 'Get far away from the LORD; this land has been given to us as a possession.' ¹⁶ Therefore say, 'Thus says the Lord GOD: "Although I have cast them far off among the Gentiles, and although I have scattered them among the countries, yet I shall be a little sanctuary for them in the countries where they have gone."' ¹⁷ Therefore say, 'Thus says the Lord GOD: "I will gather you from the peoples, assemble you from the countries where you have been scattered, and I will give you the land of Israel."' ¹⁸ And they will go there, and they will take away all its detestable things and all its abominations from there. ¹⁹ Then I will give them one heart, and I will put a new spirit within them, and take the stony heart out of their flesh, and give them a heart of flesh, ²⁰ that they may walk in My statutes and keep My judgments and do them; and they shall be My people, and I will be their God. ²¹ But *as for those* whose hearts

בִּקְרוֹב בְּנוֹת בָּתִּים הִיא הַסִּיר וַאֲנַחְנוּ הַבָּשָׂר: ⁴ לָכֵן הִנָּבֵא עֲלֵיהֶם הִנָּבֵא בֶּן־אָדָם: ⁵ וַתִּפֹּל עָלַי רוּחַ יְהוָה וַיֹּאמֶר אֵלַי אֱמֹר כֹּה־אָמַר יְהוָה כֵּן אֲמַרְתֶּם בֵּית יִשְׂרָאֵל וּמַעֲלוֹת רוּחֲכֶם אֲנִי יְדַעְתִּיהָ: ⁶ הִרְבֵּיתֶם חַלְלֵיכֶם בָּעִיר הַזֹּאת וּמִלֵּאתֶם חוּצֹתֶיהָ חָלָל: פ

⁷ לָכֵן כֹּה־אָמַר אֲדֹנָי יְהוִה חַלְלֵיכֶם אֲשֶׁר שַׂמְתֶּם בְּתוֹכָהּ הֵמָּה הַבָּשָׂר וְהִיא הַסִּיר וְאֶתְכֶם הוֹצִיא מִתּוֹכָהּ: ⁸ חֶרֶב יְרֵאתֶם וְחֶרֶב אָבִיא עֲלֵיכֶם נְאֻם אֲדֹנָי יְהוִה: ⁹ וְהוֹצֵאתִי אֶתְכֶם מִתּוֹכָהּ וְנָתַתִּי אֶתְכֶם בְּיַד־זָרִים וְעָשִׂיתִי בָכֶם שְׁפָטִים: ¹⁰ בַּחֶרֶב תִּפֹּלוּ עַל־גְּבוּל יִשְׂרָאֵל אֶשְׁפּוֹט אֶתְכֶם וִידַעְתֶּם כִּי־אֲנִי יְהוָה: ¹¹ הִיא לֹא־תִהְיֶה לָכֶם לְסִיר וְאַתֶּם תִּהְיוּ בְתוֹכָהּ לְבָשָׂר אֶל־גְּבוּל יִשְׂרָאֵל אֶשְׁפֹּט אֶתְכֶם: ¹² וִידַעְתֶּם כִּי־אֲנִי יְהוָה אֲשֶׁר בְּחֻקַּי לֹא הֲלַכְתֶּם וּמִשְׁפָּטַי לֹא עֲשִׂיתֶם וּכְמִשְׁפְּטֵי הַגּוֹיִם אֲשֶׁר סְבִיבוֹתֵיכֶם עֲשִׂיתֶם: ¹³ וַיְהִי כְּהִנָּבְאִי וּפְלַטְיָהוּ בֶן־בְּנָיָה מֵת וָאֶפֹּל עַל־פָּנַי וָאֶזְעַק קוֹל־גָּדוֹל וָאֹמַר אֲהָהּ אֲדֹנָי יְהוִה כָּלָה אַתָּה עֹשֶׂה אֵת שְׁאֵרִית יִשְׂרָאֵל: פ

¹⁴ וַיְהִי דְבַר־יְהוָה אֵלַי לֵאמֹר: ¹⁵ בֶּן־אָדָם אַחֶיךָ אַחֶיךָ אַנְשֵׁי גְאֻלָּתֶךָ וְכָל־בֵּית יִשְׂרָאֵל כֻּלֹּה אֲשֶׁר אָמְרוּ לָהֶם יֹשְׁבֵי יְרוּשָׁלִַם רַחֲקוּ מֵעַל יְהוָה לָנוּ הִיא נִתְּנָה הָאָרֶץ לְמוֹרָשָׁה: ס ¹⁶ לָכֵן אֱמֹר כֹּה־אָמַר אֲדֹנָי יְהוִה כִּי הִרְחַקְתִּים בַּגּוֹיִם וְכִי הֲפִיצוֹתִים בָּאֲרָצוֹת וָאֱהִי לָהֶם לְמִקְדָּשׁ מְעַט בָּאֲרָצוֹת אֲשֶׁר־בָּאוּ שָׁם: ס ¹⁷ לָכֵן אֱמֹר כֹּה־אָמַר אֲדֹנָי יְהוִה וְקִבַּצְתִּי אֶתְכֶם מִן־הָעַמִּים וְאָסַפְתִּי אֶתְכֶם מִן־הָאֲרָצוֹת אֲשֶׁר נְפֹצוֹתֶם בָּהֶם וְנָתַתִּי לָכֶם אֶת־אַדְמַת יִשְׂרָאֵל: ¹⁸ וּבָאוּ־שָׁמָּה וְהֵסִירוּ אֶת־כָּל־שִׁקּוּצֶיהָ וְאֶת־כָּל־תּוֹעֲבוֹתֶיהָ מִמֶּנָּה: ¹⁹ וְנָתַתִּי לָהֶם לֵב אֶחָד וְרוּחַ חֲדָשָׁה אֶתֵּן בְּקִרְבְּכֶם וַהֲסִרֹתִי לֵב הָאֶבֶן מִבְּשָׂרָם וְנָתַתִּי לָהֶם לֵב בָּשָׂר: ²⁰ לְמַעַן בְּחֻקֹּתַי יֵלֵכוּ וְאֶת־מִשְׁפָּטַי יִשְׁמְרוּ וְעָשׂוּ אֹתָם וְהָיוּ־לִי לְעָם וַאֲנִי אֶהְיֶה לָהֶם לֵאלֹהִים: ²¹ וְאֶל־לֵב שִׁקּוּצֵיהֶם וְתוֹעֲבוֹתֵיהֶם

follow the desire for their detestable things and their abominations, I will recompense their deeds on their own heads," says the Lord GOD.

22 So the cherubim lifted up their wings, with the wheels beside them, and the glory of the God of Israel *was* high above them. 23 And the glory of the LORD went up from the midst of the city and stood on the mountain, which *is* on the east side of the city.

24 Then the Spirit took me up and brought me in a vision by the Spirit of God into Chaldea, to those in captivity. And the vision that I had seen went up from me. 25 So I spoke to those in captivity of all the things the LORD had shown me.

12 Now the word of the LORD came to me, saying: 2 "Son of man, you dwell in the midst of a rebellious house, which has eyes to see but does not see, and ears to hear but does not hear; for they *are* a rebellious house.

3 "Therefore, son of man, prepare your belongings for captivity, and go into captivity by day in their sight. You shall go from your place into captivity to another place in their sight. It may be that they will consider, though they *are* a rebellious house. 4 By day you shall bring out your belongings in their sight, as though going into captivity; and at evening you shall go in their sight, like those who go into captivity. 5 Dig through the wall in their sight, and carry your belongings out through it. 6 In their sight you shall bear *them* on *your* shoulders *and* carry *them* out at twilight; you shall cover your face, so that you cannot see the ground, for I have made you a sign to the house of Israel."

7 So I did as I was commanded. I brought out my belongings by day, as though going into captivity, and at evening I dug through the wall with my hand. I brought *them* out at twilight, *and* I bore *them* on *my* shoulder in their sight.

8 And in the morning the word of the LORD came to me, saying, 9 "Son of man, has not the house of Israel, the rebellious house, said to you, 'What are you doing?' 10 Say to them, 'Thus says the Lord GOD: "This burden *concerns* the prince in Jerusalem and all the house of Israel who are among them." ' 11 Say, 'I *am* a sign to you. As I have done, so shall it be done to them; they shall be carried away into captivity.' 12 And the prince who *is* among them shall bear *his belongings* on *his* shoulder at twilight and go out. They shall dig through the wall to carry *them* out through it. He shall cover his face, so that he cannot see the ground with *his* eyes. 13 I will also spread My net over him, and he shall be caught in My snare. I will bring him to Babylon, *to* the land

לָכֶ֣ם הֹלֵ֤ךְ דַּרְכָּם֙ בְּרֹאשָׁ֣ם נָתַ֔תִּי נְאֻ֖ם אֲדֹנָ֥י
יְהֹוִֽה׃ 22 וַיִּשְׂא֤וּ הַכְּרוּבִים֙ אֶת־כַּנְפֵיהֶ֔ם וְהָאֽוֹפַנִּ֖ים
לְעֻמָּתָ֑ם וּכְב֧וֹד אֱלֹהֵֽי־יִשְׂרָאֵ֛ל עֲלֵיהֶ֖ם מִלְמָֽעְלָה׃
23 וַיַּ֙עַל֙ כְּב֣וֹד יְהֹוָ֔ה מֵעַ֖ל תּ֣וֹךְ הָעִ֑יר וַֽיַּעֲמֹד֙ עַל־
הָהָ֔ר אֲשֶׁ֥ר מִקֶּ֖דֶם לָעִֽיר׃ 24 וְר֣וּחַ נְשָׂאַ֗תְנִי וַתְּבִיאֵ֤נִי
כַשְׂדִּ֙ימָה֙ אֶל־הַגּוֹלָ֔ה בַּמַּרְאֶ֖ה בְּר֣וּחַ אֱלֹהִ֑ים וַיַּ֙עַל֙
מֵֽעָלַ֔י הַמַּרְאֶ֖ה אֲשֶׁ֥ר רָאִֽיתִי׃ 25 וָֽאֲדַבֵּ֤ר אֶל־הַגּוֹלָ֔ה
אֵ֛ת כָּל־דִּבְרֵ֥י יְהֹוָ֖ה אֲשֶׁ֥ר הֶרְאָֽנִי׃
פ

יב וַיְהִ֥י דְבַר־יְהֹוָ֖ה אֵלַ֥י לֵאמֹֽר׃ 2 בֶּן־אָדָ֗ם בְּת֤וֹךְ
בֵּית־הַמֶּ֙רִי֙ אַתָּ֣ה יֹשֵׁ֔ב אֲשֶׁ֙ר עֵינַ֤יִם לָהֶם֙ לִרְאוֹת֙
וְלֹ֣א רָא֔וּ אָזְנַ֤יִם לָהֶם֙ לִשְׁמֹ֣עַ וְלֹ֣א שָׁמֵ֔עוּ כִּ֛י בֵּ֥ית
מְרִ֖י הֵֽם׃ 3 וְאַתָּ֣ה בֶן־אָדָ֗ם עֲשֵׂ֤ה לְךָ֙ כְּלֵ֣י גוֹלָ֔ה
וּגְלֵ֥ה יוֹמָ֖ם לְעֵֽינֵיהֶ֑ם וְגָלִ֜יתָ מִמְּקֽוֹמְךָ֙ אֶל־מָק֣וֹם
אַחֵ֙ר֙ לְעֵ֣ינֵיהֶ֔ם אוּלַ֣י יִרְא֔וּ כִּ֛י בֵּ֥ית מְרִ֖י הֵֽמָּה׃

4 וְהוֹצֵאתָ֙ כֵלֶ֜יךָ כִּכְלֵ֥י גוֹלָ֛ה יוֹמָ֖ם לְעֵֽינֵיהֶ֑ם וְאַתָּ֗ה
תֵּצֵ֤א בָעֶ֙רֶב֙ לְעֵ֣ינֵיהֶ֔ם כְּמוֹצָאֵ֖י גוֹלָֽה׃ 5 לְעֵינֵיהֶ֛ם
חֲתׇר־לְךָ֥ בַקִּ֖יר וְהוֹצֵאתָ֥ בּֽוֹ׃ 6 לְעֵ֙ינֵיהֶ֜ם עַל־כָּתֵ֤ף
תִּשָּׂא֙ בָּעֲלָטָ֣ה תוֹצִ֔יא פָּנֶ֣יךָ תְכַסֶּ֔ה וְלֹ֥א תִרְאֶ֖ה אֶת־
הָאָ֑רֶץ כִּֽי־מוֹפֵ֥ת נְתַתִּ֖יךָ לְבֵ֥ית יִשְׂרָאֵֽל׃ 7 וָאַ֣עַשׂ כֵּן֮
כַּאֲשֶׁ֣ר צֻוֵּ֒יתִי֒ כֵּלַ֜י הוֹצֵ֤אתִי כִּכְלֵ֤י גוֹלָה֙ יוֹמָ֔ם וּבָעֶ֗רֶב
חָתַ֥רְתִּי־לִ֛י בַקִּ֖יר בְּיָ֑ד בָּעֲלָטָ֤ה הוֹצֵ֙אתִי֙ עַל־כָּתֵ֔ף
נָשָׂ֖אתִי לְעֵינֵיהֶֽם׃
פ

8 וַיְהִ֥י דְבַר־יְהֹוָ֖ה אֵלַ֣י בַּבֹּ֥קֶר לֵאמֹֽר׃ 9 בֶּן־אָדָ֗ם
הֲלֹ֙א אָמְר֤וּ אֵלֶ֙יךָ֙ בֵּ֣ית יִשְׂרָאֵ֔ל בֵּ֖ית הַמֶּ֑רִי מָ֥ה אַתָּ֖ה
עֹשֶֽׂה׃ 10 אֱמֹ֣ר אֲלֵיהֶ֗ם כֹּ֤ה אָמַר֙ אֲדֹנָ֣י יְהֹוִ֔ה הַנָּשִׂ֙יא
הַמַּשָּׂ֤א הַזֶּה֙ בִּיר֣וּשָׁלַ֔͏ִם וְכׇל־בֵּ֥ית יִשְׂרָאֵ֖ל אֲשֶׁר־
הֵ֥מָּה בְתוֹכָֽם׃ 11 אֱמֹ֗ר אֲנִ֤י מֽוֹפֶתְכֶם֙ כַּאֲשֶׁ֣ר עָשִׂ֔יתִי
כֵּ֖ן יֵעָשֶׂ֣ה לָהֶ֑ם בַּגּוֹלָ֥ה בַשְּׁבִ֖י יֵלֵֽכוּ׃ 12 וְהַנָּשִׂ֙יא
אֲשֶׁר־בְּתוֹכָ֜ם אֶל־כָּתֵ֤ף יִשָּׂא֙ בָּעֲלָטָ֣ה וְיֵצֵ֔א בַּקִּ֖יר
יַחְתְּר֣וּ לְה֣וֹצִיא ב֑וֹ פָּנָ֣יו יְכַסֶּ֔ה יַ֗עַן אֲשֶׁ֤ר לֹֽא־
יִרְאֶ֥ה לַעַ֛יִן ה֖וּא אֶת־הָאָֽרֶץ׃ 13 וּפָרַשְׂתִּ֤י אֶת־רִשְׁתִּי֙
עָלָ֔יו וְנִתְפַּ֖שׂ בִּמְצֽוּדָתִ֑י וְהֵבֵאתִ֤י אֹתוֹ֙ בָבֶ֙לָה֙ אֶ֣רֶץ

of the Chaldeans; yet he shall not see it, though he shall die there. 14 I will scatter to every wind all who *are* around him to help him, and all his troops; and I will draw out the sword after them.

15 "Then they shall know that I *am* the LORD, when I scatter them among the nations and disperse them throughout the countries. 16 But I will spare a few of their men from the sword, from famine, and from pestilence, that they may declare all their abominations among the Gentiles wherever they go. Then they shall know that I *am* the LORD."

17 Moreover the word of the LORD came to me, saying, 18 "Son of man, eat your bread with quaking, and drink your water with trembling and anxiety. 19 And say to the people of the land, 'Thus says the Lord GOD to the inhabitants of Jerusalem *and* to the land of Israel: "They shall eat their bread with anxiety, and drink their water with dread, so that her land may be emptied of all who are in it, because of the violence of all those who dwell in it. 20 Then the cities that are inhabited shall be laid waste, and the land shall become desolate; and you shall know that I *am* the LORD." ' "

21 And the word of the LORD came to me, saying, 22 "Son of man, what *is* this proverb *that* you *people* have about the land of Israel, which says, 'The days are prolonged, and every vision fails'? 23 Tell them therefore, 'Thus says the Lord GOD: "I will lay this proverb to rest, and they shall no more use it as a proverb in Israel." But say to them, "The days are at hand, and the fulfillment of every vision. 24 For no more shall there be any false vision or flattering divination within the house of Israel. 25 For I *am* the LORD. I speak, and the word which I speak will come to pass; it will no more be postponed; for in your days, O rebellious house, I will say the word and perform it," says the Lord GOD.' "

26 Again the word of the LORD came to me, saying, 27 "Son of man, look, the house of Israel is saying, 'The vision that he sees *is* for many days *from now,* and he prophesies of times far off.' 28 Therefore say to them, 'Thus says the Lord GOD: "None of My words will be postponed any more, but the word which I speak will be done," says the Lord GOD.' "

13 And the word of the LORD came to me, saying, 2 "Son of man, prophesy against the prophets of Israel who prophesy, and say to those who prophesy out of their own heart, 'Hear the word of the LORD!' "

3 Thus says the Lord GOD: "Woe to the foolish prophets, who follow their own spirit and have seen nothing! 4 O Israel, your prophets are like foxes in

כַּשְׂדִּ֔ים וְאוֹתָ֥הּ לֹֽא־יִרְאֶ֖ה וְשָׁ֥ם יָמֽוּת: 14 וְכֹל֩ אֲשֶׁ֨ר סְבִיבֹתָ֤יו עֶזְרֹה֙ וְכָל־אֲגַפָּ֔יו אֱזָרֶ֥ה לְכָל־ר֖וּחַ וְחֶ֣רֶב אָרִ֥יק אַחֲרֵיהֶֽם: 15 וְיָדְע֖וּ כִּֽי־אֲנִ֣י יְהֹוָ֑ה בַּהֲפִיצִ֤י אוֹתָם֙ בַּגּוֹיִ֔ם וְזֵרִיתִ֥י אוֹתָ֖ם בָּאֲרָצֽוֹת: 16 וְהוֹתַרְתִּ֣י מֵהֶ֞ם אַנְשֵׁ֣י מִסְפָּ֗ר מֵחֶ֙רֶב֙ מֵרָעָ֣ב וּמִדָּ֔בֶר לְמַ֙עַן֙ יְסַפְּר֣וּ אֶת־כָּל־תּוֹעֲבֽוֹתֵיהֶ֔ם בַּגּוֹיִ֖ם אֲשֶׁר־בָּ֣אוּ שָׁ֑ם וְיָדְע֖וּ כִּֽי־אֲנִ֥י יְהֹוָֽה:

17 וַיְהִ֥י דְבַר־יְהֹוָ֖ה אֵלַ֥י לֵאמֹֽר: 18 בֶּן־אָדָ֕ם לַחְמְךָ֙ בְּרַ֣עַשׁ תֹּאכֵ֔ל וּמֵימֶ֕יךָ בְּרָגְזָ֥ה וּבִדְאָגָ֖ה תִּשְׁתֶּֽה: 19 וְאָמַרְתָּ֣ אֶל־עַ֣ם הָאָ֡רֶץ כֹּֽה־אָמַר֩ אֲדֹנָ֨י יְהֹוִ֜ה לְיוֹשְׁבֵ֤י יְרֽוּשָׁלִַ֙ם֙ אֶל־אַדְמַ֣ת יִשְׂרָאֵ֔ל לַחְמָם֙ בִּדְאָגָ֣ה יֹאכֵ֔לוּ וּמֵֽימֵיהֶ֖ם בְּשִׁמָּמ֣וֹן יִשְׁתּ֑וּ לְמַ֜עַן תֵּשַׁ֤ם אַרְצָהּ֙ מִמְּלֹאָ֔הּ מֵחֲמַ֖ס כָּל־הַיֹּֽשְׁבִ֥ים בָּֽהּ: 20 וְהֶעָרִ֣ים הַנּֽוֹשָׁבוֹת֙ תֶּחֱרַ֔בְנָה וְהָאָ֖רֶץ שְׁמָמָ֣ה תִֽהְיֶ֑ה וִֽידַעְתֶּ֖ם כִּֽי־אֲנִ֥י יְהֹוָֽה:

21 וַיְהִ֥י דְבַר־יְהֹוָ֖ה אֵלַ֥י לֵאמֹֽר: 22 בֶּן־אָדָ֗ם מָ֣ה הַמָּשָׁ֤ל הַזֶּה֙ לָכֶ֔ם עַל־אַדְמַ֥ת יִשְׂרָאֵ֖ל לֵאמֹ֑ר יַֽאַרְכוּ֙ הַיָּמִ֔ים וְאָבַ֖ד כָּל־חָזֽוֹן: 23 לָכֵ֞ן אֱמֹ֣ר אֲלֵיהֶ֗ם כֹּֽה־אָמַר֮ אֲדֹנָ֣י יְהֹוִה֒ הִשְׁבַּ֙תִּי֙ אֶת־הַמָּשָׁ֣ל הַזֶּ֔ה וְלֹֽא־יִמְשְׁל֥וּ אֹת֛וֹ ע֖וֹד בְּיִשְׂרָאֵ֑ל כִּ֚י אִם־דַּבֵּ֣ר אֲלֵיהֶ֔ם קָֽרְבוּ֙ הַיָּמִ֔ים וּדְבַ֖ר כָּל־חָזֽוֹן: 24 כִּ֠י לֹ֣א יִֽהְיֶ֥ה ע֛וֹד כָּל־חֲז֥וֹן שָׁ֖וְא וּמִקְסַ֣ם חָלָ֑ק בְּת֖וֹךְ בֵּ֥ית יִשְׂרָאֵֽל: 25 כִּ֣י ׀ אֲנִ֣י יְהֹוָ֗ה אֲדַבֵּר֙ אֵת֩ אֲשֶׁ֨ר אֲדַבֵּ֤ר דָּבָר֙ וְיֵ֣עָשֶׂ֔ה לֹ֥א תִמָּשֵׁ֖ךְ ע֑וֹד כִּ֣י בִֽימֵיכֶ֞ם בֵּ֣ית הַמֶּ֗רִי אֲדַבֵּ֤ר דָּבָר֙ וַֽעֲשִׂיתִ֔יו נְאֻ֖ם אֲדֹנָ֥י יְהֹוָֽה:

26 וַיְהִ֥י דְבַר־יְהֹוָ֖ה אֵלַ֥י לֵאמֹֽר: 27 בֶּן־אָדָ֗ם הִנֵּ֤ה בֵֽית־יִשְׂרָאֵל֙ אֹֽמְרִ֔ים הֶחָז֛וֹן אֲשֶׁר־ה֥וּא חֹזֶ֖ה לְיָמִ֣ים רַבִּ֑ים וּלְעִתִּ֥ים רְחוֹק֖וֹת ה֥וּא נִבָּֽא: 28 לָכֵ֞ן אֱמֹ֣ר אֲלֵיהֶ֗ם כֹּ֤ה אָמַר֙ אֲדֹנָ֣י יְהֹוִ֔ה לֹֽא־תִמָּשֵׁ֥ךְ ע֖וֹד כָּל־דְּבָרָ֑י אֲשֶׁ֨ר אֲדַבֵּ֤ר דָּבָר֙ וְיֵ֣עָשֶׂ֔ה נְאֻ֖ם אֲדֹנָ֥י יְהֹוִֽה:

יג וַיְהִ֥י דְבַר־יְהֹוָ֖ה אֵלַ֥י לֵאמֹֽר: 2 בֶּן־אָדָ֕ם הִנָּבֵ֛א אֶל־נְבִיאֵ֥י יִשְׂרָאֵ֖ל הַנִּבָּאִ֑ים וְאָ֣מַרְתָּ֗ לִנְבִיאֵי֙ מִלִּבָּ֔ם שִׁמְע֖וּ דְּבַר־יְהֹוָֽה: 3 כֹּ֤ה אָמַר֙ אֲדֹנָ֣י יְהֹוִ֔ה ה֖וֹי עַל־הַנְּבִיאִ֣ים הַנְּבָלִ֑ים אֲשֶׁ֥ר הֹֽלְכִ֛ים אַחַ֥ר רוּחָ֖ם וּלְבִלְתִּ֥י רָאֽוּ: 4 כְּשֻֽׁעָלִ֖ים בׇּחֳרָב֑וֹת נְבִיאֶ֛יךָ יִשְׂרָאֵ֖ל

the deserts. ⁵You have not gone up into the gaps to build a wall for the house of Israel to stand in battle on the day of the LORD. ⁶They have envisioned futility and false divination, saying, 'Thus says the LORD!' But the LORD has not sent them; yet they hope that the word may be confirmed. ⁷Have you not seen a futile vision, and have you not spoken false divination? You say, 'The LORD says,' but I have not spoken."

⁸Therefore thus says the Lord GOD: "Because you have spoken nonsense and envisioned lies, therefore I *am* indeed against you," says the Lord GOD. ⁹"My hand will be against the prophets who envision futility and who divine lies; they shall not be in the assembly of My people, nor be written in the record of the house of Israel, nor shall they enter into the land of Israel. Then you shall know that I *am* the Lord GOD.

¹⁰"Because, indeed, because they have seduced My people, saying, 'Peace!' when *there is* no peace—and one builds a wall, and they plaster it with untempered *mortar*— ¹¹say to those who plaster *it* with untempered *mortar,* that it will fall. There will be flooding rain, and you, O great hailstones, shall fall; and a stormy wind shall tear *it* down. ¹²Surely, when the wall has fallen, will it not be said to you, 'Where *is* the mortar with which you plastered *it?*'"

¹³Therefore thus says the Lord GOD: "I will cause a stormy wind to break forth in My fury; and there shall be a flooding rain in My anger, and great hailstones in fury to consume *it.* ¹⁴So I will break down the wall you have plastered with untempered *mortar,* and bring it down to the ground, so that its foundation will be uncovered; it will fall, and you shall be consumed in the midst of it. Then you shall know that I *am* the LORD.

¹⁵"Thus will I accomplish My wrath on the wall and on those who have plastered it with untempered *mortar;* and I will say to you, 'The wall *is* no more, nor those who plastered it, ¹⁶*that is,* the prophets of Israel who prophesy concerning Jerusalem, and who see visions of peace for her when *there is* no peace,'" says the Lord GOD.

¹⁷"Likewise, son of man, set your face against the daughters of your people, who prophesy out of their own heart; prophesy against them, ¹⁸and say, 'Thus says the Lord GOD: "Woe to the *women* who sew *magic* charms on their sleeves and make veils for the heads of people of every height to hunt souls! Will you hunt the souls of My people, and keep yourselves alive? ¹⁹And will you profane Me among My people for handfuls of barley and for

הָיוּ: 5 לֹא עֲלִיתֶם בַּפְּרָצוֹת וַתִּגְדְּרוּ גָדֵר עַל־בֵּית יִשְׂרָאֵל לַעֲמֹד בַּמִּלְחָמָה בְּיוֹם יְהוָה: 6 חָזוּ שָׁוְא וְקֶסֶם כָּזָב הָאֹמְרִים נְאֻם־יְהוָה וַיהוָה לֹא שְׁלָחָם וְיִחֲלוּ לְקַיֵּם דָּבָר: 7 הֲלוֹא מַחֲזֵה־שָׁוְא חֲזִיתֶם וּמִקְסַם כָּזָב אֲמַרְתֶּם וְאֹמְרִים נְאֻם־יְהוָה וַאֲנִי לֹא דִבַּרְתִּי: ס 8 לָכֵן כֹּה אָמַר אֲדֹנָי יְהוִֹה יַעַן דַּבֶּרְכֶם שָׁוְא וַחֲזִיתֶם כָּזָב לָכֵן הִנְנִי אֲלֵיכֶם נְאֻם אֲדֹנָי יְהוִֹה: 9 וְהָיְתָה יָדִי אֶל־הַנְּבִיאִים הַחֹזִים שָׁוְא וְהַקֹּסְמִים כָּזָב בְּסוֹד עַמִּי לֹא־יִהְיוּ וּבִכְתָב בֵּית־יִשְׂרָאֵל לֹא יִכָּתֵבוּ וְאֶל־אַדְמַת יִשְׂרָאֵל לֹא יָבֹאוּ וִידַעְתֶּם כִּי אֲנִי אֲדֹנָי יְהוִֹה: 10 יַעַן וּבְיַעַן הִטְעוּ אֶת־עַמִּי לֵאמֹר שָׁלוֹם וְאֵין שָׁלוֹם וְהוּא בֹּנֶה חַיִץ וְהִנָּם טָחִים אֹתוֹ תָּפֵל: 11 אֱמֹר אֶל־טָחֵי תָפֵל וְיִפֹּל הָיָה | גֶּשֶׁם שׁוֹטֵף וְאַתֵּנָה אַבְנֵי אֶלְגָּבִישׁ תִּפֹּלְנָה וְרוּחַ סְעָרוֹת תְּבַקֵּעַ: 12 וְהִנֵּה נָפַל הַקִּיר הֲלוֹא יֵאָמֵר אֲלֵיכֶם אַיֵּה הַטִּיחַ אֲשֶׁר טַחְתֶּם: ס 13 לָכֵן כֹּה אָמַר אֲדֹנָי יְהוִֹה וּבִקַּעְתִּי רוּחַ־סְעָרוֹת בַּחֲמָתִי וְגֶשֶׁם שֹׁטֵף בְּאַפִּי יִהְיֶה וְאַבְנֵי אֶלְגָּבִישׁ בְּחֵמָה לְכָלָה: 14 וְהָרַסְתִּי אֶת־הַקִּיר אֲשֶׁר־טַחְתֶּם תָּפֵל וְהִגַּעְתִּיהוּ אֶל־הָאָרֶץ וְנִגְלָה יְסֹדוֹ וְנָפְלָה וּכְלִיתֶם בְּתוֹכָהּ וִידַעְתֶּם כִּי־אֲנִי יְהוָה: 15 וְכִלֵּיתִי אֶת־חֲמָתִי בַּקִּיר וּבַטָּחִים אֹתוֹ תָּפֵל וְאֹמַר לָכֶם אֵין הַקִּיר וְאֵין הַטָּחִים אֹתוֹ: 16 נְבִיאֵי יִשְׂרָאֵל הַנִּבְּאִים אֶל־יְרוּשָׁלַםִ וְהַחֹזִים לָהּ חֲזוֹן שָׁלֵם וְאֵין שָׁלֵם נְאֻם אֲדֹנָי יְהוִֹה: פ

17 וְאַתָּה בֶן־אָדָם שִׂים פָּנֶיךָ אֶל־בְּנוֹת עַמְּךָ הַמִּתְנַבְּאוֹת מִלִּבְּהֶן וְהִנָּבֵא עֲלֵיהֶן: 18 וְאָמַרְתָּ כֹּה־אָמַר | אֲדֹנָי יְהוִֹה הוֹי לִמְתַפְּרוֹת כְּסָתוֹת עַל | כָּל־אַצִּילֵי יָדַי וְעֹשׂוֹת הַמִּסְפָּחוֹת עַל־רֹאשׁ כָּל־קוֹמָה לְצוֹדֵד נְפָשׁוֹת הַנְּפָשׁוֹת תְּצוֹדֵדְנָה לְעַמִּי וּנְפָשׁוֹת לָכֶנָה תְחַיֶּינָה: 19 וַתְּחַלֶּלְנָה אֹתִי אֶל־עַמִּי בְּשַׁעֲלֵי שְׂעֹרִים וּבִפְתוֹתֵי לֶחֶם לְהָמִית נְפָשׁוֹת אֲשֶׁר לֹא־תְמוּתֶנָה וּלְחַיּוֹת

pieces of bread, killing people who should not die, and keeping people alive who should not live, by your lying to My people who listen to lies?"

20 'Therefore thus says the Lord GOD: "Behold, I *am* against your *magic* charms by which you hunt souls there like birds. I will tear them from your arms, and let the souls go, the souls you hunt like birds. 21 I will also tear off your veils and deliver My people out of your hand, and they shall no longer be as prey in your hand. Then you shall know that I *am* the LORD.

22 "Because with lies you have made the heart of the righteous sad, whom I have not made sad; and you have strengthened the hands of the wicked, so that he does not turn from his wicked way to save his life. 23 Therefore you shall no longer envision futility nor practice divination; for I will deliver My people out of your hand, and you shall know that I *am* the LORD." ' "

14 Now some of the elders of Israel came to me and sat before me. 2 And the word of the LORD came to me, saying, 3 "Son of man, these men have set up their idols in their hearts, and put before them that which causes them to stumble into iniquity. Should I let Myself be inquired of at all by them?

4 "Therefore speak to them, and say to them, 'Thus says the Lord GOD: "Everyone of the house of Israel who sets up his idols in his heart, and puts before him what causes him to stumble into iniquity, and then comes to the prophet, I the LORD will answer him who comes, according to the multitude of his idols, 5 that I may seize the house of Israel by their heart, because they are all estranged from Me by their idols." '

6 "Therefore say to the house of Israel, 'Thus says the Lord GOD: "Repent, turn away from your idols, and turn your faces away from all your abominations. 7 For anyone of the house of Israel, or of the strangers who dwell in Israel, who separates himself from Me and sets up his idols in his heart and puts before him what causes him to stumble into iniquity, then comes to a prophet to inquire of him concerning Me, I the LORD will answer him by Myself. 8 I will set My face against that man and make him a sign and a proverb, and I will cut him off from the midst of My people. Then you shall know that I *am* the LORD.

9 "And if the prophet is induced to speak anything, I the LORD have induced that prophet, and I will stretch out My hand against him and destroy him from among My people Israel. 10 And they shall bear their iniquity; the punishment of the

נְפָשׁוֹת אֲשֶׁר לֹא־תְחַיֶּינָה בְּכַזֶּבְכֶם לְעַמִּי שֹׁמְעֵי כָזָב: ס 20 לָכֵן כֹּה־אָמַר ׀ אֲדֹנָי יְהֹוִה הִנְנִי אֶל־כִּסְּתוֹתֵיכֶנָה אֲשֶׁר אַתֵּנָה מְצֹדְדוֹת שָׁם אֶת־הַנְּפָשׁוֹת לְפֹרְחוֹת וְקָרַעְתִּי אֹתָם מֵעַל זְרוֹעֹתֵיכֶם וְשִׁלַּחְתִּי אֶת־הַנְּפָשׁוֹת אֲשֶׁר אַתֶּם מְצֹדְדוֹת אֶת־נְפָשִׁים לְפֹרְחֹת: 21 וְקָרַעְתִּי אֶת־מִסְפְּחֹתֵיכֶם וְהִצַּלְתִּי אֶת־עַמִּי מִיֶּדְכֶן וְלֹא־יִהְיוּ עוֹד בְּיֶדְכֶן לִמְצוּדָה וִידַעְתֶּן כִּי־אֲנִי יְהֹוָה: 22 יַעַן הַכְאוֹת לֵב־צַדִּיק שֶׁקֶר וַאֲנִי לֹא הִכְאַבְתִּיו וּלְחַזֵּק יְדֵי רָשָׁע לְבִלְתִּי־שׁוּב מִדַּרְכּוֹ הָרָע לְהַחֲיֹתוֹ: 23 לָכֵן שָׁוְא לֹא תֶחֱזֶינָה וְקֶסֶם לֹא־תִקְסַמְנָה עוֹד וְהִצַּלְתִּי אֶת־עַמִּי מִיֶּדְכֶן וִידַעְתֶּן כִּי־אֲנִי יְהֹוָה: ס

יד וַיָּבוֹא אֵלַי אֲנָשִׁים מִזִּקְנֵי יִשְׂרָאֵל וַיֵּשְׁבוּ לְפָנָי: פ 2 וַיְהִי דְבַר־יְהֹוָה אֵלַי לֵאמֹר: 3 בֶּן־אָדָם הָאֲנָשִׁים הָאֵלֶּה הֶעֱלוּ גִלּוּלֵיהֶם עַל־לִבָּם וּמִכְשׁוֹל עֲוֹנָם נָתְנוּ נֹכַח פְּנֵיהֶם הַאִדָּרֹשׁ אִדָּרֵשׁ לָהֶם: ס 4 לָכֵן דַּבֵּר־אוֹתָם וְאָמַרְתָּ אֲלֵיהֶם כֹּה־אָמַר ׀ אֲדֹנָי יְהֹוִה אִישׁ אִישׁ מִבֵּית יִשְׂרָאֵל אֲשֶׁר יַעֲלֶה אֶת־גִּלֻּלָיו אֶל־לִבּוֹ וּמִכְשׁוֹל עֲוֹנוֹ יָשִׂים נֹכַח פָּנָיו וּבָא אֶל־הַנָּבִיא אֲנִי יְהֹוָה נַעֲנֵיתִי לוֹ בָהּ בְּרֹב גִּלּוּלָיו: 5 לְמַעַן תְּפֹשׂ אֶת־בֵּית־יִשְׂרָאֵל בְּלִבָּם אֲשֶׁר נָזֹרוּ מֵעָלַי בְּגִלּוּלֵיהֶם כֻּלָּם: ס 6 לָכֵן אֱמֹר ׀ אֶל־בֵּית יִשְׂרָאֵל כֹּה אָמַר אֲדֹנָי יְהֹוִה שׁוּבוּ וְהָשִׁיבוּ מֵעַל גִּלּוּלֵיכֶם וּמֵעַל כָּל־תּוֹעֲבֹתֵיכֶם הָשִׁיבוּ פְנֵיכֶם: 7 כִּי אִישׁ אִישׁ מִבֵּית יִשְׂרָאֵל וּמֵהַגֵּר אֲשֶׁר־יָגוּר בְּיִשְׂרָאֵל וְיִנָּזֵר מֵאַחֲרַי וְיַעַל גִּלּוּלָיו אֶל־לִבּוֹ וּמִכְשׁוֹל עֲוֹנוֹ יָשִׂים נֹכַח פָּנָיו וּבָא אֶל־הַנָּבִיא לִדְרָשׁ־לוֹ בִי אֲנִי יְהֹוָה נַעֲנֶה־לּוֹ בִּי: 8 וְנָתַתִּי פָנַי בָּאִישׁ הַהוּא וַהֲשִׂמֹתִיהוּ לְאוֹת וְלִמְשָׁלִים וְהִכְרַתִּיו מִתּוֹךְ עַמִּי וִידַעְתֶּם כִּי־אֲנִי יְהֹוָה: 9 וְהַנָּבִיא כִּי־יְפֻתֶּה וְדִבֶּר דָּבָר אֲנִי יְהֹוָה פִּתֵּיתִי אֵת הַנָּבִיא הַהוּא וְנָטִיתִי אֶת־יָדִי עָלָיו וְהִשְׁמַדְתִּיו מִתּוֹךְ עַמִּי יִשְׂרָאֵל: 10 וְנָשְׂאוּ

יד 4 בא

prophet shall be the same as the punishment of the one who inquired, [11] that the house of Israel may no longer stray from Me, nor be profaned anymore with all their transgressions, but that they may be My people and I may be their God," says the Lord GOD.' "

[12] The word of the LORD came again to me, saying: [13] "Son of man, when a land sins against Me by persistent unfaithfulness, I will stretch out My hand against it; I will cut off its supply of bread, send famine on it, and cut off man and beast from it. [14] Even if these three men, Noah, Daniel, and Job, were in it, they would deliver *only* themselves by their righteousness," says the Lord GOD.

[15] "If I cause wild beasts to pass through the land, and they empty it, and make it so desolate that no man may pass through because of the beasts, [16] *even though* these three men *were* in it, *as* I live," says the Lord GOD, "they would deliver neither sons nor daughters; only they would be delivered, and the land would be desolate.

[17] "Or *if* I bring a sword on that land, and say, 'Sword, go through the land,' and I cut off man and beast from it, [18] *even though* these three men *were* in it, *as* I live," says the Lord GOD, "they would deliver neither sons nor daughters, but only they themselves would be delivered.

[19] "Or *if* I send a pestilence into that land and pour out My fury on it in blood, and cut off from it man and beast, [20] *even though* Noah, Daniel, and Job *were* in it, *as* I live," says the Lord GOD, "they would deliver neither son nor daughter; they would deliver *only* themselves by their righteousness."

[21] For thus says the Lord GOD: "How much more it shall be when I send My four severe judgments on Jerusalem—the sword and famine and wild beasts and pestilence—to cut off man and beast from it? [22] Yet behold, there shall be left in it a remnant who will be brought out, *both* sons and daughters; surely they will come out to you, and you will see their ways and their doings. Then you will be comforted concerning the disaster that I have brought upon Jerusalem, all that I have brought upon it. [23] And they will comfort you, when you see their ways and their doings; and you shall know that I have done nothing without cause that I have done in it," says the Lord GOD.

15

Then the word of the LORD came to me, saying: [2] "Son of man, how is the wood of the vine *better* than any other wood, the vine branch which is among the trees of the forest? [3] Is wood taken from it to make any object? Or can *men* make a peg from it to hang any vessel on? [4] Instead, it is thrown

עָוֹן כַּעֲוֹן הַדֹּרֵשׁ כַּעֲוֹן הַנָּבִיא יִהְיֶה: 11 לְמַעַן לֹא־יִתְעוּ עוֹד בֵּית־יִשְׂרָאֵל מֵאַחֲרַי וְלֹא־יִטַּמְּאוּ עוֹד בְּכָל־פִּשְׁעֵיהֶם וְהָיוּ לִי לְעָם וַאֲנִי אֶהְיֶה לָהֶם לֵאלֹהִים נְאֻם אֲדֹנָי יֱהוִֹה: פ

12 וַיְהִי דְבַר־יְהוָֹה אֵלַי לֵאמֹר: 13 בֶּן־אָדָם אֶרֶץ כִּי תֶחֱטָא־לִי לִמְעָל־מַעַל וְנָטִיתִי יָדִי עָלֶיהָ וְשָׁבַרְתִּי לָהּ מַטֵּה־לָחֶם וְהִשְׁלַחְתִּי־בָהּ רָעָב וְהִכְרַתִּי מִמֶּנָּה אָדָם וּבְהֵמָה: 14 וְהָיוּ שְׁלֹשֶׁת הָאֲנָשִׁים הָאֵלֶּה בְּתוֹכָהּ נֹחַ דָּנִאֵל וְאִיּוֹב הֵמָּה בְצִדְקָתָם יְנַצְּלוּ נַפְשָׁם נְאֻם אֲדֹנָי יֱהוִֹה: 15 לוּ־חַיָּה רָעָה אַעֲבִיר בָּאָרֶץ וְשִׁכְּלָתָּה וְהָיְתָה שְׁמָמָה מִבְּלִי עוֹבֵר מִפְּנֵי הַחַיָּה: 16 שְׁלֹשֶׁת הָאֲנָשִׁים הָאֵלֶּה בְּתוֹכָהּ חַי־אָנִי נְאֻם אֲדֹנָי יֱהוִֹה אִם־בָּנִים וְאִם־בָּנוֹת יַצִּילוּ הֵמָּה לְבַדָּם יִנָּצֵלוּ וְהָאָרֶץ תִּהְיֶה שְׁמָמָה: 17 אוֹ חֶרֶב אָבִיא עַל־הָאָרֶץ הַהִיא וְאָמַרְתִּי חֶרֶב תַּעֲבֹר בָּאָרֶץ וְהִכְרַתִּי מִמֶּנָּה אָדָם וּבְהֵמָה: 18 וּשְׁלֹשֶׁת הָאֲנָשִׁים הָאֵלֶּה בְּתוֹכָהּ חַי־אָנִי נְאֻם אֲדֹנָי יֱהוִֹה לֹא יַצִּילוּ בָּנִים וּבָנוֹת כִּי הֵם לְבַדָּם יִנָּצֵלוּ: 19 אוֹ דֶבֶר אֲשַׁלַּח אֶל־הָאָרֶץ הַהִיא וְשָׁפַכְתִּי חֲמָתִי עָלֶיהָ בְּדָם לְהַכְרִית מִמֶּנָּה אָדָם וּבְהֵמָה: 20 וְנֹחַ דָּנִאֵל וְאִיּוֹב בְּתוֹכָהּ חַי־אָנִי נְאֻם אֲדֹנָי יֱהוִֹה אִם־בֵּן אִם־בַּת יַצִּילוּ הֵמָּה בְצִדְקָתָם יַצִּילוּ נַפְשָׁם: פ

21 כִּי כֹה אָמַר אֲדֹנָי יֱהוִֹה אַף כִּי־אַרְבַּעַת שְׁפָטַי הָרָעִים חֶרֶב וְרָעָב וְחַיָּה רָעָה וָדֶבֶר שִׁלַּחְתִּי אֶל־יְרוּשָׁלִָם לְהַכְרִית מִמֶּנָּה אָדָם וּבְהֵמָה: 22 וְהִנֵּה נוֹתְרָה־בָּהּ פְּלֵטָה הַמּוּצָאִים בָּנִים וּבָנוֹת הִנָּם יוֹצְאִים אֲלֵיכֶם וּרְאִיתֶם אֶת־דַּרְכָּם וְאֶת־עֲלִילוֹתָם וְנִחַמְתֶּם עַל־הָרָעָה אֲשֶׁר הֵבֵאתִי עַל־יְרוּשָׁלִַם אֵת כָּל־אֲשֶׁר הֵבֵאתִי עָלֶיהָ: 23 וְנִחֲמוּ אֶתְכֶם כִּי־תִרְאוּ אֶת־דַּרְכָּם וְאֶת־עֲלִילוֹתָם וִידַעְתֶּם כִּי לֹא חִנָּם עָשִׂיתִי אֵת כָּל־אֲשֶׁר־עָשִׂיתִי בָהּ נְאֻם אֲדֹנָי יֱהוִֹה: פ

טו וַיְהִי דְבַר־יְהוָֹה אֵלַי לֵאמֹר: 2 בֶּן־אָדָם מַה־יִּהְיֶה עֵץ־הַגֶּפֶן מִכָּל־עֵץ הַזְּמוֹרָה אֲשֶׁר הָיָה בַּעֲצֵי הַיָּעַר: 3 הֲיֻקַּח מִמֶּנּוּ עֵץ לַעֲשׂוֹת לִמְלָאכָה אִם־יִקְחוּ מִמֶּנּוּ יָתֵד לִתְלוֹת עָלָיו כָּל־כֶּלִי: 4 הִנֵּה לָאֵשׁ

יד 14 דָּנִאֵל   20 דָּנִאֵל

into the fire for fuel; the fire devours both ends of it, and its middle is burned. Is it useful for *any* work? ⁵Indeed, when it was whole, no object could be made from it. How much less will it be useful for *any* work when the fire has devoured it, and it is burned?

⁶"Therefore thus says the Lord GOD: 'Like the wood of the vine among the trees of the forest, which I have given to the fire for fuel, so I will give up the inhabitants of Jerusalem; ⁷and I will set My face against them. They will go out from *one* fire, but *another* fire shall devour them. Then you shall know that I *am* the LORD, when I set My face against them. ⁸Thus I will make the land desolate, because they have persisted in unfaithfulness,' says the Lord GOD."

16 Again the word of the LORD came to me, saying, ²"Son of man, cause Jerusalem to know her abominations, ³and say, 'Thus says the Lord GOD to Jerusalem: "Your birth and your nativity *are* from the land of Canaan; your father *was* an Amorite and your mother a Hittite. ⁴*As for* your nativity, on the day you were born your navel cord was not cut, nor were you washed in water to cleanse *you;* you were not rubbed with salt nor wrapped in swaddling cloths. ⁵No eye pitied you, to do any of these things for you, to have compassion on you; but you were thrown out into the open field, when you yourself were loathed on the day you were born.

⁶"And when I passed by you and saw you struggling in your own blood, I said to you in your blood, 'Live!' Yes, I said to you in your blood, 'Live!' ⁷I made you thrive like a plant in the field; and you grew, matured, and became very beautiful. *Your* breasts were formed, your hair grew, but you *were* naked and bare.

⁸"When I passed by you again and looked upon you, indeed your time *was* the time of love; so I spread My wing over you and covered your nakedness. Yes, I swore an oath to you and entered into a covenant with you, and you became Mine," says the Lord GOD.

⁹"Then I washed you in water; yes, I thoroughly washed off your blood, and I anointed you with oil. ¹⁰I clothed you in embroidered cloth and gave you sandals of badger skin; I clothed you with fine linen and covered you with silk. ¹¹I adorned you with ornaments, put bracelets on your wrists, and a chain on your neck. ¹²And I put a jewel in your nose, earrings in your ears, and a beautiful crown on your head. ¹³Thus you were adorned with gold and silver, and your clothing *was of* fine linen, silk,

נָתַן לְאָכְלָה אֵת שְׁנֵי קְצוֹתָיו אֲכָלָה הָאֵשׁ וְתוֹכוֹ נָחָר הֲיִצְלַח לִמְלָאכָה: 5 הִנֵּה בִּהְיוֹתוֹ תָמִים לֹא יֵעָשֶׂה לִמְלָאכָה אַף כִּי־אֵשׁ אֲכָלַתְהוּ וַיֵּחָר וְנַעֲשָׂה עוֹד לִמְלָאכָה: ס 6 לָכֵן כֹּה אָמַר אֲדֹנָי יְהֹוִה כַּאֲשֶׁר עֵץ־הַגֶּפֶן בְּעֵץ הַיַּעַר אֲשֶׁר־נְתַתִּיו לָאֵשׁ לְאָכְלָה כֵּן נָתַתִּי אֶת־יֹשְׁבֵי יְרוּשָׁלָ‍ִם: 7 וְנָתַתִּי אֶת־פָּנַי בָּהֶם מֵהָאֵשׁ יָצָאוּ וְהָאֵשׁ תֹּאכְלֵם וִידַעְתֶּם כִּי־אֲנִי יְהֹוָה בְּשׂוּמִי אֶת־פָּנַי בָּהֶם: 8 וְנָתַתִּי אֶת־הָאָרֶץ שְׁמָמָה יַעַן מָעֲלוּ מַעַל נְאֻם אֲדֹנָי יְהֹוִה: פ

טז וַיְהִי דְבַר־יְהֹוָה אֵלַי לֵאמֹר: 2 בֶּן־אָדָם הוֹדַע אֶת־יְרוּשָׁלַ‍ִם אֶת־תּוֹעֲבֹתֶיהָ: 3 וְאָמַרְתָּ כֹּה־אָמַר אֲדֹנָי יְהֹוִה לִירוּשָׁלַ‍ִם מְכֹרֹתַיִךְ וּמֹלְדֹתַיִךְ מֵאֶרֶץ הַכְּנַעֲנִי אָבִיךְ הָאֱמֹרִי וְאִמֵּךְ חִתִּית: 4 וּמוֹלְדוֹתַיִךְ בְּיוֹם הוּלֶּדֶת אֹתָךְ לֹא־כָרַּת שָׁרֵּךְ וּבְמַיִם לֹא־רֻחַצְתְּ לְמִשְׁעִי וְהָמְלֵחַ לֹא הֻמְלַחַתְּ וְהָחְתֵּל לֹא חֻתָּלְתְּ: 5 לֹא־חָסָה עָלַיִךְ עַיִן לַעֲשׂוֹת לָךְ אַחַת מֵאֵלֶּה לְחֻמְלָה עָלָיִךְ וַתֻּשְׁלְכִי אֶל־פְּנֵי הַשָּׂדֶה בְּגֹעַל נַפְשֵׁךְ בְּיוֹם הֻלֶּדֶת אֹתָךְ: 6 וָאֶעֱבֹר עָלַיִךְ וָאֶרְאֵךְ מִתְבּוֹסֶסֶת בְּדָמָיִךְ וָאֹמַר לָךְ בְּדָמַיִךְ חֲיִי וָאֹמַר לָךְ בְּדָמַיִךְ חֲיִי: 7 רְבָבָה כְּצֶמַח הַשָּׂדֶה נְתַתִּיךְ וַתִּרְבִּי וַתִּגְדְּלִי וַתָּבֹאִי בַּעֲדִי עֲדָיִים שָׁדַיִם נָכֹנוּ וּשְׂעָרֵךְ צִמֵּחַ וְאַתְּ עֵרֹם וְעֶרְיָה: 8 וָאֶעֱבֹר עָלַיִךְ וָאֶרְאֵךְ וְהִנֵּה עִתֵּךְ עֵת דֹּדִים וָאֶפְרֹשׂ כְּנָפִי עָלַיִךְ וָאֲכַסֶּה עֶרְוָתֵךְ וָאֶשָּׁבַע לָךְ וָאָבוֹא בִבְרִית אֹתָךְ נְאֻם אֲדֹנָי יְהֹוִה וַתִּהְיִי לִי: 9 וָאֶרְחָצֵךְ בַּמַּיִם וָאֶשְׁטֹף דָּמַיִךְ מֵעָלָיִךְ וָאֲסֻכֵךְ בַּשָּׁמֶן: 10 וָאַלְבִּישֵׁךְ רִקְמָה וָאֶנְעֲלֵךְ תָּחַשׁ וָאֶחְבְּשֵׁךְ בַּשֵּׁשׁ וַאֲכַסֵּךְ מֶשִׁי: 11 וָאֶעְדֵּךְ עֶדִי וָאֶתְּנָה צְמִידִים עַל־יָדַיִךְ וְרָבִיד עַל־גְּרוֹנֵךְ: 12 וָאֶתֵּן נֶזֶם עַל־אַפֵּךְ וַעֲגִילִים עַל־אָזְנָיִךְ וַעֲטֶרֶת תִּפְאֶרֶת בְּרֹאשֵׁךְ: 13 וַתַּעְדִּי זָהָב וָכֶסֶף וּמַלְבֻּשֵׁךְ שֵׁשׁᴾ וָמֶשִׁי וְרִקְמָה סֹלֶת וּדְבַשׁ וָשֶׁמֶן אָכָלְתִּ‍ᴾ וַתִּיפִ‍ᴾ בִּמְאֹד מְאֹד וַתִּצְלְחִי

and embroidered cloth. You ate *pastry of* fine flour, honey, and oil. You were exceedingly beautiful, and succeeded to royalty. ¹⁴ Your fame went out among the nations because of your beauty, for it *was* perfect through My splendor which I had bestowed on you," says the Lord GOD.

¹⁵ "But you trusted in your own beauty, played the harlot because of your fame, and poured out your harlotry on everyone passing by who *would have* it. ¹⁶ You took some of your garments and adorned multicolored high places for yourself, and played the harlot on them. *Such* things should not happen, nor be. ¹⁷ You have also taken your beautiful jewelry from My gold and My silver, which I had given you, and made for yourself male images and played the harlot with them. ¹⁸ You took your embroidered garments and covered them, and you set My oil and My incense before them. ¹⁹ Also My food which I gave you—the pastry of fine flour, oil, and honey *which* I fed you—you set it before them as sweet incense; and *so* it was," says the Lord GOD.

²⁰ "Moreover you took your sons and your daughters, whom you bore to Me, and these you sacrificed to them to be devoured. *Were* your *acts* of harlotry a small matter, ²¹ that you have slain My children and offered them up to them by causing them to pass through *the fire?* ²² And in all your abominations and acts of harlotry you did not remember the days of your youth, when you were naked and bare, struggling in your blood.

²³ "Then it was so, after all your wickedness— 'Woe, woe to you!' says the Lord GOD— ²⁴ *that* you also built for yourself a shrine, and made a high place for yourself in every street. ²⁵ You built your high places at the head of every road, and made your beauty to be abhorred. You offered yourself to everyone who passed by, and multiplied your acts of harlotry. ²⁶ You also committed harlotry with the Egyptians, your very fleshly neighbors, and increased your acts of harlotry to provoke Me to anger.

²⁷ "Behold, therefore, I stretched out My hand against you, diminished your allotment, and gave you up to the will of those who hate you, the daughters of the Philistines, who were ashamed of your lewd behavior. ²⁸ You also played the harlot with the Assyrians, because you were insatiable; indeed you played the harlot with them and still were not satisfied. ²⁹ Moreover you multiplied your acts of harlotry as far as the land of the trader, Chaldea; and even then you were not satisfied.

לִמְלוּכָה: 14 וַיֵּצֵא לָךְ שֵׁם בַּגּוֹיִם בְּיָפְיֵךְ כִּי | כָּלִיל
הוּא בַּהֲדָרִי אֲשֶׁר־שַׂמְתִּי עָלַיִךְ נְאֻם אֲדֹנָי יְהוִה:
15 וַתִּבְטְחִי בְיָפְיֵךְ וַתִּזְנִי עַל־שְׁמֵךְ וַתִּשְׁפְּכִי אֶת־
תַּזְנוּתַיִךְ עַל־כָּל־עוֹבֵר לוֹ־יֶהִי: 16 וַתִּקְחִי מִבְּגָדַיִךְ
וַתַּעֲשִׂי־לָךְ בָּמוֹת טְלֻאוֹת וַתִּזְנִי עֲלֵיהֶם לֹא בָאוֹת
וְלֹא יִהְיֶה: 17 וַתִּקְחִי כְּלֵי תִפְאַרְתֵּךְ מִזְּהָבִי וּמִכַּסְפִּי
אֲשֶׁר נָתַתִּי לָךְ וַתַּעֲשִׂי־לָךְ צַלְמֵי זָכָר וַתִּזְנִי־
בָם: 18 וַתִּקְחִי אֶת־בִּגְדֵי רִקְמָתֵךְ וַתְּכַסִּים וְשַׁמְנִי
וּקְטָרְתִּי נָתַתְּ לִפְנֵיהֶם: 19 וְלַחְמִי אֲשֶׁר־נָתַתִּי לָךְ
סֹלֶת וָשֶׁמֶן וּדְבַשׁ הֶאֱכַלְתִּיךְ וּנְתַתִּיהוּ לִפְנֵיהֶם
לְרֵיחַ נִיחֹחַ וַיֶּהִי נְאֻם אֲדֹנָי יְהוִה: 20 וַתִּקְחִי
אֶת־בָּנַיִךְ וְאֶת־בְּנוֹתַיִךְ אֲשֶׁר יָלַדְתְּ לִי וַתִּזְבָּחִים
לָהֶם לֶאֱכוֹל הַמְעַט מִתַּזְנוּתֵךְ: 21 וַתִּשְׁחֲטִי אֶת־
בָּנַי וַתִּתְּנִים בְּהַעֲבִיר אוֹתָם לָהֶם: 22 וְאֵת כָּל־
תּוֹעֲבֹתַיִךְ וְתַזְנֻתַיִךְ לֹא זָכַרְתְּ אֶת־יְמֵי נְעוּרַיִךְ
בִּהְיוֹתֵךְ עֵרֹם וְעֶרְיָה מִתְבּוֹסֶסֶת בְּדָמֵךְ הָיִית:
23 וַיְהִי אַחֲרֵי כָּל־רָעָתֵךְ אוֹי אוֹי לָךְ נְאֻם אֲדֹנָי
יְהוִה: 24 וַתִּבְנִי־לָךְ גֶּב וַתַּעֲשִׂי־לָךְ רָמָה בְּכָל־
רְחוֹב: 25 אֶל־כָּל־רֹאשׁ דֶּרֶךְ בָּנִית רָמָתֵךְ וַתְּתַעֲבִי
אֶת־יָפְיֵךְ וַתְּפַשְּׂקִי אֶת־רַגְלַיִךְ לְכָל־עוֹבֵר וַתַּרְבִּי
אֶת־תַּזְנֻתֵךְ: 26 וַתִּזְנִי אֶל־בְּנֵי־מִצְרַיִם שְׁכֵנַיִךְ גִּדְלֵי
בָשָׂר וַתַּרְבִּי אֶת־תַּזְנֻתֵךְ לְהַכְעִיסֵנִי: 27 וְהִנֵּה נָטִיתִי
יָדִי עָלַיִךְ וָאֶגְרַע חֻקֵּךְ וָאֶתְּנֵךְ בְּנֶפֶשׁ שֹׂנְאוֹתַיִךְ
בְּנוֹת פְּלִשְׁתִּים הַנִּכְלָמוֹת מִדַּרְכֵּךְ זִמָּה: 28 וַתִּזְנִי
אֶל־בְּנֵי אַשּׁוּר מִבִּלְתִּי שָׂבְעָתֵךְ וַתִּזְנִים וְגַם לֹא
שָׂבָעַתְּ: 29 וַתַּרְבִּי אֶת־תַּזְנוּתֵךְ אֶל־אֶרֶץ

מו 18 נָתַתְּ 20 מִתַּזְנוּתֵךְ 22 זָכַרְתְּ 25 תַּזְנוּתַיִךְ

30 "How degenerate is your heart!" says the Lord GOD, "seeing you do all these *things*, the deeds of a brazen harlot.

31 "You erected your shrine at the head of every road, and built your high place in every street. Yet you were not like a harlot, because you scorned payment. 32 *You are* an adulterous wife, *who* takes strangers instead of her husband. 33 Men make payment to all harlots, but you made your payments to all your lovers, and hired them to come to you from all around for your harlotry. 34 You are the opposite of *other* women in your harlotry, because no one solicited you to be a harlot. In that you gave payment but no payment was given you, therefore you are the opposite."

35 'Now then, O harlot, hear the word of the LORD! 36 Thus says the Lord GOD: "Because your filthiness was poured out and your nakedness uncovered in your harlotry with your lovers, and with all your abominable idols, and because of the blood of your children which you gave to them, 37 surely, therefore, I will gather all your lovers with whom you took pleasure, all those you loved, *and* all those you hated; I will gather them from all around against you and will uncover your nakedness to them, that they may see all your nakedness. 38 And I will judge you as women who break wedlock or shed blood are judged; I will bring blood upon you in fury and jealousy. 39 I will also give you into their hand, and they shall throw down your shrines and break down your high places. They shall also strip you of your clothes, take your beautiful jewelry, and leave you naked and bare.

40 "They shall also bring up an assembly against you, and they shall stone you with stones and thrust you through with their swords. 41 They shall burn your houses with fire, and execute judgments on you in the sight of many women; and I will make you cease playing the harlot, and you shall no longer hire lovers. 42 So I will lay to rest My fury toward you, and My jealousy shall depart from you. I will be quiet, and be angry no more. 43 Because you did not remember the days of your youth, but agitated Me with all these *things*, surely I will also recompense your deeds on *your own* head," says the Lord GOD. "And you shall not commit lewdness in addition to all your abominations.

44 "Indeed everyone who quotes proverbs will use *this* proverb against you: 'Like mother, like daughter!' 45 You *are* your mother's daughter, loathing husband and children; and you *are* the sister of your sisters, who loathed their husbands and children; your mother *was* a Hittite and your father an Amorite.

כְּנַעַן כַּשְׁדִּימָה וְגַם־בְּזֹאת לֹא שָׂבָעַתְּ: 30 מָה אֲמֻלָה לִבָּתֵךְ נְאֻם אֲדֹנָי יְהוִֹה בַּעֲשׂוֹתֵךְ אֶת־כָּל־ אֵלֶּה מַעֲשֵׂה אִשָּׁה־זוֹנָה שַׁלָּטֶת: 31 בִּבְנוֹתַיִךְ גַּבֵּךְ בְּרֹאשׁ כָּל־דֶּרֶךְ וְרָמָתֵךְ עָשִׂיתִי בְּכָל־רְחוֹב וְלֹא־ הָיִיתִי כַּזּוֹנָה לְקַלֵּס אֶתְנָן: 32 הָאִשָּׁה הַמְּנָאָפֶת תַּחַת אִישָׁהּ תִּקַּח אֶת־זָרִים: 33 לְכָל־זֹנוֹת יִתְּנוּ־ נֵדֶה וְאַתְּ נָתַתְּ אֶת־נְדָנַיִךְ לְכָל־מְאַהֲבַיִךְ וַתִּשְׁחֳדִי אוֹתָם לָבוֹא אֵלַיִךְ מִסָּבִיב בְּתַזְנוּתָיִךְ: 34 וַיְהִי־ בָךְ הֵפֶךְ מִן־הַנָּשִׁים בְּתַזְנוּתַיִךְ וְאַחֲרַיִךְ לֹא זוּנָּה וּבְתִתֵּךְ אֶתְנָן וְאֶתְנַן לֹא נִתַּן־לָךְ וַתְּהִי לְהֶפֶךְ: 35 לָכֵן זוֹנָה שִׁמְעִי דְּבַר־יְהוָֹה: פ

36 כֹּה־אָמַר אֲדֹנָי יְהוִֹה יַעַן הִשָּׁפֵךְ נְחֻשְׁתֵּךְ וַתִּגָּלֶה עֶרְוָתֵךְ בְּתַזְנוּתַיִךְ עַל־מְאַהֲבָיִךְ וְעַל כָּל־ גִּלּוּלֵי תוֹעֲבוֹתַיִךְ וְכִדְמֵי בָנַיִךְ אֲשֶׁר נָתַתְּ לָהֶם: 37 לָכֵן הִנְנִי מְקַבֵּץ אֶת־כָּל־מְאַהֲבַיִךְ אֲשֶׁר עָרַבְתְּ עֲלֵיהֶם וְאֵת כָּל־אֲשֶׁר אָהַבְתְּ עַל כָּל־אֲשֶׁר שָׂנֵאת וְקִבַּצְתִּי אֹתָם עָלַיִךְ מִסָּבִיב וְגִלֵּיתִי עֶרְוָתֵךְ אֲלֵהֶם וְרָאוּ אֶת־כָּל־עֶרְוָתֵךְ: 38 וּשְׁפַטְתִּיךְ מִשְׁפְּטֵי נֹאֲפוֹת וְשֹׁפְכֹת דָּם וּנְתַתִּיךְ דַּם חֵמָה וְקִנְאָה: 39 וְנָתַתִּי אוֹתָךְ בְּיָדָם וְהָרְסוּ גַבֵּךְ וְנִתְּצוּ רָמֹתַיִךְ וְהִפְשִׁיטוּ אוֹתָךְ בְּגָדַיִךְ וְלָקְחוּ כְּלֵי תִפְאַרְתֵּךְ וְהִנִּיחוּךְ עֵירֹם וְעֶרְיָה: 40 וְהֶעֱלוּ עָלַיִךְ קָהָל וְרָגְמוּ אוֹתָךְ בָּאָבֶן וּבִתְּקוּךְ בְּחַרְבוֹתָם: 41 וְשָׂרְפוּ בָתַּיִךְ בָּאֵשׁ וְעָשׂוּ־בָךְ שְׁפָטִים לְעֵינֵי נָשִׁים רַבּוֹת וְהִשְׁבַּתִּיךְ מִזּוֹנָה וְגַם־אֶתְנַן לֹא תִתְּנִי־עוֹד: 42 וַהֲנִחֹתִי חֲמָתִי בָּךְ וְסָרָה קִנְאָתִי מִמֵּךְ וְשָׁקַטְתִּי וְלֹא אֶכְעַס עוֹד: 43 יַעַן אֲשֶׁר לֹא־זָכַרְתִּי אֶת־ יְמֵי נְעוּרַיִךְ וַתִּרְגְּזִי־לִי בְּכָל־אֵלֶּה וְגַם־אֲנִי הֵא דַרְכֵּךְ | בְּרֹאשׁ נָתַתִּי נְאֻם אֲדֹנָי יְהוִֹה וְלֹא עָשִׂיתִי אֶת־הַזִּמָּה עַל כָּל־תּוֹעֲבֹתָיִךְ: 44 הִנֵּה כָּל־ הַמֹּשֵׁל עָלַיִךְ יִמְשֹׁל לֵאמֹר כְּאִמָּה בִּתָּהּ: 45 בַּת־ אִמֵּךְ אַתְּ גֹּעֶלֶת אִישָׁהּ וּבָנֶיהָ וַאֲחוֹת אֲחוֹתֵךְ אַתְּ אֲשֶׁר גָּעֲלוּ אַנְשֵׁיהֶן וּבְנֵיהֶן אִמְּכֶן חִתִּית

טז 31 עָשִׂית הָיִית 43 זָכַרְתְּ 43 עָשִׂית

46 "Your elder sister *is* Samaria, who dwells with her daughters to the north of you; and your younger sister, who dwells to the south of you, *is* Sodom and her daughters. 47 You did not walk in their ways nor act according to their abominations; but, as *if that were* too little, you became more corrupt than they in all your ways.

48 "*As* I live," says the Lord GOD, "neither your sister Sodom nor her daughters have done as you and your daughters have done. 49 Look, this was the iniquity of your sister Sodom: She and her daughter had pride, fullness of food, and abundance of idleness; neither did she strengthen the hand of the poor and needy. 50 And they were haughty and committed abomination before Me; therefore I took them away as I saw *fit.*

51 "Samaria did not commit half of your sins; but you have multiplied your abominations more than they, and have justified your sisters by all the abominations which you have done. 52 You who judged your sisters, bear your own shame also, because the sins which you committed were more abominable than theirs; they are more righteous than you. Yes, be disgraced also, and bear your own shame, because you justified your sisters.

53 "When I bring back their captives, the captives of Sodom and her daughters, and the captives of Samaria and her daughters, then *I will also bring back* the captives of your captivity among them, 54 that you may bear your own shame and be disgraced by all that you did when you comforted them. 55 When your sisters, Sodom and her daughters, return to their former state, and Samaria and her daughters return to their former state, then you and your daughters will return to your former state. 56 For your sister Sodom was not a byword in your mouth in the days of your pride, 57 before your wickedness was uncovered. It was like the time of the reproach of the daughters of Syria and all *those* around her, and of the daughters of the Philistines, who despise you everywhere. 58 You have paid for your lewdness and your abominations," says the LORD. 59 For thus says the Lord GOD: "I will deal with you as you have done, who despised the oath by breaking the covenant.

60 "Nevertheless I will remember My covenant with you in the days of your youth, and I will establish an everlasting covenant with you. 61 Then you will remember your ways and be ashamed, when you receive your older and your younger sisters; for I will give them to you for daughters, but not because of My covenant with you. 62 And I will establish My covenant with you. Then you shall know that I *am* the LORD, 63 that you may

וְאָבִיךְ אֱמֹרִי׃ 46 וַאֲחוֹתֵךְ הַגְּדוֹלָה שֹׁמְרוֹן הִיא וּבְנוֹתֶיהָ הַיּוֹשֶׁבֶת עַל־שְׂמֹאולֵךְ וַאֲחוֹתֵךְ הַקְּטַנָּה מִמֵּךְ הַיּוֹשֶׁבֶת מִימִינֵךְ סְדֹם וּבְנוֹתֶיהָ׃ 47 וְלֹא בְדַרְכֵיהֶן הָלַכְתְּ וּבְתוֹעֲבוֹתֵיהֶן עָשִׂיתִ כִּמְעַט קָט וַתַּשְׁחִתִי מֵהֵן בְּכָל־דְּרָכָיִךְ׃ 48 חַי־אָנִי נְאֻם אֲדֹנָי יְהוִה אִם־עָשְׂתָה סְדֹם אֲחוֹתֵךְ הִיא וּבְנוֹתֶיהָ כַּאֲשֶׁר עָשִׂית אַתְּ וּבְנוֹתָיִךְ׃ 49 הִנֵּה־זֶה הָיָה עֲוֹן סְדֹם אֲחוֹתֵךְ גָּאוֹן שִׂבְעַת־לֶחֶם וְשַׁלְוַת הַשְׁקֵט הָיָה לָהּ וְלִבְנוֹתֶיהָ וְיַד־עָנִי וְאֶבְיוֹן לֹא הֶחֱזִיקָה׃ 50 וַתִּגְבְּהֶינָה וַתַּעֲשֶׂינָה תוֹעֵבָה לְפָנָי וָאָסִיר אֶתְהֶן כַּאֲשֶׁר רָאִיתִי׃ ס 51 וְשֹׁמְרוֹן כַּחֲצִי חַטֹּאתַיִךְ לֹא חָטָאָה וַתַּרְבִּי אֶת־תּוֹעֲבוֹתַיִךְ מֵהֵנָּה וַתְּצַדְּקִי אֶת־אֲחוֹתֵךְ בְּכָל־תּוֹעֲבוֹתַיִךְ אֲשֶׁר עָשִׂיתִי׃ 52 גַּם־אַתְּ שְׂאִי כְלִמָּתֵךְ אֲשֶׁר פִּלַּלְתְּ לַאֲחוֹתֵךְ בְּחַטֹּאתַיִךְ אֲשֶׁר־הִתְעַבְתְּ מֵהֵן תִּצְדַּקְנָה מִמֵּךְ וְגַם־אַתְּ בּוֹשִׁי וּשְׂאִי כְלִמָּתֵךְ בְּצַדֶּקְתֵּךְ אֲחוֹתֵךְ׃ 53 וְשַׁבְתִּי אֶת־שְׁבִיתְהֶן אֶת־שְׁבִית סְדֹם וּבְנוֹתֶיהָ וְאֶת־שְׁבִית שֹׁמְרוֹן וּבְנוֹתֶיהָ וּשְׁבִית שְׁבִיתַיִךְ בְּתוֹכָהְנָה׃ 54 לְמַעַן תִּשְׂאִי כְלִמָּתֵךְ וְנִכְלַמְתְּ מִכֹּל אֲשֶׁר עָשִׂית בְּנַחֲמֵךְ אֹתָן׃ 55 וַאֲחוֹתַיִךְ סְדֹם וּבְנוֹתֶיהָ תָּשֹׁבְןָ לְקַדְמָתָן וְשֹׁמְרוֹן וּבְנוֹתֶיהָ תָּשֹׁבְןָ לְקַדְמָתָן וְאַתְּ וּבְנוֹתַיִךְ תְּשֻׁבֶינָה לְקַדְמַתְכֶן׃ 56 וְלוֹא הָיְתָה סְדֹם אֲחוֹתֵךְ לִשְׁמוּעָה בְּפִיךְ בְּיוֹם גְּאוֹנָיִךְ׃ 57 בְּטֶרֶם תִּגָּלֶה רָעָתֵךְ כְּמוֹ עֵת חֶרְפַּת בְּנוֹת־אֲרָם וְכָל־סְבִיבוֹתֶיהָ בְּנוֹת פְּלִשְׁתִּים הַשָּׁאטוֹת אוֹתָךְ מִסָּבִיב׃ 58 אֶת־זִמָּתֵךְ וְאֶת־תּוֹעֲבוֹתַיִךְ אַתְּ נְשָׂאתִים נְאֻם יְהוָה׃ ס 59 כִּי כֹה אָמַר אֲדֹנָי יְהוִה וְעָשִׂית אוֹתָךְ כַּאֲשֶׁר עָשִׂית אֲשֶׁר בָּזִית אָלָה לְהָפֵר בְּרִית׃ 60 וְזָכַרְתִּי אֲנִי אֶת־בְּרִיתִי אוֹתָךְ בִּימֵי נְעוּרָיִךְ וַהֲקִמוֹתִי לָךְ בְּרִית עוֹלָם׃ 61 וְזָכַרְתְּ אֶת־דְּרָכַיִךְ וְנִכְלַמְתְּ בְּקַחְתֵּךְ אֶת־אֲחוֹתַיִךְ הַגְּדֹלוֹת מִמֵּךְ אֶל־הַקְּטַנּוֹת מִמֵּךְ וְנָתַתִּי אֶתְהֶן לָךְ לְבָנוֹת וְלֹא מִבְּרִיתֵךְ׃ 62 וַהֲקִמוֹתִי אֲנִי אֶת־בְּרִיתִי אִתָּךְ וְיָדַעַתְּ כִּי־אֲנִי יְהוָה׃ 63 לְמַעַן

47 טז עָשִׂית, 51 אֲחוֹתֵךְ 53 עָשִׂית שְׁבוּת וּשְׁבוּת 59 וְעָשִׂיתִי

remember and be ashamed, and never open your mouth anymore because of your shame, when I provide you an atonement for all you have done," says the Lord GOD.' "

17 And the word of the LORD came to me, saying, ²"Son of man, pose a riddle, and speak a parable to the house of Israel, ³and say, 'Thus says the Lord GOD:

"A great eagle with large wings and long pinions,
Full of feathers of various colors,
Came to Lebanon
And took from the cedar the highest branch.
⁴ He cropped off its topmost young twig
And carried it to a land of trade;
He set it in a city of merchants.
⁵ Then he took some of the seed of the land
And planted it in a fertile field;
He placed *it* by abundant waters
And set it like a willow tree.
⁶ And it grew and became a spreading vine of low stature;
Its branches turned toward him,
But its roots were under it.
So it became a vine,
Brought forth branches,
And put forth shoots.

⁷ "But there was another great eagle with large wings and many feathers;
And behold, this vine bent its roots toward him,
And stretched its branches toward him,
From the garden terrace where it had been planted,
That he might water it.
⁸ It was planted in good soil by many waters,
To bring forth branches, bear fruit,
And become a majestic vine." '

⁹ "Say, 'Thus says the Lord GOD:

"Will it thrive?
Will he not pull up its roots,
Cut off its fruit,
And leave it to wither?
All of its spring leaves will wither,
And no great power or many people
Will be needed to pluck it up by its roots.
¹⁰ Behold, *it is* planted,
Will it thrive?
Will it not utterly wither when the east wind touches it?
It will wither in the garden terrace where it grew." ' "

¹¹ Moreover the word of the LORD came to me, saying, ¹²"Say now to the rebellious house: 'Do you not know what these *things mean?*' Tell *them,* 'Indeed the king of Babylon went to Jerusalem and took its king and princes, and led them with him to Babylon. ¹³ And he took the king's offspring, made

---

תִּזְכְּרִי וָבֹשְׁתְּ וְלֹא יִהְיֶה־לָּךְ עוֹד פִּתְחוֹן פֶּה מִפְּנֵי כְּלִמָּתֵךְ בְּכַפְּרִי־לָךְ לְכָל־אֲשֶׁר עָשִׂית נְאֻם אֲדֹנָי יְהֹוִה: ס

יז וַיְהִי דְבַר־יְהֹוָה אֵלַי לֵאמֹר: 2 בֶּן־אָדָם חוּד חִידָה וּמְשֹׁל מָשָׁל אֶל־בֵּית יִשְׂרָאֵל: 3 וְאָמַרְתָּ כֹּה־אָמַר אֲדֹנָי יְהֹוִה הַנֶּשֶׁר הַגָּדוֹל גְּדוֹל הַכְּנָפַיִם אֶרֶךְ הָאֵבֶר מָלֵא הַנּוֹצָה אֲשֶׁר־לוֹ הָרִקְמָה בָּא אֶל־הַלְּבָנוֹן וַיִּקַּח אֶת־צַמֶּרֶת הָאָרֶז: 4 אֵת רֹאשׁ יְנִיקוֹתָיו קָטָף וַיְבִיאֵהוּ אֶל־אֶרֶץ כְּנַעַן בְּעִיר רֹכְלִים שָׂמוֹ: 5 וַיִּקַּח מִזֶּרַע הָאָרֶץ וַיִּתְּנֵהוּ בִּשְׂדֵה־זָרַע קָח עַל־מַיִם רַבִּים צַפְצָפָה שָׂמוֹ: 6 וַיִּצְמַח וַיְהִי לְגֶפֶן סֹרַחַת שִׁפְלַת קוֹמָה לִפְנוֹת דָּלִיּוֹתָיו אֵלָיו וְשָׁרָשָׁיו תַּחְתָּיו יִהְיוּ וַתְּהִי לְגֶפֶן וַתַּעַשׂ בַּדִּים וַתְּשַׁלַּח פֹּארוֹת: 7 וַיְהִי נֶשֶׁר־אֶחָד גָּדוֹל גְּדוֹל כְּנָפַיִם וְרַב־נוֹצָה וְהִנֵּה הַגֶּפֶן הַזֹּאת כָּפְנָה שָׁרָשֶׁיהָ עָלָיו וְדָלִיּוֹתָיו שִׁלְחָה־לּוֹ לְהַשְׁקוֹת אוֹתָהּ מֵעֲרֻגוֹת מַטָּעָהּ: 8 אֶל־שָׂדֶה טּוֹב אֶל־מַיִם רַבִּים הִיא שְׁתוּלָה לַעֲשׂוֹת עָנָף וְלָשֵׂאת פֶּרִי לִהְיוֹת לְגֶפֶן אַדָּרֶת: ס 9 אֱמֹר כֹּה אָמַר אֲדֹנָי יְהֹוִה תִּצְלָח הֲלוֹא אֶת־שָׁרָשֶׁיהָ יְנַתֵּק וְאֶת־פִּרְיָהּ | יְקוֹסֵס וְיָבֵשׁ כָּל־טַרְפֵּי צִמְחָהּ תִּיבָשׁ וְלֹא־בִזְרֹעַ גְּדוֹלָה וּבְעַם־רָב לְמַשְׂאוֹת אוֹתָהּ מִשָּׁרָשֶׁיהָ: 10 וְהִנֵּה שְׁתוּלָה הֲתִצְלָח הֲלוֹא כְגַעַת בָּהּ רוּחַ הַקָּדִים תִּיבַשׁ יָבֹשׁ עַל־עֲרֻגֹת צִמְחָהּ תִּיבָשׁ: ס 11 וַיְהִי דְבַר־יְהֹוָה אֵלַי לֵאמֹר: 12 אֱמָר־נָא לְבֵית הַמֶּרִי הֲלֹא יְדַעְתֶּם מָה־אֵלֶּה אֱמֹר הִנֵּה־בָא מֶלֶךְ־בָּבֶל יְרוּשָׁלַם וַיִּקַּח אֶת־מַלְכָּהּ וְאֶת־שָׂרֶיהָ וַיָּבֵא אוֹתָם אֵלָיו בָּבֶלָה: 13 וַיִּקַּח מִזֶּרַע הַמְּלוּכָה וַיִּכְרֹת

a covenant with him, and put him under oath. He also took away the mighty of the land, [14]that the kingdom might be brought low and not lift itself up, *but* that by keeping his covenant it might stand. [15]But he rebelled against him by sending his ambassadors to Egypt, that they might give him horses and many people. Will he prosper? Will he who does such *things* escape? Can he break a covenant and still be delivered?

[16]'*As* I live,' says the Lord GOD, 'surely in the place *where* the king *dwells* who made him king, whose oath he despised and whose covenant he broke—with him in the midst of Babylon he shall die. [17]Nor will Pharaoh with *his* mighty army and great company do anything in the war, when they heap up a siege mound and build a wall to cut off many persons. [18]Since he despised the oath by breaking the covenant, and in fact gave his hand and still did all these *things,* he shall not escape.'"

[19]Therefore thus says the Lord GOD: "*As* I live, surely My oath which he despised, and My covenant which he broke, I will recompense on his own head. [20]I will spread My net over him, and he shall be taken in My snare. I will bring him to Babylon and try him there for the treason which he committed against Me. [21]All his fugitives with all his troops shall fall by the sword, and those who remain shall be scattered to every wind; and you shall know that I, the LORD, have spoken."

[22]Thus says the Lord GOD: "I will take also *one* of the highest branches of the high cedar and set *it* out. I will crop off from the topmost of its young twigs a tender one, and will plant *it* on a high and prominent mountain. [23]On the mountain height of Israel I will plant it; and it will bring forth boughs, and bear fruit, and be a majestic cedar. Under it will dwell birds of every sort; in the shadow of its branches they will dwell. [24]And all the trees of the field shall know that I, the LORD, have brought down the high tree and exalted the low tree, dried up the green tree and made the dry tree flourish; I, the LORD, have spoken and have done *it.*"

18 The word of the LORD came to me again, saying, [2]"What do you mean when you use this proverb concerning the land of Israel, saying:

'The fathers have eaten sour grapes,
And the children's teeth are set on edge'?

[3]"*As* I live," says the Lord GOD, "you shall no longer use this proverb in Israel.

[4] "Behold, all souls are Mine;
The soul of the father
As well as the soul of the son is Mine;

אִתּוֹ בְּרִית וַיָּבֵא אֹתוֹ בְּאָלָה וְאֶת־אֵילֵי הָאָרֶץ לָקָח: 14 לִהְיוֹת מַמְלָכָה שְׁפָלָה לְבִלְתִּי הִתְנַשֵּׂא לִשְׁמֹר אֶת־בְּרִיתוֹ לְעָמְדָהּ: 15 וַיִּמְרָד־בּוֹ לִשְׁלֹחַ מַלְאָכָיו מִצְרַיִם לָתֶת־לוֹ סוּסִים וְעַם־רָב הֲיִצְלָח הֲיִמָּלֵט הָעֹשֵׂה אֵלֶּה וְהֵפֵר בְּרִית וְנִמְלָט: 16 חַי־אָנִי נְאֻם אֲדֹנָי יְהוִה אִם־לֹא בִּמְקוֹם הַמֶּלֶךְ הַמַּמְלִיךְ אֹתוֹ אֲשֶׁר בָּזָה אֶת־אָלָתוֹ וַאֲשֶׁר הֵפֵר אֶת־בְּרִיתוֹ אִתּוֹ בְתוֹךְ־בָּבֶל יָמוּת: 17 וְלֹא בְחַיִל גָּדוֹל וּבְקָהָל רָב יַעֲשֶׂה אוֹתוֹ פַרְעֹה בַּמִּלְחָמָה בִּשְׁפֹּךְ סֹלְלָה וּבִבְנוֹת דָּיֵק לְהַכְרִית נְפָשׁוֹת רַבּוֹת: 18 וּבָזָה אָלָה לְהָפֵר בְּרִית וְהִנֵּה נָתַן יָדוֹ וְכָל־אֵלֶּה עָשָׂה לֹא יִמָּלֵט: ס 19 לָכֵן כֹּה־אָמַר אֲדֹנָי יְהוִה חַי־אָנִי אִם־לֹא אָלָתִי אֲשֶׁר בָּזָה וּבְרִיתִי אֲשֶׁר הֵפִיר וּנְתַתִּיו בְּרֹאשׁוֹ: 20 וּפָרַשְׂתִּי עָלָיו רִשְׁתִּי וְנִתְפַּשׂ בִּמְצוּדָתִי וַהֲבִיאוֹתִיהוּ בָבֶלָה וְנִשְׁפַּטְתִּי אִתּוֹ שָׁם מַעֲלוֹ אֲשֶׁר מָעַל־בִּי: 21 וְאֵת כָּל־מִבְרָחָו בְּכָל־אֲגַפָּיו בַּחֶרֶב יִפֹּלוּ וְהַנִּשְׁאָרִים לְכָל־רוּחַ יִפָּרֵשׂוּ וִידַעְתֶּם כִּי אֲנִי יְהוִה דִּבַּרְתִּי: ס 22 כֹּה אָמַר אֲדֹנָי יְהוִה וְלָקַחְתִּי אָנִי מִצַּמֶּרֶת הָאֶרֶז הָרָמָה וְנָתָתִּי מֵרֹאשׁ יֹנְקוֹתָיו רַךְ אֶקְטֹף וְשָׁתַלְתִּי אָנִי עַל הַר־גָּבֹהַּ וְתָלוּל: 23 בְּהַר מְרוֹם יִשְׂרָאֵל אֶשְׁתֳּלֶנּוּ וְנָשָׂא עָנָף וְעָשָׂה פֶרִי וְהָיָה לְאֶרֶז אַדִּיר וְשָׁכְנוּ תַחְתָּיו כֹּל צִפּוֹר כָּל־כָּנָף בְּצֵל דָּלִיּוֹתָיו תִּשְׁכֹּנָּה: 24 וְיָדְעוּ כָּל־עֲצֵי הַשָּׂדֶה כִּי אֲנִי יְהוִה הִשְׁפַּלְתִּי עֵץ גָּבֹהַּ הִגְבַּהְתִּי עֵץ שָׁפָל הוֹבַשְׁתִּי עֵץ לָח וְהִפְרַחְתִּי עֵץ יָבֵשׁ אֲנִי יְהוִה דִּבַּרְתִּי וְעָשִׂיתִי: פ

יח וַיְהִי דְבַר־יְהוָה אֵלַי לֵאמֹר: 2 מַה־לָכֶם אַתֶּם מֹשְׁלִים אֶת־הַמָּשָׁל הַזֶּה עַל־אַדְמַת יִשְׂרָאֵל לֵאמֹר אָבוֹת יֹאכְלוּ בֹסֶר וְשִׁנֵּי הַבָּנִים תִּקְהֶינָה: 3 חַי־אָנִי נְאֻם אֲדֹנָי יְהוִה אִם־יִהְיֶה לָכֶם עוֹד מְשֹׁל הַמָּשָׁל הַזֶּה בְּיִשְׂרָאֵל: 4 הֵן כָּל־הַנְּפָשׁוֹת לִי הֵנָּה כְּנֶפֶשׁ הָאָב וּכְנֶפֶשׁ הַבֵּן לִי־הֵנָּה הַנֶּפֶשׁ הַחֹטֵאת הִיא

The soul who sins shall die.

5 But if a man is just
And does what is lawful and right;
6 If he has not eaten on the mountains,
Nor lifted up his eyes to the idols of the house of
    Israel,
Nor defiled his neighbor's wife,
Nor approached a woman during her impurity;
7 If he has not oppressed anyone,
But has restored to the debtor his pledge;
Has robbed no one by violence,
But has given his bread to the hungry
And covered the naked with clothing;
8 If he has not exacted usury
Nor taken any increase,
But has withdrawn his hand from iniquity
And executed true judgment between man and
    man;
9 *If* he has walked in My statutes
And kept My judgments faithfully—
He *is* just;
He shall surely live!"
Says the Lord God.

10 "If he begets a son *who is* a robber
Or a shedder of blood,
Who does any of these *things*
11 And does none of those *duties,*
But has eaten on the mountains
Or defiled his neighbor's wife;
12 If he has oppressed the poor and needy,
Robbed by violence,
Not restored the pledge,
Lifted his eyes to the idols,
Or committed abomination;
13 If he has exacted usury
Or taken increase—
Shall he then live?
He shall not live!
If he has done any of these abominations,
He shall surely die;
His blood shall be upon him.

14 "*If,* however, he begets a son
Who sees all the sins which his father has done,
And considers but does not do likewise;
15 *Who* has not eaten on the mountains,
Nor lifted his eyes to the idols of the house of
    Israel,
Nor defiled his neighbor's wife;
16 Has not oppressed anyone,
Nor withheld a pledge,
Nor robbed by violence,
But has given his bread to the hungry
And covered the naked with clothing;
17 *Who* has withdrawn his hand from the poor
And not received usury or increase,
But has executed My judgments
And walked in My statutes—
He shall not die for the iniquity of his father;
He shall surely live!

18 "*As for* his father,
Because he cruelly oppressed,

תָּמֽוּת: ס 5 וְאִישׁ כִּי־יִהְיֶה צַדִּיק וְעָשָׂה

מִשְׁפָּט וּצְדָקָה: 6 אֶל־הֶֽהָרִים לֹא אָכָל וְעֵינָיו לֹא

נָשָׂא אֶל־גִּלּוּלֵי בֵּית יִשְׂרָאֵל וְאֶת־אֵשֶׁת רֵעֵהוּ לֹא

טִמֵּא וְאֶל־אִשָּׁה נִדָּה לֹא יִקְרָב: 7 וְאִישׁ לֹא יוֹנֶה

חֲבֹֽלָתוֹ חוֹב יָשִׁיב גְּזֵלָה לֹא יִגְזֹל לַחְמוֹ לְרָעֵב

יִתֵּן וְעֵירֹם יְכַסֶּה־בָּֽגֶד: 8 בַּנֶּשֶׁךְ לֹא־יִתֵּן וְתַרְבִּית

לֹא יִקָּח מֵעָוֶל יָשִׁיב יָדוֹ מִשְׁפַּט אֱמֶת יַעֲשֶׂה

בֵּין אִישׁ לְאִישׁ: 9 בְּחֻקּוֹתַי יְהַלֵּךְ וּמִשְׁפָּטַי שָׁמַר

לַעֲשׂוֹת אֱמֶת צַדִּיק הוּא חָיֹה יִֽחְיֶה נְאֻם אֲדֹנָי

יְהוִֹה: 10 וְהוֹלִיד בֵּן־פָּרִיץ שֹׁפֵךְ דָּם וְעָשָׂה אָח

מֵאַחַד מֵאֵֽלֶּה: 11 וְהוּא אֶת־כָּל־אֵלֶּה לֹא עָשָׂה

כִּי גַם אֶל־הֶֽהָרִים אָכַל וְאֶת־אֵשֶׁת רֵעֵהוּ טִמֵּא:

12 עָנִי וְאֶבְיוֹן הוֹנָה גְּזֵלוֹת גָּזָל חֲבֹל לֹא יָשִׁיב

וְאֶל־הַגִּלּוּלִים נָשָׂא עֵינָיו תּוֹעֵבָה עָשָׂה: 13 בַּנֶּשֶׁךְ

נָתַן וְתַרְבִּית לָקַח וָחָי לֹא יִֽחְיֶה אֵת כָּל־הַתּוֹעֵבוֹת

הָאֵלֶּה עָשָׂה מוֹת יוּמָת דָּמָיו בּוֹ יִהְיֶה: 14 וְהִנֵּה

הוֹלִיד בֵּן וַיַּרְא אֶת־כָּל־חַטֹּאת אָבִיו אֲשֶׁר עָשָׂה

וַיִּרְאֶה וְלֹא יַעֲשֶׂה כָּהֵן: 15 עַל־הֶהָרִים לֹא אָכָל

וְעֵינָיו לֹא נָשָׂא אֶל־גִּלּוּלֵי בֵּית יִשְׂרָאֵל אֶת־אֵשֶׁת

רֵעֵהוּ לֹא טִמֵּא: 16 וְאִישׁ לֹא הוֹנָה חֲבֹל לֹא חָבָל

וּגְזֵלָה לֹא גָזָל לַחְמוֹ לְרָעֵב נָתָן וְעֵרוֹם כִּסָּה־

בָֽגֶד: 17 מֵעָנִי הֵשִׁיב יָדוֹ נֶשֶׁךְ וְתַרְבִּית לֹא לָקָח

מִשְׁפָּטַי עָשָׂה בְּחֻקּוֹתַי הָלָךְ הוּא לֹא יָמוּת בַּעֲוֹן

אָבִיו חָיֹה יִֽחְיֶה: 18 אָבִיו כִּי־עָשַׁק עֹשֶׁק גָּזַל גֵּזֶל אָח

Robbed his brother by violence,
And did what *is* not good among his people,
Behold, he shall die for his iniquity.

19 "Yet you say, 'Why should the son not bear the guilt of the father?' Because the son has done what is lawful and right, and has kept all My statutes and observed them, he shall surely live. 20 The soul who sins shall die. The son shall not bear the guilt of the father, nor the father bear the guilt of the son. The righteousness of the righteous shall be upon himself, and the wickedness of the wicked shall be upon himself.

21 "But if a wicked man turns from all his sins which he has committed, keeps all My statutes, and does what is lawful and right, he shall surely live; he shall not die. 22 None of the transgressions which he has committed shall be remembered against him; because of the righteousness which he has done, he shall live. 23 Do I have any pleasure at all that the wicked should die?" says the Lord GOD, "*and* not that he should turn from his ways and live?

24 "But when a righteous man turns away from his righteousness and commits iniquity, and does according to all the abominations that the wicked *man* does, shall he live? All the righteousness which he has done shall not be remembered; because of the unfaithfulness of which he is guilty and the sin which he has committed, because of them he shall die.

25 "Yet you say, 'The way of the Lord is not fair.' Hear now, O house of Israel, is it not My way which is fair, and your ways which are not fair? 26 When a righteous *man* turns away from his righteousness, commits iniquity, and dies in it, it is because of the iniquity which he has done that he dies. 27 Again, when a wicked *man* turns away from the wickedness which he committed, and does what is lawful and right, he preserves himself alive. 28 Because he considers and turns away from all the transgressions which he committed, he shall surely live; he shall not die. 29 Yet the house of Israel says, 'The way of the Lord is not fair.' O house of Israel, is it not My ways which are fair, and your ways which are not fair?

30 "Therefore I will judge you, O house of Israel, every one according to his ways," says the Lord GOD. "Repent, and turn from all your transgressions, so that iniquity will not be your ruin. 31 Cast away from you all the transgressions which you have committed, and get yourselves a new heart and a new spirit. For why should you die, O house of Israel? 32 For I have no pleasure in the death of one who dies," says the Lord GOD. "Therefore turn and live!"

וַאֲשֶׁ֣ר לֹא־ט֗וֹב עָשָׂה֙ בְּת֣וֹךְ עַמָּ֔יו וְהִנֵּה־מֵ֖ת בַּעֲוֺנֽוֹ׃

19 וַאֲמַרְתֶּ֕ם מַדֻּ֛עַ לֹא־נָשָׂ֥א הַבֵּ֖ן בַּעֲוֺ֣ן הָאָ֑ב וְהַבֵּ֞ן מִשְׁפָּ֧ט וּצְדָקָ֣ה עָשָׂ֗ה אֵ֣ת כָּל־חֻקּוֹתַ֥י שָׁמַ֛ר וַיַּעֲשֶׂ֥ה אֹתָ֖ם חָיֹ֥ה יִחְיֶֽה׃ 20 הַנֶּ֥פֶשׁ הַחֹטֵ֖את הִ֣יא תָמ֑וּת בֵּ֞ן לֹא־יִשָּׂ֣א ׀ בַּעֲוֺ֣ן הָאָ֗ב וְאָב֙ לֹ֤א יִשָּׂא֙ בַּעֲוֺ֣ן הַבֵּ֔ן צִדְקַ֤ת הַצַּדִּיק֙ עָלָ֣יו תִּֽהְיֶ֔ה וְרִשְׁעַ֥ת רָשָׁ֖ע עָלָ֥יו תִּֽהְיֶֽה׃ ס 21 וְהָ֣רָשָׁ֗ע כִּ֤י יָשׁוּב֙ מִכָּל־חַטֹּאתָו֙ אֲשֶׁ֣ר עָשָׂ֔ה וְשָׁמַר֙ אֶת־כָּל־חֻקּוֹתַ֔י וְעָשָׂ֥ה מִשְׁפָּ֖ט וּצְדָקָ֑ה חָיֹ֥ה יִחְיֶ֖ה לֹ֥א יָמֽוּת׃ 22 כָּל־פְּשָׁעָיו֙ אֲשֶׁ֣ר עָשָׂ֔ה לֹ֥א יִזָּכְר֖וּ ל֑וֹ בְּצִדְקָת֥וֹ אֲשֶׁר־עָשָׂ֖ה יִחְיֶֽה׃ 23 הֶחָפֹ֤ץ אֶחְפֹּץ֙ מ֣וֹת רָשָׁ֔ע נְאֻ֖ם אֲדֹנָ֣י יְהוִ֑ה הֲל֛וֹא בְּשׁוּב֥וֹ מִדְּרָכָ֖יו וְחָיָֽה׃ ס 24 וּבְשׁ֣וּב צַדִּ֣יק מִצִּדְקָתוֹ֮ וְעָ֣שָׂה עָוֶל֒ כְּכֹ֣ל הַתּוֹעֵב֗וֹת אֲשֶׁר־עָשָׂ֤ה הָרָשָׁע֙ יַעֲשֶׂ֔ה וָחָ֑י כָּל־צִדְקֹתָ֤ו אֲשֶׁר־עָשָׂה֙ לֹ֣א תִזָּכַ֔רְנָה בְּמַעֲל֧וֹ אֲשֶׁר־מָעַ֛ל וּבְחַטָּאת֥וֹ אֲשֶׁר־חָטָ֖א בָּ֥ם יָמֽוּת׃ 25 וַאֲמַרְתֶּ֕ם לֹ֥א יִתָּכֵ֖ן דֶּ֣רֶךְ אֲדֹנָ֑י שִׁמְעוּ־נָא֙ בֵּ֣ית יִשְׂרָאֵ֔ל הֲדַרְכִּ֣י לֹ֣א יִתָּכֵ֔ן הֲלֹ֥א דַרְכֵיכֶ֖ם לֹ֥א יִתָּכֵֽנוּ׃ 26 בְּשׁוּב־צַדִּ֧יק מִצִּדְקָת֛וֹ וְעָ֥שָׂה עָ֖וֶל וּמֵ֣ת עֲלֵיהֶ֑ם בְּעַוְל֥וֹ אֲשֶׁר־עָשָׂ֖ה יָמֽוּת׃ ס 27 וּבְשׁ֣וּב רָשָׁ֗ע מֵֽרִשְׁעָתוֹ֙ אֲשֶׁ֣ר עָשָׂ֔ה וַיַּ֥עַשׂ מִשְׁפָּ֖ט וּצְדָקָ֑ה ה֖וּא אֶת־נַפְשׁ֥וֹ יְחַיֶּֽה׃ 28 וַיִּרְאֶ֣ה וַיָּשׁוֹב֙ מִכָּל־פְּשָׁעָ֖יו אֲשֶׁ֣ר עָשָׂ֑ה חָי֥וֹ יִחְיֶ֖ה לֹ֥א יָמֽוּת׃ 29 וְאָֽמְרוּ֙ בֵּ֣ית יִשְׂרָאֵ֔ל לֹ֥א יִתָּכֵ֖ן דֶּ֣רֶךְ אֲדֹנָ֑י הַדְּרָכַ֞י לֹ֤א יִתָּֽכְנוּ֙ בֵּ֣ית יִשְׂרָאֵ֔ל הֲלֹ֥א דַרְכֵיכֶ֖ם לֹ֥א יִתָּכֵֽן׃ 30 לָכֵן֩ אִ֨ישׁ כִּדְרָכָ֜יו אֶשְׁפֹּ֤ט אֶתְכֶם֙ בֵּ֣ית יִשְׂרָאֵ֔ל נְאֻ֖ם אֲדֹנָ֣י יְהוִ֑ה שׁ֤וּבוּ וְהָשִׁ֙יבוּ֙ מִכָּל־פִּשְׁעֵיכֶ֔ם וְלֹֽא־יִהְיֶ֥ה לָכֶ֛ם לְמִכְשׁ֖וֹל עָוֺֽן׃ 31 הַשְׁלִ֣יכוּ מֵעֲלֵיכֶ֗ם אֶת־כָּל־פִּשְׁעֵיכֶם֙ אֲשֶׁ֣ר פְּשַׁעְתֶּ֣ם בָּ֔ם וַעֲשׂ֥וּ לָכֶ֛ם לֵ֥ב חָדָ֖שׁ וְר֣וּחַ חֲדָשָׁ֑ה וְלָ֥מָּה תָמֻ֖תוּ בֵּ֥ית יִשְׂרָאֵֽל׃ 32 כִּ֣י לֹ֤א אֶחְפֹּץ֙ בְּמ֣וֹת הַמֵּ֔ת נְאֻ֖ם אֲדֹנָ֣י יְהוִ֑ה וְהָשִׁ֖יבוּ וִֽחְיֽוּ׃ פ

יח 20 הָרָשָׁע   21 חַטֹּאתָיו   24 צִדְקֹתָיו   28 וַיָּשׁב

19 "Moreover take up a lamentation for the princes of Israel, ²and say:

'What *is* your mother? A lioness:
She lay down among the lions;
Among the young lions she nourished her cubs.
³ She brought up one of her cubs,
And he became a young lion;
He learned to catch prey,
And he devoured men.
⁴ The nations also heard of him;
He was trapped in their pit,
And they brought him with chains to the land of Egypt.
⁵ 'When she saw that she waited, *that* her hope was lost,
She took another of her cubs *and* made him a young lion.
⁶ He roved among the lions,
And became a young lion;
He learned to catch prey;
He devoured men.
⁷ He knew their desolate places,
And laid waste their cities;
The land with its fullness was desolated
By the noise of his roaring.
⁸ Then the nations set against him from the provinces on every side,
And spread their net over him;
He was trapped in their pit.
⁹ They put him in a cage with chains,
And brought him to the king of Babylon;
They brought him in nets,
That his voice should no longer be heard on the mountains of Israel.

¹⁰ 'Your mother *was* like a vine in your bloodline,
Planted by the waters,
Fruitful and full of branches
Because of many waters.
¹¹ She had strong branches for scepters of rulers.
She towered in stature above the thick branches,
And was seen in her height amid the dense foliage.
¹² But she was plucked up in fury,
She was cast down to the ground,
And the east wind dried her fruit.
Her strong branches were broken and withered;
The fire consumed them.
¹³ And now she *is* planted in the wilderness,
In a dry and thirsty land.
¹⁴ Fire has come out from a rod of her branches
And devoured her fruit,
So that she has no strong branch— a scepter for ruling.' "

This *is* a lamentation, and has become a lamentation.

20 It came to pass in the seventh year, in the fifth *month,* on the tenth *day* of the month, *that* certain of the elders of Israel came to inquire of the LORD,

יט וְאַתָּה שָׂא קִינָה אֶל־נְשִׂיאֵי יִשְׂרָאֵל: ² וְאָמַרְתָּ

מָה אִמְּךָ לְבִיָּא בֵּין אֲרָיוֹת רָבָצָה בְּתוֹךְ כְּפִרִים

רִבְּתָה גוּרֶיהָ: ³ וַתַּעַל אֶחָד מִגֻּרֶיהָ כְּפִיר הָיָה

וַיִּלְמַד לִטְרָף־טֶרֶף אָדָם אָכָל: ⁴ וַיִּשְׁמְעוּ אֵלָיו

גּוֹיִם בְּשַׁחְתָּם נִתְפָּשׂ וַיְבִאֻהוּ בַחַחִים אֶל־אֶרֶץ

מִצְרָיִם: ⁵ וַתֵּרֶא כִּי נוֹחֲלָה אָבְדָה תִּקְוָתָהּ וַתִּקַּח

אֶחָד מִגֻּרֶיהָ כְּפִיר שָׂמָתְהוּ: ⁶ וַיִּתְהַלֵּךְ בְּתוֹךְ־

אֲרָיוֹת כְּפִיר הָיָה וַיִּלְמַד לִטְרָף־טֶרֶף אָדָם אָכָל:

⁷ וַיֵּדַע אַלְמְנוֹתָיו וְעָרֵיהֶם הֶחֱרִיב וַתֵּשַׁם אֶרֶץ

וּמְלֹאָהּ מִקּוֹל שַׁאֲגָתוֹ: ⁸ וַיִּתְּנוּ עָלָיו גּוֹיִם סָבִיב

מִמְּדִינוֹת וַיִּפְרְשׂוּ עָלָיו רִשְׁתָּם בְּשַׁחְתָּם נִתְפָּשׂ:

⁹ וַיִּתְּנֻהוּ בַסּוּגַר בַּחַחִים וַיְבִאֻהוּ אֶל־מֶלֶךְ בָּבֶל

יְבִאֻהוּ בַּמְּצֹדוֹת לְמַעַן לֹא־יִשָּׁמַע קוֹלוֹ עוֹד אֶל־

הָרֵי יִשְׂרָאֵל:
    פ

¹⁰ אִמְּךָ כַגֶּפֶן בְּדָמְךָ עַל־מַיִם שְׁתוּלָה פֹּרִיָּה וַעֲנֵפָה

הָיְתָה מִמַּיִם רַבִּים: ¹¹ וַיִּהְיוּ־לָהּ מַטּוֹת עֹז אֶל־

שִׁבְטֵי מֹשְׁלִים וַתִּגְבַּהּ קוֹמָתוֹ עַל־בֵּין עֲבֹתִים

וַיֵּרָא בְגָבְהוֹ בְּרֹב דָּלִיֹּתָיו: ¹² וַתֻּתַּשׁ בְּחֵמָה לָאָרֶץ

הֻשְׁלָכָה וְרוּחַ הַקָּדִים הוֹבִישׁ פִּרְיָהּ הִתְפָּרְקוּ וְיָבֵשׁוּ

מַטֵּה עֻזָּהּ אֵשׁ אֲכָלָתְהוּ: ¹³ וְעַתָּה שְׁתוּלָה בַמִּדְבָּר

בְּאֶרֶץ צִיָּה וְצָמָא: ¹⁴ וַתֵּצֵא אֵשׁ מִמַּטֵּה בַדֶּיהָ

פִּרְיָהּ אָכָלָה וְלֹא־הָיָה בָהּ מַטֵּה־עֹז שֵׁבֶט לִמְשׁוֹל

קִינָה הִיא וַתְּהִי לְקִינָה:
    פ

כ וַיְהִי בַּשָּׁנָה הַשְּׁבִיעִית בַּחֲמִשִׁי בֶּעָשׂוֹר לַחֹדֶשׁ

בָּאוּ אֲנָשִׁים מִזִּקְנֵי יִשְׂרָאֵל לִדְרֹשׁ אֶת־יְהוָה וַיֵּשְׁבוּ

and sat before me. ²Then the word of the LORD
came to me, saying, ³"Son of man, speak to the
elders of Israel, and say to them, 'Thus says the
Lord GOD: "Have you come to inquire of Me? *As* I
live," says the Lord GOD, "I will not be inquired of
by you." ' ⁴Will you judge them, son of man, will
you judge *them?* Then make known to them the
abominations of their fathers.

⁵"Say to them, 'Thus says the Lord GOD: "On
the day when I chose Israel and raised My hand in
an oath to the descendants of the house of Jacob,
and made Myself known to them in the land of
Egypt, I raised My hand in an oath to them, saying,
'I *am* the LORD your God.' ⁶On that day I raised
My hand in an oath to them, to bring them out of
the land of Egypt into a land that I had searched
out for them, 'flowing with milk and honey,' the
glory of all lands. ⁷Then I said to them, 'Each of
you, throw away the abominations which are before
his eyes, and do not defile yourselves with the idols
of Egypt. I *am* the LORD your God.' ⁸But they
rebelled against Me and would not obey Me. They
did not all cast away the abominations which were
before their eyes, nor did they forsake the idols of
Egypt. Then I said, 'I will pour out My fury on
them and fulfill My anger against them in the midst
of the land of Egypt.' ⁹But I acted for My name's
sake, that it should not be profaned before the
Gentiles among whom they *were,* in whose sight I
had made Myself known to them, to bring them out
of the land of Egypt.

¹⁰"Therefore I made them go out of the land of
Egypt and brought them into the wilderness. ¹¹And
I gave them My statutes and showed them My
judgments, 'which, *if* a man does, he shall live by
them.' ¹²Moreover I also gave them My Sabbaths,
to be a sign between them and Me, that they might
know that I *am* the LORD who sanctifies them.
¹³Yet the house of Israel rebelled against Me in the
wilderness; they did not walk in My statutes; they
despised My judgments, 'which, *if* a man does, he
shall live by them'; and they greatly defiled My
Sabbaths. Then I said I would pour out My fury on
them in the wilderness, to consume them. ¹⁴But I
acted for My name's sake, that it should not be
profaned before the Gentiles, in whose sight I had
brought them out. ¹⁵So I also raised My hand in an
oath to them in the wilderness, that I would not
bring them into the land which I had given *them,*
'flowing with milk and honey,' the glory of all
lands, ¹⁶because they despised My judgments and
did not walk in My statutes, but profaned My
Sabbaths; for their heart went after their idols.

לְפָנָֽי׃ ס ² וַיְהִ֥י דְבַר־יְהֹוָ֖ה אֵלַ֥י לֵאמֹֽר׃

³ בֶּן־אָדָ֗ם דַּבֵּ֞ר אֶת־זִקְנֵ֤י יִשְׂרָאֵל֙ וְאָמַרְתָּ֣ אֲלֵהֶ֔ם כֹּ֤ה
אָמַר֙ אֲדֹנָ֣י יְהֹוִ֔ה הֲלִדְרֹ֥שׁ אֹתִ֖י אַתֶּ֣ם בָּאִ֑ים חַי־אָ֙נִי֙
אִם־אִדָּרֵ֣שׁ לָכֶ֔ם נְאֻ֖ם אֲדֹנָ֥י יְהֹוִֽה׃ ⁴ הֲתִשְׁפֹּ֥ט אֹתָ֛ם
הֲתִשְׁפּ֖וֹט בֶּן־אָדָ֑ם אֶת־תּוֹעֲבֹ֥ת אֲבוֹתָ֖ם הוֹדִיעֵֽם׃

⁵ וְאָמַרְתָּ֣ אֲלֵיהֶ֗ם כֹּֽה־אָמַר֮ אֲדֹנָ֣י יְהֹוִה֒ בְּיוֹם֙ בׇּחֳרִ֣י
בְיִשְׂרָאֵ֔ל וָאֶשָּׂ֣א יָדִ֗י לְזֶ֙רַע֙ בֵּ֣ית יַעֲקֹ֔ב וָאִוָּדַ֤ע
לָהֶם֙ בְּאֶ֣רֶץ מִצְרָ֔יִם וָאֶשָּׂ֧א יָדִ֛י לָהֶ֖ם לֵאמֹ֑ר אֲנִ֖י
יְהֹוָ֥ה אֱלֹהֵיכֶֽם׃ ⁶ בַּיּ֣וֹם הַה֗וּא נָשָׂ֤אתִי יָדִי֙ לָהֶ֔ם
לְהֽוֹצִיאָ֖ם מֵאֶ֣רֶץ מִצְרָ֑יִם אֶל־אֶ֜רֶץ אֲשֶׁר־תַּ֣רְתִּי
לָהֶ֗ם זָבַ֤ת חָלָב֙ וּדְבַ֔שׁ צְבִ֥י הִ֖יא לְכׇל־הָאֲרָצֽוֹת׃

⁷ וָאֹמַ֣ר אֲלֵהֶ֗ם אִ֣ישׁ שִׁקּוּצֵ֤י עֵינָיו֙ הַשְׁלִ֔יכוּ וּבְגִלּוּלֵ֥י
מִצְרַ֖יִם אַל־תִּטַּמָּ֑אוּ אֲנִ֖י יְהֹוָ֥ה אֱלֹהֵיכֶֽם׃ ⁸ וַיַּמְרוּ־
בִ֗י וְלֹ֤א אָבוּ֙ לִשְׁמֹ֣עַ אֵלַ֔י אִ֣ישׁ אֶת־שִׁקּוּצֵ֤י עֵֽינֵיהֶם֙
לֹ֣א הִשְׁלִ֔יכוּ וְאֶת־גִּלּוּלֵ֥י מִצְרַ֖יִם לֹ֣א עָזָ֑בוּ וָאֹמַ֞ר
לִשְׁפֹּ֧ךְ חֲמָתִ֣י עֲלֵיהֶ֗ם לְכַלּ֤וֹת אַפִּי֙ בָּהֶ֔ם בְּת֖וֹךְ אֶ֣רֶץ
מִצְרָֽיִם׃ ⁹ וָאַ֙עַשׂ֙ לְמַ֣עַן שְׁמִ֔י לְבִלְתִּ֥י הֵחֵ֖ל לְעֵינֵ֣י
הַגּוֹיִ֗ם אֲשֶׁר־הֵ֙מָּה֙ בְתוֹכָ֔ם אֲשֶׁ֛ר נוֹדַ֥עְתִּי אֲלֵיהֶ֖ם
לְעֵ֣ינֵיהֶ֑ם לְהוֹצִיאָ֖ם מֵאֶ֥רֶץ מִצְרָֽיִם׃ ¹⁰ וָאֽוֹצִיאֵ֖ם
מֵאֶ֣רֶץ מִצְרָ֑יִם וָאֲבִאֵ֖ם אֶל־הַמִּדְבָּֽר׃ ¹¹ וָאֶתֵּ֤ן לָהֶם֙
אֶת־חֻקּוֹתַ֔י וְאֶת־מִשְׁפָּטַ֖י הוֹדַ֣עְתִּי אוֹתָ֑ם אֲשֶׁ֨ר
יַעֲשֶׂ֥ה אוֹתָ֛ם הָאָדָ֖ם וָחַ֥י בָּהֶֽם׃ ¹² וְגַ֤ם אֶת־
שַׁבְּתוֹתַי֙ נָתַ֣תִּי לָהֶ֔ם לִֽהְי֣וֹת לְא֔וֹת בֵּינִ֖י וּבֵֽינֵיהֶ֑ם
לָדַ֕עַת כִּ֛י אֲנִ֥י יְהֹוָ֖ה מְקַדְּשָֽׁם׃ ¹³ וַיַּמְרוּ־בִ֣י בֵית־
יִשְׂרָאֵ֣ל בַּמִּדְבָּ֗ר בְּחֻקּוֹתַ֣י לֹא־הָלָ֡כוּ וְאֶת־מִשְׁפָּטַ֣י
מָאָ֡סוּ אֲשֶׁר֩ יַעֲשֶׂ֙ה אֹתָ֤ם הָֽאָדָם֙ וָחַ֣י בָּהֶ֔ם וְאֶת־
שַׁבְּתֹתַ֖י חִלְּל֣וּ מְאֹ֑ד וָאֹמַ֞ר לִשְׁפֹּ֤ךְ חֲמָתִ֤י עֲלֵיהֶם֙
בַּמִּדְבָּ֖ר לְכַלּוֹתָֽם׃ ¹⁴ וָאֶעֱשֶׂ֖ה לְמַ֣עַן שְׁמִ֑י לְבִלְתִּ֤י
הֵחֵל֙ לְעֵינֵ֣י הַגּוֹיִ֔ם אֲשֶׁ֥ר הוֹצֵאתִ֖ים לְעֵינֵיהֶֽם׃
¹⁵ וְגַם־אֲנִ֗י נָשָׂ֧אתִי יָדִ֛י לָהֶ֖ם בַּמִּדְבָּ֑ר לְבִלְתִּי֩ הָבִ֙יא
אוֹתָ֜ם אֶל־הָאָ֣רֶץ אֲשֶׁר־נָתַ֗תִּי זָבַ֤ת חָלָב֙ וּדְבַ֔שׁ
צְבִ֥י הִ֖יא לְכׇל־הָאֲרָצֽוֹת׃ ¹⁶ יַ֜עַן בְּמִשְׁפָּטַ֣י מָאָ֗סוּ
וְאֶת־חֻקּוֹתַי֙ לֹא־הָלְכ֣וּ בָהֶ֔ם וְאֶת־שַׁבְּתוֹתַ֖י חִלֵּ֑לוּ

[17]Nevertheless My eye spared them from destruction. I did not make an end of them in the wilderness.

[18]"But I said to their children in the wilderness, 'Do not walk in the statutes of your fathers, nor observe their judgments, nor defile yourselves with their idols. [19]I am the LORD your God: Walk in My statutes, keep My judgments, and do them; [20]hallow My Sabbaths, and they will be a sign between Me and you, that you may know that I am the LORD your God.'

[21]"Notwithstanding, the children rebelled against Me; they did not walk in My statutes, and were not careful to observe My judgments, 'which, if a man does, he shall live by them'; but they profaned My Sabbaths. Then I said I would pour out My fury on them and fulfill My anger against them in the wilderness. [22]Nevertheless I withdrew My hand and acted for My name's sake, that it should not be profaned in the sight of the Gentiles, in whose sight I had brought them out. [23]Also I raised My hand in an oath to those in the wilderness, that I would scatter them among the Gentiles and disperse them throughout the countries, [24]because they had not executed My judgments, but had despised My statutes, profaned My Sabbaths, and their eyes were fixed on their fathers' idols.

[25]"Therefore I also gave them up to statutes that were not good, and judgments by which they could not live; [26]and I pronounced them unclean because of their ritual gifts, in that they caused all their firstborn to pass through the fire, that I might make them desolate and that they might know that I am the LORD."'

[27]"Therefore, son of man, speak to the house of Israel, and say to them, 'Thus says the Lord GOD: "In this too your fathers have blasphemed Me, by being unfaithful to Me. [28]When I brought them into the land concerning which I had raised My hand in an oath to give them, and they saw all the high hills and all the thick trees, there they offered their sacrifices and provoked Me with their offerings. There they also sent up their sweet aroma and poured out their drink offerings. [29]Then I said to them, 'What is this high place to which you go?' So its name is called Bamah to this day."' [30]Therefore say to the house of Israel, 'Thus says the Lord GOD: "Are you defiling yourselves in the manner of your fathers, and committing harlotry according to their abominations? [31]For when you offer your gifts and make your sons pass through the fire, you defile yourselves with all your idols, even to this day. So shall I be inquired of by you, O house of Israel? As I

כִּי אַחֲרֵי גִלּוּלֵיהֶם לִבָּם הֹלֵךְ: 17 וַתָּחָס עֵינִי
עֲלֵיהֶם מִשַּׁחֲתָם וְלֹא־עָשִׂיתִי אוֹתָם כָּלָה בַּמִּדְבָּר:

18 וָאֹמַר אֶל־בְּנֵיהֶם בַּמִּדְבָּר בְּחוּקֵּי אֲבוֹתֵיכֶם
אַל־תֵּלֵכוּ וְאֶת־מִשְׁפְּטֵיהֶם אַל־תִּשְׁמֹרוּ וּבְגִלּוּלֵיהֶם
אַל־תִּטַּמָּאוּ: 19 אֲנִי יְהֹוָה אֱלֹהֵיכֶם בְּחֻקּוֹתַי לֵכוּ
וְאֶת־מִשְׁפָּטַי שִׁמְרוּ וַעֲשׂוּ אוֹתָם: 20 וְאֶת־שַׁבְּתוֹתַי
קַדֵּשׁוּ וְהָיוּ לְאוֹת בֵּינִי וּבֵינֵיכֶם לָדַעַת כִּי אֲנִי
יְהֹוָה אֱלֹהֵיכֶם: 21 וַיַּמְרוּ־בִי הַבָּנִים בְּחֻקּוֹתַי לֹא־
הָלָכוּ וְאֶת־מִשְׁפָּטַי לֹא־שָׁמְרוּ לַעֲשׂוֹת אוֹתָם אֲשֶׁר
יַעֲשֶׂה אוֹתָם הָאָדָם וָחַי בָּהֶם אֶת־שַׁבְּתוֹתַי חִלֵּלוּ
וָאֹמַר לִשְׁפֹּךְ חֲמָתִי עֲלֵיהֶם לְכַלּוֹת אַפִּי בָּם
בַּמִּדְבָּר: 22 וַהֲשִׁבֹתִי אֶת־יָדִי וָאַעַשׂ לְמַעַן שְׁמִי
לְבִלְתִּי הֵחֵל לְעֵינֵי הַגּוֹיִם אֲשֶׁר־הוֹצֵאתִי אוֹתָם
לְעֵינֵיהֶם: 23 גַּם־אֲנִי נָשָׂאתִי אֶת־יָדִי לָהֶם בַּמִּדְבָּר
לְהָפִיץ אֹתָם בַּגּוֹיִם וּלְזָרוֹת אוֹתָם בָּאֲרָצוֹת: 24 יַעַן
מִשְׁפָּטַי לֹא־עָשׂוּ וְחֻקּוֹתַי מָאָסוּ וְאֶת־שַׁבְּתוֹתַי
חִלֵּלוּ וְאַחֲרֵי גִּלּוּלֵי אֲבוֹתָם הָיוּ עֵינֵיהֶם: 25 וְגַם־
אֲנִי נָתַתִּי לָהֶם חֻקִּים לֹא טוֹבִים וּמִשְׁפָּטִים לֹא
יִחְיוּ בָּהֶם: 26 וָאֲטַמֵּא אוֹתָם בְּמַתְּנוֹתָם בְּהַעֲבִיר
כָּל־פֶּטֶר רָחַם לְמַעַן אֲשִׁמֵּם לְמַעַן אֲשֶׁר יֵדְעוּ
אֲשֶׁר אֲנִי יְהֹוָה: ס   27 לָכֵן דַּבֵּר אֶל־בֵּית
יִשְׂרָאֵל בֶּן־אָדָם וְאָמַרְתָּ אֲלֵיהֶם כֹּה אָמַר אֲדֹנָי
יְהֹוִה עוֹד זֹאת גִּדְּפוּ אוֹתִי אֲבוֹתֵיכֶם בְּמַעֲלָם
בִּי מָעַל: 28 וָאֲבִיאֵם אֶל־הָאָרֶץ אֲשֶׁר נָשָׂאתִי
אֶת־יָדִי לָתֵת אוֹתָהּ לָהֶם וַיִּרְאוּ כָל־גִּבְעָה רָמָה
וְכָל־עֵץ עָבֹת וַיִּזְבְּחוּ־שָׁם אֶת־זִבְחֵיהֶם וַיִּתְּנוּ־שָׁם
כַּעַס קָרְבָּנָם וַיָּשִׂימוּ שָׁם רֵיחַ נִיחוֹחֵיהֶם וַיַּסִּיכוּ
שָׁם אֶת־נִסְכֵּיהֶם: 29 וָאֹמַר אֲלֵהֶם מָה הַבָּמָה
אֲשֶׁר־אַתֶּם הַבָּאִים שָׁם וַיִּקָּרֵא שְׁמָהּ בָּמָה עַד
הַיּוֹם הַזֶּה: 30 לָכֵן אֱמֹר | אֶל־בֵּית יִשְׂרָאֵל
כֹּה אָמַר אֲדֹנָי יְהֹוִה הַבְּדֶרֶךְ אֲבוֹתֵיכֶם אַתֶּם
נִטְמָאִים וְאַחֲרֵי שִׁקּוּצֵיהֶם אַתֶּם זֹנִים: 31 וּבִשְׂאֵת
מַתְּנֹתֵיכֶם בְּהַעֲבִיר בְּנֵיכֶם בָּאֵשׁ אַתֶּם נִטְמְאִים
לְכָל־גִּלּוּלֵיכֶם עַד־הַיּוֹם וַאֲנִי אִדָּרֵשׁ לָכֶם בֵּית
יִשְׂרָאֵל חַי־אָנִי נְאֻם אֲדֹנָי יְהֹוִה אִם־אִדָּרֵשׁ לָכֶם:

live," says the Lord GOD, "I will not be inquired of by you. ³² What you have in your mind shall never be, when you say, 'We will be like the Gentiles, like the families in other countries, serving wood and stone.'

³³ "As I live," says the Lord GOD, "surely with a mighty hand, with an outstretched arm, and with fury poured out, I will rule over you. ³⁴ I will bring you out from the peoples and gather you out of the countries where you are scattered, with a mighty hand, with an outstretched arm, and with fury poured out. ³⁵ And I will bring you into the wilderness of the peoples, and there I will plead My case with you face to face. ³⁶ Just as I pleaded My case with your fathers in the wilderness of the land of Egypt, so I will plead My case with you," says the Lord GOD.

³⁷ "I will make you pass under the rod, and I will bring you into the bond of the covenant; ³⁸ I will purge the rebels from among you, and those who transgress against Me; I will bring them out of the country where they dwell, but they shall not enter the land of Israel. Then you will know that I am the LORD.

³⁹ "As for you, O house of Israel," thus says the Lord GOD: "Go, serve every one of you his idols— and hereafter—if you will not obey Me; but profane My holy name no more with your gifts and your idols. ⁴⁰ For on My holy mountain, on the mountain height of Israel," says the Lord GOD, "there all the house of Israel, all of them in the land, shall serve Me; there I will accept them, and there I will require your offerings and the firstfruits of your sacrifices, together with all your holy things. ⁴¹ I will accept you as a sweet aroma when I bring you out from the peoples and gather you out of the countries where you have been scattered; and I will be hallowed in you before the Gentiles. ⁴² Then you shall know that I am the LORD, when I bring you into the land of Israel, into the country for which I raised My hand in an oath to give to your fathers. ⁴³ And there you shall remember your ways and all your doings with which you were defiled; and you shall loathe yourselves in your own sight because of all the evils that you have committed. ⁴⁴ Then you shall know that I am the LORD, when I have dealt with you for My name's sake, not according to your wicked ways nor according to your corrupt doings, O house of Israel," says the Lord GOD.' "

⁴⁵ Furthermore the word of the LORD came to me, saying, ⁴⁶ "Son of man, set your face toward the south; preach against the south and prophesy against the forest land, the South, ⁴⁷ and say to the forest of the South, 'Hear the word of the LORD!

---

³² וְהָעֹלָה֙ עַל־ר֣וּחֲכֶ֔ם הָי֖וֹ לֹ֣א תִֽהְיֶ֑ה אֲשֶׁ֣ר ׀ אַתֶּ֣ם אֹֽמְרִ֗ים נִֽהְיֶ֣ה כַגּוֹיִ֔ם כְּמִשְׁפְּח֖וֹת הָאֲרָצ֑וֹת לְשָׁרֵ֖ת עֵ֥ץ וָאָֽבֶן׃ ³³ חַי־אָ֗נִי נְאֻם֙ אֲדֹנָ֣י יְהֹוִ֔ה אִם־לֹ֠א בְּיָ֣ד חֲזָקָ֞ה וּבִזְר֧וֹעַ נְטוּיָ֛ה וּבְחֵמָ֥ה שְׁפוּכָ֖ה אֶמְל֥וֹךְ עֲלֵיכֶֽם׃ ³⁴ וְהֽוֹצֵאתִ֤י אֶתְכֶם֙ מִן־הָ֣עַמִּ֔ים וְקִבַּצְתִּ֣י אֶתְכֶ֔ם מִן־הָ֣אֲרָצ֔וֹת אֲשֶׁ֥ר נְפוֹצֹתֶ֖ם בָּ֑ם בְּיָ֤ד חֲזָקָה֙ וּבִזְר֣וֹעַ נְטוּיָ֔ה וּבְחֵמָ֖ה שְׁפוּכָֽה׃ ³⁵ וְהֵבֵאתִ֣י אֶתְכֶ֔ם אֶל־מִדְבַּ֖ר הָֽעַמִּ֑ים וְנִשְׁפַּטְתִּ֤י אִתְּכֶם֙ שָׁ֔ם פָּנִ֖ים אֶל־פָּנִֽים׃ ³⁶ כַּאֲשֶׁ֤ר נִשְׁפַּ֙טְתִּי֙ אֶת־אֲב֣וֹתֵיכֶ֔ם בְּמִדְבַּ֖ר אֶ֣רֶץ מִצְרָ֑יִם כֵּ֚ן אִשָּׁפֵ֣ט אִתְּכֶ֔ם נְאֻ֖ם אֲדֹנָ֥י יְהֹוִֽה׃ ³⁷ וְהַֽעֲבַרְתִּ֥י אֶתְכֶ֖ם תַּ֣חַת הַשָּׁ֑בֶט וְהֵבֵאתִ֥י אֶתְכֶ֖ם בְּמָסֹ֥רֶת הַבְּרִֽית׃ ³⁸ וּבָרוֹתִ֣י מִכֶּ֣ם הַמֹּרְדִ֗ים וְהַפּֽוֹשְׁעִים֙ בִּ֔י מֵאֶ֤רֶץ מְגֽוּרֵיהֶם֙ אוֹצִ֣יא אוֹתָ֔ם וְאֶל־אַדְמַ֥ת יִשְׂרָאֵ֖ל לֹ֣א יָב֑וֹא וִֽידַעְתֶּ֖ם כִּֽי־אֲנִ֥י יְהֹוָֽה׃ ³⁹ וְאַתֶּ֨ם בֵּֽית־יִשְׂרָאֵ֜ל כֹּֽה־אָמַ֣ר ׀ אֲדֹנָ֣י יְהֹוִ֗ה אִ֤ישׁ גִּלּוּלָיו֙ לְכ֣וּ עֲבֹ֔דוּ וְאַחַ֕ר אִם־אֵֽינְכֶ֖ם שֹׁמְעִ֣ים אֵלָ֑י וְאֶת־שֵׁ֤ם קׇדְשִׁי֙ לֹ֣א תְחַלְּלוּ־ע֔וֹד בְּמַתְּנֽוֹתֵיכֶ֖ם וּבְגִלּוּלֵיכֶֽם׃ ⁴⁰ כִּ֣י בְהַר־קׇדְשִׁ֞י בְּהַ֣ר ׀ מְר֣וֹם יִשְׂרָאֵ֗ל נְאֻם֙ אֲדֹנָ֣י יְהֹוִ֔ה שָׁ֣ם יַֽעַבְדֻ֜נִי כׇּל־בֵּ֤ית יִשְׂרָאֵל֙ כֻּלֹּ֣ה בָּאָ֔רֶץ שָׁ֖ם אֶרְצֵ֑ם וְשָׁ֣ם אֶדְר֗וֹשׁ אֶת־תְּרוּמֹֽתֵיכֶ֛ם וְאֶת־רֵאשִׁ֥ית מַשְׂאֽוֹתֵיכֶ֖ם בְּכׇל־קׇדְשֵׁיכֶֽם׃ ⁴¹ בְּרֵ֣יחַ נִיחֹ֘חַ֮ אֶרְצֶ֣ה אֶתְכֶם֒ בְּהוֹצִיאִ֤י אֶתְכֶם֙ מִן־הָ֣עַמִּ֔ים וְקִבַּצְתִּ֣י אֶתְכֶ֔ם מִן־הָ֣אֲרָצ֔וֹת אֲשֶׁ֥ר נְפֹצֹתֶ֖ם בָּ֑ם וְנִקְדַּשְׁתִּ֥י בָכֶ֖ם לְעֵינֵ֥י הַגּוֹיִֽם׃ ⁴² וִֽידַעְתֶּם֙ כִּֽי־אֲנִ֣י יְהֹוָ֔ה בַּהֲבִיאִ֥י אֶתְכֶ֖ם אֶל־אַדְמַ֣ת יִשְׂרָאֵ֑ל אֶל־הָאָ֗רֶץ אֲשֶׁ֤ר נָשָׂ֙אתִי֙ אֶת־יָדִ֔י לָתֵ֥ת אוֹתָ֖הּ לַאֲבֽוֹתֵיכֶֽם׃ ⁴³ וּזְכַרְתֶּם־שָׁ֗ם אֶת־דַּרְכֵיכֶם֙ וְאֵת֙ כׇּל־עֲלִיל֣וֹתֵיכֶ֔ם אֲשֶׁ֥ר נִטְמֵאתֶ֖ם בָּ֑ם וּנְקֹֽטֹתֶם֙ בִּפְנֵיכֶ֔ם בְּכׇל־רָעֽוֹתֵיכֶ֖ם אֲשֶׁ֥ר עֲשִׂיתֶֽם׃ ⁴⁴ וִֽידַעְתֶּ֞ם כִּֽי־אֲנִ֣י יְהֹוָ֗ה בַּעֲשׂוֹתִ֤י אִתְּכֶם֙ לְמַ֣עַן שְׁמִ֔י לֹ֧א כְדַרְכֵיכֶ֣ם הָרָעִ֗ים וְכַעֲלִילֽוֹתֵיכֶם֙ הַנִּשְׁחָת֔וֹת בֵּ֖ית יִשְׂרָאֵ֑ל נְאֻ֖ם אֲדֹנָ֥י יְהֹוִֽה׃ פ

כא וַיְהִ֥י דְבַר־יְהֹוָ֖ה אֵלַ֥י לֵאמֹֽר׃ ² בֶּן־אָדָ֗ם שִׂ֤ים פָּנֶ֙יךָ֙ דֶּ֣רֶךְ תֵּימָ֔נָה וְהַטֵּ֖ף אֶל־דָּר֑וֹם וְהִנָּבֵ֛א אֶל־יַ֥עַר הַשָּׂדֶ֖ה נֶֽגֶב׃ ³ וְאָֽמַרְתָּ֙ לְיַ֣עַר הַנֶּ֔גֶב שְׁמַ֖ע דְּבַר־יְהֹוָ֑ה כֹּֽה־אָמַ֣ר אֲדֹנָ֣י יְהֹוִ֗ה הִנְנִ֤י מַצִּֽית־בְּךָ֙ ׀ אֵ֔שׁ

Thus says the Lord God: "Behold, I will kindle a fire in you, and it shall devour every green tree and every dry tree in you; the blazing flame shall not be quenched, and all faces from the south to the north shall be scorched by it. 48 All flesh shall see that I, the Lord, have kindled it; it shall not be quenched." ' "

49 Then I said, "Ah, Lord God! They say of me, 'Does he not speak parables?' "

21 And the word of the Lord came to me, saying, 2 "Son of man, set your face toward Jerusalem, preach against the holy places, and prophesy against the land of Israel; 3 and say to the land of Israel, 'Thus says the Lord: "Behold, I am against you, and I will draw My sword out of its sheath and cut off both righteous and wicked from you. 4 Because I will cut off both righteous and wicked from you, therefore My sword shall go out of its sheath against all flesh from south to north, 5 that all flesh may know that I, the Lord, have drawn My sword out of its sheath; it shall not return anymore." ' 6 Sigh therefore, son of man, with a breaking heart, and sigh with bitterness before their eyes. 7 And it shall be when they say to you, 'Why are you sighing?' that you shall answer, 'Because of the news; when it comes, every heart will melt, all hands will be feeble, every spirit will faint, and all knees will be weak as water. Behold, it is coming and shall be brought to pass,' says the Lord God."

8 Again the word of the Lord came to me, saying, 9 "Son of man, prophesy and say, 'Thus says the Lord!' Say:

'A sword, a sword is sharpened
And also polished!
10   Sharpened to make a dreadful slaughter,
Polished to flash like lightning!
Should we then make mirth?
It despises the scepter of My son,
As it does all wood.
11   And He has given it to be polished,
That it may be handled;
This sword is sharpened, and it is polished
To be given into the hand of the slayer.'

12   "Cry and wail, son of man;
For it will be against My people,
Against all the princes of Israel.
Terrors including the sword will be against My people;
Therefore strike your thigh.

13   "Because it is a testing,
And what if the sword despises even the scepter?
The scepter shall be no more,"

says the Lord God.

וְאָכְלָה בָךְ כָּל־עֵץ־לַח וְכָל־עֵץ יָבֵשׁ לֹא־תִכְבֶּה לַהֶבֶת שַׁלְהֶבֶת וְנִצְרְבוּ־בָהּ כָּל־פָּנִים מִנֶּגֶב צָפוֹנָה:
4 וְרָאוּ כָּל־בָּשָׂר כִּי אֲנִי יְהוָה בִּעַרְתִּיהָ לֹא תִכְבֶּה:
5 וָאֹמַר אֲהָהּ אֲדֹנָי יְהוִה הֵמָּה אֹמְרִים לִי הֲלֹא מְמַשֵּׁל מְשָׁלִים הוּא: פ
6 וַיְהִי דְבַר־יְהוָה אֵלַי לֵאמֹר: 7 בֶּן־אָדָם שִׂים פָּנֶיךָ אֶל־יְרוּשָׁלַ͏ִם וְהַטֵּף אֶל־מִקְדָּשִׁים וְהִנָּבֵא אֶל־אַדְמַת יִשְׂרָאֵל: 8 וְאָמַרְתָּ לְאַדְמַת יִשְׂרָאֵל כֹּה אָמַר יְהוָה הִנְנִי אֵלַיִךְ וְהוֹצֵאתִי חַרְבִּי מִתַּעְרָהּ וְהִכְרַתִּי מִמֵּךְ צַדִּיק וְרָשָׁע: 9 יַעַן אֲשֶׁר־הִכְרַתִּי מִמֵּךְ צַדִּיק וְרָשָׁע לָכֵן תֵּצֵא חַרְבִּי מִתַּעְרָהּ אֶל־כָּל־בָּשָׂר מִנֶּגֶב צָפוֹן:
10 וְיָדְעוּ כָּל־בָּשָׂר כִּי אֲנִי יְהוָה הוֹצֵאתִי חַרְבִּי מִתַּעְרָהּ לֹא תָשׁוּב עוֹד: ס 11 וְאַתָּה בֶן־אָדָם הֵאָנַח בְּשִׁבְרוֹן מָתְנַיִם וּבִמְרִירוּת תֵּאָנַח לְעֵינֵיהֶם: 12 וְהָיָה כִּי־יֹאמְרוּ אֵלֶיךָ עַל־מָה אַתָּה נֶאֱנָח וְאָמַרְתָּ אֶל־שְׁמוּעָה כִי־בָאָה וְנָמֵס כָּל־לֵב וְרָפוּ כָל־יָדַיִם וְכִהֲתָה כָל־רוּחַ וְכָל־בִּרְכַּיִם תֵּלַכְנָה מַּיִם הִנֵּה בָאָה וְנִהְיָתָה נְאֻם אֲדֹנָי יְהוִה: פ
13 וַיְהִי דְבַר־יְהוָה אֵלַי לֵאמֹר: 14 בֶּן־אָדָם הִנָּבֵא וְאָמַרְתָּ כֹּה אָמַר אֲדֹנָי אֱמֹר חֶרֶב חֶרֶב הוּחַדָּה וְגַם־מְרוּטָה: 15 לְמַעַן טְבֹחַ טֶבַח הוּחַדָּה לְמַעַן הֱיֵה־לָהּ בָּרָק מֹרָטָּה אוֹ נָשִׂישׂ שֵׁבֶט בְּנִי מֹאֶסֶת כָּל־עֵץ: 16 וַיִּתֵּן אֹתָהּ לְמָרְטָה לִתְפֹּשׂ בַּכָּף הִיא הוּחַדָּה חֶרֶב וְהִיא מֹרָטָּה לָתֵת אוֹתָהּ בְּיַד־הוֹרֵג:
17 זְעַק וְהֵילֵל בֶּן־אָדָם כִּי־הִיא הָיְתָה בְעַמִּי הִיא בְּכָל־נְשִׂיאֵי יִשְׂרָאֵל מְגוּרֵי אֶל־חֶרֶב הָיוּ אֶת־עַמִּי לָכֵן סְפֹק אֶל־יָרֵךְ: 18 כִּי בֹחַן וּמָה אִם־גַּם־שֵׁבֶט מֹאֶסֶת לֹא יִהְיֶה נְאֻם אֲדֹנָי יְהוִה: פ

14 "You therefore, son of man, prophesy,
And strike *your* hands together.
The third time let the sword do double *damage*.
It *is* the sword *that* slays,
The sword that slays the great *men,*
That enters their private chambers.

15 I have set the point of the sword against all their gates,
That the heart may melt and many may stumble.
Ah! *It is* made bright;
It is grasped for slaughter:

16 "Swords at the ready!
Thrust right!
Set your blade!
Thrust left—
Wherever your edge is ordered!

17 "I also will beat My fists together,
And I will cause My fury to rest;
I, the LORD, have spoken."

18 The word of the LORD came to me again, saying: 19 "And son of man, appoint for yourself two ways for the sword of the king of Babylon to go; both of them shall go from the same land. Make a sign; put *it* at the head of the road to the city. 20 Appoint a road for the sword to go to Rabbah of the Ammonites, and to Judah, into fortified Jerusalem. 21 For the king of Babylon stands at the parting of the road, at the fork of the two roads, to use divination: he shakes the arrows, he consults the images, he looks at the liver. 22 In his right hand is the divination for Jerusalem: to set up battering rams, to call for a slaughter, to lift the voice with shouting, to set battering rams against the gates, to heap up a *siege* mound, and to build a wall. 23 And it will be to them like a false divination in the eyes of those who have sworn oaths with them; but he will bring their iniquity to remembrance, that they may be taken.

24 "Therefore thus says the Lord GOD: 'Because you have made your iniquity to be remembered, in that your transgressions are uncovered, so that in all your doings your sins appear—because you have come to remembrance, you shall be taken in hand.

25 'Now to you, O profane, wicked prince of Israel, whose day has come, whose iniquity *shall* end, 26 thus says the Lord GOD:

"Remove the turban, and take off the crown;
Nothing *shall* remain the same.
Exalt the humble, and humble the exalted.

27 Overthrown, overthrown,
I will make it overthrown!
It shall be no *longer,*
Until He comes whose right it is,
And I will give it *to Him.*"'

19 וְאַתָּה בֶן־אָדָם הִנָּבֵא וְהַךְ כַּף אֶל־כָּף וְתִכָּפֵ֖ל חֶרֶב שְׁלִישִׁתָה חֶרֶב חֲלָלִים הִיא חֶרֶב חָלָל הַגָּדוֹל הַחֹדֶרֶת לָהֶם: 20 לְמַעַן ׀ לָמוּג לֵב וְהַרְבֵּה הַמִּכְשֹׁלִים עַל כָּל־שַׁעֲרֵיהֶם נָתַתִּי אִבְחַת־חָרֶב אָח עֲשׂוּיָה לְבָרָק מְעֻטָּה לְטָבַח: 21 הִתְאַחֲדִי הֵימִנִי הָשִׂימִי הַשְׂמִילִי אָנָה פָּנַיִךְ מֻעָדוֹת: 22 וְגַם־ אֲנִי אַכֶּה כַפִּי אֶל־כַּפִּי וַהֲנִחֹתִי חֲמָתִי אֲנִי יְהוָה דִּבַּרְתִּי: פ

23 וַיְהִי דְבַר־יְהוָה אֵלַי לֵאמֹר: 24 וְאַתָּה בֶן־אָדָם שִׂים־לְךָ ׀ שְׁנַיִם דְּרָכִים לָבוֹא חֶרֶב מֶלֶךְ־בָּבֶל מֵאֶרֶץ אֶחָד יֵצְאוּ שְׁנֵיהֶם וְיָד בָּרֵא בְּרֹאשׁ דֶּרֶךְ־עִיר בָּרֵא: 25 דֶּרֶךְ תָּשִׂים לָבוֹא חֶרֶב אֵת רַבַּת בְּנֵי־עַמּוֹן וְאֶת־יְהוּדָה בִירוּשָׁלַ͏ִם בְּצוּרָה: 26 כִּי־עָמַד מֶלֶךְ־ בָּבֶל אֶל־אֵם הַדֶּרֶךְ בְּרֹאשׁ שְׁנֵי הַדְּרָכִים לִקְסָם־ קָסֶם קִלְקַל בַּחִצִּים שָׁאַל בַּתְּרָפִים רָאָה בַּכָּבֵד: 27 בִּימִינוֹ הָיָה ׀ הַקֶּסֶם יְרוּשָׁלַ͏ִם לָשׂוּם כָּרִים לִפְתֹּחַ פֶּה בְּרֶצַח לְהָרִים קוֹל בִּתְרוּעָה לָשׂוּם כָּרִים עַל־שְׁעָרִים לִשְׁפֹּךְ סֹלְלָה לִבְנוֹת דָּיֵק: 28 וְהָיָה לָהֶם כִּקְסָם־שָׁוְא בְּעֵינֵיהֶם שְׁבֻעֵי שְׁבֻעוֹת לָהֶם וְהוּא־מַזְכִּיר עָוֹן לְהִתָּפֵשׂ: פ

29 לָכֵן כֹּה־אָמַר אֲדֹנָי יְהוִה יַעַן הַזְכַּרְכֶם עֲוֹנְכֶם בְּהִגָּלוֹת פִּשְׁעֵיכֶם לְהֵרָאוֹת חַטֹּאותֵיכֶם בְּכֹל עֲלִילוֹתֵיכֶם יַעַן הִזָּכֶרְכֶם בַּכַּף תִּתָּפֵשׂוּ: פ

30 וְאַתָּה חָלָל רָשָׁע נְשִׂיא יִשְׂרָאֵל אֲשֶׁר־בָּא יוֹמוֹ בְּעֵת עֲוֹן קֵץ: ס 31 כֹּה אָמַר אֲדֹנָי יְהוִה הָסִיר הַמִּצְנֶפֶת וְהָרִים הָעֲטָרָה זֹאת לֹא־ זֹאת הַשָּׁפָלָה הַגְבֵּהַ וְהַגָּבֹהַ הַשְׁפִּיל: 32 עַוָּה עַוָּה

28 "And you, son of man, prophesy and say,
'Thus says the Lord GOD concerning the
Ammonites and concerning their reproach,' and
say:

'A sword, a sword *is* drawn,
Polished for slaughter,
For consuming, for flashing—

29 While they see false visions for you,
While they divine a lie to you,
To bring you on the necks of the wicked, the slain
Whose day has come,
Whose iniquity *shall* end.

30 'Return *it* to its sheath.
I will judge you
In the place where you were created,
In the land of your nativity.

31 I will pour out My indignation on you;
I will blow against you with the fire of My wrath,
And deliver you into the hands of brutal men *who*
are skillful to destroy.

32 You shall be fuel for the fire;
Your blood shall be in the midst of the land.
You shall not be remembered,
For I the LORD have spoken.'"

22 Moreover the word of the LORD came to me,
saying, 2 "Now, son of man, will you judge, will you
judge the bloody city? Yes, show her all her
abominations! 3 Then say, 'Thus says the Lord
GOD: "The city sheds blood in her own midst, that
her time may come; and she makes idols within
herself to defile herself. 4 You have become guilty
by the blood which you have shed, and have defiled
yourself with the idols which you have made. You
have caused your days to draw near, and have come
to *the end of* your years; therefore I have made you
a reproach to the nations, and a mockery to all
countries. 5 *Those* near and *those* far from you will
mock you as infamous *and* full of tumult.

6 "Look, the princes of Israel: each one has used
his power to shed blood in you. 7 In you they have
made light of father and mother; in your midst they
have oppressed the stranger; in you they have
mistreated the fatherless and the widow. 8 You have
despised My holy things and profaned My
Sabbaths. 9 In you are men who slander to cause
bloodshed; in you are those who eat on the
mountains; in your midst they commit lewdness.
10 In you men uncover their fathers' nakedness; in
you they violate women who are set apart during
their impurity. 11 One commits abomination with
his neighbor's wife; another lewdly defiles his
daughter-in-law; and another in you violates his
sister, his father's daughter. 12 In you they take
bribes to shed blood; you take usury and increase;

עֲוֹה אֲשִׁימֶנָּה גַּם־זֹאת לֹא הָיָה עַד־בֹּא אֲשֶׁר־לֹו
הַמִּשְׁפָּט וּנְתַתִּיו: פ

33 וְאַתָּה בֶן־אָדָם הִנָּבֵא וְאָמַרְתָּ כֹּה אָמַר אֲדֹנָי
יְהֹוִה אֶל־בְּנֵי עַמֹּון וְאֶל־חֶרְפָּתָם וְאָמַרְתָּ חֶרֶב
חֶרֶב פְּתוּחָה לְטֶבַח מְרוּטָה לְהָכִיל לְמַעַן בָּרָק:
34 בַּחֲזוֹת לָךְ שָׁוְא בִּקְסָם־לָךְ כָּזָב לָתֵת אוֹתָךְ אֶל־
צַוְּארֵי חַלְלֵי רְשָׁעִים אֲשֶׁר־בָּא יוֹמָם בְּעֵת עֲוֹן קֵץ:
35 הָשַׁב אֶל־תַּעְרָהּ בִּמְקוֹם אֲשֶׁר־נִבְרֵאת בְּאֶרֶץ
מְכֻרוֹתַיִךְ אֶשְׁפֹּט אֹתָךְ: 36 וְשָׁפַכְתִּי עָלַיִךְ זַעְמִי
בְּאֵשׁ עֶבְרָתִי אָפִיחַ עָלָיִךְ וּנְתַתִּיךְ בְּיַד אֲנָשִׁים
בֹּעֲרִים חָרָשֵׁי מַשְׁחִית: 37 לָאֵשׁ תִּהְיֶה לְאָכְלָה
דָּמֵךְ יִהְיֶה בְּתוֹךְ הָאָרֶץ לֹא תִזָּכֵרִי כִּי אֲנִי יְהֹוָה
דִּבַּרְתִּי: פ

כב וַיְהִי דְבַר־יְהֹוָה אֵלַי לֵאמֹר: 2 וְאַתָּה בֶן־אָדָם
הֲתִשְׁפֹּט הֲתִשְׁפֹּט אֶת־עִיר הַדָּמִים וְהוֹדַעְתָּהּ אֵת
כָּל־תּוֹעֲבוֹתֶיהָ: 3 וְאָמַרְתָּ כֹּה אָמַר אֲדֹנָי יְהֹוִה
עִיר שֹׁפֶכֶת דָּם בְּתוֹכָהּ לָבוֹא עִתָּהּ וְעָשְׂתָה
גִלּוּלִים עָלֶיהָ לְטָמְאָה: 4 בְּדָמֵךְ אֲשֶׁר־שָׁפַכְתְּ
אָשַׁמְתְּ וּבְגִלּוּלַיִךְ אֲשֶׁר־עָשִׂית טָמֵאת וַתַּקְרִיבִי
יָמַיִךְ וַתָּבוֹא עַד־שְׁנוֹתָיִךְ עַל־כֵּן נְתַתִּיךְ חֶרְפָּה
לַגּוֹיִם וְקַלָּסָה לְכָל־הָאֲרָצוֹת: 5 הַקְּרֹבוֹת וְהָרְחֹקוֹת
מִמֵּךְ יִתְקַלְּסוּ־בָךְ טְמֵאַת הַשֵּׁם רַבַּת הַמְּהוּמָה:
6 הִנֵּה נְשִׂיאֵי יִשְׂרָאֵל אִישׁ לִזְרֹעוֹ הָיוּ בָךְ לְמַעַן
שְׁפָךְ־דָּם: 7 אָב וָאֵם הֵקַלּוּ בָךְ לַגֵּר עָשׂוּ בַעֹשֶׁק
בְּתוֹכֵךְ יָתוֹם וְאַלְמָנָה הוֹנוּ בָךְ: 8 קָדָשַׁי בָּזִית
וְאֶת־שַׁבְּתֹתַי חִלָּלְתְּ: 9 אַנְשֵׁי רָכִיל הָיוּ בָךְ לְמַעַן
שְׁפָךְ־דָּם וְאֶל־הֶהָרִים אָכְלוּ בָךְ זִמָּה עָשׂוּ בְתוֹכֵךְ:
10 עֶרְוַת־אָב גִּלָּה־בָךְ טְמֵאַת הַנִּדָּה עִנּוּ־בָךְ:
11 וְאִישׁ ׀ אֶת־אֵשֶׁת רֵעֵהוּ עָשָׂה תּוֹעֵבָה וְאִישׁ
אֶת־כַּלָּתוֹ טִמֵּא בְזִמָּה וְאִישׁ אֶת־אֲחֹתוֹ בַת־אָבִיו
עִנָּה־בָךְ: 12 שֹׁחַד לָקְחוּ־בָךְ לְמַעַן שְׁפָךְ־דָּם נֶשֶׁךְ

you have made profit from your neighbors by extortion, and have forgotten Me," says the Lord GOD.

13 "Behold, therefore, I beat My fists at the dishonest profit which you have made, and at the bloodshed which has been in your midst. 14 Can your heart endure, or can your hands remain strong, in the days when I shall deal with you? I, the LORD, have spoken, and will do *it.* 15 I will scatter you among the nations, disperse you throughout the countries, and remove your filthiness completely from you. 16 You shall defile yourself in the sight of the nations; then you shall know that I *am* the LORD." ' "

17 The word of the LORD came to me, saying, 18 "Son of man, the house of Israel has become dross to Me; they *are* all bronze, tin, iron, and lead, in the midst of a furnace; they have become dross from silver. 19 Therefore thus says the Lord GOD: 'Because you have all become dross, therefore behold, I will gather you into the midst of Jerusalem. 20 *As men* gather silver, bronze, iron, lead, and tin into the midst of a furnace, to blow fire on it, to melt *it;* so I will gather *you* in My anger and in My fury, and I will leave *you there* and melt you. 21 Yes, I will gather you and blow on you with the fire of My wrath, and you shall be melted in its midst. 22 As silver is melted in the midst of a furnace, so shall you be melted in its midst; then you shall know that I, the LORD, have poured out My fury on you.' "

23 And the word of the LORD came to me, saying, 24 "Son of man, say to her: 'You *are* a land that is not cleansed or rained on in the day of indignation.' 25 The conspiracy of her prophets in her midst is like a roaring lion tearing the prey; they have devoured people; they have taken treasure and precious things; they have made many widows in her midst. 26 Her priests have violated My law and profaned My holy things; they have not distinguished between the holy and unholy, nor have they made known *the difference* between the unclean and the clean; and they have hidden their eyes from My Sabbaths, so that I am profaned among them. 27 Her princes in her midst *are* like wolves tearing the prey, to shed blood, to destroy people, and to get dishonest gain. 28 Her prophets plastered them with untempered *mortar,* seeing false visions, and divining lies for them, saying, 'Thus says the Lord GOD,' when the LORD had not spoken. 29 The people of the land have used oppressions, committed robbery, and mistreated the poor and needy; and they wrongfully oppress the stranger. 30 So I sought for a man among them who would make a

וְתַרְבִּית לָקַחַתְּ וַתְּבַצְּעִי רֵעַיִךְ בַּעֹשֶׁק וְאֹתִי שָׁכַחַתְּ
נְאֻם אֲדֹנָי יְהֹוִה: 13 וְהִנֵּה הִכֵּיתִי כַפִּי אֶל־בִּצְעֵךְ
אֲשֶׁר עָשִׂית וְעַל־דָּמֵךְ אֲשֶׁר הָיוּ בְּתוֹכֵךְ: 14 הֲיַעֲמֹד
לִבֵּךְ אִם־תֶּחֱזַקְנָה יָדַיִךְ לַיָּמִים אֲשֶׁר אֲנִי עֹשֶׂה
אוֹתָךְ אֲנִי יְהֹוָה דִּבַּרְתִּי וְעָשִׂיתִי: 15 וַהֲפִיצוֹתִי
אוֹתָךְ בַּגּוֹיִם וְזֵרִיתִיךְ בָּאֲרָצוֹת וַהֲתִמֹּתִי טֻמְאָתֵךְ
מִמֵּךְ: 16 וְנִחַלְתְּ בָּךְ לְעֵינֵי גוֹיִם וְיָדַעַתְּ כִּי־אֲנִי
יְהֹוָה: פ

17 וַיְהִי דְבַר־יְהֹוָה אֵלַי לֵאמֹר: 18 בֶּן־אָדָם הָיוּ־
לִי בֵית־יִשְׂרָאֵל לְסוּג כֻּלָּם נְחֹשֶׁת וּבְדִיל
וּבַרְזֶל וְעוֹפֶרֶת בְּתוֹךְ כּוּר סִגִים כֶּסֶף
הָיוּ:   ס   19 לָכֵן כֹּה אָמַר אֲדֹנָי יְהֹוִה יַעַן
הֱיוֹת כֻּלְּכֶם לְסִגִים לָכֵן הִנְנִי קֹבֵץ אֶתְכֶם אֶל־תּוֹךְ
יְרוּשָׁלָ͏ִם: 20 קְבֻצַת כֶּסֶף וּנְחֹשֶׁת וּבַרְזֶל וְעוֹפֶרֶת
וּבְדִיל אֶל־תּוֹךְ כּוּר לָפַחַת־עָלָיו אֵשׁ לְהַנְתִּיךְ כֵּן
אֶקְבֹּץ בְּאַפִּי וּבַחֲמָתִי וְהִנַּחְתִּי וְהִתַּכְתִּי אֶתְכֶם:
21 וְכִנַּסְתִּי אֶתְכֶם וְנָפַחְתִּי עֲלֵיכֶם בְּאֵשׁ עֶבְרָתִי
וְנִתַּכְתֶּם בְּתוֹכָהּ: 22 כְּהִתּוּךְ כֶּסֶף בְּתוֹךְ כּוּר כֵּן
תֻּתְּכוּ בְתוֹכָהּ וִידַעְתֶּם כִּי־אֲנִי יְהֹוָה שָׁפַכְתִּי חֲמָתִי
עֲלֵיכֶם: פ

23 וַיְהִי דְבַר־יְהֹוָה אֵלַי לֵאמֹר: 24 בֶּן־אָדָם אֱמָר־
לָהּ אַתְּ אֶרֶץ לֹא מְטֹהָרָה הִיא לֹא גֻשְׁמָהּ בְּיוֹם
זָעַם: 25 קֶשֶׁר נְבִיאֶיהָ בְּתוֹכָהּ כַּאֲרִי שׁוֹאֵג טֹרֵף
טָרֶף נֶפֶשׁ אָכָלוּ חֹסֶן וִיקָר יִקָּחוּ אַלְמְנוֹתֶיהָ הִרְבּוּ
בְתוֹכָהּ: 26 כֹּהֲנֶיהָ חָמְסוּ תוֹרָתִי וַיְחַלְּלוּ קָדָשַׁי
בֵּין־קֹדֶשׁ לְחֹל לֹא הִבְדִּילוּ וּבֵין־הַטָּמֵא לְטָהוֹר לֹא
הוֹדִיעוּ וּמִשַׁבְּתוֹתַי הֶעְלִימוּ עֵינֵיהֶם וָאֵחַל בְּתוֹכָם:
27 שָׂרֶיהָ בְקִרְבָּהּ כִּזְאֵבִים טֹרְפֵי טָרֶף לִשְׁפָּךְ־דָּם
לְאַבֵּד נְפָשׁוֹת לְמַעַן בְּצֹעַ בָּצַע: 28 וּנְבִיאֶיהָ טָחוּ
לָהֶם תָּפֵל חֹזִים שָׁוְא וְקֹסְמִים לָהֶם כָּזָב אֹמְרִים
כֹּה אָמַר אֲדֹנָי יְהֹוִה וַיהֹוָה לֹא דִבֵּר: 29 עַם הָאָרֶץ
עָשְׁקוּ עֹשֶׁק וְגָזְלוּ גָּזֵל וְעָנִי וְאֶבְיוֹן הוֹנוּ וְאֶת־הַגֵּר
עָשְׁקוּ בְּלֹא מִשְׁפָּט: 30 וָאֲבַקֵּשׁ מֵהֶם אִישׁ גֹּדֵר־

wall, and stand in the gap before Me on behalf of the land, that I should not destroy it; but I found no one. 31 Therefore I have poured out My indignation on them; I have consumed them with the fire of My wrath; and I have recompensed their deeds on their own heads," says the Lord GOD.

גָּדֵר וְעֹמֵד בַּפֶּרֶץ לְפָנַי בְּעַד הָאָרֶץ לְבִלְתִּי שַׁחֲתָהּ וְלֹא מָצָאתִי: 31 וָאֶשְׁפֹּךְ עֲלֵיהֶם זַעְמִי בְּאֵשׁ עֶבְרָתִי כִּלִּיתִים דַּרְכָּם בְּרֹאשָׁם נָתַתִּי נְאֻם אֲדֹנָי יְהוִה: פ

23

The word of the LORD came again to me, saying:

2 "Son of man, there were two women, The daughters of one mother.
3 They committed harlotry in Egypt, They committed harlotry in their youth; Their breasts were there embraced, Their virgin bosom was there pressed.
4 Their names: Oholah the elder and Oholibah her sister; They were Mine, And they bore sons and daughters. As for their names, Samaria is Oholah, and Jerusalem is Oholibah.
5 "Oholah played the harlot even though she was Mine; And she lusted for her lovers, the neighboring Assyrians,
6 Who were clothed in purple, Captains and rulers, All of them desirable young men, Horsemen riding on horses.
7 Thus she committed her harlotry with them, All of them choice men of Assyria; And with all for whom she lusted, With all their idols, she defiled herself.
8 She has never given up her harlotry brought from Egypt, For in her youth they had lain with her, Pressed her virgin bosom, And poured out their immorality upon her.
9 "Therefore I have delivered her Into the hand of her lovers, Into the hand of the Assyrians, For whom she lusted.
10 They uncovered her nakedness, Took away her sons and daughters, And slew her with the sword; She became a byword among women, For they had executed judgment on her.

11 "Now although her sister Oholibah saw this, she became more corrupt in her lust than she, and in her harlotry more corrupt than her sister's harlotry.

12 "She lusted for the neighboring Assyrians, Captains and rulers, Clothed most gorgeously, Horsemen riding on horses, All of them desirable young men.
13 Then I saw that she was defiled; Both took the same way.

כג וַיְהִי דְבַר־יְהוָה אֵלַי לֵאמֹר: 2 בֶּן־אָדָם שְׁתַּיִם נָשִׁים בְּנוֹת אֵם־אַחַת הָיוּ: 3 וַתִּזְנֶינָה בְמִצְרַיִם בִּנְעוּרֵיהֶן זָנוּ שָׁמָּה מֹעֲכוּ שְׁדֵיהֶן וְשָׁם עִשּׂוּ דַּדֵּי בְּתוּלֵיהֶן: 4 וּשְׁמוֹתָן אָהֳלָה הַגְּדוֹלָה וְאָהֳלִיבָה אֲחוֹתָהּ וַתִּהְיֶינָה לִי וַתֵּלַדְנָה בָּנִים וּבָנוֹת וּשְׁמוֹתָן שֹׁמְרוֹן אָהֳלָה וִירוּשָׁלַםִ אָהֳלִיבָה: 5 וַתִּזֶן אָהֳלָה תַּחְתָּי וַתַּעְגַּב עַל־מְאַהֲבֶיהָ אֶל־אַשּׁוּר קְרוֹבִים: 6 לְבֻשֵׁי תְכֵלֶת פַּחוֹת וּסְגָנִים בַּחוּרֵי חֶמֶד כֻּלָּם פָּרָשִׁים רֹכְבֵי סוּסִים: 7 וַתִּתֵּן תַּזְנוּתֶיהָ עֲלֵיהֶם מִבְחַר בְּנֵי־אַשּׁוּר כֻּלָּם וּבְכֹל אֲשֶׁר־עָגְבָה בְּכָל־גִּלּוּלֵיהֶם נִטְמָאָה: 8 וְאֶת־תַּזְנוּתֶיהָ מִמִּצְרַיִם לֹא עָזָבָה כִּי אוֹתָהּ שָׁכְבוּ בִנְעוּרֶיהָ וְהֵמָּה עִשּׂוּ דַּדֵּי בְתוּלֶיהָ וַיִּשְׁפְּכוּ תַזְנוּתָם עָלֶיהָ: 9 לָכֵן נְתַתִּיהָ בְּיַד־מְאַהֲבֶיהָ בְּיַד בְּנֵי אַשּׁוּר אֲשֶׁר עָגְבָה עֲלֵיהֶם: 10 הֵמָּה גִּלּוּ עֶרְוָתָהּ בָּנֶיהָ וּבְנוֹתֶיהָ לָקָחוּ וְאוֹתָהּ בַּחֶרֶב הָרָגוּ וַתְּהִי־שֵׁם לַנָּשִׁים וּשְׁפוּטִים עָשׂוּ בָהּ: ס 11 וַתֵּרֶא אֲחוֹתָהּ אָהֳלִיבָה וַתַּשְׁחֵת עַגְבָתָהּ מִמֶּנָּה וְאֶת־תַּזְנוּתֶיהָ מִזְּנוּנֵי אֲחוֹתָהּ: 12 אֶל־בְּנֵי אַשּׁוּר עָגָבָה פַּחוֹת וּסְגָנִים קְרֹבִים לְבֻשֵׁי מִכְלוֹל פָּרָשִׁים רֹכְבֵי סוּסִים בַּחוּרֵי חֶמֶד כֻּלָּם: 13 וָאֵרֶא כִּי נִטְמָאָה דֶּרֶךְ

14 But she increased her harlotry;
She looked at men portrayed on the wall,
Images of Chaldeans portrayed in vermilion,

15 Girded with belts around their waists,
Flowing turbans on their heads,
All of them looking like captains,
In the manner of the Babylonians of Chaldea,
The land of their nativity.

16 As soon as her eyes saw them,
She lusted for them
And sent messengers to them in Chaldea.

17 "Then the Babylonians came to her, into the bed
of love,
And they defiled her with their immorality;
So she was defiled by them, and alienated herself
from them.

18 She revealed her harlotry and uncovered her
nakedness.
Then I alienated Myself from her,
As I had alienated Myself from her sister.

19 "Yet she multiplied her harlotry
In calling to remembrance the days of her youth,
When she had played the harlot in the land of
Egypt.

20 For she lusted for her paramours,
Whose flesh is like the flesh of donkeys,
And whose issue is like the issue of horses.

21 Thus you called to remembrance the lewdness of
your youth,
When the Egyptians pressed your bosom
Because of your youthful breasts.

22 "Therefore, Oholibah, thus says the Lord GOD:

'Behold, I will stir up your lovers against you,
From whom you have alienated yourself,
And I will bring them against you from every
side:

23 The Babylonians,
All the Chaldeans,
Pekod, Shoa, Koa,
All the Assyrians with them,
All of them desirable young men,
Governors and rulers,
Captains and men of renown,
All of them riding on horses.

24 And they shall come against you
With chariots, wagons, and war-horses,
With a horde of people.
They shall array against you
Buckler, shield, and helmet all around.

'I will delegate judgment to them,
And they shall judge you according to their
judgments.

25 I will set My jealousy against you,
And they shall deal furiously with you;
They shall remove your nose and your ears,
And your remnant shall fall by the sword;
They shall take your sons and your daughters,
And your remnant shall be devoured by fire.

26 They shall also strip you of your clothes
And take away your beautiful jewelry.

אֶחָד לִשְׁתֵּיהֶן: 14 וַתּוֹסֶף אֶל־תַּזְנוּתֶיהָ וַתֵּרֶא
אַנְשֵׁי מְחֻקֶּה עַל־הַקִּיר צַלְמֵי כַשְׂדִּיים חֲקֻקִים
בַּשָּׁשַׁר: 15 חֲגוֹרֵי אֵזוֹר בְּמָתְנֵיהֶם סְרוּחֵי טְבוּלִים
בְּרָאשֵׁיהֶם מַרְאֵה שָׁלִשִׁים כֻּלָּם דְּמוּת בְּנֵי־בָבֶל
כַּשְׂדִּים אֶרֶץ מוֹלַדְתָּם: 16 וַתַּעְגְּב עֲלֵיהֶם לְמַרְאֵה
עֵינֶיהָ וַתִּשְׁלַח מַלְאָכִים אֲלֵיהֶם כַּשְׂדִּימָה: 17 וַיָּבֹאוּ
אֵלֶיהָ בְנֵי־בָבֶל לְמִשְׁכַּב דֹּדִים וַיְטַמְּאוּ אוֹתָהּ
בְּתַזְנוּתָם וַתִּטְמָא־בָם וַתֵּקַע נַפְשָׁהּ מֵהֶם: 18 וַתְּגַל
תַּזְנוּתֶיהָ וַתְּגַל אֶת־עֶרְוָתָהּ וַתֵּקַע נַפְשִׁי מֵעָלֶיהָ
כַּאֲשֶׁר נָקְעָה נַפְשִׁי מֵעַל אֲחוֹתָהּ: 19 וַתַּרְבֶּה אֶת־
תַּזְנוּתֶיהָ לִזְכֹּר אֶת־יְמֵי נְעוּרֶיהָ אֲשֶׁר זָנְתָה בְּאֶרֶץ
מִצְרָיִם: 20 וַתַּעְגְּבָה עַל פִּלַגְשֵׁיהֶם אֲשֶׁר בְּשַׂר־
חֲמוֹרִים בְּשָׂרָם וְזִרְמַת סוּסִים זִרְמָתָם: 21 וַתִּפְקְדִי
אֵת זִמַּת נְעוּרָיִךְ בַּעְשׂוֹת מִמִּצְרַיִם דַּדַּיִךְ לְמַעַן
שְׁדֵי נְעוּרָיִךְ: ס 22 לָכֵן אָהֳלִיבָה כֹּה־אָמַר
אֲדֹנָי יְהוִה הִנְנִי מֵעִיר אֶת־מְאַהֲבַיִךְ עָלַיִךְ אֵת
אֲשֶׁר־נָקְעָה נַפְשֵׁךְ מֵהֶם וַהֲבֵאתִים עָלַיִךְ מִסָּבִיב:
23 בְּנֵי בָבֶל וְכָל־כַּשְׂדִּים פְּקוֹד וְשׁוֹעַ וְקוֹעַ כָּל־
בְּנֵי אַשּׁוּר אוֹתָם בַּחוּרֵי חֶמֶד פַּחוֹת וּסְגָנִים כֻּלָּם
שָׁלִשִׁים וּקְרוּאִים רֹכְבֵי סוּסִים כֻּלָּם: 24 וּבָאוּ עָלַיִךְ
הֹצֶן רֶכֶב וְגַלְגַּל וּבִקְהַל עַמִּים צִנָּה וּמָגֵן וְקוֹבַע
יָשִׂימוּ עָלַיִךְ סָבִיב וְנָתַתִּי לִפְנֵיהֶם מִשְׁפָּט וּשְׁפָטוּךְ
בְּמִשְׁפְּטֵיהֶם: 25 וְנָתַתִּי קִנְאָתִי בָּךְ וְעָשׂוּ אוֹתָךְ
בְּחֵמָה אַפֵּךְ וְאָזְנַיִךְ יָסִירוּ וְאַחֲרִיתֵךְ בַּחֶרֶב תִּפּוֹל
הֵמָּה בָּנַיִךְ וּבְנוֹתַיִךְ יִקָּחוּ וְאַחֲרִיתֵךְ תֵּאָכֵל בָּאֵשׁ:
26 וְהִפְשִׁיטוּךְ אֶת־בְּגָדָיִךְ וְלָקְחוּ כְּלֵי תִפְאַרְתֵּךְ:

27 'Thus I will make you cease your lewdness and
your harlotry
Brought from the land of Egypt,
So that you will not lift your eyes to them,
Nor remember Egypt anymore.'

28 "For thus says the Lord GOD: 'Surely I will
deliver you into the hand of those you hate, into the
hand *of those* from whom you alienated yourself.
29 They will deal hatefully with you, take away all
you have worked for, and leave you naked and
bare. The nakedness of your harlotry shall be
uncovered, both your lewdness and your harlotry.
30 I will do these *things* to you because you have
gone as a harlot after the Gentiles, because you
have become defiled by their idols. 31 You have
walked in the way of your sister; therefore I will put
her cup in your hand.'

32 "Thus says the Lord GOD:

'You shall drink of your sister's cup,
The deep and wide one;
You shall be laughed to scorn
And held in derision;
It contains much.
33   You will be filled with drunkenness and sorrow,
The cup of horror and desolation,
The cup of your sister Samaria.
34   You shall drink and drain it,
You shall break its shards,
And tear at your own breasts;
For I have spoken,'
Says the Lord GOD.

35 "Therefore thus says the Lord GOD:

'Because you have forgotten Me and cast Me
behind your back,
Therefore you shall bear the *penalty*
Of your lewdness and your harlotry.' "

36 The LORD also said to me: "Son of man, will
you judge Oholah and Oholibah? Then declare to
them their abominations. 37 For they have
committed adultery, and blood *is* on their hands.
They have committed adultery with their idols, and
even sacrificed their sons whom they bore to Me,
passing them through *the fire,* to devour *them.*
38 Moreover they have done this to Me: They have
defiled My sanctuary on the same day and profaned
My Sabbaths. 39 For after they had slain their
children for their idols, on the same day they came
into My sanctuary to profane it; and indeed thus
they have done in the midst of My house.

40 "Furthermore you sent for men to come from
afar, to whom a messenger *was* sent; and there they
came. And you washed yourself for them, painted
your eyes, and adorned yourself with ornaments.
41 You sat on a stately couch, with a table prepared
before it, on which you had set My incense and My

27 וְהִשְׁבַּתִּ֤י זִמָּתֵךְ֙ מִמֵּ֔ךְ וְאֶת־זְנוּתֵ֖ךְ מֵאֶ֣רֶץ מִצְרָ֑יִם
וְלֹא־תִשְׂאִ֤י עֵינַ֨יִךְ֙ אֲלֵיהֶ֔ם וּמִצְרַ֖יִם לֹ֥א תִזְכְּרִי־
ע֖וֹד׃ ס 28 כִּ֣י כֹ֤ה אָמַר֙ אֲדֹנָ֣י יְהֹוִ֔ה הִנְנִ֤י
נֹֽתְנָךְ֙ בְּיַ֣ד אֲשֶׁ֣ר שָׂנֵ֔את בְּיַ֖ד אֲשֶׁר־נָקְעָ֥ה נַפְשֵׁ֖ךְ
מֵהֶֽם׃ 29 וְעָשׂ֨וּ אוֹתָ֜ךְ בְּשִׂנְאָ֗ה וְלָקְחוּ֙ כָּל־יְגִיעֵ֔ךְ
וַעֲזָב֖וּךְ עֵירֹ֣ם וְעֶרְיָ֑ה וְנִגְלָה֙ עֶרְוַ֣ת זְנוּנַ֔יִךְ וְזִמָּתֵ֖ךְ
וְתַזְנוּתָֽיִךְ׃ 30 עָשֹׂ֥ה אֵ֖לֶּה לָ֑ךְ בִּזְנוֹתֵךְ֙ אַחֲרֵ֣י גוֹיִ֔ם עַ֖ל
אֲשֶׁר־נִטְמֵ֥את בְּגִלּוּלֵיהֶֽם׃ 31 בְּדֶ֥רֶךְ אֲחוֹתֵ֖ךְ הָלָ֑כְתְּ
וְנָתַתִּ֥י כוֹסָ֖הּ בְּיָדֵֽךְ׃ ס 32 כֹּ֤ה אָמַר֙ אֲדֹנָ֣י
יְהֹוִ֔ה כּ֤וֹס אֲחוֹתֵךְ֙ תִּשְׁתִּ֔י הָעֲמֻקָּ֖ה וְהָרְחָבָ֑ה תִּהְיֶ֣ה
לִצְחֹ֣ק וּלְלַ֔עַג מִרְבָּ֖ה לְהָכִֽיל׃ 33 שִׁכָּר֥וֹן וְיָג֖וֹן תִּמָּלֵ֑אִי
כּ֚וֹס שַׁמָּ֣ה וּשְׁמָמָ֔ה כּ֖וֹס אֲחוֹתֵ֥ךְ שֹׁמְרֽוֹן׃ 34 וְשָׁתִ֨ית
אוֹתָ֜הּ וּמָצִ֗ית וְאֶת־חֲרָשֶׂ֛יהָ תְּגָרֵ֖מִי וְשָׁדַ֣יִךְ תְּנַתֵּ֑קִי
כִּ֚י אֲנִ֣י דִבַּ֔רְתִּי נְאֻ֖ם אֲדֹנָ֥י יְהֹוִֽה׃ ס 35 לָכֵ֗ן
כֹּ֤ה אָמַר֙ אֲדֹנָ֣י יְהֹוִ֔ה יַ֚עַן שָׁכַ֣חַתְּ אוֹתִ֔י וַתַּשְׁלִ֥יכִי
אוֹתִ֖י אַחֲרֵ֣י גַוֵּ֑ךְ וְגַם־אַ֛תְּ שְׂאִ֥י זִמָּתֵ֖ךְ וְאֶת־
תַּזְנוּתָֽיִךְ׃ ס 36 וַיֹּ֤אמֶר יְהֹוָה֙ אֵלַ֔י בֶּן־אָדָ֕ם
הֲתִשְׁפּ֥וֹט אֶת־אׇהֳלָ֖ה וְאֶת־אׇהֳלִיבָ֑ה וְהַגֵּ֣ד לָהֶ֔ן אֵ֖ת
תוֹעֲבוֹתֵיהֶֽן׃ 37 כִּ֣י נִאֵ֗פוּ וְדָם֙ בִּֽידֵיהֶ֔ן וְאֶת־גִּלּֽוּלֵיהֶ֖ן
נִאֵ֑פוּ וְגַ֤ם אֶת־בְּנֵיהֶן֙ אֲשֶׁ֣ר יָלְדוּ־לִ֔י הֶעֱבִ֥ירוּ לָהֶ֖ם
לְאׇכְלָֽה׃ 38 ע֥וֹד זֹ֖את עָ֣שׂוּ לִ֑י טִמְּא֤וּ אֶת־מִקְדָּשִׁי֙
בַּיּ֣וֹם הַה֔וּא וְאֶת־שַׁבְּתוֹתַ֖י חִלֵּֽלוּ׃ 39 וּֽבְשַׁחֲטָ֣ם אֶת־
בְּנֵיהֶם֙ לְגִלּ֣וּלֵיהֶ֔ם וַיָּבֹ֧אוּ אֶל־מִקְדָּשִׁ֛י בַּיּ֥וֹם הַה֖וּא
לְחַלְּל֑וֹ וְהִנֵּה־כֹ֥ה עָשׂ֖וּ בְּת֥וֹךְ בֵּיתִֽי׃ 40 וְאַ֣ף כִּ֤י
תִשְׁלַ֙חְנָה֙ לַֽאֲנָשִׁ֔ים בָּאִ֖ים מִמֶּרְחָ֑ק אֲשֶׁ֤ר מַלְאָךְ֙
שָׁל֣וּחַ אֲלֵיהֶ֔ם וְהִנֵּה־בָ֕אוּ לַאֲשֶׁ֥ר רָחַ֖צְתְּ כָּחַ֣לְתְּ
עֵינַ֔יִךְ וְעָדִ֖ית עֶֽדִי׃ 41 וְיָשַׁבְתְּ֙ עַל־מִטָּ֣ה כְבוּדָּ֔ה
וְשֻׁלְחָ֥ן עָר֖וּךְ לְפָנֶ֑יהָ וּקְטׇרְתִּ֥י וְשַׁמְנִ֖י שַׂ֥מְתְּ עָלֶֽיהָ׃

oil. 42 The sound of a carefree multitude *was* with her, and Sabeans *were* brought from the wilderness with men of the common sort, who put bracelets on their wrists and beautiful crowns on their heads. 43 Then I said concerning *her who had grown* old in adulteries, 'Will they commit harlotry with her now, and she *with them?*' 44 Yet they went in to her, as men go in to a woman who plays the harlot; thus they went in to Oholah and Oholibah, the lewd women. 45 But righteous men will judge them after the manner of adulteresses, and after the manner of women who shed blood, because they *are* adulteresses, and blood *is* on their hands.

46 "For thus says the Lord GOD: 'Bring up an assembly against them, give them up to trouble and plunder. 47 The assembly shall stone them with stones and execute them with their swords; they shall slay their sons and their daughters, and burn their houses with fire. 48 Thus I will cause lewdness to cease from the land, that all women may be taught not to practice your lewdness. 49 They shall repay you for your lewdness, and you shall pay for your idolatrous sins. Then you shall know that I *am* the Lord GOD.' "

24

Again, in the ninth year, in the tenth month, on the tenth *day* of the month, the word of the LORD came to me, saying, 2 "Son of man, write down the name of the day, this very day—the king of Babylon started his siege against Jerusalem this very day. 3 And utter a parable to the rebellious house, and say to them, 'Thus says the Lord GOD:

"Put on a pot, set *it* on,
And also pour water into it.
4   Gather pieces *of meat* in it,
Every good piece,
The thigh and the shoulder.
Fill *it* with choice cuts;
5   Take the choice of the flock.
Also pile *fuel* bones under it,
Make it boil well,
And let the cuts simmer in it."

6 'Therefore thus says the Lord GOD:

"Woe to the bloody city,
To the pot whose scum *is* in it,
And whose scum is not gone from it!
Bring it out piece by piece,
On which no lot has fallen.
7   For her blood is in her midst;
She set it on top of a rock;
She did not pour it on the ground,
To cover it with dust.
8   That it may raise up fury and take vengeance,
I have set her blood on top of a rock,
That it may not be covered."

42 וְקוֹל הָמוֹן שָׁלֵו בָהּ וְאֶל־אֲנָשִׁים מֵרֹב אָדָם מוּבָאִים סבאים [סָבָאִים P] מִמִּדְבָּר וַיִּתְּנוּ צְמִידִים אֶל־יְדֵיהֶן וַעֲטֶרֶת תִּפְאֶרֶת עַל־רָאשֵׁיהֶן: 43 וָאֹמַר לַבָּלָה נִאוּפִים עת [עַתָּה P] יזנה [יִזְנוּ P] תַזְנוּתֶהָ וָהִיא: 44 וַיָּבוֹא אֵלֶיהָ כְּבוֹא אֶל־אִשָּׁה זוֹנָה כֵּן בָּאוּ אֶל־אָהֳלָה וְאֶל־אָהֳלִיבָה אִשֹּׁת הַזִּמָּה: 45 וַאֲנָשִׁים צַדִּיקִם הֵמָּה יִשְׁפְּטוּ אוֹתְהֶם מִשְׁפַּט נֹאֲפוֹת וּמִשְׁפַּט שֹׁפְכוֹת דָּם כִּי נֹאֲפֹת הֵנָּה וְדָם בִּידֵיהֶן: ס 46 כִּי כֹּה אָמַר אֲדֹנָי יְהוִֹה הַעֲלֵה עֲלֵיהֶם קָהָל וְנָתֹן אֶתְהֶן לְזַעֲוָה וְלָבַז: 47 וְרָגְמוּ עֲלֵיהֶן אֶבֶן קָהָל וּבָרֵא אוֹתְהֶן בְּחַרְבוֹתָם בְּנֵיהֶם וּבְנוֹתֵיהֶם יַהֲרֹגוּ וּבָתֵּיהֶן בָּאֵשׁ יִשְׂרֹפוּ: 48 וְהִשְׁבַּתִּי זִמָּה מִן־הָאָרֶץ וְנִוַּסְּרוּ כָּל־הַנָּשִׁים וְלֹא תַעֲשֶׂינָה כְּזִמַּתְכֶנָה: 49 וְנָתְנוּ זִמַּתְכֶנָה עֲלֵיכֶן וַחֲטָאֵי גִלּוּלֵיכֶן תִּשֶּׂאינָה וִידַעְתֶּם כִּי אֲנִי אֲדֹנָי יְהוִֹה: פ

כד וַיְהִי דְבַר־יְהוָֹה אֵלַי בַּשָּׁנָה הַתְּשִׁיעִית בַּחֹדֶשׁ הָעֲשִׂירִי בֶּעָשׂוֹר לַחֹדֶשׁ לֵאמֹר: 2 בֶּן־אָדָם כתוב [כְּתָב־לְךָ P] אֶת־שֵׁם הַיּוֹם אֶת־עֶצֶם הַיּוֹם הַזֶּה סָמַךְ מֶלֶךְ־בָּבֶל אֶל־יְרוּשָׁלַ͏ִם בְּעֶצֶם הַיּוֹם הַזֶּה: 3 וּמְשֹׁל אֶל־בֵּית־הַמֶּרִי מָשָׁל וְאָמַרְתָּ אֲלֵיהֶם כֹּה אָמַר אֲדֹנָי יְהוִֹה שְׁפֹת הַסִּיר שְׁפֹת וְגַם־יְצֹק בּוֹ מָיִם: 4 אֱסֹף נְתָחֶיהָ אֵלֶיהָ כָּל־נֵתַח טוֹב יָרֵךְ וְכָתֵף מִבְחַר עֲצָמִים מַלֵּא: 5 מִבְחַר הַצֹּאן לָקוֹחַ וְגַם דּוּר הָעֲצָמִים תַּחְתֶּיהָ רַתַּח רְתָחֶיהָ גַּם־בָּשְׁלוּ עֲצָמֶיהָ בְּתוֹכָהּ: ס 6 לָכֵן כֹּה־אָמַר אֲדֹנָי יְהוִֹה אוֹי עִיר הַדָּמִים סִיר אֲשֶׁר חֶלְאָתָה בָהּ וְחֶלְאָתָהּ לֹא יָצְאָה מִמֶּנָּה לִנְתָחֶיהָ לִנְתָחֶיהָ הוֹצִיאָהּ לֹא־נָפַל עָלֶיהָ גּוֹרָל: 7 כִּי דָמָהּ בְּתוֹכָהּ הָיָה עַל־צְחִיחַ סֶלַע שָׂמָתְהוּ לֹא שְׁפָכַתְהוּ עַל־הָאָרֶץ לְכַסּוֹת עָלָיו עָפָר: 8 לְהַעֲלוֹת חֵמָה לִנְקֹם נָקָם נָתַתִּי אֶת־דָּמָהּ עַל־צְחִיחַ סָלַע לְבִלְתִּי הִכָּסוֹת: פ

9 לָכֵ֗ן כֹּ֤ה אָמַר֙ אֲדֹנָ֣י יְהוִ֔ה אֹ֖וי עִ֣יר הַדָּמִ֑ים גַּם־
אֲנִ֖י אַגְדִּ֥יל הַמְּדוּרָֽה׃ 10 הַרְבֵּ֤ה הָעֵצִים֙ הַדְלֵ֣ק
הָאֵ֔שׁ הָתֵ֖ם הַבָּשָׂ֑ר וְהַרְקַח֙ הַמֶּרְקָחָ֔ה וְהָעֲצָמֹ֖ות
יֵחָֽרוּ׃ 11 וְהַעֲמִידֶ֥הָ עַל־גֶּחָלֶ֖יהָ רֵקָ֑ה לְמַ֨עַן תֵּחַ֜ם
וְחָ֣רָה נְחֻשְׁתָּ֗הּ וְנִתְּכָ֤ה בְתֹוכָהּ֙ טֻמְאָתָ֔הּ תִּתֻּ֖ם
חֶלְאָתָֽהּ׃ 12 תְּאֻנִ֖ים הֶלְאָ֑ת וְלֹֽא־תֵצֵ֤א מִמֶּ֙נָּה֙ רַבַּ֣ת
חֶלְאָתָ֔הּ בְּאֵ֖שׁ חֶלְאָתָֽהּ׃ 13 בְּטֻמְאָתֵ֖ךְ זִמָּ֑ה יַ֤עַן
טִֽהַרְתִּיךְ֙ וְלֹ֣א טָהַ֔רְתְּ מִטֻּמְאָתֵךְ֙ לֹ֣א תִטְהֲרִי־עֹ֔וד
עַד־הֲנִיחִ֥י אֶת־חֲמָתִ֖י בָּֽךְ׃ 14 אֲנִ֧י יְהוָ֣ה דִּבַּ֗רְתִּי
בָּאָ֤ה וְעָשִׂ֙יתִי֙ לֹֽא־אֶפְרַ֔ע וְלֹא־אָח֖וּס וְלֹ֣א אֶנָּחֵ֑ם
כִּדְרָכַ֤יִךְ וְכַעֲלִילֹותַ֙יִךְ֙ שְׁפָט֔וּךְ נְאֻ֖ם אֲדֹנָ֥י יְהוִֽה׃ פ

15 וַיְהִ֥י דְבַר־יְהוָ֖ה אֵלַ֥י לֵאמֹֽר׃ 16 בֶּן־אָדָ֡ם הִנְנִ֣י
לֹקֵ֩חַ מִמְּךָ֨ אֶת־מַחְמַ֤ד עֵינֶ֙יךָ֙ בְּמַגֵּפָ֔ה וְלֹ֥א תִסְפֹּ֖ד
וְלֹ֣א תִבְכֶּ֑ה וְלֹ֥וא תָבֹ֖וא דִּמְעָתֶֽךָ׃ 17 הֵאָנֵ֣ק ׀
דֹּ֗ם מֵתִים֙ אֵ֣בֶל לֹֽא־תַעֲשֶׂ֔ה פְאֵֽרְךָ֙ חֲבֹ֣ושׁ עָלֶ֔יךָ
וּנְעָלֶ֖יךָ תָּשִׂ֣ים בְּרַגְלֶ֑יךָ וְלֹ֤א תַעְטֶה֙ עַל־שָׂפָ֔ם
וְלֶ֥חֶם אֲנָשִׁ֖ים לֹ֥א תֹאכֵֽל׃ 18 וָאֲדַבֵּ֤ר אֶל־הָעָם֙
בַּבֹּ֔קֶר וַתָּ֥מָת אִשְׁתִּ֖י בָּעָ֑רֶב וָאַ֥עַשׂ בַּבֹּ֖קֶר כַּאֲשֶׁ֥ר
צֻוֵּֽיתִי׃ 19 וַיֹּאמְר֥וּ אֵלַ֖י הָעָ֑ם הֲלֹֽא־תַגִּ֥יד לָ֙נוּ֙ מָה־
אֵ֣לֶּה לָּ֔נוּ כִּ֥י אַתָּ֖ה עֹשֶֽׂה׃ 20 וָאֹמַ֖ר אֲלֵיהֶ֑ם
דְּבַר־יְהוָ֖ה הָיָ֥ה אֵלַ֥י לֵאמֹֽר׃ 21 אֱמֹ֣ר ׀ לְבֵ֣ית
יִשְׂרָאֵ֗ל כֹּֽה־אָמַר֮ אֲדֹנָ֣י יְהוִה֒ הִנְנִ֨י מְחַלֵּ֤ל אֶת־
מִקְדָּשִׁי֙ גְּאֹ֣ון עֻזְּכֶ֔ם מַחְמַ֥ד עֵֽינֵיכֶ֖ם וּמַחְמַ֣ל
נַפְשְׁכֶ֑ם וּבְנֵיכֶ֧ם וּבְנֹֽותֵיכֶ֛ם אֲשֶׁ֥ר עֲזַבְתֶּ֖ם בַּחֶ֥רֶב
יִפֹּֽלוּ׃ 22 וַעֲשִׂיתֶ֖ם כַּאֲשֶׁ֣ר עָשִׂ֑יתִי עַל־שָׂפָם֙ לֹ֣א
תַעְט֔וּ וְלֶ֥חֶם אֲנָשִׁ֖ים לֹ֥א תֹאכֵֽלוּ׃ 23 וּפְאֵרֵכֶ֣ם
עַל־רָאשֵׁיכֶ֗ם וְנַֽעֲלֵיכֶם֙ בְּרַגְלֵיכֶ֔ם לֹ֥א תִסְפְּד֖וּ
וְלֹ֣א תִבְכּ֑וּ וּנְמַקֹּתֶם֙ בַּעֲוֹנֹ֣תֵיכֶ֔ם וּנְהַמְתֶּ֖ם אִ֥ישׁ
אֶל־אָחִֽיו׃ 24 וְהָיָ֨ה יְחֶזְקֵ֤אל לָכֶם֙ לְמֹופֵ֔ת כְּכֹ֥ל

9 'Therefore thus says the Lord GOD:

"Woe to the bloody city!
I too will make the pyre great.
10 Heap on the wood,
Kindle the fire;
Cook the meat well,
Mix in the spices,
And let the cuts be burned up.

11 "Then set the pot empty on the coals,
That it may become hot and its bronze may burn,
That its filthiness may be melted in it,
That its scum may be consumed.
12 She has grown weary with lies,
And her great scum has not gone from her.
Let her scum *be* in the fire!
13 In your filthiness *is* lewdness.
Because I have cleansed you, and you were not
cleansed,
You will not be cleansed of your filthiness
anymore,
Till I have caused My fury to rest upon you.
14 I, the LORD, have spoken *it;*
It shall come to pass, and I will do *it;*
I will not hold back,
Nor will I spare,
Nor will I relent;
According to your ways
And according to your deeds
They will judge you,"
Says the Lord GOD.' "

15 Also the word of the LORD came to me, saying,
16 "Son of man, behold, I take away from you the
desire of your eyes with one stroke; yet you shall
neither mourn nor weep, nor shall your tears run
down. 17 Sigh in silence, make no mourning for the
dead; bind your turban on your head, and put your
sandals on your feet; do not cover *your* lips, and do
not eat man's bread *of sorrow.*"

18 So I spoke to the people in the morning, and at
evening my wife died; and the next morning I did as
I was commanded.

19 And the people said to me, "Will you not tell
us what these *things signify* to us, that you behave
so?"

20 Then I answered them, "The word of the LORD
came to me, saying, 21 'Speak to the house of Israel,
"Thus says the Lord GOD: 'Behold, I will profane
My sanctuary, your arrogant boast, the desire of
your eyes, the delight of your soul; and your sons
and daughters whom you left behind shall fall by
the sword. 22 And you shall do as I have done; you
shall not cover *your* lips nor eat man's bread *of
sorrow.* 23 Your turbans shall be on your heads and
your sandals on your feet; you shall neither mourn
nor weep, but you shall pine away in your iniquities
and mourn with one another. 24 Thus Ezekiel is a

sign to you; according to all that he has done you shall do; and when this comes, you shall know that I *am* the Lord GOD.'"

²⁵'And you, son of man—*will it* not *be* in the day when I take from them their stronghold, their joy and their glory, the desire of their eyes, and that on which they set their minds, their sons and their daughters: ²⁶on that day one who escapes will come to you to let *you* hear *it* with *your* ears; ²⁷on that day your mouth will be opened to him who has escaped; you shall speak and no longer be mute. Thus you will be a sign to them, and they shall know that I *am* the LORD.'"

25

¹The word of the LORD came to me, saying, ²"Son of man, set your face against the Ammonites, and prophesy against them. ³Say to the Ammonites, 'Hear the word of the Lord GOD! Thus says the Lord GOD: "Because you said, 'Aha!' against My sanctuary when it was profaned, and against the land of Israel when it was desolate, and against the house of Judah when they went into captivity, ⁴indeed, therefore, I will deliver you as a possession to the men of the East, and they shall set their encampments among you and make their dwellings among you; they shall eat your fruit, and they shall drink your milk. ⁵And I will make Rabbah a stable for camels and Ammon a resting place for flocks. Then you shall know that I *am* the LORD."

⁶'For thus says the Lord GOD: "Because you clapped *your* hands, stamped your feet, and rejoiced in heart with all your disdain for the land of Israel, ⁷indeed, therefore, I will stretch out My hand against you, and give you as plunder to the nations; I will cut you off from the peoples, and I will cause you to perish from the countries; I will destroy you, and you shall know that I *am* the LORD."

⁸'Thus says the Lord GOD: "Because Moab and Seir say, 'Look! The house of Judah *is* like all the nations,' ⁹therefore, behold, I will clear the territory of Moab of cities, of the cities on its frontier, the glory of the country, Beth Jeshimoth, Baal Meon, and Kirjathaim. ¹⁰To the men of the East I will give it as a possession, together with the Ammonites, that the Ammonites may not be remembered among the nations. ¹¹And I will execute judgments upon Moab, and they shall know that I *am* the LORD."

¹²'Thus says the Lord GOD: "Because of what Edom did against the house of Judah by taking vengeance, and has greatly offended by avenging itself on them," ¹³therefore thus says the Lord GOD: "I will also stretch out My hand against

אֲשֶׁר־עָשָׂה תַעֲשֶׂוּ וְיִדַעְתֶּם כִּי אֲנִי אֲדֹנָי יְהֹוִה: ס 25 וְאַתָּה בֶן־אָדָם הֲלֹוא בְּיוֹם קַחְתִּי מֵהֶם אֶת־מָעוּזָּם מְשׂוֹשׂ תִּפְאַרְתָּם אֶת־מַחְמַד עֵינֵיהֶם וְאֶת־מַשָּׂא נַפְשָׁם בְּנֵיהֶם וּבְנוֹתֵיהֶם: 26 בַּיּוֹם הַהוּא יָבוֹא הַפָּלִיט אֵלֶיךָ לְהַשְׁמָעוּת אָזְנָיִם: 27 בַּיּוֹם הַהוּא יִפָּתַח פִּיךָ אֶת־הַפָּלִיט וּתְדַבֵּר וְלֹא תֵאָלֵם עוֹד וְהָיִיתָ לָהֶם לְמוֹפֵת וְיָדְעוּ כִּי־אֲנִי יְהֹוָה: ס

כה וַיְהִי דְבַר־יְהֹוָה אֵלַי לֵאמֹר: 2 בֶּן־אָדָם שִׂים פָּנֶיךָ אֶל־בְּנֵי עַמּוֹן וְהִנָּבֵא עֲלֵיהֶם: 3 וְאָמַרְתָּ לִבְנֵי עַמּוֹן שִׁמְעוּ דְּבַר־אֲדֹנָי יְהֹוִה כֹּה־אָמַר אֲדֹנָי יְהֹוִה יַעַן אָמְרֵךְ הֶאָח אֶל־מִקְדָּשִׁי כִי־נִחָל וְאֶל־אַדְמַת יִשְׂרָאֵל כִּי נָשַׁמָּה וְאֶל־בֵּית יְהוּדָה כִּי הָלְכוּ בַּגּוֹלָה: 4 לָכֵן הִנְנִי נֹתְנָךְ לִבְנֵי־קֶדֶם לְמוֹרָשָׁה וְיִשְּׁבוּ טִירוֹתֵיהֶם בָּךְ וְנָתְנוּ בָךְ מִשְׁכְּנֵיהֶם הֵמָּה יֹאכְלוּ פִרְיֵךְ וְהֵמָּה יִשְׁתּוּ חֲלָבֵךְ: 5 וְנָתַתִּי אֶת־רַבָּה לִנְוֵה גְמַלִּים וְאֶת־בְּנֵי עַמּוֹן לְמִרְבַּץ־צֹאן וִידַעְתֶּם כִּי־אֲנִי יְהֹוָה: ס 6 כִּי כֹה אָמַר אֲדֹנָי יְהֹוִה יַעַן מַחְאֲךָ יָד וְרַקְעֲךָ בְּרָגֶל וַתִּשְׂמַח בְּכָל־שָׁאטְךָ בְּנֶפֶשׁ אֶל־אַדְמַת יִשְׂרָאֵל: 7 לָכֵן הִנְנִי נָטִיתִי אֶת־יָדִי עָלֶיךָ וּנְתַתִּיךָ לְבַז לַגּוֹיִם וְהִכְרַתִּיךָ מִן־הָעַמִּים וְהַאֲבַדְתִּיךָ מִן־הָאֲרָצוֹת אַשְׁמִידְךָ וְיָדַעְתָּ כִּי־אֲנִי יְהֹוָה: ס 8 כֹּה אָמַר אֲדֹנָי יְהֹוִה יַעַן אֲמֹר מוֹאָב וְשֵׂעִיר הִנֵּה כְּכָל־הַגּוֹיִם בֵּית יְהוּדָה: 9 לָכֵן הִנְנִי פֹתֵחַ אֶת־כֶּתֶף מוֹאָב מֵהֶעָרִים מֵעָרָיו מִקָּצֵהוּ צְבִי אֶרֶץ בֵּית הַיְשִׁימֹת בַּעַל מְעוֹן וְקִרְיָתָמָה: 10 לִבְנֵי־קֶדֶם עַל־בְּנֵי עַמּוֹן וּנְתַתִּיהָ לְמוֹרָשָׁה לְמַעַן לֹא־תִזָּכֵר בְּנֵי־עַמּוֹן בַּגּוֹיִם: 11 וּבְמוֹאָב אֶעֱשֶׂה שְׁפָטִים וְיָדְעוּ כִּי־אֲנִי יְהֹוָה: ס 12 כֹּה אָמַר אֲדֹנָי יְהֹוִה יַעַן עֲשׂוֹת אֱדוֹם בִּנְקֹם נָקָם לְבֵית יְהוּדָה וַיֶּאְשְׁמוּ אָשׁוֹם וְנִקְּמוּ בָהֶם: 13 לָכֵן כֹּה אָמַר אֲדֹנָי יְהֹוִה וְנָטִתִי יָדִי עַל־אֱדוֹם וְהִכְרַתִּי

Edom, cut off man and beast from it, and make it desolate from Teman; Dedan shall fall by the sword. ¹⁴ I will lay My vengeance on Edom by the hand of My people Israel, that they may do in Edom according to My anger and according to My fury; and they shall know My vengeance," says the Lord GOD.

¹⁵ 'Thus says the Lord GOD: "Because the Philistines dealt vengefully and took vengeance with a spiteful heart, to destroy because of the old hatred," ¹⁶ therefore thus says the Lord GOD: "I will stretch out My hand against the Philistines, and I will cut off the Cherethites and destroy the remnant of the seacoast. ¹⁷ I will execute great vengeance on them with furious rebukes; and they shall know that I *am* the LORD, when I lay My vengeance upon them." ' "

26 And it came to pass in the eleventh year, on the first *day* of the month, *that* the word of the LORD came to me, saying, ² "Son of man, because Tyre has said against Jerusalem, 'Aha! She is broken who *was* the gateway of the peoples; now she is turned over to me; I shall be filled; she is laid waste.'

³ "Therefore thus says the Lord GOD: 'Behold, I *am* against you, O Tyre, and will cause many nations to come up against you, as the sea causes its waves to come up. ⁴ And they shall destroy the walls of Tyre and break down her towers; I will also scrape her dust from her, and make her like the top of a rock. ⁵ It shall be *a place for* spreading nets in the midst of the sea, for I have spoken,' says the Lord GOD; 'it shall become plunder for the nations. ⁶ Also her daughter *villages* which *are* in the fields shall be slain by the sword. Then they shall know that I am the LORD.'

⁷ "For thus says the Lord GOD: 'Behold, I will bring against Tyre from the north Nebuchadnezzar king of Babylon, king of kings, with horses, with chariots, and with horsemen, and an army with many people. ⁸ He will slay with the sword your daughter *villages* in the fields; he will heap up a siege mound against you, build a wall against you, and raise a defense against you. ⁹ He will direct his battering rams against your walls, and with his axes he will break down your towers. ¹⁰ Because of the abundance of his horses, their dust will cover you; your walls will shake at the noise of the horsemen, the wagons, and the chariots, when he enters your gates, as men enter a city that has been breached. ¹¹ With the hooves of his horses he will trample all your streets; he will slay your people by the sword, and your strong pillars will fall to the ground.

מִמֶּנָּה אָדָם וּבְהֵמָה וּנְתַתֶּיהָ חָרְבָּה מִתֵּימָן וּדְדָנֶה
בַּחֶרֶב יִפֹּלוּ: 14 וְנָתַתִּי אֶת־נִקְמָתִי בֶּאֱדוֹם בְּיַד עַמִּי
יִשְׂרָאֵל וְעָשׂוּ בֶאֱדוֹם כְּאַפִּי וְכַחֲמָתִי וְיָדְעוּ אֶת־
נִקְמָתִי נְאֻם אֲדֹנָי יְהוִה: פ

15 כֹּה אָמַר אֲדֹנָי יְהוִה יַעַן עֲשׂוֹת פְּלִשְׁתִּים
בִּנְקָמָה וַיִּנָּקְמוּ נָקָם בִּשְׁאָט בְּנֶפֶשׁ לְמַשְׁחִית אֵיבַת
עוֹלָם: 16 לָכֵן כֹּה אָמַר אֲדֹנָי יְהוִה הִנְנִי נוֹטֶה יָדִי
עַל־פְּלִשְׁתִּים וְהִכְרַתִּי אֶת־כְּרֵתִים וְהַאֲבַדְתִּי אֶת־
שְׁאֵרִית חוֹף הַיָּם: 17 וְעָשִׂיתִי בָם נְקָמוֹת גְּדֹלוֹת
בְּתוֹכְחוֹת חֵמָה וְיָדְעוּ כִּי־אֲנִי יְהוִה בְּתִתִּי אֶת־
נִקְמָתִי בָּם: ס

כו וַיְהִי בְּעַשְׁתֵּי־עֶשְׂרֵה שָׁנָה בְּאֶחָד לַחֹדֶשׁ הָיָה
דְבַר־יְהוָה אֵלַי לֵאמֹר: 2 בֶּן־אָדָם יַעַן אֲשֶׁר־אָמְרָה
צֹר עַל־יְרוּשָׁלִַם הֶאָח נִשְׁבְּרָה דַּלְתוֹת הָעַמִּים
נָסֵבָּה אֵלָי אִמָּלְאָה הָחֳרָבָה: 3 לָכֵן כֹּה אָמַר
אֲדֹנָי יְהוִה הִנְנִי עָלַיִךְ צֹר וְהַעֲלֵיתִי עָלַיִךְ גּוֹיִם
רַבִּים כְּהַעֲלוֹת הַיָּם לְגַלָּיו: 4 וְשִׁחֲתוּ חֹמוֹת צֹר
וְהָרְסוּ מִגְדָּלֶיהָ וְסִחֵיתִי עֲפָרָהּ מִמֶּנָּה וְנָתַתִּי אוֹתָהּ
לִצְחִיחַ סָלַע: 5 מִשְׁטַח חֲרָמִים תִּהְיֶה בְּתוֹךְ הַיָּם
כִּי אֲנִי דִבַּרְתִּי נְאֻם אֲדֹנָי יְהוִה וְהָיְתָה לְבַז לַגּוֹיִם:
6 וּבְנוֹתֶיהָ אֲשֶׁר בַּשָּׂדֶה בַּחֶרֶב תֵּהָרַגְנָה וְיָדְעוּ כִּי־
אֲנִי יְהוָה: פ

7 כִּי כֹה אָמַר אֲדֹנָי יְהוִה הִנְנִי מֵבִיא אֶל־צֹר
נְבוּכַדְרֶאצַּר מֶלֶךְ־בָּבֶל מִצָּפוֹן מֶלֶךְ מְלָכִים בְּסוּס
וּבְרֶכֶב וּבְפָרָשִׁים וְקָהָל וְעַם־רָב: 8 בְּנוֹתַיִךְ בַּשָּׂדֶה
בַּחֶרֶב יַהֲרֹג וְנָתַן עָלַיִךְ דָּיֵק וְשָׁפַךְ עָלַיִךְ סֹלְלָה
וְהֵקִים עָלַיִךְ צִנָּה: 9 וּמְחִי קָבָלּוֹ יִתֵּן בְּחֹמוֹתָיִךְ
וּמִגְדְּלֹתַיִךְ יִתֹּץ בְּחַרְבוֹתָיו: 10 מִשִּׁפְעַת סוּסָיו
יְכַסֵּךְ אֲבָקָם מִקּוֹל פָּרַשׁ וְגַלְגַּל וָרֶכֶב תִּרְעַשְׁנָה
חוֹמוֹתַיִךְ בְּבֹאוֹ בִּשְׁעָרַיִךְ כִּמְבוֹאֵי עִיר מְבֻקָּעָה:
11 בְּפַרְסוֹת סוּסָיו יִרְמֹס אֶת־כָּל־חוּצוֹתָיִךְ עַמֵּךְ

12 They will plunder your riches and pillage your merchandise; they will break down your walls and destroy your pleasant houses; they will lay your stones, your timber, and your soil in the midst of the water. 13 I will put an end to the sound of your songs, and the sound of your harps shall be heard no more. 14 I will make you like the top of a rock; you shall be *a place for* spreading nets, and you shall never be rebuilt, for I the LORD have spoken,' says the Lord GOD.

15 "Thus says the Lord GOD to Tyre: 'Will the coastlands not shake at the sound of your fall, when the wounded cry, when slaughter is made in the midst of you? 16 Then all the princes of the sea will come down from their thrones, lay aside their robes, and take off their embroidered garments; they will clothe themselves with trembling; they will sit on the ground, tremble *every* moment, and be astonished at you. 17 And they will take up a lamentation for you, and say to you:

"How you have perished,
　O one inhabited by seafaring men,
　O renowned city,
　Who was strong at sea,
　She and her inhabitants,
　Who caused their terror *to be* on all her
　　inhabitants!
18　Now the coastlands tremble on the day of your
　　fall;
　Yes, the coastlands by the sea are troubled at
　　your departure." '

19 "For thus says the Lord GOD: 'When I make you a desolate city, like cities that are not inhabited, when I bring the deep upon you, and great waters cover you, 20 then I will bring you down with those who descend into the Pit, to the people of old, and I will make you dwell in the lowest part of the earth, in places desolate from antiquity, with those who go down to the Pit, so that you may never be inhabited; and I shall establish glory in the land of the living. 21 I will make you a terror, and you *shall be* no *more;* though you are sought for, you will never be found again,' says the Lord GOD. "

27 The word of the LORD came again to me, saying, 2 "Now, son of man, take up a lamentation for Tyre, 3 and say to Tyre, 'You who are situated at the entrance of the sea, merchant of the peoples on many coastlands, thus says the Lord GOD:

"O Tyre, you have said,
　'I *am* perfect in beauty.'
4　Your borders *are* in the midst of the seas.
　Your builders have perfected your beauty.
5　They made all *your* planks of fir trees from Senir;

12 וְשָׁלְלוּ תֵרֶד: לָאָרֶץ עֻזֵּךְ וּמַצְּבוֹת יַהֲרֹג בַּחֶרֶב
חֵילֵךְ וּבָזְזוּ רְכֻלָּתֵךְ וְהָרְסוּ חוֹמוֹתַיִךְ וּבָתֵּי חֶמְדָּתֵךְ
יִתֹּצוּ וַאֲבָנַיִךְ וְעֵצַיִךְ וַעֲפָרֵךְ בְּתוֹךְ מַיִם יָשִׂימוּ:
13 וְהִשְׁבַּתִּי הֲמוֹן שִׁירָיִךְ וְקוֹל כִּנּוֹרַיִךְ לֹא יִשָּׁמַע
עוֹד: 14 וּנְתַתִּיךְ לִצְחִיחַ סֶלַע מִשְׁטַח חֲרָמִים
תִּהְיֶה לֹא תִבָּנֶה עוֹד כִּי אֲנִי יְהוָה דִּבַּרְתִּי
נְאֻם אֲדֹנָי יְהוִה: ס 15 כֹּה אָמַר אֲדֹנָי
יְהוִה לְצוֹר הֲלֹא | מִקּוֹל מַפַּלְתֵּךְ בֶּאֱנֹק חָלָל
בֵּהָרֵג הֶרֶג בְּתוֹכֵךְ יִרְעֲשׁוּ הָאִיִּים: 16 וְיָרְדוּ מֵעַל
כִּסְאוֹתָם כֹּל נְשִׂיאֵי הַיָּם וְהֵסִירוּ אֶת־מְעִילֵיהֶם
וְאֶת־בִּגְדֵי רִקְמָתָם יִפְשֹׁטוּ חֲרָדוֹת | יִלְבָּשׁוּ
עַל־הָאָרֶץ יֵשֵׁבוּ וְחָרְדוּ לִרְגָעִים וְשָׁמְמוּ עָלָיִךְ:
17 וְנָשְׂאוּ עָלַיִךְ קִינָה וְאָמְרוּ לָךְ אֵיךְ אָבַדְתְּ נוֹשֶׁבֶת
מִיַּמִּים הָעִיר הַהֻלָּלָה אֲשֶׁר הָיְתָה חֲזָקָה בַיָּם הִיא
וְיֹשְׁבֶיהָ אֲשֶׁר־נָתְנוּ חִתִּיתָם לְכָל־יוֹשְׁבֶיהָ: 18 עַתָּה
יֶחְרְדוּ הָאִיִּן יוֹם מַפַּלְתֵּךְ וְנִבְהֲלוּ הָאִיִּים אֲשֶׁר־
בַּיָּם מִצֵּאתֵךְ: ס 19 כִּי כֹה אָמַר אֲדֹנָי
יְהוִה בְּתִתִּי אֹתָךְ עִיר נֶחֱרֶבֶת כֶּעָרִים אֲשֶׁר לֹא־
נוֹשָׁבוּ בְּהַעֲלוֹת עָלַיִךְ אֶת־תְּהוֹם וְכִסּוּךְ הַמַּיִם
הָרַבִּים: 20 וְהוֹרַדְתִּיךְ אֶת־יוֹרְדֵי בוֹר אֶל־עַם עוֹלָם
וְהוֹשַׁבְתִּיךְ בְּאֶרֶץ תַּחְתִּיּוֹת כָּחֳרָבוֹת מֵעוֹלָם אֶת־
יוֹרְדֵי בוֹר לְמַעַן לֹא תֵשֵׁבִי וְנָתַתִּי צְבִי בְּאֶרֶץ חַיִּים:
21 בַּלָּהוֹת אֶתְּנֵךְ וְאֵינֵךְ וּתְבֻקְשִׁי וְלֹא־תִמָּצְאִי עוֹד
לְעוֹלָם נְאֻם אֲדֹנָי יְהוִה: ס

כז וַיְהִי דְבַר־יְהוָה אֵלַי לֵאמֹר: 2 וְאַתָּה בֶן־אָדָם
שָׂא עַל־צֹר קִינָה: 3 וְאָמַרְתָּ לְצוֹר הַיּשֶׁבְתִּ עַל־
מְבוֹאֹת יָם רֹכֶלֶת הָעַמִּים אֶל־אִיִּים רַבִּים כֹּה אָמַר
אֲדֹנָי יְהוִה צוֹר אַתְּ אָמַרְתְּ אֲנִי כְּלִילַת יֹפִי: 4 בְּלֵב
יַמִּים גְּבוּלָיִךְ בֹּנַיִךְ כָּלְלוּ יָפְיֵךְ: 5 בְּרוֹשִׁים מִשְּׂנִיר
בָּנוּ לָךְ אֵת כָּל־לֻחֹתָיִם אֶרֶז מִלְּבָנוֹן לָקָחוּ לַעֲשׂוֹת

קמ 3 הַיֹּשֶׁבֶת

They took a cedar from Lebanon to make you a
mast.

6 *Of* oaks from Bashan they made your oars;
The company of Ashurites have inlaid your
planks
With ivory from the coasts of Cyprus.

7 Fine embroidered linen from Egypt was what you
spread for your sail;
Blue and purple from the coasts of Elishah was
what covered you.

8 "Inhabitants of Sidon and Arvad were your
oarsmen;
Your wise men, O Tyre, were in you;
They became your pilots.

9 Elders of Gebal and its wise men
Were in you to caulk your seams;
All the ships of the sea
And their oarsmen were in you
To market your merchandise.

10 "Those from Persia, Lydia, and Libya
Were in your army as men of war;
They hung shield and helmet in you;
They gave splendor to you.

11 Men of Arvad with your army *were* on your walls
all around,
And the men of Gammad were in your towers;
They hung their shields on your walls *all* around;
They made your beauty perfect.

12 "Tarshish *was* your merchant because of your
many luxury goods. They gave you silver, iron, tin,
and lead for your goods. 13 Javan, Tubal, and
Meshech *were* your traders. They bartered human
lives and vessels of bronze for your merchandise.
14 Those from the house of Togarmah traded for
your wares with horses, steeds, and mules. 15 The
men of Dedan *were* your traders; many isles *were*
the market of your hand. They brought you ivory
tusks and ebony as payment. 16 Syria *was* your
merchant because of the abundance of goods you
made. They gave you for your wares emeralds,
purple, embroidery, fine linen, corals, and rubies.
17 Judah and the land of Israel *were* your traders.
They traded for your merchandise wheat of
Minnith, millet, honey, oil, and balm. 18 Damascus
was your merchant because of the abundance of
goods you made, because of your many luxury
items, with the wine of Helbon and with white
wool. 19 Dan and Javan paid for your wares,
traversing back and forth. Wrought iron, cassia,
and cane were among your merchandise. 20 Dedan
was your merchant in saddlecloths for riding.
21 Arabia and all the princes of Kedar *were* your
regular merchants. They traded with you in lambs,
rams, and goats. 22 The merchants of Sheba and
Raamah *were* your merchants. They traded for
your wares the choicest spices, all kinds of precious
stones, and gold. 23 Haran, Canneh, Eden, the

תֹּרֶן עָלָיִךְ: 6 אַלּוֹנִים מִבָּשָׁן עָשׂוּ מִשּׁוֹטָיִךְ קַרְשֵׁךְ
עָשׂוּ־שֵׁן בַּת־אֲשֻׁרִים מֵאִיֵּי כִּתִּיִּם פ: 7 שֵׁשׁ־בְּרִקְמָה
מִמִּצְרַיִם הָיָה מִפְרָשֵׂךְ לִהְיוֹת לָךְ לְנֵס תְּכֵלֶת
וְאַרְגָּמָן מֵאִיֵּי אֱלִישָׁה הָיָה מְכַסֵּךְ: 8 יֹשְׁבֵי צִידוֹן
וְאַרְוַד הָיוּ שָׁטִים לָךְ חֲכָמַיִךְ צוֹר הָיוּ בָךְ הֵמָּה
חֹבְלָיִךְ: 9 זִקְנֵי גְבַל וַחֲכָמֶיהָ הָיוּ בָךְ מַחֲזִיקֵי בִּדְקֵךְ
כָּל־אֳנִיּוֹת הַיָּם וּמַלָּחֵיהֶם הָיוּ בָךְ לַעֲרֹב מַעֲרָבֵךְ:
10 פָּרַס וְלוּד וּפוּט הָיוּ בְחֵילֵךְ אַנְשֵׁי מִלְחַמְתֵּךְ מָגֵן
וְכוֹבַע תִּלּוּ־בָךְ הֵמָּה נָתְנוּ הֲדָרֵךְ: 11 בְּנֵי אַרְוַד
וְחֵילֵךְ עַל־חוֹמוֹתַיִךְ סָבִיב וְגַמָּדִים בְּמִגְדְּלוֹתַיִךְ
הָיוּ שִׁלְטֵיהֶם תִּלּוּ עַל־חוֹמוֹתַיִךְ סָבִיב הֵמָּה כָּלְלוּ
יָפְיֵךְ: 12 תַּרְשִׁישׁ סֹחַרְתֵּךְ מֵרֹב כָּל־הוֹן בְּכֶסֶף בַּרְזֶל
בְּדִיל וְעוֹפֶרֶת נָתְנוּ עִזְבוֹנָיִךְ: 13 יָוָן תֻּבַל וָמֶשֶׁךְ
הֵמָּה רֹכְלָיִךְ בְּנֶפֶשׁ אָדָם וּכְלֵי נְחֹשֶׁת נָתְנוּ מַעֲרָבֵךְ:
14 מִבֵּית תּוֹגַרְמָה סוּסִים וּפָרָשִׁים וּפְרָדִים נָתְנוּ
עִזְבוֹנָיִךְ: 15 בְּנֵי דְדָן רֹכְלַיִךְ אִיִּים רַבִּים סְחֹרַת
יָדֵךְ קַרְנוֹת שֵׁן וְהוֹבְנִים פ הֵשִׁיבוּ אֶשְׁכָּרֵךְ: 16 אֲרָם
סֹחַרְתֵּךְ מֵרֹב מַעֲשָׂיִךְ בְּנֹפֶךְ אַרְגָּמָן וְרִקְמָה וּבוּץ
וְרָאמֹת וְכַדְכֹּד נָתְנוּ בְּעִזְבוֹנָיִךְ: 17 יְהוּדָה וְאֶרֶץ
יִשְׂרָאֵל הֵמָּה רֹכְלָיִךְ בְּחִטֵּי מִנִּית וּפַנַּג וּדְבַשׁ
וָשֶׁמֶן וָצֹרִי נָתְנוּ מַעֲרָבֵךְ: 18 דַּמֶּשֶׂק סֹחַרְתֵּךְ בְּרֹב
מַעֲשַׂיִךְ מֵרֹב כָּל־הוֹן בְּיֵין חֶלְבּוֹן וְצֶמֶר צָחַר:
19 וְדָן וְיָוָן מְאוּזָּל בְּעִזְבוֹנַיִךְ נָתָנּוּ בַּרְזֶל עָשׁוֹת
קִדָּה וְקָנֶה בְּמַעֲרָבֵךְ הָיָה: 20 דְּדָן רֹכַלְתֵּךְ בְּבִגְדֵי־
חֹפֶשׁ לְרִכְבָּה: 21 עֲרַב וְכָל־נְשִׂיאֵי קֵדָר הֵמָּה סֹחֲרֵי
יָדֵךְ בְּכָרִים וְאֵילִם וְעַתּוּדִים בָּם סֹחֲרָיִךְ: 22 רֹכְלֵי
שְׁבָא וְרַעְמָה הֵמָּה רֹכְלָיִךְ בְּרֹאשׁ כָּל־בֹּשֶׂם וּבְכָל־
אֶבֶן יְקָרָה וְזָהָב נָתְנוּ עִזְבוֹנָיִךְ: 23 חָרָן וְכַנֵּה וָעֶדֶן

merchants of Sheba, Assyria, *and* Chilmad *were* your merchants. ²⁴ These *were* your merchants in choice items—in purple clothes, in embroidered garments, in chests of multicolored apparel, in sturdy woven cords, which were in your marketplace.

²⁵ "The ships of Tarshish were carriers of your merchandise.
　　You were filled and very glorious in the midst of the seas.
²⁶ Your oarsmen brought you into many waters,
　　But the east wind broke you in the midst of the seas.

²⁷ "Your riches, wares, and merchandise,
　　Your mariners and pilots,
　　Your caulkers and merchandisers,
　　All your men of war who *are* in you,
　　And the entire company which *is* in your midst,
　　Will fall into the midst of the seas on the day of your ruin.
²⁸ The common-land will shake at the sound of the cry of your pilots.

²⁹ "All who handle the oar,
　　The mariners,
　　All the pilots of the sea
　　Will come down from their ships *and* stand on the shore.
³⁰ They will make their voice heard because of you;
　　They will cry bitterly and cast dust on their heads;
　　They will roll about in ashes;
³¹ They will shave themselves completely bald because of you,
　　Gird themselves with sackcloth,
　　And weep for you
　　With bitterness of heart *and* bitter wailing.
³² In their wailing for you
　　They will take up a lamentation,
　　And lament for you:
　　'What *city is* like Tyre,
　　Destroyed in the midst of the sea?

³³ 'When your wares went out by sea,
　　You satisfied many people;
　　You enriched the kings of the earth
　　With your many luxury goods and your merchandise.
³⁴ But you are broken by the seas in the depths of the waters;
　　Your merchandise and the entire company will fall in your midst.
³⁵ All the inhabitants of the isles will be astonished at you;
　　Their kings will be greatly afraid,
　　And *their* countenance will be troubled.
³⁶ The merchants among the peoples will hiss at you;
　　You will become a horror, and *be* no more forever.' " "

רֹכְלֵי שְׁבָא אַשּׁוּר כִּלְמַד רֹכַלְתֵּךְ: 24 הֵמָּה רֹכְלַיִךְ בְּמַכְלֻלִים בִּגְלוֹמֵי תְּכֵלֶת וְרִקְמָה וּבְגִנְזֵי בְּרֹמִים בַּחֲבָלִים חֲבֻשִׁים וַאֲרֻזִים בְּמַרְכֻלְתֵּךְ: 25 אֳנִיּוֹת תַּרְשִׁישׁ שָׁרוֹתַיִךְ מַעֲרָבֵךְ וַתִּמָּלְאִי וַתִּכְבְּדִי מְאֹד בְּלֵב יַמִּים: 26 בְּמַיִם רַבִּים הֱבִיאוּךְ הַשָּׁטִים אֹתָךְ רוּחַ הַקָּדִים שְׁבָרֵךְ בְּלֵב יַמִּים: 27 הוֹנֵךְ וְעִזְבוֹנַיִךְ מַעֲרָבֵךְ מַלָּחַיִךְ וְחֹבְלָיִךְ מַחֲזִיקֵי בִדְקֵךְ וְעֹרְבֵי מַעֲרָבֵךְ וְכָל־אַנְשֵׁי מִלְחַמְתֵּךְ אֲשֶׁר־בָּךְ וּבְכָל־קְהָלֵךְ אֲשֶׁר בְּתוֹכֵךְ יִפְּלוּ בְּלֵב יַמִּים בְּיוֹם מַפַּלְתֵּךְ: 28 לְקוֹל זַעֲקַת חֹבְלָיִךְ יִרְעֲשׁוּ מִגְרֹשׁוֹת: 29 וְיָרְדוּ מֵאֳנִיּוֹתֵיהֶם כֹּל תֹּפְשֵׂי מָשׁוֹט מַלָּחִים כֹּל חֹבְלֵי הַיָּם אֶל־הָאָרֶץ יַעֲמֹדוּ: 30 וְהִשְׁמִיעוּ עָלַיִךְ בְּקוֹלָם וְיִזְעֲקוּ מָרָה וְיַעֲלוּ עָפָר עַל־רָאשֵׁיהֶם בָּאֵפֶר יִתְפַּלָּשׁוּ: 31 וְהִקְרִיחוּ אֵלַיִךְ קָרְחָה וְחָגְרוּ שַׂקִּים וּבָכוּ אֵלַיִךְ בְּמַר־נֶפֶשׁ מִסְפֵּד מָר: 32 וְנָשְׂאוּ אֵלַיִךְ בְּנִיהֶם קִינָה וְקוֹנְנוּ עָלָיִךְ מִי כְצוֹר כְּדֻמָּה בְּתוֹךְ הַיָּם: 33 בְּצֵאת עִזְבוֹנַיִךְ מִיַּמִּים הִשְׂבַּעַתְּ עַמִּים רַבִּים בְּרֹב הוֹנַיִךְ וּמַעֲרָבַיִךְ הֶעֱשַׁרְתְּ מַלְכֵי־אָרֶץ: 34 עֵת נִשְׁבֶּרֶת מִיַּמִּים בְּמַעֲמַקֵּי־מָיִם מַעֲרָבֵךְ וְכָל־קְהָלֵךְ בְּתוֹכֵךְ נָפָלוּ: 35 כֹּל יֹשְׁבֵי הָאִיִּם שָׁמְמוּ עָלָיִךְ וּמַלְכֵיהֶם שָׂעֲרוּ שַׂעַר רָעֲמוּ פָּנִים: 36 סֹחֲרִים בָּעַמִּים שָׁרְקוּ עָלָיִךְ בַּלָּהוֹת הָיִית וְאֵינֵךְ עַד־עוֹלָם: ס

28 The word of the LORD came to me again, saying, [2] "Son of man, say to the prince of Tyre, 'Thus says the Lord GOD:

> "Because your heart *is* lifted up,
> And you say, 'I *am* a god,
> I sit *in* the seat of gods,
> In the midst of the seas,'
> Yet you *are* a man, and not a god,
> Though you set your heart as the heart of a god
> [3] (Behold, you *are* wiser than Daniel!
> There is no secret that can be hidden from you!
> [4] With your wisdom and your understanding
> You have gained riches for yourself,
> And gathered gold and silver into your treasuries;
> [5] By your great wisdom in trade you have increased your riches,
> And your heart is lifted up because of your riches),"

[6] Therefore thus says the Lord GOD:

> "Because you have set your heart as the heart of a god,
> [7] Behold, therefore, I will bring strangers against you,
> The most terrible of the nations;
> And they shall draw their swords against the beauty of your wisdom,
> And defile your splendor.
> [8] They shall throw you down into the Pit,
> And you shall die the death of the slain
> In the midst of the seas.
> [9] "Will you still say before him who slays you,
> 'I *am* a god'?
> But you *shall be* a man, and not a god,
> In the hand of him who slays you.
> [10] You shall die the death of the uncircumcised
> By the hand of aliens;
> For I have spoken," says the Lord GOD.' "

[11] Moreover the word of the LORD came to me, saying, [12] "Son of man, take up a lamentation for the king of Tyre, and say to him, 'Thus says the Lord GOD:

> "You *were* the seal of perfection,
> Full of wisdom and perfect in beauty.
> [13] You were in Eden, the garden of God;
> Every precious stone *was* your covering:
> The sardius, topaz, and diamond,
> Beryl, onyx, and jasper,
> Sapphire, turquoise, and emerald with gold.
> The workmanship of your timbrels and pipes
> Was prepared for you on the day you were created.
> [14] "You *were* the anointed cherub who covers;
> I established you;
> You were on the holy mountain of God;
> You walked back and forth in the midst of fiery stones.
> [15] You *were* perfect in your ways from the day you were created,
> Till iniquity was found in you.

כח וַיְהִי דְבַר־יְהֹוָה אֵלַי לֵאמֹר: [2] בֶּן־אָדָם
אֱמֹר לִנְגִיד צֹר כֹּה־אָמַר ׀ אֲדֹנָי יְהֹוִה יַעַן
גָּבַהּ לִבְּךָ וַתֹּאמֶר אֵל אָנִי מוֹשַׁב אֱלֹהִים יָשַׁבְתִּי
בְּלֵב יַמִּים וְאַתָּה אָדָם וְלֹא־אֵל וַתִּתֵּן לִבְּךָ
כְּלֵב אֱלֹהִים: [3] הִנֵּה חָכָם אַתָּה מִדָּנִאֵל כָּל־
סָתוּם לֹא עֲמָמוּךָ: [4] בְּחָכְמָתְךָ וּבִתְבוּנָתְךָ עָשִׂיתָ
לְּךָ חָיִל וַתַּעַשׂ זָהָב וָכֶסֶף בְּאוֹצְרוֹתֶיךָ: [5] בְּרֹב
חָכְמָתְךָ בִּרְכֻלָּתְךָ הִרְבִּיתָ חֵילֶךָ וַיִּגְבַּהּ לְבָבְךָ
בְּחֵילֶךָ: ס [6] לָכֵן כֹּה אָמַר אֲדֹנָי יְהֹוִה
יַעַן תִּתְּךָ אֶת־לְבָבְךָ כְּלֵב אֱלֹהִים: [7] לָכֵן הִנְנִי
מֵבִיא עָלֶיךָ זָרִים עָרִיצֵי גּוֹיִם וְהֵרִיקוּ חַרְבוֹתָם
עַל־יְפִי חָכְמָתֶךָ וְחִלְּלוּ יִפְעָתֶךָ: [8] לַשַּׁחַת יוֹרִדוּךָ
וָמַתָּה מְמוֹתֵי חָלָל בְּלֵב יַמִּים: [9] הֶאָמֹר תֹּאמַר
אֱלֹהִים אָנִי לִפְנֵי הֹרְגֶךָ וְאַתָּה אָדָם וְלֹא־אֵל בְּיַד
מְחַלְלֶיךָ: [10] מוֹתֵי עֲרֵלִים תָּמוּת בְּיַד־זָרִים כִּי אֲנִי
דִבַּרְתִּי נְאֻם אֲדֹנָי יְהֹוִה: ס [11] וַיְהִי דְבַר־
יְהֹוָה אֵלַי לֵאמֹר: [12] בֶּן־אָדָם שָׂא קִינָה עַל־מֶלֶךְ
צוֹר וְאָמַרְתָּ לּוֹ כֹּה אָמַר אֲדֹנָי יְהֹוִה אַתָּה חוֹתֵם
תָּכְנִית מָלֵא חָכְמָה וּכְלִיל יֹפִי: [13] בְּעֵדֶן גַּן־אֱלֹהִים
הָיִיתָ כָּל־אֶבֶן יְקָרָה מְסֻכָתֶךָ אֹדֶם פִּטְדָה וְיָהֲלֹם
תַּרְשִׁישׁ שֹׁהַם וְיָשְׁפֵה סַפִּיר נֹפֶךְ וּבָרְקַת וְזָהָב
מְלֶאכֶת תֻּפֶּיךָ וּנְקָבֶיךָ בָּךְ בְּיוֹם הִבָּרַאֲךָ כּוֹנָנוּ:
[14] אַתְּ־כְּרוּב מִמְשַׁח הַסּוֹכֵךְ וּנְתַתִּיךָ בְּהַר קֹדֶשׁ
אֱלֹהִים הָיִיתָ בְּתוֹךְ אַבְנֵי־אֵשׁ הִתְהַלָּכְתָּ: [15] תָּמִים
אַתָּה בִּדְרָכֶיךָ מִיּוֹם הִבָּרְאָךְ עַד־נִמְצָא עַוְלָתָה

כח [3] מִדָּנִאֵל

16 "By the abundance of your trading
    You became filled with violence within,
    And you sinned;
    Therefore I cast you as a profane thing
    Out of the mountain of God;
    And I destroyed you, O covering cherub,
    From the midst of the fiery stones.

17 "Your heart was lifted up because of your beauty;
    You corrupted your wisdom for the sake of your
        splendor;
    I cast you to the ground,
    I laid you before kings,
    That they might gaze at you.

18 "You defiled your sanctuaries
    By the multitude of your iniquities,
    By the iniquity of your trading;
    Therefore I brought fire from your midst;
    It devoured you,
    And I turned you to ashes upon the earth
    In the sight of all who saw you.

19 All who knew you among the peoples are
        astonished at you;
    You have become a horror,
    And *shall be* no more forever."'"

20 Then the word of the LORD came to me, saying, 21 "Son of man, set your face toward Sidon, and prophesy against her, 22 and say, 'Thus says the Lord GOD:

    "Behold, I *am* against you, O Sidon;
    I will be glorified in your midst;
    And they shall know that I *am* the LORD,
    When I execute judgments in her and am
        hallowed in her.
23 For I will send pestilence upon her,
    And blood in her streets;
    The wounded shall be judged in her midst
    By the sword against her on every side;
    Then they shall know that I *am* the LORD.

24 "And there shall no longer be a pricking brier or a painful thorn for the house of Israel from among all *who are* around them, who despise them. Then they shall know that I *am* the Lord GOD."

25 'Thus says the Lord GOD: "When I have gathered the house of Israel from the peoples among whom they are scattered, and am hallowed in them in the sight of the Gentiles, then they will dwell in their own land which I gave to My servant Jacob. 26 And they will dwell safely there, build houses, and plant vineyards; yes, they will dwell securely, when I execute judgments on all those around them who despise them. Then they shall know that I *am* the LORD their God."'"

29 In the tenth year, in the tenth *month,* on the twelfth *day* of the month, the word of the LORD came to me, saying, 2 "Son of man, set your face

בָּךְ׃ 16 בְּרֹב רְכֻלָּתְךָ מָלוּ תוֹכְךָ חָמָס וַתֶּחֱטָא וָאֶחַלֶּלְךָ מֵהַר אֱלֹהִים וָאַבֶּדְךָ כְּרוּב הַסֹּכֵךְ מִתּוֹךְ אַבְנֵי־אֵשׁ׃ 17 גָּבַהּ לִבְּךָ בְּיָפְיֶךָ שִׁחַתָּ חָכְמָתְךָ עַל־ יִפְעָתֶךָ עַל־אֶרֶץ הִשְׁלַכְתִּיךָ לִפְנֵי מְלָכִים נְתַתִּיךָ לְרַאֲוָה בָךְ׃ 18 מֵרֹב עֲוֺנֶיךָ בְּעֶוֶל רְכֻלָּתְךָ חִלַּלְתָּ מִקְדָּשֶׁיךָ וָאוֹצִא־אֵשׁ מִתּוֹכְךָ הִיא אֲכָלַתְךָ וָאֶתֶּנְךָ לְאֵפֶר עַל־הָאָרֶץ לְעֵינֵי כָּל־רֹאֶיךָ׃ 19 כָּל־יוֹדְעֶיךָ בָּעַמִּים שָׁמְמוּ עָלֶיךָ בַּלָּהוֹת הָיִיתָ וְאֵינְךָ עַד־ עוֹלָם׃
פ

20 וַיְהִי דְבַר־יְהֹוָה אֵלַי לֵאמֹר׃ 21 בֶּן־אָדָם שִׂים פָּנֶיךָ אֶל־צִידוֹן וְהִנָּבֵא עָלֶיהָ׃ 22 וְאָמַרְתָּ כֹּה אָמַר אֲדֹנָי יֱהֹוִה הִנְנִי עָלַיִךְ צִידוֹן וְנִכְבַּדְתִּי בְּתוֹכֵךְ וְיָדְעוּ כִּי־אֲנִי יְהֹוָה בַּעֲשׂוֹתִי בָהּ שְׁפָטִים וְנִקְדַּשְׁתִּי בָהּ׃ 23 וְשִׁלַּחְתִּי־בָהּ דֶּבֶר וָדָם בְּחוּצוֹתֶיהָ וְנִפְלַל חָלָל בְּתוֹכָהּ בְּחֶרֶב עָלֶיהָ מִסָּבִיב וְיָדְעוּ כִּי־אֲנִי יְהֹוָה׃ 24 וְלֹא־יִהְיֶה עוֹד לְבֵית יִשְׂרָאֵל סִלּוֹן מַמְאִיר וְקוֹץ מַכְאִב מִכֹּל סְבִיבֹתָם הַשָּׁאטִים אוֹתָם וְיָדְעוּ כִּי אֲנִי אֲדֹנָי יְהֹוִה׃ ס 25 כֹּה־אָמַר אֲדֹנָי יֱהֹוִה בְּקַבְּצִי ׀ אֶת־בֵּית יִשְׂרָאֵל מִן־הָעַמִּים אֲשֶׁר נָפֹצוּ בָם וְנִקְדַּשְׁתִּי בָם לְעֵינֵי הַגּוֹיִם וְיָשְׁבוּ עַל־ אַדְמָתָם אֲשֶׁר נָתַתִּי לְעַבְדִּי לְיַעֲקֹב׃ 26 וְיָשְׁבוּ עָלֶיהָ לָבֶטַח וּבָנוּ בָתִּים וְנָטְעוּ כְרָמִים וְיָשְׁבוּ לָבֶטַח בַּעֲשׂוֹתִי שְׁפָטִים בְּכֹל הַשָּׁאטִים אֹתָם מִסְּבִיבוֹתָם וְיָדְעוּ כִּי אֲנִי יְהֹוָה אֱלֹהֵיהֶם׃ ס

כט בַּשָּׁנָה הָעֲשִׂירִית בָּעֲשִׂרִי בִּשְׁנֵים עָשָׂר לַחֹדֶשׁ הָיָה דְבַר־יְהֹוָה אֵלַי לֵאמֹר׃ 2 בֶּן־אָדָם שִׂים

against Pharaoh king of Egypt, and prophesy against him, and against all Egypt. ³Speak, and say, 'Thus says the Lord GOD:

"Behold, I *am* against you,
O Pharaoh king of Egypt,
O great monster who lies in the midst of his rivers,
Who has said, 'My River *is* my own;
I have made *it* for myself.'

⁴ But I will put hooks in your jaws,
And cause the fish of your rivers to stick to your scales;
I will bring you up out of the midst of your rivers,
And all the fish in your rivers will stick to your scales.

⁵ I will leave you in the wilderness,
You and all the fish of your rivers;
You shall fall on the open field;
You shall not be picked up or gathered.
I have given you as food
To the beasts of the field
And to the birds of the heavens.

⁶ "Then all the inhabitants of Egypt
Shall know that I *am* the LORD,
Because they have been a staff of reed to the house of Israel.

⁷ When they took hold of you with the hand,
You broke and tore all their shoulders;
When they leaned on you,
You broke and made all their backs quiver."

⁸'Therefore thus says the Lord GOD: "Surely I will bring a sword upon you and cut off from you man and beast. ⁹And the land of Egypt shall become desolate and waste; then they will know that I *am* the LORD, because he said, 'The River *is* mine, and I have made *it*.' ¹⁰Indeed, therefore, I *am* against you and against your rivers, and I will make the land of Egypt utterly waste and desolate, from Migdol *to* Syene, as far as the border of Ethiopia. ¹¹Neither foot of man shall pass through it nor foot of beast pass through it, and it shall be uninhabited forty years. ¹²I will make the land of Egypt desolate in the midst of the countries *that are* desolate; and among the cities *that are* laid waste, her cities shall be desolate forty years; and I will scatter the Egyptians among the nations and disperse them throughout the countries. "

¹³'Yet, thus says the Lord GOD: "At the end of forty years I will gather the Egyptians from the peoples among whom they were scattered. ¹⁴I will bring back the captives of Egypt and cause them to return to the land of Pathros, to the land of their origin, and there they shall be a lowly kingdom. ¹⁵It shall be the lowliest of kingdoms; it shall never again exalt itself above the nations, for I will diminish them so that they will not rule over the

פָּנֶיךָ עַל־פַּרְעֹה מֶלֶךְ מִצְרָיִם וְהִנָּבֵא עָלָיו וְעַל־
מִצְרַיִם כֻּלָּהּ: 3 דַּבֵּר וְאָמַרְתָּ כֹּה־אָמַר ׀ אֲדֹנָי
יְהוִה הִנְנִי עָלֶיךָ פַּרְעֹה מֶלֶךְ־מִצְרַיִם הַתַּנִּים הַגָּדוֹל
הָרֹבֵץ בְּתוֹךְ יְאֹרָיו אֲשֶׁר אָמַר לִי יְאֹרִי וַאֲנִי
עֲשִׂיתִנִי: 4 וְנָתַתִּי חַחִיִּ°ים בִּלְחָיֶיךָ וְהִדְבַּקְתִּי דְגַת־
יְאֹרֶיךָ בְּקַשְׂקְשֹׂתֶיךָ וְהַעֲלִיתִ֫יךָ מִתּוֹךְ יְאֹרֶיךָ וְאֵת
כָּל־דְּגַת יְאֹרֶיךָ בְּקַשְׂקְשֹׂתֶיךָ תִּדְבָּק: 5 וּנְטַשְׁתִּיךָ
הַמִּדְבָּרָה אוֹתְךָ וְאֵת כָּל־דְּגַת יְאֹרֶיךָ עַל־פְּנֵי
הַשָּׂדֶה תִּפּוֹל לֹא תֵאָסֵף וְלֹא תִקָּבֵץ לְחַיַּת הָאָרֶץ
וּלְעוֹף הַשָּׁמַיִם נְתַתִּיךָ לְאָכְלָה: 6 וְיָדְעוּ כָּל־יֹשְׁבֵי
מִצְרַיִם כִּי אֲנִי יְהוָה יַעַן הֱיוֹתָם מִשְׁעֶנֶת קָנֶה
לְבֵית יִשְׂרָאֵל: 7 בְּתָפְשָׂם בְּךָ בַכַּפֹּ°ך תֵּרוֹץ וּבָקַעְתָּ
לָהֶם כָּל־כָּתֵף וּבְהִשָּׁעֲנָם עָלֶיךָ תִּשָּׁבֵר וְהַעֲמַדְתָּ
לָהֶם כָּל־מָתְנָיִם: ס 8 לָכֵן כֹּה אָמַר אֲדֹנָי
יְהוִה הִנְנִי מֵבִיא עָלַיִךְ חָרֶב וְהִכְרַתִּי מִמֵּךְ אָדָם
וּבְהֵמָה: 9 וְהָיְתָה אֶרֶץ־מִצְרַיִם לִשְׁמָמָה וְחָרְבָּה
וְיָדְעוּ כִּי־אֲנִי יְהוָה יַעַן אָמַר יְאֹר לִי וַאֲנִי עָשִׂיתִי:
10 לָכֵן הִנְנִי אֵלֶיךָ וְאֶל־יְאֹרֶיךָ וְנָתַתִּי אֶת־אֶרֶץ
מִצְרַיִם לְחָרְבוֹת חֹרֶב שְׁמָמָה מִמִּגְדֹּל סְוֵנֵה וְעַד־
גְּבוּל כּוּשׁ: 11 לֹא תַעֲבָר־בָּהּ רֶגֶל אָדָם וְרֶגֶל
בְּהֵמָה לֹא תַעֲבָר־בָּהּ וְלֹא תֵשֵׁב אַרְבָּעִים שָׁנָה:
12 וְנָתַתִּי אֶת־אֶרֶץ מִצְרַיִם שְׁמָמָה בְּתוֹךְ ׀ אֲרָצוֹת
נְשַׁמּוֹת וְעָרֶיהָ בְּתוֹךְ עָרִים מָחֳרָבוֹת תִּהְיֶיןָ שְׁמָמָה
אַרְבָּעִים שָׁנָה וַהֲפִצֹתִי אֶת־מִצְרַיִם בַּגּוֹיִם וְזֵרִיתִים
בָּאֲרָצוֹת: פ
13 כִּי כֹּה אָמַר אֲדֹנָי יְהוִה מִקֵּץ אַרְבָּעִים שָׁנָה
אֲקַבֵּץ אֶת־מִצְרַיִם מִן־הָעַמִּים אֲשֶׁר־נָפֹצוּ שָׁמָּה:
14 וְשַׁבְתִּי אֶת־שְׁבוּת מִצְרַיִם וַהֲשִׁבֹתִי אֹתָם אֶרֶץ
פַּתְרוֹס עַל־אֶרֶץ מְכוּרָתָם וְהָיוּ שָׁם מַמְלָכָה
שְׁפָלָה: 15 מִן־הַמַּמְלָכוֹת תִּהְיֶה שְׁפָלָה וְלֹא־
תִתְנַשֵּׂא עוֹד עַל־הַגּוֹיִם וְהִמְעַטְתִּים לְבִלְתִּי רְדוֹת

nations anymore. [16] No longer shall it be the confidence of the house of Israel, but will remind them of *their* iniquity when they turned to follow them. Then they shall know that I *am* the Lord GOD.' ' "

[17] And it came to pass in the twenty-seventh year, in the first *month*, on the first *day* of the month, *that* the word of the LORD came to me, saying, [18] "Son of man, Nebuchadnezzar king of Babylon caused his army to labor strenuously against Tyre; every head *was* made bald, and every shoulder rubbed raw; yet neither he nor his army received wages from Tyre, for the labor which they expended on it. [19] Therefore thus says the Lord GOD: 'Surely I will give the land of Egypt to Nebuchadnezzar king of Babylon; he shall take away her wealth, carry off her spoil, and remove her pillage; and that will be the wages for his army. [20] I have given him the land of Egypt *for* his labor, because they worked for Me,' says the Lord GOD.

[21] 'In that day I will cause the horn of the house of Israel to spring forth, and I will open your mouth to speak in their midst. Then they shall know that I *am* the LORD.' "

30 The word of the LORD came to me again, saying, [2] "Son of man, prophesy and say, 'Thus says the Lord GOD:

"Wail, 'Woe to the day!'
[3]　For the day *is* near,
　　Even the day of the LORD *is* near;
　　It will be a day of clouds, the time of the Gentiles.
[4]　The sword shall come upon Egypt,
　　And great anguish shall be in Ethiopia,
　　When the slain fall in Egypt,
　　And they take away her wealth,
　　And her foundations are broken down.

[5] "Ethiopia, Libya, Lydia, all the mingled people, Chub, and the men of the lands who are allied, shall fall with them by the sword. "

[6] 'Thus says the LORD:

"Those who uphold Egypt shall fall,
　And the pride of her power shall come down.
　From Migdol *to* Syene
　Those within her shall fall by the sword,"
　Says the Lord GOD.
[7]　"They shall be desolate in the midst of the desolate countries,
　　And her cities shall be in the midst of the cities *that are* laid waste.
[8]　Then they will know that I *am* the LORD,
　　When I have set a fire in Egypt
　　And all her helpers are destroyed.
[9]　On that day messengers shall go forth from Me in ships

בַּגּוֹיִם: 16 וְלֹא יִהְיֶה־עוֹד לְבֵית יִשְׂרָאֵל לְמִבְטָח מַזְכִּיר עָוֹן בִּפְנוֹתָם אַחֲרֵיהֶם וְיָדְעוּ כִּי אֲנִי אֲדֹנָי יְהוִה: ס

17 וַיְהִי בְּעֶשְׂרִים וָשֶׁבַע שָׁנָה בָּרִאשׁוֹן בְּאֶחָד לַחֹדֶשׁ הָיָה דְבַר־יְהוָה אֵלַי לֵאמֹר: 18 בֶּן־אָדָם נְבוּכַדְרֶאצַּר מֶלֶךְ־בָּבֶל הֶעֱבִיד אֶת־חֵילוֹ עֲבֹדָה גְדֹלָה אֶל־צֹר כָּל־רֹאשׁ מֻקְרָח וְכָל־כָּתֵף מְרוּטָה וְשָׂכָר לֹא־הָיָה לוֹ וּלְחֵילוֹ מִצֹּר עַל־הָעֲבֹדָה אֲשֶׁר־עָבַד עָלֶיהָ: ס 19 לָכֵן כֹּה אָמַר אֲדֹנָי יְהוִה הִנְנִי נֹתֵן לִנְבוּכַדְרֶאצַּר מֶלֶךְ־בָּבֶל אֶת־אֶרֶץ מִצְרָיִם וְנָשָׂא הֲמֹנָהּ וְשָׁלַל שְׁלָלָהּ וּבָזַז בִּזָּהּ וְהָיְתָה שָׂכָר לְחֵילוֹ: 20 פְּעֻלָּתוֹ אֲשֶׁר־עָבַד בָּהּ נָתַתִּי לוֹ אֶת־אֶרֶץ מִצְרָיִם אֲשֶׁר עָשׂוּ לִי נְאֻם אֲדֹנָי יְהוִה: ס 21 בַּיּוֹם הַהוּא אַצְמִיחַ קֶרֶן לְבֵית יִשְׂרָאֵל וּלְךָ אֶתֵּן פִּתְחוֹן־פֶּה בְּתוֹכָם וְיָדְעוּ כִּי־אֲנִי יְהוָה: פ

ל וַיְהִי דְבַר־יְהוָה אֵלַי לֵאמֹר: 2 בֶּן־אָדָם הִנָּבֵא וְאָמַרְתָּ כֹּה אָמַר אֲדֹנָי יְהוִה הֵילִילוּ הָהּ לַיּוֹם: 3 כִּי־קָרוֹב יוֹם וְקָרוֹב יוֹם לַיהוָה יוֹם עָנָן עֵת גּוֹיִם יִהְיֶה: 4 וּבָאָה חֶרֶב בְּמִצְרַיִם וְהָיְתָה חַלְחָלָה בְּכוּשׁ בִּנְפֹל חָלָל בְּמִצְרַיִם וְלָקְחוּ הֲמוֹנָהּ וְנֶהֶרְסוּ יְסוֹדֹתֶיהָ: 5 כּוּשׁ וּפוּט וְלוּד וְכָל־הָעֶרֶב וְכוּב וּבְנֵי אֶרֶץ הַבְּרִית אִתָּם בַּחֶרֶב יִפֹּלוּ: פ

6 כֹּה אָמַר יְהוָה וְנָפְלוּ סֹמְכֵי מִצְרַיִם וְיָרַד גְּאוֹן עֻזָּהּ מִמִּגְדֹּל סְוֵנֵה בַּחֶרֶב יִפְּלוּ־בָהּ נְאֻם אֲדֹנָי יְהוִה: 7 וְנָשַׁמּוּ בְּתוֹךְ אֲרָצוֹת נְשַׁמּוֹת וְעָרָיו בְּתוֹךְ־עָרִים נַחֲרָבוֹת תִּהְיֶינָה: 8 וְיָדְעוּ כִּי־אֲנִי יְהוָה בְּתִתִּי־אֵשׁ בְּמִצְרַיִם וְנִשְׁבְּרוּ כָּל־עֹזְרֶיהָ: 9 בַּיּוֹם הַהוּא יֵצְאוּ מַלְאָכִים מִלְּפָנַי בַּצִּים לְהַחֲרִיד אֶת־כּוּשׁ בֶּטַח וְהָיְתָה חַלְחָלָה בָהֶם בְּיוֹם מִצְרַיִם כִּי

To make the careless Ethiopians afraid,
And great anguish shall come upon them,
As on the day of Egypt;
For indeed it is coming!"

10 'Thus says the Lord GOD:

"I will also make a multitude of Egypt to cease
By the hand of Nebuchadnezzar king of Babylon.
11 He and his people with him, the most terrible of
    the nations,
Shall be brought to destroy the land;
They shall draw their swords against Egypt,
And fill the land with the slain.
12 I will make the rivers dry,
And sell the land into the hand of the wicked;
I will make the land waste, and all that is in it,
By the hand of aliens.
I, the LORD, have spoken."

13 'Thus says the Lord GOD:

"I will also destroy the idols,
And cause the images to cease from Noph;
There shall no longer be princes from the land of
    Egypt;
I will put fear in the land of Egypt.
14 I will make Pathros desolate,
Set fire to Zoan,
And execute judgments in No.
15 I will pour My fury on Sin, the strength of Egypt;
I will cut off the multitude of No,
16 And set a fire in Egypt;
Sin shall have great pain,
No shall be split open,
And Noph *shall be in* distress daily.
17 The young men of Aven and Pi Beseth shall fall
    by the sword,
And these *cities* shall go into captivity.
18 At Tehaphnehes the day shall also be darkened,
When I break the yokes of Egypt there.
And her arrogant strength shall cease in her;
As for her, a cloud shall cover her,
And her daughters shall go into captivity.
19 Thus I will execute judgments on Egypt,
Then they shall know that I *am* the LORD." ' "

20 And it came to pass in the eleventh year, in the
first *month*, on the seventh *day* of the month, *that*
the word of the LORD came to me, saying, 21 "Son
of man, I have broken the arm of Pharaoh king of
Egypt; and see, it has not been bandaged for
healing, nor a splint put on to bind it, to make it
strong enough to hold a sword. 22 Therefore thus
says the Lord GOD: 'Surely I *am* against Pharaoh
king of Egypt, and will break his arms, both the
strong one and the one that was broken; and I will
make the sword fall out of his hand. 23 I will scatter
the Egyptians among the nations, and disperse
them throughout the countries. 24 I will strengthen
the arms of the king of Babylon and put My sword
in his hand; but I will break Pharaoh's arms, and he

10 כֹּה אָמַר אֲדֹנָי יְהוִה ס הִנֵּה בָאָה:
וְהִשְׁבַּתִּי אֶת־הֲמוֹן מִצְרַיִם בְּיַד נְבוּכַדְרֶאצַּר מֶלֶךְ־
בָּבֶל: 11 הוּא וְעַמּוֹ אִתּוֹ עָרִיצֵי גוֹיִם מוּבָאִים
לְשַׁחֵת הָאָרֶץ וְהֵרִיקוּ חַרְבוֹתָם עַל־מִצְרַיִם וּמָלְאוּ
אֶת־הָאָרֶץ חָלָל: 12 וְנָתַתִּי יְאֹרִים חָרָבָה וּמָכַרְתִּי
אֶת־הָאָרֶץ בְּיַד־רָעִים וַהֲשִׁמֹּתִי אֶרֶץ וּמְלֹאָהּ בְּיַד־
זָרִים אֲנִי יְהוָה דִּבַּרְתִּי: ס 13 כֹּה־אָמַר
אֲדֹנָי יְהוִה וְהַאֲבַדְתִּי גִלּוּלִים וְהִשְׁבַּתִּי אֱלִילִים מִנֹּף
וְנָשִׂיא מֵאֶרֶץ־מִצְרַיִם לֹא יִהְיֶה־עוֹד וְנָתַתִּי יִרְאָה
בְּאֶרֶץ מִצְרָיִם: 14 וַהֲשִׁמֹּתִי אֶת־פַּתְרוֹס וְנָתַתִּי אֵשׁ
בְּצֹעַן וְעָשִׂיתִי שְׁפָטִים בְּנֹא: 15 וְשָׁפַכְתִּי חֲמָתִי עַל־
סִין מָעוֹז מִצְרָיִם וְהִכְרַתִּי אֶת־הֲמוֹן נֹא: 16 וְנָתַתִּי
אֵשׁ בְּמִצְרַיִם חוּל תָּחִיל ᵖ סִין וְנֹא תִּהְיֶה לְהִבָּקֵעַ
וְנֹף צָרֵי יוֹמָם: 17 בַּחוּרֵי אָוֶן וּפִי־בֶסֶת בַּחֶרֶב יִפֹּלוּ
וְהֵנָּה בַּשְּׁבִי תֵלַכְנָה: 18 וּבִתְחַפְנְחֵס חָשַׂךְ הַיּוֹם
בְּשִׁבְרִי־שָׁם אֶת־מֹטוֹת מִצְרַיִם וְנִשְׁבַּת־בָּהּ גְּאוֹן
עֻזָּהּ הִיא עָנָן יְכַסֶּנָּה וּבְנוֹתֶיהָ בַּשְּׁבִי תֵלַכְנָה:
19 וְעָשִׂיתִי שְׁפָטִים בְּמִצְרָיִם וְיָדְעוּ כִּי־אֲנִי יְהוָה: פ
20 וַיְהִי בְּאַחַת עֶשְׂרֵה שָׁנָה בָּרִאשׁוֹן בְּשִׁבְעָה
לַחֹדֶשׁ הָיָה דְבַר־יְהוָה אֵלַי לֵאמֹר: 21 בֶּן־אָדָם
אֶת־זְרוֹעַ פַּרְעֹה מֶלֶךְ־מִצְרַיִם שָׁבָרְתִּי וְהִנֵּה לֹא־
חֻבְּשָׁה לָתֵת רְפֻאוֹת לָשׂוּם חִתּוּל לְחָבְשָׁהּ לְחָזְקָהּ
לִתְפֹּשׂ בֶּחָרֶב: ס 22 לָכֵן כֹּה־אָמַר
אֲדֹנָי יְהוִה הִנְנִי אֶל־פַּרְעֹה מֶלֶךְ־מִצְרַיִם וְשָׁבַרְתִּי
אֶת־זְרֹעֹתָיו אֶת־הַחֲזָקָה וְאֶת־הַנִּשְׁבָּרֶת וְהִפַּלְתִּי
אֶת־הַחֶרֶב מִיָּדוֹ: 23 וַהֲפִצוֹתִי אֶת־מִצְרַיִם בַּגּוֹיִם
וְזֵרִיתִם בָּאֲרָצוֹת: 24 וְחִזַּקְתִּי אֶת־זְרֹעוֹת מֶלֶךְ בָּבֶל

will groan before him with the groanings of a mortally wounded *man.* 25 Thus I will strengthen the arms of the king of Babylon, but the arms of Pharaoh shall fall down; they shall know that I *am* the Lord, when I put My sword into the hand of the king of Babylon and he stretches it out against the land of Egypt. 26 I will scatter the Egyptians among the nations and disperse them throughout the countries. Then they shall know that I *am* the Lord.' "

31 Now it came to pass in the eleventh year, in the third *month,* on the first *day* of the month, *that* the word of the Lord came to me, saying, 2 "Son of man, say to Pharaoh king of Egypt and to his multitude:

'Whom are you like in your greatness?
3   Indeed Assyria *was* a cedar in Lebanon,
      With fine branches that shaded the forest,
      And of high stature;
      And its top was among the thick boughs.
4   The waters made it grow;
      Underground waters gave it height,
      With their rivers running around the place where
          it was planted,
      And sent out rivulets to all the trees of the field.
5   'Therefore its height was exalted above all the
          trees of the field;
      Its boughs were multiplied,
      And its branches became long because of the
          abundance of water,
      As it sent them out.
6   All the birds of the heavens made their nests in its
          boughs;
      Under its branches all the beasts of the field
          brought forth their young;
      And in its shadow all great nations made their
          home.
7   'Thus it was beautiful in greatness and in the
          length of its branches,
      Because its roots reached to abundant waters.
8   The cedars in the garden of God could not hide it;
      The fir trees were not like its boughs,
      And the chestnut trees were not like its branches;
      No tree in the garden of God was like it in
          beauty.
9   I made it beautiful with a multitude of branches,
      So that all the trees of Eden envied it,
      That *were* in the garden of God.'

10 "Therefore thus says the Lord God: 'Because you have increased in height, and it set its top among the thick boughs, and its heart was lifted up in its height, 11 therefore I will deliver it into the hand of the mighty one of the nations, and he shall surely deal with it; I have driven it out for its wickedness. 12 And aliens, the most terrible of the nations, have cut it down and left it; its branches

וְנָתַתִּי אֶת־חַרְבִּי בְּיָדוֹ וְשָׁבַרְתִּי אֶת־זְרֹעוֹת פַּרְעֹה
וְנָאַק נַאֲקוֹת חָלָל לְפָנָיו: 25 וְהַחֲזַקְתִּי אֶת־זְרֹעוֹת
מֶלֶךְ בָּבֶל וּזְרֹעוֹת פַּרְעֹה תִּפֹּלְנָה וְיָדְעוּ כִּי־אֲנִי
יְהוָה בְּתִתִּי חַרְבִּי בְּיַד מֶלֶךְ־בָּבֶל וְנָטָה אוֹתָהּ אֶל־
אֶרֶץ מִצְרָיִם: 26 וַהֲפִצוֹתִי אֶת־מִצְרַיִם בַּגּוֹיִם וְזֵרִיתִי
אוֹתָם בָּאֲרָצוֹת וְיָדְעוּ כִּי־אֲנִי יְהוָה: ס

לא וַיְהִי בְּאַחַת עֶשְׂרֵה שָׁנָה בַּשְּׁלִישִׁי בְּאֶחָד
לַחֹדֶשׁ הָיָה דְבַר־יְהוָה אֵלַי לֵאמֹר: 2 בֶּן־אָדָם אֱמֹר
אֶל־פַּרְעֹה מֶלֶךְ־מִצְרַיִם וְאֶל־הֲמוֹנוֹ אֶל־מִי דָּמִיתָ
בְגָדְלֶךָ: 3 הִנֵּה אַשּׁוּר אֶרֶז בַּלְּבָנוֹן יְפֵה עָנָף וְחֹרֶשׁ
מֵצַל וּגְבַהּ קוֹמָה וּבֵין עֲבֹתִים הָיְתָה צַמַּרְתּוֹ:
4 מַיִם גִּדְּלוּהוּ תְּהוֹם רֹמְמָתְהוּ אֶת־נַהֲרֹתֶיהָ הֹלֵךְ
סְבִיבוֹת מַטָּעָהּ וְאֶת־תְּעָלֹתֶיהָ שִׁלְּחָה אֶל כָּל־עֲצֵי
הַשָּׂדֶה: 5 עַל־כֵּן גָּבְהָא קֹמָתוֹ מִכֹּל עֲצֵי הַשָּׂדֶה
וַתִּרְבֶּינָה סַרְעַפֹּתָיו וַתֶּאֱרַכְנָה פֹארֹתָו מִמַּיִם רַבִּים
בְּשַׁלְּחוֹ: 6 בִּסְעַפֹּתָיו קִנְנוּ כָּל־עוֹף הַשָּׁמַיִם וְתַחַת
פֹארֹתָיו יָלְדוּ כֹּל חַיַּת הַשָּׂדֶה וּבְצִלּוֹ יֵשְׁבוּ כֹּל גּוֹיִם
רַבִּים: 7 וַיְּיִף בְּגָדְלוֹ בְּאֹרֶךְ דָּלִיּוֹתָיו כִּי־הָיָה שָׁרְשׁוֹ
אֶל־מַיִם רַבִּים: 8 אֲרָזִים לֹא־עֲמָמֻהוּ בְּגַן־אֱלֹהִים
בְּרוֹשִׁים לֹא דָמוּ אֶל־סְעַפֹּתָיו וְעַרְמֹנִים לֹא־הָיוּ
כְּפֹארֹתָיו כָּל־עֵץ בְּגַן־אֱלֹהִים לֹא־דָמָה אֵלָיו בְּיָפְיוֹ:
9 יָפֶה עֲשִׂיתִיו בְּרֹב דָּלִיּוֹתָיו וַיְקַנְאֻהוּ כָּל־עֲצֵי־
עֵדֶן אֲשֶׁר בְּגַן הָאֱלֹהִים: ס 10 לָכֵן כֹּה אָמַר
אֲדֹנָי יְהוִה יַעַן אֲשֶׁר גָּבַהְתָּ בְּקוֹמָה וַיִּתֵּן צַמַּרְתּוֹ
אֶל־בֵּין עֲבוֹתִים וְרָם לְבָבוֹ בְּגָבְהוֹ: 11 וְאֶתְּנֵהוּ
בְּיַד אֵיל גּוֹיִם עָשׂוֹ יַעֲשֶׂה לוֹ כְּרִשְׁעוֹ גֵּרַשְׁתִּהוּ:
12 וַיִּכְרְתֻהוּ זָרִים עָרִיצֵי גוֹיִם וַיִּטְּשֻׁהוּ אֶל־הֶהָרִים
וּבְכָל־גֵּאָיוֹת נָפְלוּ דָלִיּוֹתָיו וַתִּשָּׁבַרְנָה פֹארֹתָיו בְּכָל־

לא 5 פֹארֹתָיו

have fallen on the mountains and in all the valleys; its boughs lie broken by all the rivers of the land; and all the peoples of the earth have gone from under its shadow and left it.

13 'On its ruin will remain all the birds of the heavens,
And all the beasts of the field will come to its branches—

14 So that no trees by the waters may ever again exalt themselves for their height, nor set their tops among the thick boughs, that no tree which drinks water may ever be high enough to reach up to them.

'For they have all been delivered to death,
To the depths of the earth,
Among the children of men who go down to the Pit.'

15 "Thus says the Lord GOD: 'In the day when it went down to hell, I caused mourning. I covered the deep because of it. I restrained its rivers, and the great waters were held back. I caused Lebanon to mourn for it, and all the trees of the field wilted because of it. 16 I made the nations shake at the sound of its fall, when I cast it down to hell together with those who descend into the Pit; and all the trees of Eden, the choice and best of Lebanon, all that drink water, were comforted in the depths of the earth. 17 They also went down to hell with it, with those *slain* by the sword; and *those who were* its *strong* arm dwelt in its shadows among the nations.

18 'To which of the trees in Eden will you then be likened in glory and greatness? Yet you shall be brought down with the trees of Eden to the depths of the earth; you shall lie in the midst of the uncircumcised, with *those* slain by the sword. This *is* Pharaoh and all his multitude,' says the Lord GOD."

32 And it came to pass in the twelfth year, in the twelfth *month,* on the first *day* of the month, *that* the word of the LORD came to me, saying, 2 "Son of man, take up a lamentation for Pharaoh king of Egypt, and say to him:

'You are like a young lion among the nations,
And you *are* like a monster in the seas,
Bursting forth in your rivers,
Troubling the waters with your feet,
And fouling their rivers.'

3 "Thus says the Lord GOD:

'I will therefore spread My net over you with a company of many people,
And they will draw you up in My net.
4 Then I will leave you on the land;
I will cast you out on the open fields,

אֲפִיקֵי הָאָרֶץ וַיֵּרְדוּ מִצִּלּוֹ כָּל־עַמֵּי הָאָרֶץ וַיִּטְּשֻׁהוּ:
13 עַל־מַפַּלְתּוֹ יִשְׁכְּנוּ כָּל־עוֹף הַשָּׁמָיִם וְאֶל־פֹּארֹתָיו
הָיוּ כָּל חַיַּת הַשָּׂדֶה: 14 לְמַעַן אֲשֶׁר לֹא־יִגְבְּהוּ
בְקוֹמָתָם כָּל־עֲצֵי־מַיִם וְלֹא־יִתְּנוּ אֶת־צַמַּרְתָּם אֶל־
בֵּין עֲבֹתִים וְלֹא־יַעַמְדוּ אֲלֵיהֶם בְּגָבְהָם כָּל־שֹׁתֵי
מָיִם כִּי־כֻלָּם נִתְּנוּ לַמָּוֶת אֶל־אֶרֶץ תַּחְתִּית בְּתוֹךְ
בְּנֵי אָדָם אֶל־יוֹרְדֵי בוֹר: ס 15 כֹּה־אָמַר אֲדֹנָי
יְהוִה בְּיוֹם רִדְתּוֹ שְׁאוֹלָה הֶאֱבַלְתִּי כִּסֵּתִי עָלָיו
אֶת־תְּהוֹם וָאֶמְנַע נַהֲרוֹתֶיהָ וַיִּכָּלְאוּ מַיִם רַבִּים
וָאַקְדִּר עָלָיו לְבָנוֹן וְכָל־עֲצֵי הַשָּׂדֶה עָלָיו עֻלְּפֶּה:
16 מִקּוֹל מַפַּלְתּוֹ הִרְעַשְׁתִּי גוֹיִם בְּהוֹרִדִי אֹתוֹ
שְׁאוֹלָה אֶת־יוֹרְדֵי בוֹר וַיִּנָּחֲמוּ בְּאֶרֶץ תַּחְתִּית כָּל־
עֲצֵי־עֵדֶן מִבְחַר וְטוֹב־לְבָנוֹן כָּל־שֹׁתֵי מָיִם: 17 גַּם־
הֵם אִתּוֹ יָרְדוּ שְׁאוֹלָה אֶל־חַלְלֵי־חָרֶב וּזְרֹעוֹ יָשְׁבוּ
בְצִלּוֹ בְּתוֹךְ גּוֹיִם: 18 אֶל־מִי דָמִיתָ כָּכָה בְּכָבוֹד
וּבְגֹדֶל בַּעֲצֵי־עֵדֶן וְהוֹרַדְתָּ אֶת־עֲצֵי־עֵדֶן אֶל־אֶרֶץ
תַּחְתִּית בְּתוֹךְ עֲרֵלִים תִּשְׁכַּב אֶת־חַלְלֵי־חֶרֶב הוּא
פַרְעֹה וְכָל־הֲמוֹנֹהP נְאֻם אֲדֹנָי יְהוִה: ס

לב וַיְהִי בִּשְׁתֵּי עֶשְׂרֵה שָׁנָה בִּשְׁנֵי־עָשָׂר חֹדֶשׁ
בְּאֶחָד לַחֹדֶשׁ הָיָה דְבַר־יְהוָה אֵלַי לֵאמֹר: 2 בֶּן־
אָדָם שָׂא קִינָה עַל־פַּרְעֹה מֶלֶךְ־מִצְרַיִם וְאָמַרְתָּ
אֵלָיו כְּפִיר גּוֹיִם נִדְמֵיתָ וְאַתָּה כַּתַּנִּים בַּיַּמִּים וַתָּגַח
בְּנַהֲרוֹתֶיךָ וַתִּדְלַח־מַיִם בְּרַגְלֶיךָ וַתִּרְפָּס נַהֲרוֹתָם:
3 כֹּה אָמַר אֲדֹנָי יְהוִה וּפָרַשְׂתִּי עָלֶיךָ אֶת־רִשְׁתִּי
בִּקְהַל עַמִּים רַבִּים וְהֶעֱלוּךָ בְּחֶרְמִי: 4 וּנְטַשְׁתִּיךָ
בָאָרֶץ עַל־פְּנֵי הַשָּׂדֶה אֲטִילֶךָ וְהִשְׁכַּנְתִּי עָלֶיךָ
כָּל־עוֹף הַשָּׁמָיִם וְהִשְׂבַּעְתִּי מִמְּךָ חַיַּת כָּל־הָאָרֶץ:

And cause to settle on you all the birds of the
heavens.
And with you I will fill the beasts of the whole
earth.

5 I will lay your flesh on the mountains,
And fill the valleys with your carcass.

6 'I will also water the land with the flow of your
blood,
Even to the mountains;
And the riverbeds will be full of you.

7 When *I* put out your light,
I will cover the heavens, and make its stars dark;
I will cover the sun with a cloud,
And the moon shall not give her light.

8 All the bright lights of the heavens I will make
dark over you,
And bring darkness upon your land,'
Says the Lord GOD.

9 'I will also trouble the hearts of many peoples,
when I bring your destruction among the nations,
into the countries which you have not known.
10 Yes, I will make many peoples astonished at you,
and their kings shall be horribly afraid of you when
I brandish My sword before them; and they shall
tremble *every* moment, every man for his own life,
in the day of your fall.'

11 "For thus says the Lord GOD: 'The sword of
the king of Babylon shall come upon you. 12 By the
swords of the mighty warriors, all of them the most
terrible of the nations, I will cause your multitude
to fall.

'They shall plunder the pomp of Egypt,
And all its multitude shall be destroyed.

13 Also I will destroy all its animals
From beside its great waters,
The foot of man shall muddy them no more,
Nor shall the hooves of animals muddy them.

14 Then I will make their waters clear,
And make their rivers run like oil,'
Says the Lord GOD.

15 'When I make the land of Egypt desolate,
And the country is destitute of all that once filled
it,
When I strike all who dwell in it,
Then they shall know that I *am* the LORD.

16 'This *is* the lamentation
With which they shall lament her;
The daughters of the nations shall lament her;
They shall lament for her, for Egypt,
And for all her multitude,'
Says the Lord GOD."

17 It came to pass also in the twelfth year, on the
fifteenth *day* of the month, *that* the word of the
LORD came to me, saying:

18 "Son of man, wail over the multitude of Egypt,
And cast them down to the depths of the earth,
Her and the daughters of the famous nations,

5 וְנָתַתִּי אֶת־בְּשָׂרְךָ עַל־הֶהָרִים וּמִלֵּאתִי הַגֵּאָיוֹת
רָמוּתֶךָ: 6 וְהִשְׁקֵיתִי אֶרֶץ צָפָתְךָ מִדָּמְךָ אֶל־הֶהָרִים
וַאֲפִקִים יִמָּלְאוּן מִמֶּךָּ: 7 וְכִסֵּיתִי בְכַבּוֹתְךָ שָׁמַיִם
וְהִקְדַּרְתִּי אֶת־כֹּכְבֵיהֶם שֶׁמֶשׁ בֶּעָנָן אֲכַסֶּנּוּ וְיָרֵחַ
לֹא־יָאִיר אוֹרוֹ: 8 כָּל־מְאוֹרֵי אוֹר בַּשָּׁמַיִם אַקְדִּירֵם
עָלֶיךָ וְנָתַתִּי חֹשֶׁךְ עַל־אַרְצְךָ נְאֻם אֲדֹנָי יְהוִה:

9 וְהִכְעַסְתִּי לֵב עַמִּים רַבִּים בַּהֲבִיאִי שִׁבְרְךָ בַּגּוֹיִם
עַל־אֲרָצוֹת אֲשֶׁר לֹא־יְדַעְתָּם: 10 וַהֲשִׁמּוֹתִי עָלֶיךָ
עַמִּים רַבִּים וּמַלְכֵיהֶם יִשְׂעֲרוּ עָלֶיךָ שַׂעַר בְּעוֹפְפִי
חַרְבִּי עַל־פְּנֵיהֶם וְחָרְדוּ לִרְגָעִים אִישׁ לְנַפְשׁוֹ
בְּיוֹם מַפַּלְתֶּךָ:   ס   11 כִּי כֹּה אָמַר אֲדֹנָי
יְהוִה חֶרֶב מֶלֶךְ־בָּבֶל תְּבוֹאֶךָ: 12 בְּחַרְבוֹת גִּבּוֹרִים
אַפִּיל הֲמוֹנֶךָ עָרִיצֵי גוֹיִם כֻּלָּם וְשָׁדְדוּ אֶת־גְּאוֹן
מִצְרַיִם וְנִשְׁמַד כָּל־הֲמוֹנָהּ: 13 וְהַאֲבַדְתִּי אֶת־כָּל־
בְּהֶמְתָּהּ מֵעַל מַיִם רַבִּים וְלֹא תִדְלָחֵם רֶגֶל־אָדָם
עוֹד וּפַרְסוֹת בְּהֵמָה לֹא תִדְלָחֵם: 14 אָז אַשְׁקִיעַ
מֵימֵיהֶם וְנַהֲרוֹתָם כַּשֶּׁמֶן אוֹלִיךְ נְאֻם אֲדֹנָי יְהוִה:

15 בְּתִתִּי אֶת־אֶרֶץ מִצְרַיִם שְׁמָמָה וּנְשַׁמָּה אֶרֶץ
מִמְּלֹאָהּ בְּהַכּוֹתִי אֶת־כָּל־יוֹשְׁבֵי בָהּ וְיָדְעוּ כִּי־אֲנִי
יְהוִה: 16 קִינָה הִיא וְקוֹנְנוּהָ בְּנוֹת הַגּוֹיִם תְּקוֹנֵנָּה
אוֹתָהּ עַל־מִצְרַיִם וְעַל־כָּל־הֲמוֹנָהּ תְּקוֹנֵנָּה אוֹתָהּ
נְאֻם אֲדֹנָי יְהוִה: פ

17 וַיְהִי בִּשְׁתֵּי עֶשְׂרֵה שָׁנָה בַּחֲמִשָּׁה עָשָׂר לַחֹדֶשׁ
הָיָה דְבַר־יְהוָה אֵלַי לֵאמֹר: 18 בֶּן־אָדָם נְהֵה

עַל־הֲמוֹן מִצְרַיִם וְהוֹרִדֻהוּ אוֹתָהּ וּבְנוֹת גּוֹיִם

אַדִּרִם אֶל־אֶרֶץ תַּחְתִּיּוֹת אֶת־יוֹרְדֵי בוֹר: 19 מִמִּי

נָעַמְתָּ רְדָה וְהָשְׁכְּבָה אֶת־עֲרֵלִים: 20 בְּתוֹךְ חַלְלֵי־

חֶרֶב יִפֹּלוּ חֶרֶב נִתָּנָה מָשְׁכוּ אוֹתָהּ וְכָל־הֲמוֹנֶיהָ:

21 יְדַבְּרוּ־לוֹ אֵלֵי גִבּוֹרִים מִתּוֹךְ שְׁאוֹל אֶת־עֹזְרָיו

יָרְדוּ שָׁכְבוּ הָעֲרֵלִים חַלְלֵי־חָרֶב: 22 שָׁם אַשּׁוּר

וְכָל־קְהָלָהּ סְבִיבוֹתָיו קִבְרֹתָיו כֻּלָּם חֲלָלִים הַנֹּפְלִים

בֶּחָרֶב: 23 אֲשֶׁר נִתְּנוּ קִבְרֹתֶיהָ בְּיַרְכְּתֵי־בוֹר וַיְהִי

קְהָלָהּ סְבִיבוֹת קְבֻרָתָהּ כֻּלָּם חֲלָלִים נֹפְלִים בַּחֶרֶב

אֲשֶׁר־נָתְנוּ חִתִּית בְּאֶרֶץ חַיִּים: 24 שָׁם עֵילָם וְכָל־

הֲמוֹנָהּ סְבִיבוֹת קְבֻרָתָהּ כֻּלָּם חֲלָלִים הַנֹּפְלִים

בַּחֶרֶב אֲשֶׁר־יָרְדוּ עֲרֵלִים ׀ אֶל־אֶרֶץ תַּחְתִּיּוֹת

אֲשֶׁר נָתְנוּ חִתִּיתָם בְּאֶרֶץ חַיִּים וַיִּשְׂאוּ כְלִמָּתָם

אֶת־יוֹרְדֵי בוֹר: 25 בְּתוֹךְ חֲלָלִים נָתְנוּ מִשְׁכָּב לָהּ

בְּכָל־הֲמוֹנָהּ סְבִיבוֹתָיו קִבְרֹתֶהָ כֻּלָּם עֲרֵלִים חַלְלֵי־

חֶרֶב כִּי־נִתַּן חִתִּיתָם בְּאֶרֶץ חַיִּים וַיִּשְׂאוּ כְלִמָּתָם

אֶת־יוֹרְדֵי בוֹר בְּתוֹךְ חֲלָלִים נִתָּן: 26 שָׁם מֶשֶׁךְ

תֻּבַל וְכָל־הֲמוֹנָהּ סְבִיבוֹתָיו קִבְרוֹתֶיהָ כֻּלָּם עֲרֵלִים

מְחֻלְלֵי חֶרֶב כִּי־נָתְנוּ חִתִּיתָם בְּאֶרֶץ חַיִּים: 27 וְלֹא

יִשְׁכְּבוּ אֶת־גִּבּוֹרִים נֹפְלִים מֵעֲרֵלִים אֲשֶׁר יָרְדוּ־

שְׁאוֹל בִּכְלֵי־מִלְחַמְתָּם וַיִּתְּנוּ אֶת־חַרְבוֹתָם תַּחַת

רָאשֵׁיהֶם וַתְּהִי עֲוֹנֹתָם עַל־עַצְמוֹתָם כִּי־חִתִּית

גִּבּוֹרִים בְּאֶרֶץ חַיִּים: 28 וְאַתָּה בְּתוֹךְ עֲרֵלִים תִּשָּׁבֵר

וְתִשְׁכַּב אֶת־חַלְלֵי־חָרֶב: 29 שָׁמָּה אֱדוֹם מְלָכֶיהָ

וְכָל־נְשִׂיאֶיהָ אֲשֶׁר־נִתְּנוּ בִגְבוּרָתָם אֶת־חַלְלֵי־חָרֶב

English (left column)

With those who go down to the Pit:
19 'Whom do you surpass in beauty?
   Go down, be placed with the uncircumcised.'

20 "They shall fall in the midst of *those* slain by the sword;
   She is delivered to the sword,
   Drawing her and all her multitudes.
21 The strong among the mighty
   Shall speak to him out of the midst of hell
   With those who help him:
   'They have gone down,
   They lie with the uncircumcised, slain by the sword.'

22 "Assyria *is* there, and all her company,
   With their graves all around her,
   All of them slain, fallen by the sword.
23 Her graves are set in the recesses of the Pit,
   And her company is all around her grave,
   All of them slain, fallen by the sword,
   Who caused terror in the land of the living.

24 "There *is* Elam and all her multitude,
   All around her grave,
   All of them slain, fallen by the sword,
   Who have gone down uncircumcised to the lower
      parts of the earth,
   Who caused their terror in the land of the living;
   Now they bear their shame with those who go
      down to the Pit.
25 They have set her bed in the midst of the slain,
   With all her multitude,
   With her graves all around it,
   All of them uncircumcised, slain by the sword;
   Though their terror was caused
   In the land of the living,
   Yet they bear their shame
   With those who go down to the Pit;
   It was put in the midst of the slain.

26 "There *are* Meshech and Tubal and all their
      multitudes,
   With all their graves around it,
   All of them uncircumcised, slain by the sword,
   Though they caused their terror in the land of the
      living.
27 They do not lie with the mighty
   Who are fallen of the uncircumcised,
   Who have gone down to hell with their weapons
      of war;
   They have laid their swords under their heads,
   But their iniquities will be on their bones,
   Because of the terror of the mighty in the land of
      the living.
28 Yes, you shall be broken in the midst of the
      uncircumcised,
   And lie with *those* slain by the sword.

29 "There *is* Edom,
   Her kings and all her princes,
   Who despite their might
   Are laid beside *those* slain by the sword;
   They shall lie with the uncircumcised,
   And with those who go down to the Pit.

30 There *are* the princes of the north,
All of them, and all the Sidonians,
Who have gone down with the slain
In shame at the terror which they caused by their
might;
They lie uncircumcised with *those* slain by the
sword,
And bear their shame with those who go down to
the Pit.

31 "Pharaoh will see them
And be comforted over all his multitude,
Pharaoh and all his army,
Slain by the sword,"
Says the Lord GOD.

32 "For I have caused My terror in the land of the
living;
And he shall be placed in the midst of the
uncircumcised
With *those* slain by the sword,
Pharaoh and all his multitude,"
Says the Lord GOD.

33 Again the word of the LORD came to me,
saying, 2 "Son of man, speak to the children of your
people, and say to them: 'When I bring the sword
upon a land, and the people of the land take a man
from their territory and make him their watchman,
3 when he sees the sword coming upon the land, if
he blows the trumpet and warns the people, 4 then
whoever hears the sound of the trumpet and does
not take warning, if the sword comes and takes him
away, his blood shall be on his *own* head. 5 He heard
the sound of the trumpet, but did not take warning;
his blood shall be upon himself. But he who takes
warning will save his life. 6 But if the watchman sees
the sword coming and does not blow the trumpet,
and the people are not warned, and the sword
comes and takes *any* person from among them, he is
taken away in his iniquity; but his blood I will
require at the watchman's hand.'

7 "So you, son of man: I have made you a
watchman for the house of Israel; therefore you
shall hear a word from My mouth and warn them
for Me. 8 When I say to the wicked, 'O wicked *man*,
you shall surely die!' and you do not speak to warn
the wicked from his way, that wicked *man* shall die
in his iniquity; but his blood I will require at your
hand. 9 Nevertheless if you warn the wicked to turn
from his way, and he does not turn from his way, he
shall die in his iniquity; but you have delivered your
soul.

10 "Therefore you, O son of man, say to the
house of Israel: 'Thus you say, "If our transgressions and our sins *lie* upon us, and we pine away in
them, how can we then live?" ' 11 Say to them: 'As I
live,' says the Lord GOD, 'I have no pleasure in the

הֵ֣מָּה אֶת־עֲרֵלִ֑ים יִשְׁכְּב֖וּ וְאֶת־יֹרְדֵ֥י בֽוֹר׃ 30 שָׁ֣מָּה

נְסִיכֵ֨י צָפ֤וֹן כֻּלָּם֙ וְכָל־צִ֣דֹנִ֔י אֲשֶׁר־יָרְד֖וּ אֶת־

חֲלָלִ֑ים בְּחִתִּיתָ֣ם מִגְבֽוּרָתָ֣ם בּוֹשִׁ֔ים וַיִּשְׁכְּב֣וּ עֲרֵלִ֗ים

אֶת־חַלְלֵי־חֶ֔רֶב וַיִּשְׂא֥וּ כְלִמָּתָ֖ם אֶת־יֹ֥רְדֵי בֽוֹר׃

31 אוֹתָם֙ יִרְאֶ֣ה פַרְעֹ֔ה וְנִחַ֖ם עַל־כָּל־הֲמוֹנֹ֑הP חַלְלֵי־

חֶ֛רֶב פַּרְעֹ֥ה וְכָל־חֵיל֖וֹ נְאֻ֥ם אֲדֹנָ֥י יְהוִֽה׃ 32 כִּֽי־

נָתַ֥תִּי אֶת־חִתִּיתִיP בְּאֶ֣רֶץ חַיִּ֑ים וְהֻשְׁכַּב֩ בְּת֨וֹךְ

עֲרֵלִ֜ים אֶת־חַלְלֵי־חֶ֗רֶב פַּרְעֹה֙ וְכָל־הֲמוֹנֹהP֔ נְאֻ֖ם

אֲדֹנָ֥י יְהוִֽה׃

P

לג וַיְהִ֥י דְבַר־יְהוָ֖ה אֵלַ֥י לֵאמֹֽר׃ 2 בֶּן־אָדָ֗ם דַּבֵּ֤ר

אֶל־בְּנֵֽי־עַמְּךָ֙ וְאָמַרְתָּ֣ אֲלֵיהֶ֔ם אֶ֕רֶץ כִּֽי־אָבִ֥יא עָלֶ֖יהָ

חָ֑רֶב וְלָקְח֣וּ עַם־הָאָ֩רֶץ֩ אִ֨ישׁ אֶחָ֤ד מִקְצֵיהֶם֙ וְנָתְנ֤וּ

אֹתוֹ֙ לָהֶ֣ם לְצֹפֶֽה׃ 3 וְרָאָ֥ה אֶת־הַחֶ֖רֶב בָּאָ֣ה עַל־

הָאָ֑רֶץ וְתָקַ֥ע בַּשּׁוֹפָ֖ר וְהִזְהִ֥יר אֶת־הָעָֽם׃ 4 וְשָׁמַ֣ע

הַשֹּׁמֵ֣עַ אֶת־ק֣וֹל הַשּׁוֹפָר֮ וְלֹ֣א נִזְהָר֒ וַתָּב֤וֹא חֶ֙רֶב֙

וַתִּקָּחֵ֔הוּ דָּמ֖וֹ בְרֹאשׁ֥וֹ יִהְיֶֽה׃ 5 אֵת֩ ק֨וֹל הַשּׁוֹפָ֤ר

שָׁמַע֙ וְלֹ֣א נִזְהָ֔ר דָּמ֖וֹ בּ֣וֹ יִהְיֶ֑ה וְה֥וּא נִזְהָ֖ר נַפְשׁ֥וֹ

מִלֵּֽט׃ 6 וְ֠הַצֹּפֶה כִּֽי־יִרְאֶ֨ה אֶת־הַחֶ֜רֶב בָּאָ֗ה וְלֹֽא־

תָקַ֤ע בַּשּׁוֹפָר֙ וְהָעָ֣ם לֹֽא־נִזְהָ֔ר וַתָּב֣וֹא חֶ֗רֶב וַתִּקַּ֤ח

מֵהֶם֙ נָ֔פֶשׁ ה֖וּא בַּעֲוֺנ֣וֹ נִלְקָ֑ח וְדָמ֖וֹ מִיַּֽד־הַצֹּפֶ֥ה

אֶדְרֹֽשׁ׃ ס 7 וְאַתָּ֣ה בֶן־אָדָ֗ם צֹפֶ֥ה נְתַתִּ֖יךָ

לְבֵ֣ית יִשְׂרָאֵ֑ל וְשָׁמַעְתָּ֤ מִפִּי֙ דָּבָ֔ר וְהִזְהַרְתָּ֥ אֹתָ֖ם

מִמֶּֽנִּי׃ 8 בְּאָמְרִ֣י לָרָשָׁ֗ע רָשָׁע֙ מ֣וֹת תָּמ֔וּת וְלֹ֣א

דִבַּ֔רְתָּ לְהַזְהִ֥יר רָשָׁ֖ע מִדַּרְכּ֑וֹ ה֤וּא רָשָׁע֙ בַּעֲוֺנ֣וֹ

יָמ֔וּת וְדָמ֖וֹ מִיָּדְךָ֥ אֲבַקֵּֽשׁ׃ 9 וְ֠אַתָּה כִּֽי־הִזְהַ֨רְתָּ רָשָׁ֤ע

מִדַּרְכּוֹ֙ לָשׁ֣וּב מִמֶּ֔נָּה וְלֹא־שָׁ֖ב מִדַּרְכּ֑וֹ ה֤וּא בַּעֲוֺנ֣וֹ

יָמ֔וּת וְאַתָּ֖ה נַפְשְׁךָ֥ הִצַּֽלְתָּ׃ ס 10 וְאַתָּ֣ה

בֶן־אָדָ֗ם אֱמֹר֙ אֶל־בֵּ֣ית יִשְׂרָאֵ֔ל כֵּ֤ן אֲמַרְתֶּם֙ לֵאמֹ֔ר

כִּֽי־פְשָׁעֵ֤ינוּ וְחַטֹּאתֵ֙ינוּ֙ עָלֵ֔ינוּ וּבָ֖ם אֲנַ֣חְנוּ נְמַקִּ֑ים

וְאֵ֖יךְ נִֽחְיֶֽה׃ 11 אֱמֹ֨ר אֲלֵיהֶ֜ם חַי־אָ֣נִי ׀ נְאֻ֣ם ׀

אֲדֹנָ֣י יְהוִ֗ה אִם־אֶחְפֹּץ֙ בְּמ֣וֹת הָרָשָׁ֔ע כִּ֣י אִם־בְּשׁ֨וּב

לב 31 הֲמוֹנֹו 32 חִתִּיתִי הֲמוֹנֹו

death of the wicked, but that the wicked turn from his way and live. Turn, turn from your evil ways! For why should you die, O house of Israel?'

12 "Therefore you, O son of man, say to the children of your people: 'The righteousness of the righteous man shall not deliver him in the day of his transgression; as for the wickedness of the wicked, he shall not fall because of it in the day that he turns from his wickedness; nor shall the righteous be able to live because of *his righteousness* in the day that he sins.' 13 When I say to the righteous *that* he shall surely live, but he trusts in his own righteousness and commits iniquity, none of his righteous works shall be remembered; but because of the iniquity that he has committed, he shall die. 14 Again, when I say to the wicked, 'You shall surely die,' if he turns from his sin and does what is lawful and right, 15 *if* the wicked restores the pledge, gives back what he has stolen, and walks in the statutes of life without committing iniquity, he shall surely live; he shall not die. 16 None of his sins which he has committed shall be remembered against him; he has done what is lawful and right; he shall surely live.

17 "Yet the children of your people say, 'The way of the LORD is not fair.' But it is their way which is not fair! 18 When the righteous turns from his righteousness and commits iniquity, he shall die because of it. 19 But when the wicked turns from his wickedness and does what is lawful and right, he shall live because of it. 20 Yet you say, 'The way of the LORD is not fair.' O house of Israel, I will judge every one of you according to his own ways."

21 And it came to pass in the twelfth year of our captivity, in the tenth *month,* on the fifth *day* of the month, *that* one who had escaped from Jerusalem came to me and said, "The city has been captured!"

22 Now the hand of the LORD had been upon me the evening before the man came who had escaped. And He had opened my mouth; so when he came to me in the morning, my mouth was opened, and I was no longer mute.

23 Then the word of the LORD came to me, saying: 24 "Son of man, they who inhabit those ruins in the land of Israel are saying, 'Abraham was only one, and he inherited the land. But we *are* many; the land has been given to us as a possession.'

25 "Therefore say to them, 'Thus says the Lord GOD: "You eat *meat* with blood, you lift up your eyes toward your idols, and shed blood. Should you then possess the land? 26 You rely on your sword, you commit abominations, and you defile one another's wives. Should you then possess the land?" '

רָשָׁע מִדַּרְכּוֹ וְחָיָה שׁוּבוּ שׁוּבוּ מִדַּרְכֵיכֶם הָרָעִים
וְלָמָּה תָמוּתוּ בֵּית יִשְׂרָאֵל: פ

12 וְאַתָּה בֶן־אָדָם אֱמֹר אֶל־בְּנֵי־עַמְּךָ צִדְקַת הַצַּדִּיק
לֹא תַצִּילֶנּוּ בְּיוֹם פִּשְׁעוֹ וְרִשְׁעַת הָרָשָׁע לֹא־יִכָּשֶׁל
בָּהּ בְּיוֹם שׁוּבוֹ מֵרִשְׁעוֹ וְצַדִּיק לֹא יוּכַל לִחְיוֹת
בָּהּ בְּיוֹם חֲטֹאתוֹ: 13 בְּאָמְרִי לַצַּדִּיק חָיֹה יִחְיֶה
וְהוּא־בָטַח עַל־צִדְקָתוֹ וְעָשָׂה עָוֶל כָּל־צִדְקֹתָו לֹא
תִזָּכַרְנָה וּבְעַוְלוֹ אֲשֶׁר־עָשָׂה בּוֹ יָמוּת: 14 וּבְאָמְרִי
לָרָשָׁע מוֹת תָּמוּת וְשָׁב מֵחַטָּאתוֹ וְעָשָׂה מִשְׁפָּט
וּצְדָקָה: 15 חֲבֹל יָשִׁיב רָשָׁע גְּזֵלָה יְשַׁלֵּם בְּחֻקּוֹת
הַחַיִּים הָלַךְ לְבִלְתִּי עֲשׂוֹת עָוֶל חָיוֹ יִחְיֶה לֹא
יָמוּת: 16 כָּל־חַטֹּאתָו אֲשֶׁר חָטָא לֹא תִזָּכַרְנָה
לוֹ מִשְׁפָּט וּצְדָקָה עָשָׂה חָיוֹ יִחְיֶה: 17 וְאָמְרוּ בְּנֵי
עַמְּךָ לֹא יִתָּכֵן דֶּרֶךְ אֲדֹנָי וְהֵמָּה דַּרְכָּם לֹא־יִתָּכֵן:
18 בְּשׁוּב־צַדִּיק מִצִּדְקָתוֹ וְעָשָׂה עָוֶל וּמֵת בָּהֶם:
19 וּבְשׁוּב רָשָׁע מֵרִשְׁעָתוֹ וְעָשָׂה מִשְׁפָּט וּצְדָקָה
עֲלֵיהֶם הוּא יִחְיֶה: 20 וַאֲמַרְתֶּם לֹא יִתָּכֵן דֶּרֶךְ
אֲדֹנָי אִישׁ כִּדְרָכָיו אֶשְׁפּוֹט אֶתְכֶם בֵּית יִשְׂרָאֵל: פ

21 וַיְהִי בִּשְׁתֵּי עֶשְׂרֵה שָׁנָה בָּעֲשִׂרִי בַּחֲמִשָּׁה לַחֹדֶשׁ
לְגָלוּתֵנוּ בָּא־אֵלַי הַפָּלִיט מִירוּשָׁלַ͏ִם לֵאמֹר הֻכְּתָה
הָעִיר: 22 וְיַד־יְהֹוָה הָיְתָה אֵלַי בָּעֶרֶב לִפְנֵי בּוֹא
הַפָּלִיט וַיִּפְתַּח אֶת־פִּי עַד־בּוֹא אֵלַי בַּבֹּקֶר וַיִּפָּתַח
פִּי וְלֹא נֶאֱלַמְתִּי עוֹד: פ

23 וַיְהִי דְבַר־יְהֹוָה אֵלַי לֵאמֹר: 24 בֶּן־אָדָם יֹשְׁבֵי
הֶחֳרָבוֹת הָאֵלֶּה עַל־אַדְמַת יִשְׂרָאֵל אֹמְרִים לֵאמֹר
אֶחָד הָיָה אַבְרָהָם וַיִּירַשׁ אֶת־הָאָרֶץ וַאֲנַחְנוּ רַבִּים
לָנוּ נִתְּנָה הָאָרֶץ לְמוֹרָשָׁה: ס 25 לָכֵן
אֱמֹר אֲלֵהֶם כֹּה־אָמַר אֲדֹנָי יְהֹוִה עַל־הַדָּם
תֹּאכֵלוּ וְעֵינֵכֶם תִּשְׂאוּ אֶל־גִּלּוּלֵיכֶם וְדָם תִּשְׁפֹּכוּ
וְהָאָרֶץ תִּירָשׁוּ: 26 עֲמַדְתֶּם עַל־חַרְבְּכֶם עֲשִׂיתֶן
תּוֹעֵבָה וְאִישׁ אֶת־אֵשֶׁת רֵעֵהוּ טִמֵּאתֶם וְהָאָרֶץ

לג 13 צִדְקֹתָיו   16 חַטֹּאתָיו

27 "Say thus to them, 'Thus says the Lord GOD: "*As* I live, surely those who *are* in the ruins shall fall by the sword, and the one who *is* in the open field I will give to the beasts to be devoured, and those who *are* in the strongholds and caves shall die of the pestilence. 28 For I will make the land most desolate, her arrogant strength shall cease, and the mountains of Israel shall be so desolate that no one will pass through. 29 Then they shall know that I *am* the LORD, when I have made the land most desolate because of all their abominations which they have committed." '

30 "As for you, son of man, the children of your people are talking about you beside the walls and in the doors of the houses; and they speak to one another, everyone saying to his brother, 'Please come and hear what the word is that comes from the LORD.' 31 So they come to you as people do, they sit before you *as* My people, and they hear your words, but they do not do them; for with their mouth they show much love, *but* their hearts pursue their *own* gain. 32 Indeed you *are* to them as a very lovely song of one who has a pleasant voice and can play well on an instrument; for they hear your words, but they do not do them. 33 And when this comes to pass—surely it will come—then they will know that a prophet has been among them."

34 And the word of the LORD came to me, saying, 2 "Son of man, prophesy against the shepherds of Israel, prophesy and say to them, 'Thus says the Lord GOD to the shepherds: "Woe to the shepherds of Israel who feed themselves! Should not the shepherds feed the flocks? 3 You eat the fat and clothe yourselves with the wool; you slaughter the fatlings, *but* you do not feed the flock. 4 The weak you have not strengthened, nor have you healed those who were sick, nor bound up the broken, nor brought back what was driven away, nor sought what was lost; but with force and cruelty you have ruled them. 5 So they were scattered because *there was* no shepherd; and they became food for all the beasts of the field when they were scattered. 6 My sheep wandered through all the mountains, and on every high hill; yes, My flock was scattered over the whole face of the earth, and no one was seeking or searching *for them.*"

7 'Therefore, you shepherds, hear the word of the LORD: 8 "*As* I live," says the Lord GOD, "surely because My flock became a prey, and My flock became food for every beast of the field, because *there was* no shepherd, nor did My shepherds search for My flock, but the shepherds fed themselves and did not feed My flock"— 9 there-

27 כֹּה־תֹאמַר אֲלֵהֶם כֹּה־אָמַר ס תִּירָשׁוּ:

אֲדֹנָי יְהוִה חַי־אָנִי אִם־לֹא אֲשֶׁר בֶּחֳרָבוֹת בַּחֶרֶב

יִפֹּלוּ וַאֲשֶׁר עַל־פְּנֵי הַשָּׂדֶה לַחַיָּה נְתַתִּיו לְאָכְלוֹ

וַאֲשֶׁר בַּמְּצָדוֹת וּבַמְּעָרוֹת בַּדֶּבֶר יָמוּתוּ: 28 וְנָתַתִּי

אֶת־הָאָרֶץ שְׁמָמָה וּמְשַׁמָּה וְנִשְׁבַּת גְּאוֹן עֻזָּהּ

וְשָׁמְמוּ הָרֵי יִשְׂרָאֵל מֵאֵין עוֹבֵר: 29 וְיָדְעוּ כִּי־

אֲנִי יְהוָה בְּתִתִּי אֶת־הָאָרֶץ שְׁמָמָה וּמְשַׁמָּה עַל

כָּל־תּוֹעֲבֹתָם אֲשֶׁר עָשׂוּ: ס 30 וְאַתָּה בֶן־

אָדָם בְּנֵי עַמְּךָ הַנִּדְבָּרִים בְּךָ אֵצֶל הַקִּירוֹת וּבְפִתְחֵי

הַבָּתִּים וְדִבֶּר־חַד אֶת־אַחַד אִישׁ אֶת־אָחִיו לֵאמֹר

בֹּאוּ־נָא וְשִׁמְעוּ מָה הַדָּבָר הַיּוֹצֵא מֵאֵת יְהוָה:

31 וְיָבוֹאוּ אֵלֶיךָ כִּמְבוֹא־עָם וְיֵשְׁבוּ לְפָנֶיךָ עַמִּי

וְשָׁמְעוּ אֶת־דְּבָרֶיךָ וְאוֹתָם לֹא יַעֲשׂוּ כִּי־עֲגָבִים

בְּפִיהֶם הֵמָּה עֹשִׂים אַחֲרֵי בִצְעָם לִבָּם הֹלֵךְ:

32 וְהִנְּךָ לָהֶם כְּשִׁיר עֲגָבִים יְפֵה קוֹל וּמֵטִב נַגֵּן

וְשָׁמְעוּ אֶת־דְּבָרֶיךָ וְעֹשִׂים אֵינָם אוֹתָם: 33 וּבְבֹאָהּ

הִנֵּה בָאָה וְיָדְעוּ כִּי נָבִיא הָיָה בְתוֹכָם: ס

לד וַיְהִי דְבַר־יְהוָה אֵלַי לֵאמֹר: 2 בֶּן־אָדָם הִנָּבֵא

עַל־רוֹעֵי יִשְׂרָאֵל הִנָּבֵא וְאָמַרְתָּ אֲלֵיהֶם לָרֹעִים

כֹּה־אָמַר אֲדֹנָי יְהוִה הוֹי רֹעֵי־יִשְׂרָאֵל אֲשֶׁר

הָיוּ רֹעִים אוֹתָם הֲלוֹא הַצֹּאן יִרְעוּ הָרֹעִים:

3 אֶת־הַחֵלֶב תֹּאכֵלוּ וְאֶת־הַצֶּמֶר תִּלְבָּשׁוּ הַבְּרִיאָה

תִּזְבָּחוּ הַצֹּאן לֹא תִרְעוּ: 4 אֶת־הַנַּחְלוֹת לֹא

חִזַּקְתֶּם וְאֶת־הַחוֹלָה לֹא־רִפֵּאתֶם וְלַנִּשְׁבֶּרֶת לֹא

חֲבַשְׁתֶּם וְאֶת־הַנִּדַּחַת לֹא הֲשֵׁבֹתֶם וְאֶת־הָאֹבֶדֶת

לֹא בִקַּשְׁתֶּם וּבְחָזְקָה רְדִיתֶם אֹתָם וּבְפָרֶךְ:

5 וַתְּפוּצֶינָה מִבְּלִי רֹעֶה וַתִּהְיֶינָה לְאָכְלָה לְכָל־

חַיַּת הַשָּׂדֶה וַתְּפוּצֶינָה: 6 יִשְׁגּוּ צֹאנִי בְּכָל־הֶהָרִים

וְעַל כָּל־גִּבְעָה רָמָה וְעַל כָּל־פְּנֵי הָאָרֶץ נָפֹצוּ

צֹאנִי וְאֵין דּוֹרֵשׁ וְאֵין מְבַקֵּשׁ: 7 לָכֵן רֹעִים שִׁמְעוּ

אֶת־דְּבַר יְהוָה: 8 חַי־אָנִי נְאֻם אֲדֹנָי יְהוִה

אִם־לֹא יַעַן הֱיוֹת־צֹאנִי לָבַז וַתִּהְיֶינָה צֹאנִי

לְאָכְלָה לְכָל־חַיַּת הַשָּׂדֶה מֵאֵין רֹעֶה וְלֹא־דָרְשׁוּ

רֹעַי אֶת־צֹאנִי וַיִּרְעוּ הָרֹעִים אוֹתָם וְאֶת־צֹאנִי

לֹא רָעוּ: 9 לָכֵן הָרֹעִים שִׁמְעוּ דְּבַר־ ס

fore, O shepherds, hear the word of the LORD! ¹⁰Thus says the Lord GOD: "Behold, I *am* against the shepherds, and I will require My flock at their hand; I will cause them to cease feeding the sheep, and the shepherds shall feed themselves no more; for I will deliver My flock from their mouths, that they may no longer be food for them."

¹¹'For thus says the Lord GOD: "Indeed I Myself will search for My sheep and seek them out. ¹²As a shepherd seeks out his flock on the day he is among his scattered sheep, so will I seek out My sheep and deliver them from all the places where they were scattered on a cloudy and dark day. ¹³And I will bring them out from the peoples and gather them from the countries, and will bring them to their own land; I will feed them on the mountains of Israel, in the valleys and in all the inhabited places of the country. ¹⁴I will feed them in good pasture, and their fold shall be on the high mountains of Israel. There they shall lie down in a good fold and feed in rich pasture on the mountains of Israel. ¹⁵I will feed My flock, and I will make them lie down," says the Lord GOD. ¹⁶"I will seek what was lost and bring back what was driven away, bind up the broken and strengthen what was sick; but I will destroy the fat and the strong, and feed them in judgment."

¹⁷'And *as for* you, O My flock, thus says the Lord GOD: "Behold, I shall judge between sheep and sheep, between rams and goats. ¹⁸*Is it* too little for you to have eaten up the good pasture, that you must tread down with your feet the residue of your pasture—and to have drunk of the clear waters, that you must foul the residue with your feet? ¹⁹And *as for* My flock, they eat what you have trampled with your feet, and they drink what you have fouled with your feet."

²⁰'Therefore thus says the Lord GOD to them: "Behold, I Myself will judge between the fat and the lean sheep. ²¹Because you have pushed with side and shoulder, butted all the weak ones with your horns, and scattered them abroad, ²²therefore I will save My flock, and they shall no longer be a prey; and I will judge between sheep and sheep. ²³I will establish one shepherd over them, and he shall feed them—My servant David. He shall feed them and be their shepherd. ²⁴And I, the LORD, will be their God, and My servant David a prince among them; I, the LORD, have spoken.

²⁵"I will make a covenant of peace with them, and cause wild beasts to cease from the land; and they will dwell safely in the wilderness and sleep in the woods. ²⁶I will make them and the places all around My hill a blessing; and I will cause showers to come down in their season; there shall be

showers of blessing. ²⁷ Then the trees of the field shall yield their fruit, and the earth shall yield her increase. They shall be safe in their land; and they shall know that I *am* the LORD, when I have broken the bands of their yoke and delivered them from the hand of those who enslaved them. ²⁸ And they shall no longer be a prey for the nations, nor shall beasts of the land devour them; but they shall dwell safely, and no one shall make *them* afraid. ²⁹ I will raise up for them a garden of renown, and they shall no longer be consumed with hunger in the land, nor bear the shame of the Gentiles anymore. ³⁰ Thus they shall know that I, the LORD their God, *am* with them, and they, the house of Israel, *are* My people," says the Lord GOD.' "

³¹ "You are My flock, the flock of My pasture; you *are* men, *and* I *am* your God," says the Lord GOD.

35 Moreover the word of the LORD came to me, saying, ² "Son of man, set your face against Mount Seir and prophesy against it, ³ and say to it, 'Thus says the Lord GOD:

> "Behold, O Mount Seir, I *am* against you;
> I will stretch out My hand against you,
> And make you most desolate;
> ⁴ I shall lay your cities waste,
> And you shall be desolate.
> Then you shall know that I *am* the LORD.

⁵ "Because you have had an ancient hatred, and have shed *the blood of* the children of Israel by the power of the sword at the time of their calamity, *when* their iniquity *came to an* end, ⁶ therefore, *as* I live," says the Lord GOD, "I will prepare you for blood, and blood shall pursue you; since you have not hated blood, therefore blood shall pursue you. ⁷ Thus I will make Mount Seir most desolate, and cut off from it the one who leaves and the one who returns. ⁸ And I will fill its mountains with the slain; on your hills and in your valleys and in all your ravines those who are slain by the sword shall fall. ⁹ I will make you perpetually desolate, and your cities shall be uninhabited; then you shall know that I *am* the LORD.

¹⁰ "Because you have said, 'These two nations and these two countries shall be mine, and we will possess them,' although the LORD was there, ¹¹ therefore, *as* I live," says the Lord GOD, "I will do according to your anger and according to the envy which you showed in your hatred against them; and I will make Myself known among them when I judge you. ¹² Then you shall know that I *am* the LORD. I have heard all your blasphemies which you have spoken against the mountains of Israel,

וְהוֹרַדְתִּי הַגֶּשֶׁם בְּעִתּוֹ גִּשְׁמֵי בְרָכָה יִהְיוּ: 27 וְנָתַן עֵץ הַשָּׂדֶה אֶת־פִּרְיוֹ וְהָאָרֶץ תִּתֵּן יְבוּלָהּ וְהָיוּ עַל־אַדְמָתָם לָבֶטַח וְיָדְעוּ כִּי־אֲנִי יְהוָה בְּשִׁבְרִי אֶת־מֹטוֹת עֻלָּם וְהִצַּלְתִּים מִיַּד הָעֹבְדִים בָּהֶם: 28 וְלֹא־יִהְיוּ עוֹד בַּז לַגּוֹיִם וְחַיַּת הָאָרֶץ לֹא תֹאכְלֵם וְיָשְׁבוּ לָבֶטַח וְאֵין מַחֲרִיד: 29 וַהֲקִמֹתִי לָהֶם מַטָּע לְשֵׁם וְלֹא־יִהְיוּ עוֹד אֲסֻפֵי רָעָב בָּאָרֶץ וְלֹא־יִשְׂאוּ עוֹד כְּלִמַּת הַגּוֹיִם: 30 וְיָדְעוּ כִּי אֲנִי יְהוָה אֱלֹהֵיהֶם אִתָּם וְהֵמָּה עַמִּי בֵּית יִשְׂרָאֵל נְאֻם אֲדֹנָי יְהוָה: 31 וְאַתֵּן צֹאנִי צֹאן מַרְעִיתִי אָדָם אַתֶּם אֲנִי אֱלֹהֵיכֶם נְאֻם אֲדֹנָי יְהוָה: פ

לה וַיְהִי דְבַר־יְהוָה אֵלַי לֵאמֹר: 2 בֶּן־אָדָם שִׂים פָּנֶיךָ עַל־הַר שֵׂעִיר וְהִנָּבֵא עָלָיו: 3 וְאָמַרְתָּ לּוֹ כֹּה אָמַר אֲדֹנָי יְהוָה הִנְנִי אֵלֶיךָ הַר־שֵׂעִיר וְנָטִיתִי יָדִי עָלֶיךָ וּנְתַתִּיךָ שְׁמָמָה וּמְשַׁמָּה: 4 עָרֶיךָ חָרְבָּה אָשִׂים וְאַתָּה שְׁמָמָה תִהְיֶה וְיָדַעְתָּ כִּי־אֲנִי יְהוָה:

5 יַעַן הֱיוֹת לְךָ אֵיבַת עוֹלָם וַתַּגֵּר אֶת־בְּנֵי־יִשְׂרָאֵל עַל־יְדֵי־חָרֶב בְּעֵת אֵידָם בְּעֵת עֲוֹן קֵץ: 6 לָכֵן חַי־אָנִי נְאֻם אֲדֹנָי יְהוָה כִּי־לְדָם אֶעֶשְׂךָ וְדָם יִרְדֳּפֶךָ אִם־לֹא דָם שָׂנֵאתָ וְדָם יִרְדֳּפֶךָ: 7 וְנָתַתִּי אֶת־הַר שֵׂעִיר לְשִׁמְמָה וּשְׁמָמָה וְהִכְרַתִּי מִמֶּנּוּ עֹבֵר וָשָׁב: 8 וּמִלֵּאתִי אֶת־הָרָיו חֲלָלָיו גִּבְעוֹתֶיךָ וְגֵאוֹתֶיךָ וְכָל־אֲפִיקֶיךָ חַלְלֵי־חֶרֶב יִפְּלוּ בָהֶם: 9 שִׁמְמוֹת עוֹלָם אֶתֶּנְךָ וְעָרֶיךָ לֹא תֵשַׁבְנָה וִידַעְתֶּם כִּי־אֲנִי יְהוָה: 10 יַעַן אֲמָרְךָ אֶת־שְׁנֵי הַגּוֹיִם וְאֶת־שְׁתֵּי הָאֲרָצוֹת לִי תִהְיֶינָה וִירַשְׁנוּהָ וַיהוָה שָׁם הָיָה: 11 לָכֵן חַי־אָנִי נְאֻם אֲדֹנָי יְהוִה וְעָשִׂיתִי כְּאַפְּךָ וּכְקִנְאָתְךָ אֲשֶׁר עָשִׂיתָה מִשִּׂנְאָתֶיךָ בָּם וְנוֹדַעְתִּי בָם כַּאֲשֶׁר אֶשְׁפְּטֶךָ: 12 וְיָדַעְתָּ כִּי־אֲנִי יְהוָה שָׁמַעְתִּי אֶת־כָּל־נָאֲצוֹתֶיךָ אֲשֶׁר אָמַרְתָּ עַל־הָרֵי יִשְׂרָאֵל לֵאמֹר שָׁמֵמוּ לָנוּ נִתְּנוּ

saying, 'They are desolate; they are given to us to consume.' 13 Thus with your mouth you have boasted against Me and multiplied your words against Me; I have heard *them*."

14 'Thus says the Lord GOD: "The whole earth will rejoice when I make you desolate. 15 As you rejoiced because the inheritance of the house of Israel was desolate, so I will do to you; you shall be desolate, O Mount Seir, as well as all of Edom—all of it! Then they shall know that I *am* the LORD."'

36 "And you, son of man, prophesy to the mountains of Israel, and say, 'O mountains of Israel, hear the word of the LORD! 2 Thus says the Lord GOD: "Because the enemy has said of you, 'Aha! The ancient heights have become our possession,'"' 3 therefore prophesy, and say, 'Thus says the Lord GOD: "Because they made *you* desolate and swallowed you up on every side, so that you became the possession of the rest of the nations, and you are taken up by the lips of talkers and slandered by the people"— 4 therefore, O mountains of Israel, hear the word of the Lord GOD! Thus says the Lord GOD to the mountains, the hills, the rivers, the valleys, the desolate wastes, and the cities that have been forsaken, which became plunder and mockery to the rest of the nations all around— 5 therefore thus says the Lord GOD: "Surely I have spoken in My burning jealousy against the rest of the nations and against all Edom, who gave My land to themselves as a possession, with wholehearted joy *and* spiteful minds, in order to plunder its open country."'

6 "Therefore prophesy concerning the land of Israel, and say to the mountains, the hills, the rivers, and the valleys, 'Thus says the Lord GOD: "Behold, I have spoken in My jealousy and My fury, because you have borne the shame of the nations." 7 Therefore thus says the Lord GOD: "I have raised My hand in an oath that surely the nations that *are* around you shall bear their own shame. 8 But you, O mountains of Israel, you shall shoot forth your branches and yield your fruit to My people Israel, for they are about to come. 9 For indeed I *am* for you, and I will turn to you, and you shall be tilled and sown. 10 I will multiply men upon you, all the house of Israel, all of it; and the cities shall be inhabited and the ruins rebuilt. 11 I will multiply upon you man and beast; and they shall increase and bear young; I will make you inhabited as in former times, and do better *for you* than at your beginnings. Then you shall know that I *am* the LORD. 12 Yes, I will cause men to walk on you, My

לְאָכְלָה: 13 וַתַּגְדִּילוּ עָלַי בְּפִיכֶם וְהַעְתַּרְתֶּם עָלַי דִּבְרֵיכֶם אֲנִי שָׁמָעְתִּי: ס 14 כֹּה אָמַר אֲדֹנָי יְהוִה כִּשְׂמֹחַ כָּל־הָאָרֶץ שְׁמָמָה אֶעֱשֶׂה־לָּךְ: 15 כְּשִׂמְחָתְךָ לְנַחְלַת בֵּית־יִשְׂרָאֵל עַל אֲשֶׁר־שָׁמֵמָה כֵּן אֶעֱשֶׂה־לָּךְ שְׁמָמָה תִהְיֶה הַר־שֵׂעִיר וְכָל־אֱדוֹם כֻּלָּהּ וְיָדְעוּ כִּי־אֲנִי יְהוָה: פ

לו 1 וְאַתָּה בֶן־אָדָם הִנָּבֵא אֶל־הָרֵי יִשְׂרָאֵל וְאָמַרְתָּ הָרֵי יִשְׂרָאֵל שִׁמְעוּ דְּבַר־יְהוָה: 2 כֹּה אָמַר אֲדֹנָי יְהוִה יַעַן אָמַר הָאוֹיֵב עֲלֵיכֶם הֶאָח וּבָמוֹת עוֹלָם לְמוֹרָשָׁה הָיְתָה לָּנוּ: 3 לָכֵן הִנָּבֵא וְאָמַרְתָּ כֹּה אָמַר אֲדֹנָי יְהוִה יַעַן בְּיַעַן שַׁמּוֹת וְשָׁאֹף אֶתְכֶם מִסָּבִיב לִהְיוֹתְכֶם מוֹרָשָׁה לִשְׁאֵרִית הַגּוֹיִם וַתֵּעֲלוּ עַל־שְׂפַת לָשׁוֹן וְדִבַּת־עָם: 4 לָכֵן הָרֵי יִשְׂרָאֵל שִׁמְעוּ דְּבַר־אֲדֹנָי יְהוִה כֹּה־אָמַר אֲדֹנָי יְהוִה לֶהָרִים וְלַגְּבָעוֹת לָאֲפִיקִים וְלַגֵּאָיוֹת וְלֶחֳרָבוֹת הַשֹּׁמְמוֹת וְלֶעָרִים הַנֶּעֱזָבוֹת אֲשֶׁר הָיוּ לְבַז וּלְלַעַג לִשְׁאֵרִית הַגּוֹיִם אֲשֶׁר מִסָּבִיב: ס 5 לָכֵן כֹּה־אָמַר אֲדֹנָי יְהוִה אִם־לֹא בְּאֵשׁ קִנְאָתִי דִבַּרְתִּי עַל־שְׁאֵרִית הַגּוֹיִם וְעַל־אֱדוֹם כֻּלָּא אֲשֶׁר נָתְנוּ־אֶת־אַרְצִי ׀ לָהֶם לְמוֹרָשָׁה בְּשִׂמְחַת כָּל־לֵבָב בִּשְׁאָט נֶפֶשׁ לְמַעַן מִגְרָשָׁהּ לָבַז: 6 לָכֵן הִנָּבֵא עַל־אַדְמַת יִשְׂרָאֵל וְאָמַרְתָּ לֶהָרִים וְלַגְּבָעוֹת לָאֲפִיקִים וְלַגֵּאָיוֹת כֹּה־אָמַר ׀ אֲדֹנָי יְהוִה הִנְנִי בְקִנְאָתִי וּבַחֲמָתִי דִּבַּרְתִּי יַעַן כְּלִמַּת גּוֹיִם נְשָׂאתֶם: 7 לָכֵן כֹּה אָמַר אֲדֹנָי יְהוִה אֲנִי נָשָׂאתִי אֶת־יָדִי אִם־לֹא הַגּוֹיִם אֲשֶׁר לָכֶם מִסָּבִיב הֵמָּה כְּלִמָּתָם יִשָּׂאוּ: 8 וְאַתֶּם הָרֵי יִשְׂרָאֵל עַנְפְּכֶם תִּתֵּנוּ וּפֶרְיְכֶם תִּשְׂאוּ לְעַמִּי יִשְׂרָאֵל כִּי קֵרְבוּ לָבוֹא: 9 כִּי הִנְנִי אֲלֵיכֶם וּפָנִיתִי אֲלֵיכֶם וְנֶעֱבַדְתֶּם וְנִזְרַעְתֶּם: 10 וְהִרְבֵּיתִי עֲלֵיכֶם אָדָם כָּל־בֵּית יִשְׂרָאֵל כֻּלֹּה וְנֹשְׁבוּ הֶעָרִים וְהֶחֳרָבוֹת תִּבָּנֶינָה: 11 וְהִרְבֵּיתִי עֲלֵיכֶם אָדָם וּבְהֵמָה וְרָבוּ וּפָרוּ וְהוֹשַׁבְתִּי אֶתְכֶם כְּקַדְמוֹתֵיכֶם וְהֵטִבֹתִי מֵרִאשֹׁתֵיכֶם וִידַעְתֶּם כִּי־אֲנִי יְהוָה: 12 וְהוֹלַכְתִּי עֲלֵיכֶם אָדָם אֶת־עַמִּי

people Israel; they shall take possession of you, and you shall be their inheritance; no more shall you bereave them *of children*."

13 'Thus says the Lord GOD: "Because they say to you, 'You devour men and bereave your nation *of children*,' 14 therefore you shall devour men no more, nor bereave your nation anymore," says the Lord GOD. 15 Nor will I let you hear the taunts of the nations anymore, nor bear the reproach of the peoples anymore, nor shall you cause your nation to stumble anymore," says the Lord GOD.' "

16 Moreover the word of the LORD came to me, saying: 17 "Son of man, when the house of Israel dwelt in their own land, they defiled it by their own ways and deeds; to Me their way was like the uncleanness of a woman in her customary impurity. 18 Therefore I poured out My fury on them for the blood they had shed on the land, and for their idols *with which* they had defiled it. 19 So I scattered them among the nations, and they were dispersed throughout the countries; I judged them according to their ways and their deeds. 20 When they came to the nations, wherever they went, they profaned My holy name—when they said of them, 'These *are* the people of the LORD, *and yet* they have gone out of His land.' 21 But I had concern for My holy name, which the house of Israel had profaned among the nations wherever they went.

22 "Therefore say to the house of Israel, 'Thus says the Lord GOD: "I do not do *this* for your sake, O house of Israel, but for My holy name's sake, which you have profaned among the nations wherever you went. 23 And I will sanctify My great name, which has been profaned among the nations, which you have profaned in their midst; and the nations shall know that I *am* the LORD," says the Lord GOD, "when I am hallowed in you before their eyes. 24 For I will take you from among the nations, gather you out of all countries, and bring you into your own land. 25 Then I will sprinkle clean water on you, and you shall be clean; I will cleanse you from all your filthiness and from all your idols. 26 I will give you a new heart and put a new spirit within you; I will take the heart of stone out of your flesh and give you a heart of flesh. 27 I will put My Spirit within you and cause you to walk in My statutes, and you will keep My judgments and do *them*. 28 Then you shall dwell in the land that I gave to your fathers; you shall be My people, and I will be your God. 29 I will deliver you from all your uncleannesses. I will call for the grain and multiply it, and bring no famine upon you. 30 And I will multiply the fruit of your trees and the increase of your fields, so that you need never again bear the

יִשְׂרָאֵל וִירֵשׁוּךָ וְהָיִיתָ לָהֶם לְנַחֲלָה וְלֹא־תוֹסִף
עוֹד לְשַׁכְּלָם: ס 13 כֹּה אָמַר אֲדֹנָי יְהוִֹה
יַעַן אֹמְרִים לָכֶם אֹכֶלֶת אָדָם אָתְּי וּמְשַׁכֶּלֶת
גּוֹיַךְ הָיִית: 14 לָכֵן אָדָם לֹא־תֹאכְלִי עוֹד
וְגוֹיַךְ לֹא תְכַשְּׁלִי־עוֹד נְאֻם אֲדֹנָי
יְהוִֹה: 15 וְלֹא־אַשְׁמִיעַ אֵלַיִךְ עוֹד כְּלִמַּת הַגּוֹיִם
וְחֶרְפַּת עַמִּים לֹא תִשְׂאִי־עוֹד וְגוֹיַךְ לֹא־תַכְשִׁלִי
עוֹד נְאֻם אֲדֹנָי יְהוִֹה: ס 16 וַיְהִי דְבַר־
יְהוָֹה אֵלַי לֵאמֹר: 17 בֶּן־אָדָם בֵּית יִשְׂרָאֵל יֹשְׁבִים
עַל־אַדְמָתָם וַיְטַמְּאוּ אוֹתָהּ בְּדַרְכָּם וּבַעֲלִילוֹתָם
כְּטֻמְאַת הַנִּדָּה הָיְתָה דַרְכָּם לְפָנָי: 18 וָאֶשְׁפֹּךְ
חֲמָתִי עֲלֵיהֶם עַל־הַדָּם אֲשֶׁר־שָׁפְכוּ עַל־הָאָרֶץ
וּבְגִלּוּלֵיהֶם טִמְּאוּהָ: 19 וָאָפִיץ אֹתָם בַּגּוֹיִם וַיִּזָּרוּ
בָּאֲרָצוֹת כְּדַרְכָּם וְכַעֲלִילוֹתָם שְׁפַטְתִּים: 20 וַיָּבוֹא
אֶל־הַגּוֹיִם אֲשֶׁר־בָּאוּ שָׁם וַיְחַלְּלוּ אֶת־שֵׁם קָדְשִׁי
בֶּאֱמֹר לָהֶם עַם־יְהוָֹה אֵלֶּה וּמֵאַרְצוֹ יָצָאוּ:
21 וָאֶחְמֹל עַל־שֵׁם קָדְשִׁי אֲשֶׁר חִלְּלוּהוּ בֵּית
יִשְׂרָאֵל בַּגּוֹיִם אֲשֶׁר־בָּאוּ שָׁמָּה: ס 22 לָכֵן
אֱמֹר לְבֵית־יִשְׂרָאֵל כֹּה אָמַר אֲדֹנָי יְהוִֹה לֹא
לְמַעַנְכֶם אֲנִי עֹשֶׂה בֵּית יִשְׂרָאֵל כִּי אִם־לְשֵׁם־
קָדְשִׁי אֲשֶׁר חִלַּלְתֶּם בַּגּוֹיִם אֲשֶׁר־בָּאתֶם שָׁם:
23 וְקִדַּשְׁתִּי אֶת־שְׁמִי הַגָּדוֹל הַמְחֻלָּל בַּגּוֹיִם אֲשֶׁר
חִלַּלְתֶּם בְּתוֹכָם וְיָדְעוּ הַגּוֹיִם כִּי־אֲנִי יְהוָֹה נְאֻם
אֲדֹנָי יְהוִֹה בְּהִקָּדְשִׁי בָכֶם לְעֵינֵיהֶם: 24 וְלָקַחְתִּי
אֶתְכֶם מִן־הַגּוֹיִם וְקִבַּצְתִּי אֶתְכֶם מִכָּל־הָאֲרָצוֹת
וְהֵבֵאתִי אֶתְכֶם אֶל־אַדְמַתְכֶם: 25 וְזָרַקְתִּי עֲלֵיכֶם
מַיִם טְהוֹרִים וּטְהַרְתֶּם מִכֹּל טֻמְאוֹתֵיכֶם וּמִכָּל־
גִּלּוּלֵיכֶם אֲטַהֵר אֶתְכֶם: 26 וְנָתַתִּי לָכֶם לֵב חָדָשׁ
וְרוּחַ חֲדָשָׁה אֶתֵּן בְּקִרְבְּכֶם וַהֲסִרֹתִי אֶת־לֵב הָאֶבֶן
מִבְּשַׂרְכֶם וְנָתַתִּי לָכֶם לֵב בָּשָׂר: 27 וְאֶת־רוּחִי אֶתֵּן
בְּקִרְבְּכֶם וְעָשִׂיתִי אֵת אֲשֶׁר־בְּחֻקַּי תֵּלֵכוּ וּמִשְׁפָּטַי
תִּשְׁמְרוּ וַעֲשִׂיתֶם: 28 וִישַׁבְתֶּם בָּאָרֶץ אֲשֶׁר נָתַתִּי
לַאֲבֹתֵיכֶם וִהְיִיתֶם לִי לְעָם וְאָנֹכִי אֶהְיֶה לָכֶם
לֵאלֹהִים: 29 וְהוֹשַׁעְתִּי אֶתְכֶם מִכֹּל טֻמְאוֹתֵיכֶם
וְקָרָאתִי אֶל־הַדָּגָן וְהִרְבֵּיתִי אֹתוֹ וְלֹא־אֶתֵּן עֲלֵיכֶם
רָעָב: 30 וְהִרְבֵּיתִי אֶת־פְּרִי הָעֵץ וּתְנוּבַת הַשָּׂדֶה

לֹ 13 אֶת גּוֹיַיִךְ 14 וְגוֹיַיִךְ 15 וְגוֹיַיִךְ

reproach of famine among the nations. ³¹ Then you will remember your evil ways and your deeds that *were* not good; and you will loathe yourselves in your own sight, for your iniquities and your abominations. ³² Not for your sake do I do *this*," says the Lord GOD, "let it be known to you. Be ashamed and confounded for your own ways, O house of Israel!"

³³ 'Thus says the Lord GOD: "On the day that I cleanse you from all your iniquities, I will also enable *you* to dwell in the cities, and the ruins shall be rebuilt. ³⁴ The desolate land shall be tilled instead of lying desolate in the sight of all who pass by. ³⁵ So they will say, 'This land that was desolate has become like the garden of Eden; and the wasted, desolate, and ruined cities *are now* fortified *and* inhabited.' ³⁶ Then the nations which are left all around you shall know that I, the LORD, have rebuilt the ruined places *and* planted what was desolate. I, the LORD, have spoken *it*, and I will do *it*."

³⁷ 'Thus says the Lord GOD: "I will also let the house of Israel inquire of Me to do this for them: I will increase their men like a flock. ³⁸ Like a flock *offered as* holy *sacrifices*, like the flock at Jerusalem on its feast days, so shall the ruined cities be filled with flocks of men. Then they shall know that I *am* the LORD." ' "

37 The hand of the LORD came upon me and brought me out in the Spirit of the LORD, and set me down in the midst of the valley; and it *was* full of bones. ² Then He caused me to pass by them all around, and behold, *there were* very many in the open valley; and indeed *they were* very dry. ³ And He said to me, "Son of man, can these bones live?"

So I answered, "O Lord GOD, You know."

⁴ Again He said to me, "Prophesy to these bones, and say to them, 'O dry bones, hear the word of the LORD! ⁵ Thus says the Lord GOD to these bones: "Surely I will cause breath to enter into you, and you shall live. ⁶ I will put sinews on you and bring flesh upon you, cover you with skin and put breath in you; and you shall live. Then you shall know that I *am* the LORD." ' "

⁷ So I prophesied as I was commanded; and as I prophesied, there was a noise, and suddenly a rattling; and the bones came together, bone to bone. ⁸ Indeed, as I looked, the sinews and the flesh came upon them, and the skin covered them over; but *there was* no breath in them.

⁹ Also He said to me, "Prophesy to the breath, prophesy, son of man, and say to the breath, 'Thus says the Lord GOD: "Come from the four winds, O

לְמַעַן אֲשֶׁר לֹא תִקְחוּ עוֹד חֶרְפַּת רָעָב בַּגּוֹיִם: 31 וּזְכַרְתֶּם אֶת־דַּרְכֵיכֶם הָרָעִים וּמַעַלְלֵיכֶם אֲשֶׁר לֹא־טוֹבִים וּנְקֹטֹתֶם בִּפְנֵיכֶם עַל עֲוֺנֹתֵיכֶם וְעַל תּוֹעֲבֹתֵיכֶם: 32 לֹא לְמַעַנְכֶם אֲנִי־עֹשֶׂה נְאֻם אֲדֹנָי יְהֹוִה יִוָּדַע לָכֶם בּוֹשׁוּ וְהִכָּלְמוּ מִדַּרְכֵיכֶם בֵּית יִשְׂרָאֵל: ס 33 כֹּה אָמַר אֲדֹנָי יְהֹוִה בְּיוֹם טַהֲרִי אֶתְכֶם מִכֹּל עֲוֺנוֹתֵיכֶם וְהוֹשַׁבְתִּי אֶת־הֶעָרִים וְנִבְנוּ הֶחֳרָבוֹת: 34 וְהָאָרֶץ הַנְּשַׁמָּה תֵּעָבֵד תַּחַת אֲשֶׁר הָיְתָה שְׁמָמָה לְעֵינֵי כָּל־עוֹבֵר: 35 וְאָמְרוּ הָאָרֶץ הַלֵּזוּ הַנְּשַׁמָּה הָיְתָה כְּגַן־עֵדֶן וְהֶעָרִים הֶחֳרֵבוֹת וְהַנְּשַׁמּוֹת וְהַנֶּהֱרָסוֹת בְּצוּרוֹת יָשָׁבוּ: 36 וְיָדְעוּ הַגּוֹיִם אֲשֶׁר יִשָּׁאֲרוּ סְבִיבוֹתֵיכֶם כִּי | אֲנִי יְהֹוָה בָּנִיתִי הַנֶּהֱרָסוֹת נָטַעְתִּי הַנְּשַׁמָּה אֲנִי יְהֹוָה דִּבַּרְתִּי וְעָשִׂיתִי: 37 ס כֹּה אָמַר אֲדֹנָי יְהֹוִה עוֹד זֹאת אִדָּרֵשׁ לְבֵית־יִשְׂרָאֵל לַעֲשׂוֹת לָהֶם אַרְבֶּה אֹתָם כַּצֹּאן אָדָם: 38 כְּצֹאן קָדָשִׁים כְּצֹאן יְרוּשָׁלַ͏ִם בְּמוֹעֲדֶיהָ כֵּן תִּהְיֶינָה הֶעָרִים הֶחֳרֵבוֹת מְלֵאוֹת צֹאן אָדָם וְיָדְעוּ כִּי־אֲנִי יְהֹוָה: ס

לז הָיְתָה עָלַי יַד־יְהֹוָה וַיּוֹצִאֵנִי בְרוּחַ יְהֹוָה וַיְנִיחֵנִי בְּתוֹךְ הַבִּקְעָה וְהִיא מְלֵאָה עֲצָמוֹת: 2 וְהֶעֱבִירַנִי עֲלֵיהֶם סָבִיב | סָבִיב וְהִנֵּה רַבּוֹת מְאֹד עַל־פְּנֵי הַבִּקְעָה וְהִנֵּה יְבֵשׁוֹת מְאֹד: 3 וַיֹּאמֶר אֵלַי בֶּן־אָדָם הֲתִחְיֶינָה הָעֲצָמוֹת הָאֵלֶּה וָאֹמַר אֲדֹנָי יְהֹוִה אַתָּה יָדָעְתָּ: 4 וַיֹּאמֶר אֵלַי הִנָּבֵא עַל־הָעֲצָמוֹת הָאֵלֶּה וְאָמַרְתָּ אֲלֵיהֶם הָעֲצָמוֹת הַיְבֵשׁוֹת שִׁמְעוּ דְּבַר־יְהֹוָה: 5 כֹּה אָמַר אֲדֹנָי יְהֹוִה לָעֲצָמוֹת הָאֵלֶּה הִנֵּה אֲנִי מֵבִיא בָכֶם רוּחַ וִחְיִיתֶם: 6 וְנָתַתִּי עֲלֵיכֶם גִּדִים וְהַעֲלֵתִי עֲלֵיכֶם בָּשָׂר וְקָרַמְתִּי עֲלֵיכֶם עוֹר וְנָתַתִּי בָכֶם רוּחַ וִחְיִיתֶם וִידַעְתֶּם כִּי־אֲנִי יְהֹוָה: 7 וְנִבֵּאתִי כַּאֲשֶׁר צֻוֵּיתִי וַיְהִי־קוֹל כְּהִנָּבְאִי וְהִנֵּה־רַעַשׁ וַתִּקְרְבוּ עֲצָמוֹת עֶצֶם אֶל־עַצְמוֹ: 8 וְרָאִיתִי וְהִנֵּה־עֲלֵיהֶם גִּדִים וּבָשָׂר עָלָה וַיִּקְרַם עֲלֵיהֶם עוֹר מִלְמָעְלָה וְרוּחַ אֵין בָּהֶם: 9 וַיֹּאמֶר אֵלַי הִנָּבֵא אֶל־הָרוּחַ הִנָּבֵא בֶן־אָדָם וְאָמַרְתָּ אֶל־הָרוּחַ כֹּה־אָמַר | אֲדֹנָי יְהֹוִה מֵאַרְבַּע רוּחוֹת בֹּאִי הָרוּחַ

breath, and breathe on these slain, that they may live." ' " 10 So I prophesied as He commanded me, and breath came into them, and they lived, and stood upon their feet, an exceedingly great army.

11 Then He said to me, "Son of man, these bones are the whole house of Israel. They indeed say, 'Our bones are dry, our hope is lost, and we ourselves are cut off!' 12 Therefore prophesy and say to them, 'Thus says the Lord GOD: "Behold, O My people, I will open your graves and cause you to come up from your graves, and bring you into the land of Israel. 13 Then you shall know that I am the LORD, when I have opened your graves, O My people, and brought you up from your graves. 14 I will put My Spirit in you, and you shall live, and I will place you in your own land. Then you shall know that I, the LORD, have spoken it and performed it," says the LORD.' "

15 Again the word of the LORD came to me, saying, 16 "As for you, son of man, take a stick for yourself and write on it: 'For Judah and for the children of Israel, his companions.' Then take another stick and write on it, 'For Joseph, the stick of Ephraim, and for all the house of Israel, his companions.' 17 Then join them one to another for yourself into one stick, and they will become one in your hand.

18 "And when the children of your people speak to you, saying, 'Will you not show us what you mean by these?'— 19 say to them, 'Thus says the Lord GOD: "Surely I will take the stick of Joseph, which is in the hand of Ephraim, and the tribes of Israel, his companions; and I will join them with it, with the stick of Judah, and make them one stick, and they will be one in My hand." ' 20 And the sticks on which you write will be in your hand before their eyes.

21 "Then say to them, 'Thus says the Lord GOD: "Surely I will take the children of Israel from among the nations, wherever they have gone, and will gather them from every side and bring them into their own land; 22 and I will make them one nation in the land, on the mountains of Israel; and one king shall be king over them all; they shall no longer be two nations, nor shall they ever be divided into two kingdoms again. 23 They shall not defile themselves anymore with their idols, nor with their detestable things, nor with any of their transgressions; but I will deliver them from all their dwelling places in which they have sinned, and will cleanse them. Then they shall be My people, and I will be their God.

וּפְחִי בַּהֲרוּגִים הָאֵלֶּה וְיִחְיוּ: 10 וְהִנַּבֵּאתִי כַּאֲשֶׁר צִוָּנִי וַתָּבוֹא בָהֶם הָרוּחַ וַיִּחְיוּ וַיַּעַמְדוּ עַל־רַגְלֵיהֶם חַיִל גָּדוֹל מְאֹד־מְאֹד: ס 11 וַיֹּאמֶר אֵלַי בֶּן־אָדָם הָעֲצָמוֹת הָאֵלֶּה כָּל־בֵּית יִשְׂרָאֵל הֵמָּה הִנֵּה אֹמְרִים יָבְשׁוּ עַצְמוֹתֵינוּ וְאָבְדָה תִקְוָתֵנוּ נִגְזַרְנוּ לָנוּ: 12 לָכֵן הִנָּבֵא וְאָמַרְתָּ אֲלֵיהֶם כֹּה־אָמַר אֲדֹנָי יְהוִה הִנֵּה אֲנִי פֹתֵחַ אֶת־קִבְרוֹתֵיכֶם וְהַעֲלֵיתִי אֶתְכֶם מִקִּבְרוֹתֵיכֶם עַמִּי וְהֵבֵאתִי אֶתְכֶם אֶל־אַדְמַת יִשְׂרָאֵל: ס 13 וִידַעְתֶּם כִּי־אֲנִי יְהוָה בְּפִתְחִי אֶת־קִבְרוֹתֵיכֶם וּבְהַעֲלוֹתִי אֶתְכֶם מִקִּבְרוֹתֵיכֶם עַמִּי: 14 וְנָתַתִּי רוּחִי בָכֶם וִחְיִיתֶם וְהִנַּחְתִּי אֶתְכֶם עַל־אַדְמַתְכֶם וִידַעְתֶּם כִּי־אֲנִי יְהוָה דִּבַּרְתִּי וְעָשִׂיתִי נְאֻם־יְהוָה: פ

15 וַיְהִי דְבַר־יְהוָה אֵלַי לֵאמֹר: 16 וְאַתָּה בֶן־אָדָם קַח־לְךָ עֵץ אֶחָד וּכְתֹב עָלָיו לִיהוּדָה וְלִבְנֵי יִשְׂרָאֵל חֲבֵרָו וּלְקַח עֵץ אֶחָד וּכְתוֹב עָלָיו לְיוֹסֵף עֵץ אֶפְרַיִם וְכָל־בֵּית יִשְׂרָאֵל חֲבֵרָו: 17 וְקָרַב אֹתָם אֶחָד אֶל־אֶחָד לְךָ לְעֵץ אֶחָד וְהָיוּ לַאֲחָדִים בְּיָדֶךָ: 18 וְכַאֲשֶׁר יֹאמְרוּ אֵלֶיךָ בְּנֵי עַמְּךָ לֵאמֹר הֲלוֹא־תַגִּיד לָנוּ מָה־אֵלֶּה לָּךְ: 19 דַּבֵּר אֲלֵהֶם כֹּה־אָמַר אֲדֹנָי יְהוִה הִנֵּה אֲנִי לֹקֵחַ אֶת־עֵץ יוֹסֵף אֲשֶׁר בְּיַד־אֶפְרַיִם וְשִׁבְטֵי יִשְׂרָאֵל חֲבֵרָו וְנָתַתִּי אוֹתָם עָלָיו אֶת־עֵץ יְהוּדָה וַעֲשִׂיתִם לְעֵץ אֶחָד וְהָיוּ אֶחָד בְּיָדִי: 20 וְהָיוּ הָעֵצִים אֲשֶׁר־תִּכְתֹּב עֲלֵיהֶם בְּיָדְךָ לְעֵינֵיהֶם: 21 וְדַבֵּר אֲלֵיהֶם כֹּה־אָמַר אֲדֹנָי יְהוִה הִנֵּה אֲנִי לֹקֵחַ אֶת־בְּנֵי יִשְׂרָאֵל מִבֵּין הַגּוֹיִם אֲשֶׁר הָלְכוּ־שָׁם וְקִבַּצְתִּי אֹתָם מִסָּבִיב וְהֵבֵאתִי אוֹתָם אֶל־אַדְמָתָם: 22 וְעָשִׂיתִי אֹתָם לְגוֹי אֶחָד בָּאָרֶץ בְּהָרֵי יִשְׂרָאֵל וּמֶלֶךְ אֶחָד יִהְיֶה לְכֻלָּם לְמֶלֶךְ וְלֹא יִהְיוּ־עוֹד לִשְׁנֵי גוֹיִם וְלֹא יֵחָצוּ עוֹד לִשְׁתֵּי מַמְלָכוֹת עוֹד: 23 וְלֹא יִטַּמְּאוּ עוֹד בְּגִלּוּלֵיהֶם וּבְשִׁקּוּצֵיהֶם וּבְכֹל פִּשְׁעֵיהֶם וְהוֹשַׁעְתִּי אֹתָם מִכֹּל מוֹשְׁבֹתֵיהֶם אֲשֶׁר חָטְאוּ בָהֶם וְטִהַרְתִּי אוֹתָם וְהָיוּ־לִי לְעָם וַאֲנִי אֶהְיֶה לָהֶם

24 "David My servant *shall be* king over them, and they shall all have one shepherd; they shall also walk in My judgments and observe My statutes, and do them. 25 Then they shall dwell in the land that I have given to Jacob My servant, where your fathers dwelt; and they shall dwell there, they, their children, and their children's children, forever; and My servant David *shall be* their prince forever. 26 Moreover I will make a covenant of peace with them, and it shall be an everlasting covenant with them; I will establish them and multiply them, and I will set My sanctuary in their midst forevermore. 27 My tabernacle also shall be with them; indeed I will be their God, and they shall be My people. 28 The nations also will know that I, the Lord, sanctify Israel, when My sanctuary is in their midst forevermore." ' "

38 Now the word of the Lord came to me, saying, 2 "Son of man, set your face against Gog, of the land of Magog, the prince of Rosh, Meshech, and Tubal, and prophesy against him, 3 and say, 'Thus says the Lord God: "Behold, I *am* against you, O Gog, the prince of Rosh, Meshech, and Tubal. 4 I will turn you around, put hooks into your jaws, and lead you out, with all your army, horses, and horsemen, all splendidly clothed, a great company *with* bucklers and shields, all of them handling swords. 5 Persia, Ethiopia, and Libya are with them, all of them *with* shield and helmet; 6 Gomer and all its troops; the house of Togarmah *from* the far north and all its troops—many people *are* with you.

7 "Prepare yourself and be ready, you and all your companies that are gathered about you; and be a guard for them. 8 After many days you will be visited. In the latter years you will come into the land of those brought back from the sword *and* gathered from many people on the mountains of Israel, which had long been desolate; they were brought out of the nations, and now all of them dwell safely. 9 You will ascend, coming like a storm, covering the land like a cloud, you and all your troops and many peoples with you."

10 'Thus says the Lord God: "On that day it shall come to pass *that* thoughts will arise in your mind, and you will make an evil plan: 11 You will say, 'I will go up against a land of unwalled villages; I will go to a peaceful people, who dwell safely, all of them dwelling without walls, and having neither bars nor gates'— 12 to take plunder and to take booty, to stretch out your hand against the waste places *that are again* inhabited, and against a people gathered from the nations, who have acquired

לֵאלֹהִ֑ים: 24 וְעַבְדִּ֤י דָוִד֙ מֶ֣לֶךְ עֲלֵיהֶ֔ם וְרוֹעֶ֥ה אֶחָ֖ד יִהְיֶ֣ה לְכֻלָּ֑ם וּבְמִשְׁפָּטַ֣י יֵלֵ֔כוּ וְחֻקֹּתַ֥י יִשְׁמְר֖וּ וְעָשׂ֥וּ אוֹתָֽם: 25 וְיָשְׁב֣וּ עַל־הָאָ֗רֶץ אֲשֶׁ֤ר נָתַ֙תִּי֙ לְעַבְדִּ֣י לְיַעֲקֹ֔ב אֲשֶׁ֥ר יָ֥שְׁבוּ־בָ֖הּ אֲבֽוֹתֵיכֶ֑ם וְיָשְׁב֣וּ עָלֶ֡יהָ הֵ֠מָּה וּבְנֵיהֶ֞ם וּבְנֵ֤י בְנֵיהֶם֙ עַד־עוֹלָ֔ם וְדָוִ֣ד עַבְדִּ֔י נָשִׂ֥יא לָהֶ֖ם לְעוֹלָֽם: 26 וְכָרַתִּ֤י לָהֶם֙ בְּרִ֣ית שָׁל֔וֹם בְּרִ֥ית עוֹלָ֖ם יִהְיֶ֣ה אוֹתָ֑ם וּנְתַתִּים֙ וְהִרְבֵּיתִ֣י אוֹתָ֔ם וְנָתַתִּ֧י אֶת־מִקְדָּשִׁ֛י בְּתוֹכָ֖ם לְעוֹלָֽם: 27 וְהָיָ֤ה מִשְׁכָּנִי֙ עֲלֵיהֶ֔ם וְהָיִ֥יתִי לָהֶ֖ם לֵאלֹהִ֑ים וְהֵ֖מָּה יִֽהְיוּ־לִ֥י לְעָֽם: 28 וְיָֽדְעוּ֙ הַגּוֹיִ֔ם כִּ֚י אֲנִ֣י יְהֹוָ֔ה מְקַדֵּ֖שׁ אֶת־יִשְׂרָאֵ֑ל בִּהְי֧וֹת מִקְדָּשִׁ֛י בְּתוֹכָ֖ם לְעוֹלָֽם: ס

לח וַיְהִ֥י דְבַר־יְהֹוָ֖ה אֵלַ֥י לֵאמֹֽר: 2 בֶּן־אָדָ֗ם שִׂ֤ים פָּנֶ֙יךָ֙ אֶל־גּוֹג֙ אֶ֣רֶץ הַמָּג֔וֹג נְשִׂ֕יא רֹ֖אשׁ מֶ֣שֶׁךְ וְתֻבָ֑ל וְהִנָּבֵ֖א עָלָֽיו: 3 וְאָ֣מַרְתָּ֔ כֹּ֥ה אָמַ֖ר אֲדֹנָ֣י יֱהֹוִ֑ה הִנְנִ֤י אֵלֶ֙יךָ֙ גּ֔וֹג נְשִׂ֕יא רֹ֖אשׁ מֶ֥שֶׁךְ וְתֻבָֽל: 4 וְשׁ֣וֹבַבְתִּ֔יךָ וְנָתַתִּ֤י חַחִים֙ בִּלְחָיֶ֔יךָ וְהֽוֹצֵאתִי֙ אֽוֹתְךָ֣ וְאֶת־כָּל־חֵילֶ֗ךָ סוּסִים֙ וּפָ֣רָשִׁ֔ים לְבֻשֵׁ֥י מִכְל֖וֹל כֻּלָּ֑ם קָהָ֥ל רָב֙ צִנָּ֣ה וּמָגֵ֔ן תֹּפְשֵׂ֥י חֲרָב֖וֹת כֻּלָּֽם: 5 פָּרַ֛ס כּ֥וּשׁ וּפ֖וּט אִתָּ֑ם כֻּלָּ֖ם מָגֵ֥ן וְכוֹבָֽע: 6 גֹּ֚מֶר וְכָל־אֲגַפֶּ֔יהָ בֵּ֚ית תּֽוֹגַרְמָ֔ה יַרְכְּתֵ֥י צָפ֖וֹן וְאֶת־כָּל־אֲגַפָּ֑יו עַמִּ֥ים רַבִּ֖ים אִתָּֽךְ: 7 הִכֹּן֙ וְהָכֵ֣ן לְךָ֔ אַתָּ֕ה וְכָל־קְהָלֶ֖ךָ הַנִּקְהָלִ֣ים עָלֶ֑יךָ וְהָיִ֥יתָ לָהֶ֖ם לְמִשְׁמָֽר: 8 מִיָּמִ֣ים רַבִּים֮ תִּפָּקֵד֒ בְּאַחֲרִ֣ית הַשָּׁנִ֗ים תָּב֣וֹא ׀ אֶל־אֶ֣רֶץ ׀ מְשׁוֹבֶ֣בֶת מֵחֶ֡רֶב מְקֻבֶּ֩צֶת֩ מֵֽעַמִּ֨ים רַבִּ֜ים עַ֣ל הָרֵ֤י יִשְׂרָאֵל֙ אֲשֶׁר־הָי֥וּ לְחָרְבָּ֖ה תָּמִ֑יד וְהִיא֙ מֵֽעַמִּ֣ים הוּצָ֔אָה וְיָשְׁב֥וּ לָבֶ֖טַח כֻּלָּֽם: 9 וְעָלִ֙יתָ֙ כַּשֹּׁאָ֣ה תָב֔וֹא כֶּֽעָנָ֛ן לְכַסּ֥וֹת הָאָ֖רֶץ תִּֽהְיֶ֑ה אַתָּה֙ וְכָל־אֲגַפֶּ֔יךָ וְעַמִּ֥ים רַבִּ֖ים אוֹתָֽךְ: ס 10 כֹּ֥ה אָמַ֖ר אֲדֹנָ֣י יֱהֹוִ֑ה וְהָיָ֣ה ׀ בַּיּ֣וֹם הַה֗וּא יַֽעֲל֤וּ דְבָרִים֙ עַל־לְבָ֣בֶ֔ךָ וְחָשַׁבְתָּ֖ מַחֲשֶׁ֥בֶת רָעָֽה: 11 וְאָֽמַרְתָּ֗ אֶֽעֱלֶה֙ עַל־אֶ֣רֶץ פְּרָז֔וֹת אָבוֹא֙ הַשֹּׁ֣קְטִ֔ים יֹשְׁבֵ֖י לָבֶ֑טַח כֻּלָּ֗ם יֹֽשְׁבִים֙ בְּאֵ֣ין חוֹמָ֔ה וּבְרִ֥יחַ וּדְלָתַ֖יִם אֵ֥ין לָהֶֽם: 12 לִשְׁלֹ֤ל שָׁלָל֙ וְלָבֹ֣ז בַּ֔ז לְהָשִׁ֤יב יָֽדְךָ֙ עַל־חֳרָב֣וֹת נוֹשָׁב֔וֹת וְאֶל־עַ֗ם מְאֻסָּף֙ מִגּוֹיִ֔ם עֹשֶׂ֖ה מִקְנֶ֣ה וְקִנְיָ֑ן יֹשְׁבֵ֖י עַל־

livestock and goods, who dwell in the midst of the land. [13] Sheba, Dedan, the merchants of Tarshish, and all their young lions will say to you, 'Have you come to take plunder? Have you gathered your army to take booty, to carry away silver and gold, to take away livestock and goods, to take great plunder?' "'

[14] "Therefore, son of man, prophesy and say to Gog, 'Thus says the Lord GOD: "On that day when My people Israel dwell safely, will you not know *it?* [15] Then you will come from your place out of the far north, you and many peoples with you, all of them riding on horses, a great company and a mighty army. [16] You will come up against My people Israel like a cloud, to cover the land. It will be in the latter days that I will bring you against My land, so that the nations may know Me, when I am hallowed in you, O Gog, before their eyes." [17] Thus says the Lord GOD: "Are *you* he of whom I have spoken in former days by My servants the prophets of Israel, who prophesied for years in those days that I would bring you against them?

[18] "And it will come to pass at the same time, when Gog comes against the land of Israel," says the Lord GOD, "*that* My fury will show in My face. [19] For in My jealousy *and* in the fire of My wrath I have spoken: 'Surely in that day there shall be a great earthquake in the land of Israel, [20] so that the fish of the sea, the birds of the heavens, the beasts of the field, all creeping things that creep on the earth, and all men who *are* on the face of the earth shall shake at My presence. The mountains shall be thrown down, the steep places shall fall, and every wall shall fall to the ground.' [21] I will call for a sword against Gog throughout all My mountains," says the Lord GOD. "Every man's sword will be against his brother. [22] And I will bring him to judgment with pestilence and bloodshed; I will rain down on him, on his troops, and on the many peoples who *are* with him, flooding rain, great hailstones, fire, and brimstone. [23] Thus I will magnify Myself and sanctify Myself, and I will be known in the eyes of many nations. Then they shall know that I *am* the LORD." '

39 "And you, son of man, prophesy against Gog, and say, 'Thus says the Lord GOD: "Behold, I *am* against you, O Gog, the prince of Rosh, Meshech, and Tubal; [2] and I will turn you around and lead you on, bringing you up from the far north, and bring you against the mountains of Israel. [3] Then I will knock the bow out of your left hand, and cause the arrows to fall out of your right hand. [4] You shall fall upon the mountains of Israel, you and all your

טַבּוּר הָאָרֶץ: 13 שְׁבָא וּדְדָן וְסֹחֲרֵי תַרְשִׁישׁ וְכָל־
כְּפִרֶיהָ יֹאמְרוּ לְךָ הֲלִשְׁלֹל שָׁלָל אַתָּה בָא הֲלִבֹז
בַּז הִקְהַלְתָּ קָהָלֶךָ לָשֵׂאת ׀ כֶּסֶף וְזָהָב לָקַחַת
מִקְנֶה וְקִנְיָן לִשְׁלֹל שָׁלָל גָּדוֹל: ס 14 לָכֵן
הִנָּבֵא בֶן־אָדָם וְאָמַרְתָּ לְגוֹג כֹּה אָמַר אֲדֹנָי יְהוִה
הֲלוֹא ׀ בַּיּוֹם הַהוּא בְּשֶׁבֶת עַמִּי יִשְׂרָאֵל לָבֶטַח
תֵּדָע: 15 וּבָאתָ מִמְּקוֹמְךָ מִיַּרְכְּתֵי צָפוֹן אַתָּה
וְעַמִּים רַבִּים אִתָּךְ רֹכְבֵי סוּסִים כֻּלָּם קָהָל גָּדוֹל
וְחַיִל רָב: 16 וְעָלִיתָ עַל־עַמִּי יִשְׂרָאֵל כֶּעָנָן לְכַסּוֹת
הָאָרֶץ בְּאַחֲרִית הַיָּמִים תִּהְיֶה וַהֲבִאוֹתִיךָ עַל־אַרְצִי
לְמַעַן דַּעַת הַגּוֹיִם אֹתִי בְּהִקָּדְשִׁי בְךָ לְעֵינֵיהֶם
גּוֹג: ס 17 כֹּה־אָמַר אֲדֹנָי יְהוִה הַאַתָּה־
הוּא אֲשֶׁר־דִּבַּרְתִּי בְּיָמִים קַדְמוֹנִים בְּיַד עֲבָדַי
נְבִיאֵי יִשְׂרָאֵל הַנִּבְּאִים בַּיָּמִים הָהֵם שָׁנִים לְהָבִיא
אֹתְךָ עֲלֵיהֶם: ס 18 וְהָיָה ׀ בַּיּוֹם הַהוּא
בְּיוֹם בּוֹא גוֹג עַל־אַדְמַת יִשְׂרָאֵל נְאֻם אֲדֹנָי יְהוִה
תַּעֲלֶה חֲמָתִי בְּאַפִּי: 19 וּבְקִנְאָתִי בְאֵשׁ־עֶבְרָתִי
דִּבַּרְתִּי אִם־לֹא ׀ בַּיּוֹם הַהוּא יִהְיֶה רַעַשׁ גָּדוֹל
עַל אַדְמַת יִשְׂרָאֵל: 20 וְרָעֲשׁוּ מִפָּנַי דְּגֵי הַיָּם וְעוֹף
הַשָּׁמַיִם וְחַיַּת הַשָּׂדֶה וְכָל־הָרֶמֶשׂ הָרֹמֵשׂ עַל־
הָאֲדָמָה וְכֹל הָאָדָם אֲשֶׁר עַל־פְּנֵי הָאֲדָמָה וְנֶהֶרְסוּ
הֶהָרִים וְנָפְלוּ הַמַּדְרֵגוֹת וְכָל־חוֹמָה לָאָרֶץ תִּפּוֹל:
21 וְקָרָאתִי עָלָיו לְכָל־הָרַי חֶרֶב נְאֻם אֲדֹנָי יְהוִה
חֶרֶב אִישׁ בְּאָחִיו תִּהְיֶה: 22 וְנִשְׁפַּטְתִּי אִתּוֹ בְּדֶבֶר
וּבְדָם וְגֶשֶׁם שׁוֹטֵף וְאַבְנֵי אֶלְגָּבִישׁ אֵשׁ וְגָפְרִית
אַמְטִיר עָלָיו וְעַל־אֲגַפָּיו וְעַל־עַמִּים רַבִּים אֲשֶׁר
אִתּוֹ: 23 וְהִתְגַּדִּלְתִּי וְהִתְקַדִּשְׁתִּי וְנוֹדַעְתִּי לְעֵינֵי
גּוֹיִם רַבִּים וְיָדְעוּ כִּי־אֲנִי יְהוָה: ס

לט וְאַתָּה בֶן־אָדָם הִנָּבֵא עַל־גּוֹג וְאָמַרְתָּ כֹּה
אָמַר אֲדֹנָי יְהוִה הִנְנִי אֵלֶיךָ גּוֹג נְשִׂיא רֹאשׁ מֶשֶׁךְ
וְתֻבָל: 2 וְשֹׁבַבְתִּיךָ וְשִׁשֵּׁאתִיךָ וְהַעֲלִיתִיךָ מִיַּרְכְּתֵי
צָפוֹן וַהֲבִאוֹתִךָ עַל־הָרֵי יִשְׂרָאֵל: 3 וְהִכֵּיתִי קַשְׁתְּךָ
מִיַּד שְׂמֹאולֶךָ וְחִצֶּיךָ מִיַּד יְמִינְךָ אַפִּיל: 4 עַל־הָרֵי
יִשְׂרָאֵל תִּפּוֹל אַתָּה וְכָל־אֲגַפֶּיךָ וְעַמִּים אֲשֶׁר אִתָּךְ

troops and the peoples who *are* with you; I will give you to birds of prey of every sort and *to* the beasts of the field to be devoured. ⁵ You shall fall on the open field; for I have spoken," says the Lord GOD. ⁶ "And I will send fire on Magog and on those who live in security in the coastlands. Then they shall know that I *am* the LORD. ⁷ So I will make My holy name known in the midst of My people Israel, and I will not *let them* profane My holy name anymore. Then the nations shall know that *I am* the LORD, the Holy One in Israel. ⁸ Surely it is coming, and it shall be done," says the Lord GOD. "This *is* the day of which I have spoken.

⁹ "Then those who dwell in the cities of Israel will go out and set on fire and burn the weapons, both the shields and bucklers, the bows and arrows, the javelins and spears; and they will make fires with them for seven years. ¹⁰ They will not take wood from the field nor cut down *any* from the forests, because they will make fires with the weapons; and they will plunder those who plundered them, and pillage those who pillaged them," says the Lord GOD.

¹¹ "It will come to pass in that day *that* I will give Gog a burial place there in Israel, the valley of those who pass by east of the sea; and it will obstruct travelers, because there they will bury Gog and all his multitude. Therefore they will call *it* the Valley of Hamon Gog. ¹² For seven months the house of Israel will be burying them, in order to cleanse the land. ¹³ Indeed all the people of the land will be burying, and they will gain renown for it on the day that I am glorified," says the Lord GOD. ¹⁴ "They will set apart men regularly employed, with the help of a search party, to pass through the land and bury those bodies remaining on the ground, in order to cleanse it. At the end of seven months they will make a search. ¹⁵ The search party will pass through the land; and *when anyone* sees a man's bone, he shall set up a marker by it, till the buriers have buried it in the Valley of Hamon Gog. ¹⁶ *The* name of *the* city *will* also *be* Hamonah. Thus they shall cleanse the land." '

¹⁷ "And as for you, son of man, thus says the Lord GOD, 'Speak to every sort of bird and to every beast of the field:

"Assemble yourselves and come;
    Gather together from all sides to My sacrificial meal
Which I am sacrificing for you,
A great sacrificial meal on the mountains of Israel,
That you may eat flesh and drink blood.
¹⁸   You shall eat the flesh of the mighty,
    Drink the blood of the princes of the earth,

לְעֵיט צִפּוֹר כָּל־כָּנָף וְחַיַּת הַשָּׂדֶה נְתַתִּיךָ לְאָכְלָה: 5 עַל־פְּנֵי הַשָּׂדֶה תִּפּוֹל כִּי אֲנִי דִבַּרְתִּי נְאֻם אֲדֹנָי יְהוִֹה: 6 וְשִׁלַּחְתִּי־אֵשׁ בְּמָגוֹג וּבְיֹשְׁבֵי הָאִיִּים לָבֶטַח וְיָדְעוּ כִּי־אֲנִי יְהוָֹה: 7 וְאֶת־שֵׁם קָדְשִׁי אוֹדִיעַ בְּתוֹךְ עַמִּי יִשְׂרָאֵל וְלֹא־אַחֵל אֶת־שֵׁם־קָדְשִׁי עוֹד וְיָדְעוּ הַגּוֹיִם כִּי־אֲנִי יְהוָֹה קָדוֹשׁ בְּיִשְׂרָאֵל: 8 הִנֵּה בָאָה וְנִהְיָתָה נְאֻם אֲדֹנָי יְהוִֹה הוּא הַיּוֹם אֲשֶׁר דִּבַּרְתִּי: 9 וְיָצְאוּ יֹשְׁבֵי | עָרֵי יִשְׂרָאֵל וּבִעֲרוּ וְהִשִּׂיקוּ בְּנֶשֶׁק וּמָגֵן וְצִנָּה בְּקֶשֶׁת וּבְחִצִּים וּבְמַקֵּל יָד וּבְרֹמַח וּבִעֲרוּ בָהֶם אֵשׁ שֶׁבַע שָׁנִים: 10 וְלֹא־יִשְׂאוּ עֵצִים מִן־הַשָּׂדֶה וְלֹא יַחְטְבוּ מִן־הַיְעָרִים כִּי בַנֶּשֶׁק יְבַעֲרוּ־אֵשׁ וְשָׁלְלוּ אֶת־שֹׁלְלֵיהֶם וּבָזְזוּ אֶת־בֹּזְזֵיהֶם נְאֻם אֲדֹנָי יְהוִֹה: ס 11 וְהָיָה בַיּוֹם הַהוּא אֶתֵּן לְגוֹג | מְקוֹם־שָׁם קֶבֶר בְּיִשְׂרָאֵל גֵּי הָעֹבְרִים קִדְמַת הַיָּם וְחֹסֶמֶת הִיא אֶת־הָעֹבְרִים וְקָבְרוּ שָׁם אֶת־גּוֹג וְאֶת־כָּל־הֲמוֹנֹהּ וְקָרְאוּ גֵּיא הֲמוֹן גּוֹג: 12 וּקְבָרוּם בֵּית יִשְׂרָאֵל לְמַעַן טַהֵר אֶת־הָאָרֶץ שִׁבְעָה חֳדָשִׁים: 13 וְקָבְרוּ כָּל־עַם הָאָרֶץ וְהָיָה לָהֶם לְשֵׁם יוֹם הִכָּבְדִי נְאֻם אֲדֹנָי יְהוִֹה: 14 וְאַנְשֵׁי תָמִיד יַבְדִּילוּ עֹבְרִים בָּאָרֶץ מְקַבְּרִים אֶת־הָעֹבְרִים אֶת־הַנּוֹתָרִים עַל־פְּנֵי הָאָרֶץ לְטַהֲרָהּ מִקְצֵה שִׁבְעָה־חֳדָשִׁים יַחְקֹרוּ: 15 וְעָבְרוּ הָעֹבְרִים בָּאָרֶץ וְרָאָה עֶצֶם אָדָם וּבָנָה אֶצְלוֹ צִיּוּן עַד קָבְרוּ אֹתוֹ הַמְקַבְּרִים אֶל־גֵּיא הֲמוֹן גּוֹג: 16 וְגַם שֶׁם־עִיר הֲמוֹנָה וְטִהֲרוּ הָאָרֶץ: ס 17 וְאַתָּה בֶן־אָדָם כֹּה־אָמַר | אֲדֹנָי יְהוִֹה אֱמֹר לְצִפּוֹר כָּל־כָּנָף וּלְכֹל | חַיַּת הַשָּׂדֶה הִקָּבְצוּ וָבֹאוּ הֵאָסְפוּ מִסָּבִיב עַל־זִבְחִי אֲשֶׁר אֲנִי זֹבֵחַ לָכֶם זֶבַח גָּדוֹל עַל הָרֵי יִשְׂרָאֵל וַאֲכַלְתֶּם בָּשָׂר וּשְׁתִיתֶם דָּם: 18 בְּשַׂר גִּבּוֹרִים תֹּאכֵלוּ וְדַם־נְשִׂיאֵי הָאָרֶץ תִּשְׁתּוּ אֵילִים כָּרִים וְעַתּוּדִים פָּרִים מְרִיאֵי בָשָׁן כֻּלָּם:

Of rams and lambs,
Of goats and bulls,
All of them fatlings of Bashan.
19 You shall eat fat till you are full,
And drink blood till you are drunk,
At My sacrificial meal
Which I am sacrificing for you.
20 You shall be filled at My table
With horses and riders,
With mighty men
And with all the men of war," says the Lord GOD.

21 "I will set My glory among the nations; all the nations shall see My judgment which I have executed, and My hand which I have laid on them. 22 So the house of Israel shall know that I *am* the LORD their God from that day forward. 23 The Gentiles shall know that the house of Israel went into captivity for their iniquity; because they were unfaithful to Me, therefore I hid My face from them. I gave them into the hand of their enemies, and they all fell by the sword. 24 According to their uncleanness and according to their transgressions I have dealt with them, and hidden My face from them.'"

25 "Therefore thus says the Lord GOD: 'Now I will bring back the captives of Jacob, and have mercy on the whole house of Israel; and I will be jealous for My holy name— 26 after they have borne their shame, and all their unfaithfulness in which they were unfaithful to Me, when they dwelt safely in their *own* land and no one made *them* afraid. 27 When I have brought them back from the peoples and gathered them out of their enemies' lands, and I am hallowed in them in the sight of many nations, 28 then they shall know that I *am* the LORD their God, who sent them into captivity among the nations, but also brought them back to their land, and left none of them captive any longer. 29 And I will not hide My face from them anymore; for I shall have poured out My Spirit on the house of Israel,' says the Lord GOD."

40 In the twenty-fifth year of our captivity, at the beginning of the year, on the tenth *day* of the month, in the fourteenth year after the city was captured, on the very same day the hand of the LORD was upon me; and He took me there. 2 In the visions of God He took me into the land of Israel and set me on a very high mountain; on it toward the south *was* something like the structure of a city. 3 He took me there, and behold, *there was* a man whose appearance *was* like the appearance of bronze. He had a line of flax and a measuring rod in his hand, and he stood in the gateway.

וַאֲכַלְתֶּם־חֵלֶב לְשָׂבְעָה וּשְׁתִיתֶם דָּם לְשִׁכָּרוֹן 19
מִזִּבְחִי אֲשֶׁר־זָבַחְתִּי לָכֶם: 20 וּשְׂבַעְתֶּם עַל־שֻׁלְחָנִי
סוּס וָרֶכֶב גִּבּוֹר וְכָל־אִישׁ מִלְחָמָה נְאֻם אֲדֹנָי
יְהוִֹה: 21 וְנָתַתִּי אֶת־כְּבוֹדִי בַּגּוֹיִם וְרָאוּ כָל־הַגּוֹיִם
אֶת־מִשְׁפָּטִי אֲשֶׁר עָשִׂיתִי וְאֶת־יָדִי אֲשֶׁר־שַׂמְתִּי
בָהֶם: 22 וְיָדְעוּ בֵּית יִשְׂרָאֵל כִּי אֲנִי יְהוָֹה אֱלֹהֵיהֶם
מִן־הַיּוֹם הַהוּא וָהָלְאָה: 23 וְיָדְעוּ הַגּוֹיִם כִּי בַעֲוֹנָם
גָּלוּ בֵית־יִשְׂרָאֵל עַל אֲשֶׁר מָעֲלוּ־בִי וָאַסְתִּר פָּנַי
מֵהֶם וָאֶתְּנֵם בְּיַד צָרֵיהֶם וַיִּפְּלוּ בַחֶרֶב כֻּלָּם:
24 כְּטֻמְאָתָם וּכְפִשְׁעֵיהֶם עָשִׂיתִי אֹתָם וָאַסְתִּר פָּנַי
מֵהֶם: ס 25 לָכֵן כֹּה אָמַר אֲדֹנָי יְהוִֹה
עַתָּה אָשִׁיב אֶת־שְׁבִית יַעֲקֹב וְרִחַמְתִּי כָּל־בֵּית
יִשְׂרָאֵל וְקִנֵּאתִי לְשֵׁם קָדְשִׁי: 26 וְנָשׂוּ אֶת־כְּלִמָּתָם
וְאֶת־כָּל־מַעֲלָם אֲשֶׁר מָעֲלוּ־בִי בְּשִׁבְתָּם עַל־
אַדְמָתָם לָבֶטַח וְאֵין מַחֲרִיד: 27 בְּשׁוֹבְבִי אוֹתָם מִן־
הָעַמִּים וְקִבַּצְתִּי אֹתָם מֵאַרְצוֹת אֹיְבֵיהֶם וְנִקְדַּשְׁתִּי
בָם לְעֵינֵי הַגּוֹיִם רַבִּים: 28 וְיָדְעוּ כִּי אֲנִי יְהוָֹה
אֱלֹהֵיהֶם בְּהַגְלוֹתִי אֹתָם אֶל־הַגּוֹיִם וְכִנַּסְתִּים עַל־
אַדְמָתָם וְלֹא־אוֹתִיר עוֹד מֵהֶם שָׁם: 29 וְלֹא־
אַסְתִּיר עוֹד פָּנַי מֵהֶם אֲשֶׁר שָׁפַכְתִּי אֶת־רוּחִי
עַל־בֵּית יִשְׂרָאֵל נְאֻם אֲדֹנָי יְהוִֹה: פ

מ בְּעֶשְׂרִים וְחָמֵשׁ שָׁנָה לְגָלוּתֵנוּ בְּרֹאשׁ הַשָּׁנָה
בֶּעָשׂוֹר לַחֹדֶשׁ בְּאַרְבַּע עֶשְׂרֵה שָׁנָה אַחַר אֲשֶׁר
הֻכְּתָה הָעִיר בְּעֶצֶם הַיּוֹם הַזֶּה הָיְתָה עָלַי יַד־
יְהוָֹה וַיָּבֵא אֹתִי שָׁמָּה: 2 בְּמַרְאוֹת אֱלֹהִים הֱבִיאַנִי
אֶל־אֶרֶץ יִשְׂרָאֵל וַיְנִיחֵנִי אֶל־הַר גָּבֹהַּ מְאֹד וְעָלָיו
כְּמִבְנֵה־עִיר מִנֶּגֶב: 3 וַיָּבִיא אוֹתִי שָׁמָּה וְהִנֵּה־אִישׁ
מַרְאֵהוּ כְּמַרְאֵה נְחֹשֶׁת וּפְתִיל־פִּשְׁתִּים בְּיָדוֹ וּקָנֶה

⁴And the man said to me, "Son of man, look with your eyes and hear with your ears, and fix your mind on everything I show you; for you *were* brought here so that I might show *them* to you. Declare to the house of Israel everything you see." ⁵Now there was a wall all around the outside of the temple. In the man's hand was a measuring rod six cubits *long, each being a* cubit and a handbreadth; and he measured the width of the wall structure, one rod; and the height, one rod.

⁶Then he went to the gateway which faced east; and he went up its stairs and measured the threshold of the gateway, *which was* one rod wide, and the other threshold *was* one rod wide. ⁷Each gate chamber *was* one rod long and one rod wide; between the gate chambers *was a space of* five cubits; and the threshold of the gateway by the vestibule of the inside gate *was* one rod. ⁸He also measured the vestibule of the inside gate, one rod. ⁹Then he measured the vestibule of the gateway, eight cubits; and the gateposts, two cubits. The vestibule of the gate *was* on the inside. ¹⁰In the eastern gateway *were* three gate chambers on one side and three on the other; the three *were* all the same size; also the gateposts were of the same size on this side and that side.

¹¹He measured the width of the entrance to the gateway, ten cubits; *and* the length of the gate, thirteen cubits. ¹²*There was* a space in front of the gate chambers, one cubit *on this side* and one cubit on that side; the gate chambers *were* six cubits on this side and six cubits on that side. ¹³Then he measured the gateway from the roof of *one* gate chamber to the roof of the other; the width *was* twenty-five cubits, as door faces door. ¹⁴He measured the gateposts, sixty cubits high, and the court all around the gateway *extended* to the gatepost. ¹⁵*From* the front of the entrance gate to the front of the vestibule of the inner gate *was* fifty cubits. ¹⁶*There were* beveled window *frames* in the gate chambers and in their intervening archways on the inside of the gateway all around, and likewise in the vestibules. *There were* windows all around on the inside. And on each gatepost *were* palm trees.

¹⁷Then he brought me into the outer court; and *there were* chambers and a pavement made all around the court; thirty chambers faced the pavement. ¹⁸The pavement was by the side of the gateways, corresponding to the length of the gateways; *this was* the lower pavement. ¹⁹Then he measured the width from the front of the lower gateway to the front of the inner court exterior, one hundred cubits toward the east and the north.

הַמִּדָּה וְהוּא עֹמֵד בַּשָּׁעַר: 4 וַיְדַבֵּר אֵלַי הָאִישׁ בֶּן־אָדָם רְאֵה בְעֵינֶיךָ וּבְאָזְנֶיךָ שְׁמָע וְשִׂים לִבְּךָ לְכֹל אֲשֶׁר־אֲנִי מַרְאֶה אוֹתָךְ כִּי לְמַעַן הַרְאוֹתְכָה הֻבָאתָה הֵנָּה הַגֵּד אֶת־כָּל־אֲשֶׁר־אַתָּה רֹאֶה לְבֵית יִשְׂרָאֵל: 5 וְהִנֵּה חוֹמָה מִחוּץ לַבַּיִת סָבִיב | סָבִיב וּבְיַד הָאִישׁ קְנֵה הַמִּדָּה שֵׁשׁ־אַמּוֹת בָּאַמָּה וָטֹפַח וַיָּמָד אֶת־רֹחַב הַבִּנְיָן קָנֶה אֶחָד וְקוֹמָה קָנֶה אֶחָד: 6 וַיָּבוֹא אֶל־שַׁעַר אֲשֶׁר פָּנָיו דֶּרֶךְ הַקָּדִימָה וַיַּעַל בְּמַעֲלוֹתָו | וַיָּמָד אֶת־סַף הַשַּׁעַר קָנֶה אֶחָד רֹחַב וְאֵת סַף אֶחָד קָנֶה אֶחָד רֹחַב:

7 וְהַתָּא קָנֶה אֶחָד אֹרֶךְ וְקָנֶה אֶחָד רֹחַב וּבֵין הַתָּאִים חָמֵשׁ אַמּוֹת וְסַף הַשַּׁעַר מֵאֵצֶל אוּלָם הַשַּׁעַר מֵהַבַּיִת קָנֶה אֶחָד: 8 וַיָּמָד אֶת־אֻלָם הַשַּׁעַר מֵהַבַּיִת קָנֶה אֶחָד: 9 וַיָּמָד אֶת־אֻלָם הַשַּׁעַר שְׁמֹנֶה אַמּוֹת וְאֵילָו שְׁתַּיִם אַמּוֹת וְאֻלָם הַשַּׁעַר מֵהַבָּיִת:

10 וְתָאֵי הַשַּׁעַר דֶּרֶךְ הַקָּדִים שְׁלֹשָׁה מִפֹּה וּשְׁלֹשָׁה מִפֹּה מִדָּה אַחַת לִשְׁלָשְׁתָּם וּמִדָּה אַחַת לָאֵילִם מִפֹּה וּמִפּוֹ: 11 וַיָּמָד אֶת־רֹחַב פֶּתַח־הַשַּׁעַר עֶשֶׂר אַמּוֹת אֹרֶךְ הַשַּׁעַר שְׁלוֹשׁ עֶשְׂרֵה אַמּוֹת: 12 וּגְבוּל לִפְנֵי הַתָּאוֹת אַמָּה אֶחָת וְאַמָּה־אַחַת גְּבוּל מִפֹּה וְהַתָּא שֵׁשׁ־אַמּוֹת מִפּוֹ וְשֵׁשׁ אַמּוֹת מִפֹּה:

13 וַיָּמָד אֶת־הַשַּׁעַר מִגַּג הַתָּא לְגַגּוֹ רֹחַב עֶשְׂרִים וְחָמֵשׁ אַמּוֹת פֶּתַח נֶגֶד פָּתַח: 14 וַיַּעַשׂ אֶת־אֵילִים שִׁשִּׁים אַמָּה וְאֶל־אֵיל הֶחָצֵר הַשַּׁעַר סָבִיב | סָבִיב: 15 וְעַל פְּנֵי הַשַּׁעַר הַיְאָתוֹן עַל־לִפְנֵי אֻלָם הַשַּׁעַר הַפְּנִימִי חֲמִשִּׁים אַמָּה: 16 וְחַלֹּנוֹת אֲטֻמוֹת אֶל־הַתָּאִים וְאֶל אֵלֵיהֵמָה לִפְנִימָה לַשַּׁעַר סָבִיב | סָבִיב וְכֵן לָאֵלַמּוֹת וְחַלּוֹנוֹת סָבִיב | סָבִיב לִפְנִימָה וְאֶל־אַיִל תִּמֹרִים: 17 וַיְבִיאֵנִי אֶל־הֶחָצֵר הַחִיצוֹנָה וְהִנֵּה לְשָׁכוֹת וְרִצְפָה עָשׂוּי לֶחָצֵר סָבִיב | סָבִיב שְׁלֹשִׁים לְשָׁכוֹת אֶל־הָרִצְפָה: 18 וְהָרִצְפָה אֶל־כֶּתֶף הַשְּׁעָרִים לְעֻמַּת אֹרֶךְ הַשְּׁעָרִים הָרִצְפָה הַתַּחְתּוֹנָה: 19 וַיָּמָד רֹחַב מִלִּפְנֵי הַשַּׁעַר הַתַּחְתּוֹנָה לִפְנֵי הֶחָצֵר הַפְּנִימִי

²⁰On the outer court was also a gateway facing north, and he measured its length and its width. ²¹Its gate chambers, three on this side and three on that side, its gateposts and its archways, had the same measurements as the first gate; its length *was* fifty cubits and its width twenty-five cubits. ²²Its windows and those of its archways, and also its palm trees, *had* the same measurements as the gateway facing east; it was ascended by seven steps, and its archway *was* in front of it. ²³A gate of the inner court was opposite the northern gateway, just as the eastern *gateway;* and he measured from gateway to gateway, one hundred cubits.

²⁴After that he brought me toward the south, and there a gateway was facing south; and he measured its gateposts and archways according to these same measurements. ²⁵*There were* windows in it and in its archways all around like those windows; its length *was* fifty cubits and its width twenty-five cubits. ²⁶Seven steps led up to it, and its archway *was* in front of them; and it had palm trees on its gateposts, one on this side and one on that side. ²⁷*There was* also a gateway on the inner court, facing south; and he measured from gateway to gateway toward the south, one hundred cubits.

²⁸Then he brought me to the inner court through the southern gateway; he measured the southern gateway according to these same measurements. ²⁹Also its gate chambers, its gateposts, and its archways *were* according to these same measurements; *there were* windows in it and in its archways all around; *it was* fifty cubits long and twenty-five cubits wide. ³⁰*There were* archways all around, twenty-five cubits long and five cubits wide. ³¹Its archways faced the outer court, palm trees *were* on its gateposts, and going up to it *were* eight steps.

³²And he brought me into the inner court facing east; he measured the gateway according to these same measurements. ³³Also its gate chambers, its gateposts, and its archways *were* according to these same measurements; and *there were* windows in it and in its archways all around; *it was* fifty cubits long and twenty-five cubits wide. ³⁴Its archways faced the outer court, and palm trees *were* on its gateposts on this side and on that side; and going up to it *were* eight steps.

³⁵Then he brought me to the north gateway and measured *it* according to these same measurements— ³⁶also its gate chambers, its gateposts, and its archways. It had windows all around; its length *was* fifty cubits and its width twenty-five cubits. ³⁷Its gateposts faced the outer court, palm trees *were* on its gateposts on this side and on that side, and going up to it *were* eight steps.

20 וְהַשַּׁעַר מְחוּץ מֵאָה אַמָּה הַקָּדִים וְהַצָּפוֹן: אֲשֶׁר פָּנָיו דֶּרֶךְ הַצָּפוֹן לֶחָצֵר הַחִיצוֹנָה מָדַד אָרְכּוֹ וְרָחְבּוֹ: 21 וְתָאָו שְׁלוֹשָׁה מִפּוֹ וּשְׁלֹשָׁה מִפּוֹ וְאֵילָו וְאֵלַמָּו הָיָה כְּמִדַּת הַשַּׁעַר הָרִאשׁוֹן חֲמִשִּׁים אַמָּה אָרְכּוֹ וְרֹחַב חָמֵשׁ וְעֶשְׂרִים בָּאַמָּה: 22 וְחַלּוֹנָו וְאֵלַמָּו וְתִמֹרָו כְּמִדַּת הַשַּׁעַר אֲשֶׁר פָּנָיו דֶּרֶךְ הַקָּדִים וּבְמַעֲלוֹת שֶׁבַע יַעֲלוּ בוֹ וְאֵילַמָּו לִפְנֵיהֶם: 23 וְשַׁעַר לֶחָצֵר הַפְּנִימִי נֶגֶד הַשַּׁעַר לַצָּפוֹן וְלַקָּדִים וַיָּמָד מִשַּׁעַר אֶל־שַׁעַר מֵאָה אַמָּה: 24 וַיּוֹלִכֵנִי דֶּרֶךְ הַדָּרוֹם וְהִנֵּה־שַׁעַר דֶּרֶךְ הַדָּרוֹם וּמָדַד אֵילָו וְאֵילַמָּו כַּמִּדּוֹת הָאֵלֶּה: 25 וְחַלּוֹנִים לוֹ וּלְאֵילַמָּו סָבִיב סָבִיב כְּהַחֲלֹנוֹת הָאֵלֶּה חֲמִשִּׁים אַמָּה אֹרֶךְ וְרֹחַב חָמֵשׁ וְעֶשְׂרִים אַמָּה: 26 וּמַעֲלוֹת שִׁבְעָה עֹלוֹתָו וְאֵלַמָּו לִפְנֵיהֶם וְתִמֹרִים לוֹ אֶחָד מִפּוֹ וְאֶחָד מִפּוֹ אֶל־אֵילָו: 27 וְשַׁעַר לֶחָצֵר הַפְּנִימִי דֶּרֶךְ הַדָּרוֹם וַיָּמָד מִשַּׁעַר אֶל־הַשַּׁעַר דֶּרֶךְ הַדָּרוֹם מֵאָה אַמּוֹת: 28 וַיְבִיאֵנִי אֶל־חָצֵר הַפְּנִימִי בְּשַׁעַר הַדָּרוֹם וַיָּמָד אֶת־הַשַּׁעַר הַדָּרוֹם כַּמִּדּוֹת הָאֵלֶּה: 29 וְתָאָו וְאֵילָו וְאֵלַמָּו כַּמִּדּוֹת הָאֵלֶּה וְחַלּוֹנוֹת לוֹ וּלְאֵלַמָּו סָבִיב סָבִיב חֲמִשִּׁים אַמָּה אֹרֶךְ וְרֹחַב עֶשְׂרִים וְחָמֵשׁ אַמּוֹת: 30 וְאֵלַמּוֹת סָבִיב סָבִיב אֹרֶךְ חָמֵשׁ וְעֶשְׂרִים אַמָּה וְרֹחַב חָמֵשׁ אַמּוֹת: 31 וְאֵלַמָּו אֶל־חָצֵר הַחִצוֹנָה וְתִמֹרִים אֶל־אֵילָו וּמַעֲלוֹת שְׁמוֹנֶה מַעֲלָו: 32 וַיְבִיאֵנִי אֶל־הֶחָצֵר הַפְּנִימִי דֶּרֶךְ הַקָּדִים וַיָּמָד אֶת־הַשַּׁעַר כַּמִּדּוֹת הָאֵלֶּה: 33 וְתָאָו וְאֵילָו וְאֵלַמָּו כַּמִּדּוֹת הָאֵלֶּה וְחַלּוֹנוֹת לוֹ וּלְאֵלַמָּו סָבִיב סָבִיב אֹרֶךְ חֲמִשִּׁים אַמָּה וְרֹחַב חָמֵשׁ וְעֶשְׂרִים אַמָּה: 34 וְאֵלַמָּו לֶחָצֵר הַחִיצוֹנָה וְתִמֹרִים אֶל־אֵילָו מִפּוֹ וּמִפּוֹ וּשְׁמֹנֶה מַעֲלוֹת מַעֲלָו: 35 וַיְבִיאֵנִי אֶל־שַׁעַר הַצָּפוֹן וּמָדַד כַּמִּדּוֹת הָאֵלֶּה: 36 תָּאָו אֵלָו וְאֵלַמָּו וְחַלּוֹנוֹת לוֹ סָבִיב סָבִיב אֹרֶךְ חֲמִשִּׁים אַמָּה וְרֹחַב חָמֵשׁ וְעֶשְׂרִים אַמָּה: 37 וְאֵילָו לֶחָצֵר הַחִיצוֹנָה וְתִמֹרִים אֶל־אֵילָו מִפּוֹ וּמִפּוֹ וּשְׁמֹנֶה מַעֲלוֹת מַעֲלָו:

ם 6 בְּמַעֲלוֹתָו 9 וְאֵלָו 15 הָאִיתוֹן

21 וְתָאָיו וְאֵלַמָּיו
22 וְחַלּוֹנָיו וְאֵלַמָּיו וְתִמֹרָיו וְאֵילַמָּו 24 אֵילָיו וְאֵילַמָּיו
25 וּלְאֵילַמָּיו 26 עֹלוֹתָיו וְאֵלַמָּיו אֵילָיו
29 וְתָאָיו וְאֵילָיו וְאֵלַמָּיו וּלְאֵלַמָּיו
31 אֵילָיו מַעֲלָיו 33 וְאֵלָיו וְתָאָיו וְאֵלַמָּיו וּלְאֵלַמָּיו
34 וְאֵלַמָּיו אֵלָיו מַעֲלָיו 36 תָּאָיו אֵלָיו וְאֵלַמָּיו
37 וְאֵילָיו אֵילָיו מַעֲלָיו

38 *There was* a chamber and its entrance by the gateposts of the gateway, where they washed the burnt offering. 39 In the vestibule of the gateway *were* two tables on this side and two tables on that side, on which to slay the burnt offering, the sin offering, and the trespass offering. 40 At the outer side of the vestibule, as one goes up to the entrance of the northern gateway, *were* two tables; and on the other side of the vestibule of the gateway *were* two tables. 41 Four tables *were* on this side and four tables on that side, by the side of the gateway, eight tables on which they slaughtered *the sacrifices.* 42 *There were* also four tables of hewn stone for the burnt offering, one cubit and a half long, one cubit and a half wide, and one cubit high; on these they laid the instruments with which they slaughtered the burnt offering and the sacrifice. 43 Inside *were* hooks, a handbreadth wide, fastened all around; and the flesh of the sacrifices *was* on the tables.

44 Outside the inner gate *were* the chambers for the singers in the inner court, one facing south at the side of the northern gateway, and the other facing north at the side of the southern gateway. 45 Then he said to me, "This chamber which faces south *is* for the priests who have charge of the temple. 46 The chamber which faces north *is* for the priests who have charge of the altar; these *are* the sons of Zadok, from the sons of Levi, who come near the LORD to minister to Him."

47 And he measured the court, one hundred cubits long and one hundred cubits wide, foursquare. The altar *was* in front of the temple. 48 Then he brought me to the vestibule of the temple and measured the doorposts of the vestibule, five cubits on this side and five cubits on that side; and the width of the gateway was three cubits on this side and three cubits on that side. 49 The length of the vestibule *was* twenty cubits, and the width eleven cubits; and by the steps which led up to it *there were* pillars by the doorposts, one on this side and another on that side.

41 Then he brought me into the sanctuary and measured the doorposts, six cubits wide on one side and six cubits wide on the other side—the width of the tabernacle. 2 The width of the entryway *was* ten cubits, and the side walls of the entrance *were* five cubits on this side and five cubits on the other side; and he measured its length, forty cubits, and its width, twenty cubits.

3 Also he went inside and measured the doorposts, two cubits; and the entrance, six cubits *high;* and the width of the entrance, seven cubits. 4 He

38 וְלִשְׁכָּה וּפִתְחָהּ בְּאֵילִים הַשְּׁעָרִים שָׁם יָדִיחוּ אֶת־הָעֹלָה: 39 וּבְאֻלָם הַשַּׁעַר שְׁנַיִם שֻׁלְחָנוֹת מִפּוֹ וּשְׁנַיִם שֻׁלְחָנוֹת מִפֹּה לִשְׁחוֹט אֲלֵיהֶם הָעוֹלָה וְהַחַטָּאת וְהָאָשָׁם: 40 וְאֶל־הַכָּתֵף מִחוּצָה לָעוֹלֶה לְפֶתַח הַשַּׁעַר הַצָּפוֹנָה שְׁנַיִם שֻׁלְחָנוֹת וְאֶל־הַכָּתֵף הָאַחֶרֶת אֲשֶׁר לְאֻלָם הַשַּׁעַר שְׁנַיִם שֻׁלְחָנוֹת: 41 אַרְבָּעָה שֻׁלְחָנוֹת מִפֹּה וְאַרְבָּעָה שֻׁלְחָנוֹת מִפֹּה לְכֶתֶף הַשַּׁעַר שְׁמוֹנָה שֻׁלְחָנוֹת אֲלֵיהֶם יִשְׁחָטוּ: 42 וְאַרְבָּעָה שֻׁלְחָנוֹת לָעוֹלָה אַבְנֵי גָזִית אֹרֶךְ אַמָּה אַחַת וָחֵצִי וְרֹחַב אַמָּה אַחַת וָחֵצִי וְגֹבַהּ אַמָּה אֶחָת אֲלֵיהֶם וְיַנִּיחוּ אֶת־הַכֵּלִים אֲשֶׁר יִשְׁחֲטוּ אֶת־הָעוֹלָה בָּם וְהַזָּבַח: 43 וְהַשְׁפַתַּיִם טֹפַח אֶחָד מוּכָנִים בַּבַּיִת סָבִיב | סָבִיב וְאֶל־הַשֻּׁלְחָנוֹת בְּשַׂר הַקָּרְבָן: 44 וּמִחוּצָה לַשַּׁעַר הַפְּנִימִי לִשְׁכוֹת שָׁרִים בֶּחָצֵר הַפְּנִימִי אֲשֶׁר אֶל־כֶּתֶף שַׁעַר הַצָּפוֹן וּפְנֵיהֶם דֶּרֶךְ הַדָּרוֹם אֶחָד אֶל־כֶּתֶף שַׁעַר הַקָּדִים פְּנֵי דֶּרֶךְ הַצָּפֹן: 45 וַיְדַבֵּר אֵלָי זֹה הַלִּשְׁכָּה אֲשֶׁר פָּנֶיהָ דֶּרֶךְ הַדָּרוֹם לַכֹּהֲנִים שֹׁמְרֵי מִשְׁמֶרֶת הַבָּיִת: 46 וְהַלִּשְׁכָּה אֲשֶׁר פָּנֶיהָ דֶּרֶךְ הַצָּפוֹן לַכֹּהֲנִים שֹׁמְרֵי מִשְׁמֶרֶת הַמִּזְבֵּחַ הֵמָּה בְנֵי־צָדוֹק הַקְּרֵבִים מִבְּנֵי־לֵוִי אֶל־יְהֹוָה לְשָׁרְתוֹ: 47 וַיָּמָד אֶת־הֶחָצֵר אֹרֶךְ | מֵאָה אַמָּה וְרֹחַב מֵאָה אַמָּה מְרֻבָּעַת וְהַמִּזְבֵּחַ לִפְנֵי הַבָּיִת: 48 וַיְבִיאֵנִי אֶל־אֻלָם הַבַּיִת וַיָּמָד אֵל אֻלָם חָמֵשׁ אַמּוֹת מִפֹּה וְחָמֵשׁ אַמּוֹת מִפֹּה וְרֹחַב הַשַּׁעַר שָׁלֹשׁ אַמּוֹת מִפּוֹ וְשָׁלֹשׁ אַמּוֹת מִפֹּה: 49 אֹרֶךְ הָאֻלָם עֶשְׂרִים אַמָּה וְרֹחַב עַשְׁתֵּי עֶשְׂרֵה אַמָּה וּבַמַּעֲלוֹת אֲשֶׁר יַעֲלוּ אֵלָיו וְעַמֻּדִים אֶל־הָאֵילִים אֶחָד מִפֹּה וְאֶחָד מִפֹּה:

מא וַיְבִיאֵנִי אֶל־הַהֵיכָל וַיָּמָד אֶת־הָאֵילִים שֵׁשׁ־אַמּוֹת רֹחַב־מִפּוֹ וְשֵׁשׁ־אַמּוֹת־רֹחַב מִפּוֹ רֹחַב הָאֹהֶל: 2 וְרֹחַב הַפֶּתַח עֶשֶׂר אַמּוֹת וְכִתְפוֹת הַפֶּתַח חָמֵשׁ אַמּוֹת מִפּוֹ וְחָמֵשׁ אַמּוֹת מִפּוֹ וַיָּמָד אָרְכּוֹ אַרְבָּעִים אַמָּה וְרֹחַב עֶשְׂרִים אַמָּה: 3 וּבָא לִפְנִימָה וַיָּמָד אֵיל־הַפֶּתַח שְׁתַּיִם אַמּוֹת וְהַפֶּתַח שֵׁשׁ אַמּוֹת וְרֹחַב הַפֶּתַח שֶׁבַע אַמּוֹת: 4 וַיָּמָד

measured the length, twenty cubits; and the width, twenty cubits, beyond the sanctuary; and he said to me, "This *is* the Most Holy *Place*."

⁵ Next, he measured the wall of the temple, six cubits. The width of each side chamber all around the temple *was* four cubits on every side. ⁶ The side chambers *were* in three stories, one above the other, thirty chambers in each story; they rested on ledges which *were* for the side chambers all around, that they might be supported, but not fastened to the wall of the temple. ⁷ As one went up from story to story, the side chambers became wider all around, because their supporting ledges in the wall of the temple ascended like steps; therefore the width of the structure increased as one went up *from* the lowest *story* to the highest by way of the middle one. ⁸ I also saw an elevation all around the temple; it was the foundation of the side chambers, a full rod, *that is,* six cubits *high*. ⁹ The thickness of the outer wall of the side chambers *was* five cubits, and so also the remaining terrace by the place of the side chambers of the temple. ¹⁰ And between *it and the wall* chambers was a width of twenty cubits all around the temple on every side. ¹¹ The doors of the side chambers opened on the terrace, one door toward the north and another toward the south; and the width of the terrace *was* five cubits all around.

¹² The building that faced the separating courtyard at its western end *was* seventy cubits wide; the wall of the building *was* five cubits thick all around, and its length ninety cubits.

¹³ So he measured the temple, one hundred cubits long; and the separating courtyard with the building and its walls *was* one hundred cubits long; ¹⁴ also the width of the eastern face of the temple, including the separating courtyard, *was* one hundred cubits. ¹⁵ He measured the length of the building behind it, facing the separating courtyard, with its galleries on the one side and on the other side, one hundred cubits, as well as the inner temple and the porches of the court, ¹⁶ their doorposts and the beveled window frames. And the galleries all around their three stories opposite the threshold were paneled with wood from the ground to the windows—the windows were covered— ¹⁷ from the space above the door, even to the inner room, as well as outside, and on every wall all around, inside and outside, by measure.

¹⁸ And *it was* made with cherubim and palm trees, a palm tree between cherub and cherub. *Each* cherub had two faces, ¹⁹ so that the face of a man *was* toward a palm tree on one side, and the face of a young lion toward a palm tree on the other side;

אֶת־אָרְכּוֹ עֶשְׂרִים אַמָּה וְרֹחַב עֶשְׂרִים אַמָּה אֶל־
פְּנֵי הַהֵיכָל וַיֹּאמֶר אֵלַי זֶה קֹדֶשׁ הַקֳּדָשִׁים: 5 וַיָּמָד
קִיר־הַבַּיִת שֵׁשׁ אַמּוֹת וְרֹחַב הַצֵּלָע אַרְבַּע אַמּוֹת
סָבִיב ׀ סָבִיב לַבַּיִת סָבִיב: 6 וְהַצְּלָעוֹת צֵלָע אֶל־
צֵלָע שָׁלוֹשׁ וּשְׁלֹשִׁים פְּעָמִים וּבָאוֹת בַּקִּיר אֲשֶׁר־
לַבַּיִת לַצְּלָעוֹת סָבִיב ׀ סָבִיב לִהְיוֹת אֲחוּזִים וְלֹא־
יִהְיוּ אֲחוּזִים בְּקִיר הַבָּיִת: 7 וְרָחֲבָה וְנָסְבָה לְמַעְלָה
לְמַעְלָה לַצְּלָעוֹת כִּי מוּסַב־הַבַּיִת לְמַעְלָה לְמַעְלָה
סָבִיב ׀ סָבִיב לַבַּיִת עַל־כֵּן רֹחַב־לַבַּיִת לְמָעְלָה וְכֵן
הַתַּחְתּוֹנָה יַעֲלֶה עַל־הָעֶלְיוֹנָה לַתִּיכוֹנָה: 8 וְרָאִיתִי
לַבַּיִת גֹּבַהּ סָבִיב ׀ סָבִיב מיסדות הַצְּלָעוֹת מְלוֹ
הַקָּנֶה שֵׁשׁ אַמּוֹת אַצִּילָה: 9 רֹחַב הַקִּיר אֲשֶׁר־
לַצֵּלָע אֶל־הַחוּץ חָמֵשׁ אַמּוֹת וַאֲשֶׁר מֻנָּח בֵּית
צְלָעוֹת אֲשֶׁר לַבָּיִת: 10 וּבֵין הַלְּשָׁכוֹת רֹחַב עֶשְׂרִים
אַמָּה סָבִיב לַבַּיִת סָבִיב ׀ סָבִיב: 11 וּפֶתַח הַצֵּלָע
לַמֻּנָּח פֶּתַח אֶחָד דֶּרֶךְ הַצָּפוֹן וּפֶתַח אֶחָד לַדָּרוֹם
וְרֹחַב מְקוֹם הַמֻּנָּח חָמֵשׁ אַמּוֹת סָבִיב ׀ סָבִיב:

12 וְהַבִּנְיָן אֲשֶׁר אֶל־פְּנֵי הַגִּזְרָה פְּאַת דֶּרֶךְ־הַיָּם
רֹחַב שִׁבְעִים אַמָּה וְקִיר הַבִּנְיָן חָמֵשׁ־אַמּוֹת רֹחַב
סָבִיב ׀ סָבִיב וְאָרְכּוֹ תִּשְׁעִים אַמָּה: 13 וּמָדַד אֶת־
הַבַּיִת אֹרֶךְ מֵאָה אַמָּה וְהַגִּזְרָה וְהַבִּנְיָה וְקִירוֹתֶיהָ
אֹרֶךְ מֵאָה אַמָּה: 14 וְרֹחַב פְּנֵי הַבַּיִת וְהַגִּזְרָה
לַקָּדִים מֵאָה אַמָּה: 15 וּמָדַד אֹרֶךְ־הַבִּנְיָן אֶל־
פְּנֵי הַגִּזְרָה אֲשֶׁר עַל־אַחֲרֶיהָ ואתוקיהא מִפּוֹ
וּמִפּוֹ מֵאָה אַמָּה וְהַהֵיכָל הַפְּנִימִי וְאֻלַמֵּי הֶחָצֵר:

16 הַסִּפִּים וְהַחַלּוֹנִים הָאֲטֻמוֹת וְהָאַתִּיקִים ׀ סָבִיב
לִשְׁלָשְׁתָּם נֶגֶד הַסַּף שְׂחִיף עֵץ סָבִיב ׀ סָבִיב
וְהָאָרֶץ עַד־הַחַלֹּנוֹת וְהַחַלֹּנוֹת מְכֻסּוֹת: 17 עַל־
מֵעַל הַפֶּתַח וְעַד־הַבַּיִת הַפְּנִימִי וְלַחוּץ וְאֶל־כָּל־
הַקִּיר סָבִיב ׀ סָבִיב בַּפְּנִימִי וּבַחִיצוֹן מִדּוֹת:

18 וְעָשׂוּי כְּרוּבִים וְתִמֹרִים וְתִמֹרָה בֵּין־כְּרוּב לִכְרוּב
וּשְׁנַיִם פָּנִים לַכְּרוּב: 19 וּפְנֵי אָדָם אֶל־הַתִּמֹרָה
מִפּוֹ וּפְנֵי־כְפִיר אֶל־הַתִּמֹרָה מִפּוֹ עָשׂוּי אֶל־

thus *it was* made throughout the temple all around. ²⁰ From the floor to the space above the door, and on the wall of the sanctuary, cherubim and palm trees *were* carved.

²¹ The doorposts of the temple *were* square, *as was* the front of the sanctuary; their appearance was similar. ²² The altar *was* of wood, three cubits high, and its length two cubits. Its corners, its length, and its sides *were* of wood; and he said to me, "This *is* the table that *is* before the LORD."

²³ The temple and the sanctuary had two doors. ²⁴ The doors had two panels *apiece*, two folding panels: two *panels* for one door and two panels for the other *door*. ²⁵ Cherubim and palm trees *were* carved on the doors of the temple just as they were carved on the walls. A wooden canopy *was* on the front of the vestibule outside. ²⁶ *There were* beveled window *frames* and palm trees on one side and on the other, on the sides of the vestibule—also on the side chambers of the temple and on the canopies.

42 Then he brought me out into the outer court, by the way toward the north; and he brought me into the chamber which *was* opposite the separating courtyard, and which *was* opposite the building toward the north. ² Facing the length, *which was* one hundred cubits (the width was fifty cubits), was the north door. ³ Opposite the inner court of twenty *cubits,* and opposite the pavement of the outer court, *was* gallery against gallery in three *stories.* ⁴ In front of the chambers, toward the inside, *was* a walk ten cubits wide, at a distance of one cubit; and their doors faced north. ⁵ Now the upper chambers *were* shorter, because the galleries took away *space* from them more than from the lower and middle stories of the building. ⁶ For they *were* in three *stories* and did not have pillars like the pillars of the courts; therefore *the upper level* was shortened more than the lower and middle levels from the ground up. ⁷ And a wall which *was* outside ran parallel to the chambers, at the front of the chambers, toward the outer court; its length *was* fifty cubits. ⁸ The length of the chambers toward the outer court *was* fifty cubits, whereas that facing the temple *was* one hundred cubits. ⁹ At the lower chambers *was* the entrance on the east side, as one goes into them from the outer court.

¹⁰ Also *there were* chambers in the thickness of the wall of the court toward the east, opposite separating courtyard and opposite the building. ¹¹ *There was* a walk in front of them also, and their appearance *was* like the chambers which *were* toward the north; they *were* as long and as wide as the others, and all their exits and entrances *were*

כָּל־הַבַּ֤יִת סָבִ֨יב ׀ סָבִ֔יב 20 מֵהָאָ֖רֶץ עַד־מֵעַ֣ל הַפֶּ֔תַח הַכְּרוּבִ֥ים וְהַתִּמֹרִ֖ים עֲשׂוּיִ֑ם וְקִ֖יר הַהֵיכָֽל׃ 21 הַֽהֵיכָ֖ל מְזוּזַ֣ת רְבֻעָ֑ה וּפְנֵ֣י הַקֹּ֔דֶשׁ הַמַּרְאֶ֖ה כַּמַּרְאֶֽה׃ 22 הַמִּזְבֵּ֣חַ עֵ֣ץ שָׁל֣וֹשׁ אַמּ֣וֹת גָּבֹ֗הַּ וְאָרְכּ֣וֹ שְׁתַּֽיִם־אַמּ֗וֹת וּמִקְצֹעוֹתָיו֙ ל֔וֹ וְאָרְכּ֥וֹ וְקִירֹתָ֖יו עֵ֑ץ וַיְדַבֵּ֣ר אֵלַ֔י זֶ֚ה הַשֻּׁלְחָ֔ן אֲשֶׁ֖ר לִפְנֵ֥י יְהוָֽה׃ 23 וּשְׁתַּ֥יִם דְּלָת֖וֹת לַהֵיכָ֥ל וְלַקֹּֽדֶשׁ׃ 24 וּשְׁתַּ֧יִם דְּלָת֣וֹת לַדְּלָת֑וֹת שְׁתַּ֜יִם מוּסַבּ֣וֹת דְּלָת֗וֹת שְׁתַּ֨יִם֙ לְדֶ֣לֶת אֶחָ֔ת וּשְׁתֵּ֥י דְלָת֖וֹת לָאַחֶֽרֶת׃ 25 וַעֲשׂוּיָ֨ה אֲלֵיהֶ֜ן אֶֽל־דַּלְת֤וֹת הַֽהֵיכָל֙ כְּרוּבִ֣ים וְתִֽמֹרִ֔ים כַּאֲשֶׁ֥ר עֲשׂוּיִ֖ם לַקִּיר֑וֹת וְעָ֥ב עֵ֛ץ אֶל־פְּנֵ֥י הָאוּלָ֖ם מֵהַחֽוּץ׃ 26 וְחַלּוֹנִ֣ים אֲטֻמ֗וֹת וְתִֽמֹרִ֛ים מִפּ֥וֹ וּמִפּ֖וֹ אֶל־כִּתְפ֣וֹת הָאוּלָ֑ם וְצַלְע֥וֹת הַבַּ֖יִת וְהָעֻבִּֽים׃

מב וַיּוֹצִאֵ֗נִי אֶל־הֶֽחָצֵר֙ הַחִ֣יצוֹנָ֔ה הַדֶּ֖רֶךְ דֶּ֣רֶךְ הַצָּפ֑וֹן וַיְבִאֵ֣נִי אֶל־הַלִּשְׁכָּ֗ה אֲשֶׁ֨ר נֶ֧גֶד הַגִּזְרָ֛ה וַאֲשֶֽׁר־נֶ֥גֶד הַבִּנְיָ֖ן אֶל־הַצָּפֽוֹן׃ 2 אֶל־פְּנֵי־אֹ֙רֶךְ֙ אַמּ֣וֹת הַמֵּאָ֔ה פֶּ֖תַח הַצָּפ֑וֹן וְהָרֹ֖חַב חֲמִשִּׁ֥ים אַמּֽוֹת׃ 3 נֶ֣גֶד הָעֶשְׂרִ֗ים אֲשֶׁ֤ר לֶֽחָצֵר֙ הַפְּנִימִ֔י וְנֶ֣גֶד רִֽצְפָ֔ה אֲשֶׁ֖ר לֶחָצֵ֣ר הַחִֽיצוֹנָ֑ה אַתִּ֥יק אֶל־פְּנֵֽי־אַתִּ֖יק בַּשְּׁלִשִֽׁים׃ 4 וְלִפְנֵ֨י הַלְּשָׁכ֜וֹת מַהֲלַךְ֩ עֶ֨שֶׂר אַמּ֥וֹת רֹ֙חַב֙ אֶל־הַפְּנִימִ֔ית דֶּ֖רֶךְ אַמָּ֣ה אֶחָ֑ת וּפִתְחֵיהֶ֖ם לַצָּפֽוֹן׃ 5 וְהַלְּשָׁכ֥וֹת הָעֶלְיוֹנֹ֖ת קְצֻר֑וֹת כִּֽי־יוֹכְל֨וּ אַתִּיקִ֤ים מֵהֵ֙נָה֙ מֵהַתַּחְתֹּנ֣וֹת וּמֵהַתִּֽכֹנ֔וֹת בִּנְיָֽן׃ 6 כִּ֤י מְשֻׁלָּשׁוֹת֙ הֵ֔נָּה וְאֵ֤ין לָהֶן֙ עַמּוּדִ֔ים כְּעַמּוּדֵ֖י הַחֲצֵר֑וֹת עַל־כֵּ֣ן נֶאֱצַ֗ל מֵהַתַּחְתּוֹנ֛וֹת וּמֵהַתִּֽיכֹנ֖וֹת מֵהָאָֽרֶץ׃ 7 וְגָדֵ֤ר אֲשֶׁר־לַחוּץ֙ לְעֻמַּ֣ת הַלְּשָׁכ֔וֹת דֶּ֛רֶךְ הֶחָצֵ֥ר הַחִֽצוֹנָ֖ה אֶל־פְּנֵ֣י הַלְּשָׁכ֑וֹת אָרְכּ֖וֹ חֲמִשִּׁ֥ים אַמָּֽה׃ 8 כִּֽי־אֹ֣רֶךְ הַלְּשָׁכ֗וֹת אֲשֶׁ֛ר לֶחָצֵ֥ר הַחִֽצוֹנָ֖ה חֲמִשִּׁ֣ים אַמָּ֑ה וְהִנֵּ֧ה עַל־פְּנֵ֛י הַהֵיכָ֖ל מֵאָ֥ה אַמָּֽה׃ 9 וּמִתַּ֖חַת לִּשְׁכ֣וֹתP וּמִתַּ֣חַת הָאֵ֑לֶּה הַמֵּבִיאP הַמֵּבִ֣יא מֵֽהַקָּדִ֔ים בְּבֹא֣וֹ לָהֵ֖נָּה מֵֽהֶחָצֵֽר׃ 10 בְּרֹ֣חַב ׀ גֶּ֣דֶר הֶחָצֵ֗ר דֶּ֤רֶךְ הַקָּדִים֙ אֶל־פְּנֵ֣י הַגִּזְרָ֔ה וְאֶל־פְּנֵ֥י הַבִּנְיָ֖ן לְשָׁכֽוֹת׃ 11 וְדֶ֙רֶךְ֙ לִפְנֵיהֶ֔ם כְּמַרְאֵ֣ה הַלְּשָׁכ֗וֹת אֲשֶׁר֙ דֶּ֣רֶךְ הַצָּפ֔וֹן כְּאָרְכָּ֖ן כֵּ֣ן רָחְבָּ֑ן

according to plan. [12] And corresponding to the doors of the chambers that *were* facing south, as one enters them, *there was* a door in front of the walk, the way directly in front of the wall toward the east.

[13] Then he said to me, "The north chambers *and* the south chambers, which *are* opposite the separating courtyard, *are* the holy chambers where the priests who approach the LORD shall eat the most holy offerings. There they shall lay the most holy offerings—the grain offering, the sin offering, and the trespass offering—for the place *is* holy. [14] When the priests enter them, they shall not go out of the holy *chamber* into the outer court; but there they shall leave their garments in which they minister, for they *are* holy. They shall put on other garments; then they may approach *that* which *is* for the people."

[15] Now when he had finished measuring the inner temple, he brought me out through the gateway that faces toward the east, and measured it all around. [16] He measured the east side with the measuring rod, five hundred rods by the measuring rod all around. [17] He measured the north side, five hundred rods by the measuring rod all around. [18] He measured the south side, five hundred rods by the measuring rod. [19] He came around to the west side *and* measured five hundred rods by the measuring rod. [20] He measured it on the four sides; it had a wall all around, five hundred *cubits* long and five hundred wide, to separate the holy areas from the common.

43 Afterward he brought me to the gate, the gate that faces toward the east. [2] And behold, the glory of the God of Israel came from the way of the east. His voice *was* like the sound of many waters; and the earth shone with His glory. [3] *It was* like the appearance of the vision which I saw—like the vision which I saw when I came to destroy the city. The visions *were* like the vision which I saw by the River Chebar; and I fell on my face. [4] And the glory of the LORD came into the temple by way of the gate which faces toward the east. [5] The Spirit lifted me up and brought me into the inner court; and behold, the glory of the LORD filled the temple.

[6] Then I heard *Him* speaking to me from the temple, while a man stood beside me. [7] And He said to me, "Son of man, *this is* the place of My throne and the place of the soles of My feet, where I will dwell in the midst of the children of Israel forever. No more shall the house of Israel defile My holy name, they nor their kings, by their harlotry or with the carcasses of their kings on their high places.

וְכָל מוֹצָאֵיהֶן וּכְמִשְׁפְּטֵיהֶן וּכְפִתְחֵיהֶן: 12 וּכְפִתְחֵי הַלְּשָׁכוֹת אֲשֶׁר דֶּרֶךְ הַדָּרוֹם פֶּתַח בְּרֹאשׁ דָּרֶךְ דֶּרֶךְ בִּפְנֵי הַגְּדֶרֶת הַגִּנָה דֶּרֶךְ הַקָּדִים בְּבוֹאָן: 13 וַיֹּאמֶר אֵלַי לִשְׁכוֹת הַצָּפוֹן לִשְׁכוֹת הַדָּרוֹם אֲשֶׁר אֶל פְּנֵי הַגִּזְרָה הֵנָה | לִשְׁכוֹת הַקֹּדֶשׁ אֲשֶׁר יֹאכְלוּ שָׁם הַכֹּהֲנִים אֲשֶׁר קְרוֹבִים לַיהוָה קָדְשֵׁי הַקֳּדָשִׁים שָׁם יַנִּיחוּ | קָדְשֵׁי הַקֳּדָשִׁים וְהַמִּנְחָה וְהַחַטָּאת וְהָאָשָׁם כִּי הַמָּקוֹם קָדֹשׁ: 14 בְּבֹאָם הַכֹּהֲנִים וְלֹא יֵצְאוּ מֵהַקֹּדֶשׁ אֶל הֶחָצֵר הַחִיצוֹנָה וְשָׁם יַנִּיחוּ בִגְדֵיהֶם אֲשֶׁר יְשָׁרְתוּ בָהֶן כִּי קֹדֶשׁ הֵנָה יִלְבְּשׁוּ בְּגָדִים אֲחֵרִים וְקָרְבוּ אֶל אֲשֶׁר לָעָם: 15 וְכִלָּה אֶת מִדּוֹת הַבַּיִת הַפְּנִימִי וְהוֹצִיאַנִי דֶּרֶךְ הַשַּׁעַר אֲשֶׁר פָּנָיו דֶּרֶךְ הַקָּדִים וּמְדָדוֹ סָבִיב | סָבִיב: 16 מָדַד רוּחַ הַקָּדִים בִּקְנֵה הַמִּדָּה חֲמֵשׁ אֵמוֹת קָנִים בִּקְנֵה הַמִּדָּה סָבִיב: 17 מָדַד רוּחַ הַצָּפוֹן חֲמֵשׁ מֵאוֹת קָנִים בִּקְנֵה הַמִּדָּה סָבִיב: 18 אֵת רוּחַ הַדָּרוֹם מָדַד חֲמֵשׁ מֵאוֹת קָנִים בִּקְנֵה הַמִּדָּה: 19 סָבַב אֶל רוּחַ הַיָּם מָדַד חֲמֵשׁ מֵאוֹת קָנִים בִּקְנֵה הַמִּדָּה: 20 לְאַרְבַּע רוּחוֹת מְדָדוֹ חוֹמָה לוֹ סָבִיב | סָבִיב אֹרֶךְ חֲמֵשׁ מֵאוֹת וְרֹחַב חֲמֵשׁ מֵאוֹת לְהַבְדִּיל בֵּין הַקֹּדֶשׁ לְחֹל:

מג וַיּוֹלִכֵנִי אֶל הַשַּׁעַר שַׁעַר אֲשֶׁר פֹּנֶה דֶּרֶךְ הַקָּדִים: 2 וְהִנֵּה כְּבוֹד אֱלֹהֵי יִשְׂרָאֵל בָּא מִדֶּרֶךְ הַקָּדִים וְקוֹלוֹ כְּקוֹל מַיִם רַבִּים וְהָאָרֶץ הֵאִירָה מִכְּבֹדוֹ: 3 וּכְמַרְאֵה הַמַּרְאֶה אֲשֶׁר רָאִיתִי כַּמַּרְאֶה אֲשֶׁר רָאִיתִי בְּבֹאִי לְשַׁחֵת אֶת הָעִיר וּמַרְאוֹת כַּמַּרְאֶה אֲשֶׁר רָאִיתִי אֶל נְהַר כְּבָר וָאֶפֹּל אֶל פָּנָי: 4 וּכְבוֹד יְהוָה בָּא אֶל הַבָּיִת דֶּרֶךְ שַׁעַר אֲשֶׁר פָּנָיו דֶּרֶךְ הַקָּדִים: 5 וַתִּשָּׂאֵנִי רוּחַ וַתְּבִיאֵנִי אֶל הֶחָצֵר הַפְּנִימִי וְהִנֵּה מָלֵא כְבוֹד יְהוָה הַבָּיִת: 6 וָאֶשְׁמַע מִדַּבֵּר אֵלַי מֵהַבָּיִת וְאִישׁ הָיָה עֹמֵד אֶצְלִי: 7 וַיֹּאמֶר אֵלַי בֶּן אָדָם אֶת מְקוֹם כִּסְאִי וְאֶת מְקוֹם כַּפּוֹת רַגְלַי אֲשֶׁר אֶשְׁכָּן שָׁם בְּתוֹךְ בְּנֵי יִשְׂרָאֵל לְעוֹלָם וְלֹא יְטַמְּאוּ עוֹד בֵּית יִשְׂרָאֵל שֵׁם קָדְשִׁי הֵמָּה וּמַלְכֵיהֶם בִּזְנוּתָם וּבְפִגְרֵי מַלְכֵיהֶם בָּמוֹתָם:

מב 14 וְלָבְשׁוּ   16 מֵאוֹת

8 When they set their threshold by My threshold, and their doorpost by My doorpost, with a wall between them and Me, they defiled My holy name by the abominations which they committed; therefore I have consumed them in My anger. 9 Now let them put their harlotry and the carcasses of their kings far away from Me, and I will dwell in their midst forever.

10 "Son of man, describe the temple to the house of Israel, that they may be ashamed of their iniquities; and let them measure the pattern. 11 And if they are ashamed of all that they have done, make known to them the design of the temple and its arrangement, its exits and its entrances, its entire design and all its ordinances, all its forms and all its laws. Write it down in their sight, so that they may keep its whole design and all its ordinances, and perform them. 12 This is the law of the temple: The whole area surrounding the mountaintop is most holy. Behold, this is the law of the temple.

13 "These are the measurements of the altar in cubits (the cubit is one cubit and a handbreadth): the base one cubit high and one cubit wide, with a rim all around its edge of one span. This is the height of the altar: 14 from the base on the ground to the lower ledge, two cubits; the width of the ledge, one cubit; from the smaller ledge to the larger ledge, four cubits; and the width of the ledge, one cubit. 15 The altar hearth is four cubits high, with four horns extending upward from the hearth. 16 The altar hearth is twelve cubits long, twelve wide, square at its four corners; 17 the ledge, fourteen cubits long and fourteen wide on its four sides, with a rim of half a cubit around it; its base, one cubit all around; and its steps face toward the east."

18 And He said to me, "Son of man, thus says the Lord GOD: 'These are the ordinances for the altar on the day when it is made, for sacrificing burnt offerings on it, and for sprinkling blood on it. 19 You shall give a young bull for a sin offering to the priests, the Levites, who are of the seed of Zadok, who approach Me to minister to Me,' says the Lord GOD. 20 You shall take some of its blood and put it on the four horns of the altar, on the four corners of the ledge, and on the rim around it; thus you shall cleanse it and make atonement for it. 21 Then you shall also take the bull of the sin offering, and burn it in the appointed place of the temple, outside the sanctuary. 22 On the second day you shall offer a kid of the goats without blemish for a sin offering; and they shall cleanse the altar, as they cleansed it with the bull. 23 When you have finished cleansing it, you shall offer a young bull without blemish, and a ram from the flock without

8 בְּתִתָּם סִפָּם אֶת־סִפִּי וּמְזוּזָתָם אֵצֶל מְזוּזָתִי וְהַקִּיר בֵּינִי וּבֵינֵיהֶם וְטִמְּאוּ | אֶת־שֵׁם קָדְשִׁי בְּתוֹעֲבוֹתָם אֲשֶׁר עָשׂוּ וָאֲכַל אֹתָם בְּאַפִּי: 9 עַתָּה יְרַחֲקוּ אֶת־זְנוּתָם וּפִגְרֵי מַלְכֵיהֶם מִמֶּנִּי וְשָׁכַנְתִּי בְתוֹכָם לְעוֹלָם: ס 10 אַתָּה בֶן־אָדָם הַגֵּד אֶת־בֵּית יִשְׂרָאֵל אֶת־הַבַּיִת וְיִכָּלְמוּ מֵעֲוֺנוֹתֵיהֶם וּמָדְדוּ אֶת־תָּכְנִית: 11 וְאִם־נִכְלְמוּ מִכֹּל אֲשֶׁר־ עָשׂוּ צוּרַת הַבַּיִת וּתְכוּנָתוֹ וּמוֹצָאָיו וּמוֹבָאָיו וְכָל־צוּרֹתָו וְאֵת כָּל־חֻקֹּתָיו וְכָל־צוּרֹתָו וְכָל־ תּוֹרֹתָו הוֹדַע אוֹתָם וּכְתֹב לְעֵינֵיהֶם וְיִשְׁמְרוּ אֶת־ כָּל־צוּרָתוֹ וְאֶת־כָּל־חֻקֹּתָיו וְעָשׂוּ אוֹתָם: 12 זֹאת תּוֹרַת הַבָּיִת עַל־רֹאשׁ הָהָר כָּל־גְּבֻלוֹ סָבִיב | סָבִיב קֹדֶשׁ קָדָשִׁים הִנֵּה־זֹאת תּוֹרַת הַבָּיִת: 13 וְאֵלֶּה מִדּוֹת הַמִּזְבֵּחַ בָּאַמּוֹת אַמָּה אַמָּה וָטֹפַח וְחֵיק הָאַמָּה וְאַמָּה־רֹחַב וּגְבוּלָהּ אֶל־שְׂפָתָהּ סָבִיב זֶרֶת הָאֶחָד וְזֶה גַּב הַמִּזְבֵּחַ: 14 וּמֵחֵיק הָאָרֶץ עַד־הָעֲזָרָה הַתַּחְתּוֹנָה שְׁתַּיִם אַמּוֹת וְרֹחַב אַמָּה אֶחָת וּמֵהָעֲזָרָה הַקְּטַנָּה עַד־הָעֲזָרָה הַגְּדוֹלָה אַרְבַּע אַמּוֹת וְרֹחַב הָאַמָּה: 15 וְהַהַרְאֵל אַרְבַּע אַמּוֹת וּמֵהָאֲרִאֵיל וּלְמַעְלָה הַקְּרָנוֹת אַרְבַּע: 16 וְהָאֲרִאֵיל שְׁתֵּים עֶשְׂרֵה אֹרֶךְ בִּשְׁתֵּים עֶשְׂרֵה רֹחַב רָבוּעַ אֶל אַרְבַּעַת רְבָעָיו: 17 וְהָעֲזָרָה אַרְבַּע עֶשְׂרֵה אֹרֶךְ בְּאַרְבַּע עֶשְׂרֵה רֹחַב אֶל אַרְבַּעַת רְבָעֶיהָ וְהַגְּבוּל סָבִיב אוֹתָהּ חֲצִי הָאַמָּה וְהַחֵיק־ לָהּ אַמָּה סָבִיב וּמַעֲלֹתֵהוּ פְּנוֹת קָדִים: 18 וַיֹּאמֶר אֵלַי בֶּן־אָדָם כֹּה אָמַר אֲדֹנָי יְהֹוִה אֵלֶּה חֻקּוֹת הַמִּזְבֵּחַ בְּיוֹם הֵעָשׂוֹתוֹ לְהַעֲלוֹת עָלָיו עוֹלָה וְלִזְרֹק עָלָיו דָּם: 19 וְנָתַתָּה אֶל־הַכֹּהֲנִים הַלְוִיִּם אֲשֶׁר הֵם מִזֶּרַע צָדוֹק הַקְּרֹבִים אֵלַי נְאֻם אֲדֹנָי יְהֹוִה לְשָׁרְתֵנִי פַּר בֶּן־בָּקָר לְחַטָּאת: 20 וְלָקַחְתָּ מִדָּמוֹ וְנָתַתָּה עַל־אַרְבַּע קַרְנֹתָיו וְאֶל־אַרְבַּע פִּנּוֹת הָעֲזָרָה וְאֶל־ הַגְּבוּל סָבִיב וְחִטֵּאתָ אוֹתוֹ וְכִפַּרְתָּהוּ: 21 וְלָקַחְתָּ אֵת הַפָּר הַחַטָּאת וּשְׂרָפוֹ בְּמִפְקַד הַבַּיִת מִחוּץ לַמִּקְדָּשׁ: 22 וּבַיּוֹם הַשֵּׁנִי תַּקְרִיב שְׂעִיר־עִזִּים תָּמִים לְחַטָּאת וְחִטְּאוּ אֶת־הַמִּזְבֵּחַ כַּאֲשֶׁר חִטְּאוּ בַּפָּר: 23 בְּכַלּוֹתְךָ מֵחַטֵּא תַּקְרִיב פַּר בֶּן־בָּקָר תָּמִים

מג 11 צוּרֹתָיו תּוֹרֹתָיו 15 וּמֵהָאֲרִאֵיל 16 וְהָאֲרִאֵל

blemish. 24 When you offer them before the LORD, the priests shall throw salt on them, and they will offer them up *as* a burnt offering to the LORD. 25 Every day for seven days you shall prepare a goat *for* a sin offering; they shall also prepare a young bull and a ram from the flock, both without blemish. 26 Seven days they shall make atonement for the altar and purify it, and so consecrate *it*. 27 When these days are over it shall be, on the eighth day and thereafter, that the priests shall offer your burnt offerings and your peace offerings on the altar; and I will accept you,' says the Lord GOD."

44 Then He brought me back to the outer gate of the sanctuary which faces toward the east, but it *was* shut. 2 And the LORD said to me, "This gate shall be shut; it shall not be opened, and no man shall enter by it, because the LORD God of Israel has entered by it; therefore it shall be shut. 3 *As for* the prince, *because* he *is* the prince, he may sit in it to eat bread before the LORD; he shall enter by way of the vestibule of the gateway, and go out the same way."

4 Also He brought me by way of the north gate to the front of the temple; so I looked, and behold, the glory of the LORD filled the house of the LORD; and I fell on my face. 5 And the LORD said to me, "Son of man, mark well, see with your eyes and hear with your ears, all that I say to you concerning all the ordinances of the house of the LORD and all its laws. Mark well who may enter the house and all who go out from the sanctuary.

6 "Now say to the rebellious, to the house of Israel, 'Thus says the Lord GOD: "O house of Israel, let Us have no more of all your abominations. 7 When you brought in foreigners, uncircumcised in heart and uncircumcised in flesh, to be in My sanctuary to defile it—My house—and when you offered My food, the fat and the blood, then they broke My covenant because of all your abominations. 8 And you have not kept charge of My holy things, but you have set *others* to keep charge of My sanctuary for you." 9 Thus says the Lord GOD: "No foreigner, uncircumcised in heart or uncircumcised in flesh, shall enter My sanctuary, including any foreigner who *is* among the children of Israel.

10 "And the Levites who went far from Me, when Israel went astray, who strayed away from Me after their idols, they shall bear their iniquity. 11 Yet they shall be ministers in My sanctuary, *as* gatekeepers of the house and ministers of the house; they shall slay the burnt offering and the sacrifice for the people, and they shall stand before them to minister

וְאַ֨יִל מִן־הַצֹּ֖אן תְּמִימִֽם: 24 וְהִקְרַבְתֶּ֣ם לִפְנֵ֣י יְהֹוָ֗ה וְהִשְׁלִ֤יכוּ הַכֹּֽהֲנִים֙ עֲלֵיהֶ֣ם מֶ֔לַח וְהֶעֱל֥וּ אוֹתָ֛ם עֹלָ֖ה לַֽיהֹוָֽה: 25 שִׁבְעַ֣ת יָמִ֗ים תַּֽעֲשֶׂ֥ה שְׂעִיר־חַטָּאת֙ לַיּ֔וֹם וּפַ֧ר בֶּן־בָּקָ֛ר וְאַ֥יִל מִן־הַצֹּ֖אן תְּמִימִ֥ם יַֽעֲשֽׂוּ: 26 שִׁבְעַ֣ת יָמִ֔ים יְכַפְּר֖וּ אֶת־הַמִּזְבֵּ֑חַ וְטִֽהֲר֖וּ אֹת֑וֹ וּמִלְא֖וּ יָדָֽו: 27 וִֽיכַלּ֖וּ אֶת־הַיָּמִ֑ים ס וְהָיָ֣ה בַיּ֣וֹם הַשְּׁמִינִ֣י וָהָ֗לְאָה יַֽעֲשׂ֤וּ הַכֹּֽהֲנִים֙ עַל־הַמִּזְבֵּ֔חַ אֶת־עֽוֹלֽוֹתֵיכֶם֙ וְאֶת־שַׁלְמֵיכֶ֔ם וְרָצִ֥אתִי אֶתְכֶ֖ם נְאֻ֛ם אֲדֹנָ֥י יְהֹוִֽה: ס

מד וַיָּ֣שֶׁב אֹתִ֗י דֶּ֛רֶךְ שַׁ֥עַר הַמִּקְדָּ֖שׁ הַֽחִיצ֑וֹן הַפֹּנֶ֣ה קָדִ֑ים וְה֖וּא סָגֽוּר: 2 וַיֹּ֨אמֶר אֵלַ֜י יְהֹוָ֗ה הַשַּׁ֣עַר הַזֶּ֤ה סָגוּר֙ יִֽהְיֶ֔ה לֹ֣א יִפָּתֵ֔חַ וְאִ֖ישׁ לֹֽא־יָ֣בֹא ב֑וֹ כִּ֣י יְהֹוָ֧ה אֱלֹהֵֽי־יִשְׂרָאֵ֛ל בָּ֥א ב֖וֹ וְהָיָ֥ה סָגֽוּר: 3 אֶת־הַנָּשִׂ֗יא נָשִׂ֣יא ה֡וּא יֵֽשֶׁב־בּ֩וֹ לֶֽאֱכָל־לֶ֨חֶם לִפְנֵ֣י יְהֹוָ֔ה מִדֶּ֨רֶךְ אֻלָ֤ם הַשַּׁ֨עַר֙ יָב֔וֹא וּמִדַּרְכּ֖וֹ יֵצֵֽא: 4 וַיְבִיאֵ֣נִי דֶּֽרֶךְ־שַׁ֣עַר הַצָּפוֹן֮ אֶל־פְּנֵ֣י הַבַּ֒יִת֒ וָאֵ֕רֶא וְהִנֵּ֛ה מָלֵ֥א כְבֽוֹד־יְהֹוָ֖ה אֶת־בֵּ֣ית יְהֹוָ֑ה וָֽאֶפֹּ֖ל אֶל־פָּנָֽי: 5 וַיֹּ֨אמֶר אֵלַ֜י יְהֹוָ֗ה בֶּן־אָדָ֞ם שִׂ֧ים לִבְּךָ֣ וּרְאֵ֣ה בְעֵינֶ֗יךָ וּבְאָזְנֶ֨יךָ שְּׁמָ֜ע אֵ֣ת כָּל־אֲשֶׁ֣ר אֲנִ֣י מְדַבֵּ֣ר אֹתָ֗ךְ לְכָל־חֻקּ֤וֹת בֵּֽית־יְהֹוָה֙ וּלְכָל־תּ֣וֹרֹתָ֔יו וְשַׂמְתָּ֤ לִבְּךָ֙ לִמְב֣וֹא הַבַּ֔יִת בְּכֹ֖ל מוֹצָאֵ֥י הַמִּקְדָּֽשׁ: 6 וְאָֽמַרְתָּ֤ אֶל־מֶ֨רִי֙ אֶל־בֵּ֣ית יִשְׂרָאֵ֔ל כֹּ֥ה אָמַ֖ר אֲדֹנָ֣י יְהֹוִ֑ה רַב־לָכֶ֛ם מִכָּל־תּֽוֹעֲבֽוֹתֵיכֶ֖ם בֵּ֥ית יִשְׂרָאֵֽל: 7 בַּֽהֲבִֽיאֲכֶ֣ם בְּנֵֽי־נֵכָ֗ר עַרְלֵי־לֵב֙ וְעַרְלֵ֣י בָשָׂ֔ר לִֽהְי֥וֹת בְּמִקְדָּשִׁ֖י לְחַלְּל֣וֹ אֶת־בֵּיתִ֑י בְּהַקְרִֽיבְכֶ֤ם אֶת־לַחְמִי֙ חֵ֣לֶב וָדָ֔ם וַיָּפֵ֨רוּ֙ אֶת־בְּרִיתִ֔י אֶ֖ל כָּל־תּֽוֹעֲבֽוֹתֵיכֶֽם: 8 וְלֹ֥א שְׁמַרְתֶּ֖ם מִשְׁמֶ֣רֶת קָֽדָשָׁ֑י וַתְּשִׂימ֗וּן לְשֹֽׁמְרֵ֧י מִשְׁמַרְתִּ֛י בְּמִקְדָּשִׁ֖י לָכֶֽם: 9 כֹּֽה־אָמַר֮ אֲדֹנָ֣י יְהֹוִה֒ כָּל־בֶּן־נֵכָ֗ר עֶ֤רֶל לֵב֙ וְעֶ֣רֶל בָּשָׂ֔ר לֹ֥א יָב֖וֹא אֶל־מִקְדָּשִׁ֑י לְכָל־בֶּן־נֵכָ֔ר אֲשֶׁ֖ר בְּת֥וֹךְ בְּנֵ֥י יִשְׂרָאֵֽל: 10 כִּ֣י אִם־הַלְוִיִּ֗ם אֲשֶׁ֤ר רָֽחֲקוּ֙ מֵֽעָלַ֔י בִּתְע֤וֹת יִשְׂרָאֵל֙ אֲשֶׁ֣ר תָּע֣וּ מֵֽעָלַ֔י אַֽחֲרֵ֖י גִּלּֽוּלֵיהֶ֑ם וְנָֽשְׂא֖וּ עֲוֺנָֽם: 11 וְהָי֤וּ בְמִקְדָּשִׁי֙ מְשָׁ֣רְתִ֔ים פְּקֻדּוֹת֙ אֶל־שַֽׁעֲרֵ֣י הַבַּ֔יִת וּמְשָֽׁרְתִ֖ים אֶת־הַבָּ֑יִת הֵ֠מָּה יִשְׁחֲט֨וּ אֶת־הָֽעֹלָ֤ה וְאֶת־הַזֶּ֨בַח֙ לָעָ֔ם וְהֵ֛מָּה יַֽעַמְד֥וּ לִפְנֵיהֶ֖ם לְשָֽׁרְתָֽם:

מג 26 יָדָ֖ו
מד 5 תּֽוֹרֹתָֽיו

to them. 12 Because they ministered to them before their idols and caused the house of Israel to fall into iniquity, therefore I have raised My hand in an oath against them," says the Lord GOD, "that they shall bear their iniquity. 13 And they shall not come near Me to minister to Me as priest, nor come near any of My holy things, nor into the Most Holy *Place;* but they shall bear their shame and their abominations which they have committed. 14 Nevertheless I will make them keep charge of the temple, for all its work, and for all that has to be done in it.

15 "But the priests, the Levites, the sons of Zadok, who kept charge of My sanctuary when the children of Israel went astray from Me, they shall come near Me to minister to Me; and they shall stand before Me to offer to Me the fat and the blood," says the Lord GOD. 16 "They shall enter My sanctuary, and they shall come near My table to minister to Me, and they shall keep My charge. 17 And it shall be, whenever they enter the gates of the inner court, that they shall put on linen garments; no wool shall come upon them while they minister within the gates of the inner court or within the house. 18 They shall have linen turbans on their heads and linen trousers on their bodies; they shall not clothe themselves with *anything that causes* sweat. 19 When they go out to the outer court, to the *outer* court to the people, they shall take off their garments in which they have ministered, leave them in the holy chambers, and put on other garments; and in their holy garments they shall not sanctify the people.

20 "They shall neither shave their heads, nor let their hair grow long, but they shall keep their hair well trimmed. 21 No priest shall drink wine when he enters the inner court. 22 They shall not take as wife a widow or a divorced woman, but take virgins of the descendants of the house of Israel, or widows of priests.

23 "And they shall teach My people *the difference* between the holy and the unholy, and cause them to discern between the unclean and the clean. 24 In controversy they shall stand as judges, *and* judge it according to My judgments. They shall keep My laws and My statutes in all My appointed meetings, and they shall hallow My Sabbaths.

25 "They shall not defile *themselves* by coming near a dead person. Only for father or mother, for son or daughter, for brother or unmarried sister may they defile themselves. 26 After he is cleansed, they shall count seven days for him. 27 And on the day that he goes to the sanctuary to minister in the sanctuary, he must offer his sin offering in the inner court," says the Lord GOD.

12 יַ֣עַן אֲשֶׁ֣ר יְשָׁרְת֣וּ אוֹתָם֩ לִפְנֵ֨י גִלּֽוּלֵיהֶ֜ם וְהָי֣וּ לְבֵֽית־יִשְׂרָאֵ֗ל לְמִכְשׁ֣וֹל עָוֺ֑ן עַל־כֵּ֨ן נָשָׂ֤אתִי יָדִי֙ עֲלֵיהֶ֔ם נְאֻם֙ אֲדֹנָ֣י יְהֹוִ֔ה וְנָשְׂא֖וּ עֲוֺנָֽם׃ 13 וְלֹֽא־יִגְּשׁ֤וּ אֵלַי֙ לְכַהֵ֣ן לִ֔י וְלָגֶ֙שֶׁת֙ עַל־כׇּל־קׇדָשַׁ֔י אֶל־קׇדְשֵׁ֖י הַקֳּדָשִׁ֑ים וְנָֽשְׂאוּ֙ כְּלִמָּתָ֔ם וְתוֹעֲבוֹתָ֖ם אֲשֶׁ֥ר עָשֽׂוּ׃ 14 וְנָתַתִּ֣י אוֹתָ֔ם שֹׁמְרֵ֖י מִשְׁמֶ֣רֶת הַבָּ֑יִת לְכֹל֙ עֲבֹ֣דָת֔וֹ וּלְכֹ֛ל אֲשֶׁ֥ר יֵעָשֶׂ֖ה בּֽוֹ׃ פ

15 וְהַכֹּהֲנִ֨ים הַלְוִיִּ֜ם בְּנֵ֣י צָד֗וֹק אֲשֶׁ֣ר שָֽׁמְרוּ֩ אֶת־מִשְׁמֶ֨רֶת מִקְדָּשִׁ֜י בִּתְע֤וֹת בְּנֵֽי־יִשְׂרָאֵל֙ מֵֽעָלַ֔י הֵ֛מָּה יִקְרְב֥וּ אֵלַ֖י לְשָׁרְתֵ֑נִי וְעָמְד֣וּ לְפָנַ֗י לְהַקְרִ֥יב לִי֙ חֵ֣לֶב וָדָ֔ם נְאֻ֖ם אֲדֹנָ֥י יְהֹוִֽה׃ 16 הֵ֜מָּה יָבֹ֣אוּ אֶל־מִקְדָּשִׁ֗י וְהֵ֛מָּה יִקְרְב֥וּ אֶל־שֻׁלְחָנִ֖י לְשָׁרְתֵ֑נִי וְשָׁמְר֖וּ אֶת־מִשְׁמַרְתִּֽי׃ 17 וְהָיָ֗ה בְּבוֹאָם֙ אֶל־שַֽׁעֲרֵי֙ הֶחָצֵ֣ר הַפְּנִימִ֔ית בִּגְדֵ֥י פִשְׁתִּ֖ים יִלְבָּ֑שׁוּ וְלֹֽא־יַעֲלֶ֤ה עֲלֵיהֶם֙ צֶ֔מֶר בְּשָֽׁרְתָ֗ם בְּשַׁעֲרֵ֛י הֶחָצֵ֥ר הַפְּנִימִ֖ית וָבָֽיְתָה׃ 18 פַּאֲרֵ֤י פִשְׁתִּים֙ יִהְי֣וּ עַל־רֹאשָׁ֔ם וּמִכְנְסֵ֣י פִשְׁתִּ֔ים יִהְי֖וּ עַל־מׇתְנֵיהֶ֑ם לֹ֥א יַחְגְּר֖וּ בַּיָּֽזַע׃ 19 וּֽבְצֵאתָ֞ם אֶל־הֶחָצֵ֣ר הַחִיצוֹנָ֗ה אֶל־הֶחָצֵ֤ר הַחִֽיצוֹנָה֙ אֶל־הָעָ֔ם יִפְשְׁטוּ֙ אֶת־בִּגְדֵיהֶ֔ם אֲשֶׁר־הֵ֖מָּה מְשָׁרְתִ֣ם בָּ֑ם וְהִנִּ֤יחוּ אוֹתָם֙ בְּלִֽשְׁכֹ֣ת הַקֹּ֔דֶשׁ וְלָֽבְשׁוּ֙ בְּגָדִ֣ים אֲחֵרִ֔ים וְלֹֽא־יְקַדְּשׁ֥וּ אֶת־הָעָ֖ם בְּבִגְדֵיהֶֽם׃ 20 וְרֹאשָׁם֙ לֹ֣א יְגַלֵּ֔חוּ וּפֶ֖רַע לֹ֣א יְשַׁלֵּ֑חוּ כָּס֥וֹם יִכְסְמ֖וּ אֶת־רָֽאשֵׁיהֶֽם׃ 21 וְיַ֥יִן לֹֽא־יִשְׁתּ֖וּ כׇּל־כֹּהֵ֑ן בְּבוֹאָ֖ם אֶל־הֶחָצֵ֥ר הַפְּנִימִֽית׃ 22 וְאַלְמָנָה֙ וּגְרוּשָׁ֔ה לֹֽא־יִקְח֥וּ לָהֶ֖ם לְנָשִׁ֑ים כִּ֣י אִם־בְּתוּלֹ֗ת מִזֶּ֙רַע֙ בֵּ֣ית יִשְׂרָאֵ֔ל וְהָֽאַלְמָנָה֙ אֲשֶׁ֣ר תִּֽהְיֶ֣ה אַלְמָנָ֔ה מִכֹּהֵ֖ן יִקָּֽחוּ׃ 23 וְאֶת־עַמִּ֣י יוֹר֔וּ בֵּ֥ין קֹ֖דֶשׁ לְחֹ֑ל וּבֵין־טָמֵ֥א לְטָה֖וֹר יֽוֹדִעֻֽם׃ 24 וְעַל־רִ֗יב הֵ֚מָּה יַעַמְד֣וּ לְשָׁפֹ֔ט בְּמִשְׁפָּטַ֖י (שפטהו) יִשְׁפְּט֑וּהוּ וְאֶת־תּוֹרֹתַ֤י וְאֶת־חֻקֹּתַי֙ בְּכׇל־מוֹעֲדַ֣י יִשְׁמֹ֔רוּ וְאֶת־שַׁבְּתוֹתַ֖י יְקַדֵּֽשׁוּ׃ 25 וְאֶל־מֵ֣ת אָדָ֔ם לֹ֥א יָב֖וֹא לְטׇמְאָ֑ה כִּ֣י אִם־לְאָ֡ב וּ֠לְאֵ֠ם וּלְבֵ֨ן וּלְבַ֜ת לְאָ֗ח וּלְאָח֛וֹת אֲשֶׁר־לֹֽא־הָיְתָ֥ה לְאִ֖ישׁ יִטַּמָּֽאוּ׃ 26 וְאַחֲרֵ֖י טׇהֳרָת֑וֹ שִׁבְעַ֥ת יָמִ֖ים יִסְפְּרוּ־לֽוֹ׃ 27 וּבְיוֹם֩ בֹּא֨וֹ אֶל־הַקֹּ֜דֶשׁ אֶל־הֶחָצֵ֤ר הַפְּנִימִית֙ לְשָׁרֵ֣ת בַּקֹּ֔דֶשׁ יַקְרִ֖יב חַטָּאת֑וֹ נְאֻ֖ם

28 "It shall be, in regard to their inheritance, *that* I *am* their inheritance. You shall give them no possession in Israel, for I *am* their possession. 29 They shall eat the grain offering, the sin offering, and the trespass offering; every dedicated thing in Israel shall be theirs. 30 The best of all firstfruits of any kind, and every sacrifice of any kind from all your sacrifices, shall be the priest's; also you shall give to the priest the first of your ground meal, to cause a blessing to rest on your house. 31 The priests shall not eat anything, bird or beast, that died naturally or was torn *by wild beasts*.

45 "Moreover, when you divide the land by lot into inheritance, you shall set apart a district for the LORD, a holy section of the land; its length *shall be* twenty-five thousand *cubits,* and the width ten thousand. It *shall be* holy throughout its territory all around. 2 Of this there shall be a square plot for the sanctuary, five hundred by five hundred *rods,* with fifty cubits around it for an open space. 3 So this is the district you shall measure: twenty-five thousand *cubits* long and ten thousand wide; in it shall be the sanctuary, the Most Holy *Place.* 4 It shall be a holy *section* of the land, belonging to the priests, the ministers of the sanctuary, who come near to minister to the LORD; it shall be a place for their houses and a holy place for the sanctuary. 5 *An area* twenty-five thousand *cubits* long and ten thousand wide shall belong to the Levites, the ministers of the temple; they shall have twenty chambers as a possession.

6 "You shall appoint as the property of the city an area five thousand *cubits* wide and twenty-five thousand long, adjacent to the district of the holy *section;* it shall belong to the whole house of Israel.

7 "The prince shall have *a section* on one side and the other of the holy district and the city's property; and bordering on the holy district and the city's property, extending westward on the west side and eastward on the east side, the length *shall he* side by side with one of the *tribal* portions, from the west border to the east border. 8 The land shall be his possession in Israel; and My princes shall no more oppress My people, but they shall give *the rest of* the land to the house of Israel, according to their tribes."

9 'Thus says the Lord GOD: "Enough, O princes of Israel! Remove violence and plundering, execute justice and righteousness, and stop dispossessing My people," says the Lord GOD. 10 "You shall have honest scales, an honest ephah, and an honest bath. 11 The ephah and the bath shall be of the same measure, so that the bath contains one-tenth of a

אֲדֹנָי יְהֹוִה: 28 וְהָיְתָה לָהֶם לְנַחֲלָה אֲנִי נַחֲלָתָם
וַאֲחֻזָּה לֹא־תִתְּנוּ לָהֶם בְּיִשְׂרָאֵל אֲנִי אֲחֻזָּתָם:
29 הַמִּנְחָה וְהַחַטָּאת וְהָאָשָׁם הֵמָּה יֹאכְלוּם וְכָל־
חֵרֶם בְּיִשְׂרָאֵל לָהֶם יִהְיֶה: 30 וְרֵאשִׁית כָּל־בִּכּוּרֵי
כֹל וְכָל־תְּרוּמַת כֹּל מִכֹּל תְּרוּמוֹתֵיכֶם לַכֹּהֲנִים
יִהְיֶה וְרֵאשִׁית עֲרִסוֹתֵיכֶם תִּתְּנוּ לַכֹּהֵן לְהָנִיחַ
בְּרָכָה אֶל־בֵּיתֶךָ: 31 כָּל־נְבֵלָה וּטְרֵפָה מִן־הָעוֹף
וּמִן־הַבְּהֵמָה לֹא יֹאכְלוּ הַכֹּהֲנִים: פ

מה וּבְהַפִּילְכֶם אֶת־הָאָרֶץ בְּנַחֲלָה תָּרִימוּ
תְרוּמָה לַיהֹוָה ׀ קֹדֶשׁ מִן־הָאָרֶץ אֹרֶךְ חֲמִשָּׁה
וְעֶשְׂרִים אֶלֶף אֹרֶךְ וְרֹחַב עֲשָׂרָה אֶלֶף קֹדֶשׁ־הוּא
בְכָל־גְּבוּלָהּ סָבִיב: 2 יִהְיֶה מִזֶּה אֶל־הַקֹּדֶשׁ חֲמֵשׁ
מֵאוֹת בַּחֲמֵשׁ מֵאוֹת מְרֻבָּע סָבִיב וַחֲמִשִּׁים אַמָּה
מִגְרָשׁ לוֹ סָבִיב: 3 וּמִן־הַמִּדָּה הַזֹּאת תָּמוֹד אֹרֶךְ
חֲמֵשׁ וְעֶשְׂרִים אֶלֶף וְרֹחַב עֲשֶׂרֶת אֲלָפִים וּבוֹ־
יִהְיֶה הַמִּקְדָּשׁ קֹדֶשׁ קָדָשִׁים: 4 קֹדֶשׁ מִן־הָאָרֶץ
הוּא לַכֹּהֲנִים מְשָׁרְתֵי הַמִּקְדָּשׁ יִהְיֶה הַקְּרֵבִים
לְשָׁרֵת אֶת־יְהֹוָה וְהָיָה לָהֶם מָקוֹם לְבָתִּים וּמִקְדָּשׁ
לַמִּקְדָּשׁ: 5 וַחֲמִשָּׁה וְעֶשְׂרִים אֶלֶף אֹרֶךְ וַעֲשֶׂרֶת
אֲלָפִים רֹחַב יִהְיֶה לַלְוִיִּם מְשָׁרְתֵי הַבַּיִת לָהֶם
לַאֲחֻזָּה עֶשְׂרִים לְשָׁכֹת: 6 וַאֲחֻזַּת הָעִיר תִּתְּנוּ
חֲמֵשֶׁת אֲלָפִים רֹחַב וְאֹרֶךְ חֲמִשָּׁה וְעֶשְׂרִים
אֶלֶף לְעֻמַּת תְּרוּמַת הַקֹּדֶשׁ לְכָל־בֵּית יִשְׂרָאֵל
יִהְיֶה: 7 וְלַנָּשִׂיא מִזֶּה וּמִזֶּה לִתְרוּמַת הַקֹּדֶשׁ
וְלַאֲחֻזַּת הָעִיר אֶל־פְּנֵי תְרוּמַת־הַקֹּדֶשׁ וְאֶל־פְּנֵי
אֲחֻזַּת הָעִיר מִפְּאַת־יָם יָמָּה וּמִפְּאַת־קֵדְמָה קָדִימָה
וְאֹרֶךְ לְעֻמּוֹת אַחַד הַחֲלָקִים מִגְּבוּל יָם אֶל־גְּבוּל
קָדִימָה: 8 לָאָרֶץ יִהְיֶה־לּוֹ לַאֲחֻזָּה בְּיִשְׂרָאֵל וְלֹא־
יוֹנוּ עוֹד נְשִׂיאַי אֶת־עַמִּי וְהָאָרֶץ יִתְּנוּ לְבֵית־
יִשְׂרָאֵל לְשִׁבְטֵיהֶם: ס 9 כֹּה־אָמַר אֲדֹנָי
יְהֹוִה רַב־לָכֶם נְשִׂיאֵי יִשְׂרָאֵל חָמָס וָשֹׁד הָסִירוּ
וּמִשְׁפָּט וּצְדָקָה עֲשׂוּ הָרִימוּ גְרֻשֹׁתֵיכֶם מֵעַל עַמִּי
נְאֻם אֲדֹנָי יְהֹוִה: 10 מֹאזְנֵי־צֶדֶק וְאֵיפַת־צֶדֶק וּבַת־
צֶדֶק יְהִי לָכֶם: 11 הָאֵיפָה וְהַבַּת תֹּכֶן אֶחָד יִהְיֶה

מה 3 חֲמִשָּׁה 5 וְהָיָה

homer, and the ephah one-tenth of a homer; their measure shall be according to the homer. 12The shekel *shall be* twenty gerahs; twenty shekels, twenty-five shekels, *and* fifteen shekels shall be your mina.

13 "This *is* the offering which you shall offer: you shall give one-sixth of an ephah from a homer of wheat, and one-sixth of an ephah from a homer of barley. 14The ordinance concerning oil, the bath of oil, *is* one-tenth of a bath from a kor. A kor *is* a homer or ten baths, for ten baths *are* a homer. 15And one lamb shall be given from a flock of two hundred, from the rich pastures of Israel. These shall be for grain offerings, burnt offerings, and peace offerings, to make atonement for them," says the Lord God. 16"All the people of the land shall give this offering for the prince in Israel. 17Then it shall be the prince's part *to give* burnt offerings, grain offerings, and drink offerings, at the feasts, the New Moons, the Sabbaths, and at all the appointed seasons of the house of Israel. He shall prepare the sin offering, the grain offering, the burnt offering, and the peace offerings to make atonement for the house of Israel."

18 'Thus says the Lord God: "In the first *month,* on the first *day* of the month, you shall take a young bull without blemish and cleanse the sanctuary. 19The priest shall take some of the blood of the sin offering and put *it* on the doorposts of the temple, on the four corners of the ledge of the altar, and on the gateposts of the gate of the inner court. 20And so you shall do on the seventh *day* of the month for everyone who has sinned unintentionally or in ignorance. Thus you shall make atonement for the temple.

21 "In the first *month,* on the fourteenth day of the month, you shall observe the Passover, a feast of seven days; unleavened bread shall be eaten. 22And on that day the prince shall prepare for himself and for all the people of the land a bull *for* a sin offering. 23On the seven days of the feast he shall prepare a burnt offering to the Lord, seven bulls and seven rams without blemish, daily for seven days, and a kid of the goats daily *for* a sin offering. 24And he shall prepare a grain offering of one ephah for each bull and one ephah for each ram, together with a hin of oil for each ephah.

25 "In the seventh *month,* on the fifteenth day of the month, at the feast, he shall do likewise for seven days, according to the sin offering, the burnt offering, the grain offering, and the oil."

לָשֵׂאת מַעְשַׂר הַחֹמֶר הַבַּת וַעֲשִׂירִת הַחֹמֶר הָאֵיפָה אֶל־הַחֹמֶר יִהְיֶה מַתְכֻּנְתּוֹ: 12 וְהַשֶּׁקֶל עֶשְׂרִים גֵּרָה עֶשְׂרִים שְׁקָלִים חֲמִשָּׁה וְעֶשְׂרִים שְׁקָלִים עֲשָׂרָה וַחֲמִשָּׁה שֶׁקֶל הַמָּנֶה יִהְיֶה לָכֶם: 13 זֹאת הַתְּרוּמָה אֲשֶׁר תָּרִימוּ שִׁשִּׁית הָאֵיפָה מֵחֹמֶר הַחִטִּים וְשִׁשִּׁיתֶם הָאֵיפָה מֵחֹמֶר הַשְּׂעֹרִים: 14 וְחֹק הַשֶּׁמֶן הַבַּת הַשֶּׁמֶן מַעְשַׂר הַבַּת מִן־הַכֹּר עֲשֶׂרֶת הַבַּתִּים חֹמֶר כִּי־עֲשֶׂרֶת הַבַּתִּים חֹמֶר: 15 וְשֶׂה־אַחַת מִן־הַצֹּאן מִן־הַמָּאתַיִם מִמַּשְׁקֵה יִשְׂרָאֵל לְמִנְחָה וּלְעוֹלָה וְלִשְׁלָמִים לְכַפֵּר עֲלֵיהֶם נְאֻם אֲדֹנָי יְהוִה: 16 כֹּל הָעָם הָאָרֶץ יִהְיוּ אֶל־הַתְּרוּמָה הַזֹּאת לַנָּשִׂיא בְּיִשְׂרָאֵל: 17 וְעַל־הַנָּשִׂיא יִהְיֶה הָעוֹלוֹת וְהַמִּנְחָה וְהַנֵּסֶךְ בַּחַגִּים וּבֶחֳדָשִׁים וּבַשַּׁבָּתוֹת בְּכָל־מוֹעֲדֵי בֵּית יִשְׂרָאֵל הוּא־יַעֲשֶׂה אֶת־הַחַטָּאת וְאֶת־הַמִּנְחָה וְאֶת־הָעוֹלָה וְאֶת־הַשְּׁלָמִים לְכַפֵּר בְּעַד בֵּית־יִשְׂרָאֵל: ס 18 כֹּה־אָמַר אֲדֹנָי יְהוִה בָּרִאשׁוֹן בְּאֶחָד לַחֹדֶשׁ תִּקַּח פַּר־בֶּן־בָּקָר תָּמִים וְחִטֵּאתָ אֶת־הַמִּקְדָּשׁ: 19 וְלָקַח הַכֹּהֵן מִדַּם הַחַטָּאת וְנָתַן אֶל־מְזוּזַת הַבַּיִת וְאֶל־אַרְבַּע פִּנּוֹת הָעֲזָרָה לַמִּזְבֵּחַ וְעַל־מְזוּזַת שַׁעַר הֶחָצֵר הַפְּנִימִית: 20 וְכֵן תַּעֲשֶׂה בְּשִׁבְעָה בַחֹדֶשׁ מֵאִישׁ שֹׁגֶה וּמִפֶּתִי וְכִפַּרְתֶּם אֶת־הַבָּיִת: 21 בָּרִאשׁוֹן בְּאַרְבָּעָה עָשָׂר יוֹם לַחֹדֶשׁ יִהְיֶה לָכֶם הַפָּסַח חָג שְׁבֻעוֹת יָמִים מַצּוֹת יֵאָכֵל: 22 וְעָשָׂה הַנָּשִׂיא בַּיּוֹם הַהוּא בַּעֲדוֹ וּבְעַד כָּל־עַם הָאָרֶץ פַּר חַטָּאת: 23 וְשִׁבְעַת יְמֵי־הֶחָג יַעֲשֶׂה עוֹלָה לַיהוָה שִׁבְעַת פָּרִים וְשִׁבְעַת אֵילִים תְּמִימִם לַיּוֹם שִׁבְעַת הַיָּמִים וְחַטָּאת שְׂעִיר עִזִּים לַיּוֹם: 24 וּמִנְחָה אֵיפָה לַפָּר וְאֵיפָה לָאַיִל יַעֲשֶׂה וְשֶׁמֶן הִין לָאֵיפָה: 25 בַּשְּׁבִיעִי בַּחֲמִשָּׁה עָשָׂר יוֹם לַחֹדֶשׁ בֶּחָג יַעֲשֶׂה כָאֵלֶּה שִׁבְעַת הַיָּמִים כַּחַטָּאת כָּעֹלָה וְכַמִּנְחָה וְכַשָּׁמֶן: ס

46 ¹Thus says the Lord GOD: "The gateway of the inner court that faces toward the east shall be shut the six working days; but on the Sabbath it shall be opened, and on the day of the New Moon it shall be opened. ²The prince shall enter by way of the vestibule of the gateway from the outside, and stand by the gatepost. The priests shall prepare his burnt offering and his peace offerings. He shall worship at the threshold of the gate. Then he shall go out, but the gate shall not be shut until evening. ³Likewise the people of the land shall worship at the entrance to this gateway before the LORD on the Sabbaths and the New Moons. ⁴The burnt offering that the prince offers to the LORD on the Sabbath day *shall be* six lambs without blemish, and a ram without blemish; ⁵and the grain offering *shall be one* ephah for a ram, and the grain offering for the lambs, as much as he wants to give, as well as a hin of oil with every ephah. ⁶On the day of the New Moon *it shall be* a young bull without blemish, six lambs, and a ram; they shall be without blemish. ⁷He shall prepare a grain offering of an ephah for a bull, an ephah for a ram, as much as he wants to give for the lambs, and a hin of oil with every ephah. ⁸When the prince enters, he shall go in by way of the vestibule of the gateway, and go out the same way.

⁹"But when the people of the land come before the LORD on the appointed feast days, whoever enters by way of the north gate to worship shall go out by way of the south gate; and whoever enters by way of the south gate shall go out by way of the north gate. He shall not return by way of the gate through which he came, but shall go out through the opposite gate. ¹⁰The prince shall then be in their midst. When they go in, he shall go in; and when they go out, he shall go out. ¹¹At the festivals and the appointed feast days the grain offering shall be an ephah for a bull, an ephah for a ram, as much as he wants to give for the lambs, and a hin of oil with every ephah.

¹²"Now when the prince makes a voluntary burnt offering or voluntary peace offering to the LORD, the gate that faces toward the east shall then be opened for him; and he shall prepare his burnt offering and his peace offerings as he did on the Sabbath day. Then he shall go out, and after he goes out the gate shall be shut.

¹³"You shall daily make a burnt offering to the LORD *of* a lamb of the first year without blemish; you shall prepare it every morning. ¹⁴And you shall prepare a grain offering with it every morning, a sixth of an ephah, and a third of a hin of oil to moisten the fine flour. This grain offering is a perpetual ordinance, to be made regularly to the

מו כֹּה־אָמַר אֲדֹנָי יְהֹוִה שַׁעַר הֶחָצֵר הַפְּנִימִית הַפֹּנֶה קָדִים יִהְיֶה סָגוּר שֵׁשֶׁת יְמֵי הַמַּעֲשֶׂה וּבְיוֹם הַשַּׁבָּת יִפָּתֵחַ וּבְיוֹם הַחֹדֶשׁ יִפָּתֵחַ: ² וּבָא הַנָּשִׂיא דֶּרֶךְ אוּלָם הַשַּׁעַר מִחוּץ וְעָמַד עַל־מְזוּזַת הַשַּׁעַר וְעָשׂוּ הַכֹּהֲנִים אֶת־עוֹלָתוֹ וְאֶת־שְׁלָמָיו וְהִשְׁתַּחֲוָה עַל־מִפְתַּן הַשַּׁעַר וְיָצָא וְהַשַּׁעַר לֹא־יִסָּגֵר עַד־הָעָרֶב: ³ וְהִשְׁתַּחֲווּ עַם־הָאָרֶץ פֶּתַח הַשַּׁעַר הַהוּא בַּשַּׁבָּתוֹת וּבֶחֳדָשִׁים לִפְנֵי יְהֹוָה: ⁴ וְהָעֹלָה אֲשֶׁר־יַקְרִב הַנָּשִׂיא לַיהֹוָה בְּיוֹם הַשַּׁבָּת שִׁשָּׁה כְבָשִׂים תְּמִימִם וְאַיִל תָּמִים: ⁵ וּמִנְחָה אֵיפָה לָאַיִל וְלַכְּבָשִׂים מִנְחָה מַתַּת יָדוֹ וְשֶׁמֶן הִין לָאֵיפָה: ⁶ וּבְיוֹם הַחֹדֶשׁ פַּר בֶּן־בָּקָר תְּמִימִם וְשֵׁשֶׁת כְּבָשִׂים וָאַיִל תְּמִימִם יִהְיוּ: ⁷ וְאֵיפָה לַפָּר וְאֵיפָה לָאַיִל יַעֲשֶׂה מִנְחָה וְלַכְּבָשִׂים כַּאֲשֶׁר תַּשִּׂיג יָדוֹ וְשֶׁמֶן הִין לָאֵיפָה: ⁸ וּבְבוֹא הַנָּשִׂיא דֶּרֶךְ אוּלָם הַשַּׁעַר יָבוֹא וּבְדַרְכּוֹ יֵצֵא: ⁹ וּבְבוֹא עַם־הָאָרֶץ לִפְנֵי יְהֹוָה בַּמּוֹעֲדִים הַבָּא דֶּרֶךְ־שַׁעַר צָפוֹן לְהִשְׁתַּחֲוֹת יֵצֵא דֶּרֶךְ־שַׁעַר נֶגֶב וְהַבָּא דֶּרֶךְ־שַׁעַר נֶגֶב יֵצֵא דֶּרֶךְ־שַׁעַר צָפוֹנָה לֹא יָשׁוּב דֶּרֶךְ הַשַּׁעַר אֲשֶׁר־בָּא בוֹ כִּי נִכְחוֹ יֵצֵאוּ: ¹⁰ וְהַנָּשִׂיא בְּתוֹכָם בְּבוֹאָם יָבוֹא וּבְצֵאתָם יֵצֵאוּ: ¹¹ וּבַחַגִּים וּבַמּוֹעֲדִים תִּהְיֶה הַמִּנְחָה אֵיפָה לַפָּר וְאֵיפָה לָאַיִל וְלַכְּבָשִׂים מַתַּת יָדוֹ וְשֶׁמֶן הִין לָאֵיפָה: ס ¹² וְכִי־יַעֲשֶׂה הַנָּשִׂיא נְדָבָה עוֹלָה אוֹ־שְׁלָמִים נְדָבָה לַיהֹוָה וּפָתַח לוֹ אֶת־הַשַּׁעַר הַפֹּנֶה קָדִים וְעָשָׂה אֶת־עֹלָתוֹ וְאֶת־שְׁלָמָיו כַּאֲשֶׁר יַעֲשֶׂה בְּיוֹם הַשַּׁבָּת וְיָצָא וְסָגַר אֶת־הַשַּׁעַר אַחֲרֵי צֵאתוֹ: ¹³ וְכֶבֶשׂ בֶּן־שְׁנָתוֹ תָּמִים תַּעֲשֶׂה עוֹלָה לַיּוֹם לַיהֹוָה בַּבֹּקֶר בַּבֹּקֶר תַּעֲשֶׂה אֹתוֹ: ¹⁴ וּמִנְחָה תַעֲשֶׂה עָלָיו בַּבֹּקֶר בַּבֹּקֶר שִׁשִּׁית הָאֵיפָה וְשֶׁמֶן שְׁלִישִׁית הַהִין לָרֹס אֶת־הַסֹּלֶת

LORD. ¹⁵Thus they shall prepare the lamb, the grain offering, and the oil, *as* a regular burnt offering every morning."

¹⁶'Thus says the Lord GOD: "If the prince gives a gift *of some* of his inheritance to any of his sons, it shall belong to his sons; it is their possession by inheritance. ¹⁷But if he gives a gift of some of his inheritance to one of his servants, it shall be his until the year of liberty, after which it shall return to the prince. But his inheritance shall belong to his sons; it shall become theirs. ¹⁸Moreover the prince shall not take any of the people's inheritance by evicting them from their property; he shall provide an inheritance for his sons from his own property, so that none of My people may be scattered from his property." ' "

¹⁹Now he brought me through the entrance, which *was* at the side of the gate, into the holy chambers of the priests which face toward the north; and there a place *was* situated at their extreme western end. ²⁰And he said to me, "This *is* the place where the priests shall boil the trespass offering and the sin offering, *and* where they shall bake the grain offering, so that they do not bring *them* out into the outer court to sanctify the people."

²¹Then he brought me out into the outer court and caused me to pass by the four corners of the court; and in fact, in every corner of the court *there was another* court. ²²In the four corners of the court *were* enclosed courts, forty *cubits* long and thirty wide; all four corners *were* the same size. ²³*There was* a row *of building stones* all around in them, all around the four of them; and cooking hearths were made under the rows of stones all around. ²⁴And he said to me, "These *are* the kitchens where the ministers of the temple shall boil the sacrifices of the people."

47 Then he brought me back to the door of the temple; and there was water, flowing from under the threshold of the temple toward the east, for the front of the temple faced east; the water was flowing from under the right side of the temple, south of the altar. ²He brought me out by way of the north gate, and led me around on the outside to the outer gateway that faces east; and there was water, running out on the right side.

³And when the man went out to the east with the line in his hand, he measured one thousand cubits, and he brought me through the waters; the water *came up to my* ankles. ⁴Again he measured one thousand and brought me through the waters; the water *came up to my* knees. Again he measured one

מִנְחָה לַיהוָה חֻקּוֹת עוֹלָם תָּמִיד: 15 וַעֲשׂוּ אֶת־
הַכֶּבֶשׂ וְאֶת־הַמִּנְחָה וְאֶת־הַשֶּׁמֶן בַּבֹּקֶר בַּבֹּקֶר
עוֹלַת תָּמִיד: פ

16 כֹּה־אָמַר אֲדֹנָי יְהוִה כִּי־יִתֵּן הַנָּשִׂיא מַתָּנָה
לְאִישׁ מִבָּנָיו נַחֲלָתוֹ הִיא לְבָנָיו תִּהְיֶה אֲחֻזָּתָם
הִיא בְּנַחֲלָה: 17 וְכִי־יִתֵּן מַתָּנָה מִנַּחֲלָתוֹ לְאַחַד
מֵעֲבָדָיו וְהָיְתָה לּוֹ עַד־שְׁנַת הַדְּרוֹר וְשָׁבַת לַנָּשִׂיא
אַךְ נַחֲלָתוֹ בָּנָיו לָהֶם תִּהְיֶה: 18 וְלֹא־יִקַּח הַנָּשִׂיא
מִנַּחֲלַת הָעָם לְהוֹנֹתָם מֵאֲחֻזָּתָם מֵאֲחֻזָּתוֹ יַנְחִל
אֶת־בָּנָיו לְמַעַן אֲשֶׁר לֹא־יָפֻצוּ עַמִּי אִישׁ מֵאֲחֻזָּתוֹ:
19 וַיְבִיאֵנִי בַמָּבוֹא אֲשֶׁר עַל־כֶּתֶף הַשַּׁעַר אֶל־
הַלִּשְׁכוֹת הַקֹּדֶשׁ אֶל־הַכֹּהֲנִים הַפֹּנוֹת צָפוֹנָה וְהִנֵּה־
שָׁם מָקוֹם בַּיַּרְכָתָם ק יָמָּה: ס 20 וַיֹּאמֶר
אֵלַי זֶה הַמָּקוֹם אֲשֶׁר יְבַשְּׁלוּ־שָׁם הַכֹּהֲנִים אֶת־
הָאָשָׁם וְאֶת־הַחַטָּאת אֲשֶׁר יֹאפוּ אֶת־הַמִּנְחָה
לְבִלְתִּי הוֹצִיא אֶל־הֶחָצֵר הַחִיצוֹנָה לְקַדֵּשׁ אֶת־
הָעָם: 21 וַיּוֹצִיאֵנִי אֶל־הֶחָצֵר הַחִיצֹנָה וַיַּעֲבִירֵנִי
אֶל־אַרְבַּעַת מִקְצוֹעֵי הֶחָצֵר וְהִנֵּה חָצֵר בְּמִקְצֹעַ
הֶחָצֵר חָצֵר בְּמִקְצֹעַ הֶחָצֵר: 22 בְּאַרְבַּעַת מִקְצֹעוֹת
הֶחָצֵר חֲצֵרוֹת קְטֻרוֹת אַרְבָּעִים אֹרֶךְ וּשְׁלֹשִׁים
רֹחַב מִדָּה אַחַת לְאַרְבַּעְתָּם מְהֻקְצָעוֹת: 23 וְטוּר
סָבִיב בָּהֶם סָבִיב לְאַרְבַּעְתָּם וּמְבַשְּׁלוֹת עָשׂוּי
מִתַּחַת הַטִּירוֹת סָבִיב: 24 וַיֹּאמֶר אֵלַי אֵלֶּה בֵּית
הַמְבַשְּׁלִים אֲשֶׁר יְבַשְּׁלוּ־שָׁם מְשָׁרְתֵי הַבַּיִת אֶת־
זֶבַח הָעָם:

מז וַיְשִׁבֵנִי אֶל־פֶּתַח הַבַּיִת וְהִנֵּה־מַיִם יֹצְאִים
מִתַּחַת מִפְתַּן הַבַּיִת קָדִימָה כִּי־פְנֵי הַבַּיִת קָדִים
וְהַמַּיִם יֹרְדִים מִתַּחַת מִכֶּתֶף הַבַּיִת הַיְמָנִית מִנֶּגֶב
לַמִּזְבֵּחַ: 2 וַיּוֹצִאֵנִי דֶּרֶךְ־שַׁעַר צָפוֹנָה וַיְסִבֵּנִי דֶּרֶךְ
חוּץ אֶל־שַׁעַר הַחוּץ דֶּרֶךְ הַפּוֹנֶה קָדִים וְהִנֵּה־
מַיִם מְפַכִּים מִן־הַכָּתֵף הַיְמָנִית: 3 בְּצֵאת־הָאִישׁ
קָדִים וְקָו בְּיָדוֹ וַיָּמָד אֶלֶף בָּאַמָּה וַיַּעֲבִרֵנִי בַמַּיִם
מֵי אָפְסָיִם: 4 וַיָּמָד אֶלֶף וַיַּעֲבִרֵנִי בַמַּיִם מַיִם

thousand and brought me through; the water *came up to my* waist. 5 Again he measured one thousand, *and it was* a river that I could not cross; for the water was too deep, water in which one must swim, a river that could not be crossed. 6 He said to me, "Son of man, have you seen *this?*" Then he brought me and returned me to the bank of the river.

7 When I returned, there, along the bank of the river, *were* very many trees on one side and the other. 8 Then he said to me: "This water flows toward the eastern region, goes down into the valley, and enters the sea. *When it* reaches the sea, *its* waters are healed. 9 And it shall be *that* every living thing that moves, wherever the rivers go, will live. There will be a very great multitude of fish, because these waters go there; for they will be healed, and everything will live wherever the river goes. 10 It shall be *that* fishermen will stand by it from En Gedi to En Eglaim; they will be *places* for spreading their nets. Their fish will be of the same kinds as the fish of the Great Sea, exceedingly many. 11 But its swamps and marshes will not be healed; they will be given over to salt. 12 Along the bank of the river, on this side and that, will grow all *kinds of* trees used for food; their leaves will not wither, and their fruit will not fail. They will bear fruit every month, because their water flows from the sanctuary. Their fruit will be for food, and their leaves for medicine."

13 Thus says the Lord GOD: "These *are* the borders by which you shall divide the land as an inheritance among the twelve tribes of Israel. Joseph *shall have two* portions. 14 You shall inherit it equally with one another; for I raised My hand in an oath to give it to your fathers, and this land shall fall to you as your inheritance.

15 "This *shall be* the border of the land on the north: from the Great Sea, *by* the road to Hethlon, as one goes to Zedad, 16 Hamath, Berothah, Sibraim (which *is* between the border of Damascus and the border of Hamath), to Hazar Hatticon (which *is* on the border of Hauran). 17 Thus the boundary shall be from the Sea to Hazar Enan, the border of Damascus; and as for the north, northward, it is the border of Hamath. *This is* the north side.

18 "On the east side you shall mark out the border from between Hauran and Damascus, and between Gilead and the land of Israel, along the Jordan, and along the eastern side of the sea. *This is* the east side.

5 וַיָּ֣מָד בְּרְכַּ֗יִם וַיַּעֲבִרֵ֖נִי מֵ֥י מָתְנָֽיִם׃ וַיָּ֣מָד אֶ֗לֶף נַ֕חַל אֲשֶׁ֤ר לֹֽא־אוּכַל֙ לַעֲבֹ֔ר כִּֽי־גָא֥וּ הַמַּ֖יִם מֵ֣י שָׂ֔חוּ נַ֖חַל אֲשֶׁ֥ר לֹֽא־יֵעָבֵֽר׃ 6 וַיֹּ֖אמֶר אֵלַ֑י הֲרָאִ֣יתָ בֶן־אָדָ֑ם וַיּוֹלִכֵ֥נִי וַיְשִׁבֵ֖נִי שְׂפַ֥ת הַנָּֽחַל׃ 7 בְּשׁוּבֵ֕נִי וְהִנֵּה֙ אֶל־שְׂפַ֣ת הַנַּ֔חַל עֵ֖ץ רַ֣ב מְאֹ֑ד מִזֶּ֖ה וּמִזֶּֽה׃ 8 וַיֹּ֣אמֶר אֵלַ֗י הַמַּ֤יִם הָאֵ֙לֶּה֙ יוֹצְאִ֗ים אֶל־הַגְּלִילָ֣ה הַקַּדְמוֹנָ֔ה וְיָרְד֖וּ עַל־הָעֲרָבָ֑ה וּבָ֣אוּ הַיָּ֗מָּה אֶל־הַיָּ֙מָּה֙ הַמּֽוּצָאִ֔ים וְנִרְפְּא֖וּ הַמָּֽיִם׃ 9 וְהָיָ֣ה כָל־נֶ֣פֶשׁ חַיָּ֣ה ׀ אֲשֶׁר־יִשְׁרֹ֡ץ אֶל֩ כָּל־אֲשֶׁ֨ר יָב֜וֹא שָׁ֣ם נַחֲלַ֗יִם יִֽחְיֶ֔ה וְהָיָ֤ה הַדָּגָה֙ רַבָּ֣ה מְאֹ֔ד כִּ֣י בָ֤אוּ שָׁ֙מָּה֙ הַמַּ֣יִם הָאֵ֔לֶּה וְיֵרָ֣פְא֔וּ וָחָ֑י כֹּ֛ל אֲשֶׁר־יָ֥בוֹא שָׁ֖מָּה הַנָּֽחַל׃ 10 וְהָיָה֩ וְעָמְד֨וּ עָלָ֜יו דַּוָּגִ֗ים מֵעֵ֥ין גֶּ֙דִי֙ וְעַד־עֵ֣ין עֶגְלַ֔יִם מִשְׁט֥וֹחַ לַֽחֲרָמִ֖ים יִהְי֑וּ לְמִינָה֙ תִּהְיֶ֣ה דְגָתָ֔ם כִּדְגַ֛ת הַיָּ֥ם הַגָּד֖וֹל רַבָּ֥ה מְאֹֽד׃ 11 בִּצֹּאתָ֧ו וּגְבָאָ֛יו וְלֹ֥א יֵרָֽפְא֖וּ לְמֶ֥לַח נִתָּֽנוּ׃ 12 וְעַל־הַנַּ֣חַל יַעֲלֶ֣ה עַל־שְׂפָת֣וֹ מִזֶּ֣ה ׀ וּמִזֶּ֣ה ׀ כָּל־עֵֽץ־מַאֲכָ֗ל לֹֽא־יִבּ֤וֹל עָלֵ֙הוּ֙ וְלֹֽא־יִתֹּ֣ם פִּרְי֔וֹ לָחֳדָשָׁיו֙ יְבַכֵּ֔ר כִּ֣י מֵימָ֗יו מִן־הַמִּקְדָּשׁ֙ הֵ֣מָּה יֽוֹצְאִ֔ים וְהָיָ֤ה פִרְיוֹ֙ לְמַֽאֲכָ֔ל וְעָלֵ֖הוּ לִתְרוּפָֽה׃ ס

13 כֹּ֤ה אָמַר֙ אֲדֹנָ֣י יְהוִ֔ה גֵּ֤ה גְבוּל֙ אֲשֶׁ֣ר תִּתְנַחֲל֣וּ אֶת־הָאָ֔רֶץ לִשְׁנֵ֥י עָשָׂ֖ר שִׁבְטֵ֣י יִשְׂרָאֵ֑ל יוֹסֵ֖ף חֲבָלִֽים׃ 14 וּנְחַלְתֶּ֣ם אוֹתָ֗הּ אִ֤ישׁ כְּאָחִ֔יו אֲשֶׁ֤ר נָשָׂ֙אתִי֙ אֶת־יָדִ֔י לְתִתָּ֖הּ לַאֲבֹֽתֵיכֶ֑ם וְנָפְלָ֞ה הָאָ֧רֶץ הַזֹּ֛את לָכֶ֖ם בְּנַחֲלָֽה׃ 15 וְזֶ֖ה גְּב֣וּל הָאָ֑רֶץ לִפְאַ֣ת צָפ֗וֹנָה מִן־הַיָּ֤ם הַגָּדוֹל֙ הַדֶּ֣רֶךְ חֶתְלֹ֔ן לְב֖וֹא צְדָֽדָה׃ 16 חֲמָ֣ת ׀ בֵּר֗וֹתָה סִבְרַ֙יִם֙ אֲשֶׁר֙ בֵּֽין־גְּב֣וּל דַּמֶּ֔שֶׂק וּבֵ֖ין גְּב֣וּל חֲמָ֑ת חָצֵר֙ הַתִּיכ֔וֹן אֲשֶׁ֥ר אֶל־גְּב֖וּל חַוְרָֽן׃ 17 וְהָיָ֨ה גְב֜וּל מִן־הַיָּ֗ם חֲצַ֤ר עֵינוֹן֙ גְּב֣וּל דַּמֶּ֔שֶׂק וְצָפ֥וֹן ׀ צָפ֖וֹנָה וּגְב֣וּל חֲמָ֑ת וְאֵ֖ת פְּאַ֥ת צָפֽוֹן׃ 18 וּפְאַ֣ת קָדִ֡ים מִבֵּ֣ין חַוְרָ֣ן וּמִבֵּין־דַּמֶּ֡שֶׂק וּמִבֵּ֣ין הַגִּלְעָד֩ וּמִבֵּ֨ין אֶ֤רֶץ יִשְׂרָאֵל֙ הַיַּרְדֵּ֔ן מִגְּב֛וּל עַל־הַיָּ֥ם הַקַּדְמוֹנִ֖י תָּמֹ֑דּוּ וְאֵ֖ת פְּאַ֥ת קָדִֽימָה׃

מז 8 וְנִרְפּוּ   10 עֹמְדוּ   11 בִּצֹּאתָו   12 וְהָיָה

¹⁹"The south side, toward the South, *shall be* from Tamar to the waters of Meribah by Kadesh, along the brook to the Great Sea. *This is* the south side, toward the South.

²⁰"The west side *shall be* the Great Sea, from the *southern* boundary until one comes to a point opposite Hamath. This *is* the west side.

²¹"Thus you shall divide this land among yourselves according to the tribes of Israel. ²²It shall be that you will divide it by lot as an inheritance for yourselves, and for the strangers who dwell among you and who bear children among you. They shall be to you as native-born among the children of Israel; they shall have an inheritance with you among the tribes of Israel. ²³And it shall be *that* in whatever tribe the stranger dwells, there you shall give *him* his inheritance," says the Lord GOD.

48 "Now these *are* the names of the tribes: From the northern border along the road to Hethlon at the entrance of Hamath, to Hazar Enan, the border of Damascus northward, in the direction of Hamath, *there shall be* one *section for* Dan from its east to its west side; ²by the border of Dan, from the east side to the west, one *section for* Asher; ³by the border of Asher, from the east side to the west, one *section for* Naphtali; ⁴by the border of Naphtali, from the east side to the west, one *section for* Manasseh; ⁵by the border of Manasseh, from the east side to the west, one *section for* Ephraim; ⁶by the border of Ephraim, from the east side to the west, one *section for* Reuben; ⁷by the border of Reuben, from the east side to the west, one *section for* Judah; ⁸by the border of Judah, from the east side to the west, shall be the district which you shall set apart, twenty-five thousand *cubits* in width, and *in* length the same as one of the *other* portions, from the east side to the west, with the sanctuary in the center.

⁹"The district that you shall set apart for the LORD *shall be* twenty-five thousand *cubits* in length and ten thousand in width. ¹⁰To these—to the priests—the holy district shall belong: on the north twenty-five thousand *cubits in length*, on the west ten thousand in width, on the east ten thousand in width, and on the south twenty-five thousand in length. The sanctuary of the LORD shall be in the center. ¹¹*It shall be* for the priests of the sons of Zadok, who are sanctified, who have kept My charge, who did not go astray when the children of Israel went astray, as the Levites went astray.

19 וּפְאַת נֶגֶב תֵּימָנָה מִתָּמָר עַד־מֵי מְרִיבוֹת קָדֵשׁ נַחֲלָה אֶל־הַיָּם הַגָּדוֹל וְאֵת פְּאַת־תֵּימָנָה נֶגְבָּה: 20 וּפְאַת־יָם הַיָּם הַגָּדוֹל מִגְּבוּל עַד־נֹכַח לְבוֹא חֲמָת זֹאת פְּאַת־יָם: 21 וְחִלַּקְתֶּם אֶת־הָאָרֶץ הַזֹּאת לָכֶם לְשִׁבְטֵי יִשְׂרָאֵל: 22 וְהָיָה תַּפִּלוּ אוֹתָהּ בְּנַחֲלָה לָכֶם וּלְהַגֵּרִים הַגָּרִים בְּתוֹכְכֶם אֲשֶׁר־הוֹלִדוּ בָנִים בְּתוֹכְכֶם וְהָיוּ לָכֶם כְּאֶזְרָח בִּבְנֵי יִשְׂרָאֵל אִתְּכֶם יִפְּלוּ בְנַחֲלָה בְּתוֹךְ שִׁבְטֵי יִשְׂרָאֵל: 23 וְהָיָה בַשֵּׁבֶט אֲשֶׁר־גָּר הַגֵּר אִתּוֹ שָׁם תִּתְּנוּ נַחֲלָתוֹ נְאֻם אֲדֹנָי יְהֹוִה: ס

מח וְאֵלֶּה שְׁמוֹת הַשְּׁבָטִים מִקְצֵה צָפוֹנָה אֶל־יַד דֶּרֶךְ־חֶתְלֹן ׀ לְבוֹא־חֲמָת חֲצַר עֵינָן גְּבוּל דַּמֶּשֶׂק צָפוֹנָה אֶל־יַד חֲמָת וְהָיוּ־לוֹ פְאַת־קָדִים הַיָּם דָּן אֶחָד: 2 וְעַל ׀ גְּבוּל דָּן מִפְּאַת קָדִים עַד־פְּאַת־יָמָּה אָשֵׁר אֶחָד: 3 וְעַל ׀ גְּבוּל אָשֵׁר מִפְּאַת קָדִימָה וְעַד־פְּאַת־יָמָּה נַפְתָּלִי אֶחָד: 4 וְעַל ׀ גְּבוּל נַפְתָּלִי מִפְּאַת קָדִמָה עַד־פְּאַת־יָמָּה מְנַשֶּׁה אֶחָד: 5 וְעַל ׀ גְּבוּל מְנַשֶּׁה מִפְּאַת קָדִמָה עַד־פְּאַת־יָמָּה אֶפְרַיִם אֶחָד: 6 וְעַל ׀ גְּבוּל אֶפְרַיִם מִפְּאַת קָדִים וְעַד־פְּאַת־יָמָּה רְאוּבֵן אֶחָד: 7 וְעַל ׀ גְּבוּל רְאוּבֵן מִפְּאַת קָדִים עַד־פְּאַת־יָמָּה יְהוּדָה אֶחָד: 8 וְעַל ׀ גְּבוּל יְהוּדָה מִפְּאַת קָדִים עַד־פְּאַת־יָמָּה תִּהְיֶה הַתְּרוּמָה אֲשֶׁר־תָּרִימוּ חֲמִשָּׁה וְעֶשְׂרִים אֶלֶף רֹחַב וְאֹרֶךְ כְּאַחַד הַחֲלָקִים מִפְּאַת קָדִימָה עַד־פְּאַת־יָמָּה וְהָיָה הַמִּקְדָּשׁ בְּתוֹכוֹ: 9 הַתְּרוּמָה אֲשֶׁר תָּרִימוּ לַיהֹוָה אֹרֶךְ חֲמִשָּׁה וְעֶשְׂרִים אֶלֶף וְרֹחַב עֲשֶׂרֶת אֲלָפִים: 10 וּלְאֵלֶּה תִּהְיֶה תְרוּמַת־הַקֹּדֶשׁ לַכֹּהֲנִים צָפוֹנָה חֲמִשָּׁה וְעֶשְׂרִים אֶלֶף וְיָמָּה רֹחַב עֲשֶׂרֶת אֲלָפִים וְקָדִימָה רֹחַב עֲשֶׂרֶת אֲלָפִים וְנֶגְבָּה אֹרֶךְ חֲמִשָּׁה וְעֶשְׂרִים אָלֶף וְהָיָה מִקְדַּשׁ־יְהֹוָה בְּתוֹכוֹ: 11 לַכֹּהֲנִים הַמְקֻדָּשׁ מִבְּנֵי צָדוֹק אֲשֶׁר שָׁמְרוּ מִשְׁמַרְתִּי אֲשֶׁר לֹא־תָעוּ בִּתְעוֹת בְּנֵי יִשְׂרָאֵל

12 And *this* district of land that is set apart shall be to them a thing most holy by the border of the Levites.

13 "Opposite the border of the priests, the Levites *shall have an area* twenty-five thousand *cubits* in length and ten thousand in width; its entire length *shall be* twenty-five thousand and its width ten thousand. 14 And they shall not sell or exchange any of it; they may not alienate this best *part* of the land, for *it is* holy to the LORD.

15 "The five thousand *cubits* in width that remain, along the edge of the twenty-five thousand, shall be for general use by the city, for dwellings and common-land; and the city shall be in the center. 16 These *shall be* its measurements: the north side four thousand five hundred *cubits,* the south side four thousand five hundred, the east side four thousand five hundred, and the west side four thousand five hundred. 17 The common-land of the city shall be: to the north two hundred and fifty *cubits,* to the south two hundred and fifty, to the east two hundred and fifty, and to the west two hundred and fifty. 18 The rest of the length, alongside the district of the holy *section, shall be* ten thousand *cubits* to the east and ten thousand to the west. It shall be adjacent to the district of the holy *section,* and its produce shall be food for the workers of the city. 19 The workers of the city, from all the tribes of Israel, shall cultivate it. 20 The entire district *shall be* twenty-five thousand *cubits* by twenty-five thousand *cubits,* foursquare. You shall set apart the holy district with the property of the city.

21 "The rest *shall belong* to the prince, on one side and on the other of the holy district and of the city's property, next to the twenty-five thousand *cubits* of the *holy* district as far as the eastern border, and westward next to the twenty-five thousand as far as the western border, adjacent to the *tribal* portions; *it shall belong* to the prince. It shall be the holy district, and the sanctuary of the temple *shall be* in the center. 22 Moreover, apart from the possession of the Levites and the possession of the city *which are* in the midst of what *belongs* to the prince, *the area* between the border of Judah and the border of Benjamin shall belong to the prince.

23 "As for the rest of the tribes, from the east side to the west, Benjamin *shall have* one *section;* 24 by the border of Benjamin, from the east side to the west, Simeon *shall have* one *section;* 25 by the border of Simeon, from the east side to the west, Issachar *shall have* one *section;* 26 by the border of Issachar, from the east side to the west, Zebulun *shall have* one *section;* 27 by the border of Zebulun, from the

12 וְהָיְתָה לָהֶם ס כַּאֲשֶׁר תָּעוּ הַלְוִיִּם:
תְּרוּמִיָּה מִתְּרוּמַת הָאָרֶץ קֹדֶשׁ קָדָשִׁים אֶל־גְּבוּל
הַלְוִיִּם: 13 וְהַלְוִיִּם לְעֻמַּת גְּבוּל הַכֹּהֲנִים חֲמִשָּׁה
וְעֶשְׂרִים אֶלֶף אֹרֶךְ וְרֹחַב עֲשֶׂרֶת אֲלָפִים כָּל־
אֹרֶךְ חֲמִשָּׁה וְעֶשְׂרִים אֶלֶף וְרֹחַב עֲשֶׂרֶת אֲלָפִים:
14 וְלֹא־יִמְכְּרוּ מִמֶּנּוּ וְלֹא יָמֵר וְלֹא יַעֲבוֹר רֵאשִׁית
הָאָרֶץ כִּי־קֹדֶשׁ לַיהוָה: 15 וַחֲמֵשֶׁת אֲלָפִים הַנּוֹתָר
בָּרֹחַב עַל־פְּנֵי חֲמִשָּׁה וְעֶשְׂרִים אֶלֶף חֹל־הוּא
לָעִיר לְמוֹשָׁב וּלְמִגְרָשׁ וְהָיְתָה הָעִיר בְּתוֹכֹה:
16 וְאֵלֶּה מִדּוֹתֶיהָ פְּאַת צָפוֹן חֲמֵשׁ מֵאוֹת וְאַרְבַּעַת
אֲלָפִים וּפְאַת־נֶגֶב חֲמֵשׁ חֲמֵשׁ מֵאוֹת וְאַרְבַּעַת
אֲלָפִים וּמִפְּאַת קָדִים חֲמֵשׁ מֵאוֹת וְאַרְבַּעַת
אֲלָפִים וּפְאַת־יָמָּה חֲמֵשׁ מֵאוֹת וְאַרְבַּעַת אֲלָפִים:
17 וְהָיָה מִגְרָשׁ לָעִיר צָפוֹנָה חֲמִשִּׁים וּמָאתַיִם
וְנֶגְבָּה חֲמִשִּׁים וּמָאתַיִם וְקָדִימָה חֲמִשִּׁים וּמָאתַיִם
וְיָמָּה חֲמִשִּׁים וּמָאתַיִם: 18 וְהַנּוֹתָר בָּאֹרֶךְ לְעֻמַּת
תְּרוּמַת הַקֹּדֶשׁ עֲשֶׂרֶת אֲלָפִים קָדִימָה וַעֲשֶׂרֶת
אֲלָפִים יָמָּה וְהָיָה לְעֻמַּת תְּרוּמַת הַקֹּדֶשׁ וְהָיְתָה
תְבוּאָתֹה לְלֶחֶם לְעֹבְדֵי הָעִיר: 19 וְהָעֹבֵד הָעִיר
יַעַבְדוּהוּ מִכֹּל שִׁבְטֵי יִשְׂרָאֵל: 20 כָּל־הַתְּרוּמָה
חֲמִשָּׁה וְעֶשְׂרִים אֶלֶף בַּחֲמִשָּׁה וְעֶשְׂרִים אֶלֶף
רְבִיעִית תָּרִימוּ אֶת־תְּרוּמַת הַקֹּדֶשׁ אֶל־אֲחֻזַּת
הָעִיר: 21 וְהַנּוֹתָר לַנָּשִׂיא מִזֶּה וּמִזֶּה לִתְרוּמַת־
הַקֹּדֶשׁ וְלַאֲחֻזַּת הָעִיר אֶל־פְּנֵי חֲמִשָּׁה וְעֶשְׂרִים
אֶלֶף תְּרוּמָה עַד־גְּבוּל קָדִימָה וְיָמָּה עַל־פְּנֵי
חֲמִשָּׁה וְעֶשְׂרִים אֶלֶף עַל־גְּבוּל יָמָּה לְעֻמַּת חֲלָקִים
לַנָּשִׂיא וְהָיְתָה תְּרוּמַת הַקֹּדֶשׁ וּמִקְדַּשׁ הַבַּיִת
בְּתוֹכֹה: 22 וּמֵאֲחֻזַּת הַלְוִיִּם וּמֵאֲחֻזַּת הָעִיר בְּתוֹךְ
אֲשֶׁר לַנָּשִׂיא יִהְיֶה בֵּין גְּבוּל יְהוּדָה וּבֵין גְּבוּל
בִּנְיָמִן לַנָּשִׂיא יִהְיֶה: 23 וְיֶתֶר הַשְּׁבָטִים מִפְּאַת
קָדִימָה עַד־פְּאַת־יָמָּה בִּנְיָמִן אֶחָד: 24 וְעַל גְּבוּל
בִּנְיָמִן מִפְּאַת קָדִימָה עַד־פְּאַת־יָמָּה שִׁמְעוֹן אֶחָד:
25 וְעַל גְּבוּל שִׁמְעוֹן מִפְּאַת קָדִימָה עַד־פְּאַת־
יָמָּה יִשָּׂשכָר אֶחָד: 26 וְעַל גְּבוּל יִשָּׂשכָר מִפְּאַת
קָדִימָה עַד־פְּאַת־יָמָּה זְבוּלֻן אֶחָד: 27 וְעַל גְּבוּל
זְבוּלֻן מִפְּאַת קָדִמָה עַד־פְּאַת־יָמָּה גָּד אֶחָד:

east side to the west, Gad *shall have* one *section;* [28] by the border of Gad, on the south side, toward the South, the border shall be from Tamar *to the* waters of Meribah *by* Kadesh, along the brook to the Great Sea. [29] This *is* the land which you shall divide by lot as an inheritance among the tribes of Israel, and these *are* their portions," says the Lord GOD.

[30] "These *are* the exits of the city. On the north side, measuring four thousand five hundred *cubits* [31] (the gates of the city *shall be* named after the tribes of Israel), the three gates northward: one gate for Reuben, one gate for Judah, and one gate for Levi; [32] on the east side, four thousand five hundred *cubits,* three gates: one gate for Joseph, one gate for Benjamin, and one gate for Dan; [33] on the south side, measuring four thousand five hundred *cubits,* three gates: one gate for Simeon, one gate for Issachar, and one gate for Zebulun; [34] on the west side, four thousand five hundred *cubits* with their three gates: one gate for Gad, one gate for Asher, and one gate for Naphtali. [35] All the way around *shall be* eighteen thousand *cubits;* and the name of the city from *that* day *shall be:* THE LORD *IS* THERE."

28 וְעַל גְּבוּל גָּד אֶל־פְּאַת נֶגֶב תֵּימָנָה וְהָיָה גְבוּל מִתָּמָר מֵי מְרִיבַת קָדֵשׁ נַחֲלָה עַל־הַיָּם הַגָּדוֹל: 29 זֹאת הָאָרֶץ אֲשֶׁר־תַּפִּילוּ מִנַּחֲלָה לְשִׁבְטֵי יִשְׂרָאֵל וְאֵלֶּה מַחְלְקוֹתָם נְאֻם אֲדֹנָי יְהוִה: פ

30 וְאֵלֶּה תּוֹצְאֹת הָעִיר מִפְּאַת צָפוֹן חֲמֵשׁ מֵאוֹת וְאַרְבַּעַת אֲלָפִים מִדָּה: 31 וְשַׁעֲרֵי הָעִיר עַל־ שְׁמוֹת שִׁבְטֵי יִשְׂרָאֵל שְׁעָרִים שְׁלוֹשָׁה צָפוֹנָה שַׁעַר רְאוּבֵן אֶחָד שַׁעַר יְהוּדָה אֶחָד שַׁעַר לֵוִי אֶחָד: 32 וְאֶל־פְּאַת קָדִימָה חֲמֵשׁ מֵאוֹת וְאַרְבַּעַת אֲלָפִים וּשְׁעָרִים שְׁלֹשָׁה וְשַׁעַר יוֹסֵף אֶחָד שַׁעַר בִּנְיָמִן אֶחָד שַׁעַר דָּן אֶחָד: 33 וּפְאַת־נֶגְבָּה חֲמֵשׁ מֵאוֹת וְאַרְבַּעַת אֲלָפִים מִדָּה וּשְׁעָרִים שְׁלֹשָׁה שַׁעַר שִׁמְעוֹן אֶחָד שַׁעַר יִשָּׂשׂכָר אֶחָד שַׁעַר זְבוּלֻן אֶחָד: 34 פְּאַת־יָמָּה חֲמֵשׁ מֵאוֹת וְאַרְבַּעַת אֲלָפִים שַׁעֲרֵיהֶם שְׁלֹשָׁה שַׁעַר גָּד אֶחָד שַׁעַר אָשֵׁר אֶחָד שַׁעַר נַפְתָּלִי אֶחָד: 35 סָבִיב שְׁמֹנָה עָשָׂר אָלֶף וְשֵׁם־הָעִיר מִיּוֹם יְהוָה ׀ שָׁמָּה:

The Book of
HOSEA

1 The word of the LORD that came to Hosea the son of Beeri, in the days of Uzziah, Jotham, Ahaz, *and* Hezekiah, kings of Judah, and in the days of Jeroboam the son of Joash, king of Israel.

²When the LORD began to speak by Hosea, the LORD said to Hosea:

> "Go, take yourself a wife of harlotry
> And children of harlotry,
> For the land has committed great harlotry
> *By departing* from the LORD."

³So he went and took Gomer the daughter of Diblaim, and she conceived and bore him a son. ⁴Then the LORD said to him:

> "Call his name Jezreel,
> For in a little *while*
> I will avenge the bloodshed of Jezreel on the
>   house of Jehu,
> And bring an end to the kingdom of the house of
>   Israel.
> 5   It shall come to pass in that day
>   That I will break the bow of Israel in the Valley
>   of Jezreel."

⁶And she conceived again and bore a daughter. Then *God* said to him:

> "Call her name Lo-Ruhamah,
> For I will no longer have mercy on the house of
>   Israel,
> But I will utterly take them away.
> 7   Yet I will have mercy on the house of Judah,
>   Will save them by the LORD their God,
>   And will not save them by bow,
>   Nor by sword or battle,
>   By horses or horsemen."

⁸Now when she had weaned Lo-Ruhamah, she conceived and bore a son. ⁹Then *God* said:

> "Call his name Lo-Ammi,
> For you *are* not My people,
> And I will not be your *God*.

> 10 "Yet the number of the children of Israel
>   Shall be as the sand of the sea,
>   Which cannot be measured or numbered.
>   And it shall come to pass
>   In the place where it was said to them,
>   'You *are* not My people,'
>   *There* it shall be said to them,
>   '*You are* sons of the living God.'
> 11 Then the children of Judah and the children of
>   Israel
>   Shall be gathered together,

א דְּבַר־יְהֹוָה ׀ אֲשֶׁר הָיָה אֶל־הוֹשֵׁעַ בֶּן־בְּאֵרִי בִּימֵי עֻזִּיָּה יוֹתָם אָחָז יְחִזְקִיָּה מַלְכֵי יְהוּדָה וּבִימֵי יָרָבְעָם בֶּן־יוֹאָשׁ מֶלֶךְ יִשְׂרָאֵל: 2 תְּחִלַּת דִּבֶּר־יְהֹוָה בְּהוֹשֵׁעַ פ וַיֹּאמֶר יְהֹוָה אֶל־הוֹשֵׁעַ לֵךְ קַח־לְךָ אֵשֶׁת זְנוּנִים וְיַלְדֵי זְנוּנִים כִּי־זָנֹה תִזְנֶה הָאָרֶץ מֵאַחֲרֵי יְהֹוָה: 3 וַיֵּלֶךְ וַיִּקַּח אֶת־גֹּמֶר בַּת־דִּבְלָיִם וַתַּהַר וַתֵּלֶד־לוֹ בֵּן: 4 וַיֹּאמֶר יְהֹוָה אֵלָיו קְרָא שְׁמוֹ יִזְרְעֶאל כִּי־עוֹד מְעַט וּפָקַדְתִּי אֶת־דְּמֵי יִזְרְעֶאל עַל־בֵּית יֵהוּא וְהִשְׁבַּתִּי מַמְלְכוּת בֵּית יִשְׂרָאֵל: 5 וְהָיָה בַּיּוֹם הַהוּא וְשָׁבַרְתִּי אֶת־קֶשֶׁת יִשְׂרָאֵל בְּעֵמֶק יִזְרְעֶאל: 6 וַתַּהַר עוֹד וַתֵּלֶד בַּת וַיֹּאמֶר לוֹ קְרָא שְׁמָהּ לֹא רֻחָמָה כִּי לֹא אוֹסִיף עוֹד אֲרַחֵם אֶת־בֵּית יִשְׂרָאֵל כִּי־נָשֹׂא אֶשָּׂא לָהֶם: 7 וְאֶת־ בֵּית יְהוּדָה אֲרַחֵם וְהוֹשַׁעְתִּים בַּיהֹוָה אֱלֹהֵיהֶם וְלֹא אוֹשִׁיעֵם בְּקֶשֶׁת וּבְחֶרֶב וּבְמִלְחָמָה בְּסוּסִים וּבְפָרָשִׁים: 8 וַתִּגְמֹל אֶת־לֹא רֻחָמָה וַתַּהַר וַתֵּלֶד בֵּן: 9 וַיֹּאמֶר קְרָא שְׁמוֹ לֹא עַמִּי כִּי אַתֶּם לֹא עַמִּי וְאָנֹכִי לֹא־אֶהְיֶה לָכֶם: ס

ב וְהָיָה מִסְפַּר בְּנֵי־יִשְׂרָאֵל כְּחוֹל הַיָּם אֲשֶׁר לֹא־יִמַּד וְלֹא יִסָּפֵר וְהָיָה בִּמְקוֹם אֲשֶׁר־יֵאָמֵר לָהֶם לֹא־עַמִּי אַתֶּם יֵאָמֵר לָהֶם בְּנֵי אֵל־חָי: 2 וְנִקְבְּצוּ בְּנֵי־יְהוּדָה וּבְנֵי־יִשְׂרָאֵל יַחְדָּו וְשָׂמוּ לָהֶם רֹאשׁ

And appoint for themselves one head;
And they shall come up out of the land,
For great *will be* the day of Jezreel!

2   Say to your brethren, 'My people,'
And to your sisters, 'Mercy *is shown*.'

2 "Bring charges against your mother, bring
    charges;
    For she *is* not My wife, nor *am* I her
    Husband!
    Let her put away her harlotries from her
    sight,
    And her adulteries from between her breasts;
3 Lest I strip her naked
    And expose her, as in the day she was born,
    And make her like a wilderness,
    And set her like a dry land,
    And slay her with thirst.

4 "I will not have mercy on her children,
    For they *are* the children of harlotry.
5 For their mother has played the harlot;
    She who conceived them has behaved
    shamefully.
    For she said, 'I will go after my lovers,
    Who give *me* my bread and my water,
    My wool and my linen,
    My oil and my drink.'

6 "Therefore, behold,
    I will hedge up your way with thorns,
    And wall her in,
    So that she cannot find her paths.
7 She will chase her lovers,
    But not overtake them;
    Yes, she will seek them, but not find *them*.
    Then she will say,
    'I will go and return to my first husband,
    For then *it was* better for me than now.'
8 For she did not know
    That I gave her grain, new wine, and oil,
    And multiplied her silver and gold—
    Which they prepared for Baal.

9 "Therefore I will return and take away
    My grain in its time
    And My new wine in its season,
    And will take back My wool and My linen,
    Given to cover her nakedness.
10 Now I will uncover her lewdness in the sight
    of her lovers,
    And no one shall deliver her from My hand.
11 I will also cause all her mirth to cease,
    Her feast days,
    Her New Moons,
    Her Sabbaths—
    All her appointed feasts.
12 "And I will destroy her vines and her fig trees,
    Of which she has said,

אֶחָד וְעָלוּ מִן־הָאָרֶץ כִּי גָדוֹל יוֹם יִזְרְעֶאל: 3 אִמְרוּ
לַאֲחֵיכֶם עַמִּי וְלַאֲחוֹתֵיכֶם רֻחָמָה:

4 רִיבוּ בְאִמְּכֶם רִיבוּ
כִּי־הִיא לֹא אִשְׁתִּי
וְאָנֹכִי לֹא אִישָׁהּ
וְתָסֵר זְנוּנֶיהָ מִפָּנֶיהָ
וְנַאֲפוּפֶיהָ מִבֵּין שָׁדֶיהָ:
5 פֶּן־אַפְשִׁיטֶנָּה עֲרֻמָּה
וְהִצַּגְתִּיהָ כְּיוֹם הִוָּלְדָהּ
וְשַׂמְתִּיהָ כַמִּדְבָּר
וְשַׁתִּהָ כְּאֶרֶץ צִיָּה
וַהֲמִתִּיהָ בַּצָּמָא:
6 וְאֶת־בָּנֶיהָ לֹא אֲרַחֵם
כִּי־בְנֵי זְנוּנִים הֵמָּה:
7 כִּי זָנְתָה אִמָּם הֹבִישָׁה הוֹרָתָם
כִּי אָמְרָה אֵלְכָה אַחֲרֵי מְאַהֲבַי
נֹתְנֵי לַחְמִי וּמֵימַי
צַמְרִי וּפִשְׁתִּי שַׁמְנִי וְשִׁקּוּיָי:
8 לָכֵן הִנְנִי־שָׂךְ אֶת־דַּרְכֵּךְ בַּסִּירִים
וְגָדַרְתִּי אֶת־גְּדֵרָהּ וּנְתִיבוֹתֶיהָ לֹא תִמְצָא:
9 וְרִדְּפָה אֶת־מְאַהֲבֶיהָ
וְלֹא־תַשִּׂיג אֹתָם
וּבִקְשָׁתַם וְלֹא תִמְצָא
וְאָמְרָה אֵלְכָה וְאָשׁוּבָה
אֶל־אִישִׁי הָרִאשׁוֹן
כִּי טוֹב לִי אָז מֵעָתָּה:
10 וְהִיא לֹא יָדְעָה כִּי אָנֹכִי נָתַתִּי לָהּ
הַדָּגָן וְהַתִּירוֹשׁ וְהַיִּצְהָר
וְכֶסֶף הִרְבֵּיתִי לָהּ
וְזָהָב עָשׂוּ לַבָּעַל:
11 לָכֵן אָשׁוּב וְלָקַחְתִּי דְגָנִי בְּעִתּוֹ
וְתִירוֹשִׁי בְּמוֹעֲדוֹ
וְהִצַּלְתִּי צַמְרִי וּפִשְׁתִּי
לְכַסּוֹת אֶת־עֶרְוָתָהּ:
12 וְעַתָּה אֲגַלֶּה אֶת־נַבְלֻתָהּ
לְעֵינֵי מְאַהֲבֶיהָ
וְאִישׁ לֹא־יַצִּילֶנָּה מִיָּדִי:
13 וְהִשְׁבַּתִּי כָּל־מְשׂוֹשָׂהּ
חַגָּהּ חָדְשָׁהּ וְשַׁבַּתָּהּ
וְכֹל מוֹעֲדָהּ:
14 וַהֲשִׁמֹּתִי גַּפְנָהּ וּתְאֵנָתָהּ
אֲשֶׁר אָמְרָה אֶתְנָה הֵמָּה לִי

'These *are* my wages that my lovers have
    given me.'
So I will make them a forest,
And the beasts of the field shall eat them.

13 I will punish her
For the days of the Baals to which she
    burned incense.
She decked herself with her earrings and
    jewelry,
And went after her lovers;
But Me she forgot," says the LORD.

14 "Therefore, behold, I will allure her,
Will bring her into the wilderness,
And speak comfort to her.

15 I will give her her vineyards from there,
And the Valley of Achor as a door of hope;
She shall sing there,
As in the days of her youth,
As in the day when she came up from the
    land of Egypt.

16 "And it shall be, in that day,"
Says the LORD,
"*That* you will call Me 'My Husband,'
And no longer call Me 'My Master,'

17 For I will take from her mouth the names of
    the Baals,
And they shall be remembered by their name
    no more.

18 In that day I will make a covenant for them
With the beasts of the field,
With the birds of the air,
And *with* the creeping things of the ground.
Bow and sword of battle I will shatter from
    the earth,
To make them lie down safely.

19 "I will betroth you to Me forever;
Yes, I will betroth you to Me
In righteousness and justice,
In lovingkindness and mercy;

20 I will betroth you to Me in faithfulness,
And you shall know the LORD.

21 "It shall come to pass in that day
That I will answer," says the LORD;
"I will answer the heavens,
And they shall answer the earth.

22 The earth shall answer
With grain,
With new wine,
And with oil;
They shall answer Jezreel.

23 Then I will sow her for Myself in the earth,

אֲשֶׁר נָתְנוּ־לִי מְאַהֲבָי
וְשַׂמְתִּים לְיַעַר
וַאֲכָלָתַם חַיַּת הַשָּׂדֶה׃

15 וּפָקַדְתִּי עָלֶיהָ אֶת־יְמֵי הַבְּעָלִים
אֲשֶׁר תַּקְטִיר לָהֶם
וַתַּעַד נִזְמָהּ וְחֶלְיָתָהּ
וַתֵּלֶךְ אַחֲרֵי מְאַהֲבֶיהָ
וְאֹתִי שָׁכְחָה נְאֻם־יְהוָה׃ פ

16 לָכֵן הִנֵּה אָנֹכִי מְפַתֶּיהָ
וְהֹלַכְתִּיהָ הַמִּדְבָּר
וְדִבַּרְתִּי עַל־לִבָּהּ׃

17 וְנָתַתִּי לָהּ אֶת־כְּרָמֶיהָ מִשָּׁם
וְאֶת־עֵמֶק עָכוֹר לְפֶתַח תִּקְוָה
וְעָנְתָה שָּׁמָּה כִּימֵי נְעוּרֶיהָ
וּכְיוֹם עֲלֹתָהּ מֵאֶרֶץ־מִצְרָיִם׃ ס

18 וְהָיָה בַיּוֹם־הַהוּא נְאֻם־יְהוָה
תִּקְרְאִי אִישִׁי
וְלֹא־תִקְרְאִי־לִי עוֹד בַּעְלִי׃

19 וַהֲסִרֹתִי אֶת־שְׁמוֹת הַבְּעָלִים מִפִּיהָ
וְלֹא־יִזָּכְרוּ עוֹד בִּשְׁמָם׃

20 וְכָרַתִּי לָהֶם בְּרִית בַּיּוֹם הַהוּא
עִם־חַיַּת הַשָּׂדֶה וְעִם־עוֹף הַשָּׁמַיִם
וְרֶמֶשׂ הָאֲדָמָה
וְקֶשֶׁת וְחֶרֶב וּמִלְחָמָה
אֶשְׁבּוֹר מִן־הָאָרֶץ
וְהִשְׁכַּבְתִּים לָבֶטַח׃

21 וְאֵרַשְׂתִּיךְ לִי לְעוֹלָם
וְאֵרַשְׂתִּיךְ לִי בְּצֶדֶק וּבְמִשְׁפָּט
וּבְחֶסֶד וּבְרַחֲמִים׃

22 וְאֵרַשְׂתִּיךְ לִי בֶּאֱמוּנָה
וְיָדַעַתְּ אֶת־יְהוָה׃ ס

23 וְהָיָה בַּיּוֹם הַהוּא
אֶעֱנֶה נְאֻם־יְהוָה אֶעֱנֶה אֶת־הַשָּׁמָיִם
וְהֵם יַעֲנוּ אֶת־הָאָרֶץ׃

24 וְהָאָרֶץ תַּעֲנֶה אֶת־הַדָּגָן
וְאֶת־הַתִּירוֹשׁ וְאֶת־הַיִּצְהָר
וְהֵם יַעֲנוּ אֶת־יִזְרְעֶאל׃

25 וּזְרַעְתִּיהָ לִּי בָּאָרֶץ

And I will have mercy on *her who had* not
    obtained mercy;
Then I will say to *those who were* not My
    people,
    'You *are* My people!'
And they shall say, '*You are* my God!' "

וְרִחַמְתִּי אֶת־לֹא רֻחָמָה
וְאָמַרְתִּי לְלֹא־עַמִּי עַמִּי־אַתָּה
וְהוּא יֹאמַר אֱלֹהָי: פ

3 Then the LORD said to me, "Go again, love a
woman *who is* loved by a lover and is committing
adultery, just like the love of the LORD for the
children of Israel, who look to other gods and love
the raisin cakes *of the pagans.*"

² So I bought her for myself for fifteen *shekels* of
silver, and one and one-half homers of barley. ³ And
I said to her, "You shall stay with me many days;
you shall not play the harlot, nor shall you have a
man—so, too, *will* I *be* toward you."

⁴ For the children of Israel shall abide many days
without king or prince, without sacrifice or sacred
pillar, without ephod or teraphim. ⁵ Afterward the
children of Israel shall return and seek the LORD
their God and David their king. They shall fear the
LORD and His goodness in the latter days.

ג וַיֹּאמֶר יְהוָה אֵלַי עוֹד לֵךְ אֱהַב־אִשָּׁה אֲהֻבַת
רֵעַ וּמְנָאָפֶת כְּאַהֲבַת יְהוָה אֶת־בְּנֵי יִשְׂרָאֵל וְהֵם
פֹּנִים אֶל־אֱלֹהִים אֲחֵרִים וְאֹהֲבֵי אֲשִׁישֵׁי עֲנָבִים:
² וָאֶכְּרֶהָ לִּי בַּחֲמִשָּׁה עָשָׂר כָּסֶף וְחֹמֶר שְׂעֹרִים
וְלֵתֶךְ שְׂעֹרִים: ³ וָאֹמַר אֵלֶיהָ יָמִים רַבִּים תֵּשְׁבִי לִי
לֹא תִזְנִי וְלֹא תִהְיִי לְאִישׁ וְגַם־אֲנִי אֵלָיִךְ: ⁴ כִּי |
יָמִים רַבִּים יֵשְׁבוּ בְּנֵי יִשְׂרָאֵל אֵין מֶלֶךְ וְאֵין שָׂר
וְאֵין זֶבַח וְאֵין מַצֵּבָה וְאֵין אֵפוֹד וּתְרָפִים: ⁵ אַחַר
יָשֻׁבוּ בְּנֵי יִשְׂרָאֵל וּבִקְשׁוּ אֶת־יְהוָה אֱלֹהֵיהֶם וְאֵת
דָּוִד מַלְכָּם וּפָחֲדוּ אֶל־יְהוָה וְאֶל־טוּבוֹ בְּאַחֲרִית
הַיָּמִים: פ

4 Hear the word of the LORD,
    You children of Israel,
For the LORD *brings* a charge against the
    inhabitants of the land:

"There is no truth or mercy
Or knowledge of God in the land.
² *By* swearing and lying,
Killing and stealing and committing adul-
    tery,
They break all restraint,
With bloodshed upon bloodshed.
³ Therefore the land will mourn;
And everyone who dwells there will waste
    away
With the beasts of the field
And the birds of the air;
Even the fish of the sea will be taken away.

⁴ "Now let no man contend, or rebuke another;
For your people *are* like those who contend
    with the priest.
⁵ Therefore you shall stumble in the day;
The prophet also shall stumble with you in
    the night;
And I will destroy your mother.
⁶ My people are destroyed for lack of
    knowledge.
Because you have rejected knowledge,
I also will reject you from being priest for
    Me;

ד שִׁמְעוּ דְבַר־יְהוָה בְּנֵי יִשְׂרָאֵל
כִּי רִיב לַיהוָה עִם־יוֹשְׁבֵי הָאָרֶץ
כִּי אֵין־אֱמֶת וְאֵין־חֶסֶד
וְאֵין־דַּעַת אֱלֹהִים בָּאָרֶץ:
² אָלֹה וְכַחֵשׁ וְרָצֹחַ וְגָנֹב וְנָאֹף
פָּרָצוּ וְדָמִים בְּדָמִים נָגָעוּ:
³ עַל־כֵּן | תֶּאֱבַל הָאָרֶץ
וְאֻמְלַל כָּל־יוֹשֵׁב בָּהּ
בְּחַיַּת הַשָּׂדֶה וּבְעוֹף הַשָּׁמָיִם
וְגַם־דְּגֵי הַיָּם יֵאָסֵפוּ:
⁴ אַךְ אִישׁ אַל־יָרֵב וְאַל־יוֹכַח אִישׁ
וְעַמְּךָ כִּמְרִיבֵי כֹהֵן:
⁵ וְכָשַׁלְתָּ הַיּוֹם
וְכָשַׁל גַּם־נָבִיא עִמְּךָ לָיְלָה
וְדָמִיתִי אִמֶּךָ:
⁶ נִדְמוּ עַמִּי מִבְּלִי הַדָּעַת
כִּי־אַתָּה הַדַּעַת מָאַסְתָּ
וְאֶמְאָסְאֶךָ[p] מִכַּהֵן לִי

ד 6 וְאֶמְאָסְךָ

Because you have forgotten the law of your
    God,
  I also will forget your children.

7 "The more they increased,
  The more they sinned against Me;
  I will change their glory into shame.

8 They eat up the sin of My people;
  They set their heart on their iniquity.

9 And it shall be: like people, like priest.
  So I will punish them for their ways,
  And reward them for their deeds.

10 For they shall eat, but not have enough;
  They shall commit harlotry, but not increase;
  Because they have ceased obeying the LORD.

11 "Harlotry, wine, and new wine enslave the
    heart.
12 My people ask counsel from their wooden
    idols,
  And their staff informs them.
  For the spirit of harlotry has caused *them* to
    stray,
  And they have played the harlot against their
    God.
13 They offer sacrifices on the mountaintops,
  And burn incense on the hills,
  Under oaks, poplars, and terebinths,
  Because their shade *is* good.
  Therefore your daughters commit harlotry,
  And your brides commit adultery.

14 "I will not punish your daughters when they
    commit harlotry,
  Nor your brides when they commit adultery;
  For *the men* themselves go apart with
    harlots,
  And offer sacrifices with a ritual harlot.
  Therefore people *who* do not understand will
    be trampled.

15 "Though you, Israel, play the harlot,
  Let not Judah offend.
  Do not come up to Gilgal,
  Nor go up to Beth Aven,
  Nor swear an oath, *saying,* 'As the LORD
    lives'—

16 "For Israel is stubborn
  Like a stubborn calf;
  Now the LORD will let them forage
  Like a lamb in open country.

17 "Ephraim *is* joined to idols,
  Let him alone.
18 Their drink is rebellion,
  They commit harlotry continually.

וַתִּשְׁכַּח תּוֹרַת אֱלֹהֶיךָ
אֶשְׁכַּח בָּנֶיךָ גַּם־אָנִי:

7 כְּרֻבָּם כֵּן חָטְאוּ־לִי
כְּבוֹדָם בְּקָלוֹן אָמִיר:

8 חַטַּאת עַמִּי יֹאכֵלוּ
וְאֶל־עֲוֺנָם יִשְׂאוּ נַפְשׁוֹ:

9 וְהָיָה כָעָם כַּכֹּהֵן
וּפָקַדְתִּי עָלָיו דְּרָכָיו
וּמַעֲלָלָיו אָשִׁיב לוֹ:

10 וְאָכְלוּ וְלֹא יִשְׂבָּעוּ
הִזְנוּ וְלֹא יִפְרֹצוּ
כִּי־אֶת־יְהֹוָה עָזְבוּ לִשְׁמֹר:

11 זְנוּת וְיַיִן וְתִירוֹשׁ יִקַּח־לֵב:

12 עַמִּי בְּעֵצוֹ יִשְׁאָל
וּמַקְלוֹ יַגִּיד לוֹ
כִּי רוּחַ זְנוּנִים הִתְעָה
וַיִּזְנוּ מִתַּחַת אֱלֹהֵיהֶם:

13 עַל־רָאשֵׁי הֶהָרִים יְזַבֵּחוּ
וְעַל־הַגְּבָעוֹת יְקַטֵּרוּ
תַּחַת אַלּוֹן וְלִבְנֶה וְאֵלָה
כִּי טוֹב צִלָּהּ
עַל־כֵּן תִּזְנֶינָה בְּנוֹתֵיכֶם
וְכַלּוֹתֵיכֶם תְּנָאַפְנָה:

14 לֹא־אֶפְקוֹד עַל־בְּנוֹתֵיכֶם
כִּי תִזְנֶינָה
וְעַל־כַּלּוֹתֵיכֶם כִּי תְנָאַפְנָה
כִּי־הֵם עִם־הַזֹּנוֹת יְפָרֵדוּ
וְעִם־הַקְּדֵשׁוֹת יְזַבֵּחוּ
וְעָם לֹא־יָבִין יִלָּבֵט:

15 אִם־זֹנֶה אַתָּה יִשְׂרָאֵל
אַל־יֶאְשַׁם יְהוּדָה
וְאַל־תָּבֹאוּ הַגִּלְגָּל
וְאַל־תַּעֲלוּ בֵּית אָוֶן
וְאַל־תִּשָּׁבְעוּ חַי־יְהֹוָה:

16 כִּי כְּפָרָה סֹרֵרָה סָרַר יִשְׂרָאֵל
עַתָּה יִרְעֵם יְהֹוָה כְּכֶבֶשׂ בַּמֶּרְחָב:

17 חֲבוּר עֲצַבִּים אֶפְרָיִם
הַנַּח־לוֹ:

18 סָר סָבְאָם
הַזְנֵה הִזְנוּ

Her rulers dearly love dishonor.
19 The wind has wrapped her up in its wings,
And they shall be ashamed because of their
    sacrifices.

אָהֲבוּ הֵבוּ קָלוֹן מָגִנֶּיהָ׃
19 צָרַר רוּחַ אוֹתָהּ בִּכְנָפֶיהָ
וְיֵבֹשׁוּ מִזִּבְחוֹתָם׃ ס

5 "Hear this, O priests!
Take heed, O house of Israel!
Give ear, O house of the king!
For yours *is* the judgment,
Because you have been a snare to Mizpah
And a net spread on Tabor.
2 The revolters are deeply involved in
    slaughter,
Though I rebuke them all.
3 I know Ephraim,
And Israel is not hidden from Me;
For now, O Ephraim, you commit harlotry;
Israel is defiled.
4 "They do not direct their deeds
Toward turning to their God,
For the spirit of harlotry is in their midst,
And they do not know the LORD.
5 The pride of Israel testifies to his face;
Therefore Israel and Ephraim stumble in
    their iniquity;
Judah also stumbles with them.
6 "With their flocks and herds
They shall go to seek the LORD,
But they will not find *Him;*
He has withdrawn Himself from them.
7 They have dealt treacherously with the
    LORD,
For they have begotten pagan children.
Now a New Moon shall devour them and
    their heritage.
8 "Blow the ram's horn in Gibeah,
The trumpet in Ramah!
Cry aloud *at* Beth Aven,
'*Look* behind you, O Benjamin!'
9 Ephraim shall be desolate in the day of
    rebuke;
Among the tribes of Israel I make known
    what is sure.
10 "The princes of Judah are like those who
    remove a landmark;
I will pour out my wrath on them like water.
11 Ephraim is oppressed *and* broken in judg-
    ment,
Because he willingly walked by *human*
    precept.
12 Therefore I *will be* to Ephraim like a moth,
And to the house of Judah like rottenness.

ה שִׁמְעוּ־זֹאת הַכֹּהֲנִים
וְהַקְשִׁיבוּ | בֵּית יִשְׂרָאֵל
וּבֵית הַמֶּלֶךְ הַאֲזִינוּ
כִּי לָכֶם הַמִּשְׁפָּט
כִּי־פַח הֱיִיתֶם לְמִצְפָּה
וְרֶשֶׁת פְּרוּשָׂה עַל־תָּבוֹר׃
2 וְשַׁחֲטָה שֵׂטִים הֶעְמִיקוּ
וַאֲנִי מוּסָר לְכֻלָּם׃
3 אֲנִי יָדַעְתִּי אֶפְרַיִם
וְיִשְׂרָאֵל לֹא־נִכְחַד מִמֶּנִּי
כִּי עַתָּה הִזְנֵיתָ אֶפְרַיִם
נִטְמָא יִשְׂרָאֵל׃
4 לֹא יִתְּנוּ מַעַלְלֵיהֶם
לָשׁוּב אֶל־אֱלֹהֵיהֶם
כִּי רוּחַ זְנוּנִים בְּקִרְבָּם
וְאֶת־יְהֹוָה לֹא יָדָעוּ׃
5 וְעָנָה גְאוֹן־יִשְׂרָאֵל בְּפָנָיו
וְיִשְׂרָאֵל וְאֶפְרַיִם יִכָּשְׁלוּ בַּעֲוֹנָם
כָּשַׁל גַּם־יְהוּדָה עִמָּם׃
6 בְּצֹאנָם וּבִבְקָרָם יֵלְכוּ
לְבַקֵּשׁ אֶת־יְהֹוָה וְלֹא יִמְצָאוּ
חָלַץ מֵהֶם׃
7 בַּיהֹוָה בָּגָדוּ
כִּי־בָנִים זָרִים יָלָדוּ
עַתָּה יֹאכְלֵם חֹדֶשׁ אֶת־חֶלְקֵיהֶם׃ ס
8 תִּקְעוּ שׁוֹפָר בַּגִּבְעָה
חֲצֹצְרָה בָּרָמָה
הָרִיעוּ בֵּית אָוֶן
אַחֲרֶיךָ בִּנְיָמִין׃
9 אֶפְרַיִם לְשַׁמָּה תִהְיֶה בְּיוֹם תּוֹכֵחָה
בְּשִׁבְטֵי יִשְׂרָאֵל הוֹדַעְתִּי נֶאֱמָנָה׃
10 הָיוּ שָׂרֵי יְהוּדָה כְּמַסִּיגֵי גְּבוּל
עֲלֵיהֶם אֶשְׁפּוֹךְ כַּמַּיִם עֶבְרָתִי׃
11 עָשׁוּק אֶפְרַיִם רְצוּץ מִשְׁפָּט
כִּי הוֹאִיל הָלַךְ אַחֲרֵי־צָו׃
12 וַאֲנִי כָעָשׁ לְאֶפְרָיִם
וְכָרָקָב לְבֵית יְהוּדָה׃

13 "When Ephraim saw his sickness,
    And Judah *saw* his wound,
    Then Ephraim went to Assyria
    And sent to King Jareb;
    Yet he cannot cure you,
    Nor heal you of your wound.

14 For I *will be* like a lion to Ephraim,
    And like a young lion to the house of Judah.
    I, *even* I, will tear *them* and go away;
    I will take *them* away, and no one shall
        rescue.

15 I will return again to My place
    Till they acknowledge their offense.
    Then they will seek My face;
    In their affliction they will earnestly seek
        Me."

6   Come, and let us return to the LORD;
    For He has torn, but He will heal us;
    He has stricken, but He will bind us up.

2   After two days He will revive us;
    On the third day He will raise us up,
    That we may live in His sight.

3   Let us know,
    Let us pursue the knowledge of the LORD.
    His going forth is established as the morning;
    He will come to us like the rain,
    Like the latter *and* former rain to the earth.

4   "O Ephraim, what shall I do to you?
    O Judah, what shall I do to you?
    For your faithfulness is like a morning cloud,
    And like the early dew it goes away.

5   Therefore I have hewn *them* by the prophets,
    I have slain them by the words of My mouth;
    And your judgments *are like* light *that* goes
        forth.

6   For I desire mercy and not sacrifice,
    And the knowledge of God more than burnt
        offerings.

7   "But like men they transgressed the covenant;
    There they dealt treacherously with Me.

8   Gilead *is* a city of evildoers
    And defiled with blood.

9   As bands of robbers lie in wait for a man,
    So the company of priests murder on the way
        to Shechem;
    Surely they commit lewdness.

10 I have seen a horrible thing in the house of
        Israel:
    There *is* the harlotry of Ephraim;
    Israel is defiled.

11 Also, O Judah, a harvest is appointed for
        you,

וַיַּרְא אֶפְרַיִם אֶת־חָלְיוֹ 13
וִיהוּדָה אֶת־מְזֹרוֹ
וַיֵּלֶךְ אֶפְרַיִם אֶל־אַשּׁוּר
וַיִּשְׁלַח אֶל־מֶלֶךְ יָרֵב
וְהוּא לֹא יוּכַל לִרְפֹּא לָכֶם
וְלֹא־יִגְהֶה מִכֶּם מָזוֹר׃
כִּי אָנֹכִי כַשַּׁחַל לְאֶפְרַיִם 14
וְכַכְּפִיר לְבֵית יְהוּדָה
אֲנִי אֲנִי אֶטְרֹף וְאֵלֵךְ
אֶשָּׂא וְאֵין מַצִּיל׃
אֵלֵךְ אָשׁוּבָה אֶל־מְקוֹמִי 15
עַד אֲשֶׁר־יֶאְשְׁמוּ וּבִקְשׁוּ פָנָי
בַּצַּר לָהֶם יְשַׁחֲרֻנְנִי׃

לְכוּ וְנָשׁוּבָה אֶל־יְהוָה 1
כִּי הוּא טָרָף וְיִרְפָּאֵנוּ
יַךְ וְיַחְבְּשֵׁנוּ׃
יְחַיֵּנוּ מִיֹּמָיִם בַּיּוֹם הַשְּׁלִישִׁי 2
יְקִמֵנוּ וְנִחְיֶה לְפָנָיו׃
וְנֵדְעָה נִרְדְּפָה לָדַעַת אֶת־יְהוָה 3
כְּשַׁחַר נָכוֹן מוֹצָאוֹ
וְיָבוֹא כַגֶּשֶׁם לָנוּ
כְּמַלְקוֹשׁ יוֹרֶה אָרֶץ׃
מָה אֶעֱשֶׂה־לְּךָ אֶפְרַיִם מָה אֶעֱשֶׂה־לְּךָ יְהוּדָה 4
וְחַסְדְּכֶם כַּעֲנַן־בֹּקֶר וְכַטַּל מַשְׁכִּים הֹלֵךְ׃
עַל־כֵּן חָצַבְתִּי בַּנְּבִיאִים 5
הֲרַגְתִּים בְּאִמְרֵי־פִי
וּמִשְׁפָּטֶיךָ אוֹר יֵצֵא׃
כִּי חֶסֶד חָפַצְתִּי וְלֹא־זָבַח 6
וְדַעַת אֱלֹהִים מֵעֹלוֹת׃
וְהֵמָּה כְּאָדָם עָבְרוּ בְרִית 7
שָׁם בָּגְדוּ בִי׃
גִּלְעָד קִרְיַת פֹּעֲלֵי אָוֶן 8
עֲקֻבָּה מִדָּם׃
וּכְחַכֵּי אִישׁ גְּדוּדִים חֶבֶר כֹּהֲנִים 9
דֶּרֶךְ יְרַצְּחוּ־שֶׁכְמָה
כִּי זִמָּה עָשׂוּ׃
בְּבֵית יִשְׂרָאֵל רָאִיתִי שַׁעֲרִירִיָּה 10
שָׁם זְנוּת לְאֶפְרַיִם נִטְמָא יִשְׂרָאֵל׃
גַּם־יְהוּדָה שָׁת קָצִיר לָךְ 11

When I return the captives of My people.　　ס　　　בְּשׁוּבִי שְׁבוּת עַמִּי:

7 "When I would have healed Israel,　　　　ז　כְּרָפְאִי לְיִשְׂרָאֵל
　　　Then the iniquity of Ephraim was uncovered,　　וְנִגְלָה עֲוֹן אֶפְרַיִם וְרָעוֹת שֹׁמְרוֹן
　　　And the wickedness of Samaria.
　　　For they have committed fraud;　　　　כִּי פָעֲלוּ שָׁקֶר
　　　A thief comes in;　　　　וְגַנָּב יָבוֹא
　　　A band of robbers takes spoil outside.　　פָּשַׁט גְּדוּד בַּחוּץ:

2　They do not consider in their hearts　　2　וּבַל־יֹאמְרוּ לִלְבָבָם
　　That I remember all their wickedness;　　כָּל־רָעָתָם זָכָרְתִּי
　　Now their own deeds have surrounded them;　עַתָּה סְבָבוּם מַעַלְלֵיהֶם
　　They are before My face.　　　　נֶגֶד פָּנַי הָיוּ:

3　They make a king glad with their wickedness,　3　בְּרָעָתָם יְשַׂמְּחוּ־מֶלֶךְ
　　And princes with their lies.　　　וּבְכַחֲשֵׁיהֶם שָׂרִים:

4　"They *are* all adulterers.　　　4　כֻּלָּם מְנָאֲפִים
　　Like an oven heated by a baker—　　כְּמוֹ תַנּוּר בֹּעֵרָה מֵאֹפֶה
　　He ceases stirring *the fire* after kneading the
　　　dough,
　　Until it is leavened.　　　　יַשְׁבּוֹת מֵעִיר
5　In the day of our king　　　5
　　Princes have made *him* sick, inflamed with　מִלּוּשׁ בָּצֵק עַד־חֻמְצָתוֹ:
　　　wine;
　　He stretched out his hand with scoffers.　　יוֹם מַלְכֵּנוּ

6　They prepare their heart like an oven,　　הֶחֱלוּ שָׂרִים חֲמַת מִיָּיִן
　　While they lie in wait;　　　מָשַׁךְ יָדוֹ אֶת־לֹצְצִים:
　　Their baker sleeps all night;
　　In the morning it burns like a flaming fire.　6　כִּי־קֵרְבוּ כַתַּנּוּר לִבָּם בְּאָרְבָּם
7　They are all hot, like an oven,　　כָּל־הַלַּיְלָה יָשֵׁן אֹפֵהֶם
　　And have devoured their judges;　　בֹּקֶר הוּא בֹעֵר כְּאֵשׁ לֶהָבָה:
　　All their kings have fallen.
　　None among them calls upon Me.　　7　כֻּלָּם יֵחַמּוּ כַּתַּנּוּר
　　　　　　　וְאָכְלוּ אֶת־שֹׁפְטֵיהֶם
8　"Ephraim has mixed himself among the　　כָּל־מַלְכֵיהֶם נָפָלוּ
　　　peoples;　　　　אֵין־קֹרֵא בָהֶם אֵלָי:
　　Ephraim is a cake unturned.
9　Aliens have devoured his strength,　　8　אֶפְרַיִם בָּעַמִּים הוּא יִתְבּוֹלָל
　　But he does not know *it;*　　אֶפְרַיִם הָיָה עֻגָה בְּלִי הֲפוּכָה:
　　Yes, gray hairs are here and there on him,
　　Yet he does not know *it.*　　9　אָכְלוּ זָרִים כֹּחוֹ
10　And the pride of Israel testifies to his face,　וְהוּא לֹא יָדָע
　　But they do not return to the LORD their　גַּם־שֵׂיבָה זָרְקָה בּוֹ
　　　God,　　　　וְהוּא לֹא יָדָע:
　　Nor seek Him for all this.
　　　　　　　　10　וְעָנָה גְאוֹן־יִשְׂרָאֵל בְּפָנָיו
11　"Ephraim also is like a silly dove, without　וְלֹא־שָׁבוּ אֶל־יְהוָה אֱלֹהֵיהֶם
　　　sense—　　　　וְלֹא בִקְשֻׁהוּ בְּכָל־זֹאת:
　　They call to Egypt,
　　They go to Assyria.　　　11　וַיְהִי אֶפְרַיִם כְּיוֹנָה פוֹתָה אֵין לֵב
12　Wherever they go, I will spread My net on　מִצְרַיִם קָרָאוּ אַשּׁוּר הָלָכוּ:
　　　them;
　　I will bring them down like birds of the air;　12　כַּאֲשֶׁר יֵלֵכוּ אֶפְרוֹשׁ עֲלֵיהֶם רִשְׁתִּי
　　I will chastise them　　　כְּעוֹף הַשָּׁמַיִם אוֹרִידֵם
　　According to what their congregation has　ס　אַיְסִרֵם כְּשֵׁמַע לַעֲדָתָם:
　　　heard.

13 "Woe to them, for they have fled from Me!
Destruction to them,
Because they have transgressed against Me!
Though I redeemed them,
Yet they have spoken lies against Me.

14 They did not cry out to Me with their heart
When they wailed upon their beds.

"They assemble together for grain and new
wine,
They rebel against Me;

15 Though I disciplined *and* strengthened their
arms,
Yet they devise evil against Me;

16 They return, *but* not to the Most High;
They are like a treacherous bow.
Their princes shall fall by the sword
For the cursings of their tongue.
This *shall be* their derision in the land of
Egypt.

8 "*Set* the trumpet to your mouth!
He shall come like an eagle against the house
of the LORD,
Because they have transgressed My covenant
And rebelled against My law.

2 Israel will cry to Me,
'My God, we know You!'

3 Israel has rejected the good;
The enemy will pursue him.

4 "They set up kings, but not by Me;
They made princes, but I did not
acknowledge *them*.
From their silver and gold
They made idols for themselves—
That they might be cut off.

5 Your calf is rejected, O Samaria!
My anger is aroused against them—
How long until they attain to innocence?

6 For from Israel *is* even this:
A workman made it, and it *is* not God;
But the calf of Samaria shall be broken to
pieces.

7 "They sow the wind,
And reap the whirlwind.
The stalk has no bud;
It shall never produce meal.
If it should produce,
Aliens would swallow it up.

8 Israel is swallowed up;
Now they are among the Gentiles
Like a vessel in which *is* no pleasure.

9 For they have gone up to Assyria,

13 אוֹי לָהֶם כִּי־נָדְדוּ מִמֶּנִּי
שֹׁד לָהֶם כִּי־פָשְׁעוּ בִי
וְאָנֹכִי אֶפְדֵּם
וְהֵמָּה דִּבְּרוּ עָלַי כְּזָבִים׃

14 וְלֹא־זָעֲקוּ אֵלַי בְּלִבָּם
כִּי יְיֵלִילוּ עַל־מִשְׁכְּבוֹתָם
עַל־דָּגָן וְתִירוֹשׁ
יִתְגּוֹרָרוּ יָסוּרוּ בִי׃

15 וַאֲנִי יִסַּרְתִּי חִזַּקְתִּי זְרוֹעֹתָם
וְאֵלַי יְחַשְּׁבוּ־רָע׃

16 יָשׁוּבוּ ׀ לֹא עָל
הָיוּ כְּקֶשֶׁת רְמִיָּה
יִפְּלוּ בַחֶרֶב
שָׂרֵיהֶם מִזַּעַם לְשׁוֹנָם
זוֹ לַעְגָּם בְּאֶרֶץ מִצְרָיִם׃

ח אֶל־חִכְּךָ שֹׁפָר
כַּנֶּשֶׁר עַל־בֵּית יְהוָה
יַעַן עָבְרוּ בְרִיתִי
וְעַל־תּוֹרָתִי פָּשָׁעוּ׃

2 לִי יִזְעָקוּ
אֱלֹהַי יְדַעֲנוּךָ יִשְׂרָאֵל׃

3 זָנַח יִשְׂרָאֵל טוֹב
אוֹיֵב יִרְדְּפוֹ׃

4 הֵם הִמְלִיכוּ וְלֹא מִמֶּנִּי
הֵשִׂירוּ וְלֹא יָדָעְתִּי
כַּסְפָּם וּזְהָבָם עָשׂוּ לָהֶם עֲצַבִּים
לְמַעַן יִכָּרֵת׃

5 זָנַח עֶגְלֵךְ שֹׁמְרוֹן
חָרָה אַפִּי בָּם
עַד־מָתַי לֹא יוּכְלוּ נִקָּיֹן׃

6 כִּי מִיִּשְׂרָאֵל וְהוּא
חָרָשׁ עָשָׂהוּ וְלֹא אֱלֹהִים הוּא
כִּי־שְׁבָבִים יִהְיֶה עֵגֶל שֹׁמְרוֹן׃

7 כִּי רוּחַ יִזְרָעוּ וְסוּפָתָה יִקְצֹרוּ
קָמָה אֵין־לוֹ צֶמַח בְּלִי יַעֲשֶׂה־קֶּמַח
אוּלַי יַעֲשֶׂה זָרִים יִבְלָעֻהוּ׃

8 נִבְלַע יִשְׂרָאֵל
עַתָּה הָיוּ בַגּוֹיִם
כִּכְלִי אֵין־חֵפֶץ בּוֹ׃

9 כִּי־הֵמָּה עָלוּ אַשּׁוּר

Like a wild donkey alone by itself;
Ephraim has hired lovers.

10 Yes, though they have hired among the
nations,
Now I will gather them;
And they shall sorrow a little,
Because of the burden of the king of princes.

11 "Because Ephraim has made many altars for
sin,
They have become for him altars for sinning.

12 I have written for him the great things of My
law,
But they were considered a strange thing.

13 *For* the sacrifices of My offerings they
sacrifice flesh and eat *it*,
But the LORD does not accept them.
Now He will remember their iniquity and
punish their sins.
They shall return to Egypt.

14 "For Israel has forgotten his Maker,
And has built temples;
Judah also has multiplied fortified cities;
But I will send fire upon his cities,
And it shall devour his palaces."

פֶּרֶא בּוֹדֵד לוֹ
אֶפְרַיִם הִתְנוּ אֲהָבִים:
10 גַּם כִּי־יִתְנוּ בַגּוֹיִם עַתָּה אֲקַבְּצֵם
וַיָּחֵלּוּ מְּעָט
מִמַּשָּׂא מֶלֶךְ שָׂרִים:
11 כִּי־הִרְבָּה אֶפְרַיִם מִזְבְּחֹת לַחֲטֹא
הָיוּ־לוֹ מִזְבְּחוֹת לַחֲטֹא:
12 אֶכְתָּוב־לוֹ רֻבֵּו תּוֹרָתִי
כְּמוֹ־זָר נֶחְשָׁבוּ:
13 זִבְחֵי הַבְהָבַי יִזְבְּחוּ בָשָׂר וַיֹּאכֵלוּ
יְהוָה לֹא רָצָם
עַתָּה יִזְכֹּר עֲוֹנָם וְיִפְקֹד חַטֹּאותָם
הֵמָּה מִצְרַיִם יָשׁוּבוּ:
14 וַיִּשְׁכַּח יִשְׂרָאֵל אֶת־עֹשֵׂהוּ
וַיִּבֶן הֵיכָלוֹת
וִיהוּדָה הִרְבָּה עָרִים בְּצֻרוֹת
וְשִׁלַּחְתִּי־אֵשׁ בְּעָרָיו
וְאָכְלָה אַרְמְנֹתֶיהָ: ס

9 Do not rejoice, O Israel, with joy like *other*
peoples,
For you have played the harlot against your
God.
You have made love *for* hire on every
threshing floor.

2 The threshing floor and the winepress
Shall not feed them,
And the new wine shall fail in her.

3 They shall not dwell in the LORD's land,
But Ephraim shall return to Egypt,
And shall eat unclean *things* in Assyria.

4 They shall not offer wine *offerings* to the
LORD,
Nor shall their sacrifices be pleasing to Him.
It shall be like bread of mourners to them;
All who eat it shall be defiled.
For their bread *shall be* for their *own* life;
It shall not come into the house of the LORD.

5 What will you do in the appointed day,
And in the day of the feast of the LORD?

6 For indeed they are gone because of
destruction.
Egypt shall gather them up;
Memphis shall bury them.
Nettles shall possess their valuables of silver;
Thorns *shall be* in their tents.

ט אַל־תִּשְׂמַח יִשְׂרָאֵל ׀
אֶל־גִּיל כָּעַמִּים
כִּי זָנִיתָ מֵעַל אֱלֹהֶיךָ
אָהַבְתָּ אֶתְנָן עַל כָּל־גָּרְנוֹת דָּגָן:
2 גֹּרֶן וָיֶקֶב לֹא יִרְעֵם
וְתִירוֹשׁ יְכַחֶשׁ בָּהּ:
3 לֹא יֵשְׁבוּ בְּאֶרֶץ יְהוָה
וְשָׁב אֶפְרַיִם מִצְרַיִם
וּבְאַשּׁוּר טָמֵא יֹאכֵלוּ:
4 לֹא־יִסְּכוּ לַיהוָה ׀ יַיִן וְלֹא יֶעֶרְבוּ־לוֹ
זִבְחֵיהֶם כְּלֶחֶם אוֹנִים לָהֶם
כָּל־אֹכְלָיו יִטַּמָּאוּ
כִּי־לַחְמָם לְנַפְשָׁם לֹא יָבוֹא בֵּית יְהוָה:
5 מַה־תַּעֲשׂוּ לְיוֹם מוֹעֵד
וּלְיוֹם חַג־יְהוָה:
6 כִּי־הִנֵּה הָלְכוּ מִשֹּׁד מִצְרַיִם תְּקַבְּצֵם
מֹף תְּקַבְּרֵם
מַחְמַד לְכַסְפָּם קִמּוֹשׂ יִירָשֵׁם חוֹחַ בְּאָהֳלֵיהֶם:

7 The days of punishment have come;
　The days of recompense have come.
　Israel knows!
　The prophet *is* a fool,
　The spiritual man *is* insane,
　Because of the greatness of your iniquity and
　　great enmity.
8 The watchman of Ephraim *is* with my God;
　But the prophet *is* a fowler's snare in all his
　　ways—
　Enmity in the house of his God.
9 They are deeply corrupted,
　As in the days of Gibeah.
　He will remember their iniquity;
　He will punish their sins.

10 "I found Israel
　Like grapes in the wilderness;
　I saw your fathers
　As the firstfruits on the fig tree in its first
　　season.
　But they went to Baal Peor,
　And separated themselves *to that* shame;
　They became an abomination like the thing
　　they loved.
11 *As for* Ephraim, their glory shall fly away
　　like a bird—
　No birth, no pregnancy, and no conception!
12 Though they bring up their children,
　Yet I will bereave them to the last man.
　Yes, woe to them when I depart from them!
13 Just as I saw Ephraim like Tyre, planted in a
　　pleasant place,
　So Ephraim will bring out his children to the
　　murderer."

14 Give them, O Lord—
　What will You give?
　Give them a miscarrying womb
　And dry breasts!

15 "All their wickedness *is* in Gilgal,
　For there I hated them.
　Because of the evil of their deeds
　I will drive them from My house;
　I will love them no more.
　All their princes *are* rebellious.
16 Ephraim is stricken,
　Their root is dried up;
　They shall bear no fruit.
　Yes, were they to bear children,
　I would kill the darlings of their womb."

17 My God will cast them away,
　Because they did not obey Him;

7 בָּאוּ ׀ יְמֵי הַפְּקֻדָּה
בָּאוּ יְמֵי הַשִּׁלֻּם
יֵדְעוּ יִשְׂרָאֵל
אֱוִיל הַנָּבִיא מְשֻׁגָּע אִישׁ הָרוּחַ
עַל רֹב עֲוֹנְךָ
וְרַבָּה מַשְׂטֵמָה:
8 צֹפֶה אֶפְרַיִם עִם־אֱלֹהָי
נָבִיא פַּח יָקוֹשׁ עַל־כָּל־דְּרָכָיו
מַשְׂטֵמָה בְּבֵית אֱלֹהָיו:
9 הֶעְמִיקוּ־שִׁחֵתוּ כִּימֵי הַגִּבְעָה
יִזְכּוֹר עֲוֹנָם
יִפְקוֹד חַטֹּאותָם: ס

10 כַּעֲנָבִים בַּמִּדְבָּר מָצָאתִי יִשְׂרָאֵל
כְּבִכּוּרָה בִתְאֵנָה בְּרֵאשִׁיתָהּ
רָאִיתִי אֲבוֹתֵיכֶם
הֵמָּה בָּאוּ בַעַל־פְּעוֹר
וַיִּנָּזְרוּ לַבֹּשֶׁת
וַיִּהְיוּ שִׁקּוּצִים כְּאָהֳבָם:
11 אֶפְרַיִם כָּעוֹף יִתְעוֹפֵף כְּבוֹדָם
מִלֵּדָה וּמִבֶּטֶן וּמֵהֵרָיוֹן:
12 כִּי אִם־יְגַדְּלוּ אֶת־בְּנֵיהֶם
וְשִׁכַּלְתִּים מֵאָדָם
כִּי־גַם־אוֹי לָהֶם בְּשׂוּרִי מֵהֶם:
13 אֶפְרַיִם כַּאֲשֶׁר־רָאִיתִי לְצוֹר
שְׁתוּלָה בְנָוֶה
וְאֶפְרַיִם לְהוֹצִיא אֶל־הֹרֵג בָּנָיו:
14 תֵּן־לָהֶם יְהוָה מַה־תִּתֵּן
תֵּן־לָהֶם רֶחֶם מַשְׁכִּיל
וְשָׁדַיִם צֹמְקִים:

15 כָּל־רָעָתָם בַּגִּלְגָּל
כִּי־שָׁם שְׂנֵאתִים
עַל רֹעַ מַעַלְלֵיהֶם
מִבֵּיתִי אֲגָרְשֵׁם
לֹא אוֹסֵף אַהֲבָתָם
כָּל־שָׂרֵיהֶם סֹרְרִים:
16 הֻכָּה אֶפְרַיִם שָׁרְשָׁם יָבֵשׁ
פְּרִי בְלִי־ק עֲשׂוּן
גַּם כִּי יֵלֵדוּן וְהֵמַתִּי מַחֲמַדֵּי בִטְנָם: ס
17 יִמְאָסֵם אֱלֹהַי

And they shall be wanderers among the
nations.

כִּי לֹא שָׁמְעוּ לוֹ
וְיִהְיוּ נֹדְדִים בַּגּוֹיִם: ס

10 Israel empties *his* vine;
He brings forth fruit for himself.
According to the multitude of his fruit
He has increased the altars;
According to the bounty of his land
They have embellished *his* sacred pillars.

י גֶּפֶן בּוֹקֵק יִשְׂרָאֵל
פְּרִי יְשַׁוֶּה־לּוֹ כְּרֹב לְפִרְיוֹ
הִרְבָּה לַמִּזְבְּחוֹת
כְּטוֹב לְאַרְצוֹ
הֵיטִיבוּ מַצֵּבוֹת:

2 Their heart is divided;
Now they are held guilty.
He will break down their altars;
He will ruin their sacred pillars.

2 חָלַק לִבָּם עַתָּה יֶאְשָׁמוּ
הוּא יַעֲרֹף מִזְבְּחוֹתָם
יְשֹׁדֵד מַצֵּבוֹתָם:

3 For now they say,
"We have no king,
Because we did not fear the LORD.
And as for a king, what would he do for us?"

3 כִּי עַתָּה יֹאמְרוּ אֵין מֶלֶךְ לָנוּ
כִּי לֹא יָרֵאנוּ אֶת־יְהֹוָה
וְהַמֶּלֶךְ מַה־יַּעֲשֶׂה־לָּנוּ:

4 They have spoken words,
Swearing falsely in making a covenant.
Thus judgment springs up like hemlock in
the furrows of the field.

4 דִּבְּרוּ דְבָרִים
אָלוֹת שָׁוְא כָּרֹת בְּרִית
וּפָרַח כָּרֹאשׁ מִשְׁפָּט
עַל תַּלְמֵי שָׂדָי:

5 The inhabitants of Samaria fear
Because of the calf of Beth Aven.
For its people mourn for it,
And its priests shriek for it—
Because its glory has departed from it.

5 לְעֶגְלוֹת בֵּית אָוֶן
יָגוּרוּ שְׁכַן שֹׁמְרוֹן
כִּי־אָבַל עָלָיו עַמּוֹ
וּכְמָרָיו עָלָיו יָגִילוּ
עַל־כְּבוֹדוֹ כִּי־גָלָה מִמֶּנּוּ:

6 *The idol* also shall be carried to Assyria
As a present for King Jareb.
Ephraim shall receive shame,
And Israel shall be ashamed of his own
counsel.

6 גַּם־אוֹתוֹ לְאַשּׁוּר יוּבָל
מִנְחָה לְמֶלֶךְ יָרֵב
בָּשְׁנָה אֶפְרַיִם יִקָּח
וְיֵבוֹשׁ יִשְׂרָאֵל מֵעֲצָתוֹ:

7 *As for* Samaria, her king is cut off
Like a twig on the water.

8 Also the high places of Aven, the sin of
Israel,
Shall be destroyed.
The thorn and thistle shall grow on their
altars;
They shall say to the mountains, "Cover us!"
And to the hills, "Fall on us!"

7 נִדְמֶה שֹׁמְרוֹן מַלְכָּהּ
כְּקֶצֶף עַל־פְּנֵי־מָיִם:

8 וְנִשְׁמְדוּ בָּמוֹת אָוֶן
חַטַּאת יִשְׂרָאֵל
קוֹץ וְדַרְדַּר יַעֲלֶה עַל־מִזְבְּחוֹתָם
וְאָמְרוּ לֶהָרִים כַּסּוּנוּ
וְלַגְּבָעוֹת נִפְלוּ עָלֵינוּ: ס

9 "O Israel, you have sinned from the days of
Gibeah;
There they stood.
The battle in Gibeah against the children of
iniquity
Did not overtake them.

9 מִימֵי הַגִּבְעָה חָטָאתָ יִשְׂרָאֵל
שָׁם עָמָדוּ
לֹא־תַשִּׂיגֵם בַּגִּבְעָה
מִלְחָמָה עַל־בְּנֵי עַלְוָה:

10 When *it is* My desire, I will chasten them.
Peoples shall be gathered against them
When I bind them for their two
transgressions.

10 בְּאַוָּתִי וְאֶסֳּרֵם
וְאֻסְּפוּ עֲלֵיהֶם עַמִּים
בְּאָסְרָם לִשְׁתֵּי עֵינֹתָם:ק

11 Ephraim *is* a trained heifer
That loves to thresh *grain;*

י 10 עֲוֹנֹתָם

But I harnessed her fair neck,
I will make Ephraim pull *a plow*.
Judah shall plow;
Jacob shall break his clods."

וְאֶפְרַיִם עֶגְלָה מְלֻמָּדָה אֹהַבְתִּי לָדוּשׁ 11
וַאֲנִי עָבַרְתִּי עַל־טוּב צַוָּארָהּ
אַרְכִּיב אֶפְרַיִם יַחֲרוֹשׁ יְהוּדָה
יְשַׂדֶּד־לוֹ יַעֲקֹב׃

12 Sow for yourselves righteousness;
Reap in mercy;
Break up your fallow ground,
For *it is* time to seek the LORD,
Till He comes and rains righteousness on
you.

זִרְעוּ לָכֶם לִצְדָקָה קִצְרוּ לְפִי־חֶסֶד 12
נִירוּ לָכֶם נִיר
וְעֵת לִדְרוֹשׁ אֶת־יְהוָה
עַד־יָבוֹא וְיֹרֶה צֶדֶק לָכֶם׃

13 You have plowed wickedness;
You have reaped iniquity.
You have eaten the fruit of lies,
Because you trusted in your own way,
In the multitude of your mighty men.

חֲרַשְׁתֶּם־רֶשַׁע עַוְלָתָה קְצַרְתֶּם 13
אֲכַלְתֶּם פְּרִי־כָחַשׁ
כִּי־בָטַחְתָּ בְדַרְכְּךָ
בְּרֹב גִּבּוֹרֶיךָ׃

14 Therefore tumult shall arise among your
people,
And all your fortresses shall be plundered
As Shalman plundered Beth Arbel in the day
of battle—
A mother dashed in pieces upon *her* children.

וְקָאם שָׁאוֹן בְּעַמֶּךָ וְכָל־מִבְצָרֶיךָ יוּשַּׁד 14
כְּשֹׁד שַׁלְמַן
בֵּית אַרְבֵאל בְּיוֹם מִלְחָמָה
אֵם עַל־בָּנִים רֻטָּשָׁה׃

15 Thus it shall be done to you, O Bethel,
Because of your great wickedness.
At dawn the king of Israel
Shall be cut off utterly.

כָּכָה עָשָׂה לָכֶם בֵּית־אֵל 15
מִפְּנֵי רָעַת רָעַתְכֶם
בַּשַּׁחַר נִדְמֹה נִדְמָה מֶלֶךְ יִשְׂרָאֵל׃

11 "When Israel *was* a child, I loved him,
And out of Egypt I called My son.

יא כִּי נַעַר יִשְׂרָאֵל וָאֹהֲבֵהוּ
וּמִמִּצְרַיִם קָרָאתִי לִבְנִי׃

2 *As* they called them,
So they went from them;
They sacrificed to the Baals,
And burned incense to carved images.

קָרְאוּ לָהֶם כֵּן הָלְכוּ מִפְּנֵיהֶם 2
לַבְּעָלִים יְזַבֵּחוּ וְלַפְּסִלִים יְקַטֵּרוּן׃

3 "I taught Ephraim to walk,
Taking them by their arms;
But they did not know that I healed them.

וְאָנֹכִי תִרְגַּלְתִּי לְאֶפְרַיִם 3
קָחָם עַל־זְרוֹעֹתָיו
וְלֹא יָדְעוּ כִּי רְפָאתִים׃

4 I drew them with gentle cords,
With bands of love,
And I was to them as those who take the
yoke from their neck.
I stooped *and* fed them.

בְּחַבְלֵי אָדָם אֶמְשְׁכֵם בַּעֲבֹתוֹת אַהֲבָה 4
וָאֶהְיֶה לָהֶם כִּמְרִימֵי עֹל עַל לְחֵיהֶם
וְאַט אֵלָיו אוֹכִיל׃

5 "He shall not return to the land of Egypt;
But the Assyrian shall be his king,
Because they refused to repent.

לֹא יָשׁוּב אֶל־אֶרֶץ מִצְרַיִם 5
וְאַשּׁוּר הוּא מַלְכּוֹ כִּי מֵאֲנוּ לָשׁוּב׃

6 And the sword shall slash in his cities,
Devour his districts,
And consume *them*,
Because of their own counsels.

וְחָלָה חֶרֶב בְּעָרָיו 6
וְכִלְּתָה בַדָּיו וְאָכֵלָה
מִמֹּעֲצוֹתֵיהֶם׃

7 My people are bent on backsliding from Me.
Though they call to the Most High,
None at all exalt *Him*.

וְעַמִּי תְלוּאִים לִמְשׁוּבָתִי 7
וְאֶל־עַל יִקְרָאֻהוּ
יַחַד לֹא יְרוֹמֵם׃

8 "How can I give you up, Ephraim?
How can I hand you over, Israel?

אֵיךְ אֶתֶּנְךָ אֶפְרַיִם 8
אֲמַגֶּנְךָ יִשְׂרָאֵל

How can I make you like Admah?   אֵיךְ אֶתֶּנְךָ כְאַדְמָה
How can I set you like Zeboiim?   אֲשִׂימְךָ כִּצְבֹאיִם
My heart churns within Me;   נֶהְפַּךְ עָלַי לִבִּי
My sympathy is stirred.   יַחַד נִכְמְרוּ נִחוּמָי:

9 I will not execute the fierceness of My anger;   לֹא אֶעֱשֶׂה חֲרוֹן אַפִּי   9
  I will not again destroy Ephraim.   לֹא אָשׁוּב לְשַׁחֵת אֶפְרָיִם
  For I *am* God, and not man,   כִּי אֵל אָנֹכִי וְלֹא־אִישׁ
  The Holy One in your midst;   בְּקִרְבְּךָ קָדוֹשׁ
  And I will not come with terror.   וְלֹא אָבוֹא בְּעִיר:

10 "They shall walk after the LORD.   אַחֲרֵי יְהוָה   10
  He will roar like a lion.   יֵלְכוּ כְּאַרְיֵה יִשְׁאָג
  When He roars,   כִּי־הוּא יִשְׁאַג
  Then *His* sons shall come trembling from the west;   וְיֶחֶרְדוּ בָנִים מִיָּם:

11 They shall come trembling like a bird from Egypt,   יֶחֶרְדוּ כְצִפּוֹר מִמִּצְרַיִם   11
  Like a dove from the land of Assyria.   וּכְיוֹנָה מֵאֶרֶץ אַשּׁוּר
  And I will let them dwell in their houses,"   וְהוֹשַׁבְתִּים עַל־בָּתֵּיהֶם
  Says the LORD.   נְאֻם־יְהוָה: ס

12 "Ephraim has encircled Me with lies,   יב סְבָבֻנִי בְכַחַשׁ אֶפְרַיִם
  And the house of Israel with deceit;   וּבְמִרְמָה בֵּית יִשְׂרָאֵל
  But Judah still walks with God,   וִיהוּדָה עֹד רָד עִם־אֵל
  Even with the Holy One *who is* faithful.   וְעִם־קְדוֹשִׁים נֶאֱמָן:

12 "Ephraim feeds on the wind,   אֶפְרַיִם רֹעֶה רוּחַ וְרֹדֵף קָדִים   2
  And pursues the east wind;   כָּל־הַיּוֹם כָּזָב וָשֹׁד יַרְבֶּה
  He daily increases lies and desolation.   וּבְרִית עִם־אַשּׁוּר יִכְרֹתוּ
  Also they make a covenant with the Assyrians,   וְשֶׁמֶן לְמִצְרַיִם יוּבָל:
  And oil is carried to Egypt.

2 "The LORD also *brings* a charge against Judah,   וְרִיב לַיהוָה עִם־יְהוּדָה   3
  And will punish Jacob according to his ways;   וְלִפְקֹד עַל־יַעֲקֹב כִּדְרָכָיו
  According to his deeds He will recompense him.   כְּמַעֲלָלָיו יָשִׁיב לוֹ:

3 He took his brother by the heel in the womb,   בַּבֶּטֶן עָקַב אֶת־אָחִיו   4
  And in his strength he struggled with God.   וּבְאוֹנוֹ שָׂרָה אֶת־אֱלֹהִים:

4 Yes, he struggled with the Angel and prevailed;   וַיָּשַׂר אֶל־מַלְאָךְ וַיֻּכָל בָּכָה וַיִּתְחַנֶּן־לוֹ   5
  He wept, and sought favor from Him.   בֵּית־אֵל יִמְצָאֶנּוּ וְשָׁם יְדַבֵּר עִמָּנוּ:
  He found Him *in* Bethel,
  And there He spoke to us—

5 That is, the LORD God of hosts.   וַיהוָה אֱלֹהֵי הַצְּבָאוֹת יְהוָה זִכְרוֹ:   6
  The LORD *is* His memorable name.

6 So you, by *the help of* your God, return;   וְאַתָּה בֵּאלֹהֶיךָ תָשׁוּב   7
  Observe mercy and justice,   חֶסֶד וּמִשְׁפָּט שְׁמֹר
  And wait on your God continually.   וְקַוֵּה אֶל־אֱלֹהֶיךָ תָּמִיד:

7 "A cunning Canaanite!   כְּנַעַן בְּיָדוֹ מֹאזְנֵי מִרְמָה   8
  Deceitful scales *are* in his hand;   לַעֲשֹׁק אָהֵב:
  He loves to oppress.

8 And Ephraim said,   וַיֹּאמֶר אֶפְרַיִם אַךְ עָשַׁרְתִּי   9
  'Surely I have become rich,   מָצָאתִי אוֹן לִי

I have found wealth for myself;
In all my labors
They shall find in me no iniquity that *is* sin.'

9 "But I *am* the LORD your God,
Ever since the land of Egypt;
I will again make you dwell in tents,
As in the days of the appointed feast.

10 I have also spoken by the prophets,
And have multiplied visions;
I have given symbols through the witness of
the prophets."

11 Though Gilead *has* idols—
Surely they are vanity—
Though they sacrifice bulls in Gilgal,
Indeed their altars *shall be* heaps in the
furrows of the field.

12 Jacob fled to the country of Syria;
Israel served for a spouse,
And for a wife he tended *sheep.*

13 By a prophet the LORD brought Israel out of
Egypt,
And by a prophet he was preserved.

14 Ephraim provoked *Him* to anger most
bitterly;
Therefore his Lord will leave the guilt of his
bloodshed upon him,
And return his reproach upon him.

13

When Ephraim spoke, trembling,
He exalted *himself* in Israel;
But when he offended through Baal *worship*,
he died.

2 Now they sin more and more,
And have made for themselves molded
images,
Idols of their silver, according to their skill;
All of it *is* the work of craftsmen.
They say of them,
"Let the men who sacrifice kiss the calves!"

3 Therefore they shall be like the morning
cloud
And like the early dew that passes away,
Like chaff blown off from a threshing floor
And like smoke from a chimney.

4 "Yet I *am* the LORD your God
Ever since the land of Egypt,
And you shall know no God but Me;
For *there is* no savior besides Me.

5 I knew you in the wilderness,
In the land of great drought.

6 When they had pasture, they were filled;
They were filled and their heart was exalted;

כָּל־יְגִיעַי לֹא יִמְצְאוּ־לִי
עָוֺן אֲשֶׁר־חֵטְא:

10 וְאָנֹכִי יְהֹוָה אֱלֹהֶיךָ
מֵאֶרֶץ מִצְרָיִם
עֹד אוֹשִׁיבְךָ בָאֳהָלִים
כִּימֵי מוֹעֵד:

11 וְדִבַּרְתִּי עַל־הַנְּבִיאִים
וְאָנֹכִי חָזוֹן הִרְבֵּיתִי
וּבְיַד הַנְּבִיאִים אֲדַמֶּה:

12 אִם־גִּלְעָד אָוֶן אַךְ־שָׁוְא הָיוּ
בַּגִּלְגָּל שְׁוָרִים זִבֵּחוּ
גַּם מִזְבְּחוֹתָם כְּגַלִּים עַל תַּלְמֵי שָׂדָי:

13 וַיִּבְרַח יַעֲקֹב שְׂדֵה אֲרָם
וַיַּעֲבֹד יִשְׂרָאֵל בְּאִשָּׁה
וּבְאִשָּׁה שָׁמָר:

14 וּבְנָבִיא הֶעֱלָה יְהֹוָה
אֶת־יִשְׂרָאֵל מִמִּצְרָיִם
וּבְנָבִיא נִשְׁמָר:

15 הִכְעִיס אֶפְרַיִם תַּמְרוּרִים
וְדָמָיו עָלָיו יִטּוֹשׁ
וְחֶרְפָּתוֹ יָשִׁיב לוֹ אֲדֹנָיו:

יג כְּדַבֵּר אֶפְרַיִם רְתֵת
נָשָׂא הוּא בְּיִשְׂרָאֵל
וַיֶּאְשַׁם בַּבַּעַל וַיָּמֹת:

2 וְעַתָּה ׀ יוֹסִפוּ לַחֲטֹא
וַיַּעֲשׂוּ לָהֶם מַסֵּכָה מִכַּסְפָּם
כִּתְבוּנָם עֲצַבִּים מַעֲשֵׂה חָרָשִׁים כֻּלֹּה
לָהֶם הֵם אֹמְרִים זֹבְחֵי אָדָם עֲגָלִים יִשָּׁקוּן:

3 לָכֵן יִהְיוּ כַּעֲנַן־בֹּקֶר
וְכַטַּל מַשְׁכִּים הֹלֵךְ
כְּמֹץ יְסֹעֵר מִגֹּרֶן
וּכְעָשָׁן מֵאֲרֻבָּה:

4 וְאָנֹכִי יְהֹוָה אֱלֹהֶיךָ
מֵאֶרֶץ מִצְרָיִם
וֵאלֹהִים זוּלָתִי לֹא תֵדָע
וּמוֹשִׁיעַ אַיִן בִּלְתִּי:

5 אֲנִי יְדַעְתִּיךָ בַּמִּדְבָּר
בְּאֶרֶץ תַּלְאֻבוֹת:

6 כְּמַרְעִיתָם וַיִּשְׂבָּעוּ
שָׂבְעוּ וַיָּרָם לִבָּם

Therefore they forgot Me.

עַל־כֵּ֖ן שְׁכֵחֽוּנִי׃

7 "So I will be to them like a lion;
Like a leopard by the road I will lurk;

7 וָאֱהִ֥י לָהֶ֖ם כְּמוֹ־שָׁ֑חַל
כְּנָמֵ֖ר עַל־דֶּ֥רֶךְ אָשֽׁוּר׃

8 I will meet them like a bear deprived *of her
cubs;*
I will tear open their rib cage,
And there I will devour them like a lion.
The wild beast shall tear them.

8 אֶפְגְּשֵׁם֙ כְּדֹ֣ב שַׁכּ֔וּל וְאֶקְרַ֖ע סְג֣וֹר לִבָּ֑ם
וְאֹכְלֵ֥ם שָׁם֙ כְּלָבִ֔יא חַיַּ֥ת הַשָּׂדֶ֖ה תְּבַקְּעֵֽם׃

9 "O Israel, you are destroyed,
But your help *is* from Me.

9 שִׁחֶתְךָ֥ יִשְׂרָאֵ֖ל כִּֽי־בִ֥י בְעֶזְרֶֽךָ׃

10 I will be your King;
Where *is any other,*
That he may save you in all your cities?
And your judges to whom you said,
'Give me a king and princes'?

10 אֱהִ֤י מַלְכְּךָ֙ אֵפ֔וֹא
וְיוֹשִֽׁיעֲךָ֖ בְּכָל־עָרֶ֑יךָ
וְשֹׁ֣פְטֶ֔יךָ אֲשֶׁ֣ר אָמַ֔רְתָּ
תְּנָה־לִּ֥י מֶ֖לֶךְ וְשָׂרִֽים׃

11 I gave you a king in My anger,
And took *him* away in My wrath.

11 אֶֽתֶּן־לְךָ֥ מֶ֙לֶךְ֙ בְּאַפִּ֔י
וְאֶקַּ֖ח בְּעֶבְרָתִֽי׃ ס

12 "The iniquity of Ephraim *is* bound up;
His sin *is* stored up.

12 צָרוּר֙ עֲוֺ֣ן אֶפְרָ֔יִם
צְפוּנָ֖ה חַטָּאתֽוֹ׃

13 The sorrows of a woman in childbirth shall
come upon him.
He *is* an unwise son,
For he should not stay long where children
are born.

13 חֶבְלֵ֥י יֽוֹלֵדָ֖ה יָבֹ֣אוּ ל֑וֹ
הוּא־בֵן֙ לֹ֣א חָכָ֔ם
כִּֽי־עֵ֥ת לֹֽא־יַעֲמֹ֖ד בְּמִשְׁבַּ֥ר בָּנִֽים׃

14 "I will ransom them from the power of the
grave;
I will redeem them from death.
O Death, I will be your plagues!
O Grave, I will be your destruction!
Pity is hidden from My eyes."

14 מִיַּ֤ד שְׁאוֹל֙ אֶפְדֵּ֔ם
מִמָּ֖וֶת אֶגְאָלֵ֑ם
אֱהִ֨י דְבָרֶ֜יךָ מָ֗וֶת
אֱהִ֤י קָֽטָבְךָ֙ שְׁא֔וֹל
נֹ֖חַם יִסָּתֵ֥ר מֵעֵינָֽי׃

15 Though he is fruitful among *his* brethren,
An east wind shall come;
The wind of the LORD shall come up from
the wilderness.
Then his spring shall become dry,
And his fountain shall be dried up.
He shall plunder the treasury of every
desirable prize.

15 כִּ֣י ה֔וּא בֵּ֥ן אַחִ֖ים יַפְרִ֑יא
יָב֣וֹא קָדִים֩ ר֨וּחַ יְהֹוָ֜ה
מִמִּדְבָּ֣ר עֹלֶ֗ה
וְיֵב֤וֹשׁ מְקוֹרוֹ֙ וְיֶחֱרַ֣ב מַעְיָנ֔וֹ
ה֣וּא יִשְׁסֶ֔ה אוֹצַ֖ר כָּל־כְּלִ֥י חֶמְדָּֽה׃

16 Samaria is held guilty,
For she has rebelled against her God.
They shall fall by the sword,
Their infants shall be dashed in pieces,
And their women with child ripped open.

יד תֶּאְשַׁם֙ שֹֽׁמְר֔וֹן
כִּ֥י מָרְתָ֖ה בֵּֽאלֹהֶ֑יהָ
בַּחֶ֣רֶב יִפֹּ֔לוּ
עֹלְלֵיהֶ֣ם יְרֻטָּ֔שׁוּ
וְהָרִיּוֹתָ֖יו יְבֻקָּֽעוּ׃ פ

14 O Israel, return to the LORD your God,
For you have stumbled because of your
iniquity;

2 שׁ֚וּבָה יִשְׂרָאֵ֔ל עַ֖ד יְהֹוָ֣ה אֱלֹהֶ֑יךָ
כִּ֥י כָשַׁ֖לְתָּ בַּעֲוֺנֶֽךָ׃

2 Take words with you,
And return to the LORD.
Say to Him,
"Take away all iniquity;
Receive *us* graciously,

3 קְח֤וּ עִמָּכֶם֙ דְּבָרִ֔ים
וְשׁ֖וּבוּ אֶל־יְהֹוָ֑ה
אִמְר֣וּ אֵלָ֗יו כָּל־תִּשָּׂ֤א עָוֺן֙

For we will offer the sacrifices of our lips.

3 Assyria shall not save us,
We will not ride on horses,
Nor will we say anymore to the work of our
    hands, '*You are* our gods.'
For in You the fatherless finds mercy."

4 "I will heal their backsliding,
I will love them freely,
For My anger has turned away from him.

5 I will be like the dew to Israel;
He shall grow like the lily,
And lengthen his roots like Lebanon.

6 His branches shall spread;
His beauty shall be like an olive tree,
And his fragrance like Lebanon.

7 Those who dwell under his shadow shall
    return;
They shall be revived *like* grain,
And grow like a vine.
Their scent *shall be* like the wine of Lebanon.

8 "Ephraim *shall say,* 'What have I to do
    anymore with idols?'
I have heard and observed him.
I *am* like a green cypress tree;
Your fruit is found in Me."

9 Who *is* wise?
Let him understand these things.
Who is prudent?
Let him know them.
For the ways of the LORD *are* right;
The righteous walk in them,
But transgressors stumble in them.

וְקַח־טֹוב

וּנְשַׁלְּמָה פָרִים שְׂפָתֵינוּ׃

4 אַשּׁוּר ׀ לֹא יֹושִׁיעֵנוּ עַל־סוּס לֹא נִרְכָּב
וְלֹא־נֹאמַר עֹוד
אֱלֹהֵינוּ לְמַעֲשֵׂה יָדֵינוּ
אֲשֶׁר־בְּךָ יְרֻחַם יָתֹום׃

5 אֶרְפָּא מְשׁוּבָתָם אֹהֲבֵם נְדָבָה
כִּי שָׁב אַפִּי מִמֶּנּוּ׃

6 אֶהְיֶה כַטַּל לְיִשְׂרָאֵל
יִפְרַח כַּשּׁוֹשַׁנָּה
וְיַךְ שָׁרָשָׁיו כַּלְּבָנֹון׃

7 יֵלְכוּ יֹנְקֹותָיו
וִיהִי כַזַּיִת הֹודֹו
וְרֵיחַ לֹו כַּלְּבָנֹון׃

8 יָשֻׁבוּ יֹשְׁבֵי בְצִלֹּו יְחַיּוּ דָגָן
וְיִפְרְחוּ כַגָּפֶן
זִכְרֹו כְּיֵין לְבָנֹון׃ ס

9 אֶפְרַיִם מַה־לִּי עֹוד לָעֲצַבִּים
אֲנִי עָנִיתִי וַאֲשׁוּרֶנּוּ
אֲנִי כִּבְרֹושׁ רַעֲנָן
מִמֶּנִּי פֶּרְיְךָ נִמְצָא׃

10 מִי חָכָם וְיָבֵן אֵלֶּה
נָבֹון וְיֵדָעֵם
כִּי־יְשָׁרִים דַּרְכֵי יְהוָה
וְצַדִּקִים יֵלְכוּ בָם
וּפֹשְׁעִים יִכָּשְׁלוּ בָם׃

The Book of

JOEL

יוֹאֵל

א דְּבַר־יְהוָֹה אֲשֶׁר הָיָה
אֶל־יוֹאֵל בֶּן־פְּתוּאֵל:

1 The word of the LORD that came to Joel the son
of Pethuel.

2 שִׁמְעוּ־זֹאת הַזְּקֵנִים
וְהַאֲזִינוּ כֹּל יוֹשְׁבֵי הָאָרֶץ
הֶהָיְתָה זֹּאת בִּימֵיכֶם
וְאִם בִּימֵי אֲבֹתֵיכֶם:

2 Hear this, you elders,
And give ear, all you inhabitants of the land!
Has *anything like* this happened in your days,
Or even in the days of your fathers?

3 עָלֶיהָ לִבְנֵיכֶם סַפֵּרוּ
וּבְנֵיכֶם לִבְנֵיהֶם
וּבְנֵיהֶם לְדוֹר אַחֵר:

3 Tell your children about it,
Let your children *tell* their children,
And their children another generation.

4 יֶתֶר הַגָּזָם אָכַל הָאַרְבֶּה
וְיֶתֶר הָאַרְבֶּה אָכַל הַיָּלֶק
וְיֶתֶר הַיֶּלֶק אָכַל הֶחָסִיל:

4 What the chewing locust left, the swarming
    locust has eaten;
What the swarming locust left, the crawling
    locust has eaten;
And what the crawling locust left, the
    consuming locust has eaten.

5 הָקִיצוּ שִׁכּוֹרִים וּבְכוּ
וְהֵילִלוּ כָּל־שֹׁתֵי יָיִן
עַל־עָסִיס כִּי נִכְרַת מִפִּיכֶם:

5 Awake, you drunkards, and weep;
And wail, all you drinkers of wine,
Because of the new wine,
For it has been cut off from your mouth.

6 כִּי־גוֹי עָלָה עַל־אַרְצִי
עָצוּם וְאֵין מִסְפָּר
שִׁנָּיו שִׁנֵּי אַרְיֵה
וּמְתַלְּעוֹת לָבִיא לוֹ:

6 For a nation has come up against My land,
Strong, and without number;
His teeth *are* the teeth of a lion,
And he has the fangs of a fierce lion.

7 שָׂם גַּפְנִי לְשַׁמָּה וּתְאֵנָתִי לִקְצָפָה
חָשֹׂף חֲשָׂפָהּ וְהִשְׁלִיךְ הִלְבִּינוּ שָׂרִיגֶיהָ:

7 He has laid waste My vine,
And ruined My fig tree;
He has stripped it bare and thrown *it* away;
Its branches are made white.

8 אֱלִי כִּבְתוּלָה חֲגֻרַת־שַׂק
עַל־בַּעַל נְעוּרֶיהָ:

8 Lament like a virgin girded with sackcloth
For the husband of her youth.

9 הָכְרַת מִנְחָה וָנֶסֶךְ מִבֵּית יְהוָֹה
אָבְלוּ הַכֹּהֲנִים מְשָׁרְתֵי יְהוָה:

9 The grain offering and the drink offering
Have been cut off from the house of the
    LORD;
The priests mourn, who minister to the
    LORD.

10 שֻׁדַּד שָׂדֶה אָבְלָה אֲדָמָה
כִּי שֻׁדַּד דָּגָן
הוֹבִישׁ תִּירוֹשׁ אֻמְלַל יִצְהָר:

10 The field is wasted,
The land mourns;
For the grain is ruined,
The new wine is dried up,
The oil fails.

11 הֹבִישׁוּ אִכָּרִים
הֵילִילוּ כֹּרְמִים
עַל־חִטָּה וְעַל־שְׂעֹרָה
כִּי אָבַד קְצִיר שָׂדֶה:

11 Be ashamed, you farmers,
Wail, you vinedressers,
For the wheat and the barley;
Because the harvest of the field has perished.

12 הַגֶּפֶן הוֹבִישָׁה
וְהַתְּאֵנָה אֻמְלָלָה

12 The vine has dried up,
And the fig tree has withered;

The pomegranate tree,
The palm tree also,
And the apple tree—
All the trees of the field are withered;
Surely joy has withered away from the sons
    of men.

רִמּוֹן גַּם־תָּמָר וְתַפּוּחַ
כָּל־עֲצֵי הַשָּׂדֶה יָבֵשׁוּ
כִּי־הֹבִישׁ שָׂשׂוֹן מִן־בְּנֵי אָדָם: ס

13 Gird yourselves and lament, you priests;
Wail, you who minister before the altar;
Come, lie all night in sackcloth,
You who minister to my God;
For the grain offering and the drink offering
Are withheld from the house of your God.

13 חִגְרוּ וְסִפְדוּ הַכֹּהֲנִים
הֵילִילוּ מְשָׁרְתֵי מִזְבֵּחַ
בֹּאוּ לִינוּ בַשַּׂקִּים
מְשָׁרְתֵי אֱלֹהָי
כִּי נִמְנַע מִבֵּית אֱלֹהֵיכֶם
מִנְחָה וָנָסֶךְ:

14 Consecrate a fast,
Call a sacred assembly;
Gather the elders
And all the inhabitants of the land
Into the house of the LORD your God,
And cry out to the LORD.

14 קַדְּשׁוּ־צוֹם קִרְאוּ עֲצָרָה
אִסְפוּ זְקֵנִים כֹּל יֹשְׁבֵי הָאָרֶץ
בֵּית יְהוָה אֱלֹהֵיכֶם
וְזַעֲקוּ אֶל־יְהוָה:

15 Alas for the day!
For the day of the LORD *is* at hand;
It shall come as destruction from the
    Almighty.

15 אֲהָהּ לַיּוֹם כִּי קָרוֹב יוֹם יְהוָה
וּכְשֹׁד מִשַּׁדַּי יָבוֹא:

16 Is not the food cut off before our eyes,
Joy and gladness from the house of our God?

16 הֲלוֹא נֶגֶד עֵינֵינוּ אֹכֶל נִכְרָת
מִבֵּית אֱלֹהֵינוּ שִׂמְחָה וָגִיל:

17 The seed shrivels under the clods,
Storehouses are in shambles;
Barns are broken down,
For the grain has withered.

17 עָבְשׁוּ פְרֻדוֹת תַּחַת מֶגְרְפֹתֵיהֶם
נָשַׁמּוּ אֹצָרוֹת נֶהֶרְסוּ מַמְּגֻרוֹת
כִּי הֹבִישׁ דָּגָן:

18 How the animals groan!
The herds of cattle are restless,
Because they have no pasture;
Even the flocks of sheep suffer punishment.

18 מַה־נֶּאֶנְחָה בְהֵמָה נָבֹכוּ עֶדְרֵי בָקָר
כִּי אֵין מִרְעֶה לָהֶם
גַּם־עֶדְרֵי הַצֹּאן נֶאְשָׁמוּ:

19 O LORD, to You I cry out;
For fire has devoured the open pastures,
And a flame has burned all the trees of the
    field.

19 אֵלֶיךָ יְהוָה אֶקְרָא
כִּי אֵשׁ אָכְלָה נְאוֹת מִדְבָּר
וְלֶהָבָה לִהֲטָה כָּל־עֲצֵי הַשָּׂדֶה:

20 The beasts of the field also cry out to You,
For the water brooks are dried up,
And fire has devoured the open pastures.

20 גַּם־בַּהֲמוֹת שָׂדֶה תַּעֲרוֹג אֵלֶיךָ
כִּי יָבְשׁוּ אֲפִיקֵי מָיִם
וְאֵשׁ אָכְלָה נְאוֹת הַמִּדְבָּר: פ

2

Blow the trumpet in Zion,
And sound an alarm in My holy mountain!
Let all the inhabitants of the land tremble;
For the day of the LORD is coming,
For it is at hand:

ב תִּקְעוּ שׁוֹפָר בְּצִיּוֹן
וְהָרִיעוּ בְּהַר קָדְשִׁי
יִרְגְּזוּ כֹּל יֹשְׁבֵי הָאָרֶץ
כִּי־בָא יוֹם־יְהוָה כִּי קָרוֹב:

2 A day of darkness and gloominess,
A day of clouds and thick darkness,
Like the morning *clouds* spread over the
    mountains.
A people *come,* great and strong,
The like of whom has never been;
Nor will there ever be any *such* after them,

2 יוֹם חֹשֶׁךְ וַאֲפֵלָה
יוֹם עָנָן וַעֲרָפֶל
כְּשַׁחַר פָּרֻשׂ עַל־הֶהָרִים
עַם רַב וְעָצוּם

Even for many successive generations.

3 A fire devours before them,
And behind them a flame burns;
The land *is* like the Garden of Eden before them,
And behind them a desolate wilderness;
Surely nothing shall escape them.

4 Their appearance is like the appearance of horses;
And like swift steeds, so they run.

5 With a noise like chariots
Over mountaintops they leap,
Like the noise of a flaming fire that devours the stubble,
Like a strong people set in battle array.

6 Before them the people writhe in pain;
All faces are drained of color.

7 They run like mighty men,
They climb the wall like men of war;
Every one marches in formation,
And they do not break ranks.

8 They do not push one another;
Every one marches in his own column.
Though they lunge between the weapons,
They are not cut down.

9 They run to and fro in the city,
They run on the wall;
They climb into the houses,
They enter at the windows like a thief.

10 The earth quakes before them,
The heavens tremble;
The sun and moon grow dark,
And the stars diminish their brightness.

11 The LORD gives voice before His army,
For His camp is very great;
For strong *is the One* who executes His word.
For the day of the LORD *is* great and very terrible;
Who can endure it?

12 "Now, therefore," says the LORD,
"Turn to Me with all your heart,
With fasting, with weeping, and with mourning."

13 So rend your heart, and not your garments;
Return to the LORD your God,
For He *is* gracious and merciful,
Slow to anger, and of great kindness;
And He relents from doing harm.

14 Who knows *if* He will turn and relent,
And leave a blessing behind Him—
A grain offering and a drink offering
For the LORD your God?

כְּמֹהוּ לֹא נִהְיָה מִן־הָעוֹלָם
וְאַחֲרָיו לֹא יוֹסֵף עַד־שְׁנֵי דּוֹר וָדוֹר:
3 לְפָנָיו אָכְלָה אֵשׁ וְאַחֲרָיו תְּלַהֵט לֶהָבָה
כְּגַן־עֵדֶן הָאָרֶץ לְפָנָיו וְאַחֲרָיו מִדְבַּר שְׁמָמָה
וְגַם־פְּלֵיטָה לֹא־הָיְתָה לּוֹ:
4 כְּמַרְאֵה סוּסִים מַרְאֵהוּ
וּכְפָרָשִׁים כֵּן יְרוּצוּן:
5 כְּקוֹל מַרְכָּבוֹת עַל־רָאשֵׁי הֶהָרִים יְרַקֵּדוּן
כְּקוֹל לַהַב אֵשׁ אֹכְלָה קָשׁ
כְּעַם עָצוּם עֱרוּךְ מִלְחָמָה:
6 מִפָּנָיו יָחִילוּ עַמִּים
כָּל־פָּנִים קִבְּצוּ פָארוּר:
7 כְּגִבּוֹרִים יְרֻצוּן
כְּאַנְשֵׁי מִלְחָמָה יַעֲלוּ חוֹמָה
וְאִישׁ בִּדְרָכָיו יֵלֵכוּן
וְלֹא יְעַבְּטוּן אֹרְחוֹתָם:
8 וְאִישׁ אָחִיו לֹא יִדְחָקוּן
גֶּבֶר בִּמְסִלָּתוֹ יֵלֵכוּן
וּבְעַד הַשֶּׁלַח יִפֹּלוּ לֹא יִבְצָעוּ:
9 בָּעִיר יָשֹׁקּוּ בַּחוֹמָה יְרֻצוּן
בַּבָּתִּים יַעֲלוּ
בְּעַד הַחַלּוֹנִים יָבֹאוּ כַּגַּנָּב:
10 לְפָנָיו רָגְזָה אֶרֶץ רָעֲשׁוּ שָׁמָיִם
שֶׁמֶשׁ וְיָרֵחַ קָדָרוּ
וְכוֹכָבִים אָסְפוּ נָגְהָם:
11 וַיהֹוָה נָתַן קוֹלוֹ לִפְנֵי חֵילוֹ
כִּי רַב מְאֹד מַחֲנֵהוּ
כִּי עָצוּם עֹשֵׂה דְבָרוֹ
כִּי־גָדוֹל יוֹם־יְהֹוָה
וְנוֹרָא מְאֹד וּמִי יְכִילֶנּוּ:
12 וְגַם־עַתָּה נְאֻם־יְהֹוָה
שֻׁבוּ עָדַי בְּכָל־לְבַבְכֶם
וּבְצוֹם וּבִבְכִי וּבְמִסְפֵּד:
13 וְקִרְעוּ לְבַבְכֶם וְאַל־בִּגְדֵיכֶם
וְשׁוּבוּ אֶל־יְהֹוָה אֱלֹהֵיכֶם
כִּי־חַנּוּן וְרַחוּם הוּא
אֶרֶךְ אַפַּיִם וְרַב־חֶסֶד
וְנִחָם עַל־הָרָעָה:
14 מִי יוֹדֵעַ יָשׁוּב וְנִחָם
וְהִשְׁאִיר אַחֲרָיו בְּרָכָה
מִנְחָה וָנֶסֶךְ לַיהֹוָה אֱלֹהֵיכֶם:

פ

¹⁵ Blow the trumpet in Zion,
　　Consecrate a fast,
　　Call a sacred assembly;
¹⁶ Gather the people,
　　Sanctify the congregation,
　　Assemble the elders,
　　Gather the children and nursing babes;
　　Let the bridegroom go out from his chamber,
　　And the bride from her dressing room.
¹⁷ Let the priests, who minister to the LORD,
　　Weep between the porch and the altar;
　　Let them say, "Spare Your people, O LORD,
　　And do not give Your heritage to reproach,
　　That the nations should rule over them.
　　Why should they say among the peoples,
　　'Where *is* their God?'"

¹⁸ Then the LORD will be zealous for His land,
　　And pity His people.
¹⁹ The LORD will answer and say to His people,
　　"Behold, I will send you grain and new wine
　　　　and oil,
　　And you will be satisfied by them;
　　I will no longer make you a reproach among
　　　　the nations.

²⁰ "But I will remove far from you the northern
　　　　army,
　　And will drive him away into a barren and
　　　　desolate land,
　　With his face toward the eastern sea
　　And his back toward the western sea;
　　His stench will come up,
　　And his foul odor will rise,
　　Because he has done monstrous things."

²¹ Fear not, O land;
　　Be glad and rejoice,
　　For the LORD has done marvelous things!
²² Do not be afraid, you beasts of the field;
　　For the open pastures are springing up,
　　And the tree bears its fruit;
　　The fig tree and the vine yield their strength.
²³ Be glad then, you children of Zion,
　　And rejoice in the LORD your God;
　　For He has given you the former rain
　　　　faithfully,
　　And He will cause the rain to come down for
　　　　you—
　　The former rain,
　　And the latter rain in the first *month*.
²⁴ The threshing floors shall be full of wheat,
　　And the vats shall overflow with new wine
　　　　and oil.

תִּקְע֤וּ שׁוֹפָר֙ בְּצִיּ֔וֹן 15
קַדְּשׁוּ־צ֖וֹם קִרְא֥וּ עֲצָרָֽה׃
אִסְפוּ־עָ֞ם 16
קַדְּשׁ֣וּ קָהָ֗ל
קִבְצ֣וּ זְקֵנִ֔ים
אִסְפוּ֙ עֽוֹלָלִ֔ים
וְיֹנְקֵ֖י שָׁדָ֑יִם
יֵצֵ֤א חָתָן֙ מֵֽחֶדְר֔וֹ
וְכַלָּ֖ה מֵחֻפָּתָֽהּ׃
בֵּ֤ין הָאוּלָם֙ וְלַמִּזְבֵּ֔חַ 17
יִבְכּוּ֙ הַכֹּ֣הֲנִ֔ים מְשָׁרְתֵ֖י יְהוָ֑ה
וְֽיֹאמְר֡וּ ח֣וּסָה יְהוָ֣ה עַל־עַמֶּ֗ךָ
וְאַל־תִּתֵּ֨ן נַחֲלָתְךָ֤ לְחֶרְפָּה֙
לִמְשָׁל־בָּ֣ם גּוֹיִ֔ם
לָ֚מָּה יֹאמְר֣וּ בָֽעַמִּ֔ים
אַיֵּ֖ה אֱלֹהֵיהֶֽם׃

וַיְקַנֵּ֥א יְהוָ֖ה לְאַרְצ֑וֹ 18
וַיַּחְמֹ֖ל עַל־עַמּֽוֹ׃
וַיַּ֨עַן יְהוָ֜ה וַיֹּ֣אמֶר לְעַמּ֗וֹ 19
הִנְנִ֨י שֹׁלֵ֤חַ לָכֶם֙ אֶת־הַדָּגָ֔ן
וְהַתִּיר֖וֹשׁ וְהַיִּצְהָ֑ר
וּשְׂבַעְתֶּ֖ם אֹת֑וֹ
וְלֹא־אֶתֵּ֨ן אֶתְכֶ֥ם ע֛וֹד חֶרְפָּ֖ה בַּגּוֹיִֽם׃

וְֽאֶת־הַצְּפוֹנִ֞י אַרְחִ֣יק מֵעֲלֵיכֶ֗ם 20
וְהִדַּחְתִּיו֮ אֶל־אֶ֣רֶץ צִיָּ֣ה וּשְׁמָמָה֒
אֶת־פָּנָ֗יו אֶל־הַיָּם֙ הַקַּדְמֹנִ֔י
וְסֹפ֖וֹ אֶל־הַיָּ֣ם הָאַֽחֲר֑וֹן
וְעָלָ֣ה בָאְשׁ֗וֹ וְתַ֙עַל֙ צַחֲנָת֔וֹ
כִּ֥י הִגְדִּ֖יל לַעֲשֽׂוֹת׃

אַל־תִּֽירְאִ֖י אֲדָמָ֑ה גִּ֥ילִי וּשְׂמָ֔חִי 21
כִּֽי־הִגְדִּ֥יל יְהוָ֖ה לַעֲשֽׂוֹת׃
אַל־תִּֽירְאוּ֙ בַּהֲמ֣וֹת שָׂדַ֔י 22
כִּ֥י דָשְׁא֖וּ נְא֣וֹת מִדְבָּ֑ר
כִּֽי־עֵץ֙ נָשָׂ֣א פִרְי֔וֹ
תְּאֵנָ֥ה וָגֶ֖פֶן נָתְנ֥וּ חֵילָֽם׃
וּבְנֵ֣י צִיּ֗וֹן גִּ֤ילוּ וְשִׂמְחוּ֙ 23
בַּיהוָ֣ה אֱלֹֽהֵיכֶ֔ם
כִּֽי־נָתַ֥ן לָכֶ֛ם אֶת־הַמּוֹרֶ֖ה לִצְדָקָ֑ה
וַיּ֣וֹרֶד לָכֶ֗ם גֶּ֛שֶׁם
מוֹרֶ֥ה וּמַלְק֖וֹשׁ בָּרִאשֽׁוֹן׃
וּמָלְא֥וּ הַגֳּרָנ֖וֹת בָּ֑ר 24
וְהֵשִׁ֥יקוּ הַיְקָבִ֖ים תִּיר֥וֹשׁ וְיִצְהָֽר׃

²⁵ "So I will restore to you the years that the
    swarming locust has eaten,
The crawling locust,
The consuming locust,
And the chewing locust,
My great army which I sent among you.

²⁶ You shall eat in plenty and be satisfied,
And praise the name of the LORD your God,
Who has dealt wondrously with you;
And My people shall never be put to shame.

²⁷ Then you shall know that I *am* in the midst
    of Israel:
I *am* the LORD your God
And there is no other.
My people shall never be put to shame.

²⁸ "And it shall come to pass afterward
That I will pour out My Spirit on all flesh;
Your sons and your daughters shall pro-
    phesy,
Your old men shall dream dreams,
Your young men shall see visions.

²⁹ And also on *My* menservants and on *My*
    maidservants
I will pour out My Spirit in those days.

³⁰ "And I will show wonders in the heavens and
    in the earth:
Blood and fire and pillars of smoke.

³¹ The sun shall be turned into darkness,
And the moon into blood,
Before the coming of the great and awesome
    day of the LORD.

³² And it shall come to pass
That whoever calls on the name of the LORD
Shall be saved.
For in Mount Zion and in Jerusalem there
    shall be deliverance,
As the LORD has said,
Among the remnant whom the LORD calls.

3 "For behold, in those days and at that time,
When I bring back the captives of Judah and
    Jerusalem,

² I will also gather all nations,
And bring them down to the Valley of
    Jehoshaphat;
And I will enter into judgment with them
    there
On account of My people, My heritage
    Israel,
Whom they have scattered among the
    nations;
They have also divided up My land.

³ They have cast lots for My people,

וְשִׁלַּמְתִּי לָכֶם אֶת־הַשָּׁנִים 25
אֲשֶׁר אָכַל הָאַרְבֶּה
הַיֶּלֶק וְהֶחָסִיל וְהַגָּזָם
חֵילִי הַגָּדוֹל אֲשֶׁר שִׁלַּחְתִּי בָּכֶם:
וַאֲכַלְתֶּם אָכוֹל וְשָׂבוֹעַ 26
וְהִלַּלְתֶּם אֶת־שֵׁם יְהֹוָה אֱלֹהֵיכֶם
אֲשֶׁר־עָשָׂה עִמָּכֶם לְהַפְלִיא
וְלֹא־יֵבֹשׁוּ עַמִּי לְעוֹלָם:
וִידַעְתֶּם כִּי בְקֶרֶב יִשְׂרָאֵל אָנִי 27
וַאֲנִי יְהֹוָה אֱלֹהֵיכֶם וְאֵין עוֹד
וְלֹא־יֵבֹשׁוּ עַמִּי לְעוֹלָם: ס

וְהָיָה אַחֲרֵי־כֵן **ג**
אֶשְׁפּוֹךְ אֶת־רוּחִי עַל־כָּל־בָּשָׂר
וְנִבְּאוּ בְּנֵיכֶם וּבְנוֹתֵיכֶם
זִקְנֵיכֶם חֲלֹמוֹת יַחֲלֹמוּן
בַּחוּרֵיכֶם חֶזְיֹנוֹת יִרְאוּ:
וְגַם עַל־הָעֲבָדִים וְעַל־הַשְּׁפָחוֹת 2
בַּיָּמִים הָהֵמָּה אֶשְׁפּוֹךְ אֶת־רוּחִי:
וְנָתַתִּי מוֹפְתִים בַּשָּׁמַיִם וּבָאָרֶץ 3
דָּם וָאֵשׁ וְתִימֲרוֹת עָשָׁן:
הַשֶּׁמֶשׁ יֵהָפֵךְ לְחֹשֶׁךְ 4
וְהַיָּרֵחַ לְדָם
לִפְנֵי בּוֹא יוֹם יְהֹוָה הַגָּדוֹל וְהַנּוֹרָא:
וְהָיָה כֹּל אֲשֶׁר־יִקְרָא 5
בְּשֵׁם יְהֹוָה יִמָּלֵט
כִּי בְּהַר־צִיּוֹן וּבִירוּשָׁלִַם
תִּהְיֶה פְלֵיטָה
כַּאֲשֶׁר אָמַר יְהֹוָה
וּבַשְּׂרִידִים אֲשֶׁר יְהֹוָה קֹרֵא:

כִּי הִנֵּה בַּיָּמִים הָהֵמָּה וּבָעֵת הַהִיא **ד**
אֲשֶׁר אָשׁוּב אֶת־שְׁבוּת יְהוּדָה וִירוּשָׁלִָם:
וְקִבַּצְתִּי אֶת־כָּל־הַגּוֹיִם 2
וְהוֹרַדְתִּים אֶל־עֵמֶק יְהוֹשָׁפָט
וְנִשְׁפַּטְתִּי עִמָּם שָׁם
עַל־עַמִּי וְנַחֲלָתִי יִשְׂרָאֵל
אֲשֶׁר פִּזְּרוּ בַגּוֹיִם
וְאֶת־אַרְצִי חִלֵּקוּ:
וְאֶל־עַמִּי יַדּוּ גוֹרָל 3

Have given a boy *as payment* for a harlot,
And sold a girl for wine, that they may drink.

4 "Indeed, what have you to do with Me,
  O Tyre and Sidon, and all the coasts of Philistia?
  Will you retaliate against Me?
  But if you retaliate against Me,
  Swiftly and speedily I will return your retaliation
    upon your own head;
5 Because you have taken My silver and My gold,
  And have carried into your temples My prized
    possessions.
6 Also the people of Judah and the people of
    Jerusalem
  You have sold to the Greeks,
  That you may remove them far from their
    borders.

7 "Behold, I will raise them
  Out of the place to which you have sold them,
  And will return your retaliation upon your own
    head.
8 I will sell your sons and your daughters
  Into the hand of the people of Judah,
  And they will sell them to the Sabeans,
  To a people far off;
  For the LORD has spoken."

9 Proclaim this among the nations:
  "Prepare for war!
  Wake up the mighty men,
  Let all the men of war draw near,
  Let them come up.
10 Beat your plowshares into swords
   And your pruning hooks into spears;
   Let the weak say, 'I *am* strong.' "

11 Assemble and come, all you nations,
   And gather together all around.
   Cause Your mighty ones to go down there, O
     LORD.

12 "Let the nations be wakened, and come up to
     the Valley of Jehoshaphat;
   For there I will sit to judge all the
     surrounding nations.
13 Put in the sickle, for the harvest is ripe.
   Come, go down;
   For the winepress is full,
   The vats overflow—
   For their wickedness *is* great."

14 Multitudes, multitudes in the valley of
     decision!
   For the day of the LORD *is* near in the valley
     of decision.
15 The sun and moon will grow dark,
   And the stars will diminish their brightness.
16 The LORD also will roar from Zion,
   And utter His voice from Jerusalem;
   The heavens and earth will shake;

וַיִּתְּנוּ הַיֶּלֶד בַּזּוֹנָה
וְהַיַּלְדָּה מָכְרוּ בַיַּיִן וַיִּשְׁתּוּ:

4 וְגַם מָה־אַתֶּם לִי צֹר וְצִידוֹן וְכֹל גְּלִילוֹת פְּלָשֶׁת
הַגְּמוּל אַתֶּם מְשַׁלְּמִים עָלָי וְאִם־גֹּמְלִים אַתֶּם
עָלַי קַל מְהֵרָה אָשִׁיב גְּמֻלְכֶם בְּרֹאשְׁכֶם: 5 אֲשֶׁר־
כַּסְפִּי וּזְהָבִי לְקַחְתֶּם וּמַחֲמַדַּי הַטֹּבִים הֲבֵאתֶם
לְהֵיכְלֵיכֶם: 6 וּבְנֵי יְהוּדָה וּבְנֵי יְרוּשָׁלַ͏ִם מְכַרְתֶּם
לִבְנֵי הַיְּוָנִים לְמַעַן הַרְחִיקָם מֵעַל גְּבוּלָם: 7 הִנְנִי
מְעִירָם מִן־הַמָּקוֹם אֲשֶׁר־מְכַרְתֶּם אֹתָם שָׁמָּה
וַהֲשִׁבֹתִי גְמֻלְכֶם בְּרֹאשְׁכֶם: 8 וּמָכַרְתִּי אֶת־בְּנֵיכֶם
וְאֶת־בְּנוֹתֵיכֶם בְּיַד בְּנֵי יְהוּדָה וּמְכָרוּם לִשְׁבָאיִם
אֶל־גּוֹי רָחוֹק כִּי יְהוָה דִּבֵּר: ס

9 קִרְאוּ־זֹאת בַּגּוֹיִם
קַדְּשׁוּ מִלְחָמָה
הָעִירוּ הַגִּבּוֹרִים
יִגְּשׁוּ יַעֲלוּ
כֹּל אַנְשֵׁי הַמִּלְחָמָה:

10 כֹּתּוּ אִתֵּיכֶם לַחֲרָבוֹת
וּמַזְמְרֹתֵיכֶם לִרְמָחִים
הַחַלָּשׁ יֹאמַר גִּבּוֹר אָנִי:

11 עוּשׁוּ וָבֹאוּ כָל־הַגּוֹיִם
מִסָּבִיב וְנִקְבָּצוּ
שָׁמָּה הַנְחַת יְהוָה גִּבּוֹרֶיךָ:

12 יֵעוֹרוּ וְיַעֲלוּ הַגּוֹיִם
אֶל־עֵמֶק יְהוֹשָׁפָט
כִּי שָׁם אֵשֵׁב
לִשְׁפֹּט אֶת־כָּל־הַגּוֹיִם מִסָּבִיב:

13 שִׁלְחוּ מַגָּל
כִּי בָשַׁל קָצִיר
בֹּאוּ רְדוּ כִּי־מָלְאָה גַּת
הֵשִׁיקוּ הַיְקָבִים
כִּי רַבָּה רָעָתָם:

14 הֲמוֹנִים הֲמוֹנִים בְּעֵמֶק הֶחָרוּץ
כִּי קָרוֹב יוֹם יְהוָה בְּעֵמֶק הֶחָרוּץ:

15 שֶׁמֶשׁ וְיָרֵחַ קָדָרוּ
וְכוֹכָבִים אָסְפוּ נָגְהָם:

16 וַיהוָה מִצִּיּוֹן יִשְׁאָג
וּמִירוּשָׁלַ͏ִם יִתֵּן קוֹלוֹ
וְרָעֲשׁוּ שָׁמַיִם וָאָרֶץ

But the LORD will be a shelter for His people,
And the strength of the children of Israel.

וַיהוָֹה מַחֲסֶה לְעַמּוֹ
וּמָעוֹז לִבְנֵי יִשְׂרָאֵל׃

17 "So you shall know that I *am* the LORD your God,
Dwelling in Zion My holy mountain.
Then Jerusalem shall be holy,
And no aliens shall ever pass through her again."

17 וִידַעְתֶּם כִּי אֲנִי יְהוָה אֱלֹהֵיכֶם
שֹׁכֵן בְּצִיּוֹן הַר־קָדְשִׁי
וְהָיְתָה יְרוּשָׁלַם קֹדֶשׁ
וְזָרִים לֹא־יַעַבְרוּ־בָהּ עוֹד׃ ס

18 And it will come to pass in that day
That the mountains shall drip with new wine,
The hills shall flow with milk,
And all the brooks of Judah shall be flooded with water;
A fountain shall flow from the house of the LORD
And water the Valley of Acacias.

18 וְהָיָה בַיּוֹם הַהוּא
יִטְּפוּ הֶהָרִים עָסִיס
וְהַגְּבָעוֹת תֵּלַכְנָה חָלָב
וְכָל־אֲפִיקֵי יְהוּדָה יֵלְכוּ מָיִם
וּמַעְיָן מִבֵּית יְהוָה יֵצֵא
וְהִשְׁקָה אֶת־נַחַל הַשִּׁטִּים׃

19 "Egypt shall be a desolation,
And Edom a desolate wilderness,
Because of violence *against* the people of Judah,
For they have shed innocent blood in their land.

19 מִצְרַיִם לִשְׁמָמָה תִהְיֶה
וֶאֱדוֹם לְמִדְבַּר שְׁמָמָה תִהְיֶה
מֵחֲמַס בְּנֵי יְהוּדָה
אֲשֶׁר־שָׁפְכוּ דָם־נָקִיא בְּאַרְצָם׃

20 But Judah shall abide forever,
And Jerusalem from generation to generation.

20 וִיהוּדָה לְעוֹלָם תֵּשֵׁב
וִירוּשָׁלַם לְדוֹר וָדוֹר׃

21 For I will acquit them of the guilt of bloodshed, whom I had not acquitted;
For the LORD dwells in Zion."

21 וְנִקֵּיתִי דָּמָם לֹא־נִקֵּיתִי
וַיהוָה שֹׁכֵן בְּצִיּוֹן׃

The Book of

AMOS

עמום

1 The words of Amos, who was among the
sheepbreeders of Tekoa, which he saw concerning
Israel in the days of Uzziah king of Judah, and in
the days of Jeroboam the son of Joash, king of
Israel, two years before the earthquake.

² And he said:

"The LORD roars from Zion,
And utters His voice from Jerusalem;
The pastures of the shepherds mourn,
And the top of Carmel withers."

³ Thus says the LORD:

"For three transgressions of Damascus, and
for four,
I will not turn away its *punishment,*
Because they have threshed Gilead with
implements of iron.
⁴ But I will send a fire into the house of
Hazael,
Which shall devour the palaces of Ben-
Hadad.
⁵ I will also break the *gate* bar of Damascus,
And cut off the inhabitant from the Valley of
Aven,
And the one who holds the scepter from Beth
Eden.
The people of Syria shall go captive to Kir,"
Says the LORD.

⁶ Thus says the LORD:

"For three transgressions of Gaza, and for
four,
I will not turn away its *punishment,*
Because they took captive the whole
captivity
To deliver *them* up to Edom.
⁷ But I will send a fire upon the wall of Gaza,
Which shall devour its palaces.
⁸ I will cut off the inhabitant from Ashdod,
And the one who holds the scepter from
Ashkelon;
I will turn My hand against Ekron,
And the remnant of the Philistines shall
perish,"
Says the Lord GOD.

⁹ Thus says the LORD:

א דִּבְרֵי עָמוֹס אֲשֶׁר־הָיָה בַנֹּקְדִים מִתְּקוֹעַ אֲשֶׁר
חָזָה עַל־יִשְׂרָאֵל בִּימֵי ׀ עֻזִּיָּה מֶלֶךְ־יְהוּדָה וּבִימֵי
יָרָבְעָם בֶּן־יוֹאָשׁ מֶלֶךְ יִשְׂרָאֵל שְׁנָתַיִם לִפְנֵי הָרָעַשׁ:

2 וַיֹּאמַר ׀ יְהֹוָה מִצִּיּוֹן יִשְׁאָג
וּמִירוּשָׁלַ͏ִם יִתֵּן קוֹלוֹ
וְאָבְלוּ נְאוֹת הָרֹעִים
וְיָבֵשׁ רֹאשׁ הַכַּרְמֶל: פ

3 כֹּה אָמַר יְהֹוָה
עַל־שְׁלֹשָׁה פִּשְׁעֵי דַמֶּשֶׂק
וְעַל־אַרְבָּעָה לֹא אֲשִׁיבֶנּוּ
עַל־דּוּשָׁם בַּחֲרֻצוֹת הַבַּרְזֶל
אֶת־הַגִּלְעָד:

4 וְשִׁלַּחְתִּי אֵשׁ בְּבֵית חֲזָאֵל
וְאָכְלָה אַרְמְנוֹת בֶּן־הֲדָד:

5 וְשָׁבַרְתִּי בְּרִיחַ דַּמֶּשֶׂק
וְהִכְרַתִּי יוֹשֵׁב מִבִּקְעַת־אָוֶן
וְתוֹמֵךְ שֵׁבֶט מִבֵּית עֶדֶן
וְגָלוּ עַם־אֲרָם קִירָה
אָמַר יְהֹוָה: פ

6 כֹּה אָמַר יְהֹוָה
עַל־שְׁלֹשָׁה פִּשְׁעֵי עַזָּה
וְעַל־אַרְבָּעָה לֹא אֲשִׁיבֶנּוּ
עַל־הַגְלוֹתָם גָּלוּת שְׁלֵמָה
לְהַסְגִּיר לֶאֱדוֹם:

7 וְשִׁלַּחְתִּי אֵשׁ בְּחוֹמַת עַזָּה
וְאָכְלָה אַרְמְנֹתֶיהָ:

8 וְהִכְרַתִּי יוֹשֵׁב מֵאַשְׁדּוֹד
וְתוֹמֵךְ שֵׁבֶט מֵאַשְׁקְלוֹן
וַהֲשִׁיבוֹתִי יָדִי עַל־עֶקְרוֹן
וְאָבְדוּ שְׁאֵרִית פְּלִשְׁתִּים
אָמַר אֲדֹנָי יְהֹוִה: פ

9 כֹּה אָמַר יְהֹוָה

"For three transgressions of Tyre, and for
four,
I will not turn away its *punishment,*
Because they delivered up the whole captivity
to Edom,
And did not remember the covenant of
brotherhood.

10 But I will send a fire upon the wall of Tyre,
Which shall devour its palaces."

11 Thus says the LORD:

"For three transgressions of Edom, and for
four,
I will not turn away its *punishment,*
Because he pursued his brother with the
sword,
And cast off all pity;
His anger tore perpetually,
And he kept his wrath forever.

12 But I will send a fire upon Teman,
Which shall devour the palaces of Bozrah."

13 Thus says the LORD:

"For three transgressions of the people of
Ammon, and for four,
I will not turn away its *punishment,*
Because they ripped open the women with
child in Gilead,
That they might enlarge their territory.

14 But I will kindle a fire in the wall of Rabbah,
And it shall devour its palaces,
Amid shouting in the day of battle,
And a tempest in the day of the whirlwind.

15 Their king shall go into captivity,
He and his princes together,"
Says the LORD.

2 Thus says the LORD:

"For three transgressions of Moab, and for
four,
I will not turn away its *punishment,*
Because he burned the bones of the king of
Edom to lime.

2 But I will send a fire upon Moab,
And it shall devour the palaces of Kerioth;
Moab shall die with tumult,
With shouting *and* trumpet sound.

3 And I will cut off the judge from its midst,
And slay all its princes with him,"
Says the LORD.

4 Thus says the LORD:

"For three transgressions of Judah, and for
four,

עַל־שְׁלֹשָׁה פִּשְׁעֵי־צֹר
וְעַל־אַרְבָּעָה לֹא אֲשִׁיבֶנּוּ
עַל־הַסְגִּירָם גָּלוּת שְׁלֵמָה לֶאֱדוֹם
וְלֹא זָכְרוּ בְּרִית אַחִים׃
10 וְשִׁלַּחְתִּי אֵשׁ בְּחוֹמַת צֹר
וְאָכְלָה אַרְמְנֹתֶיהָ׃ פ
11 כֹּה אָמַר יְהֹוָה
עַל־שְׁלֹשָׁה פִּשְׁעֵי אֱדוֹם
וְעַל־אַרְבָּעָה לֹא אֲשִׁיבֶנּוּ
עַל־רׇדְפוֹ בַחֶרֶב אָחִיו
וְשִׁחֵת רַחֲמָיו
וַיִּטְרֹף לָעַד אַפּוֹ
וְעֶבְרָתוֹ שְׁמָרָה נֶצַח׃
12 וְשִׁלַּחְתִּי אֵשׁ בְּתֵימָן
וְאָכְלָה אַרְמְנוֹת בׇּצְרָה׃ פ
13 כֹּה אָמַר יְהֹוָה
עַל־שְׁלֹשָׁה פִּשְׁעֵי בְנֵי־עַמּוֹן
וְעַל־אַרְבָּעָה לֹא אֲשִׁיבֶנּוּ
עַל־בִּקְעָם הָרוֹת הַגִּלְעָד
לְמַעַן הַרְחִיב אֶת־גְּבוּלָם׃
14 וְהִצַּתִּי אֵשׁ בְּחוֹמַת רַבָּה
וְאָכְלָה אַרְמְנוֹתֶיהָ
בִּתְרוּעָה בְּיוֹם מִלְחָמָה
בְּסַעַר בְּיוֹם סוּפָה׃
15 וְהָלַךְ מַלְכָּם בַּגּוֹלָה
הוּא וְשָׂרָיו יַחְדָּו אָמַר יְהֹוָה׃ פ

ב כֹּה אָמַר יְהֹוָה
עַל־שְׁלֹשָׁה פִּשְׁעֵי מוֹאָב
וְעַל־אַרְבָּעָה לֹא אֲשִׁיבֶנּוּ
עַל־שָׂרְפוֹ עַצְמוֹת מֶלֶךְ־אֱדוֹם לַשִּׂיד׃
2 וְשִׁלַּחְתִּי־אֵשׁ בְּמוֹאָב
וְאָכְלָה אַרְמְנוֹת הַקְּרִיּוֹת
וּמֵת בְּשָׁאוֹן מוֹאָב
בִּתְרוּעָה בְּקוֹל שׁוֹפָר׃
3 וְהִכְרַתִּי שׁוֹפֵט מִקִּרְבָּהּ
וְכׇל־שָׂרֶיהָ אֶהֱרוֹג עִמּוֹ אָמַר יְהֹוָה׃ פ
4 כֹּה אָמַר יְהֹוָה
עַל־שְׁלֹשָׁה פִּשְׁעֵי יְהוּדָה
וְעַל־אַרְבָּעָה לֹא אֲשִׁיבֶנּוּ

I will not turn away its *punishment,*
Because they have despised the law of the
LORD,
And have not kept His commandments.
Their lies lead them astray,
Lies which their fathers followed.
5 But I will send a fire upon Judah,
And it shall devour the palaces of
Jerusalem."

6 Thus says the LORD:

"For three transgressions of Israel, and for
four,
I will not turn away its *punishment,*
Because they sell the righteous for silver,
And the poor for a pair of sandals.
7 They pant after the dust of the earth *which is*
on the head of the poor,
And pervert the way of the humble.
A man and his father go in to the *same* girl,
To defile My holy name.
8 They lie down by every altar on clothes taken
in pledge,
And drink the wine of the condemned *in* the
house of their god.
9 "Yet *it was* I who destroyed the Amorite
before them,
Whose height *was* like the height of the
cedars,
And he *was as* strong as the oaks;
Yet I destroyed his fruit above
And his roots beneath.
10 Also *it was* I *who* brought you up from the
land of Egypt,
And led you forty years through the
wilderness,
To possess the land of the Amorite.
11 I raised up some of your sons as prophets,
And some of your young men as Nazirites.
Is it not so, O you children of Israel?"
Says the LORD.
12 "But you gave the Nazirites wine to drink,
And commanded the prophets saying,
'Do not prophesy!'
13 "Behold, I am weighed down by you,
As a cart full of sheaves is weighed down.
14 Therefore flight shall perish from the swift,
The strong shall not strengthen his power,
Nor shall the mighty deliver himself;
15 He shall not stand who handles the bow,
The swift of foot shall not escape,
Nor shall he who rides a horse deliver
himself."

עַל־מָאֳסָם אֶת־תּוֹרַת יְהֹוָה
וְחֻקָּיו לֹא שָׁמָרוּ וַיַּתְעוּם כִּזְבֵיהֶם
אֲשֶׁר־הָלְכוּ אֲבוֹתָם אַחֲרֵיהֶם:
5 וְשִׁלַּחְתִּי אֵשׁ בִּיהוּדָה
וְאָכְלָה אַרְמְנוֹת יְרוּשָׁלָ͏ִם: פ

6 כֹּה אָמַר יְהֹוָה
עַל־שְׁלֹשָׁה פִּשְׁעֵי יִשְׂרָאֵל
וְעַל־אַרְבָּעָה לֹא אֲשִׁיבֶנּוּ
עַל־מִכְרָם בַּכֶּסֶף צַדִּיק
וְאֶבְיוֹן בַּעֲבוּר נַעֲלָיִם:

7 הַשֹּׁאֲפִים עַל־עֲפַר־אֶרֶץ בְּרֹאשׁ דַּלִּים
וְדֶרֶךְ עֲנָוִים יַטּוּ
וְאִישׁ וְאָבִיו יֵלְכוּ אֶל־הַנַּעֲרָה
לְמַעַן חַלֵּל אֶת־שֵׁם קָדְשִׁי:

8 וְעַל־בְּגָדִים חֲבֻלִים יַטּוּ אֵצֶל כָּל־מִזְבֵּחַ
וְיֵין עֲנוּשִׁים יִשְׁתּוּ בֵּית אֱלֹהֵיהֶם:

9 וְאָנֹכִי הִשְׁמַדְתִּי
אֶת־הָאֱמֹרִי מִפְּנֵיהֶם
אֲשֶׁר כְּגֹבַהּ אֲרָזִים גָּבְהוֹ
וְחָסֹן הוּא כָּאַלּוֹנִים
וָאַשְׁמִיד פִּרְיוֹ מִמַּעַל
וְשָׁרָשָׁיו מִתָּחַת:

10 וְאָנֹכִי הֶעֱלֵיתִי אֶתְכֶם
מֵאֶרֶץ מִצְרָיִם
וָאוֹלֵךְ אֶתְכֶם בַּמִּדְבָּר
אַרְבָּעִים שָׁנָה
לָרֶשֶׁת אֶת־אֶרֶץ הָאֱמֹרִי:

11 וָאָקִים מִבְּנֵיכֶם לִנְבִיאִים
וּמִבַּחוּרֵיכֶם לִנְזִרִים
הַאַף אֵין־זֹאת בְּנֵי יִשְׂרָאֵל נְאֻם־יְהֹוָה:

12 וַתַּשְׁקוּ אֶת־הַנְּזִרִים יָיִן
וְעַל־הַנְּבִיאִים צִוִּיתֶם לֵאמֹר לֹא תִּנָּבְאוּ:

13 הִנֵּה אָנֹכִי מֵעִיק תַּחְתֵּיכֶם
כַּאֲשֶׁר תָּעִיק הָעֲגָלָה
הַמְלֵאָה לָהּ עָמִיר:

14 וְאָבַד מָנוֹס מִקָּל
וְחָזָק לֹא־יְאַמֵּץ כֹּחוֹ
וְגִבּוֹר לֹא־יְמַלֵּט נַפְשׁוֹ:

15 וְתֹפֵשׂ הַקֶּשֶׁת לֹא יַעֲמֹד
וְקַל בְּרַגְלָיו לֹא יְמַלֵּט
וְרֹכֵב הַסּוּס לֹא יְמַלֵּט נַפְשׁוֹ:

16 The most courageous men of might
Shall flee naked in that day,"
Says the LORD.

16 וְאַמִּיץ לִבּוֹ בַּגִּבּוֹרִים
עָרוֹם יָנוּס בַּיּוֹם־הַהוּא נְאֻם־יְהוָֹה: פ

3 Hear this word that the LORD has spoken against
you, O children of Israel, against the whole family
which I brought up from the land of Egypt, saying:

ג שִׁמְעוּ אֶת־הַדָּבָר הַזֶּה אֲשֶׁר דִּבֶּר יְהוָֹה עֲלֵיכֶם
בְּנֵי יִשְׂרָאֵל עַל כָּל־הַמִּשְׁפָּחָה אֲשֶׁר הֶעֱלֵיתִי מֵאֶרֶץ
מִצְרַיִם לֵאמֹר:

2 "You only have I known of all the families of
the earth;
Therefore I will punish you for all your
iniquities."

2 רַק אֶתְכֶם יָדַעְתִּי
מִכֹּל מִשְׁפְּחוֹת הָאֲדָמָה
עַל־כֵּן אֶפְקֹד עֲלֵיכֶם
אֵת כָּל־עֲוֺנֹתֵיכֶם:

3 Can two walk together, unless they are
agreed?

3 הֲיֵלְכוּ שְׁנַיִם יַחְדָּו
בִּלְתִּי אִם־נוֹעָדוּ:

4 Will a lion roar in the forest, when he has no
prey?
Will a young lion cry out of his den, if he has
caught nothing?

4 הֲיִשְׁאַג אַרְיֵה בַּיַּעַר וְטֶרֶף אֵין לוֹ
הֲיִתֵּן כְּפִיר קוֹלוֹ מִמְּעֹנָתוֹ
בִּלְתִּי אִם־לָכָד:

5 Will a bird fall into a snare on the earth,
where there is no trap for it?
Will a snare spring up from the earth, if it
has caught nothing at all?

5 הֲתִפֹּל צִפּוֹר עַל־פַּח הָאָרֶץ
וּמוֹקֵשׁ אֵין לָהּ
הֲיַעֲלֶה־פַּח מִן־הָאֲדָמָה
וְלָכוֹד לֹא יִלְכּוֹד:

6 If a trumpet is blown in a city, will not the
people be afraid?
If there is calamity in a city, will not the
LORD have done it?

6 אִם־יִתָּקַע שׁוֹפָר בְּעִיר
וְעָם לֹא יֶחֱרָדוּ
אִם־תִּהְיֶה רָעָה בְּעִיר
וַיהוָֹה לֹא עָשָׂה:

7 Surely the Lord GOD does nothing,
Unless He reveals His secret to His servants
the prophets.

7 כִּי לֹא יַעֲשֶׂה אֲדֹנָי יְהוִֹה דָּבָר
כִּי אִם־גָּלָה סוֹדוֹ
אֶל־עֲבָדָיו הַנְּבִיאִים:

8 A lion has roared!
Who will not fear?
The Lord GOD has spoken!
Who can but prophesy?

8 אַרְיֵה שָׁאָג מִי לֹא יִירָא
אֲדֹנָי יְהוִֹה דִּבֶּר מִי לֹא יִנָּבֵא:

9 "Proclaim in the palaces at Ashdod,
And in the palaces in the land of Egypt, and
say:
'Assemble on the mountains of Samaria;
See great tumults in her midst,
And the oppressed within her.

9 הַשְׁמִיעוּ עַל־אַרְמְנוֹת בְּאַשְׁדּוֹד
וְעַל־אַרְמְנוֹת בְּאֶרֶץ מִצְרָיִם
וְאִמְרוּ הֵאָסְפוּ עַל־הָרֵי שֹׁמְרוֹן
וּרְאוּ מְהוּמֹת רַבּוֹת בְּתוֹכָהּ
וַעֲשׁוּקִים בְּקִרְבָּהּ:

10 For they do not know to do right,'
Says the LORD,
'Who store up violence and robbery in their
palaces.'"

10 וְלֹא־יָדְעוּ עֲשׂוֹת־נְכֹחָה נְאֻם־יְהוָֹה
הָאוֹצְרִים חָמָס וָשֹׁד בְּאַרְמְנוֹתֵיהֶם: פ

11 Therefore thus says the Lord GOD:

"An adversary *shall be* all around the land;
He shall sap your strength from you,
And your palaces shall be plundered."

11 לָכֵן כֹּה אָמַר אֲדֹנָי יְהוִֹה צַר וּסְבִיב הָאָרֶץ
וְהוֹרִד מִמֵּךְ עֻזֵּךְ וְנָבֹזּוּ אַרְמְנוֹתָיִךְ:

12 Thus says the LORD:

"As a shepherd takes from the mouth of a lion
Two legs or a piece of an ear,
So shall the children of Israel be taken out
Who dwell in Samaria—

12 כֹּה אָמַר יְהוָֹה
כַּאֲשֶׁר יַצִּיל הָרֹעֶה מִפִּי הָאֲרִי
שְׁתֵּי כְרָעַיִם אוֹ בְדַל־אֹזֶן
כֵּן יִנָּצְלוּ בְּנֵי יִשְׂרָאֵל

In the corner of a bed and on the edge of a
couch!

13 Hear and testify against the house of Jacob,"
Says the Lord GOD, the God of hosts,

14 "That in the day I punish Israel for their
transgressions,
I will also visit *destruction* on the altars of
Bethel;
And the horns of the altar shall be cut off
And fall to the ground.

15 I will destroy the winter house along with the
summer house;
The houses of ivory shall perish,
And the great houses shall have an end,"
Says the LORD.

4 Hear this word, you cows of Bashan, who
are on the mountain of Samaria,
Who oppress the poor,
Who crush the needy,
Who say to your husbands, "Bring *wine,* let
us drink!"

2 The Lord GOD has sworn by His holiness:
"Behold, the days shall come upon you
When He will take you away with fishhooks,
And your posterity with fishhooks.

3 You will go out *through* broken *walls,*
Each one straight ahead of her,
And you will be cast into Harmon,"
Says the LORD.

4 "Come to Bethel and transgress,
At Gilgal multiply transgression;
Bring your sacrifices every morning,
Your tithes every three days.

5 Offer a sacrifice of thanksgiving with leaven,
Proclaim *and* announce the freewill offerings;
For this you love,
You children of Israel!"
Says the Lord GOD.

6 "Also I gave you cleanness of teeth in all your
cities.
And lack of bread in all your places;
Yet you have not returned to Me,"
Says the LORD.

7 "I also withheld rain from you,
When *there were* still three months to the
harvest.
I made it rain on one city,
I withheld rain from another city.
One part was rained upon,
And where it did not rain the part withered.

8 So two *or* three cities wandered to another
city to drink water,

הַיֹּשְׁבִים֙ בְּשֹׁמְר֔וֹן
בִּפְאַ֥ת מִטָּ֖ה וּבִדְמֶ֥שֶׁק עָֽרֶשׂ׃

13 שִׁמְע֤וּ וְהָעִ֙ידוּ֙ בְּבֵ֣ית יַֽעֲקֹ֔ב
נְאֻם־אֲדֹנָ֥י יְהֹוִ֖ה אֱלֹהֵ֥י הַצְּבָאֽוֹת׃

14 כִּ֗י בְּי֛וֹם פׇּקְדִ֥י פִשְׁעֵֽי־יִשְׂרָאֵ֖ל עָלָ֑יו
וּפָקַדְתִּי֙ עַל־מִזְבְּח֣וֹת בֵּֽית־אֵ֔ל
וְנִגְדְּעוּ֙ קַרְנ֣וֹת הַמִּזְבֵּ֔חַ
וְנָפְל֖וּ לָאָֽרֶץ׃

15 וְהִכֵּיתִ֥י בֵית־הַחֹ֖רֶף עַל־בֵּ֣ית הַקָּ֑יִץ
וְאָבְד֞וּ בָּתֵּ֣י הַשֵּׁ֗ן וְסָפ֛וּ בָּתִּ֥ים רַבִּ֖ים נְאֻם־
יְהֹוָֽה׃ ס

ד שִׁמְע֞וּ הַדָּבָ֣ר הַזֶּ֗ה פָּר֤וֹת הַבָּשָׁן֙
אֲשֶׁר֙ בְּהַ֣ר שֹׁמְר֔וֹן
הָעֹשְׁק֣וֹת דַּלִּ֔ים הָרֹצְצ֖וֹת אֶבְיוֹנִ֑ים
הָאֹמְרֹ֥ת לַאֲדֹֽנֵיהֶ֖ם הָבִ֥יאָה וְנִשְׁתֶּֽה׃

2 נִשְׁבַּ֨ע אֲדֹנָ֤י יְהֹוִה֙ בְּקׇדְשׁ֔וֹ
כִּ֛י הִנֵּ֥ה יָמִ֖ים בָּאִ֣ים עֲלֵיכֶ֑ם
וְנִשָּׂ֤א אֶתְכֶם֙ בְּצִנּ֔וֹת
וְאַחֲרִֽיתְכֶ֖ן בְּסִיר֥וֹת דּוּגָֽה׃

3 וּפְרָצִ֥ים תֵּצֶ֖אנָה אִשָּׁ֣ה נֶגְדָּ֑הּ
וְהִשְׁלַכְתֶּ֥נָה הַהַרְמ֖וֹנָה נְאֻם־יְהֹוָֽה׃

4 בֹּ֤אוּ בֵֽית־אֵל֙ וּפִשְׁע֔וּ
הַגִּלְגָּ֖ל הַרְבּ֣וּ לִפְשֹׁ֑עַ
וְהָבִ֤יאוּ לַבֹּ֙קֶר֙ זִבְחֵיכֶ֔ם
לִשְׁלֹ֥שֶׁת יָמִ֖ים מַעְשְׂרֹֽתֵיכֶֽם׃

5 וְקַטֵּ֤ר מֵֽחָמֵץ֙ תּוֹדָ֔ה
וְקִרְא֥וּ נְדָב֖וֹת הַשְׁמִ֑יעוּ
כִּ֣י כֵ֤ן אֲהַבְתֶּם֙ בְּנֵ֣י יִשְׂרָאֵ֔ל
נְאֻ֖ם אֲדֹנָ֥י יְהֹוִֽה׃

6 וְגַם־אֲנִ֞י נָתַ֧תִּי לָכֶ֛ם
נִקְי֥וֹן שִׁנַּ֖יִם בְּכׇל־עָרֵיכֶ֑ם
וְחֹ֤סֶר לֶ֙חֶם֙ בְּכֹ֣ל מְקוֹמֹֽתֵיכֶ֔ם
וְלֹא־שַׁבְתֶּ֥ם עָדַ֖י נְאֻם־יְהֹוָֽה׃

7 וְגַ֣ם אָנֹכִ֞י מָנַ֣עְתִּי מִכֶּ֣ם אֶת־הַגֶּ֗שֶׁם
בְּע֨וֹד שְׁלֹשָׁ֤ה חֳדָשִׁים֙ לַקָּצִ֔יר
וְהִמְטַרְתִּי֙ עַל־עִ֣יר אֶחָ֔ת
וְעַל־עִ֥יר אַחַ֖ת לֹ֣א אַמְטִ֑יר
חֶלְקָ֤ה אַחַת֙ תִּמָּטֵ֔ר
וְחֶלְקָ֛ה אֲשֶֽׁר־לֹֽא־תַמְטִ֥יר עָלֶ֖יהָ תִּיבָֽשׁ׃

8 וְנָע֡וּ שְׁתַּ֩יִם֩ שָׁלֹ֨שׁ עָרִ֜ים

But they were not satisfied;
Yet you have not returned to Me,"
Says the LORD.

אֶל־עִיר אַחַת
לִשְׁתּוֹת מַיִם וְלֹא יִשְׂבָּעוּ
וְלֹא־שַׁבְתֶּם עָדַי

9 "I blasted you with blight and mildew.
When your gardens increased,
Your vineyards,
Your fig trees,
And your olive trees,
The locust devoured *them;*
Yet you have not returned to Me,"
Says the LORD.

9 נְאֻם־יְהוָה:
הִכֵּיתִי אֶתְכֶם בַּשִּׁדָּפוֹן וּבַיֵּרָקוֹן
הַרְבּוֹת גַּנּוֹתֵיכֶם וְכַרְמֵיכֶם
וּתְאֵנֵיכֶם וְזֵיתֵיכֶם יֹאכַל הַגָּזָם
וְלֹא־שַׁבְתֶּם עָדַי
נְאֻם־יְהוָה:

10 "I sent among you a plague after the manner
of Egypt;
Your young men I killed with a sword,
Along with your captive horses;
I made the stench of your camps come up
into your nostrils;
Yet you have not returned to Me,"
Says the LORD.

10 שִׁלַּחְתִּי בָכֶם דֶּבֶר בְּדֶרֶךְ מִצְרַיִם
הָרַגְתִּי בַחֶרֶב בַּחוּרֵיכֶם
עִם שְׁבִי סוּסֵיכֶם
וָאַעֲלֶה בְּאֹשׁ מַחֲנֵיכֶם וּבְאַפְּכֶם
וְלֹא־שַׁבְתֶּם עָדַי
נְאֻם־יְהוָה:

11 "I overthrew *some* of you,
As God overthrew Sodom and Gomorrah,
And you were like a firebrand plucked from
the burning;
Yet you have not returned to Me,"
Says the LORD.

11 הָפַכְתִּי בָכֶם
כְּמַהְפֵּכַת אֱלֹהִים
אֶת־סְדֹם וְאֶת־עֲמֹרָה
וַתִּהְיוּ כְּאוּד מֻצָּל מִשְּׂרֵפָה
וְלֹא־שַׁבְתֶּם עָדַי
נְאֻם־יְהוָה:

12 "Therefore thus will I do to you, O Israel;
Because I will do this to you,
Prepare to meet your God, O Israel!"

12 לָכֵן כֹּה אֶעֱשֶׂה־לְּךָ יִשְׂרָאֵל
עֵקֶב כִּי־זֹאת אֶעֱשֶׂה־לָּךְ
הִכּוֹן לִקְרַאת־אֱלֹהֶיךָ יִשְׂרָאֵל:

13 For behold,
He who forms mountains,
And creates the wind,
Who declares to man what his thought *is,*
And makes the morning darkness,
Who treads the high places of the earth—
The LORD God of hosts *is* His name.

13 כִּי הִנֵּה יוֹצֵר הָרִים וּבֹרֵא רוּחַ
וּמַגִּיד לְאָדָם מַה־שֵּׂחוֹ
עֹשֵׂה שַׁחַר עֵיפָה
וְדֹרֵךְ עַל־בָּמֳתֵי אָרֶץ
יְהוָה אֱלֹהֵי־צְבָאוֹת שְׁמוֹ:

5 Hear this word which I take up against you, a
lamentation, O house of Israel:

ה שִׁמְעוּ אֶת־הַדָּבָר הַזֶּה אֲשֶׁר אָנֹכִי
נֹשֵׂא עֲלֵיכֶם קִינָה בֵּית יִשְׂרָאֵל:

2 The virgin of Israel has fallen;
She will rise no more.
She lies forsaken on her land;
There is no one to raise her up.

2 נָפְלָה לֹא־תוֹסִיף קוּם
בְּתוּלַת יִשְׂרָאֵל
נִטְּשָׁה עַל־אַדְמָתָהּ
אֵין מְקִימָהּ:

3 For thus says the Lord GOD:

"The city that goes out by a thousand
Shall have a hundred left,
And that which goes out by a hundred
Shall have ten left to the house of Israel."

3 כִּי כֹה אָמַר אֲדֹנָי יְהוִה הָעִיר הַיֹּצֵאת אֶלֶף
תַּשְׁאִיר מֵאָה וְהַיּוֹצֵאת מֵאָה תַּשְׁאִיר עֲשָׂרָה לְבֵית
יִשְׂרָאֵל: 4 כִּי כֹה אָמַר יְהוָה לְבֵית
יִשְׂרָאֵל

4 For thus says the LORD to the house of Israel:

"Seek Me and live;
5 But do not seek Bethel,

דִּרְשׁוּנִי וִחְיוּ:
5 וְאַל־תִּדְרְשׁוּ בֵּית־אֵל

Nor enter Gilgal,
Nor pass over to Beersheba;
For Gilgal shall surely go into captivity,
And Bethel shall come to nothing.

וְהַגִּלְגָּל לֹא תָבֹאוּ
וּבְאֵר שֶׁבַע לֹא תַעֲבֹרוּ
כִּי הַגִּלְגָּל גָּלֹה יִגְלֶה
וּבֵית־אֵל יִהְיֶה לְאָוֶן:

6 Seek the LORD and live,
Lest He break out like fire *in the house of Joseph,*
And devour *it,*
With no one to quench *it* in Bethel—

6 דִּרְשׁוּ אֶת־יְהוָה וִחְיוּ
פֶּן־יִצְלַח כָּאֵשׁ בֵּית יוֹסֵף
וְאָכְלָה וְאֵין־מְכַבֶּה לְבֵית־אֵל:

7 You who turn justice to wormwood,
And lay righteousness to rest in the earth!"

7 הַהֹפְכִים לְלַעֲנָה מִשְׁפָּט
וּצְדָקָה לָאָרֶץ הִנִּיחוּ:

8 He made the Pleiades and Orion;
He turns the shadow of death into morning
And makes the day dark as night;
He calls for the waters of the sea
And pours them out on the face of the earth;
The LORD *is* His name.

8 עֹשֵׂה כִימָה וּכְסִיל
וְהֹפֵךְ לַבֹּקֶר צַלְמָוֶת
וְיוֹם לַיְלָה הֶחְשִׁיךְ
הַקּוֹרֵא לְמֵי־הַיָּם
וַיִּשְׁפְּכֵם עַל־פְּנֵי הָאָרֶץ
יְהוָה שְׁמוֹ: ס

9 He rains ruin upon the strong,
So that fury comes upon the fortress.

9 הַמַּבְלִיג שֹׁד עַל־עָז
וְשֹׁד עַל־מִבְצָר יָבוֹא:

10 They hate the one who rebukes in the gate,
And they abhor the one who speaks uprightly.

10 שָׂנְאוּ בַשַּׁעַר מוֹכִיחַ
וְדֹבֵר תָּמִים יְתָעֵבוּ:

11 Therefore, because you tread down the poor
And take grain taxes from him,
Though you have built houses of hewn stone,
Yet you shall not dwell in them;
You have planted pleasant vineyards,
But you shall not drink wine from them.

11 לָכֵן יַעַן בּוֹשַׁסְכֶם עַל־דָּל
וּמַשְׂאַת־בַּר תִּקְחוּ מִמֶּנּוּ
בָּתֵּי גָזִית בְּנִיתֶם וְלֹא־תֵשְׁבוּ בָם
כַּרְמֵי־חֶמֶד נְטַעְתֶּם
וְלֹא תִשְׁתּוּ אֶת־יֵינָם:

12 For I know your manifold transgressions
And your mighty sins:
Afflicting the just *and* taking bribes;
Diverting the poor *from justice* at the gate.

12 כִּי יָדַעְתִּי רַבִּים פִּשְׁעֵיכֶם
וַעֲצֻמִים חַטֹּאתֵיכֶם
צֹרְרֵי צַדִּיק לֹקְחֵי כֹפֶר
וְאֶבְיוֹנִים בַּשַּׁעַר הִטּוּ:

13 Therefore the prudent keep silent at that time,
For it *is* an evil time.

13 לָכֵן הַמַּשְׂכִּיל בָּעֵת הַהִיא יִדֹּם
כִּי עֵת רָעָה הִיא:

14 Seek good and not evil,
That you may live;
So the LORD God of hosts will be with you,
As you have spoken.

14 דִּרְשׁוּ־טוֹב וְאַל־רָע לְמַעַן תִּחְיוּ
וִיהִי־כֵן יְהוָה אֱלֹהֵי־צְבָאוֹת
אִתְּכֶם כַּאֲשֶׁר אֲמַרְתֶּם:

15 Hate evil, love good;
Establish justice in the gate.
It may be that the LORD God of hosts
Will be gracious to the remnant of Joseph.

15 שִׂנְאוּ־רָע וְאֶהֱבוּ טוֹב
וְהַצִּיגוּ בַשַּׁעַר מִשְׁפָּט
אוּלַי יֶחֱנַן יְהוָה אֱלֹהֵי־צְבָאוֹת
שְׁאֵרִית יוֹסֵף: ס

16 Therefore the LORD God of hosts, the Lord, says this:

16 לָכֵן כֹּה־אָמַר יְהוָה אֱלֹהֵי צְבָאוֹת אֲדֹנָי
בְּכָל־רְחֹבוֹת מִסְפֵּד

"*There shall be* wailing in all streets,
And they shall say in all the highways,
'Alas! Alas!'
They shall call the farmer to mourning,
And skillful lamenters to wailing.

וּבְכָל־חוּצוֹת יֹאמְרוּ הוֹ־הוֹ
וְקָרְאוּ אִכָּר אֶל־אֵבֶל

17 In all vineyards *there shall be* wailing,
For I will pass through you,"

17 וּמִסְפֵּד אֶל־יוֹדְעֵי נֶהִי:

Says the LORD.

18 Woe to you who desire the day of the LORD!
For what good *is* the day of the LORD to
you?
It *will be* darkness, and not light.

19 It *will be* as though a man fled from a lion,
And a bear met him!
Or *as though* he went into the house,
Leaned his hand on the wall,
And a serpent bit him!

20 *Is* not the day of the LORD darkness, and not
light?
Is it not very dark, with no brightness in it?

21 "I hate, I despise your feast days,
And I do not savor your sacred assemblies.

22 Though you offer Me burnt offerings and
your grain offerings,
I will not accept *them,*
Nor will I regard your fattened peace
offerings.

23 Take away from Me the noise of your songs,
For I will not hear the melody of your
stringed instruments.

24 But let justice run down like water,
And righteousness like a mighty stream.

25 "Did you offer Me sacrifices and offerings
In the wilderness forty years, O house of Israel?

26 You also carried Sikkuth your king
And Chiun, your idols,
The star of your gods,
Which you made for yourselves.

27 Therefore I will send you into captivity beyond
Damascus,"
Says the LORD, whose name *is* the God of hosts.

6 Woe to you *who are* at ease in Zion,
And trust in Mount Samaria,
Notable persons in the chief nation,
To whom the house of Israel comes!

2 Go over to Calneh and see;
And from there go to Hamath the great;
Then go down to Gath of the Philistines.
Are you better than these kingdoms?
Or is their territory greater than your
territory?

3 *Woe to* you who put far off the day of doom,
Who cause the seat of violence to come near;

4 Who lie on beds of ivory,
Stretch out on your couches,
Eat lambs from the flock
And calves from the midst of the stall;

5 Who sing idly to the sound of stringed
instruments,

17 וּבְכָל־כְּרָמִים מִסְפֵּד
כִּי־אֶעֱבֹר בְּקִרְבְּךָ
אָמַר יְהֹוָה: ס

18 הוֹי הַמִּתְאַוִּים אֶת־יוֹם יְהֹוָה
לָמָּה־זֶּה לָכֶם יוֹם יְהֹוָה
הוּא־חֹשֶׁךְ וְלֹא־אוֹר:

19 כַּאֲשֶׁר יָנוּס אִישׁ מִפְּנֵי הָאֲרִי
וּפְגָעוֹ הַדֹּב
וּבָא הַבַּיִת וְסָמַךְ יָדוֹ עַל־הַקִּיר
וּנְשָׁכוֹ הַנָּחָשׁ:

20 הֲלֹא־חֹשֶׁךְ יוֹם יְהֹוָה וְלֹא־אוֹר
וְאָפֵל וְלֹא־נֹגַהּ לוֹ:

21 שָׂנֵאתִי מָאַסְתִּי חַגֵּיכֶם
וְלֹא אָרִיחַ בְּעַצְּרֹתֵיכֶם:

22 כִּי אִם־תַּעֲלוּ־לִי עֹלוֹת
וּמִנְחֹתֵיכֶם לֹא אֶרְצֶה
וְשֶׁלֶם מְרִיאֵיכֶם לֹא אַבִּיט:

23 הָסֵר מֵעָלַי הֲמוֹן שִׁרֶיךָ
וְזִמְרַת נְבָלֶיךָ לֹא אֶשְׁמָע:

24 וְיִגַּל כַּמַּיִם מִשְׁפָּט
וּצְדָקָה כְּנַחַל אֵיתָן:

25 הַזְּבָחִים וּמִנְחָה הִגַּשְׁתֶּם־לִי בַּמִּדְבָּר אַרְבָּעִים
שָׁנָה בֵּית יִשְׂרָאֵל: 26 וּנְשָׂאתֶם אֵת סִכּוּת מַלְכְּכֶם
וְאֵת כִּיּוּן צַלְמֵיכֶם כּוֹכַב אֱלֹהֵיכֶם אֲשֶׁר עֲשִׂיתֶם
לָכֶם: 27 וְהִגְלֵיתִי אֶתְכֶם מֵהָלְאָה לְדַמָּשֶׂק אָמַר
יְהֹוָה אֱלֹהֵי־צְבָאוֹת שְׁמוֹ: פ

ו הוֹי הַשַּׁאֲנַנִּים בְּצִיּוֹן וְהַבֹּטְחִים בְּהַר שֹׁמְרוֹן
נְקֻבֵי רֵאשִׁית הַגּוֹיִם וּבָאוּ לָהֶם בֵּית יִשְׂרָאֵל:

2 עִבְרוּ כַלְנֵה וּרְאוּ
וּלְכוּ מִשָּׁם חֲמַת רַבָּה
וּרְדוּ גַת־פְּלִשְׁתִּים
הֲטוֹבִים מִן־הַמַּמְלָכוֹת הָאֵלֶּה
אִם־רַב גְּבוּלָם מִגְּבֻלְכֶם:

3 הַמְנַדִּים לְיוֹם רָע
וַתַּגִּישׁוּן שֶׁבֶת חָמָס:

4 הַשֹּׁכְבִים עַל־מִטּוֹת שֵׁן
וּסְרֻחִים עַל־עַרְשׂוֹתָם
וְאֹכְלִים כָּרִים מִצֹּאן
וַעֲגָלִים מִתּוֹךְ מַרְבֵּק:

5 הַפֹּרְטִים עַל־פִּי הַנָּבֶל

And invent for yourselves musical instruments like David;

6   Who drink wine from bowls,
And anoint yourselves with the best
ointments,
But are not grieved for the affliction of
Joseph.

7   Therefore they shall now go captive as the
first of the captives,
And those who recline at banquets shall be
removed.

8   The Lord GOD has sworn by Himself,
The LORD God of hosts says:
"I abhor the pride of Jacob,
And hate his palaces;
Therefore I will deliver up *the* city
And all that is in it."

9 Then it shall come to pass, that if ten men
remain in one house, they shall die. 10 And when a
relative *of the dead,* with one who will burn *the
bodies,* picks up the bodies to take them out of the
house, he will say to one inside the house, "*Are
there* any more with you?"

Then someone will say, "None."

And he will say, "Hold your tongue! For we dare
not mention the name of the LORD."

11   For behold, the LORD gives a command:
He will break the great house into bits,
And the little house into pieces.

12   Do horses run on rocks?
Does *one* plow *there* with oxen?
Yet you have turned justice into gall,
And the fruit of righteousness into worm-
wood,

13   You who rejoice over Lo Debar,
Who say, "Have we not taken Karnaim for
ourselves
By our own strength?"

14   "But, behold, I will raise up a nation against you,
O house of Israel,"
Says the LORD God of hosts;
"And they will afflict you from the entrance of
Hamath
To the Valley of the Arabah."

7 Thus the Lord GOD showed me: Behold, He
formed locust swarms at the beginning of the late
crop; indeed *it was* the late crop after the king's
mowings. 2 And so it was, when they had finished
eating the grass of the land, that I said:

"O Lord GOD, forgive, I pray!
Oh, that Jacob may stand,

כְּדָוִיד חָשְׁבוּ לָהֶם כְּלֵי־שִׁיר:
6 הַשֹּׁתִים בְּמִזְרְקֵי יַיִן
וְרֵאשִׁית שְׁמָנִים יִמְשָׁחוּ
וְלֹא נֶחְלוּ עַל־שֵׁבֶר יוֹסֵף:
7 לָכֵן עַתָּה יִגְלוּ בְּרֹאשׁ גֹּלִים
וְסָר מִרְזַח סְרוּחִים: פ

8 נִשְׁבַּע אֲדֹנָי יְהוִה בְּנַפְשׁוֹ
נְאֻם־יְהוָה אֱלֹהֵי צְבָאוֹת
מְתָאֵב אָנֹכִי אֶת־גְּאוֹן יַעֲקֹב
וְאַרְמְנֹתָיו שָׂנֵאתִי
וְהִסְגַּרְתִּי עִיר וּמְלֹאָהּ:

9 וְהָיָה אִם־יִוָּתְרוּ עֲשָׂרָה אֲנָשִׁים בְּבַיִת אֶחָד וָמֵתוּ:
10 וּנְשָׂאוֹ דּוֹדוֹ וּמְסָרְפוֹ לְהוֹצִיא עֲצָמִים מִן־הַבַּיִת
וְאָמַר לַאֲשֶׁר בְּיַרְכְּתֵי הַבַּיִת הַעוֹד עִמָּךְ וְאָמַר
אָפֶס וְאָמַר הָס כִּי לֹא לְהַזְכִּיר בְּשֵׁם יְהוָה:

11 כִּי־הִנֵּה יְהוָה מְצַוֶּה
וְהִכָּה הַבַּיִת הַגָּדוֹל רְסִיסִים
וְהַבַּיִת הַקָּטֹן בְּקִעִים:
12 הַיְרֻצוּן בַּסֶּלַע סוּסִים
אִם־יַחֲרוֹשׁ בַּבְּקָרִים
כִּי־הֲפַכְתֶּם לְרֹאשׁ מִשְׁפָּט
וּפְרִי צְדָקָה לְלַעֲנָה:
13 הַשְּׂמֵחִים לְלֹא דָבָר
הָאֹמְרִים הֲלוֹא בְחָזְקֵנוּ
לָקַחְנוּ לָנוּ קַרְנָיִם:

14 כִּי הִנְנִי מֵקִים עֲלֵיכֶם בֵּית יִשְׂרָאֵל נְאֻם־יְהוָה
אֱלֹהֵי הַצְּבָאוֹת גּוֹי וְלָחֲצוּ אֶתְכֶם מִלְּבוֹא חֲמָת
עַד־נַחַל הָעֲרָבָה: ס

ז כֹּה הִרְאַנִי אֲדֹנָי יְהוִה וְהִנֵּה יוֹצֵר גֹּבַי בִּתְחִלַּת
עֲלוֹת הַלָּקֶשׁ וְהִנֵּה־לֶקֶשׁ אַחַר גִּזֵּי הַמֶּלֶךְ: 2 וְהָיָה
אִם־כִּלָּה לֶאֱכוֹל אֶת־עֵשֶׂב הָאָרֶץ וָאֹמַר
אֲדֹנָי יְהוִה סְלַח־נָא
מִי יָקוּם יַעֲקֹב

For he *is* small!"

3   *So* the Lord relented concerning this.
"It shall not be," said the Lord.

4 Thus the Lord God showed me: Behold, the Lord God called for conflict by fire, and it consumed the great deep and devoured the territory. 5 Then I said:

"O Lord God, cease, I pray!
Oh, that Jacob may stand,
For he *is* small!"

6   *So* the Lord relented concerning this.
"This also shall not be," said the Lord God.

7 Thus He showed me: Behold, the Lord stood on a wall *made* with a plumb line, with a plumb line in His hand. 8 And the Lord said to me, "Amos, what do you see?"

And I said, "A plumb line."

Then the Lord said:

"Behold, I am setting a plumb line
In the midst of My people Israel;
I will not pass by them anymore.
9   The high places of Isaac shall be desolate,
And the sanctuaries of Israel shall be laid waste.
I will rise with the sword against the house of Jeroboam."

10 Then Amaziah the priest of Bethel sent to Jeroboam king of Israel, saying, "Amos has conspired against you in the midst of the house of Israel. The land is not able to bear all his words. 11 For thus Amos has said:

'Jeroboam shall die by the sword,
And Israel shall surely be led away captive
From their own land.'"

12 Then Amaziah said to Amos:

"Go, you seer!
Flee to the land of Judah.
There eat bread,
And there prophesy.
13   But never again prophesy at Bethel,
For it *is* the king's sanctuary,
And it *is* the royal residence."

14 Then Amos answered, and said to Amaziah:

"I *was* no prophet,
Nor *was* I a son of a prophet,
But I *was* a sheepbreeder
And a tender of sycamore fruit.
15   Then the Lord took me as I followed the flock,
And the Lord said to me,
'Go, prophesy to My people Israel.'
16 Now therefore, hear the word of the Lord:
You say, 'Do not prophesy against Israel,
And do not spout against the house of Isaac.'

כִּי קָטֹן הוּא:

3 נִחַם יְהֹוָה עַל־זֹאת
לֹא תִהְיֶה אָמַר יְהֹוָה:

4 כֹּה הִרְאַנִי אֲדֹנָי יְהֹוִה וְהִנֵּה קֹרֵא לָרִב בָּאֵשׁ
אֲדֹנָי יְהֹוִה וַתֹּאכַל אֶת־תְּהוֹם רַבָּה וְאָכְלָה אֶת־
הַחֵלֶק:

5 וָאֹמַר אֲדֹנָי יְהֹוִה חֲדַל־נָא
מִי יָקוּם יַעֲקֹב כִּי קָטֹן הוּא:

6 נִחַם יְהֹוָה עַל־זֹאת
גַּם־הִיא לֹא תִהְיֶה אָמַר אֲדֹנָי יְהֹוִה: ס

7 כֹּה הִרְאַנִי וְהִנֵּה אֲדֹנָי נִצָּב עַל־חוֹמַת אֲנָךְ וּבְיָדוֹ
אֲנָךְ: 8 וַיֹּאמֶר יְהֹוָה אֵלַי מָה־אַתָּה רֹאֶה עָמוֹס
וָאֹמַר אֲנָךְ וַיֹּאמֶר אֲדֹנָי
הִנְנִי שָׂם אֲנָךְ בְּקֶרֶב עַמִּי יִשְׂרָאֵל
לֹא־אוֹסִיף עוֹד עֲבוֹר לוֹ:
9 וְנָשַׁמּוּ בָּמוֹת יִשְׂחָק
וּמִקְדְּשֵׁי יִשְׂרָאֵל יֶחֱרָבוּ
וְקַמְתִּי עַל־בֵּית יָרָבְעָם בֶּחָרֶב: פ

10 וַיִּשְׁלַח אֲמַצְיָה כֹּהֵן בֵּית־אֵל אֶל־יָרָבְעָם מֶלֶךְ־
יִשְׂרָאֵל לֵאמֹר קָשַׁר עָלֶיךָ עָמוֹס בְּקֶרֶב בֵּית יִשְׂרָאֵל
לֹא־תוּכַל הָאָרֶץ לְהָכִיל אֶת־כָּל־דְּבָרָיו: 11 כִּי־כֹה
אָמַר עָמוֹס
בַּחֶרֶב יָמוּת יָרָבְעָם
וְיִשְׂרָאֵל גָּלֹה יִגְלֶה מֵעַל אַדְמָתוֹ: ס

12 וַיֹּאמֶר אֲמַצְיָה אֶל־עָמוֹס חֹזֶה לֵךְ בְּרַח־לְךָ אֶל־
אֶרֶץ יְהוּדָה וֶאֱכָל־שָׁם לֶחֶם וְשָׁם תִּנָּבֵא: 13 וּבֵית־
אֵל לֹא־תוֹסִיף עוֹד לְהִנָּבֵא כִּי מִקְדַּשׁ־מֶלֶךְ הוּא
וּבֵית מַמְלָכָה הוּא: ס 14 וַיַּעַן עָמוֹס וַיֹּאמֶר
אֶל־אֲמַצְיָה לֹא־נָבִיא אָנֹכִי וְלֹא בֶן־נָבִיא אָנֹכִי כִּי־
בוֹקֵר אָנֹכִי וּבוֹלֵס שִׁקְמִים: 15 וַיִּקָּחֵנִי יְהֹוָה מֵאַחֲרֵי
הַצֹּאן וַיֹּאמֶר אֵלַי יְהֹוָה לֵךְ הִנָּבֵא אֶל־עַמִּי יִשְׂרָאֵל:

16 וְעַתָּה שְׁמַע דְּבַר־יְהֹוָה
אַתָּה אֹמֵר לֹא תִנָּבֵא עַל־יִשְׂרָאֵל
וְלֹא תַטִּיף עַל־בֵּית יִשְׂחָק:

17 "Therefore thus says the LORD:

'Your wife shall be a harlot in the city;
Your sons and daughters shall fall by the
    sword;
Your land shall be divided by *survey* line;
You shall die in a defiled land;
And Israel shall surely be led away captive
From his own land.' "

8 Thus the Lord GOD showed me: Behold, a
basket of summer fruit. ² And He said, "Amos,
what do you see?"

So I said, "A basket of summer fruit."

Then the LORD said to me:

"The end has come upon My people Israel;
I will not pass by them anymore.
3 And the songs of the temple
Shall be wailing in that day,"
Says the Lord GOD—
"Many dead bodies everywhere,
They shall be thrown out in silence."

4 Hear this, you who swallow up the needy,
And make the poor of the land fail,

⁵ Saying:

"When will the New Moon be past,
That we may sell grain?
And the Sabbath,
That we may trade wheat?
Making the ephah small and the shekel large,
Falsifying the scales by deceit,
6 That we may buy the poor for silver,
And the needy for a pair of sandals—
Even sell the bad wheat?"

7 The LORD has sworn by the pride of Jacob:
"Surely I will never forget any of their works.
8 Shall the land not tremble for this,
And everyone mourn who dwells in it?
All of it shall swell like the River,
Heave and subside
Like the River of Egypt.

9 "And it shall come to pass in that day," says
    the Lord GOD,
"That I will make the sun go down at noon,
And I will darken the earth in broad
    daylight;
10 I will turn your feasts into mourning,
And all your songs into lamentation;
I will bring sackcloth on every waist,
And baldness on every head;
I will make it like mourning for an only *son*,
And its end like a bitter day.

לָכֵ֞ן כֹּה־אָמַ֣ר יְהוָ֗ה 17
אֶשְׁתְּךָ֞ בָּעִ֣יר תִּזְנֶ֗ה
וּבָנֶ֤יךָ וּבְנֹתֶ֙יךָ֙ בַּחֶ֣רֶב יִפֹּ֔לוּ
וְאַדְמָתְךָ֖ בַּחֶ֣בֶל תְּחֻלָּ֑ק
וְאַתָּ֗ה עַל־אֲדָמָ֤ה טְמֵאָה֙ תָּמ֔וּת
וְיִשְׂרָאֵ֕ל גָּלֹ֥ה יִגְלֶ֖ה מֵעַ֥ל אַדְמָתֽוֹ׃ ס

ח כֹּ֤ה הִרְאַ֙נִי֙ אֲדֹנָ֣י יְהוִ֔ה וְהִנֵּ֖ה כְּל֣וּב קָ֑יִץ וַיֹּ֗אמֶר 2
מָֽה־אַתָּ֤ה רֹאֶה֙ עָמ֔וֹס וָאֹמַ֖ר כְּל֣וּב קָ֑יִץ וַיֹּ֤אמֶר
יְהוָה֙ אֵלַ֔י בָּ֥א הַקֵּ֖ץ אֶל־עַמִּ֣י יִשְׂרָאֵ֔ל לֹא־אוֹסִ֥יף
ע֖וֹד עֲב֥וֹר לֽוֹ׃

וְהֵילִ֜ילוּ שִׁיר֤וֹת הֵיכָל֙ בַּיּ֣וֹם הַה֔וּא 3
נְאֻ֖ם אֲדֹנָ֣י יְהוִ֑ה
רַ֣ב הַפֶּ֔גֶר
בְּכָל־מָק֖וֹם הִשְׁלִ֥יךְ הָֽס׃ פ

שִׁמְעוּ־זֹ֕את הַשֹּׁאֲפִ֖ים אֶבְי֑וֹן 4
וְלַשְׁבִּ֖ית עֲנִיֵּי־אָֽרֶץ׃

לֵאמֹ֗ר מָתַ֞י יַעֲבֹ֤ר הַחֹ֙דֶשׁ֙ 5
וְנַשְׁבִּ֣ירָה שֶּׁ֔בֶר
וְהַשַּׁבָּ֖ת וְנִפְתְּחָה־בָּ֑ר
לְהַקְטִ֤ין אֵיפָה֙ וּלְהַגְדִּ֣יל שֶׁ֔קֶל
וּלְעַוֵּ֖ת מֹאזְנֵ֥י מִרְמָֽה׃

לִקְנ֤וֹת בַּכֶּ֙סֶף֙ דַּלִּ֔ים 6
וְאֶבְי֖וֹן בַּעֲב֣וּר נַעֲלָ֑יִם
וּמַפַּ֥ל בַּ֖ר נַשְׁבִּֽיר׃

נִשְׁבַּ֥ע יְהוָ֖ה בִּגְא֣וֹן יַעֲקֹ֑ב 7
אִם־אֶשְׁכַּ֥ח לָנֶ֖צַח כָּל־מַעֲשֵׂיהֶֽם׃

הַ֤עַל זֹאת֙ לֹא־תִרְגַּ֣ז הָאָ֔רֶץ 8
וְאָבַ֖ל כָּל־יוֹשֵׁ֣ב בָּ֑הּ
וְעָלְתָ֤ה כָאֹר֙ כֻּלָּ֔הּ
וְנִגְרְשָׁ֥ה וְנִשְׁקְעָ֖ה כִּיא֥וֹר מִצְרָֽיִם׃ ס

וְהָיָ֣ה ׀ בַּיּ֣וֹם הַה֗וּא 9
נְאֻם֙ אֲדֹנָ֣י יְהוִ֔ה
וְהֵבֵאתִ֥י הַשֶּׁ֖מֶשׁ בַּֽצָּהֳרָ֑יִם
וְהַחֲשַׁכְתִּ֥י לָאָ֖רֶץ בְּי֥וֹם אֽוֹר׃

וְהָפַכְתִּ֨י חַגֵּיכֶ֜ם לְאֵ֗בֶל 10
וְכָל־שִׁירֵיכֶם֙ לְקִינָ֔ה
וְהַעֲלֵיתִ֤י עַל־כָּל־מָתְנַ֙יִם֙ שָׂ֔ק
וְעַל־כָּל־רֹ֖אשׁ קָרְחָ֑ה
וְשַׂמְתִּ֙יהָ֙ כְּאֵ֣בֶל יָחִ֔יד
וְאַחֲרִיתָ֖הּ כְּי֥וֹם מָֽר׃

8 וְנִשְׁקְעָה ח

11 "Behold, the days are coming," says the Lord
God,
"That I will send a famine on the land,
Not a famine of bread,
Nor a thirst for water,
But of hearing the words of the LORD.
12 They shall wander from sea to sea,
And from north to east;
They shall run to and fro, seeking the word
of the LORD,
But shall not find *it.*
13 "In that day the fair virgins
And strong young men
Shall faint from thirst.
14 Those who swear by the sin of Samaria,
Who say,
'As your god lives, O Dan!'
And, 'As the way of Beersheba lives!'
They shall fall and never rise again."

9 I saw the Lord standing by the altar, and He
said:

"Strike the doorposts, that the thresholds may
shake,
And break them on the heads of them all.
I will slay the last of them with the sword.
He who flees from them shall not get away,
And he who escapes from them shall not be
delivered.
2 "Though they dig into hell,
From there My hand shall take them;
Though they climb up to heaven,
From there I will bring them down;
3 And though they hide themselves on top of
Carmel,
From there I will search and take them;
Though they hide from My sight at the
bottom of the sea,
From there I will command the serpent, and
it shall bite them;
4 Though they go into captivity before their
enemies,
From there I will command the sword,
And it shall slay them.
I will set My eyes on them for harm and not
for good."
5 The Lord GOD of hosts,
He who touches the earth and it melts,
And all who dwell there mourn;
All of it shall swell like the River,
And subside like the River of Egypt.
6 He who builds His layers in the sky,

11 הִנֵּה ׀ יָמִים בָּאִים נְאֻם אֲדֹנָי יְהֹוִה
וְהִשְׁלַחְתִּי רָעָב בָּאָרֶץ
לֹא־רָעָב לַלֶּחֶם וְלֹא־צָמָא לַמַּיִם
כִּי אִם־לִשְׁמֹעַ אֵת דִּבְרֵי יְהֹוָה:
12 וְנָעוּ מִיָּם עַד־יָם
וּמִצָּפוֹן וְעַד־מִזְרָח
יְשׁוֹטְטוּ לְבַקֵּשׁ אֶת־דְּבַר־יְהֹוָה
וְלֹא יִמְצָאוּ:
13 בַּיּוֹם הַהוּא תִּתְעַלַּפְנָה
הַבְּתוּלֹת הַיָּפוֹת וְהַבַּחוּרִים בַּצָּמָא:
14 הַנִּשְׁבָּעִים בְּאַשְׁמַת שֹׁמְרוֹן
וְאָמְרוּ חֵי אֱלֹהֶיךָ דָּן
וְחֵי דֶּרֶךְ בְּאֵר־שָׁבַע
וְנָפְלוּ וְלֹא־יָקוּמוּ עוֹד: ס

ט רָאִיתִי אֶת־אֲדֹנָי
נִצָּב עַל־הַמִּזְבֵּחַ וַיֹּאמֶר
הַךְ הַכַּפְתּוֹר וְיִרְעֲשׁוּ הַסִּפִּים
וּבְצַעַם בְּרֹאשׁ כֻּלָּם
וְאַחֲרִיתָם בַּחֶרֶב אֶהֱרֹג
לֹא־יָנוּס לָהֶם נָס
וְלֹא־יִמָּלֵט לָהֶם פָּלִיט:
2 אִם־יַחְתְּרוּ בִשְׁאוֹל
מִשָּׁם יָדִי תִקָּחֵם
וְאִם־יַעֲלוּ הַשָּׁמַיִם
מִשָּׁם אוֹרִידֵם:
3 וְאִם־יֵחָבְאוּ בְּרֹאשׁ הַכַּרְמֶל
מִשָּׁם אֲחַפֵּשׂ וּלְקַחְתִּים
וְאִם־יִסָּתְרוּ מִנֶּגֶד עֵינַי בְּקַרְקַע הַיָּם
מִשָּׁם אֲצַוֶּה אֶת־הַנָּחָשׁ וּנְשָׁכָם:
4 וְאִם־יֵלְכוּ בַשְּׁבִי לִפְנֵי אֹיְבֵיהֶם
מִשָּׁם אֲצַוֶּה אֶת־הַחֶרֶב וַהֲרָגָתַם
וְשַׂמְתִּי עֵינִי עֲלֵיהֶם
לְרָעָה וְלֹא לְטוֹבָה:
5 וַאדֹנָי יְהֹוִה הַצְּבָאוֹת
הַנּוֹגֵעַ בָּאָרֶץ וַתָּמוֹג
וְאָבְלוּ כָּל־יוֹשְׁבֵי בָהּ
וְעָלְתָה כַיְאֹר כֻּלָּהּ
וְשָׁקְעָה כִּיאֹר מִצְרָיִם:
6 הַבּוֹנֶה בַשָּׁמַיִם מַעֲלוֹתוֹº

And has founded His strata in the earth;
Who calls for the waters of the sea,
And pours them out on the face of the
    earth—
The LORD *is* His name.

וַאֲגֻדָּתוֹ עַל־אֶרֶץ יְסָדָהּ
הַקֹּרֵא לְמֵי־הַיָּם
וַיִּשְׁפְּכֵם עַל־פְּנֵי הָאָרֶץ
יְהוָה שְׁמוֹ׃

7 *"Are* you not like the people of Ethiopia to
    Me,
    O children of Israel?" says the LORD.
  "Did I not bring up Israel from the land of
    Egypt,
    The Philistines from Caphtor,
    And the Syrians from Kir?

7 הֲלוֹא כִבְנֵי כֻשִׁיִּים אַתֶּם לִי
בְּנֵי יִשְׂרָאֵל נְאֻם־יְהוָה
הֲלוֹא אֶת־יִשְׂרָאֵל
הֶעֱלֵיתִי מֵאֶרֶץ מִצְרַיִם
וּפְלִשְׁתִּיִּים מִכַּפְתּוֹר וַאֲרָם מִקִּיר׃

8 "Behold, the eyes of the Lord GOD *are* on the
    sinful kingdom,
    And I will destroy it from the face of the
    earth;
    Yet I will not utterly destroy the house of
    Jacob,"
  Says the LORD.

8 הִנֵּה עֵינֵי ׀ אֲדֹנָי יְהוִה
בַּמַּמְלָכָה הַחַטָּאָה
וְהִשְׁמַדְתִּי אֹתָהּ מֵעַל פְּנֵי הָאֲדָמָה
אֶפֶס כִּי לֹא הַשְׁמֵיד אַשְׁמִיד
אֶת־בֵּית יַעֲקֹב נְאֻם־יְהוָה׃

9 "For surely I will command,
    And will sift the house of Israel among all
    nations,
    As *grain* is sifted in a sieve;
    Yet not the smallest grain shall fall to the
    ground.

9 כִּי־הִנֵּה אָנֹכִי מְצַוֶּה וַהֲנִעוֹתִי
בְכָל־הַגּוֹיִם אֶת־בֵּית יִשְׂרָאֵל
כַּאֲשֶׁר יִנּוֹעַ בַּכְּבָרָה
וְלֹא־יִפּוֹל צְרוֹר אָרֶץ׃

10 All the sinners of My people shall die by the
    sword,
    Who say, 'The calamity shall not overtake
    nor confront us.'

10 בַּחֶרֶב יָמוּתוּ כֹּל חַטָּאֵי עַמִּי
הָאֹמְרִים לֹא־תַגִּישׁ וְתַקְדִּים
בַּעֲדֵינוּ הָרָעָה׃

11 "On that day I will raise up
    The tabernacle of David, which has fallen
    down,
    And repair its damages;
    I will raise up its ruins,
    And rebuild it as in the days of old;

11 בַּיּוֹם הַהוּא אָקִים
אֶת־סֻכַּת דָּוִיד הַנֹּפֶלֶת
וְגָדַרְתִּי אֶת־פִּרְצֵיהֶן
וַהֲרִסֹתָיו אָקִים
וּבְנִיתִיהָ כִּימֵי עוֹלָם׃

12 That they may possess the remnant of Edom,
    And all the Gentiles who are called by My
    name,"
  Says the LORD who does this thing.

12 לְמַעַן יִירְשׁוּ
אֶת־שְׁאֵרִית אֱדוֹם וְכָל־הַגּוֹיִם
אֲשֶׁר־נִקְרָא שְׁמִי עֲלֵיהֶם
נְאֻם־יְהוָה עֹשֶׂה זֹּאת׃ פ

13 "Behold, the days are coming," says the
    LORD,
  "When the plowman shall overtake the
    reaper,
    And the treader of grapes him who sows
    seed;
    The mountains shall drip with sweet wine,
    And all the hills shall flow *with it.*

13 הִנֵּה יָמִים בָּאִים נְאֻם־יְהוָה
וְנִגַּשׁ חוֹרֵשׁ בַּקֹּצֵר
וְדֹרֵךְ עֲנָבִים בְּמֹשֵׁךְ הַזָּרַע
וְהִטִּיפוּ הֶהָרִים עָסִיס
וְכָל־הַגְּבָעוֹת תִּתְמוֹגַגְנָה׃

14 I will bring back the captives of My people
    Israel;
    They shall build the waste cities and inhabit
    them;

14 וְשַׁבְתִּי אֶת־שְׁבוּת עַמִּי יִשְׂרָאֵל
וּבָנוּ עָרִים נְשַׁמּוֹת וְיָשָׁבוּ

They shall plant vineyards and drink wine
    from them;
They shall also make gardens and eat fruit
    from them.
15 I will plant them in their land,
    And no longer shall they be pulled up
From the land I have given them,"
Says the LORD your God.

וְנָטְעוּ כְרָמִים וְשָׁתוּ אֶת־יֵינָם
וְעָשׂוּ גַנּוֹת וְאָכְלוּ אֶת־פְּרִיהֶם:
15 וּנְטַעְתִּים עַל־אַדְמָתָם
וְלֹא יִנָּתְשׁוּ עוֹד
מֵעַל אַדְמָתָם אֲשֶׁר נָתַתִּי לָהֶם
אָמַר יְהוָה אֱלֹהֶיךָ:

The Book of

OBADIAH

1 The vision of Obadiah.

אֶ חֲזֹון עֹבַדְיָה

Thus says the Lord GOD concerning Edom
(We have heard a report from the LORD,
And a messenger has been sent among the
nations, *saying,*
"Arise, and let us rise up against her for
battle"):

כֹּה־אָמַר אֲדֹנָי יְהוִֹה לֶאֱדֹום
שְׁמוּעָה שָׁמַעְנוּ מֵאֵת יְהוָֹה
וְצִיר בַּגֹּויִם שֻׁלָּח
קוּמוּ וְנָקוּמָה עָלֶיהָ לַמִּלְחָמָה:

2 "Behold, I will make you small among the
nations;
You shall be greatly despised.

2 הִנֵּה קָטֹן נְתַתִּיךָ בַּגֹּויִם
בָּזוּי אַתָּה מְאֹד:

3 The pride of your heart has deceived you,
You who dwell in the clefts of the rock,
Whose habitation is high;
You who say in your heart, 'Who will bring
me down to the ground?'

3 זְדֹון לִבְּךָ הִשִּׁיאֶךָ
שֹׁכְנִי בְחַגְוֵי־סֶלַע
מְרֹום שִׁבְתֹּו אֹמֵר בְּלִבֹּו
מִי יֹורִדֵנִי אָרֶץ:

4 Though you ascend *as* high as the eagle,
And though you set your nest among the
stars,
From there I will bring you down," says the
LORD.

4 אִם־תַּגְבִּיהַּ כַּנֶּשֶׁר
וְאִם־בֵּין כֹּוכָבִים שִׂים קִנֶּךָ
מִשָּׁם אֹורִידְךָ נְאֻם־יְהוָֹה:

5 "If thieves had come to you,
If robbers by night—
Oh, how you will be cut off!—
Would they not have stolen till they had
enough?
If grape-gatherers had come to you,
Would they not have left *some* gleanings?

5 אִם־גַּנָּבִים בָּאוּ־לְךָ
אִם־שֹׁודְדֵי לַיְלָה
אֵיךְ נִדְמֵיתָה
הֲלֹוא יִגְנְבוּ דַּיָּם
אִם־בֹּצְרִים בָּאוּ לָךְ
הֲלֹוא יַשְׁאִירוּ עֹלֵלֹות:

6 "Oh, how Esau shall be searched out!
How his hidden treasures shall be sought
after!

6 אֵיךְ נֶחְפְּשׂוּ עֵשָׂו
נִבְעוּ מַצְפֻּנָיו:

7 All the men in your confederacy
Shall force you to the border;
The men at peace with you
Shall deceive you *and* prevail against you.
Those who eat your bread shall lay a trap for
you.
No one is aware of it.

7 עַד־הַגְּבוּל שִׁלְּחוּךָ
כֹּל אַנְשֵׁי בְרִיתֶךָ
הִשִּׁיאוּךָ יָכְלוּ לְךָ
אַנְשֵׁי שְׁלֹמֶךָ
לַחְמְךָ יָשִׂימוּ מָזֹור תַּחְתֶּיךָ
אֵין תְּבוּנָה בֹּו:

8 "Will I not in that day," says the LORD,
"Even destroy the wise *men* from Edom,
And understanding from the mountains of
Esau?

8 הֲלֹוא בַּיֹּום הַהוּא נְאֻם יְהוָֹה
וְהַאֲבַדְתִּי חֲכָמִים מֵאֱדֹום
וּתְבוּנָה מֵהַר עֵשָׂו:

9 Then your mighty men, O Teman, shall be
dismayed,
To the end that everyone from the mountains
of Esau

9 וְחַתּוּ גִבֹּורֶיךָ תֵּימָן

May be cut off by slaughter.

10 "For violence against your brother Jacob,
Shame shall cover you,
And you shall be cut off forever.

11 In the day that you stood on the other side—
In the day that strangers carried captive his
forces,
When foreigners entered his gates
And cast lots for Jerusalem—
Even you *were* as one of them.

12 "But you should not have gazed on the day of
your brother
In the day of his captivity;
Nor should you have rejoiced over the
children of Judah
In the day of their destruction;
Nor should you have spoken proudly
In the day of distress.

13 You should not have entered the gate of My
people
In the day of their calamity.
Indeed, you should not have gazed on their
affliction
In the day of their calamity,
Nor laid *hands* on their substance
In the day of their calamity.

14 You should not have stood at the crossroads
To cut off those among them who escaped;
Nor should you have delivered up those
among them who remained
In the day of distress.

15 "For the day of the LORD upon all the nations
is near;
As you have done, it shall be done to you;
Your reprisal shall return upon your own
head.

16 For as you drank on My holy mountain,
So shall all the nations drink continually;
Yes, they shall drink, and swallow,
And they shall be as though they had never
been.

17 "But on Mount Zion there shall be
deliverance,
And there shall be holiness;
The house of Jacob shall possess their
possessions.

18 The house of Jacob shall be a fire,
And the house of Joseph a flame;
But the house of Esau *shall be* stubble;
They shall kindle them and devour them,
And no survivor shall *remain* of the house of
Esau,"

לְמַעַן יִכָּרֶת־אִישׁ
מֵהַר עֵשָׂו מִקָּטֶל׃

10 מֵחֲמַס אָחִיךָ יַעֲקֹב
תְּכַסְּךָ בוּשָׁה
וְנִכְרַתָּ לְעוֹלָם׃

11 בְּיוֹם עֲמָדְךָ מִנֶּגֶד
בְּיוֹם שְׁבוֹת זָרִים חֵילוֹ
וְנָכְרִים בָּאוּ שְׁעָרָו
וְעַל־יְרוּשָׁלַ͏ִם יַדּוּ גוֹרָל
גַּם־אַתָּה כְּאַחַד מֵהֶם׃

12 וְאַל־תֵּרֶא בְיוֹם־אָחִיךָ
בְּיוֹם נָכְרוֹ
וְאַל־תִּשְׂמַח לִבְנֵי־יְהוּדָה
בְּיוֹם אָבְדָם
וְאַל־תַּגְדֵּל פִּיךָ
בְּיוֹם צָרָה׃

13 אַל־תָּבוֹא בְשַׁעַר־עַמִּי
בְּיוֹם אֵידָם
אַל־תֵּרֶא גַם־אַתָּה בְּרָעָתוֹ
בְּיוֹם אֵידוֹ
וְאַל־תִּשְׁלַחְנָה בְחֵילוֹ
בְּיוֹם אֵידוֹ׃

14 וְאַל־תַּעֲמֹד עַל־הַפֶּרֶק
לְהַכְרִית אֶת־פְּלִיטָיו
וְאַל־תַּסְגֵּר שְׂרִידָיו בְּיוֹם צָרָה׃

15 כִּי־קָרוֹב יוֹם־יְהוָה
עַל־כָּל־הַגּוֹיִם
כַּאֲשֶׁר עָשִׂיתָ יֵעָשֶׂה לָּךְ
גְּמֻלְךָ יָשׁוּב בְּרֹאשֶׁךָ׃

16 כִּי כַּאֲשֶׁר שְׁתִיתֶם עַל־הַר קָדְשִׁי
יִשְׁתּוּ כָל־הַגּוֹיִם תָּמִיד
וְשָׁתוּ וְלָעוּ
וְהָיוּ כְּלוֹא הָיוּ׃

17 וּבְהַר צִיּוֹן תִּהְיֶה פְלֵיטָה
וְהָיָה קֹדֶשׁ
וְיָרְשׁוּ בֵּית יַעֲקֹב אֵת מוֹרָשֵׁיהֶם׃

18 וְהָיָה בֵית־יַעֲקֹב אֵשׁ
וּבֵית יוֹסֵף לֶהָבָה
וּבֵית עֵשָׂו לְקַשׁ
וְדָלְקוּ בָהֶם וַאֲכָלוּם

For the LORD has spoken.

19 The South shall possess the mountains of
   Esau,
   And the Lowland shall possess Philistia.
   They shall possess the fields of Ephraim
   And the fields of Samaria.
   Benjamin *shall possess* Gilead.

20 And the captives of this host of the children
   of Israel
   Shall possess the land of the Canaanites
   As far as Zarephath.
   The captives of Jerusalem who are in
   Sepharad
   Shall possess the cities of the South.

21 Then saviors shall come to Mount Zion
   To judge the mountains of Esau,
   And the kingdom shall be the LORD's.

וְלֹא־יִהְיֶה שָׂרִיד לְבֵית עֵשָׂו
כִּי יְהוָה דִּבֵּר:
19 וְיָרְשׁוּ הַנֶּגֶב אֶת־הַר עֵשָׂו
וְהַשְּׁפֵלָה אֶת־פְּלִשְׁתִּים
וְיָרְשׁוּ אֶת־שְׂדֵה אֶפְרַיִם
וְאֵת שְׂדֵה שֹׁמְרוֹן
וּבִנְיָמִן אֶת־הַגִּלְעָד:
20 וְגָלֻת הַחֵל־הַזֶּה לִבְנֵי יִשְׂרָאֵל
אֲשֶׁר־כְּנַעֲנִים עַד־צָרְפַת
וְגָלֻת יְרוּשָׁלַ͏ִם אֲשֶׁר בִּסְפָרַד
יָרְשׁוּ אֵת עָרֵי הַנֶּגֶב:
21 וְעָלוּ מוֹשִׁעִים בְּהַר צִיּוֹן
לִשְׁפֹּט אֶת־הַר עֵשָׂו
וְהָיְתָה לַיהוָה הַמְּלוּכָה:

The Book of
JONAH

1 Now the word of the LORD came to Jonah the son of Amittai, saying, 2 "Arise, go to Nineveh, that great city, and cry out against it; for their wickedness has come up before Me." 3 But Jonah arose to flee to Tarshish from the presence of the LORD. He went down to Joppa, and found a ship going to Tarshish; so he paid the fare, and went down into it, to go with them to Tarshish from the presence of the LORD.

4 But the LORD sent out a great wind on the sea, and there was a mighty tempest on the sea, so that the ship was about to be broken up.

5 Then the mariners were afraid; and every man cried out to his god, and threw the cargo that *was* in the ship into the sea, to lighten the load. But Jonah had gone down into the lowest parts of the ship, had lain down, and was fast asleep.

6 So the captain came to him, and said to him, "What do you mean, sleeper? Arise, call on your God; perhaps your God will consider us, so that we may not perish."

7 And they said to one another, "Come, let us cast lots, that we may know for whose cause this trouble *has come* upon us." So they cast lots, and the lot fell on Jonah. 8 Then they said to him, "Please tell us! For whose cause *is* this trouble upon us? What is your occupation? And where do you come from? What is your country? And of what people are you?"

9 So he said to them, "I *am* a Hebrew; and I fear the LORD, the God of heaven, who made the sea and the dry *land*."

10 Then the men were exceedingly afraid, and said to him, "Why have you done this?" For the men knew that he fled from the presence of the LORD, because he had told them. 11 Then they said to him, "What shall we do to you that the sea may be calm for us?"—for the sea was growing more tempestuous.

12 And he said to them, "Pick me up and throw me into the sea; then the sea will become calm for you. For I know that this great tempest *is* because of me."

13 Nevertheless the men rowed hard to return to land, but they could not, for the sea continued to grow more tempestuous against them. 14 Therefore they cried out to the LORD and said, "We pray, O

א וַיְהִי דְּבַר־יְהֹוָה אֶל־יוֹנָה בֶן־אֲמִתַּי לֵאמֹר:
2 קוּם לֵךְ אֶל־נִינְוֵה הָעִיר הַגְּדוֹלָה וּקְרָא עָלֶיהָ כִּי־
עָלְתָה רָעָתָם לְפָנָי: 3 וַיָּקָם יוֹנָה לִבְרֹחַ תַּרְשִׁישָׁה
מִלִּפְנֵי יְהֹוָה וַיֵּרֶד יָפוֹ וַיִּמְצָא אֳנִיָּה | בָּאָה
תַרְשִׁישׁ וַיִּתֵּן שְׂכָרָהּ וַיֵּרֶד בָּהּ לָבוֹא עִמָּהֶם
תַּרְשִׁישָׁה מִלִּפְנֵי יְהֹוָה: 4 וַיהֹוָה הֵטִיל רוּחַ־גְּדוֹלָה
אֶל־הַיָּם וַיְהִי סַעַר־גָּדוֹל בַּיָּם וְהָאֳנִיָּה חִשְּׁבָה
לְהִשָּׁבֵר: 5 וַיִּירְאוּ הַמַּלָּחִים וַיִּזְעֲקוּ אִישׁ אֶל־אֱלֹהָיו
וַיָּטִלוּ אֶת־הַכֵּלִים אֲשֶׁר בָּאֳנִיָּה אֶל־הַיָּם לְהָקֵל
מֵעֲלֵיהֶם וְיוֹנָה יָרַד אֶל־יַרְכְּתֵי הַסְּפִינָה וַיִּשְׁכַּב
וַיֵּרָדַם: 6 וַיִּקְרַב אֵלָיו רַב הַחֹבֵל וַיֹּאמֶר לוֹ מַה־
לְּךָ נִרְדָּם קוּם קְרָא אֶל־אֱלֹהֶיךָ אוּלַי יִתְעַשֵּׁת
הָאֱלֹהִים לָנוּ וְלֹא נֹאבֵד: 7 וַיֹּאמְרוּ אִישׁ אֶל־רֵעֵהוּ
לְכוּ וְנַפִּילָה גוֹרָלוֹת וְנֵדְעָה בְּשֶׁלְּמִי הָרָעָה הַזֹּאת
לָנוּ וַיַּפִּלוּ גּוֹרָלוֹת וַיִּפֹּל הַגּוֹרָל עַל־יוֹנָה: 8 וַיֹּאמְרוּ
אֵלָיו הַגִּידָה־נָּא לָנוּ בַּאֲשֶׁר לְמִי־הָרָעָה הַזֹּאת לָנוּ
מַה־מְּלַאכְתְּךָ וּמֵאַיִן תָּבוֹא מָה אַרְצֶךָ וְאֵי־מִזֶּה
עַם אָתָּה: 9 וַיֹּאמֶר אֲלֵיהֶם עִבְרִי אָנֹכִי וְאֶת־יְהֹוָה
אֱלֹהֵי הַשָּׁמַיִם אֲנִי יָרֵא אֲשֶׁר־עָשָׂה אֶת־הַיָּם וְאֶת־
הַיַּבָּשָׁה: 10 וַיִּירְאוּ הָאֲנָשִׁים יִרְאָה גְדוֹלָה וַיֹּאמְרוּ
אֵלָיו מַה־זֹּאת עָשִׂיתָ כִּי־יָדְעוּ הָאֲנָשִׁים כִּי־מִלִּפְנֵי
יְהֹוָה הוּא בֹרֵחַ כִּי הִגִּיד לָהֶם: 11 וַיֹּאמְרוּ אֵלָיו
מַה־נַּעֲשֶׂה לָּךְ וְיִשְׁתֹּק הַיָּם מֵעָלֵינוּ כִּי הַיָּם הוֹלֵךְ
וְסֹעֵר: 12 וַיֹּאמֶר אֲלֵיהֶם שָׂאוּנִי וַהֲטִילֻנִי אֶל־הַיָּם
וְיִשְׁתֹּק הַיָּם מֵעֲלֵיכֶם כִּי יוֹדֵעַ אָנִי כִּי בְשֶׁלִּי
הַסַּעַר הַגָּדוֹל הַזֶּה עֲלֵיכֶם: 13 וַיַּחְתְּרוּ הָאֲנָשִׁים
לְהָשִׁיב אֶל־הַיַּבָּשָׁה וְלֹא יָכֹלוּ כִּי הַיָּם הוֹלֵךְ וְסֹעֵר
עֲלֵיהֶם: 14 וַיִּקְרְאוּ אֶל־יְהֹוָה וַיֹּאמְרוּ אָנָּה יְהֹוָה
אַל־נָא נֹאבְדָה בְּנֶפֶשׁ הָאִישׁ הַזֶּה וְאַל־תִּתֵּן עָלֵינוּ
דָּם נָקִיא כִּי־אַתָּה יְהֹוָה כַּאֲשֶׁר חָפַצְתָּ עָשִׂיתָ:

LORD, please do not let us perish for this man's life, and do not charge us with innocent blood; for You, O LORD, have done as it pleased You." ¹⁵So they picked up Jonah and threw him into the sea, and the sea ceased from its raging. ¹⁶Then the men feared the LORD exceedingly, and offered a sacrifice to the LORD and took vows.

¹⁷Now the LORD had prepared a great fish to swallow Jonah. And Jonah was in the belly of the fish three days and three nights.

2 Then Jonah prayed to the LORD his God from the fish's belly. ²And he said:

"I cried out to the LORD because of my
    affliction,
And He answered me.

"Out of the belly of Sheol I cried,
And You heard my voice.
³ For You cast me into the deep,
Into the heart of the seas,
And the floods surrounded me;
All Your billows and Your waves passed
    over me.
⁴ Then I said, 'I have been cast out of Your
    sight;
Yet I will look again toward Your holy
    temple.'
⁵ The waters surrounded me, *even* to my soul;
The deep closed around me;
Weeds were wrapped around my head.
⁶ I went down to the moorings of the
    mountains;
The earth with its bars *closed* behind me
    forever;
Yet You have brought up my life from the
    pit,
O LORD, my God.
⁷ "When my soul fainted within me,
I remembered the LORD;
And my prayer went *up* to You,
Into Your holy temple.
⁸ "Those who regard worthless idols
Forsake their own Mercy.
⁹ But I will sacrifice to You
With the voice of thanksgiving;
I will pay what I have vowed.
Salvation *is* of the LORD."

¹⁰So the LORD spoke to the fish, and it vomited Jonah onto dry *land.*

15 וַיִּשְׂאוּ֙ אֶת־יוֹנָ֔ה וַיְטִלֻ֖הוּ אֶל־הַיָּ֑ם וַיַּעֲמֹ֥ד הַיָּ֖ם מִזַּעְפּֽוֹ: 16 וַיִּֽירְא֧וּ הָאֲנָשִׁ֛ים יִרְאָ֥ה גְדוֹלָ֖ה אֶת־יְהוָ֑ה וַיִּזְבְּחוּ־זֶ֙בַח֙ לַֽיהוָ֔ה וַיִּדְּר֖וּ נְדָרִֽים:

ב וַיְמַ֤ן יְהוָה֙ דָּ֣ג גָּד֔וֹל לִבְלֹ֖עַ אֶת־יוֹנָ֑ה וַיְהִ֤י יוֹנָה֙ בִּמְעֵ֣י הַדָּ֔ג שְׁלֹשָׁ֥ה יָמִ֖ים וּשְׁלֹשָׁ֥ה לֵילֽוֹת: 2 וַיִּתְפַּלֵּ֣ל יוֹנָ֔ה אֶל־יְהוָ֖ה אֱלֹהָ֑יו מִמְּעֵ֖י הַדָּגָֽה:

3 וַיֹּ֗אמֶר קָרָ֠אתִי מִצָּ֥רָה לִ֛י
אֶל־יְהוָ֖ה וַֽיַּעֲנֵ֑נִי
מִבֶּ֧טֶן שְׁא֛וֹל שִׁוַּ֖עְתִּי שָׁמַ֥עְתָּ קוֹלִֽי:
4 וַתַּשְׁלִיכֵ֤נִי מְצוּלָה֙ בִּלְבַ֣ב יַמִּ֔ים
וְנָהָ֖ר יְסֹבְבֵ֑נִי
כָּל־מִשְׁבָּרֶ֥יךָ וְגַלֶּ֖יךָ עָלַ֥י עָבָֽרוּ:
5 וַאֲנִ֣י אָמַ֔רְתִּי נִגְרַ֖שְׁתִּי מִנֶּ֣גֶד עֵינֶ֑יךָ
אַ֚ךְ אוֹסִ֣יף לְהַבִּ֔יט
אֶל־הֵיכַ֥ל קָדְשֶֽׁךָ:
6 אֲפָפ֤וּנִי מַ֙יִם֙ עַד־נֶ֔פֶשׁ
תְּה֖וֹם יְסֹבְבֵ֑נִי
ס֖וּף חָב֥וּשׁ לְרֹאשִֽׁי:
7 לְקִצְבֵ֤י הָרִים֙ יָרַ֔דְתִּי
הָאָ֛רֶץ בְּרִחֶ֥יהָ בַעֲדִ֖י לְעוֹלָ֑ם
וַתַּ֧עַל מִשַּׁ֛חַת חַיַּ֖י יְהוָ֥ה אֱלֹהָֽי:
8 בְּהִתְעַטֵּ֤ף עָלַי֙ נַפְשִׁ֔י
אֶת־יְהוָ֖ה זָכָ֑רְתִּי
וַתָּב֤וֹא אֵלֶ֙יךָ֙ תְּפִלָּתִ֔י
אֶל־הֵיכַ֖ל קָדְשֶֽׁךָ:
9 מְשַׁמְּרִ֖ים הַבְלֵי־שָׁ֑וְא חַסְדָּ֖ם יַעֲזֹֽבוּ:
10 וַאֲנִ֗י בְּק֤וֹל תּוֹדָה֙ אֶזְבְּחָה־לָּ֔ךְ
אֲשֶׁ֥ר נָדַ֖רְתִּי אֲשַׁלֵּ֑מָה
יְשׁוּעָ֖תָה לַיהוָֽה: ס

11 וַיֹּ֥אמֶר יְהוָ֖ה לַדָּ֑ג וַיָּקֵ֥א אֶת־יוֹנָ֖ה אֶל־הַיַּבָּשָֽׁה: פ

3 Now the word of the LORD came to Jonah the second time, saying, [2] "Arise, go to Nineveh, that great city, and preach to it the message that I tell you." [3] So Jonah arose and went to Nineveh, according to the word of the LORD. Now Nineveh was an exceedingly great city, a three-day journey *in extent.* [4] And Jonah began to enter the city on the first day's walk. Then he cried out and said, "Yet forty days, and Nineveh shall be overthrown!"

[5] So the people of Nineveh believed God, proclaimed a fast, and put on sackcloth, from the greatest to the least of them. [6] Then word came to the king of Nineveh; and he arose from his throne and laid aside his robe, covered *himself* with sackcloth and sat in ashes. [7] And he caused *it* to be proclaimed and published throughout Nineveh by the decree of the king and his nobles, saying,

Let neither man nor beast, herd nor flock, taste anything; do not let them eat, or drink water. [8] But let man and beast be covered with sackcloth, and cry mightily to God; yes, let every one turn from his evil way and from the violence that is in his hands. [9] Who can tell *if* God will turn and relent, and turn away from His fierce anger, so that we may not perish?

[10] Then God saw their works, that they turned from their evil way; and God relented from the disaster that He had said He would bring upon them, and He did not do it.

4 But it displeased Jonah exceedingly, and he became angry. [2] So he prayed to the LORD, and said, "Ah, LORD, was not this what I said when I was still in my country? Therefore I fled previously to Tarshish; for I know that You *are* a gracious and merciful God, slow to anger and abundant in lovingkindness, One who relents from doing harm. [3] Therefore now, O LORD, please take my life from me, for *it is* better for me to die than to live!"

[4] Then the LORD said, "*Is it* right for you to be angry?"

[5] So Jonah went out of the city and sat on the east side of the city. There he made himself a shelter and sat under it in the shade, till he might see what would become of the city. [6] And the LORD God prepared a plant and made it come up over Jonah, that it might be shade for his head to deliver him from his misery. So Jonah was very grateful for the plant. [7] But as morning dawned the next day God prepared a worm, and it *so* damaged the plant that it withered. [8] And it happened, when the sun arose, that God prepared a vehement east wind; and the

ג וַיְהִי דְבַר־יְהֹוָה אֶל־יוֹנָה שֵׁנִית לֵאמֹר: 2 קוּם לֵךְ אֶל־נִינְוֵה הָעִיר הַגְּדוֹלָה וּקְרָא אֵלֶיהָ אֶת־הַקְּרִיאָה אֲשֶׁר אָנֹכִי דֹּבֵר אֵלֶיךָ: 3 וַיָּקָם יוֹנָה וַיֵּלֶךְ אֶל־נִינְוֵה כִּדְבַר יְהֹוָה וְנִינְוֵה הָיְתָה עִיר־גְּדוֹלָה לֵאלֹהִים מַהֲלַךְ שְׁלֹשֶׁת יָמִים: 4 וַיָּחֶל יוֹנָה לָבוֹא בָעִיר מַהֲלַךְ יוֹם אֶחָד וַיִּקְרָא וַיֹּאמַר עוֹד אַרְבָּעִים יוֹם וְנִינְוֵה נֶהְפָּכֶת: 5 וַיַּאֲמִינוּ אַנְשֵׁי נִינְוֵה בֵּאלֹהִים וַיִּקְרְאוּ־צוֹם וַיִּלְבְּשׁוּ שַׂקִּים מִגְּדוֹלָם וְעַד־קְטַנָּם: 6 וַיִּגַּע הַדָּבָר אֶל־מֶלֶךְ נִינְוֵה וַיָּקָם מִכִּסְאוֹ וַיַּעֲבֵר אַדַּרְתּוֹ מֵעָלָיו וַיְכַס שַׂק וַיֵּשֶׁב עַל־הָאֵפֶר:

7 וַיַּזְעֵק וַיֹּאמֶר בְּנִינְוֵה מִטַּעַם הַמֶּלֶךְ וּגְדֹלָיו לֵאמֹר הָאָדָם וְהַבְּהֵמָה הַבָּקָר וְהַצֹּאן אַל־יִטְעֲמוּ מְאוּמָה אַל־יִרְעוּ וּמַיִם אַל־יִשְׁתּוּ: 8 וְיִתְכַּסּוּ שַׂקִּים הָאָדָם וְהַבְּהֵמָה וְיִקְרְאוּ אֶל־אֱלֹהִים בְּחָזְקָה וְיָשֻׁבוּ אִישׁ מִדַּרְכּוֹ הָרָעָה וּמִן־הֶחָמָס אֲשֶׁר בְּכַפֵּיהֶם: 9 מִי־יוֹדֵעַ יָשׁוּב וְנִחַם הָאֱלֹהִים וְשָׁב מֵחֲרוֹן אַפּוֹ וְלֹא נֹאבֵד: 10 וַיַּרְא הָאֱלֹהִים אֶת־מַעֲשֵׂיהֶם כִּי־שָׁבוּ מִדַּרְכָּם הָרָעָה וַיִּנָּחֶם הָאֱלֹהִים עַל־הָרָעָה אֲשֶׁר־דִּבֶּר לַעֲשׂוֹת־לָהֶם וְלֹא עָשָׂה:

ד וַיֵּרַע אֶל־יוֹנָה רָעָה גְדוֹלָה וַיִּחַר לוֹ: 2 וַיִּתְפַּלֵּל אֶל־יְהֹוָה וַיֹּאמַר אָנָּה יְהֹוָה הֲלוֹא־זֶה דְבָרִי עַד־הֱיוֹתִי עַל־אַדְמָתִי עַל־כֵּן קִדַּמְתִּי לִבְרֹחַ תַּרְשִׁישָׁה כִּי יָדַעְתִּי כִּי אַתָּה אֵל־חַנּוּן וְרַחוּם אֶרֶךְ אַפַּיִם וְרַב־חֶסֶד וְנִחָם עַל־הָרָעָה: 3 וְעַתָּה יְהֹוָה קַח־נָא אֶת־נַפְשִׁי מִמֶּנִּי כִּי טוֹב מוֹתִי מֵחַיָּי: 4 וַיֹּאמֶר יְהֹוָה הַהֵיטֵב חָרָה לָךְ: ס

5 וַיֵּצֵא יוֹנָה מִן־הָעִיר וַיֵּשֶׁב מִקֶּדֶם לָעִיר וַיַּעַשׂ לוֹ שָׁם סֻכָּה וַיֵּשֶׁב תַּחְתֶּיהָ בַּצֵּל עַד אֲשֶׁר יִרְאֶה מַה־יִּהְיֶה בָּעִיר: 6 וַיְמַן יְהֹוָה־אֱלֹהִים קִיקָיוֹן וַיַּעַל מֵעַל לְיוֹנָה לִהְיוֹת צֵל עַל־רֹאשׁוֹ לְהַצִּיל לוֹ מֵרָעָתוֹ וַיִּשְׂמַח יוֹנָה עַל־הַקִּיקָיוֹן שִׂמְחָה גְדוֹלָה: 7 וַיְמַן הָאֱלֹהִים תּוֹלַעַת בַּעֲלוֹת הַשַּׁחַר לַמָּחֳרָת וַתַּךְ אֶת־הַקִּיקָיוֹן וַיִּיבָשׁ: 8 וַיְהִי כִּזְרֹחַ הַשֶּׁמֶשׁ וַיְמַן אֱלֹהִים רוּחַ קָדִים חֲרִישִׁית וַתַּךְ הַשֶּׁמֶשׁ עַל־רֹאשׁ

sun beat on Jonah's head, so that he grew faint.
Then he wished death for himself, and said, "*It is*
better for me to die than to live."

⁹ Then God said to Jonah, "*Is it* right for you to
be angry about the plant?"

And he said, "*It is* right for me to be angry, even
to death!"

¹⁰ But the LORD said, "You have had pity on the
plant for which you have not labored, nor made it
grow, which came up in a night and perished in a
night. ¹¹ And should I not pity Nineveh, that great
city, in which are more than one hundred and
twenty thousand persons who cannot discern
between their right hand and their left—and much
livestock?"

יוֹנָה וַיִּתְעַלָּף וַיִּשְׁאַל אֶת־נַפְשׁוֹ לָמוּת וַיֹּאמֶר טוֹב
מוֹתִי מֵחַיָּי: 9 וַיֹּאמֶר אֱלֹהִים אֶל־יוֹנָה הַהֵיטֵב
חָרָה־לְךָ עַל־הַקִּיקָיוֹן וַיֹּאמֶר הֵיטֵב חָרָה־לִי עַד־
מָוֶת: 10 וַיֹּאמֶר יְהוָה אַתָּה חַסְתָּ עַל־הַקִּיקָיוֹן אֲשֶׁר
לֹא־עָמַלְתָּ בּוֹ וְלֹא גִדַּלְתּוֹ שֶׁבִּן־לַיְלָה הָיָה וּבִן־
לַיְלָה אָבָד: 11 וַאֲנִי לֹא אָחוּס עַל־נִינְוֵה הָעִיר
הַגְּדוֹלָה אֲשֶׁר יֶשׁ־בָּהּ הַרְבֵּה מִשְׁתֵּים־עֶשְׂרֵה רִבּוֹ
אָדָם אֲשֶׁר לֹא־יָדַע בֵּין־יְמִינוֹ לִשְׂמֹאלוֹ וּבְהֵמָה
רַבָּה:

The Book of

MICAH

מיכה

א דְּבַר־יְהוָה ׀ אֲשֶׁר הָיָה אֶל־מִיכָה הַמֹּרַשְׁתִּי
בִּימֵי יוֹתָם אָחָז יְחִזְקִיָּה מַלְכֵי יְהוּדָה אֲשֶׁר־חָזָה
עַל־שֹׁמְרוֹן וִירוּשָׁלָ͏ִם:

1 The word of the LORD that came to Micah of Moresheth in the days of Jotham, Ahaz, *and* Hezekiah, kings of Judah, which he saw concerning Samaria and Jerusalem.

2 שִׁמְעוּ עַמִּים כֻּלָּם
הַקְשִׁיבִי אֶרֶץ וּמְלֹאָהּ
וִיהִי אֲדֹנָי יְהוִה בָּכֶם לְעֵד
אֲדֹנָי מֵהֵיכַל קָדְשׁוֹ:

2 Hear, all you peoples!
Listen, O earth, and all that is in it!
Let the Lord GOD be a witness against you,
The Lord from His holy temple.

3 כִּי־הִנֵּה יְהוָה יֹצֵא מִמְּקוֹמוֹ
וְיָרַד וְדָרַךְ עַל־בָּמֳותֵי אָרֶץ:

3 For behold, the LORD is coming out of His place;
He will come down
And tread on the high places of the earth.

4 וְנָמַסּוּ הֶהָרִים תַּחְתָּיו וְהָעֲמָקִים יִתְבַּקָּעוּ
כַּדּוֹנַג מִפְּנֵי הָאֵשׁ כְּמַיִם מֻגָּרִים בְּמוֹרָד:

4 The mountains will melt under Him,
And the valleys will split
Like wax before the fire,
Like waters poured down a steep place.

5 בְּפֶשַׁע יַעֲקֹב כָּל־זֹאת
וּבְחַטֹּאות בֵּית יִשְׂרָאֵל
מִי־פֶשַׁע יַעֲקֹב הֲלוֹא שֹׁמְרוֹן
וּמִי בָּמוֹת יְהוּדָה הֲלוֹא יְרוּשָׁלָ͏ִם:

5 All this is for the transgression of Jacob
And for the sins of the house of Israel.
What *is* the transgression of Jacob?
Is it not Samaria?
And what *are* the high places of Judah?
Are they not Jerusalem?

6 וְשַׂמְתִּי שֹׁמְרוֹן לְעִי הַשָּׂדֶה
לְמַטָּעֵי כָרֶם
וְהִגַּרְתִּי לַגַּי אֲבָנֶיהָ
וִיסֹדֶיהָ אֲגַלֶּה:

6 "Therefore I will make Samaria a heap of
ruins in the field,
Places for planting a vineyard;
I will pour down her stones into the valley,
And I will uncover her foundations.

7 וְכָל־פְּסִילֶיהָ יֻכַּתּוּ
וְכָל־אֶתְנַנֶּיהָ יִשָּׂרְפוּ בָאֵשׁ
וְכָל־עֲצַבֶּיהָ אָשִׂים שְׁמָמָה
כִּי מֵאֶתְנַן זוֹנָה קִבָּצָה
וְעַד־אֶתְנַן זוֹנָה יָשׁוּבוּ:

7 All her carved images shall be beaten to
pieces,
And all her pay as a harlot shall be burned
with the fire;
All her idols I will lay desolate,
For she gathered *it* from the pay of a harlot,
And they shall return to the pay of a harlot."

8 עַל־זֹאת אֶסְפְּדָה וְאֵילִילָה
אֵילְכָה שילַל וְעָרוֹם
אֶעֱשֶׂה מִסְפֵּד כַּתַּנִּים
וְאֵבֶל כִּבְנוֹת יַעֲנָה:

8 Therefore I will wail and howl,
I will go stripped and naked;
I will make a wailing like the jackals
And a mourning like the ostriches,

9 כִּי אֲנוּשָׁה מַכּוֹתֶיהָ
כִּי־בָאָה עַד־יְהוּדָה
נָגַע עַד־שַׁעַר עַמִּי עַד־יְרוּשָׁלָ͏ִם:

9 For her wounds *are* incurable.
For it has come to Judah;
It has come to the gate of My people—
To Jerusalem.

10 בְּגַת אַל־תַּגִּידוּ בָּכוֹ אַל־תִּבְכּוּ
בְּבֵית לְעַפְרָה עָפָר התפלשתי:

10 Tell *it* not in Gath,
Weep not at all;
In Beth Aphrah

א 3 בָּמֳתֵי 8 שׁולָל 10 הִתְפַּלָּשִׁי

Roll yourself in the dust.

11 Pass by in naked shame, you inhabitant of
  Shaphir;
  The inhabitant of Zaanan does not go out.
  Beth Ezel mourns;
  Its place to stand is taken away from you.

12 For the inhabitant of Maroth pined for
  good,
  But disaster came down from the LORD
  To the gate of Jerusalem.

13 O inhabitant of Lachish,
  Harness the chariot to the swift steeds
  (She *was* the beginning of sin to the daughter
  of Zion),
  For the transgressions of Israel were found in
  you.

14 Therefore you shall give presents to
  Moresheth Gath;
  The houses of Achzib *shall be* a lie to the
  kings of Israel.

15 I will yet bring an heir to you, O inhabitant
  of Mareshah;
  The glory of Israel shall come to Adullam.

16 Make yourself bald and cut off your hair,
  Because of your precious children;
  Enlarge your baldness like an eagle,
  For they shall go from you into captivity.

2 Woe to those who devise iniquity,
  And work out evil on their beds!
  At morning light they practice it,
  Because it is in the power of their hand.

2 They covet fields and take *them* by violence,
  Also houses, and seize *them*.
  So they oppress a man and his house,
  A man and his inheritance.

3 Therefore thus says the LORD:

  "Behold, against this family I am devising
  disaster,
  From which you cannot remove your necks;
  Nor shall you walk haughtily,
  For this *is* an evil time.

4 In that day *one* shall take up a proverb
  against you,
  And lament with a bitter lamentation,
  saying:
  'We are utterly destroyed!
  He has changed the heritage of my people;
  How He has removed *it* from me!
  To a turncoat He has divided our fields.' "

5 Therefore you will have no one to determine
  boundaries by lot

עִבְרִי לָכֶם יוֹשֶׁבֶת שָׁפִיר 11
עֶרְיָה־בֹשֶׁת
לֹא יָצְאָה יוֹשֶׁבֶת צַאֲנָן
מִסְפַּד בֵּית הָאֵצֶל
יִקַּח מִכֶּם עֶמְדָּתוֹ:

כִּי־חָלָה לְטוֹב יוֹשֶׁבֶת מָרוֹת 12
כִּי־יָרַד רָע מֵאֵת יְהֹוָה
לְשַׁעַר יְרוּשָׁלָ͏ִם:

רְתֹם הַמֶּרְכָּבָה לָרֶכֶשׁ 13
יוֹשֶׁבֶת לָכִישׁ
רֵאשִׁית חַטָּאת הִיא לְבַת־צִיּוֹן
כִּי־בָךְ נִמְצְאוּ פִּשְׁעֵי יִשְׂרָאֵל:

לָכֵן תִּתְּנִי שִׁלּוּחִים עַל מוֹרֶשֶׁת גַּת 14
בָּתֵּי אַכְזִיב לְאַכְזָב
לְמַלְכֵי יִשְׂרָאֵל:

עֹד הַיֹּרֵשׁ אָבִי לָךְ 15
יוֹשֶׁבֶת מָרֵשָׁה
עַד־עֲדֻלָּם יָבוֹא כְּבוֹד יִשְׂרָאֵל:

קָרְחִי וָגֹזִּי עַל־בְּנֵי תַּעֲנוּגָיִךְ 16
הַרְחִבִי קָרְחָתֵךְ כַּנֶּשֶׁר
כִּי גָלוּ מִמֵּךְ: ס

ב הוֹי חֹשְׁבֵי־אָוֶן
וּפֹעֲלֵי רָע עַל־מִשְׁכְּבוֹתָם
בְּאוֹר הַבֹּקֶר יַעֲשׂוּהָ
כִּי יֶשׁ־לְאֵל יָדָם:

וְחָמְדוּ שָׂדוֹת וְגָזָלוּ 2
וּבָתִּים וְנָשָׂאוּ
וְעָשְׁקוּ גֶּבֶר וּבֵיתוֹ
וְאִישׁ וְנַחֲלָתוֹ:

לָכֵן כֹּה אָמַר יְהֹוָה 3
הִנְנִי חֹשֵׁב עַל־הַמִּשְׁפָּחָה הַזֹּאת רָעָה
אֲשֶׁר לֹא־תָמִישׁוּ מִשָּׁם צַוְּארֹתֵיכֶם
וְלֹא תֵלְכוּ רוֹמָה כִּי עֵת רָעָה הִיא:

בַּיּוֹם הַהוּא יִשָּׂא עֲלֵיכֶם מָשָׁל 4
וְנָהָה נְהִי נִהְיָה
אָמַר שָׁדוֹד נְשַׁדֻּנוּ
חֵלֶק עַמִּי יָמִיר
אֵיךְ יָמִישׁ לִי
לְשׁוֹבֵב שָׂדֵינוּ יְחַלֵּק:

לָכֵן לֹא־יִהְיֶה לְךָ 5

In the assembly of the LORD.

מַשְׁלֵ֣יךְ חֶ֑בֶל בְּגוֹרָ֖ל
בִּקְהַ֥ל יְהוָֽה:

6 "Do not prattle," *you say to those* who
    prophesy.
  So they shall not prophesy to you;
  They shall not return insult for insult.

6 אַל־תַּטִּ֖פוּ יַטִּיפ֑וּן
  לֹֽא־יַטִּ֣פוּ לָאֵ֔לֶּה
  לֹ֥א יִסַּ֖ג כְּלִמּֽוֹת:

7 *You who are* named the house of Jacob:
  "Is the Spirit of the LORD restricted?
  Are these His doings?
  Do not My words do good
  To him who walks uprightly?

7 הֶאָמ֣וּר בֵּֽית־יַעֲקֹ֗ב
  הֲקָצַר֙ ר֣וּחַ יְהוָ֔ה
  אִם־אֵ֖לֶּה מַעֲלָלָ֑יו
  הֲל֤וֹא דְבָרַי֙ יֵיטִ֔יבוּ עִ֖ם הַיָּשָׁ֥ר הוֹלֵֽךְ:

8 "Lately My people have risen up as an
    enemy—
  You pull off the robe with the garment
  From those who trust *you,* as they pass by,
  Like men returned from war.

8 וְאֶתְמ֗וּל עַמִּי֙ לְאוֹיֵ֣ב יְקוֹמֵ֔ם
  מִמּ֣וּל שַׂלְמָ֔ה אֶ֖דֶר תַּפְשִׁט֑וּן
  מֵעֹבְרִ֣ים בֶּ֔טַח שׁוּבֵ֖י מִלְחָמָֽה:

9 The women of My people you cast out
  From their pleasant houses;
  From their children
  You have taken away My glory forever.

9 נְשֵׁ֤י עַמִּי֙ תְּגָ֣רְשׁ֔וּן מִבֵּ֖ית תַּֽעֲנֻגֶ֑יהָ
  מֵעַל֙ עֹֽלָלֶ֔יהָ תִּקְח֥וּ הֲדָרִ֖י לְעוֹלָֽם:

10 "Arise and depart,
  For this *is* not *your* rest;
  Because it is defiled, it shall destroy,
  Yes, with utter destruction.

10 ק֣וּמוּ וּלְכ֔וּ כִּ֥י לֹא־זֹ֖את הַמְּנוּחָ֑ה
  בַּעֲב֥וּר טָמְאָ֛ה
  תְּחַבֵּ֖ל וְחֶ֥בֶל נִמְרָֽץ:

11 If a man should walk in a false spirit
  And speak a lie, *saying,*
  'I will prophesy to you of wine and drink,'
  Even he would be the prattler of this people.

11 לוּ־אִ֞ישׁ הֹלֵ֥ךְ ר֙וּחַ֙ וָשֶׁ֣קֶר כִּזֵּ֔ב
  אַטִּ֣ף לְךָ֔ לַיַּ֖יִן וְלַשֵּׁכָ֑ר
  וְהָיָ֥ה מַטִּ֖יף הָעָ֥ם הַזֶּֽה:

12 "I will surely assemble all of you, O Jacob,
  I will surely gather the remnant of Israel;
  I will put them together like sheep of the
    fold,
  Like a flock in the midst of their pasture;
  They shall make a loud noise because of *so*
    many people.

12 אָסֹ֨ף אֶאֱסֹ֤ף יַעֲקֹב֙ כֻּלָּ֔ךְ
  קַבֵּ֥ץ אֲקַבֵּ֖ץ שְׁאֵרִ֣ית יִשְׂרָאֵ֑ל
  יַ֣חַד אֲשִׂימֶ֔נּוּ כְּצֹ֖אן בָּצְרָ֑ה
  כְּעֵ֙דֶר֙ בְּת֣וֹךְ הַדָּֽבְר֔וֹ
  תְּהִימֶ֖נָה מֵאָדָֽם:

13 The one who breaks open will come up
    before them;
  They will break out,
  Pass through the gate,
  And go out by it;
  Their king will pass before them,
  With the LORD at their head."

13 עָלָ֤ה הַפֹּרֵץ֙ לִפְנֵיהֶ֔ם
  פָּֽרְצ֖וּ וַֽיַּעֲבֹ֑רוּ
  שַׁ֖עַר וַיֵּ֣צְאוּ ב֑וֹ
  וַיַּעֲבֹ֤ר מַלְכָּם֙ לִפְנֵיהֶ֔ם
  וַיהוָ֖ה בְּרֹאשָֽׁם: פ

3 And I said:

  "Hear now, O heads of Jacob,
  And you rulers of the house of Israel:
  Is it not for you to know justice?

ג וָאֹמַ֕ר
  שִׁמְעוּ־נָ֖א רָאשֵׁ֣י יַעֲקֹ֑ב
  וּקְצִינֵ֖י בֵּ֣ית יִשְׂרָאֵ֑ל
  הֲל֣וֹא לָכֶ֔ם לָדַ֖עַת אֶת־הַמִּשְׁפָּֽט:

2 You who hate good and love evil;
  Who strip the skin from My people,
  And the flesh from their bones;

2 שֹׂנְאֵ֥י ט֖וֹב וְאֹ֣הֲבֵי רָעָ֑ה
  גֹּזְלֵ֤י עוֹרָם֙ מֵֽעֲלֵיהֶ֔ם
  וּשְׁאֵרָ֖ם מֵעַ֥ל עַצְמוֹתָֽם:

3 Who also eat the flesh of My people,
  Flay their skin from them,
  Break their bones,

3 וַאֲשֶׁ֣ר אָכְלוּ֮ שְׁאֵ֣ר עַמִּי֒
  וְעוֹרָ֛ם מֵעֲלֵיהֶ֖ם הִפְשִׁ֑יטוּ

ג רָע 2

And chop *them* in pieces
Like *meat* for the pot,
Like flesh in the caldron."

4 Then they will cry to the LORD,
But He will not hear them;
He will even hide His face from them at that
time,
Because they have been evil in their deeds.

5 Thus says the LORD concerning the prophets
Who make my people stray;
Who chant "Peace"
While they chew with their teeth,
But who prepare war against him
Who puts nothing into their mouths:

6 "Therefore you shall have night without
vision,
And you shall have darkness without
divination;
The sun shall go down on the prophets,
And the day shall be dark for them.

7 So the seers shall be ashamed,
And the diviners abashed;
Indeed they shall all cover their lips;
For *there is* no answer from God."

8 But truly I am full of power by the Spirit of
the LORD,
And of justice and might,
To declare to Jacob his transgression
And to Israel his sin.

9 Now hear this,
You heads of the house of Jacob
And rulers of the house of Israel,
Who abhor justice
And pervert all equity,

10 Who build up Zion with bloodshed
And Jerusalem with iniquity:

11 Her heads judge for a bribe,
Her priests teach for pay,
And her prophets divine for money.
Yet they lean on the LORD, and say,
"Is not the LORD among us?
No harm can come upon us."

12 Therefore because of you
Zion shall be plowed *like* a field,
Jerusalem shall become heaps of ruins,
And the mountain of the temple
Like the bare hills of the forest.

4 Now it shall come to pass in the latter days
That the mountain of the LORD's house
Shall be established on the top of the
mountains,

וְאֵת־עַצְמֹתֵיהֶם פִּצֵּחוּ
וּפָרְשׂוּ כַּאֲשֶׁר בַּסִּיר
וּכְבָשָׂר בְּתוֹךְ קַלָּחַת׃

4 אָז יִזְעֲקוּ אֶל־יְהוָה
וְלֹא יַעֲנֶה אוֹתָם
וְיַסְתֵּר פָּנָיו מֵהֶם בָּעֵת הַהִיא
כַּאֲשֶׁר הֵרֵעוּ מַעַלְלֵיהֶם׃ פ

5 כֹּה אָמַר יְהוָה
עַל־הַנְּבִיאִים הַמַּתְעִים אֶת־עַמִּי
הַנֹּשְׁכִים בְּשִׁנֵּיהֶם וְקָרְאוּ שָׁלוֹם
וַאֲשֶׁר לֹא־יִתֵּן עַל־פִּיהֶם
וְקִדְּשׁוּ עָלָיו מִלְחָמָה׃

6 לָכֵן לַיְלָה לָכֶם מֵחָזוֹן
וְחָשְׁכָה לָכֶם מִקְּסֹם
וּבָאָה הַשֶּׁמֶשׁ עַל־הַנְּבִיאִים
וְקָדַר עֲלֵיהֶם הַיּוֹם׃

7 וּבֹשׁוּ הַחֹזִים וְחָפְרוּ הַקֹּסְמִים
וְעָטוּ עַל־שָׂפָם כֻּלָּם
כִּי אֵין מַעֲנֵה אֱלֹהִים׃

8 וְאוּלָם אָנֹכִי מָלֵאתִי כֹחַ
אֶת־רוּחַ יְהוָה
וּמִשְׁפָּט וּגְבוּרָה
לְהַגִּיד לְיַעֲקֹב פִּשְׁעוֹ
וּלְיִשְׂרָאֵל חַטָּאתוֹ׃ ס

9 שִׁמְעוּ־נָא זֹאת רָאשֵׁי בֵּית יַעֲקֹב
וּקְצִינֵי בֵּית יִשְׂרָאֵל
הַמֲתַעֲבִים מִשְׁפָּט
וְאֵת כָּל־הַיְשָׁרָה יְעַקֵּשׁוּ׃

10 בֹּנֶה צִיּוֹן בְּדָמִים
וִירוּשָׁלִַם בְּעַוְלָה׃

11 רָאשֶׁיהָ בְּשֹׁחַד יִשְׁפֹּטוּ
וְכֹהֲנֶיהָ בִּמְחִיר יוֹרוּ
וּנְבִיאֶיהָ בְּכֶסֶף יִקְסֹמוּ
וְעַל־יְהוָה יִשָּׁעֵנוּ לֵאמֹר
הֲלוֹא יְהוָה בְּקִרְבֵּנוּ
לֹא־תָבוֹא עָלֵינוּ רָעָה׃

12 לָכֵן בִּגְלַלְכֶם צִיּוֹן שָׂדֶה תֵחָרֵשׁ
וִירוּשָׁלִַם עִיִּין תִּהְיֶה
וְהַר הַבַּיִת לְבָמוֹת יָעַר׃ פ

ד וְהָיָה בְּאַחֲרִית הַיָּמִים יִהְיֶה
הַר בֵּית־יְהוָה נָכוֹן בְּרֹאשׁ הֶהָרִים

And shall be exalted above the hills;
And peoples shall flow to it.

וְנִשָּׂא הוּא מִגְּבָעֹות
וְנָהֲרוּ עָלָיו עַמִּים׃

2 Many nations shall come and say,
"Come, and let us go up to the mountain of
the LORD,
To the house of the God of Jacob;
He will teach us His ways,
And we shall walk in His paths."
For out of Zion the law shall go forth,
And the word of the LORD from Jerusalem.

וְהָלְכוּ גֹּויִם רַבִּים וְאָמְרוּ
לְכוּ ׀ וְנַעֲלֶה אֶל־הַר־יְהֹוָה
וְאֶל־בֵּית אֱלֹהֵי יַעֲקֹב
וְיֹורֵנוּ מִדְּרָכָיו
וְנֵלְכָה בְּאֹרְחֹתָיו
כִּי מִצִּיֹּון תֵּצֵא תֹורָה
וּדְבַר־יְהֹוָה מִירוּשָׁלָ͏ִם׃

3 He shall judge between many peoples,
And rebuke strong nations afar off;
They shall beat their swords into plowshares,
And their spears into pruning hooks;
Nation shall not lift up sword against nation,
Neither shall they learn war anymore.

וְשָׁפַט בֵּין עַמִּים רַבִּים
וְהֹוכִיחַ לְגֹויִם עֲצֻמִים עַד־רָחֹוק
וְכִתְּתוּ חַרְבֹתֵיהֶם לְאִתִּים
וַחֲנִיתֹתֵיהֶם לְמַזְמֵרֹות
לֹא־יִשְׂאוּ גֹּוי אֶל־גֹּוי חֶרֶב
וְלֹא־יִלְמְדוּן עֹוד מִלְחָמָה׃

4 But everyone shall sit under his vine and
under his fig tree,
And no one shall make *them* afraid;
For the mouth of the LORD of hosts has
spoken.

וְיָשְׁבוּ אִישׁ תַּחַת גַּפְנֹו
וְתַחַת תְּאֵנָתֹו וְאֵין מַחֲרִיד
כִּי־פִי יְהֹוָה צְבָאֹות דִּבֵּר׃

5 For all people walk each in the name of his
god,
But we will walk in the name of the LORD
our God
Forever and ever.

כִּי כָּל־הָעַמִּים יֵלְכוּ
אִישׁ בְּשֵׁם אֱלֹהָיו
וַאֲנַחְנוּ נֵלֵךְ בְּשֵׁם־יְהֹוָה אֱלֹהֵינוּ
לְעֹולָם וָעֶד׃

6 "In that day," says the LORD,
"I will assemble the lame,
I will gather the outcast
And those whom I have afflicted;

בַּיֹּום הַהוּא נְאֻם־יְהֹוָה
אֹסְפָה הַצֹּלֵעָה
וְהַנִּדָּחָה אֲקַבֵּצָה
וַאֲשֶׁר הֲרֵעֹתִי׃

7 I will make the lame a remnant,
And the outcast a strong nation;
So the LORD will reign over them in Mount
Zion
From now on, even forever.

וְשַׂמְתִּי אֶת־הַצֹּלֵעָה לִשְׁאֵרִית
וְהַנַּהֲלָאָה לְגֹוי עָצוּם
וּמָלַךְ יְהֹוָה עֲלֵיהֶם בְּהַר צִיֹּון
מֵעַתָּה וְעַד־עֹולָם׃

8 And you, O tower of the flock,
The stronghold of the daughter of Zion,
To you shall it come,
Even the former dominion shall come,
The kingdom of the daughter of Jerusalem."

וְאַתָּה מִגְדַּל־עֵדֶר עֹפֶל
בַּת־צִיֹּון עָדֶיךָ תֵּאתֶה
וּבָאָה הַמֶּמְשָׁלָה הָרִאשֹׁנָה
מַמְלֶכֶת לְבַת־יְרוּשָׁלָ͏ִם׃

9 Now why do you cry aloud?
Is there no king in your midst?
Has your counselor perished?
For pangs have seized you like a woman in
labor.

עַתָּה לָמָּה תָרִיעִי רֵעַ
הֲמֶלֶךְ אֵין־בָּךְ
אִם־יֹועֲצֵךְ אָבָד
כִּי־הֶחֱזִיקֵךְ חִיל כַּיֹּולֵדָה׃

10 Be in pain, and labor to bring forth,
O daughter of Zion,
Like a woman in birth pangs.
For now you shall go forth from the city,
You shall dwell in the field,
And to Babylon you shall go.
There you shall be delivered;
There the LORD will redeem you

חוּלִי וָגֹחִי
בַּת־צִיֹּון כַּיֹּולֵדָה

From the hand of your enemies.

כִּי־עַתָּה תֵּצְאִי מִקִּרְיָה

11 Now also many nations have gathered
against you,
Who say, "Let her be defiled,
And let our eye look upon Zion."

וְשָׁכַנְתְּ בַּשָּׂדֶה
וּבָאת עַד־בָּבֶל
שָׁם תִּנָּצֵלִי
שָׁם יִגְאָלֵךְ יְהוָה מִכַּף אֹיְבָיִךְ:

12 But they do not know the thoughts of the
LORD,
Nor do they understand His counsel;
For He will gather them like sheaves to the
threshing floor.

11 וְעַתָּה נֶאֶסְפוּ עָלַיִךְ גּוֹיִם רַבִּים
הָאֹמְרִים תֶּחֱנָף וְתַחַז בְּצִיּוֹן עֵינֵינוּ:

12 וְהֵמָּה לֹא יָדְעוּ מַחְשְׁבוֹת יְהוָה

13 "Arise and thresh, O daughter of Zion;
For I will make your horn iron,
And I will make your hooves bronze;
You shall beat in pieces many peoples;
I will consecrate their gain to the LORD,
And their substance to the Lord of the whole
earth."

וְלֹא הֵבִינוּ עֲצָתוֹ
כִּי קִבְּצָם כֶּעָמִיר גֹּרְנָה:

13 קוּמִי וָדוֹשִׁי בַת־צִיּוֹן
כִּי־קַרְנֵךְ אָשִׂים בַּרְזֶל
וּפַרְסֹתַיִךְ אָשִׂים נְחוּשָׁה
וַהֲדִקּוֹת עַמִּים רַבִּים
וְהַחֲרַמְתִּי לַיהוָה בִּצְעָם
וְחֵילָם לַאֲדוֹן כָּל־הָאָרֶץ:

5 Now gather yourself in troops,
O daughter of troops;
He has laid siege against us;
They will strike the judge of Israel with a rod
on the cheek.

14 עַתָּה תִּתְגֹּדְדִי בַת־גְּדוּד
מָצוֹר שָׂם עָלֵינוּ
בַּשֵּׁבֶט יַכּוּ עַל־הַלְּחִי
אֵת שֹׁפֵט יִשְׂרָאֵל: ס

2 "But you, Bethlehem Ephrathah,
Though you are little among the thousands of
Judah,
Yet out of you shall come forth to Me
The One to be Ruler in Israel,
Whose goings forth *are* from of old,
From everlasting."

ה וְאַתָּה בֵּית־לֶחֶם אֶפְרָתָה
צָעִיר לִהְיוֹת בְּאַלְפֵי יְהוּדָה
מִמְּךָ לִי יֵצֵא לִהְיוֹת מוֹשֵׁל בְּיִשְׂרָאֵל
וּמוֹצָאֹתָיו מִקֶּדֶם מִימֵי עוֹלָם:

3 Therefore He shall give them up,
Until the time *that* she who is in labor has
given birth;
Then the remnant of His brethren
Shall return to the children of Israel.

2 לָכֵן יִתְּנֵם
עַד־עֵת יוֹלֵדָה יָלָדָה
וְיֶתֶר אֶחָיו יְשׁוּבוּן עַל־בְּנֵי יִשְׂרָאֵל:

4 And He shall stand and feed *His flock*
In the strength of the LORD,
In the majesty of the name of the LORD His
God;
And they shall abide,
For now He shall be great
To the ends of the earth;

3 וְעָמַד וְרָעָה בְּעֹז יְהוָה
בִּגְאוֹן שֵׁם יְהוָה אֱלֹהָיו
וְיָשָׁבוּ כִּי־עַתָּה יִגְדַּל
עַד־אַפְסֵי־אָרֶץ:

5 And this *One* shall be peace.

When the Assyrian comes into our land,
And when he treads in our palaces,
Then we will raise against him
Seven shepherds and eight princely men.

4 וְהָיָה זֶה שָׁלוֹם
אַשּׁוּר ׀ כִּי־יָבוֹא בְאַרְצֵנוּ
וְכִי יִדְרֹךְ בְּאַרְמְנֹתֵינוּ
וַהֲקֵמֹנוּ עָלָיו שִׁבְעָה רֹעִים
וּשְׁמֹנָה נְסִיכֵי אָדָם:

6 They shall waste with the sword the land of
Assyria,
And the land of Nimrod at its entrances;
Thus He shall deliver *us* from the Assyrian,
When he comes into our land

5 וְרָעוּ אֶת־אֶרֶץ אַשּׁוּר בַּחֶרֶב
וְאֶת־אֶרֶץ נִמְרֹד בִּפְתָחֶיהָ

And when he treads within our borders.

וְהִצִּיל מֵֽאַשּׁוּר כִּֽי־יָב֣וֹא בְאַרְצֵ֔נוּ

7 Then the remnant of Jacob
Shall be in the midst of many peoples,
Like dew from the LORD,
Like showers on the grass,
That tarry for no man
Nor wait for the sons of men.

וְכִ֥י יִדְרֹ֖ךְ בִּגְבוּלֵֽנוּ׃ ס

6 וְהָיָ֣ה ׀ שְׁאֵרִ֣ית יַעֲקֹ֗ב בְּקֶ֙רֶב֙ עַמִּ֣ים רַבִּ֔ים

כְּטַל֙ מֵאֵ֣ת יְהֹוָ֔ה כִּרְבִיבִ֖ים עֲלֵי־עֵ֑שֶׂב

אֲשֶׁ֤ר לֹֽא־יְקַוֶּה֙ לְאִ֔ישׁ וְלֹ֥א יְיַחֵ֖ל לִבְנֵ֥י אָדָֽם׃

8 And the remnant of Jacob
Shall be among the Gentiles,
In the midst of many peoples,
Like a lion among the beasts of the forest,
Like a young lion among flocks of sheep,
Who, if he passes through,
Both treads down and tears in pieces,
And none can deliver.

7 וְהָיָה֩ שְׁאֵרִ֨ית יַעֲקֹ֜ב בַּגּוֹיִ֗ם

בְּקֶ֙רֶב֙ עַמִּ֣ים רַבִּ֔ים

כְּאַרְיֵה֙ בְּבַהֲמ֣וֹת יַ֔עַר

כִּכְפִ֖יר בְּעֶדְרֵי־צֹ֑אן

אֲשֶׁ֧ר אִ֣ם עָבַ֗ר

וְרָמַ֥ס וְטָרַ֖ף וְאֵ֥ין מַצִּֽיל׃

9 Your hand shall be lifted against your
adversaries,
And all your enemies shall be cut off.

8 תָּרֹ֥ם יָדְךָ֖ עַל־צָרֶ֑יךָ

וְכָל־אֹיְבֶ֖יךָ יִכָּרֵֽתוּ׃ פ

10 "And it shall be in that day," says the LORD,
"That I will cut off your horses from your
midst
And destroy your chariots.

9 וְהָיָ֤ה בַיּוֹם־הַהוּא֙ נְאֻם־יְהֹוָ֔ה

וְהִכְרַתִּ֥י סוּסֶ֖יךָ מִקִּרְבֶּ֑ךָ

וְהַאֲבַדְתִּ֖י מַרְכְּבֹתֶֽיךָ׃

11 I will cut off the cities of your land
And throw down all your strongholds.

10 וְהִכְרַתִּ֖י עָרֵ֣י אַרְצֶ֑ךָ

וְהָרַסְתִּ֖י כָּל־מִבְצָרֶֽיךָ׃

12 I will cut off sorceries from your hand,
And you shall have no soothsayers.

11 וְהִכְרַתִּ֥י כְשָׁפִ֖ים מִיָּדֶ֑ךָ

וּמְעוֹנְנִ֖ים לֹ֥א יִֽהְיוּ־לָֽךְ׃

13 Your carved images I will also cut off,
And your sacred pillars from your midst;
You shall no more worship the work of your
hands;

12 וְהִכְרַתִּ֧י פְסִילֶ֛יךָ וּמַצֵּבוֹתֶ֖יךָ מִקִּרְבֶּ֑ךָ

וְלֹֽא־תִשְׁתַּחֲוֶ֥ה ע֖וֹד לְמַעֲשֵׂ֥ה יָדֶֽיךָ׃

14 I will pluck your wooden images from your
midst;
Thus I will destroy your cities.

13 וְנָתַשְׁתִּ֥י אֲשֵׁירֶ֖יךָ מִקִּרְבֶּ֑ךָ

וְהִשְׁמַדְתִּ֖י עָרֶֽיךָ׃

15 And I will execute vengeance in anger and
fury
On the nations that have not heard."

14 וְעָשִׂ֜יתִי בְּאַ֧ף וּבְחֵמָ֛ה נָקָ֖ם אֶת־הַגּוֹיִ֑ם

אֲשֶׁ֖ר לֹ֥א שָׁמֵֽעוּ׃ ס

6 Hear now what the LORD says:

"Arise, plead your case before the mountains,
And let the hills hear your voice.

ו שִׁמְעוּ־נָ֕א אֵ֥ת אֲשֶׁר־יְהֹוָ֖ה אֹמֵ֑ר

ק֚וּם רִ֣יב אֶת־הֶֽהָרִ֔ים

2 Hear, O you mountains, the LORD's
complaint,
And you strong foundations of the earth;
For the LORD has a complaint against His
people,
And He will contend with Israel.

וְתִשְׁמַ֖עְנָה הַגְּבָע֥וֹת קוֹלֶֽךָ׃

2 שִׁמְע֤וּ הָרִים֙ אֶת־רִ֣יב יְהֹוָ֔ה

וְהָאֵֽתָנִ֖ים מֹ֣סְדֵי אָ֑רֶץ

כִּ֣י רִ֤יב לַֽיהֹוָה֙ עִם־עַמּ֔וֹ

וְעִם־יִשְׂרָאֵ֖ל יִתְוַכָּֽח׃

3 "O My people, what have I done to you?
And how have I wearied you?
Testify against Me.

3 עַמִּ֛י מֶה־עָשִׂ֥יתִי לְךָ֖

וּמָ֣ה הֶלְאֵתִ֑יךָ

עֲנֵ֥ה בִֽי׃

4 For I brought you up from the land of
Egypt,
I redeemed you from the house of bondage;

4 כִּ֤י הֶעֱלִתִ֙יךָ֙ מֵאֶ֣רֶץ מִצְרַ֔יִם

And I sent before you Moses, Aaron, and
  Miriam.

5 O My people, remember now
  What Balak king of Moab counseled,
  And what Balaam the son of Beor answered
    him,
  From Acacia Grove to Gilgal,
  That you may know the righteousness of the
    LORD."

6 With what shall I come before the LORD,
  And bow myself before the High God?
  Shall I come before Him with burnt
    offerings,
  With calves a year old?
7 Will the LORD be pleased with thousands of
    rams,
  Ten thousand rivers of oil?
  Shall I give my firstborn *for* my
    transgression,
  The fruit of my body *for* the sin of my soul?

8 He has shown you, O man, what *is* good;
  And what does the LORD require of you
  But to do justly,
  To love mercy,
  And to walk humbly with your God?

9 The LORD's voice cries to the city—
  Wisdom shall see Your name:

  "Hear the rod!
  Who has appointed it?
10 Are there yet the treasures of wickedness
  In the house of the wicked,
  And the short measure *that is* an
    abomination?
11 Shall I count pure *those* with the wicked
    scales,
  And with the bag of deceitful weights?
12 For her rich men are full of violence,
  Her inhabitants have spoken lies,
  And their tongue is deceitful in their mouth.

13 "Therefore I will also make *you* sick by
    striking you,
  By making *you* desolate because of your sins.
14 You shall eat, but not be satisfied;
  Hunger *shall be* in your midst.
  You may carry *some* away, but shall not save
    them;
  And what you do rescue I will give over to
    the sword.

15 "You shall sow, but not reap;
  You shall tread the olives, but not anoint
    yourselves with oil;

וּמִבֵּ֥ית עֲבָדִ֖ים פְּדִיתִ֑יךָ
וָאֶשְׁלַ֣ח לְפָנֶ֔יךָ
אֶת־מֹשֶׁ֖ה אַהֲרֹ֥ן וּמִרְיָֽם׃

5 עַמִּ֗י זְכָר־נָא֙ מַה־יָּעַ֗ץ
בָּלָק֙ מֶ֣לֶךְ מוֹאָ֔ב
וּמֶה־עָנָ֥ה אֹת֖וֹ בִּלְעָ֣ם בֶּן־בְּע֑וֹר
מִן־הַשִּׁטִּים֙ עַד־הַגִּלְגָּ֔ל
לְמַ֕עַן דַּ֖עַת צִדְק֥וֹת יְהוָֽה׃

6 בַּמָּה֙ אֲקַדֵּ֣ם יְהוָ֔ה
אִכַּ֖ף לֵאלֹהֵ֣י מָר֑וֹם
הַאֲקַדְּמֶ֣נּוּ בְעוֹל֔וֹת
בַּעֲגָלִ֖ים בְּנֵ֥י שָׁנָֽה׃

7 הֲיִרְצֶ֤ה יְהוָה֙ בְּאַלְפֵ֣י אֵילִ֔ים
בְּרִֽבְב֖וֹת נַֽחֲלֵי־שָׁ֑מֶן
הַאֶתֵּ֤ן בְּכוֹרִי֙ פִּשְׁעִ֔י
פְּרִ֥י בִטְנִ֖י חַטַּ֥את נַפְשִֽׁי׃

8 הִגִּ֥יד לְךָ֛ אָדָ֖ם מַה־טּ֑וֹב
וּמָֽה־יְהוָ֞ה דּוֹרֵ֣שׁ מִמְּךָ֗
כִּ֣י אִם־עֲשׂ֤וֹת מִשְׁפָּט֙ וְאַ֣הֲבַת חֶ֔סֶד
וְהַצְנֵ֥עַ לֶ֖כֶת עִם־אֱלֹהֶֽיךָ׃ פ

9 ק֤וֹל יְהוָה֙ לָעִ֣יר יִקְרָ֔א
וְתוּשִׁיָּ֖ה יִרְאֶ֣ה שְׁמֶ֑ךָ
שִׁמְע֥וּ מַטֶּ֖ה וּמִ֥י יְעָדָֽהּ׃

10 ע֗וֹד הַאִשׁ֙ בֵּ֣ית רָשָׁ֔ע אֹצְר֖וֹת רֶ֑שַׁע
וְאֵיפַ֥ת רָז֖וֹן זְעוּמָֽה׃

11 הַאֶזְכֶּ֖ה בְּמֹ֣אזְנֵי רֶ֑שַׁע
וּבְכִ֖יס אַבְנֵ֥י מִרְמָֽה׃

12 אֲשֶׁ֤ר עֲשִׁירֶ֙יהָ֙ מָלְא֣וּ חָמָ֔ס
וְיֹשְׁבֶ֖יהָ דִּבְּרוּ־שָׁ֑קֶר
וּלְשׁוֹנָ֖ם רְמִיָּ֥ה בְּפִיהֶֽם׃

13 וְגַם־אֲנִ֖י הֶחֱלֵ֣יתִי הַכּוֹתֶ֑ךָ
הַשְׁמֵ֖ם עַל־חַטֹּאתֶֽךָ׃

14 אַתָּ֤ה תֹאכַל֙ וְלֹ֣א תִשְׂבָּ֔ע
וְיֶשְׁחֲךָ֖ בְּקִרְבֶּ֑ךָ
וְתַסֵּג֙ וְלֹ֣א תַפְלִ֔יט
וַאֲשֶׁ֥ר תְּפַלֵּ֖ט לַחֶ֥רֶב אֶתֵּֽן׃

15 אַתָּ֥ה תִזְרַ֖ע וְלֹ֣א תִקְצ֑וֹר
אַתָּ֤ה תִדְרֹךְ־זַ֙יִת֙

And *make* sweet wine, but not drink wine.
16 For the statutes of Omri are kept;
All the works of Ahab's house *are done;*
And you walk in their counsels,
That I may make you a desolation,
And your inhabitants a hissing.
Therefore you shall bear the reproach of My
   people."

וְלֹא־תָסוּךְ שֶׁמֶן
וְתִירוֹשׁ וְלֹא תִשְׁתֶּה־יָּיִן:

16 וְיִשְׁתַּמֵּר חֻקּוֹת עָמְרִי
וְכֹל מַעֲשֵׂה בֵית־אַחְאָב
וַתֵּלְכוּ בְּמֹעֲצוֹתָם
לְמַעַן תִּתִּי אֹתְךָ לְשַׁמָּה
וְיֹשְׁבֶיהָ לִשְׁרֵקָה
וְחֶרְפַּת עַמִּי תִּשָּׂאוּ: פ

7 Woe is me!
For I am like those who gather summer
   fruits,
Like those who glean vintage grapes;
There is no cluster to eat
Of the first-ripe fruit *which* my soul desires.
2 The faithful *man* has perished from the earth,
And *there is* no one upright among men.
They all lie in wait for blood;
Every man hunts his brother with a net.
3 That they may successfully do evil with both
   hands—
The prince asks *for gifts,*
The judge *seeks* a bribe,
And the great *man* utters his evil desire;
So they scheme together.
4 The best of them *is* like a brier;
The most upright *is sharper* than a thorn
   hedge;
The day of your watchman and your
   punishment comes;
Now shall be their perplexity.
5 Do not trust in a friend;
Do not put your confidence in a companion;
Guard the doors of your mouth
From her who lies in your bosom.
6 For son dishonors father,
Daughter rises against her mother,
Daughter-in-law against her mother-in-law;
A man's enemies *are* the men of his own
   household.
7 Therefore I will look to the LORD;
I will wait for the God of my salvation;
My God will hear me.
8 Do not rejoice over me, my enemy;
When I fall, I will arise;
When I sit in darkness,
The LORD *will be* a light to me.
9 I will bear the indignation of the LORD,
Because I have sinned against Him,
Until He pleads my case
And executes justice for me.
He will bring me forth to the light;

ז אַלְלַי לִי כִּי הָיִיתִי כְּאָסְפֵּי־קַיִץ
כְּעֹלֲלֹת בָּצִיר
אֵין־אֶשְׁכּוֹל לֶאֱכוֹל
בִּכּוּרָה אִוְּתָה נַפְשִׁי:

2 אָבַד חָסִיד מִן־הָאָרֶץ
וְיָשָׁר בָּאָדָם אָיִן
כֻּלָּם לְדָמִים יֶאֱרֹבוּ
אִישׁ אֶת־אָחִיהוּ יָצוּדוּ חֵרֶם:

3 עַל־הָרַע כַּפַּיִם לְהֵיטִיב
הַשַּׂר שֹׁאֵל וְהַשֹּׁפֵט בַּשִּׁלּוּם
וְהַגָּדוֹל דֹּבֵר הַוַּת נַפְשׁוֹ
הוּא וַיְעַבְּתוּהָ:

4 טוֹבָם כְּחֵדֶק
יָשָׁר מִמְּסוּכָה
יוֹם מְצַפֶּיךָ פְּקֻדָּתְךָ בָאָה
עַתָּה תִהְיֶה מְבוּכָתָם:

5 אַל־תַּאֲמִינוּ בְרֵעַ
אַל־תִּבְטְחוּ בְּאַלּוּף
מִשֹּׁכֶבֶת חֵיקֶךָ שְׁמֹר פִּתְחֵי־פִיךָ:

6 כִּי־בֵן מְנַבֵּל אָב
בַּת קָמָה בְאִמָּהּ
כַּלָּה בַּחֲמֹתָהּ
אֹיְבֵי אִישׁ אַנְשֵׁי בֵיתוֹ:

7 וַאֲנִי בַּיהוָה אֲצַפֶּה
אוֹחִילָה לֵאלֹהֵי יִשְׁעִי
יִשְׁמָעֵנִי אֱלֹהָי:

8 אַל־תִּשְׂמְחִי אֹיַבְתִּי לִי
כִּי נָפַלְתִּי קָמְתִּי
כִּי־אֵשֵׁב בַּחֹשֶׁךְ יְהוָה אוֹר לִי: ס

9 זַעַף יְהוָה אֶשָּׂא

I will see His righteousness.
10 Then *she who is* my enemy will see,
And shame will cover her who said to me,
"Where is the LORD your God?"
My eyes will see her;
Now she will be trampled down
Like mud in the streets.

11 *In* the day when your walls are to be built,
In that day the decree shall go far and wide.

12 *In* that day they shall come to you
From Assyria and the fortified cities,
From the fortress to the River,
From sea to sea,
And mountain *to* mountain.

13 Yet the land shall be desolate
Because of those who dwell in it,
And for the fruit of their deeds.

14 Shepherd Your people with Your staff,
The flock of Your heritage,
Who dwell solitarily *in* a woodland,
In the midst of Carmel;
Let them feed *in* Bashan and Gilead,
As in days of old.

15 "As in the days when you came out of the land
of Egypt,
I will show them wonders."

16 The nations shall see and be ashamed of all
their might;
They shall put *their* hand over *their* mouth;
Their ears shall be deaf.

17 They shall lick the dust like a serpent;
They shall crawl from their holes like snakes
of the earth.
They shall be afraid of the LORD our God,
And shall fear because of You.

18 Who *is* a God like You,
Pardoning iniquity
And passing over the transgression of the
remnant of His heritage?

He does not retain His anger forever,
Because He delights *in* mercy.

19 He will again have compassion on us,
And will subdue our iniquities.

You will cast all our sins
Into the depths of the sea.

20 You will give truth to Jacob
And mercy to Abraham,
Which You have sworn to our fathers
From days of old.

כִּי חָטָאתִי לֽוֹ
עַד אֲשֶׁר יָרִיב רִיבִי וְעָשָׂה מִשְׁפָּטִי
יוֹצִיאֵנִי לָאוֹר
אֶרְאֶה בְּצִדְקָתֽוֹ׃
10 וְתֵרֶא אֹיַבְתִּי וּתְכַסֶּהָ בוּשָׁה
הָאֹמְרָה אֵלַי אַיּוֹ יְהוָה אֱלֹהָיִךְ
עֵינַי תִּרְאֶינָּה בָּהּ
עַתָּה תִּהְיֶה לְמִרְמָס כְּטִיט חוּצֽוֹת׃
11 יוֹם לִבְנוֹת גְּדֵרָיִךְ
יוֹם הַהוּא יִרְחַק־חֹֽק׃
12 יוֹם הוּא וְעָדֶיךָ יָבוֹא
לְמִנִּי אַשּׁוּר וְעָרֵי מָצוֹר
וּלְמִנִּי מָצוֹר וְעַד־נָהָר
וְיָם מִיָּם וְהַר הָהָֽר׃
13 וְהָיְתָה הָאָרֶץ לִשְׁמָמָה עַל־יֹשְׁבֶיהָ
מִפְּרִי מַעַלְלֵיהֶֽם׃ ס
14 רְעֵה עַמְּךָ בְשִׁבְטֶךָ צֹאן נַחֲלָתֶךָ
שֹׁכְנִי לְבָדָד יַעַר בְּתוֹךְ כַּרְמֶל
יִרְעוּ בָשָׁן וְגִלְעָד כִּימֵי עוֹלָֽם׃
15 כִּימֵי צֵאתְךָ מֵאֶרֶץ מִצְרָיִם
אַרְאֶנּוּ נִפְלָאֽוֹת׃
16 יִרְאוּ גוֹיִם וְיֵבֹשׁוּ מִכֹּל גְּבוּרָתָם
יָשִׂימוּ יָד עַל־פֶּה
אָזְנֵיהֶם תֶּחֱרַֽשְׁנָה׃
17 יְלַחֲכוּ עָפָר כַּנָּחָשׁ
כְּזֹחֲלֵי אֶרֶץ יִרְגְּזוּ מִמִּסְגְּרֹתֵיהֶם
אֶל־יְהוָה אֱלֹהֵינוּ יִפְחָדוּ
וְיִרְאוּ מִמֶּֽךָּ׃
18 מִי־אֵל כָּמוֹךָ
נֹשֵׂא עָוֹן וְעֹבֵר עַל־פֶּשַׁע
לִשְׁאֵרִית נַחֲלָתוֹ
לֹא־הֶחֱזִיק לָעַד אַפּוֹ
כִּי־חָפֵץ חֶסֶד הֽוּא׃
19 יָשׁוּב יְרַחֲמֵנוּ יִכְבֹּשׁ עֲוֺנֹתֵינוּ
וְתַשְׁלִיךְ בִּמְצֻלוֹת יָם כָּל־חַטֹּאותָֽם׃
20 תִּתֵּן אֱמֶת לְיַעֲקֹב חֶסֶד לְאַבְרָהָם
אֲשֶׁר־נִשְׁבַּעְתָּ לַאֲבֹתֵינוּ מִימֵי קֶֽדֶם׃

The Book of

NAHUM

נחום

1 The burden against Nineveh. The book of the vision of Nahum the Elkoshite.

2   God *is* jealous, and the LORD avenges;
     The LORD avenges and *is* furious.
     The LORD will take vengeance on His
       adversaries,
     And He reserves *wrath* for His enemies;
3   The LORD *is* slow to anger and great in
      power,
     And will not at all acquit *the wicked*.

     The LORD has His way
     In the whirlwind and in the storm,
     And the clouds *are* the dust of His feet.
4   He rebukes the sea and makes it dry,
     And dries up all the rivers.
     Bashan and Carmel wither,
     And the flower of Lebanon wilts.
5   The mountains quake before Him,
     The hills melt,
     And the earth heaves at His presence,
     Yes, the world and all who dwell in it.

6   Who can stand before His indignation?
     And who can endure the fierceness of His
      anger?
     His fury is poured out like fire,
     And the rocks are thrown down by Him.

7   The LORD *is* good,
     A stronghold in the day of trouble;
     And He knows those who trust in Him.
8   But with an overflowing flood
     He will make an utter end of its place,
     And darkness will pursue His enemies.

9   What do you conspire against the LORD?
     He will make an utter end *of it*.
     Affliction will not rise up a second time.
10   For while tangled *like* thorns,
     And while drunken *like* drunkards,
     They shall be devoured like stubble fully
      dried.
11   From you comes forth *one*
     Who plots evil against the LORD,
     A wicked counselor.

12 Thus says the LORD:

     "Though *they are* safe, and likewise many,

א מַשָּׂא נִינְוֵה סֵפֶר חֲזוֹן נַחוּם הָאֶלְקֹשִׁי:

2 אֵל קַנּוֹא וְנֹקֵם יְהֹוָה נֹקֵם יְהֹוָה וּבַעַל חֵמָה
נֹקֵם יְהֹוָה לְצָרָיו וְנוֹטֵר הוּא לְאֹיְבָיו:

3 יְהֹוָה אֶרֶךְ אַפַּיִם וּגְדָל־כֹּחַ
וְנַקֵּה לֹא יְנַקֶּה
יְהֹוָה בְּסוּפָה וּבִשְׂעָרָה דַּרְכּוֹ
וְעָנָן אֲבַק רַגְלָיו:

4 גּוֹעֵר בַּיָּם וַיַּבְּשֵׁהוּ וְכָל־הַנְּהָרוֹת הֶחֱרִיב
אֻמְלַל בָּשָׁן וְכַרְמֶל וּפֶרַח לְבָנוֹן אֻמְלָל:

5 הָרִים רָעֲשׁוּ מִמֶּנּוּ וְהַגְּבָעוֹת הִתְמֹגָגוּ
וַתִּשָּׂא הָאָרֶץ מִפָּנָיו וְתֵבֵל וְכָל־יֹשְׁבֵי בָהּ:

6 לִפְנֵי זַעְמוֹ מִי יַעֲמוֹד וּמִי יָקוּם בַּחֲרוֹן אַפּוֹ
חֲמָתוֹ נִתְּכָה כָאֵשׁ וְהַצֻּרִים נִתְּצוּ מִמֶּנּוּ:

7 טוֹב יְהֹוָה
לְמָעוֹז בְּיוֹם צָרָה
וְיֹדֵעַ חֹסֵי בוֹ:

8 וּבְשֶׁטֶף עֹבֵר
כָּלָה יַעֲשֶׂה מְקוֹמָהּ
וְאֹיְבָיו יְרַדֶּף־חֹשֶׁךְ:

9 מַה־תְּחַשְּׁבוּן אֶל־יְהֹוָה
כָּלָה הוּא עֹשֶׂה
לֹא־תָקוּם פַּעֲמַיִם צָרָה:

10 כִּי עַד־סִירִים סְבֻכִים
וּכְסָבְאָם סְבוּאִים
אֻכְּלוּ כְּקַשׁ יָבֵשׁ מָלֵא:

11 מִמֵּךְ יָצָא
חֹשֵׁב עַל־יְהֹוָה רָעָה
יֹעֵץ בְּלִיָּעַל: ס

12 כֹּה | אָמַר יְהֹוָה
אִם־שְׁלֵמִים וְכֵן רַבִּים

Yet in this manner they will be cut down
　　When he passes through.
Though I have afflicted you,
　　I will afflict you no more;
13　For now I will break off his yoke from you,
　　And burst your bonds apart."

14　The LORD has given a command concerning
　　　you:

"Your name shall be perpetuated no longer.
Out of the house of your gods
　　I will cut off the carved image and the
　　　molded image.
I will dig your grave,
　　For you are vile."

15　Behold, on the mountains
　　The feet of him who brings good tidings,
Who proclaims peace!
O Judah, keep your appointed feasts,
　　Perform your vows.
For the wicked one shall no more pass
　　　through you;
　　He is utterly cut off.

2　He who scatters has come up before your
　　　face.
Man the fort!
Watch the road!
Strengthen *your* flanks!
Fortify *your* power mightily.

2　For the LORD will restore the excellence of
　　　Jacob
Like the excellence of Israel,
For the emptiers have emptied them out
　　And ruined their vine branches.

3　The shields of his mighty men *are* made red,
The valiant men *are* in scarlet.
The chariots *come* with flaming torches
　　In the day of his preparation,
And the spears are brandished.

4　The chariots rage in the streets,
They jostle one another in the broad roads;
They seem like torches,
　　They run like lightning.

5　He remembers his nobles;
They stumble in their walk;
They make haste to her walls,
　　And the defense is prepared.

6　The gates of the rivers are opened,
　　And the palace is dissolved.

7　It is decreed:
　　She shall be led away captive,

וְכֵן נָגֹזּוּ וְעָבָר
וְעִנִּתִךְ לֹא אֲעַנֵּךְ עוֹד׃
13 וְעַתָּה אֶשְׁבֹּר מֹטֵהוּ מֵעָלָיִךְ
וּמוֹסְרֹתַיִךְ אֲנַתֵּק׃
14 וְצִוָּה עָלֶיךָ יְהוָה
לֹא־יִזָּרַע מִשִּׁמְךָ עוֹד
מִבֵּית אֱלֹהֶיךָ
אַכְרִית פֶּסֶל וּמַסֵּכָה
אָשִׂים קִבְרֶךָ כִּי קַלּוֹתָ׃　פ

ב הִנֵּה עַל־הֶהָרִים
רַגְלֵי מְבַשֵּׂר מַשְׁמִיעַ שָׁלוֹם
חָגִּי יְהוּדָה חַגַּיִךְ
שַׁלְּמִי נְדָרָיִךְ
כִּי לֹא יוֹסִיף עוֹד
לַעֲבֹור־P בָּךְ בְּלִיַּעַל
כֻּלֹּה נִכְרָת׃
2 עָלָה מֵפִיץ עַל־פָּנַיִךְ נָצוֹר מְצֻרָה
צַפֵּה־דֶרֶךְ חַזֵּק מָתְנַיִם אַמֵּץ כֹּחַ מְאֹד׃
3 כִּי שָׁב יְהוָה אֶת־גְּאוֹן יַעֲקֹב
כִּגְאוֹן יִשְׂרָאֵל
כִּי בְקָקוּם בֹּקְקִים
וּזְמֹרֵיהֶם שִׁחֵתוּ׃
4 מָגֵן גִּבֹּרֵיהוּ מְאָדָּם
אַנְשֵׁי־חַיִל מְתֻלָּעִים
בְּאֵשׁ־פְּלָדוֹת הָרֶכֶב בְּיוֹם הֲכִינוֹ
וְהַבְּרֹשִׁים הָרְעָלוּ׃
5 בַּחוּצוֹת יִתְהוֹלְלוּ הָרֶכֶב
יִשְׁתַּקְשְׁקוּן בָּרְחֹבוֹת
מַרְאֵיהֶן כַּלַּפִּידִם
כַּבְּרָקִים יְרוֹצֵצוּ׃
6 יִזְכֹּר אַדִּירָיו יִכָּשְׁלוּ בַהֲלִכוֹתָםP
יְמַהֲרוּ חוֹמָתָהּ וְהֻכַן הַסֹּכֵךְ׃
7 שַׁעֲרֵי הַנְּהָרוֹת נִפְתָּחוּ
וְהַהֵיכָל נָמוֹג׃
8 וְהֻצַּב גֻּלְּתָה הֹעֲלָתָה

ב 1 לַעֲבָר־ 6 בַּהֲלִיכָתְם

She shall be brought up;
And her maidservants shall lead *her* as with
    the voice of doves,
Beating their breasts.

8 Though Nineveh of old *was* like a pool of
    water,
Now they flee away.
"Halt! Halt!" *they cry;*
But no one turns back.

9 Take spoil of silver!
Take spoil of gold!
There is no end of treasure,
Or wealth of every desirable prize.

10 She is empty, desolate, and waste!
The heart melts, and the knees shake;
Much pain *is* in every side,
And all their faces are drained of color.

11 Where *is* the dwelling of the lions,
And the feeding place of the young lions,
Where the lion walked, the lioness *and* lion's
    cub,
And no one made *them* afraid?

12 The lion tore in pieces enough for his cubs,
Killed for his lionesses,
Filled his caves with prey,
And his dens with flesh.

13 "Behold, I *am* against you," says the LORD of
hosts, "I will burn your chariots in smoke, and the
sword shall devour your young lions; I will cut off
your prey from the earth, and the voice of your
messengers shall be heard no more."

3 Woe to the bloody city!
It *is* all full of lies *and* robbery.
Its victim never departs.

2 The noise of a whip
And the noise of rattling wheels,
Of galloping horses,
Of clattering chariots!

3 Horsemen charge with bright sword and
    glittering spear.
There is a multitude of slain,
A great number of bodies,
Countless corpses—
They stumble over the corpses—

4 Because of the multitude of harlotries of the
    seductive harlot,
The mistress of sorceries,
Who sells nations through her harlotries,
And families through her sorceries.

5 "Behold, I *am* against you," says the LORD of
    hosts;

וְאַמְהֹתֶ֗יהָ מְנַהֲג֣וֹת כְּק֣וֹל יוֹנִ֔ים
מְתֹפְפֹ֖ת עַל־לִבְבֵהֶֽן׃

9 וְנִֽינְוֵ֥ה כִבְרֵכַת־מַ֖יִם מִ֣ימֵי הִ֑יא
וְהֵ֣מָּה נָסִ֔ים
עִמְד֥וּ עֲמֹ֖דוּ וְאֵ֥ין מַפְנֶֽה׃

10 בֹּ֥זּוּ כֶ֖סֶף בֹּ֣זּוּ זָהָ֑ב
וְאֵ֥ין קֵ֙צֶה֙ לַתְּכוּנָ֔ה
כָּבֹ֕ד מִכֹּ֖ל כְּלִ֥י חֶמְדָּֽה׃

11 בּוּקָ֥ה וּמְבוּקָ֖ה וּמְבֻלָּקָ֑ה
וְלֵ֨ב נָמֵ֜ס וּפִ֣ק בִּרְכַּ֗יִם
וְחַלְחָלָה֙ בְּכָל־מָתְנַ֔יִם
וּפְנֵ֥י כֻלָּ֖ם קִבְּצ֥וּ פָארֽוּר׃

12 אַיֵּה֙ מְע֣וֹן אֲרָי֔וֹת
וּמִרְעֶ֥ה ה֖וּא לַכְּפִרִ֑ים
אֲשֶׁ֣ר הָלַ֡ךְ אַרְיֵה֩ לָבִ֨יא שָׁ֜ם
גּ֥וּר אַרְיֵ֖ה וְאֵ֥ין מַחֲרִֽיד׃

13 אַרְיֵ֤ה טֹרֵף֙ בְּדֵ֣י גֹֽרוֹתָ֔יו וּמְחַנֵּ֖ק לְלִבְאֹתָ֑יו
וַיְמַלֵּא־טֶ֣רֶף חֹרָ֔יו וּמְעֹֽנֹתָ֖יו טְרֵפָֽה׃

14 הִנְנִ֣י אֵלַ֗יִךְ נְאֻם֙ יְהֹוָ֣ה צְבָא֔וֹת
וְהִבְעַרְתִּ֤י בֶֽעָשָׁן֙ רִכְבָּ֔הּ
וּכְפִירַ֖יִךְ תֹּ֣אכַל חָ֑רֶב
וְהִכְרַתִּ֤י מֵאֶ֙רֶץ֙ טַרְפֵּ֔ךְ
וְלֹֽא־יִשָּׁמַ֥ע ע֖וֹד ק֥וֹל מַלְאָכֵֽכֵה׃ ס

ג 1 ה֤וֹי עִ֣יר דָּמִ֔ים
כֻּלָּ֖הּ כַּ֣חַשׁ פֶּ֣רֶק מְלֵאָ֑ה
לֹ֥א יָמִ֖ישׁ טָֽרֶף׃

2 ק֣וֹל שׁ֔וֹט וְק֖וֹל רַ֣עַשׁ אוֹפָ֑ן
וְס֣וּס דֹּהֵ֔ר וּמֶרְכָּבָ֖ה מְרַקֵּדָֽה׃

3 פָּרָ֣שׁ מַעֲלֶ֗ה וְלַ֤הַב חֶ֙רֶב֙ וּבְרַ֣ק חֲנִ֔ית
וְרֹ֥ב חָלָ֖ל וְכֹ֣בֶד פָּ֑גֶר
וְאֵ֥ין קֵ֙צֶה֙ לַגְּוִיָּ֔ה יִכְשְׁל֖וּ בִּגְוִיָּתָֽם׃

4 מֵרֹב֙ זְנוּנֵ֣י זוֹנָ֔ה
ט֥וֹבַת חֵ֖ן בַּעֲלַ֣ת כְּשָׁפִ֑ים
הַמֹּכֶ֤רֶת גּוֹיִם֙ בִּזְנוּנֶ֔יהָ
וּמִשְׁפָּח֖וֹת בִּכְשָׁפֶֽיהָ׃

5 הִנְנִ֣י אֵלַ֗יִךְ נְאֻם֙ יְהֹוָ֣ה צְבָא֔וֹת
וְגִלֵּיתִ֥י שׁוּלַ֖יִךְ עַל־פָּנָ֑יִךְ

ג 3 וְכָשְׁלֽוּ

"I will lift your skirts over your face,
I will show the nations your nakedness,
And the kingdoms your shame.

6 I will cast abominable filth upon you,
Make you vile,
And make you a spectacle.

7 It shall come to pass *that* all who look upon you
Will flee from you, and say,
'Nineveh is laid waste!
Who will bemoan her?'
Where shall I seek comforters for you?"

8 Are you better than No Amon
That was situated by the River,
That had the waters around her,
Whose rampart *was* the sea,
Whose wall *was* the sea?

9 Ethiopia and Egypt *were* her strength,
And *it was* boundless;
Put and Lubim were your helpers.

10 Yet she *was* carried away,
She went into captivity;
Her young children also were dashed to pieces
At the head of every street;
They cast lots for her honorable men,
And all her great men were bound in chains.

11 You also will be drunk;
You will be hidden;
You also will seek refuge from the enemy.

12 All your strongholds *are* fig trees with ripened figs:
If they are shaken,
They fall into the mouth of the eater.

13 Surely, your people in your midst *are* women!
The gates of your land are wide open for your enemies;
Fire shall devour the bars of your *gates*.

14 Draw your water for the siege!
Fortify your strongholds!
Go into the clay and tread the mortar!
Make strong the brick kiln!

15 There the fire will devour you,
The sword will cut you off;
It will eat you up like a locust.

Make yourself many—like the locust!
Make yourself many— like the *swarming* locusts!

16 You have multiplied your merchants more than the stars of heaven.
The locust plunders and flies away.

וְהַרְאֵיתִי גוֹיִם מַעְרֵךְ
וּמַמְלָכוֹת קְלוֹנֵךְ׃

6 וְהִשְׁלַכְתִּי עָלַיִךְ
שִׁקֻּצִים וְנִבַּלְתִּיךְ
וְשַׂמְתִּיךְ כְּרֹאִי׃

7 וְהָיָה כָל־רֹאַיִךְ יִדּוֹד מִמֵּךְ
וְאָמַר שָׁדְּדָה נִינְוֵה
מִי יָנוּד לָהּ
מֵאַיִן אֲבַקֵּשׁ מְנַחֲמִים לָךְ׃

8 הֲתֵיטְבִי מִנֹּא אָמוֹן
הַיֹּשְׁבָה בַּיְאֹרִים מַיִם סָבִיב לָהּ
אֲשֶׁר־חֵיל יָם מִיָּם חוֹמָתָהּ׃

9 כּוּשׁ עָצְמָה וּמִצְרַיִם וְאֵין קֵצֶה
פּוּט וְלוּבִים הָיוּ בְּעֶזְרָתֵךְ׃

10 גַּם־הִיא לַגֹּלָה הָלְכָה בַשֶּׁבִי
גַּם עֹלָלֶיהָ
יְרֻטְּשׁוּ בְּרֹאשׁ כָּל־חוּצוֹת
וְעַל־נִכְבַּדֶּיהָ יַדּוּ גוֹרָל
וְכָל־גְּדוֹלֶיהָ רֻתְּקוּ בַזִּקִּים׃

11 גַּם־אַתְּ תִּשְׁכְּרִי תְּהִי נַעֲלָמָה
גַּם־אַתְּ תְּבַקְשִׁי מָעוֹז מֵאוֹיֵב׃

12 כָּל־מִבְצָרַיִךְ
תְּאֵנִים עִם־בִּכּוּרִים אִם־יִנּוֹעוּ
וְנָפְלוּ עַל־פִּי אוֹכֵל׃

13 הִנֵּה עַמֵּךְ נָשִׁים בְּקִרְבֵּךְ
לְאֹיְבַיִךְ פָּתוֹחַ נִפְתְּחוּ
שַׁעֲרֵי אַרְצֵךְ
אָכְלָה אֵשׁ בְּרִיחָיִךְ׃

14 מֵי מָצוֹר שַׁאֲבִי־לָךְ
חַזְּקִי מִבְצָרָיִךְ
בֹּאִי בַטִּיט וְרִמְסִי בַחֹמֶר
הַחֲזִיקִי מַלְבֵּן׃

15 שָׁם תֹּאכְלֵךְ אֵשׁ
תַּכְרִיתֵךְ חֶרֶב
תֹּאכְלֵךְ כַּיָּלֶק
הִתְכַּבֵּד כַּיֶּלֶק
הִתְכַּבְּדִי כָּאַרְבֶּה׃

16 הִרְבֵּית רֹכְלַיִךְ
מִכּוֹכְבֵי הַשָּׁמָיִם
יֶלֶק פָּשַׁט וַיָּעֹף׃

17 Your commanders *are* like *swarming* locusts,
  And your generals like great grasshoppers,
  Which camp in the hedges on a cold day;
  When the sun rises they flee away,
  And the place where they *are* is not known.

18 Your shepherds slumber, O king of Assyria;
  Your nobles rest *in the dust.*
  Your people are scattered on the mountains,
  And no one gathers them.

19 Your injury *has* no healing,
  Your wound is severe.
  All who hear news of you
  Will clap *their* hands over you,
  For upon whom has not your wickedness
    passed continually?

17 מִנְּזָרַיִךְ כָּאַרְבֶּה
וְטַפְסְרַיִךְ כְּגוֹב גֹּבָי
הַחוֹנִים בַּגְּדֵרוֹת בְּיוֹם קָרָה
שֶׁמֶשׁ זָרְחָה וְנוֹדַד
וְלֹא־נוֹדַע מְקוֹמוֹ אַיָּם:

18 נָמוּ רֹעֶיךָ מֶלֶךְ אַשּׁוּר
יִשְׁכְּנוּ אַדִּירֶיךָ
נָפֹשׁוּ עַמְּךָ עַל־הֶהָרִים וְאֵין מְקַבֵּץ:

19 אֵין־כֵּהָה לְשִׁבְרֶךָ נַחְלָה מַכָּתֶךָ
כֹּל ׀ שֹׁמְעֵי שִׁמְעֲךָ תָּקְעוּ כַף עָלֶיךָ
כִּי עַל־מִי לֹא־עָבְרָה רָעָתְךָ תָּמִיד:

The Book of

HABAKKUK

חבקוק

1 The burden which the prophet Habakkuk saw.

א הַמַּשָּׂא אֲשֶׁר חָזָה חֲבַקּוּק הַנָּבִיא:

2 O LORD, how long shall I cry,
And You will not hear?
Even cry out to You, "Violence!"
And You will not save.

2 עַד־אָנָה יְהֹוָה שִׁוַּעְתִּי וְלֹא תִשְׁמָע
אֶזְעַק אֵלֶיךָ חָמָס וְלֹא תוֹשִׁיעַ:

3 Why do You show me iniquity,
And cause *me* to see trouble?
For plundering and violence *are* before me;
There is strife, and contention arises.

3 לָמָּה תַרְאֵנִי אָוֶן וְעָמָל תַּבִּיט
וְשֹׁד וְחָמָס לְנֶגְדִּי
וַיְהִי רִיב וּמָדוֹן יִשָּׂא:

4 Therefore the law is powerless,
And justice never goes forth.
For the wicked surround the righteous;
Therefore perverse judgment proceeds.

4 עַל־כֵּן תָּפוּג תּוֹרָה
וְלֹא־יֵצֵא לָנֶצַח מִשְׁפָּט
כִּי רָשָׁע מַכְתִּיר אֶת־הַצַּדִּיק
עַל־כֵּן יֵצֵא מִשְׁפָּט מְעֻקָּל:

5 "Look among the nations and watch—
Be utterly astounded!
For *I will* work a work in your days
Which you would not believe, though it were
told *you*.

5 רְאוּ בַגּוֹיִם וְהַבִּיטוּ
וְהִתַּמְּהוּ תְּמָהוּ
כִּי־פֹעַל פֹּעֵל בִּימֵיכֶם
לֹא תַאֲמִינוּ כִּי יְסֻפָּר:

6 For indeed I am raising up the Chaldeans,
A bitter and hasty nation
Which marches through the breadth of the
earth,
To possess dwelling places *that are* not theirs.

6 כִּי־הִנְנִי מֵקִים אֶת־הַכַּשְׂדִּים
הַגּוֹי הַמַּר וְהַנִּמְהָר
הַהוֹלֵךְ לְמֶרְחֲבֵי־אֶרֶץ
לָרֶשֶׁת מִשְׁכָּנוֹת לֹא־לוֹ:

7 They are terrible and dreadful;
Their judgment and their dignity proceed
from themselves.

7 אָיֹם וְנוֹרָא הוּא
מִמֶּנּוּ מִשְׁפָּטוֹ וּשְׂאֵתוֹ יֵצֵא:

8 Their horses also are swifter than leopards,
And more fierce than evening wolves.
Their chargers charge ahead;
Their cavalry comes from afar;
They fly as the eagle *that* hastens to eat.

8 וְקַלּוּ מִנְּמֵרִים סוּסָיו
וְחַדּוּ מִזְּאֵבֵי עֶרֶב
וּפָשׁוּ פָּרָשָׁיו
וּפָרָשָׁיו מֵרָחוֹק יָבֹאוּ
יָעֻפוּ כְּנֶשֶׁר חָשׁ לֶאֱכוֹל:

9 "They all come for violence;
Their faces are set *like* the east wind.
They gather captives like sand.

9 כֻּלֹּה לְחָמָס יָבוֹא
מְגַמַּת פְּנֵיהֶם קָדִימָה
וַיֶּאֱסֹף כַּחוֹל שֶׁבִי:

10 They scoff at kings,
And princes are scorned by them.
They deride every stronghold,
For they heap up earthen *mounds* and seize
it.

10 וְהוּא בַּמְּלָכִים יִתְקַלָּס
וְרֹזְנִים מִשְׂחָק לוֹ
הוּא לְכָל־מִבְצָר יִשְׂחָק
וַיִּצְבֹּר עָפָר וַיִּלְכְּדָהּ:

11 Then *his* mind changes, and he transgresses;
He commits offense,
Ascribing this power to his god."

11 אָז חָלַף רוּחַ וַיַּעֲבֹר וְאָשֵׁם
זוּ כֹחוֹ לֵאלֹהוֹ:

12 Are You not from everlasting,
O LORD my God, my Holy One?
We shall not die.

12 הֲלוֹא אַתָּה מִקֶּדֶם
יְהֹוָה אֱלֹהַי

O Lᴏʀᴅ, You have appointed them for judgment;
O Rock, You have marked them for correction.

קָדְשִׁי לֹא נָמוּת
יְהֹוָה לְמִשְׁפָּט שַׂמְתּוֹ
וְצוּר לְהוֹכִיחַ יְסַדְתּוֹ׃

13 *You are* of purer eyes than to behold evil,
And cannot look on wickedness.
Why do You look on those who deal treacherously,
And hold Your tongue when the wicked devours
A *person* more righteous than he?

13 טְהוֹר עֵינַיִם מֵרְאוֹת רָע וְהַבִּיט אֶל־עָמָל לֹא
תוּכָל
לָמָּה תַבִּיט בּוֹגְדִים
תַּחֲרִישׁ בְּבַלַּע רָשָׁע צַדִּיק מִמֶּנּוּ׃

14 *Why* do You make men like fish of the sea,
Like creeping things *that have* no ruler over them?

14 וַתַּעֲשֶׂה אָדָם כִּדְגֵי הַיָּם
כְּרֶמֶשׂ לֹא־מֹשֵׁל בּוֹ׃

15 They take up all of them with a hook,
They catch them in their net,
And gather them in their dragnet.
Therefore they rejoice and are glad.

15 כֻּלֹּה בְּחַכָּה הֵעֲלָה
יְגֹרֵהוּ בְחֶרְמוֹ
וְיַאַסְפֵהוּ בְּמִכְמַרְתּוֹ
עַל־כֵּן יִשְׂמַח וְיָגִיל׃

16 Therefore they sacrifice to their net,
And burn incense to their dragnet;
Because by them their share *is* sumptuous
And their food plentiful.

16 עַל־כֵּן יְזַבֵּחַ לְחֶרְמוֹ
וִיקַטֵּר לְמִכְמַרְתּוֹ
כִּי בָהֵמָּה שָׁמֵן חֶלְקוֹ
וּמַאֲכָלוֹ בְּרִאָה׃

17 Shall they therefore empty their net,
And continue to slay nations without pity?

17 הַעַל כֵּן יָרִיק חֶרְמוֹ
וְתָמִיד לַהֲרֹג גּוֹיִם לֹא יַחְמוֹל׃ ס

2 I will stand my watch
And set myself on the rampart,
And watch to see what He will say to me,
And what I will answer when I am corrected.

ב עַל־מִשְׁמַרְתִּי אֶעֱמֹדָה
וְאֶתְיַצְּבָה עַל־מָצוֹר
וַאֲצַפֶּה לִרְאוֹת מַה־יְדַבֶּר־בִּי
וּמָה אָשִׁיב עַל־תּוֹכַחְתִּי׃

2 Then the Lᴏʀᴅ answered me and said:

2 וַיַּעֲנֵנִי יְהֹוָה וַיֹּאמֶר

"Write the vision
And make *it* plain on tablets,
That he may run who reads it.

כְּתוֹב חָזוֹן
וּבָאֵר עַל־הַלֻּחוֹת
לְמַעַן יָרוּץ קוֹרֵא בוֹ׃

3 For the vision *is* yet for an appointed time;
But at the end it will speak, and it will not lie.
Though it tarries, wait for it;
Because it will surely come,
It will not tarry.

3 כִּי עוֹד חָזוֹן לַמּוֹעֵד
וְיָפֵחַ לַקֵּץ וְלֹא יְכַזֵּב
אִם־יִתְמַהְמָהּ חַכֵּה־לוֹ
כִּי־בֹא יָבֹא לֹא יְאַחֵר׃

4 "Behold the proud,
His soul is not upright in him;
But the just shall live by his faith.

4 הִנֵּה עֻפְּלָה לֹא־יָשְׁרָה נַפְשׁוֹ בּוֹ
וְצַדִּיק בֶּאֱמוּנָתוֹ יִחְיֶה׃

5 "Indeed, because he transgresses by wine,
He is a proud man,
And he does not stay at home.
Because he enlarges his desire as hell,
And he *is* like death, and cannot be satisfied,
He gathers to himself all nations
And heaps up for himself all peoples.

5 וְאַף כִּי־הַיַּיִן בּוֹגֵד
גֶּבֶר יָהִיר וְלֹא יִנְוֶה
אֲשֶׁר הִרְחִיב כִּשְׁאוֹל נַפְשׁוֹ
וְהוּא כַמָּוֶת וְלֹא יִשְׂבָּע
וַיֶּאֱסֹף אֵלָיו כָּל־הַגּוֹיִם
וַיִּקְבֹּץ אֵלָיו כָּל־הָעַמִּים׃

6 "Will not all these take up a proverb against him,
And a taunting riddle against him, and say,
'Woe to him who increases

6 הֲלוֹא־אֵלֶּה כֻלָּם עָלָיו מָשָׁל יִשָּׂאוּ
וּמְלִיצָה חִידוֹת לוֹ

What is not his—how long?
And to him who loads himself with many
　　pledges"?

7　Will not your creditors rise up suddenly?
Will they not awaken who oppress you?
And you will become their booty.

8　Because you have plundered many nations,
All the remnant of the people shall plunder
　　you,
Because of men's blood
And the violence of the land *and* the city,
And of all who dwell in it.

9　"Woe to him who covets evil gain for his
　　house,
That he may set his nest on high,
That he may be delivered from the power of
　　disaster!

10　You give shameful counsel to your house,
Cutting off many peoples,
And sin *against* your soul.

11　For the stone will cry out from the wall,
And the beam from the timbers will answer
　　it.

12　"Woe to him who builds a town with
　　bloodshed,
Who establishes a city by iniquity!

13　Behold, *is it* not of the Lord of hosts
That the peoples labor to feed the fire,
And nations weary themselves in vain?

14　For the earth will be filled
With the knowledge of the glory of the
　　Lord,
As the waters cover the sea.

15　"Woe to him who gives drink to his neighbor,
Pressing *him to* your bottle,
Even to make *him* drunk,
That you may look on his nakedness!

16　You are filled with shame instead of glory.
You also—drink!
And be exposed as uncircumcised!
The cup of the Lord's right hand *will be*
　　turned against you,
And utter shame will be on your glory.

17　For the violence *done to* Lebanon will cover
　　you,
And the plunder of beasts *which* made them
　　afraid,
Because of men's blood
And the violence of the land *and* the city,
And of all who dwell in it.

18　"What profit is the image, that its maker
　　should carve it,

וַיֹּאמַ֗ר הֲלֹא־אֵ֙לֶּה֙ הַמַּרְבֶּ֣ה לֹּא־ל֔וֹ
עַד־מָתַ֕י וּמַכְבִּ֥יד עָלָ֖יו עַבְטִֽיט׃
7 הֲל֣וֹא פֶ֗תַע יָק֙וּמוּ֙ נֹשְׁכֶ֔יךָ
וְיִקְצ֖וּ מְזַעְזְעֶ֑יךָ
וְהָיִ֥יתָ לִמְשִׁסּ֖וֹת לָֽמוֹ׃
8 כִּ֤י אַתָּה֙ שַׁלּ֙וֹתָ֙ גּוֹיִ֣ם רַבִּ֔ים
יְשָׁלּ֖וּךָ כָּל־יֶ֣תֶר עַמִּ֑ים
מִדְּמֵ֤י אָדָם֙ וַחֲמַס־אֶ֔רֶץ
קִרְיָ֖ה וְכָל־יֹ֥שְׁבֵי בָֽהּ׃　ף
9 ה֗וֹי בֹּצֵ֛עַ בֶּ֥צַע רָ֖ע לְבֵית֑וֹ
לָשׂ֤וּם בַּמָּרוֹם֙ קִנּ֔וֹ
לְהִנָּצֵ֖ל מִכַּף־רָֽע׃
10 יָעַ֣צְתָּ בֹּ֖שֶׁת לְבֵיתֶ֑ךָ
קְצוֹת־עַמִּ֥ים רַבִּ֖ים
וְחוֹטֵ֥א נַפְשֶֽׁךָ׃
11 כִּי־אֶ֖בֶן מִקִּ֣יר תִּזְעָ֑ק
וְכָפִ֖יס מֵעֵ֥ץ יַעֲנֶֽנָּה׃　ף
12 ה֗וֹי בֹּנֶ֥ה עִ֖יר בְּדָמִ֑ים
וְכוֹנֵ֥ן קִרְיָ֖ה בְּעַוְלָֽה׃
13 הֲל֣וֹא הִנֵּ֔ה מֵאֵ֖ת יְהוָ֣ה צְבָא֑וֹת
וְיִֽיגְע֤וּ עַמִּים֙ בְּדֵי־אֵ֔שׁ
וּלְאֻמִּ֥ים בְּדֵי־רִ֖יק יִעָֽפוּ׃
14 כִּ֚י תִּמָּלֵ֣א הָאָ֔רֶץ
לָדַ֖עַת אֶת־כְּב֣וֹד יְהוָ֑ה
כַּמַּ֖יִם יְכַסּ֥וּ עַל־יָֽם׃　ס
15 ה֗וֹי מַשְׁקֵ֤ה רֵעֵ֙הוּ֙
מְסַפֵּ֤חַ חֲמָֽתְךָ֙ וְאַ֣ף שַׁכֵּ֔ר
לְמַ֥עַן הַבִּ֖יט עַל־מְעוֹרֵיהֶֽם׃
16 שָׂבַ֤עְתָּ קָלוֹן֙ מִכָּב֔וֹד
שְׁתֵ֥ה גַם־אַ֖תָּה וְהֵעָרֵ֑ל
תִּסּ֣וֹב עָלֶ֗יךָ כּ֚וֹס יְמִ֣ין יְהוָ֔ה
וְקִיקָל֖וֹן עַל־כְּבוֹדֶֽךָ׃
17 כִּ֣י חֲמַ֤ס לְבָנוֹן֙ יְכַסֶּ֔ךָּ
וְשֹׁ֥ד בְּהֵמ֖וֹת יְחִיתַ֑ן
מִדְּמֵ֤י אָדָם֙ וַחֲמַס־אֶ֔רֶץ
קִרְיָ֖ה וְכָל־יֹ֥שְׁבֵי בָֽהּ׃　ס
18 מָֽה־הוֹעִ֣יל פֶּ֔סֶל
כִּ֥י פְסָל֖וֹ יֹֽצְר֑וֹ

The molded image, a teacher of lies,
That the maker of its mold should trust in it,
To make mute idols?

19 Woe to him who says to wood, 'Awake!'
To silent stone, 'Arise! It shall teach!'
Behold, it is overlaid with gold and silver,
Yet in it there is no breath at all.

20 "But the LORD is in His holy temple.
Let all the earth keep silence before Him."

3 A prayer of Habakkuk the prophet, on
Shigionoth.

2 O LORD, I have heard Your speech *and* was
afraid;
O LORD, revive Your work in the midst of
the years!
In the midst of the years make *it* known;
In wrath remember mercy.

3 God came from Teman,
The Holy One from Mount Paran.   Selah

His glory covered the heavens,
And the earth was full of His praise.

4 *His* brightness was like the light;
He had rays *flashing* from His hand,
And there His power *was* hidden.

5 Before Him went pestilence,
And fever followed at His feet.

6 He stood and measured the earth;
He looked and startled the nations.
And the everlasting mountains were scat-
tered,
The perpetual hills bowed.
His ways *are* everlasting.

7 I saw the tents of Cushan in affliction;
The curtains of the land of Midian trembled.

8 O LORD, were *You* displeased with the rivers,
Was Your anger against the rivers,
Was Your wrath against the sea,
That You rode on Your horses,
Your chariots of salvation?

9 Your bow was made quite ready;
Oaths were sworn over *Your* arrows.   Selah

You divided the earth with rivers.

10 The mountains saw You *and* trembled;
The overflowing of the water passed by.
The deep uttered its voice,
And lifted its hands on high.

11 The sun and moon stood still in their
habitation;
At the light of Your arrows they went,
At the shining of Your glittering spear.

מַסֵּכָה וּמוֹרֶה שָׁקֶר
כִּי בָטַח יֹצֵר יִצְרוֹ עָלָיו
לַעֲשׂוֹת אֱלִילִים אִלְּמִים: ס
19 הוֹי אֹמֵר לָעֵץ הָקִיצָה
עוּרִי לְאֶבֶן דּוּמָם
הוּא יוֹרֶה
הִנֵּה־הוּא תָּפוּשׂ זָהָב וָכֶסֶף
וְכָל־רוּחַ אֵין בְּקִרְבּוֹ:
20 וַיהוָה בְּהֵיכַל קָדְשׁוֹ
הַס מִפָּנָיו כָּל־הָאָרֶץ: פ

ג תְּפִלָּה לַחֲבַקּוּק הַנָּבִיא עַל שִׁגְיֹנוֹת:
2 יְהוָה שָׁמַעְתִּי שִׁמְעֲךָ יָרֵאתִי
יְהוָה פָּעָלְךָ בְּקֶרֶב שָׁנִים חַיֵּיהוּ
בְּקֶרֶב שָׁנִים תּוֹדִיעַ
בְּרֹגֶז רַחֵם תִּזְכּוֹר:
3 אֱלוֹהַּ מִתֵּימָן יָבוֹא
וְקָדוֹשׁ מֵהַר־פָּארָן סֶלָה
כִּסָּה שָׁמַיִם הוֹדוֹ
וּתְהִלָּתוֹ מָלְאָה הָאָרֶץ:
4 וְנֹגַהּ כָּאוֹר תִּהְיֶה
קַרְנַיִם מִיָּדוֹ לוֹ
וְשָׁם חֶבְיוֹן עֻזֹּה:
5 לְפָנָיו יֵלֶךְ דָּבֶר
וְיֵצֵא רֶשֶׁף לְרַגְלָיו:
6 עָמַד ׀ וַיְמֹדֶד אֶרֶץ רָאָה וַיַּתֵּר גּוֹיִם
וַיִּתְפֹּצְצוּ הַרְרֵי־עַד שַׁחוּ גִּבְעוֹת עוֹלָם
הֲלִיכוֹת עוֹלָם לוֹ:
7 תַּחַת אָוֶן רָאִיתִי אָהֳלֵי כוּשָׁן
יִרְגְּזוּן יְרִיעוֹת אֶרֶץ מִדְיָן: ס
8 הֲבִנְהָרִים חָרָה יְהוָה
אִם בַּנְּהָרִים אַפֶּךָ
אִם־בַּיָּם עֶבְרָתֶךָ
כִּי תִרְכַּב עַל־סוּסֶיךָ
מַרְכְּבֹתֶיךָ יְשׁוּעָה:
9 עֶרְיָה תֵעוֹר קַשְׁתֶּךָ
שְׁבֻעוֹת מַטּוֹת אֹמֶר סֶלָה
נְהָרוֹת תְּבַקַּע־אָרֶץ:
10 רָאוּךָ יָחִילוּ הָרִים זֶרֶם מַיִם עָבָר
נָתַן תְּהוֹם קוֹלוֹ רוֹם יָדֵיהוּ נָשָׂא:
11 שֶׁמֶשׁ יָרֵחַ עָמַד זְבֻלָה

12 You marched through the land in
    indignation;
  You trampled the nations in anger.
13 You went forth for the salvation of Your
    people,
  For salvation with Your Anointed.
  You struck the head from the house of the
    wicked,
  By laying bare from foundation to neck.
                      Selah

14 You thrust through with his own arrows
  The head of his villages.
  They came out like a whirlwind to scatter
    me;
  Their rejoicing was like feasting on the poor
    in secret.
15 You walked through the sea with Your
    horses,
  Through the heap of great waters.

16 When I heard, my body trembled;
  My lips quivered at *the* voice;
  Rottenness entered my bones;
  And I trembled in myself,
  That I might rest in the day of trouble.
  When he comes up to the people,
  He will invade them with his troops.

17 Though the fig tree may not blossom,
  Nor fruit be on the vines;
  Though the labor of the olive may fail,
  And the fields yield no food;
  Though the flock may be cut off from the
    fold,
  And there be no herd in the stalls—
18 Yet I will rejoice in the LORD,
  I will joy in the God of my salvation.

19 The LORD God is my strength;
  He will make my feet like deer's *feet,*
  And He will make me walk on my high hills.

To the Chief Musician. With my stringed
instruments.

לְאוֹר חִצֶּיךָ יְהַלֵּכוּ
לְנֹגַהּ בְּרַק חֲנִיתֶךָ׃
12 בְּזַעַם תִּצְעַד־אָרֶץ
בְּאַף תָּדוּשׁ גּוֹיִם׃
13 יָצָאתָ לְיֵשַׁע עַמֶּךָ
לְיֵשַׁע אֶת־מְשִׁיחֶךָ
מָחַצְתָּ רֹּאשׁ מִבֵּית רָשָׁע
עָרוֹת יְסוֹד עַד־צַוָּאר סֶלָה׃ פ
14 נָקַבְתָּ בְמַטָּיו רֹאשׁ פְּרָזָו
יִסְעֲרוּ לַהֲפִיצֵנִי
עֲלִיצֻתָם כְּמוֹ־לֶאֱכֹל עָנִי
בַּמִּסְתָּר׃
15 דָּרַכְתָּ בַיָּם סוּסֶיךָ
חֹמֶר מַיִם רַבִּים׃
16 שָׁמַעְתִּי ׀ וַתִּרְגַּז בִּטְנִי
לְקוֹל צָלֲלוּ שְׂפָתַי
יָבוֹא רָקָב בַּעֲצָמַי
וְתַחְתַּי אֶרְגָּז
אֲשֶׁר אָנוּחַ לְיוֹם צָרָה
לַעֲלוֹת לְעַם יְגוּדֶנּוּ׃
17 כִּי־תְאֵנָה לֹא־תִפְרָח
וְאֵין יְבוּל בַּגְּפָנִים
כִּחֵשׁ מַעֲשֵׂה־זַיִת
וּשְׁדֵמוֹת לֹא־עָשָׂה אֹכֶל
גָּזַר מִמִּכְלָה צֹאן
וְאֵין בָּקָר בָּרְפָתִים׃
18 וַאֲנִי בַּיהוָה אֶעְלוֹזָה
אָגִילָה בֵּאלֹהֵי יִשְׁעִי׃
19 יְהוִה אֲדֹנָי חֵילִי
וַיָּשֶׂם רַגְלַי כָּאַיָּלוֹת
וְעַל בָּמוֹתַי יַדְרִכֵנִי
לַמְנַצֵּחַ בִּנְגִינוֹתָי׃

The Book of
ZEPHANIAH

1 The word of the LORD which came to Zephaniah the son of Cushi, the son of Gedaliah, the son of Amariah, the son of Hezekiah, in the days of Josiah the son of Amon, king of Judah.

2 "I will utterly consume everything
From the face of the land,"
Says the LORD;

3 "I will consume man and beast;
I will consume the birds of the heavens,
The fish of the sea,
And the stumbling blocks along with the wicked.
I will cut off man from the face of the land,"
Says the LORD.

4 "I will stretch out My hand against Judah,
And against all the inhabitants of Jerusalem.
I will cut off every trace of Baal from this place,
The names of the idolatrous priests with the *pagan* priests—

5 Those who worship the host of heaven on the housetops;
Those who worship and swear *oaths* by the LORD,
But who *also* swear by Milcom;

6 Those who have turned back from *following* the LORD,
And have not sought the LORD, nor inquired of Him."

7 Be silent in the presence of the Lord GOD;
For the day of the LORD *is* at hand,
For the LORD has prepared a sacrifice;
He has invited His guests.

8 "And it shall be,
In the day of the LORD's sacrifice,
That I will punish the princes and the king's children,
And all such as are clothed with foreign apparel.

9 In the same day I will punish
All those who leap over the threshold,
Who fill their masters' houses with violence and deceit.

10 "And there shall be on that day," says the LORD,

צפניה

א דְּבַר־יְהוָה ׀ אֲשֶׁר הָיָה אֶל־צְפַנְיָה בֶּן־כּוּשִׁי
בֶן־גְּדַלְיָה בֶּן־אֲמַרְיָה בֶּן־חִזְקִיָּה בִּימֵי יֹאשִׁיָּהוּ בֶן־
אָמוֹן מֶלֶךְ יְהוּדָה:

2 אָסֹף אָסֵף כֹּל מֵעַל פְּנֵי הָאֲדָמָה
נְאֻם־יְהוָה:

3 אָסֵף אָדָם וּבְהֵמָה
אָסֵף עוֹף־הַשָּׁמַיִם וּדְגֵי הַיָּם
וְהַמַּכְשֵׁלוֹת אֶת־הָרְשָׁעִים
וְהִכְרַתִּי אֶת־הָאָדָם
מֵעַל פְּנֵי הָאֲדָמָה
נְאֻם־יְהוָה:

4 וְנָטִיתִי יָדִי עַל־יְהוּדָה
וְעַל כָּל־יוֹשְׁבֵי יְרוּשָׁלָ͏ִם
וְהִכְרַתִּי מִן־הַמָּקוֹם הַזֶּה
אֶת־שְׁאָר הַבַּעַל
אֶת־שֵׁם הַכְּמָרִים עִם־הַכֹּהֲנִים:

5 וְאֶת־הַמִּשְׁתַּחֲוִים עַל־הַגַּגּוֹת
לִצְבָא הַשָּׁמָיִם
וְאֶת־הַמִּשְׁתַּחֲוִים הַנִּשְׁבָּעִים לַיהוָה
וְהַנִּשְׁבָּעִים בְּמַלְכָּם:

6 וְאֶת־הַנְּסוֹגִים מֵאַחֲרֵי יְהוָה
וַאֲשֶׁר לֹא־בִקְשׁוּ אֶת־יְהוָה
וְלֹא דְרָשֻׁהוּ:

7 הַס מִפְּנֵי אֲדֹנָי יְהוִה
כִּי קָרוֹב יוֹם יְהוָה
כִּי־הֵכִין יְהוָה זֶבַח הִקְדִּישׁ קְרֻאָיו:

8 וְהָיָה בְּיוֹם זֶבַח יְהוָה
וּפָקַדְתִּי עַל־הַשָּׂרִים וְעַל־בְּנֵי הַמֶּלֶךְ
וְעַל כָּל־הַלֹּבְשִׁים מַלְבּוּשׁ נָכְרִי:

9 וּפָקַדְתִּי עַל כָּל־הַדּוֹלֵג
עַל־הַמִּפְתָּן בַּיּוֹם הַהוּא
הַמְמַלְאִים בֵּית אֲדֹנֵיהֶם
חָמָס וּמִרְמָה: ס

10 וְהָיָה בַיּוֹם הַהוּא נְאֻם־יְהוָה

"The sound of a mournful cry from the Fish
   Gate,
A wailing from the Second Quarter,
And a loud crashing from the hills.
11 Wail, you inhabitants of Maktesh!
For all the merchant people are cut down;
All those who handle money are cut off.

12 "And it shall come to pass at that time
That I will search Jerusalem with lamps,
And punish the men
Who are settled in complacency,
Who say in their heart,
'The LORD will not do good,
Nor will He do evil.'
13 Therefore their goods shall become booty,
And their houses a desolation;
They shall build houses, but not inhabit
   them;
They shall plant vineyards, but not drink
   their wine."

14 The great day of the LORD *is* near;
It is near and hastens quickly.
The noise of the day of the LORD is bitter;
There the mighty men shall cry out.
15 That day *is* a day of wrath,
A day of trouble and distress,
A day of devastation and desolation,
A day of darkness and gloominess,
A day of clouds and thick darkness,
16 A day of trumpet and alarm
Against the fortified cities
And against the high towers.

17 "I will bring distress upon men,
And they shall walk like blind men,
Because they have sinned against the LORD;
Their blood shall be poured out like dust,
And their flesh like refuse."

18 Neither their silver nor their gold
Shall be able to deliver them
In the day of the LORD's wrath;
But the whole land shall be devoured
By the fire of His jealousy,
For He will make speedy riddance
Of all those who dwell in the land.

2 Gather yourselves together, yes, gather
   together,
O undesirable nation,
2 Before the decree is issued,
Or the day passes like chaff,
Before the LORD's fierce anger comes upon
   you,

קוֹל צְעָקָה מִשַּׁעַר הַדָּגִים
וִילָלָה מִן־הַמִּשְׁנֶה
וְשֶׁבֶר גָּדוֹל מֵהַגְּבָעוֹת:
11 הֵילִילוּ יֹשְׁבֵי הַמַּכְתֵּשׁ
כִּי נִדְמָה כָּל־עַם כְּנַעַן
נִכְרְתוּ כָּל־נְטִילֵי כָסֶף:
12 וְהָיָה בָּעֵת הַהִיא
אֲחַפֵּשׂ אֶת־יְרוּשָׁלַ͏ִם בַּנֵּרוֹת
וּפָקַדְתִּי עַל־הָאֲנָשִׁים
הַקֹּפְאִים עַל־שִׁמְרֵיהֶם
הָאֹמְרִים בִּלְבָבָם
לֹא־יֵיטִיב יְהֹוָה וְלֹא יָרֵעַ:
13 וְהָיָה חֵילָם לִמְשִׁסָּה
וּבָתֵּיהֶם לִשְׁמָמָה
וּבָנוּ בָתִּים וְלֹא יֵשֵׁבוּ
וְנָטְעוּ כְרָמִים וְלֹא יִשְׁתּוּ אֶת־יֵינָם:
14 קָרוֹב יוֹם־יְהֹוָה הַגָּדוֹל
קָרוֹב וּמַהֵר מְאֹד קוֹל יוֹם יְהֹוָה
מַר צֹרֵחַ שָׁם גִּבּוֹר:
15 יוֹם עֶבְרָה הַיּוֹם הַהוּא
יוֹם צָרָה וּמְצוּקָה יוֹם שֹׁאָה וּמְשׁוֹאָה
יוֹם חֹשֶׁךְ וַאֲפֵלָה יוֹם עָנָן וַעֲרָפֶל:
16 יוֹם שׁוֹפָר וּתְרוּעָה
עַל הֶעָרִים הַבְּצֻרוֹת
וְעַל הַפִּנּוֹת הַגְּבֹהוֹת:
17 וַהֲצֵרֹתִי לָאָדָם וְהָלְכוּ כַּעִוְרִים
כִּי לַיהֹוָה חָטָאוּ
וְשֻׁפַּךְ דָּמָם כֶּעָפָר
וּלְחֻמָם כַּגְּלָלִים:
18 גַּם־כַּסְפָּם גַּם־זְהָבָם
לֹא־יוּכַל לְהַצִּילָם
בְּיוֹם עֶבְרַת יְהֹוָה
וּבְאֵשׁ קִנְאָתוֹ תֵּאָכֵל כָּל־הָאָרֶץ
כִּי־כָלָה אַךְ־נִבְהָלָה יַעֲשֶׂה
אֵת כָּל־יֹשְׁבֵי הָאָרֶץ: ס

ב הִתְקוֹשְׁשׁוּ וָקוֹשּׁוּ הַגּוֹי לֹא נִכְסָף:
2 בְּטֶרֶם לֶדֶת חֹק
כְּמֹץ עָבַר יוֹם
בְּטֶרֶם ׀ לֹא־יָבוֹא עֲלֵיכֶם
חֲרוֹן אַף־יְהֹוָה

Before the day of the LORD's anger comes
upon you!

3 Seek the LORD, all you meek of the earth,
Who have upheld His justice.
Seek righteousness, seek humility.
It may be that you will be hidden
In the day of the LORD's anger.

4 For Gaza shall be forsaken,
And Ashkelon desolate;
They shall drive out Ashdod at noonday,
And Ekron shall be uprooted.

5 Woe to the inhabitants of the seacoast,
The nation of the Cherethites!
The word of the LORD is against you,
O Canaan, land of the Philistines:
"I will destroy you;
So there shall be no inhabitant."

6 The seacoast shall be pastures,
With shelters for shepherds and folds for
flocks.

7 The coast shall be for the remnant of the
house of Judah;
They shall feed *their* flocks there;
In the houses of Ashkelon they shall lie down
at evening.
For the LORD their God will intervene for
them,
And return their captives.

8 "I have heard the reproach of Moab,
And the insults of the people of Ammon,
With which they have reproached My
people,
And made arrogant threats against their
borders.

9 Therefore, as I live,"
Says the LORD of hosts, the God of Israel,
"Surely Moab shall be like Sodom,
And the people of Ammon like Gomorrah—
Overrun with weeds and saltpits,
And a perpetual desolation.
The residue of My people shall plunder them,
And the remnant of My people shall possess
them."

10 This they shall have for their pride,
Because they have reproached and made
arrogant threats
Against the people of the LORD of hosts.

11 The LORD *will be* awesome to them,
For He will reduce to nothing all the gods of
the earth;
People shall worship Him,
Each one from his place,

בְּטֶרֶם ׀ לֹא־יָבוֹא עֲלֵיכֶם
חֲרוֹן אַף־יְהֹוָה
בְּטֶרֶם לֹא־יָבוֹא עֲלֵיכֶם
יוֹם אַף־יְהֹוָה:
3 בַּקְּשׁוּ אֶת־יְהֹוָה כָּל־עַנְוֵי הָאָרֶץ
אֲשֶׁר מִשְׁפָּטוֹ פָּעָלוּ
בַּקְּשׁוּ־צֶדֶק בַּקְּשׁוּ עֲנָוָה
אוּלַי תִּסָּתְרוּ בְּיוֹם אַף־יְהֹוָה:
4 כִּי עַזָּה עֲזוּבָה תִהְיֶה
וְאַשְׁקְלוֹן לִשְׁמָמָה
אַשְׁדּוֹד בַּצָּהֳרַיִם יְגָרְשׁוּהָ
וְעֶקְרוֹן תֵּעָקֵר: ס
5 הוֹי יֹשְׁבֵי חֶבֶל הַיָּם
גּוֹי כְּרֵתִים
דְּבַר־יְהֹוָה עֲלֵיכֶם
כְּנַעַן אֶרֶץ פְּלִשְׁתִּים
וְהַאֲבַדְתִּיךְ מֵאֵין יוֹשֵׁב:
6 וְהָיְתָה חֶבֶל הַיָּם נְוֹת
כְּרֹת רֹעִים וְגִדְרוֹת צֹאן:
7 וְהָיָה חֶבֶל לִשְׁאֵרִית
בֵּית יְהוּדָה עֲלֵיהֶם יִרְעוּן
בְּבָתֵּי אַשְׁקְלוֹן בָּעֶרֶב יִרְבָּצוּן
כִּי יִפְקְדֵם יְהֹוָה אֱלֹהֵיהֶם וְשָׁב שְׁבוּתָם׃ף
8 שָׁמַעְתִּי חֶרְפַּת מוֹאָב
וְגִדּוּפֵי בְּנֵי עַמּוֹן
אֲשֶׁר חֵרְפוּ אֶת־עַמִּי
וַיַּגְדִּילוּ עַל־גְּבוּלָם:
9 לָכֵן חַי־אָנִי
נְאֻם יְהֹוָה צְבָאוֹת אֱלֹהֵי יִשְׂרָאֵל
כִּי־מוֹאָב כִּסְדֹם תִּהְיֶה
וּבְנֵי עַמּוֹן כַּעֲמֹרָה
מִמְשַׁק חָרוּל
וּמִכְרֵה־מֶלַח וּשְׁמָמָה עַד־עוֹלָם
שְׁאֵרִית עַמִּי יְבָזּוּם
וְיֶתֶר גּוֹיִ יִנְחָלוּם:
10 זֹאת לָהֶם תַּחַת גְּאוֹנָם
כִּי חֵרְפוּ וַיַּגְדִּלוּ
עַל־עַם יְהֹוָה צְבָאוֹת:
11 נוֹרָא יְהֹוָה עֲלֵיהֶם
כִּי רָזָה אֵת כָּל־אֱלֹהֵי הָאָרֶץ

ב 7 שְׁבִיתָם 9 גּוֹיִי

Indeed all the shores of the nations.

12 "You Ethiopians also,
You shall be slain by My sword."

13 And He will stretch out His hand against the
    north,
Destroy Assyria,
And make Nineveh a desolation,
As dry as the wilderness.

14 The herds shall lie down in her midst,
Every beast of the nation.
Both the pelican and the bittern
Shall lodge on the capitals *of* her *pillars;*
Their voice shall sing in the windows;
Desolation *shall be* at the threshold;
For He will lay bare the cedar work.

15 This is the rejoicing city
That dwelt securely,
That said in her heart,
"I *am it, and there is* none besides me."
How has she become a desolation,
A place for beasts to lie down!
Everyone who passes by her
Shall hiss and shake his fist.

3   Woe to her who is rebellious and polluted,
    To the oppressing city!

2   She has not obeyed *His* voice,
    She has not received correction;
    She has not trusted in the LORD,
    She has not drawn near to her God.

3   Her princes in her midst *are* roaring lions;
    Her judges *are* evening wolves
    That leave not a bone till morning.

4   Her prophets are insolent, treacherous peo-
    ple;
    Her priests have polluted the sanctuary,
    They have done violence to the law.

5   The LORD *is* righteous in her midst,
    He will do no unrighteousness.
    Every morning He brings His justice to light;
    He never fails,
    But the unjust knows no shame.

6   "I have cut off nations,
    Their fortresses are devastated;
    I have made their streets desolate,
    With none passing by.
    Their cities are destroyed;
    There is no one, no inhabitant.

7   I said, 'Surely you will fear Me,
    You will receive instruction'—
    So that her dwelling would not be cut off,
    Despite everything for which I punished her.

וְיִשְׁתַּחֲווּ־לוֹ אִישׁ מִמְּקוֹמוֹ
כֹּל אִיֵּי הַגּוֹיִם:

12 גַּם־אַתֶּם כּוּשִׁים
חַלְלֵי חַרְבִּי הֵמָּה:

13 וְיֵט יָדוֹ עַל־צָפוֹן וִיאַבֵּד אֶת־אַשּׁוּר
וְיָשֵׂם אֶת־נִינְוֵה לִשְׁמָמָה צִיָּה כַּמִּדְבָּר:

14 וְרָבְצוּ בְתוֹכָהּ עֲדָרִים
כָּל־חַיְתוֹ־גוֹי
גַּם־קָאַת גַּם־קִפֹּד
בְּכַפְתֹּרֶיהָ יָלִינוּ
קוֹל יְשׁוֹרֵר בַּחַלּוֹן חֹרֶב בַּסַּף
כִּי אַרְזָה עֵרָה:

15 זֹאת הָעִיר הָעַלִּיזָה
הַיּוֹשֶׁבֶת לָבֶטַח
הָאֹמְרָה בִּלְבָבָהּ
אֲנִי וְאַפְסִי עוֹד
אֵיךְ ׀ הָיְתָה לְשַׁמָּה
מַרְבֵּץ לַחַיָּה כֹּל עוֹבֵר עָלֶיהָ
יִשְׁרֹק יָנִיעַ יָדוֹ: ס

ג הוֹי מֹרְאָה וְנִגְאָלָה
הָעִיר הַיּוֹנָה:

2 לֹא שָׁמְעָה בְּקוֹל לֹא לָקְחָה מוּסָר
בַּיהוָה לֹא בָטָחָה אֶל־אֱלֹהֶיהָ לֹא קָרֵבָה:

3 שָׂרֶיהָ בְקִרְבָּהּ אֲרָיוֹת שֹׁאֲגִים
שֹׁפְטֶיהָ זְאֵבֵי עֶרֶב
לֹא גָרְמוּ לַבֹּקֶר:

4 נְבִיאֶיהָ פֹּחֲזִים אַנְשֵׁי בֹּגְדוֹת
כֹּהֲנֶיהָ חִלְּלוּ־קֹדֶשׁ חָמְסוּ תוֹרָה:

5 יְהוָה צַדִּיק בְּקִרְבָּהּ
לֹא יַעֲשֶׂה עַוְלָה
בַּבֹּקֶר בַּבֹּקֶר
מִשְׁפָּטוֹ יִתֵּן לָאוֹר לֹא נֶעְדָּר
וְלֹא־יוֹדֵעַ עַוָּל בֹּשֶׁת:

6 הִכְרַתִּי גוֹיִם
נָשַׁמּוּ פִּנּוֹתָם
הֶחֱרַבְתִּי חוּצוֹתָם
מִבְּלִי עוֹבֵר
נִצְדּוּ עָרֵיהֶם
מִבְּלִי־אִישׁ מֵאֵין יוֹשֵׁב:

7 אָמַרְתִּי אַךְ־תִּירְאִי אוֹתִי

But they rose early and corrupted all their deeds.

8 "Therefore wait for Me," says the LORD,
"Until the day I rise up for plunder;
My determination *is* to gather the nations
To My assembly of kingdoms,
To pour on them My indignation,
All My fierce anger;
All the earth shall be devoured
With the fire of My jealousy.

9 "For then I will restore to the peoples a pure language,
That they all may call on the name of the LORD,
To serve Him with one accord.

10 From beyond the rivers of Ethiopia
My worshipers,
The daughter of My dispersed ones,
Shall bring My offering.

11 In that day you shall not be shamed for any of your deeds
In which you transgress against Me;
For then I will take away from your midst
Those who rejoice in your pride,
And you shall no longer be haughty
In My holy mountain.

12 I will leave in your midst
A meek and humble people,
And they shall trust in the name of the LORD.

13 The remnant of Israel shall do no unrighteousness
And speak no lies,
Nor shall a deceitful tongue be found in their mouth;
For they shall feed *their* flocks and lie down,
And no one shall make *them* afraid."

14 Sing, O daughter of Zion!
Shout, O Israel!
Be glad and rejoice with all *your* heart,
O daughter of Jerusalem!

15 The LORD has taken away your judgments,
He has cast out your enemy.
The King of Israel, the LORD, *is* in your midst;
You shall see disaster no more.

16 In that day it shall be said to Jerusalem:
"Do not fear;
Zion, let not your hands be weak.

17 The LORD your God in your midst,
The Mighty One, will save;
He will rejoice over you with gladness,
He will quiet *you* with His love,

תִּקְחִי מוּסָר
וְלֹא־יִכָּרֵת מְעוֹנָהּ

8 לָכֵן חַכּוּ־לִי נְאֻם־יְהֹוָה לְיוֹם קוּמִי לְעַד
כִּי מִשְׁפָּטִי לֶאֱסֹף גּוֹיִם לְקָבְצִי מַמְלָכוֹת
לִשְׁפֹּךְ עֲלֵיהֶם זַעְמִי כֹּל חֲרוֹן אַפִּי
כִּי בְּאֵשׁ קִנְאָתִי תֵּאָכֵל כָּל־הָאָרֶץ׃

9 כִּי־אָז אֶהְפֹּךְ אֶל־עַמִּים שָׂפָה בְרוּרָה
לִקְרֹא כֻלָּם בְּשֵׁם יְהֹוָה לְעָבְדוֹ שְׁכֶם אֶחָד׃

10 מֵעֵבֶר לְנַהֲרֵי־כוּשׁ עֲתָרַי בַּת־פּוּצַי
יוֹבִלוּן מִנְחָתִי׃

11 בַּיּוֹם הַהוּא לֹא תֵבוֹשִׁי מִכֹּל עֲלִילֹתַיִךְ
אֲשֶׁר פָּשַׁעַתְּ בִּי
כִּי־אָז אָסִיר מִקִּרְבֵּךְ עַלִּיזֵי גַּאֲוָתֵךְ
וְלֹא־תוֹסִפִי לְגָבְהָה עוֹד בְּהַר קָדְשִׁי׃

12 וְהִשְׁאַרְתִּי בְקִרְבֵּךְ עַם עָנִי וָדָל
וְחָסוּ בְּשֵׁם יְהֹוָה׃

13 שְׁאֵרִית יִשְׂרָאֵל לֹא־יַעֲשׂוּ עַוְלָה
וְלֹא־יְדַבְּרוּ כָזָב
וְלֹא־יִמָּצֵא בְּפִיהֶם לְשׁוֹן תַּרְמִית
כִּי־הֵמָּה יִרְעוּ וְרָבְצוּ וְאֵין מַחֲרִיד׃ ס

14 רָנִּי בַּת־צִיּוֹן הָרִיעוּ יִשְׂרָאֵל
שִׂמְחִי וְעָלְזִי בְּכָל־לֵב בַּת יְרוּשָׁלָ͏ִם׃

15 הֵסִיר יְהֹוָה מִשְׁפָּטַיִךְ פִּנָּה אֹיְבֵךְ
מֶלֶךְ יִשְׂרָאֵל יְהֹוָה בְּקִרְבֵּךְ
לֹא־תִירְאִי רָע עוֹד׃

16 בַּיּוֹם הַהוּא יֵאָמֵר לִירוּשָׁלַ͏ִם אַל־תִּירָאִי
צִיּוֹן אַל־יִרְפּוּ יָדָיִךְ׃

17 יְהֹוָה אֱלֹהַיִךְ בְּקִרְבֵּךְ גִּבּוֹר יוֹשִׁיעַ

He will rejoice over you with singing."

18 "I will gather those who sorrow over the
       appointed assembly,
    Who are among you,
    To whom its reproach *is* a burden.
19 Behold, at that time
    I will deal with all who afflict you;
    I will save the lame,
    And gather those who were driven out;
    I will appoint them for praise and fame
    In every land where they were put to shame.
20 At that time I will bring you back,
    Even at the time I gather you;
    For I will give you fame and praise
    Among all the peoples of the earth,
    When I return your captives before your
       eyes,"
    Says the LORD.

יָשִׂישׂ עָלַיִךְ בְּשִׂמְחָה
יַחֲרִישׁ בְּאַהֲבָתוֹ
יָגִיל עָלַיִךְ בְּרִנָּה:
18 נוּגֵי מִמּוֹעֵד אָסַפְתִּי מִמֵּךְ הָיוּ
מַשְׂאֵת עָלֶיהָ חֶרְפָּה:
19 הִנְנִי עֹשֶׂה אֶת־כָּל־מְעַנַּיִךְ בָּעֵת הַהִיא
וְהוֹשַׁעְתִּי אֶת־הַצֹּלֵעָה וְהַנִּדָּחָה אֲקַבֵּץ
וְשַׂמְתִּים לִתְהִלָּה וּלְשֵׁם
בְּכָל־הָאָרֶץ בָּשְׁתָּם:
20 בָּעֵת הַהִיא אָבִיא אֶתְכֶם
וּבָעֵת קַבְּצִי אֶתְכֶם
כִּי־אֶתֵּן אֶתְכֶם לְשֵׁם וְלִתְהִלָּה
בְּכֹל עַמֵּי הָאָרֶץ
בְּשׁוּבִי אֶת־שְׁבוּתֵיכֶם לְעֵינֵיכֶם אָמַר יְהֹוָה:

The Book of

HAGGAI

1 In the second year of King Darius, in the sixth
month, on the first day of the month, the word of
the LORD came by Haggai the prophet to
Zerubbabel the son of Shealtiel, governor of Judah,
and to Joshua the son of Jehozadak, the high priest,
saying, ² "Thus speaks the LORD of hosts, saying:
'This people says, "The time has not come, the time
that the LORD's house should be built." ' "

³ Then the word of the LORD came by Haggai the
prophet, saying, ⁴ "Is it time for you yourselves to
dwell in your paneled houses, and this temple to lie
in ruins?" ⁵ Now therefore, thus says the LORD of
hosts: "Consider your ways!

6   "You have sown much, and bring in little;
      You eat, but do not have enough;
      You drink, but you are not filled with drink;
      You clothe yourselves, but no one is warm;
      And he who earns wages,
      Earns wages to put into a bag with holes."

⁷ Thus says the LORD of hosts: "Consider your
ways! ⁸ Go up to the mountains and bring wood
and build the temple, that I may take pleasure in it
and be glorified," says the LORD. ⁹ "You looked for
much, but indeed it came to little; and when you
brought it home, I blew it away. Why?" says the
LORD of hosts. "Because of My house that is in
ruins, while every one of you runs to his own house.
¹⁰ Therefore the heavens above you withhold the
dew, and the earth withholds its fruit. ¹¹ For I called
for a drought on the land and the mountains, on the
grain and the new wine and the oil, on whatever the
ground brings forth, on men and livestock, and on
all the labor of your hands."

¹² Then Zerubbabel the son of Shealtiel, and
Joshua the son of Jehozadak, the high priest, with
all the remnant of the people, obeyed the voice of
the LORD their God, and the words of Haggai the
prophet, as the LORD their God had sent him; and
the people feared the presence of the LORD. ¹³ Then
Haggai, the LORD's messenger, spoke the LORD's
message to the people, saying, "I am with you, says
the LORD." ¹⁴ So the LORD stirred up the spirit of
Zerubbabel the son of Shealtiel, governor of Judah,
and the spirit of Joshua the son of Jehozadak, the
high priest, and the spirit of all the remnant of the
people; and they came and worked on the house of

א בִּשְׁנַת שְׁתַּיִם לְדָרְיָוֶשׁ הַמֶּלֶךְ בַּחֹדֶשׁ הַשִּׁשִּׁי
בְּיוֹם אֶחָד לַחֹדֶשׁ הָיָה דְבַר־יְהֹוָה בְּיַד־חַגַּי הַנָּבִיא
אֶל־זְרֻבָּבֶל בֶּן־שְׁאַלְתִּיאֵל פַּחַת יְהוּדָה וְאֶל־יְהוֹשֻׁעַ
בֶּן־יְהוֹצָדָק הַכֹּהֵן הַגָּדוֹל לֵאמֹר: ² כֹּה אָמַר יְהֹוָה
צְבָאוֹת לֵאמֹר הָעָם הַזֶּה אָמְרוּ לֹא עֶת־בֹּא עֶת־
בֵּית יְהֹוָה לְהִבָּנוֹת: פ
³ וַיְהִי דְּבַר־יְהֹוָה בְּיַד־חַגַּי הַנָּבִיא לֵאמֹר: ⁴ הַעֵת
לָכֶם אַתֶּם לָשֶׁבֶת בְּבָתֵּיכֶם סְפוּנִים וְהַבַּיִת הַזֶּה
חָרֵב: ⁵ וְעַתָּה כֹּה אָמַר יְהֹוָה צְבָאוֹת שִׂימוּ לְבַבְכֶם
עַל־דַּרְכֵיכֶם:
6   זְרַעְתֶּם הַרְבֵּה וְהָבֵא מְעָט
      אָכוֹל וְאֵין־לְשָׂבְעָה
      שָׁתוֹ וְאֵין־לְשָׁכְרָה
      לָבוֹשׁ וְאֵין־לְחֹם לוֹ
      וְהַמִּשְׂתַּכֵּר מִשְׂתַּכֵּר
      אֶל־צְרוֹר נָקוּב: פ
⁷ כֹּה אָמַר יְהֹוָה צְבָאוֹת שִׂימוּ לְבַבְכֶם עַל־
דַּרְכֵיכֶם: ⁸ עֲלוּ הָהָר וַהֲבֵאתֶם עֵץ וּבְנוּ הַבָּיִת
וְאֶרְצֶה־בּוֹ ַ וְאֶכָּבֵדפ אָמַר יְהֹוָה: ⁹ פָּנֹה אֶל־הַרְבֵּה
וְהִנֵּה לִמְעָט וַהֲבֵאתֶם הַבַּיִת וְנָפַחְתִּי בוֹ יַעַן מֶה
נְאֻם יְהֹוָה צְבָאוֹת יַעַן בֵּיתִי אֲשֶׁר־הוּא חָרֵב וְאַתֶּם
רָצִים אִישׁ לְבֵיתוֹ: ¹⁰ עַל־כֵּן עֲלֵיכֶם כָּלְאוּ שָׁמַיִם
מִטָּל וְהָאָרֶץ כָּלְאָה יְבוּלָהּ: ¹¹ וָאֶקְרָא חֹרֶב עַל־
הָאָרֶץ וְעַל־הֶהָרִים וְעַל־הַדָּגָן וְעַל־הַתִּירוֹשׁ וְעַל־
הַיִּצְהָר וְעַל אֲשֶׁר תּוֹצִיא הָאֲדָמָה וְעַל־הָאָדָם וְעַל־
הַבְּהֵמָה וְעַל כָּל־יְגִיעַ כַּפָּיִם: ס ¹² וַיִּשְׁמַע
זְרֻבָּבֶל ׀ בֶּן־שַׁלְתִּיאֵל וִיהוֹשֻׁעַ בֶּן־יְהוֹצָדָק הַכֹּהֵן
הַגָּדוֹל ׀ וְכֹל ׀ שְׁאֵרִית הָעָם בְּקוֹל יְהֹוָה אֱלֹהֵיהֶם
וְעַל־דִּבְרֵי חַגַּי הַנָּבִיא כַּאֲשֶׁר שְׁלָחוֹ יְהֹוָה אֱלֹהֵיהֶם
וַיִּירְאוּ הָעָם מִפְּנֵי יְהֹוָה: ¹³ וַיֹּאמֶר חַגַּי מַלְאַךְ יְהֹוָה
בְּמַלְאֲכוּת יְהֹוָה לָעָם לֵאמֹר אֲנִי אִתְּכֶם נְאֻם־
יְהֹוָה: ¹⁴ וַיָּעַר יְהֹוָה אֶת־רוּחַ זְרֻבָּבֶל בֶּן־שַׁלְתִּיאֵל
פַּחַת יְהוּדָה וְאֶת־רוּחַ יְהוֹשֻׁעַ בֶּן־יְהוֹצָדָק הַכֹּהֵן
הַגָּדוֹל וְאֶת־רוּחַ כֹּל שְׁאֵרִית הָעָם וַיָּבֹאוּ וַיַּעֲשׂוּ
מְלָאכָה בְּבֵית־יְהֹוָה צְבָאוֹת אֱלֹהֵיהֶם: פ

the LORD of hosts, their God, ¹⁵ on the twenty-fourth day of the sixth month, in the second year of King Darius.

2 In the seventh *month,* on the twenty-first of the month, the word of the LORD came by Haggai the prophet, saying: ² "Speak now to Zerubbabel the son of Shealtiel, governor of Judah, and to Joshua the son of Jehozadak, the high priest, and to the remnant of the people, saying: ³ 'Who is left among you who saw this temple in its former glory? And how do you see it now? In comparison with it, *is this* not in your eyes as nothing? ⁴ Yet now be strong, Zerubbabel,' says the LORD; 'and be strong, Joshua, son of Jehozadak, the high priest; and be strong, all you people of the land,' says the LORD, 'and work; for I *am* with you,' says the LORD of hosts. ⁵ 'According to the word that I covenanted with you when you came out of Egypt, so My Spirit remains among you; do not fear!'

⁶ "For thus says the LORD of hosts: 'Once more (it *is* a little while) I will shake heaven and earth, the sea and dry land; ⁷ and I will shake all nations, and they shall come to the Desire of All Nations, and I will fill this temple with glory,' says the LORD of hosts. ⁸ 'The silver *is* Mine, and the gold *is* Mine,' says the LORD of hosts. ⁹ 'The glory of this latter temple shall be greater than the former,' says the LORD of hosts. 'And in this place I will give peace,' says the LORD of hosts."

¹⁰ On the twenty-fourth *day* of the ninth *month,* in the second year of Darius, the word of the LORD came by Haggai the prophet, saying, ¹¹ "Thus says the LORD of hosts: 'Now, ask the priests *concerning the* law, saying, ¹² "If one carries holy meat in the fold of his garment, and with the edge he touches bread or stew, wine or oil, or any food, will it become holy?" ' "

Then the priests answered and said, "No."

¹³ And Haggai said, "If *one who is* unclean *because* of a dead body touches any of these, will it be unclean?"

So the priests answered and said, "It shall be unclean."

¹⁴ Then Haggai answered and said, " 'So is this people, and so is this nation before Me,' says the LORD, 'and so is every work of their hands; and what they offer there is unclean.

¹⁵ 'And now, carefully consider from this day forward: from before stone was laid upon stone in the temple of the LORD— ¹⁶ since those *days,* when *one* came to a heap of twenty ephahs, there were *but* ten; when *one* came to the wine vat to draw out fifty baths from the press, there were *but* twenty. ¹⁷ I

¹⁵ בְּיוֹם עֶשְׂרִים וְאַרְבָּעָה לַחֹדֶשׁ בַּשִּׁשִּׁי בִּשְׁנַת שְׁתַּיִם לְדָרְיָוֶשׁ הַמֶּלֶךְ:

ב בַּשְּׁבִיעִי בְּעֶשְׂרִים וְאֶחָד לַחֹדֶשׁ הָיָה דְבַר־יְהוָה בְּיַד־חַגַּי הַנָּבִיא לֵאמֹר: ² אֱמָר־נָא אֶל־זְרֻבָּבֶל בֶּן־שַׁלְתִּיאֵל פַּחַת יְהוּדָה וְאֶל־יְהוֹשֻׁעַ בֶּן־יְהוֹצָדָק הַכֹּהֵן הַגָּדוֹל וְאֶל־שְׁאֵרִית הָעָם לֵאמֹר: ³ מִי בָכֶם הַנִּשְׁאָר אֲשֶׁר רָאָה אֶת־הַבַּיִת הַזֶּה בִּכְבוֹדוֹ הָרִאשׁוֹן וּמָה אַתֶּם רֹאִים אֹתוֹ עַתָּה הֲלוֹא כָמֹהוּ כְּאַיִן בְּעֵינֵיכֶם: ⁴ וְעַתָּה חֲזַק זְרֻבָּבֶל | נְאֻם־יְהוָה וַחֲזַק יְהוֹשֻׁעַ בֶּן־יְהוֹצָדָק הַכֹּהֵן הַגָּדוֹל וַחֲזַק כָּל־עַם הָאָרֶץ נְאֻם־יְהוָה וַעֲשׂוּ כִּי־אֲנִי אִתְּכֶם נְאֻם יְהוָה צְבָאוֹת: ⁵ אֶת־הַדָּבָר אֲשֶׁר־כָּרַתִּי אִתְּכֶם בְּצֵאתְכֶם מִמִּצְרַיִם וְרוּחִי עֹמֶדֶת בְּתוֹכְכֶם אַל־תִּירָאוּ: ס ⁶ כִּי כֹה אָמַר יְהוָה צְבָאוֹת עוֹד אַחַת מְעַט הִיא וַאֲנִי מַרְעִישׁ אֶת־הַשָּׁמַיִם וְאֶת־הָאָרֶץ וְאֶת־הַיָּם וְאֶת־הֶחָרָבָה: ⁷ וְהִרְעַשְׁתִּי אֶת־כָּל־הַגּוֹיִם וּבָאוּ חֶמְדַּת כָּל־הַגּוֹיִם וּמִלֵּאתִי אֶת־הַבַּיִת הַזֶּה כָּבוֹד אָמַר יְהוָה צְבָאוֹת: ⁸ לִי הַכֶּסֶף וְלִי הַזָּהָב נְאֻם יְהוָה צְבָאוֹת: ⁹ גָּדוֹל יִהְיֶה כְּבוֹד הַבַּיִת הַזֶּה הָאַחֲרוֹן מִן־הָרִאשׁוֹן אָמַר יְהוָה צְבָאוֹת וּבַמָּקוֹם הַזֶּה אֶתֵּן שָׁלוֹם נְאֻם יְהוָה צְבָאוֹת: פ

¹⁰ בְּעֶשְׂרִים וְאַרְבָּעָה לַתְּשִׁיעִי בִּשְׁנַת שְׁתַּיִם לְדָרְיָוֶשׁ הָיָה דְּבַר־יְהוָה אֶל־חַגַּי הַנָּבִיא לֵאמֹר: ¹¹ כֹּה אָמַר יְהוָה צְבָאוֹת שְׁאַל־נָא אֶת־הַכֹּהֲנִים תּוֹרָה לֵאמֹר: ¹² הֵן | יִשָּׂא־אִישׁ בְּשַׂר־קֹדֶשׁ בִּכְנַף בִּגְדוֹ וְנָגַע בִּכְנָפוֹ אֶל־הַלֶּחֶם וְאֶל־הַנָּזִיד וְאֶל־הַיַּיִן וְאֶל־שֶׁמֶן וְאֶל־כָּל־מַאֲכָל הֲיִקְדָּשׁ וַיַּעֲנוּ הַכֹּהֲנִים וַיֹּאמְרוּ לֹא: ¹³ וַיֹּאמֶר חַגַּי אִם־יִגַּע טְמֵא־נֶפֶשׁ בְּכָל־אֵלֶּה הֲיִטְמָא וַיַּעֲנוּ הַכֹּהֲנִים וַיֹּאמְרוּ יִטְמָא: ¹⁴ וַיַּעַן חַגַּי וַיֹּאמֶר כֵּן הָעָם־הַזֶּה וְכֵן הַגּוֹי הַזֶּה לְפָנַי נְאֻם־יְהוָה וְכֵן כָּל־מַעֲשֵׂה יְדֵיהֶם וַאֲשֶׁר יַקְרִיבוּ שָׁם טָמֵא הוּא: ¹⁵ וְעַתָּה שִׂימוּ־נָא לְבַבְכֶם מִן־הַיּוֹם הַזֶּה וָמָעְלָה מִטֶּרֶם שׂוּם־אֶבֶן אֶל־אֶבֶן בְּהֵיכַל יְהוָה: ¹⁶ מִהְיוֹתָם בָּא אֶל־עֲרֵמַת עֶשְׂרִים וְהָיְתָה עֲשָׂרָה בָּא אֶל־הַיֶּקֶב לַחְשֹׂף חֲמִשִּׁים פּוּרָה וְהָיְתָה עֶשְׂרִים: ¹⁷ הִכֵּיתִי

struck you with blight and mildew and hail in all the labors of your hands; yet you did not *turn* to Me,' says the LORD. 18 'Consider now from this day forward, from the twenty-fourth day of the ninth month, from the day that the foundation of the LORD's temple was laid—consider it: 19 Is the seed still in the barn? As yet the vine, the fig tree, the pomegranate, and the olive tree have not yielded *fruit*. *But* from this day I will bless *you*.' "

20 And again the word of the LORD came to Haggai on the twenty-fourth day of the month, saying, 21 "Speak to Zerubbabel, governor of Judah, saying:

'I will shake heaven and earth.
22 I will overthrow the throne of kingdoms;
I will destroy the strength of the Gentile
     kingdoms.
I will overthrow the chariots
And those who ride in them;
The horses and their riders shall come down,
Every one by the sword of his brother.

23 'In that day,' says the LORD of hosts, 'I will take you, Zerubbabel My servant, the son of Shealtiel,' says the LORD, 'and will make you like a signet *ring;* for I have chosen you,' says the LORD of hosts."

אֶתְכֶ֜ם בַּשִּׁדָּפ֤וֹן וּבַיֵּֽרָקוֹן֙ וּבַבָּרָ֔ד אֵ֖ת כָּל־מַעֲשֵׂ֣ה יְדֵיכֶ֑ם וְאֵין־אֶתְכֶ֥ם אֵלַ֖י נְאֻם־יְהוָֽה: 18 שִֽׂימוּ־נָ֣א לְבַבְכֶ֔ם מִן־הַיּ֥וֹם הַזֶּ֖ה וָמָ֑עְלָה מִיּ֣וֹם עֶשְׂרִ֤ים וְאַרְבָּעָה֙ לַתְּשִׁיעִ֔י לְמִן־הַיּ֗וֹם אֲשֶׁר־יֻסַּ֛ד הֵֽיכַל־יְהוָ֖ה שִׂ֥ימוּ לְבַבְכֶֽם: 19 הַע֤וֹד הַזֶּ֨רַע֙ בַּמְּגוּרָ֔ה וְעַד־הַגֶּ֨פֶן וְהַתְּאֵנָ֧ה וְהָרִמּ֛וֹן וְעֵ֥ץ הַזַּ֖יִת לֹ֣א נָשָׂ֑א מִן־הַיּ֥וֹם הַזֶּ֖ה אֲבָרֵֽךְ: ס 20 וַיְהִ֨י דְבַר־יְהוָ֤ה ׀ שֵׁנִית֙ אֶל־חַגַּ֔י בְּעֶשְׂרִ֥ים וְאַרְבָּעָ֖ה לַחֹ֑דֶשׁ לֵאמֹֽר: 21 אֱמֹ֕ר אֶל־זְרֻבָּבֶ֥ל פַּֽחַת־יְהוּדָ֖ה לֵאמֹ֑ר אֲנִ֣י מַרְעִ֔ישׁ אֶת־הַשָּׁמַ֖יִם וְאֶת־הָאָֽרֶץ: 22 וְהָֽפַכְתִּי֙ כִּסֵּ֣א מַמְלָכ֔וֹת וְהִ֨שְׁמַדְתִּ֔י חֹ֖זֶק מַמְלְכ֣וֹת הַגּוֹיִ֑ם וְהָפַכְתִּ֤י מֶרְכָּבָה֙ וְרֹ֣כְבֶ֔יהָ וְיָרְד֤וּ סוּסִים֙ וְרֹ֣כְבֵיהֶ֔ם אִ֖ישׁ בְּחֶ֥רֶב אָחִֽיו: 23 בַּיּ֣וֹם הַה֣וּא נְאֻם־יְהוָ֣ה צְבָא֗וֹת אֶקָּחֲךָ֞ זְרֻבָּבֶ֥ל בֶּן־שְׁאַלְתִּיאֵ֤ל עַבְדִּי֙ נְאֻם־יְהוָ֔ה וְשַׂמְתִּ֖יךָ כַּֽחוֹתָ֑ם כִּֽי־בְךָ֣ בָחַ֔רְתִּי נְאֻ֖ם יְהוָ֥ה צְבָאֽוֹת:

The Book of

ZECHARIAH

1 In the eighth month of the second year of Darius, the word of the LORD came to Zechariah the son of Berechiah, the son of Iddo the prophet, saying, 2 "The LORD has been very angry with your fathers. 3 Therefore say to them, 'Thus says the LORD of hosts: "Return to Me," says the LORD of hosts, "and I will return to you," says the LORD of hosts. 4 "Do not be like your fathers, to whom the former prophets preached, saying, 'Thus says the LORD of hosts: "Turn now from your evil ways and your evil deeds."' But they did not hear nor heed Me," says the LORD.

5 "Your fathers, where are they?
    And the prophets, do they live forever?
6 Yet surely My words and My statutes,
    Which I commanded My servants the prophets,
    Did they not overtake your fathers?

"So they returned and said:

'Just as the LORD of hosts determined to do to us,
    According to our ways and according to our deeds,
    So He has dealt with us.'"'"

7 On the twenty-fourth day of the eleventh month, which is the month Shebat, in the second year of Darius, the word of the LORD came to Zechariah the son of Berechiah, the son of Iddo the prophet: 8 I saw by night, and behold, a man riding on a red horse, and it stood among the myrtle trees in the hollow; and behind him were horses: red, sorrel, and white. 9 Then I said, "My lord, what are these?" So the angel who talked with me said to me, "I will show you what they are."

10 And the man who stood among the myrtle trees answered and said, "These are the ones whom the LORD has sent to walk to and fro throughout the earth."

11 So they answered the Angel of the LORD, who stood among the myrtle trees, and said, "We have walked to and fro throughout the earth, and behold, all the earth is resting quietly."

12 Then the Angel of the LORD answered and said, "O LORD of hosts, how long will You not have mercy on Jerusalem and on the cities of Judah, against which You were angry these seventy years?"

בְּחֹדֶשׁ הַשְּׁמִינִי בִּשְׁנַת שְׁתַּיִם לְדָרְיָוֶשׁ הָיָה א
דְבַר־יְהֹוָה אֶל־זְכַרְיָה בֶּן־בֶּרֶכְיָה בֶּן־עִדּוֹ הַנָּבִיא
לֵאמֹר: 2 קָצַף יְהֹוָה עַל־אֲבוֹתֵיכֶם קָצֶף: 3 וְאָמַרְתָּ
אֲלֵהֶם כֹּה אָמַר יְהֹוָה צְבָאוֹת שׁוּבוּ אֵלַי נְאֻם יְהֹוָה
צְבָאוֹת וְאָשׁוּב אֲלֵיכֶם אָמַר יְהֹוָה צְבָאוֹת: 4 אַל־
תִּהְיוּ כַאֲבֹתֵיכֶם אֲשֶׁר קָרְאוּ־אֲלֵיהֶם הַנְּבִיאִים
הָרִאשֹׁנִים לֵאמֹר כֹּה אָמַר יְהֹוָה צְבָאוֹת שׁוּבוּ
נָא מִדַּרְכֵיכֶם הָרָעִים וּמַעֲלִילֵיכֶם הָרָעִים וְלֹא
שָׁמְעוּ וְלֹא־הִקְשִׁיבוּ אֵלַי נְאֻם־יְהֹוָה: 5 אֲבוֹתֵיכֶם
אַיֵּה־הֵם וְהַנְּבִאִים הַלְעוֹלָם יִחְיוּ: 6 אַךְ דְּבָרַי
וְחֻקַּי אֲשֶׁר צִוִּיתִי אֶת־עֲבָדַי הַנְּבִיאִים הֲלוֹא
הִשִּׂיגוּ אֲבֹתֵיכֶם וַיָּשׁוּבוּ וַיֹּאמְרוּ כַּאֲשֶׁר זָמַם
יְהֹוָה צְבָאוֹת לַעֲשׂוֹת לָנוּ כִּדְרָכֵינוּ וּכְמַעֲלָלֵינוּ כֵּן
עָשָׂה אִתָּנוּ: ס 7 בְּיוֹם עֶשְׂרִים וְאַרְבָּעָה
לְעַשְׁתֵּי־עָשָׂר חֹדֶשׁ הוּא־חֹדֶשׁ שְׁבָט בִּשְׁנַת שְׁתַּיִם
לְדָרְיָוֶשׁ הָיָה דְבַר־יְהֹוָה אֶל־זְכַרְיָה בֶּן־בֶּרֶכְיָהוּ בֶּן־
עִדּוֹא הַנָּבִיא לֵאמֹר: 8 רָאִיתִי הַלַּיְלָה וְהִנֵּה־אִישׁ
רֹכֵב עַל־סוּס אָדֹם וְהוּא עֹמֵד בֵּין הַהֲדַסִּים אֲשֶׁר
בַּמְּצֻלָה וְאַחֲרָיו סוּסִים אֲדֻמִּים שְׂרֻקִּים וּלְבָנִים:
9 וָאֹמַר מָה־אֵלֶּה אֲדֹנִי וַיֹּאמֶר אֵלַי הַמַּלְאָךְ הַדֹּבֵר
בִּי אֲנִי אַרְאֶךָּ מָה־הֵמָּה אֵלֶּה: 10 וַיַּעַן הָאִישׁ
הָעֹמֵד בֵּין־הַהֲדַסִּים וַיֹּאמַר אֵלֶּה אֲשֶׁר שָׁלַח יְהֹוָה
לְהִתְהַלֵּךְ בָּאָרֶץ: 11 וַיַּעֲנוּ אֶת־מַלְאַךְ יְהֹוָה הָעֹמֵד
בֵּין הַהֲדַסִּים וַיֹּאמְרוּ הִתְהַלַּכְנוּ בָאָרֶץ וְהִנֵּה כָל־
הָאָרֶץ יֹשֶׁבֶת וְשֹׁקָטֶת: 12 וַיַּעַן מַלְאַךְ־יְהֹוָה וַיֹּאמַר
יְהֹוָה צְבָאוֹת עַד־מָתַי אַתָּה לֹא־תְרַחֵם אֶת
יְרוּשָׁלַ͏ִם וְאֵת עָרֵי יְהוּדָה אֲשֶׁר זָעַמְתָּה זֶה שִׁבְעִים

13 And the LORD answered the angel who talked to me, *with good and* comforting words. 14 So the angel who spoke with me said to me, "Proclaim, saying, 'Thus says the LORD of hosts:

> "I am zealous for Jerusalem
> And for Zion with great zeal.
> 15 I am exceedingly angry with the nations at ease;
> For I was a little angry,
> And they helped—*but* with evil *intent*."

16 'Therefore thus says the LORD:

> "I am returning to Jerusalem with mercy;
> My house shall be built in it," says the LORD of hosts,
> "And a *surveyor's* line shall be stretched out over Jerusalem."'

17 "Again proclaim, saying, 'Thus says the LORD of hosts:

> "My cities shall again spread out through prosperity;
> The LORD will again comfort Zion,
> And will again choose Jerusalem."'"

18 Then I raised my eyes and looked, and there *were* four horns. 19 And I said to the angel who talked with me, "What *are* these?"

So he answered me, "These *are* the horns that have scattered Judah, Israel, and Jerusalem."

20 Then the LORD showed me four craftsmen. 21 And I said, "What are these coming to do?"

So he said, "These *are* the horns that scattered Judah, so that no one could lift up his head; but the craftsmen are coming to terrify them, to cast out the horns of the nations that lifted up *their* horn against the land of Judah to scatter it."

2 Then I raised my eyes and looked, and behold, a man with a measuring line in his hand. 2 So I said, "Where are you going?"

And he said to me, "To measure Jerusalem, to see what *is* its width and what *is* its length."

3 And there *was* the angel who talked with me, going out; and another angel was coming out to meet him, 4 who said to him, "Run, speak to this young man, saying: 'Jerusalem shall be inhabited *as* towns without walls, because of the multitude of men and livestock in it. 5 For I,' says the LORD, 'will be a wall of fire all around her, and I will be the glory in her midst.'"

6 "Up, up! Flee from the land of the north," says the LORD; "for I have spread you abroad like the four winds of heaven," says the LORD. 7 "Up, Zion! Escape, you who dwell with the daughter of Babylon."

שָׁנָה: 13 וַיַּעַן יְהֹוָה אֶת־הַמַּלְאָךְ הַדֹּבֵר בִּי דְּבָרִים
טוֹבִים דְּבָרִים נִחֻמִים: 14 וַיֹּאמֶר אֵלַי הַמַּלְאָךְ
הַדֹּבֵר בִּי קְרָא לֵאמֹר כֹּה אָמַר יְהֹוָה צְבָאוֹת
קִנֵּאתִי לִירוּשָׁלַ͏ִם וּלְצִיּוֹן קִנְאָה גְדוֹלָה: 15 וְקֶצֶף
גָּדוֹל אֲנִי קֹצֵף עַל־הַגּוֹיִם הַשַּׁאֲנַנִּים אֲשֶׁר אֲנִי
קָצַפְתִּי מְּעָט וְהֵמָּה עָזְרוּ לְרָעָה: 16 לָכֵן כֹּה־אָמַר
יְהֹוָה שַׁבְתִּי לִירוּשָׁלַ͏ִם בְּרַחֲמִים בֵּיתִי יִבָּנֶה בָּהּ נְאֻם
יְהֹוָה צְבָאוֹת וְקָוֻה יִנָּטֶה עַל־יְרוּשָׁלָ͏ִם: 17 עוֹד |
קְרָא לֵאמֹר כֹּה אָמַר יְהֹוָה צְבָאוֹת עוֹד תְּפוּצֶינָה
עָרַי מִטּוֹב וְנִחַם יְהֹוָה עוֹד אֶת־צִיּוֹן וּבָחַר עוֹד
בִּירוּשָׁלָ͏ִם: ס

ב וָאֶשָּׂא אֶת־עֵינַי וָאֵרֶא וְהִנֵּה אַרְבַּע קְרָנוֹת:
2 וָאֹמַר אֶל־הַמַּלְאָךְ הַדֹּבֵר בִּי מָה־אֵלֶּה וַיֹּאמֶר אֵלַי
אֵלֶּה הַקְּרָנוֹת אֲשֶׁר זֵרוּ אֶת־יְהוּדָה אֶת־יִשְׂרָאֵל
וִירוּשָׁלָ͏ִם: ס 3 וַיַּרְאֵנִי יְהֹוָה אַרְבָּעָה
חָרָשִׁים: 4 וָאֹמַר מָה אֵלֶּה בָאִים לַעֲשׂוֹת וַיֹּאמֶר
לֵאמֹר אֵלֶּה הַקְּרָנוֹת אֲשֶׁר־זֵרוּ אֶת־יְהוּדָה כְּפִי־
אִישׁ לֹא־נָשָׂא רֹאשׁוֹ וַיָּבֹאוּ אֵלֶּה לְהַחֲרִיד אֹתָם
לְיַדּוֹת אֶת־קַרְנוֹת הַגּוֹיִם הַנֹּשְׂאִים קֶרֶן אֶל־אֶרֶץ
יְהוּדָה לְזָרוֹתָהּ: ס 5 וָאֶשָּׂא עֵינַי וָאֵרֶא
וְהִנֵּה־אִישׁ וּבְיָדוֹ חֶבֶל מִדָּה: 6 וָאֹמַר אָנָה אַתָּה
הֹלֵךְ וַיֹּאמֶר אֵלַי לָמֹד אֶת־יְרוּשָׁלַ͏ִם לִרְאוֹת כַּמָּה־
רָחְבָּהּ וְכַמָּה אָרְכָּהּ: 7 וְהִנֵּה הַמַּלְאָךְ הַדֹּבֵר בִּי
יֹצֵא וּמַלְאָךְ אַחֵר יֹצֵא לִקְרָאתוֹ: 8 וַיֹּאמֶר אֵלָו רֻץ
דַּבֵּר אֶל־הַנַּעַר הַלָּז לֵאמֹר פְּרָזוֹת תֵּשֵׁב יְרוּשָׁלַ͏ִם
מֵרֹב אָדָם וּבְהֵמָה בְּתוֹכָהּ: 9 וַאֲנִי אֶהְיֶה־לָּהּ נְאֻם־
יְהֹוָה חוֹמַת אֵשׁ סָבִיב וּלְכָבוֹד אֶהְיֶה בְתוֹכָהּ: פ

10 הוֹי הוֹי וְנֻסוּ מֵאֶרֶץ צָפוֹן נְאֻם־יְהֹוָה כִּי כְּאַרְבַּע
רוּחוֹת הַשָּׁמַיִם פֵּרַשְׂתִּי אֶתְכֶם נְאֻם־יְהֹוָה: 11 הוֹי

8 For thus says the LORD of hosts: "He sent Me after glory, to the nations which plunder you; for he who touches you touches the apple of His eye. 9 For surely I will shake My hand against them, and they shall become spoil for their servants. Then you will know that the LORD of hosts has sent Me.

10 "Sing and rejoice, O daughter of Zion! For behold, I am coming and I will dwell in your midst," says the LORD. 11 "Many nations shall be joined to the LORD in that day, and they shall become My people. And I will dwell in your midst. Then you will know that the LORD of hosts has sent Me to you. 12 And the LORD will take possession of Judah as His inheritance in the Holy Land, and will again choose Jerusalem. 13 Be silent, all flesh, before the LORD, for He is aroused from His holy habitation!"

3 Then he showed me Joshua the high priest standing before the Angel of the LORD, and Satan standing at his right hand to oppose him. 2 And the LORD said to Satan, "The LORD rebuke you, Satan! The LORD who has chosen Jerusalem rebuke you! *Is* this not a brand plucked from the fire?"

3 Now Joshua was clothed with filthy garments, and was standing before the Angel.

4 Then He answered and spoke to those who stood before Him, saying, "Take away the filthy garments from him." And to him He said, "See, I have removed your iniquity from you, and I will clothe you with rich robes."

5 And I said, "Let them put a clean turban on his head."

So they put a clean turban on his head, and they put the clothes on him. And the Angel of the LORD stood by.

6 Then the Angel of the LORD admonished Joshua, saying, 7 "Thus says the LORD of hosts:

'If you will walk in My ways,
And if you will keep My command,
Then you shall also judge My house,
And likewise have charge of My courts;
I will give you places to walk
Among these who stand here.

8   'Hear, O Joshua, the high priest,
You and your companions who sit before you,
For they are a wondrous sign;
For behold, I am bringing forth My Servant the BRANCH.

9   For behold, the stone
That I have laid before Joshua:
Upon the stone *are* seven eyes.
Behold, I will engrave its inscription,'
Says the LORD of hosts,

צִיּוֹן הַמְלְטִי יוֹשֶׁבֶת בַּת־בָּבֶל: ס 12 כִּי כֹה אָמַר יְהֹוָה צְבָאוֹת אַחַר כָּבוֹד שְׁלָחַנִי אֶל־הַגּוֹיִם הַשֹּׁלְלִים אֶתְכֶם כִּי הַנֹּגֵעַ בָּכֶם נֹגֵעַ בְּבָבַת עֵינוֹ: 13 כִּי הִנְנִי מֵנִיף אֶת־יָדִי עֲלֵיהֶם וְהָיוּ שָׁלָל לְעַבְדֵיהֶם וִידַעְתֶּם כִּי־יְהֹוָה צְבָאוֹת שְׁלָחַנִי: ס 14 רָנִּי וְשִׂמְחִי בַּת־צִיּוֹן כִּי הִנְנִי־בָא וְשָׁכַנְתִּי בְתוֹכֵךְ נְאֻם־יְהֹוָה: 15 וְנִלְווּ גוֹיִם רַבִּים אֶל־יְהֹוָה בַּיּוֹם הַהוּא וְהָיוּ לִי לְעָם וְשָׁכַנְתִּי בְתוֹכֵךְ וְיָדַעַתְּ כִּי־יְהֹוָה צְבָאוֹת שְׁלָחַנִי אֵלָיִךְ: 16 וְנָחַל יְהֹוָה אֶת־יְהוּדָה חֶלְקוֹ עַל אַדְמַת הַקֹּדֶשׁ וּבָחַר עוֹד בִּירוּשָׁלָם: 17 הַס כָּל־בָּשָׂר מִפְּנֵי יְהֹוָה כִּי נֵעוֹר מִמְּעוֹן קָדְשׁוֹ: ס

ג וַיַּרְאֵנִי אֶת־יְהוֹשֻׁעַ הַכֹּהֵן הַגָּדוֹל עֹמֵד לִפְנֵי מַלְאַךְ יְהֹוָה וְהַשָּׂטָן עֹמֵד עַל־יְמִינוֹ לְשִׂטְנוֹ: 2 וַיֹּאמֶר יְהֹוָה אֶל־הַשָּׂטָן יִגְעַר יְהֹוָה בְּךָ הַשָּׂטָן וְיִגְעַר יְהֹוָה בְּךָ הַבֹּחֵר בִּירוּשָׁלָם הֲלוֹא זֶה אוּד מֻצָּל מֵאֵשׁ: 3 וִיהוֹשֻׁעַ הָיָה לָבֻשׁ בְּגָדִים צוֹאִים וְעֹמֵד לִפְנֵי הַמַּלְאָךְ: 4 וַיַּעַן וַיֹּאמֶר אֶל־הָעֹמְדִים לְפָנָיו לֵאמֹר הָסִירוּ הַבְּגָדִים הַצֹּאִים מֵעָלָיו וַיֹּאמֶר אֵלָיו רְאֵה הֶעֱבַרְתִּי מֵעָלֶיךָ עֲוֺנֶךָ וְהַלְבֵּשׁ אֹתְךָ מַחֲלָצוֹת: 5 וָאֹמַר יָשִׂימוּ צָנִיף טָהוֹר עַל־רֹאשׁוֹ וַיָּשִׂימוּ הַצָּנִיף הַטָּהוֹר עַל־רֹאשׁוֹ וַיַּלְבִּשֻׁהוּ בְּגָדִים וּמַלְאַךְ יְהֹוָה עֹמֵד: 6 וַיָּעַד מַלְאַךְ יְהֹוָה בִּיהוֹשֻׁעַ לֵאמֹר: 7 כֹּה־אָמַר יְהֹוָה צְבָאוֹת אִם־בִּדְרָכַי תֵּלֵךְ וְאִם אֶת־מִשְׁמַרְתִּי תִשְׁמֹר וְגַם־אַתָּה תָּדִין אֶת־בֵּיתִי וְגַם תִּשְׁמֹר אֶת־חֲצֵרָי וְנָתַתִּי לְךָ מַהְלְכִים בֵּין הָעֹמְדִים הָאֵלֶּה: 8 שְׁמַע־נָא יְהוֹשֻׁעַ הַכֹּהֵן הַגָּדוֹל אַתָּה וְרֵעֶיךָ הַיֹּשְׁבִים לְפָנֶיךָ כִּי־אַנְשֵׁי מוֹפֵת הֵמָּה כִּי־הִנְנִי מֵבִיא אֶת־עַבְדִּי צֶמַח: 9 כִּי הִנֵּה הָאֶבֶן אֲשֶׁר נָתַתִּי לִפְנֵי יְהוֹשֻׁעַ עַל־אֶבֶן אַחַת שִׁבְעָה עֵינָיִם הִנְנִי מְפַתֵּחַ פִּתֻּחָהּ נְאֻם יְהֹוָה

'And I will remove the iniquity of that land in one day.

10 In that day,' says the LORD of hosts, 'Everyone will invite his neighbor Under his vine and under his fig tree.'"

4

Now the angel who talked with me came back and wakened me, as a man who is wakened out of his sleep. ²And he said to me, "What do you see?"

So I said, "I am looking, and there *is* a lampstand of solid gold with a bowl on top of it, and on the *stand* seven lamps with seven pipes to the seven lamps. ³Two olive trees *are* by it, one at the right of the bowl and the other at its left." ⁴So I answered and spoke to the angel who talked with me, saying, "What *are* these, my lord?"

⁵Then the angel who talked with me answered and said to me, "Do you not know what these are?"

And I said, "No, my lord."

⁶So he answered and said to me:

"This *is* the word of the LORD to Zerubbabel:
'Not by might nor by power, but by My Spirit,'
Says the LORD of hosts.
⁷ 'Who *are* you, O great mountain?
Before Zerubbabel *you shall become* a plain!
And he shall bring forth the capstone
With shouts of "Grace, grace to it!" ' "

⁸Moreover the word of the LORD came to me, saying:

⁹ "The hands of Zerubbabel
Have laid the foundation of this temple;
His hands shall also finish *it*.
Then you will know
That the LORD of hosts has sent Me to you.
10 For who has despised the day of small things?
For these seven rejoice to see
The plumb line in the hand of Zerubbabel.
They are the eyes of the LORD,
Which scan to and fro throughout the whole earth."

¹¹Then I answered and said to him, "What *are* these two olive trees—at the right of the lampstand and at its left?" ¹²And I further answered and said to him, "What *are these* two olive branches that *drip* into the receptacles of the two gold pipes from which the golden *oil* drains?"

¹³Then he answered me and said, "Do you not know what these *are?*"

And I said, "No, my lord."

¹⁴So he said, "These *are* the two anointed ones, who stand beside the Lord of the whole earth."

5

Then I turned and raised my eyes, and saw there a flying scroll.

²And he said to me, "What do you see?"

צְבָא֔וֹת וּמַשְׁתִּ֛י אֶת־עֲוֹ֥ן הָאָֽרֶץ־הַהִ֖יא בְּי֥וֹם אֶחָֽד׃
10 בַּיּ֣וֹם הַה֗וּא נְאֻם֙ יְהֹוָ֣ה צְבָא֔וֹת תִּקְרְא֖וּ אִ֣ישׁ לְרֵעֵ֑הוּ אֶל־תַּ֥חַת גֶּ֖פֶן וְאֶל־תַּ֥חַת תְּאֵנָֽה׃

ד וַיָּ֕שׇׁב הַמַּלְאָ֖ךְ הַדֹּבֵ֣ר בִּ֑י וַיְעִירֵ֕נִי כְּאִ֖ישׁ אֲשֶׁר־יֵע֥וֹר מִשְּׁנָתֽוֹ׃ 2 וַיֹּ֣אמֶר אֵלַ֔י מָ֥ה אַתָּ֖ה רֹאֶ֑ה וָאֹמַ֡ר רָאִ֣יתִי ׀ וְהִנֵּ֣ה מְנוֹרַת֩ זָהָ֨ב כֻּלָּ֜הּ וְגֻלָּ֣הּ עַל־רֹאשָׁ֗הּ וְשִׁבְעָ֤ה נֵרֹתֶ֙יהָ֙ עָלֶ֔יהָ שִׁבְעָ֤ה וְשִׁבְעָה֙ מֽוּצָק֔וֹת לַנֵּר֖וֹת אֲשֶׁ֥ר עַל־רֹאשָֽׁהּ׃ 3 וּשְׁנַ֥יִם זֵיתִ֖ים עָלֶ֑יהָ אֶחָד֙ מִימִ֣ין הַגֻּלָּ֔ה וְאֶחָ֖ד עַל־שְׂמֹאלָֽהּ׃ 4 וָאַ֙עַן֙ וָֽאֹמַ֔ר אֶל־הַמַּלְאָ֛ךְ הַדֹּבֵ֥ר בִּ֖י לֵאמֹ֑ר מָה־אֵ֖לֶּה אֲדֹנִֽי׃ 5 וַ֠יַּ֠עַן הַמַּלְאָ֞ךְ הַדֹּבֵ֥ר בִּ֛י וַיֹּ֥אמֶר אֵלַ֖י הֲל֣וֹא יָדַ֔עְתָּ מָה־הֵ֖מָּה אֵ֑לֶּה וָאֹמַ֖ר לֹ֥א אֲדֹנִֽי׃ 6 וַיַּ֜עַן וַיֹּ֤אמֶר אֵלַי֙ לֵאמֹ֔ר זֶ֚ה דְּבַר־יְהֹוָ֔ה אֶל־זְרֻבָּבֶ֖ל לֵאמֹ֑ר לֹ֤א בְחַ֙יִל֙ וְלֹ֣א בְכֹ֔חַ כִּ֣י אִם־בְּרוּחִ֔י אָמַ֖ר יְהֹוָ֥ה צְבָאֽוֹת׃ 7 מִֽי־אַתָּ֧ה הַֽר־הַגָּד֛וֹל לִפְנֵ֥י זְרֻבָּבֶ֖ל לְמִישֹׁ֑ר וְהוֹצִיא֙ אֶת־הָאֶ֣בֶן הָרֹאשָׁ֔ה תְּשֻׁא֕וֹת חֵ֥ן חֵ֖ן לָֽהּ׃ פ
8 וַיְהִ֥י דְבַר־יְהֹוָ֖ה אֵלַ֥י לֵאמֹֽר׃ 9 יְדֵ֣י זְרֻבָּבֶ֗ל יִסְּדוּ֙ הַבַּ֣יִת הַזֶּ֔ה וְיָדָ֖יו תְּבַצַּ֑עְנָה וְ֣יָדַעְתָּ֔ כִּֽי־יְהֹוָ֥ה צְבָא֖וֹת שְׁלָחַ֥נִי אֲלֵיכֶֽם׃ 10 כִּ֣י מִ֣י בַז֮ לְי֣וֹם קְטַנּוֹת֒ וְשָׂמְח֗וּ וְרָא֞וּ אֶת־הָאֶ֧בֶן הַבְּדִ֛יל בְּיַ֥ד זְרֻבָּבֶ֖ל שִׁבְעָה־אֵ֑לֶּה עֵינֵ֣י יְהֹוָ֔ה הֵ֥מָּה מְשׁוֹטְטִ֖ים בְּכׇל־הָאָֽרֶץ׃ 11 וָאַ֖עַן וָאֹמַ֣ר אֵלָ֑יו מַה־שְּׁנֵ֤י הַזֵּיתִים֙ הָאֵ֔לֶּה עַל־יְמִ֥ין הַמְּנוֹרָ֖ה וְעַל־שְׂמֹאולָֽהּ׃ 12 וָאַ֣עַן שֵׁנִ֔ית וָאֹמַ֖ר אֵלָ֑יו מַה־שְׁתֵּ֞י שִׁבְּלֵ֣י הַזֵּיתִ֗ים אֲשֶׁר֙ בְּיַ֗ד שְׁנֵי֙ צַנְתְּר֣וֹת הַזָּהָ֔ב הַֽמְרִיקִ֥ים מֵעֲלֵיהֶ֖ם הַזָּהָֽב׃ 13 וַיֹּ֤אמֶר אֵלַי֙ לֵאמֹ֔ר הֲל֥וֹא יָדַ֖עְתָּ מָה־אֵ֑לֶּה וָאֹמַ֖ר לֹ֥א אֲדֹנִֽי׃ 14 וַיֹּ֕אמֶר אֵ֖לֶּה שְׁנֵ֣י בְנֵֽי־הַיִּצְהָ֑ר הָעֹמְדִ֖ים עַל־אֲד֥וֹן כׇּל־הָאָֽרֶץ׃

ה וָאָשׁ֕וּב וָאֶשָּׂ֥א עֵינַ֖י וָאֶרְאֶ֑ה וְהִנֵּ֖ה מְגִלָּ֥ה עָפָֽה׃ 2 וַיֹּ֣אמֶר אֵלַ֔י מָ֥ה אַתָּ֖ה רֹאֶ֑ה וָאֹמַ֕ר אֲנִ֥י רֹאֶה֙

So I answered, "I see a flying scroll. Its length *is* twenty cubits and its width ten cubits."

3 Then he said to me, "This *is* the curse that goes out over the face of the whole earth: 'Every thief shall be expelled,' according *to* this side of *the scroll;* and, 'Every perjurer shall be expelled,' according *to* that side of it."

4   "I will send out *the curse*," says the LORD of hosts;
    "It shall enter the house of the thief
      And the house of the one who swears falsely by
      My name.
    It shall remain in the midst of his house
    And consume it, with its timber and stones."

5 Then the angel who talked with me came out and said to me, "Lift your eyes now, and see what this *is* that goes forth."

6 So I asked, "What *is* it?" And he said, "It *is* a basket that is going forth."

He also said, "This *is* their resemblance throughout the earth: 7 Here *is* a lead disc lifted up, and this *is* a woman sitting inside the basket"; 8 then he said, "This *is* Wickedness!" And he thrust her down into the basket, and threw the lead cover over its mouth. 9 Then I raised my eyes and looked, and there *were* two women, coming with the wind in their wings; for they had wings like the wings of a stork, and they lifted up the basket between earth and heaven.

10 So I said to the angel who talked with me, "Where are they carrying the basket?"

11 And he said to me, "To build a house for it in the land of Shinar; when it is ready, *the basket* will be set there on its base."

6 Then I turned and raised my eyes and looked, and behold, four chariots *were* coming from between two mountains, and the mountains *were* mountains of bronze. 2 With the first chariot *were* red horses, with the second chariot black horses, 3 with the third chariot white horses, and with the fourth chariot dappled horses—strong *steeds.* 4 Then I answered and said to the angel who talked with me, "What *are* these, my lord?"

5 And the angel answered and said to me, "These *are* four spirits of heaven, who go out from *their* station before the Lord of all the earth. 6 The one with the black horses is going to the north country, the white are going after them, and the dappled are going toward the south country." 7 Then the strong *steeds* went out, eager to go, that they might walk to and fro throughout the earth. And He said, "Go, walk to and fro throughout the earth." So they walked to and fro throughout the earth. 8 And He

מְגִלָּה עָפָה אָרְכָּהּ עֶשְׂרִים בָּאַמָּה וְרָחְבָּהּ עֶשֶׂר
בָּאַמָּה: 3 וַיֹּאמֶר אֵלַי זֹאת הָאָלָה הַיּוֹצֵאת עַל־
פְּנֵי כָל־הָאָרֶץ כִּי כָל־הַגֹּנֵב מִזֶּה כָּמוֹהָ נִקָּה וְכָל־
הַנִּשְׁבָּע מִזֶּה כָּמוֹהָ נִקָּה: 4 הוֹצֵאתִיהָ נְאֻם יְהוָה
צְבָאוֹת וּבָאָה אֶל־בֵּית הַגַּנָּב וְאֶל־בֵּית הַנִּשְׁבָּע
בִּשְׁמִי לַשָּׁקֶר וְלָנֶה בְּתוֹךְ בֵּיתוֹ וְכִלַּתּוּ וְאֶת־עֵצָיו
וְאֶת־אֲבָנָיו: 5 וַיֵּצֵא הַמַּלְאָךְ הַדֹּבֵר בִּי וַיֹּאמֶר אֵלַי
שָׂא נָא עֵינֶיךָ וּרְאֵה מָה הַיּוֹצֵאת הַזֹּאת: 6 וָאֹמַר
מַה־הִיא וַיֹּאמֶר זֹאת הָאֵיפָה הַיּוֹצֵאת וַיֹּאמֶר זֹאת
עֵינָם בְּכָל־הָאָרֶץ: 7 וְהִנֵּה כִּכַּר עֹפֶרֶת נִשֵּׂאת וְזֹאת
אִשָּׁה אַחַת יוֹשֶׁבֶת בְּתוֹךְ הָאֵיפָה: 8 וַיֹּאמֶר זֹאת
הָרִשְׁעָה וַיַּשְׁלֵךְ אֹתָהּ אֶל־תּוֹךְ הָאֵיפָה וַיַּשְׁלֵךְ אֶת־
אֶבֶן הָעֹפֶרֶת אֶל־פִּיהָ: ס 9 וָאֶשָּׂא עֵינַי
וָאֵרֶא וְהִנֵּה שְׁתַּיִם נָשִׁים יוֹצְאוֹת וְרוּחַ בְּכַנְפֵיהֶם
וְלָהֵנָּה כְנָפַיִם כְּכַנְפֵי הַחֲסִידָה וַתִּשֶּׂאנָה אֶת־
הָאֵיפָה בֵּין הָאָרֶץ וּבֵין הַשָּׁמָיִם: 10 וָאֹמַר אֶל־
הַמַּלְאָךְ הַדֹּבֵר בִּי אָנָה הֵמָּה מוֹלִכוֹת אֶת־הָאֵיפָה:
11 וַיֹּאמֶר אֵלַי לִבְנוֹת־לָהּ בַיִת בְּאֶרֶץ שִׁנְעָר וְהוּכַן
וְהֻנִּיחָה שָּׁם עַל־מְכֻנָתָהּ: ס

ו וָאָשֻׁב וָאֶשָּׂא עֵינַי וָאֶרְאֶה וְהִנֵּה אַרְבַּע מַרְכָּבוֹת
יֹצְאוֹת מִבֵּין שְׁנֵי הֶהָרִים וְהֶהָרִים הָרֵי נְחֹשֶׁת:
2 בַּמֶּרְכָּבָה הָרִאשֹׁנָה סוּסִים אֲדֻמִּים וּבַמֶּרְכָּבָה
הַשֵּׁנִית סוּסִים שְׁחֹרִים: 3 וּבַמֶּרְכָּבָה הַשְּׁלִשִׁית
סוּסִים לְבָנִים וּבַמֶּרְכָּבָה הָרְבִעִית סוּסִים בְּרֻדִּים
אֲמֻצִּים: 4 וָאַעַן וָאֹמַר אֶל־הַמַּלְאָךְ הַדֹּבֵר בִּי מָה
אֵלֶּה אֲדֹנִי: 5 וַיַּעַן הַמַּלְאָךְ וַיֹּאמֶר אֵלָי אֵלֶּה אַרְבַּע
רֻחוֹת הַשָּׁמַיִם יוֹצְאוֹת מֵהִתְיַצֵּב עַל־אֲדוֹן כָּל־
הָאָרֶץ: 6 אֲשֶׁר־בָּהּ הַסּוּסִים הַשְּׁחֹרִים יֹצְאִים אֶל־
אֶרֶץ צָפוֹן וְהַלְּבָנִים יָצְאוּ אֶל־אַחֲרֵיהֶם וְהַבְּרֻדִּים
יָצְאוּ אֶל־אֶרֶץ הַתֵּימָן: 7 וְהָאֲמֻצִּים יָצְאוּ וַיְבַקְשׁוּ
לָלֶכֶת לְהִתְהַלֵּךְ בָּאָרֶץ וַיֹּאמֶר לְכוּ הִתְהַלְּכוּ בָאָרֶץ
וַתִּתְהַלַּכְנָה בָּאָרֶץ: 8 וַיַּזְעֵק אֹתִי וַיְדַבֵּר אֵלַי לֵאמֹר

called to me, and spoke to me, saying, "See, those who go toward the north country have given rest to My Spirit in the north country."

9 Then the word of the LORD came to me, saying: 10 "Receive *the gift* from the captives—from Heldai, Tobijah, and Jedaiah, who have come from Babylon—and go the same day and enter the house of Josiah the son of Zephaniah. 11 Take the silver and gold, make an elaborate crown, and set *it* on the head of Joshua the son of Jehozadak, the high priest. 12 Then speak to him, saying, 'Thus says the LORD of hosts, saying:

"Behold, the Man whose name *is* the BRANCH!
From His place He shall branch out,
And He shall build the temple of the LORD;
13 Yes, He shall build the temple of the LORD.
He shall bear the glory,
And shall sit and rule on His throne;
So He shall be a priest on His throne,
And the counsel of peace shall be between them both.'"

14 "Now the elaborate crown shall be for a memorial in the temple of the LORD for Helem, Tobijah, Jedaiah, and Hen the son of Zephaniah. 15 Even those from afar shall come and build the temple of the LORD. Then you shall know that the LORD of hosts has sent Me to you. And *this* shall come to pass if you diligently obey the voice of the LORD your God."

7 Now in the fourth year of King Darius it came to pass *that* the word of the LORD came to Zechariah, on the fourth day of the ninth month, Chislev, 2 when *the people* sent Sherezer, with Regem-Melech and his men, *to* the house of God, to pray before the LORD, 3 *and* to ask the priests who *were* in the house of the LORD of hosts, and the prophets, saying, "Should I weep in the fifth month and fast as I have done for so many years?"

4 Then the word of the LORD of hosts came to me, saying, 5 "Say to all the people of the land, and to the priests: 'When you fasted and mourned in the fifth and seventh *months* during those seventy years, did you really fast for Me—for Me? 6 When you eat and when you drink, do you not eat and drink *for yourselves*? 7 *Should you* not *have obeyed* the words which the LORD proclaimed through the former prophets when Jerusalem and the cities around it were inhabited and prosperous, and the South and the Lowland were inhabited?' "

8 Then the word of the LORD came to Zechariah, saying, 9 "Thus says the LORD of hosts:

'Execute true justice,
Show mercy and compassion

רָאֵה הַיּוֹצְאִים אֶל־אֶרֶץ צָפוֹן הֵנִיחוּ אֶת־רוּחִי
בְּאֶרֶץ צָפוֹן: ס 9 וַיְהִי דְבַר־יְהֹוָה אֵלַי
לֵאמֹר: 10 לָקוֹחַ מֵאֵת הַגּוֹלָה מֵחֶלְדַּי וּמֵאֵת טוֹבִיָּה
וּמֵאֵת יְדַעְיָה וּבָאתָ אַתָּה בַּיּוֹם הַהוּא וּבָאתָ
בֵּית יֹאשִׁיָּה בֶן־צְפַנְיָה אֲשֶׁר־בָּאוּ מִבָּבֶל: 11 וְלָקַחְתָּ
כֶסֶף־וְזָהָב וְעָשִׂיתָ עֲטָרוֹת וְשַׂמְתָּ בְּרֹאשׁ יְהוֹשֻׁעַ
בֶּן־יְהוֹצָדָק הַכֹּהֵן הַגָּדוֹל: 12 וְאָמַרְתָּ אֵלָיו לֵאמֹר
כֹּה אָמַר יְהֹוָה צְבָאוֹת לֵאמֹר הִנֵּה־אִישׁ צֶמַח שְׁמוֹ
וּמִתַּחְתָּיו יִצְמָח וּבָנָה אֶת־הֵיכַל יְהֹוָה: 13 וְהוּא
יִבְנֶה אֶת־הֵיכַל יְהֹוָה וְהוּא־יִשָּׂא הוֹד וְיָשַׁב וּמָשַׁל
עַל־כִּסְאוֹ וְהָיָה כֹהֵן עַל־כִּסְאוֹ וַעֲצַת שָׁלוֹם תִּהְיֶה
בֵּין שְׁנֵיהֶם: 14 וְהָעֲטָרֹת תִּהְיֶה לְחֵלֶם וּלְטוֹבִיָּה
וְלִידַעְיָה וּלְחֵן בֶּן־צְפַנְיָה לְזִכָּרוֹן בְּהֵיכַל יְהֹוָה:
15 וּרְחוֹקִים | יָבֹאוּ וּבָנוּ בְּהֵיכַל יְהֹוָה וִידַעְתֶּם
כִּי־יְהֹוָה צְבָאוֹת שְׁלָחַנִי אֲלֵיכֶם וְהָיָה אִם־שָׁמוֹעַ
תִּשְׁמְעוּן בְּקוֹל יְהֹוָה אֱלֹהֵיכֶם: ס

ז וַיְהִי בִּשְׁנַת אַרְבַּע לְדָרְיָוֶשׁ הַמֶּלֶךְ הָיָה דְבַר־
יְהֹוָה אֶל־זְכַרְיָה בְּאַרְבָּעָה לַחֹדֶשׁ הַתְּשִׁעִי בְּכִסְלֵו:
2 וַיִּשְׁלַח בֵּית־אֵל שַׂר־אֶצֶר וְרֶגֶם מֶלֶךְ וַאֲנָשָׁיו
לְחַלּוֹת אֶת־פְּנֵי יְהֹוָה: 3 לֵאמֹר אֶל־הַכֹּהֲנִים אֲשֶׁר
לְבֵית־יְהֹוָה צְבָאוֹת וְאֶל־הַנְּבִיאִים לֵאמֹר הַאֶבְכֶּה
בַּחֹדֶשׁ הַחֲמִשִׁי הִנָּזֵר כַּאֲשֶׁר עָשִׂיתִי זֶה כַּמֶּה
שָׁנִים: פ
4 וַיְהִי דְּבַר־יְהֹוָה צְבָאוֹת אֵלַי לֵאמֹר: 5 אֱמֹר
אֶל־כָּל־עַם הָאָרֶץ וְאֶל־הַכֹּהֲנִים לֵאמֹר כִּי־צַמְתֶּם
וְסָפוֹד בַּחֲמִשִׁי וּבַשְּׁבִיעִי וְזֶה שִׁבְעִים שָׁנָה הֲצוֹם
צַמְתֻּנִי אָנִי: 6 וְכִי תֹאכְלוּ וְכִי תִשְׁתּוּ הֲלוֹא אַתֶּם
הָאֹכְלִים וְאַתֶּם הַשֹּׁתִים: 7 הֲלוֹא אֶת־הַדְּבָרִים
אֲשֶׁר קָרָא יְהֹוָה בְּיַד הַנְּבִיאִים הָרִאשֹׁנִים בִּהְיוֹת
יְרוּשָׁלַםִ יֹשֶׁבֶת וּשְׁלֵוָה וְעָרֶיהָ סְבִיבֹתֶיהָ וְהַנֶּגֶב
וְהַשְּׁפֵלָה יֹשֵׁב: פ
8 וַיְהִי דְּבַר־יְהֹוָה אֶל־זְכַרְיָה לֵאמֹר: 9 כֹּה אָמַר
יְהֹוָה צְבָאוֹת לֵאמֹר מִשְׁפַּט אֱמֶת שְׁפֹטוּ וְחֶסֶד

Everyone to his brother.
10 Do not oppress the widow or the fatherless,
    The alien or the poor.
    Let none of you plan evil in his heart
    Against his brother.'

11 But they refused to heed, shrugged their shoulders, and stopped their ears so that they could not hear. 12 Yes, they made their hearts like flint, refusing to hear the law and the words which the LORD of hosts had sent by His Spirit through the former prophets. Thus great wrath came from the LORD of hosts. 13 Therefore it happened, *that* just as He proclaimed and they would not hear, so they called out and I would not listen," says the LORD of hosts. 14 "But I scattered them with a whirlwind among all the nations which they had not known. Thus the land became desolate after them, so that no one passed through or returned; for they made the pleasant land desolate."

8 Again the word of the LORD of hosts came, saying, 2 "Thus says the LORD of hosts:

    'I am zealous for Zion with great zeal;
    With great fervor I am zealous for her.'

3 "Thus says the LORD:

    'I will return to Zion,
    And dwell in the midst of Jerusalem.
    Jerusalem shall be called the City of Truth,
    The Mountain of the LORD of hosts,
    The Holy Mountain.'

4 "Thus says the LORD of hosts:

    'Old men and old women shall again sit
    In the streets of Jerusalem,
    Each one with his staff in his hand
    Because of great age.
5   The streets of the city
    Shall be full of boys and girls
    Playing in its streets.'

6 "Thus says the LORD of hosts:

    'If it is marvelous in the eyes of the remnant of
      this people in these days,
    Will it also be marvelous in My eyes?'
    Says the LORD of hosts.

7 "Thus says the LORD of hosts:

    'Behold, I will save My people from the land of
      the east
    And from the land of the west;
8   I will bring them *back,*
    And they shall dwell in the midst of Jerusalem.
    They shall be My people
    And I will be their God,
    In truth and righteousness.'

9 "Thus says the LORD of hosts:

וְרַחֲמִים עֲשׂוּ אִישׁ אֶת־אָחִיו: 10 וְאַלְמָנָה וְיָתוֹם
גֵּר וְעָנִי אַל־תַּעֲשֹׁקוּ וְרָעַת אִישׁ אָחִיו אַל־תַּחְשְׁבוּ
בִּלְבַבְכֶם: 11 וַיְמָאֲנוּ לְהַקְשִׁיב וַיִּתְּנוּ כָּתֵף סֹרָרֶת
וְאָזְנֵיהֶם הִכְבִּידוּ מִשְּׁמוֹעַ: 12 וְלִבָּם שָׂמוּ שָׁמִיר
מִשְּׁמוֹעַ אֶת־הַתּוֹרָה וְאֶת־הַדְּבָרִים אֲשֶׁר שָׁלַח
יְהוָה צְבָאוֹת בְּרוּחוֹ בְּיַד הַנְּבִיאִים הָרִאשֹׁנִים וַיְהִי
קֶצֶף גָּדוֹל מֵאֵת יְהוָה צְבָאוֹת: 13 וַיְהִי כַאֲשֶׁר־
קָרָא וְלֹא שָׁמֵעוּ כֵּן יִקְרְאוּ וְלֹא אֶשְׁמָע אָמַר
יְהוָה צְבָאוֹת: 14 וְאֶסָעֲרֵם עַל כָּל־הַגּוֹיִם אֲשֶׁר
לֹא־יְדָעוּם וְהָאָרֶץ נָשַׁמָּה אַחֲרֵיהֶם מֵעֹבֵר וּמִשָּׁב
ס   וַיָּשִׂימוּ אֶרֶץ־חֶמְדָּה לְשַׁמָּה:

ח וַיְהִי דְּבַר־יְהוָה צְבָאוֹת לֵאמֹר: 2 כֹּה אָמַר
יְהוָה צְבָאוֹת קִנֵּאתִי לְצִיּוֹן קִנְאָה גְדוֹלָה וְחֵמָה
גְדוֹלָה קִנֵּאתִי לָהּ: 3 כֹּה אָמַר יְהוָה שַׁבְתִּי אֶל־
צִיּוֹן וְשָׁכַנְתִּי בְּתוֹךְ יְרוּשָׁלִָם וְנִקְרְאָה יְרוּשָׁלִַם עִיר־
הָאֱמֶת וְהַר־יְהוָה צְבָאוֹת הַר הַקֹּדֶשׁ: ס 4 כֹּה
אָמַר יְהוָה צְבָאוֹת עֹד יֵשְׁבוּ זְקֵנִים וּזְקֵנוֹת
בִּרְחֹבוֹת יְרוּשָׁלִָם וְאִישׁ מִשְׁעַנְתּוֹ בְּיָדוֹ מֵרֹב יָמִים:
5 וּרְחֹבוֹת הָעִיר יִמָּלְאוּ יְלָדִים וִילָדוֹת מְשַׂחֲקִים
בִּרְחֹבֹתֶיהָ: ס 6 כֹּה אָמַר יְהוָה צְבָאוֹת כִּי
יִפָּלֵא בְּעֵינֵי שְׁאֵרִית הָעָם הַזֶּה בַּיָּמִים הָהֵם גַּם־
בְּעֵינַי יִפָּלֵא נְאֻם יְהוָה צְבָאוֹת: ס

7 כֹּה אָמַר יְהוָה צְבָאוֹת הִנְנִי מוֹשִׁיעַ אֶת־
עַמִּי מֵאֶרֶץ מִזְרָח וּמֵאֶרֶץ מְבוֹא הַשָּׁמֶשׁ:
8 וְהֵבֵאתִי אֹתָם וְשָׁכְנוּ בְּתוֹךְ יְרוּשָׁלִָם וְהָיוּ־
לִי לְעָם וַאֲנִי אֶהְיֶה לָהֶם לֵאלֹהִים בֶּאֱמֶת
וּבִצְדָקָה: ס 9 כֹּה־אָמַר יְהוָה צְבָאוֹת תֶּחֱזַקְנָה

'Let your hands be strong,
You who have been hearing in these days
These words by the mouth of the prophets,
Who *spoke* in the day the foundation was laid
For the house of the LORD of hosts,
That the temple might be built.
10 For before these days
   There were no wages for man nor any hire for
       beast;
   There was no peace from the enemy for whoever
       went out or came in;
   For I set all men, everyone, against his neighbor.

11 But now I *will* not *treat* the remnant of this
people as in the former days,' says the LORD of
hosts.

12 'For the seed *shall be* prosperous,
   The vine shall give its fruit,
   The ground shall give her increase,
   And the heavens shall give their dew—
   I will cause the remnant of this people
   To possess all these.
13 And it shall come to pass
   That just as you were a curse among the nations,
   O house of Judah and house of Israel,
   So I will save you, and you shall be a blessing.
   Do not fear,
   Let your hands be strong.'

14 "For thus says the LORD of hosts:

   'Just as I determined to punish you
   When your fathers provoked Me to wrath,'
   Says the LORD of hosts,
   'And I would not relent,
15 So again in these days
   I am determined to do good
   To Jerusalem and to the house of Judah.
   Do not fear.
16 These *are* the things you shall do:
   Speak each man the truth to his neighbor;
   Give judgment in your gates for truth, justice,
       and peace;
17 Let none of you think evil in your heart against
       your neighbor;
   And do not love a false oath.
   For all these *are things* that I hate,'
   Says the LORD."

18 Then the word of the LORD of hosts came to
me, saying, 19 "Thus says the LORD of hosts:

   'The fast of the fourth *month,*
   The fast of the fifth,
   The fast of the seventh,
   And the fast of the tenth,
   Shall be joy and gladness and cheerful feasts
   For the house of Judah.
   Therefore love truth and peace.'

20 "Thus says the LORD of hosts:

   'Peoples shall yet come,
   Inhabitants of many cities;

יְדֵיכֶם הַשֹּׁמְעִים בַּיָּמִים הָאֵלֶּה אֵת הַדְּבָרִים

הָאֵלֶּה מִפִּי הַנְּבִיאִים אֲשֶׁר בְּיוֹם יֻסַּד בֵּית־יְהֹוָה

צְבָאוֹת הַהֵיכָל לְהִבָּנוֹת: 10 כִּי לִפְנֵי הַיָּמִים הָהֵם

שְׂכַר הָאָדָם לֹא נִהְיָה וּשְׂכַר הַבְּהֵמָה אֵינֶנָּה

וְלַיּוֹצֵא וְלַבָּא אֵין־שָׁלוֹם מִן־הַצָּר וַאֲשַׁלַּח אֶת־

כָּל־הָאָדָם אִישׁ בְּרֵעֵהוּ: 11 וְעַתָּה לֹא כַיָּמִים

הָרִאשֹׁנִים אֲנִי לִשְׁאֵרִית הָעָם הַזֶּה נְאֻם יְהֹוָה

צְבָאוֹת: 12 כִּי־זֶרַע הַשָּׁלוֹם הַגֶּפֶן תִּתֵּן פִּרְיָהּ

וְהָאָרֶץ תִּתֵּן אֶת־יְבוּלָהּ וְהַשָּׁמַיִם יִתְּנוּ טַלָּם

וְהִנְחַלְתִּי אֶת־שְׁאֵרִית הָעָם הַזֶּה אֶת־כָּל־אֵלֶּה:

13 וְהָיָה כַּאֲשֶׁר הֱיִיתֶם קְלָלָה בַּגּוֹיִם בֵּית יְהוּדָה

וּבֵית יִשְׂרָאֵל כֵּן אוֹשִׁיעַ אֶתְכֶם וִהְיִיתֶם בְּרָכָה

אַל־תִּירָאוּ תֶּחֱזַקְנָה יְדֵיכֶם: ס 14 כִּי כֹה אָמַר

יְהֹוָה צְבָאוֹת כַּאֲשֶׁר זָמַמְתִּי לְהָרַע לָכֶם בְּהַקְצִיף

אֲבֹתֵיכֶם אֹתִי אָמַר יְהֹוָה צְבָאוֹת וְלֹא נִחָמְתִּי:

15 כֵּן שַׁבְתִּי זָמַמְתִּי בַּיָּמִים הָאֵלֶּה לְהֵיטִיב אֶת־

יְרוּשָׁלַ͏ִם וְאֶת־בֵּית יְהוּדָה אַל־תִּירָאוּ: 16 אֵלֶּה

הַדְּבָרִים אֲשֶׁר תַּעֲשׂוּ דַּבְּרוּ אֱמֶת אִישׁ אֶת־רֵעֵהוּ

אֱמֶת וּמִשְׁפַּט שָׁלוֹם שִׁפְטוּ בְּשַׁעֲרֵיכֶם: 17 וְאִישׁ |

אֶת־רָעַת רֵעֵהוּ אַל־תַּחְשְׁבוּ בִּלְבַבְכֶם וּשְׁבֻעַת

שֶׁקֶר אַל־תֶּאֱהָבוּ כִּי אֶת־כָּל־אֵלֶּה אֲשֶׁר שָׂנֵאתִי

נְאֻם־יְהֹוָה: ס 18 וַיְהִי דְּבַר־יְהֹוָה צְבָאוֹת אֵלַי

לֵאמֹר: 19 כֹּה־אָמַר יְהֹוָה צְבָאוֹת צוֹם הָרְבִיעִי

וְצוֹם הַחֲמִישִׁי וְצוֹם הַשְּׁבִיעִי וְצוֹם הָעֲשִׂירִי יִהְיֶה

לְבֵית־יְהוּדָה לְשָׂשׂוֹן וּלְשִׂמְחָה וּלְמֹעֲדִים טוֹבִים

וְהָאֱמֶת וְהַשָּׁלוֹם אֱהָבוּ:   פ

20 כֹּה אָמַר יְהֹוָה צְבָאוֹת עֹד אֲשֶׁר יָבֹאוּ עַמִּים

21 The inhabitants of one *city* shall go to another,
    saying,
  "Let us continue to go and pray before the LORD,
  And seek the LORD of hosts.
  I myself will go also."
22 Yes, many peoples and strong nations
  Shall come to seek the LORD of hosts in
    Jerusalem,
  And to pray before the LORD.'

23 "Thus says the LORD of hosts: 'In those days
ten men from every language of the nations shall
grasp the sleeve of a Jewish man, saying, "Let us go
with you, for we have heard *that* God *is* with
you."'"

9 The burden of the word of the LORD
  Against the land of Hadrach,
  And Damascus its resting place
  (For the eyes of men
  And all the tribes of Israel
  Are on the LORD);
2 Also *against* Hamath, *which* borders on it,
  And *against* Tyre and Sidon, though they are
    very wise.
3 For Tyre built herself a tower,
  Heaped up silver like the dust,
  And gold like the mire of the streets.
4 Behold, the LORD will cast her out;
  He will destroy her power in the sea,
  And she will be devoured by fire.
5 Ashkelon shall see *it* and fear;
  Gaza also shall be very sorrowful;
  And Ekron, for He dried up her expectation.
  The king shall perish from Gaza,
  And Ashkelon shall not be inhabited.
6 "A mixed race shall settle in Ashdod,
  And I will cut off the pride of the Philistines.
7 I will take away the blood from his mouth,
  And the abominations from between his
    teeth.
  But he who remains, even he *shall be* for our
    God,
  And shall be like a leader in Judah,
  And Ekron like a Jebusite.
8 I will camp around My house
  Because of the army,
  Because of him who passes by and him who
    returns.
  No more shall an oppressor pass through
    them,
  For now I have seen with My eyes.
9 "Rejoice greatly, O daughter of Zion!
  Shout, O daughter of Jerusalem!

וְיֹשְׁבֵי עָרִים רַבּוֹת: 21 וְהָלְכוּ יֹשְׁבֵי אַחַת אֶל־אַחַת
לֵאמֹר נֵלְכָה הָלוֹךְ לְחַלּוֹת אֶת־פְּנֵי יְהוָה וּלְבַקֵּשׁ
אֶת־יְהוָה צְבָאוֹת אֵלְכָה גַּם־אָנִי: 22 וּבָאוּ עַמִּים
רַבִּים וְגוֹיִם עֲצוּמִים לְבַקֵּשׁ אֶת־יְהוָה צְבָאוֹת
בִּירוּשָׁלִָם וּלְחַלּוֹת אֶת־פְּנֵי יְהוָה: ס 23 כֹּה־
אָמַר יְהוָה צְבָאוֹת בַּיָּמִים הָהֵמָּה אֲשֶׁר יַחֲזִיקוּ
עֲשָׂרָה אֲנָשִׁים מִכֹּל לְשֹׁנוֹת הַגּוֹיִם וְהֶחֱזִיקוּ בִּכְנַף
אִישׁ יְהוּדִי לֵאמֹר נֵלְכָה עִמָּכֶם כִּי שָׁמַעְנוּ אֱלֹהִים
עִמָּכֶם: ס

ט מַשָּׂא דְבַר־יְהוָה
בְּאֶרֶץ חַדְרָךְ
וְדַמֶּשֶׂק מְנֻחָתוֹ
כִּי לַיהוָה עֵין אָדָם
וְכֹל שִׁבְטֵי יִשְׂרָאֵל:
2 וְגַם־חֲמָת תִּגְבָּל־בָּהּ
צֹר וְצִידוֹן כִּי חָכְמָה מְאֹד:
3 וַתִּבֶן צֹר מָצוֹר לָהּ
וַתִּצְבָּר־כֶּסֶף כֶּעָפָר
וְחָרוּץ כְּטִיט חוּצוֹת:
4 הִנֵּה אֲדֹנָי יוֹרִשֶׁנָּה
וְהִכָּה בַיָּם חֵילָהּ
וְהִיא בָּאֵשׁ תֵּאָכֵל:
5 תֵּרֶא אַשְׁקְלוֹן וְתִירָא
וְעַזָּה וְתָחִיל מְאֹד
וְעֶקְרוֹן כִּי־הֹבִישׁ מֶבָּטָהּ
וְאָבַד מֶלֶךְ מֵעַזָּה
וְאַשְׁקְלוֹן לֹא תֵשֵׁב:
6 וְיָשַׁב מַמְזֵר בְּאַשְׁדּוֹד
וְהִכְרַתִּי גְּאוֹן פְּלִשְׁתִּים:
7 וַהֲסִרֹתִי דָמָיו מִפִּיו
וְשִׁקֻּצָיו מִבֵּין שִׁנָּיו
וְנִשְׁאַר גַּם־הוּא לֵאלֹהֵינוּ
וְהָיָה כְּאַלֻּף בִּיהוּדָה
וְעֶקְרוֹן כִּיבוּסִי:
8 וְחָנִיתִי לְבֵיתִי מִצָּבָה
מֵעֹבֵר וּמִשָּׁב
וְלֹא־יַעֲבֹר עֲלֵיהֶם עוֹד נֹגֵשׂ
כִּי עַתָּה רָאִיתִי בְעֵינָי: ס
9 גִּילִי מְאֹד בַּת־צִיּוֹן
הָרִיעִי בַּת יְרוּשָׁלִַם

Behold, your King is coming to you;   הִנֵּה מַלְכֵּךְ יָבוֹא לָךְ
He *is* just and having salvation,   צַדִּיק וְנוֹשָׁע הוּא
Lowly and riding on a donkey,   עָנִי וְרֹכֵב עַל־חֲמוֹר
A colt, the foal of a donkey.   וְעַל־עַיִר בֶּן־אֲתֹנוֹת׃

10   I will cut off the chariot from Ephraim   10   וְהִכְרַתִּי־רֶכֶב מֵאֶפְרַיִם
And the horse from Jerusalem;   וְסוּס מִירוּשָׁלַͅם
The battle bow shall be cut off.   וְנִכְרְתָה קֶשֶׁת מִלְחָמָה
He shall speak peace to the nations;   וְדִבֶּר שָׁלוֹם לַגּוֹיִם
His dominion *shall be* 'from sea to sea,   וּמָשְׁלוֹ מִיָּם עַד־יָם
And from the River to the ends of the earth.'   וּמִנָּהָר עַד־אַפְסֵי־אָרֶץ׃

11   "As for you also,
Because of the blood of your covenant,   11   גַּם־אַתְּ בְּדַם־בְּרִיתֵךְ
I will set your prisoners free from the
     waterless pit.   שִׁלַּחְתִּי אֲסִירַיִךְ מִבּוֹר אֵין מַיִם בּוֹ׃

12   Return to the stronghold,   12   שׁוּבוּ לְבִצָּרוֹן אֲסִירֵי הַתִּקְוָה
You prisoners of hope.
Even today I declare   גַּם־הַיּוֹם מַגִּיד מִשְׁנֶה אָשִׁיב לָךְ׃
That I will restore double to you.

13   For I have bent Judah, My *bow,*   13   כִּי־דָרַכְתִּי לִי יְהוּדָה
Fitted the bow with Ephraim,   קֶשֶׁת מִלֵּאתִי אֶפְרַיִם
And raised up your sons, O Zion,   וְעוֹרַרְתִּי בָנַיִךְ צִיּוֹן
Against your sons, O Greece,   עַל־בָּנַיִךְ יָוָן
And made you like the sword of a mighty
     man."   וְשַׂמְתִּיךְ כְּחֶרֶב גִּבּוֹר׃

14   Then the LORD will be seen over them,   14   וַיהֹוָה עֲלֵיהֶם יֵרָאֶה
And His arrow will go forth like lightning.   וְיָצָא כַבָּרָק חִצּוֹ
The Lord GOD will blow the trumpet,   וַאדֹנָי יְהֹוִה בַּשּׁוֹפָר יִתְקָע
And go with whirlwinds from the south.   וְהָלַךְ בְּסַעֲרוֹת תֵּימָן׃

15   The LORD of hosts will defend them;   15   יְהֹוָה צְבָאוֹת יָגֵן עֲלֵיהֶם
They shall devour and subdue with sling-
     stones.   וְאָכְלוּ וְכָבְשׁוּ אַבְנֵי־קֶלַע
They shall drink *and* roar as if with wine;   וְשָׁתוּ הָמוּ כְּמוֹ־יָיִן
They shall be filled *with blood* like basins,   וּמָלְאוּ כַּמִּזְרָק כְּזָוִיּוֹת מִזְבֵּחַ׃
Like the corners of the altar.

16   The LORD their God will save them in that
     day,   16   וְהוֹשִׁיעָם יְהֹוָה אֱלֹהֵיהֶם
As the flock of His people.   בַּיּוֹם הַהוּא כְּצֹאן עַמּוֹ
For they *shall be* like the jewels of a crown,   כִּי אַבְנֵי־נֵזֶר
Lifted like a banner over His land—   מִתְנוֹסְסוֹת עַל־אַדְמָתוֹ׃

17   For how great is its goodness   17   כִּי מַה־טּוּבוֹ וּמַה־יָפְיוֹ
And how great its beauty!   דָּגָן בַּחוּרִים
Grain shall make the young men thrive,
And new wine the young women.   וְתִירוֹשׁ יְנוֹבֵב בְּתֻלוֹת׃

10   Ask the LORD for rain   י   שַׁאֲלוּ מֵיְהֹוָה מָטָר בְּעֵת מַלְקוֹשׁ
In the time of the latter rain.   יְהֹוָה עֹשֶׂה חֲזִיזִים
The LORD will make flashing clouds;   וּמְטַר־גֶּשֶׁם יִתֵּן לָהֶם
He will give them showers of rain,   לְאִישׁ עֵשֶׂב בַּשָּׂדֶה׃
Grass in the field for everyone.

2   For the idols speak delusion;   2   כִּי הַתְּרָפִים דִּבְּרוּ־אָוֶן
The diviners envision lies,   וְהַקּוֹסְמִים חָזוּ שֶׁקֶר
And tell false dreams;   וַחֲלֹמוֹת הַשָּׁוְא יְדַבֵּרוּ

They comfort in vain.
Therefore *the people* wend their way like
    sheep;
They are in trouble because *there is* no
    shepherd.

הֶבֶל יְנַחֵמוּן
עַל־כֵּן נָסְעוּ כְמוֹ־צֹאן
יַעֲנוּ כִּי־אֵין רֹעֶה: פ

3 "My anger is kindled against the shepherds,
And I will punish the goatherds.
For the LORD of hosts will visit His flock,
The house of Judah,
And will make them as His royal horse in the
    battle.

עַל־הָרֹעִים חָרָה אַפִּי
וְעַל־הָעַתּוּדִים אֶפְקוֹד
כִּי־פָקַד יְהוָה צְבָאוֹת אֶת־עֶדְרוֹ
אֶת־בֵּית יְהוּדָה
וְשָׂם אוֹתָם כְּסוּס הוֹדוֹ בַּמִּלְחָמָה:

4 From him comes the cornerstone,
From him the tent peg,
From him the battle bow,
From him every ruler together.

מִמֶּנּוּ פִנָּה
מִמֶּנּוּ יָתֵד
מִמֶּנּוּ קֶשֶׁת מִלְחָמָה
מִמֶּנּוּ יֵצֵא כָל־נוֹגֵשׂ יַחְדָּו:

5 They shall be like mighty men,
Who tread down *their enemies*
In the mire of the streets in the battle.
They shall fight because the LORD is with
    them,
And the riders on horses shall be put to
    shame.

וְהָיוּ כְגִבֹּרִים בּוֹסִים
בְּטִיט חוּצוֹת בַּמִּלְחָמָה
וְנִלְחֲמוּ כִּי יְהוָה עִמָּם
וְהֹבִישׁוּ רֹכְבֵי סוּסִים:

6 "I will strengthen the house of Judah,
And I will save the house of Joseph.
I will bring them back,
Because I have mercy on them.
They shall be as though I had not cast them
    aside;
For I *am* the LORD their God,
And I will hear them.

וְגִבַּרְתִּי | אֶת־בֵּית יְהוּדָה
וְאֶת־בֵּית יוֹסֵף אוֹשִׁיעַ
וְהוֹשְׁבוֹתִים כִּי רִחַמְתִּים
וְהָיוּ כַּאֲשֶׁר לֹא־זְנַחְתִּים
כִּי אֲנִי יְהוָה אֱלֹהֵיהֶם וְאֶעֱנֵם:

7 *Those of* Ephraim shall be like a mighty man,
And their heart shall rejoice as if with wine.
Yes, their children shall see *it* and be glad;
Their heart shall rejoice in the LORD.

וְהָיוּ כְגִבּוֹר אֶפְרַיִם
וְשָׂמַח לִבָּם כְּמוֹ־יָיִן
וּבְנֵיהֶם יִרְאוּ וְשָׂמֵחוּ
יָגֵל לִבָּם בַּיהוָה:

8 I will whistle for them and gather them,
For I will redeem them;
And they shall increase as they once
    increased.

אֶשְׁרְקָה לָהֶם
וַאֲקַבְּצֵם כִּי פְדִיתִים
וְרָבוּ כְּמוֹ רָבוּ:

9 "I will sow them among the peoples,
And they shall remember Me in far
    countries;
They shall live, together with their children,
And they shall return.

וְאֶזְרָעֵם בָּעַמִּים
וּבַמֶּרְחַקִּים יִזְכְּרוּנִי
וְחָיוּ אֶת־בְּנֵיהֶם וָשָׁבוּ:

10 I will also bring them back from the land of
    Egypt,
And gather them from Assyria.
I will bring them into the land of Gilead and
    Lebanon,
Until no *more room* is found for them.

וַהֲשִׁיבוֹתִים מֵאֶרֶץ מִצְרַיִם
וּמֵאַשּׁוּר אֲקַבְּצֵם
וְאֶל־אֶרֶץ גִּלְעָד וּלְבָנוֹן אֲבִיאֵם
וְלֹא יִמָּצֵא לָהֶם:

11 He shall pass through the sea with affliction,
And strike the waves of the sea:
All the depths of the River shall dry up.

וְעָבַר בַּיָּם צָרָה
וְהִכָּה בַיָּם גַּלִּים

Then the pride of Assyria shall be brought
down,
And the scepter of Egypt shall depart.

12 "So I will strengthen them in the LORD,
And they shall walk up and down in His
name,"
Says the LORD.

11 Open your doors, O Lebanon,
That fire may devour your cedars.
2 Wail, O cypress, for the cedar has fallen,
Because the mighty *trees* are ruined.
Wail, O oaks of Bashan,
For the thick forest has come down.
3 *There is* the sound of wailing shepherds!
For their glory is in ruins.
There is the sound of roaring lions!
For the pride of the Jordan is in ruins.

4 Thus says the LORD my God, "Feed the flock
for slaughter, 5 whose owners slaughter them and
feel no guilt; those who sell them say, 'Blessed be
the LORD, for I am rich'; and their shepherds do not
pity them. 6 For I will no longer pity the inhabitants
of the land," says the LORD. "But indeed I will give
everyone into his neighbor's hand and into the hand
of his king. They shall attack the land, and I will
not deliver *them* from their hand."

7 So I fed the flock for slaughter, in particular the
poor of the flock. I took for myself two staffs: the
one I called Beauty, and the other I called Bonds;
and I fed the flock. 8 I dismissed the three shepherds
in one month. My soul loathed them, and their soul
also abhorred me. 9 Then I said, "I will not feed
you. Let what is dying die, and what is perishing
perish. Let those that are left eat each other's flesh."
10 And I took my staff, Beauty, and cut it in two,
that I might break the covenant which I had made
with all the peoples. 11 So it was broken on that day.
Thus the poor of the flock, who were watching me,
knew that it *was* the word of the LORD. 12 Then I
said to them, "If it is agreeable to you, give *me* my
wages; and if not, refrain." So they weighed out for
my wages thirty *pieces* of silver.

13 And the LORD said to me, "Throw it to the
potter"—that princely price they set on me. So I
took the thirty *pieces* of silver and threw them into
the house of the LORD for the potter. 14 Then I cut
in two my other staff, Bonds, that I might break the
brotherhood between Judah and Israel.

15 And the LORD said to me, "Next, take for
yourself the implements of a foolish shepherd.
16 For indeed I will raise up a shepherd in the land
who will not care for those who are cut off, nor seek

וְהֹבִישׁוּ כֹּל מְצוּלוֹת יְאֹר
וְהוּרַד גְּאוֹן אַשּׁוּר
וְשֵׁבֶט מִצְרַיִם יָסוּר:
12 וְגִבַּרְתִּים בַּיהוָֹה
וּבִשְׁמוֹ יִתְהַלָּכוּ
נְאֻם יְהוָֹה: ס

יא פְּתַח לְבָנוֹן דְּלָתֶיךָ
וְתֹאכַל אֵשׁ בַּאֲרָזֶיךָ:
2 הֵילֵל בְּרוֹשׁ כִּי־נָפַל אֶרֶז
אֲשֶׁר אַדִּרִים שֻׁדָּדוּ
הֵילִילוּ אַלּוֹנֵי בָשָׁן
כִּי יָרַד יַעַר הַבָּצוּרᵏ:
3 קוֹל יִלְלַת הָרֹעִים
כִּי שֻׁדְּדָה אַדַּרְתָּם
קוֹל שַׁאֲגַת כְּפִירִים
כִּי שֻׁדַּד גְּאוֹן הַיַּרְדֵּן: ס
4 כֹּה אָמַר יְהוָֹה אֱלֹהָי רְעֵה אֶת־צֹאן הַהֲרֵגָה:
5 אֲשֶׁר קֹנֵיהֶן יַהֲרֻגְן וְלֹא יֶאְשָׁמוּ וּמֹכְרֵיהֶן יֹאמַר
בָּרוּךְ יְהוָֹה וַאעְשִׁר וְרֹעֵיהֶם לֹא יַחְמוֹל עֲלֵיהֶן:
6 כִּי לֹא אֶחְמוֹל עוֹד עַל־יֹשְׁבֵי הָאָרֶץ נְאֻם־יְהוָֹה
וְהִנֵּה אָנֹכִי מַמְצִיא אֶת־הָאָדָם אִישׁ בְּיַד־רֵעֵהוּ
וּבְיַד מַלְכּוֹ וְכִתְּתוּ אֶת־הָאָרֶץ וְלֹא אַצִּיל מִיָּדָם:
7 וָאֶרְעֶה אֶת־צֹאן הַהֲרֵגָה לָכֵן עֲנִיֵּי הַצֹּאן וָאֶקַּח־
לִי שְׁנֵי מַקְלוֹת לְאַחַד קָרָאתִי נֹעַם וּלְאַחַד קָרָאתִי
חֹבְלִים וָאֶרְעֶה אֶת־הַצֹּאן: 8 וָאַכְחִד אֶת־שְׁלֹשֶׁת
הָרֹעִים בְּיֶרַח אֶחָד וַתִּקְצַר נַפְשִׁי בָּהֶם וְגַם־נַפְשָׁם
בָּחֲלָה בִי: 9 וָאֹמַר לֹא אֶרְעֶה אֶתְכֶם הַמֵּתָה תָמוּת
וְהַנִּכְחֶדֶת תִּכָּחֵד וְהַנִּשְׁאָרוֹת תֹּאכַלְנָה אִשָּׁה אֶת־
בְּשַׂר רְעוּתָהּ: 10 וָאֶקַּח אֶת־מַקְלִי אֶת־נֹעַם וָאֶגְדַּע
אֹתוֹ לְהָפֵיר אֶת־בְּרִיתִי אֲשֶׁר כָּרַתִּי אֶת־כָּל־
הָעַמִּים: 11 וַתֻּפַר בַּיּוֹם הַהוּא וַיֵּדְעוּ כֵן עֲנִיֵּי
הַצֹּאן הַשֹּׁמְרִים אֹתִי כִּי דְבַר־יְהוָֹה הוּא: 12 וָאֹמַר
אֲלֵיהֶם אִם־טוֹב בְּעֵינֵיכֶם הָבוּ שְׂכָרִי וְאִם־לֹא |
חֲדָלוּ וַיִּשְׁקְלוּ אֶת־שְׂכָרִי שְׁלֹשִׁים כָּסֶף: 13 וַיֹּאמֶר
יְהוָֹה אֵלַי הַשְׁלִיכֵהוּ אֶל־הַיּוֹצֵר אֶדֶר הַיְקָר אֲשֶׁר
יָקַרְתִּי מֵעֲלֵיהֶם וָאֶקְחָה שְׁלֹשִׁים הַכֶּסֶף וָאַשְׁלִיךְ
אֹתוֹ בֵּית יְהוָֹה אֶל־הַיּוֹצֵר: 14 וָאֶגְדַּע אֶת־מַקְלִי
הַשֵּׁנִי אֵת הַחֹבְלִים לְהָפֵר אֶת־הָאַחֲוָה בֵּין יְהוּדָה
וּבֵין יִשְׂרָאֵל: ס 15 וַיֹּאמֶר יְהוָֹה אֵלַי עוֹד
קַח־לְךָ כְּלִי רֹעֶה אֱוִלִי: 16 כִּי הִנֵּה־אָנֹכִי מֵקִים

the young, nor heal those that are broken, nor feed those that still stand. But he will eat the flesh of the fat and tear their hooves in pieces.

17 "Woe to the worthless shepherd,
Who leaves the flock!
A sword *shall be* against his arm
And against his right eye;
His arm shall completely wither,
And his right eye shall be totally blinded."

12 The burden of the word of the LORD against Israel. Thus says the LORD, who stretches out the heavens, lays the foundation of the earth, and forms the spirit of man within him: 2 "Behold, I will make Jerusalem a cup of drunkenness to all the surrounding peoples, when they lay siege against Judah and Jerusalem. 3 And it shall happen in that day that I will make Jerusalem a very heavy stone for all peoples; all who would heave it away will surely be cut in pieces, though all nations of the earth are gathered against it. 4 In that day," says the LORD, "I will strike every horse with confusion, and its rider with madness; I will open My eyes on the house of Judah, and will strike every horse of the peoples with blindness. 5 And the governors of Judah shall say in their heart, 'The inhabitants of Jerusalem *are* my strength in the LORD of hosts, their God.' 6 In that day I will make the governors of Judah like a firepan in the woodpile, and like a fiery torch in the sheaves; they shall devour all the surrounding peoples on the right hand and on the left, but Jerusalem shall be inhabited again in her own place—Jerusalem.

7 "The LORD will save the tents of Judah first, so that the glory of the house of David and the glory of the inhabitants of Jerusalem shall not become greater than that of Judah. 8 In that day the LORD will defend the inhabitants of Jerusalem; the one who is feeble among them in that day shall be like David, and the house of David *shall be* like God, like the Angel of the LORD before them. 9 It shall be in that day *that* I will seek to destroy all the nations that come against Jerusalem.

10 "And I will pour on the house of David and on the inhabitants of Jerusalem the Spirit of grace and supplication; then they will look on Me whom they pierced. Yes, they will mourn for Him as one mourns for *his* only *son,* and grieve for Him as one grieves for a firstborn. 11 In that day there shall be a great mourning in Jerusalem, like the mourning at Hadad Rimmon in the plain of Megiddo. 12 And the land shall mourn, every family by itself: the family of the house of David by itself, and their wives by

רֹעֶ֤ה בָאָ֙רֶץ֙ הַנִּכְחָד֣וֹת לֹֽא־יִפְקֹ֔ד הַנַּ֖עַר לֹֽא־יְבַקֵּ֑שׁ
וְהַנִּשְׁבֶּ֣רֶת לֹ֣א יְרַפֵּ֔א הַנִּצָּבָ֖ה לֹ֣א יְכַלְכֵּ֑ל וּבְשַׂ֤ר
הַבְּרִיאָה֙ יֹאכַ֔ל וּפַרְסֵיהֶ֖ן יְפָרֵֽק׃ ס

17 ה֤וֹי רֹעִי֙ הָֽאֱלִ֔יל עֹזְבִ֖י הַצֹּ֑אן
חֶ֥רֶב עַל־זְרוֹע֖וֹ
וְעַל־עֵ֣ין יְמִינ֑וֹ
זְרֹעוֹ֙ יָב֣וֹשׁ תִּיבָ֔שׁ
וְעֵ֥ין יְמִינ֖וֹ כָּהֹ֥ה תִכְהֶֽה׃ ס

יב מַשָּׂ֥א דְבַר־יְהוָ֖ה עַל־יִשְׂרָאֵ֑ל נְאֻם־יְהוָ֗ה נֹטֶ֤ה
שָׁמַ֙יִם֙ וְיֹסֵ֣ד אָ֔רֶץ וְיֹצֵ֥ר רֽוּחַ־אָדָ֖ם בְּקִרְבּֽוֹ׃ פ
2 הִנֵּ֣ה אָ֠נֹכִי שָׂ֣ם אֶת־יְרוּשָׁלִַ֧ם סַף־רַ֛עַל לְכָל־
הָעַמִּ֖ים סָבִ֑יב וְגַ֧ם עַל־יְהוּדָ֛ה יִֽהְיֶ֥ה בַמָּצ֖וֹר עַל־
יְרוּשָׁלִָֽם׃ 3 וְהָיָ֣ה בַיּוֹם־הַה֠וּא אָשִׂ֨ים אֶת־יְרוּשָׁלִַ֜ם
אֶ֤בֶן מַֽעֲמָסָה֙ לְכָל־הָ֣עַמִּ֔ים כָּל־עֹמְסֶ֖יהָ שָׂר֣וֹט
יִשָּׂרֵ֑טוּ וְנֶֽאֶסְפ֣וּ עָלֶ֔יהָ כֹּ֖ל גּוֹיֵ֥י הָאָֽרֶץ׃ 4 בַּיּ֨וֹם הַה֜וּא
נְאֻם־יְהוָ֗ה אַכֶּ֤ה כָל־סוּס֙ בַּתִּמָּה֔וֹן וְרֹכְב֖וֹ בַּשִּׁגָּע֑וֹן
וְעַל־בֵּ֤ית יְהוּדָה֙ אֶפְקַ֣ח אֶת־עֵינַ֔י וְכֹל֙ ס֣וּס הָֽעַמִּ֔ים
אַכֶּ֖ה בַּֽעִוָּרֽוֹן׃ 5 וְאָֽמְר֛וּ אַלֻּפֵ֥י יְהוּדָ֖ה בְּלִבָּ֑ם אַמְצָ֣ה
לִ֗י יֹֽשְׁבֵי֙ יְר֣וּשָׁלִַ֔ם בַּֽיהוָ֥ה צְבָא֖וֹת אֱלֹֽהֵיהֶֽם׃ 6 בַּיּ֣וֹם
הַה֡וּא אָשִׂים֩ אֶת־אַלֻּפֵ֨י יְהוּדָ֜ה כְּֽכִיּ֥וֹר אֵשׁ֙ בְּעֵצִ֔ים
וּכְלַפִּ֥יד אֵשׁ֙ בְּעָמִ֔יר וְאָֽכְל֗וּ עַל־יָמִ֧ין וְעַל־שְׂמֹ֛אול
אֶת־כָּל־הָֽעַמִּ֖ים סָבִ֑יב וְיָשְׁבָ֧ה יְרוּשָׁלִַ֛ם ע֖וֹד תַּחְתֶּ֑יהָ
בִּירוּשָׁלִָֽם׃ פ

7 וְהוֹשִׁ֧יעַ יְהוָ֛ה אֶת־אָֽהֳלֵ֥י יְהוּדָ֖ה בָּרִֽאשֹׁנָ֑ה לְמַ֙עַן
לֹֽא־תִגְדַּ֜ל תִּפְאֶ֤רֶת בֵּית־דָּוִיד֙ וְתִפְאֶ֙רֶת֙ יֹשֵׁ֣ב
יְרוּשָׁלִַ֔ם עַל־יְהוּדָֽה׃ 8 בַּיּ֣וֹם הַה֗וּא יָגֵ֤ן יְהוָה֙
בְּעַד֙ יוֹשֵׁ֣ב יְרוּשָׁלִַ֔ם וְהָיָ֞ה הַנִּכְשָׁ֥ל בָּהֶ֛ם בַּיּ֥וֹם
הַה֖וּא כְּדָוִ֑יד וּבֵ֤ית דָּוִיד֙ כֵּֽאלֹהִ֔ים כְּמַלְאַ֥ךְ יְהוָ֖ה
לִפְנֵיהֶֽם׃ 9 וְהָיָ֖ה בַּיּ֣וֹם הַה֑וּא אֲבַקֵּ֣שׁ לְהַשְׁמִ֔יד
אֶת־כָּל־הַגּוֹיִ֖ם הַבָּאִ֣ים עַל־יְרוּשָׁלִָֽם׃ 10 וְשָׁפַכְתִּי֩
עַל־בֵּ֨ית דָּוִ֜יד וְעַ֣ל ׀ יוֹשֵׁ֣ב יְרוּשָׁלִַ֗ם ר֤וּחַ חֵן֙
וְתַ֣חֲנוּנִ֔ים וְהִבִּ֥יטוּ אֵלַ֖י אֵ֣ת אֲשֶׁר־דָּקָ֑רוּ וְסָֽפְד֣וּ
עָלָ֗יו כְּמִסְפֵּד֙ עַל־הַיָּחִ֔יד וְהָמֵ֥ר עָלָ֖יו כְּהָמֵ֥ר עַֽל־
הַבְּכֽוֹר׃ 11 בַּיּ֣וֹם הַה֗וּא יִגְדַּ֤ל הַמִּסְפֵּד֙ בִּיר֣וּשָׁלִַ֔ם
כְּמִסְפַּ֥ד הֲדַדְרִמּ֖וֹן בְּבִקְעַ֥ת מְגִדּֽוֹן׃ 12 וְסָֽפְדָ֣ה
הָאָ֗רֶץ מִשְׁפָּח֤וֹת מִשְׁפָּחוֹת֙ לְבָ֔ד מִשְׁפַּ֣חַת בֵּֽית־

themselves; the family of the house of Nathan by itself, and their wives by themselves; [13] the family of the house of Levi by itself, and their wives by themselves; the family of Shimei by itself, and their wives by themselves; [14] all the families that remain, every family by itself, and their wives by themselves.

13 "In that day a fountain shall be opened for the house of David and for the inhabitants of Jerusalem, for sin and for uncleanness.

[2] "It shall be in that day," says the LORD of hosts, "that I will cut off the names of the idols from the land, and they shall no longer be remembered. I will also cause the prophets and the unclean spirit to depart from the land. [3] It shall come to pass that if anyone still prophesies, then his father and mother who begot him will say to him, 'You shall not live, because you have spoken lies in the name of the LORD.' And his father and mother who begot him shall thrust him through when he prophesies.

[4] "And it shall be in that day that every prophet will be ashamed of his vision when he prophesies; they will not wear a robe of coarse hair to deceive. [5] But he will say, 'I am no prophet, I am a farmer; for a man taught me to keep cattle from my youth.' [6] And one will say to him, 'What are these wounds between your arms?' Then he will answer, 'Those with which I was wounded in the house of my friends.'

[7]   "Awake, O sword, against My Shepherd, Against the Man who is My Companion," Says the LORD of hosts.

   "Strike the Shepherd, And the sheep will be scattered; Then I will turn My hand against the little ones.

[8]   And it shall come to pass in all the land," Says the LORD, "That two-thirds in it shall be cut off and die, But one-third shall be left in it:

[9]   I will bring the one-third through the fire, Will refine them as silver is refined, And test them as gold is tested. They will call on My name, And I will answer them. I will say, 'This is My people'; And each one will say, 'The LORD is my God.'"

14 Behold, the day of the LORD is coming, And your spoil will be divided in your midst.

[2]   For I will gather all the nations to battle against Jerusalem;

דָּוִיד לְבָד וּנְשֵׁיהֶם לְבָד מִשְׁפַּחַת בֵּית־נָתָן לְבָד
וּנְשֵׁיהֶם לְבָד: 13 מִשְׁפַּחַת בֵּית־לֵוִי לְבָד וּנְשֵׁיהֶם
לְבָד מִשְׁפַּחַת הַשִּׁמְעִי לְבָד וּנְשֵׁיהֶם לְבָד: 14 כֹּל
הַמִּשְׁפָּחוֹת הַנִּשְׁאָרוֹת מִשְׁפַּחַת מִשְׁפַּחַת לְבָד
וּנְשֵׁיהֶם לְבָד: ס

יג בַּיּוֹם הַהוּא יִהְיֶה מָקוֹר נִפְתָּח לְבֵית דָּוִיד
וּלְיֹשְׁבֵי יְרוּשָׁלָ͏ִם לְחַטַּאת וּלְנִדָּה: 2 וְהָיָה בַיּוֹם
הַהוּא נְאֻם ׀ יְהֹוָה צְבָאוֹת אַכְרִית אֶת־שְׁמוֹת
הָעֲצַבִּים מִן־הָאָרֶץ וְלֹא יִזָּכְרוּ עוֹד וְגַם אֶת־
הַנְּבִיאִים וְאֶת־רוּחַ הַטֻּמְאָה אַעֲבִיר מִן־הָאָרֶץ:
3 וְהָיָה כִּי־יִנָּבֵא אִישׁ עוֹד וְאָמְרוּ אֵלָיו אָבִיו וְאִמּוֹ
יֹלְדָיו לֹא תִחְיֶה כִּי שֶׁקֶר דִּבַּרְתָּ בְּשֵׁם יְהֹוָה
וּדְקָרֻהוּ אָבִיהוּ וְאִמּוֹ יֹלְדָיו בְּהִנָּבְאוֹ: 4 וְהָיָה ׀
בַּיּוֹם הַהוּא יֵבֹשׁוּ הַנְּבִיאִים אִישׁ מֵחֶזְיֹנוֹ בְּהִנָּבְאֹתוֹ
וְלֹא יִלְבְּשׁוּ אַדֶּרֶת שֵׂעָר לְמַעַן כַּחֵשׁ: 5 וְאָמַר לֹא
נָבִיא אָנֹכִי אִישׁ־עֹבֵד אֲדָמָה אָנֹכִי כִּי אָדָם הִקְנַנִי
מִנְּעוּרָי: 6 וְאָמַר אֵלָיו מָה הַמַּכּוֹת הָאֵלֶּה בֵּין יָדֶיךָ
וְאָמַר אֲשֶׁר הֻכֵּיתִי בֵּית מְאַהֲבָי: ס

7 חֶרֶב עוּרִי עַל־רֹעִי
  וְעַל־גֶּבֶר עֲמִיתִי
  נְאֻם יְהֹוָה צְבָאוֹת
  הַךְ אֶת־הָרֹעֶה וּתְפוּצֶיןָ הַצֹּאן
  וַהֲשִׁבֹתִי יָדִי עַל־הַצֹּעֲרִים:

8 וְהָיָה בְכָל־הָאָרֶץ נְאֻם־יְהֹוָה
  פִּי־שְׁנַיִם בָּהּ יִכָּרְתוּ יִגְוָעוּ
  וְהַשְּׁלִשִׁית יִוָּתֶר בָּהּ:

9 וְהֵבֵאתִי אֶת־הַשְּׁלִשִׁית בָּאֵשׁ
  וּצְרַפְתִּים כִּצְרֹף אֶת־הַכֶּסֶף
  וּבְחַנְתִּים כִּבְחֹן אֶת־הַזָּהָב
  הוּא ׀ יִקְרָא בִשְׁמִי
  וַאֲנִי אֶעֱנֶה אֹתוֹ
  אָמַרְתִּי עַמִּי הוּא
  וְהוּא יֹאמַר יְהֹוָה אֱלֹהָי: ס

יד הִנֵּה יוֹם־בָּא לַיהֹוָה
  וְחֻלַּק שְׁלָלֵךְ בְּקִרְבֵּךְ:
2 וְאָסַפְתִּי אֶת־כָּל־הַגּוֹיִם ׀

The city shall be taken,
The houses rifled,
And the women ravished.
Half of the city shall go into captivity,
But the remnant of the people shall not be
    cut off from the city.

3 Then the LORD will go forth
And fight against those nations,
As He fights in the day of battle.

4 And in that day His feet will stand on the
    Mount of Olives,
Which faces Jerusalem on the east.
And the Mount of Olives shall be split in
    two,
From east to west,
Making a very large valley;
Half of the mountain shall move toward the
    north
And half of it toward the south.

5 Then you shall flee *through* My mountain
    valley,
For the mountain valley shall reach to Azal.
Yes, you shall flee
As you fled from the earthquake
In the days of Uzziah king of Judah.

Thus the LORD my God will come,
And all the saints with You.

6 It shall come to pass in that day
That there will be no light;
The lights will diminish.

7 It shall be one day
Which is known to the LORD—
Neither day nor night.
But at evening time it shall happen
That it will be light.

8 And in that day it shall be
That living waters shall flow from Jerusalem,
Half of them toward the eastern sea
And half of them toward the western sea;
In both summer and winter it shall occur.

9 And the LORD shall be King over all the
    earth.
In that day it shall be—

"The LORD *is* one,"
And His name one.

10 All the land shall be turned into a plain from
Geba to Rimmon south of Jerusalem. *Jerusalem*
shall be raised up and inhabited in her place from
Benjamin's Gate to the place of the First Gate and
the Corner Gate, and *from* the Tower of Hananel to
the king's winepresses.

אֶל־יְרוּשָׁלַ֖͏ִם לַמִּלְחָמָ֑ה
וְנִלְכְּדָ֣ה הָעִ֗יר וְנָשַׁ֙סּוּ֙ הַבָּ֣תִּ֔ים
וְהַנָּשִׁ֖ים תשגלנה
וְיָצָ֞א חֲצִ֤י הָעִיר֙ בַּגּוֹלָ֔ה
וְיֶ֣תֶר הָעָ֔ם לֹ֥א יִכָּרֵ֖ת מִן־הָעִֽיר׃

3 וְיָצָ֣א יְהוָ֔ה
וְנִלְחַ֖ם בַּגּוֹיִ֣ם הָהֵ֑ם
כְּי֥וֹם הִלָּחֲמ֖וֹ בְּי֥וֹם קְרָֽב׃

4 וְעָמְד֣וּ רַגְלָ֣יו בַּיּוֹם־הַה֗וּא
עַל־הַ֤ר הַזֵּיתִים֙
אֲשֶׁ֨ר עַל־פְּנֵ֤י יְרוּשָׁלַ֙͏ִם֙ מִקֶּ֔דֶם
וְנִבְקַע֩ הַ֨ר הַזֵּיתִ֤ים מֵֽחֶצְיוֹ֙
מִזְרָ֣חָה וָיָ֔מָּה
גֵּ֖יא גְּדוֹלָ֣ה מְאֹ֑ד
וּמָ֨שׁ חֲצִ֤י הָהָר֙
צָפ֔וֹנָה וְחֶצְיוֹ־נֶֽגְבָּה׃

5 וְנַסְתֶּ֣ם גֵּיא־הָרַ֗י
כִּֽי־יַגִּ֣יעַ גֵּי־הָרִים֮ אֶל־אָצַל֒
וְנַסְתֶּ֗ם כַּאֲשֶׁ֤ר נַסְתֶּם֙ מִפְּנֵ֣י הָרַ֔עַשׁ
בִּימֵ֖י עֻזִּיָּ֣ה מֶֽלֶךְ־יְהוּדָ֑ה
וּבָא֙ יְהוָ֣ה אֱלֹהַ֔י
כָּל־קְדֹשִׁ֖ים עִמָּֽךְ׃

6 וְהָיָ֖ה בַּיּ֣וֹם הַה֑וּא לֹֽא־יִהְיֶ֣ה א֔וֹר
יְקָר֖וֹת יקפאון׃

7 וְהָיָ֣ה יוֹם־אֶחָ֗ד
ה֛וּא יִוָּדַ֥ע לַֽיהוָ֖ה
לֹא־י֣וֹם וְלֹא־לָ֑יְלָה
וְהָיָ֥ה לְעֵת־עֶ֖רֶב יִֽהְיֶה־אֽוֹר׃

8 וְהָיָ֣ה ׀ בַּיּ֣וֹם הַה֗וּא
יֵצְא֤וּ מַֽיִם־חַיִּים֙ מִיר֣וּשָׁלַ֔͏ִם
חֶצְיָ֗ם אֶל־הַיָּם֙ הַקַּדְמוֹנִ֔י
וְחֶצְיָ֖ם אֶל־הַיָּ֣ם הָאַחֲר֑וֹן
בַּקַּ֥יִץ וּבָחֹ֖רֶף יִהְיֶֽה׃

9 וְהָיָ֧ה יְהוָ֛ה לְמֶ֖לֶךְ עַל־כָּל־הָאָ֑רֶץ
בַּיּ֣וֹם הַה֗וּא יִהְיֶ֧ה יְהוָ֛ה
אֶחָ֖ד וּשְׁמ֥וֹ אֶחָֽד׃

10 יִסּ֣וֹב כָּל־הָאָ֤רֶץ כָּעֲרָבָה֙ מִגֶּ֣בַע לְרִמּ֔וֹן נֶ֖גֶב
יְרֽוּשָׁלָ֑͏ִם וְֽרָאֲמָ֡ה וְיָשְׁבָ֣ה תַחְתֶּ֩יהָ֩ לְמִשַּׁ֨עַר בִּנְיָמִ֜ן
עַד־מְק֣וֹם שַׁ֣עַר הָרִאשׁ֗וֹן עַד־שַׁ֙עַר֙ הַפִּנִּ֔ים וּמִגְדַּ֣ל
חֲנַנְאֵ֔ל עַ֖ד יִקְבֵ֥י הַמֶּֽלֶךְ׃

11 *The people* shall dwell in it;
And no longer shall there be utter
    destruction,
But Jerusalem shall be safely inhabited.

11 וְיָשְׁבוּ בָהּ
וְחֵרֶם לֹא יִהְיֶה־עֹוד
וְיָשְׁבָה יְרוּשָׁלַ͏ִם לָבֶטַח:

12 And this shall be the plague with which the
LORD will strike all the people who fought against
Jerusalem:

12 וְזֹאת | תִּהְיֶה הַמַּגֵּפָה

    Their flesh shall dissolve while they stand on
      their feet,
    Their eyes shall dissolve in their sockets,
    And their tongues shall dissolve in their
      mouths.

אֲשֶׁר יִגֹּף יְהוָה אֶת־כָּל־הָעַמִּים
אֲשֶׁר צָבְאוּ עַל־יְרוּשָׁלָ͏ִם
הָמֵק | בְּשָׂרֹו וְהוּא עֹמֵד עַל־רַגְלָיו
וְעֵינָיו תִּמַּקְנָה בְחֹרֵיהֶן
וּלְשֹׁונֹו תִּמַּק בְּפִיהֶם:

13 It shall come to pass in that day
That a great panic from the LORD will be
    among them.
Everyone will seize the hand of his neighbor,
And raise his hand against his neighbor's
    hand;

13 וְהָיָה בַּיֹּום הַהוּא
תִּהְיֶה מְהוּמַת־יְהוָה רַבָּה בָּהֶם
וְהֶחֱזִיקוּ אִישׁ יַד רֵעֵהוּ
וְעָלְתָה יָדֹו עַל־יַד רֵעֵהוּ:

14 Judah also will fight at Jerusalem.
And the wealth of all the surrounding
    nations
Shall be gathered together:
Gold, silver, and apparel in great abundance.

14 וְגַם־יְהוּדָה תִּלָּחֵם בִּירוּשָׁלָ͏ִם
וְאֻסַּף חֵיל כָּל־הַגֹּויִם סָבִיב
זָהָב וָכֶסֶף וּבְגָדִים לָרֹב מְאֹד:

15 Such also shall be the plague
On the horse *and* the mule,
On the camel and the donkey,
And on all the cattle that will be in those
    camps.
So *shall* this plague *be*.

15 וְכֵן תִּהְיֶה מַגֵּפַת הַסּוּס
הַפֶּרֶד הַגָּמָל וְהַחֲמֹור
וְכָל־הַבְּהֵמָה אֲשֶׁר יִהְיֶה
בַּמַּחֲנֹות הָהֵמָּה כַּמַּגֵּפָה הַזֹּאת:

16 And it shall come to pass *that* everyone who is
left of all the nations which came against Jerusalem
shall go up from year to year to worship the King,
the LORD of hosts, and to keep the Feast of
Tabernacles. 17 And it shall be *that* whichever of the
families of the earth do not come up to Jerusalem to
worship the King, the LORD of hosts, on them there
will be no rain. 18 If the family of Egypt will not
come up and enter in, they *shall have* no *rain;* they
shall receive the plague with which the LORD strikes
the nations who do not come up to keep the Feast
of Tabernacles. 19 This shall be the punishment of
Egypt and the punishment of all the nations that do
not come up to keep the Feast of Tabernacles.

20 In that day "HOLINESS TO THE LORD"
shall be *engraved* on the bells of the horses. The pots
in the LORD's house shall be like the bowls before
the altar. 21 Yes, every pot in Jerusalem and Judah
shall be holiness to the LORD of hosts. Everyone
who sacrifices shall come and take them and cook
in them. In that day there shall no longer be a
Canaanite in the house of the LORD of hosts.

16 וְהָיָה כָּל־הַנֹּותָר מִכָּל־הַגֹּויִם הַבָּאִים עַל־
יְרוּשָׁלָ͏ִם וְעָלוּ מִדֵּי שָׁנָה בְשָׁנָה לְהִשְׁתַּחֲוֹת לְמֶלֶךְ
יְהוָה צְבָאֹות וְלָחֹג אֶת־חַג הַסֻּכֹּות: 17 וְהָיָה
אֲשֶׁר לֹא־יַעֲלֶה מֵאֵת מִשְׁפְּחֹות הָאָרֶץ אֶל־יְרוּשָׁלַ͏ִם
לְהִשְׁתַּחֲוֹת לְמֶלֶךְ יְהוָה צְבָאֹות וְלֹא עֲלֵיהֶם יִהְיֶה
הַגָּשֶׁם: 18 וְאִם־מִשְׁפַּחַת מִצְרַיִם לֹא־תַעֲלֶה וְלֹא
בָאָה וְלֹא עֲלֵיהֶם תִּהְיֶה הַמַּגֵּפָה אֲשֶׁר יִגֹּף יְהוָה
אֶת־הַגֹּויִם אֲשֶׁר לֹא יַעֲלוּ לָחֹג אֶת־חַג הַסֻּכֹּות:
19 זֹאת תִּהְיֶה חַטַּאת מִצְרָיִם וְחַטַּאת כָּל־הַגֹּויִם
אֲשֶׁר לֹא יַעֲלוּ לָחֹג אֶת־חַג הַסֻּכֹּות: 20 בַּיֹּום הַהוּא
יִהְיֶה עַל־מְצִלֹּות הַסּוּס קֹדֶשׁ לַיהוָה וְהָיָה הַסִּירֹות
בְּבֵית יְהוָה כַּמִּזְרָקִים לִפְנֵי הַמִּזְבֵּחַ: 21 וְהָיָה כָּל־
סִיר בִּירוּשָׁלַ͏ִם וּבִיהוּדָה קֹדֶשׁ לַיהוָה צְבָאֹות וּבָאוּ
כָּל־הַזֹּבְחִים וְלָקְחוּ מֵהֶם וּבִשְּׁלוּ בָהֶם וְלֹא־יִהְיֶה
כְנַעֲנִי עֹוד בְּבֵית־יְהוָה צְבָאֹות בַּיֹּום הַהוּא:

The Book of
MALACHI

מַלְאָכִי

1 The burden of the word of the LORD to Israel by Malachi.

א מַשָּׂא דְבַר־יְהוָה אֶל־יִשְׂרָאֵל
בְּיַד מַלְאָכִי:

2 "I have loved you," says the LORD.
"Yet you say, 'In what way have You loved us?'
Was not Esau Jacob's brother?"
Says the LORD.
"Yet Jacob I have loved;
3 But Esau I have hated,
And laid waste his mountains and his heritage
For the jackals of the wilderness."

2 אָהַבְתִּי אֶתְכֶם אָמַר יְהוָה
וַאֲמַרְתֶּם בַּמָּה אֲהַבְתָּנוּ
הֲלוֹא־אָח עֵשָׂו לְיַעֲקֹב
נְאֻם־יְהוָה
וָאֹהַב אֶת־יַעֲקֹב:

3 וְאֶת־עֵשָׂו שָׂנֵאתִי
וָאָשִׂים אֶת־הָרָיו שְׁמָמָה
וְאֶת־נַחֲלָתוֹ לְתַנּוֹת מִדְבָּר:

4 Even though Edom has said,
"We have been impoverished,
But we will return and build the desolate places,"
Thus says the LORD of hosts:

"They may build, but I will throw down;
They shall be called the Territory of Wickedness,
And the people against whom the LORD will have indignation forever.
5 Your eyes shall see,
And you shall say,
'The LORD is magnified beyond the border of Israel.'

4 כִּי־תֹאמַר אֱדוֹם רֻשַּׁשְׁנוּ
וְנָשׁוּב וְנִבְנֶה חֳרָבוֹת
כֹּה אָמַר יְהוָה צְבָאוֹת
הֵמָּה יִבְנוּ וַאֲנִי אֶהֱרוֹס
וְקָרְאוּ לָהֶם גְּבוּל רִשְׁעָה
וְהָעָם אֲשֶׁר־זָעַם יְהוָה עַד־עוֹלָם:

5 וְעֵינֵיכֶם תִּרְאֶינָה
וְאַתֶּם תֹּאמְרוּ יִגְדַּל יְהוָה
מֵעַל לִגְבוּל יִשְׂרָאֵל:

6 "A son honors *his* father,
And a servant *his* master.
If then I am the Father,
Where *is* My honor?
And if I *am* a Master,
Where *is* My reverence?
Says the LORD of hosts
To you priests who despise My name.
Yet you say, 'In what way have we despised Your name?'

6 בֵּן יְכַבֵּד אָב וְעֶבֶד אֲדֹנָיו
וְאִם־אָב אָנִי אַיֵּה כְבוֹדִי
וְאִם־אֲדוֹנִים אָנִי אַיֵּה מוֹרָאִי
אָמַר ׀ יְהוָה צְבָאוֹת
לָכֶם הַכֹּהֲנִים בּוֹזֵי שְׁמִי
וַאֲמַרְתֶּם בַּמֶּה בָזִינוּ אֶת־שְׁמֶךָ:

7 "You offer defiled food on My altar,
But say,
'In what way have we defiled You?'
By saying,
'The table of the LORD is contemptible.'
8 And when you offer the blind as a sacrifice,
Is it not evil?
And when you offer the lame and sick,
Is it not evil?

7 מַגִּישִׁים עַל־מִזְבְּחִי לֶחֶם מְגֹאָל
וַאֲמַרְתֶּם בַּמֶּה גֵאַלְנוּךָ
בֶּאֱמָרְכֶם שֻׁלְחַן יְהוָה נִבְזֶה הוּא:

8 וְכִי־תַגִּשׁוּן עִוֵּר לִזְבֹּחַ אֵין רָע
וְכִי תַגִּישׁוּ פִּסֵּחַ וְחֹלֶה אֵין רָע
הַקְרִיבֵהוּ נָא לְפֶחָתֶךָ

Offer it then to your governor!
Would he be pleased with you?
Would he accept you favorably?"
Says the LORD of hosts.

9 "But now entreat God's favor,
That He may be gracious to us.
While this is being *done* by your hands,
Will He accept you favorably?"
Says the LORD of hosts.

10 "Who *is there* even among you who would
shut the doors,
So that you would not kindle fire *on* My altar
in vain?
I have no pleasure in you,"
Says the LORD of hosts,
"Nor will I accept an offering from your
hands.

11 For from the rising of the sun, even to its
going down,
My name *shall be* great among the Gentiles;
In every place incense *shall be* offered to My
name,
And a pure offering;
For My name shall be great among the
nations,"
Says the LORD of hosts.

12 "But you profane it,
In that you say,
'The table of the LORD is defiled;
And its fruit, its food, *is* contemptible.'

13 You also say,
'Oh, what a weariness!'
And you sneer at it,"
Says the LORD of hosts.
"And you bring the stolen, the lame, and the
sick;
Thus you bring an offering!
Should I accept this from your hand?"
Says the LORD.

14 "But cursed *be* the deceiver
Who has in his flock a male,
And takes a vow,
But sacrifices to the Lord what is
blemished—
For I *am* a great King,"
Says the LORD of hosts,
"And My name *is to be* feared among the
nations.

2 "And now, O priests, this commandment is
for you.

2 If you will not hear,
And if you will not take *it* to heart,

הֲיִרְצְךָ֙ א֣וֹ הֲיִשָּׂ֣א פָנֶ֔יךָ
אָמַ֖ר יְהֹוָ֥ה צְבָאֽוֹת׃
9 וְעַתָּ֛ה חַלּוּ־נָ֥א פְנֵי־אֵ֖ל וִֽיחׇנֵּ֑נוּ
מִיֶּדְכֶם֙ הָ֣יְתָה זֹּ֔את
הֲיִשָּׂ֤א מִכֶּם֙ פָּנִ֔ים
אָמַ֖ר יְהֹוָ֥ה צְבָאֽוֹת׃
10 מִ֤י גַם־בָּכֶם֙ וְיִסְגֹּ֣ר דְּלָתַ֔יִם
וְלֹא־תָאִ֥ירוּ מִזְבְּחִ֖י חִנָּ֑ם
אֵ֣ין־לִ֞י חֵ֗פֶץ בָּכֶ֔ם
אָמַר֙ יְהֹוָ֣ה צְבָא֔וֹת
וּמִנְחָ֖ה לֹא־אֶרְצֶ֥ה מִיֶּדְכֶֽם׃
11 כִּ֣י מִמִּזְרַח־שֶׁ֜מֶשׁ וְעַד־מְבוֹא֗וֹ
גָּד֤וֹל שְׁמִי֙ בַּגּוֹיִ֔ם
וּבְכׇל־מָק֗וֹם מֻקְטָ֥ר מֻגָּ֛שׁ
לִשְׁמִ֖י וּמִנְחָ֣ה טְהוֹרָ֑ה
כִּֽי־גָד֤וֹל שְׁמִי֙ בַּגּוֹיִ֔ם
אָמַ֖ר יְהֹוָ֥ה צְבָאֽוֹת׃
12 וְאַתֶּ֖ם מְחַלְּלִ֣ים אוֹת֑וֹ
בֶּאֱמׇרְכֶ֗ם
שֻׁלְחַ֤ן אֲדֹנָי֙ מְגֹאָ֣ל ה֔וּא
וְנִיב֖וֹ נִבְזֶ֥ה אׇכְלֽוֹ׃
13 וַאֲמַרְתֶּם֩ הִנֵּ֨ה מַתְּלָאָ֜ה
וְהִפַּחְתֶּ֣ם אוֹת֗וֹ אָמַר֙ יְהֹוָ֣ה צְבָא֔וֹת
וַהֲבֵאתֶ֣ם גָּז֗וּל
וְאֶת־הַפִּסֵּ֙חַ֙ וְאֶת־הַ֣חוֹלֶ֔ה
וַהֲבֵאתֶ֖ם אֶת־הַמִּנְחָ֑ה
הַאֶרְצֶ֥ה אוֹתָ֛הּ
מִיֶּדְכֶ֖ם אָמַ֥ר יְהֹוָֽה׃ ס
14 וְאָר֣וּר נוֹכֵ֗ל וְיֵ֤שׁ בְּעֶדְרוֹ֙ זָכָ֔ר
וְנֹדֵ֕ר וְזֹבֵ֥חַ מׇשְׁחָ֖ת לַֽאדֹנָ֑י
כִּי֩ מֶ֨לֶךְ גָּד֜וֹל אָ֗נִי אָמַר֙ יְהֹוָ֣ה צְבָא֔וֹת
וּשְׁמִ֖י נוֹרָ֥א בַגּוֹיִֽם׃

ב וְעַתָּ֗ה אֲלֵיכֶ֛ם
הַמִּצְוָ֥ה הַזֹּ֖את הַכֹּהֲנִֽים׃
2 אִם־לֹ֣א תִשְׁמְע֗וּ
וְאִם־לֹא֩ תָשִׂ֨ימוּ עַל־לֵ֜ב

To give glory to My name,"
Says the LORD of hosts,
"I will send a curse upon you,
And I will curse your blessings.
Yes, I have cursed them already,
Because you do not take *it* to heart.

3 "Behold, I will rebuke your descendants
And spread refuse on your faces,
The refuse of your solemn feasts;
And *one* will take you away with it.

4 Then you shall know that I have sent this
    commandment to you,
That My covenant with Levi may continue,"
Says the LORD of hosts.

5 "My covenant was with him, *one* of life and
    peace,
And I gave them to him *that he might* fear
    Me;
So he feared Me
And was reverent before My name.

6 The law of truth was in his mouth,
And injustice was not found on his lips.
He walked with Me in peace and equity,
And turned many away from iniquity.

7 "For the lips of a priest should keep
    knowledge,
And *people* should seek the law from his
    mouth;
For he is the messenger of the LORD of hosts.

8 But you have departed from the way;
You have caused many to stumble at the law.
You have corrupted the covenant of Levi,"
Says the LORD of hosts.

9 "Therefore I also have made you contemptible
    and base
Before all the people,
Because you have not kept My ways
But have shown partiality in the law."

10 Have we not all one Father?
Has not one God created us?
Why do we deal treacherously with one
    another
By profaning the covenant of the fathers?

11 Judah has dealt treacherously,
And an abomination has been committed in
    Israel and in Jerusalem,
For Judah has profaned
The LORD's holy *institution* which He loves:
He has married the daughter of a foreign
    god.

12 May the LORD cut off from the tents of
    Jacob

לָתֵת כָּבוֹד לִשְׁמִי
אָמַר יְהֹוָה צְבָאוֹת
וְשִׁלַּחְתִּי בָכֶם אֶת־הַמְּאֵרָה
וְאָרוֹתִי אֶת־בִּרְכוֹתֵיכֶם
וְגַם אָרוֹתִיהָ
כִּי אֵינְכֶם שָׂמִים עַל־לֵב:

3 הִנְנִי גֹעֵר לָכֶם אֶת־הַזֶּרַע
וְזֵרִיתִי פֶרֶשׁ עַל־פְּנֵיכֶם פֶּרֶשׁ חַגֵּיכֶם
וְנָשָׂא אֶתְכֶם אֵלָיו:

4 וִידַעְתֶּם כִּי שִׁלַּחְתִּי אֲלֵיכֶם
אֵת הַמִּצְוָה הַזֹּאת
לִהְיוֹת בְּרִיתִי אֶת־לֵוִי
אָמַר יְהֹוָה צְבָאוֹת:

5 בְּרִיתִי ׀ הָיְתָה אִתּוֹ
הַחַיִּים וְהַשָּׁלוֹם
וָאֶתְּנֵם־לוֹ מוֹרָא וַיִּירָאֵנִי
וּמִפְּנֵי שְׁמִי נִחַת הוּא:

6 תּוֹרַת אֱמֶת הָיְתָה בְּפִיהוּ
וְעַוְלָה לֹא־נִמְצָא בִשְׂפָתָיו
בְּשָׁלוֹם וּבְמִישׁוֹר הָלַךְ אִתִּי
וְרַבִּים הֵשִׁיב מֵעָוֹן:

7 כִּי־שִׂפְתֵי כֹהֵן יִשְׁמְרוּ־דַעַת
וְתוֹרָה יְבַקְשׁוּ מִפִּיהוּ
כִּי מַלְאַךְ יְהֹוָה־צְבָאוֹת הוּא:

8 וְאַתֶּם סַרְתֶּם מִן־הַדֶּרֶךְ
הִכְשַׁלְתֶּם רַבִּים בַּתּוֹרָה
שִׁחַתֶּם בְּרִית הַלֵּוִי
אָמַר יְהֹוָה צְבָאוֹת:

9 וְגַם־אֲנִי נָתַתִּי אֶתְכֶם
נִבְזִים וּשְׁפָלִים לְכָל־הָעָם
כְּפִי אֲשֶׁר אֵינְכֶם שֹׁמְרִים אֶת־דְּרָכַי
וְנֹשְׂאִים פָּנִים בַּתּוֹרָה:
פ

10 הֲלוֹא אָב אֶחָד לְכֻלָּנוּ
הֲלוֹא אֵל אֶחָד בְּרָאָנוּ
מַדּוּעַ נִבְגַּד אִישׁ בְּאָחִיו
לְחַלֵּל בְּרִית אֲבֹתֵינוּ:

11 בָּגְדָה יְהוּדָה
וְתוֹעֵבָה נֶעֶשְׂתָה בְיִשְׂרָאֵל וּבִירוּשָׁלָ‍ִם
כִּי ׀ חִלֵּל יְהוּדָה קֹדֶשׁ יְהֹוָה אֲשֶׁר אָהֵב
וּבָעַל בַּת־אֵל נֵכָר:

12 יַכְרֵת יְהֹוָה לָאִישׁ אֲשֶׁר יַעֲשֶׂנָּה

The man who does this, being awake and aware,
Yet who brings an offering to the LORD of hosts!

עֵר וְעֹנֶ֔ה מֵאָהֳלֵ֖י יַעֲקֹ֑ב
וּמַגִּ֣ישׁ מִנְחָ֔ה לַיהֹוָ֖ה צְבָאֽוֹת׃

13 And this is the second thing you do:
You cover the altar of the LORD with tears,
With weeping and crying;
So He does not regard the offering anymore,
Nor receive *it* with goodwill from your hands.

13 וְזֹ֣את שֵׁנִית֮ תַּעֲשׂוּ֒
כַּסּ֤וֹת דִּמְעָה֙ אֶת־מִזְבַּ֣ח יְהֹוָ֔ה
בְּכִ֖י וַאֲנָקָ֑ה
מֵאֵ֣ין ע֗וֹד פְּנוֹת֙ אֶל־הַמִּנְחָ֔ה
וְלָקַ֥חַת רָצ֖וֹן מִיֶּדְכֶֽם׃

14 Yet you say, "For what reason?"
Because the LORD has been witness
Between you and the wife of your youth,
With whom you have dealt treacherously;
Yet she is your companion
And your wife by covenant.

14 וַאֲמַרְתֶּ֖ם עַל־מָ֑ה
עַ֡ל כִּי־יְהֹוָה֩ הֵעִ֨יד בֵּינְךָ֜
וּבֵ֣ין ׀ אֵ֣שֶׁת נְעוּרֶ֗יךָ
אֲשֶׁ֤ר אַתָּה֙ בָּגַ֣דְתָּה בָּ֔הּ
וְהִ֥יא חֲבֶרְתְּךָ֖ וְאֵ֥שֶׁת בְּרִיתֶֽךָ׃

15 But did He not make *them* one,
Having a remnant of the Spirit?
And why one?
He seeks godly offspring.
Therefore take heed to your spirit,
And let none deal treacherously with the wife of his youth.

15 וְלֹא־אֶחָ֣ד עָשָׂ֗ה וּשְׁאָ֥ר ר֨וּחַ֙ ל֔וֹ
וּמָה֙ הָֽאֶחָ֔ד מְבַקֵּ֖שׁ זֶ֣רַע אֱלֹהִ֑ים
וְנִשְׁמַרְתֶּם֙ בְּרֽוּחֲכֶ֔ם
וּבְאֵ֥שֶׁת נְעוּרֶ֖יךָ אַל־יִבְגֹּֽד׃

16 "For the LORD God of Israel says
That He hates divorce,
For it covers one's garment with violence,"
Says the LORD of hosts.
"Therefore take heed to your spirit,
That you do not deal treacherously."

16 כִּֽי־שָׂנֵ֣א שַׁלַּ֗ח אָמַ֤ר יְהֹוָה֙ אֱלֹהֵ֣י יִשְׂרָאֵ֔ל
וְכִסָּ֤ה חָמָס֙ עַל־לְבוּשׁ֔וֹ
אָמַ֖ר יְהֹוָ֣ה צְבָא֑וֹת
וְנִשְׁמַרְתֶּ֥ם בְּרֽוּחֲכֶ֖ם וְלֹ֥א תִבְגֹּֽדוּ׃

17 You have wearied the LORD with your words;
Yet you say,
"In what way have we wearied *Him?*"
In that you say,
"Everyone who does evil
Is good in the sight of the LORD,
And He delights in them,"
Or, "Where *is* the God of justice?"

17 הוֹגַעְתֶּ֤ם יְהֹוָה֙ בְּדִבְרֵיכֶ֔ם
וַאֲמַרְתֶּ֖ם בַּמָּ֣ה הוֹגָ֑עְנוּ
בֶּאֱמׇרְכֶ֗ם כׇּל־עֹ֨שֵׂה רָ֜ע
ט֣וֹב ׀ בְּעֵינֵ֣י יְהֹוָ֗ה
וּבָהֶם֙ ה֣וּא חָפֵ֔ץ
א֖וֹ אַיֵּ֥ה אֱלֹהֵ֖י הַמִּשְׁפָּֽט׃

3 "Behold, I send My messenger,
And he will prepare the way before Me.
And the Lord, whom you seek,
Will suddenly come to His temple,
Even the Messenger of the covenant,
In whom you delight.
Behold, He is coming,"
Says the LORD of hosts.

ג הִנְנִ֤י שֹׁלֵ֙חַ֙ מַלְאָכִ֔י וּפִנָּה־דֶ֖רֶךְ לְפָנָ֑י
וּפִתְאֹם֩ יָב֨וֹא אֶל־הֵיכָל֜וֹ
הָאָד֣וֹן ׀ אֲשֶׁר־אַתֶּ֣ם מְבַקְשִׁ֗ים
וּמַלְאַ֤ךְ הַבְּרִית֙
אֲשֶׁר־אַתֶּ֣ם חֲפֵצִ֔ים הִנֵּה־בָ֔א
אָמַ֖ר יְהֹוָ֥ה צְבָאֽוֹת׃

2 "But who can endure the day of His coming?
And who can stand when He appears?
For He *is* like a refiner's fire
And like launderers' soap.

2 וּמִ֤י מְכַלְכֵּל֙ אֶת־י֣וֹם בּוֹא֔וֹ
וּמִ֥י הָעֹמֵ֖ד בְּהֵרָֽאוֹת֑וֹ
כִּי־הוּא֙ כְּאֵ֣שׁ מְצָרֵ֔ף
וּכְבֹרִ֖ית מְכַבְּסִֽים׃

3 He will sit as a refiner and a purifier of silver;

3 וְיָשַׁ֨ב מְצָרֵ֤ף וּמְטַהֵר֙ כֶּ֔סֶף

He will purify the sons of Levi,
And purge them as gold and silver,
That they may offer to the LORD
An offering in righteousness.

4 "Then the offering of Judah and Jerusalem
Will be pleasant to the LORD,
As in the days of old,
As in former years.

5 And I will come near you for judgment;
I will be a swift witness
Against sorcerers,
Against adulterers,
Against perjurers,
Against those who exploit wage earners and
    widows and orphans,
And against those who turn away an alien—
Because they do not fear Me,"
Says the LORD of hosts.

6 "For I *am* the LORD, I do not change;
Therefore you are not consumed, O sons of
    Jacob.

7 Yet from the days of your fathers
You have gone away from My ordinances
And have not kept *them.*
Return to Me, and I will return to you,"
Says the LORD of hosts.
"But you said,
'In what way shall we return?'

8 "Will a man rob God?
Yet you have robbed Me!
But you say,
'In what way have we robbed You?'
In tithes and offerings.

9 You are cursed with a curse,
For you have robbed Me,
Even this whole nation.

10 Bring all the tithes into the storehouse,
That there may be food in My house,
And try Me now in this,"
Says the LORD of hosts,
"If I will not open for you the windows of
    heaven
And pour out for you *such* blessing
That *there will* not *be room* enough *to receive
    it.*

11 "And I will rebuke the devourer for your
    sakes,
So that he will not destroy the fruit of your
    ground,
Nor shall the vine fail to bear fruit for you in
    the field,"
Says the LORD of hosts;

וְטִהַר אֶת־בְּנֵי־לֵוִי וְזִקַּק אֹתָם
כַּזָּהָב וְכַכָּסֶף וְהָיוּ לַיהוָה
מַגִּישֵׁי מִנְחָה בִּצְדָקָה׃

4 וְעָרְבָה לַיהוָה
מִנְחַת יְהוּדָה וִירוּשָׁלָ͏ִם
כִּימֵי עוֹלָם
וּכְשָׁנִים קַדְמֹנִיֹּת׃

5 וְקָרַבְתִּי אֲלֵיכֶם לַמִּשְׁפָּט
וְהָיִיתִי ׀ עֵד מְמַהֵר
בַּמְכַשְּׁפִים וּבַמְנָאֲפִים
וּבַנִּשְׁבָּעִים לַשָּׁקֶר
וּבְעֹשְׁקֵי שְׂכַר־שָׂכִיר
אַלְמָנָה וְיָתוֹם וּמַטֵּי־גֵר
וְלֹא יְרֵאוּנִי
אָמַר יְהוָה צְבָאוֹת׃

6 כִּי אֲנִי יְהוָה לֹא שָׁנִיתִי
וְאַתֶּם בְּנֵי־יַעֲקֹב לֹא כְלִיתֶם׃

7 לְמִימֵי אֲבֹתֵיכֶם
סַרְתֶּם מֵחֻקַּי וְלֹא שְׁמַרְתֶּם
שׁוּבוּ אֵלַי וְאָשׁוּבָה אֲלֵיכֶם
אָמַר יְהוָה צְבָאוֹת
וַאֲמַרְתֶּם בַּמֶּה נָשׁוּב׃

8 הֲיִקְבַּע אָדָם אֱלֹהִים
כִּי אַתֶּם קֹבְעִים אֹתִי
וַאֲמַרְתֶּם בַּמֶּה קְבַעֲנוּךָ
הַמַּעֲשֵׂר וְהַתְּרוּמָה׃

9 בַּמְּאֵרָה אַתֶּם נֵאָרִים
וְאֹתִי אַתֶּם קֹבְעִים הַגּוֹי כֻּלּוֹ׃

10 הָבִיאוּ אֶת־כָּל־הַמַּעֲשֵׂר
אֶל־בֵּית הָאוֹצָר וִיהִי טֶרֶף בְּבֵיתִי
וּבְחָנוּנִי נָא בָּזֹאת
אָמַר יְהוָה צְבָאוֹת
אִם־לֹא אֶפְתַּח לָכֶם
אֵת אֲרֻבּוֹת הַשָּׁמַיִם
וַהֲרִיקֹתִי לָכֶם
בְּרָכָה עַד־בְּלִי־דָי׃

11 וְגָעַרְתִּי לָכֶם בָּאֹכֵל
וְלֹא־יַשְׁחִת לָכֶם אֶת־פְּרִי הָאֲדָמָה
וְלֹא־תְשַׁכֵּל לָכֶם הַגֶּפֶן בַּשָּׂדֶה
אָמַר יְהוָה צְבָאוֹת׃

12 And all nations will call you blessed,
For you will be a delightful land,"
Says the LORD of hosts.

13 "Your words have been harsh against Me,"
Says the LORD,
"Yet you say,
'What have we spoken against You?'

14 You have said,
'It is useless to serve God;
What profit is it that we have kept His
ordinance,
And that we have walked as mourners
Before the LORD of hosts?

15 So now we call the proud blessed,
For those who do wickedness are raised up;
They even tempt God and go free.' "

16 Then those who feared the LORD spoke to
one another,
And the LORD listened and heard them;
So a book of remembrance was written
before Him
For those who fear the LORD
And who meditate on His name.

17 "They shall be Mine," says the LORD of hosts,
"On the day that I make them My jewels.
And I will spare them
As a man spares his own son who serves
him."

18 Then you shall again discern
Between the righteous and the wicked,
Between one who serves God
And one who does not serve Him.

4 "For behold, the day is coming,
Burning like an oven,
And all the proud, yes, all who do wickedly
will be stubble.
And the day which is coming shall burn them
up,"
Says the LORD of hosts,
"That will leave them neither root nor branch.

2 But to you who fear My name
The Sun of Righteousness shall arise
With healing in His wings;
And you shall go out
And grow fat like stall-fed calves.

3 You shall trample the wicked,
For they shall be ashes under the soles of
your feet
On the day that I do this,"
Says the LORD of hosts.

4 "Remember the Law of Moses, My servant,

וְאִשְּׁר֤וּ אֶתְכֶם֙ כָּל־הַגּוֹיִ֔ם 12
כִּי־תִהְי֥וּ אַתֶּ֖ם אֶ֣רֶץ חֵ֑פֶץ
אָמַ֖ר יְהוָ֥ה צְבָאֽוֹת׃ ס

חָזְק֥וּ עָלַ֛י דִּבְרֵיכֶ֖ם אָמַ֣ר יְהוָ֑ה 13
וַאֲמַרְתֶּ֕ם מַה־נִּדְבַּ֖רְנוּ עָלֶֽיךָ׃

אֲמַרְתֶּ֕ם שָׁ֖וְא עֲבֹ֣ד אֱלֹהִ֑ים 14
וּמַה־בֶּ֗צַע כִּ֤י שָׁמַ֙רְנוּ֙ מִשְׁמַרְתּ֔וֹ
וְכִ֤י הָלַ֙כְנוּ֙ קְדֹ֣רַנִּ֔ית
מִפְּנֵ֖י יְהוָ֥ה צְבָאֽוֹת׃

וְעַתָּ֕ה אֲנַ֖חְנוּ מְאַשְּׁרִ֣ים זֵדִ֑ים 15
גַּם־נִבְנוּ֙ עֹשֵׂ֣י רִשְׁעָ֔ה
גַּ֧ם בָּחֲנ֛וּ אֱלֹהִ֖ים וַיִּמָּלֵֽטוּ׃

אָ֧ז נִדְבְּר֛וּ יִרְאֵ֥י יְהוָ֖ה 16
אִ֣ישׁ אֶת־רֵעֵ֑הוּ
וַיַּקְשֵׁ֤ב יְהוָה֙ וַיִּשְׁמָ֔ע
וַ֠יִּכָּתֵ֠ב סֵ֣פֶר זִכָּר֤וֹן לְפָנָיו֙
לְיִרְאֵ֣י יְהוָ֔ה וּלְחֹשְׁבֵ֖י שְׁמֽוֹ׃

וְהָ֣יוּ לִ֗י אָמַר֙ יְהוָ֣ה צְבָא֔וֹת 17
לַיּ֕וֹם אֲשֶׁ֥ר אֲנִ֖י עֹשֶׂ֣ה סְגֻלָּ֑ה
וְחָמַלְתִּ֣י עֲלֵיהֶ֔ם כַּאֲשֶׁ֛ר יַחְמֹ֥ל אִ֖ישׁ
עַל־בְּנ֥וֹ הָעֹבֵ֖ד אֹתֽוֹ׃

וְשַׁבְתֶּם֙ וּרְאִיתֶ֔ם בֵּ֥ין צַדִּ֖יק לְרָשָׁ֑ע 18
בֵּ֚ין עֹבֵ֣ד אֱלֹהִ֔ים
לַאֲשֶׁ֖ר לֹ֥א עֲבָדֽוֹ׃ ס

כִּֽי־הִנֵּ֤ה הַיּוֹם֙ בָּ֔א 19
בֹּעֵ֖ר כַּתַּנּ֑וּר וְהָי֨וּ כָל־זֵדִ֜ים
וְכָל־עֹשֵׂ֤ה רִשְׁעָה֙ קַ֔שׁ
וְלִהַ֧ט אֹתָ֛ם הַיּ֥וֹם הַבָּ֖א
אָמַ֖ר יְהוָ֣ה צְבָא֑וֹת
אֲשֶׁ֛ר לֹא־יַעֲזֹ֥ב לָהֶ֖ם שֹׁ֥רֶשׁ וְעָנָֽף׃

וְזָרְחָ֨ה לָכֶ֜ם 20
יִרְאֵ֤י שְׁמִי֙ שֶׁ֣מֶשׁ צְדָקָ֔ה
וּמַרְפֵּ֖א בִּכְנָפֶ֑יהָ
וִיצָאתֶ֥ם וּפִשְׁתֶּ֖ם כְּעֶגְלֵ֥י מַרְבֵּֽק׃

וְעַסּוֹתֶ֣ם רְשָׁעִ֔ים כִּֽי־יִהְי֣וּ אֵ֔פֶר 21
תַּ֖חַת כַּפּ֣וֹת רַגְלֵיכֶ֑ם
בַּיּוֹם֙ אֲשֶׁ֣ר אֲנִ֣י עֹשֶׂ֔ה
אָמַ֖ר יְהוָ֥ה צְבָאֽוֹת׃ פ

זִכְר֕וּ תּוֹרַ֖ת מֹשֶׁ֣ה עַבְדִּ֑י 22
אֲשֶׁר֩ צִוִּ֨יתִי אוֹת֤וֹ בְחֹרֵב֙

Which I commanded him in Horeb for all
  Israel,
With the statutes and judgments.
5 Behold, I will send you Elijah the prophet
Before the coming of the great and dreadful
  day of the LORD.
6 And he will turn
The hearts of the fathers to the children,
And the hearts of the children to their
  fathers,
Lest I come and strike the earth with a
  curse."

עַל־כָּל־יִשְׂרָאֵל
חֻקִּים וּמִשְׁפָּטִים:
23 הִנֵּה אָנֹכִי שֹׁלֵחַ לָכֶם
אֵת אֵלִיָּה הַנָּבִיא
לִפְנֵי בּוֹא יוֹם יְהֹוָה
הַגָּדוֹל וְהַנּוֹרָא:
24 וְהֵשִׁיב לֵב־אָבוֹת עַל־בָּנִים
וְלֵב בָּנִים עַל־אֲבוֹתָם
פֶּן־אָבוֹא וְהִכֵּיתִי אֶת־הָאָרֶץ חֵרֶם:

The Book of

PSALMS

Book One: Psalms 1—41

תהלים

1 Blessed *is* the man
  Who walks not in the counsel of the ungodly,
    Nor stands in the path of sinners,
    Nor sits in the seat of the scornful;
2 But his delight *is* in the law of the LORD,
    And in His law he meditates day and night.
3 He shall be like a tree
    Planted by the rivers of water,
    That brings forth its fruit in its season,
    Whose leaf also shall not wither;
  And whatever he does shall prosper.

4 The ungodly *are* not so,
  But *are* like the chaff which the wind drives
    away.
5 Therefore the ungodly shall not stand in the
    judgment,
  Nor sinners in the congregation of the
    righteous.

6 For the LORD knows the way of the righteous,
  But the way of the ungodly shall perish.

א אַשְׁרֵי־הָאִישׁ
אֲשֶׁר ׀ לֹא הָלַךְ בַּעֲצַת רְשָׁעִים
וּבְדֶרֶךְ חַטָּאִים לֹא עָמָד
וּבְמוֹשַׁב לֵצִים לֹא יָשָׁב:
2 כִּי אִם בְּתוֹרַת יְהוָה חֶפְצוֹ
וּבְתוֹרָתוֹ יֶהְגֶּה יוֹמָם וָלָיְלָה:
3 וְהָיָה כְּעֵץ שָׁתוּל עַל־פַּלְגֵי מָיִם
אֲשֶׁר פִּרְיוֹ ׀ יִתֵּן בְּעִתּוֹ וְעָלֵהוּ לֹא־יִבּוֹל
וְכֹל אֲשֶׁר־יַעֲשֶׂה יַצְלִיחַ:
4 לֹא־כֵן הָרְשָׁעִים
כִּי אִם־כַּמֹּץ אֲשֶׁר־תִּדְּפֶנּוּ רוּחַ:
5 עַל־כֵּן ׀ לֹא־יָקֻמוּ רְשָׁעִים בַּמִּשְׁפָּט
וְחַטָּאִים בַּעֲדַת צַדִּיקִים:
6 כִּי־יוֹדֵעַ יְהוָה דֶּרֶךְ צַדִּיקִים
וְדֶרֶךְ רְשָׁעִים תֹּאבֵד:

2 Why do the nations rage,
  And the people plot a vain thing?
2 The kings of the earth set themselves,
  And the rulers take counsel together,
  Against the LORD and against His Anointed,
    saying,
3 "Let us break Their bonds in pieces
  And cast away Their cords from us."

4 He who sits in the heavens shall laugh;
  The LORD shall hold them in derision.
5 Then He shall speak to them in His wrath,
  And distress them in His deep displeasure:
6 "Yet I have set My King
  On My holy hill of Zion."

7 "I will declare the decree:
  The LORD has said to Me,
  'You *are* My Son,
  Today I have begotten You.
8 Ask of Me, and I will give *You*
  The nations *for* Your inheritance,
  And the ends of the earth *for* Your possession.
9 You shall break them with a rod of iron;

ב לָמָּה רָגְשׁוּ גוֹיִם
וּלְאֻמִּים יֶהְגּוּ־רִיק:
2 יִתְיַצְּבוּ ׀ מַלְכֵי־אֶרֶץ
וְרוֹזְנִים נוֹסְדוּ־יָחַד
עַל־יְהוָה וְעַל־מְשִׁיחוֹ:
3 נְנַתְּקָה אֶת־מוֹסְרוֹתֵימוֹ
וְנַשְׁלִיכָה מִמֶּנּוּ עֲבֹתֵימוֹ:
4 יוֹשֵׁב בַּשָּׁמַיִם יִשְׂחָק
אֲדֹנָי יִלְעַג־לָמוֹ:
5 אָז יְדַבֵּר אֵלֵימוֹ בְאַפּוֹ
וּבַחֲרוֹנוֹ יְבַהֲלֵמוֹ:
6 וַאֲנִי נָסַכְתִּי מַלְכִּי
עַל־צִיּוֹן הַר־קָדְשִׁי:
7 אֲסַפְּרָה אֶל חֹק
יְהוָה אָמַר אֵלַי בְּנִי אַתָּה אֲנִי הַיּוֹם יְלִדְתִּיךָ:
8 שְׁאַל מִמֶּנִּי וְאֶתְּנָה גוֹיִם נַחֲלָתֶךָ
וַאֲחֻזָּתְךָ אַפְסֵי־אָרֶץ:
9 תְּרֹעֵם בְּשֵׁבֶט בַּרְזֶל

You shall dash them to pieces like a potter's
vessel.'"

כִּכְלִי יוֹצֵר תְּנַפְּצֵם:

10 Now therefore, be wise, O kings;
Be instructed, you judges of the earth.

10 וְעַתָּה מְלָכִים הַשְׂכִּילוּ
הִוָּסְרוּ שֹׁפְטֵי אָרֶץ:

11 Serve the LORD with fear,
And rejoice with trembling.

11 עִבְדוּ אֶת־יְהֹוָה בְּיִרְאָה
וְגִילוּ בִּרְעָדָה:

12 Kiss the Son, lest He be angry,
And you perish *in* the way,
When His wrath is kindled but a little.
Blessed *are* all those who put their trust in
Him.

12 נַשְּׁקוּ־בַר פֶּן־יֶאֱנַף ׀ וְתֹאבְדוּ דֶרֶךְ
כִּי־יִבְעַר כִּמְעַט אַפּוֹ
אַשְׁרֵי כָּל־חוֹסֵי בוֹ:

3 A Psalm of David when he fled from Absalom his
son.

Lord, how they have increased who trouble
me!
Many *are* they who rise up against me.

ג מִזְמוֹר לְדָוִד
בְּבָרְחוֹ מִפְּנֵי ׀ אַבְשָׁלוֹם בְּנוֹ:

2 יְהֹוָה מָה־רַבּוּ צָרָי
רַבִּים קָמִים עָלָי:

2 Many *are* they who say of me,
"There is no help for him in God."   Selah

3 רַבִּים אֹמְרִים לְנַפְשִׁי
אֵין יְשׁוּעָתָה לּוֹ בֵאלֹהִים סֶלָה:

3 But You, O LORD, *are* a shield for me,
My glory and the One who lifts up my head.

4 וְאַתָּה יְהֹוָה מָגֵן בַּעֲדִי
כְּבוֹדִי וּמֵרִים רֹאשִׁי:

4 I cried to the LORD with my voice,
And He heard me from His holy hill.   Selah

5 קוֹלִי אֶל־יְהֹוָה אֶקְרָא
וַיַּעֲנֵנִי מֵהַר קָדְשׁוֹ סֶלָה:

5 I lay down and slept;
I awoke, for the LORD sustained me.

6 אֲנִי שָׁכַבְתִּי וָאִישָׁנָה
הֱקִיצוֹתִי כִּי יְהֹוָה יִסְמְכֵנִי:

6 I will not be afraid of ten thousands of people
Who have set *themselves* against me all around.

7 לֹא־אִירָא מֵרִבְבוֹת עָם
אֲשֶׁר סָבִיב שָׁתוּ עָלָי:

7 Arise, O LORD;
Save me, O my God!
For You have struck all my enemies on the
cheekbone;
You have broken the teeth of the ungodly.

8 קוּמָה יְהֹוָה ׀ הוֹשִׁיעֵנִי אֱלֹהַי
כִּי־הִכִּיתָ אֶת־כָּל־אֹיְבַי לֶחִי
שִׁנֵּי רְשָׁעִים שִׁבַּרְתָּ:

8 Salvation *belongs* to the LORD.
Your blessing *is* upon Your people.   Selah

9 לַיהֹוָה הַיְשׁוּעָה
עַל־עַמְּךָ בִרְכָתֶךָ סֶּלָה:

4 To the Chief Musician. With stringed instruments. A
Psalm of David.

Hear me when I call, O God of my
righteousness!
You have relieved me in *my* distress;
Have mercy on me, and hear my prayer.

ד לַמְנַצֵּחַ בִּנְגִינוֹת מִזְמוֹר לְדָוִד:

2 בְּקָרְאִי עֲנֵנִי ׀ אֱלֹהֵי צִדְקִי בַּצָּר הִרְחַבְתָּ לִּי
חָנֵּנִי וּשְׁמַע תְּפִלָּתִי:

2 How long, O you sons of men,
Will you turn my glory to shame?
How long will you love worthlessness
And seek falsehood?   Selah

3 בְּנֵי אִישׁ עַד־מֶה כְבוֹדִי לִכְלִמָּה תֶּאֱהָבוּן רִיק
תְּבַקְשׁוּ כָזָב סֶלָה:

3 But know that the LORD has set apart for
Himself him who is godly;
The LORD will hear when I call to Him.

4 וּדְעוּ כִּי־הִפְלָה יְהֹוָה חָסִיד לוֹ
יְהֹוָה יִשְׁמַע בְּקָרְאִי אֵלָיו:

4 Be angry, and do not sin.
Meditate within your heart on your bed, and
be still.   Selah

5 רִגְזוּ וְאַל־תֶּחֱטָאוּ
אִמְרוּ בִלְבַבְכֶם עַל־מִשְׁכַּבְכֶם וְדֹמּוּ סֶלָה:

5 Offer the sacrifices of righteousness,
And put your trust in the LORD.

6 *There are* many who say,
"Who will show us *any* good?"
LORD, lift up the light of Your countenance
upon us.

7 You have put gladness in my heart,
More than in the season that their grain and
wine increased.

8 I will both lie down in peace, and sleep;
For You alone, O LORD, make me dwell in
safety.

5 To the Chief Musician. With flutes. A Psalm of
David.
Give ear to my words, O LORD,
Consider my meditation.

2 Give heed to the voice of my cry,
My King and my God,
For to You I will pray.

3 My voice You shall hear in the morning, O
LORD;
In the morning I will direct *it* to You,
And I will look up.

4 For You *are* not a God who takes pleasure in
wickedness,
Nor shall evil dwell with You.

5 The boastful shall not stand in Your sight;
You hate all workers of iniquity.

6 You shall destroy those who speak falsehood;
The LORD abhors the bloodthirsty and
deceitful man.

7 But as for me, I will come into Your house in
the multitude of Your mercy;
In fear of You I will worship toward Your holy
temple.

8 Lead me, O LORD, in Your righteousness
because of my enemies;
Make Your way straight before my face.

9 For *there is* no faithfulness in their mouth;
Their inward part *is* destruction;
Their throat *is* an open tomb;
They flatter with their tongue.

10 Pronounce them guilty, O God!
Let them fall by their own counsels;
Cast them out in the multitude of their
transgressions,
For they have rebelled against You.

11 But let all those rejoice who put their trust in
You;
Let them ever shout for joy, because You
defend them;

זִבְחוּ זִבְחֵי־צֶדֶק 6
וּבִטְחוּ אֶל־יְהֹוָה:

רַבִּים אֹמְרִים מִי־יַרְאֵנוּ טוֹב 7
נְסָה־עָלֵינוּ אוֹר פָּנֶיךָ יְהֹוָה:

נָתַתָּה שִׂמְחָה בְלִבִּי 8
מֵעֵת דְּגָנָם וְתִירוֹשָׁם רָבּוּ:

בְּשָׁלוֹם יַחְדָּו אֶשְׁכְּבָה וְאִישָׁן 9
כִּי־אַתָּה יְהֹוָה לְבָדָד לָבֶטַח תּוֹשִׁיבֵנִי:

ה לַמְנַצֵּחַ אֶל־הַנְּחִילוֹת
מִזְמוֹר לְדָוִד:

אֲמָרַי הַאֲזִינָה ׀ יְהֹוָה 2
בִּינָה הֲגִיגִי:

הַקְשִׁיבָה ׀ לְקוֹל שַׁוְעִי מַלְכִּי וֵאלֹהָי 3
כִּי־אֵלֶיךָ אֶתְפַּלָּל:

יְהֹוָה בֹּקֶר תִּשְׁמַע קוֹלִי 4
בֹּקֶר אֶעֱרָךְ־לְךָ וַאֲצַפֶּה:

כִּי ׀ לֹא אֵל־חָפֵץ רֶשַׁע ׀ אָתָּה 5
לֹא יְגֻרְךָ רָע:

לֹא־יִתְיַצְּבוּ הוֹלְלִים לְנֶגֶד עֵינֶיךָ 6
שָׂנֵאתָ כָּל־פֹּעֲלֵי אָוֶן:

תְּאַבֵּד דֹּבְרֵי כָזָב 7
אִישׁ־דָּמִים וּמִרְמָה יְתָעֵב ׀ יְהֹוָה:

וַאֲנִי בְּרֹב חַסְדְּךָ אָבוֹא בֵיתֶךָ 8
אֶשְׁתַּחֲוֶה אֶל־הֵיכַל־קָדְשְׁךָ בְּיִרְאָתֶךָ:

יְהֹוָה ׀ נְחֵנִי בְצִדְקָתֶךָ לְמַעַן שׁוֹרְרָי 9
הוֹשַׁרק לְפָנַי דַּרְכֶּךָ:

כִּי אֵין בְּפִיהוּ נְכוֹנָה קִרְבָּם הַוּוֹת 10
קֶבֶר־פָּתוּחַ גְּרוֹנָם לְשׁוֹנָם יַחֲלִיקוּן:

הַאֲשִׁימֵם ׀ אֱלֹהִים 11
יִפְּלוּ מִמֹּעֲצוֹתֵיהֶם
בְּרֹב פִּשְׁעֵיהֶם הַדִּיחֵמוֹ
כִּי־מָרוּ בָךְ:

ה 9 הַיְשַׁר

Let those also who love Your name
Be joyful in You.

12 For You, O LORD, will bless the righteous;
With favor You will surround him as *with* a
shield.

6 To the Chief Musician. With stringed instruments.
On an eight-stringed harp. A Psalm of David.
O LORD, do not rebuke me in Your anger,
Nor chasten me in Your hot displeasure.

2 Have mercy on me, O LORD, for I *am* weak;
O LORD, heal me, for my bones are troubled.

3 My soul also is greatly troubled;
But You, O LORD—how long?

4 Return, O LORD, deliver me!
Oh, save me for Your mercies' sake!

5 For in death *there is* no remembrance of You;
In the grave who will give You thanks?

6 I am weary with my groaning;
All night I make my bed swim;
I drench my couch with my tears.

7 My eye wastes away because of grief;
It grows old because of all my enemies.

8 Depart from me, all you workers of iniquity;
For the LORD has heard the voice of my
weeping.

9 The LORD has heard my supplication;
The LORD will receive my prayer.

10 Let all my enemies be ashamed and greatly
troubled;
Let them turn back *and* be ashamed suddenly.

7 A Meditation of David, which he sang to the LORD
concerning the words of Cush, a Benjamite.
O LORD my God, in You I put my trust;
Save me from all those who persecute me;
And deliver me,

2 Lest they tear me like a lion,
Rending *me* in pieces, while *there is* none to
deliver.

3 O LORD my God, if I have done this:
If there is iniquity in my hands,

4 If I have repaid evil to him who was at peace
with me,
Or have plundered my enemy without cause,

5 Let the enemy pursue me and overtake *me;*
Yes, let him trample my life to the earth,
And lay my honor in the dust.   Selah

6 Arise, O LORD, in Your anger;
Lift Yourself up because of the rage of my
enemies;

12 וְיִשְׂמְח֣וּ כָל־ח֣וֹסֵי בָ֭ךְ לְעוֹלָ֣ם יְרַנֵּ֑נוּ
וְתָסֵ֥ךְ עָלֵ֑ימוֹ
וְיַעְלְצ֥וּ בְךָ֗
אֹהֲבֵ֥י שְׁמֶֽךָ׃

13 כִּֽי־אַתָּה֮ תְּבָרֵ֢ךְ צַ֫דִּ֥יק
יְהֹוָ֑ה כַּ֝צִּנָּ֗ה רָצ֥וֹן תַּעְטְרֶֽנּוּ׃

ו לַמְנַצֵּ֣חַ בִּנְגִינוֹת֮ עַֽל־הַשְּׁמִינִ֥ית
מִזְמ֥וֹר לְדָוִֽד׃
2 יְֽהֹוָ֗ה אַל־בְּאַפְּךָ֥ תוֹכִיחֵ֑נִי
וְֽאַל־בַּחֲמָתְךָ֥ תְיַסְּרֵֽנִי׃
3 חָנֵּ֥נִי יְהֹוָה֮ כִּ֤י אֻמְלַ֫ל אָ֥נִי
רְפָאֵ֥נִי יְהֹוָ֑ה כִּ֖י נִבְהֲל֣וּ עֲצָמָֽי׃
4 וְ֭נַפְשִׁי נִבְהֲלָ֣ה מְאֹ֑ד
וְאַ֥תְּ יְ֝הֹוָ֗ה עַד־מָתָֽי׃
5 שׁוּבָ֣ה יְ֭הֹוָה חַלְּצָ֣ה נַפְשִׁ֑י
ה֝וֹשִׁיעֵ֗נִי לְמַ֣עַן חַסְדֶּֽךָ׃
6 כִּ֤י אֵ֣ין בַּמָּ֣וֶת זִכְרֶ֑ךָ
בִּ֝שְׁא֗וֹל מִ֣י יֽוֹדֶה־לָּֽךְ׃
7 יָגַ֤עְתִּי ׀ בְּֽאַנְחָתִ֗י אַשְׂחֶ֣ה בְכָל־לַ֭יְלָה מִטָּתִ֑י
בְּ֝דִמְעָתִ֗י עַרְשִׂ֥י אַמְסֶֽה׃
8 עָֽשְׁשָׁ֣ה מִכַּ֣עַס עֵינִ֑י
עָֽ֝תְקָ֗ה בְּכָל־צוֹרְרָֽי׃
9 ס֣וּרוּ מִ֭מֶּנִּי כָּל־פֹּ֣עֲלֵי אָ֑וֶן
כִּֽי־שָׁמַ֥ע יְ֝הֹוָ֗ה ק֣וֹל בִּכְיִֽי׃
10 שָׁמַ֣ע יְ֭הֹוָה תְּחִנָּתִ֑י
יְ֝הֹוָ֗ה תְּֽפִלָּתִ֥י יִקָּֽח׃
11 יֵבֹ֤שׁוּ ׀ וְיִבָּהֲל֣וּ מְ֭אֹד כָּל־אֹיְבָ֑י
יָ֝שֻׁ֗בוּ יֵבֹ֥שׁוּ רָֽגַע׃

ז שִׁגָּי֗וֹן לְדָ֫וִ֥ד
אֲשֶׁר־שָׁ֥ר לַיהֹוָ֑ה עַל־דִּבְרֵי־כ֝֗וּשׁ בֶּן־יְמִינִֽי׃
2 יְהֹוָ֣ה אֱ֭לֹהַי בְּךָ֣ חָסִ֑יתִי
הוֹשִׁיעֵ֥נִי מִכָּל־רֹ֝דְפַ֗י וְהַצִּילֵֽנִי׃
3 פֶּן־יִטְרֹ֣ף כְּאַרְיֵ֣ה נַפְשִׁ֑י
פֹּ֝רֵ֗ק וְאֵ֣ין מַצִּֽיל׃
4 יְהֹוָ֣ה אֱ֭לֹהַי אִם־עָשִׂ֣יתִי זֹ֑את
אִם־יֶשׁ־עָ֥וֶל בְּכַפָּֽי׃
5 אִם־גָּ֭מַלְתִּי שֽׁוֹלְמִ֥י רָ֑ע
וָאֲחַלְּצָ֖ה צוֹרְרִ֣י רֵיקָֽם׃
6 יִֽרַדֹּ֥ף אוֹיֵ֨ב ׀ נַפְשִׁ֡י וְיַשֵּׂ֗ג וְיִרְמֹ֣ס לָאָ֣רֶץ חַיָּ֑י
וּכְבוֹדִ֓י ׀ לֶעָפָ֖ר יַשְׁכֵּ֣ן סֶֽלָה׃

Rise up for me *to* the judgment You have commanded!

קוּמָה יְהֹוָה ׀ בְּאַפֶּךָ הִנָּשֵׂא בְּעַבְרוֹת צוֹרְרָי

7 So the congregation of the peoples shall surround You;
For their sakes, therefore, return on high.

וְעוּרָה אֵלַי מִשְׁפָּט צִוִּיתָ:
8 וַעֲדַת לְאֻמִּים תְּסוֹבְבֶךָּ
וְעָלֶיהָ לַמָּרוֹם שׁוּבָה:

8 The LORD shall judge the peoples;
Judge me, O LORD, according to my righteousness,
And according to my integrity within me.

9 יְהֹוָה יָדִין עַמִּים
שָׁפְטֵנִי יְהֹוָה כְּצִדְקִי וּכְתֻמִּי עָלָי:

9 Oh, let the wickedness of the wicked come to an end,
But establish the just;
For the righteous God tests the hearts and minds.

10 יִגְמָר־נָא רַע ׀ רְשָׁעִים
וּתְכוֹנֵן צַדִּיק
וּבֹחֵן לִבּוֹת וּכְלָיוֹת
אֱלֹהִים צַדִּיק:

10 My defense *is* of God,
Who saves the upright in heart.

11 מָגִנִּי עַל־אֱלֹהִים
מוֹשִׁיעַ יִשְׁרֵי־לֵב:

11 God *is* a just judge,
And God is angry *with the wicked* every day.

12 אֱלֹהִים שׁוֹפֵט צַדִּיק
וְאֵל זֹעֵם בְּכָל־יוֹם:

12 If he does not turn back,
He will sharpen His sword;
He bends His bow and makes it ready.

13 אִם־לֹא יָשׁוּב חַרְבּוֹ יִלְטוֹשׁ
קַשְׁתּוֹ דָרַךְ וַיְכוֹנְנֶהָ:

13 He also prepares for Himself instruments of death;
He makes His arrows into fiery shafts.

14 וְלוֹ הֵכִין כְּלֵי־מָוֶת
חִצָּיו לְדֹלְקִים יִפְעָל:

14 Behold, *the wicked* brings forth iniquity;
Yes, he conceives trouble and brings forth falsehood.

15 הִנֵּה יְחַבֶּל־אָוֶן
וְהָרָה עָמָל וְיָלַד שָׁקֶר:

15 He made a pit and dug it out,
And has fallen into the ditch *which* he made.

16 בּוֹר כָּרָה וַיַּחְפְּרֵהוּ
וַיִּפֹּל בְּשַׁחַת יִפְעָל:

16 His trouble shall return upon his own head,
And his violent dealing shall come down on his own crown.

17 יָשׁוּב עֲמָלוֹ בְרֹאשׁוֹ
וְעַל קָדְקֳדוֹ חֲמָסוֹ יֵרֵד:

17 I will praise the LORD according to His righteousness,
And will sing praise to the name of the LORD Most High.

18 אוֹדֶה יְהֹוָה כְּצִדְקוֹ
וַאֲזַמְּרָה שֵׁם־יְהֹוָה עֶלְיוֹן:

8 To the Chief Musician. On the instrument of Gath. A Psalm of David.

ח לַמְנַצֵּחַ עַל־הַגִּתִּית
מִזְמוֹר לְדָוִד:

O LORD, our Lord,
How excellent *is* Your name in all the earth,
Who have set Your glory above the heavens!

2 יְהֹוָה אֲדֹנֵינוּ
מָה־אַדִּיר שִׁמְךָ בְּכָל־הָאָרֶץ
אֲשֶׁר תְּנָה הוֹדְךָ
עַל־הַשָּׁמָיִם:

2 Out of the mouth of babes and nursing infants You have ordained strength,
Because of Your enemies,
That You may silence the enemy and the avenger.

3 מִפִּי עוֹלְלִים ׀ וְיֹנְקִים
יִסַּדְתָּ עֹז
לְמַעַן צוֹרְרֶיךָ
לְהַשְׁבִּית אוֹיֵב וּמִתְנַקֵּם:

3 When I consider Your heavens, the work of Your fingers,
The moon and the stars, which You have ordained,

4 כִּי־אֶרְאֶה שָׁמֶיךָ מַעֲשֵׂי אֶצְבְּעֹתֶיךָ
יָרֵחַ וְכוֹכָבִים אֲשֶׁר כּוֹנָנְתָּה:

4 What is man that You are mindful of him,
And the son of man that You visit him?

5 For You have made him a little lower than the angels,
And You have crowned him with glory and honor.

6 You have made him to have dominion over the works of Your hands;
You have put all *things* under his feet,

7 All sheep and oxen—
Even the beasts of the field,

8 The birds of the air,
And the fish of the sea
That pass through the paths of the seas.

9 O LORD, our Lord,
How excellent *is* Your name in all the earth!

9 To the Chief Musician. To *the tune of* "Death of the Son." A Psalm of David.

 I will praise *You,* O LORD, with my whole heart;
I will tell of all Your marvelous works.

2 I will be glad and rejoice in You;
I will sing praise to Your name, O Most High.

3 When my enemies turn back,
They shall fall and perish at Your presence.

4 For You have maintained my right and my cause;
You sat on the throne judging in righteousness.

5 You have rebuked the nations,
You have destroyed the wicked;
You have blotted out their name forever and ever.

6 O enemy, destructions are finished forever!
And you have destroyed cities;
Even their memory has perished.

7 But the LORD shall endure forever;
He has prepared His throne for judgment.

8 He shall judge the world in righteousness,
And He shall administer judgment for the peoples in uprightness.

9 The LORD also will be a refuge for the oppressed,
A refuge in times of trouble.

10 And those who know Your name will put their trust in You;
For You, LORD, have not forsaken those who seek You.

11 Sing praises to the LORD, who dwells in Zion!
Declare His deeds among the people.

12 When He avenges blood, He remembers them;

5 מָה־אֱנוֹשׁ כִּי־תִזְכְּרֶנּוּ
וּבֶן־אָדָם כִּי תִפְקְדֶנּוּ:

6 וַתְּחַסְּרֵהוּ מְּעַט מֵאֱלֹהִים
וְכָבוֹד וְהָדָר תְּעַטְּרֵהוּ:

7 תַּמְשִׁילֵהוּ בְּמַעֲשֵׂי יָדֶיךָ
כֹּל שַׁתָּה תַחַת־רַגְלָיו:

8 צֹנֶה וַאֲלָפִים כֻּלָּם
וְגַם בַּהֲמוֹת שָׂדָי:

9 צִפּוֹר שָׁמַיִם וּדְגֵי הַיָּם
עֹבֵר אָרְחוֹת יַמִּים:

10 יְהֹוָה אֲדֹנֵינוּ
מָה־אַדִּיר שִׁמְךָ בְּכָל־הָאָרֶץ:

ט לַמְנַצֵּחַ עַל־מוּת לַבֵּן מִזְמוֹר לְדָוִד:

2 אוֹדֶה יְהֹוָה בְּכָל־לִבִּי
אֲסַפְּרָה כָּל־נִפְלְאוֹתֶיךָ:

3 אֶשְׂמְחָה וְאֶעֶלְצָה בָךְ
אֲזַמְּרָה שִׁמְךָ עֶלְיוֹן:

4 בְּשׁוּב־אוֹיְבַי אָחוֹר
יִכָּשְׁלוּ וְיֹאבְדוּ מִפָּנֶיךָ:

5 כִּי־עָשִׂיתָ מִשְׁפָּטִי וְדִינִי
יָשַׁבְתָּ לְכִסֵּא שׁוֹפֵט צֶדֶק:

6 גָּעַרְתָּ גוֹיִם אִבַּדְתָּ רָשָׁע
שְׁמָם מָחִיתָ לְעוֹלָם וָעֶד:

7 הָאוֹיֵב תַּמּוּ חֳרָבוֹת לָנֶצַח
וְעָרִים נָתַשְׁתָּ אָבַד זִכְרָם הֵמָּה:

8 וַיהֹוָה לְעוֹלָם יֵשֵׁב
כּוֹנֵן לַמִּשְׁפָּט כִּסְאוֹ:

9 וְהוּא יִשְׁפֹּט־תֵּבֵל בְּצֶדֶק
יָדִין לְאֻמִּים בְּמֵישָׁרִים:

10 וִיהִי יְהֹוָה מִשְׂגָּב לַדָּךְ
מִשְׂגָּב לְעִתּוֹת בַּצָּרָה:

11 וְיִבְטְחוּ בְךָ יוֹדְעֵי שְׁמֶךָ
כִּי לֹא־עָזַבְתָּ דֹרְשֶׁיךָ יְהֹוָה:

12 זַמְּרוּ לַיהֹוָה יֹשֵׁב צִיּוֹן
הַגִּידוּ בָעַמִּים עֲלִילוֹתָיו:

13 כִּי־דֹרֵשׁ דָּמִים אוֹתָם זָכָר

He does not forget the cry of the humble.

13 Have mercy on me, O LORD!
Consider my trouble from those who hate me,
You who lift me up from the gates of death,

14 That I may tell of all Your praise
In the gates of the daughter of Zion.
I will rejoice in Your salvation.

15 The nations have sunk down in the pit *which*
they made;
In the net which they hid, their own foot is
caught.

16 The LORD is known *by* the judgment He
executes;
The wicked is snared in the work of his own
hands.
         Meditation.   Selah

17 The wicked shall be turned into hell,
And all the nations that forget God.

18 For the needy shall not always be forgotten;
The expectation of the poor shall *not* perish
forever.

19 Arise, O LORD,
Do not let man prevail;
Let the nations be judged in Your sight.

20 Put them in fear, O LORD,
That the nations may know themselves *to be*
but men.   Selah

10 Why do You stand afar off, O LORD?
Why do You hide in times of trouble?

2 The wicked in *his* pride persecutes the poor;
Let them be caught in the plots which they
have devised.

3 For the wicked boasts of his heart's desire;
He blesses the greedy *and* renounces the LORD.

4 The wicked in his proud countenance does not
seek *God;*
God *is* in none of his thoughts.

5 His ways are always prospering;
Your judgments *are* far above, out of his sight;
As for all his enemies, he sneers at them.

6 He has said in his heart, "I shall not be moved;
I shall never be in adversity."

7 His mouth is full of cursing and deceit and
oppression;
Under his tongue *is* trouble and iniquity.

8 He sits in the lurking places of the villages;
In the secret places he murders the innocent;
His eyes are secretly fixed on the helpless.

9 He lies in wait secretly, as a lion in his den;
He lies in wait to catch the poor;

לֹא־שָׁכַח צַעֲקַת עֲנָיִיםᵖ:

14 חׇנְנֵנִי יְהֹוָה רְאֵה עׇנְיִי מִשֹּׂנְאָי
מְרוֹמְמִי מִשַּׁעֲרֵי מָוֶת:

15 לְמַעַן אֲסַפְּרָה כׇּל־תְּהִלָּתֶיךָ
בְּשַׁעֲרֵי בַת־צִיּוֹן אָגִילָה בִּישׁוּעָתֶךָ:

16 טָבְעוּ גוֹיִם בְּשַׁחַת עָשׂוּ
בְּרֶשֶׁת־זוּ טָמָנוּ נִלְכְּדָה רַגְלָם:

17 נוֹדַע ׀ יְהֹוָה מִשְׁפָּט עָשָׂה
בְּפֹעַל כַּפָּיו נוֹקֵשׁ רָשָׁע הִגָּיוֹן סֶלָה:

18 יָשׁוּבוּ רְשָׁעִים לִשְׁאוֹלָה
כׇּל־גּוֹיִם שְׁכֵחֵי אֱלֹהִים:

19 כִּי לֹא לָנֶצַח יִשָּׁכַח אֶבְיוֹן
תִּקְוַת עֲנָוִיםᵖ תֹּאבַד לָעַד:

20 קוּמָה יְהֹוָה אַל־יָעֹז אֱנוֹשׁ
יִשָּׁפְטוּ גוֹיִם עַל־פָּנֶיךָ:

21 שִׁיתָה יְהֹוָה ׀ מוֹרָה לָהֶם
יֵדְעוּ גוֹיִם אֱנוֹשׁ הֵמָּה סֶּלָה:

י לָמָה יְהֹוָה תַּעֲמֹד בְּרָחוֹק
תַּעְלִים לְעִתּוֹת בַּצָּרָה:

2 בְּגַאֲוַת רָשָׁע יִדְלַק עָנִי
יִתָּפְשׂוּ ׀ בִּמְזִמּוֹת זוּ חָשָׁבוּ:

3 כִּי־הִלֵּל רָשָׁע עַל־תַּאֲוַת נַפְשׁוֹ
וּבֹצֵעַ בֵּרֵךְ נִאֵץ ׀ יְהֹוָה:

4 רָשָׁע כְּגֹבַהּ אַפּוֹ בַּל־יִדְרֹשׁ
אֵין אֱלֹהִים כׇּל־מְזִמּוֹתָיו:

5 יָחִילוּ דְרָכָוᵖ ׀ בְּכׇל־עֵת
מָרוֹם מִשְׁפָּטֶיךָ מִנֶּגְדּוֹ
כׇּל־צוֹרְרָיו יָפִיחַ בָּהֶם:

6 אָמַר בְּלִבּוֹ בַּל־אֶמּוֹט
לְדֹר וָדֹר אֲשֶׁר לֹא־בְרָע:

7 אָלָה פִּיהוּ מָלֵא וּמִרְמוֹת וָתֹךְ
תַּחַת לְשׁוֹנוֹ עָמָל וָאָוֶן:

8 יֵשֵׁב ׀ בְּמַאְרַב חֲצֵרִים בַּמִּסְתָּרִים יַהֲרֹג נָקִי
עֵינָיו לְחֵלְכָה יִצְפֹּנוּ:

9 יֶאֱרֹב בַּמִּסְתָּר ׀ כְּאַרְיֵה בְסֻכֹּה
יֶאֱרֹב לַחֲטוֹף עָנִי

He catches the poor when he draws him into
   his net.

יַחְטֹף עָנִי
בְּמָשְׁכוֹ בְרִשְׁתּוֹ:

10 So he crouches, he lies low,
   That the helpless may fall by his strength.

10 וְדָכָה יָשֹׁחַ
וְנָפַל בַּעֲצוּמָיו חֵלְכָּאִים:

11 He has said in his heart,
   "God has forgotten;
   He hides His face;
   He will never see."

11 אָמַר בְּלִבּוֹ שָׁכַח אֵל
הִסְתִּיר פָּנָיו בַּל־רָאָה לָנֶצַח:

12 Arise, O LORD!
   O God, lift up Your hand!
   Do not forget the humble.

12 קוּמָה יְהוָה אֵל נְשָׂא יָדֶךָ
אַל־תִּשְׁכַּח עֲנָוִים:

13 Why do the wicked renounce God?
   He has said in his heart,
   "You will not require *an account*."

13 עַל־מֶה נִאֵץ רָשָׁע אֱלֹהִים
אָמַר בְּלִבּוֹ לֹא תִּדְרֹשׁ:

14 But You have seen, for You observe trouble
   and grief,
   To repay *it* by Your hand.
   The helpless commits himself to You;
   You are the helper of the fatherless.

14 רָאִתָה כִּי־אַתָּה עָמָל וָכַעַס תַּבִּיט
לָתֵת בְּיָדֶךָ
עָלֶיךָ יַעֲזֹב חֵלְכָה
יָתוֹם אַתָּה הָיִיתָ עוֹזֵר:

15 Break the arm of the wicked and the evil *man;*
   Seek out his wickedness *until* You find none.

15 שְׁבֹר זְרוֹעַ רָשָׁע
וָרָע תִּדְרוֹשׁ־רִשְׁעוֹ בַל־תִּמְצָא:

16 The LORD *is* King forever and ever;
   The nations have perished out of His land.

16 יְהוָה מֶלֶךְ עוֹלָם וָעֶד
אָבְדוּ גוֹיִם מֵאַרְצוֹ:

17 LORD, You have heard the desire of the
   humble;
   You will prepare their heart;
   You will cause Your ear to hear,

17 תַּאֲוַת עֲנָוִים שָׁמַעְתָּ יְהוָה
תָּכִין לִבָּם תַּקְשִׁיב אָזְנֶךָ:

18 To do justice to the fatherless and the
   oppressed,
   That the man of the earth may oppress no
   more.

18 לִשְׁפֹּט יָתוֹם וָדָךְ
בַּל־יוֹסִיף עוֹד לַעֲרֹץ אֱנוֹשׁ מִן־הָאָרֶץ:

11 To the Chief Musician. A Psalm of David.
   In the LORD I put my trust;
   How can you say to my soul,
   "Flee *as* a bird to your mountain"?

יא לַמְנַצֵּחַ לְדָוִד
בַּיהוָה חָסִיתִי אֵיךְ תֹּאמְרוּ לְנַפְשִׁי
נוּדוּ הַרְכֶם צִפּוֹר:

2 For look! The wicked bend *their* bow,
   They make ready their arrow on the string,
   That they may shoot secretly at the upright in
   heart.

2 כִּי הִנֵּה הָרְשָׁעִים יִדְרְכוּן קֶשֶׁת
כּוֹנְנוּ חִצָּם עַל־יֶתֶר
לִירוֹת בְּמוֹ־אֹפֶל
לְיִשְׁרֵי־לֵב:

3 If the foundations are destroyed,
   What can the righteous do?

3 כִּי הַשָּׁתוֹת יֵהָרֵסוּן
צַדִּיק מַה־פָּעָל:

4 The LORD *is* in His holy temple,
   The LORD's throne *is* in heaven;
   His eyes behold,
   His eyelids test the sons of men.

4 יְהוָה בְּהֵיכַל קָדְשׁוֹ
יְהוָה בַּשָּׁמַיִם כִּסְאוֹ
עֵינָיו יֶחֱזוּ
עַפְעַפָּיו יִבְחֲנוּ בְּנֵי אָדָם:

5 The LORD tests the righteous,
   But the wicked and the one who loves violence
   His soul hates.

5 יְהוָה צַדִּיק יִבְחָן
וְרָשָׁע וְאֹהֵב חָמָס שָׂנְאָה נַפְשׁוֹ:

6 Upon the wicked He will rain coals;
   Fire and brimstone and a burning wind
   Shall be the portion of their cup.

6 יַמְטֵר עַל־רְשָׁעִים פַּחִים
אֵשׁ וְגָפְרִית וְרוּחַ זִלְעָפוֹת מְנָת כּוֹסָם:

7 For the LORD *is* righteous,
He loves righteousness;
His countenance beholds the upright.

12 To the Chief Musician. On an eight-stringed harp.
A Psalm of David.
Help, LORD, for the godly man ceases!
For the faithful disappear from among the sons
of men.

2 They speak idly everyone with his neighbor;
With flattering lips *and* a double heart they
speak.

3 May the LORD cut off all flattering lips,
And the tongue that speaks proud things,

4 Who have said,
"With our tongue we will prevail;
Our lips *are* our own;
Who *is* lord over us?"

5 "For the oppression of the poor, for the sighing
of the needy,
Now I will arise," says the LORD;
"I will set *him* in the safety for which he yearns."

6 The words of the LORD *are* pure words,
Like silver tried in a furnace of earth,
Purified seven times.

7 You shall keep them, O LORD,
You shall preserve them from this generation
forever.

8 The wicked prowl on every side,
When vileness is exalted among the sons of
men.

13 To the Chief Musician. A Psalm of David.
How long, O LORD? Will You forget me
forever?
How long will You hide Your face from me?

2 How long shall I take counsel in my soul,
Having sorrow in my heart daily?
How long will my enemy be exalted over me?

3 Consider *and* hear me, O LORD my God;
Enlighten my eyes,
Lest I sleep the *sleep of* death;

4 Lest my enemy say,
"I have prevailed against him";
Lest those who trouble me rejoice when I am
moved.

5 But I have trusted in Your mercy;
My heart shall rejoice in Your salvation.

6 I will sing to the LORD,
Because He has dealt bountifully with me.

7 כִּי־צַדִּיק יְהֹוָה צְדָקוֹת אָהֵב
יָשָׁר יֶחֱזוּ פָנֵימוֹ:

יב לַמְנַצֵּחַ עַל־הַשְּׁמִינִית
מִזְמוֹר לְדָוִד:
2 הוֹשִׁיעָה יְהֹוָה כִּי־גָמַר חָסִיד
כִּי־פַסּוּ אֱמוּנִים מִבְּנֵי אָדָם:
3 שָׁוְא ׀ יְדַבְּרוּ אִישׁ אֶת־רֵעֵהוּ
שְׂפַת חֲלָקוֹת בְּלֵב וָלֵב יְדַבֵּרוּ:
4 יַכְרֵת יְהֹוָה כָּל־שִׂפְתֵי חֲלָקוֹת
לָשׁוֹן מְדַבֶּרֶת גְּדֹלוֹת:
5 אֲשֶׁר אָמְרוּ ׀ לִלְשֹׁנֵנוּ נַגְבִּיר שְׂפָתֵינוּ אִתָּנוּ
מִי אָדוֹן לָנוּ:
6 מִשֹּׁד עֲנִיִּים
מֵאֶנְקַת אֶבְיוֹנִים
עַתָּה אָקוּם יֹאמַר יְהֹוָה
אָשִׁית בְּיֵשַׁע יָפִיחַ לוֹ:
7 אִמֲרוֹת יְהֹוָה
אֲמָרוֹת טְהֹרוֹת
כֶּסֶף צָרוּף בַּעֲלִיל לָאָרֶץ
מְזֻקָּק שִׁבְעָתָיִם:
8 אַתָּה־יְהֹוָה תִּשְׁמְרֵם
תִּצְּרֶנּוּ ׀ מִן־הַדּוֹר זוּ לְעוֹלָם:
9 סָבִיב רְשָׁעִים יִתְהַלָּכוּן
כְּרֻם זֻלּוּת לִבְנֵי אָדָם:

יג לַמְנַצֵּחַ מִזְמוֹר לְדָוִד:
2 עַד־אָנָה יְהֹוָה תִּשְׁכָּחֵנִי נֶצַח
עַד־אָנָה ׀ תַּסְתִּיר אֶת־פָּנֶיךָ מִמֶּנִּי:
3 עַד־אָנָה אָשִׁית עֵצוֹת בְּנַפְשִׁי
יָגוֹן בִּלְבָבִי יוֹמָם
עַד־אָנָה ׀
יָרוּם אֹיְבִי עָלָי:
4 הַבִּיטָה עֲנֵנִי יְהֹוָה אֱלֹהָי
הָאִירָה עֵינַי פֶּן־אִישַׁן הַמָּוֶת:
5 פֶּן־יֹאמַר אֹיְבִי יְכָלְתִּיו
צָרַי יָגִילוּ כִּי אֶמּוֹט:
6 וַאֲנִי ׀ בְּחַסְדְּךָ בָטַחְתִּי
יָגֵל לִבִּי בִּישׁוּעָתֶךָ
אָשִׁירָה לַיהֹוָה
כִּי גָמַל עָלָי:

14

To the Chief Musician. A Psalm of David.
The fool has said in his heart,
"*There is* no God."
They are corrupt,
They have done abominable works,
There is none who does good.

2 The LORD looks down from heaven upon the
  children of men,
  To see if there are any who understand, who
   seek God.

3 They have all turned aside,
  They have together become corrupt;
  There is none who does good,
  No, not one.

4 Have all the workers of iniquity no knowledge,
  Who eat up my people *as* they eat bread,
  And do not call on the LORD?

5 There they are in great fear,
  For God *is* with the generation of the
   righteous.

6 You shame the counsel of the poor,
  But the LORD *is* his refuge.

7 Oh, that the salvation of Israel *would come* out
  of Zion!
  When the LORD brings back the captivity of
   His people,
  Let Jacob rejoice *and* Israel be glad.

15

A Psalm of David.
LORD, who may abide in Your tabernacle?
Who may dwell in Your holy hill?

2 He who walks uprightly,
  And works righteousness,
  And speaks the truth in his heart;

3 He *who* does not backbite with his tongue,
  Nor does evil to his neighbor,
  Nor does he take up a reproach against his
   friend;

4 In whose eyes a vile person is despised,
  But he honors those who fear the LORD;
  He *who* swears to his own hurt and does not
   change;

5 He *who* does not put out his money at usury,
  Nor does he take a bribe against the
   innocent.

He who does these *things* shall never be moved.

16

A Michtam of David.
Preserve me, O God, for in You I put my trust.

2 *O my soul,* you have said to the LORD,
  "You *are* my Lord,

יד לַמְנַצֵּחַ לְדָוִד
אָמַר נָבָל בְּלִבּוֹ
אֵין אֱלֹהִים
הִשְׁחִיתוּ הִתְעִיבוּ עֲלִילָה
אֵין עֹשֵׂה־טוֹב׃

2 יְהֹוָה
מִשָּׁמַיִם הִשְׁקִיף עַל־בְּנֵי־אָדָם
לִרְאוֹת הֲיֵשׁ מַשְׂכִּיל
דֹּרֵשׁ אֶת־אֱלֹהִים׃

3 הַכֹּל סָר יַחְדָּו נֶאֱלָחוּ
אֵין עֹשֵׂה־טוֹב אֵין גַּם־אֶחָד׃

4 הֲלֹא יָדְעוּ כָּל־פֹּעֲלֵי אָוֶן
אֹכְלֵי עַמִּי אָכְלוּ לֶחֶם יְהֹוָה לֹא קָרָאוּ׃

5 שָׁם ׀ פָּחֲדוּ פָחַד
כִּי־אֱלֹהִים בְּדוֹר צַדִּיק׃

6 עֲצַת־עָנִי תָבִישׁוּ
כִּי יְהֹוָה מַחְסֵהוּ׃

7 מִי יִתֵּן מִצִּיּוֹן
יְשׁוּעַת יִשְׂרָאֵל
בְּשׁוּב יְהֹוָה שְׁבוּת עַמּוֹ
יָגֵל יַעֲקֹב יִשְׂמַח יִשְׂרָאֵל׃

טו מִזְמוֹר לְדָוִד
יְהֹוָה מִי־יָגוּר בְּאׇהֳלֶךָ מִי־יִשְׁכֹּן בְּהַר קׇדְשֶׁךָ׃

2 הוֹלֵךְ תָּמִים וּפֹעֵל צֶדֶק
וְדֹבֵר אֱמֶת בִּלְבָבוֹ׃

3 לֹא־רָגַל ׀ עַל־לְשֹׁנוֹ לֹא־עָשָׂה לְרֵעֵהוּ רָעָה
וְחֶרְפָּה לֹא־נָשָׂא עַל־קְרֹבוֹ׃

4 נִבְזֶה ׀ בְּעֵינָיו נִמְאָס
וְאֶת־יִרְאֵי יְהֹוָה יְכַבֵּד
נִשְׁבַּע לְהָרַע
וְלֹא יָמִר׃

5 כַּסְפּוֹ ׀ לֹא־נָתַן בְּנֶשֶׁךְ
וְשֹׁחַד עַל־נָקִי לֹא לָקָח
עֹשֵׂה־אֵלֶּה
לֹא יִמּוֹט לְעוֹלָם׃

טז מִכְתָּם לְדָוִד
שָׁמְרֵנִי אֵל כִּי־חָסִיתִי בָךְ׃

2 אָמַרְתְּ לַיהֹוָה אֲדֹנָי אָתָּה
טוֹבָתִי בַּל־עָלֶיךָ׃

My goodness is nothing apart from You."

3 As for the saints who *are* on the earth,
"They are the excellent ones, in whom is all my
delight."

4 Their sorrows shall be multiplied who hasten
after another *god;*
Their drink offerings of blood I will not offer,
Nor take up their names on my lips.

5 O LORD, *You are* the portion of my inheritance
and my cup;
You maintain my lot.

6 The lines have fallen to me in pleasant *places;*
Yes, I have a good inheritance.

7 I will bless the LORD who has given me counsel;
My heart also instructs me in the night seasons.

8 I have set the LORD always before me;
Because *He is* at my right hand I shall not be
moved.

9 Therefore my heart is glad, and my glory
rejoices;
My flesh also will rest in hope.

10 For You will not leave my soul in Sheol,
Nor will You allow Your Holy One to see
corruption.

11 You will show me the path of life;
In Your presence *is* fullness of joy;
At Your right hand *are* pleasures forevermore.

17 A Prayer of David.
Hear a just cause, O LORD,
Attend to my cry;
Give ear to my prayer *which is* not from
deceitful lips.

2 Let my vindication come from Your presence;
Let Your eyes look on the things that are
upright.

3 You have tested my heart;
You have visited *me* in the night;
You have tried me and have found nothing;
I have purposed that my mouth shall not
transgress.

4 Concerning the works of men,
By the word of Your lips,
I have kept away from the paths of the
destroyer.

5 Uphold my steps in Your paths,
That my footsteps may not slip.

6 I have called upon You, for You will hear me,
O God;
Incline Your ear to me, *and* hear my speech.

3 לִקְדוֹשִׁים אֲשֶׁר־בָּאָרֶץ הֵמָּה
וְאַדִּירֵי כָּל־חֶפְצִי־בָם:
4 יִרְבּוּ עַצְּבוֹתָם
אַחֵר מָהָרוּ
בַּל־אַסִּיךְ נִסְכֵּיהֶם מִדָּם
וּבַל־אֶשָּׂא אֶת־שְׁמוֹתָם עַל־שְׂפָתָי:
5 יְהֹוָה מְנָת־חֶלְקִי וְכוֹסִי
אַתָּה תּוֹמִיךְ גּוֹרָלִי:
6 חֲבָלִים נָפְלוּ־לִי בַּנְּעִמִים
אַף־נַחֲלָת שָׁפְרָה עָלָי:
7 אֲבָרֵךְ אֶת־יְהֹוָה אֲשֶׁר יְעָצָנִי
אַף־לֵילוֹת יִסְּרוּנִי כִלְיוֹתָי:
8 שִׁוִּיתִי יְהֹוָה לְנֶגְדִּי תָמִיד
כִּי מִימִינִי בַּל־אֶמּוֹט:
9 לָכֵן ׀ שָׂמַח לִבִּי וַיָּגֶל כְּבוֹדִי
אַף־בְּשָׂרִי יִשְׁכֹּן לָבֶטַח:
10 כִּי ׀ לֹא־תַעֲזֹב נַפְשִׁי לִשְׁאוֹל
לֹא־תִתֵּן חֲסִידְךָ לִרְאוֹת שָׁחַת:
11 תּוֹדִיעֵנִי
אֹרַח חַיִּים
שֹׂבַע שְׂמָחוֹת אֶת־פָּנֶיךָ
נְעִמוֹת בִּימִינְךָ נֶצַח:

יז תְּפִלָּה לְדָוִד
שִׁמְעָה יְהֹוָה ׀ צֶדֶק
הַקְשִׁיבָה רִנָּתִי הַאֲזִינָה תְפִלָּתִי
בְּלֹא
שִׂפְתֵי מִרְמָה:
2 מִלְּפָנֶיךָ מִשְׁפָּטִי יֵצֵא
עֵינֶיךָ תֶּחֱזֶינָה מֵישָׁרִים:
3 בָּחַנְתָּ לִבִּי ׀ פָּקַדְתָּ לַּיְלָה
צְרַפְתַּנִי בַל־תִּמְצָא
זַמֹּתִי
בַּל־יַעֲבָר־פִּי:
4 לִפְעֻלּוֹת אָדָם בִּדְבַר שְׂפָתֶיךָ
אֲנִי שָׁמַרְתִּי אָרְחוֹת פָּרִיץ:
5 תָּמֹךְ אֲשֻׁרַי בְּמַעְגְּלוֹתֶיךָ
בַּל־נָמוֹטוּ פְעָמָי:
6 אֲנִי־קְרָאתִיךָ כִי־תַעֲנֵנִי אֵל
הַט־אָזְנְךָ לִי שְׁמַע אִמְרָתִי:

⁷ Show Your marvelous lovingkindness by Your
right hand,
O You who save those who trust *in You*
From those who rise up *against them.*
⁸ Keep me as the apple of Your eye;
Hide me under the shadow of Your wings,
⁹ From the wicked who oppress me,
From my deadly enemies who surround me.

¹⁰ They have closed up their fat *hearts;*
With their mouths they speak proudly.
¹¹ They have now surrounded us in our steps;
They have set their eyes, crouching down to the
earth,
¹² As a lion is eager to tear his prey,
And like a young lion lurking in secret places.

¹³ Arise, O LORD,
Confront him, cast him down;
Deliver my life from the wicked with Your
sword,
¹⁴ With Your hand from men, O LORD,
From men of the world *who have* their portion
in *this* life,
And whose belly You fill with Your hidden
treasure.
They are satisfied with children,
And leave the rest of their *possession* for their
babes.

¹⁵ As for me, I will see Your face in righteousness;
I shall be satisfied when I awake in Your
likeness.

18 To the Chief Musician. A Psalm of David the
servant of the LORD, who spoke to the LORD the words of
this song on the day that the LORD delivered him from
the hand of all his enemies and from the hand of Saul.
And he said:
I will love You, O LORD, my strength.
² The LORD is my rock and my fortress and my
deliverer;
My God, my strength, in whom I will trust;
My shield and the horn of my salvation, my
stronghold.
³ I will call upon the LORD, *who is worthy* to be
praised;
So shall I be saved from my enemies.
⁴ The pangs of death surrounded me,
And the floods of ungodliness made me afraid.
⁵ The sorrows of Sheol surrounded me;
The snares of death confronted me.
⁶ In my distress I called upon the LORD,
And cried out to my God;
He heard my voice from His temple,
And my cry came before Him, *even* to His ears.

הַפְלֵה חֲסָדֶיךָ מוֹשִׁיעַ חוֹסִים 7
מִמִּתְקוֹמְמִים בִּימִינֶךָ:
שָׁמְרֵנִי כְּאִישׁוֹן בַּת־עָיִן 8
בְּצֵל כְּנָפֶיךָ תַּסְתִּירֵנִי:
מִפְּנֵי רְשָׁעִים זוּ שַׁדּוּנִי 9
אֹיְבַי בְּנֶפֶשׁ יַקִּיפוּ עָלָי:
חֶלְבָּמוֹ סָגְרוּ 10
פִּימוֹ דִּבְּרוּ בְגֵאוּת:
אַשֻּׁרֵינוּ עַתָּה סְבָבוּנִי 11
עֵינֵיהֶם יָשִׁיתוּ לִנְטוֹת בָּאָרֶץ:
דִּמְיֹנוֹ כְּאַרְיֵה יִכְסוֹף לִטְרוֹף 12
וְכִכְפִיר יֹשֵׁב בְּמִסְתָּרִים:
קוּמָה יְהֹוָה 13
קַדְּמָה פָנָיו הַכְרִיעֵהוּ
פַּלְּטָה נַפְשִׁי
מֵרָשָׁע חַרְבֶּךָ:
מִמְתִים יָדְךָ | יְהֹוָה 14
מִמְתִים מֵחֶלֶד
חֶלְקָם בַּחַיִּים
וּצְפִינְךָ תְּמַלֵּא בִטְנָם
יִשְׂבְּעוּ בָנִים
וְהִנִּיחוּ יִתְרָם לְעוֹלְלֵיהֶם:
אֲנִי בְּצֶדֶק אֶחֱזֶה פָנֶיךָ 15
אֶשְׂבְּעָה בְהָקִיץ תְּמוּנָתֶךָ:

יח לַמְנַצֵּחַ | לְעֶבֶד יְהֹוָה לְדָוִד אֲשֶׁר דִּבֶּר |
לַיהֹוָה אֶת־דִּבְרֵי הַשִּׁירָה הַזֹּאת בְּיוֹם הִצִּיל־יְהֹוָה
אוֹתוֹ מִכַּף כָּל־אֹיְבָיו וּמִיַּד שָׁאוּל:
וַיֹּאמַר אֶרְחָמְךָ יְהֹוָה חִזְקִי: 2
יְהֹוָה | סַלְעִי וּמְצוּדָתִי 3
וּמְפַלְטִי אֵלִי צוּרִי אֶחֱסֶה־בּוֹ
מָגִנִּי וְקֶרֶן־יִשְׁעִי מִשְׂגַּבִּי:
מְהֻלָּל אֶקְרָא יְהֹוָה 4
וּמִן־אֹיְבַי אִוָּשֵׁעַ:
אֲפָפוּנִי חֶבְלֵי־מָוֶת 5
וְנַחֲלֵי בְלִיַּעַל יְבַעֲתוּנִי:
חֶבְלֵי שְׁאוֹל סְבָבוּנִי 6
קִדְּמוּנִי מוֹקְשֵׁי מָוֶת:
בַּצַּר־לִי | אֶקְרָא יְהֹוָה 7
וְאֶל־אֱלֹהַי אֲשַׁוֵּעַ
יִשְׁמַע מֵהֵיכָלוֹ קוֹלִי
וְשַׁוְעָתִי לְפָנָיו | תָּבוֹא בְאָזְנָיו:

ר 11 סְבָבוּנִי 14 וּצְפִינְךָ

8 וַתִּגְעַ֬שׁ וַתִּרְעַ֙שׁ ׀ הָאָ֗רֶץ
וּמוֹסְדֵ֣י הָרִ֣ים יִרְגָּ֑זוּ
וַ֝יִּֽתְגָּֽעֲשׁ֗וּ כִּי־חָ֥רָה לֽוֹ׃

9 עָ֘לָ֤ה עָשָׁ֙ן ׀ בְּאַפּ֗וֹ
וְאֵשׁ־מִפִּ֥יו תֹּאכֵ֑ל
גֶּ֝חָלִ֗ים בָּעֲר֥וּ מִמֶּֽנּוּ׃

10 וַיֵּ֣ט שָׁ֭מַיִם וַיֵּרַ֑ד
וַ֝עֲרָפֶ֗ל תַּ֣חַת רַגְלָֽיו׃

11 וַיִּרְכַּ֣ב עַל־כְּ֭רוּב וַיָּעֹ֑ף
וַ֝יֵּ֗דֶא עַל־כַּנְפֵי־רֽוּחַ׃

12 יָ֤שֶׁת חֹ֨שֶׁךְ ׀ סִתְר֗וֹ סְבִ֣יבוֹתָ֣יו סֻכָּת֑וֹ
חֶשְׁכַת־מַ֝֗יִם עָבֵ֥י שְׁחָקִֽים׃

13 מִנֹּ֗גַהּ נֶ֫גְדּ֥וֹ
עָבָ֥יו עָבְר֑וּ בָּ֝רָ֗ד וְגַֽחֲלֵי־אֵֽשׁ׃

14 וַיַּרְעֵ֬ם בַּשָּׁמַ֙יִם ׀ יְהֹוָ֗ה וְעֶלְי֗וֹן יִתֵּ֣ן קֹל֑וֹ
בָּ֝רָ֗ד וְגַֽחֲלֵי־אֵֽשׁ׃

15 וַיִּשְׁלַ֣ח חִ֭צָּיו וַיְפִיצֵ֑ם
וּבְרָקִ֥ים רָ֝֗ב וַיְהֻמֵּֽם׃

16 וַיֵּ֤רָא֙וּ ׀ אֲפִ֪יקֵי מַ֡יִם
וַיִּגָּלוּ֮ מוֹסְד֢וֹת תֵּ֫בֵ֥ל
מִגַּעֲרָ֣תְךָ֣ יְהֹוָ֑ה
מִ֝נִּשְׁמַ֗ת ר֣וּחַ אַפֶּֽךָ׃

17 יִשְׁלַ֣ח מִ֭מָּרוֹם יִקָּחֵ֑נִי
יַֽ֝מְשֵׁ֗נִי מִמַּ֥יִם רַבִּֽים׃

18 יַצִּילֵ֗נִי מֵאֹיְבִ֥י עָ֑ז
וּ֝מִשֹּׂנְאַ֗י כִּֽי־אָמְצ֥וּ מִמֶּֽנִּי׃

19 יְקַדְּמ֥וּנִי בְיוֹם־אֵידִ֑י
וַֽיְהִי־יְהֹוָ֖ה לְמִשְׁעָ֣ן לִֽי׃

20 וַיּוֹצִיאֵ֥נִי לַמֶּרְחָ֑ב
יְ֝חַלְּצֵ֗נִי כִּ֘י חָ֥פֵֽץ בִּֽי׃

21 יִגְמְלֵ֣נִי יְהֹוָ֣ה כְּצִדְקִ֑י
כְּבֹ֥ר יָ֝דַ֗י יָשִׁ֥יב לִֽי׃

22 כִּֽי־שָׁ֭מַרְתִּי דַּרְכֵ֣י יְהֹוָ֑ה
וְלֹֽא־רָ֝שַׁ֗עְתִּי מֵאֱלֹהָֽי׃

23 כִּ֣י כׇל־מִשְׁפָּטָ֣יו לְנֶגְדִּ֑י
וְ֝חֻקֹּתָ֗יו לֹֽא־אָסִ֥יר מֶֽנִּי׃

24 וָאֱהִ֣י תָמִ֣ים עִמּ֑וֹ
וָ֝אֶשְׁתַּמֵּ֗ר מֵעֲוֺנִֽי׃

25 וַיָּֽשֶׁב־יְהֹוָ֣ה לִ֣י כְצִדְקִ֑י
כְּבֹ֥ר יָ֝דַ֗י לְנֶ֣גֶד עֵינָֽיו׃

26 עִם־חָסִ֥יד תִּתְחַסָּ֑ד
עִם־גְּבַ֖ר תָּמִ֣ים תִּתַּמָּֽם׃

7 Then the earth shook and trembled;
The foundations of the hills also quaked and were shaken,
Because He was angry.

8 Smoke went up from His nostrils,
And devouring fire from His mouth;
Coals were kindled by it.

9 He bowed the heavens also, and came down
With darkness under His feet.

10 And He rode upon a cherub, and flew;
He flew upon the wings of the wind.

11 He made darkness His secret place;
His canopy around Him *was* dark waters
And thick clouds of the skies.

12 From the brightness before Him,
His thick clouds passed with hailstones and coals of fire.

13 The LORD thundered from heaven,
And the Most High uttered His voice,
Hailstones and coals of fire.

14 He sent out His arrows and scattered the foe,
Lightnings in abundance, and He vanquished them.

15 Then the channels of the sea were seen,
The foundations of the world were uncovered
At Your rebuke, O LORD,
At the blast of the breath of Your nostrils.

16 He sent from above, He took me;
He drew me out of many waters.

17 He delivered me from my strong enemy,
From those who hated me,
For they were too strong for me.

18 They confronted me in the day of my calamity,
But the LORD was my support.

19 He also brought me out into a broad place;
He delivered me because He delighted in me.

20 The LORD rewarded me according to my righteousness;
According to the cleanness of my hands
He has recompensed me.

21 For I have kept the ways of the LORD,
And have not wickedly departed from my God.

22 For all His judgments *were* before me,
And I did not put away His statutes from me.

23 I was also blameless before Him,
And I kept myself from my iniquity.

24 Therefore the LORD has recompensed me
according to my righteousness,
According to the cleanness of my hands in His sight.

25 With the merciful You will show Yourself merciful;

With a blameless man You will show Yourself
blameless;

26 With the pure You will show Yourself pure;
And with the devious You will show Yourself
shrewd.

27 For You will save the humble people,
But will bring down haughty looks.

28 For You will light my lamp;
The LORD my God will enlighten my darkness.

29 For by You I can run against a troop,
By my God I can leap over a wall.

30 As for God, His way is perfect;
The word of the LORD is proven;
He is a shield to all who trust in Him.

31 For who is God, except the LORD?
And who is a rock, except our God?

32 It is God who arms me with strength,
And makes my way perfect.

33 He makes my feet like the feet of deer,
And sets me on my high places.

34 He teaches my hands to make war,
So that my arms can bend a bow of bronze.

35 You have also given me the shield of Your
salvation;
Your right hand has held me up,
Your gentleness has made me great.

36 You enlarged my path under me,
So my feet did not slip.

37 I have pursued my enemies and overtaken
them;
Neither did I turn back again till they were
destroyed.

38 I have wounded them,
So that they could not rise;
They have fallen under my feet.

39 For You have armed me with strength for the
battle;
You have subdued under me those who rose up
against me.

40 You have also given me the necks of my
enemies,
So that I destroyed those who hated me.

41 They cried out, but there was none to save;
Even to the LORD, but He did not answer them.

42 Then I beat them as fine as the dust before the
wind;
I cast them out like dirt in the streets.

43 You have delivered me from the strivings of the
people;
You have made me the head of the nations;
A people I have not known shall serve me.

44 As soon as they hear of me they obey me;

עִם־נָבָר תִּתְבָּרָר 27
וְעִם־עִקֵּשׁ תִּתְפַּתָּל:

כִּי־אַתָּה עַם־עָנִי תוֹשִׁיעַ 28
וְעֵינַיִם רָמוֹת תַּשְׁפִּיל:

כִּי־אַתָּה תָּאִיר נֵרִי 29
יְהוָה אֱלֹהַי יַגִּיהַּ חָשְׁכִּי:

כִּי־בְךָ אָרֻץ גְּדוּד 30
וּבֵאלֹהַי אֲדַלֶּג־שׁוּר:

הָאֵל 31
תָּמִים דַּרְכּוֹ
אִמְרַת־יְהוָה צְרוּפָה
מָגֵן הוּא לְכֹל ׀ הַחֹסִים בּוֹ:

כִּי מִי אֱלוֹהַּ מִבַּלְעֲדֵי יְהוָה 32
וּמִי צוּר זוּלָתִי אֱלֹהֵינוּ:

הָאֵל הַמְאַזְּרֵנִי חָיִל 33
וַיִּתֵּן תָּמִים דַּרְכִּי:

מְשַׁוֶּה רַגְלַי כָּאַיָּלוֹת 34
וְעַל בָּמֹתַי יַעֲמִידֵנִי:

מְלַמֵּד יָדַי לַמִּלְחָמָה 35
וְנִחֲתָה קֶשֶׁת־נְחוּשָׁה זְרוֹעֹתָי:

וַתִּתֶּן־לִי מָגֵן יִשְׁעֶךָ 36
וִימִינְךָ תִסְעָדֵנִי וְעַנְוַתְךָ תַרְבֵּנִי:

תַּרְחִיב צַעֲדִי תַחְתָּי 37
וְלֹא מָעֲדוּ קַרְסֻלָּי:

אֶרְדּוֹף אוֹיְבַי וְאַשִּׂיגֵם 38
וְלֹא־אָשׁוּב עַד־כַּלּוֹתָם:

אֶמְחָצֵם וְלֹא־יֻכְלוּ קוּם 39
יִפְּלוּ תַּחַת רַגְלָי:

וַתְּאַזְּרֵנִי חַיִל לַמִּלְחָמָה 40
תַּכְרִיעַ קָמַי תַּחְתָּי:

וְאֹיְבַי נָתַתָּה לִּי עֹרֶף 41
וּמְשַׂנְאַי אַצְמִיתֵם:

יְשַׁוְּעוּ וְאֵין־מוֹשִׁיעַ 42
עַל־יְהוָה וְלֹא עָנָם:

וְאֶשְׁחָקֵם כְּעָפָר עַל־פְּנֵי־רוּחַ 43
כְּטִיט חוּצוֹת אֲרִיקֵם:

תְּפַלְּטֵנִי מֵרִיבֵי עָם 44
תְּשִׂימֵנִי לְרֹאשׁ גּוֹיִם עַם לֹא־יָדַעְתִּי יַעַבְדוּנִי:

לְשֵׁמַע אֹזֶן יִשָּׁמְעוּ לִי 45
בְּנֵי־נֵכָר יְכַחֲשׁוּ־לִי:

The foreigners submit to me.

45 The foreigners fade away,
And come frightened from their hideouts.

46 The LORD lives!
Blessed *be* my Rock!
Let the God of my salvation be exalted.

47 *It is* God who avenges me,
And subdues the peoples under me;

48 He delivers me from my enemies.
You also lift me up above those who rise
against me;
You have delivered me from the violent man.

49 Therefore I will give thanks to You, O LORD,
among the Gentiles,
And sing praises to Your name.

50 Great deliverance He gives to His king,
And shows mercy to His anointed,
To David and his descendants forevermore.

19 To the Chief Musician. A Psalm of David.
The heavens declare the glory of God;
And the firmament shows His handiwork.

2 Day unto day utters speech,
And night unto night reveals knowledge.

3 *There is* no speech nor language
Where their voice is not heard.

4 Their line has gone out through all the earth,
And their words to the end of the world.

In them He has set a tabernacle for the sun,

5 Which *is* like a bridegroom coming out of his
chamber,
And rejoices like a strong man to run its race.

6 Its rising *is* from one end of heaven,
And its circuit to the other end;
And there is nothing hidden from its heat.

7 The law of the LORD *is* perfect, converting the
soul;
The testimony of the LORD *is* sure, making wise
the simple;

8 The statutes of the LORD *are* right, rejoicing the
heart;
The commandment of the LORD *is* pure,
enlightening the eyes;

9 The fear of the LORD *is* clean, enduring forever;
The judgments of the LORD *are* true *and*
righteous altogether.

10 More to be desired *are they* than gold,
Yea, than much fine gold;
Sweeter also than honey and the honeycomb.

11 Moreover by them Your servant is warned,
And in keeping them *there is* great reward.

12 Who can understand *his* errors?

46 בְּנֵי־נֵכָר יִבֹּלוּ
וְיַחְרְגוּ מִמִּסְגְּרוֹתֵיהֶם:

47 חַי־יְהוָה וּבָרוּךְ צוּרִי
וְיָרוּם אֱלוֹהֵי יִשְׁעִי:

48 הָאֵל הַנּוֹתֵן נְקָמוֹת לִי
וַיַּדְבֵּר עַמִּים תַּחְתָּי:

49 מְפַלְּטִי מֵאֹיְבָי
אַף מִן־קָמַי תְּרוֹמְמֵנִי מֵאִישׁ חָמָס תַּצִּילֵנִי:

50 עַל־כֵּן אוֹדְךָ בַגּוֹיִם יְהוָה
וּלְשִׁמְךָ אֲזַמֵּרָה:

51 מַגְדִּל יְשׁוּעוֹת מַלְכּוֹ
וְעֹשֶׂה חֶסֶד לִמְשִׁיחוֹ לְדָוִד וּלְזַרְעוֹ
עַד־עוֹלָם:

יט לַמְנַצֵּחַ מִזְמוֹר לְדָוִד:

2 הַשָּׁמַיִם מְסַפְּרִים כְּבוֹד־אֵל
וּמַעֲשֵׂה יָדָיו מַגִּיד הָרָקִיעַ:

3 יוֹם לְיוֹם יַבִּיעַ אֹמֶר
וְלַיְלָה לְּלַיְלָה יְחַוֶּה־דָּעַת:

4 אֵין־אֹמֶר וְאֵין דְּבָרִים
בְּלִי נִשְׁמָע קוֹלָם:

5 בְּכָל־הָאָרֶץ יָצָא קַוָּם
וּבִקְצֵה תֵבֵל מִלֵּיהֶם
לַשֶּׁמֶשׁ
שָׂם־אֹהֶל בָּהֶם:

6 וְהוּא כְּחָתָן יֹצֵא מֵחֻפָּתוֹ
יָשִׂישׂ כְּגִבּוֹר לָרוּץ אֹרַח:

7 מִקְצֵה הַשָּׁמַיִם מוֹצָאוֹ
וּתְקוּפָתוֹ עַל־קְצוֹתָם
וְאֵין נִסְתָּר מֵחַמָּתוֹ:

8 תּוֹרַת יְהוָה תְּמִימָה מְשִׁיבַת נָפֶשׁ
עֵדוּת יְהוָה נֶאֱמָנָה מַחְכִּימַת פֶּתִי:

9 פִּקּוּדֵי יְהוָה יְשָׁרִים מְשַׂמְּחֵי־לֵב
מִצְוַת יְהוָה בָּרָה מְאִירַת עֵינָיִם:

10 יִרְאַת יְהוָה טְהוֹרָה עוֹמֶדֶת לָעַד
מִשְׁפְּטֵי־יְהוָה אֱמֶת צָדְקוּ יַחְדָּו:

11 הַנֶּחֱמָדִים מִזָּהָב וּמִפַּז רָב
וּמְתוּקִים מִדְּבַשׁ וְנֹפֶת צוּפִים:

12 גַּם־עַבְדְּךָ נִזְהָר בָּהֶם
בְּשָׁמְרָם עֵקֶב רָב:

13 שְׁגִיאוֹת מִי־יָבִין

Cleanse me from secret *faults.*

13 Keep back Your servant also from
presumptuous *sins;*
Let them not have dominion over me.
Then I shall be blameless,
And I shall be innocent of great transgression.

14 Let the words of my mouth and the meditation
of my heart
Be acceptable in Your sight,
O Lord, my strength and my Redeemer.

20 To the Chief Musician. A Psalm of David.
May the Lord answer you in the day of
trouble;
May the name of the God of Jacob defend you;

2 May He send you help from the sanctuary,
And strengthen you out of Zion;

3 May He remember all your offerings,
And accept your burnt sacrifice.   Selah

4 May He grant you according to your heart's
desire,
And fulfill all your purpose.

5 We will rejoice in your salvation,
And in the name of our God we will set up *our*
banners!
May the Lord fulfill all your petitions.

6 Now I know that the Lord saves His anointed;
He will answer him from His holy heaven
With the saving strength of His right hand.

7 Some *trust* in chariots, and some in horses;
But we will remember the name of the Lord
our God.

8 They have bowed down and fallen;
But we have risen and stand upright.

9 Save, Lord!
May the King answer us when we call.

21 To the Chief Musician. A Psalm of David.
The king shall have joy in Your strength, O
Lord;
And in Your salvation how greatly shall he
rejoice!

2 You have given him his heart's desire,
And have not withheld the request of his lips.
Selah

3 For You meet him with the blessings of
goodness;
You set a crown of pure gold upon his head.

4 He asked life from You, *and* You gave *it* to
him—
Length of days forever and ever.

מִנִּסְתָּרוֹת נַקֵּנִי:

14 גַּם מִזֵּדִים ׀ חֲשֹׂךְ עַבְדֶּךָ
אַל־יִמְשְׁלוּ־בִי אָז אֵיתָם
וְנִקֵּיתִי
מִפֶּשַׁע רָב:

15 יִהְיוּ לְרָצוֹן ׀ אִמְרֵי־פִי וְהֶגְיוֹן לִבִּי
לְפָנֶיךָ
יְהֹוָה
צוּרִי וְגֹאֲלִי:

כ לַמְנַצֵּחַ מִזְמוֹר לְדָוִד:

2 יַעַנְךָ יְהֹוָה בְּיוֹם צָרָה
יְשַׂגֶּבְךָ שֵׁם ׀ אֱלֹהֵי יַעֲקֹב:

3 יִשְׁלַח־עֶזְרְךָ מִקֹּדֶשׁ
וּמִצִּיּוֹן יִסְעָדֶךָּ:

4 יִזְכֹּר כָּל־מִנְחֹתֶךָ
וְעוֹלָתְךָ יְדַשְּׁנֶה סֶלָה:

5 יִתֶּן־לְךָ כִלְבָבֶךָ
וְכָל־עֲצָתְךָ יְמַלֵּא:

6 נְרַנְּנָה ׀ בִּישׁוּעָתֶךָ וּבְשֵׁם־אֱלֹהֵינוּ נִדְגֹּל
יְמַלֵּא יְהֹוָה כָּל־מִשְׁאֲלוֹתֶיךָ:

7 עַתָּה יָדַעְתִּי כִּי הוֹשִׁיעַ ׀ יְהֹוָה מְשִׁיחוֹ
יַעֲנֵהוּ מִשְּׁמֵי קָדְשׁוֹ
בִּגְבֻרוֹת יֵשַׁע יְמִינוֹ:

8 אֵלֶּה בָרֶכֶב וְאֵלֶּה בַסּוּסִים
וַאֲנַחְנוּ ׀
בְּשֵׁם־יְהֹוָה אֱלֹהֵינוּ נַזְכִּיר:

9 הֵמָּה כָּרְעוּ וְנָפָלוּ
וַאֲנַחְנוּ קַּמְנוּ וַנִּתְעוֹדָד:

10 יְהֹוָה הוֹשִׁיעָה
הַמֶּלֶךְ יַעֲנֵנוּ בְיוֹם־קָרְאֵנוּ:

כא לַמְנַצֵּחַ מִזְמוֹר לְדָוִד:

2 יְהֹוָה בְּעָזְּךָ יִשְׂמַח־מֶלֶךְ
וּבִישׁוּעָתְךָ מַה־יָּגֶיל מְאֹד:

3 תַּאֲוַת לִבּוֹ נָתַתָּה לּוֹ
וַאֲרֶשֶׁת שְׂפָתָיו בַּל־מָנַעְתָּ סֶּלָה:

4 כִּי־תְקַדְּמֶנּוּ בִּרְכוֹת טוֹב
תָּשִׁית לְרֹאשׁוֹ עֲטֶרֶת פָּז:

5 חַיִּים ׀ שָׁאַל מִמְּךָ נָתַתָּה לּוֹ
אֹרֶךְ יָמִים עוֹלָם וָעֶד:

5 His glory *is* great in Your salvation;
  Honor and majesty You have placed upon
    him.
6 For You have made him most blessed forever;
  You have made him exceedingly glad with
    Your presence.
7 For the king trusts in the LORD,
  And through the mercy of the Most High he
    shall not be moved.
8 Your hand will find all Your enemies;
  Your right hand will find those who hate You.
9 You shall make them as a fiery oven in the time
    of Your anger;
  The LORD shall swallow them up in His wrath,
  And the fire shall devour them.
10 Their offspring You shall destroy from the
    earth,
  And their descendants from among the sons of
    men.
11 For they intended evil against You;
  They devised a plot *which* they are not able *to*
    perform.
12 Therefore You will make them turn their back;
  You will make ready *Your arrows* on Your
    string toward their faces.

13 Be exalted, O LORD, in Your own strength!
  We will sing and praise Your power.

22 To the Chief Musician. Set to "The Deer of the
Dawn." A Psalm of David.
  My God, My God, why have You forsaken
    Me?
  Why are You so far from helping Me,
  And from the words of My groaning?
2 O My God, I cry in the daytime, but You do
    not hear;
  And in the night season, and am not silent.

3 But You *are* holy,
  Enthroned in the praises of Israel.
4 Our fathers trusted in You;
  They trusted, and You delivered them.
5 They cried to You, and were delivered;
  They trusted in You, and were not ashamed.

6 But I *am* a worm, and no man;
  A reproach of men, and despised by the people.
7 All those who see Me ridicule Me;
  They shoot out the lip, they shake the head,
    saying,
8 "He trusted in the LORD, let Him rescue Him;
  Let Him deliver Him, since He delights in
    Him!"

6 גָּדוֹל כְּבוֹדוֹ בִּישׁוּעָתֶךָ
  הוֹד וְהָדָר תְּשַׁוֶּה עָלָיו:
7 כִּי־תְשִׁיתֵהוּ בְרָכוֹת לָעַד
  תְּחַדֵּהוּ בְשִׂמְחָה אֶת־פָּנֶיךָ:
8 כִּי־הַמֶּלֶךְ בֹּטֵחַ בַּיהֹוָה
  וּבְחֶסֶד עֶלְיוֹן בַּל־יִמּוֹט:
9 תִּמְצָא יָדְךָ לְכָל־אֹיְבֶיךָ
  יְמִינְךָ תִּמְצָא שֹׂנְאֶיךָ:
10 תְּשִׁיתֵמוֹ | כְּתַנּוּר אֵשׁ
  לְעֵת פָּנֶיךָ
  יְהֹוָה בְּאַפּוֹ יְבַלְּעֵם
  וְתֹאכְלֵם אֵשׁ:
11 פִּרְיָמוֹ מֵאֶרֶץ תְּאַבֵּד
  וְזַרְעָם מִבְּנֵי אָדָם:
12 כִּי־נָטוּ עָלֶיךָ רָעָה
  חָשְׁבוּ מְזִמָּה בַּל־יוּכָלוּ:
13 כִּי תְּשִׁיתֵמוֹ שֶׁכֶם
  בְּמֵיתָרֶיךָ תְּכוֹנֵן עַל־פְּנֵיהֶם:
14 רוּמָה יְהֹוָה בְּעֻזֶּךָ
  נָשִׁירָה וּנְזַמְּרָה גְּבוּרָתֶךָ:

כב לַמְנַצֵּחַ עַל־אַיֶּלֶת הַשַּׁחַר
  מִזְמוֹר לְדָוִד:
2 אֵלִי אֵלִי לָמָה עֲזַבְתָּנִי
  רָחוֹק מִישׁוּעָתִי דִּבְרֵי שַׁאֲגָתִי:
3 אֱלֹהַי אֶקְרָא יוֹמָם וְלֹא תַעֲנֶה
  וְלַיְלָה וְלֹא־דוּמִיָּה לִי:
4 וְאַתָּה קָדוֹשׁ
  יוֹשֵׁב תְּהִלּוֹת יִשְׂרָאֵל:
5 בְּךָ בָּטְחוּ אֲבֹתֵינוּ
  בָּטְחוּ וַתְּפַלְּטֵמוֹ:
6 אֵלֶיךָ זָעֲקוּ וְנִמְלָטוּ
  בְּךָ בָטְחוּ וְלֹא־בוֹשׁוּ:
7 וְאָנֹכִי תוֹלַעַת וְלֹא־אִישׁ
  חֶרְפַּת אָדָם וּבְזוּי עָם:
8 כָּל־רֹאַי יַלְעִגוּ לִי
  יַפְטִירוּ בְשָׂפָה יָנִיעוּ רֹאשׁ:
9 גֹּל אֶל־יְהֹוָה יְפַלְּטֵהוּ
  יַצִּילֵהוּ כִּי חָפֵץ בּוֹ:

9 But You *are* He who took Me out of the womb;
You made Me trust *while* on My mother's breasts.

10 I was cast upon You from birth.
From My mother's womb
You *have been* My God.

11 Be not far from Me,
For trouble *is* near;
For *there is* none to help.

12 Many bulls have surrounded Me;
Strong *bulls* of Bashan have encircled Me.

13 They gape at Me *with* their mouths,
Like a raging and roaring lion.

14 I am poured out like water,
And all My bones are out of joint;
My heart is like wax;
It has melted within Me.

15 My strength is dried up like a potsherd,
And My tongue clings to My jaws;
You have brought Me to the dust of death.

16 For dogs have surrounded Me;
The congregation of the wicked has enclosed Me.
They pierced My hands and My feet;

17 I can count all My bones.
They look *and* stare at Me.

18 They divide My garments among them,
And for My clothing they cast lots.

19 But You, O LORD, do not be far from Me;
O My Strength, hasten to help Me!

20 Deliver Me from the sword,
My precious *life* from the power of the dog.

21 Save Me from the lion's mouth
And from the horns of the wild oxen!

You have answered Me.

22 I will declare Your name to My brethren;
In the midst of the assembly I will praise You.

23 You who fear the LORD, praise Him!
All you descendants of Jacob, glorify Him,
And fear Him, all you offspring of Israel!

24 For He has not despised nor abhorred the affliction of the afflicted;
Nor has He hidden His face from Him;
But when He cried to Him, He heard.

25 My praise *shall be* of You in the great assembly;
I will pay My vows before those who fear Him.

26 The poor shall eat and be satisfied;
Those who seek Him will praise the LORD.
Let your heart live forever!

10 כִּי־אַתָּה גֹחִי מִבָּטֶן
מַבְטִיחִי עַל־שְׁדֵי אִמִּי:

11 עָלֶיךָ הָשְׁלַכְתִּי מֵרָחֶם
מִבֶּטֶן אִמִּי אֵלִי אָתָּה:

12 אַל־תִּרְחַק מִמֶּנִּי כִּי־צָרָה קְרוֹבָה
כִּי־אֵין עוֹזֵר:

13 סְבָבוּנִי פָּרִים רַבִּים
אַבִּירֵי בָשָׁן כִּתְּרוּנִי:

14 פָּצוּ עָלַי פִּיהֶם
אַרְיֵה טֹרֵף וְשֹׁאֵג:

15 כַּמַּיִם נִשְׁפַּכְתִּי
וְהִתְפָּרְדוּ כָּל־עַצְמוֹתָי
הָיָה לִבִּי כַּדּוֹנָג
נָמֵס בְּתוֹךְ מֵעָי:

16 יָבֵשׁ כַּחֶרֶשׂ ׀ כֹּחִי וּלְשׁוֹנִי מֻדְבָּק מַלְקוֹחָי
וְלַעֲפַר־מָוֶת תִּשְׁפְּתֵנִי:

17 כִּי סְבָבוּנִי כְּלָבִים
עֲדַת מְרֵעִים הִקִּיפוּנִי כָּאֲרִי יָדַי וְרַגְלָי:

18 אֲסַפֵּר כָּל־עַצְמוֹתָי
הֵמָּה יַבִּיטוּ יִרְאוּ־בִי:

19 יְחַלְּקוּ בְגָדַי לָהֶם
וְעַל־לְבוּשִׁי יַפִּילוּ גוֹרָל:

20 וְאַתָּה יְהֹוָה אַל־תִּרְחָק
אֱיָלוּתִי לְעֶזְרָתִי חוּשָׁה:

21 הַצִּילָה מֵחֶרֶב נַפְשִׁי
מִיַּד־כֶּלֶב יְחִידָתִי:

22 הוֹשִׁיעֵנִי מִפִּי אַרְיֵה
וּמִקַּרְנֵי רֵמִים עֲנִיתָנִי:

23 אֲסַפְּרָה שִׁמְךָ לְאֶחָי
בְּתוֹךְ קָהָל אֲהַלְלֶךָּ:

24 יִרְאֵי יְהֹוָה ׀ הַלְלוּהוּ
כָּל־זֶרַע יַעֲקֹב כַּבְּדוּהוּ
וְגוּרוּ מִמֶּנּוּ כָּל־זֶרַע יִשְׂרָאֵל:

25 כִּי לֹא־בָזָה וְלֹא שִׁקַּץ עֱנוּת עָנִי
וְלֹא־הִסְתִּיר פָּנָיו מִמֶּנּוּ
וּבְשַׁוְּעוֹ אֵלָיו שָׁמֵעַ:

26 מֵאִתְּךָ תְהִלָּתִי
בְּקָהָל רָב נְדָרַי אֲשַׁלֵּם נֶגֶד יְרֵאָיו:

27 יֹאכְלוּ עֲנָוִים ׀ וְיִשְׂבָּעוּ
יְהַלְלוּ יְהֹוָה דֹּרְשָׁיו

²⁷ All the ends of the world
Shall remember and turn to the L<small>ORD</small>,
And all the families of the nations
Shall worship before You.

²⁸ For the kingdom *is* the L<small>ORD</small>'s,
And He rules over the nations.

²⁹ All the prosperous of the earth
Shall eat and worship;
All those who go down to the dust
Shall bow before Him,
Even he who cannot keep himself alive.

³⁰ A posterity shall serve Him.
It will be recounted of the Lord to the *next*
   generation,

³¹ They will come and declare His righteousness
   to a people who will be born,
That He has done *this*.

יְחִי לְבַבְכֶם לָעַד:
²⁸ יִזְכְּרוּ ׀ וְיָשֻׁבוּ אֶל־יְהֹוָה
כָּל־אַפְסֵי־אָרֶץ
וְיִשְׁתַּחֲווּ לְפָנֶיךָ
כָּל־מִשְׁפְּחוֹת גּוֹיִם:
²⁹ כִּי לַיהֹוָה הַמְּלוּכָה
וּמֹשֵׁל בַּגּוֹיִם:
³⁰ אָכְלוּ וַיִּשְׁתַּחֲווּ ׀ כָּל־דִּשְׁנֵי־אָרֶץ
לְפָנָיו יִכְרְעוּ כָּל־יוֹרְדֵי עָפָר
וְנַפְשׁוֹ לֹא חִיָּה:
³¹ זֶרַע יַעַבְדֶנּוּ
יְסֻפַּר לַאדֹנָי לַדּוֹר:
³² יָבֹאוּ וְיַגִּידוּ צִדְקָתוֹ
לְעַם נוֹלָד כִּי עָשָׂה:

23 A Psalm of David.

The L<small>ORD</small> *is* my shepherd;
I shall not want.

² He makes me to lie down in green pastures;
He leads me beside the still waters.

³ He restores my soul;
He leads me in the paths of righteousness
For His name's sake.

⁴ Yea, though I walk through the valley of the
   shadow of death,
I will fear no evil;
For You *are* with me;
Your rod and Your staff, they comfort me.

⁵ You prepare a table before me in the presence
   of my enemies;
You anoint my head with oil;
My cup runs over.

⁶ Surely goodness and mercy shall follow me
All the days of my life;
And I will dwell in the house of the L<small>ORD</small>
Forever.

כג מִזְמוֹר לְדָוִד
יְהֹוָה רֹעִי לֹא אֶחְסָר:
² בִּנְאוֹת דֶּשֶׁא יַרְבִּיצֵנִי
עַל־מֵי מְנֻחוֹת יְנַהֲלֵנִי:
³ נַפְשִׁי יְשׁוֹבֵב
יַנְחֵנִי בְמַעְגְּלֵי־צֶדֶק לְמַעַן שְׁמוֹ:
⁴ גַּם כִּי־אֵלֵךְ בְּגֵיא צַלְמָוֶת לֹא־אִירָא רָע
כִּי־אַתָּה עִמָּדִי
שִׁבְטְךָ וּמִשְׁעַנְתֶּךָ הֵמָּה יְנַחֲמֻנִי:
⁵ תַּעֲרֹךְ לְפָנַי ׀ שֻׁלְחָן נֶגֶד צֹרְרָי
דִּשַּׁנְתָּ בַשֶּׁמֶן רֹאשִׁי כּוֹסִי רְוָיָה:
⁶ אַךְ ׀ טוֹב וָחֶסֶד יִרְדְּפוּנִי
כָּל־יְמֵי חַיָּי
וְשַׁבְתִּי בְּבֵית־יְהֹוָה
לְאֹרֶךְ יָמִים:

24 A Psalm of David.

The earth *is* the L<small>ORD</small>'s, and all its fullness,
The world and those who dwell therein.

² For He has founded it upon the seas,
And established it upon the waters.

³ Who may ascend into the hill of the L<small>ORD</small>?
Or who may stand in His holy place?

⁴ He who has clean hands and a pure heart,
Who has not lifted up his soul to an idol,
Nor sworn deceitfully.

⁵ He shall receive blessing from the L<small>ORD</small>,

כד לְדָוִד מִזְמוֹר
לַיהֹוָה הָאָרֶץ וּמְלוֹאָהּ
תֵּבֵל וְיֹשְׁבֵי בָהּ:
² כִּי־הוּא עַל־יַמִּים יְסָדָהּ
וְעַל־נְהָרוֹת יְכוֹנְנֶהָ:
³ מִי־יַעֲלֶה בְהַר־יְהֹוָה
וּמִי־יָקוּם בִּמְקוֹם קָדְשׁוֹ:
⁴ נְקִי כַפַּיִם וּבַר־לֵבָב
אֲשֶׁר ׀ לֹא־נָשָׂא לַשָּׁוְא נַפְשִׁי
וְלֹא נִשְׁבַּע לְמִרְמָה:
⁵ יִשָּׂא בְרָכָה מֵאֵת יְהֹוָה

And righteousness from the God of his
  salvation.

6 This *is* Jacob, the generation of those who seek
    Him,
    Who seek Your face.   Selah

7 Lift up your heads, O you gates!
    And be lifted up, you everlasting doors!
    And the King of glory shall come in.

8 Who *is* this King of glory?
    The LORD strong and mighty,
    The LORD mighty in battle.

9 Lift up your heads, O you gates!
    Lift up, you everlasting doors!
    And the King of glory shall come in.

10 Who is this King of glory?
    The LORD of hosts,
    He *is* the King of glory.   Selah

25 A Psalm of David.
    To You, O LORD, I lift up my soul.

2 O my God, I trust in You;
    Let me not be ashamed;
    Let not my enemies triumph over me.

3 Indeed, let no one who waits on You be
    ashamed;
    Let those be ashamed who deal treacherously
    without cause.

4 Show me Your ways, O LORD;
    Teach me Your paths.

5 Lead me in Your truth and teach me,
    For You *are* the God of my salvation;
    On You I wait all the day.

6 Remember, O LORD, Your tender mercies and
    Your lovingkindnesses,
    For they *are* from of old.

7 Do not remember the sins of my youth, nor my
    transgressions;
    According to Your mercy remember me,
    For Your goodness' sake, O LORD.

8 Good and upright *is* the LORD;
    Therefore He teaches sinners in the way.

9 The humble He guides in justice,
    And the humble He teaches His way.

10 All the paths of the LORD *are* mercy and truth,
    To such as keep His covenant and His
    testimonies.

11 For Your name's sake, O LORD,
    Pardon my iniquity, for it *is* great.

12 Who *is* the man that fears the LORD?
    Him shall He teach in the way He chooses.

13 He himself shall dwell in prosperity,
    And his descendants shall inherit the earth.

וּצְדָקָה מֵאֱלֹהֵי יִשְׁעוֹ:
6 זֶה דּוֹר דֹּרְשָׁיו
מְבַקְשֵׁי פָנֶיךָ יַעֲקֹב סֶלָה:
7 שְׂאוּ שְׁעָרִים ׀ רָאשֵׁיכֶם וְהִנָּשְׂאוּ פִּתְחֵי עוֹלָם
וְיָבוֹא מֶלֶךְ הַכָּבוֹד:
8 מִי זֶה מֶלֶךְ הַכָּבוֹד
יְהֹוָה עִזּוּז וְגִבּוֹר
יְהֹוָה גִּבּוֹר מִלְחָמָה:
9 שְׂאוּ שְׁעָרִים ׀ רָאשֵׁיכֶם וּשְׂאוּ פִּתְחֵי עוֹלָם
וְיָבֹא מֶלֶךְ הַכָּבוֹד:
10 מִי הוּא זֶה מֶלֶךְ הַכָּבוֹד
יְהֹוָה צְבָאוֹת
הוּא מֶלֶךְ הַכָּבוֹד סֶלָה:

כה לְדָוִד
אֵלֶיךָ יְהֹוָה נַפְשִׁי אֶשָּׂא:
2 אֱלֹהַי בְּךָ בָטַחְתִּי אַל־אֵבוֹשָׁה
אַל־יַעַלְצוּ אֹיְבַי לִי:
3 גַּם כָּל־קֹוֶיךָ לֹא יֵבֹשׁוּ
יֵבֹשׁוּ הַבּוֹגְדִים רֵיקָם:
4 דְּרָכֶיךָ יְהֹוָה הוֹדִיעֵנִי
אֹרְחוֹתֶיךָ לַמְּדֵנִי:
5 הַדְרִיכֵנִי בַאֲמִתֶּךָ ׀ וְלַמְּדֵנִי
כִּי־אַתָּה אֱלֹהֵי יִשְׁעִי
אוֹתְךָ קִוִּיתִי כָּל־הַיּוֹם:
6 זְכֹר־רַחֲמֶיךָ יְהֹוָה וַחֲסָדֶיךָ
כִּי מֵעוֹלָם הֵמָּה:
7 חַטֹּאות נְעוּרַי ׀ וּפְשָׁעַי
אַל־תִּזְכֹּר כְּחַסְדְּךָ זְכָר־לִי־אַתָּה
לְמַעַן טוּבְךָ יְהֹוָה:
8 טוֹב־וְיָשָׁר יְהֹוָה
עַל־כֵּן יוֹרֶה חַטָּאִים בַּדָּרֶךְ:
9 יַדְרֵךְ עֲנָוִים בַּמִּשְׁפָּט
וִילַמֵּד עֲנָוִים דַּרְכּוֹ:
10 כָּל־אָרְחוֹת יְהֹוָה חֶסֶד וֶאֱמֶת
לְנֹצְרֵי בְרִיתוֹ וְעֵדֹתָיו:
11 לְמַעַן־שִׁמְךָ יְהֹוָה
וְסָלַחְתָּ לַעֲוֹנִי כִּי רַב־הוּא:
12 מִי־זֶה הָאִישׁ יְרֵא יְהֹוָה
יוֹרֶנּוּ בְּדֶרֶךְ יִבְחָר:
13 נַפְשׁוֹ בְּטוֹב תָּלִין
וְזַרְעוֹ יִירַשׁ אָרֶץ:

כד 6 דֹּרְשָׁיו

14 The secret of the LORD *is* with those who fear
   Him,
   And He will show them His covenant.
15 My eyes *are* ever toward the LORD,
   For He shall pluck my feet out of the net.
16 Turn Yourself to me, and have mercy on me,
   For I *am* desolate and afflicted.
17 The troubles of my heart have enlarged;
   Bring me out of my distresses!
18 Look on my affliction and my pain,
   And forgive all my sins.
19 Consider my enemies, for they are many;
   And they hate me with cruel hatred.
20 Keep my soul, and deliver me;
   Let me not be ashamed, for I put my trust in
   You.
21 Let integrity and uprightness preserve me,
   For I wait for You.

22 Redeem Israel, O God,
   Out of all their troubles!

26 A Psalm of David.
   Vindicate me, O LORD,
   For I have walked in my integrity.
   I have also trusted in the LORD;
   I shall not slip.
2 Examine me, O LORD, and prove me;
   Try my mind and my heart.
3 For Your lovingkindness *is* before my eyes,
   And I have walked in Your truth.
4 I have not sat with idolatrous mortals,
   Nor will I go in with hypocrites.
5 I have hated the assembly of evildoers,
   And will not sit with the wicked.

6 I will wash my hands in innocence;
   So I will go about Your altar, O LORD,
7 That I may proclaim with the voice of
   thanksgiving,
   And tell of all Your wondrous works.
8 LORD, I have loved the habitation of Your
   house,
   And the place where Your glory dwells.

9 Do not gather my soul with sinners,
   Nor my life with bloodthirsty men,
10 In whose hands *is* a sinister scheme,
   And whose right hand is full of bribes.

11 But as for me, I will walk in my integrity;
   Redeem me and be merciful to me.
12 My foot stands in an even place;
   In the congregations I will bless the LORD.

14 סוֹד יְהוָה לִירֵאָיו
וּבְרִיתוֹ לְהוֹדִיעָם:
15 עֵינַי תָּמִיד אֶל־יְהוָה
כִּי הוּא־יוֹצִיא מֵרֶשֶׁת רַגְלָי:
16 פְּנֵה־אֵלַי וְחָנֵּנִי
כִּי־יָחִיד וְעָנִי אָנִי:
17 צָרוֹת לְבָבִי הִרְחִיבוּ
מִמְּצוּקוֹתַי הוֹצִיאֵנִי:
18 רְאֵה עָנְיִי וַעֲמָלִי
וְשָׂא לְכָל־חַטּאותָי:
19 רְאֵה־אוֹיְבַי כִּי־רָבּוּ
וְשִׂנְאַת חָמָס שְׂנֵאוּנִי:
20 שָׁמְרָה נַפְשִׁי וְהַצִּילֵנִי
אַל־אֵבוֹשׁ כִּי־חָסִיתִי בָךְ:
21 תֹּם־וָיֹשֶׁר יִצְּרוּנִי
כִּי קִוִּיתִיךָ:
22 פְּדֵה אֱלֹהִים אֶת־יִשְׂרָאֵל
מִכֹּל צָרוֹתָיו:

כו לְדָוִד ׀ שָׁפְטֵנִי יְהוָה כִּי־אֲנִי בְּתֻמִּי הָלַכְתִּי
וּבַיהוָה בָּטַחְתִּי לֹא אֶמְעָד:
2 בְּחָנֵנִי יְהוָה וְנַסֵּנִי
צרופה כִלְיוֹתַי וְלִבִּי:
3 כִּי־חַסְדְּךָ לְנֶגֶד עֵינָי
וְהִתְהַלַּכְתִּי בַּאֲמִתֶּךָ:
4 לֹא־יָשַׁבְתִּי עִם־מְתֵי־שָׁוְא
וְעִם נַעֲלָמִים לֹא אָבוֹא:
5 שָׂנֵאתִי קְהַל מְרֵעִים
וְעִם־רְשָׁעִים לֹא אֵשֵׁב:
6 אֶרְחַץ בְּנִקָּיוֹן כַּפָּי
וַאֲסֹבְבָה אֶת־מִזְבַּחֲךָ יְהוָה:
7 לַשְׁמִעַ בְּקוֹל תּוֹדָה
וּלְסַפֵּר כָּל־נִפְלְאוֹתֶיךָ:
8 יְהוָה אָהַבְתִּי מְעוֹן בֵּיתֶךָ
וּמְקוֹם מִשְׁכַּן כְּבוֹדֶךָ:
9 אַל־תֶּאֱסֹף עִם־חַטָּאִים נַפְשִׁי
וְעִם־אַנְשֵׁי דָמִים חַיָּי:
10 אֲשֶׁר־בִּידֵיהֶם זִמָּה
וִימִינָם מָלְאָה שֹּׁחַד:
11 וַאֲנִי בְּתֻמִּי אֵלֵךְ פְּדֵנִי וְחָנֵּנִי:
12 רַגְלִי עָמְדָה בְמִישׁוֹר
בְּמַקְהֵלִים אֲבָרֵךְ יְהוָה:

27 A Psalm of David.

The LORD *is* my light and my salvation;
Whom shall I fear?
The LORD *is* the strength of my life;
Of whom shall I be afraid?

2 When the wicked came against me
To eat up my flesh,
My enemies and foes,
They stumbled and fell.

3 Though an army may encamp against me,
My heart shall not fear;
Though war may rise against me,
In this I *will be* confident.

4 One *thing* I have desired of the LORD,
That will I seek:
That I may dwell in the house of the LORD
All the days of my life,
To behold the beauty of the LORD,
And to inquire in His temple.

5 For in the time of trouble
He shall hide me in His pavilion;
In the secret place of His tabernacle
He shall hide me;
He shall set me high upon a rock.

6 And now my head shall be lifted up above my
    enemies all around me;
Therefore I will offer sacrifices of joy in His
    tabernacle;
I will sing, yes, I will sing praises to the LORD.

7 Hear, O LORD, *when* I cry with my voice!
Have mercy also upon me, and answer me.

8 *When You said,* "Seek My face,"
My heart said to You, "Your face, LORD, I will
    seek."

9 Do not hide Your face from me;
Do not turn Your servant away in anger;
You have been my help;
Do not leave me nor forsake me,
O God of my salvation.

10 When my father and my mother forsake me,
Then the LORD will take care of me.

11 Teach me Your way, O LORD,
And lead me in a smooth path, because of my
    enemies.

12 Do not deliver me to the will of my adversaries;
For false witnesses have risen against me,
And such as breathe out violence.

13 *I would have lost heart,* unless I had believed
That I would see the goodness of the LORD
In the land of the living.

14 Wait on the LORD;
Be of good courage,

כז לְדָוִד │
יְהֹוָה │ אוֹרִי וְיִשְׁעִי מִמִּי אִירָא
יְהֹוָה מָעוֹז־חַיַּי
מִמִּי אֶפְחָד:

2 בִּקְרֹב עָלַי │ מְרֵעִים
לֶאֱכֹל אֶת־בְּשָׂרִי
צָרַי וְאֹיְבַי לִי
הֵמָּה כָשְׁלוּ וְנָפָלוּ:

3 אִם־תַּחֲנֶה עָלַי │ מַחֲנֶה
לֹא־יִירָא לִבִּי
אִם־תָּקוּם עָלַי מִלְחָמָה
בְּזֹאת אֲנִי בוֹטֵחַ:

4 אַחַת │ שָׁאַלְתִּי מֵאֵת־יְהֹוָה
אוֹתָהּ אֲבַקֵּשׁ
שִׁבְתִּי בְּבֵית־יְהֹוָה
כָּל־יְמֵי חַיַּי
לַחֲזוֹת בְּנֹעַם־יְהֹוָה
וּלְבַקֵּר בְּהֵיכָלוֹ:

5 כִּי יִצְפְּנֵנִי │ בְּסֻכֹּה
בְּיוֹם רָעָה
יַסְתִּרֵנִי בְּסֵתֶר אָהֳלוֹ
בְּצוּר יְרוֹמְמֵנִי:

6 וְעַתָּה יָרוּם רֹאשִׁי עַל אֹיְבַי סְבִיבוֹתַי
וְאֶזְבְּחָה בְאָהֳלוֹ זִבְחֵי תְרוּעָה
אָשִׁירָה וַאֲזַמְּרָה לַיהֹוָה:

7 שְׁמַע־יְהֹוָה קוֹלִי אֶקְרָא
וְחָנֵּנִי וַעֲנֵנִי:

8 לְךָ │ אָמַר לִבִּי בַּקְּשׁוּ פָנָי
אֶת־פָּנֶיךָ יְהֹוָה אֲבַקֵּשׁ:

9 אַל־תַּסְתֵּר פָּנֶיךָ │ מִמֶּנִּי
אַל־תַּט־בְּאַף עַבְדֶּךָ
עֶזְרָתִי הָיִיתָ
אַל־תִּטְּשֵׁנִי וְאַל־תַּעַזְבֵנִי אֱלֹהֵי יִשְׁעִי:

10 כִּי־אָבִי וְאִמִּי עֲזָבוּנִי
וַיהֹוָה יַאַסְפֵנִי:

11 הוֹרֵנִי יְהֹוָה דַּרְכֶּךָ
וּנְחֵנִי בְּאֹרַח מִישׁוֹר לְמַעַן שׁוֹרְרָי:

12 אַל־תִּתְּנֵנִי בְּנֶפֶשׁ צָרָי
כִּי קָמוּ־בִי עֵדֵי־שֶׁקֶר וִיפֵחַ חָמָס:

13 לוּלֵא הֶאֱמַנְתִּי לִרְאוֹת בְּטוּב־יְהֹוָה
בְּאֶרֶץ חַיִּים:

14 קַוֵּה אֶל־יְהֹוָה

And He shall strengthen your heart;
Wait, I say, on the LORD!

חֲזַק וְיַאֲמֵץ לִבֶּךָ וְקַוֵּה אֶל־יְהֹוָה:

28 A Psalm of David.
To You I will cry, O LORD my Rock:
Do not be silent to me,
Lest, if You *are* silent to me,
I become like those who go down to the pit.

2 Hear the voice of my supplications
When I cry to You,
When I lift up my hands toward Your holy
sanctuary.

3 Do not take me away with the wicked
And with the workers of iniquity,
Who speak peace to their neighbors,
But evil *is* in their hearts.

4 Give them according to their deeds,
And according to the wickedness of their
endeavors;
Give them according to the work of their
hands;
Render to them what they deserve.

5 Because they do not regard the works of the
LORD,
Nor the operation of His hands,
He shall destroy them
And not build them up.

6 Blessed *be* the LORD,
Because He has heard the voice of my
supplications!

7 The LORD *is* my strength and my shield;
My heart trusted in Him, and I am helped;
Therefore my heart greatly rejoices,
And with my song I will praise Him.

8 The LORD *is* their strength,
And He *is* the saving refuge of His anointed.

9 Save Your people,
And bless Your inheritance;
Shepherd them also,
And bear them up forever.

כח לְדָוִד אֵלֶיךָ יְהֹוָה | אֶקְרָא
צוּרִי אַל־תֶּחֱרַשׁ מִמֶּנִּי
פֶּן־תֶּחֱשֶׁה מִמֶּנִּי
וְנִמְשַׁלְתִּי עִם־יוֹרְדֵי בוֹר:
2 שְׁמַע קוֹל תַּחֲנוּנַי
בְּשַׁוְּעִי אֵלֶיךָ
בְּנָשְׂאִי יָדַי
אֶל־דְּבִיר קָדְשֶׁךָ:
3 אַל־תִּמְשְׁכֵנִי עִם־רְשָׁעִים
וְעִם־פֹּעֲלֵי אָוֶן
דֹּבְרֵי שָׁלוֹם עִם־רֵעֵיהֶם
וְרָעָה בִּלְבָבָם:
4 תֶּן־לָהֶם כְּפָעֳלָם
וּכְרֹעַ מַעַלְלֵיהֶם
כְּמַעֲשֵׂה יְדֵיהֶם תֵּן לָהֶם
הָשֵׁב גְּמוּלָם לָהֶם:
5 כִּי לֹא יָבִינוּ אֶל־פְּעֻלֹּת יְהֹוָה
וְאֶל־מַעֲשֵׂה יָדָיו
יֶהֶרְסֵם וְלֹא יִבְנֵם:
6 בָּרוּךְ יְהֹוָה
כִּי־שָׁמַע קוֹל תַּחֲנוּנָי:
7 יְהֹוָה | עֻזִּי וּמָגִנִּי
בּוֹ בָטַח לִבִּי וְנֶעֱזָרְתִּי
וַיַּעֲלֹז לִבִּי
וּמִשִּׁירִי אֲהוֹדֶנּוּ:
8 יְהֹוָה עֹז־לָמוֹ
וּמָעוֹז יְשׁוּעוֹת מְשִׁיחוֹ הוּא:
9 הוֹשִׁיעָה | אֶת־עַמֶּךָ
וּבָרֵךְ אֶת־נַחֲלָתֶךָ
וּרְעֵם וְנַשְּׂאֵם
עַד־הָעוֹלָם:

29 A Psalm of David.
Give unto the LORD, O you mighty ones,
Give unto the LORD glory and strength.

2 Give unto the LORD the glory due to His name;
Worship the LORD in the beauty of holiness.

3 The voice of the LORD *is* over the waters;
The God of glory thunders;
The LORD *is* over many waters.

4 The voice of the LORD *is* powerful;
The voice of the LORD *is* full of majesty.

כט מִזְמוֹר לְדָוִד
הָבוּ לַיהֹוָה בְּנֵי אֵלִים הָבוּ לַיהֹוָה כָּבוֹד וָעֹז:
2 הָבוּ לַיהֹוָה כְּבוֹד שְׁמוֹ
הִשְׁתַּחֲווּ לַיהֹוָה בְּהַדְרַת־קֹדֶשׁ:
3 קוֹל יְהֹוָה עַל־הַמָּיִם
אֵל־הַכָּבוֹד הִרְעִים
יְהֹוָה עַל־מַיִם רַבִּים:
4 קוֹל־יְהֹוָה בַּכֹּחַ
קוֹל יְהֹוָה בֶּהָדָר:

5   The voice of the LORD breaks the cedars,
    Yes, the LORD splinters the cedars of Lebanon.
6   He makes them also skip like a calf,
    Lebanon and Sirion like a young wild ox.
7   The voice of the LORD divides the flames of
    fire.
8   The voice of the LORD shakes the wilderness;
    The LORD shakes the Wilderness of Kadesh.
9   The voice of the LORD makes the deer give
    birth,
    And strips the forests bare;
    And in His temple everyone says, "Glory!"

10   The LORD sat *enthroned* at the Flood,
    And the LORD sits as King forever.
11   The LORD will give strength to His people;
    The LORD will bless His people with peace.

30 A Psalm. A Song at the dedication of the house of David.

    I will extol You, O LORD, for You have lifted
    me up,
    And have not let my foes rejoice over me.
2   O LORD my God, I cried out to You,
    And You healed me.
3   O LORD, You brought my soul up from the
    grave;
    You have kept me alive, that I should not go
    down to the pit.

4   Sing praise to the LORD, you saints of His,
    And give thanks at the remembrance of His
    holy name.
5   For His anger *is but for* a moment,
    His favor *is for* life;
    Weeping may endure for a night,
    But joy *comes* in the morning.

6   Now in my prosperity I said,
    "I shall never be moved."
7   LORD, by Your favor You have made my
    mountain stand strong;
    You hid Your face, *and* I was troubled.

8   I cried out to You, O LORD;
    And to the LORD I made supplication:
9   "What profit *is there* in my blood,
    When I go down to the pit?
    Will the dust praise You?
    Will it declare Your truth?
10   Hear, O LORD, and have mercy on me;
    LORD, be my helper!"

11   You have turned for me my mourning into
    dancing;

5 קוֹל־יְהוָה שֹׁבֵר אֲרָזִים
וַיְשַׁבֵּר יְהוָה אֶת־אַרְזֵי הַלְּבָנוֹן:
6 וַיַּרְקִידֵם כְּמוֹ־עֵגֶל
לְבָנוֹן וְשִׂרְיֹן כְּמוֹ בֶן־רְאֵמִים:
7 קוֹל־יְהוָה חֹצֵב
לַהֲבוֹת אֵשׁ:
8 קוֹל יְהוָה יָחִיל מִדְבָּר
יָחִיל יְהוָה מִדְבַּר קָדֵשׁ:
9 קוֹל יְהוָה ׀ יְחוֹלֵל אַיָּלוֹת
וַיֶּחֱשֹׂף יְעָרוֹת
וּבְהֵיכָלוֹ
כֻּלּוֹ אֹמֵר כָּבוֹד:
10 יְהוָה לַמַּבּוּל יָשָׁב
וַיֵּשֶׁב יְהוָה מֶלֶךְ לְעוֹלָם:
11 יְהוָה עֹז לְעַמּוֹ יִתֵּן
יְהוָה ׀ יְבָרֵךְ אֶת־עַמּוֹ בַשָּׁלוֹם:

ל מִזְמוֹר שִׁיר־חֲנֻכַּת הַבַּיִת לְדָוִד:
2 אֲרוֹמִמְךָ יְהוָה כִּי דִלִּיתָנִי
וְלֹא־שִׂמַּחְתָּ אֹיְבַי לִי:
3 יְהוָה אֱלֹהָי
שִׁוַּעְתִּי אֵלֶיךָ וַתִּרְפָּאֵנִי:
4 יְהוָה הֶעֱלִיתָ מִן־שְׁאוֹל נַפְשִׁי
חִיִּיתַנִי מִיָּרְדִי־ק בוֹר:
5 זַמְּרוּ לַיהוָה חֲסִידָיו
וְהוֹדוּ לְזֵכֶר קָדְשׁוֹ:
6 כִּי רֶגַע ׀ בְּאַפּוֹ חַיִּים בִּרְצוֹנוֹ
בָּעֶרֶב יָלִין בֶּכִי וְלַבֹּקֶר רִנָּה:
7 וַאֲנִי אָמַרְתִּי בְשַׁלְוִי
בַּל־אֶמּוֹט לְעוֹלָם:
8 יְהוָה בִּרְצוֹנְךָ הֶעֱמַדְתָּה לְהַרְרִי עֹז
הִסְתַּרְתָּ פָנֶיךָ הָיִיתִי נִבְהָל:
9 אֵלֶיךָ יְהוָה אֶקְרָא
וְאֶל־אֲדֹנָי אֶתְחַנָּן:
10 מַה־בֶּצַע בְּדָמִי
בְּרִדְתִּי אֶל־שָׁחַת
הֲיוֹדְךָ עָפָר
הֲיַגִּיד אֲמִתֶּךָ:
11 שְׁמַע־יְהוָה וְחָנֵּנִי
יְהוָה הֱיֵה־עֹזֵר לִי:
12 הָפַכְתָּ מִסְפְּדִי לְמָחוֹל לִי

ל 4 מֵיָדִי

You have put off my sackcloth and clothed me
  with gladness,

פִּתַּחְתָּ שַׂקִּי וַתְּאַזְּרֵנִי שִׂמְחָה:

12 To the end that *my* glory may sing praise to
  You and not be silent.

13 לְמַעַן ׀ יְזַמֶּרְךָ כָבוֹד וְלֹא יִדֹּם

O LORD my God, I will give thanks to You
  forever.

יְהֹוָה אֱלֹהַי לְעוֹלָם אוֹדֶךָּ:

31 To the Chief Musician. A Psalm of David.

לא לַמְנַצֵּחַ מִזְמוֹר לְדָוִד:

In You, O LORD, I put my trust;
Let me never be ashamed;
Deliver me in Your righteousness.

2 בְּךָ יְהֹוָה חָסִיתִי אַל־אֵבוֹשָׁה לְעוֹלָם
בְּצִדְקָתְךָ פַלְּטֵנִי:

2 Bow down Your ear to me,
Deliver me speedily;
Be my rock of refuge,
A fortress of defense to save me.

3 הַטֵּה אֵלַי ׀ אָזְנְךָ
מְהֵרָה הַצִּילֵנִי הֱיֵה לִי ׀ לְצוּר־מָעוֹז לְבֵית
מְצוּדוֹת לְהוֹשִׁיעֵנִי:

3 For You *are* my rock and my fortress;
Therefore, for Your name's sake,
Lead me and guide me.

4 כִּי־סַלְעִי וּמְצוּדָתִי אָתָּה
וּלְמַעַן שִׁמְךָ תַּנְחֵנִי וּתְנַהֲלֵנִי:

4 Pull me out of the net which they have secretly
  laid for me,
For You *are* my strength.

5 תּוֹצִיאֵנִי מֵרֶשֶׁת זוּ טָמְנוּ לִי
כִּי־אַתָּה מָעוּזִּי:

5 Into Your hand I commit my spirit;
You have redeemed me, O LORD God of truth.

6 בְּיָדְךָ אַפְקִיד רוּחִי
פָּדִיתָה אוֹתִי יְהֹוָה אֵל אֱמֶת:

6 I have hated those who regard useless idols;
But I trust in the LORD.

7 שָׂנֵאתִי הַשֹּׁמְרִים הַבְלֵי־שָׁוְא
וַאֲנִי אֶל־יְהֹוָה בָּטָחְתִּי:

7 I will be glad and rejoice in Your mercy,
For You have considered my trouble;
You have known my soul in adversities,

8 אָגִילָה וְאֶשְׂמְחָה בְּחַסְדֶּךָ
אֲשֶׁר רָאִיתָ אֶת־עָנְיִי
יָדַעְתָּ בְּצָרוֹת נַפְשִׁי:

8 And have not shut me up into the hand of the
  enemy;
You have set my feet in a wide place.

9 וְלֹא הִסְגַּרְתַּנִי בְּיַד־אוֹיֵב
הֶעֱמַדְתָּ בַמֶּרְחָב רַגְלָי:

9 Have mercy on me, O LORD, for I am in
  trouble;
My eye wastes away with grief,
Yes, my soul and my body!

10 חָנֵּנִי יְהֹוָה כִּי צַר־לִי
עָשְׁשָׁה בְכַעַס עֵינִי
נַפְשִׁי וּבִטְנִי:

10 For my life is spent with grief,
And my years with sighing;
My strength fails because of my iniquity,
And my bones waste away.

11 כִּי כָלוּ בְיָגוֹן חַיַּי
וּשְׁנוֹתַי בַּאֲנָחָה
כָּשַׁל בַּעֲוֹנִי כֹחִי
וַעֲצָמַי עָשֵׁשׁוּ:

11 I am a reproach among all my enemies,
But especially among my neighbors,
And *am* repulsive to my acquaintances;
Those who see me outside flee from me.

12 מִכָּל־צֹרְרַי הָיִיתִי חֶרְפָּה וְלִשְׁכֵנַי ׀ מְאֹד
וּפַחַד לִמְיֻדָּעָי רֹאַי בַּחוּץ
נָדְדוּ מִמֶּנִּי:

12 I am forgotten like a dead man, out of mind;
I am like a broken vessel.

13 נִשְׁכַּחְתִּי כְּמֵת מִלֵּב
הָיִיתִי כִּכְלִי אֹבֵד:

13 For I hear the slander of many;
Fear *is* on every side;
While they take counsel together against me,
They scheme to take away my life.

14 כִּי שָׁמַעְתִּי ׀ דִּבַּת רַבִּים
מָגוֹר מִסָּבִיב
בְּהִוָּסְדָם יַחַד עָלַי
לָקַחַת נַפְשִׁי זָמָמוּ:

14 But as for me, I trust in You, O LORD;
I say, "You *are* my God."

15 וַאֲנִי ׀ עָלֶיךָ בָטַחְתִּי יְהֹוָה
אָמַרְתִּי אֱלֹהַי אָתָּה:

15 My times *are* in Your hand;

16 בְּיָדְךָ עִתֹּתָי

Deliver me from the hand of my enemies,
And from those who persecute me.

16 Make Your face shine upon Your servant;
Save me for Your mercies' sake.

17 Do not let me be ashamed, O LORD, for I have
    called upon You;
Let the wicked be ashamed;
Let them be silent in the grave.

18 Let the lying lips be put to silence,
Which speak insolent things proudly and
    contemptuously against the righteous.

19 Oh, how great *is* Your goodness,
Which You have laid up for those who fear
    You,
Which You have prepared for those who trust
    in You
In the presence of the sons of men!

20 You shall hide them in the secret place of Your
    presence
From the plots of man;
You shall keep them secretly in a pavilion
From the strife of tongues.

21 Blessed *be* the LORD,
For He has shown me His marvelous kindness
    in a strong city!

22 For I said in my haste,
"I am cut off from before Your eyes";
Nevertheless You heard the voice of my
    supplications
When I cried out to You.

23 Oh, love the LORD, all you His saints!
For the LORD preserves the faithful,
And fully repays the proud person.

24 Be of good courage,
And He shall strengthen your heart,
All you who hope in the LORD.

32 A Psalm of David. A Contemplation.
Blessed *is he whose* transgression *is* forgiven,
Whose sin *is* covered.

2 Blessed *is* the man to whom the LORD does not
    impute iniquity,
And in whose spirit *there is* no deceit.

3 When I kept silent, my bones grew old
Through my groaning all the day long.

4 For day and night Your hand was heavy upon
    me;
My vitality was turned into the drought of
    summer.   Selah

5 I acknowledged my sin to You,
And my iniquity I have not hidden.

הַצִּילֵנִי מִיַּד־אוֹיְבַי וּמֵרֹדְפָי׃

17 הָאִירָה פָנֶיךָ עַל־עַבְדֶּךָ
הוֹשִׁיעֵנִי בְחַסְדֶּךָ׃

18 יְהֹוָה אַל־אֵבוֹשָׁה כִּי קְרָאתִיךָ
יֵבֹשׁוּ רְשָׁעִים יִדְּמוּ לִשְׁאוֹל׃

19 תֵּאָלַמְנָה שִׂפְתֵי שָׁקֶר
הַדֹּבְרוֹת עַל־צַדִּיק עָתָק בְּגַאֲוָה וָבוּז׃

20 מָה רַב־טוּבְךָ
אֲשֶׁר־צָפַנְתָּ לִּירֵאֶיךָ
פָּעַלְתָּ לַחֹסִים בָּךְ
נֶגֶד בְּנֵי אָדָם׃

21 תַּסְתִּירֵם ׀ בְּסֵתֶר פָּנֶיךָ
מֵרֻכְסֵי אִישׁ
תִּצְפְּנֵם בְּסֻכָּה
מֵרִיב לְשֹׁנוֹת׃

22 בָּרוּךְ יְהֹוָה
כִּי הִפְלִיא חַסְדּוֹ לִי בְּעִיר מָצוֹר׃

23 וַאֲנִי ׀ אָמַרְתִּי בְחׇפְזִי
נִגְרַזְתִּי מִנֶּגֶד עֵינֶיךָ
אָכֵן שָׁמַעְתָּ קוֹל תַּחֲנוּנַי
בְּשַׁוְּעִי אֵלֶיךָ׃

24 אֶהֱבוּ אֶת־יְהֹוָה כׇּל־חֲסִידָיו
אֱמוּנִים נֹצֵר יְהֹוָה
וּמְשַׁלֵּם עַל־יֶתֶר עֹשֵׂה גַאֲוָה׃

25 חִזְקוּ וְיַאֲמֵץ לְבַבְכֶם
כׇּל־הַמְיַחֲלִים לַיהֹוָה׃

לב לְדָוִד מַשְׂכִּיל
אַשְׁרֵי נְשׂוּי־פֶּשַׁע כְּסוּי חֲטָאָה׃

2 אַשְׁרֵי אָדָם לֹא יַחְשֹׁב יְהֹוָה לוֹ עָוֺן
וְאֵין בְּרוּחוֹ רְמִיָּה׃

3 כִּי־הֶחֱרַשְׁתִּי בָּלוּ עֲצָמָי
בְּשַׁאֲגָתִי כׇּל־הַיּוֹם׃

4 כִּי ׀ יוֹמָם וָלַיְלָה
תִּכְבַּד עָלַי יָדֶךָ
נֶהְפַּךְ לְשַׁדִּי
בְּחַרְבֹנֵי קַיִץ סֶלָה׃

5 חַטָּאתִי אוֹדִיעֲךָ
וַעֲוֺנִי לֹא־כִסִּיתִי

I said, "I will confess my transgressions to the LORD,"
And You forgave the iniquity of my sin.
    Selah

6 For this cause everyone who is godly shall pray to You
In a time when You may be found;
Surely in a flood of great waters
They shall not come near him.

7 You *are* my hiding place;
You shall preserve me from trouble;
You shall surround me with songs of deliverance. Selah

8 I will instruct you and teach you in the way you should go;
I will guide you with My eye.

9 Do not be like the horse *or* like the mule,
Which have no understanding,
Which must be harnessed with bit and bridle,
Else they will not come near you.

10 Many sorrows *shall be* to the wicked;
But he who trusts in the LORD, mercy shall surround him.

11 Be glad in the LORD and rejoice, you righteous;
And shout for joy, all *you* upright in heart!

33 Rejoice in the LORD, O you righteous!
For praise from the upright is beautiful.

2 Praise the LORD with the harp;
Make melody to Him with an instrument of ten strings.

3 Sing to Him a new song;
Play skillfully with a shout of joy.

4 For the word of the LORD *is* right,
And all His work *is done* in truth.

5 He loves righteousness and justice;
The earth is full of the goodness of the LORD.

6 By the word of the LORD the heavens were made,
And all the host of them by the breath of His mouth.

7 He gathers the waters of the sea together as a heap;
He lays up the deep in storehouses.

8 Let all the earth fear the LORD;
Let all the inhabitants of the world stand in awe of Him.

9 For He spoke, and it was *done;*
He commanded, and it stood fast.

10 The LORD brings the counsel of the nations to nothing;

אָמַרְתִּי אוֹדֶה עֲלֵי פְשָׁעַי לַיהוָה
וְאַתָּה נָשָׂאתָ עֲוֹן חַטָּאתִי סֶלָה:
6 עַל־זֹאת יִתְפַּלֵּל כָּל־חָסִיד ׀ אֵלֶיךָ
לְעֵת מְצֹא
רַק לְשֵׁטֶף מַיִם רַבִּים
אֵלָיו לֹא יַגִּיעוּ:
7 אַתָּה ׀ סֵתֶר לִי
מִצַּר תִּצְּרֵנִי
רָנֵּי פַלֵּט
תְּסוֹבְבֵנִי סֶלָה:
8 אַשְׂכִּילְךָ ׀ וְאוֹרְךָ בְּדֶרֶךְ־זוּ תֵלֵךְ
אִיעֲצָה עָלֶיךָ עֵינִי:
9 אַל־תִּהְיוּ ׀ כְּסוּס כְּפֶרֶד
אֵין הָבִין
בְּמֶתֶג־וָרֶסֶן עֶדְיוֹ לִבְלוֹם
בַּל קְרֹב אֵלֶיךָ:
10 רַבִּים מַכְאוֹבִים לָרָשָׁע
וְהַבּוֹטֵחַ בַּיהוָה חֶסֶד יְסוֹבְבֶנּוּ:
11 שִׂמְחוּ בַיהוָה וְגִילוּ צַדִּיקִים
וְהַרְנִינוּ כָּל־יִשְׁרֵי־לֵב:

לג רַנְּנוּ צַדִּיקִים בַּיהוָה
לַיְשָׁרִים נָאוָה תְהִלָּה:
2 הוֹדוּ לַיהוָה בְּכִנּוֹר
בְּנֵבֶל עָשׂוֹר זַמְּרוּ־לוֹ:
3 שִׁירוּ־לוֹ שִׁיר חָדָשׁ
הֵיטִיבוּ נַגֵּן בִּתְרוּעָה:
4 כִּי־יָשָׁר דְּבַר־יְהוָה
וְכָל־מַעֲשֵׂהוּ בֶּאֱמוּנָה:
5 אֹהֵב צְדָקָה וּמִשְׁפָּט
חֶסֶד יְהוָה מָלְאָה הָאָרֶץ:
6 בִּדְבַר יְהוָה שָׁמַיִם נַעֲשׂוּ
וּבְרוּחַ פִּיו כָּל־צְבָאָם:
7 כֹּנֵס כַּנֵּד מֵי הַיָּם
נֹתֵן בְּאֹצָרוֹת תְּהוֹמוֹת:
8 יִירְאוּ מֵיהוָה כָּל־הָאָרֶץ
מִמֶּנּוּ יָגוּרוּ כָּל־יֹשְׁבֵי תֵבֵל:
9 כִּי הוּא אָמַר וַיֶּהִי
הוּא־צִוָּה וַיַּעֲמֹד:
10 יְהוָה הֵפִיר עֲצַת־גּוֹיִם
הֵנִיא מַחְשְׁבוֹת עַמִּים:

He makes the plans of the peoples of no effect.

11 The counsel of the LORD stands forever,
   The plans of His heart to all generations.

12 Blessed *is* the nation whose God *is* the LORD,
   The people He has chosen as His own
      inheritance.

13 The LORD looks from heaven;
   He sees all the sons of men.

14 From the place of His dwelling He looks
   On all the inhabitants of the earth;

15 He fashions their hearts individually;
   He considers all their works.

16 No king *is* saved by the multitude of an army;
   A mighty man is not delivered by great
      strength.

17 A horse *is* a vain hope for safety;
   Neither shall it deliver *any* by its great strength.

18 Behold, the eye of the LORD *is* on those who
      fear Him,
   On those who hope in His mercy,

19 To deliver their soul from death,
   And to keep them alive in famine.

20 Our soul waits for the LORD;
   He *is* our help and our shield.

21 For our heart shall rejoice in Him,
   Because we have trusted in His holy name.

22 Let Your mercy, O LORD, be upon us,
   Just as we hope in You.

34 A Psalm of David when he pretended madness
before Abimelech, who drove him away, and he
departed.
   I will bless the LORD at all times;
   His praise *shall* continually *be* in my mouth.

2 My soul shall make its boast in the LORD;
   The humble shall hear *of it* and be glad.

3 Oh, magnify the LORD with me,
   And let us exalt His name together.

4 I sought the LORD, and He heard me,
   And delivered me from all my fears.

5 They looked to Him and were radiant,
   And their faces were not ashamed.

6 This poor man cried out, and the LORD heard
      him,
   And saved him out of all his troubles.

7 The angel of the LORD encamps all around
      those who fear Him,
   And delivers them.

8 Oh, taste and see that the LORD *is* good;
   Blessed *is* the man *who* trusts in Him!

9 Oh, fear the LORD, you His saints!

11 עֲצַת יְהוָה לְעוֹלָם תַּעֲמֹד
   מַחְשְׁבוֹת לִבּוֹ לְדֹר וָדֹר:

12 אַשְׁרֵי הַגּוֹי אֲשֶׁר־יְהוָה אֱלֹהָיו
   הָעָם ׀ בָּחַר לְנַחֲלָה לוֹ:

13 מִשָּׁמַיִם הִבִּיט יְהוָה
   רָאָה אֶת־כָּל־בְּנֵי הָאָדָם:

14 מִמְּכוֹן־שִׁבְתּוֹ הִשְׁגִּיחַ
   אֶל כָּל־יֹשְׁבֵי הָאָרֶץ:

15 הַיֹּצֵר יַחַד לִבָּם
   הַמֵּבִין אֶל־כָּל־מַעֲשֵׂיהֶם:

16 אֵין־הַמֶּלֶךְ נוֹשָׁע בְּרָב־חָיִל
   גִּבּוֹר לֹא־יִנָּצֵל בְּרָב־כֹּחַ:

17 שֶׁקֶר הַסּוּס לִתְשׁוּעָה
   וּבְרֹב חֵילוֹ לֹא יְמַלֵּט:

18 הִנֵּה עֵין יְהוָה אֶל־יְרֵאָיו
   לַמְיַחֲלִים לְחַסְדּוֹ:

19 לְהַצִּיל מִמָּוֶת נַפְשָׁם
   וּלְחַיּוֹתָם בָּרָעָב:

20 נַפְשֵׁנוּ חִכְּתָה לַיהוָה
   עֶזְרֵנוּ וּמָגִנֵּנוּ הוּא:

21 כִּי־בוֹ יִשְׂמַח לִבֵּנוּ
   כִּי בְשֵׁם קָדְשׁוֹ בָטָחְנוּ:

22 יְהִי־חַסְדְּךָ יְהוָה עָלֵינוּ
   כַּאֲשֶׁר יִחַלְנוּ לָךְ:

לד לְדָוִד בְּשַׁנּוֹתוֹ אֶת־טַעְמוֹ לִפְנֵי אֲבִימֶלֶךְ
   וַיְגָרֲשֵׁהוּ וַיֵּלַךְ:

2 אֲבָרֲכָה אֶת־יְהוָה בְּכָל־עֵת
   תָּמִיד תְּהִלָּתוֹ בְּפִי:

3 בַּיהוָה תִּתְהַלֵּל נַפְשִׁי
   יִשְׁמְעוּ עֲנָוִים וְיִשְׂמָחוּ:

4 גַּדְּלוּ לַיהוָה אִתִּי
   וּנְרוֹמְמָה שְׁמוֹ יַחְדָּו:

5 דָּרַשְׁתִּי אֶת־יְהוָה וְעָנָנִי
   וּמִכָּל־מְגוּרוֹתַי הִצִּילָנִי:

6 הִבִּיטוּ אֵלָיו וְנָהָרוּ
   וּפְנֵיהֶם אַל־יֶחְפָּרוּ:

7 זֶה עָנִי קָרָא וַיהוָה שָׁמֵעַ
   וּמִכָּל־צָרוֹתָיו הוֹשִׁיעוֹ:

8 חֹנֶה מַלְאַךְ־יְהוָה סָבִיב לִירֵאָיו וַיְחַלְּצֵם:

9 טַעֲמוּ וּרְאוּ כִּי־טוֹב יְהוָה
   אַשְׁרֵי הַגֶּבֶר יֶחֱסֶה־בּוֹ:

10 יְראוּ אֶת־יְהוָה קְדֹשָׁיו

There *is* no want to those who fear Him.

10 The young lions lack and suffer hunger;
But those who seek the LORD shall not lack any good *thing*.

11 Come, you children, listen to me;
I will teach you the fear of the LORD.

12 Who *is* the man *who* desires life,
And loves *many* days, that he may see good?

13 Keep your tongue from evil,
And your lips from speaking deceit.

14 Depart from evil and do good;
Seek peace and pursue it.

15 The eyes of the LORD *are* on the righteous,
And His ears *are* open to their cry.

16 The face of the LORD *is* against those who do evil,
To cut off the remembrance of them from the earth.

17 *The righteous* cry out, and the LORD hears,
And delivers them out of all their troubles.

18 The LORD *is* near to those who have a broken heart,
And saves such as have a contrite spirit.

19 Many *are* the afflictions of the righteous,
But the LORD delivers him out of them all.

20 He guards all his bones;
Not one of them is broken.

21 Evil shall slay the wicked,
And those who hate the righteous shall be condemned.

22 The LORD redeems the soul of His servants,
And none of those who trust in Him shall be condemned.

35 A Psalm of David.

Plead *my cause,* O LORD, with those who strive with me;
Fight against those who fight against me.

2 Take hold of shield and buckler,
And stand up for my help.

3 Also draw out the spear,
And stop those who pursue me.
Say to my soul,
"I *am* your salvation."

4 Let those be put to shame and brought to dishonor
Who seek after my life;
Let those be turned back and brought to confusion
Who plot my hurt.

5 Let them be like chaff before the wind,
And let the angel of the LORD chase *them*.

כִּי־אֵין מַחְסוֹר לִירֵאָיו:

11 כְּפִירִים רָשׁוּ וְרָעֵבוּ
וְדֹרְשֵׁי יְהֹוָה לֹא־יַחְסְרוּ כָל־טוֹב:

12 לְכוּ־בָנִים שִׁמְעוּ־לִי
יִרְאַת יְהֹוָה אֲלַמֶּדְכֶם:

13 מִי־הָאִישׁ הֶחָפֵץ חַיִּים
אֹהֵב יָמִים לִרְאוֹת טוֹב:

14 נְצֹר לְשׁוֹנְךָ מֵרָע
וּשְׂפָתֶיךָ מִדַּבֵּר מִרְמָה:

15 סוּר מֵרָע וַעֲשֵׂה־טוֹב
בַּקֵּשׁ שָׁלוֹם וְרָדְפֵהוּ:

16 עֵינֵי יְהֹוָה אֶל־צַדִּיקִים
וְאָזְנָיו אֶל־שַׁוְעָתָם:

17 פְּנֵי יְהֹוָה בְּעֹשֵׂי רָע
לְהַכְרִית מֵאֶרֶץ זִכְרָם:

18 צָעֲקוּ וַיהֹוָה שָׁמֵעַ
וּמִכָּל־צָרוֹתָם הִצִּילָם:

19 קָרוֹב יְהֹוָה לְנִשְׁבְּרֵי־לֵב
וְאֶת־דַּכְּאֵי־רוּחַ יוֹשִׁיעַ:

20 רַבּוֹת רָעוֹת צַדִּיק
וּמִכֻּלָּם יַצִּילֶנּוּ יְהֹוָה:

21 שֹׁמֵר כָּל־עַצְמוֹתָיו
אַחַת מֵהֵנָּה לֹא נִשְׁבָּרָה:

22 תְּמוֹתֵת רָשָׁע רָעָה
וְשֹׂנְאֵי צַדִּיק יֶאְשָׁמוּ:

23 פּוֹדֶה יְהֹוָה נֶפֶשׁ עֲבָדָיו
וְלֹא יֶאְשְׁמוּ כָּל־הַחֹסִים בּוֹ:

לה לְדָוִד ׀ רִיבָה יְהֹוָה אֶת־יְרִיבַי
לְחַם אֶת־לֹחֲמָי:

2 הַחֲזֵק מָגֵן וְצִנָּה
וְקוּמָה בְּעֶזְרָתִי:

3 וְהָרֵק חֲנִית וּסְגֹר לִקְרַאת רֹדְפָי
אֱמֹר לְנַפְשִׁי יְשֻׁעָתֵךְ אָנִי:

4 יֵבֹשׁוּ וְיִכָּלְמוּ מְבַקְשֵׁי נַפְשִׁי
יִסֹּגוּ אָחוֹר וְיַחְפְּרוּ חֹשְׁבֵי רָעָתִי:

5 יִהְיוּ כְּמֹץ לִפְנֵי־רוּחַ
וּמַלְאַךְ יְהֹוָה דּוֹחֶה:

6   Let their way be dark and slippery,
     And let the angel of the LORD pursue them.
7   For without cause they have hidden their net
       for me *in* a pit,
     Which they have dug without cause for my life.
8   Let destruction come upon him unexpectedly,
     And let his net that he has hidden catch
       himself;
     Into that very destruction let him fall.
9   And my soul shall be joyful in the LORD;
     It shall rejoice in His salvation.
10   All my bones shall say,
     "LORD, who *is* like You,
     Delivering the poor from him who is too strong
       for him,
     Yes, the poor and the needy from him who
       plunders him?"

11   Fierce witnesses rise up;
     They ask me *things* that I do not know.
12   They reward me evil for good,
     To the sorrow of my soul.
13   But as for me, when they were sick,
     My clothing *was* sackcloth;
     I humbled myself with fasting;
     And my prayer would return to my own heart.
14   I paced about as though *he were* my friend *or*
       brother;
     I bowed down heavily, as one who mourns *for*
       his mother.
15   But in my adversity they rejoiced
     And gathered together;
     Attackers gathered against me,
     And I did not know *it;*
     They tore *at me* and did not cease;
16   With ungodly mockers at feasts
     They gnashed at me with their teeth.
17   Lord, how long will You look on?
     Rescue me from their destructions,
     My precious *life* from the lions.
18   I will give You thanks in the great assembly;
     I will praise You among many people.

19   Let them not rejoice over me who are
       wrongfully my enemies;
     Nor let them wink with the eye who hate me
       without a cause.
20   For they do not speak peace,
     But they devise deceitful matters
     Against *the* quiet ones in the land.
21   They also opened their mouth wide against me,
     And said, "Aha, aha!
     Our eyes have seen *it.*"

6   יְהִי־דַרְכָּם חֹשֶׁךְ וַחֲלַקְלַקּוֹת
     וּמַלְאַךְ יְהֹוָה רֹדְפָם:
7   כִּי־חִנָּם טָמְנוּ־לִי שַׁחַת רִשְׁתָּם
     חִנָּם חָפְרוּ לְנַפְשִׁי:
8   תְּבוֹאֵהוּ שׁוֹאָה לֹא־יֵדָע
     וְרִשְׁתּוֹ אֲשֶׁר־טָמַן תִּלְכְּדוֹ
     בְּשׁוֹאָה יִפָּל־בָּהּ:
9   וְנַפְשִׁי תָּגִיל בַּיהֹוָה
     תָּשִׂישׂ בִּישׁוּעָתוֹ:
10   כָּל עַצְמוֹתַי | תֹּאמַרְנָה
     יְהֹוָה מִי כָמוֹךָ
     מַצִּיל עָנִי מֵחָזָק מִמֶּנּוּ
     וְעָנִי וְאֶבְיוֹן מִגֹּזְלוֹ:
11   יְקוּמוּן עֵדֵי חָמָס
     אֲשֶׁר לֹא־יָדַעְתִּי יִשְׁאָלוּנִי:
12   יְשַׁלְּמוּנִי רָעָה תַּחַת טוֹבָה
     שְׁכוֹל לְנַפְשִׁי:
13   וַאֲנִי | בַּחֲלוֹתָם לְבוּשִׁי שָׂק
     עִנֵּיתִי בַצּוֹם נַפְשִׁי
     וּתְפִלָּתִי עַל־חֵיקִי תָשׁוּב:
14   כְּרֵעַ־כְּאָח לִי הִתְהַלָּכְתִּי
     כַּאֲבֶל־אֵם קֹדֵר שַׁחוֹתִי:
15   וּבְצַלְעִי
     שָׂמְחוּ וְנֶאֱסָפוּ
     נֶאֶסְפוּ עָלַי נֵכִים
     וְלֹא יָדַעְתִּי
     קָרְעוּ
     וְלֹא־דָמּוּ:
16   בְּחַנְפֵי לַעֲגֵי מָעוֹג
     חָרֹק עָלַי שִׁנֵּימוֹ:
17   אֲדֹנָי
     כַּמָּה תִּרְאֶה
     הָשִׁיבָה נַפְשִׁי מִשֹּׁאֵיהֶם
     מִכְּפִירִים יְחִידָתִי:
18   אוֹדְךָ בְּקָהָל רָב
     בְּעַם עָצוּם אֲהַלְלֶךָּ:
19   אַל־יִשְׂמְחוּ־לִי אֹיְבַי שֶׁקֶר
     שֹׂנְאַי חִנָּם יִקְרְצוּ־עָיִן:
20   כִּי לֹא שָׁלוֹם יְדַבֵּרוּ
     וְעַל רִגְעֵי־אֶרֶץ דִּבְרֵי מִרְמוֹת יַחֲשֹׁבוּן:
21   וַיַּרְחִיבוּ עָלַי פִּיהֶם
     אָמְרוּ הֶאָח | הֶאָח רָאֲתָה עֵינֵינוּ:

22 *This* You have seen, O LORD;
Do not keep silence.
O Lord, do not be far from me.

23 Stir up Yourself, and awake to my vindication,
To my cause, my God and my Lord.

24 Vindicate me, O LORD my God, according to
Your righteousness;
And let them not rejoice over me.

25 Let them not say in their hearts, "Ah, so we
would have it!"
Let them not say, "We have swallowed him
up."

26 Let them be ashamed and brought to mutual
confusion
Who rejoice at my hurt;
Let them be clothed with shame and dishonor
Who exalt themselves against me.

27 Let them shout for joy and be glad,
Who favor my righteous cause;
And let them say continually,
"Let the LORD be magnified,
Who has pleasure in the prosperity of His
servant."

28 And my tongue shall speak of Your
righteousness
And of Your praise all the day long.

רָאִיתָה יְהוָה אַל־תֶּחֱרַשׁ 22
אֲדֹנָי אַל־תִּרְחַק מִמֶּנִּי:
הָעִירָה וְהָקִיצָה לְמִשְׁפָּטִי 23
אֱלֹהַי וַאדֹנָי לְרִיבִי:
שָׁפְטֵנִי כְצִדְקְךָ יְהוָה אֱלֹהָי 24
וְאַל־יִשְׂמְחוּ־לִי:
אַל־יֹאמְרוּ בְלִבָּם הֶאָח נַפְשֵׁנוּ 25
אַל־יֹאמְרוּ בִּלַּעֲנוּהוּ:
יֵבֹשׁוּ וְיַחְפְּרוּ | יַחְדָּו 26
שְׂמֵחֵי רָעָתִי
יִלְבְּשׁוּ־בֹשֶׁת וּכְלִמָּה
הַמַּגְדִּילִים עָלָי:
יָרֹנּוּ וְיִשְׂמְחוּ 27
חֲפֵצֵי צִדְקִי
וְיֹאמְרוּ תָמִיד יִגְדַּל יְהוָה
הֶחָפֵץ שְׁלוֹם עַבְדּוֹ:
וּלְשׁוֹנִי תֶּהְגֶּה צִדְקֶךָ 28
כָּל־הַיּוֹם תְּהִלָּתֶךָ:

36 To the Chief Musician. A Psalm of David the
servant of the LORD.
An oracle within my heart concerning the
transgression of the wicked:
There is no fear of God before his eyes.

2 For he flatters himself in his own eyes,
When he finds out his iniquity *and* when he
hates.

3 The words of his mouth *are* wickedness and
deceit;
He has ceased to be wise *and* to do good.

4 He devises wickedness on his bed;
He sets himself in a way *that is* not good;
He does not abhor evil.

5 Your mercy, O LORD, *is* in the heavens;
Your faithfulness *reaches* to the clouds.

6 Your righteousness *is* like the great mountains;
Your judgments *are* a great deep;
O LORD, You preserve man and beast.

7 How precious *is* Your lovingkindness, O God!
Therefore the children of men put their trust
under the shadow of Your wings.

8 They are abundantly satisfied with the fullness
of Your house,

לַמְנַצֵּחַ | לְעֶבֶד־יְהוָה לְדָוִד: לו
נְאֻם־פֶּשַׁע לָרָשָׁע בְּקֶרֶב לִבִּי 2
אֵין־פַּחַד אֱלֹהִים לְנֶגֶד עֵינָיו:
כִּי־הֶחֱלִיק אֵלָיו בְּעֵינָיו 3
לִמְצֹא עֲוֹנוֹ לִשְׂנֹא:
דִּבְרֵי־פִיו אָוֶן וּמִרְמָה 4
חָדַל לְהַשְׂכִּיל לְהֵיטִיב:
אָוֶן | יַחְשֹׁב עַל־מִשְׁכָּבוֹ 5
יִתְיַצֵּב עַל־דֶּרֶךְ לֹא־טוֹב רָע לֹא יִמְאָס:
יְהוָה בְּהַשָּׁמַיִם חַסְדֶּךָ 6
אֱמוּנָתְךָ עַד־שְׁחָקִים:
צִדְקָתְךָ | כְּהַרְרֵי־אֵל מִשְׁפָּטֶךָ תְּהוֹם רַבָּה 7
אָדָם־וּבְהֵמָה תוֹשִׁיעַ יְהוָה:
מַה־יָּקָר חַסְדְּךָ אֱלֹהִים 8
וּבְנֵי אָדָם בְּצֵל כְּנָפֶיךָ יֶחֱסָיוּן:
יִרְוְיֻן מִדֶּשֶׁן בֵּיתֶךָ 9
וְנַחַל עֲדָנֶיךָ תַשְׁקֵם:

And You give them drink from the river of
    Your pleasures.

9 For with You *is* the fountain of life;
    In Your light we see light.

10 Oh, continue Your lovingkindness to those
    who know You,
    And Your righteousness to the upright in
    heart.

11 Let not the foot of pride come against me,
    And let not the hand of the wicked drive me
    away.

12 There the workers of iniquity have fallen;
    They have been cast down and are not able to
    rise.

37 A Psalm of David.

Do not fret because of evildoers,
    Nor be envious of the workers of iniquity.

2 For they shall soon be cut down like the grass,
    And wither as the green herb.

3 Trust in the LORD, and do good;
    Dwell in the land, and feed on His faithfulness.

4 Delight yourself also in the LORD,
    And He shall give you the desires of your heart.

5 Commit your way to the LORD,
    Trust also in Him,
    And He shall bring *it* to pass.

6 He shall bring forth your righteousness as the
    light,
    And your justice as the noonday.

7 Rest in the LORD, and wait patiently for Him;
    Do not fret because of him who prospers in his
    way,
    Because of the man who brings wicked schemes
    to pass.

8 Cease from anger, and forsake wrath;
    Do not fret—it only *causes* harm.

9 For evildoers shall be cut off;
    But those who wait on the LORD,
    They shall inherit the earth.

10 For yet a little while and the wicked *shall be* no
    more;
    Indeed, you will look carefully for his place,
    But it *shall be* no more.

11 But the meek shall inherit the earth,
    And shall delight themselves in the abundance
    of peace.

12 The wicked plots against the just,
    And gnashes at him with his teeth.

13 The Lord laughs at him,
    For He sees that his day is coming.

10 כִּי־עִמְּךָ מְקוֹר חַיִּים
בְּאוֹרְךָ נִרְאֶה־אוֹר:

11 מְשֹׁךְ חַסְדְּךָ לְיֹדְעֶיךָ
וְצִדְקָתְךָ לְיִשְׁרֵי־לֵב:

12 אַל־תְּבוֹאֵנִי רֶגֶל גַּאֲוָה
וְיַד־רְשָׁעִים אַל־תְּנִדֵנִי:

13 שָׁם נָפְלוּ פֹּעֲלֵי אָוֶן
דֹּחוּ וְלֹא־יָכְלוּ קוּם:

לז לְדָוִד ׀ אַל־תִּתְחַר בַּמְּרֵעִים
אַל־תְּקַנֵּא בְּעֹשֵׂי עַוְלָה:

2 כִּי כֶחָצִיר מְהֵרָה יִמָּלוּ
וּכְיֶרֶק דֶּשֶׁא יִבּוֹלוּן:

3 בְּטַח בַּיהוָה וַעֲשֵׂה־טוֹב
שְׁכָן־אֶרֶץ וּרְעֵה אֱמוּנָה:

4 וְהִתְעַנַּג עַל־יְהוָה
וְיִתֶּן־לְךָ מִשְׁאֲלֹת לִבֶּךָ:

5 גּוֹל עַל־יְהוָה דַּרְכֶּךָ
וּבְטַח עָלָיו וְהוּא יַעֲשֶׂה:

6 וְהוֹצִיא כָאוֹר צִדְקֶךָ
וּמִשְׁפָּטֶךָ כַּצָּהֳרָיִם:

7 דּוֹם לַיהוָה
וְהִתְחוֹלֵל לוֹ
אַל־תִּתְחַר בְּמַצְלִיחַ דַּרְכּוֹ
בְּאִישׁ עֹשֶׂה מְזִמּוֹת:

8 הֶרֶף מֵאַף וַעֲזֹב חֵמָה
אַל־תִּתְחַר אַךְ־לְהָרֵעַ:

9 כִּי־מְרֵעִים יִכָּרֵתוּן
וְקֹוֵי יְהוָה הֵמָּה יִירְשׁוּ־אָרֶץ:

10 וְעוֹד מְעַט וְאֵין רָשָׁע
וְהִתְבּוֹנַנְתָּ עַל־מְקוֹמוֹ וְאֵינֶנּוּ:

11 וַעֲנָוִים יִירְשׁוּ־אָרֶץ
וְהִתְעַנְּגוּ עַל־רֹב שָׁלוֹם:

12 זֹמֵם רָשָׁע לַצַּדִּיק
וְחֹרֵק עָלָיו שִׁנָּיו:

13 אֲדֹנָי יִשְׂחַק־לוֹ
כִּי־רָאָה כִּי־יָבֹא יוֹמוֹ:

14 The wicked have drawn the sword
And have bent their bow,
To cast down the poor and needy,
To slay those who are of upright conduct.

14 חֶ֤רֶב ׀ פָּֽתְח֬וּ רְשָׁעִ֗ים וְדָרְכ֥וּ קַשְׁתָּ֑ם
לְ֭הַפִּיל עָנִ֣י וְאֶבְי֑וֹן
לִ֝טְב֗וֹחַ יִשְׁרֵי־דָֽרֶךְ׃

15 Their sword shall enter their own heart,
And their bows shall be broken.

15 חַ֭רְבָּם תָּב֣וֹא בְלִבָּ֑ם
וְ֝קַשְּׁתוֹתָ֗ם תִּשָּׁבַֽרְנָה׃

16 A little that a righteous man has
Is better than the riches of many wicked.

16 טוֹב־מְ֭עַט לַצַּדִּ֑יק
מֵ֝הֲמ֗וֹן רְשָׁעִ֥ים רַבִּֽים׃

17 For the arms of the wicked shall be broken,
But the LORD upholds the righteous.

17 כִּ֤י זְרוֹע֣וֹת רְ֭שָׁעִים תִּשָּׁבַ֑רְנָה
וְסוֹמֵ֖ךְ צַדִּיקִ֣ים יְהוָֽה׃

18 The LORD knows the days of the upright,
And their inheritance shall be forever.

18 יוֹדֵ֣עַ יְ֭הוָה יְמֵ֣י תְמִימִ֑ם
וְ֝נַחֲלָתָ֗ם לְעוֹלָ֥ם תִּהְיֶֽה׃

19 They shall not be ashamed in the evil time,
And in the days of famine they shall be
satisfied.

19 לֹֽא־יֵ֭בֹשׁוּ בְּעֵ֣ת רָעָ֑ה
וּבִימֵ֖י רְעָב֣וֹן יִשְׂבָּֽעוּ׃

20 But the wicked shall perish;
And the enemies of the LORD,
Like the splendor of the meadows, shall vanish.
Into smoke they shall vanish away.

20 כִּ֤י רְשָׁעִ֨ים ׀ יֹאבֵ֗דוּ וְאֹיְבֵ֣י יְ֭הוָה כִּיקַ֣ר כָּרִ֑ים
כָּל֖וּ בֶעָשָׁ֣ן כָּֽלוּ׃

21 The wicked borrows and does not repay,
But the righteous shows mercy and gives.

21 לֹוֶ֣ה רָ֭שָׁע וְלֹ֣א יְשַׁלֵּ֑ם
וְ֝צַדִּ֗יק חוֹנֵ֥ן וְנוֹתֵֽן׃

22 For *those* blessed by Him shall inherit the
earth,
But *those* cursed by Him shall be cut off.

22 כִּ֣י מְ֭בֹרָכָיו יִ֣ירְשׁוּ אָ֑רֶץ
וּ֝מְקֻלָּלָ֗יו יִכָּרֵֽתוּ׃

23 The steps of a *good* man are ordered by the
LORD,
And He delights in his way.

23 מֵ֭יְהוָה מִֽצְעֲדֵי־גֶ֣בֶר כּוֹנָ֑נוּ
וְדַרְכּ֥וֹ יֶחְפָּֽץ׃

24 Though he fall, he shall not be utterly cast
down;
For the LORD upholds *him* with His hand.

24 כִּֽי־יִפֹּ֥ל לֹֽא־יוּטָ֑ל
כִּֽי־יְ֝הוָ֗ה סוֹמֵ֥ךְ יָדֽוֹ׃

25 I have been young, and *now* am old;
Yet I have not seen the righteous forsaken,
Nor his descendants begging bread.

25 נַ֤עַר ׀ הָיִ֗יתִי גַּם־זָ֫קַ֥נְתִּי
וְֽלֹא־רָ֭אִיתִי צַדִּ֣יק נֶעֱזָ֑ב
וְ֝זַרְע֗וֹ מְבַקֶּשׁ־לָֽחֶם׃

26 *He is* ever merciful, and lends;
And his descendants *are* blessed.

26 כָּל־הַ֭יּוֹם חוֹנֵ֣ן וּמַלְוֶ֑ה
וְ֝זַרְע֗וֹ לִבְרָכָֽה׃

27 Depart from evil, and do good;
And dwell forevermore.

27 ס֣וּר מֵ֭רָע וַעֲשֵׂה־ט֗וֹב
וּשְׁכֹ֥ן לְעוֹלָֽם׃

28 For the LORD loves justice,
And does not forsake His saints;
They are preserved forever,
But the descendants of the wicked shall be cut
off.

28 כִּ֤י יְהוָ֨ה ׀ אֹ֘הֵ֤ב מִשְׁפָּ֗ט
וְלֹא־יַעֲזֹ֣ב אֶת־חֲ֭סִידָיו לְעוֹלָ֣ם נִשְׁמָ֑רוּ
וְזֶ֖רַע רְשָׁעִ֣ים נִכְרָֽת׃

29 The righteous shall inherit the land,
And dwell in it forever.

29 צַדִּיקִ֥ים יִֽירְשׁוּ־אָ֑רֶץ
וְיִשְׁכְּנ֖וּ לָעַ֣ד עָלֶֽיהָ׃

30 The mouth of the righteous speaks wisdom,
And his tongue talks of justice.

30 פִּֽי־צַ֭דִּיק יֶהְגֶּ֣ה חָכְמָ֑ה
וּ֝לְשׁוֹנ֗וֹ תְּדַבֵּ֥ר מִשְׁפָּֽט׃

31 The law of his God *is* in his heart;
None of his steps shall slide.

31 תּוֹרַ֣ת אֱלֹהָ֣יו בְּלִבּ֑וֹ
לֹ֖א תִמְעַ֣ד אֲשֻׁרָֽיו׃

32 The wicked watches the righteous,
And seeks to slay him.

32 צוֹפֶ֣ה רָ֭שָׁע לַצַּדִּ֑יק
וּ֝מְבַקֵּ֗שׁ לַהֲמִיתֽוֹ׃

33 The LORD will not leave him in his hand,

33 יְ֭הוָה לֹא־יַעַזְבֶ֣נּוּ בְיָד֑וֹ

Nor condemn him when he is judged.

34 Wait on the LORD,
And keep His way,
And He shall exalt you to inherit the land;
When the wicked are cut off, you shall see *it.*

35 I have seen the wicked in great power,
And spreading himself like a native green tree.

36 Yet he passed away, and behold, he *was* no more;
Indeed I sought him, but he could not be found.

37 Mark the blameless *man,* and observe the upright;
For the future of *that* man *is* peace.

38 But the transgressors shall be destroyed together;
The future of the wicked shall be cut off.

39 But the salvation of the righteous *is* from the LORD;
He is their strength in the time of trouble.

40 And the LORD shall help them and deliver them;
He shall deliver them from the wicked,
And save them,
Because they trust in Him.

38 A Psalm of David. To bring to remembrance.
O LORD, do not rebuke me in Your wrath,
Nor chasten me in Your hot displeasure!

2 For Your arrows pierce me deeply,
And Your hand presses me down.

3 *There is* no soundness in my flesh
Because of Your anger,
Nor *any* health in my bones
Because of my sin.

4 For my iniquities have gone over my head;
Like a heavy burden they are too heavy for me.

5 My wounds are foul *and* festering
Because of my foolishness.

6 I am troubled, I am bowed down greatly;
I go mourning all the day long.

7 For my loins are full of inflammation,
And *there is* no soundness in my flesh.

8 I am feeble and severely broken;
I groan because of the turmoil of my heart.

9 Lord, all my desire *is* before You;
And my sighing is not hidden from You.

10 My heart pants, my strength fails me;
As for the light of my eyes, it also has gone from me.

וְלֹא יַרְשִׁיעֻנּוּ בְּהִשָּׁפְטוֹ:

34 קַוֵּה אֶל־יְהֹוָה ׀ וּשְׁמֹר דַּרְכּוֹ
וִירוֹמִמְךָ לָרֶשֶׁת אָרֶץ
בְּהִכָּרֵת רְשָׁעִים תִּרְאֶה:

35 רָאִיתִי רָשָׁע עָרִיץ
וּמִתְעָרֶה כְּאֶזְרָח רַעֲנָן:

36 וַיַּעֲבֹר וְהִנֵּה אֵינֶנּוּ
וָאֲבַקְשֵׁהוּ וְלֹא נִמְצָא:

37 שְׁמָר־תָּם וּרְאֵה יָשָׁר
כִּי־אַחֲרִית לְאִישׁ שָׁלוֹם:

38 וּפֹשְׁעִים נִשְׁמְדוּ יַחְדָּו
אַחֲרִית רְשָׁעִים נִכְרָתָה:

39 וּתְשׁוּעַת צַדִּיקִים מֵיְהֹוָה
מָעוּזָּם בְּעֵת צָרָה:

40 וַיַּעְזְרֵם יְהֹוָה וַיְפַלְּטֵם
יְפַלְּטֵם מֵרְשָׁעִים וְיוֹשִׁיעֵם כִּי־חָסוּ בוֹ:

לח מִזְמוֹר לְדָוִד לְהַזְכִּיר:

2 יְהֹוָה אַל־בְּקֶצְפְּךָ תוֹכִיחֵנִי
וּבַחֲמָתְךָ תְיַסְּרֵנִי:

3 כִּי־חִצֶּיךָ נִחֲתוּ בִי
וַתִּנְחַת עָלַי יָדֶךָ:

4 אֵין־מְתֹם בִּבְשָׂרִי מִפְּנֵי זַעְמֶךָ
אֵין־שָׁלוֹם בַּעֲצָמַי מִפְּנֵי חַטָּאתִי:

5 כִּי עֲוֹנֹתַי עָבְרוּ רֹאשִׁי
כְּמַשָּׂא כָבֵד יִכְבְּדוּ מִמֶּנִּי:

6 הִבְאִישׁוּ נָמַקּוּ חַבּוּרֹתָי
מִפְּנֵי אִוַּלְתִּי:

7 נַעֲוֵיתִי שַׁחֹתִי עַד־מְאֹד
כָּל־הַיּוֹם קֹדֵר הִלָּכְתִּי:

8 כִּי־כְסָלַי מָלְאוּ נִקְלֶה
וְאֵין מְתֹם בִּבְשָׂרִי:

9 נְפוּגוֹתִי וְנִדְכֵּיתִי עַד־מְאֹד
שָׁאַגְתִּי מִנַּהֲמַת לִבִּי:

10 אֲדֹנָי נֶגְדְּךָ כָל־תַּאֲוָתִי
וְאַנְחָתִי מִמְּךָ לֹא־נִסְתָּרָה:

11 לִבִּי סְחַרְחַר עֲזָבַנִי כֹחִי
וְאוֹר־עֵינַי גַּם־הֵם אֵין אִתִּי:

11 My loved ones and my friends stand aloof from
   my plague,
   And my relatives stand afar off.

12 Those also who seek my life lay snares *for me;*
   Those who seek my hurt speak of destruction,
   And plan deception all the day long.

13 But I, like a deaf *man,* do not hear;
   And *I am* like a mute *who* does not open his
   mouth.

14 Thus I am like a man who does not hear,
   And in whose mouth *is* no response.

15 For in You, O LORD, I hope;
   You will hear, O Lord my God.

16 For I said, *"Hear me,* lest they rejoice over me,
   Lest, when my foot slips, they exalt *themselves*
   against me."

17 For I *am* ready to fall,
   And my sorrow *is* continually before me.

18 For I will declare my iniquity;
   I will be in anguish over my sin.

19 But my enemies *are* vigorous, *and* they are
   strong;
   And those who hate me wrongfully have
   multiplied.

20 Those also who render evil for good,
   They are my adversaries, because I follow *what
   is* good.

21 Do not forsake me, O LORD;
   O my God, be not far from me!

22 Make haste to help me,
   O Lord, my salvation!

39 To the Chief Musician. To Jeduthun. A Psalm of
David.
   I said, "I will guard my ways,
   Lest I sin with my tongue;
   I will restrain my mouth with a muzzle,
   While the wicked are before me."

2 I was mute with silence,
   I held my peace *even* from good;
   And my sorrow was stirred up.

3 My heart was hot within me;
   While I was musing, the fire burned.
   Then I spoke with my tongue:

4 "LORD, make me to know my end,
   And what *is* the measure of my days,
   That I may know how frail I *am.*

5 Indeed, You have made my days *as* hand-
   breadths,
   And my age *is* as nothing before You;
   Certainly every man at his best state *is* but
   vapor.   Selah

12 אֹהֲבַי ׀ וְרֵעַי מִנֶּגֶד נִגְעִי יַעֲמֹדוּ
   וּקְרוֹבַי מֵרָחֹק עָמָדוּ:
13 וַיְנַקְשׁוּ ׀ מְבַקְשֵׁי נַפְשִׁי וְדֹרְשֵׁי רָעָתִי דִּבְּרוּ
   הַוּוֹת
   וּמִרְמוֹת כָּל־הַיּוֹם יֶהְגּוּ:
14 וַאֲנִי כְחֵרֵשׁ לֹא אֶשְׁמָע
   וּכְאִלֵּם לֹא יִפְתַּח־פִּיו:
15 וָאֱהִי כְּאִישׁ אֲשֶׁר לֹא־שֹׁמֵעַ
   וְאֵין בְּפִיו תּוֹכָחוֹת:
16 כִּי־לְךָ יְהוָה הוֹחָלְתִּי
   אַתָּה תַעֲנֶה אֲדֹנָי אֱלֹהָי:
17 כִּי־אָמַרְתִּי פֶּן־יִשְׂמְחוּ־לִי
   בְּמוֹט רַגְלִי עָלַי הִגְדִּילוּ:
18 כִּי־אֲנִי לְצֶלַע נָכוֹן
   וּמַכְאוֹבִי נֶגְדִּי תָמִיד:
19 כִּי־עֲוֹנִי אַגִּיד
   אֶדְאַג מֵחַטָּאתִי:
20 וְאֹיְבַי חַיִּים עָצֵמוּ
   וְרַבּוּ שֹׂנְאַי שָׁקֶר:
21 וּמְשַׁלְּמֵי רָעָה תַּחַת טוֹבָה
   יִשְׂטְנוּנִי תַּחַת רָדְפִי־ᵖ טוֹב:
22 אַל־תַּעַזְבֵנִי יְהוָה
   אֱלֹהַי אַל־תִּרְחַק מִמֶּנִּי:
23 חוּשָׁה לְעֶזְרָתִי
   אֲדֹנָי תְּשׁוּעָתִי:

לט לַמְנַצֵּחַ לִידִיתוּןᵖ מִזְמוֹר לְדָוִד:
2 אָמַרְתִּי
   אֶשְׁמְרָה דְרָכַיᵏ מֵחֲטוֹא בִלְשׁוֹנִי
   אֶשְׁמְרָה לְפִי מַחְסוֹם
   בְּעֹד רָשָׁע לְנֶגְדִּי:
3 נֶאֱלַמְתִּי דוּמִיָּה הֶחֱשֵׁיתִי מִטּוֹב
   וּכְאֵבִי נֶעְכָּר:
4 חַם־לִבִּי ׀ בְּקִרְבִּי בַּהֲגִיגִי תִבְעַר־אֵשׁ
   דִּבַּרְתִּי בִּלְשׁוֹנִי:
5 הוֹדִיעֵנִי יְהוָה ׀ קִצִּי וּמִדַּת יָמַי מַה־הִיא
   אֵדְעָה מֶה־חָדֵל אָנִי:
6 הִנֵּה טְפָחוֹת ׀ נָתַתָּה יָמַי
   וְחֶלְדִּי כְאַיִן נֶגְדֶּךָ
   אַךְ כָּל־הֶבֶל כָּל־אָדָם
   נִצָּב סֶלָה:

לח 21 רָדְפִיᵖ   לט 1 לִידִיתוּן

6   Surely every man walks about like a shadow;
    Surely they busy themselves in vain;
    He heaps up *riches*,
    And does not know who will gather them.

7   "And now, Lord, what do I wait for?
    My hope *is* in You.

8   Deliver me from all my transgressions;
    Do not make me the reproach of the foolish.

9   I was mute, I did not open my mouth,
    Because it was You who did *it*.

10   Remove Your plague from me;
    I am consumed by the blow of Your hand.

11   When with rebukes You correct man for
      iniquity,
    You make his beauty melt away like a moth;
    Surely every man *is* vapor.   Selah

12   "Hear my prayer, O LORD,
    And give ear to my cry;
    Do not be silent at my tears;
    For I *am* a stranger with You,
    A sojourner, as all my fathers *were*.

13   Remove Your gaze from me, that I may regain
      strength,
    Before I go away and am no more."

40 To the Chief Musician. A Psalm of David.
    I waited patiently for the LORD;
    And He inclined to me,
    And heard my cry.

2   He also brought me up out of a horrible pit,
    Out of the miry clay,
    And set my feet upon a rock,
    And established my steps.

3   He has put a new song in my mouth—
    Praise to our God;
    Many will see *it* and fear,
    And will trust in the LORD.

4   Blessed *is* that man who makes the LORD his
      trust,
    And does not respect the proud, nor such as
      turn aside to lies.

5   Many, O LORD my God, *are* Your wonderful
      works
    Which You have done;
    And Your thoughts toward us
    Cannot be recounted to You in order;
    If I would declare and speak *of them*,
    They are more than can be numbered.

6   Sacrifice and offering You did not desire;
    My ears You have opened.
    Burnt offering and sin offering You did not
      require.

אַךְ־בְּצֶ֨לֶם ׀ יִתְהַלֶּךְ־אִ֗ישׁ   7
אַךְ־הֶ֥בֶל יֶהֱמָי֑וּן
יִ֝צְבֹּ֗ר וְֽלֹא־יֵדַ֥ע מִי־אֹסְפָֽם׃

וְעַתָּ֣ה מַה־קִּוִּ֣יתִי אֲדֹנָ֑י   8
תּ֝וֹחַלְתִּ֗י לְךָ֥ הִֽיא׃

מִכָּל־פְּשָׁעַ֥י הַצִּילֵ֑נִי   9
חֶרְפַּ֥ת נָ֝בָ֗ל אַל־תְּשִׂימֵֽנִי׃

נֶ֭אֱלַמְתִּי לֹ֣א אֶפְתַּח־פִּ֑י   10
כִּ֖י אַתָּ֣ה עָשִֽׂיתָ׃

הָסֵ֣ר מֵעָלַ֣י נִגְעֶ֑ךָ   11
מִתִּגְרַ֥ת יָ֝דְךָ֗ אֲנִ֣י כָלִֽיתִי׃

בְּֽתוֹכָ֘ח֤וֹת עַל־עָוֺ֨ן ׀ יִסַּ֬רְתָּ אִ֗ישׁ   12
וַתֶּ֣מֶס כָּעָ֣שׁ חֲמוּד֑וֹ
אַ֤ךְ הֶ֖בֶל כָּל־אָדָ֣ם סֶֽלָה׃

שִֽׁמְעָ֥ה־תְפִלָּתִ֨י ׀ יְהֹוָ֡ה   13
וְשַׁוְעָתִ֨י ׀ הַאֲזִ֗ינָה
אֶֽל־דִּמְעָתִ֗י אַֽל־תֶּ֫חֱרַ֥שׁ
כִּ֤י גֵ֣ר אָנֹכִ֣י עִמָּ֑ךְ
תּ֝וֹשָׁ֗ב כְּכָל־אֲבוֹתָֽי׃

הָשַׁ֣ע מִמֶּ֣נִּי וְאַבְלִ֑יגָה   14
בְּטֶ֖רֶם אֵלֵ֣ךְ וְאֵינֶֽנִּי׃

מ   לַמְנַצֵּ֗חַ לְדָוִ֥ד מִזְמֽוֹר׃

קַוֺּ֣ה קִוִּ֣יתִי יְהֹוָ֑ה   2
וַיֵּ֥ט אֵ֝לַ֗י וַיִּשְׁמַ֥ע שַׁוְעָתִֽי׃

וַיַּעֲלֵ֤נִי ׀ מִבּ֥וֹר שָׁאוֹן֮   3
מִטִּ֪יט הַיָּ֫וֵ֥ן
וַיָּ֖קֶם עַל־סֶ֥לַע רַגְלַ֗י
כּוֹנֵ֥ן אֲשֻׁרָֽי׃

וַיִּתֵּ֬ן בְּפִ֨י ׀ שִׁ֥יר חָדָשׁ֮   4
תְּהִלָּ�֥ה לֵֽאלֹהֵ֫ינוּ
יִרְא֣וּ רַבִּ֣ים וְיִירָ֑אוּ
וְ֝יִבְטְח֗וּ בַּיהֹוָֽה׃

אַ֥שְֽׁרֵי הַגֶּ֗בֶר אֲשֶׁר־שָׂ֣ם יְ֭הֹוָה מִבְטַח֑וֹ   5
וְֽלֹא־פָנָ֥ה אֶל־רְ֝הָבִ֗ים וְשָׂטֵ֥י כָזָֽב׃

רַבּ֤וֹת עָשִׂ֨יתָ ׀ אַתָּ֣ה ׀ יְהֹוָ֣ה אֱלֹהַי֮   6
נִֽפְלְאֹתֶ֥יךָ וּמַחְשְׁבֹתֶ֗יךָ אֵ֫לֵ֥ינוּ
אֵ֤ין ׀ עֲרֹ֬ךְ אֵלֶ֗יךָ אַגִּ֥ידָה וַאֲדַבֵּ֑רָה
עָ֝צְמ֗וּ מִסַּפֵּֽר׃

זֶ֤בַח וּמִנְחָ֨ה ׀ לֹֽא־חָפַ֗צְתָּ   7
אָ֭זְנַיִם כָּרִ֣יתָ לִּ֑י
עוֹלָ֥ה וַ֝חֲטָאָ֗ה לֹ֣א שָׁאָֽלְתָּ׃

7 Then I said, "Behold, I come;
In the scroll of the book *it is* written of me.
8 I delight to do Your will, O my God,
And Your law *is* within my heart."
9 I have proclaimed the good news of right-
eousness
In the great assembly;
Indeed, I do not restrain my lips,
O Lord, You Yourself know.
10 I have not hidden Your righteousness within
my heart;
I have declared Your faithfulness and Your
salvation;
I have not concealed Your lovingkindness and
Your truth
From the great assembly.
11 Do not withhold Your tender mercies from me,
O Lord;
Let Your lovingkindness and Your truth
continually preserve me.
12 For innumerable evils have surrounded me;
My iniquities have overtaken me, so that I am
not able to look up;
They are more than the hairs of my head;
Therefore my heart fails me.
13 Be pleased, O Lord, to deliver me;
O Lord, make haste to help me!
14 Let them be ashamed and brought to mutual
confusion
Who seek to destroy my life;
Let them be driven backward and brought to
dishonor
Who wish me evil.
15 Let them be confounded because of their
shame,
Who say to me, "Aha, aha!"
16 Let all those who seek You rejoice and be glad
in You;
Let such as love Your salvation say
continually,
"The Lord be magnified!"
17 But I *am* poor and needy;
Yet the Lord thinks upon me.
You *are* my help and my deliverer;
Do not delay, O my God.

41

To the Chief Musician. A Psalm of David.
Blessed *is* he who considers the poor;
The Lord will deliver him in time of trouble.
2 The Lord will preserve him and keep him
alive,

8 אָז אָמַרְתִּי הִנֵּה־בָאתִי
בִּמְגִלַּת־סֵפֶר כָּתוּב עָלָי:
9 לַעֲשׂוֹת־רְצוֹנְךָ אֱלֹהַי חָפָצְתִּי
וְתוֹרָתְךָ בְּתוֹךְ מֵעָי:
10 בִּשַּׂרְתִּי צֶדֶק ׀ בְּקָהָל רָב
הִנֵּה שְׂפָתַי לֹא אֶכְלָא
יְהֹוָה אַתָּה יָדָעְתָּ:
11 צִדְקָתְךָ לֹא־כִסִּיתִי ׀ בְּתוֹךְ לִבִּי
אֱמוּנָתְךָ וּתְשׁוּעָתְךָ אָמַרְתִּי
לֹא־כִחַדְתִּי חַסְדְּךָ וַאֲמִתְּךָ
לְקָהָל רָב:
12 אַתָּה יְהֹוָה
לֹא־תִכְלָא רַחֲמֶיךָ מִמֶּנִּי
חַסְדְּךָ וַאֲמִתְּךָ
תָּמִיד יִצְּרוּנִי:
13 כִּי אָפְפוּ־עָלַי ׀ רָעוֹת
עַד־אֵין מִסְפָּר
הִשִּׂיגוּנִי עֲוֹנֹתַי
וְלֹא־יָכֹלְתִּי לִרְאוֹת
עָצְמוּ מִשַּׂעֲרוֹת רֹאשִׁי
וְלִבִּי עֲזָבָנִי:
14 רְצֵה יְהֹוָה לְהַצִּילֵנִי
יְהֹוָה לְעֶזְרָתִי חוּשָׁה:
15 יֵבֹשׁוּ וְיַחְפְּרוּ ׀ יַחַד
מְבַקְשֵׁי נַפְשִׁי לִסְפּוֹתָהּ
יִסֹּגוּ אָחוֹר וְיִכָּלְמוּ
חֲפֵצֵי רָעָתִי:
16 יָשֹׁמּוּ עַל־עֵקֶב בָּשְׁתָּם
הָאֹמְרִים לִי הֶאָח ׀ הֶאָח:
17 יָשִׂישׂוּ וְיִשְׂמְחוּ ׀ בְּךָ כָּל־מְבַקְשֶׁיךָ
יֹאמְרוּ תָמִיד יִגְדַּל יְהֹוָה
אֹהֲבֵי תְּשׁוּעָתֶךָ:
18 וַאֲנִי ׀ עָנִי וְאֶבְיוֹן
אֲדֹנָי יַחֲשָׁב לִי
עֶזְרָתִי וּמְפַלְטִי אַתָּה
אֱלֹהַי אַל־תְּאַחַר:

מא לַמְנַצֵּחַ מִזְמוֹר לְדָוִד:
2 אַשְׁרֵי מַשְׂכִּיל אֶל־דָּל
בְּיוֹם רָעָה יְמַלְּטֵהוּ יְהֹוָה:
3 יְהֹוָה ׀ יִשְׁמְרֵהוּ וִיחַיֵּהוּ יְאֻשַּׁרק בָּאָרֶץ

And he will be blessed on the earth;
You will not deliver him to the will of his
   enemies.

3 The LORD will strengthen him on his bed of
      illness;
   You will sustain him on his sickbed.

4 I said, "LORD, be merciful to me;
   Heal my soul, for I have sinned against You."

5 My enemies speak evil of me:
   "When will he die, and his name perish?"

6 And if he comes to see *me,* he speaks lies;
   His heart gathers iniquity to itself;
   When he goes out, he tells *it.*

7 All who hate me whisper together against me;
   Against me they devise my hurt.

8 "An evil disease," *they say,* "clings to him.
   And *now* that he lies down, he will rise up no
      more."

9 Even my own familiar friend in whom I
      trusted,
   Who ate my bread,
   Has lifted up *his* heel against me.

10 But You, O LORD, be merciful to me, and raise
      me up,
   That I may repay them.

11 By this I know that You are well pleased with
      me,
   Because my enemy does not triumph over me.

12 As for me, You uphold me in my integrity,
   And set me before Your face forever.

13 Blessed *be* the LORD God of Israel
   From everlasting to everlasting!
   Amen and Amen.

Book Two: Psalms 42—72

42 To the Chief Musician. A Contemplation of the
sons of Korah.
   As the deer pants for the water brooks,
   So pants my soul for You, O God.

2 My soul thirsts for God, for the living God.
   When shall I come and appear before God?

3 My tears have been my food day and night,
   While they continually say to me,
   "Where *is* your God?"

4 When I remember these *things,*
   I pour out my soul within me.
   For I used to go with the multitude;
   I went with them to the house of God,
   With the voice of joy and praise,
   With a multitude that kept a pilgrim feast.

וְאַל־תִּתְּנֵהוּ בְּנֶפֶשׁ אֹיְבָיו׃

4 יְהֹוָה יִסְעָדֶנּוּ עַל־עֶרֶשׂ דְּוָי
כָּל־מִשְׁכָּבוֹ הָפַכְתָּ בְחָלְיוֹ׃

5 אֲנִי־אָמַרְתִּי יְהֹוָה חָנֵּנִי
רְפָאָה נַפְשִׁי כִּי־חָטָאתִי לָךְ׃

6 אוֹיְבַי יֹאמְרוּ רַע לִי
מָתַי יָמוּת וְאָבַד שְׁמוֹ׃

7 וְאִם־בָּא לִרְאוֹת ׀ שָׁוְא יְדַבֵּר
לִבּוֹ יִקְבָּץ־אָוֶן לוֹ
יֵצֵא לַחוּץ יְדַבֵּר׃

8 יַחַד עָלַי יִתְלַחֲשׁוּ כָּל־שֹׂנְאָי
עָלַי ׀ יַחְשְׁבוּ רָעָה לִי׃

9 דְּבַר־בְּלִיַּעַל יָצוּק בּוֹ
וַאֲשֶׁר שָׁכַב לֹא־יוֹסִיף לָקוּם׃

10 גַּם־אִישׁ שְׁלוֹמִי ׀ אֲשֶׁר־בָּטַחְתִּי בוֹ
אוֹכֵל לַחְמִי
הִגְדִּיל עָלַי עָקֵב׃

11 וְאַתָּה יְהֹוָה חָנֵּנִי וַהֲקִימֵנִי
וַאֲשַׁלְּמָה לָהֶם׃

12 בְּזֹאת יָדַעְתִּי כִּי־חָפַצְתָּ בִּי
כִּי לֹא־יָרִיעַ אֹיְבִי עָלָי׃

13 וַאֲנִי בְּתֻמִּי תָּמַכְתָּ בִּי
וַתַּצִּיבֵנִי לְפָנֶיךָ לְעוֹלָם׃

14 בָּרוּךְ יְהֹוָה ׀ אֱלֹהֵי יִשְׂרָאֵל
מֵהָעוֹלָם וְעַד הָעוֹלָם אָמֵן ׀ וְאָמֵן׃

מב לַמְנַצֵּחַ מַשְׂכִּיל לִבְנֵי־קֹרַח׃

2 כְּאַיָּל תַּעֲרֹג עַל־אֲפִיקֵי־מָיִם
כֵּן נַפְשִׁי תַעֲרֹג אֵלֶיךָ אֱלֹהִים׃

3 צָמְאָה נַפְשִׁי ׀ לֵאלֹהִים לְאֵל חָי
מָתַי אָבוֹא
וְאֵרָאֶה פְּנֵי אֱלֹהִים׃

4 הָיְתָה־לִּי דִמְעָתִי לֶחֶם
יוֹמָם וָלַיְלָה
בֶּאֱמֹר אֵלַי כָּל־הַיּוֹם
אַיֵּה אֱלֹהֶיךָ׃

5 אֵלֶּה אֶזְכְּרָה ׀
וְאֶשְׁפְּכָה עָלַי ׀ נַפְשִׁי
כִּי אֶעֱבֹר ׀ בַּסָּךְ
אֶדַּדֵּם עַד־בֵּית אֱלֹהִים
בְּקוֹל־רִנָּה וְתוֹדָה
הָמוֹן חוֹגֵג׃

5   Why are you cast down, O my soul?
    And *why* are you disquieted within me?
    Hope in God, for I shall yet praise Him
    For the help of His countenance.

6   O my God, my soul is cast down within me;
    Therefore I will remember You from the land
       of the Jordan,
    And from the heights of Hermon,
    From the Hill Mizar.

7   Deep calls unto deep at the noise of Your
       waterfalls;
    All Your waves and billows have gone over me.

8   The LORD will command His lovingkindness in
       the daytime,
    And in the night His song *shall be* with me—
    A prayer to the God of my life.

9   I will say to God my Rock,
    "Why have You forgotten me?
    Why do I go mourning because of the
       oppression of the enemy?"

10 *As* with a breaking of my bones,
    My enemies reproach me,
    While they say to me all day long,
    "Where *is* your God?"

11 Why are you cast down, O my soul?
    And why are you disquieted within me?
    Hope in God;
    For I shall yet praise Him,
    The help of my countenance and my God.

43 Vindicate me, O God,
    And plead my cause against an ungodly nation;
    Oh, deliver me from the deceitful and unjust
       man!

2   For You *are* the God of my strength;
    Why do You cast me off?
    Why do I go mourning because of the
       oppression of the enemy?

3   Oh, send out Your light and Your truth!
    Let them lead me;
    Let them bring me to Your holy hill
    And to Your tabernacle.

4   Then I will go to the altar of God,
    To God my exceeding joy;
    And on the harp I will praise You,
    O God, my God.

5   Why are you cast down, O my soul?
    And why are you disquieted within me?
    Hope in God;
    For I shall yet praise Him,
    The help of my countenance and my God.

מַה־תִּשְׁתּוֹחֲחִי ׀ נַפְשִׁי וַתֶּהֱמִי עָלָי   6
הוֹחִ֫ילִי לֵאלֹהִים כִּי־ע֥וֹד אוֹדֶ֑נּוּ יְשׁוּע֥וֹת פָּנָֽיו׃
אֱלֹהַ֗י עָלַי֮ נַפְשִׁ֪י תִשְׁתּ֫וֹחָ֥ח   7
עַל־כֵּ֗ן אֶ֭זְכׇּרְךָ מֵאֶ֣רֶץ יַרְדֵּ֑ן
וְ֝חֶרְמוֹנִ֗ים מֵהַ֥ר מִצְעָֽר׃
תְּהוֹם־אֶל־תְּה֣וֹם ק֭וֹרֵא   8
לְק֣וֹל צִנּוֹרֶ֑יךָ
כׇּֽל־מִשְׁבָּרֶ֥יךָ וְ֝גַלֶּ֗יךָ עָלַ֥י עָבָֽרוּ׃
יוֹמָ֤ם ׀ יְצַוֶּ֬ה יְהֹוָ֨ה ׀ חַסְדּ֗וֹ   9
וּ֭בַלַּיְלָה שִׁירֹ֣ה עִמִּ֑י
תְּ֝פִלָּ֗ה לְאֵ֣ל חַיָּֽי׃
אוֹמְרָ֤ה ׀ לְאֵ֥ל סַלְעִי֮ לָמָ֢ה שְׁכַ֫חְתָּ֥נִי   10
לָֽמָּה־קֹדֵ֥ר אֵלֵ֗ךְ בְּלַ֣חַץ אוֹיֵֽב׃
בְּרֶ֤צַח ׀ בְּֽעַצְמוֹתַ֗י חֵרְפ֥וּנִי צוֹרְרָ֑י   11
בְּאׇמְרָ֥ם אֵלַ֥י כׇּל־הַ֝יּ֗וֹם אַיֵּ֥ה אֱלֹהֶֽיךָ׃
מַה־תִּשְׁתּ֬וֹחֲחִ֨י ׀ נַפְשִׁי֮ וּֽמַה־תֶּהֱמִ֢י עָ֫לָ֥י   12
הוֹחִ֣ילִי לֵ֭אלֹהִים כִּי־ע֣וֹד אוֹדֶ֑נּוּ
יְשׁוּעֹ֥ת פָּ֝נַ֗י וֵאלֹהָֽי׃

מג שׇׁפְטֵ֤נִי אֱלֹהִ֨ים ׀ וְרִ֘יבָ֤ה רִיבִ֗י
מִגּ֥וֹי לֹא־חָסִ֑יד
מֵ֤אִישׁ־מִרְמָ֖ה וְעַוְלָ֣ה
תְפַלְּטֵֽנִי׃
כִּֽי־אַתָּ֤ה ׀ אֱלֹהֵ֣י מָֽעוּזִּי֮   2
לָמָ֪ה זְנַ֫חְתָּ֥נִי
לָֽמָּה־קֹדֵ֥ר אֶתְהַלֵּ֗ךְ
בְּלַ֣חַץ אוֹיֵֽב׃
שְׁלַח־אוֹרְךָ֣ וַ֭אֲמִתְּךָ   3
הֵ֣מָּה יַנְח֑וּנִי
יְבִיא֥וּנִי אֶל־הַֽר־קׇ֝דְשְׁךָ֗
וְאֶל־מִשְׁכְּנוֹתֶֽיךָ׃
וְאָב֤וֹאָה ׀ אֶל־מִזְבַּ֬ח אֱלֹהִ֗ים   4
אֶל־אֵל֮ שִׂמְחַ֢ת גִּ֫ילִ֥י
וְאוֹדְךָ֥ בְכִנּ֗וֹר
אֱלֹהִ֥ים אֱלֹהָֽי׃
מַה־תִּשְׁתּ֬וֹחֲחִ֨י ׀ נַפְשִׁי֮   5
וּֽמַה־תֶּהֱמִ֢י עָ֫לָ֥י
הוֹחִ֣ילִי לֵ֭אלֹהִים כִּי־ע֣וֹד אוֹדֶ֑נּוּ
יְשׁוּעֹ֥ת פָּ֝נַ֗י וֵאלֹהָֽי׃

44 To the Chief Musician. A Contemplation of the sons of Korah.

We have heard with our ears, O God,
Our fathers have told us,
The deeds You did in their days,
In days of old:

2 You drove out the nations with Your hand,
But them You planted;
You afflicted the peoples, and cast them out.

3 For they did not gain possession of the land by
their own sword,
Nor did their own arm save them;
But it was Your right hand, Your arm, and the
light of Your countenance,
Because You favored them.

4 You are my King, O God;
Command victories for Jacob.

5 Through You we will push down our enemies;
Through Your name we will trample those who
rise up against us.

6 For I will not trust in my bow,
Nor shall my sword save me.

7 But You have saved us from our enemies,
And have put to shame those who hated us.

8 In God we boast all day long,
And praise Your name forever.   Selah

9 But You have cast us off and put us to shame,
And You do not go out with our armies.

10 You make us turn back from the enemy,
And those who hate us have taken spoil for
themselves.

11 You have given us up like sheep *intended* for
food,
And have scattered us among the nations.

12 You sell Your people for *next to* nothing,
And are not enriched by selling them.

13 You make us a reproach to our neighbors,
A scorn and a derision to those all around us.

14 You make us a byword among the nations,
A shaking of the head among the peoples.

15 My dishonor *is* continually before me,
And the shame of my face has covered me,

16 Because of the voice of him who reproaches
and reviles,
Because of the enemy and the avenger.

17 All this has come upon us;
But we have not forgotten You,
Nor have we dealt falsely with Your covenant.

18 Our heart has not turned back,
Nor have our steps departed from Your way;

19 But You have severely broken us in the place of
jackals,

מד לַמְנַצֵּחַ לִבְנֵי־קֹרַח מַשְׂכִּיל:

2 אֱלֹהִים ׀ בְּאָזְנֵינוּ שָׁמַעְנוּ
אֲבוֹתֵינוּ סִפְּרוּ־לָנוּ
פֹּעַל פָּעַלְתָּ בִימֵיהֶם
בִּימֵי קֶדֶם:

3 אַתָּה ׀ יָדְךָ גוֹיִם הוֹרַשְׁתָּ וַתִּטָּעֵם
תָּרַע לְאֻמִּים וַתְּשַׁלְּחֵם:

4 כִּי לֹא בְחַרְבָּם יָרְשׁוּ אָרֶץ
וּזְרוֹעָם לֹא־הוֹשִׁיעָה לָּמוֹ
כִּי־יְמִינְךָ וּזְרוֹעֲךָ וְאוֹר פָּנֶיךָ
כִּי רְצִיתָם:

5 אַתָּה־הוּא מַלְכִּי אֱלֹהִים
צַוֵּה יְשׁוּעוֹת יַעֲקֹב:

6 בְּךָ צָרֵינוּ נְנַגֵּחַ
בְּשִׁמְךָ נָבוּס קָמֵינוּ:

7 כִּי לֹא בְקַשְׁתִּי אֶבְטָח
וְחַרְבִּי לֹא תוֹשִׁיעֵנִי:

8 כִּי הוֹשַׁעְתָּנוּ מִצָּרֵינוּ
וּמְשַׂנְאֵינוּ הֱבִישׁוֹתָ:

9 בֵּאלֹהִים הִלַּלְנוּ כָל־הַיּוֹם
וְשִׁמְךָ ׀ לְעוֹלָם נוֹדֶה סֶלָה:

10 אַף־זָנַחְתָּ וַתַּכְלִימֵנוּ
וְלֹא־תֵצֵא בְּצִבְאוֹתֵינוּ:

11 תְּשִׁיבֵנוּ אָחוֹר מִנִּי־צָר
וּמְשַׂנְאֵינוּ שָׁסוּ לָמוֹ:

12 תִּתְּנֵנוּ כְּצֹאן מַאֲכָל
וּבַגּוֹיִם זֵרִיתָנוּ:

13 תִּמְכֹּר־עַמְּךָ בְלֹא־הוֹן
וְלֹא־רִבִּיתָ בִּמְחִירֵיהֶם:

14 תְּשִׂימֵנוּ חֶרְפָּה לִשְׁכֵנֵינוּ
לַעַג וָקֶלֶס לִסְבִיבוֹתֵינוּ:

15 תְּשִׂימֵנוּ מָשָׁל בַּגּוֹיִם
מְנוֹד־רֹאשׁ בַּל־אֻמִּים:

16 כָּל־הַיּוֹם כְּלִמָּתִי נֶגְדִּי
וּבֹשֶׁת פָּנַי כִּסָּתְנִי:

17 מִקּוֹל מְחָרֵף וּמְגַדֵּף
מִפְּנֵי אוֹיֵב וּמִתְנַקֵּם:

18 כָּל־זֹאת בָּאַתְנוּ וְלֹא שְׁכַחֲנוּךָ
וְלֹא־שִׁקַּרְנוּ בִּבְרִיתֶךָ:

19 לֹא־נָסוֹג אָחוֹר לִבֵּנוּ
וַתֵּט אֲשֻׁרֵינוּ מִנִּי אָרְחֶךָ:

20 כִּי דִכִּיתָנוּ בִּמְקוֹם תַּנִּים

And covered us with the shadow of death.   וַתְּכַס עָלֵינוּ בְצַלְמָוֶת:

20   If we had forgotten the name of our God,   21 אִם־שָׁכַחְנוּ שֵׁם אֱלֹהֵינוּ
Or stretched out our hands to a foreign god,   וַנִּפְרֹשׂ כַּפֵּינוּ לְאֵל זָר:

21   Would not God search this out?   22 הֲלֹא אֱלֹהִים יַחֲקָר־זֹאת
For He knows the secrets of the heart.   כִּי־הוּא יֹדֵעַ תַּעֲלֻמוֹת לֵב:

22   Yet for Your sake we are killed all day long;   23 כִּי־עָלֶיךָ הֹרַגְנוּ כָל־הַיּוֹם
We are accounted as sheep for the slaughter.   נֶחְשַׁבְנוּ כְּצֹאן טִבְחָה:

23   Awake! Why do You sleep, O Lord?   24 עוּרָה לָמָּה תִישַׁן אֲדֹנָי
Arise! Do not cast us off forever.   הָקִיצָה אַל־תִּזְנַח לָנֶצַח:

24   Why do You hide Your face,   25 לָמָּה־פָנֶיךָ תַסְתִּיר
And forget our affliction and our oppression?   תִּשְׁכַּח עָנְיֵנוּ וְלַחֲצֵנוּ:

25   For our soul is bowed down to the dust;   26 כִּי שָׁחָה לֶעָפָר נַפְשֵׁנוּ
Our body clings to the ground.   דָּבְקָה לָאָרֶץ בִּטְנֵנוּ:

26   Arise for our help,   27 קוּמָה עֶזְרָתָה לָּנוּ
And redeem us for Your mercies' sake.   וּפְדֵנוּ לְמַעַן חַסְדֶּךָ:

45 To the Chief Musician. Set to "The Lilies." A
Contemplation of the sons of Korah. A Song of Love.   מה לַמְנַצֵּחַ עַל־שֹׁשַׁנִּים
My heart is overflowing with a good theme;   לִבְנֵי־קֹרַח מַשְׂכִּיל שִׁיר יְדִידֹת:
I recite my composition concerning the King;
My tongue is the pen of a ready writer.   2 רָחַשׁ לִבִּי דָּבָר טוֹב

2   You are fairer than the sons of men;   אֹמֵר אָנִי מַעֲשַׂי לְמֶלֶךְ
Grace is poured upon Your lips;   לְשׁוֹנִי עֵט סוֹפֵר מָהִיר:
Therefore God has blessed You forever.

3   Gird Your sword upon Your thigh, O Mighty   3 יָפְיָפִיתָ מִבְּנֵי אָדָם
One,   הוּצַק חֵן בְּשְׂפְתוֹתֶיךָ
With Your glory and Your majesty.   עַל־כֵּן בֵּרַכְךָ אֱלֹהִים לְעוֹלָם:

4   And in Your majesty ride prosperously because   4 חֲגוֹר־חַרְבְּךָ עַל־יָרֵךְ גִּבּוֹר
of truth, humility, and righteousness;   הוֹדְךָ וַהֲדָרֶךָ:
And Your right hand shall teach You awesome
things.

5   Your arrows are sharp in the heart of the   5 וַהֲדָרְךָ צְלַח רְכַב
King's enemies;   עַל־דְּבַר־אֱמֶת וְעַנְוָה־צֶדֶק
The peoples fall under You.   וְתוֹרְךָ נוֹרָאוֹת יְמִינֶךָ:

6   Your throne, O God, is forever and ever;   6 חִצֶּיךָ שְׁנוּנִים
A scepter of righteousness is the scepter of   עַמִּים תַּחְתֶּיךָ יִפְּלוּ בְּלֵב אוֹיְבֵי הַמֶּלֶךְ:
Your kingdom.

7   You love righteousness and hate wickedness;   7 כִּסְאֲךָ אֱלֹהִים עוֹלָם וָעֶד
Therefore God, Your God, has anointed You   שֵׁבֶט מִישֹׁר שֵׁבֶט מַלְכוּתֶךָ:
With the oil of gladness more than Your
companions.

8   All Your garments are scented with myrrh and   8 אָהַבְתָּ צֶּדֶק
aloes and cassia,   וַתִּשְׂנָא רֶשַׁע
Out of the ivory palaces, by which they have   עַל־כֵּן מְשָׁחֲךָ אֱלֹהִים אֱלֹהֶיךָ
made You glad.   שֶׁמֶן שָׂשׂוֹן מֵחֲבֵרֶיךָ:

9   Kings' daughters are among Your honorable   9 מֹר־וַאֲהָלוֹת קְצִיעוֹת כָּל־בִּגְדֹתֶיךָ
women;   מִן־הֵיכְלֵי שֵׁן מִנִּי שִׂמְּחוּךָ:
At Your right hand stands the queen in gold
from Ophir.   10 בְּנוֹת מְלָכִים בְּיִקְּרוֹתֶיךָ
     נִצְּבָה שֵׁגַל לִימִינְךָ בְּכֶתֶם אוֹפִיר:

10   Listen, O daughter,   11 שִׁמְעִי־בַת וּרְאִי וְהַטִּי אָזְנֵךְ
Consider and incline your ear;

Forget your own people also, and your father's house;

11 So the King will greatly desire your beauty;
Because He *is* your Lord, worship Him.

12 And the daughter of Tyre *will come* with a gift;
The rich among the people will seek your favor.

13 The royal daughter *is* all glorious within *the palace;*
Her clothing *is* woven with gold.

14 She shall be brought to the King in robes of many colors;
The virgins, her companions who follow her, shall be brought to You.

15 With gladness and rejoicing they shall be brought;
They shall enter the King's palace.

16 Instead of Your fathers shall be Your sons,
Whom You shall make princes in all the earth.

17 I will make Your name to be remembered in all generations;
Therefore the people shall praise You forever and ever.

46 To the Chief Musician. A Psalm of the sons of Korah. A Song for Alamoth.
God *is* our refuge and strength,
A very present help in trouble.

2 Therefore we will not fear,
Even though the earth be removed,
And though the mountains be carried into the midst of the sea;

3 *Though* its waters roar *and* be troubled,
Though the mountains shake with its swelling. Selah

4 *There is* a river whose streams shall make glad the city of God,
The holy *place* of the tabernacle of the Most High.

5 God *is* in the midst of her, she shall not be moved;
God shall help her, just at the break of dawn.

6 The nations raged, the kingdoms were moved;
He uttered His voice, the earth melted.

7 The LORD of hosts *is* with us;
The God of Jacob *is* our refuge. Selah

8 Come, behold the works of the LORD,
Who has made desolations in the earth.

9 He makes wars cease to the end of the earth;
He breaks the bow and cuts the spear in two;
He burns the chariot in the fire.

וְשִׁכְחִי עַמֵּךְ וּבֵית אָבִיךְ:

12 וְיִתְאָו הַמֶּלֶךְ יָפְיֵךְ
כִּי־הוּא אֲדֹנַיִךְ וְהִשְׁתַּחֲוִי־לוֹ:

13 וּבַת־צֹר ׀
בְּמִנְחָה פָּנַיִךְ יְחַלּוּ עֲשִׁירֵי עָם:

14 כָּל־כְּבוּדָּה בַת־מֶלֶךְ פְּנִימָה
מִמִּשְׁבְּצוֹת זָהָב לְבוּשָׁהּ:

15 לִרְקָמוֹת תּוּבַל לַמֶּלֶךְ
בְּתוּלוֹת אַחֲרֶיהָ רֵעוֹתֶיהָ מוּבָאוֹת לָךְ:

16 תּוּבַלְנָה בִּשְׂמָחֹת וָגִיל
תְּבֹאֶינָה בְּהֵיכַל מֶלֶךְ:

17 תַּחַת אֲבֹתֶיךָ יִהְיוּ בָנֶיךָ
תְּשִׁיתֵמוֹ לְשָׂרִים בְּכָל־הָאָרֶץ:

18 אַזְכִּירָה שִׁמְךָ בְּכָל־דֹּר וָדֹר
עַל־כֵּן עַמִּים יְהוֹדֻךָ לְעֹלָם וָעֶד:

מו לַמְנַצֵּחַ לִבְנֵי־קֹרַח
עַל־עֲלָמוֹת שִׁיר:

2 אֱלֹהִים לָנוּ מַחֲסֶה וָעֹז
עֶזְרָה בְצָרוֹת נִמְצָא מְאֹד:

3 עַל־כֵּן לֹא־נִירָא בְּהָמִיר אָרֶץ
וּבְמוֹט הָרִים בְּלֵב יַמִּים:

4 יֶהֱמוּ יֶחְמְרוּ מֵימָיו
יִרְעֲשׁוּ־הָרִים בְּגַאֲוָתוֹ סֶלָה:

5 נָהָר פְּלָגָיו יְשַׂמְּחוּ עִיר־אֱלֹהִים
קְדֹשׁ מִשְׁכְּנֵי עֶלְיוֹן:

6 אֱלֹהִים בְּקִרְבָּהּ בַּל־תִּמּוֹט
יַעְזְרֶהָ אֱלֹהִים לִפְנוֹת בֹּקֶר:

7 הָמוּ גוֹיִם מָטוּ מַמְלָכוֹת
נָתַן בְּקוֹלוֹ תָּמוּג אָרֶץ:

8 יְהוָה צְבָאוֹת עִמָּנוּ
מִשְׂגָּב־לָנוּ אֱלֹהֵי יַעֲקֹב סֶלָה:

9 לְכוּ־חֲזוּ מִפְעֲלוֹת יְהוָה
אֲשֶׁר־שָׂם שַׁמּוֹת בָּאָרֶץ:

10 מַשְׁבִּית מִלְחָמוֹת
עַד־קְצֵה הָאָרֶץ
קֶשֶׁת יְשַׁבֵּר וְקִצֵּץ חֲנִית
עֲגָלוֹת יִשְׂרֹף בָּאֵשׁ:

10 Be still, and know that I *am* God;
I will be exalted among the nations,
I will be exalted in the earth!

11 הַרְפּ֣וּ וּ֭דְעוּ כִּי־אָנֹכִ֣י אֱלֹהִ֑ים
אָר֥וּם בַּ֝גּוֹיִ֗ם אָר֥וּם בָּאָֽרֶץ׃

11 The LORD of hosts *is* with us;
The God of Jacob *is* our refuge.   Selah

12 יְהֹוָ֣ה צְבָא֣וֹת עִמָּ֑נוּ
מִשְׂגָּֽב־לָ֝֔נוּ אֱלֹהֵ֖י יַעֲקֹ֣ב סֶֽלָה׃

47 To the Chief Musician. A Psalm of the sons of Korah.

מז לַמְנַצֵּ֬חַ ׀ לִבְנֵי־קֹ֬רַח מִזְמֽוֹר׃

Oh, clap your hands, all you peoples!
Shout to God with the voice of triumph!

2 כָּֽל־הָ֭עַמִּים תִּקְעוּ־כָ֑ף
הָרִ֥יעוּ לֵ֝אלֹהִ֗ים בְּק֣וֹל רִנָּֽה׃

2 For the LORD Most High *is* awesome;
He is a great King over all the earth.

3 כִּֽי־יְהֹוָ֣ה עֶלְי֣וֹן נוֹרָ֑א
מֶ֥לֶךְ גָּ֝ד֗וֹל עַל־כָּל־הָאָֽרֶץ׃

3 He will subdue the peoples under us,
And the nations under our feet.

4 יַדְבֵּ֣ר עַמִּ֣ים תַּחְתֵּ֑ינוּ
וּ֝לְאֻמִּ֗ים תַּ֣חַת רַגְלֵֽינוּ׃

4 He will choose our inheritance for us,
The excellence of Jacob whom He loves.
                                        Selah

5 יִבְחַר־לָ֥נוּ אֶת־נַחֲלָתֵ֑נוּ
אֶ֥ת גְּא֨וֹן יַעֲקֹ֖ב אֲשֶׁר־אָהֵ֣ב סֶֽלָה׃

6 עָלָ֣ה אֱ֭לֹהִים בִּתְרוּעָ֑ה

5 God has gone up with a shout,
The LORD with the sound of a trumpet.

יְ֝הֹוָ֗ה בְּק֣וֹל שׁוֹפָֽר׃

6 Sing praises to God, sing praises!
Sing praises to our King, sing praises!

7 זַמְּר֣וּ אֱלֹהִ֣ים זַמֵּ֑רוּ
זַמְּר֖וּ לְמַלְכֵּ֣נוּ זַמֵּֽרוּ׃

7 For God *is* the King of all the earth;
Sing praises with understanding.

8 כִּ֤י מֶ֖לֶךְ כָּל־הָאָ֥רֶץ אֱלֹהִ֗ים
זַמְּר֥וּ מַשְׂכִּֽיל׃

8 God reigns over the nations;
God sits on His holy throne.

9 מָלַ֣ךְ אֱ֭לֹהִים עַל־גּוֹיִ֑ם
אֱלֹהִ֗ים ׀ יָשַׁ֤ב ׀ עַל־כִּסֵּ֬א קָדְשֽׁוֹ׃

9 The princes of the people have gathered
    together,
The people of the God of Abraham.
For the shields of the earth *belong* to God;
He is greatly exalted.

10 נְדִ֘יבֵ֤י עַמִּ֨ים ׀ נֶאֱסָ֗פוּ עַם֮ אֱלֹהֵ֢י אַבְרָ֫הָ֥ם
כִּ֣י לֵֽ֭אלֹהִים מָֽגִנֵּי־אֶ֗רֶץ מְאֹ֣ד נַעֲלָֽה׃

מח שִׁ֥יר מִ֝זְמ֗וֹר לִבְנֵי־קֹֽרַח׃

48 A Song. A Psalm of the sons of Korah.
Great *is* the LORD, and greatly to be praised
In the city of our God,
In His holy mountain.

2 גָּ֘ד֤וֹל יְהֹוָ֣ה וּמְהֻלָּ֣ל מְאֹ֑ד
בְּעִ֥יר אֱ֝לֹהֵ֗ינוּ הַר־קָדְשֽׁוֹ׃

2 Beautiful in elevation,
The joy of the whole earth,
Is Mount Zion *on* the sides of the north,
The city of the great King.

3 יְפֵ֥ה נוֹף֮ מְשׂ֢וֹשׂ כָּל־הָ֫אָ֥רֶץ
הַר־צִ֭יּוֹן יַרְכְּתֵ֣י צָפ֑וֹן
קִ֝רְיַ֗ת מֶ֣לֶךְ רָֽב׃

3 God *is* in her palaces;
He is known as her refuge.

4 אֱלֹהִ֥ים בְּאַרְמְנוֹתֶ֗יהָ
נוֹדַ֥ע לְמִשְׂגָּֽב׃

4 For behold, the kings assembled,
They passed by together.

5 כִּֽי־הִנֵּ֣ה הַ֭מְּלָכִים נֽוֹעֲד֑וּ
עָבְר֥וּ יַחְדָּֽו׃

5 They saw *it, and* so they marveled;
They were troubled, they hastened away.

6 הֵ֣מָּה רָ֭אוּ כֵּ֣ן תָּמָ֑הוּ
נִבְהֲל֥וּ נֶחְפָּֽזוּ׃

6 Fear took hold of them there,
And pain, as of a woman in birth pangs,

7 רְ֭עָדָה אֲחָזָ֣תַם שָׁ֑ם
חִ֝֗יל כַּיּוֹלֵדָֽה׃

7 *As when* You break the ships of Tarshish
With an east wind.

8 בְּר֥וּחַ קָדִ֑ים
תְּ֝שַׁבֵּ֗ר אֳנִיּ֥וֹת תַּרְשִֽׁישׁ׃

8 As we have heard,
So we have seen

9 כַּאֲשֶׁ֤ר שָׁמַ֨עְנוּ ׀
כֵּ֤ן רָאִ֨ינוּ

In the city of the LORD of hosts,
In the city of our God:
God will establish it forever.   Selah

בְּעִיר־יְהֹוָה צְבָאוֹת
בְּעִיר אֱלֹהֵינוּ
אֱלֹהִים יְכוֹנְנֶהָ עַד־עוֹלָם סֶלָה:

9 We have thought, O God, on Your
lovingkindness,
In the midst of Your temple.

דִּמִּינוּ אֱלֹהִים חַסְדֶּךָ 10
בְּקֶרֶב הֵיכָלֶךָ:

10 According to Your name, O God,
So is Your praise to the ends of the earth;
Your right hand is full of righteousness.

כְּשִׁמְךָ אֱלֹהִים 11
כֵּן תְּהִלָּתְךָ עַל־קַצְוֵי־אֶרֶץ
צֶדֶק מָלְאָה יְמִינֶךָ:

11 Let Mount Zion rejoice,
Let the daughters of Judah be glad,
Because of Your judgments.

יִשְׂמַח | הַר־צִיּוֹן תָּגֵלְנָה בְּנוֹת יְהוּדָה 12
לְמַעַן מִשְׁפָּטֶיךָ:

12 Walk about Zion,
And go all around her.
Count her towers;

סֹבּוּ צִיּוֹן וְהַקִּיפוּהָ 13
סִפְרוּ מִגְדָּלֶיהָ:

13 Mark well her bulwarks;
Consider her palaces;
That you may tell it to the generation
following.

שִׁיתוּ לִבְּכֶם | לְחֵילָה פַּסְּגוּ אַרְמְנוֹתֶיהָ 14
לְמַעַן תְּסַפְּרוּ לְדוֹר אַחֲרוֹן:

14 For this is God,
Our God forever and ever;
He will be our guide
Even to death.

כִּי זֶה | אֱלֹהִים אֱלֹהֵינוּ עוֹלָם וָעֶד 15
הוּא יְנַהֲגֵנוּ עַל־מוּת:

49 To the Chief Musician. A Psalm of the sons of
Korah.
Hear this, all peoples;
Give ear, all inhabitants of the world,

מט לַמְנַצֵּחַ | לִבְנֵי־קֹרַח מִזְמוֹר:
שִׁמְעוּ־זֹאת כָּל־הָעַמִּים 2
הַאֲזִינוּ כָּל־יֹשְׁבֵי חָלֶד:

2 Both low and high,
Rich and poor together.

גַּם־בְּנֵי אָדָם גַּם־בְּנֵי־אִישׁ 3
יַחַד עָשִׁיר וְאֶבְיוֹן:

3 My mouth shall speak wisdom,
And the meditation of my heart shall give
understanding.

פִּי יְדַבֵּר חָכְמוֹת 4
וְהָגוּת לִבִּי תְבוּנוֹת:

4 I will incline my ear to a proverb;
I will disclose my dark saying on the harp.

אַטֶּה לְמָשָׁל אָזְנִי 5
אֶפְתַּח בְּכִנּוֹר חִידָתִי:

5 Why should I fear in the days of evil,
When the iniquity at my heels surrounds me?

לָמָּה אִירָא בִּימֵי רָע 6
עֲוֹן עֲקֵבַי יְסוּבֵּנִי:

6 Those who trust in their wealth
And boast in the multitude of their riches,

הַבֹּטְחִים עַל־חֵילָם 7
וּבְרֹב עָשְׁרָם יִתְהַלָּלוּ:

7 None of them can by any means redeem his
brother,
Nor give to God a ransom for him—

אָח לֹא־פָדֹה יִפְדֶּה אִישׁ 8
לֹא־יִתֵּן לֵאלֹהִים כָּפְרוֹ:

8 For the redemption of their souls is costly,
And it shall cease forever—

וְיֵקַר פִּדְיוֹן נַפְשָׁם 9
וְחָדַל לְעוֹלָם:

9 That he should continue to live eternally,
And not see the Pit.

וִיחִי־עוֹד לָנֶצַח 10
לֹא יִרְאֶה הַשָּׁחַת:

10 For he sees wise men die;
Likewise the fool and the senseless person
perish,
And leave their wealth to others.

כִּי יִרְאֶה | חֲכָמִים יָמוּתוּ 11
יַחַד כְּסִיל וָבַעַר יֹאבֵדוּ
וְעָזְבוּ לַאֲחֵרִים חֵילָם:

11 Their inner thought is that their houses will last
forever,

קִרְבָּם בָּתֵּימוֹ | לְעוֹלָם 12
מִשְׁכְּנֹתָם לְדֹר וָדֹר

Their dwelling places to all generations;
They call *their* lands after their own names.

קָרְאוּ בִשְׁמוֹתָם
עֲלֵי אֲדָמוֹת:

12 Nevertheless man, *though* in honor, does not
    remain;
He is like the beasts *that* perish.

13 וְאָדָם בִּיקָר בַּל־יָלִין
נִמְשַׁל כַּבְּהֵמוֹת נִדְמוּ:

13 This is the way of those who *are* foolish,
And of their posterity who approve their
    sayings.   Selah

14 זֶה דַרְכָּם כֵּסֶל לָמוֹ
וְאַחֲרֵיהֶם ׀ בְּפִיהֶם יִרְצוּ סֶלָה:

14 Like sheep they are laid in the grave;
Death shall feed on them;
The upright shall have dominion over them in
    the morning;
And their beauty shall be consumed in the
    grave, far from their dwelling.

15 כַּצֹּאן ׀ לִשְׁאוֹל שַׁתּוּ
מָוֶת יִרְעֵם
וַיִּרְדּוּ בָם יְשָׁרִים ׀ לַבֹּקֶר וְצִירָם ᴾ לְבַלּוֹת
שְׁאוֹל מִזְּבֻל לוֹ:

15 But God will redeem my soul from the power
    of the grave,
For He shall receive me.   Selah

16 אַךְ־אֱלֹהִים יִפְדֶּה נַפְשִׁי מִיַּד־שְׁאוֹל
כִּי יִקָּחֵנִי סֶלָה:

16 Do not be afraid when one becomes rich,
When the glory of his house is increased;

17 אַל־תִּירָא כִּי־יַעֲשִׁר אִישׁ
כִּי־יִרְבֶּה כְּבוֹד בֵּיתוֹ:

17 For when he dies he shall carry nothing away;
His glory shall not descend after him.

18 כִּי לֹא בְמוֹתוֹ יִקַּח הַכֹּל
לֹא־יֵרֵד אַחֲרָיו כְּבוֹדוֹ:

18 Though while he lives he blesses himself
(For *men* will praise you when you do well for
    yourself),

19 כִּי־נַפְשׁוֹ בְּחַיָּיו יְבָרֵךְ
וְיוֹדֻךָ כִּי־תֵיטִיב לָךְ:

19 He shall go to the generation of his fathers;
They shall never see light.

20 תָּבוֹא עַד־דּוֹר אֲבוֹתָיו
עַד־נֵצַח לֹא יִרְאוּ־אוֹר:

20 A man *who is* in honor, yet does not
    understand,
Is like the beasts *that* perish.

21 אָדָם בִּיקָר וְלֹא יָבִין
נִמְשַׁל כַּבְּהֵמוֹת נִדְמוּ:

50 A Psalm of Asaph.

The Mighty One, God the LORD,
Has spoken and called the earth
From the rising of the sun to its going down.

נ מִזְמוֹר לְאָסָף
אֵל ׀ אֱלֹהִים יְהֹוָה דִּבֶּר וַיִּקְרָא־אָרֶץ
מִמִּזְרַח־שֶׁמֶשׁ עַד־מְבֹאוֹ:

2 Out of Zion, the perfection of beauty,
God will shine forth.

2 מִצִּיּוֹן מִכְלַל־יֹפִי
אֱלֹהִים הוֹפִיעַ:

3 Our God shall come, and shall not keep silent;
A fire shall devour before Him,
And it shall be very tempestuous all around
    Him.

3 יָבֹא אֱלֹהֵינוּ וְאַל־יֶחֱרַשׁ
אֵשׁ־לְפָנָיו תֹּאכֵל
וּסְבִיבָיו נִשְׂעֲרָה מְאֹד:

4 He shall call to the heavens from above,
And to the earth, that He may judge His
    people:

4 יִקְרָא אֶל־הַשָּׁמַיִם מֵעָל
וְאֶל־הָאָרֶץ לָדִין עַמּוֹ:

5 "Gather My saints together to Me,
Those who have made a covenant with Me by
    sacrifice."

5 אִסְפוּ־לִי חֲסִידָי
כֹּרְתֵי בְרִיתִי עֲלֵי־זָבַח:

6 Let the heavens declare His righteousness,
For God Himself *is* Judge.   Selah

6 וַיַּגִּידוּ שָׁמַיִם צִדְקוֹ
כִּי־אֱלֹהִים ׀ שֹׁפֵט הוּא סֶלָה:

7 "Hear, O My people, and I will speak,
O Israel, and I will testify against you;
I *am* God, your God!

7 שִׁמְעָה עַמִּי ׀ וַאֲדַבֵּרָה
יִשְׂרָאֵל וְאָעִידָה בָּךְ
אֱלֹהִים אֱלֹהֶיךָ אָנֹכִי:

8 I will not rebuke you for your sacrifices

8 לֹא עַל־זְבָחֶיךָ אוֹכִיחֶךָ
וְעוֹלֹתֶיךָ לְנֶגְדִּי תָמִיד:

Or your burnt offerings,
Which are continually before Me.
9   I will not take a bull from your house,
Nor goats out of your folds.
10   For every beast of the forest *is* Mine,
And the cattle on a thousand hills.
11   I know all the birds of the mountains,
And the wild beasts of the field *are* Mine.

12   "If I were hungry, I would not tell you;
For the world *is* Mine, and all its fullness.
13   Will I eat the flesh of bulls,
Or drink the blood of goats?
14   Offer to God thanksgiving,
And pay your vows to the Most High.
15   Call upon Me in the day of trouble;
I will deliver you, and you shall glorify Me."

16   But to the wicked God says:
"What *right* have you to declare My statutes,
Or take My covenant in your mouth,
17   Seeing you hate instruction
And cast My words behind you?
18   When you saw a thief, you consented with him,
And have been a partaker with adulterers.
19   You give your mouth to evil,
And your tongue frames deceit.
20   You sit *and* speak against your brother;
You slander your own mother's son.
21   These *things* you have done, and I kept silent;
You thought that I was altogether like you;
But I will rebuke you,
And set *them* in order before your eyes.

22   "Now consider this, you who forget God,
Lest I tear *you* in pieces,
And *there be* none to deliver:
23   Whoever offers praise glorifies Me;
And to him who orders *his* conduct *aright*
I will show the salvation of God."

51 To the Chief Musician. A Psalm of David when
Nathan the prophet went to him, after he had gone in to
Bathsheba.
Have mercy upon me, O God,
According to Your lovingkindness;
According to the multitude of Your tender
mercies,
Blot out my transgressions.
2   Wash me thoroughly from my iniquity,
And cleanse me from my sin.
3   For I acknowledge my transgressions,
And my sin *is* always before me.
4   Against You, You only, have I sinned,
And done *this* evil in Your sight—

9 לֹא־אֶקַּח מִבֵּיתְךָ פָר
מִמִּכְלְאֹתֶיךָ עַתּוּדִים׃
10 כִּי־לִי כָל־חַיְתוֹ־יָעַר
בְּהֵמוֹת בְּהַרְרֵי־אָלֶף׃
11 יָדַעְתִּי כָּל־עוֹף הָרִים
וְזִיז שָׂדַי עִמָּדִי׃
12 אִם־אֶרְעַב לֹא־אֹמַר לָךְ
כִּי־לִי תֵבֵל וּמְלֹאָהּ׃
13 הַאוֹכַל בְּשַׂר אַבִּירִים
וְדַם עַתּוּדִים אֶשְׁתֶּה׃
14 זְבַח לֵאלֹהִים תּוֹדָה
וְשַׁלֵּם לְעֶלְיוֹן נְדָרֶיךָ׃
15 וּקְרָאֵנִי בְּיוֹם צָרָה
אֲחַלֶּצְךָ וּתְכַבְּדֵנִי׃
16 וְלָרָשָׁע ׀ אָמַר אֱלֹהִים מַה־לְּךָ לְסַפֵּר חֻקָּי
וַתִּשָּׂא בְרִיתִי עֲלֵי־פִיךָ׃
17 וְאַתָּה שָׂנֵאתָ מוּסָר
וַתַּשְׁלֵךְ דְּבָרַי אַחֲרֶיךָ׃
18 אִם־רָאִיתָ גַנָּב וַתִּרֶץ עִמּוֹ
וְעִם מְנָאֲפִים חֶלְקֶךָ׃
19 פִּיךָ שָׁלַחְתָּ בְרָעָה
וּלְשׁוֹנְךָ תַּצְמִיד מִרְמָה׃
20 תֵּשֵׁב בְּאָחִיךָ תְדַבֵּר
בְּבֶן־אִמְּךָ תִּתֶּן־דֹּפִי׃
21 אֵלֶּה עָשִׂיתָ ׀ וְהֶחֱרַשְׁתִּי
דִּמִּיתָ הֱיוֹת־אֶהְיֶה כָמוֹךָ
אוֹכִיחֲךָ וְאֶעֶרְכָה לְעֵינֶיךָ׃
22 בִּינוּ־נָא זֹאת שֹׁכְחֵי אֱלוֹהַּ
פֶּן־אֶטְרֹף וְאֵין מַצִּיל׃
23 זֹבֵחַ תּוֹדָה יְכַבְּדָנְנִי
וְשָׂם דֶּרֶךְ אַרְאֶנּוּ בְּיֵשַׁע אֱלֹהִים׃

נא לַמְנַצֵּחַ מִזְמוֹר לְדָוִד׃
2 בְּבוֹא־אֵלָיו נָתָן הַנָּבִיא כַּאֲשֶׁר־בָּא אֶל־בַּת־
שָׁבַע׃
3 חָנֵּנִי אֱלֹהִים כְּחַסְדֶּךָ
כְּרֹב רַחֲמֶיךָ מְחֵה פְשָׁעָי׃
4 הַרְבֵּהֿ כַּבְּסֵנִי מֵעֲוֹנִי
וּמֵחַטָּאתִי טַהֲרֵנִי׃
5 כִּי־פְשָׁעַי אֲנִי אֵדָע
וְחַטָּאתִי נֶגְדִּי תָמִיד׃
6 לְךָ לְבַדְּךָ ׀ חָטָאתִי וְהָרַע בְּעֵינֶיךָ עָשִׂיתִי

נא 4 הֶרֶב

That You may be found just when You speak,
And blameless when You judge.

לְמַעַן תִּצְדַּק בְּדָבְרֶךָ תִּזְכֶּה בְשָׁפְטֶךָ:

7 הֵן־בְּעָווֹן חוֹלָלְתִּי
וּבְחֵטְא יֶחֱמַתְנִי אִמִּי:

5 Behold, I was brought forth in iniquity,
And in sin my mother conceived me.

8 הֵן־אֱמֶת חָפַצְתָּ בַטֻּחוֹת
וּבְסָתֻם חָכְמָה תוֹדִיעֵנִי:

6 Behold, You desire truth in the inward parts,
And in the hidden *part* You will make me to
   know wisdom.

9 תְּחַטְּאֵנִי בְאֵזוֹב וְאֶטְהָר
תְּכַבְּסֵנִי וּמִשֶּׁלֶג אַלְבִּין:

7 Purge me with hyssop, and I shall be clean;
Wash me, and I shall be whiter than snow.

10 תַּשְׁמִיעֵנִי שָׂשׂוֹן וְשִׂמְחָה
תָּגֵלְנָה עֲצָמוֹת דִּכִּיתָ:

8 Make me hear joy and gladness,
That the bones You have broken may rejoice.

11 הַסְתֵּר פָּנֶיךָ מֵחֲטָאָי
וְכָל־עֲוֹנֹתַי מְחֵה:

9 Hide Your face from my sins,
And blot out all my iniquities.

12 לֵב טָהוֹר בְּרָא־לִי אֱלֹהִים
וְרוּחַ נָכוֹן חַדֵּשׁ בְּקִרְבִּי:

10 Create in me a clean heart, O God,
And renew a steadfast spirit within me.

13 אַל־תַּשְׁלִיכֵנִי מִלְּפָנֶיךָ
וְרוּחַ קָדְשְׁךָ אַל־תִּקַּח מִמֶּנִּי:

11 Do not cast me away from Your presence,
And do not take Your Holy Spirit from me.

14 הָשִׁיבָה לִּי שְׂשׂוֹן יִשְׁעֶךָ
וְרוּחַ נְדִיבָה תִסְמְכֵנִי:

12 Restore to me the joy of Your salvation,
And uphold me *by Your* generous Spirit.

15 אֲלַמְּדָה פֹשְׁעִים דְּרָכֶיךָ
וְחַטָּאִים אֵלֶיךָ יָשׁוּבוּ:

13 *Then* I will teach transgressors Your ways,
And sinners shall be converted to You.

16 הַצִּילֵנִי מִדָּמִים אֱלֹהִים אֱלֹהֵי תְּשׁוּעָתִי
תְּרַנֵּן לְשׁוֹנִי צִדְקָתֶךָ:

14 Deliver me from the guilt of bloodshed, O
   God,
The God of my salvation,
And my tongue shall sing aloud of Your
   righteousness.

17 אֲדֹנָי שְׂפָתַי תִּפְתָּח
וּפִי יַגִּיד תְּהִלָּתֶךָ:

15 O Lord, open my lips,
And my mouth shall show forth Your praise.

18 כִּי לֹא־תַחְפֹּץ זֶבַח וְאֶתֵּנָה
עוֹלָה לֹא תִרְצֶה:

16 For You do not desire sacrifice, or else I would
   give *it;*
You do not delight in burnt offering.

19 זִבְחֵי אֱלֹהִים רוּחַ נִשְׁבָּרָה לֵב־נִשְׁבָּר וְנִדְכֶּה
אֱלֹהִים לֹא תִבְזֶה:

17 The sacrifices of God *are* a broken spirit,
A broken and a contrite heart—
These, O God, You will not despise.

20 הֵיטִיבָה בִרְצוֹנְךָ אֶת־צִיּוֹן
תִּבְנֶה חוֹמוֹת יְרוּשָׁלָ͏ִם:

18 Do good in Your good pleasure to Zion;
Build the walls of Jerusalem.

21 אָז תַּחְפֹּץ זִבְחֵי־צֶדֶק עוֹלָה וְכָלִיל
אָז יַעֲלוּ עַל־מִזְבַּחֲךָ פָרִים:

19 Then You shall be pleased with the sacrifices of
   righteousness,
With burnt offering and whole burnt offering;
Then they shall offer bulls on Your altar.

נב לַמְנַצֵּחַ מַשְׂכִּיל לְדָוִד:

2 בְּבוֹא דּוֹאֵג הָאֲדֹמִי וַיַּגֵּד לְשָׁאוּל וַיֹּאמֶר לוֹ
בָּא דָוִד אֶל־בֵּית אֲחִימֶלֶךְ:

52 To the Chief Musician. A Contemplation of David
when Doeg the Edomite went and told Saul, and said to
him, "David has gone to the house of Ahimelech."
Why do you boast in evil, O mighty man?
The goodness of God *endures* continually.

3 מַה־תִּתְהַלֵּל בְּרָעָה הַגִּבּוֹר
חֶסֶד אֵל כָּל־הַיּוֹם:

2 Your tongue devises destruction,
Like a sharp razor, working deceitfully.

4 הַוּוֹת תַּחְשֹׁב לְשׁוֹנֶךָ
כְּתַעַר מְלֻטָּשׁ עֹשֵׂה רְמִיָּה:

3 You love evil more than good,
Lying rather than speaking righteousness.
               Selah

5 אָהַבְתָּ רָּע מִטּוֹב
שֶׁקֶר מִדַּבֵּר צֶדֶק סֶלָה:

4 You love all devouring words,
  You deceitful tongue.

5 God shall likewise destroy you forever;
  He shall take you away, and pluck you out of
      your dwelling place,
  And uproot you from the land of the living.
                                    Selah

6 The righteous also shall see and fear,
  And shall laugh at him, *saying,*

7 "Here is the man *who* did not make God his
      strength,
  But trusted in the abundance of his riches,
  And strengthened himself in his wickedness."

8 But I *am* like a green olive tree in the house of
      God;
  I trust in the mercy of God forever and ever.

9 I will praise You forever,
  Because You have done *it;*
  And in the presence of Your saints
  I will wait on Your name, for *it is* good.

6 אָהַבְתָּ כָל־דִּבְרֵי־בָלַע
לְשׁוֹן מִרְמָה:

7 גַּם־אֵל יִתָּצְךָ לָנֶצַח
יַחְתְּךָ וְיִסָּחֲךָ מֵאֹהֶל
וְשֵׁרֶשְׁךָ מֵאֶרֶץ חַיִּים סֶלָה:

8 וְיִרְאוּ צַדִּיקִים וְיִירָאוּ
וְעָלָיו יִשְׂחָקוּ:

9 הִנֵּה הַגֶּבֶר
לֹא יָשִׂים אֱלֹהִים מָעוּזּוֹ
וַיִּבְטַח בְּרֹב עָשְׁרוֹ
יָעֹז בְּהַוָּתוֹ:

10 וַאֲנִי כְּזַיִת רַעֲנָן
בְּבֵית אֱלֹהִים
בָּטַחְתִּי בְחֶסֶד־אֱלֹהִים עוֹלָם וָעֶד:

11 אוֹדְךָ לְעוֹלָם כִּי עָשִׂיתָ
וַאֲקַוֶּה שִׁמְךָ כִי־טוֹב נֶגֶד חֲסִידֶיךָ:

53 To the Chief Musician. Set to "Mahalath." A
Contemplation of David.
      The fool has said in his heart,
  "*There is* no God."
      They are corrupt, and have done abominable
          iniquity;
  There is none who does good.

2 God looks down from heaven upon the
      children of men,
  To see if there are *any* who understand, who
      seek God.

3 Every one of them has turned aside;
  They have together become corrupt;
  There is none who does good,
  No, not one.

4 Have the workers of iniquity no knowledge,
  Who eat up my people *as* they eat bread,
  And do not call upon God?

5 There they are in great fear
  Where no fear was,
  For God has scattered the bones of him who
      encamps against you;
  You have put *them* to shame,
  Because God has despised them.

6 Oh, that the salvation of Israel would come out
      of Zion!
  When God brings back the captivity of His
      people,
  Let Jacob rejoice *and* Israel be glad.

נג לַמְנַצֵּחַ עַל־מָחֲלַת מַשְׂכִּיל לְדָוִד:

2 אָמַר נָבָל בְּלִבּוֹ
אֵין אֱלֹהִים
הִשְׁחִיתוּ וְהִתְעִיבוּ עָוֶל
אֵין עֹשֵׂה־טוֹב:

3 אֱלֹהִים
מִשָּׁמַיִם הִשְׁקִיף עַל־בְּנֵי אָדָם
לִרְאוֹת הֲיֵשׁ מַשְׂכִּיל
דֹּרֵשׁ אֶת־אֱלֹהִים:

4 כֻּלּוֹ סָג יַחְדָּו נֶאֱלָחוּ
אֵין עֹשֵׂה־טוֹב אֵין גַּם־אֶחָד:

5 הֲלֹא יָדְעוּ פֹּעֲלֵי אָוֶן
אֹכְלֵי עַמִּי אָכְלוּ לֶחֶם אֱלֹהִים לֹא קָרָאוּ:

6 שָׁם פָּחֲדוּ־פַחַד
לֹא־הָיָה פָחַד
כִּי־אֱלֹהִים פִּזַּר עַצְמוֹת חֹנָךְ
הֱבִשֹׁתָה כִּי־אֱלֹהִים מְאָסָם:

7 מִי יִתֵּן מִצִּיּוֹן
יְשֻׁעוֹת יִשְׂרָאֵל
בְּשׁוּב אֱלֹהִים שְׁבוּת עַמּוֹ
יָגֵל יַעֲקֹב יִשְׂמַח יִשְׂרָאֵל:

54 To the Chief Musician. With stringed instruments.
A Contemplation of David when the Ziphites went and
said to Saul, "Is David not hiding with us?"
    Save me, O God, by Your name,
    And vindicate me by Your strength.
2 Hear my prayer, O God;
    Give ear to the words of my mouth.
3 For strangers have risen up against me,
    And oppressors have sought after my life;
    They have not set God before them.   Selah

4 Behold, God *is* my helper;
    The Lord *is* with those who uphold my life.
5 He will repay my enemies for their evil.
    Cut them off in Your truth.

6 I will freely sacrifice to You;
    I will praise Your name, O LORD, for *it is* good.
7 For He has delivered me out of all trouble;
    And my eye has seen *its desire* upon my
       enemies.

55 To the Chief Musician. With stringed instruments.
A Contemplation of David.
    Give ear to my prayer, O God,
    And do not hide Yourself from my
       supplication.
2 Attend to me, and hear me;
    I am restless in my complaint, and moan
       noisily,
3 Because of the voice of the enemy,
    Because of the oppression of the wicked;
    For they bring down trouble upon me,
    And in wrath they hate me.

4 My heart is severely pained within me,
    And the terrors of death have fallen upon me.
5 Fearfulness and trembling have come upon me,
    And horror has overwhelmed me.
6 So I said, "Oh, that I had wings like a dove!
    I would fly away and be at rest.
7 Indeed, I would wander far off,
    And remain in the wilderness.   Selah
8 I would hasten my escape
    From the windy storm *and* tempest."

9 Destroy, O Lord, *and* divide their tongues,
    For I have seen violence and strife in the city.
10 Day and night they go around it on its walls;
    Iniquity and trouble *are* also in the midst of it.
11 Destruction *is* in its midst;
    Oppression and deceit do not depart from its
       streets.

12 For *it is* not an enemy *who* reproaches me;
    Then I could bear *it.*

נד לַמְנַצֵּחַ בִּנְגִינֹת מַשְׂכִּיל לְדָוִד׃
2 בְּבֹא הַזִּיפִים וַיֹּאמְרוּ לְשָׁאוּל
הֲלֹא דָוִד מִסְתַּתֵּר עִמָּנוּ׃
3 אֱלֹהִים בְּשִׁמְךָ הוֹשִׁיעֵנִי
וּבִגְבוּרָתְךָ תְדִינֵנִי׃
4 אֱלֹהִים שְׁמַע תְּפִלָּתִי
הַאֲזִינָה לְאִמְרֵי־פִי׃
5 כִּי זָרִים ׀ קָמוּ עָלַי וְעָרִיצִים בִּקְשׁוּ נַפְשִׁי
לֹא שָׂמוּ אֱלֹהִים לְנֶגְדָּם סֶלָה׃
6 הִנֵּה אֱלֹהִים עֹזֵר לִי
אֲדֹנָי בְּסֹמְכֵי נַפְשִׁי׃
7 יָשׁוֹב הָרַע לְשֹׁרְרָי
בַּאֲמִתְּךָ הַצְמִיתֵם׃
8 בִּנְדָבָה אֶזְבְּחָה־לָּךְ
אוֹדֶה שִּׁמְךָ יְהֹוָה כִּי־טוֹב׃
9 כִּי מִכָּל־צָרָה הִצִּילָנִי
וּבְאֹיְבַי רָאֲתָה עֵינִי׃

נה לַמְנַצֵּחַ בִּנְגִינֹת מַשְׂכִּיל לְדָוִד׃
2 הַאֲזִינָה אֱלֹהִים תְּפִלָּתִי
וְאַל־תִּתְעַלַּם מִתְּחִנָּתִי׃
3 הַקְשִׁיבָה לִּי וַעֲנֵנִי
אָרִיד בְּשִׂיחִי וְאָהִימָה׃
4 מִקּוֹל אוֹיֵב מִפְּנֵי עָקַת רָשָׁע
כִּי־יָמִיטוּ עָלַי אָוֶן וּבְאַף יִשְׂטְמוּנִי׃
5 לִבִּי יָחִיל בְּקִרְבִּי
וְאֵימוֹת מָוֶת נָפְלוּ עָלָי׃
6 יִרְאָה וָרַעַד יָבֹא בִי
וַתְּכַסֵּנִי פַּלָּצוּת׃
7 וָאֹמַר מִי־יִתֶּן־לִּי אֵבֶר כַּיּוֹנָה
אָעוּפָה וְאֶשְׁכֹּנָה׃
8 הִנֵּה אַרְחִיק נְדֹד
אָלִין בַּמִּדְבָּר סֶלָה׃
9 אָחִישָׁה מִפְלָט לִי
מֵרוּחַ סֹעָה מִסָּעַר׃
10 בַּלַּע אֲדֹנָי פַּלַּג לְשׁוֹנָם
כִּי־רָאִיתִי חָמָס וְרִיב בָּעִיר׃
11 יוֹמָם וָלַיְלָה יְסוֹבְבֻהָ עַל־חוֹמֹתֶיהָ
וְאָוֶן וְעָמָל בְּקִרְבָּהּ׃
12 הַוּוֹת בְּקִרְבָּהּ
וְלֹא־יָמִישׁ מֵרְחֹבָהּ תֹּךְ וּמִרְמָה׃
13 כִּי לֹא־אוֹיֵב יְחָרְפֵנִי וְאֶשָּׂא
נד 7 יָשֻׁב

Nor *is it* one *who* hates me who has exalted
   himself against me;
Then I could hide from him.

13 But *it was* you, a man my equal,
   My companion and my acquaintance.

14 We took sweet counsel together,
   And walked to the house of God in the throng.

15 Let death seize them;
   Let them go down alive into hell,
   For wickedness *is* in their dwellings *and* among
      them.

16 As for me, I will call upon God,
   And the LORD shall save me.

17 Evening and morning and at noon
   I will pray, and cry aloud,
   And He shall hear my voice.

18 He has redeemed my soul in peace from the
      battle *that was* against me,
   For there were many against me.

19 God will hear, and afflict them,
   Even He who abides from of old.   Selah
   Because they do not change,
   Therefore they do not fear God.

20 He has put forth his hands against those who
      were at peace with him;
   He has broken his covenant.

21 *The words* of his mouth were smoother than
      butter,
   But war *was* in his heart;
   His words were softer than oil,
   Yet they *were* drawn swords.

22 Cast your burden on the LORD,
   And He shall sustain you;
   He shall never permit the righteous to be
      moved.

23 But You, O God, shall bring them down to the
      pit of destruction;
   Bloodthirsty and deceitful men shall not live
      out half their days;
   But I will trust in You.

56
To the Chief Musician. Set to "The Silent Dove in
Distant Lands." A Michtam of David when the
Philistines captured him in Gath.

   Be merciful to me, O God, for man would
      swallow me up;
   Fighting all day he oppresses me.

2 My enemies would hound *me* all day,
   For *there are* many who fight against me, O
      Most High.

3 Whenever I am afraid,

לֹא־מְשַׂנְאִי עָלַי הִגְדִּיל
וְאֶסָּתֵר מִמֶּנּוּ׃
וְאַתָּה אֱנוֹשׁ כְּעֶרְכִּי 14
אַלּוּפִי וּמְיֻדָּעִי׃
אֲשֶׁר יַחְדָּו נַמְתִּיק סוֹד 15
בְּבֵית אֱלֹהִים נְהַלֵּךְ בְּרָגֶשׁ׃
יַשִּׁימָוֶת ׀ עָלֵימוֹ יֵרְדוּ שְׁאוֹל חַיִּים 16
כִּי־רָעוֹת בִּמְגוּרָם בְּקִרְבָּם׃
אֲנִי אֶל־אֱלֹהִים אֶקְרָא 17
וַיהֹוָה יוֹשִׁיעֵנִי׃
עֶרֶב וָבֹקֶר וְצָהֳרַיִם אָשִׂיחָה וְאֶהֱמֶה 18
וַיִּשְׁמַע קוֹלִי׃
פָּדָה בְשָׁלוֹם נַפְשִׁי מִקְּרָב־לִי 19
כִּי־בְרַבִּים הָיוּ עִמָּדִי׃
יִשְׁמַע ׀ אֵל ׀ וְיַעֲנֵם 20
וְיֹשֵׁב קֶדֶם סֶלָה
אֲשֶׁר אֵין חֲלִיפוֹת לָמוֹ
וְלֹא יָרְאוּ אֱלֹהִים׃
שָׁלַח יָדָיו בִּשְׁלֹמָיו 21
חִלֵּל בְּרִיתוֹ׃
חָלְקוּ ׀ מַחְמָאֹת פִּיו 22
וּקֲרָב־לִבּוֹ
רַכּוּ דְבָרָיו מִשֶּׁמֶן
וְהֵמָּה פְתִחוֹת׃
הַשְׁלֵךְ עַל־יְהֹוָה ׀ יְהָבְךָ 23
וְהוּא יְכַלְכְּלֶךָ
לֹא־יִתֵּן לְעוֹלָם מוֹט
לַצַּדִּיק׃
וְאַתָּה אֱלֹהִים ׀ 24
תּוֹרִדֵם ׀ לִבְאֵר שַׁחַת
אַנְשֵׁי דָמִים וּמִרְמָה
לֹא־יֶחֱצוּ יְמֵיהֶם
וַאֲנִי אֶבְטַח־בָּךְ׃

נו לַמְנַצֵּחַ ׀ עַל־יוֹנַת אֵלֶם רְחֹקִים
לְדָוִד מִכְתָּם
בֶּאֱחֹז אֹתוֹ פְלִשְׁתִּים בְּגַת׃
חָנֵּנִי אֱלֹהִים כִּי־שְׁאָפַנִי אֱנוֹשׁ 2
כָּל־הַיּוֹם לֹחֵם יִלְחָצֵנִי׃
שָׁאֲפוּ שׁוֹרְרַי כָּל־הַיּוֹם 3
כִּי־רַבִּים לֹחֲמִים לִי מָרוֹם׃
יוֹם אִירָא 4
נה 16 יֵשׁ מָוֶת

I will trust in You.

4 In God (I will praise His word),
In God I have put my trust;
I will not fear.
What can flesh do to me?

5 All day they twist my words;
All their thoughts *are* against me for evil.

6 They gather together,
They hide, they mark my steps,
When they lie in wait for my life.

7 Shall they escape by iniquity?
In anger cast down the peoples, O God!

8 You number my wanderings;
Put my tears into Your bottle;
Are they not in Your book?

9 When I cry out *to You,*
Then my enemies will turn back;
This I know, because God *is* for me.

10 In God (I will praise *His* word),
In the LORD (I will praise *His* word),

11 In God I have put my trust;
I will not be afraid.
What can man do to me?

12 Vows *made* to You *are binding* upon me, O
God;
I will render praises to You,

13 For You have delivered my soul from death.
Have You not *kept* my feet from falling,
That I may walk before God
In the light of the living?

אֲנִי אֵלֶיךָ אֶבְטָח׃

5 בֵּאלֹהִים אֲהַלֵּל דְּבָרוֹ
בֵּאלֹהִים בָּטַחְתִּי לֹא אִירָא
מַה־יַּעֲשֶׂה בָשָׂר לִי׃

6 כָּל־הַיּוֹם דְּבָרַי יְעַצֵּבוּ
עָלַי כָּל־מַחְשְׁבֹתָם לָרָע׃

7 יָגוּרוּ ׀ יִצְפּוֹנוּ הֵמָּה עֲקֵבַי יִשְׁמֹרוּ
כַּאֲשֶׁר קִוּוּ נַפְשִׁי׃

8 עַל־אָוֶן פַּלֶּט־לָמוֹ
בְּאַף עַמִּים ׀ הוֹרֵד אֱלֹהִים׃

9 נֹדִי סָפַרְתָּה אָתָּה
שִׂימָה דִמְעָתִי בְנֹאדֶךָ הֲלֹא בְּסִפְרָתֶךָ׃

10 אָז יָשׁוּבוּ אוֹיְבַי אָחוֹר בְּיוֹם אֶקְרָא
זֶה־יָדַעְתִּי כִּי־אֱלֹהִים לִי׃

11 בֵּאלֹהִים אֲהַלֵּל דָּבָר
בַּיהוָה אֲהַלֵּל דָּבָר׃

12 בֵּאלֹהִים בָּטַחְתִּי לֹא אִירָא
מַה־יַּעֲשֶׂה אָדָם לִי׃

13 עָלַי אֱלֹהִים נְדָרֶיךָ
אֲשַׁלֵּם תּוֹדֹת לָךְ׃

14 כִּי הִצַּלְתָּ נַפְשִׁי מִמָּוֶת
הֲלֹא רַגְלַי מִדֶּחִי
לְהִתְהַלֵּךְ לִפְנֵי אֱלֹהִים
בְּאוֹר הַחַיִּים׃

57 To the Chief Musician. Set to "Do Not Destroy."
A Michtam of David when he fled from Saul into the
cave.

Be merciful to me, O God, be merciful to me!
For my soul trusts in You;
And in the shadow of Your wings I will make
my refuge,
Until *these* calamities have passed by.

2 I will cry out to God Most High,
To God who performs *all things* for me.

3 He shall send from heaven and save me;
He reproaches the one who would swallow me
up.   Selah
God shall send forth His mercy and His truth.

4 My soul *is* among lions;
I lie *among* the sons of men
Who are set on fire,
Whose teeth *are* spears and arrows,
And their tongue a sharp sword.

5 Be exalted, O God, above the heavens;
Let Your glory *be* above all the earth.

נז לַמְנַצֵּחַ אַל־תַּשְׁחֵת לְדָוִד מִכְתָּם
בְּבָרְחוֹ מִפְּנֵי־שָׁאוּל בַּמְּעָרָה׃

2 חָנֵּנִי אֱלֹהִים ׀ חָנֵּנִי
כִּי בְךָ חָסָיָה נַפְשִׁי
וּבְצֵל־כְּנָפֶיךָ אֶחְסֶה
עַד יַעֲבֹר הַוּוֹת׃

3 אֶקְרָא לֵאלֹהִים עֶלְיוֹן
לָאֵל גֹּמֵר עָלָי׃

4 יִשְׁלַח מִשָּׁמַיִם ׀ וְיוֹשִׁיעֵנִי חֵרֵף שֹׁאֲפִי סֶלָה
יִשְׁלַח אֱלֹהִים חַסְדּוֹ וַאֲמִתּוֹ׃

5 נַפְשִׁי ׀ בְּתוֹךְ לְבָאִם
אֶשְׁכְּבָה לֹהֲטִים
בְּנֵי־אָדָם שִׁנֵּיהֶם חֲנִית וְחִצִּים
וּלְשׁוֹנָם חֶרֶב חַדָּה׃

6 רוּמָה עַל־הַשָּׁמַיִם אֱלֹהִים
עַל כָּל־הָאָרֶץ כְּבוֹדֶךָ׃

6   They have prepared a net for my steps;
     My soul is bowed down;
     They have dug a pit before me;
     Into the midst of it they *themselves* have fallen.
                    Selah

7   My heart is steadfast, O God, my heart is
       steadfast;
     I will sing and give praise.
8   Awake, my glory!
     Awake, lute and harp!
     I will awaken the dawn.
9   I will praise You, O Lord, among the peoples;
     I will sing to You among the nations.
10   For Your mercy reaches unto the heavens,
     And Your truth unto the clouds.
11   Be exalted, O God, above the heavens;
     Let Your glory *be* above all the earth.

58 To the Chief Musician. Set to "Do Not Destroy."
A Michtam of David.

     Do you indeed speak righteousness, you silent
       ones?
     Do you judge uprightly, you sons of men?
2   No, in heart you work wickedness;
     You weigh out the violence of your hands in
       the earth.
3   The wicked are estranged from the womb;
     They go astray as soon as they are born,
       speaking lies.
4   Their poison *is* like the poison of a serpent;
     They are like the deaf cobra *that* stops its ear,
5   Which will not heed the voice of charmers,
     Charming ever so skillfully.
6   Break their teeth in their mouth, O God!
     Break out the fangs of the young lions, O
       LORD!
7   Let them flow away as waters *which* run
       continually;
     When he bends *his* bow,
     Let his arrows be as if cut in pieces.
8   *Let them be* like a snail which melts away as it
       goes,
     Like a stillborn child of a woman, that they
       may not see the sun.
9   Before your pots can feel *the burning* thorns,
     He shall take them away as with a whirlwind,
     As in His living and burning wrath.
10   The righteous shall rejoice when he sees the
       vengeance;
     He shall wash his feet in the blood of the
       wicked,

רֶשֶׁת ׀ הֵכִינוּ לִפְעָמַי 7
כָּפַף נַפְשִׁי
כָּרוּ לְפָנַי שִׁיחָה
נָפְלוּ בְתוֹכָהּ סֶלָה׃

נָכוֹן לִבִּי אֱלֹהִים נָכוֹן לִבִּי 8
אָשִׁירָה וַאֲזַמֵּרָה׃

עוּרָה כְבוֹדִי עוּרָה הַנֵּבֶל וְכִנּוֹר 9
אָעִירָה שָּׁחַר׃

אוֹדְךָ בָעַמִּים ׀ אֲדֹנָי 10
אֲזַמֶּרְךָ בַּל־אֻמִּים׃

כִּי־גָדֹל עַד־שָׁמַיִם חַסְדֶּךָ 11
וְעַד־שְׁחָקִים אֲמִתֶּךָ׃

רוּמָה עַל־שָׁמַיִם אֱלֹהִים 12
עַל כָּל־הָאָרֶץ כְּבוֹדֶךָ׃

נח לַמְנַצֵּחַ אַל־תַּשְׁחֵת לְדָוִד מִכְתָּם׃

הַאֻמְנָם אֵלֶם צֶדֶק תְּדַבֵּרוּן 2
מֵישָׁרִים תִּשְׁפְּטוּ בְּנֵי אָדָם׃

אַף־בְּלֵב עוֹלֹת תִּפְעָלוּן 3
בָּאָרֶץ חֲמַס יְדֵיכֶם תְּפַלֵּסוּן׃

זֹרוּ רְשָׁעִים מֵרָחֶם 4
תָּעוּ מִבֶּטֶן דֹּבְרֵי כָזָב׃

חֲמַת־לָמוֹ כִּדְמוּת חֲמַת־נָחָשׁ 5
כְּמוֹ־פֶתֶן חֵרֵשׁ יַאְטֵם אָזְנוֹ׃

אֲשֶׁר לֹא־יִשְׁמַע לְקוֹל מְלַחֲשִׁים 6
חוֹבֵר חֲבָרִים מְחֻכָּם׃

אֱלֹהִים הֲרָס־שִׁנֵּימוֹ בְּפִימוֹ 7
מַלְתְּעוֹת כְּפִירִים נְתֹץ ׀ יְהוָה׃

יִמָּאֲסוּ כְמוֹ־מַיִם 8
יִתְהַלְּכוּ־לָמוֹ
יִדְרֹךְ חִצָּו
כְּמוֹ יִתְמֹלָלוּ׃

כְּמוֹ שַׁבְּלוּל תֶּמֶס יַהֲלֹךְ 9
נֵפֶל אֵשֶׁת בַּל־חָזוּ שָׁמֶשׁ׃

בְּטֶרֶם יָבִינוּ סִּירֹתֵיכֶם אָטָד 10
כְּמוֹ־חַי כְּמוֹ־חָרוֹן יִשְׂעָרֶנּוּ׃

יִשְׂמַח צַדִּיק כִּי־חָזָה נָקָם 11
פְּעָמָיו יִרְחַץ בְּדַם הָרָשָׁע׃

11　So that men will say,
　　"Surely *there is* a reward for the righteous;
　　Surely He is God who judges in the earth."

59 To the Chief Musician. Set to "Do Not Destroy."
A Michtam of David when Saul sent men, and they
watched the house in order to kill him.
　　Deliver me from my enemies, O my God;
　　Defend me from those who rise up against me.
2　Deliver me from the workers of iniquity,
　　And save me from bloodthirsty men.

3　For look, they lie in wait for my life;
　　The mighty gather against me,
　　Not *for* my transgression nor *for* my sin, O
　　　　LORD.
4　They run and prepare themselves through no
　　　　fault *of* mine.

　　Awake to help me, and behold!
5　You therefore, O LORD God of hosts, the God
　　　　of Israel,
　　Awake to punish all the nations;
　　Do not be merciful to any wicked
　　　　transgressors.　　　　　　　　　Selah

6　At evening they return,
　　They growl like a dog,
　　And go all around the city.
7　Indeed, they belch with their mouth;
　　Swords *are* in their lips;
　　For *they say,* "Who hears?"

8　But You, O LORD, shall laugh at them;
　　You shall have all the nations in derision.
9　I will wait for You, O You his Strength;
　　For God *is* my defense.
10　My God of mercy shall come to meet me;
　　God shall let me see *my desire* on my enemies.

11　Do not slay them, lest my people forget;
　　Scatter them by Your power,
　　And bring them down,
　　O Lord our shield.
12　*For* the sin of their mouth *and* the words of
　　　　their lips,
　　Let them even be taken in their pride,
　　And for the cursing and lying *which* they speak.
13　Consume *them* in wrath, consume *them,*
　　That they *may* not *be;*
　　And let them know that God rules in Jacob
　　To the ends of the earth.　　　　　Selah

14　And at evening they return,
　　They growl like a dog,
　　And go all around the city.
15　They wander up and down for food,

12　וְיֹאמַר אָדָם אַךְ־פְּרִי לַצַּדִּיק
　　אַךְ יֵשׁ־אֱלֹהִים שֹׁפְטִים בָּאָרֶץ׃

נט לַמְנַצֵּחַ אַל־תַּשְׁחֵת לְדָוִד מִכְתָּם בִּשְׁלֹחַ שָׁאוּל
　　וַיִּשְׁמְרוּ אֶת־הַבַּיִת לַהֲמִיתוֹ׃
2　הַצִּילֵנִי מֵאֹיְבַי ׀ אֱלֹהָי
　　מִמִּתְקוֹמְמַי תְּשַׂגְּבֵנִי׃
3　הַצִּילֵנִי מִפֹּעֲלֵי אָוֶן
　　וּמֵאַנְשֵׁי דָמִים הוֹשִׁיעֵנִי׃
4　כִּי הִנֵּה אָרְבוּ לְנַפְשִׁי
　　יָגוּרוּ עָלַי עַזִּים
　　לֹא־פִשְׁעִי וְלֹא־חַטָּאתִי יְהוָה׃
5　בְּלִי־עָוֹן יְרוּצוּן וְיִכּוֹנָנוּ
　　עוּרָה לִקְרָאתִי וּרְאֵה׃
6　וְאַתָּה יְהוָה־אֱלֹהִים ׀ צְבָאוֹת אֱלֹהֵי יִשְׂרָאֵל
　　הָקִיצָה לִפְקֹד כָּל־הַגּוֹיִם
　　אַל־תָּחֹן כָּל־בֹּגְדֵי אָוֶן סֶלָה׃
7　יָשׁוּבוּ לָעֶרֶב יֶהֱמוּ כַכָּלֶב
　　וִיסוֹבְבוּ עִיר׃
8　הִנֵּה ׀ יַבִּיעוּן בְּפִיהֶם חֲרָבוֹת בְּשִׂפְתוֹתֵיהֶם
　　כִּי־מִי שֹׁמֵעַ׃
9　וְאַתָּה יְהוָה תִּשְׂחַק־לָמוֹ
　　תִּלְעַג לְכָל־גּוֹיִם׃
10　עֻזּוֹ אֵלֶיךָ אֶשְׁמֹרָה
　　כִּי־אֱלֹהִים מִשְׂגַּבִּי׃
11　אֱלֹהֵי חַסְדּוֹ° יְקַדְּמֵנִי
　　אֱלֹהִים יַרְאֵנִי בְשֹׁרְרָי׃
12　אַל־תַּהַרְגֵם ׀ פֶּן־יִשְׁכְּחוּ עַמִּי
　　הֲנִיעֵמוֹ בְחֵילְךָ וְהוֹרִידֵמוֹ
　　מָגִנֵּנוּ אֲדֹנָי׃
13　חַטַּאת־פִּימוֹ
　　דְּבַר־שְׂפָתֵימוֹ
　　וְיִלָּכְדוּ בִגְאוֹנָם
　　וּמֵאָלָה וּמִכַּחַשׁ יְסַפֵּרוּ׃
14　כַּלֵּה בְחֵמָה
　　כַּלֵּה וְאֵינֵמוֹ
　　וְיֵדְעוּ כִּי־אֱלֹהִים מֹשֵׁל בְּיַעֲקֹב
　　לְאַפְסֵי הָאָרֶץ סֶלָה׃
15　וְיָשֻׁבוּ לָעֶרֶב יֶהֱמוּ כַכָּלֶב
　　וִיסוֹבְבוּ עִיר׃
16　הֵמָּה יְנִועוּן° לֶאֱכֹל

נם 11 חַסְדִּי　16 יְנִיעוּן

And howl if they are not satisfied.

16   But I will sing of Your power;
     Yes, I will sing aloud of Your mercy in the
       morning;
     For You have been my defense
     And refuge in the day of my trouble.
17   To You, O my Strength, I will sing praises;
     For God *is* my defense,
     My God of mercy.

אִם־לֹא יִשְׂבְּעוּ וַיָּלִינוּ׃
וַאֲנִי ׀ אָשִׁיר עֻזֶּךָ   17
וַאֲרַגֵּן לַבֹּקֶר חַסְדֶּךָ
כִּי־הָיִיתָ מִשְׂגָּב לִי
וּמָנוֹס בְּיוֹם צַר־לִי׃
עֻזִּי אֵלֶיךָ אֲזַמֵּרָה   18
כִּי־אֱלֹהִים מִשְׂגַּבִּי אֱלֹהֵי חַסְדִּי׃

60 To the Chief Musician. Set to "Lily of the
Testimony." A Michtam of David. For teaching. When
he fought against Mesopotamia and Syria of Zobah, and
Joab returned and killed twelve thousand Edomites in
the Valley of Salt.

     O God, You have cast us off;
     You have broken us down;
     You have been displeased;
     Oh, restore us again!
2   You have made the earth tremble;
     You have broken it;
     Heal its breaches, for it is shaking.
3   You have shown Your people hard things;
     You have made us drink the wine of confusion.

4   You have given a banner to those who fear
       You,
     That it may be displayed because of the truth.
                    Selah

5   That Your beloved may be delivered,
     Save *with* Your right hand, and hear me.

6   God has spoken in His holiness:
     "I will rejoice;
     I will divide Shechem
     And measure out the Valley of Succoth.
7   Gilead *is* Mine, and Manasseh *is* Mine;
     Ephraim also *is* the helmet for My head;
     Judah *is* My lawgiver.
8   Moab *is* My washpot;
     Over Edom I will cast My shoe;
     Philistia, shout in triumph because of Me."

9   Who will bring me *to* the strong city?
     Who will lead me to Edom?
10 *Is it* not You, O God, *who* cast us off?
     And You, O God, *who* did not go out with our
       armies?
11 Give us help from trouble,
     For the help of man *is* useless.
12 Through God we will do valiantly,
     For *it is* He *who* shall tread down our enemies.

ס לַמְנַצֵּחַ עַל־שׁוּשַׁן עֵדוּת
מִכְתָּם לְדָוִד לְלַמֵּד׃
בְּהַצּוֹתוֹ ׀ אֶת אֲרַם נַהֲרַיִם   2
וְאֶת־אֲרַם צוֹבָה
וַיָּשָׁב יוֹאָב וַיַּךְ אֶת־אֱדוֹם בְּגֵיא־מֶלַח
שְׁנֵים עָשָׂר אָלֶף׃
אֱלֹהִים זְנַחְתָּנוּ פְרַצְתָּנוּ   3
אָנַפְתָּ תְּשׁוֹבֵב לָנוּ׃
הִרְעַשְׁתָּה אֶרֶץ פְּצַמְתָּהּ   4
רְפָה שְׁבָרֶיהָ כִי־מָטָה׃
הִרְאִיתָה עַמְּךָ קָשָׁה   5
הִשְׁקִיתָנוּ יַיִן תַּרְעֵלָה׃
נָתַתָּה לִּירֵאֶיךָ נֵּס לְהִתְנוֹסֵס   6
מִפְּנֵי קֹשֶׁט סֶלָה׃
לְמַעַן יֵחָלְצוּן יְדִידֶיךָ   7
הוֹשִׁיעָה יְמִינְךָ וַעֲנֵנִי׃
אֱלֹהִים ׀ דִּבֶּר בְּקָדְשׁוֹ אֶעְלֹזָה   8
אֲחַלְּקָה שְׁכֶם וְעֵמֶק סֻכּוֹת אֲמַדֵּד׃
לִי גִלְעָד ׀ וְלִי מְנַשֶּׁה וְאֶפְרַיִם מָעוֹז רֹאשִׁי   9
יְהוּדָה מְחֹקְקִי׃
מוֹאָב ׀ סִיר רַחְצִי עַל־אֱדוֹם אַשְׁלִיךְ נַעֲלִי   10
עָלַי פְּלֶשֶׁת הִתְרֹעָעִי׃
מִי יֹבִלֵנִי עִיר מָצוֹר   11
מִי נָחַנִי עַד־אֱדוֹם׃
הֲלֹא־אַתָּה אֱלֹהִים זְנַחְתָּנוּ   12
וְלֹא־תֵצֵא אֱלֹהִים בְּצִבְאוֹתֵינוּ׃
הָבָה־לָּנוּ עֶזְרָת מִצָּר   13
וְשָׁוְא תְּשׁוּעַת אָדָם׃
בֵּאלֹהִים נַעֲשֶׂה־חָיִל   14
וְהוּא יָבוּס צָרֵינוּ׃

61 To the Chief Musician. On a stringed instrument.
A Psalm of David.

סא לַמְנַצֵּחַ ׀ עַל־נְגִינַת לְדָוִד׃

ס   7 וְעַנֵּנִי

Hear my cry, O God;
Attend to my prayer.
2 From the end of the earth I will cry to You,
When my heart is overwhelmed;
Lead me to the rock that is higher than I.

3 For You have been a shelter for me,
A strong tower from the enemy.
4 I will abide in Your tabernacle forever;
I will trust in the shelter of Your wings.
                      Selah

5 For You, O God, have heard my vows;
You have given *me* the heritage of those who
     fear Your name.
6 You will prolong the king's life,
His years as many generations.
7 He shall abide before God forever.
Oh, prepare mercy and truth, *which* may
     preserve him!

8 So I will sing praise to Your name forever,
That I may daily perform my vows.

62 To the Chief Musician. To Jeduthun. A Psalm of
David.
Truly my soul silently *waits* for God;
From Him *comes* my salvation.

2 He only *is* my rock and my salvation;
He is my defense;
I shall not be greatly moved.

3 How long will you attack a man?
You shall be slain, all of you,
Like a leaning wall and a tottering fence.
4 They only consult to cast *him* down from his
     high position;
They delight in lies;
They bless with their mouth,
But they curse inwardly.   Selah

5 My soul, wait silently for God alone,
For my expectation *is* from Him.
6 He only *is* my rock and my salvation;
He is my defense;
I shall not be moved.
7 In God *is* my salvation and my glory;
The rock of my strength,
And my refuge, *is* in God.

8 Trust in Him at all times, you people;
Pour out your heart before Him;
God *is* a refuge for us.   Selah
9 Surely men of low degree *are* a vapor,
Men of high degree *are* a lie;
If they are weighed on the scales,
They *are* altogether *lighter* than vapor.

2 שִׁמְעָה אֱלֹהִים רִנָּתִי
הַקְשִׁיבָה תְּפִלָּתִי:
3 מִקְצֵה הָאָרֶץ ׀ אֵלֶיךָ אֶקְרָא בַּעֲטֹף לִבִּי
בְּצוּר־יָרוּם מִמֶּנִּי תַנְחֵנִי:
4 כִּי־הָיִיתָ מַחְסֶה לִי
מִגְדַּל־עֹז מִפְּנֵי אוֹיֵב:
5 אָגוּרָה בְאָהָלְךָ עוֹלָמִים
אֶחֱסֶה בְסֵתֶר כְּנָפֶיךָ סֶּלָה:
6 כִּי־אַתָּה אֱלֹהִים שָׁמַעְתָּ לִנְדָרַי
נָתַתָּ יְרֻשַּׁת יִרְאֵי שְׁמֶךָ:
7 יָמִים עַל־יְמֵי־מֶלֶךְ תּוֹסִיף
שְׁנוֹתָיו כְּמוֹ־דֹר וָדֹר:
8 יֵשֵׁב עוֹלָם לִפְנֵי אֱלֹהִים
חֶסֶד וֶאֱמֶת מַן יִנְצְרֻהוּ:
9 כֵּן אֲזַמְּרָה שִׁמְךָ לָעַד
לְשַׁלְּמִי נְדָרַי יוֹם ׀ יוֹם:

סב לַמְנַצֵּחַ עַל־יְדוּתוּן
מִזְמוֹר לְדָוִד:
2 אַךְ אֶל־אֱלֹהִים דּוּמִיָּה נַפְשִׁי
מִמֶּנּוּ יְשׁוּעָתִי:
3 אַךְ־הוּא צוּרִי וִישׁוּעָתִי
מִשְׂגַּבִּי לֹא־אֶמּוֹט רַבָּה:
4 עַד־אָנָה ׀ תְּהוֹתְתוּ עַל־אִישׁ
תְּרָצְּחוּ כֻלְּכֶם
כְּקִיר נָטוּי
גָּדֵר הַדְּחוּיָה:
5 אַךְ מִשְּׂאֵתוֹ ׀ יָעֲצוּ לְהַדִּיחַ
יִרְצוּ כָזָב
בְּפִיו יְבָרֵכוּ
וּבְקִרְבָּם יְקַלְלוּ־סֶלָה:
6 אַךְ לֵאלֹהִים דּוֹמִּי נַפְשִׁי
כִּי־מִמֶּנּוּ תִּקְוָתִי:
7 אַךְ־הוּא צוּרִי וִישׁוּעָתִי
מִשְׂגַּבִּי לֹא אֶמּוֹט:
8 עַל־אֱלֹהִים יִשְׁעִי וּכְבוֹדִי
צוּר־עֻזִּי מַחְסִי בֵּאלֹהִים:
9 בִּטְחוּ בוֹ בְכָל־עֵת ׀ עָם
שִׁפְכוּ־לְפָנָיו לְבַבְכֶם
אֱלֹהִים מַחֲסֶה־לָּנוּ סֶלָה:
10 אַךְ ׀ הֶבֶל בְּנֵי־אָדָם
כָּזָב בְּנֵי אִישׁ בְּמֹאזְנַיִם לַעֲלוֹת
הֵמָּה מֵהֶבֶל יָחַד:

10 Do not trust in oppression,
    Nor vainly hope in robbery;
    If riches increase,
    Do not set *your* heart *on them.*

11 God has spoken once,
    Twice I have heard this:
    That power *belongs* to God.

12 Also to You, O Lord, *belongs* mercy;
    For You render to each one according to his
       work.

אַל־תִּבְטְח֪וּ בְעֹ֡שֶׁק 11
וּבְגָזֵ֗ל אַל־תֶּ֫הְבָּ֥לוּ
חַ֤יִל ׀ כִּֽי־יָנ֑וּב
אַל־תָּשִׁ֥יתוּ לֵֽב׃

אַחַ֤ת ׀ דִּבֶּ֬ר אֱלֹהִ֗ים שְׁתַּֽיִם־ז֥וּ שָׁמָ֑עְתִּי 12
כִּ֤י עֹ֝֗ז לֵֽאלֹהִֽים׃

וּֽלְךָ־אֲדֹנָ֥י חָ֑סֶד 13
כִּֽי־אַתָּ֤ה תְשַׁלֵּ֖ם לְאִ֣ישׁ כְּמַֽעֲשֵֽׂהוּ׃

63 A Psalm of David when he was in the wilderness of
Judah.
    O God, You *are* my God;
    Early will I seek You;
    My soul thirsts for You;
    My flesh longs for You
    In a dry and thirsty land
    Where there is no water.

2   So I have looked for You in the sanctuary,
    To see Your power and Your glory.

3   Because Your lovingkindness *is* better than life,
    My lips shall praise You.

4   Thus I will bless You while I live;
    I will lift up my hands in Your name.

5   My soul shall be satisfied as with marrow and
       fatness,
    And my mouth shall praise You with joyful
       lips.

6   When I remember You on my bed,
    I meditate on You in the *night* watches.

7   Because You have been my help,
    Therefore in the shadow of Your wings I will
       rejoice.

8   My soul follows close behind You;
    Your right hand upholds me.

9   But those *who* seek my life, to destroy *it,*
    Shall go into the lower parts of the earth.

10 They shall fall by the sword;
    They shall be a portion for jackals.

11 But the king shall rejoice in God;
    Everyone who swears by Him shall glory;
    But the mouth of those who speak lies shall be
       stopped.

סג מִזְמ֥וֹר לְדָוִ֑ד בִּ֝הְיוֹת֗וֹ בְּמִדְבַּ֥ר יְהוּדָֽה׃

אֱלֹהִ֤ים ׀ אֵלִ֥י אַתָּ֗ה אֲ‍ֽשַׁחֲ֫רֶ֥ךָּ 2
צָמְאָ֬ה לְךָ֨ ׀ נַפְשִׁ֗י כָּמַ֣הּ לְךָ֣ בְשָׂרִ֑י
בְּאֶֽרֶץ־צִיָּ֖ה וְעָיֵ֣ף בְּלִי־מָֽיִם׃

כֵּ֭ן בַּקֹּ֣דֶשׁ חֲזִיתִ֑יךָ 3
לִרְא֥וֹת עֻ֝זְּךָ֗ וּכְבוֹדֶֽךָ׃

כִּי־ט֣וֹב חַ֭סְדְּךָ מֵֽחַיִּ֗ים 4
שְׂפָתַ֥י יְשַׁבְּחֽוּנְךָ׃

כֵּ֭ן אֲבָרֶכְךָ֣ בְחַיָּ֑י 5
בְּ֝שִׁמְךָ֗ אֶשָּׂ֥א כַפָּֽי׃

כְּמ֤וֹ חֵ֣לֶב וָ֭דֶשֶׁן תִּשְׂבַּ֣ע נַפְשִׁ֑י 6
וְשִׂפְתֵ֥י רְ֝נָנ֗וֹת יְהַלֶּל־פִּֽי׃

אִם־זְכַרְתִּ֥יךָ עַל־יְצוּעָ֑י 7
בְּ֝אַשְׁמֻר֗וֹת אֶהְגֶּה־בָּֽךְ׃

כִּֽי־הָיִ֣יתָ עֶזְרָ֣תָה לִּ֑י 8
וּבְצֵ֖ל כְּנָפֶ֣יךָ אֲרַנֵּֽן׃

דָּֽבְקָ֣ה נַפְשִׁ֣י אַחֲרֶ֑יךָ 9
בִּ֝֗י תָּמְכָ֥ה יְמִינֶֽךָ׃

וְהֵ֗מָּה לְ֭שׁוֹאָה יְבַקְשׁ֣וּ נַפְשִׁ֑י 10
יָ֝בֹ֗אוּ בְּֽתַחְתִּיּ֥וֹת הָאָֽרֶץ׃

יַגִּירֻ֥הוּ עַל־יְדֵי־חָ֑רֶב 11
מְנָ֖ת שֻֽׁעָלִ֣ים יִהְיֽוּ׃

וְהַמֶּלֶךְ֮ 12
יִשְׂמַ֪ח בֵּֽאלֹ֫הִ֥ים
יִ֭תְהַלֵּל כָּל־הַנִּשְׁבָּ֣ע בּ֑וֹ
כִּ֥י יִ֝סָּכֵ֗ר פִּ֣י דֽוֹבְרֵי־שָֽׁקֶר׃

64 To the Chief Musician. A Psalm of David.
    Hear my voice, O God, in my meditation;
    Preserve my life from fear of the enemy.

2   Hide me from the secret plots of the wicked,
    From the rebellion of the workers of iniquity,

3   Who sharpen their tongue like a sword,

סד לַמְנַצֵּ֗חַ מִזְמ֥וֹר לְדָוִֽד׃

שְׁמַע־אֱלֹהִ֣ים קוֹלִ֣י בְשִׂיחִ֑י 2
מִפַּ֥חַד א֝וֹיֵ֗ב תִּצֹּ֥ר חַיָּֽי׃

תַּ֭סְתִּירֵנִי מִסּ֣וֹד מְרֵעִ֑ים 3
מֵ֝רִגְשַׁ֗ת פֹּ֣עֲלֵי אָֽוֶן׃

אֲשֶׁ֤ר שָׁנְנ֣וּ כַחֶ֣רֶב לְשׁוֹנָ֑ם 4

And bend *their bows to shoot* their arrows—
bitter words,

⁴ That they may shoot in secret at the blameless;
Suddenly they shoot at him and do not fear.

⁵ They encourage themselves *in* an evil matter;
They talk of laying snares secretly;
They say, "Who will see them?"

⁶ They devise iniquities:
"We have perfected a shrewd scheme."
Both the inward thought and the heart of man
are deep.

⁷ But God shall shoot at them *with* an arrow;
Suddenly they shall be wounded.

⁸ So He will make them stumble over their own
tongue;
All who see them shall flee away.

⁹ All men shall fear,
And shall declare the work of God;
For they shall wisely consider His doing.

¹⁰ The righteous shall be glad in the LORD, and
trust in Him.
And all the upright in heart shall glory.

65 To the Chief Musician. A Psalm of David. A Song.
Praise is awaiting You, O God, in Zion;
And to You the vow shall be performed.

² O You who hear prayer,
To You all flesh will come.

³ Iniquities prevail against me;
As for our transgressions,
You will provide atonement for them.

⁴ Blessed *is the man* You choose,
And cause to approach *You,*
That he may dwell in Your courts.
We shall be satisfied with the goodness of Your
house,
Of Your holy temple.

⁵ *By* awesome deeds in righteousness You will
answer us,
O God of our salvation,
You who are the confidence of all the ends of
the earth,
And of the far-off seas;

⁶ Who established the mountains by His
strength,
Being clothed with power;

⁷ You who still the noise of the seas,
The noise of their waves,
And the tumult of the peoples.

⁸ They also who dwell in the farthest parts are
afraid of Your signs;

דַּרְכוּ חִצָּם דָּבָר מָר׃
לִירוֹת בַּמִּסְתָּרִים תָּם ⁵
פִּתְאֹם יֹרֻהוּ וְלֹא יִירָאוּ׃
יְחַזְּקוּ־לָמוֹ ׀ דָּבָר רָע ⁶
יְסַפְּרוּ לִטְמוֹן מוֹקְשִׁים
אָמְרוּ מִי יִרְאֶה־לָּמוֹ׃
יַחְפְּשׂוּ־עוֹלֹת ⁷
תַּמְנוּ חֵפֶשׂ מְחֻפָּשׂ
וְקֶרֶב אִישׁ
וְלֵב עָמֹק׃
וַיֹּרֵם אֱלֹהִים ⁸
חֵץ פִּתְאוֹם הָיוּ מַכּוֹתָם׃
וַיַּכְשִׁילוּהוּ עָלֵימוֹ לְשׁוֹנָם ⁹
יִתְנֹדְדוּ כָּל־רֹאֵה בָם׃
וַיִּירְאוּ כָּל־אָדָם ¹⁰
וַיַּגִּידוּ פֹּעַל אֱלֹהִים וּמַעֲשֵׂהוּ הִשְׂכִּילוּ׃
יִשְׂמַח צַדִּיק בַּיהוָה וְחָסָה בוֹ ¹¹
וְיִתְהַלְלוּ כָּל־יִשְׁרֵי־לֵב׃

סה לַמְנַצֵּחַ מִזְמוֹר לְדָוִד שִׁיר׃
לְךָ דֻמִיָּה תְהִלָּה אֱלֹהִים בְּצִיּוֹן ²
וּלְךָ יְשֻׁלַּם־נֶדֶר׃
שֹׁמֵעַ תְּפִלָּה ³
עָדֶיךָ כָּל־בָּשָׂר יָבֹאוּ׃
דִּבְרֵי עֲוֹנֹת גָּבְרוּ מֶנִּי ⁴
פְּשָׁעֵינוּ אַתָּה תְכַפְּרֵם׃
אַשְׁרֵי ׀ תִּבְחַר וּתְקָרֵב ⁵
יִשְׁכֹּן חֲצֵרֶיךָ
נִשְׂבְּעָה בְּטוּב בֵּיתֶךָ
קְדֹשׁ הֵיכָלֶךָ׃
נוֹרָאוֹת ׀ בְּצֶדֶק תַּעֲנֵנוּ ⁶
אֱלֹהֵי יִשְׁעֵנוּ
מִבְטָח כָּל־קַצְוֵי־אֶרֶץ
וְיָם רְחֹקִים׃
מֵכִין הָרִים בְּכֹחוֹ ⁷
נֶאְזָר בִּגְבוּרָה׃
מַשְׁבִּיחַ ׀ שְׁאוֹן יַמִּים שְׁאוֹן גַּלֵּיהֶם ⁸
וַהֲמוֹן לְאֻמִּים׃
וַיִּירְאוּ ׀ יֹשְׁבֵי קְצָוֹת מֵאוֹתֹתֶיךָ ⁹

You make the outgoings of the morning and
evening rejoice.

9   You visit the earth and water it,
    You greatly enrich it;
    The river of God is full of water;
    You provide their grain,
    For so You have prepared it.

10 You water its ridges abundantly,
    You settle its furrows;
    You make it soft with showers,
    You bless its growth.

11 You crown the year with Your goodness,
    And Your paths drip *with* abundance.

12 They drop *on* the pastures of the wilderness,
    And the little hills rejoice on every side.

13 The pastures are clothed with flocks;
    The valleys also are covered with grain;
    They shout for joy, they also sing.

66 To the Chief Musician. A Song. A Psalm.
    Make a joyful shout to God, all the earth!

2   Sing out the honor of His name;
    Make His praise glorious.

3   Say to God,
    "How awesome are Your works!
    Through the greatness of Your power
    Your enemies shall submit themselves to You.

4   All the earth shall worship You
    And sing praises to You;
    They shall sing praises *to* Your name."
                                    Selah

5   Come and see the works of God;
    He is awesome *in His* doing toward the sons of
    men.

6   He turned the sea into dry *land;*
    They went through the river on foot.
    There we will rejoice in Him.

7   He rules by His power forever;
    His eyes observe the nations;
    Do not let the rebellious exalt themselves.
                                    Selah

8   Oh, bless our God, you peoples!
    And make the voice of His praise to be heard,

9   Who keeps our soul among the living,
    And does not allow our feet to be moved.

10 For You, O God, have tested us;
    You have refined us as silver is refined.

11 You brought us into the net;
    You laid affliction on our backs.

12 You have caused men to ride over our heads;
    We went through fire and through water;
    But You brought us out to rich *fulfillment.*

מוֹצָאֵי־בֹקֶר וָעֶרֶב תַּרְנִין:

10 פָּקַדְתָּ הָאָרֶץ ׀ וַתְּשֹׁקְקֶהָ רַבַּת תַּעְשְׁרֶנָּה
    פֶּלֶג אֱלֹהִים מָלֵא מָיִם
    תָּכִין דְּגָנָם
    כִּי־כֵן תְּכִינֶהָ:

11 תְּלָמֶיהָ רַוֵּה נַחֵת גְּדוּדֶיהָ
    בִּרְבִיבִים תְּמֹגְגֶנָּה צִמְחָהּ תְּבָרֵךְ:

12 עִטַּרְתָּ שְׁנַת טוֹבָתֶךָ
    וּמַעְגָּלֶיךָ יִרְעֲפוּן דָּשֶׁן:

13 יִרְעֲפוּ נְאוֹת מִדְבָּר
    וְגִיל גְּבָעוֹת תַּחְגֹּרְנָה:

14 לָבְשׁוּ כָרִים ׀ הַצֹּאן
    וַעֲמָקִים יַעַטְפוּ־בָר
    יִתְרוֹעֲעוּ אַף־יָשִׁירוּ:

סו לַמְנַצֵּחַ שִׁיר מִזְמוֹר
    הָרִיעוּ לֵאלֹהִים כָּל־הָאָרֶץ:

2   זַמְּרוּ כְבוֹד־שְׁמוֹ
    שִׂימוּ כָבוֹד תְּהִלָּתוֹ:

3   אִמְרוּ לֵאלֹהִים מַה־נּוֹרָא מַעֲשֶׂיךָ
    בְּרֹב עֻזְּךָ יְכַחֲשׁוּ לְךָ אֹיְבֶיךָ:

4   כָּל־הָאָרֶץ ׀ יִשְׁתַּחֲווּ לְךָ וִיזַמְּרוּ־לָךְ
    יְזַמְּרוּ שִׁמְךָ סֶלָה:

5   לְכוּ וּרְאוּ מִפְעֲלוֹת אֱלֹהִים
    נוֹרָא עֲלִילָה עַל־בְּנֵי אָדָם:

6   הָפַךְ יָם ׀ לְיַבָּשָׁה בַּנָּהָר יַעַבְרוּ בְרָגֶל
    שָׁם נִשְׂמְחָה־בּוֹ:

7   מֹשֵׁל בִּגְבוּרָתוֹ ׀ עוֹלָם
    עֵינָיו בַּגּוֹיִם תִּצְפֶּינָה
    הַסּוֹרְרִים ׀
    אַל־יָרִימוּ לָמוֹ סֶלָה:

8   בָּרְכוּ עַמִּים ׀ אֱלֹהֵינוּ
    וְהַשְׁמִיעוּ קוֹל תְּהִלָּתוֹ:

9   הַשָּׂם נַפְשֵׁנוּ בַּחַיִּים
    וְלֹא־נָתַן לַמּוֹט רַגְלֵנוּ:

10 כִּי־בְחַנְתָּנוּ אֱלֹהִים
    צְרַפְתָּנוּ כִּצְרָף־כָּסֶף:

11 הֲבֵאתָנוּ בַמְּצוּדָה
    שַׂמְתָּ מוּעָקָה בְמָתְנֵינוּ:

12 הִרְכַּבְתָּ אֱנוֹשׁ לְרֹאשֵׁנוּ
    בָּאנוּ־בָאֵשׁ וּבַמַּיִם וַתּוֹצִיאֵנוּ לָרְוָיָה:

סו 7 יָרִימוּ

13 I will go into Your house with burnt offerings;
    I will pay You my vows,

14 Which my lips have uttered
    And my mouth has spoken when I was in
      trouble.

15 I will offer You burnt sacrifices of fat animals,
    With the sweet aroma of rams;
    I will offer bulls with goats.   Selah

16 Come *and* hear, all you who fear God,
    And I will declare what He has done for my
      soul.

17 I cried to Him with my mouth,
    And He was extolled with my tongue.

18 If I regard iniquity in my heart,
    The Lord will not hear.

19 *But* certainly God has heard *me;*
    He has attended to the voice of my prayer.

20 Blessed *be* God,
    Who has not turned away my prayer,
    Nor His mercy from me!

67 To the Chief Musician. On stringed instruments. A
Psalm. A Song.
    God be merciful to us and bless us,
    And cause His face to shine upon us,
         Selah

2 That Your way may be known on earth,
    Your salvation among all nations.

3 Let the peoples praise You, O God;
    Let all the peoples praise You.

4 Oh, let the nations be glad and sing for joy!
    For You shall judge the people righteously,
    And govern the nations on earth.   Selah

5 Let the peoples praise You, O God;
    Let all the peoples praise You.

6 *Then* the earth shall yield her increase;
    God, our own God, shall bless us.

7 God shall bless us,
    And all the ends of the earth shall fear Him.

68 To the Chief Musician. A Psalm of David. A Song.
    Let God arise,
    Let His enemies be scattered;
    Let those also who hate Him flee before Him.

2 As smoke is driven away,
    So drive *them* away;
    As wax melts before the fire,
    So let the wicked perish at the presence of God.

3 But let the righteous be glad;
    Let them rejoice before God;
    Yes, let them rejoice exceedingly.

13 אָבוֹא בֵיתְךָ בְעוֹלוֹת
אֲשַׁלֵּם לְךָ נְדָרָי:

14 אֲשֶׁר־פָּצוּ שְׂפָתָי
וְדִבֶּר־פִּי בַּצַּר־לִי:

15 עֹלוֹת מֵחִים אַעֲלֶה־לָּךְ
עִם־קְטֹרֶת אֵילִים
אֶעֱשֶׂה בָקָר עִם־עַתּוּדִים סֶלָה:

16 לְכוּ־שִׁמְעוּ וַאֲסַפְּרָה כָּל־יִרְאֵי אֱלֹהִים
אֲשֶׁר עָשָׂה לְנַפְשִׁי:

17 אֵלָיו פִּי־קָרָאתִי
וְרוֹמַם תַּחַת לְשׁוֹנִי:

18 אָוֶן אִם־רָאִיתִי בְלִבִּי
לֹא יִשְׁמַע ׀ אֲדֹנָי:

19 אָכֵן שָׁמַע אֱלֹהִים
הִקְשִׁיב בְּקוֹל תְּפִלָּתִי:

20 בָּרוּךְ אֱלֹהִים
אֲשֶׁר לֹא־הֵסִיר תְּפִלָּתִי וְחַסְדּוֹ מֵאִתִּי:

סז לַמְנַצֵּחַ בִּנְגִינֹת מִזְמוֹר שִׁיר:

2 אֱלֹהִים יְחָנֵּנוּ וִיבָרְכֵנוּ
יָאֵר פָּנָיו אִתָּנוּ סֶלָה:

3 לָדַעַת בָּאָרֶץ דַּרְכֶּךָ
בְּכָל־גּוֹיִם יְשׁוּעָתֶךָ:

4 יוֹדוּךָ עַמִּים ׀ אֱלֹהִים
יוֹדוּךָ עַמִּים כֻּלָּם:

5 יִשְׂמְחוּ וִירַנְּנוּ לְאֻמִּים
כִּי־תִשְׁפֹּט עַמִּים מִישׁוֹר
וּלְאֻמִּים ׀ בָּאָרֶץ תַּנְחֵם סֶלָה:

6 יוֹדוּךָ עַמִּים ׀ אֱלֹהִים
יוֹדוּךָ עַמִּים כֻּלָּם:

7 אֶרֶץ נָתְנָה יְבוּלָהּ
יְבָרְכֵנוּ אֱלֹהִים אֱלֹהֵינוּ:

8 יְבָרְכֵנוּ אֱלֹהִים
וְיִירְאוּ אֹתוֹ כָּל־אַפְסֵי־אָרֶץ:

סח לַמְנַצֵּחַ לְדָוִד מִזְמוֹר שִׁיר:

2 יָקוּם אֱלֹהִים יָפוּצוּ אוֹיְבָיו
וְיָנוּסוּ מְשַׂנְאָיו מִפָּנָיו:

3 כְּהִנְדֹּף עָשָׁן תִּנְדֹּף
כְּהִמֵּס דּוֹנַג מִפְּנֵי־אֵשׁ
יֹאבְדוּ רְשָׁעִים מִפְּנֵי אֱלֹהִים:

4 וְצַדִּיקִים יִשְׂמְחוּ יַעַלְצוּ לִפְנֵי אֱלֹהִים
וְיָשִׂישׂוּ בְשִׂמְחָה:

4   Sing to God, sing praises to His name;
   Extol Him who rides on the clouds,
   By His name YAH,
   And rejoice before Him.

5   A father of the fatherless, a defender of
      widows,
   Is God in His holy habitation.

6   God sets the solitary in families;
   He brings out those who are bound into
      prosperity;
   But the rebellious dwell in a dry *land*.

7   O God, when You went out before Your
      people,
   When You marched through the wilderness,
                      Selah

8   The earth shook;
   The heavens also dropped *rain* at the presence
      of God;
   Sinai itself *was moved* at the presence of God,
      the God of Israel.

9   You, O God, sent a plentiful rain,
   Whereby You confirmed Your inheritance,
   When it was weary.

10   Your congregation dwelt in it;
   You, O God, provided from Your goodness
      for the poor.

11   The Lord gave the word;
   Great *was* the company of those who
      proclaimed *it:*

12   "Kings of armies flee, they flee,
   And she who remains at home divides the
      spoil.

13   Though you lie down among the sheepfolds,
   You will be like the wings of a dove covered
      with silver,
   And her feathers with yellow gold."

14   When the Almighty scattered kings in it,
   It was *white* as snow in Zalmon.

15   A mountain of God *is* the mountain of Bashan;
   A mountain *of many* peaks is the mountain of
      Bashan.

16   Why do you fume with envy, you mountains of
      many peaks?
   This is the mountain *which* God desires to
      dwell in;
   Yes, the LORD will dwell *in it* forever.

17   The chariots of God *are* twenty thousand,
   Even thousands of thousands;
   The Lord is among them *as in* Sinai, in the
      Holy *Place.*

18   You have ascended on high,
   You have led captivity captive;

שִׁירוּ ׀ לֵאלֹהִים 5
זַמְּרוּ שְׁמוֹ
סֹלּוּ לָרֹכֵב בָּעֲרָבוֹת בְּיָהּ שְׁמוֹ
וְעִלְזוּ לְפָנָיו:

אֲבִי יְתוֹמִים וְדַיַּן אַלְמָנוֹת 6
אֱלֹהִים בִּמְעוֹן קָדְשׁוֹ:

אֱלֹהִים ׀ מוֹשִׁיב יְחִידִים ׀ בַּיְתָה 7
מוֹצִיא אֲסִירִים בַּכּוֹשָׁרוֹת
אַךְ סוֹרֲרִים
שָׁכְנוּ צְחִיחָה:

אֱלֹהִים בְּצֵאתְךָ לִפְנֵי עַמֶּךָ 8
בְּצַעְדְּךָ בִישִׁימוֹן סֶלָה:

אֶרֶץ רָעָשָׁה ׀ אַף־שָׁמַיִם נָטְפוּ 9
מִפְּנֵי אֱלֹהִים
זֶה סִינַי
מִפְּנֵי אֱלֹהִים אֱלֹהֵי יִשְׂרָאֵל:

גֶּשֶׁם נְדָבוֹת תָּנִיף אֱלֹהִים 10
נַחֲלָתְךָ וְנִלְאָה אַתָּה כוֹנַנְתָּהּ:

חַיָּתְךָ יָשְׁבוּ־בָהּ 11
תָּכִין בְּטוֹבָתְךָ לֶעָנִי אֱלֹהִים:

אֲדֹנָי יִתֶּן־אֹמֶר 12
הַמְבַשְּׂרוֹת צָבָא רָב:

מַלְכֵי צְבָאוֹת יִדֹּדוּן יִדֹּדוּן 13
וּנְוַת בַּיִת תְּחַלֵּק שָׁלָל:

אִם־תִּשְׁכְּבוּן 14
בֵּין שְׁפַתָּיִם
כַּנְפֵי יוֹנָה נֶחְפָּה בַכֶּסֶף
וְאֶבְרוֹתֶיהָ בִּירַקְרַק חָרוּץ:

בְּפָרֵשׂ שַׁדַּי מְלָכִים בָּהּ 15
תַּשְׁלֵג בְּצַלְמוֹן:

הַר־אֱלֹהִים הַר־בָּשָׁן 16
הַר גַּבְנֻנִּים הַר־בָּשָׁן:

לָמָּה ׀ תְּרַצְּדוּן 17
הָרִים גַּבְנֻנִּים
הָהָר חָמַד אֱלֹהִים לְשִׁבְתּוֹ
אַף־יְהוָה יִשְׁכֹּן לָנֶצַח:

רֶכֶב אֱלֹהִים רִבֹּתַיִם אַלְפֵי שִׁנְאָן 18
אֲדֹנָי בָם סִינַי בַּקֹּדֶשׁ:

עָלִיתָ לַמָּרוֹם ׀ שָׁבִיתָ שֶּׁבִי 19

You have received gifts among men,
Even *from* the rebellious,
That the LORD God might dwell *there*.

19 Blessed *be* the Lord,
Who daily loads us *with benefits*,
The God of our salvation!   Selah

20 Our God *is* the God of salvation;
And to GOD the Lord *belong* escapes from
    death.

21 But God will wound the head of His enemies,
The hairy scalp of the one who still goes on in
    his trespasses.

22 The Lord said, "I will bring back from Bashan,
I will bring *them* back from the depths of the
    sea,

23 That your foot may crush *them* in blood,
And the tongues of your dogs *may have* their
    portion from *your* enemies."

24 They have seen Your procession, O God,
The procession of my God, my King, into the
    sanctuary.

25 The singers went before, the players on
    instruments *followed* after;
Among *them* were the maidens playing
    timbrels.

26 Bless God in the congregations,
The Lord, from the fountain of Israel.

27 There *is* little Benjamin, their leader,
The princes of Judah *and* their company,
The princes of Zebulun *and* the princes of
    Naphtali.

28 Your God has commanded your strength;
Strengthen, O God, what You have done for
    us.

29 Because of Your temple at Jerusalem,
Kings will bring presents to You.

30 Rebuke the beasts of the reeds,
The herd of bulls with the calves of the peoples,
Till everyone submits himself with pieces of
    silver.
Scatter the peoples *who* delight in war.

31 Envoys will come out of Egypt;
Ethiopia will quickly stretch out her hands to
    God.

32 Sing to God, you kingdoms of the earth;
Oh, sing praises to the Lord,   Selah

33 To Him who rides on the heaven of heavens,
which were of old!
Indeed, He sends out His voice, a mighty voice.

34 Ascribe strength to God;
His excellence *is* over Israel,
And His strength *is* in the clouds.

לָקַחְתָּ מַתָּנוֹת בָּאָדָם
וְאַף סוֹרְרִים
לִשְׁכֹּן ׀ יָהּ אֱלֹהִים:

20 בָּרוּךְ אֲדֹנָי יוֹם ׀ יוֹם
יַעֲמָס־לָנוּ הָאֵל יְשׁוּעָתֵנוּ סֶלָה:

21 הָאֵל ׀ לָנוּ אֵל לְמוֹשָׁעוֹת
וְלֵיהוִֹה אֲדֹנָי לַמָּוֶת תּוֹצָאוֹת:

22 אַךְ־אֱלֹהִים יִמְחַץ רֹאשׁ אֹיְבָיו
קָדְקֹד שֵׂעָר מִתְהַלֵּךְ בַּאֲשָׁמָיו:

23 אָמַר אֲדֹנָי מִבָּשָׁן אָשִׁיב
אָשִׁיב מִמְּצֻלוֹת יָם:

24 לְמַעַן ׀ תִּמְחַץ רַגְלְךָ בְּדָם
לְשׁוֹן כְּלָבֶיךָ מֵאֹיְבִים מִנֵּהוּ:

25 רָאוּ הֲלִיכוֹתֶיךָ אֱלֹהִים
הֲלִיכוֹת אֵלִי מַלְכִּי בַקֹּדֶשׁ:

26 קִדְּמוּ שָׁרִים אַחַר נֹגְנִים
בְּתוֹךְ עֲלָמוֹת תּוֹפֵפוֹת:

27 בְּמַקְהֵלוֹת בָּרְכוּ אֱלֹהִים
יְהוָֹה מִמְּקוֹר יִשְׂרָאֵל:

28 שָׁם בִּנְיָמִן ׀ צָעִיר רֹדֵם שָׂרֵי יְהוּדָה רִגְמָתָם
שָׂרֵי זְבֻלוּן שָׂרֵי נַפְתָּלִי:

29 צִוָּה אֱלֹהֶיךָ עֻזֶּךָ
עוּזָּה אֱלֹהִים זוּ פָּעַלְתָּ לָּנוּ:

30 מֵהֵיכָלֶךָ עַל־יְרוּשָׁלִָם
לְךָ יוֹבִילוּ מְלָכִים שָׁי:

31 גְּעַר חַיַּת קָנֶה עֲדַת אַבִּירִים ׀ בְּעֶגְלֵי עַמִּים
מִתְרַפֵּס בְּרַצֵּי־כָסֶף
בִּזַּר עַמִּים
קְרָבוֹת יֶחְפָּצוּ:

32 יֶאֱתָיוּ חַשְׁמַנִּים מִנִּי מִצְרָיִם
כּוּשׁ תָּרִיץ יָדָיו לֵאלֹהִים:

33 מַמְלְכוֹת הָאָרֶץ שִׁירוּ לֵאלֹהִים
זַמְּרוּ אֲדֹנָי סֶלָה:

34 לָרֹכֵב בִּשְׁמֵי שְׁמֵי־קֶדֶם
הֵן יִתֵּן בְּקוֹלוֹ קוֹל עֹז:

35 תְּנוּ עֹז לֵאלֹהִים
עַל־יִשְׂרָאֵל גַּאֲוָתוֹ וְעֻזּוֹ בַּשְּׁחָקִים:

35 O God, *You are* more awesome than Your holy
       places.
    The God of Israel *is* He who gives strength and
       power to *His* people.
    Blessed *be* God!

69 To the Chief Musician. Set to "The Lilies." A
Psalm of David.

    Save me, O God!
    For the waters have come up to *my* neck.
2   I sink in deep mire,
    Where *there is* no standing;
    I have come into deep waters,
    Where the floods overflow me.
3   I am weary with my crying;
    My throat is dry;
    My eyes fail while I wait for my God.

4   Those who hate me without a cause
    Are more than the hairs of my head;
    They are mighty who would destroy me,
    Being my enemies wrongfully;
    Though I have stolen nothing,
    I *still* must restore *it*.
5   O God, You know my foolishness;
    And my sins are not hidden from You.
6   Let not those who wait for You, O Lord GOD
       of hosts, be ashamed because of me;
    Let not those who seek You be confounded
       because of me, O God of Israel.
7   Because for Your sake I have borne reproach;
    Shame has covered my face.
8   I have become a stranger to my brothers,
    And an alien to my mother's children;
9   Because zeal for Your house has eaten me up,
    And the reproaches of those who reproach
       You have fallen on me.
10 When I wept *and chastened* my soul with
       fasting,
    That became my reproach.
11 I also made sackcloth my garment;
    I became a byword to them.
12 Those who sit in the gate speak against me,
    And I *am* the song of the drunkards.

13 But as for me, my prayer *is* to You,
    O LORD, *in* the acceptable time;
    O God, in the multitude of Your mercy,
    Hear me in the truth of Your salvation.
14 Deliver me out of the mire,
    And let me not sink;
    Let me be delivered from those who hate me,
    And out of the deep waters.
15 Let not the floodwater overflow me,
    Nor let the deep swallow me up;

נוֹרָא אֱלֹהִים מִמִּקְדָּשֶׁיךָ 36
אֵל יִשְׂרָאֵל הוּא נֹתֵן ׀ עֹז וְתַעֲצֻמוֹת לָעָם
בָּרוּךְ אֱלֹהִים:

סט לַמְנַצֵּחַ עַל־שׁוֹשַׁנִּים לְדָוִד:
הוֹשִׁיעֵנִי אֱלֹהִים 2
כִּי בָאוּ מַיִם עַד־נָפֶשׁ:
טָבַעְתִּי ׀ בִּיוֵן מְצוּלָה 3
וְאֵין מָעֳמָד
בָּאתִי בְמַעֲמַקֵּי־מַיִם
וְשִׁבֹּלֶת שְׁטָפָתְנִי:
יָגַעְתִּי בְקָרְאִי נִחַר גְּרוֹנִי 4
כָּלוּ עֵינַי מְיַחֵל לֵאלֹהָי:
רַבּוּ ׀ מִשַּׂעֲרוֹת רֹאשִׁי 5
שֹׂנְאַי חִנָּם
עָצְמוּ מַצְמִיתַי אֹיְבַי שֶׁקֶר
אֲשֶׁר לֹא־גָזַלְתִּי אָז אָשִׁיב:
אֱלֹהִים אַתָּה יָדַעְתָּ לְאִוַּלְתִּי 6
וְאַשְׁמוֹתַי מִמְּךָ לֹא־נִכְחָדוּ:
אַל־יֵבֹשׁוּ בִי ׀ קֹוֶיךָ 7
אֲדֹנָי יְהֹוִה צְבָאוֹת
אַל־יִכָּלְמוּ בִי מְבַקְשֶׁיךָ
אֱלֹהֵי יִשְׂרָאֵל:
כִּי־עָלֶיךָ נָשָׂאתִי חֶרְפָּה 8
כִּסְּתָה כְלִמָּה פָנָי:
מוּזָר הָיִיתִי לְאֶחָי 9
וְנָכְרִי לִבְנֵי אִמִּי:
כִּי־קִנְאַת בֵּיתְךָ אֲכָלָתְנִי 10
וְחֶרְפּוֹת חוֹרְפֶיךָ נָפְלוּ עָלָי:
וָאֶבְכֶּה בַצּוֹם נַפְשִׁי 11
וַתְּהִי לַחֲרָפוֹת לִי:
וָאֶתְּנָה לְבוּשִׁי שָׂק 12
וָאֱהִי לָהֶם לְמָשָׁל:
יָשִׂיחוּ בִי יֹשְׁבֵי שָׁעַר 13
וּנְגִינוֹת שׁוֹתֵי שֵׁכָר:
וַאֲנִי תְפִלָּתִי־לְךָ ׀ יְהֹוָה עֵת רָצוֹן 14
אֱלֹהִים בְּרָב־חַסְדֶּךָ
עֲנֵנִי בֶּאֱמֶת יִשְׁעֶךָ:
הַצִּילֵנִי מִטִּיט וְאַל־אֶטְבָּעָה 15
אִנָּצְלָה מִשֹּׂנְאַי וּמִמַּעֲמַקֵּי־מָיִם:
אַל־תִּשְׁטְפֵנִי ׀ שִׁבֹּלֶת מַיִם 16
וְאַל־תִּבְלָעֵנִי מְצוּלָה

And let not the pit shut its mouth on me.

16 Hear me, O LORD, for Your lovingkindness *is* good;
     Turn to me according to the multitude of Your tender mercies.

17 And do not hide Your face from Your servant,
     For I am in trouble;
     Hear me speedily.

18 Draw near to my soul, *and* redeem it;
     Deliver me because of my enemies.

19 You know my reproach, my shame, and my dishonor;
     My adversaries *are* all before You.

20 Reproach has broken my heart,
     And I am full of heaviness;
     I looked *for someone* to take pity, but *there was* none;
     And for comforters, but I found none.

21 They also gave me gall for my food,
     And for my thirst they gave me vinegar to drink.

22 Let their table become a snare before them,
     And their well-being a trap.

23 Let their eyes be darkened, so that they do not see;
     And make their loins shake continually.

24 Pour out Your indignation upon them,
     And let Your wrathful anger take hold of them.

25 Let their dwelling place be desolate;
     Let no one live in their tents.

26 For they persecute the *ones* You have struck,
     And talk of the grief of those You have wounded.

27 Add iniquity to their iniquity,
     And let them not come into Your righteousness.

28 Let them be blotted out of the book of the living,
     And not be written with the righteous.

29 But I *am* poor and sorrowful;
     Let Your salvation, O God, set me up on high.

30 I will praise the name of God with a song,
     And will magnify Him with thanksgiving.

31 *This* also shall please the LORD better than an ox *or* bull,
     Which has horns and hooves.

32 The humble shall see *this and* be glad;
     And you who seek God, your hearts shall live.

33 For the LORD hears the poor,
     And does not despise His prisoners.

34 Let heaven and earth praise Him,

וְאַל־תֶּאְטַר־עָלַי בְּאֵר פִּיהָ׃

17 עֲנֵנִי יְהֹוָה כִּי־טוֹב חַסְדֶּךָ כְּרֹב רַחֲמֶיךָ פְּנֵה אֵלָי׃

18 וְאַל־תַּסְתֵּר פָּנֶיךָ מֵעַבְדֶּךָ כִּי־צַר־לִי מַהֵר עֲנֵנִי׃

19 קָרְבָה אֶל־נַפְשִׁי גְאָלָהּ לְמַעַן אֹיְבַי פְּדֵנִי׃

20 אַתָּה יָדַעְתָּ חֶרְפָּתִי וּבָשְׁתִּי וּכְלִמָּתִי נֶגְדְּךָ כָּל־צוֹרְרָי׃

21 חֶרְפָּה ׀ שָׁבְרָה לִבִּי וָאָנוּשָׁה וָאֲקַוֶּה לָנוּד וָאַיִן וְלַמְנַחֲמִים וְלֹא מָצָאתִי׃

22 וַיִּתְּנוּ בְּבָרוּתִי רֹאשׁ וְלִצְמָאִי יַשְׁקוּנִי חֹמֶץ׃

23 יְהִי־שֻׁלְחָנָם לִפְנֵיהֶם לְפָח וְלִשְׁלוֹמִים לְמוֹקֵשׁ׃

24 תֶּחְשַׁכְנָה עֵינֵיהֶם מֵרְאוֹת וּמָתְנֵיהֶם תָּמִיד הַמְעַד׃

25 שְׁפָךְ־עֲלֵיהֶם זַעְמֶךָ וַחֲרוֹן אַפְּךָ יַשִּׂיגֵם׃

26 תְּהִי־טִירָתָם נְשַׁמָּה בְּאָהֳלֵיהֶם אַל־יְהִי יֹשֵׁב׃

27 כִּי־אַתָּה אֲשֶׁר־הִכִּיתָ רָדָפוּ וְאֶל־מַכְאוֹב חֲלָלֶיךָ יְסַפֵּרוּ׃

28 תְּנָה־עָוֺן עַל־עֲוֺנָם וְאַל־יָבֹאוּ בְּצִדְקָתֶךָ׃

29 יִמָּחוּ מִסֵּפֶר חַיִּים וְעִם צַדִּיקִים אַל־יִכָּתֵבוּ׃

30 וַאֲנִי עָנִי וְכוֹאֵב יְשׁוּעָתְךָ אֱלֹהִים תְּשַׂגְּבֵנִי׃

31 אֲהַלְלָה שֵׁם־אֱלֹהִים בְּשִׁיר וַאֲגַדְּלֶנּוּ בְתוֹדָה׃

32 וְתִיטַב לַיהֹוָה מִשּׁוֹר פָּר מַקְרִן מַפְרִיס׃

33 רָאוּ עֲנָוִים יִשְׂמָחוּ דֹּרְשֵׁי אֱלֹהִים וִיחִי לְבַבְכֶם׃

34 כִּי־שֹׁמֵעַ אֶל־אֶבְיוֹנִים יְהֹוָה וְאֶת־אֲסִירָיו לֹא בָזָה׃

35 יְהַלְלוּהוּ שָׁמַיִם וָאָרֶץ

The seas and everything that moves in them.

35 For God will save Zion
And build the cities of Judah,
That they may dwell there and possess it.

36 Also, the descendants of His servants shall
inherit it,
And those who love His name shall dwell in it.

70 To the Chief Musician. *A Psalm* of David. To
bring to remembrance.

Make haste, O God, to deliver me!
Make haste to help me, O LORD!

2 Let them be ashamed and confounded
Who seek my life;
Let them be turned back and confused
Who desire my hurt.

3 Let them be turned back because of their
shame,
Who say, "Aha, aha!"

4 Let all those who seek You rejoice and be glad
in You;
And let those who love Your salvation say
continually,
"Let God be magnified!"

5 But I *am* poor and needy;
Make haste to me, O God!
You *are* my help and my deliverer;
O LORD, do not delay.

71 In You, O LORD, I put my trust;
Let me never be put to shame.

2 Deliver me in Your righteousness, and cause
me to escape;
Incline Your ear to me, and save me.

3 Be my strong refuge,
To which I may resort continually;
You have given the commandment to save me,
For You *are* my rock and my fortress.

4 Deliver me, O my God, out of the hand of the
wicked,
Out of the hand of the unrighteous and cruel
man.

5 For You are my hope, O Lord GOD;
You are my trust from my youth.

6 By You I have been upheld from birth;
You are He who took me out of my mother's
womb.
My praise *shall be* continually of You.

7 I have become as a wonder to many,
But You *are* my strong refuge.

8 Let my mouth be filled *with* Your praise

יַמִּים וְכָל־רֹמֵשׂ בָּם׃

36 כִּי אֱלֹהִים ׀ יוֹשִׁיעַ צִיּוֹן וְיִבְנֶה עָרֵי יְהוּדָה
וְיָשְׁבוּ שָׁם וִירֵשׁוּהָ׃

37 וְזֶרַע עֲבָדָיו יִנְחָלוּהָ
וְאֹהֲבֵי שְׁמוֹ יִשְׁכְּנוּ־בָהּ׃

ע לַמְנַצֵּחַ לְדָוִד לְהַזְכִּיר׃

2 אֱלֹהִים לְהַצִּילֵנִי יְהוָה לְעֶזְרָתִי חוּשָׁה׃

3 יֵבֹשׁוּ וְיַחְפְּרוּ מְבַקְשֵׁי נַפְשִׁי
יִסֹּגוּ אָחוֹר וְיִכָּלְמוּ חֲפֵצֵי רָעָתִי׃

4 יָשׁוּבוּ עַל־עֵקֶב בָּשְׁתָּם
הָאֹמְרִים הֶאָח ׀ הֶאָח׃

5 יָשִׂישׂוּ וְיִשְׂמְחוּ ׀ בְּךָ
כָּל־מְבַקְשֶׁיךָ
וְיֹאמְרוּ תָמִיד יִגְדַּל אֱלֹהִים
אֹהֲבֵי יְשׁוּעָתֶךָ׃

6 וַאֲנִי ׀ עָנִי וְאֶבְיוֹן
אֱלֹהִים חוּשָׁה־לִּי
עֶזְרִי וּמְפַלְטִי אַתָּה
יְהוָה אַל־תְּאַחַר׃

עא בְּךָ־יְהוָה חָסִיתִי
אַל־אֵבוֹשָׁה לְעוֹלָם׃

2 בְּצִדְקָתְךָ תַּצִּילֵנִי וּתְפַלְּטֵנִי
הַטֵּה־אֵלַי אָזְנְךָ וְהוֹשִׁיעֵנִי׃

3 הֱיֵה לִי ׀ לְצוּר מָעוֹן לָבוֹא
תָּמִיד צִוִּיתָ לְהוֹשִׁיעֵנִי
כִּי־סַלְעִי וּמְצוּדָתִי אָתָּה׃

4 אֱלֹהַי פַּלְּטֵנִי מִיַּד רָשָׁע
מִכַּף מְעַוֵּל וְחוֹמֵץ׃

5 כִּי־אַתָּה תִקְוָתִי
אֲדֹנָי יְהוָה מִבְטַחִי מִנְּעוּרָי׃

6 עָלֶיךָ ׀ נִסְמַכְתִּי מִבֶּטֶן מִמְּעֵי אִמִּי אַתָּה גוֹזִי
בְּךָ תְהִלָּתִי תָמִיד׃

7 כְּמוֹפֵת הָיִיתִי לְרַבִּים
וְאַתָּה מַחֲסִי־עֹז׃

8 יִמָּלֵא פִי תְּהִלָּתֶךָ

And with Your glory all the day.	כָּל־הַיּוֹם תִּפְאַרְתֶּךָ׃

9 Do not cast me off in the time of old age;
Do not forsake me when my strength fails.

9 אַל־תַּשְׁלִיכֵנִי לְעֵת זִקְנָה
כִּכְלוֹת כֹּחִי אַל־תַּעַזְבֵנִי׃

10 For my enemies speak against me;
And those who lie in wait for my life take
counsel together,

10 כִּי־אָמְרוּ אוֹיְבַי לִי
וְשֹׁמְרֵי נַפְשִׁי נוֹעֲצוּ יַחְדָּו׃

11 Saying, "God has forsaken him;
Pursue and take him, for *there is* none to
deliver *him*."

11 לֵאמֹר אֱלֹהִים עֲזָבוֹ
רִדְפוּ וְתִפְשׂוּהוּ כִּי־אֵין מַצִּיל׃

12 O God, do not be far from me;
O my God, make haste to help me!

12 אֱלֹהִים אַל־תִּרְחַק מִמֶּנִּי
אֱלֹהַי לְעֶזְרָתִי חִישָׁהP׃

13 Let them be confounded *and* consumed
Who are adversaries of my life;
Let them be covered *with* reproach and
dishonor
Who seek my hurt.

13 יֵבֹשׁוּ יִכְלוּ שֹׂטְנֵי נַפְשִׁי
יַעֲטוּ חֶרְפָּה וּכְלִמָּה מְבַקְשֵׁי רָעָתִי׃

14 But I will hope continually,
And will praise You yet more and more.

14 וַאֲנִי תָּמִיד אֲיַחֵל
וְהוֹסַפְתִּי עַל־כָּל־תְּהִלָּתֶךָ׃

15 My mouth shall tell of Your righteousness
And Your salvation all the day,
For I do not know *their* limits.

15 פִּי ׀ יְסַפֵּר צִדְקָתֶךָ כָּל־הַיּוֹם תְּשׁוּעָתֶךָ
כִּי לֹא יָדַעְתִּי סְפֹרוֹת׃

16 I will go in the strength of the Lord God;
I will make mention of Your righteousness, of
Yours only.

16 אָבוֹא בִּגְבֻרוֹת אֲדֹנָי יֱהוִֹה
אַזְכִּיר צִדְקָתְךָ לְבַדֶּךָ׃

17 O God, You have taught me from my youth;
And to this *day* I declare Your wondrous
works.

17 אֱלֹהִים לִמַּדְתַּנִי מִנְּעוּרָי
וְעַד־הֵנָּה אַגִּיד נִפְלְאוֹתֶיךָ׃

18 Now also when *I am* old and grayheaded,
O God, do not forsake me,
Until I declare Your strength to *this*
generation,
Your power to everyone *who* is to come.

18 וְגַם עַד־זִקְנָה ׀ וְשֵׂיבָה
אֱלֹהִים אַל־תַּעַזְבֵנִי
עַד־אַגִּיד זְרוֹעֲךָ לְדוֹר
לְכָל־יָבוֹא גְּבוּרָתֶךָ׃

19 Also Your righteousness, O God, *is* very high,
You who have done great things;
O God, who *is* like You?

19 וְצִדְקָתְךָ אֱלֹהִים
עַד־מָרוֹם
אֲשֶׁר־עָשִׂיתָ גְדֹלוֹת
אֱלֹהִים מִי כָמוֹךָ׃

20 *You,* who have shown me great and severe
troubles,
Shall revive me again,
And bring me up again from the depths of the
earth.

20 אֲשֶׁר הִרְאִיתַנִיP ׀ צָרוֹת רַבּוֹת וְרָעוֹת
תָּשׁוּב תְּחַיֵּינִיP
וּמִתְּהֹמוֹת הָאָרֶץ תָּשׁוּב תַּעֲלֵנִי׃

21 You shall increase my greatness,
And comfort me on every side.

21 תֶּרֶב ׀ גְּדֻלָּתִי
וְתִסֹּב תְּנַחֲמֵנִי׃

22 Also with the lute I will praise You—
And Your faithfulness, O my God!
To You I will sing with the harp,
O Holy One of Israel.

22 גַּם־אֲנִי ׀ אוֹדְךָ בִכְלִי־נֶבֶל
אֲמִתְּךָ אֱלֹהָי
אֲזַמְּרָה לְךָ בְכִנּוֹר
קְדוֹשׁ יִשְׂרָאֵל׃

23 My lips shall greatly rejoice when I sing to
You,
And my soul, which You have redeemed.

23 תְּרַנֵּנָּה שְׂפָתַי כִּי אֲזַמְּרָה־לָּךְ
וְנַפְשִׁי אֲשֶׁר פָּדִיתָ׃

24 My tongue also shall talk of Your righteousness all the day long;

24 גַּם־לְשׁוֹנִי
כָּל־הַיּוֹם תֶּהְגֶּה צִדְקָתֶךָ

For they are confounded,
For they are brought to shame
Who seek my hurt.

כִּי־בֹשׁוּ כִי־חָפְרוּ
מְבַקְשֵׁי רָעָתִי:

72 A Psalm of Solomon.

Give the king Your judgments, O God,
And Your righteousness to the king's Son.

עב לִשְׁלֹמֹה |
אֱלֹהִים מִשְׁפָּטֶיךָ לְמֶלֶךְ תֵּן וְצִדְקָתְךָ לְבֶן־מֶלֶךְ:

2 He will judge Your people with righteousness,
And Your poor with justice.

2 יָדִין עַמְּךָ בְצֶדֶק
וַעֲנִיֶּיךָ בְמִשְׁפָּט:

3 The mountains will bring peace to the people,
And the little hills, by righteousness.

3 יִשְׂאוּ הָרִים שָׁלוֹם לָעָם
וּגְבָעוֹת בִּצְדָקָה:

4 He will bring justice to the poor of the people;
He will save the children of the needy,
And will break in pieces the oppressor.

4 יִשְׁפֹּט | עֲנִיֵּי־עָם יוֹשִׁיעַ לִבְנֵי אֶבְיוֹן
וִידַכֵּא עוֹשֵׁק:

5 They shall fear You
As long as the sun and moon endure,
Throughout all generations.

5 יִירָאוּךָ עִם־שָׁמֶשׁ
וְלִפְנֵי יָרֵחַ דּוֹר דּוֹרִים:

6 He shall come down like rain upon the grass
before mowing,
Like showers *that* water the earth.

6 יֵרֵד כְּמָטָר עַל־גֵּז
כִּרְבִיבִים זַרְזִיף אָרֶץ:

7 In His days the righteous shall flourish,
And abundance of peace,
Until the moon is no more.

7 יִפְרַח־בְּיָמָיו צַדִּיק
וְרֹב שָׁלוֹם עַד־בְּלִי יָרֵחַ:

8 He shall have dominion also from sea to sea,
And from the River to the ends of the earth.

8 וְיֵרְדְּ מִיָּם עַד־יָם
וּמִנָּהָר עַד־אַפְסֵי־אָרֶץ:

9 Those who dwell in the wilderness will bow
before Him,
And His enemies will lick the dust.

9 לְפָנָיו יִכְרְעוּ צִיִּים
וְאֹיְבָיו עָפָר יְלַחֵכוּ:

10 The kings of Tarshish and of the isles
Will bring presents;
The kings of Sheba and Seba
Will offer gifts.

10 מַלְכֵי תַרְשִׁישׁ וְאִיִּים
מִנְחָה יָשִׁיבוּ
מַלְכֵי שְׁבָא וּסְבָא
אֶשְׁכָּר יַקְרִיבוּ:

11 Yes, all kings shall fall down before Him;
All nations shall serve Him.

11 וְיִשְׁתַּחֲווּ־לוֹ כָל־מְלָכִים
כָּל־גּוֹיִם יַעַבְדוּהוּ:

12 For He will deliver the needy when he cries,
The poor also, and *him* who has no helper.

12 כִּי־יַצִּיל אֶבְיוֹן מְשַׁוֵּעַ
וְעָנִי וְאֵין־עֹזֵר לוֹ:

13 He will spare the poor and needy,
And will save the souls of the needy.

13 יָחֹס עַל־דַּל וְאֶבְיוֹן
וְנַפְשׁוֹת אֶבְיוֹנִים יוֹשִׁיעַ:

14 He will redeem their life from oppression and
violence;
And precious shall be their blood in His sight.

14 מִתּוֹךְ וּמֵחָמָס יִגְאַל נַפְשָׁם
וְיֵיקַר דָּמָם בְּעֵינָיו:

15 And He shall live;
And the gold of Sheba will be given to Him;
Prayer also will be made for Him continually,
And daily He shall be praised.

15 וִיחִי
וְיִתֶּן־לוֹ מִזְּהַב שְׁבָא
וְיִתְפַּלֵּל בַּעֲדוֹ תָמִיד
כָּל־הַיּוֹם יְבָרֲכֶנְהוּ:

16 There will be an abundance of grain in the
earth,
On the top of the mountains;
Its fruit shall wave like Lebanon;
And *those* of the city shall flourish like grass of
the earth.

16 יְהִי פִסַּת־בַּר | בָּאָרֶץ
בְּרֹאשׁ הָרִים
יִרְעַשׁ כַּלְּבָנוֹן פִּרְיוֹ
וְיָצִיצוּ מֵעִיר כְּעֵשֶׂב הָאָרֶץ:

17 His name shall endure forever;
    His name shall continue as long as the sun.
    And *men* shall be blessed in Him;
    All nations shall call Him blessed.

18 Blessed *be* the LORD God, the God of Israel,
    Who only does wondrous things!

19 And blessed *be* His glorious name forever!
    And let the whole earth be filled *with* His glory.
    Amen and Amen.

20 The prayers of David the son of Jesse are
    ended.

Book Three: Psalms 73—89

73 A Psalm of Asaph.

    Truly God *is* good to Israel,
    To such as are pure in heart.

2 But as for me, my feet had almost stumbled;
    My steps had nearly slipped.

3 For I *was* envious of the boastful,
    When I saw the prosperity of the wicked.

4 For *there are* no pangs in their death,
    But their strength *is* firm.

5 They *are* not in trouble *as other* men,
    Nor are they plagued like *other* men.

6 Therefore pride serves as their necklace;
    Violence covers them *like* a garment.

7 Their eyes bulge with abundance;
    They have more than heart could wish.

8 They scoff and speak wickedly *concerning*
       oppression;
    They speak loftily.

9 They set their mouth against the heavens,
    And their tongue walks through the earth.

10 Therefore his people return here,
    And waters of a full *cup* are drained by them.

11 And they say, "How does God know?
    And is there knowledge in the Most High?"

12 Behold, these *are* the ungodly,
    Who are always at ease;
    They increase *in* riches.

13 Surely I have cleansed my heart *in* vain,
    And washed my hands in innocence.

14 For all day long I have been plagued,
    And chastened every morning.

15 If I had said, "I will speak thus,"
    Behold, I would have been untrue to the
       generation of Your children.

16 When I thought *how* to understand this,
    It *was* too painful for me—

17 Until I went into the sanctuary of God;

17 יְהִי שְׁמוֹ לְעוֹלָם לִפְנֵי־שֶׁמֶשׁ יִנּוֹןᴾ שְׁמוֹ
    וְיִתְבָּרְכוּ בוֹ כָּל־גּוֹיִם יְאַשְּׁרוּהוּ:
18 בָּרוּךְ ׀ יְהֹוָה אֱלֹהִים אֱלֹהֵי יִשְׂרָאֵל
    עֹשֵׂה נִפְלָאוֹת לְבַדּוֹ:
19 וּבָרוּךְ ׀ שֵׁם כְּבוֹדוֹ לְעוֹלָם
    וְיִמָּלֵא כְבוֹדוֹ אֶת־כֹּל הָאָרֶץ אָמֵן ׀ וְאָמֵן:
20 כָּלּוּ תְפִלּוֹת דָּוִד בֶּן־יִשָׁי:

עג מִזְמוֹר לְאָסָף
    אַךְ טוֹב לְיִשְׂרָאֵל אֱלֹהִים לְבָרֵי לֵבָב:
2 וַאֲנִי כִּמְעַט נָטָוּיᴾ רַגְלָי
    כְּאַיִן שֻׁפְּכֻהᴾ אֲשֻׁרָי:
3 כִּי־קִנֵּאתִי בַּהוֹלְלִים
    שְׁלוֹם רְשָׁעִים אֶרְאֶה:
4 כִּי אֵין חַרְצֻבּוֹת לְמוֹתָם
    וּבָרִיא אוּלָם:
5 בַּעֲמַל אֱנוֹשׁ אֵינֵמוֹ
    וְעִם־אָדָם לֹא יְנֻגָּעוּ:
6 לָכֵן עֲנָקַתְמוֹ גַאֲוָה
    יַעֲטָף־שִׁית חָמָס לָמוֹ:
7 יָצָא מֵחֵלֶב עֵינֵמוֹ
    עָבְרוּ מַשְׂכִּיּוֹת לֵבָב:
8 יָמִיקוּ ׀ וִידַבְּרוּ בְרָע עֹשֶׁק
    מִמָּרוֹם יְדַבֵּרוּ:
9 שַׁתּוּ בַשָּׁמַיִם פִּיהֶם
    וּלְשׁוֹנָם תִּהֲלַךְ בָּאָרֶץ:
10 לָכֵן ׀ יָשִׁיבᴾ עַמּוֹ הֲלֹם
    וּמֵי מָלֵא יִמָּצוּ לָמוֹ:
11 וְאָמְרוּ אֵיכָה יָדַע־אֵל
    וְיֵשׁ דֵּעָה בְעֶלְיוֹן:
12 הִנֵּה־אֵלֶּה רְשָׁעִים
    וְשַׁלְוֵי עוֹלָם הִשְׂגּוּ־חָיִל:
13 אַךְ־רִיק זִכִּיתִי לְבָבִי
    וָאֶרְחַץ בְּנִקָּיוֹן כַּפָּי:
14 וָאֱהִי נָגוּעַ כָּל־הַיּוֹם
    וְתוֹכַחְתִּי לַבְּקָרִים:
15 אִם־אָמַרְתִּי אֲסַפְּרָה כְמוֹ
    הִנֵּה דוֹר בָּנֶיךָ בָגָדְתִּי:
16 וָאֲחַשְּׁבָה לָדַעַת זֹאת
    עָמָל הִיאᴾ בְעֵינָי:
17 עַד־אָבוֹא אֶל־מִקְדְּשֵׁי־אֵל

עג 17 יִנּוֹן   עג 2 נָטָיוּ שֻׁפְּכֻה   10 יָשׁוּב   16 הוּא

Then I understood their end.

18 Surely You set them in slippery places;
You cast them down to destruction.

19 Oh, how they are *brought* to desolation, as in a
moment!
They are utterly consumed with terrors.

20 As a dream when *one* awakes,
So, Lord, when You awake,
You shall despise their image.

21 Thus my heart was grieved,
And I was vexed in my mind.

22 I *was* so foolish and ignorant;
I was *like* a beast before You.

23 Nevertheless I *am* continually with You;
You hold *me* by my right hand.

24 You will guide me with Your counsel,
And afterward receive me *to* glory.

25 Whom have I in heaven *but* You?
And *there is* none upon earth *that* I desire
besides You.

26 My flesh and my heart fail;
But God *is* the strength of my heart and my
portion forever.

27 For indeed, those who are far from You shall
perish;
You have destroyed all those who desert You
for harlotry.

28 But *it is* good for me to draw near to God;
I have put my trust in the Lord GOD,
That I may declare all Your works.

74 A Contemplation of Asaph.
O God, why have You cast *us* off forever?
Why does Your anger smoke against the sheep
of Your pasture?

2 Remember Your congregation, *which* You
have purchased of old,
The tribe of Your inheritance, *which* You have
redeemed—
This Mount Zion where You have dwelt.

3 Lift up Your feet to the perpetual desolations.
The enemy has damaged everything in the
sanctuary.

4 Your enemies roar in the midst of Your
meeting place;
They set up their banners *for* signs.

5 They seem like men who lift up
Axes among the thick trees.

6 And now they break down its carved work, all
at once,
With axes and hammers.

7 They have set fire to Your sanctuary;

אָבִינָה לְאַחֲרִיתָם:

18 אַךְ בַּחֲלָקוֹת תָּשִׁית לָמוֹ
הִפַּלְתָּם לְמַשּׁוּאוֹת:

19 אֵיךְ הָיוּ לְשַׁמָּה כְרָגַע
סָפוּ תַמּוּ מִן־בַּלָּהוֹת:

20 כַּחֲלוֹם מֵהָקִיץ
אֲדֹנָי בָּעִיר ׀ צַלְמָם תִּבְזֶה:

21 כִּי יִתְחַמֵּץ לְבָבִי
וְכִלְיוֹתַי אֶשְׁתּוֹנָן:

22 וַאֲנִי־בַעַר וְלֹא אֵדָע
בְּהֵמוֹת הָיִיתִי עִמָּךְ:

23 וַאֲנִי תָמִיד עִמָּךְ
אָחַזְתָּ בְּיַד־יְמִינִי:

24 בַּעֲצָתְךָ תַנְחֵנִי
וְאַחַר כָּבוֹד תִּקָּחֵנִי:

25 מִי־לִי בַשָּׁמָיִם
וְעִמְּךָ לֹא־חָפַצְתִּי בָאָרֶץ:

26 כָּלָה שְׁאֵרִי וּלְבָבִי
צוּר־לְבָבִי וְחֶלְקִי אֱלֹהִים לְעוֹלָם:

27 כִּי־הִנֵּה רְחֵקֶיךָ יֹאבֵדוּ
הִצְמַתָּה כָּל־זוֹנֶה מִמֶּךָּ:

28 וַאֲנִי ׀ קִרֲבַת אֱלֹהִים
לִי־טוֹב
שַׁתִּי ׀ בַּאדֹנָי יְהֹוִה מַחְסִי
לְסַפֵּר כָּל־מַלְאֲכוֹתֶיךָ:

עד מַשְׂכִּיל לְאָסָף
לָמָה אֱלֹהִים זָנַחְתָּ לָנֶצַח
יֶעְשַׁן אַפְּךָ בְּצֹאן מַרְעִיתֶךָ:

2 זְכֹר עֲדָתְךָ ׀ קָנִיתָ קֶּדֶם
גָּאַלְתָּ שֵׁבֶט נַחֲלָתֶךָ
הַר־צִיּוֹן זֶה ׀ שָׁכַנְתָּ בּוֹ:

3 הָרִימָה פְעָמֶיךָ לְמַשֻּׁאוֹת נֶצַח
כָּל־הֵרַע אוֹיֵב בַּקֹּדֶשׁ:

4 שָׁאֲגוּ צֹרְרֶיךָ בְּקֶרֶב מוֹעֲדֶךָ
שָׂמוּ אוֹתֹתָם אֹתוֹת:

5 יִוָּדַע כְּמֵבִיא לְמָעְלָה
בִּסֲבָךְ־עֵץ קַרְדֻּמּוֹת:

6 וְעֵת ⁱ פִּתּוּחֶיהָ יָּחַד
בְּכַשִּׁיל וְכֵילַפֹּת יַהֲלֹמוּן:

7 שִׁלְחוּ בָאֵשׁ מִקְדָּשֶׁךָ

עד 6 וְעַתָּה

They have defiled the dwelling place of Your
    name to the ground.

8 They said in their hearts,
    "Let us destroy them altogether."
    They have burned up all the meeting places of
    God in the land.

9 We do not see our signs;
    There is no longer any prophet;
    Nor *is there* any among us who knows how
    long.

10 O God, how long will the adversary reproach?
    Will the enemy blaspheme Your name forever?

11 Why do You withdraw Your hand, even Your
    right hand?
    Take it out of Your bosom and destroy *them.*

12 For God *is* my King from of old,
    Working salvation in the midst of the earth.

13 You divided the sea by Your strength;
    You broke the heads of the sea serpents in the
    waters.

14 You broke the heads of Leviathan in pieces,
    And gave him *as* food to the people inhabiting
    the wilderness.

15 You broke open the fountain and the flood;
    You dried up mighty rivers.

16 The day *is* Yours, the night also *is* Yours;
    You have prepared the light and the sun.

17 You have set all the borders of the earth;
    You have made summer and winter.

18 Remember this, *that* the enemy has
    reproached, O Lord,
    And *that* a foolish people has blasphemed
    Your name.

19 Oh, do not deliver the life of Your turtledove to
    the wild beast!
    Do not forget the life of Your poor forever.

20 Have respect to the covenant;
    For the dark places of the earth are full of the
    haunts of cruelty.

21 Oh, do not let the oppressed return ashamed!
    Let the poor and needy praise Your name.

22 Arise, O God, plead Your own cause;
    Remember how the foolish man reproaches
    You daily.

23 Do not forget the voice of Your enemies;
    The tumult of those who rise up against You
    increases continually.

75 To the Chief Musician. Set to "Do Not Destroy."
A Psalm of Asaph. A Song.
    We give thanks to You, O God, we give
    thanks!

לָאָרֶץ חִלְּלוּ מִשְׁכַּן־שְׁמֶךָ׃

8 אָמְרוּ בְלִבָּם נִינָם יָחַד
    שָׂרְפוּ כָל־מוֹעֲדֵי־אֵל בָּאָרֶץ׃

9 אוֹתֹתֵינוּ לֹא רָאִינוּ
    אֵין־עוֹד נָבִיא וְלֹא־אִתָּנוּ יֹדֵעַ עַד־מָה׃

10 עַד־מָתַי אֱלֹהִים יְחָרֶף צָר
    יְנָאֵץ אוֹיֵב שִׁמְךָ לָנֶצַח׃

11 לָמָּה תָשִׁיב יָדְךָ וִימִינֶךָ
    מִקֶּרֶב חֵוקְךָ כַלֵּה׃

12 וֵאלֹהִים מַלְכִּי מִקֶּדֶם
    פֹּעֵל יְשׁוּעוֹת בְּקֶרֶב הָאָרֶץ׃

13 אַתָּה פוֹרַרְתָּ בְעָזְּךָ יָם
    שִׁבַּרְתָּ רָאשֵׁי תַנִּינִים עַל־הַמָּיִם׃

14 אַתָּה רִצַּצְתָּ רָאשֵׁי לִוְיָתָן
    תִּתְּנֶנּוּ מַאֲכָל לְעָם לְצִיִּים׃

15 אַתָּה בָקַעְתָּ מַעְיָן וָנָחַל
    אַתָּה הוֹבַשְׁתָּ נַהֲרוֹת אֵיתָן׃

16 לְךָ יוֹם אַף־לְךָ לָיְלָה
    אַתָּה הֲכִינוֹתָ מָאוֹר וָשָׁמֶשׁ׃

17 אַתָּה הִצַּבְתָּ כָּל־גְּבוּלוֹת אָרֶץ
    קַיִץ וָחֹרֶף אַתָּה יְצַרְתָּם׃

18 זְכָר־זֹאת אוֹיֵב חֵרֵף ׀ יְהֹוָה
    וְעַם נָבָל נִאֲצוּ שְׁמֶךָ׃

19 אַל־תִּתֵּן לְחַיַּת נֶפֶשׁ תּוֹרֶךָ
    חַיַּת עֲנִיֶּיךָ אַל־תִּשְׁכַּח לָנֶצַח׃

20 הַבֵּט לַבְּרִית
    כִּי מָלְאוּ מַחֲשַׁכֵּי־אֶרֶץ נְאוֹת חָמָס׃

21 אַל־יָשֹׁב דַּךְ נִכְלָם
    עָנִי וְאֶבְיוֹן יְהַלְלוּ שְׁמֶךָ׃

22 קוּמָה אֱלֹהִים רִיבָה רִיבֶךָ
    זְכֹר חֶרְפָּתְךָ מִנִּי־נָבָל כָּל־הַיּוֹם׃

23 אַל־תִּשְׁכַּח קוֹל צֹרְרֶיךָ
    שְׁאוֹן קָמֶיךָ עֹלֶה תָמִיד׃

עה לַמְנַצֵּחַ אַל־תַּשְׁחֵת מִזְמוֹר לְאָסָף שִׁיר׃

2 הוֹדִינוּ לְּךָ ׀ אֱלֹהִים הוֹדִינוּ וְקָרוֹב שְׁמֶךָ

עד 11 חֵיקְךָ

For Your wondrous works declare *that* Your
   name is near.

סַפְּרוּ נִפְלְאוֹתֶיךָ׃

3 כִּי אֶקַּח מוֹעֵד

2 "When I choose the proper time,
   I will judge uprightly.

אֲנִי מֵישָׁרִים אֶשְׁפֹּט׃

3 The earth and all its inhabitants are dissolved;
   I set up its pillars firmly.   Selah

4 נְמֹגִים אֶרֶץ וְכָל־יֹשְׁבֶיהָ
אָנֹכִי תִכַּנְתִּי עַמּוּדֶיהָ סֶּלָה׃

4 "I said to the boastful, 'Do not deal boastfully,'
   And to the wicked, 'Do not lift up the horn.

5 אָמַרְתִּי לַהוֹלְלִים אַל־תָּהֹלּוּ
וְלָרְשָׁעִים אַל־תָּרִימוּ קָרֶן׃

5 Do not lift up your horn on high;
   Do *not* speak with a stiff neck.' "

6 אַל־תָּרִימוּ לַמָּרוֹם קַרְנְכֶם
תְּדַבְּרוּ בְצַוָּאר עָתָק׃

6 For exaltation *comes* neither from the east
   Nor from the west nor from the south.

7 כִּי לֹא מִמּוֹצָא וּמִמַּעֲרָב
וְלֹא מִמִּדְבַּר הָרִים׃

7 But God *is* the Judge:
   He puts down one,
   And exalts another.

8 כִּי־אֱלֹהִים שֹׁפֵט
זֶה יַשְׁפִּיל וְזֶה יָרִים׃

8 For in the hand of the LORD *there is* a cup,
   And the wine is red;
   It is fully mixed, and He pours it out;
   Surely its dregs shall all the wicked of the earth
   Drain *and* drink down.

9 כִּי כוֹס בְּיַד־יְהֹוָה וְיַיִן חָמַר ׀ מָלֵא מֶסֶךְ
וַיַּגֵּר מִזֶּה
אַךְ־שְׁמָרֶיהָ יִמְצוּ יִשְׁתּוּ
כֹּל רִשְׁעֵי־אָרֶץ׃

9 But I will declare forever,
   I will sing praises to the God of Jacob.

10 וַאֲנִי אַגִּיד לְעֹלָם
אֲזַמְּרָה לֵאלֹהֵי יַעֲקֹב׃

10 "All the horns of the wicked I will also cut off,
   But the horns of the righteous shall be exalted."

11 וְכָל־קַרְנֵי רְשָׁעִים אֲגַדֵּעַ
תְּרוֹמַמְנָה קַרְנוֹת צַדִּיק׃

76 To the Chief Musician. On stringed instruments. A Psalm of Asaph. A Song.

עו לַמְנַצֵּחַ בִּנְגִינֹת מִזְמוֹר לְאָסָף שִׁיר׃

   In Judah God *is* known;
   His name *is* great in Israel.

2 נוֹדָע בִּיהוּדָה אֱלֹהִים
בְּיִשְׂרָאֵל גָּדוֹל שְׁמוֹ׃

2 In Salem also is His tabernacle,
   And His dwelling place in Zion.

3 וַיְהִי בְשָׁלֵם סֻכּוֹ
וּמְעוֹנָתוֹ בְצִיּוֹן׃

3 There He broke the arrows of the bow,
   The shield and sword of battle.   Selah

4 שָׁמָּה שִׁבַּר רִשְׁפֵי־קָשֶׁת
מָגֵן וְחֶרֶב וּמִלְחָמָה סֶּלָה׃

4 You *are* more glorious and excellent
   Than the mountains of prey.

5 נָאוֹר אַתָּה אַדִּיר
מֵהַרְרֵי־טָרֶף׃

5 The stouthearted were plundered;
   They have sunk into their sleep;
   And none of the mighty men have found the
   use of their hands.

6 אֶשְׁתּוֹלְלוּ ׀ אַבִּירֵי לֵב
נָמוּ שְׁנָתָם
וְלֹא־מָצְאוּ כָל־אַנְשֵׁי־חַיִל
יְדֵיהֶם׃

6 At Your rebuke, O God of Jacob,
   Both the chariot and horse were cast into a
   dead sleep.

7 מִגַּעֲרָתְךָ אֱלֹהֵי יַעֲקֹב
נִרְדָּם וְרֶכֶב וָסוּס׃

7 You, Yourself, *are* to be feared;
   And who may stand in Your presence
   When once You are angry?

8 אַתָּה ׀ נוֹרָא אַתָּה וּמִי־יַעֲמֹד לְפָנֶיךָ
מֵאָז אַפֶּךָ׃

8 You caused judgment to be heard from heaven;
   The earth feared and was still,

9 מִשָּׁמַיִם הִשְׁמַעְתָּ דִּין
אֶרֶץ יָרְאָה וְשָׁקָטָה׃

9 When God arose to judgment,
   To deliver all the oppressed of the earth.
                    Selah

10 בְּקוּם־לַמִּשְׁפָּט אֱלֹהִים
לְהוֹשִׁיעַ כָּל־עַנְוֵי־אֶרֶץ סֶלָה׃

¹⁰ Surely the wrath of man shall praise You;
     With the remainder of wrath You shall gird
       Yourself.

¹¹ Make vows to the LORD your God, and pay
     them;
     Let all who are around Him bring presents to
       Him who ought to be feared.

¹² He shall cut off the spirit of princes;
     He is awesome to the kings of the earth.

11 כִּי־חֲמַת אָדָם תּוֹדֶךָּ
שְׁאֵרִית חֵמֹת תַּחְגֹּר:

12 נִדְרוּ וְשַׁלְּמוּ לַיהוָה אֱלֹהֵיכֶם
כָּל־סְבִיבָיו יוֹבִילוּ שַׁי לַמּוֹרָא:

13 יִבְצֹר רוּחַ נְגִידִים
נוֹרָא לְמַלְכֵי־אָרֶץ:

77
To the Chief Musician. To Jeduthun. A Psalm of
Asaph.
     I cried out to God with my voice—
     To God with my voice;
     And He gave ear to me.

² In the day of my trouble I sought the Lord;
     My hand was stretched out in the night without
       ceasing;
     My soul refused to be comforted.

³ I remembered God, and was troubled;
     I complained, and my spirit was overwhelmed.
                   Selah

⁴ You hold my eyelids *open;*
     I am so troubled that I cannot speak.

⁵ I have considered the days of old,
     The years of ancient times.

⁶ I call to remembrance my song in the night;
     I meditate within my heart,
     And my spirit makes diligent search.

⁷ Will the Lord cast off forever?
     And will He be favorable no more?

⁸ Has His mercy ceased forever?
     Has *His* promise failed forevermore?

⁹ Has God forgotten to be gracious?
     Has He in anger shut up His tender mercies?
                   Selah

¹⁰ And I said, "This *is* my anguish;
     But I will remember the years of the right hand
       of the Most High."

¹¹ I will remember the works of the LORD;
     Surely I will remember Your wonders of old.

¹² I will also meditate on all Your work,
     And talk of Your deeds.

¹³ Your way, O God, *is* in the sanctuary;
     Who *is* so great a God as *our* God?

¹⁴ You *are* the God who does wonders;
     You have declared Your strength among the
       peoples.

¹⁵ You have with *Your* arm redeemed Your
     people,
     The sons of Jacob and Joseph.   Selah

¹⁶ The waters saw You, O God;

עז לַמְנַצֵּחַ עַל־יְדִיתוּן לְאָסָף מִזְמוֹר:

2 קוֹלִי אֶל־אֱלֹהִים וְאֶצְעָקָה
קוֹלִי אֶל־אֱלֹהִים וְהַאֲזִין אֵלָי:

3 בְּיוֹם צָרָתִי אֲדֹנָי דָּרָשְׁתִּי
יָדִי לַיְלָה נִגְּרָה וְלֹא תָפוּג
מֵאֲנָה הִנָּחֵם נַפְשִׁי:

4 אֶזְכְּרָה אֱלֹהִים וְאֶהֱמָיָה
אָשִׂיחָה וְתִתְעַטֵּף רוּחִי סֶלָה:

5 אָחַזְתָּ שְׁמֻרוֹת עֵינָי
נִפְעַמְתִּי וְלֹא אֲדַבֵּר:

6 חִשַּׁבְתִּי יָמִים מִקֶּדֶם
שְׁנוֹת עוֹלָמִים:

7 אֶזְכְּרָה נְגִינָתִי בַּלָּיְלָה
עִם־לְבָבִי אָשִׂיחָה וַיְחַפֵּשׂ רוּחִי:

8 הַלְעוֹלָמִים יִזְנַח אֲדֹנָי
וְלֹא־יֹסִיף לִרְצוֹת עוֹד:

9 הֶאָפֵס לָנֶצַח חַסְדּוֹ
גָּמַר אֹמֶר לְדֹר וָדֹר:

10 הֲשָׁכַח חַנּוֹת אֵל
אִם־קָפַץ בְּאַף רַחֲמָיו סֶלָה:

11 וָאֹמַר חַלּוֹתִי הִיא
שְׁנוֹת יְמִין עֶלְיוֹן:

12 אֶזְכּוֹר מַעַלְלֵי־יָהּ
כִּי־אֶזְכְּרָה מִקֶּדֶם פִּלְאֶךָ:

13 וְהָגִיתִי בְכָל־פָּעֳלֶךָ
וּבַעֲלִילוֹתֶיךָ אָשִׂיחָה:

14 אֱלֹהִים בַּקֹּדֶשׁ דַּרְכֶּךָ
מִי־אֵל גָּדוֹל כֵּאלֹהִים:

15 אַתָּה הָאֵל עֹשֵׂה פֶלֶא
הוֹדַעְתָּ בָעַמִּים עֻזֶּךָ:

16 גָּאַלְתָּ בִּזְרוֹעַ עַמֶּךָ
בְּנֵי־יַעֲקֹב וְיוֹסֵף סֶלָה:

17 רָאוּךָ מַּיִם אֱלֹהִים רָאוּךָ מַּיִם יָחִילוּ

The waters saw You, they were afraid;
The depths also trembled.

17 The clouds poured out water;
The skies sent out a sound;
Your arrows also flashed about.

18 The voice of Your thunder *was* in the
whirlwind;
The lightnings lit up the world;
The earth trembled and shook.

19 Your way *was* in the sea,
Your path in the great waters,
And Your footsteps were not known.

20 You led Your people like a flock
By the hand of Moses and Aaron.

אַף יִרְגְּזוּ תְהֹמוֹת:

18 זֹרְמוּ מַיִם ׀ עָבוֹת קוֹל נָתְנוּ שְׁחָקִים
אַף־חֲצָצֶיךָ יִתְהַלָּכוּ:

19 קוֹל רַעַמְךָ ׀ בַּגַּלְגַּל הֵאִירוּ בְרָקִים תֵּבֵל
רָגְזָה וַתִּרְעַשׁ הָאָרֶץ:

20 בַּיָּם דַּרְכֶּךָ וּשְׁבִילְךָ בְּמַיִם רַבִּים
וְעִקְּבוֹתֶיךָ לֹא נֹדָעוּ:

21 נָחִיתָ כַצֹּאן עַמֶּךָ
בְּיַד־מֹשֶׁה וְאַהֲרֹן:

78 A Contemplation of Asaph.

Give ear, O my people, *to* my law;
Incline your ears to the words of my mouth.

2 I will open my mouth in a parable;
I will utter dark sayings of old,

3 Which we have heard and known,
And our fathers have told us.

4 We will not hide *them* from their children,
Telling to the generation to come the praises of
the LORD,
And His strength and His wonderful works
that He has done.

5 For He established a testimony in Jacob,
And appointed a law in Israel,
Which He commanded our fathers,
That they should make them known to their
children;

6 That the generation to come might know *them,*
The children *who* would be born,
That they may arise and declare *them* to their
children,

7 That they may set their hope in God,
And not forget the works of God,
But keep His commandments;

8 And may not be like their fathers,
A stubborn and rebellious generation,
A generation *that* did not set its heart aright,
And whose spirit was not faithful to God.

9 The children of Ephraim, *being* armed *and*
carrying bows,
Turned back in the day of battle.

10 They did not keep the covenant of God;
They refused to walk in His law,

11 And forgot His works
And His wonders that He had shown them.

12 Marvelous things He did in the sight of their
fathers,

עח מַשְׂכִּיל לְאָסָף
הַאֲזִינָה עַמִּי תּוֹרָתִי
הַטּוּ אָזְנְכֶם לְאִמְרֵי־פִי:

2 אֶפְתְּחָה בְמָשָׁל פִּי
אַבִּיעָה חִידוֹת מִנִּי־קֶדֶם:

3 אֲשֶׁר שָׁמַעְנוּ וַנֵּדָעֵם
וַאֲבוֹתֵינוּ סִפְּרוּ־לָנוּ:

4 לֹא נְכַחֵד ׀ מִבְּנֵיהֶם
לְדוֹר אַחֲרוֹן מְסַפְּרִים תְּהִלּוֹת יְהֹוָה
וֶעֱזוּזוֹ וְנִפְלְאוֹתָיו אֲשֶׁר עָשָׂה:

5 וַיָּקֶם עֵדוּת ׀ בְּיַעֲקֹב
וְתוֹרָה שָׂם בְּיִשְׂרָאֵל
אֲשֶׁר צִוָּה אֶת־אֲבוֹתֵינוּ
לְהוֹדִיעָם לִבְנֵיהֶם:

6 לְמַעַן יֵדְעוּ ׀ דּוֹר אַחֲרוֹן בָּנִים יִוָּלֵדוּ
יָקֻמוּ וִיסַפְּרוּ לִבְנֵיהֶם:

7 וְיָשִׂימוּ בֵאלֹהִים כִּסְלָם
וְלֹא יִשְׁכְּחוּ מַעַלְלֵי־אֵל וּמִצְוֹתָיו יִנְצֹרוּ:

8 וְלֹא יִהְיוּ ׀ כַּאֲבוֹתָם
דּוֹר סוֹרֵר וּמֹרֶה
דּוֹר לֹא־הֵכִין לִבּוֹ
וְלֹא־נֶאֶמְנָה אֶת־אֵל רוּחוֹ:

9 בְּנֵי־אֶפְרַיִם נוֹשְׁקֵי רוֹמֵי־קָשֶׁת
הָפְכוּ בְּיוֹם קְרָב:

10 לֹא שָׁמְרוּ בְּרִית אֱלֹהִים
וּבְתוֹרָתוֹ מֵאֲנוּ לָלֶכֶת:

11 וַיִּשְׁכְּחוּ עֲלִילוֹתָיו
וְנִפְלְאוֹתָיו אֲשֶׁר הֶרְאָם:

12 נֶגֶד אֲבוֹתָם עָשָׂה פֶלֶא

עו 20 וּשְׁבִילְךָ

In the land of Egypt, *in* the field of Zoan.

13 He divided the sea and caused them to pass
through;
And He made the waters stand up like a heap.

14 In the daytime also He led them with the cloud,
And all the night with a light of fire.

15 He split the rocks in the wilderness,
And gave *them* drink in abundance like the
depths.

16 He also brought streams out of the rock,
And caused waters to run down like rivers.

17 But they sinned even more against Him
By rebelling against the Most High in the
wilderness.

18 And they tested God in their heart
By asking for the food of their fancy.

19 Yes, they spoke against God:
They said, "Can God prepare a table in the
wilderness?

20 Behold, He struck the rock,
So that the waters gushed out,
And the streams overflowed.
Can He give bread also?
Can He provide meat for His people?"

21 Therefore the LORD heard *this* and was furious;
So a fire was kindled against Jacob,
And anger also came up against Israel,

22 Because they did not believe in God,
And did not trust in His salvation.

23 Yet He had commanded the clouds above,
And opened the doors of heaven,

24 Had rained down manna on them to eat,
And given them of the bread of heaven.

25 Men ate angels' food;
He sent them food to the full.

26 He caused an east wind to blow in the heavens;
And by His power He brought in the south
wind.

27 He also rained meat on them like the dust,
Feathered fowl like the sand of the seas;

28 And He let *them* fall in the midst of their camp,
All around their dwellings.

29 So they ate and were well filled,
For He gave them their own desire.

30 They were not deprived of their craving;
But while their food *was* still in their mouths,

31 The wrath of God came against them,
And slew the stoutest of them,
And struck down the choice *men* of Israel.

32 In spite of this they still sinned,
And did not believe in His wondrous works.

33 Therefore their days He consumed in futility,

בְּאֶרֶץ מִצְרַיִם שְׂדֵה־צֹעַן:

13 בָּקַע יָם וַיַּעֲבִירֵם
וַיַּצֶּב־מַיִם כְּמוֹ־נֵד:

14 וַיַּנְחֵם בֶּעָנָן יוֹמָם
וְכָל־הַלַּיְלָה בְּאוֹר אֵשׁ:

15 יְבַקַּע צֻרִים בַּמִּדְבָּר
וַיַּשְׁקְ כִּתְהֹמוֹת רַבָּה:

16 וַיּוֹצִא נוֹזְלִים מִסָּלַע
וַיּוֹרֶד כַּנְּהָרוֹת מָיִם:

17 וַיּוֹסִיפוּ עוֹד לַחֲטֹא־לוֹ
לַמְרוֹת עֶלְיוֹן בַּצִּיָּה:

18 וַיְנַסּוּ־אֵל בִּלְבָבָם
לִשְׁאָל־אֹכֶל לְנַפְשָׁם:

19 וַיְדַבְּרוּ בֵּאלֹהִים
אָמְרוּ הֲיוּכַל אֵל לַעֲרֹךְ שֻׁלְחָן בַּמִּדְבָּר:

20 הֵן הִכָּה־צוּר ׀ וַיָּזוּבוּ מַיִם וּנְחָלִים יִשְׁטֹפוּ
הֲגַם־לֶחֶם יוּכַל תֵּת אִם־יָכִין שְׁאֵר לְעַמּוֹ:

21 לָכֵן ׀ שָׁמַע יְהֹוָה וַיִּתְעַבָּר וְאֵשׁ נִשְּׂקָה בְיַעֲקֹב
וְגַם־אַף עָלָה בְיִשְׂרָאֵל:

22 כִּי לֹא הֶאֱמִינוּ בֵּאלֹהִים
וְלֹא בָטְחוּ בִּישׁוּעָתוֹ:

23 וַיְצַו שְׁחָקִים מִמָּעַל
וְדַלְתֵי שָׁמַיִם פָּתָח:

24 וַיַּמְטֵר עֲלֵיהֶם מָן לֶאֱכֹל
וּדְגַן־שָׁמַיִם נָתַן לָמוֹ:

25 לֶחֶם אַבִּירִים אָכַל אִישׁ
צֵידָה שָׁלַח לָהֶם לָשֹׂבַע:

26 יַסַּע קָדִים בַּשָּׁמָיִם
וַיְנַהֵג בְּעֻזּוֹ תֵימָן:

27 וַיַּמְטֵר עֲלֵיהֶם כֶּעָפָר שְׁאֵר
וּכְחוֹל יַמִּים עוֹף כָּנָף:

28 וַיַּפֵּל בְּקֶרֶב מַחֲנֵהוּ
סָבִיב לְמִשְׁכְּנֹתָיו:

29 וַיֹּאכְלוּ וַיִּשְׂבְּעוּ מְאֹד
וְתַאֲוָתָם יָבִא לָהֶם:

30 לֹא־זָרוּ מִתַּאֲוָתָם
עוֹד אָכְלָם בְּפִיהֶם:

31 וְאַף אֱלֹהִים ׀ עָלָה בָהֶם וַיַּהֲרֹג בְּמִשְׁמַנֵּיהֶם
וּבַחוּרֵי יִשְׂרָאֵל הִכְרִיעַ:

32 בְּכָל־זֹאת חָטְאוּ־עוֹד
וְלֹא־הֶאֱמִינוּ בְּנִפְלְאוֹתָיו:

33 וַיְכַל־בַּהֶבֶל יְמֵיהֶם

And their years in fear.

וּשְׁנוֹתָם בַּבֶּהָלָה:

34 When He slew them, then they sought Him;
    And they returned and sought earnestly for
    God.

34 אִם־הֲרָגָם וּדְרָשׁוּהוּ

וְשָׁבוּ וְשִׁחֲרוּ־אֵל:

35 Then they remembered that God *was* their
    rock,
    And the Most High God their Redeemer.

35 וַיִּזְכְּרוּ כִּי־אֱלֹהִים צוּרָם

וְאֵל עֶלְיוֹן גֹּאֲלָם:

36 Nevertheless they flattered Him with their
    mouth,
    And they lied to Him with their tongue;

36 וַיְפַתּוּהוּ בְּפִיהֶם

וּבִלְשׁוֹנָם יְכַזְּבוּ־לוֹ:

37 For their heart was not steadfast with Him,
    Nor were they faithful in His covenant.

37 וְלִבָּם לֹא־נָכוֹן עִמּוֹ

וְלֹא נֶאֶמְנוּ בִּבְרִיתוֹ:

38 But He, *being* full of compassion, forgave *their*
    iniquity,
    And did not destroy *them*.
    Yes, many a time He turned His anger away,
    And did not stir up all His wrath;

38 וְהוּא רַחוּם ׀ יְכַפֵּר עָוֹן

וְלֹא־יַשְׁחִית

וְהִרְבָּה לְהָשִׁיב אַפּוֹ

וְלֹא־יָעִיר כָּל־חֲמָתוֹ:

39 For He remembered that they *were but* flesh,
    A breath that passes away and does not come
    again.

39 וַיִּזְכֹּר כִּי־בָשָׂר הֵמָּה

רוּחַ הוֹלֵךְ וְלֹא יָשׁוּב:

40 How often they provoked Him in the
    wilderness,
    And grieved Him in the desert!

40 כַּמָּה יַמְרוּהוּ בַמִּדְבָּר

יַעֲצִיבוּהוּ בִּישִׁימוֹן:

41 Yes, again and again they tempted God,
    And limited the Holy One of Israel.

41 וַיָּשׁוּבוּ וַיְנַסּוּ אֵל

וּקְדוֹשׁ יִשְׂרָאֵל הִתְווּ:

42 They did not remember His power:
    The day when He redeemed them from the
    enemy,

42 לֹא־זָכְרוּ אֶת־יָדוֹ

יוֹם אֲשֶׁר־פָּדָם מִנִּי־צָר:

43 When He worked His signs in Egypt,
    And His wonders in the field of Zoan;

43 אֲשֶׁר־שָׂם בְּמִצְרַיִם אֹתוֹתָיו

וּמוֹפְתָיו בִּשְׂדֵה־צֹעַן:

44 Turned their rivers into blood,
    And their streams, that they could not drink.

44 וַיַּהֲפֹךְ לְדָם יְאֹרֵיהֶם

וְנֹזְלֵיהֶם בַּל־יִשְׁתָּיוּן:

45 He sent swarms of flies among them, which
    devoured them,
    And frogs, which destroyed them.

45 יְשַׁלַּח בָּהֶם עָרֹב וַיֹּאכְלֵם

וּצְפַרְדֵּעַ וַתַּשְׁחִיתֵם:

46 He also gave their crops to the caterpillar,
    And their labor to the locust.

46 וַיִּתֵּן לֶחָסִיל יְבוּלָם

וִיגִיעָם לָאַרְבֶּה:

47 He destroyed their vines with hail,
    And their sycamore trees with frost.

47 יַהֲרֹג בַּבָּרָד גַּפְנָם

וְשִׁקְמוֹתָם בַּחֲנָמַל:

48 He also gave up their cattle to the hail,
    And their flocks to fiery lightning.

48 וַיַּסְגֵּר לַבָּרָד בְּעִירָם

וּמִקְנֵיהֶם לָרְשָׁפִים:

49 He cast on them the fierceness of His anger,
    Wrath, indignation, and trouble,
    By sending angels of destruction *among them.*

49 יְשַׁלַּח־בָּם ׀ חֲרוֹן אַפּוֹ עֶבְרָה וָזַעַם וְצָרָה

מִשְׁלַחַת מַלְאֲכֵי רָעִים:

50 He made a path for His anger;
    He did not spare their soul from death,
    But gave their life over to the plague,

50 יְפַלֵּס נָתִיב לְאַפּוֹ

לֹא־חָשַׂךְ מִמָּוֶת נַפְשָׁם וְחַיָּתָם לַדֶּבֶר הִסְגִּיר:

51 And destroyed all the firstborn in Egypt,
    The first of *their* strength in the tents of Ham.

51 וַיַּךְ כָּל־בְּכוֹר בְּמִצְרָיִם

רֵאשִׁית אוֹנִים בְּאָהֳלֵי־חָם:

52 But He made His own people go forth like
    sheep,
    And guided them in the wilderness like a flock;

52 וַיַּסַּע כַּצֹּאן עַמּוֹ

וַיְנַהֲגֵם כַּעֵדֶר בַּמִּדְבָּר:

53 And He led them on safely, so that they did not fear;
But the sea overwhelmed their enemies.

54 And He brought them to His holy border,
This mountain *which* His right hand had acquired.

55 He also drove out the nations before them,
Allotted them an inheritance by survey,
And made the tribes of Israel dwell in their tents.

56 Yet they tested and provoked the Most High God,
And did not keep His testimonies,

57 But turned back and acted unfaithfully like their fathers;
They were turned aside like a deceitful bow.

58 For they provoked Him to anger with their high places,
And moved Him to jealousy with their carved images.

59 When God heard *this,* He was furious,
And greatly abhorred Israel,

60 So that He forsook the tabernacle of Shiloh,
The tent He had placed among men,

61 And delivered His strength into captivity,
And His glory into the enemy's hand.

62 He also gave His people over to the sword,
And was furious with His inheritance.

63 The fire consumed their young men,
And their maidens were not given in marriage.

64 Their priests fell by the sword,
And their widows made no lamentation.

65 Then the Lord awoke as *from* sleep,
Like a mighty man who shouts because of wine.

66 And He beat back His enemies;
He put them to a perpetual reproach.

67 Moreover He rejected the tent of Joseph,
And did not choose the tribe of Ephraim,

68 But chose the tribe of Judah,
Mount Zion which He loved.

69 And He built His sanctuary like the heights,
Like the earth which He has established forever.

70 He also chose David His servant,
And took him from the sheepfolds;

71 From following the ewes that had young He brought him,
To shepherd Jacob His people,
And Israel His inheritance.

72 So he shepherded them according to the integrity of his heart,

53 וַיַּנְחֵם לָבֶטַח וְלֹא פָחָדוּ
וְאֶת־אוֹיְבֵיהֶם כִּסָּה הַיָּם:

54 וַיְבִיאֵם אֶל־גְּבוּל קָדְשׁוֹ
הַר־זֶה קָנְתָה יְמִינוֹ:

55 וַיְגָרֶשׁ מִפְּנֵיהֶם ׀ גּוֹיִם
וַיַּפִּילֵם בְּחֶבֶל נַחֲלָה
וַיַּשְׁכֵּן בְּאָהֳלֵיהֶם
שִׁבְטֵי יִשְׂרָאֵל:

56 וַיְנַסּוּ וַיַּמְרוּ אֶת־אֱלֹהִים עֶלְיוֹן
וְעֵדוֹתָיו לֹא שָׁמָרוּ:

57 וַיִּסֹּגוּ וַיִּבְגְּדוּ כַּאֲבוֹתָם
נֶהְפְּכוּ כְּקֶשֶׁת רְמִיָּה:

58 וַיַּכְעִיסוּהוּ בְּבָמוֹתָם
וּבִפְסִילֵיהֶם יַקְנִיאוּהוּ:

59 שָׁמַע אֱלֹהִים וַיִּתְעַבָּר
וַיִּמְאַס מְאֹד בְּיִשְׂרָאֵל:

60 וַיִּטֹּשׁ מִשְׁכַּן שִׁלוֹ
אֹהֶל שִׁכֵּן בָּאָדָם:

61 וַיִּתֵּן לַשְּׁבִי עֻזּוֹ
וְתִפְאַרְתּוֹ בְיַד־צָר:

62 וַיַּסְגֵּר לַחֶרֶב עַמּוֹ
וּבְנַחֲלָתוֹ הִתְעַבָּר:

63 בַּחוּרָיו אָכְלָה־אֵשׁ
וּבְתוּלֹתָיו לֹא הוּלָּלוּ:

64 כֹּהֲנָיו בַּחֶרֶב נָפָלוּ
וְאַלְמְנֹתָיו לֹא תִבְכֶּינָה:

65 וַיִּקַץ כְּיָשֵׁן ׀ אֲדֹנָי
כְּגִבּוֹר מִתְרוֹנֵן מִיָּיִן:

66 וַיַּךְ־צָרָיו אָחוֹר
חֶרְפַּת עוֹלָם נָתַן לָמוֹ:

67 וַיִּמְאַס בְּאֹהֶל יוֹסֵף
וּבְשֵׁבֶט אֶפְרַיִם לֹא בָחָר:

68 וַיִּבְחַר אֶת־שֵׁבֶט יְהוּדָה
אֶת־הַר צִיּוֹן אֲשֶׁר אָהֵב:

69 וַיִּבֶן כְּמוֹ־רָמִים מִקְדָּשׁוֹ
כְּאֶרֶץ יְסָדָהּ לְעוֹלָם:

70 וַיִּבְחַר בְּדָוִד עַבְדּוֹ
וַיִּקָּחֵהוּ מִמִּכְלְאֹת צֹאן:

71 מֵאַחַר עָלוֹת הֱבִיאוֹ
לִרְעוֹת בְּיַעֲקֹב עַמּוֹ וּבְיִשְׂרָאֵל נַחֲלָתוֹ:

And guided them by the skillfulness of his hands.

79 A Psalm of Asaph.

O God, the nations have come into Your inheritance;
Your holy temple they have defiled;
They have laid Jerusalem in heaps.

2 The dead bodies of Your servants
They have given *as* food for the birds of the heavens,
The flesh of Your saints to the beasts of the earth.

3 Their blood they have shed like water all around Jerusalem,
And *there was* no one to bury *them*.

4 We have become a reproach to our neighbors,
A scorn and derision to those who are around us.

5 How long, LORD?
Will You be angry forever?
Will Your jealousy burn like fire?

6 Pour out Your wrath on the nations that do not know You,
And on the kingdoms that do not call on Your name.

7 For they have devoured Jacob,
And laid waste his dwelling place.

8 Oh, do not remember former iniquities against us!
Let Your tender mercies come speedily to meet us,
For we have been brought very low.

9 Help us, O God of our salvation,
For the glory of Your name;
And deliver us, and provide atonement for our sins,
For Your name's sake!

10 Why should the nations say,
"Where *is* their God?"
Let there be known among the nations in our sight
The avenging of the blood of Your servants *which has been* shed.

11 Let the groaning of the prisoner come before You;
According to the greatness of Your power
Preserve those who are appointed to die;

12 And return to our neighbors sevenfold into their bosom
Their reproach with which they have reproached You, O Lord.

עט מִזְמוֹר לְאָסָף

אֱלֹהִים בָּאוּ גוֹיִם ׀ בְּנַחֲלָתֶךָ
טִמְּאוּ אֶת־הֵיכַל קָדְשֶׁךָ
שָׂמוּ אֶת־יְרוּשָׁלַ͏ִם
לְעִיִּים:

2 נָתְנוּ אֶת־נִבְלַת עֲבָדֶיךָ
מַאֲכָל לְעוֹף הַשָּׁמָיִם
בְּשַׂר חֲסִידֶיךָ
לְחַיְתוֹ־אָרֶץ:

3 שָׁפְכוּ דָמָם ׀ כַּמַּיִם סְבִיבוֹת יְרוּשָׁלַ͏ִם
וְאֵין קוֹבֵר:

4 הָיִינוּ חֶרְפָּה לִשְׁכֵנֵינוּ
לַעַג וָקֶלֶס לִסְבִיבוֹתֵינוּ:

5 עַד־מָה יְהוָה תֶּאֱנַף לָנֶצַח
תִּבְעַר כְּמוֹ־אֵשׁ קִנְאָתֶךָ:

6 שְׁפֹךְ חֲמָתְךָ
אֶל־הַגּוֹיִם אֲשֶׁר לֹא־יְדָעוּךָ
וְעַל מַמְלָכוֹת
אֲשֶׁר בְּשִׁמְךָ לֹא קָרָאוּ:

7 כִּי אָכַל אֶת־יַעֲקֹב
וְאֶת־נָוֵהוּ הֵשַׁמּוּ:

8 אַל־תִּזְכָּר־לָנוּ
עֲוֺנֹת רִאשֹׁנִים
מַהֵר יְקַדְּמוּנוּ רַחֲמֶיךָ
כִּי דַלּוֹנוּ מְאֹד:

9 עָזְרֵנוּ ׀ אֱלֹהֵי יִשְׁעֵנוּ
עַל־דְּבַר כְּבוֹד־שְׁמֶךָ
וְהַצִּילֵנוּ וְכַפֵּר עַל־חַטֹּאתֵינוּ
לְמַעַן שְׁמֶךָ:

10 לָמָּה ׀ יֹאמְרוּ הַגּוֹיִם
אַיֵּה אֱלֹהֵיהֶם
יִוָּדַע בַּגֹּיִם[ᵖ] לְעֵינֵינוּ
נִקְמַת דַּם־עֲבָדֶיךָ הַשָּׁפוּךְ:

11 תָּבוֹא לְפָנֶיךָ אֶנְקַת אָסִיר
כְּגֹדֶל זְרוֹעֲךָ הוֹתֵר בְּנֵי תְמוּתָה:

12 וְהָשֵׁב לִשְׁכֵנֵינוּ שִׁבְעָתַיִם
אֶל־חֵיקָם
חֶרְפָּתָם אֲשֶׁר חֵרְפוּךָ
אֲדֹנָי:

עט 10 בַּגּוֹיִם

13 So we, Your people and sheep of Your pasture,
Will give You thanks forever;
We will show forth Your praise to all
generations.

13 וַאֲנַחְנוּ עַמְּךָ ׀ וְצֹאן מַרְעִיתֶךָ
נוֹדֶה לְּךָ לְעוֹלָם
לְדֹר וָדֹר
נְסַפֵּר תְּהִלָּתֶךָ:

80 To the Chief Musician. Set to "The Lilies." A
Testimony of Asaph. A Psalm.
    Give ear, O Shepherd of Israel,
You who lead Joseph like a flock;
You who dwell *between* the cherubim, shine
forth!

פ לַמְנַצֵּחַ אֶל־שֹׁשַׁנִּים
עֵדוּת לְאָסָף מִזְמוֹר:

2 Before Ephraim, Benjamin, and Manasseh,
Stir up Your strength,
And come *and* save us!

2 רֹעֵה יִשְׂרָאֵל ׀ הַאֲזִינָה
נֹהֵג כַּצֹּאן יוֹסֵף
יֹשֵׁב הַכְּרוּבִים הוֹפִיעָה:

3 Restore us, O God;
Cause Your face to shine,
And we shall be saved!

3 לִפְנֵי אֶפְרַיִם ׀ וּבִנְיָמִן וּמְנַשֶּׁה
עוֹרְרָה אֶת־גְּבוּרָתֶךָ
וּלְכָה לִישֻׁעָתָה לָּנוּ:

4 O Lord God of hosts,
How long will You be angry
Against the prayer of Your people?

4 אֱלֹהִים הֲשִׁיבֵנוּ
וְהָאֵר פָּנֶיךָ וְנִוָּשֵׁעָה:

5 You have fed them with the bread of tears,
And given them tears to drink in great
measure.

5 יְהוָה אֱלֹהִים צְבָאוֹת
עַד־מָתַי עָשַׁנְתָּ בִּתְפִלַּת עַמֶּךָ:

6 You have made us a strife to our neighbors,
And our enemies laugh among themselves.

6 הֶאֱכַלְתָּם לֶחֶם דִּמְעָה
וַתַּשְׁקֵמוֹ בִּדְמָעוֹת שָׁלִישׁ:

7 Restore us, O God of hosts;
Cause Your face to shine,
And we shall be saved!

7 תְּשִׂימֵנוּ מָדוֹן לִשְׁכֵנֵינוּ
וְאֹיְבֵינוּ יִלְעֲגוּ־לָמוֹ:

8 You have brought a vine out of Egypt;
You have cast out the nations, and planted it.

8 אֱלֹהִים צְבָאוֹת הֲשִׁיבֵנוּ
וְהָאֵר פָּנֶיךָ וְנִוָּשֵׁעָה:

9 You prepared *room* for it,
And caused it to take deep root,
And it filled the land.

9 גֶּפֶן מִמִּצְרַיִם תַּסִּיעַ
תְּגָרֵשׁ גּוֹיִם וַתִּטָּעֶהָ:

10 The hills were covered with its shadow,
And the mighty cedars with its boughs.

10 פִּנִּיתָ לְפָנֶיהָ
וַתַּשְׁרֵשׁ שָׁרָשֶׁיהָ וַתְּמַלֵּא־אָרֶץ:

11 She sent out her boughs to the Sea,
And her branches to the River.

11 כָּסּוּ הָרִים צִלָּהּ
וַעֲנָפֶיהָ אַרְזֵי־אֵל:

12 Why have You broken down her hedges,
So that all who pass by the way pluck her *fruit?*

12 תְּשַׁלַּח קְצִירֶהָ עַד־יָם
וְאֶל־נָהָר יוֹנְקוֹתֶיהָ:

13 The boar out of the woods uproots it,
And the wild beast of the field devours it.

13 לָמָּה פָּרַצְתָּ גְדֵרֶיהָ
וְאָרוּהָ כָּל־עֹבְרֵי דָרֶךְ:

14 Return, we beseech You, O God of hosts;
Look down from heaven and see,
And visit this vine

14 יְכַרְסְמֶנָּה חֲזִיר מִיָּעַר
וְזִיז שָׂדַי יִרְעֶנָּה:

15 And the vineyard which Your right hand has
planted,
And the branch *that* You made strong for
Yourself.

15 אֱלֹהִים צְבָאוֹת שׁוּב־נָא
הַבֵּט מִשָּׁמַיִם וּרְאֵה
וּפְקֹד גֶּפֶן זֹאת:

16 *It is* burned with fire, *it is* cut down;
They perish at the rebuke of Your countenance.

16 וְכַנָּה אֲשֶׁר־נָטְעָה יְמִינֶךָ
וְעַל־בֵּן אִמַּצְתָּה לָּךְ:

17 שְׂרֻפָה בָאֵשׁ כְּסוּחָה
מִגַּעֲרַת פָּנֶיךָ יֹאבֵדוּ:

17 Let Your hand be upon the man of Your right
    hand,
    Upon the son of man *whom* You made strong
    for Yourself.
18 Then we will not turn back from You;
    Revive us, and we will call upon Your name.
19 Restore us, O LORD God of hosts;
    Cause Your face to shine,
    And we shall be saved!

81
To the Chief Musician. On an instrument of Gath.
A Psalm of Asaph.
    Sing aloud to God our strength;
    Make a joyful shout to the God of Jacob.
2   Raise a song and strike the timbrel,
    The pleasant harp with the lute.
3   Blow the trumpet at the time of the New
    Moon,
    At the full moon, on our solemn feast day.
4   For this *is* a statute for Israel,
    A law of the God of Jacob.
5   This He established in Joseph *as* a testimony,
    When He went throughout the land of Egypt,
    Where I heard a language I did not understand.
6   "I removed his shoulder from the burden;
    His hands were freed from the baskets.
7   You called in trouble, and I delivered you;
    I answered you in the secret place of thunder;
    I tested you at the waters of Meribah.
                                        Selah

8   "Hear, O My people, and I will admonish you!
    O Israel, if you will listen to Me!
9   There shall be no foreign god among you;
    Nor shall you worship any foreign god.
10 I *am* the LORD your God,
    Who brought you out of the land of Egypt;
    Open your mouth wide, and I will fill it.
11 "But My people would not heed My voice,
    And Israel would *have* none of Me.
12 So I gave them over to their own stubborn
    heart,
    To walk in their own counsels.
13 "Oh, that My people would listen to Me,
    That Israel would walk in My ways!
14 I would soon subdue their enemies,
    And turn My hand against their adversaries.
15 The haters of the LORD would pretend
    submission to Him,
    But their fate would endure forever.
16 He would have fed them also with the finest of
    wheat;

פ֥א לַמְנַצֵּ֓חַ ׀ עַֽל־הַגִּתִּ֬ית לְאָסָֽף׃
2 הַ֭רְנִינוּ לֵאלֹהִ֣ים עוּזֵּ֑נוּ
  הָ֝רִ֗יעוּ לֵאלֹהֵ֥י יַעֲקֹֽב׃
3 שְֽׂאוּ־זִ֭מְרָה וּתְנוּ־תֹ֑ף
  כִּנּ֖וֹר נָעִ֣ים עִם־נָֽבֶל׃
4 תִּקְע֣וּ בַחֹ֣דֶשׁ שׁוֹפָ֑ר
  בַּ֝כֵּ֗סֶה לְי֣וֹם חַגֵּֽנוּ׃
5 כִּ֤י חֹ֣ק לְיִשְׂרָאֵ֣ל ה֑וּא
  מִ֝שְׁפָּ֗ט לֵאלֹהֵ֥י יַעֲקֹֽב׃
6 עֵ֤דוּת ׀ בִּֽיה�‍וֹסֵ֣ף שָׂמ֗וֹ
  בְּ֭צֵאתוֹ עַל־אֶ֣רֶץ מִצְרָ֑יִם
  שְׂפַ֖ת לֹא־יָדַ֣עְתִּי אֶשְׁמָֽע׃
7 הֲסִיר֣וֹתִי מִסֵּ֣בֶל שִׁכְמ֑וֹ
  כַּ֝פָּ֗יו מִדּ֥וּד תַּעֲבֹֽרְנָה׃
8 בַּצָּרָ֥ה קָרָ֗אתָ וָאֲחַ֫לְּצֶ֥ךָּ
  אֶ֭עֶנְךָ בְּסֵ֣תֶר רַ֑עַם
  אֶבְחָֽנְךָ֨ עַל־מֵ֖י מְרִיבָ֣ה סֶֽלָה׃
9 שְׁמַ֣ע עַ֭מִּי וְאָעִ֣ידָה בָּ֑ךְ
  יִ֝שְׂרָאֵ֗ל אִם־תִּֽשְׁמַֽע־לִֽי׃
10 לֹֽא־יִהְיֶ֣ה בְ֭ךָ אֵ֣ל זָ֑ר
   וְלֹ֥א תִ֝שְׁתַּחֲוֶ֗ה לְאֵ֣ל נֵכָֽר׃
11 אָנֹכִ֨י ׀ יְה֘וָ֤ה אֱלֹהֶ֗יךָ
   הַֽ֭מַּעַלְךָ מֵאֶ֣רֶץ מִצְרָ֑יִם
   הַרְחֶב־פִּ֝֗יךָ וַאֲמַלְאֵֽהוּ׃
12 וְלֹא־שָׁמַ֣ע עַמִּ֣י לְקוֹלִ֑י
   וְ֝יִשְׂרָאֵ֗ל לֹא־אָ֥בָה לִֽי׃
13 וָֽ֭אֲשַׁלְּחֵהוּ בִּשְׁרִיר֣וּת לִבָּ֑ם
   יֵ֝לְכ֗וּ בְּֽמוֹעֲצ֖וֹתֵיהֶֽם׃
14 ל֗וּ עַ֭מִּי שֹׁמֵ֣עַֽ לִ֑י
   יִ֝שְׂרָאֵ֗ל בִּדְרָכַ֥י יְהַלֵּֽכוּ׃
15 כִּ֭מְעַט אוֹיְבֵיהֶ֣ם אַכְנִ֑יעַ
   וְעַ֥ל צָ֝רֵיהֶ֗ם אָשִׁ֥יב יָדִֽי׃
16 מְשַׂנְאֵ֣י יְ֭הוָה יְכַחֲשׁוּ־ל֑וֹ
   וִיהִ֖י עִתָּ֣ם לְעוֹלָֽם׃

And with honey from the rock I would have   17
satisfied you."

82 A Psalm of Asaph.
God stands in the congregation of the mighty;
He judges among the gods.

2 How long will you judge unjustly,
And show partiality to the wicked?   Selah

3 Defend the poor and fatherless;
Do justice to the afflicted and needy.

4 Deliver the poor and needy;
Free *them* from the hand of the wicked.

5 They do not know, nor do they understand;
They walk about in darkness;
All the foundations of the earth are unstable.

6 I said, "You *are* gods,
And all of you *are* children of the Most High.

7 But you shall die like men,
And fall like one of the princes."

8 Arise, O God, judge the earth;
For You shall inherit all nations.

83 A Song. A Psalm of Asaph.
Do not keep silent, O God!
Do not hold Your peace,
And do not be still, O God!

2 For behold, Your enemies make a tumult;
And those who hate You have lifted up their
head.

3 They have taken crafty counsel against Your
people,
And consulted together against Your sheltered
ones.

4 They have said, "Come, and let us cut them off
from *being* a nation,
That the name of Israel may be remembered no
more."

5 For they have consulted together with one
consent;
They form a confederacy against You:

6 The tents of Edom and the Ishmaelites;
Moab and the Hagrites;

7 Gebal, Ammon, and Amalek;
Philistia with the inhabitants of Tyre;

8 Assyria also has joined with them;
They have helped the children of Lot.   Selah

9 Deal with them as *with* Midian,
As *with* Sisera,
As *with* Jabin at the Brook Kishon,

10 Who perished at En Dor,
Who became *as* refuse on the earth.

---

17 וַיַּאֲכִילֵהוּ מֵחֵלֶב חִטָּה
וּמִצּוּר דְּבַשׁ אַשְׂבִּיעֶךָ:

פב מִזְמוֹר לְאָסָף
אֱלֹהִים נִצָּב בַּעֲדַת־אֵל
בְּקֶרֶב אֱלֹהִים יִשְׁפֹּט:

2 עַד־מָתַי תִּשְׁפְּטוּ־עָוֶל
וּפְנֵי רְשָׁעִים תִּשְׂאוּ־סֶלָה:

3 שִׁפְטוּ־דַל וְיָתוֹם
עָנִי וָרָשׁ הַצְדִּיקוּ:

4 פַּלְּטוּ־דַל וְאֶבְיוֹן
מִיַּד רְשָׁעִים הַצִּילוּ:

5 לֹא יָדְעוּ וְלֹא יָבִינוּ
בַּחֲשֵׁכָה יִתְהַלָּכוּ
יִמּוֹטוּ
כָּל־מוֹסְדֵי אָרֶץ:

6 אֲנִי־אָמַרְתִּי אֱלֹהִים אַתֶּם
וּבְנֵי עֶלְיוֹן כֻּלְּכֶם:

7 אָכֵן כְּאָדָם תְּמוּתוּן
וּכְאַחַד הַשָּׂרִים תִּפֹּלוּ:

8 קוּמָה אֱלֹהִים שָׁפְטָה הָאָרֶץ
כִּי־אַתָּה תִנְחַל בְּכָל־הַגּוֹיִם:

פג שִׁיר מִזְמוֹר לְאָסָף:

2 אֱלֹהִים אַל־דֳּמִי־לָךְ
אַל־תֶּחֱרַשׁ וְאַל־תִּשְׁקֹט אֵל:

3 כִּי־הִנֵּה אוֹיְבֶיךָ יֶהֱמָיוּן
וּמְשַׂנְאֶיךָ נָשְׂאוּ רֹאשׁ:

4 עַל־עַמְּךָ יַעֲרִימוּ סוֹד
וְיִתְיָעֲצוּ עַל־צְפוּנֶיךָ:

5 אָמְרוּ לְכוּ וְנַכְחִידֵם מִגּוֹי
וְלֹא־יִזָּכֵר שֵׁם־יִשְׂרָאֵל עוֹד:

6 כִּי נוֹעֲצוּ לֵב יַחְדָּו
עָלֶיךָ בְּרִית יִכְרֹתוּ:

7 אָהֳלֵי אֱדוֹם וְיִשְׁמְעֵאלִים
מוֹאָב וְהַגְרִים:

8 גְּבָל וְעַמּוֹן וַעֲמָלֵק
פְּלֶשֶׁת עִם־יֹשְׁבֵי צוֹר:

9 גַּם־אַשּׁוּר נִלְוָה עִמָּם
הָיוּ זְרוֹעַ לִבְנֵי־לוֹט סֶלָה:

10 עֲשֵׂה־לָהֶם כְּמִדְיָן
כְּסִיסְרָא כְיָבִין בְּנַחַל קִישׁוֹן:

11 נִשְׁמְדוּ בְעֵין־דֹּאר
הָיוּ דֹּמֶן לָאֲדָמָה:

11 Make their nobles like Oreb and like Zeeb,
   Yes, all their princes like Zebah and Zalmunna,
12 Who said, "Let us take for ourselves
   The pastures of God for a possession."
13 O my God, make them like the whirling dust,
   Like the chaff before the wind!
14 As the fire burns the woods,
   And as the flame sets the mountains on fire,
15 So pursue them with Your tempest,
   And frighten them with Your storm.
16 Fill their faces with shame,
   That they may seek Your name, O LORD.
17 Let them be confounded and dismayed forever;
   Yes, let them be put to shame and perish,
18 That they may know that You, whose name
       alone *is* the LORD,
   Are the Most High over all the earth.

84 To the Chief Musician. On an instrument of Gath.
A Psalm of the sons of Korah.
   How lovely *is* Your tabernacle,
   O LORD of hosts!
2 My soul longs, yes, even faints
   For the courts of the LORD;
   My heart and my flesh cry out for the living
       God.
3 Even the sparrow has found a home,
   And the swallow a nest for herself,
   Where she may lay her young—
   Even Your altars, O LORD of hosts,
   My King and my God.
4 Blessed *are* those who dwell in Your house;
   They will still be praising You.   Selah
5 Blessed *is* the man whose strength *is* in You,
   Whose heart *is* set on pilgrimage.
6 *As they* pass through the Valley of Baca,
   They make it a spring;
   The rain also covers it with pools.
7 They go from strength to strength;
   Each one appears before God in Zion.
8 O LORD God of hosts, hear my prayer;
   Give ear, O God of Jacob!   Selah
9 O God, behold our shield,
   And look upon the face of Your anointed.
10 For a day in Your courts *is* better than a
       thousand.
   I would rather be a doorkeeper in the house of
       my God
   Than dwell in the tents of wickedness.
11 For the LORD God *is* a sun and shield;
   The LORD will give grace and glory;
   No good *thing* will He withhold

12 שִׁיתֵמוֹ נְדִיבֵמוֹ כְּעֹרֵב וְכִזְאֵב
   וּכְזֶבַח וּכְצַלְמֻנָּע כָּל־נְסִיכֵמוֹ׃
13 אֲשֶׁר אָמְרוּ נִירֲשָׁה לָּנוּ
   אֵת נְאוֹת אֱלֹהִים׃
14 אֱלֹהַי שִׁיתֵמוֹ כַגַּלְגַּל
   כְּקַשׁ לִפְנֵי־רוּחַ׃
15 כְּאֵשׁ תִּבְעַר־יָעַר
   וּכְלֶהָבָה תְּלַהֵט הָרִים׃
16 כֵּן תִּרְדְּפֵם בְּסַעֲרֶךָ
   וּבְסוּפָתְךָ תְבַהֲלֵם׃
17 מַלֵּא פְנֵיהֶם קָלוֹן
   וִיבַקְשׁוּ שִׁמְךָ יְהוָה׃
18 יֵבֹשׁוּ וְיִבָּהֲלוּ עֲדֵי־עַד
   וְיַחְפְּרוּ וְיֹאבֵדוּ׃
19 וְיֵדְעוּ כִּי־אַתָּה שִׁמְךָ יְהוָה לְבַדֶּךָ
   עֶלְיוֹן עַל־כָּל־הָאָרֶץ׃

פד לַמְנַצֵּחַ עַל־הַגִּתִּית לִבְנֵי־קֹרַח מִזְמוֹר׃
2 מַה־יְּדִידוֹת מִשְׁכְּנוֹתֶיךָ יְהוָה צְבָאוֹת׃
3 נִכְסְפָה וְגַם־כָּלְתָה נַפְשִׁי לְחַצְרוֹת יְהוָה
   לִבִּי וּבְשָׂרִי יְרַנְּנוּ אֶל אֵל־חָי׃
4 גַּם־צִפּוֹר מָצְאָה בַיִת וּדְרוֹר קֵן לָהּ
   אֲשֶׁר־שָׁתָה אֶפְרֹחֶיהָ
   אֶת־מִזְבְּחוֹתֶיךָ יְהוָה צְבָאוֹת
   מַלְכִּי וֵאלֹהָי׃
5 אַשְׁרֵי יוֹשְׁבֵי בֵיתֶךָ
   עוֹד יְהַלְלוּךָ סֶּלָה׃
6 אַשְׁרֵי אָדָם עוֹז־לוֹ בָךְ
   מְסִלּוֹת בִּלְבָבָם׃
7 עֹבְרֵי בְּעֵמֶק הַבָּכָא מַעְיָן יְשִׁיתוּהוּ
   גַּם־בְּרָכוֹת יַעְטֶה מוֹרֶה׃
8 יֵלְכוּ מֵחַיִל אֶל־חָיִל
   יֵרָאֶה אֶל־אֱלֹהִים בְּצִיּוֹן׃
9 יְהוָה אֱלֹהִים צְבָאוֹת שִׁמְעָה תְפִלָּתִי
   הַאֲזִינָה אֱלֹהֵי יַעֲקֹב סֶלָה׃
10 מָגִנֵּנוּ רְאֵה אֱלֹהִים
   וְהַבֵּט פְּנֵי מְשִׁיחֶךָ׃
11 כִּי טוֹב־יוֹם בַּחֲצֵרֶיךָ מֵאָלֶף
   בָּחַרְתִּי הִסְתּוֹפֵף בְּבֵית אֱלֹהַי
   מִדּוּר בְּאָהֳלֵי־רֶשַׁע׃
12 כִּי שֶׁמֶשׁ וּמָגֵן יְהוָה אֱלֹהִים
   חֵן וְכָבוֹד יִתֵּן יְהוָה
   לֹא יִמְנַע־טוֹב

From those who walk uprightly.

לְהֹלְכִים בְּתָמִים:

12 O LORD of hosts,
Blessed *is* the man who trusts in You!

13 יְהֹוָה צְבָאוֹת
אַשְׁרֵי אָדָם בֹּטֵחַ בָּךְ:

85 To the Chief Musician. A Psalm of the sons of Korah.

פֿה לַמְנַצֵּחַ | לִבְנֵי־קֹרַח מִזְמוֹר:

LORD, You have been favorable to Your land;
You have brought back the captivity of Jacob.

2 רָצִיתָ יְהֹוָה אַרְצֶךָ
שַׁבְתָּ שְׁבוּת יַעֲקֹב:

2 You have forgiven the iniquity of Your people;
You have covered all their sin.   Selah

3 נָשָׂאתָ עֲוֹן עַמֶּךָ
כִּסִּיתָ כָל־חַטָּאתָם סֶלָה:

3 You have taken away all Your wrath;
You have turned from the fierceness of Your anger.

4 אָסַפְתָּ כָל־עֶבְרָתֶךָ
הֱשִׁיבוֹתָ מֵחֲרוֹן אַפֶּךָ:

4 Restore us, O God of our salvation,
And cause Your anger toward us to cease.

5 שׁוּבֵנוּ אֱלֹהֵי יִשְׁעֵנוּ
וְהָפֵר כַּעַסְךָ עִמָּנוּ:

5 Will You be angry with us forever?
Will You prolong Your anger to all generations?

6 הַלְעוֹלָם תֶּאֱנַף־בָּנוּ
תִּמְשֹׁךְ אַפְּךָ לְדֹר וָדֹר:

6 Will You not revive us again,
That Your people may rejoice in You?

7 הֲלֹא־אַתָּה תָּשׁוּב תְּחַיֵּנוּ
וְעַמְּךָ יִשְׂמְחוּ־בָךְ:

7 Show us Your mercy, LORD,
And grant us Your salvation.

8 הַרְאֵנוּ יְהֹוָה חַסְדֶּךָ
וְיֶשְׁעֲךָ תִּתֶּן־לָנוּ:

8 I will hear what God the LORD will speak,
For He will speak peace
To His people and to His saints;
But let them not turn back to folly.

9 אֶשְׁמְעָה מַה־יְדַבֵּר הָאֵל | יְהֹוָה
כִּי | יְדַבֵּר שָׁלוֹם אֶל־עַמּוֹ וְאֶל־חֲסִידָיו
וְאַל־יָשׁוּבוּ לְכִסְלָה:

9 Surely His salvation *is* near to those who fear Him,
That glory may dwell in our land.

10 אַךְ | קָרוֹב לִירֵאָיו יִשְׁעוֹ
לִשְׁכֹּן כָּבוֹד בְּאַרְצֵנוּ:

10 Mercy and truth have met together;
Righteousness and peace have kissed.

11 חֶסֶד־וֶאֱמֶת נִפְגָּשׁוּ
צֶדֶק וְשָׁלוֹם נָשָׁקוּ:

11 Truth shall spring out of the earth,
And righteousness shall look down from heaven.

12 אֱמֶת מֵאֶרֶץ תִּצְמָח
וְצֶדֶק מִשָּׁמַיִם נִשְׁקָף:

12 Yes, the LORD will give *what is* good;
And our land will yield its increase.

13 גַּם־יְהֹוָה יִתֵּן הַטּוֹב
וְאַרְצֵנוּ תִּתֵּן יְבוּלָהּ:

13 Righteousness will go before Him,
And shall make His footsteps *our* pathway.

14 צֶדֶק לְפָנָיו יְהַלֵּךְ
וְיָשֵׂם לְדֶרֶךְ פְּעָמָיו:

86 A Prayer of David.

פֿו תְּפִלָּה לְדָוִד

Bow down Your ear, O LORD, hear me;
For I *am* poor and needy.

הַטֵּה־יְהֹוָה אָזְנְךָ עֲנֵנִי כִּי־עָנִי וְאֶבְיוֹן אָנִי:

2 Preserve my life, for I *am* holy;
You are my God;
Save Your servant who trusts in You!

2 שָׁמְרָה נַפְשִׁי כִּי־חָסִיד אָנִי
הוֹשַׁע עַבְדְּךָ אַתָּה אֱלֹהַי הַבּוֹטֵחַ אֵלֶיךָ:

3 Be merciful to me, O Lord,
For I cry to You all day long.

3 חָנֵּנִי אֲדֹנָי
כִּי אֵלֶיךָ אֶקְרָא כָּל־הַיּוֹם:

4 Rejoice the soul of Your servant,
For to You, O Lord, I lift up my soul.

4 שַׂמֵּחַ נֶפֶשׁ עַבְדֶּךָ
כִּי אֵלֶיךָ אֲדֹנָי נַפְשִׁי אֶשָּׂא:

5 For You, Lord, *are* good, and ready to forgive,
And abundant in mercy to all those who call upon You.

5 כִּי־אַתָּה אֲדֹנָי טוֹב וְסַלָּח
וְרַב־חֶסֶד לְכָל־קֹרְאֶיךָ:

6 Give ear, O LORD, to my prayer;
And attend to the voice of my supplications.

7 In the day of my trouble I will call upon You,
For You will answer me.

8 Among the gods *there is* none like You, O
Lord;
Nor *are there any works* like Your works.

9 All nations whom You have made
Shall come and worship before You, O Lord,
And shall glorify Your name.

10 For You *are* great, and do wondrous things;
You alone *are* God.

11 Teach me Your way, O LORD;
I will walk in Your truth;
Unite my heart to fear Your name.

12 I will praise You, O Lord my God, with all my
heart,
And I will glorify Your name forevermore.

13 For great *is* Your mercy toward me,
And You have delivered my soul from the
depths of Sheol.

14 O God, the proud have risen against me,
And a mob of violent *men* have sought my life,
And have not set You before them.

15 But You, O Lord, *are* a God full of
compassion, and gracious,
Longsuffering and abundant in mercy and
truth.

16 Oh, turn to me, and have mercy on me!
Give Your strength to Your servant,
And save the son of Your maidservant.

17 Show me a sign for good,
That those who hate me may see *it* and be
ashamed,
Because You, LORD, have helped me and
comforted me.

87

A Psalm of the sons of Korah. A Song.
His foundation *is* in the holy mountains.

2 The LORD loves the gates of Zion
More than all the dwellings of Jacob.

3 Glorious things are spoken of you,
O city of God!   Selah

4 "I will make mention of Rahab and Babylon to
those who know Me;
Behold, O Philistia and Tyre, with Ethiopia:
'This *one* was born there.'"

5 And of Zion it will be said,
"This *one* and that *one* were born in her;
And the Most High Himself shall establish
her."

---

6 הַאֲזִינָה יְהֹוָה תְּפִלָּתִי
וְהַקְשִׁיבָה בְּקוֹל תַּחֲנוּנוֹתָי:

7 בְּיוֹם צָרָתִי אֶקְרָאֶךָּ
כִּי תַעֲנֵנִי:

8 אֵין־כָּמוֹךָ בָאֱלֹהִים ׀ אֲדֹנָי
וְאֵין כְּמַעֲשֶׂיךָ:

9 כָּל־גּוֹיִם ׀ אֲשֶׁר עָשִׂיתָ יָבוֹאוּ ׀ וְיִשְׁתַּחֲווּ
לְפָנֶיךָ אֲדֹנָי
וִיכַבְּדוּ לִשְׁמֶךָ:

10 כִּי־גָדוֹל אַתָּה וְעֹשֵׂה נִפְלָאוֹת
אַתָּה אֱלֹהִים לְבַדֶּךָ:

11 הוֹרֵנִי יְהֹוָה ׀ דַּרְכֶּךָ
אֲהַלֵּךְ בַּאֲמִתֶּךָ
יַחֵד לְבָבִי
לְיִרְאָה שְׁמֶךָ:

12 אוֹדְךָ ׀ אֲדֹנָי אֱלֹהַי בְּכָל־לְבָבִי
וַאֲכַבְּדָה שִׁמְךָ לְעוֹלָם:

13 כִּי־חַסְדְּךָ גָּדוֹל עָלָי
וְהִצַּלְתָּ נַפְשִׁי מִשְּׁאוֹל תַּחְתִּיָּה:

14 אֱלֹהִים ׀ זֵדִים קָמוּ־עָלַי
וַעֲדַת עָרִיצִים בִּקְשׁוּ נַפְשִׁי
וְלֹא שָׂמוּךָ לְנֶגְדָּם:

15 וְאַתָּה אֲדֹנָי אֵל־רַחוּם וְחַנּוּן
אֶרֶךְ אַפַּיִם וְרַב־חֶסֶד וֶאֱמֶת:

16 פְּנֵה אֵלַי וְחָנֵּנִי
תְּנָה־עֻזְּךָ לְעַבְדֶּךָ וְהוֹשִׁיעָה לְבֶן־אֲמָתֶךָ:

17 עֲשֵׂה־עִמִּי אוֹת לְטוֹבָה
וְיִרְאוּ שֹׂנְאַי וְיֵבֹשׁוּ
כִּי־אַתָּה יְהֹוָה עֲזַרְתַּנִי וְנִחַמְתָּנִי:

פז לִבְנֵי־קֹרַח מִזְמוֹר שִׁיר
יְסוּדָתוֹ בְּהַרְרֵי־קֹדֶשׁ:

2 אֹהֵב יְהֹוָה שַׁעֲרֵי צִיּוֹן
מִכֹּל מִשְׁכְּנוֹת יַעֲקֹב:

3 נִכְבָּדוֹת מְדֻבָּר בָּךְ
עִיר הָאֱלֹהִים סֶלָה:

4 אַזְכִּיר ׀ רַהַב וּבָבֶל לְיֹדְעָי
הִנֵּה פְלֶשֶׁת וְצוֹר עִם־כּוּשׁ
זֶה יֻלַּד־שָׁם:

5 וּלֲצִיּוֹן ׀ יֵאָמַר
אִישׁ וְאִישׁ יֻלַּד־בָּהּ
וְהוּא יְכוֹנְנֶהָ עֶלְיוֹן:

6 The LORD will record,
When He registers the peoples:
"This *one* was born there."　　　Selah

7 Both the singers and the players on instruments
say,
"All my springs *are* in you."

88 A Song. A Psalm of the sons of Korah. To the
Chief Musician. Set to "Mahalath Leannoth." A
Contemplation of Heman the Ezrahite.
O LORD, God of my salvation,
I have cried out day and night before You.
2 Let my prayer come before You;
Incline Your ear to my cry.

3 For my soul is full of troubles,
And my life draws near to the grave.
4 I am counted with those who go down to the
pit;
I am like a man *who has* no strength,
5 Adrift among the dead,
Like the slain who lie in the grave,
Whom You remember no more,
And who are cut off from Your hand.

6 You have laid me in the lowest pit,
In darkness, in the depths.
7 Your wrath lies heavy upon me,
And You have afflicted *me* with all Your
waves.　　　Selah
8 You have put away my acquaintances far from
me;
You have made me an abomination to them;
I am shut up, and I cannot get out;
9 My eye wastes away because of affliction.

LORD, I have called daily upon You;
I have stretched out my hands to You.
10 Will You work wonders for the dead?
Shall the dead arise *and* praise You?　　Selah
11 Shall Your lovingkindness be declared in the
grave?
Or Your faithfulness in the place of
destruction?
12 Shall Your wonders be known in the dark?
And Your righteousness in the land of
forgetfulness?

13 But to You I have cried out, O LORD,
And in the morning my prayer comes before
You.
14 LORD, why do You cast off my soul?
Why do You hide Your face from me?
15 I *have been* afflicted and ready to die from *my*
youth;
I suffer Your terrors;

6 יְהֹוָה יִסְפֹּר בִּכְתוֹב עַמִּים
זֶה יֻלַּד־שָׁם סֶלָה:

7 וְשָׁרִים כְּחֹלְלִים
כָּל־מַעְיָנַי בָּךְ:

פח שִׁיר מִזְמוֹר לִבְנֵי קֹרַח
לַמְנַצֵּחַ עַל־מָחֲלַת לְעַנּוֹת
מַשְׂכִּיל לְהֵימָן הָאֶזְרָחִי:
2 יְהֹוָה אֱלֹהֵי יְשׁוּעָתִי
יוֹם־צָעַקְתִּי בַלַּיְלָה נֶגְדֶּךָ:

3 תָּבוֹא לְפָנֶיךָ תְּפִלָּתִי
הַטֵּה־אָזְנְךָ לְרִנָּתִי:
4 כִּי־שָׂבְעָה בְרָעוֹת נַפְשִׁי
וְחַיַּי לִשְׁאוֹל הִגִּיעוּ:
5 נֶחְשַׁבְתִּי עִם־יוֹרְדֵי בוֹר
הָיִיתִי כְּגֶבֶר אֵין־אֱיָל:

6 בַּמֵּתִים חָפְשִׁי
כְּמוֹ חֲלָלִים שֹׁכְבֵי קֶבֶר
אֲשֶׁר לֹא זְכַרְתָּם עוֹד
וְהֵמָּה
מִיָּדְךָ נִגְזָרוּ:

7 שַׁתַּנִי בְּבוֹר תַּחְתִּיּוֹת
בְּמַחֲשַׁכִּים בִּמְצֹלוֹת:
8 עָלַי סָמְכָה חֲמָתֶךָ
וְכָל־מִשְׁבָּרֶיךָ עִנִּיתָ סֶּלָה:
9 הִרְחַקְתָּ מְיֻדָּעַי מִמֶּנִּי
שַׁתַּנִי תוֹעֵבוֹת לָמוֹ כָּלֻא וְלֹא אֵצֵא:
10 עֵינִי דָאֲבָה

מִנִּי עֹנִי קְרָאתִיךָ יְהֹוָה בְּכָל־יוֹם
שִׁטַּחְתִּי אֵלֶיךָ כַפָּי:
11 הֲלַמֵּתִים תַּעֲשֶׂה־פֶּלֶא
אִם־רְפָאִים יָקוּמוּ יוֹדוּךָ סֶּלָה:
12 הַיְסֻפַּר בַּקֶּבֶר חַסְדֶּךָ
אֱמוּנָתְךָ בָּאֲבַדּוֹן:
13 הֲיִוָּדַע בַּחֹשֶׁךְ פִּלְאֶךָ
וְצִדְקָתְךָ בְּאֶרֶץ נְשִׁיָּה:

14 וַאֲנִי אֵלֶיךָ יְהֹוָה שִׁוַּעְתִּי
וּבַבֹּקֶר תְּפִלָּתִי תְקַדְּמֶךָּ:
15 לָמָה יְהֹוָה תִּזְנַח נַפְשִׁי
תַּסְתִּיר פָּנֶיךָ מִמֶּנִּי:
16 עָנִי אֲנִי וְגֹוֵעַ מִנֹּעַר
נָשָׂאתִי אֵמֶיךָ אָפוּנָה:

I am distraught.

16 Your fierce wrath has gone over me;
Your terrors have cut me off.

17 They came around me all day long like water;
They engulfed me altogether.

18 Loved one and friend You have put far from me,
And my acquaintances into darkness.

89 A Contemplation of Ethan the Ezrahite.

I will sing of the mercies of the LORD forever;
With my mouth will I make known Your
faithfulness to all generations.

2 For I have said, "Mercy shall be built up
forever;
Your faithfulness You shall establish in the
very heavens."

3 "I have made a covenant with My chosen,
I have sworn to My servant David:

4 'Your seed I will establish forever,
And build up your throne to all generations.'"
Selah

5 And the heavens will praise Your wonders, O
LORD;
Your faithfulness also in the assembly of the
saints.

6 For who in the heavens can be compared to the
LORD?
Who among the sons of the mighty can be
likened to the LORD?

7 God is greatly to be feared in the assembly of
the saints,
And to be held in reverence by all *those* around
Him.

8 O LORD God of hosts,
Who *is* mighty like You, O LORD?
Your faithfulness also surrounds You.

9 You rule the raging of the sea;
When its waves rise, You still them.

10 You have broken Rahab in pieces, as one who
is slain;
You have scattered Your enemies with Your
mighty arm.

11 The heavens *are* Yours, the earth also *is* Yours;
The world and all its fullness, You have
founded them.

12 The north and the south, You have created
them;
Tabor and Hermon rejoice in Your name.

13 You have a mighty arm;
Strong is Your hand, *and* high is Your right
hand.

17 עָלַי עָבְרוּ חֲרוֹנֶיךָ
בְּעִוּתֶיךָ צִמְּתוּתֻנִי:

18 סַבּוּנִי כַמַּיִם כָּל־הַיּוֹם
הִקִּיפוּ עָלַי יָחַד:

19 הִרְחַקְתָּ מִמֶּנִּי אֹהֵב וָרֵעַ
מְיֻדָּעַי מַחְשָׁךְ:

פט מַשְׂכִּיל לְאֵיתָן הָאֶזְרָחִי:

2 חַסְדֵי יְהוָה עוֹלָם אָשִׁירָה
לְדֹר וָדֹר ׀ אוֹדִיעַ אֱמוּנָתְךָ בְּפִי:

3 כִּי־אָמַרְתִּי עוֹלָם חֶסֶד יִבָּנֶה
שָׁמַיִם ׀ תָּכִן אֱמוּנָתְךָ בָהֶם:

4 כָּרַתִּי בְרִית לִבְחִירִי
נִשְׁבַּעְתִּי לְדָוִד עַבְדִּי:

5 עַד־עוֹלָם אָכִין זַרְעֶךָ
וּבָנִיתִי לְדֹר־וָדוֹר כִּסְאֲךָ סֶלָה:

6 וְיוֹדוּ שָׁמַיִם פִּלְאֲךָ יְהוָה
אַף־אֱמוּנָתְךָ בִּקְהַל קְדֹשִׁים:

7 כִּי מִי בַשַּׁחַק יַעֲרֹךְ לַיהוָה
יִדְמֶה לַיהוָה בִּבְנֵי אֵלִים:

8 אֵל נַעֲרָץ בְּסוֹד־קְדֹשִׁים רַבָּה
וְנוֹרָא עַל־כָּל־סְבִיבָיו:

9 יְהוָה ׀ אֱלֹהֵי צְבָאוֹת מִי־כָמוֹךָ חֲסִין ׀ יָהּ
וֶאֱמוּנָתְךָ סְבִיבוֹתֶיךָ:

10 אַתָּה מוֹשֵׁל בְּגֵאוּת הַיָּם
בְּשׂוֹא גַלָּיו אַתָּה תְשַׁבְּחֵם:

11 אַתָּה דִכִּאתָ כֶחָלָל רָהַב
בִּזְרוֹעַ עֻזְּךָ פִּזַּרְתָּ אוֹיְבֶיךָ:

12 לְךָ שָׁמַיִם אַף־לְךָ אָרֶץ
תֵּבֵל וּמְלֹאָהּ אַתָּה יְסַדְתָּם:

13 צָפוֹן וְיָמִין אַתָּה בְרָאתָם
תָּבוֹר וְחֶרְמוֹן בְּשִׁמְךָ יְרַנֵּנוּ:

14 לְךָ זְרוֹעַ עִם־גְּבוּרָה
תָּעֹז יָדְךָ תָּרוּם יְמִינֶךָ:

15 צֶדֶק וּמִשְׁפָּט מְכוֹן כִּסְאֶךָ
חֶסֶד וֶאֱמֶת יְקַדְּמוּ פָנֶיךָ:

16 אַשְׁרֵי הָעָם יוֹדְעֵי תְרוּעָה
יְהוָה בְּאוֹר־פָּנֶיךָ יְהַלֵּכוּן:

¹⁴ Righteousness and justice *are* the foundation of
    Your throne;
    Mercy and truth go before Your face.

¹⁵ Blessed *are* the people who know the joyful
    sound!
    They walk, O LORD, in the light of Your
    countenance.

¹⁶ In Your name they rejoice all day long,
    And in Your righteousness they are exalted.

¹⁷ For You *are* the glory of their strength,
    And in Your favor our horn is exalted.

¹⁸ For our shield *belongs* to the LORD,
    And our king to the Holy One of Israel.

¹⁹ Then You spoke in a vision to Your holy one,
    And said: "I have given help to *one who is*
    mighty;
    I have exalted one chosen from the people.

²⁰ I have found My servant David;
    With My holy oil I have anointed him,

²¹ With whom My hand shall be established;
    Also My arm shall strengthen him.

²² The enemy shall not outwit him,
    Nor the son of wickedness afflict him.

²³ I will beat down his foes before his face,
    And plague those who hate him.

²⁴ "But My faithfulness and My mercy *shall be*
    with him,
    And in My name his horn shall be exalted.

²⁵ Also I will set his hand over the sea,
    And his right hand over the rivers.

²⁶ He shall cry to Me, 'You *are* my Father,
    My God, and the rock of my salvation.'

²⁷ Also I will make him *My* firstborn,
    The highest of the kings of the earth.

²⁸ My mercy I will keep for him forever,
    And My covenant shall stand firm with him.

²⁹ His seed also I will make *to endure* forever,
    And his throne as the days of heaven.

³⁰ "If his sons forsake My law
    And do not walk in My judgments,

³¹ If they break My statutes
    And do not keep My commandments,

³² Then I will punish their transgression with the
    rod,
    And their iniquity with stripes.

³³ Nevertheless My lovingkindness I will not
    utterly take from him,
    Nor allow My faithfulness to fail.

³⁴ My covenant I will not break,
    Nor alter the word that has gone out of My
    lips.

³⁵ Once I have sworn by My holiness;
    I will not lie to David:

17 בִּשְׁמְךָ יְגִילוּן כָּל־הַיּוֹם
וּבְצִדְקָתְךָ יָרוּמוּ:

18 כִּי־תִפְאֶרֶת עֻזָּמוֹ אָתָּה
וּבִרְצֹנְךָ תָּרִים° קַרְנֵנוּ:

19 כִּי לַיהוָה מָגִנֵּנוּ
וְלִקְדוֹשׁ יִשְׂרָאֵל מַלְכֵּנוּ:

20 אָז דִּבַּרְתָּ־בְחָזוֹן לַחֲסִידֶיךָ
וַתֹּאמֶר שִׁוִּיתִי עֵזֶר עַל־גִּבּוֹר
הֲרִימוֹתִי בָחוּר מֵעָם:

21 מָצָאתִי דָּוִד עַבְדִּי
בְּשֶׁמֶן קָדְשִׁי מְשַׁחְתִּיו:

22 אֲשֶׁר יָדִי תִּכּוֹן עִמּוֹ
אַף־זְרוֹעִי תְאַמְּצֶנּוּ:

23 לֹא־יַשִּׁא אוֹיֵב בּוֹ
וּבֶן־עַוְלָה לֹא יְעַנֶּנּוּ:

24 וְכַתּוֹתִי מִפָּנָיו צָרָיו
וּמְשַׂנְאָיו אֶגּוֹף:

25 וֶאֱמוּנָתִי וְחַסְדִּי עִמּוֹ
וּבִשְׁמִי תָּרוּם קַרְנוֹ:

26 וְשַׂמְתִּי בַיָּם יָדוֹ
וּבַנְּהָרוֹת יְמִינוֹ:

27 הוּא יִקְרָאֵנִי אָבִי אָתָּה
אֵלִי וְצוּר יְשׁוּעָתִי:

28 אַף־אָנִי בְּכוֹר אֶתְּנֵהוּ
עֶלְיוֹן לְמַלְכֵי־אָרֶץ:

29 לְעוֹלָם אֶשְׁמוֹר־° לוֹ חַסְדִּי
וּבְרִיתִי נֶאֱמֶנֶת לוֹ:

30 וְשַׂמְתִּי לָעַד זַרְעוֹ
וְכִסְאוֹ כִּימֵי שָׁמָיִם:

31 אִם־יַעַזְבוּ בָנָיו תּוֹרָתִי
וּבְמִשְׁפָּטַי לֹא יֵלֵכוּן:

32 אִם־חֻקֹּתַי יְחַלֵּלוּ
וּמִצְוֹתַי לֹא יִשְׁמֹרוּ:

33 וּפָקַדְתִּי בְשֵׁבֶט פִּשְׁעָם
וּבִנְגָעִים עֲוֹנָם:

34 וְחַסְדִּי לֹא־אָפִיר מֵעִמּוֹ
וְלֹא־אֲשַׁקֵּר בֶּאֱמוּנָתִי:

35 לֹא־אֲחַלֵּל בְּרִיתִי
וּמוֹצָא שְׂפָתַי לֹא אֲשַׁנֶּה:

36 אַחַת נִשְׁבַּעְתִּי בְקָדְשִׁי
אִם־לְדָוִד אֲכַזֵּב:

36 His seed shall endure forever,
And his throne as the sun before Me;
37 It shall be established forever like the moon,
Even *like* the faithful witness in the sky."
Selah

38 But You have cast off and abhorred,
You have been furious with Your anointed.
39 You have renounced the covenant of Your
servant;
You have profaned his crown *by casting it* to
the ground.
40 You have broken down all his hedges;
You have brought his strongholds to ruin.
41 All who pass by the way plunder him;
He is a reproach to his neighbors.
42 You have exalted the right hand of his
adversaries;
You have made all his enemies rejoice.
43 You have also turned back the edge of his
sword,
And have not sustained him in the battle.
44 You have made his glory cease,
And cast his throne down to the ground.
45 The days of his youth You have shortened;
You have covered him with shame.　　Selah

46 How long, LORD?
Will You hide Yourself forever?
Will Your wrath burn like fire?
47 Remember how short my time is;
For what futility have You created all the
children of men?
48 What man can live and not see death?
Can he deliver his life from the power of the
grave?　　Selah

49 Lord, where *are* Your former lovingkindnesses,
Which You swore to David in Your truth?
50 Remember, Lord, the reproach of Your
servants—
How I bear in my bosom *the reproach of* all the
many peoples,
51 With which Your enemies have reproached, O
LORD,
With which they have reproached the footsteps
of Your anointed.

52 Blessed *be* the LORD forevermore!
Amen and Amen.

Book Four: Psalms 90—106

90 A Prayer of Moses the man of God.
LORD, You have been our dwelling place in all
generations.

זַרְעוֹ לְעוֹלָם יִהְיֶה 37
וְכִסְאוֹ כַשֶּׁמֶשׁ נֶגְדִּי:
כְּיָרֵחַ יִכּוֹן עוֹלָם 38
וְעֵד בַּשַּׁחַק נֶאֱמָן סֶלָה:
וְאַתָּה זָנַחְתָּ וַתִּמְאָס 39
הִתְעַבַּרְתָּ עִם־מְשִׁיחֶךָ:
נֵאַרְתָּה בְּרִית עַבְדֶּךָ 40
חִלַּלְתָּ לָאָרֶץ נִזְרוֹ:
פָּרַצְתָּ כָל־גְּדֵרֹתָיו 41
שַׂמְתָּ מִבְצָרָיו מְחִתָּה:
שַׁסֻּהוּ כָּל־עֹבְרֵי דָרֶךְ 42
הָיָה חֶרְפָּה לִשְׁכֵנָיו:
הֲרִימוֹתָ יְמִין צָרָיו 43
הִשְׂמַחְתָּ כָּל־אוֹיְבָיו:
אַף־תָּשִׁיב צוּר חַרְבּוֹ 44
וְלֹא הֲקֵימֹתוֹ בַּמִּלְחָמָה:
הִשְׁבַּתָּ מִטְּהָרוֹ 45
וְכִסְאוֹ לָאָרֶץ מִגַּרְתָּה:
הִקְצַרְתָּ יְמֵי עֲלוּמָיו 46
הֶעֱטִיתָ עָלָיו בּוּשָׁה סֶלָה:
עַד־מָה יְהֹוָה תִּסָּתֵר לָנֶצַח 47
תִּבְעַר כְּמוֹ־אֵשׁ חֲמָתֶךָ:
זְכָר־אֲנִי מֶה־חָלֶד 48
עַל־מַה־שָּׁוְא בָּרָאתָ כָל־בְּנֵי־אָדָם:
מִי גֶבֶר יִחְיֶה וְלֹא יִרְאֶה־מָּוֶת 49
יְמַלֵּט נַפְשׁוֹ מִיַּד־שְׁאוֹל סֶלָה:
אַיֵּה חֲסָדֶיךָ הָרִאשֹׁנִים אֲדֹנָי 50
נִשְׁבַּעְתָּ לְדָוִד בֶּאֱמוּנָתֶךָ:
זְכֹר אֲדֹנָי חֶרְפַּת עֲבָדֶיךָ 51
שְׂאֵתִי בְחֵיקִי כָּל־רַבִּים עַמִּים:
אֲשֶׁר חֵרְפוּ אוֹיְבֶיךָ יְהֹוָה 52
אֲשֶׁר חֵרְפוּ עִקְּבוֹת מְשִׁיחֶךָ:
בָּרוּךְ יְהֹוָה לְעוֹלָם 53
אָמֵן וְאָמֵן:

צ תְּפִלָּה לְמֹשֶׁה אִישׁ־הָאֱלֹהִים
אֲדֹנָי מָעוֹן אַתָּה הָיִיתָ לָּנוּ
בְּדֹר וָדֹר:

2 Before the mountains were brought forth,
Or ever You had formed the earth and the
   world,
Even from everlasting to everlasting, You *are*
   God.

3 You turn man to destruction,
And say, "Return, O children of men."

4 For a thousand years in Your sight
Are like yesterday when it is past,
And *like* a watch in the night.

5 You carry them away *like* a flood;
They are like a sleep.
In the morning they are like grass *which* grows
   up:

6 In the morning it flourishes and grows up;
In the evening it is cut down and withers.

7 For we have been consumed by Your anger,
And by Your wrath we are terrified.

8 You have set our iniquities before You,
Our secret *sins* in the light of Your
   countenance.

9 For all our days have passed away in Your
   wrath;
We finish our years like a sigh.

10 The days of our lives *are* seventy years;
And if by reason of strength *they are* eighty
   years,
Yet their boast *is* only labor and sorrow;
For it is soon cut off, and we fly away.

11 Who knows the power of Your anger?
For as the fear of You, *so is* Your wrath.

12 So teach *us* to number our days,
That we may gain a heart of wisdom.

13 Return, O LORD!
How long?
And have compassion on Your servants.

14 Oh, satisfy us early with Your mercy,
That we may rejoice and be glad all our days!

15 Make us glad according to the days *in which*
   You have afflicted us,
The years *in which* we have seen evil.

16 Let Your work appear to Your servants,
And Your glory to their children.

17 And let the beauty of the LORD our God be
   upon us,
And establish the work of our hands for us;
Yes, establish the work of our hands.

91 He who dwells in the secret place of the Most
   High

Shall abide under the shadow of the Almighty.

2 בְּטֶ֤רֶם ׀ הָ֘רִ֤ים יֻלָּ֗דוּ
וַתְּח֣וֹלֵֽל אֶ֣רֶץ וְתֵבֵ֑ל
וּֽמֵעוֹלָ֥ם עַד־עֹ֝ולָ֗ם
אַתָּ֥ה אֵֽל׃

3 תָּשֵׁ֣ב אֱ֭נוֹשׁ עַד־דַּכָּ֑א
וַ֝תֹּ֗אמֶר שׁ֣וּבוּ בְנֵי־אָדָֽם׃

4 כִּ֤י אֶ֪לֶף שָׁנִ֡ים בְּֽעֵינֶ֗יךָ
כְּי֣וֹם אֶ֭תְמוֹל כִּ֣י יַעֲבֹ֑ר
וְאַשְׁמוּרָ֥ה בַלָּֽיְלָה׃

5 זְ֭רַמְתָּם שֵׁנָ֣ה יִהְי֑וּ
בַּ֝בֹּ֗קֶר כֶּחָצִ֥יר יַחֲלֹֽף׃

6 בַּ֭בֹּקֶר יָצִ֣יץ וְחָלָ֑ף
לָ֝עֶ֗רֶב יְמוֹלֵ֥ל וְיָבֵֽשׁ׃

7 כִּֽי־כָלִ֥ינוּ בְאַפֶּ֑ךָ
וּֽבַחֲמָתְךָ֥ נִבְהָֽלְנוּ׃

8 שַׁתָּ֣ה עֲוֺנֹתֵ֣ינוּ לְנֶגְדֶּ֑ךָ
עֲ֝לֻמֵ֗נוּ לִמְא֥וֹר פָּנֶֽיךָ׃

9 כִּ֣י כָל־יָ֭מֵינוּ פָּנ֣וּ בְעֶבְרָתֶ֑ךָ
כִּלִּ֖ינוּ שָׁנֵ֣ינוּ כְמוֹ־הֶֽגֶה׃

10 יְמֵֽי־שְׁנוֹתֵ֨ינוּ בָהֶ֥ם שִׁבְעִ֣ים שָׁנָ֗ה
וְאִ֤ם בִּגְבוּרֹ֨ת ׀ שְׁמ֘וֹנִ֤ים שָׁנָ֗ה
וְ֭רָהְבָּם עָמָ֣ל וָאָ֑וֶן כִּי־גָ֥ז חִ֝֗ישׁ וַנָּעֻֽפָה׃

11 מִֽי־י֭וֹדֵעַ עֹ֣ז אַפֶּ֑ךָ
וּ֝כְיִרְאָתְךָ֗ עֶבְרָתֶֽךָ׃

12 לִמְנ֣וֹת יָ֭מֵינוּ כֵּ֣ן הוֹדַ֑ע
וְ֝נָבִ֗א לְבַ֣ב חָכְמָֽה׃

13 שׁוּבָ֣ה יְ֭הֹוָה עַד־מָתָ֑י
וְ֝הִנָּחֵ֗ם עַל־עֲבָדֶֽיךָ׃

14 שַׂבְּעֵ֣נוּ בַבֹּ֣קֶר חַסְדֶּ֑ךָ
וּֽנְרַנְּנָ֥ה וְ֝נִשְׂמְחָ֗ה בְּכׇל־יָמֵֽינוּ׃

15 שַׂ֭מְּחֵנוּ כִּימ֣וֹת עִנִּיתָ֑נוּ
שְׁ֝נ֗וֹת רָאִ֥ינוּ רָעָֽה׃

16 יֵרָאֶ֣ה אֶל־עֲבָדֶ֣יךָ פׇעֳלֶ֑ךָ
וַ֝הֲדָרְךָ֗ עַל־בְּנֵיהֶֽם׃

17 וִיהִ֤י ׀ נֹ֤עַם אֲדֹנָ֥י אֱלֹהֵ֗ינוּ עָ֫לֵ֥ינוּ
וּמַעֲשֵׂ֣ה יָ֭דֵינוּ כּוֹנְנָ֥ה עָלֵ֑ינוּ
וּֽמַעֲשֵׂ֥ה יָ֝דֵ֗ינוּ כּוֹנְנֵֽהוּ׃

צא יֹ֭שֵׁב בְּסֵ֣תֶר עֶלְי֑וֹן
בְּצֵ֥ל שַׁ֝דַּ֗י יִתְלוֹנָֽן׃

2   I will say of the LORD, "*He is* my refuge and
        my fortress;
    My God, in Him I will trust."

3   Surely He shall deliver you from the snare of
        the fowler
    And from the perilous pestilence.

4   He shall cover you with His feathers,
    And under His wings you shall take refuge;
    His truth *shall be your* shield and buckler.

5   You shall not be afraid of the terror by night,
    Nor of the arrow *that* flies by day,

6   *Nor* of the pestilence *that* walks in darkness,
    Nor of the destruction *that* lays waste at
        noonday.

7   A thousand may fall at your side,
    And ten thousand at your right hand;
    But it shall not come near you.

8   Only with your eyes shall you look,
    And see the reward of the wicked.

9   Because you have made the LORD, *who is* my
        refuge,
    Even the Most High, your dwelling place,

10 No evil shall befall you,
    Nor shall any plague come near your dwelling;

11 For He shall give His angels charge over you,
    To keep you in all your ways.

12 In *their* hands they shall bear you up,
    Lest you dash your foot against a stone.

13 You shall tread upon the lion and the cobra,
    The young lion and the serpent you shall
        trample underfoot.

14 "Because he has set his love upon Me, therefore
        I will deliver him;
    I will set him on high, because he has known
        My name.

15 He shall call upon Me, and I will answer him;
    I *will be* with him in trouble;
    I will deliver him and honor him.

16 With long life I will satisfy him,
    And show him My salvation."

92 A Psalm. A Song for the Sabbath day.
    It is good to give thanks to the LORD,
    And to sing praises to Your name, O Most
        High;

2   To declare Your lovingkindness in the
        morning,
    And Your faithfulness every night,

3   On an instrument of ten strings,
    On the lute,
    And on the harp,
    With harmonious sound.

אֹמַר לַיהוָה מַחְסִי וּמְצוּדָתִי
אֱלֹהַי אֶבְטַח־בּוֹ:

כִּי הוּא יַצִּילְךָ מִפַּח יָקוּשׁ
מִדֶּבֶר הַוּוֹת:

בְּאֶבְרָתוֹ ׀ יָסֶךְ לָךְ וְתַחַת־כְּנָפָיו תֶּחְסֶה
צִנָּה וְסֹחֵרָה אֲמִתּוֹ:

לֹא־תִירָא מִפַּחַד לָיְלָה
מֵחֵץ יָעוּף יוֹמָם:

מִדֶּבֶר בָּאֹפֶל יַהֲלֹךְ
מִקֶּטֶב יָשׁוּד צָהֳרָיִם:

יִפֹּל מִצִּדְּךָ ׀ אֶלֶף וּרְבָבָה מִימִינֶךָ
אֵלֶיךָ לֹא יִגָּשׁ:

רַק בְּעֵינֶיךָ תַבִּיט
וְשִׁלֻּמַת רְשָׁעִים תִּרְאֶה:

כִּי־אַתָּה יְהוָה מַחְסִי
עֶלְיוֹן שַׂמְתָּ מְעוֹנֶךָ:

לֹא־תְאֻנֶּה אֵלֶיךָ רָעָה
וְנֶגַע לֹא־יִקְרַב בְּאָהֳלֶךָ:

כִּי מַלְאָכָיו יְצַוֶּה־לָּךְ
לִשְׁמָרְךָ בְּכָל־דְּרָכֶיךָ:

עַל־כַּפַּיִם יִשָּׂאוּנְךָ
פֶּן־תִּגֹּף בָּאֶבֶן רַגְלֶךָ:

עַל־שַׁחַל וָפֶתֶן תִּדְרֹךְ
תִּרְמֹס כְּפִיר וְתַנִּין:

כִּי בִי חָשַׁק וַאֲפַלְּטֵהוּ
אֲשַׂגְּבֵהוּ כִּי־יָדַע שְׁמִי:

יִקְרָאֵנִי ׀ וְאֶעֱנֵהוּ עִמּוֹ־אָנֹכִי בְצָרָה
אֲחַלְּצֵהוּ וַאֲכַבְּדֵהוּ:

אֹרֶךְ יָמִים אַשְׂבִּיעֵהוּ
וְאַרְאֵהוּ בִּישׁוּעָתִי:

צב מִזְמוֹר שִׁיר לְיוֹם הַשַּׁבָּת:

טוֹב לְהֹדוֹת לַיהוָה
וּלְזַמֵּר לְשִׁמְךָ עֶלְיוֹן:

לְהַגִּיד בַּבֹּקֶר חַסְדֶּךָ
וֶאֱמוּנָתְךָ בַּלֵּילוֹת:

עֲלֵי־עָשׂוֹר וַעֲלֵי־נָבֶל
עֲלֵי הִגָּיוֹן בְּכִנּוֹר:

4 For You, LORD, have made me glad through
   Your work;
I will triumph in the works of Your hands.

5 O LORD, how great are Your works!
Your thoughts are very deep.

6 A senseless man does not know,
Nor does a fool understand this.

7 When the wicked spring up like grass,
And when all the workers of iniquity flourish,
It is that they may be destroyed forever.

8 But You, LORD, *are* on high forevermore.
9 For behold, Your enemies, O LORD,
For behold, Your enemies shall perish;
All the workers of iniquity shall be scattered.

10 But my horn You have exalted like a wild ox;
I have been anointed with fresh oil.

11 My eye also has seen *my desire* on my enemies;
My ears hear *my desire* on the wicked
Who rise up against me.

12 The righteous shall flourish like a palm tree,
He shall grow like a cedar in Lebanon.
13 Those who are planted in the house of the
   LORD
Shall flourish in the courts of our God.
14 They shall still bear fruit in old age;
They shall be fresh and flourishing,
15 To declare that the LORD is upright;
He is my rock, and *there is* no unrighteousness
   in Him.

93 The LORD reigns, He is clothed with majesty;
The LORD is clothed,
He has girded Himself with strength.
Surely the world is established, so that it
   cannot be moved.
2 Your throne *is* established from of old;
You *are* from everlasting.

3 The floods have lifted up, O LORD,
The floods have lifted up their voice;
The floods lift up their waves.
4 The LORD on high *is* mightier
Than the noise of many waters,
Than the mighty waves of the sea.

5 Your testimonies are very sure;
Holiness adorns Your house,
O LORD, forever.

94 O LORD God, to whom vengeance belongs—
O God, to whom vengeance belongs, shine
   forth!

5 כִּי שִׂמַּחְתַּנִי יְהֹוָה בְּפָעֳלֶךָ
בְּמַעֲשֵׂי יָדֶיךָ אֲרַנֵּן:
6 מַה־גָּדְלוּ מַעֲשֶׂיךָ יְהֹוָה
מְאֹד עָמְקוּ מַחְשְׁבֹתֶיךָ:
7 אִישׁ־בַּעַר לֹא יֵדָע
וּכְסִיל לֹא־יָבִין אֶת־זֹאת:
8 בִּפְרֹחַ רְשָׁעִים ׀ כְּמוֹ עֵשֶׂב
וַיָּצִיצוּ כָּל־פֹּעֲלֵי אָוֶן
לְהִשָּׁמְדָם עֲדֵי־עַד:
9 וְאַתָּה מָרוֹם
לְעֹלָם יְהֹוָה:
10 כִּי הִנֵּה אֹיְבֶיךָ ׀ יְהֹוָה
כִּי־הִנֵּה אֹיְבֶיךָ יֹאבֵדוּ
יִתְפָּרְדוּ כָּל־פֹּעֲלֵי אָוֶן:
11 וַתָּרֶם כִּרְאֵים קַרְנִי
בַּלֹּתִי בְּשֶׁמֶן רַעֲנָן:
12 וַתַּבֵּט עֵינִי בְּשׁוּרָי
בַּקָּמִים עָלַי מְרֵעִים
תִּשְׁמַעְנָה אָזְנָי:
13 צַדִּיק כַּתָּמָר יִפְרָח
כְּאֶרֶז בַּלְּבָנוֹן יִשְׂגֶּה:
14 שְׁתוּלִים בְּבֵית יְהֹוָה
בְּחַצְרוֹת אֱלֹהֵינוּ יַפְרִיחוּ:
15 עוֹד יְנוּבוּן בְּשֵׂיבָה
דְּשֵׁנִים וְרַעֲנַנִּים יִהְיוּ:
16 לְהַגִּיד כִּי־יָשָׁר יְהֹוָה
צוּרִי וְלֹא־עַוְלָתָה ᵖ בּוֹ:

צג יְהֹוָה מָלָךְ גֵּאוּת לָבֵשׁ
לָבֵשׁ יְהֹוָה עֹז הִתְאַזָּר
אַף־תִּכּוֹן תֵּבֵל בַּל־תִּמּוֹט:
2 נָכוֹן כִּסְאֲךָ מֵאָז
מֵעוֹלָם אָתָּה:
3 נָשְׂאוּ נְהָרוֹת ׀ יְהֹוָה נָשְׂאוּ נְהָרוֹת קוֹלָם
יִשְׂאוּ נְהָרוֹת דָּכְיָם:
4 מִקֹּלוֹת ׀ מַיִם רַבִּים אַדִּירִים מִשְׁבְּרֵי־יָם
אַדִּיר בַּמָּרוֹם יְהֹוָה:
5 עֵדֹתֶיךָ ׀ נֶאֶמְנוּ מְאֹד לְבֵיתְךָ נַאֲוָה־קֹּדֶשׁ
יְהֹוָה לְאֹרֶךְ יָמִים:

צד אֵל־נְקָמוֹת יְהֹוָה
אֵל נְקָמוֹת הוֹפִיעַ:

צב 16 עֲוְלָתָה

2 Rise up, O Judge of the earth;
   Render punishment to the proud.
3 LORD, how long will the wicked,
   How long will the wicked triumph?
4 They utter speech, *and* speak insolent things;
   All the workers of iniquity boast in themselves.
5 They break in pieces Your people, O LORD,
   And afflict Your heritage.
6 They slay the widow and the stranger,
   And murder the fatherless.
7 Yet they say, "The LORD does not see,
   Nor does the God of Jacob understand."

8 Understand, you senseless among the people;
   And *you* fools, when will you be wise?
9 He who planted the ear, shall He not hear?
   He who formed the eye, shall He not see?
10 He who instructs the nations, shall He not
      correct,
   He who teaches man knowledge?
11 The LORD knows the thoughts of man,
   That they *are* futile.

12 Blessed *is* the man whom You instruct, O
      LORD,
   And teach out of Your law,
13 That You may give him rest from the days of
      adversity,
   Until the pit is dug for the wicked.
14 For the LORD will not cast off His people,
   Nor will He forsake His inheritance.
15 But judgment will return to righteousness,
   And all the upright in heart will follow it.

16 Who will rise up for me against the evildoers?
   Who will stand up for me against the workers
      of iniquity?
17 Unless the LORD *had been* my help,
   My soul would soon have settled in silence.
18 If I say, "My foot slips,"
   Your mercy, O LORD, will hold me up.
19 In the multitude of my anxieties within me,
   Your comforts delight my soul.

20 Shall the throne of iniquity, which devises evil
      by law,
   Have fellowship with You?
21 They gather together against the life of the
      righteous,
   And condemn innocent blood.
22 But the LORD has been my defense,
   And my God the rock of my refuge.
23 He has brought on them their own iniquity,
   And shall cut them off in their own wickedness;
   The LORD our God shall cut them off.

הִנָּשֵׂא שֹׁפֵט הָאָרֶץ 2
הָשֵׁב גְּמוּל עַל־גֵּאִים:
עַד־מָתַי רְשָׁעִים ׀ יְהֹוָה 3
עַד־מָתַי רְשָׁעִים יַעֲלֹזוּ:
יַבִּיעוּ יְדַבְּרוּ עָתָק 4
יִתְאַמְּרוּ כָּל־פֹּעֲלֵי אָוֶן:
עַמְּךָ יְהֹוָה יְדַכְּאוּ וְנַחֲלָתְךָ יְעַנּוּ: 5
אַלְמָנָה וְגֵר יַהֲרֹגוּ וִיתוֹמִים יְרַצֵּחוּ: 6
וַיֹּאמְרוּ לֹא יִרְאֶה־יָּהּ 7
וְלֹא־יָבִין אֱלֹהֵי יַעֲקֹב:
בִּינוּ בֹּעֲרִים בָּעָם 8
וּכְסִילִים מָתַי תַּשְׂכִּילוּ:
הֲנֹטַע אֹזֶן הֲלֹא יִשְׁמָע 9
אִם־יֹצֵר עַיִן הֲלֹא יַבִּיט:
הֲיֹסֵר גּוֹיִם הֲלֹא יוֹכִיחַ 10
הַמְלַמֵּד אָדָם דָּעַת:
יְהֹוָה יֹדֵעַ מַחְשְׁבוֹת אָדָם 11
כִּי־הֵמָּה הָבֶל:
אַשְׁרֵי ׀ הַגֶּבֶר אֲשֶׁר־תְּיַסְּרֶנּוּ יָּהּ 12
וּמִתּוֹרָתְךָ תְלַמְּדֶנּוּ:
לְהַשְׁקִיט לוֹ מִימֵי רָע 13
עַד יִכָּרֶה לָרָשָׁע שָׁחַת:
כִּי ׀ לֹא־יִטֹּשׁ יְהֹוָה עַמּוֹ 14
וְנַחֲלָתוֹ לֹא יַעֲזֹב:
כִּי־עַד־צֶדֶק יָשׁוּב מִשְׁפָּט 15
וְאַחֲרָיו כָּל־יִשְׁרֵי־לֵב:
מִי־יָקוּם לִי עִם־מְרֵעִים 16
מִי־יִתְיַצֵּב לִי עִם־פֹּעֲלֵי אָוֶן:
לוּלֵי יְהֹוָה עֶזְרָתָה לִּי 17
כִּמְעַט ׀ שָׁכְנָה דוּמָה נַפְשִׁי:
אִם־אָמַרְתִּי מָטָה רַגְלִי 18
חַסְדְּךָ יְהֹוָה יִסְעָדֵנִי:
בְּרֹב שַׂרְעַפַּי בְּקִרְבִּי 19
תַּנְחוּמֶיךָ יְשַׁעַשְׁעוּ נַפְשִׁי:
הַיְחָבְרְךָ כִּסֵּא הַוּוֹת 20
יֹצֵר עָמָל עֲלֵי־חֹק:
יָגוֹדּוּ עַל־נֶפֶשׁ צַדִּיק 21
וְדָם נָקִי יַרְשִׁיעוּ:
וַיְהִי יְהֹוָה לִי לְמִשְׂגָּב 22
וֵאלֹהַי לְצוּר מַחְסִי:
וַיָּשֶׁב עֲלֵיהֶם ׀ אֶת־אוֹנָם וּבְרָעָתָם יַצְמִיתֵם 23
יַצְמִיתֵם יְהֹוָה אֱלֹהֵינוּ:

95 Oh come, let us sing to the LORD!
Let us shout joyfully to the Rock of our
salvation.

צֵה לְכוּ נְרַנְּנָה לַיהוָה נָרִיעָה לְצוּר יִשְׁעֵנוּ:

2 Let us come before His presence with
thanksgiving;
Let us shout joyfully to Him with psalms.

2 נְקַדְּמָה פָנָיו בְּתוֹדָה
בִּזְמִרוֹת נָרִיעַ לוֹ:

3 For the LORD is the great God,
And the great King above all gods.

3 כִּי אֵל גָּדוֹל יְהוָה
וּמֶלֶךְ גָּדוֹל עַל־כָּל־אֱלֹהִים:

4 In His hand are the deep places of the earth;
The heights of the hills are His also.

4 אֲשֶׁר בְּיָדוֹ מֶחְקְרֵי־אָרֶץ
וְתוֹעֲפוֹת הָרִים לוֹ:

5 The sea is His, for He made it;
And His hands formed the dry land.

5 אֲשֶׁר־לוֹ הַיָּם וְהוּא עָשָׂהוּ
וְיַבֶּשֶׁת יָדָיו יָצָרוּ:

6 Oh come, let us worship and bow down;
Let us kneel before the LORD our Maker.

6 בֹּאוּ נִשְׁתַּחֲוֶה וְנִכְרָעָה
נִבְרְכָה לִפְנֵי־יְהוָה עֹשֵׂנוּ:

7 For He is our God,
And we are the people of His pasture,
And the sheep of His hand.
Today, if you will hear His voice:

7 כִּי הוּא אֱלֹהֵינוּ וַאֲנַחְנוּ עַם מַרְעִיתוֹ וְצֹאן יָדוֹ
הַיּוֹם אִם־בְּקֹלוֹ תִשְׁמָעוּ:

8 "Do not harden your hearts, as in the rebellion,
As in the day of trial in the wilderness,

8 אַל־תַּקְשׁוּ לְבַבְכֶם כִּמְרִיבָה
כְּיוֹם מַסָּה בַּמִּדְבָּר:

9 When your fathers tested Me;
They tried Me, though they saw My work.

9 אֲשֶׁר נִסּוּנִי אֲבוֹתֵיכֶם
בְּחָנוּנִי גַּם־רָאוּ פָעֳלִי:

10 For forty years I was grieved with that
generation,
And said, 'It is a people who go astray in their
hearts,
And they do not know My ways.'

10 אַרְבָּעִים שָׁנָה אָקוּט בְּדוֹר
וָאֹמַר עַם תֹּעֵי לֵבָב הֵם
וְהֵם לֹא־יָדְעוּ דְרָכָי:

11 So I swore in My wrath,
'They shall not enter My rest.' "

11 אֲשֶׁר נִשְׁבַּעְתִּי בְאַפִּי
אִם־יְבֹאוּן אֶל־מְנוּחָתִי:

96 Oh, sing to the LORD a new song!
Sing to the LORD, all the earth.

צֵו שִׁירוּ לַיהוָה שִׁיר חָדָשׁ
שִׁירוּ לַיהוָה כָּל־הָאָרֶץ:

2 Sing to the LORD, bless His name;
Proclaim the good news of His salvation from
day to day.

2 שִׁירוּ לַיהוָה בָּרְכוּ שְׁמוֹ
בַּשְּׂרוּ מִיּוֹם־לְיוֹם יְשׁוּעָתוֹ:

3 Declare His glory among the nations,
His wonders among all peoples.

3 סַפְּרוּ בַגּוֹיִם כְּבוֹדוֹ
בְּכָל־הָעַמִּים נִפְלְאוֹתָיו:

4 For the LORD is great and greatly to be praised;
He is to be feared above all gods.

4 כִּי גָדוֹל יְהוָה וּמְהֻלָּל מְאֹד
נוֹרָא הוּא עַל־כָּל־אֱלֹהִים:

5 For all the gods of the peoples are idols,
But the LORD made the heavens.

5 כִּי כָּל־אֱלֹהֵי הָעַמִּים אֱלִילִים
וַיהוָה שָׁמַיִם עָשָׂה:

6 Honor and majesty are before Him;
Strength and beauty are in His sanctuary.

6 הוֹד־וְהָדָר לְפָנָיו
עֹז וְתִפְאֶרֶת בְּמִקְדָּשׁוֹ:

7 Give to the LORD, O families of the peoples,
Give to the LORD glory and strength.

7 הָבוּ לַיהוָה מִשְׁפְּחוֹת עַמִּים
הָבוּ לַיהוָה כָּבוֹד וָעֹז:

8 Give to the LORD the glory due His name;
Bring an offering, and come into His courts.

8 הָבוּ לַיהוָה כְּבוֹד שְׁמוֹ
שְׂאוּ־מִנְחָה וּבֹאוּ לְחַצְרוֹתָיו:

9 Oh, worship the LORD in the beauty of
holiness!
Tremble before Him, all the earth.

9 הִשְׁתַּחֲווּ לַיהוָה בְּהַדְרַת־קֹדֶשׁ
חִילוּ מִפָּנָיו כָּל־הָאָרֶץ:

10 Say among the nations, "The LORD reigns;
The world also is firmly established,

10 אִמְרוּ בַגּוֹיִם יְהוָה מָלָךְ
אַף־תִּכּוֹן תֵּבֵל בַּל־תִּמּוֹט

It shall not be moved;
He shall judge the peoples righteously."

11 Let the heavens rejoice, and let the earth be
glad;
Let the sea roar, and all its fullness;

12 Let the field be joyful, and all that *is* in it.
Then all the trees of the woods will rejoice
before the LORD.

13 For He is coming, for He is coming to judge the
earth.
He shall judge the world with righteousness,
And the peoples with His truth.

97 The LORD reigns;
Let the earth rejoice;
Let the multitude of isles be glad!

2 Clouds and darkness surround Him;
Righteousness and justice *are* the foundation
of His throne.

3 A fire goes before Him,
And burns up His enemies round about.

4 His lightnings light the world;
The earth sees and trembles.

5 The mountains melt like wax at the presence of
the LORD,
At the presence of the Lord of the whole earth.

6 The heavens declare His righteousness,
And all the peoples see His glory.

7 Let all be put to shame who serve carved
images,
Who boast of idols.
Worship Him, all *you* gods.

8 Zion hears and is glad,
And the daughters of Judah rejoice
Because of Your judgments, O LORD.

9 For You, LORD, *are* most high above all the
earth;
You are exalted far above all gods.

10 You who love the LORD, hate evil!
He preserves the souls of His saints;
He delivers them out of the hand of the wicked.

11 Light is sown for the righteous,
And gladness for the upright in heart.

12 Rejoice in the LORD, you righteous,
And give thanks at the remembrance of His
holy name.

98 A Psalm.
Oh, sing to the LORD a new song!
For He has done marvelous things;
His right hand and His holy arm have gained
Him the victory.

יָדִין עַמִּים בְּמֵישָׁרִים:

11 יִשְׂמְחוּ הַשָּׁמַיִם וְתָגֵל הָאָרֶץ
יִרְעַם הַיָּם וּמְלֹאוֹ:

12 יַעֲלֹז שָׂדַי וְכָל־אֲשֶׁר־בּוֹ
אָז יְרַנְּנוּ כָּל־עֲצֵי־יָעַר:

13 לִפְנֵי יְהוָה כִּי בָא
כִּי בָא לִשְׁפֹּט הָאָרֶץ
יִשְׁפֹּט־תֵּבֵל בְּצֶדֶק
וְעַמִּים בֶּאֱמוּנָתוֹ:

צז יְהוָה מָלָךְ תָּגֵל הָאָרֶץ
יִשְׂמְחוּ אִיִּים רַבִּים:

2 עָנָן וַעֲרָפֶל סְבִיבָיו
צֶדֶק וּמִשְׁפָּט מְכוֹן כִּסְאוֹ:

3 אֵשׁ לְפָנָיו תֵּלֵךְ
וּתְלַהֵט סָבִיב צָרָיו:

4 הֵאִירוּ בְרָקָיו תֵּבֵל
רָאֲתָה וַתָּחֵל הָאָרֶץ:

5 הָרִים כַּדּוֹנַג נָמַסּוּ מִלִּפְנֵי יְהוָה
מִלִּפְנֵי אֲדוֹן כָּל־הָאָרֶץ:

6 הִגִּידוּ הַשָּׁמַיִם צִדְקוֹ
וְרָאוּ כָל־הָעַמִּים כְּבוֹדוֹ:

7 יֵבֹשׁוּ כָּל־עֹבְדֵי פֶסֶל
הַמִּתְהַלְלִים בָּאֱלִילִים
הִשְׁתַּחֲווּ־לוֹ כָּל־אֱלֹהִים:

8 שָׁמְעָה וַתִּשְׂמַח צִיּוֹן
וַתָּגֵלְנָה בְּנוֹת יְהוּדָה
לְמַעַן מִשְׁפָּטֶיךָ יְהוָה:

9 כִּי־אַתָּה יְהוָה
עֶלְיוֹן עַל־כָּל־הָאָרֶץ
מְאֹד נַעֲלֵיתָ
עַל־כָּל־אֱלֹהִים:

10 אֹהֲבֵי יְהוָה שִׂנְאוּ רָע
שֹׁמֵר נַפְשׁוֹת חֲסִידָיו
מִיַּד רְשָׁעִים יַצִּילֵם:

11 אוֹר זָרֻעַ לַצַּדִּיק
וּלְיִשְׁרֵי־לֵב שִׂמְחָה:

12 שִׂמְחוּ צַדִּיקִים בַּיהוָה
וְהוֹדוּ לְזֵכֶר קָדְשׁוֹ:

צח מִזְמוֹר שִׁירוּ לַיהוָה שִׁיר חָדָשׁ
כִּי־נִפְלָאוֹת עָשָׂה
הוֹשִׁיעָה־לּוֹ יְמִינוֹ וּזְרוֹעַ קָדְשׁוֹ:

2 The LORD has made known His salvation;   הוֹדִיעַ יְהוָה יְשׁוּעָתוֹ 2
His righteousness He has revealed in the sight
of the nations.   לְעֵינֵי הַגּוֹיִם גִּלָּה צִדְקָתוֹ:

3 He has remembered His mercy and His   זָכַר חַסְדּוֹ ׀ וֶאֱמוּנָתוֹ 3
faithfulness to the house of Israel;   לְבֵית יִשְׂרָאֵל
All the ends of the earth have seen the salvation
of our God.   רָאוּ כָל־אַפְסֵי־אָרֶץ אֵת יְשׁוּעַת אֱלֹהֵינוּ:

4 Shout joyfully to the LORD, all the earth;   הָרִיעוּ לַיהוָה כָּל־הָאָרֶץ 4
Break forth in song, rejoice, and sing praises.   פִּצְחוּ וְרַנְּנוּ וְזַמֵּרוּ:

5 Sing to the LORD with the harp,   זַמְּרוּ לַיהוָה בְּכִנּוֹר 5
With the harp and the sound of a psalm,   בְּכִנּוֹר וְקוֹל זִמְרָה:

6 With trumpets and the sound of a horn;   בַּחֲצֹצְרוֹת וְקוֹל שׁוֹפָר 6
Shout joyfully before the LORD, the King.   הָרִיעוּ לִפְנֵי ׀ הַמֶּלֶךְ יְהוָה:

7 Let the sea roar, and all its fullness,   יִרְעַם הַיָּם וּמְלֹאוֹ 7
The world and those who dwell in it;   תֵּבֵל וְיֹשְׁבֵי בָהּ:

8 Let the rivers clap *their* hands;   נְהָרוֹת יִמְחֲאוּ־כָף 8
Let the hills be joyful together before the
LORD,   יַחַד הָרִים יְרַנֵּנוּ:

9 For He is coming to judge the earth.   לִפְנֵי־יְהוָה כִּי בָא לִשְׁפֹּט הָאָרֶץ 9
With righteousness He shall judge the world,   יִשְׁפֹּט־תֵּבֵל בְּצֶדֶק
And the peoples with equity.   וְעַמִּים בְּמֵישָׁרִים:

99 The LORD reigns;
Let the peoples tremble!   צט יְהוָה מָלָךְ יִרְגְּזוּ עַמִּים
He dwells *between* the cherubim;   יֹשֵׁב כְּרוּבִים תָּנוּט הָאָרֶץ:
Let the earth be moved!

2 The LORD *is* great in Zion,   יְהוָה בְּצִיּוֹן גָּדוֹל 2
And He *is* high above all the peoples.   וְרָם הוּא עַל־כָּל־הָעַמִּים:

3 Let them praise Your great and awesome   יוֹדוּ שִׁמְךָ גָּדוֹל וְנוֹרָא 3
name—
He *is* holy.   קָדוֹשׁ הוּא:

4 The King's strength also loves justice;   וְעֹז מֶלֶךְ 4
You have established equity;   מִשְׁפָּט אָהֵב
You have executed justice and righteousness in   אַתָּה כּוֹנַנְתָּ מֵישָׁרִים
Jacob.   מִשְׁפָּט וּצְדָקָה בְּיַעֲקֹב ׀ אַתָּה עָשִׂיתָ:

5 Exalt the LORD our God,   רוֹמְמוּ יְהוָה אֱלֹהֵינוּ וְהִשְׁתַּחֲווּ לַהֲדֹם רַגְלָיו 5
And worship at His footstool—   קָדוֹשׁ הוּא:
He *is* holy.

6 Moses and Aaron were among His priests,   מֹשֶׁה וְאַהֲרֹן ׀ בְּכֹהֲנָיו 6
And Samuel was among those who called upon   וּשְׁמוּאֵל בְּקֹרְאֵי שְׁמוֹ
His name;
They called upon the LORD, and He answered   קֹרִאים אֶל־יְהוָה וְהוּא יַעֲנֵם:
them.

7 He spoke to them in the cloudy pillar;   בְּעַמּוּד עָנָן יְדַבֵּר אֲלֵיהֶם 7
They kept His testimonies and the ordinance   שָׁמְרוּ עֵדֹתָיו וְחֹק נָתַן־לָמוֹ:
He gave them.

8 You answered them, O LORD our God;   יְהוָה אֱלֹהֵינוּ אַתָּה עֲנִיתָם 8
You were to them God-Who-Forgives,   אֵל נֹשֵׂא הָיִיתָ לָהֶם
Though You took vengeance on their deeds.   וְנֹקֵם עַל־עֲלִילוֹתָם:

9 Exalt the LORD our God,   רוֹמְמוּ יְהוָה אֱלֹהֵינוּ 9
And worship at His holy hill;   וְהִשְׁתַּחֲווּ לְהַר קָדְשׁוֹ
For the LORD our God *is* holy.   כִּי־קָדוֹשׁ יְהוָה אֱלֹהֵינוּ:

100 A Psalm of Thanksgiving.

Make a joyful shout to the LORD, all you lands!
2 Serve the LORD with gladness;
Come before His presence with singing.
3 Know that the LORD, He *is* God;
It is He *who* has made us, and not we ourselves;
We are His people and the sheep of His
pasture.

4 Enter into His gates with thanksgiving,
And into His courts with praise.
Be thankful to Him, *and* bless His name.
5 For the LORD *is* good;
His mercy *is* everlasting,
And His truth *endures* to all generations.

101 A Psalm of David.

I will sing of mercy and justice;
To You, O LORD, I will sing praises.
2 I will behave wisely in a perfect way.
Oh, when will You come to me?
I will walk within my house with a perfect
heart.
3 I will set nothing wicked before my eyes;
I hate the work of those who fall away;
It shall not cling to me.
4 A perverse heart shall depart from me;
I will not know wickedness.
5 Whoever secretly slanders his neighbor,
Him I will destroy;
The one who has a haughty look and a proud
heart,
Him I will not endure.
6 My eyes *shall be* on the faithful of the land,
That they may dwell with me;
He who walks in a perfect way,
He shall serve me.
7 He who works deceit shall not dwell within my
house;
He who tells lies shall not continue in my
presence.
8 Early I will destroy all the wicked of the land,
That I may cut off all the evildoers from the
city of the LORD.

102 A Prayer of the afflicted, when he is overwhelmed and pours out his complaint before the LORD.

Hear my prayer, O LORD,
And let my cry come to You.
2 Do not hide Your face from me in the day of
my trouble;
Incline Your ear to me;

ק מִזְמוֹר לְתוֹדָה
הָרִיעוּ לַיהוָה כָּל־הָאָרֶץ׃
2 עִבְדוּ אֶת־יְהוָה בְּשִׂמְחָה
בֹּאוּ לְפָנָיו בִּרְנָנָה׃
3 דְּעוּ כִּי־יְהוָה הוּא אֱלֹהִים
הוּא־עָשָׂנוּ וְלֹא אֲנַחְנוּ
עַמּוֹ וְצֹאן מַרְעִיתוֹ׃
4 בֹּאוּ שְׁעָרָיו ׀ בְּתוֹדָה חֲצֵרֹתָיו בִּתְהִלָּה
הוֹדוּ־לוֹ בָּרְכוּ שְׁמוֹ׃
5 כִּי־טוֹב יְהוָה לְעוֹלָם חַסְדּוֹ
וְעַד־דֹּר וָדֹר אֱמוּנָתוֹ׃

קא לְדָוִד מִזְמוֹר
חֶסֶד־וּמִשְׁפָּט אָשִׁירָה לְךָ יְהוָה אֲזַמֵּרָה׃
2 אַשְׂכִּילָה ׀ בְּדֶרֶךְ תָּמִים
מָתַי תָּבוֹא אֵלָי
אֶתְהַלֵּךְ בְּתָם־לְבָבִי בְּקֶרֶב בֵּיתִי׃
3 לֹא־אָשִׁית ׀ לְנֶגֶד עֵינַי
דְּבַר־בְּלִיָּעַל
עֲשֹׂה־סֵטִים שָׂנֵאתִי
לֹא יִדְבַּק בִּי׃
4 לֵבָב עִקֵּשׁ יָסוּר מִמֶּנִּי
רָע לֹא אֵדָע׃
5 מְלָשְׁנִי בַסֵּתֶר ׀ רֵעֵהוּ
אוֹתוֹ אַצְמִית גְּבַהּ־עֵינַיִם וּרְחַב לֵבָב
אֹתוֹ לֹא אוּכָל׃
6 עֵינַי ׀ בְּנֶאֶמְנֵי־אֶרֶץ
לָשֶׁבֶת עִמָּדִי הֹלֵךְ בְּדֶרֶךְ תָּמִים
הוּא יְשָׁרְתֵנִי׃
7 לֹא־יֵשֵׁב ׀ בְּקֶרֶב בֵּיתִי
עֹשֵׂה רְמִיָּה דֹּבֵר שְׁקָרִים
לֹא־יִכּוֹן לְנֶגֶד עֵינָי׃
8 לַבְּקָרִים אַצְמִית כָּל־רִשְׁעֵי־אָרֶץ
לְהַכְרִית מֵעִיר־יְהוָה
כָּל־פֹּעֲלֵי אָוֶן׃

קב תְּפִלָּה לְעָנִי כִי־יַעֲטֹף
וְלִפְנֵי יְהוָה יִשְׁפֹּךְ שִׂיחוֹ׃
2 יְהוָה שִׁמְעָה תְפִלָּתִי
וְשַׁוְעָתִי אֵלֶיךָ תָבוֹא׃
3 אַל־תַּסְתֵּר פָּנֶיךָ ׀ מִמֶּנִּי
בְּיוֹם צַר לִי הַטֵּה־אֵלַי אָזְנֶךָ

קא 5 מְלָשְׁנִי　　ק 3 וְלֹו

	English	Hebrew	

In the day that I call, answer me speedily.

בְּיוֹם אֶקְרָא מַהֵר עֲנֵנִי׃

3 For my days are consumed like smoke,
And my bones are burned like a hearth.

כִּי־כָלוּ בְעָשָׁן יָמָי   4
וְעַצְמוֹתַי כְּמוֹ־קֵד נִחָרוּ׃

4 My heart is stricken and withered like grass,
So that I forget to eat my bread.

הוּכָּה־כָעֵשֶׂב וַיִּבַשׁ לִבִּי   5
כִּי־שָׁכַחְתִּי מֵאֲכֹל לַחְמִי׃

5 Because of the sound of my groaning
My bones cling to my skin.

מִקּוֹל אַנְחָתִי   6
דָּבְקָה עַצְמִי לִבְשָׂרִי׃

6 I am like a pelican of the wilderness;
I am like an owl of the desert.

דָּמִיתִי לִקְאַת מִדְבָּר   7

7 I lie awake,
And am like a sparrow alone on the housetop.

הָיִיתִי כְּכוֹס חֳרָבוֹת׃

8 My enemies reproach me all day long;
Those who deride me swear an oath against me.

שָׁקַדְתִּי וָאֶהְיֶה כְּצִפּוֹר בּוֹדֵד עַל־גָּג׃   8

9 For I have eaten ashes like bread,
And mingled my drink with weeping,

כָּל־הַיּוֹם חֵרְפוּנִי אוֹיְבָי מְהוֹלָלַי בִּי נִשְׁבָּעוּ׃   9

10 Because of Your indignation and Your wrath;
For You have lifted me up and cast me away.

כִּי־אֵפֶר כַּלֶּחֶם אָכָלְתִּי   10
וְשִׁקֻּוַי בִּבְכִי מָסָכְתִּי׃

11 My days are like a shadow that lengthens,
And I wither away like grass.

מִפְּנֵי־זַעַמְךָ וְקִצְפֶּךָ   11
כִּי נְשָׂאתַנִי וַתַּשְׁלִיכֵנִי׃

12 But You, O LORD, shall endure forever,
And the remembrance of Your name to all generations.

יָמַי כְּצֵל נָטוּי וַאֲנִי כָּעֵשֶׂב אִיבָשׁ׃   12

13 You will arise and have mercy on Zion;
For the time to favor her,
Yes, the set time, has come.

וְאַתָּה יְהוָה לְעוֹלָם תֵּשֵׁב   13
וְזִכְרְךָ לְדֹר וָדֹר׃

14 For Your servants take pleasure in her stones,
And show favor to her dust.

אַתָּה תָקוּם תְּרַחֵם צִיּוֹן   14
כִּי־עֵת לְחֶנְנָהּ כִּי־בָא מוֹעֵד׃

15 So the nations shall fear the name of the LORD,
And all the kings of the earth Your glory.

כִּי־רָצוּ עֲבָדֶיךָ אֶת־אֲבָנֶיהָ   15
וְאֶת־עֲפָרָהּ יְחֹנֵנוּ׃

16 For the LORD shall build up Zion;
He shall appear in His glory.

וְיִירְאוּ גוֹיִם אֶת־שֵׁם יְהוָה   16
וְכָל־מַלְכֵי הָאָרֶץ אֶת־כְּבוֹדֶךָ׃

17 He shall regard the prayer of the destitute,
And shall not despise their prayer.

כִּי־בָנָה יְהוָה צִיּוֹן נִרְאָה בִּכְבוֹדוֹ׃   17

18 This will be written for the generation to come,
That a people yet to be created may praise the LORD.

פָּנָה אֶל־תְּפִלַּת הָעַרְעָר   18
וְלֹא־בָזָה אֶת־תְּפִלָּתָם׃

19 For He looked down from the height of His sanctuary;
From heaven the LORD viewed the earth,

תִּכָּתֶב זֹאת לְדוֹר אַחֲרוֹן   19
וְעַם נִבְרָא יְהַלֶּל־יָהּ׃

20 To hear the groaning of the prisoner,
To release those appointed to death,

כִּי־הִשְׁקִיף מִמְּרוֹם קָדְשׁוֹ   20
יְהוָה מִשָּׁמַיִם ׀ אֶל־אֶרֶץ הִבִּיט׃

21 To declare the name of the LORD in Zion,
And His praise in Jerusalem,

לִשְׁמֹעַ אֶנְקַת אָסִיר   21
לְפַתֵּחַ בְּנֵי תְמוּתָה׃

22 When the peoples are gathered together,
And the kingdoms, to serve the LORD.

לְסַפֵּר בְּצִיּוֹן שֵׁם יְהוָה   22
וּתְהִלָּתוֹ בִּירוּשָׁלָ͏ִם׃

23 He weakened my strength in the way;
He shortened my days.

בְּהִקָּבֵץ עַמִּים יַחְדָּו   23
וּמַמְלָכוֹת לַעֲבֹד אֶת־יְהוָה׃

24 I said, "O my God,
Do not take me away in the midst of my days;
Your years are throughout all generations.

עִנָּה בַדֶּרֶךְ כֹּחוֹ‍ק קִצַּר יָמָי׃   24

25 Of old You laid the foundation of the earth,

אֹמַר אֵלִי אַל־תַּעֲלֵנִי בַּחֲצִי יָמָי   25
בְּדוֹר דּוֹרִים שְׁנוֹתֶיךָ׃

לְפָנִים הָאָרֶץ יָסַדְתָּ   26

And the heavens *are* the work of Your hands. וּמַעֲשֵׂה יָדֶיךָ שָׁמָיִם:

26 They will perish, but You will endure; הֵמָּה ׀ יֹאבֵדוּ 27
Yes, they will all grow old like a garment; וְאַתָּה תַעֲמֹד וְכֻלָּם כַּבֶּגֶד יִבְלוּ
Like a cloak You will change them, כַּלְּבוּשׁ תַּחֲלִיפֵם וְיַחֲלֹפוּ:
And they will be changed.

27 But You *are* the same, וְאַתָּה־הוּא 28
And Your years will have no end. וּשְׁנוֹתֶיךָ לֹא יִתָּמּוּ:

28 The children of Your servants will continue, בְּנֵי־עֲבָדֶיךָ יִשְׁכּוֹנוּ 29
And their descendants will be established וְזַרְעָם לְפָנֶיךָ יִכּוֹן:
before You."

103 *A Psalm* of David.

לְדָוִד ׀ בָּרְכִי נַפְשִׁי אֶת־יְהוָה קג

Bless the LORD, O my soul; וְכָל־קְרָבַי אֶת־שֵׁם קָדְשׁוֹ:
And all that is within me, *bless* His holy name!

2 Bless the LORD, O my soul, בָּרְכִי נַפְשִׁי אֶת־יְהוָה 2
And forget not all His benefits: וְאַל־תִּשְׁכְּחִי כָּל־גְּמוּלָיו:

3 Who forgives all your iniquities, הַסֹּלֵחַ לְכָל־עֲוֹנֵכִי 3
Who heals all your diseases, הָרֹפֵא לְכָל־תַּחֲלֻאָיְכִי:

4 Who redeems your life from destruction, הַגּוֹאֵל מִשַּׁחַת חַיָּיְכִי 4
Who crowns you with lovingkindness and הַמְעַטְּרֵכִי חֶסֶד וְרַחֲמִים:
tender mercies,

5 Who satisfies your mouth with good *things*, הַמַּשְׂבִּיעַ בַּטּוֹב עֶדְיֵךְ 5
So *that* your youth is renewed like the eagle's. תִּתְחַדֵּשׁ כַּנֶּשֶׁר נְעוּרָיְכִי:

6 The LORD executes righteousness עֹשֵׂה צְדָקוֹת יְהוָה 6
And justice for all who are oppressed. וּמִשְׁפָּטִים לְכָל־עֲשׁוּקִים:

7 He made known His ways to Moses, יוֹדִיעַ דְּרָכָיו לְמֹשֶׁה 7
His acts to the children of Israel. לִבְנֵי יִשְׂרָאֵל עֲלִילוֹתָיו:

8 The LORD *is* merciful and gracious, רַחוּם וְחַנּוּן יְהוָה אֶרֶךְ אַפַּיִם וְרַב־חָסֶד: 8
Slow to anger, and abounding in mercy.

9 He will not always strive *with us*, לֹא־לָנֶצַח יָרִיב וְלֹא לְעוֹלָם יִטּוֹר: 9
Nor will He keep *His anger* forever.

10 He has not dealt with us according to our sins, לֹא כַחֲטָאֵינוּ עָשָׂה לָנוּ 10
Nor punished us according to our iniquities. וְלֹא כַעֲוֹנֹתֵינוּ גָּמַל עָלֵינוּ:

11 For as the heavens are high above the earth, כִּי כִגְבֹהַּ שָׁמַיִם עַל־הָאָרֶץ 11
So great is His mercy toward those who fear גָּבַר חַסְדּוֹ עַל־יְרֵאָיו:
Him;

12 As far as the east is from the west, כִּרְחֹק מִזְרָח מִמַּעֲרָב 12
So far has He removed our transgressions from הִרְחִיק מִמֶּנּוּ אֶת־פְּשָׁעֵינוּ:
us.

13 As a father pities *his* children, כְּרַחֵם אָב עַל־בָּנִים 13
So the LORD pities those who fear Him. רִחַם יְהוָה עַל־יְרֵאָיו:

14 For He knows our frame; כִּי־הוּא יָדַע יִצְרֵנוּ 14
He remembers that we *are* dust. זָכוּר כִּי־עָפָר אֲנָחְנוּ:

15 *As for* man, his days *are* like grass; אֱנוֹשׁ כֶּחָצִיר יָמָיו 15
As a flower of the field, so he flourishes. כְּצִיץ הַשָּׂדֶה כֵּן יָצִיץ:

16 For the wind passes over it, and it is gone, כִּי רוּחַ עָבְרָה־בּוֹ וְאֵינֶנּוּ 16
And its place remembers it no more. וְלֹא־יַכִּירֶנּוּ עוֹד מְקוֹמוֹ:

17 But the mercy of the LORD *is* from everlasting וְחֶסֶד יְהוָה ׀ מֵעוֹלָם וְעַד־עוֹלָם עַל־יְרֵאָיו 17
to everlasting וְצִדְקָתוֹ
On those who fear Him,
And His righteousness to children's children, לִבְנֵי בָנִים:

18 To such as keep His covenant, לְשֹׁמְרֵי בְרִיתוֹ 18

And to those who remember His
commandments to do them.

וּלְזֹכְרֵי פִקֻּדָיו לַעֲשׂוֹתָם:

19 The LORD has established His throne in
heaven,
And His kingdom rules over all.

19 יְהֹוָה בַּשָּׁמַיִם הֵכִין כִּסְאוֹ
וּמַלְכוּתוֹ בַּכֹּל מָשָׁלָה:

20 Bless the LORD, you His angels,
Who excel in strength, who do His word,
Heeding the voice of His word.

20 בָּרְכוּ יְהֹוָה מַלְאָכָיו
גִּבֹּרֵי כֹחַ עֹשֵׂי דְבָרוֹ
לִשְׁמֹעַ בְּקוֹל דְּבָרוֹ:

21 Bless the LORD, all *you* His hosts,
You ministers of His, who do His pleasure.

21 בָּרְכוּ יְהֹוָה כָּל־צְבָאָיו
מְשָׁרְתָיו עֹשֵׂי רְצוֹנוֹ:

22 Bless the LORD, all His works,
In all places of His dominion.
Bless the LORD, O my soul!

22 בָּרְכוּ יְהֹוָה כָּל־מַעֲשָׂיו
בְּכָל־מְקֹמוֹת מֶמְשַׁלְתּוֹ
בָּרְכִי נַפְשִׁי אֶת־יְהֹוָה:

104 Bless the LORD, O my soul!

O LORD my God, You are very great:
You are clothed with honor and majesty,

קד בָּרְכִי נַפְשִׁי אֶת־יְהֹוָה
יְהֹוָה אֱלֹהַי גָּדַלְתָּ מְּאֹד
הוֹד וְהָדָר לָבָשְׁתָּ:

2 Who cover *Yourself* with light as *with* a
garment,
Who stretch out the heavens like a curtain.

2 עֹטֶה־אוֹר כַּשַּׂלְמָה
נוֹטֶה שָׁמַיִם כַּיְרִיעָה:

3 He lays the beams of His upper chambers in the
waters,
Who makes the clouds His chariot,
Who walks on the wings of the wind,

3 הַמְקָרֶה בַמַּיִם עֲלִיּוֹתָיו
הַשָּׂם־עָבִים רְכוּבוֹ
הַמְהַלֵּךְ עַל־כַּנְפֵי־רוּחַ:

4 Who makes His angels spirits,
His ministers a flame of fire.

4 עֹשֶׂה מַלְאָכָיו רוּחוֹת
מְשָׁרְתָיו אֵשׁ לֹהֵט:

5 *You who* laid the foundations of the earth,
So *that* it should not be moved forever,

5 יָסַד־אֶרֶץ עַל־מְכוֹנֶיהָ
בַּל־תִּמּוֹט עוֹלָם וָעֶד:

6 You covered it with the deep as *with* a garment;
The waters stood above the mountains.

6 תְּהוֹם כַּלְּבוּשׁ כִּסִּיתוֹ
עַל־הָרִים יַעַמְדוּ־מָיִם:

7 At Your rebuke they fled;
At the voice of Your thunder they hastened
away.

7 מִן־גַּעֲרָתְךָ יְנוּסוּן
מִן־קוֹל רַעַמְךָ יֵחָפֵזוּן:

8 They went up over the mountains;
They went down into the valleys,
To the place which You founded for them.

8 יַעֲלוּ הָרִים יֵרְדוּ בְקָעוֹת
אֶל־מְקוֹם זֶה יָסַדְתָּ לָהֶם:

9 You have set a boundary that they may not
pass over,
That they may not return to cover the earth.

9 גְּבוּל־שַׂמְתָּ בַּל־יַעֲבֹרוּן
בַּל־יְשׁוּבוּן לְכַסּוֹת הָאָרֶץ:

10 He sends the springs into the valleys;
They flow among the hills.

10 הַמְשַׁלֵּחַ מַעְיָנִים בַּנְּחָלִים
בֵּין הָרִים יְהַלֵּכוּן:

11 They give drink to every beast of the field;
The wild donkeys quench their thirst.

11 יַשְׁקוּ כָּל־חַיְתוֹ שָׂדָי
יִשְׁבְּרוּ פְרָאִים צְמָאָם:

12 By them the birds of the heavens have their
home;
They sing among the branches.

12 עֲלֵיהֶם עוֹף־הַשָּׁמַיִם יִשְׁכּוֹן
מִבֵּין עֳפָאיִם יִתְּנוּ־קוֹל:

13 He waters the hills from His upper chambers;
The earth is satisfied with the fruit of Your
works.

13 מַשְׁקֶה הָרִים מֵעֲלִיּוֹתָיו
מִפְּרִי מַעֲשֶׂיךָ תִּשְׂבַּע הָאָרֶץ:

14 He causes the grass to grow for the cattle,
And vegetation for the service of man,

14 מַצְמִיחַ חָצִיר לַבְּהֵמָה
וְעֵשֶׂב לַעֲבֹדַת הָאָדָם

That he may bring forth food from the earth,

15 And wine *that* makes glad the heart of man,
   Oil to make *his* face shine,
   And bread *which* strengthens man's heart.

16 The trees of the LORD are full *of sap,*
   The cedars of Lebanon which He planted,

17 Where the birds make their nests;
   The stork has her home in the fir trees.

18 The high hills *are* for the wild goats;
   The cliffs are a refuge for the rock badgers.

19 He appointed the moon for seasons;
   The sun knows its going down.

20 You make darkness, and it is night,
   In which all the beasts of the forest creep
      about.

21 The young lions roar after their prey,
   And seek their food from God.

22 *When* the sun rises, they gather together
   And lie down in their dens.

23 Man goes out to his work
   And to his labor until the evening.

24 O LORD, how manifold are Your works!
   In wisdom You have made them all.
   The earth is full of Your possessions—

25 This great and wide sea,
   In which *are* innumerable teeming things,
   Living things both small and great.

26 There the ships sail about;
   There is that Leviathan
   Which You have made to play there.

27 These all wait for You,
   That You may give *them* their food in due
      season.

28 *What* You give them they gather in;
   You open Your hand, they are filled with
      good.

29 You hide Your face, they are troubled;
   You take away their breath, they die and
      return to their dust.

30 You send forth Your Spirit, they are created;
   And You renew the face of the earth.

31 May the glory of the LORD endure forever;
   May the LORD rejoice in His works.

32 He looks on the earth, and it trembles;
   He touches the hills, and they smoke.

33 I will sing to the LORD as long as I live;
   I will sing praise to my God while I have my
      being.

34 May my meditation be sweet to Him;
   I will be glad in the LORD.

35 May sinners be consumed from the earth,
   And the wicked be no more.

לְהוֹצִיא לֶחֶם מִן־הָאָרֶץ:

15 וְיַיִן ׀ יְשַׂמַּח לְבַב־אֱנוֹשׁ
לְהַצְהִיל פָּנִים מִשָּׁמֶן
וְלֶחֶם לְבַב־אֱנוֹשׁ יִסְעָד:

16 יִשְׂבְּעוּ עֲצֵי יְהוָה
אַרְזֵי לְבָנוֹן אֲשֶׁר נָטָע:

17 אֲשֶׁר־שָׁם צִפֳּרִים יְקַנֵּנוּ
חֲסִידָה בְּרוֹשִׁים בֵּיתָהּ:

18 הָרִים הַגְּבֹהִים לַיְּעֵלִים
סְלָעִים מַחְסֶה לַשְׁפַנִּים:

19 עָשָׂה יָרֵחַ לְמוֹעֲדִים שֶׁמֶשׁ יָדַע מְבוֹאוֹ:

20 תָּשֶׁת־חֹשֶׁךְ וִיהִי לָיְלָה
בּוֹ־תִרְמֹשׂ כָּל־חַיְתוֹ־יָעַר:

21 הַכְּפִירִים שֹׁאֲגִים לַטָּרֶף
וּלְבַקֵּשׁ מֵאֵל אָכְלָם:

22 תִּזְרַח הַשֶּׁמֶשׁ יֵאָסֵפוּן
וְאֶל־מְעוֹנֹתָם יִרְבָּצוּן:

23 יֵצֵא אָדָם לְפָעֳלוֹ וְלַעֲבֹדָתוֹ עֲדֵי־עָרֶב:

24 מָה־רַבּוּ מַעֲשֶׂיךָ ׀ יְהוָה
כֻּלָּם בְּחָכְמָה עָשִׂיתָ
מָלְאָה הָאָרֶץ קִנְיָנֶךָ:

25 זֶה ׀ הַיָּם גָּדוֹל וּרְחַב יָדָיִם
שָׁם־רֶמֶשׂ וְאֵין מִסְפָּר
חַיּוֹת קְטַנּוֹת עִם־גְּדֹלוֹת:

26 שָׁם אֳנִיּוֹת יְהַלֵּכוּן
לִוְיָתָן זֶה־יָצַרְתָּ לְשַׂחֶק־בּוֹ:

27 כֻּלָּם אֵלֶיךָ יְשַׂבֵּרוּן לָתֵת אָכְלָם בְּעִתּוֹ:

28 תִּתֵּן לָהֶם יִלְקֹטוּן
תִּפְתַּח יָדְךָ יִשְׂבְּעוּן טוֹב:

29 תַּסְתִּיר פָּנֶיךָ יִבָּהֵלוּן תֹּסֵף רוּחָם יִגְוָעוּן
וְאֶל־עֲפָרָם יְשׁוּבוּן:

30 תְּשַׁלַּח רוּחֲךָ יִבָּרֵאוּן
וּתְחַדֵּשׁ פְּנֵי אֲדָמָה:

31 יְהִי כְבוֹד יְהוָה לְעוֹלָם
יִשְׂמַח יְהוָה בְּמַעֲשָׂיו:

32 הַמַּבִּיט לָאָרֶץ וַתִּרְעָד
יִגַּע בֶּהָרִים וְיֶעֱשָׁנוּ:

33 אָשִׁירָה לַיהוָה בְּחַיָּי
אֲזַמְּרָה לֵאלֹהַי בְּעוֹדִי:

34 יֶעֱרַב עָלָיו שִׂיחִי אָנֹכִי אֶשְׂמַח בַּיהוָה:

35 יִתַּמּוּ חַטָּאִים ׀ מִן־הָאָרֶץ

Bless the LORD, O my soul!
Praise the LORD!

וּרְשָׁעִים ׀ עוֹד אֵינָם
בָּרְכִי נַפְשִׁי אֶת־יְהֹוָה הַלְלוּ־יָהּ׃

105 Oh, give thanks to the LORD!
Call upon His name;
Make known His deeds among the peoples!

קה הוֹדוּ לַיהֹוָה קִרְאוּ בִשְׁמוֹ
הוֹדִיעוּ בָעַמִּים עֲלִילוֹתָיו׃

2 Sing to Him, sing psalms to Him;
Talk of all His wondrous works!

2 שִׁירוּ־לוֹ זַמְּרוּ־לוֹ
שִׂיחוּ בְּכָל־נִפְלְאוֹתָיו׃

3 Glory in His holy name;
Let the hearts of those rejoice who seek the
LORD!

3 הִתְהַלְלוּ בְּשֵׁם קָדְשׁוֹ
יִשְׂמַח לֵב ׀ מְבַקְשֵׁי יְהֹוָה׃

4 Seek the LORD and His strength;
Seek His face evermore!

4 דִּרְשׁוּ יְהֹוָה וְעֻזּוֹ בַּקְּשׁוּ פָנָיו תָּמִיד׃

5 Remember His marvelous works which He has
done,
His wonders, and the judgments of His mouth,

5 זִכְרוּ נִפְלְאוֹתָיו אֲשֶׁר־עָשָׂה
מֹפְתָיו וּמִשְׁפְּטֵי־פִיו׃

6 O seed of Abraham His servant,
You children of Jacob, His chosen ones!

6 זֶרַע אַבְרָהָם עַבְדּוֹ
בְּנֵי יַעֲקֹב בְּחִירָיו׃

7 He *is* the LORD our God;
His judgments *are* in all the earth.

7 הוּא יְהֹוָה אֱלֹהֵינוּ
בְּכָל־הָאָרֶץ מִשְׁפָּטָיו׃

8 He remembers His covenant forever,
The word *which* He commanded, for a
thousand generations,

8 זָכַר לְעוֹלָם בְּרִיתוֹ דָּבָר צִוָּה לְאֶלֶף דּוֹר׃

9 *The covenant* which He made with Abraham,
And His oath to Isaac,

9 אֲשֶׁר כָּרַת אֶת־אַבְרָהָם
וּשְׁבוּעָתוֹ לְיִשְׂחָק׃

10 And confirmed it to Jacob for a statute,
To Israel *as* an everlasting covenant,

10 וַיַּעֲמִידֶהָ לְיַעֲקֹב לְחֹק
לְיִשְׂרָאֵל בְּרִית עוֹלָם׃

11 Saying, "To you I will give the land of Canaan
As the allotment of your inheritance,"

11 לֵאמֹר לְךָ אֶתֵּן אֶת־אֶרֶץ־כְּנָעַן
חֶבֶל נַחֲלַתְכֶם׃

12 When they were few in number,
Indeed very few, and strangers in it.

12 בִּהְיוֹתָם מְתֵי מִסְפָּר
כִּמְעַט וְגָרִים בָּהּ׃

13 When they went from one nation to another,
From *one* kingdom to another people,

13 וַיִּתְהַלְּכוּ מִגּוֹי אֶל־גּוֹי
מִמַּמְלָכָה אֶל־עַם אַחֵר׃

14 He permitted no one to do them wrong;
Yes, He rebuked kings for their sakes,

14 לֹא־הִנִּיחַ אָדָם לְעָשְׁקָם
וַיּוֹכַח עֲלֵיהֶם מְלָכִים׃

15 *Saying,* "Do not touch My anointed ones,
And do My prophets no harm."

15 אַל־תִּגְּעוּ בִמְשִׁיחָי וְלִנְבִיאַי אַל־תָּרֵעוּ׃

16 Moreover He called for a famine in the land;
He destroyed all the provision of bread.

16 וַיִּקְרָא רָעָב עַל־הָאָרֶץ
כָּל־מַטֵּה־לֶחֶם שָׁבָר׃

17 He sent a man before them—
Joseph—*who* was sold as a slave.

17 שָׁלַח לִפְנֵיהֶם אִישׁ
לְעֶבֶד נִמְכַּר יוֹסֵף׃

18 They hurt his feet with fetters,
He was laid in irons.

18 עִנּוּ בַכֶּבֶל רַגְלוֹ בַּרְזֶל בָּאָה נַפְשׁוֹ׃

19 Until the time that his word came to pass,
The word of the LORD tested him.

19 עַד־עֵת בֹּא־דְבָרוֹ
אִמְרַת יְהֹוָה צְרָפָתְהוּ׃

20 The king sent and released him,
The ruler of the people let him go free.

20 שָׁלַח מֶלֶךְ וַיַּתִּירֵהוּ
מֹשֵׁל עַמִּים וַיְפַתְּחֵהוּ׃

21 He made him lord of his house,
And ruler of all his possessions,

21 שָׂמוֹ אָדוֹן לְבֵיתוֹ
וּמֹשֵׁל בְּכָל־קִנְיָנוֹ׃

22 To bind his princes at his pleasure,
And teach his elders wisdom.

22 לֶאְסֹר שָׂרָיו בְּנַפְשׁוֹ וּזְקֵנָיו יְחַכֵּם׃

23 Israel also came into Egypt,

קה 18 רַגְלָו

And Jacob dwelt in the land of Ham.   וַיָּבֹא יִשְׂרָאֵל מִצְרָיִם 23

24 He increased His people greatly,   וְיַעֲקֹב גָּר בְּאֶרֶץ־חָם:
    And made them stronger than their enemies.

25 He turned their heart to hate His people,   וַיֶּפֶר אֶת־עַמּוֹ מְאֹד וַיַּעֲצִמֵהוּ מִצָּרָיו: 24
    To deal craftily with His servants.   הָפַךְ לִבָּם לִשְׂנֹא עַמּוֹ 25

26 He sent Moses His servant,   לְהִתְנַכֵּל בַּעֲבָדָיו:
    And Aaron whom He had chosen.   שָׁלַח מֹשֶׁה עַבְדּוֹ 26

27 They performed His signs among them,   אַהֲרֹן אֲשֶׁר בָּחַר־בּוֹ:
    And wonders in the land of Ham.   שָׂמוּ־בָם דִּבְרֵי אֹתוֹתָיו 27

28 He sent darkness, and made it dark;   וּמֹפְתִים בְּאֶרֶץ חָם:
    And they did not rebel against His word.   שָׁלַח חֹשֶׁךְ וַיַּחְשִׁךְ 28

29 He turned their waters into blood,   וְלֹא־מָרוּ אֶת־דְּבָרָיו:
    And killed their fish.

30 Their land abounded with frogs,   הָפַךְ אֶת־מֵימֵיהֶם לְדָם וַיָּמֶת אֶת־דְּגָתָם: 29
    Even in the chambers of their kings.

31 He spoke, and there came swarms of flies,   שָׁרַץ אַרְצָם צְפַרְדְּעִים בְּחַדְרֵי מַלְכֵיהֶם: 30
    And lice in all their territory.   אָמַר וַיָּבֹא עָרֹב כִּנִּים בְּכָל־גְּבוּלָם: 31

32 He gave them hail for rain,   נָתַן גִּשְׁמֵיהֶם בָּרָד אֵשׁ לֶהָבוֹת בְּאַרְצָם: 32
    And flaming fire in their land.

33 He struck their vines also, and their fig trees,   וַיַּךְ גַּפְנָם וּתְאֵנָתָם וַיְשַׁבֵּר עֵץ גְּבוּלָם: 33
    And splintered the trees of their territory.   אָמַר וַיָּבֹא אַרְבֶּה וְיֶלֶק וְאֵין מִסְפָּר: 34

34 He spoke, and locusts came,   וַיֹּאכַל כָּל־עֵשֶׂב בְּאַרְצָם 35
    Young locusts without number,

35 And ate up all the vegetation in their land,   וַיֹּאכַל פְּרִי אַדְמָתָם:
    And devoured the fruit of their ground.

36 He also destroyed all the firstborn in their land,   וַיַּךְ כָּל־בְּכוֹר בְּאַרְצָם 36
    The first of all their strength.   רֵאשִׁית לְכָל־אוֹנָם:

37 He also brought them out with silver and gold,   וַיּוֹצִיאֵם בְּכֶסֶף וְזָהָב 37
    And there was none feeble among His tribes.   וְאֵין בִּשְׁבָטָיו כּוֹשֵׁל:

38 Egypt was glad when they departed,   שָׂמַח מִצְרַיִם בְּצֵאתָם 38
    For the fear of them had fallen upon them.   כִּי־נָפַל פַּחְדָּם עֲלֵיהֶם:

39 He spread a cloud for a covering,   פָּרַשׂ עָנָן לְמָסָךְ וְאֵשׁ לְהָאִיר לָיְלָה: 39
    And fire to give light in the night.

40 The people asked, and He brought quail,   שָׁאַל וַיָּבֵא שְׂלָו וְלֶחֶם שָׁמַיִם יַשְׂבִּיעֵם: 40
    And satisfied them with the bread of heaven.

41 He opened the rock, and water gushed out;   פָּתַח צוּר וַיָּזוּבוּ מָיִם 41
    It ran in the dry places like a river.   הָלְכוּ בַּצִּיּוֹת נָהָר:

42 For He remembered His holy promise,   כִּי־זָכַר אֶת־דְּבַר קָדְשׁוֹ 42
    And Abraham His servant.   אֶת־אַבְרָהָם עַבְדּוֹ:

43 He brought out His people with joy,   וַיּוֹצִא עַמּוֹ בְשָׂשׂוֹן בְּרִנָּה אֶת־בְּחִירָיו: 43
    His chosen ones with gladness.   וַיִּתֵּן לָהֶם אַרְצוֹת גּוֹיִם 44

44 He gave them the lands of the Gentiles,   וַעֲמַל לְאֻמִּים יִירָשׁוּ:
    And they inherited the labor of the nations,

45 That they might observe His statutes   בַּעֲבוּר יִשְׁמְרוּ חֻקָּיו 45
    And keep His laws.   וְתוֹרֹתָיו יִנְצֹרוּ הַלְלוּ־יָהּ:

Praise the LORD!

106 Praise the LORD!   קו הַלְלוּיָהּ ׀ הוֹדוּ לַיהוָה כִּי־טוֹב
    Oh, give thanks to the LORD, for He is good!   כִּי לְעוֹלָם חַסְדּוֹ:
    For His mercy endures forever.   מִי יְמַלֵּל גְּבוּרוֹת יְהוָה 2

2 Who can utter the mighty acts of the LORD?   יַשְׁמִיעַ כָּל־תְּהִלָּתוֹ:
    Who can declare all His praise?

3 Blessed *are* those who keep justice,
And he who does righteousness at all times!

4 Remember me, O LORD, with the favor *You
have toward* Your people.
Oh, visit me with Your salvation,

5 That I may see the benefit of Your chosen
ones,
That I may rejoice in the gladness of Your
nation,
That I may glory with Your inheritance.

6 We have sinned with our fathers,
We have committed iniquity,
We have done wickedly.

7 Our fathers in Egypt did not understand Your
wonders;
They did not remember the multitude of Your
mercies,
But rebelled by the sea—the Red Sea.

8 Nevertheless He saved them for His name's
sake,
That He might make His mighty power known.

9 He rebuked the Red Sea also, and it dried up;
So He led them through the depths,
As through the wilderness.

10 He saved them from the hand of him who
hated *them,*
And redeemed them from the hand of the
enemy.

11 The waters covered their enemies;
There was not one of them left.

12 Then they believed His words;
They sang His praise.

13 They soon forgot His works;
They did not wait for His counsel,

14 But lusted exceedingly in the wilderness,
And tested God in the desert.

15 And He gave them their request,
But sent leanness into their soul.

16 When they envied Moses in the camp,
And Aaron the saint of the LORD,

17 The earth opened up and swallowed Dathan,
And covered the faction of Abiram.

18 A fire was kindled in their company;
The flame burned up the wicked.

19 They made a calf in Horeb,
And worshiped the molded image.

20 Thus they changed their glory
Into the image of an ox that eats grass.

21 They forgot God their Savior,
Who had done great things in Egypt,

22 Wondrous works in the land of Ham,

3 אַשְׁרֵי שֹׁמְרֵי מִשְׁפָּט
עֹשֵׂה צְדָקָה בְכָל־עֵת:

4 זָכְרֵנִי יְהֹוָה בִּרְצוֹן עַמֶּךָ
פָּקְדֵנִי בִּישׁוּעָתֶךָ:

5 לִרְאוֹת | בְּטוֹבַת בְּחִירֶיךָ
לִשְׂמֹחַ בְּשִׂמְחַת גּוֹיֶךָ
לְהִתְהַלֵּל עִם־נַחֲלָתֶךָ:

6 חָטָאנוּ עִם־אֲבוֹתֵינוּ
הֶעֱוִינוּ הִרְשָׁעְנוּ:

7 אֲבוֹתֵינוּ בְמִצְרַיִם |
לֹא־הִשְׂכִּילוּ נִפְלְאוֹתֶיךָ לֹא זָכְרוּ
אֶת־רֹב חֲסָדֶיךָ
וַיַּמְרוּ עַל־יָם בְּיַם־סוּף:

8 וַיּוֹשִׁיעֵם לְמַעַן שְׁמוֹ
לְהוֹדִיעַ אֶת־גְּבוּרָתוֹ:

9 וַיִּגְעַר בְּיַם־סוּף וַיֶּחֱרָב
וַיּוֹלִיכֵם בַּתְּהֹמוֹת כַּמִּדְבָּר:

10 וַיּוֹשִׁיעֵם מִיַּד שׂוֹנֵא
וַיִּגְאָלֵם מִיַּד אוֹיֵב:

11 וַיְכַסּוּ־מַיִם צָרֵיהֶם
אֶחָד מֵהֶם לֹא נוֹתָר:

12 וַיַּאֲמִינוּ בִדְבָרָיו
יָשִׁירוּ תְּהִלָּתוֹ:

13 מִהֲרוּ שָׁכְחוּ מַעֲשָׂיו
לֹא־חִכּוּ לַעֲצָתוֹ:

14 וַיִּתְאַוּוּ תַאֲוָה בַּמִּדְבָּר
וַיְנַסּוּ־אֵל בִּישִׁימוֹן:

15 וַיִּתֵּן לָהֶם שֶׁאֱלָתָם
וַיְשַׁלַּח רָזוֹן בְּנַפְשָׁם:

16 וַיְקַנְאוּ לְמֹשֶׁה בַּמַּחֲנֶה
לְאַהֲרֹן קְדוֹשׁ יְהֹוָה:

17 תִּפְתַּח־אֶרֶץ וַתִּבְלַע דָּתָן
וַתְּכַס עַל־עֲדַת אֲבִירָם:

18 וַתִּבְעַר־אֵשׁ בַּעֲדָתָם
לֶהָבָה תְּלַהֵט רְשָׁעִים:

19 יַעֲשׂוּ־עֵגֶל בְּחֹרֵב
וַיִּשְׁתַּחֲווּ לְמַסֵּכָה:

20 וַיָּמִירוּ אֶת־כְּבוֹדָם
בְּתַבְנִית שׁוֹר אֹכֵל עֵשֶׂב:

21 שָׁכְחוּ אֵל מוֹשִׁיעָם
עֹשֶׂה גְדֹלוֹת בְּמִצְרָיִם:

22 נִפְלָאוֹת בְּאֶרֶץ חָם

Awesome things by the Red Sea.

23 Therefore He said that He would destroy them,
Had not Moses His chosen one stood before
Him in the breach,
To turn away His wrath, lest He destroy *them*.

24 Then they despised the pleasant land;
They did not believe His word,

25 But complained in their tents,
And did not heed the voice of the LORD.

26 Therefore He raised His hand *in an oath*
against them,
To overthrow them in the wilderness,

27 To overthrow their descendants among the
nations,
And to scatter them in the lands.

28 They joined themselves also to Baal of Peor,
And ate sacrifices made to the dead.

29 Thus they provoked *Him* to anger with their
deeds,
And the plague broke out among them.

30 Then Phinehas stood up and intervened,
And the plague was stopped.

31 And that was accounted to him for righteousness
To all generations forevermore.

32 They angered *Him* also at the waters of strife,
So that it went ill with Moses on account of
them;

33 Because they rebelled against His Spirit,
So that he spoke rashly with his lips.

34 They did not destroy the peoples,
Concerning whom the LORD had commanded
them,

35 But they mingled with the Gentiles
And learned their works;

36 They served their idols,
Which became a snare to them.

37 They even sacrificed their sons
And their daughters to demons,

38 And shed innocent blood,
The blood of their sons and daughters,
Whom they sacrificed to the idols of Canaan;
And the land was polluted with blood.

39 Thus they were defiled by their own works,
And played the harlot by their own deeds.

40 Therefore the wrath of the LORD was kindled
against His people,
So that He abhorred His own inheritance.

41 And He gave them into the hand of the
Gentiles,
And those who hated them ruled over them.

42 Their enemies also oppressed them,

נוֹרָאוֹת עַל־יַם־סוּף:

23 וַיֹּאמֶר לְהַשְׁמִידָם
לוּלֵי מֹשֶׁה בְחִירוֹ עָמַד בַּפֶּרֶץ לְפָנָיו
לְהָשִׁיב חֲמָתוֹ מֵהַשְׁחִית:

24 וַיִּמְאֲסוּ בְּאֶרֶץ חֶמְדָּה
לֹא־הֶאֱמִינוּ לִדְבָרוֹ:

25 וַיֵּרָגְנוּ בְאָהֳלֵיהֶם
לֹא שָׁמְעוּ בְּקוֹל יְהֹוָה:

26 וַיִּשָּׂא יָדוֹ לָהֶם
לְהַפִּיל אוֹתָם בַּמִּדְבָּר:

27 וּלְהַפִּיל זַרְעָם בַּגּוֹיִם
וּלְזָרוֹתָם בָּאֲרָצוֹת:

28 וַיִּצָּמְדוּ לְבַעַל פְּעוֹר
וַיֹּאכְלוּ זִבְחֵי מֵתִים:

29 וַיַּכְעִיסוּ בְּמַעַלְלֵיהֶם
וַתִּפְרָץ־בָּם מַגֵּפָה:

30 וַיַּעֲמֹד פִּינְחָס וַיְפַלֵּל
וַתֵּעָצַר הַמַּגֵּפָה:

31 וַתֵּחָשֶׁב לוֹ לִצְדָקָה
לְדֹר וָדֹר עַד־עוֹלָם:

32 וַיַּקְצִיפוּ עַל־מֵי מְרִיבָה
וַיֵּרַע לְמֹשֶׁה בַּעֲבוּרָם:

33 כִּי־הִמְרוּ אֶת־רוּחוֹ
וַיְבַטֵּא בִּשְׂפָתָיו:

34 לֹא־הִשְׁמִידוּ אֶת־הָעַמִּים
אֲשֶׁר אָמַר יְהֹוָה לָהֶם:

35 וַיִּתְעָרְבוּ בַגּוֹיִם
וַיִּלְמְדוּ מַעֲשֵׂיהֶם:

36 וַיַּעַבְדוּ אֶת־עֲצַבֵּיהֶם
וַיִּהְיוּ לָהֶם לְמוֹקֵשׁ:

37 וַיִּזְבְּחוּ אֶת־בְּנֵיהֶם
וְאֶת־בְּנוֹתֵיהֶם לַשֵּׁדִים:

38 וַיִּשְׁפְּכוּ דָם נָקִי דַּם־בְּנֵיהֶם וּבְנוֹתֵיהֶם
אֲשֶׁר זִבְּחוּ לַעֲצַבֵּי כְנָעַן
וַתֶּחֱנַף הָאָרֶץ בַּדָּמִים:

39 וַיִּטְמְאוּ בְמַעֲשֵׂיהֶם
וַיִּזְנוּ בְּמַעַלְלֵיהֶם:

40 וַיִּחַר־אַף יְהֹוָה בְּעַמּוֹ
וַיְתָעֵב אֶת־נַחֲלָתוֹ:

41 וַיִּתְּנֵם בְּיַד־גּוֹיִם
וַיִּמְשְׁלוּ בָהֶם שֹׂנְאֵיהֶם:

42 וַיִּלְחָצוּם אוֹיְבֵיהֶם

And they were brought into subjection under
their hand.

43 Many times He delivered them;
But they rebelled in their counsel,
And were brought low for their iniquity.

44 Nevertheless He regarded their affliction,
When He heard their cry;

45 And for their sake He remembered His
covenant,
And relented according to the multitude of His
mercies.

46 He also made them to be pitied
By all those who carried them away captive.

47 Save us, O LORD our God,
And gather us from among the Gentiles,
To give thanks to Your holy name,
To triumph in Your praise.

48 Blessed be the LORD God of Israel
From everlasting to everlasting!
And let all the people say, "Amen!"

Praise the LORD!

וַיִּכָּנְעוּ תַּחַת יָדָם׃

43 פְּעָמִים רַבּוֹת יַצִּילֵם
וְהֵמָּה יַמְרוּ בַעֲצָתָם
וַיָּמֹכּוּ בַּעֲוֺנָם׃

44 וַיַּרְא בַּצַּר לָהֶם
בְּשָׁמְעוֹ אֶת־רִנָּתָם׃

45 וַיִּזְכֹּר לָהֶם בְּרִיתוֹ
וַיִּנָּחֵם כְּרֹב חֲסָדָֽיק׃

46 וַיִּתֵּן אוֹתָם לְרַחֲמִים
לִפְנֵי כָּל־שׁוֹבֵיהֶם׃

47 הוֹשִׁיעֵנוּ ׀ יְהוָה אֱלֹהֵינוּ
וְקַבְּצֵנוּ מִן־הַגּוֹיִם
לְהֹדוֹת לְשֵׁם קָדְשֶׁךָ
לְהִשְׁתַּבֵּחַ בִּתְהִלָּתֶךָ׃

48 בָּרוּךְ־יְהוָה אֱלֹהֵי יִשְׂרָאֵל
מִן־הָעוֹלָם ׀ וְעַד הָעוֹלָם
וְאָמַר כָּל־הָעָם
אָמֵן הַלְלוּ־יָהּ׃

Book Five: Psalms 107—150

107 Oh, give thanks to the LORD, for He is
good!

For His mercy endures forever.

2 Let the redeemed of the LORD say so,
Whom He has redeemed from the hand of the
enemy,

3 And gathered out of the lands,
From the east and from the west,
From the north and from the south.

4 They wandered in the wilderness in a desolate
way;
They found no city to dwell in.

5 Hungry and thirsty,
Their soul fainted in them.

6 Then they cried out to the LORD in their
trouble,
And He delivered them out of their distresses.

7 And He led them forth by the right way,
That they might go to a city for a dwelling
place.

8 Oh, that men would give thanks to the LORD
for His goodness,
And for His wonderful works to the children of
men!

9 For He satisfies the longing soul,
And fills the hungry soul with goodness.

קז הֹדוּ לַיהוָה כִּי־טוֹב
כִּי לְעוֹלָם חַסְדּֽוֹ׃

2 יֹאמְרוּ גְּאוּלֵי יְהוָה
אֲשֶׁר גְּאָלָם מִיַּד־צָר׃

3 וּמֵאֲרָצוֹת קִבְּצָם
מִמִּזְרָח וּמִמַּעֲרָב מִצָּפוֹן וּמִיָּם׃

4 תָּעוּ בַמִּדְבָּר בִּישִׁימוֹן דָּרֶךְ
עִיר מוֹשָׁב לֹא מָצָֽאוּ׃

5 רְעֵבִים גַּם־צְמֵאִים
נַפְשָׁם בָּהֶם תִּתְעַטָּֽף׃

6 וַיִּצְעֲקוּ אֶל־יְהוָה בַּצַּר לָהֶם
מִמְּצוּקוֹתֵיהֶם יַצִּילֵֽם׃

7 וַיַּדְרִיכֵם בְּדֶרֶךְ יְשָׁרָה
לָלֶכֶת אֶל־עִיר מוֹשָׁב׃

8 יוֹדוּ לַיהוָה חַסְדּוֹ
וְנִפְלְאוֹתָיו לִבְנֵי אָדָם׃

9 כִּי־הִשְׂבִּיעַ נֶפֶשׁ שֹׁקֵקָה
וְנֶפֶשׁ רְעֵבָה מִלֵּא־טֽוֹב׃

10 Those who sat in darkness and in the shadow
of death,
Bound in affliction and irons—
11 Because they rebelled against the words of
God,
And despised the counsel of the Most High,
12 Therefore He brought down their heart with
labor;
They fell down, and *there was* none to help.
13 Then they cried out to the LORD in their
trouble,
And He saved them out of their distresses.
14 He brought them out of darkness and the
shadow of death,
And broke their chains in pieces.
15 Oh, that *men* would give thanks to the LORD
for His goodness,
And *for* His wonderful works to the children of
men!
16 For He has broken the gates of bronze,
And cut the bars of iron in two.
17 Fools, because of their transgression,
And because of their iniquities, were afflicted.
18 Their soul abhorred all manner of food,
And they drew near to the gates of death.
19 Then they cried out to the LORD in their
trouble,
And He saved them out of their distresses.
20 He sent His word and healed them,
And delivered *them* from their destructions.
21 Oh, that *men* would give thanks to the LORD
for His goodness,
And *for* His wonderful works to the children of
men!
22 Let them sacrifice the sacrifices of
thanksgiving,
And declare His works with rejoicing.
23 Those who go down to the sea in ships,
Who do business on great waters,
24 They see the works of the LORD,
And His wonders in the deep.
25 For He commands and raises the stormy wind,
Which lifts up the waves of the sea.
26 They mount up to the heavens,
They go down again to the depths;
Their soul melts because of trouble.
27 They reel to and fro, and stagger like a drunken
man,
And are at their wits' end.
28 Then they cry out to the LORD in their trouble,
And He brings them out of their distresses.
29 He calms the storm,
So that its waves are still.

10 יֹשְׁבֵי חֹשֶׁךְ וְצַלְמָוֶת
אֲסִירֵי עֳנִי וּבַרְזֶל:
11 כִּי־הִמְרוּ אִמְרֵי־אֵל
וַעֲצַת עֶלְיוֹן נָאָצוּ:
12 וַיַּכְנַע בֶּעָמָל לִבָּם
כָּשְׁלוּ וְאֵין עֹזֵר:
13 וַיִּזְעֲקוּ אֶל־יְהוָה בַּצַּר לָהֶם
מִמְּצֻקוֹתֵיהֶם יוֹשִׁיעֵם:
14 יוֹצִיאֵם מֵחֹשֶׁךְ וְצַלְמָוֶת
וּמוֹסְרוֹתֵיהֶם יְנַתֵּק:
15 יוֹדוּ לַיהוָה חַסְדּוֹ
וְנִפְלְאוֹתָיו לִבְנֵי אָדָם:
16 כִּי־שִׁבַּר דַּלְתוֹת נְחֹשֶׁת
וּבְרִיחֵי בַרְזֶל גִּדֵּעַ:
17 אֱוִלִים מִדֶּרֶךְ פִּשְׁעָם
וּמֵעֲוֹנֹתֵיהֶם יִתְעַנּוּ:
18 כָּל־אֹכֶל תְּתַעֵב נַפְשָׁם
וַיַּגִּיעוּ עַד־שַׁעֲרֵי מָוֶת:
19 וַיִּזְעֲקוּ אֶל־יְהוָה בַּצַּר לָהֶם
מִמְּצֻקוֹתֵיהֶם יוֹשִׁיעֵם:
20 יִשְׁלַח דְּבָרוֹ וְיִרְפָּאֵם
וִימַלֵּט מִשְּׁחִיתוֹתָם:
21 יוֹדוּ לַיהוָה חַסְדּוֹ
וְנִפְלְאוֹתָיו לִבְנֵי אָדָם:
22 וְיִזְבְּחוּ זִבְחֵי תוֹדָה
וִיסַפְּרוּ מַעֲשָׂיו בְּרִנָּה:
23 יוֹרְדֵי הַיָּם בָּאֳנִיּוֹת
עֹשֵׂי מְלָאכָה בְּמַיִם רַבִּים:
24 הֵמָּה רָאוּ מַעֲשֵׂי יְהוָה
וְנִפְלְאוֹתָיו בִּמְצוּלָה:
25 וַיֹּאמֶר וַיַּעֲמֵד רוּחַ סְעָרָה
וַתְּרוֹמֵם גַּלָּיו:
26 יַעֲלוּ שָׁמַיִם יֵרְדוּ תְהוֹמוֹת
נַפְשָׁם בְּרָעָה תִתְמוֹגָג:
27 יָחוֹגּוּ וְיָנוּעוּ כַּשִּׁכּוֹר
וְכָל־חָכְמָתָם תִּתְבַּלָּע:
28 וַיִּצְעֲקוּ אֶל־יְהוָה בַּצַּר לָהֶם
וּמִמְּצוּקֹתֵיהֶם יוֹצִיאֵם:
29 יָקֵם סְעָרָה לִדְמָמָה
וַיֶּחֱשׁוּ גַּלֵּיהֶם:

³⁰ Then they are glad because they are quiet;
    So He guides them to their desired haven.

וַיִּשְׂמְחוּ כִי־יִשְׁתֹּקוּ   30
וַיַּנְחֵם אֶל־מְחוֹז חֶפְצָם:

³¹ Oh, that *men* would give thanks to the L<small>ORD</small>
    for His goodness,
    And *for* His wonderful works to the children of
    men!

יוֹדוּ לַיהֹוָה חַסְדּוֹ   31
וְנִפְלְאוֹתָיו לִבְנֵי אָדָם:

³² Let them exalt Him also in the assembly of the
    people,
    And praise Him in the company of the elders.

וִירֹמְמוּהוּ בִּקְהַל־עָם   32
וּבְמוֹשַׁב זְקֵנִים יְהַלְלוּהוּ:

³³ He turns rivers into a wilderness,
    And the watersprings into dry ground;

יָשֵׂם נְהָרוֹת לְמִדְבָּר   33
וּמֹצָאֵי מַיִם לְצִמָּאוֹן:

³⁴ A fruitful land into barrenness,
    For the wickedness of those who dwell in it.

אֶרֶץ פְּרִי לִמְלֵחָה   34
מֵרָעַת יֹשְׁבֵי בָהּ:

³⁵ He turns a wilderness into pools of water,
    And dry land into watersprings.

יָשֵׂם מִדְבָּר לַאֲגַם־מַיִם   35
וְאֶרֶץ צִיָּה לְמֹצָאֵי מָיִם:

³⁶ There He makes the hungry dwell,
    That they may establish a city for a dwelling
    place,

וַיּוֹשֶׁב שָׁם רְעֵבִים   36
וַיְכוֹנְנוּ עִיר מוֹשָׁב:

³⁷ And sow fields and plant vineyards,
    That they may yield a fruitful harvest.

וַיִּזְרְעוּ שָׂדוֹת וַיִּטְּעוּ כְרָמִים   37
וַיַּעֲשׂוּ פְּרִי תְבוּאָה:

³⁸ He also blesses them, and they multiply greatly;
    And He does not let their cattle decrease.

וַיְבָרֲכֵם וַיִּרְבּוּ מְאֹד   38
וּבְהֶמְתָּם לֹא יַמְעִיט:

³⁹ When they are diminished and brought low
    Through oppression, affliction and sorrow,

וַיִּמְעֲטוּ וַיָּשֹׁחוּ   39
מֵעֹצֶר רָעָה וְיָגוֹן:

⁴⁰ He pours contempt on princes,
    And causes them to wander in the wilderness
    where there is no way;

שֹׁפֵךְ בּוּז עַל־נְדִיבִים   40
וַיַּתְעֵם בְּתֹהוּ לֹא־דָרֶךְ:

⁴¹ Yet He sets the poor on high, far from
    affliction,
    And makes *their* families like a flock.

וַיְשַׂגֵּב אֶבְיוֹן מֵעוֹנִי   41
וַיָּשֶׂם כַּצֹּאן מִשְׁפָּחוֹת:

⁴² The righteous see *it* and rejoice,
    And all iniquity stops its mouth.

יִרְאוּ יְשָׁרִים וְיִשְׂמָחוּ   42
וְכָל־עַוְלָה קָפְצָה פִּיהָ:

⁴³ Whoever *is* wise will observe these *things,*
    And they will understand the lovingkindness of
    the L<small>ORD</small>.

מִי־חָכָם וְיִשְׁמָר־אֵלֶּה   43
וְיִתְבּוֹנְנוּ חַסְדֵי יְהֹוָה:

108 A Song. A Psalm of David.

שִׁיר מִזְמוֹר לְדָוִד: קח

    O God, my heart is steadfast;
    I will sing and give praise, even with my glory.

נָכוֹן לִבִּי אֱלֹהִים אָשִׁירָה וַאֲזַמְּרָה אַף־כְּבוֹדִי: 2

² Awake, lute and harp!
    I will awaken the dawn.

עוּרָה הַנֵּבֶל וְכִנּוֹר   3
אָעִירָה שָּׁחַר:

³ I will praise You, O L<small>ORD</small>, among the peoples,
    And I will sing praises to You among the
    nations.

אוֹדְךָ בָעַמִּים | יְהֹוָה   4
וַאֲזַמֶּרְךָ בַּל־אֻמִּים:

⁴ For Your mercy *is* great above the heavens,
    And Your truth *reaches* to the clouds.

כִּי־גָדוֹל מֵעַל־שָׁמַיִם חַסְדֶּךָ   5
וְעַד־שְׁחָקִים אֲמִתֶּךָ:

⁵ Be exalted, O God, above the heavens,
    And Your glory above all the earth;

רוּמָה עַל־שָׁמַיִם אֱלֹהִים   6
וְעַל כָּל־הָאָרֶץ כְּבוֹדֶךָ:

⁶ That Your beloved may be delivered,
    Save *with* Your right hand, and hear me.

לְמַעַן יֵחָלְצוּן יְדִידֶיךָ   7
הוֹשִׁיעָה יְמִינְךָ וַעֲנֵנִי:

⁷ God has spoken in His holiness:
    "I will rejoice;

אֱלֹהִים | דִּבֶּר בְּקָדְשׁוֹ אֶעְלֹזָה   8

I will divide Shechem
And measure out the Valley of Succoth.

8 Gilead *is* Mine; Manasseh *is* Mine;
Ephraim also *is* the helmet for My head;
Judah *is* My lawgiver.

9 Moab *is* My washpot;
Over Edom I will cast My shoe;
Over Philistia I will triumph."

10 Who will bring me *into* the strong city?
Who will lead me to Edom?

11 *Is it* not You, O God, *who* cast us off?
And *You,* O God, *who* did not go out with our
armies?

12 Give us help from trouble,
For the help of man is useless.

13 Through God we will do valiantly,
For *it is* He *who* shall tread down our enemies.

109 To the Chief Musician. A Psalm of David.
Do not keep silent,
O God of my praise!

2 For the mouth of the wicked and the mouth of
the deceitful
Have opened against me;
They have spoken against me with a lying
tongue.

3 They have also surrounded me with words of
hatred,
And fought against me without a cause.

4 In return for my love they are my accusers,
But I *give myself to* prayer.

5 Thus they have rewarded me evil for good,
And hatred for my love.

6 Set a wicked man over him,
And let an accuser stand at his right hand.

7 When he is judged, let him be found guilty,
And let his prayer become sin.

8 Let his days be few,
And let another take his office.

9 Let his children be fatherless,
And his wife a widow.

10 Let his children continually be vagabonds, and
beg;
Let them seek *their bread* also from their
desolate places.

11 Let the creditor seize all that he has,
And let strangers plunder his labor.

12 Let there be none to extend mercy to him,
Nor let there be any to favor his fatherless
children.

13 Let his posterity be cut off,

אֲחַלְּקָה שְׁכֶם וְעֵמֶק סֻכּוֹת אֲמַדֵּד:

9 לִי גִלְעָד ׀ לִי מְנַשֶּׁה וְאֶפְרַיִם מָעוֹז רֹאשִׁי
יְהוּדָה מְחֹקְקִי:

10 מוֹאָב ׀ סִיר רַחְצִי עַל־אֱדוֹם אַשְׁלִיךְ נַעֲלִי
עָלַי־פְּלֶשֶׁת אֶתְרוֹעָע:

11 מִי יֹבִלֵנִי עִיר מִבְצָר
מִי נָחַנִי עַד־אֱדוֹם:

12 הֲלֹא־אֱלֹהִים זְנַחְתָּנוּ
וְלֹא־תֵצֵא אֱלֹהִים בְּצִבְאוֹתֵינוּ:

13 הָבָה־לָּנוּ עֶזְרָת מִצָּר
וְשָׁוְא תְּשׁוּעַת אָדָם:

14 בֵּאלֹהִים נַעֲשֶׂה־חָיִל
וְהוּא יָבוּס צָרֵינוּ:

קט לַמְנַצֵּחַ לְדָוִד מִזְמוֹר
אֱלֹהֵי תְהִלָּתִי
אַל־תֶּחֱרַשׁ:

2 כִּי פִי רָשָׁע וּפִי־מִרְמָה עָלַי פָּתָחוּ
דִּבְּרוּ אִתִּי לְשׁוֹן שָׁקֶר:

3 וְדִבְרֵי שִׂנְאָה סְבָבוּנִי
וַיִּלָּחֲמוּנִי חִנָּם:

4 תַּחַת־אַהֲבָתִי יִשְׂטְנוּנִי
וַאֲנִי תְפִלָּה:

5 וַיָּשִׂימוּ עָלַי רָעָה תַּחַת טוֹבָה
וְשִׂנְאָה תַּחַת אַהֲבָתִי:

6 הַפְקֵד עָלָיו רָשָׁע
וְשָׂטָן יַעֲמֹד עַל־יְמִינוֹ:

7 בְּהִשָּׁפְטוֹ יֵצֵא רָשָׁע
וּתְפִלָּתוֹ תִּהְיֶה לַחֲטָאָה:

8 יִהְיוּ־יָמָיו מְעַטִּים
פְּקֻדָּתוֹ יִקַּח אַחֵר:

9 יִהְיוּ־בָנָיו יְתוֹמִים
וְאִשְׁתּוֹ אַלְמָנָה:

10 וְנוֹעַ יָנוּעוּ בָנָיו וְשִׁאֵלוּ
וְדָרְשׁוּ מֵחָרְבוֹתֵיהֶם:

11 יְנַקֵּשׁ נוֹשֶׁה לְכָל־אֲשֶׁר־לוֹ
וְיָבֹזּוּ זָרִים יְגִיעוֹ:

12 אַל־יְהִי־לוֹ מֹשֵׁךְ חָסֶד
וְאַל־יְהִי חוֹנֵן לִיתוֹמָיו:

13 יְהִי־אַחֲרִיתוֹ לְהַכְרִית

And in the generation following let their name be blotted out.

14 Let the iniquity of his fathers be remembered before the LORD,
And let not the sin of his mother be blotted out.

15 Let them be continually before the LORD,
That He may cut off the memory of them from the earth;

16 Because he did not remember to show mercy,
But persecuted the poor and needy man,
That he might even slay the broken in heart.

17 As he loved cursing, so let it come to him;
As he did not delight in blessing, so let it be far from him.

18 As he clothed himself with cursing as with his garment,
So let it enter his body like water,
And like oil into his bones.

19 Let it be to him like the garment which covers him,
And for a belt with which he girds himself continually.

20 *Let* this *be* the LORD's reward to my accusers,
And to those who speak evil against my person.

21 But You, O GOD the Lord,
Deal with me for Your name's sake;
Because Your mercy *is* good, deliver me.

22 For I *am* poor and needy,
And my heart is wounded within me.

23 I am gone like a shadow when it lengthens;
I am shaken off like a locust.

24 My knees are weak through fasting,
And my flesh is feeble from lack of fatness.

25 I also have become a reproach to them;
When they look at me, they shake their heads.

26 Help me, O LORD my God!
Oh, save me according to Your mercy,

27 That they may know that this *is* Your hand—
That You, LORD, have done it!

28 Let them curse, but You bless;
When they arise, let them be ashamed,
But let Your servant rejoice.

29 Let my accusers be clothed with shame,
And let them cover themselves with their own disgrace as with a mantle.

30 I will greatly praise the LORD with my mouth;
Yes, I will praise Him among the multitude.

31 For He shall stand at the right hand of the poor,
To save *him* from those who condemn him.

בְּדוֹר אַחֵר יִמַּח שְׁמָם:

14 יִזָּכֵר ׀ עֲוֺן אֲבֹתָיו אֶל־יְהֹוָה
וְחַטַּאת אִמּוֹ אַל־תִּמָּח:

15 יִהְיוּ נֶגֶד־יְהֹוָה תָּמִיד
וְיַכְרֵת מֵאֶרֶץ זִכְרָם:

16 יַעַן אֲשֶׁר ׀ לֹא זָכַר עֲשׂוֹת חָסֶד
וַיִּרְדֹּף אִישׁ־עָנִי וְאֶבְיוֹן וְנִכְאֵה לֵבָב
לְמוֹתֵת:

17 וַיֶּאֱהַב קְלָלָה וַתְּבוֹאֵהוּ
וְלֹא־חָפֵץ בִּבְרָכָה וַתִּרְחַק מִמֶּנּוּ:

18 וַיִּלְבַּשׁ קְלָלָה כְּמַדּוֹ
וַתָּבֹא כַמַּיִם בְּקִרְבּוֹ וְכַשֶּׁמֶן בְּעַצְמוֹתָיו:

19 תְּהִי־לוֹ כְּבֶגֶד יַעְטֶה
וּלְמֵזַח תָּמִיד יַחְגְּרֶהָ:

20 זֹאת פְּעֻלַּת שֹׂטְנַי מֵאֵת יְהֹוָה
וְהַדֹּבְרִים רָע עַל־נַפְשִׁי:

21 וְאַתָּה ׀ יְהֹוִה אֲדֹנָי
עֲשֵׂה־אִתִּי לְמַעַן שְׁמֶךָ
כִּי־טוֹב חַסְדְּךָ
הַצִּילֵנִי:

22 כִּי־עָנִי וְאֶבְיוֹן אָנֹכִי
וְלִבִּי חָלַל בְּקִרְבִּי:

23 כְּצֵל־כִּנְטוֹתוֹ נֶהֱלָכְתִּי
נִנְעַרְתִּי כָּאַרְבֶּה:

24 בִּרְכַּי כָּשְׁלוּ מִצּוֹם
וּבְשָׂרִי כָּחַשׁ מִשָּׁמֶן:

25 וַאֲנִי ׀ הָיִיתִי חֶרְפָּה לָהֶם
יִרְאוּנִי יְנִיעוּן רֹאשָׁם:

26 עָזְרֵנִי יְהֹוָה אֱלֹהָי
הוֹשִׁיעֵנִי כְחַסְדֶּךָ:

27 וְיֵדְעוּ כִּי־יָדְךָ זֹּאת
אַתָּה יְהֹוָה עֲשִׂיתָהּ:

28 יְקַלְלוּ־הֵמָּה וְאַתָּה תְבָרֵךְ
קָמוּ ׀ וַיֵּבֹשׁוּ וְעַבְדְּךָ יִשְׂמָח:

29 יִלְבְּשׁוּ שׂוֹטְנַי כְּלִמָּה
וְיַעֲטוּ כַמְעִיל בָּשְׁתָּם:

30 אוֹדֶה יְהֹוָה מְאֹד בְּפִי
וּבְתוֹךְ רַבִּים אֲהַלְלֶנּוּ:

31 כִּי־יַעֲמֹד לִימִין אֶבְיוֹן
לְהוֹשִׁיעַ מִשֹּׁפְטֵי נַפְשׁוֹ:

110 A Psalm of David.

The LORD said to my Lord,
"Sit at My right hand,
Till I make Your enemies Your footstool."

2 The LORD shall send the rod of Your strength
out of Zion.
Rule in the midst of Your enemies!

3 Your people *shall be* volunteers
In the day of Your power;
In the beauties of holiness, from the womb of
the morning,
You have the dew of Your youth.

4 The LORD has sworn
And will not relent,
"You *are* a priest forever
According to the order of Melchizedek."

5 The Lord *is* at Your right hand;
He shall execute kings in the day of His wrath.

6 He shall judge among the nations,
He shall fill *the places* with dead bodies,
He shall execute the heads of many countries.

7 He shall drink of the brook by the wayside;
Therefore He shall lift up the head.

111 Praise the LORD!

I will praise the LORD with *my* whole heart,
In the assembly of the upright and *in the*
congregation.

2 The works of the LORD *are* great,
Studied by all who have pleasure in them.

3 His work *is* honorable and glorious,
And His righteousness endures forever.

4 He has made His wonderful works to be
remembered;
The LORD *is* gracious and full of compassion.

5 He has given food to those who fear Him;
He will ever be mindful of His covenant.

6 He has declared to His people the power of His
works,
In giving them the heritage of the nations.

7 The works of His hands *are* verity and justice;
All His precepts *are* sure.

8 They stand fast forever and ever,
And are done in truth and uprightness.

9 He has sent redemption to His people;
He has commanded His covenant forever:
Holy and awesome *is* His name.

10 The fear of the LORD *is* the beginning of
wisdom;
A good understanding have all those who do
His commandments.
His praise endures forever.

קי לְדָוִד מִזְמוֹר
נְאֻם יְהֹוָה ׀ לַאדֹנִי שֵׁב לִימִינִי
עַד־אָשִׁית אֹיְבֶיךָ הֲדֹם לְרַגְלֶיךָ׃

2 מַטֵּה־עֻזְּךָ יִשְׁלַח יְהֹוָה מִצִּיּוֹן
רְדֵה בְּקֶרֶב אֹיְבֶיךָ׃

3 עַמְּךָ נְדָבֹת בְּיוֹם חֵילֶךָ
בְּהַדְרֵי־קֹדֶשׁ מֵרֶחֶם מִשְׁחָר
לְךָ טַל יַלְדֻתֶיךָ׃

4 נִשְׁבַּע יְהֹוָה ׀ וְלֹא יִנָּחֵם
אַתָּה־כֹהֵן לְעוֹלָם
עַל־דִּבְרָתִי מַלְכִּי־צֶדֶק׃

5 אֲדֹנָי עַל־יְמִינְךָ
מָחַץ בְּיוֹם־אַפּוֹ מְלָכִים׃

6 יָדִין בַּגּוֹיִם מָלֵא גְוִיּוֹת
מָחַץ רֹאשׁ עַל־אֶרֶץ רַבָּה׃

7 מִנַּחַל בַּדֶּרֶךְ יִשְׁתֶּה
עַל־כֵּן יָרִים רֹאשׁ׃

קיא הַלְלוּ יָהּ ׀ אוֹדֶה יְהֹוָה בְּכָל־לֵבָב
בְּסוֹד יְשָׁרִים וְעֵדָה׃

2 גְּדֹלִים מַעֲשֵׂי יְהֹוָה
דְּרוּשִׁים לְכָל־חֶפְצֵיהֶם׃

3 הוֹד־וְהָדָר פָּעֳלוֹ
וְצִדְקָתוֹ עֹמֶדֶת לָעַד׃

4 זֵכֶר עָשָׂה לְנִפְלְאֹתָיו
חַנּוּן וְרַחוּם יְהֹוָה׃

5 טֶרֶף נָתַן לִירֵאָיו
יִזְכֹּר לְעוֹלָם בְּרִיתוֹ׃

6 כֹּחַ מַעֲשָׂיו הִגִּיד לְעַמּוֹ
לָתֵת לָהֶם נַחֲלַת גּוֹיִם׃

7 מַעֲשֵׂי יָדָיו אֱמֶת וּמִשְׁפָּט
נֶאֱמָנִים כָּל־פִּקּוּדָיו׃

8 סְמוּכִים לָעַד לְעוֹלָם
עֲשׂוּיִם בֶּאֱמֶת וְיָשָׁר׃

9 פְּדוּת ׀ שָׁלַח לְעַמּוֹ
צִוָּה־לְעוֹלָם בְּרִיתוֹ
קָדוֹשׁ וְנוֹרָא שְׁמוֹ׃

10 רֵאשִׁית חָכְמָה ׀ יִרְאַת יְהֹוָה
שֵׂכֶל טוֹב לְכָל־עֹשֵׂיהֶם
תְּהִלָּתוֹ עֹמֶדֶת לָעַד׃

112 Praise the LORD!

Blessed *is* the man *who* fears the LORD,
Who delights greatly in His commandments.

2 His descendants will be mighty on earth;
The generation of the upright will be blessed.

3 Wealth and riches *will be* in his house,
And his righteousness endures forever.

4 Unto the upright there arises light in the
darkness;
He is gracious, and full of compassion, and
righteous.

5 A good man deals graciously and lends;
He will guide his affairs with discretion.

6 Surely he will never be shaken;
The righteous will be in everlasting remembrance.

7 He will not be afraid of evil tidings;
His heart is steadfast, trusting in the LORD.

8 His heart *is* established;
He will not be afraid,
Until he sees *his desire* upon his enemies.

9 He has dispersed abroad,
He has given to the poor;
His righteousness endures forever;
His horn will be exalted with honor.

10 The wicked will see *it* and be grieved;
He will gnash his teeth and melt away;
The desire of the wicked shall perish.

113 Praise the LORD!

Praise, O servants of the LORD,
Praise the name of the LORD!

2 Blessed be the name of the LORD
From this time forth and forevermore!

3 From the rising of the sun to its going down
The LORD's name *is* to be praised.

4 The LORD *is* high above all nations,
His glory above the heavens.

5 Who *is* like the LORD our God,
Who dwells on high,

6 Who humbles Himself to behold
The things that are in the heavens and in the
earth?

7 He raises the poor out of the dust,
And lifts the needy out of the ash heap,

8 That He may seat *him* with princes—
With the princes of His people.

9 He grants the barren woman a home,
Like a joyful mother of children.

Praise the LORD!

קיב הַלְלוּ יָהּ ׀ אַשְׁרֵי־אִישׁ יָרֵא אֶת־יְהֹוָה
בְּמִצְוֺתָיו חָפֵץ מְאֹד:
2 גִּבּוֹר בָּאָרֶץ יִהְיֶה זַרְעוֹ
דּוֹר יְשָׁרִים יְבֹרָךְ:
3 הוֹן־וָעֹשֶׁר בְּבֵיתוֹ
וְצִדְקָתוֹ עֹמֶדֶת לָעַד:
4 זָרַח בַּחֹשֶׁךְ אוֹר לַיְשָׁרִים
חַנּוּן וְרַחוּם וְצַדִּיק:
5 טוֹב־אִישׁ חוֹנֵן וּמַלְוֶה
יְכַלְכֵּל דְּבָרָיו בְּמִשְׁפָּט:
6 כִּי־לְעוֹלָם לֹא־יִמּוֹט
לְזֵכֶר עוֹלָם יִהְיֶה צַדִּיק:
7 מִשְּׁמוּעָה רָעָה לֹא יִירָא
נָכוֹן לִבּוֹ בָּטֻחַ בַּיהֹוָה:
8 סָמוּךְ לִבּוֹ לֹא יִירָא
עַד אֲשֶׁר־יִרְאֶה בְצָרָיו:
9 פִּזַּר ׀ נָתַן לָאֶבְיוֹנִים
צִדְקָתוֹ עֹמֶדֶת לָעַד
קַרְנוֹ תָּרוּם בְּכָבוֹד:
10 רָשָׁע יִרְאֶה ׀ וְכָעָס
שִׁנָּיו יַחֲרֹק וְנָמָס
תַּאֲוַת רְשָׁעִים תֹּאבֵד:

קיג הַלְלוּ יָהּ ׀ הַלְלוּ עַבְדֵי יְהֹוָה
הַלְלוּ אֶת־שֵׁם יְהֹוָה:
2 יְהִי שֵׁם יְהֹוָה מְבֹרָךְ
מֵעַתָּה וְעַד־עוֹלָם:
3 מִמִּזְרַח־שֶׁמֶשׁ עַד־מְבוֹאוֹ
מְהֻלָּל שֵׁם יְהֹוָה:
4 רָם עַל־כָּל־גּוֹיִם ׀ יְהֹוָה
עַל הַשָּׁמַיִם כְּבוֹדוֹ:
5 מִי כַּיהֹוָה אֱלֹהֵינוּ
הַמַּגְבִּיהִי לָשָׁבֶת:
6 הַמַּשְׁפִּילִי לִרְאוֹת
בַּשָּׁמַיִם וּבָאָרֶץ:
7 מְקִימִי מֵעָפָר דָּל
מֵאַשְׁפֹּת יָרִים אֶבְיוֹן:
8 לְהוֹשִׁיבִי עִם־נְדִיבִים
עִם נְדִיבֵי עַמּוֹ:
9 מוֹשִׁיבִי ׀ עֲקֶרֶת הַבַּיִת
אֵם־הַבָּנִים שְׂמֵחָה
הַלְלוּ־יָהּ:

114 When Israel went out of Egypt,
The house of Jacob from a people of strange
    language,
2 Judah became His sanctuary,
And Israel His dominion.

3 The sea saw *it* and fled;
Jordan turned back.
4 The mountains skipped like rams,
The little hills like lambs.
5 What ails you, O sea, that you fled?
O Jordan, *that* you turned back?
6 O mountains, *that* you skipped like rams?
O little hills, like lambs?

7 Tremble, O earth, at the presence of the Lord,
At the presence of the God of Jacob,
8 Who turned the rock *into* a pool of water,
The flint into a fountain of waters.

115 Not unto us, O LORD, not unto us,
But to Your name give glory,
Because of Your mercy,
Because of Your truth.
2 Why should the Gentiles say,
"So where *is* their God?"

3 But our God *is* in heaven;
He does whatever He pleases.
4 Their idols *are* silver and gold,
The work of men's hands.
5 They have mouths, but they do not speak;
Eyes they have, but they do not see;
6 They have ears, but they do not hear;
Noses they have, but they do not smell;
7 They have hands, but they do not handle;
Feet they have, but they do not walk;
Nor do they mutter through their throat.
8 Those who make them are like them;
So is everyone who trusts in them.

9 O Israel, trust in the LORD;
He *is* their help and their shield.
10 O house of Aaron, trust in the LORD;
He *is* their help and their shield.
11 You who fear the LORD, trust in the LORD;
He *is* their help and their shield.

12 The LORD has been mindful of *us;*
He will bless us;
He will bless the house of Israel;
He will bless the house of Aaron.
13 He will bless those who fear the LORD,
Both small and great.

14 May the LORD give you increase more and
    more,

קיד בְּצֵאת יִשְׂרָאֵל מִמִּצְרָיִם
בֵּית יַעֲקֹב מֵעַם לֹעֵז:
2 הָיְתָה יְהוּדָה לְקָדְשׁוֹ
יִשְׂרָאֵל מַמְשְׁלוֹתָיו:
3 הַיָּם רָאָה וַיָּנֹס
הַיַּרְדֵּן יִסֹּב לְאָחוֹר:
4 הֶהָרִים רָקְדוּ כְאֵילִים
גְּבָעוֹת כִּבְנֵי־צֹאן:
5 מַה־לְּךָ הַיָּם כִּי תָנוּס
הַיַּרְדֵּן תִּסֹּב לְאָחוֹר:
6 הֶהָרִים תִּרְקְדוּ כְאֵילִים
גְּבָעוֹת כִּבְנֵי־צֹאן:
7 מִלִּפְנֵי אָדוֹן חוּלִי אָרֶץ
מִלִּפְנֵי אֱלוֹהַּ יַעֲקֹב:
8 הַהֹפְכִי הַצּוּר אֲגַם־מָיִם
חַלָּמִישׁ לְמַעְיְנוֹ־מָיִם:

קטו לֹא לָנוּ יְהוָה לֹא לָנוּ
כִּי־לְשִׁמְךָ תֵּן כָּבוֹד עַל־חַסְדְּךָ עַל־אֲמִתֶּךָ:
2 לָמָּה יֹאמְרוּ הַגּוֹיִם
אַיֵּה־נָא אֱלֹהֵיהֶם:
3 וֵאלֹהֵינוּ בַשָּׁמָיִם
כֹּל אֲשֶׁר־חָפֵץ עָשָׂה:
4 עֲצַבֵּיהֶם כֶּסֶף וְזָהָב
מַעֲשֵׂה יְדֵי אָדָם:
5 פֶּה־לָהֶם וְלֹא יְדַבֵּרוּ
עֵינַיִם לָהֶם וְלֹא יִרְאוּ:
6 אָזְנַיִם לָהֶם וְלֹא יִשְׁמָעוּ
אַף לָהֶם וְלֹא יְרִיחוּן:
7 יְדֵיהֶם וְלֹא יְמִישׁוּן רַגְלֵיהֶם וְלֹא יְהַלֵּכוּ
לֹא־יֶהְגּוּ בִּגְרוֹנָם:
8 כְּמוֹהֶם יִהְיוּ עֹשֵׂיהֶם
כֹּל אֲשֶׁר־בֹּטֵחַ בָּהֶם:
9 יִשְׂרָאֵל בְּטַח בַּיהוָה
עֶזְרָם וּמָגִנָּם הוּא:
10 בֵּית אַהֲרֹן בִּטְחוּ בַיהוָה
עֶזְרָם וּמָגִנָּם הוּא:
11 יִרְאֵי יְהוָה בִּטְחוּ בַיהוָה
עֶזְרָם וּמָגִנָּם הוּא:
12 יְהוָה זְכָרָנוּ יְבָרֵךְ יְבָרֵךְ אֶת־בֵּית יִשְׂרָאֵל
יְבָרֵךְ אֶת־בֵּית אַהֲרֹן:
13 יְבָרֵךְ יִרְאֵי יְהוָה הַקְּטַנִּים עִם־הַגְּדֹלִים:
14 יֹסֵף יְהוָה עֲלֵיכֶם

You and your children.

15 *May* you *be* blessed by the LORD,
Who made heaven and earth.

עֲלֵיכֶם וְעַל־בְּנֵיכֶם:
15 בְּרוּכִים אַתֶּם לַיהֹוָה
עֹשֵׂה שָׁמַיִם וָאָרֶץ:

16 The heaven, *even* the heavens, *are* the LORD's;
But the earth He has given to the children of
men.

16 הַשָּׁמַיִם שָׁמַיִם לַיהֹוָה
וְהָאָרֶץ נָתַן לִבְנֵי־אָדָם:

17 The dead do not praise the LORD,
Nor any who go down into silence.

17 לֹא הַמֵּתִים יְהַלְלוּ־יָהּ
וְלֹא כָּל־יֹרְדֵי דוּמָה:

18 But we will bless the LORD
From this time forth and forevermore.
Praise the LORD!

18 וַאֲנַחְנוּ ׀ נְבָרֵךְ יָהּ
מֵעַתָּה וְעַד־עוֹלָם הַלְלוּ־יָהּ:

116 I love the LORD, because He has heard
My voice *and* my supplications.

קטז אָהַבְתִּי כִּי־יִשְׁמַע ׀ יְהֹוָה
אֶת־קוֹלִי תַּחֲנוּנָי:

2 Because He has inclined His ear to me,
Therefore I will call *upon Him* as long as I live.

2 כִּי־הִטָּה אָזְנוֹ לִי
וּבְיָמַי אֶקְרָא:

3 The pains of death surrounded me,
And the pangs of Sheol laid hold of me;
I found trouble and sorrow.

3 אֲפָפוּנִי ׀ חֶבְלֵי־מָוֶת וּמְצָרֵי שְׁאוֹל מְצָאוּנִי
צָרָה וְיָגוֹן אֶמְצָא:

4 Then I called upon the name of the LORD:
"O LORD, I implore You, deliver my soul!"

4 וּבְשֵׁם־יְהֹוָה אֶקְרָא
אָנָּה יְהֹוָה מַלְּטָה נַפְשִׁי:

5 Gracious *is* the LORD, and righteous;
Yes, our God *is* merciful.

5 חַנּוּן יְהֹוָה וְצַדִּיק
וֵאלֹהֵינוּ מְרַחֵם:

6 The LORD preserves the simple;
I was brought low, and He saved me.

6 שֹׁמֵר פְּתָאיִם יְהֹוָה
דַּלּוֹתִי וְלִי יְהוֹשִׁיעַ:

7 Return to your rest, O my soul,
For the LORD has dealt bountifully with you.

7 שׁוּבִי נַפְשִׁי לִמְנוּחָיְכִי
כִּי־יְהֹוָה גָּמַל עָלָיְכִי:

8 For You have delivered my soul from death,
My eyes from tears,
And my feet from falling.

8 כִּי חִלַּצְתָּ נַפְשִׁי מִמָּוֶת
אֶת־עֵינִי מִן־דִּמְעָה אֶת־רַגְלִי מִדֶּחִי:

9 I will walk before the LORD
In the land of the living.

9 אֶתְהַלֵּךְ לִפְנֵי יְהֹוָה
בְּאַרְצוֹת הַחַיִּים:

10 I believed, therefore I spoke,
"I am greatly afflicted."

10 הֶאֱמַנְתִּי כִּי אֲדַבֵּר אֲנִי עָנִיתִי מְאֹד:

11 I said in my haste,
"All men *are* liars."

11 אֲנִי אָמַרְתִּי בְחָפְזִי
כָּל־הָאָדָם כֹּזֵב:

12 What shall I render to the LORD
For all His benefits toward me?

12 מָה־אָשִׁיב לַיהֹוָה
כָּל־תַּגְמוּלוֹהִי עָלָי:

13 I will take up the cup of salvation,
And call upon the name of the LORD.

13 כּוֹס־יְשׁוּעוֹת אֶשָּׂא
וּבְשֵׁם יְהֹוָה אֶקְרָא:

14 I will pay my vows to the LORD
Now in the presence of all His people.

14 נְדָרַי לַיהֹוָה אֲשַׁלֵּם
נֶגְדָה־נָּא לְכָל־עַמּוֹ:

15 Precious in the sight of the LORD
Is the death of His saints.

15 יָקָר בְּעֵינֵי יְהֹוָה הַמָּוְתָה לַחֲסִידָיו:

16 O LORD, truly I *am* Your servant;
I *am* Your servant, the son of Your
maidservant;
You have loosed my bonds.

16 אָנָּה יְהֹוָה כִּי־אֲנִי עַבְדֶּךָ
אֲנִי־עַבְדְּךָ בֶּן־אֲמָתֶךָ
פִּתַּחְתָּ לְמוֹסֵרָי:

17 I will offer to You the sacrifice of thanksgiving,
And will call upon the name of the LORD.

17 לְךָ־אֶזְבַּח זֶבַח תּוֹדָה
וּבְשֵׁם יְהֹוָה אֶקְרָא:

18 I will pay my vows to the LORD
   Now in the presence of all His people,

19 In the courts of the LORD's house,
   In the midst of you, O Jerusalem.

Praise the LORD!

18 נְדָרַי לַיהֹוָה אֲשַׁלֵּם
נֶגְדָה־נָּא לְכָל־עַמּוֹ:

19 בְּחַצְרוֹת ׀ בֵּית יְהֹוָה
בְּתוֹכֵכִי יְרוּשָׁלָ͏ִם הַלְלוּ־יָהּ:

117 Praise the LORD, all you Gentiles!
   Laud Him, all you peoples!

2 For His merciful kindness is great toward us,
   And the truth of the LORD *endures* forever.

Praise the LORD!

קיז הַלְלוּ אֶת־יְהֹוָה כָּל־גּוֹיִם
שַׁבְּחוּהוּ כָּל־הָאֻמִּים:

2 כִּי גָבַר עָלֵינוּ ׀ חַסְדּוֹ
וֶאֱמֶת־יְהֹוָה לְעוֹלָם הַלְלוּ־יָהּ:

118 Oh, give thanks to the LORD, for *He is* good!
   For His mercy *endures* forever.

2 Let Israel now say,
   "His mercy *endures* forever."

3 Let the house of Aaron now say,
   "His mercy *endures* forever."

4 Let those who fear the LORD now say,
   "His mercy *endures* forever."

5 I called on the LORD in distress;
   The LORD answered me *and set me* in a broad place.

6 The LORD *is* on my side;
   I will not fear.
   What can man do to me?

7 The LORD is for me among those who help me;
   Therefore I shall see *my desire* on those who hate me.

8 *It is* better to trust in the LORD
   Than to put confidence in man.

9 *It is* better to trust in the LORD
   Than to put confidence in princes.

10 All nations surrounded me,
   But in the name of the LORD I will destroy them.

11 They surrounded me,
   Yes, they surrounded me;
   But in the name of the LORD I will destroy them.

12 They surrounded me like bees;
   They were quenched like a fire of thorns;
   For in the name of the LORD I will destroy them.

13 You pushed me violently, that I might fall,
   But the LORD helped me.

14 The LORD *is* my strength and song,
   And He has become my salvation.

15 The voice of rejoicing and salvation
   Is in the tents of the righteous;

קיח הוֹדוּ לַיהֹוָה כִּי־טוֹב
כִּי לְעוֹלָם חַסְדּוֹ:

2 יֹאמַר־נָא יִשְׂרָאֵל
כִּי לְעוֹלָם חַסְדּוֹ:

3 יֹאמְרוּ־נָא בֵית־אַהֲרֹן
כִּי לְעוֹלָם חַסְדּוֹ:

4 יֹאמְרוּ־נָא יִרְאֵי יְהֹוָה
כִּי לְעוֹלָם חַסְדּוֹ:

5 מִן־הַמֵּצַר קָרָאתִי יָּהּ
עָנָנִי בַמֶּרְחָב יָהּ:

6 יְהֹוָה לִי לֹא אִירָא
מַה־יַּעֲשֶׂה לִי אָדָם:

7 יְהֹוָה לִי בְּעֹזְרָי
וַאֲנִי אֶרְאֶה בְשֹׂנְאָי:

8 טוֹב לַחֲסוֹת בַּיהֹוָה
מִבְּטֹחַ בָּאָדָם:

9 טוֹב לַחֲסוֹת בַּיהֹוָה
מִבְּטֹחַ בִּנְדִיבִים:

10 כָּל־גּוֹיִם סְבָבוּנִי
בְּשֵׁם יְהֹוָה כִּי אֲמִילַם:

11 סַבּוּנִי גַם־סְבָבוּנִי
בְּשֵׁם יְהֹוָה כִּי אֲמִילַם:

12 סַבּוּנִי כִדְבוֹרִים דֹּעֲכוּ כְּאֵשׁ קוֹצִים
בְּשֵׁם יְהֹוָה כִּי אֲמִילַם:

13 דַּחֹה דְחִיתַנִי לִנְפֹּל
וַיהֹוָה עֲזָרָנִי:

14 עָזִּי וְזִמְרָת יָהּ
וַיְהִי־לִי לִישׁוּעָה:

15 קוֹל ׀ רִנָּה וִישׁוּעָה בְּאָהֳלֵי צַדִּיקִים

The right hand of the LORD does valiantly.

יְמִין יְהֹוָה עֹשָׂה חָיִל׃

16 The right hand of the LORD is exalted;
The right hand of the LORD does valiantly.

16 יְמִין יְהֹוָה רוֹמֵמָה
יְמִין יְהֹוָה עֹשָׂה חָיִל׃

17 I shall not die, but live,
And declare the works of the LORD.

17 לֹא אָמוּת כִּי־אֶחְיֶה
וַאֲסַפֵּר מַעֲשֵׂי יָהּ׃

18 The LORD has chastened me severely,
But He has not given me over to death.

18 יַסֹּר יִסְּרַנִּי יָּהּ וְלַמָּוֶת לֹא נְתָנָנִי׃

19 Open to me the gates of righteousness;
I will go through them,
And I will praise the LORD.

19 פִּתְחוּ־לִי שַׁעֲרֵי־צֶדֶק
אָבֹא־בָם אוֹדֶה יָהּ׃

20 This is the gate of the LORD,
Through which the righteous shall enter.

20 זֶה־הַשַּׁעַר לַיהֹוָה
צַדִּיקִים יָבֹאוּ בוֹ׃

21 I will praise You,
For You have answered me,
And have become my salvation.

21 אוֹדְךָ כִּי עֲנִיתָנִי
וַתְּהִי־לִי לִישׁוּעָה׃

22 The stone *which* the builders rejected
Has become the chief cornerstone.

22 אֶבֶן מָאֲסוּ הַבּוֹנִים
הָיְתָה לְרֹאשׁ פִּנָּה׃

23 This was the LORD's doing;
It *is* marvelous in our eyes.

23 מֵאֵת יְהֹוָה הָיְתָה זֹּאת
הִיא נִפְלָאת בְּעֵינֵינוּ׃

24 This *is* the day the LORD has made;
We will rejoice and be glad in it.

24 זֶה־הַיּוֹם עָשָׂה יְהֹוָה
נָגִילָה וְנִשְׂמְחָה בוֹ׃

25 Save now, I pray, O LORD;
O LORD, I pray, send now prosperity.

25 אָנָּא יְהֹוָה הוֹשִׁיעָה נָּא
אָנָּא יְהֹוָה הַצְלִיחָה נָּא׃

26 Blessed *is* he who comes in the name of the LORD!
We have blessed you from the house of the LORD.

26 בָּרוּךְ הַבָּא בְּשֵׁם יְהֹוָה
בֵּרַכְנוּכֶם מִבֵּית יְהֹוָה׃

27 God *is* the LORD,
And He has given us light;
Bind the sacrifice with cords to the horns of the altar.

27 אֵל יְהֹוָה וַיָּאֶר לָנוּ
אִסְרוּ־חַג בַּעֲבֹתִים עַד־קַרְנוֹת הַמִּזְבֵּחַ׃

28 You *are* my God, and I will praise You;
You are my God, I will exalt You.

28 אֵלִי אַתָּה וְאוֹדֶךָּ
אֱלֹהַי אֲרוֹמְמֶךָּ׃

29 Oh, give thanks to the LORD, for *He is* good!
For His mercy *endures* forever.

29 הוֹדוּ לַיהֹוָה כִּי־טוֹב
כִּי לְעוֹלָם חַסְדּוֹ׃

119 Blessed *are* the undefiled in the way,
Who walk in the law of the LORD!

קיט אַשְׁרֵי תְמִימֵי־דָרֶךְ הַהֹלְכִים בְּתוֹרַת יְהֹוָה׃

2 Blessed *are* those who keep His testimonies,
Who seek Him with the whole heart!

2 אַשְׁרֵי נֹצְרֵי עֵדֹתָיו בְּכָל־לֵב יִדְרְשׁוּהוּ׃

3 They also do no iniquity;
They walk in His ways.

3 אַף לֹא־פָעֲלוּ עַוְלָה
בִּדְרָכָיו הָלָכוּ׃

4 You have commanded *us*
To keep Your precepts diligently.

4 אַתָּה צִוִּיתָה פִקֻּדֶיךָ
לִשְׁמֹר מְאֹד׃

5 Oh, that my ways were directed
To keep Your statutes!

5 אַחֲלַי יִכֹּנוּ דְרָכָי
לִשְׁמֹר חֻקֶּיךָ׃

6 Then I would not be ashamed,
When I look into all Your commandments.

6 אָז לֹא־אֵבוֹשׁ
בְּהַבִּיטִי אֶל־כָּל־מִצְוֹתֶיךָ׃

7 I will praise You with uprightness of heart,
When I learn Your righteous judgments.

7 אוֹדְךָ בְּיֹשֶׁר לֵבָב
בְּלָמְדִי מִשְׁפְּטֵי צִדְקֶךָ׃

8 I will keep Your statutes;
Oh, do not forsake me utterly!

8 אֶת־חֻקֶּיךָ אֶשְׁמֹר
אַל־תַּעַזְבֵנִי עַד־מְאֹד׃

9　How can a young man cleanse his way? By taking heed according to Your word.	9　בַּמֶּה יְזַכֶּה־נַּעַר אֶת־אָרְחוֹ לִשְׁמֹר כִּדְבָרֶךָ׃
10　With my whole heart I have sought You; Oh, let me not wander from Your commandments!	10　בְּכָל־לִבִּי דְרַשְׁתִּיךָ אַל־תַּשְׁגֵּנִי מִמִּצְוֺתֶיךָ׃
11　Your word I have hidden in my heart, That I might not sin against You.	11　בְּלִבִּי צָפַנְתִּי אִמְרָתֶךָ לְמַעַן לֹא אֶחֱטָא־לָךְ׃
12　Blessed *are* You, O LORD! Teach me Your statutes.	12　בָּרוּךְ אַתָּה יְהֹוָה לַמְּדֵנִי חֻקֶּיךָ׃
13　With my lips I have declared All the judgments of Your mouth.	13　בִּשְׂפָתַי סִפַּרְתִּי כֹּל מִשְׁפְּטֵי־פִיךָ׃
14　I have rejoiced in the way of Your testimonies, As *much as* in all riches.	14　בְּדֶרֶךְ עֵדְוֺתֶיךָ שַׂשְׂתִּי כְּעַל כָּל־הוֹן׃
15　I will meditate on Your precepts, And contemplate Your ways.	15　בְּפִקֻּדֶיךָ אָשִׂיחָה וְאַבִּיטָה אֹרְחֹתֶיךָ׃
16　I will delight myself in Your statutes; I will not forget Your word.	16　בְּחֻקֹּתֶיךָ אֶשְׁתַּעֲשָׁע לֹא אֶשְׁכַּח דְּבָרֶךָ׃
17　Deal bountifully with Your servant, *That* I may live and keep Your word.	17　גְּמֹל עַל־עַבְדְּךָ אֶחְיֶה וְאֶשְׁמְרָה דְבָרֶךָ׃
18　Open my eyes, that I may see Wondrous things from Your law.	18　גַּל־עֵינַי וְאַבִּיטָה נִפְלָאוֹת מִתּוֹרָתֶךָ׃
19　I *am* a stranger in the earth; Do not hide Your commandments from me.	19　גֵּר אָנֹכִי בָאָרֶץ אַל־תַּסְתֵּר מִמֶּנִּי מִצְוֺתֶיךָ׃
20　My soul breaks with longing For Your judgments at all times.	20　גָּרְסָה נַפְשִׁי לְתַאֲבָה אֶל־מִשְׁפָּטֶיךָ בְכָל־עֵת׃
21　You rebuke the proud—the cursed, Who stray from Your commandments.	21　גָּעַרְתָּ זֵדִים אֲרוּרִים הַשֹּׁגִים מִמִּצְוֺתֶיךָ׃
22　Remove from me reproach and contempt, For I have kept Your testimonies.	22　גַּל מֵעָלַי חֶרְפָּה וָבוּז כִּי עֵדֹתֶיךָ נָצָרְתִּי׃
23　Princes also sit *and* speak against me, *But* Your servant meditates on Your statutes.	23　גַּם יָשְׁבוּ שָׂרִים בִּי נִדְבָּרוּ עַבְדְּךָ יָשִׂיחַ בְּחֻקֶּיךָ׃
24　Your testimonies also *are* my delight *And* my counselors.	24　גַּם־עֵדֹתֶיךָ שַׁעֲשֻׁעָי אַנְשֵׁי עֲצָתִי׃
25　My soul clings to the dust; Revive me according to Your word.	25　דָּבְקָה לֶעָפָר נַפְשִׁי חַיֵּנִי כִּדְבָרֶךָ׃
26　I have declared my ways, and You answered me; Teach me Your statutes.	26　דְּרָכַי סִפַּרְתִּי וַתַּעֲנֵנִי לַמְּדֵנִי חֻקֶּיךָ׃
27　Make me understand the way of Your precepts; So shall I meditate on Your wonderful works.	27　דֶּרֶךְ־פִּקּוּדֶיךָ הֲבִינֵנִי וְאָשִׂיחָה בְּנִפְלְאוֹתֶיךָ׃
28　My soul melts from heaviness; Strengthen me according to Your word.	28　דָּלְפָה נַפְשִׁי מִתּוּגָה קַיְּמֵנִי כִּדְבָרֶךָ׃
29　Remove from me the way of lying, And grant me Your law graciously.	29　דֶּרֶךְ־שֶׁקֶר הָסֵר מִמֶּנִּי וְתוֹרָתְךָ חָנֵּנִי׃
30　I have chosen the way of truth; Your judgments I have laid *before me*.	30　דֶּרֶךְ־אֱמוּנָה בָחָרְתִּי מִשְׁפָּטֶיךָ שִׁוִּיתִי׃
31　I cling to Your testimonies; O LORD, do not put me to shame!	31　דָּבַקְתִּי בְעֵדְוֺתֶיךָ יְהֹוָה אַל־תְּבִישֵׁנִי׃
32　I will run the course of Your commandments, For You shall enlarge my heart.	32　דֶּרֶךְ־מִצְוֺתֶיךָ אָרוּץ כִּי תַרְחִיב לִבִּי׃
33　Teach me, O LORD, the way of Your statutes, And I shall keep it *to* the end.	33　הוֹרֵנִי יְהֹוָה דֶּרֶךְ חֻקֶּיךָ וְאֶצְּרֶנָּה עֵקֶב׃

34 Give me understanding, and I shall keep Your law;
Indeed, I shall observe it with *my* whole heart.

35 Make me walk in the path of Your commandments,
For I delight in it.

36 Incline my heart to Your testimonies,
And not to covetousness.

37 Turn away my eyes from looking at worthless things,
And revive me in Your way.

38 Establish Your word to Your servant,
Who *is* devoted to fearing You.

39 Turn away my reproach which I dread,
For Your judgments *are* good.

40 Behold, I long for Your precepts;
Revive me in Your righteousness.

41 Let Your mercies come also to me, O Lord—
Your salvation according to Your word.

42 So shall I have an answer for him who reproaches me,
For I trust in Your word.

43 And take not the word of truth utterly out of my mouth,
For I have hoped in Your ordinances.

44 So shall I keep Your law continually,
Forever and ever.

45 And I will walk at liberty,
For I seek Your precepts.

46 I will speak of Your testimonies also before kings,
And will not be ashamed.

47 And I will delight myself in Your commandments,
Which I love.

48 My hands also I will lift up to Your commandments,
Which I love,
And I will meditate on Your statutes.

49 Remember the word to Your servant,
Upon which You have caused me to hope.

50 This *is* my comfort in my affliction,
For Your word has given me life.

51 The proud have me in great derision,
Yet I do not turn aside from Your law.

52 I remembered Your judgments of old, O Lord,
And have comforted myself.

53 Indignation has taken hold of me
Because of the wicked, who forsake Your law.

54 Your statutes have been my songs
In the house of my pilgrimage.

55 I remember Your name in the night, O Lord,
And I keep Your law.

34 הֲבִינֵנִי וְאֶצְּרָה תוֹרָתֶךָ
וְאֶשְׁמְרֶנָּה בְכָל־לֵב:

35 הַדְרִיכֵנִי בִּנְתִיב מִצְוֹתֶיךָ
כִּי־בוֹ חָפָצְתִּי:

36 הַט־לִבִּי אֶל־עֵדְוֹתֶיךָ
וְאַל אֶל־בָּצַע:

37 הַעֲבֵר עֵינַי מֵרְאוֹת שָׁוְא
בִּדְרָכֶךָ חַיֵּנִי:

38 הָקֵם לְעַבְדְּךָ אִמְרָתֶךָ
אֲשֶׁר לְיִרְאָתֶךָ:

39 הַעֲבֵר חֶרְפָּתִי אֲשֶׁר יָגֹרְתִּי
כִּי מִשְׁפָּטֶיךָ טוֹבִים:

40 הִנֵּה תָּאַבְתִּי לְפִקֻּדֶיךָ
בְּצִדְקָתְךָ חַיֵּנִי:

41 וִיבֹאֻנִי חֲסָדֶךָ יְהֹוָה
תְּשׁוּעָתְךָ כְּאִמְרָתֶךָ:

42 וְאֶעֱנֶה חֹרְפִי דָבָר
כִּי־בָטַחְתִּי בִּדְבָרֶךָ:

43 וְאַל־תַּצֵּל מִפִּי דְבַר־אֱמֶת עַד־מְאֹד
כִּי לְמִשְׁפָּטֶךָ יִחָלְתִּי:

44 וְאֶשְׁמְרָה תוֹרָתְךָ תָמִיד
לְעוֹלָם וָעֶד:

45 וְאֶתְהַלְּכָה בָרְחָבָה
כִּי פִקֻּדֶיךָ דָרָשְׁתִּי:

46 וַאֲדַבְּרָה בְעֵדֹתֶיךָ נֶגֶד מְלָכִים
וְלֹא אֵבוֹשׁ:

47 וְאֶשְׁתַּעֲשַׁע בְּמִצְוֹתֶיךָ
אֲשֶׁר אָהָבְתִּי:

48 וְאֶשָּׂא־כַפַּי אֶל־מִצְוֹתֶיךָ אֲשֶׁר אָהָבְתִּי
וְאָשִׂיחָה בְחֻקֶּיךָ:

49 זְכֹר־דָּבָר לְעַבְדֶּךָ עַל אֲשֶׁר יִחַלְתָּנִי:

50 זֹאת נֶחָמָתִי בְעָנְיִי כִּי אִמְרָתְךָ חִיָּתְנִי:

51 זֵדִים הֱלִיצֻנִי עַד־מְאֹד
מִתּוֹרָתְךָ לֹא נָטִיתִי:

52 זָכַרְתִּי מִשְׁפָּטֶיךָ מֵעוֹלָם ׀ יְהֹוָה
וָאֶתְנֶחָם:

53 זַלְעָפָה אֲחָזַתְנִי מֵרְשָׁעִים
עֹזְבֵי תוֹרָתֶךָ:

54 זְמִרוֹת הָיוּ־לִי חֻקֶּיךָ
בְּבֵית מְגוּרָי:

55 זָכַרְתִּי בַלַּיְלָה שִׁמְךָ יְהֹוָה
וָאֶשְׁמְרָה תוֹרָתֶךָ:

56　This has become mine,
Because I kept Your precepts.

57　*You are* my portion, O LORD;
I have said that I would keep Your words.

58　I entreated Your favor with *my* whole heart;
Be merciful to me according to Your word.

59　I thought about my ways,
And turned my feet to Your testimonies.

60　I made haste, and did not delay
To keep Your commandments.

61　The cords of the wicked have bound me,
But I have not forgotten Your law.

62　At midnight I will rise to give thanks to You,
Because of Your righteous judgments.

63　I *am* a companion of all who fear You,
And of those who keep Your precepts.

64　The earth, O LORD, is full of Your mercy;
Teach me Your statutes.

65　You have dealt well with Your servant,
O LORD, according to Your word.

66　Teach me good judgment and knowledge,
For I believe Your commandments.

67　Before I was afflicted I went astray,
But now I keep Your word.

68　You *are* good, and do good;
Teach me Your statutes.

69　The proud have forged a lie against me,
But I will keep Your precepts with *my* whole
heart.

70　Their heart is as fat as grease,
But I delight in Your law.

71　*It is* good for me that I have been afflicted,
That I may learn Your statutes.

72　The law of Your mouth *is* better to me
Than thousands of *coins of* gold and silver.

73　Your hands have made me and fashioned me;
Give me understanding, that I may learn Your
commandments.

74　Those who fear You will be glad when they see
me,
Because I have hoped in Your word.

75　I know, O LORD, that Your judgments *are*
right,
And *that* in faithfulness You have afflicted me.

76　Let, I pray, Your merciful kindness be for my
comfort,
According to Your word to Your servant.

77　Let Your tender mercies come to me, that I
may live;
For Your law *is* my delight.

78　Let the proud be ashamed,
For they treated me wrongfully with falsehood;
But I will meditate on Your precepts.

56　זֹאת הָיְתָה־לִּי כִּי פִקֻּדֶיךָ נָצָרְתִּי:
57　חֶלְקִי יְהֹוָה אָמַרְתִּי לִשְׁמֹר דְּבָרֶיךָ:
58　חִלִּיתִי פָנֶיךָ בְכָל־לֵב
　　חָנֵּנִי כְּאִמְרָתֶךָ:
59　חִשַּׁבְתִּי דְרָכָי
　　וָאָשִׁיבָה רַגְלַי אֶל־עֵדֹתֶיךָ:
60　חַשְׁתִּי וְלֹא הִתְמַהְמָהְתִּי
　　לִשְׁמֹר מִצְוֹתֶיךָ:
61　חֶבְלֵי רְשָׁעִים עִוְּדֻנִי
　　תּוֹרָתְךָ לֹא שָׁכָחְתִּי:
62　חֲצוֹת־לַיְלָה אָקוּם לְהוֹדוֹת לָךְ
　　עַל מִשְׁפְּטֵי צִדְקֶךָ:
63　חָבֵר אָנִי לְכָל־אֲשֶׁר יְרֵאוּךָ
　　וּלְשֹׁמְרֵי פִּקּוּדֶיךָ:
64　חַסְדְּךָ יְהֹוָה מָלְאָה הָאָרֶץ חֻקֶּיךָ לַמְּדֵנִי:
65　טוֹב עָשִׂיתָ עִם־עַבְדְּךָ
　　יְהֹוָה כִּדְבָרֶךָ:
66　טוּב טַעַם וָדַעַת לַמְּדֵנִי
　　כִּי בְמִצְוֹתֶיךָ הֶאֱמָנְתִּי:
67　טֶרֶם אֶעֱנֶה אֲנִי שֹׁגֵג
　　וְעַתָּה אִמְרָתְךָ שָׁמָרְתִּי:
68　טוֹב־אַתָּה וּמֵטִיב לַמְּדֵנִי חֻקֶּיךָ:
69　טָפְלוּ עָלַי שֶׁקֶר זֵדִים
　　אֲנִי בְּכָל־לֵב ׀ אֶצֹּר פִּקּוּדֶיךָ:
70　טָפַשׁ כַּחֵלֶב לִבָּם
　　אֲנִי תּוֹרָתְךָ שִׁעֲשָׁעְתִּי:
71　טוֹב־לִי כִי־עֻנֵּיתִי
　　לְמַעַן אֶלְמַד חֻקֶּיךָ:
72　טוֹב־לִי תוֹרַת־פִּיךָ
　　מֵאַלְפֵי זָהָב וָכָסֶף:
73　יָדֶיךָ עָשׂוּנִי וַיְכוֹנְנוּנִי
　　הֲבִינֵנִי וְאֶלְמְדָה מִצְוֹתֶיךָ:
74　יְרֵאֶיךָ יִרְאוּנִי וְיִשְׂמָחוּ
　　כִּי לִדְבָרְךָ יִחָלְתִּי:
75　יָדַעְתִּי יְהֹוָה כִּי־צֶדֶק מִשְׁפָּטֶיךָ
　　וֶאֱמוּנָה עִנִּיתָנִי:
76　יְהִי־נָא חַסְדְּךָ לְנַחֲמֵנִי
　　כְּאִמְרָתְךָ לְעַבְדֶּךָ:
77　יְבֹאוּנִי רַחֲמֶיךָ וְאֶחְיֶה
　　כִּי־תוֹרָתְךָ שַׁעֲשֻׁעָי:
78　יֵבֹשׁוּ זֵדִים כִּי־שֶׁקֶר עִוְּתוּנִי
　　אֲנִי אָשִׂיחַ בְּפִקּוּדֶיךָ:

79   Let those who fear You turn to me,
Those who know Your testimonies.

80   Let my heart be blameless regarding Your statutes,
That I may not be ashamed.

81   My soul faints for Your salvation,
But I hope in Your word.

82   My eyes fail *from searching* Your word,
Saying, "When will You comfort me?"

83   For I have become like a wineskin in smoke,
Yet I do not forget Your statutes.

84   How many *are* the days of Your servant?
When will You execute judgment on those who persecute me?

85   The proud have dug pits for me,
Which *is* not according to Your law.

86   All Your commandments *are* faithful;
They persecute me wrongfully;
Help me!

87   They almost made an end of me on earth,
But I did not forsake Your precepts.

88   Revive me according to Your lovingkindness,
So that I may keep the testimony of Your mouth.

89   Forever, O LORD,
Your word is settled in heaven.

90   Your faithfulness *endures* to all generations;
You established the earth, and it abides.

91   They continue this day according to Your ordinances,
For all *are* Your servants.

92   Unless Your law *had been* my delight,
I would then have perished in my affliction.

93   I will never forget Your precepts,
For by them You have given me life.

94   I *am* Yours, save me;
For I have sought Your precepts.

95   The wicked wait for me to destroy me,
But I will consider Your testimonies.

96   I have seen the consummation of all perfection,
But Your commandment *is* exceedingly broad.

97   Oh, how I love Your law!
It *is* my meditation all the day.

98   You, through Your commandments, make me wiser than my enemies;
For they *are* ever with me.

99   I have more understanding than all my teachers,
For Your testimonies *are* my meditation.

100   I understand more than the ancients,
Because I keep Your precepts.

101   I have restrained my feet from every evil way,
That I may keep Your word.

79 יָשׁוּבוּ לִי יְרֵאֶיךָ וְיֹדְעֵי עֵדֹתֶיךָ׃
80 יְהִי־לִבִּי תָמִים בְּחֻקֶּיךָ לְמַעַן לֹא אֵבוֹשׁ׃
81 כָּלְתָה לִתְשׁוּעָתְךָ נַפְשִׁי לִדְבָרְךָ יִחָלְתִּי׃
82 כָּלוּ עֵינַי לְאִמְרָתֶךָ לֵאמֹר מָתַי תְּנַחֲמֵנִי׃
83 כִּי־הָיִיתִי כְּנֹאד בְּקִיטוֹר חֻקֶּיךָ לֹא שָׁכָחְתִּי׃
84 כַּמָּה יְמֵי־עַבְדֶּךָ מָתַי תַּעֲשֶׂה בְרֹדְפַי מִשְׁפָּט׃
85 כָּרוּ־לִי זֵדִים שִׁיחוֹת אֲשֶׁר לֹא כְתוֹרָתֶךָ׃
86 כָּל־מִצְוֹתֶיךָ אֱמוּנָה שֶׁקֶר רְדָפוּנִי עָזְרֵנִי׃
87 כִּמְעַט כִּלּוּנִי בָאָרֶץ וַאֲנִי לֹא־עָזַבְתִּי פִקֻּדֶיךָ׃
88 כְּחַסְדְּךָ חַיֵּנִי וְאֶשְׁמְרָה עֵדוּת פִּיךָ׃
89 לְעוֹלָם יְהוָה דְּבָרְךָ נִצָּב בַּשָּׁמָיִם׃
90 לְדֹר וָדֹר אֱמוּנָתֶךָ כּוֹנַנְתָּ אֶרֶץ וַתַּעֲמֹד׃
91 לְמִשְׁפָּטֶיךָ עָמְדוּ הַיּוֹם כִּי הַכֹּל עֲבָדֶיךָ׃
92 לוּלֵי תוֹרָתְךָ שַׁעֲשֻׁעָי אָז אָבַדְתִּי בְעָנְיִי׃
93 לְעוֹלָם לֹא־אֶשְׁכַּח פִּקּוּדֶיךָ כִּי בָם חִיִּיתָנִי׃
94 לְךָ־אֲנִי הוֹשִׁיעֵנִי כִּי פִקּוּדֶיךָ דָרָשְׁתִּי׃
95 לִי קִוּוּ רְשָׁעִים לְאַבְּדֵנִי עֵדֹתֶיךָ אֶתְבּוֹנָן׃
96 לְכָל תִּכְלָה רָאִיתִי קֵץ רְחָבָה מִצְוָתְךָ מְאֹד׃
97 מָה־אָהַבְתִּי תוֹרָתֶךָ כָּל־הַיּוֹם הִיא שִׂיחָתִי׃
98 מֵאֹיְבַי תְּחַכְּמֵנִי מִצְוֹתֶךָ כִּי לְעוֹלָם הִיא־לִי׃
99 מִכָּל־מְלַמְּדַי הִשְׂכַּלְתִּי כִּי עֵדְוֹתֶיךָ שִׂיחָה לִי׃
100 מִזְּקֵנִים אֶתְבּוֹנָן כִּי פִקּוּדֶיךָ נָצָרְתִּי׃
101 מִכָּל־אֹרַח רָע כָּלִאתִי רַגְלָי לְמַעַן אֶשְׁמֹר דְּבָרֶךָ׃

102   I have not departed from Your judgments,
      For You Yourself have taught me.

103   How sweet are Your words to my taste,
      Sweeter than honey to my mouth!

104   Through Your precepts I get understanding;
      Therefore I hate every false way.

105   Your word *is* a lamp to my feet
      And a light to my path.

106   I have sworn and confirmed
      That I will keep Your righteous judgments.

107   I am afflicted very much;
      Revive me, O LORD, according to Your word.

108   Accept, I pray, the freewill offerings of my
      mouth, O LORD,
      And teach me Your judgments.

109   My life *is* continually in my hand,
      Yet I do not forget Your law.

110   The wicked have laid a snare for me,
      Yet I have not strayed from Your precepts.

111   Your testimonies I have taken as a heritage
      forever,
      For they *are* the rejoicing of my heart.

112   I have inclined my heart to perform Your
      statutes
      Forever, to the very end.

113   I hate the double-minded,
      But I love Your law.

114   You *are* my hiding place and my shield;
      I hope in Your word.

115   Depart from me, you evildoers,
      For I will keep the commandments of my God!

116   Uphold me according to Your word, that I
      may live;
      And do not let me be ashamed of my hope.

117   Hold me up, and I shall be safe,
      And I shall observe Your statutes continually.

118   You reject all those who stray from Your
      statutes,
      For their deceit *is* falsehood.

119   You put away all the wicked of the earth *like*
      dross;
      Therefore I love Your testimonies.

120   My flesh trembles for fear of You,
      And I am afraid of Your judgments.

121   I have done justice and righteousness;
      Do not leave me to my oppressors.

122   Be surety for Your servant for good;
      Do not let the proud oppress me.

123   My eyes fail *from seeking* Your salvation
      And Your righteous word.

124   Deal with Your servant according to Your
      mercy,
      And teach me Your statutes.

מִמִּשְׁפָּטֶיךָ לֹא־סָרְתִּי 102
כִּי־אַתָּה הוֹרֵתָנִי:

מַה־נִּמְלְצוּ לְחִכִּי אִמְרָתֶךָ מִדְּבַשׁ לְפִי: 103

מִפִּקּוּדֶיךָ אֶתְבּוֹנָן 104
עַל־כֵּן שָׂנֵאתִי ׀ כָּל־אֹרַח שָׁקֶר:

נֵר־לְרַגְלִי דְבָרֶךָ וְאוֹר לִנְתִיבָתִי: 105

נִשְׁבַּעְתִּי וָאֲקַיֵּמָה 106
לִשְׁמֹר מִשְׁפְּטֵי צִדְקֶךָ:

נַעֲנֵיתִי עַד־מְאֹד 107
יְהֹוָה חַיֵּנִי כִדְבָרֶךָ:

נִדְבוֹת פִּי רְצֵה־נָא יְהֹוָה 108
וּמִשְׁפָּטֶיךָ לַמְּדֵנִי:

נַפְשִׁי בְכַפִּי תָמִיד 109
וְתוֹרָתְךָ לֹא שָׁכָחְתִּי:

נָתְנוּ רְשָׁעִים פַּח לִי 110
וּמִפִּקּוּדֶיךָ לֹא תָעִיתִי:

נָחַלְתִּי עֵדְוֹתֶיךָ לְעוֹלָם 111
כִּי־שְׂשׂוֹן לִבִּי הֵמָּה:

נָטִיתִי לִבִּי לַעֲשׂוֹת חֻקֶּיךָ 112
לְעוֹלָם עֵקֶב:

סֵעֲפִים שָׂנֵאתִי וְתוֹרָתְךָ אָהָבְתִּי: 113

סִתְרִי וּמָגִנִּי אָתָּה 114
לִדְבָרְךָ יִחָלְתִּי:

סוּרוּ־מִמֶּנִּי מְרֵעִים 115
וְאֶצְּרָה מִצְוֹת אֱלֹהָי:

סָמְכֵנִי כְאִמְרָתְךָ וְאֶחְיֶה 116
וְאַל־תְּבִישֵׁנִי מִשִּׂבְרִי:

סְעָדֵנִי וְאִוָּשֵׁעָה 117
וְאֶשְׁעָה בְחֻקֶּיךָ תָמִיד:

סָלִיתָ כָּל־שׁוֹגִים מֵחֻקֶּיךָ 118
כִּי־שֶׁקֶר תַּרְמִיתָם:

סִגִים הִשְׁבַּתָּ כָל־רִשְׁעֵי־אָרֶץ 119
לָכֵן אָהַבְתִּי עֵדֹתֶיךָ:

סָמַר מִפַּחְדְּךָ בְשָׂרִי 120
וּמִמִּשְׁפָּטֶיךָ יָרֵאתִי:

עָשִׂיתִי מִשְׁפָּט וָצֶדֶק 121
בַּל־תַּנִּיחֵנִי לְעֹשְׁקָי:

עֲרֹב עַבְדְּךָ לְטוֹב 122
אַל־יַעַשְׁקֻנִי זֵדִים:

עֵינַי כָּלוּ לִישׁוּעָתֶךָ וּלְאִמְרַת צִדְקֶךָ: 123

עֲשֵׂה עִם־עַבְדְּךָ כְחַסְדֶּךָ 124
וְחֻקֶּיךָ לַמְּדֵנִי:

125 I *am* Your servant;
Give me understanding,
That I may know Your testimonies.

עַבְדְּךָ־אָנִי הֲבִינֵנִי 125
וְאֵדְעָה עֵדֹתֶיךָ׃

126 *It is* time for *You* to act, O LORD,
For they have regarded Your law as void.

עֵת לַעֲשׂוֹת לַיהֹוָה 126
הֵפֵרוּ תּוֹרָתֶךָ׃

127 Therefore I love Your commandments
More than gold, yes, than fine gold!

עַל־כֵּן אָהַבְתִּי מִצְוֺתֶיךָ 127
מִזָּהָב וּמִפָּז׃

128 Therefore all *Your* precepts *concerning* all
    things
I consider *to be* right;
I hate every false way.

עַל־כֵּן ׀ כָּל־פִּקּוּדֵי כֹל יִשָּׁרְתִּי 128
כָּל־אֹרַח שֶׁקֶר שָׂנֵאתִי׃

129 Your testimonies are wonderful;
Therefore my soul keeps them.

פְּלָאוֹת עֵדְוֺתֶיךָ 129
עַל־כֵּן נְצָרָתַם נַפְשִׁי׃

130 The entrance of Your words gives light;
It gives understanding to the simple.

פֵּתַח דְּבָרֶיךָ יָאִיר מֵבִין פְּתָיִים׃ 130

131 I opened my mouth and panted,
For I longed for Your commandments.

פִּי־פָעַרְתִּי וָאֶשְׁאָפָה 131
כִּי לְמִצְוֺתֶיךָ יָאָבְתִּי׃

132 Look upon me and be merciful to me,
As Your custom *is* toward those who love
    Your name.

פְּנֵה־אֵלַי וְחָנֵּנִי 132
כְּמִשְׁפָּט לְאֹהֲבֵי שְׁמֶךָ׃

133 Direct my steps by Your word,
And let no iniquity have dominion over me.

פְּעָמַי הָכֵן בְּאִמְרָתֶךָ 133
וְאַל־תַּשְׁלֶט־בִּי כָל־אָוֶן׃

134 Redeem me from the oppression of man,
That I may keep Your precepts.

פְּדֵנִי מֵעֹשֶׁק אָדָם 134
וְאֶשְׁמְרָה פִּקּוּדֶיךָ׃

135 Make Your face shine upon Your servant,
And teach me Your statutes.

פָּנֶיךָ הָאֵר בְּעַבְדֶּךָ 135
וְלַמְּדֵנִי אֶת־חֻקֶּיךָ׃

136 Rivers of water run down from my eyes,
Because *men* do not keep Your law.

פַּלְגֵי־מַיִם יָרְדוּ עֵינָי 136
עַל לֹא־שָׁמְרוּ תוֹרָתֶךָ׃

137 Righteous *are* You, O LORD,
And upright *are* Your judgments.

צַדִּיק אַתָּה יְהֹוָה 137
וְיָשָׁר מִשְׁפָּטֶיךָ׃

138 Your testimonies, *which* You have
    commanded,
Are righteous and very faithful.

צִוִּיתָ צֶדֶק עֵדֹתֶיךָ 138
וֶאֱמוּנָה מְאֹד׃

139 My zeal has consumed me,
Because my enemies have forgotten Your
    words.

צִמְּתַתְנִי קִנְאָתִי 139
כִּי־שָׁכְחוּ דְבָרֶיךָ צָרָי׃

140 Your word *is* very pure;
Therefore Your servant loves it.

צְרוּפָה אִמְרָתְךָ מְאֹד וְעַבְדְּךָ אֲהֵבָהּ׃ 140

141 I *am* small and despised,
Yet I do not forget Your precepts.

צָעִיר אָנֹכִי וְנִבְזֶה 141
פִּקֻּדֶיךָ לֹא שָׁכָחְתִּי׃

142 Your righteousness *is* an everlasting
    righteousness,
And Your law *is* truth.

צִדְקָתְךָ צֶדֶק לְעוֹלָם 142
וְתוֹרָתְךָ אֱמֶת׃

143 Trouble and anguish have overtaken me,
Yet Your commandments *are* my delights.

צַר־וּמָצוֹק מְצָאוּנִי 143
מִצְוֺתֶיךָ שַׁעֲשֻׁעָי׃

144 The righteousness of Your testimonies *is*
    everlasting;
Give me understanding, and I shall live.

צֶדֶק עֵדְוֺתֶיךָ לְעוֹלָם הֲבִינֵנִי וְאֶחְיֶה׃ 144

145 I cry out with *my* whole heart;
Hear me, O LORD!
I will keep Your statutes.

קָרָאתִי בְכָל־לֵב עֲנֵנִי יְהֹוָה 145
חֻקֶּיךָ אֶצֹּרָה׃

146 I cry out to You;
Save me, and I will keep Your testimonies.

קְרָאתִיךָ הוֹשִׁיעֵנִי 146
וְאֶשְׁמְרָה עֵדֹתֶיךָ׃

147 I rise before the dawning of the morning,
    And cry for help;
    I hope in Your word.

148 My eyes are awake through the *night* watches,
    That I may meditate on Your word.

149 Hear my voice according to Your
        lovingkindness;
    O LORD, revive me according to Your justice.

150 They draw near who follow after wickedness;
    They are far from Your law.

151 You *are* near, O LORD,
    And all Your commandments *are* truth.

152 Concerning Your testimonies,
    I have known of old that You have founded
        them forever.

153 Consider my affliction and deliver me,
    For I do not forget Your law.

154 Plead my cause and redeem me;
    Revive me according to Your word.

155 Salvation *is* far from the wicked,
    For they do not seek Your statutes.

156 Great *are* Your tender mercies, O LORD;
    Revive me according to Your judgments.

157 Many *are* my persecutors and my enemies,
    Yet I do not turn from Your testimonies.

158 I see the treacherous, and am disgusted,
    Because they do not keep Your word.

159 Consider how I love Your precepts;
    Revive me, O LORD, according to Your
        lovingkindness.

160 The entirety of Your word *is* truth,
    And every one of Your righteous judgments
        endures forever.

161 Princes persecute me without a cause,
    But my heart stands in awe of Your word.

162 I rejoice at Your word
    As one who finds great treasure.

163 I hate and abhor lying,
    But I love Your law.

164 Seven times a day I praise You,
    Because of Your righteous judgments.

165 Great peace have those who love Your law,
    And nothing causes them to stumble.

166 LORD, I hope for Your salvation,
    And I do Your commandments.

167 My soul keeps Your testimonies,
    And I love them exceedingly.

168 I keep Your precepts and Your testimonies,
    For all my ways *are* before You.

169 Let my cry come before You, O LORD;
    Give me understanding according to Your
        word.

170 Let my supplication come before You;

147 קִדַּמְתִּי בַנֶּשֶׁף וָאֲשַׁוֵּעָה
    לִדְבָרְךָ יִחָלְתִּי:
148 קִדְּמוּ עֵינַי אַשְׁמֻרוֹת
    לָשִׂיחַ בְּאִמְרָתֶךָ:
149 קוֹלִי שִׁמְעָה כְחַסְדֶּךָ
    יְהוָה כְּמִשְׁפָּטֶךָ חַיֵּנִי:
150 קָרְבוּ רֹדְפֵי זִמָּה מִתּוֹרָתְךָ רָחָקוּ:
151 קָרוֹב אַתָּה יְהוָה וְכָל־מִצְוֺתֶיךָ אֱמֶת:
152 קֶדֶם יָדַעְתִּי מֵעֵדֹתֶיךָ
    כִּי לְעוֹלָם יְסַדְתָּם:
153 רְאֵה־עָנְיִי וְחַלְּצֵנִי
    כִּי־תוֹרָתְךָ לֹא שָׁכָחְתִּי:
154 רִיבָה רִיבִי וּגְאָלֵנִי
    לְאִמְרָתְךָ חַיֵּנִי:
155 רָחוֹק מֵרְשָׁעִים יְשׁוּעָה
    כִּי־חֻקֶּיךָ לֹא דָרָשׁוּ:
156 רַחֲמֶיךָ רַבִּים יְהוָה
    כְּמִשְׁפָּטֶיךָ חַיֵּנִי:
157 רַבִּים רֹדְפַי וְצָרָי
    מֵעֵדְוֺתֶיךָ לֹא נָטִיתִי:
158 רָאִיתִי בֹגְדִים וָאֶתְקוֹטָטָה
    אֲשֶׁר אִמְרָתְךָ לֹא שָׁמָרוּ:
159 רְאֵה כִּי־פִקּוּדֶיךָ אָהָבְתִּי
    יְהוָה כְּחַסְדְּךָ חַיֵּנִי:
160 רֹאשׁ־דְּבָרְךָ אֱמֶת
    וּלְעוֹלָם כָּל־מִשְׁפַּט צִדְקֶךָ:
161 שָׂרִים רְדָפוּנִי חִנָּם וּמִדְּבָרְךָ פָּחַד לִבִּי:
162 שָׂשׂ אָנֹכִי עַל־אִמְרָתֶךָ
    כְּמוֹצֵא שָׁלָל רָב:
163 שֶׁקֶר שָׂנֵאתִי וָאֲתַעֵבָה
    תּוֹרָתְךָ אָהָבְתִּי:
164 שֶׁבַע בַּיּוֹם הִלַּלְתִּיךָ
    עַל מִשְׁפְּטֵי צִדְקֶךָ:
165 שָׁלוֹם רָב לְאֹהֲבֵי תוֹרָתֶךָ וְאֵין־לָמוֹ מִכְשׁוֹל:
166 שִׂבַּרְתִּי לִישׁוּעָתְךָ יְהוָה וּמִצְוֺתֶיךָ עָשִׂיתִי:
167 שָׁמְרָה נַפְשִׁי עֵדֹתֶיךָ וָאֹהֲבֵם מְאֹד:
168 שָׁמַרְתִּי פִקּוּדֶיךָ וְעֵדֹתֶיךָ
    כִּי כָל־דְּרָכַי נֶגְדֶּךָ:
169 תִּקְרַב רִנָּתִי לְפָנֶיךָ יְהוָה
    כִּדְבָרְךָ הֲבִינֵנִי:
170 תָּבוֹא תְּחִנָּתִי לְפָנֶיךָ

קיט   147 לִדְבָרֶךָ   161 וּמִדְּבָרֶךָ

Deliver me according to Your word.
171 My lips shall utter praise,
    For You teach me Your statutes.
172 My tongue shall speak of Your word,
    For all Your commandments *are*
       righteousness.
173 Let Your hand become my help,
    For I have chosen Your precepts.
174 I long for Your salvation, O LORD,
    And Your law *is* my delight.
175 Let my soul live, and it shall praise You;
    And let Your judgments help me.
176 I have gone astray like a lost sheep;
    Seek Your servant,
    For I do not forget Your commandments.

כְּאִמְרָתְךָ הַצִּילֵנִי:
171 תַּבַּעְנָה שְׂפָתַי תְּהִלָּה
כִּי תְלַמְּדֵנִי חֻקֶּיךָ:
172 תַּעַן לְשׁוֹנִי אִמְרָתֶךָ
כִּי כָל־מִצְוֺתֶיךָ צֶּדֶק:
173 תְּהִי־יָדְךָ לְעָזְרֵנִי
כִּי פִקּוּדֶיךָ בָחָרְתִּי:
174 תָּאַבְתִּי לִישׁוּעָתְךָ יְהֹוָה
וְתוֹרָתְךָ שַׁעֲשֻׁעָי:
175 תְּחִי־נַפְשִׁי וּתְהַלְלֶךָּ וּמִשְׁפָּטֶךָ יַעְזְרֻנִי:
176 תָּעִיתִי כְּשֶׂה אֹבֵד בַּקֵּשׁ עַבְדֶּךָ
כִּי מִצְוֺתֶיךָ לֹא שָׁכָחְתִּי:

120 A Song of Ascents.

In my distress I cried to the LORD,
    And He heard me.
2 Deliver my soul, O LORD, from lying lips
    And from a deceitful tongue.

3 What shall be given to you,
    Or what shall be done to you,
    You false tongue?
4 Sharp arrows of the warrior,
    With coals of the broom tree!

5 Woe is me, that I dwell in Meshech,
    That I dwell among the tents of Kedar!
6 My soul has dwelt too long
    With one who hates peace.
7 I *am for* peace;
    But when I speak, they *are* for war.

קכ שִׁיר הַמַּעֲלוֹת
אֶל־יְהֹוָה בַּצָּרָתָה לִּי
קָרָאתִי וַיַּעֲנֵנִי:
2 יְהֹוָה הַצִּילָה נַפְשִׁי מִשְּׂפַת־שֶׁקֶר
מִלָּשׁוֹן רְמִיָּה:
3 מַה־יִּתֵּן לְךָ וּמַה־יֹּסִיף לָךְ לָשׁוֹן רְמִיָּה:
4 חִצֵּי גִבּוֹר שְׁנוּנִים
עִם גַּחֲלֵי רְתָמִים:
5 אוֹיָה־לִי כִּי־גַרְתִּי מֶשֶׁךְ
שָׁכַנְתִּי עִם־אָהֳלֵי קֵדָר:
6 רַבַּת שָׁכְנָה־לָּהּ נַפְשִׁי
עִם שׂוֹנֵא שָׁלוֹם:
7 אֲנִי־שָׁלוֹם וְכִי אֲדַבֵּר
הֵמָּה לַמִּלְחָמָה:

121 A Song of Ascents.

I will lift up my eyes to the hills—
    From whence comes my help?
2 My help *comes* from the LORD,
    Who made heaven and earth.

3 He will not allow your foot to be moved;
    He who keeps you will not slumber.
4 Behold, He who keeps Israel
    Shall neither slumber nor sleep.

5 The LORD *is* your keeper;
    The LORD *is* your shade at your right hand.
6 The sun shall not strike you by day,
    Nor the moon by night.

7 The LORD shall preserve you from all evil;
    He shall preserve your soul.
8 The LORD shall preserve your going out and
       your coming in
    From this time forth, and even forevermore.

קכא שִׁיר לַמַּעֲלוֹת
אֶשָּׂא עֵינַי אֶל־הֶהָרִים
מֵאַיִן יָבֹא עֶזְרִי:
2 עֶזְרִי מֵעִם יְהֹוָה
עֹשֵׂה שָׁמַיִם וָאָרֶץ:
3 אַל־יִתֵּן לַמּוֹט רַגְלֶךָ
אַל־יָנוּם שֹׁמְרֶךָ:
4 הִנֵּה לֹא־יָנוּם וְלֹא יִישָׁן
שׁוֹמֵר יִשְׂרָאֵל:
5 יְהֹוָה שֹׁמְרֶךָ יְהֹוָה צִלְּךָ עַל־יַד יְמִינֶךָ:
6 יוֹמָם הַשֶּׁמֶשׁ לֹא־יַכֶּכָּה וְיָרֵחַ בַּלָּיְלָה:
7 יְהֹוָה יִשְׁמָרְךָ מִכָּל־רָע
יִשְׁמֹר אֶת־נַפְשֶׁךָ:
8 יְהֹוָה יִשְׁמָר־צֵאתְךָ וּבוֹאֶךָ
מֵעַתָּה וְעַד־עוֹלָם:

122 A Song of Ascents. Of David.

I was glad when they said to me,
"Let us go into the house of the LORD."

2 Our feet have been standing
Within your gates, O Jerusalem!

3 Jerusalem is built
As a city that is compact together,

4 Where the tribes go up,
The tribes of the LORD,
To the Testimony of Israel,
To give thanks to the name of the LORD.

5 For thrones are set there for judgment,
The thrones of the house of David.

6 Pray for the peace of Jerusalem:
"May they prosper who love you.

7 Peace be within your walls,
Prosperity within your palaces."

8 For the sake of my brethren and companions,
I will now say, "Peace be within you."

9 Because of the house of the LORD our God
I will seek your good.

123 A Song of Ascents.

Unto You I lift up my eyes,
O You who dwell in the heavens.

2 Behold, as the eyes of servants *look* to the hand
of their masters,
As the eyes of a maid to the hand of her
mistress,
So our eyes *look* to the LORD our God,
Until He has mercy on us.

3 Have mercy on us, O LORD, have mercy on us!
For we are exceedingly filled with contempt.

4 Our soul is exceedingly filled
With the scorn of those who are at ease,
With the contempt of the proud.

124 A Song of Ascents. Of David.

"If it had not been the LORD who was on our
side,"
Let Israel now say—

2 "If it had not been the LORD who was on our
side,
When men rose up against us,

3 Then they would have swallowed us alive,
When their wrath was kindled against us;

4 Then the waters would have overwhelmed us,
The stream would have gone over our soul;

5 Then the swollen waters
Would have gone over our soul."

6 Blessed be the LORD,
Who has not given us as prey to their teeth.

קכב שִׁיר הַמַּעֲלוֹת לְדָוִד
שָׂמַחְתִּי בְּאֹמְרִים לִי
בֵּית יְהוָה נֵלֵךְ:
2 עֹמְדוֹת הָיוּ רַגְלֵינוּ בִּשְׁעָרַיִךְ יְרוּשָׁלָ͏ִם:
3 יְרוּשָׁלַ͏ִם הַבְּנוּיָה כְּעִיר שֶׁחֻבְּרָה־לָּהּ יַחְדָּו:
4 שֶׁשָּׁם עָלוּ שְׁבָטִים שִׁבְטֵי־יָהּ עֵדוּת לְיִשְׂרָאֵל
לְהֹדוֹת לְשֵׁם יְהוָה:
5 כִּי שָׁמָּה ׀ יָשְׁבוּ כִסְאוֹת לְמִשְׁפָּט
כִּסְאוֹת לְבֵית דָּוִיד:
6 שַׁאֲלוּ שְׁלוֹם יְרוּשָׁלָ͏ִם יִשְׁלָיוּ אֹהֲבָיִךְ:
7 יְהִי־שָׁלוֹם בְּחֵילֵךְ
שַׁלְוָה בְּאַרְמְנוֹתָיִךְ:
8 לְמַעַן אַחַי וְרֵעָי
אֲדַבְּרָה־נָּא שָׁלוֹם בָּךְ:
9 לְמַעַן בֵּית־יְהוָה אֱלֹהֵינוּ
אֲבַקְשָׁה טוֹב לָךְ:

קכג שִׁיר הַמַּעֲלוֹת
אֵלֶיךָ נָשָׂאתִי אֶת־עֵינַי
הַיֹּשְׁבִי בַּשָּׁמָיִם:
2 הִנֵּה כְעֵינֵי עֲבָדִים אֶל־יַד אֲדוֹנֵיהֶם
כְּעֵינֵי שִׁפְחָה אֶל־יַד גְּבִרְתָּהּ
כֵּן עֵינֵינוּ אֶל־יְהוָה אֱלֹהֵינוּ
עַד שֶׁיְּחָנֵּנוּ:
3 חָנֵּנוּ יְהוָה חָנֵּנוּ
כִּי־רַב שָׂבַעְנוּ בוּז:
4 רַבַּת שָׂבְעָה־לָּהּ נַפְשֵׁנוּ הַלַּעַג הַשַּׁאֲנַנִּים
הַבּוּז לִגְאֵיוֹנִים:

קכד שִׁיר הַמַּעֲלוֹת לְדָוִד
לוּלֵי יְהוָה שֶׁהָיָה לָנוּ
יֹאמַר־נָא יִשְׂרָאֵל:
2 לוּלֵי יְהוָה שֶׁהָיָה לָנוּ
בְּקוּם עָלֵינוּ אָדָם:
3 אֲזַי חַיִּים בְּלָעוּנוּ
בַּחֲרוֹת אַפָּם בָּנוּ:
4 אֲזַי הַמַּיִם שְׁטָפוּנוּ
נַחְלָה עָבַר עַל־נַפְשֵׁנוּ:
5 אֲזַי עָבַר עַל־נַפְשֵׁנוּ
הַמַּיִם הַזֵּידוֹנִים:
6 בָּרוּךְ יְהוָה
שֶׁלֹּא נְתָנָנוּ טֶרֶף לְשִׁנֵּיהֶם:

7   Our soul has escaped as a bird from the snare
of the fowlers;
The snare is broken, and we have escaped.

8   Our help *is* in the name of the LORD,
Who made heaven and earth.

נַפְשֵׁנוּ כְּצִפּוֹר נִמְלְטָה֮ מִפַּ֪ח י֫וֹקְשִׁ֥ים 7
הַפַּ֥ח נִשְׁבָּ֑ר וַאֲנַ֥חְנוּ נִמְלָֽטְנוּ׃
עֶ֭זְרֵנוּ בְּשֵׁ֣ם יְהֹוָ֑ה 8
עֹ֝שֵׂ֗ה שָׁמַ֥יִם וָאָֽרֶץ׃

125   A Song of Ascents.
Those who trust in the LORD
Are like Mount Zion,
Which cannot be moved, *but* abides forever.

2   As the mountains surround Jerusalem,
So the LORD surrounds His people
From this time forth and forever.

3   For the scepter of wickedness shall not rest
On the land allotted to the righteous,
Lest the righteous reach out their hands to
iniquity.

4   Do good, O LORD, to *those who are* good,
And to *those who are* upright in their hearts.

5   As for such as turn aside to their crooked ways,
The LORD shall lead them away
With the workers of iniquity.

Peace *be* upon Israel!

קכה שִׁ֗יר הַֽמַּ֫עֲל֥וֹת
הַבֹּטְחִ֥ים בַּיהֹוָ֑ה
כְּֽהַר־צִיּ֥וֹן לֹא־יִ֝מּ֗וֹט לְעוֹלָ֥ם יֵשֵֽׁב׃
יְֽרוּשָׁלִַ֗ם הָרִים֮ סָבִ֪יב לָ֥֫הּ 2
וַ֭יהֹוָה סָבִ֣יב לְעַמּ֑וֹ
מֵֽ֝עַתָּ֗ה וְעַד־עוֹלָֽם׃
כִּ֤י לֹ֪א יָנ֡וּחַ שֵׁ֤בֶט הָרֶ֗שַׁע 3
עַ֭ל גּוֹרַ֣ל הַֽצַּדִּיקִ֑ים
לְמַ֡עַן לֹא־יִשְׁלְח֖וּ הַצַּדִּיקִ֥ים בְּעַוְלָ֗תָה יְדֵיהֶֽם׃
הֵיטִ֣יבָה יְ֭הֹוָה לַטּוֹבִ֑ים 4
וְ֝לִישָׁרִ֗ים בְּלִבּוֹתָֽם׃
וְהַמַּטִּ֤ים עֲֽקַלְקַלּוֹתָ֗ם 5
יוֹלִיכֵ֣ם יְ֭הֹוָה אֶת־פֹּֽעֲלֵ֣י הָאָ֑וֶן
שָׁ֝ל֗וֹם עַל־יִשְׂרָאֵֽל׃

126   A Song of Ascents.
When the LORD brought back the captivity of
Zion,
We were like those who dream.

2   Then our mouth was filled with laughter,
And our tongue with singing.
Then they said among the nations,
"The LORD has done great things for them."

3   The LORD has done great things for us,
And we are glad.

4   Bring back our captivity, O LORD,
As the streams in the South.

5   Those who sow in tears
Shall reap in joy.

6   He who continually goes forth weeping,
Bearing seed for sowing,
Shall doubtless come again with rejoicing,
Bringing his sheaves *with him.*

קכו שִׁ֗יר הַֽמַּ֫עֲל֥וֹת
בְּשׁ֣וּב יְ֭הֹוָה אֶת־שִׁיבַ֣ת צִיּ֑וֹן
הָ֝יִ֗ינוּ כְּחֹלְמִֽים׃
אָ֤ז יִמָּלֵ֪א שְׂח֡וֹק פִּינוּ֮ וּלְשׁוֹנֵ֪נוּ רִ֫נָּ֥ה 2
אָ֭ז יֹאמְר֣וּ בַגּוֹיִ֑ם
הִגְדִּ֥יל יְ֝הֹוָ֗ה לַעֲשׂ֥וֹת עִם־אֵֽלֶּה׃
הִגְדִּ֣יל יְ֭הֹוָה לַעֲשׂ֣וֹת עִמָּ֑נוּ 3
הָ֝יִ֗ינוּ שְׂמֵחִֽים׃
שׁוּבָ֣ה יְ֭הֹוָה אֶת־שְׁבִיתֵ֑נוּ 4
כַּאֲפִיקִ֥ים בַּנֶּֽגֶב׃
הַזֹּרְעִ֥ים בְּדִמְעָ֗ה בְּרִנָּ֥ה יִקְצֹֽרוּ׃ 5
הָ֘ל֤וֹךְ יֵלֵ֨ךְ ׀ וּבָכֹה֮ נֹשֵׂ֪א מֶֽשֶׁךְ־הַ֫זָּ֥רַע 6
בֹּא־יָב֥וֹא בְרִנָּ֑ה
נֹ֝שֵׂ֗א אֲלֻמֹּתָֽיו׃

127   A Song of Ascents. Of Solomon.
Unless the LORD builds the house,
They labor in vain who build it;
Unless the LORD guards the city,
The watchman stays awake in vain.

2   *It is* vain for you to rise up early,
To sit up late,
To eat the bread of sorrows;

קכז שִׁ֥יר הַֽמַּעֲל֗וֹת לִשְׁלֹ֫מֹ֥ה
אִם־יְהֹוָ֤ה ׀ לֹא־יִבְנֶ֬ה בַ֗יִת
שָׁ֤וְא ׀ עָמְל֣וּ בוֹנָ֣יו בּ֑וֹ
אִם־יְהֹוָ֥ה לֹא־יִשְׁמׇר־עִ֝֗יר
שָׁ֤וְא ׀ שָׁקַ֬ד שׁוֹמֵֽר׃
שָׁ֤וְא לָכֶ֨ם ׀ מַשְׁכִּ֪ימֵי ק֡וּם 2
מְאַֽחֲרֵי־שֶׁ֗בֶת
אֹ֭כְלֵי לֶ֣חֶם הָעֲצָבִ֑ים

For so He gives His beloved sleep.

3 Behold, children *are* a heritage from the LORD,
The fruit of the womb *is* a reward.

4 Like arrows in the hand of a warrior,
So *are* the children of one's youth.

5 Happy *is* the man who has his quiver full of
them;
They shall not be ashamed,
But shall speak with their enemies in the gate.

כֵּן יִתֵּן לִידִידוֹ שֵׁנָא׃
3 הִנֵּה נַחֲלַת יְהֹוָה בָּנִים
שָׂכָר פְּרִי הַבָּֽטֶן׃
4 כְּחִצִּים בְּיַד־גִּבּוֹר
כֵּן בְּנֵי הַנְּעוּרִֽים׃
5 אַשְׁרֵי הַגֶּבֶר אֲשֶׁר מִלֵּא אֶת־אַשְׁפָּתוֹ מֵהֶם
לֹא־יֵבֹשׁוּ
כִּֽי־יְדַבְּרוּ אֶת־אוֹיְבִים בַּשָּֽׁעַר׃

קכח 128 A Song of Ascents.

שִׁיר הַֽמַּעֲלוֹת

Blessed *is* every one who fears the LORD,
Who walks in His ways.

2 When you eat the labor of your hands,
You *shall be* happy, and *it shall be* well with
you.

3 Your wife *shall be* like a fruitful vine
In the very heart of your house,
Your children like olive plants
All around your table.

4 Behold, thus shall the man be blessed
Who fears the LORD.

5 The LORD bless you out of Zion,
And may you see the good of Jerusalem
All the days of your life.

6 Yes, may you see your children's children.

Peace *be* upon Israel!

אַשְׁרֵי כָּל־יְרֵא יְהֹוָה
הַהֹלֵךְ בִּדְרָכָֽיו׃
2 יְגִיעַ כַּפֶּיךָ כִּי תֹאכֵל
אַשְׁרֶיךָ וְטוֹב לָֽךְ׃
3 אֶשְׁתְּךָ ׀ כְּגֶפֶן פֹּרִיָּה בְּיַרְכְּתֵי בֵיתֶךָ
בָּנֶיךָ כִּשְׁתִלֵי זֵיתִים
סָבִיב לְשֻׁלְחָנֶֽךָ׃
4 הִנֵּה כִי־כֵן יְבֹרַךְ גָּבֶר יְרֵא יְהֹוָֽה׃
5 יְבָרֶכְךָ יְהֹוָה מִצִּיּוֹן
וּרְאֵה בְּטוּב יְרוּשָׁלָ͏ִם כֹּל יְמֵי חַיֶּֽיךָ׃
6 וּרְאֵה־בָנִים לְבָנֶיךָ
שָׁלוֹם עַל־יִשְׂרָאֵֽל׃

קכט 129 A Song of Ascents.

שִׁיר הַֽמַּעֲלוֹת

"Many a time they have afflicted me from my
youth,"
Let Israel now say—

2 "Many a time they have afflicted me from my
youth;
Yet they have not prevailed against me.

3 The plowers plowed on my back;
They made their furrows long."

4 The LORD *is* righteous;
He has cut in pieces the cords of the wicked.

5 Let all those who hate Zion
Be put to shame and turned back.

6 Let them be as the grass *on* the housetops,
Which withers before it grows up,

7 With which the reaper does not fill his hand,
Nor he who binds sheaves, his arms.

8 Neither let those who pass by them say,
"The blessing of the LORD *be* upon you;
We bless you in the name of the LORD!"

רַבַּת צְרָרוּנִי מִנְּעוּרַי
יֹֽאמַר־נָא יִשְׂרָאֵֽל׃
2 רַבַּת צְרָרוּנִי מִנְּעוּרָי
גַּם לֹא־יָכְלוּ לִֽי׃
3 עַל־גַּבִּי חָרְשׁוּ חֹרְשִׁים
הֶאֱרִיכוּ לְמַעֲנוֹתָֽם׃ ק
4 יְהֹוָה צַדִּיק
קִצֵּץ עֲבוֹת רְשָׁעִֽים׃
5 יֵבֹשׁוּ וְיִסֹּגוּ אָחוֹר
כֹּל שֹׂנְאֵי צִיּֽוֹן׃
6 יִהְיוּ כַּחֲצִיר גַּגּוֹת
שֶׁקַּדְמַת שָׁלַף יָבֵֽשׁ׃
7 שֶׁלֹּא מִלֵּא כַפּוֹ קוֹצֵר וְחִצְנוֹ מְעַמֵּֽר׃
8 וְלֹא אָמְרוּ ׀ הָעֹבְרִים בִּרְכַּת־יְהֹוָה אֲלֵיכֶם
בֵּרַכְנוּ אֶתְכֶם בְּשֵׁם יְהֹוָֽה׃

קל 130 A Song of Ascents.

שִׁיר הַֽמַּעֲלוֹת

Out of the depths I have cried to You, O LORD;

מִמַּעֲמַקִּים קְרָאתִיךָ יְהֹוָֽה׃

קכט 3 לְמַעֲנוֹתָם

2 Lord, hear my voice!
Let Your ears be attentive
To the voice of my supplications.

3 If You, LORD, should mark iniquities,
O Lord, who could stand?

4 But *there is* forgiveness with You,
That You may be feared.

5 I wait for the LORD, my soul waits,
And in His word I do hope.

6 My soul *waits* for the Lord
More than those who watch for the morning—
Yes, more than those who watch for the
morning.

7 O Israel, hope in the LORD;
For with the LORD *there is* mercy,
And with Him *is* abundant redemption.

8 And He shall redeem Israel
From all his iniquities.

131 A Song of Ascents. Of David.
LORD, my heart is not haughty,
Nor my eyes lofty.
Neither do I concern myself with great matters,
Nor with things too profound for me.

2 Surely I have calmed and quieted my soul,
Like a weaned child with his mother;
Like a weaned child *is* my soul within me.

3 O Israel, hope in the LORD
From this time forth and forever.

132 A Song of Ascents.
LORD, remember David
And all his afflictions;

2 How he swore to the LORD,
And vowed to the Mighty One of Jacob:

3 "Surely I will not go into the chamber of my
house,
Or go up to the comfort of my bed;

4 I will not give sleep to my eyes
Or slumber to my eyelids,

5 Until I find a place for the LORD,
A dwelling place for the Mighty One of Jacob."

6 Behold, we heard of it in Ephrathah;
We found it in the fields of the woods.

7 Let us go into His tabernacle;
Let us worship at His footstool.

8 Arise, O LORD, to Your resting place,
You and the ark of Your strength.

9 Let Your priests be clothed with righteousness,
And let Your saints shout for joy.

אֲדֹנָי֮ שִׁמְעָ֪ה בְק֫וֹלִ֥י תִּהְיֶ֣ינָה אָ֭זְנֶיךָ קַשֻּׁב֑וֹת
לְ֝ק֗וֹל תַּחֲנוּנָֽי׃ 2

אִם־עֲוֺנ֥וֹת תִּשְׁמָר־יָ֑הּ
אֲ֝דֹנָ֗י מִ֣י יַעֲמֹֽד׃ 3

כִּֽי־עִמְּךָ֥ הַסְּלִיחָ֑ה
לְ֝מַ֗עַן תִּוָּרֵֽא׃ 4

קִוִּ֣יתִי יְ֭הֹוָה קִוְּתָ֣ה נַפְשִׁ֑י
וְֽלִדְבָר֥וֹ הוֹחָֽלְתִּי׃ 5

נַפְשִׁ֥י לַֽאדֹנָ֑י 6
מִשֹּׁמְרִ֥ים לַ֝בֹּ֗קֶר שֹׁמְרִ֥ים לַבֹּֽקֶר׃

יַחֵ֥ל יִשְׂרָאֵ֗ל אֶל־יְ֫הֹוָ֥ה 7
כִּֽי־עִם־יְהֹוָ֥ה הַחֶ֑סֶד וְהַרְבֵּ֖ה עִמּ֣וֹ פְדֽוּת׃

וְ֭הוּא יִפְדֶּ֣ה אֶת־יִשְׂרָאֵ֑ל 8
מִ֝כֹּ֗ל עֲוֺנוֹתָֽיו׃

קלא שִׁ֥יר הַֽמַּעֲל֗וֹת לְדָ֫וִ֥ד
יְהֹוָ֤ה ׀ לֹא־גָבַ֣הּ לִ֭בִּי וְלֹא־רָמ֣וּ עֵינַ֑י וְלֹא־
הִלַּ֓כְתִּי ׀ בִּגְדֹל֖וֹת וּבְנִפְלָא֣וֹת מִמֶּֽנִּי׃

אִם־לֹ֤א שִׁוִּ֨יתִי ׀ וְדוֹמַ֗מְתִּי נַ֫פְשִׁ֥י 2
כְּ֭גָמֻל עֲלֵ֣י אִמּ֑וֹ
כַּגָּמֻ֖ל עָלַ֣י נַפְשִֽׁי׃

יַחֵ֣ל יִ֭שְׂרָאֵל אֶל־יְהֹוָ֑ה 3
מֵ֝עַתָּ֗ה וְעַד־עוֹלָֽם׃

קלב שִׁ֗יר הַֽמַּ֫עֲל֥וֹת
זְכוֹר־יְהֹוָ֥ה לְדָוִ֑ד
אֵ֝֗ת כָּל־עֻנּוֹתֽוֹ׃

אֲשֶׁ֣ר נִ֭שְׁבַּע לַיהֹוָ֑ה 2
נָ֝דַ֗ר לַאֲבִ֥יר יַעֲקֹֽב׃

אִם־אָ֭בֹא בְּאֹ֣הֶל בֵּיתִ֑י 3
אִם־אֶ֝עֱלֶ֗ה עַל־עֶ֣רֶשׂ יְצוּעָֽי׃

אִם־אֶתֵּ֣ן שְׁנַ֣ת לְעֵינָ֑י 4
לְֽעַפְעַפַּ֥י תְּנוּמָֽה׃

עַד־אֶמְצָ֣א מָ֭קוֹם לַיהֹוָ֑ה 5
מִ֝שְׁכָּנ֗וֹת לַאֲבִ֥יר יַעֲקֹֽב׃

הִנֵּֽה־שְׁמַעֲנ֥וּהָ בְאֶפְרָ֑תָה 6
מְ֝צָאנ֗וּהָ בִּשְׂדֵי־יָֽעַר׃

נָב֥וֹאָה לְמִשְׁכְּנוֹתָ֑יו 7
נִ֝שְׁתַּחֲוֶ֗ה לַהֲדֹ֥ם רַגְלָֽיו׃

קוּמָ֣ה יְ֭הֹוָה לִמְנוּחָתֶ֑ךָ 8
אַ֝תָּ֗ה וַאֲר֥וֹן עֻזֶּֽךָ׃

כֹּהֲנֶ֥יךָ יִלְבְּשׁוּ־צֶ֑דֶק 9
וַחֲסִידֶ֥יךָ יְרַנֵּֽנוּ׃

10 For Your servant David's sake,
Do not turn away the face of Your Anointed.

11 The LORD has sworn *in* truth to David;
He will not turn from it:
"I will set upon your throne the fruit of your
body.

12 If your sons will keep My covenant
And My testimony which I shall teach them,
Their sons also shall sit upon your throne
forevermore."

13 For the LORD has chosen Zion;
He has desired *it* for His dwelling place:

14 "This *is* My resting place forever;
Here I will dwell, for I have desired it.

15 I will abundantly bless her provision;
I will satisfy her poor with bread.

16 I will also clothe her priests with salvation,
And her saints shall shout aloud for joy.

17 There I will make the horn of David grow;
I will prepare a lamp for My Anointed.

18 His enemies I will clothe with shame,
But upon Himself His crown shall flourish."

133 A Song of Ascents. Of David.
Behold, how good and how pleasant *it is*
For brethren to dwell together in unity!

2 *It is* like the precious oil upon the head,
Running down on the beard,
The beard of Aaron,
Running down on the edge of his garments.

3 *It is* like the dew of Hermon,
Descending upon the mountains of Zion;
For there the LORD commanded the blessing—
Life forevermore.

134 A Song of Ascents.
Behold, bless the LORD,
All *you* servants of the LORD,
Who by night stand in the house of the LORD!

2 Lift up your hands *in* the sanctuary,
And bless the LORD.

3 The LORD who made heaven and earth
Bless you from Zion!

135 Praise the LORD!
Praise the name of the LORD;
Praise *Him*, O you servants of the LORD!

2 You who stand in the house of the LORD,
In the courts of the house of our God,

3 Praise the LORD, for the LORD *is* good;
Sing praises to His name, for *it is* pleasant:

10 בַּעֲבוּר דָּוִד עַבְדֶּךָ
אַל־תָּשֵׁב פְּנֵי מְשִׁיחֶךָ׃

11 נִשְׁבַּע־יְהֹוָה ׀ לְדָוִד אֱמֶת לֹא־יָשׁוּב מִמֶּנָּה
מִפְּרִי בִטְנְךָ אָשִׁית לְכִסֵּא־לָךְ׃

12 אִם־יִשְׁמְרוּ בָנֶיךָ ׀ בְּרִיתִי
וְעֵדֹתִי זוֹ אֲלַמְּדֵם גַּם־בְּנֵיהֶם עֲדֵי־עַד
יֵשְׁבוּ לְכִסֵּא־לָךְ׃

13 כִּי־בָחַר יְהֹוָה בְּצִיּוֹן
אִוָּהּ לְמוֹשָׁב לוֹ׃

14 זֹאת־מְנוּחָתִי עֲדֵי־עַד
פֹּה־אֵשֵׁב כִּי אִוִּתִיהָ׃

15 צֵידָהּ בָּרֵךְ אֲבָרֵךְ
אֶבְיוֹנֶיהָ אַשְׂבִּיעַ לָחֶם׃

16 וְכֹהֲנֶיהָ אַלְבִּישׁ יֶשַׁע
וַחֲסִידֶיהָ רַנֵּן יְרַנֵּנוּ׃

17 שָׁם אַצְמִיחַ קֶרֶן לְדָוִד
עָרַכְתִּי נֵר לִמְשִׁיחִי׃

18 אוֹיְבָיו אַלְבִּישׁ בֹּשֶׁת
וְעָלָיו יָצִיץ נִזְרוֹ׃

קלג שִׁיר הַמַּעֲלוֹת לְדָוִד
הִנֵּה מַה־טּוֹב וּמַה־נָּעִים
שֶׁבֶת אַחִים גַּם־יָחַד׃

2 כַּשֶּׁמֶן הַטּוֹב ׀ עַל־הָרֹאשׁ יֹרֵד
עַל־הַזָּקָן זְקַן־אַהֲרֹן
שֶׁיֹּרֵד עַל־פִּי מִדּוֹתָיו׃

3 כְּטַל־חֶרְמוֹן שֶׁיֹּרֵד עַל־הַרְרֵי צִיּוֹן
כִּי שָׁם ׀ צִוָּה יְהֹוָה אֶת־הַבְּרָכָה
חַיִּים עַד־הָעוֹלָם׃

קלד שִׁיר הַמַּעֲלוֹת
הִנֵּה ׀ בָּרְכוּ אֶת־יְהֹוָה כָּל־עַבְדֵי יְהֹוָה
הָעֹמְדִים בְּבֵית־יְהֹוָה בַּלֵּילוֹת׃

2 שְׂאוּ־יְדֵכֶם קֹדֶשׁ וּבָרְכוּ אֶת־יְהֹוָה׃

3 יְבָרֶכְךָ יְהֹוָה מִצִּיּוֹן
עֹשֵׂה שָׁמַיִם וָאָרֶץ׃

קלה הַלְלוּ יָהּ ׀ הַלְלוּ אֶת־שֵׁם יְהֹוָה
הַלְלוּ עַבְדֵי יְהֹוָה׃

2 שֶׁעֹמְדִים בְּבֵית יְהֹוָה
בְּחַצְרוֹת בֵּית אֱלֹהֵינוּ׃

3 הַלְלוּ־יָהּ כִּי־טוֹב יְהֹוָה
זַמְּרוּ לִשְׁמוֹ כִּי נָעִים׃

4 For the Lord has chosen Jacob for Himself, Israel for His special treasure.	כִּי־יַעֲקֹב בָּחַר לוֹ יָהּ 4 יִשְׂרָאֵל לִסְגֻלָּתוֹ:
5 For I know that the Lord *is* great, And our Lord *is* above all gods.	כִּי אֲנִי יָדַעְתִּי כִּי־גָדוֹל יְהֹוָה 5 וַאֲדֹנֵינוּ מִכָּל־אֱלֹהִים:
6 Whatever the Lord pleases He does, In heaven and in earth, In the seas and in all deep places.	כֹּל אֲשֶׁר־חָפֵץ יְהֹוָה עָשָׂה 6 בַּשָּׁמַיִם וּבָאָרֶץ בַּיַּמִּים וְכָל־תְּהֹמוֹת:
7 He causes the vapors to ascend from the ends of the earth; He makes lightning for the rain; He brings the wind out of His treasuries.	מַעֲלֶה נְשִׂאִים מִקְצֵה הָאָרֶץ 7 בְּרָקִים לַמָּטָר עָשָׂה מוֹצֵא־רוּחַ מֵאוֹצְרוֹתָיו:
8 He destroyed the firstborn of Egypt, Both of man and beast.	שֶׁהִכָּה בְּכוֹרֵי מִצְרָיִם 8 מֵאָדָם עַד־בְּהֵמָה:
9 He sent signs and wonders into the midst of you, O Egypt, Upon Pharaoh and all his servants.	שָׁלַח אֹתוֹת וּמֹפְתִים בְּתוֹכֵכִי מִצְרָיִם 9 בְּפַרְעֹה וּבְכָל־עֲבָדָיו:
10 He defeated many nations And slew mighty kings—	שֶׁהִכָּה גּוֹיִם רַבִּים 10 וְהָרַג מְלָכִים עֲצוּמִים:
11 Sihon king of the Amorites, Og king of Bashan, And all the kingdoms of Canaan—	לְסִיחוֹן מֶלֶךְ הָאֱמֹרִי וּלְעוֹג מֶלֶךְ הַבָּשָׁן 11 וּלְכֹל מַמְלְכוֹת כְּנָעַן:
12 And gave their land *as* a heritage, A heritage to Israel His people.	וְנָתַן אַרְצָם נַחֲלָה 12 נַחֲלָה לְיִשְׂרָאֵל עַמּוֹ:
13 Your name, O Lord, *endures* forever, Your fame, O Lord, throughout all generations.	יְהֹוָה שִׁמְךָ לְעוֹלָם יְהֹוָה זִכְרְךָ לְדֹר־וָדֹר: 13
14 For the Lord will judge His people, And He will have compassion on His servants.	כִּי־יָדִין יְהֹוָה עַמּוֹ 14 וְעַל־עֲבָדָיו יִתְנֶחָם:
15 The idols of the nations *are* silver and gold, The work of men's hands.	עֲצַבֵּי הַגּוֹיִם כֶּסֶף וְזָהָב 15 מַעֲשֵׂה יְדֵי אָדָם:
16 They have mouths, but they do not speak; Eyes they have, but they do not see;	פֶּה־לָהֶם וְלֹא יְדַבֵּרוּ 16 עֵינַיִם לָהֶם וְלֹא יִרְאוּ:
17 They have ears, but they do not hear; Nor is there *any* breath in their mouths.	אָזְנַיִם לָהֶם וְלֹא יַאֲזִינוּ 17 אַף אֵין־יֶשׁ־רוּחַ בְּפִיהֶם:
18 Those who make them are like them; *So is* everyone who trusts in them.	כְּמוֹהֶם יִהְיוּ עֹשֵׂיהֶם 18 כֹּל אֲשֶׁר־בֹּטֵחַ בָּהֶם:
19 Bless the Lord, O house of Israel! Bless the Lord, O house of Aaron!	בֵּית יִשְׂרָאֵל בָּרְכוּ אֶת־יְהֹוָה 19 בֵּית אַהֲרֹן בָּרְכוּ אֶת־יְהֹוָה:
20 Bless the Lord, O house of Levi! You who fear the Lord, bless the Lord!	בֵּית הַלֵּוִי בָּרְכוּ אֶת־יְהֹוָה 20 יִרְאֵי יְהֹוָה בָּרְכוּ אֶת־יְהֹוָה:
21 Blessed be the Lord out of Zion, Who dwells in Jerusalem! Praise the Lord!	בָּרוּךְ יְהֹוָה מִצִּיּוֹן שֹׁכֵן יְרוּשָׁלָ͏ִם הַלְלוּ־יָהּ: 21

136 Oh, give thanks to the Lord, for *He is* good!
    For His mercy *endures* forever.

2 Oh, give thanks to the God of gods!
    For His mercy *endures* forever.

3 Oh, give thanks to the Lord of lords!

קלו   הוֹדוּ לַיהֹוָה כִּי־טוֹב
כִּי לְעוֹלָם חַסְדּוֹ:
הוֹדוּ לֵאלֹהֵי הָאֱלֹהִים   2
כִּי לְעוֹלָם חַסְדּוֹ:
הוֹדוּ לַאֲדֹנֵי הָאֲדֹנִים   3
כִּי לְעוֹלָם חַסְדּוֹ:

For His mercy *endures* forever:	לְעֹשֵׂה נִפְלָאוֹת גְּדֹלוֹת לְבַדּוֹ 4
	כִּי לְעוֹלָם חַסְדּוֹ:
4 To Him who alone does great wonders,	לְעֹשֵׂה הַשָּׁמַיִם בִּתְבוּנָה 5
For His mercy *endures* forever;	כִּי לְעוֹלָם חַסְדּוֹ:
5 To Him who by wisdom made the heavens,	לְרֹקַע הָאָרֶץ עַל־הַמָּיִם 6
For His mercy *endures* forever;	כִּי לְעוֹלָם חַסְדּוֹ:
6 To Him who laid out the earth above the	לְעֹשֵׂה אוֹרִים גְּדֹלִים 7
waters,	כִּי לְעוֹלָם חַסְדּוֹ:
For His mercy *endures* forever;	אֶת־הַשֶּׁמֶשׁ לְמֶמְשֶׁלֶת בַּיּוֹם 8
7 To Him who made great lights,	כִּי לְעוֹלָם חַסְדּוֹ:
For His mercy *endures* forever—	אֶת־הַיָּרֵחַ וְכוֹכָבִים לְמֶמְשְׁלוֹת בַּלָּיְלָה 9
8 The sun to rule by day,	כִּי לְעוֹלָם חַסְדּוֹ:
For His mercy *endures* forever;	לְמַכֵּה מִצְרַיִם בִּבְכוֹרֵיהֶם 10
9 The moon and stars to rule by night,	כִּי לְעוֹלָם חַסְדּוֹ:
For His mercy *endures* forever.	וַיּוֹצֵא יִשְׂרָאֵל מִתּוֹכָם 11
	כִּי לְעוֹלָם חַסְדּוֹ:
10 To Him who struck Egypt in their firstborn,	בְּיָד חֲזָקָה וּבִזְרוֹעַ נְטוּיָה 12
For His mercy *endures* forever;	כִּי לְעוֹלָם חַסְדּוֹ:
11 And brought out Israel from among them,	לְגֹזֵר יַם־סוּף לִגְזָרִים 13
For His mercy *endures* forever;	כִּי לְעוֹלָם חַסְדּוֹ:
12 With a strong hand, and with an outstretched	וְהֶעֱבִיר יִשְׂרָאֵל בְּתוֹכוֹ 14
arm,	כִּי לְעוֹלָם חַסְדּוֹ:
For His mercy *endures* forever;	וְנִעֵר פַּרְעֹה וְחֵילוֹ בְיַם־סוּף 15
13 To Him who divided the Red Sea in two,	כִּי לְעוֹלָם חַסְדּוֹ:
For His mercy *endures* forever;	לְמוֹלִיךְ עַמּוֹ בַּמִּדְבָּר 16
14 And made Israel pass through the midst of it,	כִּי לְעוֹלָם חַסְדּוֹ:
For His mercy *endures* forever;	לְמַכֵּה מְלָכִים גְּדֹלִים 17
15 But overthrew Pharaoh and his army in the	כִּי לְעוֹלָם חַסְדּוֹ:
Red Sea,	וַיַּהֲרֹג מְלָכִים אַדִּירִים 18
For His mercy *endures* forever;	כִּי לְעוֹלָם חַסְדּוֹ:
16 To Him who led His people through the	לְסִיחוֹן מֶלֶךְ הָאֱמֹרִי 19
wilderness,	כִּי לְעוֹלָם חַסְדּוֹ:
For His mercy *endures* forever;	וּלְעוֹג מֶלֶךְ הַבָּשָׁן 20
17 To Him who struck down great kings,	כִּי לְעוֹלָם חַסְדּוֹ:
For His mercy *endures* forever;	וְנָתַן אַרְצָם לְנַחֲלָה 21
18 And slew famous kings,	כִּי לְעוֹלָם חַסְדּוֹ:
For His mercy *endures* forever—	נַחֲלָה לְיִשְׂרָאֵל עַבְדּוֹ 22
19 Sihon king of the Amorites,	כִּי לְעוֹלָם חַסְדּוֹ:
For His mercy *endures* forever;	שֶׁבְּשִׁפְלֵנוּ זָכַר לָנוּ 23
20 And Og king of Bashan,	כִּי לְעוֹלָם חַסְדּוֹ:
For His mercy *endures* forever—	וַיִּפְרְקֵנוּ מִצָּרֵינוּ 24
21 And gave their land as a heritage,	כִּי לְעוֹלָם חַסְדּוֹ:
For His mercy *endures* forever;	נֹתֵן לֶחֶם לְכָל־בָּשָׂר 25
22 A heritage to Israel His servant,	כִּי לְעוֹלָם חַסְדּוֹ:
For His mercy *endures* forever.	הוֹדוּ לְאֵל הַשָּׁמָיִם 26
	כִּי לְעוֹלָם חַסְדּוֹ:
23 Who remembered us in our lowly state,	
For His mercy *endures* forever;	
24 And rescued us from our enemies,	
For His mercy *endures* forever;	
25 Who gives food to all flesh,	
For His mercy *endures* forever.	
26 Oh, give thanks to the God of heaven!	
For His mercy *endures* forever.	

137 By the rivers of Babylon,
There we sat down, yea, we wept
When we remembered Zion.
2 We hung our harps
Upon the willows in the midst of it.
3 For there those who carried us away captive
  asked of us a song,
And those who plundered us *requested* mirth,
Saying, "Sing us *one* of the songs of Zion!"

4 How shall we sing the LORD's song
In a foreign land?
5 If I forget you, O Jerusalem,
Let my right hand forget *its skill!*
6 If I do not remember you,
Let my tongue cling to the roof of my mouth—
If I do not exalt Jerusalem
Above my chief joy.

7 Remember, O LORD, against the sons of Edom
The day of Jerusalem,
Who said, "Raze *it,* raze *it,*
To its very foundation!"

8 O daughter of Babylon, who are to be
  destroyed,
Happy the one who repays you as you have
  served us!
9 Happy the one who takes and dashes
Your little ones against the rock!

138 *A Psalm* of David.
I will praise You with my whole heart;
Before the gods I will sing praises to You.
2 I will worship toward Your holy temple,
And praise Your name
For Your lovingkindness and Your truth;
For You have magnified Your word above all
  Your name.
3 In the day when I cried out, You answered me,
And made me bold *with* strength in my soul.

4 All the kings of the earth shall praise You, O
  LORD,
When they hear the words of Your mouth.
5 Yes, they shall sing of the ways of the LORD,
For great *is* the glory of the LORD.
6 Though the LORD *is* on high,
Yet He regards the lowly;
But the proud He knows from afar.

7 Though I walk in the midst of trouble, You will
  revive me;
You will stretch out Your hand
Against the wrath of my enemies,
And Your right hand will save me.
8 The LORD will perfect *that which* concerns me;

Your mercy, O LORD, *endures* forever;
Do not forsake the works of Your hands.

139 For the Chief Musician. A Psalm of David.
O LORD, You have searched me and known
me.

2   You know my sitting down and my rising up;
You understand my thought afar off.
3   You comprehend my path and my lying down,
And are acquainted with all my ways.
4   For *there is* not a word on my tongue,
But behold, O LORD, You know it altogether.
5   You have hedged me behind and before,
And laid Your hand upon me.
6   *Such* knowledge *is* too wonderful for me;
It is high, I cannot *attain* it.

7   Where can I go from Your Spirit?
Or where can I flee from Your presence?
8   If I ascend into heaven, You *are* there;
If I make my bed in hell, behold, You *are* there.
9   *If* I take the wings of the morning,
And dwell in the uttermost parts of the sea,
10   Even there Your hand shall lead me,
And Your right hand shall hold me.
11   If I say, "Surely the darkness shall fall on me,"
Even the night shall be light about me;
12   Indeed, the darkness shall not hide from You,
But the night shines as the day;
The darkness and the light *are* both alike *to*
You.

13   For You formed my inward parts;
You covered me in my mother's womb.
14   I will praise You, for I am fearfully *and*
wonderfully made;
Marvelous are Your works,
And *that* my soul knows very well.
15   My frame was not hidden from You,
When I was made in secret,
And skillfully wrought in the lowest parts of the
earth.
16   Your eyes saw my substance, being yet
unformed.
And in Your book they all were written,
The days fashioned for me,
When *as yet there were* none of them.

17   How precious also are Your thoughts to me, O
God!
How great is the sum of them!
18   *If* I should count them, they would be more in
number than the sand;
When I awake, I am still with You.

19   Oh, that You would slay the wicked, O God!

יְהוָה חַסְדְּךָ לְעוֹלָם מַעֲשֵׂי יָדֶיךָ אַל־תֶּרֶף:

קלט לַמְנַצֵּחַ לְדָוִד מִזְמוֹר
יְהוָה חֲקַרְתַּנִי וַתֵּדָע:
2   אַתָּה יָדַעְתָּ שִׁבְתִּי וְקוּמִי
בַּנְתָּה לְרֵעִי מֵרָחוֹק:
3   אָרְחִי וְרִבְעִי זֵרִיתָ
וְכָל־דְּרָכַי הִסְכַּנְתָּה:
4   כִּי אֵין מִלָּה בִּלְשׁוֹנִי
הֵן יְהוָה יָדַעְתָּ כֻלָּהּ:
5   אָחוֹר וָקֶדֶם צַרְתָּנִי
וַתָּשֶׁת עָלַי כַּפֶּכָה:
6   פְּלִיאָה דַעַת מִמֶּנִּי
נִשְׂגְּבָה לֹא־אוּכַל לָהּ:
7   אָנָה אֵלֵךְ מֵרוּחֶךָ
וְאָנָה מִפָּנֶיךָ אֶבְרָח:
8   אִם־אֶסַּק שָׁמַיִם שָׁם אָתָּה
וְאַצִּיעָה שְּׁאוֹל הִנֶּךָּ:
9   אֶשָּׂא כַנְפֵי־שָׁחַר
אֶשְׁכְּנָה בְּאַחֲרִית יָם:
10   גַּם־שָׁם יָדְךָ תַנְחֵנִי
וְתֹאחֲזֵנִי יְמִינֶךָ:
11   וָאֹמַר אַךְ־חֹשֶׁךְ יְשׁוּפֵנִי
וְלַיְלָה אוֹר בַּעֲדֵנִי:
12   גַּם־חֹשֶׁךְ לֹא־יַחְשִׁיךְ מִמֶּךָּ
וְלַיְלָה כַּיּוֹם יָאִיר
כַּחֲשֵׁיכָה כָּאוֹרָה:
13   כִּי־אַתָּה קָנִיתָ כִלְיֹתָי
תְּסֻכֵּנִי בְּבֶטֶן אִמִּי:
14   אוֹדְךָ עַל כִּי נוֹרָאוֹת נִפְלֵיתִי
נִפְלָאִים מַעֲשֶׂיךָ
וְנַפְשִׁי יֹדַעַת מְאֹד:
15   לֹא־נִכְחַד עָצְמִי מִמֶּךָ
אֲשֶׁר־עֻשֵּׂיתִי בַסֵּתֶר
רֻקַּמְתִּי בְּתַחְתִּיּוֹת אָרֶץ:
16   גָּלְמִי רָאוּ עֵינֶיךָ
וְעַל־סִפְרְךָ כֻּלָּם יִכָּתֵבוּ יָמִים יֻצָּרוּ
וְלֹא אֶחָד בָּהֶם:
17   וְלִי מַה־יָּקְרוּ רֵעֶיךָ אֵל
מֶה עָצְמוּ רָאשֵׁיהֶם:
18   אֶסְפְּרֵם מֵחוֹל יִרְבּוּן
הֱקִיצֹתִי וְעוֹדִי עִמָּךְ:

קלט 6 פְּלִיאָה   16 וְלוֹ

Depart from me, therefore, you bloodthirsty
  men.

20 For they speak against You wickedly;
  Your enemies take *Your name* in vain.

21 Do I not hate them, O LORD, who hate You?
  And do I not loathe those who rise up against
  You?

22 I hate them with perfect hatred;
  I count them my enemies.

23 Search me, O God, and know my heart;
  Try me, and know my anxieties;

24 And see if *there is any* wicked way in me,
  And lead me in the way everlasting.

140 To the Chief Musician. A Psalm of David.

Deliver me, O LORD, from evil men;
  Preserve me from violent men,

2 Who plan evil things in *their* hearts;
  They continually gather together *for* war.

3 They sharpen their tongues like a serpent;
  The poison of asps *is* under their lips.   Selah

4 Keep me, O LORD, from the hands of the
  wicked;
  Preserve me from violent men,
  Who have purposed to make my steps stumble.

5 The proud have hidden a snare for me, and
  cords;
  They have spread a net by the wayside;
  They have set traps for me.   Selah

6 I said to the LORD: "You *are* my God;
  Hear the voice of my supplications, O LORD.

7 O GOD the Lord, the strength of my salvation,
  You have covered my head in the day of battle.

8 Do not grant, O LORD, the desires of the
  wicked;
  Do not further his *wicked* scheme,
  Lest they be exalted.   Selah

9 "*As for* the head of those who surround me,
  Let the evil of their lips cover them;

10 Let burning coals fall upon them;
  Let them be cast into the fire,
  Into deep pits, that they rise not up again.

11 Let not a slanderer be established in the earth;
  Let evil hunt the violent man to overthrow
  him."

12 I know that the LORD will maintain
  The cause of the afflicted,
  And justice for the poor.

13 Surely the righteous shall give thanks to Your
  name;
  The upright shall dwell in Your presence.

---

19 אִם־תִּקְטֹל אֱלוֹהַּ ׀ רָשָׁע
  וְאַנְשֵׁי דָמִים סוּרוּ מֶנִּי:

20 אֲשֶׁר יֹאמְרֻךָ לִמְזִמָּה
  נָשֻׂא לַשָּׁוְא עָרֶיךָ:

21 הֲלוֹא־מְשַׂנְאֶיךָ יְהוָה ׀ אֶשְׂנָא
  וּבִתְקוֹמְמֶיךָ אֶתְקוֹטָט:

22 תַּכְלִית שִׂנְאָה שְׂנֵאתִים
  לְאוֹיְבִים הָיוּ לִי:

23 חָקְרֵנִי אֵל וְדַע לְבָבִי
  בְּחָנֵנִי וְדַע שַׂרְעַפָּי:

24 וּרְאֵה אִם־דֶּרֶךְ־עֹצֶב בִּי
  וּנְחֵנִי בְּדֶרֶךְ עוֹלָם:

קמ לַמְנַצֵּחַ מִזְמוֹר לְדָוִד:

2 חַלְּצֵנִי יְהוָה מֵאָדָם רָע
  מֵאִישׁ חֲמָסִים תִּנְצְרֵנִי:

3 אֲשֶׁר חָשְׁבוּ רָעוֹת בְּלֵב
  כָּל־יוֹם יָגוּרוּ מִלְחָמוֹת:

4 שָׁנֲנוּ לְשׁוֹנָם כְּמוֹ־נָחָשׁ
  חֲמַת עַכְשׁוּב תַּחַת שְׂפָתֵימוֹ סֶלָה:

5 שָׁמְרֵנִי יְהוָה ׀ מִידֵי רָשָׁע
  מֵאִישׁ חֲמָסִים תִּנְצְרֵנִי
  אֲשֶׁר חָשְׁבוּ לִדְחוֹת פְּעָמָי:

6 טָמְנוּ־גֵאִים ׀ פַּח לִי
  וַחֲבָלִים פָּרְשׂוּ רֶשֶׁת לְיַד־מַעְגָּל
  מֹקְשִׁים שָׁתוּ־לִי סֶלָה:

7 אָמַרְתִּי לַיהוָה אֵלִי אָתָּה
  הַאֲזִינָה יְהוָה קוֹל תַּחֲנוּנָי:

8 יְהוִה אֲדֹנָי עֹז יְשׁוּעָתִי
  סַכֹּתָה לְרֹאשִׁי בְּיוֹם נָשֶׁק:

9 אַל־תִּתֵּן יְהוָה מַאֲוַיֵּי רָשָׁע
  זְמָמוֹ אַל־תָּפֵק יָרוּמוּ סֶלָה:

10 רֹאשׁ מְסִבָּי
  עֲמַל שְׂפָתֵימוֹ יְכַסּוּמוֹ^P:

11 יִמּוֹטוּ^P עֲלֵיהֶם גֶּחָלִים
  בָּאֵשׁ יַפִּלֵם בְּמַהֲמֹרוֹת בַּל־יָקוּמוּ:

12 אִישׁ לָשׁוֹן בַּל־יִכּוֹן בָּאָרֶץ
  אִישׁ־חָמָס רָע יְצוּדֶנּוּ לְמַדְחֵפֹת:

13 יָדַעְתִּי^P כִּי־יַעֲשֶׂה יְהוָה דִּין עָנִי
  מִשְׁפַּט אֶבְיֹנִים:

14 אַךְ צַדִּיקִים יוֹדוּ לִשְׁמֶךָ
  יֵשְׁבוּ יְשָׁרִים אֶת־פָּנֶיךָ:

קמ 10 יְכַסּוּמוֹ‎ 11 יִמּוֹטוּ‎ 13 יָדַעְתִּי‎

141 A Psalm of David.

LORD, I cry out to You;
Make haste to me!
Give ear to my voice when I cry out to You.

2 Let my prayer be set before You *as* incense,
The lifting up of my hands *as* the evening
sacrifice.

3 Set a guard, O LORD, over my mouth;
Keep watch over the door of my lips.

4 Do not incline my heart to any evil thing,
To practice wicked works
With men who work iniquity;
And do not let me eat of their delicacies.

5 Let the righteous strike me;
It shall be a kindness.
And let him rebuke me;
It shall be as excellent oil;
Let my head not refuse it.
For still my prayer *is* against the deeds of the
wicked.

6 Their judges are overthrown by the sides of the
cliff,
And they hear my words, for they are sweet.

7 Our bones are scattered at the mouth of the
grave,
As when one plows and breaks up the earth.

8 But my eyes *are* upon You, O GOD the Lord;
In You I take refuge;
Do not leave my soul destitute.

9 Keep me from the snares they have laid for me,
And from the traps of the workers of iniquity.

10 Let the wicked fall into their own nets,
While I escape safely.

142 A Contemplation of David. A Prayer when he
was in the cave.

I cry out to the LORD with my voice;
With my voice to the LORD I make my
supplication.

2 I pour out my complaint before Him;
I declare before Him my trouble.

3 When my spirit was overwhelmed within me,
Then You knew my path.
In the way in which I walk
They have secretly set a snare for me.

4 Look on *my* right hand and see,
For *there is* no one who acknowledges me;
Refuge has failed me;
No one cares for my soul.

5 I cried out to You, O LORD:
I said, "You *are* my refuge,
My portion in the land of the living.

קמא מִזְמוֹר לְדָוִד

יְהוָה קְרָאתִיךָ חוּשָׁה לִּי
הַאֲזִינָה קוֹלִי בְּקָרְאִי־לָךְ:

2 תִּכּוֹן תְּפִלָּתִי קְטֹרֶת לְפָנֶיךָ
מַשְׂאַת כַּפַּי מִנְחַת־עָרֶב:

3 שִׁיתָה יְהוָה שָׁמְרָה לְפִי
נִצְּרָה עַל־דַּל שְׂפָתָי:

4 אַל־תַּט־לִבִּי לְדָבָר רָע
לְהִתְעוֹלֵל עֲלִלוֹת בְּרֶשַׁע
אֶת־אִישִׁים פֹּעֲלֵי־אָוֶן
וּבַל־אֶלְחַם בְּמַנְעַמֵּיהֶם:

5 יֶהֶלְמֵנִי־צַדִּיק חֶסֶד וְיוֹכִיחֵנִי
שֶׁמֶן רֹאשׁ אַל־יָנִי רֹאשִׁי
כִּי־עוֹד וּתְפִלָּתִי בְּרָעוֹתֵיהֶם:

6 נִשְׁמְטוּ בִידֵי־סֶלַע שֹׁפְטֵיהֶם
וְשָׁמְעוּ אֲמָרַי כִּי נָעֵמוּ:

7 כְּמוֹ פֹלֵחַ וּבֹקֵעַ בָּאָרֶץ
נִפְזְרוּ עֲצָמֵינוּ לְפִי שְׁאוֹל:

8 כִּי אֵלֶיךָ יְהוָה אֲדֹנָי עֵינָי
בְּכָה חָסִיתִי אַל־תְּעַר נַפְשִׁי:

9 שָׁמְרֵנִי מִידֵי פַח יָקְשׁוּ לִי
וּמֹקְשׁוֹת פֹּעֲלֵי אָוֶן:

10 יִפְּלוּ בְמַכְמֹרָיו רְשָׁעִים
יַחַד אָנֹכִי עַד־אֶעֱבוֹר:

קמב מַשְׂכִּיל לְדָוִד
בִּהְיוֹתוֹ בַמְּעָרָה
תְפִלָּה:

2 קוֹלִי אֶל־יְהוָה אֶזְעָק
קוֹלִי אֶל־יְהוָה אֶתְחַנָּן:

3 אֶשְׁפֹּךְ לְפָנָיו שִׂיחִי
צָרָתִי לְפָנָיו אַגִּיד:

4 בְּהִתְעַטֵּף עָלַי רוּחִי
וְאַתָּה יָדַעְתָּ נְתִיבָתִי
בְּאֹרַח־זוּ אֲהַלֵּךְ
טָמְנוּ פַח לִי:

5 הַבֵּיט יָמִין וּרְאֵה וְאֵין־לִי מַכִּיר
אָבַד מָנוֹס מִמֶּנִּי
אֵין דּוֹרֵשׁ לְנַפְשִׁי:

6 זָעַקְתִּי אֵלֶיךָ יְהוָה
אָמַרְתִּי אַתָּה מַחְסִי
חֶלְקִי בְּאֶרֶץ הַחַיִּים:

6 Attend to my cry,
For I am brought very low;
Deliver me from my persecutors,
For they are stronger than I.

7 Bring my soul out of prison,
That I may praise Your name;
The righteous shall surround me,
For You shall deal bountifully with me."

הַקְשִׁיבָה ׀ אֶל־רִנָּתִי֮ כִּי־דַלּ֢וֹתִ֫י מְאֹ֥ד 7
הַצִּילֵנִי מֵרֹדְפַ֑י
כִּ֖י אָמְצ֣וּ מִמֶּֽנִּי׃

ה֘וֹצִ֤יאָה מִמַּסְגֵּ֨ר ׀ נַפְשִׁי֮ לְהוֹד֢וֹת אֶת־שְׁ֫מֶ֥ךָ 8
בִּ֭י יַכְתִּ֣רוּ צַדִּיקִ֑ים
כִּ֖י תִגְמֹ֣ל עָלָֽי׃

143 A Psalm of David.
Hear my prayer, O LORD,
Give ear to my supplications!
In Your faithfulness answer me,
And in Your righteousness.

2 Do not enter into judgment with Your servant,
For in Your sight no one living is righteous.

3 For the enemy has persecuted my soul;
He has crushed my life to the ground;
He has made me dwell in darkness,
Like those who have long been dead.

4 Therefore my spirit is overwhelmed within me;
My heart within me is distressed.

5 I remember the days of old;
I meditate on all Your works;
I muse on the work of Your hands.

6 I spread out my hands to You;
My soul *longs* for You like a thirsty land.
                   Selah

7 Answer me speedily, O LORD;
My spirit fails!
Do not hide Your face from me,
Lest I be like those who go down into the pit.

8 Cause me to hear Your lovingkindness in the
     morning,
For in You do I trust;
Cause me to know the way in which I should
     walk,
For I lift up my soul to You.

9 Deliver me, O LORD, from my enemies;
In You I take shelter.

10 Teach me to do Your will,
For You *are* my God;
Your Spirit *is* good.
Lead me in the land of uprightness.

11 Revive me, O LORD, for Your name's sake!
For Your righteousness' sake bring my soul
     out of trouble.

12 In Your mercy cut off my enemies,
And destroy all those who afflict my soul;
For I *am* Your servant.

קָמֵג מִזְמ֗וֹר לְדָ֫וִ֥ד
יְהֹוָ֤ה ׀ שְׁמַ֬ע תְּפִלָּתִ֗י
הַאֲזִ֥ינָה אֶל־תַּחֲנוּנַ֑י
בֶּאֱמֻנָתְךָ֥ עֲ֝נֵ֗נִי בְּצִדְקָתֶֽךָ׃

וְאַל־תָּב֣וֹא בְ֭מִשְׁפָּט 2
אֶת־עַבְדֶּ֑ךָ
כִּ֤י לֹא־יִצְדַּ֖ק לְפָנֶ֣יךָ כׇל־חָֽי׃

כִּ֥י רָדַ֪ף אוֹיֵ֨ב ׀ נַפְשִׁ֗י 3
דִּכָּ֣א לָ֭אָרֶץ חַיָּתִ֑י
הוֹשִׁיבַ֥נִי בְ֝מַחֲשַׁכִּ֗ים כְּמֵתֵ֥י עוֹלָֽם׃

וַתִּתְעַטֵּ֣ף עָלַ֣י רוּחִ֑י 4
בְּ֝תוֹכִ֗י יִשְׁתּוֹמֵ֥ם לִבִּֽי׃

זָ֘כַ֤רְתִּי יָמִ֨ים ׀ מִקֶּ֗דֶם הָ֭גִיתִי בְכׇל־פׇּעֳלֶ֑ךָ 5
בְּֽמַעֲשֵׂ֖ה יָדֶ֣יךָ אֲשׂוֹחֵֽחַ׃

פֵּרַ֣שְׂתִּי יָדַ֣י אֵלֶ֑יךָ 6
נַ֝פְשִׁ֗י כְּאֶֽרֶץ־עֲיֵפָ֖ה לְךָ֣ סֶֽלָה׃

מַ֘הֵ֤ר עֲנֵ֨נִי ׀ יְהֹוָה֮ כָּלְתָ֢ה ר֫וּחִ֥י 7
אַל־תַּסְתֵּ֣ר פָּנֶ֣יךָ מִמֶּ֑נִּי
וְ֝נִמְשַׁ֗לְתִּי עִם־יֹ֥רְדֵי בֽוֹר׃

הַשְׁמִ֘יעֵ֤נִי בַבֹּ֨קֶר ׀ חַסְדֶּךָ֮ כִּֽי־בְךָ֢ בָ֫טָ֥חְתִּי 8
הוֹדִיעֵ֗נִי דֶּֽרֶךְ־ז֥וּ אֵלֵ֑ךְ
כִּֽי־אֵ֝לֶ֗יךָ נָשָׂ֥אתִי נַפְשִֽׁי׃

הַצִּילֵ֖נִי מֵאֹיְבַ֥י ׀ יְהֹוָ֗ה 9
אֵלֶ֥יךָ כִסִּֽתִי׃

לַמְּדֵ֨נִי ׀ לַ֥עֲשׂ֣וֹת רְצוֹנֶךָ֮ כִּֽי־אַתָּ֢ה אֱל֫וֹהָ֥י 10
רוּחֲךָ֥ טוֹבָ֑ה
תַּ֝נְחֵ֗נִי בְּאֶ֣רֶץ מִישֽׁוֹר׃

לְמַֽעַן־שִׁמְךָ֣ יְהֹוָ֣ה תְּחַיֵּ֑נִי 11
בְּצִדְקָתְךָ֓ ׀ תּוֹצִ֖יא מִצָּרָ֣ה נַפְשִֽׁי׃

וּֽבְחַסְדְּךָ֮ תַּצְמִ֢ית אֹ֫יְבָ֥י 12
וְֽ֭הַאֲבַדְתָּ כׇּל־צֹרְרֵ֣י נַפְשִׁ֑י כִּ֝֗י אֲנִ֣י עַבְדֶּֽךָ׃

144 A Psalm of David.
　　Blessed *be* the LORD my Rock,
　　Who trains my hands for war,
　　And my fingers for battle—

2　My lovingkindness and my fortress,
　　My high tower and my deliverer,
　　My shield and *the One* in whom I take refuge,
　　Who subdues my people under me.

3　LORD, what *is* man, that You take knowledge
　　　of him?
　　Or the son of man, that You are mindful of
　　　him?

4　Man is like a breath;
　　His days *are* like a passing shadow.

5　Bow down Your heavens, O LORD, and come
　　　down;
　　Touch the mountains, and they shall smoke.

6　Flash forth lightning and scatter them;
　　Shoot out Your arrows and destroy them.

7　Stretch out Your hand from above;
　　Rescue me and deliver me out of great waters,
　　From the hand of foreigners,

8　Whose mouth speaks lying words,
　　And whose right hand *is* a right hand of
　　　falsehood.

9　I will sing a new song to You, O God;
　　On a harp of ten strings I will sing praises to
　　　You,

10　*The One* who gives salvation to kings,
　　Who delivers David His servant
　　From the deadly sword.

11　Rescue me and deliver me from the hand of
　　　foreigners,
　　Whose mouth speaks lying words,
　　And whose right hand *is* a right hand of
　　　falsehood—

12　That our sons *may be* as plants grown up in
　　　their youth;
　　That our daughters *may be* as pillars,
　　Sculptured in palace style;

13　*That* our barns *may be* full,
　　Supplying all kinds of produce;
　　That our sheep may bring forth thousands
　　And ten thousands in our fields;

14　*That* our oxen *may be* well laden;
　　That there be no breaking in or going out;
　　That there be no outcry in our streets.

15　Happy *are* the people who are in such a state;
　　Happy *are* the people whose God *is* the LORD!

145 A Praise of David.
　　I will extol You, my God, O King;

קמד לְדָוִד ׀ בָּרוּךְ יְהֹוָה ׀ צוּרִי
הַמְלַמֵּד יָדַי לַקְרָב
אֶצְבְּעוֹתַי לַמִּלְחָמָה:
2 חַסְדִּי וּמְצוּדָתִי
מִשְׂגַּבִּי וּמְפַלְטִי לִי
מָגִנִּי וּבוֹ חָסִיתִי
הָרוֹדֵד עַמִּי תַחְתָּי:
3 יְהֹוָה מָה־אָדָם וַתֵּדָעֵהוּ
בֶּן־אֱנוֹשׁ וַתְּחַשְּׁבֵהוּ:
4 אָדָם לַהֶבֶל דָּמָה
יָמָיו כְּצֵל עוֹבֵר:
5 יְהֹוָה הַט־שָׁמֶיךָ וְתֵרֵד
גַּע בֶּהָרִים וְיֶעֱשָׁנוּ:
6 בְּרוֹק בָּרָק וּתְפִיצֵם
שְׁלַח חִצֶּיךָ וּתְהֻמֵּם:
7 שְׁלַח יָדֶיךָ מִמָּרוֹם
פְּצֵנִי וְהַצִּילֵנִי מִמַּיִם רַבִּים מִיַּד בְּנֵי נֵכָר:
8 אֲשֶׁר פִּיהֶם דִּבֶּר־שָׁוְא
וִימִינָם יְמִין שָׁקֶר:
9 אֱלֹהִים שִׁיר חָדָשׁ אָשִׁירָה לָּךְ
בְּנֵבֶל עָשׂוֹר אֲזַמְּרָה־לָּךְ:
10 הַנּוֹתֵן תְּשׁוּעָה לַמְּלָכִים
הַפּוֹצֶה אֶת־דָּוִד עַבְדּוֹ מֵחֶרֶב רָעָה:
11 פְּצֵנִי וְהַצִּילֵנִי
מִיַּד בְּנֵי־נֵכָר
אֲשֶׁר פִּיהֶם דִּבֶּר־שָׁוְא
וִימִינָם יְמִין שָׁקֶר:
12 אֲשֶׁר בָּנֵינוּ ׀ כִּנְטִעִים
מְגֻדָּלִים בִּנְעוּרֵיהֶם
בְּנוֹתֵינוּ כְזָוִיֹּת
מְחֻטָּבוֹת תַּבְנִית הֵיכָל:
13 מְזָוֵינוּ מְלֵאִים
מְפִיקִים מִזַּן אֶל־זַן
צֹאונֵנוּ מַאֲלִיפוֹת מְרֻבָּבוֹת
בְּחוּצוֹתֵינוּ:
14 אַלּוּפֵינוּ מְסֻבָּלִים
אֵין־פֶּרֶץ וְאֵין יוֹצֵאת וְאֵין צְוָחָה בִּרְחֹבֹתֵינוּ:
15 אַשְׁרֵי הָעָם שֶׁכָּכָה לּוֹ
אַשְׁרֵי הָעָם שֶׁיְהֹוָה אֱלֹהָיו:

קמה תְּהִלָּה לְדָוִד
אֲרוֹמִמְךָ אֱלוֹהַי הַמֶּלֶךְ

And I will bless Your name forever and ever.

2 Every day I will bless You,
And I will praise Your name forever and ever.

3 Great *is* the LORD, and greatly to be praised;
And His greatness *is* unsearchable.

4 One generation shall praise Your works to another,
And shall declare Your mighty acts.

5 I will meditate on the glorious splendor of Your majesty,
And on Your wondrous works.

6 *Men* shall speak of the might of Your awesome acts,
And I will declare Your greatness.

7 They shall utter the memory of Your great goodness,
And shall sing of Your righteousness.

8 The LORD *is* gracious and full of compassion,
Slow to anger and great in mercy.

9 The LORD *is* good to all,
And His tender mercies *are* over all His works.

10 All Your works shall praise You, O LORD,
And Your saints shall bless You.

11 They shall speak of the glory of Your kingdom,
And talk of Your power,

12 To make known to the sons of men His mighty acts,
And the glorious majesty of His kingdom.

13 Your kingdom *is* an everlasting kingdom,
And Your dominion *endures* throughout all generations.

14 The LORD upholds all who fall,
And raises up all *who are* bowed down.

15 The eyes of all look expectantly to You,
And You give them their food in due season.

16 You open Your hand
And satisfy the desire of every living thing.

17 The LORD *is* righteous in all His ways,
Gracious in all His works.

18 The LORD *is* near to all who call upon Him,
To all who call upon Him in truth.

19 He will fulfill the desire of those who fear Him;
He also will hear their cry and save them.

20 The LORD preserves all who love Him,
But all the wicked He will destroy.

21 My mouth shall speak the praise of the LORD,
And all flesh shall bless His holy name
Forever and ever.

146 Praise the LORD!

Praise the LORD, O my soul!

2 While I live I will praise the LORD;

וַאֲבָרֲכָה שִׁמְךָ לְעוֹלָם וָעֶד׃

2 בְּכָל־יוֹם אֲבָרֲכֶךָּ
וַאֲהַלֲלָה שִׁמְךָ לְעוֹלָם וָעֶד׃

3 גָּדוֹל יְהוָה וּמְהֻלָּל מְאֹד
וְלִגְדֻלָּתוֹ אֵין חֵקֶר׃

4 דּוֹר לְדוֹר יְשַׁבַּח מַעֲשֶׂיךָ
וּגְבוּרֹתֶיךָ יַגִּידוּ׃

5 הֲדַר כְּבוֹד הוֹדֶךָ
וְדִבְרֵי נִפְלְאֹתֶיךָ אָשִׂיחָה׃

6 וֶעֱזוּז נוֹרְאֹתֶיךָ יֹאמֵרוּ וּגְדוּלָּתְךָ ק אֲסַפְּרֶנָּה׃

7 זֵכֶר רַב־טוּבְךָ יַבִּיעוּ וְצִדְקָתְךָ יְרַנֵּנוּ׃

8 חַנּוּן וְרַחוּם יְהוָה
אֶרֶךְ אַפַּיִם וּגְדָל־חָסֶד׃

9 טוֹב־יְהוָה לַכֹּל
וְרַחֲמָיו עַל־כָּל־מַעֲשָׂיו׃

10 יוֹדוּךָ יְהוָה כָּל־מַעֲשֶׂיךָ
וַחֲסִידֶיךָ יְבָרֲכוּכָה׃

11 כְּבוֹד מַלְכוּתְךָ יֹאמֵרוּ
וּגְבוּרָתְךָ יְדַבֵּרוּ׃

12 לְהוֹדִיעַ לִבְנֵי הָאָדָם גְּבוּרֹתָיו
וּכְבוֹד הֲדַר מַלְכוּתוֹ׃

13 מַלְכוּתְךָ מַלְכוּת כָּל־עֹלָמִים
וּמֶמְשֶׁלְתְּךָ בְּכָל־דּוֹר וָדֹר׃

14 סוֹמֵךְ יְהוָה לְכָל־הַנֹּפְלִים
וְזוֹקֵף לְכָל־הַכְּפוּפִים׃

15 עֵינֵי־כֹל אֵלֶיךָ יְשַׂבֵּרוּ
וְאַתָּה נוֹתֵן־לָהֶם אֶת־אָכְלָם בְּעִתּוֹ׃

16 פּוֹתֵחַ אֶת־יָדֶךָ
וּמַשְׂבִּיעַ לְכָל־חַי רָצוֹן׃

17 צַדִּיק יְהוָה בְּכָל־דְּרָכָיו
וְחָסִיד בְּכָל־מַעֲשָׂיו׃

18 קָרוֹב יְהוָה לְכָל־קֹרְאָיו
לְכֹל אֲשֶׁר יִקְרָאֻהוּ בֶאֱמֶת׃

19 רְצוֹן־יְרֵאָיו יַעֲשֶׂה
וְאֶת־שַׁוְעָתָם יִשְׁמַע וְיוֹשִׁיעֵם׃

20 שׁוֹמֵר יְהוָה אֶת־כָּל־אֹהֲבָיו
וְאֵת כָּל־הָרְשָׁעִים יַשְׁמִיד׃

21 תְּהִלַּת יְהוָה יְדַבֶּר־פִּי
וִיבָרֵךְ כָּל־בָּשָׂר שֵׁם קָדְשׁוֹ לְעוֹלָם וָעֶד׃

קמו הַלְלוּ־יָהּ הַלְלִי נַפְשִׁי אֶת־יְהוָה׃

2 אֲהַלֲלָה יְהוָה בְּחַיָּי

I will sing praises to my God while I have my being.

3 Do not put your trust in princes,
Nor in a son of man, in whom *there is* no help.

4 His spirit departs, he returns to his earth;
In that very day his plans perish.

5 Happy *is* he who *has* the God of Jacob for his help,
Whose hope *is* in the LORD his God,

6 Who made heaven and earth,
The sea, and all that *is* in them;
Who keeps truth forever,

7 Who executes justice for the oppressed,
Who gives food to the hungry.
The LORD gives freedom to the prisoners.

8 The LORD opens *the eyes of* the blind;
The LORD raises those who are bowed down;
The LORD loves the righteous.

9 The LORD watches over the strangers;
He relieves the fatherless and widow;
But the way of the wicked He turns upside down.

10 The LORD shall reign forever—
Your God, O Zion, to all generations.

Praise the LORD!

147 Praise the LORD!
For *it is* good to sing praises to our God;
For *it is* pleasant, *and* praise is beautiful.

2 The LORD builds up Jerusalem;
He gathers together the outcasts of Israel.

3 He heals the brokenhearted
And binds up their wounds.

4 He counts the number of the stars;
He calls them all by name.

5 Great *is* our Lord, and mighty in power;
His understanding *is* infinite.

6 The LORD lifts up the humble;
He casts the wicked down to the ground.

7 Sing to the LORD with thanksgiving;
Sing praises on the harp to our God,

8 Who covers the heavens with clouds,
Who prepares rain for the earth,
Who makes grass to grow on the mountains.

9 He gives to the beast its food,
And to the young ravens that cry.

10 He does not delight in the strength of the horse;
He takes no pleasure in the legs of a man.

11 The LORD takes pleasure in those who fear Him,

אֲזַמְּרָה לֵאלֹהַי בְּעוֹדִי:

3 אַל־תִּבְטְחוּ בִנְדִיבִים
בְּבֶן־אָדָם ׀ שֶׁאֵין לוֹ תְשׁוּעָה:

4 תֵּצֵא רוּחוֹ יָשֻׁב לְאַדְמָתוֹ
בַּיּוֹם הַהוּא אָבְדוּ עֶשְׁתֹּנֹתָיו:

5 אַשְׁרֵי שֶׁאֵל יַעֲקֹב בְּעֶזְרוֹ
שִׂבְרוֹ עַל־יְהוָה אֱלֹהָיו:

6 עֹשֶׂה ׀ שָׁמַיִם וָאָרֶץ
אֶת־הַיָּם וְאֶת־כָּל־אֲשֶׁר־בָּם
הַשֹּׁמֵר אֱמֶת לְעוֹלָם:

7 עֹשֶׂה מִשְׁפָּט ׀ לָעֲשׁוּקִים נֹתֵן לֶחֶם לָרְעֵבִים
יְהוָה מַתִּיר אֲסוּרִים:

8 יְהוָה ׀ פֹּקֵחַ עִוְרִים יְהוָה זֹקֵף כְּפוּפִים
יְהוָה אֹהֵב צַדִּיקִים:

9 יְהוָה ׀ שֹׁמֵר אֶת־גֵּרִים יָתוֹם וְאַלְמָנָה יְעוֹדֵד
וְדֶרֶךְ רְשָׁעִים יְעַוֵּת:

10 יִמְלֹךְ יְהוָה ׀ לְעוֹלָם
אֱלֹהַיִךְ צִיּוֹן לְדֹר וָדֹר
הַלְלוּ־יָהּ:

קמז הַלְלוּ יָהּ ׀ כִּי־טוֹב זַמְּרָה אֱלֹהֵינוּ
כִּי־נָעִים נָאוָה תְהִלָּה:

2 בּוֹנֵה יְרוּשָׁלִַם יְהוָה
נִדְחֵי יִשְׂרָאֵל יְכַנֵּס:

3 הָרֹפֵא לִשְׁבוּרֵי לֵב
וּמְחַבֵּשׁ לְעַצְּבוֹתָם:

4 מוֹנֶה מִסְפָּר לַכּוֹכָבִים
לְכֻלָּם שֵׁמוֹת יִקְרָא:

5 גָּדוֹל אֲדוֹנֵינוּ וְרַב־כֹּחַ
לִתְבוּנָתוֹ אֵין מִסְפָּר:

6 מְעוֹדֵד עֲנָוִים יְהוָה
מַשְׁפִּיל רְשָׁעִים עֲדֵי־אָרֶץ:

7 עֱנוּ לַיהוָה בְּתוֹדָה
זַמְּרוּ לֵאלֹהֵינוּ בְכִנּוֹר:

8 הַמְכַסֶּה שָׁמַיִם ׀ בְּעָבִים
הַמֵּכִין לָאָרֶץ מָטָר
הַמַּצְמִיחַ הָרִים חָצִיר:

9 נוֹתֵן לִבְהֵמָה לַחְמָהּ
לִבְנֵי עֹרֵב אֲשֶׁר יִקְרָאוּ:

10 לֹא בִגְבוּרַת הַסּוּס יֶחְפָּץ
לֹא־בְשׁוֹקֵי הָאִישׁ יִרְצֶה:

11 רוֹצֶה יְהוָה אֶת־יְרֵאָיו

In those who hope in His mercy.　　אֶת־הַֽמְיַחֲלִ֥ים לְחַסְדּֽוֹ׃

12　Praise the LORD, O Jerusalem!
　　Praise your God, O Zion!　　שַׁבְּחִ֣י יְ֭רוּשָׁלִַם אֶת־יְהֹוָ֑ה　12
　　הַֽלְלִ֖י אֱלֹהַ֣יִךְ צִיּֽוֹן׃

13　For He has strengthened the bars of your gates;
　　He has blessed your children within you.　　כִּֽי־חִ֭זַּק בְּרִיחֵ֣י שְׁעָרָ֑יִךְ　13
　　בֵּרַ֖ךְ בָּנַ֣יִךְ בְּקִרְבֵּֽךְ׃

14　He makes peace in your borders,
　　And fills you with the finest wheat.　　הַשָּׂם־גְּבוּלֵ֥ךְ שָׁל֑וֹם　14
　　חֵ֥לֶב חִ֝טִּ֗ים יַשְׂבִּיעֵֽךְ׃

15　He sends out His command to the earth;
　　His word runs very swiftly.　　הַשֹּׁלֵ֣חַ אִמְרָת֣וֹ אָ֑רֶץ　15
　　עַד־מְ֝הֵרָ֗ה יָר֥וּץ דְּבָרֽוֹ׃

16　He gives snow like wool;
　　He scatters the frost like ashes;　　הַנֹּתֵ֣ן שֶׁ֣לֶג כַּצָּ֑מֶר　16
　　כְּ֝פ֗וֹר כָּאֵ֥פֶר יְפַזֵּֽר׃

17　He casts out His hail like morsels;
　　Who can stand before His cold?　　מַשְׁלִ֣יךְ קַֽרְח֣וֹ כְפִתִּ֑ים　17
　　לִפְנֵ֥י קָ֝רָת֗וֹ מִ֣י יַעֲמֹֽד׃

18　He sends out His word and melts them;
　　He causes His wind to blow, and the waters
　　　flow.　　יִשְׁלַ֣ח דְּבָר֣וֹ וְיַמְסֵ֑ם　18
　　יַשֵּׁ֥ב ר֝וּח֗וֹ יִזְּלוּ־מָֽיִם׃

19　He declares His word to Jacob,
　　His statutes and His judgments to Israel.　　מַגִּ֣יד דְּבָרָ֣ו לְיַעֲקֹ֑ב　19
　　חֻקָּ֥יו וּ֝מִשְׁפָּטָ֗יו לְיִשְׂרָאֵֽל׃

20　He has not dealt thus with any nation;
　　And as for His judgments, they have not
　　　known them.　　לֹ֘א עָ֤שָׂה כֵ֨ן ׀ לְכׇל־גּ֗וֹי　20
　　וּמִשְׁפָּטִ֥ים בַּל־יְ֝דָע֗וּם הַֽלְלוּ־יָֽהּ׃

　　Praise the LORD!

148
Praise the LORD!
Praise the LORD from the heavens;
Praise Him in the heights!

2　Praise Him, all His angels;
　　Praise Him, all His hosts!

3　Praise Him, sun and moon;
　　Praise Him, all you stars of light!

4　Praise Him, you heavens of heavens,
　　And you waters above the heavens!

5　Let them praise the name of the LORD,
　　For He commanded and they were created.

6　He also established them forever and ever;
　　He made a decree which shall not pass away.

7　Praise the LORD from the earth,
　　You great sea creatures and all the depths;

8　Fire and hail, snow and clouds;
　　Stormy wind, fulfilling His word;

9　Mountains and all hills;
　　Fruitful trees and all cedars;

10　Beasts and all cattle;
　　Creeping things and flying fowl;

11　Kings of the earth and all peoples;
　　Princes and all judges of the earth;

12　Both young men and maidens;
　　Old men and children.

13　Let them praise the name of the LORD,
　　For His name alone is exalted;
　　His glory is above the earth and heaven.

קמח
הַ֥לְלוּ יָ֨הּ ׀ הַֽלְל֣וּ אֶת־יְ֭הֹוָה מִן־הַשָּׁמַ֑יִם
הַֽ֝לְל֗וּהוּ בַּמְּרוֹמִֽים׃

הַֽלְל֣וּהוּ כׇל־מַלְאָכָ֑יו הַֽ֝לְל֗וּהוּ כׇּל־צְבָאָֽו׃　2

הַֽלְל֣וּהוּ שֶׁ֣מֶשׁ וְיָרֵ֑חַ　3
הַֽ֝לְל֗וּהוּ כׇּל־כּ֥וֹכְבֵי אֽוֹר׃

הַֽ֭לְלוּהוּ שְׁמֵ֣י הַשָּׁמָ֑יִם　4
וְ֝הַמַּ֗יִם אֲשֶׁ֤ר ׀ מֵעַ֬ל הַשָּׁמָֽיִם׃

יְֽ֭הַלְלוּ אֶת־שֵׁ֣ם יְהֹוָ֑ה כִּ֤י ה֭וּא צִוָּ֣ה וְנִבְרָֽאוּ׃　5

וַיַּעֲמִידֵ֣ם לָעַ֣ד לְעוֹלָ֑ם　6
חׇק־נָ֝תַ֗ן וְלֹ֣א יַעֲבֽוֹר׃

הַֽלְל֣וּ אֶת־יְ֭הֹוָה מִן־הָאָ֑רֶץ　7
תַּ֝נִּינִ֗ים וְכׇל־תְּהֹמֽוֹת׃

אֵ֣שׁ וּ֭בָרָד שֶׁ֣לֶג וְקִיט֑וֹר　8
ר֥וּחַ סְ֝עָרָ֗ה עֹשָׂ֥ה דְבָרֽוֹ׃

הֶהָרִ֥ים וְכׇל־גְּבָע֑וֹת עֵ֥ץ פְּ֝רִ֗י וְכׇל־אֲרָזִֽים׃　9

הַֽחַיָּ֥ה וְכׇל־בְּהֵמָ֑ה　10
רֶ֝֗מֶשׂ וְצִפּ֥וֹר כָּנָֽף׃

מַלְכֵי־אֶ֭רֶץ וְכׇל־לְאֻמִּ֑ים　11
שָׂ֝רִ֗ים וְכׇל־שֹׁ֥פְטֵי אָֽרֶץ׃

בַּחוּרִ֥ים וְגַם־בְּתוּל֑וֹת　12
זְ֝קֵנִ֗ים עִם־נְעָרִֽים׃

יְהַלְל֤וּ ׀ אֶת־שֵׁ֬ם יְהֹוָ֗ה כִּֽי־נִשְׂגָּ֣ב שְׁמ֣וֹ לְבַדּ֑וֹ　13
ה֝וֹד֗וֹ עַל־אֶ֥רֶץ וְשָׁמָֽיִם׃

14 And He has exalted the horn of His people,
The praise of all His saints—
Of the children of Israel,
A people near to Him.
Praise the LORD!

14 וַיָּרֶם קֶרֶן ׀ לְעַמּוֹ תְּהִלָּה לְכָל־חֲסִידָיו
לִבְנֵי יִשְׂרָאֵל עַם־קְרֹבוֹ
הַלְלוּ־יָהּ:

קמט הַלְלוּ יָהּ ׀

149 Praise the LORD!
Sing to the LORD a new song,
And His praise in the assembly of saints.

שִׁירוּ לַיהוָה שִׁיר חָדָשׁ
תְּהִלָּתוֹ בִּקְהַל חֲסִידִים:

2 Let Israel rejoice in their Maker;
Let the children of Zion be joyful in their King.

2 יִשְׂמַח יִשְׂרָאֵל בְּעֹשָׂיו
בְּנֵי־צִיּוֹן יָגִילוּ בְמַלְכָּם:

3 Let them praise His name with the dance;
Let them sing praises to Him with the timbrel
and harp.

3 יְהַלְלוּ שְׁמוֹ בְמָחוֹל
בְּתֹף וְכִנּוֹר יְזַמְּרוּ־לוֹ:

4 For the LORD takes pleasure in His people;
He will beautify the humble with salvation.

4 כִּי־רוֹצֶה יְהוָה בְּעַמּוֹ
יְפָאֵר עֲנָוִים בִּישׁוּעָה:

5 Let the saints be joyful in glory;
Let them sing aloud on their beds.

5 יַעְלְזוּ חֲסִידִים בְּכָבוֹד
יְרַנְּנוּ עַל־מִשְׁכְּבוֹתָם:

6 *Let* the high praises of God *be* in their mouth,
And a two-edged sword in their hand,

6 רוֹמְמוֹת אֵל בִּגְרוֹנָם
וְחֶרֶב פִּיפִיּוֹת בְּיָדָם:

7 To execute vengeance on the nations,
And punishments on the peoples;

7 לַעֲשׂוֹת נְקָמָה בַּגּוֹיִם
תּוֹכֵחֹת בַּל־אֻמִּים:

8 To bind their kings with chains,
And their nobles with fetters of iron;

8 לֶאְסֹר מַלְכֵיהֶם בְּזִקִּים
וְנִכְבְּדֵיהֶם בְּכַבְלֵי בַרְזֶל:

9 To execute on them the written judgment—
This honor have all His saints.

9 לַעֲשׂוֹת בָּהֶם ׀ מִשְׁפָּט כָּתוּב
הָדָר הוּא לְכָל־חֲסִידָיו

Praise the LORD!

הַלְלוּ־יָהּ:

קן הַלְלוּ יָהּ ׀

150 Praise the LORD!
Praise God in His sanctuary;
Praise Him in His mighty firmament!

הַלְלוּ־אֵל בְּקָדְשׁוֹ
הַלְלוּהוּ בִּרְקִיעַ עֻזּוֹ:

2 Praise Him for His mighty acts;
Praise Him according to His excellent
greatness!

2 הַלְלוּהוּ בִגְבוּרֹתָיו
הַלְלוּהוּ כְּרֹב גֻּדְלוֹ:

3 Praise Him with the sound of the trumpet;
Praise Him with the lute and harp!

3 הַלְלוּהוּ בְּתֵקַע שׁוֹפָר
הַלְלוּהוּ בְּנֵבֶל וְכִנּוֹר:

4 Praise Him with the timbrel and dance;
Praise Him with stringed instruments and
flutes!

4 הַלְלוּהוּ בְתֹף וּמָחוֹל
הַלְלוּהוּ בְּמִנִּים וְעוּגָב:

5 Praise Him with loud cymbals;
Praise Him with clashing cymbals!

5 הַלְלוּהוּ בְצִלְצְלֵי־שָׁמַע
הַלְלוּהוּ בְּצִלְצְלֵי תְרוּעָה:

6 Let everything that has breath praise the LORD.

6 כֹּל הַנְּשָׁמָה תְּהַלֵּל יָהּ
הַלְלוּ־יָהּ:

Praise the LORD!

The Book of

PROVERBS

מִשְׁלֵי

1 The proverbs of Solomon the son of David, king of Israel:

2 To know wisdom and instruction,
To perceive the words of understanding,
3 To receive the instruction of wisdom,
Justice, judgment, and equity;
4 To give prudence to the simple,
To the young man knowledge and discretion—
5 A wise *man* will hear and increase learning,
And a man of understanding will attain wise counsel,
6 To understand a proverb and an enigma,
The words of the wise and their riddles.

7 The fear of the LORD *is* the beginning of knowledge,
But fools despise wisdom and instruction.

8 My son, hear the instruction of your father,
And do not forsake the law of your mother;
9 For they *will be* a graceful ornament on your head,
And chains about your neck.

10 My son, if sinners entice you,
Do not consent.
11 If they say, "Come with us,
Let us lie in wait to *shed* blood;
Let us lurk secretly for the innocent without cause;
12 Let us swallow them alive like Sheol,
And whole, like those who go down to the Pit;
13 We shall find all *kinds* of precious possessions,
We shall fill our houses with spoil;
14 Cast in your lot among us,
Let us all have one purse"—
15 My son, do not walk in the way with them,
Keep your foot from their path;
16 For their feet run to evil,
And they make haste to shed blood.
17 Surely, in vain the net is spread
In the sight of any bird;
18 But they lie in wait for their *own* blood,
They lurk secretly for their *own* lives.

א מִשְׁלֵי שְׁלֹמֹה בֶן־דָּוִד מֶלֶךְ יִשְׂרָאֵל:
2 לָדַעַת חָכְמָה וּמוּסָר
לְהָבִין אִמְרֵי בִינָה:
3 לָקַחַת מוּסַר הַשְׂכֵּל
צֶדֶק וּמִשְׁפָּט וּמֵישָׁרִים:
4 לָתֵת לִפְתָאיִם עָרְמָה
לְנַעַר דַּעַת וּמְזִמָּה:
5 יִשְׁמַע חָכָם וְיוֹסֶף לֶקַח
וְנָבוֹן תַּחְבֻּלוֹת יִקְנֶה:
6 לְהָבִין מָשָׁל וּמְלִיצָה
דִּבְרֵי חֲכָמִים וְחִידֹתָם:
7 יִרְאַת יְהֹוָה רֵאשִׁית דָּעַת
פ חָכְמָה וּמוּסָר אֱוִילִים בָּזוּ:
8 שְׁמַע בְּנִי מוּסַר אָבִיךָ
וְאַל־תִּטֹּשׁ תּוֹרַת אִמֶּךָ:
9 כִּי | לִוְיַת חֵן הֵם לְרֹאשֶׁךָ
וַעֲנָקִים לְגַרְגְּרֹתֶיךָ:
10 בְּנִי אִם־יְפַתּוּךָ חַטָּאִים אַל־תֹּבֵא:
11 אִם־יֹאמְרוּ
לְכָה אִתָּנוּ
נֶאֶרְבָה לְדָם
נִצְפְּנָה לְנָקִי חִנָּם:
12 נִבְלָעֵם כִּשְׁאוֹל חַיִּים
וּתְמִימִים כְּיוֹרְדֵי בוֹר:
13 כָּל־הוֹן יָקָר נִמְצָא
נְמַלֵּא בָתֵּינוּ שָׁלָל:
14 גּוֹרָלְךָ תַּפִּיל בְּתוֹכֵנוּ
כִּיס אֶחָד יִהְיֶה לְכֻלָּנוּ:
15 בְּנִי אַל־תֵּלֵךְ בְּדֶרֶךְ אִתָּם
מְנַע רַגְלְךָ מִנְּתִיבָתָם:
16 כִּי רַגְלֵיהֶם לָרַע יָרוּצוּ
וִימַהֲרוּ לִשְׁפָּךְ־דָּם:
17 כִּי־חִנָּם מְזֹרָה הָרָשֶׁת
בְּעֵינֵי כָל־בַּעַל כָּנָף:
18 וְהֵם לְדָמָם יֶאֱרֹבוּ
יִצְפְּנוּ לְנַפְשֹׁתָם:

¹⁹ So *are* the ways of everyone who is greedy for gain;
It takes away the life of its owners.

²⁰ Wisdom calls aloud outside;
She raises her voice in the open squares.

²¹ She cries out in the chief concourses,
At the openings of the gates in the city
She speaks her words:

²² "How long, you simple ones, will you love simplicity?
For scorners delight in their scorning,
And fools hate knowledge.

²³ Turn at my rebuke;
Surely I will pour out my spirit on you;
I will make my words known to you.

²⁴ Because I have called and you refused,
I have stretched out my hand and no one regarded,

²⁵ Because you disdained all my counsel,
And would have none of my rebuke,

²⁶ I also will laugh at your calamity;
I will mock when your terror comes,

²⁷ When your terror comes like a storm,
And your destruction comes like a whirlwind,
When distress and anguish come upon you.

²⁸ "Then they will call on me, but I will not answer;
They will seek me diligently, but they will not find me.

²⁹ Because they hated knowledge
And did not choose the fear of the LORD,

³⁰ They would have none of my counsel
And despised my every rebuke.

³¹ Therefore they shall eat the fruit of their own way,
And be filled to the full with their own fancies.

³² For the turning away of the simple will slay them,
And the complacency of fools will destroy them;

³³ But whoever listens to me will dwell safely,
And will be secure, without fear of evil."

2 My son, if you receive my words,
And treasure my commands within you,

² So that you incline your ear to wisdom,
And apply your heart to understanding;

³ Yes, if you cry out for discernment,
And lift up your voice for understanding,

⁴ If you seek her as silver,
And search for her as *for* hidden treasures;

---

19 כֵּ֗ן אָ֭רְחוֹת כָּל־בֹּ֣צֵֽעַ בָּ֑צַע
אֶת־נֶ֖פֶשׁ בְּעָלָ֣יו יִקָּֽח׃   פ

20 חָ֭כְמוֹת בַּח֣וּץ תָּרֹ֑נָּה
בָּ֝רְחֹב֗וֹת תִּתֵּ֥ן קוֹלָֽהּ׃

21 בְּרֹ֥אשׁ הֹמִיּ֗וֹת תִּ֫קְרָ֥א
בְּפִתְחֵ֖י שְׁעָרִ֥ים בָּעִ֗יר אֲמָרֶ֥יהָ תֹאמֵֽר׃

22 עַד־מָתַ֣י ׀ פְּתָיִם֮ תְּֽאֵהֲב֫וּ פֶ֥תִי
וְלֵצִ֗ים לָ֭צוֹן חָמְד֣וּ לָהֶ֑ם
וּ֝כְסִילִ֗ים יִשְׂנְאוּ־דָֽעַת׃

23 תָּשׁ֗וּבוּ לְֽתוֹכַ֫חְתִּ֥י
הִנֵּ֤ה אַבִּ֣יעָה לָכֶ֣ם רוּחִ֑י אוֹדִ֖יעָה דְבָרַ֣י אֶתְכֶֽם׃

24 יַ֣עַן קָ֭רָאתִי וַתְּמָאֵ֑נוּ
נָטִ֥יתִי יָ֝דִ֗י וְאֵ֣ין מַקְשִֽׁיב׃

25 וַתִּפְרְע֥וּ כָל־עֲצָתִ֑י
וְ֝תוֹכַחְתִּ֗י לֹ֣א אֲבִיתֶֽם׃

26 גַּם־אֲ֭נִי בְּאֵידְכֶ֣ם אֶשְׂחָ֑ק
אֶ֝לְעַ֗ג בְּבֹ֣א פַחְדְּכֶֽם׃

27 בְּבֹ֤א כְשַׁאֲוָ֨ה ׀ פַּחְדְּכֶ֗ם
וְֽאֵידְכֶ֗ם כְּסוּפָ֥ה יֶאֱתֶ֑ה
בְּבֹ֥א עֲלֵיכֶ֗ם צָרָ֥ה וְצוּקָֽה׃

28 אָ֣ז יִ֭קְרָאֻנְנִי וְלֹ֣א אֶֽעֱנֶ֑ה
יְ֝שַׁחֲרֻ֗נְנִי וְלֹ֣א יִמְצָאֻֽנְנִי׃

29 תַּ֭חַת כִּי־שָׂ֣נְאוּ דָ֑עַת
וְיִרְאַ֥ת יְ֝הֹוָ֗ה לֹ֣א בָחָֽרוּ׃

30 לֹא־אָב֥וּ לַעֲצָתִ֑י
נָ֝אֲצ֗וּ כָּל־תּוֹכַחְתִּֽי׃

31 וְֽ֭יֹאכְלוּ מִפְּרִ֣י דַרְכָּ֑ם
וּֽמִמֹּעֲצֹ֖תֵיהֶ֣ם יִשְׂבָּֽעוּ׃

32 כִּ֤י מְשׁוּבַ֣ת פְּתָיִ֣ם תַּֽהַרְגֵ֑ם
וְשַׁלְוַ֖ת כְּסִילִ֣ים תְּאַבְּדֵֽם׃

33 וְשֹׁמֵ֣עַֽ לִ֭י יִשְׁכָּן־בֶּ֑טַח
וְ֝שַׁאֲנַ֗ן מִפַּ֥חַד רָעָֽה׃   פ

ב בְּ֭נִי אִם־תִּקַּ֣ח אֲמָרָ֑י
וּ֝מִצְוֺתַ֗י תִּצְפֹּ֥ן אִתָּֽךְ׃

2 לְהַקְשִׁ֣יב לַֽחָכְמָ֣ה אָזְנֶ֑ךָ
תַּטֶּ֥ה לִ֝בְּךָ֗ לַתְּבוּנָֽה׃

3 כִּ֤י אִ֣ם לַבִּינָ֣ה תִקְרָ֑א
לַ֝תְּבוּנָ֗ה תִּתֵּ֥ן קוֹלֶֽךָ׃

4 אִם־תְּבַקְשֶׁ֥נָּה כַכָּ֑סֶף
וְֽכַמַּטְמוֹנִ֥ים תַּחְפְּשֶֽׂנָּה׃

א 27 כְשׁוֹאָה

⁵ Then you will understand the fear of the
    LORD,
    And find the knowledge of God.
⁶ For the LORD gives wisdom;
    From His mouth *come* knowledge and
    understanding;
⁷ He stores up sound wisdom for the upright;
    He is a shield to those who walk uprightly;
⁸ He guards the paths of justice,
    And preserves the way of His saints.
⁹ Then you will understand righteousness and
    justice,
    Equity *and* every good path.

¹⁰ When wisdom enters your heart,
    And knowledge is pleasant to your soul,
¹¹ Discretion will preserve you;
    Understanding will keep you,
¹² To deliver you from the way of evil,
    From the man who speaks perverse things,
¹³ From those who leave the paths of upright-
    ness
    To walk in the ways of darkness;
¹⁴ Who rejoice in doing evil,
    And delight in the perversity of the wicked;
¹⁵ Whose ways *are* crooked,
    And *who are* devious in their paths;
¹⁶ To deliver you from the immoral woman,
    From the seductress *who* flatters with her
    words,
¹⁷ Who forsakes the companion of her youth,
    And forgets the covenant of her God.
¹⁸ For her house leads down to death,
    And her paths to the dead;
¹⁹ None who go to her return,
    Nor do they regain the paths of life—
²⁰ So you may walk in the way of goodness,
    And keep *to* the paths of righteousness.
²¹ For the upright will dwell in the land,
    And the blameless will remain in it;
²² But the wicked will be cut off from the earth,
    And the unfaithful will be uprooted from it.

3 My son, do not forget my law,
    But let your heart keep my commands;
² For length of days and long life
    And peace they will add to you.

³ Let not mercy and truth forsake you;
    Bind them around your neck,
    Write them on the tablet of your heart,
⁴ *And* so find favor and high esteem
    In the sight of God and man.

⁵ Trust in the LORD with all your heart,

5 אָז תָּבִין יִרְאַת יְהֹוָה
וְדַעַת אֱלֹהִים תִּמְצָא:
6 כִּי־יְהֹוָה יִתֵּן חָכְמָה
מִפִּיו דַּעַת וּתְבוּנָה:
7 וְצָפַ֣ן לַיְשָׁרִים תּוּשִׁיָּה
מָגֵן לְהֹלְכֵי תֹם:
8 לִנְצֹר אָרְחוֹת מִשְׁפָּט
וְדֶרֶךְ חֲסִידָו יִשְׁמֹר:
9 אָז תָּבִין צֶדֶק וּמִשְׁפָּט
וּמֵישָׁרִים כָּל־מַעְגַּל־טוֹב:
10 כִּי־תָבוֹא חָכְמָה בְלִבֶּךָ
וְדַעַת לְנַפְשְׁךָ יִנְעָם:
11 מְזִמָּה תִּשְׁמֹר עָלֶיךָ תְּבוּנָה תִנְצְרֶכָּה:
12 לְהַצִּילְךָ מִדֶּרֶךְ רָע
מֵאִישׁ מְדַבֵּר תַּהְפֻּכוֹת:
13 הַעֹזְבִים אָרְחוֹת יֹשֶׁר
לָלֶכֶת בְּדַרְכֵי־חֹשֶׁךְ:
14 הַשְּׂמֵחִים לַעֲשׂוֹת רָע
יָגִילוּ בְּתַהְפֻּכוֹת רָע:
15 אֲשֶׁר אָרְחֹתֵיהֶם עִקְּשִׁים
וּנְלוֹזִים בְּמַעְגְּלוֹתָם:
16 לְהַצִּילְךָ מֵאִשָּׁה זָרָה
מִנָּכְרִיָּה אֲמָרֶיהָ הֶחֱלִיקָה:
17 הַעֹזֶבֶת אַלּוּף נְעוּרֶיהָ
וְאֶת־בְּרִית אֱלֹהֶיהָ שָׁכֵחָה:
18 כִּי שָׁחָה אֶל־מָוֶת בֵּיתָהּ
וְאֶל־רְפָאִים מַעְגְּלֹתֶיהָ:
19 כָּל־בָּאֶיהָ לֹא יְשׁוּבוּן
וְלֹא־יַשִּׂיגוּ אָרְחוֹת חַיִּים:
20 לְמַעַן תֵּלֵךְ בְּדֶרֶךְ טוֹבִים
וְאָרְחוֹת צַדִּיקִים תִּשְׁמֹר:
21 כִּי־יְשָׁרִים יִשְׁכְּנוּ־אָרֶץ
וּתְמִימִים יִוָּתְרוּ בָהּ:
22 וּרְשָׁעִים מֵאֶרֶץ יִכָּרֵתוּ
וּבוֹגְדִים יִסְּחוּ מִמֶּנָּה: פ

ג בְּנִי תּוֹרָתִי אַל־תִּשְׁכָּח וּמִצְוֹתַי יִצֹּר לִבֶּךָ:
2 כִּי אֹרֶךְ יָמִים וּשְׁנוֹת חַיִּים
וְשָׁלוֹם יוֹסִיפוּ לָךְ:
3 חֶסֶד וֶאֱמֶת אַל־יַעַזְבֻךָ
קָשְׁרֵם עַל־גַּרְגְּרוֹתֶיךָ
כָּתְבֵם עַל־לוּחַ לִבֶּךָ:
4 וּמְצָא־חֵן וְשֵׂכֶל־טוֹב
בְּעֵינֵי אֱלֹהִים וְאָדָם: פ
5 בְּטַח אֶל־יְהֹוָה בְּכָל־לִבֶּךָ

And lean not on your own understanding;
6 In all your ways acknowledge Him,
And He shall direct your paths.

7 Do not be wise in your own eyes;
Fear the LORD and depart from evil.
8 It will be health to your flesh,
And strength to your bones.

9 Honor the LORD with your possessions,
And with the firstfruits of all your increase;
10 So your barns will be filled with plenty,
And your vats will overflow with new wine.

11 My son, do not despise the chastening of the
LORD,
Nor detest His correction;
12 For whom the LORD loves He corrects,
Just as a father the son *in whom* he delights.

13 Happy *is* the man *who* finds wisdom,
And the man *who* gains understanding;
14 For her proceeds *are* better than the profits
of silver,
And her gain than fine gold.
15 She *is* more precious than rubies,
And all the things you may desire cannot
compare with her.
16 Length of days *is* in her right hand,
In her left hand riches and honor.
17 Her ways *are* ways of pleasantness,
And all her paths *are* peace.
18 She *is* a tree of life to those who take hold of
her,
And happy *are* all who retain her.

19 The LORD by wisdom founded the earth;
By understanding He established the
heavens;
20 By His knowledge the depths were broken
up,
And clouds drop down the dew.

21 My son, let them not depart from your
eyes—
Keep sound wisdom and discretion;
22 So they will be life to your soul
And grace to your neck.
23 Then you will walk safely in your way,
And your foot will not stumble.
24 When you lie down, you will not be afraid;
Yes, you will lie down and your sleep will be
sweet.
25 Do not be afraid of sudden terror,
Nor of trouble from the wicked when it
comes;
26 For the LORD will be your confidence,

וְאֶל־בִּינָתְךָ אַל־תִּשָּׁעֵן׃
6 בְּכָל־דְּרָכֶיךָ דָעֵהוּ
וְהוּא יְיַשֵּׁר אֹרְחֹתֶיךָ׃
7 אַל־תְּהִי חָכָם בְּעֵינֶיךָ
יְרָא אֶת־יְהוָה וְסוּר מֵרָע׃
8 רִפְאוּת תְּהִי לְשָׁרֶּךָ
וְשִׁקּוּי לְעַצְמוֹתֶיךָ׃
9 כַּבֵּד אֶת־יְהוָה מֵהוֹנֶךָ
וּמֵרֵאשִׁית כָּל־תְּבוּאָתֶךָ׃
10 וְיִמָּלְאוּ אֲסָמֶיךָ שָׂבָע
וְתִירוֹשׁ יְקָבֶיךָ יִפְרֹצוּ׃   פ
11 מוּסַר יְהוָה בְּנִי אַל־תִּמְאָס
וְאַל־תָּקֹץ בְּתוֹכַחְתּוֹ׃
12 כִּי אֶת אֲשֶׁר יֶאֱהַב יְהוָה יוֹכִיחַ
וּכְאָב אֶת־בֵּן יִרְצֶה׃
13 אַשְׁרֵי אָדָם מָצָא חָכְמָה
וְאָדָם יָפִיק תְּבוּנָה׃
14 כִּי טוֹב סַחְרָהּ מִסְּחַר־כָּסֶף
וּמֵחָרוּץ תְּבוּאָתָהּ׃
15 יְקָרָה הִיא מִפְּנִינִים׃פ
וְכָל־חֲפָצֶיךָ לֹא יִשְׁווּ־בָהּ׃
16 אֹרֶךְ יָמִים בִּימִינָהּ
בִּשְׂמֹאולָהּ עֹשֶׁר וְכָבוֹד׃
17 דְּרָכֶיהָ דַרְכֵי־נֹעַם
וְכָל־נְתִיבוֹתֶיהָ שָׁלוֹם׃
18 עֵץ־חַיִּים הִיא לַמַּחֲזִיקִים בָּהּ
וְתֹמְכֶיהָ מְאֻשָּׁר׃   פ
19 יְהוָה בְּחָכְמָה יָסַד־אָרֶץ
כּוֹנֵן שָׁמַיִם בִּתְבוּנָה׃
20 בְּדַעְתּוֹ תְּהוֹמוֹת נִבְקָעוּ
וּשְׁחָקִים יִרְעֲפוּ־טָל׃
21 בְּנִי אַל־יָלֻזוּ מֵעֵינֶיךָ
נְצֹר תֻּשִׁיָּה וּמְזִמָּה׃
22 וְיִהְיוּ חַיִּים לְנַפְשֶׁךָ
וְחֵן לְגַרְגְּרֹתֶיךָ׃
23 אָז תֵּלֵךְ לָבֶטַח דַּרְכֶּךָ
וְרַגְלְךָ לֹא תִגּוֹף׃
24 אִם־תִּשְׁכַּב לֹא־תִפְחָד
וְשָׁכַבְתָּ וְעָרְבָה שְׁנָתֶךָ׃
25 אַל־תִּירָא מִפַּחַד פִּתְאֹם
וּמִשֹּׁאַת רְשָׁעִים כִּי תָבֹא׃
26 כִּי־יְהוָה יִהְיֶה בְכִסְלֶךָ

ג 15 מִפְּנִינִים

And will keep your foot from being caught.

27 Do not withhold good from those to whom
it is due,
When it is in the power of your hand to do
so.

28 Do not say to your neighbor,
"Go, and come back,
And tomorrow I will give *it,*"
When *you have* it with you.

29 Do not devise evil against your neighbor,
For he dwells by you for safety's sake.

30 Do not strive with a man without cause,
If he has done you no harm.

31 Do not envy the oppressor,
And choose none of his ways;

32 For the perverse *person is* an abomination to
the LORD,
But His secret counsel *is* with the upright.

33 The curse of the LORD *is* on the house of the
wicked,
But He blesses the home of the just.

34 Surely He scorns the scornful,
But gives grace to the humble.

35 The wise shall inherit glory,
But shame shall be the legacy of fools.

4 Hear, *my* children, the instruction of a
father,
And give attention to know understanding;

2 For I give you good doctrine:
Do not forsake my law.

3 When I was my father's son,
Tender and the only one in the sight of my
mother,

4 He also taught me, and said to me:
"Let your heart retain my words;
Keep my commands, and live.

5 Get wisdom! Get understanding!
Do not forget, nor turn away from the
words of my mouth.

6 Do not forsake her, and she will preserve
you;
Love her, and she will keep you.

7 Wisdom *is* the principal thing;
Therefore get wisdom.
And in all your getting, get understanding.

8 Exalt her, and she will promote you;
She will bring you honor, when you embrace
her.

9 She will place on your head an ornament of
grace;
A crown of glory she will deliver to you."

10 Hear, my son, and receive my sayings,

וְשָׁמַר רַגְלְךָ מִלָּכֶד׃

27 אַל־תִּמְנַע־טוֹב מִבְּעָלָיו
בִּהְיוֹת לְאֵל יָדְךָ לַעֲשׂוֹת׃

28 אַל־תֹּאמַר לְרֵעֲךָ ׀ לֵךְ וָשׁוּב וּמָחָר אֶתֵּן
וְיֵשׁ אִתָּךְ׃

29 אַל־תַּחֲרֹשׁ עַל־רֵעֲךָ רָעָה
וְהוּא־יוֹשֵׁב לָבֶטַח אִתָּךְ׃

30 אַל־תָּרִיב עִם־אָדָם חִנָּם
אִם־לֹא גְמָלְךָ רָעָה׃

31 אַל־תְּקַנֵּא בְּאִישׁ חָמָס
וְאַל־תִּבְחַר בְּכָל־דְּרָכָיו׃

32 כִּי תוֹעֲבַת יְהוָה נָלוֹז
וְאֶת־יְשָׁרִים סוֹדוֹ׃

33 מְאֵרַת יְהוָה בְּבֵית רָשָׁע
וּנְוֵה צַדִּיקִים יְבָרֵךְ׃

34 אִם־לַלֵּצִים הוּא־יָלִיץ
וְלַעֲנָיִים יִתֶּן־חֵן׃

35 כָּבוֹד חֲכָמִים יִנְחָלוּ
וּכְסִילִים מֵרִים קָלוֹן׃   פ

ד שִׁמְעוּ בָנִים מוּסַר אָב
וְהַקְשִׁיבוּ לָדַעַת בִּינָה׃

2 כִּי לֶקַח טוֹב נָתַתִּי לָכֶם
תּוֹרָתִי אַל־תַּעֲזֹבוּ׃

3 כִּי־בֵן הָיִיתִי לְאָבִי
רַךְ וְיָחִיד לִפְנֵי אִמִּי׃

4 וַיֹּרֵנִי וַיֹּאמֶר לִי יִתְמָךְ־דְּבָרַי לִבֶּךָ
שְׁמֹר מִצְוֺתַי וֶחְיֵה׃

5 קְנֵה חָכְמָה קְנֵה בִינָה
אַל־תִּשְׁכַּח וְאַל־תֵּט מֵאִמְרֵי־פִי׃

6 אַל־תַּעַזְבֶהָ וְתִשְׁמְרֶךָּ
אֱהָבֶהָ וְתִצְּרֶךָּ׃

7 רֵאשִׁית חָכְמָה קְנֵה חָכְמָה
וּבְכָל־קִנְיָנְךָ קְנֵה בִינָה׃

8 סַלְסְלֶהָ וּתְרוֹמְמֶךָּ
תְּכַבֵּדְךָ כִּי תְחַבְּקֶנָּה׃

9 תִּתֵּן לְרֹאשְׁךָ לִוְיַת־חֵן
עֲטֶרֶת תִּפְאֶרֶת תְּמַגְּנֶךָּ׃

10 שְׁמַע בְּנִי וְקַח אֲמָרָי

ג 27 יָדְךָ 28 לְרֵעֲךָ 30 תָּרִיב 34 וְלַעֲנָיִים

And the years of your life will be many.

וְיִרְבּוּ לְּךָ שְׁנוֹת חַיִּים׃

11 I have taught you in the way of wisdom;
I have led you in right paths.

11 בְּדֶרֶךְ חָכְמָה הֹרֵתִיךָ
הִדְרַכְתִּיךָ בְּמַעְגְּלֵי־יֹשֶׁר׃

12 When you walk, your steps will not be hindered,
And when you run, you will not stumble.

12 בְּלֶכְתְּךָ לֹא־יֵצַר צַעֲדֶךָ
וְאִם־תָּרוּץ לֹא תִכָּשֵׁל׃

13 Take firm hold of instruction, do not let go;
Keep her, for she *is* your life.

13 הַחֲזֵק בַּמּוּסָר אַל־תֶּרֶף
נִצְּרֶהָ כִּי־הִיא חַיֶּיךָ׃

14 Do not enter the path of the wicked,
And do not walk in the way of evil.

14 בְּאֹרַח רְשָׁעִים אַל־תָּבֹא
וְאַל־תְּאַשֵּׁר בְּדֶרֶךְ רָעִים׃

15 Avoid it, do not travel on it;
Turn away from it and pass on.

15 פְּרָעֵהוּ אַל־תַּעֲבָר־בּוֹ
שְׂטֵה מֵעָלָיו וַעֲבוֹר׃

16 For they do not sleep unless they have done evil;
And their sleep is taken away unless they make *someone* fall.

16 כִּי לֹא יִשְׁנוּ אִם־לֹא יָרֵעוּ
וְנִגְזְלָה שְׁנָתָם אִם־לֹא יַכְשׁוֹלוּ׃ ק

17 For they eat the bread of wickedness,
And drink the wine of violence.

17 כִּי לָחֲמוּ לֶחֶם רֶשַׁע
וְיֵין חֲמָסִים יִשְׁתּוּ׃

18 But the path of the just *is* like the shining sun,
That shines ever brighter unto the perfect day.

18 וְאֹרַח צַדִּיקִים כְּאוֹר נֹגַהּ
הוֹלֵךְ וָאוֹר עַד־נְכוֹן הַיּוֹם׃

19 The way of the wicked *is* like darkness;
They do not know what makes them stumble.

19 דֶּרֶךְ רְשָׁעִים כָּאֲפֵלָה
לֹא יָדְעוּ בַּמֶּה יִכָּשֵׁלוּ׃ פ

20 My son, give attention to my words;
Incline your ear to my sayings.

20 בְּנִי לִדְבָרַי הַקְשִׁיבָה
לַאֲמָרַי הַט־אָזְנֶךָ׃

21 Do not let them depart from your eyes;
Keep them in the midst of your heart;

21 אַל־יַלִּיזוּ מֵעֵינֶיךָ
שָׁמְרֵם בְּתוֹךְ לְבָבֶךָ׃

22 For they *are* life to those who find them,
And health to all their flesh.

22 כִּי־חַיִּים הֵם לְמֹצְאֵיהֶם
וּלְכָל־בְּשָׂרוֹ מַרְפֵּא׃

23 Keep your heart with all diligence,
For out of it *spring* the issues of life.

23 מִכָּל־מִשְׁמָר נְצֹר לִבֶּךָ
כִּי־מִמֶּנּוּ תּוֹצְאוֹת חַיִּים׃

24 Put away from you a deceitful mouth,
And put perverse lips far from you.

24 הָסֵר מִמְּךָ עִקְּשׁוּת פֶּה
וּלְזוּת שְׂפָתַיִם הַרְחֵק מִמֶּךָּ׃

25 Let your eyes look straight ahead,
And your eyelids look right before you.

25 עֵינֶיךָ לְנֹכַח יַבִּיטוּ
וְעַפְעַפֶּיךָ יַיְשִׁרוּ נֶגְדֶּךָ׃

26 Ponder the path of your feet,
And let all your ways be established.

26 פַּלֵּס מַעְגַּל רַגְלֶךָ
וְכָל־דְּרָכֶיךָ יִכֹּנוּ׃

27 Do not turn to the right or the left;
Remove your foot from evil.

27 אַל־תֵּט־יָמִין וּשְׂמֹאול
הָסֵר רַגְלְךָ מֵרָע׃

5 My son, pay attention to my wisdom;
Lend your ear to my understanding,

ה בְּנִי לְחָכְמָתִי הַקְשִׁיבָה לִתְבוּנָתִי הַט־אָזְנֶךָ׃

2 That you may preserve discretion,
And your lips may keep knowledge.

2 לִשְׁמֹר מְזִמּוֹת
וְדַעַת שְׂפָתֶיךָ יִנְצֹרוּ׃

3 For the lips of an immoral woman drip honey,
And her mouth *is* smoother than oil;

3 כִּי נֹפֶת תִּטֹּפְנָה שִׂפְתֵי זָרָה
וְחָלָק מִשֶּׁמֶן חִכָּהּ׃

4 But in the end she is bitter as wormwood,
Sharp as a two-edged sword.

4 וְאַחֲרִיתָהּ מָרָה כַלַּעֲנָה
חַדָּה כְּחֶרֶב פִּיּוֹת׃

5 Her feet go down to death,

5 רַגְלֶיהָ יֹרְדוֹת מָוֶת

ד 16 יַכְשׁוֹלוּ

Her steps lay hold of hell.

6 Lest you ponder *her* path of life—
Her ways are unstable;
You do not know *them*.

7 Therefore hear me now, *my* children,
And do not depart from the words of my mouth.

8 Remove your way far from her,
And do not go near the door of her house,

9 Lest you give your honor to others,
And your years to the cruel *one;*

10 Lest aliens be filled with your wealth,
And your labors *go* to the house of a foreigner;

11 And you mourn at last,
When your flesh and your body are consumed,

12 And say:
"How I have hated instruction,
And my heart despised correction!

13 I have not obeyed the voice of my teachers,
Nor inclined my ear to those who instructed me!

14 I was on the verge of total ruin,
In the midst of the assembly and congregation."

15 Drink water from your own cistern,
And running water from your own well.

16 Should your fountains be dispersed abroad,
Streams of water in the streets?

17 Let them be only your own,
And not for strangers with you.

18 Let your fountain be blessed,
And rejoice with the wife of your youth.

19 *As a* loving deer and a graceful doe,
Let her breasts satisfy you at all times;
And always be enraptured with her love.

20 For why should you, my son, be enraptured by an immoral woman,
And be embraced in the arms of a seductress?

21 For the ways of man *are* before the eyes of the LORD,
And He ponders all his paths.

22 His own iniquities entrap the wicked *man,*
And he is caught in the cords of his sin.

23 He shall die for lack of instruction,
And in the greatness of his folly he shall go astray.

6 My son, if you become surety for your friend,

שְׁאוֹל צְעָדֶיהָ יִתְמֹכוּ׃
6 אֹרַח חַיִּים פֶּן־תְּפַלֵּס
נָעוּ מַעְגְּלֹתֶיהָ לֹא תֵדָע׃
7 וְעַתָּה בָנִים שִׁמְעוּ־לִי
וְאַל־תָּסוּרוּ מֵאִמְרֵי־פִי׃
8 הַרְחֵק מֵעָלֶיהָ דַרְכֶּךָ
וְאַל־תִּקְרַב אֶל־פֶּתַח בֵּיתָהּ׃
9 פֶּן־תִּתֵּן לַאֲחֵרִים הוֹדֶךָ
וּשְׁנֹתֶיךָ לְאַכְזָרִי׃
10 פֶּן־יִשְׂבְּעוּ זָרִים כֹּחֶךָ
וַעֲצָבֶיךָ בְּבֵית נָכְרִי׃
11 וְנָהַמְתָּ בְאַחֲרִיתֶךָ
בִּכְלוֹת בְּשָׂרְךָ וּשְׁאֵרֶךָ׃
12 וְאָמַרְתָּ אֵיךְ שָׂנֵאתִי מוּסָר
וְתוֹכַחַת נָאַץ לִבִּי׃
13 וְלֹא־שָׁמַעְתִּי בְּקוֹל מוֹרָי
וְלִמְלַמְּדַי לֹא־הִטִּיתִי אָזְנִי׃
14 כִּמְעַט הָיִיתִי בְכָל־רָע
בְּתוֹךְ קָהָל וְעֵדָה׃
15 שְׁתֵה־מַיִם מִבּוֹרֶךָ
וְנֹזְלִים מִתּוֹךְ בְּאֵרֶךָ׃
16 יָפוּצוּ מַעְיְנֹתֶיךָ חוּצָה
בָּרְחֹבוֹת פַּלְגֵי־מָיִם׃
17 יִהְיוּ־לְךָ לְבַדֶּךָ
וְאֵין לְזָרִים אִתָּךְ׃
18 יְהִי־מְקוֹרְךָ בָרוּךְ
וּשְׂמַח מֵאֵשֶׁת נְעוּרֶךָ׃
19 אַיֶּלֶת אֲהָבִים
וְיַעֲלַת־חֵן
דַּדֶּיהָ יְרַוֻּךָ בְכָל־עֵת
בְּאַהֲבָתָהּ תִּשְׁגֶּה תָמִיד׃
20 וְלָמָּה תִשְׁגֶּה בְנִי בְזָרָה
וּתְחַבֵּק חֵק נָכְרִיָּה׃
21 כִּי נֹכַח ׀ עֵינֵי יְהֹוָה דַּרְכֵי־אִישׁ
וְכָל־מַעְגְּלֹתָיו מְפַלֵּס׃
22 עַווֹנוֹתָיו יִלְכְּדֻנוֹ אֶת־הָרָשָׁע
וּבְחַבְלֵי חַטָּאתוֹ יִתָּמֵךְ׃
23 הוּא יָמוּת בְּאֵין מוּסָר
וּבְרֹב אִוַּלְתּוֹ יִשְׁגֶּה׃
ו בְּנִי אִם־עָרַבְתָּ לְרֵעֶךָ
תָּקַעְתָּ לַזָּר כַּפֶּיךָ׃

If you have shaken hands in pledge for a stranger,	נוֹקַ֖שְׁתָּ בְאִמְרֵי־פִ֑יךָ 2
2 You are snared by the words of your mouth; You are taken by the words of your mouth.	נִ֝לְכַּ֗דְתָּ בְּאִמְרֵי־פִֽיךָ׃ עֲשֵׂ֨ה זֹ֥את אֵפ֪וֹא ׀ בְּנִ֡י וְֽהִנָּצֵ֗ל 3
3 So do this, my son, and deliver yourself; For you have come into the hand of your friend: Go and humble yourself; Plead with your friend.	כִּ֥י בָ֪אתָ בְכַף־רֵעֶ֥ךָ לֵ֥ךְ הִ֝תְרַפֵּ֗ס וּרְהַ֥ב רֵעֶֽיךָ׃ אַל־תִּתֵּ֣ן שֵׁנָ֣ה לְעֵינֶ֑יךָ 4 וּ֝תְנוּמָ֗ה לְעַפְעַפֶּֽיךָ׃
4 Give no sleep to your eyes, Nor slumber to your eyelids.	הִ֭נָּצֵל כִּצְבִ֣י מִיָּ֑ד 5
5 Deliver yourself like a gazelle from the hand *of the hunter,* And like a bird from the hand of the fowler.	וּ֝כְצִפּ֗וֹר מִיַּ֥ד יָקֽוּשׁ׃ ס לֵֽךְ־אֶל־נְמָלָ֥ה עָצֵ֑ל 6 רְאֵ֖ה דְרָכֶ֣יהָ וַחֲכָֽם׃
6 Go to the ant, you sluggard! Consider her ways and be wise,	אֲשֶׁ֖ר אֵֽין־לָ֥הּ קָצִ֗ין שֹׁטֵ֥ר וּמֹשֵֽׁל׃ 7
7 Which, having no captain, Overseer or ruler,	תָּכִ֣ין בַּקַּ֣יִץ לַחְמָ֑הּ 8 אָגְרָ֥ה בַ֝קָּצִ֗יר מַאֲכָלָֽהּ׃
8 Provides her supplies in the summer, *And* gathers her food in the harvest.	עַד־מָתַ֖י עָצֵ֥ל ׀ תִּשְׁכָּ֑ב 9 מָ֝תַ֗י תָּק֥וּם מִשְּׁנָתֶֽךָ׃
9 How long will you slumber, O sluggard? When will you rise from your sleep?	מְעַ֣ט שֵׁ֭נוֹת מְעַ֣ט תְּנוּמ֑וֹת 10
10 A little sleep, a little slumber, A little folding of the hands to sleep—	מְעַ֓ט ׀ חִבֻּ֖ק יָדַ֣יִם לִשְׁכָּֽב׃ וּבָֽא־כִמְהַלֵּ֥ךְ רֵאשֶׁ֑ךָ 11
11 So shall your poverty come on you like a prowler, And your need like an armed man.	וּ֝מַחְסֹֽרְךָ֗ כְּאִ֣ישׁ מָגֵֽן׃ ס אָדָ֣ם בְּ֭לִיַּעַל אִ֣ישׁ אָ֑וֶן 12
12 A worthless person, a wicked man, Walks with a perverse mouth;	הֽ֝וֹלֵ֗ךְ עִקְּשׁ֥וּת פֶּֽה׃ קֹרֵ֣ץ בְּ֭עֵינָיו מֹלֵ֣ל בְּרַגְלָ֑ו 13
13 He winks with his eyes, He shuffles his feet, He points with his fingers;	מֹ֝רֶ֗ה בְּאֶצְבְּעֹתָֽיו׃ תַּֽהְפֻּכ֨וֹת ׀ בְּלִבּ֗וֹ חֹרֵ֣שׁ רָ֣ע בְּכָל־עֵ֑ת 14 מדינים֑ יְשַׁלֵּֽחַ׃
14 Perversity *is* in his heart, He devises evil continually, He sows discord.	עַל־כֵּ֗ן פִּ֭תְאֹם יָב֣וֹא אֵיד֑וֹ 15 פֶּ֥תַע יִ֝שָּׁבֵ֗ר וְאֵ֣ין מַרְפֵּֽא׃ ס
15 Therefore his calamity shall come suddenly; Suddenly he shall be broken without remedy.	שֶׁשׁ־הֵ֭נָּה שָׂנֵ֣א יְהֹוָ֑ה וְשֶׁ֗בַע 16 תועבות֥ נַפְשֽׁוֹ׃
16 These six *things* the LORD hates, Yes, seven *are* an abomination to Him:	עֵינַ֣יִם רָ֭מוֹת לְשׁ֣וֹן שָׁ֑קֶר 17 וְ֝יָדַ֗יִם שֹׁפְכ֥וֹת דָּם־נָקִֽי׃
17 A proud look, A lying tongue, Hands that shed innocent blood,	לֵ֗ב חֹ֭רֵשׁ מַחְשְׁב֣וֹת אָ֑וֶן 18 רַ֝גְלַ֗יִם מְֽמַהֲר֥וֹת לָר֥וּץ לָֽרָעָֽה׃
18 A heart that devises wicked plans, Feet that are swift in running to evil,	יָפִ֣יחַ כְּ֭זָבִים עֵ֣ד שָׁ֑קֶר 19 וּמְשַׁלֵּ֥חַ מְ֝דָנִ֗ים בֵּ֣ין אַחִֽים׃
19 A false witness *who* speaks lies, And one who sows discord among brethren.	נְצֹ֣ר בְּ֭נִי מִצְוַ֣ת אָבִ֑יךָ 20 וְאַל־תִּ֝טֹּ֗שׁ תּוֹרַ֥ת אִמֶּֽךָ׃
20 My son, keep your father's command, And do not forsake the law of your mother.	קָשְׁרֵ֥ם עַל־לִבְּךָ֣ תָמִ֑יד 21 עׇ֝נְדֵ֗ם עַל־גַּרְגְּרֹתֶֽךָ׃
21 Bind them continually upon your heart; Tie them around your neck.	בְּהִתְהַלֶּכְךָ֨ ׀ תַּנְחֶ֬ה אֹתָ֗ךְ 22
22 When you roam, they will lead you;	

14 1 מדינים 16 תועבת

When you sleep, they will keep you;
And *when* you awake, they will speak with you.

בְּשָׁכְבְּךָ תִּשְׁמֹר עָלֶיךָ
וַהֲקִיצוֹתָ הִיא תְשִׂיחֶךָ:

23 For the commandment *is* a lamp,
And the law a light;
Reproofs of instruction *are* the way of life,

23 כִּי נֵר מִצְוָה וְתוֹרָה אוֹר
וְדֶרֶךְ חַיִּים תּוֹכְחוֹת מוּסָר:

24 To keep you from the evil woman,
From the flattering tongue of a seductress.

24 לִשְׁמָרְךָ מֵאֵשֶׁת רָע
מֵחֶלְקַת לָשׁוֹן נָכְרִיָּה:

25 Do not lust after her beauty in your heart,
Nor let her allure you with her eyelids.

25 אַל־תַּחְמֹד יָפְיָהּ בִּלְבָבֶךָ
וְאַל־תִּקָּחֲךָ בְּעַפְעַפֶּיהָ:

26 For by means of a harlot
A man is reduced to a crust of bread;
And an adulteress will prey upon his precious life.

26 כִּי בְעַד־אִשָּׁה זוֹנָה
עַד־כִּכַּר לָחֶם
וְאֵשֶׁת אִישׁ
נֶפֶשׁ יְקָרָה תָצוּד: פ

27 Can a man take fire to his bosom,
And his clothes not be burned?

27 הֲיַחְתֶּה אִישׁ אֵשׁ בְּחֵיקוֹ
וּבְגָדָיו לֹא תִשָּׂרַפְנָה:

28 Can one walk on hot coals,
And his feet not be seared?

28 אִם־יְהַלֵּךְ אִישׁ עַל־הַגֶּחָלִים
וְרַגְלָיו לֹא תִכָּוֶינָה:

29 So *is* he who goes in to his neighbor's wife;
Whoever touches her shall not be innocent.

29 כֵּן הַבָּא אֶל־אֵשֶׁת רֵעֵהוּ
לֹא יִנָּקֶה כָּל־הַנֹּגֵעַ בָּהּ:

30 *People* do not despise a thief
If he steals to satisfy himself when he is starving.

30 לֹא־יָבוּזוּ לַגַּנָּב כִּי יִגְנוֹב
לְמַלֵּא נַפְשׁוֹ כִּי יִרְעָב:

31 Yet *when* he is found, he must restore sevenfold;
He may have to give up all the substance of his house.

31 וְנִמְצָא יְשַׁלֵּם שִׁבְעָתָיִם
אֶת־כָּל־הוֹן בֵּיתוֹ יִתֵּן:

32 Whoever commits adultery with a woman lacks understanding;
He *who* does so destroys his own soul.

32 נֹאֵף אִשָּׁה חֲסַר־לֵב
מַשְׁחִית נַפְשׁוֹ הוּא יַעֲשֶׂנָּה:

33 Wounds and dishonor he will get,
And his reproach will not be wiped away.

33 נֶגַע־וְקָלוֹן יִמְצָא
וְחֶרְפָּתוֹ לֹא תִמָּחֶה:

34 For jealousy *is* a husband's fury;
Therefore he will not spare in the day of vengeance.

34 כִּי־קִנְאָה חֲמַת־גָּבֶר
וְלֹא־יַחְמוֹל בְּיוֹם נָקָם:

35 He will accept no recompense,
Nor will he be appeased though you give many gifts.

35 לֹא־יִשָּׂא פְּנֵי כָל־כֹּפֶר
וְלֹא־יֹאבֶה כִּי תַרְבֶּה־שֹׁחַד: פ

7

My son, keep my words,
And treasure my commands within you.

ז בְּנִי שְׁמֹר אֲמָרָי
וּמִצְוֹתַי תִּצְפֹּן אִתָּךְ:

2 Keep my commands and live,
And my law as the apple of your eye.

2 שְׁמֹר מִצְוֹתַי וֶחְיֵה
וְתוֹרָתִי כְּאִישׁוֹן עֵינֶיךָ:

3 Bind them on your fingers;
Write them on the tablet of your heart.

3 קָשְׁרֵם עַל־אֶצְבְּעֹתֶיךָ
כָּתְבֵם עַל־לוּחַ לִבֶּךָ:

4 Say to wisdom, "You *are* my sister,"
And call understanding *your* nearest kin,

4 אֱמֹר לַחָכְמָה אֲחֹתִי אָתְּ
וּמֹדָע לַבִּינָה תִקְרָא:

5 That they may keep you from the immoral woman,
From the seductress *who* flatters with her words.

5 לִשְׁמָרְךָ מֵאִשָּׁה זָרָה
מִנָּכְרִיָּה אֲמָרֶיהָ הֶחֱלִיקָה:

6 For at the window of my house
I looked through my lattice,

6 כִּי בְּחַלּוֹן בֵּיתִי
בְּעַד אֶשְׁנַבִּי נִשְׁקָפְתִּי:

7 And saw among the simple,
I perceived among the youths,
A young man devoid of understanding,

8 Passing along the street near her corner;
And he took the path to her house

9 In the twilight, in the evening,
In the black and dark night.

10 And there a woman met him,
With the attire of a harlot, and a crafty heart.

11 She *was* loud and rebellious,
Her feet would not stay at home.

12 At times *she was* outside, at times in the open square,
Lurking at every corner.

13 So she caught him and kissed him;
With an impudent face she said to him:

14 "*I have* peace offerings with me;
Today I have paid my vows.

15 So I came out to meet you,
Diligently to seek your face,
And I have found you.

16 I have spread my bed with tapestry,
Colored coverings of Egyptian linen.

17 I have perfumed my bed
With myrrh, aloes, and cinnamon.

18 Come, let us take our fill of love until morning;
Let us delight ourselves with love.

19 For my husband *is* not at home;
He has gone on a long journey;

20 He has taken a bag of money with him,
And will come home on the appointed day."

21 With her enticing speech she caused him to yield,
With her flattering lips she seduced him.

22 Immediately he went after her, as an ox goes to the slaughter,
Or as a fool to the correction of the stocks,

23 Till an arrow struck his liver.
As a bird hastens to the snare,
He did not know it *would cost* his life.

24 Now therefore, listen to me, *my* children;
Pay attention to the words of my mouth:

25 Do not let your heart turn aside to her ways,
Do not stray into her paths;

26 For she has cast down many wounded,
And all who were slain by her were strong *men.*

27 Her house *is* the way to hell,
Descending to the chambers of death.

וָאֵרֶא בַפְּתָאיִם אָבִינָה בַבָּנִים 7
נַעַר חֲסַר־לֵב:

עֹבֵר בַּשׁוּק אֵצֶל פִּנָּהּ 8
וְדֶרֶךְ בֵּיתָהּ יִצְעָד:

בְּנֶשֶׁף־בְּעֶרֶב יוֹם 9
בְּאִישׁוֹן לַיְלָה וַאֲפֵלָה:

וְהִנֵּה אִשָּׁה לִקְרָאתוֹ 10
שִׁית זוֹנָה וּנְצֻרַת לֵב:

הֹמִיָּה הִיא וְסֹרָרֶת 11
בְּבֵיתָהּ לֹא־יִשְׁכְּנוּ רַגְלֶיהָ:

פַּעַם ׀ בַּחוּץ פַּעַם בָּרְחֹבוֹת 12
וְאֵצֶל כָּל־פִּנָּה תֶאֱרֹב:

וְהֶחֱזִיקָה בּוֹ וְנָשְׁקָה־לּוֹ 13
הֵעֵזָה פָנֶיהָ וַתֹּאמַר לוֹ:

זִבְחֵי שְׁלָמִים עָלָי 14
הַיּוֹם שִׁלַּמְתִּי נְדָרָי:

עַל־כֵּן יָצָאתִי לִקְרָאתֶךָ 15
לְשַׁחֵר פָּנֶיךָ וָאֶמְצָאֶךָּ:

מַרְבַדִּים רָבַדְתִּי עַרְשִׂי 16
חֲטֻבוֹת אֵטוּן מִצְרָיִם:

נַפְתִּי מִשְׁכָּבִי 17
מֹר אֲהָלִים וְקִנָּמוֹן:

לְכָה נִרְוֶה דֹדִים עַד־הַבֹּקֶר 18
נִתְעַלְּסָה בָּאֳהָבִים:

כִּי אֵין הָאִישׁ בְּבֵיתוֹ 19
הָלַךְ בְּדֶרֶךְ מֵרָחוֹק:

צְרוֹר־הַכֶּסֶף לָקַח בְּיָדוֹ 20
לְיוֹם הַכֵּסֶא יָבֹא בֵיתוֹ:

הִטַּתּוּ בְּרֹב לִקְחָהּ 21
בְּחֵלֶק שְׂפָתֶיהָ תַּדִּיחֶנּוּ:

הוֹלֵךְ אַחֲרֶיהָ פִּתְאֹם 22
כְּשׁוֹר אֶל־טֶבַח יָבוֹא וּכְעֶכֶס אֶל־מוּסַר אֱוִיל:

עַד יְפַלַּח חֵץ כְּבֵדוֹ כְּמַהֵר צִפּוֹר אֶל־פָּח 23
וְלֹא־יָדַע כִּי־בְנַפְשׁוֹ הוּא: פ

וְעַתָּה בָנִים שִׁמְעוּ־לִי 24
וְהַקְשִׁיבוּ לְאִמְרֵי־פִי:

אַל־יֵשְׂטְ אֶל־דְּרָכֶיהָ לִבֶּךָ 25
אַל־תֵּתַע בִּנְתִיבוֹתֶיהָ:

כִּי־רַבִּים חֲלָלִים הִפִּילָה 26
וַעֲצֻמִים כָּל־הֲרֻגֶיהָ:

דַּרְכֵי שְׁאוֹל בֵּיתָהּ 27
יֹרְדוֹת אֶל־חַדְרֵי־מָוֶת: פ

8 Does not wisdom cry out,
And understanding lift up her voice?

2 She takes her stand on the top of the high hill,
Beside the way, where the paths meet.

3 She cries out by the gates, at the entry of the city,
At the entrance of the doors:

4 "To you, O men, I call,
And my voice *is* to the sons of men.

5 O you simple ones, understand prudence,
And you fools, be of an understanding heart.

6 Listen, for I will speak of excellent things,
And from the opening of my lips *will come* right things;

7 For my mouth will speak truth;
Wickedness *is* an abomination to my lips.

8 All the words of my mouth *are* with righteousness;
Nothing crooked or perverse *is* in them.

9 They *are* all plain to him who understands,
And right to those who find knowledge.

10 Receive my instruction, and not silver,
And knowledge rather than choice gold;

11 For wisdom *is* better than rubies,
And all the things one may desire cannot be compared with her.

12 "I, wisdom, dwell with prudence,
And find out knowledge *and* discretion.

13 The fear of the LORD *is* to hate evil;
Pride and arrogance and the evil way
And the perverse mouth I hate.

14 Counsel *is* mine, and sound wisdom;
I *am* understanding, I have strength.

15 By me kings reign,
And rulers decree justice.

16 By me princes rule, and nobles,
All the judges of the earth.

17 I love those who love me,
And those who seek me diligently will find me.

18 Riches and honor *are* with me,
Enduring riches and righteousness.

19 My fruit *is* better than gold, yes, than fine gold,
And my revenue than choice silver.

20 I traverse the way of righteousness,
In the midst of the paths of justice,

21 That I may cause those who love me to inherit wealth,
That I may fill their treasuries.

משלי ח

ח הֲלֹא־חָכְמָה תִקְרָא וּתְבוּנָה תִּתֵּן קוֹלָהּ:
2 בְּרֹאשׁ־מְרוֹמִים עֲלֵי־דָרֶךְ
בֵּית נְתִיבוֹת נִצָּבָה:
3 לְיַד־שְׁעָרִים לְפִי־קָרֶת
מְבוֹא פְתָחִים תָּרֹנָּה:
4 אֲלֵיכֶם אִישִׁים אֶקְרָא
וְקוֹלִי אֶל־בְּנֵי אָדָם:
5 הָבִינוּ פְתָאיִם עָרְמָה
וּכְסִילִים הָבִינוּ לֵב:
6 שִׁמְעוּ כִּי־נְגִידִים אֲדַבֵּר
וּמִפְתַּח שְׂפָתַי מֵישָׁרִים:
7 כִּי־אֱמֶת יֶהְגֶּה חִכִּי
וְתוֹעֲבַת שְׂפָתַי רֶשַׁע:
8 בְּצֶדֶק כָּל־אִמְרֵי־פִי
אֵין בָּהֶם נִפְתָּל וְעִקֵּשׁ:
9 כֻּלָּם נְכֹחִים לַמֵּבִין
וִישָׁרִים לְמֹצְאֵי דָעַת:
10 קְחוּ־מוּסָרִי וְאַל־כָּסֶף
וְדַעַת מֵחָרוּץ נִבְחָר:
11 כִּי־טוֹבָה חָכְמָה מִפְּנִינִים
וְכָל־חֲפָצִים לֹא יִשְׁווּ־בָהּ:
12 אֲנִי־חָכְמָה שָׁכַנְתִּי עָרְמָה
וְדַעַת מְזִמּוֹת אֶמְצָא:
13 יִרְאַת יְהֹוָה שְׂנֹאת רָע
גֵּאָה וְגָאוֹן ׀ וְדֶרֶךְ רָע וּפִי תַהְפֻּכוֹת שָׂנֵאתִי:
14 לִי־עֵצָה וְתוּשִׁיָּה
אֲנִי בִינָה לִי גְבוּרָה:
15 בִּי מְלָכִים יִמְלֹכוּ
וְרוֹזְנִים יְחֹקְקוּ צֶדֶק:
16 בִּי שָׂרִים יָשֹׂרוּ
וּנְדִיבִים כָּל־שֹׁפְטֵי צֶדֶק:
17 אֲנִי אֹהֲבֶיהָ אֵהָב
וּמְשַׁחֲרַי יִמְצָאֻנְנִי:
18 עֹשֶׁר־וְכָבוֹד אִתִּי
הוֹן עָתֵק וּצְדָקָה:
19 טוֹב פִּרְיִי מֵחָרוּץ וּמִפָּז
וּתְבוּאָתִי מִכֶּסֶף נִבְחָר:
20 בְּאֹרַח־צְדָקָה אֲהַלֵּךְ
בְּתוֹךְ נְתִיבוֹת מִשְׁפָּט:
21 לְהַנְחִיל אֹהֲבַי ׀ יֵשׁ
וְאֹצְרֹתֵיהֶם אֲמַלֵּא: פ

22 "The LORD possessed me at the beginning of
    His way,
    Before His works of old.
23 I have been established from everlasting,
    From the beginning, before there was ever
    an earth.
24 When *there were* no depths I was brought
    forth,
    When *there were* no fountains abounding
    with water.
25 Before the mountains were settled,
    Before the hills, I was brought forth;
26 While as yet He had not made the earth or
    the fields,
    Or the primal dust of the world.
27 When He prepared the heavens, I *was* there,
    When He drew a circle on the face of the
    deep,
28 When He established the clouds above,
    When He strengthened the fountains of the
    deep,
29 When He assigned to the sea its limit,
    So that the waters would not transgress His
    command,
    When He marked out the foundations of the
    earth,
30 Then I was beside Him *as* a master
    craftsman;
    And I was daily *His* delight,
    Rejoicing always before Him,
31 Rejoicing in His inhabited world,
    And my delight *was* with the sons of men.
32 "Now therefore, listen to me, *my* children,
    For blessed *are those* who keep my ways.
33 Hear instruction and be wise,
    And do not disdain *it*.
34 Blessed is the man who listens to me,
    Watching daily at my gates,
    Waiting at the posts of my doors.
35 For whoever finds me finds life,
    And obtains favor from the LORD;
36 But he who sins against me wrongs his own
    soul;
    All those who hate me love death."

9 Wisdom has built her house,
    She has hewn out her seven pillars;
2 She has slaughtered her meat,
    She has mixed her wine,
    She has also furnished her table.
3 She has sent out her maidens,
    She cries out from the highest places of the
    city,

22 יְהֹוָה קָנָנִי רֵאשִׁית דַּרְכּוֹ
קֶדֶם מִפְעָלָיו מֵאָז:
23 מֵעוֹלָם נִסַּכְתִּי מֵרֹאשׁ
מִקַּדְמֵי־אָרֶץ:
24 בְּאֵין־תְּהֹמוֹת חוֹלָלְתִּי
בְּאֵין מַעְיָנוֹת נִכְבַּדֵּי־מָיִם:
25 בְּטֶרֶם הָרִים הָטְבָּעוּ
לִפְנֵי גְבָעוֹת חוֹלָלְתִּי:
26 עַד־לֹא עָשָׂה אֶרֶץ וְחוּצוֹת
וְרֹאשׁ עַפְרוֹת תֵּבֵל:
27 בַּהֲכִינוֹ שָׁמַיִם שָׁם אָנִי
בְּחוּקוֹ חוּג עַל־פְּנֵי תְהוֹם:
28 בְּאַמְּצוֹ שְׁחָקִים מִמָּעַל
בַּעֲזוֹז עִינוֹת תְּהוֹם:
29 בְּשׂוּמוֹ לַיָּם ׀ חֻקּוֹ וּמַיִם לֹא יַעַבְרוּ־פִיו
בְּחוּקוֹ מוֹסְדֵי אָרֶץ:
30 וָאֶהְיֶה אֶצְלוֹ אָמוֹן
וָאֶהְיֶה שַׁעֲשֻׁעִים יוֹם ׀ יוֹם מְשַׂחֶקֶת לְפָנָיו
בְּכָל־עֵת:
31 מְשַׂחֶקֶת בְּתֵבֵל אַרְצוֹ
וְשַׁעֲשֻׁעַי אֶת־בְּנֵי אָדָם:
32 וְעַתָּה בָנִים שִׁמְעוּ־לִי
וְאַשְׁרֵי דְּרָכַי יִשְׁמֹרוּ:
33 שִׁמְעוּ מוּסָר וַחֲכָמוּ
וְאַל־תִּפְרָעוּ:
34 אַשְׁרֵי אָדָם שֹׁמֵעַ לִי
לִשְׁקֹד עַל־דַּלְתֹתַי יוֹם ׀ יוֹם לִשְׁמֹר מְזוּזֹת
פְּתָחָי:
35 כִּי מֹצְאִי מָצָא חַיִּים
וַיָּפֶק רָצוֹן מֵיְהֹוָה:
36 וְחֹטְאִי חֹמֵס נַפְשׁוֹ
כָּל־מְשַׂנְאַי אָהֲבוּ מָוֶת:

ט חָכְמוֹת בָּנְתָה בֵיתָהּ
חָצְבָה עַמּוּדֶיהָ שִׁבְעָה:
2 טָבְחָה טִבְחָהּ מָסְכָה יֵינָהּ
אַף עָרְכָה שֻׁלְחָנָהּ:
3 שָׁלְחָה נַעֲרֹתֶיהָ תִקְרָא
עַל־גַּפֵּי מְרֹמֵי קָרֶת:

English	Hebrew

4 "Whoever *is* simple, let him turn in here!"
    As for him who lacks understanding, she
    says to him,
	4 מִי־פֶ֭תִי יָסֻ֣ר הֵ֑נָּה
	 חֲסַר־לֵ֝֗ב אָ֣מְרָה לּֽוֹ׃

5 "Come, eat of my bread And drink of the wine I have mixed.	5 לְ֭כוּ לַחֲמ֣וּ בְֽלַחֲמִ֑י וּ֝שְׁת֗וּ בְּיַ֣יִן מָסָֽכְתִּי׃
6 Forsake foolishness and live, And go in the way of understanding.	6 עִזְב֣וּ פְתָאיִ֣ם וִֽחְי֑וּ וְ֝אִשְׁר֗וּ בְּדֶ֣רֶךְ בִּינָֽה׃

7 "He who corrects a scoffer gets shame for
    himself,
    And he who rebukes a wicked *man only*
    harms himself.
	7 יֹ֤סֵ֨ר ׀ לֵ֗ץ לֹקֵ֣חַֽ ל֣וֹ קָל֑וֹן
	 וּמוֹכִ֖יחַ לְרָשָׁ֣ע מוּמֽוֹ׃

8 Do not correct a scoffer, lest he hate you; Rebuke a wise *man,* and he will love you.	8 אַל־תּ֣וֹכַח לֵ֭ץ פֶּן־יִשְׂנָאֶ֑ךָּ הוֹכַ֥ח לְ֝חָכָ֗ם וְיֶאֱהָבֶֽךָ׃

9 Give *instruction* to a wise *man,* and he will be
    still wiser;
    Teach a just *man,* and he will increase in
    learning.
	9 תֵּ֣ן לְ֭חָכָם וְיֶחְכַּם־ע֑וֹד
	 הוֹדַ֥ע לְ֝צַדִּ֗יק וְי֣וֹסֶף לֶֽקַח׃ פ

10 "The fear of the LORD *is* the beginning of
    wisdom,
    And the knowledge of the Holy One *is*
    understanding.
	10 תְּחִלַּ֣ת חָ֭כְמָה יִרְאַ֣ת יְהוָ֑ה
	 וְדַ֖עַת קְדֹשִׁ֣ים בִּינָֽה׃

11 For by me your days will be multiplied, And years of life will be added to you.	11 כִּי־בִ֭י יִרְבּ֣וּ יָמֶ֑יךָ וְיוֹסִ֖יפוּ לְּךָ֣ שְׁנ֣וֹת חַיִּֽים׃
12 If you are wise, you are wise for yourself, And *if* you scoff, you will bear *it* alone."	12 אִם־חָ֭כַמְתָּ חָכַ֣מְתָּ לָּ֑ךְ וְ֝לַ֗צְתָּ לְֽבַדְּךָ֥ תִשָּֽׂא׃
13 A foolish woman is clamorous; *She is* simple, and knows nothing.	13 אֵ֣שֶׁת כְּ֭סִילוּת הֹמִיָּ֑ה פְּ֝תַיּ֗וּת וּבַל־יָ֥דְעָה מָּֽה׃
14 For she sits at the door of her house, On a seat *by* the highest places of the city,	14 וְֽ֭יָשְׁבָה לְפֶ֣תַח בֵּיתָ֑הּ עַל־כִּ֝סֵּ֗א מְרֹ֣מֵי קָֽרֶת׃
15 To call to those who pass by, Who go straight on their way:	15 לִקְרֹ֥א לְעֹֽבְרֵי־דָ֑רֶךְ הַֽ֝מְיַשְּׁרִ֗ים אֹֽרְחוֹתָֽם׃

16 "Whoever *is* simple, let him turn in here";
    And *as for* him who lacks understanding,
    she says to him,
	16 מִי־פֶ֭תִי יָסֻ֣ר הֵ֑נָּה
	 וַחֲסַר־לֵ֝֗ב וְאָ֣מְרָה לּֽוֹ׃

17 "Stolen water is sweet, And bread *eaten* in secret is pleasant."	17 מַֽיִם־גְּנוּבִ֥ים יִמְתָּ֑קוּ וְלֶ֖חֶם סְתָרִ֣ים יִנְעָֽם׃

18 But he does not know that the dead *are*
    there,
    That her guests *are* in the depths of hell.
	18 וְֽלֹא־יָ֭דַע כִּֽי־רְפָאִ֣ים שָׁ֑ם
	 בְּעִמְקֵ֖י שְׁא֣וֹל קְרֻאֶֽיהָ׃ פ

10 The proverbs of Solomon:
    A wise son makes a glad father,
    But a foolish son *is* the grief of his mother.
	י מִשְׁלֵ֗י שְׁלֹ֫מֹ֥ה
	 בֵּ֣ן חָ֭כָם יְשַׂמַּח־אָ֑ב
	 וּבֵ֥ן כְּ֝סִ֗יל תּוּגַ֥ת אִמּֽוֹ׃

2 Treasures of wickedness profit nothing, But righteousness delivers from death.	2 לֹא־י֭וֹעִילוּ אוֹצְר֣וֹת רֶ֑שַׁע וּ֝צְדָקָ֗ה תַּצִּ֥יל מִמָּֽוֶת׃

3 The LORD will not allow the righteous soul
    to famish,
    But He casts away the desire of the wicked.
	3 לֹֽא־יַרְעִ֣יב יְ֭הוָה נֶ֣פֶשׁ צַדִּ֑יק
	 וְהַוַּ֖ת רְשָׁעִ֣ים יֶהְדֹּֽף׃

4 He who has a slack hand becomes poor, But the hand of the diligent makes rich.	4 רָ֗אשׁ עֹשֶׂ֥ה כַף־רְמִיָּ֑ה וְיַ֖ד חָרוּצִ֣ים תַּעֲשִֽׁיר׃
5 He who gathers in summer *is* a wise son;	5 אֹגֵ֣ר בַּ֭קַּיִץ בֵּ֣ן מַשְׂכִּ֑יל

He who sleeps in harvest *is* a son who causes shame.

6 Blessings *are* on the head of the righteous,
But violence covers the mouth of the wicked.

7 The memory of the righteous *is* blessed,
But the name of the wicked will rot.

8 The wise in heart will receive commands,
But a prating fool will fall.

9 He who walks with integrity walks securely,
But he who perverts his ways will become known.

10 He who winks with the eye causes trouble,
But a prating fool will fall.

11 The mouth of the righteous *is* a well of life,
But violence covers the mouth of the wicked.

12 Hatred stirs up strife,
But love covers all sins.

13 Wisdom is found on the lips of him who has understanding,
But a rod *is* for the back of him who is devoid of understanding.

14 Wise *people* store up knowledge,
But the mouth of the foolish *is* near destruction.

15 The rich man's wealth *is* his strong city;
The destruction of the poor *is* their poverty.

16 The labor of the righteous *leads* to life,
The wages of the wicked to sin.

17 He who keeps instruction *is* in the way of life,
But he who refuses correction goes astray.

18 Whoever hides hatred *has* lying lips,
And whoever spreads slander *is* a fool.

19 In the multitude of words sin is not lacking,
But he who restrains his lips *is* wise.

20 The tongue of the righteous *is* choice silver;
The heart of the wicked *is worth* little.

21 The lips of the righteous feed many,
But fools die for lack of wisdom.

22 The blessing of the LORD makes *one* rich,
And He adds no sorrow with it.

23 To do evil *is* like sport to a fool,
But a man of understanding has wisdom.

24 The fear of the wicked will come upon him,
And the desire of the righteous will be granted.

25 When the whirlwind passes by, the wicked *is* no *more,*

נִרְדָּם בַּקָּצִיר בֵּן מֵבִישׁ׃

6 בְּרָכוֹת לְרֹאשׁ צַדִּיק
וּפִי רְשָׁעִים יְכַסֶּה חָמָס׃

7 זֵכֶר צַדִּיק לִבְרָכָה
וְשֵׁם רְשָׁעִים יִרְקָב׃

8 חֲכַם־לֵב יִקַּח מִצְוֺת
וֶאֱוִיל שְׂפָתַיִם יִלָּבֵט׃

9 הוֹלֵךְ בַּתֹּם יֵלֶךְ בֶּטַח
וּמְעַקֵּשׁ דְּרָכָיו יִוָּדֵעַ׃

10 קֹרֵץ עַיִן יִתֵּן עַצָּבֶת
וֶאֱוִיל שְׂפָתַיִם יִלָּבֵט׃

11 מְקוֹר חַיִּים פִּי צַדִּיק
וּפִי רְשָׁעִים יְכַסֶּה חָמָס׃

12 שִׂנְאָה תְּעוֹרֵר מְדָנִים
וְעַל כָּל־פְּשָׁעִים תְּכַסֶּה אַהֲבָה׃

13 בְּשִׂפְתֵי נָבוֹן תִּמָּצֵא חָכְמָה
וְשֵׁבֶט לְגֵו חֲסַר־לֵב׃

14 חֲכָמִים יִצְפְּנוּ־דָעַת
וּפִי־אֱוִיל מְחִתָּה קְרֹבָה׃

15 הוֹן עָשִׁיר קִרְיַת עֻזּוֹ
מְחִתַּת דַּלִּים רֵישָׁם׃

16 פְּעֻלַּת צַדִּיק לְחַיִּים
תְּבוּאַת רָשָׁע לְחַטָּאת׃

17 אֹרַח לְחַיִּים שׁוֹמֵר מוּסָר
וְעוֹזֵב תּוֹכַחַת מַתְעֶה׃

18 מְכַסֶּה שִׂנְאָה שִׂפְתֵי־שָׁקֶר
וּמוֹצִא דִבָּה הוּא כְסִיל׃

19 בְּרֹב דְּבָרִים לֹא יֶחְדַּל־פָּשַׁע
וְחֹשֵׂךְ שְׂפָתָיו מַשְׂכִּיל׃

20 כֶּסֶף נִבְחָר לְשׁוֹן צַדִּיק
לֵב רְשָׁעִים כִּמְעָט׃

21 שִׂפְתֵי צַדִּיק יִרְעוּ רַבִּים
וֶאֱוִילִים בַּחֲסַר־לֵב יָמוּתוּ׃

22 בִּרְכַּת יְהֹוָה הִיא תַעֲשִׁיר
וְלֹא־יוֹסִף עֶצֶב עִמָּהּ׃

23 כִּשְׂחוֹק לִכְסִיל עֲשׂוֹת זִמָּה
וְחָכְמָה לְאִישׁ תְּבוּנָה׃

24 מְגוֹרַת רָשָׁע הִיא תְבוֹאֶנּוּ
וְתַאֲוַת צַדִּיקִים יִתֵּן׃

25 כַּעֲבוֹר סוּפָה וְאֵין רָשָׁע

But the righteous *has* an everlasting foundation.

וְצַדִּיק יְסוֹד עוֹלָם:

26 As vinegar to the teeth and smoke to the eyes,
So *is* the lazy *man* to those who send him.

26 כַּחֹמֶץ ׀ לַשִּׁנַּיִם וְכֶעָשָׁן לָעֵינָיִם
כֵּן הֶעָצֵל לְשֹׁלְחָיו:

27 The fear of the LORD prolongs days,
But the years of the wicked will be shortened.

27 יִרְאַת יְהֹוָה תּוֹסִיף יָמִים
וּשְׁנוֹת רְשָׁעִים תִּקְצֹרְנָה:

28 The hope of the righteous *will be* gladness,
But the expectation of the wicked will perish.

28 תּוֹחֶלֶת צַדִּיקִים שִׂמְחָה
וְתִקְוַת רְשָׁעִים תֹּאבֵד:

29 The way of the LORD *is* strength for the upright,
But destruction *will come* to the workers of iniquity.

29 מָעוֹז לַתֹּם דֶּרֶךְ יְהֹוָה
וּמְחִתָּה לְפֹעֲלֵי אָוֶן:

30 The righteous will never be removed,
But the wicked will not inhabit the earth.

30 צַדִּיק לְעוֹלָם בַּל־יִמּוֹט
וּרְשָׁעִים לֹא יִשְׁכְּנוּ־אָרֶץ:

31 The mouth of the righteous brings forth wisdom,
But the perverse tongue will be cut out.

31 פִּי־צַדִּיק יָנוּב חָכְמָה
וּלְשׁוֹן תַּהְפֻּכוֹת תִּכָּרֵת:

32 The lips of the righteous know what is acceptable,
But the mouth of the wicked *what is* perverse.

32 שִׂפְתֵי צַדִּיק יֵדְעוּן רָצוֹן
וּפִי רְשָׁעִים תַּהְפֻּכוֹת:

11 Dishonest scales *are* an abomination to the LORD,
But a just weight *is* His delight.

יא מֹאזְנֵי מִרְמָה תּוֹעֲבַת יְהֹוָה
וְאֶבֶן שְׁלֵמָה רְצוֹנוֹ:

2 When pride comes, then comes shame;
But with the humble *is* wisdom.

2 בָּא־זָדוֹן וַיָּבֹא קָלוֹן
וְאֶת־צְנוּעִים חָכְמָה:

3 The integrity of the upright will guide them,
But the perversity of the unfaithful will destroy them.

3 תֻּמַּת יְשָׁרִים תַּנְחֵם
וְסֶלֶף בּוֹגְדִים וְשַׁדָּֽם:

4 Riches do not profit in the day of wrath,
But righteousness delivers from death.

4 לֹא־יוֹעִיל הוֹן בְּיוֹם עֶבְרָה
וּצְדָקָה תַּצִּיל מִמָּוֶת:

5 The righteousness of the blameless will direct his way aright,
But the wicked will fall by his own wickedness.

5 צִדְקַת תָּמִים תְּיַשֵּׁר דַּרְכּוֹ
וּבְרִשְׁעָתוֹ יִפֹּל רָשָׁע:

6 The righteousness of the upright will deliver them,
But the unfaithful will be caught by *their* lust.

6 צִדְקַת יְשָׁרִים תַּצִּילֵם
וּבְהַוַּת בֹּגְדִים יִלָּכֵדוּ:

7 When a wicked man dies, *his* expectation will perish,
And the hope of the unjust perishes.

7 בְּמוֹת אָדָם רָשָׁע תֹּאבַד תִּקְוָה
וְתוֹחֶלֶת אוֹנִים אָבָדָה:

8 The righteous is delivered from trouble,
And it comes to the wicked instead.

8 צַדִּיק מִצָּרָה נֶחֱלָץ
וַיָּבֹא רָשָׁע תַּחְתָּיו:

9 The hypocrite with *his* mouth destroys his neighbor,
But through knowledge the righteous will be delivered.

9 בְּפֶה חָנֵף יַשְׁחִת רֵעֵהוּ
וּבְדַעַת צַדִּיקִים יֵחָלֵצוּ:

10 When it goes well with the righteous, the city
    rejoices;
    And when the wicked perish, *there is*
    jubilation.

11 By the blessing of the upright the city is
    exalted,
    But it is overthrown by the mouth of the
    wicked.

12 He who is devoid of wisdom despises his
    neighbor,
    But a man of understanding holds his peace.

13 A talebearer reveals secrets,
    But he who is of a faithful spirit conceals a
    matter.

14 Where *there is* no counsel, the people fall;
    But in the multitude of counselors *there is*
    safety.

15 He who is surety for a stranger will suffer,
    But one who hates being surety is secure.

16 A gracious woman retains honor,
    But ruthless *men* retain riches.

17 The merciful man does good for his own
    soul,
    But *he who is* cruel troubles his own flesh.

18 The wicked *man* does deceptive work,
    But he who sows righteousness *will have* a
    sure reward.

19 As righteousness *leads* to life,
    So he who pursues evil *pursues it* to his own
    death.

20 Those who are of a perverse heart *are* an
    abomination to the LORD,
    But *the* blameless in their ways *are* His
    delight.

21 *Though they join* forces, the wicked will not
    go unpunished;
    But the posterity of the righteous will be
    delivered.

22 *As* a ring of gold in a swine's snout,
    So is a lovely woman who lacks discretion.

23 The desire of the righteous *is* only good,
    But the expectation of the wicked *is* wrath.

24 There is *one* who scatters, yet increases
    more;
    And there is *one* who withholds more than is
    right,
    But it *leads* to poverty.

25 The generous soul will be made rich,
    And he who waters will also be watered
    himself.

10 בְּטוּב צַדִּיקִים תַּעֲלֹץ קִרְיָה
   וּבַאֲבֹד רְשָׁעִים רִנָּה׃

11 בְּבִרְכַּת יְשָׁרִים תָּרוּם קָרֶת
   וּבְפִי רְשָׁעִים תֵּהָרֵס׃

12 בָּז־לְרֵעֵהוּ חֲסַר־לֵב
   וְאִישׁ תְּבוּנוֹת יַחֲרִישׁ׃

13 הוֹלֵךְ רָכִיל מְגַלֶּה־סּוֹד
   וְנֶאֱמַן־רוּחַ מְכַסֶּה דָבָר׃

14 בְּאֵין תַּחְבֻּלוֹת יִפָּל־עָם
   וּתְשׁוּעָה בְּרֹב יוֹעֵץ׃

15 רַע־יֵרוֹעַ כִּי־עָרַב זָר
   וְשֹׂנֵא תֹקְעִים בּוֹטֵחַ׃

16 אֵשֶׁת־חֵן תִּתְמֹךְ כָּבוֹד
   וְעָרִיצִים יִתְמְכוּ־עֹשֶׁר׃

17 גֹּמֵל נַפְשׁוֹ אִישׁ חָסֶד
   וְעֹכֵר שְׁאֵרוֹ אַכְזָרִי׃

18 רָשָׁע עֹשֶׂה פְעֻלַּת־שָׁקֶר
   וְזֹרֵעַ צְדָקָה שֶׂכֶר אֱמֶת׃

19 כֵּן־צְדָקָה לְחַיִּים
   וּמְרַדֵּף רָעָה לְמוֹתוֹ׃

20 תּוֹעֲבַת יְהוָה עִקְּשֵׁי־לֵב
   וּרְצוֹנוֹ תְּמִימֵי דָרֶךְ׃

21 יָד לְיָד לֹא־יִנָּקֶה רָּע
   וְזֶרַע צַדִּיקִים נִמְלָט׃

22 נֶזֶם זָהָב בְּאַף חֲזִיר
   אִשָּׁה יָפָה וְסָרַת טָעַם׃

23 תַּאֲוַת צַדִּיקִים אַךְ־טוֹב
   תִּקְוַת רְשָׁעִים עֶבְרָה׃

24 יֵשׁ מְפַזֵּר וְנוֹסָף עוֹד
   וְחוֹשֵׂךְ מִיֹּשֶׁר אַךְ־לְמַחְסוֹר׃

25 נֶפֶשׁ־בְּרָכָה תְדֻשָּׁן
   וּמַרְוֶה גַּם־הוּא יוֹרֶא׃

26 The people will curse him who withholds
    grain,
    But blessing *will be* on the head of him who
    sells *it*.

27 He who earnestly seeks good finds favor,
    But trouble will come to him who seeks *evil*.

28 He who trusts in his riches will fall,
    But the righteous will flourish like foliage.

29 He who troubles his own house will inherit
    the wind,
    And the fool *will be* servant to the wise of
    heart.

30 The fruit of the righteous *is a* tree of life,
    And he who wins souls *is* wise.

31 If the righteous will be recompensed on the
    earth,
    How much more the ungodly and the sinner.

12 Whoever loves instruction loves knowledge,
    But he who hates correction *is* stupid.

2 A good *man* obtains favor from the LORD,
    But a man of wicked intentions He will
    condemn.

3 A man is not established by wickedness,
    But the root of the righteous cannot be
    moved.

4 An excellent wife *is* the crown of her
    husband,
    But she who causes shame *is* like rottenness
    in his bones.

5 The thoughts of the righteous *are* right,
    But the counsels of the wicked *are* deceitful.

6 The words of the wicked *are,* "Lie in wait for
    blood,"
    But the mouth of the upright will deliver
    them.

7 The wicked are overthrown and *are* no
    more,
    But the house of the righteous will stand.

8 A man will be commended according to his
    wisdom,
    But he who is of a perverse heart will be
    despised.

9 Better *is the one* who is slighted but has a
    servant,
    Than he who honors himself but lacks
    bread.

26 מֹנֵעַ בָּר יִקְּבֻהוּ לְאֹם
וּבְרָכָה לְרֹאשׁ מַשְׁבִּיר׃

27 לֹא־יַחֲרֹךְ רְמִיָּה צֵידֹו שָׁחַר טֹוב יְבַקֵּשׁ רָצֹון
וְדֹרֵשׁ רָעָה תְבֹואֶנּוּ׃

28 בֹּטֵחַ בְּעָשְׁרֹו הוּא יִפֹּל
וְכֶעָלֶה צַדִּיקִים יִפְרָחוּ׃

29 עֹכֵר בֵּיתֹו יִנְחַל־רוּחַ
וְעֶבֶד אֱוִיל לַחֲכַם־לֵב׃

30 פְּרִי־צַדִּיק עֵץ חַיִּים
וְלֹקֵחַ נְפָשֹׁות חָכָם׃

31 הֵן צַדִּיק בָּאָרֶץ יְשֻׁלָּם
אַף כִּי־רָשָׁע וְחֹוטֵא׃

יב אֹהֵב מוּסָר אֹהֵב דָּעַת
וְשֹׂנֵא תֹוכַחַת בָּעַר׃

2 טֹוב יָפִיק רָצֹון מֵיְהוָה
וְאִישׁ מְזִמֹּות יַרְשִׁיעַ׃

3 לֹא־יִכֹּון אָדָם בְּרֶשַׁע
וְשֹׁרֶשׁ צַדִּיקִים בַּל־יִמֹּוט׃

4 אֵשֶׁת־חַיִל עֲטֶרֶת בַּעְלָהּ
וּכְרָקָב בְּעַצְמֹותָיו מְבִישָׁה׃

5 מַחְשְׁבֹות צַדִּיקִים מִשְׁפָּט
תַּחְבֻּלֹות רְשָׁעִים מִרְמָה׃

6 דִּבְרֵי רְשָׁעִים אֱרָב־דָּם
וּפִי יְשָׁרִים יַצִּילֵם׃

7 הָפֹוךְ רְשָׁעִים וְאֵינָם
וּבֵית צַדִּיקִים יַעֲמֹד׃

8 לְפִי־שִׂכְלֹו יְהֻלַּל־אִישׁ
וְנַעֲוֵה־לֵב יִהְיֶה לָבוּז׃

9 טֹוב נִקְלֶה וְעֶבֶד לֹו
מִמְּתַכַּבֵּד וַחֲסַר־לָחֶם׃

10 A righteous *man* regards the life of his
　　animal,
　　But the tender mercies of the wicked *are*
　　cruel.

11 He who tills his land will be satisfied with
　　bread,
　　But he who follows frivolity *is* devoid of
　　understanding.

12 The wicked covet the catch of evil *men,*
　　But the root of the righteous yields *fruit.*

13 The wicked is ensnared by the transgression
　　of *his* lips,
　　But the righteous will come through trouble.

14 A man will be satisfied with good by the fruit
　　of *his* mouth,
　　And the recompense of a man's hands will
　　be rendered to him.

15 The way of a fool *is* right in his own eyes,
　　But he who heeds counsel *is* wise.

16 A fool's wrath is known at once,
　　But a prudent *man* covers shame.

17 He *who* speaks truth declares righteousness,
　　But a false witness, deceit.

18 There is one who speaks like the piercings of
　　a sword,
　　But the tongue of the wise *promotes* health.

19 The truthful lip shall be established forever,
　　But a lying tongue *is* but for a moment.

20 Deceit is in the heart of those who devise
　　evil,
　　But counselors of peace have joy.

21 No grave trouble will overtake the righteous,
　　But the wicked shall be filled with evil.

22 Lying lips *are* an abomination to the LORD,
　　But those who deal truthfully *are* His
　　delight.

23 A prudent man conceals knowledge,
　　But the heart of fools proclaims foolishness.

24 The hand of the diligent will rule,
　　But the lazy *man* will be put to forced labor.

25 Anxiety in the heart of man causes depres-
　　sion,
　　But a good word makes it glad.

26 The righteous should choose his friends
　　carefully,
　　For the way of the wicked leads them astray.

27 The lazy *man* does not roast what he took in
　　hunting,
　　But diligence *is* man's precious possession.

28 In the way of righteousness *is* life,

10 יוֹדֵעַ צַדִּיק נֶפֶשׁ בְּהֶמְתּוֹ
וְרַחֲמֵי רְשָׁעִים אַכְזָרִי:

11 עֹבֵד אַדְמָתוֹ יִשְׂבַּע־לָחֶם וּמְרַדֵּף רֵיקִים חֲסַר־
לֵב:

12 חָמַד רָשָׁע מְצוֹד רָעִים
וְשֹׁרֶשׁ צַדִּיקִים יִתֵּן:

13 בְּפֶשַׁע שְׂפָתַיִם מוֹקֵשׁ רָע
וַיֵּצֵא מִצָּרָה צַדִּיק:

14 מִפְּרִי פִי־אִישׁ יִשְׂבַּע־טוֹב
וּגְמוּל יְדֵי־אָדָם יָשׁוּב לוֹ:

15 דֶּרֶךְ אֱוִיל יָשָׁר בְּעֵינָיו
וְשֹׁמֵעַ לְעֵצָה חָכָם:

16 אֱוִיל בַּיּוֹם יִוָּדַע כַּעְסוֹ
וְכֹסֶה קָלוֹן עָרוּם:

17 יָפִיחַ אֱמוּנָה יַגִּיד צֶדֶק
וְעֵד שְׁקָרִים מִרְמָה:

18 יֵשׁ בּוֹטֶה כְּמַדְקְרוֹת חָרֶב
וּלְשׁוֹן חֲכָמִים מַרְפֵּא:

19 שְׂפַת־אֱמֶת תִּכּוֹן לָעַד
וְעַד־אַרְגִּיעָה לְשׁוֹן שָׁקֶר:

20 מִרְמָה בְּלֶב־חֹרְשֵׁי רָע
וּלְיֹעֲצֵי שָׁלוֹם שִׂמְחָה:

21 לֹא־יְאֻנֶּה לַצַּדִּיק כָּל־אָוֶן
וּרְשָׁעִים מָלְאוּ רָע:

22 תּוֹעֲבַת יְהֹוָה שִׂפְתֵי־שָׁקֶר
וְעֹשֵׂי אֱמוּנָה רְצוֹנוֹ:

23 אָדָם עָרוּם כֹּסֶה דָּעַת
וְלֵב כְּסִילִים יִקְרָא אִוֶּלֶת:

24 יַד־חָרוּצִים תִּמְשׁוֹל
וּרְמִיָּה תִּהְיֶה לָמַס:

25 דְּאָגָה בְלֶב־אִישׁ יַשְׁחֶנָּה
וְדָבָר טוֹב יְשַׂמְּחֶנָּה:

26 יָתֵר מֵרֵעֵהוּ צַדִּיק
וְדֶרֶךְ רְשָׁעִים תַּתְעֵם:

27 לֹא־יַחֲרֹךְ רְמִיָּה צֵידוֹ
וְהוֹן־אָדָם יָקָר חָרוּץ:

28 בְּאֹרַח־צְדָקָה חַיִּים

And in *its* pathway *there is* no death.   וְדֶרֶךְ נְתִיבָה אַל־מָוֶת:

13 A wise son *heeds* his father's instruction,
But a scoffer does not listen to rebuke.

יג בֵּן חָכָם מוּסַר אָב
וְלֵץ לֹא־שָׁמַע גְּעָרָה:

2 A man shall eat well by the fruit of *his* mouth,
But the soul of the unfaithful feeds on violence.

2 מִפְּרִי פִי־אִישׁ יֹאכַל טוֹב
וְנֶפֶשׁ בֹּגְדִים חָמָס:

3 He who guards his mouth preserves his life,
But he who opens wide his lips shall have destruction.

3 נֹצֵר פִּיו שֹׁמֵר נַפְשׁוֹ
פֹּשֵׂק שְׂפָתָיו מְחִתָּה־לוֹ:

4 The soul of a lazy *man* desires, and *has* nothing;
But the soul of the diligent shall be made rich.

4 מִתְאַוָּה וָאַיִן נַפְשׁוֹ עָצֵל
וְנֶפֶשׁ חָרֻצִים תְּדֻשָּׁן:

5 A righteous *man* hates lying,
But a wicked *man* is loathsome and comes to shame.

5 דְּבַר־שֶׁקֶר יִשְׂנָא צַדִּיק
וְרָשָׁע יַבְאִישׁ וְיַחְפִּיר:

6 Righteousness guards *him whose* way is blameless,
But wickedness overthrows the sinner.

6 צְדָקָה תִּצֹּר תָּם־דָּרֶךְ
וְרִשְׁעָה תְּסַלֵּף חַטָּאת:

7 There is one who makes himself rich, yet *has* nothing;
And one who makes himself poor, yet *has* great riches.

7 יֵשׁ מִתְעַשֵּׁר וְאֵין כֹּל
מִתְרוֹשֵׁשׁ וְהוֹן רָב:

8 The ransom of a man's life *is* his riches,
But the poor does not hear rebuke.

8 כֹּפֶר נֶפֶשׁ־אִישׁ עָשְׁרוֹ
וְרָשׁ לֹא־שָׁמַע גְּעָרָה:

9 The light of the righteous rejoices,
But the lamp of the wicked will be put out.

9 אוֹר־צַדִּיקִים יִשְׂמָח
וְנֵר רְשָׁעִים יִדְעָךְ:

10 By pride comes nothing but strife,
But with the well-advised *is* wisdom.

10 רַק־בְּזָדוֹן יִתֵּן מַצָּה
וְאֶת־נוֹעָצִים חָכְמָה:

11 Wealth *gained by* dishonesty will be diminished,
But he who gathers by labor will increase.

11 הוֹן מֵהֶבֶל יִמְעָט
וְקֹבֵץ עַל־יָד יַרְבֶּה:

12 Hope deferred makes the heart sick,
But *when* the desire comes, *it is* a tree of life.

12 תּוֹחֶלֶת מְמֻשָּׁכָה מַחֲלָה־לֵב
וְעֵץ חַיִּים תַּאֲוָה בָאָה:

13 He who despises the word will be destroyed,
But he who fears the commandment will be rewarded.

13 בָּז לְדָבָר יֵחָבֶל לוֹ
וִירֵא מִצְוָה הוּא יְשֻׁלָּם:

14 The law of the wise *is* a fountain of life,
To turn *one* away from the snares of death.

14 תּוֹרַת חָכָם מְקוֹר חַיִּים
לָסוּר מִמֹּקְשֵׁי מָוֶת:

15 Good understanding gains favor,
But the way of the unfaithful *is* hard.

15 שֵׂכֶל־טוֹב יִתֶּן־חֵן
וְדֶרֶךְ בֹּגְדִים אֵיתָן:

16 Every prudent *man* acts with knowledge,
But a fool lays open *his* folly.

16 כָּל־עָרוּם יַעֲשֶׂה בְדָעַת
וּכְסִיל יִפְרֹשׂ אִוֶּלֶת:

17 A wicked messenger falls into trouble,
But a faithful ambassador *brings* health.

17 מַלְאָךְ רָשָׁע יִפֹּל בְּרָע
וְצִיר אֱמוּנִים מַרְפֵּא:

18 Poverty and shame *will come* to him who
disdains correction,
But he who regards a rebuke will be
honored.

19 A desire accomplished is sweet to the soul,
But *it is* an abomination to fools to depart
from evil.

20 He who walks with wise *men* will be wise,
But the companion of fools will be
destroyed.

21 Evil pursues sinners,
But to the righteous, good shall be repaid.

22 A good *man* leaves an inheritance to his
children's children,
But the wealth of the sinner is stored up for
the righteous.

23 Much food *is in* the fallow *ground* of the
poor,
And for lack of justice there is waste.

24 He who spares his rod hates his son,
But he who loves him disciplines him
promptly.

25 The righteous eats to the satisfying of his
soul,
But the stomach of the wicked shall be in
want.

14 The wise woman builds her house,
But the foolish pulls it down with her hands.

2 He who walks in his uprightness fears the
LORD,
But *he who is* perverse in his ways despises
Him.

3 In the mouth of a fool *is* a rod of pride,
But the lips of the wise will preserve them.

4 Where no oxen *are*, the trough *is* clean;
But much increase *comes* by the strength of
an ox.

5 A faithful witness does not lie,
But a false witness will utter lies.

6 A scoffer seeks wisdom and does not *find it*,
But knowledge *is* easy to him who
understands.

7 Go from the presence of a foolish man,
When you do not perceive *in him* the lips of
knowledge.

8 The wisdom of the prudent *is* to understand
his way,
But the folly of fools *is* deceit.

רֵישׁ וְקָלוֹן פּוֹרֵעַ מוּסָר 18
וְשׁוֹמֵר תּוֹכַחַת יְכֻבָּד:

תַּאֲוָה נִהְיָה תֶּעֱרַב לְנָפֶשׁ 19
וְתוֹעֲבַת כְּסִילִים סוּר מֵרָע:

הֹלֵךְ אֶת־חֲכָמִים וַחֲכָם 20
וְרֹעֶה כְסִילִים יֵרוֹעַ:

חַטָּאִים תְּרַדֵּף רָעָה 21
וְאֶת־צַדִּיקִים יְשַׁלֶּם־טוֹב:

טוֹב יַנְחִיל בְּנֵי־בָנִים 22
וְצָפוּן לַצַּדִּיק חֵיל חוֹטֵא:

רָב־אֹכֶל נִיר רָאשִׁים 23
וְיֵשׁ נִסְפֶּה בְּלֹא מִשְׁפָּט:

חוֹשֵׂךְ שִׁבְטוֹ שׂוֹנֵא בְנוֹ 24
וְאֹהֲבוֹ שִׁחֲרוֹ מוּסָר:

צַדִּיק אֹכֵל לְשֹׂבַע נַפְשׁוֹ 25
וּבֶטֶן רְשָׁעִים תֶּחְסָר:

יד חַכְמוֹת נָשִׁים בָּנְתָה בֵיתָהּ
וְאִוֶּלֶת בְּיָדֶיהָ תֶהֶרְסֶנּוּ:

הוֹלֵךְ בְּיָשְׁרוֹ יְרֵא יְהוָה 2
וּנְלוֹז דְּרָכָיו בּוֹזֵהוּ:

בְּפִי־אֱוִיל חֹטֶר גַּאֲוָה 3
וְשִׂפְתֵי חֲכָמִים תִּשְׁמוּרֵם:

בְּאֵין אֲלָפִים אֵבוּס בָּר 4
וְרָב־תְּבוּאוֹת בְּכֹחַ שׁוֹר:

עֵד אֱמוּנִים לֹא יְכַזֵּב 5
וְיָפִיחַ כְּזָבִים עֵד שָׁקֶר:

בִּקֶּשׁ־לֵץ חָכְמָה וָאָיִן 6
וְדַעַת לְנָבוֹן נָקָל:

לֵךְ מִנֶּגֶד לְאִישׁ כְּסִיל 7
וּבַל־יָדַעְתָּ שִׂפְתֵי־דָעַת:

חָכְמַת עָרוּם הָבִין דַּרְכּוֹ 8
וְאִוֶּלֶת כְּסִילִים מִרְמָה:

ט 20 הֹלֵךְ יָחְכָּם

9   Fools mock at sin,
     But among the upright *there is* favor.

אֱוִלִים יָלִיץ אָשָׁם 9
וּבֵין יְשָׁרִים רָצוֹן׃

10   The heart knows its own bitterness,
     And a stranger does not share its joy.

לֵב יוֹדֵעַ מָרַת נַפְשׁוֹ 10
וּבְשִׂמְחָתוֹ לֹא־יִתְעָרַב זָר׃

11   The house of the wicked will be overthrown,
     But the tent of the upright will flourish.

בֵּית רְשָׁעִים יִשָּׁמֵד 11
וְאֹהֶל יְשָׁרִים יַפְרִיחַ׃

12   There is a way *that seems* right to a man,
     But its end *is* the way of death.

יֵשׁ דֶּרֶךְ יָשָׁר לִפְנֵי־אִישׁ 12
וְאַחֲרִיתָהּ דַּרְכֵי־מָוֶת׃

13   Even in laughter the heart may sorrow,
     And the end of mirth *may be* grief.

גַּם־בִּשְׂחוֹק יִכְאַב־לֵב 13
וְאַחֲרִיתָהּ שִׂמְחָה תוּגָה׃

14   The backslider in heart will be filled with his
       own ways,
     But a good man *will be satisfied* from above.

מִדְּרָכָיו יִשְׂבַּע סוּג לֵב 14
וּמֵעָלָיו אִישׁ טוֹב׃

15   The simple believes every word,
     But the prudent considers well his steps.

פֶּתִי יַאֲמִין לְכָל־דָּבָר 15
וְעָרוּם יָבִין לַאֲשֻׁרוֹ׃

16   A wise *man* fears and departs from evil,
     But a fool rages and is self-confident.

חָכָם יָרֵא וְסָר מֵרָע 16
וּכְסִיל מִתְעַבֵּר וּבוֹטֵחַ׃

17   A quick-tempered *man* acts foolishly,
     And a man of wicked intentions is hated.

קְצַר־אַפַּיִם יַעֲשֶׂה אִוֶּלֶת 17
וְאִישׁ מְזִמּוֹת יִשָּׂנֵא׃

18   The simple inherit folly,
     But the prudent are crowned with
       knowledge.

נָחֲלוּ פְתָאיִם אִוֶּלֶת 18
וַעֲרוּמִים יַכְתִּרוּ דָעַת׃

19   The evil will bow before the good,
     And the wicked at the gates of the righteous.

שַׁחוּ רָעִים לִפְנֵי טוֹבִים 19
וּרְשָׁעִים עַל־שַׁעֲרֵי צַדִּיק׃

20   The poor *man* is hated even by his own
       neighbor,
     But the rich *has* many friends.

גַּם־לְרֵעֵהוּ יִשָּׂנֵא רָשׁ 20
וְאֹהֲבֵי עָשִׁיר רַבִּים׃

21   He who despises his neighbor sins;
     But he who has mercy on the poor, happy *is*
       he.

בָּז־לְרֵעֵהוּ חוֹטֵא 21
וּמְחוֹנֵן עֲנִיִּים אַשְׁרָיו׃

22   Do they not go astray who devise evil?
     But mercy and truth *belong* to those who
       devise good.

הֲלוֹא־יִתְעוּ חֹרְשֵׁי רָע 22
וְחֶסֶד וֶאֱמֶת חֹרְשֵׁי טוֹב׃

23   In all labor there is profit,
     But idle chatter *leads* only to poverty.

בְּכָל־עֶצֶב יִהְיֶה מוֹתָר 23
וּדְבַר־שְׂפָתַיִם אַךְ־לְמַחְסוֹר׃

24   The crown of the wise is their riches,
     But the foolishness of fools is folly.

עֲטֶרֶת חֲכָמִים עָשְׁרָם 24
אִוֶּלֶת כְּסִילִים אִוֶּלֶת׃

25   A true witness delivers souls,
     But a deceitful *witness* speaks lies.

מַצִּיל נְפָשׁוֹת עֵד אֱמֶת 25
וְיָפִחַ כְּזָבִים מִרְמָה׃

26   In the fear of the LORD *there is* strong
       confidence,
     And His children will have a place of refuge.

בְּיִרְאַת יְהֹוָה מִבְטַח־עֹז 26
וּלְבָנָיו יִהְיֶה מַחְסֶה׃

27   The fear of the LORD *is* a fountain of life,
     To turn *one* away from the snares of death.

יִרְאַת יְהֹוָה מְקוֹר חַיִּים 27
לָסוּר מִמֹּקְשֵׁי מָוֶת׃

28   In a multitude of people *is* a king's honor,
     But in the lack of people *is* the downfall of a
       prince.

בְּרָב־עָם הַדְרַת־מֶלֶךְ 28
וּבְאֶפֶס לְאֹם מְחִתַּת רָזוֹן׃

יד 21 עֲנִיִּים

29   *He who is* slow to wrath has great understanding,
But *he who is* impulsive exalts folly.

אֶרֶךְ אַפַּיִם רַב־תְּבוּנָה 29
וּקְצַר־רוּחַ מֵרִים אִוֶּלֶת:

30   A sound heart *is* life to the body,
But envy *is* rottenness to the bones.

מְאוֹר־עֵינַיִם יְשַׂמַּח־לֵב 30
שְׁמוּעָה טוֹבָה תְּדַשֶּׁן־עָצֶם:

31   He who oppresses the poor reproaches his
Maker,
But he who honors Him has mercy on the
needy.

אֹזֶן שֹׁמַעַת תּוֹכַחַת חַיִּים 31
בְּקֶרֶב חֲכָמִים תָּלִין:

32   The wicked is banished in his wickedness,
But the righteous has a refuge in his death.

פּוֹרֵעַ מוּסָר מוֹאֵס נַפְשׁוֹ 32
וְשׁוֹמֵעַ תּוֹכַחַת קוֹנֶה לֵּב:

33   Wisdom rests in the heart of him who has
understanding,
But *what is* in the heart of fools is made
known.

יִרְאַת יְהוָה מוּסַר חָכְמָה 33
וְלִפְנֵי כָבוֹד עֲנָוָה:

34   Righteousness exalts a nation,
But sin *is* a reproach to *any* people.

צְדָקָה תְרוֹמֵם־גּוֹי 34
וְחֶסֶד לְאֻמִּים חַטָּאת:

35   The king's favor *is* toward a wise servant,
But his wrath *is against* him who causes
shame.

רְצוֹן־מֶלֶךְ לְעֶבֶד מַשְׂכִּיל 35
וְעֶבְרָתוֹ תִּהְיֶה מֵבִישׁ:

15
A soft answer turns away wrath,
But a harsh word stirs up anger.

טו מַעֲנֶה־רַּךְ יָשִׁיב חֵמָה
וּדְבַר־עֶצֶב יַעֲלֶה־אָף:

2   The tongue of the wise uses knowledge
rightly,
But the mouth of fools pours forth
foolishness.

לְשׁוֹן חֲכָמִים תֵּיטִיב דָּעַת 2
וּפִי כְסִילִים יַבִּיעַ אִוֶּלֶת:

3   The eyes of the LORD *are* in every place,
Keeping watch on the evil and the good.

בְּכָל־מָקוֹם עֵינֵי יְהוָה 3
צֹפוֹת רָעִים וְטוֹבִים:

4   A wholesome tongue *is* a tree of life,
But perverseness in it breaks the spirit.

מַרְפֵּא לָשׁוֹן עֵץ חַיִּים 4
וְסֶלֶף בָּהּ שֶׁבֶר בְּרוּחַ:

5   A fool despises his father's instruction,
But he who receives correction is prudent.

אֱוִיל יִנְאַץ מוּסַר אָבִיו 5
וְשֹׁמֵר תּוֹכַחַת יַעְרִם:

6   *In* the house of the righteous *there is* much
treasure,
But in the revenue of the wicked is trouble.

בֵּית צַדִּיק חֹסֶן רָב 6
וּבִתְבוּאַת רָשָׁע נֶעְכָּרֶת:

7   The lips of the wise disperse knowledge,
But the heart of the fool *does* not *do* so.

שִׂפְתֵי חֲכָמִים יְזָרוּ דָעַת 7
וְלֵב כְּסִילִים לֹא־כֵן:

8   The sacrifice of the wicked *is* an abomination to the LORD,
But the prayer of the upright *is* His delight.

זֶבַח רְשָׁעִים תּוֹעֲבַת יְהוָה 8
וּתְפִלַּת יְשָׁרִים רְצוֹנוֹ:

9   The way of the wicked *is* an abomination to
the LORD,
But He loves him who follows righteousness.

תּוֹעֲבַת יְהוָה דֶּרֶךְ רָשָׁע 9
וּמְרַדֵּף צְדָקָה יֶאֱהָב:

10   Harsh discipline *is* for him who forsakes the
way,
And he who hates correction will die.

מוּסָר רָע לְעֹזֵב אֹרַח 10
שׂוֹנֵא תוֹכַחַת יָמוּת:

11   Hell and Destruction *are* before the LORD;

שְׁאוֹל וַאֲבַדּוֹן נֶגֶד יְהוָה 11

So how much more the hearts of the sons of men.

אַף כִּי־לִבּוֹת בְּנֵי־אָדָם:

12 A scoffer does not love one who corrects him,
Nor will he go to the wise.

12 לֹא יֶאֱהַב־לֵץ הוֹכֵחַ לוֹ
אֶל־חֲכָמִים לֹא יֵלֵךְ:

13 A merry heart makes a cheerful countenance,
But by sorrow of the heart the spirit is broken.

13 לֵב שָׂמֵחַ יֵיטִב פָּנִים
וּבְעַצְּבַת־לֵב רוּחַ נְכֵאָה:

14 The heart of him who has understanding seeks knowledge,
But the mouth of fools feeds on foolishness.

14 לֵב נָבוֹן יְבַקֶּשׁ־דָּעַת
וּפְנֵי כְסִילִים יִרְעֶה אִוֶּלֶת:

15 All the days of the afflicted are evil,
But he who is of a merry heart has a continual feast.

15 כָּל־יְמֵי עָנִי רָעִים
וְטוֹב־לֵב מִשְׁתֶּה תָמִיד:

16 Better is a little with the fear of the LORD,
Than great treasure with trouble.

16 טוֹב־מְעַט בְּיִרְאַת יְהוָה
מֵאוֹצָר רָב וּמְהוּמָה בוֹ:

17 Better is a dinner of herbs where love is,
Than a fatted calf with hatred.

17 טוֹב אֲרֻחַת יָרָק וְאַהֲבָה־שָׁם
מִשּׁוֹר אָבוּס וְשִׂנְאָה־בוֹ:

18 A wrathful man stirs up strife,
But he who is slow to anger allays contention.

18 אִישׁ חֵמָה יְגָרֶה מָדוֹן
וְאֶרֶךְ אַפַּיִם יַשְׁקִיט רִיב:

19 The way of the lazy man is like a hedge of thorns,
But the way of the upright is a highway.

19 דֶּרֶךְ עָצֵל כִּמְשֻׂכַת חָדֶק
וְאֹרַח יְשָׁרִים סְלֻלָה:

20 A wise son makes a father glad,
But a foolish man despises his mother.

20 בֵּן חָכָם יְשַׂמַּח־אָב
וּכְסִיל אָדָם בּוֹזֶה אִמּוֹ:

21 Folly is joy to him who is destitute of discernment,
But a man of understanding walks uprightly.

21 אִוֶּלֶת שִׂמְחָה לַחֲסַר־לֵב
וְאִישׁ תְּבוּנָה יְיַשֶּׁר־לָכֶת:

22 Without counsel, plans go awry,
But in the multitude of counselors they are established.

22 הָפֵר מַחֲשָׁבוֹת בְּאֵין סוֹד
וּבְרֹב יוֹעֲצִים תָּקוּם:

23 A man has joy by the answer of his mouth,
And a word spoken in due season, how good it is!

23 שִׂמְחָה לָאִישׁ בְּמַעֲנֵה־פִיו
וְדָבָר בְּעִתּוֹ מַה־טּוֹב:

24 The way of life winds upward for the wise,
That he may turn away from hell below.

24 אֹרַח חַיִּים לְמַעְלָה לְמַשְׂכִּיל
לְמַעַן סוּר מִשְּׁאוֹל מָטָּה:

25 The LORD will destroy the house of the proud,
But He will establish the boundary of the widow.

25 בֵּית גֵּאִים יִסַּח יְהוָה
וְיַצֵּב גְּבוּל אַלְמָנָה:

26 The thoughts of the wicked are an abomination to the LORD,
But the words of the pure are pleasant.

26 תּוֹעֲבַת יְהוָה מַחְשְׁבוֹת רָע
וּטְהֹרִים אִמְרֵי־נֹעַם:

27 He who is greedy for gain troubles his own house,
But he who hates bribes will live.

27 עֹכֵר בֵּיתוֹ בּוֹצֵעַ בָּצַע
וְשׂוֹנֵא מַתָּנֹת יִחְיֶה:

28 The heart of the righteous studies how to
      answer,
      But the mouth of the wicked pours forth
      evil.

29 The LORD *is* far from the wicked,
      But He hears the prayer of the righteous.

30 The light of the eyes rejoices the heart,
      And a good report makes the bones healthy.

31 The ear that hears the rebukes of life
      Will abide among the wise.

32 He who disdains instruction despises his own
      soul,
      But he who heeds rebuke gets
      understanding.

33 The fear of the LORD *is* the instruction of
      wisdom,
      And before honor *is* humility.

16 The preparations of the heart *belong* to man,
      But the answer of the tongue *is* from the
      LORD.

2 All the ways of a man *are* pure in his own
      eyes,
      But the LORD weighs the spirits.

3 Commit your works to the LORD,
      And your thoughts will be established.

4 The LORD has made all for Himself,
      Yes, even the wicked for the day of doom.

5 Everyone proud in heart *is* an abomination
      to the LORD;
      Though they join forces, none will go
      unpunished.

6 In mercy and truth
      Atonement is provided for iniquity;
      And by the fear of the LORD *one* departs
      from evil.

7 When a man's ways please the LORD,
      He makes even his enemies to be at peace
      with him.

8 Better *is* a little with righteousness,
      Than vast revenues without justice.

9 A man's heart plans his way,
      But the LORD directs his steps.

10 Divination *is* on the lips of the king;
      His mouth must not transgress in judgment.

11 Honest weights and scales *are* the LORD's;
      All the weights in the bag *are* His work.

12 *It is* an abomination for kings to commit
      wickedness,

28 לֵב צַדִּיק יֶהְגֶּה לַעֲנוֹת
וּפִי רְשָׁעִים יַבִּיעַ רָעוֹת׃

29 רָחוֹק יְהוָה מֵרְשָׁעִים
וּתְפִלַּת צַדִּיקִים יִשְׁמָע׃

30 מְאוֹר־עֵינַיִם יְשַׂמַּח־לֵב
שְׁמוּעָה טוֹבָה תְּדַשֶּׁן־עָצֶם׃

31 אֹזֶן שֹׁמַעַת תּוֹכַחַת חַיִּים
בְּקֶרֶב חֲכָמִים תָּלִין׃

32 פּוֹרֵעַ מוּסָר מוֹאֵס נַפְשׁוֹ
וְשׁוֹמֵעַ תּוֹכַחַת קוֹנֶה לֵּב׃

33 יִרְאַת יְהוָה מוּסַר חָכְמָה
וְלִפְנֵי כָבוֹד עֲנָוָה׃

טז לְאָדָם מַעַרְכֵי־לֵב
וּמֵיְהוָה מַעֲנֵה לָשׁוֹן׃

2 כָּל־דַּרְכֵי־אִישׁ זַךְ בְּעֵינָיו
וְתֹכֵן רוּחוֹת יְהוָה׃

3 גֹּל אֶל־יְהוָה מַעֲשֶׂיךָ
וְיִכֹּנוּ מַחְשְׁבֹתֶיךָ׃

4 כֹּל פָּעַל יְהוָה לַמַּעֲנֵהוּ
וְגַם־רָשָׁע לְיוֹם רָעָה׃

5 תּוֹעֲבַת יְהוָה כָּל־גְּבַהּ־לֵב
יָד לְיָד לֹא יִנָּקֶה׃

6 בְּחֶסֶד וֶאֱמֶת יְכֻפַּר עָוֹן
וּבְיִרְאַת יְהוָה סוּר מֵרָע׃

7 בִּרְצוֹת יְהוָה דַּרְכֵי־אִישׁ
גַּם־אוֹיְבָיו יַשְׁלִם אִתּוֹ׃

8 טוֹב־מְעַט בִּצְדָקָה
מֵרֹב תְּבוּאוֹת בְּלֹא מִשְׁפָּט׃

9 לֵב אָדָם יְחַשֵּׁב דַּרְכּוֹ
וַיהוָה יָכִין צַעֲדוֹ׃

10 קֶסֶם ׀ עַל־שִׂפְתֵי־מֶלֶךְ
בְּמִשְׁפָּט לֹא יִמְעַל־פִּיו׃

11 פֶּלֶס ׀ וּמֹאזְנֵי מִשְׁפָּט לַיהוָה
מַעֲשֵׂהוּ כָּל־אַבְנֵי־כִיס׃

12 תּוֹעֲבַת מְלָכִים עֲשׂוֹת רֶשַׁע

For a throne is established by righteousness.

13 Righteous lips *are* the delight of kings,
And they love him who speaks *what is* right.

14 As messengers of death *is* the king's wrath,
But a wise man will appease it.

15 In the light of the king's face *is* life,
And his favor *is* like a cloud of the latter
rain.

16 How much better to get wisdom than gold!
And to get understanding is to be chosen
rather than silver.

17 The highway of the upright *is* to depart from
evil;
He who keeps his way preserves his soul.

18 Pride *goes* before destruction,
And a haughty spirit before a fall.

19 Better *to be* of a humble spirit with the lowly,
Than to divide the spoil with the proud.

20 He who heeds the word wisely will find
good,
And whoever trusts in the Lord, happy *is*
he.

21 The wise in heart will be called prudent,
And sweetness of the lips increases learning.

22 Understanding *is* a wellspring of life to him
who has it.
But the correction of fools *is* folly.

23 The heart of the wise teaches his mouth,
And adds learning to his lips.

24 Pleasant words *are* like a honeycomb,
Sweetness to the soul and health to the
bones.

25 There is a way *that seems* right to a man,
But its end *is* the way of death.

26 The person who labors, labors for himself,
For his *hungry* mouth drives him *on.*

27 An ungodly man digs up evil,
And *it is* on his lips like a burning fire.

28 A perverse man sows strife,
And a whisperer separates the best of
friends.

29 A violent man entices his neighbor,
And leads him in a way *that is* not good.

30 He winks his eye to devise perverse things;
He purses his lips *and* brings about evil.

31 The silver-haired head *is* a crown of glory,
If it is found in the way of righteousness.

כִּי בִצְדָקָה יִכּוֹן כִּסֵּא:
13 רְצוֹן מְלָכִים שִׂפְתֵי־צֶדֶק
וְדֹבֵר יְשָׁרִים יֶאֱהָב:
14 חֲמַת־מֶלֶךְ מַלְאֲכֵי־מָוֶת
וְאִישׁ חָכָם יְכַפְּרֶנָּה:
15 בְּאוֹר־פְּנֵי־מֶלֶךְ חַיִּים
וּרְצוֹנוֹ כְּעָב מַלְקוֹשׁ:
16 קְנֹה־חָכְמָה מַה־טּוֹב מֵחָרוּץ
וּקְנוֹת בִּינָה נִבְחָר מִכָּסֶף:
17 מְסִלַּת יְשָׁרִים סוּר מֵרָע
שֹׁמֵר נַפְשׁוֹ נֹצֵר דַּרְכּוֹ:
18 לִפְנֵי־שֶׁבֶר גָּאוֹן
וְלִפְנֵי כִשָּׁלוֹן גֹּבַהּ רוּחַ:
19 טוֹב שְׁפַל־רוּחַ אֶת־עֲנָוִים
מֵחַלֵּק שָׁלָל אֶת־גֵּאִים:
20 מַשְׂכִּיל עַל־דָּבָר יִמְצָא־טוֹב
וּבוֹטֵחַ בַּיהוָה אַשְׁרָיו:
21 לַחֲכַם־לֵב יִקָּרֵא נָבוֹן
וּמֶתֶק שְׂפָתַיִם יֹסִיף לֶקַח:
22 מְקוֹר חַיִּים שֵׂכֶל בְּעָלָיו
וּמוּסַר אֱוִלִים אִוֶּלֶת:
23 לֵב חָכָם יַשְׂכִּיל פִּיהוּ
וְעַל־שְׂפָתָיו יֹסִיף לֶקַח:
24 צוּף־דְּבַשׁ אִמְרֵי־נֹעַם
מָתוֹק לַנֶּפֶשׁ וּמַרְפֵּא לָעָצֶם:
25 יֵשׁ דֶּרֶךְ יָשָׁר לִפְנֵי־אִישׁ
וְאַחֲרִיתָהּ דַּרְכֵי־מָוֶת:
26 נֶפֶשׁ עָמֵל עָמְלָה לּוֹ
כִּי־אָכַף עָלָיו פִּיהוּ:
27 אִישׁ בְּלִיַּעַל כֹּרֶה רָעָה
וְעַל־שְׂפָתוֹ כְּאֵשׁ צָרָבֶת:
28 אִישׁ תַּהְפֻּכוֹת יְשַׁלַּח מָדוֹן
וְנִרְגָּן מַפְרִיד אַלּוּף:
29 אִישׁ חָמָס יְפַתֶּה רֵעֵהוּ
וְהוֹלִיכוֹ בְּדֶרֶךְ לֹא־טוֹב:
30 עֹצֶה עֵינָיו לַחְשֹׁב תַּהְפֻּכוֹת
קֹרֵץ שְׂפָתָיו כִּלָּה רָעָה:

31 He who *is* slow to anger *is* better than the
   mighty,
   And he who rules his spirit than he who
   takes a city.

עֲטֶרֶת תִּפְאֶרֶת שֵׂיבָה 31
בְּדֶרֶךְ צְדָקָה תִּמָּצֵא:

33 The lot is cast into the lap,
   But its every decision *is* from the LORD.

טוֹב אֶרֶךְ אַפַּיִם מִגִּבּוֹר 32
וּמֹשֵׁל בְּרוּחוֹ מִלֹּכֵד עִיר:

בַּחֵיק יוּטַל אֶת־הַגּוֹרָל 33
וּמֵיְהֹוָה כָּל־מִשְׁפָּטוֹ:

17 Better *is* a dry morsel with quietness,
   Than a house full of feasting *with* strife.

2 A wise servant will rule over a son who
   causes shame,
   And will share an inheritance among the
   brothers.

יז טוֹב פַּת חֲרֵבָה וְשַׁלְוָה־בָהּ
מִבַּיִת מָלֵא זִבְחֵי־רִיב:

3 The refining pot *is* for silver and the furnace
   for gold,
   But the LORD tests the hearts.

עֶבֶד־מַשְׂכִּיל יִמְשֹׁל בְּבֵן מֵבִישׁ 2
וּבְתוֹךְ אַחִים יַחֲלֹק נַחֲלָה:

4 An evildoer gives heed to false lips;
   A liar listens eagerly to a spiteful tongue.

מַצְרֵף לַכֶּסֶף וְכוּר לַזָּהָב 3
וּבֹחֵן לִבּוֹת יְהֹוָה:

5 He who mocks the poor reproaches his
   Maker;
   He who is glad at calamity will not go
   unpunished.

מֵרַע מַקְשִׁיב עַל־שְׂפַת־אָוֶן 4
שֶׁקֶר מֵזִין עַל־לְשׁוֹן הַוֹּת:

6 Children's children *are* the crown of old
   men,
   And the glory of children *is* their father.

לֹעֵג לָרָשׁ חֵרֵף עֹשֵׂהוּ 5
שָׂמֵחַ לְאֵיד לֹא יִנָּקֶה:

7 Excellent speech is not becoming to a fool,
   Much less lying lips to a prince.

עֲטֶרֶת זְקֵנִים בְּנֵי בָנִים 6
וְתִפְאֶרֶת בָּנִים אֲבוֹתָם:

8 A present *is* a precious stone in the eyes of its
   possessor;
   Wherever he turns, he prospers.

לֹא־נָאוָה לְנָבָל שְׂפַת־יֶתֶר 7
אַף כִּי־לְנָדִיב שְׂפַת־שָׁקֶר:

9 He who covers a transgression seeks love,
   But he who repeats a matter separates
   friends.

אֶבֶן־חֵן הַשֹּׁחַד בְּעֵינֵי בְעָלָיו 8
אֶל־כָּל־אֲשֶׁר יִפְנֶה יַשְׂכִּיל:

10 Rebuke is more effective for a wise *man*
    Than a hundred blows on a fool.

מְכַסֶּה־פֶּשַׁע מְבַקֵּשׁ אַהֲבָה 9
וְשֹׁנֶה בְדָבָר מַפְרִיד אַלּוּף:

11 An evil *man* seeks only rebellion;
    Therefore a cruel messenger will be sent
    against him.

תֵּחַת גְּעָרָה בְמֵבִין 10
מֵהַכּוֹת כְּסִיל מֵאָה:

12 Let a man meet a bear robbed of her cubs,
    Rather than a fool in his folly.

אַךְ־מְרִי יְבַקֶּשׁ־רָע 11
וּמַלְאָךְ אַכְזָרִי יְשֻׁלַּח־בּוֹ:

13 Whoever rewards evil for good,
    Evil will not depart from his house.

פָּגוֹשׁ דֹּב שַׁכּוּל בְּאִישׁ 12
וְאַל־כְּסִיל בְּאִוַּלְתּוֹ:

14 The beginning of strife *is like* releasing
    water;
    Therefore stop contention before a quarrel
    starts.

מֵשִׁיב רָעָה תַּחַת טוֹבָה 13
לֹא־תָמִישׁᴾ רָעָה מִבֵּיתוֹ:

פּוֹטֵר מַיִם רֵאשִׁית מָדוֹן 14
וְלִפְנֵי הִתְגַּלַּע הָרִיב נְטוֹשׁ:

15 He who justifies the wicked, and he who
condemns the just,
Both of them alike *are* an abomination to
the LORD.

16 Why *is there* in the hand of a fool the
purchase price of wisdom,
Since *he has* no heart *for it?*

17 A friend loves at all times,
And a brother is born for adversity.

18 A man devoid of understanding shakes
hands in a pledge,
And becomes surety for his friend.

19 He who loves transgression loves strife,
And he who exalts his gate seeks
destruction.

20 He who has a deceitful heart finds no good,
And he who has a perverse tongue falls into
evil.

21 He who begets a scoffer *does so* to his
sorrow,
And the father of a fool has no joy.

22 A merry heart does good, *like* medicine,
But a broken spirit dries the bones.

23 A wicked *man* accepts a bribe behind the
back
To pervert the ways of justice.

24 Wisdom *is* in the sight of him who has
understanding,
But the eyes of a fool *are* on the ends of the
earth.

25 A foolish son *is* a grief to his father,
And bitterness to her who bore him.

26 Also, to punish the righteous *is* not good,
Nor to strike princes for *their* uprightness.

27 He who has knowledge spares his words,
And a man of understanding is of a calm
spirit.

28 Even a fool is counted wise when he holds
his peace;
When he shuts his lips, *he is considered*
perceptive.

18 A man who isolates himself seeks his own
desire;

He rages against all wise judgment.

2 A fool has no delight in understanding,
But in expressing his own heart.

15 מַצְדִּיק רָשָׁע וּמַרְשִׁיעַ צַדִּיק
תּוֹעֲבַת יְהֹוָה גַּם־שְׁנֵיהֶם:

16 לָמָּה־זֶּה מְחִיר בְּיַד־כְּסִיל
לִקְנוֹת חָכְמָה וְלֶב־אָיִן:

17 בְּכָל־עֵת אֹהֵב הָרֵעַ
וְאָח לְצָרָה יִוָּלֵד:

18 אָדָם חֲסַר־לֵב תּוֹקֵעַ כָּף
עֹרֵב עֲרֻבָּה לִפְנֵי רֵעֵהוּ:

19 אֹהֵב פֶּשַׁע אֹהֵב מַצָּה
מַגְבִּיהַּ פִּתְחוֹ מְבַקֶּשׁ־שָׁבֶר:

20 עִקֶּשׁ־לֵב לֹא יִמְצָא־טוֹב
וְנֶהְפָּךְ בִּלְשׁוֹנוֹ יִפּוֹל בְּרָעָה:

21 יֹלֵד כְּסִיל לְתוּגָה לוֹ
וְלֹא־יִשְׂמַח אֲבִי נָבָל:

22 לֵב שָׂמֵחַ יֵיטִב גֵּהָה
וְרוּחַ נְכֵאָה תְּיַבֶּשׁ־גָּרֶם:

23 שֹׁחַד מֵחֵיק רָשָׁע יִקָּח
לְהַטּוֹת אָרְחוֹת מִשְׁפָּט:

24 אֶת־פְּנֵי מֵבִין חָכְמָה
וְעֵינֵי כְסִיל בִּקְצֵה־אָרֶץ:

25 כַּעַס לְאָבִיו בֵּן כְּסִיל
וּמֶמֶר לְיוֹלַדְתּוֹ:

26 גַּם עֲנוֹשׁ לַצַּדִּיק לֹא־טוֹב
לְהַכּוֹת נְדִיבִים עַל־יֹשֶׁר:

27 חוֹשֵׂךְ אֲמָרָיו יוֹדֵעַ דָּעַת
וְקַר ק רוּחַ אִישׁ תְּבוּנָה:

28 גַּם אֱוִיל מַחֲרִישׁ חָכָם יֵחָשֵׁב
אֹטֵם שְׂפָתָיו נָבוֹן:

יח לְתַאֲוָה יְבַקֵּשׁ נִפְרָד
בְּכָל־תּוּשִׁיָּה יִתְגַּלָּע:

2 לֹא־יַחְפֹּץ כְּסִיל בִּתְבוּנָה
כִּי אִם־בְּהִתְגַּלּוֹת לִבּוֹ:

3 When the wicked comes, contempt comes also;
And with dishonor *comes* reproach.

4 The words of a man's mouth *are* deep waters;
The wellspring of wisdom *is* a flowing brook.

5 *It is* not good to show partiality to the wicked,
Or to overthrow the righteous in judgment.

6 A fool's lips enter into contention,
And his mouth calls for blows.

7 A fool's mouth *is* his destruction,
And his lips *are* the snare of his soul.

8 The words of a talebearer *are* like tasty trifles,
And they go down into the inmost body.

9 He who is slothful in his work
Is a brother to him who is a great destroyer.

10 The name of the LORD *is* a strong tower;
The righteous run to it and are safe.

11 The rich man's wealth *is* his strong city,
And like a high wall in his own esteem.

12 Before destruction the heart of a man is haughty,
And before honor *is* humility.

13 He who answers a matter before he hears *it,*
It *is* folly and shame to him.

14 The spirit of a man will sustain him in sickness,
But who can bear a broken spirit?

15 The heart of the prudent acquires knowledge,
And the ear of the wise seeks knowledge.

16 A man's gift makes room for him,
And brings him before great men.

17 The first *one* to plead his cause *seems* right,
Until his neighbor comes and examines him.

18 Casting lots causes contentions to cease,
And keeps the mighty apart.

19 A brother offended *is harder to win* than a strong city,
And contentions *are* like the bars of a castle.

20 A man's stomach shall be satisfied from the fruit of his mouth;
From the produce of his lips he shall be filled.

כִּֽי־ב֣וֹא רָ֭שָׁע בָּ֣א גַם־בּ֑וּז
וְֽעִם־קָל֥וֹן חֶרְפָּֽה׃ 3

מַ֣יִם עֲ֭מֻקִּים דִּבְרֵ֣י פִי־אִ֑ישׁ
נַ֥חַל נֹ֝בֵ֗עַ מְק֣וֹר חָכְמָֽה׃ 4

שְׂאֵ֣ת פְּנֵי־רָשָׁ֣ע לֹא־ט֑וֹב
לְהַטּ֥וֹת צַ֝דִּ֗יק בַּמִּשְׁפָּֽט׃ 5

שִׂפְתֵ֣י כְ֭סִיל יָבֹ֣אוּ בְרִ֑יב
וּ֝פִ֗יו לְֽמַהֲלֻמ֥וֹת יִקְרָֽא׃ 6

פִּֽי־כְ֭סִיל מְחִתָּה־ל֑וֹ
וּ֝שְׂפָתָ֗יו מוֹקֵ֥שׁ נַפְשֽׁוֹ׃ 7

דִּבְרֵ֣י נִ֭רְגָּן כְּמִֽתְלַהֲמִ֑ים
וְ֝הֵ֗ם יָרְד֥וּ חַדְרֵי־בָֽטֶן׃ 8

גַּ֭ם מִתְרַפֶּ֣ה בִמְלַאכְתּ֑וֹ
אָ֥ח ה֝֗וּא לְבַ֣עַל מַשְׁחִֽית׃ 9

מִגְדַּל־עֹ֭ז שֵׁ֣ם יְהוָ֑ה
בּֽוֹ־יָר֖וּץ צַדִּ֣יק וְנִשְׂגָּֽב׃ 10

ה֣וֹן עָ֭שִׁיר קִרְיַ֣ת עֻזּ֑וֹ
וּכְחוֹמָ֥ה נִ֝שְׂגָּבָ֗ה בְּמַשְׂכִּיתֽוֹ׃ 11

לִפְנֵי־שֶׁ֭בֶר יִגְבַּ֣הּ לֵב־אִ֑ישׁ
וְלִפְנֵ֖י כָב֣וֹד עֲנָוָֽה׃ 12

מֵשִׁ֣יב דָּ֭בָר בְּטֶ֣רֶם יִשְׁמָ֑ע
אִוֶּ֥לֶת הִיא־ל֝֗וֹ וּכְלִמָּֽה׃ 13

רֽוּחַ־אִ֭ישׁ יְכַלְכֵּ֣ל מַחֲלֵ֑הוּ
וְר֥וּחַ נְ֝כֵאָ֗ה מִ֣י יִשָּׂאֶֽנָּה׃ 14

לֵ֣ב נָ֭בוֹן יִקְנֶה־דָּ֑עַת
וְאֹ֥זֶן חֲ֝כָמִ֗ים תְּבַקֶּשׁ־דָּֽעַת׃ 15

מַתָּ֣ן אָ֭דָם יַרְחִ֣יב ל֑וֹ
וְלִפְנֵ֖י גְדֹלִ֣ים יַנְחֶֽנּוּ׃ 16

צַדִּ֣יק הָרִאשׁ֣וֹן בְּרִיב֑וֹ
יָבֹֽא־רֵ֝עֵ֗הוּ וַחֲקָרֽוֹ׃ 17

מִ֭דְיָנִים יַשְׁבִּ֣ית הַגּוֹרָ֑ל
וּבֵ֖ין עֲצוּמִ֣ים יַפְרִֽיד׃ 18

אָ֗ח נִפְשָׁ֥ע מִקִּרְיַת־עֹ֑ז
וּמִדְיָנִים כִּבְרִ֥יחַ אַרְמֽוֹן׃ 19

מִפְּרִ֣י פִי־אִ֭ישׁ תִּשְׂבַּ֣ע בִּטְנ֑וֹ
תְּבוּאַ֖ת שְׂפָתָ֣יו יִשְׂבָּֽע׃ 20

יח 17 וּבָ־   19 וּמִדְיָנִ֗ים

21 Death and life *are* in the power of the tongue, And those who love it will eat its fruit.	מֶוֶת וְחַיִּים בְּיַד־לָשׁוֹן 21 וְאֹהֲבֶיהָ יֹאכַל פִּרְיָהּ:
22 *He who* finds a wife finds a good *thing,* And obtains favor from the LORD.	מָצָא אִשָּׁה מָצָא טוֹב 22 וַיָּפֶק רָצוֹן מֵיְהֹוָה:
23 The poor *man* uses entreaties, But the rich answers roughly.	תַּחֲנוּנִים יְדַבֶּר־רָשׁ 23 וְעָשִׁיר יַעֲנֶה עַזּוֹת:
24 A man *who has* friends must himself be friendly, But there is a friend *who* sticks closer than a brother.	אִישׁ רֵעִים לְהִתְרֹעֵעַ 24 וְיֵשׁ אֹהֵב דָּבֵק מֵאָח:

19 Better *is* the poor who walks in his integrity Than *one who is* perverse in his lips, and is a fool.	**יט** טוֹב־רָשׁ הוֹלֵךְ בְּתֻמּוֹ מֵעִקֵּשׁ שְׂפָתָיו וְהוּא כְסִיל:
2 Also it is not good *for* a soul *to be* without knowledge, And he sins who hastens with *his* feet.	גַּם בְּלֹא־דַעַת נֶפֶשׁ לֹא־טוֹב 2 וְאָץ בְּרַגְלַיִם חוֹטֵא:
3 The foolishness of a man twists his way, And his heart frets against the LORD.	אִוֶּלֶת אָדָם תְּסַלֵּף דַּרְכּוֹ 3 וְעַל־יְהֹוָה יִזְעַף לִבּוֹ:
4 Wealth makes many friends, But the poor is separated from his friend.	הוֹן יֹסִיף רֵעִים רַבִּים 4 וְדָל מֵרֵעֵהוּ יִפָּרֵד:
5 A false witness will not go unpunished, And *he who* speaks lies will not escape.	עֵד שְׁקָרִים לֹא יִנָּקֶה 5 וְיָפִיחַ כְּזָבִים לֹא יִמָּלֵט:
6 Many entreat the favor of the nobility, And every man *is* a friend to one who gives gifts.	רַבִּים יְחַלּוּ פְנֵי־נָדִיב 6 וְכָל־הָרֵעַ לְאִישׁ מַתָּן:
7 All the brothers of the poor hate him; How much more do his friends go far from him! He may pursue *them with* words, *yet* they abandon *him.*	כָּל אֲחֵי־רָשׁ ׀ שְׂנֵאֻהוּ 7 אַף כִּי מְרֵעֵהוּ רָחֲקוּ מִמֶּנּוּ מְרַדֵּף אֲמָרִים לֹא־ ᵖ הֵמָּה:
8 He who gets wisdom loves his own soul; He who keeps understanding will find good.	קֹנֶה־לֵּב אֹהֵב נַפְשׁוֹ 8 שֹׁמֵר תְּבוּנָה לִמְצֹא־טוֹב:
9 A false witness will not go unpunished, And *he who* speaks lies shall perish.	עֵד שְׁקָרִים לֹא יִנָּקֶה 9 וְיָפִיחַ כְּזָבִים יֹאבֵד: פ
10 Luxury is not fitting for a fool, Much less for a servant to rule over princes.	לֹא־נָאוֶה לִכְסִיל תַּעֲנוּג 10 אַף כִּי־לְעֶבֶד ׀ מְשֹׁל בְּשָׂרִים:
11 The discretion of a man makes him slow to anger, And his glory *is* to overlook a transgression.	שֵׂכֶל אָדָם הֶאֱרִיךְ אַפּוֹ 11 וְתִפְאַרְתּוֹ עֲבֹר עַל־פָּשַׁע:
12 The king's wrath *is* like the roaring of a lion, But his favor *is* like dew on the grass.	נַהַם כַּכְּפִיר זַעַף מֶלֶךְ 12 וּכְטַל עַל־עֵשֶׂב רְצוֹנוֹ:
13 A foolish son *is* the ruin of his father, And the contentions of a wife *are* a continual dripping.	הַוֹּת לְאָבִיו בֵּן כְּסִיל 13 יט 7 לֹ־

14   Houses and riches *are* an inheritance from
      fathers,
      But a prudent wife *is* from the LORD.

15   Laziness casts *one* into a deep sleep,
      And an idle person will suffer hunger.

16   He who keeps the commandment keeps his
      soul,
      But he who is careless of his ways will die.

17   He who has pity on the poor lends to the
      LORD,
      And He will pay back what he has given.

18   Chasten your son while there is hope,
      And do not set your heart on his
      destruction.

19   *A man of* great wrath will suffer punishment;
      For if you rescue *him,* you will have to do it
      again.

20   Listen to counsel and receive instruction,
      That you may be wise in your latter days.

21   There are many plans in a man's heart,
      Nevertheless the LORD's counsel—that will
      stand.

22   What is desired in a man is kindness,
      And a poor man is better than a liar.

23   The fear of the LORD *leads* to life,
      And *he who has it* will abide in satisfaction;
      He will not be visited with evil.

24   A lazy *man* buries his hand in the bowl,
      And will not so much as bring it to his
      mouth again.

25   Strike a scoffer, and the simple will become
      wary;
      Rebuke one who has understanding, *and* he
      will discern knowledge.

26   He who mistreats *his* father *and* chases away
      his mother
      Is a son who causes shame and brings
      reproach.

27   Cease listening to instruction, my son,
      And you will stray from the words of
      knowledge.

28   A disreputable witness scorns justice,
      And the mouth of the wicked devours
      iniquity.

29   Judgments are prepared for scoffers,
      And beatings for the backs of fools.

וְרֹדֵף שַׁלְמֹנִים מִדְיְנֵי אִשָּׁה׃

14 בַּיִת וָהוֹן נַחֲלַת אָבוֹת
וּמֵיְהֹוָה אִשָּׁה מַשְׂכָּלֶת׃

15 עַצְלָה תַּפִּיל תַּרְדֵּמָה
וְנֶפֶשׁ רְמִיָּה תִרְעָב׃

16 שֹׁמֵר מִצְוָה שֹׁמֵר נַפְשׁוֹ
בּוֹזֵה דְרָכָיו יָמוּת׃ᴾ

17 מַלְוֵה יְהֹוָה חוֹנֵן דָּל
וּגְמֻלוֹ יְשַׁלֶּם־לוֹ׃

18 יַסֵּר בִּנְךָ כִּי־יֵשׁ תִּקְוָה
וְאֶל־הֲמִיתוֹ אַל־תִּשָּׂא נַפְשֶׁךָ׃

19 גְּרָל־ᴾ חֵמָה נֹשֵׂא עֹנֶשׁ
כִּי אִם־תַּצִּיל וְעוֹד תּוֹסִף׃

20 שְׁמַע עֵצָה וְקַבֵּל מוּסָר
לְמַעַן תֶּחְכַּם בְּאַחֲרִיתֶךָ׃

21 רַבּוֹת מַחֲשָׁבוֹת בְּלֶב־אִישׁ
וַעֲצַת יְהֹוָה הִיא תָקוּם׃

22 תַּאֲוַת אָדָם חַסְדּוֹ
וְטוֹב־רָשׁ מֵאִישׁ כָּזָב׃

23 יִרְאַת יְהֹוָה לְחַיִּים
וְשָׂבֵעַ יָלִין בַּל־יִפָּקֶד רָע׃

24 טָמַן עָצֵל יָדוֹ בַּצַּלָּחַת
גַּם־אֶל־פִּיהוּ לֹא יְשִׁיבֶנָּה׃

25 לֵץ תַּכֶּה וּפֶתִי יַעְרִם
וְהוֹכִיחַ לְנָבוֹן יָבִין דָּעַת׃

26 מְשַׁדֶּד־אָב יַבְרִיחַ אֵם
בֵּן מֵבִישׁ וּמַחְפִּיר׃

27 חֲדַל־בְּנִי לִשְׁמֹעַ מוּסָר
לִשְׁגוֹת מֵאִמְרֵי־דָעַת׃

28 עֵד בְּלִיַּעַל יָלִיץ מִשְׁפָּט
וּפִי רְשָׁעִים יְבַלַּע־אָוֶן׃

29 נָכוֹנוּ לַלֵּצִים שְׁפָטִים
וּמַהֲלֻמוֹת לְגֵו כְּסִילִים׃

20 Wine *is* a mocker,
Strong drink *is* a brawler,
And whoever is led astray by it is not wise.

כ לֵץ הַיַּיִן הֹמֶה שֵׁכָר
וְכָל־שֹׁגֶה בּוֹ לֹא יֶחְכָּם:

2 The wrath of a king *is* like the roaring of a lion;
Whoever provokes him to anger sins *against* his own life.

2 נַהַם כַּכְּפִיר אֵימַת מֶלֶךְ
מִתְעַבְּרוֹ חוֹטֵא נַפְשׁוֹ:

3 *It is* honorable for a man to stop striving,
Since any fool can start a quarrel.

3 כָּבוֹד לָאִישׁ שֶׁבֶת מֵרִיב
וְכָל־אֱוִיל יִתְגַּלָּע:

4 The lazy *man* will not plow because of winter;
He will beg during harvest and *have* nothing.

4 מֵחֹרֶף עָצֵל לֹא־יַחֲרֹשׁ
יִשְׁאַל בַּקָּצִיר וָאָיִן:

5 Counsel in the heart of man *is like* deep water,
But a man of understanding will draw it out.

5 מַיִם עֲמֻקִּים עֵצָה בְלֶב־אִישׁ
וְאִישׁ תְּבוּנָה יִדְלֶנָּה:

6 Most men will proclaim each his own goodness,
But who can find a faithful man?

6 רָב־אָדָם יִקְרָא אִישׁ חַסְדּוֹ
וְאִישׁ אֱמוּנִים מִי יִמְצָא:

7 The righteous *man* walks in his integrity;
His children *are* blessed after him.

7 מִתְהַלֵּךְ בְּתֻמּוֹ צַדִּיק
אַשְׁרֵי בָנָיו אַחֲרָיו:

8 A king who sits on the throne of judgment
Scatters all evil with his eyes.

8 מֶלֶךְ יוֹשֵׁב עַל־כִּסֵּא־דִין
מְזָרֶה בְעֵינָיו כָּל־רָע:

9 Who can say, "I have made my heart clean,
I am pure from my sin"?

9 מִי־יֹאמַר זִכִּיתִי לִבִּי
טָהַרְתִּי מֵחַטָּאתִי:

10 Diverse weights *and* diverse measures,
They *are* both alike, an abomination to the LORD.

10 אֶבֶן וָאֶבֶן אֵיפָה וְאֵיפָה
תּוֹעֲבַת יְהוָה גַּם־שְׁנֵיהֶם:

11 Even a child is known by his deeds,
Whether what he does *is* pure and right.

11 גַּם בְּמַעֲלָלָיו יִתְנַכֶּר־נָעַר
אִם־זַךְ וְאִם־יָשָׁר פָּעֳלוֹ:

12 The hearing ear and the seeing eye,
The LORD has made them both.

12 אֹזֶן שֹׁמַעַת וְעַיִן רֹאָה
יְהוָה עָשָׂה גַם־שְׁנֵיהֶם:

13 Do not love sleep, lest you come to poverty;
Open your eyes, *and* you will be satisfied with bread.

13 אַל־תֶּאֱהַב שֵׁנָה פֶּן־תִּוָּרֵשׁ
פְּקַח עֵינֶיךָ שְׂבַע־לָחֶם:

14 "*It is* good for nothing," cries the buyer;
But when he has gone his way, then he boasts.

14 רַע רַע יֹאמַר הַקּוֹנֶה
וְאֹזֵל לוֹ אָז יִתְהַלָּל:

15 There is gold and a multitude of rubies,
But the lips of knowledge *are* a precious jewel.

15 יֵשׁ זָהָב וְרָב־פְּנִינִים
וּכְלִי יְקָר שִׂפְתֵי־דָעַת:

16 Take the garment of one who is surety *for* a stranger,
And hold it as a pledge *when it* is for a seductress.

16 לְקַח־בִּגְדוֹ כִּי־עָרַב זָר
וּבְעַד נָכְרִים חַבְלֵהוּ:

17 Bread gained by deceit *is* sweet to a man,
But afterward his mouth will be filled with gravel.

17 עָרֵב לָאִישׁ לֶחֶם שָׁקֶר
וְאַחַר יִמָּלֵא־פִיהוּ חָצָץ:

18 Plans are established by counsel;
By wise counsel wage war.

19 He who goes about *as* a talebearer reveals
secrets;
Therefore do not associate with one who
flatters with his lips.

20 Whoever curses his father or his mother,
His lamp will be put out in deep darkness.

21 An inheritance gained hastily at the beginning
Will not be blessed at the end.

22 Do not say, "I will recompense evil";
Wait for the LORD, and He will save you.

23 Diverse weights *are* an abomination to the
LORD,
And dishonest scales *are* not good.

24 A man's steps *are* of the LORD;
How then can a man understand his own
way?

25 *It is* a snare for a man to devote rashly
something as holy,
And afterward to reconsider *his* vows.

26 A wise king sifts out the wicked,
And brings the threshing wheel over them.

27 The spirit of a man *is* the lamp of the LORD,
Searching all the inner depths of his heart.

28 Mercy and truth preserve the king,
And by lovingkindness he upholds his
throne.

29 The glory of young men *is* their strength,
And the splendor of old men *is* their gray
head.

30 Blows that hurt cleanse away evil,
As *do* stripes the inner depths of the heart.

21 The king's heart *is* in the hand of the LORD,
Like the rivers of water; He turns it wherever
He wishes.

2 Every way of a man *is* right in his own eyes,
But the LORD weighs the hearts.

3 To do righteousness and justice
Is more acceptable to the LORD than
sacrifice.

4 A haughty look, a proud heart,
And the plowing of the wicked *are* sin.

5 The plans of the diligent *lead* surely to
plenty,

18 מַחֲשָׁבוֹת בְּעֵצָה תִּכּוֹן
וּבְתַחְבֻּלוֹת עֲשֵׂה מִלְחָמָה׃

19 גּוֹלֶה־סּוֹד הוֹלֵךְ רָכִיל
וּלְפֹתֶה שְׂפָתָיו לֹא תִתְעָרָב׃

20 מְקַלֵּל אָבִיו וְאִמּוֹ
יִדְעַךְ נֵרוֹ בֶּאֱשׁוּןᴾ חֹשֶׁךְ׃

21 נַחֲלָה מְבֹהֶלֶתᴾ בָּרִאשֹׁנָה
וְאַחֲרִיתָהּ לֹא תְבֹרָךְ׃

22 אַל־תֹּאמַר אֲשַׁלְּמָה־רָע
קַוֵּה לַיהוָה וְיֹשַׁע לָךְ׃

23 תּוֹעֲבַת יְהוָה אֶבֶן וָאָבֶן
וּמֹאזְנֵי מִרְמָה לֹא־טוֹב׃

24 מֵיהוָה מִצְעֲדֵי־גָבֶר
וְאָדָם מַה־יָּבִין דַּרְכּוֹ׃

25 מוֹקֵשׁ אָדָם יָלַע קֹדֶשׁ
וְאַחַר נְדָרִים לְבַקֵּר׃

26 מְזָרֶה רְשָׁעִים מֶלֶךְ חָכָם
וַיָּשֶׁב עֲלֵיהֶם אוֹפָן׃

27 נֵר יְהוָה נִשְׁמַת אָדָם
חֹפֵשׂ כָּל־חַדְרֵי־בָטֶן׃

28 חֶסֶד וֶאֱמֶת יִצְּרוּ־מֶלֶךְ
וְסָעַד בַּחֶסֶד כִּסְאוֹ׃

29 תִּפְאֶרֶת בַּחוּרִים כֹּחָם
וַהֲדַר זְקֵנִים שֵׂיבָה׃

30 חַבֻּרוֹת פֶּצַע תַּמְרִיקᴾ בְּרָע
וּמַכּוֹת חַדְרֵי־בָטֶן׃

כא פַּלְגֵי־מַיִם לֶב־מֶלֶךְ בְּיַד־יְהוָה
עַל־כָּל־אֲשֶׁר יַחְפֹּץ יַטֶּנּוּ׃

2 כָּל־דֶּרֶךְ־אִישׁ יָשָׁר בְּעֵינָיו
וְתֹכֵן לִבּוֹת יְהוָה׃

3 עֲשֹׂה צְדָקָה וּמִשְׁפָּט
נִבְחָר לַיהוָה מִזָּבַח׃

4 רוּם־עֵינַיִם וּרְחַב־לֵב
נֵר רְשָׁעִים חַטָּאת׃

5 מַחְשְׁבוֹת חָרוּץ אַךְ־לְמוֹתָר

כ 20. בֶּאֱשׁוּן   21 מְבֹהֶלֶת   30 תַּמְרִיק

But *those of* everyone *who is* hasty, surely to poverty.

וְכָל־אָ֝֗ץ אַךְ־לְמַחְסֽוֹר׃

6 פֹּ֣עַל א֭וֹצָרוֹת בִּלְשׁ֣וֹן שָׁ֑קֶר

6 Getting treasures by a lying tongue
Is the fleeting fantasy of those who seek death.

הֶ֥בֶל נִ֝דָּ֗ף מְבַקְשֵׁי־מָֽוֶת׃

7 שֹׁד־רְשָׁעִ֥ים יְגוֹרֵ֑ם

7 The violence of the wicked will destroy them,
Because they refuse to do justice.

כִּ֥י מֵ֝אֲנ֗וּ לַעֲשׂ֥וֹת מִשְׁפָּֽט׃

8 הֲפַכְפַּ֬ךְ דֶּ֣רֶךְ אִ֣ישׁ וָזָ֑ר

8 The way of a guilty man *is* perverse;
But *as for* the pure, his work *is* right.

וְ֝זַ֗ךְ יָשָׁ֥ר פָּעֳלֽוֹ׃

9 ט֗וֹב לָשֶׁ֥בֶת עַל־פִּנַּת־גָּ֑ג

9 Better to dwell in a corner of a housetop,
Than in a house shared with a contentious woman.

מֵאֵ֥שֶׁת מִ֝דְיָנִ֗ים וּבֵ֥ית חָֽבֶר׃

10 נֶ֣פֶשׁ רָ֭שָׁע אִוְּתָה־רָ֑ע

10 The soul of the wicked desires evil;
His neighbor finds no favor in his eyes.

לֹא־יֻחַ֖ן בְּעֵינָ֣יו רֵעֵֽהוּ׃

11 בַּעְנָשׁ־לֵ֭ץ יֶחְכַּם־פֶּ֑תִי

11 When the scoffer is punished, the simple is made wise;
But when the wise is instructed, he receives knowledge.

וּבְהַשְׂכִּ֥יל לְ֝חָכָ֗ם יִקַּח־דָּֽעַת׃

12 מַשְׂכִּ֥יל צַ֭דִּיק לְבֵ֣ית רָשָׁ֑ע

12 The righteous *God* wisely considers the house of the wicked,
Overthrowing the wicked for *their* wickedness.

מְסַלֵּ֖ף רְשָׁעִ֣ים לָרָֽע׃

13 אֹטֵ֣ם אָ֭זְנוֹ מִזַּעֲקַת־דָּ֑ל

13 Whoever shuts his ears to the cry of the poor
Will also cry himself and not be heard.

גַּֽם־ה֥וּא יִ֝קְרָ֗א וְלֹ֣א יֵעָנֶֽה׃

14 מַתָּ֣ן בַּ֭סֵּתֶר יִכְפֶּה־אָ֑ף

14 A gift in secret pacifies anger,
And a bribe behind the back, strong wrath.

וְשֹׁ֥חַד בַּ֝חֵ֗ק חֵמָ֥ה עַזָּֽה׃

15 שִׂמְחָ֣ה לַ֭צַּדִּיק עֲשׂ֣וֹת מִשְׁפָּ֑ט

15 *It is* a joy for the just to do justice,
But destruction *will come* to the workers of iniquity.

וּ֝מְחִתָּ֗ה לְפֹ֣עֲלֵי אָֽוֶן׃

16 אָדָ֗ם תּ֭וֹעֶה מִדֶּ֣רֶךְ הַשְׂכֵּ֑ל

16 A man who wanders from the way of understanding
Will rest in the assembly of the dead.

בִּקְהַ֖ל רְפָאִ֣ים יָנֽוּחַ׃

17 אִ֣ישׁ מַ֭חְסוֹר אֹהֵ֣ב שִׂמְחָ֑ה

17 He who loves pleasure *will be* a poor man;
He who loves wine and oil will not be rich.

אֹהֵ֥ב יַֽיִן־וָ֝שֶׁ֗מֶן לֹ֣א יַעֲשִֽׁיר׃

18 כֹּ֣פֶר לַצַּדִּ֣יק רָשָׁ֑ע

18 The wicked *shall be* a ransom for the righteous,
And the unfaithful for the upright.

וְתַ֖חַת יְשָׁרִ֣ים בּוֹגֵֽד׃

19 ט֗וֹב שֶׁ֥בֶת בְּאֶֽרֶץ־מִדְבָּ֑ר

19 Better to dwell in the wilderness,
Than with a contentious and angry woman.

מֵאֵ֖שֶׁת מִדְיָנִ֣ים ᵖ וָכָֽעַס׃

20 אוֹצָ֤ר ׀ נֶחְמָ֣ד וָ֭שֶׁמֶן בִּנְוֵ֣ה חָכָ֑ם

20 *There is* desirable treasure,
And oil in the dwelling of the wise,
But a foolish man squanders it.

וּכְסִ֖יל אָדָ֣ם יְבַלְּעֶֽנּוּ׃

21 רֹ֭דֵף צְדָקָ֣ה וָחָ֑סֶד

21 He who follows righteousness and mercy
Finds life, righteousness and honor.

יִמְצָ֥א חַ֝יִּ֗ים צְדָקָ֥ה וְכָבֽוֹד׃

22 עִ֣יר גִּ֭בֹּרִים עָלָ֣ה חָכָ֑ם

22 A wise *man* scales the city of the mighty,
And brings down the trusted stronghold.

וַ֝יֹּ֗רֶד עֹ֣ז מִבְטֶחָֽה׃

23 Whoever guards his mouth and tongue
    Keeps his soul from troubles.

24 A proud *and* haughty *man*—"Scoffer" *is* his name;
    He acts with arrogant pride.

25 The desire of the lazy *man* kills him,
    For his hands refuse to labor.

26 He covets greedily all day long,
    But the righteous gives and does not spare.

27 The sacrifice of the wicked *is* an abomination;
    How much more *when* he brings it with wicked intent!

28 A false witness shall perish,
    But the man who hears *him* will speak endlessly.

29 A wicked man hardens his face,
    But *as for* the upright, he establishes his way.

30 *There is* no wisdom or understanding
    Or counsel against the LORD.

31 The horse *is* prepared for the day of battle,
    But deliverance *is* of the LORD.

22 A *good* name is to be chosen rather than great riches,
    Loving favor rather than silver and gold.

2 The rich and the poor have this in common,
    The LORD *is* the maker of them all.

3 A prudent *man* foresees evil and hides himself,
    But the simple pass on and are punished.

4 By humility *and* the fear of the LORD
    Are riches and honor and life.

5 Thorns *and* snares *are* in the way of the perverse;
    He who guards his soul will be far from them.

6 Train up a child in the way he should go,
    And when he is old he will not depart from it.

7 The rich rules over the poor,
    And the borrower *is* servant to the lender.

8 He who sows iniquity will reap sorrow,
    And the rod of his anger will fail.

9 He who has a generous eye will be blessed,
    For he gives of his bread to the poor.

שֹׁמֵ֣ר פִּ֭יו וּלְשׁוֹנ֑וֹ 23
שֹׁמֵ֖ר מִצָּר֣וֹת נַפְשֽׁוֹ׃

זֵ֣ד יָ֭הִיר לֵ֣ץ שְׁמ֑וֹ 24
עֹ֝ושֶׂ֗ה בְּעֶבְרַ֥ת זָדֽוֹן׃

תַּאֲוַ֣ת עָצֵ֣ל תְּמִיתֶ֑נּוּ 25
כִּֽי־מֵאֲנ֖וּ יָדָ֣יו לַעֲשֽׂוֹת׃

כָּל־הַ֭יּוֹם הִתְאַוָּ֣ה תַאֲוָ֑ה 26
וְצַדִּ֥יק יִ֝תֵּ֗ן וְלֹ֣א יַחְשֹֽׂךְ׃

זֶ֣בַח רְ֭שָׁעִים תּוֹעֵבָ֑ה 27
אַ֝֗ף כִּֽי־בְזִמָּ֥ה יְבִיאֶֽנּוּ׃

עֵד־כְּזָבִ֥ים יֹאבֵ֑ד 28
וְאִ֥ישׁ שׁ֝וֹמֵ֗עַ לָנֶ֥צַח יְדַבֵּֽר׃

הֵעֵ֬ז אִ֣ישׁ רָשָׁ֣ע בְּפָנָ֑יו 29
וְ֝יָשָׁ֗ר ה֤וּא ׀ יָכִ֬ין דְּרָכֽוֹ ׀ דַּרְכּֽוֹ׃

אֵ֣ין חָ֭כְמָה וְאֵ֣ין תְּבוּנָ֑ה 30
וְאֵ֥ין עֵ֝צָ֗ה לְנֶ֣גֶד יְהוָֽה׃   ס

ס֗וּס מ֭וּכָן לְי֣וֹם מִלְחָמָ֑ה 31
וְ֝לַֽיהוָ֗ה הַתְּשׁוּעָֽה׃

נִבְחָ֣ר שֵׁ֭ם מֵעֹ֣שֶׁר רָ֑ב **כב**
מִכֶּ֥סֶף וּ֝מִזָּהָ֗ב חֵ֣ן טֽוֹב׃

עָשִׁ֣יר וָרָ֣שׁ נִפְגָּ֑שׁוּ 2
עֹשֵׂ֖ה כֻלָּ֣ם יְהוָֽה׃

עָר֤וּם ׀ רָאָ֣ה רָעָ֣ה וְיִסָּתֵ֑ר ק 3
וּ֝פְתָיִ֗ים עָבְר֥וּ וְֽנֶעֱנָֽשׁוּ׃

עֵ֣קֶב עֲ֭נָוָה יִרְאַ֣ת יְהוָ֑ה 4
עֹ֖שֶׁר וְכָב֣וֹד וְחַיִּֽים׃

צִנִּ֣ים פַּ֭חִים בְּדֶ֣רֶךְ עִקֵּ֑שׁ 5
שׁוֹמֵ֥ר נַ֝פְשׁ֗וֹ יִרְחַ֥ק מֵהֶֽם׃

חֲנֹ֣ךְ לַ֭נַּעַר עַל־פִּ֣י דַרְכּ֑וֹ 6
גַּ֥ם כִּֽי־יַ֝זְקִ֗ין לֹֽא־יָס֥וּר מִמֶּֽנָּה׃

עָשִׁ֥יר בְּרָשִׁ֥ים יִמְשׁ֑וֹל 7
וְעֶ֥בֶד לֹ֝וֶ֗ה לְאִ֣ישׁ מַלְוֶֽה׃

זוֹרֵ֣עַ עַ֭וְלָה יִקְצׇר־ ק אָ֑וֶן 8
וְשֵׁ֖בֶט עֶבְרָת֣וֹ יִכְלֶֽה׃

טֽוֹב־עַ֭יִן ה֣וּא יְבֹרָ֑ךְ 9
כִּֽי־נָתַ֖ן מִלַּחְמ֣וֹ לַדָּֽל׃

כא 29 יָכִ֬ין   דַּרְכּֽוֹ

10 Cast out the scoffer, and contention will
    leave;
    Yes, strife and reproach will cease.

11 He who loves purity of heart
    And has grace on his lips,
    The king *will be* his friend.

12 The eyes of the LORD preserve knowledge,
    But He overthrows the words of the
    faithless.

13 The lazy *man* says, "*There is* a lion outside!
    I shall be slain in the streets!"

14 The mouth of an immoral woman *is* a deep
    pit;
    He who is abhorred by the LORD will fall
    there.

15 Foolishness *is* bound up in the heart of a
    child;
    The rod of correction will drive it far from
    him.

16 He who oppresses the poor to increase his
    riches,
    And he who gives to the rich, *will* surely
    come to poverty.

17 Incline your ear and hear the words of the
    wise,
    And apply your heart to my knowledge;

18 For *it is* a pleasant thing if you keep them
    within you;
    Let them all be fixed upon your lips,

19 So that your trust may be in the LORD;
    I have instructed you today, even you.

20 Have I not written to you excellent things
    Of counsels and knowledge,

21 That I may make you know the certainty of
    the words of truth,
    That you may answer words of truth
    To those who send to you?

22 Do not rob the poor because he *is* poor,
    Nor oppress the afflicted at the gate;

23 For the LORD will plead their cause,
    And plunder the soul of those who plunder
    them.

24 Make no friendship with an angry man,
    And with a furious man do not go,

25 Lest you learn his ways
    And set a snare for your soul.

26 Do not be one of those who shakes hands in
    a pledge,
    One of those who is surety for debts;

27 If you have nothing *with which* to pay,

גָּרֵשׁ לֵץ וְיֵצֵא מָדֹון 10
וְיִשְׁבֹּת דִּין וְקָלֹון׃

אֹהֵב טְהוֹר־לֵב 11
חֵן שְׂפָתָיו רֵעֵהוּ מֶלֶךְ׃

עֵינֵי יְהוָה נָצְרוּ דָעַת 12
וַיְסַלֵּף דִּבְרֵי בֹגֵד׃

אָמַר עָצֵל אֲרִי בַחוּץ 13
בְּתֹוךְ רְחֹבֹות אֵרָצֵחַ׃

שׁוּחָה עֲמֻקָּה פִּי זָרֹות 14
זְעוּם יְהוָה יִפּוֹל־שָׁם׃

אִוֶּלֶת קְשׁוּרָה בְלֶב־נָעַר 15
שֵׁבֶט מוּסָר יַרְחִיקֶנָּה מִמֶּנּוּ׃

עֹשֵׁק דָּל לְהַרְבֹּות לֹו 16
נֹתֵן לְעָשִׁיר אַךְ־לְמַחְסֹור׃

הַט אָזְנְךָ וּשְׁמַע דִּבְרֵי חֲכָמִים 17
וְלִבְּךָ תָּשִׁית לְדַעְתִּי׃

כִּי־נָעִים כִּי־תִשְׁמְרֵם בְּבִטְנֶךָ 18
יִכֹּנוּ יַחְדָּו עַל־שְׂפָתֶיךָ׃

לִהְיֹות בַּיהוָה מִבְטַחֶךָ 19
הֹודַעְתִּיךָ הַיֹּום אַף־אָתָּה׃

הֲלֹא כָתַבְתִּי לְךָ שָׁלִישׁוֹם 20
בְּמוֹעֵצֹת וָדָעַת׃

לְהֹודִיעֲךָ קֹשְׁטְ אִמְרֵי אֱמֶת 21
לְהָשִׁיב אֲמָרִים אֱמֶת לְשֹׁלְחֶיךָ׃ פ

אַל־תִּגְזָל־דָּל כִּי דַל־הוּא 22
וְאַל־תְּדַכֵּא עָנִי בַשָּׁעַר׃

כִּי־יְהוָה יָרִיב רִיבָם 23
וְקָבַע אֶת־קֹבְעֵיהֶם נָפֶשׁ׃

אַל־תִּתְרַע אֶת־בַּעַל אָף 24
וְאֶת־אִישׁ חֵמֹות לֹא תָבֹוא׃

פֶּן־תֶּאֱלַף אֹרְחֹתֹו 25
וְלָקַחְתָּ מֹוקֵשׁ לְנַפְשֶׁךָ׃

אַל־תְּהִי בְתֹקְעֵי־כָף 26
בַּעֹרְבִים מַשָּׁאֹות׃

אִם־אֵין לְךָ לְשַׁלֵּם 27
לָמָּה יִקַּח מִשְׁכָּבְךָ מִתַּחְתֶּיךָ׃

Why should he take away your bed from
  under you?

אַל־תַּסֵּג גְּבוּל עוֹלָם 28
אֲשֶׁר עָשׂוּ אֲבוֹתֶיךָ:

28 Do not remove the ancient landmark
  Which your fathers have set.

חֲזִיתָ אִישׁ ׀ מָהִיר בִּמְלַאכְתּוֹ 29
לִפְנֵי־מְלָכִים יִתְיַצָּב
בַּל־יִתְיַצֵּב
לִפְנֵי חֲשֻׁכִּים: פ

29 Do you see a man who excels in his work?
  He will stand before kings;
  He will not stand before unknown men.

כג כִּי־תֵשֵׁב לִלְחוֹם אֶת־מוֹשֵׁל
בִּין תָּבִין אֶת־אֲשֶׁר לְפָנֶיךָ:

23 When you sit down to eat with a ruler,
  Consider carefully what is before you;

וְשַׂמְתָּ שַׂכִּין בְּלֹעֶךָ 2
אִם־בַּעַל נֶפֶשׁ אָתָּה:

2 And put a knife to your throat
  If you are a man given to appetite.

אַל־תִּתְאָו לְמַטְעַמּוֹתָיו 3
וְהוּא לֶחֶם כְּזָבִים:

3 Do not desire his delicacies,
  For they are deceptive food.

אַל־תִּיגַע לְהַעֲשִׁיר 4
מִבִּינָתְךָ חֲדָל:

4 Do not overwork to be rich;
  Because of your own understanding, cease!

הֲתָעוֹף עֵינֶיךָ בּוֹ וְאֵינֶנּוּ 5
כִּי עָשֹׂה יַעֲשֶׂה־לּוֹ כְנָפַיִם
כְּנֶשֶׁר וְעָיֵף הַשָּׁמָיִם: פ

5 Will you set your eyes on that which is not?
  For riches certainly make themselves wings;
  They fly away like an eagle toward heaven.

אַל־תִּלְחַם אֶת־לֶחֶם רַע עָיִן 6
וְאַל־תִּתְאָו לְמַטְעַמֹּתָיו:

6 Do not eat the bread of a miser,
  Nor desire his delicacies;

כִּי ׀ כְּמוֹ־שָׁעַר בְּנַפְשׁוֹ כֶּן־הוּא 7
אֱכֹל וּשְׁתֵה יֹאמַר לָךְ
וְלִבּוֹ בַּל־עִמָּךְ:

7 For as he thinks in his heart, so is he.
  "Eat and drink!" he says to you,
  But his heart is not with you.

פִּתְּךָ־אָכַלְתָּ תְקִיאֶנָּה 8
וְשִׁחַתָּ דְּבָרֶיךָ הַנְּעִימִים:

8 The morsel you have eaten, you will vomit
  up,
  And waste your pleasant words.

בְּאָזְנֵי כְסִיל אַל־תְּדַבֵּר 9
כִּי־יָבוּז לְשֵׂכֶל מִלֶּיךָ:

9 Do not speak in the hearing of a fool,
  For he will despise the wisdom of your
  words.

אַל־תַּסֵּג גְּבוּל עוֹלָם 10
וּבִשְׂדֵי יְתוֹמִים אַל־תָּבֹא:

10 Do not remove the ancient landmark,
  Nor enter the fields of the fatherless;

כִּי־גֹאֲלָם חָזָק 11
הוּא־יָרִיב אֶת־רִיבָם אִתָּךְ:

11 For their Redeemer is mighty;
  He will plead their cause against you.

הָבִיאָה לַמּוּסָר לִבֶּךָ 12
וְאָזְנְךָ לְאִמְרֵי־דָעַת:

12 Apply your heart to instruction,
  And your ears to words of knowledge.

אַל־תִּמְנַע מִנַּעַר מוּסָר 13
כִּי־תַכֶּנּוּ בַשֵּׁבֶט לֹא יָמוּת:

13 Do not withhold correction from a child,
  For if you beat him with a rod, he will not
  die.

אַתָּה בַּשֵּׁבֶט תַּכֶּנּוּ 14
וְנַפְשׁוֹ מִשְּׁאוֹל תַּצִּיל:

14 You shall beat him with a rod,
  And deliver his soul from hell.

בְּנִי אִם־חָכַם לִבֶּךָ 15
יִשְׂמַח לִבִּי גַם־אָנִי:

15 My son, if your heart is wise,
  My heart will rejoice—indeed, I myself;

וְתַעְלֹזְנָה כִלְיוֹתָי 16
בְּדַבֵּר שְׂפָתֶיךָ מֵישָׁרִים:

16 Yes, my inmost being will rejoice
  When your lips speak right things.

אַל־יְקַנֵּא לִבְּךָ בַּחַטָּאִים 17
כִּי אִם־בְּיִרְאַת־יְהוָה כָּל־הַיּוֹם:

17 Do not let your heart envy sinners,
  But be zealous for the fear of the LORD all
  the day;

כִּי אִם־יֵשׁ אַחֲרִית 18

18 For surely there is a hereafter,

כג 5 הֲתָעִיף יָעוּף 6 תִּתְאָיו

And your hope will not be cut off.   וְתִקְוָתְךָ֥ לֹ֣א תִכָּרֵֽת׃

19 Hear, my son, and be wise;
And guide your heart in the way.
      19 שְׁמַֽע־אַתָּ֣ה בְנִ֣י וַחֲכָ֑ם
וְאַשֵּׁ֖ר בַּדֶּ֣רֶךְ לִבֶּֽךָ׃

20 Do not mix with winebibbers,
Or with gluttonous eaters of meat;
      20 אַל־תְּהִ֥י בְסֹֽבְאֵי־יָ֑יִן
בְּזֹלֲלֵ֖י בָשָׂ֣ר לָֽמוֹ׃

21 For the drunkard and the glutton will come
to poverty,
And drowsiness will clothe *a man* with rags.
      21 כִּי־סֹבֵ֣א וְ֭זוֹלֵל יִוָּרֵ֑שׁ
וּקְרָעִ֥ים תַּלְבִּ֥ישׁ נוּמָֽה׃

22 Listen to your father who begot you,
And do not despise your mother when she is
old.
      22 שְׁמַ֣ע לְ֭אָבִיךָ זֶ֣ה יְלָדֶ֑ךָ
וְאַל־תָּ֝ב֗וּז כִּֽי־זָקְנָ֥ה אִמֶּֽךָ׃

23 Buy the truth, and do not sell *it,*
Also wisdom and instruction and
understanding.
      23 אֱמֶ֣ת קְ֭נֵה וְאַל־תִּמְכֹּ֑ר
חָכְמָ֖ה וּמוּסָ֣ר וּבִינָֽה׃

24 The father of the righteous will greatly
rejoice,
And he who begets a wise *child* will delight
in him.
      24 גִּיל יָג֣וּל אֲבִ֣י צַדִּ֑יק
יוֹלֵ֥ד חָ֝כָ֗ם וְיִשְׂמַח־בּֽוֹ׃

25 Let your father and your mother be glad,
And let her who bore you rejoice.
      25 יִֽשְׂמַח־אָבִ֥יךָ וְאִמֶּ֑ךָ
וְ֝תָגֵ֗ל יֽוֹלַדְתֶּֽךָ׃

26 My son, give me your heart,
And let your eyes observe my ways.
      26 תְּנָֽה־בְנִ֣י לִבְּךָ֣ לִ֑י
וְ֝עֵינֶ֗יךָ דְּרָכַ֥י תִּרְצֶֽנָה׃

27 For a harlot *is* a deep pit,
And a seductress *is* a narrow well.
      27 כִּֽי־שׁוּחָ֣ה עֲמֻקָּ֣ה זוֹנָ֑ה
וּבְאֵ֥ר צָרָ֝֗ה נָכְרִיָּֽה׃

28 She also lies in wait as *for* a victim,
And increases the unfaithful among men.
      28 אַף־הִ֭יא כְּחֶ֣תֶף תֶּֽאֱרֹ֑ב
וּבוֹגְדִ֥ים בְּאָדָ֣ם תּוֹסִֽף׃

29 Who has woe?
Who has sorrow?
Who has contentions?
Who has complaints?
Who has wounds without cause?
Who has redness of eyes?
      29 לְמִ֨י א֥וֹי לְמִ֪י אֲב֡וֹי לְמִ֤י מִדְיָנִ֨ים ׀ לְמִ֥י שִׂ֗יחַ
לְ֭מִי פְּצָעִ֣ים חִנָּ֑ם
לְ֝מִ֗י חַכְלִל֥וּת עֵינָֽיִם׃

30 Those who linger long at the wine,
Those who go in search of mixed wine.
      30 לַֽמְאַחֲרִ֥ים עַל־הַיָּ֑יִן
לַ֝בָּאִ֗ים לַחְקֹ֥ר מִמְסָֽךְ׃

31 Do not look on the wine when it is red,
When it sparkles in the cup,
When it swirls around smoothly;
      31 אַל־תֵּ֥רֶא יַיִן֮ כִּ֤י יִתְאַ֫דָּ֥ם
כִּֽי־יִתֵּ֣ן בַּכּ֣וֹס עֵינ֑וֹ יִ֝תְהַלֵּ֗ךְ בְּמֵישָׁרִֽים׃

32 At the last it bites like a serpent,
And stings like a viper.
      32 אַ֭חֲרִיתוֹ כְּנָחָ֣שׁ יִשָּׁ֑ךְ
וּֽכְצִפְעֹנִ֥י יַפְרִֽשׁ׃

33 Your eyes will see strange things,
And your heart will utter perverse things.
      33 עֵ֭ינֶיךָ יִרְא֣וּ זָר֑וֹת
וְ֝לִבְּךָ֗ יְדַבֵּ֥ר תַּהְפֻּכֽוֹת׃

34 Yes, you will be like one who lies down in
the midst of the sea,
Or like one who lies at the top of the mast,
saying:
      34 וְ֭הָיִיתָ כְּשֹׁכֵ֣ב בְּלֶב־יָ֑ם
וּ֝כְשֹׁכֵ֗ב בְּרֹ֣אשׁ חִבֵּֽל׃

35 "They have struck me, *but* I was not hurt;
They have beaten me, but I did not feel *it.*
When shall I awake, that I may seek another
drink?"
      35 הִכּ֥וּנִי בַל־חָלִיתִי֮
הֲלָמ֗וּנִי בַּל־יָ֫דָ֥עְתִּי
מָתַ֥י אָקִ֑יץ
א֝וֹסִ֗יף אֲבַקְשֶׁ֥נּוּ עֽוֹד׃

כג 24 גִּיל יָגֵל וְיוֹלֵד יִשְׂמַח־ 26 תִּצֹּרְנָה 29 מִדְיָנִים
31 בַּכּוֹס

24 Do not be envious of evil men,
Nor desire to be with them;
2 For their heart devises violence,
And their lips talk of troublemaking.

3 Through wisdom a house is built,
And by understanding it is established;
4 By knowledge the rooms are filled
With all precious and pleasant riches.

5 A wise man *is* strong,
Yes, a man of knowledge increases strength;
6 For by wise counsel you will wage your own war,
And in a multitude of counselors *there is* safety.

7 Wisdom *is* too lofty for a fool;
He does not open his mouth in the gate.

8 He who plots to do evil
Will be called a schemer.
9 The devising of foolishness *is* sin,
And the scoffer *is* an abomination to men.

10 *If* you faint in the day of adversity,
Your strength *is* small.

11 Deliver *those who* are drawn toward death,
And hold back *those* stumbling to the slaughter.
12 If you say, "Surely we did not know this,"
Does not He who weighs the hearts consider *it?*
He who keeps your soul, does He *not* know *it?*
And will He *not* render to *each* man according to his deeds?

13 My son, eat honey because *it is* good,
And the honeycomb *which is* sweet to your taste;
14 So *shall* the knowledge of wisdom *be* to your soul;
If you have found *it,* there is a prospect,
And your hope will not be cut off.

15 Do not lie in wait, O wicked *man,* against the dwelling of the righteous;
Do not plunder his resting place;
16 For a righteous *man* may fall seven times And rise again,
But the wicked shall fall by calamity.

17 Do not rejoice when your enemy falls,
And do not let your heart be glad when he stumbles;
18 Lest the LORD see *it,* and it displease Him,
And He turn away His wrath from him.

כד אַל־תְּקַנָּא בְּאַנְשֵׁי רָעָה
וְאַל־תִּתְאָו לִהְיוֹת אִתָּם:
2 כִּי־שֹׁד יֶהְגֶּה לִבָּם
וְעָמָל שִׂפְתֵיהֶם תְּדַבֵּרְנָה:
3 בְּחָכְמָה יִבָּנֶה בָּיִת
וּבִתְבוּנָה יִתְכּוֹנָן:
4 וּבְדַעַת חֲדָרִים יִמָּלְאוּ
כָּל־הוֹן יָקָר וְנָעִים:
5 גֶּבֶר־חָכָם בַּעוֹז
וְאִישׁ־דַּעַת מְאַמֶּץ־כֹּחַ:
6 כִּי בְתַחְבֻּלוֹת תַּעֲשֶׂה־לְּךָ מִלְחָמָה
וּתְשׁוּעָה בְּרֹב יוֹעֵץ:
7 רָאמוֹת לֶאֱוִיל חָכְמוֹת
בַּשַּׁעַר לֹא יִפְתַּח־פִּיהוּ:
8 מְחַשֵּׁב לְהָרֵעַ
לוֹ בַּעַל־מְזִמּוֹת יִקְרָאוּ:
9 זִמַּת אִוֶּלֶת חַטָּאת
וְתוֹעֲבַת לְאָדָם לֵץ:
10 הִתְרַפִּיתָ בְּיוֹם צָרָה
צַר כֹּחֶכָה:
11 הַצֵּל לְקֻחִים לַמָּוֶת
וּמָטִים לַהֶרֶג אִם־תַּחְשׂוֹךְ:
12 כִּי־תֹאמַר
הֵן לֹא־יָדַעְנוּ זֶה
הֲלֹא־תֹכֵן לִבּוֹת | הוּא־יָבִין
וְנֹצֵר נַפְשְׁךָ הוּא יֵדָע
וְהֵשִׁיב לְאָדָם כְּפָעֳלוֹ:
13 אֱכָל־בְּנִי דְבַשׁ כִּי־טוֹב
וְנֹפֶת מָתוֹק עַל־חִכֶּךָ:
14 כֵּן | דְּעֶה חָכְמָה לְנַפְשֶׁךָ
אִם־מָצָאתָ וְיֵשׁ אַחֲרִית וְתִקְוָתְךָ לֹא תִכָּרֵת: פ
15 אַל־תֶּאֱרֹב רָשָׁע לִנְוֵה צַדִּיק
אַל־תְּשַׁדֵּד רִבְצוֹ:
16 כִּי שֶׁבַע | יִפּוֹל צַדִּיק וָקָם
וּרְשָׁעִים יִכָּשְׁלוּ בְרָעָה:
17 בִּנְפֹל אוֹיִבְךָ אַל־תִּשְׂמָח
וּבִכָּשְׁלוֹ אַל־יָגֵל לִבֶּךָ:
18 פֶּן־יִרְאֶה יְהוָה וְרַע בְּעֵינָיו
וְהֵשִׁיב מֵעָלָיו אַפּוֹ:

כד 1 תִּתְאָיו 17 אוֹיִבְךָ

19 Do not fret because of evildoers,
Nor be envious of the wicked;

20 For there will be no prospect for the evil *man;*
The lamp of the wicked will be put out.

21 My son, fear the LORD and the king;
Do not associate with those given to change;

22 For their calamity will rise suddenly,
And who knows the ruin those two can bring?

23 These *things* also *belong* to the wise:
It is not good to show partiality in judgment.

24 He who says to the wicked, "You *are* righteous,"
Him the people will curse;
Nations will abhor him.

25 But those who rebuke *the wicked* will have delight,
And a good blessing will come upon them.

26 He who gives a right answer kisses the lips.

27 Prepare your outside work,
Make it fit for yourself in the field;
And afterward build your house.

28 Do not be a witness against your neighbor without cause,
For would you deceive with your lips?

29 Do not say, "I will do to him just as he has done to me;
I will render to the man according to his work."

30 I went by the field of the lazy *man,*
And by the vineyard of the man devoid of understanding;

31 And there it was, all overgrown with thorns;
Its surface was covered with nettles;
Its stone wall was broken down.

32 When I saw *it,* I considered *it* well;
I looked on *it and* received instruction:

33 A little sleep, a little slumber,
A little folding of the hands to rest;

34 So shall your poverty come *like* a prowler,
And your need like an armed man.

25 These also *are* proverbs of Solomon which the men of Hezekiah king of Judah copied:

2 *It is* the glory of God to conceal a matter,
But the glory of kings *is* to search out a matter.

3 *As* the heavens for height and the earth for depth,

---

19 אַל־תִּתְחַר בַּמְּרֵעִים
אַל־תְּקַנֵּא בָּרְשָׁעִים:

20 כִּי ׀ לֹא־תִהְיֶה אַחֲרִית לָרָע
נֵר רְשָׁעִים יִדְעָךְ:

21 יְרָא־אֶת־יְהֹוָה בְּנִי וָמֶלֶךְ
עִם־שׁוֹנִים אַל־תִּתְעָרָב:

22 כִּי־פִתְאֹם יָקוּם אֵידָם
וּפִיד שְׁנֵיהֶם מִי יוֹדֵעַ: ס

23 גַּם־אֵלֶּה לַחֲכָמִים
הַכֵּר־פָּנִים בְּמִשְׁפָּט בַּל־טוֹב:

24 אֹמֵר ׀ לְרָשָׁע צַדִּיק אָתָּה
יִקְּבֻהוּ עַמִּים יִזְעָמוּהוּ לְאֻמִּים:

25 וְלַמּוֹכִיחִים יִנְעָם
וַעֲלֵיהֶם תָּבוֹא בִרְכַּת־טוֹב:

26 שְׂפָתַיִם יִשָּׁק
מֵשִׁיב דְּבָרִים נְכֹחִים:

27 הָכֵן בַּחוּץ ׀ מְלַאכְתֶּךָ וְעַתְּדָהּ בַּשָּׂדֶה לָךְ
אַחַר וּבָנִיתָ בֵיתֶךָ: פ

28 אַל־תְּהִי עֵד־חִנָּם בְּרֵעֶךָ
וַהֲפִתִּיתָ בִּשְׂפָתֶיךָ:

29 אַל־תֹּאמַר כַּאֲשֶׁר עָשָׂה־לִי כֵּן אֶעֱשֶׂה־לּוֹ
אָשִׁיב לָאִישׁ כְּפָעֳלוֹ:

30 עַל־שְׂדֵה אִישׁ־עָצֵל עָבַרְתִּי
וְעַל־כֶּרֶם אָדָם חֲסַר־לֵב:

31 וְהִנֵּה עָלָה כֻלּוֹ ׀ קִמְּשֹׂנִים כָּסּוּ פָנָיו חֲרֻלִּים
וְגֶדֶר אֲבָנָיו נֶהֱרָסָה:

32 וָאֶחֱזֶה אָנֹכִי אָשִׁית לִבִּי
רָאִיתִי לָקַחְתִּי מוּסָר:

33 מְעַט שֵׁנוֹת מְעַט תְּנוּמוֹת
מְעַט ׀ חִבֻּק יָדַיִם לִשְׁכָּב:

34 וּבָא־מִתְהַלֵּךְ רֵישֶׁךָ
וּמַחְסֹרֶיךָ כְּאִישׁ מָגֵן: פ

כה גַּם־אֵלֶּה מִשְׁלֵי שְׁלֹמֹה
אֲשֶׁר הֶעְתִּיקוּ אַנְשֵׁי ׀ חִזְקִיָּה מֶלֶךְ־יְהוּדָה:

2 כְּבֹד אֱלֹהִים הַסְתֵּר דָּבָר
וּכְבֹד מְלָכִים חֲקֹר דָּבָר:

3 שָׁמַיִם לָרוּם וָאָרֶץ לָעֹמֶק

	So the heart of kings *is* unsearchable.	וְלֵב מְלָכִים אֵין חֵקֶר׃
4	Take away the dross from silver,	4 הָגוֹ סִיגִים מִכָּסֶף
	And it will go to the silversmith *for* jewelry.	וַיֵּצֵא לַצֹּרֵף כֶּלִי׃
5	Take away the wicked from before the king,	5 הָגוֹ רָשָׁע לִפְנֵי־מֶלֶךְ
	And his throne will be established in righteousness.	וְיִכּוֹן בַּצֶּדֶק כִּסְאוֹ׃
6	Do not exalt yourself in the presence of the king,	6 אַל־תִּתְהַדַּר לִפְנֵי־מֶלֶךְ
	And do not stand in the place of the great;	וּבִמְקוֹם גְּדֹלִים אַל־תַּעֲמֹד׃
7	For *it is* better that he say to you, "Come up here,"	7 כִּי טוֹב אֲמָר־לְךָ עֲלֵה הֵנָּה
	Than that you should be put lower in the presence of the prince, Whom your eyes have seen.	מֵהַשְׁפִּילְךָ לִפְנֵי נָדִיב אֲשֶׁר רָאוּ עֵינֶיךָ׃
8	Do not go hastily to court;	8 אַל־תֵּצֵא לָרִב מַהֵר
	For what will you do in the end, When your neighbor has put you to shame?	פֶּן מַה־תַּעֲשֶׂה בְּאַחֲרִיתָהּ בְּהַכְלִים אֹתְךָ רֵעֶךָ׃
9	Debate your case with your neighbor,	9 רִיבְךָ רִיב אֶת־רֵעֶךָ
	And do not disclose the secret to another;	וְסוֹד אַחֵר אַל־תְּגָל׃
10	Lest he who hears *it* expose your shame,	10 פֶּן־יְחַסֶּדְךָ שֹׁמֵעַ
	And your reputation be ruined.	וְדִבָּתְךָ לֹא תָשׁוּב׃
11	A word fitly spoken *is like* apples of gold In settings of silver.	11 תַּפּוּחֵי זָהָב בְּמַשְׂכִּיּוֹת כָּסֶף דָּבָר דָּבֻר עַל־אָפְנָיו׃
12	*Like* an earring of gold and an ornament of fine gold *Is* a wise rebuker to an obedient ear.	12 נֶזֶם זָהָב וַחֲלִי־כָתֶם מוֹכִיחַ חָכָם עַל־אֹזֶן שֹׁמָעַת׃
13	Like the cold of snow in time of harvest *Is* a faithful messenger to those who send him, For he refreshes the soul of his masters.	13 כְּצִנַּת־שֶׁלֶג ׀ בְּיוֹם קָצִיר צִיר נֶאֱמָן לְשֹׁלְחָיו וְנֶפֶשׁ אֲדֹנָיו יָשִׁיב׃ פ
14	Whoever falsely boasts of giving *Is like* clouds and wind without rain.	14 נְשִׂיאִים וְרוּחַ וְגֶשֶׁם אָיִן אִישׁ מִתְהַלֵּל בְּמַתַּת־שָׁקֶר׃
15	By long forbearance a ruler is persuaded, And a gentle tongue breaks a bone.	15 בְּאֹרֶךְ אַפַּיִם יְפֻתֶּה קָצִין וְלָשׁוֹן רַכָּה תִּשְׁבָּר־גָּרֶם׃
16	Have you found honey? Eat only as much as you need, Lest you be filled with it and vomit.	16 דְּבַשׁ מָצָאתָ אֱכֹל דַּיֶּךָ פֶּן־תִּשְׂבָּעֶנּוּ וַהֲקֵאתוֹ׃
17	Seldom set foot in your neighbor's house, Lest he become weary of you and hate you.	17 הֹקַר רַגְלְךָ מִבֵּית רֵעֶךָ פֶּן־יִשְׂבָּעֲךָ וּשְׂנֵאֶךָ׃
18	A man who bears false witness against his neighbor *Is like* a club, a sword, and a sharp arrow.	18 מֵפִיץ וְחֶרֶב וְחֵץ שָׁנוּן אִישׁ עֹנֶה בְרֵעֵהוּ עֵד שָׁקֶר׃
19	Confidence in an unfaithful *man* in time of trouble *Is like* a bad tooth and a foot out of joint.	19 שֵׁן רֹעָה וְרֶגֶל מוּעָדֶת מִבְטָח בּוֹגֵד בְּיוֹם צָרָה׃
20	*Like* one who takes away a garment in cold weather, *And like* vinegar on soda, *Is* one who sings songs to a heavy heart.	20 מַעֲדֶה בֶּגֶד ׀ בְּיוֹם קָרָה חֹמֶץ עַל־נָתֶר וְשָׁר בַּשִּׁרִים עַל לֶב־רָע׃ פ

21 If your enemy is hungry, give him bread to
eat;
And if he is thirsty, give him water to drink;
22 For *so* you will heap coals of fire on his
head,
And the LORD will reward you.

23 The north wind brings forth rain,
And a backbiting tongue an angry
countenance.

24 *It is* better to dwell in a corner of a housetop,
Than in a house shared with a contentious
woman.

25 *As* cold water to a weary soul,
So *is* good news from a far country.

26 A righteous *man* who falters before the
wicked
Is like a murky spring and a polluted well.

27 *It is* not good to eat much honey;
So to seek one's own glory *is not* glory.

28 Whoever *has* no rule over his own spirit
Is like a city broken down, without walls.

26 As snow in summer and rain in harvest,
So honor is not fitting for a fool.

2 Like a flitting sparrow, like a flying swallow,
So a curse without cause shall not alight.

3 A whip for the horse,
A bridle for the donkey,
And a rod for the fool's back.

4 Do not answer a fool according to his folly,
Lest you also be like him.

5 Answer a fool according to his folly,
Lest he be wise in his own eyes.

6 He who sends a message by the hand of a
fool
Cuts off *his own* feet *and* drinks violence.

7 *Like* the legs of the lame that hang limp
Is a proverb in the mouth of fools.

8 Like one who binds a stone in a sling
Is he who gives honor to a fool.

9 *Like* a thorn *that* goes into the hand of a
drunkard
Is a proverb in the mouth of fools.

10 The great *God* who formed everything
Gives the fool *his* hire and the transgressor
his wages.

11 As a dog returns to his own vomit,
So a fool repeats his folly.

12 Do you see a man wise in his own eyes?
There is more hope for a fool than for him.

אִם־רָעֵב שֹׂנַאֲךָ הַאֲכִלֵהוּ לָחֶם 21
וְאִם־צָמֵא הַשְׁקֵהוּ מָיִם:
כִּי גֶחָלִים אַתָּה חֹתֶה עַל־רֹאשׁוֹ 22
וַיהוָה יְשַׁלֶּם־לָךְ:
רוּחַ צָפוֹן תְּחוֹלֵל גָּשֶׁם 23
וּפָנִים נִזְעָמִים לְשׁוֹן סָתֶר:
טוֹב שֶׁבֶת עַל־פִּנַּת־גָּג 24
מֵאֵשֶׁת מִדְוָנִים וּבֵית חָבֶר:
מַיִם קָרִים עַל־נֶפֶשׁ עֲיֵפָה 25
וּשְׁמוּעָה טוֹבָה מֵאֶרֶץ מֶרְחָק:
מַעְיָן נִרְפָּשׂ וּמָקוֹר מָשְׁחָת 26
צַדִּיק מָט לִפְנֵי־רָשָׁע:
אָכֹל דְּבַשׁ הַרְבּוֹת לֹא־טוֹב 27
וְחֵקֶר כְּבֹדָם כָּבוֹד:
עִיר פְּרוּצָה אֵין חוֹמָה 28
אִישׁ אֲשֶׁר אֵין מַעְצָר לְרוּחוֹ:

כ כַּשֶּׁלֶג ׀ בַּקַּיִץ וְכַמָּטָר בַּקָּצִיר
כֵּן לֹא־נָאוֶה לִכְסִיל כָּבוֹד:
כַּצִּפּוֹר לָנוּד כַּדְּרוֹר לָעוּף 2
כֵּן קִלְלַת חִנָּם לֹא תָבֹא:
שׁוֹט לַסּוּס מֶתֶג לַחֲמוֹר 3
וְשֵׁבֶט לְגֵו כְּסִילִים:
אַל־תַּעַן כְּסִיל כְּאִוַּלְתּוֹ 4
פֶּן־תִּשְׁוֶה־לּוֹ גַם־אָתָּה:
עֲנֵה כְסִיל כְּאִוַּלְתּוֹ 5
פֶּן־יִהְיֶה חָכָם בְּעֵינָיו:
מְקַצֶּה רַגְלַיִם חָמָס שֹׁתֶה 6
שֹׁלֵחַ דְּבָרִים בְּיַד־כְּסִיל:
דַּלְיוּ שֹׁקַיִם מִפִּסֵּחַ 7
וּמָשָׁל בְּפִי כְסִילִים:
כִּצְרוֹר אֶבֶן בְּמַרְגֵּמָה 8
כֵּן־נוֹתֵן לִכְסִיל כָּבוֹד:
חוֹחַ עָלָה בְיַד־שִׁכּוֹר 9
וּמָשָׁל בְּפִי כְסִילִים:
רַב מְחוֹלֵל־כֹּל 10
וְשֹׂכֵר כְּסִיל וְשֹׂכֵר עֹבְרִים:
כְּכֶלֶב שָׁב עַל־קֵאוֹ 11
כְּסִיל שׁוֹנֶה בְאִוַּלְתּוֹ:
רָאִיתָ אִישׁ חָכָם בְּעֵינָיו 12
תִּקְוָה לִכְסִיל מִמֶּנּוּ:

כה 24 מִדְיָנִים
כו 2 לוֹ

13	The lazy *man* says, "*There is* a lion in the road! A fierce lion *is* in the streets!"
14	*As* a door turns on its hinges, So *does* the lazy *man* on his bed.
15	The lazy *man* buries his hand in the bowl; It wearies him to bring it back to his mouth.
16	The lazy *man is* wiser in his own eyes Than seven men who can answer sensibly.
17	He who passes by *and* meddles in a quarrel not his own *Is like* one who takes a dog by the ears.
18	Like a madman who throws firebrands, arrows, and death,
19	*Is* the man *who* deceives his neighbor, And says, "I was only joking!"
20	Where *there is* no wood, the fire goes out; And where *there is* no talebearer, strife ceases.
21	*As* charcoal *is* to burning coals, and wood to fire, So *is* a contentious man to kindle strife.
22	The words of a talebearer *are* like tasty trifles, And they go down into the inmost body.
23	Fervent lips with a wicked heart *Are like* earthenware covered with silver dross.
24	He who hates, disguises *it* with his lips, And lays up deceit within himself;
25	When he speaks kindly, do not believe him, For *there are* seven abominations in his heart;
26	*Though his* hatred is covered by deceit, His wickedness will be revealed before the assembly.
27	Whoever digs a pit will fall into it, And he who rolls a stone will have it roll back on him.
28	A lying tongue hates *those who are* crushed by it, And a flattering mouth works ruin.

27
1	Do not boast about tomorrow, For you do not know what a day may bring forth.
2	Let another man praise you, and not your own mouth; A stranger, and not your own lips.
3	A stone *is* heavy and sand *is* weighty,

אָמַר עָצֵל שַׁחַל בַּדָּרֶךְ 13
אֲרִי בֵּין הָרְחֹבוֹת׃
הַדֶּלֶת תִּסּוֹב עַל־צִירָהּ 14
וְעָצֵל עַל־מִטָּתוֹ׃
טָמַן עָצֵל יָדוֹ בַּצַּלָּחַת 15
נִלְאָה לַהֲשִׁיבָהּ אֶל־פִּיו׃
חָכָם עָצֵל בְּעֵינָיו 16
מִשִּׁבְעָה מְשִׁיבֵי טָעַם׃
מַחֲזִיק בְּאָזְנֵי־כָלֶב 17
עֹבֵר מִתְעַבֵּר עַל־רִיב לֹּא־לוֹ׃
כְּמִתְלַהְלֵהַּ הַיֹּרֶה זִקִּים 18
חִצִּים וָמָוֶת׃
כֵּן־אִישׁ רִמָּה אֶת־רֵעֵהוּ 19
וְאָמַר הֲלֹא־מְשַׂחֵק אָנִי׃
בְּאֶפֶס עֵצִים תִּכְבֶּה־אֵשׁ 20
וּבְאֵין נִרְגָּן יִשְׁתֹּק מָדוֹן׃
פֶּחָם לְגֶחָלִים וְעֵצִים לְאֵשׁ 21
וְאִישׁ מדונים מִדְיָנִים לְחַרְחַר־רִיב׃ פ
דִּבְרֵי נִרְגָּן כְּמִתְלַהֲמִים 22
וְהֵם יָרְדוּ חַדְרֵי־בָטֶן׃
כֶּסֶף סִיגִים מְצֻפֶּה עַל־חָרֶשׂ 23
שְׂפָתַיִם דֹּלְקִים וְלֶב־רָע׃
בשפתו בִּשְׂפָתָו יִנָּכֵר שׂוֹנֵא 24
וּבְקִרְבּוֹ יָשִׁית מִרְמָה׃
כִּי־יְחַנֵּן קוֹלוֹ אַל־תַּאֲמֶן־בּוֹ 25
כִּי שֶׁבַע תּוֹעֵבוֹת בְּלִבּוֹ׃
תִּכַּסֶּה שִׂנְאָה בְּמַשָּׁאוֹן 26
תִּגָּלֶה רָעָתוֹ בְקָהָל׃
כֹּרֶה־שַּׁחַת בָּהּ יִפֹּל 27
וְגֹלֵל אֶבֶן אֵלָיו תָּשׁוּב׃
לְשׁוֹן־שֶׁקֶר יִשְׂנָא דַכָּיו 28
וּפֶה חָלָק יַעֲשֶׂה מִדְחֶה׃

כז אַל־תִּתְהַלֵּל בְּיוֹם מָחָר
כִּי לֹא־תֵדַע מַה־יֵּלֶד יוֹם׃
יְהַלֶּלְךָ זָר וְלֹא־פִיךָ 2
נָכְרִי וְאַל־שְׂפָתֶיךָ׃
כֹּבֶד־אֶבֶן וְנֵטֶל הַחוֹל 3

כו 21 מדינים 24 בשפתיו

But a fool's wrath *is* heavier than both of
them.

4 Wrath *is* cruel and anger a torrent,
But who *is* able to stand before jealousy?

5 Open rebuke *is* better
Than love carefully concealed.

6 Faithful *are* the wounds of a friend,
But the kisses of an enemy *are* deceitful.

7 A satisfied soul loathes the honeycomb,
But to a hungry soul every bitter thing *is*
sweet.

8 Like a bird that wanders from its nest
Is a man who wanders from his place.

9 Ointment and perfume delight the heart,
And the sweetness of a man's friend *gives*
delight by hearty counsel.

10 Do not forsake your own friend or your
father's friend,
Nor go to your brother's house in the day of
your calamity;
Better *is* a neighbor nearby than a brother
far away.

11 My son, be wise, and make my heart glad,
That I may answer him who reproaches me.

12 A prudent *man* foresees evil *and* hides
himself;
The simple pass on *and* are punished.

13 Take the garment of him who is surety for a
stranger,
And hold it in pledge *when* he is surety for a
seductress.

14 He who blesses his friend with a loud voice,
rising early in the morning,
It will be counted a curse to him.

15 A continual dripping on a very rainy day
And a contentious woman are alike;

16 Whoever restrains her restrains the wind,
And grasps oil with his right hand.

17 *As* iron sharpens iron,
So a man sharpens the countenance of his
friend.

18 Whoever keeps the fig tree will eat its fruit;
So he who waits on his master will be
honored.

19 As in water face *reflects* face,
So a man's heart *reveals* the man.

20 Hell and Destruction are never full;

וְכַעַס אֱוִיל כָּבֵד מִשְּׁנֵיהֶם:

4 אַכְזְרִיּוּת חֵמָה וְשֶׁטֶף אָף
וּמִי יַעֲמֹד לִפְנֵי קִנְאָה:

5 טוֹבָה תּוֹכַחַת מְגֻלָּה
מֵאַהֲבָה מְסֻתָּרֶת:

6 נֶאֱמָנִים פִּצְעֵי אוֹהֵב
וְנַעְתָּרוֹת נְשִׁיקוֹת שׂוֹנֵא:

7 נֶפֶשׁ שְׂבֵעָה תָּבוּס נֹפֶת
וְנֶפֶשׁ רְעֵבָה כָּל־מַר מָתוֹק:

8 כְּצִפּוֹר נוֹדֶדֶת מִן־קִנָּהּ
כֵּן־אִישׁ נוֹדֵד מִמְּקוֹמוֹ:

9 שֶׁמֶן וּקְטֹרֶת יְשַׂמַּח־לֵב
וּמֶתֶק רֵעֵהוּ מֵעֲצַת־נָפֶשׁ:

10 רֵעֲךָ וְרֵעֶה אָבִיךָ אַל־תַּעֲזֹב
וּבֵית אָחִיךָ אַל־תָּבוֹא בְּיוֹם אֵידֶךָ
טוֹב שָׁכֵן קָרוֹב
מֵאָח רָחוֹק:

11 חֲכַם בְּנִי וְשַׂמַּח לִבִּי
וְאָשִׁיבָה חֹרְפִי דָבָר:

12 עָרוּם רָאָה רָעָה נִסְתָּר
פְּתָאיִם עָבְרוּ נֶעֱנָשׁוּ:

13 קַח־בִּגְדוֹ כִּי־עָרַב זָר
וּבְעַד נָכְרִיָּה חַבְלֵהוּ:

14 מְבָרֵךְ רֵעֵהוּ ׀ בְּקוֹל גָּדוֹל בַּבֹּקֶר הַשְׁכֵּים
קְלָלָה תֵּחָשֶׁב לוֹ:

15 דֶּלֶף טוֹרֵד בְּיוֹם סַגְרִיר
וְאֵשֶׁת מִדְיָנִים נִשְׁתָּוָה:

16 צֹפְנֶיהָ צָפַן־רוּחַ
וְשֶׁמֶן יְמִינוֹ יִקְרָא:

17 בַּרְזֶל בְּבַרְזֶל יָחַד
וְאִישׁ יַחַד פְּנֵי־רֵעֵהוּ:

18 נֹצֵר תְּאֵנָה יֹאכַל פִּרְיָהּ
וְשֹׁמֵר אֲדֹנָיו יְכֻבָּד:

19 כַּמַּיִם הַפָּנִים לַפָּנִים
כֵּן לֵב־הָאָדָם לָאָדָם:

20 שְׁאוֹל וַאֲבַדֹּה לֹא תִשְׂבַּעְנָה

כז 10 וְרֵעֶ 15 מִדְיָנִים 20 וַאֲבַדּוֹ

So the eyes of man are never satisfied.

וְעֵינֵי הָאָדָם לֹא תִשְׂבַּעְנָה:

21 The refining pot *is* for silver and the furnace
   for gold,
   And a man *is valued* by what others say of
   him.

21 מַצְרֵף לַכֶּסֶף וְכוּר לַזָּהָב
וְאִישׁ לְפִי מַהֲלָלוֹ:

22 Though you grind a fool in a mortar with a
   pestle along with crushed grain,
   Yet his foolishness will not depart from him.

22 אִם תִּכְתּוֹשׁ־אֶת־הָאֱוִיל ׀ בַּמַּכְתֵּשׁ בְּתוֹךְ
הָרִיפוֹת
בַּעֲלִי לֹא־תָסוּר מֵעָלָיו אִוַּלְתּוֹ: פ

23 Be diligent to know the state of your flocks,
   And attend to your herds;

23 יָדֹעַ תֵּדַע פְּנֵי צֹאנֶךָ
שִׁית לִבְּךָ לַעֲדָרִים:

24 For riches *are* not forever,
   Nor does a crown *endure* to all generations.

24 כִּי לֹא לְעוֹלָם חֹסֶן
וְאִם־נֵזֶר לְדוֹר דּוֹרP:

25 *When* the hay is removed, and the tender
   grass shows itself,
   And the herbs of the mountains are gathered
   in,

25 גָּלָה חָצִיר וְנִרְאָה־דֶשֶׁא
וְנֶאֶסְפוּ עִשְּׂבוֹת הָרִים:

26 The lambs *will provide* your clothing,
   And the goats the price of a field;

26 כְּבָשִׂים לִלְבוּשֶׁךָ
וּמְחִיר שָׂדֶה עַתּוּדִים:

27 *You shall have* enough goats' milk for your
   food,
   For the food of your household,
   And the nourishment of your maidservants.

27 וְדֵי ׀ חֲלֵב עִזִּים לְלַחְמְךָ לְלֶחֶם בֵּיתֶךָ
וְחַיִּים לְנַעֲרוֹתֶיךָ:

28 The wicked flee when no one pursues,
   But the righteous are bold as a lion.

כח נָסוּ וְאֵין־רֹדֵף רָשָׁע
וְצַדִּיקִים כִּכְפִיר יִבְטָח:

2 Because of the transgression of a land, many
   are its princes;
   But by a man of understanding *and*
   knowledge
   Right will be prolonged.

2 בְּפֶשַׁע אֶרֶץ רַבִּים שָׂרֶיהָ
וּבְאָדָם מֵבִין יֹדֵעַ כֵּן יַאֲרִיךְ:

3 A poor man who oppresses the poor
   Is like a driving rain which leaves no food.

3 גֶּבֶר רָשׁ וְעֹשֵׁק דַּלִּים
מָטָר סֹחֵף וְאֵין לָחֶם:

4 Those who forsake the law praise the
   wicked,
   But such as keep the law contend with them.

4 עֹזְבֵי תוֹרָה יְהַלְלוּ רָשָׁע
וְשֹׁמְרֵי תוֹרָה יִתְגָּרוּ בָם: פ

5 Evil men do not understand justice,
   But those who seek the LORD understand all.

5 אַנְשֵׁי־רָע לֹא־יָבִינוּ מִשְׁפָּט
וּמְבַקְשֵׁי יְהֹוָה יָבִינוּ כֹל:

6 Better *is* the poor who walks in his integrity
   Than one perverse *in his* ways, though he *be*
   rich.

6 טוֹב־רָשׁ הוֹלֵךְ בְּתֻמּוֹ
מֵעִקֵּשׁ דְּרָכַיִם וְהוּא עָשִׁיר:

7 Whoever keeps the law *is* a discerning son,
   But a companion of gluttons shames his
   father.

7 נוֹצֵר תּוֹרָה בֵּן מֵבִין
וְרֹעֶה זוֹלְלִים יַכְלִים אָבִיו:

8 One who increases his possessions by usury
   and extortion
   Gathers it for him who will pity the poor.

8 מַרְבֶּה הוֹנוֹ בְּנֶשֶׁךְ וּבְתַרְבִּיתP
לְחוֹנֵן דַּלִּים יִקְבְּצֶנּוּ:

9 One who turns away his ear from hearing
   the law,
   Even his prayer *is* an abomination.

9 מֵסִיר אָזְנוֹ מִשְּׁמֹעַ תּוֹרָה
גַּם־תְּפִלָּתוֹ תּוֹעֵבָה:

10 Whoever causes the upright to go astray in an evil way,
He himself will fall into his own pit;
But the blameless will inherit good.

11 The rich man *is* wise in his own eyes,
But the poor who has understanding searches him out.

12 When the righteous rejoice, *there is* great glory;
But when the wicked arise, men hide themselves.

13 He who covers his sins will not prosper,
But whoever confesses and forsakes *them* will have mercy.

14 Happy *is* the man who is always reverent,
But he who hardens his heart will fall into calamity.

15 *Like* a roaring lion and a charging bear
Is a wicked ruler over poor people.

16 A ruler who lacks understanding *is* a great oppressor,
But he who hates covetousness will prolong *his* days.

17 A man burdened with bloodshed will flee into a pit;
Let no one help him.

18 Whoever walks blamelessly will be saved,
But *he who is* perverse *in his* ways will suddenly fall.

19 He who tills his land will have plenty of bread,
But he who follows frivolity will have poverty enough!

20 A faithful man will abound with blessings,
But he who hastens to be rich will not go unpunished.

21 To show partiality *is* not good,
Because for a piece of bread a man will transgress.

22 A man with an evil eye hastens after riches,
And does not consider that poverty will come upon him.

23 He who rebukes a man will find more favor afterward
Than he who flatters with the tongue.

24 Whoever robs his father or his mother,
And says, "*It is* no transgression,"
The same *is* companion to a destroyer.

10 מַשְׁגֶּה יְשָׁרִים ׀ בְּדֶרֶךְ רָע בִּשְׁחוּתוֹ הוּא־
יִפּוֹל
וּתְמִימִים יִנְחֲלוּ־טוֹב:

11 חָכָם בְּעֵינָיו אִישׁ עָשִׁיר
וְדַל מֵבִין יַחְקְרֶנּוּ:

12 בַּעֲלֹץ צַדִּיקִים רַבָּה תִפְאָרֶת
וּבְקוּם רְשָׁעִים יְחֻפַּשׂ אָדָם:

13 מְכַסֶּה פְשָׁעָיו לֹא יַצְלִיחַ
וּמוֹדֶה וְעֹזֵב יְרֻחָם:

14 אַשְׁרֵי אָדָם מְפַחֵד תָּמִיד
וּמַקְשֶׁה לִבּוֹ יִפּוֹל בְּרָעָה:

15 אֲרִי־נֹהֵם וְדֹב שׁוֹקֵק
מֹשֵׁל רָשָׁע עַל עַם־דָּל:

16 נָגִיד חֲסַר תְּבוּנוֹת וְרַב מַעֲשַׁקּוֹת
שֹׂנֵאפ בֶצַע יַאֲרִיךְ יָמִים: ‪פ‬

17 אָדָם עָשֻׁק בְּדַם־נָפֶשׁ
עַד־בּוֹר יָנוּס אַל־יִתְמְכוּ־בוֹ:

18 הוֹלֵךְ תָּמִים יִוָּשֵׁעַ
וְנֶעְקַשׁ דְּרָכַיִם יִפּוֹל בְּאֶחָת:

19 עֹבֵד אַדְמָתוֹ יִשְׂבַּע־לָחֶם
וּמְרַדֵּף רֵקִים יִשְׂבַּע־רִישׁ:

20 אִישׁ אֱמוּנוֹת רַב־בְּרָכוֹת
וְאָץ לְהַעֲשִׁיר לֹא יִנָּקֶה:

21 הַכֵּר־פָּנִים לֹא־טוֹב
וְעַל־פַּת־לֶחֶם יִפְשַׁע־גָּבֶר:

22 נִבְהָל לַהוֹן אִישׁ רַע עָיִן
וְלֹא־יֵדַע כִּי־חֶסֶר יְבֹאֶנּוּ:

23 מוֹכִיחַ אָדָם אַחֲרַי חֵן יִמְצָא
מִמַּחֲלִיק לָשׁוֹן:

24 גּוֹזֵל ׀ אָבִיו וְאִמּוֹ וְאֹמֵר אֵין־פָּשַׁע
חָבֵר הוּא לְאִישׁ מַשְׁחִית:

25 He who is of a proud heart stirs up strife, But he who trusts in the LORD will be prospered.	רְחַב־נֶ֭פֶשׁ יְגָרֶ֣ה מָד֑וֹן 25 וּבוֹטֵ֖חַ עַל־יְהֹוָ֣ה יְדֻשָּֽׁן׃
26 He who trusts in his own heart is a fool, But whoever walks wisely will be delivered.	בּוֹטֵ֣חַ בְּ֭לִבּוֹ ה֣וּא כְסִ֑יל 26 וְהוֹלֵ֥ךְ בְּ֝חׇכְמָ֗ה ה֣וּא יִמָּלֵֽט׃
27 He who gives to the poor will not lack, But he who hides his eyes will have many curses.	נוֹתֵ֣ן לָ֭רָשׁ אֵ֣ין מַחְס֑וֹר 27 וּמַעְלִ֥ים עֵ֝ינָ֗יו רַב־מְאֵרֽוֹת׃
28 When the wicked arise, men hide themselves; But when they perish, the righteous increase.	בְּק֣וּם רְ֭שָׁעִים יִסָּתֵ֣ר אָדָ֑ם 28 וּ֝בְאׇבְדָ֗ם יִרְבּ֥וּ צַדִּיקִֽים׃

29 He who is often rebuked, *and* hardens *his*
   neck,
Will suddenly be destroyed, and that
   without remedy.
	כט אִ֣ישׁ תּ֭וֹכָחוֹת מַקְשֶׁה־עֹ֑רֶף
	פֶּ֥תַע יִ֝שָּׁבֵ֗ר וְאֵ֣ין מַרְפֵּֽא׃

2 When the righteous are in authority, the
   people rejoice;
But when a wicked *man* rules, the people
   groan.
	בִּרְב֣וֹת צַ֭דִּיקִים יִשְׂמַ֣ח הָעָ֑ם 2
	וּבִמְשֹׁ֥ל רָ֝שָׁ֗ע יֵאָ֥נַֽח עָֽם׃

3 Whoever loves wisdom makes his father
   rejoice,
But a companion of harlots wastes *his*
   wealth.
	אִֽישׁ־אֹהֵ֣ב חׇ֭כְמָה יְשַׂמַּ֣ח אָבִ֑יו 3
	וְרֹעֶ֥ה ז֝וֹנ֗וֹת יְאַבֶּד־הֽוֹן׃

4 The king establishes the land by justice, But he who receives bribes overthrows it.	מֶ֗לֶךְ בְּ֭מִשְׁפָּט יַעֲמִ֣יד אָ֑רֶץ 4 וְאִ֖ישׁ תְּרוּמ֣וֹת יֶהֶרְסֶֽנָּה׃
5 A man who flatters his neighbor Spreads a net for his feet.	גֶּ֭בֶר מַחֲלִ֣יק עַל־רֵעֵ֑הוּ 5 רֶ֝֗שֶׁת פּוֹרֵ֥שׂ עַל־פְּעָמָֽיו׃
6 By transgression an evil man is snared, But the righteous sings and rejoices.	בְּפֶ֤שַֽׁע אִ֣ישׁ רָ֣ע מוֹקֵ֑שׁ 6 וְ֝צַדִּ֗יק יָר֥וּן וְשָׂמֵֽחַ׃

7 The righteous considers the cause of the
   poor,
But the wicked does not understand *such*
   knowledge.
	יֹדֵ֣עַ צַ֭דִּיק דִּ֣ין דַּלִּ֑ים 7
	רָ֝שָׁ֗ע לֹא־יָבִ֥ין דָּֽעַת׃

8 Scoffers set a city aflame, But wise *men* turn away wrath.	אַנְשֵׁ֣י לָ֭צוֹן יָפִ֣יחוּ קִרְיָ֑ה 8 וַ֝חֲכָמִ֗ים יָשִׁ֥יבוּ אָֽף׃
9 *If* a wise man contends with a foolish man, Whether *the fool* rages or laughs, *there is* no peace.	אִֽישׁ־חָכָ֗ם נִ֭שְׁפָּט אֶת־אִ֣ישׁ אֱוִ֑יל 9 וְרָגַ֥ז וְ֝שָׂחַ֗ק וְאֵ֣ין נָֽחַת׃
10 The bloodthirsty hate the blameless, But the upright seek his well-being.	אַנְשֵׁ֣י דָ֭מִים יִשְׂנְאוּ־תָ֑ם 10 וִ֝ישָׁרִ֗ים יְבַקְשׁ֥וּ נַפְשֽׁוֹ׃
11 A fool vents all his feelings, But a wise *man* holds them back.	כׇּל־ר֭וּחוֹ יוֹצִ֣יא כְסִ֑יל 11 וְ֝חָכָ֗ם בְּאָח֥וֹר יְשַׁבְּחֶֽנָּה׃
12 If a ruler pays attention to lies, All his servants *become* wicked.	מֹ֭שֵׁל מַקְשִׁ֣יב עַל־דְּבַר־שָׁ֑קֶר 12 כׇּֽל־מְשָׁרְתָ֥יו רְשָׁעִֽים׃
13 The poor *man* and the oppressor have this in common: The LORD gives light to the eyes of both.	רָ֤שׁ וְאִ֣ישׁ תְּכָכִ֣ים נִפְגָּ֑שׁוּ 13 מֵ֤אִיר־עֵינֵ֖י שְׁנֵיהֶ֣ם יְהֹוָֽה׃

14 The king who judges the poor with truth,
His throne will be established forever.

מֶלֶךְ שׁוֹפֵט בֶּאֱמֶת דַּלִּים 14
כִּסְאוֹ לָעַד יִכּוֹן:

15 The rod and rebuke give wisdom,
But a child left *to himself* brings shame to his
mother.

שֵׁבֶט וְתוֹכַחַת יִתֵּן חָכְמָה 15
וְנַעַר מְשֻׁלָּח מֵבִישׁ אִמּוֹ:

16 When the wicked are multiplied, transgression increases;
But the righteous will see their fall.

בִּרְבוֹת רְשָׁעִים יִרְבֶּה־פָּשַׁע 16
וְצַדִּיקִים בְּמַפַּלְתָּם יִרְאוּ:

17 Correct your son, and he will give you rest;
Yes, he will give delight to your soul.

יַסֵּר בִּנְךָ וִינִיחֶךָ 17
וְיִתֵּן מַעֲדַנִּים לְנַפְשֶׁךָ: פ

18 Where *there is* no revelation, the people cast
off restraint;
But happy *is* he who keeps the law.

בְּאֵין חָזוֹן יִפָּרַע עָם 18
וְשֹׁמֵר תּוֹרָה אַשְׁרֵהוּ:

19 A servant will not be corrected by mere
words;
For though he understands, he will not
respond.

בִּדְבָרִים לֹא־יִוָּסֶר עָבֶד 19
כִּי־יָבִין וְאֵין מַעֲנֶה:

20 Do you see a man hasty in his words?
There is more hope for a fool than for him.

חָזִיתָ אִישׁ אָץ בִּדְבָרָיו 20
תִּקְוָה לִכְסִיל מִמֶּנּוּ:

21 He who pampers his servant from childhood
Will have him as a son in the end.

מְפַנֵּק מִנֹּעַר עַבְדּוֹ 21
וְאַחֲרִיתוֹ יִהְיֶה מָנוֹן:

22 An angry man stirs up strife,
And a furious man abounds in
transgression.

אִישׁ־אַף יְגָרֶה מָדוֹן 22
וּבַעַל חֵמָה רַב־פָּשַׁע:

23 A man's pride will bring him low,
But the humble in spirit will retain honor.

גַּאֲוַת אָדָם תַּשְׁפִּילֶנּוּ 23
וּשְׁפַל־רוּחַ יִתְמֹךְ כָּבוֹד:

24 Whoever is a partner with a thief hates his
own life;
He swears to tell the truth, but reveals
nothing.

חוֹלֵק עִם־גַּנָּב שׂוֹנֵא נַפְשׁוֹ 24
אָלָה יִשְׁמַע וְלֹא יַגִּיד:

25 The fear of man brings a snare,
But whoever trusts in the LORD shall be safe.

חֶרְדַּת אָדָם יִתֵּן מוֹקֵשׁ 25
וּבוֹטֵחַ בַּיהוָה יְשֻׂגָּב:

26 Many seek the ruler's favor,
But justice for man *comes* from the LORD.

רַבִּים מְבַקְשִׁים פְּנֵי־מוֹשֵׁל 26
וּמֵיהוָה מִשְׁפַּט־אִישׁ:

27 An unjust man *is* an abomination to the
righteous,
And he who is upright in the way *is* an
abomination to the wicked.

תּוֹעֲבַת צַדִּיקִים אִישׁ עָוֶל 27
וְתוֹעֲבַת רָשָׁע יְשַׁר־דָּרֶךְ: פ

30

The words of Agur the son of Jakeh, *his*
utterance. This man declared to Ithiel—to Ithiel
and Ucal:

דִּבְרֵי | אָגוּר בִּן־יָקֶה הַמַּשָּׂא ל
נְאֻם הַגֶּבֶר לְאִיתִיאֵל לְאִיתִיאֵל וְאֻכָל:

2 Surely I *am* more stupid than *any* man,
And do not have the understanding of a
man.

כִּי בַעַר אָנֹכִי מֵאִישׁ 2
וְלֹא־בִינַת אָדָם לִי:

3 I neither learned wisdom
Nor have knowledge of the Holy One.

וְלֹא־לָמַדְתִּי חָכְמָה 3
וְדַעַת קְדֹשִׁים אֵדָע:

4 Who has ascended into heaven, or descended?
Who has gathered the wind in His fists?
Who has bound the waters in a garment?
Who has established all the ends of the earth?
What *is* His name, and what *is* His Son's name,
If you know?

5 Every word of God *is* pure;
He *is* a shield to those who put their trust in Him.

6 Do not add to His words,
Lest He rebuke you, and you be found a liar.

7 Two *things* I request of You
(Deprive me not before I die):

8 Remove falsehood and lies far from me;
Give me neither poverty nor riches—
Feed me with the food allotted to me;

9 Lest I be full and deny *You,*
And say, "Who *is* the LORD?"
Or lest I be poor and steal,
And profane the name of my God.

10 Do not malign a servant to his master,
Lest he curse you, and you be found guilty.

11 *There is* a generation *that* curses its father,
And does not bless its mother.

12 *There is* a generation *that is* pure in its own eyes,
Yet is not washed from its filthiness.

13 *There is* a generation— oh, how lofty are their eyes!
And their eyelids are lifted up.

14 *There is* a generation whose teeth *are like* swords,
And whose fangs *are like* knives,
To devour the poor from off the earth,
And the needy from *among* men.

15 The leech has two daughters—
Give *and* Give!
There are three *things that* are never satisfied,
Four never say, "Enough!":

16 The grave,
The barren womb,
The earth *that* is not satisfied with water—
And the fire never says, "Enough!"

17 The eye *that* mocks *his* father,
And scorns obedience to *his* mother,
The ravens of the valley will pick it out,
And the young eagles will eat it.

מִי עָלָה־שָׁמַיִם ׀ וַיֵּרַד 4
מִי אָסַף־רוּחַ ׀ בְּחָפְנָיו
מִי צָרַר־מַיִם ׀ בַּשִּׂמְלָה
מִי הֵקִים כָּל־אַפְסֵי־אָרֶץ
מַה־שְּׁמוֹ וּמַה־שֶּׁם־בְּנוֹ
כִּי תֵדָע:

כָּל־אִמְרַת אֱלוֹהַּ צְרוּפָה 5
מָגֵן הוּא לַחֹסִים בּוֹ:

אַל־תּוֹסְףְּ עַל־דְּבָרָיו 6
פֶּן־יוֹכִיחַ בְּךָ וְנִכְזָבְתָּ: ס

שְׁתַּיִם שָׁאַלְתִּי מֵאִתָּךְ 7
אַל־תִּמְנַע מִמֶּנִּי בְּטֶרֶם אָמוּת:

שָׁוְא ׀ וּדְבַר־כָּזָב הַרְחֵק מִמֶּנִּי 8
רֵאשׁ וָעֹשֶׁר אַל־תִּתֶּן־לִי
הַטְרִיפֵנִי לֶחֶם חֻקִּי:

פֶּן אֶשְׂבַּע ׀ וְכִחַשְׁתִּי 9
וְאָמַרְתִּי מִי יְהֹוָה
וּפֶן־אִוָּרֵשׁ וְגָנַבְתִּי
וְתָפַשְׂתִּי שֵׁם אֱלֹהָי: ס

אַל־תַּלְשֵׁן עֶבֶד אֶל־אֲדֹנָו 10
פֶּן־יְקַלֶּלְךָ וְאָשָׁמְתָּ:

דּוֹר אָבִיו יְקַלֵּל 11
וְאֶת־אִמּוֹ לֹא יְבָרֵךְ:

דּוֹר טָהוֹר בְּעֵינָיו 12
וּמִצֹּאָתוֹ לֹא רֻחָץ:

דּוֹר מָה־רָמוּ עֵינָיו 13
וְעַפְעַפָּיו יִנָּשֵׂאוּ:

דּוֹר ׀ חֲרָבוֹת שִׁנָּיו 14
וּמַאֲכָלוֹת מְתַלְּעֹתָיו
לֶאֱכֹל עֲנִיִּים מֵאֶרֶץ
וְאֶבְיוֹנִים מֵאָדָם:

לַעֲלוּקָה ׀ שְׁתֵּי בָנוֹת 15
הַב ׀ הַב
שָׁלוֹשׁ הֵנָּה לֹא תִשְׂבַּעְנָה
אַרְבַּע לֹא־אָמְרוּ הוֹן:

שְׁאוֹל וְעֹצֶר רָחַם 16
אֶרֶץ לֹא־שָׂבְעָה מַּיִם וְאֵשׁ לֹא־אָמְרָה הוֹן:

עַיִן ׀ תִּלְעַג לְאָב 17
וְתָבוּז לִיקֲּהַת־אֵם
יִקְּרוּהָ עֹרְבֵי־נַחַל
וְיֹאכְלוּהָ בְנֵי־נָשֶׁר: ס

18 There are three *things which* are too wonderful for me, Yes, four *which* I do not understand:	18 שְׁלֹשָׁה הֵמָּה נִפְלְאוּ מִמֶּנִּי וְאַרְבָּעָ֖ה לֹא יְדַעְתִּים:
19 The way of an eagle in the air, The way of a serpent on a rock, The way of a ship in the midst of the sea, And the way of a man with a virgin.	19 דֶּרֶךְ הַנֶּשֶׁר ׀ בַּשָּׁמַיִם דֶּרֶךְ נָחָשׁ עֲלֵי צוּר דֶּרֶךְ־אֳנִיָּה בְלֶב־יָם וְדֶרֶךְ גֶּבֶר בְּעַלְמָה:
20 This *is* the way of an adulterous woman: She eats and wipes her mouth, And says, "I have done no wickedness."	20 כֵּן ׀ דֶּרֶךְ אִשָּׁה מְנָאָפֶת אָכְלָה וּמָחֲתָה פִיהָ וְאָמְרָה לֹא־פָעַלְתִּי אָוֶן:
21 For three *things* the earth is perturbed, Yes, for four it cannot bear up:	21 תַּחַת שָׁלוֹשׁ רָגְזָה אֶרֶץ וְתַחַת אַרְבַּע לֹא־תוּכַל שְׂאֵת:
22 For a servant when he reigns, A fool when he is filled with food,	22 תַּחַת־עֶבֶד כִּי יִמְלוֹךְ וְנָבָל כִּי יִשְׂבַּע־לָחֶם:
23 A hateful *woman* when she is married, And a maidservant who succeeds her mistress.	23 תַּחַת שְׂנוּאָה כִּי תִבָּעֵל וְשִׁפְחָה כִּי־תִירַשׁ גְּבִרְתָּהּ:
24 There are four *things which* are little on the earth, But they *are* exceedingly wise:	24 אַרְבָּעָה הֵם קְטַנֵּי־אָרֶץ וְהֵמָּה חֲכָמִים מְחֻכָּמִים:
25 The ants *are* a people not strong, Yet they prepare their food in the summer;	25 הַנְּמָלִים עַם לֹא־עָז וַיָּכִינוּ בַקַּיִץ לַחְמָם:
26 The rock badgers are a feeble folk, Yet they make their homes in the crags;	26 שְׁפַנִּים עַם לֹא־עָצוּם וַיָּשִׂימוּ בַסֶּלַע בֵּיתָם:
27 The locusts have no king, Yet they all advance in ranks;	27 מֶלֶךְ אֵין לָאַרְבֶּה וַיֵּצֵא חֹצֵץ כֻּלּוֹ:
28 The spider skillfully grasps with its hands, And it is in kings' palaces.	28 שְׂמָמִית בְּיָדַיִם תְּתַפֵּשׂ וְהִיא בְּהֵיכְלֵי מֶלֶךְ:
29 There are three *things which* are majestic in pace, Yes, four *which* are stately in walk:	29 שְׁלֹשָׁה הֵמָּה מֵיטִיבֵי צָעַד וְאַרְבָּעָה מֵיטִבֵי לָכֶת:
30 A lion, *which is* mighty among beasts And does not turn away from any;	30 לַיִשׁ גִּבּוֹר בַּבְּהֵמָה וְלֹא־יָשׁוּב מִפְּנֵי־כֹל:
31 A greyhound, A male goat also, And a king *whose* troops *are* with him.	31 זַרְזִיר מָתְנַיִם אוֹ־תָיִשׁ וּמֶלֶךְ אַלְקוּם עִמּוֹ:
32 If you have been foolish in exalting yourself, Or if you have devised evil, *put your* hand on *your* mouth.	32 אִם־נָבַלְתָּ בְהִתְנַשֵּׂא וְאִם־זַמּוֹתָ יָד לְפֶה:
33 For *as* the churning of milk produces butter, And wringing the nose produces blood, So the forcing of wrath produces strife.	33 כִּי מִיץ חָלָב יוֹצִיא חֶמְאָה וּמִיץ־אַף יוֹצִיא דָם וּמִיץ אַפַּיִם יוֹצִיא רִיב:
31 The words of King Lemuel, the utterance which his mother taught him:	**לא** דִּבְרֵי לְמוֹאֵל מֶלֶךְ מַשָּׂא אֲשֶׁר־יִסְּרַתּוּ אִמּוֹ:
2 What, my son? And what, son of my womb? And what, son of my vows?	2 מַה־בְּרִי וּמַה־בַּר־בִּטְנִי וּמֶה בַּר־נְדָרָי:
3 Do not give your strength to women, Nor your ways to that which destroys kings.	3 אַל־תִּתֵּן לַנָּשִׁים חֵילֶךָ וּדְרָכֶיךָ לַמְחוֹת מְלָכִין:
4 *It is* not for kings, O Lemuel,	4 אַל לַמְלָכִים ׀ לְמוֹאֵל אַל לַמְלָכִים שְׁתוֹ־יָיִן

It is not for kings to drink wine,
Nor for princes intoxicating drink;

5 Lest they drink and forget the law,
And pervert the justice of all the afflicted.

6 Give strong drink to him who is perishing,
And wine to those who are bitter of heart.

7 Let him drink and forget his poverty,
And remember his misery no more.

8 Open your mouth for the speechless,
In the cause of all *who are* appointed to die.

9 Open your mouth, judge righteously,
And plead the cause of the poor and needy.

10 Who can find a virtuous wife?
For her worth *is* far above rubies.

11 The heart of her husband safely trusts her;
So he will have no lack of gain.

12 She does him good and not evil
All the days of her life.

13 She seeks wool and flax,
And willingly works with her hands.

14 She is like the merchant ships,
She brings her food from afar.

15 She also rises while it is yet night,
And provides food for her household,
And a portion for her maidservants.

16 She considers a field and buys it;
From her profits she plants a vineyard.

17 She girds herself with strength,
And strengthens her arms.

18 She perceives that her merchandise *is* good,
And her lamp does not go out by night.

19 She stretches out her hands to the distaff,
And her hand holds the spindle.

20 She extends her hand to the poor,
Yes, she reaches out her hands to the needy.

21 She is not afraid of snow for her household,
For all her household *is* clothed with scarlet.

22 She makes tapestry for herself;
Her clothing *is* fine linen and purple.

23 Her husband is known in the gates,
When he sits among the elders of the land.

24 She makes linen garments and sells *them*,
And supplies sashes for the merchants.

25 Strength and honor *are* her clothing;
She shall rejoice in time to come.

26 She opens her mouth with wisdom,
And on her tongue *is* the law of kindness.

27 She watches over the ways of her household,
And does not eat the bread of idleness.

28 Her children rise up and call her blessed;
Her husband *also*, and he praises her:

29 "Many daughters have done well,
But you excel them all."

וְלָרוֹזְנִים אֵ[p] שֵׁכָר׃

5 פֶּן־יִשְׁתֶּה וְיִשְׁכַּח מְחֻקָּק
וִישַׁנֶּה דִּין כָּל־בְּנֵי־עֹנִי׃

6 תְּנוּ־שֵׁכָר לְאוֹבֵד
וְיַיִן לְמָרֵי נָפֶשׁ׃

7 יִשְׁתֶּה וְיִשְׁכַּח רִישׁוֹ
וַעֲמָלוֹ לֹא יִזְכָּר־עוֹד׃

8 פְּתַח־פִּיךָ לְאִלֵּם
אֶל־דִּין כָּל־בְּנֵי חֲלוֹף׃

9 פְּתַח־פִּיךָ שְׁפָט־צֶדֶק
וְדִין עָנִי וְאֶבְיוֹן׃ ס

10 אֵשֶׁת־חַיִל מִי יִמְצָא
וְרָחֹק מִפְּנִינִים מִכְרָהּ׃

11 בָּטַח בָּהּ לֵב בַּעְלָהּ
וְשָׁלָל לֹא יֶחְסָר׃

12 גְּמָלַתְהוּ טוֹב וְלֹא־רָע כֹּל יְמֵי חַיֶּיהָ׃

13 דָּרְשָׁה צֶמֶר וּפִשְׁתִּים
וַתַּעַשׂ בְּחֵפֶץ כַּפֶּיהָ׃

14 הָיְתָה כָּאֳנִיּוֹת סוֹחֵר
מִמֶּרְחָק תָּבִיא לַחְמָהּ׃

15 וַתָּקָם ׀ בְּעוֹד לַיְלָה וַתִּתֵּן טֶרֶף לְבֵיתָהּ
וְחֹק לְנַעֲרֹתֶיהָ׃

16 זָמְמָה שָׂדֶה וַתִּקָּחֵהוּ
מִפְּרִי כַפֶּיהָ נָטַע[p] כָּרֶם׃

17 חָגְרָה בְעוֹז מָתְנֶיהָ
וַתְּאַמֵּץ זְרֹעוֹתֶיהָ׃

18 טָעֲמָה כִּי־טוֹב סַחְרָהּ
לֹא־יִכְבֶּה בליל[p] נֵרָהּ׃

19 יָדֶיהָ שִׁלְּחָה בַכִּישׁוֹר
וְכַפֶּיהָ תָּמְכוּ פָלֶךְ׃

20 כַּפָּהּ פָּרְשָׂה לֶעָנִי
וְיָדֶיהָ שִׁלְּחָה לָאֶבְיוֹן׃

21 לֹא־תִירָא לְבֵיתָהּ מִשָּׁלֶג
כִּי כָל־בֵּיתָהּ לָבֻשׁ שָׁנִים׃

22 מַרְבַדִּים עָשְׂתָה־לָּהּ
שֵׁשׁ וְאַרְגָּמָן לְבוּשָׁהּ׃

23 נוֹדָע בַּשְּׁעָרִים בַּעְלָהּ
בְּשִׁבְתּוֹ עִם־זִקְנֵי־אָרֶץ׃

24 סָדִין עָשְׂתָה וַתִּמְכֹּר
וַחֲגוֹר נָתְנָה לַכְּנַעֲנִי׃

25 עֹז־וְהָדָר לְבוּשָׁהּ
וַתִּשְׂחַק לְיוֹם אַחֲרוֹן׃

26 פִּיהָ פָּתְחָה בְחָכְמָה
וְתוֹרַת־חֶסֶד עַל־לְשׁוֹנָהּ׃

27 צוֹפִיָּה הֲלִיכוֹת בֵּיתָהּ
וְלֶחֶם עַצְלוּת לֹא תֹאכֵל׃

28 קָמוּ בָנֶיהָ וַיְאַשְּׁרוּהָ
בַּעְלָהּ וַיְהַלְלָהּ׃

29 רַבּוֹת בָּנוֹת עָשׂוּ חָיִל
וְאַתְּ עָלִית עַל־כֻּלָּנָה׃

לא 4 אֵ[p] 16 נָטְעָה 18 בליל

30 Charm *is* deceitful and beauty *is* passing,
  But a woman *who* fears the LORD, she shall
   be praised.

31 Give her of the fruit of her hands,
  And let her own works praise her in the
   gates.

30 שֶׁקֶר הַחֵן וְהֶבֶל הַיֹּפִי
  אִשָּׁה יִרְאַת־יְהֹוָה הִיא תִתְהַלָּל׃

31 תְּנוּ־לָהּ מִפְּרִי יָדֶיהָ
  וִיהַלְלוּהָ בַשְּׁעָרִים מַעֲשֶׂיהָ׃

The Book of
JOB

1 There was a man in the land of Uz, whose name *was* Job; and that man was blameless and upright, and one who feared God and shunned evil. ²And seven sons and three daughters were born to him. ³Also, his possessions were seven thousand sheep, three thousand camels, five hundred yoke of oxen, five hundred female donkeys, and a very large household, so that this man was the greatest of all the people of the East.

⁴And his sons would go and feast *in their* houses, each on his *appointed* day, and would send and invite their three sisters to eat and drink with them. ⁵So it was, when the days of feasting had run their course, that Job would send and sanctify them, and he would rise early in the morning and offer burnt offerings *according to* the number of them all. For Job said, "It may be that my sons have sinned and cursed God in their hearts." Thus Job did regularly.

⁶Now there was a day when the sons of God came to present themselves before the LORD, and Satan also came among them. ⁷And the LORD said to Satan, "From where do you come?"

So Satan answered the LORD and said, "From going to and fro on the earth, and from walking back and forth on it."

⁸Then the LORD said to Satan, "Have you considered My servant Job, that *there is* none like him on the earth, a blameless and upright man, one who fears God and shuns evil?"

⁹So Satan answered the LORD and said, "Does Job fear God for nothing? ¹⁰Have You not made a hedge around him, around his household, and around all that he has on every side? You have blessed the work of his hands, and his possessions have increased in the land. ¹¹But now, stretch out Your hand and touch all that he has, and he will surely curse You to Your face!"

¹²And the LORD said to Satan, "Behold, all that he has *is* in your power; only do not lay a hand on his *person*."

So Satan went out from the presence of the LORD.

¹³Now there was a day when his sons and daughters *were* eating and drinking wine in their oldest brother's house; ¹⁴and a messenger came to Job and said, "The oxen were plowing, and the donkeys feeding beside them, ¹⁵when the Sabeans

א אִישׁ הָיָה בְאֶרֶץ־עוּץ אִיּוֹב שְׁמוֹ וְהָיָה | הָאִישׁ הַהוּא תָּם וְיָשָׁר וִירֵא אֱלֹהִים וְסָר מֵרָע: 2 וַיִּוָּלְדוּ לוֹ שִׁבְעָה בָנִים וְשָׁלוֹשׁ בָּנוֹת: 3 וַיְהִי מִקְנֵהוּ שִׁבְעַת אַלְפֵי־צֹאן וּשְׁלֹשֶׁת אַלְפֵי גְמַלִּים וַחֲמֵשׁ מֵאוֹת צֶמֶד־בָּקָר וַחֲמֵשׁ מֵאוֹת אֲתוֹנוֹת וַעֲבֻדָּה רַבָּה מְאֹד וַיְהִי הָאִישׁ הַהוּא גָּדוֹל מִכָּל־בְּנֵי־קֶדֶם: 4 וְהָלְכוּ בָנָיו וְעָשׂוּ מִשְׁתֶּה בֵּית אִישׁ יוֹמוֹ וְשָׁלְחוּ וְקָרְאוּ לִשְׁלֹשֶׁת אַחְיוֹתֵיהֶם לֶאֱכֹל וְלִשְׁתּוֹת עִמָּהֶם: 5 וַיְהִי כִּי הִקִּיפוּ יְמֵי הַמִּשְׁתֶּה וַיִּשְׁלַח אִיּוֹב וַיְקַדְּשֵׁם וְהִשְׁכִּים בַּבֹּקֶר וְהֶעֱלָה עֹלוֹת מִסְפַּר כֻּלָּם כִּי אָמַר אִיּוֹב אוּלַי חָטְאוּ בָנַי וּבֵרְכוּ אֱלֹהִים בִּלְבָבָם כָּכָה יַעֲשֶׂה אִיּוֹב כָּל־הַיָּמִים: פ

6 וַיְהִי הַיּוֹם וַיָּבֹאוּ בְּנֵי הָאֱלֹהִים לְהִתְיַצֵּב עַל־יְהֹוָה וַיָּבוֹא גַם־הַשָּׂטָן בְּתוֹכָם: 7 וַיֹּאמֶר יְהֹוָה אֶל־הַשָּׂטָן מֵאַיִן תָּבֹא וַיַּעַן הַשָּׂטָן אֶת־יְהֹוָה וַיֹּאמַר מִשּׁוּט בָּאָרֶץ וּמֵהִתְהַלֵּךְ בָּהּ: 8 וַיֹּאמֶר יְהֹוָה אֶל־הַשָּׂטָן הֲשַׂמְתָּ לִבְּךָ עַל־עַבְדִּי אִיּוֹב כִּי אֵין כָּמֹהוּ בָּאָרֶץ אִישׁ תָּם וְיָשָׁר יְרֵא אֱלֹהִים וְסָר מֵרָע: 9 וַיַּעַן הַשָּׂטָן אֶת־יְהֹוָה וַיֹּאמַר הַחִנָּם יָרֵא אִיּוֹב אֱלֹהִים: 10 הֲלֹא־אַתְּ שַׂכְתָּ בַעֲדוֹ וּבְעַד־בֵּיתוֹ וּבְעַד כָּל־אֲשֶׁר־לוֹ מִסָּבִיב מַעֲשֵׂה יָדָיו בֵּרַכְתָּ וּמִקְנֵהוּ פָּרַץ בָּאָרֶץ: 11 וְאוּלָם שְׁלַח־נָא יָדְךָ וְגַע בְּכָל־אֲשֶׁר־לוֹ אִם־לֹא עַל־פָּנֶיךָ יְבָרֲכֶךָּ: 12 וַיֹּאמֶר יְהֹוָה אֶל־הַשָּׂטָן הִנֵּה כָל־אֲשֶׁר־לוֹ בְּיָדֶךָ רַק אֵלָיו אַל־תִּשְׁלַח יָדֶךָ וַיֵּצֵא הַשָּׂטָן מֵעִם פְּנֵי יְהֹוָה: 13 וַיְהִי הַיּוֹם וּבָנָיו וּבְנֹתָיו אֹכְלִים וְשֹׁתִים יַיִן בְּבֵית אֲחִיהֶם הַבְּכוֹר: 14 וּמַלְאָךְ בָּא אֶל־אִיּוֹב וַיֹּאמַר הַבָּקָר הָיוּ חֹרְשׁוֹת וְהָאֲתֹנוֹת רֹעוֹת עַל־יְדֵיהֶם: 15 וַתִּפֹּל שְׁבָא וַתִּקָּחֵם וְאֶת־הַנְּעָרִים הִכּוּ לְפִי־חָרֶב וָאִמָּלְטָה רַק

raided *them* and took them away—indeed they have killed the servants with the edge of the sword; and I alone have escaped to tell you!"

16 While he *was* still speaking, another also came and said, "The fire of God fell from heaven and burned up the sheep and the servants, and consumed them; and I alone have escaped to tell you!"

17 While he *was* still speaking, another also came and said, "The Chaldeans formed three bands, raided the camels and took them away, yes, and killed the servants with the edge of the sword; and I alone have escaped to tell you!"

18 While he *was* still speaking, another also came and said, "Your sons and daughters *were* eating and drinking wine in their oldest brother's house,
19 and suddenly a great wind came from across the wilderness and struck the four corners of the house, -and it fell on the young people, and they are dead; and I alone have escaped to tell you!"

20 Then Job arose, tore his robe, and shaved his head; and he fell to the ground and worshiped.
21 And he said:

"Naked I came from my mother's womb,
And naked shall I return there.
The LORD gave, and the LORD has taken away;
Blessed be the name of the LORD."

22 In all this Job did not sin nor charge God with wrong.

2 Again there was a day when the sons of God came to present themselves before the LORD, and Satan came also among them to present himself before the LORD. 2 And the LORD said to Satan, "From where do you come?"

Satan answered the LORD and said, "From going to and fro on the earth, and from walking back and forth on it."

3 Then the LORD said to Satan, "Have you considered My servant Job, that *there is* none like him on the earth, a blameless and upright man, one who fears God and shuns evil? And still he holds fast to his integrity, although you incited Me against him, to destroy him without cause."

4 So Satan answered the LORD and said, "Skin for skin! Yes, all that a man has he will give for his life. 5 But stretch out Your hand now, and touch his bone and his flesh, and he will surely curse You to Your face!"

6 And the LORD said to Satan, "Behold, he *is* in your hand, but spare his life."

16 עוֹד ׀ זֶה מְדַבֵּר וְזֶה אֲנִי לְבַדִּי לְהַגִּיד לָךְ:
בָּא וַיֹּאמַר אֵשׁ אֱלֹהִים נָפְלָה מִן־הַשָּׁמַיִם וַתִּבְעַר
בַּצֹּאן וּבַנְּעָרִים וַתֹּאכְלֵם וָאִמָּלְטָה רַק־אֲנִי לְבַדִּי
לְהַגִּיד לָךְ: 17 עוֹד ׀ זֶה מְדַבֵּר וְזֶה בָּא וַיֹּאמַר
כַּשְׂדִּים שָׂמוּ ׀ שְׁלֹשָׁה רָאשִׁים וַיִּפְשְׁטוּ עַל־הַגְּמַלִּים
וַיִּקָּחוּם וְאֶת־הַנְּעָרִים הִכּוּ לְפִי־חָרֶב וָאִמָּלְטָה רַק־
אֲנִי לְבַדִּי לְהַגִּיד לָךְ: 18 עַד זֶה מְדַבֵּר וְזֶה בָּא
וַיֹּאמַר בָּנֶיךָ וּבְנוֹתֶיךָ אֹכְלִים וְשֹׁתִים יַיִן בְּבֵית
אֲחִיהֶם הַבְּכוֹר: 19 וְהִנֵּה רוּחַ גְּדוֹלָה בָּאָה ׀ מֵעֵבֶר
הַמִּדְבָּר וַיִּגַּע בְּאַרְבַּע פִּנּוֹת הַבַּיִת וַיִּפֹּל עַל־הַנְּעָרִים
וַיָּמוּתוּ וָאִמָּלְטָה רַק־אֲנִי לְבַדִּי לְהַגִּיד לָךְ: 20 וַיָּקָם
אִיּוֹב וַיִּקְרַע אֶת־מְעִלוֹ וַיָּגָז אֶת־רֹאשׁוֹ וַיִּפֹּל אַרְצָה
וַיִּשְׁתָּחוּ: 21 וַיֹּאמֶר עָרֹם יָצָתִי מִבֶּטֶן אִמִּי וְעָרֹם
אָשׁוּב שָׁמָּה יְהֹוָה נָתַן וַיהֹוָה לָקָח יְהִי שֵׁם יְהֹוָה
מְבֹרָךְ: 22 בְּכָל־זֹאת לֹא־חָטָא אִיּוֹב וְלֹא־נָתַן תִּפְלָה
לֵאלֹהִים: פ

ב וַיְהִי הַיּוֹם וַיָּבֹאוּ בְּנֵי הָאֱלֹהִים לְהִתְיַצֵּב עַל־יְהֹוָה
וַיָּבוֹא גַם־הַשָּׂטָן בְּתֹכָם לְהִתְיַצֵּב עַל־יְהֹוָה: 2 וַיֹּאמֶר
יְהֹוָה אֶל־הַשָּׂטָן אֵי מִזֶּה תָּבֹא וַיַּעַן הַשָּׂטָן אֶת־
יְהֹוָה וַיֹּאמַר מִשֻּׁט בָּאָרֶץ וּמֵהִתְהַלֵּךְ בָּהּ: 3 וַיֹּאמֶר
יְהֹוָה אֶל־הַשָּׂטָן הֲשַׂמְתָּ לִבְּךָ אֶל־עַבְדִּי אִיּוֹב כִּי אֵין
כָּמֹהוּ בָּאָרֶץ אִישׁ תָּם וְיָשָׁר יְרֵא אֱלֹהִים וְסָר מֵרָע
וְעֹדֶנּוּ מַחֲזִיק בְּתֻמָּתוֹ וַתְּסִיתֵנִי בוֹ לְבַלְּעוֹ חִנָּם:
4 וַיַּעַן הַשָּׂטָן אֶת־יְהֹוָה וַיֹּאמַר עוֹר בְּעַד־עוֹר וְכֹל
אֲשֶׁר לָאִישׁ יִתֵּן בְּעַד נַפְשׁוֹ: 5 אוּלָם שְׁלַח־נָא יָדְךָ
וְגַע אֶל־עַצְמוֹ וְאֶל־בְּשָׂרוֹ אִם־לֹא אֶל־פָּנֶיךָ יְבָרֲכֶךָּ:
6 וַיֹּאמֶר יְהֹוָה אֶל־הַשָּׂטָן הִנּוֹ בְיָדֶךָ אַךְ אֶת־נַפְשׁוֹ

א יָצָאתִי

7 So Satan went out from the presence of the LORD, and struck Job with painful boils from the sole of his foot to the crown of his head. 8 And he took for himself a potsherd with which to scrape himself while he sat in the midst of the ashes.

9 Then his wife said to him, "Do you still hold fast to your integrity? Curse God and die!"

10 But he said to her, "You speak as one of the foolish women speaks. Shall we indeed accept good from God, and shall we not accept adversity?" In all this Job did not sin with his lips.

11 Now when Job's three friends heard of all this adversity that had come upon him, each one came from his own place—Eliphaz the Temanite, Bildad the Shuhite, and Zophar the Naamathite. For they had made an appointment together to come and mourn with him, and to comfort him. 12 And when they raised their eyes from afar, and did not recognize him, they lifted their voices and wept; and each one tore his robe and sprinkled dust on his head toward heaven. 13 So they sat down with him on the ground seven days and seven nights, and no one spoke a word to him, for they saw that *his* grief was very great.

3 After this Job opened his mouth and cursed the day of his *birth*. 2 And Job spoke, and said:

3   "May the day perish on which I was born,
    And the night *in which* it was said,
    'A male child is conceived.'

4   May that day be darkness;
    May God above not seek it,
    Nor the light shine upon it.

5   May darkness and the shadow of death claim it;
    May a cloud settle on it;
    May the blackness of the day terrify it.

6   *As for* that night, may darkness seize it;
    May it not rejoice among the days of the year,
    May it not come into the number of the months.

7   Oh, may that night be barren!
    May no joyful shout come into it!

8   May those curse it who curse the day,
    Those who are ready to arouse Leviathan.

9   May the stars of its morning be dark;
    May it look for light, but *have* none,
    And not see the dawning of the day;

10 Because it did not shut up the doors of my *mother's* womb,
    Nor hide sorrow from my eyes.

11 "Why did I not die at birth?

שָׁמֹר: 7 וַיֵּצֵא הַשָּׂטָן מֵאֵת פְּנֵי יְהוָה וַיַּךְ אֶת־אִיּוֹב בִּשְׁחִין רָע מִכַּף רַגְלוֹ עַד קָדְקֳדוֹ: 8 וַיִּקַּח־לוֹ חֶרֶשׂ לְהִתְגָּרֵד בּוֹ וְהוּא יֹשֵׁב בְּתוֹךְ־הָאֵפֶר: 9 וַתֹּאמֶר לוֹ אִשְׁתּוֹ עֹדְךָ מַחֲזִיק בְּתֻמָּתֶךָ בָּרֵךְ אֱלֹהִים וָמֻת: 10 וַיֹּאמֶר אֵלֶיהָ כְּדַבֵּר אַחַת הַנְּבָלוֹת תְּדַבֵּרִי גַּם אֶת־הַטּוֹב נְקַבֵּל מֵאֵת הָאֱלֹהִים וְאֶת־הָרָע לֹא נְקַבֵּל בְּכָל־זֹאת לֹא־חָטָא אִיּוֹב בִּשְׂפָתָיו:

פ

11 וַיִּשְׁמְעוּ שְׁלֹשֶׁת ׀ רֵעֵי אִיּוֹב אֵת כָּל־הָרָעָה הַזֹּאת הַבָּאָה עָלָיו וַיָּבֹאוּ אִישׁ מִמְּקֹמוֹ אֱלִיפַז הַתֵּימָנִי וּבִלְדַּד הַשּׁוּחִי וְצוֹפַר הַנַּעֲמָתִי וַיִּוָּעֲדוּ יַחְדָּו לָבוֹא לָנוּד־לוֹ וּלְנַחֲמוֹ: 12 וַיִּשְׂאוּ אֶת־עֵינֵיהֶם מֵרָחוֹק וְלֹא הִכִּירֻהוּ וַיִּשְׂאוּ קוֹלָם וַיִּבְכּוּ וַיִּקְרְעוּ אִישׁ מְעִלוֹ וַיִּזְרְקוּ עָפָר עַל־רָאשֵׁיהֶם הַשָּׁמָיְמָה: 13 וַיֵּשְׁבוּ אִתּוֹ לָאָרֶץ שִׁבְעַת יָמִים וְשִׁבְעַת לֵילוֹת וְאֵין־דֹּבֵר אֵלָיו דָּבָר כִּי רָאוּ כִּי־גָדַל הַכְּאֵב מְאֹד:

ג 1 אַחֲרֵי־כֵן פָּתַח אִיּוֹב אֶת־פִּיהוּ וַיְקַלֵּל אֶת־יוֹמוֹ:

2 וַיַּעַן אִיּוֹב וַיֹּאמַר:

3 יֹאבַד יוֹם אִוָּלֶד בּוֹ וְהַלַּיְלָה אָמַר הֹרָה גָבֶר:

4 הַיּוֹם הַהוּא יְהִי חֹשֶׁךְ אַל־יִדְרְשֵׁהוּ אֱלוֹהַּ מִמָּעַל וְאַל־תּוֹפַע עָלָיו נְהָרָה:

5 יִגְאָלֻהוּ חֹשֶׁךְ וְצַלְמָוֶת תִּשְׁכָּן־עָלָיו עֲנָנָה יְבַעֲתֻהוּ כִּמְרִירֵי יוֹם:

6 הַלַּיְלָה הַהוּא יִקָּחֵהוּ אֹפֶל אַל־יִחַדְּ בִּימֵי שָׁנָה בְּמִסְפַּר יְרָחִים אַל־יָבֹא:

7 הִנֵּה הַלַּיְלָה הַהוּא יְהִי גַלְמוּד אַל־תָּבֹא רְנָנָה בוֹ:

8 יִקְּבֻהוּ אֹרְרֵי־יוֹם הָעֲתִידִים עֹרֵר לִוְיָתָן:

9 יֶחְשְׁכוּ כּוֹכְבֵי נִשְׁפּוֹ יְקַו־לְאוֹר וָאַיִן וְאַל־יִרְאֶה בְּעַפְעַפֵּי־שָׁחַר:

10 כִּי לֹא סָגַר דַּלְתֵי בִטְנִי וַיַּסְתֵּר עָמָל מֵעֵינָי:

11 לָמָּה לֹּא מֵרֶחֶם אָמוּת

Why did I *not* perish when I came from the womb?		מִבֶּ֥טֶן יָ֝צָ֗אתִי וְאֶגְוָֽע׃
12 Why did the knees receive me? Or why the breasts, that I should nurse?	12	מַ֭דּוּעַ קִדְּמ֣וּנִי בִרְכָּ֑יִם וּמַה־שָּׁ֝דַ֗יִם כִּ֣י אִינָֽק׃
13 For now I would have lain still and been quiet, I would have been asleep; Then I would have been at rest	13	כִּֽי־עַ֭תָּה שָׁכַ֣בְתִּי וְאֶשְׁק֑וֹט יָ֝שַׁ֗נְתִּי אָ֤ז ׀ יָנ֬וּחַֽ לִֽי׃
14 With kings and counselors of the earth, Who built ruins for themselves,	14	עִם־מְ֭לָכִים וְיֹ֣עֲצֵי אָ֑רֶץ הַבֹּנִ֖ים חֳרָב֣וֹת לָֽמוֹ׃
15 Or with princes who had gold, Who filled their houses *with* silver;	15	א֣וֹ עִם־שָׂ֭רִים זָהָ֣ב לָהֶ֑ם הַֽמְמַלְאִ֖ים בָּתֵּיהֶ֣ם כָּֽסֶף׃
16 Or *why* was I not hidden like a stillborn child, Like infants who never saw light?	16	א֤וֹ כְנֵ֣פֶל טָ֭מוּן לֹ֣א אֶהְיֶ֑ה כְּ֝עֹלְלִ֗ים לֹא־רָ֥אוּ אֽוֹר׃
17 There the wicked cease *from* troubling, And there the weary are at rest.	17	שָׁ֣ם רְ֭שָׁעִים חָ֣דְלוּ רֹ֑גֶז וְשָׁ֥ם יָ֝נ֗וּחוּ יְגִ֣יעֵי כֹֽחַ׃
18 *There* the prisoners rest together; They do not hear the voice of the oppressor.	18	יַ֭חַד אֲסִירִ֣ים שַׁאֲנָ֑נוּ לֹ֥א שָׁ֝מְע֗וּ ק֣וֹל נֹגֵֽשׂ׃
19 The small and great are there, And the servant *is* free from his master.	19	קָטֹ֣ן וְ֭גָדוֹל שָׁ֣ם ה֑וּא וְ֝עֶ֗בֶד חָפְשִׁ֥י מֵאֲדֹנָֽיו׃
20 "Why is light given to him who is in misery, And life to the bitter of soul,	20	לָ֤מָּה יִתֵּ֣ן לְעָמֵ֣ל א֑וֹר וְ֝חַיִּ֗ים לְמָ֣רֵי נָֽפֶשׁ׃
21 Who long for death, but it does not *come*, And search for it more than hidden treasures;	21	הַֽמְחַכִּ֣ים לַמָּ֣וֶת וְאֵינֶ֑נּוּ וַֽ֝יַּחְפְּרֻ֗הוּ מִמַּטְמוֹנִֽים׃
22 Who rejoice exceedingly, *And* are glad when they can find the grave?	22	הַשְּׂמֵחִ֥ים אֱלֵי־גִ֑יל יָ֝שִׂ֗ישׂוּ כִּ֣י יִמְצְאוּ־קָֽבֶר׃
23 *Why is light given* to a man whose way is hidden, And whom God has hedged in?	23	לְ֭גֶבֶר אֲשֶׁר־דַּרְכּ֣וֹ נִסְתָּ֑רָה וַיָּ֖סֶךְ אֱל֣וֹהַּ בַּעֲדֽוֹ׃
24 For my sighing comes before I eat, And my groanings pour out like water.	24	כִּֽי־לִפְנֵ֣י לַ֭חְמִי אַנְחָתִ֣י תָבֹ֑א וַֽיִּתְּכ֖וּ כַמַּ֣יִם שַׁאֲגֹתָֽי׃
25 For the thing I greatly feared has come upon me, And what I dreaded has happened to me.	25	כִּ֤י פַ֣חַד פָּ֭חַדְתִּי וַיֶּאֱתָיֵ֑נִי וַאֲשֶׁ֥ר יָ֝גֹ֗רְתִּי יָ֣בֹא לִֽי׃
26 I am not at ease, nor am I quiet; I have no rest, for trouble comes."	26	לֹ֤א שָׁלַ֨וְתִּי ׀ וְלֹ֖א שָׁקַ֥טְתִּי וְֽלֹא־נָ֗חְתִּי וַיָּ֥בֹא רֹֽגֶז׃ פ

4 Then Eliphaz the Temanite answered and said:

2 "*If* one attempts a word with you, will you become weary? But who can withhold himself from speaking?		ד וַ֭יַּעַן אֱלִיפַ֥ז הַֽתֵּימָנִ֗י וַיֹּאמַֽר׃
	2	הֲנִסָּ֬ה דָבָ֣ר אֵלֶ֣יךָ תִּלְאֶ֑ה וַעְצֹ֥ר בְּ֝מִלִּ֗ין מִ֣י יוּכָֽל׃
3 Surely you have instructed many, And you have strengthened weak hands.	3	הִ֭נֵּה יִסַּ֣רְתָּ רַבִּ֑ים וְיָדַ֖יִם רָפ֣וֹת תְּחַזֵּֽק׃
4 Your words have upheld him who was stumbling, And you have strengthened the feeble knees;	4	כּ֭וֹשֵׁל יְקִימ֣וּן מִלֶּ֑יךָ וּבִרְכַּ֖יִם כֹּרְע֣וֹת תְּאַמֵּֽץ׃
5 But now it comes upon you, and you are weary; It touches you, and you are troubled.	5	כִּ֤י עַתָּ֨ה ׀ תָּב֣וֹא אֵלֶ֣יךָ וַתֵּ֑לֶא תִּגַּ֥ע עָ֝דֶ֗יךָ וַתִּבָּהֵֽל׃
6 *Is* not your reverence your confidence?	6	הֲלֹ֣א יִ֭רְאָתְךָ כִּסְלָתֶ֑ךָ

And the integrity of your ways your hope?   תִּקְוָתְךָ וְתֹם דְּרָכֶיךָ:

7 "Remember now, who *ever* perished being innocent?   7 זְכָר־נָא מִי הוּא נָקִי אָבָד

Or where were the upright *ever* cut off?   וְאֵיפֹה יְשָׁרִים נִכְחָדוּ:

8 Even as I have seen,   8 כַּאֲשֶׁר רָאִיתִי חֹרְשֵׁי אָוֶן

Those who plow iniquity

And sow trouble reap the same.   וְזֹרְעֵי עָמָל יִקְצְרֻהוּ:

9 By the blast of God they perish,   9 מִנִּשְׁמַת אֱלוֹהַ יֹאבֵדוּ

And by the breath of His anger they are consumed.   וּמֵרוּחַ אַפּוֹ יִכְלוּ:

10 The roaring of the lion,   10 שַׁאֲגַת אַרְיֵה וְקוֹל שָׁחַל

The voice of the fierce lion,

And the teeth of the young lions are broken.   וְשִׁנֵּי כְפִירִים נִתָּעוּ:

11 The old lion perishes for lack of prey,   11 לַיִשׁ אֹבֵד מִבְּלִי־טָרֶף

And the cubs of the lioness are scattered.   וּבְנֵי לָבִיא יִתְפָּרָדוּ:

12 "Now a word was secretly brought to me,   12 וְאֵלַי דָּבָר יְגֻנָּב

And my ear received a whisper of it.   וַתִּקַּח אָזְנִי שֵׁמֶץ מֶנְהוּ:

13 In disquieting thoughts from the visions of the night,   13 בִּשְׂעִפִּים מֵחֶזְיֹנוֹת לָיְלָה

When deep sleep falls on men,   בִּנְפֹל תַּרְדֵּמָה עַל־אֲנָשִׁים:

14 Fear came upon me, and trembling,   14 פַּחַד קְרָאַנִי וּרְעָדָה

Which made all my bones shake.   וְרֹב עַצְמוֹתַי הִפְחִיד:

15 Then a spirit passed before my face;   15 וְרוּחַ עַל־פָּנַי יַחֲלֹף

The hair on my body stood up.   תְּסַמֵּר שַׂעֲרַת בְּשָׂרִי:

16 It stood still,   16 יַעֲמֹד וְלֹא־אַכִּיר מַרְאֵהוּ

But I could not discern its appearance.

A form *was* before my eyes;   תְּמוּנָה לְנֶגֶד עֵינָי

There was silence;   דְּמָמָה וָקוֹל

Then I heard a voice *saying:*   אֶשְׁמָע:

17 'Can a mortal be more righteous than God?   17 הַאֱנוֹשׁ מֵאֱלוֹהַ יִצְדָּק

Can a man be more pure than his Maker?   אִם מֵעֹשֵׂהוּ יִטְהַר־גָּבֶר:

18 If He puts no trust in His servants,   18 הֵן בַּעֲבָדָיו לֹא יַאֲמִין

If He charges His angels with error,   וּבְמַלְאָכָיו יָשִׂים תָּהֳלָה:

19 How much more those who dwell in houses of clay,   19 אַף שֹׁכְנֵי בָתֵּי־חֹמֶר אֲשֶׁר־בֶּעָפָר יְסוֹדָם

Whose foundation is in the dust,

Who are crushed before a moth?   יְדַכְּאוּם לִפְנֵי־עָשׁ:

20 They are broken in pieces from morning till evening;   20 מִבֹּקֶר לָעֶרֶב יֻכַּתּוּ

They perish forever, with no one regarding.   מִבְּלִי מֵשִׂים לָנֶצַח יֹאבֵדוּ:

21 Does not their own excellence go away?   21 הֲלֹא־נִסַּע יִתְרָם בָּם

They die, even without wisdom.'   יָמוּתוּ וְלֹא בְחָכְמָה:

---

5 "Call out now;   ה קְרָא־נָא הֲיֵשׁ עוֹנֶךָּ

Is there anyone who will answer you?

And to which of the holy ones will you turn?   וְאֶל־מִי מִקְּדֹשִׁים תִּפְנֶה:

2 For wrath kills a foolish man,   2 כִּי־לֶאֱוִיל יַהֲרָג־כָּעַשׂ

And envy slays a simple one.   וּפֹתֶה תָּמִית קִנְאָה:

3 I have seen the foolish taking root,   3 אֲנִי־רָאִיתִי אֱוִיל מַשְׁרִישׁ

But suddenly I cursed his dwelling place.   וָאֶקּוֹב נָוֵהוּ פִתְאֹם:

4 His sons are far from safety,   4 יִרְחֲקוּ בָנָיו מִיֶּשַׁע

They are crushed in the gate,

And *there is* no deliverer.   וְיִדַּכְּאוּ בַשַּׁעַר וְאֵין מַצִּיל:

5 Because the hungry eat up his harvest,
Taking it even from the thorns,
And a snare snatches their substance.

6 For affliction does not come from the dust,
Nor does trouble spring from the ground;

7 Yet man is born to trouble,
As the sparks fly upward.

8 "But as for me, I would seek God,
And to God I would commit my cause—

9 Who does great things, and unsearchable,
Marvelous things without number.

10 He gives rain on the earth,
And sends waters on the fields.

11 He sets on high those who are lowly,
And those who mourn are lifted to safety.

12 He frustrates the devices of the crafty,
So that their hands cannot carry out their
plans.

13 He catches the wise in their own craftiness,
And the counsel of the cunning comes
quickly upon them.

14 They meet with darkness in the daytime,
And grope at noontime as in the night.

15 But He saves the needy from the sword,
From the mouth of the mighty,
And from their hand.

16 So the poor have hope,
And injustice shuts her mouth.

17 "Behold, happy is the man whom God
corrects;
Therefore do not despise the chastening of
the Almighty.

18 For He bruises, but He binds up;
He wounds, but His hands make whole.

19 He shall deliver you in six troubles,
Yes, in seven no evil shall touch you.

20 In famine He shall redeem you from death,
And in war from the power of the sword.

21 You shall be hidden from the scourge of the
tongue,
And you shall not be afraid of destruction
when it comes.

22 You shall laugh at destruction and famine,
And you shall not be afraid of the beasts of
the earth.

23 For you shall have a covenant with the
stones of the field,
And the beasts of the field shall be at peace
with you.

24 You shall know that your tent is in peace;
You shall visit your dwelling and find
nothing amiss.

5 אֲשֶׁר קְצִירוֹ ׀ רָעֵב יֹאכֵל וְאֶל־מִצִּנִּים יִקָּחֵהוּ
וְשָׁאַף צַמִּים חֵילָם:

6 כִּי ׀ לֹא־יֵצֵא מֵעָפָר אָוֶן
וּמֵאֲדָמָה לֹא־יִצְמַח עָמָל:

7 כִּי־אָדָם לְעָמָל יוּלָּד
וּבְנֵי־רֶשֶׁף יַגְבִּיהוּ עוּף:

8 אוּלָם אֲנִי אֶדְרֹשׁ אֶל־אֵל
וְאֶל־אֱלֹהִים אָשִׂים דִּבְרָתִי:

9 עֹשֶׂה גְדֹלוֹת וְאֵין חֵקֶר
נִפְלָאוֹת עַד־אֵין מִסְפָּר:

10 הַנֹּתֵן מָטָר עַל־פְּנֵי־אָרֶץ
וְשֹׁלֵחַ מַיִם עַל־פְּנֵי חוּצוֹת:

11 לָשׂוּם שְׁפָלִים לְמָרוֹם
וְקֹדְרִים שָׂגְבוּ יֶשַׁע:

12 מֵפֵר מַחְשְׁבוֹת עֲרוּמִים
וְלֹא־תַעֲשֶׂינָה יְדֵיהֶם תּוּשִׁיָּה:

13 לֹכֵד חֲכָמִים בְּעָרְמָם
וַעֲצַת נִפְתָּלִים נִמְהָרָה:

14 יוֹמָם יְפַגְּשׁוּ־חֹשֶׁךְ
וְכַלַּיְלָה יְמַשְׁשׁוּ בַצָּהֳרָיִם:

15 וַיֹּשַׁע מֵחֶרֶב מִפִּיהֶם
וּמִיַּד חָזָק אֶבְיוֹן:

16 וַתְּהִי לַדַּל תִּקְוָה
וְעֹלָתָה קָפְצָה פִּיהָ:

17 הִנֵּה אַשְׁרֵי אֱנוֹשׁ יוֹכִחֶנּוּ אֱלוֹהַּ
וּמוּסַר שַׁדַּי אַל־תִּמְאָס:

18 כִּי הוּא יַכְאִיב וְיֶחְבָּשׁ
יִמְחַץ וְיָדָו ⁰ תִּרְפֶּינָה:

19 בְּשֵׁשׁ צָרוֹת יַצִּילֶךָּ
וּבְשֶׁבַע ׀ לֹא־יִגַּע בְּךָ רָע:

20 בְּרָעָב פָּדְךָ מִמָּוֶת
וּבְמִלְחָמָה מִידֵי חָרֶב:

21 בְּשׁוֹט לָשׁוֹן תֵּחָבֵא
וְלֹא־תִירָא מִשֹּׁד כִּי יָבוֹא:

22 לְשֹׁד וּלְכָפָן תִּשְׂחָק
וּמֵחַיַּת הָאָרֶץ אַל־תִּירָא:

23 כִּי עִם־אַבְנֵי הַשָּׂדֶה בְרִיתֶךָ
וְחַיַּת הַשָּׂדֶה הָשְׁלְמָה־לָךְ:

24 וְיָדַעְתָּ כִּי־שָׁלוֹם אָהֳלֶךָ
וּפָקַדְתָּ נָוְךָ וְלֹא תֶחֱטָא:

25 You shall also know that your descendants
    shall be many,
    And your offspring like the grass of the
    earth.
26 You shall come to the grave at a full age,
    As a sheaf of grain ripens in its season.
27 Behold, this we have searched out;
    It *is* true.
    Hear it, and know for yourself."

6 Then Job answered and said:

2 "Oh, that my grief were fully weighed,
    And my calamity laid with it on the scales!
3 For then it would be heavier than the sand
    of the sea—
    Therefore my words have been rash.
4 For the arrows of the Almighty *are* within
    me;
    My spirit drinks in their poison;
    The terrors of God are arrayed against me.
5 Does the wild donkey bray when it has grass,
    Or does the ox low over its fodder?
6 Can flavorless food be eaten without salt?
    Or is there *any* taste in the white of an egg?
7 My soul refuses to touch them;
    They *are* as loathsome food to me.

8 "Oh, that I might have my request,
    That God would grant *me* the thing that I
    long for!
9 That it would please God to crush me,
    That He would loose His hand and cut me
    off!
10 Then I would still have comfort;
    Though in anguish I would exult,
    He will not spare;
    For I have not concealed the words of the
    Holy One.

11 "What strength do I have, that I should hope?
    And what *is* my end, that I should prolong
    my life?
12 *Is* my strength the strength of stones?
    Or is my flesh bronze?
13 *Is* my help not within me?
    And is success driven from me?

14 "To him who is afflicted, kindness *should be*
    shown by his friend,
    Even though he forsakes the fear of the
    Almighty.
15 My brothers have dealt deceitfully like a
    brook,
    Like the streams of the brooks that pass
    away,

25 וְיָדַעְתָּ כִּי־רַב זַרְעֶךָ
וְצֶאֱצָאֶיךָ כְּעֵשֶׂב הָאָרֶץ׃
26 תָּבוֹא בְכֶלַח אֱלֵי־קָבֶר
כַּעֲלוֹת גָּדִישׁ בְּעִתּוֹ׃
27 הִנֵּה־זֹאת חֲקַרְנוּהָ כֶּן־הִיא
שְׁמָעֶנָּה וְאַתָּה דַע־לָךְ׃   פ

ו 1 וַיַּעַן אִיּוֹב וַיֹּאמַר׃
2 לוּ שָׁקוֹל יִשָּׁקֵל כַּעְשִׂי
וְהַיָּתִי בְּמֹאזְנַיִם יִשְׂאוּ־יָחַד׃
3 כִּי־עַתָּה מֵחוֹל יַמִּים יִכְבָּד
עַל־כֵּן דְּבָרַי לָעוּ׃
4 כִּי חִצֵּי שַׁדַּי עִמָּדִי אֲשֶׁר חֲמָתָם שֹׁתָה רוּחִי
בִּעוּתֵי אֱלוֹהַּ יַעַרְכוּנִי׃
5 הֲיִנְהַק־פֶּרֶא עֲלֵי־דֶשֶׁא
אִם יִגְעֶה־שּׁוֹר עַל־בְּלִילוֹ׃
6 הֲיֵאָכֵל תָּפֵל מִבְּלִי־מֶלַח
אִם־יֶשׁ־טַעַם בְּרִיר חַלָּמוּת׃
7 מֵאֲנָה לִנְגּוֹעַ נַפְשִׁי
הֵמָּה כִּדְוֵי לַחְמִי׃
8 מִי־יִתֵּן תָּבוֹא שֶׁאֱלָתִי
וְתִקְוָתִי יִתֵּן אֱלוֹהַּ׃
9 וְיֹאֵל אֱלוֹהַּ וִידַכְּאֵנִי
יַתֵּר יָדוֹ וִיבַצְּעֵנִי׃
10 וּתְהִי עוֹד ׀ נֶחָמָתִי
וַאֲסַלְּדָה בְחִילָה לֹא יַחְמוֹל
כִּי־לֹא כִחַדְתִּי אִמְרֵי קָדוֹשׁ׃
11 מַה־כֹּחִי כִי־אֲיַחֵל
וּמַה־קִּצִּי כִּי־אַאֲרִיךְ נַפְשִׁי׃
12 אִם־כֹּחַ אֲבָנִים כֹּחִי
אִם־בְּשָׂרִי נָחוּשׁ׃
13 הַאִם אֵין עֶזְרָתִי בִי
וְתֻשִׁיָּה נִדְּחָה מִמֶּנִּי׃
14 לַמָּס מֵרֵעֵהוּ חָסֶד
וְיִרְאַת שַׁדַּי יַעֲזוֹב׃
15 אַחַי בָּגְדוּ כְמוֹ־נָחַל
כַּאֲפִיק נְחָלִים יַעֲבֹרוּ׃

1 2 וְהַיָּתִי

16 Which are dark because of the ice,
   And into which the snow vanishes.
17 When it is warm, they cease to flow;
   When it is hot, they vanish from their place.
18 The paths of their way turn aside,
   They go nowhere and perish.
19 The caravans of Tema look,
   The travelers of Sheba hope for them.
20 They are disappointed because they were confident;
   They come there and are confused.
21 For now you are nothing,
   You see terror and are afraid.
22 Did I ever say, 'Bring *something* to me'?
   Or, 'Offer a bribe for me from your wealth'?
23 Or, 'Deliver me from the enemy's hand'?
   Or, 'Redeem me from the hand of oppressors'?

24 "Teach me, and I will hold my tongue;
   Cause me to understand wherein I have erred.
25 How forceful are right words!
   But what does your arguing prove?
26 Do you intend to rebuke *my* words,
   And the speeches of a desperate one, *which are* as wind?
27 Yes, you overwhelm the fatherless,
   And you undermine your friend.
28 Now therefore, be pleased to look at me;
   For I would never lie to your face.
29 Yield now, let there be no injustice!
   Yes, concede, my righteousness still stands!
30 Is there injustice on my tongue?
   Cannot my taste discern the unsavory?

7   "*Is there* not a time of hard service for man on earth?
   Are not his days also like the days of a hired man?
2 Like a servant who earnestly desires the shade,
   And like a hired man who eagerly looks for his wages,
3 So I have been allotted months of futility,
   And wearisome nights have been appointed to me.
4 When I lie down, I say, 'When shall I arise,
   And the night be ended?'
   For I have had my fill of tossing till dawn.
5 My flesh is caked with worms and dust,
   My skin is cracked and breaks out afresh.

6 "My days are swifter than a weaver's shuttle,
   And are spent without hope.

---

16 הַקֹּדְרִים מִנִּי־קָרַח
   עָלֵימוֹ יִתְעַלֶּם־שָׁלֶג:
17 בְּעֵת יְזֹרְבוּ נִצְמָתוּ
   בְּחֻמּוֹ נִדְעֲכוּ מִמְּקוֹמָם:
18 יִלָּפְתוּ אָרְחוֹת דַּרְכָּם
   יַעֲלוּ בַתֹּהוּ וְיֹאבֵדוּ:
19 הִבִּיטוּ אָרְחוֹת תֵּמָא
   הֲלִיכֹת שְׁבָא קִוּוּ־לָמוֹ:
20 בֹּשׁוּ כִּי־בָטָח
   בָּאוּ עָדֶיהָ וַיֶּחְפָּרוּ:
21 כִּי־עַתָּה הֱיִיתֶם לֹא ᵖ
   תִּרְאוּ חֲתַת וַתִּירָאוּ:
22 הֲכִי־אָמַרְתִּי הָבוּ לִי
   וּמִכֹּחֲכֶם שִׁחֲדוּ בַעֲדִי:
23 וּמַלְּטוּנִי מִיַּד־צָר
   וּמִיַּד עָרִיצִים תִּפְדּוּנִי:
24 הוֹרוּנִי וַאֲנִי אַחֲרִישׁ
   וּמַה־שָּׁגִיתִי הָבִינוּ לִי:
25 מַה־נִּמְרְצוּ אִמְרֵי־יֹשֶׁר
   וּמַה־יּוֹכִיחַ הוֹכֵחַ מִכֶּם:
26 הַלְהוֹכַח מִלִּים תַּחְשֹׁבוּ
   וּלְרוּחַ אִמְרֵי נֹאָשׁ:
27 אַף־עַל־יָתוֹם תַּפִּילוּ
   וְתִכְרוּ עַל־רֵיעֲכֶם:
28 וְעַתָּה הוֹאִילוּ פְנוּ־בִי
   וְעַל־פְּנֵיכֶם אִם־אֲכַזֵּב:
29 שֻׁבוּ־נָא אַל־תְּהִי עַוְלָה
   וְשֻׁבִי ᵖ עוֹד צִדְקִי־בָהּ:
30 הֲיֵשׁ־בִּלְשׁוֹנִי עַוְלָה
   אִם־חִכִּי לֹא־יָבִין הַוּוֹת:

ז הֲלֹא־צָבָא לֶאֱנוֹשׁ עַל־ ᵖ אָרֶץ
   וְכִימֵי שָׂכִיר יָמָיו:
2 כְּעֶבֶד יִשְׁאַף־צֵל
   וּכְשָׂכִיר יְקַוֶּה פָעֳלוֹ:
3 כֵּן הָנְחַלְתִּי לִי יַרְחֵי־שָׁוְא
   וְלֵילוֹת עָמָל מִנּוּ־לִי:
4 אִם־שָׁכַבְתִּי וְאָמַרְתִּי מָתַי אָקוּם וּמִדַּד־עָרֶב
   וְשָׂבַעְתִּי נְדֻדִים עֲדֵי־נָשֶׁף:
5 לָבַשׁ בְּשָׂרִי רִמָּה וְגִישׁ ᵖ עָפָר
   עוֹרִי רָגַע וַיִּמָּאֵס:
6 יָמַי קַלּוּ מִנִּי־אָרֶג

7 Oh, remember that my life *is* a breath!
My eye will never again see good.

8 The eye of him who sees me will see me no
more;
While your *eyes* are upon me, I shall no
longer *be.*

9 *As* the cloud disappears and vanishes away,
So he who goes down to the grave does not
come up.

10 He shall never return to his house,
Nor shall his place know him anymore.

11 "Therefore I will not restrain my mouth;
I will speak in the anguish of my spirit;
I will complain in the bitterness of my soul.

12 *Am* I a sea, or a sea serpent,
That You set a guard over me?

13 When I say, 'My bed will comfort me,
My couch will ease my complaint,'

14 Then You scare me with dreams
And terrify me with visions,

15 So that my soul chooses strangling
And death rather than my body.

16 I loathe *my life;*
I would not live forever.
Let me alone,
For my days *are but* a breath.

17 "What *is* man, that You should exalt him,
That You should set Your heart on him,

18 That You should visit him every morning,
And test him every moment?

19 How long?
Will You not look away from me,
And let me alone till I swallow my saliva?

20 Have I sinned?
What have I done to You, O watcher of
men?
Why have You set me as Your target,
So that I am a burden to myself?

21 Why then do You not pardon my trans-
gression,
And take away my iniquity?
For now I will lie down in the dust,
And You will seek me diligently,
But I *will* no longer *be.*"

8 Then Bildad the Shuhite answered and said:

2 "How long will you speak these *things,*
And the words of your mouth *be like* a
strong wind?

3 Does God subvert judgment?
Or does the Almighty pervert justice?

4 If your sons have sinned against Him,

וַיִּכְלוּ בְּאֶפֶס תִּקְוָה:

7 זְכֹר כִּי־רוּחַ חַיָּי
לֹא־תָשׁוּב עֵינִי לִרְאוֹת טוֹב:

8 לֹא־תְשׁוּרֵנִי עֵין רֹאִי
עֵינֶיךָ בִּי וְאֵינֶנִּי:

9 כָּלָה עָנָן וַיֵּלַךְ
כֵּן יוֹרֵד שְׁאוֹל לֹא יַעֲלֶה:

10 לֹא־יָשׁוּב עוֹד לְבֵיתוֹ
וְלֹא־יַכִּירֶנּוּ עוֹד מְקֹמוֹ:

11 גַּם־אֲנִי לֹא אֶחֱשָׂךְ פִּי
אֲדַבְּרָה בְּצַר רוּחִי
אָשִׂיחָה בְּמַר נַפְשִׁי:

12 הֲיָם־אָנִי אִם־תַּנִּין
כִּי־תָשִׂים עָלַי מִשְׁמָר:

13 כִּי־אָמַרְתִּי תְּנַחֲמֵנִי עַרְשִׂי
יִשָּׂא בְשִׂיחִי מִשְׁכָּבִי:

14 וְחִתַּתַּנִי בַחֲלֹמוֹת
וּמֵחֶזְיֹנוֹת תְּבַעֲתַנִּי:

15 וַתִּבְחַר מַחֲנָק נַפְשִׁי
מָוֶת מֵעַצְמוֹתָי:

16 מָאַסְתִּי לֹא־לְעֹלָם אֶחְיֶה
חֲדַל מִמֶּנִּי כִּי־הֶבֶל יָמָי:

17 מָה־אֱנוֹשׁ כִּי תְגַדְּלֶנּוּ
וְכִי־תָשִׁית אֵלָיו לִבֶּךָ:

18 וַתִּפְקְדֶנּוּ לִבְקָרִים
לִרְגָעִים תִּבְחָנֶנּוּ:

19 כַּמָּה לֹא־תִשְׁעֶה מִמֶּנִּי
לֹא־תַרְפֵּנִי עַד־בִּלְעִי רֻקִּי:

20 חָטָאתִי מָה אֶפְעַל לָךְ נֹצֵר הָאָדָם
לָמָה שַׂמְתַּנִי לְמִפְגָּע לָךְ
וָאֶהְיֶה עָלַי לְמַשָּׂא:

21 וּמֶה לֹא־תִשָּׂא פִשְׁעִי וְתַעֲבִיר אֶת־עֲוֺנִי
כִּי־עַתָּה לֶעָפָר אֶשְׁכָּב
וְשִׁחֲרְתַּנִי וְאֵינֶנִּי: פ

ח 8 וַיַּעַן בִּלְדַּד הַשּׁוּחִי וַיֹּאמַר:

2 עַד־אָן תְּמַלֶּל־אֵלֶּה
וְרוּחַ כַּבִּיר אִמְרֵי־פִיךָ:

3 הַאֵל יְעַוֵּת מִשְׁפָּט
וְאִם־שַׁדַּי יְעַוֵּת־צֶדֶק:

4 אִם־בָּנֶיךָ חָטְאוּ־לוֹ

He has cast them away for their
   transgression.

5 If you would earnestly seek God
   And make your supplication to the
     Almighty,

6 If you *were* pure and upright,
   Surely now He would awake for you,
   And prosper your rightful dwelling place.

7 Though your beginning was small,
   Yet your latter end would increase
     abundantly.

8 "For inquire, please, of the former age,
   And consider the things discovered by their
     fathers;

9 For we *were born* yesterday, and know
     nothing,
   Because our days on earth *are* a shadow.

10 Will they not teach you and tell you,
   And utter words from their heart?

11 "Can the papyrus grow up without a marsh?
   Can the reeds flourish without water?

12 While it *is* yet green *and* not cut down,
   It withers before any *other* plant.

13 So *are* the paths of all who forget God;
   And the hope of the hypocrite shall perish,

14 Whose confidence shall be cut off,
   And whose trust *is* a spider's web.

15 He leans on his house, but it does not stand.
   He holds it fast, but it does not endure.

16 He grows green in the sun,
   And his branches spread out in his garden.

17 His roots wrap around the rock heap,
   And look for a place in the stones.

18 If he is destroyed from his place,
   Then *it* will deny him, *saying,* 'I have not
     seen you.'

19 "Behold, this is the joy of His way,
   And out of the earth others will grow.

20 Behold, God will not cast away the blame-
     less,
   Nor will He uphold the evildoers.

21 He will yet fill your mouth with laughing,
   And your lips with rejoicing.

22 Those who hate you will be clothed with
     shame,
   And the dwelling place of the wicked will
     come to nothing."

9 Then Job answered and said:

2 "Truly I know *it is* so,
   But how can a man be righteous before
     God?

וַיְשַׁלְּחֵם בְּיַד־פִּשְׁעָם׃

5 אִם־אַתָּה תְּשַׁחֵר אֶל־אֵל
וְאֶל־שַׁדַּי תִּתְחַנָּן׃

6 אִם־זַךְ וְיָשָׁר אָתָּה
כִּי־עַתָּה יָעִיר עָלֶיךָ וְשִׁלַּם נְוַת צִדְקֶךָ׃

7 וְהָיָה רֵאשִׁיתְךָ מִצְעָר
וְאַחֲרִיתְךָ יִשְׂגֶּה מְאֹד׃

8 כִּי־שְׁאַל־נָא לְדֹר רִישׁוֹן
וְכוֹנֵן לְחֵקֶר אֲבוֹתָם׃

9 כִּי־תְמוֹל אֲנַחְנוּ וְלֹא נֵדָע
כִּי צֵל יָמֵינוּ עֲלֵי־אָרֶץ׃

10 הֲלֹא־הֵם יוֹרוּךָ יֹאמְרוּ לָךְ
וּמִלִּבָּם יוֹצִאוּ מִלִּים׃

11 הֲיִגְאֶה־גֹּמֶא בְּלֹא בִצָּה
יִשְׂגֶּה־אָחוּ בְלִי־מָיִם׃

12 עֹדֶנּוּ בְאִבּוֹ לֹא יִקָּטֵף
וְלִפְנֵי כָל־חָצִיר יִיבָשׁ׃

13 כֵּן אָרְחוֹת כָּל־שֹׁכְחֵי אֵל
וְתִקְוַת חָנֵף תֹּאבֵד׃

14 אֲשֶׁר־יָקוֹט כִּסְלוֹ
וּבֵית עַכָּבִישׁ מִבְטַחוֹ׃

15 יִשָּׁעֵן עַל־בֵּיתוֹ וְלֹא יַעֲמֹד
יַחֲזִיק בּוֹ וְלֹא יָקוּם׃

16 רָטֹב הוּא לִפְנֵי־שָׁמֶשׁ
וְעַל־גַּנָּתוֹ יֹנַקְתּוֹ תֵצֵא׃

17 עַל־גַּל שָׁרָשָׁיו יְסֻבָּכוּ
בֵּית אֲבָנִים יֶחֱזֶה׃

18 אִם־יְבַלְּעֶנּוּ מִמְּקוֹמוֹ
וְכִחֶשׁ בּוֹ לֹא רְאִיתִיךָ׃

19 הֶן־הוּא מְשׂוֹשׂ דַּרְכּוֹ
וּמֵעָפָר אַחֵר יִצְמָחוּ׃

20 הֶן־אֵל לֹא יִמְאַס־תָּם
וְלֹא־יַחֲזִיק בְּיַד־מְרֵעִים׃

21 עַד־יְמַלֵּה שְׂחוֹק פִּיךָ
וּשְׂפָתֶיךָ תְרוּעָה׃

22 שֹׂנְאֶיךָ יִלְבְּשׁוּ־בֹשֶׁת
וְאֹהֶל רְשָׁעִים אֵינֶנּוּ׃   פ

ט וַיַּעַן אִיּוֹב וַיֹּאמַר׃

2 אָמְנָם יָדַעְתִּי כִי־כֵן
וּמַה־יִּצְדַּק אֱנוֹשׁ עִם־אֵל׃

3   אִם־יַחְפֹּץ לָרִיב עִמּוֹ
לֹא־יַעֲנֶנּוּ אַחַת מִנִּי־אָלֶף׃

4   חֲכַם לֵבָב וְאַמִּיץ כֹּחַ
מִי־הִקְשָׁה אֵלָיו וַיִּשְׁלָם׃

5   הַמַּעְתִּיק הָרִים וְלֹא יָדָעוּ
אֲשֶׁר הֲפָכָם בְּאַפּוֹ׃

6   הַמַּרְגִּיז אֶרֶץ מִמְּקוֹמָהּ
וְעַמּוּדֶיהָ יִתְפַלָּצוּן׃

7   הָאֹמֵר לַחֶרֶס וְלֹא יִזְרָח
וּבְעַד כּוֹכָבִים יַחְתֹּם׃

8   נֹטֶה שָׁמַיִם לְבַדּוֹ
וְדוֹרֵךְ עַל־בָּמֳתֵי יָם׃

9   עֹשֶׂה־עָשׁ כְּסִיל וְכִימָה וְחַדְרֵי תֵמָן׃

10   עֹשֶׂה גְדֹלוֹת עַד־אֵין חֵקֶר
וְנִפְלָאוֹת עַד־אֵין מִסְפָּר׃

11   הֵן יַעֲבֹר עָלַי וְלֹא אֶרְאֶה
וְיַחֲלֹף וְלֹא־אָבִין לוֹ׃

12   הֵן יַחְתֹּף מִי יְשִׁיבֶנּוּ
מִי־יֹאמַר אֵלָיו מַה־תַּעֲשֶׂה׃

13   אֱלוֹהַּ לֹא־יָשִׁיב אַפּוֹ
תַּחְתָּו שָׁחֲחוּ עֹזְרֵי רָהַב׃

14   אַף כִּי־אָנֹכִי אֶעֱנֶנּוּ
אֶבְחֲרָה דְבָרַי עִמּוֹ׃

15   אֲשֶׁר אִם־צָדַקְתִּי לֹא אֶעֱנֶה
לִמְשֹׁפְטִי אֶתְחַנָּן׃

16   אִם־קָרָאתִי וַיַּעֲנֵנִי
לֹא־אַאֲמִין כִּי־יַאֲזִין קוֹלִי׃

17   אֲשֶׁר־בִּשְׂעָרָה יְשׁוּפֵנִי
וְהִרְבָּה פְצָעַי חִנָּם׃

18   לֹא־יִתְּנֵנִי הָשֵׁב רוּחִי
כִּי יַשְׂבִּעַנִי מַמְּרֹרִים׃

19   אִם־לְכֹחַ אַמִּיץ הִנֵּה
וְאִם־לְמִשְׁפָּט מִי יוֹעִידֵנִי׃

20   אִם־אֶצְדָּק פִּי יַרְשִׁיעֵנִי
תָּם־אָנִי וַיַּעְקְשֵׁנִי׃

21   תָּם־אָנִי לֹא־אֵדַע נַפְשִׁי
אֶמְאַס חַיָּי׃

22   אַחַת הִיא
עַל־כֵּן אָמַרְתִּי תָּם וְרָשָׁע הוּא מְכַלֶּה׃

23   אִם־שׁוֹט יָמִית פִּתְאֹם
לְמַסַּת נְקִיִּם יִלְעָג׃

---

3   If one wished to contend with Him,
He could not answer Him one time out of a thousand.

4   *God is* wise in heart and mighty in strength.
Who has hardened *himself* against Him and prospered?

5   He removes the mountains, and they do not know
When He overturns them in His anger;

6   He shakes the earth out of its place,
And its pillars tremble;

7   He commands the sun, and it does not rise;
He seals off the stars;

8   He alone spreads out the heavens,
And treads on the waves of the sea;

9   He made the Bear, Orion, and the Pleiades,
And the chambers of the south;

10   He does great things past finding out,
Yes, wonders without number.

11   If He goes by me, I do not see *Him;*
If He moves past, I do not perceive Him;

12   If He takes away, who can hinder Him?
Who can say to Him, 'What are You doing?'

13   God will not withdraw His anger,
The allies of the proud lie prostrate beneath Him.

14   "How then can I answer Him,
And choose my words *to reason* with Him?

15   For though I were righteous, I could not answer Him;
I would beg mercy of my Judge.

16   If I called and He answered me,
I would not believe that He was listening to my voice.

17   For He crushes me with a tempest,
And multiplies my wounds without cause.

18   He will not allow me to catch my breath,
But fills me with bitterness.

19   If *it is a matter* of strength, indeed *He is* strong;
And if of justice, who will appoint my day *in court?*

20   Though I were righteous, my own mouth would condemn me;
Though I *were* blameless, it would prove me perverse.

21   "I am blameless, yet I do not know myself;
I despise my life.

22   It *is* all one *thing;*
Therefore I say, 'He destroys the blameless and the wicked.'

23   If the scourge slays suddenly,
He laughs at the plight of the innocent.

24 The earth is given into the hand of the wicked.
He covers the faces of its judges.
If it is not *He,* who else could it be?

25 "Now my days are swifter than a runner;
They flee away, they see no good.

26 They pass by like swift ships,
Like an eagle swooping on its prey.

27 If I say, 'I will forget my complaint,
I will put off my sad face and wear a smile,'

28 I am afraid of all my sufferings;
I know that You will not hold me innocent.

29 *If* I am condemned,
Why then do I labor in vain?

30 If I wash myself with snow water,
And cleanse my hands with soap,

31 Yet You will plunge me into the pit,
And my own clothes will abhor me.

32 "For *He is* not a man, as I *am,*
That I may answer Him,
And that we should go to court together.

33 Nor is there any mediator between us,
Who may lay his hand on us both.

34 Let Him take His rod away from me,
And do not let dread of Him terrify me.

35 *Then* I would speak and not fear Him,
But it is not so with me.

10 "My soul loathes my life;
I will give free course to my complaint,
I will speak in the bitterness of my soul.

2 I will say to God, 'Do not condemn me;
Show me why You contend with me.

3 *Does it* seem good to You that You should oppress,
That You should despise the work of Your hands,
And smile on the counsel of the wicked?

4 Do You have eyes of flesh?
Or do You see as man sees?

5 *Are* Your days like the days of a mortal man?
Are Your years like the days of a mighty man,

6 That You should seek for my iniquity
And search out my sin,

7 Although You know that I am not wicked,
And *there is* no one who can deliver from Your hand?

8 'Your hands have made me and fashioned me,
An intricate unity;

כד אֶרֶץ ׀ נִתְּנָה בְיַד־רָשָׁע
פְּנֵי־שֹׁפְטֶיהָ יְכַסֶּה
אִם־לֹא אֵפוֹא מִי־הוּא׃

כה וְיָמַי קַלּוּ מִנִּי־רָץ
בָּרְחוּ לֹא־רָאוּ טוֹבָה׃

כו חָלְפוּ עִם־אֳנִיּוֹת אֵבֶה
כְּנֶשֶׁר יָטוּשׂ עֲלֵי־אֹכֶל׃

כז אִם־אָמְרִי אֶשְׁכְּחָה שִׂיחִי
אֶעֶזְבָה פָנַי וְאַבְלִיגָה׃

כח יָגֹרְתִּי כָל־עַצְּבֹתָי
יָדַעְתִּי כִּי־לֹא תְנַקֵּנִי׃

כט אָנֹכִי אֶרְשָׁע
לָמָּה־זֶּה הֶבֶל אִיגָע׃

ל אִם־הִתְרָחַצְתִּי בְמוֹ־שָׁלֶג
וַהֲזִכּוֹתִי בְּבֹר כַּפָּי׃

לא אָז בַּשַּׁחַת תִּטְבְּלֵנִי
וְתִעֲבוּנִי שַׂלְמוֹתָי׃

לב כִּי־לֹא־אִישׁ כָּמֹנִי אֶעֱנֶנּוּ
נָבוֹא יַחְדָּו בַּמִּשְׁפָּט׃

לג לֹא יֵשׁ־בֵּינֵינוּ מוֹכִיחַ
יָשֵׁת יָדוֹ עַל־שְׁנֵינוּ׃

לד יָסֵר מֵעָלַי שִׁבְטוֹ
וְאֵמָתוֹ אַל־תְּבַעֲתַנִּי׃

לה אֲדַבְּרָה וְלֹא אִירָאֶנּוּ
כִּי לֹא־כֵן אָנֹכִי עִמָּדִי׃

י נָקְטָה נַפְשִׁי בְּחַיָּי
אֶעֶזְבָה עָלַי שִׂיחִי אֲדַבְּרָה בְּמַר נַפְשִׁי׃

ב אֹמַר אֶל־אֱלוֹהַּ אַל־תַּרְשִׁיעֵנִי
הוֹדִיעֵנִי עַל מַה־תְּרִיבֵנִי׃

ג הֲטוֹב לְךָ ׀ כִּי־תַעֲשֹׁק כִּי־תִמְאַס יְגִיעַ כַּפֶּיךָ
וְעַל־עֲצַת רְשָׁעִים הוֹפָעְתָּ׃

ד הַעֵינֵי בָשָׂר לָךְ
אִם־כִּרְאוֹת אֱנוֹשׁ תִּרְאֶה׃

ה הֲכִימֵי אֱנוֹשׁ יָמֶיךָ
אִם־שְׁנוֹתֶיךָ כִּימֵי גָבֶר׃

ו כִּי־תְבַקֵּשׁ לַעֲוֺנִי
וּלְחַטָּאתִי תִדְרוֹשׁ׃

ז עַל־דַּעְתְּךָ כִּי־לֹא אֶרְשָׁע
וְאֵין מִיָּדְךָ מַצִּיל׃

ח יָדֶיךָ עִצְּבוּנִי וַיַּעֲשׂוּנִי

ט 30 בְּמֹר

Yet You would destroy me.

9 Remember, I pray, that You have made me
like clay.
And will You turn me into dust again?

10 Did You not pour me out like milk,
And curdle me like cheese,

11 Clothe me with skin and flesh,
And knit me together with bones and
sinews?

12 You have granted me life and favor,
And Your care has preserved my spirit.

13 'And these *things* You have hidden in Your
heart;
I know that this *was* with You:

14 If I sin, then You mark me,
And will not acquit me of my iniquity.

15 If I am wicked, woe to me;
Even *if* I am righteous, I cannot lift up my
head.
I am full of disgrace;
See my misery!

16 If *my head* is exalted,
You hunt me like a fierce lion,
And again You show Yourself awesome
against me.

17 You renew Your witnesses against me,
And increase Your indignation toward me;
Changes and war are *ever* with me.

18 'Why then have You brought me out of the
womb?
Oh, that I had perished and no eye had seen
me!

19 I would have been as though I had not been.
I would have been carried from the womb to
the grave.

20 Are not my days few?
Cease! Leave me alone, that I may take a
little comfort,

21 Before I go *to the place from which* I shall not
return,
To the land of darkness and the shadow of
death,

22 A land as dark as darkness *itself,*
As the shadow of death, without any order,
Where even the light *is* like darkness.'"

11 Then Zophar the Naamathite answered and
said:

2 "Should not the multitude of words be
answered?
And should a man full of talk be vindicated?

יַחַד סָבִיב וַתְּבַלְּעֵנִי׃

9 זְכָר־נָא כִּי־כַחֹמֶר עֲשִׂיתָנִי
וְאֶל־עָפָר תְּשִׁיבֵנִי׃

10 הֲלֹא כֶחָלָב תַּתִּיכֵנִי
וְכַגְּבִנָּה תַּקְפִּיאֵנִי׃

11 עוֹר וּבָשָׂר תַּלְבִּישֵׁנִי
וּבַעֲצָמוֹת וְגִידִים תְּסֹכְכֵנִי׃

12 חַיִּים וָחֶסֶד עָשִׂיתָ עִמָּדִי
וּפְקֻדָּתְךָ שָׁמְרָה רוּחִי׃

13 וְאֵלֶּה צָפַנְתָּ בִלְבָבֶךָ
יָדַעְתִּי כִּי־זֹאת עִמָּךְ׃

14 אִם־חָטָאתִי וּשְׁמַרְתָּנִי
וּמֵעֲוֺנִי לֹא תְנַקֵּנִי׃

15 אִם־רָשַׁעְתִּי אַלְלַי לִי
וְצָדַקְתִּי לֹא־אֶשָּׂא רֹאשִׁי
שְׂבַע קָלוֹן
וּרְאֵה עָנְיִי׃

16 וְיִגְאֶה כַּשַּׁחַל תְּצוּדֵנִי
וְתָשֹׁב תִּתְפַּלָּא־בִי׃

17 תְּחַדֵּשׁ עֵדֶיךָ ׀ נֶגְדִּי וְתֶרֶב כַּעַשְׂךָ עִמָּדִי
חֲלִיפוֹת וְצָבָא עִמִּי׃

18 וְלָמָּה מֵרֶחֶם הֹצֵאתָנִי
אֶגְוַע וְעַיִן לֹא־תִרְאֵנִי׃

19 כַּאֲשֶׁר לֹא־הָיִיתִי אֶהְיֶה
מִבֶּטֶן לַקֶּבֶר אוּבָל׃

20 הֲלֹא־מְעַט יָמַי יַחֲדָל ֯ק
יָשִׁית ֯ק מִמֶּנִּי וְאַבְלִיגָה מְעָט׃

21 בְּטֶרֶם אֵלֵךְ וְלֹא אָשׁוּב
אֶל־אֶרֶץ חֹשֶׁךְ וְצַלְמָוֶת׃

22 אֶרֶץ עֵיפָתָה ׀ כְּמוֹ אֹפֶל צַלְמָוֶת וְלֹא סְדָרִים
וַתֹּפַע כְּמוֹ־אֹפֶל׃　פ

יא וַיַּעַן צֹפַר הַנַּעֲמָתִי וַיֹּאמַר׃

2 הֲרֹב דְּבָרִים לֹא יֵעָנֶה
וְאִם־אִישׁ שְׂפָתַיִם יִצְדָּק׃

20 ֯י וַחֲדָל ֯ק וְשִׁית

3 Should your empty talk make men hold their
   peace?
   And when you mock, should no one rebuke
   you?
4 For you have said,
   'My doctrine *is* pure,
   And I am clean in your eyes.'
5 But oh, that God would speak,
   And open His lips against you,
6 That He would show you the secrets of
   wisdom!
   For *they would* double *your* prudence.
   Know therefore that God exacts from you
   Less than your iniquity *deserves*.

7 "Can you search out the deep things of God?
   Can you find out the limits of the Almighty?
8 *They are* higher than heaven— what can you
   do?
   Deeper than Sheol— what can you know?
9 Their measure *is* longer than the earth
   And broader than the sea.

10 "If He passes by, imprisons, and gathers *to
   judgment,*
   Then who can hinder Him?
11 For He knows deceitful men;
   He sees wickedness also.
   Will He not then consider *it?*
12 For an empty-headed man will be wise,
   When a wild donkey's colt is born a man.

13 "If you would prepare your heart,
   And stretch out your hands toward Him;
14 If iniquity *were* in your hand, *and you* put it
   far away,
   And would not let wickedness dwell in your
   tents;
15 Then surely you could lift up your face
   without spot;
   Yes, you could be steadfast, and not fear;
16 Because you would forget *your* misery,
   And remember *it* as waters *that have* passed
   away,
17 And *your* life would be brighter than noonday.
   Though you were dark, you would be like the
   morning.
18 And you would be secure, because there is
   hope;
   Yes, you would dig *around you, and* take
   your rest in safety.
19 You would also lie down, and no one would
   make *you* afraid;
   Yes, many would court your favor.
20 But the eyes of the wicked will fail,

בְּדֶּיךָ מְתִים יַחֲרִישׁוּ 3
וַתִּלְעַג וְאֵין מַכְלִם:
וַתֹּאמֶר זַךְ לִקְחִי 4
וּבַר הָיִיתִי בְעֵינֶיךָ:
וְאוּלָם מִי־יִתֵּן אֱלוֹהַּ דַּבֵּר 5
וְיִפְתַּח שְׂפָתָיו עִמָּךְ:
וְיַגֶּד־לְךָ ׀ תַּעֲלֻמוֹת חָכְמָה 6
כִּי־כִפְלַיִם לְתוּשִׁיָּה
וְדַע
כִּי־יַשֶּׁה לְךָ אֱלוֹהַּ מֵעֲוֺנֶךָ:
הַחֵקֶר אֱלוֹהַּ תִּמְצָא 7
אִם עַד־תַּכְלִית שַׁדַּי תִּמְצָא:
גָּבְהֵי שָׁמַיִם מַה־תִּפְעָל 8
עֲמֻקָּה מִשְּׁאוֹל מַה־תֵּדָע:
אֲרֻכָּה מֵאֶרֶץ מִדָּהּ 9
וּרְחָבָה מִנִּי־יָם:
אִם־יַחֲלֹף וְיַסְגִּיר 10
וְיַקְהִיל וּמִי יְשִׁיבֶנּוּ:
כִּי־הוּא יָדַע מְתֵי־שָׁוְא 11
וַיַּרְא־אָוֶן וְלֹא יִתְבּוֹנָן:
וְאִישׁ נָבוּב יִלָּבֵב 12
וְעַיִר פֶּרֶא אָדָם יִוָּלֵד:
אִם־אַתָּה הֲכִינוֹתָ לִבֶּךָ 13
וּפָרַשְׂתָּ אֵלָיו כַּפֶּךָ:
אִם־אָוֶן בְּיָדְךָ הַרְחִיקֵהוּ 14
וְאַל־תַּשְׁכֵּן בְּאֹהָלֶיךָ עַוְלָה:
כִּי־אָז ׀ תִּשָּׂא פָנֶיךָ מִמּוּם 15
וְהָיִיתָ מֻצָק וְלֹא תִירָא:
כִּי־אַתָּה עָמָל תִּשְׁכָּח 16
כְּמַיִם עָבְרוּ תִזְכֹּר:
וּמִצָּהֳרַיִם יָקוּם חָלֶד 17
תָּעֻפָה כַּבֹּקֶר תִּהְיֶה:
וּבָטַחְתָּ כִּי־יֵשׁ תִּקְוָה 18
וְחָפַרְתָּ לָבֶטַח תִּשְׁכָּב:
וְרָבַצְתָּ וְאֵין מַחֲרִיד 19
וְחִלּוּ פָנֶיךָ רַבִּים:
וְעֵינֵי רְשָׁעִים תִּכְלֶינָה 20
וּמָנוֹס אָבַד מִנְהֶם וְתִקְוָתָם מַפַּח־נָפֶשׁ:

And they shall not escape,
And their hope—loss of life!"

12

Then Job answered and said:

2 "No doubt you *are* the people,
And wisdom will die with you!

3 But I have understanding as well as you;
I *am* not inferior to you.
Indeed, who does not *know* such things as
these?

4 "I am one mocked by his friends,
Who called on God, and He answered him,
The just and blameless *who is* ridiculed.

5 A lamp is despised in the thought of one who
is at ease;
It is made ready for those whose feet slip.

6 The tents of robbers prosper,
And those who provoke God are secure—
In what God provides by His hand.

7 "But now ask the beasts, and they will teach
you;
And the birds of the air, and they will tell
you;

8 Or speak to the earth, and it will teach you;
And the fish of the sea will explain to you.

9 Who among all these does not know
That the hand of the LORD has done this,

10 In whose hand *is* the life of every living
thing,
And the breath of all mankind?

11 Does not the ear test words
And the mouth taste its food?

12 Wisdom *is* with aged men,
And with length of days, understanding.

13 "With Him *are* wisdom and strength,
He has counsel and understanding.

14 If He breaks *a thing* down, it cannot be
rebuilt;
If He imprisons a man, there can be no
release.

15 If He withholds the waters, they dry up;
If He sends them out, they overwhelm the
earth.

16 With Him *are* strength and prudence.
The deceived and the deceiver *are* His.

17 He leads counselors away plundered,
And makes fools of the judges.

18 He loosens the bonds of kings,
And binds their waist with a belt.

19 He leads princes away plundered,
And overthrows the mighty.

20 He deprives the trusted ones of speech,

יב וַיַּעַן אִיּוֹב וַיֹּאמַר:

2 אָמְנָם כִּי אַתֶּם־עָם
וְעִמָּכֶם תָּמוּת חָכְמָה:

3 גַּם־לִי לֵבָב ׀ כְּמוֹכֶם לֹא־נֹפֵל אָנֹכִי מִכֶּם
וְאֶת־מִי־אֵין כְּמוֹ־אֵלֶּה:

4 שְׂחֹק לְרֵעֵהוּ ׀ אֶהְיֶה קֹרֵא לֶאֱלוֹהַּ וַיַּעֲנֵהוּ
שְׂחוֹק צַדִּיק תָּמִים:

5 לַפִּיד בּוּז לְעַשְׁתּוּת שַׁאֲנָן
נָכוֹן לְמוֹעֲדֵי רָגֶל:

6 יִשְׁלָיוּ אֹהָלִים ׀ לְשֹׁדְדִים וּבַטֻּחוֹת לְמַרְגִּיזֵי אֵל
לַאֲשֶׁר הֵבִיא אֱלוֹהַּ בְּיָדוֹ:

7 וְאוּלָם שְׁאַל־נָא בְהֵמוֹת וְתֹרֶךָּ
וְעוֹף הַשָּׁמַיִם וְיַגֶּד־לָךְ:

8 אוֹ שִׂיחַ לָאָרֶץ וְתֹרֶךָּ
וִיסַפְּרוּ לְךָ דְּגֵי הַיָּם:

9 מִי לֹא־יָדַע בְּכָל־אֵלֶּה
כִּי יַד־יְהֹוָה עָשְׂתָה זֹּאת:

10 אֲשֶׁר בְּיָדוֹ נֶפֶשׁ כָּל־חָי
וְרוּחַ כָּל־בְּשַׂר־אִישׁ:

11 הֲלֹא־אֹזֶן מִלִּין תִּבְחָן
וְחֵךְ אֹכֶל יִטְעַם־לוֹ:

12 בִּישִׁישִׁים חָכְמָה
וְאֹרֶךְ יָמִים תְּבוּנָה:

13 עִמּוֹ חָכְמָה וּגְבוּרָה
לוֹ עֵצָה וּתְבוּנָה:

14 הֵן יַהֲרוֹס וְלֹא יִבָּנֶה
יִסְגֹּר עַל־אִישׁ וְלֹא יִפָּתֵחַ:

15 הֵן יַעְצֹר בַּמַּיִם וְיָבָשׁוּ
וִישַׁלְּחֵם וְיַהַפְכוּ אָרֶץ:

16 עִמּוֹ עֹז וְתוּשִׁיָּה
לוֹ שֹׁגֵג וּמַשְׁגֶּה:

17 מוֹלִיךְ יוֹעֲצִים שׁוֹלָל
וְשֹׁפְטִים יְהוֹלֵל:

18 מוּסַר מְלָכִים פִּתֵּחַ
וַיֶּאְסֹר אֵזוֹר בְּמָתְנֵיהֶם:

19 מוֹלִיךְ כֹּהֲנִים שׁוֹלָל
וְאֵתָנִים יְסַלֵּף:

20 מֵסִיר שָׂפָה לְנֶאֱמָנִים
וְטַעַם זְקֵנִים יִקָּח:

And takes away the discernment of the
    elders.

21 He pours contempt on princes,
    And disarms the mighty.

22 He uncovers deep things out of darkness,
    And brings the shadow of death to light.

23 He makes nations great, and destroys them;
    He enlarges nations, and guides them.

24 He takes away the understanding of the
    chiefs of the people of the earth,
    And makes them wander in a pathless
    wilderness.

25 They grope in the dark without light,
    And He makes them stagger like a drunken
    man.

13 "Behold, my eye has seen all *this,*
    My ear has heard and understood it.

2 What you know, I also know;
    I *am* not inferior to you.

3 But I would speak to the Almighty,
    And I desire to reason with God.

4 But you forgers of lies,
    You *are* all worthless physicians.

5 Oh, that you would be silent,
    And it would be your wisdom!

6 Now hear my reasoning,
    And heed the pleadings of my lips.

7 Will you speak wickedly for God,
    And talk deceitfully for Him?

8 Will you show partiality for Him?
    Will you contend for God?

9 Will it be well when He searches you out?
    Or can you mock Him as one mocks a man?

10 He will surely rebuke you
    If you secretly show partiality.

11 Will not His excellence make you afraid,
    And the dread of Him fall upon you?

12 Your platitudes *are* proverbs of ashes,
    Your defenses are defenses of clay.

13 "Hold your peace with me, and let me speak,
    Then let come on me what *may!*

14 Why do I take my flesh in my teeth,
    And put my life in my hands?

15 Though He slay me, yet will I trust Him.
    Even so, I will defend my own ways before
    Him.

16 He also *shall* be my salvation,
    For a hypocrite could not come before Him.

17 Listen carefully to my speech,
    And to my declaration with your ears.

18 See now, I have prepared *my* case,
    I know that I shall be vindicated.

21 שׁוֹפֵךְ בּוּז עַל־נְדִיבִים
    וּמְזִיחַ אֲפִיקִים רִפָּה:

22 מְגַלֶּה עֲמֻקוֹת מִנִּי־חֹשֶׁךְ
    וַיֹּצֵא לָאוֹר צַלְמָוֶת:

23 מַשְׂגִּיא לַגּוֹיִם וַיְאַבְּדֵם
    שֹׁטֵחַ לַגּוֹיִם וַיַּנְחֵם:

24 מֵסִיר לֵב רָאשֵׁי עַם־הָאָרֶץ
    וַיַּתְעֵם בְּתֹהוּ לֹא־דָרֶךְ:

25 יְמַשְׁשׁוּ־חֹשֶׁךְ וְלֹא־אוֹר וַיַּתְעֵם כַּשִּׁכּוֹר:

יג הֶן־כֹּל רָאֲתָה עֵינִי
    שָׁמְעָה אָזְנִי וַתָּבֶן לָהּ:

2 כְּדַעְתְּכֶם יָדַעְתִּי גַם־אָנִי
    לֹא־נֹפֵל אָנֹכִי מִכֶּם:

3 אוּלָם אֲנִי אֶל־שַׁדַּי אֲדַבֵּר
    וְהוֹכֵחַ אֶל־אֵל אֶחְפָּץ:

4 וְאוּלָם אַתֶּם טֹפְלֵי־שָׁקֶר
    רֹפְאֵי אֱלִל כֻּלְּכֶם:

5 מִי־יִתֵּן הַחֲרֵשׁ תַּחֲרִישׁוּן וּתְהִי לָכֶם לְחָכְמָה:

6 שִׁמְעוּ־נָא תוֹכַחְתִּי וְרִבוֹת שְׂפָתַי הַקְשִׁיבוּ:

7 הֲלְאֵל תְּדַבְּרוּ עַוְלָה וְלוֹ תְּדַבְּרוּ רְמִיָּה:

8 הֲפָנָיו תִּשָּׂאוּן אִם־לָאֵל תְּרִיבוּן:

9 הֲטוֹב כִּי־יַחְקֹר אֶתְכֶם
    אִם־כְּהָתֵל בֶּאֱנוֹשׁ תְּהָתֵלּוּ בוֹ:

10 הוֹכֵחַ יוֹכִיחַ אֶתְכֶם
    אִם־בַּסֵּתֶר פָּנִים תִּשָּׂאוּן:

11 הֲלֹא שְׂאֵתוֹ תְּבַעֵת אֶתְכֶם
    וּפַחְדּוֹ יִפֹּל עֲלֵיכֶם:

12 זִכְרֹנֵיכֶם מִשְׁלֵי־אֵפֶר
    לְגַבֵּי־חֹמֶר גַּבֵּיכֶם:

13 הַחֲרִישׁוּ מִמֶּנִּי וַאֲדַבְּרָה־אָנִי
    וְיַעֲבֹר עָלַי מָה:

14 עַל־מָה אֶשָּׂא בְשָׂרִי בְשִׁנָּי
    וְנַפְשִׁי אָשִׂים בְּכַפִּי:

15 הֵן יִקְטְלֵנִי לֹא P אֲיַחֵל
    אַךְ־דְּרָכַי אֶל־פָּנָיו אוֹכִיחַ:

16 גַּם־הוּא־לִי לִישׁוּעָה
    כִּי־לֹא לְפָנָיו חָנֵף יָבוֹא:

17 שִׁמְעוּ שָׁמוֹעַ מִלָּתִי
    וְאַחֲוָתִי בְּאָזְנֵיכֶם:

18 הִנֵּה־נָא עָרַכְתִּי מִשְׁפָּט
    יָדַעְתִּי כִּי־אֲנִי אֶצְדָּק:

19 Who *is* he *who* will contend with me?
If now I hold my tongue, I perish.

מִי־הוּא יָרִיב עִמָּדִי 19
כִּי־עַתָּה אַחֲרִישׁ וְאֶגְוָע׃

20 "Only two *things* do not do to me,
Then I will not hide myself from You:

אַךְ־שְׁתַּיִם אַל־תַּעַשׂ עִמָּדִי 20
אָז מִפָּנֶיךָ לֹא אֶסָּתֵר׃

21 Withdraw Your hand far from me,
And let not the dread of You make me afraid.

כַּפְּךָ מֵעָלַי הַרְחַק 21
וְאֵמָתְךָ אַל־תְּבַעֲתַנִּי׃

22 Then call, and I will answer;
Or let me speak, then You respond to me.

וּקְרָא וְאָנֹכִי אֶעֱנֶה 22
אוֹ־אֲדַבֵּר וַהֲשִׁיבֵנִי׃

23 How many *are* my iniquities and sins?
Make me know my transgression and my sin.

כַּמָּה לִי עֲוֹנוֹת וְחַטָּאוֹת 23
פִּשְׁעִי וְחַטָּאתִי הֹדִיעֵנִי׃

24 Why do You hide Your face,
And regard me as Your enemy?

לָמָּה־פָנֶיךָ תַסְתִּיר 24
וְתַחְשְׁבֵנִי לְאוֹיֵב לָךְ׃

25 Will You frighten a leaf driven to and fro?
And will You pursue dry stubble?

הֶעָלֶה נִדָּף תַּעֲרוֹץ 25
וְאֶת־קַשׁ יָבֵשׁ תִּרְדֹּף׃

26 For You write bitter things against me,
And make me inherit the iniquities of my youth.

כִּי־תִכְתֹּב עָלַי מְרֹרוֹת 26
וְתוֹרִישֵׁנִי עֲוֹנוֹת נְעוּרָי׃

27 You put my feet in the stocks,
And watch closely all my paths.
You set a limit for the soles of my feet.

וְתָשֵׂם בַּסַּד ׀ רַגְלַי וְתִשְׁמוֹר כָּל־אָרְחוֹתָי 27
עַל־שָׁרְשֵׁי רַגְלַי תִּתְחַקֶּה׃

28 "*Man* decays like a rotten thing,
Like a garment that is moth-eaten.

וְהוּא כְּרָקָב יִבְלֶה 28
כְּבֶגֶד אֲכָלוֹ עָשׁ׃

14 "Man *who is* born of woman
Is of few days and full of trouble.

אָדָם יְלוּד אִשָּׁה **יד**
קְצַר יָמִים וּשְׂבַע־רֹגֶז׃

2 He comes forth like a flower and fades away;
He flees like a shadow and does not continue.

כְּצִיץ יָצָא וַיִּמָּל 2
וַיִּבְרַח כַּצֵּל וְלֹא יַעֲמוֹד׃

3 And do You open Your eyes on such a one,
And bring me to judgment with Yourself?

אַף־עַל־זֶה פָּקַחְתָּ עֵינֶךָ 3
וְאֹתִי תָבִיא בְמִשְׁפָּט עִמָּךְ׃

4 Who can bring a clean *thing* out of an unclean?
No one!

מִי־יִתֵּן טָהוֹר מִטָּמֵא לֹא אֶחָד׃ 4

5 Since his days *are* determined,
The number of his months *is* with You;
You have appointed his limits, so that he cannot pass.

אִם חֲרוּצִים ׀ יָמָיו מִסְפַּר־חֳדָשָׁיו אִתָּךְ 5
חֻקָּו עָשִׂיתָ וְלֹא יַעֲבוֹר׃

6 Look away from him that he may rest,
Till like a hired man he finishes his day.

שְׁעֵה מֵעָלָיו וְיֶחְדָּל 6
עַד־יִרְצֶה כְּשָׂכִיר יוֹמוֹ׃

7 "For there is hope for a tree,
If it is cut down, that it will sprout again,
And that its tender shoots will not cease.

כִּי יֵשׁ לָעֵץ תִּקְוָה 7
אִם־יִכָּרֵת וְעוֹד יַחֲלִיף
וְיֹנַקְתּוֹ לֹא תֶחְדָּל׃

8 Though its root may grow old in the earth,
And its stump may die in the ground,

אִם־יַזְקִין בָּאָרֶץ שָׁרְשׁוֹ 8
וּבֶעָפָר יָמוּת גִּזְעוֹ׃

9 *Yet* at the scent of water it will bud
And bring forth branches like a plant.

מֵרֵיחַ מַיִם יַפְרִחַ 9
וְעָשָׂה קָצִיר כְּמוֹ־נָטַע׃

10 But man dies and is laid away;
Indeed he breathes his last
And where *is* he?

וְגֶבֶר יָמוּת וַיֶּחֱלָשׁ 10
וַיִּגְוַע אָדָם וְאַיּוֹ׃

11 *As* water disappears from the sea,
And a river becomes parched and dries up,

אָזְלוּ־מַיִם מִנִּי־יָם 11
וְנָהָר יֶחֱרַב וְיָבֵשׁ׃

יד 5 חֻקָּו

12 So man lies down and does not rise.
Till the heavens *are* no more,
They will not awake
Nor be roused from their sleep.

13 "Oh, that You would hide me in the grave,
That You would conceal me until Your
  wrath is past,
That You would appoint me a set time, and
  remember me!

14 If a man dies, shall he live *again*?
All the days of my hard service I will wait,
Till my change comes.

15 You shall call, and I will answer You;
You shall desire the work of Your hands.

16 For now You number my steps,
But do not watch over my sin.

17 My transgression *is* sealed up in a bag,
And You cover my iniquity.

18 "But *as* a mountain falls *and* crumbles away,
And *as* a rock is moved from its place;

19 *As* water wears away stones,
And as torrents wash away the soil of the
  earth;
So You destroy the hope of man.

20 You prevail forever against him, and he
  passes on;
You change his countenance and send him
  away.

21 His sons come to honor, and he does not
  know *it;*
They are brought low, and he does not
  perceive *it.*

22 But his flesh will be in pain over it,
And his soul will mourn over it."

15 Then Eliphaz the Temanite answered and said:

2 "Should a wise man answer with empty
  knowledge,
And fill himself with the east wind?

3 Should he reason with unprofitable talk,
Or by speeches with which he can do no
  good?

4 Yes, you cast off fear,
And restrain prayer before God.

5 For your iniquity teaches your mouth,
And you choose the tongue of the crafty.

6 Your own mouth condemns you, and not I;
Yes, your own lips testify against you.

7 "*Are* you the first man *who* was born?
Or were you made before the hills?

8 Have you heard the counsel of God?
Do you limit wisdom to yourself?

---

12 וְאִישׁ שָׁכַב וְלֹא־יָקוּם
עַד־בִּלְתִּי שָׁמַיִם לֹא יָקִיצוּ
וְלֹא־יֵעֹרוּ מִשְּׁנָתָם:

13 מִי יִתֵּן ׀ בִּשְׁאוֹל תַּצְפִּנֵנִי
תַּסְתִּירֵנִי עַד־שׁוּב אַפֶּךָ
תָּשִׁית לִי חֹק וְתִזְכְּרֵנִי:

14 אִם־יָמוּת גֶּבֶר הֲיִחְיֶה
כָּל־יְמֵי צְבָאִי אֲיַחֵל
עַד־בּוֹא חֲלִיפָתִי:

15 תִּקְרָא וְאָנֹכִי אֶעֱנֶךָּ
לְמַעֲשֵׂה יָדֶיךָ תִכְסֹף:

16 כִּי־עַתָּה צְעָדַי תִּסְפּוֹר
לֹא־תִשְׁמֹר עַל־חַטָּאתִי:

17 חָתֻם בִּצְרוֹר פִּשְׁעִי
וַתִּטְפֹּל עַל־עֲוֺנִי:

18 וְאוּלָם הַר־נוֹפֵל יִבּוֹל
וְצוּר יֶעְתַּק מִמְּקֹמוֹ:

19 אֲבָנִים ׀ שָׁחֲקוּ מַיִם
תִּשְׁטֹף־סְפִיחֶיהָ עֲפַר־אָרֶץ
וְתִקְוַת אֱנוֹשׁ הֶאֱבַדְתָּ:

20 תִּתְקְפֵהוּ לָנֶצַח וַיַּהֲלֹךְ
מְשַׁנֶּה פָנָיו וַתְּשַׁלְּחֵהוּ:

21 יִכְבְּדוּ בָנָיו וְלֹא יֵדָע
וְיִצְעֲרוּ וְלֹא־יָבִין לָמוֹ:

22 אַךְ־בְּשָׂרוֹ עָלָיו יִכְאָב
וְנַפְשׁוֹ עָלָיו תֶּאֱבָל:

פ

טו וַיַּעַן אֱלִיפַז הַתֵּימָנִי וַיֹּאמַר:

2 הֶחָכָם יַעֲנֶה דַעַת־רוּחַ
וִימַלֵּא קָדִים בִּטְנוֹ:

3 הוֹכֵחַ בְּדָבָר לֹא יִסְכּוֹן
וּמִלִּים לֹא־יוֹעִיל בָּם:

4 אַף־אַתָּה תָּפֵר יִרְאָה
וְתִגְרַע שִׂיחָה לִפְנֵי־אֵל:

5 כִּי יְאַלֵּף עֲוֺנְךָ פִיךָ
וְתִבְחַר לְשׁוֹן עֲרוּמִים:

6 יַרְשִׁיעֲךָ פִיךָ וְלֹא־אָנִי
וּשְׂפָתֶיךָ יַעֲנוּ־בָךְ:

7 הֲרִאישׁוֹן אָדָם תִּוָּלֵד
וְלִפְנֵי גְבָעוֹת חוֹלָלְתָּ:

8 הַבְסוֹד אֱלוֹהַּ תִּשְׁמָע
וְתִגְרַע אֵלֶיךָ חָכְמָה:

9 What do you know that we do not know?
  What do you understand that *is* not in us?

10 Both the gray-haired and the aged *are*
   among us,
   Much older than your father.

11 *Are* the consolations of God too small for
   you,
   And the word *spoken* gently with you?

12 Why does your heart carry you away,
   And what do your eyes wink at,

13 That you turn your spirit against God,
   And let *such* words go out of your mouth?

14 "What *is* man, that he could be pure?
   And *he who is* born of a woman, that he
   could be righteous?

15 If *God* puts no trust in His saints,
   And the heavens are not pure in His sight,

16 How much less man, *who is* abominable and
   filthy,
   Who drinks iniquity like water!

17 "I will tell you, hear me;
   What I have seen I will declare,

18 What wise men have told,
   Not hiding *anything received* from their
   fathers,

19 To whom alone the land was given,
   And no alien passed among them:

20 The wicked man writhes with pain all *his*
   days,
   And the number of years is hidden from the
   oppressor.

21 Dreadful sounds *are* in his ears;
   In prosperity the destroyer comes upon him.

22 He does not believe that he will return from
   darkness,
   For a sword is waiting for him.

23 He wanders about for bread, *saying*, 'Where
   is it?'
   He knows that a day of darkness is ready at
   his hand.

24 Trouble and anguish make him afraid;
   They overpower him, like a king ready for
   battle.

25 For he stretches out his hand against God,
   And acts defiantly against the Almighty,

26 Running stubbornly against Him
   With his strong, embossed shield.

27 "Though he has covered his face with his
   fatness,
   And made *his* waist heavy with fat,

28 He dwells in desolate cities,
   In houses which no one inhabits,
   Which are destined to become ruins.

9 מַה־יָּדַעְתָּ וְלֹא נֵדָע
  תָּבִין וְלֹא־עִמָּנוּ הוּא׃

10 גַּם־שָׂב גַּם־יָשִׁישׁ בָּנוּ
   כַּבִּיר מֵאָבִיךָ יָמִים׃

11 הַמְעַט מִמְּךָ תַּנְחֻמוֹת אֵל
   וְדָבָר לָאַט עִמָּךְ׃

12 מַה־יִּקָּחֲךָ לִבֶּךָ
   וּמַה־יִּרְזְמוּן עֵינֶיךָ׃

13 כִּי־תָשִׁיב אֶל־אֵל רוּחֶךָ
   וְהֹצֵאתָ מִפִּיךָ מִלִּין׃

14 מָה־אֱנוֹשׁ כִּי־יִזְכֶּה
   וְכִי־יִצְדַּק יְלוּד אִשָּׁה׃

15 הֵן בִּקְדֹשָׁו לֹא יַאֲמִין
   וְשָׁמַיִם לֹא־זַכּוּ בְעֵינָיו׃

16 אַף כִּי־נִתְעָב וְנֶאֱלָח
   אִישׁ־שֹׁתֶה כַמַּיִם עַוְלָה׃

17 אֲחַוְךָ שְׁמַע־לִי
   וְזֶה־חָזִיתִי וַאֲסַפֵּרָה׃

18 אֲשֶׁר־חֲכָמִים יַגִּידוּ
   וְלֹא כִחֲדוּ מֵאֲבוֹתָם׃

19 לָהֶם לְבַדָּם נִתְּנָה הָאָרֶץ
   וְלֹא־עָבַר זָר בְּתוֹכָם׃

20 כָּל־יְמֵי רָשָׁע הוּא מִתְחוֹלֵל
   וּמִסְפַּר שָׁנִים נִצְפְּנוּ לֶעָרִיץ׃

21 קוֹל־פְּחָדִים בְּאָזְנָיו
   בַּשָּׁלוֹם שׁוֹדֵד יְבוֹאֶנּוּ׃

22 לֹא־יַאֲמִין שׁוּב מִנִּי־חֹשֶׁךְ
   וְצָפוּי הוּא אֱלֵי־חָרֶב׃

23 נֹדֵד הוּא לַלֶּחֶם אַיֵּה
   יָדַע כִּי־נָכוֹן בְּיָדוֹ יוֹם־חֹשֶׁךְ׃

24 יְבַעֲתֻהוּ צַר וּמְצוּקָה
   תִּתְקְפֵהוּ כְּמֶלֶךְ עָתִיד לַכִּידוֹר׃

25 כִּי־נָטָה אֶל־אֵל יָדוֹ
   וְאֶל־שַׁדַּי יִתְגַּבָּר׃

26 יָרוּץ אֵלָיו בְּצַוָּאר
   בַּעֲבִי גַּבֵּי מָגִנָּיו׃

27 כִּי־כִסָּה פָנָיו בְּחֶלְבּוֹ
   וַיַּעַשׂ פִּימָה עֲלֵי־כָסֶל׃

28 וַיִּשְׁכּוֹן עָרִים נִכְחָדוֹת בָּתִּים לֹא־יֵשְׁבוּ לָמוֹ
   אֲשֶׁר הִתְעַתְּדוּ לְגַלִּים׃

טו 15 בִּקְדֹשָׁו   22 וְצָפוּי

29 He will not be rich,
   Nor will his wealth continue,
   Nor will his possessions overspread the
      earth.

30 He will not depart from darkness;
   The flame will dry out his branches,
   And by the breath of His mouth he will go
      away.

31 Let him not trust in futile *things,* deceiving
      himself,
   For futility will be his reward.

32 It will be accomplished before his time,
   And his branch will not be green.

33 He will shake off his unripe grape like a vine,
   And cast off his blossom like an olive tree.

34 For the company of hypocrites *will be*
      barren,
   And fire will consume the tents of bribery.

35 They conceive trouble and bring forth
      futility;
   Their womb prepares deceit."

16 Then Job answered and said:

2 "I have heard many such things;
   Miserable comforters *are* you all!

3 Shall words of wind have an end?
   Or what provokes you that you answer?

4 I also could speak as you *do,*
   If your soul were in my soul's place.
   I could heap up words against you,
   And shake my head at you;

5 *But* I would strengthen you with my mouth,
   And the comfort of my lips would relieve
      your grief.

6 "Though I speak, my grief is not relieved;
   And *if* I remain silent, how am I eased?

7 But now He has worn me out;
   You have made desolate all my company.

8 You have shriveled me up,
   And it is a witness *against me;*
   My leanness rises up against me
   And bears witness to my face.

9 He tears *me* in His wrath, and hates me;
   He gnashes at me with His teeth;
   My adversary sharpens His gaze on me.

10 They gape at me with their mouth,
   They strike me reproachfully on the cheek,
   They gather together against me.

11 God has delivered me to the ungodly,
   And turned me over to the hands of the
      wicked.

12 I was at ease, but He has shattered me;

29 לֹא־יֶעְשַׁר וְלֹא־יָקוּם חֵילוֹ
וְלֹא־יִטֶּה לָאָרֶץ מִנְלָם:
30 לֹא־יָסוּר ׀ מִנִּי־חֹשֶׁךְ יֹנַקְתּוֹ תְּיַבֵּשׁ שַׁלְהֶבֶת
וְיָסוּר בְּרוּחַ פִּיו:
31 אַל־יַאֲמֵן בַּשָּׁו נִתְעָה
כִּי־שָׁוְא תִּהְיֶה תְמוּרָתוֹ:
32 בְּלֹא־יוֹמוֹ תִּמָּלֵא
וְכִפָּתוֹ לֹא רַעֲנָנָה:
33 יַחְמֹס כַּגֶּפֶן בִּסְרוֹ
וְיַשְׁלֵךְ כַּזַּיִת נִצָּתוֹ:
34 כִּי־עֲדַת חָנֵף גַּלְמוּד
וְאֵשׁ אָכְלָה אָהֳלֵי־שֹׁחַד:
35 הָרֹה עָמָל וְיָלֹד אָוֶן
וּבִטְנָם תָּכִין מִרְמָה: ס

טז וַיַּעַן אִיּוֹב וַיֹּאמַר:
2 שָׁמַעְתִּי כְאֵלֶּה רַבּוֹת
מְנַחֲמֵי עָמָל כֻּלְּכֶם:
3 הֲקֵץ לְדִבְרֵי־רוּחַ
אוֹ מַה־יַּמְרִיצְךָ כִּי תַעֲנֶה:
4 גַּם ׀ אָנֹכִי
כָּכֶם אֲדַבֵּרָה
לוּ־יֵשׁ נַפְשְׁכֶם תַּחַת נַפְשִׁי
אַחְבִּירָה עֲלֵיכֶם בְּמִלִּים
וְאָנִיעָה עֲלֵיכֶם
בְּמוֹ רֹאשִׁי:
5 אֲאַמִּצְכֶם בְּמוֹ־פִי
וְנִיד שְׂפָתַי יַחְשֹׂךְ:
6 אִם־אֲדַבְּרָה לֹא־יֵחָשֵׂךְ כְּאֵבִי
וְאַחְדְּלָה מַה־מִנִּי יַהֲלֹךְ:
7 אַךְ־עַתָּה הֶלְאָנִי
הֲשִׁמּוֹתָ כָּל־עֲדָתִי:
8 וַתִּקְמְטֵנִי לְעֵד הָיָה
וַיָּקָם בִּי כַחֲשִׁי בְּפָנַי יַעֲנֶה:
9 אַפּוֹ טָרַף ׀ וַיִּשְׂטְמֵנִי חָרַק עָלַי בְּשִׁנָּיו
צָרִי ׀ יִלְטוֹשׁ עֵינָיו לִי:
10 פָּעֲרוּ עָלַי ׀ בְּפִיהֶם בְּחֶרְפָּה הִכּוּ לְחָיָי
יַחַד עָלַי יִתְמַלָּאוּן:
11 יַסְגִּירֵנִי אֵל אֶל עֲוִיל
וְעַל־יְדֵי רְשָׁעִים יִרְטֵנִי:
12 שָׁלֵו הָיִיתִי ׀ וַיְפַרְפְּרֵנִי

He also has taken *me* by my neck, and
   shaken me to pieces;
He has set me up for His target,
13 His archers surround me.
He pierces my heart and does not pity;
   He pours out my gall on the ground.
14 He breaks me with wound upon wound;
   He runs at me like a warrior.

15 "I have sewn sackcloth over my skin,
   And laid my head in the dust.
16 My face is flushed from weeping,
   And on my eyelids *is* the shadow of death;
17 Although no violence *is* in my hands,
   And my prayer *is* pure.

18 "O earth, do not cover my blood,
   And let my cry have no *resting* place!
19 Surely even now my witness *is* in heaven,
   And my evidence *is* on high.
20 My friends scorn me;
   My eyes pour out *tears* to God.
21 Oh, that one might plead for a man with
     God,
   As a man *pleads* for his neighbor!
22 For when a few years are finished,
   I shall go the way of no return.

17

"My spirit is broken,
   My days are extinguished,
   The grave *is ready* for me.
2 *Are* not mockers with me?
   And does not my eye dwell on their
     provocation?

3 "Now put down a pledge for me with
     Yourself.
   Who *is* he *who* will shake hands with me?
4 For You have hidden their heart from
     understanding;
   Therefore You will not exalt *them*.
5 He who speaks flattery to *his* friends,
   Even the eyes of his children will fail.

6 "But He has made me a byword of the people,
   And I have become one in whose face men
     spit.
7 My eye has also grown dim because of
     sorrow,
   And all my members *are* like shadows.
8 Upright *men* are astonished at this,
   And the innocent stirs himself up against the
     hypocrite.
9 Yet the righteous will hold to his way,
   And he who has clean hands will be stronger
     and stronger.

וְאָחַז בְּעָרְפִּי וַיְפַצְפְּצֵנִי
וַיְקִימֵנִי לוֹ לְמַטָּרָה:
13 יָסֹבּוּ עָלַי ׀ רַבָּיו
יְפַלַּח כִּלְיוֹתַי וְלֹא יַחְמוֹל
יִשְׁפֹּךְ לָאָרֶץ מְרֵרָתִי:
14 יִפְרְצֵנִי פֶרֶץ עַל־פְּנֵי־פָרֶץ
יָרֻץ עָלַי כְּגִבּוֹר:
15 שַׂק תָּפַרְתִּי עֲלֵי גִלְדִּי
וְעֹלַלְתִּי בֶעָפָר קַרְנִי:
16 פָּנַי חֲמַרְמְרָה° מִנִּי־בֶכִי
וְעַל עַפְעַפַּי צַלְמָוֶת:
17 עַל לֹא־חָמָס בְּכַפָּי
וּתְפִלָּתִי זַכָּה:
18 אֶרֶץ אַל־תְּכַסִּי דָמִי
וְאַל־יְהִי מָקוֹם לְזַעֲקָתִי:
19 גַּם־עַתָּה הִנֵּה־בַשָּׁמַיִם עֵדִי
וְשָׂהֲדִי בַּמְּרוֹמִים:
20 מְלִיצַי רֵעָי
אֶל־אֱלוֹהַּ דָּלְפָה עֵינִי:
21 וְיוֹכַח לְגֶבֶר עִם־אֱלוֹהַּ
וּבֶן־אָדָם לְרֵעֵהוּ:
22 כִּי־שְׁנוֹת מִסְפָּר יֶאֱתָיוּ
וְאֹרַח לֹא־אָשׁוּב אֶהֱלֹךְ:

יז רוּחִי חֻבָּלָה יָמַי נִזְעָכוּ
קְבָרִים לִי:
2 אִם־לֹא הֲתֻלִים עִמָּדִי
וּבְהַמְּרוֹתָם תָּלַן עֵינִי:
3 שִׂימָה־נָּא עָרְבֵנִי עִמָּךְ
מִי הוּא לְיָדִי יִתָּקֵעַ:
4 כִּי־לִבָּם צָפַנְתָּ מִּשָּׂכֶל
עַל־כֵּן לֹא תְרֹמֵם:
5 לְחֵלֶק יַגִּיד רֵעִים
וְעֵינֵי בָנָיו תִּכְלֶנָה:
6 וְהִצִּגַנִי לִמְשֹׁל עַמִּים
וְתֹפֶת לְפָנִים אֶהְיֶה:
7 וַתֵּכַהּ מִכַּעַשׂ עֵינִי
וִיצֻרַי כַּצֵּל כֻּלָּם:
8 יָשֹׁמּוּ יְשָׁרִים עַל־זֹאת
וְנָקִי עַל־חָנֵף יִתְעֹרָר:
9 וְיֹאחֵז צַדִּיק דַּרְכּוֹ
וּטְהָר־יָדַיִם יֹסִיף אֹמֶץ:

טז 16 חֲמַרְמְרוּ

10 "But please, come back again, all of you,
    For I shall not find *one* wise *man* among
    you.

11 My days are past,
    My purposes are broken off,
    Even the thoughts of my heart.

12 They change the night into day;
    'The light *is* near,' *they say,* in the face of
    darkness.

13 If I wait *for* the grave *as* my house,
    If I make my bed in the darkness,

14 If I say to corruption, 'You *are* my father,'
    And to the worm, 'You *are* my mother and
    my sister,'

15 Where then *is* my hope?
    As for my hope, who can see it?

16 *Will* they go down to the gates of Sheol?
    Shall *we have* rest together in the dust?"

18 Then Bildad the Shuhite answered and said:

2 "How long *till* you put an end to words?
    Gain understanding, and afterward we will
    speak.

3 Why are we counted as beasts,
    And regarded as stupid in your sight?

4 You who tear yourself in anger,
    Shall the earth be forsaken for you?
    Or shall the rock be removed from its place?

5 "The light of the wicked indeed goes out,
    And the flame of his fire does not shine.

6 The light is dark in his tent,
    And his lamp beside him is put out.

7 The steps of his strength are shortened,
    And his own counsel casts him down.

8 For he is cast into a net by his own feet,
    And he walks into a snare.

9 The net takes *him* by the heel,
    And a snare lays hold of him.

10 A noose *is* hidden for him on the ground,
    And a trap for him in the road.

11 Terrors frighten him on every side,
    And drive him to his feet.

12 His strength is starved,
    And destruction *is* ready at his side.

13 It devours patches of his skin;
    The firstborn of death devours his limbs.

14 He is uprooted from the shelter of his tent,
    And they parade him before the king of
    terrors.

15 They dwell in his tent *who are* none of his;
    Brimstone is scattered on his dwelling.

16 His roots are dried out below,
    And his branch withers above.

10 וְאוּלָם כֻּלָּם תָּשֻׁבוּ וּבֹאוּ נָא
וְלֹא־אֶמְצָא בָכֶם חָכָם:

11 יָמַי עָבְרוּ זִמֹּתַי נִתְּקוּ
מוֹרָשֵׁי לְבָבִי:

12 לַיְלָה לְיוֹם יָשִׂימוּ
אוֹר קָרוֹב מִפְּנֵי־חֹשֶׁךְ:

13 אִם־אֲקַוֶּה שְׁאוֹל בֵּיתִי
בַּחֹשֶׁךְ רִפַּדְתִּי יְצוּעָי:

14 לַשַּׁחַת קָרָאתִי אָבִי אָתָּה
אִמִּי וַאֲחֹתִי לָרִמָּה:

15 וְאַיֵּה אֵפוֹ תִקְוָתִי
וְתִקְוָתִי מִי יְשׁוּרֶנָּה:

16 בַּדֵּי שְׁאֹל תֵּרַדְנָה
אִם־יַחַד עַל־עָפָר נָחַת: ס

יח 1 וַיַּעַן בִּלְדַּד הַשֻּׁחִי וַיֹּאמַר:

2 עַד־אָנָה ׀ תְּשִׂימוּן קִנְצֵי לְמִלִּין
תָּבִינוּ וְאַחַר נְדַבֵּר:

3 מַדּוּעַ נֶחְשַׁבְנוּ כַבְּהֵמָה
נִטְמִינוּ בְּעֵינֵיכֶם:

4 טֹרֵף נַפְשׁוֹ בְּאַפּוֹ
הַלְמַעַנְךָ תֵּעָזַב אָרֶץ וְיֶעְתַּק־צוּר מִמְּקֹמוֹ:

5 גַּם אוֹר רְשָׁעִים יִדְעָךְ
וְלֹא־יִגַּהּ שְׁבִיב אִשּׁוֹ:

6 אוֹר חָשַׁךְ בְּאָהֳלוֹ
וְנֵרוֹ עָלָיו יִדְעָךְ:

7 יֵצְרוּ צַעֲדֵי אוֹנוֹ
וְתַשְׁלִיכֵהוּ עֲצָתוֹ:

8 כִּי־שֻׁלַּח בְּרֶשֶׁת בְּרַגְלָיו
וְעַל־שְׂבָכָה יִתְהַלָּךְ:

9 יֹאחֵז בְּעָקֵב פָּח
יַחֲזֵק עָלָיו צַמִּים:

10 טָמוּן בָּאָרֶץ חַבְלוֹ
וּמַלְכֻּדְתּוֹ עֲלֵי נָתִיב:

11 סָבִיב בִּעֲתֻהוּ בַלָּהוֹת
וֶהֱפִיצֻהוּ לְרַגְלָיו:

12 יְהִי־רָעֵב אֹנוֹ
וְאֵיד נָכוֹן לְצַלְעוֹ:

13 יֹאכַל בַּדֵּי עוֹרוֹ
יֹאכַל בַּדָּיו בְּכוֹר מָוֶת:

14 יִנָּתֵק מֵאָהֳלוֹ מִבְטַחוֹ
וְתַצְעִדֵהוּ לְמֶלֶךְ בַּלָּהוֹת:

15 תִּשְׁכּוֹן בְּאָהֳלוֹ מִבְּלִי־לוֹ
יְזֹרֶה עַל־נָוֵהוּ גָפְרִית:

16 מִתַּחַת שָׁרָשָׁיו יִבָשׁוּ

¹⁷ The memory of him perishes from the earth,
And he has no name among the renowned.

¹⁸ He is driven from light into darkness,
And chased out of the world.

¹⁹ He has neither son nor posterity among his
people,
Nor any remaining in his dwellings.

²⁰ Those in the west are astonished at his day,
As those in the east are frightened.

²¹ Surely such *are* the dwellings of the wicked,
And this *is* the place *of him who* does not
know God."

19 Then Job answered and said:

² "How long will you torment my soul,
And break me in pieces with words?

³ These ten times you have reproached me;
You are not ashamed *that* you have wronged
me.

⁴ And if indeed I have erred,
My error remains with me.

⁵ If indeed you exalt *yourselves* against me,
And plead my disgrace against me,

⁶ Know then that God has wronged me,
And has surrounded me with His net.

⁷ "If I cry out concerning wrong, I am not
heard.
If I cry aloud, *there is* no justice.

⁸ He has fenced up my way, so that I cannot
pass;
And He has set darkness in my paths.

⁹ He has stripped me of my glory,
And taken the crown *from* my head.

¹⁰ He breaks me down on every side,
And I am gone;
My hope He has uprooted like a tree.

¹¹ He has also kindled His wrath against me,
And He counts me as *one of* His enemies.

¹² His troops come together
And build up their road against me;
They encamp all around my tent.

¹³ "He has removed my brothers far from me,
And my acquaintances are completely
estranged from me.

¹⁴ My relatives have failed,
And my close friends have forgotten me.

¹⁵ Those who dwell in my house, and my
maidservants,
Count me as a stranger;
I am an alien in their sight.

¹⁶ I call my servant, but he gives no answer;
I beg him with my mouth.

וּמֵעַל יִמַּל קְצִירוֹ׃

17 זִכְרוֹ־אָבַד מִנִּי־אָרֶץ
וְלֹא־שֵׁם לוֹ עַל־פְּנֵי־חוּץ׃

18 יֶהְדְּפֻהוּ מֵאוֹר אֶל־חֹשֶׁךְ
וּמִתֵּבֵל יְנִדֻּהוּ׃

19 לֹא נִין לוֹ וְלֹא־נֶכֶד בְּעַמּוֹ
וְאֵין שָׂרִיד בִּמְגוּרָיו׃

20 עַל־יוֹמוֹ נָשַׁמּוּ אַחֲרֹנִים
וְקַדְמֹנִים אָחֲזוּ שָׂעַר׃

21 אַךְ־אֵלֶּה מִשְׁכְּנוֹת עַוָּל
וְזֶה מְקוֹם לֹא־יָדַע־אֵל׃ ס

יט וַיַּעַן אִיּוֹב וַיֹּאמַר׃

2 עַד־אָנָה תּוֹגְיוּן נַפְשִׁי
וּתְדַכְּאוּנַנִי בְמִלִּים׃

3 זֶה עֶשֶׂר פְּעָמִים תַּכְלִימוּנִי
לֹא־תֵבֹשׁוּ תַּהְכְּרוּ־לִי׃

4 וְאַף־אָמְנָם שָׁגִיתִי
אִתִּי תָּלִין מְשׁוּגָתִי׃

5 אִם־אָמְנָם עָלַי תַּגְדִּילוּ
וְתוֹכִיחוּ עָלַי חֶרְפָּתִי׃

6 דְּעוּ־אֵפוֹ כִּי־אֱלוֹהַּ עִוְּתָנִי
וּמְצוּדוֹ עָלַי הִקִּיף׃

7 הֵן אֶצְעַק חָמָס וְלֹא אֵעָנֶה
אֲשַׁוַּע וְאֵין מִשְׁפָּט׃

8 אָרְחִי גָדַר וְלֹא אֶעֱבוֹר
וְעַל נְתִיבוֹתַי חֹשֶׁךְ יָשִׂים׃

9 כְּבוֹדִי מֵעָלַי הִפְשִׁיט
וַיָּסַר עֲטֶרֶת רֹאשִׁי׃

10 יִתְּצֵנִי סָבִיב וָאֵלַךְ
וַיַּסַּע כָּעֵץ תִּקְוָתִי׃

11 וַיַּחַר עָלַי אַפּוֹ
וַיַּחְשְׁבֵנִי לוֹ כְצָרָיו׃

12 יַחַד ׀ יָבֹאוּ גְדוּדָיו וַיָּסֹלּוּ עָלַי דַּרְכָּם
וַיַּחֲנוּ סָבִיב לְאָהֳלִי׃

13 אַחַי מֵעָלַי הִרְחִיק
וְיֹדְעַי אַךְ־זָרוּ מִמֶּנִּי׃

14 חָדְלוּ קְרוֹבָי
וּמְיֻדָּעַי שְׁכֵחוּנִי׃

15 גָּרֵי בֵיתִי וְאַמְהֹתַי לְזָר תַּחְשְׁבֻנִי
נָכְרִי הָיִיתִי בְעֵינֵיהֶם׃

16 לְעַבְדִּי קָרָאתִי וְלֹא יַעֲנֶה
בְּמוֹ־פִי אֶתְחַנֶּן־לוֹ׃

17 My breath is offensive to my wife,
And I am repulsive to the children of my
own body.

18 Even young children despise me;
I arise, and they speak against me.

19 All my close friends abhor me,
And those whom I love have turned against
me.

20 My bone clings to my skin and to my flesh,
And I have escaped by the skin of my teeth.

21 "Have pity on me, have pity on me, O you my
friends,
For the hand of God has struck me!

22 Why do you persecute me as God *does*,
And are not satisfied with my flesh?

23 "Oh, that my words were written!
Oh, that they were inscribed in a book!

24 That they were engraved on a rock
With an iron pen and lead, forever!

25 For I know *that* my Redeemer lives,
And He shall stand at last on the earth;

26 And after my skin is destroyed, this *I know*,
That in my flesh I shall see God,

27 Whom I shall see for myself,
And my eyes shall behold, and not another.
How my heart yearns within me!

28 If you should say, 'How shall we persecute
him?'—
Since the root of the matter is found in me,

29 Be afraid of the sword for yourselves;
For wrath *brings* the punishment of the
sword,
That you may know *there is* a judgment."

20 Then Zophar the Naamathite answered and
said:

2 "Therefore my anxious thoughts make me
answer,
Because of the turmoil within me.

3 I have heard the rebuke that reproaches me,
And the spirit of my understanding causes
me to answer.

4 "Do you *not* know this of old,
Since man was placed on earth,

5 That the triumphing of the wicked is short,
And the joy of the hypocrite is *but* for a
moment?

6 Though his haughtiness mounts up to the
heavens,
And his head reaches to the clouds,

7 *Yet* he will perish forever like his own refuse;

---

17 רוּחִי זָרָה לְאִשְׁתִּי
וְחַנֹּתִי לִבְנֵי בִטְנִי:

18 גַּם־עֲוִילִים מָאֲסוּ בִי
אָקוּמָה וַיְדַבְּרוּ־בִי:

19 תִּעֲבוּנִי כָּל־מְתֵי סוֹדִי
וְזֶה־אָהַבְתִּי נֶהְפְּכוּ־בִי:

20 בְּעוֹרִי וּבִבְשָׂרִי דָּבְקָה עַצְמִי
וָאֶתְמַלְּטָה בְּעוֹר שִׁנָּי:

21 חָנֻּנִי חָנֻּנִי אַתֶּם רֵעָי
כִּי יַד־אֱלוֹהַּ נָגְעָה בִּי:

22 לָמָּה תִּרְדְּפֻנִי כְמוֹ־אֵל
וּמִבְּשָׂרִי לֹא תִשְׂבָּעוּ:

23 מִי־יִתֵּן אֵפוֹ וְיִכָּתְבוּן מִלָּי
מִי־יִתֵּן בַּסֵּפֶר וְיֻחָקוּ:

24 בְּעֵט־בַּרְזֶל וְעֹפָרֶת
לָעַד בַּצּוּר יֵחָצְבוּן:

25 וַאֲנִי יָדַעְתִּי גֹּאֲלִי חָי
וְאַחֲרוֹן עַל־עָפָר יָקוּם:

26 וְאַחַר עוֹרִי נִקְּפוּ־זֹאת
וּמִבְּשָׂרִי אֶחֱזֶה אֱלוֹהַּ:

27 אֲשֶׁר אֲנִי ׀ אֶחֱזֶה־לִּי וְעֵינַי רָאוּ וְלֹא־זָר
כָּלוּ כִלְיֹתַי בְּחֵקִי:

28 כִּי תֹאמְרוּ מַה־נִּרְדָּף־לוֹ
וְשֹׁרֶשׁ דָּבָר נִמְצָא־בִי:

29 גּוּרוּ לָכֶם ׀ מִפְּנֵי־חֶרֶב כִּי־חֵמָה עֲוֹנוֹת חָרֶב
לְמַעַן תֵּדְעוּן שַׁדִּין: ס

כ וַיַּעַן צֹפַר הַנַּעֲמָתִי וַיֹּאמַר:

2 לָכֵן שְׂעִפַּי יְשִׁיבוּנִי
וּבַעֲבוּר חוּשִׁי בִי:

3 מוּסַר כְּלִמָּתִי אֶשְׁמָע
וְרוּחַ מִבִּינָתִי יַעֲנֵנִי:

4 הֲזֹאת יָדַעְתָּ מִנִּי־עַד
מִנִּי שִׂים אָדָם עֲלֵי־אָרֶץ:

5 כִּי רִנְנַת רְשָׁעִים מִקָּרוֹב
וְשִׂמְחַת חָנֵף עֲדֵי־רָגַע:

6 אִם־יַעֲלֶה לַשָּׁמַיִם שִׂיאוֹ
וְרֹאשׁוֹ לָעָב יַגִּיעַ:

7 כְּגֶלֲלוֹ לָנֶצַח יֹאבֵד
רֹאָיו יֹאמְרוּ אַיּוֹ:

Those who have seen him will say, 'Where is he?'

8 He will fly away like a dream, and not be found;
Yes, he will be chased away like a vision of the night.

9 The eye *that* saw him will *see him* no more,
Nor will his place behold him anymore.

10 His children will seek the favor of the poor,
And his hands will restore his wealth.

11 His bones are full of his youthful vigor,
But it will lie down with him in the dust.

12 "Though evil is sweet in his mouth,
And he hides it under his tongue,

13 *Though* he spares it and does not forsake it,
But still keeps it in his mouth,

14 *Yet* his food in his stomach turns sour;
It becomes cobra venom within him.

15 He swallows down riches
And vomits them up again;
God casts them out of his belly.

16 He will suck the poison of cobras;
The viper's tongue will slay him.

17 He will not see the streams,
The rivers flowing with honey and cream.

18 He will restore that for which he labored,
And will not swallow *it* down;
From the proceeds of business
He will get no enjoyment.

19 For he has oppressed *and* forsaken the poor,
He has violently seized a house which he did not build.

20 "Because he knows no quietness in his heart,
He will not save anything he desires.

21 Nothing is left for him to eat;
Therefore his well-being will not last.

22 In his self-sufficiency he will be in distress;
Every hand of misery will come against him.

23 *When* he is about to fill his stomach,
God will cast on him the fury of His wrath,
And will rain *it* on him while he is eating.

24 He will flee from the iron weapon;
A bronze bow will pierce him through.

25 It is drawn, and comes out of the body;
Yes, the glittering *point* comes out of his gall.
Terrors *come* upon him;

26 Total darkness *is* reserved for his treasures.
An unfanned fire will consume him;
It shall go ill with him who is left in his tent.

27 The heavens will reveal his iniquity,
And the earth will rise up against him.

28 The increase of his house will depart,

8 פַּחֲלוֹם יָעוּף וְלֹא יִמְצָאוּהוּ
וְיֻדַּד כְּחֶזְיוֹן לָיְלָה:

9 עַיִן שְׁזָפַתּוּ וְלֹא תוֹסִיף
וְלֹא־עוֹד תְּשׁוּרֶנּוּ מְקוֹמוֹ:

10 בָּנָיו יְרַצּוּ דַלִּים
וְיָדָיו תָּשֵׁבְנָה אוֹנוֹ:

11 עַצְמוֹתָיו מָלְאוּ עֲלוּמָו
וְעִמּוֹ עַל־עָפָר תִּשְׁכָּב:

12 אִם־תַּמְתִּיק בְּפִיו רָעָה
יַכְחִידֶנָּה תַּחַת לְשׁוֹנוֹ:

13 יַחְמֹל עָלֶיהָ וְלֹא יַעַזְבֶנָּה
וְיִמְנָעֶנָּה בְּתוֹךְ חִכּוֹ:

14 לַחְמוֹ בְּמֵעָיו נֶהְפָּךְ
מְרוֹרַת פְּתָנִים בְּקִרְבּוֹ:

15 חַיִל בָּלַע וַיְקִאֶנּוּ
מִבִּטְנוֹ יוֹרִשֶׁנּוּ אֵל:

16 רֹאשׁ־פְּתָנִים יִינָק
תַּהַרְגֵהוּ לְשׁוֹן אֶפְעֶה:

17 אַל־יֵרֶא בִפְלַגּוֹת
נַהֲרֵי נַחֲלֵי דְּבַשׁ וְחֶמְאָה:

18 מֵשִׁיב יָגָע וְלֹא יִבְלָע
כְּחֵיל תְּמוּרָתוֹ וְלֹא יַעֲלֹס:

19 כִּי־רִצַּץ עָזַב דַּלִּים
בַּיִת גָּזַל וְלֹא יִבְנֵהוּ:

20 כִּי לֹא־יָדַע שָׁלֵו בְּבִטְנוֹ
בַּחֲמוּדוֹ לֹא יְמַלֵּט:

21 אֵין־שָׂרִיד לְאָכְלוֹ
עַל־כֵּן לֹא־יָחִיל טוּבוֹ:

22 בִּמְלֹאות שִׂפְקוֹ יֵצֶר לוֹ
כָּל־יַד עָמֵל תְּבוֹאֶנּוּ:

23 יְהִי לְמַלֵּא בִטְנוֹ יְשַׁלַּח־בּוֹ חֲרוֹן אַפּוֹ
וְיַמְטֵר עָלֵימוֹ בִּלְחוּמוֹ:

24 יִבְרַח מִנֵּשֶׁק בַּרְזֶל
תַּחְלְפֵהוּ קֶשֶׁת נְחוּשָׁה:

25 שָׁלַף וַיֵּצֵא מִגֵּוָה
וּבָרָק מִמְּרֹרָתוֹ יַהֲלֹךְ עָלָיו אֵמִים:

26 כָּל־חֹשֶׁךְ טָמוּן לִצְפּוּנָיו
תְּאָכְלֵהוּ אֵשׁ לֹא־נֻפָּח
יֵרַע שָׂרִיד בְּאָהֳלוֹ:

27 יְגַלּוּ שָׁמַיִם עֲוֺנוֹ
וְאֶרֶץ מִתְקוֹמָמָה לוֹ:

28 יִגֶל יְבוּל בֵּיתוֹ

כ 11 עֲלוּמָיו

And his goods will flow away in the day of His wrath.

29 This *is* the portion from God for a wicked man,
The heritage appointed to him by God."

נִגָּרוֹת בְּיוֹם אַפּוֹ׃
29 זֶה ׀ חֵלֶק־אָדָם רָשָׁע מֵאֱלֹהִים
וְנַחֲלַת אִמְרוֹ מֵאֵל׃   פ

21

Then Job answered and said:

כא וַיַּעַן אִיּוֹב וַיֹּאמַר׃

2 "Listen carefully to my speech,
And let this be your consolation.

2 שִׁמְעוּ שָׁמוֹעַ מִלָּתִי
וּתְהִי־זֹאת תַּנְחוּמֹתֵיכֶם׃

3 Bear with me that I may speak,
And after I have spoken, keep mocking.

3 שָׂאוּנִי וְאָנֹכִי אֲדַבֵּר
וְאַחַר דַּבְּרִי תַלְעִיג׃

4 "As for me, *is* my complaint against man?
And if *it were*, why should I not be impatient?

4 הֶאָנֹכִי לְאָדָם שִׂיחִי
וְאִם־מַדּוּעַ לֹא־תִקְצַר רוּחִי׃

5 Look at me and be astonished;
Put *your* hand over *your* mouth.

5 פְּנוּ־אֵלַי וְהָשַׁמּוּ
וְשִׂימוּ יָד עַל־פֶּה׃

6 Even when I remember I am terrified,
And trembling takes hold of my flesh.

6 וְאִם־זָכַרְתִּי וְנִבְהָלְתִּי
וְאָחַז בְּשָׂרִי פַּלָּצוּת׃

7 Why do the wicked live *and* become old,
Yes, become mighty in power?

7 מַדּוּעַ רְשָׁעִים יִחְיוּ
עָתְקוּ גַּם־גָּבְרוּ חָיִל׃

8 Their descendants are established with them in their sight,
And their offspring before their eyes.

8 זַרְעָם נָכוֹן לִפְנֵיהֶם עִמָּם
וְצֶאֱצָאֵיהֶם לְעֵינֵיהֶם׃

9 Their houses *are* safe from fear,
Neither *is* the rod of God upon them.

9 בָּתֵּיהֶם שָׁלוֹם מִפָּחַד
וְלֹא שֵׁבֶט אֱלוֹהַּ עֲלֵיהֶם׃

10 Their bull breeds without failure;
Their cow calves without miscarriage.

10 שׁוֹרוֹ עִבַּר וְלֹא יַגְעִל
תְּפַלֵּט פָּרָתוֹ וְלֹא תְשַׁכֵּל׃

11 They send forth their little ones like a flock,
And their children dance.

11 יְשַׁלְּחוּ כַצֹּאן עֲוִילֵיהֶם
וְיַלְדֵיהֶם יְרַקֵּדוּן׃

12 They sing to the tambourine and harp,
And rejoice to the sound of the flute.

12 יִשְׂאוּ כְּתֹף וְכִנּוֹר
וְיִשְׂמְחוּ לְקוֹל עוּגָב׃

13 They spend their days in wealth,
And in a moment go down to the grave.

13 יְבַלּוּ בַטּוֹב יְמֵיהֶם
וּבְרֶגַע שְׁאוֹל יֵחָתּוּ׃

14 Yet they say to God, 'Depart from us,
For we do not desire the knowledge of Your ways.

14 וַיֹּאמְרוּ לָאֵל סוּר מִמֶּנּוּ
וְדַעַת דְּרָכֶיךָ לֹא חָפָצְנוּ׃

15 Who *is* the Almighty, that we should serve Him?
And what profit do we have if we pray to Him?'

15 מַה־שַׁדַּי כִּי־נַעַבְדֶנּוּ
וּמַה־נּוֹעִיל כִּי נִפְגַּע־בּוֹ׃

16 Indeed their prosperity *is* not in their hand;
The counsel of the wicked is far from me.

16 הֵן לֹא בְיָדָם טוּבָם
עֲצַת רְשָׁעִים רָחֲקָה מֶנִּי׃

17 "How often is the lamp of the wicked put out?
How often does their destruction come upon them,
The sorrows *God* distributes in His anger?

17 כַּמָּה ׀ נֵר־רְשָׁעִים יִדְעָךְ
וְיָבֹא עָלֵימוֹ אֵידָם
חֲבָלִים יְחַלֵּק בְּאַפּוֹ׃

18 They are like straw before the wind,
And like chaff that a storm carries away.

18 יִהְיוּ כְּתֶבֶן לִפְנֵי־רוּחַ
וּכְמֹץ גְּנָבַתּוּ סוּפָה׃

19 *They say,* 'God lays up one's iniquity for his children';
Let Him recompense him, that he may know *it*.

19 אֱלוֹהַּ יִצְפֹּן־לְבָנָיו אוֹנוֹ
יְשַׁלֵּם אֵלָיו וְיֵדָע׃

20 Let his eyes see his destruction,
And let him drink of the wrath of the
   Almighty.

21 For what does he care about his household
   after him,
When the number of his months is cut in
   half?

22 "Can *anyone* teach God knowledge,
Since He judges those on high?

23 One dies in his full strength,
Being wholly at ease and secure;

24 His pails are full of milk,
And the marrow of his bones is moist.

25 Another man dies in the bitterness of his
   soul,
Never having eaten with pleasure.

26 They lie down alike in the dust,
And worms cover them.

27 "Look, I know your thoughts,
And the schemes *with which* you would
   wrong me.

28 For you say,
'Where *is* the house of the prince?
And where *is* the tent,
The dwelling place of the wicked?'

29 Have you not asked those who travel the
   road?
And do you not know their signs?

30 For the wicked are reserved for the day of
   doom;
They shall be brought out on the day of
   wrath.

31 Who condemns his way to his face?
And who repays him *for what* he has done?

32 Yet he shall be brought to the grave,
And a vigil kept over the tomb.

33 The clods of the valley shall be sweet to him;
Everyone shall follow him,
As countless *have gone* before him.

34 How then can you comfort me with empty
   words,
Since falsehood remains in your answers?"

22 Then Eliphaz the Temanite answered and said:

2 "Can a man be profitable to God,
Though he who is wise may be profitable to
   himself?

3 *Is it* any pleasure to the Almighty that you
   are righteous?
Or *is it* gain *to Him* that you make your
   ways blameless?

20 יִרְא֣וּ עֵינָ֣ו כִּיד֑וֹ
וּמֵחֲמַ֖ת שַׁדַּ֣י יִשְׁתֶּֽה׃

21 כִּ֤י מַה־חֶפְצ֣וֹ בְּבֵית֣וֹ אַחֲרָ֑יו
וּמִסְפַּ֖ר חֳדָשָׁ֣יו חֻצָּֽצוּ׃

22 הַלְאֵ֥ל יְלַמֶּד־דָּ֑עַת
וְה֗וּא רָמִ֥ים יִשְׁפּֽוֹט׃

23 זֶ֗ה יָ֭מוּת בְּעֶ֣צֶם תֻּמּ֑וֹ
כֻּ֝לּ֗וֹ שַׁלְאֲנַ֥ן וְשָׁלֵֽיו׃

24 עֲ֭טִינָיו מָלְא֣וּ חָלָ֑ב
וּמֹ֖חַ עַצְמוֹתָ֣יו יְשֻׁקֶּֽה׃

25 וְזֶ֗ה יָ֭מוּת בְּנֶ֣פֶשׁ מָרָ֑ה
וְלֹֽא־אָכַ֥ל בַּטּוֹבָֽה׃

26 יַ֭חַד עַל־עָפָ֣ר יִשְׁכָּ֑בוּ
וְ֝רִמָּ֗ה תְּכַסֶּ֥ה עֲלֵיהֶֽם׃

27 הֵ֤ן יָדַ֨עְתִּי מַחְשְׁבֽוֹתֵיכֶ֑ם
וּ֝מְזִמּ֗וֹת עָלַ֥י תַּחְמֹֽסוּ׃

28 כִּ֤י תֹֽאמְר֗וּ אַיֵּ֥ה בֵית־נָדִ֑יב
וְאַיֵּ֥ה אֹ֝הֶל ׀ מִשְׁכְּנ֥וֹת רְשָׁעִֽים׃

29 הֲלֹ֣א שְׁ֭אֶלְתֶּם עֽוֹבְרֵ֣י דָ֑רֶךְ
וְ֝אֹתֹתָ֗ם לֹ֣א תְנַכֵּֽרוּ׃

30 כִּ֤י לְי֣וֹם אֵ֭יד יֵחָ֣שֶׂךְ רָ֑ע
לְי֖וֹם עֲבָר֣וֹת יוּבָֽלוּ׃

31 מִֽי־יַגִּ֣יד עַל־פָּנָ֣יו דַּרְכּ֑וֹ
וְהֽוּא־עָ֝שָׂ֗ה מִ֣י יְשַׁלֶּם־לֽוֹ׃

32 וְ֭הוּא לִקְבָר֣וֹת יוּבָ֑ל
וְֽעַל־גָּדִ֥ישׁ יִשְׁקֽוֹד׃

33 מָֽתְקוּ־ל֗וֹ רִגְבֵ֫י נָ֥חַל
וְֽאַחֲרָ֗יו כָּל־אָדָ֥ם יִמְשֹׁ֑ךְ וּ֝לְפָנָ֗יו אֵ֣ין מִסְפָּֽר׃

34 וְ֭אֵיךְ תְּנַחֲמ֣וּנִי הָ֑בֶל
ס וּ֝תְשֽׁוּבֹתֵיכֶ֗ם נִשְׁאַר־מָֽעַל׃

כב וַ֭יַּעַן אֱלִיפַ֥ז הַֽתֵּמָנִ֗י וַיֹּאמַֽר׃

2 הַלְאֵ֥ל יִסְכָּן־גָּ֑בֶר
כִּֽי־יִסְכֹּ֥ן עָלֵ֣ימוֹ מַשְׂכִּֽיל׃

3 הַחֵ֣פֶץ לְ֭שַׁדַּי כִּ֣י תִצְדָּ֑ק
וְאִם־בֶּ֝֗צַע כִּֽי־תַתֵּ֥ם דְּרָכֶֽיךָ׃

4 "Is it because of your fear of Him that He
    corrects you,
    And enters into judgment with you?

5 *Is* not your wickedness great,
    And your iniquity without end?

6 For you have taken pledges from your
    brother for no reason,
    And stripped the naked of their clothing.

7 You have not given the weary water to
    drink,
    And you have withheld bread from the
    hungry.

8 But the mighty man possessed the land,
    And the honorable man dwelt in it.

9 You have sent widows away empty,
    And the strength of the fatherless was
    crushed.

10 Therefore snares *are* all around you,
    And sudden fear troubles you,

11 Or darkness *so that* you cannot see;
    And an abundance of water covers you.

12 "Is not God in the height of heaven?
    And see the highest stars, how lofty they are!

13 And you say, 'What does God know?
    Can He judge through the deep darkness?

14 Thick clouds cover Him, so that He cannot
    see,
    And He walks above the circle of heaven.'

15 Will you keep to the old way
    Which wicked men have trod,

16 Who were cut down before their time,
    Whose foundations were swept away by a
    flood?

17 They said to God, 'Depart from us!
    What can the Almighty do to them?'

18 Yet He filled their houses with good *things;*
    But the counsel of the wicked is far from me.

19 "The righteous see *it* and are glad,
    And the innocent laugh at them:

20 'Surely our adversaries are cut down,
    And the fire consumes their remnant.'

21 "Now acquaint yourself with Him, and be at
    peace;
    Thereby good will come to you.

22 Receive, please, instruction from His mouth,
    And lay up His words in your heart.

23 If you return to the Almighty, you will be
    built up;
    You will remove iniquity far from your
    tents.

24 Then you will lay your gold in the dust,
    And the *gold* of Ophir among the stones of
    the brooks.

4 הֲמִיִּרְאָתְךָ יֹכִיחֶךָ
  יָבוֹא עִמְּךָ בַּמִּשְׁפָּט:

5 הֲלֹא רָעָתְךָ רַבָּה
  וְאֵין־קֵץ לַעֲוֺנֹתֶיךָ:

6 כִּי־תַחְבֹּל אַחֶיךָ חִנָּם
  וּבִגְדֵי עֲרוּמִּים תַּפְשִׁיט:

7 לֹא־מַיִם עָיֵף תַּשְׁקֶה
  וּמֵרָעֵב תִּמְנַע־לָחֶם:

8 וְאִישׁ זְרוֹעַ לוֹ הָאָרֶץ
  וּנְשׂוּא פָנִים יֵשֶׁב בָּהּ:

9 אַלְמָנוֹת שִׁלַּחְתָּ רֵיקָם
  וּזְרֹעוֹת יְתֹמִים יְדֻכָּא:

10 עַל־כֵּן סְבִיבוֹתֶיךָ פַחִים
  וִיבַהֶלְךָ פַּחַד פִּתְאֹם:

11 אוֹ־חֹשֶׁךְ לֹא־תִרְאֶה
  וְשִׁפְעַת־מַיִם תְּכַסֶּךָּ:

12 הֲלֹא־אֱלוֹהַּ גֹּבַהּ שָׁמָיִם
  וּרְאֵה רֹאשׁ כּוֹכָבִים כִּי־רָמּוּ:

13 וְאָמַרְתָּ מַה־יָּדַע אֵל
  הַבְעַד עֲרָפֶל יִשְׁפּוֹט:

14 עָבִים סֵתֶר־לוֹ וְלֹא יִרְאֶה
  וְחוּג שָׁמַיִם יִתְהַלָּךְ:

15 הַאֹרַח עוֹלָם תִּשְׁמֹר
  אֲשֶׁר דָּרְכוּ מְתֵי־אָוֶן:

16 אֲשֶׁר־קֻמְּטוּ וְלֹא־עֵת
  נָהָר יוּצַק יְסוֹדָם:

17 הָאֹמְרִים לָאֵל סוּר מִמֶּנּוּ
  וּמַה־יִּפְעַל שַׁדַּי לָמוֹ:

18 וְהוּא מִלֵּא בָתֵּיהֶם טוֹב
  וַעֲצַת רְשָׁעִים רָחֲקָה מֶנִּי:

19 יִרְאוּ צַדִּיקִים וְיִשְׂמָחוּ
  וְנָקִי יִלְעַג־לָמוֹ:

20 אִם־לֹא נִכְחַד קִימָנוּ
  וְיִתְרָם אָכְלָה אֵשׁ:

21 הַסְכֶּן־נָא עִמּוֹ וּשְׁלָם
  בָּהֶם תְּבוֹאַתְךָ טוֹבָה:

22 קַח־נָא מִפִּיו תּוֹרָה
  וְשִׂים אֲמָרָיו בִּלְבָבֶךָ:

23 אִם־תָּשׁוּב עַד־שַׁדַּי תִּבָּנֶה
  תַּרְחִיק עַוְלָה מֵאָהֳלֶךָ:

24 וְשִׁית־עַל־עָפָר בָּצֶר
  וּבְצוּר נְחָלִים אוֹפִיר:

²⁵ Yes, the Almighty will be your gold
And your precious silver;
²⁶ For then you will have your delight in the
Almighty,
And lift up your face to God.
²⁷ You will make your prayer to Him,
He will hear you,
And you will pay your vows.
²⁸ You will also declare a thing,
And it will be established for you;
So light will shine on your ways.
²⁹ When they cast *you* down, and you say,
'Exaltation *will come!*'
Then He will save the humble *person*.
³⁰ He will *even* deliver one who is not innocent;
Yes, he will be delivered by the purity of
your hands."

23

Then Job answered and said:

² "Even today my complaint is bitter;
My hand is listless because of my groaning.
³ Oh, that I knew where I might find Him,
That I might come to His seat!
⁴ I would present *my* case before Him,
And fill my mouth with arguments.
⁵ I would know the words *which* He would
answer me,
And understand what He would say to me.
⁶ Would He contend with me in His great
power?
No! But He would take *note* of me.
⁷ There the upright could reason with Him,
And I would be delivered forever from my
Judge.
⁸ "Look, I go forward, but He is not *there,*
And backward, but I cannot perceive Him;
⁹ When He works on the left hand, I cannot
behold *Him;*
When He turns to the right hand, I cannot
see *Him.*
¹⁰ But He knows the way that I take;
When He has tested me, I shall come forth as
gold.
¹¹ My foot has held fast to His steps;
I have kept His way and not turned aside.
¹² I have not departed from the commandment
of His lips;
I have treasured the words of His mouth
More than my necessary *food.*
¹³ "But He *is* unique, and who can make Him
change?
And *whatever* His soul desires, *that* He does.

25 וְהָיָה שַׁדַּי בְּצָרֶיךָ
וְכֶסֶף תּוֹעָפוֹת לָךְ:
26 כִּי־אָז עַל־שַׁדַּי תִּתְעַנָּג
וְתִשָּׂא אֶל־אֱלוֹהַּ פָּנֶיךָ:
27 תַּעְתִּיר אֵלָיו וְיִשְׁמָעֶךָּ
וּנְדָרֶיךָ תְשַׁלֵּם:
28 וְתִגְזַר־אוֹמֶר וְיָקָם לָךְ
וְעַל־דְּרָכֶיךָ נָגַהּ אוֹר:
29 כִּי־הִשְׁפִּילוּ וַתֹּאמֶר גֵּוָה
וְשַׁח עֵינַיִם יוֹשִׁעַ:
30 יְמַלֵּט אִי־נָקִי
וְנִמְלַט בְּבֹר כַּפֶּיךָ:
  פ

כג וַיַּעַן אִיּוֹב וַיֹּאמַר:
2 גַּם־הַיּוֹם מְרִי שִׂחִי
יָדִי כָּבְדָה עַל־אַנְחָתִי:
3 מִי־יִתֵּן יָדַעְתִּי וְאֶמְצָאֵהוּ
אָבוֹא עַד־תְּכוּנָתוֹ:
4 אֶעֶרְכָה לְפָנָיו מִשְׁפָּט
וּפִי אֲמַלֵּא תוֹכָחוֹת:
5 אֵדְעָה מִלִּים יַעֲנֵנִי
וְאָבִינָה מַה־יֹּאמַר לִי:
6 הַבְּרָב־כֹּחַ יָרִיב עִמָּדִי
לֹא אַךְ־הוּא יָשִׂם בִּי:
7 שָׁם יָשָׁר נוֹכָח עִמּוֹ
וַאֲפַלְּטָה לָנֶצַח מִשֹּׁפְטִי:
8 הֵן קֶדֶם אֶהֱלֹךְ וְאֵינֶנּוּ
וְאָחוֹר וְלֹא־אָבִין לוֹ:
9 שְׂמֹאול בַּעֲשֹׂתוֹ וְלֹא־אָחַז
יַעְטֹף יָמִין וְלֹא אֶרְאֶה:
10 כִּי־יָדַע דֶּרֶךְ עִמָּדִי
בְּחָנַנִי כַּזָּהָב אֵצֵא:
11 בַּאֲשֻׁרוֹ אָחֲזָה רַגְלִי
דַּרְכּוֹ שָׁמַרְתִּי וְלֹא־אָט:
12 מִצְוַת שְׂפָתָיו וְלֹא אָמִישׁ
מֵחֻקִּי צָפַנְתִּי אִמְרֵי־פִיו:
13 וְהוּא בְאֶחָד וּמִי יְשִׁיבֶנּוּ
וְנַפְשׁוֹ אִוְּתָה וַיָּעַשׂ:

14 For He performs *what is* appointed for me,
And many such *things are* with Him.

15 Therefore I am terrified at His presence;
When I consider *this*, I am afraid of Him.

16 For God made my heart weak,
And the Almighty terrifies me;

17 Because I was not cut off from the presence of darkness,
And He did *not* hide deep darkness from my face.

24 "Since times are not hidden from the Almighty,
Why do those who know Him see not His days?

2 "*Some* remove landmarks;
They seize flocks violently and feed *on them;*

3 They drive away the donkey of the fatherless;
They take the widow's ox as a pledge.

4 They push the needy off the road;
All the poor of the land are forced to hide.

5 Indeed, *like* wild donkeys in the desert,
They go out to their work, searching for food.
The wilderness *yields* food for them *and for their* children.

6 They gather their fodder in the field
And glean in the vineyard of the wicked.

7 They spend the night naked, without clothing,
And have no covering in the cold.

8 They are wet with the showers of the mountains,
And huddle around the rock for want of shelter.

9 "*Some* snatch the fatherless from the breast,
And take a pledge from the poor.

10 They cause *the poor* to go naked, without clothing;
And they take away the sheaves from the hungry.

11 They press out oil within their walls,
And tread winepresses, yet suffer thirst.

12 The dying groan in the city,
And the souls of the wounded cry out;
Yet God does not charge *them* with wrong.

13 "There are those who rebel against the light;
They do not know its ways
Nor abide in its paths.

14 The murderer rises with the light;
He kills the poor and needy;
And in the night he is like a thief.

14 כִּי יַשְׁלֵם חֻקִּי
וְכָהֵנָּה רַבּוֹת עִמּוֹ׃

15 עַל־כֵּן מִפָּנָיו אֶבָּהֵל
אֶתְבּוֹנֵן וְאֶפְחַד מִמֶּנּוּ׃

16 וְאֵל הֵרַךְ לִבִּי
וְשַׁדַּי הִבְהִילָנִי׃

17 כִּי־לֹא נִצְמַתִּי מִפְּנֵי־חֹשֶׁךְ
וּמִפָּנַי כִּסָּה־אֹפֶל׃

כד מַדּוּעַ מִשַּׁדַּי לֹא־נִצְפְּנוּ עִתִּים
וְיֹדְעָו לֹא־חָזוּ יָמָיו׃

2 גְּבֻלוֹת יַשִּׂיגוּ
עֵדֶר גָּזְלוּ וַיִּרְעוּ׃

3 חֲמוֹר יְתוֹמִים יִנְהָגוּ
יַחְבְּלוּ שׁוֹר אַלְמָנָה׃

4 יַטּוּ אֶבְיוֹנִים מִדָּרֶךְ
יַחַד חֻבְּאוּ עֲנִיֵּי־אָרֶץ׃

5 הֵן פְּרָאִים ׀ בַּמִּדְבָּר
יָצְאוּ בְּפָעֳלָם מְשַׁחֲרֵי לַטָּרֶף
עֲרָבָה לוֹ לֶחֶם
לַנְּעָרִים׃

6 בַּשָּׂדֶה בְּלִילוֹ יִקְצוֹרוּ
וְכֶרֶם רָשָׁע יְלַקֵּשׁוּ׃

7 עָרוֹם יָלִינוּ מִבְּלִי לְבוּשׁ
וְאֵין כְּסוּת בַּקָּרָה׃

8 מִזֶּרֶם הָרִים יִרְטָבוּ
וּמִבְּלִי מַחְסֶה חִבְּקוּ־צוּר׃

9 יִגְזְלוּ מִשֹּׁד יָתוֹם
וְעַל־עָנִי יַחְבֹּלוּ׃

10 עָרוֹם הִלְּכוּ בְּלִי לְבוּשׁ
וּרְעֵבִים נָשְׂאוּ עֹמֶר׃

11 בֵּין־שׁוּרֹתָם יַצְהִירוּ
יְקָבִים דָּרְכוּ וַיִּצְמָאוּ׃

12 מֵעִיר מְתִים ׀ יִנְאָקוּ
וְנֶפֶשׁ־חֲלָלִים תְּשַׁוֵּעַ
וֶאֱלוֹהַּ
לֹא־יָשִׂים תִּפְלָה׃

13 הֵמָּה ׀ הָיוּ בְּמֹרְדֵי־אוֹר
לֹא־הִכִּירוּ דְרָכָיו וְלֹא יָשְׁבוּ בִּנְתִיבֹתָיו׃

14 לָאוֹר יָקוּם רוֹצֵחַ יִקְטָל־עָנִי וְאֶבְיוֹן
וּבַלַּיְלָה יְהִי כַגַּנָּב׃

כד 1 וְיֹדְעָיו   6 יִקְצוֹרוּ

15 The eye of the adulterer waits for the
        twilight,
    Saying, 'No eye will see me';
    And he disguises *his* face.
16 In the dark they break into houses
    Which they marked for themselves in the
        daytime;
    They do not know the light.
17 For the morning is the same to them as the
        shadow of death;
    If *someone* recognizes *them,*
    They are in the terrors of the shadow of
        death.
18 "They *should be* swift on the face of the
        waters,
    Their portion *should be* cursed in the earth,
    So that no *one would* turn into the way of
        their vineyards.
19 As drought and heat consume the snow
        waters,
    So the grave *consumes those who* have
        sinned.
20 The womb *should* forget him,
    The worm *should* feed sweetly on him;
    He *should* be remembered no more,
    And wickedness *should* be broken like a tree.
21 For he preys on the barren *who* do not bear,
    And does no good for the widow.
22 "But *God* draws the mighty away with His
        power;
    He rises up, but no *man* is sure of life.
23 He gives them security, and they rely *on it;*
    Yet His eyes *are* on their ways.
24 They are exalted for a little while,
    Then they are gone.
    They are brought low;
    They are taken out of the way like all *others;*
    They dry out like the heads of grain.

25 "Now if *it is* not *so,* who will prove me a liar,
    And make my speech worth nothing?"

25 Then Bildad the Shuhite answered and said:

2 "Dominion and fear *belong* to Him;
    He makes peace in His high places.
3 Is there any number to His armies?
    Upon whom does His light not rise?
4 How then can man be righteous before God?
    Or how can he be pure *who is* born of a
        woman?
5 If even the moon does not shine,
    And the stars are not pure in His sight,
6 How much less man, *who is* a maggot,

וְעֵין נֹאֵף ׀ שָׁמְרָה נֶשֶׁף לֵאמֹר 15
לֹא־תְשׁוּרֵנִי עָיִן
וְסֵתֶר פָּנִים
יָשִׂים׃

חָתַר בַּחֹשֶׁךְ בָּתִּים 16
יוֹמָם חִתְּמוּ־לָמוֹ לֹא־יָדְעוּ אוֹר׃

כִּי יַחְדָּו ׀ בֹּקֶר לָמוֹ צַלְמָוֶת 17
כִּי־יַכִּיר בַּלְהוֹת צַלְמָוֶת׃

קַל־הוּא ׀ עַל־פְּנֵי־מַיִם 18
תְּקֻלַּל חֶלְקָתָם בָּאָרֶץ
לֹא־יִפְנֶה
דֶּרֶךְ כְּרָמִים׃

צִיָּה גַם־חֹם יִגְזְלוּ מֵימֵי־שֶׁלֶג 19
שְׁאוֹל חָטָאוּ׃

יִשְׁכָּחֵהוּ רֶחֶם ׀ מְתָקוֹ רִמָּה 20
עוֹד לֹא־יִזָּכֵר
וַתִּשָּׁבֵר כָּעֵץ
עַוְלָה׃

רֹעֶה עֲקָרָה לֹא תֵלֵד 21
וְאַלְמָנָה לֹא יְיֵטִיב׃

וּמָשַׁךְ אַבִּירִים בְּכֹחוֹ 22
יָקוּם וְלֹא־יַאֲמִין בַּחַיִּין׃

יִתֶּן־לוֹ לָבֶטַח וְיִשָּׁעֵן 23
וְעֵינֵיהוּ עַל־דַּרְכֵיהֶם׃

רוֹמּוּ מְּעַט ׀ וְאֵינֶנּוּ 24
וְהֻמְּכוּ כַּכֹּל יִקָּפְצוּן
וּכְרֹאשׁ שִׁבֹּלֶת
יִמָּלוּ׃

וְאִם־לֹא אֵפוֹ מִי יַכְזִיבֵנִי 25
וְיָשֵׂם לְאַל מִלָּתִי׃ ס

כה וַיַּעַן בִּלְדַּד הַשֻּׁחִי וַיֹּאמַר׃
הַמְשֵׁל וָפַחַד עִמּוֹ 2
עֹשֶׂה שָׁלוֹם בִּמְרוֹמָיו׃
הֲיֵשׁ מִסְפָּר לִגְדוּדָיו 3
וְעַל־מִי לֹא־יָקוּם אוֹרֵהוּ׃
וּמַה־יִּצְדַּק אֱנוֹשׁ עִם־אֵל 4
וּמַה־יִּזְכֶּה יְלוּד אִשָּׁה׃
הֵן עַד־יָרֵחַ וְלֹא יַאֲהִיל 5
וְכוֹכָבִים לֹא־זַכּוּ בְעֵינָיו׃
אַף כִּי־אֱנוֹשׁ רִמָּה 6
וּבֶן־אָדָם תּוֹלֵעָה׃

And a son of man, *who is* a worm?"

26 But Job answered and said:

2 "How have you helped *him who is* without power?
How have you saved the arm *that has* no strength?

3 How have you counseled *one who has* no wisdom?
And *how* have you declared sound advice to many?

4 To whom have you uttered words?
And whose spirit came from you?

5 "The dead tremble,
Those under the waters and those inhabiting them.

6 Sheol *is* naked before Him,
And Destruction has no covering.

7 He stretches out the north over empty space;
He hangs the earth on nothing.

8 He binds up the water in His thick clouds,
Yet the clouds are not broken under it.

9 He covers the face of *His* throne,
And spreads His cloud over it.

10 He drew a circular horizon on the face of the waters,
At the boundary of light and darkness.

11 The pillars of heaven tremble,
And are astonished at His rebuke.

12 He stirs up the sea with His power,
And by His understanding He breaks up the storm.

13 By His Spirit He adorned the heavens;
His hand pierced the fleeing serpent.

14 Indeed these *are* the mere edges of His ways,
And how small a whisper we hear of Him!
But the thunder of His power who can understand?"

27 Moreover Job continued his discourse, and said:

2 "*As* God lives, *who* has taken away my justice,
And the Almighty, *who* has made my soul bitter,

3 As long as my breath *is* in me,
And the breath of God in my nostrils,

4 My lips will not speak wickedness,
Nor my tongue utter deceit.

5 Far be it from me
That I should say you are right;
Till I die I will not put away my integrity from me.

כו 1 וַיַּ֖עַן אִיּ֣וֹב וַיֹּאמַֽר׃

2 מֶה־עָזַ֥רְתָּ לְלֹא־כֹ֑חַ
הוֹשַׁ֝֗עְתָּ זְר֣וֹעַ לֹא־עֹֽז׃

3 מַה־יָּעַ֭צְתָּ לְלֹ֣א חָכְמָ֑ה
וְ֝תוּשִׁיָּ֗ה לָרֹ֥ב הוֹדָֽעְתָּ׃

4 אֶת־מִ֭י הִגַּ֣דְתָּ מִלִּ֑ין
וְנִשְׁמַת־מִ֝י יָצְאָ֥ה מִמֶּֽךָּ׃

5 הָרְפָאִ֥ים יְחוֹלָ֑לוּ
מִתַּ֥חַת מַ֝֗יִם וְשֹׁכְנֵיהֶֽם׃

6 עָר֣וֹם שְׁא֣וֹל נֶגְדּ֑וֹ
וְאֵ֥ין כְּ֝ס֗וּת לָֽאֲבַדּֽוֹן׃

7 נֹטֶ֣ה צָפ֣וֹן עַל־תֹּ֑הוּ
תֹּ֥לֶה אֶ֝֗רֶץ עַל־בְּלִי־מָֽה׃

8 צֹרֵֽר־מַ֥יִם בְּעָבָ֑יו
וְלֹא־נִבְקַ֖ע עָנָ֣ן תַּחְתָּֽם׃

9 מְאַחֵ֥ז פְּנֵי־כִסֵּ֑ה
פַּרְשֵׁ֖ז עָלָ֣יו עֲנָנֽוֹ׃

10 חֹֽק־חָ֭ג עַל־פְּנֵי־מָ֑יִם
עַד־תַּכְלִ֖ית א֣וֹר עִם־חֹֽשֶׁךְ׃

11 עַמּוּדֵ֣י שָׁמַ֣יִם יְרוֹפָ֑פוּ
וְ֝יִתְמְה֗וּ מִגַּעֲרָתֽוֹ׃

12 בְּ֭כֹחוֹ רָגַ֣ע הַיָּ֑ם
וּבִתְובֻנָת֗וֹ° מָ֣חַץ רָֽהַב׃

13 בְּ֭רוּחוֹ שָׁמַ֣יִם שִׁפְרָ֑ה
חֹֽלֲלָ֥ה יָ֝ד֗וֹ נָחָ֥שׁ בָּרִֽיחַ׃

14 הֶן־אֵ֤לֶּה ׀ קְצ֬וֹת דְּרָכָ֗ו°
וּמַה־שֵּׁ֣מֶץ דָּ֭בָר נִשְׁמַע־בּ֑וֹ
וְרַ֥עַם גְּבוּרֹתָ֗ו° מִ֣י יִתְבּוֹנָֽן׃ ס

כז 1 וַיֹּ֣סֶף אִ֭יּוֹב שְׂאֵ֥ת מְשָׁל֗וֹ וַיֹּאמַֽר׃

2 חַי־אֵ֭ל הֵסִ֣יר מִשְׁפָּטִ֑י
וְ֝שַׁדַּ֗י הֵמַ֥ר נַפְשִֽׁי׃

3 כִּֽי־כָל־ע֣וֹד נִשְׁמָתִ֣י בִ֑י
וְר֖וּחַ אֱל֣וֹהַּ בְּאַפִּֽי׃

4 אִם־תְּדַבֵּ֥רְנָה שְׂפָתַ֣י עַוְלָ֑ה
וּ֝לְשׁוֹנִ֗י אִם־יֶהְגֶּ֥ה רְמִיָּֽה׃

5 חָלִ֣ילָה לִּי֮ אִם־אַצְדִּ֪יק אֶ֫תְכֶ֥ם
עַד־אֶגְוָ֑ע
לֹא־אָסִ֖יר תֻּמָּתִ֣י מִמֶּֽנִּי׃

6	My righteousness I hold fast, and will not let it go; My heart shall not reproach *me* as long as I live.
7	"May my enemy be like the wicked, And he who rises up against me like the unrighteous.
8	For what is the hope of the hypocrite, Though he may gain *much*, If God takes away his life?
9	Will God hear his cry When trouble comes upon him?
10	Will he delight himself in the Almighty? Will he always call on God?
11	"I will teach you about the hand of God; What *is* with the Almighty I will not conceal.
12	Surely all of you have seen *it*; Why then do you behave with complete nonsense?
13	"This is the portion of a wicked man with God, And the heritage of oppressors, received from the Almighty:
14	If his children are multiplied, *it is* for the sword; And his offspring shall not be satisfied with bread.
15	Those who survive him shall be buried in death, And their widows shall not weep,
16	Though he heaps up silver like dust, And piles up clothing like clay—
17	He may pile *it* up, but the just will wear *it*, And the innocent will divide the silver.
18	He builds his house like a moth, Like a booth *which* a watchman makes.
19	The rich man will lie down, But not be gathered *up*; He opens his eyes, And he *is* no more.
20	Terrors overtake him like a flood; A tempest steals him away in the night.
21	The east wind carries him away, and he is gone; It sweeps him out of his place.
22	It hurls against him and does not spare; He flees desperately from its power.
23	*Men* shall clap their hands at him, And shall hiss him out of his place.
28	"Surely there is a mine for silver, And a place *where* gold is refined.

6 בְּצִדְקָתִי הֶחֱזַקְתִּי וְלֹא אַרְפֶּהָ
לֹא־יֶחֱרַף לְבָבִי מִיָּמָי:
7 יְהִי כְרָשָׁע אֹיְבִי
וּמִתְקוֹמְמִי כְעַוָּל:
8 כִּי מַה־תִּקְוַת חָנֵף כִּי יִבְצָע
כִּי יֵשֶׁל אֱלוֹהַּ נַפְשׁוֹ:
9 הַצַעֲקָתוֹ יִשְׁמַע ׀ אֵל
כִּי־תָבוֹא עָלָיו צָרָה:
10 אִם־עַל־שַׁדַּי יִתְעַנָּג
יִקְרָא אֱלוֹהַּ בְּכָל־עֵת:
11 אוֹרֶה אֶתְכֶם בְּיַד־אֵל
אֲשֶׁר עִם־שַׁדַּי לֹא אֲכַחֵד:
12 הֵן־אַתֶּם כֻּלְּכֶם חֲזִיתֶם
וְלָמָּה־זֶּה הֶבֶל תֶּהְבָּלוּ:
13 זֶה ׀ חֵלֶק־אָדָם רָשָׁע ׀ עִם־אֵל
וְנַחֲלַת עָרִיצִים מִשַּׁדַּי יִקָּחוּ:
14 אִם־יִרְבּוּ בָנָיו לְמוֹ־חָרֶב
וְצֶאֱצָאָיו לֹא יִשְׂבְּעוּ־לָחֶם:
15 שְׂרִידוֹ בַּמָּוֶת יִקָּבֵרוּ
וְאַלְמְנֹתָיו לֹא תִבְכֶּינָה:
16 אִם־יִצְבֹּר כֶּעָפָר כָּסֶף
וְכַחֹמֶר יָכִין מַלְבּוּשׁ:
17 יָכִין וְצַדִּיק יִלְבָּשׁ
וְכֶסֶף נָקִי יַחֲלֹק:
18 בָּנָה כָעָשׁ בֵּיתוֹ
וּכְסֻכָּה עָשָׂה נֹצֵר:
19 עָשִׁיר יִשְׁכַּב וְלֹא יֵאָסֵף
עֵינָיו פָּקַח וְאֵינֶנּוּ:
20 תַּשִּׂיגֵהוּ כַמַּיִם בַּלָּהוֹת
לַיְלָה גְּנָבַתּוּ סוּפָה:
21 יִשָּׂאֵהוּ קָדִים וְיֵלַךְ
וִישָׂעֲרֵהוּ מִמְּקֹמוֹ:
22 וְיַשְׁלֵךְ עָלָיו וְלֹא יַחְמֹל
מִיָּדוֹ בָּרוֹחַ יִבְרָח:
23 יִשְׂפֹּק עָלֵימוֹ כַפֵּימוֹ
וְיִשְׁרֹק עָלָיו מִמְּקֹמוֹ:

כח כִּי יֵשׁ לַכֶּסֶף מוֹצָא
וּמָקוֹם לַזָּהָב יָזֹקּוּ:

כו 15 שְׂרִידָיו

2	Iron is taken from the earth, And copper *is* smelted *from* ore.
3	*Man* puts an end to darkness, And searches every recess For ore in the darkness and the shadow of death.
4	He breaks open a shaft away from people; *In places* forgotten by feet They hang far away from men; They swing to and fro.
5	*As for* the earth, from it comes bread, But underneath it is turned up as by fire;
6	Its stones *are* the source of sapphires, And it contains gold dust.
7	*That* path no bird knows, Nor has the falcon's eye seen it.
8	The proud lions have not trodden it, Nor has the fierce lion passed over it.
9	He puts his hand on the flint; He overturns the mountains at the roots.
10	He cuts out channels in the rocks, And his eye sees every precious thing.
11	He dams up the streams from trickling; *What is* hidden he brings forth to light.
12	"But where can wisdom be found? And where *is* the place of understanding?
13	Man does not know its value, Nor is it found in the land of the living.
14	The deep says, '*It is* not in me'; And the sea says, '*It is* not with me.'
15	It cannot be purchased for gold, Nor can silver be weighed *for* its price.
16	It cannot be valued in the gold of Ophir, In precious onyx or sapphire.
17	Neither gold nor crystal can equal it, Nor can it be exchanged for jewelry of fine gold.
18	No mention shall be made of coral or quartz, For the price of wisdom *is* above rubies.
19	The topaz of Ethiopia cannot equal it, Nor can it be valued in pure gold.
20	"From where then does wisdom come? And where *is* the place of understanding?
21	It is hidden from the eyes of all living, And concealed from the birds of the air.
22	Destruction and Death say, 'We have heard a report about it with our ears.'
23	God understands its way, And He knows its place.
24	For He looks to the ends of the earth, *And* sees under the whole heavens,

2 בַּרְזֶל מֵעָפָר יֻקָּח
וְאֶבֶן יָצוּק נְחוּשָׁה:
3 קֵץ ׀ שָׂם לַחֹשֶׁךְ וּלְכָל־תַּכְלִית הוּא חוֹקֵר
אֶבֶן אֹפֶל וְצַלְמָוֶת:
4 פָּרַץ נַחַל ׀ מֵעִם־גָּר הַנִּשְׁכָּחִים מִנִּי־רֶגֶל
דַּלּוּ מֵאֱנוֹשׁ נָעוּ:
5 אֶרֶץ מִמֶּנָּה יֵצֵא־לָחֶם
וְתַחְתֶּיהָ נֶהְפַּךְ כְּמוֹ־אֵשׁ:
6 מְקוֹם־סַפִּיר אֲבָנֶיהָ וְעַפְרֹת זָהָב לוֹ:
7 נָתִיב לֹא־יְדָעוֹ עָיִט וְלֹא שְׁזָפַתּוּ עֵין אַיָּה:
8 לֹא־הִדְרִיכֻהוּ בְנֵי־שָׁחַץ
לֹא־עָדָה עָלָיו שָׁחַל:
9 בַּחַלָּמִישׁ שָׁלַח יָדוֹ
הָפַךְ מִשֹּׁרֶשׁ הָרִים:
10 בַּצּוּרוֹת יְאֹרִים בִּקֵּעַ וְכָל־יְקָר רָאֲתָה עֵינוֹ:
11 מִבְּכִי נְהָרוֹת חִבֵּשׁ וְתַעֲלֻמָהּ יֹצִא אוֹר: פ
12 וְהַחָכְמָה מֵאַיִן תִּמָּצֵא
וְאֵי זֶה מְקוֹם בִּינָה:
13 לֹא־יָדַע אֱנוֹשׁ עֶרְכָּהּ
וְלֹא תִמָּצֵא בְּאֶרֶץ הַחַיִּים:
14 תְּהוֹם אָמַר לֹא בִי־הִיא
וְיָם אָמַר אֵין עִמָּדִי:
15 לֹא־יֻתַּן סְגוֹר תַּחְתֶּיהָ
וְלֹא יִשָּׁקֵל כֶּסֶף מְחִירָהּ:
16 לֹא־תְסֻלֶּה בְּכֶתֶם אוֹפִיר
בְּשֹׁהַם יָקָר וְסַפִּיר:
17 לֹא־יַעַרְכֶנָּה זָהָב וּזְכוֹכִית
וּתְמוּרָתָהּ כְּלִי־פָז:
18 רָאמוֹת וְגָבִישׁ לֹא יִזָּכֵר
וּמֶשֶׁךְ חָכְמָה מִפְּנִינִים:
19 לֹא־יַעַרְכֶנָּה פִּטְדַת־כּוּשׁ
בְּכֶתֶם טָהוֹר לֹא תְסֻלֶּה: פ
20 וְהַחָכְמָה מֵאַיִן תָּבוֹא
וְאֵי זֶה מְקוֹם בִּינָה:
21 וְנֶעֶלְמָה מֵעֵינֵי כָל־חָי
וּמֵעוֹף הַשָּׁמַיִם נִסְתָּרָה:
22 אֲבַדּוֹן וָמָוֶת אָמְרוּ
בְּאָזְנֵינוּ שָׁמַעְנוּ שִׁמְעָהּ:
23 אֱלֹהִים הֵבִין דַּרְכָּהּ
וְהוּא יָדַע אֶת־מְקוֹמָהּ:
24 כִּי־הוּא לִקְצוֹת־הָאָרֶץ יַבִּיט
תַּחַת כָּל־הַשָּׁמַיִם יִרְאֶה:

25 To establish a weight for the wind,
    And apportion the waters by measure.
26 When He made a law for the rain,
    And a path for the thunderbolt,
27 Then He saw *wisdom* and declared it;
    He prepared it, indeed, He searched it out.
28 And to man He said,
    'Behold, the fear of the Lord, that *is* wisdom,
    And to depart from evil *is* understanding.'"

29

Job further continued his discourse, and said:

2 "Oh, that I were as *in* months past,
    As *in* the days *when* God watched over me;
3 When His lamp shone upon my head,
    And when by His light I walked *through*
    darkness;
4 Just as I was in the days of my prime,
    When the friendly counsel of God *was* over
    my tent;
5 When the Almighty *was* yet with me,
    When my children *were* around me;
6 When my steps were bathed with cream,
    And the rock poured out rivers of oil for me!

7 "When I went out to the gate by the city,
    When I took my seat in the open square,
8 The young men saw me and hid,
    And the aged arose *and* stood;
9 The princes refrained from talking,
    And put *their* hand on their mouth;
10 The voice of nobles was hushed,
    And their tongue stuck to the roof of their
    mouth.
11 When the ear heard, then it blessed me,
    And when the eye saw, then it approved me;
12 Because I delivered the poor who cried out,
    The fatherless and *the one who* had no
    helper.
13 The blessing of a perishing *man* came upon
    me,
    And I caused the widow's heart to sing for
    joy.
14 I put on righteousness, and it clothed me;
    My justice *was* like a robe and a turban.
15 I *was* eyes to the blind,
    And I *was* feet to the lame.
16 I *was* a father to the poor,
    And I searched out the case *that* I did not
    know.
17 I broke the fangs of the wicked,
    And plucked the victim from his teeth.
18 "Then I said, 'I shall die in my nest,
    And multiply *my* days as the sand.

25 לַעֲשׂוֹת לָר֥וּחַ מִשְׁקָ֑ל
    וּמַ֗יִם תִּכֵּ֥ן בְּמִדָּֽה׃
26 בַּעֲשֹׂת֣וֹ לַמָּטָ֣ר חֹ֑ק
    וְדֶ֗רֶךְ לַחֲזִ֥יז קֹלֽוֹת׃
27 אָ֣ז רָ֭אָהּ וַֽיְסַפְּרָ֑הּ
    הֱ֝כִינָ֗הּ וְגַם־חֲקָרָֽהּ׃
28 וַיֹּ֤אמֶר ׀ לָֽאָדָ֗ם הֵ֤ן יִרְאַ֬ת אֲדֹנָ֣י הִ֣יא חׇכְמָ֑ה
    וְס֖וּר מֵרָ֣ע בִּינָֽה׃ ס

כט וַיֹּ֣סֶף אִ֭יּוֹב שְׂאֵ֥ת מְשָׁל֗וֹ וַיֹּאמַֽר׃
2 מִֽי־יִתְּנֵ֥נִי כְיַרְחֵי־קֶ֑דֶם
    כִּ֝ימֵ֗י אֱל֣וֹהַּ יִשְׁמְרֵֽנִי׃
3 בְּהִלּ֣וֹ נֵ֭רוֹ עֲלֵ֣י רֹאשִׁ֑י
    לְ֝אוֹר֗וֹ אֵ֣לֶךְ חֹֽשֶׁךְ׃
4 כַּאֲשֶׁ֣ר הָ֭יִיתִי בִּימֵ֣י חׇרְפִּ֑י
    בְּס֥וֹד אֱ֝ל֗וֹהַּ עֲלֵ֣י אׇהֳלִֽי׃
5 בְּע֣וֹד שַׁ֭דַּי עִמָּדִ֑י
    סְבִ֖יבוֹתַ֣י נְעָרָֽי׃
6 בִּרְחֹ֣ץ הֲלִיכַ֣י בְּחֵמָ֑ה
    וְצ֥וּר יָצ֥וּק עִמָּדִ֗י פַּלְגֵי־שָֽׁמֶן׃
7 בְּצֵ֣אתִי שַׁ֣עַר עֲלֵי־קָ֑רֶת
    בָּ֝רְח֗וֹב אָכִ֥ין מוֹשָׁבִֽי׃
8 רָא֣וּנִי נְעָרִ֣ים וְנֶחְבָּ֑אוּ
    וִֽ֝ישִׁישִׁ֗ים קָ֣מוּ עָמָֽדוּ׃
9 שָׂ֭רִים עָצְר֣וּ בְמִלִּ֑ים
    וְ֝כַ֗ף יָשִׂ֥ימוּ לְפִיהֶֽם׃
10 קוֹל־נְגִידִ֥ים נֶחְבָּ֑אוּ
    וּלְשׁוֹנָ֗ם לְחִכָּ֥ם דָּבֵֽקָה׃
11 כִּ֤י אֹ֣זֶן שָׁ֭מְעָה וַֽתְּאַשְּׁרֵ֑נִי
    וְעַ֥יִן רָ֝אֲתָ֗ה וַתְּעִידֵֽנִי׃
12 כִּֽי־אֲ֭מַלֵּט עָנִ֣י מְשַׁוֵּ֑עַ
    וְ֝יָת֗וֹם וְֽלֹא־עֹזֵ֥ר לֽוֹ׃
13 בִּרְכַּ֣ת אֹ֭בֵד עָלַ֣י תָּבֹ֑א
    וְלֵ֖ב אַלְמָנָ֣ה אַרְנִֽן׃
14 צֶ֣דֶק לָ֭בַשְׁתִּי וַיִּלְבָּשֵׁ֑נִי
    כִּמְעִ֥יל וְ֝צָנִ֗יף מִשְׁפָּטִֽי׃
15 עֵינַ֣יִם הָ֭יִיתִי לַֽעִוֵּ֑ר
    וְרַגְלַ֖יִם לַפִּסֵּ֣חַ אָֽנִי׃
16 אָ֣ב אָ֭נֹכִי לָֽאֶבְיוֹנִ֑ים
    וְרִ֖ב לֹא־יָדַ֣עְתִּי אֶחְקְרֵֽהוּ׃
17 וָ֭אֲשַׁבְּרָה מְתַלְּע֣וֹת עַוָּ֑ל
    וּ֝מִשִּׁנָּ֗יו אַשְׁלִ֥יךְ טָֽרֶף׃
18 וָ֭אֹמַר עִם־קִנִּ֣י אֶגְוָ֑ע
    וְ֝כַח֗וֹל אַרְבֶּ֥ה יָמִֽים׃

19 My root *is* spread out to the waters,
And the dew lies all night on my branch.
20 My glory *is* fresh within me,
And my bow is renewed in my hand.'

שָׁרְשִׁי פָתוּחַ אֱלֵי־מָיִם 19
וְטַל יָלִין בִּקְצִירִי:
כְּבוֹדִי חָדָשׁ עִמָּדִי 20
וְקַשְׁתִּי בְּיָדִי תַחֲלִיף:

21 "*Men* listened to me and waited,
And kept silence for my counsel.
22 After my words they did not speak again,
And my speech settled on them *as* dew.
23 They waited for me *as* for the rain,
And they opened their mouth wide *as* for the
spring rain.
24 *If* I mocked at them, they did not believe *it,*
And the light of my countenance they did
not cast down.
25 I chose the way for them, and sat as chief;
So I dwelt as a king in the army,
As one *who* comforts mourners.

לִי־שָׁמְעוּ וְיִחֵלּוּ 21
וְיִדְּמוּ לְמוֹ עֲצָתִי:
אַחֲרֵי דְבָרִי לֹא יִשְׁנוּ 22
וְעָלֵימוֹ תִּטֹּף מִלָּתִי:
וְיִחֲלוּ כַמָּטָר לִי 23
וּפִיהֶם פָּעֲרוּ לְמַלְקוֹשׁ:
אֶשְׂחַק אֲלֵהֶם לֹא יַאֲמִינוּ 24
וְאוֹר פָּנַי לֹא יַפִּילוּן:
אֶבְחַר דַּרְכָּם וְאֵשֵׁב רֹאשׁ 25
וְאֶשְׁכּוֹן כְּמֶלֶךְ בַּגְּדוּד
כַּאֲשֶׁר אֲבֵלִים יְנַחֵם:

30 "But now they mock at me, *men* younger
than I,
Whose fathers I disdained to put with the
dogs of my flock.
2 Indeed, what *profit* is the strength of their
hands to me?
Their vigor has perished.
3 *They are* gaunt from want and famine,
Fleeing late to the wilderness, desolate and
waste,
4 Who pluck mallow by the bushes,
And broom tree roots *for* their food.
5 They were driven out from among *men,*
They shouted at them as *at* a thief.
6 *They had* to live in the clefts of the valleys,
In caves of the earth and the rocks.
7 Among the bushes they brayed,
Under the nettles they nestled.
8 *They were* sons of fools,
Yes, sons of vile men;
They were scourged from the land.

ל וְעַתָּה שָׂחֲקוּ עָלַי צְעִירִים מִמֶּנִּי לְיָמִים
אֲשֶׁר־מָאַסְתִּי אֲבוֹתָם
לָשִׁית עִם־כַּלְבֵי צֹאנִי:
גַּם־כֹּחַ יְדֵיהֶם לָמָּה לִּי 2
עָלֵימוֹ אָבַד כָּלַח:
בְּחֶסֶר וּבְכָפָן גַּלְמוּד 3
הַעֹרְקִים צִיָּה אֶמֶשׁ שׁוֹאָה וּמְשֹׁאָה:
הַקֹּטְפִים מַלּוּחַ עֲלֵי־שִׂיחַ 4
וְשֹׁרֶשׁ רְתָמִים לַחְמָם:
מִן־גֵּו יְגֹרָשׁוּ 5
יָרִיעוּ עָלֵימוֹ כַּגַּנָּב:
בַּעֲרוּץ נְחָלִים לִשְׁכֹּן 6
חֹרֵי עָפָר וְכֵפִים:
בֵּין־שִׂיחִים יִנְהָקוּ 7
תַּחַת חָרוּל יְסֻפָּחוּ:
בְּנֵי־נָבָל גַּם־בְּנֵי בְלִי־שֵׁם 8
נִכְּאוּ מִן־הָאָרֶץ:

9 "And now I am their taunting song;
Yes, I am their byword.
10 They abhor me, they keep far from me;
They do not hesitate to spit in my face.
11 Because He has loosed my bowstring and
afflicted me,
They have cast off restraint before me.
12 At *my* right *hand* the rabble arises;
They push away my feet,
And they raise against me their ways of
destruction.
13 They break up my path,
They promote my calamity;
They have no helper.

וְעַתָּה נְגִינָתָם הָיִיתִי 9
וָאֱהִי לָהֶם לְמִלָּה:
תִּעֲבוּנִי רָחֲקוּ מֶנִּי 10
וּמִפָּנַי לֹא־חָשְׂכוּ רֹק:
כִּי־יִתְרוֹ פִּתַּח וַיְעַנֵּנִי 11
וְרֶסֶן מִפָּנַי שִׁלֵּחוּ:
עַל־יָמִין פִּרְחַח יָקוּמוּ 12
רַגְלַי שִׁלֵּחוּ וַיָּסֹלּוּ עָלַי אָרְחוֹת אֵידָם:
נָתְסוּ נְתִיבָתִי 13
לְהַוָּתִי יֹעִילוּ לֹא עֹזֵר לָמוֹ:

ל 11 יִתְרִי

14 They come as broad breakers;
   Under the ruinous storm they roll along.
15 Terrors are turned upon me;
   They pursue my honor as the wind,
   And my prosperity has passed like a cloud.

16 "And now my soul is poured out because of
   my *plight;*
   The days of affliction take hold of me.
17 My bones are pierced in me at night,
   And my gnawing pains take no rest.
18 By great force my garment is disfigured;
   It binds me about as the collar of my coat.
19 He has cast me into the mire,
   And I have become like dust and ashes.

20 "I cry out to You, but You do not answer me;
   I stand up, and You regard me.
21 *But* You have become cruel to me;
   With the strength of Your hand You oppose
   me.
22 You lift me up to the wind and cause me to
   ride *on it;*
   You spoil my success.
23 For I know *that* You will bring me *to* death,
   And *to* the house appointed for all living.

24 "Surely He would not stretch out *His* hand
   against a heap of ruins,
   If they cry out when He destroys *it.*
25 Have I not wept for him who was in trouble?
   Has *not* my soul grieved for the poor?
26 But when I looked for good, evil came *to me;*
   And when I waited for light, then came
   darkness.
27 My heart is in turmoil and cannot rest;
   Days of affliction confront me.
28 I go about mourning, but not in the sun;
   I stand up in the assembly *and* cry out for
   help.
29 I am a brother of jackals,
   And a companion of ostriches.
30 My skin grows black and falls from me;
   My bones burn with fever.
31 My harp is *turned* to mourning,
   And my flute to the voice of those who
   weep.

31 "I have made a covenant with my eyes;
   Why then should I look upon a young
   woman?
2 For what *is* the allotment of God from
   above,
   And the inheritance of the Almighty from
   on high?

14 כְּפֶרֶץ רָחָב יֶאֱתָיוּ
תַּחַת שֹׁאָה הִתְגַּלְגָּלוּ׃
15 הָהְפַּךְ עָלַי
בַּלָּהוֹת
תִּרְדֹּף כָּרוּחַ נְדִבָתִי
וּכְעָב עָבְרָה יְשֻׁעָתִי׃
16 וְעַתָּה עָלַי תִּשְׁתַּפֵּךְ נַפְשִׁי
יֹאחֲזוּנִי יְמֵי־עֹנִי׃
17 לַיְלָה עֲצָמַי נִקַּר מֵעָלָי
וְעֹרְקַי לֹא יִשְׁכָּבוּן׃
18 בְּרָב־כֹּחַ יִתְחַפֵּשׂ לְבוּשִׁי
כְּפִי כֻתָּנְתִּי יַאַזְרֵנִי׃
19 הֹרָנִי לַחֹמֶר
וָאֶתְמַשֵּׁל כֶּעָפָר וָאֵפֶר׃
20 אֲשַׁוַּע אֵלֶיךָ וְלֹא תַעֲנֵנִי
עָמַדְתִּי וַתִּתְבֹּנֶן בִּי׃
21 תֵּהָפֵךְ לְאַכְזָר לִי
בְּעֹצֶם יָדְךָ תִשְׂטְמֵנִי׃
22 תִּשָּׂאֵנִי אֶל־רוּחַ תַּרְכִּיבֵנִי
וּתְמֹגְגֵנִי תְּשִׁיָּהׁ׃פ
23 כִּי־יָדַעְתִּי מָוֶת תְּשִׁיבֵנִי
וּבֵית מוֹעֵד לְכָל־חָי׃
24 אַךְ לֹא־בְעִי יִשְׁלַח־יָד
אִם־בְּפִידוֹ לָהֶן שׁוּעַ׃
25 אִם־לֹא בָכִיתִי לִקְשֵׁה־יוֹם
עָגְמָה נַפְשִׁי לָאֶבְיוֹן׃
26 כִּי טוֹב קִוִּיתִי וַיָּבֹא רָע
וַאֲיַחֲלָה לְאוֹר וַיָּבֹא אֹפֶל׃
27 מֵעַי רֻתְּחוּ וְלֹא־דָמּוּ
קִדְּמֻנִי יְמֵי־עֹנִי׃
28 קֹדֵר הִלַּכְתִּי בְּלֹא חַמָּה
קַמְתִּי בַקָּהָל אֲשַׁוֵּעַ׃
29 אָח הָיִיתִי לְתַנִּים
וְרֵעַ לִבְנוֹת יַעֲנָה׃
30 עוֹרִי שָׁחַר מֵעָלָי
וְעַצְמִי־חָרָה מִנִּי־חֹרֶב׃
31 וַיְהִי לְאֵבֶל כִּנֹּרִי
וְעֻגָבִי לְקוֹל בֹּכִים׃

לא בְּרִית כָּרַתִּי לְעֵינָי
וּמָה אֶתְבּוֹנֵן עַל־בְּתוּלָה׃
2 וּמֶה חֵלֶק אֱלוֹהַּ מִמָּעַל
וְנַחֲלַת שַׁדַּי מִמְּרֹמִים׃

ל 22 תּוּשִׁיָּה

3   *Is* it not destruction for the wicked,
    And disaster for the workers of iniquity?

4   Does He not see my ways,
    And count all my steps?

5   "If I have walked with falsehood,
    Or if my foot has hastened to deceit,

6   Let me be weighed on honest scales,
    That God may know my integrity.

7   If my step has turned from the way,
    Or my heart walked after my eyes,
    Or if any spot adheres to my hands,

8   *Then* let me sow, and another eat;
    Yes, let my harvest be rooted out.

9   "If my heart has been enticed by a woman,
    Or *if* I have lurked at my neighbor's door,

10   *Then* let my wife grind for another,
    And let others bow down over her.

11   For that *would be* wickedness;
    Yes, it *would be* iniquity *deserving of* judgment.

12   For that *would be* a fire *that* consumes to destruction,
    And would root out all my increase.

13   "If I have despised the cause of my male or female servant
    When they complained against me,

14   What then shall I do when God rises up?
    When He punishes, how shall I answer Him?

15   Did not He who made me in the womb make them?
    Did not the same One fashion us in the womb?

16   "If I have kept the poor from *their* desire,
    Or caused the eyes of the widow to fail,

17   Or eaten my morsel by myself,
    So that the fatherless could not eat of it

18   (But from my youth I reared him as a father,
    And from my mother's womb I guided *the widow*);

19   If I have seen anyone perish for lack of clothing,
    Or any poor *man* without covering;

20   If his heart has not blessed me,
    And *if* he was *not* warmed with the fleece of my sheep;

21   If I have raised my hand against the fatherless,
    When I saw I had help in the gate;

22   *Then* let my arm fall from my shoulder,
    Let my arm be torn from the socket.

23   For destruction *from* God *is* a terror to me,

הֲלֹא־אֵיד לְעַוָּל ‏3
וְנֵכֶר לְפֹעֲלֵי אָוֶן:

הֲלֹא־הוּא יִרְאֶה דְרָכָי ‏4
וְכָל־צְעָדַי יִסְפּוֹר:

אִם־הָלַכְתִּי עִם־שָׁוְא ‏5
וַתַּחַשׁ עַל־מִרְמָה רַגְלִי:

יִשְׁקְלֵנִי בְמֹאזְנֵי־צֶדֶק ‏6
וְיֵדַע אֱלוֹהַּ תֻּמָּתִי:

אִם תִּטֶּה אַשֻּׁרִי מִנִּי הַדֶּרֶךְ ‏7
וְאַחַר עֵינַי הָלַךְ לִבִּי
וּבְכַפַּי דָּבַק מֻאוּם: פ

אֶזְרְעָה וְאַחֵר יֹאכֵל ‏8
וְצֶאֱצָאַי יְשֹׁרָשׁוּ:

אִם־נִפְתָּה לִבִּי עַל־אִשָּׁה ‏9
וְעַל־פֶּתַח רֵעִי אָרָבְתִּי:

תִּטְחַן לְאַחֵר אִשְׁתִּי ‏10
וְעָלֶיהָ יִכְרְעוּן אֲחֵרִין:

כִּי־הוּא [Pּ] זִמָּה ‏11
וְהוּא [Pּ] עָוֹן פְּלִילִים:

כִּי אֵשׁ הִיא עַד־אֲבַדּוֹן תֹּאכֵל ‏12
וּבְכָל־תְּבוּאָתִי תְשָׁרֵשׁ:

אִם־אֶמְאַס מִשְׁפַּט עַבְדִּי וַאֲמָתִי ‏13
בְּרִבָם עִמָּדִי:

וּמָה אֶעֱשֶׂה כִּי־יָקוּם אֵל ‏14
וְכִי־יִפְקֹד מָה אֲשִׁיבֶנּוּ:

הֲלֹא־בַבֶּטֶן עֹשֵׂנִי עָשָׂהוּ ‏15
וַיְכֻנֶנּוּ בָּרֶחֶם אֶחָד:

אִם־אֶמְנַע מֵחֵפֶץ דַּלִּים ‏16
וְעֵינֵי אַלְמָנָה אֲכַלֶּה:

וְאֹכַל פִּתִּי לְבַדִּי ‏17
וְלֹא־אָכַל יָתוֹם מִמֶּנָּה:

כִּי מִנְּעוּרַי גְּדֵלַנִי כְאָב ‏18
וּמִבֶּטֶן אִמִּי אַנְחֶנָּה:

אִם־אֶרְאֶה אוֹבֵד מִבְּלִי לְבוּשׁ ‏19
וְאֵין כְּסוּת לָאֶבְיוֹן:

אִם־לֹא בֵרֲכוּנִי חֲלָצָו [Pּ] ‏20
וּמִגֵּז כְּבָשַׂי יִתְחַמָּם:

אִם־הֲנִיפוֹתִי עַל־יָתוֹם יָדִי ‏21
כִּי־אֶרְאֶה בַשַּׁעַר עֶזְרָתִי:

כְּתֵפִי מִשִּׁכְמָה תִפּוֹל ‏22
וְאֶזְרֹעִי מִקָּנָה תִשָּׁבֵר:

כִּי פַחַד אֵלַי אֵיד אֵל ‏23

And because of His magnificence I cannot
endure.

24 "If I have made gold my hope,
Or said to fine gold, 'You are my
confidence';
25 If I have rejoiced because my wealth was
great,
And because my hand had gained much;
26 If I have observed the sun when it shines,
Or the moon moving in brightness,
27 So that my heart has been secretly enticed,
And my mouth has kissed my hand;
28 This also would be an iniquity deserving of
judgment,
For I would have denied God who is above.

29 "If I have rejoiced at the destruction of him
who hated me,
Or lifted myself up when evil found him
30 (Indeed I have not allowed my mouth to sin
By asking for a curse on his soul);
31 If the men of my tent have not said,
'Who is there that has not been satisfied with
his meat?'
32 (But no sojourner had to lodge in the street,
For I have opened my doors to the traveler);
33 If I have covered my transgressions as
Adam,
By hiding my iniquity in my bosom,
34 Because I feared the great multitude,
And dreaded the contempt of families,
So that I kept silence
And did not go out of the door—
35 Oh, that I had one to hear me!
Here is my mark.
Oh, that the Almighty would answer me,
That my Prosecutor had written a book!
36 Surely I would carry it on my shoulder,
And bind it on me like a crown;
37 I would declare to Him the number of my
steps;
Like a prince I would approach Him.

38 "If my land cries out against me,
And its furrows weep together;
39 If I have eaten its fruit without money,
Or caused its owners to lose their lives;
40 Then let thistles grow instead of wheat,
And weeds instead of barley."

The words of Job are ended.

32 So these three men ceased answering Job,
because he was righteous in his own eyes. 2 Then the
wrath of Elihu, the son of Barachel the Buzite, of

וּמִשְּׂאֵתוֹ לֹא אוּכָל׃
24 אִם־שַׂמְתִּי זָהָב כִּסְלִי
וְלַכֶּתֶם אָמַרְתִּי מִבְטַחִי׃
25 אִם־אֶשְׂמַח כִּי־רַב חֵילִי
וְכִי־כַבִּיר מָצְאָה יָדִי׃
26 אִם־אֶרְאֶה אוֹר כִּי יָהֵל
וְיָרֵחַ יָקָר הֹלֵךְ׃
27 וַיִּפְתְּ בַּסֵּתֶר לִבִּי
וַתִּשַּׁק יָדִי לְפִי׃
28 גַּם־הוּא עָוֺן פְּלִילִי
כִּי־כִחַשְׁתִּי לָאֵל מִמָּעַל׃
29 אִם־אֶשְׂמַח בְּפִיד מְשַׂנְאִי
וְהִתְעֹרַרְתִּי כִּי־מְצָאוֹ רָע׃
30 וְלֹא־נָתַתִּי לַחֲטֹא חִכִּי
לִשְׁאֹל בְּאָלָה נַפְשׁוֹ׃
31 אִם־לֹא אָמְרוּ מְתֵי אָהֳלִי
מִי־יִתֵּן מִבְּשָׂרוֹ לֹא נִשְׂבָּע׃
32 בַּחוּץ לֹא־יָלִין גֵּר
דְּלָתַי לָאֹרַח אֶפְתָּח׃
33 אִם־כִּסִּיתִי כְאָדָם פְּשָׁעָי
לִטְמוֹן בְּחֻבִּי עֲוֺנִי׃
34 כִּי אֶעֱרוֹץ ׀ הָמוֹן רַבָּה
וּבוּז־מִשְׁפָּחוֹת יְחִתֵּנִי
וָאֶדֹּם לֹא־אֵצֵא פָתַח׃
35 מִי יִתֶּן־לִי ׀ שֹׁמֵעַ לִי
הֶן־תָּוִי שַׁדַּי יַעֲנֵנִי
וְסֵפֶר כָּתַב אִישׁ רִיבִי׃
36 אִם־לֹא עַל־שִׁכְמִי אֶשָּׂאֶנּוּ
אֶעֶנְדֶנּוּ עֲטָרוֹת לִי׃
37 מִסְפַּר צְעָדַי אַגִּידֶנּוּ
כְּמוֹ־נָגִיד אֲקָרֲבֶנּוּ׃
38 אִם־עָלַי אַדְמָתִי תִזְעָק
וְיַחַד תְּלָמֶיהָ יִבְכָּיוּן׃
39 אִם־כֹּחָהּ אָכַלְתִּי בְלִי־כָסֶף
וְנֶפֶשׁ בְּעָלֶיהָ הִפָּחְתִּי׃
40 תַּחַת חִטָּה ׀ יֵצֵא חוֹחַ וְתַחַת־שְׂעֹרָה בָאְשָׁה
תַּמּוּ דִּבְרֵי אִיּוֹב׃ פ

לב וַיִּשְׁבְּתוּ שְׁלֹשֶׁת הָאֲנָשִׁים הָאֵלֶּה
מֵעֲנוֹת אֶת־אִיּוֹב
כִּי הוּא צַדִּיק בְּעֵינָיו׃ פ
2 וַיִּחַר אַף ׀ אֱלִיהוּא בֶן־בַּרַכְאֵל הַבּוּזִי
לא 20 הַלָּצֵו

the family of Ram, was aroused against Job; his wrath was aroused because he justified himself rather than God. ³Also against his three friends his wrath was aroused, because they had found no answer, and *yet* had condemned Job.

⁴Now because they *were* years older than he, Elihu had waited to speak to Job. ⁵When Elihu saw that *there was* no answer in the mouth of these three men, his wrath was aroused.

⁶So Elihu, the son of Barachel the Buzite, answered and said:

"I *am* young in years, and you *are* very old;
Therefore I was afraid,
And dared not declare my opinion to you.
⁷ I said, 'Age should speak,
And multitude of years should teach wisdom.'
⁸ But *there is* a spirit in man,
And the breath of the Almighty gives him understanding.
⁹ Great men are not *always* wise,
Nor do the aged *always* understand justice.
¹⁰ "Therefore I say, 'Listen to me,
I also will declare my opinion.'
¹¹ Indeed I waited for your words,
I listened to your reasonings, while you searched out what to say.
¹² I paid close attention to you;
And surely not one of you convinced Job,
Or answered his words—
¹³ Lest you say,
'We have found wisdom';
God will vanquish him, not man.
¹⁴ Now he has not directed *his* words against me;
So I will not answer him with your words.
¹⁵ "They are dismayed and answer no more;
Words escape them.
¹⁶ And I have waited, because they did not speak,
Because they stood still *and* answered no more.
¹⁷ I also will answer my part,
I too will declare my opinion.
¹⁸ For I am full of words;
The spirit within me compels me.
¹⁹ Indeed my belly *is* like wine *that* has no vent;
It is ready to burst like new wineskins.
²⁰ I will speak, that I may find relief;
I must open my lips and answer.
²¹ Let me not, I pray, show partiality to anyone;
Nor let me flatter any man.

מִמִּשְׁפַּ֥חַת רָ֑ם
בְּאִיּ֖וֹב חָרָ֣ה אַפּ֑וֹ
עַֽל־צַדְּק֥וֹ נַפְשׁ֝֗וֹ מֵאֱלֹהִֽים׃
3 וּבִשְׁלֹ֤שֶׁת רֵעָ֨יו ׀ חָרָ֣ה אַפּ֑וֹ
עַ֤ל אֲשֶׁ֖ר לֹא־מָצְא֥וּ מַעֲנֶ֑ה
וַ֝יַּרְשִׁ֗יעוּ אֶת־אִיּֽוֹב׃
4 וֶֽאֱלִיה֗וּ חִכָּ֣ה אֶת־אִ֭יּוֹב בִּדְבָרִ֑ים
כִּ֤י זְֽקֵנִים־הֵ֖מָּה מִמֶּ֣נּוּ לְיָמִֽים׃
5 וַיַּ֤רְא אֱלִיה֗וּ כִּ֤י אֵ֣ין מַ֭עֲנֶה בְּפִ֗י שְׁלֹ֥שֶׁת
האֲנָשִׁ֗ים וַיִּ֥חַר אַפּֽוֹ׃ פ
6 וַיַּ֤עַן ׀ אֱלִיה֣וּ בֶן־בַּֽרַכְאֵ֣ל הַבּוּזִי֮ וַיֹּאמַ֒ר
צָ֘עִ֤יר אֲנִ֣י לְ֭יָמִים וְאַתֶּ֣ם יְשִׁישִׁ֑ים
עַל־כֵּ֖ן זָחַ֥לְתִּי וָֽאִירָ֓א ׀ מֵחַוֺּ֖ת דֵּעִ֣י אֶתְכֶֽם׃
7 אָ֭מַרְתִּי יָמִ֣ים יְדַבֵּ֑רוּ
וְרֹ֥ב שָׁ֝נִ֗ים יֹדִ֥יעוּ חָכְמָֽה׃
8 אָ֭כֵן רֽוּחַ־הִ֣יא בֶאֱנ֑וֹשׁ
וְנִשְׁמַ֖ת שַׁדַּ֣י תְּבִינֵֽם׃
9 לֹֽא־רַבִּ֥ים יֶחְכָּ֑מוּ
וּ֝זְקֵנִ֗ים יָבִ֥ינוּ מִשְׁפָּֽט׃
10 לָכֵ֣ן אָ֭מַרְתִּי שִׁמְעָה־לִּ֑י
אֲחַוֶּ֖ה דֵּעִ֣י אַף־אָֽנִי׃
11 הֵ֤ן הוֹחַ֨לְתִּי לְֽדִבְרֵיכֶ֗ם אָ֭זִין עַד־תְּב֥וּנֹֽתֵיכֶ֑ם
עַֽד־תַּחְקְר֥וּן מִלִּֽין׃
12 וְעָֽדֵיכֶ֗ם אֶתְבּ֫וֹנָ֥ן
וְהִנֵּ֤ה אֵ֣ין לְאִיּ֣וֹב מוֹכִ֑יחַ עוֹנֶ֖ה אֲמָרָ֣יו מִכֶּֽם׃
13 פֶּן־תֹּ֣֭אמְרוּ מָצָ֣אנוּ חָכְמָ֑ה
אֵ֖ל יִדְּפֶ֣נּוּ לֹא־אִֽישׁ׃
14 וְלֹא־עָרַ֣ךְ אֵלַ֣י מִלִּ֑ין
וּ֝בְאִמְרֵיכֶ֗ם לֹ֣א אֲשִׁיבֶֽנּוּ׃
15 חַ֭תּוּ לֹא־עָ֣נוּ ע֑וֹד
הֶעְתִּ֖יקוּ מֵהֶ֣ם מִלִּֽים׃
16 וְ֭הוֹחַלְתִּי כִּי־לֹ֣א יְדַבֵּ֑רוּ
כִּ֥י עָ֝מְד֗וּ לֹא־עָ֥נוּ עֽוֹד׃
17 אַעֲנֶ֣ה אַף־אֲנִ֣י חֶלְקִ֑י
אֲחַוֶּ֖ה דֵעִ֣י אַף־אָֽנִי׃
18 כִּ֭י מָלֵ֣תִי מִלִּ֑ים
הֱ֝צִיקַ֗תְנִי ר֣וּחַ בִּטְנִֽי׃
19 הִנֵּֽה־בִטְנִ֗י כְּיַ֥יִן לֹא־יִפָּתֵ֑חַ
כְּאֹב֥וֹת חֲ֝דָשִׁ֗ים יִבָּקֵֽעַ׃
20 אֲדַבְּרָ֥ה וְיִֽרְוַֽח־לִ֑י
אֶפְתַּ֖ח שְׂפָתַ֣י וְאֶֽעֱנֶֽה׃
21 אַל־נָ֣א אֶשָּׂ֣א פְנֵי־אִ֑ישׁ
וְאֶל־אָ֝דָ֗ם לֹ֣א אֲכַנֶּֽה׃

22 For I do not know how to flatter,
    Else my Maker would soon take me away.

כִּי לֹא יָדַעְתִּי אֲכַנֶּה 22
כִּמְעַט יִשָּׂאֵנִי עֹשֵׂנִי׃

33 "But please, Job, hear my speech,
    And listen to all my words.

לג וְאוּלָם שְׁמַע־נָא אִיּוֹב מִלָּי
וְכָל־דְּבָרַי הַאֲזִינָה׃

2 Now, I open my mouth;
    My tongue speaks in my mouth.

הִנֵּה־נָא פָּתַחְתִּי פִי 2
דִּבְּרָה לְשׁוֹנִי בְחִכִּי׃

3 My words *come* from my upright heart;
    My lips utter pure knowledge.

יֹשֶׁר־לִבִּי אֲמָרָי וְדַעַת שְׂפָתַי בָּרוּר מִלֵּלוּ׃ 3

4 The Spirit of God has made me,
    And the breath of the Almighty gives me
    life.

רוּחַ־אֵל עָשָׂתְנִי 4
וְנִשְׁמַת שַׁדַּי תְּחַיֵּנִי׃

5 If you can answer me,
    Set *your words* in order before me;
    Take your stand.

אִם־תּוּכַל הֲשִׁיבֵנִי 5
עֶרְכָה לְפָנַי הִתְיַצָּבָה׃

6 Truly I *am* as your spokesman before God;
    I also have been formed out of clay.

הֵן־אֲנִי כְפִיךָ לָאֵל 6
מֵחֹמֶר קֹרַצְתִּי גַם־אָנִי׃

7 Surely no fear of me will terrify you,
    Nor will my hand be heavy on you.

הִנֵּה אֵמָתִי לֹא תְבַעֲתֶךָּ 7
וְאַכְפִּי עָלֶיךָ לֹא־יִכְבָּד׃

8 "Surely you have spoken in my hearing,
    And I have heard the sound of *your* words,
        saying,

אַךְ אָמַרְתָּ בְאָזְנָי וְקוֹל מִלִּין אֶשְׁמָע׃ 8

9 'I *am* pure, without transgression;
    I *am* innocent, and *there is* no iniquity in me.

זַךְ אֲנִי בְּלִי פָשַׁע 9
חַף אָנֹכִי וְלֹא עָוֹן לִי׃

10 Yet He finds occasions against me,
    He counts me as His enemy;

הֵן תְּנוּאוֹת עָלַי יִמְצָא 10
יַחְשְׁבֵנִי לְאוֹיֵב לוֹ׃

11 He puts my feet in the stocks,
    He watches all my paths.'

יָשֵׂם בַּסַּד רַגְלָי 11
יִשְׁמֹר כָּל־אָרְחֹתָי׃

12 "Look, *in* this you are not righteous.
    I will answer you,
    For God is greater than man.

הֶן־זֹאת לֹא־צָדַקְתָּ אֶעֱנֶךָּ 12
כִּי־יִרְבֶּה אֱלוֹהַּ מֵאֱנוֹשׁ׃

13 Why do you contend with Him?
    For He does not give an accounting of any
        of His words.

מַדּוּעַ אֵלָיו רִיבוֹתָ 13
כִּי כָל־דְּבָרָיו לֹא־יַעֲנֶה׃

14 For God may speak in one way, or in
        another,
    Yet man does not perceive it.

כִּי־בְאַחַת יְדַבֶּר־אֵל 14
וּבִשְׁתַּיִם לֹא יְשׁוּרֶנָּה׃

15 In a dream, in a vision of the night,
    When deep sleep falls upon men,
    While slumbering on their beds,

בַּחֲלוֹם ׀ חֶזְיוֹן לַיְלָה 15
בִּנְפֹל תַּרְדֵּמָה עַל־אֲנָשִׁים
בִּתְנוּמוֹת עֲלֵי מִשְׁכָּב׃

16 Then He opens the ears of men,
    And seals their instruction.

אָז יִגְלֶה אֹזֶן אֲנָשִׁים וּבְמֹסָרָם יַחְתֹּם׃ 16

17 In order to turn man *from his* deed,
    And conceal pride from man,

לְהָסִיר אָדָם מַעֲשֶׂה 17
וְגֵוָה מִגֶּבֶר יְכַסֶּה׃

18 He keeps back his soul from the Pit,
    And his life from perishing by the sword.

יַחְשֹׂךְ נַפְשׁוֹ מִנִּי־שָׁחַת 18
וְחַיָּתוֹ מֵעֲבֹר בַּשָּׁלַח׃

19 "*Man* is also chastened with pain on his bed,
    And with strong *pain* in many of his bones,

וְהוּכַח בְּמַכְאוֹב עַל־מִשְׁכָּבוֹ 19
וְרִיב עֲצָמָיו אֵתָן׃

20 So that his life abhors bread,
    And his soul succulent food.

וְזִהֲמַתּוּ חַיָּתוֹ לָחֶם 20
וְנַפְשׁוֹ מַאֲכַל תַּאֲוָה׃

21 His flesh wastes away from sight,

יִכֶל בְּשָׂרוֹ מֵרֹאִי 21

לג 19 וְרִיב

And his bones stick out *which once* were not seen.

22 Yes, his soul draws near the Pit,
And his life to the executioners.

23 "If there is a messenger for him,
A mediator, one among a thousand,
To show man His uprightness,

24 Then He is gracious to him, and says,
'Deliver him from going down to the Pit;
I have found a ransom';

25 His flesh shall be young like a child's,
He shall return to the days of his youth.

26 He shall pray to God, and He will delight in him,
He shall see His face with joy,
For He restores to man His righteousness.

27 Then he looks at men and says,
'I have sinned, and perverted *what was* right,
And it did not profit me.'

28 He will redeem his soul from going down to the Pit,
And his life shall see the light.

29 "Behold, God works all these *things,*
Twice, *in fact,* three *times* with a man,

30 To bring back his soul from the Pit,
That he may be enlightened with the light of life.

31 "Give ear, Job, listen to me;
Hold your peace, and I will speak.

32 If you have anything to say, answer me;
Speak, for I desire to justify you.

33 If not, listen to me;
Hold your peace, and I will teach you wisdom."

34 Elihu further answered and said:

2 "Hear my words, you wise *men;*
Give ear to me, you who have knowledge.

3 For the ear tests words
As the palate tastes food.

4 Let us choose justice for ourselves;
Let us know among ourselves what *is* good.

5 "For Job has said, 'I am righteous,
But God has taken away my justice;

6 Should I lie concerning my right?
My wound *is* incurable, *though I am* without transgression.'

7 What man *is* like Job,
Who drinks scorn like water,

8 Who goes in company with the workers of iniquity,
And walks with wicked men?

וְשֻׁפּוּ עַצְמוֹתָיו לֹא רָאוּ:

22 וַתִּקְרַב לַשַּׁחַת נַפְשׁוֹ
וְחַיָּתוֹ לַמְמִתִים:

23 אִם־יֵשׁ עָלָיו ׀ מַלְאָךְ מֵלִיץ אֶחָד מִנִּי־אָלֶף
לְהַגִּיד לְאָדָם יָשְׁרוֹ:

24 וַיְחֻנֶּנּוּ וַיֹּאמֶר פְּדָעֵהוּ מֵרֶדֶת שָׁחַת
מָצָאתִי כֹפֶר:

25 רֻטֲפַשׁ בְּשָׂרוֹ מִנֹּעַר
יָשׁוּב לִימֵי עֲלוּמָיו:

26 יֶעְתַּר אֶל־אֱלוֹהַּ ׀ וַיִּרְצֵהוּ
וַיַּרְא פָּנָיו בִּתְרוּעָה
וַיָּשֶׁב לֶאֱנוֹשׁ צִדְקָתוֹ:

27 יָשֹׁר ׀ עַל־אֲנָשִׁים וַיֹּאמֶר חָטָאתִי וְיָשָׁר
הֶעֱוֵיתִי וְלֹא־שָׁוָה לִי:

28 פָּדָה נַפְשׁוֹ מֵעֲבֹר בַּשָּׁחַת
וְחַיָּתוֹ בָּאוֹר תִּרְאֶה:

29 הֶן־כָּל־אֵלֶּה יִפְעַל־אֵל
פַּעֲמַיִם שָׁלוֹשׁ עִם־גָּבֶר:

30 לְהָשִׁיב נַפְשׁוֹ מִנִּי־שָׁחַת
לֵאוֹר בְּאוֹר הַחַיִּים:

31 הַקְשֵׁב אִיּוֹב שְׁמַע־לִי
הַחֲרֵשׁ וְאָנֹכִי אֲדַבֵּר:

32 אִם־יֵשׁ־מִלִּין הֲשִׁיבֵנִי
דַּבֵּר כִּי־חָפַצְתִּי צַדְּקֶךָּ:

33 אִם־אַיִן אַתָּה שְׁמַע־לִי
הַחֲרֵשׁ וַאֲאַלֶּפְךָ חָכְמָה: ס

לד וַיַּעַן אֱלִיהוּא וַיֹּאמַר:

2 שִׁמְעוּ חֲכָמִים מִלָּי
וְיֹדְעִים הַאֲזִינוּ לִי:

3 כִּי־אֹזֶן מִלִּין תִּבְחָן
וְחֵךְ יִטְעַם לֶאֱכֹל:

4 מִשְׁפָּט נִבְחֲרָה־לָּנוּ
נֵדְעָה בֵינֵינוּ מַה־טּוֹב:

5 כִּי־אָמַר אִיּוֹב צָדַקְתִּי
וְאֵל הֵסִיר מִשְׁפָּטִי:

6 עַל־מִשְׁפָּטִי אֲכַזֵּב
אָנוּשׁ חִצִּי בְלִי־פָשַׁע:

7 מִי־גֶבֶר כְּאִיּוֹב
יִשְׁתֶּה־לַּעַג כַּמָּיִם:

8 וְאָרַח לְחֶבְרָה עִם־פֹּעֲלֵי אָוֶן
וְלָלֶכֶת עִם־אַנְשֵׁי־רֶשַׁע:

לג 21 וְשֻׁפּוּ   28 נַפְשׁוֹ, וְחַיָּתוֹ

9   For he has said, 'It profits a man nothing
       That he should delight in God.'

10   "Therefore listen to me, you men of under-
       standing:
       Far be it from God *to do* wickedness,
       And *from* the Almighty to *commit* iniquity.

11   For He repays man *according to* his work,
       And makes man to find a reward according
       to *his* way.

12   Surely God will never do wickedly,
       Nor will the Almighty pervert justice.

13   Who gave Him charge over the earth?
       Or who appointed *Him over* the whole
       world?

14   If He should set His heart on it,
       If He should gather to Himself His Spirit
       and His breath,

15   All flesh would perish together,
       And man would return to dust.

16   "If *you have* understanding, hear this;
       Listen to the sound of my words:

17   Should one who hates justice govern?
       Will you condemn *Him who is* most just?

18   *Is it fitting* to say to a king, '*You are*
       worthless,'
       And to nobles, '*You are* wicked'?

19   Yet He is not partial to princes,
       Nor does He regard the rich more than the
       poor;
       For they *are* all the work of His hands.

20   In a moment they die, in the middle of the
       night;
       The people are shaken and pass away;
       The mighty are taken away without a hand.

21   "For His eyes *are* on the ways of man,
       And He sees all his steps.

22   There is no darkness nor shadow of death
       Where the workers of iniquity may hide
       themselves.

23   For He need not further consider a man,
       That he should go before God in judgment.

24   He breaks in pieces mighty men without
       inquiry,
       And sets others in their place.

25   Therefore He knows their works;
       He overthrows *them* in the night,
       And they are crushed.

26   He strikes them as wicked *men*
       In the open sight of others,

27   Because they turned back from Him,
       And would not consider any of His ways,

28   So that they caused the cry of the poor to
       come to Him;

כִּי־אָמַר לֹא יִסְכָּן־גָּבֶר 9
בִּרְצֹתוֹ עִם־אֱלֹהִים׃

לָכֵן ׀ אַנְשֵׁי לֵבָב שִׁמְעוּ לִי 10
חָלִלָה לָאֵל מֵרֶשַׁע וְשַׁדַּי מֵעָוֶל׃

כִּי פֹעַל אָדָם יְשַׁלֶּם־לוֹ 11
וּכְאֹרַח אִישׁ יַמְצִאֶנּוּ׃

אַף־אָמְנָם אֵל לֹא־יַרְשִׁיעַ 12
וְשַׁדַּי לֹא־יְעַוֵּת מִשְׁפָּט׃

מִי־פָקַד עָלָיו אָרְצָה 13
וּמִי שָׂם תֵּבֵל כֻּלָּהּ׃

אִם־יָשִׂים אֵלָיו לִבּוֹ 14
רוּחוֹ וְנִשְׁמָתוֹ אֵלָיו יֶאֱסֹף׃

יִגְוַע כָּל־בָּשָׂר יָחַד 15
וְאָדָם עַל־עָפָר יָשׁוּב׃

וְאִם־בִּינָה שִׁמְעָה־זֹּאת 16
הַאֲזִינָה לְקוֹל מִלָּי׃

הַאַף שׂוֹנֵא מִשְׁפָּט יַחֲבוֹשׁ 17
וְאִם־צַדִּיק כַּבִּיר תַּרְשִׁיעַ׃

הַאֲמֹר לְמֶלֶךְ בְּלִיָּעַל 18
רָשָׁע אֶל־נְדִיבִים׃

אֲשֶׁר לֹא־נָשָׂא ׀ פְּנֵי שָׂרִים 19
וְלֹא נִכַּר־שׁוֹעַ לִפְנֵי־דָל
כִּי־מַעֲשֵׂה יָדָיו כֻּלָּם׃

רֶגַע ׀ יָמֻתוּ 20
וַחֲצוֹת לָיְלָה
יְגֹעֲשׁוּ עָם וְיַעֲבֹרוּ
וְיָסִירוּ אַבִּיר לֹא בְיָד׃

כִּי־עֵינָיו עַל־דַּרְכֵי־אִישׁ 21
וְכָל־צְעָדָיו יִרְאֶה׃

אֵין־חֹשֶׁךְ וְאֵין צַלְמָוֶת 22
לְהִסָּתֶר שָׁם פֹּעֲלֵי אָוֶן׃

כִּי לֹא עַל־אִישׁ יָשִׂים עוֹד 23
לַהֲלֹךְ אֶל־אֵל בַּמִּשְׁפָּט׃

יָרֹעַ כַּבִּירִים לֹא־חֵקֶר 24
וַיַּעֲמֵד אֲחֵרִים תַּחְתָּם׃

לָכֵן יַכִּיר מַעְבָּדֵיהֶם 25
וְהָפַךְ לַיְלָה וְיִדַּכָּאוּ׃

תַּחַת־רְשָׁעִים סְפָקָם 26
בִּמְקוֹם רֹאִים׃

אֲשֶׁר עַל־כֵּן סָרוּ מֵאַחֲרָיו 27
וְכָל־דְּרָכָיו לֹא הִשְׂכִּילוּ׃

לְהָבִיא עָלָיו צַעֲקַת־דָּל 28

For He hears the cry of the afflicted.

וְצַעֲקַת עֲנִיִּים יִשְׁמָע:

29 When He gives quietness, who then can
make trouble?
And when He hides *His* face, who then can
see Him,
Whether *it is* against a nation or a man
alone?—

29 וְהוּא יַשְׁקִט ׀ וּמִי יַרְשִׁעַ
וְיַסְתֵּר פָּנִים וּמִי יְשׁוּרֶנּוּ
וְעַל־גּוֹי וְעַל־אָדָם
יָחַד:

30 That the hypocrite should not reign,
Lest the people be ensnared.

30 מִמְּלֹךְ אָדָם חָנֵף
מִמֹּקְשֵׁי עָם:

31 "For has *anyone* said to God,
'I have borne *chastening;*
I will offend no more;

31 כִּי־אֶל־אֵל הֶאָמַר נָשָׂאתִי
לֹא אֶחְבֹּל:

32 Teach me *what* I do not see;
If I have done iniquity, I will do no more'?

32 בִּלְעֲדֵי אֶחֱזֶה אַתָּה הֹרֵנִי
אִם־עָוֶל פָּעַלְתִּי לֹא אֹסִיף:

33 Should He repay *it* according to your *terms,*
Just because you disavow it?
You must choose, and not I;
Therefore speak what you know.

33 הֲמֵעִמְּךָ יְשַׁלְמֶנָּה כִּי־מָאַסְתָּ כִּי־אַתָּה תִבְחַר
וְלֹא־אָנִי
וּמַה־יָדַעְתָּ דַבֵּר:

34 "Men of understanding say to me,
Wise men who listen to me:

34 אַנְשֵׁי לֵבָב יֹאמְרוּ לִי
וְגֶבֶר חָכָם שֹׁמֵעַ לִי:

35 'Job speaks without knowledge,
His words *are* without wisdom.'

35 אִיּוֹב לֹא־בְדַעַת יְדַבֵּר
וּדְבָרָיו לֹא בְהַשְׂכֵּיל:

36 Oh, that Job were tried to the utmost,
Because *his* answers *are like* those of wicked
men!

36 אָבִי יִבָּחֵן אִיּוֹב עַד־נֶצַח
עַל־תְּשֻׁבֹת בְּאַנְשֵׁי־אָוֶן:

37 For he adds rebellion to his sin;
He claps *his hands* among us,
And multiplies his words against God."

37 כִּי יֹסִיף עַל־חַטָּאתוֹ פֶּשַׁע בֵּינֵינוּ יִסְפּוֹק
וְיֶרֶב אֲמָרָיו לָאֵל: ס

35 Moreover Elihu answered and said:

לה וַיַּעַן אֱלִיהוּ וַיֹּאמַר:

2 "Do you think this is right?
Do you say,
'My righteousness is more than God's'?

2 הֲזֹאת חָשַׁבְתָּ לְמִשְׁפָּט
אָמַרְתָּ צִדְקִי מֵאֵל:

3 For you say,
'What advantage will it be to You?
What profit shall I have, more than *if* I had
sinned?'

3 כִּי־תֹאמַר מַה־יִּסְכָּן־לָךְ
מָה־אֹעִיל מֵחַטָּאתִי:

4 "I will answer you,
And your companions with you.

4 אֲנִי אֲשִׁיבְךָ מִלִּין
וְאֶת־רֵעֶיךָ עִמָּךְ:

5 Look to the heavens and see;
And behold the clouds—
They are higher than you.

5 הַבֵּט שָׁמַיִם וּרְאֵה
וְשׁוּר שְׁחָקִים גָּבְהוּ מִמֶּךָּ:

6 If you sin, what do you accomplish against
Him?
Or, *if* your transgressions are multiplied,
what do you do to Him?

6 אִם־חָטָאתָ מַה־תִּפְעָל־בּוֹ
וְרַבּוּ פְשָׁעֶיךָ מַה־תַּעֲשֶׂה־לּוֹ:

7 If you are righteous, what do you give Him?
Or what does He receive from your hand?

7 אִם־צָדַקְתָּ מַה־תִּתֶּן־לוֹ
אוֹ מַה־מִיָּדְךָ יִקָּח:

8 Your wickedness affects a man such as you,
And your righteousness a son of man.

8 לְאִישׁ־כָּמוֹךָ רִשְׁעֶךָ
וּלְבֶן־אָדָם צִדְקָתֶךָ:

9 "Because of the multitude of oppressions they
cry out;

9 מֵרֹב עֲשׁוּקִים יַזְעִיקוּ

They cry out for help because of the arm of the mighty.

10 But no one says, 'Where *is* God my Maker, Who gives songs in the night,

11 Who teaches us more than the beasts of the earth, And makes us wiser than the birds of heaven?'

12 There they cry out, but He does not answer, Because of the pride of evil men.

13 Surely God will not listen to empty *talk,* Nor will the Almighty regard it.

14 Although you say you do not see Him, *Yet* justice *is* before Him, and you must wait for Him.

15 And now, because He has not punished in His anger, Nor taken much notice of folly,

16 Therefore Job opens his mouth in vain; He multiplies words without knowledge."

36 Elihu also proceeded and said:

2 "Bear with me a little, and I will show you That *there are* yet words to speak on God's behalf.

3 I will fetch my knowledge from afar; I will ascribe righteousness to my Maker.

4 For truly my words *are* not false; One who is perfect in knowledge *is* with you.

5 "Behold, God *is* mighty, but despises *no one; He is* mighty in strength of understanding.

6 He does not preserve the life of the wicked, But gives justice to the oppressed.

7 He does not withdraw His eyes from the righteous; But *they are* on the throne with kings, For He has seated them forever, And they are exalted.

8 And if *they are* bound in fetters, Held in the cords of affliction,

9 Then He tells them their work and their transgressions— That they have acted defiantly.

10 He also opens their ear to instruction, And commands that they turn from iniquity.

11 If they obey and serve *Him,* They shall spend their days in prosperity, And their years in pleasures.

12 But if they do not obey, They shall perish by the sword, And they shall die without knowledge.

13 "But the hypocrites in heart store up wrath;

יְשַׁוְּעוּ מִזְּרוֹעַ רַבִּים׃

10 וְלֹא־אָמַר אַיֵּה אֱלוֹהַּ עֹשָׂי
נֹתֵן זְמִרוֹת בַּלָּיְלָה׃

11 מַלְּפֵנוּ מִבַּהֲמוֹת אָרֶץ
וּמֵעוֹף הַשָּׁמַיִם יְחַכְּמֵנוּ׃

12 שָׁם יִצְעֲקוּ וְלֹא יַעֲנֶה
מִפְּנֵי גְּאוֹן רָעִים׃

13 אַךְ־שָׁוְא לֹא־יִשְׁמַע ׀ אֵל
וְשַׁדַּי לֹא יְשׁוּרֶנָּה׃

14 אַף כִּי־תֹאמַר לֹא תְשׁוּרֶנּוּ
דִּין לְפָנָיו וּתְחוֹלֵל לוֹ׃

15 וְעַתָּה כִּי־אַיִן פָּקַד אַפּוֹ
וְלֹא־יָדַע בַּפַּשׁ מְאֹד׃

16 וְאִיּוֹב הֶבֶל יִפְצֶה־פִּיהוּ
בִּבְלִי־דַעַת מִלִּין יַכְבִּר׃ פ

לו וַיֹּסֶף אֱלִיהוּא וַיֹּאמַר׃

2 כַּתַּר־לִי זְעֵיר וַאֲחַוֶּךָּ
כִּי עוֹד לֶאֱלוֹהַּ מִלִּים׃

3 אֶשָּׂא דֵעִי לְמֵרָחוֹק
וּלְפֹעֲלִי אֶתֵּן־צֶדֶק׃

4 כִּי־אָמְנָם לֹא־שֶׁקֶר מִלָּי
תְּמִים דֵּעוֹת עִמָּךְ׃

5 הֶן־אֵל כַּבִּיר וְלֹא יִמְאָס
כַּבִּיר כֹּחַ לֵב׃

6 לֹא־יְחַיֶּה רָשָׁע
וּמִשְׁפַּט עֲנִיִּים יִתֵּן׃

7 לֹא־יִגְרַע מִצַּדִּיק
עֵינָיו
וְאֶת־מְלָכִים לַכִּסֵּא
וַיֹּשִׁיבֵם לָנֶצַח וַיִּגְבָּהוּ׃

8 וְאִם־אֲסוּרִים בַּזִּקִּים
יִלָּכְדוּן בְּחַבְלֵי־עֹנִי׃

9 וַיַּגֵּד לָהֶם פָּעֳלָם
וּפִשְׁעֵיהֶם כִּי יִתְגַּבָּרוּ׃

10 וַיִּגֶל אָזְנָם לַמּוּסָר
וַיֹּאמֶר כִּי־יְשֻׁבוּן מֵאָוֶן׃

11 אִם־יִשְׁמְעוּ וְיַעֲבֹדוּ
יְכַלּוּ יְמֵיהֶם בַּטּוֹב וּשְׁנֵיהֶם בַּנְּעִימִים׃

12 וְאִם־לֹא יִשְׁמְעוּ בְּשֶׁלַח יַעֲבֹרוּ
וְיִגְוְעוּ כִּבְלִי־דָעַת׃

13 וְחַנְפֵי־לֵב יָשִׂימוּ אָף

They do not cry for help when He binds them.

14 They die in youth,
And their life *ends* among the perverted persons.

15 He delivers the poor in their affliction,
And opens their ears in oppression.

16 "Indeed He would have brought you out of dire distress,
Into a broad place where *there is* no restraint;
And what is set on your table *would be* full of richness.

17 But you are filled with the judgment due the wicked;
Judgment and justice take hold *of you*.

18 Because *there is* wrath, *beware* lest He take you away with *one* blow;
For a large ransom would not help you avoid *it*.

19 Will your riches,
Or all the mighty forces,
Keep you from distress?

20 Do not desire the night,
When people are cut off in their place.

21 Take heed, do not turn to iniquity,
For you have chosen this rather than affliction.

22 "Behold, God is exalted by His power;
Who teaches like Him?

23 Who has assigned Him His way,
Or who has said, 'You have done wrong'?

24 "Remember to magnify His work,
Of which men have sung.

25 Everyone has seen it;
Man looks on *it* from afar.

26 "Behold, God *is* great, and we do not know *Him*;
Nor can the number of His years *be* discovered.

27 For He draws up drops of water,
Which distill as rain from the mist,

28 Which the clouds drop down
And pour abundantly on man.

29 Indeed, can *anyone* understand the spreading of clouds,
The thunder from His canopy?

30 Look, He scatters His light upon it,
And covers the depths of the sea.

31 For by these He judges the peoples;
He gives food in abundance.

32 He covers *His* hands with lightning,

לֹא יְשַׁוְּעוּ כִּי אֲסָרָם׃

14 תָּמֹת בַּנֹּעַר נַפְשָׁם
וְחַיָּתָם בַּקְּדֵשִׁים׃

15 יְחַלֵּץ עָנִי בְעָנְיוֹ
וְיִגֶל בַּלַּחַץ אָזְנָם׃

16 וְאַף הֲסִיתְךָ ׀ מִפִּי־צָר
רַחַב לֹא־מוּצָק תַּחְתֶּיהָ
וְנַחַת שֻׁלְחָנְךָ
מָלֵא דָשֶׁן׃

17 וְדִין־רָשָׁע מָלֵאתָ
דִּין וּמִשְׁפָּט יִתְמֹכוּ׃

18 כִּי־חֵמָה פֶּן־יְסִיתְךָ בְסָפֶק
וְרָב־כֹּפֶר אַל־יַטֶּךָ׃

19 הֲיַעֲרֹךְ שׁוּעֲךָ לֹא בְצָר
וְכֹל מַאֲמַצֵּי־כֹחַ׃

20 אַל־תִּשְׁאַף הַלָּיְלָה
לַעֲלוֹת עַמִּים תַּחְתָּם׃

21 הִשָּׁמֶר אַל־תֵּפֶן אֶל־אָוֶן
כִּי־עַל־זֶה בָּחַרְתָּ מֵעֹנִי׃

22 הֶן־אֵל יַשְׂגִּיב בְּכֹחוֹ
מִי כָמֹהוּ מוֹרֶה׃

23 מִי־פָקַד עָלָיו דַּרְכּוֹ
וּמִי־אָמַר פָּעַלְתָּ עַוְלָה׃

24 זְכֹר כִּי־תַשְׂגִּיא פָעֳלוֹ
אֲשֶׁר שֹׁרְרוּ אֲנָשִׁים׃

25 כָּל־אָדָם חָזוּ־בוֹ
אֱנוֹשׁ יַבִּיט מֵרָחוֹק׃

26 הֶן־אֵל שַׂגִּיא וְלֹא נֵדָע
מִסְפַּר שָׁנָיו וְלֹא־חֵקֶר׃

27 כִּי יְגָרַע נִטְפֵי־מָיִם
יָזֹקּוּ מָטָר לְאֵדוֹ׃

28 אֲשֶׁר־יִזְּלוּ שְׁחָקִים
יִרְעֲפוּ עֲלֵי ׀ אָדָם רָב׃

29 אַף אִם־יָבִין מִפְרְשֵׂי־עָב
תְּשֻׁאוֹת סֻכָּתוֹ׃

30 הֶן־פָּרַשׂ עָלָיו אוֹרוֹ
וְשָׁרְשֵׁי הַיָּם כִּסָּה׃

31 כִּי־בָם יָדִין עַמִּים
יִתֶּן־אֹכֶל לְמַכְבִּיר׃

32 עַל־כַּפַּיִם כִּסָּה־אוֹר

And commands it to strike.
33 His thunder declares it,
The cattle also, concerning the rising *storm*.

וִיצַ֥ו עָלֶ֗יהָ בְמַפְגִּֽיעַ׃
33 יַגִּ֣יד עָלָ֣יו רֵע֑וֹ
מִ֝קְנֶ֗ה אַ֣ף עַל־עוֹלֶֽה׃

37 "At this also my heart trembles,
And leaps from its place.
2 Hear attentively the thunder of His voice,
And the rumbling *that* comes from His
mouth.
3 He sends it forth under the whole heaven,
His lightning to the ends of the earth.
4 After it a voice roars;
He thunders with His majestic voice,
And He does not restrain them when His
voice is heard.
5 God thunders marvelously with His voice;
He does great things which we cannot
comprehend.
6 For He says to the snow, 'Fall *on* the earth';
Likewise to the gentle rain and the heavy
rain of His strength.
7 He seals the hand of every man,
That all men may know His work.
8 The beasts go into dens,
And remain in their lairs.
9 From the chamber *of the south* comes the
whirlwind,
And cold from the scattering winds *of the
north.*
10 By the breath of God ice is given,
And the broad waters are frozen.
11 Also with moisture He saturates the thick
clouds;
He scatters His bright clouds.
12 And they swirl about, being turned by His
guidance,
That they may do whatever He commands
them
On the face of the whole earth.
13 He causes it to come,
Whether for correction,
Or for His land,
Or for mercy.
14 "Listen to this, O Job;
Stand still and consider the wondrous works
of God.
15 Do you know when God dispatches them,
And causes the light of His cloud to shine?
16 Do you know how the clouds are balanced,
Those wondrous works of Him who is
perfect in knowledge?
17 Why *are* your garments hot,
When He quiets the earth by the south *wind*?

לז אַף־לְ֭זֹאת יֶחֱרַ֣ד לִבִּ֑י
וְ֝יִתַּ֗ר מִמְּקוֹמֽוֹ׃
2 שִׁמְע֤וּ שָׁמ֣וֹעַ בְּרֹ֣גֶז קֹל֑וֹ
וְ֝הֶ֗גֶה מִפִּ֥יו יֵצֵֽא׃
3 תַּֽחַת־כָּל־הַשָּׁמַ֥יִם יִשְׁרֵ֑הוּ
וְ֝אוֹר֗וֹ עַל־כַּנְפ֥וֹת הָאָֽרֶץ׃
4 אַחֲרָ֤יו ׀ יִשְׁאַג־ק֗וֹל
יַרְעֵ֥ם בְּק֣וֹל גְּאוֹנ֑וֹ
וְלֹ֥א יְ֝עַקְּבֵ֗ם כִּֽי־יִשָּׁמַ֥ע קוֹלֽוֹ׃
5 יַרְעֵ֤ם אֵ֣ל בְּקוֹל֣וֹ נִפְלָא֑וֹת
עֹשֶׂ֥ה גְ֝דֹל֗וֹת וְלֹ֣א נֵדָֽע׃
6 כִּ֤י לַשֶּׁ֨לַג ׀ יֹאמַ֗ר הֱוֵ֫א אָ֥רֶץ
וְגֶ֣שֶׁם מָטָ֑ר
וְ֝גֶ֗שֶׁם מִטְר֥וֹת עֻזּֽוֹ׃
7 בְּיַד־כָּל־אָדָ֥ם יַחְתּ֑וֹם
לָ֝דַ֗עַת כָּל־אַנְשֵׁ֥י מַעֲשֵֽׂהוּ׃
8 וַתָּבֹ֣א חַיָּ֣ה בְמוֹ־אָ֑רֶב
וּבִמְע֖וֹנֹתֶ֣יהָ תִשְׁכֹּֽן׃
9 מִן־הַ֭חֶדֶר תָּב֣וֹא סוּפָ֑ה
וּֽמִמְּזָרִ֥ים קָרָֽה׃
10 מִנִּשְׁמַת־אֵ֥ל יִתֶּן־קָ֑רַח
וְרֹ֖חַב מַ֣יִם בְּמוּצָֽק׃
11 אַף־בְּ֭רִי יַטְרִ֣יחַ עָ֑ב
יָ֝פִ֗יץ עֲנַ֣ן אוֹרֽוֹ׃
12 וְה֤וּא מְסִבּ֨וֹת ׀ מִתְהַפֵּ֣ךְ בְּתַחְבּוּלֹתָ֣ו
לְפָעֳלָ֑ם
כֹּ֖ל אֲשֶׁ֥ר יְצַוֵּ֓ם ׀ עַל־פְּנֵ֖י תֵבֵ֣ל אָֽרְצָה׃
13 אִם־לְשֵׁ֥בֶט אִם־לְאַרְצ֑וֹ
אִם־לְ֝חֶ֗סֶד יַמְצִאֵֽהוּ׃
14 הַאֲזִ֣ינָה זֹּ֣את אִיּ֑וֹב
עֲ֝מֹ֗ד וְהִתְבּוֹנֵ֓ן ׀ נִפְלְא֬וֹת אֵֽל׃
15 הֲ֭תֵדַע בְּשׂוּם־אֱל֣וֹהַּ עֲלֵיהֶ֑ם
וְ֝הוֹפִ֗יעַ א֣וֹר עֲנָנֽוֹ׃
16 הֲ֭תֵדַע עַל־מִפְלְשֵׂי־עָ֑ב
מִ֝פְלְא֗וֹת תְּמִ֣ים דֵּעִֽים׃
17 אֲשֶׁר־בְּגָדֶ֥יךָ חַמִּ֑ים
בְּהַשְׁקִ֥ט אֶ֝֗רֶץ מִדָּרֽוֹם׃

לז 12 בְּתַחְבּוּלֹתָֽיו

18 With Him, have you spread out the skies,
Strong as a cast metal mirror?

19 "Teach us what we should say to Him,
For we can prepare nothing because of the
darkness.

20 Should He be told that I *wish to* speak?
If a man were to speak, surely he would be
swallowed up.

21 Even now *men* cannot look at the light *when
it is* bright in the skies,
When the wind has passed and cleared them.

22 He comes from the north *as* golden *splendor;*
With God *is* awesome majesty.

23 *As for* the Almighty, we cannot find Him;
He is excellent in power,
In judgment and abundant justice;
He does not oppress.

24 Therefore men fear Him;
He shows no partiality to any *who are* wise
of heart."

38 Then the Lord answered Job out of the
whirlwind, and said:

2 "Who *is* this who darkens counsel
By words without knowledge?

3 Now prepare yourself like a man;
I will question you, and you shall answer
Me.

4 "Where were you when I laid the foundations
of the earth?
Tell *Me,* if you have understanding.

5 Who determined its measurements?
Surely you know!
Or who stretched the line upon it?

6 To what were its foundations fastened?
Or who laid its cornerstone,

7 When the morning stars sang together,
And all the sons of God shouted for joy?

8 "Or *who* shut in the sea with doors,
When it burst forth *and* issued from the
womb;

9 When I made the clouds its garment,
And thick darkness its swaddling band;

10 When I fixed My limit for it,
And set bars and doors;

11 When I said,
'This far you may come, but no farther,
And here your proud waves must stop!'

12 "Have you commanded the morning since
your days *began,*
And caused the dawn to know its place,

---

18 תַּרְקִיעַ עִמּוֹ לִשְׁחָקִים
חֲזָקִים כִּרְאִי מוּצָק:

19 הוֹדִיעֵנוּ מַה־נֹּאמַר לוֹ
לֹא־נַעֲרֹךְ מִפְּנֵי־חֹשֶׁךְ:

20 הַיְסֻפַּר־לוֹ כִּי אֲדַבֵּר
אִם־אָמַר אִישׁ כִּי יְבֻלָּע:

21 וְעַתָּה ׀ לֹא רָאוּ אוֹר
בָּהִיר הוּא בַּשְּׁחָקִים
וְרוּחַ עָבְרָה וַתְּטַהֲרֵם:

22 מִצָּפוֹן זָהָב יֶאֱתֶה
עַל־אֱלוֹהַּ נוֹרָא הוֹד:

23 שַׁדַּי לֹא־מְצָאנֻהוּ שַׂגִּיא־כֹחַ
וּמִשְׁפָּט וְרֹב־צְדָקָה לֹא יְעַנֶּה:

24 לָכֵן יְרֵאוּהוּ אֲנָשִׁים
לֹא־יִרְאֶה כָּל־חַכְמֵי־לֵב: פ

לח וַיַּעַן־יְהֹוָה אֶת־אִיּוֹב מִנְּ ׀ הַסְּעָרָה
וַיֹּאמַר:

2 מִי זֶה ׀ מַחְשִׁיךְ עֵצָה בְמִלִּין
בְּלִי־דָעַת:

3 אֱזָר־נָא כְגֶבֶר חֲלָצֶיךָ
וְאֶשְׁאָלְךָ וְהוֹדִיעֵנִי:

4 אֵיפֹה הָיִיתָ בְּיָסְדִי־אָרֶץ
הַגֵּד אִם־יָדַעְתָּ בִינָה:

5 מִי־שָׂם מְמַדֶּיהָ כִּי תֵדָע
אוֹ מִי־נָטָה עָלֶיהָ קָּו:

6 עַל־מָה אֲדָנֶיהָ הָטְבָּעוּ
אוֹ מִי־יָרָה אֶבֶן פִּנָּתָהּ:

7 בְּרָן־יַחַד כּוֹכְבֵי בֹקֶר
וַיָּרִיעוּ כָּל־בְּנֵי אֱלֹהִים:

8 וַיָּסֶךְ בִּדְלָתַיִם יָם
בְּגִיחוֹ מֵרֶחֶם יֵצֵא:

9 בְּשׂוּמִי עָנָן לְבֻשׁוֹ
וַעֲרָפֶל חֲתֻלָּתוֹ:

10 וָאֶשְׁבֹּר עָלָיו חֻקִּי
וָאָשִׂים בְּרִיחַ וּדְלָתָיִם:

11 וָאֹמַר עַד־פֹּה תָבוֹא וְלֹא תֹסִיף
וּפֹא־יָשִׁית בִּגְאוֹן גַּלֶּיךָ:

12 הְמִיָּמֶיךָ צִוִּיתָ בֹּקֶר
יִדַּעְתָּה שַׁחַר מְקֹמוֹ:

לח 1 מִן הַסְּעָרָה 12 יִדַּעְתָּ הַשַּׁחַר

13 That it might take hold of the ends of the
    earth,
    And the wicked be shaken out of it?

14 It takes on form like clay *under* a seal,
    And stands out like a garment.

15 From the wicked their light is withheld,
    And the upraised arm is broken.

16 "Have you entered the springs of the sea?
    Or have you walked in search of the depths?

17 Have the gates of death been revealed to
    you?
    Or have you seen the doors of the shadow of
    death?

18 Have you comprehended the breadth of the
    earth?
    Tell *Me*, if you know all this.

19 "Where *is* the way *to* the dwelling of light?
    And darkness, where *is* its place,

20 That you may take it to its territory,
    That you may know the paths *to* its home?

21 Do you know *it*, because you were born
    then,
    Or *because* the number of your days *is* great?

22 "Have you entered the treasury of snow,
    Or have you seen the treasury of hail,

23 Which I have reserved for the time of
    trouble,
    For the day of battle and war?

24 By what way is light diffused,
    Or the east wind scattered over the earth?

25 "Who has divided a channel for the over-
    flowing *water*,
    Or a path for the thunderbolt,

26 To cause it to rain on a land *where there is*
    no one,
    A wilderness in which *there is* no man;

27 To satisfy the desolate waste,
    And cause to spring forth the growth of
    tender grass?

28 Has the rain a father?
    Or who has begotten the drops of dew?

29 From whose womb comes the ice?
    And the frost of heaven, who gives it birth?

30 The waters harden like stone,
    And the surface of the deep is frozen.

31 "Can you bind the cluster of the Pleiades,
    Or loose the belt of Orion?

32 Can you bring out Mazzaroth in its season?
    Or can you guide the Great Bear with its
    cubs?

33 Do you know the ordinances of the heavens?
    Can you set their dominion over the earth?

13 לֶאֱחֹז בְּכַנְפוֹת הָאָרֶץ
וְיִנָּעֲרוּ רְשָׁעִים מִמֶּנָּה:

14 תִּתְהַפֵּךְ כְּחֹמֶר חוֹתָם
וְיִתְיַצְּבוּ כְּמוֹ לְבוּשׁ:

15 וְיִמָּנַע מֵרְשָׁעִים אוֹרָם
וּזְרוֹעַ רָמָה תִּשָּׁבֵר:

16 הֲבָאתָ עַד־נִבְכֵי־יָם
וּבְחֵקֶר תְּהוֹם הִתְהַלָּכְתָּ:

17 הֲנִגְלוּ לְךָ שַׁעֲרֵי־מָוֶת
וְשַׁעֲרֵי צַלְמָוֶת תִּרְאֶה:

18 הִתְבֹּנַנְתָּ עַד־רַחֲבֵי־אָרֶץ
הַגֵּד אִם־יָדַעְתָּ כֻלָּהּ:

19 אֵי־זֶה הַדֶּרֶךְ יִשְׁכָּן־אוֹר
וְחֹשֶׁךְ אֵי־זֶה מְקֹמוֹ:

20 כִּי תִקָּחֶנּוּ אֶל־גְּבוּלוֹ
וְכִי־תָבִין נְתִיבוֹת בֵּיתוֹ:

21 יָדַעְתָּ כִּי־אָז תִּוָּלֵד
וּמִסְפַּר יָמֶיךָ רַבִּים:

22 הֲבָאתָ אֶל־אֹצְרוֹת שָׁלֶג
וְאֹצְרוֹת בָּרָד תִּרְאֶה:

23 אֲשֶׁר־חָשַׂכְתִּי לְעֶת־צָר
לְיוֹם קְרָב וּמִלְחָמָה:

24 אֵי־זֶה הַדֶּרֶךְ יֵחָלֶק אוֹר
יָפֵץ קָדִים עֲלֵי־אָרֶץ:

25 מִי־פִלַּג לַשֶּׁטֶף תְּעָלָה
וְדֶרֶךְ לַחֲזִיז קֹלוֹת:

26 לְהַמְטִיר עַל־אֶרֶץ לֹא־אִישׁ
מִדְבָּר לֹא־אָדָם בּוֹ:

27 לְהַשְׂבִּיעַ שֹׁאָה וּמְשֹׁאָה
וּלְהַצְמִיחַ מֹצָא דֶשֶׁא:

28 הֲיֵשׁ־לַמָּטָר אָב
אוֹ מִי־הוֹלִיד אֶגְלֵי־טָל:

29 מִבֶּטֶן מִי יָצָא הַקָּרַח
וּכְפֹר שָׁמַיִם מִי יְלָדוֹ:

30 כָּאֶבֶן מַיִם יִתְחַבָּאוּ
וּפְנֵי תְהוֹם יִתְלַכָּדוּ:

31 הַתְקַשֵּׁר מַעֲדַנּוֹת כִּימָה
אוֹ־מֹשְׁכוֹת כְּסִיל תְּפַתֵּחַ:

32 הֲתֹצִיא מַזָּרוֹת בְּעִתּוֹ
וְעַיִשׁ עַל־בָּנֶיהָ תַנְחֵם:

33 הֲיָדַעְתָּ חֻקּוֹת שָׁמָיִם
אִם־תָּשִׂים מִשְׁטָרוֹ בָאָרֶץ:

34 "Can you lift up your voice to the clouds,   הֲתָרִים לָעָב קוֹלֶךָ   34
That an abundance of water may cover you?   וְשִׁפְעַת־מַיִם תְּכַסֶּךָּ:

35 Can you send out lightnings, that they may go,   הַתְשַׁלַּח בְּרָקִים וְיֵלֵכוּ   35
And say to you, 'Here we *are!*'?   וְיֹאמְרוּ לְךָ הִנֵּנוּ:

36 Who has put wisdom in the mind?   מִי־שָׁת בַּטֻּחוֹת חָכְמָה   36
Or who has given understanding to the heart?   אוֹ מִי־נָתַן לַשֶּׂכְוִי בִינָה:

37 Who can number the clouds by wisdom?   מִי־יְסַפֵּר שְׁחָקִים בְּחָכְמָה   37
Or who can pour out the bottles of heaven,   וְנִבְלֵי שָׁמַיִם מִי יַשְׁכִּיב:

38 When the dust hardens in clumps,   בְּצֶקֶת עָפָר לַמּוּצָק   38
And the clods cling together?   וּרְגָבִים יְדֻבָּקוּ:

39 "Can you hunt the prey for the lion,   הֲתָצוּד לְלָבִיא טָרֶף   39
Or satisfy the appetite of the young lions,   וְחַיַּת כְּפִירִים תְּמַלֵּא:

40 When they crouch in *their* dens,   כִּי־יָשֹׁחוּ בַמְּעוֹנוֹת   40
Or lurk in their lairs to lie in wait?   יֵשְׁבוּ בַסֻּכָּה לְמוֹ־אָרֶב:

41 Who provides food for the raven,   מִי יָכִין לָעֹרֵב צֵידוֹ   41
When its young ones cry to God,   כִּי־יְלָדָו אֶל־אֵל יְשַׁוֵּעוּ
And wander about for lack of food?   יִתְעוּ לִבְלִי־אֹכֶל:

39 "Do you know the time when the wild mountain goats bear young?   הֲיָדַעְתָּ עֵת לֶדֶת יַעֲלֵי־סָלַע   **לט**
Or can you mark when the deer gives birth?   חֹלֵל אַיָּלוֹת תִּשְׁמֹר:

2 Can you number the months *that* they fulfill?   תִּסְפֹּר יְרָחִים תְּמַלֶּאנָה   2
Or do you know the time when they bear young?   וְיָדַעְתָּ עֵת לִדְתָּנָה:

3 They bow down,   תִּכְרַעְנָה יַלְדֵיהֶן תְּפַלַּחְנָה   3
They bring forth their young,
They deliver their offspring.   חֶבְלֵיהֶם תְּשַׁלַּחְנָה:

4 Their young ones are healthy,   יַחְלְמוּ בְנֵיהֶם יִרְבּוּ בַבָּר   4
They grow strong with grain;
They depart and do not return to them.   יָצְאוּ וְלֹא־שָׁבוּ לָמוֹ:

5 "Who set the wild donkey free?   מִי־שִׁלַּח פֶּרֶא חָפְשִׁי   5
Who loosed the bonds of the onager,   וּמֹסְרוֹת עָרוֹד מִי פִתֵּחַ:

6 Whose home I have made the wilderness,   אֲשֶׁר־שַׂמְתִּי עֲרָבָה בֵיתוֹ   6
And the barren land his dwelling?   וּמִשְׁכְּנוֹתָיו מְלֵחָה:

7 He scorns the tumult of the city;   יִשְׂחַק לַהֲמוֹן קִרְיָה   7
He does not heed the shouts of the driver.   תְּשֻׁאוֹת נוֹגֵשׂ לֹא יִשְׁמָע:

8 The range of the mountains *is* his pasture,   יְתוּר הָרִים מִרְעֵהוּ   8
And he searches after every green thing.   וְאַחַר כָּל־יָרוֹק יִדְרוֹשׁ:

9 "Will the wild ox be willing to serve you?   הֲיֹאבֶה רֵּים עָבְדֶךָ   9
Will he bed by your manger?   אִם־יָלִין עַל־אֲבוּסֶךָ:

10 Can you bind the wild ox in the furrow with ropes?   הֲתִקְשָׁר־רֵים בְּתֶלֶם עֲבֹתוֹ   10
Or will he plow the valleys behind you?   אִם־יְשַׂדֵּד עֲמָקִים אַחֲרֶיךָ:

11 Will you trust him because his strength *is* great?   הֲתִבְטַח־בּוֹ כִּי־רַב כֹּחוֹ   11
Or will you leave your labor to him?   וְתַעֲזֹב אֵלָיו יְגִיעֶךָ:

12 Will you trust him to bring home your grain,   הֲתַאֲמִין בּוֹ כִּי־יָשׁוּב זַרְעֶךָ   12
And gather it to your threshing floor?   וְגָרְנְךָ יֶאֱסֹף:

13 "The wings of the ostrich wave proudly,   כְּנַף־רְנָנִים נֶעֱלָסָה   13

לח 41 יְלָדָו   לט 12 יָשִׁיב

But are her wings and pinions *like the* kindly
    stork's?

אִם־אֶבְרָה חֲסִידָה וְנֹצָה:

14 For she leaves her eggs on the ground,
    And warms them in the dust;

14 כִּי־תַעֲזֹב לָאָרֶץ בֵּצֶיהָ
וְעַל־עָפָר תְּחַמֵּם:

15 She forgets that a foot may crush them,
    Or that a wild beast may break them.

15 וַתִּשְׁכַּח כִּי־רֶגֶל תְּזוּרֶהָ
וְחַיַּת הַשָּׂדֶה תְּדוּשֶׁהָ:

16 She treats her young harshly, as though *they*
    were not hers;
    Her labor is in vain, without concern,

16 הִקְשִׁיחַ בָּנֶיהָ לְּלֹא־לָהּ
לְרִיק יְגִיעָהּ בְּלִי־פָחַד:

17 Because God deprived her of wisdom,
    And did not endow her with understanding.

17 כִּי־הִשָּׁהּ אֱלוֹהַּ חָכְמָה
וְלֹא־חָלַק לָהּ בַּבִּינָה:

18 When she lifts herself on high,
    She scorns the horse and its rider.

18 כָּעֵת בַּמָּרוֹם תַּמְרִיא
תִּשְׂחַק לַסּוּס וּלְרֹכְבוֹ:

19 "Have you given the horse strength?
    Have you clothed his neck with thunder?

19 הֲתִתֵּן לַסּוּס גְּבוּרָה
הֲתַלְבִּישׁ צַוָּארוֹ רַעְמָה:

20 Can you frighten him like a locust?
    His majestic snorting strikes terror.

20 הֲתַרְעִישֶׁנּוּ כָּאַרְבֶּה
הוֹד נַחְרוֹ אֵימָה:

21 He paws in the valley, and rejoices in *his*
    strength;
    He gallops into the clash of arms.

21 יַחְפְּרוּ בָעֵמֶק וְיָשִׂישׂ בְּכֹחַ
יֵצֵא לִקְרַאת־נָשֶׁק:

22 He mocks at fear, and is not frightened;
    Nor does he turn back from the sword.

22 יִשְׂחַק לְפַחַד וְלֹא יֵחָת
וְלֹא־יָשׁוּב מִפְּנֵי־חָרֶב:

23 The quiver rattles against him,
    The glittering spear and javelin.

23 עָלָיו תִּרְנֶה אַשְׁפָּה
לַהַב חֲנִית וְכִידוֹן:

24 He devours the distance with fierceness and
    rage;
    Nor does he come to a halt because the
    trumpet *has* sounded.

24 בְּרַעַשׁ וְרֹגֶז יְגַמֶּא־אָרֶץ
וְלֹא־יַאֲמִין כִּי־קוֹל שׁוֹפָר:

25 At *the blast of* the trumpet he says, 'Aha!'
    He smells the battle from afar,
    The thunder of captains and shouting.

25 בְּדֵי שֹׁפָר ׀ יֹאמַר הֶאָח
וּמֵרָחוֹק יָרִיחַ מִלְחָמָה
רַעַם שָׂרִים וּתְרוּעָה:

26 "Does the hawk fly by your wisdom,
    And spread its wings toward the south?

26 הֲמִבִּינָתְךָ יַאֲבֶר־נֵץ
יִפְרֹשׂ כְּנָפָו לְתֵימָן:

27 Does the eagle mount up at your command,
    And make its nest on high?

27 אִם־עַל־פִּיךָ יַגְבִּיהַּ נָשֶׁר
וְכִי יָרִים קִנּוֹ:

28 On the rock it dwells and resides,
    On the crag of the rock and the stronghold.

28 סֶלַע יִשְׁכֹּן וְיִתְלֹנָן
עַל־שֶׁן־סֶלַע וּמְצוּדָה:

29 From there it spies out the prey;
    Its eyes observe from afar.

29 מִשָּׁם חָפַר־אֹכֶל
לְמֵרָחוֹק עֵינָיו יַבִּיטוּ:

30 Its young ones suck up blood;
    And where the slain *are*, there it *is*."

30 וְאֶפְרֹחָו יְעַלְעוּ־דָם
וּבַאֲשֶׁר חֲלָלִים שָׁם הוּא:

40 Moreover the LORD answered Job, and said:

מ וַיַּעַן יְהוָה אֶת־אִיּוֹב וַיֹּאמַר:

2 "Shall the one who contends with the
    Almighty correct *Him?*
    He who rebukes God, let him answer it."

2 הֲרֹב עִם־שַׁדַּי יִסּוֹר
מוֹכִיחַ אֱלוֹהַּ יַעֲנֶנָּה:

3 Then Job answered the LORD and said:

3 וַיַּעַן אִיּוֹב אֶת־יְהוָה וַיֹּאמַר:

4 "Behold, I am vile;
    What shall I answer You?
    I lay my hand over my mouth.

4 הֵן קַלֹּתִי מָה אֲשִׁיבֶךָּ
יָדִי שַׂמְתִּי לְמוֹ־פִי:

5 Once I have spoken, but I will not answer;
    Yes, twice, but I will proceed no further."

5 אַחַת דִּבַּרְתִּי וְלֹא אֶעֱנֶה
וּשְׁתַּיִם וְלֹא אוֹסִיף:

לט 26 כְּנָפוֹ 30 וְאֶפְרֹחָיו

6 Then the LORD answered Job out of the whirlwind, and said:

וּשְׁתַּ֫יִם וְלֹ֣א אוֹסִֽיף׃   פ

6 וַיַּֽעַן־יְהֹוָ֣ה אֶת־אִיּ֗וֹב מִן ‹ס› סְעָרָ֑ה
וַיֹּאמַֽר׃

7 "Now prepare yourself like a man;
I will question you, and you shall answer Me:

7 אֱזׇר־נָ֣א כְגֶ֣בֶר חֲלָצֶ֑יךָ
אֶ֝שְׁאׇלְךָ֗ וְהוֹדִיעֵֽנִי׃

8 "Would you indeed annul My judgment?
Would you condemn Me that you may be justified?

8 הַ֭אַף תָּפֵ֣ר מִשְׁפָּטִ֑י
תַּ֝רְשִׁיעֵ֗נִי לְמַ֣עַן תִּצְדָּֽק׃

9 Have you an arm like God?
Or can you thunder with a voice like His?

9 וְאִם־זְר֖וֹעַ כָּאֵ֥ל ׀ לָ֑ךְ
וּ֝בְק֗וֹל כָּמֹ֥הוּ תַרְעֵֽם׃

10 Then adorn yourself with majesty and splendor,
And array yourself with glory and beauty.

10 עֲדֵ֥ה נָ֣א גָֽא֣וֹן וָגֹ֑בַהּ
וְה֖וֹד וְהָדָ֣ר תִּלְבָּֽשׁ׃

11 Disperse the rage of your wrath;
Look on everyone who is proud, and humble him.

11 הָ֭פֵץ עֶבְר֣וֹת אַפֶּ֑ךָ
וּרְאֵ֥ה כָל־גֵּ֝אֶ֗ה וְהַשְׁפִּילֵֽהוּ׃

12 Look on everyone who is proud, and bring him low;
Tread down the wicked in their place.

12 רְאֵ֣ה כָל־גֵּ֭אֶה הַכְנִיעֵ֑הוּ
וַהֲדֹ֖ךְ רְשָׁעִ֣ים תַּחְתָּֽם׃

13 Hide them in the dust together,
Bind their faces in hidden darkness.

13 טׇמְנֵ֣ם בֶּעָפָ֣ר יָ֑חַד
פְּ֝נֵיהֶ֗ם חֲבֹ֥שׁ בַּטָּמֽוּן׃

14 Then I will also confess to you
That your own right hand can save you.

14 וְגַם־אֲנִ֥י אוֹדֶ֑ךָּ
כִּֽי־תוֹשִׁ֖עַ לְךָ֣ יְמִינֶֽךָ׃

15 "Look now at the behemoth, which I made along with you;
He eats grass like an ox.

15 הִנֵּה־נָ֣א בְ֭הֵמוֹת אֲשֶׁר־עָשִׂ֣יתִי עִמָּ֑ךְ
חָ֝צִ֗יר כַּבָּקָ֥ר יֹאכֵֽל׃

16 See now, his strength is in his hips,
And his power is in his stomach muscles.

16 הִנֵּה־נָ֣א כֹח֣וֹ בְמׇתְנָ֑יו
וְ֝אֹנ֗וֹ בִּשְׁרִירֵ֥י בִטְנֽוֹ׃

17 He moves his tail like a cedar;
The sinews of his thighs are tightly knit.

17 יַחְפֹּ֣ץ זְנָב֣וֹ כְמוֹ־אָ֑רֶז
גִּידֵ֖י פַחֲדָ֣ו ‹ס› יְשֹׂרָֽגוּ׃

18 His bones are like beams of bronze,
His ribs like bars of iron.

18 עֲ֭צָמָיו אֲפִיקֵ֣י נְחֻשָׁ֑ה
גְּ֝רָמָ֗יו כִּמְטִ֥יל בַּרְזֶֽל׃

19 He is the first of the ways of God;
Only He who made him can bring near His sword.

19 ה֖וּא רֵאשִׁ֣ית דַּרְכֵי־אֵ֑ל
הָ֝עֹשׂוֹ יַגֵּ֥שׁ חַרְבּֽוֹ׃

20 Surely the mountains yield food for him,
And all the beasts of the field play there.

20 כִּֽי־ב֭וּל הָרִ֣ים יִשְׂאוּ־ל֑וֹ
וְֽכׇל־חַיַּ֥ת הַ֝שָּׂדֶ֗ה יְשַׂחֲקוּ־שָֽׁם׃

21 He lies under the lotus trees,
In a covert of reeds and marsh.

21 תַּֽחַת־צֶאֱלִ֥ים יִשְׁכָּ֑ב
בְּסֵ֖תֶר קָנֶ֣ה וּבִצָּֽה׃

22 The lotus trees cover him with their shade;
The willows by the brook surround him.

22 יְסֻכֻּ֣הוּ צֶאֱלִ֣ים צִֽלְל֑וֹ
יְ֝סֻבּ֗וּהוּ עַרְבֵי־נָֽחַל׃

23 Indeed the river may rage,
Yet he is not disturbed;
He is confident, though the Jordan gushes into his mouth,

23 הֵ֤ן יַעֲשֹׁ֣ק נָ֭הָר לֹ֣א יַחְפּ֑וֹז
יִבְטַ֓ח ׀ כִּֽי־יָגִ֖יחַ יַרְדֵּ֣ן אֶל־פִּֽיהוּ׃

24 Though he takes it in his eyes,
Or one pierces his nose with a snare.

24 בְּעֵינָ֥יו יִקָּחֶ֑נּוּ
בְּ֝מֽוֹקְשִׁ֗ים יִנְקׇב־אָֽף׃

25 תִּמְשֹׁ֣ךְ לִוְיָתָ֣ן בְּחַכָּ֑ה
וּ֝בְחֶ֗בֶל תַּשְׁקִ֥יעַ לְשֹׁנֽוֹ׃

41 "Can you draw out Leviathan with a hook,
Or snare his tongue with a line which you lower?

26 הֲתָשִׂ֣ים אַגְמ֣וֹן בְּאַפּ֑וֹ

2 Can you put a reed through his nose,

ס 6 מֵן ׀ סְעָרָה   17 דָּו פַחֲדָֽיו

Or pierce his jaw with a hook?

3 Will he make many supplications to you?
Will he speak softly to you?
4 Will he make a covenant with you?
Will you take him as a servant forever?
5 Will you play with him as *with* a bird,
Or will you leash him for your maidens?
6 Will *your* companions make a banquet of him?
Will they apportion him among the merchants?
7 Can you fill his skin with harpoons,
Or his head with fishing spears?
8 Lay your hand on him;
Remember the battle—
Never do it again!
9 Indeed, *any* hope of *overcoming* him is false;
Shall *one not* be overwhelmed at the sight of him?
10 No one *is* so fierce that he would dare stir him up.
Who then is able to stand against Me?
11 Who has preceded Me, that I should pay *him*?
Everything under heaven is Mine.

12 "I will not conceal his limbs,
His mighty power, or his graceful proportions.
13 Who can remove his outer coat?
Who can approach *him* with a double bridle?
14 Who can open the doors of his face,
With his terrible teeth all around?
15 *His* rows of scales are *his* pride,
Shut up tightly *as with* a seal;
16 One is so near another
That no air can come between them;
17 They are joined one to another,
They stick together and cannot be parted.
18 His sneezings flash forth light,
And his eyes *are* like the eyelids of the morning.
19 Out of his mouth go burning lights;
Sparks of fire shoot out.
20 Smoke goes out of his nostrils,
As *from* a boiling pot and burning rushes.
21 His breath kindles coals,
And a flame goes out of his mouth.
22 Strength dwells in his neck,
And sorrow dances before him.
23 The folds of his flesh are joined together;
They are firm on him and cannot be moved.
24 His heart is as hard as stone,
Even as hard as the lower *millstone*.

27 וּבְחוֹחַ תִּקּוֹב לֶחֱיוֹ:
הֲיַרְבֶּה אֵלֶיךָ תַּחֲנוּנִים
אִם־יְדַבֵּר אֵלֶיךָ רַכּוֹת:
28 הֲיִכְרֹת בְּרִית עִמָּךְ
תִּקָּחֶנּוּ לְעֶבֶד עוֹלָם:
29 הַתְשַׂחֶק־בּוֹ כַּצִּפּוֹר
וְתִקְשְׁרֶנּוּ לְנַעֲרוֹתֶיךָ:
30 יִכְרוּ עָלָיו חַבָּרִים
יֶחֱצוּהוּ בֵּין כְּנַעֲנִים:
31 הַתְמַלֵּא בְשֻׂכּוֹת עוֹרוֹ
וּבְצִלְצַל דָּגִים רֹאשׁוֹ:
32 שִׂים־עָלָיו כַּפֶּךָ
זְכֹר מִלְחָמָה אַל־תּוֹסַף:

מא הֵן־תֹּחַלְתּוֹ נִכְזָבָה
הֲגַם אֶל־מַרְאָיו יֻטָל:
2 לֹא־אַכְזָר כִּי יְעוּרֶנּוּ
וּמִי הוּא לְפָנַי יִתְיַצָּב:
3 מִי הִקְדִּימַנִי וַאֲשַׁלֵּם
תַּחַת כָּל־הַשָּׁמַיִם לִי־הוּא:
4 לֹא־ אַחֲרִישׁ בַּדָּיו
וּדְבַר־גְּבוּרוֹת וְחִין עֶרְכּוֹ:
5 מִי־גִלָּה פְּנֵי לְבוּשׁוֹ
בְּכֶפֶל רִסְנוֹ מִי יָבוֹא:
6 דַּלְתֵי פָנָיו מִי פִתֵּחַ
סְבִיבוֹת שִׁנָּיו אֵימָה:
7 גַּאֲוָה אֲפִיקֵי מָגִנִּים
סָגוּר חוֹתָם צָר:
8 אֶחָד בְּאֶחָד יִגַּשׁוּ וְרוּחַ לֹא־יָבוֹא בֵינֵיהֶם:
9 אִישׁ־בְּאָחִיהוּ יְדֻבָּקוּ
יִתְלַכְּדוּ וְלֹא יִתְפָּרָדוּ:
10 עֲטִישֹׁתָיו תָּהֶל אוֹר וְעֵינָיו כְּעַפְעַפֵּי־שָׁחַר:
11 מִפִּיו לַפִּידִים יַהֲלֹכוּ
כִּידוֹדֵי אֵשׁ יִתְמַלָּטוּ:
12 מִנְּחִירָיו יֵצֵא עָשָׁן
כְּדוּד נָפוּחַ וְאַגְמֹן:
13 נַפְשׁוֹ גֶּחָלִים תְּלַהֵט וְלַהַב מִפִּיו יֵצֵא:
14 בְּצַוָּארוֹ יָלִין עֹז וּלְפָנָיו תָּדוּץ דְּאָבָה:
15 מַפְּלֵי בְשָׂרוֹ דָבֵקוּ
יָצוּק עָלָיו בַּל־יִמּוֹט:
16 לִבּוֹ יָצוּק כְּמוֹ־אָבֶן וְיָצוּק כְּפֶלַח תַּחְתִּית:

מא 4 לד

25 When he raises himself up, the mighty are
    afraid;
    Because of his crashings they are beside
    themselves.
26 *Though* the sword reaches him, it cannot
    avail;
    Nor does spear, dart, or javelin.
27 He regards iron as straw,
    And bronze as rotten wood.
28 The arrow cannot make him flee;
    Slingstones become like stubble to him.
29 Darts are regarded as straw;
    He laughs at the threat of javelins.
30 His undersides *are* like sharp potsherds;
    He spreads pointed *marks* in the mire.
31 He makes the deep boil like a pot;
    He makes the sea like a pot of ointment.
32 He leaves a shining wake behind him;
    One would think the deep had white hair.
33 On earth there is nothing like him,
    Which is made without fear.
34 He beholds every high *thing;*
    He *is* king over all the children of pride."

42 Then Job answered the LORD and said:

2 "I know that You can do everything,
    And that no purpose *of Yours* can be
    withheld from You.
3 *You asked,* 'Who *is* this who hides counsel
    without knowledge?'
    Therefore I have uttered what I did not
    understand,
    Things too wonderful for me, which I did
    not know.
4 Listen, please, and let me speak;
    You said, 'I will question you, and you shall
    answer Me.'

5 "I have heard of You by the hearing of the
    ear,
    But now my eye sees You.
6 Therefore I abhor *myself,*
    And repent in dust and ashes."

7 And so it was, after the LORD had spoken these
words to Job, that the LORD said to Eliphaz the
Temanite, "My wrath is aroused against you and
your two friends, for you have not spoken of Me
what is right, as My servant Job *has.* 8 Now
therefore, take for yourselves seven bulls and seven
rams, go to My servant Job, and offer up for
yourselves a burnt offering; and My servant Job
shall pray for you. For I will accept him, lest I deal

17 מִשֵּׂתוֹ יָגוּרוּ אֵלִים
מִשְּׁבָרִים יִתְחַטָּאוּ:
18 מַשִּׂיגֵהוּ חֶרֶב בְּלִי תָקוּם
חֲנִית מַסָּע וְשִׁרְיָה:
19 יַחְשֹׁב לְתֶבֶן בַּרְזֶל
לְעֵץ רִקָּבוֹן נְחוּשָׁה:
20 לֹא־יַבְרִיחֶנּוּ בֶן־קָשֶׁת
לְקַשׁ נֶהְפְּכוּ־לוֹ אַבְנֵי־קָלַע:
21 כְּקַשׁ נֶחְשְׁבוּ תוֹתָח
וְיִשְׂחַק לְרַעַשׁ כִּידוֹן:
22 תַּחְתָּיו חַדּוּדֵי חָרֶשׂ
יִרְפַּד חָרוּץ עֲלֵי־טִיט:
23 יַרְתִּיחַ כַּסִּיר מְצוּלָה
יָם יָשִׂים כַּמֶּרְקָחָה:
24 אַחֲרָיו יָאִיר נָתִיב
יַחְשֹׁב תְּהוֹם לְשֵׂיבָה:
25 אֵין־עַל־עָפָר מָשְׁלוֹ
הֶעָשׂוּ לִבְלִי־חָת:
26 אֶת־כָּל־גָּבֹהַּ יִרְאֶה
הוּא מֶלֶךְ עַל־כָּל־בְּנֵי־שָׁחַץ: ס

מב וַיַּעַן אִיּוֹב אֶת־יְהֹוָה וַיֹּאמַר:
2 יָדַעְתָּ כִּי־כֹל תּוּכָל
וְלֹא־יִבָּצֵר מִמְּךָ מְזִמָּה:
3 מִי זֶה ׀ מַעְלִים עֵצָה
בְּלִי דָעַת
לָכֵן הִגַּדְתִּי וְלֹא אָבִין
נִפְלָאוֹת מִמֶּנִּי וְלֹא אֵדָע:
4 שְׁמַע־נָא וְאָנֹכִי אֲדַבֵּר
אֶשְׁאָלְךָ וְהוֹדִיעֵנִי:
5 לְשֵׁמַע־אֹזֶן שְׁמַעְתִּיךָ
וְעַתָּה עֵינִי רָאָתְךָ:
6 עַל־כֵּן אֶמְאַס וְנִחַמְתִּי
עַל־עָפָר וָאֵפֶר: פ

7 וַיְהִי אַחַר דִּבֶּר יְהֹוָה אֶת־הַדְּבָרִים הָאֵלֶּה אֶל־אִיּוֹב
וַיֹּאמֶר יְהֹוָה אֶל־אֱלִיפַז הַתֵּימָנִי חָרָה אַפִּי בְךָ וּבִשְׁנֵי
רֵעֶיךָ כִּי לֹא דִבַּרְתֶּם אֵלַי נְכוֹנָה כְּעַבְדִּי אִיּוֹב:
8 וְעַתָּה קְחוּ־לָכֶם שִׁבְעָה־פָרִים וְשִׁבְעָה אֵילִים
וּלְכוּ ׀ אֶל־עַבְדִּי אִיּוֹב וְהַעֲלִיתֶם עוֹלָה בַּעַדְכֶם

with you *according to your* folly; because you have not spoken of Me *what is* right, as My servant Job *has*."

⁹ So Eliphaz the Temanite and Bildad the Shuhite *and* Zophar the Naamathite went and did as the Lord commanded them; for the Lord had accepted Job. ¹⁰ And the Lord restored Job's losses when he prayed for his friends. Indeed the Lord gave Job twice as much as he had before. ¹¹ Then all his brothers, all his sisters, and all those who had been his acquaintances before, came to him and ate food with him in his house; and they consoled him and comforted him for all the adversity that the Lord had brought upon him. Each one gave him a piece of silver and each a ring of gold.

¹² Now the Lord blessed the latter *days* of Job more than his beginning; for he had fourteen thousand sheep, six thousand camels, one thousand yoke of oxen, and one thousand female donkeys. ¹³ He also had seven sons and three daughters. ¹⁴ And he called the name of the first Jemimah, the name of the second Keziah, and the name of the third Keren-Happuch. ¹⁵ In all the land were found no women *so* beautiful as the daughters of Job; and their father gave them an inheritance among their brothers.

¹⁶ After this Job lived one hundred and forty years, and saw his children and grandchildren *for* four generations. ¹⁷ So Job died, old and full of days.

וְאִיּוֹב עַבְדִּי יִתְפַּלֵּל עֲלֵיכֶם כִּי אִם־פָּנָיו אֶשָּׂא
לְבִלְתִּי עֲשׂוֹת עִמָּכֶם נְבָלָה כִּי לֹא דִבַּרְתֶּם אֵלַי
נְכוֹנָה כְּעַבְדִּי אִיּוֹב: 9 וַיֵּלְכוּ אֱלִיפַז הַתֵּימָנִי וּבִלְדַּד
הַשּׁוּחִי צֹפַר הַנַּעֲמָתִי וַיַּעֲשׂוּ כַּאֲשֶׁר דִּבֶּר אֲלֵיהֶם
יְהֹוָה וַיִּשָּׂא יְהֹוָה אֶת־פְּנֵי אִיּוֹב: 10 וַיהֹוָה שָׁב אֶת־
שְׁבִית אִיּוֹב בְּהִתְפַּלְלוֹ בְּעַד רֵעֵהוּ וַיֹּסֶף יְהֹוָה
אֶת־כָּל־אֲשֶׁר לְאִיּוֹב לְמִשְׁנֶה: 11 וַיָּבֹאוּ אֵלָיו כָּל־
אֶחָיו וְכָל־אַחְיֹתָיו וְכָל־יֹדְעָיו לְפָנִים וַיֹּאכְלוּ עִמּוֹ
לֶחֶם בְּבֵיתוֹ וַיָּנֻדוּ לוֹ וַיְנַחֲמוּ אֹתוֹ עַל כָּל־הָרָעָה
אֲשֶׁר־הֵבִיא יְהֹוָה עָלָיו וַיִּתְּנוּ־לוֹ אִישׁ קְשִׂיטָה אֶחָת
וְאִישׁ נֶזֶם זָהָב אֶחָד: ס   12 וַיהֹוָה בֵּרַךְ
אֶת־אַחֲרִית אִיּוֹב מֵרֵאשִׁתוֹ וַיְהִי־לוֹ אַרְבָּעָה עָשָׂר
אֶלֶף צֹאן וְשֵׁשֶׁת אֲלָפִים גְּמַלִּים וְאֶלֶף־צֶמֶד בָּקָר
וְאֶלֶף אֲתוֹנוֹת: 13 וַיְהִי־לוֹ שִׁבְעָנָה בָנִים וְשָׁלוֹשׁ
בָּנוֹת: 14 וַיִּקְרָא שֵׁם־הָאַחַת יְמִימָה וְשֵׁם הַשֵּׁנִית
קְצִיעָה וְשֵׁם הַשְּׁלִישִׁית קֶרֶן הַפּוּךְ: 15 וְלֹא נִמְצָא
נָשִׁים יָפוֹת כִּבְנוֹת אִיּוֹב בְּכָל־הָאָרֶץ וַיִּתֵּן לָהֶם
אֲבִיהֶם נַחֲלָה בְּתוֹךְ אֲחֵיהֶם: ס   16 וַיְחִי
אִיּוֹב אַחֲרֵי־זֹאת מֵאָה וְאַרְבָּעִים שָׁנָה וַיִּרְאֶה אֶת־
בָּנָיו וְאֶת־בְּנֵי בָנָיו אַרְבָּעָה דֹּרוֹת: 17 וַיָּמָת אִיּוֹב
זָקֵן וּשְׂבַע יָמִים: ס

The

SONG OF SOLOMON

1 The song of songs, which *is* Solomon's.

2   Let him kiss me with the kisses of his mouth—
    For your love *is* better than wine.

3   Because of the fragrance of your good ointments,
    Your name *is* ointment poured forth;
    Therefore the virgins love you.

4   Draw me away!
    We will run after you.
    The king has brought me into his chambers.
    We will be glad and rejoice in you.
    We will remember your love more than wine.
    Rightly do they love you.

5   I *am* dark, but lovely,
    O daughters of Jerusalem,
    Like the tents of Kedar,
    Like the curtains of Solomon.

6   Do not look upon me, because I *am* dark,
    Because the sun has tanned me.
    My mother's sons were angry with me;
    They made me the keeper of the vineyards,
    But my own vineyard I have not kept.

7   Tell me, O you whom I love,
    Where you feed *your flock,*
    Where you make *it* rest at noon.
    For why should I be as one who veils herself
    By the flocks of your companions?

8   If you do not know, O fairest among women,
    Follow in the footsteps of the flock,
    And feed your little goats
    Beside the shepherds' tents.

9   I have compared you, my love,
    To my filly among Pharaoh's chariots.

10   Your cheeks are lovely with ornaments,
    Your neck with chains *of gold.*

11   We will make you ornaments of gold
    With studs of silver.

12   While the king *is* at his table,
    My spikenard sends forth its fragrance.

13   A bundle of myrrh *is* my beloved to me,
    That lies all night between my breasts.

14   My beloved *is* to me a cluster of henna *blooms*
    In the vineyards of En Gedi.

15   Behold, you *are* fair, my love!
    Behold, you *are* fair!
    You *have* dove's eyes.

16   Behold, you *are* handsome, my beloved!
    Yes, pleasant!
    Also our bed *is* green.

17   The beams of our houses *are* cedar,
    And our rafters of fir.

2   I *am* the rose of Sharon,
    And the lily of the valleys.

שִׁיר הַשִּׁירִים אֲשֶׁר לִשְׁלֹמֹה: 2 יִשָּׁקֵנִי מִנְּשִׁיקוֹת א
פִּיהוּ כִּי־טוֹבִים דֹּדֶיךָ מִיָּיִן: 3 לְרֵיחַ שְׁמָנֶיךָ
טוֹבִים שֶׁמֶן תּוּרַק שְׁמֶךָ עַל־כֵּן עֲלָמוֹת אֲהֵבוּךָ:
4 מָשְׁכֵנִי אַחֲרֶיךָ נָּרוּצָה הֱבִיאַנִי הַמֶּלֶךְ חֲדָרָיו
נָגִילָה וְנִשְׂמְחָה בָּךְ נַזְכִּירָה דֹדֶיךָ מִיַּיִן מֵישָׁרִים
אֲהֵבוּךָ: ס 5 שְׁחוֹרָה אֲנִי וְנָאוָה בְּנוֹת
יְרוּשָׁלָ͏ִם כְּאָהֳלֵי קֵדָר כִּירִיעוֹת שְׁלֹמֹה: 6 אַל־
תִּרְאוּנִי שֶׁאֲנִי שְׁחַרְחֹרֶת שֶׁשֱּׁזָפַתְנִי הַשָּׁמֶשׁ בְּנֵי
אִמִּי נִחֲרוּ־בִי שָׂמֻנִי נֹטֵרָה אֶת־הַכְּרָמִים כַּרְמִי
שֶׁלִּי לֹא נָטָרְתִּי: 7 הַגִּידָה לִּי שֶׁאָהֲבָה נַפְשִׁי
אֵיכָה תִרְעֶה אֵיכָה תַּרְבִּיץ בַּצָּהֳרָיִם שַׁלָּמָה אֶהְיֶה
כְּעֹטְיָה עַל עֶדְרֵי חֲבֵרֶיךָ: 8 אִם־לֹא תֵדְעִי לָךְ
הַיָּפָה בַּנָּשִׁים צְאִי־לָךְ בְּעִקְבֵי הַצֹּאן וּרְעִי אֶת־
גְּדִיֹּתַיִךְ עַל מִשְׁכְּנוֹת הָרֹעִים: ס 9 לְסֻסָתִי
בְּרִכְבֵי פַרְעֹה דִּמִּיתִיךְ רַעְיָתִי: 10 נָאווּ לְחָיַיִךְ
בַּתֹּרִים צַוָּארֵךְ בַּחֲרוּזִים: 11 תּוֹרֵי זָהָב נַעֲשֶׂה־לָּךְ
עִם נְקֻדּוֹת הַכָּסֶף: 12 עַד־שֶׁהַמֶּלֶךְ בִּמְסִבּוֹ נִרְדִּי
נָתַן רֵיחוֹ: 13 צְרוֹר הַמֹּר ׀ דּוֹדִי לִי בֵּין שָׁדַי
יָלִין: 14 אֶשְׁכֹּל הַכֹּפֶר ׀ דּוֹדִי לִי בְּכַרְמֵי עֵין
גֶּדִי: ס 15 הִנָּךְ יָפָה רַעְיָתִי הִנָּךְ יָפָה
עֵינַיִךְ יוֹנִים: 16 הִנְּךָ יָפֶה דוֹדִי אַף נָעִים אַף־עַרְשֵׂנוּ
רַעֲנָנָה: 17 קֹרוֹת בָּתֵּינוּ אֲרָזִים רַחִיטֵנוּ[ק] בְּרוֹתִים:

אֲנִי חֲבַצֶּלֶת הַשָּׁרוֹן שׁוֹשַׁנַּת הָעֲמָקִים: ב

2 Like a lily among thorns,
   So is my love among the daughters.
3 Like an apple tree among the trees of the woods,
   So *is* my beloved among the sons.
   I sat down in his shade with great delight,
   And his fruit *was* sweet to my taste.
4 He brought me to the banqueting house,
   And his banner over me *was* love.
5 Sustain me with cakes of raisins,
   Refresh me with apples,
   For I *am* lovesick.
6 His left hand *is* under my head,
   And his right hand embraces me.
7 I charge you, O daughters of Jerusalem,
   By the gazelles or by the does of the field,
   Do not stir up nor awaken love
   Until it pleases.
8 The voice of my beloved!
   Behold, he comes
   Leaping upon the mountains,
   Skipping upon the hills.
9 My beloved is like a gazelle or a young stag.
   Behold, he stands behind our wall;
   He is looking through the windows,
   Gazing through the lattice.
10 My beloved spoke, and said to me:
   "Rise up, my love, my fair one,
   And come away.
11 For lo, the winter is past,
   The rain is over *and* gone.
12 The flowers appear on the earth;
   The time of singing has come,
   And the voice of the turtledove
   Is heard in our land.
13 The fig tree puts forth her green figs,
   And the vines *with* the tender grapes
   Give a good smell.
   Rise up, my love, my fair one,
   And come away!
14 "O my dove, in the clefts of the rock,
   In the secret *places* of the cliff,
   Let me see your face,
   Let me hear your voice;
   For your voice *is* sweet,
   And your face *is* lovely."
15 Catch us the foxes,
   The little foxes that spoil the vines,
   For our vines *have* tender grapes.
16 My beloved *is* mine, and I *am* his.
   He feeds *his flock* among the lilies.
17 Until the day breaks
   And the shadows flee away,
   Turn, my beloved,
   And be like a gazelle
   Or a young stag
   Upon the mountains of Bether.

3 By night on my bed I sought the one I love;
   I sought him, but I did not find him.
2 "I will rise now," *I said,*
   "And go about the city;

כְּשֽׁוֹשַׁנָּה בֵּין הַחוֹחִים כֵּן רַעְיָתִי בֵּין הַבָּנֽוֹת: 2

כְּתַפּוּחַ בַּעֲצֵי הַיַּעַר כֵּן דּוֹדִי בֵּין הַבָּנִים בְּצִלּוֹ 3
חִמַּדְתִּי וְיָשַׁבְתִּי וּפִרְיוֹ מָתוֹק לְחִכִּי: הֱבִיאַנִי אֶל־ 4
בֵּית הַיַּיִן וְדִגְלוֹ עָלַי אַהֲבָה: סַמְּכוּנִי בָּאֲשִׁישׁוֹת 5
רַפְּדוּנִי בַּתַּפּוּחִים כִּי־חוֹלַת אַהֲבָה אָנִי: שְׂמֹאלוֹ 6
תַּחַת לְרֹאשִׁי וִימִינוֹ תְּחַבְּקֵנִי: הִשְׁבַּעְתִּי אֶתְכֶם 7
בְּנוֹת יְרוּשָׁלַ͏ִם בִּצְבָאוֹת אוֹ בְּאַיְלוֹת הַשָּׂדֶה
אִם־תָּעִירוּ ׀ וְאִם־תְּעֽוֹרְרוּ אֶת־הָאַהֲבָה עַד
שֶׁתֶּחְפָּץ: ס קוֹל דּוֹדִי הִנֵּה־זֶה בָּא 8
מְדַלֵּג עַל־הֶהָרִים מְקַפֵּץ עַל־הַגְּבָעֽוֹת: דּוֹמֶה 9
דוֹדִי לִצְבִי אוֹ לְעֹפֶר הָאַיָּלִים הִנֵּה־זֶה עוֹמֵד אַחַר
כָּתְלֵנוּ מַשְׁגִּיחַ מִן־הַחַלֹּנוֹת מֵצִיץ מִן־הַחֲרַכִּֽים:
עָנָה דוֹדִי וְאָמַר לִי קוּמִי לָךְ רַעְיָתִי יָפָתִי וּלְכִי־ 10
לָךְ: כִּי־הִנֵּה הַסְּתָו עָבָר הַגֶּשֶׁם חָלַף הָלַךְ 11
לֽוֹ: הַנִּצָּנִים נִרְאוּ בָאָרֶץ עֵת הַזָּמִיר הִגִּיעַ וְקוֹל 12
הַתּוֹר נִשְׁמַע בְּאַרְצֵֽנוּ: הַתְּאֵנָה חָנְטָה פַגֶּיהָ 13
וְהַגְּפָנִים ׀ סְמָדַר נָתְנוּ רֵיחַ קוּמִי לָכְי רַעְיָתִי יָפָתִי
וּלְכִי־לָֽךְ: ס יוֹנָתִי בְּחַגְוֵי הַסֶּלַע בְּסֵתֶר 14
הַמַּדְרֵגָה הַרְאִינִי אֶת־מַרְאַיִךְ הַשְׁמִיעִנִי אֶת־קוֹלֵךְ
כִּי־קוֹלֵךְ עָרֵב וּמַרְאֵיךְ נָאוֶֽה: ס אֶחֱזוּ־ 15
לָנוּ שֽׁוּעָלִים שֻׁעָלִים קְטַנִּים מְחַבְּלִים כְּרָמִים
וּכְרָמֵינוּ סְמָדַֽר: דּוֹדִי לִי וַאֲנִי לוֹ הָרֹעֶה 16
בַּשּׁוֹשַׁנִּֽים: עַד שֶׁיָּפֽוּחַ הַיּוֹם וְנָסוּ הַצְּלָלִים סֹב 17
דְּמֵה־לְךָ דוֹדִי לִצְבִי אוֹ לְעֹפֶר הָאַיָּלִים עַל־הָרֵי
בָֽתֶר: ס

ג עַל־מִשְׁכָּבִי בַּלֵּילוֹת בִּקַּשְׁתִּי אֵת שֶׁאָהֲבָה נַפְשִׁי
בִּקַּשְׁתִּיו וְלֹא מְצָאתִֽיו: אָקֽוּמָה נָּא וַאֲסוֹבְבָה 2

ב 11 הַסְּתָיו   13 לָךְ

In the streets and in the squares
I will seek the one I love."
I sought him, but I did not find him.

3 The watchmen who go about the city found me;
I said,
"Have you seen the one I love?"

4 Scarcely had I passed by them,
When I found the one I love.
I held him and would not let him go,
Until I had brought him to the house of my
    mother,
And into the chamber of her who conceived me.

5 I charge you, O daughters of Jerusalem,
By the gazelles or by the does of the field,
Do not stir up nor awaken love
Until it pleases.

6 Who *is* this coming out of the wilderness
Like pillars of smoke,
Perfumed with myrrh and frankincense,
With all the merchant's fragrant powders?

7 Behold, it *is* Solomon's couch,
With sixty valiant men around it,
Of the valiant of Israel.

8 They all hold swords,
Being expert in war.
Every man *has* his sword on his thigh
Because of fear in the night.

9 Of the wood of Lebanon
Solomon the King
Made himself a palanquin:

10 He made its pillars *of* silver,
Its support *of* gold,
Its seat *of* purple,
Its interior paved *with* love
By the daughters of Jerusalem.

11 Go forth, O daughters of Zion,
And see King Solomon with the crown
With which his mother crowned him
On the day of his wedding,
The day of the gladness of his heart.

4

Behold, you *are* fair, my love!
Behold, you *are* fair!
You *have* dove's eyes behind your veil.
Your hair *is* like a flock of goats,
Going down from Mount Gilead.

2 Your teeth *are* like a flock of shorn *sheep*
Which have come up from the washing,
Every one of which bears twins,
And none *is* barren among them.

3 Your lips *are* like a strand of scarlet,
And your mouth is lovely.
Your temples behind your veil
Are like a piece of pomegranate.

4 Your neck *is* like the tower of David,
Built for an armory,
On which hang a thousand bucklers,
All shields of mighty men.

5 Your two breasts *are* like two fawns,
Twins of a gazelle,

בָּעִיר בַּשְּׁוָקִים וּבָרְחֹבוֹת אֲבַקְשָׁה אֵת שֶׁאָהֲבָה
נַפְשִׁי בִּקַּשְׁתִּיו וְלֹא מְצָאתִיו: 3 מְצָאוּנִי הַשֹּׁמְרִים
הַסֹּבְבִים בָּעִיר אֵת שֶׁאָהֲבָה נַפְשִׁי רְאִיתֶם:
4 כִּמְעַט שֶׁעָבַרְתִּי מֵהֶם עַד שֶׁמָּצָאתִי אֵת שֶׁאָהֲבָה
נַפְשִׁי אֲחַזְתִּיו וְלֹא אַרְפֶּנּוּ עַד־שֶׁהֲבֵיאתִיו אֶל־
בֵּית אִמִּי וְאֶל־חֶדֶר הוֹרָתִי: 5 הִשְׁבַּעְתִּי אֶתְכֶם
בְּנוֹת יְרוּשָׁלַם בִּצְבָאוֹת אוֹ בְּאַיְלוֹת הַשָּׂדֶה
אִם־תָּעִירוּ ׀ וְאִם־תְּעוֹרְרוּ אֶת־הָאַהֲבָה עַד
שֶׁתֶּחְפָּץ: ס 6 מִי זֹאת עֹלָה מִן־הַמִּדְבָּר
כְּתִימֲרוֹת עָשָׁן מְקֻטֶּרֶת מוֹר וּלְבוֹנָה מִכֹּל אַבְקַת
רוֹכֵל: 7 הִנֵּה מִטָּתוֹ שֶׁלִּשְׁלֹמֹה שִׁשִּׁים גִּבֹּרִים
סָבִיב לָהּ מִגִּבֹּרֵי יִשְׂרָאֵל: 8 כֻּלָּם אֲחֻזֵי חֶרֶב
מְלֻמְּדֵי מִלְחָמָה אִישׁ חַרְבּוֹ עַל־יְרֵכוֹ מִפַּחַד
בַּלֵּילוֹת: ס 9 אַפִּרְיוֹן עָשָׂה לוֹ הַמֶּלֶךְ
שְׁלֹמֹה מֵעֲצֵי הַלְּבָנוֹן: 10 עַמּוּדָיו עָשָׂה כֶסֶף
רְפִידָתוֹ זָהָב מֶרְכָּבוֹ אַרְגָּמָן תּוֹכוֹ רָצוּף אַהֲבָה
מִבְּנוֹת יְרוּשָׁלָם: 11 צְאֶינָה ׀ וּרְאֶינָה בְּנוֹת צִיּוֹן
בַּמֶּלֶךְ שְׁלֹמֹה בָּעֲטָרָה שֶׁעִטְּרָה־לּוֹ אִמּוֹ בְּיוֹם
חֲתֻנָּתוֹ וּבְיוֹם שִׂמְחַת לִבּוֹ: ס

ד הִנָּךְ יָפָה רַעְיָתִי הִנָּךְ יָפָה עֵינַיִךְ יוֹנִים
מִבַּעַד לְצַמָּתֵךְ שַׂעְרֵךְ כְּעֵדֶר הָעִזִּים שֶׁגָּלְשׁוּ
מֵהַר גִּלְעָד: 2 שִׁנַּיִךְ כְּעֵדֶר הַקְּצוּבוֹת שֶׁעָלוּ מִן־
הָרַחְצָה שֶׁכֻּלָּם מַתְאִימוֹת וְשַׁכֻּלָה אֵין בָּהֶם:
3 כְּחוּט הַשָּׁנִי שִׂפְתֹתַיִךְ וּמִדְבָּרֵיךְ נָאוֶה כְּפֶלַח
הָרִמּוֹן רַקָּתֵךְ מִבַּעַד לְצַמָּתֵךְ: 4 כְּמִגְדַּל דָּוִיד
צַוָּארֵךְ בָּנוּי לְתַלְפִּיּוֹת אֶלֶף הַמָּגֵן תָּלוּי עָלָיו
כֹּל שִׁלְטֵי הַגִּבֹּרִים: 5 שְׁנֵי שָׁדַיִךְ כִּשְׁנֵי עֳפָרִים

Which feed among the lilies.

6 Until the day breaks
And the shadows flee away,
I will go my way to the mountain of myrrh
And to the hill of frankincense.

7 You *are* all fair, my love,
And *there is* no spot in you.

8 Come with me from Lebanon, *my* spouse,
With me from Lebanon.
Look from the top of Amana,
From the top of Senir and Hermon,
From the lions' dens,
From the mountains of the leopards.

9 You have ravished my heart,
My sister, *my* spouse;
You have ravished my heart
With one *look* of your eyes,
With one link of your necklace.

10 How fair is your love,
My sister, *my* spouse!
How much better than wine is your love,
And the scent of your perfumes
Than all spices!

11 Your lips, O *my* spouse,
Drip as the honeycomb;
Honey and milk *are* under your tongue;
And the fragrance of your garments
Is like the fragrance of Lebanon.

12 A garden enclosed
Is my sister, *my* spouse,
A spring shut up,
A fountain sealed.

13 Your plants *are* an orchard of pomegranates
With pleasant fruits,
Fragrant henna with spikenard,

14 Spikenard and saffron,
Calamus and cinnamon,
With all trees of frankincense,
Myrrh and aloes,
With all the chief spices—

15 A fountain of gardens,
A well of living waters,
And streams from Lebanon.

16 Awake, O north *wind,*
And come, O south!
Blow upon my garden,
That its spices may flow out.
Let my beloved come to his garden
And eat its pleasant fruits.

5 I have come to my garden, my sister, *my* spouse;
I have gathered my myrrh with my spice;
I have eaten my honeycomb with my honey;
I have drunk my wine with my milk.
Eat, O friends!
Drink, yes, drink deeply,
O beloved ones!

2 I sleep, but my heart is awake;
It is the voice of my beloved!
He knocks, *saying,*

תְּאוֹמֵי צְבִיָּה הָרוֹעִים בַּשּׁוֹשַׁנִּים: 6 עַד שֶׁיָּפוּחַ
הַיּוֹם וְנָסוּ הַצְּלָלִים אֵלֶךְ לִי אֶל־הַר הַמּוֹר וְאֶל־
גִּבְעַת הַלְּבוֹנָה: 7 כֻּלָּךְ יָפָה רַעְיָתִי וּמוּם אֵין
בָּךְ: ס 8 אִתִּי מִלְּבָנוֹן כַּלָּה אִתִּי מִלְּבָנוֹן
תָּבוֹאִי תָּשׁוּרִי ׀ מֵרֹאשׁ אֲמָנָה מֵרֹאשׁ שְׂנִיר
וְחֶרְמוֹן מִמְּעֹנוֹת אֲרָיוֹת מֵהַרְרֵי נְמֵרִים: 9 לִבַּבְתִּנִי
אֲחֹתִי כַלָּה לִבַּבְתִּנִי בְּאַחַד מֵעֵינַיִךְ בְּאַחַד עֲנָק
מִצַּוְּרֹנָיִךְ: 10 מַה־יָּפוּ דֹדַיִךְ אֲחֹתִי כַלָּה מַה־טֹּבוּ
דֹדַיִךְ מִיַּיִן וְרֵיחַ שְׁמָנַיִךְ מִכָּל־בְּשָׂמִים: 11 נֹפֶת
תִּטֹּפְנָה שִׂפְתוֹתַיִךְ כַּלָּה דְּבַשׁ וְחָלָב תַּחַת לְשׁוֹנֵךְ
וְרֵיחַ שַׂלְמֹתַיִךְ כְּרֵיחַ לְבָנוֹן: ס 12 גַּן ׀
נָעוּל אֲחֹתִי כַלָּה גַּל נָעוּל מַעְיָן חָתוּם: 13 שְׁלָחַיִךְ
פַּרְדֵּס רִמּוֹנִים עִם פְּרִי מְגָדִים כְּפָרִים עִם־נְרָדִים:
14 נֵרְדְּ ׀ וְכַרְכֹּם קָנֶה וְקִנָּמוֹן עִם כָּל־עֲצֵי לְבוֹנָה
מֹר וַאֲהָלוֹת עִם כָּל־רָאשֵׁי בְשָׂמִים: 15 מַעְיַן גַּנִּים
בְּאֵר מַיִם חַיִּים וְנֹזְלִים מִן־לְבָנוֹן: 16 עוּרִי צָפוֹן
וּבוֹאִי תֵימָן הָפִיחִי גַנִּי יִזְּלוּ בְשָׂמָיו יָבֹא דוֹדִי לְגַנּוֹ
וְיֹאכַל פְּרִי מְגָדָיו:

ה בָּאתִי לְגַנִּי אֲחֹתִי כַלָּה אָרִיתִי מוֹרִי עִם־בְּשָׂמִי
אָכַלְתִּי יַעְרִי עִם־דִּבְשִׁי שָׁתִיתִי יֵינִי עִם־חֲלָבִי אִכְלוּ
רֵעִים שְׁתוּ וְשִׁכְרוּ דּוֹדִים: ס 2 אֲנִי יְשֵׁנָה
וְלִבִּי עֵר קוֹל ׀ דּוֹדִי דוֹפֵק פִּתְחִי־לִי אֲחֹתִי רַעְיָתִי

ד 9 בְּאַחַת

"Open for me, my sister, my love,
My dove, my perfect one;
For my head is covered with dew,
My locks with the drops of the night."

3 I have taken off my robe;
How can I put it on *again*?
I have washed my feet;
How can I defile them?
4 My beloved put his hand
By the latch *of the door*,
And my heart yearned for him.
5 I arose to open for my beloved,
And my hands dripped *with* myrrh,
My fingers with liquid myrrh,
On the handles of the lock.

6 I opened for my beloved,
But my beloved had turned away *and* was gone.
My heart leaped up when he spoke.
I sought him, but I could not find him;
I called him, but he gave me no answer.
7 The watchmen who went about the city found
me.
They struck me, they wounded me;
The keepers of the walls
Took my veil away from me.
8 I charge you, O daughters of Jerusalem,
If you find my beloved,
That you tell him I *am* lovesick!
9 What *is* your beloved
More than *another* beloved,
O fairest among women?
What *is* your beloved
More than *another* beloved,
That you so charge us?
10 My beloved *is* white and ruddy,
Chief among ten thousand.
11 His head *is like* the finest gold;
His locks *are* wavy,
And black as a raven.
12 His eyes *are* like doves
By the rivers of waters,
Washed with milk,
And fitly set.
13 His cheeks *are* like a bed of spices,
Banks of scented herbs.
His lips *are* lilies,
Dripping liquid myrrh.
14 His hands *are* rods of gold
Set with beryl.
His body *is* carved ivory
Inlaid *with* sapphires.
15 His legs *are* pillars of marble
Set on bases of fine gold.
His countenance *is* like Lebanon,
Excellent as the cedars.
16 His mouth *is* most sweet,
Yes, he *is* altogether lovely.
This *is* my beloved,
And this *is* my friend,
O daughters of Jerusalem!

יוֹנָתִי תַמָּתִי שֶׁרֹאשִׁי נִמְלָא־טָל קְוֻצּוֹתַי רְסִיסֵי

לָיְלָה: 3 פָּשַׁטְתִּי אֶת־כֻּתָּנְתִּי אֵיכָכָה אֶלְבָּשֶׁנָּה

רָחַצְתִּי אֶת־רַגְלַי אֵיכָכָה אֲטַנְּפֵם: 4 דּוֹדִי שָׁלַח

יָדוֹ מִן־הַחֹר וּמֵעַי הָמוּ עָלָיו: 5 קַמְתִּי אֲנִי לִפְתֹּחַ

לְדוֹדִי וְיָדַי נָטְפוּ־מוֹר וְאֶצְבְּעֹתַי מוֹר עֹבֵר עַל

כַּפּוֹת הַמַּנְעוּל: 6 פָּתַחְתִּי אֲנִי לְדוֹדִי וְדוֹדִי חָמַק

עָבָר נַפְשִׁי יָצְאָה בְדַבְּרוֹ בִּקַּשְׁתִּיהוּ וְלֹא מְצָאתִיהוּ

קְרָאתִיו וְלֹא עָנָנִי: 7 מְצָאֻנִי הַשֹּׁמְרִים הַסֹּבְבִים

בָּעִיר הִכּוּנִי פְצָעוּנִי נָשְׂאוּ אֶת־רְדִידִי מֵעָלַי שֹׁמְרֵי

הַחֹמוֹת: 8 הִשְׁבַּעְתִּי אֶתְכֶם בְּנוֹת יְרוּשָׁלִָם אִם־

תִּמְצְאוּ אֶת־דּוֹדִי מַה־תַּגִּידוּ לוֹ שֶׁחוֹלַת אַהֲבָה

אָנִי: 9 מַה־דּוֹדֵךְ מִדּוֹד הַיָּפָה בַּנָּשִׁים מַה־דּוֹדֵךְ

מִדּוֹד שֶׁכָּכָה הִשְׁבַּעְתָּנוּ: 10 דּוֹדִי צַח וְאָדוֹם דָּגוּל

מֵרְבָבָה: 11 רֹאשׁוֹ כֶּתֶם פָּז קְוֻצּוֹתָיו תַּלְתַּלִּים

שְׁחֹרוֹת כָּעוֹרֵב: 12 עֵינָיו כְּיוֹנִים עַל־אֲפִיקֵי מָיִם

רֹחֲצוֹת בֶּחָלָב יֹשְׁבוֹת עַל־מִלֵּאת: 13 לְחָיָו כַּעֲרוּגַת

הַבֹּשֶׂם מִגְדְּלוֹת מֶרְקָחִים שִׂפְתוֹתָיו שׁוֹשַׁנִּים

נֹטְפוֹת מוֹר עֹבֵר: 14 יָדָיו גְּלִילֵי זָהָב מְמֻלָּאִים

בַּתַּרְשִׁישׁ מֵעָיו עֶשֶׁת שֵׁן מְעֻלֶּפֶת סַפִּירִים:

15 שׁוֹקָיו עַמּוּדֵי שֵׁשׁ מְיֻסָּדִים עַל־אַדְנֵי־פָז מַרְאֵהוּ

כַּלְּבָנוֹן בָּחוּר כָּאֲרָזִים: 16 חִכּוֹ מַמְתַקִּים וְכֻלּוֹ

מַחֲמַדִּים זֶה דוֹדִי וְזֶה רֵעִי בְּנוֹת יְרוּשָׁלִָם:

6 Where has your beloved gone,
    O fairest among women?
    Where has your beloved turned aside,
    That we may seek him with you?

2 My beloved has gone to his garden,
    To the beds of spices,
    To feed *his flock* in the gardens,
    And to gather lilies.

3 I *am* my beloved's,
    And my beloved *is* mine.
    He feeds *his flock* among the lilies.

4 O my love, you *are as* beautiful as Tirzah,
    Lovely as Jerusalem,
    Awesome as *an army* with banners!

5 Turn your eyes away from me,
    For they have overcome me.
    Your hair *is* like a flock of goats
    Going down from Gilead.

6 Your teeth *are* like a flock of sheep
    Which have come up from the washing;
    Every one bears twins,
    And none *is* barren among them.

7 Like a piece of pomegranate
    Are your temples behind your veil.

8 There are sixty queens
    And eighty concubines,
    And virgins without number.

9 My dove, my perfect one,
    Is the only one,
    The only one of her mother,
    The favorite of the one who bore her.
    The daughters saw her
    And called her blessed,
    The queens and the concubines,
    And they praised her.

10 Who is she who looks forth as the morning,
    Fair as the moon,
    Clear as the sun,
    Awesome as *an army* with banners?

11 I went down to the garden of nuts
    To see the verdure of the valley,
    To see whether the vine had budded
    And the pomegranates had bloomed.

12 Before I was even aware,
    My soul had made me
    As the chariots of my noble people.

13 Return, return, O Shulamite,
    Return, return, that we may look upon you!
    What would you see in the Shulamite—
    As it were, the dance of the two camps?

7 How beautiful are your feet in sandals,
    O prince's daughter!
    The curves of your thighs *are* like jewels,
    The work of the hands of a skillful workman.

2 Your navel *is* a rounded goblet;
    It lacks no blended beverage.
    Your waist *is* a heap of wheat
    Set about with lilies.

3 Your two breasts *are* like two fawns,
    Twins of a gazelle.

ו אָנָה הָלַךְ דּוֹדֵךְ הַיָּפָה בַּנָּשִׁים אָנָה פָּנָה
דוֹדֵךְ וּנְבַקְשֶׁנּוּ עִמָּךְ: 2 דּוֹדִי יָרַד לְגַנּוֹ לַעֲרוּגוֹת
הַבֹּשֶׂם לִרְעוֹת בַּגַּנִּים וְלִלְקֹט שׁוֹשַׁנִּים: 3 אֲנִי לְדוֹדִי
וְדוֹדִי לִי הָרֹעֶה בַּשּׁוֹשַׁנִּים: ס 4 יָפָה אַתְּ
רַעְיָתִי כְּתִרְצָה נָאוָה כִּירוּשָׁלִָם אֲיֻמָּה כַּנִּדְגָּלוֹת:
5 הָסֵבִּי עֵינַיִךְ מִנֶּגְדִּי שֶׁהֵם הִרְהִיבֻנִי שַׂעְרֵךְ כְּעֵדֶר
הָעִזִּים שֶׁגָּלְשׁוּ מִן־הַגִּלְעָד: 6 שִׁנַּיִךְ כְּעֵדֶר הָרְחֵלִים
שֶׁעָלוּ מִן־הָרַחְצָה שֶׁכֻּלָּם מַתְאִימוֹת וְשַׁכֻּלָה אֵין
בָּהֶם: 7 כְּפֶלַח הָרִמּוֹן רַקָּתֵךְ מִבַּעַד לְצַמָּתֵךְ:

8 שִׁשִּׁים הֵמָּה מְלָכוֹת וּשְׁמֹנִים פִּילַגְשִׁים וַעֲלָמוֹת
אֵין מִסְפָּר: 9 אַחַת הִיא יוֹנָתִי תַמָּתִי אַחַת הִיא
לְאִמָּהּ בָּרָה הִיא לְיוֹלַדְתָּהּ רָאוּהָ בָנוֹת וַיְאַשְּׁרוּהָ
מְלָכוֹת וּפִילַגְשִׁים וַיְהַלְלוּהָ: ס 10 מִי־
זֹאת הַנִּשְׁקָפָה כְּמוֹ־שָׁחַר יָפָה כַלְּבָנָה בָּרָה
כַּחַמָּה אֲיֻמָּה כַּנִּדְגָּלוֹת: ס 11 אֶל־גִּנַּת
אֱגוֹז יָרַדְתִּי לִרְאוֹת בְּאִבֵּי הַנָּחַל לִרְאוֹת הֲפָרְחָה
הַגֶּפֶן הֵנֵצוּ הָרִמֹּנִים: 12 לֹא יָדַעְתִּי נַפְשִׁי שָׂמַתְנִי
מַרְכְּבוֹת עַמִּי־נָדִיב:

ז שׁוּבִי שׁוּבִי הַשּׁוּלַמִּית שׁוּבִי שׁוּבִי וְנֶחֱזֶה־
בָּךְ מַה־תֶּחֱזוּ בַּשּׁוּלַמִּית כִּמְחֹלַת הַמַּחֲנָיִם: 2 מַה־
יָּפוּ פְעָמַיִךְ בַּנְּעָלִים בַּת־נָדִיב חַמּוּקֵי יְרֵכַיִךְ כְּמוֹ
חֲלָאִים מַעֲשֵׂה יְדֵי אָמָּן: 3 שָׁרְרֵךְ אַגַּן הַסַּהַר אַל־
יֶחְסַר הַמָּזֶג בִּטְנֵךְ עֲרֵמַת חִטִּים סוּגָה בַּשּׁוֹשַׁנִּים:
4 שְׁנֵי שָׁדַיִךְ כִּשְׁנֵי עֳפָרִים תָּאֳמֵי צְבִיָּה: 5 צַוָּארֵךְ

4
Your neck *is* like an ivory tower,
Your eyes *like* the pools in Heshbon
By the gate of Bath Rabbim.
Your nose *is* like the tower of Lebanon
Which looks toward Damascus.

5
Your head crowns you like *Mount* Carmel,
And the hair of your head *is* like purple;
A king *is* held captive by *your* tresses.

6
How fair and how pleasant you are,
O love, with your delights!

7
This stature of yours is like a palm tree,
And your breasts *like* its clusters.

8
I said, "I will go up to the palm tree,
I will take hold of its branches."
Let now your breasts be like clusters of the vine,
The fragrance of your breath like apples,
And the roof of your mouth like the best wine.

9
The wine goes *down* smoothly for my beloved,
Moving gently the lips of sleepers.

10
I *am* my beloved's,
And his desire *is* toward me.

11
Come, my beloved,
Let us go forth to the field;
Let us lodge in the villages.

12
Let us get up early to the vineyards;
Let us see if the vine has budded,
Whether the grape blossoms are open,
And the pomegranates are in bloom.
There I will give you my love.

13
The mandrakes give off a fragrance,
And at our gates *are* pleasant *fruits,*
All manner, new and old,
Which I have laid up for you, my beloved.

כְּמִגְדַּל הַשֵּׁן עֵינַ֫יִךְ בְּרֵכוֹת בְּחֶשְׁבּוֹן עַל־שַׁעַר בַּת־
רַבִּים אַפֵּךְ כְּמִגְדַּל הַלְּבָנוֹן צוֹפֶה פְּנֵי דַמָּשֶׂק:
6 רֹאשֵׁךְ עָלַיִךְ כַּכַּרְמֶל וְדַלַּת רֹאשֵׁךְ כָּאַרְגָּמָן
מֶלֶךְ אָסוּר בָּרְהָטִים: 7 מַה־יָּפִית וּמַה־נָּעַמְתְּ
אַהֲבָה בַּתַּעֲנוּגִים: 8 זֹאת קוֹמָתֵךְ דָּמְתָה לְתָמָר
וְשָׁדַיִךְ לְאַשְׁכֹּלוֹת: 9 אָמַרְתִּי אֶעֱלֶה בְתָמָר אֹחֲזָה
בְּסַנְסִנָּיו וְיִהְיוּ־נָא שָׁדַיִךְ כְּאֶשְׁכְּלוֹת הַגֶּפֶן וְרֵיחַ
אַפֵּךְ כַּתַּפּוּחִים: 10 וְחִכֵּךְ כְּיֵין הַטּוֹב הוֹלֵךְ לְדוֹדִי
לְמֵישָׁרִים דּוֹבֵב שִׂפְתֵי יְשֵׁנִים: 11 אֲנִי לְדוֹדִי וְעָלַי
תְּשׁוּקָתוֹ: ס   12 לְכָה דוֹדִי נֵצֵא הַשָּׂדֶה
נָלִינָה בַּכְּפָרִים: 13 נַשְׁכִּימָה לַכְּרָמִים נִרְאֶה אִם
פָּרְחָה הַגֶּפֶן פִּתַּח הַסְּמָדַר הֵנֵצוּ הָרִמּוֹנִים שָׁם
אֶתֵּן אֶת־דֹּדַי לָךְ: 14 הַדּוּדָאִים נָתְנוּ־רֵיחַ וְעַל־
פְּתָחֵינוּ כָּל־מְגָדִים חֲדָשִׁים גַּם־יְשָׁנִים דּוֹדִי צָפַנְתִּי
לָךְ:

8

Oh, that you were like my brother,
Who nursed at my mother's breasts!
If I should find you outside,
I would kiss you;
I would not be despised.

2
I would lead you *and* bring you
Into the house of my mother,
She *who* used to instruct me.
I would cause you to drink of spiced wine,
Of the juice of my pomegranate.

3
His left hand *is* under my head,
And his right hand embraces me.

4
I charge you, O daughters of Jerusalem,
Do not stir up nor awaken love
Until it pleases.

5
Who *is* this coming up from the wilderness,
Leaning upon her beloved?

I awakened you under the apple tree.
There your mother brought you forth;
There she *who* bore you brought *you* forth.

6
Set me as a seal upon your heart,
As a seal upon your arm;
For love *is* as strong as death,
Jealousy *as* cruel as the grave;
Its flames *are* flames of fire,
A most vehement flame.

ח מִי יִתֶּנְךָ כְּאָח לִי יוֹנֵק שְׁדֵי אִמִּי אֶמְצָאֲךָ בַחוּץ
אֶשָּׁקְךָ גַּם לֹא־יָבוּזוּ לִי: 2 אֶנְהָגֲךָ אֲבִיאֲךָ אֶל־בֵּית
אִמִּי תְּלַמְּדֵנִי אַשְׁקְךָ מִיַּיִן הָרֶקַח מֵעֲסִיס רִמֹּנִי:
3 שְׂמֹאלוֹ תַּחַת רֹאשִׁי וִימִינוֹ תְּחַבְּקֵנִי: 4 הִשְׁבַּעְתִּי
אֶתְכֶם בְּנוֹת יְרוּשָׁלָ͏ִם מַה־תָּעִירוּ וּמַה־תְּעֹרְרוּ
אֶת־הָאַהֲבָה עַד שֶׁתֶּחְפָּץ: ס   5 מִי זֹאת
עֹלָה מִן־הַמִּדְבָּר מִתְרַפֶּקֶת עַל־דּוֹדָהּ תַּחַת הַתַּפּוּחַ
עוֹרַרְתִּיךָ שָׁמָּה חִבְּלַתְךָ אִמֶּךָ שָׁמָּה חִבְּלָה יְלָדַתְךָ:
6 שִׂימֵנִי כַחוֹתָם עַל־לִבֶּךָ כַּחוֹתָם עַל־זְרוֹעֶךָ כִּי־
עַזָּה כַמָּוֶת אַהֲבָה קָשָׁה כִשְׁאוֹל קִנְאָה רְשָׁפֶיהָ

7   Many waters cannot quench love,
    Nor can the floods drown it.
    If a man would give for love
    All the wealth of his house,
    It would be utterly despised.

8   We have a little sister,
    And she has no breasts.
    What shall we do for our sister
    In the day when she is spoken for?

9   If she *is* a wall,
    We will build upon her
    A battlement of silver;
    And if she *is* a door,
    We will enclose her
    With boards of cedar.

10 I *am* a wall,
    And my breasts like towers;
    Then I became in his eyes
    As one who found peace.

11 Solomon had a vineyard at Baal Hamon;
    He leased the vineyard to keepers;
    Everyone was to bring for its fruit
    A thousand silver coins.

12 My own vineyard *is* before me.
    You, O Solomon, *may have* a thousand,
    And those who tend its fruit two hundred.

13 You who dwell in the gardens,
    The companions listen for your voice—
    Let me hear it!

14 Make haste, my beloved,
    And be like a gazelle
    Or a young stag
    On the mountains of spices.

רִשְׁפֵּי אֵשׁ שַׁלְהֶבֶתְיָה: 7 מַיִם רַבִּים לֹא יוּכְלוּ
לְכַבּוֹת אֶת־הָאַהֲבָה וּנְהָרוֹת לֹא יִשְׁטְפוּהָ אִם־
יִתֵּן אִישׁ אֶת־כָּל־הוֹן בֵּיתוֹ בָּאַהֲבָה בּוֹז יָבוּזוּ
לוֹ: ס 8 אָחוֹת לָנוּ קְטַנָּה וְשָׁדַיִם אֵין לָהּ
מַה־נַּעֲשֶׂה לַאֲחֹתֵנוּ בַּיּוֹם שֶׁיְּדֻבַּר־בָּהּ: 9 אִם־חוֹמָה
הִיא נִבְנֶה עָלֶיהָ טִירַת כָּסֶף וְאִם־דֶּלֶת הִיא נָצוּר
עָלֶיהָ לוּחַ אָרֶז: 10 אֲנִי חוֹמָה וְשָׁדַי כַּמִּגְדָּלוֹת אָז
הָיִיתִי בְעֵינָיו כְּמוֹצְאֵת שָׁלוֹם:
פ

11 כֶּרֶם הָיָה לִשְׁלֹמֹה בְּבַעַל הָמוֹן נָתַן אֶת־הַכֶּרֶם
לַנֹּטְרִים אִישׁ יָבִא בְּפִרְיוֹ אֶלֶף כָּסֶף: 12 כַּרְמִי שֶׁלִּי
לְפָנָי הָאֶלֶף לְךָ שְׁלֹמֹה וּמָאתַיִם לְנֹטְרִים אֶת־
פִּרְיוֹ: 13 הַיּוֹשֶׁבֶת בַּגַּנִּים חֲבֵרִים מַקְשִׁיבִים לְקוֹלֵךְ
הַשְׁמִיעִינִי: 14 בְּרַח ׀ דּוֹדִי וּדְמֵה־לְךָ לִצְבִי אוֹ
לְעֹפֶר הָאַיָּלִים עַל הָרֵי בְשָׂמִים:

The Book of

RUTH

רות

1 Now it came to pass, in the days when the judges ruled, that there was a famine in the land. And a certain man of Bethlehem, Judah, went to dwell in the country of Moab, he and his wife and his two sons. ²The name of the man *was* Elimelech, the name of his wife *was* Naomi, and the names of his two sons *were* Mahlon and Chilion—Ephrathites of Bethlehem, Judah. And they went to the country of Moab and remained there. ³Then Elimelech, Naomi's husband, died; and she was left, and her two sons. ⁴Now they took wives of the women of Moab: the name of the one *was* Orpah, and the name of the other Ruth. And they dwelt there about ten years. ⁵Then both Mahlon and Chilion also died; so the woman survived her two sons and her husband.

⁶Then she arose with her daughters-in-law that she might return from the country of Moab, for she had heard in the country of Moab that the LORD had visited His people by giving them bread. ⁷Therefore she went out from the place where she was, and her two daughters-in-law with her; and they went on the way to return to the land of Judah. ⁸And Naomi said to her two daughters-in-law, "Go, return each to her mother's house. The LORD deal kindly with you, as you have dealt with the dead and with me. ⁹The LORD grant that you may find rest, each in the house of her husband."

So she kissed them, and they lifted up their voices and wept. ¹⁰And they said to her, "Surely we will return with you to your people."

¹¹But Naomi said, "Turn back, my daughters; why will you go with me? *Are* there still sons in my womb, that they may be your husbands? ¹²Turn back, my daughters, go—for I am too old to have a husband. If I should say I have hope, *if* I should have a husband tonight and should also bear sons, ¹³would you wait for them till they were grown? Would you restrain yourselves from having husbands? No, my daughters; for it grieves me very much for your sakes that the hand of the LORD has gone out against me!"

¹⁴Then they lifted up their voices and wept again; and Orpah kissed her mother-in-law, but Ruth clung to her.

א וַיְהִי בִּימֵי שְׁפֹט הַשֹּׁפְטִים וַיְהִי רָעָב בָּאָרֶץ וַיֵּלֶךְ אִישׁ מִבֵּית לֶחֶם יְהוּדָה לָגוּר בִּשְׂדֵי מוֹאָב הוּא וְאִשְׁתּוֹ וּשְׁנֵי בָנָיו: 2 וְשֵׁם הָאִישׁ אֱלִימֶלֶךְ וְשֵׁם אִשְׁתּוֹ נָעֳמִי וְשֵׁם שְׁנֵי־בָנָיו | מַחְלוֹן וְכִלְיוֹן אֶפְרָתִים מִבֵּית לֶחֶם יְהוּדָה וַיָּבֹאוּ שְׂדֵי־מוֹאָב וַיִּהְיוּ־שָׁם: 3 וַיָּמָת אֱלִימֶלֶךְ אִישׁ נָעֳמִי וַתִּשָּׁאֵר הִיא וּשְׁנֵי בָנֶיהָ: 4 וַיִּשְׂאוּ לָהֶם נָשִׁים מֹאֲבִיּוֹת שֵׁם הָאַחַת עָרְפָּה וְשֵׁם הַשֵּׁנִית רוּת וַיֵּשְׁבוּ שָׁם כְּעֶשֶׂר שָׁנִים: 5 וַיָּמֻתוּ גַם־שְׁנֵיהֶם מַחְלוֹן וְכִלְיוֹן וַתִּשָּׁאֵר הָאִשָּׁה מִשְּׁנֵי יְלָדֶיהָ וּמֵאִישָׁהּ:

6 וַתָּקָם הִיא וְכַלֹּתֶיהָ וַתָּשָׁב מִשְּׂדֵי מוֹאָב כִּי שָׁמְעָה בִּשְׂדֵה מוֹאָב כִּי־פָקַד יְהוָה אֶת־עַמּוֹ לָתֵת לָהֶם לָחֶם: 7 וַתֵּצֵא מִן־הַמָּקוֹם אֲשֶׁר הָיְתָה־שָּׁמָּה וּשְׁתֵּי כַלֹּתֶיהָ עִמָּהּ וַתֵּלַכְנָה בַדֶּרֶךְ לָשׁוּב אֶל־אֶרֶץ יְהוּדָה: 8 וַתֹּאמֶר נָעֳמִי לִשְׁתֵּי כַלֹּתֶיהָ לֵכְנָה שֹּׁבְנָה אִשָּׁה לְבֵית אִמָּהּ יַעֲשֶׂה יְהוָה עִמָּכֶם חֶסֶד כַּאֲשֶׁר עֲשִׂיתֶם עִם־הַמֵּתִים וְעִמָּדִי: 9 יִתֵּן יְהוָה לָכֶם וּמְצֶאןָ מְנוּחָה אִשָּׁה בֵּית אִישָׁהּ וַתִּשַּׁק לָהֶן וַתִּשֶּׂאנָה קוֹלָן וַתִּבְכֶּינָה: 10 וַתֹּאמַרְנָה־לָּהּ כִּי־אִתָּךְ נָשׁוּב לְעַמֵּךְ: 11 וַתֹּאמֶר נָעֳמִי שֹׁבְנָה בְנֹתַי לָמָּה תֵלַכְנָה עִמִּי הַעוֹד־לִי בָנִים בְּמֵעַי וְהָיוּ לָכֶם לַאֲנָשִׁים: 12 שֹׁבְנָה בְנֹתַי לֵכְןָ כִּי זָקַנְתִּי מִהְיוֹת לְאִישׁ כִּי אָמַרְתִּי יֶשׁ־לִי תִקְוָה גַּם הָיִיתִי הַלַּיְלָה לְאִישׁ וְגַם יָלַדְתִּי בָנִים: 13 הֲלָהֵן | תְּשַׂבֵּרְנָה עַד אֲשֶׁר יִגְדָּלוּ הֲלָהֵן תֵּעָגֵנָה לְבִלְתִּי הֱיוֹת לְאִישׁ אַל בְּנֹתַי כִּי־מַר־לִי מְאֹד מִכֶּם כִּי־יָצְאָה בִי יַד־יְהוָה: 14 וַתִּשֶּׂנָה קוֹלָן וַתִּבְכֶּינָה עוֹד וַתִּשַּׁק

15 And she said, "Look, your sister-in-law has gone back to her people and to her gods; return after your sister-in-law."

16 But Ruth said:

"Entreat me not to leave you,
Or to turn back from following after you;
For wherever you go, I will go;
And wherever you lodge, I will lodge;
Your people *shall be* my people,
And your God, my God.

17 Where you die, I will die,
And there will I be buried.
The LORD do so to me, and more also,
If *anything but* death parts you and me."

18 When she saw that she was determined to go with her, she stopped speaking to her.

19 Now the two of them went until they came to Bethlehem. And it happened, when they had come to Bethlehem, that all the city was excited because of them; and the women said, "*Is this Naomi?*"

20 But she said to them, "Do not call me Naomi; call me Mara, for the Almighty has dealt very bitterly with me. 21 I went out full, and the LORD has brought me home again empty. Why do you call me Naomi, since the LORD has testified against me, and the Almighty has afflicted me?"

22 So Naomi returned, and Ruth the Moabitess her daughter-in-law with her, who returned from the country of Moab. Now they came to Bethlehem at the beginning of barley harvest.

2 There was a relative of Naomi's husband, a man of great wealth, of the family of Elimelech. His name *was* Boaz. 2 So Ruth the Moabitess said to Naomi, "Please let me go to the field, and glean heads of grain after *him* in whose sight I may find favor."

And she said to her, "Go, my daughter."

3 Then she left, and went and gleaned in the field after the reapers. And she happened to come to the part of the field *belonging* to Boaz, who *was* of the family of Elimelech.

4 Now behold, Boaz came from Bethlehem, and said to the reapers, "The LORD *be* with you!"

And they answered him, "The LORD bless you!"

5 Then Boaz said to his servant who was in charge of the reapers, "Whose young woman *is* this?"

6 So the servant who was in charge of the reapers answered and said, "It *is* the young Moabite woman who came back with Naomi from the country of Moab. 7 And she said, 'Please let me glean and gather after the reapers among the

עׇרְפָּה לַחֲמוֹתָהּ וְרוּת דָּבְקָה בָּהּ׃ 15 וַתֹּאמֶר הִנֵּה שָׁבָה יְבִמְתֵּךְ אֶל־עַמָּהּ וְאֶל־אֱלֹהֶיהָ שׁוּבִי אַחֲרֵי יְבִמְתֵּךְ׃ 16 וַתֹּאמֶר רוּת אַל־תִּפְגְּעִי־בִי לְעׇזְבֵךְ לָשׁוּב מֵאַחֲרָיִךְ כִּי אֶל־אֲשֶׁר תֵּלְכִי אֵלֵךְ וּבַאֲשֶׁר תָּלִינִי אָלִין עַמֵּךְ עַמִּי וֵאלֹהַיִךְ אֱלֹהָי׃ 17 בַּאֲשֶׁר תָּמוּתִי אָמוּת וְשָׁם אֶקָּבֵר כֹּה יַעֲשֶׂה יְהֹוָה לִי וְכֹה יֹסִיף כִּי הַמָּוֶת יַפְרִיד בֵּינִי וּבֵינֵךְ׃ 18 וַתֵּרֶא כִּי־מִתְאַמֶּצֶת הִיא לָלֶכֶת אִתָּהּ וַתֶּחְדַּל לְדַבֵּר אֵלֶיהָ׃ 19 וַתֵּלַכְנָה שְׁתֵּיהֶם עַד־בֹּאָנָה בֵּית לָחֶם וַיְהִי כְּבֹאָנָה בֵּית לֶחֶם וַתֵּהֹם כׇּל־הָעִיר עֲלֵיהֶן וַתֹּאמַרְנָה הֲזֹאת נׇעֳמִי׃ 20 וַתֹּאמֶר אֲלֵיהֶן אַל־תִּקְרֶאנָה לִי נׇעֳמִי קְרֶאןָ לִי מָרָא כִּי־הֵמַר שַׁדַּי לִי מְאֹד׃ 21 אֲנִי מְלֵאָה הָלַכְתִּי וְרֵיקָם הֱשִׁיבַנִי יְהֹוָה לָמָּה תִקְרֶאנָה לִי נׇעֳמִי וַיהֹוָה עָנָה בִי וְשַׁדַּי הֵרַע לִי׃ 22 וַתָּשׇׁב נׇעֳמִי וְרוּת הַמּוֹאֲבִיָּה כַלָּתָהּ עִמָּהּ הַשָּׁבָה מִשְּׂדֵי מוֹאָב וְהֵמָּה בָּאוּ בֵּית לֶחֶם בִּתְחִלַּת קְצִיר שְׂעֹרִים׃

ב וּלְנׇעֳמִי מוֹדָע לְאִישָׁהּ אִישׁ גִּבּוֹר חַיִל מִמִּשְׁפַּחַת אֱלִימֶלֶךְ וּשְׁמוֹ בֹּעַז׃ 2 וַתֹּאמֶר רוּת הַמּוֹאֲבִיָּה אֶל־נׇעֳמִי אֵלְכָה־נָּא הַשָּׂדֶה וַאֲלַקֳטָה בַשִּׁבֳּלִים אַחַר אֲשֶׁר אֶמְצָא־חֵן בְּעֵינָיו וַתֹּאמֶר לָהּ לְכִי בִתִּי׃ 3 וַתֵּלֶךְ וַתָּבוֹא וַתְּלַקֵּט בַּשָּׂדֶה אַחֲרֵי הַקֹּצְרִים וַיִּקֶר מִקְרֶהָ חֶלְקַת הַשָּׂדֶה לְבֹעַז אֲשֶׁר מִמִּשְׁפַּחַת אֱלִימֶלֶךְ׃ 4 וְהִנֵּה־בֹעַז בָּא מִבֵּית לֶחֶם וַיֹּאמֶר לַקּוֹצְרִים יְהֹוָה עִמָּכֶם וַיֹּאמְרוּ לוֹ יְבָרֶכְךָ יְהֹוָה׃ 5 וַיֹּאמֶר בֹּעַז לְנַעֲרוֹ הַנִּצָּב עַל־הַקֹּצְרִים לְמִי הַנַּעֲרָה הַזֹּאת׃ 6 וַיַּעַן הַנַּעַר הַנִּצָּב עַל־הַקֹּצְרִים וַיֹּאמַר נַעֲרָה מוֹאֲבִיָּה הִיא הַשָּׁבָה עִם־נׇעֳמִי מִשְּׂדֵה מוֹאָב׃ 7 וַתֹּאמֶר אֲלַקֳטָה־נָּא וְאָסַפְתִּי בׇעֳמָרִים אַחֲרֵי הַקֹּצְרִים וַתָּבוֹא וַתַּעֲמֹד

sheaves.' So she came and has continued from morning until now, though she rested a little in the house."

[8] Then Boaz said to Ruth, "You will listen, my daughter, will you not? Do not go to glean in another field, nor go from here, but stay close by my young women. [9] *Let* your eyes *be* on the field which they reap, and go after them. Have I not commanded the young men not to touch you? And when you are thirsty, go to the vessels and drink from what the young men have drawn."

[10] So she fell on her face, bowed down to the ground, and said to him, "Why have I found favor in your eyes, that you should take notice of me, since I *am* a foreigner?"

[11] And Boaz answered and said to her, "It has been fully reported to me, all that you have done for your mother-in-law since the death of your husband, and *how* you have left your father and your mother and the land of your birth, and have come to a people whom you did not know before. [12] The LORD repay your work, and a full reward be given you by the LORD God of Israel, under whose wings you have come for refuge."

[13] Then she said, "Let me find favor in your sight, my lord; for you have comforted me, and have spoken kindly to your maidservant, though I am not like one of your maidservants."

[14] Now Boaz said to her at mealtime, "Come here, and eat of the bread, and dip your piece of bread in the vinegar." So she sat beside the reapers, and he passed parched *grain* to her; and she ate and was satisfied, and kept some back. [15] And when she rose up to glean, Boaz commanded his young men, saying, "Let her glean even among the sheaves, and do not reproach her. [16] Also let *grain* from the bundles fall purposely for her; leave *it* that she may glean, and do not rebuke her."

[17] So she gleaned in the field until evening, and beat out what she had gleaned, and it was about an ephah of barley. [18] Then she took *it* up and went into the city, and her mother-in-law saw what she had gleaned. So she brought out and gave to her what she had kept back after she had been satisfied.

[19] And her mother-in-law said to her, "Where have you gleaned today? And where did you work? Blessed be the one who took notice of you."

So she told her mother-in-law with whom she had worked, and said, "The man's name with whom I worked today *is* Boaz."

מֵאָז הַבֹּקֶר וְעַד־עַתָּה זֶה שִׁבְתָּהּ הַבַּיִת מְעָט: 8 וַיֹּאמֶר בֹּעַז אֶל־רוּת הֲלוֹא שָׁמַעַתְּ בִּתִּי אַל־תֵּלְכִי לִלְקֹט בְּשָׂדֶה אַחֵר וְגַם לֹא תַעֲבוּרִי מִזֶּה וְכֹה תִדְבָּקִין עִם־נַעֲרֹתָי: 9 עֵינַיִךְ בַּשָּׂדֶה אֲשֶׁר־יִקְצֹרוּן וְהָלַכְתְּ אַחֲרֵיהֶן הֲלוֹא צִוִּיתִי אֶת־הַנְּעָרִים לְבִלְתִּי נָגְעֵךְ וְצָמִת וְהָלַכְתְּ אֶל־הַכֵּלִים וְשָׁתִית מֵאֲשֶׁר יִשְׁאֲבוּן הַנְּעָרִים: 10 וַתִּפֹּל עַל־פָּנֶיהָ וַתִּשְׁתַּחוּ אָרְצָה וַתֹּאמֶר אֵלָיו מַדּוּעַ מָצָאתִי חֵן בְּעֵינֶיךָ לְהַכִּירֵנִי וְאָנֹכִי נָכְרִיָּה: 11 וַיַּעַן בֹּעַז וַיֹּאמֶר לָהּ הֻגֵּד הֻגַּד לִי כֹּל אֲשֶׁר־עָשִׂית אֶת־חֲמוֹתֵךְ אַחֲרֵי מוֹת אִישֵׁךְ וַתַּעַזְבִי אָבִיךְ וְאִמֵּךְ וְאֶרֶץ מוֹלַדְתֵּךְ וַתֵּלְכִי אֶל־עַם אֲשֶׁר לֹא־יָדַעַתְּ תְּמוֹל שִׁלְשׁוֹם: 12 יְשַׁלֵּם יְהוָה פָּעֳלֵךְ וּתְהִי מַשְׂכֻּרְתֵּךְ שְׁלֵמָה מֵעִם יְהוָה אֱלֹהֵי יִשְׂרָאֵל אֲשֶׁר־בָּאת לַחֲסוֹת תַּחַת־כְּנָפָיו:

13 וַתֹּאמֶר אֶמְצָא־חֵן בְּעֵינֶיךָ אֲדֹנִי כִּי נִחַמְתָּנִי וְכִי דִבַּרְתָּ עַל־לֵב שִׁפְחָתֶךָ וְאָנֹכִי לֹא אֶהְיֶה כְּאַחַת שִׁפְחֹתֶיךָ: 14 וַיֹּאמֶר לָה בֹעַז לְעֵת הָאֹכֶל גֹּשִׁי הֲלֹם וְאָכַלְתְּ מִן־הַלֶּחֶם וְטָבַלְתְּ פִּתֵּךְ בַּחֹמֶץ וַתֵּשֶׁב מִצַּד הַקֹּצְרִים וַיִּצְבָּט־לָהּ קָלִי וַתֹּאכַל וַתִּשְׂבַּע וַתֹּתַר: 15 וַתָּקָם לְלַקֵּט וַיְצַו בֹּעַז אֶת־נְעָרָיו לֵאמֹר גַּם בֵּין הָעֳמָרִים תְּלַקֵּט וְלֹא תַכְלִימוּהָ: 16 וְגַם שֹׁל־תָּשֹׁלּוּ לָהּ מִן־הַצְּבָתִים וַעֲזַבְתֶּם וְלִקְּטָה וְלֹא תִגְעֲרוּ־בָהּ: 17 וַתְּלַקֵּט בַּשָּׂדֶה עַד־הָעָרֶב וַתַּחְבֹּט אֵת אֲשֶׁר־לִקֵּטָה וַיְהִי כְּאֵיפָה שְׂעֹרִים: 18 וַתִּשָּׂא וַתָּבוֹא הָעִיר וַתֵּרֶא חֲמוֹתָהּ אֵת אֲשֶׁר־לִקֵּטָה וַתּוֹצֵא וַתִּתֶּן־לָהּ אֵת אֲשֶׁר־הוֹתִרָה מִשָּׂבְעָהּ: 19 וַתֹּאמֶר לָהּ חֲמוֹתָהּ אֵיפֹה לִקַּטְתְּ הַיּוֹם וְאָנָה עָשִׂית יְהִי מַכִּירֵךְ בָּרוּךְ וַתַּגֵּד לַחֲמוֹתָהּ אֵת אֲשֶׁר־עָשְׂתָה עִמּוֹ וַתֹּאמֶר שֵׁם

20 Then Naomi said to her daughter-in-law, "Blessed *be* he of the LORD, who has not forsaken His kindness to the living and the dead!" And Naomi said to her, "This man *is* a relation of ours, one of our close relatives."

21 Ruth the Moabitess said, "He also said to me, 'You shall stay close by my young men until they have finished all my harvest.'"

22 And Naomi said to Ruth her daughter-in-law, "*It is* good, my daughter, that you go out with his young women, and that people do not meet you in any other field." 23 So she stayed close by the young women of Boaz, to glean until the end of barley harvest and wheat harvest; and she dwelt with her mother-in-law.

3 Then Naomi her mother-in-law said to her, "My daughter, shall I not seek security for you, that it may be well with you? 2 Now Boaz, whose young women you were with, *is he* not our relative? In fact, he is winnowing barley tonight at the threshing floor. 3 Therefore wash yourself and anoint yourself, put on your *best* garment and go down to the threshing floor; *but* do not make yourself known to the man until he has finished eating and drinking. 4 Then it shall be, when he lies down, that you shall notice the place where he lies; and you shall go in, uncover his feet, and lie down; and he will tell you what you should do."

5 And she said to her, "All that you say to me I will do."

6 So she went down to the threshing floor and did according to all that her mother-in-law instructed her. 7 And after Boaz had eaten and drunk, and his heart was cheerful, he went to lie down at the end of the heap of grain; and she came softly, uncovered his feet, and lay down.

8 Now it happened at midnight that the man was startled, and turned himself; and there, a woman was lying at his feet. 9 And he said, "Who *are* you?"

So she answered, "I *am* Ruth, your maidservant. Take your maidservant under your wing, for you are a close relative."

10 Then he said, "Blessed *are* you of the LORD, my daughter! For you have shown more kindness at the end than at the beginning, in that you did not go after young men, whether poor or rich. 11 And now, my daughter, do not fear. I will do for you all that you request, for all the people of my town know that you *are* a virtuous woman. 12 Now it is true that I *am* a close relative; however, there is a relative closer than I. 13 Stay this night, and in the morning it shall be *that* if he will perform the duty of a close relative for you—good; let him do it. But if he does

20 וַתֹּאמֶר נָעֳמִי לְכַלָּתָהּ בָּרוּךְ הוּא לַיהוָה אֲשֶׁר לֹא־עָזַב חַסְדּוֹ אֶת־הַחַיִּים וְאֶת־הַמֵּתִים וַתֹּאמֶר לָהּ נָעֳמִי קָרוֹב לָנוּ הָאִישׁ מִגֹּאֲלֵנוּ הוּא: 21 וַתֹּאמֶר רוּת הַמּוֹאֲבִיָּה גַּם כִּי־אָמַר אֵלַי עִם־הַנְּעָרִים אֲשֶׁר־לִי תִּדְבָּקִין עַד אִם־כִּלּוּ אֵת כָּל־הַקָּצִיר אֲשֶׁר־לִי: 22 וַתֹּאמֶר נָעֳמִי אֶל־רוּת כַּלָּתָהּ טוֹב בִּתִּי כִּי תֵצְאִי עִם־נַעֲרוֹתָיו וְלֹא יִפְגְּעוּ־בָךְ בְּשָׂדֶה אַחֵר: 23 וַתִּדְבַּק בְּנַעֲרוֹת בֹּעַז לְלַקֵּט עַד־כְּלוֹת קְצִיר־הַשְּׂעֹרִים וּקְצִיר הַחִטִּים וַתֵּשֶׁב אֶת־חֲמוֹתָהּ:

ג וַתֹּאמֶר לָהּ נָעֳמִי חֲמוֹתָהּ בִּתִּי הֲלֹא אֲבַקֶּשׁ־לָךְ מָנוֹחַ אֲשֶׁר יִיטַב־לָךְ: 2 וְעַתָּה הֲלֹא בֹעַז מֹדַעְתָּנוּ אֲשֶׁר הָיִית אֶת־נַעֲרוֹתָיו הִנֵּה־הוּא זֹרֶה אֶת־גֹּרֶן הַשְּׂעֹרִים הַלָּיְלָה: 3 וְרָחַצְתְּ וָסַכְתְּ וְשַׂמְתְּ שִׂמְלֹתַיִךְ עָלַיִךְ וְיָרַדְתִּי הַגֹּרֶן אַל־תִּוָּדְעִי לָאִישׁ עַד כַּלֹּתוֹ לֶאֱכֹל וְלִשְׁתּוֹת: 4 וִיהִי בְשָׁכְבוֹ וְיָדַעַתְּ אֶת־הַמָּקוֹם אֲשֶׁר יִשְׁכַּב־שָׁם וּבָאת וְגִלִּית מַרְגְּלֹתָיו וְשָׁכָבְתִּי וְהוּא יַגִּיד לָךְ אֵת אֲשֶׁר תַּעֲשִׂין: 5 וַתֹּאמֶר אֵלֶיהָ כֹּל אֲשֶׁר־תֹּאמְרִי אֶעֱשֶׂה: 6 וַתֵּרֶד הַגֹּרֶן וַתַּעַשׂ כְּכֹל אֲשֶׁר־צִוַּתָּה חֲמוֹתָהּ:

7 וַיֹּאכַל בֹּעַז וַיֵּשְׁתְּ וַיִּיטַב לִבּוֹ וַיָּבֹא לִשְׁכַּב בִּקְצֵה הָעֲרֵמָה וַתָּבֹא בַלָּט וַתְּגַל מַרְגְּלֹתָיו וַתִּשְׁכָּב: 8 וַיְהִי בַּחֲצִי הַלַּיְלָה וַיֶּחֱרַד הָאִישׁ וַיִּלָּפֵת וְהִנֵּה אִשָּׁה שֹׁכֶבֶת מַרְגְּלֹתָיו: 9 וַיֹּאמֶר מִי־אָתְּ וַתֹּאמֶר אָנֹכִי רוּת אֲמָתֶךָ וּפָרַשְׂתָּ כְנָפֶךָ עַל־אֲמָתְךָ כִּי גֹאֵל אָתָּה: 10 וַיֹּאמֶר בְּרוּכָה אַתְּ לַיהוָה בִּתִּי הֵיטַבְתְּ חַסְדֵּךְ הָאַחֲרוֹן מִן־הָרִאשׁוֹן לְבִלְתִּי־לֶכֶת אַחֲרֵי הַבַּחוּרִים אִם־דַּל וְאִם־עָשִׁיר: 11 וְעַתָּה בִּתִּי אַל־תִּירְאִי כֹּל אֲשֶׁר־תֹּאמְרִי אֶעֱשֶׂה־לָּךְ כִּי יוֹדֵעַ כָּל־שַׁעַר עַמִּי כִּי אֵשֶׁת חַיִל אָתְּ: 12 וְעַתָּה כִּי אָמְנָם כִּי אִם גֹּאֵל אָנֹכִי וְגַם יֵשׁ גֹּאֵל קָרוֹב מִמֶּנִּי:

13 לִינִי הַלַּיְלָה וְהָיָה בַבֹּקֶר אִם־יִגְאָלֵךְ טוֹב יִגְאָל וְאִם־לֹא יַחְפֹּץ לְגָאֳלֵךְ וּגְאַלְתִּיךְ אָנֹכִי חַי־

not want to perform the duty for you, then I will perform the duty for you, *as the* LORD *lives! Lie down until morning.*"

¹⁴So she lay at his feet until morning, and she arose before one could recognize another. Then he said, "Do not let it be known that the woman came to the threshing floor." ¹⁵Also he said, "Bring the shawl that *is* on you and hold it." And when she held it, he measured six *ephahs* of barley, and laid *it* on her. Then she went into the city.

¹⁶When she came to her mother-in-law, she said, "*Is* that you, my daughter?"

Then she told her all that the man had done for her. ¹⁷And she said, "These six *ephahs* of barley he gave me; for he said to me, 'Do not go empty-handed to your mother-in-law.' "

¹⁸Then she said, "Sit still, my daughter, until you know how the matter will turn out; for the man will not rest until he has concluded the matter this day."

4 Now Boaz went up to the gate and sat down there; and behold, the close relative of whom Boaz had spoken came by. So Boaz said, "Come aside, friend, sit down here." So he came aside and sat down. ²And he took ten men of the elders of the city, and said, "Sit down here." So they sat down. ³Then he said to the close relative, "Naomi, who has come back from the country of Moab, sold the piece of land which *belonged* to our brother Elimelech. ⁴And I thought to inform you, saying, 'Buy *it* back in the presence of the inhabitants and the elders of my people. If you will redeem *it,* redeem *it;* but if you will not redeem *it, then* tell me, that I may know; for *there is* no one but you to redeem *it,* and I *am* next after you.' "

And he said, "I will redeem *it.*"

⁵Then Boaz said, "On the day you buy the field from the hand of Naomi, you must also buy *it* from Ruth the Moabitess, the wife of the dead, to perpetuate the name of the dead through his inheritance."

⁶And the close relative said, "I cannot redeem *it* for myself, lest I ruin my own inheritance. You redeem my right of redemption for yourself, for I cannot redeem *it.*"

⁷Now this *was the custom* in former times in Israel concerning redeeming and exchanging, to confirm anything: one man took off his sandal and gave *it* to the other, and this *was* a confirmation in Israel.

⁸Therefore the close relative said to Boaz, "Buy *it* for yourself." So he took off his sandal. ⁹And Boaz said to the elders and all the people, "You *are* witnesses this day that I have bought all that was

יְהוָה שִׁכְבִי עַד־הַבֹּקֶר: 14 וַתִּשְׁכַּב מַרְגְּלוֹתָוֹ עַד־
הַבֹּקֶר וַתָּקָם בְּטֶרֶוֹם יַכִּיר אִישׁ אֶת־רֵעֵהוּ וַיֹּאמֶר
אַל־יִוָּדַע כִּי־בָאָה הָאִשָּׁה הַגֹּרֶן: 15 וַיֹּאמֶר הָבִי
הַמִּטְפַּחַת אֲשֶׁר־עָלַיִךְ וְאֶחֳזִי־בָהּ וַתֹּאחֶז בָּהּ וַיָּמָד
שֵׁשׁ־שְׂעֹרִים וַיָּשֶׁת עָלֶיהָ וַיָּבֹא הָעִיר: 16 וַתָּבוֹא
אֶל־חֲמוֹתָהּ וַתֹּאמֶר מִי־אַתְּ בִּתִּי וַתַּגֶּד־לָהּ אֵת כָּל־
אֲשֶׁר עָשָׂה־לָהּ הָאִישׁ: 17 וַתֹּאמֶר שֵׁשׁ־הַשְּׂעֹרִים
הָאֵלֶּה נָתַן לִי כִּי אָמַר _ P אֵלַי־תָּבוֹאִי רֵיקָם אֶל־
חֲמוֹתֵךְ: 18 וַתֹּאמֶר שְׁבִי בִתִּי עַד אֲשֶׁר תֵּדְעִין
אֵיךְ יִפֹּל דָּבָר כִּי לֹא יִשְׁקֹט הָאִישׁ כִּי־אִם־כִּלָּה
הַדָּבָר הַיּוֹם:

ד וּבֹעַז עָלָה הַשַּׁעַר וַיֵּשֶׁב שָׁם וְהִנֵּה הַגֹּאֵל
עֹבֵר אֲשֶׁר דִּבֶּר־בֹּעַז וַיֹּאמֶר סוּרָה שְׁבָה־פֹּה פְּלֹנִי
אַלְמֹנִי וַיָּסַר וַיֵּשֵׁב: 2 וַיִּקַּח עֲשָׂרָה אֲנָשִׁים מִזִּקְנֵי
הָעִיר וַיֹּאמֶר שְׁבוּ־פֹה וַיֵּשֵׁבוּ: 3 וַיֹּאמֶר לַגֹּאֵל
חֶלְקַת הַשָּׂדֶה אֲשֶׁר לְאָחִינוּ לֶאֱלִימֶלֶךְ מָכְרָה נָעֳמִי
הַשָּׁבָה מִשְּׂדֵה מוֹאָב: 4 וַאֲנִי אָמַרְתִּי אֶגְלֶה אָזְנְךָ
לֵאמֹר קְנֵה נֶגֶד הַיֹּשְׁבִים וְנֶגֶד זִקְנֵי עַמִּי אִם־
תִּגְאַל גְּאָל וְאִם־לֹא יִגְאַל הַגִּידָה לִּי וְאֵדְעָ כִּי
אֵין זוּלָתְךָ לִגְאוֹל וְאָנֹכִי אַחֲרֶיךָ וַיֹּאמֶר אָנֹכִי
אֶגְאָל: 5 וַיֹּאמֶר בֹּעַז בְּיוֹם־קְנוֹתְךָ הַשָּׂדֶה מִיַּד נָעֳמִי
וּמֵאֵת רוּת הַמּוֹאֲבִיָּה אֵשֶׁת־הַמֵּת קָנִיתִי P לְהָקִים
שֵׁם־הַמֵּת עַל־נַחֲלָתוֹ: 6 וַיֹּאמֶר הַגֹּאֵל לֹא אוּכַל
לִגְאוֹל־ P לִי פֶּן־אַשְׁחִית אֶת־נַחֲלָתִי גְּאַל־לְךָ אַתָּה
אֶת־גְּאֻלָּתִי כִּי לֹא־אוּכַל לִגְאֹל: 7 וְזֹאת לְפָנִים
בְּיִשְׂרָאֵל עַל־הַגְּאֻלָּה וְעַל־הַתְּמוּרָה לְקַיֵּם כָּל־
דָּבָר שָׁלַף אִישׁ נַעֲלוֹ וְנָתַן לְרֵעֵהוּ וְזֹאת הַתְּעוּדָה
בְּיִשְׂרָאֵל: 8 וַיֹּאמֶר הַגֹּאֵל לְבֹעַז קְנֵה־לָךְ וַיִּשְׁלֹף
נַעֲלוֹ: 9 וַיֹּאמֶר בֹּעַז לַזְּקֵנִים וְכָל־הָעָם עֵדִים אַתֶּם
הַיּוֹם כִּי קָנִיתִי אֶת־כָּל־אֲשֶׁר לֶאֱלִימֶלֶךְ וְאֵת כָּל־

Elimelech's, and all that *was* Chilion's and Mahlon's, from the hand of Naomi. ¹⁰ Moreover, Ruth the Moabitess, the widow of Mahlon, I have acquired as my wife, to perpetuate the name of the dead through his inheritance, that the name of the dead may not be cut off from among his brethren and from his position at the gate. You *are* witnesses this day."

¹¹ And all the people who *were* at the gate, and the elders, said, "*We are* witnesses. The LORD make the woman who is coming to your house like Rachel and Leah, the two who built the house of Israel; and may you prosper in Ephrathah and be famous in Bethlehem. ¹² May your house be like the house of Perez, whom Tamar bore to Judah, because of the offspring which the LORD will give you from this young woman."

¹³ So Boaz took Ruth and she became his wife; and when he went in to her, the LORD gave her conception, and she bore a son. ¹⁴ Then the women said to Naomi, "Blessed *be* the LORD, who has not left you this day without a close relative; and may his name be famous in Israel! ¹⁵ And may he be to you a restorer of life and a nourisher of your old age; for your daughter-in-law, who loves you, who is better to you than seven sons, has borne him." ¹⁶ Then Naomi took the child and laid him on her bosom, and became a nurse to him. ¹⁷ Also the neighbor women gave him a name, saying, "There is a son born to Naomi." And they called his name Obed. He *is* the father of Jesse, the father of David.

¹⁸ Now this *is* the genealogy of Perez: Perez begot Hezron; ¹⁹ Hezron begot Ram, and Ram begot Amminadab; ²⁰ Amminadab begot Nahshon, and Nahshon begot Salmon; ²¹ Salmon begot Boaz, and Boaz begot Obed; ²² Obed begot Jesse, and Jesse begot David.

אֲשֶׁר לְכִלְיוֹן וּמַחְלוֹן מִיַּד נָעֳמִי: 10 וְגַם אֶת־רוּת הַמֹּאֲבִיָּה אֵשֶׁת מַחְלוֹן קָנִיתִי לִי לְאִשָּׁה לְהָקִים שֵׁם־הַמֵּת עַל־נַחֲלָתוֹ וְלֹא־יִכָּרֵת שֵׁם־הַמֵּת מֵעִם אֶחָיו וּמִשַּׁעַר מְקוֹמוֹ עֵדִים אַתֶּם הַיּוֹם: 11 וַיֹּאמְרוּ כָּל־הָעָם אֲשֶׁר־בַּשַּׁעַר וְהַזְּקֵנִים עֵדִים יִתֵּן יְהוָה אֶת־הָאִשָּׁה הַבָּאָה אֶל־בֵּיתֶךָ כְּרָחֵל ׀ וּכְלֵאָה אֲשֶׁר בָּנוּ שְׁתֵּיהֶם אֶת־בֵּית יִשְׂרָאֵל וַעֲשֵׂה־חַיִל בְּאֶפְרָתָה וּקְרָא־שֵׁם בְּבֵית לָחֶם: 12 וִיהִי בֵיתְךָ כְּבֵית פֶּרֶץ אֲשֶׁר־יָלְדָה תָמָר לִיהוּדָה מִן־הַזֶּרַע אֲשֶׁר יִתֵּן יְהוָה לְךָ מִן־הַנַּעֲרָה הַזֹּאת: 13 וַיִּקַּח בֹּעַז אֶת־רוּת וַתְּהִי־לוֹ לְאִשָּׁה וַיָּבֹא אֵלֶיהָ וַיִּתֵּן יְהוָה לָהּ הֵרָיוֹן וַתֵּלֶד בֵּן: 14 וַתֹּאמַרְנָה הַנָּשִׁים אֶל־נָעֳמִי בָּרוּךְ יְהוָה אֲשֶׁר לֹא הִשְׁבִּית לָךְ גֹּאֵל הַיּוֹם וְיִקָּרֵא שְׁמוֹ בְּיִשְׂרָאֵל: 15 וְהָיָה לָךְ לְמֵשִׁיב נֶפֶשׁ וּלְכַלְכֵּל אֶת־שֵׂיבָתֵךְ כִּי כַלָּתֵךְ אֲשֶׁר־אֲהֵבַתֶךְ יְלָדַתּוּ אֲשֶׁר־הִיא טוֹבָה לָךְ מִשִּׁבְעָה בָּנִים: 16 וַתִּקַּח נָעֳמִי אֶת־הַיֶּלֶד וַתְּשִׁתֵהוּ בְחֵיקָהּ וַתְּהִי־לוֹ לְאֹמֶנֶת: 17 וַתִּקְרֶאנָה לוֹ הַשְּׁכֵנוֹת שֵׁם לֵאמֹר יֻלַּד־בֵּן לְנָעֳמִי וַתִּקְרֶאנָה שְׁמוֹ עוֹבֵד הוּא אֲבִי־יִשַׁי אֲבִי דָוִד: פ 18 וְאֵלֶּה תּוֹלְדוֹת פָּרֶץ פֶּרֶץ הוֹלִיד אֶת־חֶצְרוֹן: 19 וְחֶצְרוֹן הוֹלִיד אֶת־רָם וְרָם הוֹלִיד אֶת־עַמִּינָדָב: 20 וְעַמִּינָדָב הוֹלִיד אֶת־נַחְשׁוֹן וְנַחְשׁוֹן הוֹלִיד אֶת־שַׂלְמָה: 21 וְשַׂלְמוֹן הוֹלִיד אֶת־בֹּעַז וּבֹעַז הוֹלִיד אֶת־עוֹבֵד: 22 וְעֹבֵד הוֹלִיד אֶת־יִשַׁי וְיִשַׁי הוֹלִיד אֶת־דָּוִד:

The Book of

LAMENTATIONS

אֵיכָה

1

How lonely sits the city
That was full of people!
How like a widow is she,
Who *was* great among the nations!
The princess among the provinces
Has become a slave!

2 She weeps bitterly in the night,
Her tears *are* on her cheeks;
Among all her lovers
She has none to comfort *her*.
All her friends have dealt treacherously with her;
They have become her enemies.

3 Judah has gone into captivity,
Under affliction and hard servitude;
She dwells among the nations,
She finds no rest;
All her persecutors overtake her in dire straits.

4 The roads to Zion mourn
Because no one comes to the set feasts.
All her gates are desolate;
Her priests sigh,
Her virgins are afflicted,
And she *is* in bitterness.

5 Her adversaries have become the master,
Her enemies prosper;
For the LORD has afflicted her
Because of the multitude of her transgressions.
Her children have gone into captivity before the
    enemy.

6 And from the daughter of Zion
All her splendor has departed.
Her princes have become like deer
That find no pasture,
That flee without strength
Before the pursuer.

7 In the days of her affliction and roaming,
Jerusalem remembers all her pleasant things
That she had in the days of old.
When her people fell into the hand of the enemy,
With no one to help her,
The adversaries saw her
And mocked at her downfall.

8 Jerusalem has sinned gravely,
Therefore she has become vile.
All who honored her despise her
Because they have seen her nakedness;
Yes, she sighs and turns away.

9 Her uncleanness *is* in her skirts;
She did not consider her destiny;
Therefore her collapse was awesome;
She had no comforter.

א אֵיכָה ׀ יָשְׁבָה בָדָד הָעִיר רַבָּתִי עָם הָיְתָה
כְּאַלְמָנָה רַבָּתִי בַגּוֹיִם שָׂרָתִי בַּמְּדִינוֹת הָיְתָה לָמַס:

2 בָּכוֹ תִבְכֶּה בַּלַּיְלָה וְדִמְעָתָהּ עַל לֶחֱיָהּ אֵין־לָהּ
מְנַחֵם מִכָּל־אֹהֲבֶיהָ כָּל־רֵעֶיהָ בָּגְדוּ בָהּ הָיוּ לָהּ
לְאֹיְבִים:

3 גָּלְתָה יְהוּדָה מֵעֹנִי וּמֵרֹב עֲבֹדָה הִיא יָשְׁבָה
בַגּוֹיִם לֹא מָצְאָה מָנוֹחַ כָּל־רֹדְפֶיהָ הִשִּׂיגוּהָ בֵּין
הַמְּצָרִים:

4 דַּרְכֵי צִיּוֹן אֲבֵלוֹת מִבְּלִי בָּאֵי מוֹעֵד כָּל־שְׁעָרֶיהָ
שׁוֹמֵמִין כֹּהֲנֶיהָ נֶאֱנָחִים בְּתוּלֹתֶיהָ נּוּגוֹת וְהִיא
מַר־לָהּ:

5 הָיוּ צָרֶיהָ לְרֹאשׁ אֹיְבֶיהָ שָׁלוּ כִּי־יְהֹוָה הוֹגָהּ
עַל רֹב־פְּשָׁעֶיהָ עוֹלָלֶיהָ הָלְכוּ שְׁבִי לִפְנֵי־צָר:

6 וַיֵּצֵא מִן־בַּת־צִיּוֹן כָּל־הֲדָרָהּ הָיוּ שָׂרֶיהָ
כְּאַיָּלִים לֹא־מָצְאוּ מִרְעֶה וַיֵּלְכוּ בְלֹא־כֹחַ לִפְנֵי
רוֹדֵף:

7 זָכְרָה יְרוּשָׁלִַם יְמֵי עָנְיָהּ וּמְרוּדֶיהָ כֹּל מַחֲמֻדֶיהָ
אֲשֶׁר הָיוּ מִימֵי קֶדֶם בִּנְפֹל עַמָּהּ בְּיַד־צָר וְאֵין
עוֹזֵר לָהּ רָאוּהָ צָרִים שָׂחֲקוּ עַל מִשְׁבַּתֶּהָ:

8 חֵטְא חָטְאָה יְרוּשָׁלִַם עַל־כֵּן לְנִידָה הָיָתָה
כָּל־מְכַבְּדֶיהָ הִזִּילוּהָ כִּי־רָאוּ עֶרְוָתָהּ גַּם־הִיא
נֶאֶנְחָה וַתָּשָׁב אָחוֹר:

9 טֻמְאָתָהּ בְּשׁוּלֶיהָ לֹא זָכְרָה אַחֲרִיתָהּ וַתֵּרֶד
פְּלָאִים אֵין מְנַחֵם לָהּ רְאֵה יְהֹוָה אֶת־עָנְיִי כִּי

א 6 מִבַּת־

"O Lᴏʀᴅ, behold my affliction,
For *the* enemy is exalted!"

הִגְדִּיל אוֹיֵב:

10 The adversary has spread his hand
Over all her pleasant things;
For she has seen the nations enter her sanctuary,
Those whom You commanded
Not to enter Your assembly.

10 יָדוֹ פָּרַשׂ צָר עַל כָּל־מַחֲמַדֶּיהָ כִּי־רָאֲתָה גוֹיִם
בָּאוּ מִקְדָּשָׁהּ אֲשֶׁר צִוִּיתָה לֹא־יָבֹאוּ בַקָּהָל לָךְ:

11 All her people sigh,
They seek bread;
They have given their valuables for food to
restore life.
"See, O Lᴏʀᴅ, and consider,
For I am scorned."

11 כָּל־עַמָּהּ נֶאֱנָחִים מְבַקְשִׁים לֶחֶם נָתְנוּ
מַחֲמוֹדֵּיהֶםᵖ בְּאֹכֶל לְהָשִׁיב נָפֶשׁ רְאֵה יְהוָה
וְהַבִּיטָה כִּי הָיִיתִי זוֹלֵלָה:

12 "*Is it* nothing to you, all you who pass by?
Behold and see
If there is any sorrow like my sorrow,
Which has been brought on me,
Which the Lᴏʀᴅ has inflicted
In the day of His fierce anger.

12 לוֹא אֲלֵיכֶם כָּל־עֹבְרֵי דֶרֶךְ הַבִּיטוּ וּרְאוּ אִם־
יֵשׁ מַכְאוֹב כְּמַכְאֹבִי אֲשֶׁר עוֹלַל לִי אֲשֶׁר הוֹגָה
יְהוָה בְּיוֹם חֲרוֹן אַפּוֹ:

13 "From above He has sent fire into my bones,
And it overpowered them;
He has spread a net for my feet
And turned me back;
He has made me desolate
And faint all the day.

13 מִמָּרוֹם שָׁלַח־אֵשׁ בְּעַצְמֹתַי וַיִּרְדֶּנָּה פָּרַשׂ רֶשֶׁת
לְרַגְלַי הֱשִׁיבַנִי אָחוֹר נְתָנַנִי שֹׁמֵמָה כָּל־הַיּוֹם
דָּוָה:

14 "The yoke of my transgressions was bound;
They were woven together by His hands,
And thrust upon my neck.
He made my strength fail;
The Lord delivered me into the hands of *those
whom* I am not able to withstand.

14 נִשְׂקַד עֹל פְּשָׁעַי בְּיָדוֹ יִשְׂתָּרְגוּ עָלוּ עַל־צַוָּארִי
הִכְשִׁיל כֹּחִי נְתָנַנִי אֲדֹנָי בִּידֵי לֹא־אוּכַל קוּם:

15 "The Lord has trampled underfoot all my mighty
men in my midst;
He has called an assembly against me
To crush my young men;
The Lord trampled *as* in a winepress
The virgin daughter of Judah.

15 סִלָּה כָל־אַבִּירַי ׀ אֲדֹנָי בְּקִרְבִּי קָרָא עָלַי מוֹעֵד
לִשְׁבֹּר בַּחוּרָי גַּת דָּרַךְ אֲדֹנָי לִבְתוּלַת בַּת־
יְהוּדָה:

16 "For these *things* I weep;
My eye, my eye overflows with water;
Because the comforter, who should restore my
life,
Is far from me.
My children are desolate
Because the enemy prevailed."

16 עַל־אֵלֶּה ׀ אֲנִי בוֹכִיָּה עֵינִי ׀ עֵינִי יֹרְדָה
מַּיִם כִּי־רָחַק מִמֶּנִּי מְנַחֵם מֵשִׁיב נַפְשִׁי הָיוּ בָנַי
שׁוֹמֵמִים כִּי גָבַר אוֹיֵב:

17 Zion spreads out her hands,
But no one comforts her;
The Lᴏʀᴅ has commanded concerning Jacob
That those around him *become* his adversaries;
Jerusalem has become an unclean thing among
them.

17 פֵּרְשָׂה צִיּוֹן בְּיָדֶיהָ אֵין מְנַחֵם לָהּ צִוָּה יְהוָה
לְיַעֲקֹב סְבִיבָיו צָרָיו הָיְתָה יְרוּשָׁלַ͏ִם לְנִדָּה
בֵּינֵיהֶם:

18 "The Lᴏʀᴅ is righteous,
For I rebelled against His commandment.
Hear now, all peoples,
And behold my sorrow;
My virgins and my young men
Have gone into captivity.

18 צַדִּיק הוּא יְהוָה כִּי פִיהוּ מָרִיתִי שִׁמְעוּ־נָא כָל־
עַמִּיםᵖ וּרְאוּ מַכְאֹבִי בְּתוּלֹתַי וּבַחוּרַי הָלְכוּ
בַשֶּׁבִי:

19 "I called for my lovers,
But they deceived me;

19 קָרָאתִי לַמְאַהֲבַי הֵמָּה רִמּוּנִי כֹּהֲנַי וּזְקֵנַי בָּעִיר

My priests and my elders
Breathed their last in the city,
While they sought food
To restore their life.

גָּוָעוּ כִּי־בִקְשׁוּ אֹכֶל לָמוֹ וְיָשִׁיבוּ אֶת־נַפְשָׁם:

20 "See, O LORD, that I *am* in distress;
My soul is troubled;
My heart is overturned within me,
For I have been very rebellious.
Outside the sword bereaves,
At home *it is* like death.

20 רְאֵה יְהוָה כִּי־צַר־לִי מֵעַי חֳמַרְמָרוּ נֶהְפַּךְ לִבִּי
בְּקִרְבִּי כִּי מָרוֹ מָרִיתִי מִחוּץ שִׁכְּלָה־חֶרֶב בַּבַּיִת
כַּמָּוֶת:

21 "They have heard that I sigh,
But no one comforts me.
All my enemies have heard of my trouble;
They are glad that You have done *it*.
Bring on the day You have announced,
That they may become like me.

21 שָׁמְעוּ כִּי נֶאֱנָחָה אָנִי אֵין מְנַחֵם לִי כָּל־אֹיְבַי
שָׁמְעוּ רָעָתִי שָׂשׂוּ כִּי אַתָּה עָשִׂיתָ הֵבֵאתָ יוֹם־
קָרָאתָ וְיִהְיוּ כָמֹנִי:

22 "Let all their wickedness come before You,
And do to them as You have done to me
For all my transgressions;
For my sighs *are* many,
And my heart *is* faint."

22 תָּבֹא כָל־רָעָתָם לְפָנֶיךָ וְעוֹלֵל לָמוֹ כַּאֲשֶׁר
עוֹלַלְתָּ לִי עַל כָּל־פְּשָׁעָי כִּי־רַבּוֹת אַנְחֹתַי וְלִבִּי
דַוָּי:
פ

2

How the Lord has covered the daughter of Zion
With a cloud in His anger!
He cast down from heaven to the earth
The beauty of Israel,
And did not remember His footstool
In the day of His anger.

ב אֵיכָה יָעִיב בְּאַפּוֹ | אֲדֹנָי אֶת־בַּת־צִיּוֹן הִשְׁלִיךְ
מִשָּׁמַיִם אֶרֶץ תִּפְאֶרֶת יִשְׂרָאֵל וְלֹא־זָכַר הֲדֹם־רַגְלָיו
בְּיוֹם אַפּוֹ:

2 The Lord has swallowed up and has not pitied
All the dwelling places of Jacob.
He has thrown down in His wrath
The strongholds of the daughter of Judah;
He has brought *them* down to the ground;
He has profaned the kingdom and its princes.

2 בִּלַּע אֲדֹנָי לֹא חָמַל אֵת כָּל־נְאוֹת יַעֲקֹב
הָרַס בְּעֶבְרָתוֹ מִבְצְרֵי בַת־יְהוּדָה הִגִּיעַ לָאָרֶץ
חִלֵּל מַמְלָכָה וְשָׂרֶיהָ:

3 He has cut off in fierce anger
Every horn of Israel;
He has drawn back His right hand
From before the enemy.
He has blazed against Jacob like a flaming fire
Devouring all around.

3 גָּדַע בָּחֳרִי־אַף כֹּל קֶרֶן יִשְׂרָאֵל הֵשִׁיב אָחוֹר
יְמִינוֹ מִפְּנֵי אוֹיֵב וַיִּבְעַר בְּיַעֲקֹב כְּאֵשׁ לֶהָבָה
אָכְלָה סָבִיב:

4 Standing like an enemy, He has bent His bow;
With His right hand, like an adversary,
He has slain all *who were* pleasing to His eye;
On the tent of the daughter of Zion,
He has poured out His fury like fire.

4 דָּרַךְ קַשְׁתּוֹ כְּאוֹיֵב נִצָּב יְמִינוֹ כְּצָר וַיַּהֲרֹג כֹּל
מַחֲמַדֵּי־עָיִן בְּאֹהֶל בַּת־צִיּוֹן שָׁפַךְ כָּאֵשׁ חֲמָתוֹ:

5 The Lord was like an enemy.
He has swallowed up Israel,
He has swallowed up all her palaces;
He has destroyed her strongholds,
And has increased mourning and lamentation
In the daughter of Judah.

5 הָיָה אֲדֹנָי | כְּאוֹיֵב בִּלַּע יִשְׂרָאֵל בִּלַּע כָּל־
אַרְמְנוֹתֶיהָ שִׁחֵת מִבְצָרָיו וַיֶּרֶב בְּבַת־יְהוּדָה
תַּאֲנִיָּה וַאֲנִיָּה:

6 He has done violence to His tabernacle,
As if it were a garden;
He has destroyed His place of assembly;
The LORD has caused
The appointed feasts and Sabbaths to be
forgotten in Zion.

6 וַיַּחְמֹס כַּגַּן שֻׂכּוֹ שִׁחֵת מוֹעֲדוֹ שִׁכַּח יְהוָה |

In His burning indignation He has spurned the
king and the priest.

בְּצִיּוֹן מוֹעֵד וְשַׁבָּת וַיִּנְאַץ בְּזַֽעַם־אַפּוֹ מֶלֶךְ וְכֹהֵן׃

7   The Lord has spurned His altar,
He has abandoned His sanctuary;
He has given up the walls of her palaces
Into the hand of the enemy.
They have made a noise in the house of the Lord
As on the day of a set feast.

7   זָנַח אֲדֹנָי ׀ מִזְבְּחוֹ נִאֵר מִקְדָּשׁוֹ הִסְגִּיר בְּיַד־
אוֹיֵב חוֹמֹת אַרְמְנוֹתֶיהָ קוֹל נָתְנוּ בְּבֵית־יְהֹוָה
כְּיוֹם מוֹעֵד׃

8   The Lord has purposed to destroy
The wall of the daughter of Zion.
He has stretched out a line;
He has not withdrawn His hand from destroying;
Therefore He has caused the rampart and wall to
lament;
They languished together.

8   חָשַׁב יְהֹוָה ׀ לְהַשְׁחִית חוֹמַת בַּת־צִיּוֹן נָטָה קָו
לֹא־הֵשִׁיב יָדוֹ מִבַּלֵּעַ וַיַּֽאֲבֶל־חֵל וְחוֹמָה יַחְדָּו
אֻמְלָלוּ׃

9   Her gates have sunk into the ground;
He has destroyed and broken her bars.
Her king and her princes are among the nations;
The Law is no more,
And her prophets find no vision from the Lord.

9   טָבְעוּ בָאָרֶץ שְׁעָרֶיהָ אִבַּד וְשִׁבַּר בְּרִיחֶיהָ מַלְכָּהּ
וְשָׂרֶיהָ בַגּוֹיִם אֵין תּוֹרָה גַּם־נְבִיאֶיהָ לֹא־מָצְאוּ
חָזוֹן מֵיְהֹוָה׃

10 The elders of the daughter of Zion
Sit on the ground and keep silence;
They throw dust on their heads
And gird themselves with sackcloth.
The virgins of Jerusalem
Bow their heads to the ground.

10 יֵשְׁבוּ לָאָרֶץ יִדְּמוּ זִקְנֵי בַת־צִיּוֹן הֶעֱלוּ עָפָר
עַל־רֹאשָׁם חָגְרוּ שַׂקִּים הוֹרִידוּ לָאָרֶץ רֹאשָׁן
בְּתוּלֹת יְרוּשָׁלָ͏ִם׃

11 My eyes fail with tears,
My heart is troubled;
My bile is poured on the ground
Because of the destruction of the daughter of my
people,
Because the children and the infants
Faint in the streets of the city.

11 כָּלוּ בַדְּמָעוֹת עֵינַי חֳמַרְמְרוּ מֵעַי נִשְׁפַּךְ לָאָרֶץ
כְּבֵדִי עַל־שֶׁבֶר בַּת־עַמִּי בֵּעָטֵף עוֹלֵל וְיוֹנֵק
בִּרְחֹבוֹת קִרְיָה׃

12 They say to their mothers,
"Where is grain and wine?"
As they swoon like the wounded
In the streets of the city,
As their life is poured out
In their mothers' bosom.

12 לְאִמֹּתָם יֹאמְרוּ אַיֵּה דָּגָן וָיָיִן בְּהִֽתְעַטְּפָם כֶּחָלָל
בִּרְחֹבוֹת עִיר בְּהִשְׁתַּפֵּךְ נַפְשָׁם אֶל־חֵיק אִמֹּתָם׃

13 How shall I console you?
To what shall I liken you,
O daughter of Jerusalem?
What shall I compare with you, that I may
comfort you,
O virgin daughter of Zion?
For your ruin is spread wide as the sea;
Who can heal you?

13 מָה־אֲעִידֵךְ מָה אֲדַמֶּה־לָּךְ הַבַּת יְרוּשָׁלַ͏ִם מָה
אַשְׁוֶה־לָּךְ וַאֲנַחֲמֵךְ בְּתוּלַת בַּת־צִיּוֹן כִּי־גָדוֹל
כַּיָּם שִׁבְרֵךְ מִי יִרְפָּא־לָךְ׃

14 Your prophets have seen for you
False and deceptive visions;
They have not uncovered your iniquity,
To bring back your captives,
But have envisioned for you false prophecies and
delusions.

14 נְבִיאַיִךְ חָזוּ לָךְ שָׁוְא וְתָפֵל וְלֹא־גִלּוּ עַל־
עֲוֺנֵךְ לְהָשִׁיב שְׁבִיתֵךְ[p] וַיֶּחֱזוּ לָךְ מַשְׂאוֹת שָׁוְא
וּמַדּוּחִים׃

15 All who pass by clap their hands at you;
They hiss and shake their heads
At the daughter of Jerusalem:

"Is this the city that is called
'The perfection of beauty,

15 סָפְקוּ עָלַיִךְ כַּפַּיִם כָּל־עֹבְרֵי דֶרֶךְ שָׁרְקוּ וַיָּנִעוּ
רֹאשָׁם עַל־בַּת יְרוּשָׁלָ͏ִם הֲזֹאת הָעִיר שֶׁיֹּאמְרוּ

ב   14 שְׁבִיתֵךְ

The joy of the whole earth'?"   כְּלִילַת יֹפִי מָשׂוֹשׂ לְכָל־הָאָרֶץ:

16   All your enemies have opened their mouth
     against you;
    They hiss and gnash *their* teeth.
    They say, "We have swallowed *her* up!
    Surely this *is* the day we have waited for;
    We have found *it*, we have seen *it!*"

16 פָּצוּ עָלַיִךְ פִּיהֶם כָּל־אוֹיְבַיִךְ שָׁרְקוּ וַיַּחַרְקוּ־שֵׁן
אָמְרוּ בִּלָּעְנוּ אַךְ זֶה הַיּוֹם שֶׁקִּוִּינֻהוּ מָצָאנוּ
רָאִינוּ:

17   The Lord has done what He purposed;
    He has fulfilled His word
    Which He commanded in days of old.
    He has thrown down and has not pitied,
    And He has caused an enemy to rejoice over you;
    He has exalted the horn of your adversaries.

17 עָשָׂה יְהֹוָה אֲשֶׁר זָמָם בִּצַּע אֶמְרָתוֹ אֲשֶׁר צִוָּה
מִימֵי־קֶדֶם הָרַס וְלֹא חָמָל וַיְשַׂמַּח עָלַיִךְ אוֹיֵב
הֵרִים קֶרֶן צָרָיִךְ:

18   Their heart cried out to the Lord,
    "O wall of the daughter of Zion,
    Let tears run down like a river day and night;
    Give yourself no relief;
    Give your eyes no rest.

18 צָעַק לִבָּם אֶל־אֲדֹנָי חוֹמַת בַּת־צִיּוֹן הוֹרִידִי
כַנַּחַל דִּמְעָה יוֹמָם וָלַיְלָה אַל־תִּתְּנִי פוּגַת לָךְ
אַל־תִּדֹּם בַּת־עֵינֵךְ:

19   "Arise, cry out in the night,
    At the beginning of the watches;
    Pour out your heart like water before the face of
     the Lord.
    Lift your hands toward Him
    For the life of your young children,
    Who faint from hunger at the head of every
     street."

19 קוּמִי ׀ רֹנִּי בַלַּיְלָ לְרֹאשׁ אַשְׁמֻרוֹת שִׁפְכִי
כַמַּיִם לִבֵּךְ נֹכַח פְּנֵי אֲדֹנָי שְׂאִי אֵלָיו כַּפַּיִךְ
עַל־נֶפֶשׁ עֽוֹלָלַיִךְ הָעֲטוּפִים בְּרָעָב בְּרֹאשׁ כָּל־
חוּצוֹת:

20   "See, O Lord, and consider!
    To whom have You done this?
    Should the women eat their offspring,
    The children they have cuddled?
    Should the priest and prophet be slain
    In the sanctuary of the Lord?

20 רְאֵה יְהֹוָה וְהַבִּיטָה לְמִי עוֹלַלְתָּ כֹּה אִם־
תֹּאכַלְנָה נָשִׁים פִּרְיָם עֹלֲלֵי טִפֻּחִים אִם־יֵהָרֵג
בְּמִקְדַּשׁ אֲדֹנָי כֹּהֵן וְנָבִיא:

21   "Young and old lie
    On the ground in the streets;
    My virgins and my young men
    Have fallen by the sword;
    You have slain *them* in the day of Your anger,
    You have slaughtered *and* not pitied.

21 שָׁכְבוּ לָאָרֶץ חוּצוֹת נַעַר וְזָקֵן בְּתוּלֹתַי וּבַחוּרַי
נָפְלוּ בֶחָרֶב הָרַגְתָּ בְּיוֹם אַפֶּךָ טָבַחְתָּ לֹא
חָמָלְתָּ:

22   "You have invited as to a feast day
    The terrors that surround me.
    In the day of the Lord's anger
    There was no refugee or survivor.
    Those whom I have borne and brought up
    My enemies have destroyed."

22 תִּקְרָא כְיוֹם מוֹעֵד מְגוּרַי מִסָּבִיב וְלֹא הָיָה בְּיוֹם
אַף־יְהֹוָה פָּלִיט וְשָׂרִיד אֲשֶׁר־טִפַּחְתִּי וְרִבִּיתִי
אֹיְבִי כִלָּם:
       פ

3

1   I *am* the man *who* has seen affliction by the rod
    of His wrath.

א אֲנִי הַגֶּבֶר רָאָה עֳנִי בְּשֵׁבֶט עֶבְרָתוֹ:

2   He has led me and made *me* walk
    In darkness and not *in* light.

2 אוֹתִי נָהַג וַיֹּלַךְ חֹשֶׁךְ וְלֹא־אוֹר:

3   Surely He has turned His hand against me
    Time and time again throughout the day.

3 אַךְ בִּי יָשֻׁב יַהֲפֹךְ יָדוֹ כָּל־הַיּוֹם:

4   He has aged my flesh and my skin,
    And broken my bones.

4 בִּלָּה בְשָׂרִי וְעוֹרִי שִׁבַּר עַצְמוֹתָי:

5   He has besieged me
    And surrounded *me* with bitterness and woe.

5 בָּנָה עָלַי וַיַּקַּף רֹאשׁ וּתְלָאָה:

6   He has set me in dark places
    Like the dead of long ago.

6 בְּמַחֲשַׁכִּים הוֹשִׁיבַנִי כְּמֵתֵי עוֹלָם:

7   He has hedged me in so that I cannot get out;

7 גָּדַר בַּעֲדִי וְלֹא אֵצֵא הִכְבִּיד נְחָשְׁתִּי:

ב 19 בַּלַּיְלָה

He has made my chain heavy.

8 Even when I cry and shout,
He shuts out my prayer.

9 He has blocked my ways with hewn stone;
He has made my paths crooked.

10 He *has been* to me a bear lying in wait,
Like a lion in ambush.

11 He has turned aside my ways and torn me in
pieces;
He has made me desolate.

12 He has bent His bow
And set me up as a target for the arrow.

13 He has caused the arrows of His quiver
To pierce my loins.

14 I have become the ridicule of all my people—
Their taunting song all the day.

15 He has filled me with bitterness,
He has made me drink wormwood.

16 He has also broken my teeth with gravel,
And covered me with ashes.

17 You have moved my soul far from peace;
I have forgotten prosperity.

18 And I said, "My strength and my hope
Have perished from the LORD."

19 Remember my affliction and roaming,
The wormwood and the gall.

20 My soul still remembers
And sinks within me.

21 This I recall to my mind,
Therefore I have hope.

22 *Through* the LORD's mercies we are not
consumed,
Because His compassions fail not.

23 *They are* new every morning;
Great *is* Your faithfulness.

24 "The LORD *is* my portion," says my soul,
"Therefore I hope in Him!"

25 The LORD *is* good to those who wait for Him,
To the soul *who* seeks Him.

26 *It is* good that *one* should hope and wait quietly
For the salvation of the LORD.

27 *It is* good for a man to bear
The yoke in his youth.

28 Let him sit alone and keep silent,
Because *God* has laid *it* on him;

29 Let him put his mouth in the dust—
There may yet be hope.

30 Let him give *his* cheek to the one who strikes him,
And be full of reproach.

31 For the Lord will not cast off forever.

32 Though He causes grief,
Yet He will show compassion
According to the multitude of His mercies.

33 For He does not afflict willingly,
Nor grieve the children of men.

34 To crush under one's feet
All the prisoners of the earth,

35 To turn aside the justice *due* a man
Before the face of the Most High,

גַּם כִּי אֶזְעַק וַאֲשַׁוֵּעַ שָׂתַם תְּפִלָּתִי: 8

גָּדַר דְּרָכַי בְּגָזִית נְתִיבֹתַי עִוָּה: 9

דֹּב אֹרֵב הוּא לִי אֲרִי${}^{\text{P}}$ בְּמִסְתָּרִים: 10

דְּרָכַי סוֹרֵר וַיְפַשְּׁחֵנִי שָׂמַנִי שֹׁמֵם: 11

דָּרַךְ קַשְׁתּוֹ וַיַּצִּיבֵנִי כַּמַּטָּרָא לַחֵץ: 12

הֵבִיא בְּכִלְיוֹתָי בְּנֵי אַשְׁפָּתוֹ: 13

הָיִיתִי שְּׂחֹק לְכָל־עַמִּי נְגִינָתָם כָּל־הַיּוֹם: 14

הִשְׂבִּיעַנִי בַמְּרוֹרִים הִרְוַנִי לַעֲנָה: 15

וַיַּגְרֵס בֶּחָצָץ שִׁנָּי הִכְפִּישַׁנִי בָּאֵפֶר: 16

וַתִּזְנַח מִשָּׁלוֹם נַפְשִׁי נָשִׁיתִי טוֹבָה: 17

וָאֹמַר אָבַד נִצְחִי וְתוֹחַלְתִּי מֵיְהוָה: 18

זְכָר־עָנְיִי וּמְרוּדִי לַעֲנָה וָרֹאשׁ: 19

זָכוֹר תִּזְכּוֹר וְתָשִׁיחַ${}^{\text{P}}$ עָלַי נַפְשִׁי: 20

זֹאת אָשִׁיב אֶל־לִבִּי עַל־כֵּן אוֹחִיל: 21

חַסְדֵי יְהוָה כִּי לֹא־תָמְנוּ כִּי לֹא־כָלוּ רַחֲמָיו: 22

חֲדָשִׁים לַבְּקָרִים רַבָּה אֱמוּנָתֶךָ: 23

חֶלְקִי יְהוָה אָמְרָה נַפְשִׁי עַל־כֵּן אוֹחִיל לוֹ: 24

טוֹב יְהוָה לְקֹוָו לְנֶפֶשׁ תִּדְרְשֶׁנּוּ: 25

טוֹב וְיָחִיל וְדוּמָם לִתְשׁוּעַת יְהוָה: 26

טוֹב לַגֶּבֶר כִּי־יִשָּׂא עֹל בִּנְעוּרָיו: 27

יֵשֵׁב בָּדָד וְיִדֹּם כִּי נָטַל עָלָיו: 28

יִתֵּן בֶּעָפָר פִּיהוּ אוּלַי יֵשׁ תִּקְוָה: 29

יִתֵּן לְמַכֵּהוּ לֶחִי יִשְׂבַּע בְּחֶרְפָּה: 30

כִּי לֹא יִזְנַח לְעוֹלָם אֲדֹנָי: 31

כִּי אִם־הוֹגָה וְרִחַם כְּרֹב חֲסָדָו${}^{\text{P}}$: 32

כִּי לֹא עִנָּה מִלִּבּוֹ וַיַּגֶּה בְּנֵי־אִישׁ: 33

לְדַכֵּא תַּחַת רַגְלָיו כֹּל אֲסִירֵי אָרֶץ: 34

לְהַטּוֹת מִשְׁפַּט־גָּבֶר נֶגֶד פְּנֵי עֶלְיוֹן: 35

ג 10 אֲרִי 20 וְתָשֹׁחַ 32וַחֲסָדָיו

36 Or subvert a man in his cause—
The Lord does not approve.

לְעַוֵּת אָדָם בְּרִיבוֹ אֲדֹנָי לֹא רָאָה:

37 Who *is* he *who* speaks and it comes to pass,
When the Lord has not commanded *it?*

מִי זֶה אָמַר וַתֶּהִי אֲדֹנָי לֹא צִוָּה:

38 *Is it* not from the mouth of the Most High
That woe and well-being proceed?

מִפִּי עֶלְיוֹן לֹא תֵצֵא הָרָעוֹת וְהַטּוֹב:

39 Why should a living man complain,
A man for the punishment of his sins?

מַה־יִּתְאוֹנֵן אָדָם חָי גֶּבֶר עַל־חֲטָאָו:ᵖ

40 Let us search out and examine our ways,
And turn back to the Lᴏʀᴅ;

נַחְפְּשָׂה דְרָכֵינוּ וְנַחְקֹרָה וְנָשׁוּבָה עַד־יְהוָה:

41 Let us lift our hearts and hands
To God in heaven.

נִשָּׂא לְבָבֵנוּ אֶל־כַּפָּיִם אֶל־אֵל בַּשָּׁמָיִם:

42 We have transgressed and rebelled;
You have not pardoned.

נַחְנוּ פָשַׁעְנוּ וּמָרִינוּ אַתָּה לֹא סָלָחְתָּ:

43 You have covered *Yourself* with anger
And pursued us;
You have slain *and* not pitied.

סַכֹּתָה בָאַף וַתִּרְדְּפֵנוּ הָרַגְתָּ לֹא חָמָלְתָּ:

44 You have covered Yourself with a cloud,
That prayer should not pass through.

סַכּוֹתָה בֶעָנָן לָךְ מֵעֲבוֹר תְּפִלָּה:

45 You have made us an offscouring and refuse
In the midst of the peoples.

סְחִי וּמָאוֹס תְּשִׂימֵנוּ בְּקֶרֶב הָעַמִּים:

46 All our enemies
Have opened their mouths against us.

פָּצוּ עָלֵינוּ פִּיהֶם כָּל־אֹיְבֵינוּ:

47 Fear and a snare have come upon us,
Desolation and destruction.

פַּחַד וָפַחַת הָיָה לָנוּ הַשֵּׁאת וְהַשָּׁבֶר:

48 My eyes overflow with rivers of water
For the destruction of the daughter of my people.

פַּלְגֵי־מַיִם תֵּרַד עֵינִי עַל־שֶׁבֶר בַּת־עַמִּי:

49 My eyes flow and do not cease,
Without interruption,

עֵינִי נִגְּרָה וְלֹא תִדְמֶה מֵאֵין הֲפֻגוֹת:

50 Till the Lᴏʀᴅ from heaven
Looks down and sees.

עַד־יַשְׁקִיף וְיֵרֶא יְהוָה מִשָּׁמָיִם:

51 My eyes bring suffering to my soul
Because of all the daughters of my city.

עֵינִי עוֹלְלָה לְנַפְשִׁי מִכֹּל בְּנוֹת עִירִי:

52 My enemies without cause
Hunted me down like a bird.

צוֹד צָדוּנִי כַּצִּפּוֹר אֹיְבַי חִנָּם:

53 They silenced my life in the pit
And threw stones at me.

צָמְתוּ בַבּוֹר חַיָּי וַיַּדּוּ־אֶבֶן בִּי:

54 The waters flowed over my head;
I said, "I am cut off!"

צָפוּ־מַיִם עַל־רֹאשִׁי אָמַרְתִּי נִגְזָרְתִּי:

55 I called on Your name, O Lᴏʀᴅ,
From the lowest pit.

קָרָאתִי שִׁמְךָ יְהוָה מִבּוֹר תַּחְתִּיּוֹת:

56 You have heard my voice:
"Do not hide Your ear
From my sighing, from my cry for help."

קוֹלִי שָׁמָעְתָּ אַל־תַּעְלֵם אָזְנְךָ לְרַוְחָתִי לְשַׁוְעָתִי:

57 You drew near on the day I called on You,
And said, "Do not fear!"

קָרַבְתָּ בְּיוֹם אֶקְרָאֶךָּ אָמַרְתָּ אַל־תִּירָא:

58 O Lord, You have pleaded the case for my soul;
You have redeemed my life.

רַבְתָּ אֲדֹנָי רִיבֵי נַפְשִׁי גָּאַלְתָּ חַיָּי:

59 O Lᴏʀᴅ, You have seen *how* I am wronged;
Judge my case.

רָאִיתָה יְהוָה עַוָּתָתִי שָׁפְטָה מִשְׁפָּטִי:

60 You have seen all their vengeance,
All their schemes against me.

רָאִיתָה כָּל־נִקְמָתָם כָּל־מַחְשְׁבֹתָם לִי:

61 You have heard their reproach, O Lᴏʀᴅ,
All their schemes against me,

שָׁמַעְתָּ חֶרְפָּתָם יְהוָה כָּל־מַחְשְׁבֹתָם עָלָי:

62 The lips of my enemies
And their whispering against me all the day.

שִׂפְתֵי קָמַי וְהֶגְיוֹנָם עָלַי כָּל־הַיּוֹם:

63 Look at their sitting down and their rising up;
I *am* their taunting song.

שִׁבְתָּם וְקִימָתָם הַבִּיטָה אֲנִי מַנְגִּינָתָם:

ג   39 חֲטָאָיו

64 Repay them, O LORD,
According to the work of their hands.
65 Give them a veiled heart;
Your curse *be* upon them!
66 In Your anger,
Pursue and destroy them
From under the heavens of the LORD.

תָּשִׁיב לָהֶם גְּמוּל יְהוָה כְּמַעֲשֵׂה יְדֵיהֶם: 64

תִּתֵּן לָהֶם מְגִנַּת־לֵב תַּאֲלָתְךָ לָהֶם: 65

תִּרְדֹּף בְּאַף וְתַשְׁמִידֵם מִתַּחַת שְׁמֵי יְהוָה: פ 66

4

How the gold has become dim!
How changed the fine gold!
The stones of the sanctuary are scattered
At the head of every street.

ד אֵיכָה יוּעַם זָהָב יִשְׁנֶא הַכֶּתֶם הַטּוֹב תִּשְׁתַּפֵּכְנָה אַבְנֵי־קֹדֶשׁ בְּרֹאשׁ כָּל־חוּצוֹת:

2 The precious sons of Zion,
Valuable as fine gold,
How they are regarded as clay pots,
The work of the hands of the potter!

בְּנֵי צִיּוֹן הַיְקָרִים הַמְסֻלָּאִים בַּפָּז אֵיכָה נֶחְשְׁבוּ לְנִבְלֵי־חֶרֶשׂ מַעֲשֵׂה יְדֵי יוֹצֵר: 2

3 Even the jackals present their breasts
To nurse their young;
But the daughter of my people *is* cruel,
Like ostriches in the wilderness.

גַּם־תַּנִּין חָלְצוּ שַׁד הֵינִיקוּ גּוּרֵיהֶן בַּת־עַמִּי לְאַכְזָר כִּי עֵנִים בַּמִּדְבָּר: 3

4 The tongue of the infant clings
To the roof of its mouth for thirst;
The young children ask for bread,
But no one breaks *it* for them.

דָּבַק לְשׁוֹן יוֹנֵק אֶל־חִכּוֹ בַּצָּמָא עוֹלָלִים שָׁאֲלוּ לֶחֶם פֹּרֵשׂ אֵין לָהֶם: 4

5 Those who ate delicacies
Are desolate in the streets;
Those who were brought up in scarlet
Embrace ash heaps.

הָאֹכְלִים לְמַעֲדַנִּים נָשַׁמּוּ בַּחוּצוֹת הָאֱמֻנִים עֲלֵי תוֹלָע חִבְּקוּ אַשְׁפַּתּוֹת: 5

6 The punishment of the iniquity of the daughter of
my people
Is greater than the punishment of the sin of
Sodom,
Which was overthrown in a moment,
With no hand to help her!

וַיִּגְדַּל עֲוֹן בַּת־עַמִּי מֵחַטַּאת סְדֹם הַהֲפוּכָה כְמוֹ־רָגַע וְלֹא־חָלוּ בָהּ יָדָיִם: 6

7 Her Nazirites were brighter than snow
And whiter than milk;
They were more ruddy in body than rubies,
Like sapphire in their appearance.

זַכּוּ נְזִירֶיהָ מִשֶּׁלֶג צַחוּ מֵחָלָב אָדְמוּ עֶצֶם מִפְּנִינִים סַפִּיר גִּזְרָתָם: 7

8 *Now* their appearance is blacker than soot;
They go unrecognized in the streets;
Their skin clings to their bones,
It has become as dry as wood.

חָשַׁךְ מִשְּׁחוֹר תָּאֳרָם לֹא נִכְּרוּ בַּחוּצוֹת צָפַד עוֹרָם עַל־עַצְמָם יָבֵשׁ הָיָה כָעֵץ: 8

9 *Those* slain by the sword are better off
Than *those* who die of hunger;
For these pine away,
Stricken *for lack* of the fruits of the field.

טוֹבִים הָיוּ חַלְלֵי־חֶרֶב מֵחַלְלֵי רָעָב שֶׁהֵם יָזוּבוּ מְדֻקָּרִים מִתְּנוּבֹת שָׂדָי: 9

10 The hands of the compassionate women
Have cooked their own children;
They became food for them
In the destruction of the daughter of my people.

יְדֵי נָשִׁים רַחֲמָנִיּוֹת בִּשְּׁלוּ יַלְדֵיהֶן הָיוּ לְבָרוֹת לָמוֹ בְּשֶׁבֶר בַּת־עַמִּי: 10

11 The LORD has fulfilled His fury,
He has poured out His fierce anger.
He kindled a fire in Zion,
And it has devoured its foundations.

כִּלָּה יְהוָה אֶת־חֲמָתוֹ שָׁפַךְ חֲרוֹן אַפּוֹ וַיַּצֶּת־אֵשׁ בְּצִיּוֹן וַתֹּאכַל יְסוֹדֹתֶיהָ: 11

12 The kings of the earth,
And all inhabitants of the world,
Would not have believed

לֹא הֶאֱמִינוּ מַלְכֵי־אֶרֶץ וכל יֹשְׁבֵי תֵבֵל כִּי 12

ד 3 תַּנִּים   כַּיְעֵנִים 12כֹל

That the adversary and the enemy
Could enter the gates of Jerusalem—

יָבֹא צַר וְאוֹיֵב בְּשַׁעֲרֵי יְרוּשָׁלָ͏ִם:

13 Because of the sins of her prophets
And the iniquities of her priests,
Who shed in her midst
The blood of the just.

13 מֵחַטֹּאת נְבִיאֶיהָ עֲוֺנֹת כֹּהֲנֶיהָ הַשֹּׁפְכִים
בְּקִרְבָּהּ דַּם צַדִּיקִים:

14 They wandered blind in the streets;
They have defiled themselves with blood,
So that no one would touch their garments.

14 נָעוּ עִוְרִים בַּחוּצוֹת נְגֹאֲלוּ בַּדָּם בְּלֹא יוּכְלוּ
יִגְּעוּ בִּלְבֻשֵׁיהֶם:

15 They cried out to them,
"Go away, unclean!
Go away, go away,
Do not touch us!"
When they fled and wandered,
Those among the nations said,
"They shall no longer dwell *here*."

15 סוּרוּ טָמֵא קָרְאוּ לָמוֹ סוּרוּ סוּרוּ אַל־תִּגָּעוּ כִּי
נָצוּ גַּם־נָעוּ אָמְרוּ בַּגּוֹיִם לֹא יוֹסִיפוּ לָגוּר:

16 The face of the Lord scattered them;
He no longer regards them.
The people do not respect the priests
Nor show favor to the elders.

16 פְּנֵי יְהֹוָה חִלְּקָם לֹא יוֹסִיף לְהַבִּיטָם פְּנֵי כֹהֲנִים
לֹא נָשָׂאוּ זְקֵנִיםᵖ לֹא חָנָנוּ:

17 Still our eyes failed us,
Watching vainly for our help;
In our watching we watched
For a nation *that* could not save *us*.

17 עוֹדֵינָהᵖ תִּכְלֶינָה עֵינֵינוּ אֶל־עֶזְרָתֵנוּ הָבֶל
בְּצִפִּיָּתֵנוּ צִפִּינוּ אֶל־גּוֹי לֹא יוֹשִׁעַ:

18 They tracked our steps
So that we could not walk in our streets.
Our end was near;
Our days were over,
For our end had come.

18 צָדוּ צְעָדֵינוּ מִלֶּכֶת בִּרְחֹבֹתֵינוּ קָרַב קִצֵּינוּ מָלְאוּ
יָמֵינוּ כִּי־בָא קִצֵּינוּ:

19 Our pursuers were swifter
Than the eagles of the heavens.
They pursued us on the mountains
And lay in wait for us in the wilderness.

19 קַלִּים הָיוּ רֹדְפֵינוּ מִנִּשְׁרֵי שָׁמָיִם עַל־הֶהָרִים
דְּלָקֻנוּ בַּמִּדְבָּר אָרְבוּ לָנוּ:

20 The breath of our nostrils, the anointed of the
Lord,
Was caught in their pits,
Of whom we said, "Under his shadow
We shall live among the nations."

20 רוּחַ אַפֵּינוּ מְשִׁיחַ יְהֹוָה נִלְכַּד בִּשְׁחִיתוֹתָם אֲשֶׁר
אָמַרְנוּ בְּצִלּוֹ נִחְיֶה בַגּוֹיִם:

21 Rejoice and be glad, O daughter of Edom,
You who dwell in the land of Uz!
The cup shall also pass over to you
And you shall become drunk and make yourself
naked.

21 שִׂישִׂי וְשִׂמְחִי בַּת־אֱדוֹם יוֹשַׁבְתִּיᵖ בְּאֶרֶץ עוּץ
גַּם־עָלַיִךְ תַּעֲבָר־כּוֹס תִּשְׁכְּרִי וְתִתְעָרִי:

22 *The punishment of* your iniquity is accomplished,
O daughter of Zion;
He will no longer send you into captivity.
He will punish your iniquity,
O daughter of Edom;
He will uncover your sins!

22 תַּם־עֲוֺנֵךְ בַּת־צִיּוֹן לֹא יוֹסִיף לְהַגְלוֹתֵךְ פָּקַד
עֲוֺנֵךְ בַּת־אֱדוֹם גִּלָּה עַל־חַטֹּאתָיִךְ:
פ

ה זְכֹר יְהֹוָה מֶה־הָיָה לָנוּ הַבִּיטᵖ וּרְאֵה אֶת־
חֶרְפָּתֵנוּ:

5

Remember, O Lord, what has come upon us;
Look, and behold our reproach!

2 Our inheritance has been turned over to aliens,
And our houses to foreigners.

2 נַחֲלָתֵנוּ נֶהֶפְכָה לְזָרִים בָּתֵּינוּ לְנָכְרִים:

3 We have become orphans and waifs,
Our mothers *are* like widows.

3 יְתוֹמִים הָיִינוּ אֵיןᵖ אָב אִמֹּתֵינוּ כְּאַלְמָנוֹת:

4 We pay for the water we drink,

4 מֵימֵינוּ בְּכֶסֶף שָׁתִינוּ עֵצֵינוּ בִּמְחִיר יָבֹאוּ:

ד 16 וְזָקֵנִים 17 עוֹדֵינוּ 21 יוֹשֶׁבֶת
ה 1 הַבִּיטָה 3 וְאֵין

And our wood comes at a price.
5 *They* pursue at our heels;
We labor *and* have no rest.
6 We have given our hand *to* the Egyptians
And the Assyrians, to be satisfied with bread.

7 Our fathers sinned *and are* no more,
But we bear their iniquities.
8 Servants rule over us;
There is none to deliver *us* from their hand.
9 We get our bread *at the risk* of our lives,
Because of the sword in the wilderness.

10 Our skin is hot as an oven,
Because of the fever of famine.
11 They ravished the women in Zion,
The maidens in the cities of Judah.
12 Princes were hung up by their hands,
And elders were not respected.
13 Young men ground at the millstones;
Boys staggered under *loads of* wood.
14 The elders have ceased *gathering* at the gate,
And the young men from their music.

15 The joy of our heart has ceased;
Our dance has turned into mourning.
16 The crown has fallen *from* our head.
Woe to us, for we have sinned!
17 Because of this our heart is faint;
Because of these *things* our eyes grow dim;
18 Because of Mount Zion which is desolate,
With foxes walking about on it.

19 You, O LORD, remain forever;
Your throne from generation to generation.
20 Why do You forget us forever,
And forsake us for so long a time?
21 Turn us back to You, O LORD, and we will be restored;
Renew our days as of old,
22 Unless You have utterly rejected us,
And are very angry with us!

עַל צַוָּארֵ֙נוּ֙ נִרְדָּ֔פְנוּ יָגַ֖עְנוּ [לֹא]ᵖ הֽוּנַֽח־לָֽנוּ׃ 5

מִצְרַ֙יִם֙ נָתַ֣נּוּ יָ֔ד אַשּׁ֖וּר לִשְׂבֹּ֥עַ לָֽחֶם׃ 6

אֲבֹתֵ֤ינוּ חָֽטְאוּ֙ [אֵינָ֔ם]ᵖ [אֲנַ֖חְנוּ]ᵖ עֲוֺנֹתֵיהֶ֥ם 7
סָבָֽלְנוּ׃

עֲבָדִים֙ מָ֣שְׁלוּ בָ֔נוּ פֹּרֵ֖ק אֵ֥ין מִיָּדָֽם׃ 8

בְּנַפְשֵׁ֙נוּ֙ נָבִ֣יא לַחְמֵ֔נוּ מִפְּנֵ֖י חֶ֥רֶב הַמִּדְבָּֽר׃ 9

עוֹרֵ֙נוּ֙ כְּתַנּ֣וּר נִכְמָ֔רוּ מִפְּנֵ֖י זַלְעֲפ֥וֹת רָעָֽב׃ 10

נָשִׁים֙ בְּצִיּ֣וֹן עִנּ֔וּ בְּתֻלֹ֖ת בְּעָרֵ֥י יְהוּדָֽה׃ 11

שָׂרִים֙ בְּיָדָ֣ם נִתְל֔וּ פְּנֵ֥י זְקֵנִ֖ים לֹ֥א נֶהְדָּֽרוּ׃ 12

בַּחוּרִים֙ טְח֣וֹן נָשָׂ֔אוּ וּנְעָרִ֖ים בָּעֵ֥ץ כָּשָֽׁלוּ׃ 13

זְקֵנִים֙ מִשַּׁ֣עַר שָׁבָ֔תוּ בַּחוּרִ֖ים מִנְּגִינָתָֽם׃ 14

שָׁבַת֙ מְשׂ֣וֹשׂ לִבֵּ֔נוּ נֶהְפַּ֥ךְ לְאֵ֖בֶל מְחֹלֵֽנוּ׃ 15

נָֽפְלָה֙ עֲטֶ֣רֶת רֹאשֵׁ֔נוּ אֽוֹי־נָ֥א לָ֖נוּ כִּ֥י חָטָֽאנוּ׃ 16

עַל־זֶ֗ה הָיָ֤ה דָוֶה֙ לִבֵּ֔נוּ עַל־אֵ֖לֶּה חָשְׁכ֥וּ עֵינֵֽינוּ׃ 17

עַ֤ל הַר־צִיּוֹן֙ שֶׁשָּׁמֵ֔ם שֽׁוּעָלִ֖ים הִלְּכוּ־בֽוֹ׃ פ 18

אַתָּ֤ה יְהוָה֙ לְעוֹלָ֣ם תֵּשֵׁ֔ב כִּסְאֲךָ֖ לְדֹ֥ר וָדֽוֹר׃ 19

לָ֤מָּה לָנֶ֙צַח֙ תִּשְׁכָּחֵ֔נוּ תַּֽעַזְבֵ֖נוּ לְאֹ֥רֶךְ יָמִֽים׃ 20

הֲשִׁיבֵ֙נוּ יְהוָ֤ה ׀ אֵלֶ֙יךָ֙ [וְנָשׁ֔וּבָ]ᵖ חַדֵּ֥שׁ יָמֵ֖ינוּ 21
כְּקֶֽדֶם׃

כִּ֣י אִם־מָאֹ֤ס מְאַסְתָּ֙נוּ֙ קָצַ֥פְתָּ עָלֵ֖ינוּ עַד־מְאֹֽד׃ 22

ה 5 וְלֹא 7 וְאֵינָם וַאֲנַחְנוּ 21וְנָשׁ֔וּבָה

The Book of

ECCLESIASTES

קֹהֶלֶת

1 The words of the Preacher, the son of David, king in Jerusalem.

2 "Vanity of vanities," says the Preacher;
"Vanity of vanities, all *is* vanity."

3 What profit has a man from all his labor
In which he toils under the sun?
4 *One* generation passes away, and *another* generation comes;
But the earth abides forever.
5 The sun also rises, and the sun goes down,
And hastens to the place where it arose.
6 The wind goes toward the south,
And turns around to the north;
The wind whirls about continually,
And comes again on its circuit.
7 All the rivers run into the sea,
Yet the sea *is* not full;
To the place from which the rivers come,
There they return again.
8 All things *are* full of labor;
Man cannot express *it*.
The eye is not satisfied with seeing,
Nor the ear filled with hearing.
9 That which has been *is* what will be,
That which *is* done is what will be done,
And *there is* nothing new under the sun.
10 Is there anything of which it may be said,
"See, this *is* new"?
It has already been in ancient times before us.
11 *There is* no remembrance of former *things,*
Nor will there be any remembrance of *things* that are to come
By *those* who will come after.

12 I, the Preacher, was king over Israel in Jerusalem. 13 And I set my heart to seek and search out by wisdom concerning all that is done under heaven; this burdensome task God has given to the sons of man, by which they may be exercised. 14 I have seen all the works that are done under the sun; and indeed, all *is* vanity and grasping for the wind.

15 *What is* crooked cannot be made straight,
And what is lacking cannot be numbered.

16 I communed with my heart, saying, "Look, I have attained greatness, and have gained more wisdom than all who were before me in Jerusalem. My heart has understood great wisdom and knowledge." 17 And I set my heart to know wisdom and to know madness and folly. I perceived that this also is grasping for the wind.

א דִּבְרֵי קֹהֶלֶת בֶּן־דָּוִד מֶלֶךְ בִּירוּשָׁלָ͏ִם: 2 הֲבֵל הֲבָלִים אָמַר קֹהֶלֶת הֲבֵל הֲבָלִים הַכֹּל הָבֶל: 3 מַה־יִּתְרוֹן לָאָדָם בְּכָל־עֲמָלוֹ שֶׁיַּעֲמֹל תַּחַת הַשָּׁמֶשׁ: 4 דּוֹר הֹלֵךְ וְדוֹר בָּא וְהָאָרֶץ לְעוֹלָם עֹמָדֶת: 5 וְזָרַח הַשֶּׁמֶשׁ וּבָא הַשָּׁמֶשׁ וְאֶל־מְקוֹמוֹ שׁוֹאֵף זוֹרֵחַ הוּא שָׁם: 6 הוֹלֵךְ אֶל־דָּרוֹם וְסוֹבֵב אֶל־צָפוֹן סוֹבֵב ׀ סֹבֵב הוֹלֵךְ הָרוּחַ וְעַל־סְבִיבֹתָיו שָׁב הָרוּחַ: 7 כָּל־הַנְּחָלִים הֹלְכִים אֶל־הַיָּם וְהַיָּם אֵינֶנּוּ מָלֵא אֶל־מְקוֹם שֶׁהַנְּחָלִים הֹלְכִים שָׁם הֵם שָׁבִים לָלָכֶת: 8 כָּל־הַדְּבָרִים יְגֵעִים לֹא־יוּכַל אִישׁ לְדַבֵּר לֹא־תִשְׂבַּע עַיִן לִרְאוֹת וְלֹא־תִמָּלֵא אֹזֶן מִשְּׁמֹעַ: 9 מַה־שֶּׁהָיָה הוּא שֶׁיִּהְיֶה וּמַה־שֶּׁנַּעֲשָׂה הוּא שֶׁיֵּעָשֶׂה וְאֵין כָּל־חָדָשׁ תַּחַת הַשָּׁמֶשׁ: 10 יֵשׁ דָּבָר שֶׁיֹּאמַר רְאֵה־זֶה חָדָשׁ הוּא כְּבָר הָיָה לְעֹלָמִים אֲשֶׁר הָיָה מִלְּפָנֵנוּ: 11 אֵין זִכְרוֹן לָרִאשֹׁנִים וְגַם לָאַחֲרֹנִים שֶׁיִּהְיוּ לֹא־יִהְיֶה לָהֶם זִכָּרוֹן עִם שֶׁיִּהְיוּ לָאַחֲרֹנָה: פ

12 אֲנִי קֹהֶלֶת הָיִיתִי מֶלֶךְ עַל־יִשְׂרָאֵל בִּירוּשָׁלָ͏ִם: 13 וְנָתַתִּי אֶת־לִבִּי לִדְרוֹשׁ וְלָתוּר בַּחָכְמָה עַל כָּל־אֲשֶׁר נַעֲשָׂה תַּחַת הַשָּׁמָיִם הוּא ׀ עִנְיַן רָע נָתַן אֱלֹהִים לִבְנֵי הָאָדָם לַעֲנוֹת בּוֹ: 14 רָאִיתִי אֶת־כָּל־הַמַּעֲשִׂים שֶׁנַּעֲשׂוּ תַּחַת הַשָּׁמֶשׁ וְהִנֵּה הַכֹּל הֶבֶל וּרְעוּת רוּחַ: 15 מְעֻוָּת לֹא־יוּכַל לִתְקֹן וְחֶסְרוֹן לֹא־יוּכַל לְהִמָּנוֹת: 16 דִּבַּרְתִּי אֲנִי עִם־לִבִּי לֵאמֹר אֲנִי הִנֵּה הִגְדַּלְתִּי וְהוֹסַפְתִּי חָכְמָה עַל כָּל־אֲשֶׁר־הָיָה לְפָנַי עַל־יְרוּשָׁלָ͏ִם וְלִבִּי רָאָה הַרְבֵּה חָכְמָה וָדָעַת: 17 וָאֶתְּנָה לִבִּי לָדַעַת חָכְמָה וְדַעַת הוֹלֵלוֹת

18   For in much wisdom *is* much grief,
     And he who increases knowledge increases
        sorrow.

2   I said in my heart, "Come now, I will test you with mirth; therefore enjoy pleasure"; but surely, this also *was* vanity. ²I said of laughter—"Madness!"; and of mirth, "What does it accomplish?" ³I searched in my heart *how* to gratify my flesh with wine, while guiding my heart with wisdom, and how to lay hold on folly, till I might see what *was* good for the sons of men to do under heaven all the days of their lives.

⁴I made my works great, I built myself houses, and planted myself vineyards. ⁵I made myself gardens and orchards, and I planted all *kinds* of fruit trees in them. ⁶I made myself water pools from which to water the growing trees of the grove. ⁷I acquired male and female servants, and had servants born in my house. Yes, I had greater possessions of herds and flocks than all who were in Jerusalem before me. ⁸I also gathered for myself silver and gold and the special treasures of kings and of the provinces. I acquired male and female singers, the delights of the sons of men, *and* musical instruments of all kinds.

⁹So I became great and excelled more than all who were before me in Jerusalem. Also my wisdom remained with me.

10   Whatever my eyes desired I did not keep from
       them.
     I did not withhold my heart from any pleasure,
     For my heart rejoiced in all my labor;
     And this was my reward from all my labor.
11   Then I looked on all the works that my hands
       had done
     And on the labor in which I had toiled;
     And indeed all *was* vanity and grasping for the
       wind.
     There was no profit under the sun.
12   Then I turned myself to consider wisdom and
       madness and folly;
     For what *can* the man *do* who succeeds the
       king?—
     Only what he has already done.
13   Then I saw that wisdom excels folly
     As light excels darkness.
14   The wise man's eyes *are* in his head,
     But the fool walks in darkness.
     Yet I myself perceived
     That the same event happens to them all.
15   So I said in my heart,

     "As it happens to the fool,
     It also happens to me,
     And why was I then more wise?"
     Then I said in my heart,

18 כִּי וּבְשִׂכְלוּת יָדַעְתִּי שֶׁגַּם־זֶה הוּא רַעְיוֹן רוּחַ:
בְּרֹב חָכְמָה רָב־כָּעַס וְיוֹסִיף דַּעַת יוֹסִיף מַכְאוֹב:

ב אָמַרְתִּי אֲנִי בְּלִבִּי לְכָה־נָּא אֲנַסְּכָה בְשִׂמְחָה
וּרְאֵה בְטוֹב וְהִנֵּה גַם־הוּא הָבֶל: 2 לִשְׂחוֹק אָמַרְתִּי
מְהוֹלָל וּלְשִׂמְחָה מַה־זֹּה עֹשָׂה: 3 תַּרְתִּי בְלִבִּי
לִמְשׁוֹךְ בַּיַּיִן אֶת־בְּשָׂרִי וְלִבִּי נֹהֵג בַּחָכְמָה וְלֶאֱחֹז
בְּסִכְלוּת עַד אֲשֶׁר־אֶרְאֶה אֵי־זֶה טוֹב לִבְנֵי הָאָדָם
אֲשֶׁר יַעֲשׂוּ תַּחַת הַשָּׁמַיִם מִסְפַּר יְמֵי חַיֵּיהֶם:
4 הִגְדַּלְתִּי מַעֲשָׂי בָּנִיתִי לִי בָּתִּים נָטַעְתִּי לִי כְּרָמִים:
5 עָשִׂיתִי לִי גַּנּוֹת וּפַרְדֵּסִים וְנָטַעְתִּי בָהֶם עֵץ כָּל־
פֶּרִי: 6 עָשִׂיתִי לִי בְּרֵכוֹת מָיִם לְהַשְׁקוֹת מֵהֶם
יַעַר צוֹמֵחַ עֵצִים: 7 קָנִיתִי עֲבָדִים וּשְׁפָחוֹת וּבְנֵי־
בַיִת הָיָה לִי גַּם מִקְנֶה בָקָר וָצֹאן הַרְבֵּה הָיָה
לִי מִכֹּל שֶׁהָיוּ לְפָנַי בִּירוּשָׁלִָם: 8 כָּנַסְתִּי לִי גַם־
כֶּסֶף וְזָהָב וּסְגֻלַּת מְלָכִים וְהַמְּדִינוֹת עָשִׂיתִי לִי
שָׁרִים וְשָׁרוֹת וְתַעֲנוּגֹת בְּנֵי הָאָדָם שִׁדָּה וְשִׁדּוֹת:
9 וְגָדַלְתִּי וְהוֹסַפְתִּי מִכֹּל שֶׁהָיָה לְפָנַי בִּירוּשָׁלִָם
אַף חָכְמָתִי עָמְדָה לִּי: 10 וְכֹל אֲשֶׁר שָׁאֲלוּ עֵינַי
לֹא אָצַלְתִּי מֵהֶם לֹא־מָנַעְתִּי אֶת־לִבִּי מִכָּל־שִׂמְחָה
כִּי־לִבִּי שָׂמֵחַ מִכָּל־עֲמָלִי וְזֶה־הָיָה חֶלְקִי מִכָּל־
עֲמָלִי: 11 וּפָנִיתִי אֲנִי בְּכָל־מַעֲשַׂי שֶׁעָשׂוּ יָדַי וּבֶעָמָל
שֶׁעָמַלְתִּי לַעֲשׂוֹת וְהִנֵּה הַכֹּל הֶבֶל וּרְעוּת רוּחַ
וְאֵין יִתְרוֹן תַּחַת הַשָּׁמֶשׁ: 12 וּפָנִיתִי אֲנִי לִרְאוֹת
חָכְמָה וְהוֹלֵלוֹת וְסִכְלוּת כִּי | מֶה הָאָדָם שֶׁיָּבוֹא
אַחֲרֵי הַמֶּלֶךְ אֵת אֲשֶׁר־כְּבָר עָשׂוּהוּ: 13 וְרָאִיתִי
אָנִי שֶׁיֵּשׁ יִתְרוֹן לַחָכְמָה מִן־הַסִּכְלוּת כִּיתְרוֹן הָאוֹר
מִן־הַחֹשֶׁךְ: 14 הֶחָכָם עֵינָיו בְּרֹאשׁוֹ וְהַכְּסִיל בַּחֹשֶׁךְ
הוֹלֵךְ וְיָדַעְתִּי גַם־אָנִי שֶׁמִּקְרֶה אֶחָד יִקְרֶה אֶת־
כֻּלָּם: 15 וְאָמַרְתִּי אֲנִי בְּלִבִּי כְּמִקְרֵה הַכְּסִיל גַּם־
אֲנִי יִקְרֵנִי וְלָמָּה חָכַמְתִּי אֲנִי אָז יוֹתֵר וְדִבַּרְתִּי בְלִבִּי

"This also *is* vanity."

16 For *there is* no more remembrance of the wise
than of the fool forever,
Since all that now *is* will be forgotten in the days
to come.
And how does a wise *man* die?
As the fool!

17 Therefore I hated life because the work that was done under the sun *was* distressing to me, for all *is* vanity and grasping for the wind.

18 Then I hated all my labor in which I had toiled under the sun, because I must leave it to the man who will come after me. 19 And who knows whether he will be wise or a fool? Yet he will rule over all my labor in which I toiled and in which I have shown myself wise under the sun. This also *is* vanity. 20 Therefore I turned my heart and despaired of all the labor in which I had toiled under the sun. 21 For there is a man whose labor *is* with wisdom, knowledge, and skill; yet he must leave his heritage to a man who has not labored for it. This also *is* vanity and a great evil. 22 For what has man for all his labor, and for the striving of his heart with which he has toiled under the sun? 23 For all his days *are* sorrowful, and his work burdensome; even in the night his heart takes no rest. This also *is* vanity.

24 Nothing *is* better for a man *than* that he should eat and drink, and *that* his soul should enjoy good in his labor. This also, I saw, was from the hand of God. 25 For who can eat, or who can have enjoyment, more than I? 26 For *God* gives wisdom and knowledge and joy to a man who *is* good in His sight; but to the sinner He gives the work of gathering and collecting, that he may give to *him* who *is* good before God. This also *is* vanity and grasping for the wind.

3 To everything *there is* a season,
A time for every purpose under heaven:

2 A time to be born,
And a time to die;
A time to plant,
And a time to pluck *what is* planted;

3 A time to kill,
And a time to heal;
A time to break down,
And a time to build up;

4 A time to weep,
And a time to laugh;
A time to mourn,
And a time to dance;

5 A time to cast away stones,
And a time to gather stones;

שֶׁגַּם־זֶה הָבֶל: 16 כִּי אֵין זִכְרוֹן לֶחָכָם עִם־הַכְּסִיל
לְעוֹלָם בְּשֶׁכְּבָר הַיָּמִים הַבָּאִים הַכֹּל נִשְׁכָּח וְאֵיךְ
יָמוּת הֶחָכָם עִם־הַכְּסִיל: 17 וְשָׂנֵאתִי אֶת־הַחַיִּים
כִּי רַע עָלַי הַמַּעֲשֶׂה שֶׁנַּעֲשָׂה תַּחַת הַשָּׁמֶשׁ כִּי־הַכֹּל
הֶבֶל וּרְעוּת רוּחַ: 18 וְשָׂנֵאתִי אֲנִי אֶת־כָּל־עֲמָלִי
שֶׁאֲנִי עָמֵל תַּחַת הַשָּׁמֶשׁ שֶׁאַנִּיחֶנּוּ לָאָדָם שֶׁיִּהְיֶה
אַחֲרָי: 19 וּמִי יוֹדֵעַ הֶחָכָם יִהְיֶה אוֹ סָכָל וְיִשְׁלַט
בְּכָל־עֲמָלִי שֶׁעָמַלְתִּי וְשֶׁחָכַמְתִּי תַּחַת הַשָּׁמֶשׁ גַּם־
זֶה הָבֶל: 20 וְסַבּוֹתִי אֲנִי לְיַאֵשׁ אֶת־לִבִּי עַל כָּל־
הֶעָמָל שֶׁעָמַלְתִּי תַּחַת הַשָּׁמֶשׁ: 21 כִּי־יֵשׁ אָדָם
שֶׁעֲמָלוֹ בְּחָכְמָה וּבְדַעַת וּבְכִשְׁרוֹן וּלְאָדָם שֶׁלֹּא
עָמַל־בּוֹ יִתְּנֶנּוּ חֶלְקוֹ גַּם־זֶה הֶבֶל וְרָעָה רַבָּה:
22 כִּי מֶה־הֹוֶה לָאָדָם בְּכָל־עֲמָלוֹ וּבְרַעְיוֹן לִבּוֹ
שֶׁהוּא עָמֵל תַּחַת הַשָּׁמֶשׁ: 23 כִּי כָל־יָמָיו מַכְאֹבִים
וָכַעַס עִנְיָנוֹ גַּם־בַּלַּיְלָה לֹא־שָׁכַב לִבּוֹ גַּם־זֶה הֶבֶל
הוּא: 24 אֵין־טוֹב בָּאָדָם שֶׁיֹּאכַל וְשָׁתָה וְהֶרְאָה
אֶת־נַפְשׁוֹ טוֹב בַּעֲמָלוֹ גַּם־זֹה רָאִיתִי אָנִי כִּי מִיַּד
הָאֱלֹהִים הִיא: 25 כִּי מִי יֹאכַל וּמִי יָחוּשׁ חוּץ
מִמֶּנִּי: 26 כִּי לְאָדָם שֶׁטּוֹב לְפָנָיו נָתַן חָכְמָה וְדַעַת
וְשִׂמְחָה וְלַחוֹטֶא נָתַן עִנְיָן לֶאֱסוֹף וְלִכְנוֹס לָתֵת
לְטוֹב לִפְנֵי הָאֱלֹהִים גַּם־זֶה הֶבֶל וּרְעוּת רוּחַ:

ג לַכֹּל זְמָן וְעֵת לְכָל־חֵפֶץ תַּחַת הַשָּׁמָיִם: ס
2 עֵת לָלֶדֶת
וְעֵת לָמוּת
עֵת לָטַעַת
וְעֵת לַעֲקוֹר נָטוּעַ:
3 עֵת לַהֲרוֹג
וְעֵת לִרְפּוֹא
עֵת לִפְרוֹץ
וְעֵת לִבְנוֹת:
4 עֵת לִבְכּוֹת
וְעֵת לִשְׂחוֹק
עֵת סְפוֹד
וְעֵת רְקוֹד:
5 עֵת לְהַשְׁלִיךְ אֲבָנִים
וְעֵת כְּנוֹס אֲבָנִים

A time to embrace,
And a time to refrain from embracing;
6 A time to gain,
And a time to lose;
A time to keep,
And a time to throw away;
7 A time to tear,
And a time to sew;
A time to keep silence,
And a time to speak;
8 A time to love,
And a time to hate;
A time of war,
And a time of peace.

9 What profit has the worker from that in which he labors? 10 I have seen the God-given task with which the sons of men are to be occupied. 11 He has made everything beautiful in its time. Also He has put eternity in their hearts, except that no one can find out the work that God does from beginning to end.

12 I know that nothing *is* better for them than to rejoice, and to do good in their lives, 13 and also that every man should eat and drink and enjoy the good of all his labor—it *is* the gift of God.

14 I know that whatever God does,
It shall be forever.
Nothing can be added to it,
And nothing taken from it.
God does *it*, that men should fear before Him.
15 That which is has already been,
And what is to be has already been;
And God requires an account of what is past.

16 Moreover I saw under the sun:

In the place of judgment,
Wickedness *was* there;
And *in* the place of righteousness,
Iniquity *was* there.

17 I said in my heart,

"God shall judge the righteous and the wicked,
For *there is* a time there for every purpose and for
every work."

18 I said in my heart, "Concerning the condition of the sons of men, God tests them, that they may see that they themselves are *like* animals." 19 For what happens to the sons of men also happens to animals; one thing befalls them: as one dies, so dies the other. Surely, they all have one breath; man has no advantage over animals, for all *is* vanity. 20 All go to one place: all are from the dust, and all return to dust. 21 Who knows the spirit of the sons of men, which goes upward, and the spirit of the animal, which goes down to the earth? 22 So I perceived that

עֵת לַחֲבוֹק
וְעֵת לִרְחֹק מֵחַבֵּק:
6 עֵת לְבַקֵּשׁ
וְעֵת לְאַבֵּד
עֵת לִשְׁמוֹר
וְעֵת לְהַשְׁלִיךְ:
7 עֵת לִקְרוֹעַ
וְעֵת לִתְפּוֹר
עֵת לַחֲשׁוֹת
וְעֵת לְדַבֵּר:
8 עֵת לֶאֱהֹב
וְעֵת לִשְׂנֹא
עֵת מִלְחָמָה
וְעֵת שָׁלוֹם: ס

9 מַה־יִּתְרוֹן הָעוֹשֶׂה בַּאֲשֶׁר הוּא עָמֵל: 10 רָאִיתִי
אֶת־הָעִנְיָן אֲשֶׁר נָתַן אֱלֹהִים לִבְנֵי הָאָדָם לַעֲנוֹת
בּוֹ: 11 אֶת־הַכֹּל עָשָׂה יָפֶה בְעִתּוֹ גַּם אֶת־הָעֹלָם
נָתַן בְּלִבָּם מִבְּלִי אֲשֶׁר לֹא־יִמְצָא הָאָדָם אֶת־
הַמַּעֲשֶׂה אֲשֶׁר־עָשָׂה הָאֱלֹהִים מֵרֹאשׁ וְעַד־סוֹף:

12 יָדַעְתִּי כִּי אֵין טוֹב בָּם כִּי אִם־לִשְׂמוֹחַ וְלַעֲשׂוֹת
טוֹב בְּחַיָּיו: 13 וְגַם כָּל־הָאָדָם שֶׁיֹּאכַל וְשָׁתָה וְרָאָה
טוֹב בְּכָל־עֲמָלוֹ מַתַּת אֱלֹהִים הִיא: 14 יָדַעְתִּי
כִּי כָּל־אֲשֶׁר יַעֲשֶׂה הָאֱלֹהִים הוּא יִהְיֶה לְעוֹלָם
עָלָיו אֵין לְהוֹסִיף וּמִמֶּנּוּ אֵין לִגְרֹעַ וְהָאֱלֹהִים
עָשָׂה שֶׁיִּרְאוּ מִלְּפָנָיו: 15 מַה־שֶּׁהָיָה כְּבָר הוּא
וַאֲשֶׁר לִהְיוֹת כְּבָר הָיָה וְהָאֱלֹהִים יְבַקֵּשׁ אֶת־נִרְדָּף:

16 וְעוֹד רָאִיתִי תַּחַת הַשָּׁמֶשׁ מְקוֹם הַמִּשְׁפָּט שָׁמָּה
הָרֶשַׁע וּמְקוֹם הַצֶּדֶק שָׁמָּה הָרָשַׁע: 17 אָמַרְתִּי אֲנִי
בְּלִבִּי אֶת־הַצַּדִּיק וְאֶת־הָרָשָׁע יִשְׁפֹּט הָאֱלֹהִים כִּי
עֵת לְכָל־חֵפֶץ וְעַל כָּל־הַמַּעֲשֶׂה שָׁם: 18 אָמַרְתִּי
אֲנִי בְּלִבִּי עַל־דִּבְרַת בְּנֵי הָאָדָם לְבָרָם הָאֱלֹהִים
וְלִרְאוֹת שְׁהֶם־בְּהֵמָה הֵמָּה לָהֶם: 19 כִּי מִקְרֶה
בְנֵי־הָאָדָם וּמִקְרֶה הַבְּהֵמָה וּמִקְרֶה אֶחָד לָהֶם
כְּמוֹת זֶה כֵּן מוֹת זֶה וְרוּחַ אֶחָד לַכֹּל וּמוֹתַר
הָאָדָם מִן־הַבְּהֵמָה אָיִן כִּי הַכֹּל הָבֶל: 20 הַכֹּל
הוֹלֵךְ אֶל־מָקוֹם אֶחָד הַכֹּל הָיָה מִן־הֶעָפָר וְהַכֹּל
שָׁב אֶל־הֶעָפָר: 21 מִי יוֹדֵעַ רוּחַ בְּנֵי הָאָדָם הָעֹלָה
הִיא לְמָעְלָה וְרוּחַ הַבְּהֵמָה הַיֹּרֶדֶת הִיא לְמַטָּה
לָאָרֶץ: 22 וְרָאִיתִי כִּי אֵין טוֹב מֵאֲשֶׁר יִשְׂמַח הָאָדָם

nothing *is* better than that a man should rejoice in his own works, for that *is* his heritage. For who can bring him to see what will happen after him?

בְּמַעֲשָׂיו כִּי־הוּא חֶלְקוֹ כִּי מִי יְבִיאֶנּוּ לִרְאוֹת בְּמֶה שֶׁיִּהְיֶה אַחֲרָיו:

4 Then I returned and considered all the oppression that is done under the sun:

    And look! The tears of the oppressed,
    But they have no comforter—
    On the side of their oppressors *there is* power,
    But they have no comforter.

2   Therefore I praised the dead who were already dead,
    More than the living who are still alive.

3   Yet, better than both *is he* who has never existed,
    Who has not seen the evil work that is done under the sun.

4 Again, I saw that for all toil and every skillful work a man is envied by his neighbor. This also *is* vanity and grasping for the wind.

5   The fool folds his hands
    And consumes his own flesh.

6   Better a handful *with* quietness
    Than both hands full, *together with* toil and grasping for the wind.

7 Then I returned, and I saw vanity under the sun:

8   There is one alone, without companion:
    He has neither son nor brother.
    Yet *there is* no end to all his labors,
    Nor is his eye satisfied with riches.
    But he never asks,
    "For whom do I toil and deprive myself of good?"
    This also *is* vanity and a grave misfortune.

9   Two *are* better than one,
    Because they have a good reward for their labor.

10   For if they fall, one will lift up his companion.
    But woe to him *who is* alone when he falls,
    For *he has* no one to help him up.

11   Again, if two lie down together, they will keep warm;
    But how can one be warm *alone*?

12   Though one may be overpowered by another,
    two can withstand him.
    And a threefold cord is not quickly broken.

13   Better a poor and wise youth
    Than an old and foolish king who will be admonished no more.

14   For he comes out of prison to be king,
    Although he was born poor in his kingdom.

15   I saw all the living who walk under the sun;
    They were with the second youth who stands in his place.

16   *There was* no end of all the people over whom he was made king;
    Yet those who come afterward will not rejoice in him.
    Surely this also *is* vanity and grasping for the wind.

ד וְשַׁבְתִּי אֲנִי וָאֶרְאֶה אֶת־כָּל־הָעֲשֻׁקִים אֲשֶׁר נַעֲשִׂים תַּחַת הַשָּׁמֶשׁ וְהִנֵּה ׀ דִּמְעַת הָעֲשֻׁקִים וְאֵין לָהֶם מְנַחֵם וּמִיַּד עֹשְׁקֵיהֶם כֹּחַ וְאֵין לָהֶם מְנַחֵם:

2 וְשַׁבֵּחַ אֲנִי אֶת־הַמֵּתִים שֶׁכְּבָר מֵתוּ מִן־הַחַיִּים אֲשֶׁר הֵמָּה חַיִּים עֲדֶנָה: 3 וְטוֹב מִשְּׁנֵיהֶם אֵת אֲשֶׁר־עֲדֶן לֹא הָיָה אֲשֶׁר לֹא־רָאָה אֶת־הַמַּעֲשֶׂה הָרָע אֲשֶׁר נַעֲשָׂה תַּחַת הַשָּׁמֶשׁ: 4 וְרָאִיתִי אֲנִי אֶת־כָּל־עָמָל וְאֵת כָּל־כִּשְׁרוֹן הַמַּעֲשֶׂה כִּי הִיא קִנְאַת־אִישׁ מֵרֵעֵהוּ גַּם־זֶה הֶבֶל וּרְעוּת רוּחַ:

5 הַכְּסִיל חֹבֵק אֶת־יָדָיו וְאֹכֵל אֶת־בְּשָׂרוֹ: 6 טוֹב מְלֹא כַף נָחַת מִמְּלֹא חָפְנַיִם עָמָל וּרְעוּת רוּחַ:

7 וְשַׁבְתִּי אֲנִי וָאֶרְאֶה הֶבֶל תַּחַת הַשָּׁמֶשׁ: 8 יֵשׁ אֶחָד וְאֵין שֵׁנִי גַּם בֵּן וָאָח אֵין־לוֹ וְאֵין קֵץ לְכָל־עֲמָלוֹ גַּם־עֵינָיו לֹא־תִשְׂבַּע עֹשֶׁר וּלְמִי ׀ אֲנִי עָמֵל וּמְחַסֵּר אֶת־נַפְשִׁי מִטּוֹבָה גַּם־זֶה הֶבֶל וְעִנְיַן רָע הוּא: 9 טוֹבִים הַשְּׁנַיִם מִן־הָאֶחָד אֲשֶׁר יֵשׁ־לָהֶם שָׂכָר טוֹב בַּעֲמָלָם: 10 כִּי אִם־יִפֹּלוּ הָאֶחָד יָקִים אֶת־חֲבֵרוֹ וְאִילוֹ הָאֶחָד שֶׁיִּפּוֹל וְאֵין שֵׁנִי לַהֲקִימוֹ:

11 גַּם אִם־יִשְׁכְּבוּ שְׁנַיִם וְחַם לָהֶם וּלְאֶחָד אֵיךְ יֵחָם: 12 וְאִם־יִתְקְפוֹ הָאֶחָד הַשְּׁנַיִם יַעַמְדוּ נֶגְדּוֹ וְהַחוּט הַמְשֻׁלָּשׁ לֹא בִמְהֵרָה יִנָּתֵק: 13 טוֹב יֶלֶד מִסְכֵּן וְחָכָם מִמֶּלֶךְ זָקֵן וּכְסִיל אֲשֶׁר לֹא־יָדַע לְהִזָּהֵר עוֹד: 14 כִּי־מִבֵּית הָסוּרִים יָצָא לִמְלֹךְ כִּי גַּם בְּמַלְכוּתוֹ נוֹלַד רָשׁ: 15 רָאִיתִי אֶת־כָּל־הַחַיִּים הַמְהַלְּכִים תַּחַת הַשָּׁמֶשׁ עִם הַיֶּלֶד הַשֵּׁנִי אֲשֶׁר יַעֲמֹד תַּחְתָּיו: 16 אֵין־קֵץ לְכָל־הָעָם לְכֹל אֲשֶׁר־הָיָה לִפְנֵיהֶם גַּם הָאַחֲרוֹנִים לֹא יִשְׂמְחוּ־בוֹ כִּי־גַם־

5 Walk prudently when you go to the house of God; and draw near to hear rather than to give the sacrifice of fools, for they do not know that they do evil.

2   Do not be rash with your mouth,
And let not your heart utter anything hastily before God.
For God *is* in heaven, and you on earth;
Therefore let your words be few.

3   For a dream comes through much activity,
And a fool's voice *is known* by *his* many words.

4   When you make a vow to God, do not delay to pay it;
For *He has* no pleasure in fools.
Pay what you have vowed—

5   Better not to vow than to vow and not pay.

6 Do not let your mouth cause your flesh to sin, nor say before the messenger *of God* that it *was* an error. Why should God be angry at your excuse and destroy the work of your hands? 7 For in the multitude of dreams and many words *there is* also vanity. But fear God.

8 If you see the oppression of the poor, and the violent perversion of justice and righteousness in a province, do not marvel at the matter; for high official watches over high official, and higher officials are over them. 9 Moreover the profit of the land is for all; *even* the king is served from the field.

10   He who loves silver will not be satisfied with silver;
Nor he who loves abundance, with increase.
This also *is* vanity.

11   When goods increase,
They increase who eat them;
So what profit have the owners
Except to see *them* with their eyes?

12   The sleep of a laboring man *is* sweet,
Whether he eats little or much;
But the abundance of the rich will not permit him to sleep.

13   There is a severe evil *which* I have seen under the sun:
Riches kept for their owner to his hurt.

14   But those riches perish through misfortune;
When he begets a son, *there is* nothing in his hand.

15   As he came from his mother's womb, naked shall he return,
To go as he came;
And he shall take nothing from his labor
Which he may carry away in his hand.

16   And this also *is* a severe evil—
Just exactly as he came, so shall he go.
And what profit has he who has labored for the wind?

זֶה הֶבֶל וּרְעְיוֹן רוּחַ: 17 שְׁמֹר רַגְלְךָ כַּאֲשֶׁר תֵּלֵךְ אֶל־בֵּית הָאֱלֹהִים וְקָרוֹב לִשְׁמֹעַ מִתֵּת הַכְּסִילִים זָבַח כִּי־אֵינָם יוֹדְעִים לַעֲשׂוֹת רָע:

ה אַל־תְּבַהֵל עַל־פִּיךָ וְלִבְּךָ אַל־יְמַהֵר לְהוֹצִיא דָבָר לִפְנֵי הָאֱלֹהִים כִּי הָאֱלֹהִים בַּשָּׁמַיִם וְאַתָּה עַל־הָאָרֶץ עַל־כֵּן יִהְיוּ דְבָרֶיךָ מְעַטִּים: 2 כִּי בָּא הַחֲלוֹם בְּרֹב עִנְיָן וְקוֹל כְּסִיל בְּרֹב דְּבָרִים: 3 כַּאֲשֶׁר תִּדֹּר נֶדֶר לֵאלֹהִים אַל־תְּאַחֵר לְשַׁלְּמוֹ כִּי אֵין חֵפֶץ בַּכְּסִילִים אֵת אֲשֶׁר־תִּדֹּר שַׁלֵּם: 4 טוֹב אֲשֶׁר לֹא־תִדֹּר מִשֶּׁתִּדּוֹר וְלֹא תְשַׁלֵּם: 5 אַל־תִּתֵּן אֶת־פִּיךָ לַחֲטִיא אֶת־בְּשָׂרֶךָ וְאַל־תֹּאמַר לִפְנֵי הַמַּלְאָךְ כִּי שְׁגָגָה הִיא לָמָּה יִקְצֹף הָאֱלֹהִים עַל־קוֹלֶךָ וְחִבֵּל אֶת־מַעֲשֵׂה יָדֶיךָ: 6 כִּי בְרֹב חֲלֹמוֹת וַהֲבָלִים וּדְבָרִים הַרְבֵּה כִּי אֶת־הָאֱלֹהִים יְרָא: 7 אִם־עֹשֶׁק רָשׁ וְגֵזֶל מִשְׁפָּט וָצֶדֶק תִּרְאֶה בַמְּדִינָה אַל־תִּתְמַהּ עַל־הַחֵפֶץ כִּי גָבֹהַּ מֵעַל גָּבֹהַּ שֹׁמֵר וּגְבֹהִים עֲלֵיהֶם:

8 וְיִתְרוֹן אֶרֶץ בַּכֹּל הִיא מֶלֶךְ לְשָׂדֶה נֶעֱבָד: 9 אֹהֵב כֶּסֶף לֹא־יִשְׂבַּע כֶּסֶף וּמִי־אֹהֵב בֶּהָמוֹן לֹא תְבוּאָה גַּם־זֶה הָבֶל: 10 בִּרְבוֹת הַטּוֹבָה רַבּוּ אוֹכְלֶיהָ וּמַה־כִּשְׁרוֹן לִבְעָלֶיהָ כִּי אִם־רְאִית עֵינָיו: 11 מְתוּקָה שְׁנַת הָעֹבֵד אִם־מְעַט וְאִם־הַרְבֵּה יֹאכֵל וְהַשָּׂבָע לֶעָשִׁיר אֵינֶנּוּ מַנִּיחַ לוֹ לִישׁוֹן: 12 יֵשׁ רָעָה חוֹלָה רָאִיתִי תַּחַת הַשָּׁמֶשׁ עֹשֶׁר שָׁמוּר לִבְעָלָיו לְרָעָתוֹ: 13 וְאָבַד הָעֹשֶׁר הַהוּא בְּעִנְיַן רָע וְהוֹלִיד בֵּן וְאֵין בְּיָדוֹ מְאוּמָה: 14 כַּאֲשֶׁר יָצָא מִבֶּטֶן אִמּוֹ עָרוֹם יָשׁוּב לָלֶכֶת כְּשֶׁבָּא וּמְאוּמָה לֹא־יִשָּׂא בַעֲמָלוֹ שֶׁיֹּלֵךְ בְּיָדוֹ: 15 וְגַם־זֹה רָעָה חוֹלָה כָּל־עֻמַּת שֶׁבָּא כֵּן יֵלֵךְ וּמַה־יִּתְרוֹן לוֹ שֶׁיַּעֲמֹל

ד 17 רַגְלֶיךָ   ה 8 הִיא 10 רָאוֹת

17 All his days he also eats in darkness,
   And *he has* much sorrow and sickness and anger.

18 Here is what I have seen: *It is* good and fitting
for one to eat and drink, and to enjoy the good of all
his labor in which he toils under the sun all the days
of his life which God gives him; for it *is* his heritage.
19 As for every man to whom God has given riches
and wealth, and given him power to eat of it, to
receive his heritage and rejoice in his labor—this *is*
the gift of God. 20 For he will not dwell unduly on
the days of his life, because God keeps *him* busy
with the joy of his heart.

6 There is an evil which I have seen under the sun,
and it *is* common among men: 2 A man to whom
God has given riches and wealth and honor, so that
he lacks nothing for himself of all he desires; yet
God does not give him power to eat of it, but a
foreigner consumes it. This *is* vanity, and it *is* an
evil affliction.

3 If a man begets a hundred *children* and lives
many years, so that the days of his years are many,
but his soul is not satisfied with goodness, or indeed
he has no burial, I say *that* a stillborn child *is* better
than he— 4 for it comes in vanity and departs in
darkness, and its name is covered with darkness.
5 Though it has not seen the sun or known *anything,*
this has more rest than that man, 6 even if he lives a
thousand years twice—but has not seen goodness.
Do not all go to one place?

7   All the labor of man *is* for his mouth,
     And yet the soul is not satisfied.
8   For what more has the wise *man* than the fool?
     What does the poor man have,
     Who knows *how* to walk before the living?
9   Better *is* the sight of the eyes than the wandering
         of desire.
     This also *is* vanity and grasping for the wind.

10 Whatever one is, he has been named already,
     For it is known that he *is* man;
     And he cannot contend with Him who is mightier
         than he.
11 Since there are many things that increase vanity,
     How *is* man the better?

12 For who knows what *is* good for man in life, all
the days of his vain life which he passes like a
shadow? Who can tell a man what will happen after
him under the sun?

7 A good name *is* better than precious ointment,
     And the day of death than the day of one's birth;
2   Better to go to the house of mourning
     Than to go to the house of feasting,
     For that *is* the end of all men;
     And the living will take *it* to heart.

לָר֑וּחַ 16 גַּם כָּל־יָמָ֛יו בַּחֹ֥שֶׁךְ יֹאכֵ֖ל וְכָעַ֣ס הַרְבֵּ֑ה
וְחָלְי֖וֹ וָקָֽצֶף׃ 17 הִנֵּ֞ה אֲשֶׁר־רָאִ֣יתִי אָ֗נִי ט֣וֹב אֲשֶׁר־
יָפֶ֡ה לֶֽאֱכוֹל־וְ֠לִשְׁתּוֹת וְלִרְא֨וֹת טוֹבָ֜ה בְּכָל־עֲמָל֣וֹ ׀
שֶׁיַּעֲמֹ֣ל תַּֽחַת־הַשֶּׁ֗מֶשׁ מִסְפַּ֧ר יְמֵי־חַיָּ֛ו אֲשֶׁר־נָֽתַן־
ל֥וֹ הָאֱלֹהִ֖ים כִּי־ה֥וּא חֶלְקֽוֹ׃ 18 גַּ֣ם כָּֽל־הָאָדָ֡ם אֲשֶׁ֣ר
נָֽתַן־ל֣וֹ הָאֱלֹהִ֡ים עֹ֣שֶׁר וּנְכָסִים֩ וְהִשְׁלִיט֨וֹ לֶאֱכֹ֤ל
מִמֶּ֙נּוּ֙ וְלָשֵׂ֣את אֶת־חֶלְק֔וֹ וְלִשְׂמֹ֖חַ בַּעֲמָל֑וֹ זֹ֕ה מַתַּ֥ת
אֱלֹהִ֖ים הִֽיא׃ 19 כִּ֚י לֹ֣א הַרְבֵּ֣ה יִזְכֹּ֔ר אֶת־יְמֵ֖י חַיָּ֑יו
כִּ֚י הָאֱלֹהִ֣ים מַעֲנֶ֔ה בְּשִׂמְחַ֖ת לִבּֽוֹ׃

ו יֵ֣שׁ רָעָ֔ה אֲשֶׁ֥ר רָאִ֖יתִי תַּ֣חַת הַשָּׁ֑מֶשׁ וְרַבָּ֥ה הִ֖יא
עַל־הָאָדָֽם׃ 2 אִ֣ישׁ אֲשֶׁ֣ר יִתֶּן־ל֣וֹ הָאֱלֹהִ֡ים עֹשֶׁר֩
וּנְכָסִ֨ים וְכָב֜וֹד וְֽאֵינֶ֥נּוּ חָסֵ֣ר לְנַפְשׁ֣וֹ ׀ מִכֹּ֣ל אֲשֶׁר־
יִתְאַוֶּ֗ה וְלֹֽא־יַשְׁלִיטֶ֤נּוּ הָֽאֱלֹהִים֙ לֶאֱכֹ֣ל מִמֶּ֔נּוּ כִּ֣י
אִ֥ישׁ נָכְרִ֖י יֹֽאכֲלֶ֑נּוּ זֶ֥ה הֶ֛בֶל וָחֳלִ֥י רָ֖ע הֽוּא׃ 3 אִם־
יוֹלִ֨יד אִ֜ישׁ מֵאָ֗ה וְשָׁנִ֣ים רַבּוֹת֮ יִֽחְיֶה֒ וְרַ֣ב ׀ שֶׁיִּהְי֣וּ
יְמֵֽי־שָׁנָ֗יו וְנַפְשׁוֹ֙ לֹא־תִשְׂבַּ֣ע מִן־הַטּוֹבָ֔ה וְגַם־קְבוּרָ֖ה
לֹא־הָ֣יְתָה לּ֑וֹ אָמַ֕רְתִּי ט֥וֹב מִמֶּ֖נּוּ הַנָּֽפֶל׃ 4 כִּֽי־בַהֶ֣בֶל
בָּ֔א וּבַחֹ֣שֶׁךְ יֵלֵ֑ךְ וּבַחֹ֖שֶׁךְ שְׁמ֥וֹ יְכֻסֶּֽה׃ 5 גַּם־שֶׁ֥מֶשׁ
לֹא־רָאָ֖ה וְלֹ֣א יָדָ֑ע נַ֥חַת לָזֶ֖ה מִזֶּֽה׃ 6 וְאִלּ֣וּ חָיָ֗ה
אֶ֤לֶף שָׁנִים֙ פַּעֲמַ֔יִם וְטוֹבָ֖ה לֹ֣א רָאָ֑ה הֲלֹ֛א אֶל־
מָק֥וֹם אֶחָ֖ד הַכֹּ֥ל הוֹלֵֽךְ׃ 7 כָּל־עֲמַ֥ל הָאָדָ֖ם לְפִ֑יהוּ
וְגַם־הַנֶּ֖פֶשׁ לֹ֥א תִמָּלֵֽא׃ 8 כִּ֛י מַה־יּוֹתֵ֥ר לֶחָכָ֖ם מִן־
הַכְּסִ֑יל מַה־לֶּעָנִ֣י יוֹדֵ֔עַ לַהֲלֹ֖ךְ נֶ֥גֶד הַחַיִּֽים׃ 9 ט֛וֹב
מַרְאֵ֥ה עֵינַ֖יִם מֵֽהֲלָךְ־נָ֑פֶשׁ גַּם־זֶ֥ה הֶ֖בֶל וּרְע֥וּת רֽוּחַ׃
10 מַה־שֶּֽׁהָיָ֗ה כְּבָר֙ נִקְרָ֣א שְׁמ֔וֹ וְנוֹדָ֖ע אֲשֶׁר־ה֣וּא
אָדָ֑ם וְלֹֽא־יוּכַ֣ל לָדִ֔ין עִ֥ם שֶׁהַתְּקִיף֖ מִמֶּֽנּוּ׃ 11 כִּ֛י
יֵשׁ־דְּבָרִ֥ים הַרְבֵּ֖ה מַרְבִּ֣ים הָ֑בֶל מַה־יֹּתֵ֖ר לָאָדָֽם׃
12 כִּ֣י מִֽי־יוֹדֵעַ֩ מַה־טּ֨וֹב לָֽאָדָ֜ם בַּֽחַיִּ֗ים מִסְפַּ֛ר יְמֵי־
חַיֵּ֥י הֶבְל֖וֹ וְיַעֲשֵׂ֣ם כַּצֵּ֑ל אֲשֶׁ֣ר מִֽי־יַגִּ֣יד לָֽאָדָ֔ם מַה־
יִּהְיֶ֥ה אַחֲרָ֖יו תַּ֥חַת הַשָּֽׁמֶשׁ׃

ז ט֥וֹב שֵׁ֖ם מִשֶּׁ֣מֶן ט֑וֹב וְי֣וֹם הַמָּ֔וֶת מִיּ֖וֹם הִוָּלְדֽוֹ׃
2 ט֞וֹב לָלֶ֣כֶת אֶל־בֵּֽית־אֵ֗בֶל מִלֶּ֙כֶת֙ אֶל־בֵּ֣ית מִשְׁתֶּ֔ה
בַּאֲשֶׁ֕ר ה֖וּא ס֣וֹף כָּל־הָאָדָ֑ם וְהַחַ֖י יִתֵּ֥ן אֶל־לִבּֽוֹ׃

3 Sorrow *is* better than laughter,
   For by a sad countenance the heart is made
      better.
4 The heart of the wise *is* in the house of mourning,
   But the heart of fools *is* in the house of mirth.
5 *It is* better to hear the rebuke of the wise
   Than for a man to hear the song of fools.
6 For like the crackling of thorns under a pot,
   So *is* the laughter of the fool.
   This also is vanity.
7 Surely oppression destroys a wise *man's* reason,
   And a bribe debases the heart.
8 The end of a thing *is* better than its beginning;
   The patient in spirit *is* better than the proud in
      spirit.
9 Do not hasten in your spirit to be angry,
   For anger rests in the bosom of fools.
10 Do not say,

"Why were the former days better than these?"
For you do not inquire wisely concerning this.

11 Wisdom *is* good with an inheritance,
   And profitable to those who see the sun.
12 For wisdom *is* a defense *as* money *is* a defense,
   But the excellence of knowledge *is that* wisdom
      gives life to those who have it.
13 Consider the work of God;
   For who can make straight what He has made
      crooked?
14 In the day of prosperity be joyful,
   But in the day of adversity consider:
   Surely God has appointed the one as well as the
      other,
   So that man can find out nothing *that will come*
      after him.

15 I have seen everything in my days of vanity:

There is a just *man* who perishes in his
   righteousness,
And there is a wicked *man* who prolongs *life* in
   his wickedness.

16 Do not be overly righteous,
   Nor be overly wise:
   Why should you destroy yourself?
17 Do not be overly wicked,
   Nor be foolish:
   Why should you die before your time?
18 *It is* good that you grasp this,
   And also not remove your hand from the other;
   For he who fears God will escape them all.
19 Wisdom strengthens the wise
   More than ten rulers of the city.
20 For *there is* not a just man on earth who does
     good
   And does not sin.
21 Also do not take to heart everything people say,
   Lest you hear your servant cursing you.
22 For many times, also, your own heart has known
   That even you have cursed others.

3 טוֹב כַּעַס מִשְּׂחֹק כִּי־בְרֹעַ פָּנִים יִיטַב לֵב: 4 לֵב
חֲכָמִים בְּבֵית אֵבֶל וְלֵב כְּסִילִים בְּבֵית שִׂמְחָה:
5 טוֹב לִשְׁמֹעַ גַּעֲרַת חָכָם מֵאִישׁ שֹׁמֵעַ שִׁיר
כְּסִילִים: 6 כִּי כְקוֹל הַסִּירִים תַּחַת הַסִּיר כֵּן
שְׂחֹק הַכְּסִיל וְגַם־זֶה הָבֶל: 7 כִּי הָעֹשֶׁק יְהוֹלֵל
חָכָם וִיאַבֵּד אֶת־לֵב מַתָּנָה: 8 טוֹב אַחֲרִית דָּבָר
מֵרֵאשִׁיתוֹ טוֹב אֶרֶךְ־רוּחַ מִגְּבַהּ־רוּחַ: 9 אַל־תְּבַהֵל
בְּרוּחֲךָ לִכְעוֹס כִּי כַעַס בְּחֵיק כְּסִילִים יָנוּחַ: 10 אַל־
תֹּאמַר מֶה הָיָה שֶׁהַיָּמִים הָרִאשֹׁנִים הָיוּ טוֹבִים
מֵאֵלֶּה כִּי לֹא מֵחָכְמָה שָׁאַלְתָּ עַל־זֶה: 11 טוֹבָה
חָכְמָה עִם־נַחֲלָה וְיֹתֵר לְרֹאֵי הַשָּׁמֶשׁ: 12 כִּי בְּצֵל
הַחָכְמָה בְּצֵל הַכָּסֶף וְיִתְרוֹן דַּעַת הַחָכְמָה תְּחַיֶּה
בְעָלֶיהָ: 13 רְאֵה אֶת־מַעֲשֵׂה הָאֱלֹהִים כִּי מִי יוּכַל
לְתַקֵּן אֵת אֲשֶׁר עִוְּתוֹ: 14 בְּיוֹם טוֹבָה הֱיֵה בְטוֹב
וּבְיוֹם רָעָה רְאֵה גַּם אֶת־זֶה לְעֻמַּת־זֶה עָשָׂה
הָאֱלֹהִים עַל־דִּבְרַת שֶׁלֹּא יִמְצָא הָאָדָם אַחֲרָיו
מְאוּמָה: 15 אֶת־הַכֹּל רָאִיתִי בִּימֵי הֶבְלִי יֵשׁ צַדִּיק
אֹבֵד בְּצִדְקוֹ וְיֵשׁ רָשָׁע מַאֲרִיךְ בְּרָעָתוֹ: 16 אַל־תְּהִי
צַדִּיק הַרְבֵּה וְאַל־תִּתְחַכַּם יוֹתֵר לָמָּה תִּשּׁוֹמֵם:
17 אַל־תִּרְשַׁע הַרְבֵּה וְאַל־תְּהִי סָכָל לָמָּה תָמוּת
בְּלֹא עִתֶּךָ: 18 טוֹב אֲשֶׁר תֶּאֱחֹז בָּזֶה וְגַם־מִזֶּה
אַל־תַּנַּח אֶת־יָדֶךָ כִּי־יְרֵא אֱלֹהִים יֵצֵא אֶת־כֻּלָּם:
19 הַחָכְמָה תָּעֹז לֶחָכָם מֵעֲשָׂרָה שַׁלִּיטִים אֲשֶׁר
הָיוּ בָּעִיר: 20 כִּי אָדָם אֵין צַדִּיק בָּאָרֶץ אֲשֶׁר
יַעֲשֶׂה־טּוֹב וְלֹא יֶחֱטָא: 21 גַּם לְכָל־הַדְּבָרִים אֲשֶׁר
יְדַבֵּרוּ אַל־תִּתֵּן לִבֶּךָ אֲשֶׁר לֹא־תִשְׁמַע אֶת־עַבְדְּךָ
מְקַלְלֶךָ: 22 כִּי גַּם־פְּעָמִים רַבּוֹת יָדַע לִבֶּךָ אֲשֶׁר

23 All this I have proved by wisdom.
I said, "I will be wise";
But it *was* far from me.
24 As for that which is far off and exceedingly deep,
Who can find it out?
25 I applied my heart to know,
To search and seek out wisdom and the reason *of things,*
To know the wickedness of folly,
Even of foolishness *and* madness.
26 And I find more bitter than death
The woman whose heart *is* snares and nets,
Whose hands *are* fetters.
He who pleases God shall escape from her,
But the sinner shall be trapped by her.
27 "Here is what I have found," says the Preacher,
"*Adding* one thing to the other to find out the reason,
28 Which my soul still seeks but I cannot find:
One man among a thousand I have found,
But a woman among all these I have not found.
29 Truly, this only I have found:
That God made man upright,
But they have sought out many schemes."

8 Who *is* like a wise *man?*
And who knows the interpretation of a thing?
A man's wisdom makes his face shine,
And the sternness of his face is changed.

2 I say, "Keep the king's commandment for the sake of your oath to God. 3 Do not be hasty to go from his presence. Do not take your stand for an evil thing, for he does whatever pleases him."

4 Where the word of a king *is, there is* power;
And who may say to him, "What are you doing?"
5 He who keeps his command will experience nothing harmful;
And a wise man's heart discerns both time and judgment,
6 Because for every matter there is a time and judgment,
Though the misery of man increases greatly.
7 For he does not know what will happen;
So who can tell him when it will occur?
8 No one has power over the spirit to retain the spirit,
And no one has power in the day of death.
There is no release from that war,
And wickedness will not deliver those who are given to it.

9 All this I have seen, and applied my heart to every work that is done under the sun: *There is* a time in which one man rules over another to his own hurt.

10 Then I saw the wicked buried, who had come and gone from the place of holiness, and they were forgotten in the city where they had so done. This also *is* vanity. 11 Because the sentence against an evil

גַּם־אַתְּ קִלֲלַתְ אֲחֵרִים: 23 כָּל־זֹה נִסִּיתִי בַחָכְמָה
אָמַרְתִּי אֶחְכָּמָה וְהִיא רְחוֹקָה מִמֶּנִּי: 24 רָחוֹק
מַה־שֶּׁהָיָה וְעָמֹק ׀ עָמֹק מִי יִמְצָאֶנּוּ: 25 סַבּוֹתִי
אֲנִי וְלִבִּי לָדַעַת וְלָתוּר וּבַקֵּשׁ חָכְמָה וְחֶשְׁבּוֹן
וְלָדַעַת רֶשַׁע כֶּסֶל וְהַסִּכְלוּת הוֹלֵלוֹת: 26 וּמוֹצֶא
אֲנִי מַר מִמָּוֶת אֶת־הָאִשָּׁה אֲשֶׁר־הִיא מְצוֹדִים
וַחֲרָמִים לִבָּהּ אֲסוּרִים יָדֶיהָ טוֹב לִפְנֵי הָאֱלֹהִים
יִמָּלֵט מִמֶּנָּה וְחוֹטֵא יִלָּכֶד בָּהּ: 27 רְאֵה זֶה מָצָאתִי
אָמְרָה קֹהֶלֶת אַחַת לְאַחַת לִמְצֹא חֶשְׁבּוֹן: 28 אֲשֶׁר
עוֹד־בִּקְשָׁה נַפְשִׁי וְלֹא מָצָאתִי אָדָם אֶחָד מֵאֶלֶף
מָצָאתִי וְאִשָּׁה בְכָל־אֵלֶּה לֹא מָצָאתִי: 29 לְבַד
רְאֵה־זֶה מָצָאתִי אֲשֶׁר עָשָׂה הָאֱלֹהִים אֶת־הָאָדָם
יָשָׁר וְהֵמָּה בִקְשׁוּ חִשְּׁבֹנוֹת רַבִּים:

ח מִי כְּהֶחָכָם וּמִי יוֹדֵעַ פֵּשֶׁר דָּבָר חָכְמַת אָדָם
תָּאִיר פָּנָיו וְעֹז פָּנָיו יְשֻׁנֶּא: 2 אֲנִי פִּי־מֶלֶךְ שְׁמֹר
וְעַל דִּבְרַת שְׁבוּעַת אֱלֹהִים: 3 אַל־תִּבָּהֵל מִפָּנָיו
תֵּלֵךְ אַל־תַּעֲמֹד בְּדָבָר רָע כִּי כָּל־אֲשֶׁר יַחְפֹּץ
יַעֲשֶׂה: 4 בַּאֲשֶׁר דְּבַר־מֶלֶךְ שִׁלְטוֹן וּמִי יֹאמַר־לוֹ
מַה־תַּעֲשֶׂה: 5 שׁוֹמֵר מִצְוָה לֹא יֵדַע דָּבָר רָע
וְעֵת וּמִשְׁפָּט יֵדַע לֵב חָכָם: 6 כִּי לְכָל־חֵפֶץ יֵשׁ
עֵת וּמִשְׁפָּט כִּי־רָעַת הָאָדָם רַבָּה עָלָיו: 7 כִּי־
אֵינֶנּוּ יֹדֵעַ מַה־שֶּׁיִּהְיֶה כִּי כַּאֲשֶׁר יִהְיֶה מִי יַגִּיד
לוֹ: 8 אֵין אָדָם שַׁלִּיט בָּרוּחַ לִכְלוֹא אֶת־הָרוּחַ
וְאֵין שִׁלְטוֹן בְּיוֹם הַמָּוֶת וְאֵין מִשְׁלַחַת בַּמִּלְחָמָה
וְלֹא־יְמַלֵּט רֶשַׁע אֶת־בְּעָלָיו: 9 אֶת־כָּל־זֶה רָאִיתִי
וְנָתוֹן אֶת־לִבִּי לְכָל־מַעֲשֶׂה אֲשֶׁר נַעֲשָׂה תַּחַת
הַשָּׁמֶשׁ עֵת אֲשֶׁר שָׁלַט הָאָדָם בְּאָדָם לְרַע לוֹ:
10 וּבְכֵן רָאִיתִי רְשָׁעִים קְבֻרִים וָבָאוּ וּמִמְּקוֹם קָדוֹשׁ
יְהַלֵּכוּ וְיִשְׁתַּכְּחוּ בָעִיר אֲשֶׁר כֵּן עָשׂוּ גַּם־זֶה הָבֶל:
11 אֲשֶׁר אֵין־נַעֲשָׂה פִתְגָם מַעֲשֵׂה הָרָעָה מְהֵרָה

work is not executed speedily, therefore the heart of the sons of men is fully set in them to do evil. ¹²Though a sinner does evil a hundred *times,* and his *days* are prolonged, yet I surely know that it will be well with those who fear God, who fear before Him. ¹³But it will not be well with the wicked; nor will he prolong *his* days, *which are* as a shadow, because he does not fear before God.

¹⁴There is a vanity which occurs on earth, that there are just *men* to whom it happens according to the work of the wicked; again, there are wicked *men* to whom it happens according to the work of the righteous. I said that this also *is* vanity.

¹⁵So I commended enjoyment, because a man has nothing better under the sun than to eat, drink, and be merry; for this will remain with him in his labor *all* the days of his life which God gives him under the sun.

¹⁶When I applied my heart to know wisdom and to see the business that is done on earth, even though one sees no sleep day or night, ¹⁷then I saw all the work of God, that a man cannot find out the work that is done under the sun. For though a man labors to discover *it,* yet he will not find *it;* moreover, though a wise *man* attempts to know *it,* he will not be able to find *it.*

9 For I considered all this in my heart, so that I could declare it all: that the righteous and the wise and their works *are* in the hand of God. People know neither love nor hatred *by* anything *they see* before them. ²All things *come* alike to all:

> One event *happens* to the righteous and the
>   wicked;
> To the good, the clean, and the unclean;
> To him who sacrifices and him who does not
>   sacrifice.
> As is the good, so *is* the sinner;
> He who takes an oath as *he* who fears an oath.

³This *is* an evil in all that is done under the sun: that one thing *happens* to all. Truly the hearts of the sons of men are full of evil; madness *is* in their hearts while they live, and after that *they go* to the dead. ⁴But for him who is joined to all the living there is hope, for a living dog is better than a dead lion.

> 5   For the living know that they will die;
>   But the dead know nothing,
>   And they have no more reward,
>   For the memory of them is forgotten.
> 6   Also their love, their hatred, and their envy have
>   now perished;
>   Nevermore will they have a share
>   In anything done under the sun.

7   Go, eat your bread with joy,

עַל־כֵּ֗ן מָלֵ֛א לֵ֥ב בְּנֵֽי־הָאָדָ֖ם בָּהֶ֥ם לַעֲשׂ֥וֹת רָֽע׃ 12 אֲשֶׁ֣ר חֹטֶ֗א עֹשֶׂ֥ה רָ֛ע מְאַ֖ת וּמַאֲרִ֣יךְ ל֑וֹ כִּ֣י גַם־ יוֹדֵ֣עַ אָ֗נִי אֲשֶׁ֤ר יִהְיֶה־טּוֹב֙ לְיִרְאֵ֣י הָאֱלֹהִ֔ים אֲשֶׁ֥ר יִֽירְא֖וּ מִלְּפָנָֽיו׃ 13 וְטוֹב֙ לֹא־יִֽהְיֶ֣ה לָֽרָשָׁ֔ע וְלֹֽא־יַאֲרִ֥יךְ יָמִ֖ים כַּצֵּ֑ל אֲשֶׁ֛ר אֵינֶ֥נּוּ יָרֵ֖א מִלִּפְנֵ֥י אֱלֹהִֽים׃ 14 יֶשׁ־ הֶ֨בֶל֙ אֲשֶׁ֣ר נַעֲשָׂ֣ה עַל־הָאָ֔רֶץ אֲשֶׁ֣ר ׀ יֵ֣שׁ צַדִּיקִ֗ים אֲשֶׁ֨ר מַגִּ֤יעַ אֲלֵהֶם֙ כְּמַעֲשֵׂ֣ה הָרְשָׁעִ֔ים וְיֵ֣שׁ רְשָׁעִ֔ים שֶׁמַּגִּ֤יעַ אֲלֵהֶם֙ כְּמַעֲשֵׂ֣ה הַצַּדִּיקִ֔ים אָמַ֖רְתִּי שֶׁגַּם־ זֶ֥ה הָֽבֶל׃ 15 וְשִׁבַּ֤חְתִּֽי אֲנִי֙ אֶת־הַשִּׂמְחָ֔ה אֲשֶׁ֨ר אֵֽין־ ט֤וֹב לָֽאָדָם֙ תַּ֣חַת הַשֶּׁ֔מֶשׁ כִּ֛י אִם־לֶאֱכ֥וֹל וְלִשְׁתּ֖וֹת וְלִשְׂמ֑וֹחַ וְה֞וּא יִלְוֶ֣נּוּ בַעֲמָל֗וֹ יְמֵ֧י חַיָּ֛יו אֲשֶׁר־נָֽתַן־ ל֥וֹ הָאֱלֹהִ֖ים תַּ֥חַת הַשָּֽׁמֶשׁ׃ 16 כַּאֲשֶׁ֨ר נָתַ֤תִּי אֶת־ לִבִּי֙ לָדַ֣עַת חָכְמָ֔ה וְלִרְאוֹת֙ אֶת־הָ֣עִנְיָ֔ן אֲשֶׁ֥ר נַעֲשָׂ֖ה עַל־הָאָ֑רֶץ כִּ֣י גַ֤ם בַּיּוֹם֙ וּבַלַּ֔יְלָה שֵׁנָ֕ה בְּעֵינָ֖יו אֵינֶ֥נּוּ רֹאֶֽה׃ 17 וְרָאִ֨יתִי֙ אֶת־כָּל־מַעֲשֵׂ֣ה הָאֱלֹהִ֔ים כִּ֣י לֹ֥א יוּכַ֣ל הָאָדָ֗ם לִמְצוֹא֙ אֶת־הַֽמַּעֲשֶׂה֙ אֲשֶׁ֣ר נַעֲשָׂ֣ה תַֽחַת־הַשֶּׁ֔מֶשׁ בְּ֠שֶׁל אֲשֶׁ֨ר יַעֲמֹ֧ל הָאָדָ֛ם לְבַקֵּ֖שׁ וְלֹ֣א יִמְצָ֑א וְגַ֨ם אִם־יֹאמַ֤ר הֶֽחָכָם֙ לָדַ֔עַת לֹ֥א יוּכַ֖ל לִמְצֹֽא׃

ט כִּ֣י אֶת־כָּל־זֶ֗ה נָתַ֤תִּי אֶל־לִבִּי֙ וְלָב֣וּר אֶת־ כָּל־זֶ֔ה אֲשֶׁ֨ר הַצַּדִּיקִ֧ים וְהַחֲכָמִ֛ים וַעֲבָדֵיהֶ֖ם בְּיַ֣ד הָאֱלֹהִ֑ים גַּֽם־אַהֲבָ֣ה גַם־שִׂנְאָ֗ה אֵ֤ין יוֹדֵ֙עַ֙ הָֽאָדָ֔ם הַכֹּ֖ל לִפְנֵיהֶֽם׃ 2 הַכֹּ֞ל כַּאֲשֶׁ֣ר לַכֹּ֗ל מִקְרֶ֣ה אֶחָ֡ד לַצַּדִּ֣יק וְלָרָשָׁ֩ע לַטּוֹב֩ וְלַטָּה֨וֹר וְלַטָּמֵ֜א וְלַזֹּבֵ֗חַ וְלַאֲשֶׁ֣ר אֵינֶ֣נּוּ זֹבֵ֔חַ כַּטּוֹב֙ כַּֽחֹטֶ֔א הַנִּשְׁבָּ֕ע כַּאֲשֶׁ֖ר שְׁבוּעָ֥ה יָרֵֽא׃ 3 זֶ֣ה ׀ רָ֗ע בְּכֹ֤ל אֲשֶֽׁר־נַעֲשָׂה֙ תַּ֣חַת הַשֶּׁ֔מֶשׁ כִּֽי־מִקְרֶ֥ה אֶחָ֖ד לַכֹּ֑ל וְגַ֣ם לֵ֥ב בְּֽנֵי־הָֽאָדָ֡ם מָֽלֵא־רָ֞ע וְהוֹלֵל֤וֹת בִּלְבָבָם֙ בְּחַיֵּיהֶ֔ם וְאַחֲרָ֖יו אֶל־ הַמֵּתִֽים׃ 4 כִּי־מִי֙ אֲשֶׁ֣ר יְבֻחַ֔רᵖ אֶ֥ל כָּל־הַֽחַיִּ֖ים יֵ֣שׁ בִּטָּח֑וֹן כִּֽי־לְכֶ֤לֶב חַי֙ ה֣וּא ט֔וֹב מִן־הָאַרְיֵ֖ה הַמֵּֽת׃ 5 כִּ֧י הַֽחַיִּ֛ים יוֹדְעִ֖ים שֶׁיָּמֻ֑תוּ וְהַמֵּתִ֞ים אֵינָ֣ם יוֹדְעִ֣ים מְא֗וּמָה וְאֵֽין־ע֤וֹד לָהֶם֙ שָׂכָ֔ר כִּ֥י נִשְׁכַּ֖ח זִכְרָֽם׃ 6 גַּ֣ם אַהֲבָתָ֧ם גַּם־שִׂנְאָתָ֛ם גַּם־קִנְאָתָ֖ם כְּבָ֣ר אָבָ֑דָה וְחֵ֨לֶק אֵין־לָהֶ֥ם עוֹד֙ לְעוֹלָ֔ם בְּכֹ֥ל אֲשֶׁ֖ר נַעֲשָׂ֥ה תַּ֥חַת הַשָּֽׁמֶשׁ׃ 7 לֵ֣ךְ אֱכֹ֤ל בְּשִׂמְחָה֙ לַחְמֶ֔ךָ

And drink your wine with a merry heart;
For God has already accepted your works.

8 Let your garments always be white,
And let your head lack no oil.

9 Live joyfully with the wife whom you love all the days of your vain life which He has given you under the sun, all your days of vanity; for that *is* your portion in life, and in the labor which you perform under the sun.

10 Whatever your hand finds to do, do *it* with your might; for *there is* no work or device or knowledge or wisdom in the grave where you are going.

11 I returned and saw under the sun that—

The race *is* not to the swift,
Nor the battle to the strong,
Nor bread to the wise,
Nor riches to men of understanding,
Nor favor to men of skill;
But time and chance happen to them all.

12 For man also does not know his time:
Like fish taken in a cruel net,
Like birds caught in a snare,
So the sons of men *are* snared in an evil time,
When it falls suddenly upon them.

13 This wisdom I have also seen under the sun, and it *seemed* great to me: 14 *There was* a little city with few men in it; and a great king came against it, besieged it, and built great snares around it. 15 Now there was found in it a poor wise man, and he by his wisdom delivered the city. Yet no one remembered that same poor man.

16 Then I said:

"Wisdom *is* better than strength.
Nevertheless the poor man's wisdom *is* despised,
And his words are not heard.

17 Words of the wise, *spoken quietly, should be heard*
Rather than the shout of a ruler of fools.

18 Wisdom *is* better than weapons of war;
But one sinner destroys much good."

10

Dead flies putrefy the perfumer's ointment,
And cause it to give off a foul odor;
So does a little folly to one respected for wisdom *and* honor.

2 A wise man's heart *is* at his right hand,
But a fool's heart at his left.

3 Even when a fool walks along the way,
He lacks wisdom,
And he shows everyone *that* he *is* a fool.

4 If the spirit of the ruler rises against you,
Do not leave your post;
For conciliation pacifies great offenses.

5 There is an evil I have seen under the sun,
As an error proceeding from the ruler:

6 Folly is set in great dignity,

וְשֵׁתָה בְלֶב־טוֹב יֵינֶךָ כִּי כְבָר רָצָה הָאֱלֹהִים אֶת־
מַעֲשֶׂיךָ: 8 בְּכָל־עֵת יִהְיוּ בְגָדֶיךָ לְבָנִים וְשֶׁמֶן עַל־
רֹאשְׁךָ אַל־יֶחְסָר: 9 רְאֵה חַיִּים עִם־אִשָּׁה אֲשֶׁר־
אָהַבְתָּ כָּל־יְמֵי חַיֵּי הֶבְלֶךָ אֲשֶׁר נָתַן־לְךָ תַּחַת
הַשֶּׁמֶשׁ כֹּל יְמֵי הֶבְלֶךָ כִּי הוּא חֶלְקְךָ בַּחַיִּים
וּבַעֲמָלְךָ אֲשֶׁר־אַתָּה עָמֵל תַּחַת הַשָּׁמֶשׁ: 10 כֹּל
אֲשֶׁר תִּמְצָא יָדְךָ לַעֲשׂוֹת בְּכֹחֲךָ עֲשֵׂה כִּי אֵין
מַעֲשֶׂה וְחֶשְׁבּוֹן וְדַעַת וְחָכְמָה בִּשְׁאוֹל אֲשֶׁר אַתָּה
הֹלֵךְ שָׁמָּה: ס 11 שַׁבְתִּי וְרָאֹה תַחַת־
הַשֶּׁמֶשׁ כִּי לֹא לַקַּלִּים הַמֵּרוֹץ וְלֹא לַגִּבּוֹרִים
הַמִּלְחָמָה וְגַם לֹא לַחֲכָמִים לֶחֶם וְגַם לֹא לַנְּבֹנִים
עֹשֶׁר וְגַם לֹא לַיֹּדְעִים חֵן כִּי־עֵת וָפֶגַע יִקְרֶה אֶת־
כֻּלָּם: 12 כִּי גַּם לֹא־יֵדַע הָאָדָם אֶת־עִתּוֹ כַּדָּגִים
שֶׁנֶּאֱחָזִים בִּמְצוֹדָה רָעָה וְכַצִּפֳּרִים הָאֲחֻזוֹת בַּפָּח
כָּהֵם יוּקָשִׁים בְּנֵי הָאָדָם לְעֵת רָעָה כְּשֶׁתִּפּוֹל
עֲלֵיהֶם פִּתְאֹם: 13 גַּם־זֹה רָאִיתִי חָכְמָה תַּחַת
הַשָּׁמֶשׁ וּגְדוֹלָה הִיא אֵלָי: 14 עִיר קְטַנָּה וַאֲנָשִׁים
בָּהּ מְעָט וּבָא־אֵלֶיהָ מֶלֶךְ גָּדוֹל וְסָבַב אֹתָהּ וּבָנָה
עָלֶיהָ מְצוֹדִים גְּדֹלִים: 15 וּמָצָא בָהּ אִישׁ מִסְכֵּן
חָכָם וּמִלַּט־הוּא אֶת־הָעִיר בְּחָכְמָתוֹ וְאָדָם לֹא זָכַר
אֶת־הָאִישׁ הַמִּסְכֵּן הַהוּא: 16 וְאָמַרְתִּי אָנִי טוֹבָה
חָכְמָה מִגְּבוּרָה וְחָכְמַת הַמִּסְכֵּן בְּזוּיָה וּדְבָרָיו
אֵינָם נִשְׁמָעִים: 17 דִּבְרֵי חֲכָמִים בְּנַחַת נִשְׁמָעִים
מִזַּעֲקַת מוֹשֵׁל בַּכְּסִילִים: 18 טוֹבָה חָכְמָה מִכְּלֵי
קְרָב וְחוֹטֶא אֶחָד יְאַבֵּד טוֹבָה הַרְבֵּה:

י 1 זְבוּבֵי מָוֶת יַבְאִישׁ יַבִּיעַ שֶׁמֶן רוֹקֵחַ יָקָר מֵחָכְמָה
מִכָּבוֹד סִכְלוּת מְעָט: 2 לֵב חָכָם לִימִינוֹ וְלֵב כְּסִיל
לִשְׂמֹאלוֹ: 3 וְגַם־בַּדֶּרֶךְ כְּשֶׁהַסָּכָל הֹלֵךְ לִבּוֹ חָסֵר
וְאָמַר לַכֹּל סָכָל הוּא: 4 אִם־רוּחַ הַמּוֹשֵׁל תַּעֲלֶה
עָלֶיךָ מְקוֹמְךָ אַל־תַּנַּח כִּי מַרְפֵּא יַנִּיחַ חֲטָאִים
גְּדוֹלִים: 5 יֵשׁ רָעָה רָאִיתִי תַּחַת הַשָּׁמֶשׁ כִּשְׁגָגָה
שֶׁיֹּצָא מִלִּפְנֵי הַשַּׁלִּיט: 6 נִתַּן הַסֶּכֶל בַּמְּרוֹמִים

While the rich sit in a lowly place.

7 I have seen servants on horses,
While princes walk on the ground like servants.

8 He who digs a pit will fall into it,
And whoever breaks through a wall will be bitten
   by a serpent.

9 He who quarries stones may be hurt by them,
And he who splits wood may be endangered by it.

10 If the ax is dull,
And one does not sharpen the edge,
Then he must use more strength;
But wisdom brings success.

11 A serpent may bite when *it is* not charmed;
The babbler is no different.

12 The words of a wise man's mouth *are* gracious,
But the lips of a fool shall swallow him up;

13 The words of his mouth begin with foolishness,
And the end of his talk *is* raving madness.

14 A fool also multiplies words.
No man knows what is to be;
Who can tell him what will be after him?

15 The labor of fools wearies them,
For they do not even know how to go to the city!

16 Woe to you, O land, when your king *is* a child,
And your princes feast in the morning!

17 Blessed *are* you, O land, when your king *is* the
   son of nobles,
And your princes feast at the proper time—
For strength and not for drunkenness!

18 Because of laziness the building decays,
And through idleness of hands the house leaks.

19 A feast is made for laughter,
And wine makes merry;
But money answers everything.

20 Do not curse the king, even in your thought;
Do not curse the rich, even in your bedroom;
For a bird of the air may carry your voice,
And a bird in flight may tell the matter.

11

Cast your bread upon the waters,
For you will find it after many days.

2 Give a serving to seven, and also to eight,
For you do not know what evil will be on the
   earth.

3 If the clouds are full of rain,
They empty *themselves* upon the earth;
And if a tree falls to the south or the north,
In the place where the tree falls, there it shall lie.

4 He who observes the wind will not sow,
And he who regards the clouds will not reap.

5 As you do not know what *is* the way of the wind,
Or how the bones *grow* in the womb of her who is
   with child,
So you do not know the works of God who
   makes everything.

6 In the morning sow your seed,
And in the evening do not withhold your hand;
For you do not know which will prosper,
Either this or that,

רַבִּים וַעֲשִׁירִים בַּשֵּׁפֶל יֵשֵׁבוּ: 7 רָאִיתִי עֲבָדִים
עַל־סוּסִים וְשָׂרִים הֹלְכִים כַּעֲבָדִים עַל־הָאָרֶץ:
8 חֹפֵר גּוּמָּץ בּוֹ יִפּוֹל וּפֹרֵץ גָּדֵר יִשְּׁכֶנּוּ נָחָשׁ:
9 מַסִּיעַ אֲבָנִים יֵעָצֵב בָּהֶם בּוֹקֵעַ עֵצִים יִסָּכֶן בָּם:
10 אִם־קֵהָה הַבַּרְזֶל וְהוּא לֹא־פָנִים קִלְקַל וַחֲיָלִים
יְגַבֵּר וְיִתְרוֹן הַכְשֵׁיר חָכְמָה: 11 אִם־יִשֹּׁךְ הַנָּחָשׁ
בְּלוֹא־לָחַשׁ וְאֵין יִתְרוֹן לְבַעַל הַלָּשׁוֹן: 12 דִּבְרֵי
פִי־חָכָם חֵן וְשִׂפְתוֹת כְּסִיל תְּבַלְּעֶנּוּ: 13 תְּחִלַּת
דִּבְרֵי־פִיהוּ סִכְלוּת וְאַחֲרִית פִּיהוּ הוֹלֵלוּת רָעָה:
14 וְהַסָּכָל יַרְבֶּה דְבָרִים לֹא־יֵדַע הָאָדָם מַה־
שֶׁיִּהְיֶה וַאֲשֶׁר יִהְיֶה מֵאַחֲרָיו מִי יַגִּיד לוֹ: 15 עֲמַל
הַכְּסִילִים תְּיַגְּעֶנּוּ אֲשֶׁר לֹא־יָדַע לָלֶכֶת אֶל־עִיר:
16 אִי־לָךְ אֶרֶץ שֶׁמַּלְכֵּךְ נָעַר וְשָׂרַיִךְ בַּבֹּקֶר יֹאכֵלוּ:
17 אַשְׁרֵיךְ אֶרֶץ שֶׁמַּלְכֵּךְ בֶּן־חוֹרִים וְשָׂרַיִךְ בָּעֵת
יֹאכֵלוּ בִּגְבוּרָה וְלֹא בַשְּׁתִי: 18 בַּעֲצַלְתַּיִם יִמַּךְ
הַמְּקָרֶה וּבְשִׁפְלוּת יָדַיִם יִדְלֹף הַבָּיִת: 19 לִשְׂחוֹק
עֹשִׂים לֶחֶם וְיַיִן יְשַׂמַּח חַיִּים וְהַכֶּסֶף יַעֲנֶה אֶת־
הַכֹּל: 20 גַּם בְּמַדָּעֲךָ מֶלֶךְ אַל־תְּקַלֵּל וּבְחַדְרֵי
מִשְׁכָּבְךָ אַל־תְּקַלֵּל עָשִׁיר כִּי עוֹף הַשָּׁמַיִם יוֹלִיךְ
אֶת־הַקּוֹל וּבַעַל הַכְּנָפַיִם יַגִּיד דָּבָר:

יא שַׁלַּח לַחְמְךָ עַל־פְּנֵי הַמָּיִם כִּי־בְרֹב הַיָּמִים
תִּמְצָאֶנּוּ: 2 תֶּן־חֵלֶק לְשִׁבְעָה וְגַם לִשְׁמוֹנָה כִּי
לֹא תֵדַע מַה־יִּהְיֶה רָעָה עַל־הָאָרֶץ: 3 אִם־יִמָּלְאוּ
הֶעָבִים גֶּשֶׁם עַל־הָאָרֶץ יָרִיקוּ וְאִם־יִפּוֹל עֵץ בַּדָּרוֹם
וְאִם בַּצָּפוֹן מְקוֹם שֶׁיִּפּוֹל הָעֵץ שָׁם יְהוּא: 4 שֹׁמֵר
רוּחַ לֹא יִזְרָע וְרֹאֶה בֶעָבִים לֹא יִקְצוֹר: 5 כַּאֲשֶׁר
אֵינְךָ יוֹדֵעַ מַה־דֶּרֶךְ הָרוּחַ כַּעֲצָמִים בְּבֶטֶן הַמְּלֵאָה
כָּכָה לֹא תֵדַע אֶת־מַעֲשֵׂה הָאֱלֹהִים אֲשֶׁר יַעֲשֶׂה
אֶת־הַכֹּל: 6 בַּבֹּקֶר זְרַע אֶת־זַרְעֶךָ וְלָעֶרֶב אַל־
תַּנַּח יָדֶךָ כִּי אֵינְךָ יוֹדֵעַ אֵי זֶה יִכְשָׁר הֲזֶה אוֹ־

Or whether both alike *will be* good.

7 Truly the light is sweet,
And *it is* pleasant for the eyes to behold the sun;
8 But if a man lives many years
And rejoices in them all,
Yet let him remember the days of darkness,
For they will be many.
All that is coming *is* vanity.

9 Rejoice, O young man, in your youth,
And let your heart cheer you in the days of your youth;
Walk in the ways of your heart,
And in the sight of your eyes;
But know that for all these
God will bring you into judgment.

10 Therefore remove sorrow from your heart,
And put away evil from your flesh,
For childhood and youth *are* vanity.

12 Remember now your Creator in the days of your youth,
Before the difficult days come,
And the years draw near when you say,
"I have no pleasure in them":
2 While the sun and the light,
The moon and the stars,
Are not darkened,
And the clouds do not return after the rain;
3 In the day when the keepers of the house tremble,
And the strong men bow down;
When the grinders cease because they are few,
And those that look through the windows grow dim;
4 When the doors are shut in the streets,
And the sound of grinding is low;
When one rises up at the sound of a bird,
And all the daughters of music are brought low.
5 Also they are afraid of height,
And of terrors in the way;
When the almond tree blossoms,
The grasshopper is a burden,
And desire fails.
For man goes to his eternal home,
And the mourners go about the streets.

6 *Remember your Creator* before the silver cord is loosed,
Or the golden bowl is broken,
Or the pitcher shattered at the fountain,
Or the wheel broken at the well.
7 Then the dust will return to the earth as it was,
And the spirit will return to God who gave it.

8 "Vanity of vanities," says the Preacher,
"All *is* vanity."

9 And moreover, because the Preacher was wise, he still taught the people knowledge; yes, he pondered and sought out *and* set in order many proverbs. 10 The Preacher sought to find acceptable words; and *what was* written *was* upright—words of truth. 11 The words of the wise are like goads, and

זֶה וְאִם־שְׁנֵיהֶם כְּאֶחָד טוֹבִים: 7 וּמָתוֹק הָאוֹר
וְטוֹב לַעֵינַיִם לִרְאוֹת אֶת־הַשָּׁמֶשׁ: 8 כִּי אִם־שָׁנִים
הַרְבֵּה יִחְיֶה הָאָדָם בְּכֻלָּם יִשְׂמָח וְיִזְכֹּר אֶת־יְמֵי
הַחֹשֶׁךְ כִּי־הַרְבֵּה יִהְיוּ כָּל־שֶׁבָּא הָבֶל: 9 שְׂמַח
בָּחוּר בְּיַלְדוּתֶיךָ וִיטִיבְךָ לִבְּךָ בִּימֵי בְחוּרוֹתֶךָ וְהַלֵּךְ
בְּדַרְכֵי לִבְּךָ וּבְמַרְאֵי עֵינֶיךָ וְדָע כִּי עַל־כָּל־אֵלֶּה
יְבִיאֲךָ הָאֱלֹהִים בַּמִּשְׁפָּט: 10 וְהָסֵר כַּעַס מִלִּבֶּךָ
וְהַעֲבֵר רָעָה מִבְּשָׂרֶךָ כִּי־הַיַּלְדוּת וְהַשַּׁחֲרוּת הָבֶל:

יב וּזְכֹר אֶת־בּוֹרְאֶיךָ בִּימֵי בְּחוּרֹתֶיךָ עַד אֲשֶׁר
לֹא־יָבֹאוּ יְמֵי הָרָעָה וְהִגִּיעוּ שָׁנִים אֲשֶׁר תֹּאמַר
אֵין־לִי בָהֶם חֵפֶץ: 2 עַד אֲשֶׁר לֹא־תֶחְשַׁךְ הַשֶּׁמֶשׁ
וְהָאוֹר וְהַיָּרֵחַ וְהַכּוֹכָבִים וְשָׁבוּ הֶעָבִים אַחַר
הַגָּשֶׁם: 3 בַּיּוֹם שֶׁיָּזֻעוּ שֹׁמְרֵי הַבַּיִת וְהִתְעַוְּתוּ
אַנְשֵׁי הֶחָיִל וּבָטְלוּ הַטֹּחֲנוֹת כִּי מִעֵטוּ וְחָשְׁכוּ
הָרֹאוֹת בָּאֲרֻבּוֹת: 4 וְסֻגְּרוּ דְלָתַיִם בַּשּׁוּק בִּשְׁפַל
קוֹל הַטַּחֲנָה וְיָקוּם לְקוֹל הַצִּפּוֹר וְיִשַּׁחוּ כָּל־בְּנוֹת
הַשִּׁיר: 5 גַּם מִגָּבֹהַּ יִרָאוּ וְחַתְחַתִּים בַּדֶּרֶךְ וְיָנֵאץ
הַשָּׁקֵד וְיִסְתַּבֵּל הֶחָגָב וְתָפֵר הָאֲבִיּוֹנָה כִּי־הֹלֵךְ
הָאָדָם אֶל־בֵּית עוֹלָמוֹ וְסָבְבוּ בַשּׁוּק הַסֹּפְדִים:
6 עַד אֲשֶׁר לֹא־יֵרָחֵק חֶבֶל הַכֶּסֶף וְתָרֻץ גֻּלַּת
הַזָּהָב וְתִשָּׁבֶר כַּד עַל־הַמַּבּוּעַ וְנָרֹץ הַגַּלְגַּל אֶל־
הַבּוֹר: 7 וְיָשֹׁב הֶעָפָר עַל־הָאָרֶץ כְּשֶׁהָיָה וְהָרוּחַ
תָּשׁוּב אֶל־הָאֱלֹהִים אֲשֶׁר נְתָנָהּ: 8 הֲבֵל הֲבָלִים
אָמַר הַקּוֹהֶלֶת הַכֹּל הָבֶל: 9 וְיֹתֵר שֶׁהָיָה קֹהֶלֶת
חָכָם עוֹד לִמַּד־דַּעַת אֶת־הָעָם וְאִזֵּן וְחִקֵּר תִּקֵּן
מְשָׁלִים הַרְבֵּה: 10 בִּקֵּשׁ קֹהֶלֶת לִמְצֹא דִּבְרֵי־חֵפֶץ
וְכָתוּב יֹשֶׁר דִּבְרֵי אֱמֶת: 11 דִּבְרֵי חֲכָמִים כַּדָּרְבֹנוֹת

the words of scholars are like well-driven nails, given by one Shepherd. ¹² And further, my son, be admonished by these. Of making many books *there is* no end, and much study *is* wearisome to the flesh.

¹³ Let us hear the conclusion of the whole matter:

Fear God and keep His commandments,
For this is man's all.
¹⁴   For God will bring every work into judgment,
Including every secret thing,
Whether good or evil.

וּכְמַשְׂמְרוֹת נְטוּעִים בַּעֲלֵי אֲסֻפּוֹת נִתְּנוּ מֵרֹעֶה אֶחָד: ¹² וְיֹתֵר מֵהֵמָּה בְּנִי הִזָּהֵר עֲשׂוֹת סְפָרִים הַרְבֵּה אֵין קֵץ וְלַהַג הַרְבֵּה יְגִעַת בָּשָׂר: ¹³ סוֹף דָּבָר הַכֹּל נִשְׁמָע אֶת־הָאֱלֹהִים יְרָא וְאֶת־מִצְוֹתָיו שְׁמוֹר כִּי־זֶה כָּל־הָאָדָם: ¹⁴ כִּי אֶת־כָּל־מַעֲשֶׂה הָאֱלֹהִים יָבֵא בְמִשְׁפָּט עַל כָּל־נֶעְלָם אִם־טוֹב וְאִם־רָע:

The Book of
ESTHER

1 Now it came to pass in the days of Ahasuerus (this *was* the Ahasuerus who reigned over one hundred and twenty-seven provinces, from India to Ethiopia), ²in those days when King Ahasuerus sat on the throne of his kingdom, which *was* in Shushan the citadel, ³ *that* in the third year of his reign he made a feast for all his officials and servants—the powers of Persia and Media, the nobles, and the princes of the provinces *being* before him— ⁴when he showed the riches of his glorious kingdom and the splendor of his excellent majesty for many days, one hundred and eighty days *in all.*

⁵And when these days were completed, the king made a feast lasting seven days for all the people who were present in Shushan the citadel, from great to small, in the court of the garden of the king's palace. ⁶ *There were* white and blue linen *curtains* fastened with cords of fine linen and purple on silver rods and marble pillars; *and the* couches *were* of gold and silver on a *mosaic* pavement of alabaster, turquoise, and white and black marble. ⁷And they served drinks in golden vessels, each vessel being different from the other, with royal wine in abundance, according to the generosity of the king. ⁸In accordance with the law, the drinking was not compulsory; for so the king had ordered all the officers of his household, that they should do according to each man's pleasure.

⁹Queen Vashti also made a feast for the women *in* the royal palace which *belonged* to King Ahasuerus.

¹⁰On the seventh day, when the heart of the king was merry with wine, he commanded Mehuman, Biztha, Harbona, Bigtha, Abagtha, Zethar, and Carcas, seven eunuchs who served in the presence of King Ahasuerus, ¹¹to bring Queen Vashti before the king, *wearing* her royal crown, in order to show her beauty to the people and the officials, for she *was* beautiful to behold. ¹²But Queen Vashti refused to come at the king's command *brought* by *his* eunuchs; therefore the king was furious, and his anger burned within him.

¹³Then the king said to the wise men who understood the times (for this *was* the king's manner toward all who knew law and justice, ¹⁴those closest to him *being* Carshena, Shethar,

א וַיְהִ֖י בִּימֵ֣י אֲחַשְׁוֵר֑וֹשׁ ה֣וּא אֲחַשְׁוֵר֗וֹשׁ הַמֹּלֵ֞ךְ מֵהֹ֣דּוּ וְעַד־כּ֗וּשׁ שֶׁ֧בַע וְעֶשְׂרִ֛ים וּמֵאָ֖ה מְדִינָֽה׃ ² בַּיָּמִ֣ים הָהֵ֔ם כְּשֶׁ֣בֶת ׀ הַמֶּ֣לֶךְ אֲחַשְׁוֵר֗וֹשׁ עַ֚ל כִּסֵּ֣א מַלְכוּת֔וֹ אֲשֶׁ֖ר בְּשׁוּשַׁ֥ן הַבִּירָֽה׃ ³ בִּשְׁנַ֤ת שָׁלוֹשׁ֙ לְמָלְכ֔וֹ עָשָׂ֣ה מִשְׁתֶּ֔ה לְכָל־שָׂרָ֖יו וַעֲבָדָ֑יו חֵ֣יל ׀ פָּרַ֣ס וּמָדַ֗י הַֽפַּרְתְּמִ֛ים וְשָׂרֵ֥י הַמְּדִינ֖וֹת לְפָנָֽיו׃ ⁴ בְּהַרְאֹת֗וֹ אֶת־עֹ֙שֶׁר֙ כְּב֣וֹד מַלְכוּת֔וֹ וְאֶ֨ת־יְקָ֔ר תִּפְאֶ֖רֶת גְּדוּלָּת֑וֹ יָמִ֣ים רַבִּ֔ים שְׁמוֹנִ֥ים וּמְאַ֖ת יֽוֹם׃ ⁵ וּבִמְל֣וֹאת ׀ הַיָּמִ֣ים הָאֵ֗לֶּה עָשָׂ֣ה הַמֶּ֡לֶךְ לְכָל־הָעָ֣ם הַנִּמְצְאִים֩ בְּשׁוּשַׁ֨ן הַבִּירָ֜ה לְמִגָּד֧וֹל וְעַד־קָטָ֛ן מִשְׁתֶּ֖ה שִׁבְעַ֣ת יָמִ֑ים בַּחֲצַ֕ר גִּנַּ֥ת בִּיתַ֖ן הַמֶּֽלֶךְ׃ ⁶ ח֣וּר ׀ כַּרְפַּ֣ס וּתְכֵ֗לֶת אָחוּז֙ בְּחַבְלֵי־ב֣וּץ וְאַרְגָּמָ֔ן עַל־גְּלִ֥ילֵי כֶ֖סֶף וְעַמּ֣וּדֵי שֵׁ֑שׁ מִטּ֣וֹת ׀ זָהָ֣ב וָכֶ֗סֶף עַ֛ל רִֽצְפַ֥ת בַּהַט־וָשֵׁ֖שׁ וְדַ֥ר וְסֹחָֽרֶת׃

⁷ וְהַשְׁק֗וֹת בִּכְלֵ֣י זָהָ֔ב וְכֵלִ֖ים מִכֵּלִ֣ים שׁוֹנִ֑ים וְיֵ֥ין מַלְכ֛וּת רָ֖ב כְּיַ֥ד הַמֶּֽלֶךְ׃ ⁸ וְהַשְּׁתִיָּ֥ה כַדָּ֖ת אֵ֣ין אֹנֵ֑ס כִּי־כֵ֣ן ׀ יִסַּ֣ד הַמֶּ֗לֶךְ עַ֚ל כָּל־רַ֣ב בֵּית֔וֹ לַעֲשׂ֖וֹת כִּרְצ֥וֹן אִישׁ־וָאִֽישׁ׃ ⁹ גַּ֚ם וַשְׁתִּ֣י הַמַּלְכָּ֔ה עָשְׂתָ֖ה מִשְׁתֵּ֣ה נָשִׁ֑ים בֵּ֚ית הַמַּלְכ֔וּת אֲשֶׁ֖ר לַמֶּ֥לֶךְ אֲחַשְׁוֵרֽוֹשׁ׃ ס ¹⁰ בַּיּוֹם֙ הַשְּׁבִיעִ֔י כְּט֥וֹב לֵב־הַמֶּ֖לֶךְ בַּיָּ֑יִן אָמַ֡ר לִ֠מְהוּמָ֠ן בִּזְּתָ֨א חַֽרְבוֹנָ֜א בִּגְתָ֤א וַאֲבַגְתָא֙ זֵתַ֣ר וְכַרְכַּ֔ס שִׁבְעַת֙ הַסָּ֣רִיסִ֔ים הַמְשָׁ֣רְתִ֔ים אֶת־פְּנֵ֖י הַמֶּ֥לֶךְ אֲחַשְׁוֵרֽוֹשׁ׃ ¹¹ לְ֠הָבִיא אֶת־וַשְׁתִּ֧י הַמַּלְכָּ֛ה לִפְנֵ֥י הַמֶּ֖לֶךְ בְּכֶ֣תֶר מַלְכ֑וּת לְהַרְא֨וֹת הָֽעַמִּ֤ים וְהַשָּׂרִים֙ אֶת־יָפְיָ֔הּ כִּֽי־טוֹבַ֥ת מַרְאֶ֖ה הִֽיא׃ ¹² וַתְּמָאֵ֞ן הַמַּלְכָּ֣ה וַשְׁתִּ֗י לָבוֹא֙ בִּדְבַ֣ר הַמֶּ֔לֶךְ אֲשֶׁ֖ר בְּיַ֣ד הַסָּרִיסִ֑ים וַיִּקְצֹ֤ף הַמֶּ֙לֶךְ֙ מְאֹ֔ד וַחֲמָת֖וֹ בָּעֲרָ֥ה בֽוֹ׃ ¹³ וַיֹּ֣אמֶר הַמֶּ֔לֶךְ לַחֲכָמִ֖ים יֹדְעֵ֣י הָֽעִתִּ֑ים כִּי־כֵן֙ דְּבַ֣ר הַמֶּ֔לֶךְ לִפְנֵ֕י כָּל־יֹדְעֵ֖י דָּ֥ת וָדִֽין׃ ¹⁴ וְהַקָּרֹ֣ב אֵלָ֗יו כַּרְשְׁנָ֤א שֵׁתָר֙ אַדְמָ֣תָא תַרְשִׁ֔ישׁ מֶ֥רֶס מַרְסְנָ֖א מְמוּכָ֑ן שִׁבְעַ֣ת שָׂרֵ֣י ׀

Admatha, Tarshish, Meres, Marsena, and Memucan, the seven princes of Persia and Media, who
had access to the king's presence, *and* who ranked
highest in the kingdom): [15] "What *shall we* do to
Queen Vashti, according to law, because she did not
obey the command of King Ahasuerus *brought to
her* by the eunuchs?"

[16] And Memucan answered before the king and
the princes: "Queen Vashti has not only wronged
the king, but also all the princes, and all the people
who *are* in all the provinces of King Ahasuerus.
[17] For the queen's behavior will become known to
all women, so that they will despise their husbands
in their eyes, when they report, 'King Ahasuerus
commanded Queen Vashti to be brought in before
him, but she did not come.' [18] This very day the
noble ladies of Persia and Media will say to all the
king's officials that they have heard of the behavior
of the queen. Thus *there will be* excessive contempt
and wrath. [19] If it pleases the king, let a royal decree
go out from him, and let it be recorded in the laws
of the Persians and the Medes, so that it will not be
altered, that Vashti shall come no more before King
Ahasuerus; and let the king give her royal position
to another who is better than she. [20] When the
king's decree which he will make is proclaimed
throughout all his empire (for it is great), all wives
will honor their husbands, both great and small."

[21] And the reply pleased the king and the princes,
and the king did according to the word of
Memucan. [22] Then he sent letters to all the king's
provinces, to each province in its own script, and to
every people in their own language, that each man
should be master in his own house, and speak in the
language of his own people.

2 After these things, when the wrath of King
Ahasuerus subsided, he remembered Vashti, what
she had done, and what had been decreed against
her. [2] Then the king's servants who attended him
said: "Let beautiful young virgins be sought for the
king; [3] and let the king appoint officers in all the
provinces of his kingdom, that they may gather all
the beautiful young virgins to Shushan the citadel,
into the women's quarters, under the custody of
Hegai the king's eunuch, custodian of the women.
And let beauty preparations be given *them*. [4] Then
let the young woman who pleases the king be queen
instead of Vashti."

This thing pleased the king, and he did so.

[5] In Shushan the citadel there was a certain Jew
whose name *was* Mordecai the son of Jair, the son
of Shimei, the son of Kish, a Benjamite. [6] *Kish* had
been carried away from Jerusalem with the captives

פָּרַ֗ס וּמָדַי֙ רֹאֵ֣י פְּנֵ֣י הַמֶּ֔לֶךְ הַיֹּשְׁבִ֥ים רִאשֹׁנָ֖ה
בַּמַּלְכֽוּת׃ 15 כְּדָת֙ מַֽה־לַּעֲשׂ֔וֹת בַּמַּלְכָּ֖ה וַשְׁתִּ֑י עַ֣ל ׀
אֲשֶׁ֣ר לֹֽא־עָשְׂתָ֗ה אֶֽת־מַאֲמַר֙ הַמֶּ֣לֶךְ אֲחַשְׁוֵר֔וֹשׁ
בְּיַ֖ד הַסָּרִיסִֽים׃ ס 16 וַיֹּ֣אמֶר מְמוּכָ֗ן לִפְנֵ֤י
הַמֶּ֙לֶךְ֙ וְהַשָּׂרִ֔ים לֹ֤א עַל־הַמֶּ֙לֶךְ֙ לְבַדּ֔וֹ עָוְתָ֖ה וַשְׁתִּ֣י
הַמַּלְכָּ֑ה כִּ֤י עַל־כָּל־הַשָּׂרִים֙ וְעַל־כָּל־הָ֣עַמִּ֔ים אֲשֶׁ֕ר
בְּכָל־מְדִינ֖וֹת הַמֶּ֥לֶךְ אֲחַשְׁוֵרֽוֹשׁ׃ 17 כִּֽי־יֵצֵ֤א דְבַר־
הַמַּלְכָּה֙ עַל־כָּל־הַנָּשִׁ֔ים לְהַבְז֥וֹת בַּעְלֵיהֶ֖ן בְּעֵינֵיהֶ֑ן
בְּאָמְרָ֗ם הַמֶּ֣לֶךְ אֲחַשְׁוֵר֡וֹשׁ אָמַ֞ר לְהָבִ֨יא אֶת־
וַשְׁתִּ֧י הַמַּלְכָּ֛ה לְפָנָ֖יו וְלֹא־בָֽאָה׃ 18 וְֽהַיּ֨וֹם הַזֶּ֜ה
תֹּאמַ֣רְנָה ׀ שָׂר֣וֹת פָּֽרַס־וּמָדַ֗י אֲשֶׁ֤ר שָֽׁמְעוּ֙ אֶת־
דְּבַ֣ר הַמַּלְכָּ֔ה לְכֹ֖ל שָׂרֵ֣י הַמֶּ֑לֶךְ וּכְדַ֖י בִּזָּי֥וֹן וָקָֽצֶף׃
19 אִם־עַל־הַמֶּ֣לֶךְ ט֗וֹב יֵצֵ֤א דְבַר־מַלְכוּת֙ מִלְּפָנָ֔יו
וְיִכָּתֵ֛ב בְּדָתֵ֥י פָֽרַס־וּמָדַ֖י וְלֹ֣א יַעֲב֑וֹר אֲשֶׁ֨ר לֹֽא־
תָב֜וֹא וַשְׁתִּ֗י לִפְנֵי֙ הַמֶּ֣לֶךְ אֲחַשְׁוֵר֔וֹשׁ וּמַלְכוּתָהּ֙ יִתֵּ֣ן
הַמֶּ֔לֶךְ לִרְעוּתָ֖הּ הַטּוֹבָ֥ה מִמֶּֽנָּה׃ 20 וְנִשְׁמַע֩ פִּתְגָ֨ם
הַמֶּ֤לֶךְ אֲשֶֽׁר־יַעֲשֶׂה֙ בְּכָל־מַלְכוּת֔וֹ כִּ֥י רַבָּ֖ה הִ֑יא
וְכָל־הַנָּשִׁ֗ים יִתְּנ֤וּ יְקָר֙ לְבַעְלֵיהֶ֔ן לְמִגָּד֖וֹל וְעַד־קָטָֽן׃
21 וַיִּיטַב֙ הַדָּבָ֔ר בְּעֵינֵ֥י הַמֶּ֖לֶךְ וְהַשָּׂרִ֑ים וַיַּ֥עַשׂ הַמֶּ֖לֶךְ
כִּדְבַ֥ר מְמוּכָֽן׃ 22 וַיִּשְׁלַ֤ח סְפָרִים֙ אֶל־כָּל־מְדִינ֣וֹת
הַמֶּ֔לֶךְ אֶל־מְדִינָ֤ה וּמְדִינָה֙ כִּכְתָבָ֔הּ וְאֶל־עַ֥ם וָעָ֖ם
כִּלְשׁוֹנ֑וֹ לִהְי֤וֹת כָּל־אִישׁ֙ שֹׂרֵ֣ר בְּבֵית֔וֹ וּמְדַבֵּ֖ר כִּלְשׁ֥וֹן
עַמּֽוֹ׃ פ

ב אַחַר֙ הַדְּבָרִ֣ים הָאֵ֔לֶּה כְּשֹׁ֕ךְ חֲמַ֖ת הַמֶּ֣לֶךְ
אֲחַשְׁוֵר֑וֹשׁ זָכַ֤ר אֶת־וַשְׁתִּי֙ וְאֵ֣ת אֲשֶׁר־עָשָׂ֔תָה וְאֵ֥ת
אֲשֶׁר־נִגְזַ֖ר עָלֶֽיהָ׃ 2 וַיֹּאמְר֥וּ נַעֲרֵֽי־הַמֶּ֖לֶךְ מְשָׁרְתָ֑יו
יְבַקְשׁ֥וּ לַמֶּ֛לֶךְ נְעָר֥וֹת בְּתוּל֖וֹת טוֹב֥וֹת מַרְאֶֽה׃
3 וְיַפְקֵ֨ד הַמֶּ֜לֶךְ פְּקִידִ֗ים בְּכָל־מְדִינ֣וֹת מַלְכוּת֒וֹ
וְיִקְבְּצ֣וּ אֶת־כָּל־נַעֲרָֽה־בְ֠תוּלָה טוֹבַ֨ת מַרְאֶ֜ה אֶל־
שׁוּשַׁ֤ן הַבִּירָה֙ אֶל־בֵּ֣ית הַנָּשִׁ֔ים אֶל־יַ֥ד הֵגֶ֛א סְרִ֥יס
הַמֶּ֖לֶךְ שֹׁמֵ֣ר הַנָּשִׁ֑ים וְנָת֖וֹן תַּמְרוּקֵיהֶֽן׃ 4 וְהַֽנַּעֲרָ֗ה
אֲשֶׁ֤ר תִּיטַב֙ בְּעֵינֵ֣י הַמֶּ֔לֶךְ תִּמְלֹ֖ךְ תַּ֣חַת וַשְׁתִּ֑י וַיִּיטַ֥ב
הַדָּבָ֛ר בְּעֵינֵ֥י הַמֶּ֖לֶךְ וַיַּ֥עַשׂ כֵּֽן׃ ס 5 אִ֣ישׁ
יְהוּדִ֔י הָיָ֖ה בְּשׁוּשַׁ֣ן הַבִּירָ֑ה וּשְׁמ֣וֹ מָרְדֳּכַ֗י בֶּ֣ן
יָאִ֧יר בֶּן־שִׁמְעִ֛י בֶּן־קִ֖ישׁ אִ֥ישׁ יְמִינִֽי׃ 6 אֲשֶׁ֤ר הָגְלָה֙

who had been captured with Jeconiah king of
Judah, whom Nebuchadnezzar the king of Babylon
had carried away. 7 And *Mordecai* had brought up
Hadassah, that *is,* Esther, his uncle's daughter, for
she had neither father nor mother. The young
woman *was* lovely and beautiful. When her father
and mother died, Mordecai took her as his own
daughter.

8 So it was, when the king's command and decree
were heard, and when many young women were
gathered at Shushan the citadel, *under* the custody
of Hegai, that Esther also was taken to the king's
palace, into the care of Hegai the custodian of the
women. 9 Now the young woman pleased him, and
she obtained his favor; so he readily gave beauty
preparations to her, besides her allowance. Then
seven choice maidservants were provided for her
from the king's palace, and he moved her and her
maidservants to the best *place* in the house of the
women.

10 Esther had not revealed her people or family,
for Mordecai had charged her not to reveal *it.*
11 And every day Mordecai paced in front of the
court of the women's quarters, to learn of Esther's
welfare and what was happening to her.

12 Each young woman's turn came to go in to
King Ahasuerus after she had completed twelve
months' preparation, according to the regulations
for the women, for thus were the days of their
preparation apportioned: six months with oil of
myrrh, and six months with perfumes and preparations for beautifying women. 13 Thus *prepared, each*
young woman went to the king, and she was given
whatever she desired to take with her from the
women's quarters to the king's palace. 14 In the
evening she went, and in the morning she returned
to the second house of the women, to the custody of
Shaashgaz, the king's eunuch who kept the
concubines. She would not go in to the king again
unless the king delighted in her and called for her by
name.

15 Now when the turn came for Esther the
daughter of Abihail the uncle of Mordecai, who
had taken her as his daughter, to go in to the king,
she requested nothing but what Hegai the king's
eunuch, the custodian of the women, advised. And
Esther obtained favor in the sight of all who saw
her. 16 So Esther was taken to King Ahasuerus, into
his royal palace, in the tenth month, which *is* the
month of Tebeth, in the seventh year of his reign.
17 The king loved Esther more than all the *other*
women, and she obtained grace and favor in his
sight more than all the virgins; so he set the royal
crown upon her head and made her queen instead

מִירוּשָׁלַיִם עִם־הַגֹּלָה אֲשֶׁר הָגְלְתָה עִם יְכָנְיָה
מֶלֶךְ־יְהוּדָה אֲשֶׁר הֶגְלָה נְבוּכַדְנֶאצַּר מֶלֶךְ בָּבֶל:

7 וַיְהִי אֹמֵן אֶת־הֲדַסָּה הִיא אֶסְתֵּר בַּת־דֹּדוֹ כִּי
אֵין לָהּ אָב וָאֵם וְהַנַּעֲרָה יְפַת־תֹּאַר וְטוֹבַת
מַרְאֶה וּבְמוֹת אָבִיהָ וְאִמָּהּ לְקָחָהּ מָרְדֳּכַי לוֹ
לְבַת: 8 וַיְהִי בְּהִשָּׁמַע דְּבַר־הַמֶּלֶךְ וְדָתוֹ וּבְהִקָּבֵץ
נְעָרוֹת רַבּוֹת אֶל־שׁוּשַׁן הַבִּירָה אֶל־יַד הֵגָי וַתִּלָּקַח
אֶסְתֵּר אֶל־בֵּית הַמֶּלֶךְ אֶל־יַד הֵגַי שֹׁמֵר הַנָּשִׁים:

9 וַתִּיטַב הַנַּעֲרָה בְעֵינָיו וַתִּשָּׂא חֶסֶד לְפָנָיו וַיְבַהֵל
אֶת־תַּמְרוּקֶיהָ וְאֶת־מָנוֹתֶהָ לָתֵת לָהּ וְאֵת שֶׁבַע
הַנְּעָרוֹת הָרְאֻיוֹת לָתֶת־לָהּ מִבֵּית הַמֶּלֶךְ וַיְשַׁנֶּהָ
וְאֶת־נַעֲרוֹתֶיהָ לְטוֹב בֵּית הַנָּשִׁים: 10 לֹא־הִגִּידָה
אֶסְתֵּר אֶת־עַמָּהּ וְאֶת־מוֹלַדְתָּהּ כִּי מָרְדֳּכַי צִוָּה
עָלֶיהָ אֲשֶׁר לֹא־תַגִּיד: 11 וּבְכָל־יוֹם וָיוֹם מָרְדֳּכַי
מִתְהַלֵּךְ לִפְנֵי חֲצַר בֵּית־הַנָּשִׁים לָדַעַת אֶת־שְׁלוֹם
אֶסְתֵּר וּמַה־יֵּעָשֶׂה בָּהּ: 12 וּבְהַגִּיעַ תֹּר נַעֲרָה
וְנַעֲרָה לָבוֹא | אֶל־הַמֶּלֶךְ אֲחַשְׁוֵרוֹשׁ מִקֵּץ הֱיוֹת
לָהּ כְּדָת הַנָּשִׁים שְׁנֵים עָשָׂר חֹדֶשׁ כִּי כֵּן יִמְלְאוּ יְמֵי
מְרוּקֵיהֶן שִׁשָּׁה חֳדָשִׁים בְּשֶׁמֶן הַמֹּר וְשִׁשָּׁה חֳדָשִׁים
בַּבְּשָׂמִים וּבְתַמְרוּקֵי הַנָּשִׁים: 13 וּבָזֶה הַנַּעֲרָה בָּאָה
אֶל־הַמֶּלֶךְ אֵת כָּל־אֲשֶׁר תֹּאמַר יִנָּתֵן לָהּ לָבוֹא
עִמָּהּ מִבֵּית הַנָּשִׁים עַד־בֵּית הַמֶּלֶךְ: 14 בָּעֶרֶב |
הִיא בָאָה וּבַבֹּקֶר הִיא שָׁבָה אֶל־בֵּית הַנָּשִׁים שֵׁנִי
אֶל־יַד שַׁעַשְׁגַז סְרִיס הַמֶּלֶךְ שֹׁמֵר הַפִּילַגְשִׁים לֹא־
תָבוֹא עוֹד אֶל־הַמֶּלֶךְ כִּי אִם־חָפֵץ בָּהּ הַמֶּלֶךְ
וְנִקְרְאָה בְשֵׁם: 15 וּבְהַגִּיעַ תֹּר־אֶסְתֵּר בַּת־אֲבִיחַיִל
דֹּד מָרְדֳּכַי אֲשֶׁר לָקַח־לוֹ לְבַת לָבוֹא אֶל־הַמֶּלֶךְ
לֹא בִקְשָׁה דָּבָר כִּי אִם אֶת־אֲשֶׁר יֹאמַר הֵגַי סְרִיס־
הַמֶּלֶךְ שֹׁמֵר הַנָּשִׁים וַתְּהִי אֶסְתֵּר נֹשֵׂאת חֵן בְּעֵינֵי
כָּל־רֹאֶיהָ: 16 וַתִּלָּקַח אֶסְתֵּר אֶל־הַמֶּלֶךְ אֲחַשְׁוֵרוֹשׁ
אֶל־בֵּית מַלְכוּתוֹ בַּחֹדֶשׁ הָעֲשִׂירִי הוּא־חֹדֶשׁ טֵבֵת
בִּשְׁנַת־שֶׁבַע לְמַלְכוּתוֹ: 17 וַיֶּאֱהַב הַמֶּלֶךְ אֶת־
אֶסְתֵּר מִכָּל־הַנָּשִׁים וַתִּשָּׂא־חֵן וָחֶסֶד לְפָנָיו מִכָּל־
הַבְּתוּלֹת וַיָּשֶׂם כֶּתֶר־מַלְכוּת בְּרֹאשָׁהּ וַיַּמְלִיכֶהָ

of Vashti. 18 Then the king made a great feast, the Feast of Esther, for all his officials and servants; and he proclaimed a holiday in the provinces and gave gifts according to the generosity of a king.

19 When virgins were gathered together a second time, Mordecai sat within the king's gate. 20 Now Esther had not revealed her family and her people, just as Mordecai had charged her, for Esther obeyed the command of Mordecai as when she was brought up by him.

21 In those days, while Mordecai sat within the king's gate, two of the king's eunuchs, Bigthan and Teresh, doorkeepers, became furious and sought to lay hands on King Ahasuerus. 22 So the matter became known to Mordecai, who told Queen Esther, and Esther informed the king in Mordecai's name. 23 And when an inquiry was made into the matter, it was confirmed, and both were hanged on a gallows; and it was written in the book of the chronicles in the presence of the king.

3 After these things King Ahasuerus promoted Haman, the son of Hammedatha the Agagite, and advanced him and set his seat above all the princes who *were* with him. 2 And all the king's servants who *were* within the king's gate bowed and paid homage to Haman, for so the king had commanded concerning him. But Mordecai would not bow or pay homage. 3 Then the king's servants who *were* within the king's gate said to Mordecai, "Why do you transgress the king's command?" 4 Now it happened, when they spoke to him daily and he would not listen to them, that they told *it* to Haman, to see whether Mordecai's words would stand; for *Mordecai* had told them that he *was* a Jew. 5 When Haman saw that Mordecai did not bow or pay him homage, Haman was filled with wrath. 6 But he disdained to lay hands on Mordecai alone, for they had told him of the people of Mordecai. Instead, Haman sought to destroy all the Jews who *were* throughout the whole kingdom of Ahasuerus—the people of Mordecai.

7 In the first month, which is the month of Nisan, in the twelfth year of King Ahasuerus, they cast Pur (that *is,* the lot), before Haman to determine the day and the month, until *it fell on the* twelfth *month,* which *is* the month of Adar.

8 Then Haman said to King Ahasuerus, "There is a certain people scattered and dispersed among the people in all the provinces of your kingdom; their laws *are* different from all *other* people's, and they do not keep the king's laws. Therefore it *is* not fitting for the king to let them remain. 9 If it pleases the king, let *a decree* be written that they be

destroyed, and I will pay ten thousand talents of silver into the hands of those who do the work, to bring *it* into the king's treasuries."

¹⁰ So the king took his signet ring from his hand and gave it to Haman, the son of Hammedatha the Agagite, the enemy of the Jews. ¹¹ And the king said to Haman, "The money and the people *are* given to you, to do with them as seems good to you."

¹² Then the king's scribes were called on the thirteenth day of the first month, and *a decree* was written according to all that Haman commanded— to the king's satraps, to the governors who *were* over each province, to the officials of all people, to every province according to its script, and to every people in their language. In the name of King Ahasuerus it was written, and sealed with the king's signet ring. ¹³ And the letters were sent by couriers into all the king's provinces, to destroy, to kill, and to annihilate all the Jews, both young and old, little children and women, in one day, on the thirteenth *day* of the twelfth *month,* which *is* the month of Adar, and to plunder their possessions. ¹⁴ A copy of the document was to be issued as law in every province, being published for all people, that they should be ready for that day. ¹⁵ The couriers went out, hastened by the king's command; and the decree was proclaimed in Shushan the citadel. So the king and Haman sat down to drink, but the city of Shushan was perplexed.

4 When Mordecai learned all that had happened, he tore his clothes and put on sackcloth and ashes, and went out into the midst of the city. He cried out with a loud and bitter cry. ² He went as far as the front of the king's gate, for no one *might* enter the king's gate clothed with sackcloth. ³ And in every province where the king's command and decree arrived, *there was* great mourning among the Jews, with fasting, weeping, and wailing; and many lay in sackcloth and ashes.

⁴ So Esther's maids and eunuchs came and told her, and the queen was deeply distressed. Then she sent garments to clothe Mordecai and take his sackcloth away from him, but he would not accept *them.* ⁵ Then Esther called Hathach, *one of* the king's eunuchs whom he had appointed to attend her, and she gave him a command concerning Mordecai, to learn what and why this *was.* ⁶ So Hathach went out to Mordecai in the city square that *was* in front of the king's gate. ⁷ And Mordecai told him all that had happened to him, and the sum of money that Haman had promised to pay into the king's treasuries to destroy the Jews. ⁸ He also gave him a copy of the written decree for their

לְאַבְּדָם וַעֲשֶׂרֶת אֲלָפִים כִּכַּר־כֶּסֶף אֶשְׁקוֹל עַל־יְדֵי עֹשֵׂי הַמְּלָאכָה לְהָבִיא אֶל־גִּנְזֵי הַמֶּלֶךְ: 10 וַיָּסַר הַמֶּלֶךְ אֶת־טַבַּעְתּוֹ מֵעַל יָדוֹ וַיִּתְּנָהּ לְהָמָן בֶּן־ הַמְּדָתָא הָאֲגָגִי צֹרֵר הַיְּהוּדִים: 11 וַיֹּאמֶר הַמֶּלֶךְ לְהָמָן הַכֶּסֶף נָתוּן לָךְ וְהָעָם לַעֲשׂוֹת בּוֹ כַּטּוֹב בְּעֵינֶיךָ: 12 וַיִּקָּרְאוּ סֹפְרֵי הַמֶּלֶךְ בַּחֹדֶשׁ הָרִאשׁוֹן בִּשְׁלוֹשָׁה עָשָׂר יוֹם בּוֹ וַיִּכָּתֵב כְּכָל־אֲשֶׁר־צִוָּה הָמָן אֶל אֲחַשְׁדַּרְפְּנֵי־הַמֶּלֶךְ וְאֶל־הַפַּחוֹת אֲשֶׁר | עַל־ מְדִינָה וּמְדִינָה וְאֶל־שָׂרֵי עַם וָעָם מְדִינָה וּמְדִינָה כִּכְתָבָהּ וְעַם וָעָם כִּלְשׁוֹנוֹ בְּשֵׁם הַמֶּלֶךְ אֲחַשְׁוֵרֹשׁ נִכְתָּב וְנֶחְתָּם בְּטַבַּעַת הַמֶּלֶךְ: 13 וְנִשְׁלוֹחַ סְפָרִים בְּיַד הָרָצִים אֶל־כָּל־מְדִינוֹת הַמֶּלֶךְ לְהַשְׁמִיד לַהֲרֹג וּלְאַבֵּד אֶת־כָּל־הַיְּהוּדִים מִנַּעַר וְעַד־זָקֵן טַף וְנָשִׁים בְּיוֹם אֶחָד בִּשְׁלוֹשָׁה עָשָׂר לְחֹדֶשׁ שְׁנֵים־עָשָׂר הוּא־חֹדֶשׁ אֲדָר וּשְׁלָלָם לָבוֹז: 14 פַּתְשֶׁגֶן הַכְּתָב לְהִנָּתֵן דָּת בְּכָל־מְדִינָה וּמְדִינָה גָּלוּי לְכָל־הָעַמִּים לִהְיוֹת עֲתִדִים לַיּוֹם הַזֶּה: 15 הָרָצִים יָצְאוּ דְחוּפִים בִּדְבַר הַמֶּלֶךְ וְהַדָּת נִתְּנָה בְּשׁוּשַׁן הַבִּירָה וְהַמֶּלֶךְ וְהָמָן יָשְׁבוּ לִשְׁתּוֹת וְהָעִיר שׁוּשָׁן נָבוֹכָה: פ

ד וּמָרְדֳּכַי יָדַע אֶת־כָּל־אֲשֶׁר נַעֲשָׂה וַיִּקְרַע מָרְדֳּכַי אֶת־בְּגָדָיו וַיִּלְבַּשׁ שַׂק וָאֵפֶר וַיֵּצֵא בְּתוֹךְ הָעִיר וַיִּזְעַק זְעָקָה גְדֹלָה וּמָרָה: 2 וַיָּבוֹא עַד לִפְנֵי שַׁעַר־ הַמֶּלֶךְ כִּי אֵין לָבוֹא אֶל־שַׁעַר הַמֶּלֶךְ בִּלְבוּשׁ שָׂק: 3 וּבְכָל־מְדִינָה וּמְדִינָה מְקוֹם אֲשֶׁר דְּבַר־ הַמֶּלֶךְ וְדָתוֹ מַגִּיעַ אֵבֶל גָּדוֹל לַיְּהוּדִים וְצוֹם וּבְכִי וּמִסְפֵּד שַׂק וָאֵפֶר יֻצַּע לָרַבִּים: 4 וַתָּבוֹאינָה נַעֲרוֹת אֶסְתֵּר וְסָרִיסֶיהָ וַיַּגִּידוּ לָהּ וַתִּתְחַלְחַל הַמַּלְכָּה מְאֹד וַתִּשְׁלַח בְּגָדִים לְהַלְבִּישׁ אֶת־מָרְדֳּכַי וּלְהָסִיר שַׂקּוֹ מֵעָלָיו וְלֹא קִבֵּל: 5 וַתִּקְרָא אֶסְתֵּר לַהֲתָךְ מִסָּרִיסֵי הַמֶּלֶךְ אֲשֶׁר הֶעֱמִיד לְפָנֶיהָ וַתְּצַוֵּהוּ עַל־ מָרְדֳּכָי לָדַעַת מַה־זֶּה וְעַל־מַה־זֶּה: 6 וַיֵּצֵא הֲתָךְ אֶל־מָרְדֳּכָי אֶל־רְחוֹב הָעִיר אֲשֶׁר לִפְנֵי שַׁעַר־ הַמֶּלֶךְ: 7 וַיַּגֶּד־לוֹ מָרְדֳּכַי אֵת כָּל־אֲשֶׁר קָרָהוּ וְאֵת | פָּרָשַׁת הַכֶּסֶף אֲשֶׁר אָמַר הָמָן לִשְׁקוֹל עַל־גִּנְזֵי הַמֶּלֶךְ בַּיְּהוּדִיים לְאַבְּדָם: 8 וְאֶת־פַּתְשֶׁגֶן

ד 4 וַתָּבוֹאנָה 7 בַּיְּהוּדִים

destruction, which was given at Shushan, that he might show it to Esther and explain it to her, and that he might command her to go in to the king to make supplication to him and plead before him for her people. 9 So Hathach returned and told Esther the words of Mordecai.

10 Then Esther spoke to Hathach, and gave him a command for Mordecai: 11 "All the king's servants and the people of the king's provinces know that any man or woman who goes into the inner court to the king, who has not been called, *he has* but one law: put *all* to death, except the one to whom the king holds out the golden scepter, that he may live. Yet I myself have not been called to go in to the king these thirty days." 12 So they told Mordecai Esther's words.

13 And Mordecai told *them* to answer Esther: "Do not think in your heart that you will escape in the king's palace any more than all the other Jews. 14 For if you remain completely silent at this time, relief and deliverance will arise for the Jews from another place, but you and your father's house will perish. Yet who knows whether you have come to the kingdom for *such* a time as this?"

15 Then Esther told *them* to reply to Mordecai: 16 "Go, gather all the Jews who are present in Shushan, and fast for me; neither eat nor drink for three days, night or day. My maids and I will fast likewise. And so I will go to the king, which *is* against the law; and if I perish, I perish!"

17 So Mordecai went his way and did according to all that Esther commanded him.

5 Now it happened on the third day that Esther put on *her* royal *robes* and stood in the inner court of the king's palace, across from the king's house, while the king sat on his royal throne in the royal house, facing the entrance of the house. 2 So it was, when the king saw Queen Esther standing in the court, *that* she found favor in his sight, and the king held out to Esther the golden scepter that *was* in his hand. Then Esther went near and touched the top of the scepter.

3 And the king said to her, "What do you wish, Queen Esther? What *is* your request? It shall be given to you—up to half the kingdom!"

4 So Esther answered, "If it pleases the king, let the king and Haman come today to the banquet that I have prepared for him."

5 Then the king said, "Bring Haman quickly, that he may do as Esther has said." So the king and Haman went to the banquet that Esther had prepared.

כְּתָב־הַדָּת אֲשֶׁר־נִתַּן בְּשׁוּשָׁן לְהַשְׁמִידָם נָתַן לוֹ
לְהַרְאוֹת אֶת־אֶסְתֵּר וּלְהַגִּיד לָהּ וּלְצַוּוֹת עָלֶיהָ
לָבוֹא אֶל־הַמֶּלֶךְ לְהִתְחַנֶּן־לוֹ וּלְבַקֵּשׁ מִלְּפָנָיו עַל־
עַמָּהּ: 9 וַיָּבוֹא הֲתָךְ וַיַּגֵּד לְאֶסְתֵּר אֵת דִּבְרֵי
מָרְדֳּכָי: 10 וַתֹּאמֶר אֶסְתֵּר לַהֲתָךְ וַתְּצַוֵּהוּ אֶל־
מָרְדֳּכָי: 11 כָּל־עַבְדֵי הַמֶּלֶךְ וְעַם־מְדִינוֹת הַמֶּלֶךְ
יֹדְעִים אֲשֶׁר כָּל־אִישׁ וְאִשָּׁה אֲשֶׁר־יָבוֹא־אֶל־הַמֶּלֶךְ
אֶל־הֶחָצֵר הַפְּנִימִית אֲשֶׁר לֹא־יִקָּרֵא אַחַת דָּתוֹ
לְהָמִית לְבַד מֵאֲשֶׁר יוֹשִׁיט־לוֹ הַמֶּלֶךְ אֶת־שַׁרְבִיט
הַזָּהָב וְחָיָה וַאֲנִי לֹא נִקְרֵאתִי לָבוֹא אֶל־הַמֶּלֶךְ
זֶה שְׁלוֹשִׁים יוֹם: 12 וַיַּגִּידוּ לְמָרְדֳּכָי אֵת דִּבְרֵי
אֶסְתֵּר: פ
13 וַיֹּאמֶר מָרְדֳּכַי לְהָשִׁיב אֶל־אֶסְתֵּר אַל־תְּדַמִּי
בְנַפְשֵׁךְ לְהִמָּלֵט בֵּית־הַמֶּלֶךְ מִכָּל־הַיְּהוּדִים: 14 כִּי
אִם־הַחֲרֵשׁ תַּחֲרִישִׁי בָּעֵת הַזֹּאת רֶוַח וְהַצָּלָה
יַעֲמוֹד לַיְּהוּדִים מִמָּקוֹם אַחֵר וְאַתְּ וּבֵית־אָבִיךְ
תֹּאבֵדוּ וּמִי יוֹדֵעַ אִם־לְעֵת כָּזֹאת הִגַּעַתְּ לַמַּלְכוּת:
15 וַתֹּאמֶר אֶסְתֵּר לְהָשִׁיב אֶל־מָרְדֳּכָי: 16 לֵךְ כְּנוֹס
אֶת־כָּל־הַיְּהוּדִים הַנִּמְצְאִים בְּשׁוּשָׁן וְצוּמוּ עָלַי
וְאַל־תֹּאכְלוּ וְאַל־תִּשְׁתּוּ שְׁלֹשֶׁת יָמִים לַיְלָה וָיוֹם
גַּם־אֲנִי וְנַעֲרֹתַי אָצוּם כֵּן וּבְכֵן אָבוֹא אֶל־הַמֶּלֶךְ
אֲשֶׁר לֹא־כַדָּת וְכַאֲשֶׁר אָבַדְתִּי אָבָדְתִּי: 17 וַיַּעֲבֹר
מָרְדֳּכָי וַיַּעַשׂ כְּכֹל אֲשֶׁר־צִוְּתָה עָלָיו אֶסְתֵּר: ס

ה וַיְהִי בַּיּוֹם הַשְּׁלִישִׁי וַתִּלְבַּשׁ אֶסְתֵּר
מַלְכוּת וַתַּעֲמֹד בַּחֲצַר בֵּית־הַמֶּלֶךְ הַפְּנִימִית נֹכַח
בֵּית הַמֶּלֶךְ וְהַמֶּלֶךְ יוֹשֵׁב עַל־כִּסֵּא מַלְכוּתוֹ
בְּבֵית הַמַּלְכוּת נֹכַח פֶּתַח הַבָּיִת: 2 וַיְהִי כִרְאוֹת
הַמֶּלֶךְ אֶת־אֶסְתֵּר הַמַּלְכָּה עֹמֶדֶת בֶּחָצֵר נָשְׂאָה
חֵן בְּעֵינָיו וַיּוֹשֶׁט הַמֶּלֶךְ לְאֶסְתֵּר אֶת־שַׁרְבִיט
הַזָּהָב אֲשֶׁר בְּיָדוֹ וַתִּקְרַב אֶסְתֵּר וַתִּגַּע בְּרֹאשׁ
הַשַּׁרְבִיט: ס 3 וַיֹּאמֶר לָהּ הַמֶּלֶךְ מַה־לָּךְ
אֶסְתֵּר הַמַּלְכָּה וּמַה־בַּקָּשָׁתֵךְ עַד־חֲצִי הַמַּלְכוּת
וְיִנָּתֵן לָךְ: 4 וַתֹּאמֶר אֶסְתֵּר אִם־עַל־הַמֶּלֶךְ טוֹב
יָבוֹא הַמֶּלֶךְ וְהָמָן הַיּוֹם אֶל־הַמִּשְׁתֶּה אֲשֶׁר־עָשִׂיתִי
לוֹ: 5 וַיֹּאמֶר הַמֶּלֶךְ מַהֲרוּ אֶת־הָמָן לַעֲשׂוֹת אֶת־
דְּבַר אֶסְתֵּר וַיָּבֹא הַמֶּלֶךְ וְהָמָן אֶל־הַמִּשְׁתֶּה אֲשֶׁר־

⁶At the banquet of wine the king said to Esther, "What *is* your petition? It shall be granted you. What *is* your request, up to half the kingdom? It shall be done!"

⁷Then Esther answered and said, "My petition and request *is this:* ⁸If I have found favor in the sight of the king, and if it pleases the king to grant my petition and fulfill my request, then let the king and Haman come to the banquet which I will prepare for them, and tomorrow I will do as the king has said."

⁹So Haman went out that day joyful and with a glad heart; but when Haman saw Mordecai in the king's gate, and that he did not stand or tremble before him, he was filled with indignation against Mordecai. ¹⁰Nevertheless Haman restrained himself and went home, and he sent and called for his friends and his wife Zeresh. ¹¹Then Haman told them of his great riches, the multitude of his children, everything in which the king had promoted him, and how he had advanced him above the officials and servants of the king.

¹²Moreover Haman said, "Besides, Queen Esther invited no one but me to come in with the king to the banquet that she prepared; and tomorrow I am again invited by her, along with the king. ¹³Yet all this avails me nothing, so long as I see Mordecai the Jew sitting at the king's gate."

¹⁴Then his wife Zeresh and all his friends said to him, "Let a gallows be made, fifty cubits high, and in the morning suggest to the king that Mordecai be hanged on it; then go merrily with the king to the banquet."

And the thing pleased Haman; so he had the gallows made.

6 That night the king could not sleep. So one was commanded to bring the book of the records of the chronicles; and they were read before the king. ²And it was found written that Mordecai had told of Bigthana and Teresh, two of the king's eunuchs, the doorkeepers who had sought to lay hands on King Ahasuerus. ³Then the king said, "What honor or dignity has been bestowed on Mordecai for this?"

And the king's servants who attended him said, "Nothing has been done for him."

⁴So the king said, "Who *is* in the court?" Now Haman had *just* entered the outer court of the king's palace to suggest that the king hang Mordecai on the gallows that he had prepared for him.

⁵The king's servants said to him, "Haman is there, standing in the court."

וַיֹּ֨אמֶר הַמֶּ֤לֶךְ לְאֶסְתֵּר֙ בְּמִשְׁתֵּ֣ה 6 :עֲשָׂ֖תָה אֶסְתֵּ֑ר
הַיַּ֗יִן מַה־שְּׁאֵלָתֵ֛ךְ וְיִנָּ֥תֵֽן לָ֖ךְ וּמַה־בַּקָּשָׁתֵ֛ךְ עַד־חֲצִ֥י
הַמַּלְכ֖וּת וְתֵעָֽשׂ׃ 7 וַתַּ֥עַן אֶסְתֵּ֖ר וַתֹּאמַ֑ר שְׁאֵלָתִ֖י
וּבַקָּשָׁתִֽי׃ 8 אִם־מָצָ֨אתִי חֵ֜ן בְּעֵינֵ֣י הַמֶּ֗לֶךְ וְאִם־
עַל־הַמֶּ֨לֶךְ֙ ט֔וֹב לָתֵת֙ אֶת־שְׁאֵ֣לָתִ֔י וְלַעֲשׂ֖וֹת אֶת־
בַּקָּשָׁתִ֑י יָב֧וֹא הַמֶּ֣לֶךְ וְהָמָ֗ן אֶל־הַמִּשְׁתֶּה֙ אֲשֶׁ֣ר
אֶֽעֱשֶׂ֣ה לָהֶ֔ם וּמָחָ֥ר אֶֽעֱשֶׂ֖ה כִּדְבַ֥ר הַמֶּֽלֶךְ׃ 9 וַיֵּצֵ֤א
הָמָן֙ בַּיּ֣וֹם הַה֔וּא שָׂמֵ֖חַ וְט֣וֹב לֵ֑ב וְכִרְא֨וֹת הָמָ֜ן
אֶֽת־מָרְדֳּכַ֣י בְּשַֽׁעַר הַמֶּ֗לֶךְ וְלֹא־קָם֙ וְלֹא־זָ֣ע מִמֶּ֔נּוּ
וַיִּמָּלֵ֥א הָמָ֛ן עַֽל־מָרְדֳּכַ֖י חֵמָֽה׃ 10 וַיִּתְאַפַּ֣ק הָמָ֗ן
וַיָּב֣וֹא אֶל־בֵּית֔וֹ וַיִּשְׁלַ֖ח וַיָּבֵ֣א אֶת־אֹֽהֲבָ֑יו וְאֶת־
זֶ֖רֶשׁ אִשְׁתּֽוֹ׃ 11 וַיְסַפֵּ֨ר לָהֶ֥ם הָמָ֛ן אֶת־כְּב֥וֹד עָשְׁר֖וֹ
וְרֹ֣ב בָּנָ֑יו וְאֵת֩ כָּל־אֲשֶׁ֨ר גִּדְּל֤וֹ הַמֶּ֨לֶךְ֙ וְאֵ֣ת אֲשֶׁ֣ר
נִשְּׂא֔וֹ עַל־הַשָּׂרִ֖ים וְעַבְדֵ֥י הַמֶּֽלֶךְ׃ 12 וַיֹּ֨אמֶר֙ הָמָ֔ן
אַ֣ף לֹא־הֵבִיאָה֩ אֶסְתֵּ֨ר הַמַּלְכָּ֧ה עִם־הַמֶּ֛לֶךְ אֶל־
הַמִּשְׁתֶּ֥ה אֲשֶׁר־עָשָׂ֖תָה כִּ֣י אִם־אוֹתִ֑י וְגַם־לְמָחָ֛ר
אֲנִ֥י קָֽרוּא־לָ֖הּ עִם־הַמֶּֽלֶךְ׃ 13 וְכָל־זֶ֕ה אֵינֶ֥נּוּ שֹׁוֶ֖ה
לִ֑י בְּכָל־עֵ֗ת אֲשֶׁ֨ר אֲנִ֤י רֹאֶה֙ אֶת־מָרְדֳּכַ֣י הַיְּהוּדִ֔י
יוֹשֵׁ֖ב בְּשַׁ֥עַר הַמֶּֽלֶךְ׃ 14 וַתֹּ֣אמֶר לוֹ֩ זֶ֨רֶשׁ אִשְׁתּ֜וֹ
וְכָל־אֹֽהֲבָ֗יו יַֽעֲשׂוּ־עֵץ֮ גָּבֹ֣הַּ חֲמִשִּׁ֣ים אַמָּה֒ וּבַבֹּ֣קֶר ׀
אֱמֹ֣ר לַמֶּ֗לֶךְ וְיִתְל֤וּ אֶֽת־מָרְדֳּכַי֙ עָלָ֔יו וּבֹֽא־עִם־הַמֶּ֥לֶךְ
אֶל־הַמִּשְׁתֶּ֖ה שָׂמֵ֑חַ וַיִּיטַ֧ב הַדָּבָ֛ר לִפְנֵ֥י הָמָ֖ן וַיַּ֥עַשׂ
הָעֵֽץ׃ פ

בַּלַּ֣יְלָה הַה֔וּא נָֽדְדָ֖ה שְׁנַ֣ת הַמֶּ֑לֶךְ וַיֹּ֗אמֶר לְהָבִ֞יא ו
אֶת־סֵ֤פֶר הַזִּכְרֹנוֹת֙ דִּבְרֵ֣י הַיָּמִ֔ים וַיִּֽהְי֥וּ נִקְרָאִ֖ים
לִפְנֵ֥י הַמֶּֽלֶךְ׃ 2 וַיִּמָּצֵ֣א כָת֗וּב אֲשֶׁר֩ הִגִּ֨יד מָרְדֳּכַ֜י
עַל־בִּגְתָ֣נָא וָתֶ֗רֶשׁ שְׁנֵי֙ סָֽרִיסֵ֣י הַמֶּ֔לֶךְ מִשֹּֽׁמְרֵ֖י הַסַּ֑ף
אֲשֶׁ֤ר בִּקְשׁוּ֙ לִשְׁלֹ֣חַ יָ֔ד בַּמֶּ֖לֶךְ אֲחַשְׁוֵרֽוֹשׁ׃ 3 וַיֹּ֣אמֶר
הַמֶּ֔לֶךְ מַֽה־נַּֽעֲשָׂ֞ה יְקָ֧ר וּגְדוּלָ֛ה לְמָרְדֳּכַ֖י עַל־זֶ֑ה
וַיֹּ֨אמְר֜וּ נַֽעֲרֵ֤י הַמֶּ֨לֶךְ֙ מְשָׁ֣רְתָ֔יו לֹֽא־נַֽעֲשָׂ֥ה עִמּ֖וֹ דָּבָֽר׃
4 וַיֹּ֣אמֶר הַמֶּ֔לֶךְ מִ֖י בֶֽחָצֵ֑ר וְהָמָ֣ן בָּ֗א לַֽחֲצַ֤ר בֵּית־
הַמֶּ֨לֶךְ֙ הַחִ֣יצוֹנָ֔ה לֵאמֹ֣ר לַמֶּ֔לֶךְ לִתְל֙וֹת֙ אֶֽת־מָרְדֳּכַ֔י
עַל־הָעֵ֖ץ אֲשֶׁר־הֵכִ֥ין לֽוֹ׃ 5 וַיֹּ֨אמְר֜וּ נַֽעֲרֵ֤י הַמֶּ֨לֶךְ֙
אֵלָ֔יו הִנֵּ֥ה הָמָ֖ן עֹמֵ֣ד בֶּֽחָצֵ֑ר וַיֹּ֥אמֶר הַמֶּ֖לֶךְ יָבֽוֹא׃

And the king said, "Let him come in."

6 So Haman came in, and the king asked him, "What shall be done for the man whom the king delights to honor?"

Now Haman thought in his heart, "Whom would the king delight to honor more than me?" 7 And Haman answered the king, "*For* the man whom the king delights to honor, 8 let a royal robe be brought which the king has worn, and a horse on which the king has ridden, which has a royal crest placed on its head. 9 Then let this robe and horse be delivered to the hand of one of the king's most noble princes, that he may array the man whom the king delights to honor. Then parade him on horseback through the city square, and proclaim before him: 'Thus shall it be done to the man whom the king delights to honor!' "

10 Then the king said to Haman, "Hurry, take the robe and the horse, as you have suggested, and do so for Mordecai the Jew who sits within the king's gate! Leave nothing undone of all that you have spoken."

11 So Haman took the robe and the horse, arrayed Mordecai and led him on horseback through the city square, and proclaimed before him, "Thus shall it be done to the man whom the king delights to honor!"

12 Afterward Mordecai went back to the king's gate. But Haman hurried to his house, mourning and with his head covered. 13 When Haman told his wife Zeresh and all his friends everything that had happened to him, his wise men and his wife Zeresh said to him, "If Mordecai, before whom you have begun to fall, is of Jewish descent, you will not prevail against him but will surely fall before him."

14 While they *were* still talking with him, the king's eunuchs came, and hastened to bring Haman to the banquet which Esther had prepared.

7 So the king and Haman went to dine with Queen Esther. 2 And on the second day, at the banquet of wine, the king again said to Esther, "What *is* your petition, Queen Esther? It shall be granted you. And what *is* your request, up to half the kingdom? It shall be done!"

3 Then Queen Esther answered and said, "If I have found favor in your sight, O king, and if it pleases the king, let my life be given me at my petition, and my people at my request. 4 For we have been sold, my people and I, to be destroyed, to be killed, and to be annihilated. Had we been sold as male and female slaves, I would have held my tongue, although the enemy could never compensate for the king's loss."

6 וַיָּבוֹא הָמָן וַיֹּאמֶר לוֹ הַמֶּלֶךְ מַה־לַעֲשׂוֹת בָּאִישׁ אֲשֶׁר הַמֶּלֶךְ חָפֵץ בִּיקָרוֹ וַיֹּאמֶר הָמָן בְּלִבּוֹ לְמִי יַחְפֹּץ הַמֶּלֶךְ לַעֲשׂוֹת יְקָר יוֹתֵר מִמֶּנִּי׃ 7 וַיֹּאמֶר הָמָן אֶל־הַמֶּלֶךְ אִישׁ אֲשֶׁר הַמֶּלֶךְ חָפֵץ בִּיקָרוֹ׃ 8 יָבִיאוּ לְבוּשׁ מַלְכוּת אֲשֶׁר לָבַשׁ־בּוֹ הַמֶּלֶךְ וְסוּס אֲשֶׁר רָכַב עָלָיו הַמֶּלֶךְ וַאֲשֶׁר נִתַּן כֶּתֶר מַלְכוּת בְּרֹאשׁוֹ׃ 9 וְנָתוֹן הַלְּבוּשׁ וְהַסּוּס עַל־יַד־אִישׁ מִשָּׂרֵי הַמֶּלֶךְ הַפַּרְתְּמִים וְהִלְבִּישׁוּ אֶת־הָאִישׁ אֲשֶׁר הַמֶּלֶךְ חָפֵץ בִּיקָרוֹ וְהִרְכִּיבֻהוּ עַל־הַסּוּס בִּרְחוֹב הָעִיר וְקָרְאוּ לְפָנָיו כָּכָה יֵעָשֶׂה לָאִישׁ אֲשֶׁר הַמֶּלֶךְ חָפֵץ בִּיקָרוֹ׃ 10 וַיֹּאמֶר הַמֶּלֶךְ לְהָמָן מַהֵר קַח אֶת־הַלְּבוּשׁ וְאֶת־הַסּוּס כַּאֲשֶׁר דִּבַּרְתָּ וַעֲשֵׂה־כֵן לְמָרְדֳּכַי הַיְּהוּדִי הַיּוֹשֵׁב בְּשַׁעַר הַמֶּלֶךְ אַל־תַּפֵּל דָּבָר מִכֹּל אֲשֶׁר דִּבַּרְתָּ׃ 11 וַיִּקַּח הָמָן אֶת־הַלְּבוּשׁ וְאֶת־הַסּוּס וַיַּלְבֵּשׁ אֶת־מָרְדֳּכָי וַיַּרְכִּיבֵהוּ בִּרְחוֹב הָעִיר וַיִּקְרָא לְפָנָיו כָּכָה יֵעָשֶׂה לָאִישׁ אֲשֶׁר הַמֶּלֶךְ חָפֵץ בִּיקָרוֹ׃ 12 וַיָּשָׁב מָרְדֳּכַי אֶל־שַׁעַר הַמֶּלֶךְ וְהָמָן נִדְחַף אֶל־בֵּיתוֹ אָבֵל וַחֲפוּי רֹאשׁ׃ 13 וַיְסַפֵּר הָמָן לְזֶרֶשׁ אִשְׁתּוֹ וּלְכָל־אֹהֲבָיו אֵת כָּל־אֲשֶׁר קָרָהוּ וַיֹּאמְרוּ לוֹ חֲכָמָיו וְזֶרֶשׁ אִשְׁתּוֹ אִם מִזֶּרַע הַיְּהוּדִים מָרְדֳּכַי אֲשֶׁר הַחִלּוֹתָ לִנְפֹּל לְפָנָיו לֹא־תוּכַל לוֹ כִּי־נָפוֹל תִּפּוֹל לְפָנָיו׃ 14 עוֹדָם מְדַבְּרִים עִמּוֹ וְסָרִיסֵי הַמֶּלֶךְ הִגִּיעוּ וַיַּבְהִלוּ לְהָבִיא אֶת־הָמָן אֶל־הַמִּשְׁתֶּה אֲשֶׁר־עָשְׂתָה אֶסְתֵּר׃

ז וַיָּבֹא הַמֶּלֶךְ וְהָמָן לִשְׁתּוֹת עִם־אֶסְתֵּר הַמַּלְכָּה׃ 2 וַיֹּאמֶר הַמֶּלֶךְ לְאֶסְתֵּר גַּם בַּיּוֹם הַשֵּׁנִי בְּמִשְׁתֵּה הַיַּיִן מַה־שְּׁאֵלָתֵךְ אֶסְתֵּר הַמַּלְכָּה וְתִנָּתֵן לָךְ וּמַה־בַּקָּשָׁתֵךְ עַד־חֲצִי הַמַּלְכוּת וְתֵעָשׂ׃ 3 וַתַּעַן אֶסְתֵּר הַמַּלְכָּה וַתֹּאמַר אִם־מָצָאתִי חֵן בְּעֵינֶיךָ הַמֶּלֶךְ וְאִם־עַל־הַמֶּלֶךְ טוֹב תִּנָּתֶן־לִי נַפְשִׁי בִּשְׁאֵלָתִי וְעַמִּי בְּבַקָּשָׁתִי׃ 4 כִּי נִמְכַּרְנוּ אֲנִי וְעַמִּי לְהַשְׁמִיד לַהֲרוֹג וּלְאַבֵּד וְאִלּוּ לַעֲבָדִים וְלִשְׁפָחוֹת נִמְכַּרְנוּ הֶחֱרַשְׁתִּי

⁵So King Ahasuerus answered and said to Queen Esther, "Who is he, and where is he, who would dare presume in his heart to do such a thing?"

⁶And Esther said, "The adversary and enemy *is* this wicked Haman!"

So Haman was terrified before the king and queen.

⁷Then the king arose in his wrath from the banquet of wine *and went* into the palace garden; but Haman stood before Queen Esther, pleading for his life, for he saw that evil was determined against him by the king. ⁸When the king returned from the palace garden to the place of the banquet of wine, Haman had fallen across the couch where Esther *was*. Then the king said, "Will he also assault the queen while I *am* in the house?"

As the word left the king's mouth, they covered Haman's face. ⁹Now Harbonah, one of the eunuchs, said to the king, "Look! The gallows, fifty cubits high, which Haman made for Mordecai, who spoke good on the king's behalf, is standing at the house of Haman."

Then the king said, "Hang him on it!"

¹⁰So they hanged Haman on the gallows that he had prepared for Mordecai. Then the king's wrath subsided.

8 On that day King Ahasuerus gave Queen Esther the house of Haman, the enemy of the Jews. And Mordecai came before the king, for Esther had told how he *was related* to her. ²So the king took off his signet ring, which he had taken from Haman, and gave it to Mordecai; and Esther appointed Mordecai over the house of Haman.

³Now Esther spoke again to the king, fell down at his feet, and implored him with tears to counteract the evil of Haman the Agagite, and the scheme which he had devised against the Jews. ⁴And the king held out the golden scepter toward Esther. So Esther arose and stood before the king, ⁵and said, "If it pleases the king, and if I have found favor in his sight and the thing *seems* right to the king and I am pleasing in his eyes, let it be written to revoke the letters devised by Haman, the son of Hammedatha the Agagite, which he wrote to annihilate the Jews who *are* in all the king's provinces. ⁶For how can I endure to see the evil that will come to my people? Or how can I endure to see the destruction of my countrymen?"

⁷Then King Ahasuerus said to Queen Esther and Mordecai the Jew, "Indeed, I have given Esther the house of Haman, and they have hanged him on the gallows because he *tried to* lay his hand on the Jews. ⁸You yourselves write *a decree* concerning the Jews,

---

5 ס וַיֹּאמֶר כִּי אֵין הַצָּר שֹׁוֶה בְּנֵזֶק הַמֶּלֶךְ:
הַמֶּלֶךְ אֲחַשְׁוֵרוֹשׁ וַיֹּאמֶר לְאֶסְתֵּר הַמַּלְכָּה מִי הוּא
זֶה וְאֵי־זֶה הוּא אֲשֶׁר־מְלָאוֹ לִבּוֹ לַעֲשׂוֹת כֵּן:
6 וַתֹּאמֶר אֶסְתֵּר אִישׁ צַר וְאוֹיֵב הָמָן הָרָע הַזֶּה
וְהָמָן נִבְעַת מִלִּפְנֵי הַמֶּלֶךְ וְהַמַּלְכָּה: 7 וְהַמֶּלֶךְ
קָם בַּחֲמָתוֹ מִמִּשְׁתֵּה הַיַּיִן אֶל־גִּנַּת הַבִּיתָן וְהָמָן
עָמַד לְבַקֵּשׁ עַל־נַפְשׁוֹ מֵאֶסְתֵּר הַמַּלְכָּה כִּי רָאָה
כִּי־כָלְתָה אֵלָיו הָרָעָה מֵאֵת הַמֶּלֶךְ: 8 וְהַמֶּלֶךְ
שָׁב מִגִּנַּת הַבִּיתָן אֶל־בֵּית ׀ מִשְׁתֵּה הַיַּיִן וְהָמָן
נֹפֵל עַל־הַמִּטָּה אֲשֶׁר אֶסְתֵּר עָלֶיהָ וַיֹּאמֶר הַמֶּלֶךְ
הֲגַם לִכְבּוֹשׁ אֶת־הַמַּלְכָּה עִמִּי בַּבָּיִת הַדָּבָר יָצָא
מִפִּי הַמֶּלֶךְ וּפְנֵי הָמָן חָפוּ: ס 9 וַיֹּאמֶר
חַרְבוֹנָה אֶחָד מִן־הַסָּרִיסִים לִפְנֵי הַמֶּלֶךְ גַּם הִנֵּה־
הָעֵץ אֲשֶׁר־עָשָׂה הָמָן לְמָרְדֳּכַי אֲשֶׁר דִּבֶּר־טוֹב
עַל־הַמֶּלֶךְ עֹמֵד בְּבֵית הָמָן גָּבֹהַּ חֲמִשִּׁים אַמָּה
וַיֹּאמֶר הַמֶּלֶךְ תְּלֻהוּ עָלָיו: 10 וַיִּתְלוּ אֶת־הָמָן עַל־
הָעֵץ אֲשֶׁר־הֵכִין לְמָרְדֳּכָי וַחֲמַת הַמֶּלֶךְ שָׁכָכָה: פ

ח בַּיּוֹם הַהוּא נָתַן הַמֶּלֶךְ אֲחַשְׁוֵרוֹשׁ לְאֶסְתֵּר
הַמַּלְכָּה אֶת־בֵּית הָמָן צֹרֵר הַיְּהוּדִיים וּמָרְדֳּכַי
בָּא לִפְנֵי הַמֶּלֶךְ כִּי־הִגִּידָה אֶסְתֵּר מַה הוּא־לָהּ:
2 וַיָּסַר הַמֶּלֶךְ אֶת־טַבַּעְתּוֹ אֲשֶׁר הֶעֱבִיר מֵהָמָן
וַיִּתְּנָהּ לְמָרְדֳּכָי וַתָּשֶׂם אֶסְתֵּר אֶת־מָרְדֳּכַי עַל־בֵּית
הָמָן: פ

3 וַתּוֹסֶף אֶסְתֵּר וַתְּדַבֵּר לִפְנֵי הַמֶּלֶךְ וַתִּפֹּל לִפְנֵי
רַגְלָיו וַתֵּבְךְּ וַתִּתְחַנֶּן־לוֹ לְהַעֲבִיר אֶת־רָעַת הָמָן
הָאֲגָגִי וְאֵת מַחֲשַׁבְתּוֹ אֲשֶׁר חָשַׁב עַל־הַיְּהוּדִים:
4 וַיּוֹשֶׁט הַמֶּלֶךְ לְאֶסְתֵּר אֵת שַׁרְבִט הַזָּהָב וַתָּקָם
אֶסְתֵּר וַתַּעֲמֹד לִפְנֵי הַמֶּלֶךְ: 5 וַתֹּאמֶר אִם־עַל־
הַמֶּלֶךְ טוֹב וְאִם־מָצָאתִי חֵן לְפָנָיו וְכָשֵׁר הַדָּבָר
לִפְנֵי הַמֶּלֶךְ וְטוֹבָה אֲנִי בְּעֵינָיו יִכָּתֵב לְהָשִׁיב
אֶת־הַסְּפָרִים מַחֲשֶׁבֶת הָמָן בֶּן־הַמְּדָתָא הָאֲגָגִי
אֲשֶׁר כָּתַב לְאַבֵּד אֶת־הַיְּהוּדִים אֲשֶׁר בְּכָל־מְדִינוֹת
הַמֶּלֶךְ: 6 כִּי אֵיכָכָה אוּכַל וְרָאִיתִי בָּרָעָה אֲשֶׁר־
יִמְצָא אֶת־עַמִּי וְאֵיכָכָה אוּכַל וְרָאִיתִי בְּאָבְדַן
מוֹלַדְתִּי: 7 ס וַיֹּאמֶר הַמֶּלֶךְ אֲחַשְׁוֵרוֹשׁ
לְאֶסְתֵּר הַמַּלְכָּה וּלְמָרְדֳּכַי הַיְּהוּדִי הִנֵּה בֵית־
הָמָן נָתַתִּי לְאֶסְתֵּר וְאֹתוֹ תָּלוּ עַל־הָעֵץ עַל
אֲשֶׁר־שָׁלַח יָדוֹ בַּיְּהוּדִיִּים: 8 וְאַתֶּם כִּתְבוּ עַל־

as you please, in the king's name, and seal *it* with the king's signet ring; for whatever is written in the king's name and sealed with the king's signet ring no one can revoke."

⁹ So the king's scribes were called at that time, in the third month, which *is* the month of Sivan, on the twenty-third *day;* and it was written, according to all that Mordecai commanded, to the Jews, the satraps, the governors, and the princes of the provinces from India to Ethiopia, one hundred and twenty-seven provinces *in all,* to every province in its own script, to every people in their own language, and to the Jews in their own script and language. ¹⁰ And he wrote in the name of King Ahasuerus, sealed *it* with the king's signet ring, and sent letters by couriers on horseback, riding on royal horses bred from swift steeds.

¹¹ By these letters the king permitted the Jews who *were* in every city to gather together and protect their lives—to destroy, kill, and annihilate all the forces of any people or province that would assault them, *both* little children and women, and to plunder their possessions, ¹² on one day in all the provinces of King Ahasuerus, on the thirteenth *day* of the twelfth month, which *is* the month of Adar. ¹³ A copy of the document was to be issued as a decree in every province and published for all people, so that the Jews would be ready on that day to avenge themselves on their enemies. ¹⁴ The couriers who rode on royal horses went out, hastened and pressed on by the king's command. And the decree was issued in Shushan the citadel.

¹⁵ So Mordecai went out from the presence of the king in royal apparel of blue and white, with a great crown of gold and a garment of fine linen and purple; and the city of Shushan rejoiced and was glad. ¹⁶ The Jews had light and gladness, joy and honor. ¹⁷ And in every province and city, wherever the king's command and decree came, the Jews had joy and gladness, a feast and a holiday. Then many of the people of the land became Jews, because fear of the Jews fell upon them.

9 Now in the twelfth month, that *is,* the month of Adar, on the thirteenth day, *the time* came for the king's command and his decree to be executed. On the day that the enemies of the Jews had hoped to overpower them, the opposite occurred, in that the Jews themselves overpowered those who hated them. ² The Jews gathered together in their cities throughout all the provinces of King Ahasuerus to lay hands on those who sought their harm. And no one could withstand them, because fear of them fell upon all people. ³ And all the officials of the

הַיְּהוּדִים כַּטּוֹב בְּעֵינֵיכֶם בְּשֵׁם הַמֶּלֶךְ וְחִתְמוּ בְּטַבַּעַת הַמֶּלֶךְ כִּי־כְתָב אֲשֶׁר־נִכְתָּב בְּשֵׁם־הַמֶּלֶךְ וְנַחְתּוֹם בְּטַבַּעַת הַמֶּלֶךְ אֵין לְהָשִׁיב: ⁹ וַיִּקָּרְאוּ סֹפְרֵי־הַמֶּלֶךְ בָּעֵת־הַהִיא בַּחֹדֶשׁ הַשְּׁלִישִׁי הוּא־ חֹדֶשׁ סִיוָן בִּשְׁלוֹשָׁה וְעֶשְׂרִים בּוֹ וַיִּכָּתֵב כְּכָל־אֲשֶׁר־ צִוָּה מָרְדֳּכַי אֶל־הַיְּהוּדִים וְאֶל הָאֲחַשְׁדַּרְפְּנִים־ וְהַפַּחוֹת וְשָׂרֵי הַמְּדִינוֹת אֲשֶׁר | מֵהֹדּוּ וְעַד־ כּוּשׁ שֶׁבַע וְעֶשְׂרִים וּמֵאָה מְדִינָה מְדִינָה וּמְדִינָה כִּכְתָבָהּ וְעַם וָעָם כִּלְשֹׁנוֹ וְאֶל־הַיְּהוּדִים כִּכְתָבָם וְכִלְשׁוֹנָם: ¹⁰ וַיִּכְתֹּב בְּשֵׁם הַמֶּלֶךְ אֲחַשְׁוֵרֹשׁ וַיַּחְתֹּם בְּטַבַּעַת הַמֶּלֶךְ וַיִּשְׁלַח סְפָרִים בְּיַד הָרָצִים בַּסּוּסִים רֹכְבֵי הָרֶכֶשׁ הָאֲחַשְׁתְּרָנִים בְּנֵי הָרַמָּכִים: ¹¹ אֲשֶׁר נָתַן הַמֶּלֶךְ לַיְּהוּדִים | אֲשֶׁר בְּכָל־עִיר־ וָעִיר לְהִקָּהֵל וְלַעֲמֹד עַל־נַפְשָׁם לְהַשְׁמִיד וְלַהֲרֹג וּלְאַבֵּד אֶת־כָּל־חֵיל עַם וּמְדִינָה הַצָּרִים אֹתָם טַף וְנָשִׁים וּשְׁלָלָם לָבוֹז: ¹² בְּיוֹם אֶחָד בְּכָל־ מְדִינוֹת הַמֶּלֶךְ אֲחַשְׁוֵרוֹשׁ בִּשְׁלוֹשָׁה עָשָׂר לְחֹדֶשׁ שְׁנֵים־עָשָׂר הוּא־חֹדֶשׁ אֲדָר: ¹³ פַּתְשֶׁגֶן הַכְּתָב לְהִנָּתֵן דָּת בְּכָל־מְדִינָה וּמְדִינָה גָּלוּי לְכָל־הָעַמִּים וְלִהְיוֹת הַיְּהוּדִיים עֲתִידִים לַיּוֹם הַזֶּה לְהִנָּקֵם מֵאֹיְבֵיהֶם: ¹⁴ הָרָצִים רֹכְבֵי הָרֶכֶשׁ הָאֲחַשְׁתְּרָנִים יָצְאוּ מְבֹהָלִים וּדְחוּפִים בִּדְבַר הַמֶּלֶךְ וְהַדָּת נִתְּנָה בְּשׁוּשַׁן הַבִּירָה: פ

¹⁵ וּמָרְדֳּכַי יָצָא | מִלִּפְנֵי הַמֶּלֶךְ בִּלְבוּשׁ מַלְכוּת תְּכֵלֶת וָחוּר וַעֲטֶרֶת זָהָב גְּדוֹלָה וְתַכְרִיךְ בּוּץ וְאַרְגָּמָן וְהָעִיר שׁוּשָׁן צָהֲלָה וְשָׂמֵחָה: ¹⁶ לַיְּהוּדִים הָיְתָה אוֹרָה וְשִׂמְחָה וְשָׂשֹׂן וִיקָר: ¹⁷ וּבְכָל־מְדִינָה וּמְדִינָה וּבְכָל־עִיר וָעִיר מְקוֹם אֲשֶׁר דְּבַר־הַמֶּלֶךְ וְדָתוֹ מַגִּיעַ שִׂמְחָה וְשָׂשׂוֹן לַיְּהוּדִים מִשְׁתֶּה וְיוֹם טוֹב וְרַבִּים מֵעַמֵּי הָאָרֶץ מִתְיַהֲדִים כִּי־נָפַל פַּחַד־ הַיְּהוּדִים עֲלֵיהֶם:

ט וּבִשְׁנֵים עָשָׂר חֹדֶשׁ הוּא־חֹדֶשׁ אֲדָר בִּשְׁלוֹשָׁה עָשָׂר יוֹם בּוֹ אֲשֶׁר הִגִּיעַ דְּבַר־הַמֶּלֶךְ וְדָתוֹ לְהֵעָשׂוֹת בַּיּוֹם אֲשֶׁר שִׂבְּרוּ אֹיְבֵי הַיְּהוּדִים לִשְׁלוֹט בָּהֶם וְנַהֲפוֹךְ הוּא אֲשֶׁר יִשְׁלְטוּ הַיְּהוּדִים הֵמָּה בְּשֹׂנְאֵיהֶם: ² נִקְהֲלוּ הַיְּהוּדִים בְּעָרֵיהֶם בְּכָל־ מְדִינוֹת הַמֶּלֶךְ אֲחַשְׁוֵרוֹשׁ לִשְׁלֹחַ יָד בִּמְבַקְשֵׁי רָעָתָם וְאִישׁ לֹא־עָמַד לִפְנֵיהֶם כִּי־נָפַל פַּחְדָּם עַל־ כָּל־הָעַמִּים: ³ וְכָל־שָׂרֵי הַמְּדִינוֹת וְהָאֲחַשְׁדַּרְפְּנִים

ח 13 הַיְּהוּדִים, עֲתִידִים

provinces, the satraps, the governors, and all those doing the king's work, helped the Jews, because the fear of Mordecai fell upon them. [4] For Mordecai *was* great in the king's palace, and his fame spread throughout all the provinces; for this man Mordecai became increasingly prominent. [5] Thus the Jews defeated all their enemies with the stroke of the sword, with slaughter and destruction, and did what they pleased with those who hated them.

[6] And in Shushan the citadel the Jews killed and destroyed five hundred men. [7] Also Parshandatha, Dalphon, Aspatha, [8] Poratha, Adalia, Aridatha, [9] Parmashta, Arisai, Aridai, and Vajezatha— [10] the ten sons of Haman the son of Hammedatha, the enemy of the Jews—they killed; but they did not lay a hand on the plunder.

[11] On that day the number of those who were killed in Shushan the citadel was brought to the king. [12] And the king said to Queen Esther, "The Jews have killed and destroyed five hundred men in Shushan the citadel, and the ten sons of Haman. What have they done in the rest of the king's provinces? Now what *is* your petition? It shall be granted to you. Or what *is* your further request? It shall be done."

[13] Then Esther said, "If it pleases the king, let it be granted to the Jews who *are* in Shushan to do again tomorrow according to today's decree, and let Haman's ten sons be hanged on the gallows."

[14] So the king commanded this to be done; the decree was issued in Shushan, and they hanged Haman's ten sons.

[15] And the Jews who *were* in Shushan gathered together again on the fourteenth day of the month of Adar and killed three hundred men at Shushan; but they did not lay a hand on the plunder.

[16] The remainder of the Jews in the king's provinces gathered together and protected their lives, had rest from their enemies, and killed seventy-five thousand of their enemies; but they did not lay a hand on the plunder. [17] *This was* on the thirteenth day of the month of Adar. And on the fourteenth of *the month* they rested and made it a day of feasting and gladness.

[18] But the Jews who *were* at Shushan assembled together on the thirteenth *day*, as well as on the fourteenth; and on the fifteenth of *the month* they rested, and made it a day of feasting and gladness. [19] Therefore the Jews of the villages who dwelt in the unwalled towns celebrated the fourteenth day of the month of Adar *with* gladness and feasting, as a holiday, and for sending presents to one another.

וְהַפַּחוֹת וְעֹשֵׂי הַמְּלָאכָה אֲשֶׁר לַמֶּלֶךְ מְנַשְּׂאִים אֶת־הַיְּהוּדִים כִּי־נָפַל פַּחַד־מָרְדֳּכַי עֲלֵיהֶם: 4 כִּי־גָדוֹל מָרְדֳּכַי בְּבֵית הַמֶּלֶךְ וְשָׁמְעוֹ הוֹלֵךְ בְּכָל־הַמְּדִינוֹת כִּי־הָאִישׁ מָרְדֳּכַי הוֹלֵךְ וְגָדוֹל: פ 5 וַיַּכּוּ הַיְּהוּדִים בְּכָל־אֹיְבֵיהֶם מַכַּת־חֶרֶב וְהֶרֶג וְאַבְדָן וַיַּעֲשׂוּ בְשֹׂנְאֵיהֶם כִּרְצוֹנָם: 6 וּבְשׁוּשַׁן הַבִּירָה הָרְגוּ הַיְּהוּדִים וְאַבֵּד חֲמֵשׁ מֵאוֹת אִישׁ:

7 וְאֵת ׀ פַּרְשַׁנְדָּתָא	וְאֵת ׀
דַּלְפוֹן	וְאֵת ׀
8 אַסְפָּתָא:	וְאֵת ׀
פּוֹרָתָא	וְאֵת ׀
אֲדַלְיָא	וְאֵת ׀
9 אֲרִידָתָא:	וְאֵת ׀
פַּרְמַשְׁתָּא	וְאֵת ׀
אֲרִיסַי	וְאֵת ׀
אֲרִדַי	וְאֵת ׀
וַיְזָתָא:	

10 עֲשֶׂרֶת בְּנֵי הָמָן בֶּן־הַמְּדָתָא צֹרֵר הַיְּהוּדִים הָרָגוּ וּבַבִּזָּה לֹא שָׁלְחוּ אֶת־יָדָם: 11 בַּיּוֹם הַהוּא בָּא מִסְפַּר הַהֲרוּגִים בְּשׁוּשַׁן הַבִּירָה לִפְנֵי הַמֶּלֶךְ: ס 12 וַיֹּאמֶר הַמֶּלֶךְ לְאֶסְתֵּר הַמַּלְכָּה בְּשׁוּשַׁן הַבִּירָה הָרְגוּ הַיְּהוּדִים וְאַבֵּד חֲמֵשׁ מֵאוֹת אִישׁ וְאֵת עֲשֶׂרֶת בְּנֵי־הָמָן בִּשְׁאָר מְדִינוֹת הַמֶּלֶךְ מֶה עָשׂוּ וּמַה־שְּׁאֵלָתֵךְ וְיִנָּתֵן לָךְ וּמַה־בַּקָּשָׁתֵךְ עוֹד וְתֵעָשׂ: 13 וַתֹּאמֶר אֶסְתֵּר אִם־עַל־הַמֶּלֶךְ טוֹב יִנָּתֵן גַּם־מָחָר לַיְּהוּדִים אֲשֶׁר בְּשׁוּשָׁן לַעֲשׂוֹת כְּדָת הַיּוֹם וְאֵת עֲשֶׂרֶת בְּנֵי־הָמָן יִתְלוּ עַל־הָעֵץ: 14 וַיֹּאמֶר הַמֶּלֶךְ לְהֵעָשׂוֹת כֵּן וַתִּנָּתֵן דָּת בְּשׁוּשָׁן וְאֵת עֲשֶׂרֶת בְּנֵי־הָמָן תָּלוּ: 15 וַיִּקָּהֲלוּ הַיְּהוּדִיים[P] אֲשֶׁר־בְּשׁוּשָׁן גַּם בְּיוֹם אַרְבָּעָה עָשָׂר לְחֹדֶשׁ אֲדָר וַיַּהַרְגוּ בְשׁוּשָׁן שְׁלֹשׁ מֵאוֹת אִישׁ וּבַבִּזָּה לֹא שָׁלְחוּ אֶת־יָדָם: 16 וּשְׁאָר הַיְּהוּדִים אֲשֶׁר בִּמְדִינוֹת הַמֶּלֶךְ נִקְהֲלוּ ׀ וְעָמֹד עַל־נַפְשָׁם וְנוֹחַ מֵאֹיְבֵיהֶם וְהָרֹג בְּשֹׂנְאֵיהֶם חֲמִשָּׁה וְשִׁבְעִים אָלֶף וּבַבִּזָּה לֹא שָׁלְחוּ אֶת־יָדָם: 17 בְּיוֹם־שְׁלֹשָׁה עָשָׂר לְחֹדֶשׁ אֲדָר וְנוֹחַ בְּאַרְבָּעָה עָשָׂר בּוֹ וְעָשֹׂה אֹתוֹ יוֹם מִשְׁתֶּה וְשִׂמְחָה: 18 וְהַיְּהוּדִיים[P] אֲשֶׁר־בְּשׁוּשָׁן נִקְהֲלוּ בִּשְׁלֹשָׁה עָשָׂר בּוֹ וּבְאַרְבָּעָה עָשָׂר בּוֹ וְנוֹחַ בַּחֲמִשָּׁה עָשָׂר בּוֹ וְעָשֹׂה אֹתוֹ יוֹם מִשְׁתֶּה

20 And Mordecai wrote these things and sent letters to all the Jews, near and far, who *were* in all the provinces of King Ahasuerus, 21 to establish among them that they should celebrate yearly the fourteenth and fifteenth days of the month of Adar, 22 as the days on which the Jews had rest from their enemies, as the month which was turned from sorrow to joy for them, and from mourning to a holiday; that they should make them days of feasting and joy, of sending presents to one another and gifts to the poor. 23 So the Jews accepted the custom which they had begun, as Mordecai had written to them, 24 because Haman, the son of Hammedatha the Agagite, the enemy of all the Jews, had plotted against the Jews to annihilate them, and had cast Pur (that *is,* the lot), to consume them and destroy them; 25 but when *Esther* came before the king, he commanded by letter that this wicked plot which *Haman* had devised against the Jews should return on his own head, and that he and his sons should be hanged on the gallows.

26 So they called these days Purim, after the name Pur. Therefore, because of all the words of this letter, what they had seen concerning this matter, and what had happened to them, 27 the Jews established and imposed it upon themselves and their descendants and all who would join them, that without fail they should celebrate these two days every year, according to the written *instructions* and according to the *prescribed* time, 28 *that* these days *should be* remembered and kept throughout every generation, every family, every province, and every city, that these days of Purim should not fail *to be observed* among the Jews, and *that* the memory of them should not perish among their descendants.

29 Then Queen Esther, the daughter of Abihail, with Mordecai the Jew, wrote with full authority to confirm this second letter about Purim. 30 And *Mordecai* sent letters to all the Jews, to the one hundred and twenty-seven provinces of the kingdom of Ahasuerus, *with* words of peace and truth, 31 to confirm these days of Purim at their *appointed* time, as Mordecai the Jew and Queen Esther had prescribed for them, and as they had decreed for themselves and their descendants concerning matters of their fasting and lamenting. 32 So the decree of Esther confirmed these matters of Purim, and it was written in the book.

10 And King Ahasuerus imposed tribute on the land and *on* the islands of the sea. 2 Now all the acts of his power and his might, and the account of the greatness of Mordecai, to which the king advanced him, *are* they not written in the book of the

וְשִׂמְחָה: 19 עַל־כֵּן הַיְּהוּדִים הַפְּרָזִים הַיֹּשְׁבִים בְּעָרֵי הַפְּרָזוֹת עֹשִׂים אֵת יוֹם אַרְבָּעָה עָשָׂר לְחֹדֶשׁ אֲדָר שִׂמְחָה וּמִשְׁתֶּה וְיוֹם טוֹב וּמִשְׁלוֹחַ מָנוֹת אִישׁ לְרֵעֵהוּ: פ

20 וַיִּכְתֹּב מָרְדֳּכַי אֶת־הַדְּבָרִים הָאֵלֶּה וַיִּשְׁלַח סְפָרִים אֶל־כָּל־הַיְּהוּדִים אֲשֶׁר בְּכָל־מְדִינוֹת הַמֶּלֶךְ אֲחַשְׁוֵרוֹשׁ הַקְּרוֹבִים וְהָרְחוֹקִים: 21 לְקַיֵּם עֲלֵיהֶם לִהְיוֹת עֹשִׂים אֵת יוֹם אַרְבָּעָה עָשָׂר לְחֹדֶשׁ אֲדָר וְאֵת יוֹם־חֲמִשָּׁה עָשָׂר בּוֹ בְּכָל־שָׁנָה וְשָׁנָה: 22 כַּיָּמִים אֲשֶׁר־נָחוּ בָהֶם הַיְּהוּדִים מֵאוֹיְבֵיהֶם וְהַחֹדֶשׁ אֲשֶׁר נֶהְפַּךְ לָהֶם מִיָּגוֹן לְשִׂמְחָה וּמֵאֵבֶל לְיוֹם טוֹב לַעֲשׂוֹת אוֹתָם יְמֵי מִשְׁתֶּה וְשִׂמְחָה וּמִשְׁלוֹחַ מָנוֹת אִישׁ לְרֵעֵהוּ וּמַתָּנוֹת לָאֶבְיוֹנִים: 23 וְקִבֵּל הַיְּהוּדִים אֵת אֲשֶׁר־הֵחֵלּוּ לַעֲשׂוֹת וְאֵת אֲשֶׁר־כָּתַב מָרְדֳּכַי אֲלֵיהֶם: 24 כִּי הָמָן בֶּן־הַמְּדָתָא הָאֲגָגִי צֹרֵר כָּל־הַיְּהוּדִים חָשַׁב עַל־הַיְּהוּדִים לְאַבְּדָם וְהִפִּיל פּוּר הוּא הַגּוֹרָל לְהֻמָּם וּלְאַבְּדָם: 25 וּבְבֹאָהּ לִפְנֵי הַמֶּלֶךְ אָמַר עִם־הַסֵּפֶר יָשׁוּב מַחֲשַׁבְתּוֹ הָרָעָה אֲשֶׁר־חָשַׁב עַל־הַיְּהוּדִים עַל־רֹאשׁוֹ וְתָלוּ אֹתוֹ וְאֶת־בָּנָיו עַל־הָעֵץ: 26 עַל־כֵּן קָרְאוּ לַיָּמִים הָאֵלֶּה פוּרִים עַל־שֵׁם הַפּוּר עַל־כֵּן עַל־כָּל־דִּבְרֵי הָאִגֶּרֶת הַזֹּאת וּמָה־רָאוּ עַל־כָּכָה וּמָה הִגִּיעַ אֲלֵיהֶם: 27 קִיְּמוּ וְקִבְּלוּ הַיְּהוּדִים עֲלֵיהֶם וְעַל־זַרְעָם וְעַל כָּל־הַנִּלְוִים עֲלֵיהֶם וְלֹא יַעֲבוֹר לִהְיוֹת עֹשִׂים אֵת שְׁנֵי הַיָּמִים הָאֵלֶּה כִּכְתָבָם וְכִזְמַנָּם בְּכָל־שָׁנָה וְשָׁנָה: 28 וְהַיָּמִים הָאֵלֶּה נִזְכָּרִים וְנַעֲשִׂים בְּכָל־דּוֹר וָדוֹר מִשְׁפָּחָה וּמִשְׁפָּחָה מְדִינָה וּמְדִינָה וְעִיר וָעִיר וִימֵי הַפּוּרִים הָאֵלֶּה לֹא יַעַבְרוּ מִתּוֹךְ הַיְּהוּדִים וְזִכְרָם לֹא־יָסוּף מִזַּרְעָם: ס 29 וַתִּכְתֹּב אֶסְתֵּר הַמַּלְכָּה בַת־אֲבִיחַיִל וּמָרְדֳּכַי הַיְּהוּדִי אֶת־כָּל־תֹּקֶף לְקַיֵּם אֵת אִגֶּרֶת הַפֻּרִים הַזֹּאת הַשֵּׁנִית: 30 וַיִּשְׁלַח סְפָרִים אֶל־כָּל־הַיְּהוּדִים אֶל־שֶׁבַע וְעֶשְׂרִים וּמֵאָה מְדִינָה מַלְכוּת אֲחַשְׁוֵרוֹשׁ דִּבְרֵי שָׁלוֹם וֶאֱמֶת: 31 לְקַיֵּם אֶת־יְמֵי הַפֻּרִים הָאֵלֶּה בִּזְמַנֵּיהֶם כַּאֲשֶׁר קִיַּם עֲלֵיהֶם מָרְדֳּכַי הַיְּהוּדִי וְאֶסְתֵּר הַמַּלְכָּה וְכַאֲשֶׁר קִיְּמוּ עַל־נַפְשָׁם וְעַל־זַרְעָם דִּבְרֵי הַצֹּמוֹת וְזַעֲקָתָם: 32 וּמַאֲמַר אֶסְתֵּר קִיַּם דִּבְרֵי הַפֻּרִים הָאֵלֶּה וְנִכְתָּב בַּסֵּפֶר: פ

י וַיָּשֶׂם הַמֶּלֶךְ אֲחַשְׁוֵרוֹשׁ מַס עַל־הָאָרֶץ וְאִיֵּי הַיָּם: 2 וְכָל־מַעֲשֵׂה תָקְפּוֹ וּגְבוּרָתוֹ וּפָרָשַׁת גְּדֻלַּת מָרְדֳּכַי אֲשֶׁר גִּדְּלוֹ הַמֶּלֶךְ הֲלוֹא־הֵם כְּתוּבִים עַל־

chronicles of the kings of Media and Persia? ³ For Mordecai the Jew *was* second to King Ahasuerus, and was great among the Jews and well received by the multitude of his brethren, seeking the good of his people and speaking peace to all his country-men.

סֵפֶר דִּבְרֵי הַיָּמִים לְמַלְכֵי מָדַי וּפָרָס: 3 כִּי |
מָרְדֳּכַי הַיְּהוּדִי מִשְׁנֶה לַמֶּלֶךְ אֲחַשְׁוֵרוֹשׁ וְגָדוֹל
לַיְּהוּדִים וְרָצוּי לְרֹב אֶחָיו דֹּרֵשׁ טוֹב לְעַמּוֹ וְדֹבֵר
שָׁלוֹם לְכָל־זַרְעוֹ:

The Book of

DANIEL

1 In the third year of the reign of Jehoiakim king of Judah, Nebuchadnezzar king of Babylon came to Jerusalem and besieged it. ²And the Lord gave Jehoiakim king of Judah into his hand, with some of the articles of the house of God, which he carried into the land of Shinar to the house of his god; and he brought the articles into the treasure house of his god.

³Then the king instructed Ashpenaz, the master of his eunuchs, to bring some of the children of Israel and some of the king's descendants and some of the nobles, ⁴young men in whom *there was* no blemish, but good-looking, gifted in all wisdom, possessing knowledge and quick to understand, who *had* ability to serve in the king's palace, and whom they might teach the language and literature of the Chaldeans. ⁵And the king appointed for them a daily provision of the king's delicacies and of the wine which he drank, and three years of training for them, so that at the end of *that time* they might serve before the king. ⁶Now from among those of the sons of Judah were Daniel, Hananiah, Mishael, and Azariah. ⁷To them the chief of the eunuchs gave names: he gave Daniel *the name* Belteshazzar; to Hananiah, Shadrach; to Mishael, Meshach; and to Azariah, Abed-Nego.

⁸But Daniel purposed in his heart that he would not defile himself with the portion of the king's delicacies, nor with the wine which he drank; therefore he requested of the chief of the eunuchs that he might not defile himself. ⁹Now God had brought Daniel into the favor and goodwill of the chief of the eunuchs. ¹⁰And the chief of the eunuchs said to Daniel, "I fear my lord the king, who has appointed your food and drink. For why should he see your faces looking worse than the young men who *are* your age? Then you would endanger my head before the king."

¹¹So Daniel said to the steward whom the chief of the eunuchs had set over Daniel, Hananiah, Mishael, and Azariah, ¹²"Please test your servants for ten days, and let them give us vegetables to eat and water to drink. ¹³Then let our appearance be examined before you, and the appearance of the young men who eat the portion of the king's

דניאל

א בִּשְׁנַת שָׁלוֹשׁ לְמַלְכוּת יְהוֹיָקִים מֶלֶךְ־יְהוּדָה
בָּא נְבוּכַדְנֶאצַּר מֶלֶךְ־בָּבֶל יְרוּשָׁלַ͏ִם וַיָּצַר עָלֶיהָ:
2 וַיִּתֵּן אֲדֹנָי בְּיָדוֹ אֶת־יְהוֹיָקִים מֶלֶךְ־יְהוּדָה וּמִקְצָת
כְּלֵי בֵית־הָאֱלֹהִים וַיְבִיאֵם אֶרֶץ־שִׁנְעָר בֵּית אֱלֹהָיו
וְאֶת־הַכֵּלִים הֵבִיא בֵּית אוֹצַר אֱלֹהָיו: 3 וַיֹּאמֶר
הַמֶּלֶךְ לְאַשְׁפְּנַז רַב סָרִיסָיו לְהָבִיא מִבְּנֵי יִשְׂרָאֵל
וּמִזֶּרַע הַמְּלוּכָה וּמִן־הַפַּרְתְּמִים: 4 יְלָדִים אֲשֶׁר
אֵין־בָּהֶם כָּל־מֹאוּם וְטוֹבֵי מַרְאֶה וּמַשְׂכִּילִים
בְּכָל־חָכְמָה וְיֹדְעֵי דַעַת וּמְבִינֵי מַדָּע וַאֲשֶׁר כֹּחַ
בָּהֶם לַעֲמֹד בְּהֵיכַל הַמֶּלֶךְ וּלֲלַמְּדָם סֵפֶר וּלְשׁוֹן
כַּשְׂדִּים: 5 וַיְמַן לָהֶם הַמֶּלֶךְ דְּבַר־יוֹם בְּיוֹמוֹ מִפַּת־
בַּג הַמֶּלֶךְ וּמִיֵּין מִשְׁתָּיו וּלְגַדְּלָם שָׁנִים שָׁלוֹשׁ
וּמִקְצָתָם יַעַמְדוּ לִפְנֵי הַמֶּלֶךְ: 6 וַיְהִי בָהֶם מִבְּנֵי
יְהוּדָה דָּנִיֵּאל חֲנַנְיָה מִישָׁאֵל וַעֲזַרְיָה: 7 וַיָּשֶׂם לָהֶם
שַׂר הַסָּרִיסִים שֵׁמוֹת וַיָּשֶׂם לְדָנִיֵּאל בֵּלְטְשַׁאצַּר
וְלַחֲנַנְיָה שַׁדְרַךְ וּלְמִישָׁאֵל מֵישַׁךְ וְלַעֲזַרְיָה עֲבֵד
נְגוֹ: 8 וַיָּשֶׂם דָּנִיֵּאל עַל־לִבּוֹ אֲשֶׁר לֹא־יִתְגָּאַל
בְּפַתְבַּג הַמֶּלֶךְ וּבְיֵין מִשְׁתָּיו וַיְבַקֵּשׁ מִשַּׂר הַסָּרִיסִים
אֲשֶׁר לֹא יִתְגָּאָל: 9 וַיִּתֵּן הָאֱלֹהִים אֶת־דָּנִיֵּאל
לְחֶסֶד וּלְרַחֲמִים לִפְנֵי שַׂר הַסָּרִיסִים: 10 וַיֹּאמֶר
שַׂר הַסָּרִיסִים לְדָנִיֵּאל יָרֵא אֲנִי אֶת־אֲדֹנִי הַמֶּלֶךְ
אֲשֶׁר מִנָּה אֶת־מַאֲכַלְכֶם וְאֶת־מִשְׁתֵּיכֶם אֲשֶׁר
לָמָּה יִרְאֶה אֶת־פְּנֵיכֶם זֹעֲפִים מִן־הַיְלָדִים אֲשֶׁר
כְּגִילְכֶם וְחִיַּבְתֶּם אֶת־רֹאשִׁי לַמֶּלֶךְ: 11 וַיֹּאמֶר
דָּנִיֵּאל אֶל־הַמֶּלְצַר אֲשֶׁר מִנָּה שַׂר הַסָּרִיסִים עַל־
דָּנִיֵּאל חֲנַנְיָה מִישָׁאֵל וַעֲזַרְיָה: 12 נַס־נָא אֶת־
עֲבָדֶיךָ יָמִים עֲשָׂרָה וְיִתְּנוּ־לָנוּ מִן־הַזֵּרֹעִים וְנֹאכְלָה
וּמַיִם וְנִשְׁתֶּה: 13 וְיֵרָאוּ לְפָנֶיךָ מַרְאֵינוּ וּמַרְאֵה
הַיְלָדִים הָאֹכְלִים אֵת פַּתְבַּג הַמֶּלֶךְ וְכַאֲשֶׁר תִּרְאֵה

delicacies; and as you see fit, *so* deal with your servants." 14So he consented with them in this matter, and tested them ten days.

15And at the end of ten days their features appeared better and fatter in flesh than all the young men who ate the portion of the king's delicacies. 16Thus the steward took away their portion of delicacies and the wine that they were to drink, and gave them vegetables.

17As for these four young men, God gave them knowledge and skill in all literature and wisdom; and Daniel had understanding in all visions and dreams.

18Now at the end of the days, when the king had said that they should be brought in, the chief of the eunuchs brought them in before Nebuchadnezzar. 19Then the king interviewed them, and among them all none was found like Daniel, Hananiah, Mishael, and Azariah; therefore they served before the king. 20And in all matters of wisdom *and* understanding about which the king examined them, he found them ten times better than all the magicians *and* astrologers who *were* in all his realm. 21Thus Daniel continued until the first year of King Cyrus.

2 Now in the second year of Nebucmhadnezzar's reign, Nebuchadnezzar had dreams; and his spirit was *so* troubled that his sleep left him. 2Then the king gave the command to call the magicians, the astrologers, the sorcerers, and the Chaldeans to tell the king his dreams. So they came and stood before the king. 3And the king said to them, "I have had a dream, and my spirit is anxious to know the dream."

4Then the Chaldeans spoke to the king in Aramaic, "O king, live forever! Tell your servants the dream, and we will give the interpretation."

5The king answered and said to the Chaldeans, "My decision is firm: if you do not make known the dream to me, and its interpretation, you shall be cut in pieces, and your houses shall be made an ash heap. 6However, if you tell the dream and its interpretation, you shall receive from me gifts, rewards, and great honor. Therefore tell me the dream and its interpretation."

7They answered again and said, "Let the king tell his servants the dream, and we will give its interpretation."

8The king answered and said, "I know for certain that you would gain time, because you see that my decision is firm: 9if you do not make known the dream to me, *there is only* one decree for you! For you have agreed to speak lying and

עֲשֵׂה עִם־עֲבָדֶיךָ: 14 וַיִּשְׁמַע לָהֶם לַדָּבָר הַזֶּה
וַיְנַסֵּם יָמִים עֲשָׂרָה: 15 וּמִקְצָת יָמִים עֲשָׂרָה
נִרְאָה מַרְאֵיהֶם טוֹב וּבְרִיאֵי בָּשָׂר מִן־כָּל־הַיְלָדִים
הָאֹכְלִים אֵת פַּתְבַּג הַמֶּלֶךְ: 16 וַיְהִי הַמֶּלְצַר נֹשֵׂא
אֶת־פַּתְבָּגָם וְיֵין מִשְׁתֵּיהֶם וְנֹתֵן לָהֶם זֵרְעֹנִים:
17 וְהַיְלָדִים הָאֵלֶּה אַרְבַּעְתָּם נָתַן לָהֶם הָאֱלֹהִים
מַדָּע וְהַשְׂכֵּל בְּכָל־סֵפֶר וְחָכְמָה וְדָנִיֵּאל הֵבִין
בְּכָל־חָזוֹן וַחֲלֹמוֹת: 18 וּלְמִקְצָת הַיָּמִים אֲשֶׁר־
אָמַר הַמֶּלֶךְ לַהֲבִיאָם וַיְבִיאֵם שַׂר הַסָּרִיסִים לִפְנֵי
נְבֻכַדְנֶצַּר: 19 וַיְדַבֵּר אִתָּם הַמֶּלֶךְ וְלֹא נִמְצָא מִכֻּלָּם
כְּדָנִיֵּאל חֲנַנְיָה מִישָׁאֵל וַעֲזַרְיָה וַיַּעַמְדוּ לִפְנֵי הַמֶּלֶךְ:
20 וְכֹל דְּבַר חָכְמַת בִּינָה אֲשֶׁר־בִּקֵּשׁ מֵהֶם הַמֶּלֶךְ
וַיִּמְצָאֵם עֶשֶׂר יָדוֹת עַל כָּל־הַחַרְטֻמִּים הָאַשָּׁפִים
אֲשֶׁר בְּכָל־מַלְכוּתוֹ: 21 וַיְהִי דָּנִיֵּאל עַד־שְׁנַת אַחַת
לְכוֹרֶשׁ הַמֶּלֶךְ:   פ

ב וּבִשְׁנַת שְׁתַּיִם לְמַלְכוּת נְבֻכַדְנֶצַּר חָלַם
נְבֻכַדְנֶצַּר חֲלֹמוֹת וַתִּתְפָּעֶם רוּחוֹ וּשְׁנָתוֹ נִהְיְתָה
עָלָיו: 2 וַיֹּאמֶר הַמֶּלֶךְ לִקְרֹא לַחַרְטֻמִּים וְלָאַשָּׁפִים
וְלַמְכַשְּׁפִים וְלַכַּשְׂדִּים לְהַגִּיד לַמֶּלֶךְ חֲלֹמֹתָיו וַיָּבֹאוּ
וַיַּעַמְדוּ לִפְנֵי הַמֶּלֶךְ: 3 וַיֹּאמֶר לָהֶם הַמֶּלֶךְ חֲלוֹם
חָלָמְתִּי וַתִּפָּעֶם רוּחִי לָדַעַת אֶת־הַחֲלוֹם: 4 וַיְדַבְּרוּ
הַכַּשְׂדִּים לַמֶּלֶךְ אֲרָמִית מַלְכָּא לְעָלְמִין חֱיִי אֱמַר
חֶלְמָא לְעַבְדָךְ וּפִשְׁרָא נְחַוֵּא: 5 עָנֵה מַלְכָּא וְאָמַר
לְכַשְׂדָּיֵא מִלְּתָא מִנִּי אַזְדָּא הֵן לָא תְהוֹדְעוּנַּנִי
חֶלְמָא וּפִשְׁרֵהּ הַדָּמִין תִּתְעַבְדוּן וּבָתֵּיכוֹן נְוָלִי
יִתְּשָׂמוּן: 6 וְהֵן חֶלְמָא וּפִשְׁרֵהּ תְּהַחֲוֺן מַתְּנָן וּנְבִזְבָּה
וִיקָר שַׂגִּיא תְּקַבְּלוּן מִן־קֳדָמָי לָהֵן חֶלְמָא וּפִשְׁרֵהּ
הַחֲוֹנִי: 7 עֲנוֹ תִנְיָנוּת וְאָמְרִין מַלְכָּא חֶלְמָא יֵאמַר
לְעַבְדוֹהִי וּפִשְׁרָה נְהַחֲוֵה: 8 עָנֵה מַלְכָּא וְאָמַר מִן־
יַצִּיב יָדַע אֲנָה דִּי עִדָּנָא אַנְתּוּן זָבְנִין כָּל־קֳבֵל דִּי
חֲזֵיתוֹן דִּי אַזְדָּא מִנִּי מִלְּתָא: 9 דִּי הֵן חֶלְמָא לָא
תְהוֹדְעֻנַּנִי חֲדָה־הִיא דָתְכוֹן וּמִלָּה כִדְבָה וּשְׁחִיתָה
הִזְמִנְתֻּן לְמֵאמַר קֳדָמַי עַד דִּי עִדָּנָא יִשְׁתַּנֵּא

corrupt words before me till the time has changed. Therefore tell me the dream, and I shall know that you can give me its interpretation."

10 The Chaldeans answered the king, and said, "There is not a man on earth who can tell the king's matter; therefore no king, lord, or ruler has *ever* asked such things of any magician, astrologer, or Chaldean. 11 *It is* a difficult thing that the king requests, and there is no other who can tell it to the king except the gods, whose dwelling is not with flesh."

12 For this reason the king was angry and very furious, and gave the command to destroy all the wise *men* of Babylon. 13 So the decree went out, and they began killing the wise *men;* and they sought Daniel and his companions, to kill *them.*

14 Then with counsel and wisdom Daniel answered Arioch, the captain of the king's guard, who had gone out to kill the wise *men* of Babylon; 15 he answered and said to Arioch the king's captain, "Why is the decree from the king so urgent?" Then Arioch made the decision known to Daniel.

16 So Daniel went in and asked the king to give him time, that he might tell the king the interpretation. 17 Then Daniel went to his house, and made the decision known to Hananiah, Mishael, and Azariah, his companions, 18 that they might seek mercies from the God of heaven concerning this secret, so that Daniel and his companions might not perish with the rest of the wise *men* of Babylon. 19 Then the secret was revealed to Daniel in a night vision. So Daniel blessed the God of heaven.

20 Daniel answered and said:

"Blessed be the name of God forever and ever,
For wisdom and might are His.
21 And He changes the times and the seasons;
He removes kings and raises up kings;
He gives wisdom to the wise
And knowledge to those who have understanding.
22 He reveals deep and secret things;
He knows what *is* in the darkness,
And light dwells with Him.

23 "I thank You and praise You,
O God of my fathers;
You have given me wisdom and might,
And have now made known to me what we asked of You,
For You have made known to us the king's demand."

לְהֵן חֶלְמָא אֱמַרוּ לִי וְאֶנְדַּע דִּי פִשְׁרֵהּ תְּהַחֲוֻנַּנִי:
10 עֲנוֹ כַשְׂדָּיֵא קֳדָם־מַלְכָּא וְאָמְרִין לָא־אִיתַי אֱנָשׁ עַל־יַבֶּשְׁתָּא דִּי מִלַּת מַלְכָּא יוּכַל לְהַחֲוָיָה כָּל־קֳבֵל דִּי כָּל־מֶלֶךְ רַב וְשַׁלִּיט מִלָּה כִדְנָה לָא שְׁאֵל לְכָל־חַרְטֹם וְאָשַׁף וְכַשְׂדָּי: 11 וּמִלְּתָא דִי־מַלְכָּה שָׁאֵל יַקִּירָה וְאָחֳרָן לָא אִיתַי דִּי יְחַוִּנַּהּ קֳדָם מַלְכָּא לָהֵן אֱלָהִין דִּי מְדָרְהוֹן עִם־בִּשְׂרָא לָא אִיתוֹהִי: 12 כָּל־קֳבֵל דְּנָה מַלְכָּא בְּנַס וּקְצַף שַׂגִּיא וַאֲמַר לְהוֹבָדָה לְכֹל חַכִּימֵי בָבֶל: 13 וְדָתָא נֶפְקַת וְחַכִּימַיָּא מִתְקַטְּלִין וּבְעוֹ דָנִיֵּאל וְחַבְרוֹהִי לְהִתְקְטָלָה:
ס

14 בֵּאדַיִן דָּנִיֵּאל הֲתִיב עֵטָא וּטְעֵם לְאַרְיוֹךְ רַב־טַבָּחַיָּא דִּי מַלְכָּא דִּי נְפַק לְקַטָּלָה לְחַכִּימֵי בָּבֶל: 15 עָנֵה וְאָמַר לְאַרְיוֹךְ שַׁלִּיטָא דִי־מַלְכָּא עַל־מָה דָתָא מְהַחְצְפָה מִן־קֳדָם מַלְכָּא אֱדַיִן מִלְּתָא הוֹדַע אַרְיוֹךְ לְדָנִיֵּאל: 16 וְדָנִיֵּאל עַל וּבְעָה מִן־מַלְכָּא דִּי זְמָן יִנְתֶּן־לֵהּ וּפִשְׁרָא לְהַחֲוָיָה לְמַלְכָּא:
ס

17 אֱדַיִן דָּנִיֵּאל לְבַיְתֵהּ אֲזַל וְלַחֲנַנְיָה מִישָׁאֵל וַעֲזַרְיָה חַבְרוֹהִי מִלְּתָא הוֹדַע: 18 וְרַחֲמִין לְמִבְעֵא מִן־קֳדָם אֱלָהּ שְׁמַיָּא עַל־רָזָה דְּנָה דִּי לָא יְהֹבְדוּן דָּנִיֵּאל וְחַבְרוֹהִי עִם־שְׁאָר חַכִּימֵי בָבֶל: 19 אֱדַיִן לְדָנִיֵּאל בְּחֶזְוָא דִי־לֵילְיָא רָזָה גֲלִי אֱדַיִן דָּנִיֵּאל בָּרִךְ לֶאֱלָהּ שְׁמַיָּא: 20 עָנֵה דָנִיֵּאל וְאָמַר לֶהֱוֵא שְׁמֵהּ דִּי־אֱלָהָא מְבָרַךְ מִן־עָלְמָא וְעַד־עָלְמָא דִּי חָכְמְתָא וּגְבוּרְתָא דִּי לֵהּ־הִיא: 21 וְהוּא מְהַשְׁנֵא עִדָּנַיָּא וְזִמְנַיָּא מְהַעְדֵּה מַלְכִין וּמְהָקֵים מַלְכִין יָהֵב חָכְמְתָא לְחַכִּימִין וּמַנְדְּעָא לְיָדְעֵי בִינָה: 22 הוּא גָּלֵא עֲמִיקָתָא וּמְסַתְּרָתָא יָדַע מָה בַחֲשׁוֹכָא וּנְהוֹרָא עִמֵּהּ שְׁרֵא: 23 לָךְ אֱלָהּ אֲבָהָתִי מְהוֹדֵא וּמְשַׁבַּח אֲנָה דִּי חָכְמְתָא וּגְבוּרְתָא יְהַבְתְּ לִי וּכְעַן הוֹדַעְתַּנִי דִּי־בְעֵינָא מִנָּךְ דִּי־מִלַּת מַלְכָּא הוֹדַעְתֶּנָא: 24 כָּל־קֳבֵל דְּנָה דָּנִיֵּאל עַל עַל־אַרְיוֹךְ

24 Therefore Daniel went to Arioch, whom the king had appointed to destroy the wise *men* of Babylon. He went and said thus to him: "Do not destroy the wise *men* of Babylon; take me before the king, and I will tell the king the interpretation."

25 Then Arioch quickly brought Daniel before the king, and said thus to him, "I have found a man of the captives of Judah, who will make known to the king the interpretation."

26 The king answered and said to Daniel, whose name *was* Belteshazzar, "Are you able to make known to me the dream which I have seen, and its interpretation?"

27 Daniel answered in the presence of the king, and said, "The secret which the king has demanded, the wise *men,* the astrologers, the magicians, and the soothsayers cannot declare to the king. 28 But there is a God in heaven who reveals secrets, and He has made known to King Nebuchadnezzar what will be in the latter days. Your dream, and the visions of your head upon your bed, were these: 29 As for you, O king, thoughts came *to* your *mind while* on your bed, *about* what would come to pass after this; and He who reveals secrets has made known to you what will be. 30 But as for me, this secret has not been revealed to me because I have more wisdom than anyone living, but for *our* sakes who make known the interpretation to the king, and that you may know the thoughts of your heart.

31 "You, O king, were watching; and behold, a great image! This great image, whose splendor *was* excellent, stood before you; and its form *was* awesome. 32 This image's head *was* of fine gold, its chest and arms of silver, its belly and thighs of bronze, 33 its legs of iron, its feet partly of iron and partly of clay. 34 You watched while a stone was cut out without hands, which struck the image on its feet of iron and clay, and broke them in pieces. 35 Then the iron, the clay, the bronze, the silver, and the gold were crushed together, and became like chaff from the summer threshing floors; the wind carried them away so that no trace of them was found. And the stone that struck the image became a great mountain and filled the whole earth.

36 "This *is* the dream. Now we will tell the interpretation of it before the king. 37 You, O king, *are* a king of kings. For the God of heaven has given you a kingdom, power, strength, and glory; 38 and wherever the children of men dwell, or the beasts of the field and the birds of the heaven, He has given *them* into your hand, and has made you ruler over them all—you *are* this head of gold. 39 But after you shall arise another kingdom inferior to yours; then another, a third kingdom of bronze,

דִּי מַנִּי מַלְכָּא לְהוֹבָדָה לְחַכִּימֵי בָבֶל אֲזַל | וְכֵן
אֲמַר־לֵהּ לְחַכִּימֵי בָבֶל אַל־תְּהוֹבֵד הַעֵלְנִי קֳדָם
מַלְכָּא וּפִשְׁרָא לְמַלְכָּא אֲחַוֵּא׃ ס 25 אֱדַיִן
אַרְיוֹךְ בְּהִתְבְּהָלָה הַנְעֵל לְדָנִיֵּאל קֳדָם מַלְכָּא
וְכֵן אֲמַר־לֵהּ דִּי־הַשְׁכַּחַת גְּבַר מִן־בְּנֵי גָלוּתָא דִּי
יְהוּד דִּי פִשְׁרָא לְמַלְכָּא יְהוֹדַע׃ 26 עָנֵה מַלְכָּא
וְאָמַר לְדָנִיֵּאל דִּי שְׁמֵהּ בֵּלְטְשַׁאצַּר הַאִיתָיךְ כָּהֵל
לְהוֹדָעֻתַנִי חֶלְמָא דִי־חֲזֵית וּפִשְׁרֵהּ׃ 27 עָנֵה דָנִיֵּאל
קֳדָם מַלְכָּא וְאָמַר רָזָה דִּי־מַלְכָּא שָׁאֵל לָא חַכִּימִין
אָשְׁפִין חַרְטֻמִּין גָּזְרִין יָכְלִין לְהַחֲוָיָה לְמַלְכָּא׃
28 בְּרַם אִיתַי אֱלָהּ בִּשְׁמַיָּא גָּלֵא רָזִין וְהוֹדַע
לְמַלְכָּא נְבוּכַדְנֶצַּר מָה דִּי לֶהֱוֵא בְּאַחֲרִית יוֹמַיָּא
חֶלְמָךְ וְחֶזְוֵי רֵאשָׁךְ עַל־מִשְׁכְּבָךְ דְּנָה הוּא׃ פ
29 אנתה^P מַלְכָּא רַעְיוֹנָךְ עַל־מִשְׁכְּבָךְ סְלִקוּ מָה דִּי
לֶהֱוֵא אַחֲרֵי דְנָה וְגָלֵא רָזַיָּא הוֹדְעָךְ מָה־דִי לֶהֱוֵא׃
30 וַאֲנָה לָא בְחָכְמָה דִּי־אִיתַי בִּי מִן־כָּל־חַיַּיָּא רָזָא
דְנָה גֱּלִי לִי לָהֵן עַל־דִּבְרַת דִּי פִשְׁרָא לְמַלְכָּא
יְהוֹדְעוּן וְרַעְיוֹנֵי לִבְבָךְ תִּנְדַּע׃ 31 אנתה^P מַלְכָּא
חָזֵה הֲוַיְתָ וַאֲלוּ צְלֵם חַד שַׂגִּיא צַלְמָא דִּכֵּן רַב
וְזִיוֵהּ יַתִּיר קָאֵם לְקָבְלָךְ וְרֵוֵהּ דְּחִיל׃ 32 הוּא
צַלְמָא רֵאשֵׁהּ דִּי־דְהַב טָב חֲדוֹהִי וּדְרָעוֹהִי דִּי
כְסַף מְעוֹהִי וְיַרְכָתֵהּ דִּי נְחָשׁ׃ 33 שָׁקוֹהִי דִּי פַרְזֶל
רַגְלוֹהִי מנהון^P דִּי פַרְזֶל וּמנהון^P דִּי חֲסַף׃ 34 חָזֵה
הֲוַיְתָ עַד דִּי הִתְגְּזֶרֶת אֶבֶן דִּי־לָא בִידַיִן וּמְחָת
לְצַלְמָא עַל־רַגְלוֹהִי דִּי פַרְזְלָא וְחַסְפָּא וְהַדֵּקֶת
הִמּוֹן׃ 35 בֵּאדַיִן דָּקוּ כַחֲדָה פַּרְזְלָא חַסְפָּא נְחָשָׁא
כַּסְפָּא וְדַהֲבָא וַהֲווֹ כְּעוּר מִן־אִדְּרֵי־קַיִט וּנְשָׂא
הִמּוֹן רוּחָא וְכָל־אֲתַר לָא־הִשְׁתְּכַח לְהוֹן וְאַבְנָא |
דִּי־מְחָת לְצַלְמָא הֲוָת לְטוּר רַב וּמְלָת כָּל־
אַרְעָא׃ 36 דְּנָה חֶלְמָא וּפִשְׁרֵהּ נֵאמַר קֳדָם־מַלְכָּא׃
37 אנתה^P מַלְכָּא מֶלֶךְ מַלְכַיָּא דִּי אֱלָהּ שְׁמַיָּא
מַלְכוּתָא חִסְנָא וְתָקְפָּא וִיקָרָא יְהַב־לָךְ׃ 38 וּבְכָל־
דִּי דארין^P בְּנֵי־אֲנָשָׁא חֵיוַת בָּרָא וְעוֹף־שְׁמַיָּא
יְהַב בִּידָךְ וְהַשְׁלְטָךְ בְּכָלְּהוֹן אנתה־הוא^P רֵאשָׁה
דִּי דַהֲבָא׃ 39 וּבָתְרָךְ תְּקוּם מַלְכוּ אָחֳרִי

ב 26 הָאִיתָךְ   29 אַנְתְּ   31 אַנְתְּ   33 מִנְּהֵין
33 וּמִנְּהֵין   37 אַנְתְּ   38 דָּיְרִין

which shall rule over all the earth. ⁴⁰ And the fourth kingdom shall be as strong as iron, inasmuch as iron breaks in pieces and shatters everything; and like iron that crushes, *that kingdom* will break in pieces and crush all the others. ⁴¹ Whereas you saw the feet and toes, partly of potter's clay and partly of iron, the kingdom shall be divided; yet the strength of the iron shall be in it, just as you saw the iron mixed with ceramic clay. ⁴² And *as* the toes of the feet *were* partly of iron and partly of clay, *so* the kingdom shall be partly strong and partly fragile. ⁴³ As you saw iron mixed with ceramic clay, they will mingle with the seed of men; but they will not adhere to one another, just as iron does not mix with clay. ⁴⁴ And in the days of these kings the God of heaven will set up a kingdom which shall never be destroyed; and the kingdom shall not be left to other people; it shall break in pieces and consume all these kingdoms, and it shall stand forever. ⁴⁵ Inasmuch as you saw that the stone was cut out of the mountain without hands, and that it broke in pieces the iron, the bronze, the clay, the silver, and the gold—the great God has made known to the king what will come to pass after this. The dream is certain, and its interpretation is sure."

⁴⁶ Then King Nebuchadnezzar fell on his face, prostrate before Daniel, and commanded that they should present an offering and incense to him. ⁴⁷ The king answered Daniel, and said, "Truly your God *is* the God of gods, the Lord of kings, and a revealer of secrets, since you could reveal this secret." ⁴⁸ Then the king promoted Daniel and gave him many great gifts; and he made him ruler over the whole province of Babylon, and chief administrator over all the wise *men* of Babylon. ⁴⁹ Also Daniel petitioned the king, and he set Shadrach, Meshach, and Abed-Nego over the affairs of the province of Babylon; but Daniel *sat* in the gate of the king.

3 Nebuchadnezzar the king made an image of gold, whose height *was* sixty cubits *and* its width six cubits. He set it up in the plain of Dura, in the province of Babylon. ² And King Nebuchadnezzar sent *word* to gather together the satraps, the administrators, the governors, the counselors, the treasurers, the judges, the magistrates, and all the officials of the provinces, to come to the dedication of the image which King Nebuchadnezzar had set up. ³ So the satraps, the administrators, the governors, the counselors, the treasurers, the judges, the magistrates, and all the officials of the provinces gathered together for the dedication of the image that King Nebuchadnezzar had set up;

and they stood before the image that Nebuchadnezzar had set up. 4 Then a herald cried aloud: "To you it is commanded, O peoples, nations, and languages, 5 *that* at the time you hear the sound of the horn, flute, harp, lyre, *and* psaltery, in symphony with all kinds of music, you shall fall down and worship the gold image that King Nebuchadnezzar has set up; 6 and whoever does not fall down and worship shall be cast immediately into the midst of a burning fiery furnace."

7 So at that time, when all the people heard the sound of the horn, flute, harp, *and* lyre, in symphony with all kinds of music, all the people, nations, and languages fell down *and* worshiped the gold image which King Nebuchadnezzar had set up.

8 Therefore at that time certain Chaldeans came forward and accused the Jews. 9 They spoke and said to King Nebuchadnezzar, "O king, live forever! 10 You, O king, have made a decree that everyone who hears the sound of the horn, flute, harp, lyre, *and* psaltery, in symphony with all kinds of music, shall fall down and worship the gold image; 11 and whoever does not fall down and worship shall be cast into the midst of a burning fiery furnace. 12 There are certain Jews whom you have set over the affairs of the province of Babylon: Shadrach, Meshach, and Abed-Nego; these men, O king, have not paid due regard to you. They do not serve your gods or worship the gold image which you have set up."

13 Then Nebuchadnezzar, in rage and fury, gave the command to bring Shadrach, Meshach, and Abed-Nego. So they brought these men before the king. 14 Nebuchadnezzar spoke, saying to them, "*Is it* true, Shadrach, Meshach, and Abed-Nego, *that* you do not serve my gods or worship the gold image which I have set up? 15 Now if you are ready at the time you hear the sound of the horn, flute, harp, lyre, *and* psaltery, in symphony with all kinds of music, and you fall down and worship the image which I have made, *good!* But if you do not worship, you shall be cast immediately into the midst of a burning fiery furnace. And who *is the* god who will deliver you from my hands?"

16 Shadrach, Meshach, and Abed-Nego answered and said to the king, "O Nebuchadnezzar, we have no need to answer you in this matter. 17 If that *is the* case, our God whom we serve is able to deliver us from the burning fiery furnace, and He will deliver *us* from your hand, O king. 18 But if not, let it be known to you, O king, that we do not serve your gods, nor will we worship the gold image which you have set up."

וְכָרוֹזָא קָרֵא בְחָיִל לְכוֹן אָמְרִין עַמְמַיָּא ⁴
אֻמַּיָּא וְלִשָּׁנַיָּא: ⁵ בְּעִדָּנָא דִּי־תִשְׁמְעוּן קָל קַרְנָא
מַשְׁרוֹקִיתָא קַיתְרֹסᵖ סַבְּכָא פְּסַנְתֵּרִין סוּמְפֹּנְיָה
וְכֹל זְנֵי זְמָרָא תִּפְּלוּן וְתִסְגְּדוּן לְצֶלֶם דַּהֲבָא דִּי
הֲקֵים נְבוּכַדְנֶצַּר מַלְכָּא: ⁶ וּמַן־דִּי־לָא יִפֵּל וְיִסְגֻּד
בַּהּ־שַׁעֲתָא יִתְרְמֵא לְגוֹא־אַתּוּן נוּרָא יָקִדְתָּא:
⁷ כָּל־קֳבֵל דְּנָה בֵּהּ־זִמְנָא כְּדִי שָׁמְעִין כָּל־
עַמְמַיָּא קָל קַרְנָא מַשְׁרוֹקִיתָא קַיתְרֹסᵖ שַׂבְּכָא
פְּסַנְטֵרִין וְכֹל זְנֵי זְמָרָא נָפְלִין כָּל־עַמְמַיָּא אֻמַּיָּא
וְלִשָּׁנַיָּא סָגְדִין לְצֶלֶם דַּהֲבָא דִּי הֲקֵים נְבוּכַדְנֶצַּר
מַלְכָּא: ⁸ כָּל־קֳבֵל דְּנָה בֵּהּ־זִמְנָא קְרִבוּ גֻּבְרִין
כַּשְׂדָּאִין וַאֲכַלוּ קַרְצֵיהוֹן דִּי יְהוּדָיֵא: ⁹ עֲנוֹ
וְאָמְרִין לִנְבוּכַדְנֶצַּר מַלְכָּא מַלְכָּא לְעָלְמִין חֱיִי:
¹⁰ אַנְתְּᵖ מַלְכָּא שָׂמְתָּ טְעֵם דִּי כָל־אֱנָשׁ דִּי־
יִשְׁמַע קָל קַרְנָא מַשְׁרוֹקִיתָא קַיתְרֹסᵖ שַׂבְּכָא
פְּסַנְטֵרִין וְסִיפֹּנְיָהᵖ וְכֹל זְנֵי זְמָרָא יִפֵּל וְיִסְגֻּד לְצֶלֶם
דַּהֲבָא: ¹¹ וּמַן־דִּי־לָא יִפֵּל וְיִסְגֻּד יִתְרְמֵא לְגוֹא־
אַתּוּן נוּרָא יָקִדְתָּא: ¹² אִיתַי גֻּבְרִין יְהוּדָאיִן דִּי־
מַנִּיתָ יָתְהוֹן עַל־עֲבִידַת מְדִינַת בָּבֶל שַׁדְרַךְ מֵישַׁךְ
וַעֲבֵד נְגוֹ גֻּבְרַיָּא אִלֵּךְ לָא־שָׂמוּ עֲלָיךְᵖ מַלְכָּא טְעֵם
לֵאלָהָיךְᵖ לָא פָלְחִין וּלְצֶלֶם דַּהֲבָא דִּי הֲקֵימְתָּ לָא
סָגְדִין: ס ¹³ בֵּאדַיִן נְבוּכַדְנֶצַּר בִּרְגַז וַחֲמָה
אֲמַר לְהַיְתָיָה לְשַׁדְרַךְ מֵישַׁךְ וַעֲבֵד נְגוֹ בֵּאדַיִן
גֻּבְרַיָּא אִלֵּךְ הֵיתָיוּ קֳדָם מַלְכָּא: ¹⁴ עָנֵה נְבֻכַדְנֶצַּר
וְאָמַר לְהוֹן הַצְדָּא שַׁדְרַךְ מֵישַׁךְ וַעֲבֵד נְגוֹ לֵאלָהַי
לָא אִיתֵיכוֹן פָּלְחִין וּלְצֶלֶם דַּהֲבָא דִּי הֲקֵימֶת לָא
סָגְדִין: ¹⁵ כְּעַן הֵן אִיתֵיכוֹן עֲתִידִין דִּי בְעִדָּנָא דִּי־
תִשְׁמְעוּן קָל קַרְנָא מַשְׁרוֹקִיתָא קַיתְרֹסᵖ שַׂבְּכָא
פְּסַנְטֵרִין וְסוּמְפֹּנְיָה וְכֹל | זְנֵי זְמָרָא תִּפְּלוּן
וְתִסְגְּדוּן לְצַלְמָא דִי־עַבְדֵת וְהֵן לָא תִסְגְּדוּן בַּהּ־
שַׁעֲתָה תִתְרְמוֹן לְגוֹא־אַתּוּן נוּרָא יָקִדְתָּא וּמַן־
הוּא אֱלָהּ דִּי יְשֵׁיזְבִנְכוֹן מִן־יְדָי: ¹⁶ עֲנוֹ שַׁדְרַךְ
מֵישַׁךְ וַעֲבֵד נְגוֹ וְאָמְרִין לְמַלְכָּא נְבוּכַדְנֶצַּר לָא־
חַשְׁחִין אֲנַחְנָה עַל־דְּנָה פִּתְגָם לַהֲתָבוּתָךְ: ¹⁷ הֵן
אִיתַי אֱלָהַנָא דִּי־אֲנַחְנָא פָלְחִין יָכִל לְשֵׁיזָבוּתַנָא
מִן־אַתּוּן נוּרָא יָקִדְתָּא וּמִן־יְדָךְ מַלְכָּא יְשֵׁיזִב:
¹⁸ וְהֵן לָא יְדִיעַ לֶהֱוֵא־לָךְ מַלְכָּא דִּי לֵאלָהָיךְᵖ לָא־
אִיתַנָאᵖ פָלְחִין וּלְצֶלֶם דַּהֲבָא דִּי הֲקֵימְתָּ לָא

19 Then Nebuchadnezzar was full of fury, and the expression on his face changed toward Shadrach, Meshach, and Abed-Nego. He spoke and commanded that they heat the furnace seven times more than it was usually heated. 20 And he commanded certain mighty men of valor who *were* in his army to bind Shadrach, Meshach, and Abed-Nego, *and* cast *them* into the burning fiery furnace. 21 Then these men were bound in their coats, their trousers, their turbans, and their *other* garments, and were cast into the midst of the burning fiery furnace. 22 Therefore, because the king's command was urgent, and the furnace exceedingly hot, the flame of the fire killed those men who took up Shadrach, Meshach, and Abed-Nego. 23 And these three men, Shadrach, Meshach, and Abed-Nego, fell down bound into the midst of the burning fiery furnace.

24 Then King Nebuchadnezzar was astonished; and he rose in haste *and* spoke, saying to his counselors, "Did we not cast three men bound into the midst of the fire?"

They answered and said to the king, "True, O king."

25 "Look!" he answered, "I see four men loose, walking in the midst of the fire; and they are not hurt, and the form of the fourth is like the Son of God."

26 Then Nebuchadnezzar went near the mouth of the burning fiery furnace *and* spoke, saying, "Shadrach, Meshach, and Abed-Nego, servants of the Most High God, come out, and come *here*." Then Shadrach, Meshach, and Abed-Nego came from the midst of the fire. 27 And the satraps, administrators, governors, and the king's counselors gathered together, and they saw these men on whose bodies the fire had no power; the hair of their head was not singed nor were their garments affected, and the smell of fire was not on them.

28 Nebuchadnezzar spoke, saying, "Blessed be the God of Shadrach, Meshach, and Abed-Nego, who sent His Angel and delivered His servants who trusted in Him, and they have frustrated the king's word, and yielded their bodies, that they should not serve nor worship any god except their own God! 29 Therefore I make a decree that any people, nation, or language which speaks anything amiss against the God of Shadrach, Meshach, and Abed-Nego shall be cut in pieces, and their houses shall be made an ash heap; because there is no other God who can deliver like this."

30 Then the king promoted Shadrach, Meshach, and Abed-Nego in the province of Babylon.

---

19 בֵּאדַ֗יִן נְבוּכַדְנֶצַּר֙ הִתְמְלִ֤י
חֱמָא֙ וּצְלֵ֣ם אַנְפּ֔וֹהִי אֶשְׁתַּנִּ֗י עַל־שַׁדְרַ֤ךְ מֵישַׁךְ֙
וַעֲבֵ֣ד נְג֔וֹ עָנֵ֤ה וְאָמַר֙ לְמֵזֵ֣א לְאַתּוּנָ֔א חַד־שִׁבְעָ֕ה
עַ֛ל דִּ֥י חֲזֵ֖ה לְמֵזְיֵֽהּ׃ 20 וּלְגֻבְרִ֤ין גִּבָּֽרֵי־חַ֙יִל֙ דִּ֣י
בְחַיְלֵ֔הּ אֲמַר֙ לְכַפָּתָ֔ה לְשַׁדְרַ֥ךְ מֵישַׁ֖ךְ וַעֲבֵ֣ד נְג֑וֹ
לְמִרְמֵ֕א לְאַתּ֥וּן נוּרָ֖א יָקִֽדְתָּֽא׃ 21 בֵּאדַ֜יִן גֻּבְרַיָּ֣א
אִלֵּ֗ךְ כְּפִ֙תוּ֙ בְּסַרְבָּלֵיה֔וֹן פַּטְּשֵׁיהוֹן֙ וְכַרְבְּלָתְה֔וֹן
וּלְבֻשֵׁיה֑וֹן וּרְמִ֕יו לְגֽוֹא־אַתּ֥וּן נוּרָ֖א יָקִֽדְתָּֽא׃ 22 כָּל־
קֳבֵ֣ל דְּנָ֗ה מִן־דִּ֞י מִלַּ֤ת מַלְכָּא֙ מַחְצְפָ֔ה וְאַתּוּנָ֖א אֵזֵ֣ה
יַתִּ֑ירָא גֻּבְרַיָּ֣א אִלֵּ֗ךְ דִּ֤י הַסִּ֙קוּ֙ לְשַׁדְרַ֤ךְ מֵישַׁךְ֙ וַעֲבֵ֣ד
נְג֔וֹ קַטִּ֣ל הִמּ֔וֹן שְׁבִיבָ֖א דִּ֥י נוּרָֽא׃ 23 וְגֻבְרַיָּ֤א אִלֵּךְ֙
תְּלָֽתֵּה֔וֹן שַׁדְרַ֥ךְ מֵישַׁ֖ךְ וַעֲבֵ֣ד נְג֑וֹ נְפַ֛לוּ לְגֽוֹא־אַתּ֥וּן־
נוּרָ֖א יָקִֽדְתָּ֥א מְכַפְּתִֽין׃ פ

24 אֱדַ֙יִן֙ נְבוּכַדְנֶצַּ֣ר מַלְכָּ֔א תְּוַ֖הּ וְקָ֣ם בְּהִתְבְּהָלָ֑ה
עָנֵ֣ה וְאָמַ֗ר לְהַדָּֽבְר֙וֹהִי֙ הֲלָ֣א גֻבְרִ֤ין תְּלָתָא֙ רְמֵ֣ינָא
לְגֽוֹא־נוּרָא֙ מְכַפְּתִ֔ין עָנַ֥יִן וְאָמְרִ֖ין לְמַלְכָּ֑א יַצִּיבָ֖א
מַלְכָּֽא׃ 25 עָנֵ֣ה וְאָמַ֗ר הָֽא־אֲנָ֤ה חָזֵה֙ גֻּבְרִ֣ין
אַרְבְּעָ֗ה שְׁרַ֙יִן֙ מַהְלְכִ֣ין בְּגֽוֹא־נוּרָ֔א וַחֲבָ֖ל לָֽא־
אִיתַ֣י בְּה֑וֹן וְרֵוֵהּ֙ דִּ֣י רְבִיעָאָ֔ה דָּמֵ֖ה לְבַר־
אֱלָהִֽין׃ 26 בֵּאדַ֜יִן קְרֵ֣ב נְבוּכַדְנֶצַּ֗ר
לִתְרַ֣ע אַתּ֣וּן נוּרָא֮ יָקִֽדְתָּא֒ עָנֵ֣ה וְאָמַ֗ר שַׁדְרַ֨ךְ מֵישַׁ֜ךְ
וַעֲבֵד־נְג֗וֹ עַבְד֙וֹהִי֙ דִּֽי־אֱלָהָ֤א עִלָּאָה֙ פֻּ֣קוּ וֶאֱת֑וֹ
בֵּאדַ֣יִן נָֽפְקִ֗ין שַׁדְרַ֥ךְ מֵישַׁ֛ךְ וַעֲבֵ֥ד נְג֖וֹ מִן־גּ֥וֹא נוּרָֽא׃
27 וּֽמִתְכַּנְּשִׁ֞ין אֲחַשְׁדַּרְפְּנַיָּ֣א סִגְנַיָּ֗א וּפַחֲוָתָא֙ וְהַדָּֽבְרֵ֣י
מַלְכָּ֔א חָזַ֙יִן֙ לְגֻבְרַיָּ֣א אִלֵּ֔ךְ דִּ֡י לָֽא־שְׁלֵט֩ נוּרָ֨א
בְּגֶשְׁמְה֜וֹן וּשְׂעַ֤ר רֵֽאשְׁהוֹן֙ לָ֣א הִתְחָרַ֔ךְ וְסַרְבָּֽלֵיה֖וֹן
לָ֣א שְׁנ֑וֹ וְרֵ֣יחַ נ֔וּר לָ֥א עֲדָ֖ת בְּהֽוֹן׃ 28 עָנֵ֤ה נְבֽוּכַדְנֶצַּר֙
וְאָמַ֗ר בְּרִ֤יךְ אֱלָֽהֲהוֹן֙ דִּֽי־שַׁדְרַ֤ךְ מֵישַׁךְ֙ וַעֲבֵ֣ד נְג֔וֹ
דִּֽי־שְׁלַ֣ח מַלְאֲכֵ֗הּ וְשֵׁיזִ֤ב לְעַבְד֙וֹהִי֙ דִּ֣י הִתְרְחִ֣צוּ
עֲל֔וֹהִי וּמִלַּ֤ת מַלְכָּא֙ שַׁנִּ֔יו וִיהַ֣בוּ גֶשְׁמֵיה֗וֹן דִּ֠י
לָֽא־יִפְלְחֻ֤ן וְלָֽא־יִסְגְּדוּן֙ לְכָל־אֱלָ֔הּ לָהֵ֖ן לֵאלָֽהֲהֽוֹן׃
29 וּמִנִּי֮ שִׂ֣ים טְעֵם֒ דִּי֩ כָל־עַ֨ם אֻמָּ֜ה וְלִשָּׁ֗ן דִּֽי־יֵאמַ֤ר
שָׁלוּ֙ עַ֣ל אֱלָֽהֲה֗וֹן דִּֽי־שַׁדְרַ֤ךְ מֵישַׁךְ֙ וַעֲבֵ֣ד נְג֔וֹא
הַדָּמִ֣ין יִתְעֲבֵ֔ד וּבַיְתֵ֖הּ נְוָלִ֣י יִשְׁתַּוֵּ֑ה כָּל־קֳבֵ֗ל דִּ֣י לָ֤א
אִיתַ֙י אֱלָ֤ה אָֽחֳרָן֙ דִּֽי־יִכֻּ֣ל לְהַצָּלָ֖ה כִּדְנָֽה׃ 30 בֵּאדַ֣יִן

ג 19 אִשְׁתַּנִּ֑י   21 פַּטְּשֵׁיה֑וֹן   25 רְבִיעָאָ֑ה   26 עִלָּאָ֑ה
28 נִשְׁמְתֽוֹן   29 שָׁלֽוּ

4 Nebuchadnezzar the king,

To all peoples, nations, and languages that dwell in all the earth:

Peace be multiplied to you.

2 I thought it good to declare the signs and wonders that the Most High God has worked for me.

3 How great *are* His signs,
And how mighty His wonders!
His kingdom *is* an everlasting kingdom,
And His dominion *is* from generation to generation.

4 I, Nebuchadnezzar, was at rest in my house, and flourishing in my palace. 5 I saw a dream which made me afraid, and the thoughts on my bed and the visions of my head troubled me. 6 Therefore I issued a decree to bring in all the wise *men* of Babylon before me, that they might make known to me the interpretation of the dream. 7 Then the magicians, the astrologers, the Chaldeans, and the soothsayers came in, and I told them the dream; but they did not make known to me its interpretation. 8 But at last Daniel came before me (his name *is* Belteshazzar, according to the name of my god; in him *is* the Spirit of the Holy God), and I told the dream before him, *saying:* 9 "Belteshazzar, chief of the magicians, because I know that the Spirit of the Holy God *is* in you, and no secret troubles you, explain to me the visions of my dream that I have seen, and its interpretation.

10 "These *were* the visions of my head *while* on my bed:

I was looking, and behold,
A tree in the midst of the earth,
And its height was great.

11 The tree grew and became strong;
Its height reached to the heavens,
And it could be seen to the ends of all the earth.

12 Its leaves *were* lovely,
Its fruit abundant,
And in it *was* food for all.
The beasts of the field found shade under it,
The birds of the heavens dwelt in its branches,
And all flesh was fed from it.

13 "I saw in the visions of my head *while* on my bed, and there was a watcher, a holy one, coming down from heaven. 14 He cried aloud and said thus:

'Chop down the tree and cut off its branches,
Strip off its leaves and scatter its fruit.

מַלְכָּא הַצְלַח לְשַׁדְרַךְ מֵישַׁךְ וַעֲבֵד נְגוֹ בִּמְדִינַת
בָּבֶל: פ

31 נְבוּכַדְנֶצַּר מַלְכָּא לְכָל־עַמְמַיָּא אֻמַּיָּא וְלִשָּׁנַיָּא
דִּי־דָאֲרִין בְּכָל־אַרְעָא שְׁלָמְכוֹן יִשְׂגֵּא: 32 אָתַיָּא
וְתִמְהַיָּא דִּי עֲבַד עִמִּי אֱלָהָא עִלָּיָא שְׁפַר קָדָמַי
לְהַחֲוָיָה: 33 אָתוֹהִי כְּמָה רַבְרְבִין וְתִמְהוֹהִי כְּמָה
תַקִּיפִין מַלְכוּתֵהּ מַלְכוּת עָלַם וְשָׁלְטָנֵהּ עִם־דָּר
וְדָר:

ד אֲנָה נְבוּכַדְנֶצַּר שְׁלֵה הֲוֵית בְּבֵיתִי וְרַעְנַן
בְּהֵיכְלִי: 2 חֵלֶם חֲזֵית וִידַחֲלִנַּנִי וְהַרְהֹרִין עַל־
מִשְׁכְּבִי וְחֶזְוֵי רֵאשִׁי יְבַהֲלֻנַּנִי: 3 וּמִנִּי שִׂים טְעֵם
לְהַנְעָלָה קָדָמַי לְכֹל חַכִּימֵי בָבֶל דִּי־פְשַׁר חֶלְמָא
יְהוֹדְעֻנַּנִי: 4 בֵּאדַיִן עָלֲלִין חַרְטֻמַיָּא אָשְׁפַיָּא
כַּשְׂדָּיֵא וְגָזְרַיָּא וְחֶלְמָא אָמַר אֲנָה קָדָמֵיהוֹן
וּפִשְׁרֵהּ לָא־מְהוֹדְעִין לִי: 5 וְעַד אָחֳרֵין עַל קָדָמַי
דָּנִיֵּאל דִּי־שְׁמֵהּ בֵּלְטְשַׁאצַּר כְּשֻׁם אֱלָהִי וְדִי
רוּחַ־אֱלָהִין קַדִּישִׁין בֵּהּ וְחֶלְמָא קָדָמוֹהִי אַמְרֵת:
6 בֵּלְטְשַׁאצַּר רַב חַרְטֻמַיָּא דִּי | אֲנָה יִדְעֵת דִּי
רוּחַ אֱלָהִין קַדִּישִׁין בָּךְ וְכָל־רָז לָא־אָנֵס לָךְ חֶזְוֵי
חֶלְמִי דִי־חֲזֵית וּפִשְׁרֵהּ אֱמַר: 7 וְחֶזְוֵי רֵאשִׁי עַל־
מִשְׁכְּבִי חָזֵה הֲוֵית וַאֲלוּ אִילָן בְּגוֹא אַרְעָא וְרוּמֵהּ
שַׂגִּיא: 8 רְבָה אִילָנָא וּתְקִף וְרוּמֵהּ יִמְטֵא לִשְׁמַיָּא
וַחֲזוֹתֵהּ לְסוֹף כָּל־אַרְעָא: 9 עָפְיֵהּ שַׁפִּיר וְאִנְבֵּהּ
שַׂגִּיא וּמָזוֹן לְכֹלָּא־בֵהּ תְּחֹתוֹהִי תַּטְלֵל | חֵיוַת
בָּרָא וּבְעַנְפוֹהִי יְדֻרָון צִפְּרֵי שְׁמַיָּא וּמִנֵּהּ יִתְּזִין
כָּל־בִּשְׂרָא: 10 חָזֵה הֲוֵית בְּחֶזְוֵי רֵאשִׁי עַל־מִשְׁכְּבִי
וַאֲלוּ עִיר וְקַדִּישׁ מִן־שְׁמַיָּא נָחִת: 11 קָרֵא בְחַיִל
וְכֵן אָמַר גֹּדּוּ אִילָנָא וְקַצִּצוּ עַנְפוֹהִי אַתַּרוּ עָפְיֵהּ
וּבַדַּרוּ אִנְבֵּהּ תְּנֻד חֵיוְתָא מִן־תַּחְתּוֹהִי וְצִפְּרַיָּא

Let the beasts get out from under it,
And the birds from its branches.

15 Nevertheless leave the stump and roots in the earth,
Bound with a band of iron and bronze,
In the tender grass of the field.
Let it be wet with the dew of heaven,
And *let* him graze with the beasts
On the grass of the earth.

16 Let his heart be changed from *that of* a man,
Let him be given the heart of a beast,
And let seven times pass over him.

17 'This decision *is* by the decree of the watchers,
And the sentence by the word of the holy ones,
In order that the living may know
That the Most High rules in the kingdom of men,
Gives it to whomever He will,
And sets over it the lowest of men.'

18 "This dream I, King Nebuchadnezzar, have seen. Now you, Belteshazzar, declare its interpretation, since all the wise *men* of my kingdom are not able to make known to me the interpretation; but you *are* able, for the Spirit of the Holy God *is* in you."

19 Then Daniel, whose name was Belteshazzar, was astonished for a time, and his thoughts troubled him. *So* the king spoke, and said, "Belteshazzar, do not let the dream or its interpretation trouble you."

Belteshazzar answered and said, "My lord, *may* the dream concern those who hate you, and its interpretation concern your enemies!

20 "The tree that you saw, which grew and became strong, whose height reached to the heavens and which *could be seen* by all the earth, 21 whose leaves *were* lovely and its fruit abundant, in which *was* food for all, under which the beasts of the field dwelt, and in whose branches the birds of the heaven had their home— 22 it *is* you, O king, who have grown and become strong; for your greatness has grown and reaches to the heavens, and your dominion to the end of the earth.

23 "And inasmuch as the king saw a watcher, a holy one, coming down from heaven and saying, 'Chop down the tree and destroy it, but leave its stump and roots in the earth, *bound* with a band of iron and bronze in the tender grass of the field; let it be wet with the dew of heaven, and let him graze with the beasts of the field, till seven times pass over him'; 24 this is the interpretation, O king, and this is the decree of the Most High, which

מִן־עַנְפּוֹהִי: 12 בְּרַם עִקַּר שָׁרְשׁוֹהִי בְּאַרְעָא שְׁבֻקוּ
וּבֶאֱסוּר דִּי־פַרְזֶל וּנְחָשׁ בְּדִתְאָא דִּי בָרָא וּבְטַל
שְׁמַיָּא יִצְטַבַּע וְעִם־חֵיוְתָא חֲלָקֵהּ בַּעֲשַׂב אַרְעָא:
13 לִבְבֵהּ מִן־אֲנָשָׁא יְשַׁנּוֹן וּלְבַב חֵיוָה יִתְיְהִב
לֵהּ וְשִׁבְעָה עִדָּנִין יַחְלְפוּן עֲלוֹהִי: 14 בִּגְזֵרַת
עִירִין פִּתְגָמָא וּמֵאמַר קַדִּישִׁין שְׁאֵלְתָא עַד־
דִּבְרַת דִּי יִנְדְּעוּן חַיַּיָּא דִּי־שַׁלִּיט עִלָּיָא בְּמַלְכוּת
אֲנָשָׁא וּלְמַן־דִּי יִצְבֵּא יִתְּנִנַּהּ וּשְׁפַל אֲנָשִׁים יְקִים
עֲלַיהּ: 15 דְּנָה חֶלְמָא חֲזֵית אֲנָה מַלְכָּא נְבוּכַדְנֶצַּר
וְאַנְתְּה בֵּלְטְשַׁאצַּר פִּשְׁרֵא אֱמַר | כָּל־קֳבֵל דִּי |
כָּל־חַכִּימֵי מַלְכוּתִי לָא־יָכְלִין פִּשְׁרָא לְהוֹדָעֻתַנִי
וְאַנְתְּה כָּהֵל דִּי רוּחַ־אֱלָהִין קַדִּישִׁין בָּךְ: 16 אֱדַיִן
דָּנִיֵּאל דִּי־שְׁמֵהּ בֵּלְטְשַׁאצַּר אֶשְׁתּוֹמַם כְּשָׁעָה חֲדָה
וְרַעְיֹנֹהִי יְבַהֲלֻנֵּהּ עָנֵה מַלְכָּא וְאָמַר בֵּלְטְשַׁאצַּר
חֶלְמָא וּפִשְׁרֵא אַל־יְבַהֲלָךְ עָנֵה בֵלְטְשַׁאצַּר וְאָמַר
מָרִאי חֶלְמָא לְשָׂנְאָיךְ וּפִשְׁרֵהּ לְעָרָיךְ: 17 אִילָנָא
דִּי חֲזַיְתָ דִּי רְבָה וּתְקִף וְרוּמֵהּ יִמְטֵא לִשְׁמַיָּא
וַחֲזוֹתֵהּ לְכָל־אַרְעָא: 18 וְעָפְיֵהּ שַׁפִּיר וְאִנְבֵּהּ
שַׂגִּיא וּמָזוֹן לְכֹלָּא־בֵהּ תְּחֹתוֹהִי תְּדוּר חֵיוַת בָּרָא
וּבְעַנְפוֹהִי יִשְׁכְּנָן צִפֲּרֵי שְׁמַיָּא: 19 אַנְתְּה הוּא אַנְתְּ־
הוּא מַלְכָּא דִּי רְבַית וּתְקֵפְתְּ וּרְבוּתָךְ רְבָת
וּמְטָת לִשְׁמַיָּא וְשָׁלְטָנָךְ לְסוֹף אַרְעָא: 20 וְדִי חֲזָה
מַלְכָּא עִיר וְקַדִּישׁ נָחִת | מִן־שְׁמַיָּא וְאָמַר גֹּדּוּ
אִילָנָא וְחַבְּלוּהִי בְּרַם עִקַּר שָׁרְשׁוֹהִי בְּאַרְעָא שְׁבֻקוּ
וּבֶאֱסוּר דִּי־פַרְזֶל וּנְחָשׁ בְּדִתְאָא דִּי בָרָא וּבְטַל
שְׁמַיָּא יִצְטַבַּע וְעִם־חֵיוַת בָּרָא חֲלָקֵהּ עַד דִּי־
שִׁבְעָה עִדָּנִין יַחְלְפוּן עֲלוֹהִי: 21 דְּנָה פִשְׁרָא מַלְכָּא
וּגְזֵרַת עִלָּיָא הִיא דִּי מְטָת עַל־מָרִאי מַלְכָּא:

ד 13 אֲנָשָׁא   14 עִלָּאָה אֲנָשָׁא עֲלַהּ   15 וְאַנְתְּ וְאַנְתְּ
16 מָרִי לְשָׂנְאָךְ לְעָרָךְ   19 רְבַת   21 עִלָּאָה מָרִי

has come upon my lord the king: ²⁵ They shall drive you from men, your dwelling shall be with the beasts of the field, and they shall make you eat grass like oxen. They shall wet you with the dew of heaven, and seven times shall pass over you, till you know that the Most High rules in the kingdom of men, and gives it to whomever He chooses.

26 "And inasmuch as they gave the command to leave the stump *and* roots of the tree, your kingdom shall be assured to you, after you come to know that Heaven rules. ²⁷ Therefore, O king, let my advice be acceptable to you; break off your sins by *being* righteous, and your iniquities by showing mercy to *the* poor. Perhaps there may be a lengthening of your prosperity."

28 All *this* came upon King Nebuchadnezzar. ²⁹ At the end of the twelve months he was walking about the royal palace of Babylon. ³⁰ The king spoke, saying, "Is not this great Babylon, that I have built for a royal dwelling by my mighty power and for the honor of my majesty?"

31 While the word *was still* in the king's mouth, a voice fell from heaven: "King Nebuchadnezzar, to you it is spoken: the kingdom has departed from you! ³² And they shall drive you from men, and your dwelling *shall be* with the beasts of the field. They shall make you eat grass like oxen; and seven times shall pass over you, until you know that the Most High rules in the kingdom of men, and gives it to whomever He chooses."

33 That very hour the word was fulfilled concerning Nebuchadnezzar; he was driven from men and ate grass like oxen; his body was wet with the dew of heaven till his hair had grown like eagles' *feathers* and his nails like birds' *claws*.

34 And at the end of the time I, Nebuchadnezzar, lifted my eyes to heaven, and my understanding returned to me; and I blessed the Most High and praised and honored Him who lives forever:

For His dominion *is* an everlasting dominion,
And His kingdom *is* from generation to generation.

35 All the inhabitants of the earth *are* reputed as nothing;
He does according to His will in the army of heaven

וְלָ֣ךְ טָֽרְדִ֣ין מִן־אֲנָשָׁ֗א וְעִם־חֵיוַ֤ת בָּרָא֙ לֶהֱוֵ֣ה
מְדֹרָ֔ךְ וְעִשְׂבָּ֤א כְתוֹרִין֙ ׀ לָ֣ךְ יְטַעֲמ֗וּן וּמִטַּ֤ל שְׁמַיָּא֙
לָ֣ךְ מְצַבְּעִ֔ין וְשִׁבְעָ֥ה עִדָּנִ֖ין יַחְלְפ֣וּן עֲלָ֑ךְP עַ֣ד
דִּֽי־תִנְדַּ֗ע דִּֽי־שַׁלִּ֤יט עִלָּיָא֙P בְּמַלְכ֣וּת אֲנָשָׁ֔א וּלְמַן־
דִּ֥י יִצְבֵּ֖א יִתְּנִנַּֽהּ: ²³ וְדִ֣י אֲמַ֗רוּ לְמִשְׁבַּ֞ק עִקַּ֤ר
שָׁרְשׁ֙וֹהִי֙ דִּ֣י אִֽילָנָ֔א מַלְכוּתָ֖ךְ לָ֣ךְ קַיָּמָ֑ה מִן־דִּ֣י
תִנְדַּ֔ע דִּ֥י שַׁלִּטִ֖ן שְׁמַיָּֽא: ²⁴ לָהֵ֣ן מַלְכָּ֗א מִלְכִּי֙ יִשְׁפַּ֣ר
עֲלָ֔ךְP וַחֲטָיָךְ֙P בְּצִדְקָ֣ה פְרֻ֔ק וַעֲוָֽיָתָ֖ךְ בְּמִחַ֣ן עֲנָ֑יִן
הֵ֛ן תֶּהֱוֵ֥א אַרְכָ֖ה לִשְׁלֵוְתָֽךְP: ²⁵ כֹּ֖לָּא מְטָ֣א עַל־
נְבוּכַדְנֶצַּ֥ר מַלְכָּֽא: פ

²⁶ לִקְצָ֥ת יַרְחִ֖ין תְּרֵֽי־עֲשַׂ֑ר עַל־הֵיכַ֛ל מַלְכוּתָ֥א דִּ֥י
בָבֶ֖ל מְהַלֵּ֥ךְ הֲוָֽה: ²⁷ עָנֵ֤ה מַלְכָּא֙ וְאָמַ֔ר הֲלָ֥א דָֽא־
הִ֤יא בָּבֶ֣ל רַבְּתָ֔א דִּֽי־אֲנָ֥ה בֱנַיְתַ֛הּ לְבֵ֥ית מַלְכ֖וּ
בִּתְקַ֣ף חִסְנִ֑י וְלִיקָ֖ר הַדְרִֽי: ²⁸ ע֗וֹד מִלְּתָא֙ בְּפֻ֣ם
מַלְכָּ֔א קָ֖ל מִן־שְׁמַיָּ֣א נְפַ֑ל לָ֣ךְ אָֽמְרִ֗ין נְבוּכַדְנֶצַּ֤ר
מַלְכָּא֙ מַלְכוּתָ֖ה עֲדָ֥ת מִנָּֽךְ: ²⁹ וּמִן־אֲנָשָׁא֩ לָ֨ךְ
טָֽרְדִ֜ין וְעִם־חֵיוַ֤ת בָּרָא֙ מְדֹרָ֔ךְ עִשְׂבָּ֤א כְתוֹרִין֙ לָ֣ךְ
יְטַעֲמ֗וּן וְשִׁבְעָ֤ה עִדָּנִין֙ יַחְלְפ֣וּן עֲלָ֔ךְP עַ֣ד דִּֽי־
תִנְדַּ֗ע דִּֽי־שַׁלִּ֤יט עִלָּיָא֙P בְּמַלְכ֣וּת אֲנָשָׁ֔א וּלְמַן־
דִּ֥י יִצְבֵּ֖א יִתְּנִנַּֽהּ: ³⁰ בַּהּ־שַׁעֲתָ֗א מִלְּתָא֮ סָ֣פַת עַל־
נְבוּכַדְנֶצַּר֒ וּמִן־אֲנָשָׁ֣א טְרִ֔יד וְעִשְׂבָּ֤א כְתוֹרִין֙ יֵאכֻ֔ל
וּמִטַּ֤ל שְׁמַיָּא֙ גִּשְׁמֵ֣הּ יִצְטַבַּ֔ע עַ֛ד דִּ֥י שַׂעְרֵ֖הּ כְּנִשְׁרִ֣ין
רְבָ֑ה וְטִפְר֖וֹהִי כְצִפְּרִֽין: ³¹ וְלִקְצָ֣ת יֽוֹמַיָּה֩ אֲנָ֨ה
נְבוּכַדְנֶצַּ֜ר עַיְנַ֣י ׀ לִשְׁמַיָּ֣א נִטְלֵ֗ת וּמַנְדְּעִי֙ עֲלַ֣י
יְת֔וּב וּלְעִלָּיָא֙P בָּרְכֵ֔ת וּלְחַ֥י עָֽלְמָ֖א שַׁבְּחֵ֣ת וְהַדְּרֵ֑ת
דִּ֤י שָׁלְטָנֵהּ֙ שָׁלְטָ֣ן עָלַ֔ם וּמַלְכוּתֵ֖הּ עִם־דָּ֥ר וְדָֽר:
³² וְכָל־דָּֽאֲרֵי֙P אַרְעָ֔א כְּלָ֖ה חֲשִׁיבִ֑ין וּֽכְמִצְבְּיֵ֗הּ עָבֵד֙
בְּחֵ֣יל שְׁמַיָּ֔א וְדָֽאֲרֵ֖יP אַרְעָ֑א וְלָ֤א אִיתַי֙ דִּֽי־יְמַחֵ֣א

And *among* the inhabitants of the earth.
No one can restrain His hand
Or say to Him, "What have You done?"

36 At the same time my reason returned to me,
and for the glory of my kingdom, my honor
and splendor returned to me. My counselors
and nobles resorted to me, I was restored to
my kingdom, and excellent majesty was
added to me. 37 Now I, Nebuchadnezzar,
praise and extol and honor the King of
heaven, all of whose works *are* truth, and
His ways justice. And those who walk in
pride He is able to put down.

5 Belshazzar the king made a great feast for a
thousand of his lords, and drank wine in the
presence of the thousand. 2 While he tasted the
wine, Belshazzar gave the command to bring the
gold and silver vessels which his father Nebuchadnezzar had taken from the temple which *had been* in
Jerusalem, that the king and his lords, his wives,
and his concubines might drink from them. 3 Then
they brought the gold vessels that had been taken
from the temple of the house of God which *had been*
in Jerusalem; and the king and his lords, his wives,
and his concubines drank from them. 4 They drank
wine, and praised the gods of gold and silver,
bronze and iron, wood and stone.

5 In the same hour the fingers of a man's hand
appeared and wrote opposite the lampstand on the
plaster of the wall of the king's palace; and the king
saw the part of the hand that wrote. 6 Then the
king's countenance changed, and his thoughts
troubled him, so that the joints of his hips were
loosened and his knees knocked against each other.
7 The king cried aloud to bring in the astrologers,
the Chaldeans, and the soothsayers. The king
spoke, saying to the wise *men* of Babylon, "Whoever reads this writing, and tells me its interpretation, shall be clothed with purple and *have* a chain
of gold around his neck; and he shall be the third
ruler in the kingdom." 8 Now all the king's wise *men*
came, but they could not read the writing, or make
known to the king its interpretation. 9 Then King
Belshazzar was greatly troubled, his countenance
was changed, and his lords were astonished.

10 The queen, because of the words of the king
and his lords, came to the banquet hall. The queen
spoke, saying, "O king, live forever! Do not let your
thoughts trouble you, nor let your countenance
change. 11 There is a man in your kingdom in whom
is the Spirit of the Holy God. And in the days of
your father, light and understanding and wisdom,
like the wisdom of the gods, were found in him; and

33 בַּהּ־זִמְנָא מַנְדְּעִי | יְתוּב עֲלַי וְלִיקַר מַלְכוּתִי הַדְרִי וְזִוִי יְתוּב עֲלַי וְלִי הַדָּבְרַי וְרַבְרְבָנַי יְבַעוֹן וְעַל־מַלְכוּתִי הָתְקְנַת וּרְבוּ יַתִּירָה הוּסְפַת לִי: 34 כְּעַן אֲנָה נְבוּכַדְנֶצַּר מְשַׁבַּח וּמְרוֹמֵם וּמְהַדַּר לְמֶלֶךְ שְׁמַיָּא דִּי כָל־מַעֲבָדוֹהִי קְשֹׁט וְאֹרְחָתֵהּ דִּין וְדִי מַהְלְכִין בְּגֵוָה יָכִל לְהַשְׁפָּלָה: פ

ה בֵּלְשַׁאצַּר מַלְכָּא עֲבַד לְחֶם רַב לְרַבְרְבָנוֹהִי אֲלַף וְלָקֳבֵל אַלְפָּא חַמְרָא שָׁתֵה: 2 בֵּלְשַׁאצַּר אֲמַר | בִּטְעֵם חַמְרָא לְהַיְתָיָה לְמָאנֵי דַּהֲבָא וְכַסְפָּא דִּי הַנְפֵּק נְבוּכַדְנֶצַּר אֲבוּהִי מִן־הֵיכְלָא דִּי בִירוּשְׁלֶם וְיִשְׁתּוֹן בְּהוֹן מַלְכָּא וְרַבְרְבָנוֹהִי שֵׁגְלָתֵהּ וּלְחֵנָתֵהּ: 3 בֵּאדַיִן הַיְתִיו מָאנֵי דַהֲבָא דִּי הַנְפִּקוּ מִן־הֵיכְלָא דִּי־בֵית אֱלָהָא דִּי בִירוּשְׁלֶם וְאִשְׁתִּיו בְּהוֹן מַלְכָּא וְרַבְרְבָנוֹהִי שֵׁגְלָתֵהּ וּלְחֵנָתֵהּ: 4 אִשְׁתִּיו חַמְרָא וְשַׁבַּחוּ לֵאלָהֵי דַּהֲבָא וְכַסְפָּא נְחָשָׁא פַרְזְלָא אָעָא וְאַבְנָא: 5 בַּהּ־שַׁעֲתָה נְפַקוּ אֶצְבְּעָן דִּי יַד־אֱנָשׁ וְכָתְבָן לָקֳבֵל נֶבְרַשְׁתָּא עַל־גִּירָא דִּי־כְתַל הֵיכְלָא דִּי מַלְכָּא וּמַלְכָּא חָזֵה פַּס יְדָה דִּי כָתְבָה: 6 אֱדַיִן מַלְכָּא זִיוֹהִי שְׁנוֹהִי וְרַעְיֹנֹהִי יְבַהֲלוּנֵּהּ וְקִטְרֵי חַרְצֵהּ מִשְׁתָּרַיִן וְאַרְכֻבָּתֵהּ דָּא לְדָא נָקְשָׁן: 7 קָרֵא מַלְכָּא בְּחַיִל לְהֶעָלָה לְאָשְׁפַיָּא כַּשְׂדָּיֵאP וְגָזְרַיָּא עָנֵה מַלְכָּא וְאָמַר | לְחַכִּימֵי בָבֶל דִּי כָל־אֱנָשׁ דִּי־יִקְרֵה כְּתָבָה דְנָה וּפִשְׁרֵהּ יְחַוִּנַּנִי אַרְגְּוָנָא יִלְבַּשׁ וְהַמְונְכָאP דִּי־דַהֲבָא עַל־צַוְּארֵהּ וְתַלְתִּי בְמַלְכוּתָא יִשְׁלַט: ס 8 אֱדַיִן עָלֲלִיןP כֹּל חַכִּימֵי מַלְכָּא וְלָא־כָהֲלִין כְּתָבָא לְמִקְרֵא וּפִשְׁרֵאP לְהוֹדָעָה לְמַלְכָּא: 9 אֱדַיִן מַלְכָּא בֵּלְשַׁאצַּר שַׂגִּיא מִתְבָּהַל וְזִיוֹהִי שָׁנַיִן עֲלוֹהִי וְרַבְרְבָנוֹהִי מִשְׁתַּבְּשִׁין: 10 מַלְכְּתָא לָקֳבֵל מִלֵּי מַלְכָּא וְרַבְרְבָנוֹהִי לְבֵית מִשְׁתְּיָא עַלַּתP עֲנָת מַלְכְּתָא וַאֲמֶרֶת מַלְכָּא לְעָלְמִין חֱיִי אַל־יְבַהֲלוּךְ רַעְיוֹנָךְ וְזִיוָיךְ אַל־יִשְׁתַּנּוֹ: 11 אִיתַי גְּבַר בְּמַלְכוּתָךְ דִּי רוּחַ אֱלָהִין קַדִּישִׁין בֵּהּ וּבְיוֹמֵי אֲבוּךְ נַהִירוּ

King Nebuchadnezzar your father—your father the king—made him chief of the magicians, astrologers, Chaldeans, *and* soothsayers. [12] Inasmuch as an excellent spirit, knowledge, understanding, interpreting dreams, solving riddles, and explaining enigmas were found in this Daniel, whom the king named Belteshazzar, now let Daniel be called, and he will give the interpretation."

[13] Then Daniel was brought in before the king. The king spoke, and said to Daniel, "*Are* you that Daniel who is one of the captives from Judah, whom my father the king brought from Judah? [14] I have heard of you, that the Spirit of God *is* in you, and *that* light and understanding and excellent wisdom are found in you. [15] Now the wise *men,* the astrologers, have been brought in before me, that they should read this writing and make known to me its interpretation, but they could not give the interpretation of the thing. [16] And I have heard of you, that you can give interpretations and explain enigmas. Now if you can read the writing and make known to me its interpretation, you shall be clothed with purple and *have* a chain of gold around your neck, and shall be the third ruler in the kingdom."

[17] Then Daniel answered, and said before the king, "Let your gifts be for yourself, and give your rewards to another; yet I will read the writing to the king, and make known to him the interpretation. [18] O king, the Most High God gave Nebuchadnezzar your father a kingdom and majesty, glory and honor. [19] And because of the majesty that He gave him, all peoples, nations, and languages trembled and feared before him. Whomever he wished, he executed; whomever he wished, he kept alive; whomever he wished, he set up; and whomever he wished, he put down. [20] But when his heart was lifted up, and his spirit was hardened in pride, he was deposed from his kingly throne, and they took his glory from him. [21] Then he was driven from the sons of men, his heart was made like the beasts, and his dwelling *was* with the wild donkeys. They fed him with grass like oxen, and his body was wet with the dew of heaven, till he knew that the Most High God rules in the kingdom of men, and appoints over it whomever He chooses.

[22] "But you his son, Belshazzar, have not humbled your heart, although you knew all this. [23] And you have lifted yourself up against the Lord of heaven. They have brought the vessels of His house before you, and you and your lords, your wives and your concubines, have drunk wine from them. And you have praised the gods of silver and gold, bronze and iron, wood and stone, which do not see or hear or know; and the God who *holds*

וְשָׂכְלְתָנוּ וְחָכְמָה כְּחָכְמַת־אֱלָהִין הִשְׁתְּכַחַת בֵּהּ וּמַלְכָּא נְבֻכַדְנֶצַּר אֲבוּךְ רַב חַרְטֻמִּין אָשְׁפִין כַּשְׂדָּאִין גָּזְרִין הֲקִימֵהּ אֲבוּךְ מַלְכָּא: 12 כָּל־קֳבֵל דִּי רוּחַ ׀ יַתִּירָה וּמַנְדַּע וְשָׂכְלְתָנוּ מְפַשַּׁר חֶלְמִין וַאַחֲוָיַת אֲחִידָן וּמְשָׁרֵא קִטְרִין הִשְׁתְּכַחַת בֵּהּ בְּדָנִיֵּאל דִּי־מַלְכָּא שָׂם־שְׁמֵהּ בֵּלְטְשַׁאצַּר כְּעַן דָּנִיֵּאל יִתְקְרֵי וּפִשְׁרָה יְהַחֲוֵה: פ

13 בֵּאדַיִן דָּנִיֵּאל הֻעַל קֳדָם מַלְכָּא עָנֵה מַלְכָּא וְאָמַר לְדָנִיֵּאל אַנְתָּה־ק הוּא דָנִיֵּאל דִּי־מִן־בְּנֵי גָלוּתָא דִּי יְהוּד דִּי הַיְתִי מַלְכָּא אֲבִי מִן־ יְהוּד: 14 וְשִׁמְעֵת עֲלָיְךְק דִּי רוּחַ אֱלָהִין בָּךְ וְנַהִירוּ וְשָׂכְלְתָנוּ וְחָכְמָה יַתִּירָה הִשְׁתְּכַחַת בָּךְ: 15 וּכְעַן הֻעַלּוּ קָדָמַי חַכִּימַיָּא אָשְׁפַיָּא דִּי־כְתָבָה דְנָה יִקְרוֹן וּפִשְׁרֵהּ לְהוֹדָעֻתַנִי וְלָא־כָהֲלִין פְּשַׁר־ מִלְּתָא לְהַחֲוָיָה: 16 וַאֲנָה שִׁמְעֵת עֲלָיְךְק דִּי־תִיכּוּלק פִּשְׁרִין לְמִפְשַׁר וְקִטְרִין לְמִשְׁרֵא כְּעַן הֵן תִּיכּוּלק כְּתָבָא לְמִקְרֵא וּפִשְׁרֵהּ לְהוֹדָעֻתַנִי אַרְגְּוָנָא תִלְבַּשׁ וְהַמְנוּכָאק דִּי־דַהֲבָא עַל־צַוְּארָךְ וְתַלְתָּא בְמַלְכוּתָא תִּשְׁלַט: פ

17 בֵּאדַיִן עָנֵה דָנִיֵּאל וְאָמַר קֳדָם מַלְכָּא מַתְּנָתָךְ לָךְ לֶהֶוְיָן וּנְבָזְבְּיָתָךְ לְאָחֳרָן הַב בְּרַם כְּתָבָא אֶקְרֵא לְמַלְכָּא וּפִשְׁרָא אֲהוֹדְעִנֵּהּ: 18 אַנְתָּה ק מַלְכָּא אֱלָהָא עִלָּיָאק מַלְכוּתָא וּרְבוּתָא וִיקָרָא וְהַדְרָה יְהַב לִנְבֻכַדְנֶצַּר אֲבוּךְ: 19 וּמִן־רְבוּתָא דִּי יְהַב־לֵהּ כֹּל עַמְמַיָּא אֻמַּיָּא וְלִשָּׁנַיָּא הֲווֹ זָאֲעִיןק וְדָחֲלִין מִן־ קֳדָמוֹהִי דִּי־הֲוָה צָבֵא הֲוָא קָטֵל וְדִי־הֲוָה צָבֵא הֲוָה מַחֵא וְדִי־הֲוָה צָבֵא הֲוָה מָרִים וְדִי־הֲוָה צָבֵא הֲוָה מַשְׁפִּיל: 20 וּכְדִיק רִם לִבְבֵהּ וְרוּחֵהּ תִּקְפַת לַהֲזָדָה הָנְחַת מִן־כָּרְסֵא מַלְכוּתֵהּ וִיקָרָה הֶעְדִּיוּ מִנֵּהּ: 21 וּמִן־בְּנֵי אֲנָשָׁא טְרִיד וְלִבְבֵהּ ׀ עִם־ חֵיוְתָא שַׁוִּיק וְעִם־עֲרָדַיָּא מְדוֹרֵהּ עִשְׂבָּא כְתוֹרִין יְטַעֲמוּנֵּהּ וּמִטַּל שְׁמַיָּא גִּשְׁמֵהּ יִצְטַבַּע עַד דִּי־יְדַע דִּי־שַׁלִּיט אֱלָהָא עִלָּיָאק בְּמַלְכוּת אֲנָשָׁא וּלְמַן־דִּי יִצְבֵּה יְהָקֵים עֲלַיַּהּק: 22 וְאַנְתָּהק בְּרֵהּ בֵּלְשַׁאצַּר לָא הַשְׁפֵּלְתְּ לִבְבָךְ כָּל־קֳבֵל דִּי כָּל־דְּנָה יְדַעְתָּ: 23 וְעַל מָרֵא־שְׁמַיָּא ׀ הִתְרוֹמַמְתָּ וּלְמָאנַיָּא דִי־ בַיְתֵהּ הַיְתִיו קָדָמָיְךְק וְאַנְתָּהק וְרַבְרְבָנָיְךְ שֵׁגְלָתָךְ וּלְחֵנָתָךְ חַמְרָא שָׁתַיִן בְּהוֹן וְלֵאלָהֵי כַסְפָּא־וְדַהֲבָא

ה 13 אַנְתָּ־ק   14 עֲלָךְ   16 עֲלָךְ תִּיכּוּל תֻּכַל וְהַמְנִיכָא
18 אַנְתְּ עִלָּאָה   19 זָיְעִין   21 שַׁוִּיו עִלָּאָה עֲלַהּ
22 וְאַנְתְּ   23 קָדָמָךְ וְאַנְתְּ וְרַבְרְבָנָךְ

your breath in His hand and owns all your ways, you have not glorified. 24 Then the fingers of the hand were sent from Him, and this writing was written.

25 "And this is the inscription that was written: MENE, MENE, TEKEL, UPHARSIN.

26 This *is* the interpretation of *each* word. MENE: God has numbered your kingdom, and finished it; 27 TEKEL: You have been weighed in the balances, and found wanting; 28 PERES: Your kingdom has been divided, and given to the Medes and Persians." 29 Then Belshazzar gave the command, and they clothed Daniel with purple and *put a* chain of gold around his neck, and made a proclamation concerning him that he should be the third ruler in the kingdom.

30 That very night Belshazzar, king of the Chaldeans, was slain. 31 And Darius the Mede received the kingdom, *being* about sixty-two years old.

6 It pleased Darius to set over the kingdom one hundred and twenty satraps, to be over the whole kingdom; 2 and over these, three governors, of whom Daniel *was* one, that the satraps might give account to them, so that the king would suffer no loss. 3 Then this Daniel distinguished himself above the governors and satraps, because an excellent spirit *was* in him; and the king gave thought to setting him over the whole realm. 4 So the governors and satraps sought to find *some* charge against Daniel concerning the kingdom; but they could find no charge or fault, because he *was* faithful; nor was there any error or fault found in him. 5 Then these men said, "We shall not find any charge against this Daniel unless we find *it* against him concerning the law of his God."

6 So these governors and satraps thronged before the king, and said thus to him: "King Darius, live forever! 7 All the governors of the kingdom, the administrators and satraps, the counselors and advisors, have consulted together to establish a royal statute and to make a firm decree, that whoever petitions any god or man for thirty days, except you, O king, shall be cast into the den of lions. 8 Now, O king, establish the decree and sign the writing, so that it cannot be changed, according to the law of the Medes and Persians, which does not alter." 9 Therefore King Darius signed the written decree.

10 Now when Daniel knew that the writing was signed, he went home. And in his upper room, with his windows open toward Jerusalem, he knelt down

נְחָשָׁא פַרְזְלָא אָעָא וְאַבְנָא דִּי לָא־חָזַיִן וְלָא־שָׁמְעִין וְלָא יָדְעִין שַׁבַּחְתָּ וְלֵאלָהָא דִּי־נִשְׁמְתָךְ בִּידֵהּ וְכָל־ אֹרְחָתָךְ לֵהּ לָא הַדַּרְתָּ: 24 בֵּאדַיִן מִן־קֳדָמוֹהִי שְׁלִיחַ פַּסָּא דִי־יְדָא וּכְתָבָא דְּנָה רְשִׁים: 25 וּדְנָה כְתָבָא דִּי רְשִׁים מְנֵא מְנֵא תְקֵל וּפַרְסִין: 26 דְּנָה פְּשַׁר־מִלְּתָא מְנֵא מְנָה־אֱלָהָא מַלְכוּתָךְ וְהַשְׁלְמַהּ: 27 תְּקֵל תְּקִילְתָּה בְמֹאזַנְיָא וְהִשְׁתְּכַחַתְּ חַסִּיר: 28 פְּרֵס פְּרִיסַת מַלְכוּתָךְ וִיהִיבַת לְמָדַי וּפָרָס: 29 בֵּאדַיִן אֲמַר בֵּלְשַׁאצַּר וְהַלְבִּישׁוּ לְדָנִיֵּאל אַרְגְּוָנָא וְהַמְונְכָא דִי־דַהֲבָא עַל־צַוְּארֵהּ וְהַכְרִזוּ עֲלוֹהִי דִּי־לֶהֱוֵא שַׁלִּיט תַּלְתָּא בְּמַלְכוּתָא: 30 בֵּהּ בְּלֵילְיָא קְטִיל בֵּלְאשַׁצַּר מַלְכָּא כַשְׂדָּיָא: פ

ו וְדָרְיָוֶשׁ מָדָיָא קַבֵּל מַלְכוּתָא כְּבַר שְׁנִין שִׁתִּין וְתַרְתֵּין: 2 שְׁפַר קֳדָם דָּרְיָוֶשׁ וַהֲקִים עַל־ מַלְכוּתָא לַאֲחַשְׁדַּרְפְּנַיָּא מְאָה וְעֶשְׂרִין דִּי לֶהֱוֹן בְּכָל־מַלְכוּתָא: 3 וְעֵלָּא מִנְּהוֹן סָרְכִין תְּלָתָא דִּי דָנִיֵּאל חַד־מִנְּהוֹן דִּי־לֶהֱוֹן אֲחַשְׁדַּרְפְּנַיָּא אִלֵּין יָהֲבִין לְהוֹן טַעְמָא וּמַלְכָּא לָא־לֶהֱוֵא נָזִק: 4 אֱדַיִן דָּנִיֵּאל דְּנָה הֲוָא מִתְנַצַּח עַל־סָרְכַיָּא וַאֲחַשְׁדַּרְפְּנַיָּא כָּל־ קֳבֵל דִּי רוּחַ יַתִּירָא בֵּהּ וּמַלְכָּא עֲשִׁית לַהֲקָמוּתֵהּ עַל־כָּל־מַלְכוּתָא: 5 אֱדַיִן סָרְכַיָּא וַאֲחַשְׁדַּרְפְּנַיָּא הֲווֹ בָעַיִן עִלָּה לְהַשְׁכָּחָה לְדָנִיֵּאל מִצַּד מַלְכוּתָא וְכָל־ עִלָּה וּשְׁחִיתָה לָא־יָכְלִין לְהַשְׁכָּחָה כָּל־קֳבֵל דִּי־ מְהֵימַן הוּא וְכָל־שָׁלוּ וּשְׁחִיתָה לָא הִשְׁתְּכַחַת עֲלוֹהִי: 6 אֱדַיִן גֻּבְרַיָּא אִלֵּךְ אָמְרִין דִּי לָא נְהַשְׁכַּח לְדָנִיֵּאל דְּנָה כָּל־עִלָּא לָהֵן הַשְׁכַּחְנָא עֲלוֹהִי בְּדָת אֱלָהֵהּ: ס 7 אֱדַיִן סָרְכַיָּא וַאֲחַשְׁדַּרְפְּנַיָּא אִלֵּן הַרְגִּשׁוּ עַל־מַלְכָּא וְכֵן אָמְרִין לֵהּ דָּרְיָוֶשׁ מַלְכָּא לְעָלְמִין חֱיִי: 8 אִתְיָעַטוּ כֹּל סָרְכֵי מַלְכוּתָא סִגְנַיָּא וַאֲחַשְׁדַּרְפְּנַיָּא הַדָּבְרַיָּא וּפַחֲוָתָא לְקַיָּמָה קְיָם מַלְכָּא וּלְתַקָּפָה אֱסָר דִּי כָל־דִּי־יִבְעֵה בָעוּ מִן־כָּל־אֱלָהּ וֶאֱנָשׁ עַד־יוֹמִין תְּלָתִין לָהֵן מִנָּךְ מַלְכָּא יִתְרְמֵא לְגֹב אַרְיָוָתָא: 9 כְּעַן מַלְכָּא תְּקִים אֱסָרָא וְתִרְשֻׁם כְּתָבָא דִּי לָא לְהַשְׁנָיָה כְּדָת־מָדַי וּפָרַס דִּי־לָא תֶעְדֵּא: 10 כָּל־קֳבֵל דְּנָה מַלְכָּא דָּרְיָוֶשׁ

ה 29 וְהַמְונִכָא   ו 1 מְדָאָה   30 כַשְׂדָּאָה

on his knees three times that day, and prayed and
gave thanks before his God, as was his custom since
early days.
11 Then these men assembled and found Daniel
praying and making supplication before his God.
12 And they went before the king, and spoke
concerning the king's decree: "Have you not signed
a decree that every man who petitions any god or
man within thirty days, except you, O king, shall be
cast into the den of lions?"

The king answered and said, "The thing is true,
according to the law of the Medes and Persians,
which does not alter."

13 So they answered and said before the king,
"That Daniel, who is one of the captives from
Judah, does not show due regard for you, O king,
or for the decree that you have signed, but makes
his petition three times a day."

14 And the king, when he heard these words, was
greatly displeased with himself, and set his heart on
Daniel to deliver him; and he labored till the going
down of the sun to deliver him. 15 Then these men
approached the king, and said to the king, "Know,
O king, that it is the law of the Medes and Persians
that no decree or statute which the king establishes
may be changed."

16 So the king gave the command, and they
brought Daniel and cast him into the den of lions.
But the king spoke, saying to Daniel, "Your God,
whom you serve continually, He will deliver you."
17 Then a stone was brought and laid on the mouth
of the den, and the king sealed it with his own signet
ring and with the signets of his lords, that the
purpose concerning Daniel might not be changed.

18 Now the king went to his palace and spent the
night fasting; and no musicians were brought before
him. Also his sleep went from him. 19 Then the king
arose very early in the morning and went in haste to
the den of lions. 20 And when he came to the den, he
cried out with a lamenting voice to Daniel. The king
spoke, saying to Daniel, "Daniel, servant of the
living God, has your God, whom you serve
continually, been able to deliver you from the
lions?"

21 Then Daniel said to the king, "O king, live
forever! 22 My God sent His angel and shut the
lions' mouths, so that they have not hurt me,
because I was found innocent before Him; and also,
O king, I have done no wrong before you."

23 Now the king was exceedingly glad for him,
and commanded that they should take Daniel up
out of the den. So Daniel was taken up out of the
den, and no injury whatever was found on him,
because he believed in his God.

רְשַׁם כְּתָבָא וֶאֱסָרָא: 11 וְדָנִיֵּאל כְּדִי יְדַע דִּי־
רְשִׁים כְּתָבָא עַל לְבַיְתֵהּ וְכַוִּין פְּתִיחָן לֵהּ בְּעִלִּיתֵהּ
נֶגֶד יְרוּשְׁלֶם וְזִמְנִין תְּלָתָה בְיוֹמָא הוּא | בָּרֵךְ
עַל־בִּרְכוֹהִי וּמְצַלֵּא וּמוֹדֵא קֳדָם אֱלָהֵהּ כָּל־קֳבֵל
דִּי־הֲוָא עָבֵד מִן־קַדְמַת דְּנָה: ס 12 אֱדַיִן
גֻּבְרַיָּא אִלֵּךְ הַרְגִּשׁוּ וְהַשְׁכַּחוּ לְדָנִיֵּאל בָּעֵא וּמִתְחַנַּן
קֳדָם אֱלָהֵהּ: 13 בֵּאדַיִן קְרִיבוּ וְאָמְרִין קֳדָם־מַלְכָּא
עַל־אֱסָר מַלְכָּא הֲלָא אֱסָר רְשַׁמְתָּ דִּי כָל־אֱנָשׁ דִּי־
יִבְעֵה מִן־כָּל־אֱלָהּ וֶאֱנָשׁ עַד־יוֹמִין תְּלָתִין לָהֵן מִנָּךְ
מַלְכָּא יִתְרְמֵא לְגוֹב אַרְיָוָתָא עָנֵה מַלְכָּא וְאָמַר
יַצִּיבָא מִלְּתָא כְּדָת־מָדַי וּפָרַס דִּי־לָא תֶעְדֵּא:
14 בֵּאדַיִן עֲנוֹ וְאָמְרִין קֳדָם מַלְכָּא דִּי דָנִיֵּאל דִּי מִן־
בְּנֵי גָלוּתָא דִּי יְהוּד לָא־שָׂם עֲלָיִךְ[P] מַלְכָּא טְעֵם
וְעַל־אֱסָרָא דִּי רְשַׁמְתָּ וְזִמְנִין תְּלָתָה בְּיוֹמָא בָּעֵא
בָּעוּתֵהּ: 15 אֱדַיִן מַלְכָּא כְּדִי מִלְּתָא שְׁמַע שַׂגִּיא
בְּאֵשׁ עֲלוֹהִי וְעַל דָּנִיֵּאל שָׂם בָּל לְשֵׁיזָבוּתֵהּ וְעַד
מֶעָלֵי שִׁמְשָׁא הֲוָא מִשְׁתַּדַּר לְהַצָּלוּתֵהּ: 16 בֵּאדַיִן
גֻּבְרַיָּא אִלֵּךְ הַרְגִּשׁוּ עַל־מַלְכָּא וְאָמְרִין לְמַלְכָּא
דַּע מַלְכָּא דִּי־דָת לְמָדַי וּפָרַס דִּי־כָל־אֱסָר וּקְיָם
דִּי־מַלְכָּא יְהָקֵים לָא לְהַשְׁנָיָה: 17 בֵּאדַיִן מַלְכָּא
אֲמַר וְהַיְתִיו לְדָנִיֵּאל וּרְמוֹ לְגֻבָּא דִּי אַרְיָוָתָא עָנֵה
מַלְכָּא וְאָמַר לְדָנִיֵּאל אֱלָהָךְ דִּי אַנְתְּ[P] פָּלַח־
לֵהּ בִּתְדִירָא הוּא יְשֵׁיזְבִנָּךְ: 18 וְהֵיתָיִת אֶבֶן חֲדָה
וְשֻׂמַת עַל־פֻּם גֻּבָּא וְחַתְמַהּ מַלְכָּא בְּעִזְקְתֵהּ
וּבְעִזְקָת רַבְרְבָנוֹהִי דִּי לָא־תִשְׁנֵא צְבוּ בְּדָנִיֵּאל:
19 אֱדַיִן אֲזַל מַלְכָּא לְהֵיכְלֵהּ וּבָת טְוָת וְדַחֲוָן
לָא־הַנְעֵל קָדָמוֹהִי וְשִׁנְתֵּהּ נַדַּת עֲלוֹהִי: 20 בֵּאדַיִן
מַלְכָּא בִּשְׁפַּרְפָּרָא יְקוּם בְּנָגְהָא וּבְהִתְבְּהָלָה לְגֻבָּא
דִּי־אַרְיָוָתָא אֲזַל: 21 וּכְמִקְרְבֵהּ לְגֻבָּא לְדָנִיֵּאל בְּקָל
עֲצִיב זְעִק עָנֵה מַלְכָּא וְאָמַר לְדָנִיֵּאל דָּנִיֵּאל עֲבֵד
אֱלָהָא חַיָּא אֱלָהָךְ דִּי אַנְתְּ[P] פָּלַח־לֵהּ בִּתְדִירָא
הַיְכֵל לְשֵׁיזָבוּתָךְ מִן־אַרְיָוָתָא: 22 אֱדַיִן דָּנִיֵּאל עִם־
מַלְכָּא מַלֵּל מַלְכָּא לְעָלְמִין חֱיִי: 23 אֱלָהִי שְׁלַח
מַלְאֲכֵהּ וּסֲגַר פֻּם אַרְיָוָתָא וְלָא חַבְּלוּנִי כָּל־קֳבֵל
דִּי קָדָמוֹהִי זָכוּ הִשְׁתְּכַחַת לִי וְאַף קֳדָמָיִךְ[P] מַלְכָּא

²⁴And the king gave the command, and they brought those men who had accused Daniel, and they cast *them* into the den of lions—them, their children, and their wives; and the lions overpowered them, and broke all their bones in pieces before they ever came to the bottom of the den.

²⁵Then King Darius wrote:

To all peoples, nations, and languages that dwell in all the earth:

Peace be multiplied to you.

26 I make a decree that in every dominion of my kingdom *men must* tremble and fear before the God of Daniel.

For He *is* the living God,
And steadfast forever;
His kingdom *is the one* which shall not be destroyed,
And His dominion *shall endure* to the end.

27 He delivers and rescues,
And He works signs and wonders
In heaven and on earth,
Who has delivered Daniel from the power of the lions.

²⁸So this Daniel prospered in the reign of Darius and in the reign of Cyrus the Persian.

7 In the first year of Belshazzar king of Babylon, Daniel had a dream and visions of his head *while* on his bed. Then he wrote down the dream, telling the main facts.

²Daniel spoke, saying, "I saw in my vision by night, and behold, the four winds of heaven were stirring up the Great Sea. ³And four great beasts came up from the sea, each different from the other. ⁴The first *was* like a lion, and had eagle's wings. I watched till its wings were plucked off; and it was lifted up from the earth and made to stand on two feet like a man, and a man's heart was given to it.

⁵"And suddenly another beast, a second, like a bear. It was raised up on one side, and *had* three ribs in its mouth between its teeth. And they said thus to it: 'Arise, devour much flesh!'

⁶"After this I looked, and there was another, like a leopard, which had on its back four wings of a bird. The beast also had four heads, and dominion was given to it.

⁷"After this I saw in the night visions, and behold, a fourth beast, dreadful and terrible, exceedingly strong. It had huge iron teeth; it was devouring, breaking in pieces, and trampling the residue with its feet. It *was* different from all the beasts that *were* before it, and it had ten horns. ⁸I was considering the horns, and there was another

²⁴ בְּאדַיִן מַלְכָּא שַׂגִּיא טְאֵב עֲלוֹהִי וּלְדָנִיֵּאל אֲמַר לְהַנְסָקָה מִן־גֻּבָּא וְהֻסַּק דָּנִיֵּאל מִן־גֻּבָּא וְכָל־חֲבָל לָא־הִשְׁתְּכַח בֵּהּ דִּי הֵימִן בֵּאלָהֵהּ: ²⁵ וַאֲמַר מַלְכָּא וְהַיְתִיו גֻּבְרַיָּא אִלֵּךְ דִּי־אֲכַלוּ קַרְצוֹהִי דִּי דָנִיֵּאל וּלְגֹב אַרְיָוָתָא רְמוֹ אִנּוּן בְּנֵיהוֹן וּנְשֵׁיהוֹן וְלָא־מְטוֹ לְאַרְעִית גֻּבָּא עַד דִּי־שְׁלִטוּ בְהוֹן אַרְיָוָתָא וְכָל־גַּרְמֵיהוֹן הַדִּקוּ: ²⁶ בֵּאדַיִן דָּרְיָוֶשׁ מַלְכָּא כְּתַב לְכָל־עַמְמַיָּא אֻמַּיָּא וְלִשָּׁנַיָּא דִּי־דָאֲרִין בְּכָל־אַרְעָא שְׁלָמְכוֹן יִשְׂגֵּא: ²⁷ מִן־קֳדָמַי שִׂים טְעֵם דִּי ׀ בְּכָל־שָׁלְטָן מַלְכוּתִי לֶהֱוֹן זָאֲעִין וְדָחֲלִין מִן־קֳדָם אֱלָהֵהּ דִּי־דָנִיֵּאל דִּי־הוּא ׀ אֱלָהָא חַיָּא וְקַיָּם לְעָלְמִין וּמַלְכוּתֵהּ דִּי־לָא תִתְחַבַּל וְשָׁלְטָנֵהּ עַד־סוֹפָא: ²⁸ מְשֵׁיזִב וּמַצִּל וְעָבֵד אָתִין וְתִמְהִין בִּשְׁמַיָּא וּבְאַרְעָא דִּי שֵׁיזִב לְדָנִיֵּאל מִן־יַד אַרְיָוָתָא: ²⁹ וְדָנִיֵּאל דְּנָה הַצְלַח בְּמַלְכוּת דָּרְיָוֶשׁ וּבְמַלְכוּת כּוֹרֶשׁ פָּרְסָאָה: פ

ז בִּשְׁנַת חֲדָה לְבֵלְאשַׁצַּר מֶלֶךְ בָּבֶל דָּנִיֵּאל חֵלֶם חֲזָה וְחֶזְוֵי רֵאשֵׁהּ עַל־מִשְׁכְּבֵהּ בֵּאדַיִן חֶלְמָא כְתַב רֵאשׁ מִלִּין אֲמַר: ² עָנֵה דָנִיֵּאל וְאָמַר חָזֵה הֲוֵית בְּחֶזְוִי עִם־לֵילְיָא וַאֲרוּ אַרְבַּע רוּחֵי שְׁמַיָּא מְגִיחָן לְיַמָּא רַבָּא: ³ וְאַרְבַּע חֵיוָן רַבְרְבָן סָלְקָן מִן־יַמָּא שָׁנְיָן דָּא מִן־דָּא: ⁴ קַדְמָיְתָא כְאַרְיֵה וְגַפִּין דִּי־נְשַׁר לַהּ חָזֵה הֲוֵית עַד דִּי־מְּרִיטוּ גַפַּיהּ וּנְטִילַת מִן־אַרְעָא וְעַל־רַגְלַיִן כֶּאֱנָשׁ הֳקִימַת וּלְבַב אֱנָשׁ יְהִיב לַהּ: ⁵ וַאֲרוּ חֵיוָה אָחֳרִי תִנְיָנָה דָּמְיָה לְדֹב וְלִשְׂטַר־חַד הֳקִמַת וּתְלָת עִלְעִין בְּפֻמַּהּ בֵּין שִׁנַּהּ וְכֵן אָמְרִין לַהּ קוּמִי אֲכֻלִי בְּשַׂר שַׂגִּיא: ⁶ בָּאתַר דְּנָה חָזֵה הֲוֵית וַאֲרוּ אָחֳרִי כִּנְמַר וְלַהּ גַּפִּין אַרְבַּע דִּי־עוֹף עַל־גַּבַּיהּ וְאַרְבְּעָה רֵאשִׁין לְחֵיוְתָא וְשָׁלְטָן יְהִיב לַהּ: ⁷ בָּאתַר דְּנָה חָזֵה הֲוֵית בְּחֶזְוֵי לֵילְיָא וַאֲרוּ חֵיוָה רְבִיעָאָה דְּחִילָה וְאֵימְתָנִי וְתַקִּיפָא יַתִּירָא וְשִׁנַּיִן דִּי־פַרְזֶל לַהּ רַבְרְבָן אָכְלָה וּמַדֱּקָה וּשְׁאָרָא בְּרַגְלַיהּ רָפְסָה וְהִיא מְשַׁנְּיָה מִן־כָּל־חֵיוָתָא דִּי קָדָמַיהּ וְקַרְנַיִן עֲשַׂר לַהּ: ⁸ מִשְׂתַּכַּל

horn, a little one, coming up among them, before
whom three of the first horns were plucked out by
the roots. And there, in this horn, *were* eyes like the
eyes of a man, and a mouth speaking pompous
words.

9   "I watched till thrones were put in place,
     And the Ancient of Days was seated;
     His garment *was* white as snow,
     And the hair of His head *was* like pure wool.
     His throne *was* a fiery flame,
     Its wheels a burning fire;
10   A fiery stream issued
     And came forth from before Him.
     A thousand thousands ministered to Him;
     Ten thousand times ten thousand stood before
       Him.
     The court was seated,
     And the books were opened.

11 "I watched then because of the sound of the
pompous words which the horn was speaking; I
watched till the beast was slain, and its body
destroyed and given to the burning flame. 12 As for
the rest of the beasts, they had their dominion taken
away, yet their lives were prolonged for a season
and a time.

13   "I was watching in the night visions,
     And behold, *One* like the Son of Man,
     Coming with the clouds of heaven!
     He came to the Ancient of Days,
     And they brought Him near before Him.
14   Then to Him was given dominion and glory and a
       kingdom,
     That all peoples, nations, and languages should
       serve Him.
     His dominion *is* an everlasting dominion,
     Which shall not pass away,
     And His kingdom *the one*
     Which shall not be destroyed.

15 "I, Daniel, was grieved in my spirit within *my*
body, and the visions of my head troubled me. 16 I
came near to one of those who stood by, and asked
him the truth of all this. So he told me and made
known to me the interpretation of these things:
17 'Those great beasts, which are four, *are* four kings
which arise out of the earth. 18 But the saints of the
Most High shall receive the kingdom, and possess
the kingdom forever, even forever and ever.'

19 "Then I wished to know the truth about the
fourth beast, which was different from all the
others, exceedingly dreadful, *with* its teeth of iron
and its nails of bronze, *which* devoured, broke in
pieces, and trampled the residue with its feet; 20 and
the ten horns that *were* on its head, and the other
horn which came up, before which three fell,
namely, that horn which had eyes and a mouth
which spoke pompous words, whose appearance
was greater than his fellows.

הֲוֵית בְּקַרְנַיָּא וַאֲלוּ קֶרֶן אָחֳרִי זְעֵירָה סִלְקָת
בֵּינֵיהֵן וּתְלָת מִן־קַרְנַיָּא קַדְמָיָתָא אֶתְעֲקַרוּ מִן־
קֳדָמַהּ וַאֲלוּ עַיְנִין כְּעַיְנֵי אֲנָשָׁא בְּקַרְנָא־דָא וּפֻם
מְמַלִּל רַבְרְבָן׃ 9 חָזֵה הֲוֵית עַד דִּי כָרְסָוָן רְמִיו
וְעַתִּיק יוֹמִין יְתִב לְבוּשֵׁהּ ׀ כִּתְלַג חִוָּר וּשְׂעַר
רֵאשֵׁהּ כַּעֲמַר נְקֵא כָּרְסְיֵהּ שְׁבִיבִין דִּי־נוּר גַּלְגִּלּוֹהִי
נוּר דָּלִק׃ 10 נְהַר דִּי־נוּר נָגֵד וְנָפֵק מִן־קֳדָמוֹהִי אֶלֶף
אַלְפִים יְשַׁמְּשׁוּנֵּהּ וְרִבּוֹ רִבְבָן קָדָמוֹהִי יְקוּמוּן
דִּינָא יְתִב וְסִפְרִין פְּתִיחוּ׃ 11 חָזֵה הֲוֵית בֵּאדַיִן
מִן־קָל מִלַּיָּא רַבְרְבָתָא דִּי קַרְנָא מְמַלֱּלָה חָזֵה
הֲוֵית עַד דִּי קְטִילַת חֵיוְתָא וְהוּבַד גִּשְׁמַהּ וִיהִיבַת
לִיקֵדַת אֶשָּׁא׃ 12 וּשְׁאָר חֵיוָתָא הֶעְדִּיו שָׁלְטָנְהוֹן
וְאַרְכָה בְחַיִּין יְהִיבַת לְהוֹן עַד־זְמַן וְעִדָּן׃ 13 חָזֵה
הֲוֵית בְּחֶזְוֵי לֵילְיָא וַאֲרוּ עִם־עֲנָנֵי שְׁמַיָּא כְּבַר
אֱנָשׁ אָתֵה הֲוָה וְעַד־עַתִּיק יוֹמַיָּא מְטָה וּקְדָמוֹהִי
הַקְרְבוּהִי׃ 14 וְלֵהּ יְהִיב שָׁלְטָן וִיקָר וּמַלְכוּ וְכֹל
עַמְמַיָּא אֻמַּיָּא וְלִשָּׁנַיָּא לֵהּ יִפְלְחוּן שָׁלְטָנֵהּ שָׁלְטָן
עָלַם דִּי־לָא יֶעְדֵּה וּמַלְכוּתֵהּ דִּי־לָא תִתְחַבַּל׃ פ

15 אֶתְכְּרִיַּת רוּחִי אֲנָה דָנִיֵּאל בְּגוֹא נִדְנֶה
וְחֶזְוֵי רֵאשִׁי יְבַהֲלֻנַּנִי׃ 16 קִרְבֵת עַל־חַד מִן־
קָאֲמַיָּא וְיַצִּיבָא אֶבְעֵא־מִנֵּהּ עַל־כָּל־דְּנָה וַאֲמַר־
לִי וּפְשַׁר מִלַּיָּא יְהוֹדְעִנַּנִי׃ 17 אִלֵּין חֵיוָתָא
רַבְרְבָתָא דִּי אִנִּין אַרְבַּע אַרְבְּעָה מַלְכִין יְקוּמוּן
מִן־אַרְעָא׃ 18 וִיקַבְּלוּן מַלְכוּתָא קַדִּישֵׁי עֶלְיוֹנִין
וְיַחְסְנוּן מַלְכוּתָא עַד־עָלְמָא וְעַד עָלַם עָלְמַיָּא׃
19 אֱדַיִן צְבִית לְיַצָּבָא עַל־חֵיוְתָא רְבִיעָיְתָא דִּי־
הֲוָת שָׁנְיָה מִן־כָּלְּהֵין דְּחִילָה יַתִּירָה שִׁנַּהּ דִּי־
פַרְזֶל וְטִפְרַהּ דִּי־נְחָשׁ אָכְלָה מַדֱּקָה וּשְׁאָרָא
בְּרַגְלַהּ רָפְסָה׃ 20 וְעַל־קַרְנַיָּא עֲשַׂר דִּי בְרֵאשַׁהּ
וְאָחֳרִי דִּי סִלְקַת וּנְפַלוּ מִן־קֳדָמַיהּ תְּלָת וְקַרְנָא
דִכֵּן וְעַיְנִין לַהּ וּפֻם מְמַלִּל רַבְרְבָן וְחֶזְוַהּ רַב מִן־

ז 8 בֵּינֵיהֶן אִתְעֲקַרָה קַדְמָה   10 אַלְפִין רִבְּבָן
19 כָּלְּהֵין שֵׁנַּהּ וְטִפְרַהּ בְּרַגְלַהּ   20 וּנְפַלָה קָדָמַהּ

21 "I was watching; and the same horn was making war against the saints, and prevailing against them, 22 until the Ancient of Days came, and a judgment was made *in favor* of the saints of the Most High, and the time came for the saints to possess the kingdom.

23 "Thus he said:

'The fourth beast shall be
A fourth kingdom on earth,
Which shall be different from all *other* kingdoms,
And shall devour the whole earth,
Trample it and break it in pieces.

24 The ten horns *are* ten kings
Who shall arise from this kingdom.
And another shall rise after them;
He shall be different from the first *ones,*
And shall subdue three kings.

25 He shall speak *pompous* words against the Most High,
Shall persecute the saints of the Most High,
And shall intend to change times and law.
Then *the saints* shall be given into his hand
For a time and times and half a time.

26 'But the court shall be seated,
And they shall take away his dominion,
To consume and destroy *it* forever.

27 Then the kingdom and dominion,
And the greatness of the kingdoms under the whole heaven,
Shall be given to the people, the saints of the Most High.
His kingdom *is* an everlasting kingdom,
And all dominions shall serve and obey Him.'

28 "This *is* the end of the account. As for me, Daniel, my thoughts greatly troubled me, and my countenance changed; but I kept the matter in my heart."

8 In the third year of the reign of King Belshazzar a vision appeared *to* me—to me, Daniel—after the one that appeared to me the first time. 2 I saw in the vision, and it so happened while I was looking, that I *was* in Shushan, the citadel, which *is* in the province of Elam; and I saw in the vision that I was by the River Ulai. 3 Then I lifted my eyes and saw, and there, standing beside the river, was a ram which had two horns, and the two horns *were* high; but one *was* higher than the other, and the higher one came up last. 4 I saw the ram pushing westward, northward, and southward, so that no animal could withstand him; nor *was there any* that could deliver from his hand, but he did according to his will and became great.

5 And as I was considering, suddenly a male goat came from the west, across the surface of the whole earth, without touching the ground; and the goat

חֲבֶרְתַּהּ: 21 חָזֵה הֲוֵית וְקַרְנָא דִכֵּן עָבְדָה קְרָב עִם־
קַדִּישִׁין וְיָכְלָה לְהוֹן: 22 עַד דִּי־אֲתָה עַתִּיק יוֹמַיָּא
וְדִינָא יְהִב לְקַדִּישֵׁי עֶלְיוֹנִין וְזִמְנָא מְטָה וּמַלְכוּתָא
הֶחֱסִנוּ קַדִּישִׁין: 23 כֵּן אֲמַר חֵיוְתָא רְבִיעָיְתָא
מַלְכוּ רְבִיעָיָא תֶּהֱוֵא בְאַרְעָא דִּי תִשְׁנֵא מִן־כָּל־
מַלְכְוָתָא וְתֵאכֻל כָּל־אַרְעָא וּתְדוּשִׁנַּהּ וְתַדְּקִנַּהּ:
24 וְקַרְנַיָּא עֲשַׂר מִנַּהּ מַלְכוּתָה עַשְׂרָה מַלְכִין יְקֻמוּן
וְאָחֳרָן יְקוּם אַחֲרֵיהוֹן וְהוּא יִשְׁנֵא מִן־קַדְמָיֵא
וּתְלָתָה מַלְכִין יְהַשְׁפִּל: 25 וּמִלִּין לְצַד עִלָּיָא יְמַלִּל
וּלְקַדִּישֵׁי עֶלְיוֹנִין יְבַלֵּא וְיִסְבַּר לְהַשְׁנָיָה זִמְנִין וְדָת
וְיִתְיַהֲבוּן בִּידֵהּ עַד־עִדָּן וְעִדָּנִין וּפְלַג עִדָּן: 26 וְדִינָא
יִתִּב וְשָׁלְטָנֵהּ יְהַעְדּוֹן לְהַשְׁמָדָה וּלְהוֹבָדָה עַד־
סוֹפָא: 27 וּמַלְכוּתָה וְשָׁלְטָנָא וּרְבוּתָא דִּי מַלְכְוָת
תְּחוֹת כָּל־שְׁמַיָּא יְהִיבַת לְעַם קַדִּישֵׁי עֶלְיוֹנִין
מַלְכוּתֵהּ מַלְכוּת עָלַם וְכֹל שָׁלְטָנַיָּא לֵהּ יִפְלְחוּן
וְיִשְׁתַּמְּעוּן: 28 עַד־כָּה סוֹפָא דִי־מִלְּתָא אֲנָה דָנִיֵּאל
שַׂגִּיא רַעְיוֹנַי יְבַהֲלֻנַּנִי וְזִיוַי יִשְׁתַּנּוֹן עֲלַי וּמִלְּתָא
בְּלִבִּי נִטְרֵת:
פ

ח בִּשְׁנַת שָׁלוֹשׁ לְמַלְכוּת בֵּלְאשַׁצַּר הַמֶּלֶךְ חָזוֹן
נִרְאָה אֵלַי אֲנִי דָנִיֵּאל אַחֲרֵי הַנִּרְאָה אֵלַי בַּתְּחִלָּה:
2 וָאֶרְאֶה בֶּחָזוֹן וַיְהִי בִּרְאֹתִי וַאֲנִי בְּשׁוּשַׁן הַבִּירָה
אֲשֶׁר בְּעֵילָם הַמְּדִינָה וָאֶרְאֶה בֶּחָזוֹן וַאֲנִי הָיִיתִי
עַל־אוּבַל אוּלָי: 3 וָאֶשָּׂא עֵינַי וָאֶרְאֶה וְהִנֵּה ׀
אַיִל אֶחָד עֹמֵד לִפְנֵי הָאֻבָל וְלוֹ קְרָנָיִם וְהַקְּרָנַיִם
גְּבֹהוֹת וְהָאַחַת גְּבֹהָה מִן־הַשֵּׁנִית וְהַגְּבֹהָה עֹלָה
בָּאַחֲרֹנָה: 4 רָאִיתִי אֶת־הָאַיִל מְנַגֵּחַ יָמָּה וְצָפוֹנָה
וָנֶגְבָּה וְכָל־חַיּוֹת לֹא־יַעַמְדוּ לְפָנָיו וְאֵין מַצִּיל מִיָּדוֹ
וְעָשָׂה כִרְצֹנוֹ וְהִגְדִּיל: 5 וַאֲנִי ׀ הָיִיתִי מֵבִין וְהִנֵּה
צְפִיר־הָעִזִּים בָּא מִן־הַמַּעֲרָב עַל־פְּנֵי כָל־הָאָרֶץ
וְאֵין נוֹגֵעַ בָּאָרֶץ וְהַצָּפִיר קֶרֶן חָזוּת בֵּין עֵינָיו:

had a notable horn between his eyes. 6 Then he came to the ram that had two horns, which I had seen standing beside the river, and ran at him with furious power. 7 And I saw him confronting the ram; he was moved with rage against him, attacked the ram, and broke his two horns. There was no power in the ram to withstand him, but he cast him down to the ground and trampled him; and there was no one that could deliver the ram from his hand.

8 Therefore the male goat grew very great; but when he became strong, the large horn was broken, and in place of it four notable ones came up toward the four winds of heaven. 9 And out of one of them came a little horn which grew exceedingly great toward the south, toward the east, and toward the Glorious *Land.* 10 And it grew up to the host of heaven; and it cast down *some* of the host and *some* of the stars to the ground, and trampled them. 11 He even exalted *himself* as high as the Prince of the host; and by him the daily *sacrifices* were taken away, and the place of His sanctuary was cast down. 12 Because of transgression, an army was given over *to the horn* to oppose the daily *sacrifices;* and he cast truth down to the ground. He did *all this* and prospered.

13 Then I heard a holy one speaking; and *another* holy one said to that certain *one* who was speaking, "How long *will* the vision *be, concerning* the daily *sacrifices* and the transgression of desolation, the giving of both the sanctuary and the host to be trampled underfoot?"

14 And he said to me, "For two thousand three hundred days; then the sanctuary shall be cleansed."

15 Then it happened, when I, Daniel, had seen the vision and was seeking the meaning, that suddenly there stood before me one having the appearance of a man. 16 And I heard a man's voice between *the banks of* the Ulai, who called, and said, "Gabriel, make this *man* understand the vision." 17 So he came near where I stood, and when he came I was afraid and fell on my face; but he said to me, "Understand, son of man, that the vision *refers to* the time of the end."

18 Now, as he was speaking with me, I was in a deep sleep with my face to the ground; but he touched me, and stood me upright. 19 And he said, "Look, I am making known to you what shall happen in the latter time of the indignation; for at the appointed time the end *shall* be. 20 The ram which you saw, having the two horns—*they are* the kings of Media and Persia. 21 And the male goat *is* the kingdom of Greece. The large horn that *is*

6 וַיָּבֹא עַד־הָאַיִל בַּעַל הַקְּרָנַיִם אֲשֶׁר רָאִיתִי עֹמֵד לִפְנֵי הָאֻבָל וַיָּרָץ אֵלָיו בַּחֲמַת כֹּחוֹ: 7 וּרְאִיתִיו מַגִּיעַ ׀ אֵצֶל הָאַיִל וַיִּתְמַרְמַר אֵלָיו וַיַּךְ אֶת־ הָאַיִל וַיְשַׁבֵּר אֶת־שְׁתֵּי קְרָנָיו וְלֹא־הָיָה כֹחַ בָּאַיִל לַעֲמֹד לְפָנָיו וַיַּשְׁלִיכֵהוּ אַרְצָה וַיִּרְמְסֵהוּ וְלֹא־הָיָה מַצִּיל לָאַיִל מִיָּדוֹ: 8 וּצְפִיר הָעִזִּים הִגְדִּיל עַד־מְאֹד וּכְעָצְמוֹ נִשְׁבְּרָה הַקֶּרֶן הַגְּדוֹלָה וַתַּעֲלֶנָה חָזוּת אַרְבַּע תַּחְתֶּיהָ לְאַרְבַּע רוּחוֹת הַשָּׁמָיִם: 9 וּמִן־ הָאַחַת מֵהֶם יָצָא קֶרֶן־אַחַת מִצְּעִירָה וַתִּגְדַּל־ יֶתֶר אֶל־הַנֶּגֶב וְאֶל־הַמִּזְרָח וְאֶל־הַצֶּבִי: 10 וַתִּגְדַּל עַד־צְבָא הַשָּׁמָיִם וַתַּפֵּל אַרְצָה מִן־הַצָּבָא וּמִן־ הַכּוֹכָבִים וַתִּרְמְסֵם: 11 וְעַד שַׂר־הַצָּבָא הִגְדִּיל וּמִמֶּנּוּ הֵרִים הַתָּמִיד וְהֻשְׁלַךְ מְכוֹן מִקְדָּשׁוֹ: 12 וְצָבָא תִּנָּתֵן עַל־הַתָּמִיד בְּפָשַׁע וְתַשְׁלֵךְ אֱמֶת אַרְצָה וְעָשְׂתָה וְהִצְלִיחָה: 13 וָאֶשְׁמְעָה אֶחָד־קָדוֹשׁ מְדַבֵּר וַיֹּאמֶר אֶחָד קָדוֹשׁ לַפַּלְמוֹנִי הַמְדַבֵּר עַד־ מָתַי הֶחָזוֹן הַתָּמִיד וְהַפֶּשַׁע שֹׁמֵם תֵּת וְקֹדֶשׁ וְצָבָא מִרְמָס: 14 וַיֹּאמֶר אֵלַי עַד עֶרֶב בֹּקֶר אַלְפַּיִם וּשְׁלֹשׁ מֵאוֹת וְנִצְדַּק קֹדֶשׁ: 15 וַיְהִי בִּרְאֹתִי אֲנִי דָנִיֵּאל אֶת־הֶחָזוֹן וָאֲבַקְשָׁה בִינָה וְהִנֵּה עֹמֵד לְנֶגְדִּי כְּמַרְאֵה־גָבֶר: 16 וָאֶשְׁמַע קוֹל־אָדָם בֵּין אוּלָי וַיִּקְרָא וַיֹּאמַר גַּבְרִיאֵל הָבֵן לְהַלָּז אֶת־הַמַּרְאֶה: 17 וַיָּבֹא אֵצֶל עָמְדִי וּבְבֹאוֹ נִבְעַתִּי וָאֶפְּלָה עַל־ פָּנָי וַיֹּאמֶר אֵלַי הָבֵן בֶּן־אָדָם כִּי לְעֶת־קֵץ הֶחָזוֹן: 18 וּבְדַבְּרוֹ עִמִּי נִרְדַּמְתִּי עַל־פָּנַי אַרְצָה וַיִּגַּע־ בִּי וַיַּעֲמִידֵנִי עַל־עָמְדִי: 19 וַיֹּאמֶר הִנְנִי מוֹדִיעֲךָ אֵת אֲשֶׁר־יִהְיֶה בְּאַחֲרִית הַזָּעַם כִּי לְמוֹעֵד קֵץ: 20 הָאַיִל אֲשֶׁר־רָאִיתָ בַּעַל הַקְּרָנָיִם מַלְכֵי מָדַי וּפָרָס: 21 וְהַצָּפִיר הַשָּׂעִיר מֶלֶךְ יָוָן וְהַקֶּרֶן הַגְּדוֹלָה

between its eyes *is* the first king. 22 As for the broken *horn* and the four that stood up in its place, four kingdoms shall arise out of that nation, but not with its power.

23 "And in the latter time of their kingdom,
   When the transgressors have reached their
      fullness,
   A king shall arise,
   Having fierce features,
   Who understands sinister schemes.
24 His power shall be mighty, but not by his own
      power;
   He shall destroy fearfully,
   And shall prosper and thrive;
   He shall destroy the mighty, and *also* the holy
      people.
25 "Through his cunning
   He shall cause deceit to prosper under his rule;
   And he shall exalt *himself* in his heart.
   He shall destroy many in *their* prosperity.
   He shall even rise against the Prince of princes;
   But he shall be broken without *human* means.
26 "And the vision of the evenings and mornings
   Which was told is true;
   Therefore seal up the vision,
   For *it refers* to many days *in the future*."

27 And I, Daniel, fainted and was sick for days; afterward I arose and went about the king's business. I was astonished by the vision, but no one understood it.

9 In the first year of Darius the son of Ahasuerus, of the lineage of the Medes, who was made king over the realm of the Chaldeans— 2 in the first year of his reign I, Daniel, understood by the books the number of the years *specified* by the word of the LORD through Jeremiah the prophet, that He would accomplish seventy years in the desolations of Jerusalem.

3 Then I set my face toward the Lord God to make request by prayer and supplications, with fasting, sackcloth, and ashes. 4 And I prayed to the LORD my God, and made confession, and said, "O Lord, great and awesome God, who keeps His covenant and mercy with those who love Him, and with those who keep His commandments, 5 we have sinned and committed iniquity, we have done wickedly and rebelled, even by departing from Your precepts and Your judgments. 6 Neither have we heeded Your servants the prophets, who spoke in Your name to our kings and our princes, to our fathers and all the people of the land. 7 O Lord, righteousness *belongs* to You, but to us shame of face, as *it is* this day—to the men of Judah, to the inhabitants of Jerusalem and all Israel, those near

אֲשֶׁר בֵּין־עֵינָיו הוּא הַמֶּלֶךְ הָרִאשׁוֹן: 22 וְהַנִּשְׁבֶּרֶת
וַתַּעֲמֹדְנָה אַרְבַּע תַּחְתֶּיהָ אַרְבַּע מַלְכֻיּוֹת מִגּוֹי
יַעֲמֹדְנָה וְלֹא בְכֹחוֹ: 23 וּבְאַחֲרִית מַלְכוּתָם כְּהָתֵם
הַפֹּשְׁעִים יַעֲמֹד מֶלֶךְ עַז־פָּנִים וּמֵבִין חִידוֹת:
24 וְעָצַם כֹּחוֹ וְלֹא בְכֹחוֹ וְנִפְלָאוֹת יַשְׁחִית וְהִצְלִיחַ
וְעָשָׂה וְהִשְׁחִית עֲצוּמִים וְעַם־קְדֹשִׁים: 25 וְעַל־
שִׂכְלוֹ וְהִצְלִיחַ מִרְמָה בְּיָדוֹ וּבִלְבָבוֹ יַגְדִּיל וּבְשַׁלְוָה
יַשְׁחִית רַבִּים וְעַל־שַׂר־שָׂרִים יַעֲמֹד וּבְאֶפֶס יָד
יִשָּׁבֵר: 26 וּמַרְאֵה הָעֶרֶב וְהַבֹּקֶר אֲשֶׁר נֶאֱמַר אֱמֶת
הוּא וְאַתָּה סְתֹם הֶחָזוֹן כִּי לְיָמִים רַבִּים: 27 וַאֲנִי
דָנִיֵּאל נִהְיֵיתִי וְנֶחֱלֵיתִי יָמִים וָאָקוּם וָאֶעֱשֶׂה
אֶת־מְלֶאכֶת הַמֶּלֶךְ וָאֶשְׁתּוֹמֵם עַל־הַמַּרְאֶה וְאֵין
מֵבִין: פ

‫ט‬ בִּשְׁנַת אַחַת לְדָרְיָוֶשׁ בֶּן־אֲחַשְׁוֵרוֹשׁ מִזֶּרַע מָדָי
אֲשֶׁר הָמְלַךְ עַל מַלְכוּת כַּשְׂדִּים: 2 בִּשְׁנַת אַחַת
לְמָלְכוֹ אֲנִי דָּנִיֵּאל בִּינֹתִי בַּסְּפָרִים מִסְפַּר הַשָּׁנִים
אֲשֶׁר הָיָה דְבַר־יְהוָה אֶל־יִרְמְיָה הַנָּבִיא לְמַלֹּאות
לְחָרְבוֹת יְרוּשָׁלִַם שִׁבְעִים שָׁנָה: 3 וָאֶתְּנָה אֶת־
פָּנַי אֶל־אֲדֹנָי הָאֱלֹהִים לְבַקֵּשׁ תְּפִלָּה וְתַחֲנוּנִים
בְּצוֹם וְשַׂק וָאֵפֶר: 4 וָאֶתְפַּלְלָה לַיהוָה אֱלֹהַי
וָאֶתְוַדֶּה וָאֹמְרָה אָנָּא אֲדֹנָי הָאֵל הַגָּדוֹל וְהַנּוֹרָא
שֹׁמֵר הַבְּרִית וְהַחֶסֶד לְאֹהֲבָיו וּלְשֹׁמְרֵי מִצְוֹתָיו:
5 חָטָאנוּ וְעָוִינוּ וְהִרְשַׁעְנוּ וּמָרָדְנוּ וְסוֹר מִמִּצְוֹתֶךָ
וּמִמִּשְׁפָּטֶיךָ: 6 וְלֹא שָׁמַעְנוּ אֶל־עֲבָדֶיךָ הַנְּבִיאִים
אֲשֶׁר דִּבְּרוּ בְּשִׁמְךָ אֶל־מְלָכֵינוּ שָׂרֵינוּ וַאֲבֹתֵינוּ
וְאֶל כָּל־עַם הָאָרֶץ: 7 לְךָ אֲדֹנָי הַצְּדָקָה וְלָנוּ
בֹּשֶׁת הַפָּנִים כַּיּוֹם הַזֶּה לְאִישׁ יְהוּדָה וּלְיוֹשְׁבֵי
יְרוּשָׁלִַם וּלְכָל־יִשְׂרָאֵל הַקְּרֹבִים וְהָרְחֹקִים בְּכָל־

and those far off in all the countries to which You have driven them, because of the unfaithfulness which they have committed against You.

8 "O Lord, to us *belongs* shame of face, to our kings, our princes, and our fathers, because we have sinned against You. 9 To the Lord our God *belong* mercy and forgiveness, though we have rebelled against Him. 10 We have not obeyed the voice of the LORD our God, to walk in His laws, which He set before us by His servants the prophets. 11 Yes, all Israel has transgressed Your law, and has departed so as not to obey Your voice; therefore the curse and the oath written in the Law of Moses the servant of God have been poured out on us, because we have sinned against Him. 12 And He has confirmed His words, which He spoke against us and against our judges who judged us, by bringing upon us a great disaster; for under the whole heaven such has never been done as what has been done to Jerusalem.

13 "As *it is* written in the Law of Moses, all this disaster has come upon us; yet we have not made our prayer before the LORD our God, that we might turn from our iniquities and understand Your truth. 14 Therefore the LORD has kept the disaster in mind, and brought it upon us; for the LORD our God *is* righteous in all the works which He does, though we have not obeyed His voice. 15 And now, O Lord our God, who brought Your people out of the land of Egypt with a mighty hand, and made Yourself a name, as *it is* this day—we have sinned, we have done wickedly!

16 "O Lord, according to all Your righteousness, I pray, let Your anger and Your fury be turned away from Your city Jerusalem, Your holy mountain; because for our sins, and for the iniquities of our fathers, Jerusalem and Your people *are* a reproach to all *those* around us. 17 Now therefore, our God, hear the prayer of Your servant, and his supplications, and for the Lord's sake cause Your face to shine on Your sanctuary, which is desolate. 18 O my God, incline Your ear and hear; open Your eyes and see our desolations, and the city which is called by Your name; for we do not present our supplications before You because of our righteous deeds, but because of Your great mercies. 19 O Lord, hear! O Lord, forgive! O Lord, listen and act! Do not delay for Your own sake, my God, for Your city and Your people are called by Your name."

20 Now while I *was* speaking, praying, and confessing my sin and the sin of my people Israel, and presenting my supplication before the LORD my God for the holy mountain of my God, 21 yes, while

הָאֲרָצוֹת אֲשֶׁר הִדַּחְתָּם שָׁם בְּמַעֲלָם אֲשֶׁר מָעֲלוּ־
בָךְ: 8 יְהוָה לָנוּ בֹּשֶׁת הַפָּנִים לִמְלָכֵינוּ לְשָׂרֵינוּ
וְלַאֲבֹתֵינוּ אֲשֶׁר חָטָאנוּ לָךְ: 9 לַאדֹנָי אֱלֹהֵינוּ
הָרַחֲמִים וְהַסְּלִחוֹת כִּי מָרַדְנוּ בּוֹ: 10 וְלֹא שָׁמַעְנוּ
בְּקוֹל יְהוָה אֱלֹהֵינוּ לָלֶכֶת בְּתוֹרֹתָיו אֲשֶׁר נָתַן
לְפָנֵינוּ בְּיַד עֲבָדָיו הַנְּבִיאִים: 11 וְכָל־יִשְׂרָאֵל עָבְרוּ
אֶת־תּוֹרָתֶךָ וְסוֹר לְבִלְתִּי שְׁמוֹעַ בְּקֹלֶךָ וַתִּתַּךְ עָלֵינוּ
הָאָלָה וְהַשְּׁבֻעָה אֲשֶׁר כְּתוּבָה בְּתוֹרַת מֹשֶׁה עֶבֶד־
הָאֱלֹהִים כִּי חָטָאנוּ לוֹ: 12 וַיָּקֶם אֶת־דְּבָרָיו ׀
אֲשֶׁר־דִּבֶּר עָלֵינוּ וְעַל שֹׁפְטֵינוּ אֲשֶׁר שְׁפָטוּנוּ
לְהָבִיא עָלֵינוּ רָעָה גְדֹלָה אֲשֶׁר לֹא־נֶעֶשְׂתָה תַּחַת
כָּל־הַשָּׁמַיִם כַּאֲשֶׁר נֶעֶשְׂתָה בִּירוּשָׁלִָם: 13 כַּאֲשֶׁר
כָּתוּב בְּתוֹרַת מֹשֶׁה אֵת כָּל־הָרָעָה הַזֹּאת בָּאָה
עָלֵינוּ וְלֹא־חִלִּינוּ אֶת־פְּנֵי ׀ יְהוָה אֱלֹהֵינוּ לָשׁוּב
מֵעֲוֹנֵנוּ וּלְהַשְׂכִּיל בַּאֲמִתֶּךָ: 14 וַיִּשְׁקֹד יְהוָה עַל־
הָרָעָה וַיְבִיאֶהָ עָלֵינוּ כִּי־צַדִּיק יְהוָה אֱלֹהֵינוּ
עַל־כָּל־מַעֲשָׂיו אֲשֶׁר עָשָׂה וְלֹא שָׁמַעְנוּ בְּקֹלוֹ:
15 וְעַתָּה ׀ אֲדֹנָי אֱלֹהֵינוּ אֲשֶׁר הוֹצֵאתָ אֶת־
עַמְּךָ מֵאֶרֶץ מִצְרַיִם בְּיָד חֲזָקָה וַתַּעַשׂ־לְךָ שֵׁם
כַּיּוֹם הַזֶּה חָטָאנוּ רָשָׁעְנוּ: 16 אֲדֹנָי כְּכָל־צִדְקֹתֶךָ
יָשָׁב־נָא אַפְּךָ וַחֲמָתְךָ מֵעִירְךָ יְרוּשָׁלַםִ הַר־קָדְשֶׁךָ
כִּי בַחֲטָאֵינוּ וּבַעֲוֹנוֹת אֲבֹתֵינוּ יְרוּשָׁלַםִ וְעַמְּךָ
לְחֶרְפָּה לְכָל־סְבִיבֹתֵינוּ: 17 וְעַתָּה ׀ שְׁמַע אֱלֹהֵינוּ
אֶל־תְּפִלַּת עַבְדְּךָ וְאֶל־תַּחֲנוּנָיו וְהָאֵר פָּנֶיךָ עַל־
מִקְדָּשְׁךָ הַשָּׁמֵם לְמַעַן אֲדֹנָי: 18 הַטֵּה אֱלֹהַי ׀
אָזְנְךָ וּשֲׁמָע פְּקַח עֵינֶיךָ וּרְאֵה שֹׁמְמֹתֵינוּ וְהָעִיר
אֲשֶׁר־נִקְרָא שִׁמְךָ עָלֶיהָ כִּי ׀ לֹא עַל־צִדְקֹתֵינוּ
אֲנַחְנוּ מַפִּילִים תַּחֲנוּנֵינוּ לְפָנֶיךָ כִּי עַל־רַחֲמֶיךָ
הָרַבִּים: 19 אֲדֹנָי ׀ שְׁמָעָה אֲדֹנָי ׀ סְלָחָה אֲדֹנָי
הַקְשִׁיבָה וַעֲשֵׂה אַל־תְּאַחַר לְמַעַנְךָ אֱלֹהַי כִּי־שִׁמְךָ
נִקְרָא עַל־עִירְךָ וְעַל־עַמֶּךָ: 20 וְעוֹד אֲנִי מְדַבֵּר
וּמִתְפַּלֵּל וּמִתְוַדֶּה חַטָּאתִי וְחַטַּאת עַמִּי יִשְׂרָאֵל
וּמַפִּיל תְּחִנָּתִי לִפְנֵי יְהוָה אֱלֹהַי עַל הַר־קֹדֶשׁ
אֱלֹהָי: 21 וְעוֹד אֲנִי מְדַבֵּר בַּתְּפִלָּה וְהָאִישׁ גַּבְרִיאֵל
אֲשֶׁר רָאִיתִי בֶחָזוֹן בַּתְּחִלָּה מֻעָף בִּיעָף נֹגֵעַ אֵלַי

I *was* speaking in prayer, the man Gabriel, whom I had seen in the vision at the beginning, being caused to fly swiftly, reached me about the time of the evening offering. ²²And he informed *me,* and talked with me, and said, "O Daniel, I have now come forth to give you skill to understand. ²³At the beginning of your supplications the command went out, and I have come to tell *you,* for you *are* greatly beloved; therefore consider the matter, and understand the vision:

24 "Seventy weeks are determined
    For your people and for your holy city,
    To finish the transgression,
    To make an end of sins,
    To make reconciliation for iniquity,
    To bring in everlasting righteousness,
    To seal up vision and prophecy,
    And to anoint the Most Holy.

25 "Know therefore and understand,
    That from the going forth of the command
    To restore and build Jerusalem
    Until Messiah the Prince,
    There shall be seven weeks and sixty-two weeks;
    The street shall be built again, and the wall,
    Even in troublesome times.

26 "And after the sixty-two weeks
    Messiah shall be cut off, but not for Himself;
    And the people of the prince who is to come
    Shall destroy the city and the sanctuary.
    The end of it *shall be* with a flood,
    And till the end of the war desolations are
       determined.

27 Then he shall confirm a covenant with many for
       one week;
    But in the middle of the week
    He shall bring an end to sacrifice and offering.
    And on the wing of abominations shall be one
       who makes desolate,
    Even until the consummation, which is
       determined,
    Is poured out on the desolate."

10 In the third year of Cyrus king of Persia a message was revealed to Daniel, whose name was called Belteshazzar. The message *was* true, but the appointed time *was* long; and he understood the message, and had understanding of the vision. ²In those days I, Daniel, was mourning three full weeks. ³I ate no pleasant food, no meat or wine came into my mouth, nor did I anoint myself at all, till three whole weeks were fulfilled.

⁴Now on the twenty-fourth day of the first month, as I was by the side of the great river, that *is,* the Tigris, ⁵I lifted my eyes and looked, and behold, a certain man clothed in linen, whose waist *was* girded with gold of Uphaz! ⁶His body *was* like beryl, his face like the appearance of lightning, his

כְּעֵת מִנְחַת־עָרֶב: 22 וַיָּבֶן וַיְדַבֵּר עִמִּי וַיֹּאמַר דָּנִיֵּאל
עַתָּה יָצָאתִי לְהַשְׂכִּילְךָ בִינָה: 23 בִּתְחִלַּת תַּחֲנוּנֶיךָ
יָצָא דָבָר וַאֲנִי בָּאתִי לְהַגִּיד כִּי חֲמוּדוֹת אָתָּה
וּבִין בַּדָּבָר וְהָבֵן בַּמַּרְאֶה: 24 שָׁבֻעִים שִׁבְעִים
נֶחְתַּךְ עַל־עַמְּךָ ׀ וְעַל־עִיר קָדְשֶׁךָ לְכַלֵּא הַפֶּשַׁע
וּלְחָתֵם חַטָּאות וּלְכַפֵּר עָוֹן וּלְהָבִיא צֶדֶק עֹלָמִים
וְלַחְתֹּם חָזוֹן וְנָבִיא וְלִמְשֹׁחַ קֹדֶשׁ קָדָשִׁים: 25 וְתֵדַע
וְתַשְׂכֵּל מִן־מֹצָא דָבָר לְהָשִׁיב וְלִבְנוֹת יְרוּשָׁלִַם
עַד־מָשִׁיחַ נָגִיד שָׁבֻעִים שִׁבְעָה וְשָׁבֻעִים שִׁשִּׁים
וּשְׁנַיִם תָּשׁוּב וְנִבְנְתָה רְחוֹב וְחָרוּץ וּבְצוֹק הָעִתִּים: 26 וְאַחֲרֵי הַשָּׁבֻעִים שִׁשִּׁים וּשְׁנַיִם יִכָּרֵת מָשִׁיחַ
וְאֵין לוֹ וְהָעִיר וְהַקֹּדֶשׁ יַשְׁחִית עַם נָגִיד הַבָּא
וְקִצּוֹ בַשֶּׁטֶף וְעַד קֵץ מִלְחָמָה נֶחֱרֶצֶת שֹׁמֵמוֹת: 27 וְהִגְבִּיר בְּרִית לָרַבִּים שָׁבוּעַ אֶחָד וַחֲצִי הַשָּׁבוּעַ
יַשְׁבִּית ׀ זֶבַח וּמִנְחָה וְעַל כְּנַף שִׁקּוּצִים מְשֹׁמֵם
וְעַד־כָּלָה וְנֶחֱרָצָה תִּתַּךְ עַל־שֹׁמֵם: פ

י בִּשְׁנַת שָׁלוֹשׁ לְכוֹרֶשׁ מֶלֶךְ פָּרַס דָּבָר נִגְלָה
לְדָנִיֵּאל אֲשֶׁר־נִקְרָא שְׁמוֹ בֵּלְטְשַׁאצַּר וֶאֱמֶת הַדָּבָר
וְצָבָא גָדוֹל וּבִין אֶת־הַדָּבָר וּבִינָה לוֹ בַּמַּרְאֶה:
2 בַּיָּמִים הָהֵם אֲנִי דָנִיֵּאל הָיִיתִי מִתְאַבֵּל שְׁלֹשָׁה
שָׁבֻעִים יָמִים: 3 לֶחֶם חֲמֻדוֹת לֹא אָכַלְתִּי וּבָשָׂר
וָיַיִן לֹא־בָא אֶל־פִּי וְסוֹךְ לֹא־סָכְתִּי עַד־מְלֹאת
שְׁלֹשֶׁת שָׁבֻעִים יָמִים: פ
4 וּבְיוֹם עֶשְׂרִים וְאַרְבָּעָה לַחֹדֶשׁ הָרִאשׁוֹן וַאֲנִי
הָיִיתִי עַל יַד הַנָּהָר הַגָּדוֹל הוּא חִדָּקֶל: 5 וָאֶשָּׂא
אֶת־עֵינַי וָאֵרֶא וְהִנֵּה אִישׁ־אֶחָד לָבוּשׁ בַּדִּים
וּמָתְנָיו חֲגֻרִים בְּכֶתֶם אוּפָז: 6 וּגְוִיָּתוֹ כְתַרְשִׁישׁ
וּפָנָיו כְּמַרְאֵה בָרָק וְעֵינָיו כְּלַפִּידֵי אֵשׁ וּזְרֹעֹתָיו
וּמַרְגְּלֹתָיו כְּעֵין נְחֹשֶׁת קָלָל וְקוֹל דְּבָרָיו כְּקוֹל

eyes like torches of fire, his arms and feet like burnished bronze in color, and the sound of his words like the voice of a multitude.

7 And I, Daniel, alone saw the vision, for the men who were with me did not see the vision; but a great terror fell upon them, so that they fled to hide themselves. 8 Therefore I was left alone when I saw this great vision, and no strength remained in me; for my vigor was turned to frailty in me, and I retained no strength. 9 Yet I heard the sound of his words; and while I heard the sound of his words I was in a deep sleep on my face, with my face to the ground.

10 Suddenly, a hand touched me, which made me tremble on my knees and on the palms of my hands. 11 And he said to me, "O Daniel, man greatly beloved, understand the words that I speak to you, and stand upright, for I have now been sent to you." While he was speaking this word to me, I stood trembling.

12 Then he said to me, "Do not fear, Daniel, for from the first day that you set your heart to understand, and to humble yourself before your God, your words were heard; and I have come because of your words. 13 But the prince of the kingdom of Persia withstood me twenty-one days; and behold, Michael, one of the chief princes, came to help me, for I had been left alone there with the kings of Persia. 14 Now I have come to make you understand what will happen to your people in the latter days, for the vision *refers* to *many* days yet *to come*."

15 When he had spoken such words to me, I turned my face toward the ground and became speechless. 16 And suddenly, *one* having the likeness of the sons of men touched my lips; then I opened my mouth and spoke, saying to him who stood before me, "My lord, because of the vision my sorrows have overwhelmed me, and I have retained no strength. 17 For how can this servant of my lord talk with you, my lord? As for me, no strength remains in me now, nor is any breath left in me."

18 Then again, *the one* having the likeness of a man touched me and strengthened me. 19 And he said, "O man greatly beloved, fear not! Peace *be* to you; be strong, yes, be strong!"

So when he spoke to me I was strengthened, and said, "Let my lord speak, for you have strengthened me."

20 Then he said, "Do you know why I have come to you? And now I must return to fight with the prince of Persia; and when I have gone forth, indeed the prince of Greece will come. 21 But I will tell you

---

הָמֽוֹן: 7 וְרָאִיתִי אֲנִי דָנִיֵּאל לְבַדִּי אֶת־הַמַּרְאָה וְהָאֲנָשִׁים אֲשֶׁר הָיוּ עִמִּי לֹא רָאוּ אֶת־הַמַּרְאָה אֲבָל חֲרָדָה גְדֹלָה נָפְלָה עֲלֵיהֶם וַיִּבְרְחוּ בְּהֵחָבֵא: 8 וַאֲנִי נִשְׁאַרְתִּי לְבַדִּי וָאֶרְאֶה אֶת־הַמַּרְאָה הַגְּדֹלָה הַזֹּאת וְלֹא נִשְׁאַר־בִּי כֹּחַ וְהוֹדִי נֶהְפַּךְ עָלַי לְמַשְׁחִית וְלֹא עָצַרְתִּי כֹּחַ: 9 וָאֶשְׁמַע אֶת־קוֹל דְּבָרָיו וּכְשָׁמְעִי אֶת־קוֹל דְּבָרָיו וַאֲנִי הָיִיתִי נִרְדָּם עַל־פָּנַי וּפָנַי אָרְצָה: 10 וְהִנֵּה־יָד נָגְעָה בִּי וַתְּנִיעֵנִי עַל־בִּרְכַּי וְכַפּוֹת יָדָי: 11 וַיֹּאמֶר אֵלַי דָּנִיֵּאל אִישׁ־חֲמֻדוֹת הָבֵן בַּדְּבָרִים אֲשֶׁר אָנֹכִי דֹבֵר אֵלֶיךָ וַעֲמֹד עַל־עָמְדֶךָ כִּי עַתָּה שֻׁלַּחְתִּי אֵלֶיךָ וּבְדַבְּרוֹ עִמִּי אֶת־הַדָּבָר הַזֶּה עָמַדְתִּי מַרְעִיד: 12 וַיֹּאמֶר אֵלַי אַל־תִּירָא דָנִיֵּאל כִּי ׀ מִן־הַיּוֹם הָרִאשׁוֹן אֲשֶׁר נָתַתָּ אֶת־לִבְּךָ לְהָבִין וּלְהִתְעַנּוֹת לִפְנֵי אֱלֹהֶיךָ נִשְׁמְעוּ דְבָרֶיךָ וַאֲנִי־בָאתִי בִּדְבָרֶיךָ: 13 וְשַׂר ׀ מַלְכוּת פָּרַס עֹמֵד לְנֶגְדִּי עֶשְׂרִים וְאֶחָד יוֹם וְהִנֵּה מִיכָאֵל אַחַד הַשָּׂרִים הָרִאשֹׁנִים בָּא לְעָזְרֵנִי וַאֲנִי נוֹתַרְתִּי שָׁם אֵצֶל מַלְכֵי פָרָס: 14 וּבָאתִי לַהֲבִינְךָ אֵת אֲשֶׁר־יִקְרָה לְעַמְּךָ בְּאַחֲרִית הַיָּמִים כִּי־עוֹד חָזוֹן לַיָּמִים: 15 וּבְדַבְּרוֹ עִמִּי כַּדְּבָרִים הָאֵלֶּה נָתַתִּי פָנַי אַרְצָה וְנֶאֱלָמְתִּי: 16 וְהִנֵּה כִּדְמוּת בְּנֵי אָדָם נֹגֵעַ עַל־שְׂפָתָי וָאֶפְתַּח־פִּי וָאֲדַבְּרָה וָאֹמְרָה אֶל־הָעֹמֵד לְנֶגְדִּי אֲדֹנִי בַּמַּרְאָה נֶהֶפְכוּ צִירַי עָלַי וְלֹא עָצַרְתִּי כֹּחַ: 17 וְהֵיךְ יוּכַל עֶבֶד אֲדֹנִי זֶה לְדַבֵּר עִם־אֲדֹנִי זֶה וַאֲנִי מֵעַתָּה לֹא־יַעֲמָד־בִּי כֹחַ וּנְשָׁמָה לֹא נִשְׁאֲרָה־בִי: 18 וַיֹּסֶף וַיִּגַּע־בִּי כְּמַרְאֵה אָדָם וַיְחַזְּקֵנִי: 19 וַיֹּאמֶר אַל־תִּירָא אִישׁ־חֲמֻדוֹת שָׁלוֹם לָךְ חֲזַק וַחֲזָק וּכְדַבְּרוֹ עִמִּי הִתְחַזַּקְתִּי וָאֹמְרָה יְדַבֵּר אֲדֹנִי כִּי חִזַּקְתָּנִי: 20 וַיֹּאמֶר הֲיָדַעְתָּ לָמָּה־בָּאתִי אֵלֶיךָ וְעַתָּה אָשׁוּב לְהִלָּחֵם עִם־שַׂר פָּרָס וַאֲנִי יוֹצֵא וְהִנֵּה שַׂר־יָוָן בָּא: 21 אֲבָל אַגִּיד לְךָ

what is noted in the Scripture of Truth. (No one upholds me against these, except Michael your prince.

11 "Also in the first year of Darius the Mede, I, *even* I, stood up to confirm and strengthen him.) 2 And now I will tell you the truth: Behold, three more kings will arise in Persia, and the fourth shall be far richer than *them* all; by his strength, through his riches, he shall stir up all against the realm of Greece. 3 Then a mighty king shall arise, who shall rule with great dominion, and do according to his will. 4 And when he has arisen, his kingdom shall be broken up and divided toward the four winds of heaven, but not among his posterity nor according to his dominion with which he ruled; for his kingdom shall be uprooted, even for others besides these.

5 "Also the king of the South shall become strong, as well as *one* of his princes; and he shall gain power over him and have dominion. His dominion *shall be* a great dominion. 6 And at the end of *some* years they shall join forces, for the daughter of the king of the South shall go to the king of the North to make an agreement; but she shall not retain the power of her authority, and neither he nor his authority shall stand; but she shall be given up, with those who brought her, and with him who begot her, and with him who strengthened her in *those* times. 7 But from a branch of her roots *one* shall arise in his place, who shall come with an army, enter the fortress of the king of the North, and deal with them and prevail. 8 And he shall also carry their gods captive to Egypt, with their princes *and* their precious articles of silver and gold; and he shall continue *more* years than the king of the North.

9 "Also *the king of the North* shall come to the kingdom of the king of the South, but shall return to his own land. 10 However his sons shall stir up strife, and assemble a multitude of great forces; and *one* shall certainly come and overwhelm and pass through; then he shall return to his fortress and stir up strife.

11 "And the king of the South shall be moved with rage, and go out and fight with him, with the king of the North, who shall muster a great multitude; but the multitude shall be given into the hand of his *enemy.* 12 When he has taken away the multitude, his heart will be lifted up; and he will cast down tens of thousands, but he will not prevail. 13 For the king of the North will return and muster

אֶת־הָרָשׁוּם בִּכְתָב אֱמֶת וְאֵין אֶחָד מִתְחַזֵּק עִמִּי עַל־אֵלֶּה כִּי אִם־מִיכָאֵל שַׂרְכֶם: פ

יא וַאֲנִי בִּשְׁנַת אַחַת לְדָרְיָוֶשׁ הַמָּדִי עָמְדִי לְמַחֲזִיק וּלְמָעוֹז לוֹ: 2 וְעַתָּה אֱמֶת אַגִּיד לָךְ הִנֵּה־ עוֹד שְׁלֹשָׁה מְלָכִים עֹמְדִים לְפָרַס וְהָרְבִיעִי יַעֲשִׁיר עֹשֶׁר־גָּדוֹל מִכֹּל וּכְחֶזְקָתוֹ בְעָשְׁרוֹ יָעִיר הַכֹּל אֵת מַלְכוּת יָוָן: 3 וְעָמַד מֶלֶךְ גִּבּוֹר וּמָשַׁל מִמְשָׁל רַב וְעָשָׂה כִּרְצוֹנוֹ: 4 וּכְעָמְדוֹ תִּשָּׁבֵר מַלְכוּתוֹ וְתֵחָץ לְאַרְבַּע רוּחוֹת הַשָּׁמָיִם וְלֹא לְאַחֲרִיתוֹ וְלֹא כְמָשְׁלוֹ אֲשֶׁר מָשָׁל כִּי תִנָּתֵשׁ מַלְכוּתוֹ וְלַאֲחֵרִים מִלְּבַד־ אֵלֶּה: 5 וְיֶחֱזַק מֶלֶךְ־הַנֶּגֶב וּמִן־שָׂרָיו וְיֶחֱזַק עָלָיו וּמָשָׁל מִמְשָׁל רַב מֶמְשַׁלְתּוֹ: 6 וּלְקֵץ שָׁנִים יִתְחַבָּרוּ וּבַת מֶלֶךְ־הַנֶּגֶב תָּבוֹא אֶל־מֶלֶךְ הַצָּפוֹן לַעֲשׂוֹת מֵישָׁרִים וְלֹא־תַעְצֹר כּוֹחַ הַזְּרוֹעַ וְלֹא יַעֲמֹד וּזְרֹעוֹ וְתִנָּתֵן הִיא וּמְבִיאֶיהָ וְהַיֹּלְדָהּ וּמַחֲזִקָהּ בָּעִתִּים: 7 וְעָמַד מִנֵּצֶר שָׁרָשֶׁיהָ כַּנּוֹ וְיָבֹא אֶל־הַחַיִל וְיָבֹא בְּמָעוֹז מֶלֶךְ הַצָּפוֹן וְעָשָׂה בָהֶם וְהֶחֱזִיק: 8 וְגַם אֱלֹהֵיהֶם עִם־נְסִכֵיהֶם עִם־כְּלֵי חֶמְדָּתָם כֶּסֶף וְזָהָב בַּשְּׁבִי יָבִא מִצְרָיִם וְהוּא שָׁנִים יַעֲמֹד מִמֶּלֶךְ הַצָּפוֹן: 9 וּבָא בְּמַלְכוּת מֶלֶךְ הַנֶּגֶב וְשָׁב אֶל־ אַדְמָתוֹ: 10 וּבָנָו יִתְגָּרוּ וְאָסְפוּ הֲמוֹן חֲיָלִים רַבִּים וּבָא בוֹא וְשָׁטַף וְעָבָר וְיָשֹׁב וְיִתְגָּרוּ עַד־מָעֻזֹּה: 11 וְיִתְמַרְמַר מֶלֶךְ הַנֶּגֶב וְיָצָא וְנִלְחַם עִמּוֹ עִם־ מֶלֶךְ הַצָּפוֹן וְהֶעֱמִיד הָמוֹן רָב וְנִתַּן הֶהָמוֹן בְּיָדוֹ: 12 וְנִשָּׂא הֶהָמוֹן יָרוּם לְבָבוֹ וְהִפִּיל רִבֹּאוֹת וְלֹא יָעוֹז: 13 וְשָׁב מֶלֶךְ הַצָּפוֹן וְהֶעֱמִיד הָמוֹן רָב מִן

יא 10 וּבָנָיו וְיִתְגָּרֶה מָשָׁוֹ 12 וְרָם

a multitude greater than the former, and shall certainly come at the end of some years with a great army and much equipment.

14 "Now in those times many shall rise up against the king of the South. Also, violent men of your people shall exalt themselves in fulfillment of the vision, but they shall fall. 15 So the king of the North shall come and build a siege mound, and take a fortified city; and the forces of the South shall not withstand *him*. Even his choice troops *shall have* no strength to resist. 16 But he who comes against him shall do according to his own will, and no one shall stand against him. He shall stand in the Glorious Land with destruction in his power.

17 "He shall also set his face to enter with the strength of his whole kingdom, and upright ones with him; thus shall he do. And he shall give him the daughter of women to destroy it; but she shall not stand *with him,* or be for him. 18 After this he shall turn his face to the coastlands, and shall take many. But a ruler shall bring the reproach against them to an end; and with the reproach removed, he shall turn back on him. 19 Then he shall turn his face toward the fortress of his own land; but he shall stumble and fall, and not be found.

20 "There shall arise in his place one who imposes taxes *on* the glorious kingdom; but within a few days he shall be destroyed, but not in anger or in battle. 21 And in his place shall arise a vile person, to whom they will not give the honor of royalty; but he shall come in peaceably, and seize the kingdom by intrigue. 22 With the force of a flood they shall be swept away from before him and be broken, and also the prince of the covenant. 23 And after the league *is made* with him he shall act deceitfully, for he shall come up and become strong with a small *number of* people. 24 He shall enter peaceably, even into the richest places of the province; and he shall do *what* his fathers have not done, nor his forefathers: he shall disperse among them the plunder, spoil, and riches; and he shall devise his plans against the strongholds, but *only* for a time.

25 "He shall stir up his power and his courage against the king of the South with a great army. And the king of the South shall be stirred up to battle with a very great and mighty army; but he shall not stand, for they shall devise plans against him. 26 Yes, those who eat of the portion of his delicacies shall destroy him; his army shall be swept away, and many shall fall down slain. 27 Both these kings' hearts *shall be* bent on evil, and they shall speak lies at the same table; but it shall not prosper, for the end *will* still *be* at the appointed time.

הָרִאשׁוֹן וּלְקֵץ הָעִתִּים שָׁנִים יָבוֹא בּוֹא בְּחַיִל גָּדוֹל וּבִרְכוּשׁ רָב: 14 וּבָעִתִּים הָהֵם רַבִּים יַעַמְדוּ עַל־מֶלֶךְ הַנֶּגֶב וּבְנֵי | פָּרִיצֵי עַמְּךָ יִנַּשְּׂאוּ לְהַעֲמִיד חָזוֹן וְנִכְשָׁלוּ: 15 וְיָבֹא מֶלֶךְ הַצָּפוֹן וְיִשְׁפֹּךְ סוֹלֲלָה וְלָכַד עִיר מִבְצָרוֹת וּזְרֹעוֹת הַנֶּגֶב לֹא יַעֲמֹדוּ וְעַם מִבְחָרָיו וְאֵין כֹּחַ לַעֲמֹד: 16 וְיַעַשׂ הַבָּא אֵלָיו כִּרְצוֹנוֹ וְאֵין עוֹמֵד לְפָנָיו וְיַעֲמֹד בְּאֶרֶץ־הַצְּבִי וְכָלָה בְיָדוֹ: 17 וְיָשֵׂם | פָּנָיו לָבוֹא בְּתֹקֶף כָּל־מַלְכוּתוֹ וִישָׁרִים עִמּוֹ וְעָשָׂה וּבַת הַנָּשִׁים יִתֶּן־לוֹ לְהַשְׁחִיתָהּ וְלֹא תַעֲמֹד וְלֹא־לוֹ תִהְיֶה: 18 וְיָשֵׁב פ פָּנָיו לְאִיִּים וְלָכַד רַבִּים וְהִשְׁבִּית קָצִין חֶרְפָּתוֹ לוֹ בִּלְתִּי חֶרְפָּתוֹ יָשִׁיב לוֹ: 19 וְיָשֵׁב פָּנָיו לְמָעוּזֵּי אַרְצוֹ וְנִכְשַׁל וְנָפַל וְלֹא יִמָּצֵא: 20 וְעָמַד עַל־כַּנּוֹ מַעֲבִיר נוֹגֵשׂ הֶדֶר מַלְכוּת וּבְיָמִים אֲחָדִים יִשָּׁבֵר וְלֹא בְאַפַּיִם וְלֹא בְמִלְחָמָה: 21 וְעָמַד עַל־כַּנּוֹ נִבְזֶה וְלֹא־נָתְנוּ עָלָיו הוֹד מַלְכוּת וּבָא בְשַׁלְוָה וְהֶחֱזִיק מַלְכוּת בַּחֲלַקְלַקּוֹת: 22 וּזְרֹעוֹת הַשֶּׁטֶף יִשָּׁטְפוּ מִלְּפָנָיו וְיִשָּׁבֵרוּ וְגַם נְגִיד בְּרִית: 23 וּמִן־הִתְחַבְּרוּת אֵלָיו יַעֲשֶׂה מִרְמָה וְעָלָה וְעָצַם בִּמְעַט־גּוֹי: 24 בְּשַׁלְוָה וּבְמִשְׁמַנֵּי מְדִינָה יָבוֹא וְעָשָׂה אֲשֶׁר לֹא־עָשׂוּ אֲבֹתָיו וַאֲבוֹת אֲבֹתָיו בִּזָּה וְשָׁלָל וּרְכוּשׁ לָהֶם יִבְזוֹר וְעַל מִבְצָרִים יְחַשֵּׁב מַחְשְׁבֹתָיו וְעַד־עֵת: 25 וְיָעֵר כֹּחוֹ וּלְבָבוֹ עַל־מֶלֶךְ הַנֶּגֶב בְּחַיִל גָּדוֹל וּמֶלֶךְ הַנֶּגֶב יִתְגָּרֶה לַמִּלְחָמָה בְּחַיִל־גָּדוֹל וְעָצוּם עַד־מְאֹד וְלֹא יַעֲמֹד כִּי־יַחְשְׁבוּ עָלָיו מַחֲשָׁבוֹת: 26 וְאֹכְלֵי פַת־בָּגוֹ יִשְׁבְּרוּהוּ וְחֵילוֹ יִשְׁטוֹף וְנָפְלוּ חֲלָלִים רַבִּים: 27 וּשְׁנֵיהֶם הַמְּלָכִים לְבָבָם לְמֵרָע וְעַל־שֻׁלְחָן אֶחָד כָּזָב יְדַבֵּרוּ וְלֹא תִצְלָח כִּי־עוֹד

28 While returning to his land with great riches, his heart shall be *moved* against the holy covenant; so he shall do *damage* and return to his own land.

29 "At the appointed time he shall return and go toward the south; but it shall not be like the former or the latter. 30 For ships from Cyprus shall come against him; therefore he shall be grieved, and return in rage against the holy covenant, and do *damage*.

"So he shall return and show regard for those who forsake the holy covenant. 31 And forces shall be mustered by him, and they shall defile the sanctuary fortress; then they shall take away the daily *sacrifices*, and place *there* the abomination of desolation. 32 Those who do wickedly against the covenant he shall corrupt with flattery; but the people who know their God shall be strong, and carry out *great exploits*. 33 And those of the people who understand shall instruct many; yet *for many* days they shall fall by sword and flame, by captivity and plundering. 34 Now when they fall, they shall be aided with a little help; but many shall join with them by intrigue. 35 And *some* of those of understanding shall fall, to refine them, purify *them,* and make *them* white, *until* the time of the end; because *it is* still for the appointed time.

36 "Then the king shall do according to his own will: he shall exalt and magnify himself above every god, shall speak blasphemies against the God of gods, and shall prosper till the wrath has been accomplished; for what has been determined shall be done. 37 He shall regard neither the God of his fathers nor the desire of women, nor regard any god; for he shall exalt himself above *them* all. 38 But in their place he shall honor a god of fortresses; and a god which his fathers did not know he shall honor with gold and silver, with precious stones and pleasant things. 39 Thus he shall act against the strongest fortresses with a foreign god, which he shall acknowledge, *and* advance *its* glory; and he shall cause them to rule over many, and divide the land for gain.

40 "At the time of the end the king of the South shall attack him; and the king of the North shall come against him like a whirlwind, with chariots, horsemen, and with many ships; and he shall enter the countries, overwhelm *them,* and pass through. 41 He shall also enter the Glorious Land, and many *countries* shall be overthrown; but these shall escape from his hand: Edom, Moab, and the prominent people of Ammon. 42 He shall stretch out his hand against the countries, and the land of Egypt shall not escape. 43 He shall have power over the treasures of gold and silver, and over all the

קֵץ לַמּוֹעֵד: 28 וְיָשֹׁב אַרְצוֹ בִּרְכוּשׁ גָּדוֹל וּלְבָבוֹ עַל־בְּרִית קֹדֶשׁ וְעָשָׂה וְשָׁב לְאַרְצוֹ: 29 לַמּוֹעֵד יָשׁוּב וּבָא בַנֶּגֶב וְלֹא־תִהְיֶה כָרִאשֹׁנָה וְכָאַחֲרֹנָה: 30 וּבָאוּ בוֹ צִיִּים כִּתִּים וְנִכְאָה וְשָׁב וְזָעַם עַל־בְּרִית־קוֹדֶשׁ וְעָשָׂה וְשָׁב וְיָבֵן עַל־עֹזְבֵי בְּרִית קֹדֶשׁ: 31 וּזְרֹעִים מִמֶּנּוּ יַעֲמֹדוּ וְחִלְּלוּ הַמִּקְדָּשׁ הַמָּעוֹז וְהֵסִירוּ הַתָּמִיד וְנָתְנוּ הַשִּׁקּוּץ מְשֹׁמֵם: 32 וּמַרְשִׁיעֵי בְרִית יַחֲנִיף בַּחֲלַקּוֹת וְעַם יֹדְעֵי אֱלֹהָיו יַחֲזִקוּ וְעָשׂוּ: 33 וּמַשְׂכִּילֵי עָם יָבִינוּ לָרַבִּים וְנִכְשְׁלוּ בְּחֶרֶב וּבְלֶהָבָה בִּשְׁבִי וּבְבִזָּה יָמִים: 34 וּבְהִכָּשְׁלָם יֵעָזְרוּ עֵזֶר מְעָט וְנִלְווּ עֲלֵיהֶם רַבִּים בַּחֲלַקְלַקּוֹת: 35 וּמִן־הַמַּשְׂכִּילִים יִכָּשְׁלוּ לִצְרוֹף בָּהֶם וּלְבָרֵר וְלַלְבֵּן עַד־עֵת קֵץ כִּי־עוֹד לַמּוֹעֵד: 36 וְעָשָׂה כִרְצוֹנוֹ הַמֶּלֶךְ וְיִתְרוֹמֵם וְיִתְגַּדֵּל עַל־כָּל־אֵל וְעַל אֵל אֵלִים יְדַבֵּר נִפְלָאוֹת וְהִצְלִיחַ עַד־כָּלָה זַעַם כִּי נֶחֱרָצָה נֶעֱשָׂתָה: 37 וְעַל־אֱלֹהֵי אֲבֹתָיו לֹא יָבִין וְעַל־חֶמְדַּת נָשִׁים וְעַל־כָּל־אֱלוֹהַּ לֹא יָבִין כִּי עַל־כֹּל יִתְגַּדָּל: 38 וְלֶאֱלֹהַּ מָעֻזִּים עַל־כַּנּוֹ יְכַבֵּד וְלֶאֱלוֹהַּ אֲשֶׁר לֹא־יְדָעֻהוּ אֲבֹתָיו יְכַבֵּד בְּזָהָב וּבְכֶסֶף וּבְאֶבֶן יְקָרָה וּבַחֲמֻדוֹת: 39 וְעָשָׂה לְמִבְצְרֵי מָעֻזִּים עִם־אֱלוֹהַּ נֵכָר אֲשֶׁר הִכִּיר‏ יַרְבֶּה כָבוֹד וְהִמְשִׁילָם בָּרַבִּים וַאֲדָמָה יְחַלֵּק בִּמְחִיר: 40 וּבְעֵת קֵץ יִתְנַגַּח עִמּוֹ מֶלֶךְ הַנֶּגֶב וְיִשְׂתָּעֵר עָלָיו מֶלֶךְ הַצָּפוֹן בְּרֶכֶב וּבְפָרָשִׁים וּבָאֳנִיּוֹת רַבּוֹת וּבָא בַאֲרָצוֹת וְשָׁטַף וְעָבָר: 41 וּבָא בְּאֶרֶץ הַצְּבִי וְרַבּוֹת יִכָּשֵׁלוּ וְאֵלֶּה יִמָּלְטוּ מִיָּדוֹ אֱדוֹם וּמוֹאָב וְרֵאשִׁית בְּנֵי עַמּוֹן: 42 וְיִשְׁלַח יָדוֹ בַּאֲרָצוֹת וְאֶרֶץ מִצְרַיִם לֹא תִהְיֶה לִפְלֵיטָה: 43 וּמָשַׁל בְּמִכְמַנֵּי הַזָּהָב וְהַכֶּסֶף

precious things of Egypt; also the Libyans and Ethiopians *shall follow* at his heels. ⁴⁴But news from the east and the north shall trouble him; therefore he shall go out with great fury to destroy and annihilate many. ⁴⁵And he shall plant the tents of his palace between the seas and the glorious holy mountain; yet he shall come to his end, and no one will help him.

12 "At that time Michael shall stand up,
The great prince who stands *watch* over the sons of your people;
And there shall be a time of trouble,
Such as never was since there was a nation,
Even to that time.
And at that time your people shall be delivered,
Every one who is found written in the book.
² And many of those who sleep in the dust of the earth shall awake,
Some to everlasting life,
Some to shame *and* everlasting contempt.
³ Those who are wise shall shine
Like the brightness of the firmament,
And those who turn many to righteousness
Like the stars forever and ever.

⁴"But you, Daniel, shut up the words, and seal the book until the time of the end; many shall run to and fro, and knowledge shall increase."

⁵Then I, Daniel, looked; and there stood two others, one on this riverbank and the other on that riverbank. ⁶And *one* said to the man clothed in linen, who *was* above the waters of the river, "How long shall the fulfillment of these wonders *be?*"

⁷Then I heard the man clothed in linen, who *was* above the waters of the river, when he held up his right hand and his left hand to heaven, and swore by Him who lives forever, that *it shall be* for a time, times, and half *a time;* and when the power of the holy people has been completely shattered, all these *things* shall be finished.

⁸Although I heard, I did not understand. Then I said, "My lord, what *shall be* the end of these *things?*"

⁹And he said, "Go *your way,* Daniel, for the words *are* closed up and sealed till the time of the end. ¹⁰Many shall be purified, made white, and refined, but the wicked shall do wickedly; and none of the wicked shall understand, but the wise shall understand.

¹¹"And from the time *that* the daily *sacrifice* is taken away, and the abomination of desolation is set up, *there shall be* one thousand two hundred and ninety days. ¹²Blessed *is* he who waits, and comes to the one thousand three hundred and thirty-five days.

וּבְכֹל חֲמֻדוֹת מִצְרָיִם וְלֻבִים וְכֻשִׁים בְּמִצְעָדָיו: 44 וּשְׁמֻעוֹת יְבַהֲלֻהוּ מִמִּזְרָח וּמִצָּפוֹן וְיָצָא בְּחֵמָא גְדֹלָה לְהַשְׁמִיד וּלְהַחֲרִים רַבִּים: 45 וְיִטַּע אָהֳלֵי אַפַּדְנוֹ בֵּין יַמִּים לְהַר־צְבִי־קֹדֶשׁ וּבָא עַד־קִצּוֹ וְאֵין עוֹזֵר לוֹ:

יב וּבָעֵת הַהִיא יַעֲמֹד מִיכָאֵל הַשַּׂר הַגָּדוֹל הָעֹמֵד עַל־בְּנֵי עַמֶּךָ וְהָיְתָה עֵת צָרָה אֲשֶׁר לֹא־ נִהְיְתָה מִהְיוֹת גּוֹי עַד הָעֵת הַהִיא וּבָעֵת הַהִיא יִמָּלֵט עַמְּךָ כָּל־הַנִּמְצָא כָּתוּב בַּסֵּפֶר: 2 וְרַבִּים מִיְּשֵׁנֵי אַדְמַת־עָפָר יָקִיצוּ אֵלֶּה לְחַיֵּי עוֹלָם וְאֵלֶּה לַחֲרָפוֹת לְדִרְאוֹן עוֹלָם: ס 3 וְהַמַּשְׂכִּלִים יַזְהִרוּ כְּזֹהַר הָרָקִיעַ וּמַצְדִּיקֵי הָרַבִּים כַּכּוֹכָבִים לְעוֹלָם וָעֶד: פ

4 וְאַתָּה דָנִיֵּאל סְתֹם הַדְּבָרִים וַחֲתֹם הַסֵּפֶר עַד־ עֵת קֵץ יְשֹׁטְטוּ רַבִּים וְתִרְבֶּה הַדָּעַת: 5 וְרָאִיתִי אֲנִי דָנִיֵּאל וְהִנֵּה שְׁנַיִם אֲחֵרִים עֹמְדִים אֶחָד הֵנָּה לִשְׂפַת הַיְאֹר וְאֶחָד הֵנָּה לִשְׂפַת הַיְאֹר: 6 וַיֹּאמֶר לָאִישׁ לְבוּשׁ הַבַּדִּים אֲשֶׁר מִמַּעַל לְמֵימֵי הַיְאֹר עַד־מָתַי קֵץ הַפְּלָאוֹת: 7 וָאֶשְׁמַע אֶת־הָאִישׁ | לְבוּשׁ הַבַּדִּים אֲשֶׁר מִמַּעַל לְמֵימֵי הַיְאֹר וַיָּרֶם יְמִינוֹ וּשְׂמֹאלוֹ אֶל־הַשָּׁמַיִם וַיִּשָּׁבַע בְּחֵי הָעוֹלָם כִּי לְמוֹעֵד מוֹעֲדִים וָחֵצִי וּכְכַלּוֹת נַפֵּץ יַד־עַם־ קֹדֶשׁ תִּכְלֶינָה כָל־אֵלֶּה: 8 וַאֲנִי שָׁמַעְתִּי וְלֹא אָבִין וָאֹמְרָה אֲדֹנִי מָה אַחֲרִית אֵלֶּה: פ

9 וַיֹּאמֶר לֵךְ דָּנִיֵּאל כִּי־סְתֻמִים וַחֲתֻמִים הַדְּבָרִים עַד־עֵת קֵץ: 10 יִתְבָּרֲרוּ וְיִתְלַבְּנוּ וְיִצָּרְפוּ רַבִּים וְהִרְשִׁיעוּ רְשָׁעִים וְלֹא יָבִינוּ כָּל־רְשָׁעִים וְהַמַּשְׂכִּלִים יָבִינוּ: 11 וּמֵעֵת הוּסַר הַתָּמִיד וְלָתֵת שִׁקּוּץ שֹׁמֵם יָמִים אֶלֶף מָאתַיִם וְתִשְׁעִים: 12 אַשְׁרֵי הַמְחַכֶּה וְיַגִּיעַ לְיָמִים אֶלֶף שְׁלֹשׁ מֵאוֹת שְׁלֹשִׁים וַחֲמִשָּׁה:

13 "But you, go *your way* till the end; for you shall rest, and will arise to your inheritance at the end of the days."

13 וְאַתָּה לֵךְ לַקֵּץ וְתָנוּחַ וְתַעֲמֹד לְגֹרָלְךָ לְקֵץ הַיָּמִין:

The Book of

EZRA

עזרא

1 Now in the first year of Cyrus king of Persia, that the word of the LORD by the mouth of Jeremiah might be fulfilled, the LORD stirred up the spirit of Cyrus king of Persia, so that he made a proclamation throughout all his kingdom, and also *put it* in writing, saying,

2   Thus says Cyrus king of Persia:
All the kingdoms of the earth the LORD God of heaven has given me. And He has commanded me to build Him a house at Jerusalem which *is* in Judah. ³ Who *is* among you of all His people? May his God be with him, and let him go up to Jerusalem which *is* in Judah, and build the house of the LORD God of Israel (He *is* God), which *is* in Jerusalem. ⁴ And whoever is left in any place where he dwells, let the men of his place help him with silver and gold, with goods and livestock, besides the freewill offerings for the house of God which *is* in Jerusalem.

⁵ Then the heads of the fathers' *houses* of Judah and Benjamin, and the priests and the Levites, with all whose spirits God had moved, arose to go up and build the house of the LORD which *is* in Jerusalem. ⁶ And all those who *were* around them encouraged them with articles of silver and gold, with goods and livestock, and with precious things, besides all *that* was willingly offered.

⁷ King Cyrus also brought out the articles of the house of the LORD, which Nebuchadnezzar had taken from Jerusalem and put in the temple of his gods; ⁸ and Cyrus king of Persia brought them out by the hand of Mithredath the treasurer, and counted them out to Sheshbazzar the prince of Judah. ⁹ This *is* the number of them: thirty gold platters, one thousand silver platters, twenty-nine knives, ¹⁰ thirty gold basins, four hundred and ten silver basins of a similar *kind, and* one thousand other articles. ¹¹ All the articles of gold and silver *were* five thousand four hundred. All *these* Sheshbazzar took with the captives who were brought from Babylon to Jerusalem.

2 Now these *are* the people of the province who came back from the captivity, of those who had been carried away, whom Nebuchadnezzar the king

א וּבִשְׁנַת אַחַת לְכֹורֶשׁ מֶלֶךְ פָּרַס לִכְלֹות דְּבַר־יְהוָה מִפִּי יִרְמְיָה הֵעִיר יְהוָה אֶת־רוּחַ כֹּרֶשׁ מֶלֶךְ־פָּרַס וַיַּעֲבֶר־קֹול בְּכָל־מַלְכוּתֹו וְגַם־בְּמִכְתָּב לֵאמֹר:

2 כֹּה אָמַר כֹּרֶשׁ מֶלֶךְ פָּרַס כֹּל מַמְלְכֹות הָאָרֶץ נָתַן לִי יְהוָה אֱלֹהֵי הַשָּׁמַיִם וְהוּא־פָקַד עָלַי לִבְנֹות־לֹו בַיִת בִּירוּשָׁלַ͏ִם אֲשֶׁר בִּיהוּדָה: 3 מִי־בָכֶם מִכָּל־עַמֹּו יְהִי אֱלֹהָיו עִמֹּו וְיַעַל לִירוּשָׁלַ͏ִם אֲשֶׁר בִּיהוּדָה וְיִבֶן אֶת־בֵּית יְהוָה אֱלֹהֵי יִשְׂרָאֵל הוּא הָאֱלֹהִים אֲשֶׁר בִּירוּשָׁלָ͏ִם: 4 וְכָל־הַנִּשְׁאָר מִכָּל־הַמְּקֹמֹות אֲשֶׁר הוּא גָר־שָׁם יְנַשְּׂאוּהוּ אַנְשֵׁי מְקֹמֹו בְּכֶסֶף וּבְזָהָב וּבִרְכוּשׁ וּבִבְהֵמָה עִם־הַנְּדָבָה לְבֵית הָאֱלֹהִים אֲשֶׁר בִּירוּשָׁלָ͏ִם: 5 וַיָּקוּמוּ רָאשֵׁי הָאָבֹות לִיהוּדָה וּבִנְיָמִן וְהַכֹּהֲנִים וְהַלְוִיִּם לְכֹל הֵעִיר הָאֱלֹהִים אֶת־רוּחֹו לַעֲלֹות לִבְנֹות אֶת־בֵּית יְהוָה אֲשֶׁר בִּירוּשָׁלָ͏ִם:

6 וְכָל־סְבִיבֹתֵיהֶם חִזְּקוּ בִידֵיהֶם בִּכְלֵי־כֶסֶף בַּזָּהָב בָּרְכוּשׁ וּבַבְּהֵמָה וּבַמִּגְדָּנֹות לְבַד עַל־כָּל־הִתְנַדֵּב: ס 7 וְהַמֶּלֶךְ כֹּורֶשׁ הֹוצִיא אֶת־כְּלֵי בֵית־יְהוָה אֲשֶׁר הֹוצִיא נְבוּכַדְנֶצַּר מִירוּשָׁלַ͏ִם וַיִּתְּנֵם בְּבֵית אֱלֹהָיו: 8 וַיֹּוצִיאֵם כֹּורֶשׁ מֶלֶךְ פָּרַס עַל־יַד מִתְרְדָת הַגִּזְבָּר וַיִּסְפְּרֵם לְשֵׁשְׁבַּצַּר הַנָּשִׂיא לִיהוּדָה: 9 וְאֵלֶּה מִסְפָּרָם אֲגַרְטְלֵי זָהָב שְׁלֹשִׁים אֲגַרְטְלֵי־כֶסֶף אָלֶף מַחֲלָפִים תִּשְׁעָה וְעֶשְׂרִים: ס 10 כְּפֹורֵי זָהָב שְׁלֹשִׁים כְּפֹורֵי כֶסֶף מִשְׁנִים אַרְבַּע מֵאֹות וַעֲשָׂרָה כֵּלִים אֲחֵרִים אָלֶף: ס 11 כָּל־כֵּלִים לַזָּהָב וְלַכֶּסֶף חֲמֵשֶׁת אֲלָפִים וְאַרְבַּע מֵאֹות הַכֹּל הֶעֱלָה שֵׁשְׁבַּצַּר עִם הֵעָלֹות הַגֹּולָה מִבָּבֶל לִירוּשָׁלָ͏ִם: פ

ב וְאֵלֶּה ׀ בְּנֵי הַמְּדִינָה הָעֹלִים מִשְּׁבִי הַגֹּולָה אֲשֶׁר הֶגְלָה נְבוּכַדְנֶצֹּור מֶלֶךְ־בָּבֶל לְבָבֶל וַיָּשׁוּבוּ

ב 1 נְבוּכַדְנֶצַּר

of Babylon had carried away to Babylon, and who returned to Jerusalem and Judah, everyone to his *own* city.

2 *Those* who came with Zerubbabel *were* Jeshua, Nehemiah, Seraiah, Reelaiah, Mordecai, Bilshan, Mispar, Bigvai, Rehum, *and* Baanah. The number of the men of the people of Israel: ³ the people of Parosh, two thousand one hundred and seventy-two; ⁴ the people of Shephatiah, three hundred and seventy-two; ⁵ the people of Arah, seven hundred and seventy-five; ⁶ the people of Pahath-Moab, of the people of Jeshua *and* Joab, two thousand eight hundred and twelve; ⁷ the people of Elam, one thousand two hundred and fifty-four; ⁸ the people of Zattu, nine hundred and forty-five; ⁹ the people of Zaccai, seven hundred and sixty; ¹⁰ the people of Bani, six hundred and forty-two; ¹¹ the people of Bebai, six hundred and twenty-three; ¹² the people of Azgad, one thousand two hundred and twenty-two; ¹³ the people of Adonikam, six hundred and sixty-six; ¹⁴ the people of Bigvai, two thousand and fifty-six; ¹⁵ the people of Adin, four hundred and fifty-four; ¹⁶ the people of Ater of Hezekiah, ninety-eight; ¹⁷ the people of Bezai, three hundred and twenty-three; ¹⁸ the people of Jorah, one hundred and twelve; ¹⁹ the people of Hashum, two hundred and twenty-three; ²⁰ the people of Gibbar, ninety-five; ²¹ the people of Bethlehem, one hundred and twenty-three; ²² the men of Netophah, fifty-six; ²³ the men of Anathoth, one hundred and twenty-eight; ²⁴ the people of Azmaveth, forty-two; ²⁵ the people of Kirjath Arim, Chephirah, and Beeroth, seven hundred and forty-three; ²⁶ the people of Ramah and Geba, six hundred and twenty-one; ²⁷ the men of Michmas, one hundred and twenty-two; ²⁸ the men of Bethel and Ai, two hundred and twenty-three; ²⁹ the people of Nebo, fifty-two; ³⁰ the people of Magbish, one hundred and fifty-six; ³¹ the people of the other Elam, one thousand two hundred and fifty-four; ³² the people of Harim, three hundred and twenty; ³³ the people of Lod, Hadid, and Ono, seven hundred and twenty-five; ³⁴ the people of Jericho, three hundred and forty-five; ³⁵ the people of Senaah, three thousand six hundred and thirty.

36 The priests: the sons of Jedaiah, of the house of Jeshua, nine hundred and seventy-three; ³⁷ the sons of Immer, one thousand and fifty-two; ³⁸ the sons of Pashhur, one thousand two hundred and forty-seven; ³⁹ the sons of Harim, one thousand and seventeen.

40 The Levites: the sons of Jeshua and Kadmiel, of the sons of Hodaviah, seventy-four.

לִירוּשָׁלַ֖͏ִם וִיהוּדָ֑ה אִ֖ישׁ לְעִירֽוֹ׃ 2 אֲשֶׁר־בָּ֣אוּ עִם־ זְרֻבָּבֶ֗ל יֵשׁ֡וּעַ נְחֶמְיָ֡ה שְׂרָיָ֡ה רְֽעֵלָיָ֡ה מָרְדֳּכַ֣י בִּלְשָׁ֗ן מִסְפָּ֛ר בִּגְוַ֥י רְח֖וּם בַּעֲנָ֑ה מִסְפַּ֕ר אַנְשֵׁ֖י עַ֥ם יִשְׂרָאֵֽל׃ ס 3 בְּנֵ֣י פַרְעֹ֔שׁ אַלְפַּ֕יִם מֵאָ֖ה שִׁבְעִ֥ים וּשְׁנָֽיִם׃ 4 בְּנֵ֣י שְׁפַטְיָ֔ה שְׁלֹ֥שׁ מֵא֖וֹת שִׁבְעִ֥ים וּשְׁנָֽיִם׃

5 בְּנֵ֣י אָרַ֔ח שְׁבַ֥ע מֵא֖וֹת חֲמִשָּׁ֥ה וְשִׁבְעִֽים׃ 6 בְּנֵֽי־ פַחַ֣ת מוֹאָ֗ב לִבְנֵ֤י יֵשׁ֙וּעַ֙ יוֹאָ֔ב אַלְפַּ֕יִם שְׁמֹנֶ֥ה מֵא֖וֹת וּשְׁנֵ֥ים עָשָֽׂר׃ 7 בְּנֵ֣י עֵילָ֔ם אֶ֕לֶף מָאתַ֖יִם חֲמִשִּׁ֥ים וְאַרְבָּעָֽה׃ 8 בְּנֵ֣י זַתּ֔וּא תְּשַׁ֥ע מֵא֖וֹת וְאַרְבָּעִ֥ים וַחֲמִשָּֽׁה׃ 9 בְּנֵ֣י זַכָּ֔י שְׁבַ֥ע מֵא֖וֹת וְשִׁשִּֽׁים׃ 10 בְּנֵ֣י בָנִ֔י שֵׁ֥שׁ מֵא֖וֹת אַרְבָּעִ֥ים וּשְׁנָֽיִם׃ 11 בְּנֵ֣י בֵבָ֔י שֵׁ֥שׁ מֵא֖וֹת עֶשְׂרִ֥ים וּשְׁלֹשָֽׁה׃ 12 בְּנֵ֣י עַזְגָּ֔ד אֶ֕לֶף מָאתַ֖יִם עֶשְׂרִ֥ים וּשְׁנָֽיִם׃ 13 בְּנֵי֙ אֲדֹ֣נִיקָ֔ם שֵׁ֥שׁ מֵא֖וֹת שִׁשִּׁ֥ים וְשִׁשָּֽׁה׃ 14 בְּנֵ֣י בִגְוָ֔י אַלְפַּ֖יִם חֲמִשִּׁ֥ים וְשִׁשָּֽׁה׃ 15 בְּנֵ֣י עָדִ֔ין אַרְבַּ֥ע מֵא֖וֹת חֲמִשִּׁ֥ים וְאַרְבָּעָֽה׃ 16 בְּנֵֽי־אָטֵ֥ר לִֽיחִזְקִיָּ֖ה תִּשְׁעִ֥ים וּשְׁמֹנָֽה׃ 17 בְּנֵ֣י בֵצָ֔י שְׁלֹ֥שׁ מֵא֖וֹת עֶשְׂרִ֥ים וּשְׁלֹשָֽׁה׃ 18 בְּנֵ֣י יוֹרָ֔ה מֵאָ֖ה וּשְׁנֵ֥ים עָשָֽׂר׃

19 בְּנֵ֣י חָשֻׁ֔ם מָאתַ֖יִם עֶשְׂרִ֥ים וּשְׁלֹשָֽׁה׃ 20 בְּנֵ֥י גִבָּ֖ר תִּשְׁעִ֥ים וַחֲמִשָּֽׁה׃ 21 בְּנֵ֣י בֵֽית־לָ֔חֶם מֵאָ֖ה עֶשְׂרִ֥ים וּשְׁלֹשָֽׁה׃ 22 אַנְשֵׁ֥י נְטֹפָ֖ה חֲמִשִּׁ֥ים וְשִׁשָּֽׁה׃ 23 אַנְשֵׁ֣י עֲנָת֔וֹת מֵאָ֖ה עֶשְׂרִ֥ים וּשְׁמֹנָֽה׃ 24 בְּנֵ֥י עַזְמָ֛וֶת אַרְבָּעִ֥ים וּשְׁנָֽיִם׃ 25 בְּנֵ֣י קִרְיַ֣ת עָרִ֗ים כְּפִירָ֖ה וּבְאֵר֑וֹת שְׁבַ֥ע מֵא֖וֹת וְאַרְבָּעִ֥ים וּשְׁלֹשָֽׁה׃ 26 בְּנֵ֤י הָֽרָמָה֙ וָגָ֔בַע שֵׁ֥שׁ מֵא֖וֹת עֶשְׂרִ֥ים וְאֶחָֽד׃ 27 אַנְשֵׁ֣י מִכְמָ֔ס מֵאָ֖ה עֶשְׂרִ֥ים וּשְׁנָֽיִם׃ 28 אַנְשֵׁ֤י בֵֽית־אֵל֙ וְהָעָ֔י מָאתַ֖יִם עֶשְׂרִ֥ים וּשְׁלֹשָֽׁה׃ 29 בְּנֵ֥י נְב֖וֹ חֲמִשִּׁ֥ים וּשְׁנָֽיִם׃ 30 בְּנֵ֣י מַגְבִּ֔ישׁ מֵאָ֖ה חֲמִשִּׁ֥ים וְשִׁשָּֽׁה׃

31 בְּנֵי֙ עֵילָ֣ם אַחֵ֔ר אֶ֕לֶף מָאתַ֖יִם חֲמִשִּׁ֥ים וְאַרְבָּעָֽה׃ 32 בְּנֵ֣י חָרִ֔ם שְׁלֹ֥שׁ מֵא֖וֹת וְעֶשְׂרִֽים׃ 33 בְּנֵי־לֹ֣ד חָדִ֣יד וְאוֹנ֗וֹ שְׁבַ֥ע מֵא֖וֹת עֶשְׂרִ֥ים וַחֲמִשָּֽׁה׃ 34 בְּנֵ֣י יְרֵח֔וֹ שְׁלֹ֥שׁ מֵא֖וֹת אַרְבָּעִ֥ים וַחֲמִשָּֽׁה׃ 35 בְּנֵ֣י סְנָאָ֔ה שְׁלֹ֥שֶׁת אֲלָפִ֕ים וְשֵׁ֥שׁ מֵא֖וֹת וּשְׁלֹשִֽׁים׃ 36 הַֽכֹּהֲנִ֑ים בְּנֵ֤י יְדַֽעְיָה֙ לְבֵ֣ית יֵשׁ֔וּעַ תְּשַׁ֥ע מֵא֖וֹת שִׁבְעִ֥ים וּשְׁלֹשָֽׁה׃ ס 37 בְּנֵ֣י אִמֵּ֔ר אֶ֖לֶף חֲמִשִּׁ֥ים וּשְׁנָֽיִם׃ 38 בְּנֵ֣י פַשְׁח֔וּר אֶ֕לֶף מָאתַ֖יִם אַרְבָּעִ֥ים וְשִׁבְעָֽה׃ 39 בְּנֵ֣י חָרִ֔ם אֶ֖לֶף וְשִׁבְעָ֥ה עָשָֽׂר׃ 40 הַלְוִיִּ֑ם בְּנֵי־יֵשׁ֧וּעַ וְקַדְמִיאֵ֛ל לִבְנֵ֥י הֽוֹדַוְיָ֖ה שִׁבְעִ֥ים

41 The singers: the sons of Asaph, one hundred and twenty-eight.

42 The sons of the gatekeepers: the sons of Shallum, the sons of Ater, the sons of Talmon, the sons of Akkub, the sons of Hatita, and the sons of Shobai, one hundred and thirty-nine *in* all.

43 The Nethinim: the sons of Ziha, the sons of Hasupha, the sons of Tabbaoth, 44 the sons of Keros, the sons of Siaha, the sons of Padon, 45 the sons of Lebanah, the sons of Hagabah, the sons of Akkub, 46 the sons of Hagab, the sons of Shalmai, the sons of Hanan, 47 the sons of Giddel, the sons of Gahar, the sons of Reaiah, 48 the sons of Rezin, the sons of Nekoda, the sons of Gazzam, 49 the sons of Uzza, the sons of Paseah, the sons of Besai, 50 the sons of Asnah, the sons of Meunim, the sons of Nephusim, 51 the sons of Bakbuk, the sons of Hakupha, the sons of Harhur, 52 the sons of Bazluth, the sons of Mehida, the sons of Harsha, 53 the sons of Barkos, the sons of Sisera, the sons of Tamah, 54 the sons of Neziah, and the sons of Hatipha.

55 The sons of Solomon's servants: the sons of Sotai, the sons of Sophereth, the sons of Peruda, 56 the sons of Jaala, the sons of Darkon, the sons of Giddel, 57 the sons of Shephatiah, the sons of Hattil, the sons of Pochereth of Zebaim, and the sons of Ami. 58 All the Nethinim and the children of Solomon's servants were three hundred and ninety-two.

59 And these *were* the ones who came up from Tel Melah, Tel Harsha, Cherub, Addan, and Immer; but they could not identify their father's house or their genealogy, whether they *were* of Israel: 60 the sons of Delaiah, the sons of Tobiah, and the sons of Nekoda, six hundred and fifty-two; 61 and of the sons of the priests: the sons of Habaiah, the sons of Koz, and the sons of Barzillai, who took a wife of the daughters of Barzillai the Gileadite, and was called by their name. 62 These sought their listing *among* those who were registered by genealogy, but they were not found; therefore they *were excluded* from the priesthood as defiled. 63 And the governor said to them that they should not eat of the most holy things till a priest could consult with the Urim and Thummim.

64 The whole assembly together *was* forty-two thousand three hundred *and* sixty, 65 besides their male and female servants, of whom *there were* seven thousand three hundred and thirty-seven; and they had two hundred men and women singers. 66 Their horses *were* seven hundred and thirty-six, their

41 הַמְשֹׁרְרִים בְּנֵי אָסָף מֵאָה
עֶשְׂרִים וּשְׁמֹנָה: פ

42 בְּנֵי הַשֹּׁעֲרִים בְּנֵי־שַׁלּוּם בְּנֵי־אָטֵר בְּנֵי־טַלְמֹן
בְּנֵי־עַקּוּב בְּנֵי חֲטִיטָא בְּנֵי שֹׁבָי הַכֹּל מֵאָה שְׁלֹשִׁים
וְתִשְׁעָה: פ

43 הַנְּתִינִים בְּנֵי־צִיחָא בְנֵי־חֲשׂוּפָא
44 בְּנֵי־קֵרֹס בְּנֵי־סִיעֲהָא
45 בְּנֵי־לְבָנָה בְנֵי־חֲגָבָה
46 בְּנֵי־חָגָב בְּנֵי־שַׁמְלַ‍יP
47 בְּנֵי־גִדֵּל בְּנֵי־גַחַר
48 בְּנֵי־רְצִין בְּנֵי־נְקוֹדָא
49 בְּנֵי־עֻזָּא בְּנֵי־פָסֵחַ
50 בְּנֵי־אַסְנָה בְּנֵי־מְעוּנִיםP
51 בְּנֵי־בַקְבּוּק בְּנֵי־חֲקוּפָא
52 בְּנֵי־בַצְלוּת בְּנֵי־מְחִידָא
53 בְּנֵי־בַרְקוֹס בְּנֵי־סִיסְרָא
54 בְּנֵי נְצִיחַ בְּנֵי חֲטִיפָא:

55 בְּנֵי עַבְדֵי שְׁלֹמֹה בְּנֵי־סֹטַי בְּנֵי־הַסֹּפֶרֶת
56 בְּנֵי־יַעְלָה בְנֵי־דַרְקוֹן
57 בְּנֵי שְׁפַטְיָה בְנֵי־חַטִּיל
בְּנֵי פֹּכֶרֶת הַצְּבָיִים בְּנֵי אָמִי:

58 כָּל־הַנְּתִינִים וּבְנֵי עַבְדֵי שְׁלֹמֹה שְׁלֹשׁ מֵאוֹת
תִּשְׁעִים וּשְׁנָיִם: ס

59 וְאֵלֶּה הָעֹלִים מִתֵּל
מֶלַח תֵּל חַרְשָׁא כְּרוּב אַדָּן אִמֵּר וְלֹא יָכְלוּ
לְהַגִּיד בֵּית־אֲבוֹתָם וְזַרְעָם אִם מִיִּשְׂרָאֵל הֵם:

60 בְּנֵי־דְלָיָה בְנֵי־טוֹבִיָּה בְּנֵי נְקוֹדָא שֵׁשׁ מֵאוֹת
חֲמִשִּׁים וּשְׁנָיִם: ס

61 וּמִבְּנֵי הַכֹּהֲנִים
בְּנֵי חֳבַיָּה בְּנֵי הַקּוֹץ בְּנֵי בַרְזִלַּי אֲשֶׁר לָקַח
מִבְּנוֹת בַּרְזִלַּי הַגִּלְעָדִי אִשָּׁה וַיִּקָּרֵא עַל־שְׁמָם:

62 אֵלֶּה בִּקְשׁוּ כְתָבָם הַמִּתְיַחְשִׂים וְלֹא נִמְצָאוּ
וַיְגֹאֲלוּ מִן־הַכְּהֻנָּה: 63 וַיֹּאמֶר הַתִּרְשָׁתָא לָהֶם
אֲשֶׁר לֹא־יֹאכְלוּ מִקֹּדֶשׁ הַקֳּדָשִׁים עַד עֲמֹד כֹּהֵן
לְאוּרִים וּלְתֻמִּים: 64 כָּל־הַקָּהָל כְּאֶחָד אַרְבַּע
רִבּוֹא אַלְפַּיִם שְׁלֹשׁ־מֵאוֹת שִׁשִּׁים: 65 מִלְּבַד
עַבְדֵיהֶם וְאַמְהֹתֵיהֶם אֵלֶּה שִׁבְעַת אֲלָפִים שְׁלֹשׁ
מֵאוֹת שְׁלֹשִׁים וְשִׁבְעָה וְלָהֶם מְשֹׁרְרִים וּמְשֹׁרְרוֹת
מָאתָיִם: 66 סוּסֵיהֶם שְׁבַע מֵאוֹת שְׁלֹשִׁים וְשִׁשָּׁה

mules two hundred and forty-five, ⁶⁷ their camels four hundred and thirty-five, and *their* donkeys six thousand seven hundred and twenty.

⁶⁸ *Some* of the heads of the fathers' *houses,* when they came to the house of the LORD which *is* in Jerusalem, offered freely for the house of God, to erect it in its place: ⁶⁹ According to their ability, they gave to the treasury for the work sixty-one thousand gold drachmas, five thousand minas of silver, and one hundred priestly garments.

⁷⁰ So the priests and the Levites, *some* of the people, the singers, the gatekeepers, and the Nethinim, dwelt in their cities, and all Israel in their cities.

3 And when the seventh month had come, and the children of Israel *were* in the cities, the people gathered together as one man to Jerusalem. ² Then Jeshua the son of Jozadak and his brethren the priests, and Zerubbabel the son of Shealtiel and his brethren, arose and built the altar of the God of Israel, to offer burnt offerings on it, as *it is* written in the Law of Moses the man of God. ³ Though fear *had come* upon them because of the people of those countries, they set the altar on its bases; and they offered burnt offerings on it to the LORD, *both* the morning and evening burnt offerings. ⁴ They also kept the Feast of Tabernacles, as *it is* written, and *offered* the daily burnt offerings in the number required by ordinance for each day. ⁵ Afterwards *they offered* the regular burnt offering, and *those* for New Moons and for all the appointed feasts of the LORD that were consecrated, and *those* of everyone who willingly offered a freewill offering to the LORD. ⁶ From the first day of the seventh month they began to offer burnt offerings to the LORD, although the foundation of the temple of the LORD had not been laid. ⁷ They also gave money to the masons and the carpenters, and food, drink, and oil to the people of Sidon and Tyre to bring cedar logs from Lebanon to the sea, to Joppa, according to the permission which they had from Cyrus king of Persia.

⁸ Now in the second month of the second year of their coming to the house of God at Jerusalem, Zerubbabel the son of Shealtiel, Jeshua the son of Jozadak, and the rest of their brethren the priests and the Levites, and all those who had come out of the captivity to Jerusalem, began *work* and appointed the Levites from twenty years old and above to oversee the work of the house of the LORD. ⁹ Then Jeshua *with* his sons and brothers, Kadmiel *with* his sons, and the sons of Judah, arose

פְרָדֵיהֶם מָאתַ֫יִם אַרְבָּעִ֖ים וַחֲמִשָּֽׁה: ⁶⁷ גְּמַלֵּיהֶ֗ם אַרְבַּ֤ע מֵאוֹת שְׁלֹשִׁ֣ים וַחֲמִשָּׁ֔ה חֲמֹרִ֕ים שֵׁ֣שֶׁת אֲלָפִ֕ים שְׁבַ֥ע מֵא֖וֹת וְעֶשְׂרִֽים: ⁶⁸ וּמֵרָאשֵׁ֣י הָֽאָב֔וֹת בְּבוֹאָ֕ם לְבֵ֥ית יְהוָ֖ה אֲשֶׁ֣ר בִּירֽוּשָׁלִָ֑ם הִֽתְנַדְּבוּ֙ לְבֵ֣ית הָֽאֱלֹהִ֔ים לְהַעֲמִיד֖וֹ עַל־מְכוֹנֽוֹ: ⁶⁹ כְּכֹחָ֗ם נָתְנ֣וּ לְאוֹצַ֣ר הַמְּלָאכָה֮ זָהָ֣ב דַּרְכְּמוֹנִ֣ים שֵֽׁשׁ־רִבֹּאות֙ וָאֶ֔לֶף ס וְכֶ֕סֶף מָנִ֖ים חֲמֵ֣שֶׁת אֲלָפִ֑ים וְכָתְנֹ֥ת כֹּהֲנִ֖ים מֵאָֽה: ס ⁷⁰ וַיֵּשְׁב֣וּ הַכֹּהֲנִ֣ים וְהַלְוִיִּ֡ם וּמִן־הָעָם֩ וְהַמְשֹׁרְרִ֨ים וְהַשּׁוֹעֲרִ֜ים וְהַנְּתִינִ֗ים בְּעָרֵיהֶ֑ם וְכָל־יִשְׂרָאֵ֖ל בְּעָרֵיהֶֽם: ס

ג וַיִּגַּע֙ הַחֹ֣דֶשׁ הַשְּׁבִיעִ֔י וּבְנֵ֥י יִשְׂרָאֵ֖ל בֶּֽעָרִ֑ים ס וַיֵּאָסְפ֤וּ הָעָם֙ כְּאִ֣ישׁ אֶחָ֔ד אֶל־יְרֽוּשָׁלִָֽם: ס ² וַיָּ֣קָם יֵשׁ֣וּעַ בֶּן־יֽוֹצָדָ֗ק וְאֶחָ֣יו הַכֹּהֲנִ֜ים וּזְרֻבָּבֶ֤ל בֶּן־שְׁאַלְתִּיאֵל֙ וְאֶחָ֔יו וַיִּבְנ֕וּ אֶת־מִזְבַּ֖ח אֱלֹהֵ֣י יִשְׂרָאֵ֑ל לְהַעֲל֤וֹת עָלָיו֙ עֹל֔וֹת כַּכָּת֕וּב בְּתוֹרַ֖ת מֹשֶׁ֥ה אִישׁ־הָאֱלֹהִֽים: ³ וַיָּכִ֤ינוּ הַמִּזְבֵּ֙חַ֙ עַל־מְכ֣וֹנֹתָ֔יו כִּ֚י בְּאֵימָ֣ה עֲלֵיהֶ֔ם מֵעַמֵּ֖י הָאֲרָצ֑וֹת וַיַּ֨עַל עָלָ֤יו עֹלוֹת֙ לַֽיהוָ֔ה עֹל֖וֹת לַבֹּ֥קֶר וְלָעָֽרֶב: ⁴ וַיַּֽעֲשׂ֛וּ אֶת־חַ֥ג הַסֻּכּ֖וֹת כַּכָּת֑וּב וְעֹלַ֨ת י֤וֹם בְּיוֹם֙ בְּמִסְפָּ֔ר כְּמִשְׁפַּ֖ט דְּבַר־י֥וֹם בְּיוֹמֽוֹ: ⁵ וְאַֽחֲרֵיכֵ֞ן עֹלַ֤ת תָּמִיד֙ וְלֶ֣חֳדָשִׁ֔ים וּלְכָל־מוֹעֲדֵ֥י יְהוָ֖ה הַמְקֻדָּשִׁ֑ים וּלְכֹ֛ל מִתְנַדֵּ֥ב נְדָבָ֖ה לַֽיהוָֽה: ⁶ מִיּ֤וֹם אֶחָד֙ לַחֹ֣דֶשׁ הַשְּׁבִיעִ֔י הֵחֵ֕לּוּ לְהַעֲל֥וֹת עֹל֖וֹת לַֽיהוָ֑ה וְהֵיכַ֥ל יְהוָ֖ה לֹ֥א יֻסָּֽד: ⁷ וַיִּתְּנ֣וּ־כֶ֔סֶף לַחֹצְבִ֖ים וְלֶחָרָשִׁ֑ים וּמַֽאֲכָ֨ל וּמִשְׁתֶּ֜ה וָשֶׁ֗מֶן לַצִּֽדֹנִים֙ וְלַצֹּרִ֔ים לְהָבִיא֩ עֲצֵ֨י אֲרָזִ֤ים מִן־הַלְּבָנוֹן֙ אֶל־יָ֣ם יָפ֔וֹא כְּרִשְׁי֛וֹן כּ֥וֹרֶשׁ מֶֽלֶךְ־פָּרַ֖ס עֲלֵיהֶֽם: פ

⁸ וּבַשָּׁנָ֣ה הַשֵּׁנִ֗ית לְבוֹאָ֞ם אֶל־בֵּ֤ית הָֽאֱלֹהִים֙ לִיר֣וּשָׁלִַ֔ם בַּחֹ֖דֶשׁ הַשֵּׁנִ֑י הֵחֵ֡לּוּ זְרֻבָּבֶ֣ל בֶּן־שְׁ֠אַלְתִּיאֵל וְיֵשׁ֨וּעַ בֶּן־יֽוֹצָדָ֜ק וּשְׁאָ֥ר אֲחֵיהֶ֣ם ׀ הַכֹּהֲנִ֣ים וְהַלְוִיִּ֗ם וְכָל־הַבָּאִים֙ מֵהַשְּׁבִ֣י יְרֽוּשָׁלִַ֔ם וַיַּעֲמִ֣ידוּ אֶת־הַלְוִיִּ֗ם מִבֶּ֨ן עֶשְׂרִ֤ים שָׁנָה֙ וָמַ֔עְלָה לְנַצֵּ֖חַ עַל־מְלֶ֥אכֶת בֵּית־יְהוָֽה: פ

⁹ וַיַּעֲמֹ֣ד יֵשׁ֡וּעַ בָּנָ֣יו וְ֠אֶחָיו קַדְמִיאֵ֨ל וּבָנָ֤יו בְּנֵֽי־יְהוּדָה֙ כְּאֶחָ֔ד לְנַצֵּ֖חַ עַל־עֹשֵׂ֣ה הַמְּלָאכָ֑ה בְּבֵ֖ית

as one to oversee those working on the house of God: the sons of Henadad *with* their sons and their brethren the Levites.

[10] When the builders laid the foundation of the temple of the LORD, the priests stood in their apparel with trumpets, and the Levites, the sons of Asaph, with cymbals, to praise the LORD, according to the ordinance of David king of Israel. [11] And they sang responsively, praising and giving thanks to the LORD:

> "For *He is* good,
> For His mercy *endures* forever toward Israel."

Then all the people shouted with a great shout, when they praised the LORD, because the foundation of the house of the LORD was laid.

[12] But many of the priests and Levites and heads of the fathers' *houses,* old men who had seen the first temple, wept with a loud voice when the foundation of this temple was laid before their eyes. Yet many shouted aloud for joy, [13] so that the people could not discern the noise of the shout of joy from the noise of the weeping of the people, for the people shouted with a loud shout, and the sound was heard afar off.

4 Now when the adversaries of Judah and Benjamin heard that the descendants of the captivity were building the temple of the LORD God of Israel, [2] they came to Zerubbabel and the heads of the fathers' *houses,* and said to them, "Let us build with you, for we seek your God as you *do;* and we have sacrificed to Him since the days of Esarhaddon king of Assyria, who brought us here." [3] But Zerubbabel and Jeshua and the rest of the heads of the fathers' *houses* of Israel said to them, "You may do nothing with us to build a house for our God; but we alone will build to the LORD God of Israel, as King Cyrus the king of Persia has commanded us." [4] Then the people of the land tried to discourage the people of Judah. They troubled them in building, [5] and hired counselors against them to frustrate their purpose all the days of Cyrus king of Persia, even until the reign of Darius king of Persia.

[6] In the reign of Ahasuerus, in the beginning of his reign, they wrote an accusation against the inhabitants of Judah and Jerusalem.

[7] In the days of Artaxerxes also, Bishlam, Mithredath, Tabel, and the rest of their companions wrote to Artaxerxes king of Persia; and the letter *was* written in Aramaic script, and translated

הָאֱלֹהִ֑ים ס בְּנֵ֤י חֵנָדָד֙ בְּנֵיהֶ֣ם וַאֲחֵיהֶ֔ם הַלְוִיִּֽם׃ 10 וְיִסְּד֥וּ הַבֹּנִ֖ים אֶת־הֵיכַ֣ל יְהוָ֑ה וַיַּעֲמִידוּ֩ הַכֹּהֲנִ֨ים מְלֻבָּשִׁ֜ים בַּחֲצֹֽצְר֗וֹת וְהַלְוִיִּ֤ם בְּנֵֽי־אָסָף֙ בִּֽמְצִלְתַּ֔יִם לְהַלֵּל֙ אֶת־יְהוָ֔ה עַל־יְדֵ֖י דָּוִ֥יד מֶֽלֶךְ־יִשְׂרָאֵֽל׃ 11 וַֽיַּעֲנ֡וּ בְּהַלֵּ֣ל וּבְהוֹדֹת֩ לַֽיהוָ֨ה כִּ֣י ט֔וֹב כִּֽי־לְעוֹלָ֥ם חַסְדּ֖וֹ עַל־יִשְׂרָאֵ֑ל וְכָל־הָעָ֡ם הֵרִיעוּ֩ תְרוּעָ֨ה גְדוֹלָ֤ה בְהַלֵּל֙ לַֽיהוָ֔ה עַ֖ל הוּסַ֥ד בֵּית־יְהוָֽה׃ ס 12 וְרַבִּ֡ים מֵהַכֹּהֲנִ֣ים וְהַלְוִיִּם֩ וְרָאשֵׁ֨י הָאָב֜וֹת הַזְּקֵנִ֗ים אֲשֶׁ֨ר רָא֜וּ אֶת־הַבַּ֤יִת הָרִאשׁוֹן֙ בְּיָסְד֔וֹ זֶ֤ה הַבַּ֙יִת֙ בְּעֵ֣ינֵיהֶ֔ם בֹּכִ֖ים בְּק֣וֹל גָּד֑וֹל וְרַבִּ֛ים בִּתְרוּעָ֥ה בְשִׂמְחָ֖ה לְהָרִ֥ים ק֥וֹל׃ 13 וְאֵ֣ין הָעָ֗ם מַכִּירִים֙ ק֣וֹל תְּרוּעַ֣ת הַשִּׂמְחָ֔ה לְק֖וֹל בְּכִ֣י הָעָ֑ם כִּ֣י הָעָ֗ם מְרִיעִים֙ תְּרוּעָ֣ה גְדוֹלָ֔ה וְהַקּ֥וֹל נִשְׁמַ֖ע עַד־לְמֵרָחֽוֹק׃ פ

ד 1 וַֽיִּשְׁמְע֔וּ צָרֵ֣י יְהוּדָ֖ה וּבִנְיָמִ֑ן כִּֽי־בְנֵ֤י הַגּוֹלָה֙ בּוֹנִ֣ים הֵיכָ֔ל לַֽיהוָ֖ה אֱלֹהֵ֥י יִשְׂרָאֵֽל׃ 2 וַיִּגְּשׁ֨וּ אֶל־זְרֻבָּבֶ֜ל וְאֶל־רָאשֵׁ֣י הָֽאָב֗וֹת וַיֹּאמְר֤וּ לָהֶם֙ נִבְנֶ֣ה עִמָּכֶ֔ם כִּ֣י כָכֶ֔ם נִדְר֖וֹשׁ לֵֽאלֹֽהֵיכֶ֑ם וְלֹ֣א׀ אֲנַ֜חְנוּ זֹבְחִ֗ים מִימֵי֙ אֵסַ֣ר חַדֹּ֔ן מֶ֣לֶךְ אַשּׁ֔וּר הַמַּעֲלֶ֥ה אֹתָ֖נוּ פֹּֽה׃ 3 וַיֹּאמֶר֩ לָהֶ֨ם זְרֻבָּבֶ֜ל וְיֵשׁ֗וּעַ וּשְׁאָ֤ר רָאשֵׁ֤י הָֽאָבוֹת֙ לְיִשְׂרָאֵ֔ל לֹֽא־לָכֶ֣ם וָלָ֔נוּ לִבְנ֥וֹת בַּ֖יִת לֵֽאלֹהֵ֑ינוּ כִּי֩ אֲנַ֨חְנוּ יַ֜חַד נִבְנֶ֗ה לַֽיהוָה֙ אֱלֹהֵ֣י יִשְׂרָאֵ֔ל כַּאֲשֶׁ֣ר צִוָּ֔נוּ הַמֶּ֖לֶךְ כּ֥וֹרֶשׁ מֶֽלֶךְ־פָּרָֽס׃ 4 וַיְהִי֙ עַם־הָאָ֔רֶץ מְרַפִּ֖ים יְדֵ֣י עַם־יְהוּדָ֑ה וּֽמְבַלַּהִ֖ים אוֹתָ֥ם לִבְנֽוֹת׃ 5 וְסֹכְרִ֤ים עֲלֵיהֶם֙ יֽוֹעֲצִ֔ים לְהָפֵ֖ר עֲצָתָ֑ם כָּל־יְמֵ֗י כּ֚וֹרֶשׁ מֶ֣לֶךְ פָּרַ֔ס וְעַד־מַלְכ֖וּת דָּרְיָ֥וֶשׁ מֶֽלֶךְ־פָּרָֽס׃ 6 וּבְמַלְכוּת֙ אֲחַשְׁוֵר֔וֹשׁ בִּתְחִלַּ֖ת מַלְכוּת֑וֹ כָּתְב֣וּ שִׂטְנָ֔ה עַל־יֹשְׁבֵ֥י יְהוּדָ֖ה וִירֽוּשָׁלִָֽם׃ ס 7 וּבִימֵ֣י אַרְתַּחְשַׁ֗שְׂתָּא כָּתַ֨ב בִּשְׁלָ֜ם מִתְרְדָ֤ת טָֽבְאֵל֙ וּשְׁאָ֣ר כְּנָוֹתָ֔יו עַל־אַרְתַּחְשַׁ֖שְׂתְּא מֶ֣לֶךְ פָּרָ֑ס וּכְתָב֙ הַנִּשְׁתְּוָ֔ן כָּת֥וּב אֲרָמִ֖ית וּמְתֻרְגָּ֥ם אֲרָמִֽית׃ פ

into the Aramaic language. ⁸Rehum the commander and Shimshai the scribe wrote a letter against Jerusalem to King Artaxerxes in this fashion:

9   From Rehum the commander, Shimshai the scribe, and the rest of their companions—*representatives* of the Dinaites, the Apharsathchites, the Tarpelites, the people of Persia and Erech and Babylon and Shushan, the Dehavites, the Elamites, ¹⁰and the rest of the nations whom the great and noble Osnapper took captive and settled in the cities of Samaria and the remainder beyond the River—and so forth.

¹¹(This *is* a copy of the letter that they sent him)

To King Artaxerxes from your servants, the men *of the region* beyond the River, and so forth:

12   Let it be known to the king that the Jews who came up from you have come to us at Jerusalem, and are building the rebellious and evil city, and are finishing *its* walls and repairing the foundations. ¹³Let it now be known to the king that, if this city is built and the walls completed, they will not pay tax, tribute, or custom, and the king's treasury will be diminished. ¹⁴Now because we receive support from the palace, it was not proper for us to see the king's dishonor; therefore we have sent and informed the king, ¹⁵that search may be made in the book of the records of your fathers. And you will find in the book of the records and know that this city *is* a rebellious city, harmful to kings and provinces, and that they have incited sedition within the city in former times, for which cause this city was destroyed.

16   We inform the king that if this city is rebuilt and its walls are completed, the result will be that you will have no dominion beyond the River.

¹⁷The king sent an answer:

To Rehum the commander, *to* Shimshai the scribe, *to* the rest of their companions who dwell in Samaria, and *to* the remainder beyond the River:

Peace, and so forth.

18   The letter which you sent to us has been clearly read before me. ¹⁹And I gave the command, and a search has been made, and

רְחוּם בְּעֵל־טְעֵם וְשִׁמְשַׁי סָפְרָא כְּתַבוּ אִגְּרָה 8
חֲדָה עַל־יְרוּשְׁלֶם לְאַרְתַּחְשַׁשְׂתְּא מַלְכָּא כְּנֵמָא:
אֱדַיִן רְחוּם בְּעֵל־טְעֵם וְשִׁמְשַׁי סָפְרָא וּשְׁאָר 9
כְּנָוָתְהוֹן דִּינָיֵא וַאֲפַרְסַתְכָיֵא טַרְפְּלָיֵא אֲפָרְסָיֵא
אַרְכְּוָיֵ בָבְלָיֵ שׁוּשַׁנְכָיֵא דֶּהָוֵ עֵלְמָיֵ: וּשְׁאָר 10
אֻמַּיָּא דִּי הַגְלִי אָסְנַפַּר רַבָּא וְיַקִּירָא וְהוֹתֵב
הִמּוֹ בְּקִרְיָה דִּי שָׁמְרָיִן וּשְׁאָר עֲבַר־נַהֲרָה וּכְעֶנֶת:
דְּנָה פַּרְשֶׁגֶן אִגַּרְתָּא דִּי שְׁלַחוּ עֲלוֹהִי עַל־ 11
אַרְתַּחְשַׁשְׂתְּא מַלְכָּא עַבְדָיִךְ אֱנָשׁ עֲבַר־נַהֲרָה
וּכְעֶנֶת:
פ

יְדִיעַ לֶהֱוֵא לְמַלְכָּא דִּי יְהוּדָיֵא דִּי סְלִקוּ מִן־ 12
לְוָתָךְ עֲלֶינָא אֲתוֹ לִירוּשְׁלֶם קִרְיְתָא מָרָדְתָּא
וּבְאִישְׁתָּא בָּנַיִן וְשׁוּרַיָּ אֶשְׁכְלִלוּ וְאֻשַּׁיָּא יַחִיטוּ:
כְּעַן יְדִיעַ לֶהֱוֵא לְמַלְכָּא דִּי הֵן קִרְיְתָא דָךְ 13
תִּתְבְּנֵא וְשׁוּרַיָּה יִשְׁתַּכְלְלוּן מִנְדָּה־בְלוֹ וַהֲלָךְ לָא
יִנְתְּנוּן וְאַפְּתֹם מַלְכִים תְּהַנְזִק: כְּעַן כָּל־קֳבֵל 14
דִּי־מְלַח הֵיכְלָא מְלַחְנָא וְעַרְוַת מַלְכָּא לָא אֲרִיךְ־
לַנָא לְמֶחֱזֵא עַל־דְּנָה שְׁלַחְנָא וְהוֹדַעְנָא לְמַלְכָּא:
דִּי יְבַקַּר בִּסְפַר־דָּכְרָנַיָּא דִּי אֲבָהָתָךְ וּתְהַשְׁכַּח 15
בִּסְפַר דָּכְרָנַיָּא וְתִנְדַּע דִּי קִרְיְתָא דָךְ קִרְיָא מָרָדָא
וּמְהַנְזְקַת מַלְכִין וּמְדִנָן וְאֶשְׁתַּדּוּר עָבְדִין בְּגַוַּהּ
מִן־יוֹמָת עָלְמָא עַל־דְּנָה קִרְיְתָא דָךְ הָחָרְבַת:
מְהוֹדְעִין אֲנַחְנָה לְמַלְכָּא דִּי הֵן קִרְיְתָא דָךְ 16
תִּתְבְּנֵא וְשׁוּרַיָּה יִשְׁתַּכְלְלוּן לָקֳבֵל דְּנָה חֲלָק בַּעֲבַר
נַהֲרָא לָא אִיתַי לָךְ:
פ

פִּתְגָמָא שְׁלַח מַלְכָּא עַל־רְחוּם בְּעֵל־ 17
טְעֵם וְשִׁמְשַׁי סָפְרָא וּשְׁאָר כְּנָוָתְהוֹן דִּי
יָתְבִין בְּשָׁמְרָיִן וּשְׁאָר עֲבַר־נַהֲרָה שְׁלָם
וּכְעֶת: ס נִשְׁתְּוָנָא דִּי שְׁלַחְתּוּן עֲלֶינָא 18
מְפָרַשׁ קֱרִי קָדָמָי: וּמִנִּי שִׂים טְעֵם וּבַקַּרוּ 19
וְהַשְׁכַּחוּ דִּי קִרְיְתָא דָךְ מִן־יוֹמָת עָלְמָא עַל־

it was found that this city in former times has revolted against kings, and rebellion and sedition have been fostered in it. ²⁰There have also been mighty kings over Jerusalem, who have ruled over all *the region* beyond the River; and tax, tribute, and custom were paid to them. ²¹Now give the command to make these men cease, that this city may not be built until the command is given by me.

22   Take heed now that you do not fail to do this. Why should damage increase to the hurt of the kings?

²³Now when the copy of King Artaxerxes' letter *was* read before Rehum, Shimshai the scribe, and their companions, they went up in haste to Jerusalem against the Jews, and by force of arms made them cease. ²⁴Thus the work of the house of God which *is* at Jerusalem ceased, and it was discontinued until the second year of the reign of Darius king of Persia.

5   Then the prophet Haggai and Zechariah the son of Iddo, prophets, prophesied to the Jews who *were* in Judah and Jerusalem, in the name of the God of Israel, *who was* over them. ²So Zerubbabel the son of Shealtiel and Jeshua the son of Jozadak rose up and began to build the house of God which *is* in Jerusalem; and the prophets of God *were* with them, helping them.

³At the same time Tattenai the governor of *the region* beyond the River and Shethar-Boznai and their companions came to them and spoke thus to them: "Who has commanded you to build this temple and finish this wall?" ⁴Then, accordingly, we told them the names of the men who were constructing this building. ⁵But the eye of their God was upon the elders of the Jews, so that they could not make them cease till a report could go to Darius. Then a written answer was returned concerning this *matter*. ⁶This is a copy of the letter that Tattenai sent:

The governor of *the region* beyond the River, and Shethar-Boznai, and his companions, the Persians who *were in the region* beyond the River, to Darius the king.

⁷(They sent a letter to him, in which was written thus)

To Darius the king:

All peace.

מַלְכִין מְתְנַשְּׂאָה וּמְרַד וְאֶשְׁתַּדּוּר מִתְעֲבֶד־בַּהּ:
20 וּמַלְכִין תַּקִּיפִין הֲווֹ עַל־יְרוּשְׁלֶם וְשַׁלִּיטִין בְּכֹל
עֲבַר נַהֲרָה וּמִדָּה בְלוֹ וַהֲלָךְ מִתְיְהֵב לְהוֹן: 21 כְּעַן
שִׂימוּ טְּעֵם לְבַטָּלָא גֻּבְרַיָּא אִלֵּךְ וְקִרְיְתָא דָךְ לָא
תִתְבְּנֵא עַד־מִנִּי טַעְמָא יִתְּשָׂם: 22 וּזְהִירִין הֱווֹ
שָׁלוּ לְמֶעְבַּד עַל־דְּנָה לְמָה יִשְׂגֵּא חֲבָלָא לְהַנְזָקַת
מַלְכִין: ס 23 אֱדַיִן מִן־דִּי פַּרְשֶׁגֶן נִשְׁתְּוָנָא דִּי
אַרְתַּחְשַׁשְׁתְּא מַלְכָּא קֱרִי קֳדָם־רְחוּם וְשִׁמְשַׁי
סָפְרָא וּכְנָוָתְהוֹן אֲזַלוּ בִבְהִילוּ לִירוּשְׁלֶם
עַל־יְהוּדָיֵא וּבַטִּלוּ הִמּוֹ בְּאֶדְרָע וְחָיִל:
24 בֵּאדַיִן בְּטֵלַת עֲבִידַת בֵּית־אֱלָהָא דִּי ס
בִּירוּשְׁלֶם וַהֲוָת בָּטְלָא עַד שְׁנַת תַּרְתֵּין לְמַלְכוּת
דָּרְיָוֶשׁ מֶלֶךְ־פָּרָס: פ

ה וְהִתְנַבִּי חַגַּי נְבִיָּאה וּזְכַרְיָה בַר־עִדּוֹא
נְבִיַּאיָּא עַל־יְהוּדָיֵא דִּי בִיהוּד וּבִירוּשְׁלֶם בְּשֻׁם
אֱלָהּ יִשְׂרָאֵל עֲלֵיהוֹן: ס 2 בֵּאדַיִן קָמוּ
זְרֻבָּבֶל בַּר־שְׁאַלְתִּיאֵל וְיֵשׁוּעַ בַּר־יוֹצָדָק וְשָׁרִיו
לְמִבְנֵא בֵּית אֱלָהָא דִּי בִירוּשְׁלֶם וְעִמְּהוֹן
נְבִיַּאיָּא דִי־אֱלָהָא מְסָעֲדִין לְהוֹן: פ

3 בֵּהּ־זִמְנָא אֲתָא עֲלֵיהוֹן תַּתְּנַי פַּחַת עֲבַר־נַהֲרָה
וּשְׁתַר בּוֹזְנַי וּכְנָוָתְהוֹן וְכֵן אָמְרִין לְהֹם מַן־שָׂם
לְכֹם טְעֵם בַּיְתָא דְנָה לִבְּנֵא וְאֻשַּׁרְנָא דְנָה
לְשַׁכְלָלָה: ס 4 אֱדַיִן כְּנֵמָא אֲמַרְנָא לְהֹם
מַן־אִנּוּן שְׁמָהָת גֻּבְרַיָּא דִּי־דְנָה בִנְיָנָא בָּנַיִן: 5 וְעֵין
אֱלָהֲהֹם הֲוָת עַל־שָׂבֵי יְהוּדָיֵא וְלָא־בַטִּלוּ הִמּוֹ
עַד־טַעְמָא לְדָרְיָוֶשׁ יְהָךְ וֶאֱדַיִן יְתִיבוּן נִשְׁתְּוָנָא
עַל־דְּנָה: פ

6 פַּרְשֶׁגֶן אִגַּרְתָּא דִּי־שְׁלַח תַּתְּנַי | פַּחַת
עֲבַר־נַהֲרָה וּשְׁתַר בּוֹזְנַי וּכְנָוָתֵהּ אֲפַרְסְכָיֵא
דִּי בַּעֲבַר נַהֲרָה עַל־דָּרְיָוֶשׁ מַלְכָּא: 7 פִּתְגָמָא
שְׁלַחוּ עֲלוֹהִי וְכִדְנָה כְּתִיב בְּגַוֵּהּ לְדָרְיָוֶשׁ

ה 1 נְבִיָּא נְבִיאָה   2 נְבִיָּא

8 Let it be known to the king that we went into the province of Judea, to the temple of the great God, which is being built with heavy stones, and timber is being laid in the walls; and this work goes on diligently and prospers in their hands.

9 Then we asked those elders, *and* spoke thus to them: "Who commanded you to build this temple and to finish these walls?" 10 We also asked them their names to inform you, that we might write the names of the men who *were* chief among them.

11 And thus they returned us an answer, saying: "We are the servants of the God of heaven and earth, and we are rebuilding the temple that was built many years ago, which a great king of Israel built and completed. 12 But because our fathers provoked the God of heaven to wrath, He gave them into the hand of Nebuchadnezzar king of Babylon, the Chaldean, *who* destroyed this temple and carried the people away to Babylon. 13 However, in the first year of Cyrus king of Babylon, King Cyrus issued a decree to build this house of God. 14 Also, the gold and silver articles of the house of God, which Nebuchadnezzar had taken from the temple that *was* in Jerusalem and carried into the temple of Babylon—those King Cyrus took from the temple of Babylon, and they were given to one named Sheshbazzar, whom he had made governor. 15 And he said to him, 'Take these articles; go, carry them to the temple *site* that *is* in Jerusalem, and let the house of God be rebuilt on its former site.' 16 Then the same Sheshbazzar came *and* laid the foundation of the house of God which *is* in Jerusalem; but from that time even until now it has been under construction, and it is not finished."

17 Now therefore, if *it seems* good to the king, let a search be made in the king's treasure house, which *is* there in Babylon, whether it is *so* that a decree was issued by King Cyrus to build this house of God at Jerusalem, and let the king send us his pleasure concerning this *matter.*

8 יְדִיעַ | לֶהֱוֵא ס מַלְכָּא שְׁלָמָא כֹּלָּא׃
לְמַלְכָּא דִּי־אֲזַלְנָא לִיהוּד מְדִינְתָּא לְבֵית אֱלָהָא
רַבָּא וְהוּא מִתְבְּנֵא אֶבֶן גְּלָל וְאָע מִתְּשָׂם
בְּכֻתְלַיָּא וַעֲבִידְתָּא דָךְ אָסְפַּרְנָא מִתְעַבְדָא וּמַצְלַח
בְּיֶדְהֹם׃ ס 9 אֱדַיִן שְׁאֵלְנָא לְשָׂבַיָּא אִלֵּךְ
כְּנֵמָא אֲמַרְנָא לְהֹם מַן־שָׂם לְכֹם טְעֵם בַּיְתָא
דְנָה לְמִבְנְיָה וְאֻשַּׁרְנָא דְנָה לְשַׁכְלָלָה׃ 10 וְאַף
שְׁמָהָתְהֹם שְׁאֵלְנָא לְהֹם לְהוֹדָעוּתָךְ דִּי נִכְתֻּב
שֻׁם־גֻּבְרַיָּא דִּי בְרָאשֵׁיהֹם׃ ס 11 וּכְנֵמָא
פִתְגָמָא הֲתִיבוּנָא לְמֵמַר אֲנַחְנָא הִמּוֹ עַבְדוֹהִי דִּי־
אֱלָהּ שְׁמַיָּא וְאַרְעָא וּבָנַיִן בַּיְתָא דִּי־הֲוָא בְנֵה
מִקַּדְמַת דְּנָה שְׁנִין שַׂגִּיאָן וּמֶלֶךְ לְיִשְׂרָאֵל רַב
בְּנָהִי וְשַׁכְלְלֵהּ׃ 12 לָהֵן מִן־דִּי הַרְגִּזוּ אֲבָהָתַנָא
לֶאֱלָהּ שְׁמַיָּא יְהַב הִמּוֹ בְּיַד נְבוּכַדְנֶצַּר מֶלֶךְ־
בָּבֶל כַּסְדָּיָא וּבַיְתָה דְּנָה סַתְרֵהּ וְעַמָּה הַגְלִי
לְבָבֶל׃ ס 13 בְּרַם בִּשְׁנַת חֲדָה לְכוֹרֶשׁ
מַלְכָּא דִּי בָבֶל כּוֹרֶשׁ מַלְכָּא שָׂם טְעֵם בֵּית־אֱלָהָא
דְנָה לִבְּנֵא׃ 14 וְאַף מָאנַיָּא דִי־בֵית־אֱלָהָא דִּי
דַהֲבָה וְכַסְפָּא דִּי נְבוּכַדְנֶצַּר הַנְפֵּק מִן־הֵיכְלָא דִּי
בִירוּשְׁלֶם וְהֵיבֵל הִמּוֹ לְהֵיכְלָא דִּי בָבֶל הַנְפֵּק הִמּוֹ
כּוֹרֶשׁ מַלְכָּא מִן־הֵיכְלָא דִּי בָבֶל וִיהִיבוּ לְשֵׁשְׁבַּצַּר
שְׁמֵהּ דִּי פֶחָה שָׂמֵהּ׃ 15 וַאֲמַר־לֵהּ | אֵלֶּה מָאנַיָּא
שֵׂא אֵזֶל־אֲחֵת הִמּוֹ בְּהֵיכְלָא דִּי בִירוּשְׁלֶם וּבֵית
אֱלָהָא יִתְבְּנֵא עַל־אַתְרֵהּ׃ ס 16 אֱדַיִן
שֵׁשְׁבַּצַּר דֵּךְ אֲתָא יְהַב אֻשַּׁיָּא דִּי־בֵית אֱלָהָא דִּי
בִירוּשְׁלֶם וּמִן־אֱדַיִן וְעַד־כְּעַן מִתְבְּנֵא וְלָא שְׁלִם׃
17 וּכְעַן הֵן עַל־מַלְכָּא טָב יִתְבַּקַּר בְּבֵית גִּנְזַיָּא
דִּי־מַלְכָּא תַמָּה דִּי בְּבָבֶל הֵן אִיתַי דִּי־מִן־כּוֹרֶשׁ
מַלְכָּא שִׂים טְעֵם לְמִבְנֵא בֵּית־אֱלָהָא דֵךְ בִּירוּשְׁלֶם
וּרְעוּת מַלְכָּא עַל־דְּנָה יִשְׁלַח עֲלֶינָא׃ ס

6 Then King Darius issued a decree, and a search was made in the archives, where the treasures were stored in Babylon. ²And at Achmetha, in the palace that *is* in the province of Media, a scroll was found, and in it a record *was* written thus:

3   In the first year of King Cyrus, King Cyrus issued a decree *concerning* the house of God at Jerusalem: "Let the house be rebuilt, the place where they offered sacrifices; and let the foundations of it be firmly laid, its height sixty cubits *and* its width sixty cubits, ⁴*with* three rows of heavy stones and one row of new timber. Let the expenses be paid from the king's treasury. ⁵Also let the gold and silver articles of the house of God, which Nebuchadnezzar took from the temple which *is* in Jerusalem and brought to Babylon, be restored and taken back to the temple which *is* in Jerusalem, *each* to its place; and deposit *them* in the house of God"—

6   Now *therefore,* Tattenai, governor of *the region* beyond the River, and Shethar-Boznai, and your companions the Persians who *are* beyond the River, keep yourselves far from there. ⁷Let the work of this house of God alone; let the governor of the Jews and the elders of the Jews build this house of God on its site.

8   Moreover I issue a decree *as to* what you shall do for the elders of these Jews, for the building of this house of God: Let the cost be paid at the king's expense from taxes *on the region* beyond the River; this is to be given immediately to these men, so that they are not hindered. ⁹And whatever they need— young bulls, rams, and lambs for the burnt offerings of the God of heaven, wheat, salt, wine, and oil, according to the request of the priests who *are* in Jerusalem—let it be given them day by day without fail, ¹⁰that they may offer sacrifices of sweet aroma to the God of heaven, and pray for the life of the king and his sons.

11   Also I issue a decree that whoever alters this edict, let a timber be pulled from his house and erected, and let him be hanged on it; and let his house be made a refuse heap because of this. ¹²And may the God who causes His name to dwell there destroy any king or people who put their hand to alter it, or to

‎א בֵּאדַ֛יִן דָּרְיָ֥וֶשׁ מַלְכָּ֖א שָׂ֣ם טְעֵ֑ם וּבַקַּ֣רוּ ׀ בְּבֵ֣ית סִפְרַיָּ֗א דִּ֧י גִנְזַיָּ֛א מְהַחֲתִ֥ין תַּמָּ֖ה בְּבָבֶֽל: 2 וְהִשְׁתְּכַ֣ח בְּאַחְמְתָ֗א בְּבִֽירְתָ֛א דִּ֛י בְּמָדַ֥י מְדִינְתָּ֖ה מְגִלָּ֣ה חֲדָ֑ה וְכֵן־כְּתִ֥יב בְּגַוַּ֖הּ דִּכְרוֹנָֽה: ‪פ‬

3 בִּשְׁנַ֨ת חֲדָ֜ה לְכ֣וֹרֶשׁ מַלְכָּ֗א כּ֣וֹרֶשׁ מַלְכָּא֮ שָׂ֣ם טְעֵם֒ בֵּית־אֱלָהָ֣א בִֽירוּשְׁלֶ֗ם בַּיְתָ֤א יִתְבְּנֵא֙ אֲתַ֣ר דִּֽי־דָבְחִ֣ין דִּבְחִ֔ין וְאֻשּׁ֖וֹהִי מְסֽוֹבְלִ֑ין רוּמֵהּ֙ אַמִּ֣ין שִׁתִּ֔ין פְּתָיֵ֖הּ אַמִּ֥ין שִׁתִּֽין: 4 נִדְבָּכִ֞ין דִּֽי־אֶ֤בֶן גְּלָל֙ תְּלָתָ֔א וְנִדְבָּ֖ךְ דִּי־אָ֣ע חֲדַ֑ת וְנִ֨פְקְתָ֔א מִן־בֵּ֥ית מַלְכָּ֖א תִּתְיְהִֽב: 5 וְ֠אַף מָאנֵ֣י בֵית־אֱלָהָא�’ דִּ֣י דַהֲבָ֣ה וְכַסְפָּ֗א דִּ֤י נְבֽוּכַדְנֶצַּר֙ הַנְפֵּ֗ק מִן־הֵֽיכְלָ֤א דִי־בִירֽוּשְׁלֶם֙ וְהֵיבֵ֣ל לְבָבֶ֔ל יַהֲתִיב֗וּן וִ֠יהָךְ לְהֵיכְלָ֤א דִֽי־בִירֽוּשְׁלֶם֙ לְאַתְרֵ֔הּ וְתַחֵ֖ת בְּבֵ֥ית אֱלָהָֽא: ‪ס‬ 6 כְּעַ֡ן תַּ֠תְּנַי פַּחַ֨ת עֲבַֽר־נַהֲרָ֜ה שְׁתַ֤ר בּֽוֹזְנַי֙ וּכְנָֽוָתְה֔וֹן אֲפַרְסְכָיֵ֔א דִּ֖י בַּעֲבַ֣ר נַהֲרָ֑ה רַחִיקִ֥ין הֲו֖וֹ מִן־תַּמָּֽה: 7 שְׁבֻ֕קוּ לַעֲבִידַ֖ת בֵּית־אֱלָהָ֣א דֵ֑ךְ פַּחַ֤ת יְהוּדָיֵא֙ וּלְשָׂבֵ֣י יְהוּדָיֵ֔א בֵּית־אֱלָהָ֥א דֵ֖ךְ יִבְנ֥וֹן עַל־אַתְרֵֽהּ: 8 וּמִנִּי֮ שִׂ֣ים טְעֵם֒ לְמָ֣א דִֽי־תַֽעַבְד֗וּן עִם־שָׂבֵ֤י יְהֽוּדָיֵא֙ אִלֵּ֔ךְ לְמִבְנֵ֖א בֵּית־אֱלָהָ֣א דֵ֑ךְ וּמִנִּכְסֵ֣י מַלְכָּ֗א דִּ֚י מִדַּת֙ עֲבַ֣ר נַהֲרָ֔ה אָסְפַּ֗רְנָא נִפְקְתָ֛א תֶּהֱוֵ֧א מִֽתְיַהֲבָ֛א לְגֻבְרַיָּ֥א אִלֵּ֖ךְ דִּי־לָ֥א לְבַטָּלָֽא: 9 וּמָ֣ה חַשְׁחָ֡ן וּבְנֵ֣י תוֹרִ֣ין וְדִכְרִ֣ין וְאִמְּרִ֣ין ׀ לַעֲלָוָ֣ן ׀ לֶאֱלָ֪הּ שְׁמַיָּ֟א חִנְטִ֞ין מְלַ֣ח ׀ חֲמַ֣ר וּמְשַׁ֗ח כְּמֵאמַ֨ר כָּהֲנַיָּ֣א דִֽי־בִירֽוּשְׁלֶם֙ לֶהֱוֵ֨א מִתְיְהֵ֥ב לְהֹ֛ם י֥וֹם ׀ בְּי֖וֹם דִּי־לָ֥א שָׁלֽוּ: 10 דִּֽי־לֶהֱוֹ֧ן מְהַקְרְבִ֣ין נִיחוֹחִ֗ין לֶאֱלָ֣הּ שְׁמַיָּ֑א וּמְצַלַּ֕יִן לְחַיֵּ֥י מַלְכָּ֖א וּבְנֽוֹהִי: 11 וּמִנִּי֮ שִׂ֣ים טְעֵם֒ דִּ֣י כָל־אֱנָ֗שׁ דִּ֤י יְהַשְׁנֵא֙ פִּתְגָמָ֣א דְנָ֔ה יִתְנְסַ֥ח אָע֙ מִן־בַּיְתֵ֔הּ וּזְקִ֖יף יִתְמְחֵ֣א עֲלֹ֑הִי וּבַיְתֵ֛הּ נְוָל֥וּ יִתְעֲבֵ֖ד עַל־דְּנָֽה: 12 וֵֽאלָהָ֞א דִּ֣י שַׁכִּ֤ן שְׁמֵהּ֙ תַּמָּ֔ה יְמַגַּ֞ר כָּל־מֶ֤לֶךְ וְעַם֙ דִּ֣י ׀ יִשְׁלַ֣ח יְדֵ֗הּ לְהַשְׁנָיָ֛ה לְחַבָּלָ֥ה

destroy this house of God which is in Jerusalem. I Darius issue a decree; let it be done diligently.

13 Then Tattenai, governor of *the region* beyond the River, Shethar-Boznai, and their companions diligently did according to what King Darius had sent. 14 So the elders of the Jews built, and they prospered through the prophesying of Haggai the prophet and Zechariah the son of Iddo. And they built and finished *it,* according to the commandment of the God of Israel, and according to the command of Cyrus, Darius, and Artaxerxes king of Persia. 15 Now the temple was finished on the third day of the month of Adar, which was in the sixth year of the reign of King Darius. 16 Then the children of Israel, the priests and the Levites and the rest of the descendants of the captivity, celebrated the dedication of this house of God with joy. 17 And they offered sacrifices at the dedication of this house of God, one hundred bulls, two hundred rams, four hundred lambs, and as a sin offering for all Israel twelve male goats, according to the number of the tribes of Israel. 18 They assigned the priests to their divisions and the Levites to their divisions, over the service of God in Jerusalem, as it is written in the Book of Moses.

19 And the descendants of the captivity kept the Passover on the fourteenth *day* of the first month. 20 For the priests and the Levites had purified themselves; all of them *were ritually* clean. And they slaughtered the Passover *lambs* for all the descendants of the captivity, for their brethren the priests, and for themselves. 21 Then the children of Israel who had returned from the captivity ate together with all who had separated themselves from the filth of the nations of the land in order to seek the LORD God of Israel. 22 And they kept the Feast of Unleavened Bread seven days with joy; for the LORD made them joyful, and turned the heart of the king of Assyria toward them, to strengthen their hands in the work of the house of God, the God of Israel.

7 Now after these things, in the reign of Artaxerxes king of Persia, Ezra the son of Seraiah, the son of Azariah, the son of Hilkiah, 2 the son of Shallum, the son of Zadok, the son of Ahitub, 3 the son of Amariah, the son of Azariah, the son of Meraioth, 4 the son of Zerahiah, the son of Uzzi, the son of Bukki, 5 the son of Abishua, the son of Phinehas, the son of Eleazar, the son of Aaron the chief priest— 6 this Ezra came up from Babylon; and he *was* a skilled scribe in the Law of Moses, which the

בֵּית־אֱלָהָא דֵךְ דִּי בִירוּשְׁלֶם אֲנָה דָרְיָוֶשׁ שָׂמֵת
טְעֵם אָסְפַּרְנָא יִתְעֲבִד: פ

13 אֱדַיִן תַּתְּנַי פַּחַת עֲבַר־נַהֲרָה שְׁתַר בּוֹזְנַי
וּכְנָוָתְהוֹן לָקֳבֵל דִּי־שְׁלַח דָּרְיָוֶשׁ מַלְכָּא כְּנֵמָא
אָסְפַּרְנָא עֲבַדוּ: 14 וְשָׂבֵי יְהוּדָיֵא בָּנַיִן וּמַצְלְחִין
בִּנְבוּאַת חַגַּי נְבִיאָה וּזְכַרְיָה בַּר־עִדּוֹא וּבְנוֹ
וְשַׁכְלִלוּ מִן־טַעַם אֱלָהּ יִשְׂרָאֵל וּמִטְּעֵם כּוֹרֶשׁ
וְדָרְיָוֶשׁ וְאַרְתַּחְשַׁשְׂתְּא מֶלֶךְ פָּרָס: 15 וְשֵׁיצִיא
בַּיְתָה דְנָה עַד יוֹם תְּלָתָה לִירַח אֲדָר דִּי־הִיא
שְׁנַת־שֵׁת לְמַלְכוּת דָּרְיָוֶשׁ מַלְכָּא: פ

16 וַעֲבַדוּ בְנֵי־יִשְׂרָאֵל כָּהֲנַיָּא וְלֵוָיֵא וּשְׁאָר בְּנֵי־
גָלוּתָא חֲנֻכַּת בֵּית־אֱלָהָא דְנָה בְּחֶדְוָה: 17 וְהַקְרִבוּ
לַחֲנֻכַּת בֵּית־אֱלָהָא דְנָה תּוֹרִין מְאָה דִּכְרִין מָאתַיִן
אִמְּרִין אַרְבַּע מְאָה וּצְפִירֵי עִזִּין לְחַטָּיָא עַל־כָּל־
יִשְׂרָאֵל תְּרֵי־עֲשַׂר לְמִנְיָן שִׁבְטֵי יִשְׂרָאֵל: 18 וַהֲקִימוּ
כָהֲנַיָּא בִּפְלֻגָּתְהוֹן וְלֵוָיֵא בְּמַחְלְקָתְהוֹן עַל־עֲבִידַת
אֱלָהָא דִּי בִירוּשְׁלֶם כִּכְתָב סְפַר מֹשֶׁה: פ

19 וַיַּעֲשׂוּ בְנֵי־הַגּוֹלָה אֶת־הַפָּסַח בְּאַרְבָּעָה עָשָׂר
לַחֹדֶשׁ הָרִאשׁוֹן: 20 כִּי הִטַּהֲרוּ הַכֹּהֲנִים וְהַלְוִיִּם
כְּאֶחָד כֻּלָּם טְהוֹרִים וַיִּשְׁחֲטוּ הַפֶּסַח לְכָל־בְּנֵי
הַגּוֹלָה וְלַאֲחֵיהֶם הַכֹּהֲנִים וְלָהֶם: 21 וַיֹּאכְלוּ בְנֵי־
יִשְׂרָאֵל הַשָּׁבִים מֵהַגּוֹלָה וְכֹל הַנִּבְדָּל מִטֻּמְאַת
גּוֹיֵ־הָאָרֶץ אֲלֵהֶם לִדְרֹשׁ לַיהֹוָה אֱלֹהֵי יִשְׂרָאֵל:
22 וַיַּעֲשׂוּ חַג־מַצּוֹת שִׁבְעַת יָמִים בְּשִׂמְחָה כִּי |
שִׂמְּחָם יְהֹוָה וְהֵסֵב לֵב מֶלֶךְ־אַשּׁוּר עֲלֵיהֶם לְחַזֵּק
יְדֵיהֶם בִּמְלֶאכֶת בֵּית־הָאֱלֹהִים אֱלֹהֵי יִשְׂרָאֵל: פ

ז וְאַחַר הַדְּבָרִים הָאֵלֶּה בְּמַלְכוּת אַרְתַּחְשַׁסְתְּא
מֶלֶךְ־פָּרָס עֶזְרָא בֶּן־שְׂרָיָה בֶּן־עֲזַרְיָה בֶּן־חִלְקִיָּה:
2 בֶּן־שַׁלּוּם בֶּן־צָדוֹק בֶּן־אֲחִיטוּב: 3 בֶּן־אֲמַרְיָה בֶּן־
עֲזַרְיָה בֶּן־מְרָיוֹת: 4 בֶּן־זְרַחְיָה בֶן־עֻזִּי בֶּן־בֻּקִּי:
5 בֶּן־אֲבִישׁוּעַ בֶּן־פִּינְחָס בֶּן־אֶלְעָזָר בֶּן־אַהֲרֹן הַכֹּהֵן
הָרֹאשׁ: 6 הוּא עֶזְרָא עָלָה מִבָּבֶל וְהוּא־סֹפֵר מָהִיר

ו 14 נְבִיא   17 לְהַקְרָבָה

LORD God of Israel had given. The king granted him all his request, according to the hand of the LORD his God upon him. [7] *Some* of the children of Israel, the priests, the Levites, the singers, the gatekeepers, and the Nethinim came up to Jerusalem in the seventh year of King Artaxerxes. [8] And Ezra came to Jerusalem in the fifth month, which *was* in the seventh year of the king. [9] On the first *day* of the first month he began *his* journey from Babylon, and on the first *day* of the fifth month he came to Jerusalem, according to the good hand of his God upon him. [10] For Ezra had prepared his heart to seek the Law of the LORD, and to do *it*, and to teach statutes and ordinances in Israel.

[11] This *is* a copy of the letter that King Artaxerxes gave Ezra the priest, the scribe, expert in the words of the commandments of the LORD, and of His statutes to Israel:

[12] Artaxerxes, king of kings,

To Ezra the priest, a scribe of the Law of the God of heaven:

Perfect *peace,* and so forth.

[13] I issue a decree that all those of the people of Israel and the priests and Levites in my realm, who volunteer to go up to Jerusalem, may go with you. [14] And whereas you are being sent by the king and his seven counselors to inquire concerning Judah and Jerusalem, with regard to the Law of your God which *is* in your hand; [15] and *whereas you are* to carry the silver and gold which the king and his counselors have freely offered to the God of Israel, whose dwelling *is* in Jerusalem; [16] and *whereas* all the silver and gold that you may find in all the province of Babylon, along with the freewill offering of the people and the priests, *are to be* freely offered for the house of their God in Jerusalem— [17] now therefore, be careful to buy with this money bulls, rams, and lambs, with their grain offerings and their drink offerings, and offer them on the altar of the house of your God in Jerusalem.

[18] And whatever seems good to you and your brethren to do with the rest of the silver and the gold, do it according to the will of your God. [19] Also the articles that are given to you for the service of the house of your God, deliver in full before the God of Jerusalem. [20] And whatever more may be needed for the

בְּתוֹרַת מֹשֶׁה אֲשֶׁר־נָתַן יְהוָה אֱלֹהֵי יִשְׂרָאֵל וַיִּתֶּן־לוֹ הַמֶּלֶךְ כְּיַד־יְהוָה אֱלֹהָיו עָלָיו כֹּל בַּקָּשָׁתוֹ׃ פ

7 וַיַּעֲלוּ מִבְּנֵי־יִשְׂרָאֵל וּמִן־הַכֹּהֲנִים וְהַלְוִיִּם וְהַמְשֹׁרְרִים וְהַשֹּׁעֲרִים וְהַנְּתִינִים אֶל־יְרוּשָׁלִָם בִּשְׁנַת־שֶׁבַע לְאַרְתַּחְשַׁסְתְּא הַמֶּלֶךְ׃ 8 וַיָּבֹא יְרוּשָׁלִַם בַּחֹדֶשׁ הַחֲמִישִׁי הִיא שְׁנַת הַשְּׁבִיעִית לַמֶּלֶךְ׃ 9 כִּי בְּאֶחָד לַחֹדֶשׁ הָרִאשׁוֹן הוּא יְסֻד הַמַּעֲלָה מִבָּבֶל וּבְאֶחָד לַחֹדֶשׁ הַחֲמִישִׁי בָּא אֶל־יְרוּשָׁלִַם כְּיַד־אֱלֹהָיו הַטּוֹבָה עָלָיו׃ 10 כִּי עֶזְרָא הֵכִין לְבָבוֹ לִדְרֹשׁ אֶת־תּוֹרַת יְהוָה וְלַעֲשֹׂת וּלְלַמֵּד בְּיִשְׂרָאֵל חֹק וּמִשְׁפָּט׃ ס 11 וְזֶה ׀ פַּרְשֶׁגֶן הַנִּשְׁתְּוָן אֲשֶׁר נָתַן הַמֶּלֶךְ אַרְתַּחְשַׁסְתְּא לְעֶזְרָא הַכֹּהֵן הַסֹּפֵר סֹפֵר דִּבְרֵי מִצְוֹת־יְהוָה וְחֻקָּיו עַל־יִשְׂרָאֵל׃ פ

12 אַרְתַּחְשַׁסְתְּא מֶלֶךְ מַלְכַיָּא לְעֶזְרָא כָהֲנָא סָפַר דָּתָא דִּי־אֱלָהּ שְׁמַיָּא גְּמִיר וּכְעֶנֶת׃ 13 מִנִּי שִׂים טְעֵם דִּי כָל־מִתְנַדַּב בְּמַלְכוּתִי מִן־עַמָּה יִשְׂרָאֵל וְכָהֲנוֹהִי וְלֵוָיֵא לִמְהָךְ לִירוּשְׁלֶם עִמָּךְ יְהָךְ׃

14 כָּל־קֳבֵל דִּי מִן־קֳדָם מַלְכָּא וְשִׁבְעַת יָעֲטֹהִי שְׁלִיחַ לְבַקָּרָא עַל־יְהוּד וְלִירוּשְׁלֶם בְּדָת אֱלָהָךְ דִּי בִידָךְ׃ 15 וּלְהֵיבָלָה כְּסַף וּדְהַב דִּי־מַלְכָּא וְיָעֲטוֹהִי הִתְנַדַּבוּ לֶאֱלָהּ יִשְׂרָאֵל דִּי בִירוּשְׁלֶם מִשְׁכְּנֵהּ׃ 16 וְכֹל כְּסַף וּדְהַב דִּי תְהַשְׁכַּח בְּכֹל מְדִינַת בָּבֶל עִם הִתְנַדָּבוּת עַמָּא וְכָהֲנַיָּא מִתְנַדְּבִין לְבֵית אֱלָהֲהֹם דִּי בִירוּשְׁלֶם׃ 17 כָּל־קֳבֵל דְּנָה אָסְפַּרְנָא תִקְנֵא בְּכַסְפָּא דְנָה תּוֹרִין ׀ דִּכְרִין אִמְּרִין וּמִנְחָתְהוֹן וְנִסְכֵּיהוֹן וּתְקָרֵב הִמּוֹ עַל־מַדְבְּחָה דִּי בֵּית אֱלָהֲכֹם דִּי בִירוּשְׁלֶם׃ 18 וּמָה דִּי עֲלָיךְ וְעַל־אֶחָיךְ יֵיטַב בִּשְׁאָר כַּסְפָּא וְדַהֲבָה לְמֶעְבַּד כִּרְעוּת אֱלָהֲכֹם תַּעַבְדוּן׃ 19 וּמָאנַיָּא דִּי־מִתְיַהֲבִין לָךְ לְפָלְחָן בֵּית אֱלָהָךְ הַשְׁלֵם קֳדָם אֱלָהּ יְרוּשְׁלֶם׃ 20 וּשְׁאָר חַשְׁחוּת בֵּית אֱלָהָךְ דִּי יִפֶּל־לָךְ

house of your God, which you may have occasion to provide, pay *for it* from the king's treasury.

21 And I, *even* I, Artaxerxes the king, issue a decree to all the treasurers who *are in the region* beyond the River, that whatever Ezra the priest, the scribe of the Law of the God of heaven, may require of you, let it be done diligently, 22 up to one hundred talents of silver, one hundred kors of wheat, one hundred baths of wine, one hundred baths of oil, and salt without prescribed limit. 23 Whatever is commanded by the God of heaven, let it diligently be done for the house of the God of heaven. For why should there be wrath against the realm of the king and his sons?

24 Also we inform you that it shall not be lawful to impose tax, tribute, or custom *on any of* the priests, Levites, singers, gatekeepers, Nethinim, or servants of this house of God. 25 And you, Ezra, according to your God-given wisdom, set magistrates and judges who may judge all the people who *are in the region* beyond the River, all such as know the laws of your God; and teach those who do not know *them*. 26 Whoever will not observe the law of your God and the law of the king, let judgment be executed speedily on him, whether *it be* death, or banishment, or confiscation of goods, or imprisonment.

27 Blessed *be* the LORD God of our fathers, who has put *such a thing* as this in the king's heart, to beautify the house of the LORD which *is* in Jerusalem, 28 and has extended mercy to me before the king and his counselors, and before all the king's mighty princes.

So I was encouraged, as the hand of the LORD my God *was* upon me; and I gathered leading men of Israel to go up with me.

8 These *are* the heads of their fathers' *houses*, and *this is* the genealogy of those who went up with me from Babylon, in the reign of King Artaxerxes: 2 of the sons of Phinehas, Gershom; of the sons of Ithamar, Daniel; of the sons of David, Hattush; 3 of the sons of Shecaniah, of the sons of Parosh, Zechariah; and registered with him *were* one hundred and fifty males; 4 of the sons of Pahath-Moab, Eliehoenai the son of Zerahiah, and with him two hundred males; 5 of the sons of Shecha-niah, Ben-Jahaziel, and with him three hundred

לְמִנְתַּן תִּנְתֵּן מִן־בֵּית גִּנְזֵי מַלְכָּא: 21 וּמִנִּי אֲנָה
אַרְתַּחְשַׁסְתְּא מַלְכָּא שִׂים טְעֵם לְכֹל גִּזַּבְרַיָּא דִּי
בַּעֲבַר נַהֲרָה דִּי כָל־דִּי יִשְׁאֲלֶנְכוֹן עֶזְרָא כָהֲנָה סָפַר
דָּתָא דִּי־אֱלָהּ שְׁמַיָּא אָסְפַּרְנָא יִתְעֲבִד: 22 עַד־כְּסַף
כַּכְּרִין מְאָה וְעַד־חִנְטִין כֹּרִין מְאָה וְעַד־חֲמַר בַּתִּין
מְאָה וְעַד־בַּתִּין מְשַׁח מְאָה וּמְלַח דִּי־לָא כְתָב:
23 כָּל־דִּי מִן־טַעַם אֱלָהּ שְׁמַיָּא יִתְעֲבֵד אַדְרַזְדָּא
לְבֵית אֱלָהּ שְׁמַיָּא דִּי־לְמָה לֶהֱוֵא קְצַף עַל־מַלְכוּת
מַלְכָּא וּבְנוֹהִי: 24 וּלְכֹם מְהוֹדְעִין דִּי כָל־כָּהֲנַיָּא
וְלֵוָיֵא זַמָּרַיָּא תָרָעַיָּא נְתִינַיָּא וּפָלְחֵי בֵּית אֱלָהָא
דְנָה מִנְדָּה בְלוֹ וַהֲלָךְ לָא שַׁלִּיט לְמִרְמֵא עֲלֵיהֹם:
25 וְאַנְתְּ עֶזְרָא כְּחָכְמַת אֱלָהָךְ דִּי־בִידָךְ מֶנִּי שָׁפְטִין
וְדַיָּנִין דִּי־לֶהֱוֹן דָּאִנִין לְכָל־עַמָּה דִּי בַּעֲבַר נַהֲרָה
לְכָל־יָדְעֵי דָּתֵי אֱלָהָךְ וְדִי לָא יָדַע תְּהוֹדְעוּן:
26 וְכָל־דִּי־לָא לֶהֱוֵא עָבֵד דָּתָא דִּי־אֱלָהָךְ וְדָתָא
דִּי מַלְכָּא אָסְפַּרְנָא דִּינָה לֶהֱוֵא מִתְעֲבֵד מִנֵּהּ הֵן
לְמוֹת הֵן לִשְׁרֹשׁוּ הֵן־לַעֲנָשׁ נִכְסִין וְלֶאֱסוּרִין: פ
27 בָּרוּךְ יְהוָה אֱלֹהֵי אֲבוֹתֵינוּ אֲשֶׁר נָתַן כָּזֹאת
בְּלֵב הַמֶּלֶךְ לְפָאֵר אֶת־בֵּית יְהוָה אֲשֶׁר בִּירוּשָׁלָ͏ִם:
28 וְעָלַי הִטָּה־חֶסֶד לִפְנֵי הַמֶּלֶךְ וְיוֹעֲצָיו וּלְכָל־שָׂרֵי
הַמֶּלֶךְ הַגִּבֹּרִים וַאֲנִי הִתְחַזַּקְתִּי כְּיַד־יְהוָה אֱלֹהַי
עָלַי וָאֶקְבְּצָה מִיִּשְׂרָאֵל רָאשִׁים לַעֲלוֹת עִמִּי: פ

ח וְאֵלֶּה רָאשֵׁי אֲבֹתֵיהֶם וְהִתְיַחְשָׂם
הָעֹלִים עִמִּי בְּמַלְכוּת אַרְתַּחְשַׁסְתְּא
הַמֶּלֶךְ מִבָּבֶל: ס 2 מִבְּנֵי
פִינְחָס גֵּרְשֹׁם ס מִבְּנֵי
אִיתָמָר דָּנִיֵּאל ס מִבְּנֵי
דָוִיד חַטּוּשׁ: 3 מִבְּנֵי
שְׁכַנְיָה מִבְּנֵי פַרְעֹשׁ
זְכַרְיָה וְעִמּוֹ הִתְיַחֵשׂ לִזְכָרִים מֵאָה
וַחֲמִשִּׁים: ס 4 מִבְּנֵי פַּחַת מוֹאָב
אֶלְיְהוֹעֵינַי בֶּן־זְרַחְיָה וְעִמּוֹ מָאתַיִם
הַזְּכָרִים: ס 5 מִבְּנֵי שְׁכַנְיָה בֶּן־יַחֲזִיאֵל

וֹ 25 דָּאִנִין ‏ 26 לִשְׁרֹשׁ

males; ⁶ of the sons of Adin, Ebed the son of Jonathan, and with him fifty males; ⁷ of the sons of Elam, Jeshaiah the son of Athaliah, and with him seventy males; ⁸ of the sons of Shephatiah, Zebadiah the son of Michael, and with him eighty males; ⁹ of the sons of Joab, Obadiah the son of Jehiel, and with him two hundred and eighteen males; ¹⁰ of the sons of Shelomith, Ben-Josiphiah, and with him one hundred and sixty males; ¹¹ of the sons of Bebai, Zechariah the son of Bebai, and with him twenty-eight males; ¹² of the sons of Azgad, Johanan the son of Hakkatan, and with him one hundred and ten males; ¹³ of the last sons of Adonikam, whose names *are* these—Eliphelet, Jeiel, and Shemaiah—and with them sixty males; ¹⁴ also of the sons of Bigvai, Uthai and Zabbud, and with them seventy males.

¹⁵ Now I gathered them by the river that flows to Ahava, and we camped there three days. And I looked among the people and the priests, and found none of the sons of Levi there. ¹⁶ Then I sent for Eliezer, Ariel, Shemaiah, Elnathan, Jarib, Elnathan, Nathan, Zechariah, and Meshullam, leaders; also for Joiarib and Elnathan, men of understanding. ¹⁷ And I gave them a command for Iddo the chief man at the place Casiphia, and I told them what they should say to Iddo *and* his brethren the Nethinim at the place Casiphia—that they should bring us servants for the house of our God. ¹⁸ Then, by the good hand of our God upon us, they brought us a man of understanding, of the sons of Mahli the son of Levi, the son of Israel, namely Sherebiah, with his sons and brothers, eighteen men; ¹⁹ and Hashabiah, and with him Jeshaiah of the sons of Merari, his brothers and their sons, twenty men; ²⁰ also of the Nethinim, whom David and the leaders had appointed for the service of the Levites, two hundred and twenty Nethinim. All of them were designated by name.

²¹ Then I proclaimed a fast there at the river of Ahava, that we might humble ourselves before our God, to seek from Him the right way for us and our little ones and all our possessions. ²² For I was ashamed to request of the king an escort of soldiers and horsemen to help us against the enemy on the road, because we had spoken to the king, saying, "The hand of our God *is* upon all those for good who seek Him, but His power and His wrath *are* against all those who forsake Him." ²³ So we fasted and entreated our God for this, and He answered our prayer.

²⁴ And I separated twelve of the leaders of the priests—Sherebiah, Hashabiah, and ten of their brethren with them— ²⁵ and weighed out to them

6 וּמִבְּנֵי ס שָׁלֹשׁ מֵאוֹת הַזְּכָרִים:
עָדִין עֶבֶד בֶּן־יוֹנָתָן וְעִמּוֹ חֲמִשִּׁים
הַזְּכָרִים: ס 7 וּמִבְּנֵי עֵילָם יְשַׁעְיָה בֶּן־
עֲתַלְיָה וְעִמּוֹ שִׁבְעִים הַזְּכָרִים: ס 8 וּמִבְּנֵי
שְׁפַטְיָה זְבַדְיָה בֶּן־מִיכָאֵל וְעִמּוֹ שְׁמֹנִים
הַזְּכָרִים: 9 מִבְּנֵי יוֹאָב עֹבַדְיָה בֶּן־
יְחִיאֵל וְעִמּוֹ מָאתַיִם וּשְׁמֹנָה עָשָׂר
הַזְּכָרִים: ס 10 וּמִבְּנֵי שְׁלוֹמִית בֶּן־יוֹסִפְיָה
וְעִמּוֹ מֵאָה וְשִׁשִּׁים הַזְּכָרִים: ס 11 וּמִבְּנֵי
בֵבַי זְכַרְיָה בֶּן־בֵּבָי וְעִמּוֹ עֶשְׂרִים
וּשְׁמֹנָה הַזְּכָרִים: ס 12 וּמִבְּנֵי עַזְגָּד
יוֹחָנָן בֶּן־הַקָּטָן וְעִמּוֹ מֵאָה וַעֲשָׂרָה
הַזְּכָרִים: ס 13 וּמִבְּנֵי אֲדֹנִיקָם אַחֲרֹנִים
וְאֵלֶּה שְׁמוֹתָם אֱלִיפֶלֶט יְעִיאֵל וּשְׁמַעְיָה וְעִמָּהֶם
שִׁשִּׁים הַזְּכָרִים: ס 14 וּמִבְּנֵי בִגְוַי עוּתַי
וְזַבּוּד וְעִמּוֹ שִׁבְעִים הַזְּכָרִים:

15 וָאֶקְבְּצֵם אֶל־הַנָּהָר הַבָּא אֶל־אַהֲוָא וַנַּחֲנֶה שָׁם
יָמִים שְׁלֹשָׁה וָאָבִינָה בָעָם וּבַכֹּהֲנִים וּמִבְּנֵי לֵוִי
לֹא־מָצָאתִי שָׁם: 16 וָאֶשְׁלְחָה לֶאֱלִיעֶזֶר לַאֲרִיאֵל
לִשְׁמַעְיָה וּלְאֶלְנָתָן וּלְיָרִיב וּלְאֶלְנָתָן וּלְנָתָן וְלִזְכַרְיָה
וְלִמְשֻׁלָּם רָאשִׁים וּלְיוֹיָרִיב וּלְאֶלְנָתָן מְבִינִים:
17 וָאֲצַוֶּה אוֹתָם עַל־אִדּוֹ הָרֹאשׁ בְּכָסִפְיָא
הַמָּקוֹם וָאָשִׂימָה בְּפִיהֶם דְּבָרִים לְדַבֵּר אֶל־
אִדּוֹ אָחִיו הַנְּתוּנִים בְּכָסִפְיָא הַמָּקוֹם לְהָבִיא־
לָנוּ מְשָׁרְתִים לְבֵית אֱלֹהֵינוּ: 18 וַיָּבִיאוּ לָנוּ כְּיַד־
אֱלֹהֵינוּ הַטּוֹבָה עָלֵינוּ אִישׁ שֶׂכֶל מִבְּנֵי מַחְלִי
בֶן־לֵוִי בֶּן־יִשְׂרָאֵל וְשֵׁרֵבְיָה וּבָנָיו וְאֶחָיו שְׁמֹנָה
עָשָׂר: 19 וְאֶת־חֲשַׁבְיָה וְאִתּוֹ יְשַׁעְיָה מִבְּנֵי מְרָרִי
אֶחָיו וּבְנֵיהֶם עֶשְׂרִים: ס 20 וּמִן־הַנְּתִינִים
שֶׁנָּתַן דָּוִיד וְהַשָּׂרִים לַעֲבֹדַת הַלְוִיִּם נְתִינִים מָאתַיִם
וְעֶשְׂרִים כֻּלָּם נִקְּבוּ בְשֵׁמוֹת: 21 וָאֶקְרָא שָׁם צוֹם
עַל־הַנָּהָר אַהֲוָא לְהִתְעַנּוֹת לִפְנֵי אֱלֹהֵינוּ לְבַקֵּשׁ
מִמֶּנּוּ דֶּרֶךְ יְשָׁרָה לָנוּ וּלְטַפֵּנוּ וּלְכָל־רְכוּשֵׁנוּ:
22 כִּי בֹשְׁתִּי לִשְׁאוֹל מִן־הַמֶּלֶךְ חַיִל וּפָרָשִׁים
לְעָזְרֵנוּ מֵאוֹיֵב בַּדָּרֶךְ כִּי־אָמַרְנוּ לַמֶּלֶךְ לֵאמֹר יַד־
אֱלֹהֵינוּ עַל־כָּל־מְבַקְשָׁיו לְטוֹבָה וְעֻזּוֹ וְאַפּוֹ עַל
כָּל־עֹזְבָיו: 23 וַנָּצוּמָה וַנְּבַקְשָׁה מֵאֱלֹהֵינוּ עַל־זֹאת
וַיֵּעָתֵר לָנוּ: 24 וָאַבְדִּילָה מִשָּׂרֵי הַכֹּהֲנִים שְׁנֵים
עָשָׂר לְשֵׁרֵבְיָה חֲשַׁבְיָה וְעִמָּהֶם מֵאֲחֵיהֶם עֲשָׂרָה:
25 וָאֶשְׁקוֹלָה לָהֶם אֶת־הַכֶּסֶף וְאֶת־הַזָּהָב וְאֶת־

ח 14 וְזַבּוּד ‏ 17 וַאֲצַוֶּה, הַנְּתִינִים ‏ 25 וָאֶשְׁקְלָה

the silver, the gold, and the articles, the offering for the house of our God which the king and his counselors and his princes, and all Israel *who were* present, had offered. 26 I weighed into their hand six hundred and fifty talents of silver, silver articles *weighing* one hundred talents, one hundred talents of gold, 27 twenty gold basins *worth* a thousand drachmas, and two vessels of fine polished bronze, precious as gold. 28 And I said to them, "You *are* holy to the LORD; the articles *are* holy also; and the silver and the gold *are* a freewill offering to the LORD God of your fathers. 29 Watch and keep *them* until you weigh *them* before the leaders of the priests and the Levites and heads of the fathers' *houses* of Israel in Jerusalem, *in* the chambers of the house of the LORD." 30 So the priests and the Levites received the silver and the gold and the articles by weight, to bring *them* to Jerusalem to the house of our God.

31 Then we departed from the river of Ahava on the twelfth *day* of the first month, to go to Jerusalem. And the hand of our God was upon us, and He delivered us from the hand of the enemy and from ambush along the road. 32 So we came to Jerusalem, and stayed there three days.

33 Now on the fourth day the silver and the gold and the articles were weighed in the house of our God by the hand of Meremoth the son of Uriah the priest, and with him *was* Eleazar the son of Phinehas; with them *were* the Levites, Jozabad the son of Jeshua and Noadiah the son of Binnui, 34 with the number *and* weight of everything. All the weight was written down at that time.

35 The children of those who had been carried away captive, who had come from the captivity, offered burnt offerings to the God of Israel: twelve bulls for all Israel, ninety-six rams, seventy-seven lambs, and twelve male goats *as* a sin offering. All *this was* a burnt offering to the LORD.

36 And they delivered the king's orders to the king's satraps and the governors *in the region* beyond the River. So they gave support to the people and the house of God.

9 When these things were done, the leaders came to me, saying, "The people of Israel and the priests and the Levites have not separated themselves from the peoples of the lands, with respect to the abominations of the Canaanites, the Hittites, the Perizzites, the Jebusites, the Ammonites, the Moabites, the Egyptians, and the Amorites. 2 For they have taken some of their daughters *as wives* for themselves and their sons, so that the holy seed is mixed with the peoples of *those* lands. Indeed, the

הַכֵּלִים תְּרוּמַת בֵּית־אֱלֹהֵינוּ הֵרִימוּ הַמֶּלֶךְ וְיֹעֲצָיו וְשָׂרָיו וְכָל־יִשְׂרָאֵל הַנִּמְצָאִים: 26 וָאֶשְׁקֲלָה עַל־ יָדָם כֶּסֶף כִּכָּרִים שֵׁשׁ־מֵאוֹת וַחֲמִשִּׁים וּכְלֵי־כֶסֶף מֵאָה לְכִכָּרִים זָהָב מֵאָה כִכָּר: 27 וּכְפֹרֵי זָהָב עֶשְׂרִים לַאֲדַרְכֹנִים אָלֶף וּכְלֵי נְחֹשֶׁת מֻצְהָב טוֹבָה שְׁנַיִם חֲמוּדֹת כַּזָּהָב: 28 וָאֹמְרָה אֲלֵהֶם אַתֶּם קֹדֶשׁ לַיהֹוָה וְהַכֵּלִים קֹדֶשׁ וְהַכֶּסֶף וְהַזָּהָב נְדָבָה לַיהֹוָה אֱלֹהֵי אֲבֹתֵיכֶם: 29 שִׁקְדוּ וְשִׁמְרוּ עַד־ תִּשְׁקְלוּ לִפְנֵי שָׂרֵי הַכֹּהֲנִים וְהַלְוִיִּם וְשָׂרֵי־הָאָבוֹת לְיִשְׂרָאֵל בִּירוּשָׁלָ͏ִם הַלִּשְׁכוֹת בֵּית יְהֹוָה: 30 וְקִבְּלוּ הַכֹּהֲנִים וְהַלְוִיִּם מִשְׁקַל הַכֶּסֶף וְהַזָּהָב וְהַכֵּלִים לְהָבִיא לִירוּשָׁלַ͏ִם לְבֵית אֱלֹהֵינוּ: פ

31 וַנִּסְעָה מִנְּהַר אַהֲוָא בִּשְׁנֵים עָשָׂר לַחֹדֶשׁ הָרִאשׁוֹן לָלֶכֶת יְרוּשָׁלָ͏ִם וְיַד־אֱלֹהֵינוּ הָיְתָה עָלֵינוּ וַיַּצִּילֵנוּ מִכַּף אוֹיֵב וְאוֹרֵב עַל־הַדָּרֶךְ: 32 וַנָּבוֹא יְרוּשָׁלָ͏ִם וַנֵּשֶׁב שָׁם יָמִים שְׁלֹשָׁה: 33 וּבַיּוֹם הָרְבִיעִי נִשְׁקַל הַכֶּסֶף וְהַזָּהָב וְהַכֵּלִים בְּבֵית אֱלֹהֵינוּ עַל יַד־מְרֵמוֹת בֶּן־אוּרִיָּה הַכֹּהֵן וְעִמּוֹ אֶלְעָזָר בֶּן־פִּינְחָס וְעִמָּהֶם יוֹזָבָד בֶּן־יֵשׁוּעַ וְנוֹעַדְיָה בֶן־בִּנּוּי הַלְוִיִּם: 34 בְּמִסְפָּר בְּמִשְׁקָל לַכֹּל וַיִּכָּתֵב כָּל־הַמִּשְׁקָל בָּעֵת הַהִיא: פ

35 הַבָּאִים מֵהַשְּׁבִי בְנֵי־הַגּוֹלָה הִקְרִיבוּ עֹלוֹת ׀ לֵאלֹהֵי יִשְׂרָאֵל פָּרִים שְׁנֵים־עָשָׂר עַל־כָּל־יִשְׂרָאֵל אֵילִים ׀ תִּשְׁעִים וְשִׁשָּׁה כְּבָשִׂים שִׁבְעִים וְשִׁבְעָה צְפִירֵי חַטָּאת שְׁנֵים עָשָׂר הַכֹּל עוֹלָה לַיהֹוָה: פ 36 וַיִּתְּנוּ ׀ אֶת־דָּתֵי הַמֶּלֶךְ לַאֲחַשְׁדַּרְפְּנֵי הַמֶּלֶךְ וּפַחֲווֹת עֵבֶר הַנָּהָר וְנִשְּׂאוּ אֶת־הָעָם וְאֶת־בֵּית־ הָאֱלֹהִים: ס

ט וּכְכַלּוֹת אֵלֶּה נִגְּשׁוּ אֵלַי הַשָּׂרִים לֵאמֹר לֹא־נִבְדְּלוּ הָעָם יִשְׂרָאֵל וְהַכֹּהֲנִים וְהַלְוִיִּם מֵעַמֵּי הָאֲרָצוֹת כְּתוֹעֲבֹתֵיהֶם לַכְּנַעֲנִי הַחִתִּי הַפְּרִזִּי הַיְבוּסִי הָעַמֹּנִי הַמֹּאָבִי הַמִּצְרִי וְהָאֱמֹרִי: 2 כִּי־נָשְׂאוּ מִבְּנֹתֵיהֶם לָהֶם וְלִבְנֵיהֶם וְהִתְעָרְבוּ זֶרַע הַקֹּדֶשׁ בְּעַמֵּי הָאֲרָצוֹת וְיַד הַשָּׂרִים וְהַסְּגָנִים הָיְתָה בַּמַּעַל

hand of the leaders and rulers has been foremost in this trespass." ³So when I heard this thing, I tore my garment and my robe, and plucked out some of the hair of my head and beard, and sat down astonished. ⁴Then everyone who trembled at the words of the God of Israel assembled to me, because of the transgression of those who had been carried away captive, and I sat astonished until the evening sacrifice.

⁵At the evening sacrifice I arose from my fasting; and having torn my garment and my robe, I fell on my knees and spread out my hands to the LORD my God. ⁶And I said: "O my God, I am too ashamed and humiliated to lift up my face to You, my God; for our iniquities have risen higher than *our* heads, and our guilt has grown up to the heavens. ⁷Since the days of our fathers to this day we *have been* very guilty, and for our iniquities we, our kings, *and* our priests have been delivered into the hand of the kings of the lands, to the sword, to captivity, to plunder, and to humiliation, as *it is* this day. ⁸And now for a little while grace has been *shown* from the LORD our God, to leave us a remnant to escape, and to give us a peg in His holy place, that our God may enlighten our eyes and give us a measure of revival in our bondage. ⁹For we *were* slaves. Yet our God did not forsake us in our bondage; but He extended mercy to us in the sight of the kings of Persia, to revive us, to repair the house of our God, to rebuild its ruins, and to give us a wall in Judah and Jerusalem. ¹⁰And now, O our God, what shall we say after this? For we have forsaken Your commandments, ¹¹which You commanded by Your servants the prophets, saying, 'The land which you are entering to possess is an unclean land, with the uncleanness of the peoples of the lands, with their abominations which have filled it from one end to another with their impurity. ¹²Now therefore, do not give your daughters as wives for their sons, nor take their daughters to your sons; and never seek their peace or prosperity, that you may be strong and eat the good of the land, and leave *it* as an inheritance to your children forever.' ¹³And after all that has come upon us for our evil deeds and for our great guilt, since You our God have punished us less than our iniquities *deserve*, and have given us *such* deliverance as this, ¹⁴should we again break Your commandments, and join in marriage with the people *committing* these abominations? Would You not be angry with us until You had consumed *us*, so that *there would be* no remnant or survivor? ¹⁵O LORD God of Israel, You *are* righteous, for we are

3 וּכְשָׁמְעִי אֶת־הַדָּבָר הַזֶּה קָרַעְתִּי אֶת־בִּגְדִי וּמְעִילִי וָאֶמְרְטָה מִשְּׂעַר רֹאשִׁי וּזְקָנִי וָאֵשְׁבָה מְשׁוֹמֵם: 4 וְאֵלַי יֵאָסְפוּ כֹּל חָרֵד בְּדִבְרֵי אֱלֹהֵי־יִשְׂרָאֵל עַל מַעַל הַגּוֹלָה וַאֲנִי יֹשֵׁב מְשׁוֹמֵם עַד לְמִנְחַת הָעָרֶב: 5 וּבְמִנְחַת הָעֶרֶב קַמְתִּי מִתַּעֲנִיתִי וּבְקָרְעִי בִגְדִי וּמְעִילִי וָאֶכְרְעָה עַל־בִּרְכַּי וָאֶפְרְשָׂה כַפַּי אֶל־יְהוָה אֱלֹהָי: 6 וָאֹמְרָה אֱלֹהַי בֹּשְׁתִּי וְנִכְלַמְתִּי לְהָרִים אֱלֹהַי פָּנַי אֵלֶיךָ כִּי עֲוֹנֹתֵינוּ רָבוּ לְמַעְלָה רֹּאשׁ וְאַשְׁמָתֵנוּ גָדְלָה עַד לַשָּׁמָיִם: 7 מִימֵי אֲבֹתֵינוּ אֲנַחְנוּ בְּאַשְׁמָה גְדֹלָה עַד הַיּוֹם הַזֶּה וּבַעֲוֹנֹתֵינוּ נִתַּנּוּ אֲנַחְנוּ מְלָכֵינוּ כֹהֲנֵינוּ בְּיַד | מַלְכֵי הָאֲרָצוֹת בַּחֶרֶב בַּשְּׁבִי וּבַבִּזָּה וּבְבֹשֶׁת פָּנִים כְּהַיּוֹם הַזֶּה: 8 וְעַתָּה כִּמְעַט־רֶגַע הָיְתָה תְחִנָּה מֵאֵת | יְהוָה אֱלֹהֵינוּ לְהַשְׁאִיר לָנוּ פְּלֵיטָה וְלָתֶת־לָנוּ יָתֵד בִּמְקוֹם קָדְשׁוֹ לְהָאִיר עֵינֵינוּ אֱלֹהֵינוּ וּלְתִתֵּנוּ מִחְיָה מְעַט בְּעַבְדֻתֵנוּ: 9 כִּי־עֲבָדִים אֲנַחְנוּ וּבְעַבְדֻתֵנוּ לֹא עֲזָבָנוּ אֱלֹהֵינוּ וַיַּט־עָלֵינוּ חֶסֶד לִפְנֵי מַלְכֵי פָרַס לָתֶת־לָנוּ מִחְיָה לְרוֹמֵם אֶת־בֵּית אֱלֹהֵינוּ וּלְהַעֲמִיד אֶת־חָרְבֹתָיו וְלָתֶת־לָנוּ גָדֵר בִּיהוּדָה וּבִירוּשָׁלָ‍ִם: 10 וְעַתָּה מַה־נֹּאמַר אֱלֹהֵינוּ אַחֲרֵי־זֹאת כִּי עָזַבְנוּ מִצְוֹתֶיךָ:

11 אֲשֶׁר צִוִּיתָ בְּיַד עֲבָדֶיךָ הַנְּבִיאִים לֵאמֹר הָאָרֶץ אֲשֶׁר אַתֶּם בָּאִים לְרִשְׁתָּהּ אֶרֶץ נִדָּה הִיא בְּנִדַּת עַמֵּי הָאֲרָצוֹת בְּתוֹעֲבֹתֵיהֶם אֲשֶׁר מִלְאוּהָ מִפֶּה אֶל־פֶּה בְּטֻמְאָתָם: 12 וְעַתָּה בְּנוֹתֵיכֶם אַל־תִּתְּנוּ לִבְנֵיהֶם וּבְנֹתֵיהֶם אַל־תִּשְׂאוּ לִבְנֵיכֶם וְלֹא־תִדְרְשׁוּ שְׁלֹמָם וְטוֹבָתָם עַד־עוֹלָם לְמַעַן תֶּחֶזְקוּ וַאֲכַלְתֶּם אֶת־טוּב הָאָרֶץ וְהוֹרַשְׁתֶּם לִבְנֵיכֶם עַד־עוֹלָם: 13 וְאַחֲרֵי כָּל־הַבָּא עָלֵינוּ בְּמַעֲשֵׂינוּ הָרָעִים וּבְאַשְׁמָתֵנוּ הַגְּדֹלָה כִּי | אַתָּה אֱלֹהֵינוּ חָשַׂכְתָּ לְמַטָּה מֵעֲוֹנֵנוּ וְנָתַתָּה לָּנוּ פְּלֵיטָה כָּזֹאת: 14 הֲנָשׁוּב לְהָפֵר מִצְוֹתֶיךָ וּלְהִתְחַתֵּן בְּעַמֵּי הַתֹּעֵבוֹת הָאֵלֶּה הֲלוֹא תֶאֱנַף־בָּנוּ עַד־כַּלֵּה לְאֵין שְׁאֵרִית וּפְלֵיטָה: ס

15 יְהוָה אֱלֹהֵי יִשְׂרָאֵל צַדִּיק אַתָּה כִּי־נִשְׁאַרְנוּ

left as a remnant, as *it is* this day. Here we *are* before You, in our guilt, though no one can stand before You because of this!"

10 Now while Ezra was praying, and while he was confessing, weeping, and bowing down before the house of God, a very large assembly of men, women, and children gathered to him from Israel; for the people wept very bitterly. [2] And Shechaniah the son of Jehiel, *one* of the sons of Elam, spoke up and said to Ezra, "We have trespassed against our God, and have taken pagan wives from the peoples of the land; yet now there is hope in Israel in spite of this. [3] Now therefore, let us make a covenant with our God to put away all these wives and those who have been born to them, according to the advice of my master and of those who tremble at the commandment of our God; and let it be done according to the law. [4] Arise, for *this* matter *is* your *responsibility*. We also *are* with you. Be of good courage, and do *it*."

[5] Then Ezra arose, and made the leaders of the priests, the Levites, and all Israel swear an oath that they would do according to this word. So they swore an oath. [6] Then Ezra rose up from before the house of God, and went into the chamber of Jehohanan the son of Eliashib; and *when* he came there, he ate no bread and drank no water, for he mourned because of the guilt of those from the captivity.

[7] And they issued a proclamation throughout Judah and Jerusalem to all the descendants of the captivity, that they must gather at Jerusalem, [8] and that whoever would not come within three days, according to the instructions of the leaders and elders, all his property would be confiscated, and he himself would be separated from the assembly of those from the captivity.

[9] So all the men of Judah and Benjamin gathered at Jerusalem within three days. It *was* the ninth month, on the twentieth of the month; and all the people sat in the open square of the house of God, trembling because of *this* matter and because of heavy rain. [10] Then Ezra the priest stood up and said to them, "You have transgressed and have taken pagan wives, adding to the guilt of Israel. [11] Now therefore, make confession to the LORD God of your fathers, and do His will; separate yourselves from the peoples of the land, and from the pagan wives."

[12] Then all the assembly answered and said with a loud voice, "Yes! As you have said, so we must do. [13] But *there are* many people; *it is* the season for heavy rain, and we are not able to stand outside.

פְּלֵיטָה כְּהַיּוֹם הַזֶּה הִנְנוּ לְפָנֶיךָ בְּאַשְׁמָתֵינוּ כִּי אֵין לַעֲמוֹד לְפָנֶיךָ עַל־זֹאת: פ

[10] וּכְהִתְפַּלֵּל עֶזְרָא וּכְהִתְוַדֹּתוֹ בֹּכֶה וּמִתְנַפֵּל לִפְנֵי בֵּית הָאֱלֹהִים נִקְבְּצוּ אֵלָיו מִיִּשְׂרָאֵל קָהָל רַב־מְאֹד אֲנָשִׁים וְנָשִׁים וִילָדִים כִּי־בָכוּ הָעָם הַרְבֵּה־בֶכֶה: ס [2] וַיַּעַן שְׁכַנְיָה בֶן־יְחִיאֵל מִבְּנֵי עֵילָם וַיֹּאמֶר לְעֶזְרָא אֲנַחְנוּ מָעַלְנוּ בֵאלֹהֵינוּ וַנֹּשֶׁב נָשִׁים נָכְרִיּוֹת מֵעַמֵּי הָאָרֶץ וְעַתָּה יֵשׁ־מִקְוֶה לְיִשְׂרָאֵל עַל־זֹאת: [3] וְעַתָּה נִכְרָת־בְּרִית לֵאלֹהֵינוּ לְהוֹצִיא כָל־נָשִׁים וְהַנּוֹלָד מֵהֶם בַּעֲצַת אֲדֹנָי וְהַחֲרֵדִים בְּמִצְוַת אֱלֹהֵינוּ וְכַתּוֹרָה יֵעָשֶׂה: [4] קוּם כִּי־עָלֶיךָ הַדָּבָר וַאֲנַחְנוּ עִמָּךְ חֲזַק וַעֲשֵׂה: פ

[5] וַיָּקָם עֶזְרָא וַיַּשְׁבַּע אֶת־שָׂרֵי הַכֹּהֲנִים הַלְוִיִּם וְכָל־יִשְׂרָאֵל לַעֲשׂוֹת כַּדָּבָר הַזֶּה וַיִּשָּׁבֵעוּ: [6] וַיָּקָם עֶזְרָא מִלִּפְנֵי בֵּית הָאֱלֹהִים וַיֵּלֶךְ אֶל־לִשְׁכַּת יְהוֹחָנָן בֶּן־אֶלְיָשִׁיב וַיֵּלֶךְ שָׁם לֶחֶם לֹא־אָכַל וּמַיִם לֹא־שָׁתָה כִּי מִתְאַבֵּל עַל־מַעַל הַגּוֹלָה: ס [7] וַיַּעֲבִירוּ קוֹל בִּיהוּדָה וִירוּשָׁלִַם לְכֹל בְּנֵי הַגּוֹלָה לְהִקָּבֵץ יְרוּשָׁלִָם: [8] וְכֹל אֲשֶׁר לֹא־יָבוֹא לִשְׁלֹשֶׁת הַיָּמִים כַּעֲצַת הַשָּׂרִים וְהַזְּקֵנִים יָחֳרַם כָּל־רְכוּשׁוֹ וְהוּא יִבָּדֵל מִקְּהַל הַגּוֹלָה: ס [9] וַיִּקָּבְצוּ כָל־אַנְשֵׁי־יְהוּדָה וּבִנְיָמִן | יְרוּשָׁלִַם לִשְׁלֹשֶׁת הַיָּמִים הוּא חֹדֶשׁ הַתְּשִׁיעִי בְּעֶשְׂרִים בַּחֹדֶשׁ וַיֵּשְׁבוּ כָל־הָעָם בִּרְחוֹב בֵּית הָאֱלֹהִים מַרְעִידִים עַל־הַדָּבָר וּמֵהַגְּשָׁמִים: פ

[10] וַיָּקָם עֶזְרָא הַכֹּהֵן וַיֹּאמֶר אֲלֵהֶם אַתֶּם מְעַלְתֶּם וַתֹּשִׁיבוּ נָשִׁים נָכְרִיּוֹת לְהוֹסִיף עַל־אַשְׁמַת יִשְׂרָאֵל: [11] וְעַתָּה תְּנוּ תוֹדָה לַיהוָה אֱלֹהֵי־אֲבֹתֵיכֶם וַעֲשׂוּ רְצוֹנוֹ וְהִבָּדְלוּ מֵעַמֵּי הָאָרֶץ וּמִן־הַנָּשִׁים הַנָּכְרִיּוֹת: [12] וַיַּעֲנוּ כָל־הַקָּהָל וַיֹּאמְרוּ קוֹל גָּדוֹל כֵּן כִּדְבָרֶיךָ עָלֵינוּ לַעֲשׂוֹת: [13] אֲבָל הָעָם רָב וְהָעֵת גְּשָׁמִים וְאֵין כֹּחַ לַעֲמוֹד בַּחוּץ וְהַמְּלָאכָה לֹא־לְיוֹם אֶחָד וְלֹא לִשְׁנַיִם כִּי־הִרְבִּינוּ לִפְשֹׁעַ בַּדָּבָר

[י] [2] עֵילָם   [12] כִּדְבָרְךָ

Nor *is this* the work of one or two days, for *there are* many of us who have transgressed in this matter. [14]Please, let the leaders of our entire assembly stand; and let all those in our cities who have taken pagan wives come at appointed times, together with the elders and judges of their cities, until the fierce wrath of our God is turned away from us in this matter." [15]Only Jonathan the son of Asahel and Jahaziah the son of Tikvah opposed this, and Meshullam and Shabbethai the Levite gave them support.

[16]Then the descendants of the captivity did so. And Ezra the priest, *with* certain heads of the fathers' *households,* were set apart by the fathers' *households,* each of them by name; and they sat down on the first day of the tenth month to examine the matter. [17]By the first day of the first month they finished *questioning* all the men who had taken pagan wives.

[18]And among the sons of the priests who had taken pagan wives *the following* were found of the sons of Jeshua the son of Jozadak, and his brothers: Maaseiah, Eliezer, Jarib, and Gedaliah. [19]And they gave their promise that they would put away their wives; and *being* guilty, *they presented* a ram of the flock as their trespass offering.

[20]Also of the sons of Immer: Hanani and Zebadiah; [21]of the sons of Harim: Maaseiah, Elijah, Shemaiah, Jehiel, and Uzziah; [22]of the sons of Pashhur: Elioenai, Maaseiah, Ishmael, Nethanel, Jozabad, and Elasah.

[23]Also of the Levites: Jozabad, Shimei, Kelaiah (the same *is* Kelita), Pethahiah, Judah, and Eliezer.

[24]Also of the singers: Eliashib; and of the gatekeepers: Shallum, Telem, and Uri.

[25]And others of Israel: of the sons of Parosh: Ramiah, Jeziah, Malchiah, Mijamin, Eleazar, Malchijah, and Benaiah; [26]of the sons of Elam: Mattaniah, Zechariah, Jehiel, Abdi, Jeremoth, and Eliah; [27]of the sons of Zattu: Elioenai, Eliashib, Mattaniah, Jeremoth, Zabad, and Aziza; [28]of the sons of Bebai: Jehohanan, Hananiah, Zabbai, *and* Athlai; [29]of the sons of Bani: Meshullam, Malluch, Adaiah, Jashub, Sheal, *and* Ramoth; [30]of the sons of Pahath-Moab: Adna, Chelal, Benaiah, Maaseiah, Mattaniah, Bezalel, Binnui, and Manasseh; [31]*of* the sons of Harim: Eliezer, Ishijah, Malchijah, Shemaiah, Shimeon, [32]Benjamin, Malluch, *and* Shemariah; [33]of the sons of Hashum: Mattenai, Mattattah, Zabad, Eliphelet, Jeremai, Manasseh, *and* Shimei; [34]of the sons of Bani: Maadai, Amram, Uel, [35]Benaiah, Bedeiah, Cheluh, [36]Vaniah, Meremoth, Eliashib, [37]Mattaniah, Mattenai, Jaasai, [38]Bani, Binnui, Shimei, [39]Shelemiah, Nathan,

הַזֶּה: 14 יַעֲמְדוּ־נָא שָׂרֵינוּ לְכָל־הַקָּהָל וְכֹל ׀ אֲשֶׁר
בְּעָרֵינוּ הַהֹשִׁיב נָשִׁים נָכְרִיּוֹת יָבֹא לְעִתִּים מְזֻמָּנִים
וְעִמָּהֶם זִקְנֵי־עִיר וָעִיר וְשֹׁפְטֶיהָ עַד לְהָשִׁיב חֲרוֹן
אַף־אֱלֹהֵינוּ מִמֶּנּוּ עַד לַדָּבָר הַזֶּה: פ
15 אַךְ יוֹנָתָן בֶּן־עֲשָׂהאֵל וְיַחְזְיָה בֶן־תִּקְוָה עָמְדוּ
עַל־זֹאת וּמְשֻׁלָּם וְשַׁבְּתַי הַלֵּוִי עֲזָרֻם: 16 וַיַּעֲשׂוּ־
כֵן בְּנֵי הַגּוֹלָה וַיִּבָּדְלוּ עֶזְרָא הַכֹּהֵן אֲנָשִׁים רָאשֵׁי
הָאָבוֹת לְבֵית אֲבֹתָם וְכֻלָּם בְּשֵׁמוֹת וַיֵּשְׁבוּ בְּיוֹם
אֶחָד לַחֹדֶשׁ הָעֲשִׂירִי לְדַרְיוֹשׁ הַדָּבָר: 17 וַיְכַלּוּ
בַכֹּל אֲנָשִׁים הַהֹשִׁיבוּ נָשִׁים נָכְרִיּוֹת עַד יוֹם אֶחָד
לַחֹדֶשׁ הָרִאשׁוֹן: פ
18 וַיִּמָּצֵא מִבְּנֵי הַכֹּהֲנִים אֲשֶׁר הֹשִׁיבוּ נָשִׁים נָכְרִיּוֹת
מִבְּנֵי יֵשׁוּעַ בֶּן־יוֹצָדָק וְאֶחָיו מַעֲשֵׂיָה וֶאֱלִיעֶזֶר וְיָרִיב
וּגְדַלְיָה: 19 וַיִּתְּנוּ יָדָם לְהוֹצִיא נְשֵׁיהֶם וַאֲשֵׁמִים
אֵיל־צֹאן עַל־אַשְׁמָתָם: ס 20 וּמִבְּנֵי
אִמֵּר חֲנָנִי וּזְבַדְיָה: ס 21 וּמִבְּנֵי חָרִם
מַעֲשֵׂיָה וְאֵלִיָּה וּשְׁמַעְיָה וִיחִיאֵל וְעֻזִּיָּה:
22 וּמִבְּנֵי פַּשְׁחוּר אֶלְיוֹעֵינַי מַעֲשֵׂיָה יִשְׁמָעֵאל
נְתַנְאֵל יוֹזָבָד וְאֶלְעָשָׂה: ס 23 וּמִן־
הַלְוִיִּם יוֹזָבָד וְשִׁמְעִי וְקֵלָיָה הוּא קְלִיטָא
פְּתַחְיָה יְהוּדָה וֶאֱלִיעֶזֶר: ס 24 וּמִן־
הַמְשֹׁרְרִים אֶלְיָשִׁיב וּמִן־הַשֹּׁעֲרִים שַׁלֻּם וָטֶלֶם
וְאוּרִי: ס 25 וּמִיִּשְׂרָאֵל מִבְּנֵי פַרְעֹשׁ רַמְיָה
וְיִזִּיָּה וּמַלְכִּיָּה וּמִיָּמִן וְאֶלְעָזָר וּמַלְכִּיָּה וּבְנָיָה:
26 וּמִבְּנֵי עֵילָם מַתַּנְיָה זְכַרְיָה וִיחִיאֵל
וְעַבְדִּי וִירֵמוֹת וְאֵלִיָּה: ס 27 וּמִבְּנֵי
זַתּוּא אֶלְיוֹעֵנַי אֶלְיָשִׁיב מַתַּנְיָה וִירֵמוֹת וְזָבָד
וַעֲזִיזָא: ס 28 וּמִבְּנֵי בֵּבָי יְהוֹחָנָן חֲנַנְיָה
זַבַּי עַתְלָי: ס 29 וּמִבְּנֵי בָנִי מְשֻׁלָּם מַלּוּךְ
וַעֲדָיָה יָשׁוּב וּשְׁאָל יְרֵמוֹת: ס 30 וּמִבְּנֵי
פַּחַת מוֹאָב עַדְנָא וּכְלָל בְּנָיָה מַעֲשֵׂיָה
מַתַּנְיָה בְצַלְאֵל וּבִנּוּי וּמְנַשֶּׁה: ס 31 וּבְנֵי
חָרִם אֱלִיעֶזֶר יִשִּׁיָּה מַלְכִּיָּה שְׁמַעְיָה שִׁמְעוֹן:
32 בְּנְיָמִן מַלּוּךְ שְׁמַרְיָה: ס 33 מִבְּנֵי
חָשֻׁם מַתְּנַי מַתַּתָּה זָבָד אֱלִיפֶלֶט יְרֵמַי מְנַשֶּׁה
שִׁמְעִי: ס 34 מִבְּנֵי בָנִי מַעֲדַי עַמְרָם
וְאוּאֵל: ס 35 בְּנָיָה בֵדְיָה כְּלֻהִי: 36 וַנְיָה
מְרֵמוֹת אֶלְיָשִׁיב: 37 מַתַּנְיָה מַתְּנַי וְיַעֲשׂוּ: 38 וּבָנִי
וּבִנּוּי שִׁמְעִי: 39 וְשֶׁלֶמְיָה וְנָתָן וַעֲדָיָה: 40 מַכְנַדְבַי

Adaiah, [40] Machnadebai, Shashai, Sharai, [41] Azarel,
Shelemiah, Shemariah, [42] Shallum, Amariah, *and*
Joseph; [43] of the sons of Nebo: Jeiel, Mattithiah,
Zabad, Zebina, Jaddai, Joel, *and* Benaiah.

[44] All these had taken pagan wives, and *some* of
them had wives *by whom* they had children.

שָׁשַׁי שָׁרָי: [41] עֲזַרְאֵל וְשֶׁלֶמְיָהוּ שְׁמַרְיָה: [42] שַׁלּוּם
אֲמַרְיָה יוֹסֵף: ס [43] מִבְּנֵי נְבוֹ יְעִיאֵל
מַתִּתְיָה זָבָד זְבִינָא יַדַּי וְיוֹאֵל בְּנָיָה: [44] כָּל־אֵלֶּה
נָשְׂאִי נָשִׁים נָכְרִיּוֹת וְיֵשׁ מֵהֶם נָשִׁים וַיָּשִׂימוּ
בָּנִים:
פ

The Book of
NEHEMIAH

נחמיה

1 The words of Nehemiah the son of Hachaliah.

It came to pass in the month of Chislev, *in* the
twentieth year, as I was in Shushan the citadel,
² that Hanani one of my brethren came with men
from Judah; and I asked them concerning the Jews
who had escaped, who had survived the captivity,
and concerning Jerusalem. ³ And they said to me,
"The survivors who are left from the captivity in the
province *are* there in great distress and reproach.
The wall of Jerusalem *is* also broken down, and its
gates *are* burned with fire."

⁴ So it was, when I heard these words, that I sat
down and wept, and mourned *for many* days; I was
fasting and praying before the God of heaven.

⁵ And I said: "I pray, LORD God of heaven, O
great and awesome God, *You* who keep *Your*
covenant and mercy with those who love You and
observe Your commandments, ⁶ please let Your ear
be attentive and Your eyes open, that You may
hear the prayer of Your servant which I pray before
You now, day and night, for the children of Israel
Your servants, and confess the sins of the children
of Israel which we have sinned against You. Both
my father's house and I have sinned. ⁷ We have
acted very corruptly against You, and have not kept
the commandments, the statutes, nor the ordinances which You commanded Your servant
Moses. ⁸ Remember, I pray, the word that You
commanded Your servant Moses, saying, '*If* you
are unfaithful, I will scatter you among the nations;
⁹ but *if* you return to Me, and keep My commandments and do them, though some of you were cast
out to the farthest part of the heavens, *yet* I will
gather them from there, and bring them to the place
which I have chosen as a dwelling for My name.'
¹⁰ Now these *are* Your servants and Your people,
whom You have redeemed by Your great power,
and by Your strong hand. ¹¹ O Lord, I pray, please
let Your ear be attentive to the prayer of Your
servant, and to the prayer of Your servants who
desire to fear Your name; and let Your servant
prosper this day, I pray, and grant him mercy in the
sight of this man."

For I was the king's cupbearer.

א 1 דִּבְרֵי נְחֶמְיָה בֶּן־חֲכַלְיָה וַיְהִי בְחֹדֶשׁ־
כִּסְלֵו שְׁנַת עֶשְׂרִים וַאֲנִי הָיִיתִי בְּשׁוּשַׁן הַבִּירָה:
2 וַיָּבֹא חֲנָנִי אֶחָד מֵאַחַי הוּא וַאֲנָשִׁים מִיהוּדָה
וָאֶשְׁאָלֵם עַל־הַיְּהוּדִים הַפְּלֵיטָה אֲשֶׁר־נִשְׁאֲרוּ מִן־
הַשֶּׁבִי וְעַל־יְרוּשָׁלִָם: 3 וַיֹּאמְרוּ לִי הַנִּשְׁאָרִים אֲשֶׁר־
נִשְׁאֲרוּ מִן־הַשְּׁבִי שָׁם בַּמְּדִינָה בְּרָעָה גְדֹלָה
וּבְחֶרְפָּה וְחוֹמַת יְרוּשָׁלִַם מְפֹרָצֶת וּשְׁעָרֶיהָ נִצְּתוּ
בָאֵשׁ: 4 וַיְהִי כְּשָׁמְעִי | אֶת־הַדְּבָרִים הָאֵלֶּה
יָשַׁבְתִּי וָאֶבְכֶּה וָאֶתְאַבְּלָה יָמִים וָאֱהִי צָם וּמִתְפַּלֵּל
לִפְנֵי אֱלֹהֵי הַשָּׁמָיִם: 5 וָאֹמַר אָנָּא יְהוָה אֱלֹהֵי
הַשָּׁמַיִם הָאֵל הַגָּדוֹל וְהַנּוֹרָא שֹׁמֵר הַבְּרִית וָחֶסֶד
לְאֹהֲבָיו וּלְשֹׁמְרֵי מִצְוֹתָיו: 6 תְּהִי נָא אָזְנְךָ־קַשֶּׁבֶת
וְעֵינֶיךָ פְתֻחוֹת לִשְׁמֹעַ אֶל־תְּפִלַּת עַבְדְּךָ אֲשֶׁר
אָנֹכִי מִתְפַּלֵּל לְפָנֶיךָ הַיּוֹם יוֹמָם וָלַיְלָה עַל־בְּנֵי
יִשְׂרָאֵל עֲבָדֶיךָ וּמִתְוַדֶּה עַל־חַטֹּאות בְּנֵי־יִשְׂרָאֵל
אֲשֶׁר חָטָאנוּ לָךְ וַאֲנִי וּבֵית־אָבִי חָטָאנוּ: 7 חֲבֹל
חָבַלְנוּ לָךְ וְלֹא־שָׁמַרְנוּ אֶת־הַמִּצְוֹת וְאֶת־הַחֻקִּים
וְאֶת־הַמִּשְׁפָּטִים אֲשֶׁר צִוִּיתָ אֶת־מֹשֶׁה עַבְדֶּךָ:
8 זְכָר־נָא אֶת־הַדָּבָר אֲשֶׁר צִוִּיתָ אֶת־מֹשֶׁה עַבְדְּךָ
לֵאמֹר אַתֶּם תִּמְעָלוּ אֲנִי אָפִיץ אֶתְכֶם בָּעַמִּים:
9 וְשַׁבְתֶּם אֵלַי וּשְׁמַרְתֶּם מִצְוֹתַי וַעֲשִׂיתֶם אֹתָם
אִם־יִהְיֶה נִדַּחֲכֶם בִּקְצֵה הַשָּׁמָיִם מִשָּׁם אֲקַבְּצֵם
וַהֲבִיאוֹתִים אֶל־הַמָּקוֹם אֲשֶׁר בָּחַרְתִּי לְשַׁכֵּן אֶת־
שְׁמִי שָׁם: 10 וְהֵם עֲבָדֶיךָ וְעַמֶּךָ אֲשֶׁר פָּדִיתָ בְּכֹחֲךָ
הַגָּדוֹל וּבְיָדְךָ הַחֲזָקָה: 11 אָנָּא אֲדֹנָי תְּהִי נָא
אָזְנְךָ־קַשֶּׁבֶת אֶל־תְּפִלַּת עַבְדְּךָ וְאֶל־תְּפִלַּת עֲבָדֶיךָ
הַחֲפֵצִים לְיִרְאָה אֶת־שְׁמֶךָ וְהַצְלִיחָה־נָּא לְעַבְדְּךָ
הַיּוֹם וּתְנֵהוּ לְרַחֲמִים לִפְנֵי הָאִישׁ הַזֶּה וַאֲנִי הָיִיתִי
מַשְׁקֶה לַמֶּלֶךְ:
פ

2 And it came to pass in the month of Nisan, in the twentieth year of King Artaxerxes, *when* wine *was* before him, that I took the wine and gave it to the king. Now I had never been sad in his presence before. ² Therefore the king said to me, "Why *is* your face sad, since you *are* not sick? This *is* nothing but sorrow of heart."

So I became dreadfully afraid, ³ and said to the king, "May the king live forever! Why should my face not be sad, when the city, the place of my fathers' tombs, *lies* waste, and its gates are burned with fire?"

⁴ Then the king said to me, "What do you request?"

So I prayed to the God of heaven. ⁵ And I said to the king, "If it pleases the king, and if your servant has found favor in your sight, I ask that you send me to Judah, to the city of my fathers' tombs, that I may rebuild it."

⁶ Then the king said to me (the queen also sitting beside him), "How long will your journey be? And when will you return?" So it pleased the king to send me; and I set him a time.

⁷ Furthermore I said to the king, "If it pleases the king, let letters be given to me for the governors *of the region* beyond the River, that they must permit me to pass through till I come to Judah, ⁸ and a letter to Asaph the keeper of the king's forest, that he must give me timber to make beams for the gates of the citadel which *pertains* to the temple, for the city wall, and for the house that I will occupy." And the king granted *them* to me according to the good hand of my God upon me.

⁹ Then I went to the governors *in the region* beyond the River, and gave them the king's letters. Now the king had sent captains of the army and horsemen with me. ¹⁰ When Sanballat the Horonite and Tobiah the Ammonite official heard *of it*, they were deeply disturbed that a man had come to seek the well-being of the children of Israel.

¹¹ So I came to Jerusalem and was there three days. ¹² Then I arose in the night, I and a few men with me; I told no one what my God had put in my heart to do at Jerusalem; nor was there any animal with me, except the one on which I rode. ¹³ And I went out by night through the Valley Gate to the Serpent Well and the Refuse Gate, and viewed the walls of Jerusalem which were broken down and its gates which were burned with fire. ¹⁴ Then I went on to the Fountain Gate and to the King's Pool, but *there was* no room for the animal under me to pass. ¹⁵ So I went up in the night by the valley, and viewed the wall; then I turned back and entered by the Valley Gate, and so returned. ¹⁶ And the

ב וַיְהִי ׀ בְּחֹדֶשׁ נִיסָן שְׁנַת עֶשְׂרִים לְאַרְתַּחְשַׁסְתְּא הַמֶּלֶךְ יַיִן לְפָנָיו וָאֶשָּׂא אֶת־הַיַּיִן וָאֶתְּנָה לַמֶּלֶךְ וְלֹא־הָיִיתִי רַע לְפָנָיו׃ ² וַיֹּאמֶר לִי הַמֶּלֶךְ מַדּוּעַ ׀ פָּנֶיךָ רָעִים וְאַתָּה אֵינְךָ חוֹלֶה אֵין זֶה כִּי־ אִם רֹעַ לֵב וָאִירָא הַרְבֵּה מְאֹד׃ ³ וָאֹמַר לַמֶּלֶךְ הַמֶּלֶךְ לְעוֹלָם יִחְיֶה מַדּוּעַ לֹא־יֵרְעוּ פָנַי אֲשֶׁר הָעִיר בֵּית־קִבְרוֹת אֲבֹתַי חֲרֵבָה וּשְׁעָרֶיהָ אֻכְּלוּ בָאֵשׁ׃ ס ⁴ וַיֹּאמֶר לִי הַמֶּלֶךְ עַל־מַה־זֶּה אַתָּה מְבַקֵּשׁ וָאֶתְפַּלֵּל אֶל־אֱלֹהֵי הַשָּׁמָיִם׃ ⁵ וָאֹמַר לַמֶּלֶךְ אִם־עַל־הַמֶּלֶךְ טוֹב וְאִם־יִיטַב עַבְדְּךָ לְפָנֶיךָ אֲשֶׁר תִּשְׁלָחֵנִי אֶל־יְהוּדָה אֶל־עִיר קִבְרוֹת אֲבֹתַי וְאֶבְנֶנָּה׃ ⁶ וַיֹּאמֶר לִי הַמֶּלֶךְ וְהַשֵּׁגַל ׀ יוֹשֶׁבֶת אֶצְלוֹ עַד־מָתַי יִהְיֶה מַהֲלָכֲךָ וּמָתַי תָּשׁוּב וַיִּיטַב לִפְנֵי־הַמֶּלֶךְ וַיִּשְׁלָחֵנִי וָאֶתְּנָה לוֹ זְמָן׃ ⁷ וָאוֹמַר לַמֶּלֶךְ אִם־עַל־הַמֶּלֶךְ טוֹב אִגְּרוֹת יִתְּנוּ־לִי עַל־ פַּחֲווֹת עֵבֶר הַנָּהָר אֲשֶׁר יַעֲבִירוּנִי עַד אֲשֶׁר־אָבוֹא אֶל־יְהוּדָה׃ ⁸ וְאִגֶּרֶת אֶל־אָסָף שֹׁמֵר הַפַּרְדֵּס אֲשֶׁר לַמֶּלֶךְ אֲשֶׁר יִתֶּן־לִי עֵצִים לְקָרוֹת אֶת־שַׁעֲרֵי הַבִּירָה אֲשֶׁר־לַבַּיִת וּלְחוֹמַת הָעִיר וְלַבַּיִת אֲשֶׁר־אָבוֹא אֵלָיו וַיִּתֶּן־לִי הַמֶּלֶךְ כְּיַד־אֱלֹהַי הַטּוֹבָה עָלָי׃ ⁹ וָאָבוֹא אֶל־פַּחֲווֹת עֵבֶר הַנָּהָר וָאֶתְּנָה לָהֶם אֵת אִגְּרוֹת הַמֶּלֶךְ וַיִּשְׁלַח עִמִּי הַמֶּלֶךְ שָׂרֵי חַיִל וּפָרָשִׁים׃ פ ¹⁰ וַיִּשְׁמַע סַנְבַלַּט הַחֹרֹנִי וְטוֹבִיָּה הָעֶבֶד הָעַמֹּנִי וַיֵּרַע לָהֶם רָעָה גְדֹלָה אֲשֶׁר־בָּא אָדָם לְבַקֵּשׁ טוֹבָה לִבְנֵי יִשְׂרָאֵל׃ ¹¹ וָאָבוֹא אֶל־יְרוּשָׁלִָם וָאֱהִי־ שָׁם יָמִים שְׁלֹשָׁה׃ ¹² וָאָקוּם ׀ לַיְלָה אֲנִי וַאֲנָשִׁים ׀ מְעַט עִמִּי וְלֹא־הִגַּדְתִּי לְאָדָם מָה אֱלֹהַי נֹתֵן אֶל־לִבִּי לַעֲשׂוֹת לִירוּשָׁלִָם וּבְהֵמָה אֵין עִמִּי כִּי אִם־הַבְּהֵמָה אֲשֶׁר אֲנִי רֹכֵב בָּהּ׃ ¹³ וָאֵצְאָה בְשַׁעַר־הַגַּיְא לַיְלָה וְאֶל־פְּנֵי עֵין הַתַּנִּין וְאֶל־שַׁעַר הָאַשְׁפֹּת וָאֱהִי שֹׂבֵר בְּחֹמֹת יְרוּשָׁלִַם אֲשֶׁר־ הֵם פְּרוּצִים וּשְׁעָרֶיהָ אֻכְּלוּ בָאֵשׁ׃ ¹⁴ וָאֶעֱבֹר אֶל־ שַׁעַר הָעַיִן וְאֶל־בְּרֵכַת הַמֶּלֶךְ וְאֵין־מָקוֹם לַבְּהֵמָה לַעֲבֹר תַּחְתָּי׃ ¹⁵ וָאֱהִי עֹלֶה בַנַּחַל לַיְלָה וָאֱהִי שֹׂבֵר בַּחוֹמָה וָאָשׁוּב וָאָבוֹא בְּשַׁעַר הַגַּיְא וָאָשׁוּב׃ ¹⁶ וְהַסְּגָנִים לֹא יָדְעוּ אָנָה הָלָכְתִּי וּמָה אֲנִי עֹשֶׂה

officials did not know where I had gone or what I had done; I had not yet told the Jews, the priests, the nobles, the officials, or the others who did the work.

17 Then I said to them, "You see the distress that we *are* in, how Jerusalem *lies* waste, and its gates are burned with fire. Come and let us build the wall of Jerusalem, that we may no longer be a reproach." 18 And I told them of the hand of my God which had been good upon me, and also of the king's words that he had spoken to me.

So they said, "Let us rise up and build." Then they set their hands to *this* good *work.*

19 But when Sanballat the Horonite, Tobiah the Ammonite official, and Geshem the Arab heard *of it,* they laughed at us and despised us, and said, "What *is* this thing that you are doing? Will you rebel against the king?"

20 So I answered them, and said to them, "The God of heaven Himself will prosper us; therefore we His servants will arise and build, but you have no heritage or right or memorial in Jerusalem."

3 Then Eliashib the high priest rose up with his brethren the priests and built the Sheep Gate; they consecrated it and hung its doors. They built as far as the Tower of the Hundred, *and* consecrated it, then as far as the Tower of Hananel. 2 Next to *Eliashib* the men of Jericho built. And next to them Zaccur the son of Imri built.

3 Also the sons of Hassenaah built the Fish Gate; they laid its beams and hung its doors with its bolts and bars. 4 And next to them Meremoth the son of Urijah, the son of Koz, made repairs. Next to them Meshullam the son of Berechiah, the son of Meshezabel, made repairs. Next to them Zadok the son of Baana made repairs. 5 Next to them the Tekoites made repairs; but their nobles did not put their shoulders to the work of their Lord.

6 Moreover Jehoiada the son of Paseah and Meshullam the son of Besodeiah repaired the Old Gate; they laid its beams and hung its doors, with its bolts and bars. 7 And next to them Melatiah the Gibeonite, Jadon the Meronothite, the men of Gibeon and Mizpah, repaired the residence of the governor *of the region* beyond the River. 8 Next to him Uzziel the son of Harhaiah, one of the goldsmiths, made repairs. Also next to him Hananiah, one of the perfumers, made repairs; and they fortified Jerusalem as far as the Broad Wall. 9 And next to them Rephaiah the son of Hur, leader of half the district of Jerusalem, made repairs. 10 Next to them Jedaiah the son of

וְלַיְּהוּדִים וְלַכֹּהֲנִים וְלַחֹרִים וְלַסְּגָנִים וּלְיֶתֶר עֹשֵׂה הַמְּלָאכָה עַד־כֵּן לֹא הִגַּדְתִּי: 17 וָאוֹמַר אֲלֵהֶם אַתֶּם רֹאִים הָרָעָה אֲשֶׁר אֲנַחְנוּ בָהּ אֲשֶׁר יְרוּשָׁלַ͏ִם חֲרֵבָה וּשְׁעָרֶיהָ נִצְּתוּ בָאֵשׁ לְכוּ וְנִבְנֶה אֶת־חוֹמַת יְרוּשָׁלַ͏ִם וְלֹא־נִהְיֶה עוֹד חֶרְפָּה: 18 וָאַגִּיד לָהֶם אֶת־יַד אֱלֹהַי אֲשֶׁר־הִיא טוֹבָה עָלַי וְאַף־דִּבְרֵי הַמֶּלֶךְ אֲשֶׁר אָמַר־לִי וַיֹּאמְרוּ נָקוּם וּבָנִינוּ וַיְחַזְּקוּ יְדֵיהֶם לַטּוֹבָה: פ

19 וַיִּשְׁמַע סַנְבַלַּט הַחֹרֹנִי וְטֹבִיָּה ׀ הָעֶבֶד הָעַמּוֹנִי וְגֶשֶׁם הָעַרְבִי וַיַּלְעִגוּ לָנוּ וַיִּבְזוּ עָלֵינוּ וַיֹּאמְרוּ מָה־הַדָּבָר הַזֶּה אֲשֶׁר אַתֶּם עֹשִׂים הַעַל הַמֶּלֶךְ אַתֶּם מֹרְדִים: 20 וָאָשִׁיב אוֹתָם דָּבָר וָאוֹמַר לָהֶם אֱלֹהֵי הַשָּׁמַיִם הוּא יַצְלִיחַ לָנוּ וַאֲנַחְנוּ עֲבָדָיו נָקוּם וּבָנִינוּ וְלָכֶם אֵין־חֵלֶק וּצְדָקָה וְזִכָּרוֹן בִּירוּשָׁלָ͏ִם:

ג וַיָּקָם אֶלְיָשִׁיב הַכֹּהֵן הַגָּדוֹל וְאֶחָיו הַכֹּהֲנִים וַיִּבְנוּ אֶת־שַׁעַר הַצֹּאן הֵמָּה קִדְּשׁוּהוּ וַיַּעֲמִידוּ דַּלְתֹתָיו וְעַד־מִגְדַּל הַמֵּאָה קִדְּשׁוּהוּ עַד מִגְדַּל חֲנַנְאֵל: 2 וְעַל־יָדוֹ בָנוּ אַנְשֵׁי יְרֵחוֹ ס וְעַל־יָדוֹ בָנָה זַכּוּר בֶּן־אִמְרִי: ס 3 וְאֵת שַׁעַר הַדָּגִים בָּנוּ בְּנֵי הַסְּנָאָה הֵמָּה קֵרוּהוּ וַיַּעֲמִידוּ דַּלְתֹתָיו מַנְעוּלָיו וּבְרִיחָיו: ס 4 וְעַל־יָדָם הֶחֱזִיק מְרֵמוֹת בֶּן־אוּרִיָּה בֶּן־הַקּוֹץ ס וְעַל־יָדָם הֶחֱזִיק מְשֻׁלָּם בֶּן־בֶּרֶכְיָה בֶּן־מְשֵׁיזַבְאֵל ס וְעַל־יָדָם הֶחֱזִיק צָדוֹק בֶּן־בַּעֲנָא: ס 5 וְעַל־יָדָם הֶחֱזִיקוּ הַתְּקוֹעִים וְאַדִּירֵיהֶם לֹא־הֵבִיאוּ צַוָּרָם בַּעֲבֹדַת אֲדֹנֵיהֶם: ס 6 וְאֵת שַׁעַר הַיְשָׁנָה הֶחֱזִיקוּ יוֹיָדָע בֶּן־פָּסֵחַ וּמְשֻׁלָּם בֶּן־בְּסוֹדְיָה הֵמָּה קֵרוּהוּ וַיַּעֲמִידוּ דַּלְתֹתָיו וּמַנְעֻלָיו וּבְרִיחָיו: ס 7 וְעַל־יָדָם הֶחֱזִיק מְלַטְיָה הַגִּבְעֹנִי וְיָדוֹן הַמֵּרֹנֹתִי אַנְשֵׁי גִבְעוֹן וְהַמִּצְפָּה לְכִסֵּא פַּחַת עֵבֶר הַנָּהָר: ס 8 עַל־יָדוֹ הֶחֱזִיק עֻזִּיאֵל בֶּן־חַרְהֲיָה צוֹרְפִים ס וְעַל־יָדוֹ הֶחֱזִיק חֲנַנְיָה בֶּן־הָרַקָּחִים וַיַּעַזְבוּ יְרוּשָׁלַ͏ִם עַד הַחוֹמָה הָרְחָבָה: 9 וְעַל־יָדָם הֶחֱזִיק רְפָיָה בֶן־חוּר שַׂר חֲצִי פֶּלֶךְ יְרוּשָׁלָ͏ִם: ס 10 וְעַל־יָדָם הֶחֱזִיק יְדָיָה בֶן־

Harumaph made repairs in front of his house. And next to him Hattush the son of Hashabniah made repairs.

11 Malchijah the son of Harim and Hashub the son of Pahath-Moab repaired another section, as well as the Tower of the Ovens. 12 And next to him was Shallum the son of Hallohesh, leader of half the district of Jerusalem; he and his daughters made repairs.

13 Hanun and the inhabitants of Zanoah repaired the Valley Gate. They built it, hung its doors with its bolts and bars, and *repaired* a thousand cubits of the wall as far as the Refuse Gate.

14 Malchijah the son of Rechab, leader of the district of Beth Haccerem, repaired the Refuse Gate; he built it and hung its doors with its bolts and bars.

15 Shallun the son of Col-Hozeh, leader of the district of Mizpah, repaired the Fountain Gate; he built it, covered it, hung its doors with its bolts and bars, and repaired the wall of the Pool of Shelah by the King's Garden, as far as the stairs that go down from the City of David. 16 After him Nehemiah the son of Azbuk, leader of half the district of Beth Zur, made repairs as far as *the place* in front of the tombs of David, to the man-made pool, and as far as the House of the Mighty.

17 After him the Levites, *under* Rehum the son of Bani, made repairs. Next to him Hashabiah, leader of half the district of Keilah, made repairs for his district. 18 After him their brethren, *under* Bavai the son of Henadad, leader of the *other* half of the district of Keilah, made repairs. 19 And next to him Ezer the son of Jeshua, the leader of Mizpah, repaired another section in front of the Ascent to the Armory at the buttress. 20 After him Baruch the son of Zabbai carefully repaired the other section, from the buttress to the door of the house of Eliashib the high priest. 21 After him Meremoth the son of Urijah, the son of Koz, repaired another section, from the door of the house of Eliashib to the end of the house of Eliashib.

22 And after him the priests, the men of the plain, made repairs. 23 After him Benjamin and Hasshub made repairs opposite their house. After them Azariah the son of Maaseiah, the son of Ananiah, made repairs by his house. 24 After him Binnui the son of Henadad repaired another section, from the house of Azariah to the buttress, even as far as the corner. 25 Palal the son of Uzai *made repairs* opposite the buttress, and on the tower which projects from the king's upper house that *was* by the court of the prison. After him Pedaiah the son of Parosh *made repairs.*

ס וְעַל־יָדוֹ הֶחֱזִיק חֲרוּמַף וְנֶגֶד בֵּיתוֹ
חַטּוּשׁ בֶּן־חֲשַׁבְנְיָה: 11 מִדָּה שֵׁנִית הֶחֱזִיק
מַלְכִּיָּה בֶן־חָרִם וְחַשּׁוּב בֶּן־פַּחַת מוֹאָב וְאֵת
מִגְדַּל הַתַּנּוּרִים: ס 12 וְעַל־יָדוֹ הֶחֱזִיק
שַׁלּוּם בֶּן־הַלּוֹחֵשׁ שַׂר חֲצִי פֶּלֶךְ יְרוּשָׁלָ͏ִם
הוּא וּבְנוֹתָיו: ס 13 אֵת שַׁעַר הַגַּיְא
הֶחֱזִיק חָנוּן וְיֹשְׁבֵי זָנוֹחַ הֵמָּה בָנוּהוּ וַיַּעֲמִידוּ
דַּלְתֹתָיו מַנְעֻלָיו וּבְרִיחָיו וְאֶלֶף אַמָּה בַּחוֹמָה
עַד שַׁעַר הָשְׁפוֹת: 14 וְאֵת שַׁעַר הָאַשְׁפּוֹת
הֶחֱזִיק מַלְכִּיָּה בֶן־רֵכָב שַׂר פֶּלֶךְ בֵּית־
הַכָּרֶם הוּא יִבְנֶנּוּ וְיַעֲמִיד דַּלְתֹתָיו מַנְעֻלָיו
וּבְרִיחָיו: ס 15 וְאֵת שַׁעַר הָעַיִן הֶחֱזִיק
שַׁלּוּן בֶּן־כָּל־חֹזֶה שַׂר פֶּלֶךְ הַמִּצְפָּה הוּא יִבְנֶנּוּ
וִיטַלְלֶנּוּ וְיַעֲמִידוֹ דַּלְתֹתָיו מַנְעֻלָיו וּבְרִיחָיו וְאֵת
חוֹמַת בְּרֵכַת הַשֶּׁלַח לְגַן־הַמֶּלֶךְ וְעַד־הַמַּעֲלוֹת
הַיּוֹרְדוֹת מֵעִיר דָּוִיד: ס 16 אַחֲרָיו הֶחֱזִיק
נְחֶמְיָה בֶן־עַזְבּוּק שַׂר חֲצִי פֶּלֶךְ בֵּית־צוּר עַד־
נֶגֶד קִבְרֵי דָוִיד וְעַד־הַבְּרֵכָה הָעֲשׂוּיָה וְעַד בֵּית
הַגִּבֹּרִים: ס 17 אַחֲרָיו הֶחֱזִיקוּ הַלְוִיִּם
רְחוּם בֶּן־בָּנִי עַל־יָדוֹ הֶחֱזִיק חֲשַׁבְיָה שַׂר־
חֲצִי־פֶלֶךְ קְעִילָה לְפִלְכּוֹ: 18 אַחֲרָיו
הֶחֱזִיקוּ אֲחֵיהֶם בַּוַּי בֶּן־חֵנָדָד שַׂר חֲצִי פֶּלֶךְ
קְעִילָה: ס 19 וַיְחַזֵּק עַל־יָדוֹ עֵזֶר בֶּן־
יֵשׁוּעַ שַׂר הַמִּצְפָּה מִדָּה שֵׁנִית מִנֶּגֶד עֲלֹת הַנֶּשֶׁק
הַמִּקְצֹעַ: 20 אַחֲרָיו הֶחֱרָה הֶחֱזִיק
בָּרוּךְ בֶּן־זַבַּי מִדָּה שֵׁנִית מִן־הַמִּקְצוֹעַ עַד־פֶּתַח
בֵּית אֶלְיָשִׁיב הַכֹּהֵן הַגָּדוֹל: ס 21 אַחֲרָיו
הֶחֱזִיק מְרֵמוֹת בֶּן־אוּרִיָּה בֶּן־הַקּוֹץ מִדָּה
שֵׁנִית מִפֶּתַח בֵּית אֶלְיָשִׁיב וְעַד־תַּכְלִית בֵּית
אֶלְיָשִׁיב: ס 22 וְאַחֲרָיו הֶחֱזִיקוּ הַכֹּהֲנִים
אַנְשֵׁי הַכִּכָּר: 23 אַחֲרָיו הֶחֱזִיק בִּנְיָמִן וְחַשּׁוּב נֶגֶד
בֵּיתָם ס אַחֲרָיו הֶחֱזִיק עֲזַרְיָה בֶן־מַעֲשֵׂיָה
בֶן־עֲנָנְיָה אֵצֶל בֵּיתוֹ: ס 24 אַחֲרָיו הֶחֱזִיק
בִּנּוּי בֶּן־חֵנָדָד מִדָּה שֵׁנִית מִבֵּית עֲזַרְיָה עַד־
הַמִּקְצוֹעַ וְעַד־הַפִּנָּה: 25 פָּלָל בֶּן־אוּזַי מִנֶּגֶד
הַמִּקְצוֹעַ וְהַמִּגְדָּל הַיּוֹצֵא מִבֵּית הַמֶּלֶךְ הָעֶלְיוֹן
אֲשֶׁר לַחֲצַר הַמַּטָּרָה אַחֲרָיו פְּדָיָה

ג 15 וַיְעֲמִיד ק 20 זַבַּי

²⁶ Moreover the Nethinim who dwelt in Ophel *made repairs* as far as *the place* in front of the Water Gate toward the east, and on the projecting tower. ²⁷ After them the Tekoites repaired another section, next to the great projecting tower, and as far as the wall of Ophel.

²⁸ Beyond the Horse Gate the priests made repairs, each in front of his *own* house. ²⁹ After them Zadok the son of Immer made repairs in front of his *own* house. After him Shemaiah the son of Shechaniah, the keeper of the East Gate, made repairs. ³⁰ After him Hananiah the son of Shelemiah, and Hanun, the sixth son of Zalaph, repaired another section. After him Meshullam the son of Berechiah made repairs in front of his dwelling. ³¹ After him Malchijah, one of the goldsmiths, made repairs as far as the house of the Nethinim and of the merchants, in front of the Miphkad Gate, and as far as the upper room at the corner. ³² And between the upper room at the corner, as far as the Sheep Gate, the goldsmiths and the merchants made repairs.

4 But it so happened, when Sanballat heard that we were rebuilding the wall, that he was furious and very indignant, and mocked the Jews. ² And he spoke before his brethren and the army of Samaria, and said, "What are these feeble Jews doing? Will they fortify themselves? Will they offer sacrifices? Will they complete it in a day? Will they revive the stones from the heaps of rubbish—*stones* that are burned?"

³ Now Tobiah the Ammonite *was* beside him, and he said, "Whatever they build, if even a fox goes up *on it,* he will break down their stone wall."

⁴ Hear, O our God, for we are despised; turn their reproach on their own heads, and give them as plunder to a land of captivity! ⁵ Do not cover their iniquity, and do not let their sin be blotted out from before You; for they have provoked *You* to anger before the builders.

⁶ So we built the wall, and the entire wall was joined together up to half its *height,* for the people had a mind to work.

⁷ Now it happened, when Sanballat, Tobiah, the Arabs, the Ammonites, and the Ashdodites heard that the walls of Jerusalem were being restored and the gaps were beginning to be closed, that they became very angry, ⁸ and all of them conspired together to come *and* attack Jerusalem and create confusion. ⁹ Nevertheless we made our prayer to our God, and because of them we set a watch against them day and night.

---

²⁶ וְהַנְּתִינִים הָיוּ יֹשְׁבִים ס בָּעֹפֶל עַד נֶגֶד שַׁעַר הַמַּיִם לַמִּזְרָח וְהַמִּגְדָּל הַיּוֹצֵא: ס ²⁷ אַחֲרָיו הֶחֱזִיקוּ הַתְּקֹעִים מִדָּה שֵׁנִית מִנֶּגֶד הַמִּגְדָּל הַגָּדוֹל הַיּוֹצֵא וְעַד חוֹמַת הָעֹפֶל: ²⁸ מֵעַל שַׁעַר הַסּוּסִים הֶחֱזִיקוּ הַכֹּהֲנִים אִישׁ לְנֶגֶד בֵּיתוֹ: ס ²⁹ אַחֲרָיו הֶחֱזִיק צָדוֹק בֶּן־אִמֵּר נֶגֶד בֵּיתוֹ ס וְאַחֲרָיו הֶחֱזִיק שְׁמַעְיָה בֶן־שְׁכַנְיָה שֹׁמֵר שַׁעַר הַמִּזְרָח: ס ³⁰ אַחֲרָי* הֶחֱזִיק חֲנַנְיָה בֶן־שֶׁלֶמְיָה וְחָנוּן בֶּן־צָלָף הַשִּׁשִּׁי מִדָּה שֵׁנִי ס אַחֲרָיו הֶחֱזִיק מְשֻׁלָּם בֶּן־בֶּרֶכְיָה נֶגֶד נִשְׁכָּתוֹ: ס ³¹ אַחֲרָי* הֶחֱזִיק מַלְכִּיָּה בֶּן־הַצֹּרְפִי עַד־בֵּית הַנְּתִינִים וְהָרֹכְלִים נֶגֶד שַׁעַר הַמִּפְקָד וְעַד עֲלִיַּת הַפִּנָּה: ³² וּבֵין עֲלִיַּת הַפִּנָּה לְשַׁעַר הַצֹּאן הֶחֱזִיקוּ הַצֹּרְפִים וְהָרֹכְלִים: פ

³³ וַיְהִי כַּאֲשֶׁר שָׁמַע סַנְבַלַּט כִּי־אֲנַחְנוּ בוֹנִים אֶת־הַחוֹמָה וַיִּחַר לוֹ וַיִּכְעַס הַרְבֵּה וַיַּלְעֵג עַל־הַיְּהוּדִים: ³⁴ וַיֹּאמֶר לִפְנֵי אֶחָיו וְחֵיל שֹׁמְרוֹן וַיֹּאמֶר מָה הַיְּהוּדִים הָאֲמֵלָלִים עֹשִׂים הֲיַעַזְבוּ לָהֶם הֲיִזְבָּחוּ הַיְכַלּוּ בַיּוֹם הַיְחַיּוּ אֶת־הָאֲבָנִים מֵעֲרֵמוֹת הֶעָפָר וְהֵמָּה שְׂרוּפוֹת: ³⁵ וְטוֹבִיָּה הָעַמֹּנִי אֶצְלוֹ וַיֹּאמֶר גַּם אֲשֶׁר־הֵם בּוֹנִים אִם־יַעֲלֶה שׁוּעָל וּפָרַץ חוֹמַת אַבְנֵיהֶם: פ

³⁶ שְׁמַע אֱלֹהֵינוּ כִּי־הָיִינוּ בוּזָה וְהָשֵׁב חֶרְפָּתָם אֶל־רֹאשָׁם וּתְנֵם לְבִזָּה בְּאֶרֶץ שִׁבְיָה: ³⁷ וְאַל־תְּכַס עַל־עֲוֺנָם וְחַטָּאתָם מִלְּפָנֶיךָ אַל־תִּמָּחֶה כִּי הִכְעִיסוּ לְנֶגֶד הַבּוֹנִים: ³⁸ וַנִּבְנֶה אֶת־הַחוֹמָה וַתִּקָּשֵׁר כָּל־הַחוֹמָה עַד־חֶצְיָהּ וַיְהִי לֵב לָעָם לַעֲשׂוֹת: פ

ד וַיְהִי כַאֲשֶׁר שָׁמַע סַנְבַלַּט וְטוֹבִיָּה וְהָעַרְבִים וְהָעַמֹּנִים וְהָאַשְׁדּוֹדִים כִּי־עָלְתָה אֲרוּכָה לְחֹמוֹת יְרוּשָׁלַםִ כִּי־הֵחֵלּוּ הַפְּרֻצִים לְהִסָּתֵם וַיִּחַר לָהֶם מְאֹד: ² וַיִּקְשְׁרוּ כֻלָּם יַחְדָּו לָבוֹא לְהִלָּחֵם בִּירוּשָׁלָםִ וְלַעֲשׂוֹת לוֹ תּוֹעָה: ³ וַנִּתְפַּלֵּל אֶל־אֱלֹהֵינוּ וַנַּעֲמִיד מִשְׁמָר עֲלֵיהֶם יוֹמָם וָלַיְלָה

10 Then Judah said, "The strength of the laborers is failing, and *there is* so much rubbish that we are not able to build the wall."

11 And our adversaries said, "They will neither know nor see anything, till we come into their midst and kill them and cause the work to cease."

12 So it was, when the Jews who dwelt near them came, that they told us ten times, "From whatever place you turn, *they will be* upon us."

13 Therefore I positioned *men* behind the lower parts of the wall, at the openings; and I set the people according to their families, with their swords, their spears, and their bows. 14 And I looked, and arose and said to the nobles, to the leaders, and to the rest of the people, "Do not be afraid of them. Remember the Lord, great and awesome, and fight for your brethren, your sons, your daughters, your wives, and your houses."

15 And it happened, when our enemies heard that it was known to us, and *that* God had brought their plot to nothing, that all of us returned to the wall, everyone to his work. 16 So it was, from that time on, *that* half of my servants worked at construction, while the other half held the spears, the shields, the bows, and *wore* armor; and the leaders *were* behind all the house of Judah. 17 Those who built on the wall, and those who carried burdens, loaded themselves so that with one hand they worked at construction, and with the other held a weapon. 18 Every one of the builders had his sword girded at his side as he built. And the one who sounded the trumpet *was* beside me.

19 Then I said to the nobles, the rulers, and the rest of the people, "The work *is* great and extensive, and we are separated far from one another on the wall. 20 Wherever you hear the sound of the trumpet, rally to us there. Our God will fight for us."

21 So we labored in the work, and half of *the men* held the spears from daybreak until the stars appeared. 22 At the same time I also said to the people, "Let each man and his servant stay at night in Jerusalem, that they may be our guard by night and a working party by day." 23 So neither I, my brethren, my servants, nor the men of the guard who followed me took off our clothes, *except* that everyone took them off for washing.

5 And there was a great outcry of the people and their wives against their Jewish brethren. 2 For there were those who said, "We, our sons, and our daughters *are* many; therefore let us get grain, that we may eat and live."

מִפְּנֵיהֶֽם: 4 וַיֹּ֣אמֶר יְהוּדָ֔ה כָּשַׁל֙ כֹּ֣חַ הַסַּבָּ֔ל וְהֶעָפָ֖ר הַרְבֵּ֑ה וַאֲנַ֙חְנוּ֙ לֹ֣א נוּכַ֔ל לִבְנ֖וֹת בַּחוֹמָֽה: 5 וַיֹּאמְר֣וּ צָרֵ֗ינוּ לֹ֤א יֵֽדְעוּ֙ וְלֹ֣א יִרְא֔וּ עַ֛ד אֲשֶׁר־נָב֥וֹא אֶל־ תּוֹכָ֖ם וַהֲרַגְנ֑וּם וְהִשְׁבַּ֖תְנוּ אֶת־הַמְּלָאכָֽה: 6 וַיְהִ֞י כַּאֲשֶׁר־בָּ֣אוּ הַיְּהוּדִ֗ים הַיֹּשְׁבִים֙ אֶצְלָ֔ם וַיֹּ֥אמְרוּ לָ֖נוּ עֶ֣שֶׂר פְּעָמִ֑ים מִכָּל־הַמְּקֹמ֖וֹת אֲשֶׁר־תָּשׁ֥וּבוּ עָלֵֽינוּ: 7 וָֽאַעֲמִ֞יד מִֽתַּחְתִּיּ֧וֹת לַמָּק֛וֹם מֵאַחֲרֵ֥י לַחוֹמָ֖ה בַּצְּחִחִיִּ֑ים‡ וָֽאַעֲמִ֤יד אֶת־הָעָם֙ לְמִשְׁפָּח֔וֹת עִם־ חַרְבֹתֵיהֶ֥ם רָמְחֵיהֶ֖ם וְקַשְּׁתֹתֵיהֶֽם: 8 וָאֵ֖רֶא וָאָק֑וּם וָאֹמַ֞ר אֶל־הַחֹרִ֤ים וְאֶל־הַסְּגָנִים֙ וְאֶל־יֶ֣תֶר הָעָ֔ם אַל־תִּֽירְא֖וּ מִפְּנֵיהֶ֑ם אֶת־אֲדֹנָ֞י הַגָּד֤וֹל וְהַנּוֹרָא֙ זְכֹ֔רוּ וְהִֽלָּחֲמ֗וּ עַל־אֲחֵיכֶם֙ בְּנֵיכֶ֣ם וּבְנֹתֵיכֶ֔ם נְשֵׁיכֶ֖ם וּבָתֵּיכֶֽם: פ

9 וַיְהִ֞י כַּאֲשֶׁר־שָׁמְע֤וּ אוֹיְבֵ֙ינוּ֙ כִּי־נ֣וֹדַֽע לָ֔נוּ וַיָּ֥פֶר הָאֱלֹהִ֖ים אֶת־עֲצָתָ֑ם וַנָּ֙שָׁב֙‡ כֻּלָּ֣נוּ אֶל־הַֽחוֹמָ֔ה אִ֖ישׁ אֶל־מְלַאכְתּֽוֹ: 10 וַיְהִ֣י | מִן־הַיּ֣וֹם הַה֗וּא חֲצִ֣י נְעָרַי֮ עֹשִׂ֣ים בַּמְּלָאכָה֒ וְחֶצְיָ֗ם מַחֲזִיקִים֙ וְהָרְמָחִ֣ים הַמָּֽגִנִּ֔ים וְהַקְּשָׁת֖וֹת וְהַשִּׁרְיֹנִ֑ים וְהַשָּׂרִ֕ים אַחֲרֵ֖י כָּל־ בֵּ֥ית יְהוּדָֽה: 11 הַבּוֹנִ֧ים בַּחוֹמָ֛ה וְהַנֹּשְׂאִ֥ים בַּסֶּ֖בֶל עֹמְשִׂ֑ים בְּאַחַ֤ת יָדוֹ֙ עֹשֶׂ֣ה בַמְּלָאכָ֔ה וְאַחַ֖ת מַחֲזֶ֥קֶת הַשָּֽׁלַח: 12 וְהַבּוֹנִ֗ים אִ֚ישׁ חַרְבּ֣וֹ אֲסוּרִ֣ים עַל־מָתְנָ֔יו וּבוֹנִ֑ים וְהַתּוֹקֵ֥עַ בַּשּׁוֹפָ֖ר אֶצְלִֽי: 13 וָאֹמַ֞ר אֶל־הַחֹרִ֤ים וְאֶל־הַסְּגָנִים֙ וְאֶל־יֶ֣תֶר הָעָ֔ם הַמְּלָאכָ֥ה הַרְבֵּ֖ה וּרְחָבָ֑ה וַאֲנַ֗חְנוּ נִפְרָדִים֙ עַל־הַ֣חוֹמָ֔ה רְחוֹקִ֖ים אִ֥ישׁ מֵאָחִֽיו: 14 בִּמְק֗וֹם אֲשֶׁ֤ר תִּשְׁמְעוּ֙ אֶת־ק֣וֹל הַשּׁוֹפָ֔ר שָׁ֖מָּה תִּקָּבְצ֣וּ אֵלֵ֑ינוּ אֱלֹהֵ֖ינוּ יִלָּ֥חֶם לָֽנוּ: 15 וַאֲנַ֖חְנוּ עֹשִׂ֣ים בַּמְּלָאכָ֑ה וְחֶצְיָ֗ם מַחֲזִיקִים֙ בָּֽרְמָחִ֔ים מֵעֲל֣וֹת הַשַּׁ֔חַר עַ֖ד צֵ֥את הַכּוֹכָבִֽים: 16 גַּ֣ם בָּעֵ֤ת הַהִיא֙ אָמַ֣רְתִּי לָעָ֔ם אִ֣ישׁ וְנַעֲר֔וֹ יָלִ֖ינוּ בְּת֣וֹךְ יְרוּשָׁלָ֑͏ִם וְהָֽיוּ־ לָ֧נוּ הַלַּ֛יְלָה מִשְׁמָ֖ר וְהַיּ֥וֹם מְלָאכָֽה: 17 וְאֵ֣ין אֲנִ֗י וְאַחַ֤י וּנְעָרַי֙ וְאַנְשֵׁ֣י הַמִּשְׁמָ֔ר אֲשֶׁ֖ר אַחֲרָ֑י אֵֽין־אֲנַ֜חְנוּ פֹשְׁטִ֤ים בְּגָדֵ֙ינוּ֙ אִ֖ישׁ שִׁלְח֥וֹ הַמָּֽיִם: ס

ה וַתְּהִ֨י צַעֲקַ֥ת הָעָ֛ם וּנְשֵׁיהֶ֖ם גְּדוֹלָ֑ה אֶל־ אֲחֵיהֶ֖ם הַיְּהוּדִֽים: 2 וְיֵ֤שׁ אֲשֶׁר֙ אֹמְרִ֔ים בָּנֵ֥ינוּ וּבְנֹתֵ֖ינוּ אֲנַ֣חְנוּ רַבִּ֑ים וְנִקְחָ֥ה דָגָ֖ן וְנֹאכְלָ֥ה וְנִחְיֶֽה:

ד 7 בַּצְּחִחִיִּ֑ים   9 וַנָּ֙שָׁב֙

3There were also *some* who said, "We have mortgaged our lands and vineyards and houses, that we might buy grain because of the famine."

4There were also those who said, "We have borrowed money for the king's tax *on* our lands and vineyards. 5Yet now our flesh *is* as the flesh of our brethren, our children as their children; and indeed we are forcing our sons and our daughters to be slaves, and *some* of our daughters have been brought into slavery. *It is* not in our power *to redeem them,* for other men have our lands and vineyards."

6And I became very angry when I heard their outcry and these words. 7After serious thought, I rebuked the nobles and rulers, and said to them, "Each of you is exacting usury from his brother." So I called a great assembly against them. 8And I said to them, "According to our ability we have redeemed our Jewish brethren who were sold to the nations. Now indeed, will you even sell your brethren? Or should they be sold to us?"

Then they were silenced and found nothing *to say.* 9Then I said, "What you are doing *is* not good. Should you not walk in the fear of our God because of the reproach of the nations, our enemies? 10I also, *with* my brethren and my servants, am lending them money and grain. Please, let us stop this usury! 11Restore now to them, even this day, their lands, their vineyards, their olive groves, and their houses, also a hundredth of the money and the grain, the new wine and the oil, that you have charged them."

12So they said, "We will restore *it,* and will require nothing from them; we will do as you say."

Then I called the priests, and required an oath from them that they would do according to this promise. 13Then I shook out the fold of my garment and said, "So may God shake out each man from his house, and from his property, who does not perform this promise. Even thus may he be shaken out and emptied."

And all the assembly said, "Amen!" and praised the LORD. Then the people did according to this promise.

14Moreover, from the time that I was appointed to be governor in the land of Judah, from the twentieth year until the thirty-second year of King Artaxerxes, twelve years, neither I nor my brothers ate the governor's provisions. 15But the former governors who *were* before me laid burdens on the people, and took from them bread and wine, besides forty shekels of silver. Yes, even their servants bore rule over the people, but I did not do so, because of the fear of God. 16Indeed, I also

3 וְיֵשׁ אֲשֶׁר אֹמְרִים שְׂדֹתֵינוּ וּכְרָמֵינוּ וּבָתֵּינוּ אֲנַחְנוּ עֹרְבִים וְנִקְחָה דָגָן בָּרָעָב: 4 וְיֵשׁ אֲשֶׁר אֹמְרִים לָוִינוּ כֶסֶף לְמִדַּת הַמֶּלֶךְ שְׂדֹתֵינוּ וּכְרָמֵינוּ: 5 וְעַתָּה כִּבְשַׂר אַחֵינוּ בְּשָׂרֵנוּ כִּבְנֵיהֶם בָּנֵינוּ וְהִנֵּה אֲנַחְנוּ כֹבְשִׁים אֶת־בָּנֵינוּ וְאֶת־בְּנֹתֵינוּ לַעֲבָדִים וְיֵשׁ מִבְּנֹתֵינוּ נִכְבָּשׁוֹת וְאֵין לְאֵל יָדֵנוּ וּשְׂדֹתֵינוּ וּכְרָמֵינוּ לַאֲחֵרִים: 6 וַיִּחַר לִי מְאֹד כַּאֲשֶׁר שָׁמַעְתִּי אֶת־ זַעֲקָתָם וְאֵת הַדְּבָרִים הָאֵלֶּה: 7 וַיִּמָּלֵךְ לִבִּי עָלַי וָאָרִיבָה אֶת־הַחֹרִים וְאֶת־הַסְּגָנִים וָאֹמְרָה לָהֶם מַשָּׁא אִישׁ־בְּאָחִיו אַתֶּם נֹשִׁאיםᵖ וָאֶתֵּן עֲלֵיהֶם קְהִלָּה גְדוֹלָה: 8 וָאֹמְרָה לָהֶם אֲנַחְנוּ קָנִינוּ אֶת־ אַחֵינוּ הַיְּהוּדִים הַנִּמְכָּרִים לַגּוֹיִם כְּדֵי בָנוּ וְגַם־ אַתֶּם תִּמְכְּרוּ אֶת־אֲחֵיכֶם וְנִמְכְּרוּ־לָנוּ וַיַּחֲרִישׁוּ וְלֹא מָצְאוּ דָּבָר: ס 9 וַיֹּאמֶרᵖ לֹא־טוֹב הַדָּבָר אֲשֶׁר־אַתֶּם עֹשִׂים הֲלוֹא בְּיִרְאַת אֱלֹהֵינוּ תֵּלֵכוּ מֵחֶרְפַּת הַגּוֹיִם אוֹיְבֵינוּ: 10 וְגַם־אֲנִי אַחַי וּנְעָרַי נֹשִׁים בָּהֶם כֶּסֶף וְדָגָן נַעַזְבָה־נָּא אֶת־הַמַּשָּׁא הַזֶּה: 11 הָשִׁיבוּ נָא לָהֶם כְּהַיּוֹם שְׂדֹתֵיהֶם כַּרְמֵיהֶם זֵיתֵיהֶם וּבָתֵּיהֶם וּמְאַת הַכֶּסֶף וְהַדָּגָן הַתִּירוֹשׁ וְהַיִּצְהָר אֲשֶׁר אַתֶּם נֹשִׁים בָּהֶם: 12 וַיֹּאמְרוּ נָשִׁיב וּמֵהֶם לֹא נְבַקֵּשׁ כֵּן נַעֲשֶׂה כַּאֲשֶׁר אַתָּה אוֹמֵר וָאֶקְרָא אֶת־הַכֹּהֲנִים וָאַשְׁבִּיעֵם לַעֲשׂוֹת כַּדָּבָר הַזֶּה: 13 גַּם־חָצְנִי נָעַרְתִּי וָאֹמְרָה כָּכָה יְנַעֵר הָאֱלֹהִים אֶת־כָּל־הָאִישׁ אֲשֶׁר לֹא־יָקִים אֶת־הַדָּבָר הַזֶּה מִבֵּיתוֹ וּמִיגִיעוֹ וְכָכָה יִהְיֶה נָעוּר וָרֵק וַיֹּאמְרוּ כָל־הַקָּהָל אָמֵן וַיְהַלְלוּ אֶת־יְהוָה וַיַּעַשׂ הָעָם כַּדָּבָר הַזֶּה: 14 גַּם מִיּוֹם ׀ אֲשֶׁר־צִוָּה אֹתִי לִהְיוֹת פֶּחָם בְּאֶרֶץ יְהוּדָה מִשְּׁנַת עֶשְׂרִים וְעַד שְׁנַת שְׁלֹשִׁים וּשְׁתַּיִם לְאַרְתַּחְשַׁסְתְּא הַמֶּלֶךְ שָׁנִים שְׁתֵּים עֶשְׂרֵה אֲנִי וְאַחַי לֶחֶם הַפֶּחָה לֹא אָכַלְתִּי: 15 וְהַפַּחוֹת הָרִאשֹׁנִים אֲשֶׁר־לְפָנַי הִכְבִּידוּ עַל־הָעָם וַיִּקְחוּ מֵהֶם בְּלֶחֶם וָיַיִן אַחַר כֶּסֶף־שְׁקָלִים אַרְבָּעִים גַּם נַעֲרֵיהֶם שָׁלְטוּ עַל־הָעָם וַאֲנִי לֹא־עָשִׂיתִי כֵן מִפְּנֵי יִרְאַת אֱלֹהִים: 16 וְגַם בִּמְלֶאכֶת הַחוֹמָה הַזֹּאת הֶחֱזַקְתִּי וְשָׂדֶה לֹא קָנִינוּ וְכָל־נְעָרַי קְבוּצִים

ה 7 נֹשִׁים 9 וָאֹמַר

continued the work on this wall, and we did not buy any land. All my servants *were* gathered there for the work.

17 And at my table *were* one hundred and fifty Jews and rulers, besides those who came to us from the nations around us. 18 Now *that* which was prepared daily *was* one ox *and* six choice sheep. Also fowl were prepared for me, and once every ten days an abundance of all kinds of wine. Yet in spite of this I did not demand the governor's provisions, because the bondage was heavy on this people.

19 Remember me, my God, for good, *according to* all that I have done for this people.

6 Now it happened when Sanballat, Tobiah, Geshem the Arab, and the rest of our enemies heard that I had rebuilt the wall, and *that* there were no breaks left in it (though at that time I had not hung the doors in the gates), 2 that Sanballat and Geshem sent to me, saying, "Come, let us meet together among the villages in the plain of Ono." But they thought to do me harm.

3 So I sent messengers to them, saying, "I *am* doing a great work, so that I cannot come down. Why should the work cease while I leave it and go down to you?"

4 But they sent me this message four times, and I answered them in the same manner.

5 Then Sanballat sent his servant to me as before, the fifth time, with an open letter in his hand. 6 In it *was* written:

It is reported among the nations, and Geshem says, *that* you and the Jews plan to rebel, therefore, according to these rumors, you are rebuilding the wall, that you may be their king. 7 And you have also appointed prophets to proclaim concerning you at Jerusalem, saying, "*There is* a king in Judah!" Now these matters will be reported to the king. So come, therefore, and let us consult together.

8 Then I sent to him, saying, "No such things as you say are being done, but you invent them in your own heart."

9 For they all *were trying to* make us afraid, saying, "Their hands will be weakened in the work, and it will not be done."

Now therefore, O God, strengthen my hands.

10 Afterward I came to the house of Shemaiah the son of Delaiah, the son of Mehetabel, who *was* a secret informer; and he said, "Let us meet together in the house of God, within the temple, and let us close the doors of the temple, for they are coming to kill you; indeed, at night they will come to kill you."

שָׁם עַל־הַמְּלָאכָה: 17 וְהַיְּהוּדִים וְהַסְּגָנִים מֵאָה וַחֲמִשִּׁים אִישׁ וְהַבָּאִים אֵלֵינוּ מִן־הַגּוֹיִם אֲשֶׁר־סְבִיבֹתֵינוּ עַל־שֻׁלְחָנִי: 18 וַאֲשֶׁר הָיָה נַעֲשֶׂה לְיוֹם אֶחָד שׁוֹר אֶחָד צֹאן שֵׁשׁ־בְּרֻרוֹת וְצִפֳּרִים נַעֲשׂוּ־לִי וּבֵין עֲשֶׂרֶת יָמִים בְּכָל־יַיִן לְהַרְבֵּה וְעִם־זֶה לֶחֶם הַפֶּחָה לֹא בִקַּשְׁתִּי כִּי־כָבְדָה הָעֲבֹדָה עַל־הָעָם הַזֶּה: 19 זָכְרָה־לִּי אֱלֹהַי לְטוֹבָה כֹּל אֲשֶׁר־עָשִׂיתִי עַל־הָעָם הַזֶּה: פ

וַ וַיְהִי כַאֲשֶׁר נִשְׁמַע לְסַנְבַלַּט וְטוֹבִיָּה וּלְגֶשֶׁם הָעַרְבִי וּלְיֶתֶר אֹיְבֵינוּ כִּי בָנִיתִי אֶת־הַחוֹמָה וְלֹא־נוֹתַר בָּהּ פָּרֶץ גַּם עַד־הָעֵת הַהִיא דְּלָתוֹת לֹא־הֶעֱמַדְתִּי בַשְּׁעָרִים: 2 וַיִּשְׁלַח סַנְבַלַּט וְגֶשֶׁם אֵלַי לֵאמֹר לְכָה וְנִוָּעֲדָה יַחְדָּו בַּכְּפִירִים בְּבִקְעַת אוֹנוֹ וְהֵמָּה חֹשְׁבִים לַעֲשׂוֹת לִי רָעָה: 3 וָאֶשְׁלְחָה עֲלֵיהֶם מַלְאָכִים לֵאמֹר מְלָאכָה גְדוֹלָה אֲנִי עֹשֶׂה וְלֹא אוּכַל לָרֶדֶת לָמָּה תִשְׁבַּת הַמְּלָאכָה כַּאֲשֶׁר אַרְפֶּהָ וְיָרַדְתִּי אֲלֵיכֶם: 4 וַיִּשְׁלְחוּ אֵלַי כַּדָּבָר הַזֶּה אַרְבַּע פְּעָמִים וָאָשִׁיב אוֹתָם כַּדָּבָר הַזֶּה: ס 5 וַיִּשְׁלַח אֵלַי סַנְבַלַּט כַּדָּבָר הַזֶּה פַּעַם חֲמִישִׁית אֶת־נַעֲרוֹ וְאִגֶּרֶת פְּתוּחָה בְּיָדוֹ: 6 כָּתוּב בָּהּ בַּגּוֹיִם נִשְׁמָע וְגַשְׁמוּ אֹמֵר אַתָּה וְהַיְּהוּדִים חֹשְׁבִים לִמְרוֹד עַל־כֵּן אַתָּה בוֹנֶה הַחוֹמָה וְאַתָּה הֹוֶה לָהֶם לְמֶלֶךְ כַּדְּבָרִים הָאֵלֶּה: 7 וְגַם־נְבִיאִים הֶעֱמַדְתָּ לִקְרֹא עָלֶיךָ בִירוּשָׁלִַם לֵאמֹר מֶלֶךְ בִּיהוּדָה וְעַתָּה יִשָּׁמַע לַמֶּלֶךְ כַּדְּבָרִים הָאֵלֶּה וְעַתָּה לְכָה וְנִוָּעֲצָה יַחְדָּו: ס 8 וָאֶשְׁלְחָה אֵלָיו לֵאמֹר לֹא נִהְיָה כַּדְּבָרִים הָאֵלֶּה אֲשֶׁר אַתָּה אוֹמֵר כִּי מִלִּבְּךָ אַתָּה בוֹדָאם: 9 כִּי כֻלָּם מְיָרְאִים אוֹתָנוּ לֵאמֹר יִרְפּוּ יְדֵיהֶם מִן־הַמְּלָאכָה וְלֹא תֵעָשֶׂה וְעַתָּה חַזֵּק אֶת־יָדָי: 10 וַאֲנִי־בָאתִי בֵּית שְׁמַעְיָה בֶן־דְּלָיָה בֶּן־מְהֵיטַבְאֵל וְהוּא עָצוּר וַיֹּאמֶר נִוָּעֵד אֶל־בֵּית הָאֱלֹהִים אֶל־תּוֹךְ הַהֵיכָל וְנִסְגְּרָה דַּלְתוֹת הַהֵיכָל

ו 8 בּוֹדָם

¹¹ And I said, "Should such a man as I flee? And who *is there* such as I who would go into the temple to save his life? I will not go in!" ¹² Then I perceived that God had not sent him at all, but that he pronounced *this* prophecy against me because Tobiah and Sanballat had hired him. ¹³ For this reason he *was* hired, that I should be afraid and act that way and sin, so *that* they might have *cause* for an evil report, that they might reproach me.

¹⁴ My God, remember Tobiah and Sanballat, according to these their works, and the prophetess Noadiah and the rest of the prophets who would have made me afraid.

¹⁵ So the wall was finished on the twenty-fifth *day* of Elul, in fifty-two days. ¹⁶ And it happened, when all our enemies heard *of it,* and all the nations around us saw *these things,* that they were very disheartened in their own eyes; for they perceived that this work was done by our God.

¹⁷ Also in those days the nobles of Judah sent many letters to Tobiah, and *the letters of* Tobiah came to them. ¹⁸ For many in Judah were pledged to him, because he was the son-in-law of Shechaniah the son of Arah, and his son Jehohanan had married the daughter of Meshullam the son of Berechiah. ¹⁹ Also they reported his good deeds before me, and reported my words to him. Tobiah sent letters to frighten me.

7 Then it was, when the wall was built and I had hung the doors, when the gatekeepers, the singers, and the Levites had been appointed, ² that I gave the charge of Jerusalem to my brother Hanani, and Hananiah the leader of the citadel, for he *was* a faithful man and feared God more than many.

³ And I said to them, "Do not let the gates of Jerusalem be opened until the sun is hot; and while they stand *guard,* let them shut and bar the doors; and appoint guards from among the inhabitants of Jerusalem, one at his watch station and another in front of his own house."

⁴ Now the city *was* large and spacious, but the people in it *were* few, and the houses *were* not rebuilt. ⁵ Then my God put it into my heart to gather the nobles, the rulers, and the people, that they might be registered by genealogy. And I found a register of the genealogy of those who had come up in the first *return,* and found written in it:

⁶ These *are* the people of the province who came back from the captivity, of those who had been carried away, whom

---

כִּי בָאִים לְהָרְגֶךָ וְלַיְלָה בָּאִים לְהָרְגֶךָ: ¹¹ וָאֹמְרָה הַאִישׁ כָּמוֹנִי יִבְרָח וּמִי כָמוֹנִי אֲשֶׁר־יָבוֹא אֶל־ הַהֵיכָל וָחָי לֹא אָבוֹא: ¹² וָאַכִּירָה וְהִנֵּה לֹא־אֱלֹהִים שְׁלָחוֹ כִּי הַנְּבוּאָה דִּבֶּר עָלַי וְטוֹבִיָּה וְסַנְבַלַּט שְׂכָרוֹ: ¹³ לְמַעַן שָׂכוּר הוּא לְמַעַן־אִירָא וְאֶעֱשֶׂה־ כֵּן וְחָטָאתִי וְהָיָה לָהֶם לְשֵׁם רָע לְמַעַן יְחָרְפוּנִי: פ

¹⁴ זָכְרָה אֱלֹהַי לְטוֹבִיָּה וּלְסַנְבַלַּט כְּמַעֲשָׂיו אֵלֶּה וְגַם לְנוֹעַדְיָה הַנְּבִיאָה וּלְיֶתֶר הַנְּבִיאִים אֲשֶׁר הָיוּ מְיָרְאִים אוֹתִי: ¹⁵ וַתִּשְׁלַם הַחוֹמָה בְּעֶשְׂרִים וַחֲמִשָּׁה לֶאֱלוּל לַחֲמִשִּׁים וּשְׁנַיִם יוֹם: פ

¹⁶ וַיְהִי כַּאֲשֶׁר שָׁמְעוּ כָּל־אוֹיְבֵינוּ וַיִּרְאוּ כָּל־הַגּוֹיִם אֲשֶׁר סְבִיבֹתֵינוּ וַיִּפְּלוּ מְאֹד בְּעֵינֵיהֶם וַיֵּדְעוּ כִּי מֵאֵת אֱלֹהֵינוּ נֶעֶשְׂתָה הַמְּלָאכָה הַזֹּאת: ¹⁷ גַּם ׀ בַּיָּמִים הָהֵם מַרְבִּים חֹרֵי יְהוּדָה אִגְּרֹתֵיהֶם הוֹלְכוֹת עַל־טוֹבִיָּה וַאֲשֶׁר לְטוֹבִיָּה בָּאוֹת אֲלֵיהֶם: ¹⁸ כִּי־ רַבִּים בִּיהוּדָה בַּעֲלֵי שְׁבוּעָה לוֹ כִּי־חָתָן הוּא לִשְׁכַנְיָה בֶן־אָרַח וִיהוֹחָנָן בְּנוֹ לָקַח אֶת־בַּת־מְשֻׁלָּם בֶּן בֶּרֶכְיָה: ¹⁹ גַּם טוֹבֹתָיו הָיוּ אֹמְרִים לְפָנַי וּדְבָרַי הָיוּ מוֹצִיאִים לוֹ אִגְּרוֹת שָׁלַח טוֹבִיָּה לְיָרְאֵנִי:

ז וַיְהִי כַּאֲשֶׁר נִבְנְתָה הַחוֹמָה וָאַעֲמִיד הַדְּלָתוֹת וַיִּפָּקְדוּ הַשּׁוֹעֲרִים וְהַמְשֹׁרְרִים וְהַלְוִיִּם: ² וָאֲצַוֶּה אֶת־חֲנָנִי אָחִי וְאֶת־חֲנַנְיָה שַׂר הַבִּירָה עַל־יְרוּשָׁלִָם כִּי־הוּא כְּאִישׁ אֱמֶת וְיָרֵא אֶת־הָאֱלֹהִים מֵרַבִּים: ³ וָאֹמַר לָהֶם לֹא יִפָּתְחוּ שַׁעֲרֵי יְרוּשָׁלִַם עַד־חֹם הַשֶּׁמֶשׁ וְעַד הֵם עֹמְדִים יָגִיפוּ הַדְּלָתוֹת וֶאֱחֹזוּ וְהַעֲמֵיד מִשְׁמְרוֹת יֹשְׁבֵי יְרוּשָׁלִַם אִישׁ בְּמִשְׁמָרוֹ וְאִישׁ נֶגֶד בֵּיתוֹ: ⁴ וְהָעִיר רַחֲבַת יָדַיִם וּגְדוֹלָה וְהָעָם מְעַט בְּתוֹכָהּ וְאֵין בָּתִּים בְּנוּיִם: ⁵ וַיִּתֵּן אֱלֹהַי אֶל־לִבִּי וָאֶקְבְּצָה אֶת־הַחֹרִים וְאֶת־הַסְּגָנִים וְאֶת־הָעָם לְהִתְיַחֵשׂ וָאֶמְצָא סֵפֶר הַיַּחַשׂ הָעוֹלִים בָּרִאשׁוֹנָה וָאֶמְצָא כָּתוּב בּוֹ: פ

⁶ אֵלֶּה ׀ בְּנֵי הַמְּדִינָה הָעֹלִים מִשְּׁבִי הַגּוֹלָה אֲשֶׁר הֶגְלָה נְבוּכַדְנֶצַּר מֶלֶךְ בָּבֶל וַיָּשׁוּבוּ לִירוּשָׁלִַם

ז 3 וָאֹמַר

Nebuchadnezzar the king of Babylon had carried away, and who returned to Jerusalem and Judah, everyone to his city.

7 Those who came with Zerubbabel *were* Jeshua, Nehemiah, Azariah, Raamiah, Nahamani, Mordecai, Bilshan, Mispereth, Bigvai, Nehum, and Baanah.

The number of the men of the people of Israel: 8 the sons of Parosh, two thousand one hundred and seventy-two;

9 the sons of Shephatiah, three hundred and seventy-two;

10 the sons of Arah, six hundred and fifty-two;

11 the sons of Pahath-Moab, of the sons of Jeshua and Joab, two thousand eight hundred and eighteen;

12 the sons of Elam, one thousand two hundred and fifty-four;

13 the sons of Zattu, eight hundred and forty-five;

14 the sons of Zaccai, seven hundred and sixty;

15 the sons of Binnui, six hundred and forty-eight;

16 the sons of Bebai, six hundred and twenty-eight;

17 the sons of Azgad, two thousand three hundred and twenty-two;

18 the sons of Adonikam, six hundred and sixty-seven;

19 the sons of Bigvai, two thousand and sixty-seven;

20 the sons of Adin, six hundred and fifty-five;

21 the sons of Ater of Hezekiah, ninety-eight;

22 the sons of Hashum, three hundred and twenty-eight;

23 the sons of Bezai, three hundred and twenty-four;

24 the sons of Hariph, one hundred and twelve;

25 the sons of Gibeon, ninety-five;

26 the men of Bethlehem and Netophah, one hundred and eighty-eight;

27 the men of Anathoth, one hundred and twenty-eight;

28 the men of Beth Azmaveth, forty-two;

29 the men of Kirjath Jearim, Chephirah, and Beeroth, seven hundred and forty-three;

30 the men of Ramah and Geba, six hundred and twenty-one;

7 הַבָּאִים עִם־זְרֻבָּבֶל יֵשׁוּעַ וְלִיהוּדָה אִישׁ לְעִירוֹ:

נְחֶמְיָה עֲזַרְיָה רַעַמְיָה נַחֲמָנִי מָרְדֳּכַי בִּלְשָׁן מִסְפֶּרֶת בִּגְוַי נְחוּם בַּעֲנָה מִסְפַּר אַנְשֵׁי עַם

יִשְׂרָאֵל: ס 8 בְּנֵי פַרְעֹשׁ אַלְפַּיִם מֵאָה וְשִׁבְעִים

וּשְׁנָיִם: ס 9 בְּנֵי שְׁפַטְיָה שְׁלֹשׁ מֵאוֹת שִׁבְעִים

וּשְׁנָיִם: ס 10 בְּנֵי אָרַח שֵׁשׁ מֵאוֹת חֲמִשִּׁים

וּשְׁנָיִם: ס 11 בְּנֵי־פַחַת מוֹאָב לִבְנֵי יֵשׁוּעַ וְיוֹאָב

אַלְפַּיִם וּשְׁמֹנֶה מֵאוֹת שְׁמֹנָה עָשָׂר: ס 12 בְּנֵי

עֵילָם אֶלֶף מָאתַיִם חֲמִשִּׁים וְאַרְבָּעָה: ס 13 בְּנֵי

זַתּוּא שְׁמֹנֶה מֵאוֹת אַרְבָּעִים וַחֲמִשָּׁה: ס 14 בְּנֵי

זַכָּי שְׁבַע מֵאוֹת וְשִׁשִּׁים: ס 15 בְּנֵי בִנּוּי

שֵׁשׁ מֵאוֹת אַרְבָּעִים וּשְׁמֹנָה: ס 16 בְּנֵי בֵבָי

שֵׁשׁ מֵאוֹת עֶשְׂרִים וּשְׁמֹנָה: ס 17 בְּנֵי עַזְגָּד

אַלְפַּיִם שְׁלֹשׁ מֵאוֹת עֶשְׂרִים וּשְׁנָיִם: ס 18 בְּנֵי

אֲדֹנִיקָם שֵׁשׁ מֵאוֹת שִׁשִּׁים וְשִׁבְעָה: ס 19 בְּנֵי

בִגְוָי אַלְפַּיִם שִׁשִּׁים וְשִׁבְעָה: ס 20 בְּנֵי עָדִין

שֵׁשׁ מֵאוֹת חֲמִשִּׁים וַחֲמִשָּׁה: ס 21 בְּנֵי־אָטֵר

לְחִזְקִיָּה תִּשְׁעִים וּשְׁמֹנָה: ס 22 בְּנֵי חָשֻׁם

שְׁלֹשׁ מֵאוֹת עֶשְׂרִים וּשְׁמֹנָה: ס 23 בְּנֵי בֵצָי

שְׁלֹשׁ מֵאוֹת עֶשְׂרִים וְאַרְבָּעָה: ס 24 בְּנֵי

חָרִיף מֵאָה שְׁנֵים עָשָׂר: ס 25 בְּנֵי גִבְעוֹן

תִּשְׁעִים וַחֲמִשָּׁה: ס 26 אַנְשֵׁי בֵית־לֶחֶם וּנְטֹפָה

מֵאָה שְׁמֹנִים וּשְׁמֹנָה: ס 27 אַנְשֵׁי עֲנָתוֹת

מֵאָה עֶשְׂרִים וּשְׁמֹנָה: ס 28 אַנְשֵׁי בֵית־

עַזְמָוֶת אַרְבָּעִים וּשְׁנָיִם: ס 29 אַנְשֵׁי קִרְיַת

יְעָרִים כְּפִירָה וּבְאֵרוֹת שְׁבַע מֵאוֹת אַרְבָּעִים

וּשְׁלֹשָׁה: ס 30 אַנְשֵׁי הָרָמָה וָגֶבַע שֵׁשׁ מֵאוֹת

³¹the men of Michmas, one hundred and twenty-two;

³²the men of Bethel and Ai, one hundred and twenty-three;

³³the men of the other Nebo, fifty-two;

³⁴the sons of the other Elam, one thousand two hundred and fifty-four;

³⁵the sons of Harim, three hundred and twenty;

³⁶the sons of Jericho, three hundred and forty-five;

³⁷the sons of Lod, Hadid, and Ono, seven hundred and twenty-one;

³⁸the sons of Senaah, three thousand nine hundred and thirty.

39 The priests: the sons of Jedaiah, of the house of Jeshua, nine hundred and seventy-three;

⁴⁰the sons of Immer, one thousand and fifty-two;

⁴¹the sons of Pashhur, one thousand two hundred and forty-seven;

⁴²the sons of Harim, one thousand and seventeen.

43 The Levites: the sons of Jeshua, of Kadmiel, *and* of the sons of Hodevah, seventy-four.

44 The singers: the sons of Asaph, one hundred and forty-eight.

45 The gatekeepers: the sons of Shallum, the sons of Ater, the sons of Talmon, the sons of Akkub, the sons of Hatita, the sons of Shobai, one hundred and thirty-eight.

46 The Nethinim: the sons of Ziha, the sons of Hasupha, the sons of Tabbaoth, ⁴⁷the sons of Keros, the sons of Sia, the sons of Padon, ⁴⁸the sons of Lebana, the sons of Hagaba, the sons of Salmai, ⁴⁹the sons of Hanan, the sons of Giddel, the sons of Gahar, ⁵⁰the sons of Reaiah, the sons of Rezin, the sons of Nekoda, ⁵¹the sons of Gazzam, the sons of Uzza, the sons of Paseah,

31 אַנְשֵׁי מִכְמָס מֵאָה עֶשְׂרִים וְאֶחָד: ס 32 אַנְשֵׁי בֵית־אֵל וְהָעָי מֵאָה עֶשְׂרִים וּשְׁלֹשָׁה: ס 33 אַנְשֵׁי נְבוֹ אַחֵר חֲמִשִּׁים וּשְׁנָיִם: ס 34 בְּנֵי עֵילָם אַחֵר אֶלֶף מָאתַיִם חֲמִשִּׁים וְאַרְבָּעָה: ס 35 בְּנֵי חָרִם שְׁלֹשׁ מֵאוֹת וְעֶשְׂרִים: ס 36 בְּנֵי יְרֵחוֹ שְׁלֹשׁ מֵאוֹת אַרְבָּעִים וַחֲמִשָּׁה: ס 37 בְּנֵי־לֹד חָדִיד וְאוֹנוֹ שְׁבַע מֵאוֹת וְעֶשְׂרִים וְאֶחָד: ס 38 בְּנֵי סְנָאָה שְׁלֹשֶׁת אֲלָפִים תְּשַׁע מֵאוֹת וּשְׁלֹשִׁים: פ

39 הַכֹּהֲנִים בְּנֵי יְדַעְיָה לְבֵית יֵשׁוּעַ תְּשַׁע מֵאוֹת שִׁבְעִים וּשְׁלֹשָׁה: ס 40 בְּנֵי אִמֵּר אֶלֶף חֲמִשִּׁים וּשְׁנָיִם: ס 41 בְּנֵי פַשְׁחוּר אֶלֶף מָאתַיִם אַרְבָּעִים וְשִׁבְעָה: ס 42 בְּנֵי חָרִם אֶלֶף שִׁבְעָה עָשָׂר: פ

43 הַלְוִיִּם בְּנֵי־יֵשׁוּעַ לְקַדְמִיאֵל לִבְנֵי לְהוֹדְוָה שִׁבְעִים וְאַרְבָּעָה: ס 44 הַמְשֹׁרְרִים בְּנֵי אָסָף מֵאָה אַרְבָּעִים וּשְׁמֹנָה: ס 45 הַשֹּׁעֲרִים בְּנֵי שַׁלּוּם בְּנֵי־אָטֵר בְּנֵי־טַלְמֹן בְּנֵי־עַקּוּב בְּנֵי חֲטִיטָא בְּנֵי שֹׁבָי מֵאָה שְׁלֹשִׁים וּשְׁמֹנָה: ס 46 הַנְּתִינִים בְּנֵי־צִחָא בְנֵי־חֲשֻׂפָא בְּנֵי טַבָּעוֹת: 47 בְּנֵי־קֵירֹס בְּנֵי־סִיעָא בְּנֵי פָדוֹן: 48 בְּנֵי־לְבָנָה בְנֵי־חֲגָבָה בְּנֵי שַׁלְמָי: 49 בְּנֵי־חָנָן בְּנֵי־גִדֵּל בְּנֵי־גָחַר: 50 בְּנֵי־רְאָיָה בְנֵי־רְצִין בְּנֵי נְקוֹדָא: 51 בְּנֵי־גַזָּם בְּנֵי־עֻזָּא בְּנֵי

52 the sons of Besai,
the sons of Meunim,
the sons of Nephishesim,
53 the sons of Bakbuk,
the sons of Hakupha,
the sons of Harhur,
54 the sons of Bazlith,
the sons of Mehida,
the sons of Harsha,
55 the sons of Barkos,
the sons of Sisera,
the sons of Tamah,
56 the sons of Neziah,
and the sons of Hatipha.

57 The sons of Solomon's servants: the sons of Sotai,
the sons of Sophereth,
the sons of Perida,
58 the sons of Jaala,
the sons of Darkon,
the sons of Giddel,
59 the sons of Shephatiah,
the sons of Hattil,
the sons of Pochereth of Zebaim,
and the children of Amon.
60 All the Nethinim, and the sons of Solomon's servants, *were* three hundred and ninety-two.

61 And these *were* the ones who came up from Tel Melah, Tel Harsha, Cherub, Addon, and Immer, but they could not identify their father's house nor their lineage, whether they *were* of Israel: 62 the sons of Delaiah, the sons of Tobiah, the sons of Nekoda, six hundred and forty-two;
63 and of the priests: the sons of Habaiah, the sons of Koz, the sons of Barzillai, who took a wife of the daughters of Barzillai the Gileadite, and was called by their name.
64 These sought their listing *among* those who were registered by genealogy, but it was not found; therefore they were excluded from the priesthood as defiled. 65 And the governor said to them that they should not eat of the most holy things till a priest could consult with the Urim and Thummim.

66 Altogether the whole assembly *was* forty-two thousand three hundred and sixty, 67 besides their male and female servants, of whom *there were* seven thousand three hundred and thirty-seven; and they had two hundred and

פֶּסַח: 52 בְּנֵי־בֵסַי בְּנֵי־מְעוּנִים בְּנֵי נְפוּשְׁסִיםᴾ:

53 בְּנֵי־בַקְבּוּק בְּנֵי־חֲקוּפָא בְּנֵי חַרְחוּר:

54 בְּנֵי־בַצְלִית בְּנֵי־מְחִידָא בְּנֵי חַרְשָׁא:

55 בְּנֵי־בַרְקוֹס בְּנֵי־סִיסְרָא בְּנֵי־תָמַח:

56 בְּנֵי נְצִיחַ בְּנֵי חֲטִיפָא:

57 בְּנֵי עַבְדֵי שְׁלֹמֹה בְּנֵי־סוֹטַי

בְּנֵי־סוֹפֶרֶת בְּנֵי פְרִידָא:

58 בְּנֵי־יַעְלָא בְנֵי־דַרְקוֹן בְּנֵי גִדֵּל:

59 בְּנֵי שְׁפַטְיָה בְנֵי־חַטִּיל

בְּנֵי פֹּכֶרֶת הַצְּבָיִים בְּנֵי אָמוֹן:

60 כָּל־הַנְּתִינִים וּבְנֵי עַבְדֵי שְׁלֹמֹה שְׁלֹשׁ מֵאוֹת

תִּשְׁעִים וּשְׁנָיִם: פ

61 וְאֵלֶּה הָעוֹלִים מִתֵּל מֶלַח תֵּל חַרְשָׁא כְּרוּב

אַדּוֹן וְאִמֵּר וְלֹא יָכְלוּ לְהַגִּיד בֵּית־אֲבוֹתָם וְזַרְעָם

אִם מִיִּשְׂרָאֵל הֵם: 62 בְּנֵי־דְלָיָה בְנֵי־טוֹבִיָּה בְּנֵי

נְקוֹדָא שֵׁשׁ מֵאוֹת וְאַרְבָּעִים וּשְׁנָיִם: ס 63 וּמִן־

הַכֹּהֲנִים בְּנֵי חֳבַיָּה בְּנֵי הַקּוֹץ בְּנֵי בַרְזִלַּי אֲשֶׁר לָקַח

מִבְּנוֹת בַּרְזִלַּי הַגִּלְעָדִי אִשָּׁה וַיִּקָּרֵא עַל־שְׁמָם:

64 אֵלֶּה בִּקְשׁוּ כְתָבָם הַמִּתְיַחְשִׂים וְלֹא נִמְצָא

וַיְגֹאֲלוּ מִן־הַכְּהֻנָּה: 65 וַיֹּאמֶר הַתִּרְשָׁתָא לָהֶם

אֲשֶׁר לֹא־יֹאכְלוּ מִקֹּדֶשׁ הַקֳּדָשִׁים עַד עֲמֹד הַכֹּהֵן

לְאוּרִים וְתֻמִּים: 66 כָּל־הַקָּהָל כְּאֶחָד אַרְבַּע רִבּוֹא

אַלְפַּיִם שְׁלֹשׁ־מֵאוֹת וְשִׁשִּׁים: 67 מִלְּבַד עַבְדֵיהֶם

וְאַמְהֹתֵיהֶם אֵלֶּה שִׁבְעַת אֲלָפִים שְׁלֹשׁ מֵאוֹת

שְׁלֹשִׁים וְשִׁבְעָה וְלָהֶם מְשֹׁרְרִים וּמְשֹׁרְרוֹת מָאתָיִם:

forty-five men and women singers. ⁶⁸Their horses were seven hundred and thirty-six, their mules two hundred and forty-five, ⁶⁹ *their* camels four hundred and thirty-five, *and* donkeys six thousand seven hundred and twenty.

⁷⁰ And some of the heads of the fathers' houses gave to the work. The governor gave to the treasury one thousand gold drachmas, fifty basins, and five hundred and thirty priestly garments. ⁷¹ Some of the heads of the fathers' *houses* gave to the treasury of the work twenty thousand gold drachmas, and two thousand two hundred silver minas. ⁷² And that which the rest of the people gave *was* twenty thousand gold drachmas, two thousand silver minas, and sixty-seven priestly garments.

⁷³ So the priests, the Levites, the gatekeepers, the singers, *some* of the people, the Nethinim, and all Israel dwelt in their cities.

When the seventh month came, the children of Israel *were* in their cities.

8 Now all the people gathered together as one man in the open square that *was* in front of the Water Gate; and they told Ezra the scribe to bring the Book of the Law of Moses, which the LORD had commanded Israel. ² So Ezra the priest brought the Law before the assembly of men and women and all who *could* hear with understanding on the first day of the seventh month. ³ Then he read from it in the open square that *was* in front of the Water Gate from morning until midday, before the men and women and those who could understand; and the ears of all the people *were attentive* to the Book of the Law.

⁴ So Ezra the scribe stood on a platform of wood which they had made for the purpose; and beside him, at his right hand, stood Mattithiah, Shema, Anaiah, Urijah, Hilkiah, and Maaseiah; and at his left hand Pedaiah, Mishael, Malchijah, Hashum, Hashbadana, Zechariah, *and* Meshullam. ⁵ And Ezra opened the book in the sight of all the people, for he was *standing* above all the people; and when he opened it, all the people stood up. ⁶ And Ezra blessed the LORD, the great God.

Then all the people answered, "Amen, Amen!" while lifting up their hands. And they bowed their heads and worshiped the LORD with *their* faces to the ground.

68 גְּמַלִּים אַרְבַּע מֵאֹות ס וְאַרְבָּעִים וַחֲמִשָּׁה: ס חֲמֹרִים שֵׁשֶׁת אֲלָפִים שְׁבַע שְׁלֹשִׁים וַחֲמִשָּׁה ס מֵאֹות וְעֶשְׂרִים: 69 וּמִקְצָת רָאשֵׁי הָאָבֹות נָתְנוּ לַמְּלָאכָה הַתִּרְשָׁתָא נָתַן לָאֹוצָר זָהָב דַּרְכְּמֹנִים אֶלֶף מִזְרָקֹות חֲמִשִּׁים כָּתְנֹות כֹּהֲנִים שְׁלֹשִׁים וַחֲמֵשׁ מֵאֹות: 70 וּמֵרָאשֵׁי הָאָבֹות נָתְנוּ לְאֹוצַר הַמְּלָאכָה זָהָב דַּרְכְּמֹונִים שְׁתֵּי רִבֹּות וְכֶסֶף מָנִים אַלְפַּיִם וּמָאתָיִם: 71 וַאֲשֶׁר נָתְנוּ שְׁאֵרִית הָעָם זָהָב דַּרְכְּמֹונִים שְׁתֵּי רִבֹּוא וְכֶסֶף מָנִים אַלְפַּיִם וְכָתְנֹת כֹּהֲנִים שִׁשִּׁים וְשִׁבְעָה: פ

72 וַיֵּשְׁבוּ הַכֹּהֲנִים וְהַלְוִיִּם וְהַשֹּׁועֲרִים וְהַמְשֹׁרְרִים וּמִן־הָעָם וְהַנְּתִינִים וְכָל־יִשְׂרָאֵל בְּעָרֵיהֶם וַיִּגַּע הַחֹדֶשׁ הַשְּׁבִיעִי וּבְנֵי יִשְׂרָאֵל בְּעָרֵיהֶם:

ח 1 וַיֵּאָסְפוּ כָל־הָעָם כְּאִישׁ אֶחָד אֶל־הָרְחֹוב אֲשֶׁר לִפְנֵי שַׁעַר־הַמָּיִם וַיֹּאמְרוּ לְעֶזְרָא הַסֹּפֵר לְהָבִיא אֶת־סֵפֶר תֹּורַת מֹשֶׁה אֲשֶׁר־צִוָּה יְהוָה אֶת־יִשְׂרָאֵל: 2 וַיָּבִיא עֶזְרָא הַכֹּהֵן אֶת־הַתֹּורָה לִפְנֵי הַקָּהָל מֵאִישׁ וְעַד־אִשָּׁה וְכֹל מֵבִין לִשְׁמֹעַ בְּיֹום אֶחָד לַחֹדֶשׁ הַשְּׁבִיעִי: 3 וַיִּקְרָא־בֹו לִפְנֵי הָרְחֹוב אֲשֶׁר ׀ לִפְנֵי שַׁעַר־הַמַּיִם מִן־הָאֹור עַד־מַחֲצִית הַיֹּום נֶגֶד הָאֲנָשִׁים וְהַנָּשִׁים וְהַמְּבִינִים וְאָזְנֵי כָל־ הָעָם אֶל־סֵפֶר הַתֹּורָה: 4 וַיַּעֲמֹד עֶזְרָא הַסֹּפֵר עַל־מִגְדַּל־עֵץ אֲשֶׁר עָשׂוּ לַדָּבָר וַיַּעֲמֹד אֶצְלֹו מַתִּתְיָה וְשֶׁמַע וַעֲנָיָה וְאוּרִיָּה וְחִלְקִיָּה וּמַעֲשֵׂיָה עַל־יְמִינֹו וּמִשְּׂמֹאלֹו פְּדָיָה וּמִישָׁאֵל וּמַלְכִּיָּה וְחָשֻׁם וְחַשְׁבַּדָּנָה זְכַרְיָה מְשֻׁלָּם: פ

5 וַיִּפְתַּח עֶזְרָא הַסֵּפֶר לְעֵינֵי כָל־הָעָם כִּי־ מֵעַל כָּל־הָעָם הָיָה וּכְפִתְחֹו עָמְדוּ כָל־הָעָם: 6 וַיְבָרֶךְ עֶזְרָא אֶת־יְהוָה הָאֱלֹהִים הַגָּדֹול וַיַּעֲנוּ כָל־הָעָם אָמֵן ׀ אָמֵן בְּמֹעַל יְדֵיהֶם וַיִּקְּדוּ

7 Also Jeshua, Bani, Sherebiah, Jamin, Akkub, Shabbethai, Hodijah, Maaseiah, Kelita, Azariah, Jozabad, Hanan, Pelaiah, and the Levites, helped the people to understand the Law; and the people *stood* in their place. 8 So they read distinctly from the book, in the Law of God; and they gave the sense, and helped *them* to understand the reading.

9 And Nehemiah, who *was* the governor, Ezra the priest *and* scribe, and the Levites who taught the people said to all the people, "This day *is* holy to the LORD your God; do not mourn nor weep." For all the people wept, when they heard the words of the Law.

10 Then he said to them, "Go your way, eat the fat, drink the sweet, and send portions to those for whom nothing is prepared; for *this* day *is* holy to our Lord. Do not sorrow, for the joy of the LORD is your strength."

11 So the Levites quieted all the people, saying, "Be still, for the day *is* holy; do not be grieved." 12 And all the people went their way to eat and drink, to send portions and rejoice greatly, because they understood the words that were declared to them.

13 Now on the second day the heads of the fathers' *houses* of all the people, with the priests and Levites, were gathered to Ezra the scribe, in order to understand the words of the Law. 14 And they found written in the Law, which the LORD had commanded by Moses, that the children of Israel should dwell in booths during the feast of the seventh month, 15 and that they should announce and proclaim in all their cities and in Jerusalem, saying, "Go out to the mountain, and bring olive branches, branches of oil trees, myrtle branches, palm branches, and branches of leafy trees, to make booths, as *it is* written."

16 Then the people went out and brought *them* and made themselves booths, each one on the roof of his house, or in their courtyards or the courts of the house of God, and in the open square of the Water Gate and in the open square of the Gate of Ephraim. 17 So the whole assembly of those who had returned from the captivity made booths and sat under the booths; for since the days of Joshua the son of Nun until that day the children of Israel had not done so. And there was very great gladness. 18 Also day by day, from the first day until the last day, he read from the Book of the Law of God. And they kept the feast seven days; and on the eighth day *there was* a sacred assembly, according to the *prescribed* manner.

וַיִּשְׁתַּחֲוֻ לַיהוָה אַפַּ֣יִם אָֽרְצָה: 7 וְיֵשׁ֣וּעַ וּבָנִ֣י וְשֵׁרֵֽבְיָ֣ה ׀ יָמִ֣ין עַקּ֣וּב שַׁבְּתַ֣י ׀ הֽוֹדִיָּ֣ה מַעֲשֵׂיָ֣ה קְלִיטָ֣א עֲזַרְיָ֣ה יוֹזָבָ֣ד חָנָ֣ן פְּלָאיָ֣ה וְהַלְוִיִּ֑ם מְבִינִ֥ים אֶת־הָעָ֖ם לַתּוֹרָ֑ה וְהָעָ֖ם עַל־עָמְדָֽם: 8 וַֽיִּקְרְא֣וּ בַסֵּ֗פֶר בְּתוֹרַ֤ת הָֽאֱלֹהִים֙ מְפֹרָ֔שׁ וְשׂ֖וֹם שֶׂ֑כֶל וַיָּבִ֖ינוּ בַּמִּקְרָֽא: ס 9 וַיֹּ֣אמֶר נְחֶמְיָ֣ה ה֣וּא הַתִּרְשָׁ֡תָא וְעֶזְרָ֣א הַכֹּהֵ֣ן ׀ הַסֹּפֵ֡ר וְהַלְוִיִּ֣ם הַמְּבִינִ֣ים אֶת־הָעָם֒ לְכָל־הָעָ֗ם הַיּ֤וֹם קָדֹֽשׁ־הוּא֙ לַיהוָ֣ה אֱלֹֽהֵיכֶ֔ם אַל־תִּֽתְאַבְּל֖וּ וְאַל־תִּבְכּ֑וּ כִּ֤י בוֹכִים֙ כָּל־הָעָ֔ם כְּשָׁמְעָ֖ם אֶת־דִּבְרֵ֥י הַתּוֹרָֽה: 10 וַיֹּ֣אמֶר לָהֶ֗ם לְכוּ֩ אִכְל֨וּ מַשְׁמַנִּ֜ים וּשְׁת֣וּ מַֽמְתַקִּ֗ים וְשִׁלְח֤וּ מָנוֹת֙ לְאֵ֣ין נָכ֣וֹן ל֔וֹ כִּֽי־קָד֥וֹשׁ הַיּ֖וֹם לַֽאֲדֹנֵ֑ינוּ וְאַל־תֵּ֣עָצֵ֔בוּ כִּֽי־חֶדְוַ֥ת יְהוָ֖ה הִ֥יא מָֽעֻזְּכֶֽם: 11 וְהַלְוִיִּ֞ם מַחְשִׁ֣ים לְכָל־הָעָם֙ לֵאמֹ֣ר הַ֔סּוּ כִּ֥י הַיּ֖וֹם קָדֹ֑שׁ וְאַל־תֵּֽעָצֵֽבוּ: 12 וַיֵּֽלְכ֨וּ כָל־הָעָ֜ם לֶֽאֱכֹ֤ל וְלִשְׁתּוֹת֙ וּלְשַׁלַּ֣ח מָנ֔וֹת וְלַֽעֲשׂ֖וֹת שִׂמְחָ֣ה גְדוֹלָ֑ה כִּ֤י הֵבִ֨ינוּ֙ בַּדְּבָרִ֔ים אֲשֶׁ֥ר הוֹדִ֖יעוּ לָהֶֽם: ס 13 וּבַיּ֣וֹם הַשֵּׁנִ֡י נֶאֶסְפ֣וּ רָאשֵׁ֣י הָֽאָבוֹת֩ לְכָל־הָעָ֨ם הַכֹּֽהֲנִ֤ים וְהַלְוִיִּם֙ אֶל־עֶזְרָ֣א הַסֹּפֵ֑ר וּלְהַשְׂכִּ֖יל אֶל־דִּבְרֵ֥י הַתּוֹרָֽה: 14 וַֽיִּמְצְא֖וּ כָּת֣וּב בַּתּוֹרָ֑ה אֲשֶׁ֨ר צִוָּ֤ה יְהוָה֙ בְּיַד־מֹשֶׁ֔ה אֲשֶׁר֩ יֵֽשְׁב֨וּ בְנֵֽי־יִשְׂרָאֵ֧ל בַּסֻּכּ֛וֹת בֶּחָ֖ג בַּחֹ֥דֶשׁ הַשְּׁבִיעִֽי: 15 וַֽאֲשֶׁ֣ר יַשְׁמִ֗יעוּ וְיַֽעֲבִ֨ירוּ ק֜וֹל בְּכָל־עָֽרֵיהֶם֮ וּבִירֽוּשָׁלִַם֒ לֵאמֹ֗ר צְא֣וּ הָהָ֔ר וְהָבִ֨יאוּ֙ עֲלֵי־זַ֙יִת֙ וַעֲלֵי־עֵ֣ץ שֶׁ֔מֶן וַעֲלֵ֤י הֲדַס֙ וַעֲלֵ֣י תְמָרִ֔ים וַעֲלֵ֖י עֵ֣ץ עָבֹ֑ת לַֽעֲשֹׂ֥ת סֻכֹּ֖ת כַּכָּתֽוּב: פ

16 וַיֵּֽצְא֣וּ הָעָם֮ וַיָּבִ֒יאוּ֒ וַיַּֽעֲשׂ֨וּ לָהֶ֤ם סֻכּוֹת֙ אִ֣ישׁ עַל־גַּגּ֗וֹ וּבְחַצְרֹֽתֵיהֶם֙ וּבְחַצְר֣וֹת בֵּ֣ית הָֽאֱלֹהִ֔ים וּבִרְח֖וֹב שַׁ֣עַר הַמַּ֑יִם וּבִרְח֖וֹב שַׁ֥עַר אֶפְרָֽיִם: 17 וַיַּֽעֲשׂ֣וּ כָל־הַ֠קָּהָל הַשָּׁבִ֨ים מִן־הַשְּׁבִ֥י ׀ סֻכּוֹת֮ וַיֵּֽשְׁב֣וּ בַסֻּכּוֹת֒ כִּ֠י לֹֽא־עָשׂ֨וּ מִימֵ֜י יֵשׁ֤וּעַ בִּן־נוּן֙ כֵּ֔ן בְּנֵ֣י יִשְׂרָאֵ֔ל עַ֖ד הַיּ֣וֹם הַה֑וּא וַתְּהִ֥י שִׂמְחָ֖ה גְדוֹלָ֥ה מְאֹֽד: 18 וַ֠יִּקְרָא בְּסֵ֨פֶר תּוֹרַ֤ת הָֽאֱלֹהִים֙ י֣וֹם ׀ בְּי֔וֹם מִן־הַיּוֹם֙ הָֽרִאשׁ֔וֹן עַ֖ד הַיּ֣וֹם הָאַֽחֲר֑וֹן וַיַּֽעֲשׂוּ־חָג֙ שִׁבְעַ֣ת יָמִ֔ים וּבַיּ֧וֹם הַשְּׁמִינִ֛י עֲצֶ֖רֶת כַּמִּשְׁפָּֽט: פ

9 Now on the twenty-fourth day of this month the children of Israel were assembled with fasting, in sackcloth, and with dust on their heads. ² Then those of Israelite lineage separated themselves from all foreigners; and they stood and confessed their sins and the iniquities of their fathers. ³ And they stood up in their place and read from the Book of the Law of the LORD their God *for one*-fourth of the day; and *for another* fourth they confessed and worshiped the LORD their God.

⁴ Then Jeshua, Bani, Kadmiel, Shebaniah, Bunni, Sherebiah, Bani, *and* Chenani stood on the stairs of the Levites and cried out with a loud voice to the LORD their God. ⁵ And the Levites, Jeshua, Kadmiel, Bani, Hashabniah, Sherebiah, Hodijah, Shebaniah, *and* Pethahiah, said:

"Stand up *and* bless the LORD your God
Forever and ever!

"Blessed be Your glorious name,
Which is exalted above all blessing and praise!
6 You alone *are* the LORD;
You have made heaven,
The heaven of heavens, with all their host,
The earth and everything on it,
The seas and all that is in them,
And You preserve them all.
The host of heaven worships You.
7 "You *are* the LORD God,
Who chose Abram,
And brought him out of Ur of the Chaldeans,
And gave him the name Abraham;
8 You found his heart faithful before You,
And made a covenant with him
To give the land of the Canaanites,
The Hittites, the Amorites,
The Perizzites, the Jebusites,
And the Girgashites—
To give *it* to his descendants.
You have performed Your words,
For You *are* righteous.
9 "You saw the affliction of our fathers in Egypt,
And heard their cry by the Red Sea.
10 You showed signs and wonders against Pharaoh,
Against all his servants,
And against all the people of his land.
For You knew that they acted proudly against them.
So You made a name for Yourself, as *it is* this day.
11 And You divided the sea before them,
So that they went through the midst of the sea on the dry land;
And their persecutors You threw into the deep,
As a stone into the mighty waters.
12 Moreover You led them by day with a cloudy pillar,
And by night with a pillar of fire,
To give them light on the road

ט וּבְיוֹם עֶשְׂרִים וְאַרְבָּעָה לַחֹדֶשׁ הַזֶּה נֶאֶסְפוּ בְנֵי־יִשְׂרָאֵל בְּצוֹם וּבְשַׂקִּים וַאֲדָמָה עֲלֵיהֶם: 2 וַיִּבָּדְלוּ זֶרַע יִשְׂרָאֵל מִכֹּל בְּנֵי נֵכָר וַיַּעַמְדוּ וַיִּתְוַדּוּ עַל־חַטֹּאתֵיהֶם וַעֲוֺנוֹת אֲבֹתֵיהֶם: 3 וַיָּקוּמוּ עַל־עָמְדָם וַיִּקְרְאוּ בְּסֵפֶר תּוֹרַת יְהוָה אֱלֹהֵיהֶם רְבִעִית הַיּוֹם וּרְבִעִית מִתְוַדִּים וּמִשְׁתַּחֲוִים לַיהוָה אֱלֹהֵיהֶם: פ

4 וַיָּקָם עַל־מַעֲלֵה הַלְוִיִּם יֵשׁוּעַ וּבָנִי קַדְמִיאֵל שְׁבַנְיָה בֻּנִּי שֵׁרֵבְיָה בָּנִי כְנָנִי וַיִּזְעֲקוּ בְּקוֹל גָּדוֹל אֶל־יְהוָה אֱלֹהֵיהֶם: 5 וַיֹּאמְרוּ הַלְוִיִּם יֵשׁוּעַ וְקַדְמִיאֵל בָּנִי חֲשַׁבְנְיָה שֵׁרֵבְיָה הוֹדִיָּה שְׁבַנְיָה פְתַחְיָה קוּמוּ בָּרֲכוּ אֶת־יְהוָה אֱלֹהֵיכֶם מִן־הָעוֹלָם עַד־הָעוֹלָם וִיבָרֲכוּ שֵׁם כְּבוֹדֶךָ וּמְרוֹמַם עַל־כָּל־בְּרָכָה וּתְהִלָּה: 6 אַתָּה־הוּא יְהוָה לְבַדֶּךָ אַתָּ עָשִׂיתָ אֶת־הַשָּׁמַיִם שְׁמֵי הַשָּׁמַיִם וְכָל־צְבָאָם הָאָרֶץ וְכָל־אֲשֶׁר עָלֶיהָ הַיַּמִּים וְכָל־אֲשֶׁר בָּהֶם וְאַתָּה מְחַיֶּה אֶת־כֻּלָּם וּצְבָא הַשָּׁמַיִם לְךָ מִשְׁתַּחֲוִים: 7 אַתָּה־הוּא יְהוָה הָאֱלֹהִים אֲשֶׁר בָּחַרְתָּ בְּאַבְרָם וְהוֹצֵאתוֹ מֵאוּר כַּשְׂדִּים וְשַׂמְתָּ שְּׁמוֹ אַבְרָהָם: 8 וּמָצָאתָ אֶת־לְבָבוֹ נֶאֱמָן לְפָנֶיךָ וְכָרוֹת עִמּוֹ הַבְּרִית לָתֵת אֶת־אֶרֶץ הַכְּנַעֲנִי הַחִתִּי הָאֱמֹרִי וְהַפְּרִזִּי וְהַיְבוּסִי וְהַגִּרְגָּשִׁי לָתֵת לְזַרְעוֹ וַתָּקֶם אֶת־דְּבָרֶיךָ כִּי צַדִּיק אָתָּה: 9 וַתֵּרֶא אֶת־עֳנִי אֲבֹתֵינוּ בְּמִצְרָיִם וְאֶת־זַעֲקָתָם שָׁמַעְתָּ עַל־יַם־סוּף: 10 וַתִּתֵּן אֹתֹת וּמֹפְתִים בְּפַרְעֹה וּבְכָל־עֲבָדָיו וּבְכָל־עַם אַרְצוֹ כִּי יָדַעְתָּ כִּי הֵזִידוּ עֲלֵיהֶם וַתַּעַשׂ־לְךָ שֵׁם כְּהַיּוֹם הַזֶּה: 11 וְהַיָּם בָּקַעְתָּ לִפְנֵיהֶם וַיַּעַבְרוּ בְתוֹךְ־הַיָּם בַּיַּבָּשָׁה וְאֶת־רֹדְפֵיהֶם הִשְׁלַכְתָּ בִמְצוֹלֹת כְּמוֹ־אֶבֶן בְּמַיִם עַזִּים: 12 וּבְעַמּוּד עָנָן הִנְחִיתָם יוֹמָם וּבְעַמּוּד אֵשׁ לַיְלָה לְהָאִיר לָהֶם

Which they should travel.

13 "You came down also on Mount Sinai,
And spoke with them from heaven,
And gave them just ordinances and true laws,
Good statutes and commandments.

14 You made known to them Your holy Sabbath,
And commanded them precepts, statutes and
laws,
By the hand of Moses Your servant.

15 You gave them bread from heaven for their
hunger,
And brought them water out of the rock for their
thirst,
And told them to go in to possess the land
Which You had sworn to give them.

16 "But they and our fathers acted proudly,
Hardened their necks,
And did not heed Your commandments.

17 They refused to obey,
And they were not mindful of Your wonders
That You did among them.
But they hardened their necks,
And in their rebellion
They appointed a leader
To return to their bondage.
But You *are* God,
Ready to pardon,
Gracious and merciful,
Slow to anger,
Abundant in kindness,
And did not forsake them.

18 "Even when they made a molded calf for
themselves,
And said, 'This *is* your god
That brought you up out of Egypt,'
And worked great provocations,

19 Yet in Your manifold mercies
You did not forsake them in the wilderness.
The pillar of the cloud did not depart from them
by day,
To lead them on the road;
Nor the pillar of fire by night,
To show them light,
And the way they should go.

20 You also gave Your good Spirit to instruct them,
And did not withhold Your manna from their
mouth,
And gave them water for their thirst.

21 Forty years You sustained them in the
wilderness;
They lacked nothing;
Their clothes did not wear out
And their feet did not swell.

22 "Moreover You gave them kingdoms and nations,
And divided them into districts.
So they took possession of the land of Sihon,
The land of the king of Heshbon,
And the land of Og king of Bashan.

23 You also multiplied their children as the stars of
heaven,
And brought them into the land

אֶת־הַדֶּרֶךְ אֲשֶׁר יֵלְכוּ־בָהּ: 13 וְעַל הַר־סִינַי יָרַדְתָּ
וְדַבֵּר עִמָּהֶם מִשָּׁמָיִם וַתִּתֵּן לָהֶם מִשְׁפָּטִים יְשָׁרִים
וְתוֹרוֹת אֱמֶת חֻקִּים וּמִצְוֺת טוֹבִים: 14 וְאֶת־שַׁבַּת
קָדְשְׁךָ הוֹדַעְתָּ לָהֶם וּמִצְווֹת וְחֻקִּים וְתוֹרָה צִוִּיתָ
לָהֶם בְּיַד מֹשֶׁה עַבְדֶּךָ: 15 וְלֶחֶם מִשָּׁמַיִם נָתַתָּה
לָהֶם לִרְעָבָם וּמַיִם מִסֶּלַע הוֹצֵאתָ לָהֶם לִצְמָאָם
וַתֹּאמֶר לָהֶם לָבוֹא לָרֶשֶׁת אֶת־הָאָרֶץ אֲשֶׁר־נָשָׂאתָ
אֶת־יָדְךָ לָתֵת לָהֶם: 16 וְהֵם וַאֲבֹתֵינוּ הֵזִידוּ וַיַּקְשׁוּ
אֶת־עָרְפָּם וְלֹא שָׁמְעוּ אֶל־מִצְוֺתֶיךָ: 17 וַיְמָאֲנוּ
לִשְׁמֹעַ וְלֹא־זָכְרוּ נִפְלְאֹתֶיךָ אֲשֶׁר עָשִׂיתָ עִמָּהֶם
וַיַּקְשׁוּ אֶת־עָרְפָּם וַיִּתְּנוּ־רֹאשׁ לָשׁוּב לְעַבְדֻתָם
בְּמִרְיָם וְאַתָּה אֱלוֹהַּ סְלִיחוֹת חַנּוּן וְרַחוּם אֶרֶךְ־
אַפַּיִם וְרַב־וְחֶסֶד וְלֹא עֲזַבְתָּם: 18 אַף כִּי־עָשׂוּ
לָהֶם עֵגֶל מַסֵּכָה וַיֹּאמְרוּ זֶה אֱלֹהֶיךָ אֲשֶׁר הֶעֶלְךָ
מִמִּצְרָיִם וַיַּעֲשׂוּ נֶאָצוֹת גְּדֹלוֹת: 19 וְאַתָּה בְּרַחֲמֶיךָ
הָרַבִּים לֹא עֲזַבְתָּם בַּמִּדְבָּר אֶת־עַמּוּד הֶעָנָן לֹא־
סָר מֵעֲלֵיהֶם בְּיוֹמָם לְהַנְחֹתָם בְּהַדֶּרֶךְ וְאֶת־עַמּוּד
הָאֵשׁ בְּלַיְלָה לְהָאִיר לָהֶם וְאֶת־הַדֶּרֶךְ אֲשֶׁר יֵלְכוּ־
בָהּ: 20 וְרוּחֲךָ הַטּוֹבָה נָתַתָּ לְהַשְׂכִּילָם וּמַנְךָ
לֹא־מָנַעְתָּ מִפִּיהֶם וּמַיִם נָתַתָּה לָהֶם לִצְמָאָם:
21 וְאַרְבָּעִים שָׁנָה כִּלְכַּלְתָּם בַּמִּדְבָּר לֹא חָסֵרוּ
שַׂלְמֹתֵיהֶם לֹא בָלוּ וְרַגְלֵיהֶם לֹא בָצֵקוּ: 22 וַתִּתֵּן
לָהֶם מַמְלָכוֹת וַעֲמָמִים וַתַּחְלְקֵם לְפֵאָה וַיִּירְשׁוּ
אֶת־אֶרֶץ סִיחוֹן וְאֶת־אֶרֶץ מֶלֶךְ חֶשְׁבּוֹן וְאֶת־אֶרֶץ
עוֹג מֶלֶךְ־הַבָּשָׁן: 23 וּבְנֵיהֶם הִרְבִּיתָ כְּכֹכְבֵי הַשָּׁמָיִם
וַתְּבִיאֵם אֶל־הָאָרֶץ אֲשֶׁר־אָמַרְתָּ לַאֲבֹתֵיהֶם לָבוֹא

ט 17 חֶסֶד

Which You had told their fathers
To go in and possess.

24 So the people went in
And possessed the land;
You subdued before them the inhabitants of the
land,
The Canaanites,
And gave them into their hands,
With their kings
And the people of the land,
That they might do with them as they wished.

25 And they took strong cities and a rich land,
And possessed houses full of all goods,
Cisterns *already* dug, vineyards, olive groves,
And fruit trees in abundance.
So they ate and were filled and grew fat,
And delighted themselves in Your great
goodness.

26 "Nevertheless they were disobedient
And rebelled against You,
Cast Your law behind their backs
And killed Your prophets, who testified against
them
To turn them to Yourself;
And they worked great provocations.

27 Therefore You delivered them into the hand of
their enemies,
Who oppressed them;
And in the time of their trouble,
When they cried to You,
You heard from heaven;
And according to Your abundant mercies
You gave them deliverers who saved them
From the hand of their enemies.

28 "But after they had rest,
They again did evil before You.
Therefore You left them in the hand of their
enemies,
So that they had dominion over them;
Yet when they returned and cried out to You,
You heard from heaven;
And many times You delivered them according
to Your mercies,

29 And testified against them,
That You might bring them back to Your law.
Yet they acted proudly,
And did not heed Your commandments,
But sinned against Your judgments,
'Which if a man does, he shall live by them.'
And they shrugged their shoulders,
Stiffened their necks,
And would not hear.

30 Yet for many years You had patience with them,
And testified against them by Your Spirit in
Your prophets.
Yet they would not listen;
Therefore You gave them into the hand of the
peoples of the lands.

31 Nevertheless in Your great mercy
You did not utterly consume them nor forsake
them;
For You *are* God, gracious and merciful.

לָרָשֶׁת: 24 וַיָּבֹאוּ הַבָּנִים וַיִּירְשׁוּ אֶת־הָאָרֶץ וַתַּכְנַע

לִפְנֵיהֶם אֶת־יֹשְׁבֵי הָאָרֶץ הַכְּנַעֲנִים וַתִּתְּנֵם בְּיָדָם

וְאֶת־מַלְכֵיהֶם וְאֶת־עַמְמֵי הָאָרֶץ לַעֲשׂוֹת בָּהֶם

כִּרְצוֹנָם: 25 וַיִּלְכְּדוּ עָרִים בְּצֻרוֹת וַאֲדָמָה שְׁמֵנָה

וַיִּירְשׁוּ בָּתִּים מְלֵאִים־כָּל־טוּב בֹּרוֹת חֲצוּבִים

כְּרָמִים וְזֵיתִים וְעֵץ מַאֲכָל לָרֹב וַיֹּאכְלוּ וַיִּשְׂבְּעוּ

וַיַּשְׁמִינוּ וַיִּתְעַדְּנוּ בְּטוּבְךָ הַגָּדוֹל: 26 וַיַּמְרוּ וַיִּמְרְדוּ

בָּךְ וַיַּשְׁלִכוּ אֶת־תּוֹרָתְךָ אַחֲרֵי גַוָּם וְאֶת־נְבִיאֶיךָ

הָרָגוּ אֲשֶׁר־הֵעִידוּ בָם לַהֲשִׁיבָם אֵלֶיךָ וַיַּעֲשׂוּ

נֶאָצוֹת גְּדוֹלֹת: 27 וַתִּתְּנֵם בְּיַד צָרֵיהֶם וַיָּצֵרוּ לָהֶם

וּבְעֵת צָרָתָם יִצְעֲקוּ אֵלֶיךָ וְאַתָּה מִשָּׁמַיִם תִּשְׁמָע

וּכְרַחֲמֶיךָ הָרַבִּים תִּתֵּן לָהֶם מוֹשִׁיעִים וְיוֹשִׁיעוּם

מִיַּד צָרֵיהֶם: 28 וּכְנוֹחַ לָהֶם יָשׁוּבוּ לַעֲשׂוֹת רַע

לְפָנֶיךָ וַתַּעַזְבֵם בְּיַד אֹיְבֵיהֶם וַיִּרְדּוּ בָהֶם וַיָּשׁוּבוּ

וַיִּזְעָקוּךָ וְאַתָּה מִשָּׁמַיִם תִּשְׁמַע וְתַצִּילֵם כְּרַחֲמֶיךָ

רַבּוֹת עִתִּים: 29 וַתָּעַד בָּהֶם לַהֲשִׁיבָם אֶל־תּוֹרָתֶךָ

וְהֵמָּה הֵזִידוּ וְלֹא־שָׁמְעוּ לְמִצְוֺתֶיךָ וּבְמִשְׁפָּטֶיךָ

חָטְאוּ־בָם אֲשֶׁר־יַעֲשֶׂה אָדָם וְחָיָה בָהֶם וַיִּתְּנוּ

כָתֵף סוֹרֶרֶת וְעָרְפָּם הִקְשׁוּ וְלֹא שָׁמֵעוּ: 30 וַתִּמְשֹׁךְ

עֲלֵיהֶם שָׁנִים רַבּוֹת וַתָּעַד בָּם בְּרוּחֲךָ בְּיַד־נְבִיאֶיךָ

וְלֹא הֶאֱזִינוּ וַתִּתְּנֵם בְּיַד עַמֵּי הָאֲרָצֹת: 31 וּבְרַחֲמֶיךָ

הָרַבִּים לֹא־עֲשִׂיתָם כָּלָה וְלֹא עֲזַבְתָּם כִּי אֵל־חַנּוּן

32 "Now therefore, our God,
The great, the mighty, and awesome God,
Who keeps covenant and mercy:
Do not let all the trouble seem small before You
That has come upon us,
Our kings and our princes,
Our priests and our prophets,
Our fathers and on all Your people,
From the days of the kings of Assyria until this
day.
33 However You *are* just in all that has befallen us;
For You have dealt faithfully,
But we have done wickedly.
34 Neither our kings nor our princes,
Our priests nor our fathers,
Have kept Your law,
Nor heeded Your commandments and Your
testimonies,
With which You testified against them.
35 For they have not served You in their kingdom,
Or in the many good *things* that You gave them,
Or in the large and rich land which You set
before them;
Nor did they turn from their wicked works.

36 "Here we *are*, servants today!
And the land that You gave to our fathers,
To eat its fruit and its bounty,
Here we *are*, servants in it!
37 And it yields much increase to the kings
You have set over us,
Because of our sins;
Also they have dominion over our bodies and our
cattle
At their pleasure;
And we *are* in great distress.

38 "And because of all this,
We make a sure *covenant* and write *it*;
Our leaders, our Levites, *and* our priests seal *it*."

10 Now those who placed *their* seal on *the document were:*

Nehemiah the governor, the son of Hacaliah,
and Zedekiah, ² Seraiah, Azariah, Jeremiah,
³ Pashhur, Amariah, Malchijah, ⁴ Hattush,
Shebaniah, Malluch, ⁵ Harim, Meremoth,
Obadiah, ⁶ Daniel, Ginnethon, Baruch,
⁷ Meshullam, Abijah, Mijamin, ⁸ Maaziah,
Bilgai, *and* Shemaiah. These *were* the priests.

9 The Levites: Jeshua the son of Azaniah,
Binnui of the sons of Henadad, *and*
Kadmiel.

10 Their brethren: Shebaniah, Hodijah, Kelita,
Pelaiah, Hanan, ¹¹ Micha, Rehob,
Hashabiah, ¹² Zaccur, Sherebiah, Shebaniah,
¹³ Hodijah, Bani, *and* Beninu.

וְרַחוּם אָתָּה: 32 וְעַתָּה אֱלֹהֵינוּ הָאֵל הַגָּדוֹל הַגִּבּוֹר
וְהַנּוֹרָא שׁוֹמֵר הַבְּרִית וְהַחֶסֶד אַל־יִמְעַט לְפָנֶיךָ
אֵת כָּל־הַתְּלָאָה אֲשֶׁר־מְצָאַתְנוּ לִמְלָכֵינוּ לְשָׂרֵינוּ
וּלְכֹהֲנֵינוּ וְלִנְבִיאֵנוּ וְלַאֲבֹתֵינוּ וּלְכָל־עַמֶּךָ מִימֵי
מַלְכֵי אַשּׁוּר עַד הַיּוֹם הַזֶּה: 33 וְאַתָּה צַדִּיק עַל
כָּל־הַבָּא עָלֵינוּ כִּי־אֱמֶת עָשִׂיתָ וַאֲנַחְנוּ הִרְשָׁעְנוּ:
34 וְאֶת־מְלָכֵינוּ שָׂרֵינוּ כֹּהֲנֵינוּ וַאֲבֹתֵינוּ לֹא עָשׂוּ
תּוֹרָתֶךָ וְלֹא הִקְשִׁיבוּ אֶל־מִצְוֹתֶיךָ וּלְעֵדְוֹתֶיךָ אֲשֶׁר
הַעִידֹתָ בָּהֶם: 35 וְהֵם בְּמַלְכוּתָם וּבְטוּבְךָ הָרָב
אֲשֶׁר־נָתַתָּ לָהֶם וּבְאֶרֶץ הָרְחָבָה וְהַשְּׁמֵנָה אֲשֶׁר־
נָתַתָּ לִפְנֵיהֶם לֹא עֲבָדוּךָ וְלֹא־שָׁבוּ מִמַּעַלְלֵיהֶם
הָרָעִים: 36 הִנֵּה אֲנַחְנוּ הַיּוֹם עֲבָדִים וְהָאָרֶץ אֲשֶׁר־
נָתַתָּה לַאֲבֹתֵינוּ לֶאֱכֹל אֶת־פִּרְיָהּ וְאֶת־טוּבָהּ הִנֵּה
אֲנַחְנוּ עֲבָדִים עָלֶיהָ: 37 וּתְבוּאָתָהּ מַרְבָּה לַמְּלָכִים
אֲשֶׁר־נָתַתָּה עָלֵינוּ בְּחַטֹּאותֵינוּ וְעַל גְּוִיֹּתֵינוּ מֹשְׁלִים
וּבִבְהֶמְתֵּנוּ כִּרְצוֹנָם וּבְצָרָה גְדוֹלָה אֲנָחְנוּ: פ

י וּבְכָל־זֹאת אֲנַחְנוּ כֹּרְתִים אֲמָנָה וְכֹתְבִים וְעַל
הֶחָתוּם שָׂרֵינוּ לְוִיֵּנוּ כֹּהֲנֵינוּ: 2 וְעַל הַחֲתוּמִים
נְחֶמְיָה הַתִּרְשָׁתָא בֶּן־חֲכַלְיָה וְצִדְקִיָּה: 3 שְׂרָיָה
עֲזַרְיָה יִרְמְיָה: 4 פַּשְׁחוּר אֲמַרְיָה מַלְכִּיָּה: 5 חַטּוּשׁ
שְׁבַנְיָה מַלּוּךְ: 6 חָרִם מְרֵמוֹת עֹבַדְיָה: 7 דָּנִיֵּאל
גִּנְּתוֹן בָּרוּךְ: 8 מְשֻׁלָּם אֲבִיָּה מִיָּמִן: 9 מַעַזְיָה בִלְגַּי
שְׁמַעְיָה אֵלֶּה הַכֹּהֲנִים: ס 10 וְהַלְוִיִּם
וְיֵשׁוּעַ בֶּן־אֲזַנְיָה בִּנּוּי מִבְּנֵי חֵנָדָד קַדְמִיאֵל:
11 וַאֲחֵיהֶם שְׁבַנְיָה הוֹדִיָּה קְלִיטָא פְּלָאיָה חָנָן:
12 מִיכָא רְחוֹב חֲשַׁבְיָה: 13 זַכּוּר שֵׁרֵבְיָה שְׁבַנְיָה:
14 הוֹדִיָּה בָנִי בְּנִינוּ: ס 15 רָאשֵׁי הָעָם

14 The leaders of the people: Parosh, Pahath-Moab, Elam, Zattu, Bani, 15 Bunni, Azgad, Bebai, 16 Adonijah, Bigvai, Adin, 17 Ater, Hezekiah, Azzur, 18 Hodijah, Hashum, Bezai, 19 Hariph, Anathoth, Nebai, 20 Magpiash, Meshullam, Hezir, 21 Meshezabel, Zadok, Jaddua, 22 Pelatiah, Hanan, Anaiah, 23 Hoshea, Hananiah, Hasshub, 24 Hallohesh, Pilha, Shobek, 25 Rehum, Hashabnah, Maaseiah, 26 Ahijah, Hanan, Anan, 27 Malluch, Harim, *and* Baanah.

28 Now the rest of the people—the priests, the Levites, the gatekeepers, the singers, the Nethinim, and all those who had separated themselves from the peoples of the lands to the Law of God, their wives, their sons, and their daughters, everyone who had knowledge and understanding— 29 these joined with their brethren, their nobles, and entered into a curse and an oath to walk in God's Law, which was given by Moses the servant of God, and to observe and do all the commandments of the LORD our Lord, and His ordinances and His statutes: 30 We would not give our daughters as wives to the peoples of the land, nor take their daughters for our sons; 31 if the peoples of the land brought wares or any grain to sell on the Sabbath day, we would not buy it from them on the Sabbath, or on a holy day; and we would forego the seventh year's *produce* and the exacting of every debt.

32 Also we made ordinances for ourselves, to exact from ourselves yearly one-third of a shekel for the service of the house of our God: 33 for the showbread, for the regular grain offering, for the regular burnt offering of the Sabbaths, the New Moons, and the set feasts; for the holy things, for the sin offerings to make atonement for Israel, and all the work of the house of our God. 34 We cast lots among the priests, the Levites, and the people, for *bringing* the wood offering into the house of our God, according to our fathers' houses, at the appointed times year by year, to burn on the altar of the LORD our God as *it is* written in the Law.

35 And *we made ordinances* to bring the firstfruits of our ground and the firstfruits of all fruit of all trees, year by year, to the house of the LORD; 36 to bring the firstborn of our sons and our cattle, as *it is* written in the Law, and the firstborn of our herds and our flocks, to the house of our God, to the priests who minister in the house of our God; 37 to bring the firstfruits of our dough, our offerings, the fruit from all kinds of trees, *the* new wine and oil, to

פַּרְעֹשׁ פַּחַת מוֹאָב עֵילָם זַתּוּא בָּנִי: 16 בְּנֵי עַזְגָּד בֵּבָי: 17 אֲדֹנִיָּה בִגְוַי עָדִין: 18 אָטֵר חִזְקִיָּה עַזּוּר: 19 הוֹדִיָּה חָשֻׁם בֵּצָי: 20 חָרִיף עֲנָתוֹת נוֹבָי: 21 מַגְפִּיעָשׁ מְשֻׁלָּם חֵזִיר: 22 מְשֵׁיזַבְאֵל צָדוֹק יַדּוּעַ: 23 פְּלַטְיָה חָנָן עֲנָיָה: 24 הוֹשֵׁעַ חֲנַנְיָה חַשּׁוּב: 25 הַלּוֹחֵשׁ פִּלְחָא שׁוֹבֵק: 26 רְחוּם חֲשַׁבְנָה מַעֲשֵׂיָה: 27 וַאֲחִיָּה חָנָן עָנָן: 28 מַלּוּךְ חָרִם בַּעֲנָה: 29 וּשְׁאָר הָעָם הַכֹּהֲנִים הַלְוִיִּם הַשּׁוֹעֲרִים הַמְשֹׁרְרִים הַנְּתִינִים וְכָל־הַנִּבְדָּל מֵעַמֵּי הָאֲרָצוֹת אֶל־תּוֹרַת הָאֱלֹהִים נְשֵׁיהֶם בְּנֵיהֶם וּבְנֹתֵיהֶם כֹּל יוֹדֵעַ מֵבִין: 30 מַחֲזִיקִים עַל־אֲחֵיהֶם אַדִּירֵיהֶם וּבָאִים בְּאָלָה וּבִשְׁבוּעָה לָלֶכֶת בְּתוֹרַת הָאֱלֹהִים אֲשֶׁר נִתְּנָה בְּיַד־מֹשֶׁה עֶבֶד־הָאֱלֹהִים וְלִשְׁמוֹר וְלַעֲשׂוֹת אֶת־כָּל־מִצְוֹת יְהוָה אֲדֹנֵינוּ וּמִשְׁפָּטָיו וְחֻקָּיו: 31 וַאֲשֶׁר לֹא־נִתֵּן בְּנֹתֵינוּ לְעַמֵּי הָאָרֶץ וְאֶת־בְּנֹתֵיהֶם לֹא נִקַּח לְבָנֵינוּ: 32 וְעַמֵּי הָאָרֶץ הַמְבִיאִים אֶת־הַמַּקָּחוֹת וְכָל־שֶׁבֶר בְּיוֹם הַשַּׁבָּת לִמְכּוֹר לֹא־נִקַּח מֵהֶם בַּשַּׁבָּת וּבְיוֹם קֹדֶשׁ וְנִטֹּשׁ אֶת־הַשָּׁנָה הַשְּׁבִיעִית וּמַשָּׁא כָל־יָד: 33 וְהֶעֱמַדְנוּ עָלֵינוּ מִצְוֹת לָתֵת עָלֵינוּ שְׁלִשִׁית הַשֶּׁקֶל בַּשָּׁנָה לַעֲבֹדַת בֵּית אֱלֹהֵינוּ: 34 לְלֶחֶם הַמַּעֲרֶכֶת וּמִנְחַת הַתָּמִיד וּלְעוֹלַת הַתָּמִיד הַשַּׁבָּתוֹת הֶחֳדָשִׁים לַמּוֹעֲדִים וְלַקֳּדָשִׁים וְלַחַטָּאוֹת לְכַפֵּר עַל־יִשְׂרָאֵל וְכֹל מְלֶאכֶת בֵּית־אֱלֹהֵינוּ: ס 35 וְהַגּוֹרָלוֹת הִפַּלְנוּ עַל־קׇרְבַּן הָעֵצִים הַכֹּהֲנִים הַלְוִיִּם וְהָעָם לְהָבִיא לְבֵית אֱלֹהֵינוּ לְבֵית־אֲבֹתֵינוּ לְעִתִּים מְזֻמָּנִים שָׁנָה בְשָׁנָה לְבַעֵר עַל־מִזְבַּח יְהוָה אֱלֹהֵינוּ כַּכָּתוּב בַּתּוֹרָה: 36 וּלְהָבִיא אֶת־בִּכּוּרֵי אַדְמָתֵנוּ וּבִכּוּרֵי כָל־פְּרִי כָל־עֵץ שָׁנָה בְשָׁנָה לְבֵית יְהוָה: 37 וְאֶת־בְּכֹרוֹת בָּנֵינוּ וּבְהֶמְתֵּינוּ כַּכָּתוּב בַּתּוֹרָה וְאֶת־בְּכוֹרֵי בְקָרֵינוּ וְצֹאנֵינוּ לְהָבִיא לְבֵית אֱלֹהֵינוּ לַכֹּהֲנִים הַמְשָׁרְתִים בְּבֵית אֱלֹהֵינוּ: 38 וְאֶת־רֵאשִׁית עֲרִיסֹתֵינוּ וּתְרוּמֹתֵינוּ וּפְרִי כָל־עֵץ תִּירוֹשׁ וְיִצְהָר

the priests, to the storerooms of the house of our
God; and to bring the tithes of our land to the
Levites, for the Levites should receive the tithes in
all our farming communities. 38 And the priest, the
descendant of Aaron, shall be with the Levites when
the Levites receive tithes; and the Levites shall bring
up a tenth of the tithes to the house of our God, to
the rooms of the storehouse.

39 For the children of Israel and the children of
Levi shall bring the offering of the grain, of the new
wine and the oil, to the storerooms where the
articles of the sanctuary are, where the priests who
minister and the gatekeepers and the singers are;
and we will not neglect the house of our God.

11 Now the leaders of the people dwelt at
Jerusalem; the rest of the people cast lots to bring
one out of ten to dwell in Jerusalem, the holy city,
and nine-tenths were to dwell in other cities. 2 And
the people blessed all the men who willingly offered
themselves to dwell at Jerusalem.

3 These are the heads of the province who dwelt
in Jerusalem. (But in the cities of Judah everyone
dwelt in his own possession in their cities—
Israelites, priests, Levites, Nethinim, and descendants of Solomon's servants.) 4 Also in Jerusalem
dwelt some of the children of Judah and of the
children of Benjamin.

The children of Judah: Athaiah the son of
Uzziah, the son of Zechariah, the son of Amariah,
the son of Shephatiah, the son of Mahalalel, of the
children of Perez; 5 and Maaseiah the son of
Baruch, the son of Col-Hozeh, the son of Hazaiah,
the son of Adaiah, the son of Joiarib, the son of
Zechariah, the son of Shiloni. 6 All the sons of Perez
who dwelt at Jerusalem were four hundred and
sixty-eight valiant men.

7 And these are the sons of Benjamin: Sallu the
son of Meshullam, the son of Joed, the son of
Pedaiah, the son of Kolaiah, the son of Maaseiah,
the son of Ithiel, the son of Jeshaiah; 8 and after him
Gabbai and Sallai, nine hundred and twenty-eight.
9 Joel the son of Zichri was their overseer, and
Judah the son of Senuah was second over the city.

10 Of the priests: Jedaiah the son of Joiarib, and
Jachin; 11 Seraiah the son of Hilkiah, the son of
Meshullam, the son of Zadok, the son of Meraioth,
the son of Ahitub, was the leader of the house of
God. 12 Their brethren who did the work of the
house were eight hundred and twenty-two; and
Adaiah the son of Jeroham, the son of Pelaliah, the
son of Amzi, the son of Zechariah, the son of
Pashhur, the son of Malchijah, 13 and his brethren,
heads of the fathers' houses, were two hundred and

נְבִיא לַכֹּהֲנִים אֶל־לִשְׁכוֹת בֵּית־אֱלֹהֵינוּ וּמַעֲשַׂר
אַדְמָתֵנוּ לַלְוִיִּם וְהֵם הַלְוִיִּם הַמְעַשְּׂרִים בְּכֹל
עָרֵי עֲבֹדָתֵנוּ: 39 וְהָיָה הַכֹּהֵן בֶּן־אַהֲרֹן עִם־הַלְוִיִּם
בַּעְשֵׂר הַלְוִיִּם וְהַלְוִיִּם יַעֲלוּ אֶת־מַעֲשַׂר הַמַּעֲשֵׂר
לְבֵית אֱלֹהֵינוּ אֶל־הַלְּשָׁכוֹת לְבֵית הָאוֹצָר: 40 כִּי
אֶל־הַלְּשָׁכוֹת יָבִיאוּ בְנֵי־יִשְׂרָאֵל וּבְנֵי הַלֵּוִי אֶת־
תְּרוּמַת הַדָּגָן הַתִּירוֹשׁ וְהַיִּצְהָר וְשָׁם כְּלֵי הַמִּקְדָּשׁ
וְהַכֹּהֲנִים הַמְשָׁרְתִים וְהַשּׁוֹעֲרִים וְהַמְשֹׁרְרִים וְלֹא
נַעֲזֹב אֶת־בֵּית אֱלֹהֵינוּ:

יא וַיֵּשְׁבוּ שָׂרֵי־הָעָם בִּירוּשָׁלָ͏ִם וּשְׁאָר הָעָם
הִפִּילוּ גוֹרָלוֹת לְהָבִיא | אֶחָד מִן־הָעֲשָׂרָה לָשֶׁבֶת
בִּירוּשָׁלַ͏ִם עִיר הַקֹּדֶשׁ וְתֵשַׁע הַיָּדוֹת בֶּעָרִים:
2 וַיְבָרֲכוּ הָעָם לְכֹל הָאֲנָשִׁים הַמִּתְנַדְּבִים לָשֶׁבֶת
בִּירוּשָׁלָ͏ִם: פ

3 וְאֵלֶּה רָאשֵׁי הַמְּדִינָה אֲשֶׁר יָשְׁבוּ בִּירוּשָׁלָ͏ִם
וּבְעָרֵי יְהוּדָה יָשְׁבוּ אִישׁ בַּאֲחֻזָּתוֹ בְּעָרֵיהֶם
יִשְׂרָאֵל הַכֹּהֲנִים וְהַלְוִיִּם וְהַנְּתִינִים וּבְנֵי עַבְדֵי
שְׁלֹמֹה: 4 וּבִירוּשָׁלַ͏ִם יָשְׁבוּ מִבְּנֵי יְהוּדָה וּמִבְּנֵי
בִנְיָמִן מִבְּנֵי יְהוּדָה עֲתָיָה בֶן־עֻזִּיָּה בֶּן־זְכַרְיָה
בֶן־אֲמַרְיָה בֶּן־שְׁפַטְיָה בֶּן־מַהֲלַלְאֵל מִבְּנֵי־פָרֶץ:
5 וּמַעֲשֵׂיָה בֶן־בָּרוּךְ בֶּן־כָּל־חֹזֶה בֶּן־חֲזָיָה בֶן־
עֲדָיָה בֶן־יוֹיָרִיב בֶּן־זְכַרְיָה בֶּן־הַשִּׁלֹנִי: 6 כָּל־בְּנֵי־
פֶרֶץ הַיֹּשְׁבִים בִּירוּשָׁלָ͏ִם אַרְבַּע מֵאוֹת שִׁשִּׁים
וּשְׁמֹנָה אַנְשֵׁי־חָיִל: ס   7 וְאֵלֶּה בְּנֵי בִנְיָמִן
סַלֻּא בֶּן־מְשֻׁלָּם בֶּן־יוֹעֵד בֶּן־פְּדָיָה בֶן־קוֹלָיָה בֶּן־
מַעֲשֵׂיָה בֶּן־אִיתִיאֵל בֶּן־יְשַׁעְיָה: 8 וְאַחֲרָיו גַּבַּי סַלָּי
תְּשַׁע מֵאוֹת עֶשְׂרִים וּשְׁמֹנָה: 9 וְיוֹאֵל בֶּן־זִכְרִי פָּקִיד
עֲלֵיהֶם וִיהוּדָה בֶן־הַסְּנוּאָה עַל־הָעִיר מִשְׁנֶה: פ

10 מִן־הַכֹּהֲנִים יְדַעְיָה בֶן־יוֹיָרִיב יָכִין: 11 שְׂרָיָה
בֶן־חִלְקִיָּה בֶּן־מְשֻׁלָּם בֶּן־צָדוֹק בֶּן־מְרָיוֹת בֶּן־
אֲחִיטוּב נְגִד בֵּית הָאֱלֹהִים: 12 וַאֲחֵיהֶם עֹשֵׂי
הַמְּלָאכָה לַבַּיִת שְׁמֹנֶה מֵאוֹת עֶשְׂרִים וּשְׁנָיִם
וַעֲדָיָה בֶּן־יְרֹחָם בֶּן־פְּלַלְיָה בֶּן־אַמְצִי בֶּן־זְכַרְיָה
בֶּן־פַּשְׁחוּר בֶּן־מַלְכִּיָּה: 13 וְאֶחָיו רָאשִׁים לְאָבוֹת
מָאתַיִם אַרְבָּעִים וּשְׁנָיִם וַעֲמַשְׁסַי בֶּן־עֲזַרְאֵל בֶּן־

forty-two; and Amashai the son of Azarel, the son of Ahzai, the son of Meshillemoth, the son of Immer, [14] and their brethren, mighty men of valor, *were* one hundred and twenty-eight. Their overseer *was* Zabdiel the son of *one of* the great men.

[15] Also of the Levites: Shemaiah the son of Hasshub, the son of Azrikam, the son of Hashabiah, the son of Bunni; [16] Shabbethai and Jozabad, of the heads of the Levites, *had* the oversight of the business outside of the house of God; [17] Mattaniah the son of Micha, the son of Zabdi, the son of Asaph, the leader *who* began the thanksgiving with prayer; Bakbukiah, the second among his brethren; and Abda the son of Shammua, the son of Galal, the son of Jeduthun. [18] All the Levites in the holy city *were* two hundred and eighty-four.

[19] Moreover the gatekeepers, Akkub, Talmon, and their brethren who kept the gates, *were* one hundred and seventy-two.

[20] And the rest of Israel, of the priests *and* Levites, *were* in all the cities of Judah, everyone in his inheritance. [21] But the Nethinim dwelt in Ophel. And Ziha and Gishpa *were* over the Nethinim.

[22] Also the overseer of the Levites at Jerusalem *was* Uzzi the son of Bani, the son of Hashabiah, the son of Mattaniah, the son of Micha, of the sons of Asaph, the singers in charge of the service of the house of God. [23] For *it was* the king's command concerning them that a certain portion should be for the singers, a quota day by day. [24] Pethahiah the son of Meshezabel, of the children of Zerah the son of Judah, *was* the king's deputy in all matters concerning the people.

[25] And as for the villages with their fields, *some* of the children of Judah dwelt in Kirjath Arba and its villages, Dibon and its villages, Jekabzeel and its villages; [26] in Jeshua, Moladah, Beth Pelet, [27] Hazar Shual, and Beersheba and its villages; [28] in Ziklag and Meconah and its villages; [29] in En Rimmon, Zorah, Jarmuth, [30] Zanoah, Adullam, and their villages; in Lachish and its fields; in Azekah and its villages. They dwelt from Beersheba to the Valley of Hinnom.

[31] Also the children of Benjamin from Geba *dwelt* in Michmash, Aija, and Bethel, and their villages; [32] in Anathoth, Nob, Ananiah, [33] in Hazor, Ramah, Gittaim; [34] in Hadid, Zeboim, Neballat, [35] in Lod, Ono, *and* the Valley of Craftsmen. [36] Some of the Judean divisions of Levites *were* in Benjamin.

12 Now these *are* the priests and the Levites who came up with Zerubbabel the son of Shealtiel, and Jeshua: Seraiah, Jeremiah, Ezra, [2] Amariah, Malluch, Hattush, [3] Shechaniah, Rehum, Meremoth,

אַחְזַי בֶּן־מְשִׁלֵּמוֹת בֶּן־אִמֵּר: 14 וַאֲחֵיהֶם גִּבּוֹרֵי חַיִל מֵאָה עֶשְׂרִים וּשְׁמֹנֶה וּפָקִיד עֲלֵיהֶם זַבְדִּיאֵל בֶּן־הַגְּדוֹלִים: ס 15 וּמִן־הַלְוִיִּם שְׁמַעְיָה בֶן־חַשּׁוּב בֶּן־עַזְרִיקָם בֶּן־חֲשַׁבְיָה בֶּן־בּוּנִּי: 16 וְשַׁבְּתַי וְיוֹזָבָד עַל־הַמְּלָאכָה הַחִיצֹנָה לְבֵית הָאֱלֹהִים מֵרָאשֵׁי הַלְוִיִּם: 17 וּמַתַּנְיָה בֶן־מִיכָה בֶּן־זַבְדִּי בֶּן־אָסָף רֹאשׁ הַתְּחִלָּה יְהוֹדֶה לַתְּפִלָּה וּבַקְבֻּקְיָה מִשְׁנֶה מֵאֶחָיו וְעַבְדָּא בֶּן־שַׁמּוּעַ בֶּן־גָּלָל בֶּן־יְדִיתוּן: 18 כָּל־הַלְוִיִּם בְּעִיר הַקֹּדֶשׁ מָאתַיִם שְׁמֹנִים וְאַרְבָּעָה: פ

19 וְהַשּׁוֹעֲרִים עַקּוּב טַלְמוֹן וַאֲחֵיהֶם הַשֹּׁמְרִים בַּשְּׁעָרִים מֵאָה שִׁבְעִים וּשְׁנָיִם: 20 וּשְׁאָר יִשְׂרָאֵל הַכֹּהֲנִים הַלְוִיִּם בְּכָל־עָרֵי יְהוּדָה אִישׁ בְּנַחֲלָתוֹ: 21 וְהַנְּתִינִים יֹשְׁבִים בָּעֹפֶל וְצִיחָא וְגִשְׁפָּא עַל־הַנְּתִינִים: פ

22 וּפְקִיד הַלְוִיִּם בִּירוּשָׁלַ͏ִם עֻזִּי בֶן־בָּנִי בֶּן־חֲשַׁבְיָה בֶּן־מַתַּנְיָה בֶּן־מִיכָה מִבְּנֵי אָסָף הַמְשֹׁרְרִים לְנֶגֶד מְלֶאכֶת בֵּית־הָאֱלֹהִים: 23 כִּי־מִצְוַת הַמֶּלֶךְ עֲלֵיהֶם וַאֲמָנָה עַל־הַמְשֹׁרְרִים דְּבַר־יוֹם בְּיוֹמוֹ: 24 וּפְתַחְיָה בֶן־מְשֵׁיזַבְאֵל מִבְּנֵי־זֶרַח בֶּן־יְהוּדָה לְיַד הַמֶּלֶךְ לְכָל־דָּבָר לָעָם: 25 וְאֶל־הַחֲצֵרִים בִּשְׂדֹתָם מִבְּנֵי יְהוּדָה יָשְׁבוּ בְּקִרְיַת הָאַרְבַּע וּבְנֹתֶיהָ וּבְדִיבֹן וּבְנֹתֶיהָ וּבִיקַּבְצְאֵל וַחֲצֵרֶיהָ: 26 וּבְיֵשׁוּעַ וּבְמוֹלָדָה וּבְבֵית פָּלֶט: 27 וּבַחֲצַר שׁוּעָל וּבְבְאֵר שֶׁבַע וּבְנֹתֶיהָ: 28 וּבְצִקְלַג וּבִמְכֹנָה וּבִבְנֹתֶיהָ: 29 וּבְעֵין רִמּוֹן וּבְצָרְעָה וּבְיַרְמוּת: 30 זָנֹחַ עֲדֻלָּם וְחַצְרֵיהֶם לָכִישׁ וּשְׂדֹתֶיהָ עֲזֵקָה וּבְנֹתֶיהָ וַיַּחֲנוּ מִבְּאֵר־שֶׁבַע עַד־גֵּיא־הִנֹּם: 31 וּבְנֵי בִנְיָמִן מִגֶּבַע מִכְמָשׂ וְעַיָּה וּבֵית־אֵל וּבְנֹתֶיהָ: 32 עֲנָתוֹת נֹב עֲנָנְיָה: 33 חָצוֹר רָמָה גִּתָּיִם: 34 חָדִיד צְבֹעִים נְבַלָּט: 35 לֹד וְאוֹנוֹ גֵּי הַחֲרָשִׁים: 36 וּמִן־הַלְוִיִּם מַחְלְקוֹת יְהוּדָה לְבִנְיָמִין: פ

יב וְאֵלֶּה הַכֹּהֲנִים וְהַלְוִיִּם אֲשֶׁר עָלוּ עִם־זְרֻבָּבֶל בֶּן־שְׁאַלְתִּיאֵל וְיֵשׁוּעַ שְׂרָיָה יִרְמְיָה עֶזְרָא: 2 אֲמַרְיָה

4 Iddo, Ginnethoi, Abijah, 5 Mijamin, Maadiah, Bilgah, 6 Shemaiah, Joiarib, Jedaiah, 7 Sallu, Amok, Hilkiah, *and* Jedaiah.

These *were* the heads of the priests and their brethren in the days of Jeshua.

8 Moreover the Levites *were* Jeshua, Binnui, Kadmiel, Sherebiah, Judah, *and* Mattaniah *who* led the thanksgiving *psalms,* he and his brethren. 9 Also Bakbukiah and Unni, their brethren, *stood* across from them in *their* duties.

10 Jeshua begot Joiakim, Joiakim begot Eliashib, Eliashib begot Joiada, 11 Joiada begot Jonathan, and Jonathan begot Jaddua.

12 Now in the days of Joiakim, the priests, the heads of the fathers' *houses were:* of Seraiah, Meraiah; of Jeremiah, Hananiah; 13 of Ezra, Meshullam; of Amariah, Jehohanan; 14 of Melichu, Jonathan; of Shebaniah, Joseph; 15 of Harim, Adna; of Meraioth, Helkai; 16 of Iddo, Zechariah; of Ginnmethon, Meshullam; 17 of Abijah, Zichri; *the son* of Minjamin; of Moadiah, Piltai; 18 of Bilgah, Shammua; of Shemaiah, Jehonathan; 19 of Joiarib, Mattenai; of Jedaiah, Uzzi; 20 of Sallai, Kallai; of Amok, Eber; 21 of Hilkiah, Hashabiah; *and* of Jedaiah, Nethanel.

22 During the reign of Darius the Persian, a record *was* also kept of the Levites and priests *who had been* heads of their fathers' *houses* in the days of Eliashib, Joiada, Johanan, and Jaddua. 23 The sons of Levi, the heads of the fathers' *houses* until the days of Johanan the son of Eliashib, *were* written in the book of the chronicles.

24 And the heads of the Levites *were* Hashabiah, Sherebiah, and Jeshua the son of Kadmiel, with their brothers across from them, to praise *and* give thanks, group alternating with group, according to the command of David the man of God. 25 Mattaniah, Bakbukiah, Obadiah, Meshullam, Talmon, and Akkub *were* gatekeepers keeping the watch at the storerooms of the gates. 26 These *lived* in the days of Joiakim the son of, Jeshua, the son of Jozadak, and in the days of Nehemiah the governor, and of Ezra the priest, the scribe.

27 Now at the dedication of the wall of Jerusalem they sought out the Levites in all their places, to bring them to Jerusalem to celebrate the dedication with gladness, both with thanksgivings and singing, *with* cymbals and stringed instruments and harps. 28 And the sons of the singers gathered together from the countryside around Jerusalem, from the villages of the Netophathites, 29 from the house of Gilgal, and from the fields of Geba and Azmaveth; for the singers had built themselves villages all

מַלּוּךְ חַטּוּשׁ: 3 שְׁכַנְיָה רְחֻם מְרֵמֹת: 4 עִדּוֹא גִנְּתוֹי אֲבִיָּה: 5 מִיָּמִין מַעַדְיָה בִּלְגָּה: 6 שְׁמַעְיָה וְיוֹיָרִיב יְדַעְיָה: 7 סַלּוּ עָמוֹק חִלְקִיָּה יְדַעְיָה אֵלֶּה רָאשֵׁי הַכֹּהֲנִים וַאֲחֵיהֶם בִּימֵי יֵשׁוּעַ: פ

8 וְהַלְוִיִּם יֵשׁוּעַ בִּנּוּי קַדְמִיאֵל שֵׁרֵבְיָה יְהוּדָה מַתַּנְיָה עַל־הֻיְּדוֹת הוּא וְאֶחָיו: 9 וּבַקְבֻּקְיָה וְעֻנִּוֹ אֲחֵיהֶם לְנֶגְדָּם לְמִשְׁמָרוֹת: 10 וְיֵשׁוּעַ הוֹלִיד אֶת־יוֹיָקִים וְיוֹיָקִים הוֹלִיד אֶת־אֶלְיָשִׁיב וְאֶלְיָשִׁיב אֶת־יוֹיָדָע: 11 וְיוֹיָדָע הוֹלִיד אֶת־יוֹנָתָן וְיוֹנָתָן הוֹלִיד אֶת־יַדּוּעַ: 12 וּבִימֵי יוֹיָקִים הָיוּ כֹהֲנִים רָאשֵׁי הָאָבוֹת לִשְׂרָיָה מְרָיָה לְיִרְמְיָה חֲנַנְיָה: 13 לְעֶזְרָא מְשֻׁלָּם לַאֲמַרְיָה יְהוֹחָנָן: 14 לִמְלוּכִי יוֹנָתָן לִשְׁבַנְיָה יוֹסֵף: 15 לְחָרִם עַדְנָא לִמְרָיוֹת חֶלְקָי: 16 לְעִדּוֹא זְכַרְיָה לְגִנְּתוֹן מְשֻׁלָּם: 17 לַאֲבִיָּה זִכְרִי לְמִנְיָמִין לְמוֹעַדְיָה פִּלְטָי: 18 לְבִלְגָּה שַׁמּוּעַ לִשְׁמַעְיָה יְהוֹנָתָן: 19 וּלְיוֹיָרִיב מַתְּנַי לִידַעְיָה עֻזִּי: 20 לְסַלַּי קַלָּי לְעָמוֹק עֵבֶר: 21 לְחִלְקִיָּה חֲשַׁבְיָה לִידַעְיָה נְתַנְאֵל: 22 הַלְוִיִּם בִּימֵי אֶלְיָשִׁיב יוֹיָדָע וְיוֹחָנָן וְיַדּוּעַ כְּתוּבִים רָאשֵׁי אָבוֹת וְהַכֹּהֲנִים עַל־מַלְכוּת דָּרְיָוֶשׁ הַפָּרְסִי: 23 בְּנֵי לֵוִי רָאשֵׁי הָאָבוֹת כְּתוּבִים עַל־סֵפֶר דִּבְרֵי הַיָּמִים וְעַד־יְמֵי יוֹחָנָן בֶּן־אֶלְיָשִׁיב: 24 וְרָאשֵׁי הַלְוִיִּם חֲשַׁבְיָה שֵׁרֵבְיָה וְיֵשׁוּעַ בֶּן־קַדְמִיאֵל וַאֲחֵיהֶם לְנֶגְדָּם לְהַלֵּל לְהוֹדוֹת בְּמִצְוַת דָּוִיד אִישׁ־הָאֱלֹהִים מִשְׁמָר לְעֻמַּת מִשְׁמָר: 25 מַתַּנְיָה וּבַקְבֻּקְיָה עֹבַדְיָה מְשֻׁלָּם טַלְמוֹן עַקּוּב שֹׁמְרִים שׁוֹעֲרִים מִשְׁמָר בַּאֲסֻפֵּי הַשְּׁעָרִים: 26 אֵלֶּה בִּימֵי יוֹיָקִים בֶּן־יֵשׁוּעַ בֶּן־יוֹצָדָק וּבִימֵי נְחֶמְיָה הַפֶּחָה וְעֶזְרָא הַכֹּהֵן הַסּוֹפֵר: פ

27 וּבַחֲנֻכַּת חוֹמַת יְרוּשָׁלַ͏ִם בִּקְשׁוּ אֶת־הַלְוִיִּם מִכָּל־מְקוֹמֹתָם לַהֲבִיאָם לִירוּשָׁלָ͏ִם לַעֲשֹׂת חֲנֻכָּה וְשִׂמְחָה וּבְתוֹדוֹת וּבְשִׁיר מְצִלְתַּיִם נְבָלִים וּבְכִנֹּרוֹת: 28 וַיֵּאָסְפוּ בְּנֵי הַמְשֹׁרְרִים וּמִן־הַכִּכָּר סְבִיבוֹת יְרוּשָׁלַ͏ִם וּמִן־חַצְרֵי נְטֹפָתִי: 29 וּמִבֵּית הַגִּלְגָּל וּמִשְּׂדוֹת גֶּבַע וְעַזְמָוֶת כִּי חֲצֵרִים בָּנוּ

around Jerusalem. ³⁰ Then the priests and Levites purified themselves, and purified the people, the gates, and the wall.

³¹ So I brought the leaders of Judah up on the wall, and appointed two large thanksgiving choirs. *One* went to the right hand on the wall toward the Refuse Gate. ³² After them went Hoshaiah and half of the leaders of Judah, ³³ and Azariah, Ezra, Meshullam, ³⁴ Judah, Benjamin, Shemaiah, Jeremiah, ³⁵ and some of the priests' sons with trumpets—Zechariah the son of Jonathan, the son of Shemaiah, the son of Mattaniah, the son of Michaiah, the son of Zaccur, the son of Asaph, ³⁶ and his brethren, Shemaiah, Azarel, Milalai, Gilalai, Maai, Nethanel, Judah, *and* Hanani, with the musical instruments of David the man of God. And Ezra the scribe *went* before them. ³⁷ By the Fountain Gate, in front of them, they went up the stairs of the City of David, on the stairway of the wall, beyond the house of David, as far as the Water Gate eastward.

³⁸ The other thanksgiving choir went the opposite *way,* and I *was* behind them with half of the people on the wall, going past the Tower of the Ovens as far as the Broad Wall, ³⁹ and above the Gate of Ephraim, above the Old Gate, above the Fish Gate, the Tower of Hananel, the Tower of the Hundred, as far as the Sheep Gate; and they stopped by the Gate of the Prison.

⁴⁰ So the two thanksgiving choirs stood in the house of God, likewise I and the half of the rulers with me; ⁴¹ and the priests, Eliakim, Maaseiah, Minjamin, Michaiah, Elioenai, Zechariah, *and* Hananiah, with trumpets; ⁴² also Maaseiah, Shemaiah, Eleazar, Uzzi, Jehohanan, Malchijah, Elam, and Ezer. The singers sang loudly with Jezrahiah the director.

⁴³ Also that day they offered great sacrifices, and rejoiced, for God had made them rejoice with great joy; the women and the children also rejoiced, so that the joy of Jerusalem was heard afar off.

⁴⁴ And at the same time some were appointed over the rooms of the storehouse for the offerings, the firstfruits, and the tithes, to gather into them from the fields of the cities the portions specified by the Law for the priests and Levites; for Judah rejoiced over the priests and Levites who ministered. ⁴⁵ Both the singers and the gatekeepers kept the charge of their God and the charge of the purification, according to the command of David *and* Solomon his son. ⁴⁶ For in the days of David and Asaph of old *there were* chiefs of the singers, and songs of praise and thanksgiving to God. ⁴⁷ In the days of Zerubbabel and in the days of

לָהֶם הַמְשֹׁרְרִים סְבִיבוֹת יְרוּשָׁלָ͏ִם: 30 וַיִּטַּהֲרוּ הַכֹּהֲנִים וְהַלְוִיִּם וַיְטַהֲרוּ אֶת־הָעָם וְאֶת־הַשְּׁעָרִים וְאֶת־הַחוֹמָה: 31 וָאַעֲלֶה אֶת־שָׂרֵי יְהוּדָה מֵעַל לַחוֹמָה וָאַעֲמִידָה שְׁתֵּי תוֹדֹת גְּדוֹלֹת וְתַהֲלֻכֹת לַיָּמִין מֵעַל לַחוֹמָה לְשַׁעַר הָאַשְׁפֹּת: 32 וַיֵּלֶךְ אַחֲרֵיהֶם הוֹשַׁעְיָה וַחֲצִי שָׂרֵי יְהוּדָה: 33 וַעֲזַרְיָה עֶזְרָא וּמְשֻׁלָּם: 34 יְהוּדָה וּבִנְיָמִן וּשְׁמַעְיָה וְיִרְמְיָה: ס 35 וּמִבְּנֵי הַכֹּהֲנִים בַּחֲצֹצְרוֹת זְכַרְיָה בֶן־יוֹנָתָן בֶּן־שְׁמַעְיָה בֶּן־מַתַּנְיָה בֶּן־מִיכָיָה בֶּן־זַכּוּר בֶּן־אָסָף: 36 וְאֶחָיו שְׁמַעְיָה וַעֲזַרְאֵל מִלֲלַי גִּלֲלַי מָעַי נְתַנְאֵל וִיהוּדָה חֲנָנִי בִּכְלֵי־שִׁיר דָּוִיד אִישׁ הָאֱלֹהִים וְעֶזְרָא הַסּוֹפֵר לִפְנֵיהֶם: 37 וְעַל שַׁעַר הָעַיִן וְנֶגְדָּם עָלוּ עַל־מַעֲלוֹת עִיר דָּוִיד בַּמַּעֲלֶה לַחוֹמָה מֵעַל לְבֵית דָּוִיד וְעַד שַׁעַר הַמַּיִם מִזְרָח: 38 וְהַתּוֹדָה הַשֵּׁנִית הַהוֹלֶכֶת לְמוֹאל וַאֲנִי אַחֲרֶיהָ וַחֲצִי הָעָם מֵעַל לְהַחוֹמָה מֵעַל לְמִגְדַּל הַתַּנּוּרִים וְעַד הַחוֹמָה הָרְחָבָה: 39 וּמֵעַל לְשַׁעַר־ אֶפְרַיִם וְעַל־שַׁעַר הַיְשָׁנָה וְעַל־שַׁעַר הַדָּגִים וּמִגְדַּל חֲנַנְאֵל וּמִגְדַּל הַמֵּאָה וְעַד שַׁעַר הַצֹּאן וְעָמְדוּ בְּשַׁעַר הַמַּטָּרָה: 40 וַתַּעֲמֹדְנָה שְׁתֵּי הַתּוֹדֹת בְּבֵית הָאֱלֹהִים וַאֲנִי וַחֲצִי הַסְּגָנִים עִמִּי: 41 וְהַכֹּהֲנִים אֶלְיָקִים מַעֲשֵׂיָה מִנְיָמִין מִיכָיָה אֶלְיוֹעֵינַי זְכַרְיָה חֲנַנְיָה בַּחֲצֹצְרוֹת: 42 וּמַעֲשֵׂיָה וּשְׁמַעְיָה וְאֶלְעָזָר וְעֻזִּי וִיהוֹחָנָן וּמַלְכִּיָּה וְעֵילָם וָעָזֶר וַיַּשְׁמִיעוּ הַמְשֹׁרְרִים וְיִזְרַחְיָה הַפָּקִיד: 43 וַיִּזְבְּחוּ בַיּוֹם־הַהוּא זְבָחִים גְּדוֹלִים וַיִּשְׂמָחוּ כִּי הָאֱלֹהִים שִׂמְּחָם שִׂמְחָה גְדוֹלָה וְגַם הַנָּשִׁים וְהַיְלָדִים שָׂמֵחוּ וַתִּשָּׁמַע שִׂמְחַת יְרוּשָׁלַ͏ִם מֵרָחוֹק: 44 וַיִּפָּקְדוּ בַיּוֹם הַהוּא אֲנָשִׁים עַל־הַנְּשָׁכוֹת לָאוֹצָרוֹת לַתְּרוּמוֹת לָרֵאשִׁית וְלַמַּעַשְׂרוֹת לִכְנוֹס בָּהֶם לִשְׂדֵי הֶעָרִים מְנָאוֹת הַתּוֹרָה לַכֹּהֲנִים וְלַלְוִיִּם כִּי שִׂמְחַת יְהוּדָה עַל־ הַכֹּהֲנִים וְעַל־הַלְוִיִּם הָעֹמְדִים: 45 וַיִּשְׁמְרוּ מִשְׁמֶרֶת אֱלֹהֵיהֶם וּמִשְׁמֶרֶת הַטָּהֳרָה וְהַמְשֹׁרְרִים וְהַשֹּׁעֲרִים כְּמִצְוַת דָּוִיד שְׁלֹמֹה בְנוֹ: 46 כִּי־בִימֵי דָּוִיד וְאָסָף מִקֶּדֶם רָאשׁ הַמְשֹׁרְרִים וְשִׁיר־תְּהִלָּה וְהֹדוֹת לֵאלֹהִים: 47 וְכָל־יִשְׂרָאֵל בִּימֵי זְרֻבָּבֶל וּבִימֵי נְחֶמְיָה

Nehemiah all Israel gave the portions for the singers and the gatekeepers, a portion for each day. They also consecrated *holy things* for the Levites, and the Levites consecrated *them* for the children of Aaron.

13 On that day they read from the Book of Moses in the hearing of the people, and in it was found written that no Ammonite or Moabite should ever come into the assembly of God, [2] because they had not met the children of Israel with bread and water, but hired Balaam against them to curse them. However, our God turned the curse into a blessing. [3] So it was, when they had heard the Law, that they separated all the mixed multitude from Israel.

[4] Now before this, Eliashib the priest, having authority over the storerooms of the house of our God, *was* allied with Tobiah. [5] And he had prepared for him a large room, where previously they had stored the grain offerings, the frankincense, the articles, the tithes of grain, the new wine and oil, which were commanded *to be given* to the Levites and singers and gatekeepers, and the offerings for the priests. [6] But during all this I was not in Jerusalem, for in the thirty-second year of Artaxerxes king of Babylon I had returned to the king. Then after certain days I obtained leave from the king, [7] and I came to Jerusalem and discovered the evil that Eliashib had done for Tobiah, in preparing a room for him in the courts of the house of God. [8] And it grieved me bitterly; therefore I threw all the household goods of Tobiah out of the room. [9] Then I commanded them to cleanse the rooms; and I brought back into them the articles of the house of God, with the grain offering and the frankincense.

[10] I also realized that the portions for the Levites had not been given *them;* for each of the Levites and the singers who did the work had gone back to his field. [11] So I contended with the rulers, and said, "Why is the house of God forsaken?" And I gathered them together and set them in their place. [12] Then all Judah brought the tithe of the grain and the new wine and the oil to the storehouse. [13] And I appointed as treasurers over the storehouse Shelemiah the priest and Zadok the scribe, and of the Levites, Pedaiah; and next to them *was* Hanan the son of Zaccur, the son of Mattaniah; for they were considered faithful, and their task *was* to distribute to their brethren.

[14] Remember me, O my God, concerning this, and do not wipe out my good deeds that I have done for the house of my God, and for its services!

נְתָנִים מְנָיֹות הַמְשֹׁרְרִים וְהַשֹּׁעֲרִים דְּבַר־יֹום בְּיֹומֹו וּמַקְדִּשִׁים לַלְוִיִּם וְהַלְוִיִּם מַקְדִּשִׁים לִבְנֵי אַהֲרֹן: פ

יג בַּיֹּום הַהוּא נִקְרָא בְּסֵפֶר מֹשֶׁה בְּאָזְנֵי הָעָם וְנִמְצָא כָּתוּב בֹּו אֲשֶׁר לֹא־יָבֹוא עַמֹּנִי וּמֹאָבִי בִּקְהַל הָאֱלֹהִים עַד־עֹולָם: 2 כִּי לֹא קִדְּמוּ אֶת־בְּנֵי יִשְׂרָאֵל בַּלֶּחֶם וּבַמָּיִם וַיִּשְׂכֹּר עָלָיו אֶת־בִּלְעָם לְקַלְלֹו וַיַּהֲפֹךְ אֱלֹהֵינוּ הַקְּלָלָה לִבְרָכָה: 3 וַיְהִי כְּשָׁמְעָם אֶת־הַתֹּורָה וַיַּבְדִּילוּ כָל־עֵרֶב מִיִּשְׂרָאֵל: 4 וְלִפְנֵי מִזֶּה אֶלְיָשִׁיב הַכֹּהֵן נָתוּן בְּלִשְׁכַּת בֵּית־אֱלֹהֵינוּ קָרֹוב לְטֹובִיָּה: 5 וַיַּעַשׂ לֹו לִשְׁכָּה גְדֹולָה וְשָׁם הָיוּ לְפָנִים נֹתְנִים אֶת־הַמִּנְחָה הַלְּבֹונָה וְהַכֵּלִים וּמַעְשַׂר הַדָּגָן הַתִּירֹושׁ וְהַיִּצְהָר מִצְוַת הַלְוִיִּם וְהַמְשֹׁרְרִים וְהַשֹּׁעֲרִים וּתְרוּמַת הַכֹּהֲנִים: 6 וּבְכָל־זֶה לֹא הָיִיתִי בִּירוּשָׁלִָם כִּי בִּשְׁנַת שְׁלֹשִׁים וּשְׁתַּיִם לְאַרְתַּחְשַׁסְתְּא מֶלֶךְ־בָּבֶל בָּאתִי אֶל־הַמֶּלֶךְ וּלְקֵץ יָמִים נִשְׁאַלְתִּי מִן־הַמֶּלֶךְ: 7 וָאָבֹוא לִירוּשָׁלִָם וָאָבִינָה בָרָעָה אֲשֶׁר עָשָׂה אֶלְיָשִׁיב לְטֹובִיָּה לַעֲשֹׂות לֹו נִשְׁכָּה בְּחַצְרֵי בֵּית הָאֱלֹהִים: 8 וַיֵּרַע לִי מְאֹד וָאַשְׁלִיכָה אֶת־כָּל־כְּלֵי בֵית־טֹובִיָּה הַחוּץ מִן־הַלִּשְׁכָּה: 9 וָאֹמְרָה וַיְטַהֲרוּ הַלְּשָׁכֹות וָאָשִׁיבָה שָּׁם כְּלֵי בֵּית הָאֱלֹהִים אֶת־הַמִּנְחָה וְהַלְּבֹונָה: פ

10 וָאֵדְעָה כִּי־מְנָיֹות הַלְוִיִּם לֹא נִתָּנָה וַיִּבְרְחוּ אִישׁ־לְשָׂדֵהוּ הַלְוִיִּם וְהַמְשֹׁרְרִים עֹשֵׂי הַמְּלָאכָה: 11 וָאָרִיבָה אֶת־הַסְּגָנִים וָאֹמְרָה מַדּוּעַ נֶעֱזַב בֵּית־הָאֱלֹהִים וָאֶקְבְּצֵם וָאַעֲמִדֵם עַל־עָמְדָם: 12 וְכָל־יְהוּדָה הֵבִיאוּ מַעְשַׂר הַדָּגָן וְהַתִּירֹושׁ וְהַיִּצְהָר לָאֹוצָרֹות: 13 וָאֹוצְרָה עַל־אֹוצָרֹות שֶׁלֶמְיָה הַכֹּהֵן וְצָדֹוק הַסֹּופֵר וּפְדָיָה מִן־הַלְוִיִּם וְעַל־יָדָם חָנָן בֶּן־זַכּוּר בֶּן־מַתַּנְיָה כִּי נֶאֱמָנִים נֶחְשָׁבוּ וַעֲלֵיהֶם לַחֲלֹק לַאֲחֵיהֶם: פ

14 זָכְרָה־לִּי אֱלֹהַי עַל־זֹאת וְאַל־תֶּמַח חֲסָדַי אֲשֶׁר

15 In those days I saw *people* in Judah treading wine presses on the Sabbath, and bringing in sheaves, and loading donkeys with wine, grapes, figs, and all *kinds of* burdens, which they brought into Jerusalem on the Sabbath day. And I warned *them* about the day on which they were selling provisions. 16 Men of Tyre dwelt there also, who brought in fish and all kinds of goods, and sold *them* on the Sabbath to the children of Judah, and in Jerusalem.

17 Then I contended with the nobles of Judah, and said to them, "What evil thing *is* this that you do, by which you profane the Sabbath day? 18 Did not your fathers do thus, and did not our God bring all this disaster on us and on this city? Yet you bring added wrath on Israel by profaning the Sabbath."

19 So it was, at the gates of Jerusalem, as it began to be dark before the Sabbath, that I commanded the gates to be shut, and charged that they must not be opened till after the Sabbath. Then I posted *some* of my servants at the gates, *so that* no burdens would be brought in on the Sabbath day. 20 Now the merchants and sellers of all kinds of wares lodged outside Jerusalem once or twice.

21 Then I warned them, and said to them, "Why do you spend the night around the wall? If you do *so* again, I will lay hands on you!" From that time on they came no *more* on the Sabbath. 22 And I commanded the Levites that they should cleanse themselves, and that they should go and guard the gates, to sanctify the Sabbath day.

Remember me, O my God, *concerning* this also, and spare me according to the greatness of Your mercy!

23 In those days I also saw Jews *who* had married women of Ashdod, Ammon, *and* Moab. 24 And half of their children spoke the language of Ashdod, and could not speak the language of Judah, but spoke according to the language of one or the other people.

25 So I contended with them and cursed them, struck some of them and pulled out their hair, and made them swear by God, *saying,* "You shall not give your daughters as wives to their sons, nor take their daughters for your sons or yourselves. 26 Did not Solomon king of Israel sin by these things? Yet among many nations there was no king like him, who was beloved of his God; and God made him king over all Israel. Nevertheless pagan women caused even him to sin. 27 Should we then hear of your doing all this great evil, transgressing against our God by marrying pagan women?"

15 בַּיָּמִ֣ים הָהֵ֡מָּה עָשִׂ֣יתִי בְבֵֽית־אֱלֹהַ֣י וּבְמִשְׁמָרָ֑יו רָאִ֣יתִי בִֽיהוּדָ֣ה ׀ דֹּרְכִֽים־גִּתּ֣וֹת ׀ בַּשַּׁבָּ֗ת וּמְבִיאִ֣ים הָעֲרֵמ֡וֹת וְעֹֽמְסִ֣ים עַל־הַֽחֲמֹרִים֩ וְאַף־יַ֨יִן עֲנָבִ֤ים וּתְאֵנִים֙ וְכָל־מַשָּׂ֔א וּמְבִיאִ֥ים יְרוּשָׁלַ֖͏ִם בְּי֣וֹם הַשַּׁבָּ֑ת וָאָעִ֕יד בְּי֖וֹם מִכְרָ֥ם צָֽיִד: 16 וְהַצֹּרִים֙ יָ֣שְׁבוּ בָ֔הּ מְבִיאִ֥ים דָּ֖אג וְכָל־מֶ֑כֶר וּמֹכְרִ֧ים בַּשַּׁבָּ֛ת לִבְנֵ֥י יְהוּדָ֖ה וּבִירֽוּשָׁלָֽ͏ִם: 17 וָֽאָרִ֕יבָה אֵ֖ת חֹרֵ֣י יְהוּדָ֑ה וָאֹמְרָ֣ה לָהֶ֗ם מָֽה־הַדָּבָ֨ר הָרָ֤ע הַזֶּה֙ אֲשֶׁ֣ר אַתֶּ֣ם עֹשִׂ֔ים וּֽמְחַלְּלִ֖ים אֶת־י֥וֹם הַשַּׁבָּֽת: 18 הֲל֨וֹא כֹ֤ה עָשׂוּ֙ אֲבֹ֣תֵיכֶ֔ם וַיָּבֵ֣א אֱלֹהֵ֗ינוּ עָלֵ֨ינוּ֙ אֵ֚ת כָּל־הָֽרָעָ֣ה הַזֹּ֔את וְעַ֖ל הָעִ֣יר הַזֹּ֑את וְאַתֶּ֞ם מוֹסִיפִ֤ים חָרוֹן֙ עַל־יִשְׂרָאֵ֔ל לְחַלֵּ֖ל אֶת־הַשַּׁבָּֽת: פ

19 וַיְהִ֡י כַּאֲשֶׁ֣ר צָֽלֲלוּ֩ שַׁעֲרֵ֨י יְרוּשָׁלַ֜͏ִם לִפְנֵ֣י הַשַּׁבָּ֗ת וָאֹֽמְרָה֙ וַיִּסָּֽגְר֣וּ הַדְּלָת֔וֹת וָאֹ֣מְרָ֔ה אֲשֶׁר֙ לֹ֣א יִפְתָּח֔וּם עַ֖ד אַחַ֣ר הַשַּׁבָּ֑ת וּמִנְּעָרַ֗י הֶעֱמַ֙דְתִּי֙ עַל־הַשְּׁעָרִ֔ים לֹא־יָב֥וֹא מַשָּׂ֖א בְּי֥וֹם הַשַּׁבָּֽת: 20 וַיָּלִ֧ינוּ הָרֹכְלִ֛ים וּמֹכְרֵ֥י כָל־מִמְכָּ֖ר מִח֣וּץ לִירֽוּשָׁלָ֑͏ִם פַּ֖עַם וּשְׁתָּֽיִם: 21 וָאָעִ֣ידָה בָהֶ֗ם וָאֹמְרָ֤ה אֲלֵיהֶם֙ מַדּ֜וּעַ אַתֶּ֤ם לֵנִים֙ נֶ֣גֶד הַחוֹמָ֔ה אִם־תִּשְׁנ֕וּ יָ֖ד אֶשְׁלַ֣ח בָּכֶ֑ם מִן־הָעֵ֣ת הַהִ֔יא לֹא־בָ֖אוּ בַּשַּׁבָּֽת: ס 22 וָאֹמְרָ֣ה לַלְוִיִּ֗ם אֲשֶׁ֨ר יִֽהְי֤וּ מִֽטַּהֲרִים֙ וּבָאִים֙ שֹׁמְרִ֣ים הַשְּׁעָרִ֔ים לְקַדֵּ֖שׁ אֶת־י֣וֹם הַשַּׁבָּ֑ת גַּם־זֹאת֙ זָכְרָה־לִּ֣י אֱלֹהַ֔י וְח֥וּסָה עָלַ֖י כְּרֹ֥ב חַסְדֶּֽךָ: פ

23 גַּ֣ם ׀ בַּיָּמִ֣ים הָהֵ֗ם רָאִ֤יתִי אֶת־הַיְּהוּדִים֙ הֹשִׁ֗יבוּ נָשִׁים֙ אשדודיות עַמֳּנִיּ֖וֹת מֽוֹאֲבִיּֽוֹת: 24 וּבְנֵיהֶ֗ם חֲצִי֙ מְדַבֵּ֣ר אַשְׁדּוֹדִ֔ית וְאֵינָ֥ם מַכִּירִ֖ים לְדַבֵּ֣ר יְהוּדִ֑ית וְכִלְשׁ֖וֹן עַ֥ם וָעָֽם: 25 וָאָרִ֤יב עִמָּם֙ וָאֲקַֽלְלֵ֔ם וָאַכֶּ֥ה מֵהֶ֛ם אֲנָשִׁ֖ים וָֽאֶמְרְטֵ֑ם וָאַשְׁבִּיעֵ֣ם בֵּֽאלֹהִ֗ים אִם־תִּתְּנ֤וּ בְנֹֽתֵיכֶם֙ לִבְנֵיהֶ֔ם וְאִם־תִּשְׂאוּ֙ מִבְּנֹ֣תֵיהֶ֔ם לִבְנֵיכֶ֖ם וְלָכֶֽם: 26 הֲל֣וֹא עַל־אֵ֣לֶּה חָֽטָא־שְׁלֹמֹ֣ה מֶ֣לֶךְ יִשְׂרָאֵ֗ל וּבַגּוֹיִ֤ם הָֽרַבִּים֙ לֹא־הָיָ֣ה מֶ֣לֶךְ כָּמֹ֔הוּ וְאָה֤וּב לֵֽאלֹהָיו֙ הָיָ֔ה וַיִּתְּנֵ֣הוּ אֱלֹהִ֔ים מֶ֖לֶךְ עַל־כָּל־יִשְׂרָאֵ֑ל גַּם־אוֹת֣וֹ הֶחֱטִ֔יאוּ הַנָּשִׁ֖ים הַנָּכְרִיּֽוֹת: 27 וְלָכֶ֣ם הֲנִשְׁמַ֗ע לַעֲשֹׂת֙ אֵ֣ת כָּל־הָרָעָ֤ה הַגְּדוֹלָה֙ הַזֹּ֔את לִמְעֹ֖ל בֵּֽאלֹהֵ֑ינוּ לְהֹשִׁ֛יב

28 And *one* of the sons of Joiada, the son of
Eliashib the high priest, *was* a son-in-law of
Sanballat the Horonite; therefore I drove him from
me.

29 Remember them, O my God, because they
have defiled the priesthood and the covenant of the
priesthood and the Levites.

30 Thus I cleansed them of everything pagan. I
also assigned duties to the priests and the Levites,
each to his service, 31 and *to bringing* the wood
offering and the firstfruits at appointed times.

Remember me, O my God, for good!

נָשִׁים נָכְרִיּוֹת: 28 וּמִבְּנֵי יוֹיָדָע בֶּן־אֶלְיָשִׁיב הַכֹּהֵן
הַגָּדוֹל חָתָן לְסַנְבַלַּט הַחֹרֹנִי וָאַבְרִיחֵהוּ מֵעָלָי:
29 זָכְרָה לָהֶם אֱלֹהָי עַל גָּאֳלֵי הַכְּהֻנָּה וּבְרִית
הַכְּהֻנָּה וְהַלְוִיִּם: 30 וְטִהַרְתִּים מִכָּל־נֵכָר וָאַעֲמִידָה
מִשְׁמָרוֹת לַכֹּהֲנִים וְלַלְוִיִּם אִישׁ בִּמְלַאכְתּוֹ:
31 וּלְקֻרְבַּן הָעֵצִים בְּעִתִּים מְזֻמָּנוֹת וְלַבִּכּוּרִים
זָכְרָה־לִּי אֱלֹהַי לְטוֹבָה:

The First Book of the

CHRONICLES

1 Adam, Seth, Enosh, ²Cainan, Mahalalel, Jared, ³Enoch, Methuselah, Lamech, ⁴Noah, Shem, Ham, and Japheth.

⁵The sons of Japheth were Gomer, Magog, Madai, Javan, Tubal, Meshech, and Tiras. ⁶The sons of Gomer were Ashkenaz, Diphath, and Togarmah. ⁷The sons of Javan were Elishah, Tarshishah, Kittim, and Rodanim.

⁸The sons of Ham were Cush, Mizraim, Put, and Canaan. ⁹The sons of Cush were Seba, Havilah, Sabta, Raama, and Sabtecha. The sons of Raama were Sheba and Dedan. ¹⁰Cush begot Nimrod; he began to be a mighty one on the earth. ¹¹Mizraim begot Ludim, Anamim, Lehabim, Naphtuhim, ¹²Pathrusim, Casluhim (from whom came the Philistines and the Caphtorim). ¹³Canaan begot Sidon, his firstborn, and Heth; ¹⁴the Jebusite, the Amorite, and the Girgashite; ¹⁵the Hivite, the Arkite, and the Sinite; ¹⁶the Arvadite, the Zemarite, and the Hamathite.

¹⁷The sons of Shem were Elam, Asshur, Arphaxad, Lud, Aram, Uz, Hul, Gether, and Meshech. ¹⁸Arphaxad begot Shelah, and Shelah begot Eber. ¹⁹To Eber were born two sons: the name of one was Peleg, for in his days the earth was divided; and his brother's name was Joktan. ²⁰Joktan begot Almodad, Sheleph, Hazarmaveth, Jerah, ²¹Hadoram, Uzal, Diklah, ²²Ebal, Abimael, Sheba, ²³Ophir, Havilah, and Jobab. All these were the sons of Joktan.

²⁴Shem, Arphaxad, Shelah, ²⁵Eber, Peleg, Reu, ²⁶Serug, Nahor, Terah, ²⁷and Abram, who is Abraham. ²⁸The sons of Abraham were Isaac and Ishmael.

²⁹These are their genealogies: The firstborn of Ishmael was Nebajoth; then Kedar, Adbeel, Mibsam, ³⁰Mishma, Dumah, Massa, Hadad, Tema, ³¹Jetur, Naphish, and Kedemah. These were the sons of Ishmael.

³²Now the sons born to Keturah, Abraham's concubine, were ZIran, Jokshan, Medan, Midian, Ishbak, and Shuah. The sons of Jokshan were Sheba and Dedan. ³³The sons of Midian were Ephah, Epher, Hanoch, Abida, and Eldaah. All these were the children of Keturah.

א אָדָם שֵׁת אֱנוֹשׁ: ² קֵינָן מַהֲלַלְאֵל יָרֶד: ³ חֲנוֹךְ מְתוּשֶׁלַח לֶמֶךְ: ⁴ נֹחַ שֵׁם חָם וָיָפֶת: ס ⁵ בְּנֵי יֶפֶת גֹּמֶר וּמָגוֹג וּמָדַי וְיָוָן וְתֻבָל וּמֶשֶׁךְ וְתִירָס: ס ⁶ וּבְנֵי גֹּמֶר אַשְׁכֲּנַז וְדִיפַת וְתוֹגַרְמָה: ⁷ וּבְנֵי יָוָן אֱלִישָׁה וְתַרְשִׁישָׁה כִּתִּים וְרוֹדָנִים: ס ⁸ בְּנֵי חָם כּוּשׁ וּמִצְרַיִם פּוּט וּכְנָעַן: ⁹ וּבְנֵי כוּשׁ סְבָא וַחֲוִילָה וְסַבְתָּא וְרַעְמָא וְסַבְתְּכָא וּבְנֵי רַעְמָא שְׁבָא וּדְדָן: ס ¹⁰ וְכוּשׁ יָלַד אֶת־נִמְרוֹד הוּא הֵחֵל לִהְיוֹת גִּבּוֹר בָּאָרֶץ: ס ¹¹ וּמִצְרַיִם יָלַד אֶת־לוּדִים וְאֶת־עֲנָמִים וְאֶת־לְהָבִים וְאֶת־נַפְתֻּחִים: ¹² וְאֶת־פַּתְרֻסִים וְאֶת־כַּסְלֻחִים אֲשֶׁר יָצְאוּ מִשָּׁם פְּלִשְׁתִּים וְאֶת־כַּפְתֹּרִים: ס ¹³ וּכְנַעַן יָלַד אֶת־צִידוֹן בְּכֹרוֹ וְאֶת־חֵת: ¹⁴ וְאֶת־הַיְבוּסִי וְאֶת־הָאֱמֹרִי וְאֵת הַגִּרְגָּשִׁי: ¹⁵ וְאֶת־הַחִוִּי וְאֶת־הָעַרְקִי וְאֶת־הַסִּינִי: ¹⁶ וְאֶת־הָאַרְוָדִי וְאֶת־הַצְּמָרִי וְאֶת־הַחֲמָתִי: ס ¹⁷ בְּנֵי שֵׁם עֵילָם וְאַשּׁוּר וְאַרְפַּכְשַׁד וְלוּד וַאֲרָם וְעוּץ וְחוּל וְגֶתֶר וָמֶשֶׁךְ: ¹⁸ וְאַרְפַּכְשַׁד יָלַד אֶת־שָׁלַח וְשֶׁלַח יָלַד אֶת־עֵבֶר: ¹⁹ וּלְעֵבֶר יֻלַּד שְׁנֵי בָנִים שֵׁם הָאֶחָד פֶּלֶג כִּי בְיָמָיו נִפְלְגָה הָאָרֶץ וְשֵׁם אָחִיו יָקְטָן: ²⁰ וְיָקְטָן יָלַד אֶת־אַלְמוֹדָד וְאֶת־שָׁלֶף וְאֶת־חֲצַרְמָוֶת וְאֶת־יָרַח: ²¹ וְאֶת־הֲדוֹרָם וְאֶת־אוּזָל וְאֶת־דִּקְלָה: ²² וְאֶת־עֵיבָל וְאֶת־אֲבִימָאֵל וְאֶת־שְׁבָא: ²³ וְאֶת־אוֹפִיר וְאֶת־חֲוִילָה וְאֶת־יוֹבָב כָּל־אֵלֶּה בְּנֵי יָקְטָן: ס ²⁴ שֵׁם אַרְפַּכְשַׁד שָׁלַח: ²⁵ עֵבֶר פֶּלֶג רְעוּ: ²⁶ שְׂרוּג נָחוֹר תָּרַח: ²⁷ אַבְרָם הוּא אַבְרָהָם: ס ²⁸ בְּנֵי אַבְרָהָם יִצְחָק וְיִשְׁמָעֵאל: ס ²⁹ אֵלֶּה תֹּלְדֹתָם בְּכוֹר יִשְׁמָעֵאל נְבָיוֹת וְקֵדָר וְאַדְבְּאֵל וּמִבְשָׂם: ³⁰ מִשְׁמָע וְדוּמָה מַשָּׂא חֲדַד וְתֵימָא: ³¹ יְטוּר נָפִישׁ וָקֵדְמָה אֵלֶּה הֵם בְּנֵי יִשְׁמָעֵאל: ס ³² וּבְנֵי קְטוּרָה פִּילֶגֶשׁ אַבְרָהָם יָלְדָה אֶת־זִמְרָן וְיָקְשָׁן וּמְדָן וּמִדְיָן וְיִשְׁבָּק וְשׁוּחַ וּבְנֵי יָקְשָׁן שְׁבָא וּדְדָן: ס ³³ וּבְנֵי

³⁴And Abraham begot Isaac. The sons of Isaac *were* Esau and Israel. ³⁵The sons of Esau *were* Eliphaz, Reuel, Jeush, Jaalam, and Korah. ³⁶And the sons of Eliphaz *were* Teman, Omar, Zephi, Gatam, *and* Kenaz; and *by* Timna, Amalek. ³⁷The sons of Reuel *were* Nahath, Zerah, Shammah, and Mizzah.

³⁸The sons of Seir *were* Lotan, Shobal, Zibeon, Anah, Dishon, Ezer, and Dishan. ³⁹And the sons of Lotan *were* Hori and Homam; Lotan's sister *was* Timna. ⁴⁰The sons of Shobal *were* Alian, Manahath, Ebal, Shephi, and Onam. The sons of Zibeon *were* Ajah and Anah. ⁴¹The son of Anah *was* Dishon. The sons of Dishon *were* Hamran, Eshban, Ithran, and Cheran. ⁴²The sons of Ezer *were* Bilhan, Zaavan, *and* Jaakan. The sons of Dishan *were* Uz and Aran.

⁴³Now these *were* the kings who reigned in the land of Edom before a king reigned over the children of Israel: Bela the son of Beor, and the name of his city was Dinhabah. ⁴⁴And when Bela died, Jobab the son of Zerah of Bozrah reigned in his place. ⁴⁵When Jobab died, Husham of the land of the Temanites reigned in his place. ⁴⁶And when Husham died, Hadad the son of Bedad, who attacked Midian in the field of Moab, reigned in his place. The name of his city *was* Avith. ⁴⁷When Hadad died, Samlah of Masrekah reigned in his place. ⁴⁸And when Samlah died, Saul of Rehoboth-by-the-River reigned in his place. ⁴⁹When Saul died, Baal-Hanan the son of Achbor reigned in his place. ⁵⁰And when Baal-Hanan died, Hadad reigned in his place; and the name of his city was Pai. His wife's name was Mehetabel the daughter of Matred, the daughter of Mezahab. ⁵¹Hadad died also. And the chiefs of Edom were Chief Timnah, Chief Aliah, Chief Jetheth, ⁵²Chief Aholibamah, Chief Elah, Chief Pinon, ⁵³Chief Kenaz, Chief Teman, Chief Mibzar, ⁵⁴Chief Magdiel, and Chief Iram. These *were* the chiefs of Edom.

2 These *were* the sons of Israel: Reuben, Simeon, Levi, Judah, Issachar, Zebulun, ²Dan, Joseph, Benjamin, Naphtali, Gad, and Asher.

³The sons of Judah *were* Er, Onan, and Shelah. *These* three were born to him by the daughter of Shua, the Canaanitess. Er, the firstborn of Judah, was wicked in the sight of the LORD; so He killed him. ⁴And Tamar, his daughter-in-law, bore him Perez and Zerah. All the sons of Judah *were* five.

⁵The sons of Perez *were* Hezron and Hamul. ⁶The sons of Zerah *were* Zimri, Ethan, Heman, Calcol, and Dara—five of them in all.

מִדְיָן עֵיפָה וָעֵפֶר וַחֲנוֹךְ וַאֲבִידָע וְאֶלְדָּעָה
34 כָּל־אֵלֶּה בְּנֵי קְטוּרָה: ס
אַבְרָהָם אֶת־יִצְחָק ס בְּנֵי יִצְחָק עֵשָׂו
וְיִשְׂרָאֵל: ס 35 בְּנֵי עֵשָׂו אֱלִיפַז רְעוּאֵל
וִיעוּשׁ וְיַעְלָם וְקֹרַח: ס 36 בְּנֵי אֱלִיפַז
תֵּימָן וְאוֹמָר צְפִי וְגַעְתָּם קְנַז וְתִמְנָע
וַעֲמָלֵק: ס 37 בְּנֵי רְעוּאֵל נַחַת זֶרַח
שַׁמָּה וּמִזָּה: ס 38 וּבְנֵי שֵׂעִיר לוֹטָן
וְשׁוֹבָל וְצִבְעוֹן וַעֲנָה וְדִישֹׁן וְאֵצֶר וְדִישָׁן:
39 וּבְנֵי לוֹטָן חֹרִי וְהוֹמָם וַאֲחוֹת לוֹטָן
40 בְּנֵי שׁוֹבָל עַלְיָן וּמָנַחַת תִּמְנָע: ס
וְעֵיבָל שְׁפִי וְאוֹנָם ס וּבְנֵי צִבְעוֹן אַיָּה
וַעֲנָה: 41 בְּנֵי עֲנָה דִישׁוֹן ס וּבְנֵי דִישׁוֹן
42 בְּנֵי־אֵצֶר ס חַמְרָן וְאֶשְׁבָּן וְיִתְרָן וּכְרָן:
בִּלְהָן וְזַעֲוָן יַעֲקָן בְּנֵי דִישׁוֹן עוּץ וַאֲרָן: פ
43 וְאֵלֶּה הַמְּלָכִים אֲשֶׁר מָלְכוּ בְּאֶרֶץ אֱדוֹם לִפְנֵי
מְלָךְ־מֶלֶךְ לִבְנֵי יִשְׂרָאֵל בֶּלַע בֶּן־בְּעוֹר וְשֵׁם עִירוֹ
דִּנְהָבָה: 44 וַיָּמָת בָּלַע וַיִּמְלֹךְ תַּחְתָּיו יוֹבָב בֶּן־
זֶרַח מִבָּצְרָה: 45 וַיָּמָת יוֹבָב וַיִּמְלֹךְ תַּחְתָּיו חוּשָׁם
מֵאֶרֶץ הַתֵּימָנִי: 46 וַיָּמָת חוּשָׁם וַיִּמְלֹךְ תַּחְתָּיו
הֲדַד בֶּן־בְּדַד הַמַּכֶּה אֶת־מִדְיָן בִּשְׂדֵה מוֹאָב וְשֵׁם
עִירוֹ עֲוִית׃ק 47 וַיָּמָת הֲדָד וַיִּמְלֹךְ תַּחְתָּיו שַׂמְלָה
מִמַּשְׂרֵקָה: 48 וַיָּמָת שַׂמְלָה וַיִּמְלֹךְ תַּחְתָּיו שָׁאוּל
מֵרְחֹבוֹת הַנָּהָר: 49 וַיָּמָת שָׁאוּל וַיִּמְלֹךְ תַּחְתָּיו בַּעַל
חָנָן בֶּן־עַכְבּוֹר: 50 וַיָּמָת בַּעַל חָנָן וַיִּמְלֹךְ תַּחְתָּיו
הֲדַד וְשֵׁם עִירוֹ פָּעִי וְשֵׁם אִשְׁתּוֹ מְהֵיטַבְאֵל בַּת־
מַטְרֵד בַּת מֵי זָהָב: 51 וַיָּמָת הֲדָד ס וַיִּהְיוּ
אַלּוּפֵי אֱדוֹם אַלּוּף תִּמְנָע אַלּוּף עַלְיָהק אַלּוּף
יְתֵת: 52 אַלּוּף אָהֳלִיבָמָה אַלּוּף אֵלָה אַלּוּף פִּינֹן:
53 אַלּוּף קְנַז אַלּוּף תֵּימָן אַלּוּף מִבְצָר: 54 אַלּוּף
מַגְדִּיאֵל אַלּוּף עִירָם אֵלֶּה אַלּוּפֵי אֱדוֹם: פ

ב אֵלֶּה בְּנֵי יִשְׂרָאֵל רְאוּבֵן שִׁמְעוֹן לֵוִי
וִיהוּדָה יִשָּׂשכָר וּזְבֻלוּן: 2 דָּן יוֹסֵף וּבִנְיָמִן
נַפְתָּלִי גָּד וְאָשֵׁר: ס 3 בְּנֵי יְהוּדָה
עֵר וְאוֹנָן וְשֵׁלָה שְׁלוֹשָׁה נוֹלַד לוֹ מִבַּת־
שׁוּעַ הַכְּנַעֲנִית וַיְהִי עֵר בְּכוֹר יְהוּדָה
רַע בְּעֵינֵי יְהוָה וַיְמִיתֵהוּ: ס 4 וְתָמָר
כַּלָּתוֹ יָלְדָה לּוֹ אֶת־פֶּרֶץ וְאֶת־זָרַח כָּל־בְּנֵי
יְהוּדָה חֲמִשָּׁה: ס 5 בְּנֵי־פֶרֶץ חֶצְרוֹן
וְחָמוּל: ס 6 וּבְנֵי זֶרַח זִמְרִי וְאֵיתָן וְהֵימָן

⁷ The son of Carmi *was* Achar, the troubler of Israel, who transgressed in the accursed thing.

⁸ The son of Ethan *was* Azariah.

⁹ Also the sons of Hezron who were born to him *were* Jerahmeel, Ram, and Chelubai. ¹⁰ Ram begot Amminadab, and Amminadab begot Nahshon, leader of the children of Judah; ¹¹ Nahshon begot Salma, and Salma begot Boaz; ¹² Boaz begot Obed, and Obed begot Jesse; ¹³ Jesse begot Eliab his firstborn, Abinadab the second, Shimea the third, ¹⁴ Nethanel the fourth, Raddai the fifth, ¹⁵ Ozem the sixth, *and* David the seventh.

¹⁶ Now their sisters *were* Zeruiah and Abigail. And the sons of Zeruiah *were* Abishai, Joab, and Asahel—three. ¹⁷ Abigail bore Amasa; and the father of Amasa *was* Jether the Ishmaelite.

¹⁸ Caleb the son of Hezron had children by Azubah, *his* wife, and by Jerioth. Now these were her sons: Jesher, Shobab, and Ardon. ¹⁹ When Azubah died, Caleb took Ephrath as his wife, who bore him Hur. ²⁰ And Hur begot Uri, and Uri begot Bezalel.

²¹ Now afterward Hezron went in to the daughter of Machir the father of Gilead, whom he married when he *was* sixty years old; and she bore him Segub. ²² Segub begot Jair, who had twenty-three cities in the land of Gilead. ²³ (Geshur and Syria took from them the towns of Jair, with Kenath and its towns—sixty towns.) All these *belonged to* the sons of Machir the father of Gilead. ²⁴ After Hezron died in Caleb Ephrathah, Hezron's wife Abijah bore him Ashhur the father of Tekoa.

²⁵ The sons of Jerahmeel, the firstborn of Hezron, *were* Ram, the firstborn, and Bunah, Oren, Ozem, *and* Ahijah. ²⁶ Jerahmeel had another wife, whose name was Atarah; she was the mother of Onam. ²⁷ The sons of Ram, the firstborn of Jerahmeel, were Maaz, Jamin, and Eker. ²⁸ The sons of Onam were Shammai and Jada. The sons of Shammai *were* Nadab and Abishur.

²⁹ And the name of the wife of Abishur *was* Abihail, and she bore him Ahban and Molid. ³⁰ The sons of Nadab *were* Seled and Appaim; Seled died without children. ³¹ The son of Appaim *was* Ishi, the son of Ishi *was* Sheshan, and Sheshan's son *was* Ahlai. ³² The sons of Jada, the brother of Shammai, *were* Jether and Jonathan; Jether died without children. ³³ The sons of Jonathan *were* Peleth and Zaza. These were the sons of Jerahmeel.

³⁴ Now Sheshan had no sons, only daughters. And Sheshan had an Egyptian servant whose name *was* Jarha. ³⁵ Sheshan gave his daughter to Jarha his servant as wife, and she bore him Attai. ³⁶ Attai begot Nathan, and Nathan begot Zabad; ³⁷ Zabad

---

וְכַלְכֹּל וָדֶרַע כֻּלָּם חֲמִשָּׁה: ס ‏7 וּבְנֵי
כַרְמִי עָכָר עוֹכֵר יִשְׂרָאֵל אֲשֶׁר מָעַל
בַּחֵרֶם: ס ‏8 וּבְנֵי אֵיתָן עֲזַרְיָה: ‏9 וּבְנֵי
חֶצְרוֹן אֲשֶׁר נוֹלַד־לוֹ אֶת־יְרַחְמְאֵל וְאֶת־רָם וְאֶת־
כְּלוּבָי: ‏10 וְרָם הוֹלִיד אֶת־עַמִּינָדָב וְעַמִּינָדָב הוֹלִיד
אֶת־נַחְשׁוֹן נְשִׂיא בְּנֵי יְהוּדָה: ‏11 וְנַחְשׁוֹן הוֹלִיד
אֶת־שַׂלְמָא וְשַׂלְמָא הוֹלִיד אֶת־בֹּעַז: ‏12 וּבֹעַז הוֹלִיד
אֶת־עוֹבֵד וְעוֹבֵד הוֹלִיד אֶת־יִשָׁי: ‏13 וְאִישַׁי הוֹלִיד
אֶת־בְּכֹרוֹ אֶת־אֱלִיאָב וַאֲבִינָדָב הַשֵּׁנִי וְשִׁמְעָא
הַשְּׁלִשִׁי: ‏14 נְתַנְאֵל הָרְבִיעִי רַדַּי הַחֲמִישִׁי: ‏15 אֹצֶם
הַשִּׁשִּׁי דָּוִיד הַשְּׁבִעִי: ‏16 וְאַחְיוֹתֵיהֶם‏ם צְרוּיָה
וַאֲבִיגָיִל וּבְנֵי צְרוּיָה אַבְשַׁי וְיוֹאָב וַעֲשָׂה־אֵל
שְׁלֹשָׁה: ‏17 וַאֲבִיגַיִל יָלְדָה אֶת־עֲמָשָׂא וַאֲבִי עֲמָשָׂא
יֶתֶר הַיִּשְׁמְעֵאלִי: ‏18 וְכָלֵב בֶּן־חֶצְרוֹן הוֹלִיד אֶת־
עֲזוּבָה אִשָּׁה וְאֶת־יְרִיעוֹת וְאֵלֶּה בָנֶיהָ יֵשֶׁר וְשׁוֹבָב
וְאַרְדּוֹן: ‏19 וַתָּמָת עֲזוּבָה וַיִּקַּח־לוֹ כָלֵב אֶת־אֶפְרָת
וַתֵּלֶד לוֹ אֶת־חוּר: ‏20 וְחוּר הוֹלִיד אֶת־אוּרִי
וְאוּרִי הוֹלִיד אֶת־בְּצַלְאֵל: ס ‏21 וְאַחַר בָּא
חֶצְרוֹן אֶל־בַּת־מָכִיר אֲבִי גִלְעָד וְהוּא לְקָחָהּ וְהוּא
בֶּן־שִׁשִּׁים שָׁנָה וַתֵּלֶד לוֹ אֶת־שְׂגוּב: ‏22 וּשְׂגוּב
הוֹלִיד אֶת־יָאִיר וַיְהִי־לוֹ עֶשְׂרִים וְשָׁלוֹשׁ עָרִים
בְּאֶרֶץ הַגִּלְעָד: ‏23 וַיִּקַּח גְּשׁוּר־וַאֲרָם אֶת־חַוֹּת יָאִיר
מֵאִתָּם אֶת־קְנָת וְאֶת־בְּנֹתֶיהָ שִׁשִּׁים עִיר כָּל־אֵלֶּה
בְּנֵי מָכִיר אֲבִי־גִלְעָד: ‏24 וְאַחַר מוֹת־חֶצְרוֹן בְּכָלֵב
אֶפְרָתָה וְאֵשֶׁת חֶצְרוֹן אֲבִיָּה וַתֵּלֶד לוֹ אֶת־אַשְׁחוּר
אֲבִי תְקוֹעַ: ‏25 וַיִּהְיוּ בְנֵי־יְרַחְמְאֵל בְּכוֹר חֶצְרוֹן
הַבְּכוֹר ׀ רָם וּבוּנָה וָאֹרֶן וָאֹצֶם אֲחִיָּה: ‏26 וַתְּהִי
אִשָּׁה אַחֶרֶת לִירַחְמְאֵל וּשְׁמָהּ עֲטָרָה הִיא אֵם
אוֹנָם: ס ‏27 וַיִּהְיוּ בְנֵי־רָם בְּכוֹר יְרַחְמְאֵל
מַעַץ וְיָמִין וָעֵקֶר: ‏28 וַיִּהְיוּ בְנֵי־אוֹנָם שַׁמַּי וְיָדָע וּבְנֵי
שַׁמַּי נָדָב וַאֲבִישׁוּר: ‏29 וְשֵׁם אֵשֶׁת אֲבִישׁוּר אֲבִיהָיִל
וַתֵּלֶד לוֹ אֶת־אַחְבָּן וְאֶת־מוֹלִיד: ‏30 וּבְנֵי נָדָב סֶלֶד
וְאַפָּיִם וַיָּמָת סֶלֶד לֹא בָנִים: ס ‏31 וּבְנֵי
אַפַּיִם יִשְׁעִי וּבְנֵי יִשְׁעִי שֵׁשָׁן וּבְנֵי שֵׁשָׁן אַחְלָי:
‏32 וּבְנֵי יָדָע אֲחִי שַׁמַּי יֶתֶר וְיוֹנָתָן וַיָּמָת יֶתֶר
לֹא בָנִים: ס ‏33 וּבְנֵי יוֹנָתָן פֶּלֶת וְזָזָא
אֵלֶּה הָיוּ בְּנֵי יְרַחְמְאֵל: ‏34 וְלֹא־הָיָה לְשֵׁשָׁן בָּנִים
כִּי אִם־בָּנוֹת וּלְשֵׁשָׁן עֶבֶד מִצְרִי וּשְׁמוֹ יַרְחָע:
‏35 וַיִּתֵּן שֵׁשָׁן אֶת־בִּתּוֹ לְיַרְחָע עַבְדּוֹ לְאִשָּׁה וַתֵּלֶד
לוֹ אֶת־עַתָּי: ‏36 וְעַתַּי הוֹלִיד אֶת־נָתָן וְנָתָן הוֹלִיד
אֶת־זָבָד: ‏37 וְזָבָד הוֹלִיד אֶת־אֶפְלָל וְאֶפְלָל

ב ‏16 וְאַחְיוֹתֵיהֶם

begot Ephlal, and Ephlal begot Obed; ³⁸ Obed begot Jehu, and Jehu begot Azariah; ³⁹ Azariah begot Helez, and Helez begot Eleasah; ⁴⁰ Eleasah begot Sismai, and Sismai begot Shallum; ⁴¹ Shallum begot Jekamiah, and Jekamiah begot Elishama.

⁴² The descendants of Caleb the brother of Jerahmeel *were* Mesha, his firstborn, who was the father of Ziph, and the sons of Mareshah the father of Hebron. ⁴³ The sons of Hebron *were* Korah, Tappuah, Rekem, and Shema. ⁴⁴ Shema begot Raham the father of Jorkoam, and Rekem begot Shammai. ⁴⁵ And the son of Shammai *was* Maon, and Maon *was* the father of Beth Zur.

⁴⁶ Ephah, Caleb's concubine, bore Haran, Moza, and Gazez; and Haran begot Gazez. ⁴⁷ And the sons of Jahdai *were* Regem, Jotham, Geshan, Pelet, Ephah, and Shaaph.

⁴⁸ Maachah, Caleb's concubine, bore Sheber and Tirhanah. ⁴⁹ She also bore Shaaph the father of Madmannah, Sheva the father of Machbenah and the father of Gibea. And the daughter of Caleb *was* Achsah.

⁵⁰ These were the descendants of Caleb: The sons of Hur, the firstborn of Ephrathah, *were* Shobal the father of Kirjath Jearim, ⁵¹ Salma the father of Bethlehem, *and* Hareph the father of Beth Gader.

⁵² And Shobal the father of Kirjath Jearim had descendants: Haroeh, *and* half of the *families of* Manuhoth. ⁵³ The families of Kirjath Jearim *were* the Ithrites, the Puthites, the Shumathites, and the Mishraites. From these came the Zorathites and the Eshtaolites.

⁵⁴ The sons of Salma *were* Bethlehem, the Netophathites, Atroth Beth Joab, half of the Manahethites, and the Zorites.

⁵⁵ And the families of the scribes who dwelt at Jabez *were* the Tirathites, the Shimeathites, *and* the Suchathites. These *were* the Kenites who came from Hammath, the father of the house of Rechab.

3 Now these were the sons of David who were born to him in Hebron; The firstborn *was* Amnon, by Ahinoam the Jezreelitess; the second, Daniel, by Abigail the Carmelitess; ² the third, Absalom the son of Maacah, the daughter of Talmai, king of Geshur; the fourth, Adonijah the son of Haggith; ³ the fifth, Shephatiah, by Abital; the sixth, Ithream, by his wife Eglah.

⁴ *These* six were born to him in Hebron. There he reigned seven years and six months, and in Jerusalem he reigned thirty-three years. ⁵ And these were born to him in Jerusalem: Shimea, Shobab, Nathan, and Solomon—four by Bathshua the daughter of Ammiel. ⁶ Also *there* were Ibhar,

הוֹלִיד אֶת־עוֹבֵד: 38 וְעוֹבֵד הוֹלִיד אֶת־יֵהוּא וְיֵהוּא הוֹלִיד אֶת־עֲזַרְיָה: 39 וַעֲזַרְיָה הוֹלִיד אֶת־חָלֶץ וְחֶלֶץ הֹלִיד אֶת־אֶלְעָשָׂה: 40 וְאֶלְעָשָׂה הוֹלִיד אֶת־סִסְמָי וְסִסְמַי הֹלִיד אֶת־שַׁלּוּם: 41 וְשַׁלּוּם הוֹלִיד אֶת־יְקַמְיָה וִיקַמְיָה הֹלִיד אֶת־אֱלִישָׁמָע: 42 וּבְנֵי כָלֵב אֲחִי יְרַחְמְאֵל מֵישָׁע בְּכֹרוֹ הוּא אֲבִי־זִיף וּבְנֵי מָרֵשָׁה אֲבִי חֶבְרוֹן: 43 וּבְנֵי חֶבְרוֹן קֹרַח וְתַפֻּחַ וְרֶקֶם וָשָׁמַע: 44 וְשֶׁמַע הוֹלִיד אֶת־רַחַם אֲבִי יָרְקֳעָם וְרֶקֶם הוֹלִיד אֶת־שַׁמָּי: 45 וּבֶן־שַׁמַּי מָעוֹן וּמָעוֹן אֲבִי בֵית־צוּר: 46 וְעֵיפָה פִּילֶגֶשׁ כָּלֵב יָלְדָה אֶת־חָרָן וְאֶת־מוֹצָא וְאֶת־גָּזֵז וְחָרָן הֹלִיד אֶת־גָּזֵז: ס 47 וּבְנֵי יָהְדָּי רֶגֶם וְיוֹתָם וְגֵישָׁן וָפֶלֶט וְעֵיפָה וָשָׁעַף: 48 פִּלֶגֶשׁ כָּלֵב מַעֲכָה יָלַד שֶׁבֶר וְאֶת־תִּרְחֲנָה: 49 וַתֵּלֶד שַׁעַף אֲבִי מַדְמַנָּה אֶת־שְׁוָא אֲבִי מַכְבֵּנָה וַאֲבִי גִבְעָא וּבַת־כָּלֵב עַכְסָה: ס 50 אֵלֶּה הָיוּ בְּנֵי כָלֵב בֶּן־ חוּר בְּכוֹר אֶפְרָתָה שׁוֹבָל אֲבִי קִרְיַת יְעָרִים: 51 שַׂלְמָא אֲבִי בֵית־לָחֶם חָרֵף אֲבִי בֵית־גָּדֵר: 52 וַיִּהְיוּ בָנִים לְשׁוֹבָל אֲבִי קִרְיַת יְעָרִים הָרֹאֶה חֲצִי הַמְּנֻחוֹת: 53 וּמִשְׁפְּחוֹת קִרְיַת יְעָרִים הַיִּתְרִי וְהַפּוּתִי וְהַשֻּׁמָתִי וְהַמִּשְׁרָעִי מֵאֵלֶּה יָצְאוּ הַצָּרְעָתִי וְהָאֶשְׁתָּאֻלִי: ס 54 בְּנֵי שַׂלְמָא בֵּית לֶחֶם וּנְטוֹפָתִי עַטְרוֹת בֵּית יוֹאָב וַחֲצִי הַמָּנַחְתִּי הַצָּרְעִי: 55 וּמִשְׁפְּחוֹת סֹפְרִים יֹשְׁבוּ יַעְבֵּץ תִּרְעָתִים שִׁמְעָתִים שׂוּכָתִים הֵמָּה הַקִּינִים הַבָּאִים מֵחַמַּת אֲבִי בֵית־רֵכָב: ס

ג וְאֵלֶּה הָיוּ בְּנֵי דָוִיד אֲשֶׁר נוֹלַד־לוֹ בְּחֶבְרוֹן הַבְּכוֹר אַמְנֹן לַאֲחִינֹעַם הַיִּזְרְעֵאלִית שֵׁנִי דָּנִיֵּאל לַאֲבִיגַיִל הַכַּרְמְלִית: 2 הַשְּׁלִשִׁי לְאַבְשָׁלוֹם בֶּן־ מַעֲכָה בַּת־תַּלְמַי מֶלֶךְ גְּשׁוּר הָרְבִיעִי אֲדֹנִיָּה בֶן־ חַגִּית: 3 הַחֲמִישִׁי שְׁפַטְיָה לַאֲבִיטָל הַשִּׁשִּׁי יִתְרְעָם לְעֶגְלָה אִשְׁתּוֹ: 4 שִׁשָּׁה נוֹלַד־לוֹ בְחֶבְרוֹן וַיִּמְלָךְ־ שָׁם שֶׁבַע שָׁנִים וְשִׁשָּׁה חֳדָשִׁים וּשְׁלֹשִׁים וְשָׁלֹשׁ שָׁנָה מָלַךְ בִּירוּשָׁלִָם: 5 וְאֵלֶּה נוּלְּדוּ־ לוֹ בִּירוּשָׁלָיִם שִׁמְעָא וְשׁוֹבָב וְנָתָן וּשְׁלֹמֹה אַרְבָּעָה לְבַת־שׁוּעַ בַּת־עַמִּיאֵל: 6 וְיִבְחָר וֶאֱלִישָׁמָע

Elishama, Eliphelet, [7]Nogah, Nepheg, Japhia, [8]Elishama, Eliada, and Eliphelet—nine *in all*. [9]*These were* all the sons of David, besides the sons of the concubines, and Tamar their sister.

[10]Solomon's son *was* Rehoboam; Abijah *was* his son, Asa his son, Jehoshaphat his son, [11]Joram his son, Ahaziah his son, Joash his son, [12]Amaziah his son, Azariah his son, Jotham his son, [13]Ahaz his son, Hezekiah his son, Manasseh his son, [14]Amon his son, *and* Josiah his son. [15]The sons of Josiah *were* Johanan the firstborn, the second Jehoiakim, the third Zedekiah, and the fourth Shallum. [16]The sons of Jehoiakim *were* Jeconiah his son *and* Zedekiah his son.

[17]And the sons of Jeconiah *were* Assir, Shealtiel his son, [18]*and* Malchiram, Pedaiah, Shenazzar, Jecamiah, Hoshama, and Nedabiah. [19]The sons of Pedaiah *were* Zerubbabel and Shimei. The sons of Zerubbabel *were* Meshullam, Hananiah, Shelomith their sister, [20]and Hashubah, Ohel, Berechiah, Hasadiah, and Jushab-Hesed—five *in all*.

[21]The sons of Hananiah *were* Pelatiah and Jeshaiah, the sons of Rephaiah, the sons of Arnan, the sons of Obadiah, and the sons of Shechaniah. [22]The son of Shechaniah was Shemaiah. The sons of Shemaiah *were* Hattush, Igal, Bariah, Neariah, and Shaphat—six *in all*. [23]The sons of Neariah *were* Elioenai, Hezekiah, and Azrikam—three *in all*. [24]The sons of Elioenai *were* Hodaviah, Eliashib, Pelaiah, Akkub, Johanan, Delaiah, and Anani— seven *in all*.

4 The sons of Judah *were* Perez, Hezron, Carmi, Hur, and Shobal. [2]And Reaiah the son of Shobal begot Jahath, and Jahath begot Ahumai and Lahad. These *were* the families of the Zorathites. [3]These *were* the sons *of the father* of Etam: Jezreel, Ishma, and Idbash; and the name of their sister *was* Hazelelponi; [4]and Penuel *was* the father of Gedor, and Ezer *was the* father of Hushah.

These *were* the sons of Hur, the firstborn of Ephrathah the father of Bethlehem.

[5]And Ashhur the father of Tekoa had two wives, Helah and Naarah. [6]Naarah bore him Ahuzzam, Hepher, Temeni, and Haahashtari. These *were* the sons of Naarah. [7]The sons of Helah *were* Zereth, Zohar, and Ethnan; [8]and Koz begot Anub, Zobebah, and the families of Aharhel the son of Harum.

[9]Now Jabez was more honorable than his brothers, and his mother called his name Jabez, saying, "Because I bore *him* in pain." [10]And Jabez called on the God of Israel saying, "Oh, that You would bless me indeed, and enlarge my territory,

וֶאֱלִיפָלֶט: 7 וְנֹגַהּ וְנֶפֶג וְיָפִיעַ: 8 וֶאֱלִישָׁמָע וְאֶלְיָדָע וֶאֱלִיפָלֶט תִּשְׁעָה: 9 כֹּל בְּנֵי דָוִיד מִלְּבַד בְּנֵי־ פִילַגְשִׁים וְתָמָר אֲחוֹתָם: פ

10 וּבֶן־שְׁלֹמֹה רְחַבְעָם אֲבִיָּה בְנוֹ אָסָא בְנוֹ יְהוֹשָׁפָט בְּנוֹ: 11 יוֹרָם בְּנוֹ אֲחַזְיָהוּ בְנוֹ יוֹאָשׁ בְּנוֹ: 12 אֲמַצְיָהוּ בְנוֹ עֲזַרְיָה בְנוֹ יוֹתָם בְּנוֹ: 13 אָחָז בְּנוֹ חִזְקִיָּהוּ בְנוֹ מְנַשֶּׁה בְנוֹ: 14 אָמוֹן בְּנוֹ יֹאשִׁיָּהוּ בְנוֹ: 15 וּבְנֵי יֹאשִׁיָּהוּ הַבְּכוֹר יוֹחָנָן הַשֵּׁנִי יְהוֹיָקִים הַשְּׁלִשִׁי צִדְקִיָּהוּ הָרְבִיעִי שַׁלּוּם: 16 וּבְנֵי יְהוֹיָקִים יְכָנְיָה בְנוֹ צִדְקִיָּה בְנוֹ: 17 וּבְנֵי יְכָנְיָה אַסִּר שְׁאַלְתִּיאֵל בְּנוֹ: 18 וּמַלְכִּירָם וּפְדָיָה וְשֶׁנְאַצַּר יְקַמְיָה הוֹשָׁמָע וּנְדַבְיָה: 19 וּבְנֵי פְדָיָה זְרֻבָּבֶל וְשִׁמְעִי וּבֶן־זְרֻבָּבֶל מְשֻׁלָּם וַחֲנַנְיָה וּשְׁלֹמִית אֲחוֹתָם: 20 וַחֲשֻׁבָה וָאֹהֶל וּבֶרֶכְיָה וַחֲסַדְיָה יֻשַׁב חֶסֶד חָמֵשׁ: 21 וּבֶן־חֲנַנְיָה פְּלַטְיָה וִישַׁעְיָה בְּנֵי רְפָיָה בְּנֵי אַרְנָן בְּנֵי עֹבַדְיָה בְּנֵי שְׁכַנְיָה: ס 22 וּבְנֵי שְׁכַנְיָה שְׁמַעְיָה וּבְנֵי שְׁמַעְיָה חַטּוּשׁ וְיִגְאָל וּבָרִיחַ וּנְעַרְיָה וְשָׁפָט שִׁשָּׁה: 23 וּבֶן־נְעַרְיָה אֶלְיוֹעֵינַי וְחִזְקִיָּה וְעַזְרִיקָם שְׁלֹשָׁה: 24 וּבְנֵי אֶלְיוֹעֵינַי הֹדַיְוָהוּ וְאֶלְיָשִׁיב וּפְלָיָה וְעַקּוּב וְיוֹחָנָן וּדְלָיָה וַעֲנָנִי שִׁבְעָה: ס

ד בְּנֵי יְהוּדָה פֶּרֶץ חֶצְרוֹן וְכַרְמִי וְחוּר וְשׁוֹבָל: 2 וּרְאָיָה בֶן־שׁוֹבָל הוֹלִיד אֶת־יַחַת וְיַחַת הֹלִיד אֶת־אֲחוּמַי וְאֶת־לָהַד אֵלֶּה מִשְׁפְּחוֹת הַצָּרְעָתִי: ס 3 וְאֵלֶּה אֲבִי עֵיטָם יִזְרְעֶאל וְיִשְׁמָא וְיִדְבָּשׁ וְשֵׁם אֲחוֹתָם הַצְלֶלְפּוֹנִי: 4 וּפְנוּאֵל אֲבִי גְדֹר וְעֵזֶר אֲבִי חוּשָׁה אֵלֶּה בְנֵי־חוּר בְּכוֹר אֶפְרָתָה אֲבִי בֵּית לָחֶם: 5 וּלְאַשְׁחוּר אֲבִי תְקוֹעַ הָיוּ שְׁתֵּי נָשִׁים חֶלְאָה וְנַעֲרָה: 6 וַתֵּלֶד לוֹ נַעֲרָה אֶת־אֲחֻזָּם וְאֶת־חֵפֶר וְאֶת־תֵּימְנִי וְאֶת־הָאֲחַשְׁתָּרִי אֵלֶּה בְּנֵי נַעֲרָה: 7 וּבְנֵי חֶלְאָה צֶרֶת יִצְחָר וְאֶתְנָן: 8 וְקוֹץ הוֹלִיד אֶת־עָנוּב וְאֶת־הַצֹּבֵבָה וּמִשְׁפְּחוֹת אֲחַרְחֵל בֶּן־הָרוּם: 9 וַיְהִי יַעְבֵּץ נִכְבָּד מֵאֶחָיו וְאִמּוֹ קָרְאָה שְׁמוֹ יַעְבֵּץ לֵאמֹר כִּי יָלַדְתִּי בְּעֹצֶב: 10 וַיִּקְרָא יַעְבֵּץ לֵאלֹהֵי יִשְׂרָאֵל לֵאמֹר אִם־בָּרֵךְ

that Your hand would be with me, and that You would keep *me* from evil, that I may not cause pain!" So God granted him what he requested.

¹¹Chelub the brother of Shuhah begot Mehir, who *was* the father of Eshton. ¹²And Eshton begot Beth-Rapha, Paseah, and Tehinnah the father of Ir-Nahash. These *were* the men of Rechah.

¹³The sons of Kenaz *were* Othniel and Seraiah. The sons of Othniel *were* Hathath, ¹⁴and Meonothai *who* begot Ophrah. Seraiah begot Joab the father of Ge Harashim, for they were craftsmen. ¹⁵The sons of Caleb the son of Jephunneh *were* Iru, Elah, and Naam. The son of Elah *was* Kenaz. ¹⁶The sons of Jehallelel *were* Ziph, Ziphah, Tiria, and Asarel. ¹⁷The sons of Ezrah *were* Jether, Mered, Epher, and Jalon. And *Mered's wife bore* Miriam, Shammai, and Ishbah the father of Eshtemoa. ¹⁸(His wife Jehudijah bore Jered the father of Gedor, Heber the father of Sochoh, and Jekuthiel the father of Zanoah.) And these were the sons of Bithiah the daughter of Pharaoh, whom Mered took.

¹⁹The sons of Hodiah's wife, the sister of Naham, *were* the fathers of Keilah the Garmite and of Eshtemoa the Maachathite. ²⁰And the sons of Shimon *were* Amnon, Rinnah, Ben-Hanan, and Tilon. And the sons of Ishi *were* Zoheth and Ben-Zoheth.

²¹The sons of Shelah the son of Judah *were* Er the father of Lecah, Laadah the father of Mareshah, and the families of the house of the linen workers of the house of Ashbea; ²²also Jokim, the men of Chozeba, and Joash; Saraph, who ruled in Moab, and Jashubi-Lehem. Now the records are ancient. ²³These *were* the potters and those who dwell at Netaim and Gederah; there they dwelt with the king for his work.

²⁴The sons of Simeon *were* Nemuel, Jamin, Jarib, Zerah, *and* Shaul, ²⁵Shallum his son, Mibsam his son, and Mishma his son. ²⁶And the sons of Mishma *were* Hamuel his son, Zacchur his son, and Shimei his son. ²⁷Shimei had sixteen sons and six daughters; but his brothers did not have many children, nor did any of their families multiply as much as the children of Judah.

²⁸They dwelt at Beersheba, Moladah, Hazar Shual, ²⁹Bilhah, Ezem, Tolad, ³⁰Bethuel, Hormah, Ziklag, ³¹Beth Marcaboth, Hazar Susim, Beth Biri, and at Shaaraim. These *were* their cities until the reign of David. ³²And their villages *were* Etam, Ain, Rimmon, Tochen, and Ashan—five cities— ³³and all the villages that *were* around these cities as far as Baal. These *were* their dwelling places, and they maintained their genealogy: ³⁴Meshobab,

תְּבָרֲכֵנִי וְהִרְבִּיתָ אֶת־גְּבוּלִי וְהָיְתָה יָדְךָ עִמִּי וְעָשִׂיתָ מֵּרָעָה לְבִלְתִּי עָצְבִּי וַיָּבֵא אֱלֹהִים אֵת אֲשֶׁר־שָׁאָל: ¹¹ וּכְלוּב אֲחִי־שׁוּחָה הוֹלִיד אֶת־מְחִיר הוּא אֲבִי אֶשְׁתּוֹן: ¹² וְאֶשְׁתּוֹן הוֹלִיד אֶת־בֵּית רָפָא וְאֶת־פָּסֵחַ וְאֶת־תְּחִנָּה אֲבִי עִיר נָחָשׁ אֵלֶּה אַנְשֵׁי רֵכָה: ס ¹³ וּבְנֵי קְנַז עָתְנִיאֵל וּשְׂרָיָה וּבְנֵי עָתְנִיאֵל חֲתַת: ¹⁴ וּמְעוֹנֹתַי הוֹלִיד אֶת־עָפְרָה וּשְׂרָיָה הוֹלִיד אֶת־יוֹאָב אֲבִי גֵּיא חֲרָשִׁים כִּי חֲרָשִׁים הָיוּ: פ

¹⁵ וּבְנֵי כָּלֵב בֶּן־יְפֻנֶּה עִירוּ אֵלָה וָנָעַם וּבְנֵי אֵלָה וּקְנַז: ¹⁶ וּבְנֵי יְהַלֶּלְאֵל זִיף וְזִיפָה תִּירְיָא וַאֲשַׂרְאֵל: ¹⁷ וּבֶן־עֶזְרָה יֶתֶר וּמֶרֶד וְעֵפֶר וְיָלוֹן וַתַּהַר אֶת־מִרְיָם וְאֶת־שַׁמַּי וְאֶת־יִשְׁבָּח אֲבִי אֶשְׁתְּמֹעַ: ¹⁸ וְאִשְׁתּוֹ הַיְהֻדִיָּה יָלְדָה אֶת־יֶרֶד אֲבִי גְדוֹר וְאֶת־חֶבֶר אֲבִי שׂוֹכוֹ וְאֶת־יְקוּתִיאֵל אֲבִי זָנוֹחַ וְאֵלֶּה בְּנֵי בִתְיָה בַת־פַּרְעֹה אֲשֶׁר לָקַח מָרֶד: ¹⁹ וּבְנֵי אֵשֶׁת הוֹדִיָּה אֲחוֹת נַחַם אֲבִי קְעִילָה הַגַּרְמִי וְאֶשְׁתְּמֹעַ הַמַּעֲכָתִי: ²⁰ וּבְנֵי שִׁימוֹן אַמְנוֹן וְרִנָּה בֶּן־חָנָן וְתִילוֹן וּבְנֵי יִשְׁעִי זוֹחֵת וּבֶן־זוֹחֵת: ²¹ בְּנֵי שֵׁלָה בֶן־יְהוּדָה עֵר אֲבִי לֵכָה וְלַעְדָּה אֲבִי מָרֵשָׁה וּמִשְׁפְּחוֹת בֵּית־עֲבֹדַת הַבֻּץ לְבֵית אַשְׁבֵּעַ: ²² וְיוֹקִים וְאַנְשֵׁי כֹזֵבָא וְיוֹאָשׁ וְשָׂרָף אֲשֶׁר בָּעֲלוּ לְמוֹאָב וְיָשֻׁבִי לָחֶם וְהַדְּבָרִים עַתִּיקִים: ²³ הֵמָּה הַיּוֹצְרִים וְיֹשְׁבֵי נְטָעִים וּגְדֵרָה עִם־הַמֶּלֶךְ בִּמְלַאכְתּוֹ יָשְׁבוּ שָׁם: ס ²⁴ בְּנֵי שִׁמְעוֹן נְמוּאֵל וְיָמִין יָרִיב זֶרַח שָׁאוּל: ²⁵ שַׁלֻּם בְּנוֹ מִבְשָׂם בְּנוֹ מִשְׁמָע בְּנוֹ: ²⁶ וּבְנֵי מִשְׁמָע חַמּוּאֵל בְּנוֹ זַכּוּר בְּנוֹ שִׁמְעִי בְנוֹ: ²⁷ וּלְשִׁמְעִי בָּנִים שִׁשָּׁה עָשָׂר וּבָנוֹת שֵׁשׁ וּלְאֶחָיו אֵין בָּנִים רַבִּים וְכֹל מִשְׁפַּחְתָּם לֹא הִרְבּוּ עַד־בְּנֵי יְהוּדָה: ס ²⁸ וַיֵּשְׁבוּ בִבְאֵר־שֶׁבַע וּמוֹלָדָה וַחֲצַר שׁוּעָל: ²⁹ וּבְבִלְהָה וּבְעֶצֶם וּבְתוֹלָד: ³⁰ וּבִבְתוּאֵל וּבְחָרְמָה וּבְצִיקְלַג: ³¹ וּבְבֵית מַרְכָּבוֹת וּבַחֲצַר סוּסִים וּבְבֵית בִּרְאִי וּבְשַׁעֲרָיִם אֵלֶּה עָרֵיהֶם עַד־מְלֹךְ דָּוִיד: ³² וְחַצְרֵיהֶם עֵיטָם וָעַיִן רִמּוֹן וְתֹכֶן וְעָשָׁן עָרִים חָמֵשׁ: ³³ וְכָל־חַצְרֵיהֶם אֲשֶׁר סְבִיבוֹת הֶעָרִים הָאֵלֶּה עַד־בָּעַל זֹאת מוֹשְׁבֹתָם וְהִתְיַחְשָׂם לָהֶם: ³⁴ וּמְשׁוֹבָב וְיַמְלֵךְ

²⁰ וְתִילוֹן

Jamlech, and Joshah the son of Amaziah; ³⁵ Joel, and Jehu the son of Joshibiah, the son of Seraiah, the son of Asiel; ³⁶ Elioenai, Jaakobah, Jeshohaiah, Asaiah, Adiel, Jesimiel, and Benaiah; ³⁷ Ziza the son of Shiphi, the son of Allon, the son of Jedaiah, the son of Shimri, the son of Shemaiah— ³⁸ these mentioned by name *were* leaders in their families, and their father's house increased greatly.

³⁹ So they went to the entrance of Gedor, as far as the east side of the valley, to seek pasture for their flocks. ⁴⁰ And they found rich, good pasture, and the land *was* broad, quiet, and peaceful; for some Hamites formerly lived there.

⁴¹ These recorded by name came in the days of Hezekiah king of Judah; and they attacked their tents and the Meunites who were found there, and utterly destroyed them, as it is to this day. So they dwelt in their place, because *there was* pasture for their flocks there. ⁴² Now *some* of them, five hundred men of the sons of Simeon, went to Mount Seir, having as their captains Pelatiah, Neariah, Rephaiah, and Uzziel, the sons of Ishi. ⁴³ And they defeated the rest of the Amalekites who had escaped. They have dwelt there to this day.

5 Now the sons of Reuben the firstborn of Israel— he *was* indeed the firstborn, but because he defiled his father's bed, his birthright was given to the sons of Joseph, the son of Israel, so that the genealogy is not listed according to the birthright; ² yet Judah prevailed over his brothers, and from him *came* a ruler, although the birthright was Joseph's— ³ the sons of Reuben the firstborn of Israel were Hanoch, Pallu, Hezron, and Carmi.

⁴ The sons of Joel *were* Shemaiah his son, Gog his son, Shimei his son, ⁵ Micah his son, Reaiah his son, Baal his son, ⁶ and Beerah his son, whom Tiglath-Pileser king of Assyria carried into captivity. He *was* leader of the Reubenites. ⁷ And his brethren by their families, when the genealogy of their generations was registered: the chief, Jeiel, and Zechariah, ⁸ and Bela the son of Azaz, the son of Shema, the son of Joel, who dwelt in Aroer, as far as Nebo and Baal Meon. ⁹ Eastward they settled as far as the entrance of the wilderness this side of the River Euphrates, because their cattle had multiplied in the land of Gilead.

¹⁰ Now in the days of Saul they made war with the Hagrites, who fell by their hand; and they dwelt in their tents throughout the entire *area* east of Gilead.

¹¹ And the children of Gad dwelt next to them in the land of Bashan as far as Salcah: ¹² Joel *was* the chief, Shapham the next, then Jaanai and Shaphat

וְיוֹשָׁה בֶּן־אֲמַצְיָה: 35 וְיוֹאֵל וְיֵהוּא בֶּן־יוֹשִׁבְיָה בֶּן־ שְׂרָיָה בֶּן־עֲשִׂיאֵל: 36 וְאֶלְיוֹעֵינַי וְיַעֲקֹבָה וִישׁוֹחָיָה וַעֲשָׂיָה וַעֲדִיאֵל וִישִׂימִאֵל וּבְנָיָה: 37 וְזִיזָא בֶן־ שִׁפְעִי בֶן־אַלּוֹן בֶּן־יְדָיָה בֶּן־שִׁמְרִי בֶּן־שְׁמַעְיָה: 38 אֵלֶּה הַבָּאִים בְּשֵׁמוֹת נְשִׂיאִים בְּמִשְׁפְּחוֹתָם וּבֵית אֲבוֹתֵיהֶם פָּרְצוּ לָרוֹב: 39 וַיֵּלְכוּ לִמְבוֹא גְדֹר עַד לְמִזְרַח הַגָּיְא לְבַקֵּשׁ מִרְעֶה לְצֹאנָם: 40 וַיִּמְצְאוּ מִרְעֶה שָׁמֵן וָטוֹב וְהָאָרֶץ רַחֲבַת יָדַיִם וְשֹׁקֶטֶת וּשְׁלֵוָה כִּי מִן־חָם הַיֹּשְׁבִים שָׁם לְפָנִים: 41 וַיָּבֹאוּ אֵלֶּה הַכְּתוּבִים בְּשֵׁמוֹת בִּימֵי | יְחִזְקִיָּהוּ מֶלֶךְ־יְהוּדָה וַיַּכּוּ אֶת־אָהֳלֵיהֶם וְאֶת־ הַמְּעִינִים ᴾ אֲשֶׁר נִמְצְאוּ־שָׁמָּה וַיַּחֲרִימֻם עַד־הַיּוֹם הַזֶּה וַיֵּשְׁבוּ תַּחְתֵּיהֶם כִּי־מִרְעֶה לְצֹאנָם שָׁם: 42 וּמֵהֶם | מִן־בְּנֵי שִׁמְעוֹן הָלְכוּ לְהַר שֵׂעִיר אֲנָשִׁים חֲמֵשׁ מֵאוֹת וּפְלַטְיָה וּנְעַרְיָה וּרְפָיָה וְעֻזִּיאֵל בְּנֵי יִשְׁעִי בְּרֹאשָׁם: 43 וַיַּכּוּ אֶת־שְׁאֵרִית הַפְּלֵטָה לַעֲמָלֵק וַיֵּשְׁבוּ שָׁם עַד הַיּוֹם הַזֶּה:

ה וּבְנֵי רְאוּבֵן בְּכוֹר־יִשְׂרָאֵל כִּי הוּא הַבְּכוֹר וּבְחַלְּלוֹ יְצוּעֵי אָבִיו נִתְּנָה בְּכֹרָתוֹ לִבְנֵי יוֹסֵף בֶּן־יִשְׂרָאֵל וְלֹא לְהִתְיַחֵשׂ לַבְּכֹרָה: 2 כִּי יְהוּדָה גָּבַר בְּאֶחָיו וּלְנָגִיד מִמֶּנּוּ וְהַבְּכֹרָה לְיוֹסֵף: ס 3 בְּנֵי רְאוּבֵן בְּכוֹר יִשְׂרָאֵל חֲנוֹךְ וּפַלּוּא חֶצְרוֹן וְכַרְמִי: 4 בְּנֵי יוֹאֵל שְׁמַעְיָה בְנוֹ גּוֹג בְּנוֹ שִׁמְעִי בְנוֹ: 5 מִיכָה בְנוֹ רְאָיָה בְנוֹ בַּעַל בְּנוֹ: 6 בְּאֵרָה בְנוֹ אֲשֶׁר הֶגְלָה תִּלְּגַת פִּלְנְאֶסֶר מֶלֶךְ אַשֻּׁר הוּא נָשִׂיא לָראוּבֵנִי: 7 וְאֶחָיו לְמִשְׁפְּחֹתָיו בְּהִתְיַחֵשׂ לְתֹלְדוֹתָם הָרֹאשׁ יְעִיאֵל וּזְכַרְיָהוּ: 8 וּבֶלַע בֶּן־עָזָז בֶּן־שֶׁמַע בֶּן־יוֹאֵל הוּא יוֹשֵׁב בַּעֲרֹעֵר וְעַד־נְבוֹ וּבַעַל מְעוֹן: 9 וְלַמִּזְרָח יָשַׁב עַד־לְבוֹא מִדְבָּרָה לְמִן־הַנָּהָר פְּרָת כִּי מִקְנֵיהֶם רָבוּ בְּאֶרֶץ גִּלְעָד: 10 וּבִימֵי שָׁאוּל עָשׂוּ מִלְחָמָה עִם־הַהַגְרִאִים וַיִּפְּלוּ בְּיָדָם וַיֵּשְׁבוּ בְּאָהֳלֵיהֶם עַל־ כָּל־פְּנֵי מִזְרָח לַגִּלְעָד: ס

11 וּבְנֵי־גָד לְנֶגְדָּם יָשְׁבוּ בְּאֶרֶץ הַבָּשָׁן עַד־ סַלְכָה: 12 יוֹאֵל הָרֹאשׁ וְשָׁפָם הַמִּשְׁנֶה וְיַעְנַי

in Bashan, ¹³and their brethren of their father's house: Michael, Meshullam, Sheba, Jorai, Jachan, Zia, and Eber—seven *in all*. ¹⁴These *were* the children of Abihail the son of Huri, the son of Jaroah, the son of Gilead, the son of Michael, the son of Jeshishai, the son of Jahdo, the son of Buz; ¹⁵Ahi the son of Abdiel, the son of Guni, *was* chief of their father's house. ¹⁶And *the Gadites* dwelt in Gilead, in Bashan and in its villages, and in all the common-lands of Sharon within their borders. ¹⁷All these were registered by genealogies in the days of Jotham king of Judah, and in the days of Jeroboam king of Israel.

¹⁸The sons of Reuben, the Gadites, and half the tribe of Manasseh *had* forty-four thousand seven hundred and sixty valiant men, men able to bear shield and sword, to shoot with the bow, and skillful in war, who went to war. ¹⁹They made war with the Hagrites, Jetur, Naphish, and Nodab. ²⁰And they were helped against them, and the Hagrites were delivered into their hand, and all who *were* with them, for they cried out to God in the battle. He heeded their prayer, because they put their trust in Him. ²¹Then they took away their livestock—fifty thousand of their camels, two hundred and fifty thousand of their sheep, and two thousand of their donkeys—also one hundred thousand of their men; ²²for many fell dead, because the war *was* God's. And they dwelt in their place until the captivity.

²³So the children of the half-tribe of Manasseh dwelt in the land. Their *numbers* increased from Bashan to Baal Hermon, that is, to Senir, or Mount Hermon. ²⁴These *were* the heads of their fathers' houses: Epher, Ishi, Eliel, Azriel, Jeremiah, Hodaviah, and Jahdiel. They were mighty men of valor, famous men, *and* heads of their fathers' houses.

²⁵And they were unfaithful to the God of their fathers, and played the harlot after the gods of the peoples of the land, whom God had destroyed before them. ²⁶So the God of Israel stirred up the spirit of Pul king of Assyria, that is, Tiglath-Pileser king of Assyria. He carried the Reubenites, the Gadites, and the half-tribe of Manasseh into captivity. He took them to Halah, Habor, Hara, and the river of Gozan to this day.

6 The sons of Levi *were* Gershon, Kohath, and Merari. ²The sons of Kohath *were* Amram, Izhar, Hebron, and Uzziel. ³The children of Amram *were* Aaron, Moses, and Miriam. And the sons of Aaron *were* Nadab, Abihu, Eleazar, and Ithamar. ⁴Eleazar begot Phinehas, *and* Phinehas begot Abishua; ⁵Abishua begot Bukki, and Bukki begot Uzzi;

וְשָׁפָט בַּבָּשָׁן: 13 וַאֲחֵיהֶם לְבֵית אֲבוֹתֵיהֶם מִיכָאֵל
וּמְשֻׁלָּם וְשֶׁבַע וְיוֹרַי וְיַעְכָּן וְזִיעַ וָעֵבֶר
שִׁבְעָה: ס 14 אֵלֶּה בְּנֵי אֲבִיחַיִל בֶּן־חוּרִי
בֶּן־יָרוֹחַ בֶּן־גִּלְעָד בֶּן־מִיכָאֵל בֶּן־יְשִׁישַׁי בֶּן־יַחְדּוֹ
בֶּן־בּוּז: 15 אֲחִי בֶּן־עַבְדִּיאֵל בֶּן־גּוּנִי רֹאשׁ לְבֵית
אֲבוֹתָם: 16 וַיֵּשְׁבוּ בַּגִּלְעָד בַּבָּשָׁן וּבִבְנֹתֶיהָ וּבְכָל־
מִגְרְשֵׁי שָׁרוֹן עַל־תּוֹצְאוֹתָם: 17 כֻּלָּם הִתְיַחְשׂוּ בִּימֵי
יוֹתָם מֶלֶךְ־יְהוּדָה וּבִימֵי יָרָבְעָם מֶלֶךְ־יִשְׂרָאֵל: פ

18 בְּנֵי־רְאוּבֵן וְגָדִי וַחֲצִי שֵׁבֶט־מְנַשֶּׁה מִן־בְּנֵי־
חַיִל אֲנָשִׁים נֹשְׂאֵי מָגֵן וְחֶרֶב וְדֹרְכֵי קֶשֶׁת
וּלְמוּדֵי מִלְחָמָה אַרְבָּעִים וְאַרְבָּעָה אֶלֶף וּשְׁבַע־
מֵאוֹת וְשִׁשִּׁים יֹצְאֵי צָבָא: 19 וַיַּעֲשׂוּ מִלְחָמָה
עִם־הַהַגְרִיאִים וִיטוּר וְנָפִישׁ וְנוֹדָב: 20 וַיֵּעָזְרוּ
עֲלֵיהֶם וַיִּנָּתְנוּ בְיָדָם הַהַגְרִיאִים וְכֹל שֶׁעִמָּהֶם כִּי
לֵאלֹהִים זָעֲקוּ בַּמִּלְחָמָה וְנַעְתּוֹר לָהֶם כִּי־בָטְחוּ
בוֹ: 21 וַיִּשְׁבּוּ מִקְנֵיהֶם גְּמַלֵּיהֶם חֲמִשִּׁים אֶלֶף וְצֹאן
מָאתַיִם וַחֲמִשִּׁים אֶלֶף וַחֲמוֹרִים אַלְפָּיִם וְנֶפֶשׁ אָדָם
מֵאָה אָלֶף: 22 כִּי־חֲלָלִים רַבִּים נָפָלוּ כִּי מֵהָאֱלֹהִים
הַמִּלְחָמָה וַיֵּשְׁבוּ תַחְתֵּיהֶם עַד־הַגֹּלָה: פ

23 וּבְנֵי חֲצִי שֵׁבֶט מְנַשֶּׁה יָשְׁבוּ בָּאָרֶץ מִבָּשָׁן עַד־
בַּעַל חֶרְמוֹן וּשְׂנִיר וְהַר־חֶרְמוֹן הֵמָּה רָבוּ: 24 וְאֵלֶּה
רָאשֵׁי בֵית־אֲבוֹתָם וָעֵפֶר וְיִשְׁעִי וֶאֱלִיאֵל וְעַזְרִיאֵל
וְיִרְמְיָה וְהוֹדַוְיָה וְיַחְדִּיאֵל אֲנָשִׁים גִּבּוֹרֵי חַיִל אַנְשֵׁי
שֵׁמוֹת רָאשִׁים לְבֵית אֲבוֹתָם: 25 וַיִּמְעֲלוּ בֵּאלֹהֵי
אֲבוֹתֵיהֶם וַיִּזְנוּ אַחֲרֵי אֱלֹהֵי עַמֵּי־הָאָרֶץ אֲשֶׁר־
הִשְׁמִיד אֱלֹהִים מִפְּנֵיהֶם: 26 וַיָּעַר אֱלֹהֵי יִשְׂרָאֵל
אֶת־רוּחַ פּוּל מֶלֶךְ־אַשּׁוּר וְאֶת־רוּחַ תִּלְּגַת
פִּלְנֶסֶר מֶלֶךְ אַשּׁוּר וַיַּגְלֵם לָראוּבֵנִי וְלַגָּדִי וְלַחֲצִי
שֵׁבֶט מְנַשֶּׁה וַיְבִיאֵם לַחְלַח וְחָבוֹר וְהָרָא וּנְהַר
גּוֹזָן עַד הַיּוֹם הַזֶּה: פ

27 בְּנֵי לֵוִי גֵּרְשׁוֹן קְהָת וּמְרָרִי: 28 וּבְנֵי קְהָת עַמְרָם
יִצְהָר וְחֶבְרוֹן וְעֻזִּיאֵל: ס 29 וּבְנֵי עַמְרָם
אַהֲרֹן וּמֹשֶׁה וּמִרְיָם ס וּבְנֵי אַהֲרֹן נָדָב
וַאֲבִיהוּא אֶלְעָזָר וְאִיתָמָר: 30 אֶלְעָזָר
הוֹלִיד אֶת־פִּינְחָס פִּינְחָס הֹלִיד אֶת־אֲבִישׁוּעַ:
31 וַאֲבִישׁוּעַ הוֹלִיד אֶת־בֻּקִּי וּבֻקִּי הוֹלִיד אֶת־

⁶Uzzi begot Zerahiah, and Zerahiah begot Meraioth; ⁷Meraioth begot Amariah, and Amariah begot Ahitub; ⁸Ahitub begot Zadok, and Zadok begot Ahimaaz; ⁹Ahimaaz begot Azariah, and Azariah begot Johanan; ¹⁰Johanan begot Azariah (it was he who ministered as priest in the temple that Solomon built in Jerusalem); ¹¹Azariah begot Amariah, and Amariah begot Ahitub; ¹²Ahitub begot Zadok, and Zadok begot Shallum; ¹³Shallum begot Hilkiah, and Hilkiah begot Azariah; ¹⁴Azariah begot Seraiah, and Seraiah begot Jehozadak. ¹⁵Jehozadak went *into captivity* when the LORD carried Judah and Jerusalem into captivity by the hand of Nebuchadnezzar.

¹⁶The sons of Levi *were* Gershon, Kohath, and Merari. ¹⁷These are the names of the sons of Gershon: Libni and Shimei. ¹⁸The sons of Kohath *were* Amram, Izhar, Hebron, and Uzziel. ¹⁹The sons of Merari *were* Mahli and Mushi. Now these *are* the families of the Levites according to their fathers: ²⁰Of Gershon *were* Libni his son, Jahath his son, Zimmah his son, ²¹Joah his son, Iddo his son, Zerah his son, *and* Jeatherai his son. ²²The sons of Kohath *were* Amminadab his son, Korah his son, Assir his son, ²³Elkanah his son, Ebiasaph his son, Assir his son, ²⁴Tahath his son, Uriel his son, Uzziah his son, and Shaul his son. ²⁵The sons of Elkanah *were* Amasai and Ahimoth. ²⁶*As for* Elkanah, the sons of Elkanah *were* Zophai his son, Nahath his son, ²⁷Eliab his son, Jeroham his son, *and* Elkanah his son. ²⁸The sons of Samuel *were* Joel the firstborn, and Abijah the second. ²⁹The sons of Merari *were* Mahli, Libni his son, Shimei his son, Uzzah his son, ³⁰Shimea his son, Haggiah his son, *and* Asaiah his son.

³¹Now these are the men whom David appointed over the service of song in the house of the LORD, after the ark came to rest. ³²They were ministering with music before the dwelling place of the tabernacle of meeting, until Solomon had built the house of the LORD in Jerusalem, and they served in their office according to their order.

³³And these *are* the ones who ministered with their sons: Of the sons of the Kohathites *were* Heman the singer, the son of Joel, the son of Samuel, ³⁴the son of Elkanah, the son of Jeroham, the son of Eliel, the son of Toah, ³⁵the son of Zuph, the son of Elkanah, the son of Mahath, the son of Amasai, ³⁶the son of Elkanah, the son of Joel, the son of Azariah, the son of Zephaniah, ³⁷the son of Tahath, the son of Assir, the son of Ebiasaph, the son of Korah, ³⁸the son of Izhar, the son of Kohath, the son of Levi, the son of Israel. ³⁹And his brother Asaph, who stood at his right hand, *was*

עֻזִּי: 32 וְעֻזִּי הוֹלִיד אֶת־זְרַחְיָה וּזְרַחְיָה הוֹלִיד אֶת־מְרָיוֹת: 33 מְרָיוֹת הוֹלִיד אֶת־אֲמַרְיָה וַאֲמַרְיָה הוֹלִיד אֶת־אֲחִיטוּב: 34 וַאֲחִיטוּב הוֹלִיד אֶת־צָדוֹק וְצָדוֹק הוֹלִיד אֶת־אֲחִימָעַץ: 35 וַאֲחִימַעַץ הוֹלִיד אֶת־עֲזַרְיָה וַעֲזַרְיָה הוֹלִיד אֶת־יוֹחָנָן: 36 וְיוֹחָנָן הוֹלִיד אֶת־עֲזַרְיָה הוּא אֲשֶׁר כִּהֵן בַּבַּיִת אֲשֶׁר־בָּנָה שְׁלֹמֹה בִּירוּשָׁלָ͏ִם: 37 וַיּוֹלֶד עֲזַרְיָה אֶת־אֲמַרְיָה וַאֲמַרְיָה הוֹלִיד אֶת־אֲחִיטוּב: 38 וַאֲחִיטוּב הוֹלִיד אֶת־צָדוֹק וְצָדוֹק הוֹלִיד אֶת־שַׁלּוּם: 39 וְשַׁלּוּם הוֹלִיד אֶת־חִלְקִיָּה וְחִלְקִיָּה הוֹלִיד אֶת־עֲזַרְיָה: 40 וַעֲזַרְיָה הוֹלִיד אֶת־שְׂרָיָה וּשְׂרָיָה הוֹלִיד אֶת־יְהוֹצָדָק: 41 וִיהוֹצָדָק הָלַךְ בְּהַגְלוֹת יְהוָה אֶת־יְהוּדָה וִירוּשָׁלָ͏ִם בְּיַד נְבֻכַדְנֶאצַּר: ס

ו 1 בְּנֵי לֵוִי גֵּרְשׁוֹם קְהָת וּמְרָרִי: 2 וְאֵלֶּה שְׁמוֹת בְּנֵי־גֵרְשׁוֹם לִבְנִי וְשִׁמְעִי: 3 וּבְנֵי קְהָת עַמְרָם וְיִצְהָר וְחֶבְרוֹן וְעֻזִּיאֵל: 4 בְּנֵי מְרָרִי מַחְלִי וּמֻשִׁי וְאֵלֶּה מִשְׁפְּחוֹת הַלֵּוִי לַאֲבוֹתֵיהֶם: 5 לְגֵרְשׁוֹם לִבְנִי בְנוֹ יַחַת בְּנוֹ זִמָּה בְנוֹ: 6 יוֹאָח בְּנוֹ עִדּוֹ בְנוֹ זֶרַח בְּנוֹ יְאָתְרַי בְּנוֹ: 7 בְּנֵי קְהָת עַמִּינָדָב בְּנוֹ קֹרַח בְּנוֹ אַסִּיר בְּנוֹ: 8 אֶלְקָנָה בְנוֹ וְאֶבְיָסָף בְּנוֹ וְאַסִּיר בְּנוֹ: 9 תַּחַת בְּנוֹ אוּרִיאֵל בְּנוֹ עֻזִּיָּה בְנוֹ וְשָׁאוּל בְּנוֹ: 10 וּבְנֵי אֶלְקָנָה עֲמָשַׂי וַאֲחִימוֹת: 11 אֶלְקָנָה בְּנוֹ אֶלְקָנָה צוֹפַי בְּנוֹ וְנַחַת בְּנוֹ: 12 אֱלִיאָב בְּנוֹ יְרֹחָם בְּנוֹ אֶלְקָנָה בְנוֹ: 13 וּבְנֵי שְׁמוּאֵל הַבְּכֹר וַשְׁנִי וַאֲבִיָּה: ס 14 בְּנֵי מְרָרִי מַחְלִי לִבְנִי בְנוֹ שִׁמְעִי בְנוֹ עֻזָּה בְנוֹ: 15 שִׁמְעָא בְנוֹ חַגִּיָּה בְנוֹ עֲשָׂיָה בְנוֹ: פ

16 וְאֵלֶּה אֲשֶׁר הֶעֱמִיד דָּוִיד עַל־יְדֵי־שִׁיר בֵּית יְהוָה מִמְּנוֹחַ הָאָרוֹן: 17 וַיִּהְיוּ מְשָׁרְתִים לִפְנֵי מִשְׁכַּן אֹהֶל־מוֹעֵד בַּשִּׁיר עַד־בְּנוֹת שְׁלֹמֹה אֶת־בֵּית יְהוָה בִּירוּשָׁלָ͏ִם וַיַּעַמְדוּ כְמִשְׁפָּטָם עַל־עֲבוֹדָתָם: 18 וְאֵלֶּה הָעֹמְדִים וּבְנֵיהֶם מִבְּנֵי הַקְּהָתִי הֵימָן הַמְשׁוֹרֵר בֶּן־יוֹאֵל בֶּן־שְׁמוּאֵל: 19 בֶּן־אֶלְקָנָה בֶּן־יְרֹחָם בֶּן־אֱלִיאֵל בֶּן־תּוֹחַ: 20 בֶּן־צִיפ׳ בֶּן־אֶלְקָנָה בֶּן־מַחַת בֶּן־עֲמָשָׂי: 21 בֶּן־אֶלְקָנָה בֶּן־יוֹאֵל בֶּן־עֲזַרְיָה בֶּן־צְפַנְיָה: 22 בֶּן־תַּחַת בֶּן־אַסִּיר בֶּן־אֶבְיָסָף בֶּן־קֹרַח: 23 בֶּן־יִצְהָר בֶּן־קְהָת בֶּן־לֵוִי בֶּן־יִשְׂרָאֵל: 24 וְאָחִיו אָסָף הָעֹמֵד עַל־יְמִינוֹ אָסָף

Asaph the son of Berachiah, the son of Shimea, ⁴⁰ the son of Michael, the son of Baaseiah, the son of Malchijah, ⁴¹ the son of Ethni, the son of Zerah, the son of Adaiah, ⁴² the son of Ethan, the son of Zimmah, the son of Shimei, ⁴³ the son of Jahath, the son of Gershon, the son of Levi.

⁴⁴ Their brethren, the sons of Merari, on the left hand, *were* Ethan the son of Kishi, the son of Abdi, the son of Malluch, ⁴⁵ the son of Hashabiah, the son of Amaziah, the son of Hilkiah, ⁴⁶ the son of Amzi, the son of Bani, the son of Shamer, ⁴⁷ the son of Mahli, the son of Mushi, the son of Merari, the son of Levi.

⁴⁸ And their brethren, the Levites, *were* appointed to every kind of service of the tabernacle of the house of God.

⁴⁹ But Aaron and his sons offered sacrifices on the altar of burnt offering and on the altar of incense, for all the work of the Most Holy *Place,* and to make atonement for Israel, according to all that Moses the servant of God had commanded. ⁵⁰ Now these *are* the sons of Aaron: Eleazar his son, Phinehas his son, Abishua his son, ⁵¹ Bukki his son, Uzzi his son, Zerahiah his son, ⁵² Meraioth his son, Amariah his son, Ahitub his son, ⁵³ Zadok his son, *and* Ahimaaz his son.

⁵⁴ Now these *are* their dwelling places throughout their settlements in their territory, for they were *given* by lot to the sons of Aaron, of the family of the Kohathites: ⁵⁵ They gave them Hebron in the land of Judah, with its surrounding common-lands. ⁵⁶ But the fields of the city and its villages they gave to Caleb the son of Jephunneh. ⁵⁷ And to the sons of Aaron they gave one of the cities of refuge, Hebron; also Libnah with its common-lands, Jattir, Eshtemoa with its common-lands, ⁵⁸ Hilen with its common-lands, Debir with its common-lands, ⁵⁹ Ashan with its common-lands, and Beth Shemesh with its common-lands. ⁶⁰ And from the tribe of Benjamin: Geba with its common-lands, Alemeth with its common-lands, and Anathoth with its common-lands. All their cities among their families *were* thirteen.

⁶¹ To the rest of the family of the tribe of the Kohathites *they gave* by lot ten cities from half the tribe of Manasseh. ⁶² And to the sons of Gershon, throughout their families, *they gave* thirteen cities from the tribe of Issachar, from the tribe of Asher, from the tribe of Naphtali, and from the tribe of Manasseh in Bashan. ⁶³ To the sons of Merari, throughout their families, *they gave* twelve cities from the tribe of Reuben, from the tribe of Gad, and from the tribe of Zebulun. ⁶⁴ So the children of Israel gave *these* cities with their common-lands to

בֶּן־מִיכָאֵל בֶּן־בַּעֲשֵׂיָה 25 בֶּן־בֶּרֶכְיָהוּ בֶּן־שִׁמְעָא
בֶּן־אֶתְנִי בֶן־זֶרַח בֶּן־עֲדָיָה: 27 בֶּן־ 26 בֶּן־מַלְכִּיָּה
אֵיתָן בֶּן־זִמָּה בֶּן־שִׁמְעִי: 28 בֶּן־יַחַת בֶּן־גֵּרְשֹׁם
בֶּן־לֵוִי: ס 29 וּבְנֵי מְרָרִי אֲחֵיהֶם עַל־
הַשְּׂמֹאול אֵיתָן בֶּן־קִישִׁי בֶּן־עַבְדִּי בֶּן־מַלּוּךְ: 30 בֶּן־
חֲשַׁבְיָה בֶן־אֲמַצְיָה בֶּן־חִלְקִיָּה: 31 בֶּן־אַמְצִי בֶן־
בָּנִי בֶּן־שָׁמֶר: 32 בֶּן־מַחְלִי בֶּן־מוּשִׁי בֶּן־מְרָרִי בֶּן־
לֵוִי: ס 33 וַאֲחֵיהֶם הַלְוִיִּם נְתוּנִים לְכָל־
עֲבוֹדַת מִשְׁכַּן בֵּית הָאֱלֹהִים: 34 וְאַהֲרֹן וּבָנָיו
מַקְטִירִים עַל־מִזְבַּח הָעוֹלָה וְעַל־מִזְבַּח הַקְּטֹרֶת
לְכֹל מְלֶאכֶת קֹדֶשׁ הַקֳּדָשִׁים וּלְכַפֵּר עַל־יִשְׂרָאֵל
כְּכֹל אֲשֶׁר צִוָּה מֹשֶׁה עֶבֶד הָאֱלֹהִים: פ

35 וְאֵלֶּה בְּנֵי אַהֲרֹן אֶלְעָזָר בְּנוֹ פִּינְחָס בְּנוֹ
אֲבִישׁוּעַ בְּנוֹ: 36 בֻּקִּי בְנוֹ עֻזִּי בְנוֹ זְרַחְיָה
בְנוֹ: 37 מְרָיוֹת בְּנוֹ אֲמַרְיָה בְנוֹ אֲחִיטוּב בְּנוֹ:
38 צָדוֹק בְּנוֹ אֲחִימַעַץ בְּנוֹ: 39 וְאֵלֶּה מוֹשְׁבוֹתָם
לְטִירוֹתָם בִּגְבוּלָם לִבְנֵי אַהֲרֹן לְמִשְׁפַּחַת הַקְּהָתִי
כִּי לָהֶם הָיָה הַגּוֹרָל: 40 וַיִּתְּנוּ לָהֶם אֶת־
חֶבְרוֹן בְּאֶרֶץ יְהוּדָה וְאֶת־מִגְרָשֶׁיהָ סְבִיבֹתֶיהָ:
41 וְאֶת־שְׂדֵה הָעִיר וְאֶת־חֲצֵרֶיהָ נָתְנוּ לְכָלֵב
בֶּן־יְפֻנֶּה: ס 42 וְלִבְנֵי אַהֲרֹן נָתְנוּ אֶת־
עָרֵי הַמִּקְלָט אֶת־חֶבְרוֹן וְאֶת־לִבְנָה וְאֶת־מִגְרָשֶׁיהָ
וְאֶת־יַתִּר וְאֶת־אֶשְׁתְּמֹעַ וְאֶת־מִגְרָשֶׁיהָ: 43 וְאֶת־
חִילֵז וְאֶת־מִגְרָשֶׁיהָ אֶת־דְּבִיר וְאֶת־מִגְרָשֶׁיהָ:
44 וְאֶת־עָשָׁן וְאֶת־מִגְרָשֶׁיהָ וְאֶת־בֵּית שֶׁמֶשׁ וְאֶת־
מִגְרָשֶׁיהָ: ס 45 וּמִמַּטֵּה בִנְיָמִן אֶת־גֶּבַע
וְאֶת־מִגְרָשֶׁיהָ וְאֶת־עָלֶמֶת וְאֶת־מִגְרָשֶׁיהָ וְאֶת־
עֲנָתוֹת וְאֶת־מִגְרָשֶׁיהָ כָּל־עָרֵיהֶם שְׁלֹשׁ־עֶשְׂרֵה
עִיר בְּמִשְׁפְּחוֹתֵיהֶם: ס 46 וְלִבְנֵי קְהָת
הַנּוֹתָרִים מִמִּשְׁפַּחַת הַמַּטֶּה מִמַּחֲצִית מַטֵּה חֲצִי
מְנַשֶּׁה בַּגּוֹרָל עָרִים עָשֶׂר: ס 47 וְלִבְנֵי
גֵרְשׁוֹם לְמִשְׁפְּחוֹתָם מִמַּטֵּה יִשָּׂשכָר וּמִמַּטֵּה אָשֵׁר
וּמִמַּטֵּה נַפְתָּלִי וּמִמַּטֵּה מְנַשֶּׁה בַּבָּשָׁן עָרִים שְׁלֹשׁ
עֶשְׂרֵה: ס 48 לִבְנֵי מְרָרִי לְמִשְׁפְּחוֹתָם
מִמַּטֵּה רְאוּבֵן וּמִמַּטֵּה־גָד וּמִמַּטֵּה זְבוּלֻן בַּגּוֹרָל
עָרִים שְׁתֵּים עֶשְׂרֵה: 49 וַיִּתְּנוּ בְנֵי־יִשְׂרָאֵל לַלְוִיִּם

the Levites. ⁶⁵And they gave by lot from the tribe of the children of Judah, from the tribe of the children of Simeon, and from the tribe of the children of Benjamin these cities which are called by *their* names.

⁶⁶Now some of the families of the sons of Kohath *were given* cities as their territory from the tribe of Ephraim. ⁶⁷And they gave them *one of* the cities of refuge, Shechem with its common-lands, in the mountains of Ephraim, also Gezer with its common-lands, ⁶⁸Jokmeam with its common-lands, Beth Horon with its common-lands, ⁶⁹Aijalon with its common-lands, and Gath Rimmon with its common-lands. ⁷⁰And from the half-tribe of Manasseh: Aner with its common-lands and Bileam with its common-lands, for the rest of the family of the sons of Kohath.

⁷¹From the family of the half-tribe of Manasseh the sons of Gershon *were given* Golan in Bashan with its common-lands and Ashtaroth with its common-lands. ⁷²And from the tribe of Issachar: Kedesh with its common-lands, Daberath with its common-lands, ⁷³Ramoth with its common-lands, and Anem with its common-lands. ⁷⁴And from the tribe of Asher: Mashal with its common-lands, Abdon with its common-lands, ⁷⁵Hukok with its common-lands, and Rehob with its common-lands. ⁷⁶And from the tribe of Naphtali: Kedesh in Galilee with its common-lands, Hammon with its common-lands, and Kirjathaim with its common-lands.

⁷⁷From the tribe of Zebulun the rest of the children of Merari *were given* Rimmon with its common-lands and Tabor with its common-lands. ⁷⁸And on the other side of the Jordan, across from Jericho, on the east side of the Jordan, *they were given* from the tribe of Reuben: Bezer in the wilderness with its common-lands, Jahzah with its common-lands, ⁷⁹Kedemoth with its common-lands, and Mephaath with its common-lands. ⁸⁰And from the tribe of Gad: Ramoth in Gilead with its common-lands, Mahanaim with its common-lands, ⁸¹Heshbon with its common-lands, and Jazer with its common-lands.

7 The sons of Issachar *were* Tola, Puah, Jashub, and Shimron—four *in all*. ²The sons of Tola *were* Uzzi, Rephaiah, Jeriel, Jahmai, Jibsam, and Shemuel, heads of their father's house. *The sons* of Tola *were* mighty men of valor in their generations; their number in the days of David *was* twenty-two thousand six hundred. ³The son of Uzzi *was* Izrahiah, and the sons of Izrahiah *were* Michael, Obadiah, Joel, and Ishiah. All five of them *were* chief men. ⁴And with them, by their generations,

אֶת־הֶעָרִים וְאֶת־מִגְרְשֵׁיהֶם: 50 וַיִּתְּנוּ בַגּוֹרָל
מִמַּטֵּה בְנֵי־יְהוּדָה וּמִמַּטֵּה בְנֵי־שִׁמְעוֹן וּמִמַּטֵּה
בְּנֵי בִנְיָמִן אֵת הֶעָרִים הָאֵלֶּה אֲשֶׁר־יִקְרְאוּ אֶתְהֶם
בְּשֵׁמוֹת: ס 51 וּמִמִּשְׁפְּחוֹת בְּנֵי קְהָת
וַיְהִי עָרֵי גְבוּלָם מִמַּטֵּה אֶפְרָיִם: 52 וַיִּתְּנוּ לָהֶם
אֶת־עָרֵי הַמִּקְלָט אֶת־שְׁכֶם וְאֶת־מִגְרָשֶׁיהָ בְּהַר
אֶפְרָיִם וְאֶת־גֶּזֶר וְאֶת־מִגְרָשֶׁיהָ: 53 וְאֶת־יָקְמְעָם
וְאֶת־מִגְרָשֶׁיהָ וְאֶת־בֵּית חוֹרוֹן וְאֶת־מִגְרָשֶׁיהָ:
54 אֶת־אַיָּלוֹן וְאֶת־מִגְרָשֶׁיהָ וְאֶת־גַּת־רִמּוֹן וְאֶת־
מִגְרָשֶׁיהָ: פ
55 וּמִמַּחֲצִית מַטֵּה מְנַשֶּׁה אֶת־עָנֵר וְאֶת־מִגְרָשֶׁיהָ
וְאֶת־בִּלְעָם וְאֶת־מִגְרָשֶׁיהָ לְמִשְׁפַּחַת לִבְנֵי־קְהָת
הַנּוֹתָרִים: פ
56 לִבְנֵי גֵּרְשׁוֹם מִמִּשְׁפַּחַת חֲצִי מַטֵּה מְנַשֶּׁה אֶת־
גּוֹלָן בַּבָּשָׁן וְאֶת־מִגְרָשֶׁיהָ וְאֶת־עַשְׁתָּרוֹת וְאֶת־
מִגְרָשֶׁיהָ: ס 57 וּמִמַּטֵּה יִשָּׂשכָר אֶת־
קֶדֶשׁ וְאֶת־מִגְרָשֶׁיהָ אֶת־דָּבְרַת וְאֶת־מִגְרָשֶׁיהָ:
58 וְאֶת־רָאמוֹת וְאֶת־מִגְרָשֶׁיהָ וְאֶת־עָנֵם וְאֶת־
מִגְרָשֶׁיהָ: ס 59 וּמִמַּטֵּה אָשֵׁר אֶת־מָשָׁל
וְאֶת־מִגְרָשֶׁיהָ וְאֶת־עַבְדּוֹן וְאֶת־מִגְרָשֶׁיהָ: 60 וְאֶת־
חוּקֹק וְאֶת־מִגְרָשֶׁיהָ וְאֶת־רְחֹב וְאֶת־מִגְרָשֶׁיהָ:
61 וּמִמַּטֵּה נַפְתָּלִי אֶת־קֶדֶשׁ בַּגָּלִיל וְאֶת־מִגְרָשֶׁיהָ
וְאֶת־חַמּוֹן וְאֶת־מִגְרָשֶׁיהָ וְאֶת־קִרְיָתַיִם וְאֶת־
מִגְרָשֶׁיהָ: ס 62 לִבְנֵי מְרָרִי הַנּוֹתָרִים
מִמַּטֵּה זְבוּלֻן אֶת־רִמּוֹנוֹ וְאֶת־מִגְרָשֶׁיהָ אֶת־תָּבוֹר
וְאֶת־מִגְרָשֶׁיהָ: 63 וּמֵעֵבֶר לְיַרְדֵּן יְרֵחוֹ לְמִזְרַח הַיַּרְדֵּן
מִמַּטֵּה רְאוּבֵן אֶת־בֶּצֶר בַּמִּדְבָּר וְאֶת־מִגְרָשֶׁיהָ
וְאֶת־יַהְצָה וְאֶת־מִגְרָשֶׁיהָ: 64 וְאֶת־קְדֵמוֹת וְאֶת־
מִגְרָשֶׁיהָ וְאֶת־מֵיפַעַת וְאֶת־מִגְרָשֶׁיהָ: 65 וּמִמַּטֵּה־
גָד אֶת־רָאמוֹת בַּגִּלְעָד וְאֶת־מִגְרָשֶׁיהָ וְאֶת־מַחֲנַיִם
וְאֶת־מִגְרָשֶׁיהָ: 66 וְאֶת־חֶשְׁבּוֹן וְאֶת־מִגְרָשֶׁיהָ וְאֶת־
יַעְזֵיר וְאֶת־מִגְרָשֶׁיהָ: ס

ז וְלִבְנֵי יִשָּׂשכָר תּוֹלָע וּפוּאָה יָשׁיּבْ^P וְשִׁמְרוֹן
אַרְבָּעָה: ס 2 וּבְנֵי תוֹלָע עֻזִּי וּרְפָיָה
וִירִיאֵל וְיַחְמַי וְיִבְשָׂם וּשְׁמוּאֵל רָאשִׁים
לְבֵית־אֲבוֹתָם לְתוֹלָע גִּבּוֹרֵי חַיִל לְתֹלְדוֹתָם
מִסְפָּרָם בִּימֵי דָוִיד עֶשְׂרִים־וּשְׁנַיִם אֶלֶף וְשֵׁשׁ
מֵאוֹת: ס 3 וּבְנֵי עֻזִּי יִזְרַחְיָה וּבְנֵי יִזְרַחְיָה
מִיכָאֵל וְעֹבַדְיָה וְיוֹאֵל יִשִּׁיָּה חֲמִשָּׁה רָאשִׁים כֻּלָּם:
4 וַעֲלֵיהֶם לְתֹלְדוֹתָם לְבֵית אֲבוֹתָם גְּדוּדֵי צָבָא

according to their fathers' houses, *were* thirty-six thousand troops ready for war; for they had many wives and sons.

⁵Now their brethren among all the families of Issachar *were* mighty men of valor, listed by their genealogies, eighty-seven thousand in all.

⁶*The sons* of Benjamin *were* Bela, Becher, and Jediael—three *in all*. ⁷The sons of Bela were Ezbon, Uzzi, Uzziel, Jerimoth, and Iri—five *in all*. They *were* heads of *their* fathers' houses, and they were listed by their genealogies, twenty-two thousand and thirty-four mighty men of valor.

⁸The sons of Becher *were* Zemirah, Joash, Eliezer, Elioenai, Omri, Jerimoth, Abijah, Anathoth, and Alemeth. All these *are* the sons of Becher. ⁹And they were recorded by genealogy according to their generations, heads of their fathers' houses, twenty thousand two hundred mighty men of valor. ¹⁰The son of Jediael *was* Bilhan, and the sons of Bilhan *were* Jeush, Benjamin, Ehud, Chenaanah, Zethan, Tharshish, and Ahishahar.

¹¹All these sons of Jediael *were* heads of their fathers' houses; *there were* seventeen thousand two hundred mighty men of valor fit to go out for war *and* battle. ¹²Shuppim and Huppim *were* the sons of Ir, *and* Hushim *was* the son of Aher.

¹³The sons of Naphtali *were* Jahziel, Guni, Jezer, and Shallum, the sons of Bilhah.

¹⁴The descendants of Manasseh: his Syrian concubine bore him Machir the father of Gilead, the father of Asriel. ¹⁵Machir took as his wife *the sister* of Huppim and Shuppim, whose name *was* Maachah. The name of *Gilead's* grandson *was* Zelophehad, but Zelophehad begot only daughters. ¹⁶(Maachah the wife of Machir bore a son, and she called his name Peresh. The name of his brother *was* Sheresh, and his sons *were* Ulam and Rakem. ¹⁷The son of Ulam *was* Bedan.) These *were* the descendants of Gilead the son of Machir, the son of Manasseh.

¹⁸His sister Hammoleketh bore Ishhod, Abiezer, and Mahlah.

¹⁹And the sons of Shemida were Ahian, Shechem, Likhi, and Aniam.

²⁰The sons of Ephraim *were* Shuthelah, Bered his son, Tahath his son, Eladah his son, Tahath his son, ²¹Zabad his son, Shuthelah his son, and Ezer and Elead. The men of Gath who were born in *that* land killed *them* because they came down to take away their cattle. ²²Then Ephraim their father mourned many days, and his brethren came to comfort him.

מִלְחָמָה שְׁלֹשִׁים וְשִׁשָּׁה אֶלֶף כִּי־הִרְבּוּ נָשִׁים וּבָנִים: ⁵ וַאֲחֵיהֶם לְכֹל מִשְׁפְּחוֹת יִשָּׂשׂכָר גִּבּוֹרֵי חֲיָלִים שְׁמוֹנִים וְשִׁבְעָה אֶלֶף הִתְיַחְשָׂם לַכֹּל: פ ⁶ בִּנְיָמִן בֶּלַע וָבֶכֶר וִידִיעֲאֵל שְׁלֹשָׁה: ⁷ וּבְנֵי בֶלַע אֶצְבּוֹן וְעֻזִּי וְעֻזִּיאֵל וִירִימוֹת וְעִירִי חֲמִשָּׁה רָאשֵׁי בֵּית אָבוֹת גִּבּוֹרֵי חֲיָלִים וְהִתְיַחְשָׂם עֶשְׂרִים וּשְׁנַיִם אֶלֶף וּשְׁלֹשִׁים וְאַרְבָּעָה: ס ⁸ וּבְנֵי בֶכֶר זְמִירָה וְיוֹעָשׁ וֶאֱלִיעֶזֶר וְאֶלְיוֹעֵינַי וְעָמְרִי וִירֵמוֹת וַאֲבִיָּה וַעֲנָתוֹת וְעָלָמֶת כָּל־אֵלֶּה בְּנֵי־בָכֶר: ⁹ וְהִתְיַחְשָׂם לְתֹלְדוֹתָם רָאשֵׁי בֵּית אֲבוֹתָם גִּבּוֹרֵי חָיִל עֶשְׂרִים אֶלֶף וּמָאתָיִם: ס ¹⁰ וּבְנֵי יְדִיעֲאֵל בִּלְהָן וּבְנֵי בִלְהָן יְעִישׁ וּבִנְיָמִן וְאֵהוּד וּכְנַעֲנָה וְזֵיתָן וְתַרְשִׁישׁ וַאֲחִישָׁחַר: ¹¹ כָּל־אֵלֶּה בְּנֵי יְדִיעֲאֵל לְרָאשֵׁי הָאָבוֹת גִּבּוֹרֵי חֲיָלִים שִׁבְעָה־עָשָׂר אֶלֶף וּמָאתַיִם יֹצְאֵי צָבָא לַמִּלְחָמָה: ¹² וְשֻׁפִּם וְחֻפִּם בְּנֵי עִיר חֻשִׁם בְּנֵי אַחֵר: ¹³ בְּנֵי נַפְתָּלִי יַחֲצִיאֵל וְגוּנִי וְיֵצֶר וְשַׁלּוּם בְּנֵי בִלְהָה: פ

¹⁴ בְּנֵי מְנַשֶּׁה אַשְׂרִיאֵל אֲשֶׁר יָלְדָה פִּילַגְשׁוֹ הָאֲרַמִּיָּה יָלְדָה אֶת־מָכִיר אֲבִי גִלְעָד: ¹⁵ וּמָכִיר לָקַח אִשָּׁה לְחֻפִּים וּלְשֻׁפִּים וְשֵׁם אֲחֹתוֹ מַעֲכָה וְשֵׁם הַשֵּׁנִי צְלָפְחָד וַתִּהְיֶנָה לִצְלָפְחָד בָּנוֹת: ¹⁶ וַתֵּלֶד מַעֲכָה אֵשֶׁת־מָכִיר בֵּן וַתִּקְרָא שְׁמוֹ פֶּרֶשׁ וְשֵׁם אָחִיו שָׁרֶשׁ וּבָנָיו אוּלָם וָרָקֶם: ¹⁷ וּבְנֵי אוּלָם בְּדָן אֵלֶּה בְּנֵי גִלְעָד בֶּן־מָכִיר בֶּן־מְנַשֶּׁה: ¹⁸ וַאֲחֹתוֹ הַמֹּלֶכֶת יָלְדָה אֶת־אִישְׁהוֹד וְאֶת־אֲבִיעֶזֶר וְאֶת־מַחְלָה: ¹⁹ וַיִּהְיוּ בְּנֵי שְׁמִידָע אַחְיָן וָשֶׁכֶם וְלִקְחִי וַאֲנִיעָם: פ

²⁰ וּבְנֵי אֶפְרַיִם שׁוּתָלַח וּבֶרֶד בְּנוֹ וְתַחַת בְּנוֹ וְאֶלְעָדָה בְנוֹ וְתַחַת בְּנוֹ: ²¹ וְזָבָד בְּנוֹ וְשׁוּתֶלַח בְּנוֹ וְעֵזֶר וְאֶלְעָד וַהֲרָגוּם אַנְשֵׁי־גַת הַנּוֹלָדִים בָּאָרֶץ כִּי יָרְדוּ לָקַחַת אֶת־מִקְנֵיהֶם: ²² וַיִּתְאַבֵּל אֶפְרַיִם

יְעִישׁ 10

23 And when he went in to his wife, she conceived and bore a son; and he called his name Beriah, because tragedy had come upon his house. 24 Now his daughter *was* Sheerah, who built Lower and Upper Beth Horon and Uzzen Sheerah; 25 and Rephah *was* his son, *as well as* Resheph, and Telah his son, Tahan his son, 26 Laadan his son, Ammihud his son, Elishama his son, 27 Nun his son, and Joshua his son.

28 Now their possessions and dwelling places *were* Bethel and its towns: to the east Naaran, to the west Gezer and its towns, and Shechem and its towns, as far as Ayyah and its towns; 29 and by the borders of the children of Manasseh *were* Beth Shean and its towns, Taanach and its towns, Megiddo and its towns, Dor and its towns. In these dwelt the children of Joseph, the son of Israel.

30 The sons of Asher *were* Imnah, Ishvah, Ishvi, Beriah, and their sister Serah. 31 The sons of Beriah *were* Heber and Malchiel, who was the father of Birzaith. 32 And Heber begot Japhlet, Shomer, Hotham, and their sister Shua. 33 The sons of Japhlet *were* Pasach, Bimhal, and Ashvath. These *were* the children of Japhlet. 34 The sons of Shemer *were* Ahi, Rohgah, Jehubbah, and Aram. 35 And the sons of his brother Helem *were* Zophah, Imna, Shelesh, and Amal. 36 The sons of Zophah *were* Suah, Harnepher, Shual, Beri, Irah, 37 Bezer, Hod, Shamma, Shilshah, Jithran, and Beera. 38 The sons of Jether *were* Jephunneh, Pispah, and Ara. 39 The sons of Ulla *were* Arah, Haniel, and Rizia.

40 All these *were* the children of Asher, heads of *their* fathers' houses, choice men, mighty men of valor, chief leaders. And they were recorded by genealogies among the army fit for battle; their number *was* twenty-six thousand.

8 Now Benjamin begot Bela his firstborn, Ashbel the second, Aharah the third, 2 Nohah the fourth, and Rapha the fifth. 3 The sons of Bela *were* Addar, Gera, Abihud, 4 Abishua, Naaman, Ahoah, 5 Gera, Shephuphan, and Huram.

6 These *are* the sons of Ehud, who were the heads of the fathers' *houses* of the inhabitants of Geba, and who forced them to move to Manahath: 7 Naaman, Ahijah, and Gera who forced them to move. He begot Uzza and Ahihud.

8 Also Shaharaim had children in the country of Moab, after he had sent away Hushim and Baara his wives. 9 By Hodesh his wife he begot Jobab, Zibia, Mesha, Malcam, 10 Jeuz, Sachiah, and Mirmah. These *were* his sons, heads of their fathers' *houses*.

אֲבִיהֶם יָמִים רַבִּים וַיָּבֹאוּ אֶחָיו לְנַחֲמֽוֹ׃ 23 וַיָּבֹא אֶל־אִשְׁתּוֹ וַתַּהַר וַתֵּלֶד בֵּן וַיִּקְרָא אֶת־שְׁמוֹ בְּרִיעָה כִּי בְרָעָה הָיְתָה בְּבֵיתֽוֹ׃ 24 וּבִתּוֹ שֶׁאֱרָה וַתִּבֶן אֶת־בֵּית־חוֹרוֹן הַתַּחְתּוֹן וְאֶת־הָעֶלְיוֹן וְאֵת אֻזֵּן שֶׁאֱרָֽה׃ 25 וְרֶפַח בְּנוֹ וְרֶשֶׁף וְתֶלַח בְּנוֹ וְתַחַן בְּנֽוֹ׃ 26 לַעְדָּן בְּנוֹ עַמִּיהוּד בְּנוֹ אֱלִישָׁמָע בְּנֽוֹ׃ 27 נֹן בְּנוֹ יְהוֹשֻׁעַ בְּנֽוֹ׃ 28 וַאֲחֻזָּתָם וּמֹשְׁבוֹתָם בֵּית־אֵל וּבְנֹתֶיהָ וְלַמִּזְרָח נַעֲרָן וְלַמַּעֲרָב גֶּזֶר וּבְנֹתֶיהָ וּשְׁכֶם וּבְנֹתֶיהָ עַד־עַיָּה וּבְנֹתֶֽיהָ׃ 29 וְעַל־יְדֵי בְנֵי־מְנַשֶּׁה בֵּית־שְׁאָן וּבְנֹתֶיהָ תַּעְנַךְ וּבְנֹתֶיהָ מְגִדּוֹ וּבְנוֹתֶיהָ דּוֹר וּבְנוֹתֶיהָ בְּאֵלֶּה יָשְׁבוּ בְּנֵי יוֹסֵף בֶּן־יִשְׂרָאֵֽל׃ פ

30 בְּנֵי אָשֵׁר יִמְנָה וְיִשְׁוָה וְיִשְׁוִי וּבְרִיעָה וְשֶׂרַח אֲחוֹתָֽם׃ 31 וּבְנֵי בְרִיעָה חֶבֶר וּמַלְכִּיאֵל הוּא אֲבִי בִרְזָֽיִת׃ 32 וְחֶבֶר הוֹלִיד אֶת־יַפְלֵט וְאֶת־שׁוֹמֵר וְאֶת־חוֹתָם וְאֵת שׁוּעָא אֲחוֹתָֽם׃ 33 וּבְנֵי יַפְלֵט פָּסַךְ וּבִמְהָל וְעַשְׁוָת אֵלֶּה בְּנֵי יַפְלֵֽט׃ 34 וּבְנֵי שָׁמֶר אֲחִי וְרָהְגָּה יְחֻבָּה וַאֲרָֽם׃ 35 וּבֶן־הֵלֶם אָחִיו צוֹפַח וְיִמְנָע וְשֵׁלֶשׁ וְעָמָֽל׃ 36 בְּנֵי צוֹפַח סוּחַ וְחַרְנֶפֶר וְשׁוּעָל וּבֵרִי וְיִמְרָֽה׃ 37 בֶּצֶר וָהוֹד וְשַׁמָּא וְשִׁלְשָׁה וְיִתְרָן וּבְאֵרָֽא׃ 38 וּבְנֵי יֶתֶר יְפֻנֶּה וּפִסְפָּה וַאֲרָֽא׃ 39 וּבְנֵי עֻלָּא אָרַח וְחַנִּיאֵל וְרִֽצְיָֽא׃ 40 כָּל־אֵלֶּה בְנֵי־אָשֵׁר רָאשֵׁי בֵית־הָאָבוֹת בְּרוּרִים גִּבּוֹרֵי חֲיָלִים רָאשֵׁי הַנְּשִׂיאִים וְהִתְיַחְשָׂם בַּצָּבָא בַּמִּלְחָמָה מִסְפָּרָם אֲנָשִׁים עֶשְׂרִים וְשִׁשָּׁה אָֽלֶף׃ ס

ח וּבִנְיָמִן הוֹלִיד אֶת־בֶּלַע בְּכֹרוֹ אַשְׁבֵּל הַשֵּׁנִי וְאַחְרַח הַשְּׁלִישִֽׁי׃ 2 נוֹחָה הָרְבִיעִי וְרָפָא הַחֲמִישִֽׁי׃ 3 וַיִּהְיוּ בָנִים לְבָלַע אַדָּר וְגֵרָא וַאֲבִיהֽוּד׃ 4 וַאֲבִישׁוּעַ וְנַעֲמָן וַאֲחֽוֹחַ׃ 5 וְגֵרָא וּשְׁפוּפָן וְחוּרָֽם׃ 6 וְאֵלֶּה בְּנֵי אֵחוּד אֵלֶּה הֵם רָאשֵׁי אָבוֹת לְיוֹשְׁבֵי גֶבַע וַיַּגְלוּם אֶל־מָנָֽחַת׃ 7 וְנַעֲמָן וַאֲחִיָּה וְגֵרָא הוּא הֶגְלָם וְהוֹלִיד אֶת־עֻזָּא וְאֶת־אֲחִיחֻֽד׃ 8 וְשַׁחֲרַיִם הוֹלִיד בִּשְׂדֵה מוֹאָב מִן־שִׁלְחוֹ אֹתָם חוּשִׁים וְאֶת־בַּעֲרָא נָשָֽׁיו׃ 9 וַיּוֹלֶד מִן־חֹדֶשׁ אִשְׁתּוֹ אֶת־יוֹבָב וְאֶת־צִבְיָא וְאֶת־מֵישָׁא וְאֶת־מַלְכָּֽם׃ 10 וְאֶת־יְעוּץ וְאֶת־שָׂכְיָה וְאֶת־מִרְמָה

¹¹And by Hushim he begot Abitub and Elpaal.
¹²The sons of Elpaal were Eber, Misham, and
Shemed, who built Ono and Lod with its towns;
¹³and Beriah and Shema, who were heads of their
fathers' houses of the inhabitants of Aijalon, who
drove out the inhabitants of Gath. ¹⁴Ahio, Shashak, Jeremoth, ¹⁵Zebadiah, Arad, Eder, ¹⁶Mi-
chael, Ispah, and Joha were the sons of Beriah.
¹⁷Zebadiah, Meshullam, Hizki, Heber, ¹⁸Ishmerai,
Jizliah, and Jobab were the sons of Elpaal. ¹⁹Jakim,
Zichri, Zabdi, ²⁰Elienai, Zillethai, Eliel, ²¹Adaiah,
Beraiah, and ShIrath were the sons of Shimei.
²²Ishpan, Eber, Eliel, ²³Abdon, Zichri, Hanan,
²⁴Hananiah, Elam, Antothijah, ²⁵Iphdeiah, and
Penuel were the sons of Shashak. ²⁶Shamsherai,
Shehariah, Athaliah, ²⁷Jaareshiah, Elijah, and
Zichri were the sons of Jeroham.

²⁸These were heads of the fathers' houses by their
generations, chief men. These dwelt in Jerusalem.

²⁹Now the father of Gibeon, whose wife's name
was Maacah, dwelt at Gibeon. ³⁰And his firstborn
son was Abdon, then Zur, Kish, Baal, Nadab,
³¹Gedor, Ahio, Zecher, ³²and Mikloth, who begot
Shimeah. They also dwelt alongside their relatives
in Jerusalem, with their brethren. ³³Ner begot Kish,
Kish begot Saul, and Saul begot Jonathan, Mal-
chishua, Abinadab, and Esh-Baal. ³⁴The son of
Jonathan was Merib-Baal, and Merib-Baal begot
Micah. ³⁵The sons of Micah were Pithon, Melech,
Tarea, and Ahaz. ³⁶And Ahaz begot Jehoaddah;
Jehoaddah begot Alemeth, Azmaveth, and Zimri;
and Zimri begot Moza. ³⁷Moza begot Binea,
Raphah his son, Eleasah his son, and Azel his son.

³⁸Azel had six sons whose names were these:
Azrikam, Bocheru, Ishmael, Sheariah, Obadiah,
and Hanan. All these were the sons of Azel. ³⁹And
the sons of Eshek his brother were Ulam his
firstborn, Jeush the second, and Eliphelet the third.

⁴⁰The sons of Ulam were mighty men of valor—
archers. They had many sons and grandsons, one
hundred and fifty in all. These were all sons of
Benjamin.

9 So all Israel was recorded by genealogies, and
indeed, they were inscribed in the book of the kings
of Israel. But Judah was carried away captive to
Babylon because of their unfaithfulness. ²And the
first inhabitants who dwelt in their possessions in
their cities were Israelites, priests, Levites, and the
Nethinim.

³Now in Jerusalem the children of Judah dwelt,
and some of the children of Benjamin, and of the
children of Ephraim and Manasseh: ⁴Uthai the son
of Ammihud, the son of Omri, the son of Imri, the

11 וּמֵחֻשִׁים הוֹלִיד אֵלֶּה בָנָיו רָאשֵׁי אָבוֹת:
אֶת־אֲבִיטוּב וְאֶת־אֶלְפָּעַל: 12 וּבְנֵי אֶלְפַּעַל עֵבֶר
וּמִשְׁעָם וָשָׁמֶד הוּא בָּנָה אֶת־אוֹנוֹ וְאֶת־לֹד
וּבְנֹתֶיהָ: 13 וּבְרִעָה וָשֶׁמַע הֵמָּה רָאשֵׁי הָאָבוֹת
לְיוֹשְׁבֵי אַיָּלוֹן הֵמָּה הִבְרִיחוּ אֶת־יוֹשְׁבֵי גַת:
14 וְאַחְיוֹ שָׁשָׁק וִירֵמוֹת: 15 וּזְבַדְיָה וַעֲרָד וָעָדֶר:
16 וּמִיכָאֵל וְיִשְׁפָּה וְיוֹחָא בְּנֵי בְרִיעָה: 17 וּזְבַדְיָה
וּמְשֻׁלָּם וְחִזְקִי וָחָבֶר: 18 וְיִשְׁמְרַי וְיִזְלִיאָה וְיוֹבָב
בְּנֵי אֶלְפָּעַל: 19 וְיָקִים וְזִכְרִי וְזַבְדִּי: 20 וֶאֱלִיעֵנַי
וְצִלְּתַי וֶאֱלִיאֵל: 21 וַעֲדָיָה וּבְרָאיָה וְשִׁמְרָת בְּנֵי
שִׁמְעִי: 22 וְיִשְׁפָּן וָעֵבֶר וֶאֱלִיאֵל: 23 וְעַבְדּוֹן וְזִכְרִי
וְחָנָן: 24 וַחֲנַנְיָה וְעֵילָם וְעַנְתֹתִיָּה: 25 וְיִפְדְּיָה
וּפְנוּאֵל בְּנֵי שָׁשָׁק: 26 וְשַׁמְשְׁרַי וּשְׁחַרְיָה וַעֲתַלְיָה:
27 וְיַעֲרֶשְׁיָה וְאֵלִיָּה וְזִכְרִי בְּנֵי יְרֹחָם: 28 אֵלֶּה
רָאשֵׁי אָבוֹת לְתֹלְדוֹתָם רָאשִׁים אֵלֶּה יָשְׁבוּ
בִירוּשָׁלָ͏ִם: ס 29 וּבְגִבְעוֹן יָשְׁבוּ אֲבִי גִבְעוֹן
וְשֵׁם אִשְׁתּוֹ מַעֲכָה: 30 וּבְנוֹ הַבְּכוֹר עַבְדּוֹן
וְצוּר וְקִישׁ וּבַעַל וְנָדָב: 31 וּגְדוֹר וְאַחְיוֹ וָזָכֶר:
32 וּמִקְלוֹת הוֹלִיד אֶת־שִׁמְאָה וְאַף־הֵמָּה נֶגֶד
אֲחֵיהֶם יָשְׁבוּ בִירוּשָׁלַ͏ִם עִם־אֲחֵיהֶם: ס 33 וְנֵר הוֹלִיד
אֶת־קִישׁ וְקִישׁ הוֹלִיד אֶת־שָׁאוּל וְשָׁאוּל הוֹלִיד
אֶת־יְהוֹנָתָן וְאֶת־מַלְכִּי־שׁוּעַ וְאֶת־אֲבִינָדָב וְאֶת־
אֶשְׁבָּעַל: 34 וּבֶן־יְהוֹנָתָן מְרִיב בָּעַל וּמְרִיב בַּעַל
הוֹלִיד אֶת־מִיכָה: ס 35 וּבְנֵי מִיכָה פִּיתוֹן
וָמֶלֶךְ וְתַאְרֵעַ וְאָחָז: 36 וְאָחָז הוֹלִיד אֶת־יְהוֹעַדָּה
וִיהוֹעַדָּה הוֹלִיד אֶת־עָלֶמֶת וְאֶת־עַזְמָוֶת וְאֶת־זִמְרִי
וְזִמְרִי הוֹלִיד אֶת־מוֹצָא: 37 וּמוֹצָא הוֹלִיד אֶת־
בִּנְעָא רָפָה בְנוֹ אֶלְעָשָׂה בְנוֹ אָצֵל בְּנוֹ: 38 וּלְאָצֵל
שִׁשָּׁה בָנִים וְאֵלֶּה שְׁמוֹתָם עַזְרִיקָם ׀ בֹּכְרוּ
וְיִשְׁמָעֵאל וּשְׁעַרְיָה וְעֹבַדְיָה וְחָנָן כָּל־אֵלֶּה בְּנֵי
אָצַל: 39 וּבְנֵי עֵשֶׁק אָחִיו אוּלָם בְּכֹרוֹ יְעוּשׁ הַשֵּׁנִי
וֶאֱלִיפֶלֶט הַשְּׁלִשִׁי: 40 וַיִּהְיוּ בְנֵי־אוּלָם אֲנָשִׁים
גִּבֹּרֵי־חַיִל דֹּרְכֵי קֶשֶׁת וּמַרְבִּים בָּנִים וּבְנֵי בָנִים
מֵאָה וַחֲמִשִּׁים כָּל־אֵלֶּה מִבְּנֵי בִנְיָמִן: פ

ט וְכָל־יִשְׂרָאֵל הִתְיַחְשׂוּ וְהִנָּם כְּתוּבִים עַל־
סֵפֶר מַלְכֵי יִשְׂרָאֵל וִיהוּדָה הָגְלוּ לְבָבֶל
בְּמַעֲלָם: ס 2 וְהַיּוֹשְׁבִים הָרִאשֹׁנִים אֲשֶׁר
בַּאֲחֻזָּתָם בְּעָרֵיהֶם יִשְׂרָאֵל הַכֹּהֲנִים הַלְוִיִּם
וְהַנְּתִינִים: 3 וּבִירוּשָׁלַ͏ִם יָשְׁבוּ מִן־בְּנֵי יְהוּדָה וּמִן־
בְּנֵי בִנְיָמִן וּמִן־בְּנֵי אֶפְרַיִם וּמְנַשֶּׁה: 4 עוּתַי בֶּן־

son of Bani, of the descendants of Perez, the son of Judah. ⁵Of the Shilonites: Asaiah the firstborn and his sons. ⁶Of the sons of Zerah: Jeuel, and their brethren—six hundred and ninety. ⁷Of the sons of Benjamin: Sallu the son of Meshullam, the son of Hodaviah, the son of Hassenuah; ⁸Ibneiah the son of Jeroham; Elah the son of Uzzi, the son of Michri; Meshullam the son of Shephatiah, the son of Reuel, the son of Ibnijah; ⁹and their brethren, according to their generations—nine hundred and fifty-six. All these men *were* heads of a father's *house* in their fathers' houses.

¹⁰Of the priests: Jedaiah, Jehoiarib, and Jachin; ¹¹Azariah the son of Hilkiah, the son of Meshullam, the son of Zadok, the son of Meraioth, the son of Ahitub, the officer over the house of God; ¹²Adaiah the son of Jeroham, the son of Pashur, the son of Malchijah; Maasai the son of Adiel, the son of Jahzerah, the son of Meshullam, the son of Meshillemith, the son of Immer; ¹³and their brethren, heads of their fathers' *houses*—one thousand seven hundred and sixty. *They were* very able men for the work of the service of the house of God.

¹⁴Of the Levites: Shemaiah the son of Hasshub, the son of Azrikam, the son of Hashabiah, of the sons of Merari; ¹⁵Bakbakkar, Heresh, Galal, and Mattaniah the son of Micah, the son of Zichri, the son of Asaph; ¹⁶Obadiah the son of Shemaiah, the son of Galal, the son of Jeduthun; and Berechiah the son of Asa, the son of Elkanah, who lived in the villages of the Netophathites.

¹⁷And the gatekeepers *were* Shallum, Akkub, Talmon, Ahiman, and their brethren. Shallum *was* the chief. ¹⁸Until then *they had been* gatekeepers for the camps of the children of Levi at the King's Gate on the east.

¹⁹Shallum the son of Kore, the son of Ebiasaph, the son of Korah, and his brethren, from his father's house, the Korahites, *were* in charge of the work of the service, gatekeepers of the tabernacle. Their fathers had been keepers of the entrance to the camp of the LORD. ²⁰And Phinehas the son of Eleazar had been the officer over them in time past; the LORD *was* with him. ²¹Zechariah the son of Meshelemiah *was* keeper of the door of the tabernacle of meeting.

²²All those chosen as gatekeepers *were* two hundred and twelve. They were recorded by their genealogy, in their villages. David and Samuel the seer had appointed them to their trusted office. ²³So they and their children *were* in charge of the gates of the house of the LORD, the house of the tabernacle, by assignment. ²⁴The gatekeepers were

עֲמִיהוּד בֶּן־עָמְרִי בֶּן־אִמְרִי בֶּן־בָּנִימִן ⁱ מִן־בְּנֵי־
פֶרֶץ בֶּן־יְהוּדָה: ⁵ וּמִן־הַשִּׁילוֹנִי עֲשָׂיָה הַבְּכוֹר
וּבָנָיו: ⁶ וּמִן־בְּנֵי־זֶרַח יְעוּאֵל וַאֲחֵיהֶם שֵׁשׁ־
מֵאוֹת וְתִשְׁעִים: ⁷ וּמִן־בְּנֵי בִּנְיָמִן סַלּוּא בֶּן־
מְשֻׁלָּם בֶּן־הוֹדַוְיָה בֶּן־הַסְּנֻאָה: ⁸ וְיִבְנְיָה בֶּן־יְרֹחָם
וְאֵלָה בֶן־עֻזִּי בֶּן־מִכְרִי וּמְשֻׁלָּם בֶּן־שְׁפַטְיָה בֶּן־
רְעוּאֵל בֶּן־יִבְנִיָּה: ⁹ וַאֲחֵיהֶם לְתֹלְדוֹתָם תִּשַׁע
מֵאוֹת וַחֲמִשִּׁים וְשִׁשָּׁה כָּל־אֵלֶּה אֲנָשִׁים רָאשֵׁי
אָבוֹת לְבֵית אֲבֹתֵיהֶם: ס ¹⁰ וּמִן־הַכֹּהֲנִים
יְדַעְיָה וִיהוֹיָרִיב וְיָכִין: ¹¹ וַעֲזַרְיָה בֶן־חִלְקִיָּה בֶּן־
מְשֻׁלָּם בֶּן־צָדוֹק בֶּן־מְרָיוֹת בֶּן־אֲחִיטוּב נְגִיד
בֵּית הָאֱלֹהִים: ס ¹² וַעֲדָיָה בֶּן־יְרֹחָם בֶּן־
פַּשְׁחוּר בֶּן־מַלְכִּיָּה וּמַעְשַׂי בֶּן־עֲדִיאֵל בֶּן־יַחְזֵרָה בֶּן־
מְשֻׁלָּם בֶּן־מְשִׁלֵּמִית בֶּן־אִמֵּר: ¹³ וַאֲחֵיהֶם רָאשִׁים
לְבֵית אֲבוֹתָם אֶלֶף וּשְׁבַע מֵאוֹת וְשִׁשִּׁים גִּבּוֹרֵי
חֵיל מְלֶאכֶת עֲבוֹדַת בֵּית־הָאֱלֹהִים: ¹⁴ וּמִן־הַלְוִיִּם
שְׁמַעְיָה בֶן־חַשּׁוּב בֶּן־עַזְרִיקָם בֶּן־חֲשַׁבְיָה מִן־
בְּנֵי מְרָרִי: ¹⁵ וּבַקְבַּקַּר חֶרֶשׁ וְגָלָל וּמַתַּנְיָה בֶּן־
מִיכָא בֶּן־זִכְרִי בֶּן־אָסָף: ¹⁶ וְעֹבַדְיָה בֶּן־שְׁמַעְיָה
בֶּן־גָּלָל בֶּן־יְדוּתוּן וּבֶרֶכְיָה בֶן־אָסָא בֶּן־אֶלְקָנָה
הַיּוֹשֵׁב בְּחַצְרֵי נְטוֹפָתִי: ¹⁷ וְהַשֹּׁעֲרִים שַׁלּוּם וְעַקּוּב
וְטַלְמֹן וַאֲחִימָן וַאֲחִיהֶם שַׁלּוּם הָרֹאשׁ: ¹⁸ וְעַד־
הֵנָּה בְּשַׁעַר הַמֶּלֶךְ מִזְרָחָה הֵמָּה הַשֹּׁעֲרִים
לְמַחֲנוֹת בְּנֵי לֵוִי: ¹⁹ וְשַׁלּוּם בֶּן־קוֹרֵא בֶּן־אֶבְיָסָף
בֶּן־קֹרַח וְאֶחָיו לְבֵית־אָבִיו הַקָּרְחִים עַל מְלֶאכֶת
הָעֲבוֹדָה שֹׁמְרֵי הַסִּפִּים לָאֹהֶל וַאֲבֹתֵיהֶם עַל־
מַחֲנֵה יְהוָה שֹׁמְרֵי הַמָּבוֹא: ²⁰ וּפִינְחָס בֶּן־אֶלְעָזָר
נָגִיד הָיָה עֲלֵיהֶם לְפָנִים יְהוָה | ²¹ זְכַרְיָה עִמּוֹ:
בֶּן מְשֶׁלֶמְיָה שֹׁעֵר פֶּתַח לְאֹהֶל מוֹעֵד: ²² כֻּלָּם
הַבְּרוּרִים לְשֹׁעֲרִים בַּסִּפִּים מָאתַיִם וּשְׁנֵים עָשָׂר
הֵמָּה בְחַצְרֵיהֶם הִתְיַחְשָׂם הֵמָּה יִסַּד דָּוִיד וּשְׁמוּאֵל
הָרֹאֶה בֶּאֱמוּנָתָם: ²³ וְהֵם וּבְנֵיהֶם עַל־הַשְּׁעָרִים
לְבֵית־יְהוָה לְבֵית־הָאֹהֶל לְמִשְׁמָרוֹת: ²⁴ לְאַרְבַּע
רוּחוֹת יִהְיוּ הַשֹּׁעֲרִים מִזְרָח יָמָּה צָפוֹנָה וָנֶגְבָּה:

assigned to the four directions: the east, west, north, and south. 25 And their brethren in their villages *had* to come with them from time to time for seven days. 26 For in this trusted office *were* four chief gatekeepers; they were Levites. And they had charge over the chambers and treasuries of the house of God. 27 And they lodged *all* around the house of God because they *had* the responsibility, and they *were* in charge of opening *it* every morning.

28 Now *some* of them were in charge of the serving vessels, for they brought them in and took them out by count. 29 *Some* of them *were* appointed over the furnishings and over all the implements of the sanctuary, and over the fine flour and the wine and the oil and the incense and the spices. 30 And *some* of the sons of the priests made the ointment of the spices.

31 Mattithiah of the Levites, the firstborn of Shallum the Korahite, had the trusted office over the things that were baked in the pans. 32 And some of their brethren of the sons of the Kohathites *were* in charge of preparing the showbread for every Sabbath.

33 These are the singers, heads of the fathers' *houses* of the Levites, *who lodged* in the chambers, *and were* free *from other duties;* for they were employed in *that* work day and night. 34 These heads of the fathers' *houses* of the Levites *were* heads throughout their generations. They dwelt at Jerusalem.

35 Jeiel the father of Gibeon, whose wife's name *was* Maachah, dwelt at Gibeon. 36 His firstborn son *was* Abdon, then Zur, Kish, Baal, Ner, Nadab, 37 Gedor, Ahio, Zechariah, and Mikloth. 38 And Mikloth begot Shimeam. They also dwelt alongside their relatives in Jerusalem, with their brethren. 39 Ner begot Kish, Kish begot Saul, and Saul begot Jonathan, Malchishua, Abinadab, and Esh-Baal. 40 The son of Jonathan *was* Merib-Baal, and Merib-Baal begot Micah. 41 The sons of Micah *were* Pithon, Melech, Tahrea, *and Ahaz.* 42 And Ahaz begot Jarah; Jarah begot Alemeth, Azmaveth, and Zimri; and Zimri begot Moza; 43 Moza begot Binea, Rephaiah his son, Eleasah his son, and Azel his son.

44 And Azel had six sons whose names *were* these: Azrikam, Bocheru, Ishmael, Sheariah, Obadiah, and Hanan; these *were* the sons of Azel.

10

Now the Philistines fought against Israel; and the men of Israel fled from before the Philistines, and fell slain on Mount Gilboa. 2 Then the Philistines followed hard after Saul and his sons. And the Philistines killed Jonathan, Abinadab, and Malchishua, Saul's sons. 3 The battle became fierce

---

25 וַאֲחֵיהֶם בְּחַצְרֵיהֶם לָבוֹא לְשִׁבְעַת הַיָּמִים מֵעֵת אֶל־עֵת עִם־אֵלֶּה: 26 כִּי בֶאֱמוּנָה הֵמָּה אַרְבַּעַת גִּבֹּרֵי הַשֹּׁעֲרִים הֵם הַלְוִיִּם וְהָיוּ עַל־הַלְּשָׁכוֹת וְעַל הָאֹצְרוֹת בֵּית הָאֱלֹהִים: 27 וּסְבִיבוֹת בֵּית־הָאֱלֹהִים יָלִינוּ כִּי־עֲלֵיהֶם מִשְׁמֶרֶת וְהֵם עַל־הַמַּפְתֵּחַ וְלַבֹּקֶר לַבֹּקֶר: 28 וּמֵהֶם עַל־כְּלֵי הָעֲבוֹדָה כִּי־בְמִסְפָּר יְבִיאוּם וּבְמִסְפָּר יוֹצִיאוּם: 29 וּמֵהֶם מְמֻנִּים עַל־הַכֵּלִים וְעַל כָּל־כְּלֵי הַקֹּדֶשׁ וְעַל־הַסֹּלֶת וְהַיַּיִן וְהַשֶּׁמֶן וְהַלְּבוֹנָה וְהַבְּשָׂמִים: 30 וּמִן־בְּנֵי הַכֹּהֲנִים רֹקְחֵי הַמִּרְקַחַת לַבְּשָׂמִים: 31 וּמַתִּתְיָה מִן־הַלְוִיִּם הוּא הַבְּכוֹר לְשַׁלֻּם הַקָּרְחִי בֶּאֱמוּנָה עַל מַעֲשֵׂה הַחֲבִתִּים: 32 וּמִן־בְּנֵי הַקְּהָתִי מִן־אֲחֵיהֶם עַל־לֶחֶם הַמַּעֲרֶכֶת לְהָכִין שַׁבַּת שַׁבָּת: ס 33 וְאֵלֶּה הַמְשֹׁרְרִים רָאשֵׁי אָבוֹת לַלְוִיִּם בַּלְּשָׁכֹת פְּטוּרִים כִּי־יוֹמָם וָלַיְלָה עֲלֵיהֶם בַּמְּלָאכָה: 34 אֵלֶּה רָאשֵׁי הָאָבוֹת לַלְוִיִּם לְתֹלְדוֹתָם רָאשִׁים אֵלֶּה יָשְׁבוּ בִירוּשָׁלִָם: פ 35 וּבְגִבְעוֹן יָשְׁבוּ אֲבִי־גִבְעוֹן יְעוּאֵל וְשֵׁם אִשְׁתּוֹ מַעֲכָה: 36 וּבְנוֹ הַבְּכוֹר עַבְדּוֹן וְצוּר וְקִישׁ וּבַעַל וְנֵר וְנָדָב: 37 וּגְדוֹר וְאַחְיוֹ וּזְכַרְיָה וּמִקְלוֹת: 38 וּמִקְלוֹת הוֹלִיד אֶת־שִׁמְאָם וְאַף־הֵם נֶגֶד אֲחֵיהֶם יָשְׁבוּ בִירוּשָׁלִַם עִם־אֲחֵיהֶם: 39 וְנֵר הוֹלִיד אֶת־קִישׁ וְקִישׁ הוֹלִיד אֶת־שָׁאוּל וְשָׁאוּל הוֹלִיד אֶת־יְהוֹנָתָן וְאֶת־מַלְכִּי־שׁוּעַ וְאֶת־אֲבִינָדָב וְאֶת־אֶשְׁבָּעַל: 40 וּבֶן־יְהוֹנָתָן מְרִיב בָּעַל וּמְרִי־בַעַל הוֹלִיד אֶת־מִיכָה: 41 וּבְנֵי מִיכָה פִּיתוֹן וָמֶלֶךְ וְתַחְרֵעַ: 42 וְאָחָז הוֹלִיד אֶת־יַעְרָה וְיַעְרָה הוֹלִיד אֶת־עָלֶמֶת וְאֶת־עַזְמָוֶת וְאֶת־זִמְרִי וְזִמְרִי הוֹלִיד אֶת־מוֹצָא: 43 וּמוֹצָא הוֹלִיד אֶת־בִּנְעָא וּרְפָיָה בְנוֹ אֶלְעָשָׂה בְנוֹ אָצֵל בְּנוֹ: 44 וּלְאָצֵל שִׁשָּׁה בָנִים וְאֵלֶּה שְׁמוֹתָם עַזְרִיקָם בֹּכְרוּ וְיִשְׁמָעֵאל וּשְׁעַרְיָה וְעֹבַדְיָה וְחָנָן אֵלֶּה בְּנֵי אָצַל: פ

י וּפְלִשְׁתִּים נִלְחֲמוּ בְיִשְׂרָאֵל וַיָּנָס אִישׁ־יִשְׂרָאֵל מִפְּנֵי פְלִשְׁתִּים וַיִּפְּלוּ חֲלָלִים בְּהַר גִּלְבֹּעַ: 2 וַיַּדְבְּקוּ פְלִשְׁתִּים אַחֲרֵי שָׁאוּל וְאַחֲרֵי בָנָיו וַיַּכּוּ פְלִשְׁתִּים אֶת־יוֹנָתָן וְאֶת־אֲבִינָדָב וְאֶת־מַלְכִּי־שׁוּעַ בְּנֵי שָׁאוּל: 3 וַתִּכְבַּד הַמִּלְחָמָה עַל־שָׁאוּל וַיִּמְצָאֻהוּ

against Saul. The archers hit him, and he was wounded by the archers. ⁴Then Saul said to his armorbearer, "Draw your sword, and thrust me through with it, lest these uncircumcised men come and abuse me." But his armorbearer would not, for he was greatly afraid. Therefore Saul took a sword and fell on it. ⁵And when his armorbearer saw that Saul was dead, he also fell on his sword and died. ⁶So Saul and his three sons died, and all his house died together. ⁷And when all the men of Israel who *were* in the valley saw that they had fled and that Saul and his sons were dead, they forsook their cities and fled; then the Philistines came and dwelt in them.

⁸So it happened the next day, when the Philistines came to strip the slain, that they found Saul and his sons fallen on Mount Gilboa. ⁹And they stripped him and took his head and his armor, and sent word *throughout* the land of the Philistines to proclaim the news *in the temple* of their idols and among the people. ¹⁰Then they put his armor in the temple of their gods, and fastened his head in the temple of Dagon.

¹¹And when all Jabesh Gilead heard all that the Philistines had done to Saul, ¹²all the valiant men arose and took the body of Saul and the bodies of his sons; and they brought them to Jabesh, and buried their bones under the tamarisk tree at Jabesh, and fasted seven days.

¹³So Saul died for his unfaithfulness which he had committed against the LORD, because he did not keep the word of the LORD, and also because he consulted a medium for guidance. ¹⁴But *he* did not inquire of the LORD; therefore He killed him, and turned the kingdom over to David the son of Jesse.

11 Then all Israel came together to David at Hebron, saying, "Indeed we *are* your bone and your flesh. ²Also, in time past, even when Saul was king, you *were* the one who led Israel out and brought them in; and the LORD your God said to you, 'You shall shepherd My people Israel, and be ruler over My people Israel.'" ³Therefore all the elders of Israel came to the king at Hebron, and David made a covenant with them at Hebron before the LORD. And they anointed David king over Israel, according to the word of the LORD by Samuel.

⁴And David and all Israel went to Jerusalem, which is Jebus, where the Jebusites *were*, the inhabitants of the land. ⁵But the inhabitants of Jebus said to David, "You shall not come in here!" Nevertheless David took the stronghold of Zion (that is, the City of David). ⁶Now David said,

---

הַמּוֹרִים בַּקֶּשֶׁת וַיָּחֶל מִן־הַיּוֹרִים: 4 וַיֹּאמֶר שָׁאוּל
אֶל־נֹשֵׂא כֵלָיו שְׁלֹף חַרְבְּךָ וְדָקְרֵנִי בָהּ פֶּן־
יָבֹאוּ הָעֲרֵלִים הָאֵלֶּה וְהִתְעַלְּלוּ־בִי וְלֹא אָבָה נֹשֵׂא
כֵלָיו כִּי יָרֵא מְאֹד ס וַיִּקַּח שָׁאוּל אֶת־
הַחֶרֶב וַיִּפֹּל עָלֶיהָ: 5 וַיַּרְא נֹשֵׂא־כֵלָיו כִּי מֵת שָׁאוּל
וַיִּפֹּל גַּם־הוּא עַל־הַחֶרֶב וַיָּמֹת: ס 6 וַיָּמָת
שָׁאוּל וּשְׁלֹשֶׁת בָּנָיו וְכָל־בֵּיתוֹ יַחְדָּו מֵתוּ: 7 וַיִּרְאוּ
כָּל־אִישׁ יִשְׂרָאֵל אֲשֶׁר־בָּעֵמֶק כִּי נָסוּ וְכִי־מֵתוּ
שָׁאוּל וּבָנָיו וַיַּעַזְבוּ עָרֵיהֶם וַיָּנֻסוּ וַיָּבֹאוּ פְלִשְׁתִּים
וַיֵּשְׁבוּ בָּהֶם: ס 8 וַיְהִי מִמָּחֳרָת וַיָּבֹאוּ
פְלִשְׁתִּים לְפַשֵּׁט אֶת־הַחֲלָלִים וַיִּמְצְאוּ אֶת־שָׁאוּל
וְאֶת־בָּנָיו נֹפְלִים בְּהַר גִּלְבֹּעַ: 9 וַיַּפְשִׁיטֻהוּ וַיִּשְׂאוּ
אֶת־רֹאשׁוֹ וְאֶת־כֵּלָיו וַיְשַׁלְּחוּ בְאֶרֶץ־פְּלִשְׁתִּים
סָבִיב לְבַשֵּׂר אֶת־עֲצַבֵּיהֶם וְאֶת־הָעָם: 10 וַיָּשִׂימוּ
אֶת־כֵּלָיו בֵּית אֱלֹהֵיהֶם וְאֶת־גֻּלְגָּלְתּוֹ תָקְעוּ בֵּית
דָּגוֹן: ס 11 וַיִּשְׁמְעוּ כֹּל יָבֵישׁ גִּלְעָד אֵת
כָּל־אֲשֶׁר־עָשׂוּ פְלִשְׁתִּים לְשָׁאוּל: 12 וַיָּקוּמוּ כָּל־
אִישׁ חַיִל וַיִּשְׂאוּ אֶת־גּוּפַת שָׁאוּל וְאֵת גּוּפֹת
בָּנָיו וַיְבִיאוּם יָבֵישָׁה וַיִּקְבְּרוּ אֶת־עַצְמוֹתֵיהֶם תַּחַת
הָאֵלָה בְּיָבֵשׁ וַיָּצוּמוּ שִׁבְעַת יָמִים: 13 וַיָּמָת שָׁאוּל
בְּמַעֲלוֹ אֲשֶׁר מָעַל בַּיהוָה עַל־דְּבַר יְהוָה אֲשֶׁר
לֹא־שָׁמָר וְגַם־לִשְׁאוֹל בָּאוֹב לִדְרוֹשׁ: 14 וְלֹא־דָרַשׁ
בַּיהוָה וַיְמִיתֵהוּ וַיַּסֵּב אֶת־הַמְּלוּכָה לְדָוִיד בֶּן־
יִשָׁי: פ

יא וַיִּקָּבְצוּ כָל־יִשְׂרָאֵל אֶל־דָּוִיד חֶבְרוֹנָה לֵאמֹר
הִנֵּה עַצְמְךָ וּבְשָׂרְךָ אֲנָחְנוּ: 2 גַּם־תְּמוֹל גַּם־
שִׁלְשׁוֹם גַּם בִּהְיוֹת שָׁאוּל מֶלֶךְ אַתָּה הַמּוֹצִיא
וְהַמֵּבִיא אֶת־יִשְׂרָאֵל וַיֹּאמֶר יְהוָה אֱלֹהֶיךָ לְךָ אַתָּה
תִרְעֶה אֶת־עַמִּי אֶת־יִשְׂרָאֵל וְאַתָּה תִּהְיֶה נָגִיד
עַל עַמִּי יִשְׂרָאֵל: 3 וַיָּבֹאוּ כָּל־זִקְנֵי יִשְׂרָאֵל אֶל־
הַמֶּלֶךְ חֶבְרוֹנָה וַיִּכְרֹת לָהֶם דָּוִיד בְּרִית בְּחֶבְרוֹן
לִפְנֵי יְהוָה וַיִּמְשְׁחוּ אֶת־דָּוִיד לְמֶלֶךְ עַל־יִשְׂרָאֵל
כִּדְבַר יְהוָה בְּיַד־שְׁמוּאֵל: ס 4 וַיֵּלֶךְ דָּוִיד
וְכָל־יִשְׂרָאֵל יְרוּשָׁלַ͏ִם הִיא יְבוּס וְשָׁם הַיְבוּסִי יֹשְׁבֵי
הָאָרֶץ: 5 וַיֹּאמְרוּ יֹשְׁבֵי יְבוּס לְדָוִיד לֹא תָבוֹא
הֵנָּה וַיִּלְכֹּד דָּוִיד אֶת־מְצֻדַת צִיּוֹן הִיא עִיר דָּוִיד:
6 וַיֹּאמֶר דָּוִיד כָּל־מַכֵּה יְבוּסִי בָּרִאשׁוֹנָה יִהְיֶה

"Whoever attacks the Jebusites first shall be chief and captain." And Joab the son of Zeruiah went up first, and became chief. ⁷ Then David dwelt in the stronghold; therefore they called it the City of David. ⁸ And he built the city around it, from the Millo to the surrounding area. Joab repaired the rest of the city. ⁹ So David went on and became great, and the LORD of hosts *was* with him.

¹⁰ Now these *were* the heads of the mighty men whom David had, who strengthened themselves with him in his kingdom, with all Israel, to make him king, according to the word of the LORD concerning Israel.

¹¹ And this *is* the number of the mighty men whom David had: Jashobeam the son of a Hachmonite, chief of the captains; he had lifted up his spear against three hundred, killed *by him* at one time.

¹² After him *was* Eleazar the son of Dodo, the Ahohite, who *was* one of the three mighty men. ¹³ He was with David at Pasdammim. Now there the Philistines were gathered for battle, and there was a piece of ground full of barley. So the people fled from the Philistines. ¹⁴ But they stationed themselves in the middle of *that* field, defended it, and killed the Philistines. So the LORD brought about a great victory.

¹⁵ Now three of the thirty chief men went down to the rock to David, into the cave of Adullam; and the army of the Philistines encamped in the Valley of Rephaim. ¹⁶ David *was* then in the stronghold, and the garrison of the Philistines *was* then in Bethlehem. ¹⁷ And David said with longing, "Oh, that someone would give me a drink of water from the well of Bethlehem, which is by the gate!" ¹⁸ So the three broke through the camp of the Philistines, drew water from the well of Bethlehem that *was* by the gate, and took *it* and brought *it* to David. Nevertheless David would not drink it, but poured it out to the LORD. ¹⁹ And he said, "Far be it from me, O my God, that I should do this! Shall I drink the blood of these men *who have put* their lives *in jeopardy*? For at the risk of their lives they brought it." Therefore he would not drink it. These things were done by the three mighty men.

²⁰ Abishai the brother of Joab was chief of *another* three. He had lifted up his spear against three hundred *men*, killed *them*, and won a name among *these* three. ²¹ Of the three he was more honored than the other two men. Therefore he became their captain. However he did not attain to the *first* three.

לְרֹאשׁ וּלְשָׂר וַיַּעַל בָּרִאשׁוֹנָה יוֹאָב בֶּן־צְרוּיָה וַיְהִי לְרֹאשׁ: 7 וַיֵּשֶׁב דָּוִיד בַּמְצָד עַל־כֵּן קָרְאוּ־לוֹ עִיר דָּוִיד: 8 וַיִּבֶן הָעִיר מִסָּבִיב מִן־הַמִּלּוֹא וְעַד־הַסָּבִיב וְיוֹאָב יְחַיֶּה אֶת־שְׁאָר הָעִיר: 9 וַיֵּלֶךְ דָּוִיד הָלוֹךְ וְגָדוֹל וַיהוָה צְבָאוֹת עִמּוֹ: פ

10 וְאֵלֶּה רָאשֵׁי הַגִּבּוֹרִים אֲשֶׁר לְדָוִיד הַמִּתְחַזְּקִים עִמּוֹ בְמַלְכוּתוֹ עִם־כָּל־יִשְׂרָאֵל לְהַמְלִיכוֹ כִּדְבַר יְהוָה עַל־יִשְׂרָאֵל: ס   11 וְאֵלֶּה מִסְפַּר הַגִּבֹּרִים אֲשֶׁר לְדָוִיד יָשָׁבְעָם בֶּן־חַכְמוֹנִי רֹאשׁ הַשָּׁלִישִׁים הוּא־עוֹרֵר אֶת־חֲנִיתוֹ עַל־שְׁלֹשׁ־מֵאוֹת חָלָל בְּפַעַם אֶחָת: 12 וְאַחֲרָיו אֶלְעָזָר בֶּן־דּוֹדוֹ הָאֲחוֹחִי הוּא בִּשְׁלוֹשָׁה הַגִּבֹּרִים: 13 הוּא־הָיָה עִם־דָּוִיד בַּפַּס דַּמִּים וְהַפְּלִשְׁתִּים נֶאֶסְפוּ־שָׁם לַמִּלְחָמָה וַתְּהִי חֶלְקַת הַשָּׂדֶה מְלֵאָה שְׂעוֹרִים וְהָעָם נָסוּ מִפְּנֵי פְלִשְׁתִּים: 14 וַיִּתְיַצְּבוּ בְתוֹךְ־הַחֶלְקָה וַיַּצִּילוּהָ וַיַּכּוּ אֶת־פְּלִשְׁתִּים וַיּוֹשַׁע יְהוָה תְּשׁוּעָה גְדוֹלָה: 15 וַיֵּרְדוּ שְׁלוֹשָׁה מִן־הַשְּׁלוֹשִׁים רֹאשׁ עַל־הַצֻּר אֶל־דָּוִיד אֶל־מְעָרַת עֲדֻלָּם וּמַחֲנֵה פְלִשְׁתִּים חֹנָה בְּעֵמֶק רְפָאִים: 16 וְדָוִיד אָז בַּמְּצוּדָה וּנְצִיב פְּלִשְׁתִּים אָז בְּבֵית לָחֶם: 17 וַיִּתְאָו דָּוִיד וַיֹּאמַר מִי יַשְׁקֵנִי מַיִם מִבּוֹר בֵּית־לֶחֶם אֲשֶׁר בַּשָּׁעַר: 18 וַיִּבְקְעוּ הַשְּׁלֹשָׁה בְּמַחֲנֵה פְלִשְׁתִּים וַיִּשְׁאֲבוּ־מַיִם מִבּוֹר בֵּית־לֶחֶם אֲשֶׁר בַּשַּׁעַר וַיִּשְׂאוּ וַיָּבִאוּ אֶל־דָּוִיד וְלֹא־אָבָה דָוִיד לִשְׁתּוֹתָם וַיְנַסֵּךְ אֹתָם לַיהוָה: 19 וַיֹּאמֶר חָלִילָה לִּי מֵאֱלֹהַי מֵעֲשׂוֹת זֹאת הֲדַם הָאֲנָשִׁים הָאֵלֶּה אֶשְׁתֶּה בְנַפְשׁוֹתָם כִּי בְנַפְשׁוֹתָם הֱבִיאוּם וְלֹא אָבָה לִשְׁתּוֹתָם אֵלֶּה עָשׂוּ שְׁלֹשֶׁת הַגִּבּוֹרִים: 20 וְאַבְשַׁי אֲחִי־יוֹאָב הוּא הָיָה רֹאשׁ הַשְּׁלוֹשָׁה וְהוּא עוֹרֵר אֶת־חֲנִיתוֹ עַל־שְׁלֹשׁ מֵאוֹת חָלָל וְלֹא־שֵׁם בַּשְּׁלוֹשָׁה: 21 מִן־הַשְּׁלוֹשָׁה בַשְּׁנַיִם נִכְבָּד וַיְהִי לָהֶם לְשָׂר וְעַד־

²²Benaiah was the son of Jehoiada, the son of a valiant man from Kabzeel, who had done many deeds. He had killed two lion-like heroes of Moab. He also had gone down and killed a lion in the midst of a pit on a snowy day. ²³And he killed an Egyptian, a man of *great* height, five cubits tall. In the Egyptian's hand *there was* a spear like a weaver's beam; and he went down to him with a staff, wrested the spear out of the Egyptian's hand, and killed him with his own spear. ²⁴These *things* Benaiah the son of Jehoiada did, and won a name among three mighty men. ²⁵Indeed he was more honored than the thirty, but he did not attain to the *first* three. And David appointed him over his guard.

²⁶Also the mighty warriors *were* Asahel the brother of Joab, Elhanan the son of Dodo of Bethlehem, ²⁷Shammoth the Harorite, Helez the Pelonite, ²⁸Ira the son of Ikkesh the Tekoite, Abiezer the Anathothite, ²⁹Sibbechai the Hushathite, Ilai the Ahohite, ³⁰Maharai the Netophathite, Heled the son of Baanah the Netophathite, ³¹Ithai the son of Ribai of Gibeah, of the sons of Benjamin, Benaiah the Pirathonite, ³²Hurai of the brooks of Gaash, Abiel the Arbathite, ³³Azmaveth the Baharumite, Eliahba the Shaalbonite, ³⁴the sons of Hashem the Gizonite, Jonathan the son of Shageh the Hararite, ³⁵Ahiam the son of Sacar the Hararite, Eliphal the son of Ur, ³⁶Hepher the Mecherathite, Ahijah the Pelonite, ³⁷Hezro the Carmelite, Naarai the son of Ezbai, ³⁸Joel the brother of Nathan, Mibhar the son of Hagri, ³⁹Zelek the Ammonite, Naharai the Berothite (the armorbearer of Joab the son of Zeruiah), ⁴⁰Ira the Ithrite, Gareb the Ithrite, ⁴¹Uriah the Hittite, Zabad the son of Ahlai, ⁴²Adina the son of Shiza the Reubenite (a chief of the Reubenites) and thirty with him, ⁴³Hanan the son of Maachah, Joshaphat the Mithnite, ⁴⁴Uzzia the Ashterathite, Shama and Jeiel the sons of Hotham the Aroerite, ⁴⁵Jediael the son of Shimri, and Joha his brother, the Tizite, ⁴⁶Eliel the Mahavite, Jeribai and Joshaviah the sons of Elnaam, Ithmah the Moabite, ⁴⁷Eliel, Obed, and Jaasiel the Mezobaite.

12 Now these *were* the men who came to David at Ziklag while he was still a fugitive from Saul the son of Kish; and they *were* among the mighty men, helpers in the war, ²armed with bows, using both the right hand and the left in *hurling* stones and *shooting* arrows with the bow. *They were* of Benjamin, Saul's brethren.

ס 22 בְּנָיָה בֶן־יְהוֹיָדָע הַשְּׁלוֹשָׁה לֹא־בָא: ס
בֶּן־אִישׁ־חַיִל רַב־פְּעָלִים מִן־קַבְצְאֵל הוּא הִכָּה
אֵת שְׁנֵי אֲרִיאֵל מוֹאָב וְהוּא יָרַד וְהִכָּה אֶת־
הָאֲרִי בְּתוֹךְ הַבּוֹר בְּיוֹם הַשָּׁלֶג: 23 וְהוּא־הִכָּה
אֶת־הָאִישׁ הַמִּצְרִי אִישׁ מִדָּה | חָמֵשׁ בָּאַמָּה
וּבְיַד הַמִּצְרִי חֲנִית כִּמְנוֹר אֹרְגִים וַיֵּרֶד אֵלָיו
בַּשָּׁבֶט וַיִּגְזֹל אֶת־הַחֲנִית מִיַּד הַמִּצְרִי וַיַּהַרְגֵהוּ
בַּחֲנִיתוֹ: 24 אֵלֶּה עָשָׂה בְּנָיָהוּ בֶּן־יְהוֹיָדָע וְלוֹ־שֵׁם
בִּשְׁלוֹשָׁה הַגִּבֹּרִים: 25 מִן־הַשְּׁלוֹשִׁים הִנּוֹ נִכְבָּד
הוּא וְאֶל־הַשְּׁלוֹשָׁה לֹא־בָא וַיְשִׂימֵהוּ דָוִיד עַל־
מִשְׁמַעְתּוֹ: ס

26 וְגִבּוֹרֵי הַחֲיָלִים עֲשָׂה־אֵל
אֲחִי יוֹאָב אֶלְחָנָן בֶּן־דּוֹדוֹ מִבֵּית לָחֶם: 27 שַׁמּוֹת
הַהֲרוֹרִי חֶלֶץ הַפְּלוֹנִי: 28 עִירָא בֶן־עִקֵּשׁ הַתְּקוֹעִי
אֲבִיעֶזֶר הָעֲנְּתוֹתִי: 29 סִבְּכַי הַחֻשָׁתִי עִילַי הָאֲחוֹחִי:
30 מַהְרַי הַנְּטֹפָתִי

חֵלֶד בֶּן־בַּעֲנָה הַנְּטוֹפָתִי: 31 אִיתַי בֶּן־רִיבַי מִגִּבְעַת
בְּנֵי בִנְיָמִן בְּנָיָה הַפִּרְעָתֹנִי: 32 חוּרַי מִנַּחֲלֵי גָעַשׁ
אֲבִיאֵל הָעַרְבָתִי: 33 עַזְמָוֶת הַבַּחֲרוּמִי אֶלְיַחְבָּא
הַשַּׁעַלְבֹנִי: 34 בְּנֵי הָשֵׁם הַגִּזוֹנִי יוֹנָתָן בֶּן־שָׁגֵה
הַהֲרָרִי: 35 אֲחִיאָם בֶּן־שָׂכָר הַהֲרָרִי אֱלִיפַל בֶּן־
אוּר: 36 חֵפֶר הַמְּכֵרָתִי אֲחִיָּה הַפְּלוֹנִי: 37 חֶצְרוֹ
הַכַּרְמְלִי נַעֲרַי בֶּן־אֶזְבָּי: 38 יוֹאֵל אֲחִי נָתָן מִבְחָר
בֶּן־הַגְרִי: 39 צֶלֶק הָעַמּוֹנִי נַחְרַי הַבֵּרֹתִי נֹשֵׂא כְּלֵי
יוֹאָב בֶּן־צְרוּיָה: 40 עִירָא הַיִּתְרִי גָּרֵב הַיִּתְרִי:
41 אוּרִיָּה הַחִתִּי זָבָד בֶּן־אַחְלָי: 42 עֲדִינָא בֶן־שִׁיזָא
הָרְאוּבֵנִי רֹאשׁ לָרְאוּבֵנִי וְעָלָיו שְׁלוֹשִׁים: 43 חָנָן
בֶּן־מַעֲכָה וְיוֹשָׁפָט הַמִּתְנִי: 44 עֻזִּיָּא הָעַשְׁתְּרָתִי
שָׁמָע וִיעוּאֵל בְּנֵי חוֹתָם הָעֲרֹעֵרִי: 45 יְדִיעֲאֵל בֶּן־
שִׁמְרִי וְיֹחָא אָחִיו הַתִּיצִי: 46 אֱלִיאֵל הַמַּחֲוִים וִירִיבַי
וְיוֹשַׁוְיָה בְּנֵי אֶלְנָעַם וְיִתְמָה הַמּוֹאָבִי: 47 אֱלִיאֵל
וְעוֹבֵד וְיַעֲשִׂיאֵל הַמְּצֹבָיָה:
פ

יב וְאֵלֶּה הַבָּאִים אֶל־דָּוִיד לְצִיקְלַג עוֹד עָצוּר
מִפְּנֵי שָׁאוּל בֶּן־קִישׁ וְהֵמָּה בַּגִּבּוֹרִים עֹזְרֵי
הַמִּלְחָמָה: 2 נֹשְׁקֵי קֶשֶׁת מַיְמִינִים וּמַשְׂמִאלִים
בָּאֲבָנִים וּבַחִצִּים בַּקָּשֶׁת מֵאֲחֵי שָׁאוּל מִבִּנְיָמִן:

³The chief *was* Ahiezer, then Joash, the sons of Shemaah the Gibeathite; Jeziel and Pelet the sons of Azmaveth; Berachah, and Jehu the Anathothite; ⁴Ishmaiah the Gibeonite, a mighty man among the thirty, and over the thirty; Jeremiah, Jahaziel, Johanan, and Jozabad the Gederathite; ⁵Eluzai, Jerimoth, Bealiah, Shemariah, and Shephatiah the Haruphite; ⁶Elkanah, Jisshiah, Azarel, Joezer, and Jashobeam, the Korahites; ⁷and Joelah and Zebadiah the sons of Jeroham of Gedor.

⁸*Some* Gadites joined David at the stronghold in the wilderness, mighty men of valor, men trained for battle, who could handle shield and spear, whose faces *were like* the faces of lions, and *were* as swift as gazelles on the mountains: ⁹Ezer the first, Obadiah the second, Eliab the third, ¹⁰Mishmannah the fourth, Jeremiah the fifth, ¹¹Attai the sixth, Eliel the seventh, ¹²Johanan the eighth, Elzabad the ninth, ¹³Jeremiah the tenth, and Machbanai the eleventh. ¹⁴These *were* from the sons of Gad, captains of the army; the least was over a hundred, and the greatest was over a thousand. ¹⁵These *are* the ones who crossed the Jordan in the first month, when it had overflowed all its banks; and they put to flight all *those* in the valleys, to the east and to the west.

¹⁶Then some of the sons of Benjamin and Judah came to David at the stronghold. ¹⁷And David went out to meet them, and answered and said to them, "If you have come peaceably to me to help me, my heart will be united with you; but if to betray me to my enemies, since *there is* no wrong in my hands, may the God of our fathers look and bring judgment." ¹⁸Then the Spirit came upon Amasai, chief of the captains, *and he said:*

"*We are* yours, O David,
We *are* on your side, O son of Jesse!
Peace, peace to you,
And peace to your helpers!
For your God helps you."

So David received them, and made them captains of the troop.

¹⁹And *some* from Manasseh defected to David when he was going with the Philistines to battle against Saul; but they did not help them, for the lords of the Philistines sent him away by agreement, saying, "He may defect to his master Saul *and endanger* our heads." ²⁰When he went to Ziklag, those of Manasseh who defected to him were Adnah, Jozabad, Jediael, Michael, Jozabad, Elihu, and Zillethai, captains of the thousands who *were* from Manasseh. ²¹And they helped David against the bands *of raiders,* for they *were* all mighty men of

3 הָרֹאשׁ אֲחִיעֶזֶר וְיוֹאָשׁ בְּנֵי הַשְּׁמָעָה הַגִּבְעָתִי וִיזִיאֵל וָפֶלֶט בְּנֵי עַזְמָוֶת וּבְרָכָה וְיֵהוּא הָעֲנְתֹתִי: 4 וְיִשְׁמַעְיָה הַגִּבְעוֹנִי גִּבּוֹר בַּשְּׁלֹשִׁים וְעַל־הַשְּׁלֹשִׁים: 5 וְיִרְמְיָה וְיַחֲזִיאֵל וְיוֹחָנָן וְיוֹזָבָד הַגְּדֵרָתִי: 6 אֶלְעוּזַי וִירִימוֹת וּבְעַלְיָה וּשְׁמַרְיָהוּ וּשְׁפַטְיָהוּ הַחֲרוּפִי: 7 אֶלְקָנָה וְיִשִּׁיָּהוּ וַעֲזַרְאֵל וְיוֹעֶזֶר וְיָשָׁבְעָם הַקָּרְחִים: 8 וְיוֹעֵאלָה וּזְבַדְיָה בְּנֵי יְרֹחָם מִן־הַגְּדוֹר: 9 וּמִן־הַגָּדִי נִבְדְּלוּ אֶל־דָּוִיד לַמְּצַד מִדְבָּרָה גִּבֹּרֵי הַחַיִל אַנְשֵׁי צָבָא לַמִּלְחָמָה עֹרְכֵי צִנָּה וָרֹמַח וּפְנֵי אַרְיֵה פְּנֵיהֶם וְכִצְבָאיִם עַל־הֶהָרִים לְמַהֵר: ס 10 עֵזֶר הָרֹאשׁ עֹבַדְיָה הַשֵּׁנִי אֱלִיאָב הַשְּׁלִשִׁי: 11 מִשְׁמַנָּה הָרְבִיעִי יִרְמְיָה הַחֲמִשִׁי: 12 עַתַּי הַשִּׁשִּׁי אֱלִיאֵל הַשְּׁבִעִי: 13 יוֹחָנָן הַשְּׁמִינִי אֶלְזָבָד הַתְּשִׁיעִי: 14 יִרְמְיָהוּ הָעֲשִׂירִי ס מַכְבַּנַּי עַשְׁתֵּי עָשָׂר: 15 אֵלֶּה מִבְּנֵי־גָד רָאשֵׁי הַצָּבָא אֶחָד לְמֵאָה הַקָּטָן וְהַגָּדוֹל לְאָלֶף: 16 אֵלֶּה הֵם אֲשֶׁר עָבְרוּ אֶת־הַיַּרְדֵּן בַּחֹדֶשׁ הָרִאשׁוֹן וְהוּא מְמַלֵּא עַל־כָּל־גְּדוֹתָיו וַיַּבְרִיחוּ אֶת־כָּל־הָעֲמָקִים לַמִּזְרָח וְלַמַּעֲרָב: ס 17 וַיָּבֹאוּ מִן־בְּנֵי בִנְיָמִן וִיהוּדָה עַד־לַמְצָד לְדָוִיד: 18 וַיֵּצֵא דָוִיד לִפְנֵיהֶם וַיַּעַן וַיֹּאמֶר לָהֶם אִם־לְשָׁלוֹם בָּאתֶם אֵלַי לְעָזְרֵנִי יִהְיֶה־לִּי עֲלֵיכֶם לֵבָב לְיָחַד וְאִם־לְרַמּוֹתַנִי לְצָרַי בְּלֹא חָמָס בְּכַפַּי יֵרֶא אֱלֹהֵי אֲבוֹתֵינוּ וְיוֹכַח: ס 19 וְרוּחַ לָבְשָׁה אֶת־עֲמָשַׂי רֹאשׁ הַשְּׁלִשִׁים לְךָ דָוִיד וְעִמְּךָ בֶן־יִשַׁי שָׁלוֹם שָׁלוֹם לְךָ וְשָׁלוֹם לְעֹזְרֶךָ כִּי עֲזָרְךָ אֱלֹהֶיךָ וַיְקַבְּלֵם דָּוִיד וַיִּתְּנֵם בְּרָאשֵׁי הַגְּדוּד: פ

20 וּמִמְּנַשֶּׁה נָפְלוּ עַל־דָּוִיד בְּבֹאוֹ עִם־פְּלִשְׁתִּים עַל־שָׁאוּל לַמִּלְחָמָה וְלֹא עֲזָרֻם כִּי בְעֵצָה שִׁלְּחֻהוּ סַרְנֵי פְלִשְׁתִּים לֵאמֹר בְּרָאשֵׁינוּ יִפּוֹל אֶל־אֲדֹנָיו שָׁאוּל: 21 בְּלֶכְתּוֹ אֶל־צִיקְלַג נָפְלוּ עָלָיו מִמְּנַשֶּׁה עַדְנַח וְיוֹזָבָד וִידִיעֲאֵל וּמִיכָאֵל וְיוֹזָבָד וֶאֱלִיהוּא

יב 3 וְיזִיאֵל   6 הַחֲרוּפִי   16 גְּדוֹתָיו   19 הַשְּׁלִשִׁים

valor, and they were captains in the army. ²²For at *that* time they came to David day by day to help him, until *it was* a great army, like the army of God.

²³Now these *were* the numbers of the divisions *that were* equipped for war, *and* came to David at Hebron to turn *over* the kingdom of Saul to him, according to the word of the LORD: ²⁴of the sons of Judah bearing shield and spear, six thousand eight hundred armed for war; ²⁵of the sons of Simeon, mighty men of valor fit for war, seven thousand one hundred; ²⁶of the sons of Levi four thousand six hundred; ²⁷Jehoiada, the leader of the Aaronites, and with him three thousand seven hundred; ²⁸Zadok, a young man, a valiant warrior, and from his father's house twenty-two captains; ²⁹of the sons of Benjamin, relatives of Saul, three thousand (until then the greatest part of them had remained loyal to the house of Saul); ³⁰of the sons of Ephraim twenty thousand eight hundred, mighty men of valor, famous men throughout their father's house; ³¹of the half-tribe of Manasseh eighteen thousand, who were designated by name to come and make David king; ³²of the sons of Issachar who had understanding of the times, to know what Israel ought to do, their chiefs were two hundred; and all their brethren were at their command; ³³of Zebulun there were fifty thousand who went out to battle, expert in war with all weapons of war, stouthearted men who could keep ranks; ³⁴of Naphtali one thousand captains, and with them thirty-seven thousand with shield and spear; ³⁵of the Danites who could keep battle formation, twenty-eight thousand six hundred; ³⁶of Asher, those who could go out to war, able to keep battle formation, forty thousand; ³⁷of the Reubenites and the Gadites and the half-tribe of Manasseh, from the other side of the Jordan, one hundred and twenty thousand armed for battle with every *kind* of weapon of war.

³⁸All these men of war, who could keep ranks, came to Hebron with a loyal heart, to make David king over all Israel; and all the rest of Israel *were* of one mind to make David king. ³⁹And they were there with David three days, eating and drinking, for their brethren had prepared for them. ⁴⁰Moreover those who were near to them, from as far away as Issachar and Zebulun and Naphtali, were bringing food on donkeys and camels, on mules and oxen—provisions of flour and cakes of figs and cakes of raisins, wine and oil and oxen and sheep abundantly, for *there was* joy in Israel.

22 וְהֵ֫מָּה עָזְר֤וּ עִם־דָּוִיד֙ עַל־הַגְּד֔וּד כִּֽי־גִבּ֥וֹרֵי חַ֖יִל כֻּלָּ֑ם וַיִּהְי֥וּ שָׂרִ֖ים בַּצָּבָֽא׃ 23 כִּ֚י לְעֶת־י֣וֹם בְּי֔וֹם יָבֹ֥אוּ עַל־דָּוִ֖יד לְעָזְר֑וֹ עַד־לְמַחֲנֶ֥ה גָד֖וֹל כְּמַחֲנֵ֥ה אֱלֹהִֽים׃ פ

24 וְ֠אֵלֶּה מִסְפְּרֵ֞י רָאשֵׁ֤י הֶֽחָלוּץ֙ לַצָּבָ֔א בָּ֥אוּ עַל־דָּוִ֖יד חֶבְר֑וֹנָה לְהָסֵ֞ב מַלְכ֥וּת שָׁא֛וּל אֵלָ֖יו כְּפִ֥י יְהוָֽה׃ ס 25 בְּנֵ֣י יְהוּדָ֗ה נֹשְׂאֵ֤י צִנָּה֙ וָרֹ֔מַח שֵׁ֥שֶׁת אֲלָפִ֖ים וּשְׁמוֹנֶ֣ה מֵא֑וֹת חֲלוּצֵ֖י צָבָֽא׃ ס 26 מִן־בְּנֵ֣י שִׁמְע֔וֹן גִּבּ֥וֹרֵי חַ֖יִל לַצָּבָ֑א שִׁבְעַ֥ת אֲלָפִ֖ים וּמֵאָֽה׃ ס 27 מִן־בְּנֵ֣י הַלֵּוִ֔י אַרְבַּ֥עַת אֲלָפִ֖ים וְשֵׁ֥שׁ מֵאֽוֹת׃ ס 28 וִיהוֹיָדָ֖ע הַנָּגִ֣יד לְאַהֲרֹ֑ן וְעִמּ֕וֹ שְׁלֹ֥שֶׁת אֲלָפִ֖ים וּשְׁבַ֥ע מֵאֽוֹת׃ ס 29 וְצָד֥וֹק נַ֖עַר גִּבּ֣וֹר חָ֑יִל וּבֵית־אָבִ֥יו שָׂרִ֖ים עֶשְׂרִ֥ים וּשְׁנָֽיִם׃ ס 30 וּמִן־בְּנֵ֣י בִנְיָמִ֗ן אֲחֵ֤י שָׁאוּל֙ שְׁלֹ֣שֶׁת אֲלָפִ֔ים וְעַד־הֵ֨נָּה֙ מַרְבִּיתָ֔ם שֹׁמְרִ֖ים מִשְׁמֶ֥רֶת בֵּ֥ית שָׁאֽוּל׃ 31 וּמִן־בְּנֵ֣י אֶפְרַ֗יִם עֶשְׂרִ֥ים אֶ֨לֶף֙ וּשְׁמוֹנֶ֣ה מֵא֔וֹת גִּבּ֖וֹרֵי חַ֑יִל אַנְשֵׁ֥י שֵׁמ֖וֹת לְבֵ֥ית אֲבוֹתָֽם׃ ס 32 וּמֵחֲצִי֙ מַטֵּ֣ה מְנַשֶּׁ֔ה שְׁמוֹנָ֥ה עָשָׂ֖ר אָ֑לֶף אֲשֶׁ֤ר נִקְּבוּ֙ בְּשֵׁמ֔וֹת לָב֕וֹא לְהַמְלִ֖יךְ אֶת־דָּוִֽיד׃ ס 33 וּמִבְּנֵ֣י יִשָׂשכָ֗ר יוֹדְעֵ֤י בִינָה֙ לַֽעִתִּ֔ים לָדַ֖עַת מַה־יַּעֲשֶׂ֣ה יִשְׂרָאֵ֑ל רָאשֵׁיהֶ֣ם מָאתַ֔יִם וְכָל־אֲחֵיהֶ֖ם עַל־פִּיהֶֽם׃ ס 34 מִזְּבֻל֞וּן יוֹצְאֵ֣י צָבָ֗א עֹֽרְכֵ֧י מִלְחָמָ֛ה בְּכָל־כְּלֵ֥י מִלְחָמָ֖ה חֲמִשִּׁ֣ים אָ֑לֶף וְלַעֲדֹ֖ר בְּלֹא־לֵ֥ב וָלֵֽב׃ ס 35 וּמִנַּפְתָּלִ֖י שָׂרִ֣ים אָ֑לֶף וְעִמָּהֶ֗ם בְּצִנָּ֥ה וַחֲנִ֛ית שְׁלֹשִׁ֥ים וְשִׁבְעָ֖ה אָֽלֶף׃ ס 36 וּמִן־הַדָּנִ֗י עֹֽרְכֵ֣י מִלְחָמָ֔ה עֶשְׂרִֽים־וּשְׁמוֹנָ֥ה אֶ֖לֶף וְשֵׁ֥שׁ מֵאֽוֹת׃ ס 37 וּמֵאָשֵׁ֗ר יוֹצְאֵ֤י צָבָא֙ לַעֲרֹ֣ךְ מִלְחָמָ֔ה אַרְבָּעִ֖ים אָֽלֶף׃ ס 38 וּמֵעֵ֣בֶר לַ֠יַּרְדֵּן מִן־הָראוּבֵנִ֨י וְהַגָּדִ֜י וַחֲצִ֣י ׀ שֵׁ֣בֶט מְנַשֶּׁ֗ה בְּכֹל֙ כְּלֵ֣י צְבָ֣א מִלְחָמָ֔ה מֵאָ֥ה וְעֶשְׂרִ֖ים אָֽלֶף׃ 39 כָּל־אֵ֜לֶּה אַנְשֵׁ֣י מִלְחָמָה֮ עֹדְרֵ֣י מַעֲרָכָה֒ בְּלֵבָ֤ב שָׁלֵם֙ בָּ֣אוּ חֶבְר֔וֹנָה לְהַמְלִ֥יךְ אֶת־דָּוִ֖יד עַל־כָּל־יִשְׂרָאֵ֑ל וְ֠גַם כָּל־שֵׁרִ֧ית יִשְׂרָאֵ֛ל לֵ֥ב אֶחָ֖ד לְהַמְלִ֥יךְ אֶת־דָּוִֽיד׃ 40 וַיִּהְיוּ־שָׁ֨ם עִם־דָּוִ֜יד יָמִ֤ים שְׁלוֹשָׁה֙ אֹכְלִ֣ים וְשׁוֹתִ֔ים כִּֽי־הֵכִ֥ינוּ לָהֶ֖ם אֲחֵיהֶֽם׃ 41 וְגַ֣ם הַקְּרֽוֹבִים־אֲלֵיהֶ֗ם עַד־יִשָׂשכָ֤ר וּזְבֻלוּן֙ וְנַפְתָּלִ֔י מְבִיאִ֣ים לֶ֡חֶם בַּחֲמוֹרִ֣ים וּבַגְּמַלִּ֣ים וּבַפְּרָדִ֣ים ׀ וּֽבַבָּקָר֩ מַאֲכָ֨ל קֶ֜מַח דְּבֵלִ֣ים וְצִמּוּקִ֗ים וְיַֽיִן־וְשֶׁ֨מֶן֙ וּבָקָ֣ר וְצֹ֔אן לָרֹ֑ב כִּ֥י שִׂמְחָ֖ה בְּיִשְׂרָאֵֽל׃ פ

13 Then David consulted with the captains of thousands and hundreds, *and* with every leader. ² And David said to all the assembly of Israel, "If *it seems* good to you, and if it is of the LORD our God, let us send out to our brethren everywhere *who are* left in all the land of Israel, and with them to the priests and Levites *who are* in their cities *and* their common-lands, that they may gather together to us; ³ and let us bring the ark of our God back to us, for we have not inquired at it since the days of Saul." ⁴ Then all the assembly said that they would do so, for the thing was right in the eyes of all the people.

⁵ So David gathered all Israel together, from Shihor in Egypt to as far as the entrance of Hamath, to bring the ark of God from Kirjath Jearim. ⁶ And David and all Israel went up to Baalah, to Kirjath Jearim, which belonged to Judah, to bring up from there the ark of God the LORD, who dwells *between* the cherubim, where *His* name is proclaimed. ⁷ So they carried the ark of God on a new cart from the house of Abinadab, and Uzza and Ahio drove the cart. ⁸ Then David and all Israel played *music* before God with all *their* might, with singing, on harps, on stringed instruments, on tambourines, on cymbals, and with trumpets.

⁹ And when they came to Chidon's threshing floor, Uzza put out his hand to hold the ark, for the oxen stumbled. ¹⁰ Then the anger of the LORD was aroused against Uzza, and He struck him because he put his hand to the ark; and he died there before God. ¹¹ And David became angry because of the LORD's outbreak against Uzza; therefore that place is called Perez Uzza to this day. ¹² David was afraid of God that day, saying, "How can I bring the ark of God to me?"

¹³ So David would not move the ark with him into the City of David, but took it aside into the house of Obed-Edom the Gittite. ¹⁴ The ark of God remained with the family of Obed-Edom in his house three months. And the LORD blessed the house of Obed-Edom and all that he had.

14 Now Hiram king of Tyre sent messengers to David, and cedar trees, with masons and carpenters, to build him a house. ² So David knew that the LORD had established him as king over Israel, for his kingdom was highly exalted for the sake of His people Israel.

³ Then David took more wives in Jerusalem, and David begot more sons and daughters. ⁴ And these are the names of his children whom he had in

יג וַיִּוָּעַץ דָּוִיד עִם־שָׂרֵי הָאֲלָפִים וְהַמֵּאוֹת לְכָל־
נָגִיד: ² וַיֹּאמֶר דָּוִיד לְכֹל ׀ קְהַל יִשְׂרָאֵל אִם־
עֲלֵיכֶם טוֹב וּמִן־יְהוָה אֱלֹהֵינוּ נִפְרְצָה נִשְׁלְחָה
עַל־אַחֵינוּ הַנִּשְׁאָרִים בְּכֹל אַרְצוֹת יִשְׂרָאֵל וְעִמָּהֶם
הַכֹּהֲנִים וְהַלְוִיִּם בְּעָרֵי מִגְרְשֵׁיהֶם וְיִקָּבְצוּ אֵלֵינוּ:
³ וְנָסֵבָּה אֶת־אֲרוֹן אֱלֹהֵינוּ אֵלֵינוּ כִּי־לֹא דְרַשְׁנֻהוּ
בִּימֵי שָׁאוּל: ⁴ וַיֹּאמְרוּ כָל־הַקָּהָל לַעֲשׂוֹת כֵּן כִּי־
יָשַׁר הַדָּבָר בְּעֵינֵי כָל־הָעָם: ⁵ וַיַּקְהֵל דָּוִיד אֶת־
כָּל־יִשְׂרָאֵל מִן־שִׁיחוֹר מִצְרַיִם וְעַד־לְבוֹא חֲמָת
לְהָבִיא אֶת־אֲרוֹן הָאֱלֹהִים מִקִּרְיַת יְעָרִים: ⁶ וַיַּעַל
דָּוִיד וְכָל־יִשְׂרָאֵל בַּעֲלָתָה אֶל־קִרְיַת יְעָרִים אֲשֶׁר
לִיהוּדָה לְהַעֲלוֹת מִשָּׁם אֵת אֲרוֹן הָאֱלֹהִים ׀
יְהוָה יוֹשֵׁב הַכְּרוּבִים אֲשֶׁר־נִקְרָא שֵׁם: ⁷ וַיַּרְכִּיבוּ
אֶת־אֲרוֹן הָאֱלֹהִים עַל־עֲגָלָה חֲדָשָׁה מִבֵּית
אֲבִינָדָב וְעֻזָּא וְאַחְיוֹ נֹהֲגִים בָּעֲגָלָה: ⁸ וְדָוִיד וְכָל־
יִשְׂרָאֵל מְשַׂחֲקִים לִפְנֵי הָאֱלֹהִים בְּכָל־עֹז וּבְשִׁירִים
וּבְכִנֹּרוֹת וּבִנְבָלִים וּבְתֻפִּים וּבִמְצִלְתַּיִם וּבַחֲצֹצְרוֹת:
⁹ וַיָּבֹאוּ עַד־גֹּרֶן כִּידֹן וַיִּשְׁלַח עֻזָּא אֶת־יָדוֹ לֶאֱחֹז
אֶת־הָאָרוֹן כִּי שָׁמְטוּ הַבָּקָר: ¹⁰ וַיִּחַר־אַף יְהוָה
בְּעֻזָּא וַיַּכֵּהוּ עַל אֲשֶׁר־שָׁלַח יָדוֹ עַל־הָאָרוֹן וַיָּמָת
שָׁם לִפְנֵי אֱלֹהִים: ¹¹ וַיִּחַר לְדָוִיד כִּי־פָרַץ יְהוָה
פֶּרֶץ בְּעֻזָּא וַיִּקְרָא לַמָּקוֹם הַהוּא פֶּרֶץ עֻזָּא עַד
הַיּוֹם הַזֶּה: ¹² וַיִּירָא דָוִיד אֶת־הָאֱלֹהִים בַּיּוֹם הַהוּא
לֵאמֹר הֵיךְ אָבִיא אֵלַי אֵת אֲרוֹן הָאֱלֹהִים: ¹³ וְלֹא־
הֵסִיר דָּוִיד אֶת־הָאָרוֹן אֵלָיו אֶל־עִיר דָּוִיד וַיַּטֵּהוּ
אֶל־בֵּית עֹבֵד־אֱדֹם הַגִּתִּי: ¹⁴ וַיֵּשֶׁב אֲרוֹן הָאֱלֹהִים
עִם־בֵּית עֹבֵד אֱדֹם בְּבֵיתוֹ שְׁלֹשָׁה חֳדָשִׁים וַיְבָרֶךְ
יְהוָה אֶת־בֵּית עֹבֵד־אֱדֹם וְאֶת־כָּל־אֲשֶׁר־לוֹ: פ

יד וַיִּשְׁלַח חִירָם מֶלֶךְ־צֹר מַלְאָכִים אֶל־דָּוִיד
וַעֲצֵי אֲרָזִים וְחָרָשֵׁי קִיר וְחָרָשֵׁי עֵצִים לִבְנוֹת לוֹ
בָּיִת: ² וַיֵּדַע דָּוִיד כִּי־הֱכִינוֹ יְהוָה לְמֶלֶךְ עַל־
יִשְׂרָאֵל כִּי־נִשֵּׂאת לְמַעְלָה מַלְכוּתוֹ בַּעֲבוּר עַמּוֹ
יִשְׂרָאֵל: פ
³ וַיִּקַּח דָּוִיד עוֹד נָשִׁים בִּירוּשָׁלִָם וַיּוֹלֶד דָּוִיד עוֹד
בָּנִים וּבָנוֹת: ⁴ וְאֵלֶּה שְׁמוֹת הַיְלוּדִים אֲשֶׁר הָיוּ

Jerusalem: Shammua, Shobab, Nathan, Solomon, [5]Ibhar, Elishua, Elpelet, [6]Nogah, Nepheg, Japhia, [7]Elishama, Beeliada, and Eliphelet.

[8]Now when the Philistines heard that David had been anointed king over all Israel, all the Philistines went up to search for David. And David heard *of it* and went out against them. [9]The Philistines went and made a raid on the Valley of Rephaim. [10]And David inquired of God, saying, "Shall I go up against the Philistines? Will You deliver them into my hand?"

The LORD said to him, "Go up, for I will deliver them into your hand."

[11]So they went up to Baal Perazim, and David defeated them there. Then David said, "God has broken through my enemies by my hand like a breakthrough of water." Therefore they called the name of that place Baal Perazim. [12]And when they left their gods there, David gave a commandment, and they were burned with fire.

[13]Then the Philistines once again made a raid on the valley. [14]Therefore David inquired again of God, and God said to him, "You shall not go up after them; circle around them, and come upon them in front of the mulberry trees. [15]And it shall be, when you hear a sound of marching in the tops of the mulberry trees, then you shall go out to battle, for God has gone out before you to strike the camp of the Philistines." [16]So David did as God commanded him, and they drove back the army of the Philistines from Gibeon as far as Gezer. [17]Then the fame of David went out into all lands, and the LORD brought the fear of him upon all nations.

15 *David* built houses for himself in the City of David; and he prepared a place for the ark of God, and pitched a tent for it. [2]Then David said, "No one may carry the ark of God but the Levites, for the LORD has chosen them to carry the ark of God and to minister before Him forever." [3]And David gathered all Israel together at Jerusalem, to bring up the ark of the LORD to its place, which he had prepared for it. [4]Then David assembled the children of Aaron and the Levites: [5]of the sons of Kohath, Uriel the chief, and one hundred and twenty of his brethren; [6]of the sons of Merari, Asaiah the chief, and two hundred and twenty of his brethren; [7]of the sons of Gershom, Joel the chief, and one hundred and thirty of his brethren; [8]of the sons of Elizaphan, Shemaiah the chief, and two hundred of his brethren; [9]of the sons of Hebron, Eliel the chief, and eighty of his brethren; [10]of the sons of Uzziel, Amminadab the chief, and one hundred and twelve of his brethren.

לֹו בִירוּשָׁלָ֑͏ִם שַׁמּ֧וּעַ וְשׁוֹבָ֛ב נָתָ֥ן וּשְׁלֹמֹֽה: 5 וְיִבְחָ֣ר
וֶאֱלִישׁ֖וּעַ וְאֶלְפָּֽלֶט: 6 וְנֹ֥גַהּ וְנֶ֖פֶג וְיָפִֽיעַ: 7 וֶאֱלִישָׁמָ֥ע
וּבְעֶלְיָדָ֖ע וֶאֱלִיפָֽלֶט: 8 וַיִּשְׁמְע֣וּ פְלִשְׁתִּ֗ים כִּֽי־
נִמְשַׁ֨ח דָּוִ֤יד לְמֶ֙לֶךְ֙ עַל־כָּל־יִשְׂרָאֵ֔ל וַיַּעֲל֥וּ כָל־
פְּלִשְׁתִּ֖ים לְבַקֵּ֣שׁ אֶת־דָּוִ֑יד וַיִּשְׁמַ֣ע דָּוִ֔יד וַיֵּצֵ֖א
לִפְנֵיהֶֽם: 9 וּפְלִשְׁתִּ֖ים בָּ֑אוּ וַֽיִּפְשְׁט֖וּ בְּעֵ֥מֶק רְפָאִֽים:
10 וַיִּשְׁאַ֨ל דָּוִ֤יד בֵּֽאלֹהִים֙ לֵאמֹ֔ר הַאֶֽעֱלֶה֙ עַל־
פְּלִשְׁתִּיִ֔ים וּנְתַתָּ֖ם בְּיָדִ֑י וַיֹּ֧אמֶר ל֣וֹ יְהוָ֗ה עֲלֵ֔ה
וּנְתַתִּ֖ים בְּיָדֶֽךָ: 11 וַיַּעֲל֣וּ בְּבַֽעַל־פְּרָצִים֮ וַיַּכֵּ֣ם שָׁ֣ם
דָּוִיד֒ וַיֹּ֣אמֶר דָּוִ֔יד פָּרַ֨ץ הָאֱלֹהִ֧ים אֶת־אוֹיְבַ֛י בְּיָדִ֖י
כְּפֶ֣רֶץ מָ֑יִם עַל־כֵּ֗ן קָרְא֛וּ שֵֽׁם־הַמָּק֥וֹם הַה֖וּא בַּ֣עַל
פְּרָצִֽים: 12 וַיַּעַזְבוּ־שָׁ֖ם אֶת־אֱלֹֽהֵיהֶ֑ם וַיֹּ֣אמֶר דָּוִ֔יד
וַיִּשָּׂרְפ֖וּ בָּאֵֽשׁ: פ

13 וַיֹּסִ֤יפוּ עוֹד֙ פְּלִשְׁתִּ֔ים וַֽיִּפְשְׁט֖וּ בָּעֵֽמֶק: 14 וַיִּשְׁאַ֨ל
ע֤וֹד דָּוִיד֙ בֵּֽאלֹהִ֔ים וַיֹּ֤אמֶר ל֣וֹ הָאֱלֹהִ֔ים לֹ֥א
תַֽעֲלֶ֖ה אַֽחֲרֵיהֶ֑ם הָסֵב֙ מֵֽעֲלֵיהֶ֔ם וּבָ֥אתָ לָהֶ֖ם
מִמּ֥וּל הַבְּכָאִֽים: 15 וִ֠יהִ֞י כְּֽשָׁמְעֲךָ֞ אֶת־ק֤וֹל הַצְּעָדָה֙
בְּרָאשֵׁ֣י הַבְּכָאִ֔ים אָ֖ז תֵּצֵ֣א בַמִּלְחָמָ֑ה כִּֽי־יָצָ֤א
הָֽאֱלֹהִים֙ לְפָנֶ֔יךָ לְהַכּ֖וֹת אֶת־מַֽחֲנֵ֥ה פְלִשְׁתִּֽים:
16 וַיַּ֣עַשׂ דָּוִ֔יד כַּֽאֲשֶׁ֥ר צִוָּ֖הוּ הָֽאֱלֹהִ֑ים וַיַּכּוּ֙ אֶת־
מַֽחֲנֵ֣ה פְלִשְׁתִּ֔ים מִגִּבְע֖וֹן וְעַד־גָּֽזְרָה: 17 וַיֵּצֵ֥א שֵׁם־
דָּוִ֖יד בְּכָל־הָֽאֲרָצ֑וֹת וַֽיהוָ֗ה נָתַ֧ן אֶת־פַּחְדּ֛וֹ עַל־כָּל־
הַגּוֹיִֽם:

טו וַיַּֽעַשׂ־ל֥וֹ בָתִּ֖ים בְּעִ֣יר דָּוִ֑יד וַיָּ֤כֶן מָקוֹם֙
לַֽאֲר֣וֹן הָֽאֱלֹהִ֔ים וַיֶּט־ל֖וֹ אֹֽהֶל: 2 אָ֚ז אָמַ֣ר דָּוִ֔יד
לֹ֤א לָשֵׂאת֙ אֶת־אֲר֣וֹן הָֽאֱלֹהִ֔ים כִּ֖י אִם־הַֽלְוִיִּ֑ם כִּי־
בָ֣ם ׀ בָּחַ֣ר יְהוָ֗ה לָשֵׂ֞את אֶת־אֲר֤וֹן יְהוָה֙ וּֽלְשָֽׁרְת֖וֹ
עַד־עוֹלָֽם: 3 וַיַּקְהֵ֥ל דָּוִ֛יד אֶת־כָּל־ פ
יִשְׂרָאֵ֖ל אֶל־יְרֽוּשָׁלָ֑͏ִם לְהַֽעֲלוֹת֙ אֶת־אֲר֣וֹן יְהוָ֔ה אֶל־
מְקוֹמ֖וֹ אֲשֶׁר־הֵכִ֥ין לֽוֹ: 4 וַיֶּֽאֱסֹ֥ף דָּוִ֖יד אֶת־בְּנֵ֣י אַֽהֲרֹ֑ן
וְאֶת־הַֽלְוִיִּֽם: 5 לִבְנֵ֣י קְהָ֔ת אֽוּרִיאֵ֖ל הַשָּׂ֑ר וְאֶחָ֖יו
מֵאָ֥ה וְעֶשְׂרִֽים: 6 לִבְנֵ֣י מְרָרִ֔י עֲשָׂיָ֖ה פ
הַשָּׂ֑ר וְאֶחָ֖יו מָאתַ֥יִם וְעֶשְׂרִֽים: 7 לִבְנֵ֣י פ
גֵֽרְשׁ֔וֹם יוֹאֵ֖ל הַשָּׂ֑ר וְאֶחָ֖יו מֵאָ֥ה
וּשְׁלֹשִֽׁים: 8 לִבְנֵ֣י אֱלִֽיצָפָ֔ן שְׁמַֽעְיָ֖ה הַשָּׂ֑ר פ
וְאֶחָ֖יו מָאתָֽיִם: 9 לִבְנֵ֣י חֶבְר֔וֹן אֱלִיאֵ֖ל פ
הַשָּׂ֑ר וְאֶחָ֖יו שְׁמוֹנִֽים: 10 לִבְנֵ֣י עֻזִּיאֵ֔ל

עֲמִֽינָדָב֙ הַשָּׂ֔ר וְאֶחָ֖יו מֵאָ֥ה וּשְׁנַ֥יִם עָשָֽׂר׃ 11 וַיִּקְרָ֣א
דָוִ֔יד לְצָד֥וֹק וּלְאֶבְיָתָ֖ר הַכֹּהֲנִ֑ים וְלַלְוִיִּ֔ם לְאֽוּרִיאֵ֣ל
עֲשָׂיָ֗ה וְ֠יוֹאֵל שְׁמַֽעְיָ֧ה וֶאֱלִיאֵ֛ל וְעַמִּֽינָדָֽב׃ 12 וַיֹּ֣אמֶר
לָהֶ֔ם אַתֶּ֛ם רָאשֵׁ֥י הָאָב֖וֹת לַלְוִיִּ֑ם הִֽתְקַדְּשׁוּ֙ אַתֶּ֣ם
וַֽאֲחֵיכֶ֔ם וְהַֽעֲלִיתֶ֔ם אֵ֚ת אֲר֣וֹן יְהוָ֔ה אֱלֹהֵ֖י יִשְׂרָאֵ֑ל
אֶל־הֲכִֽינ֖וֹתִי לֽוֹ׃ 13 כִּ֚י לְמַבָּרִ֣אשׁוֹנָ֔ה לֹ֥א אַתֶּ֖ם
פָּ֗רַץ יְהוָ֤ה אֱלֹהֵ֨ינוּ֙ בָּ֔נוּ כִּֽי־לֹ֥א דְרַשְׁנֻ֖הוּ כַּמִּשְׁפָּֽט׃
14 וַיִּֽתְקַדְּשׁ֔וּ הַכֹּֽהֲנִ֖ים וְהַֽלְוִיִּ֑ם לְהַֽעֲל֕וֹת אֶת־אֲר֥וֹן
יְהוָ֖ה אֱלֹהֵ֥י יִשְׂרָאֵֽל׃ 15 וַיִּשְׂא֣וּ בְנֵֽי־הַלְוִיִּם֮ אֵ֣ת אֲר֣וֹן
הָֽאֱלֹהִים֒ כַּֽאֲשֶׁ֛ר צִוָּ֥ה מֹשֶׁ֖ה כִּדְבַ֣ר יְהוָ֑ה בִּכְתֵפָ֛ם
בַּמֹּט֖וֹת עֲלֵיהֶֽם׃ פ

16 וַיֹּ֣אמֶר דָּוִיד֮ לְשָׂרֵ֣י הַלְוִיִּם֒ לְהַֽעֲמִ֗יד אֶת־אֲחֵיהֶם֙
הַמְשֹׁ֣רְרִ֔ים בִּכְלֵי־שִׁ֛יר נְבָלִ֥ים וְכִנֹּר֖וֹת וּמְצִלְתָּ֑יִם
מַשְׁמִעִ֥ים לְהָֽרִֽים־בְּק֖וֹל לְשִׂמְחָֽה׃ פ

17 וַיַּֽעֲמִ֣ידוּ הַלְוִיִּ֗ם אֵ֚ת הֵימָ֣ן בֶּן־יוֹאֵ֔ל וּמִן־
אֶחָ֕יו אָסָ֖ף בֶּן־בֶּרֶכְיָ֑הוּ ס וּמִן־בְּנֵ֤י מְרָרִי֙
אֲחֵיהֶ֔ם אֵיתָ֖ן בֶּן־קֽוּשָׁיָֽהוּ׃ 18 וְעִמָּהֶ֖ם אֲחֵיהֶ֣ם
הַמִּשְׁנִ֑ים זְכַרְיָ֡הוּ בֵּ֡ן וְֽיַֽעֲזִיאֵ֡ל וּֽשְׁמִירָמ֡וֹת וִֽיחִיאֵ֣ל ׀
וְעֻנִּ֡י אֱלִיאָ֡ב וּבְנָיָ֡הוּ וּמַֽעֲשֵׂיָ֡הוּ וּֽמַתִּתְיָ֡הוּ
וֶֽאֱלִֽיפְלֵ֡הֻ וּמִקְנֵיָ֡הוּ וְעֹבֵ֥ד אֱדֹ֛ם וִֽיעִיאֵ֖ל הַשֹּֽׁעֲרִֽים׃
19 וְהַֽמְשֹׁ֣רְרִ֔ים הֵימָ֥ן אָסָ֖ף וְאֵיתָ֑ן בִּמְצִלְתַּ֥יִם נְחֹ֖שֶׁת
לְהַשְׁמִֽיעַ׃ 20 וּזְכַרְיָ֨ה וַֽעֲזִיאֵ֜ל וּשְׁמִֽירָמ֤וֹת וִֽיחִיאֵל֙
וְעֻנִּ֣י וֶֽאֱלִיאָ֔ב וּמַֽעֲשֵׂיָ֖הוּ וּבְנָיָ֑הוּ בִּנְבָלִ֖ים עַל־
עֲלָמֽוֹת׃ 21 וּמַתִּתְיָ֣הוּ וֶֽאֱלִֽיפְלֵ֗הֻ וּמִקְנֵיָ֨הוּ֙ וְעֹבֵ֣ד
אֱדֹ֗ם וִֽיעִיאֵ֛ל וַֽעֲזַזְיָ֖הוּ בְּכִנֹּר֥וֹת עַל־הַשְּׁמִינִ֖ית לְנַצֵּֽחַ׃
22 וּכְנַנְיָ֛הוּ שַׂר־הַלְוִיִּ֖ם בְּמַשָּׂ֑א יָסֹ֣ר בַּמַּשָּׂ֔א כִּ֥י
מֵבִ֖ין הֽוּא׃ 23 וּבֶרֶכְיָ֣ה וְאֶלְקָנָ֔ה שֹֽׁעֲרִ֖ים לָֽאָרֽוֹן׃
24 וּשְׁבַנְיָ֣הוּ וְֽיֽוֹשָׁפָ֡ט וּנְתַנְאֵ֡ל וַֽעֲמָשַׂ֡י וּֽזְכַרְיָ֡הוּ וּבְנָיָ֡הוּ
וֶֽאֱלִיעֶ֡זֶר הַכֹּֽהֲנִ֡ים מַחְצֹצְרִים֩ בַּֽחֲצֹ֨צְר֜וֹת לִפְנֵ֣י
אֲר֣וֹן הָֽאֱלֹהִ֗ים וְעֹבֵ֥ד אֱדֹ֛ם וִֽיחִיָּ֖ה שֹֽׁעֲרִ֥ים לָֽאָרֽוֹן׃
25 וַיְהִ֣י דָוִ֣יד וְזִקְנֵ֣י יִשְׂרָאֵ֡ל וְשָׂרֵ֣י הָֽאֲלָפִים֮ הַהֹֽלְכִים֒
לְהַֽעֲל֞וֹת אֶת־אֲר֧וֹן בְּרִית־יְהוָ֛ה מִן־בֵּ֥ית עֹבֵ֖ד אֱדֹ֑ם
בְּשִׂמְחָֽה׃ 26 וַֽיְהִי֙ בֶּעְזֹ֣ר הָֽאֱלֹהִ֔ים אֶת־ ס
הַ֨לְוִיִּ֔ם נֹֽשְׂאֵ֖י אֲר֣וֹן בְּרִית־יְהוָ֑ה וַיִּזְבְּח֥וּ שִׁבְעָֽה־
פָרִ֖ים וְשִׁבְעָ֥ה אֵילִֽים׃ 27 וְדָוִ֞יד מְכֻרְבָּ֣ל ׀ בִּמְעִ֣יל
בּ֗וּץ וְכָל־הַלְוִיִּם֙ הַנֹּֽשְׂאִ֣ים אֶת־הָֽאָר֔וֹן וְהַֽמְשֹׁ֣רְרִ֔ים
וּכְנַנְיָ֛ה הַשַּׂ֥ר הַמַּשָּׂ֖א הַֽמְשֹֽׁרְרִ֑ים וְעַל־דָּוִ֖יד אֵפ֥וֹד
בָּֽד׃ 28 וְכָל־יִשְׂרָאֵ֗ל מַֽעֲלִים֙ אֶת־אֲר֣וֹן בְּרִית־יְהוָ֔ה

1 CHRONICLES 15

11 And David called for Zadok and Abiathar the priests, and for the Levites: for Uriel, Asaiah, Joel, Shemaiah, Eliel, and Amminadab. 12 He said to them, "You *are* the heads of the fathers' *houses* of the Levites; sanctify yourselves, you and your brethren, that you may bring up the ark of the LORD God of Israel to *the place* I have prepared for it. 13 For because you *did* not *do it* the first *time,* the LORD our God broke out against us, because we did not consult Him about the proper order."

14 So the priests and the Levites sanctified themselves to bring up the ark of the LORD God of Israel. 15 And the children of the Levites bore the ark of God on their shoulders, by its poles, as Moses had commanded according to the word of the LORD.

16 Then David spoke to the leaders of the Levites to appoint their brethren *to be* the singers accompanied by instruments of music, stringed instruments, harps, and cymbals, by raising the voice with resounding joy. 17 So the Levites appointed Heman the son of Joel; and of his brethren, Asaph the son of Berechiah; and of their brethren, the sons of Merari, Ethan the son of Kushaiah; 18 and with them their brethren of the second *rank:* Zechariah, Ben, Jaaziel, Shemiramoth, Jehiel, Unni, Eliab, Benaiah, Maaseiah, Mattithiah, Elipheleh, Mikneiah, Obed-Edom, and Jeiel, the gatekeepers; 19 the singers, Heman, Asaph, and Ethan, *were* to sound the cymbals of bronze; 20 Zechariah, Aziel, Shemiramoth, Jehiel, Unni, Eliab, Maaseiah, and Benaiah, with strings according to Alamoth; 21 Mattithiah, Elipheleh, Mikneiah, Obed-Edom, Jeiel, and Azaziah, to direct with harps on the Sheminith; 22 Chenaniah, leader of the Levites, was instructor *in charge of* the music, because he *was* skillful; 23 Berechiah and Elkanah *were* doorkeepers for the ark; 24 Shebaniah, Joshaphat, Nethanel, Amasai, Zechariah, Benaiah, and Eliezer, the priests, were to blow the trumpets before the ark of God; and Obed-Edom and Jehiah, doorkeepers for the ark.

25 So David, the elders of Israel, and the captains over thousands went to bring up the ark of the covenant of the LORD from the house of Obed-Edom with joy. 26 And so it was, when God helped the Levites who bore the ark of the covenant of the LORD, that they offered seven bulls and seven rams. 27 David was clothed with a robe of fine linen, as were all the Levites who bore the ark, the singers, and Chenaniah the music master *with* the singers. David also wore a linen ephod. 28 Thus all Israel brought up the ark of the covenant of the LORD

with shouting and with the sound of the horn, with trumpets and with cymbals, making music with stringed instruments and harps.

²⁹ And it happened, *as* the ark of the covenant of the LORD came to the City of David, that Michal, Saul's daughter, looked through a window and saw King David whirling and playing music; and she despised him in her heart.

16 So they brought the ark of God, and set it in the midst of the tabernacle that David had erected for it. Then they offered burnt offerings and peace offerings before God. ² And when David had finished offering the burnt offerings and the peace offerings, he blessed the people in the name of the LORD. ³ Then he distributed to everyone of Israel, both man and woman, to everyone a loaf of bread, a piece *of meat,* and a cake of raisins.

⁴ And he appointed some of the Levites to minister before the ark of the LORD, to commemorate, to thank, and to praise the LORD God of Israel: ⁵ Asaph the chief, and next to him Zechariah, *then* Jeiel, Shemiramoth, Jehiel, Mattithiah, Eliab, Benaiah, and Obed-Edom: Jeiel with stringed instruments and harps, but Asaph made music with cymbals; ⁶ Benaiah and Jahaziel the priests regularly *blew* the trumpets before the ark of the covenant of God.

⁷ On that day David first delivered *this psalm* into the hand of Asaph and his brethren, to thank the LORD:

⁸   Oh, give thanks to the LORD!
     Call upon His name;
     Make known His deeds among the peoples!
⁹   Sing to Him, sing psalms to Him;
     Talk of all His wondrous works!
¹⁰   Glory in His holy name;
     Let the hearts of those rejoice who seek the LORD!
¹¹   Seek the LORD and His strength;
     Seek His face evermore!
¹²   Remember His marvelous works which He has done,
     His wonders, and the judgments of His mouth,
¹³   O seed of Israel His servant,
     You children of Jacob, His chosen ones!
¹⁴   He *is* the LORD our God;
     His judgments *are* in all the earth.
¹⁵   Remember His covenant forever,
     The word which He commanded, for a thousand generations,
¹⁶   *The covenant which* He made with Abraham,

בִּתְרוּעָה וּבְקוֹל שׁוֹפָר וּבַחֲצֹצְרוֹת וּבִמְצִלְתָּיִם מַשְׁמִעִים בִּנְבָלִים וְכִנֹּרוֹת: ²⁹ וַיְהִי אֲרוֹן בְּרִית יְהוָה בָּא עַד־עִיר דָּוִיד וּמִיכַל בַּת־שָׁאוּל נִשְׁקְפָה | בְּעַד הַחַלּוֹן וַתֵּרֶא אֶת־הַמֶּלֶךְ דָּוִיד מְרַקֵּד וּמְשַׂחֵק וַתִּבֶז לוֹ בְּלִבָּהּ: פ

טז וַיָּבִיאוּ אֶת־אֲרוֹן הָאֱלֹהִים וַיַּצִּיגוּ אֹתוֹ בְּתוֹךְ הָאֹהֶל אֲשֶׁר נָטָה־לוֹ דָּוִיד וַיַּקְרִיבוּ עֹלוֹת וּשְׁלָמִים לִפְנֵי הָאֱלֹהִים: ² וַיְכַל דָּוִיד מֵהַעֲלוֹת הָעֹלָה וְהַשְּׁלָמִים וַיְבָרֶךְ אֶת־הָעָם בְּשֵׁם יְהוָה: ³ וַיְחַלֵּק לְכָל־אִישׁ יִשְׂרָאֵל מֵאִישׁ וְעַד־אִשָּׁה לְאִישׁ כִּכַּר־לֶחֶם וְאֶשְׁפָּר וַאֲשִׁישָׁה: ⁴ וַיִּתֵּן לִפְנֵי אֲרוֹן יְהוָה מִן־הַלְוִיִּם מְשָׁרְתִים וּלְהַזְכִּיר וּלְהוֹדוֹת וּלְהַלֵּל לַיהוָה אֱלֹהֵי יִשְׂרָאֵל: פ

⁵ אָסָף הָרֹאשׁ וּמִשְׁנֵהוּ זְכַרְיָה יְעִיאֵל וּשְׁמִירָמוֹת וִיחִיאֵל וּמַתִּתְיָה וֶאֱלִיאָב וּבְנָיָהוּ וְעֹבֵד אֱדֹם וִיעִיאֵל בִּכְלֵי נְבָלִים וּבְכִנֹּרוֹת וְאָסָף בַּמְצִלְתַּיִם מַשְׁמִיעַ: ⁶ וּבְנָיָהוּ וְיַחֲזִיאֵל הַכֹּהֲנִים בַּחֲצֹצְרוֹת תָּמִיד לִפְנֵי אֲרוֹן בְּרִית־הָאֱלֹהִים: ⁷ בַּיּוֹם הַהוּא אָז נָתַן דָּוִיד בָּרֹאשׁ לְהֹדוֹת לַיהוָה בְּיַד־אָסָף וְאֶחָיו: פ

⁸ הוֹדוּ לַיהוָה קִרְאוּ בִשְׁמוֹ
הוֹדִיעוּ בָעַמִּים עֲלִילֹתָיו:
⁹ שִׁירוּ לוֹ זַמְּרוּ־לוֹ
שִׂיחוּ בְּכָל־נִפְלְאֹתָיו:
¹⁰ הִתְהַלְלוּ בְּשֵׁם קָדְשׁוֹ
יִשְׂמַח לֵב מְבַקְשֵׁי יְהוָה:
¹¹ דִּרְשׁוּ יְהוָה וְעֻזּוֹ
בַּקְּשׁוּ פָנָיו תָּמִיד:
¹² זִכְרוּ נִפְלְאֹתָיו אֲשֶׁר עָשָׂה
מֹפְתָיו וּמִשְׁפְּטֵי־פִיהוּ:
¹³ זֶרַע יִשְׂרָאֵל עַבְדּוֹ
בְּנֵי יַעֲקֹב בְּחִירָיו:
¹⁴ הוּא יְהוָה אֱלֹהֵינוּ
בְּכָל־הָאָרֶץ מִשְׁפָּטָיו:
¹⁵ זִכְרוּ לְעוֹלָם בְּרִיתוֹ
דָּבָר צִוָּה לְאֶלֶף דּוֹר:
¹⁶ אֲשֶׁר כָּרַת אֶת־אַבְרָהָם

And His oath to Isaac,

17 And confirmed it to Jacob for a statute,
To Israel *for* an everlasting covenant,

18 Saying, "To you I will give the land of
Canaan
As the allotment of your inheritance,"

19 When you were few in number,
Indeed very few, and strangers in it.

20 When they went from one nation to another,
And from *one* kingdom to another people,

21 He permitted no man to do them wrong;
Yes, He rebuked kings for their sakes,

22 *Saying*, "Do not touch My anointed ones,
And do My prophets no harm."

23 Sing to the LORD, all the earth;
Proclaim the good news of His salvation
from day to day.

24 Declare His glory among the nations,
His wonders among all peoples.

25 For the LORD *is* great and greatly to be
praised;
He *is* also to be feared above all gods.

26 For all the gods of the peoples *are* idols,
But the LORD made the heavens.

27 Honor and majesty *are* before Him;
Strength and gladness are in His place.

28 Give to the LORD, O families of the peoples,
Give to the LORD glory and strength.

29 Give to the LORD the glory *due* His name;
Bring an offering, and come before Him.
Oh, worship the LORD in the beauty of
holiness!

30 Tremble before Him, all the earth.
The world also is firmly established,
It shall not be moved.

31 Let the heavens rejoice, and let the earth be
glad;
And let them say among the nations, "The
LORD reigns."

32 Let the sea roar, and all its fullness;
Let the field rejoice, and all that *is* in it.

33 Then the trees of the woods shall rejoice
before the LORD,
For He is coming to judge the earth.

34 Oh, give thanks to the LORD, for *He is* good!
For His mercy *endures* forever.

35 And say, "Save us, O God of our salvation;
Gather us together, and deliver us from the
Gentiles,
To give thanks to Your holy name,
To triumph in Your praise."

וּשְׁבוּעָתוֹ לְיִצְחָק׃

17 וַיַּעֲמִידֶהָ לְיַעֲקֹב לְחֹק
לְיִשְׂרָאֵל בְּרִית עוֹלָם׃

18 לֵאמֹר לְךָ אֶתֵּן אֶרֶץ־כְּנָעַן
חֶבֶל נַחֲלַתְכֶם׃

19 בִּהְיוֹתְכֶם מְתֵי מִסְפָּר
כִּמְעַט וְגָרִים בָּהּ׃

20 וַיִּתְהַלְּכוּ מִגּוֹי אֶל־גּוֹי
וּמִמַּמְלָכָה אֶל־עַם אַחֵר׃

21 לֹא־הִנִּיחַ לְאִישׁ לְעָשְׁקָם
וַיּוֹכַח עֲלֵיהֶם מְלָכִים׃

22 אַל־תִּגְּעוּ בִּמְשִׁיחָי
וּבִנְבִיאַי אַל־תָּרֵעוּ׃   פ

23 שִׁירוּ לַיהוָה כָּל־הָאָרֶץ
בַּשְּׂרוּ מִיּוֹם־אֶל־יוֹם יְשׁוּעָתוֹ

24 סַפְּרוּ בַגּוֹיִם אֶת־כְּבוֹדוֹ
בְּכָל־הָעַמִּים נִפְלְאֹתָיו׃

25 כִּי גָדוֹל יְהוָה וּמְהֻלָּל מְאֹד
וְנוֹרָא הוּא עַל־כָּל־אֱלֹהִים׃

26 כִּי כָּל־אֱלֹהֵי הָעַמִּים אֱלִילִים
וַיהוָה שָׁמַיִם עָשָׂה׃

27 הוֹד וְהָדָר לְפָנָיו
עֹז וְחֶדְוָה בִּמְקֹמוֹ׃

28 הָבוּ לַיהוָה מִשְׁפְּחוֹת עַמִּים
הָבוּ לַיהוָה כָּבוֹד וָעֹז׃

29 הָבוּ לַיהוָה כְּבוֹד שְׁמוֹ
שְׂאוּ מִנְחָה וּבֹאוּ לְפָנָיו
הִשְׁתַּחֲווּ לַיהוָה בְּהַדְרַת־קֹדֶשׁ׃

30 חִילוּ מִלְּפָנָיו כָּל־הָאָרֶץ
אַף־תִּכּוֹן תֵּבֵל בַּל־תִּמּוֹט׃

31 יִשְׂמְחוּ הַשָּׁמַיִם וְתָגֵל הָאָרֶץ
וְיֹאמְרוּ בַגּוֹיִם יְהוָה מָלָךְ׃

32 יִרְעַם הַיָּם וּמְלוֹאוֹ
יַעֲלֹץ הַשָּׂדֶה וְכָל־אֲשֶׁר־בּוֹ׃

33 אָז יְרַנְּנוּ עֲצֵי הַיָּעַר
מִלִּפְנֵי יְהוָה כִּי־בָא לִשְׁפּוֹט אֶת־הָאָרֶץ׃

34 הוֹדוּ לַיהוָה כִּי טוֹב
כִּי לְעוֹלָם חַסְדּוֹ׃

35 וְאִמְרוּ הוֹשִׁיעֵנוּ אֱלֹהֵי יִשְׁעֵנוּ
וְקַבְּצֵנוּ וְהַצִּילֵנוּ מִן־הַגּוֹיִם

36 Blessed *be* the LORD God of Israel
From everlasting to everlasting!

And all the people said, "Amen!" and praised the
LORD.

37 So he left Asaph and his brothers there before
the ark of the covenant of the LORD to minister
before the ark regularly, as every day's work
required; 38 and Obed-Edom with his sixty-eight
brethren, including Obed-Edom the son of Jeduthun, and Hosah, *to be* gatekeepers; 39 and Zadok
the priest and his brethren the priests, before the
tabernacle of the LORD at the high place that *was* at
Gibeon, 40 to offer burnt offerings to the LORD on
the altar of burnt offering regularly morning and
evening, and *to do* according to all that is written in
the Law of the LORD which He commanded Israel;
41 and with them Heman and Jeduthun and the rest
who were chosen, who were designated by name, to
give thanks to the LORD, because His mercy *endures*
forever; 42 and with them Heman and Jeduthun, to
sound aloud with trumpets and cymbals and the
musical instruments of God. Now the sons of
Jeduthun *were* gatekeepers.

43 Then all the people departed, every man to his
house; and David returned to bless his house.

17 Now it came to pass, when David was
dwelling in his house, that David said to Nathan
the prophet, "See now, I dwell in a house of cedar,
but the ark of the covenant of the LORD *is* under
tent curtains."

2 Then Nathan said to David, "Do all that *is* in
your heart, for God *is* with you."

3 But it happened that night that the word of God
came to Nathan, saying, 4 "Go and tell My servant
David, 'Thus says the LORD: "You shall not build
Me a house to dwell in. 5 For I have not dwelt in a
house since the time that I brought up Israel, even
to this day, but have gone from tent to tent, and
from *one* tabernacle *to another*. 6 Wherever I have
moved about with all Israel, have I ever spoken a
word to any of the judges of Israel, whom I
commanded to shepherd My people, saying, 'Why
have you not built Me a house of cedar?' " ' 7 Now
therefore, thus shall you say to My servant David,
'Thus says the LORD of hosts: "I took you from the
sheepfold, from following the sheep, to be ruler
over My people Israel. 8 And I have been with you
wherever you have gone, and have cut off all your
enemies from before you, and have made you a
name like the name of the great men who *are* on the
earth. 9 Moreover I will appoint a place for My
people Israel, and will plant them, that they may

לְהֹד֖וֹת לְשֵׁ֣ם קָדְשֶׁ֑ךָ
לְהִשְׁתַּבֵּ֖חַ בִּתְהִלָּתֶֽךָ׃
36 בָּר֤וּךְ יְהוָה֙ אֱלֹהֵ֣י יִשְׂרָאֵ֔ל
מִן־הָעוֹלָ֖ם וְעַ֣ד הָעֹלָ֑ם וַיֹּאמְר֤וּ כָל־הָעָם֙ אָמֵ֔ן
וְהַלֵּ֖ל לַיהוָֽה׃ פ
37 וַיַּֽעֲזָב־שָׁ֗ם לִפְנֵ֛י אֲר֥וֹן בְּרִית־יְהוָ֖ה לְאָסָ֣ף וּלְאֶחָ֑יו
לְשָׁרֵ֞ת לִפְנֵ֧י הָאָר֛וֹן תָּמִ֖יד לִדְבַר־י֥וֹם בְּיוֹמֽוֹ׃
38 וְעֹבֵ֥ד אֱדֹ֛ם וַאֲחֵיהֶ֖ם שִׁשִּׁ֣ים וּשְׁמוֹנָ֑ה וְעֹבֵ֨ד אֱדֹ֧ם
בֶּן־יְדִיתֻ֛ן וְחֹסָ֖ה לְשֹׁעֲרִֽים׃ 39 וְאֵ֣ת ׀ צָד֣וֹק הַכֹּהֵ֗ן
וְאֶחָיו֙ הַכֹּ֣הֲנִ֔ים לִפְנֵ֖י מִשְׁכַּ֣ן יְהוָ֑ה בַּבָּמָ֖ה אֲשֶׁ֥ר
בְּגִבְעֽוֹן׃ 40 לְהַעֲל֨וֹת עֹל֤וֹת לַֽיהוָה֙ עַל־מִזְבַּ֣ח הָעֹלָ֔ה
תָּמִ֖יד לַבֹּ֣קֶר וְלָעָ֑רֶב וּלְכָל־הַכָּתוּב֙ בְּתוֹרַ֣ת יְהוָ֔ה
אֲשֶׁ֥ר צִוָּ֖ה עַל־יִשְׂרָאֵֽל׃ 41 וְעִמָּהֶם֙ הֵימָ֣ן וִֽידוּת֔וּן
וּשְׁאָ֣ר הַבְּרוּרִ֗ים אֲשֶׁ֤ר נִקְּבוּ֙ בְּשֵׁמ֔וֹת לְהֹד֖וֹת לַֽיהוָ֑ה
כִּ֥י לְעוֹלָ֖ם חַסְדּֽוֹ׃ 42 וְעִמָּהֶ֨ם הֵימָ֣ן וִֽידוּתוּן֮ חֲצֹצְרוֹת֒
וּמְצִלְתַּ֗יִם לְמַשְׁמִעִ֔ים וּכְלֵ֖י שִׁ֣יר הָאֱלֹהִ֑ים וּבְנֵ֥י
יְדוּת֖וּן לַשָּֽׁעַר׃ 43 וַיֵּלְכ֥וּ כָל־הָעָ֖ם אִ֣ישׁ לְבֵית֑וֹ וַיִּסֹּ֥ב
דָּוִ֖יד לְבָרֵ֥ךְ אֶת־בֵּיתֽוֹ׃ פ

יז וַיְהִ֗י כַּאֲשֶׁ֛ר יָשַׁ֥ב דָּוִ֖יד בְּבֵית֑וֹ וַיֹּ֤אמֶר דָּוִיד֙
אֶל־נָתָ֣ן הַנָּבִ֔יא הִנֵּ֨ה אָנֹכִ֤י יוֹשֵׁב֙ בְּבֵ֣ית הָֽאֲרָזִ֔ים
וַאֲר֥וֹן בְּרִית־יְהוָ֖ה תַּ֣חַת יְרִיע֑וֹת׃ 2 וַיֹּ֤אמֶר נָתָן֙
אֶל־דָּוִ֔יד כֹּ֛ל אֲשֶׁ֥ר בִּֽלְבָבְךָ֖ עֲשֵׂ֑ה כִּ֥י הָאֱלֹהִ֖ים
עִמָּֽךְ׃ 3 וַיְהִ֖י בַּלַּ֣יְלָה הַה֑וּא וַיְהִי֙ דְּבַר־ ס
אֱלֹהִ֔ים אֶל־נָתָ֖ן לֵאמֹֽר׃ 4 לֵ֤ךְ וְאָֽמַרְתָּ֙ אֶל־דָּוִ֣יד
עַבְדִּ֔י כֹּ֖ה אָמַ֣ר יְהוָ֑ה לֹ֥א אַתָּ֛ה תִּבְנֶה־לִּ֥י הַבַּ֖יִת
לָשָֽׁבֶת׃ 5 כִּ֣י לֹ֤א יָשַׁ֙בְתִּי֙ בְּבַ֔יִת מִן־הַיּ֗וֹם אֲשֶׁ֤ר
הֶעֱלֵ֙יתִי֙ אֶת־יִשְׂרָאֵ֔ל עַ֖ד הַיּ֣וֹם הַזֶּ֑ה וָאֶֽהְיֶ֙ה מֵאֹ֤הֶל
אֶל־אֹ֔הֶל וּמִמִּשְׁכָּֽן׃ 6 בְּכֹ֥ל אֲשֶֽׁר־הִתְהַלַּ֙כְתִּי֙ בְּכָל־
יִשְׂרָאֵ֔ל הֲדָבָ֣ר דִּבַּ֗רְתִּי אֶת־אַחַד֙ שֹׁפְטֵ֣י יִשְׂרָאֵ֔ל
אֲשֶׁ֣ר צִוִּ֗יתִי לִרְע֤וֹת אֶת־עַמִּי֙ לֵאמֹ֔ר לָ֥מָּה לֹֽא־
בְנִיתֶ֖ם לִ֥י בֵּ֥ית אֲרָזִֽים׃ 7 וְ֠עַתָּה כֹּֽה־תֹאמַ֞ר לְעַבְדִּ֣י
לְדָוִ֗יד ס כֹּ֤ה אָמַר֙ יְהוָ֣ה צְבָא֔וֹת אֲנִ֤י
לְקַחְתִּ֙יךָ֙ מִן־הַנָּוֶ֔ה מִֽן־אַחֲרֵ֖י הַצֹּ֑אן לִהְי֣וֹת נָגִ֔יד עַ֖ל
עַמִּ֥י יִשְׂרָאֵֽל׃ 8 וָאֶֽהְיֶ֣ה עִמְּךָ֗ בְּכֹל֙ אֲשֶׁ֣ר הָלַ֔כְתָּ
וָאַכְרִ֥ת אֶת־כָּל־אוֹיְבֶ֖יךָ מִפָּנֶ֑יךָ וְעָשִׂ֤יתִֽי לְךָ֙ שֵׁ֔ם
כְּשֵׁ֥ם הַגְּדוֹלִ֖ים אֲשֶׁ֣ר בָּאָֽרֶץ׃ 9 וְשַׂמְתִּ֣י מָק֗וֹם לְעַמִּ֙י

dwell in a place of their own and move no more; nor shall the sons of wickedness oppress them anymore, as previously, ¹⁰since the time that I commanded judges *to be* over My people Israel. Also I will subdue all your enemies. Furthermore I tell you that the LORD will build you a house. ¹¹And it shall be, when your days are fulfilled, when you must go *to be* with your fathers, that I will set up your seed after you, who will be of your sons; and I will establish his kingdom. ¹²He shall build Me a house, and I will establish his throne forever. ¹³I will be his Father, and he shall be My son; and I will not take My mercy away from him, as I took *it* from *him* who was before you. ¹⁴And I will establish him in My house and in My kingdom forever; and his throne shall be established forever.' "'

¹⁵According to all these words and according to all this vision, so Nathan spoke to David.

¹⁶Then King David went in and sat before the LORD; and he said: "Who *am* I, O LORD God? And what is my house, that You have brought me this far? ¹⁷And *yet* this was a small thing in Your sight, O God; and You have *also* spoken of Your servant's house for a great while to come, and have regarded me according to the rank of a man of high degree, O LORD God. ¹⁸What more can David *say* to You for the honor of Your servant? For You know Your servant. ¹⁹O LORD, for Your servant's sake, and according to Your own heart, You have done all this greatness, in making known all these great things. ²⁰O LORD, *there is* none like You, nor *is there any* God besides You, according to all that we have heard with our ears. ²¹And who *is* like Your people Israel, the one nation on the earth whom God went to redeem for Himself *as* a people—to make for Yourself a name by great and awesome deeds, by driving out nations from before Your people whom You redeemed from Egypt? ²²For You have made Your people Israel Your very own people forever; and You, LORD, have become their God.

²³"And now, O LORD, the word which You have spoken concerning Your servant and concerning his house, *let it* be established forever, and do as You have said. ²⁴So let it be established, that Your name may be magnified forever, saying, 'The LORD of hosts, the God of Israel, *is* Israel's God.' And let the house of Your servant David be established before You. ²⁵For You, O my God, have revealed to Your servant that You will build him a house. Therefore Your servant has found it *in his heart* to pray before You. ²⁶And now, LORD, You are God, and have promised this goodness to Your servant. ²⁷Now You have been pleased to bless the house of Your

יִשְׂרָאֵל וּנְטַעְתִּיהוּ וְשָׁכַן תַּחְתָּיו וְלֹא יִרְגַּז עֹוד
וְלֹא־יֹוסִיפוּ בְנֵי־עַוְלָה לְבַלֹּתֹו כַּאֲשֶׁר בָּרִאשֹׁונָה: 10 וּלְמִיָּמִים אֲשֶׁר צִוִּיתִי שֹׁפְטִים עַל־עַמִּי יִשְׂרָאֵל וְהִכְנַעְתִּי אֶת־כָּל־אֹויְבֶיךָ וָאַגִּד לָךְ וּבַיִת יִבְנֶה־לְּךָ יְהוָה: 11 וְהָיָה כִּי־מָלְאוּ יָמֶיךָ לָלֶכֶת עִם־אֲבֹתֶיךָ וַהֲקִימֹותִי אֶת־זַרְעֲךָ אַחֲרֶיךָ אֲשֶׁר יִהְיֶה מִבָּנֶיךָ וַהֲכִינֹותִי אֶת־מַלְכוּתֹו: 12 הוּא יִבְנֶה־לִּי בָּיִת וְכֹנַנְתִּי אֶת־כִּסְאֹו עַד־עֹולָם: 13 אֲנִי אֶהְיֶה־לֹּו לְאָב וְהוּא יִהְיֶה־לִּי לְבֵן וְחַסְדִּי לֹא־אָסִיר מֵעִמֹּו כַּאֲשֶׁר הֲסִירֹותִי מֵאֲשֶׁר הָיָה לְפָנֶיךָ: 14 וְהַעֲמַדְתִּיהוּ בְּבֵיתִי וּבְמַלְכוּתִי עַד־הָעֹולָם וְכִסְאֹו יִהְיֶה נָכֹון עַד־עֹולָם: 15 כְּכֹל הַדְּבָרִים הָאֵלֶּה וּכְכֹל הֶחָזֹון הַזֶּה כֵּן דִּבֶּר נָתָן אֶל־דָּוִיד: פ

16 וַיָּבֹא הַמֶּלֶךְ דָּוִיד וַיֵּשֶׁב לִפְנֵי יְהוָה וַיֹּאמֶר מִי־אֲנִי יְהוָה אֱלֹהִים וּמִי בֵיתִי כִּי הֲבִיאֹתַנִי עַד־הֲלֹם: 17 וַתִּקְטַן זֹאת בְּעֵינֶיךָ אֱלֹהִים וַתְּדַבֵּר עַל־בֵּית־עַבְדְּךָ לְמֵרָחֹוק וּרְאִיתַנִי כְּתֹור הָאָדָם הַמַּעֲלָה יְהוָה אֱלֹהִים: 18 מַה־יֹּוסִיף עֹוד דָּוִיד אֵלֶיךָ לְכָבֹוד אֶת־עַבְדֶּךָ וְאַתָּה אֶת־עַבְדְּךָ יָדָעְתָּ: 19 יְהוָה בַּעֲבוּר עַבְדְּךָ וּכְלִבְּךָ עָשִׂיתָ אֵת כָּל־הַגְּדוּלָּה הַזֹּאת לְהֹודִיעַ אֶת־כָּל־הַגְּדֻלֹּות: 20 יְהוָה אֵין כָּמֹוךָ וְאֵין אֱלֹהִים זוּלָתֶךָ בְּכֹל אֲשֶׁר־שָׁמַעְנוּ בְּאָזְנֵינוּ: 21 וּמִי כְּעַמְּךָ יִשְׂרָאֵל גֹּוי אֶחָד בָּאָרֶץ אֲשֶׁר הָלַךְ הָאֱלֹהִים לִפְדֹּות לֹו עָם לָשׂוּם לְךָ שֵׁם גְּדֻלֹּות וְנֹרָאֹות לְגָרֵשׁ מִפְּנֵי עַמְּךָ אֲשֶׁר־פָּדִיתָ מִמִּצְרַיִם גֹּויִם: 22 וַתִּתֵּן אֶת־עַמְּךָ יִשְׂרָאֵל לְךָ לְעָם עַד־עֹולָם וְאַתָּה יְהוָה הָיִיתָ לָהֶם לֵאלֹהִים: 23 וְעַתָּה יְהוָה הַדָּבָר אֲשֶׁר דִּבַּרְתָּ עַל־עַבְדְּךָ וְעַל־בֵּיתֹו יֵאָמֵן עַד־עֹולָם וַעֲשֵׂה כַּאֲשֶׁר דִּבַּרְתָּ: 24 וְיֵאָמֵן וְיִגְדַּל שִׁמְךָ עַד־עֹולָם לֵאמֹר יְהוָה צְבָאֹות אֱלֹהֵי יִשְׂרָאֵל אֱלֹהִים לְיִשְׂרָאֵל וּבֵית־דָּוִיד עַבְדְּךָ נָכֹון לְפָנֶיךָ: 25 כִּי אַתָּה אֱלֹהַי גָּלִיתָ אֶת־אֹזֶן עַבְדְּךָ לִבְנֹות לֹו בָּיִת עַל־כֵּן מָצָא עַבְדְּךָ לְהִתְפַּלֵּל לְפָנֶיךָ: 26 וְעַתָּה יְהוָה אַתָּה־הוּא הָאֱלֹהִים וַתְּדַבֵּר עַל־עַבְדְּךָ הַטֹּובָה הַזֹּאת: 27 וְעַתָּה הֹואַלְתָּ לְבָרֵךְ אֶת־בֵּית עַבְדְּךָ

servant, that it may continue before You forever; for You have blessed it, O LORD, and *it shall be* blessed forever."

18

After this it came to pass that David attacked the Philistines, subdued them, and took Gath and its towns from the hand of the Philistines. ² Then he defeated Moab, and the Moabites became David's servants, *and* brought tribute.

³ And David defeated Hadadezer king of Zobah *as far as* Hamath, as he went to establish his power by the River Euphrates. ⁴ David took from him one thousand chariots, seven thousand horsemen, and twenty thousand foot soldiers. Also David hamstrung all the chariot *horses,* except that he spared enough of them for one hundred chariots.

⁵ When the Syrians of Damascus came to help Hadadezer king of Zobah, David killed twenty-two thousand of the Syrians. ⁶ Then David put *garrisons* in Syria of Damascus; and the Syrians became David's servants, *and* brought tribute. So the LORD preserved David wherever he went. ⁷ And David took the shields of gold that were on the servants of Hadadezer, and brought them to Jerusalem. ⁸ Also from Tibhath and from Chun, cities of Hadadezer, David brought a large amount of bronze, with which Solomon made the bronze Sea, the pillars, and the articles of bronze.

⁹ Now when Tou king of Hamath heard that David had defeated all the army of Hadadezer king of Zobah, ¹⁰ he sent Hadoram his son to King David, to greet him and bless him, because he had fought against Hadadezer and defeated him (for Hadadezer had been at war with Tou); and *Hadoram brought with him* all kinds of articles of gold, silver, and bronze. ¹¹ King David also dedicated these to the LORD, along with the silver and gold that he had brought from all *these* nations—from Edom, from Moab, from the people of Ammon, from the Philistines, and from Amalek.

¹² Moreover Abishai the son of Zeruiah killed eighteen thousand Edomites in the Valley of Salt. ¹³ He also put garrisons in Edom, and all the Edomites became David's servants. And the LORD preserved David wherever he went.

¹⁴ So David reigned over all Israel, and administered judgment and justice to all his people. ¹⁵ Joab the son of Zeruiah *was* over the army; Jehoshaphat the son of Ahilud *was* recorder; ¹⁶ Zadok the son of Ahitub and Abimelech the son of Abiathar *were* the priests; Shavsha *was* the scribe; ¹⁷ Benaiah the son of Jehoiada *was* over the Cherethites and the Pelethites; and David's sons *were* chief ministers at the king's side.

לִהְיוֹת לְעוֹלָם לְפָנֶיךָ כִּי־אַתָּה יְהֹוָה בֵּרַכְתָּ וּמְבֹרָךְ לְעוֹלָם: פ

יח וַיְהִי אַחֲרֵי־כֵן וַיַּךְ דָּוִיד אֶת־פְּלִשְׁתִּים וַיַּכְנִיעֵם וַיִּקַּח אֶת־גַּת וּבְנֹתֶיהָ מִיַּד פְּלִשְׁתִּים: ² וַיַּךְ אֶת־מוֹאָב וַיִּהְיוּ מוֹאָב עֲבָדִים לְדָוִיד נֹשְׂאֵי מִנְחָה: ³ וַיַּךְ דָּוִיד אֶת־הֲדַדְעֶזֶר מֶלֶךְ־צוֹבָה חֲמָתָה בְּלֶכְתּוֹ לְהַצִּיב יָדוֹ בִּנְהַר־פְּרָת: ⁴ וַיִּלְכֹּד דָּוִיד מִמֶּנּוּ אֶלֶף רֶכֶב וְשִׁבְעַת אֲלָפִים פָּרָשִׁים וְעֶשְׂרִים אֶלֶף אִישׁ רַגְלִי וַיְעַקֵּר דָּוִיד אֶת־כָּל־הָרֶכֶב וַיּוֹתֵר מִמֶּנּוּ מֵאָה רָכֶב: ⁵ וַיָּבֹא אֲרַם דַּרְמֶשֶׂק לַעְזוֹר לַהֲדַדְעֶזֶר מֶלֶךְ צוֹבָה וַיַּךְ דָּוִיד בַּאֲרָם עֶשְׂרִים־וּשְׁנַיִם אֶלֶף אִישׁ: ⁶ וַיָּשֶׂם דָּוִיד בַּאֲרַם דַּרְמֶשֶׂק וַיְהִי אֲרָם לְדָוִיד עֲבָדִים נֹשְׂאֵי מִנְחָה וַיּוֹשַׁע יְהֹוָה לְדָוִיד בְּכֹל אֲשֶׁר הָלָךְ: ⁷ וַיִּקַּח דָּוִיד אֵת שִׁלְטֵי הַזָּהָב אֲשֶׁר הָיוּ עַל עַבְדֵי הֲדַדְעֶזֶר וַיְבִיאֵם יְרוּשָׁלָ͏ִם: ⁸ וּמִטִּבְחַת וּמִכּוּן עָרֵי הֲדַדְעֶזֶר לָקַח דָּוִיד נְחֹשֶׁת רַבָּה מְאֹד בָּהּ עָשָׂה שְׁלֹמֹה אֶת־יָם הַנְּחֹשֶׁת וְאֶת־הָעַמּוּדִים וְאֵת כְּלֵי הַנְּחֹשֶׁת: פ

⁹ וַיִּשְׁמַע תֹּעוּ מֶלֶךְ חֲמָת כִּי הִכָּה דָוִיד אֶת־כָּל־חֵיל הֲדַדְעֶזֶר מֶלֶךְ־צוֹבָה: ¹⁰ וַיִּשְׁלַח אֶת־הֲדוֹרָם־בְּנוֹ אֶל־הַמֶּלֶךְ־דָּוִיד לִשְׁאָול־לוֹ לְשָׁלוֹם וּלְבָרֲכוֹ עַל אֲשֶׁר נִלְחַם בַּהֲדַדְעֶזֶר וַיַּכֵּהוּ כִּי־אִישׁ מִלְחֲמוֹת תֹּעוּ הָיָה הֲדַדְעֶזֶר וְכֹל כְּלֵי זָהָב וָכֶסֶף וּנְחֹשֶׁת: ¹¹ גַּם־אֹתָם הִקְדִּישׁ הַמֶּלֶךְ דָּוִיד לַיהֹוָה עִם־הַכֶּסֶף וְהַזָּהָב אֲשֶׁר נָשָׂא מִכָּל־הַגּוֹיִם מֵאֱדוֹם וּמִמּוֹאָב וּמִבְּנֵי עַמּוֹן וּמִפְּלִשְׁתִּים וּמֵעֲמָלֵק: ¹² וְאַבְשַׁי בֶּן־צְרוּיָה הִכָּה אֶת־אֱדוֹם בְּגֵיא הַמֶּלַח שְׁמוֹנָה עָשָׂר אָלֶף: ¹³ וַיָּשֶׂם בֶּאֱדוֹם נְצִיבִים וַיִּהְיוּ כָל־אֱדוֹם עֲבָדִים לְדָוִיד וַיּוֹשַׁע יְהֹוָה אֶת־דָּוִיד בְּכֹל אֲשֶׁר הָלָךְ: ¹⁴ וַיִּמְלֹךְ דָּוִיד עַל־כָּל־יִשְׂרָאֵל וַיְהִי עֹשֶׂה מִשְׁפָּט וּצְדָקָה לְכָל־עַמּוֹ: ¹⁵ וְיוֹאָב בֶּן־צְרוּיָה עַל־הַצָּבָא וִיהוֹשָׁפָט בֶּן־אֲחִילוּד מַזְכִּיר: ¹⁶ וְצָדוֹק בֶּן־אֲחִיטוּב וַאֲבִימֶלֶךְ בֶּן־אֶבְיָתָר כֹּהֲנִים וְשַׁוְשָׁא סוֹפֵר: ¹⁷ וּבְנָיָהוּ בֶּן־יְהוֹיָדָע עַל־הַכְּרֵתִי וְהַפְּלֵתִי וּבְנֵי־דָוִיד הָרִאשֹׁנִים לְיַד הַמֶּלֶךְ: פ

לְשָׁאֵל 10

19 It happened after this that Nahash the king of the people of Ammon died, and his son reigned in his place. ² Then David said, "I will show kindness to Hanun the son of Nahash, because his father showed kindness to me." So David sent messengers to comfort him concerning his father. And David's servants came to Hanun in the land of the people of Ammon to comfort him.

³ And the princes of the people of Ammon said to Hanun, "Do you think that David really honors your father because he has sent comforters to you? Did his servants not come to you to search and to overthrow and to spy out the land?"

⁴ Therefore Hanun took David's servants, shaved them, and cut off their garments in the middle, at their buttocks, and sent them away. ⁵ Then *some* went and told David about the men; and he sent to meet them, because the men were greatly ashamed. And the king said, "Wait at Jericho until your beards have grown, and *then* return."

⁶ When the people of Ammon saw that they had made themselves repulsive to David, Hanun and the people of Ammon sent a thousand talents of silver to hire for themselves chariots and horsemen from Mesopotamia, from Syrian Maacah, and from Zobah. ⁷ So they hired for themselves thirty-two thousand chariots, with the king of Maacah and his people, who came and encamped before Medeba. Also the people of Ammon gathered together from their cities, and came to battle.

⁸ Now when David heard *of it*, he sent Joab and all the army of the mighty men. ⁹ Then the people of Ammon came out and put themselves in battle array before the gate of the city, and the kings who had come *were* by themselves in the field.

¹⁰ When Joab saw that the battle line was against him before and behind, he chose some of Israel's best, and put *them* in battle array against the Syrians. ¹¹ And the rest of the people he put under the command of Abishai his brother, and they set *themselves* in battle array against the people of Ammon. ¹² Then he said, "If the Syrians are too strong for me, then you shall help me; but if the people of Ammon are too strong for you, then I will help you. ¹³ Be of good courage, and let us be strong for our people and for the cities of our God. And may the LORD do *what is* good in His sight."

¹⁴ So Joab and the people who *were* with him drew near for the battle against the Syrians, and they fled before him. ¹⁵ When the people of Ammon saw that the Syrians were fleeing, they also fled before Abishai his brother, and entered the city. So Joab went to Jerusalem.

יט וַיְהִי אַחֲרֵי־כֵן וַיָּמָת נָחָשׁ מֶלֶךְ בְּנֵי־עַמּוֹן
וַיִּמְלֹךְ בְּנוֹ תַּחְתָּיו: 2 וַיֹּאמֶר דָּוִיד אֶעֱשֶׂה־חֶסֶד ׀
עִם־חָנוּן בֶּן־נָחָשׁ כִּי־עָשָׂה אָבִיו עִמִּי חֶסֶד וַיִּשְׁלַח
דָּוִיד מַלְאָכִים לְנַחֲמוֹ עַל־אָבִיו וַיָּבֹאוּ עַבְדֵי דָוִיד
אֶל־אֶרֶץ בְּנֵי־עַמּוֹן אֶל־חָנוּן לְנַחֲמוֹ: 3 וַיֹּאמְרוּ שָׂרֵי
בְנֵי־עַמּוֹן לְחָנוּן הַמְכַבֵּד דָּוִיד אֶת־אָבִיךָ בְּעֵינֶיךָ
כִּי־שָׁלַח לְךָ מְנַחֲמִים הֲלֹא בַּעֲבוּר לַחְקֹר וְלַהֲפֹךְ
וּלְרַגֵּל הָאָרֶץ בָּאוּ עֲבָדָיו אֵלֶיךָ:
פ
4 וַיִּקַּח חָנוּן אֶת־עַבְדֵי דָוִיד וַיְגַלְּחֵם וַיִּכְרֹת אֶת־
מַדְוֵיהֶם בַּחֵצִי עַד־הַמִּפְשָׂעָה וַיְשַׁלְּחֵם: 5 וַיֵּלְכוּ
וַיַּגִּידוּ לְדָוִיד עַל־הָאֲנָשִׁים וַיִּשְׁלַח לִקְרָאתָם כִּי־
הָיוּ הָאֲנָשִׁים נִכְלָמִים מְאֹד וַיֹּאמֶר הַמֶּלֶךְ שְׁבוּ
בִירֵחוֹ עַד אֲשֶׁר־יְצַמַּח זְקַנְכֶם וְשַׁבְתֶּם: 6 וַיִּרְאוּ
בְּנֵי עַמּוֹן כִּי הִתְבָּאֲשׁוּ עִם־דָּוִיד וַיִּשְׁלַח חָנוּן וּבְנֵי
עַמּוֹן אֶלֶף כִּכַּר־כֶּסֶף לִשְׂכֹּר לָהֶם מִן־אֲרַם נַהֲרַיִם
וּמִן־אֲרַם מַעֲכָה וּמִצּוֹבָה רֶכֶב וּפָרָשִׁים: 7 וַיִּשְׂכְּרוּ
לָהֶם שְׁנַיִם וּשְׁלֹשִׁים אֶלֶף רֶכֶב וְאֶת־מֶלֶךְ מַעֲכָה
וְאֶת־עַמּוֹ וַיָּבֹאוּ וַיַּחֲנוּ לִפְנֵי מֵידְבָא וּבְנֵי עַמּוֹן
נֶאֶסְפוּ מֵעָרֵיהֶם וַיָּבֹאוּ לַמִּלְחָמָה: 8 וַיִּשְׁמַע דָּוִיד
וַיִּשְׁלַח אֶת־יוֹאָב וְאֵת כָּל־צָבָא הַגִּבּוֹרִים: 9 וַיֵּצְאוּ
בְּנֵי עַמּוֹן וַיַּעַרְכוּ מִלְחָמָה פֶּתַח הָעִיר וְהַמְּלָכִים
אֲשֶׁר־בָּאוּ לְבַדָּם בַּשָּׂדֶה: 10 וַיַּרְא יוֹאָב כִּי־הָיְתָה
פְנֵי־הַמִּלְחָמָה אֵלָיו פָּנִים וְאָחוֹר וַיִּבְחַר מִכָּל־
בָּחוּר בְּיִשְׂרָאֵל וַיַּעֲרֹךְ לִקְרַאת אֲרָם: 11 וְאֵת יֶתֶר
הָעָם נָתַן בְּיַד אַבְשַׁי אָחִיו וַיַּעַרְכוּ לִקְרַאת בְּנֵי
עַמּוֹן: 12 וַיֹּאמֶר אִם־תֶּחֱזַק מִמֶּנִּי אֲרָם וְהָיִיתָ לִּי
לִתְשׁוּעָה   פ   וְאִם־בְּנֵי עַמּוֹן יֶחֶזְקוּ מִמְּךָ
וְהוֹשַׁעְתִּיךָ: 13 חֲזַק וְנִתְחַזְּקָה בְּעַד־עַמֵּנוּ וּבְעַד
עָרֵי אֱלֹהֵינוּ וַיהֹוָה הַטּוֹב בְּעֵינָיו יַעֲשֶׂה: 14 וַיִּגַּשׁ
יוֹאָב וְהָעָם אֲשֶׁר־עִמּוֹ לִפְנֵי אֲרָם לַמִּלְחָמָה וַיָּנוּסוּ
מִפָּנָיו: 15 וּבְנֵי עַמּוֹן רָאוּ כִּי־נָס אֲרָם וַיָּנוּסוּ גַם־
הֵם מִפְּנֵי אַבְשַׁי אָחִיו וַיָּבֹאוּ הָעִירָה וַיָּבֹא יוֹאָב
יְרוּשָׁלָם:
פ

16 Now when the Syrians saw that they had been defeated by Israel, they sent messengers and brought the Syrians who were beyond the River, and Shophach the commander of Hadadezer's army *went* before them. 17 When it was told David, he gathered all Israel, crossed over the Jordan and came upon them, and set up in battle array against them. So when David had set up in *battle* array against the Syrians, they fought with him. 18 Then the Syrians fled before Israel; and David killed seven thousand charioteers and forty thousand foot soldiers of the Syrians, and killed Shophach the commander of the army. 19 And when the servants of Hadadezer saw that they were defeated by Israel, they made peace with David and became his servants. So the Syrians were not willing to help the people of Ammon anymore.

20 It happened in the spring of the year, at the time kings go out *to battle,* that Joab led out the armed forces and ravaged the country of the people of Ammon, and came and besieged Rabbah. But David stayed at Jerusalem. And Joab defeated Rabbah and overthrew it. 2 Then David took their king's crown from his head, and found it to weigh a talent of gold, and *there were* precious stones in it. And it was set on David's head. Also he brought out the spoil of the city in great abundance. 3 And he brought out the people who *were* in it, and put *them* to work with saws, with iron picks, and with axes. So David did to all the cities of the people of Ammon. Then David and all the people returned *to* Jerusalem.

4 Now it happened afterward that war broke out at Gezer with the Philistines, at which time Sibbechai the Hushathite killed Sippai, *who was one* of the sons of the giant. And they were subdued.

5 Again there was war with the Philistines, and Elhanan the son of Jair killed Lahmi the brother of Goliath the Gittite, the shaft of whose spear *was* like a weaver's beam.

6 Yet again there was war at Gath, where there was a man of *great* stature, with twenty-four fingers and toes, six *on each hand* and six *on each foot;* and he also was born to the giant. 7 So when he defied Israel, Jonathan the son of Shimea, David's brother, killed him.

8 These were born to the giant in Gath, and they fell by the hand of David and by the hand of his servants.

16 וַיַּ֣רְא אֲרָ֗ם כִּ֤י נִגְּפוּ֙ לִפְנֵ֣י יִשְׂרָאֵ֔ל וַיִּשְׁלְחוּ֙ מַלְאָכִ֔ים וַיּוֹצִ֣יאוּ אֶת־אֲרָ֗ם אֲשֶׁר֙ מֵעֵ֣בֶר הַנָּהָ֔ר וְשׁוֹפַ֛ךְ שַׂר־צְבָ֥א הֲדַדְעֶ֖זֶר לִפְנֵיהֶֽם׃ 17 וַיֻּגַּ֣ד לְדָוִ֗יד וַיֶּאֱסֹ֤ף אֶת־כָּל־יִשְׂרָאֵל֙ וַֽיַּעֲבֹ֣ר הַיַּרְדֵּ֔ן וַיָּבֹ֣א אֲלֵהֶ֔ם וַיַּעֲרֹ֖ךְ אֲלֵהֶ֑ם וַיַּעֲרֹ֨ךְ דָּוִ֜יד לִקְרַ֤את אֲרָם֙ מִלְחָמָ֔ה וַיִּֽלָּחֲמ֖וּ עִמּֽוֹ׃ 18 וַיָּ֣נָס אֲרָם֮ מִלִּפְנֵ֣י יִשְׂרָאֵל֒ וַיַּהֲרֹ֨ג דָּוִ֜יד מֵאֲרָ֗ם שִׁבְעַ֤ת אֲלָפִים֙ רֶ֔כֶב וְאַרְבָּעִ֥ים אֶ֖לֶף אִ֣ישׁ רַגְלִ֑י וְאֵ֛ת שׁוֹפַ֥ךְ שַׂר־הַצָּבָ֖א הֵמִֽית׃ 19 וַיִּרְא֞וּ עַבְדֵ֣י הֲדַדְעֶ֗זֶר כִּ֤י נִגְּפוּ֙ לִפְנֵ֣י יִשְׂרָאֵ֔ל וַיַּשְׁלִ֥ימוּ עִם־דָּוִ֖יד וַיַּֽעַבְדֻ֑הוּ וְלֹא־אָבָ֣ה אֲרָ֔ם לְהוֹשִׁ֥יעַ אֶת־בְּנֵֽי־עַמּ֖וֹן עֽוֹד׃

כ וַיְהִ֡י לְעֵת֩ תְּשׁוּבַ֨ת הַשָּׁנָ֜ה לְעֵ֣ת ׀ צֵ֣את הַמְּלָכִ֗ים וַיִּנְהַ֣ג יוֹאָב֩ אֶת־חֵ֨יל הַצָּבָ֜א וַיַּשְׁחֵ֣ת ׀ אֶת־אֶ֣רֶץ בְּנֵֽי־עַמּ֗וֹן וַיָּבֹא֙ וַיָּ֣צַר אֶת־רַבָּ֔ה וְדָוִ֖יד יֹשֵׁ֣ב בִּירֽוּשָׁלִָ֑ם וַיַּ֥ךְ יוֹאָ֛ב אֶת־רַבָּ֖ה וַיֶּהֶרְסֶֽהָ׃ 2 וַיִּקַּ֣ח דָּוִ֣יד אֶת־עֲטֶֽרֶת־מַלְכָּם֩ מֵעַ֨ל רֹאשׁ֜וֹ וַֽיִּמְצָאָ֣הּ ׀ מִשְׁקַ֣ל כִּכַּר־זָהָ֗ב וּבָהּ֙ אֶ֣בֶן יְקָרָ֔ה וַתְּהִ֖י עַל־רֹ֣אשׁ דָּוִ֑יד וּשְׁלַ֥ל הָעִ֛יר הוֹצִ֖יא הַרְבֵּ֥ה מְאֹֽד׃ 3 וְאֶת־הָעָ֨ם אֲשֶׁר־בָּ֜הּ הוֹצִ֗יא וַיָּ֨שַׂר֙ בַּמְּגֵרָ֔ה וּבַחֲרִיצֵ֥י הַבַּרְזֶ֖ל וּבַמְּגֵר֑וֹת וְכֵ֨ן יַעֲשֶׂ֤ה דָוִיד֙ לְכֹ֣ל עָרֵ֣י בְנֵֽי־עַמּ֔וֹן וַיָּ֧שָׁב דָּוִ֛יד וְכָל־הָעָ֖ם יְרֽוּשָׁלִָֽם׃ פ

4 וַיְהִי֙ אַחֲרֵי־כֵ֔ן וַתַּעֲמֹ֧ד מִלְחָמָ֛ה בְּגֶ֖זֶר עִם־פְּלִשְׁתִּ֑ים אָ֣ז הִכָּ֞ה סִבְּכַ֣י הַחֻֽשָׁתִ֗י אֶת־סִפַּ֛י מִילִדֵ֥י הָרְפָאִ֖ים וַיִּכָּנֵֽעוּ׃ 5 וַתְּהִי־ע֥וֹד מִלְחָמָ֖ה אֶת־פְּלִשְׁתִּ֑ים וַיַּ֞ךְ אֶלְחָנָ֣ן בֶּן־יעִ֗יר אֶת־לַחְמִי֙ אֲחִי֙ גָּלְיָ֣ת הַגִּתִּ֔י וְעֵ֥ץ חֲנִית֖וֹ כִּמְנ֥וֹר אֹרְגִֽים׃ 6 וַתְּהִי־ע֥וֹד מִלְחָמָ֖ה בְּגַ֑ת וַיְהִ֣י ׀ אִ֣ישׁ מִדָּ֗ה וְאֶצְבְּעֹתָ֤יו שֵׁשׁ־וָשֵׁשׁ֙ עֶשְׂרִ֣ים וְאַרְבַּ֔ע וְגַם־ה֖וּא נוֹלַ֥ד לְהָרָפָֽא׃ 7 וַיְחָרֵ֖ף אֶת־יִשְׂרָאֵ֑ל וַיַּכֵּ֨הוּ֙ יְה֣וֹנָתָ֔ן בֶּן־שִׁמְעָ֖א אֲחִ֥י דָוִֽיד׃ 8 אֵ֛ל נוּלְּד֥וּ לְהָרָפָ֖א בְּגַ֑ת וַיִּפְּל֥וּ בְיַד־דָּוִ֖יד וּבְיַד־עֲבָדָֽיו׃ פ

21 Now Satan stood up against Israel, and moved David to number Israel. [2] So David said to Joab and to the leaders of the people, "Go, number Israel from Beersheba to Dan, and bring the number of them to me that I may know *it.*"

[3] And Joab answered, "May the LORD make His people a hundred times more than they are. But, my lord the king, *are* they not all my lord's servants? Why then does my lord require this thing? Why should he be a cause of guilt in Israel?"

[4] Nevertheless the king's word prevailed against Joab. Therefore Joab departed and went throughout all Israel and came to Jerusalem. [5] Then Joab gave the sum of the number of the people to David. All Israel *had* one million one hundred thousand men who drew the sword, and Judah *had* four hundred and seventy thousand men who drew the sword. [6] But he did not count Levi and Benjamin among them, for the king's word was abominable to Joab.

[7] And God was displeased with this thing; therefore He struck Israel. [8] So David said to God, "I have sinned greatly, because I have done this thing; but now, I pray, take away the iniquity of Your servant, for I have done very foolishly."

[9] Then the LORD spoke to Gad, David's seer, saying, [10] "Go and tell David, saying, 'Thus says the LORD: "I offer you three *things;* choose one of them for yourself, that I may do *it* to you." ' "

[11] So Gad came to David and said to him, "Thus says the LORD: 'Choose for yourself, [12] either three years of famine, or three months to be defeated by your foes with the sword of your enemies overtaking *you,* or else for three days the sword of the LORD—the plague in the land, with the angel of the LORD destroying throughout all the territory of Israel.' Now consider what answer I should take back to Him who sent me."

[13] And David said to Gad, "I am in great distress. Please let me fall into the hand of the LORD, for His mercies *are* very great; but do not let me fall into the hand of man."

[14] So the LORD sent a plague upon Israel, and seventy thousand men of Israel fell. [15] And God sent an angel to Jerusalem to destroy it. As he was destroying, the LORD looked and relented of the disaster, and said to the angel who was destroying, "It is enough; now restrain your hand." And the angel of the LORD stood by the threshing floor of Ornan the Jebusite.

[16] Then David lifted his eyes and saw the angel of the LORD standing between earth and heaven, having in his hand a drawn sword stretched out over Jerusalem. So David and the elders, clothed in

כא וַיַּעֲמֹד שָׂטָן עַל־יִשְׂרָאֵל וַיָּסֶת אֶת־דָּוִיד לִמְנוֹת אֶת־יִשְׂרָאֵל: 2 וַיֹּאמֶר דָּוִיד אֶל־יוֹאָב וְאֶל־שָׂרֵי הָעָם לְכוּ סִפְרוּ אֶת־יִשְׂרָאֵל מִבְּאֵר שֶׁבַע וְעַד־דָּן וְהָבִיאוּ אֵלַי וְאֵדְעָה אֶת־מִסְפָּרָם: 3 וַיֹּאמֶר יוֹאָב יוֹסֵף יְהוָה עַל־עַמּוֹ כָּהֵם מֵאָה פְעָמִים הֲלֹא אֲדֹנִי הַמֶּלֶךְ כֻּלָּם לַאדֹנִי לַעֲבָדִים לָמָּה יְבַקֵּשׁ זֹאת אֲדֹנִי לָמָּה יִהְיֶה לְאַשְׁמָה לְיִשְׂרָאֵל: 4 וּדְבַר־הַמֶּלֶךְ חָזַק עַל־יוֹאָב וַיֵּצֵא יוֹאָב וַיִּתְהַלֵּךְ בְּכָל־יִשְׂרָאֵל וַיָּבֹא יְרוּשָׁלִָם: 5 וַיִּתֵּן יוֹאָב אֶת־מִסְפַּר מִפְקַד־הָעָם אֶל־דָּוִיד וַיְהִי כָל־יִשְׂרָאֵל אֶלֶף אֲלָפִים וּמֵאָה אֶלֶף אִישׁ שֹׁלֵף חֶרֶב וִיהוּדָה אַרְבַּע מֵאוֹת וְשִׁבְעִים אֶלֶף אִישׁ שֹׁלֵף חָרֶב: 6 וְלֵוִי וּבִנְיָמִן לֹא פָקַד בְּתוֹכָם כִּי־נִתְעַב דְּבַר־הַמֶּלֶךְ אֶת־יוֹאָב: 7 וַיֵּרַע בְּעֵינֵי הָאֱלֹהִים עַל־הַדָּבָר הַזֶּה וַיַּךְ אֶת־יִשְׂרָאֵל: פ

8 וַיֹּאמֶר דָּוִיד אֶל־הָאֱלֹהִים חָטָאתִי מְאֹד אֲשֶׁר עָשִׂיתִי אֶת־הַדָּבָר הַזֶּה וְעַתָּה הַעֲבֶר־נָא אֶת־עֲוֹן עַבְדְּךָ כִּי נִסְכַּלְתִּי מְאֹד: פ

9 וַיְדַבֵּר יְהוָה אֶל־גָּד חֹזֵה דָוִיד לֵאמֹר: 10 לֵךְ וְדִבַּרְתָּ אֶל־דָּוִיד לֵאמֹר כֹּה אָמַר יְהוָה שָׁלוֹשׁ אֲנִי נֹטֶה עָלֶיךָ בְּחַר־לְךָ אַחַת מֵהֵנָּה וְאֶעֱשֶׂה־לָּךְ: 11 וַיָּבֹא גָד אֶל־דָּוִיד וַיֹּאמֶר לוֹ כֹּה־אָמַר יְהוָה קַבֶּל־לָךְ: 12 אִם־שָׁלוֹשׁ שָׁנִים רָעָב וְאִם־שְׁלֹשָׁה חֳדָשִׁים נִסְפֶּה מִפְּנֵי־צָרֶיךָ וְחֶרֶב אוֹיְבֶךָ לְמַשֶּׂגֶת וְאִם־שְׁלֹשֶׁת יָמִים חֶרֶב יְהוָה וְדֶבֶר בָּאָרֶץ וּמַלְאַךְ יְהוָה מַשְׁחִית בְּכָל־גְּבוּל יִשְׂרָאֵל וְעַתָּה רְאֵה מָה־אָשִׁיב אֶת־שֹׁלְחִי דָּבָר: פ

13 וַיֹּאמֶר דָּוִיד אֶל־גָּד צַר־לִי מְאֹד אֶפְּלָה־נָּא בְיַד־יְהוָה כִּי־רַבִּים רַחֲמָיו מְאֹד וּבְיַד־אָדָם אַל־אֶפֹּל: 14 וַיִּתֵּן יְהוָה דֶּבֶר בְּיִשְׂרָאֵל וַיִּפֹּל מִיִּשְׂרָאֵל שִׁבְעִים אֶלֶף אִישׁ: 15 וַיִּשְׁלַח הָאֱלֹהִים מַלְאָךְ לִירוּשָׁלִַם לְהַשְׁחִיתָהּ וּכְהַשְׁחִית רָאָה יְהוָה וַיִּנָּחֶם עַל־הָרָעָה וַיֹּאמֶר לַמַּלְאָךְ הַמַּשְׁחִית רַב עַתָּה הֶרֶף יָדֶךָ וּמַלְאַךְ יְהוָה עֹמֵד עִם־גֹּרֶן אָרְנָן הַיְבֻסִי: ס 16 וַיִּשָּׂא דָוִיד אֶת־עֵינָיו וַיַּרְא אֶת־מַלְאַךְ יְהוָה עֹמֵד בֵּין הָאָרֶץ וּבֵין הַשָּׁמַיִם

sackcloth, fell on their faces. ¹⁷And David said to God, "Was it not I who commanded the people to be numbered? I am the one who has sinned and done evil indeed; but these sheep, what have they done? Let Your hand, I pray, O LORD my God, be against me and my father's house, but not against Your people that they should be plagued."

¹⁸Therefore, the angel of the LORD commanded Gad to say to David that David should go and erect an altar to the LORD on the threshing floor of Ornan the Jebusite. ¹⁹So David went up at the word of Gad, which he had spoken in the name of the LORD. ²⁰Now Ornan turned and saw the angel; and his four sons who were with him hid themselves, but Ornan continued threshing wheat. ²¹So David came to Ornan, and Ornan looked and saw David. And he went out from the threshing floor, and bowed before David with his face to the ground. ²²Then David said to Ornan, "Grant me the place of this threshing floor, that I may build an altar on it to the LORD. You shall grant it to me at the full price, that the plague may be withdrawn from the people."

²³But Ornan said to David, "Take it to yourself, and let my lord the king do what is good in his eyes. Look, I also give you the oxen for burnt offerings, the threshing implements for wood, and the wheat for the grain offering; I give it all."

²⁴Then King David said to Ornan, "No, but I will surely buy it for the full price, for I will not take what is yours for the LORD, nor offer burnt offerings with that which costs me nothing." ²⁵So David gave Ornan six hundred shekels of gold by weight for the place. ²⁶And David built there an altar to the LORD, and offered burnt offerings and peace offerings, and called on the LORD; and He answered him from heaven by fire on the altar of burnt offering.

²⁷So the LORD commanded the angel, and he returned his sword to its sheath.

²⁸At that time, when David saw that the LORD had answered him on the threshing floor of Ornan the Jebusite, he sacrificed there. ²⁹For the tabernacle of the LORD and the altar of the burnt offering, which Moses had made in the wilderness, were at that time at the high place in Gibeon. ³⁰But David could not go before it to inquire of God, for he was afraid of the sword of the angel of the LORD.

22 Then David said, "This is the house of the LORD God, and this is the altar of burnt offering for Israel." ²So David commanded to gather the aliens who were in the land of Israel; and he appointed masons to cut hewn stones to build the house of God. ³And David prepared iron in abundance for

וְחַרְבּוֹ שְׁלוּפָה בְּיָדוֹ נְטוּיָה עַל־יְרוּשָׁלָ͏ִם וַיִּפֹּל דָּוִיד וְהַזְּקֵנִים מְכֻסִּים בַּשַּׂקִּים עַל־פְּנֵיהֶם: 17 וַיֹּאמֶר דָּוִיד אֶל־הָאֱלֹהִים הֲלֹא אֲנִי אָמַרְתִּי לִמְנוֹת בָּעָם וַאֲנִי־הוּא אֲשֶׁר־חָטָאתִי וְהָרֵעַ הֲרֵעוֹתִי וְאֵלֶּה הַצֹּאן מֶה עָשׂוּ יְהוָה אֱלֹהַי תְּהִי נָא יָדְךָ בִּי וּבְבֵית אָבִי וּבְעַמְּךָ לֹא לְמַגֵּפָה: ס 18 וּמַלְאַךְ יְהוָה אָמַר אֶל־גָּד לֵאמֹר לְדָוִיד כִּי יַעֲלֶה דָוִיד לְהָקִים מִזְבֵּחַ לַיהוָה בְּגֹרֶן אָרְנָן הַיְבֻסִי: 19 וַיַּעַל דָּוִיד בִּדְבַר־גָּד אֲשֶׁר דִּבֶּר בְּשֵׁם יְהוָה: 20 וַיָּשָׁב אָרְנָן וַיַּרְא אֶת־הַמַּלְאָךְ וְאַרְבַּעַת בָּנָיו עִמּוֹ מִתְחַבְּאִים וְאָרְנָן דָּשׁ חִטִּים: 21 וַיָּבֹא דָוִיד עַד־אָרְנָן וַיַּבֵּט אָרְנָן וַיַּרְא אֶת־דָּוִיד וַיֵּצֵא מִן־הַגֹּרֶן וַיִּשְׁתַּחוּ לְדָוִיד אַפַּיִם אָרְצָה: 22 וַיֹּאמֶר דָּוִיד אֶל־אָרְנָן תְּנָה־לִּי מְקוֹם הַגֹּרֶן וְאֶבְנֶה־בּוֹ מִזְבֵּחַ לַיהוָה בְּכֶסֶף מָלֵא תְּנֵהוּ לִי וְתֵעָצַר הַמַּגֵּפָה מֵעַל הָעָם: 23 וַיֹּאמֶר אָרְנָן אֶל־דָּוִיד קַח־לָךְ וְיַעַשׂ אֲדֹנִי הַמֶּלֶךְ הַטּוֹב בְּעֵינָיו רְאֵה נָתַתִּי הַבָּקָר לָעֹלוֹת וְהַמּוֹרִגִּים לָעֵצִים וְהַחִטִּים לַמִּנְחָה הַכֹּל נָתָתִּי: 24 וַיֹּאמֶר הַמֶּלֶךְ דָּוִיד לְאָרְנָן לֹא כִּי־קָנֹה אֶקְנֶה בְּכֶסֶף מָלֵא כִּי לֹא־אֶשָּׂא אֲשֶׁר־לְךָ לַיהוָה וְהַעֲלוֹת עוֹלָה חִנָּם: 25 וַיִּתֵּן דָּוִיד לְאָרְנָן בַּמָּקוֹם שִׁקְלֵי זָהָב מִשְׁקָל שֵׁשׁ מֵאוֹת: 26 וַיִּבֶן שָׁם דָּוִיד מִזְבֵּחַ לַיהוָה וַיַּעַל עֹלוֹת וּשְׁלָמִים וַיִּקְרָא אֶל־יְהוָה וַיַּעֲנֵהוּ בָאֵשׁ מִן־הַשָּׁמַיִם עַל מִזְבַּח הָעֹלָה: פ 27 וַיֹּאמֶר יְהוָה לַמַּלְאָךְ וַיָּשֶׁב חַרְבּוֹ אֶל־נְדָנָהּ: 28 בָּעֵת הַהִיא בִּרְאוֹת דָּוִיד כִּי־עָנָהוּ יְהוָה בְּגֹרֶן אָרְנָן הַיְבֻסִי וַיִּזְבַּח שָׁם: 29 וּמִשְׁכַּן יְהוָה אֲשֶׁר־עָשָׂה מֹשֶׁה בַמִּדְבָּר וּמִזְבַּח הָעוֹלָה בָּעֵת הַהִיא בַּבָּמָה בְּגִבְעוֹן: 30 וְלֹא־יָכֹל דָּוִיד לָלֶכֶת לְפָנָיו לִדְרֹשׁ אֱלֹהִים כִּי נִבְעַת מִפְּנֵי חֶרֶב מַלְאַךְ יְהוָה:

כב וַיֹּאמֶר דָּוִיד זֶה הוּא בֵּית יְהוָה הָאֱלֹהִים וְזֶה־מִּזְבֵּחַ לְעֹלָה לְיִשְׂרָאֵל: ס 2 וַיֹּאמֶר דָּוִיד לִכְנוֹס אֶת־הַגֵּרִים אֲשֶׁר בְּאֶרֶץ יִשְׂרָאֵל וַיַּעֲמֵד חֹצְבִים לַחְצוֹב אַבְנֵי גָזִית לִבְנוֹת בֵּית הָאֱלֹהִים: 3 וּבַרְזֶל לָרֹב לַמִּסְמְרִים לְדַלְתוֹת הַשְּׁעָרִים

the nails of the doors of the gates and for the joints, and bronze in abundance beyond measure, [4] and cedar trees in abundance; for the Sidonians and those from Tyre brought much cedar wood to David.

[5] Now David said, "Solomon my son *is* young and inexperienced, and the house to be built for the LORD *must be* exceedingly magnificent, famous and glorious throughout all countries. I will now make preparation for it." So David made abundant preparations before his death.

[6] Then he called for his son Solomon, and charged him to build a house for the LORD God of Israel. [7] And David said to Solomon: "My son, as for me, it was in my mind to build a house to the name of the LORD my God; [8] but the word of the LORD came to me, saying, 'You have shed much blood and have made great wars; you shall not build a house for My name, because you have shed much blood on the earth in My sight. [9] Behold, a son shall be born to you, who shall be a man of rest; and I will give him rest from all his enemies all around. His name shall be Solomon, for I will give peace and quietness to Israel in his days. [10] He shall build a house for My name, and he shall be My son, and I *will be* his Father; and I will establish the throne of his kingdom over Israel forever.' [11] Now, my son, may the LORD be with you; and may you prosper, and build the house of the LORD your God, as He has said to you. [12] Only may the LORD give you wisdom and understanding, and give you charge concerning Israel, that you may keep the law of the LORD your God. [13] Then you will prosper, if you take care to fulfill the statutes and judgments with which the LORD charged Moses concerning Israel. Be strong and of good courage; do not fear nor be dismayed. [14] Indeed I have taken much trouble to prepare for the house of the LORD one hundred thousand talents of gold and one million talents of silver, and bronze and iron beyond measure, for it is so abundant. I have prepared timber and stone also, and you may add to them. [15] Moreover *there are* workmen with you in abundance: woodsmen and stonecutters, and all types of skillful men for every kind of work. [16] Of gold and silver and bronze and iron *there is* no limit. Arise and begin working, and the LORD be with you."

[17] David also commanded all the leaders of Israel to help Solomon his son, *saying,* [18] "Is not the LORD your God with you? And has He *not* given you rest on every side? For He has given the inhabitants of the land into my hand, and the land is subdued before the LORD and before His people. [19] Now set

וְלַמְחַבְּרוֹת הֵכִין דָּוִיד וּנְחֹשֶׁת לָרֹב אֵין מִשְׁקָל: [4] וַעֲצֵי אֲרָזִים לְאֵין מִסְפָּר כִּי הֵבִיאוּ הַצִּידֹנִים וְהַצֹּרִים עֲצֵי אֲרָזִים לָרֹב לְדָוִיד: פ

[5] וַיֹּאמֶר דָּוִיד שְׁלֹמֹה בְנִי נַעַר וָרָךְ וְהַבַּיִת לִבְנוֹת לַיהֹוָה לְהַגְדִּיל לְמַעְלָה לְשֵׁם וּלְתִפְאֶרֶת לְכָל־הָאֲרָצוֹת אָכִינָה נָּא לוֹ וַיָּכֶן דָּוִיד לָרֹב לִפְנֵי מוֹתוֹ:

[6] וַיִּקְרָא לִשְׁלֹמֹה בְנוֹ וַיְצַוֵּהוּ לִבְנוֹת בַּיִת לַיהֹוָה אֱלֹהֵי יִשְׂרָאֵל: ס   [7] וַיֹּאמֶר דָּוִיד לִשְׁלֹמֹה בְנוֹ אֲנִי הָיָה עִם־לְבָבִי לִבְנוֹת בַּיִת לְשֵׁם יְהֹוָה אֱלֹהָי: [8] וַיְהִי עָלַי דְּבַר־יְהֹוָה לֵאמֹר דָּם לָרֹב שָׁפַכְתָּ וּמִלְחָמוֹת גְּדֹלוֹת עָשִׂיתָ לֹא־תִבְנֶה בַיִת לִשְׁמִי כִּי דָּמִים רַבִּים שָׁפַכְתָּ אַרְצָה לְפָנָי: [9] הִנֵּה־בֵן נוֹלָד לָךְ הוּא יִהְיֶה אִישׁ מְנוּחָה וַהֲנִחוֹתִי לוֹ מִכָּל־אוֹיְבָיו מִסָּבִיב כִּי שְׁלֹמֹה יִהְיֶה שְׁמוֹ וְשָׁלוֹם וָשֶׁקֶט אֶתֵּן עַל־יִשְׂרָאֵל בְּיָמָיו: [10] הוּא־יִבְנֶה בַיִת לִשְׁמִי וְהוּא יִהְיֶה־לִּי לְבֵן וַאֲנִי־לוֹ לְאָב וַהֲכִינוֹתִי כִּסֵּא מַלְכוּתוֹ עַל־יִשְׂרָאֵל עַד־עוֹלָם: [11] עַתָּה בְנִי יְהִי יְהֹוָה עִמָּךְ וְהִצְלַחְתָּ וּבָנִיתָ בֵּית יְהֹוָה אֱלֹהֶיךָ כַּאֲשֶׁר דִּבֶּר עָלֶיךָ: [12] אַךְ יִתֶּן־לְךָ יְהֹוָה שֵׂכֶל וּבִינָה וִיצַוְּךָ עַל־יִשְׂרָאֵל וְלִשְׁמוֹר אֶת־תּוֹרַת יְהֹוָה אֱלֹהֶיךָ: [13] אָז תַּצְלִיחַ אִם־תִּשְׁמוֹר לַעֲשׂוֹת אֶת־הַחֻקִּים וְאֶת־הַמִּשְׁפָּטִים אֲשֶׁר צִוָּה יְהֹוָה אֶת־מֹשֶׁה עַל־יִשְׂרָאֵל חֲזַק וֶאֱמָץ אַל־תִּירָא וְאַל־תֵּחָת: [14] וְהִנֵּה בְעָנְיִי הֲכִינוֹתִי לְבֵית־יְהֹוָה זָהָב כִּכָּרִים מֵאָה־אֶלֶף וְכֶסֶף אֶלֶף אֲלָפִים כִּכָּרִים וְלַנְּחֹשֶׁת וְלַבַּרְזֶל אֵין מִשְׁקָל כִּי לָרֹב הָיָה וְעֵצִים וַאֲבָנִים הֲכִינוֹתִי וַעֲלֵיהֶם תּוֹסִיף: [15] וְעִמְּךָ לָרֹב עֹשֵׂי מְלָאכָה חֹצְבִים וְחָרָשֵׁי אֶבֶן וָעֵץ וְכָל־חָכָם בְּכָל־מְלָאכָה: [16] לַזָּהָב לַכֶּסֶף וְלַנְּחֹשֶׁת וְלַבַּרְזֶל אֵין מִסְפָּר קוּם וַעֲשֵׂה וִיהִי יְהֹוָה עִמָּךְ: [17] וַיְצַו דָּוִיד לְכָל־שָׂרֵי יִשְׂרָאֵל לַעְזֹר לִשְׁלֹמֹה בְנוֹ: [18] הֲלֹא יְהֹוָה אֱלֹהֵיכֶם עִמָּכֶם וְהֵנִיחַ לָכֶם מִסָּבִיב כִּי נָתַן בְּיָדִי אֵת יֹשְׁבֵי הָאָרֶץ וְנִכְבְּשָׁה הָאָרֶץ לִפְנֵי יְהֹוָה וְלִפְנֵי עַמּוֹ: [19] עַתָּה תְּנוּ לְבַבְכֶם וְנַפְשְׁכֶם לִדְרוֹשׁ לַיהֹוָה אֱלֹהֵיכֶם וְקוּמוּ וּבְנוּ אֶת־מִקְדַּשׁ

כב 7 בְּנִי

your heart and your soul to seek the LORD your God. Therefore arise and build the sanctuary of the LORD God, to bring the ark of the covenant of the LORD and the holy articles of God into the house that is to be built for the name of the LORD."

23 So when David was old and full of days, he made his son Solomon king over Israel.

2 And he gathered together all the leaders of Israel, with the priests and the Levites. 3 Now the Levites were numbered from the age of thirty years and above; and the number of individual males was thirty-eight thousand. 4 Of these, twenty-four thousand *were* to look after the work of the house of the LORD, six thousand *were* officers and judges, 5 four thousand *were* gatekeepers, and four thousand praised the LORD with *musical* instruments, "which I made," *said David,* "for giving praise."

6 Also David separated them into divisions among the sons of Levi: Gershon, Kohath, and Merari.

7 Of the Gershonites: Laadan and Shimei. 8 The sons of Laadan: the first Jehiel, then Zetham and Joel—three *in all.* 9 The sons of Shimei: Shelomith, Haziel, and Haran—three *in all.* These were the heads of the fathers' *houses* of Laadan. 10 And the sons of Shimei: Jahath, Zina, Jeush, and Beriah. These *were* the four sons of Shimei. 11 Jahath was the first and Zizah the second. But Jeush and Beriah did not have many sons; therefore they were assigned as one father's house.

12 The sons of Kohath: Amram, Izhar, Hebron, and Uzziel—four *in all.* 13 The sons of Amram: Aaron and Moses; and Aaron was set apart, he and his sons forever, that he should sanctify the most holy things, to burn incense before the LORD, to minister to Him, and to give the blessing in His name forever. 14 Now concerning Moses the man of God were reckoned to the tribe of Levi. 15 The sons of Moses *were* Gershon and Eliezer. 16 Of the sons of Gershon, Shebuel *was* the first. 17 Of the descendants of Eliezer, Rehabiah was the first. And Eliezer had no other sons, but the sons of Rehabiah were very many. 18 Of the sons of Izhar, Shelomith *was* the first. 19 Of the sons of Hebron, Jeriah *was* the first, Amariah the second, Jahaziel the third, and Jekameam the fourth. 20 Of the sons of Uzziel, Michah *was* the first and Jesshiah the second.

21 The sons of Merari *were* Mahli and Mushi. The sons of Mahli *were* Eleazar and Kish. 22 And Eleazar died, and had no sons, but only daughters;

יְהוָ֣ה הָאֱלֹהִ֗ים לְהָבִיא֙ אֶת־אֲר֤וֹן בְּרִית־יְהוָה֙ וּכְלֵ֣י קֹ֔דֶשׁ הָאֱלֹהִ֑ים לַבַּ֖יִת הַנִּבְנֶ֥ה לְשֵׁם־יְהוָֽה׃ פ

כג וְדָוִ֣יד זָקֵ֔ן וְשָׂבַ֖ע יָמִ֑ים וַיַּמְלֵ֛ךְ אֶת־שְׁלֹמֹ֥ה בְנ֖וֹ עַל־יִשְׂרָאֵֽל׃ 2 וַיֶּאֱסֹף֙ אֶת־כָּל־שָׂרֵ֣י יִשְׂרָאֵ֔ל וְהַכֹּהֲנִ֖ים וְהַלְוִיִּֽם׃ 3 וַיִּסָּֽפְרוּ֙ הַלְוִיִּ֔ם מִבֶּ֛ן שְׁלֹשִׁ֥ים שָׁנָ֖ה וָמָ֑עְלָה וַיְהִ֨י מִסְפָּרָ֤ם לְגֻלְגְּלֹתָם֙ לִגְבָרִ֔ים שְׁלֹשִׁ֥ים וּשְׁמוֹנָ֖ה אָֽלֶף׃ 4 מֵאֵ֗לֶּה לְנַצֵּ֙חַ֙ עַל־מְלֶ֣אכֶת בֵּית־יְהוָ֔ה עֶשְׂרִ֥ים וְאַרְבָּעָ֖ה אָ֑לֶף וְשֹׁטְרִ֥ים וְשֹׁפְטִ֖ים שֵׁ֥שֶׁת אֲלָפִֽים׃ 5 וְאַרְבַּ֥עַת אֲלָפִים֙ שֹֽׁעֲרִ֔ים וְאַרְבַּ֣עַת אֲלָפִ֗ים מְהַֽלְלִים֙ לַיהוָ֔ה בַּכֵּלִ֕ים אֲשֶׁ֥ר עָשִׂ֖יתִי לְהַלֵּֽל׃

6 וַיֶּֽחָלְקֵ֥ם דָּוִ֖יד מַחְלְק֑וֹת לִבְנֵ֣י לֵוִ֔י לְגֵרְשׁ֖וֹן קְהָ֥ת וּמְרָרִֽי׃

7 לַגֵּרְשֻׁנִּ֖י לַעְדָּ֥ן וְשִׁמְעִֽי׃

8 בְּנֵ֣י לַעְדָּ֗ן הָרֹ֛אשׁ יְחִיאֵ֥ל וְזֵתָ֖ם וְיוֹאֵ֥ל שְׁלֹשָֽׁה׃

9 בְּנֵ֣י שִׁמְעִ֗י שְׁלֹמוֹת֙ וַחֲזִיאֵ֣ל וְהָרָ֔ן שְׁלֹשָׁ֑ה אֵ֛לֶּה רָאשֵׁ֥י הָאָב֖וֹת לְלַעְדָּֽן׃

10 וּבְנֵ֣י שִׁמְעִ֔י יַ֣חַת זִינָ֔א וִיע֖וּשׁ וּבְרִיעָ֑ה אֵ֛לֶּה בְנֵֽי־שִׁמְעִ֖י אַרְבָּעָֽה׃ 11 וַֽיְהִי־יַ֣חַת הָרֹ֔אשׁ וְזִיזָ֖ה הַשֵּׁנִ֑י וִיע֤וּשׁ וּבְרִיעָה֙ לֹֽא־הִרְבּ֣וּ בָנִ֔ים וַיִּֽהְיוּ֙ לְבֵ֣ית אָ֔ב לִפְקֻדָּ֖ה אֶחָֽת׃ 12 בְּנֵ֣י קְהָ֗ת עַמְרָ֥ם יִצְהָ֛ר חֶבְר֥וֹן וְעֻזִּיאֵ֖ל אַרְבָּעָֽה׃ ס 13 בְּנֵ֥י עַמְרָ֖ם אַהֲרֹ֣ן וּמֹשֶׁ֑ה וַיִּבָּדֵ֣ל אַהֲרֹ֡ן לְהַקְדִּישׁוֹ֩ קֹ֨דֶשׁ קָֽדָשִׁ֜ים הֽוּא־וּבָנָ֣יו עַד־עוֹלָ֗ם לְהַקְטִיר֩ לִפְנֵ֨י יְהוָ֤ה לְשָֽׁרְתוֹ֙ וּלְבָרֵ֣ךְ בִּשְׁמ֖וֹ עַד־עוֹלָֽם׃ 14 וּמֹשֶׁ֖ה אִ֣ישׁ הָאֱלֹהִ֑ים בָּנָ֕יו יִקָּרְא֖וּ עַל־שֵׁ֥בֶט הַלֵּוִֽי׃ 15 בְּנֵ֣י מֹשֶׁ֔ה גֵּרְשֹׁ֖ם וֶאֱלִיעֶֽזֶר׃ 16 בְּנֵ֥י גֵרְשׁ֛וֹם שְׁבוּאֵ֖ל הָרֹֽאשׁ׃ 17 וַיִּֽהְי֤וּ בְנֵֽי־אֱלִיעֶ֙זֶר֙ רְחַבְיָ֣ה הָרֹ֔אשׁ וְלֹֽא־הָיָ֥ה לֶאֱלִיעֶ֖זֶר בָּנִ֣ים אֲחֵרִ֑ים וּבְנֵ֥י רְחַבְיָ֖ה רָב֥וּ לְמָֽעְלָה׃ 18 בְּנֵ֥י יִצְהָ֖ר שְׁלֹמִ֥ית הָרֹֽאשׁ׃ ס 19 בְּנֵ֖י חֶבְר֑וֹן יְרִיָּ֣הוּ הָרֹ֗אשׁ אֲמַרְיָה֙ הַשֵּׁנִ֔י יַחֲזִיאֵל֙ הַשְּׁלִישִׁ֔י וִֽיקַמְעָ֖ם הָרְבִיעִֽי׃ 20 בְּנֵ֖י עֻזִּיאֵ֑ל מִיכָ֣ה הָרֹ֔אשׁ וְיִשִּׁיָּ֖ה הַשֵּׁנִֽי׃ ס 21 בְּנֵ֣י מְרָרִ֔י מַחְלִ֖י וּמוּשִׁ֑י בְּנֵ֣י מַחְלִ֔י אֶלְעָזָ֖ר וְקִֽישׁ׃ 22 וַיָּ֙מָת֙ אֶלְעָזָ֔ר וְלֹא־הָ֥יוּ ל֛וֹ בָּנִ֖ים כִּ֣י אִם־בָּנ֑וֹת וַיִּשָּׂא֥וּם בְּנֵֽי־

and their brethren, the sons of Kish, took them *as* wives. 23 The sons of Mushi *were* Mahli, Eder, and Jeremoth—three *in all.*

24 These *were* the sons of Levi by their fathers' houses—the heads of the fathers' *houses* as they were counted individually by the number of their names, who did the work for the service of the house of the LORD, from the age of twenty years and above.

25 For David said, "The LORD God of Israel has given rest to His people, that they may dwell in Jerusalem forever"; 26 and also to the Levites, "They shall no longer carry the tabernacle, or any of the articles for its service." 27 For by the last words of David the Levites *were* numbered from twenty years old and above; 28 because their duty *was* to help the sons of Aaron in the service of the house of the LORD, in the courts and in the chambers, in the purifying of all holy things and the work of the service of the house of God, 29 both with the showbread and the fine flour for the grain offering, with the unleavened cakes and *what is baked in* the pan, with what is mixed and with all kinds of measures and sizes; 30 to stand every morning to thank and praise the LORD, and likewise at evening; 31 and at every presentation of a burnt offering to the LORD on the Sabbaths and on the New Moons and on the set feasts, by number according to the ordinance governing them, regularly before the LORD; 32 and that they should attend to the needs of the tabernacle of meeting, the needs of the holy *place,* and the needs of the sons of Aaron their brethren in the work of the house of the LORD.

24 Now *these are* the divisions of the sons of Aaron. The sons of Aaron *were* Nadab, Abihu, Eleazar, and Ithamar. 2 And Nadab and Abihu died before their father, and had no children; therefore Eleazar and Ithamar ministered as priests. 3 Then David with Zadok of the sons of Eleazar, and Ahimelech of the sons of Ithamar, divided them according to the schedule of their service.

4 There were more leaders found of the sons of Eleazar than of the sons of Ithamar, and *thus* they were divided. Among the sons of Eleazar *were* sixteen heads of *their* fathers' houses, and eight heads of their fathers' houses among the sons of Ithamar. 5 Thus they were divided by lot, one group as another, for there were officials of the sanctuary and officials *of the house* of God, from the sons of Eleazar and from the sons of Ithamar. 6 And the scribe, Shemaiah the son of Nethanel, *one of the* Levites, wrote them down before the king, the

קִישׁ אֲחֵיהֶם: 23 בְּנֵי מוּשִׁי מַחְלִי וְעֵדֶר וִירֵמוֹת שְׁלֹשָׁה: 24 אֵלֶּה בְנֵי־לֵוִי לְבֵית אֲבֹתֵיהֶם רָאשֵׁי הָאָבוֹת לִפְקוּדֵיהֶם בְּמִסְפַּר שֵׁמוֹת לְגֻלְגְּלֹתָם עֹשֵׂה הַמְּלָאכָה לַעֲבֹדַת בֵּית יְהוָה מִבֶּן עֶשְׂרִים שָׁנָה וָמָעְלָה: 25 כִּי אָמַר דָּוִיד הֵנִיחַ יְהוָה אֱלֹהֵי־יִשְׂרָאֵל לְעַמּוֹ וַיִּשְׁכֹּן בִּירוּשָׁלַ͏ִם עַד־לְעוֹלָם: 26 וְגַם לַלְוִיִּם אֵין־לָשֵׂאת אֶת־הַמִּשְׁכָּן וְאֶת־כָּל־כֵּלָיו לַעֲבֹדָתוֹ: 27 כִּי בְדִבְרֵי דָוִיד הָאַחֲרֹנִים הֵמָּה מִסְפַּר בְּנֵי־לֵוִי מִבֶּן עֶשְׂרִים שָׁנָה וּלְמָעְלָה: 28 כִּי מַעֲמָדָם לְיַד־ בְּנֵי אַהֲרֹן לַעֲבֹדַת בֵּית יְהוָה עַל־הַחֲצֵרוֹת וְעַל־ הַלְּשָׁכוֹת וְעַל־טָהֳרַת לְכָל־קֹדֶשׁ וּמַעֲשֵׂה עֲבֹדַת בֵּית הָאֱלֹהִים: 29 וּלְלֶחֶם הַמַּעֲרֶכֶת וּלְסֹלֶת לְמִנְחָה וְלִרְקִיקֵי הַמַּצּוֹת וְלַמַּחֲבַת וְלַמֻּרְבָּכֶת וּלְכָל־מְשׂוּרָה וּמִדָּה: 30 וְלַעֲמֹד בַּבֹּקֶר בַּבֹּקֶר לְהֹדוֹת וּלְהַלֵּל לַיהוָה וְכֵן לָעָרֶב: 31 וּלְכֹל הַעֲלוֹת עֹלוֹת לַיהוָה לַשַּׁבָּתוֹת לֶחֳדָשִׁים וְלַמֹּעֲדִים בְּמִסְפָּר כְּמִשְׁפָּט עֲלֵיהֶם תָּמִיד לִפְנֵי יְהוָה: 32 וְשָׁמְרוּ אֶת־מִשְׁמֶרֶת אֹהֶל־מוֹעֵד וְאֵת מִשְׁמֶרֶת הַקֹּדֶשׁ וּמִשְׁמֶרֶת בְּנֵי אַהֲרֹן אֲחֵיהֶם לַעֲבֹדַת בֵּית יְהוָה: פ

כד וְלִבְנֵי אַהֲרֹן מַחְלְקוֹתָם בְּנֵי אַהֲרֹן נָדָב וַאֲבִיהוּא אֶלְעָזָר וְאִיתָמָר: 2 וַיָּמָת נָדָב וַאֲבִיהוּא לִפְנֵי אֲבִיהֶם וּבָנִים לֹא־הָיוּ לָהֶם וַיְכַהֲנוּ אֶלְעָזָר וְאִיתָמָר: 3 וַיֶּחָלְקֵם דָּוִיד וְצָדוֹק מִן־בְּנֵי אֶלְעָזָר וַאֲחִימֶלֶךְ מִן־בְּנֵי אִיתָמָר לִפְקֻדָּתָם בַּעֲבֹדָתָם: 4 וַיִּמָּצְאוּ בְנֵי־אֶלְעָזָר רַבִּים לְרָאשֵׁי הַגְּבָרִים מִן־ בְּנֵי אִיתָמָר וַיַּחְלְקוּם לִבְנֵי אֶלְעָזָר רָאשִׁים לְבֵית־ אָבוֹת שִׁשָּׁה עָשָׂר וְלִבְנֵי אִיתָמָר לְבֵית אֲבוֹתָם שְׁמוֹנָה: 5 וַיַּחְלְקוּם בְּגוֹרָלוֹת אֵלֶּה עִם־אֵלֶּה כִּי־ הָיוּ שָׂרֵי־קֹדֶשׁ וְשָׂרֵי הָאֱלֹהִים מִבְּנֵי אֶלְעָזָר וּבִבְנֵי אִיתָמָר: ס 6 וַיִּכְתְּבֵם שְׁמַעְיָה בֶן־נְתַנְאֵל הַסּוֹפֵר מִן־הַלֵּוִי לִפְנֵי הַמֶּלֶךְ וְהַשָּׂרִים וְצָדוֹק הַכֹּהֵן וַאֲחִימֶלֶךְ בֶּן־אֶבְיָתָר וְרָאשֵׁי הָאָבוֹת לַכֹּהֲנִים וְלַלְוִיִּם בֵּית־אָב אֶחָד אָחֻז לְאֶלְעָזָר וְאָחֻז | אָחֻז לְאִיתָמָר: פ

leaders, Zadok the priest, Ahimelech the son of Abiathar, and the heads of the fathers' *houses* of the priests and Levites, one father's house taken for Eleazar and *one* for Ithamar.

[7] Now the first lot fell to Jehoiarib, the second to Jedaiah, [8] the third to Harim, the fourth to Seorim, [9] the fifth to Malchijah, the sixth to Mijamin, [10] the seventh to Hakkoz, the eighth to Abijah, [11] the ninth to Jeshua, the tenth to Shecaniah, [12] the eleventh to Eliashib, the twelfth to Jakim, [13] the thirteenth to Huppah, the fourteenth to Jeshebeab, [14] the fifteenth to Bilgah, the sixteenth to Immer, [15] the seventeenth to Hezir, the eighteenth to Happizzez, [16] the nineteenth to Pethahiah, the twentieth to Jehezekel, [17] the twenty-first to Jachin, the twenty-second to Gamul, [18] the twenty-third to Delaiah, the twenty-fourth to Maaziah.

[19] This *was* the schedule of their service for coming into the house of the LORD according to their ordinance by the hand of Aaron their father, as the LORD God of Israel had commanded him.

[20] And the rest of the sons of Levi: of the sons of Amram, Shubael; of the sons of Shubael, Jehdeiah. [21] Concerning Rehabiah, of the sons of Rehabiah, the first *was* Isshiah. [22] Of the Izharites, Shelomoth; of the sons of Shelomoth, Jahath. [23] Of the sons *of Hebron,* Jeriah *was the first,* Amariah the second, Jahaziel the third, *and* Jekameam the fourth. [24] *Of* the sons of Uzziel, Michah; of the sons of Michah, Shamir. [25] The brother of Michah, Isshiah; of the sons of Isshiah, Zechariah. [26] The sons of Merari *were* Mahli and Mushi; the son of Jaaziah, Beno. [27] The sons of Merari by Jaaziah *were* Beno, Shoham, Zaccur, and Ibri. [28] Of Mahli: Eleazar, who had no sons. [29] Of Kish: the son of Kish, Jerahmeel.

[30] Also the sons of Mushi *were* Mahli, Eder, and Jerimoth. These *were* the sons of the Levites according to their fathers' houses.

[31] These also cast lots just as their brothers the sons of Aaron did, in the presence of King David, Zadok, Ahimelech, and the heads of the fathers' *houses* of the priests and Levites. The chief fathers *did* just as their younger brethren.

25 Moreover David and the captains of the army separated for the service *some* of the sons of Asaph, of Heman, and of Jeduthun, who *should* prophesy with harps, stringed instruments, and cymbals. And the number of the skilled men performing their service was: [2] Of the sons of Asaph: Zaccur, Joseph, Nethaniah, and Asharelah; the sons of Asaph *were* under the direction of Asaph, who prophesied according to the order of the king. [3] Of Jeduthun,

7 וַיֵּצֵא הַגּוֹרָל הָרִאשׁוֹן לִיהוֹיָרִיב לִידַעְיָה הַשֵּׁנִי: 8 לְחָרִם הַשְּׁלִשִׁי לִשְׂעֹרִים הָרְבִעִי: 9 לְמַלְכִּיָּה הַחֲמִישִׁי לְמִיָּמִן הַשִּׁשִּׁי: 10 לְהַקּוֹץ הַשְּׁבִעִי לַאֲבִיָּה הַשְּׁמִינִי: 11 לְיֵשׁוּעַ הַתְּשִׁעִי לִשְׁכַנְיָהוּ הָעֲשִׂרִי: 12 לְאֶלְיָשִׁיב עַשְׁתֵּי עָשָׂר לְיָקִים שְׁנֵים עָשָׂר: 13 לְחֻפָּה שְׁלֹשָׁה עָשָׂר לְיֶשֶׁבְאָב אַרְבָּעָה עָשָׂר: 14 לְבִלְגָּה חֲמִשָּׁה עָשָׂר לְאִמֵּר שִׁשָּׁה עָשָׂר: 15 לְחֵזִיר שִׁבְעָה עָשָׂר לְהַפִּצֵּץ שְׁמוֹנָה עָשָׂר: 16 לִפְתַחְיָה תִּשְׁעָה עָשָׂר לִיחֶזְקֵאל הָעֶשְׂרִים: 17 לְיָכִין אֶחָד וְעֶשְׂרִים לְגָמוּל שְׁנַיִם וְעֶשְׂרִים: 18 לִדְלָיָהוּ שְׁלֹשָׁה וְעֶשְׂרִים לְמַעַזְיָהוּ אַרְבָּעָה וְעֶשְׂרִים: פ

19 אֵלֶּה פְקֻדָּתָם לַעֲבֹדָתָם לָבוֹא לְבֵית־יְהוָה כְּמִשְׁפָּטָם בְּיַד אַהֲרֹן אֲבִיהֶם כַּאֲשֶׁר צִוָּהוּ יְהוָה אֱלֹהֵי יִשְׂרָאֵל: פ

20 וְלִבְנֵי לֵוִי הַנּוֹתָרִים לִבְנֵי עַמְרָם שׁוּבָאֵל לִבְנֵי שׁוּבָאֵל יֶחְדְּיָהוּ: 21 לִרְחַבְיָהוּ לִבְנֵי רְחַבְיָהוּ הָרֹאשׁ יִשִּׁיָּה: 22 לַיִּצְהָרִי שְׁלֹמוֹת לִבְנֵי שְׁלֹמוֹת יָחַת: 23 וּבְנָי יְרִיָּהוּ אֲמַרְיָהוּ הַשֵּׁנִי יַחֲזִיאֵל הַשְּׁלִישִׁי יְקַמְעָם הָרְבִיעִי: 24 בְּנֵי עֻזִּיאֵל מִיכָה לִבְנֵי מִיכָה שָׁמִיר: 25 אֲחִי מִיכָה יִשִּׁיָּה לִבְנֵי יִשִּׁיָּה זְכַרְיָהוּ: 26 בְּנֵי מְרָרִי מַחְלִי וּמוּשִׁי בְּנֵי יַעֲזִיָּהוּ בְנוֹ: 27 בְּנֵי מְרָרִי לְיַעֲזִיָּהוּ בְנוֹ וְשֹׁהַם וְזַכּוּר וְעִבְרִי: 28 לְמַחְלִי אֶלְעָזָר וְלֹא־הָיָה לוֹ בָּנִים: 29 לְקִישׁ בְּנֵי־קִישׁ יְרַחְמְאֵל: 30 וּבְנֵי מוּשִׁי מַחְלִי וְעֵדֶר וִירִימוֹת אֵלֶּה בְּנֵי הַלְוִיִּם לְבֵית אֲבֹתֵיהֶם: 31 וַיַּפִּילוּ גַם־הֵם גּוֹרָלוֹת לְעֻמַּת אֲחֵיהֶם בְּנֵי־אַהֲרֹן לִפְנֵי דָוִיד הַמֶּלֶךְ וְצָדוֹק וַאֲחִימֶלֶךְ וְרָאשֵׁי הָאָבוֹת לַכֹּהֲנִים וְלַלְוִיִּם אָבוֹת הָרֹאשׁ לְעֻמַּת אָחִיו הַקָּטָן: ס

כה וַיַּבְדֵּל דָּוִיד וְשָׂרֵי הַצָּבָא לַעֲבֹדָה לִבְנֵי אָסָף וְהֵימָן וִידוּתוּן הַנִּבְּאִים בְּכִנֹּרוֹת בִּנְבָלִים וּבִמְצִלְתָּיִם וַיְהִי מִסְפָּרָם אַנְשֵׁי מְלָאכָה לַעֲבֹדָתָם: 2 לִבְנֵי אָסָף זַכּוּר וְיוֹסֵף וּנְתַנְיָה וַאֲשַׂרְאֵלָה בְּנֵי אָסָף עַל יַד־אָסָף הַנִּבָּא עַל־יְדֵי הַמֶּלֶךְ: 3 לִידוּתוּן

כד 24 שָׁמִיר   כה 1 הַנִּבְּאִים

the sons of Jeduthun: Gedaliah, Zeri, Jeshaiah, Shimei, Hashabiah, and Mattithiah, six, under the direction of their father Jeduthun, who prophesied with a harp to give thanks and to praise the LORD. [4]Of Heman, the sons of Heman: Bukkiah, Mattaniah, Uzziel, Shebuel, Jerimoth, Hananiah, Hanani, Eliathah, Giddalti, Romamti-Ezer, Joshbekashah, Mallothi, Hothir, *and* Mahazioth. [5]All these *were* the sons of Heman the king's seer in the words of God, to exalt his horn. For God gave Heman fourteen sons and three daughters.

[6]All these *were* under the direction of their father for the music *in* the house of the LORD, with cymbals, stringed instruments, and harps, for the service of the house of God. Asaph, Jeduthun, and Heman *were* under the authority of the king. [7]So the number of them, with their brethren who were instructed in the songs of the LORD, all who were skillful, *was* two hundred and eighty-eight.

[8]And they cast lots for their duty, the small as well as the great, the teacher with the student.

[9]Now the first lot for Asaph came out for Joseph; the second for Gedaliah, him with his brethren and sons, twelve; [10]the third for Zaccur, his sons and his brethren, twelve; [11]the fourth for Jizri, his sons and his brethren, twelve; [12]the fifth for Nethaniah, his sons and his brethren, twelve; [13]the sixth for Bukkiah, his sons and his brethren, twelve; [14]the seventh for Jesharelah, his sons and his brethren, twelve; [15]the eighth for Jeshaiah, his sons and his brethren, twelve; [16]the ninth for Mattaniah, his sons and his brethren, twelve; [17]the tenth for Shimei, his sons and his brethren, twelve; [18]the eleventh for Azarel, his sons and his brethren, twelve; [19]the twelfth for Hashabiah, his sons and his brethren, twelve; [20]the thirteenth for Shubael, his sons and his brethren, twelve; [21]the fourteenth for Mattithiah, his sons and his brethren, twelve; [22]the fifteenth for Jeremoth, his sons and his brethren, twelve; [23]the sixteenth for Hananiah, his sons and his brethren, twelve; [24]the seventeenth for Joshbekashah, his sons and his brethren, twelve; [25]the eighteenth for Hanani, his sons and his brethren, twelve; [26]the nineteenth for Mallothi, his sons and his brethren, twelve; [27]the twentieth for Eliathah, his sons and his brethren, twelve; [28]the twenty-first for Hothir, his sons and his brethren, twelve; [29]the twenty-second for Giddalti, his sons and his brethren, twelve; [30]the twenty-third for Mahazioth, his sons and his brethren, twelve; [31]the twenty-fourth for Romamti-Ezer, his sons and his brethren, twelve.

בְּנֵי יְדוּתוּן גְּדַלְיָהוּ וּצְרִי וִישַׁעְיָהוּ חֲשַׁבְיָהוּ וּמַתִּתְיָהוּ שִׁשָּׁה עַל יְדֵי אֲבִיהֶם יְדוּתוּן בַּכִּנּוֹר הַנִּבָּא עַל־הֹדוֹת וְהַלֵּל לַיהוָה: ס 4 לְהֵימָן בְּנֵי הֵימָן בֻּקִּיָּהוּ מַתַּנְיָהוּ עֻזִּיאֵל שְׁבוּאֵל וִירִימוֹת חֲנַנְיָה חֲנָנִי אֱלִיאָתָה גִּדַּלְתִּי וְרֹמַמְתִּי עֶזֶר יָשְׁבְּקָשָׁה מַלּוֹתִי הוֹתִיר מַחֲזִיאוֹת: 5 כָּל־אֵלֶּה בָנִים לְהֵימָן חֹזֵה הַמֶּלֶךְ בְּדִבְרֵי הָאֱלֹהִים לְהָרִים קָרֶן וַיִּתֵּן הָאֱלֹהִים לְהֵימָן בָּנִים אַרְבָּעָה עָשָׂר וּבָנוֹת שָׁלוֹשׁ: 6 כָּל־אֵלֶּה עַל־יְדֵי אֲבִיהֶם בַּשִּׁיר בֵּית יְהוָה בִּמְצִלְתַּיִם נְבָלִים וְכִנֹּרוֹת לַעֲבֹדַת בֵּית הָאֱלֹהִים עַל יְדֵי הַמֶּלֶךְ ס אָסָף וִידוּתוּן וְהֵימָן: 7 וַיְהִי מִסְפָּרָם עִם־אֲחֵיהֶם מְלֻמְּדֵי־שִׁיר לַיהוָה כָּל־הַמֵּבִין מָאתַיִם שְׁמוֹנִים וּשְׁמוֹנָה: 8 וַיַּפִּילוּ גּוֹרָלוֹת מִשְׁמֶרֶת לְעֻמַּת כַּקָּטֹן כַּגָּדוֹל מֵבִין עִם־תַּלְמִיד: פ 9 וַיֵּצֵא הַגּוֹרָל הָרִאשׁוֹן לְאָסָף לְיוֹסֵף גְּדַלְיָהוּ הַשֵּׁנִי הוּא־וְאֶחָיו וּבָנָיו שְׁנֵים עָשָׂר: 10 הַשְּׁלִשִׁי זַכּוּר בָּנָיו וְאֶחָיו שְׁנֵים עָשָׂר: 11 הָרְבִיעִי לַיִּצְרִי בָּנָיו וְאֶחָיו שְׁנֵים עָשָׂר: 12 הַחֲמִישִׁי נְתַנְיָהוּ בָּנָיו וְאֶחָיו שְׁנֵים עָשָׂר: 13 הַשִּׁשִּׁי בֻקִּיָּהוּ בָּנָיו וְאֶחָיו שְׁנֵים עָשָׂר: 14 הַשְּׁבִעִי יְשַׂרְאֵלָה בָּנָיו וְאֶחָיו שְׁנֵים עָשָׂר: 15 הַשְּׁמִינִי יְשַׁעְיָהוּ בָּנָיו וְאֶחָיו שְׁנֵים עָשָׂר: 16 הַתְּשִׁיעִי מַתַּנְיָהוּ בָּנָיו וְאֶחָיו שְׁנֵים עָשָׂר: 17 הָעֲשִׂירִי שִׁמְעִי בָּנָיו וְאֶחָיו שְׁנֵים עָשָׂר: 18 עַשְׁתֵּי־עָשָׂר עֲזַרְאֵל בָּנָיו וְאֶחָיו שְׁנֵים עָשָׂר: 19 הַשְּׁנֵים עָשָׂר לַחֲשַׁבְיָה בָּנָיו וְאֶחָיו שְׁנֵים עָשָׂר: 20 לִשְׁלֹשָׁה עָשָׂר שׁוּבָאֵל בָּנָיו וְאֶחָיו שְׁנֵים עָשָׂר: 21 לְאַרְבָּעָה עָשָׂר מַתִּתְיָהוּ בָּנָיו וְאֶחָיו שְׁנֵים עָשָׂר: 22 לַחֲמִשָּׁה עָשָׂר לִירֵמוֹת בָּנָיו וְאֶחָיו שְׁנֵים עָשָׂר: 23 לְשִׁשָּׁה עָשָׂר לַחֲנַנְיָהוּ בָּנָיו וְאֶחָיו שְׁנֵים עָשָׂר: 24 לְשִׁבְעָה עָשָׂר לְיָשְׁבְּקָשָׁה בָּנָיו וְאֶחָיו שְׁנֵים עָשָׂר: 25 לִשְׁמוֹנָה עָשָׂר לַחֲנָנִי בָּנָיו וְאֶחָיו שְׁנֵים עָשָׂר: 26 לְתִשְׁעָה עָשָׂר לְמַלּוֹתִי בָּנָיו וְאֶחָיו שְׁנֵים עָשָׂר: 27 לְעֶשְׂרִים לֶאֱלִיָּתָה בָּנָיו וְאֶחָיו שְׁנֵים עָשָׂר: 28 לְאֶחָד וְעֶשְׂרִים לְהוֹתִיר בָּנָיו וְאֶחָיו שְׁנֵים עָשָׂר: 29 לִשְׁנַיִם וְעֶשְׂרִים לְגִדַּלְתִּי בָּנָיו וְאֶחָיו שְׁנֵים עָשָׂר: 30 לִשְׁלֹשָׁה וְעֶשְׂרִים לְמַחֲזִיאוֹת בָּנָיו וְאֶחָיו שְׁנֵים עָשָׂר: 31 לְאַרְבָּעָה וְעֶשְׂרִים לְרוֹמַמְתִּי עָזֶר בָּנָיו וְאֶחָיו שְׁנֵים עָשָׂר: פ

26 Concerning the divisions of the gatekeepers: of the Korahites, Meshelemiah the son of Kore, of the sons of Asaph. ²And the sons of Meshelemiah *were* Zechariah the firstborn, Jediael the second, Zebadiah the third, Jathniel the fourth, ³Elam the fifth, Jehohanan the sixth, Eliehoenai the seventh.

⁴Moreover the sons of Obed-Edom *were* Shemaiah the firstborn, Jehozabad the second, Joah the third, Sacar the fourth, Nethanel the fifth, ⁵Ammiel the sixth, Issachar the seventh, Peulthai the eighth; for God blessed him.

⁶Also to Shemaiah his son were sons born who governed their fathers' houses, because they *were* men of great ability. ⁷The sons of Shemaiah *were* Othni, Rephael, Obed, and Elzabad, whose brothers Elihu and Semachiah *were* able men.

⁸All these *were* of the sons of Obed-Edom, they and their sons and their brethren, able men with strength for the work: sixty-two of Obed-Edom.

⁹And Meshelemiah had sons and brethren, eighteen able men.

¹⁰Also Hosah, of the children of Merari, had sons: Shimri the first (for *though* he was not the firstborn, his father made him the first), ¹¹Hilkiah the second, Tebaliah the third, Zechariah the fourth; all the sons and brethren of Hosah *were* thirteen.

¹²Among these *were* the divisions of the gatekeepers, among the chief men, *having* duties just like their brethren, to serve in the house of the LORD. ¹³And they cast lots for each gate, the small as well as the great, according to their father's house. ¹⁴The lot for the East *Gate* fell to Shelemiah. Then they cast lots *for* his son Zechariah, a wise counselor, and his lot came out for the North Gate; ¹⁵to Obed-Edom the South Gate, and to his sons the storehouse. ¹⁶To Shuppim and Hosah *the lot came out* for the West Gate, with the Shallecheth Gate on the ascending highway—watchman opposite watchman. ¹⁷On the east were *six* Levites, on the north four each day, on the south four each day, and for the storehouse two by two. ¹⁸As for the Parbar on the west, *there were* four on the highway *and* two at the Parbar. ¹⁹These were the divisions of the gatekeepers among the sons of Korah and among the sons of Merari.

²⁰Of the Levites, Ahijah *was* over the treasuries of the house of God and over the treasuries of the dedicated things. ²¹The sons of Laadan, the descendants of the Gershonites of Laadan, heads of their fathers' *houses,* of Laadan the Gershonite: Jehieli. ²²The sons of Jehieli, Zetham and Joel his brother, *were* over the treasuries of the house of the LORD. ²³Of the Amramites, the Izharites, the

כו לְמַחְלְק֣וֹת לְשֹׁעֲרִ֔ים לַקָּרְחִ֖ים מְשֶֽׁלֶמְיָ֣הוּ בֶן־
קֹרֵ֖א מִן־בְּנֵ֥י אָסָֽף׃ ²וְלִמְשֶֽׁלֶמְיָ֖הוּ בָּנִ֑ים זְכַרְיָ֣הוּ
הַבְּכ֗וֹר יְדִֽיעֲאֵ֤ל הַשֵּׁנִי֙ זְבַדְיָ֣הוּ הַשְּׁלִישִׁ֔י יַתְנִיאֵ֖ל
הָרְבִיעִֽי׃ ³עֵילָ֤ם הַֽחֲמִישִׁי֙ יְהֽוֹחָנָ֣ן הַשִּׁשִּׁ֔י אֶלְיְהֽוֹעֵינַ֖י
הַשְּׁבִיעִֽי׃ ⁴וּלְעֹבֵ֥ד אֱדֹ֖ם בָּנִ֑ים שְׁמַֽעְיָ֣ה הַבְּכ֗וֹר
יְהוֹזָבָ֤ד הַשֵּׁנִי֙ יוֹאָ֣ח הַשְּׁלִשִׁ֔י וְשָׂכָ֣ר הָֽרְבִיעִ֔י וּנְתַנְאֵ֖ל
הַֽחֲמִישִֽׁי׃ ⁵עַמִּיאֵ֣ל הַשִּׁשִּׁ֗י יִשָּׂשכָר֙ הַשְּׁבִיעִ֔י פְּעֻלְּתַ֖י
הַשְּׁמִינִ֑י כִּ֥י בֵֽרֲכ֖וֹ אֱלֹהִֽים׃ פ

⁶וְלִשְׁמַֽעְיָ֤ה בְנוֹ֙ נוֹלַ֣ד בָּנִ֔ים הַמִּמְשָׁלִ֖ים לְבֵ֣ית
אֲבִיהֶ֑ם כִּֽי־גִבּ֥וֹרֵי חַ֖יִל הֵֽמָּה׃ ⁷בְּנֵ֣י שְׁמַֽעְיָ֗ה עָתְנִ֤י
וּרְפָאֵ֣ל וְעוֹבֵ֗ד אֶלְזָבָד֙ אֶחָ֔יו בְּנֵי־חָ֑יִל אֱלִיה֖וּ אֵלֶ֑יהוּ
וּסְמַכְיָֽהוּ׃ ⁸כׇּל־אֵ֜לֶּה מִבְּנֵ֣י ׀ עֹבֵ֣ד אֱדֹ֗ם הֵ֤מָּה
וּבְנֵיהֶם֙ וַֽאֲחֵיהֶ֔ם אִֽישׁ־חַ֖יִל בַּכֹּ֣חַ לַֽעֲבֹדָ֑ה שִׁשִּׁ֥ים
וּשְׁנַ֖יִם לְעֹבֵ֥ד אֱדֹֽם׃ ⁹וְלִמְשֶֽׁלֶמְיָ֗הוּ בָּנִ֣ים וְאַחִ֔ים
בְּנֵי־חָ֖יִל שְׁמוֹנָ֥ה עָשָֽׂר׃ ס ¹⁰וּלְחֹסָ֥ה מִן־
בְּנֵי־מְרָרִ֖י בָּנִ֑ים שִׁמְרִ֤י הָרֹאשׁ֙ כִּ֣י לֹֽא־הָיָ֣ה בְכ֔וֹר
וַיְשִׂימֵ֥הוּ אָבִ֖יהוּ לְרֹֽאשׁ׃ ¹¹חִלְקִיָּ֨הוּ֙ הַשֵּׁנִ֔י טְבַלְיָ֙הוּ֙
הַשְּׁלִשִׁ֔י זְכַרְיָ֖הוּ הָֽרְבִעִ֑י כׇּל־בָּנִ֤ים וְאַחִים֙ לְחֹסָ֔ה
שְׁלֹשָׁ֥ה עָשָֽׂר׃ ¹²לְ֠אֵ֠לֶּה מַחְלְק֨וֹת הַשֹּֽׁעֲרִ֜ים לְרָאשֵׁ֣י
הַגְּבָרִ֗ים מִשְׁמָרוֹת֙ לְעֻמַּ֣ת אֲחֵיהֶ֔ם לְשָׁרֵ֖ת בְּבֵ֥ית
יְהֹוָֽה׃ ¹³וַיַּפִּ֤ילוּ גֽוֹרָלוֹת֙ כַּקָּטֹ֣ן כַּגָּד֔וֹל לְבֵ֖ית אֲבוֹתָ֑ם
לְשַׁ֖עַר וָשָֽׁעַר׃ פ

¹⁴וַיִּפֹּ֧ל הַגּוֹרָ֛ל מִזְרָ֖חָה לְשֶֽׁלֶמְיָ֑הוּ וּזְכַרְיָ֣הוּ בְנ֗וֹ
יוֹעֵץ֙ ׀ בְּשֶׂ֔כֶל הִפִּ֙ילוּ֙ גֽוֹרָל֔וֹת וַיֵּצֵ֥א גוֹרָל֖וֹ צָפֽוֹנָה׃
¹⁵לְעֹבֵ֥ד אֱדֹ֖ם נֶ֑גְבָּה וּלְבָנָ֖יו בֵּ֥ית הָֽאֲסֻפִּֽים׃
¹⁶לְשֻׁפִּ֣ים וּלְחֹסָ֗ה לַֽמַּעֲרָ֛ב עִ֚ם שַׁ֣עַר שַׁלֶּ֔כֶת
בַּֽמְסִלָּ֖ה הָֽעוֹלָ֑ה מִשְׁמָ֖ר לְעֻמַּ֥ת מִשְׁמָֽר׃ ¹⁷לַמִּזְרָח֙
הַֽלְוִיִּ֣ם שִׁשָּׁ֔ה לַצָּפ֥וֹנָה לַיּ֖וֹם אַרְבָּעָ֑ה לַנֶּ֙גְבָּה֙
לַיּ֣וֹם אַרְבָּעָ֔ה וְלָֽאֲסֻפִּ֖ים שְׁנַ֥יִם שְׁנָֽיִם׃ ¹⁸לַפַּרְבָּ֖ר
לַֽמַּעֲרָ֑ב אַרְבָּעָה֙ לַֽמְסִלָּ֔ה שְׁנַ֖יִם לַפַּרְבָּֽר׃ ¹⁹אֵ֣לֶּה
מַחְלְק֖וֹת הַשֹּֽׁעֲרִ֑ים לִבְנֵ֥י הַקׇּרְחִ֖י וְלִבְנֵ֥י מְרָרִֽי׃

²⁰וְהַ֨לְוִיִּ֔ם אֲחִיָּ֕ה עַל־אֽוֹצְרוֹת֙ בֵּ֣ית הָֽאֱלֹהִ֔ים
וּלְאֹֽצְר֖וֹת הַקֳּדָשִֽׁים׃ ²¹בְּנֵ֣י לַעְדָּ֗ן בְּנֵ֤י הַגֵּֽרְשֻׁנִּי֙
לְלַעְדָּ֔ן רָאשֵׁ֧י הָֽאָב֛וֹת לְלַעְדָּ֥ן הַגֵּֽרְשֻׁנִּ֖י יְחִֽיאֵלִֽי׃
²²בְּנֵ֖י יְחִֽיאֵלִ֑י זֵתָם֙ וְיוֹאֵ֣ל אָחִ֔יו עַל־אֹֽצְר֖וֹת בֵּ֥ית
יְהֹוָֽה׃ ²³לַֽעַמְרָמִי֙ לַיִּצְהָרִ֔י לַֽחֶבְרוֹנִ֖י לָֽעׇזִּיאֵלִֽי׃

Hebronites, and the Uzzielites: ²⁴Shebuel the son of Gershom, the son of Moses, *was* overseer of the treasuries. ²⁵And his brethren by Eliezer *were* Rehabiah his son, Jeshaiah his son, Joram his son, Zichri his son, and Shelomith his son.

²⁶This Shelomith and his brethren *were* over all the treasuries of the dedicated things which King David and the heads of fathers' *houses,* the captains over thousands and hundreds, and the captains of the army, had dedicated. ²⁷Some of the spoils won in battles they dedicated to maintain the house of the LORD. ²⁸And all that Samuel the seer, Saul the son of Kish, Abner the son of Ner, and Joab the son of Zeruiah had dedicated, every dedicated *thing,* was under the hand of Shelomith and his brethren.

²⁹Of the Izharites, Chenaniah and his sons *performed* duties as officials and judges over Israel outside Jerusalem.

³⁰Of the Hebronites, Hashabiah and his brethren, one thousand seven hundred able men, had the oversight of Israel on the west side of the Jordan for all the business of the LORD, and in the service of the king. ³¹Among the Hebronites, Jerijah *was* head of the Hebronites according to his genealogy of the fathers. In the fortieth year of the reign of David they were sought, and there were found among them capable men at Jazer of Gilead. ³²And his brethren *were* two thousand seven hundred able men, heads of fathers' *houses,* whom King David made officials over the Reubenites, the Gadites, and the half-tribe of Manasseh, for every matter pertaining to God and the affairs of the king.

27 And the children of Israel, according to their number, the heads of fathers' *houses,* the captains of thousands and hundreds and their officers, served the king in every matter of the *military* divisions. *These divisions* came in and went out month by month throughout all the months of the year, each division *having* twenty-four thousand.

²Over the first division for the first month *was* Jashobeam the son of Zabdiel, and in his division *were* twenty-four thousand; ³he *was* of the children of Perez, and the chief of all the captains of the army for the first month. ⁴Over the division of the second month *was* Dodai an Ahohite, and of his division Mikloth also *was* the leader; in his division *were* twenty-four thousand. ⁵The third captain of the army for the third month *was* Benaiah, the son of Jehoiada the priest, who was chief; in his division *were* twenty-four thousand. ⁶This was the Benaiah *who was* mighty *among* the thirty, and was over the thirty; in his division *was* Ammizabad his son. ⁷The

24 וּשְׁבָאֵל בֶּן־גֵּרְשׁוֹם בֶּן־מֹשֶׁה נָגִיד עַל־הָאֹצָרוֹת:
25 וְאֶחָיו לֶאֱלִיעֶזֶר רְחַבְיָהוּ בְנוֹ וִישַׁעְיָהוּ בְנוֹ וְיֹרָם
בְּנוֹ וְזִכְרִי בְנוֹ וּשְׁלֹמוֹתᴾ בְּנוֹ: 26 הוּא שְׁלֹמוֹת
וְאֶחָיו עַל כָּל־אֹצְרוֹת הַקֳּדָשִׁים אֲשֶׁר הִקְדִּישׁ דָּוִיד
הַמֶּלֶךְ וְרָאשֵׁי הָאָבוֹת לְשָׂרֵי־הָאֲלָפִים וְהַמֵּאוֹת
וְשָׂרֵי הַצָּבָא: 27 מִן־הַמִּלְחָמוֹת וּמִן־הַשָּׁלָל הִקְדִּישׁוּ
לְחַזֵּק לְבֵית יְהוָה: 28 וְכֹל הַהִקְדִּישׁ שְׁמוּאֵל הָרֹאֶה
וְשָׁאוּל בֶּן־קִישׁ וְאַבְנֵר בֶּן־נֵר וְיוֹאָב בֶּן־צְרוּיָה כֹּל
הַמַּקְדִּישׁ עַל יַד־שְׁלֹמִית וְאֶחָיו: פ
29 לַיִּצְהָרִי כְּנַנְיָהוּ וּבָנָיו לַמְּלָאכָה הַחִיצוֹנָה עַל־
יִשְׂרָאֵל לְשֹׁטְרִים וּלְשֹׁפְטִים: 30 לַחֶבְרוֹנִי חֲשַׁבְיָהוּ
וְאֶחָיו בְּנֵי־חַיִל אֶלֶף וּשְׁבַע־מֵאוֹת עַל פְּקֻדַּת
יִשְׂרָאֵל מֵעֵבֶר לַיַּרְדֵּן מַעְרָבָה לְכֹל מְלֶאכֶת יְהוָה
וְלַעֲבֹדַת הַמֶּלֶךְ: 31 לַחֶבְרוֹנִי יְרִיָּה הָרֹאשׁ לַחֶבְרוֹנִי
לְתֹלְדֹתָיו לְאָבוֹת בִּשְׁנַת הָאַרְבָּעִים לְמַלְכוּת דָּוִיד
נִדְרָשׁוּ וַיִּמָּצֵא בָהֶם גִּבּוֹרֵי חַיִל בְּיַעְזֵיר גִּלְעָד:
32 וְאֶחָיו בְּנֵי־חַיִל אַלְפַּיִם וּשְׁבַע מֵאוֹת רָאשֵׁי
הָאָבוֹת וַיַּפְקִידֵם דָּוִיד הַמֶּלֶךְ עַל־הָראוּבֵנִי וְהַגָּדִי
וַחֲצִי שֵׁבֶט הַמְנַשִּׁי לְכָל־דְּבַר הָאֱלֹהִים וּדְבַר
הַמֶּלֶךְ: פ

כז וּבְנֵי יִשְׂרָאֵל ׀ לְמִסְפָּרָם רָאשֵׁי הָאָבוֹת וְשָׂרֵי
הָאֲלָפִים ׀ וְהַמֵּאוֹת וְשֹׁטְרֵיהֶם הַמְשָׁרְתִים אֶת־
הַמֶּלֶךְ לְכֹל ׀ דְּבַר הַמַּחְלְקוֹת הַבָּאָה וְהַיֹּצֵאת
חֹדֶשׁ בְּחֹדֶשׁ לְכֹל חָדְשֵׁי הַשָּׁנָה הַמַּחֲלֹקֶת הָאַחַת
עֶשְׂרִים וְאַרְבָּעָה אָלֶף: ס 2 עַל הַמַּחֲלֹקֶת
הָרִאשׁוֹנָה לַחֹדֶשׁ הָרִאשׁוֹן יָשָׁבְעָם בֶּן־זַבְדִּיאֵל
וְעַל מַחֲלֻקְתּוֹ עֶשְׂרִים וְאַרְבָּעָה אָלֶף: 3 מִן־בְּנֵי־
פֶרֶץ הָרֹאשׁ לְכָל־שָׂרֵי הַצְּבָאוֹת לַחֹדֶשׁ הָרִאשׁוֹן:
4 וְעַל מַחֲלֹקֶת ׀ הַחֹדֶשׁ הַשֵּׁנִי דּוֹדַי הָאֲחוֹחִי
וּמַחֲלֻקְתּוֹ וּמִקְלוֹת הַנָּגִיד וְעַל מַחֲלֻקְתּוֹ עֶשְׂרִים
וְאַרְבָּעָה אָלֶף: ס 5 שַׂר הַצָּבָא הַשְּׁלִישִׁי לַחֹדֶשׁ
הַשְּׁלִישִׁי בְּנָיָהוּ בֶן־יְהוֹיָדָע הַכֹּהֵן רֹאשׁ וְעַל
מַחֲלֻקְתּוֹ עֶשְׂרִים וְאַרְבָּעָה אָלֶף: 6 הוּא בְנָיָהוּ
גִּבּוֹר הַשְּׁלֹשִׁים וְעַל־הַשְּׁלֹשִׁים וּמַחֲלֻקְתּוֹ עֲמִיזָבָד
בְּנוֹ: ס 7 הָרְבִיעִי לַחֹדֶשׁ הָרְבִיעִי עֲשָׂה־אֵל

כז 25 וּשְׁלֹמִית

fourth *captain* for the fourth month *was* Asahel the brother of Joab, and Zebadiah his son after him; in his division *were* twenty-four thousand. ⁸ The fifth *captain* for the fifth month *was* Shamhuth the Izrahite; in his division were twenty-four thousand. ⁹ The sixth *captain* for the sixth month *was* Ira the son of Ikkesh the Tekoite; in his division *were* twenty-four thousand. ¹⁰ The seventh *captain* for the seventh month *was* Helez the Pelonite, of the children of Ephraim; in his division *were* twenty-four thousand. ¹¹ The eighth *captain* for the eighth month *was* Sibbechai the Hushathite, of the Zarhites; in his division *were* twenty-four thousand. ¹² The ninth *captain* for the ninth month *was* Abiezer the Anathothite, of the Benjamites; in his division *were* twenty-four thousand. ¹³ The tenth *captain* for the tenth month *was* Maharai the Netophathite, of the Zarhites; in his division *were* twenty-four thousand. ¹⁴ The eleventh *captain* for the eleventh month *was* Benaiah the Pirathonite, of the children of Ephraim; in his division *were* twenty-four thousand. ¹⁵ The twelfth *captain* for the twelfth month *was* Heldai the Netophathite, of Othniel; in his division *were* twenty-four thousand.

¹⁶ Furthermore, over the tribes of Israel: the officer over the Reubenites *was* Eliezer the son of Zichri; over the Simeonites, Shephatiah the son of Maachah; ¹⁷ over the Levites, Hashabiah the son of Kemuel; over the Aaronites, Zadok; ¹⁸ over Judah, Elihu, *one* of David's brothers; over Issachar, Omri the son of Michael; ¹⁹ over Zebulun, Ishmaiah the son of Obadiah; *over* Naphtali, Jerimoth the son of Azriel; ²⁰ over the children of Ephraim, Hoshea the son of Azaziah; *over* the half-tribe of Manasseh, Joel the son of Pedaiah; ²¹ over the half-*tribe* of Manasseh in Gilead, Iddo the son of Zechariah; *over* Benjamin, Jaasiel the son of Abner; ²² over Dan, Azarel the son of Jeroham. These *were* the leaders of the tribes of Israel.

²³ But David did not take the number of those twenty years old and under, because the LORD had said He would multiply Israel like the stars of the heavens. ²⁴ Joab the son of Zeruiah began a census, but he did not finish, for wrath came upon Israel because of this census; nor was the number recorded in the account of the chronicles of King David.

²⁵ And Azmaveth the son of Adiel *was* over the king's treasuries; and Jehonathan the son of Uzziah was over the storehouses in the field, in the cities, in the villages, and in the fortresses. ²⁶ Ezri the son of Chelub was over those who did the work of the field for tilling the ground. ²⁷ And Shimei the Ramathite *was* over the vineyards, and Zabdi the Shiphmite

אֲחִי יוֹאָב וּזְבַדְיָה בְנוֹ אַחֲרָיו וְעַל מַחֲלֻקְתּוֹ עֶשְׂרִים וְאַרְבָּעָה אָלֶף: ⁸ הַחֲמִישִׁי לַחֹדֶשׁ הַחֲמִישִׁי הַשַּׂר שַׁמְהוּת הַיִּזְרָח וְעַל מַחֲלֻקְתּוֹ עֶשְׂרִים וְאַרְבָּעָה אָלֶף: ס ⁹ הַשִּׁשִּׁי לַחֹדֶשׁ הַשִּׁשִּׁי עִירָא בֶן־עִקֵּשׁ הַתְּקוֹעִי וְעַל מַחֲלֻקְתּוֹ עֶשְׂרִים וְאַרְבָּעָה אָלֶף: ס ¹⁰ הַשְּׁבִיעִי לַחֹדֶשׁ הַשְּׁבִיעִי חֶלֶץ הַפְּלוֹנִי מִן־בְּנֵי אֶפְרָיִם וְעַל מַחֲלֻקְתּוֹ עֶשְׂרִים וְאַרְבָּעָה אָלֶף: ס ¹¹ הַשְּׁמִינִי לַחֹדֶשׁ הַשְּׁמִינִי סִבְּכַי הַחֻשָׁתִי לַזַּרְחִי וְעַל מַחֲלֻקְתּוֹ עֶשְׂרִים וְאַרְבָּעָה אָלֶף: ס ¹² הַתְּשִׁיעִי לַחֹדֶשׁ הַתְּשִׁיעִי אֲבִיעֶזֶר הָעַנְּתֹתִי לַבֶּנְיְמִינִי וְעַל מַחֲלֻקְתּוֹ עֶשְׂרִים וְאַרְבָּעָה אָלֶף: ס ¹³ הָעֲשִׂירִי לַחֹדֶשׁ הָעֲשִׂירִי מַהְרַי הַנְּטוֹפָתִי לַזַּרְחִי וְעַל מַחֲלֻקְתּוֹ עֶשְׂרִים וְאַרְבָּעָה אָלֶף: ס ¹⁴ עַשְׁתֵּי־עָשָׂר לְעַשְׁתֵּי־עָשָׂר הַחֹדֶשׁ בְּנָיָה הַפִּרְעָתוֹנִי מִן־בְּנֵי אֶפְרָיִם וְעַל מַחֲלֻקְתּוֹ עֶשְׂרִים וְאַרְבָּעָה אָלֶף: ס ¹⁵ הַשְּׁנֵים עָשָׂר לִשְׁנֵים עָשָׂר הַחֹדֶשׁ חֶלְדַּי הַנְּטוֹפָתִי לְעָתְנִיאֵל וְעַל מַחֲלֻקְתּוֹ עֶשְׂרִים וְאַרְבָּעָה אָלֶף: פ ¹⁶ וְעַל שִׁבְטֵי יִשְׂרָאֵל לָראוּבֵנִי נָגִיד אֱלִיעֶזֶר בֶּן־זִכְרִי לַשִּׁמְעוֹנִי שְׁפַטְיָהוּ בֶּן־מַעֲכָה: ¹⁷ לְלֵוִי חֲשַׁבְיָה בֶן־קְמוּאֵל לְאַהֲרֹן צָדוֹק: ¹⁸ לִיהוּדָה אֱלִיהוּ מֵאֲחֵי דָוִיד לְיִשָׂשכָר עָמְרִי בֶּן־מִיכָאֵל: ¹⁹ לִזְבוּלֻן יִשְׁמַעְיָהוּ בֶן־עֹבַדְיָהוּ לְנַפְתָּלִי יְרִימוֹת בֶּן־עַזְרִיאֵל: ²⁰ לִבְנֵי אֶפְרַיִם הוֹשֵׁעַ בֶּן־עֲזַזְיָהוּ לַחֲצִי שֵׁבֶט מְנַשֶּׁה יוֹאֵל בֶּן־פְּדָיָהוּ: ²¹ לַחֲצִי הַמְנַשֶּׁה גִּלְעָדָה יִדּוֹ בֶּן־זְכַרְיָהוּ לְבִנְיָמִן יַעֲשִׂיאֵל בֶּן־אַבְנֵר: ²² לְדָן עֲזַרְאֵל בֶּן־יְרֹחָם אֵלֶּה שָׂרֵי שִׁבְטֵי יִשְׂרָאֵל: ²³ וְלֹא־נָשָׂא דָוִיד מִסְפָּרָם לְמִבֶּן עֶשְׂרִים שָׁנָה וּלְמָטָּה כִּי אָמַר יְהֹוָה לְהַרְבּוֹת אֶת־יִשְׂרָאֵל כְּכוֹכְבֵי הַשָּׁמָיִם: ²⁴ יוֹאָב בֶּן־צְרוּיָה הֵחֵל לִמְנוֹת וְלֹא כִלָּה וַיְהִי בָזֹאת קֶצֶף עַל־יִשְׂרָאֵל וְלֹא עָלָה הַמִּסְפָּר בְּמִסְפַּר דִּבְרֵי־הַיָּמִים לַמֶּלֶךְ דָּוִיד: ס ²⁵ וְעַל אֹצְרוֹת הַמֶּלֶךְ עַזְמָוֶת בֶּן־עֲדִיאֵל וְעַל הָאֹצָרוֹת בַּשָּׂדֶה בֶּעָרִים וּבַכְּפָרִים וּבַמִּגְדָּלוֹת יְהוֹנָתָן בֶּן־עֻזִּיָּהוּ: ²⁶ וְעַל עֹשֵׂי מְלֶאכֶת הַשָּׂדֶה לַעֲבֹדַת הָאֲדָמָה עֶזְרִי בֶּן־כְּלוּב: ²⁷ וְעַל־הַכְּרָמִים שִׁמְעִי

was over the produce of the vineyards for the supply of wine. 28 Baal-Hanan the Gederite was over the olive trees and the sycamore trees that *were* in the lowlands, and Joash *was* over the store of oil. 29 And Shitrai the Sharonite *was* over the herds that fed in Sharon, and Shaphat the son of Adlai was over the herds *that were* in the valleys. 30 Obil the Ishmaelite *was* over the camels, Jehdeiah the Meronothite *was* over the donkeys, 31 and Jaziz the Hagrite *was* over the flocks. All these *were* the officials over King David's property.

32 Also Jehonathan, David's uncle, *was* a counselor, a wise man, and a scribe; and Jehiel the son of Hachmoni *was* with the king's sons. 33 Ahithophel *was* the king's counselor, and Hushai the Archite *was* the king's companion. 34 After Ahithophel *was* Jehoiada the son of Benaiah, then Abiathar. And the general of the king's army *was* Joab.

28 Now David assembled at Jerusalem all the leaders of Israel: the officers of the tribes and the captains of the divisions who served the king, the captains over thousands and captains over hundreds, and the stewards over all the substance and possessions of the king and his sons, with the officials, the valiant men, and all the mighty men of valor.

2 Then King David rose to his feet and said, "Hear me, my brethren and my people: I *had* it in my heart to build a house of rest for the ark of the covenant of the LORD, and for the footstool of our God, and had made preparations to build it. 3 But God said to me, 'You shall not build a house for My name, because you *have been* a man of war and have shed blood.' 4 However the LORD God of Israel chose me above all the house of my father to be king over Israel forever, for He has chosen Judah *to be* the ruler. And of the house of Judah, the house of my father, and among the sons of my father, He was pleased with me to make *me* king over all Israel. 5 And of all my sons (for the LORD has given me many sons) He has chosen my son Solomon to sit on the throne of the kingdom of the LORD over Israel. 6 Now He said to me, 'It is your son Solomon *who* shall build My house and My courts; for I have chosen him *to be* My son, and I will be his Father. 7 Moreover I will establish his kingdom forever, if he is steadfast to observe My commandments and My judgments, as it is this day.' 8 Now therefore, in the sight of all Israel, the assembly of the LORD, and in the hearing of our God, be careful to seek out all the commandments

הָרָמָתִ֑י וְעַ֤ל שֶׁבַּכְּרָמִים֙ לְאֹצְר֣וֹת הַיַּ֔יִן זַבְדִּ֖י הַשִּׁפְמִֽי׃ 28 וְעַל־הַזֵּיתִ֣ים וְהַשִּׁקְמִ֗ים אֲשֶׁר֙ בַּשְּׁפֵלָ֔ה בַּ֥עַל חָנָ֖ן הַגְּדֵרִ֑י וְעַל־אֹצְר֥וֹת הַשֶּׁ֖מֶן יוֹעָֽשׁ׃ 29 וְעַל־הַבָּקָ֞ר הָרֹעִ֣ים בַּשָּׁר֗וֹן שִׁטְרַ֣י הַשָּׁרוֹנִ֔י וְעַל־הַבָּקָר֙ בָּעֲמָקִ֔ים שָׁפָ֖ט בֶּן־עַדְלָֽי׃ 30 וְעַל־הַגְּמַלִּ֔ים אוֹבִ֖יל הַיִּשְׁמְעֵלִ֑י וְעַל־הָאֲתֹנ֖וֹת יֶחְדְּיָ֥הוּ הַמֵּרֹנֹתִֽי׃ 31 וְעַל־הַצֹּ֖אן יָזִ֣יז הַֽהַגְרִ֑י כָּל־אֵ֙לֶּה֙ שָׂרֵ֣י הָרְכ֔וּשׁ אֲשֶׁ֖ר לַמֶּ֥לֶךְ דָּוִֽיד׃ 32 וִיהוֹנָתָ֤ן דּוֹד־דָּוִיד֙ יוֹעֵ֔ץ אִישׁ־מֵבִ֥ין וְסוֹפֵ֖ר ה֑וּא וִֽיחִיאֵ֥ל בֶּן־חַכְמוֹנִ֖י עִם־בְּנֵ֥י הַמֶּֽלֶךְ׃ 33 וַאֲחִיתֹ֥פֶל יוֹעֵ֖ץ לַמֶּ֑לֶךְ וְחוּשַׁ֥י הָאַרְכִּ֖י רֵ֥עַ הַמֶּֽלֶךְ׃ 34 וְאַחֲרֵ֣י אֲחִיתֹ֗פֶל יְהוֹיָדָ֤ע בֶּן־בְּנָיָ֙הוּ֙ וְאֶבְיָתָ֔ר וְשַׂר־צָבָ֥א לַמֶּ֖לֶךְ יוֹאָֽב׃

כח וַיַּקְהֵ֣ל דָּוִ֗יד אֶת־כָּל־שָׂרֵ֣י יִשְׂרָאֵל֮ שָׂרֵ֣י הַשְּׁבָטִ֣ים וְשָׂרֵ֣י הַמַּחְלְק֣וֹת הַמְשָׁרְתִ֣ים אֶת־הַמֶּ֡לֶךְ וְשָׂרֵ֣י הָאֲלָפִ֣ים וְשָׂרֵ֣י הַמֵּא֡וֹת וְשָׂרֵ֣י כָל־רְכוּשׁ־וּמִקְנֶ֣ה ׀ לַמֶּ֣לֶךְ וּלְבָנָ֗יו עִם־הַסָּרִיסִ֣ים וְהַגִּבּוֹרִ֑ים וּֽלְכָל־גִּבּ֥וֹר חָ֖יִל אֶל־יְרוּשָׁלָֽ͏ִם׃ 2 וַיָּ֜קָם דָּוִ֣יד הַמֶּ֗לֶךְ עַל־רַגְלָיו֮ וַיֹּ֣אמֶר שְׁמָע֣וּנִי אַחַ֣י וְעַמִּ֒י אֲנִ֣י עִם־לְבָבִ֗י לִבְנ֜וֹת בֵּ֣ית מְנוּחָ֗ה לַאֲרוֹן֙ בְּרִית־יְהֹוָ֔ה וְלַהֲדֹ֖ם רַגְלֵ֣י אֱלֹהֵ֑ינוּ וַהֲכִינ֖וֹתִי לִבְנֽוֹת׃ 3 וְהָאֱלֹהִים֙ אָ֣מַר לִ֔י לֹא־תִבְנֶ֥ה בַ֖יִת לִשְׁמִ֑י כִּ֣י אִ֧ישׁ מִלְחָמ֛וֹת אַ֖תָּה וְדָמִ֥ים שָׁפָֽכְתָּ׃ 4 וַיִּבְחַ֡ר יְהֹוָ֣ה אֱלֹהֵ֣י יִשְׂרָאֵל֮ בִּי֒ מִכֹּל֙ בֵּית־אָבִ֔י לִהְי֥וֹת לְמֶ֛לֶךְ עַל־יִשְׂרָאֵ֖ל לְעוֹלָ֑ם כִּ֤י בִֽיהוּדָה֙ בָּחַ֣ר לְנָגִ֔יד וּבְבֵ֥ית יְהוּדָ֖ה בֵּ֣ית אָבִ֑י וּבִבְנֵ֣י אָבִ֔י בִּ֣י רָצָ֔ה לְהַמְלִ֖יךְ עַל־כָּל־יִשְׂרָאֵֽל׃ 5 וּמִכָּל־בָּנַ֕י כִּ֚י רַבִּ֣ים בָּנִ֔ים נָ֥תַן לִ֖י יְהֹוָ֑ה וַיִּבְחַר֙ בִּשְׁלֹמֹ֣ה בְנִ֔י לָשֶׁ֗בֶת עַל־כִּסֵּ֛א מַלְכ֥וּת יְהֹוָ֖ה עַל־יִשְׂרָאֵֽל׃ 6 וַיֹּ֣אמֶר לִ֔י שְׁלֹמֹ֣ה בִנְךָ֔ הֽוּא־יִבְנֶ֥ה בֵיתִ֖י וַחֲצֵרוֹתָ֑י כִּֽי־בָחַ֧רְתִּי ב֣וֹ לִ֗י לְבֵ֔ן וַאֲנִ֖י אֶהְיֶה־לּ֥וֹ לְאָֽב׃ 7 וַהֲכִינוֹתִ֥י אֶת־מַלְכוּת֖וֹ עַד־לְעוֹלָ֑ם אִם־יֶ֣חֱזַ֔ק לַעֲשׂ֛וֹת מִצְוֺתַ֥י וּמִשְׁפָּטַ֖י כַּיּ֥וֹם הַזֶּֽה׃ 8 וְעַתָּ֡ה לְעֵינֵ֣י כָל־יִשְׂרָאֵ֣ל קְהַל־יְהֹוָה֩ וּבְאׇזְנֵ֨י אֱלֹהֵ֜ינוּ שִׁמְר֣וּ וְדִרְשׁ֗וּ כָּל־מִצְוֺ֛ת יְהֹוָ֥ה אֱלֹהֵיכֶ֖ם לְמַ֙עַן֙ תִּֽירְשׁוּ֙ אֶת־הָאָ֣רֶץ הַטּוֹבָ֔ה וְהִנְחַלְתֶּ֛ם לִבְנֵיכֶ֥ם אַחֲרֵיכֶ֖ם עַד־עוֹלָֽם׃ פ

of the LORD your God, that you may possess this good land, and leave *it* as an inheritance for your children after you forever.

9 "As for you, my son Solomon, know the God of your father, and serve Him with a loyal heart and with a willing mind; for the LORD searches all hearts and understands all the intent of the thoughts. If you seek Him, He will be found by you; but if you forsake Him, He will cast you off forever. 10 Consider now, for the LORD has chosen you to build a house for the sanctuary; be strong, and do it."

11 Then David gave his son Solomon the plans for the vestibule, its houses, its treasuries, its upper chambers, its inner chambers, and the place of the mercy seat; 12 and the plans for all that he had by the Spirit, of the courts of the house of the LORD, of all the chambers all around, of the treasuries of the house of God, and of the treasuries for the dedicated things; 13 also for the division of the priests and the Levites, for all the work of the service of the house of the LORD, and for all the articles of service in the house of the LORD. 14 *He* gave gold by weight for *things* of gold, for all articles used in every kind of service; also *silver* for all articles of silver by weight, for all articles used in every kind of service; 15 the weight for the lampstands of gold, and their lamps of gold, by weight for each lampstand and its lamps; for the lampstands of silver by weight, for the lampstand and its lamps, according to the use of each lampstand. 16 And by weight *he gave* gold for the tables of the showbread, for each table, and silver for the tables of silver; 17 also pure gold for the forks, the basins, the pitchers of pure gold, and the golden bowls—*he gave* gold by weight for every bowl; and for the silver bowls, *silver* by weight for every bowl; 18 and refined gold by weight for the altar of incense, and for the construction of the chariot, that is, the gold cherubim that spread *their wings* and overshadowed the ark of the covenant of the LORD. 19 "All *this*," said David, "the LORD made me understand in writing, by *His* hand upon me, all the works of these plans."

20 And David said to his son Solomon, "Be strong and of good courage, and do *it;* do not fear nor be dismayed, for the LORD God—my God— *will be* with you. He will not leave you nor forsake you, until you have finished all the work for the service of the house of the LORD. 21 *Here are* the divisions of the priests and the Levites for all the service of the house of God; and every willing craftsman *will be* with you for all manner of

9 וְאַתָּ֣ה שְׁלֹמֹֽה־בְנִ֡י דַּע֩ אֶת־אֱלֹהֵ֨י אָבִ֜יךָ וְעׇבְדֵ֗הוּ בְּלֵ֤ב שָׁלֵם֙ וּבְנֶ֣פֶשׁ חֲפֵצָ֔ה כִּ֤י כׇל־לְבָבוֹת֙ דּוֹרֵ֣שׁ יְהֹוָ֔ה וְכׇל־יֵ֥צֶר מַחֲשָׁב֖וֹת מֵבִ֑ין אִֽם־תִּדְרְשֶׁ֙נּוּ֙ יִמָּ֣צֵא לָ֔ךְ וְאִם־תַּֽעַזְבֶ֖נּוּ יַזְנִיחֲךָ֥ לָעַֽד׃ 10 רְאֵ֣ה ׀ עַתָּ֗ה כִּֽי־יְהֹוָ֞ה בָּ֣חַר בְּךָ֗ לִבְנֽוֹת־בַּ֛יִת לַמִּקְדָּ֖שׁ חֲזַ֥ק וַעֲשֵֽׂה׃ פ

11 וַיִּתֵּ֣ן דָּוִ֣יד לִשְׁלֹמֹ֣ה בְנ֡וֹ אֶת־תַּבְנִ֣ית הָאוּלָם֩ וְֽאֶת־בָּ֨תָּ֜יו וְגׇנְזַכָּ֧יו וַעֲלִֽיֹּתָ֛יו וַחֲדָרָ֥יו הַפְּנִימִ֖ים וּבֵ֥ית הַכַּפֹּֽרֶת׃ 12 וְתַבְנִ֗ית כֹּל֩ אֲשֶׁ֨ר הָיָ֤ה בָר֙וּחַ֙ עִמּ֔וֹ לְחַצְר֧וֹת בֵּית־יְהֹוָ֛ה וּֽלְכׇל־הַלְּשָׁכ֖וֹת סָבִ֑יב לְאֹֽצְרוֹת֙ בֵּ֣ית הָֽאֱלֹהִ֔ים וּלְאֹצְר֖וֹת הַקֳּדָשִֽׁים׃ 13 וּֽלְמַחְלְק֖וֹת הַכֹּהֲנִ֣ים וְהַלְוִיִּ֑ם וּֽלְכׇל־מְלֶ֙אכֶת֙ עֲבוֹדַ֣ת בֵּית־יְהֹוָ֔ה וּֽלְכׇל־כְּלֵ֖י עֲבוֹדַ֥ת בֵּית־יְהֹוָֽה׃ 14 לַזָּהָ֤ב בַּמִּשְׁקָל֙ לַזָּהָ֔ב לְכׇל־כְּלֵ֖י עֲבוֹדָ֣ה וַעֲבוֹדָ֑ה לְכֹ֜ל כְּלֵ֤י הַכֶּ֙סֶף֙ בְּמִשְׁקָ֔ל לְכׇל־כְּלֵ֖י עֲבוֹדָ֥ה וַעֲבוֹדָֽה׃ 15 וּמִשְׁקָ֞ל לִמְנֹר֣וֹת הַזָּהָ֗ב וְנֵרֹֽתֵיהֶם֙ זָהָ֔ב בְּמִשְׁקַל־מְנוֹרָ֥ה וּמְנוֹרָ֖ה וְנֵרֹתֶ֑יהָ וְלִמְנֹר֨וֹת הַכֶּ֤סֶף בְּמִשְׁקָל֙ לִמְנוֹרָ֣ה וְנֵרֹתֶ֔יהָ כַּעֲבוֹדַ֖ת מְנוֹרָ֥ה וּמְנוֹרָֽה׃ 16 וְאֶת־הַזָּהָ֥ב מִשְׁקָל֙ לְשֻׁלְחֲנ֣וֹת הַֽמַּעֲרֶ֔כֶת לְשֻׁלְחַ֖ן וְשֻׁלְחָ֑ן וְכֶ֖סֶף לְשֻׁלְחֲנ֥וֹת הַכָּֽסֶף׃ 17 וְהַמִּזְלָג֧וֹת וְהַמִּזְרָק֛וֹת וְהַקְּשָׂוֺ֖ת זָהָ֣ב טָה֑וֹר וְלִכְפוֹרֵ֨י הַזָּהָ֤ב בְּמִשְׁקָל֙ לִכְפ֣וֹר וּכְפ֔וֹר וְלִכְפוֹרֵ֥י הַכֶּ֛סֶף בְּמִשְׁקָ֖ל לִכְפ֥וֹר וּכְפֽוֹר׃ 18 וּלְמִזְבַּ֧ח הַקְּטֹ֛רֶת זָהָ֥ב מְזֻקָּ֖ק בַּמִּשְׁקָ֑ל וּלְתַבְנִ֣ית הַמֶּרְכָּבָ֗ה הַכְּרֻבִ֤ים זָהָב֙ לְפֹ֣רְשִׂ֔ים וְסֹכְכִ֖ים עַל־אֲר֥וֹן בְּרִית־יְהֹוָֽה׃ 19 הַכֹּ֥ל בִּכְתָ֛ב מִיַּ֥ד יְהֹוָ֖ה עָלַ֣י הִשְׂכִּ֑יל כֹּ֖ל מַלְאֲכ֥וֹת הַתַּבְנִֽית׃ 20 וַיֹּ֨אמֶר דָּוִ֜יד לִשְׁלֹמֹ֣ה בְנ֗וֹ חֲזַ֤ק וֶאֱמַץ֙ וַעֲשֵׂ֔ה אַל־תִּירָ֖א וְאַל־תֵּחָ֑ת כִּי֩ יְהֹוָ֨ה אֱלֹהִ֤ים אֱלֹהַי֙ עִמָּ֔ךְ לֹ֤א יַרְפְּךָ֙ וְלֹ֣א יַֽעַזְבֶ֔ךָ עַד־לִכְל֕וֹת כׇּל־מְלֶ֖אכֶת עֲבוֹדַ֥ת בֵּית־יְהֹוָֽה׃ 21 וְהִנֵּ֗ה מַחְלְקוֹת֙ הַכֹּהֲנִ֣ים וְהַלְוִיִּ֔ם לְכׇל־עֲבוֹדַ֖ת בֵּ֣ית הָאֱלֹהִ֑ים וְעִמְּךָ֙ בְכׇל־מְלָאכָ֜ה לְכׇל־

workmanship, for every kind of service; also the leaders and all the people *will be* completely at your command."

29 Furthermore King David said to all the assembly: "My son Solomon, whom alone God has chosen, *is* young and inexperienced; and the work *is* great, because the temple *is* not for man but for the LORD God. ²Now for the house of my God I have prepared with all my might: gold for *things to be made of* gold, silver for *things of* silver, bronze for *things of* bronze, iron for *things of* iron, wood for *things of* wood, onyx stones, *stones* to be set, glistening stones of various colors, all kinds of precious stones, and marble slabs in abundance. ³Moreover, because I have set my affection on the house of my God, I have given to the house of my God, over and above all that I have prepared for the holy house, my own special treasure of gold and silver: ⁴three thousand talents of gold, of the gold of Ophir, and seven thousand talents of refined silver, to overlay the walls of the houses; ⁵the gold for *things of* gold and the silver for *things of* silver, and for all kinds of work *to be done* by the hands of craftsmen. Who *then* is willing to consecrate himself this day to the LORD?"

⁶Then the leaders of the fathers' *houses,* leaders of the tribes of Israel, the captains of thousands and of hundreds, with the officers over the king's work, offered willingly. ⁷They gave for the work of the house of God five thousand talents and ten thousand darics of gold, ten thousand talents of silver, eighteen thousand talents of bronze, and one hundred thousand talents of iron. ⁸And whoever had *precious* stones gave *them* to the treasury of the house of the LORD, into the hand of Jehiel the Gershonite. ⁹Then the people rejoiced, for they had offered willingly, because with a loyal heart they had offered willingly to the LORD; and King David also rejoiced greatly.

¹⁰Therefore David blessed the LORD before all the assembly; and David said:

"Blessed are You, LORD God of Israel, our Father, forever and ever.
¹¹ Yours, O LORD, *is* the greatness,
The power and the glory,
The victory and the majesty;
For all *that is* in heaven and in earth *is Yours;*
Yours *is* the kingdom, O LORD,
And You are exalted as head over all.
¹² Both riches and honor *come* from You,
And You reign over all.
In Your hand *is* power and might;
In Your hand *it is* to make great
And to give strength to all.

נָדִיב בְּחָכְמָה לְכָל־עֲבוֹדָה וְהַשָּׂרִים וְכָל־הָעָם לְכָל־דְּבָרֶיךָ: פ

כט וַיֹּאמֶר דָּוִיד הַמֶּלֶךְ לְכָל־הַקָּהָל שְׁלֹמֹה בְנִי אֶחָד בָּחַר־בּוֹ אֱלֹהִים נַעַר וָרָךְ וְהַמְּלָאכָה גְדוֹלָה כִּי לֹא לְאָדָם הַבִּירָה כִּי לַיהֹוָה אֱלֹהִים: ²וּכְכָל־כֹּחִי הֲכִינוֹתִי לְבֵית־אֱלֹהַי הַזָּהָב | לַזָּהָב וְהַכֶּסֶף לַכֶּסֶף וְהַנְּחֹשֶׁת לַנְּחֹשֶׁת הַבַּרְזֶל לַבַּרְזֶל וְהָעֵצִים לָעֵצִים אַבְנֵי־שֹׁהַם וּמִלּוּאִים אַבְנֵי־פוּךְ וְרִקְמָה וְכֹל אֶבֶן יְקָרָה וְאַבְנֵי־שַׁיִשׁ לָרֹב: ³וְעוֹד בִּרְצוֹתִי בְּבֵית אֱלֹהַי יֶשׁ־לִי סְגֻלָּה זָהָב וָכָסֶף נָתַתִּי לְבֵית־אֱלֹהַי לְמַעְלָה מִכָּל־הֲכִינוֹתִי לְבֵית הַקֹּדֶשׁ: ⁴שְׁלֹשֶׁת אֲלָפִים כִּכְּרֵי זָהָב מִזְּהַב אוֹפִיר וְשִׁבְעַת אֲלָפִים כִּכַּר־כֶּסֶף מְזֻקָּק לָטוּחַ קִירוֹת הַבָּתִּים: ⁵לַזָּהָב לַזָּהָב וְלַכֶּסֶף לַכֶּסֶף וּלְכָל־מְלָאכָה בְּיַד חָרָשִׁים וּמִי מִתְנַדֵּב לְמַלֹּאות יָדוֹ הַיּוֹם לַיהֹוָה: ⁶וַיִּתְנַדְּבוּ שָׂרֵי הָאָבוֹת וְשָׂרֵי | שִׁבְטֵי יִשְׂרָאֵל וְשָׂרֵי הָאֲלָפִים וְהַמֵּאוֹת וּלְשָׂרֵי מְלֶאכֶת הַמֶּלֶךְ: ⁷וַיִּתְּנוּ לַעֲבוֹדַת בֵּית־הָאֱלֹהִים זָהָב כִּכָּרִים חֲמֵשֶׁת־אֲלָפִים וַאֲדַרְכֹנִים רִבּוֹ וְכֶסֶף כִּכָּרִים עֲשֶׂרֶת אֲלָפִים וּנְחֹשֶׁת רִבּוֹ וּשְׁמוֹנַת אֲלָפִים כִּכָּרִים וּבַרְזֶל מֵאָה־אֶלֶף כִּכָּרִים: ⁸וְהַנִּמְצָא אִתּוֹ אֲבָנִים נָתְנוּ לְאוֹצַר בֵּית־יְהֹוָה עַל יַד־יְחִיאֵל הַגֵּרְשֻׁנִּי: ⁹וַיִּשְׂמְחוּ הָעָם עַל־הִתְנַדְּבָם כִּי בְּלֵב שָׁלֵם הִתְנַדְּבוּ לַיהֹוָה וְגַם דָּוִיד הַמֶּלֶךְ שָׂמַח שִׂמְחָה גְדוֹלָה: פ

¹⁰וַיְבָרֶךְ דָּוִיד אֶת־יְהֹוָה לְעֵינֵי כָּל־הַקָּהָל וַיֹּאמֶר דָּוִיד בָּרוּךְ אַתָּה יְהֹוָה אֱלֹהֵי יִשְׂרָאֵל אָבִינוּ מֵעוֹלָם וְעַד־עוֹלָם: ¹¹לְךָ יְהֹוָה הַגְּדֻלָּה וְהַגְּבוּרָה וְהַתִּפְאֶרֶת וְהַנֵּצַח וְהַהוֹד כִּי־כֹל בַּשָּׁמַיִם וּבָאָרֶץ לְךָ יְהֹוָה הַמַּמְלָכָה וְהַמִּתְנַשֵּׂא לְכֹל | לְרֹאשׁ: ¹²וְהָעֹשֶׁר וְהַכָּבוֹד מִלְּפָנֶיךָ וְאַתָּה מוֹשֵׁל בַּכֹּל וּבְיָדְךָ כֹּחַ וּגְבוּרָה וּבְיָדְךָ לְגַדֵּל וּלְחַזֵּק לַכֹּל:

13 "Now therefore, our God,
We thank You
And praise Your glorious name.
14 But who *am* I, and who *are* my people,
That we should be able to offer so willingly as
this?
For all things *come* from You,
And of Your own we have given You.
15 For we *are* aliens and pilgrims before You,
As *were* all our fathers;
Our days on earth *are* as a shadow,
And without hope.

16 "O LORD our God, all this abundance that we
have prepared to build You a house for Your holy
name is from Your hand, and *is* all Your own. 17 I
know also, my God, that You test the heart and
have pleasure in uprightness. As for me, in the
uprightness of my heart I have willingly offered all
these *things;* and now with joy I have seen Your
people, who are present here to offer willingly to
You. 18 O LORD God of Abraham, Isaac, and Israel,
our fathers, keep this forever in the intent of the
thoughts of the heart of Your people, and fix their
heart toward You. 19 And give my son Solomon a
loyal heart to keep Your commandments and Your
testimonies and Your statutes, to do all *these things,*
and to build the temple for which I have made
provision."

20 Then David said to all the assembly, "Now
bless the LORD your God." So all the assembly
blessed the LORD God of their fathers, and bowed
their heads and prostrated themselves before the
LORD and the king.

21 And they made sacrifices to the LORD and
offered burnt offerings to the LORD on the next day:
a thousand bulls, a thousand rams, a thousand
lambs, with their drink offerings, and sacrifices in
abundance for all Israel. 22 So they ate and drank
before the LORD with great gladness on that day.
And they made Solomon the son of David king the
second time, and anointed *him* before the LORD *to
be* the leader, and Zadok *to be* priest. 23 Then
Solomon sat on the throne of the LORD as king
instead of David his father, and prospered; and all
Israel obeyed him. 24 All the leaders and the mighty
men, and also all the sons of King David, submitted
themselves to King Solomon. 25 So the LORD
exalted Solomon exceedingly in the sight of all
Israel, and bestowed on him *such* royal majesty as
had not been on any king before him in Israel.

26 Thus David the son of Jesse reigned over all
Israel. 27 And the period that he reigned over Israel
was forty years; seven years he reigned in Hebron,
and thirty-three *years* he reigned in Jerusalem. 28 So
he died in a good old age, full of days and riches

13 וְעַתָּה אֱלֹהֵינוּ מוֹדִים אֲנַחְנוּ לָךְ וּמְהַלְלִים לְשֵׁם
תִּפְאַרְתֶּךָ: 14 וְכִי מִי אֲנִי וּמִי עַמִּי כִּי־נַעְצֹר כֹּחַ
לְהִתְנַדֵּב כָּזֹאת כִּי־מִמְּךָ הַכֹּל וּמִיָּדְךָ נָתַנּוּ לָךְ:
15 כִּי־גֵרִים אֲנַחְנוּ לְפָנֶיךָ וְתוֹשָׁבִים כְּכָל־אֲבֹתֵינוּ
כַּצֵּל ׀ יָמֵינוּ עַל־הָאָרֶץ וְאֵין מִקְוֶה: 16 יְהוָה
אֱלֹהֵינוּ כֹל הֶהָמוֹן הַזֶּה אֲשֶׁר הֲכִינֹנוּ לִבְנוֹת־
לְךָ בַיִת לְשֵׁם קָדְשֶׁךָ מִיָּדְךָ הִיאP וּלְךָ הַכֹּל:
17 וְיָדַעְתִּי אֱלֹהַי כִּי אַתָּה בֹּחֵן לֵבָב וּמֵישָׁרִים
תִּרְצֶה אֲנִי בְּיֹשֶׁר לְבָבִי הִתְנַדַּבְתִּי כָל־אֵלֶּה וְעַתָּה
עַמְּךָ הַנִּמְצְאוּ־פֹה רָאִיתִי בְשִׂמְחָה לְהִתְנַדֶּב־לָךְ:
18 יְהוָה אֱלֹהֵי אַבְרָהָם יִצְחָק וְיִשְׂרָאֵל אֲבֹתֵינוּ
שָׁמְרָה־זֹּאת לְעוֹלָם לְיֵצֶר מַחְשְׁבוֹת לְבַב עַמֶּךָ
וְהָכֵן לְבָבָם אֵלֶיךָ: 19 וְלִשְׁלֹמֹה בְנִי תֵּן לֵבָב שָׁלֵם
לִשְׁמוֹר מִצְוֹתֶיךָ עֵדְוֹתֶיךָ וְחֻקֶּיךָ וְלַעֲשׂוֹת הַכֹּל
וְלִבְנוֹת הַבִּירָה אֲשֶׁר־הֲכִינוֹתִי: ף
20 וַיֹּאמֶר דָּוִיד לְכָל־הַקָּהָל בָּרְכוּ־נָא אֶת־יְהוָה
אֱלֹהֵיכֶם וַיְבָרְכוּ כָל־הַקָּהָל לַיהוָה אֱלֹהֵי אֲבֹתֵיהֶם
וַיִּקְּדוּ וַיִּשְׁתַּחֲווּ לַיהוָה וְלַמֶּלֶךְ: 21 וַיִּזְבְּחוּ לַיהוָה ׀
זְבָחִים וַיַּעֲלוּ עֹלוֹת לַיהוָה לְמָחֳרַת הַיּוֹם הַהוּא
פָּרִים אֶלֶף אֵילִים אֶלֶף כְּבָשִׂים אֶלֶף וְנִסְכֵּיהֶם
וּזְבָחִים לָרֹב לְכָל־יִשְׂרָאֵל: 22 וַיֹּאכְלוּ וַיִּשְׁתּוּ לִפְנֵי
יְהוָה בַּיּוֹם הַהוּא בְּשִׂמְחָה גְדוֹלָה וַיַּמְלִיכוּ שֵׁנִית
לִשְׁלֹמֹה בֶן־דָּוִיד וַיִּמְשְׁחוּ לַיהוָה לְנָגִיד וּלְצָדוֹק
לְכֹהֵן: 23 וַיֵּשֶׁב שְׁלֹמֹה עַל־כִּסֵּא יְהוָה ׀ לְמֶלֶךְ
תַּחַת־דָּוִיד אָבִיו וַיַּצְלַח וַיִּשְׁמְעוּ אֵלָיו כָּל־יִשְׂרָאֵל:
24 וְכָל־הַשָּׂרִים וְהַגִּבֹּרִים וְגַם כָּל־בְּנֵי הַמֶּלֶךְ דָּוִיד
נָתְנוּ יָד תַּחַת שְׁלֹמֹה הַמֶּלֶךְ: 25 וַיְגַדֵּל יְהוָה אֶת־
שְׁלֹמֹה לְמַעְלָה לְעֵינֵי כָּל־יִשְׂרָאֵל וַיִּתֵּן עָלָיו הוֹד
מַלְכוּת אֲשֶׁר לֹא־הָיָה עַל־כָּל־מֶלֶךְ לְפָנָיו עַל־
יִשְׂרָאֵל: ף
26 וְדָוִיד בֶּן־יִשָׁי מָלַךְ עַל־כָּל־יִשְׂרָאֵל: 27 וְהַיָּמִים
אֲשֶׁר מָלַךְ עַל־יִשְׂרָאֵל אַרְבָּעִים שָׁנָה בְּחֶבְרוֹן
מָלַךְ שֶׁבַע שָׁנִים וּבִירוּשָׁלַ͏ִם מָלַךְ שְׁלֹשִׁים וְשָׁלוֹשׁ:
28 וַיָּמָת בְּשֵׂיבָה טוֹבָה שְׂבַע יָמִים עֹשֶׁר וְכָבוֹד
וַיִּמְלֹךְ שְׁלֹמֹה בְנוֹ תַּחְתָּיו: 29 וְדִבְרֵי דָּוִיד הַמֶּלֶךְ

and honor; and Solomon his son reigned in his place. 29 Now the acts of King David, first and last, indeed they *are* written in the book of Samuel the seer, in the book of Nathan the prophet, and in the book of Gad the seer, 30 with all his reign and his might, and the events that happened to him, to Israel, and to all the kingdoms of the lands.

הָרִאשֹׁנִ֖ים וְהָאַחֲרֹנִ֑ים הִנָּ֣ם כְּתוּבִ֗ים עַל־דִּבְרֵי֙ שְׁמוּאֵ֣ל הָרֹאֶ֔ה וְעַל־דִּבְרֵי֙ נָתָ֣ן הַנָּבִ֔יא וְעַל־דִּבְרֵ֖י גָּ֣ד הַחֹזֶֽה׃ 30 עִ֥ם כָּל־מַלְכוּת֖וֹ וּגְבוּרָת֑וֹ וְהָעִתִּ֗ים אֲשֶׁ֤ר עָבְרוּ֙ עָלָ֔יו וְעַל־יִשְׂרָאֵ֔ל וְעַ֖ל כָּל־מַמְלְכ֥וֹת הָאֲרָצֽוֹת׃

The Second Book of the

CHRONICLES

דברי הימים ב

1 Now Solomon the son of David was strengthened in his kingdom, and the LORD his God *was* with him and exalted him exceedingly.

² And Solomon spoke to all Israel, to the captains of thousands and of hundreds, to the judges, and to every leader in all Israel, the heads of the fathers' *houses.* ³ Then Solomon, and all the assembly with him, went to the high place that *was* at Gibeon; for the tabernacle of meeting with God was there, which Moses the servant of the LORD had made in the wilderness. ⁴ But David had brought up the ark of God from Kirjath Jearim to *the place* David had prepared for it, for he had pitched a tent for it at Jerusalem. ⁵ Now the bronze altar that Bezalel the son of Uri, the son of Hur, had made, he put before the tabernacle of the LORD; Solomon and the assembly sought Him *there.* ⁶ And Solomon went up there to the bronze altar before the LORD, which *was* at the tabernacle of meeting, and offered a thousand burnt offerings on it.

⁷ On that night God appeared to Solomon, and said to him, "Ask! What shall I give you?"

⁸ And Solomon said to God: "You have shown great mercy to David my father, and have made me king in his place. ⁹ Now, O LORD God, let Your promise to David my father be established, for You have made me king over a people like the dust of the earth in multitude. ¹⁰ Now give me wisdom and knowledge, that I may go out and come in before this people; for who can judge this great people of Yours?"

¹¹ Then God said to Solomon: "Because this was in your heart, and you have not asked riches or wealth or honor or the life of your enemies, nor have you asked long life—but have asked wisdom and knowledge for yourself, that you may judge My people over whom I have made you king— ¹² wisdom and knowledge *are* granted to you; and I will give you riches and wealth and honor, such as none of the kings have had who *were* before you, nor shall any after you have the like."

¹³ So Solomon came to Jerusalem from the high place that *was* at Gibeon, from before the tabernacle of meeting, and reigned over Israel. ¹⁴ And Solomon gathered chariots and horsemen; he had one thousand four hundred chariots and twelve thousand horsemen, whom he stationed in

א וַיִּתְחַזֵּק שְׁלֹמֹה בֶן־דָּוִיד עַל־מַלְכוּתוֹ וַיהוָה אֱלֹהָיו עִמּוֹ וַיְגַדְּלֵהוּ לְמָעְלָה: 2 וַיֹּאמֶר שְׁלֹמֹה לְכָל־יִשְׂרָאֵל לְשָׂרֵי הָאֲלָפִים וְהַמֵּאוֹת וְלַשֹּׁפְטִים וּלְכֹל נָשִׂיא לְכָל־יִשְׂרָאֵל רָאשֵׁי הָאָבוֹת: 3 וַיֵּלְכוּ שְׁלֹמֹה וְכָל־הַקָּהָל עִמּוֹ לַבָּמָה אֲשֶׁר בְּגִבְעוֹן כִּי־שָׁם הָיָה אֹהֶל מוֹעֵד הָאֱלֹהִים אֲשֶׁר עָשָׂה מֹשֶׁה עֶבֶד־יְהוָה בַּמִּדְבָּר: 4 אֲבָל אֲרוֹן הָאֱלֹהִים הֶעֱלָה דָוִיד מִקִּרְיַת יְעָרִים בַּהֵכִין לוֹ דָּוִיד כִּי נָטָה־לוֹ אֹהֶל בִּירוּשָׁלִָם: 5 וּמִזְבַּח הַנְּחֹשֶׁת אֲשֶׁר עָשָׂה בְּצַלְאֵל בֶּן־אוּרִי בֶן־חוּר שָׂם לִפְנֵי מִשְׁכַּן יְהוָה וַיִּדְרְשֵׁהוּ שְׁלֹמֹה וְהַקָּהָל: 6 וַיַּעַל שְׁלֹמֹה שָׁם עַל־מִזְבַּח הַנְּחֹשֶׁת לִפְנֵי יְהוָה אֲשֶׁר לְאֹהֶל מוֹעֵד וַיַּעַל עָלָיו עֹלוֹת אָלֶף: 7 בַּלַּיְלָה הַהוּא נִרְאָה אֱלֹהִים לִשְׁלֹמֹה וַיֹּאמֶר לוֹ שְׁאַל מָה אֶתֶּן־לָךְ: 8 וַיֹּאמֶר שְׁלֹמֹה לֵאלֹהִים אַתָּה עָשִׂיתָ עִם־דָּוִיד אָבִי חֶסֶד גָּדוֹל וְהִמְלַכְתַּנִי תַּחְתָּיו: 9 עַתָּה יְהוָה אֱלֹהִים יֵאָמֵן דְּבָרְךָ עִם דָּוִיד אָבִי כִּי אַתָּה הִמְלַכְתַּנִי עַל־עַם רַב כַּעֲפַר הָאָרֶץ: 10 עַתָּה חָכְמָה וּמַדָּע תֶּן־לִי וְאֵצְאָה לִפְנֵי הָעָם־הַזֶּה וְאָבוֹאָה כִּי־מִי יִשְׁפֹּט אֶת־עַמְּךָ הַזֶּה הַגָּדוֹל: ס 11 וַיֹּאמֶר־אֱלֹהִים | לִשְׁלֹמֹה יַעַן אֲשֶׁר הָיְתָה זֹאת עִם־לְבָבְךָ וְלֹא־שָׁאַלְתָּ עֹשֶׁר נְכָסִים וְכָבוֹד וְאֵת נֶפֶשׁ שֹׂנְאֶיךָ וְגַם־יָמִים רַבִּים לֹא שָׁאָלְתָּ וַתִּשְׁאַל־לְךָ חָכְמָה וּמַדָּע אֲשֶׁר תִּשְׁפּוֹט אֶת־עַמִּי אֲשֶׁר הִמְלַכְתִּיךָ עָלָיו: 12 הַחָכְמָה וְהַמַּדָּע נָתוּן לָךְ וְעֹשֶׁר וּנְכָסִים וְכָבוֹד אֶתֶּן־לָךְ אֲשֶׁר | לֹא־הָיָה כֵן לַמְּלָכִים אֲשֶׁר לְפָנֶיךָ וְאַחֲרֶיךָ לֹא יִהְיֶה־כֵּן: 13 וַיָּבֹא שְׁלֹמֹה לַבָּמָה אֲשֶׁר־בְּגִבְעוֹן יְרוּשָׁלִַם מִלִּפְנֵי אֹהֶל מוֹעֵד וַיִּמְלֹךְ עַל־יִשְׂרָאֵל: פ

14 וַיֶּאֱסֹף שְׁלֹמֹה רֶכֶב וּפָרָשִׁים וַיְהִי־לוֹ אֶלֶף וְאַרְבַּע־מֵאוֹת רֶכֶב וּשְׁנֵים־עָשָׂר אֶלֶף פָּרָשִׁים

the chariot cities and with the king in Jerusalem.
15 Also the king made silver and gold as common in Jerusalem as stones, and he made cedars as abundant as the sycamores which *are* in the lowland. 16 And Solomon had horses imported from Egypt and Keveh; the king's merchants bought them in Keveh at the *current* price. 17 They also acquired and imported from Egypt a chariot for six hundred *shekels* of silver, and a horse for one hundred and fifty; thus, through their agents, they exported them to all the kings of the Hittites and the kings of Syria.

2 Then Solomon determined to build a temple for the name of the LORD, and a royal house for himself. 2 Solomon selected seventy thousand men to bear burdens, eighty thousand to quarry *stone* in the mountains, and three thousand six hundred to oversee them.

3 Then Solomon sent to Hiram king of Tyre, saying:

As you have dealt with David my father, and sent him cedars to build himself a house to dwell in, *so deal with me.* 4 Behold, I am building a temple for the name of the LORD my God, to dedicate *it* to Him, to burn before Him sweet incense, for the continual showbread, for the burnt offerings morning and evening, on the Sabbaths, on the New Moons, and on the set feasts of the LORD our God. This *is an ordinance* forever to Israel.

5 And the temple which I build *will be* great, for our God is greater than all gods. 6 But who is able to build Him a temple, since heaven and the heaven of heavens cannot contain Him? Who *am* I then, that I should build Him a temple, except to burn sacrifice before Him?

7 Therefore send me at once a man skillful to work in gold and silver, in bronze and iron, in purple and crimson and blue, who has skill to engrave with the skillful men who are with me in Judah and Jerusalem, whom David my father provided. 8 Also send me cedar and cypress and algum logs from Lebanon, for I know that your servants have skill to cut timber in Lebanon; and indeed my servants *will be* with your servants, 9 to prepare timber for me in abundance, for the temple which I am about to build *shall be* great and wonderful.

וַיַּנִּיחֵם בְּעָרֵי הָרֶכֶב וְעִם־הַמֶּלֶךְ בִּירוּשָׁלָ͏ִם: 15 וַיִּתֵּן הַמֶּלֶךְ אֶת־הַכֶּסֶף וְאֶת־הַזָּהָב בִּירוּשָׁלַ͏ִם כָּאֲבָנִים וְאֵת הָאֲרָזִים נָתַן כַּשִּׁקְמִים אֲשֶׁר־בַּשְּׁפֵלָה לָרֹב: 16 וּמוֹצָא הַסּוּסִים אֲשֶׁר לִשְׁלֹמֹה מִמִּצְרָיִם וּמִקְוֵא סֹחֲרֵי הַמֶּלֶךְ מִקְוֵא יִקְחוּ בִּמְחִיר: 17 וַיַּעֲלוּ וַיּוֹצִיאוּ מִמִּצְרַיִם מֶרְכָּבָה בְּשֵׁשׁ מֵאוֹת כֶּסֶף וְסוּס בַּחֲמִשִּׁים וּמֵאָה וְכֵן לְכָל־מַלְכֵי הַחִתִּים וּמַלְכֵי אֲרָם בְּיָדָם יוֹצִיאוּ: 18 וַיֹּאמֶר שְׁלֹמֹה לִבְנוֹת בַּיִת לְשֵׁם יְהֹוָה וּבַיִת לְמַלְכוּתוֹ:

ב וַיִּסְפֹּר שְׁלֹמֹה שִׁבְעִים אֶלֶף אִישׁ סַבָּל וּשְׁמוֹנִים אֶלֶף אִישׁ חֹצֵב בָּהָר וּמְנַצְּחִים עֲלֵיהֶם שְׁלֹשֶׁת אֲלָפִים וְשֵׁשׁ מֵאוֹת: פ

2 וַיִּשְׁלַח שְׁלֹמֹה אֶל־חוּרָם מֶלֶךְ־צֹר לֵאמֹר כַּאֲשֶׁר עָשִׂיתָ עִם־דָּוִיד אָבִי וַתִּשְׁלַח־לוֹ אֲרָזִים לִבְנוֹת־לוֹ בַיִת לָשֶׁבֶת בּוֹ: 3 הִנֵּה אֲנִי בוֹנֶה־בַּיִת לְשֵׁם | יְהֹוָה אֱלֹהַי לְהַקְדִּישׁ לוֹ לְהַקְטִיר לְפָנָיו קְטֹרֶת־סַמִּים וּמַעֲרֶכֶת תָּמִיד וְעֹלוֹת לַבֹּקֶר וְלָעֶרֶב לַשַּׁבָּתוֹת וְלֶחֳדָשִׁים וּלְמוֹעֲדֵי יְהֹוָה אֱלֹהֵינוּ לְעוֹלָם זֹאת עַל־ יִשְׂרָאֵל: 4 וְהַבַּיִת אֲשֶׁר־אֲנִי בוֹנֶה גָּדוֹל כִּי־גָדוֹל אֱלֹהֵינוּ מִכָּל־הָאֱלֹהִים: 5 וּמִי יַעֲצָר־כֹּחַ לִבְנוֹת־לוֹ בַיִת כִּי הַשָּׁמַיִם וּשְׁמֵי הַשָּׁמַיִם לֹא יְכַלְכְּלֻהוּ וּמִי אֲנִי אֲשֶׁר אֶבְנֶה־לּוֹ בַיִת כִּי אִם־לְהַקְטִיר לְפָנָיו: 6 וְעַתָּה שְׁלַח־לִי אִישׁ־חָכָם לַעֲשׂוֹת בַּזָּהָב וּבַכֶּסֶף וּבַנְּחֹשֶׁת וּבַבַּרְזֶל וּבָאַרְגְּוָן וְכַרְמִיל וּתְכֵלֶת וְיֹדֵעַ לְפַתֵּחַ פִּתּוּחִים עִם־הַחֲכָמִים אֲשֶׁר עִמִּי בִּיהוּדָה וּבִירוּשָׁלַ͏ִם אֲשֶׁר הֵכִין דָּוִיד אָבִי: 7 וּשְׁלַח־לִי עֲצֵי אֲרָזִים בְּרוֹשִׁים וְאַלְגּוּמִּים מֵהַלְּבָנוֹן כִּי אֲנִי יָדַעְתִּי אֲשֶׁר עֲבָדֶיךָ יוֹדְעִים לִכְרוֹת עֲצֵי לְבָנוֹן וְהִנֵּה עֲבָדַי עִם־עֲבָדֶיךָ: 8 וּלְהָכִין לִי עֵצִים לָרֹב כִּי הַבַּיִת אֲשֶׁר־אֲנִי בוֹנֶה גָּדוֹל וְהַפְלֵא: 9 וְהִנֵּה לַחֹטְבִים | לְכֹרְתֵי | הָעֵצִים נָתַתִּי חִטִּים | מַכּוֹת לַעֲבָדֶיךָ כֹּרִים עֶשְׂרִים אֶלֶף וּשְׂעֹרִים כֹּרִים עֶשְׂרִים אֶלֶף וְיַיִן בַּתִּים עֶשְׂרִים אֶלֶף וְשֶׁמֶן בַּתִּים עֶשְׂרִים אֶלֶף: פ

¹⁰ And indeed I will give to your servants, the woodsmen who cut timber, twenty thousand kors of ground wheat, twenty thousand kors of barley, twenty thousand baths of wine, and twenty thousand baths of oil.

¹¹ Then Hiram king of Tyre answered in writing, which he sent to Solomon:

> Because the LORD loves His people, He has made you king over them.

¹² Hiram also said:

> Blessed *be* the LORD God of Israel, who made heaven and earth, for He has given King David a wise son, endowed with prudence and understanding, who will build a temple for the LORD and a royal house for himself!

¹³ And now I have sent a skillful man, endowed with understanding, Huram my master *craftsman* ¹⁴ (the son of a woman of the daughters of Dan, and his father was a man of Tyre), skilled to work in gold and silver, bronze and iron, stone and wood, purple and blue, fine linen and crimson, and to make any engraving and to accomplish any plan which may be given to him, with your skillful men and with the skillful men of my lord David your father.

¹⁵ Now therefore, the wheat, the barley, the oil, and the wine which my lord has spoken of, let him send to his servants. ¹⁶ And we will cut wood from Lebanon, as much as you need; we will bring it to you in rafts by sea to Joppa, and you will carry it up to Jerusalem.

¹⁷ Then Solomon numbered all the aliens who *were* in the land of Israel, after the census in which David his father had numbered them; and there were found to be one hundred and fifty-three thousand six hundred. ¹⁸ And he made seventy thousand of them bearers of burdens, eighty thousand stonecutters in the mountain, and three thousand six hundred overseers to make the people work.

3 Now Solomon began to build the house of the LORD at Jerusalem on Mount Moriah, where *the* LORD had appeared to his father David, at the place that David had prepared on the threshing floor of Ornan the Jebusite. ² And he began to build on the second *day* of the second month in the fourth year of his reign.

10 וַיֹּאמֶר חוּרָם מֶלֶךְ־צֹר בִּכְתָב וַיִּשְׁלַח אֶל־שְׁלֹמֹה בְּאַהֲבַת יְהוָה אֶת־עַמּוֹ נְתָנְךָ עֲלֵיהֶם מֶלֶךְ:

11 וַיֹּאמֶר חוּרָם בָּרוּךְ יְהוָה אֱלֹהֵי יִשְׂרָאֵל אֲשֶׁר עָשָׂה אֶת־הַשָּׁמַיִם וְאֶת־הָאָרֶץ אֲשֶׁר נָתַן לְדָוִיד הַמֶּלֶךְ בֵּן חָכָם יוֹדֵעַ שֵׂכֶל וּבִינָה אֲשֶׁר יִבְנֶה־בַּיִת לַיהוָה וּבַיִת לְמַלְכוּתוֹ:

12 וְעַתָּה שָׁלַחְתִּי אִישׁ־חָכָם יוֹדֵעַ בִּינָה לְחוּרָם אָבִי:

13 בֶּן־אִשָּׁה מִן־בְּנוֹת דָּן וְאָבִיו אִישׁ־צֹרִי יוֹדֵעַ לַעֲשׂוֹת בַּזָּהָב־וּבַכֶּסֶף בַּנְּחֹשֶׁת בַּבַּרְזֶל בָּאֲבָנִים וּבָעֵצִים בָּאַרְגָּמָן בַּתְּכֵלֶת וּבַבּוּץ וּבַכַּרְמִיל וּלְפַתֵּחַ כָּל־פִּתּוּחַ וְלַחְשֹׁב כָּל־מַחֲשָׁבֶת אֲשֶׁר יִנָּתֶן־לוֹ עִם־חֲכָמֶיךָ וְחַכְמֵי אֲדֹנִי דָּוִיד אָבִיךָ:

14 וְעַתָּה הַחִטִּים וְהַשְּׂעֹרִים הַשֶּׁמֶן וְהַיַּיִן אֲשֶׁר אָמַר אֲדֹנִי יִשְׁלַח לַעֲבָדָיו:

15 וַאֲנַחְנוּ נִכְרֹת עֵצִים מִן־הַלְּבָנוֹן כְּכָל־צָרְכֶּךָ וּנְבִיאֵם לְךָ רַפְסֹדוֹת עַל־יָם יָפוֹ וְאַתָּה תַּעֲלֶה אֹתָם יְרוּשָׁלִָם: פ

16 וַיִּסְפֹּר שְׁלֹמֹה כָּל־הָאֲנָשִׁים הַגֵּירִים אֲשֶׁר בְּאֶרֶץ יִשְׂרָאֵל אַחֲרֵי הַסְּפָר אֲשֶׁר סְפָרָם דָּוִיד אָבִיו וַיִּמָּצְאוּ מֵאָה וַחֲמִשִּׁים אֶלֶף וּשְׁלֹשֶׁת אֲלָפִים וְשֵׁשׁ מֵאוֹת:

17 וַיַּעַשׂ מֵהֶם שִׁבְעִים אֶלֶף סַבָּל וּשְׁמֹנִים אֶלֶף חֹצֵב בָּהָר וּשְׁלֹשֶׁת אֲלָפִים וְשֵׁשׁ מֵאוֹת מְנַצְּחִים לְהַעֲבִיד אֶת־הָעָם:

ג וַיָּחֶל שְׁלֹמֹה לִבְנוֹת אֶת־בֵּית־יְהוָה בִּירוּשָׁלִַם בְּהַר הַמּוֹרִיָּה אֲשֶׁר נִרְאָה לְדָוִיד אָבִיהוּ אֲשֶׁר הֵכִין בִּמְקוֹם דָּוִיד בְּגֹרֶן אָרְנָן הַיְבוּסִי: 2 וַיָּחֶל לִבְנוֹת בַּחֹדֶשׁ הַשֵּׁנִי בַּשֵּׁנִי בִּשְׁנַת אַרְבַּע לְמַלְכוּתוֹ:

³ This is the foundation which Solomon laid for building the house of God: The length *was* sixty cubits (by cubits according to the former measure) and the width twenty cubits. ⁴ And the vestibule that *was* in front *of the sanctuary* was twenty cubits long across the width of the house, and the height *was* one hundred and twenty. He overlaid the inside with pure gold. ⁵ The larger room he paneled with cypress which he overlaid with fine gold, and he carved palm trees and chainwork on it. ⁶ And he decorated the house with precious stones for beauty, and the gold *was* gold from Parvaim. ⁷ He also overlaid the house—the beams and doorposts, its walls and doors—with gold; and he carved cherubim on the walls.

⁸ And he made the Most Holy Place. Its length was according to the width of the house, twenty cubits, and its width twenty cubits. He overlaid it with six hundred talents of fine gold. ⁹ The weight of the nails *was* fifty shekels of gold; and he overlaid the upper area with gold. ¹⁰ In the Most Holy Place he made two cherubim, fashioned by carving, and overlaid them with gold. ¹¹ The wings of the cherubim *were* twenty cubits in *overall* length: one wing *of the one cherub was* five cubits, touching the wall of the room, and the other wing *was* five cubits, touching the wing of the other cherub; ¹² *one* wing of the other cherub *was* five cubits, touching the wall of the room, and the other wing *also was* five cubits, touching the wing of the other cherub. ¹³ The wings of these cherubim spanned twenty cubits overall. They stood on their feet, and they faced inward. ¹⁴ And he made the veil of blue, purple, crimson, and fine linen, and wove cherubim into it.

¹⁵ Also he made in front of the temple two pillars thirty-five cubits high, and the capital that *was* on the top of each of *them* was five cubits. ¹⁶ He made wreaths of chainwork, as in the inner sanctuary, and put *them* on top of the pillars; and he made one hundred pomegranates, and put *them* on the wreaths of chainwork. ¹⁷ Then he set up the pillars before the temple, one on the right hand and the other on the left; he called the name of the one on the right hand Jachin, and the name of the one on the left Boaz.

4 Moreover he made a bronze altar: twenty cubits was its length, twenty cubits its width, and ten cubits its height.

² Then he made the Sea of cast *bronze,* ten cubits from one brim to the other; *it was* completely round. Its height *was* five cubits, and a line of thirty cubits measured its circumference. ³ And under it *was* the likeness of oxen encircling it all around, ten

וְאֵ֣לֶּה הוּסַ֣ד שְׁלֹמֹ֗ה לִבְנוֹת֙ אֶת־בֵּ֣ית הָֽאֱלֹהִ֔ים הָאֹ֤רֶךְ אַמּוֹת֙ בַּמִּדָּ֣ה הָרִֽאשׁוֹנָ֔ה אַמּ֖וֹת שִׁשִּׁ֑ים וְרֹ֖חַב אַמּ֥וֹת עֶשְׂרִֽים׃ 4 וְהָֽאוּלָ֡ם אֲשֶׁר֩ עַל־פְּנֵ֨י הָאֹ֜רֶךְ עַל־פְּנֵ֤י רֹֽחַב־הַבַּ֨יִת֙ אַמּ֣וֹת עֶשְׂרִ֔ים וְהַגֹּ֖בַהּ מֵאָ֣ה וְעֶשְׂרִ֑ים וַיְצַפֵּ֥הוּ מִפְּנִ֖ימָה זָהָ֥ב טָהֽוֹר׃ 5 וְאֵת֙ הַבַּ֣יִת הַגָּד֔וֹל חִפָּ֖ה עֵ֣ץ בְּרוֹשִׁ֑ים וַיְחַפֵּ֖הוּ זָהָ֣ב ט֑וֹב וַיַּ֧עַל עָלָ֛יו תִּמֹרִ֖ים וְשַׁרְשְׁרֽוֹת׃ 6 וַיְצַ֧ף אֶת־הַבַּ֛יִת אֶ֥בֶן יְקָרָ֖ה לְתִפְאָ֑רֶת וְהַזָּהָ֖ב זְהַ֥ב פַּרְוָֽיִם׃ 7 וַיְחַ֣ף אֶת־הַבַּ֡יִת הַקֹּר֣וֹת הַסִּפִּים֩ וְקִֽירוֹתָ֨יו וְדַלְתוֹתָ֜יו זָהָ֗ב וּפִתַּ֥ח כְּרוּבִ֖ים עַל־הַקִּירֽוֹת׃ ס 8 וַיַּ֖עַשׂ אֶת־בֵּֽית־קֹ֣דֶשׁ הַקֳּדָשִׁ֑ים אָרְכּ֞וֹ עַל־פְּנֵ֤י רֹֽחַב־הַבַּ֨יִת֙ אַמּ֣וֹת עֶשְׂרִ֔ים וְרָחְבּ֖וֹ אַמּ֣וֹת עֶשְׂרִ֑ים וַיְחַפֵּ֨הוּ֙ זָהָ֣ב ט֔וֹב לְכִכָּרִ֖ים שֵׁ֥שׁ מֵאֽוֹת׃ 9 וּמִשְׁקָ֛ל לְמִסְמְר֥וֹת לִשְׁקָלִ֖ים חֲמִשִּׁ֣ים זָהָ֑ב וְהָעֲלִיּ֖וֹת חִפָּ֥ה זָהָֽב׃ 10 וַיַּ֜עַשׂ בְּבֵֽית־קֹ֤דֶשׁ הַקֳּדָשִׁים֙ כְּרוּבִ֣ים שְׁנַ֔יִם מַעֲשֵׂ֖ה צַעֲצֻעִ֑ים וַיְצַפּ֥וּ אֹתָ֖ם זָהָֽב׃ 11 וְכַנְפֵ֣י הַכְּרוּבִ֗ים אָרְכָּם֮ אַמּ֣וֹת עֶשְׂרִים֒ כְּנַ֣ף הָאֶחָ֡ד לְאַמּ֣וֹת חָמֵשׁ֩ מַגַּ֨עַת לְקִ֤יר הַבַּ֨יִת֙ וְהַכָּנָ֣ף הָאַחֶ֔רֶת אַמּ֣וֹת חָמֵ֔שׁ מַגִּ֖יעַ לִכְנַ֥ף הַכְּר֖וּב הָאַחֵֽר׃ 12 וּכְנַ֨ף הַכְּר֤וּב הָֽאֶחָד֙ אַמּ֣וֹת חָמֵ֔שׁ מַגִּ֖יעַ לְקִ֣יר הַבָּ֑יִת וְהַכָּנָ֤ף הָאַחֶ֨רֶת֙ אַמּ֣וֹת חָמֵ֔שׁ דְּבֵקָ֕ה לִכְנַ֥ף הַכְּר֖וּב הָאַחֵֽר׃ 13 כַּנְפֵי֙ הַכְּרוּבִ֣ים הָאֵ֔לֶּה פֹּרְשִׂ֖ים אַמּ֣וֹת עֶשְׂרִ֑ים וְהֵ֛ם עֹמְדִ֥ים עַל־רַגְלֵיהֶ֖ם וּפְנֵיהֶ֥ם לַבָּֽיִת׃ ס 14 וַיַּ֨עַשׂ֙ אֶת־הַפָּרֹ֔כֶת תְּכֵ֥לֶת וְאַרְגָּמָ֖ן וְכַרְמִ֣יל וּב֑וּץ וַיַּ֥עַל עָלָ֖יו כְּרוּבִֽים׃ ס 15 וַיַּ֜עַשׂ לִפְנֵ֤י הַבַּ֨יִת֙ עַמּוּדִ֣ים שְׁנַ֔יִם אַמּ֕וֹת שְׁלֹשִׁ֥ים וְחָמֵ֖שׁ אֹ֑רֶךְ וְהַצֶּ֧פֶת אֲשֶׁר־עַל־רֹאשׁ֛וֹ אַמּ֥וֹת חָמֵֽשׁ׃ ס 16 וַיַּ֤עַשׂ שַׁרְשְׁרוֹת֙ בַּדְּבִ֔יר וַיִּתֵּ֖ן עַל־רֹ֣אשׁ הָעַמֻּדִ֑ים וַיַּ֤עַשׂ רִמּוֹנִים֙ מֵאָ֔ה וַיִּתֵּ֖ן בַּֽשַּׁרְשְׁרֽוֹת׃ 17 וַיָּ֤קֶם אֶת־הָֽעַמּוּדִים֙ עַל־פְּנֵ֣י הַהֵיכָ֔ל אֶחָ֥ד מִיָּמִ֖ין וְאֶחָ֣ד מֵֽהַשְּׂמֹ֑אול וַיִּקְרָ֤א שֵׁם־הַיְמָנִי֙ יָכִ֔ין וְשֵׁ֥ם הַשְּׂמָאלִ֖י בֹּֽעַז׃ ס

ד וַיַּ֨עַשׂ מִזְבַּ֣ח נְחֹ֔שֶׁת עֶשְׂרִ֤ים אַמָּה֙ אָרְכּ֔וֹ וְעֶשְׂרִ֥ים אַמָּ֖ה רָחְבּ֑וֹ וְעֶ֥שֶׂר אַמּ֖וֹת קֽוֹמָתֽוֹ׃ ס 2 וַיַּ֥עַשׂ אֶת־הַיָּ֖ם מוּצָ֣ק עֶ֣שֶׂר בָּֽאַמָּ֞ה מִשְּׂפָת֣וֹ אֶל־שְׂפָת֗וֹ עָג֣וֹל ׀ סָבִ֛יב וְחָמֵ֤שׁ בָּֽאַמָּה֙ קֽוֹמָת֔וֹ וְקָו֙ שְׁלֹשִׁ֣ים בָּֽאַמָּ֔ה יָסֹ֥ב אֹת֖וֹ סָבִֽיב׃ 3 וּדְמ֣וּת בְּקָרִים֩ תַּ֨חַת ל֜וֹ סָבִ֤יב ׀ סָבִיב֙ סוֹבְבִ֣ים אֹת֔וֹ עֶ֚שֶׂר בָּֽאַמָּ֔ה מַקִּיפִ֥ים אֶת־הַיָּ֖ם סָבִ֑יב

to a cubit, all the way around the Sea. The oxen *were* cast in two rows, when it was cast. ⁴It stood on twelve oxen: three looking toward the north, three looking toward the west, three looking toward the south, and three looking toward the east; the Sea *was set* upon them, and all their back parts *pointed* inward. ⁵It *was* a handbreadth thick; and its brim was shaped like the brim of a cup, *like* a lily blossom. It contained three thousand baths.

⁶He also made ten lavers, and put five on the right side and five on the left, to wash in them; such things as they offered for the burnt offering they would wash in them, but the Sea *was* for the priests to wash in. ⁷And he made ten lampstands of gold according to their design, and set *them* in the temple, five on the right side and five on the left. ⁸He also made ten tables, and placed *them* in the temple, five on the right side and five on the left. And he made one hundred bowls of gold.

⁹Furthermore he made the court of the priests, and the great court and doors for the court; and he overlaid these doors with bronze. ¹⁰He set the Sea on the right side, toward the southeast.

¹¹Then Huram made the pots and the shovels and the bowls. So Huram finished doing the work that he was to do for King Solomon for the house of God: ¹²the two pillars and the bowl-shaped capitals *that were* on top of the two pillars; the two networks covering the two bowl-shaped capitals which *were* on top of the pillars; ¹³four hundred pomegranates for the two networks (two rows of pomegranates for each network, to cover the two bowl-shaped capitals that *were* on the pillars); ¹⁴he also made carts and the lavers on the carts; ¹⁵one Sea and twelve oxen under it; ¹⁶also the pots, the shovels, the forks—and all their articles Huram his master *craftsman* made of burnished bronze for King Solomon for the house of the LORD.

¹⁷In the plain of Jordan the king had them cast in clay molds, between Succoth and Zeredah. ¹⁸And Solomon had all these articles made in such great abundance that the weight of the bronze was not determined.

¹⁹Thus Solomon had all the furnishings made for the house of God: the altar of gold and the tables on which *was* the showbread; ²⁰the lampstands with their lamps of pure gold, to burn in the prescribed manner in front of the inner sanctuary, ²¹with the flowers and the lamps and the wick-trimmers of gold, of purest gold; ²²the trimmers, the bowls, the ladles, and the censers of pure gold. As for the entry of the sanctuary, its inner doors to the Most Holy *Place,* and the doors of the main hall of the temple, *were* gold.

שְׁנַיִם טוּרִים הַבָּקָר יְצוּקִים בְּמֻצַקְתּוֹ: 4 עוֹמֵד
עַל־שְׁנֵים עָשָׂר בָּקָר שְׁלֹשָׁה פֹנִים ׀ צָפוֹנָה
וּשְׁלוֹשָׁה פֹנִים ׀ יָמָּה וּשְׁלֹשָׁה ׀ פֹּנִים נֶגְבָּה
וּשְׁלֹשָׁה פֹּנִים מִזְרָחָה וְהַיָּם עֲלֵיהֶם מִלְמָעְלָה וְכָל־
אֲחֹרֵיהֶם בָּיְתָה: 5 וְעָבְיוֹ טֶפַח וּשְׂפָתוֹ כְּמַעֲשֵׂה
שְׂפַת־כּוֹס פֶּרַח שׁוֹשַׁנָּה מַחֲזִיק בַּתִּים שְׁלֹשֶׁת
אֲלָפִים יָכִיל: ס 6 וַיַּעַשׂ כִּיּוֹרִים עֲשָׂרָה
וַיִּתֵּן חֲמִשָּׁה מִיָּמִין וַחֲמִשָּׁה מִשְּׂמֹאול לְרָחְצָה
בָּהֶם אֶת־מַעֲשֵׂה הָעוֹלָה יָדִיחוּ בָם וְהַיָּם לְרָחְצָה
לַכֹּהֲנִים בּוֹ: ס 7 וַיַּעַשׂ אֶת־מְנֹרוֹת הַזָּהָב
עֶשֶׂר כְּמִשְׁפָּטָם וַיִּתֵּן בַּהֵיכָל חָמֵשׁ מִיָּמִין וְחָמֵשׁ
מִשְּׂמֹאול: ס 8 וַיַּעַשׂ שֻׁלְחָנוֹת עֲשָׂרָה
וַיַּנַּח בַּהֵיכָל חֲמִשָּׁה מִיָּמִין וַחֲמִשָּׁה מִשְּׂמֹאול וַיַּעַשׂ
מִזְרְקֵי זָהָב מֵאָה: 9 וַיַּעַשׂ חֲצַר הַכֹּהֲנִים וְהָעֲזָרָה
הַגְּדוֹלָה וּדְלָתוֹת לָעֲזָרָה וְדַלְתוֹתֵיהֶם צִפָּה נְחֹשֶׁת:
10 וְאֶת־הַיָּם נָתַן מִכֶּתֶף הַיְמָנִית קֵדְמָה מִמּוּל
נֶגְבָּה: 11 וַיַּעַשׂ חוּרָם אֶת־הַסִּירוֹת וְאֶת־הַיָּעִים
וְאֶת־הַמִּזְרָקוֹת ס וַיְכַל חירָם לַעֲשׂוֹת
אֶת־הַמְּלָאכָה אֲשֶׁר עָשָׂה לַמֶּלֶךְ שְׁלֹמֹה בְּבֵית
הָאֱלֹהִים: 12 עַמּוּדִים שְׁנַיִם וְהַגֻּלּוֹת וְהַכֹּתָרוֹת עַל־
רֹאשׁ הָעַמּוּדִים שְׁתַּיִם וְהַשְּׂבָכוֹת שְׁתַּיִם לְכַסּוֹת
אֶת־שְׁתֵּי גֻּלּוֹת הַכֹּתָרוֹת אֲשֶׁר עַל־רֹאשׁ הָעַמּוּדִים:
13 וְאֶת־הָרִמּוֹנִים אַרְבַּע מֵאוֹת לִשְׁתֵּי הַשְּׂבָכוֹת
שְׁנַיִם טוּרִים רִמּוֹנִים לַשְּׂבָכָה הָאֶחָת לְכַסּוֹת אֶת־
שְׁתֵּי גֻּלּוֹת הַכֹּתָרוֹת אֲשֶׁר עַל־פְּנֵי הָעַמּוּדִים:
14 וְאֶת־הַמְּכֹנוֹת עָשָׂה וְאֶת־הַכִּיֹּרוֹת עָשָׂה עַל־
הַמְּכֹנוֹת: 15 אֶת־הַיָּם אֶחָד וְאֶת־הַבָּקָר שְׁנֵים־
עָשָׂר תַּחְתָּיו: 16 וְאֶת־הַסִּירוֹת וְאֶת־הַיָּעִים וְאֶת־
הַמִּזְלָגוֹת וְאֶת־כָּל־כְּלֵיהֶם עָשָׂה חוּרָם אָבִיו לַמֶּלֶךְ
שְׁלֹמֹה לְבֵית יְהוָה נְחֹשֶׁת מָרוּק: 17 בְּכִכַּר הַיַּרְדֵּן
יְצָקָם הַמֶּלֶךְ בַּעֲבִי הָאֲדָמָה בֵּין סֻכּוֹת וּבֵין
צְרֵדָתָה: 18 וַיַּעַשׂ שְׁלֹמֹה כָּל־הַכֵּלִים הָאֵלֶּה לָרֹב
מְאֹד כִּי לֹא נֶחְקַר מִשְׁקַל הַנְּחֹשֶׁת: פ
19 וַיַּעַשׂ שְׁלֹמֹה אֵת כָּל־הַכֵּלִים אֲשֶׁר בֵּית
הָאֱלֹהִים וְאֵת מִזְבַּח הַזָּהָב וְאֶת־הַשֻּׁלְחָנוֹת
וַעֲלֵיהֶם לֶחֶם הַפָּנִים: 20 וְאֶת־הַמְּנֹרוֹת וְנֵרֹתֵיהֶם
לְבַעֲרָם כַּמִּשְׁפָּט לִפְנֵי הַדְּבִיר זָהָב סָגוּר: 21 וְהַפֶּרַח
וְהַנֵּרוֹת וְהַמֶּלְקַחַיִם זָהָב הוּא מִכְלוֹת זָהָב:
22 וְהַמְזַמְּרוֹת וְהַמִּזְרָקוֹת וְהַכַּפּוֹת וְהַמַּחְתּוֹת זָהָב
סָגוּר וּפֶתַח הַבַּיִת דַּלְתוֹתָיו הַפְּנִימִיּוֹת לְקֹדֶשׁ
הַקֳּדָשִׁים וְדַלְתֵי הַבַּיִת לַהֵיכָל זָהָב:

5 So all the work that Solomon had done for the house of the LORD was finished; and Solomon brought in the things which his father David had dedicated: the silver and the gold and all the furnishings. And he put *them* in the treasuries of the house of God.

2 Now Solomon assembled the elders of Israel and all the heads of the tribes, the chief fathers of the children of Israel, in Jerusalem, that they might bring the ark of the covenant of the LORD up from the City of David, which *is* Zion. 3 Therefore all the men of Israel assembled with the king at the feast, which *was* in the seventh month. 4 So all the elders of Israel came, and the Levites took up the ark. 5 Then they brought up the ark, the tabernacle of meeting, and all the holy furnishings that *were* in the tabernacle. The priests and the Levites brought them up. 6 Also King Solomon, and all the congregation of Israel who were assembled with him before the ark, were sacrificing sheep and oxen that could not be counted or numbered for multitude. 7 Then the priests brought in the ark of the covenant of the LORD to its place, into the inner sanctuary of the temple, to the Most Holy *Place,* under the wings of the cherubim. 8 For the cherubim spread *their* wings over the place of the ark, and the cherubim overshadowed the ark and its poles. 9 The poles extended so that the ends of the poles of the ark could be seen from *the holy place,* in front of the inner sanctuary; but they could not be seen from outside. And they are there to this day. 10 Nothing was in the ark except the two tablets which Moses put *there* at Horeb, when the LORD made *a* covenant with the children of Israel, when they had come out of Egypt.

11 And it came to pass when the priests came out of the *Most* Holy *Place* (for all the priests who *were* present had sanctified themselves, without keeping to their divisions), 12 and the Levites who *were* the singers, all those of Asaph and Heman and Jeduthun, with their sons and their brethren, stood at the east end of the altar, clothed in white linen, having cymbals, stringed instruments and harps, and with them one hundred and twenty priests sounding with trumpets— 13 indeed it came to pass, when the trumpeters and singers *were* as one, to make one sound to be heard in praising and thanking the LORD, and when they lifted up their voice with the trumpets and cymbals and instruments of music, and praised the LORD, *saying:*

"*For He is* good,
For His mercy *endures* forever,"

ה וַתִּשְׁלַם כָּל־הַמְּלָאכָה אֲשֶׁר־עָשָׂה שְׁלֹמֹה לְבֵית יְהוָה ס וַיָּבֵא שְׁלֹמֹה אֶת־קָדְשֵׁי ׀ דָּוִיד אָבִיו וְאֶת־הַכֶּסֶף וְאֶת־הַזָּהָב וְאֶת־כָּל־הַכֵּלִים נָתַן בְּאֹצְרוֹת בֵּית הָאֱלֹהִים: פ

2 אָז יַקְהֵיל שְׁלֹמֹה אֶת־זִקְנֵי יִשְׂרָאֵל וְאֶת־כָּל־רָאשֵׁי הַמַּטּוֹת נְשִׂיאֵי הָאָבוֹת לִבְנֵי יִשְׂרָאֵל אֶל־יְרוּשָׁלִָם לְהַעֲלוֹת אֶת־אֲרוֹן בְּרִית־יְהוָה מֵעִיר דָּוִיד הִיא צִיּוֹן: 3 וַיִּקָּהֲלוּ אֶל־הַמֶּלֶךְ כָּל־אִישׁ יִשְׂרָאֵל בֶּחָג הוּא הַחֹדֶשׁ הַשְּׁבִעִי: 4 וַיָּבֹאוּ כֹּל זִקְנֵי יִשְׂרָאֵל וַיִּשְׂאוּ הַלְוִיִּם אֶת־הָאָרוֹן: 5 וַיַּעֲלוּ אֶת־הָאָרוֹן וְאֶת־אֹהֶל מוֹעֵד וְאֶת־כָּל־כְּלֵי הַקֹּדֶשׁ אֲשֶׁר בָּאֹהֶל הֶעֱלוּ אֹתָם הַכֹּהֲנִים הַלְוִיִּם: 6 וְהַמֶּלֶךְ שְׁלֹמֹה וְכָל־עֲדַת יִשְׂרָאֵל הַנּוֹעָדִים עָלָיו לִפְנֵי הָאָרוֹן מְזַבְּחִים צֹאן וּבָקָר אֲשֶׁר לֹא־יִסָּפְרוּ וְלֹא יִמָּנוּ מֵרֹב: 7 וַיָּבִיאוּ הַכֹּהֲנִים אֶת־אֲרוֹן בְּרִית־יְהוָה אֶל־מְקוֹמוֹ אֶל־דְּבִיר הַבַּיִת אֶל־קֹדֶשׁ הַקֳּדָשִׁים אֶל־תַּחַת כַּנְפֵי הַכְּרוּבִים: 8 וַיִּהְיוּ הַכְּרוּבִים פֹּרְשִׂים כְּנָפַיִם עַל־מְקוֹם הָאָרוֹן וַיְכַסּוּ הַכְּרוּבִים עַל־הָאָרוֹן וְעַל־בַּדָּיו מִלְמָעְלָה: 9 וַיַּאֲרִיכוּ הַבַּדִּים וַיֵּרָאוּ רָאשֵׁי הַבַּדִּים מִן־הָאָרוֹן עַל־פְּנֵי הַדְּבִיר וְלֹא יֵרָאוּ הַחוּצָה וַיְהִי שָׁם עַד הַיּוֹם הַזֶּה: 10 אֵין בָּאָרוֹן רַק שְׁנֵי הַלֻּחוֹת אֲשֶׁר־נָתַן מֹשֶׁה בְּחֹרֵב אֲשֶׁר כָּרַת יְהוָה עִם־בְּנֵי יִשְׂרָאֵל בְּצֵאתָם מִמִּצְרָיִם: פ

11 וַיְהִי בְּצֵאת הַכֹּהֲנִים מִן־הַקֹּדֶשׁ כִּי כָּל־הַכֹּהֲנִים הַנִּמְצְאִים הִתְקַדָּשׁוּ אֵין לִשְׁמוֹר לְמַחְלְקוֹת: 12 וְהַלְוִיִּם הַמְשֹׁרֲרִים לְכֻלָּם לְאָסָף לְהֵימָן לִידֻתוּן וְלִבְנֵיהֶם וְלַאֲחֵיהֶם מְלֻבָּשִׁים בּוּץ בִּמְצִלְתַּיִם וּבִנְבָלִים וְכִנֹּרוֹת עֹמְדִים מִזְרָח לַמִּזְבֵּחַ וְעִמָּהֶם כֹּהֲנִים לְמֵאָה וְעֶשְׂרִים מַחְצְרִיםᴾ בַּחֲצֹצְרוֹת: 13 וַיְהִי כְאֶחָד לַמַחְצְצרִיםᴾ וְלַמְשֹׁרֲרִים לְהַשְׁמִיעַ קוֹל־אֶחָד לְהַלֵּל וּלְהֹדוֹת לַיהוָה וּכְהָרִים קוֹל בַּחֲצֹצְרוֹת וּבִמְצִלְתַּיִם וּבִכְלֵי הַשִּׁיר וּבְהַלֵּל לַיהוָה

ה 12 מַחְצְרִים   13 לַמְחַצְּרִים

that the house, the house of the LORD, was filled with a cloud, 14 so that the priests could not continue ministering because of the cloud; for the glory of the LORD filled the house of God.

6 Then Solomon spoke:

"The LORD said
He would dwell in the dark cloud.
2   I have surely built You an exalted house,
And a place for You to dwell in forever."

3 Then the king turned around and blessed the whole assembly of Israel, while all the assembly of Israel was standing. 4 And he said: "Blessed *be* the LORD God of Israel, who has fulfilled with His hands *what* He spoke with His mouth to my father David, saying, 5 'Since the day that I brought My people out of the land of Egypt, I have chosen no city from any tribe of Israel *in which* to build a house, that My name might be there, nor did I choose any man to be a ruler over My people Israel. 6 Yet I have chosen Jerusalem, that My name may be there, and I have chosen David to be over My people Israel.' 7 Now it was in the heart of my father David to build a temple for the name of the LORD God of Israel. 8 But the LORD said to my father David, 'Whereas it was in your heart to build a temple for My name, you did well in that it was in your heart. 9 Nevertheless you shall not build the temple, but your son who will come from your body, he shall build the temple for My name.' 10 So the LORD has fulfilled His word which He spoke, and I have filled the position of my father David, and sit on the throne of Israel, as the LORD promised; and I have built the temple for the name of the LORD God of Israel. 11 And there I have put the ark, in which *is* the covenant of the LORD which He made with the children of Israel."

12 Then *Solomon* stood before the altar of the LORD in the presence of all the assembly of Israel, and spread out his hands 13 (for Solomon had made a bronze platform five cubits long, five cubits wide, and three cubits high, and had set it in the midst of the court; and he stood on it, knelt down on his knees before all the assembly of Israel, and spread out his hands toward heaven) 14 and he said: "LORD God of Israel, *there is* no God in heaven or on earth like You, who keep *Your* covenant and mercy with Your servants who walk before You with all their hearts. 15 You have kept what You promised Your servant David my father; You have both spoken with Your mouth and fulfilled *it* with Your hand, as *it is* this day. 16 Therefore, LORD God of Israel, now keep what You promised Your

כִּי־ט֖וֹב כִּ֣י לְעוֹלָ֣ם חַסְדּ֑וֹ וְהַבַּ֙יִת֙ מָלֵ֣א עָנָ֔ן בֵּ֖ית יְהוָֽה: 14 וְלֹא־יָכְל֧וּ הַכֹּהֲנִ֛ים לַעֲמ֥וֹד לְשָׁרֵ֖ת מִפְּנֵ֣י הֶֽעָנָ֑ן כִּֽי־מָלֵ֥א כְבוֹד־יְהוָ֖ה אֶת־בֵּ֥ית הָאֱלֹהִֽים: פ

ו אָ֣ז אָמַ֣ר שְׁלֹמֹ֑ה יְהוָ֣ה אָמַ֔ר לִשְׁכּ֖וֹן בָּעֲרָפֶֽל: 2 וַאֲנִ֛י בָּנִ֥יתִי בֵית־זְבֻ֖ל לָ֑ךְ וּמָכ֥וֹן לְשִׁבְתְּךָ֖ עוֹלָמִֽים: 3 וַיַּסֵּ֤ב הַמֶּ֙לֶךְ֙ אֶת־פָּנָ֔יו וַיְבָ֕רֶךְ אֵ֖ת כָּל־קְהַ֣ל יִשְׂרָאֵ֑ל וְכָל־קְהַ֥ל יִשְׂרָאֵ֖ל עוֹמֵֽד: 4 וַיֹּ֗אמֶר בָּר֤וּךְ יְהוָה֙ אֱלֹהֵ֣י יִשְׂרָאֵ֔ל אֲשֶׁר֙ דִּבֶּ֣ר בְּפִ֔יו אֵ֖ת דָּוִ֣יד אָבִ֑י וּבְיָדָ֥יו מִלֵּ֖א לֵאמֹֽר: 5 מִן־הַיּ֗וֹם אֲשֶׁ֨ר הוֹצֵ֣אתִי אֶת־עַמִּי֮ מֵאֶ֣רֶץ מִצְרַיִם֒ לֹא־בָחַ֣רְתִּֽי בְעִ֗יר מִכֹּל֙ שִׁבְטֵ֣י יִשְׂרָאֵ֔ל לִבְנ֣וֹת בַּ֔יִת לִהְי֥וֹת שְׁמִ֖י שָׁ֑ם וְלֹא־בָחַ֣רְתִּֽי בְאִ֔ישׁ לִהְי֥וֹת נָגִ֖יד עַל־עַמִּ֥י יִשְׂרָאֵֽל: 6 וָאֶבְחַ֣ר בִּירוּשָׁלִַ֔ם לִהְי֥וֹת שְׁמִ֖י שָׁ֑ם וָאֶבְחַ֣ר בְּדָוִ֔יד לִהְי֖וֹת עַל־עַמִּ֥י יִשְׂרָאֵֽל: 7 וַיְהִ֕י עִם־לְבַ֖ב דָּוִ֣יד אָבִ֑י לִבְנ֣וֹת בַּ֔יִת לְשֵׁ֖ם יְהוָ֥ה אֱלֹהֵ֖י יִשְׂרָאֵֽל: 8 וַיֹּ֤אמֶר יְהוָה֙ אֶל־דָּוִ֣יד אָבִ֔י יַ֗עַן אֲשֶׁ֤ר הָיָה֙ עִם־לְבָ֣בְךָ֔ לִבְנ֥וֹת בַּ֖יִת לִשְׁמִ֑י הֱטִיב֔וֹתָ כִּ֥י הָיָ֖ה עִם־לְבָבֶֽךָ: 9 רַ֣ק אַתָּ֔ה לֹ֥א תִבְנֶ֖ה הַבָּ֑יִת כִּ֤י בִנְךָ֙ הַיּוֹצֵ֣א מֵחֲלָצֶ֔יךָ הֽוּא־יִבְנֶ֥ה הַבַּ֖יִת לִשְׁמִֽי: 10 וַיָּ֣קֶם יְהוָ֗ה אֶת־דְּבָרוֹ֙ אֲשֶׁ֣ר דִּבֵּ֔ר וָאָק֡וּם תַּ֩חַת֩ דָּוִ֨יד אָבִ֜י וָאֵשֵׁ֣ב ׀ עַל־כִּסֵּ֣א יִשְׂרָאֵ֗ל כַּֽאֲשֶׁר֙ דִּבֶּ֣ר יְהוָ֔ה וָאֶבְנֶ֣ה הַבַּ֔יִת לְשֵׁ֥ם יְהוָ֖ה אֱלֹהֵ֥י יִשְׂרָאֵֽל: 11 וָאָשִׂ֥ים שָׁם֙ אֶת־הָ֣אָר֔וֹן אֲשֶׁר־שָׁ֖ם בְּרִ֣ית יְהוָ֑ה אֲשֶׁ֥ר כָּרַ֖ת עִם־בְּנֵ֥י יִשְׂרָאֵֽל: 12 וַֽיַּעֲמֹ֗ד לִפְנֵי֙ מִזְבַּ֣ח יְהוָ֔ה נֶ֖גֶד כָּל־קְהַ֣ל יִשְׂרָאֵ֑ל וַיִּפְרֹ֖שׂ כַּפָּֽיו: 13 כִּֽי־עָשָׂ֨ה שְׁלֹמֹ֜ה כִּיּ֣וֹר נְחֹ֗שֶׁת וַֽיִּתְּנֵהוּ֮ בְּת֣וֹךְ הָעֲזָרָה֒ חָמֵ֨שׁ אַמּ֜וֹת אָרְכּ֗וֹ וְחָמֵ֤שׁ אַמּוֹת֙ רָחְבּ֔וֹ וְאַמּ֥וֹת שָׁל֖וֹשׁ קֽוֹמָת֑וֹ וַיַּעֲמֹ֣ד עָלָ֗יו וַיִּבְרַ֤ךְ עַל־בִּרְכָּיו֙ נֶ֚גֶד כָּל־קְהַ֣ל יִשְׂרָאֵ֔ל וַיִּפְרֹ֥שׂ כַּפָּ֖יו הַשָּׁמָֽיְמָה: 14 וַיֹּאמַ֗ר יְהוָ֞ה אֱלֹהֵ֤י יִשְׂרָאֵל֙ אֵין־כָּמ֣וֹךָ אֱלֹהִ֔ים בַּשָּׁמַ֖יִם וּבָאָ֑רֶץ שֹׁמֵ֤ר הַבְּרִית֙ וְהַחֶ֔סֶד לַעֲבָדֶ֕יךָ הַהֹלְכִ֥ים לְפָנֶ֖יךָ בְּכָל־לִבָּֽם: 15 אֲשֶׁ֣ר שָׁמַ֗רְתָּ לְעַבְדְּךָ֙ דָּוִ֣יד אָבִ֔י אֵ֥ת אֲשֶׁר־דִּבַּ֖רְתָּ ל֑וֹ וַתְּדַבֵּ֥ר בְּפִ֛יךָ וּבְיָדְךָ֥ מִלֵּ֖אתָ כַּיּ֥וֹם הַזֶּֽה: 16 וְעַתָּ֞ה ׀ יְהוָ֣ה ׀ אֱלֹהֵ֣י יִשְׂרָאֵ֗ל שְׁ֠מֹר לְעַבְדְּךָ֨ דָוִ֤יד אָבִי֙ אֵת֩ אֲשֶׁ֨ר דִּבַּ֤רְתָּ לּוֹ֙ לֵאמֹ֔ר לֹא־יִכָּרֵ֨ת לְךָ֥ אִ֛ישׁ מִלְּפָנַ֖י יוֹשֵׁ֥ב עַל־כִּסֵּ֖א יִשְׂרָאֵ֑ל

servant David my father, saying, 'You shall not fail to have a man sit before Me on the throne of Israel, only if your sons take heed to their way, that they walk in My law as you have walked before Me.' 17 And now, O LORD God of Israel, let Your word come true, which You have spoken to Your servant David.

18 "But will God indeed dwell with men on the earth? Behold, heaven and the heaven of heavens cannot contain You. How much less this temple which I have built! 19 Yet regard the prayer of Your servant and his supplication, O LORD my God, and listen to the cry and the prayer which Your servant is praying before You: 20 that Your eyes may be open toward this temple day and night, toward the place where *You* said *You would* put Your name, that You may hear the prayer which Your servant makes toward this place. 21 And may You hear the supplications of Your servant and of Your people Israel, when they pray toward this place. Hear from heaven Your dwelling place, and when You hear, forgive.

22 "If anyone sins against his neighbor, and is forced to take an oath, and comes *and* takes an oath before Your altar in this temple, 23 then hear from heaven, and act, and judge Your servants, bringing retribution on the wicked by bringing his way on his own head, and justifying the righteous by giving him according to his righteousness.

24 "Or if Your people Israel are defeated before an enemy because they have sinned against You, and return and confess Your name, and pray and make supplication before You in this temple, 25 then hear from heaven and forgive the sin of Your people Israel, and bring them back to the land which You gave to them and their fathers.

26 "When the heavens are shut up and there is no rain because they have sinned against You, when they pray toward this place and confess Your name, and turn from their sin because You afflict them, 27 then hear *in* heaven, and forgive the sin of Your servants, Your people Israel, that You may teach them the good way in which they should walk; and send rain on Your land which You have given to Your people as an inheritance.

28 "When there is famine in the land, pestilence or blight or mildew, locusts or grasshoppers; when their enemies besiege them in the land of their cities; whatever plague or whatever sickness *there is;* 29 whatever prayer, whatever supplication is *made* by anyone, or by all Your people Israel, when each one knows his own burden and his own grief, and spreads out his hands to this temple: 30 then hear from heaven Your dwelling place, and forgive, and

רַק אִם־יִשְׁמְרוּ בָנֶיךָ אֶת־דַּרְכָּם לָלֶכֶת בְּתוֹרָתִי כַּאֲשֶׁר הָלַכְתָּ לְפָנָי: 17 וְעַתָּה יְהוָה אֱלֹהֵי יִשְׂרָאֵל יֵאָמֵן דְּבָרְךָ אֲשֶׁר דִּבַּרְתָּ לְעַבְדְּךָ לְדָוִיד: 18 כִּי הַאֻמְנָם יֵשֵׁב אֱלֹהִים אֶת־הָאָדָם עַל־הָאָרֶץ הִנֵּה שָׁמַיִם וּשְׁמֵי הַשָּׁמַיִם לֹא יְכַלְכְּלוּךָ אַף כִּי־הַבַּיִת הַזֶּה אֲשֶׁר בָּנִיתִי: 19 וּפָנִיתָ אֶל־תְּפִלַּת עַבְדְּךָ וְאֶל־תְּחִנָּתוֹ יְהוָה אֱלֹהָי לִשְׁמֹעַ אֶל־הָרִנָּה וְאֶל־הַתְּפִלָּה אֲשֶׁר עַבְדְּךָ מִתְפַּלֵּל לְפָנֶיךָ: 20 לִהְיוֹת עֵינֶיךָ פְתֻחוֹת אֶל־הַבַּיִת הַזֶּה יוֹמָם וָלַיְלָה אֶל־הַמָּקוֹם אֲשֶׁר אָמַרְתָּ לָשׂוּם שִׁמְךָ שָׁם לִשְׁמוֹעַ אֶל־הַתְּפִלָּה אֲשֶׁר יִתְפַּלֵּל עַבְדְּךָ אֶל־הַמָּקוֹם הַזֶּה: 21 וְשָׁמַעְתָּ אֶל־תַּחֲנוּנֵי עַבְדְּךָ וְעַמְּךָ יִשְׂרָאֵל אֲשֶׁר יִתְפַּלְלוּ אֶל־הַמָּקוֹם הַזֶּה וְאַתָּה תִּשְׁמַע מִמְּקוֹם שִׁבְתְּךָ מִן־הַשָּׁמַיִם וְשָׁמַעְתָּ וְסָלָחְתָּ: 22 אִם־יֶחֱטָא אִישׁ לְרֵעֵהוּ וְנָשָׁא־בוֹ אָלָה לְהַאֲלֹתוֹ וּבָא אָלָה לִפְנֵי מִזְבַּחֲךָ בַּבַּיִת הַזֶּה: 23 וְאַתָּה ׀ תִּשְׁמַע מִן־הַשָּׁמַיִם וְעָשִׂיתָ וְשָׁפַטְתָּ אֶת־עֲבָדֶיךָ לְהָשִׁיב לְרָשָׁע לָתֵת דַּרְכּוֹ בְּרֹאשׁוֹ וּלְהַצְדִּיק צַדִּיק לָתֶת לוֹ כְּצִדְקָתוֹ: ס 24 וְאִם־יִנָּגֵף עַמְּךָ יִשְׂרָאֵל לִפְנֵי אוֹיֵב כִּי יֶחֶטְאוּ־לָךְ וְשָׁבוּ וְהוֹדוּ אֶת־שְׁמֶךָ וְהִתְפַּלְלוּ וְהִתְחַנְּנוּ לְפָנֶיךָ בַּבַּיִת הַזֶּה: 25 וְאַתָּה תִּשְׁמַע מִן־הַשָּׁמַיִם וְסָלַחְתָּ לְחַטַּאת עַמְּךָ יִשְׂרָאֵל וַהֲשֵׁיבוֹתָם אֶל־הָאֲדָמָה אֲשֶׁר־נָתַתָּה לָהֶם וְלַאֲבֹתֵיהֶם: פ

26 בְּהֵעָצֵר הַשָּׁמַיִם וְלֹא־יִהְיֶה מָטָר כִּי יֶחֶטְאוּ־לָךְ וְהִתְפַּלְלוּ אֶל־הַמָּקוֹם הַזֶּה וְהוֹדוּ אֶת־שְׁמֶךָ מֵחַטָּאתָם יְשׁוּבוּן כִּי תַעֲנֵם: 27 וְאַתָּה ׀ תִּשְׁמַע הַשָּׁמַיִם וְסָלַחְתָּ לְחַטַּאת עֲבָדֶיךָ וְעַמְּךָ יִשְׂרָאֵל כִּי תוֹרֵם אֶל־הַדֶּרֶךְ הַטּוֹבָה אֲשֶׁר יֵלְכוּ־בָהּ וְנָתַתָּה מָטָר עַל־אַרְצְךָ אֲשֶׁר־נָתַתָּה לְעַמְּךָ לְנַחֲלָה: ס 28 רָעָב כִּי־יִהְיֶה בָאָרֶץ דֶּבֶר כִּי־יִהְיֶה שִׁדָּפוֹן וְיֵרָקוֹן אַרְבֶּה וְחָסִיל כִּי יִהְיֶה כִּי יָצַר־לוֹ אוֹיְבָיו בְּאֶרֶץ שְׁעָרָיו כָּל־נֶגַע וְכָל־מַחֲלָה: 29 כָּל־תְּפִלָּה כָל־תְּחִנָּה אֲשֶׁר יִהְיֶה לְכָל־הָאָדָם וּלְכֹל עַמְּךָ יִשְׂרָאֵל אֲשֶׁר יֵדְעוּ אִישׁ נִגְעוֹ וּמַכְאֹבוֹ וּפָרַשׂ כַּפָּיו אֶל־הַבַּיִת הַזֶּה: 30 וְאַתָּה תִּשְׁמַע

give to everyone according to all his ways, whose heart You know (for You alone know the hearts of the sons of men), [31] that they may fear You, to walk in Your ways as long as they live in the land which You gave to our fathers.

[32] "Moreover, concerning a foreigner, who is not of Your people Israel, but has come from a far country for the sake of Your great name and Your mighty hand and Your outstretched arm, when they come and pray in this temple; [33] then hear from heaven Your dwelling place, and do according to all for which the foreigner calls to You, that all peoples of the earth may know Your name and fear You, as *do* Your people Israel, and that they may know that this temple which I have built is called by Your name.

[34] "When Your people go out to battle against their enemies, wherever You send them, and when they pray to You toward this city which You have chosen and the temple which I have built for Your name, [35] then hear from heaven their prayer and their supplication, and maintain their cause.

[36] "When they sin against You (for *there is* no one who does not sin), and You become angry with them and deliver them to the enemy, and they take them captive to a land far or near; [37] *yet* when they come to themselves in the land where they were carried captive, and repent, and make supplication to You in the land of their captivity, saying, 'We have sinned, we have done wrong, and have committed wickedness'; [38] and *when* they return to You with all their heart and with all their soul in the land of their captivity, where they have been carried captive, and pray toward their land which You gave to their fathers, the city which You have chosen, and toward the temple which I have built for Your name; [39] then hear from heaven Your dwelling place their prayer and their supplications, and maintain their cause, and forgive Your people who have sinned against You. [40] Now, my God, I pray, let Your eyes be open and *let* Your ears *be* attentive to the prayer *made* in this place.

[41] "Now therefore,
　Arise, O LORD God, to Your resting place,
　You and the ark of Your strength.
　Let Your priests, O LORD God, be clothed with
　　salvation,
　And let Your saints rejoice in goodness.

[42] "O LORD God, do not turn away the face of Your Anointed;
　Remember the mercies of Your servant David."

מִן־הַשָּׁמַיִם מְכוֹן שִׁבְתֶּךָ וְסָלַחְתָּ וְנָתַתָּה לָאִישׁ
כְּכָל־דְּרָכָיו אֲשֶׁר תֵּדַע אֶת־לְבָבוֹ כִּי אַתָּה לְבַדְּךָ
יָדַעְתָּ אֶת־לְבַב בְּנֵי הָאָדָם: 31 לְמַעַן יִירָאוּךָ
לָלֶכֶת בִּדְרָכֶיךָ כָּל־הַיָּמִים אֲשֶׁר־הֵם חַיִּים עַל־
פְּנֵי הָאֲדָמָה אֲשֶׁר נָתַתָּה לַאֲבֹתֵינוּ: ס 32 וְגַם
אֶל־הַנָּכְרִי אֲשֶׁר לֹא מֵעַמְּךָ יִשְׂרָאֵל הוּא וּבָא |
מֵאֶרֶץ רְחוֹקָה לְמַעַן שִׁמְךָ הַגָּדוֹל וְיָדְךָ הַחֲזָקָה
וּזְרוֹעֲךָ הַנְּטוּיָה וּבָאוּ וְהִתְפַּלְלוּ אֶל־הַבַּיִת הַזֶּה:
33 וְאַתָּה תִּשְׁמַע מִן־הַשָּׁמַיִם מִמְּכוֹן שִׁבְתֶּךָ וְעָשִׂיתָ
כְּכֹל אֲשֶׁר־יִקְרָא אֵלֶיךָ הַנָּכְרִי לְמַעַן יֵדְעוּ כָל־
עַמֵּי הָאָרֶץ אֶת־שְׁמֶךָ וּלְיִרְאָה אֹתְךָ כְּעַמְּךָ יִשְׂרָאֵל
וְלָדַעַת כִּי־שִׁמְךָ נִקְרָא עַל־הַבַּיִת הַזֶּה אֲשֶׁר בָּנִיתִי:
34 כִּי־יֵצֵא עַמְּךָ לַמִּלְחָמָה עַל־אוֹיְבָיו בַּדֶּרֶךְ אֲשֶׁר
תִּשְׁלָחֵם וְהִתְפַּלְלוּ אֵלֶיךָ דֶּרֶךְ הָעִיר הַזֹּאת אֲשֶׁר
בָּחַרְתָּ בָּהּ וְהַבַּיִת אֲשֶׁר־בָּנִיתִי לִשְׁמֶךָ: 35 וְשָׁמַעְתָּ
מִן־הַשָּׁמַיִם אֶת־תְּפִלָּתָם וְאֶת־תְּחִנָּתָם וְעָשִׂיתָ
מִשְׁפָּטָם: 36 כִּי יֶחֶטְאוּ־לָךְ כִּי אֵין אָדָם אֲשֶׁר
לֹא־יֶחֱטָא וְאָנַפְתָּ בָם וּנְתַתָּם לִפְנֵי אוֹיֵב וְשָׁבוּם
שׁוֹבֵיהֶם אֶל־אֶרֶץ רְחוֹקָה אוֹ קְרוֹבָה: 37 וְהֵשִׁיבוּ
אֶל־לְבָבָם בָּאָרֶץ אֲשֶׁר נִשְׁבּוּ־שָׁם וְשָׁבוּ | וְהִתְחַנְּנוּ
אֵלֶיךָ בְּאֶרֶץ שִׁבְיָם לֵאמֹר חָטָאנוּ הֶעֱוִינוּ וְרָשָׁעְנוּ:
38 וְשָׁבוּ אֵלֶיךָ בְּכָל־לִבָּם וּבְכָל־נַפְשָׁם בְּאֶרֶץ שִׁבְיָם
אֲשֶׁר־שָׁבוּ אֹתָם וְהִתְפַּלְלוּ דֶּרֶךְ אַרְצָם אֲשֶׁר נָתַתָּה
לַאֲבוֹתָם וְהָעִיר אֲשֶׁר בָּחַרְתָּ וְלַבַּיִת אֲשֶׁר־בָּנִיתִי
לִשְׁמֶךָ: 39 וְשָׁמַעְתָּ מִן־הַשָּׁמַיִם מִמְּכוֹן שִׁבְתְּךָ אֶת־
תְּפִלָּתָם וְאֶת־תְּחִנֹּתֵיהֶם וְעָשִׂיתָ מִשְׁפָּטָם וְסָלַחְתָּ
לְעַמְּךָ אֲשֶׁר חָטְאוּ־לָךְ: 40 עַתָּה אֱלֹהַי יִהְיוּ־נָא
עֵינֶיךָ פְּתֻחוֹת וְאָזְנֶיךָ קַשֻּׁבוֹת לִתְפִלַּת הַמָּקוֹם
הַזֶּה: ס 41 וְעַתָּה קוּמָה יְהוָה אֱלֹהִים לְנוּחֶךָ
אַתָּה וַאֲרוֹן עֻזֶּךָ כֹּהֲנֶיךָ יְהוָה אֱלֹהִים יִלְבְּשׁוּ
תְשׁוּעָה וַחֲסִידֶיךָ יִשְׂמְחוּ בַטּוֹב: 42 יְהוָה אֱלֹהִים
אַל־תָּשֵׁב פְּנֵי מְשִׁיחֶיךָ זָכְרָה לְחַסְדֵי דָּוִיד עַבְדֶּךָ: פ

7 When Solomon had finished praying, fire came down from heaven and consumed the burnt offering and the sacrifices; and the glory of the LORD filled the temple. ² And the priests could not enter the house of the LORD, because the glory of the LORD had filled the LORD's house. ³ When all the children of Israel saw how the fire came down, and the glory of the LORD on the temple, they bowed their faces to the ground on the pavement, and worshiped and praised the LORD, *saying:*

"For *He is* good,
For His mercy *endures* forever."

⁴ Then the king and all the people offered sacrifices before the LORD. ⁵ King Solomon offered a sacrifice of twenty-two thousand bulls and one hundred and twenty thousand sheep. So the king and all the people dedicated the house of God. ⁶ And the priests attended to their services; the Levites also with instruments of the music of the LORD, which King David had made to praise the LORD, saying, "For His mercy *endures* forever," whenever David offered praise by their ministry. The priests sounded trumpets opposite them, while all Israel stood.

⁷ Furthermore Solomon consecrated the middle of the court that *was* in front of the house of the LORD; for there he offered burnt offerings and the fat of the peace offerings, because the bronze altar which Solomon had made was not able to receive the burnt offerings, the grain offerings, and the fat.

⁸ At that time Solomon kept the feast seven days, and all Israel with him, a very great assembly, from the entrance of Hamath to the Brook of Egypt. ⁹ And on the eighth day they held a sacred assembly, for they observed the dedication of the altar seven days, and the feast seven days. ¹⁰ On the twenty-third day of the seventh month he sent the people away to their tents, joyful and glad of heart for the good that the LORD had done for David, for Solomon, and for His people Israel. ¹¹ Thus Solomon finished the house of the LORD and the king's house; and Solomon successfully accomplished all that came into his heart to make in the house of the LORD and in his own house.

¹² Then the LORD appeared to Solomon by night, and said to him: "I have heard your prayer, and have chosen this place for Myself as a house of sacrifice. ¹³ When I shut up heaven and there is no rain, or command the locusts to devour the land, or send pestilence among My people, ¹⁴ if My people who are called by My name will humble themselves, and pray and seek My face, and turn from their wicked ways, then I will hear from heaven, and will

ז וּכְכַלּ֣וֹת שְׁלֹמֹה֮ לְהִתְפַּלֵּל֒ וְהָאֵ֗שׁ יָרְדָה֙ מֵֽהַשָּׁמַ֔יִם וַתֹּ֙אכַל֙ הָעֹלָ֣ה וְהַזְּבָחִ֔ים וּכְב֥וֹד יְהוָ֖ה מָלֵ֥א אֶת־הַבָּֽיִת: ² וְלֹ֤א יָֽכְלוּ֙ הַכֹּ֣הֲנִ֔ים לָב֖וֹא אֶל־בֵּ֣ית יְהוָ֑ה כִּֽי־מָלֵ֥א כְבוֹד־יְהוָ֖ה אֶת־בֵּ֥ית יְהוָֽה: ³ וְכֹ֣ל | בְּנֵ֣י יִשְׂרָאֵ֡ל רֹאִים֩ בְּרֶ֨דֶת הָאֵ֜שׁ וּכְב֧וֹד יְהוָ֣ה עַל־הַבָּ֗יִת וַיִּכְרְעוּ֩ אַפַּ֨יִם אַ֤רְצָה עַל־הָרִֽצְפָה֙ וַיִּֽשְׁתַּ֣חֲו֔וּ וְהוֹד֤וֹת לַֽיהוָה֙ כִּ֣י ט֔וֹב כִּ֥י לְעוֹלָ֖ם חַסְדּֽוֹ: ⁴ וְהַמֶּ֥לֶךְ וְכָל־הָעָ֖ם זֹבְחִ֣ים זֶ֑בַח לִפְנֵ֖י יְהוָֽה: ס

⁵ וַיִּזְבַּ֞ח הַמֶּ֣לֶךְ שְׁלֹמֹה֮ אֶת־זֶ֣בַח הַבָּקָר֒ עֶשְׂרִ֤ים וּשְׁנַ֙יִם֙ אֶ֔לֶף וְצֹ֕אן מֵאָ֥ה וְעֶשְׂרִ֖ים אָ֑לֶף וַֽיַּחְנְכוּ֙ אֶת־בֵּ֣ית הָֽאֱלֹהִ֔ים הַמֶּ֖לֶךְ וְכָל־הָעָֽם: ⁶ וְהַכֹּֽהֲנִ֞ים עַל־מִשְׁמְרוֹתָ֣ם עֹֽמְדִ֗ים וְהַֽלְוִיִּ֞ם בִּכְלֵי־שִׁ֣יר יְהוָ֗ה אֲשֶׁ֨ר עָשָׂ֜ה דָּוִ֣יד הַמֶּ֗לֶךְ לְהֹד֤וֹת לַֽיהוָה֙ כִּֽי־לְעוֹלָ֣ם חַסְדּ֔וֹ בְּהַלֵּ֥ל דָּוִ֖יד בְּיָדָ֑ם וְהַכֹּֽהֲנִים֙ מַחְצְרִ֣יםP נֶגְדָּ֔ם וְכָל־יִשְׂרָאֵ֖ל עֹמְדִֽים: ס ⁷ וַיְקַדֵּ֣שׁ שְׁלֹמֹ֗ה אֶת־תּ֣וֹךְ הֶֽחָצֵ֞ר אֲשֶׁר֙ לִפְנֵ֣י בֵית־יְהוָ֔ה כִּֽי־עָ֤שָׂה שָׁם֙ הָֽעֹל֔וֹת וְאֵ֖ת חֶלְבֵ֣י הַשְּׁלָמִ֑ים כִּֽי־מִזְבַּ֤ח הַנְּחֹ֙שֶׁת֙ אֲשֶׁ֣ר עָשָׂ֣ה שְׁלֹמֹ֔ה לֹ֣א יָכ֔וֹל לְהָכִ֖יל אֶת־הָֽעֹלָ֛ה וְאֶת־הַמִּנְחָ֖ה וְאֶת־הַחֲלָבִֽים: ⁸ וַיַּ֣עַשׂ שְׁלֹמֹ֣ה אֶת־הֶ֠חָג בָּעֵ֨ת הַהִ֜יא שִׁבְעַ֤ת יָמִים֙ וְכָל־יִשְׂרָאֵ֣ל עִמּ֔וֹ קָהָ֖ל גָּד֣וֹל מְאֹ֑ד מִלְּב֥וֹא חֲמָ֖ת עַד־נַ֥חַל מִצְרָֽיִם: ⁹ וַֽיַּעֲשׂ֛וּ בַּיּ֥וֹם הַשְּׁמִינִ֖י עֲצָ֑רֶת כִּ֣י | חֲנֻכַּ֣ת הַמִּזְבֵּ֗חַ עָשׂוּ֙ שִׁבְעַ֣ת יָמִ֔ים וְהֶחָ֖ג שִׁבְעַ֥ת יָמִֽים: ¹⁰ וּבְי֨וֹם עֶשְׂרִ֤ים וּשְׁלֹשָׁה֙ לַחֹ֣דֶשׁ הַשְּׁבִיעִ֔י שִׁלַּ֥ח אֶת־הָעָ֖ם לְאָֽהֳלֵיהֶ֑ם שְׂמֵחִים֙ וְט֣וֹבֵי לֵ֔ב עַל־הַטּוֹבָ֗ה אֲשֶׁ֨ר עָשָׂ֤ה יְהוָה֙ לְדָוִ֣יד וְלִשְׁלֹמֹ֔ה וּלְיִשְׂרָאֵ֖ל עַמּֽוֹ: ¹¹ וַיְכַ֧ל שְׁלֹמֹ֛ה אֶת־בֵּ֥ית יְהוָ֖ה וְאֶת־בֵּ֣ית הַמֶּ֑לֶךְ וְאֵ֣ת כָּל־הַבָּ֣א עַל־לֵ֣ב שְׁלֹמֹ֗ה לַֽעֲשׂ֛וֹת בְּבֵית־יְהוָ֥ה וּבְבֵית֖וֹ הִצְלִֽיחַ: פ

¹² וַיֵּרָ֧א יְהוָ֛ה אֶל־שְׁלֹמֹ֖ה בַּלָּ֑יְלָה וַיֹּ֣אמֶר ל֗וֹ שָׁמַ֙עְתִּי֙ אֶת־תְּפִלָּתֶ֔ךָ וּבָחַ֛רְתִּי בַּמָּק֥וֹם הַזֶּ֖ה לִ֥י לְבֵ֥ית זָֽבַח: ¹³ הֵ֣ן אֶֽעֱצֹ֤ר הַשָּׁמַ֙יִם֙ וְלֹֽא־יִהְיֶ֣ה מָטָ֔ר וְהֵן־אֲצַוֶּ֥ה עַל־חָגָ֖ב לֶֽאֱכ֣וֹל הָאָ֑רֶץ וְאִם־אֲשַׁלַּ֥ח דֶּ֖בֶר בְּעַמִּֽי: ¹⁴ וְיִכָּֽנְע֨וּ עַמִּ֜י אֲשֶׁ֧ר נִקְרָֽא־שְׁמִ֣י עֲלֵיהֶ֗ם וְיִֽתְפַּֽלְלוּ֙ וִֽיבַקְשׁ֣וּ פָנַ֔י וְיָשֻׁ֖בוּ מִדַּרְכֵיהֶ֣ם הָרָעִ֑ים וַֽאֲנִי֙ אֶשְׁמַ֣ע

forgive their sin and heal their land. 15 Now My eyes will be open and My ears attentive to prayer *made* in this place. 16 For now I have chosen and sanctified this house, that My name may be there forever; and My eyes and My heart will be there perpetually. 17 As for you, if you walk before Me as your father David walked, and do according to all that I have commanded you, and if you keep My statutes and My judgments, 18 then I will establish the throne of your kingdom, as I covenanted with David your father, saying, 'You shall not fail *to have* a man as ruler in Israel.'

19 "But if you turn away and forsake My statutes and My commandments which I have set before you, and go and serve other gods, and worship them, 20 then I will uproot them from My land which I have given them; and this house which I have sanctified for My name I will cast out of My sight, and will make it a proverb and a byword among all peoples.

21 "And *as for* this house, which is exalted, everyone who passes by it will be astonished and say, 'Why has the LORD done thus to this land and this house?' 22 Then they will answer, 'Because they forsook the LORD God of their fathers, who brought them out of the land of Egypt, and embraced other gods, and worshiped them and served them; therefore He has brought all this calamity on them.' "

8 It came to pass at the end of twenty years, when Solomon had built the house of the LORD and his own house, 2 that the cities which Hiram had given to Solomon, Solomon built them; and he settled the children of Israel there. 3 And Solomon went to Hamath Zobah and seized it. 4 He also built Tadmor in the wilderness, and all the storage cities which he built in Hamath. 5 He built Upper Beth Horon and Lower Beth Horon, fortified cities *with* walls, gates, and bars, 6 also Baalath and all the storage cities that Solomon had, and all the chariot cities and the cities of the cavalry, and all that Solomon desired to build in Jerusalem, in Lebanon, and in all the land of his dominion.

7 All the people *who were* left of the Hittites, Amorites, Perizzites, Hivites, and Jebusites, who *were* not of Israel— 8 that is, their descendants who were left in the land after them, whom the children of Israel did not destroy—from these Solomon raised forced labor, as it is to this day. 9 But Solomon did not make the children of Israel servants for his work. Some *were* men of war, captains of his officers, captains of his chariots, and

מִן־הַשָּׁמַיִם וְאֶסְלַח לְחַטָּאתָם וְאֶרְפָּא אֶת־אַרְצָם: 15 עַתָּה עֵינַי יִהְיוּ פְתֻחוֹת וְאָזְנַי קַשֻּׁבוֹת לִתְפִלַּת הַמָּקוֹם הַזֶּה: 16 וְעַתָּה בָּחַרְתִּי וְהִקְדַּשְׁתִּי אֶת־הַבַּיִת הַזֶּה לִהְיוֹת־שְׁמִי שָׁם עַד־עוֹלָם וְהָיוּ עֵינַי וְלִבִּי שָׁם כָּל־הַיָּמִים: 17 וְאַתָּה אִם־תֵּלֵךְ לְפָנַי כַּאֲשֶׁר הָלַךְ דָּוִיד אָבִיךָ וְלַעֲשׂוֹת כְּכֹל אֲשֶׁר צִוִּיתִיךָ וְחֻקַּי וּמִשְׁפָּטַי תִּשְׁמוֹר: 18 וַהֲקִימוֹתִי אֵת כִּסֵּא מַלְכוּתֶךָ כַּאֲשֶׁר כָּרַתִּי לְדָוִיד אָבִיךָ לֵאמֹר לֹא־יִכָּרֵת לְךָ אִישׁ מוֹשֵׁל בְּיִשְׂרָאֵל: 19 וְאִם־תְּשׁוּבוּן אַתֶּם וַעֲזַבְתֶּם חֻקּוֹתַי וּמִצְוֹתַי אֲשֶׁר נָתַתִּי לִפְנֵיכֶם וַהֲלַכְתֶּם וַעֲבַדְתֶּם אֱלֹהִים אֲחֵרִים וְהִשְׁתַּחֲוִיתֶם לָהֶם: 20 וּנְתַשְׁתִּים מֵעַל אַדְמָתִי אֲשֶׁר נָתַתִּי לָהֶם וְאֶת־הַבַּיִת הַזֶּה אֲשֶׁר הִקְדַּשְׁתִּי לִשְׁמִי אַשְׁלִיךְ מֵעַל פָּנָי וְאֶתְּנֶנּוּ לְמָשָׁל וְלִשְׁנִינָה בְּכָל־הָעַמִּים: 21 וְהַבַּיִת הַזֶּה אֲשֶׁר הָיָה עֶלְיוֹן לְכָל־עֹבֵר עָלָיו יִשֹּׁם וְאָמַר בַּמֶּה עָשָׂה יְהוָה כָּכָה לָאָרֶץ הַזֹּאת וְלַבַּיִת הַזֶּה: 22 וְאָמְרוּ עַל אֲשֶׁר עָזְבוּ אֶת־יְהוָה ׀ אֱלֹהֵי אֲבֹתֵיהֶם אֲשֶׁר הוֹצִיאָם מֵאֶרֶץ מִצְרַיִם וַיַּחֲזִיקוּ בֵּאלֹהִים אֲחֵרִים וַיִּשְׁתַּחֲווּ לָהֶם וַיַּעַבְדֻם עַל־כֵּן הֵבִיא עֲלֵיהֶם אֵת כָּל־הָרָעָה הַזֹּאת: פ

ח וַיְהִי מִקֵּץ ׀ עֶשְׂרִים שָׁנָה אֲשֶׁר בָּנָה שְׁלֹמֹה אֶת־בֵּית יְהוָה וְאֶת־בֵּיתוֹ: 2 וְהֶעָרִים אֲשֶׁר נָתַן חוּרָם לִשְׁלֹמֹה בָּנָה שְׁלֹמֹה אֹתָם וַיּוֹשֶׁב שָׁם אֶת־בְּנֵי יִשְׂרָאֵל: 3 וַיֵּלֶךְ שְׁלֹמֹה חֲמָת צוֹבָה וַיֶּחֱזַק עָלֶיהָ: 4 וַיִּבֶן אֶת־תַּדְמֹר בַּמִּדְבָּר וְאֵת כָּל־עָרֵי הַמִּסְכְּנוֹת אֲשֶׁר בָּנָה בַּחֲמָת: 5 וַיִּבֶן אֶת־בֵּית חוֹרוֹן הָעֶלְיוֹן וְאֶת־בֵּית חוֹרוֹן הַתַּחְתּוֹן עָרֵי מָצוֹר חוֹמוֹת דְּלָתַיִם וּבְרִיחַ: 6 וְאֶת־בַּעֲלָת וְאֵת כָּל־עָרֵי הַמִּסְכְּנוֹת אֲשֶׁר הָיוּ לִשְׁלֹמֹה וְאֵת כָּל־עָרֵי הָרֶכֶב וְאֵת עָרֵי הַפָּרָשִׁים וְאֵת ׀ כָּל־חֵשֶׁק שְׁלֹמֹה אֲשֶׁר חָשַׁק לִבְנוֹת בִּירוּשָׁלַםִ וּבַלְּבָנוֹן וּבְכֹל אֶרֶץ מֶמְשַׁלְתּוֹ: 7 כָּל־הָעָם הַנּוֹתָר מִן־הַחִתִּי וְהָאֱמֹרִי וְהַפְּרִזִּי וְהַחִוִּי וְהַיְבוּסִי אֲשֶׁר לֹא מִיִּשְׂרָאֵל הֵמָּה: 8 מִן־בְּנֵיהֶם אֲשֶׁר נוֹתְרוּ אַחֲרֵיהֶם בָּאָרֶץ אֲשֶׁר לֹא־כִלּוּם בְּנֵי יִשְׂרָאֵל וַיַּעֲלֵם שְׁלֹמֹה לְמַס עַד הַיּוֹם הַזֶּה: 9 וּמִן־בְּנֵי יִשְׂרָאֵל אֲשֶׁר לֹא־נָתַן שְׁלֹמֹה

his cavalry. ¹⁰And others *were* chiefs of the officials of King Solomon: two hundred and fifty, who ruled over the people.

¹¹Now Solomon brought the daughter of Pharaoh up from the City of David to the house he had built for her, for he said, "My wife shall not dwell in the house of David king of Israel, because *the places* to which the ark of the LORD has come are holy."

¹²Then Solomon offered burnt offerings to the LORD on the altar of the LORD which he had built before the vestibule, ¹³according to the daily rate, offering according to the commandment of Moses, for the Sabbaths, the New Moons, and the three appointed yearly feasts—the Feast of Unleavened Bread, the Feast of Weeks, and the Feast of Tabernacles. ¹⁴And, according to the order of David his father, he appointed the divisions of the priests for their service, the Levites for their duties (to praise and serve before the priests) as the duty of each day required, and the gatekeepers by their divisions at each gate; for so David the man of God had commanded. ¹⁵They did not depart from the command of the king to the priests and Levites concerning any matter or concerning the treasuries.

¹⁶Now all the work of Solomon was well-ordered from the day of the foundation of the house of the LORD until it was finished. So the house of the LORD was completed.

¹⁷Then Solomon went to Ezion Geber and Elath on the seacoast, in the land of Edom. ¹⁸And Hiram sent him ships by the hand of his servants, and servants who knew the sea. They went with the servants of Solomon to Ophir, and acquired four hundred and fifty talents of gold from there, and brought it to King Solomon.

9 Now when the queen of Sheba heard of the fame of Solomon, she came to Jerusalem to test Solomon with hard questions, *having* a very great retinue, camels that bore spices, gold in abundance, and precious stones; and when she came to Solomon, she spoke with him about all that was in her heart. ²So Solomon answered all her questions; there was nothing so difficult for Solomon that he could not explain it to her. ³And when the queen of Sheba had seen the wisdom of Solomon, the house that he had built, ⁴the food on his table, the seating of his servants, the service of his waiters and their apparel, his cupbearers and their apparel, and his entryway by which he went up to the house of the LORD, there was no more spirit in her.

⁵Then she said to the king: "*It was* a true report which I heard in my own land about your words and your wisdom. ⁶However I did not believe their

לַעֲבָדִים לִמְלַאכְתּוֹ כִּי־הֵמָּה אַנְשֵׁי מִלְחָמָה וְשָׂרֵי
שָׁלִישָׁיו וְשָׂרֵי רִכְבּוֹ וּפָרָשָׁיו: פ

¹⁰ וְאֵלֶּה שָׂרֵי הַנִּצָּבִים אֲשֶׁר־לַמֶּלֶךְ שְׁלֹמֹה
חֲמִשִּׁים וּמָאתָיִם הָרֹדִים בָּעָם: ¹¹ וְאֶת־בַּת־פַּרְעֹה
הֶעֱלָה שְׁלֹמֹה מֵעִיר דָּוִיד לַבַּיִת אֲשֶׁר בָּנָה־לָהּ כִּי
אָמַר לֹא־תֵשֵׁב אִשָּׁה לִי בְּבֵית דָּוִיד מֶלֶךְ־יִשְׂרָאֵל
כִּי־קֹדֶשׁ הֵמָּה אֲשֶׁר־בָּאָה אֲלֵיהֶם אֲרוֹן יְהֹוָה: פ

¹² אָז הֶעֱלָה שְׁלֹמֹה עֹלוֹת לַיהֹוָה עַל מִזְבַּח
יְהֹוָה אֲשֶׁר בָּנָה לִפְנֵי הָאוּלָם: ¹³ וּבִדְבַר־יוֹם
בְּיוֹם לְהַעֲלוֹת כְּמִצְוַת מֹשֶׁה לַשַּׁבָּתוֹת וְלֶחֳדָשִׁים
וְלַמּוֹעֲדוֹת שָׁלוֹשׁ פְּעָמִים בַּשָּׁנָה בְּחַג הַמַּצּוֹת
וּבְחַג הַשָּׁבֻעוֹת וּבְחַג הַסֻּכּוֹת: ¹⁴ וַיַּעֲמֵד כְּמִשְׁפַּט
דָּוִיד־אָבִיו אֶת־מַחְלְקוֹת הַכֹּהֲנִים עַל־עֲבֹדָתָם
וְהַלְוִיִּם עַל־מִשְׁמְרוֹתָם לְהַלֵּל וּלְשָׁרֵת נֶגֶד הַכֹּהֲנִים
לִדְבַר־יוֹם בְּיוֹמוֹ וְהַשּׁוֹעֲרִים בְּמַחְלְקוֹתָם לְשַׁעַר
וָשָׁעַר כִּי כֵן מִצְוַת דָּוִיד אִישׁ־הָאֱלֹהִים: ¹⁵ וְלֹא
סָרוּ מִצְוַת הַמֶּלֶךְ עַל־הַכֹּהֲנִים וְהַלְוִיִּם לְכָל־
דָּבָר וְלָאֹצָרוֹת: ¹⁶ וַתִּכֹּן כָּל־מְלֶאכֶת שְׁלֹמֹה עַד־
הַיּוֹם מוּסַד בֵּית־יְהֹוָה וְעַד־כְּלֹתוֹ שָׁלֵם בֵּית
יְהֹוָה: ס ¹⁷ אָז הָלַךְ שְׁלֹמֹה לְעֶצְיוֹן־
גֶּבֶר וְאֶל־אֵילוֹת עַל־שְׂפַת הַיָּם בְּאֶרֶץ אֱדוֹם:
¹⁸ וַיִּשְׁלַח־לוֹ חוּרָם בְּיַד־עֲבָדָיו אֳנִיּוֹת וַעֲבָדִים
יוֹדְעֵי יָם וַיָּבֹאוּ עִם־עַבְדֵי שְׁלֹמֹה אוֹפִירָה וַיִּקְחוּ
מִשָּׁם אַרְבַּע־מֵאוֹת וַחֲמִשִּׁים כִּכַּר זָהָב וַיָּבִיאוּ אֶל־
הַמֶּלֶךְ שְׁלֹמֹה: פ

ט וּמַלְכַּת־שְׁבָא שָׁמְעָה אֶת־שֵׁמַע שְׁלֹמֹה וַתָּבוֹא
לְנַסּוֹת אֶת־שְׁלֹמֹה בְחִידוֹת בִּירוּשָׁלַ͏ִם בְּחַיִל כָּבֵד
מְאֹד וּגְמַלִּים נֹשְׂאִים בְּשָׂמִים וְזָהָב לָרֹב וְאֶבֶן
יְקָרָה וַתָּבוֹא אֶל־שְׁלֹמֹה וַתְּדַבֵּר עִמּוֹ אֵת כָּל־אֲשֶׁר
הָיָה עִם־לְבָבָהּ: ² וַיַּגֶּד־לָהּ שְׁלֹמֹה אֶת־כָּל־דְּבָרֶיהָ
וְלֹא־נֶעְלַם דָּבָר מִשְּׁלֹמֹה אֲשֶׁר לֹא הִגִּיד לָהּ:
³ וַתֵּרֶא מַלְכַּת־שְׁבָא אֵת חָכְמַת שְׁלֹמֹה וְהַבַּיִת
אֲשֶׁר בָּנָה: ⁴ וּמַאֲכַל שֻׁלְחָנוֹ וּמוֹשַׁב עֲבָדָיו וּמַעֲמַד
מְשָׁרְתָיו וּמַלְבּוּשֵׁיהֶם וּמַשְׁקָיו וּמַלְבּוּשֵׁיהֶם וַעֲלִיָּתוֹ
אֲשֶׁר יַעֲלֶה בֵּית יְהֹוָה וְלֹא־הָיָה עוֹד בָּהּ רוּחַ:
⁵ וַתֹּאמֶר אֶל־הַמֶּלֶךְ אֱמֶת הַדָּבָר אֲשֶׁר שָׁמַעְתִּי
בְּאַרְצִי עַל־דְּבָרֶיךָ וְעַל־חָכְמָתֶךָ: ⁶ וְלֹא־הֶאֱמַנְתִּי

אֲנִיּוֹת 18 הַנִּצָּבִים 10 ח

words until I came and saw with my own eyes; and indeed the half of the greatness of your wisdom was not told me. You exceed the fame of which I heard. [7]Happy *are* your men and happy *are* these your servants, who stand continually before you and hear your wisdom! [8]Blessed be the LORD your God, who delighted in you, setting you on His throne *to be* king for the LORD your God! Because your God has loved Israel, to establish them forever, therefore He made you king over them, to do justice and righteousness."

[9]And she gave the king one hundred and twenty talents of gold, spices in great abundance, and precious stones; there never were any spices such as those the queen of Sheba gave to King Solomon.

[10]Also, the servants of Hiram and the servants of Solomon, who brought gold from Ophir, brought algum wood and precious stones. [11]And the king made walkways *of* the algum wood for the house of the LORD and for the king's house, also harps and stringed instruments for singers; and there were none such *as these* seen before in the land of Judah.

[12]Now King Solomon gave to the queen of Sheba all she desired, whatever she asked, *much more* than she had brought to the king. So she turned and went to her own country, she and her servants.

[13]The weight of gold that came to Solomon yearly was six hundred and sixty-six talents of gold, [14]besides *what* the traveling merchants and traders brought. And all the kings of Arabia and governors of the country brought gold and silver to Solomon. [15]And King Solomon made two hundred large shields of hammered gold; six hundred *shekels* of hammered gold went into each shield. [16]*He also made* three hundred shields of hammered gold; three hundred *shekels* of gold went into each shield. The king put them in the House of the Forest of Lebanon.

[17]Moreover the king made a great throne of ivory, and overlaid it with pure gold. [18]The throne *had* six steps, with a footstool of gold, *which were* fastened to the throne; there were armrests on either side of the place of the seat, and two lions stood beside the armrests. [19]Twelve lions stood there, one on each side of the six steps; nothing like *this* had been made for any *other* kingdom.

[20]All King Solomon's drinking vessels *were* gold, and all the vessels of the House of the Forest of Lebanon *were* pure gold. Not *one was* silver, for this was accounted as nothing in the days of Solomon. [21]For the king's ships went to Tarshish with the

לִדְבָרֶיהֶם עַד אֲשֶׁר־בָּאתִי וַתִּרְאֶינָה עֵינַי וְהִנֵּה לֹא הֻגַּד־לִי חֲצִי מַרְבִּית חָכְמָתֶךָ יָסַפְתָּ עַל־הַשְּׁמוּעָה אֲשֶׁר שָׁמָעְתִּי: 7 אַשְׁרֵי אֲנָשֶׁיךָ וְאַשְׁרֵי עֲבָדֶיךָ אֵלֶּה הָעֹמְדִים לְפָנֶיךָ תָּמִיד וְשֹׁמְעִים אֶת־חָכְמָתֶךָ: 8 יְהִי יְהֹוָה אֱלֹהֶיךָ בָּרוּךְ אֲשֶׁר | חָפֵץ בְּךָ לְתִתְּךָ עַל־כִּסְאוֹ לְמֶלֶךְ לַיהֹוָה אֱלֹהֶיךָ בְּאַהֲבַת אֱלֹהֶיךָ אֶת־יִשְׂרָאֵל לְהַעֲמִידוֹ לְעוֹלָם וַיִּתֶּנְךָ עֲלֵיהֶם לְמֶלֶךְ לַעֲשׂוֹת מִשְׁפָּט וּצְדָקָה:

9 וַתִּתֵּן לַמֶּלֶךְ מֵאָה וְעֶשְׂרִים | כִּכַּר זָהָב וּבְשָׂמִים לָרֹב מְאֹד וְאֶבֶן יְקָרָה וְלֹא הָיָה כַּבֹּשֶׂם הַהוּא אֲשֶׁר־נָתְנָה מַלְכַּת־שְׁבָא לַמֶּלֶךְ שְׁלֹמֹה: 10 וְגַם־עַבְדֵי חִירָם וְעַבְדֵי שְׁלֹמֹה אֲשֶׁר־הֵבִיאוּ זָהָב מֵאוֹפִיר הֵבִיאוּ עֲצֵי אַלְגּוּמִּים וְאֶבֶן יְקָרָה: 11 וַיַּעַשׂ הַמֶּלֶךְ אֶת־עֲצֵי הָאַלְגּוּמִּים מְסִלּוֹת לְבֵית־יְהֹוָה וּלְבֵית הַמֶּלֶךְ וְכִנֹּרוֹת וּנְבָלִים לַשָּׁרִים וְלֹא־נִרְאוּ כָהֵם לְפָנִים בְּאֶרֶץ יְהוּדָה: 12 וְהַמֶּלֶךְ שְׁלֹמֹה נָתַן לְמַלְכַּת־שְׁבָא אֶת־כָּל־חֶפְצָהּ אֲשֶׁר שָׁאָלָה מִלְּבַד אֲשֶׁר־הֵבִיאָה אֶל־הַמֶּלֶךְ וַתַּהֲפֹךְ וַתֵּלֶךְ לְאַרְצָהּ הִיא וַעֲבָדֶיהָ: פ

13 וַיְהִי מִשְׁקַל הַזָּהָב אֲשֶׁר־בָּא לִשְׁלֹמֹה בְּשָׁנָה אֶחָת שֵׁשׁ מֵאוֹת וְשִׁשִּׁים וָשֵׁשׁ כִּכְּרֵי זָהָב: 14 לְבַד מֵאַנְשֵׁי הַתָּרִים וְהַסֹּחֲרִים מְבִיאִים וְכָל־מַלְכֵי עֲרַב וּפַחוֹת הָאָרֶץ מְבִיאִים זָהָב וָכֶסֶף לִשְׁלֹמֹה: 15 וַיַּעַשׂ הַמֶּלֶךְ שְׁלֹמֹה מָאתַיִם צִנָּה זָהָב שָׁחוּט שֵׁשׁ מֵאוֹת זָהָב שָׁחוּט יַעֲלֶה עַל־הַצִּנָּה הָאֶחָת: 16 וּשְׁלֹשׁ־מֵאוֹת מָגִנִּים זָהָב שָׁחוּט שְׁלֹשׁ מֵאוֹת זָהָב יַעֲלֶה עַל הַמָּגֵן הָאֶחָת וַיִּתְּנֵם הַמֶּלֶךְ בְּבֵית יַעַר הַלְּבָנוֹן: פ

17 וַיַּעַשׂ הַמֶּלֶךְ כִּסֵּא־שֵׁן גָּדוֹל וַיְצַפֵּהוּ זָהָב טָהוֹר: 18 וְשֵׁשׁ מַעֲלוֹת לַכִּסֵּא וְכֶבֶשׁ בַּזָּהָב לַכִּסֵּא מׇאֳחָזִים וְיָדוֹת מִזֶּה וּמִזֶּה עַל־מְקוֹם הַשָּׁבֶת וּשְׁנַיִם אֲרָיוֹת עֹמְדִים אֵצֶל הַיָּדוֹת: 19 וּשְׁנֵים עָשָׂר אֲרָיוֹת עֹמְדִים שָׁם עַל־שֵׁשׁ הַמַּעֲלוֹת מִזֶּה וּמִזֶּה וְלֹא־נַעֲשָׂה כֵן לְכָל־מַמְלָכָה: 20 וְכֹל כְּלֵי מַשְׁקֵה הַמֶּלֶךְ שְׁלֹמֹה זָהָב וְכֹל כְּלֵי בֵּית־יַעַר הַלְּבָנוֹן זָהָב סָגוּר אֵין כֶּסֶף נֶחְשָׁב בִּימֵי שְׁלֹמֹה לִמְאוּמָה: 21 כִּי־אֳנִיּוֹת לַמֶּלֶךְ

servants of Hiram. Once every three years the merchant ships came, bringing gold, silver, ivory, apes, and monkeys.

22 So King Solomon surpassed all the kings of the earth in riches and wisdom. 23 And all the kings of the earth sought the presence of Solomon to hear his wisdom, which God had put in his heart. 24 Each man brought his present: articles of silver and gold, garments, armor, spices, horses, and mules, at a set rate year by year.

25 Solomon had four thousand stalls for horses and chariots, and twelve thousand horsemen whom he stationed in the chariot cities and with the king at Jerusalem.

26 So he reigned over all the kings from the River to the land of the Philistines, as far as the border of Egypt. 27 The king made silver *as common* in Jerusalem as stones, and he made cedar trees as abundant as the sycamores which *are* in the lowland. 28 And they brought horses to Solomon from Egypt and from all lands.

29 Now the rest of the acts of Solomon, first and last, *are* they not written in the book of Nathan the prophet, in the prophecy of Ahijah the Shilonite, and in the visions of Iddo the seer concerning Jeroboam the son of Nebat? 30 Solomon reigned in Jerusalem over all Israel forty years. 31 Then Solomon rested with his fathers, and was buried in the City of David his father. And Rehoboam his son reigned in his place.

10

And Rehoboam went to Shechem, for all Israel had gone to Shechem to make him king. 2 So it happened, when Jeroboam the son of Nebat heard *it* (he was in Egypt, where he had fled from the presence of King Solomon), that Jeroboam returned from Egypt. 3 Then they sent for him and called him. And Jeroboam and all Israel came and spoke to Rehoboam, saying, 4 "Your father made our yoke heavy; now therefore, lighten the burdensome service of your father and his heavy yoke which he put on us, and we will serve you."

5 So he said to them, "Come back to me after three days." And the people departed.

6 Then King Rehoboam consulted the elders who stood before his father Solomon while he still lived, saying, "How do you advise *me* to answer these people?"

7 And they spoke to him, saying, "If you are kind to these people, and please them, and speak good words to them, they will be your servants forever."

8 But he rejected the advice which the elders had given him, and consulted the young men who had grown up with him, who stood before him. 9 And he

הַלְכוֹת תַּרְשִׁישׁ עִם עַבְדֵי חוּרָם אַחַת לְשָׁלוֹשׁ שָׁנִים תָּבוֹאנָה ׀ אֳנִיּוֹת תַּרְשִׁישׁ נֹשְׂאוֹת זָהָב וָכֶסֶף שֶׁנְהַבִּים וְקוֹפִים וְתוּכִּיִּים: פ

22 וַיִּגְדַּל הַמֶּלֶךְ שְׁלֹמֹה מִכֹּל מַלְכֵי הָאָרֶץ לְעֹשֶׁר וְחָכְמָה: 23 וְכֹל מַלְכֵי הָאָרֶץ מְבַקְשִׁים אֶת־פְּנֵי שְׁלֹמֹה לִשְׁמֹעַ אֶת־חָכְמָתוֹ אֲשֶׁר־נָתַן הָאֱלֹהִים בְּלִבּוֹ: 24 וְהֵם מְבִיאִים אִישׁ מִנְחָתוֹ כְּלֵי כֶסֶף וּכְלֵי זָהָב וּשְׂלָמוֹת נֵשֶׁק וּבְשָׂמִים סוּסִים וּפְרָדִים דְּבַר־שָׁנָה בְּשָׁנָה: פ

25 וַיְהִי לִשְׁלֹמֹה אַרְבַּעַת אֲלָפִים אֻרְיוֹת סוּסִים וּמַרְכָּבוֹת וּשְׁנֵים־עָשָׂר אֶלֶף פָּרָשִׁים וַיַּנִּיחֵם בְּעָרֵי הָרֶכֶב וְעִם־הַמֶּלֶךְ בִּירוּשָׁלָ͏ִם: 26 וַיְהִי מוֹשֵׁל בְּכָל־הַמְּלָכִים מִן־הַנָּהָר וְעַד־אֶרֶץ פְּלִשְׁתִּים וְעַד גְּבוּל מִצְרָיִם: 27 וַיִּתֵּן הַמֶּלֶךְ אֶת־הַכֶּסֶף בִּירוּשָׁלַ͏ִם כָּאֲבָנִים וְאֵת הָאֲרָזִים נָתַן כַּשִּׁקְמִים אֲשֶׁר־בַּשְּׁפֵלָה לָרֹב: 28 וּמוֹצִיאִים סוּסִים מִמִּצְרַיִם לִשְׁלֹמֹה וּמִכָּל־הָאֲרָצוֹת: 29 וּשְׁאָר דִּבְרֵי שְׁלֹמֹה הָרִאשֹׁנִים וְהָאַחֲרוֹנִים הֲלֹא־הֵם כְּתוּבִים עַל־דִּבְרֵי נָתָן הַנָּבִיא וְעַל־נְבוּאַת אֲחִיָּה הַשִּׁילוֹנִי וּבַחֲזוֹת יֶעְדִּי הַחֹזֶה עַל־יָרָבְעָם בֶּן־נְבָט: 30 וַיִּמְלֹךְ שְׁלֹמֹה בִירוּשָׁלַ͏ִם עַל־כָּל־יִשְׂרָאֵל אַרְבָּעִים שָׁנָה: 31 וַיִּשְׁכַּב שְׁלֹמֹה עִם־אֲבֹתָיו וַיִּקְבְּרֻהוּ בְּעִיר דָּוִיד אָבִיו וַיִּמְלֹךְ רְחַבְעָם בְּנוֹ תַּחְתָּיו: פ

י וַיֵּלֶךְ רְחַבְעָם שְׁכֶמָה כִּי שְׁכֶם בָּאוּ כָל־יִשְׂרָאֵל לְהַמְלִיךְ אֹתוֹ: 2 וַיְהִי כִּשְׁמֹעַ יָרָבְעָם בֶּן־נְבָט וְהוּא בְמִצְרַיִם אֲשֶׁר בָּרַח מִפְּנֵי שְׁלֹמֹה הַמֶּלֶךְ וַיָּשָׁב יָרָבְעָם מִמִּצְרָיִם: 3 וַיִּשְׁלְחוּ וַיִּקְרְאוּ־לוֹ וַיָּבֹא יָרָבְעָם וְכָל־יִשְׂרָאֵל וַיְדַבְּרוּ אֶל־רְחַבְעָם לֵאמֹר: 4 אָבִיךָ הִקְשָׁה אֶת־עֻלֵּנוּ וְעַתָּה הָקֵל מֵעֲבֹדַת אָבִיךָ הַקָּשָׁה וּמֵעֻלּוֹ הַכָּבֵד אֲשֶׁר־נָתַן עָלֵינוּ וְנַעַבְדֶךָּ: 5 וַיֹּאמֶר אֲלֵהֶם עוֹד שְׁלֹשֶׁת יָמִים וְשׁוּבוּ אֵלָי וַיֵּלֶךְ הָעָם: ס 6 וַיִּוָּעַץ הַמֶּלֶךְ רְחַבְעָם אֶת־הַזְּקֵנִים אֲשֶׁר־הָיוּ עֹמְדִים לִפְנֵי שְׁלֹמֹה אָבִיו בִּהְיֹתוֹ חַי לֵאמֹר אֵיךְ אַתֶּם נוֹעָצִים לְהָשִׁיב לָעָם־הַזֶּה דָּבָר: 7 וַיְדַבְּרוּ אֵלָיו לֵאמֹר אִם־תִּהְיֶה לְטוֹב לְהָעָם הַזֶּה וּרְצִיתָם וְדִבַּרְתָּ אֲלֵהֶם דְּבָרִים טוֹבִים וְהָיוּ לְךָ עֲבָדִים כָּל־הַיָּמִים: 8 וַיַּעֲזֹב אֶת־עֲצַת הַזְּקֵנִים אֲשֶׁר יְעָצֻהוּ וַיִּוָּעַץ אֶת־הַיְלָדִים אֲשֶׁר גָּדְלוּ אִתּוֹ הָעֹמְדִים לְפָנָיו: 9 וַיֹּאמֶר אֲלֵהֶם מָה אַתֶּם נוֹעָצִים וְנָשִׁיב

said to them, "What advice do you give? How should we answer this people who have spoken to me, saying, 'Lighten the yoke which your father put on us'?"

10 Then the young men who had grown up with him spoke to him, saying, "Thus you should speak to the people who have spoken to you, saying, 'Your father made our yoke heavy, but you make *it* lighter on us'—thus you shall say to them: 'My little *finger* shall be thicker than my father's waist! 11 And now, whereas my father put a heavy yoke on you, I will add to your yoke; my father chastised you with whips, but I *will chastise you* with scourges!'"

12 So Jeroboam and all the people came to Rehoboam on the third day, as the king had directed, saying, "Come back to me the third day." 13 Then the king answered them roughly. King Rehoboam rejected the advice of the elders, 14 and he spoke to them according to the advice of the young men, saying, "My father made your yoke heavy, but I will add to it; my father chastised you with whips, but I *will chastise you* with scourges!" 15 So the king did not listen to the people; for the turn *of events* was from God, that the LORD might fulfill His word, which He had spoken by the hand of Ahijah the Shilonite to Jeroboam the son of Nebat.

16 Now when all Israel *saw* that the king did not listen to them, the people answered the king, saying:

"What share have we in David?
We have no inheritance in the son of Jesse.
Every man to your tents, O Israel!
Now see to your own house, O David!"

So all Israel departed to their tents. 17 But Rehoboam reigned over the children of Israel who dwelt in the cities of Judah.

18 Then King Rehoboam sent Hadoram, who *was* in charge of revenue; but the children of Israel stoned him with stones, and he died. Therefore King Rehoboam mounted *his* chariot in haste to flee to Jerusalem. 19 So Israel has been in rebellion against the house of David to this day.

11 Now when Rehoboam came to Jerusalem, he assembled from the house of Judah and Benjamin one hundred and eighty thousand chosen *men* who were warriors, to fight against Israel, that he might restore the kingdom to Rehoboam.

2 But the word of the LORD came to Shemaiah the man of God, saying, 3 "Speak to Rehoboam the son of Solomon, king of Judah, and to all Israel in Judah and Benjamin, saying, 4 'Thus says the LORD: "You shall not go up or fight against your brethren!

דִּבֶּר אֶת־הָעָם הַזֶּה אֲשֶׁר דִּבְּרוּ אֵלַי לֵאמֹר הָקֵל
מִן־הָעֹל אֲשֶׁר־נָתַן אָבִיךָ עָלֵינוּ: 10 וַיְדַבְּרוּ אִתּוֹ
הַיְלָדִים אֲשֶׁר גָּדְלוּ אִתּוֹ לֵאמֹר כֹּה־תֹאמַר לָעָם
אֲשֶׁר־דִּבְּרוּ אֵלֶיךָ לֵאמֹר אָבִיךָ הִכְבִּיד אֶת־עֻלֵּנוּ
וְאַתָּה הָקֵל מֵעָלֵינוּ כֹּה תֹּאמַר אֲלֵהֶם קָטָנִּי עָבָה
מִמָּתְנֵי אָבִי: 11 וְעַתָּה אָבִי הֶעְמִיס עֲלֵיכֶם עֹל כָּבֵד
וַאֲנִי אֹסִיף עַל־עֻלְּכֶם אָבִי יִסַּר אֶתְכֶם בַּשּׁוֹטִים
וַאֲנִי בָּעַקְרַבִּים: ס 12 וַיָּבֹא יָרָבְעָם וְכָל־
הָעָם אֶל־רְחַבְעָם בַּיּוֹם הַשְּׁלִשִׁי כַּאֲשֶׁר דִּבֶּר הַמֶּלֶךְ
לֵאמֹר שׁוּבוּ אֵלַי בַּיּוֹם הַשְּׁלִשִׁי: 13 וַיַּעֲנֵם הַמֶּלֶךְ
קָשָׁה וַיַּעֲזֹב הַמֶּלֶךְ רְחַבְעָם אֵת עֲצַת הַזְּקֵנִים:
14 וַיְדַבֵּר אֲלֵהֶם כַּעֲצַת הַיְלָדִים לֵאמֹר אַכְבִּיד אֶת־
עֻלְּכֶם וַאֲנִי אֹסִיף עָלָיו אָבִי יִסַּר אֶתְכֶם בַּשּׁוֹטִים
וַאֲנִי בָּעַקְרַבִּים: 15 וְלֹא־שָׁמַע הַמֶּלֶךְ אֶל־הָעָם כִּי־
הָיְתָה נְסִבָּה מֵעִם הָאֱלֹהִים לְמַעַן הָקִים יְהוָה
אֶת־דְּבָרוֹ אֲשֶׁר דִּבֶּר בְּיַד אֲחִיָּהוּ הַשִּׁלוֹנִי אֶל־
יָרָבְעָם בֶּן־נְבָט: 16 וְכָל־יִשְׂרָאֵל כִּי לֹא־שָׁמַע הַמֶּלֶךְ
לָהֶם וַיָּשִׁיבוּ הָעָם אֶת־הַמֶּלֶךְ ׀ לֵאמֹר מַה־לָּנוּ
חֵלֶק בְּדָוִיד וְלֹא־נַחֲלָה בְּבֶן־יִשַׁי אִישׁ לְאֹהָלֶיךָ
יִשְׂרָאֵל עַתָּה רְאֵה בֵיתְךָ דָּוִיד וַיֵּלֶךְ כָּל־יִשְׂרָאֵל
לְאֹהָלָיו: ס 17 וּבְנֵי יִשְׂרָאֵל הַיֹּשְׁבִים בְּעָרֵי
יְהוּדָה וַיִּמְלֹךְ עֲלֵיהֶם רְחַבְעָם: 18 וַיִּשְׁלַח הַמֶּלֶךְ
רְחַבְעָם אֶת־הֲדֹרָם אֲשֶׁר עַל־הַמַּס וַיִּרְגְּמוּ־בוֹ בְנֵי־
יִשְׂרָאֵל אֶבֶן וַיָּמֹת וְהַמֶּלֶךְ רְחַבְעָם הִתְאַמֵּץ לַעֲלוֹת
בַּמֶּרְכָּבָה לָנוּס יְרוּשָׁלִָם: ס 19 וַיִּפְשְׁעוּ
יִשְׂרָאֵל בְּבֵית דָּוִיד עַד הַיּוֹם הַזֶּה: ס

יא וַיָּבֹא רְחַבְעָם יְרוּשָׁלַםִ וַיַּקְהֵל אֶת־בֵּית
יְהוּדָה וּבִנְיָמִן מֵאָה וּשְׁמוֹנִים אֶלֶף בָּחוּר
עֹשֵׂה מִלְחָמָה לְהִלָּחֵם עִם־יִשְׂרָאֵל לְהָשִׁיב אֶת־
הַמַּמְלָכָה לִרְחַבְעָם:
פ
2 וַיְהִי דְּבַר־יְהוָה אֶל־שְׁמַעְיָהוּ אִישׁ־הָאֱלֹהִים
לֵאמֹר: 3 אֱמֹר אֶל־רְחַבְעָם בֶּן־שְׁלֹמֹה מֶלֶךְ יְהוּדָה
וְאֶל כָּל־יִשְׂרָאֵל בִּיהוּדָה וּבִנְיָמִן לֵאמֹר: 4 כֹּה אָמַר
יְהוָה לֹא־תַעֲלוּ וְלֹא־תִלָּחֲמוּ עִם־אֲחֵיכֶם שׁוּבוּ

Let every man return to his house, for this thing is from Me.'"' Therefore they obeyed the words of the LORD, and turned back from attacking Jeroboam.

⁵So Rehoboam dwelt in Jerusalem, and built cities for defense in Judah. ⁶And he built Bethlehem, Etam, Tekoa, ⁷Beth Zur, Sochoh, Adullam, ⁸Gath, Mareshah, Ziph, ⁹Adoraim, Lachish, Azekah, ¹⁰Zorah, Aijalon, and Hebron, which are in Judah and Benjamin, fortified cities. ¹¹And he fortified the strongholds, and put captains in them, and stores of food, oil, and wine. ¹²Also in every city *he put* shields and spears, and made them very strong, having Judah and Benjamin on his side.

¹³And from all their territories the priests and the Levites who *were* in all Israel took their stand with him. ¹⁴For the Levites left their common-lands and their possessions and came to Judah and Jerusalem, for Jeroboam and his sons had rejected them from serving as priests to the LORD. ¹⁵Then he appointed for himself priests for the high places, for the demons, and the calf idols which he had made. ¹⁶And after *the Levites left,* those from all the tribes of Israel, such as set their heart to seek the LORD God of Israel, came to Jerusalem to sacrifice to the LORD God of their fathers. ¹⁷So they strengthened the kingdom of Judah, and made Rehoboam the son of Solomon strong for three years, because they walked in the way of David and Solomon for three years.

¹⁸Then Rehoboam took for himself as wife Mahalath the daughter of Jerimoth the son of David, *and of* Abihail the daughter of Eliah the son of Jesse. ¹⁹And she bore him children: Jeush, Shamariah, and Zaham. ²⁰After her he took Maachah the granddaughter of Absalom; and she bore him Abijah, Attai, Ziza, and Shelomith. ²¹Now Rehoboam loved Maachah the granddaughter of Absalom more than all his wives and his concubines; for he took eighteen wives and sixty concubines, and begot twenty-eight sons and sixty daughters. ²²And Rehoboam appointed Abijah the son of Maachah as chief, *to be* leader among his brothers; for he *intended* to make him king. ²³He dealt wisely, and dispersed some of his sons throughout all the territories of Judah and Benjamin, to every fortified city; and he gave them provisions in abundance. He also sought many wives *for them.*

12 Now it came to pass, when Rehoboam had established the kingdom and had strengthened himself, that he forsook the law of the LORD, and all Israel along with him. ²And it happened in the

אִישׁ לְבֵיתוֹ כִּי מֵאִתִּי נִהְיָה הַדָּבָר הַזֶּה וַיִּשְׁמְעוּ
אֶת־דִּבְרֵי יְהֹוָה וַיָּשֻׁבוּ מִלֶּכֶת אֶל־יָרָבְעָם: פ
5 וַיֵּשֶׁב רְחַבְעָם בִּירוּשָׁלָ͏ִם וַיִּבֶן עָרִים לְמָצוֹר
בִּיהוּדָה: 6 וַיִּבֶן אֶת־בֵּית־לֶחֶם וְאֶת־עֵיטָם וְאֶת־
תְּקוֹעַ: 7 וְאֶת־בֵּית־צוּר וְאֶת־שׂוֹכוֹ וְאֶת־עֲדֻלָּם:
8 וְאֶת־גַּת וְאֶת־מָרֵשָׁה וְאֶת־זִיף: 9 וְאֶת־אֲדוֹרַיִם
וְאֶת־לָכִישׁ וְאֶת־עֲזֵקָה: 10 וְאֶת־צָרְעָה וְאֶת־אַיָּלוֹן
וְאֶת־חֶבְרוֹן אֲשֶׁר בִּיהוּדָה וּבְבִנְיָמִן עָרֵי מְצֻרוֹת:
11 וַיְחַזֵּק אֶת־הַמְּצֻרוֹת וַיִּתֵּן בָּהֶם נְגִידִים וְאֹצְרוֹת
מַאֲכָל וְשֶׁמֶן וָיָיִן: 12 וּבְכָל־עִיר וָעִיר צִנּוֹת
וּרְמָחִים וַיְחַזְּקֵם לְהַרְבֵּה מְאֹד וַיְהִי־לוֹ יְהוּדָה
וּבִנְיָמִן: ס 13 וְהַכֹּהֲנִים וְהַלְוִיִּם אֲשֶׁר
בְּכָל־יִשְׂרָאֵל הִתְיַצְּבוּ עָלָיו מִכָּל־גְּבוּלָם: 14 כִּי־
עָזְבוּ הַלְוִיִּם אֶת־מִגְרְשֵׁיהֶם וַאֲחֻזָּתָם וַיֵּלְכוּ לִיהוּדָה
וְלִירוּשָׁלָ͏ִם כִּי־הִזְנִיחָם יָרָבְעָם וּבָנָיו מִכַּהֵן לַיהֹוָה:
15 וַיַּעֲמֶד־לוֹ כֹּהֲנִים לַבָּמוֹת וְלַשְּׂעִירִים וְלָעֲגָלִים
אֲשֶׁר עָשָׂה: 16 וְאַחֲרֵיהֶם מִכֹּל שִׁבְטֵי יִשְׂרָאֵל
הַנֹּתְנִים אֶת־לְבָבָם לְבַקֵּשׁ אֶת־יְהֹוָה אֱלֹהֵי יִשְׂרָאֵל
בָּאוּ יְרוּשָׁלַ͏ִם לִזְבּוֹחַ לַיהֹוָה אֱלֹהֵי אֲבוֹתֵיהֶם:
17 וַיְחַזְּקוּ אֶת־מַלְכוּת יְהוּדָה וַיְאַמְּצוּ אֶת־רְחַבְעָם
בֶּן־שְׁלֹמֹה לְשָׁנִים שָׁלוֹשׁ כִּי הָלְכוּ בְּדֶרֶךְ דָּוִיד
וּשְׁלֹמֹה לְשָׁנִים שָׁלוֹשׁ: 18 וַיִּקַּח־לוֹ רְחַבְעָם אִשָּׁה
אֶת־מָחֲלַת בֶּן־ק יְרִימוֹת בֶּן־דָּוִיד אֲבִיהַיִל בַּת־
אֱלִיאָב בֶּן־יִשָׁי: 19 וַתֵּלֶד לוֹ בָּנִים אֶת־יְעוּשׁ
וְאֶת־שְׁמַרְיָה וְאֶת־זָהַם: 20 וְאַחֲרֶיהָ לָקַח אֶת־
מַעֲכָה בַּת־אַבְשָׁלוֹם וַתֵּלֶד לוֹ אֶת־אֲבִיָּה וְאֶת־
עַתַּי וְאֶת־זִיזָא וְאֶת־שְׁלֹמִית: 21 וַיֶּאֱהַב רְחַבְעָם
אֶת־מַעֲכָה בַת־אַבְשָׁלוֹם מִכָּל־נָשָׁיו וּפִילַגְשָׁיו כִּי
נָשִׁים שְׁמוֹנֶה־עֶשְׂרֵה נָשָׂא וּפִילַגְשִׁים שִׁשִּׁים וַיּוֹלֶד
עֶשְׂרִים וּשְׁמוֹנָה בָּנִים וְשִׁשִּׁים בָּנוֹת: 22 וַיַּעֲמֵד
לָרֹאשׁ רְחַבְעָם אֶת־אֲבִיָּה בֶן־מַעֲכָה לְנָגִיד בְּאֶחָיו
כִּי לְהַמְלִיכוֹ: 23 וַיָּבֶן וַיִּפְרֹץ מִכָּל־בָּנָיו לְכָל־אַרְצוֹת
יְהוּדָה וּבִנְיָמִן לְכֹל עָרֵי הַמְּצֻרוֹת וַיִּתֵּן לָהֶם הַמָּזוֹן
לָרֹב וַיִּשְׁאַל הֲמוֹן נָשִׁים:

יב וַיְהִי כְּהָכִין מַלְכוּת רְחַבְעָם וּכְחֶזְקָתוֹ עָזַב
אֶת־תּוֹרַת יְהֹוָה וְכָל־יִשְׂרָאֵל עִמּוֹ: פ
2 וַיְהִי בַּשָּׁנָה הַחֲמִישִׁית לַמֶּלֶךְ רְחַבְעָם עָלָה

יא 18 בֶּת־

fifth year of King Rehoboam *that* Shishak king of Egypt came up against Jerusalem, because they had transgressed against the LORD, [3]with twelve hundred chariots, sixty thousand horsemen, and people without number who came with him out of Egypt—the Lubim and the Sukkiim and the Ethiopians. [4]And he took the fortified cities of Judah and came to Jerusalem.

[5]Then Shemaiah the prophet came to Rehoboam and the leaders of Judah, who were gathered together in Jerusalem because of Shishak, and said to them, "Thus says the LORD: 'You have forsaken Me, and therefore I also have left you in the hand of Shishak.'"

[6]So the leaders of Israel and the king humbled themselves; and they said, "The LORD *is* righteous."

[7]Now when the LORD saw that they humbled themselves, the word of the LORD came to Shemaiah, saying, "They have humbled themselves; *therefore* I will not destroy them, but I will grant them some deliverance. My wrath shall not be poured out on Jerusalem by the hand of Shishak. [8]Nevertheless they will be his servants, that they may distinguish My service from the service of the kingdoms of the nations."

[9]So Shishak king of Egypt came up against Jerusalem, and took away the treasures of the house of the LORD and the treasures of the king's house; he took everything. He also carried away the gold shields which Solomon had made. [10]Then King Rehoboam made bronze shields in their place, and committed *them* to the hands of the captains of the guard, who guarded the doorway of the king's house. [11]And whenever the king entered the house of the LORD, the guard would go and bring them out; then they would take them back into the guardroom. [12]When he humbled himself, the wrath of the LORD turned from him, so as not to destroy *him* completely; and things also went well in Judah.

[13]Thus King Rehoboam strengthened himself in Jerusalem and reigned. Now Rehoboam *was* forty-one years old when he became king; and he reigned seventeen years in Jerusalem, the city which the LORD had chosen out of all the tribes of Israel, to put His name there. His mother's name *was* Naamah, an Ammonitess. [14]And he did evil, because he did not prepare his heart to seek the LORD.

[15]The acts of Rehoboam, first and last, *are* they not written in the book of Shemaiah the prophet, and of Iddo the seer concerning genealogies? And *there were* wars between Rehoboam and Jeroboam

שִׁישַׁק מֶלֶךְ־מִצְרַיִם עַל־יְרוּשָׁלִָם כִּי מָעֲלוּ בַּיהוָה: [3] בְּאֶלֶף וּמָאתַיִם רֶכֶב וּבְשִׁשִּׁים אֶלֶף פָּרָשִׁים וְאֵין מִסְפָּר לָעָם אֲשֶׁר־בָּאוּ עִמּוֹ מִמִּצְרַיִם לוּבִים סֻכִּיִּים וְכוּשִׁים: [4] וַיִּלְכֹּד אֶת־עָרֵי הַמְּצֻרוֹת אֲשֶׁר לִיהוּדָה וַיָּבֹא עַד־יְרוּשָׁלִָם: ס [5] וּשְׁמַעְיָה הַנָּבִיא בָּא אֶל־רְחַבְעָם וְשָׂרֵי יְהוּדָה אֲשֶׁר־נֶאֶסְפוּ אֶל־יְרוּשָׁלִַם מִפְּנֵי שִׁישָׁק וַיֹּאמֶר לָהֶם כֹּה־אָמַר יְהוָה אַתֶּם עֲזַבְתֶּם אֹתִי וְאַף־אֲנִי עָזַבְתִּי אֶתְכֶם בְּיַד־שִׁישָׁק: [6] וַיִּכָּנְעוּ שָׂרֵי־יִשְׂרָאֵל וְהַמֶּלֶךְ וַיֹּאמְרוּ צַדִּיק יְהוָה: [7] וּבִרְאוֹת יְהוָה כִּי נִכְנָעוּ הָיָה דְבַר־יְהוָה אֶל־שְׁמַעְיָה לֵאמֹר נִכְנְעוּ לֹא אַשְׁחִיתֵם וְנָתַתִּי לָהֶם כִּמְעַט לִפְלֵיטָה וְלֹא־תִתַּךְ חֲמָתִי בִּירוּשָׁלִַם בְּיַד־שִׁישָׁק: [8] כִּי יִהְיוּ־לוֹ לַעֲבָדִים וְיֵדְעוּ עֲבוֹדָתִי וַעֲבוֹדַת מַמְלְכוֹת הָאֲרָצוֹת: ס [9] וַיַּעַל שִׁישַׁק מֶלֶךְ־מִצְרַיִם עַל־יְרוּשָׁלִַם וַיִּקַּח אֶת־אֹצְרוֹת בֵּית־יְהוָה וְאֶת־אֹצְרוֹת בֵּית הַמֶּלֶךְ אֶת־הַכֹּל לָקָח וַיִּקַּח אֶת־מָגִנֵּי הַזָּהָב אֲשֶׁר עָשָׂה שְׁלֹמֹה: [10] וַיַּעַשׂ הַמֶּלֶךְ רְחַבְעָם תַּחְתֵּיהֶם מָגִנֵּי נְחֹשֶׁת וְהִפְקִיד עַל־יַד שָׂרֵי הָרָצִים הַשֹּׁמְרִים פֶּתַח בֵּית הַמֶּלֶךְ: [11] וַיְהִי מִדֵּי־בוֹא הַמֶּלֶךְ בֵּית יְהוָה בָּאוּ הָרָצִים וּנְשָׂאוּם וֶהֱשִׁבוּם אֶל־תָּא הָרָצִים: [12] וּבְהִכָּנְעוֹ שָׁב מִמֶּנּוּ אַף־יְהוָה וְלֹא לְהַשְׁחִית לְכָלָה וְגַם בִּיהוּדָה הָיָה דְּבָרִים טוֹבִים: ס [13] וַיִּתְחַזֵּק הַמֶּלֶךְ רְחַבְעָם בִּירוּשָׁלִַם וַיִּמְלֹךְ כִּי בֶן־אַרְבָּעִים וְאַחַת שָׁנָה רְחַבְעָם בְּמָלְכוֹ וּשְׁבַע עֶשְׂרֵה שָׁנָה מָלַךְ בִּירוּשָׁלִַם הָעִיר אֲשֶׁר־בָּחַר יְהוָה לָשׂוּם אֶת־שְׁמוֹ שָׁם מִכֹּל שִׁבְטֵי יִשְׂרָאֵל וְשֵׁם אִמּוֹ נַעֲמָה הָעַמֹּנִית: [14] וַיַּעַשׂ הָרָע כִּי לֹא הֵכִין לִבּוֹ לִדְרוֹשׁ אֶת־יְהוָה: ס [15] וְדִבְרֵי רְחַבְעָם הָרִאשֹׁנִים וְהָאַחֲרוֹנִים הֲלֹא־הֵם כְּתוּבִים בְּדִבְרֵי שְׁמַעְיָה הַנָּבִיא וְעִדּוֹ הַחֹזֶה לְהִתְיַחֵשׂ וּמִלְחֲמוֹת רְחַבְעָם

all their days. 16 So Rehoboam rested with his fathers, and was buried in the City of David. Then Abijah his son reigned in his place.

13 In the eighteenth year of King Jeroboam, Abijah became king over Judah. 2 He reigned three years in Jerusalem. His mother's name *was* Michaiah the daughter of Uriel of Gibeah.

And there was war between Abijah and Jeroboam. 3 Abijah set the battle in order with an army of valiant warriors, four hundred thousand choice men. Jeroboam also drew up in battle formation against him with eight hundred thousand choice men, mighty men of valor.

4 Then Abijah stood on Mount Zemaraim, which *is* in the mountains of Ephraim, and said, "Hear me, Jeroboam and all Israel: 5 Should you not know that the LORD God of Israel gave the dominion over Israel to David forever, to him and his sons, by a covenant of salt? 6 Yet Jeroboam the son of Nebat, the servant of Solomon the son of David, rose up and rebelled against his lord. 7 Then worthless rogues gathered to him, and strengthened themselves against Rehoboam the son of Solomon, when Rehoboam was young and inexperienced and could not withstand them. 8 And now you think to withstand the kingdom of the LORD, which is in the hand of the sons of David; and you *are* a great multitude, and with you are the gold calves which Jeroboam made for you as gods. 9 Have you not cast out the priests of the LORD, the sons of Aaron, and the Levites, and made for yourselves priests, like the peoples of *other* lands, so that whoever comes to consecrate himself with a young bull and seven rams may be a priest of *things that are* not gods? 10 But as for us, the LORD *is* our God, and we have not forsaken Him; and the priests who minister to the LORD *are* the sons of Aaron, and the Levites *attend* to *their* duties. 11 And they burn to the LORD every morning and every evening burnt sacrifices and sweet incense; *they* also *set* the showbread *in order on* the pure *gold* table, and the lampstand of gold with its lamps to burn every evening; for we keep the command of the LORD our God, but you have forsaken Him. 12 Now look, God Himself is with us as *our* head, and His priests with sounding trumpets to sound the alarm against you. O children of Israel, do not fight against the LORD God of your fathers, for you shall not prosper!"

13 But Jeroboam caused an ambush to go around behind them; so they were in front of Judah, and the ambush *was* behind them. 14 And when Judah looked around, to their surprise the battle line *was*

16 וַיִּשְׁכַּב רְחַבְעָם עִם־אֲבֹתָיו וַיִּקָּבֵר בְּעִיר דָּוִיד וַיִּמְלֹךְ אֲבִיָּה בְנוֹ תַּחְתָּיו: פ

יג בִּשְׁנַת שְׁמוֹנֶה עֶשְׂרֵה לַמֶּלֶךְ יָרָבְעָם וַיִּמְלֹךְ אֲבִיָּה עַל־יְהוּדָה: 2 שָׁלוֹשׁ שָׁנִים מָלַךְ בִּירוּשָׁלִָם וְשֵׁם אִמּוֹ מִיכָיָהוּ בַת־אוּרִיאֵל מִן־גִּבְעָה וּמִלְחָמָה הָיְתָה בֵּין אֲבִיָּה וּבֵין יָרָבְעָם: 3 וַיֶּאְסֹר אֲבִיָּה אֶת־הַמִּלְחָמָה בְּחַיִל גִּבּוֹרֵי מִלְחָמָה אַרְבַּע־מֵאוֹת אֶלֶף אִישׁ בָּחוּר ס וְיָרָבְעָם עָרַךְ עִמּוֹ מִלְחָמָה בִּשְׁמוֹנֶה מֵאוֹת אֶלֶף אִישׁ בָּחוּר גִּבּוֹר חָיִל: ס 4 וַיָּקָם אֲבִיָּה מֵעַל לְהַר צְמָרַיִם אֲשֶׁר בְּהַר אֶפְרָיִם וַיֹּאמֶר שְׁמָעוּנִי יָרָבְעָם וְכָל־יִשְׂרָאֵל: 5 הֲלֹא לָכֶם לָדַעַת כִּי יְהוָה אֱלֹהֵי יִשְׂרָאֵל נָתַן מַמְלָכָה לְדָוִיד עַל־יִשְׂרָאֵל לְעוֹלָם לוֹ וּלְבָנָיו בְּרִית מֶלַח: ס 6 וַיָּקָם יָרָבְעָם בֶּן־נְבָט עֶבֶד שְׁלֹמֹה בֶן־דָּוִיד וַיִּמְרֹד עַל־אֲדֹנָיו: 7 וַיִּקָּבְצוּ עָלָיו אֲנָשִׁים רֵקִים בְּנֵי בְלִיַּעַל וַיִּתְאַמְּצוּ עַל־רְחַבְעָם בֶּן־שְׁלֹמֹה וּרְחַבְעָם הָיָה נַעַר וְרַךְ־לֵבָב וְלֹא הִתְחַזַּק לִפְנֵיהֶם: 8 וְעַתָּה אַתֶּם אֹמְרִים לְהִתְחַזֵּק לִפְנֵי מַמְלֶכֶת יְהוָה בְּיַד בְּנֵי דָוִיד וְאַתֶּם הָמוֹן רָב וְעִמָּכֶם עֶגְלֵי זָהָב אֲשֶׁר עָשָׂה לָכֶם יָרָבְעָם לֵאלֹהִים: 9 הֲלֹא הִדַּחְתֶּם אֶת־כֹּהֲנֵי יְהוָה אֶת־בְּנֵי אַהֲרֹן וְהַלְוִיִּם וַתַּעֲשׂוּ לָכֶם כֹּהֲנִים כְּעַמֵּי הָאֲרָצוֹת כָּל־הַבָּא לְמַלֵּא יָדוֹ בְּפַר בֶּן־בָּקָר וְאֵילִם שִׁבְעָה וְהָיָה כֹהֵן לְלֹא אֱלֹהִים: ס 10 וַאֲנַחְנוּ יְהוָה אֱלֹהֵינוּ וְלֹא עֲזַבְנֻהוּ וְכֹהֲנִים מְשָׁרְתִים לַיהוָה בְּנֵי אַהֲרֹן וְהַלְוִיִּם בַּמְּלָאכֶת: 11 וּמַקְטִרִים לַיהוָה עֹלוֹת בַּבֹּקֶר־בַּבֹּקֶר וּבָעֶרֶב־בָּעֶרֶב וּקְטֹרֶת־סַמִּים וּמַעֲרֶכֶת לֶחֶם עַל־הַשֻּׁלְחָן הַטָּהוֹר וּמְנוֹרַת הַזָּהָב וְנֵרֹתֶיהָ לְבָעֵר בָּעֶרֶב בָּעֶרֶב כִּי־שֹׁמְרִים אֲנַחְנוּ אֶת־מִשְׁמֶרֶת יְהוָה אֱלֹהֵינוּ וְאַתֶּם עֲזַבְתֶּם אֹתוֹ: 12 וְהִנֵּה עִמָּנוּ בָרֹאשׁ הָאֱלֹהִים וְכֹהֲנָיו וַחֲצֹצְרוֹת הַתְּרוּעָה לְהָרִיעַ עֲלֵיכֶם בְּנֵי יִשְׂרָאֵל אַל־תִּלָּחֲמוּ עִם־יְהוָה אֱלֹהֵי־אֲבֹתֵיכֶם כִּי־לֹא תַצְלִיחוּ: 13 וְיָרָבְעָם הֵסֵב אֶת־הַמַּאְרָב לָבוֹא מֵאַחֲרֵיהֶם וַיִּהְיוּ לִפְנֵי יְהוּדָה וְהַמַּאְרָב מֵאַחֲרֵיהֶם: 14 וַיִּפְנוּ יְהוּדָה וְהִנֵּה לָהֶם

at both front and rear; and they cried out to the LORD, and the priests sounded the trumpets. 15 Then the men of Judah gave a shout; and as the men of Judah shouted, it happened that God struck Jeroboam and all Israel before Abijah and Judah. 16 And the children of Israel fled before Judah, and God delivered them into their hand. 17 Then Abijah and his people struck them with a great slaughter; so five hundred thousand choice men of Israel fell slain. 18 Thus the children of Israel were subdued at that time; and the children of Judah prevailed, because they relied on the LORD God of their fathers.

19 And Abijah pursued Jeroboam and took cities from him: Bethel with its villages, Jeshanah with its villages, and Ephrain with its villages. 20 So Jeroboam did not recover strength again in the days of Abijah; and the LORD struck him, and he died.

21 But Abijah grew mighty, married fourteen wives, and begot twenty-two sons and sixteen daughters. 22 Now the rest of the acts of Abijah, his ways, and his sayings *are* written in the annals of the prophet Iddo.

14 So Abijah rested with his fathers, and they buried him in the City of David. Then Asa his son reigned in his place. In his days the land was quiet for ten years.

2 Asa did *what was* good and right in the eyes of the LORD his God, 3 for he removed the altars of the foreign *gods* and the high places, and broke down the *sacred* pillars and cut down the wooden images. 4 He commanded Judah to seek the LORD God of their fathers, and to observe the law and the commandment. 5 He also removed the high places and the incense altars from all the cities of Judah, and the kingdom was quiet under him. 6 And he built fortified cities in Judah, for the land had rest; he had no war in those years, because the LORD had given him rest. 7 Therefore he said to Judah, "Let us build these cities and make walls around *them,* and towers, gates, and bars, *while* the land *is* yet before us, because we have sought the LORD our God; we have sought *Him,* and He has given us rest on every side." So they built and prospered. 8 And Asa had an army of three hundred thousand from Judah who carried shields and spears, and from Benjamin two hundred and eighty thousand men who carried shields and drew bows; all these *were* mighty men of valor.

9 Then Zerah the Ethiopian came out against them with an army of a million men and three hundred chariots, and he came to Mareshah. 10 So

הַמִּלְחָמָה פָּנִים וְאָחוֹר וַיִּצְעֲקוּ לַיהוָה וְהַכֹּהֲנִים
מַחֲצֹצְרִיםP בַּחֲצֹצְרוֹת: 15 וַיָּרִיעוּ אִישׁ יְהוּדָה
וַיְהִי בְּהָרִיעַ אִישׁ יְהוּדָה וְהָאֱלֹהִים נָגַף אֶת־
יָרָבְעָם וְכָל־יִשְׂרָאֵל לִפְנֵי אֲבִיָּה וִיהוּדָה: 16 וַיָּנוּסוּ
בְנֵי־יִשְׂרָאֵל מִפְּנֵי יְהוּדָה וַיִּתְּנֵם אֱלֹהִים בְּיָדָם:
17 וַיַּכּוּ בָהֶם אֲבִיָּה וְעַמּוֹ מַכָּה רַבָּה וַיִּפְּלוּ
חֲלָלִים מִיִּשְׂרָאֵל חֲמֵשׁ־מֵאוֹת אֶלֶף אִישׁ בָּחוּר:
18 וַיִּכָּנְעוּ בְנֵי־יִשְׂרָאֵל בָּעֵת הַהִיא וַיֶּאֶמְצוּ בְּנֵי
יְהוּדָה כִּי נִשְׁעֲנוּ עַל־יְהוָה אֱלֹהֵי אֲבוֹתֵיהֶם:
19 וַיִּרְדֹּף אֲבִיָּה אַחֲרֵי יָרָבְעָם וַיִּלְכֹּד מִמֶּנּוּ עָרִים
אֶת־בֵּית־אֵל וְאֶת־בְּנוֹתֶיהָ וְאֶת־יְשָׁנָה וְאֶת־בְּנוֹתֶיהָ
וְאֶת־עֶפְרוֹןP וּבְנֹתֶיהָ: 20 וְלֹא־עָצַר כֹּחַ־יָרָבְעָם עוֹד
בִּימֵי אֲבִיָּהוּ וַיִּגְּפֵהוּ יְהוָה וַיָּמֹת: פ
21 וַיִּתְחַזֵּק אֲבִיָּהוּ וַיִּשָּׂא־לוֹ נָשִׁים אַרְבַּע עֶשְׂרֵה
וַיּוֹלֶד עֶשְׂרִים וּשְׁנַיִם בָּנִים וְשֵׁשׁ עֶשְׂרֵה
בָּנוֹת: ס 22 וְיֶתֶר דִּבְרֵי אֲבִיָּה וּדְרָכָיו
וּדְבָרָיו כְּתוּבִים בְּמִדְרַשׁ הַנָּבִיא עִדּוֹ: 23 וַיִּשְׁכַּב
אֲבִיָּה עִם־אֲבֹתָיו וַיִּקְבְּרוּ אֹתוֹ בְּעִיר דָּוִיד וַיִּמְלֹךְ
אָסָא בְנוֹ תַּחְתָּיו בְּיָמָיו שָׁקְטָה הָאָרֶץ עֶשֶׂר
שָׁנִים: פ

יד וַיַּעַשׂ אָסָא הַטּוֹב וְהַיָּשָׁר בְּעֵינֵי יְהוָה אֱלֹהָיו:
2 וַיָּסַר אֶת־מִזְבְּחוֹת הַנֵּכָר וְהַבָּמוֹת וַיְשַׁבֵּר אֶת־
הַמַּצֵּבוֹת וַיְגַדַּע אֶת־הָאֲשֵׁרִים: 3 וַיֹּאמֶר לִיהוּדָה
לִדְרוֹשׁ אֶת־יְהוָה אֱלֹהֵי אֲבוֹתֵיהֶם וְלַעֲשׂוֹת הַתּוֹרָה
וְהַמִּצְוָה: 4 וַיָּסַר מִכָּל־עָרֵי יְהוּדָה אֶת־הַבָּמוֹת
וְאֶת־הַחַמָּנִים וַתִּשְׁקֹט הַמַּמְלָכָה לְפָנָיו: 5 וַיִּבֶן
עָרֵי מְצוּרָה בִּיהוּדָה כִּי־שָׁקְטָה הָאָרֶץ וְאֵין־עִמּוֹ
מִלְחָמָה בַּשָּׁנִים הָאֵלֶּה כִּי־הֵנִיחַ יְהוָה לוֹ: 6 וַיֹּאמֶר
לִיהוּדָה נִבְנֶה | אֶת־הֶעָרִים הָאֵלֶּה וְנָסֵב חוֹמָה
וּמִגְדָּלִים דְּלָתַיִם וּבְרִיחִים עוֹדֶנּוּ הָאָרֶץ לְפָנֵינוּ כִּי
דָרַשְׁנוּ אֶת־יְהוָה אֱלֹהֵינוּ דָּרַשְׁנוּ וַיָּנַח לָנוּ מִסָּבִיב
וַיִּבְנוּ וַיַּצְלִיחוּ: פ
7 וַיְהִי לְאָסָא חַיִל נֹשֵׂא צִנָּה וָרֹמַח מִיהוּדָה שְׁלֹשׁ
מֵאוֹת אֶלֶף ס וּמִבִּנְיָמִן נֹשְׂאֵי מָגֵן וְדֹרְכֵי
קֶשֶׁת מָאתַיִם וּשְׁמוֹנִים אֶלֶף כָּל־אֵלֶּה גִּבּוֹרֵי חָיִל:
8 וַיֵּצֵא אֲלֵיהֶם זֶרַח הַכּוּשִׁי בְּחַיִל אֶלֶף אֲלָפִים
וּמַרְכָּבוֹת שְׁלֹשׁ מֵאוֹת וַיָּבֹא עַד־מָרֵשָׁה: 9 וַיֵּצֵא
אָסָא לְפָנָיו וַיַּעַרְכוּ מִלְחָמָה בְּגֵיא צְפַתָה לְמָרֵשָׁה:
10 וַיִּקְרָא אָסָא אֶל־יְהוָה אֱלֹהָיו וַיֹּאמַר

Asa went out against him, and they set the troops in battle array in the Valley of Zephathah at Mareshah. ¹¹ And Asa cried out to the LORD his God, and said, "LORD, *it is* nothing for You to help, whether with many or with those who have no power; help us, O LORD our God, for we rest on You, and in Your name we go against this multitude. O LORD, You *are* our God; do not let man prevail against You!"

¹² So the LORD struck the Ethiopians before Asa and Judah, and the Ethiopians fled. ¹³ And Asa and the people who *were* with him pursued them to Gerar. So the Ethiopians were overthrown, and they could not recover, for they were broken before the LORD and His army. And they carried away very much spoil. ¹⁴ Then they defeated all the cities around Gerar, for the fear of the LORD came upon them; and they plundered all the cities, for there was exceedingly much spoil in them. ¹⁵ They also attacked the livestock enclosures, and carried off sheep and camels in abundance, and returned to Jerusalem.

15 Now the Spirit of God came upon Azariah the son of Oded. ² And he went out to meet Asa, and said to him: "Hear me, Asa, and all Judah and Benjamin. The LORD *is* with you while you are with Him. If you seek Him, He will be found by you; but if you forsake Him, He will forsake you. ³ For a long time Israel *has been* without the true God, without a teaching priest, and without law; ⁴ but when in their trouble they turned to the LORD God of Israel, and sought Him, He was found by them. ⁵ And in those times *there was* no peace to the one who went out, nor to the one who came in, but great turmoil *was* on all the inhabitants of the lands. ⁶ So nation was destroyed by nation, and city by city, for God troubled them with every adversity. ⁷ But you, be strong and do not let your hands be weak, for your work shall be rewarded!"

⁸ And when Asa heard these words and the prophecy of Oded the prophet, he took courage, and removed the abominable idols from all the land of Judah and Benjamin and from the cities which he had taken in the mountains of Ephraim; and he restored the altar of the LORD that *was* before the vestibule of the LORD. ⁹ Then he gathered all Judah and Benjamin, and those who dwelt with them from Ephraim, Manasseh, and Simeon, for they came over to him in great numbers from Israel when they saw that the LORD his God was with him.

¹⁰ So they gathered together at Jerusalem in the third month, in the fifteenth year of the reign of Asa. ¹¹ And they offered to the LORD at that time

יְהוָה אֵין־עִמְּךָ לַעְזוֹר בֵּין רַב לְאֵין כֹּחַ עָזְרֵנוּ יְהוָה אֱלֹהֵינוּ כִּי־עָלֶיךָ נִשְׁעַנּוּ וּבְשִׁמְךָ בָאנוּ עַל־ הֶהָמוֹן הַזֶּה יְהוָה אֱלֹהֵינוּ אַתָּה אַל־יַעְצֹר עִמְּךָ אֱנוֹשׁ: ס ¹¹ וַיִּגֹּף יְהוָה אֶת־הַכּוּשִׁים לִפְנֵי אָסָא וְלִפְנֵי יְהוּדָה וַיָּנֻסוּ הַכּוּשִׁים: ¹² וַיִּרְדְּפֵם אָסָא וְהָעָם אֲשֶׁר־עִמּוֹ עַד־לִגְרָר וַיִּפֹּל מִכּוּשִׁים לְאֵין לָהֶם מִחְיָה כִּי־נִשְׁבְּרוּ לִפְנֵי־יְהוָה וְלִפְנֵי מַחֲנֵהוּ וַיִּשְׂאוּ שָׁלָל הַרְבֵּה מְאֹד: ¹³ וַיַּכּוּ אֵת כָּל־הֶעָרִים סְבִיבוֹת גְּרָר כִּי־הָיָה פַחַד־יְהוָה עֲלֵיהֶם וַיָּבֹזּוּ אֶת־כָּל־הֶעָרִים כִּי־בִזָּה רַבָּה הָיְתָה בָהֶם: ¹⁴ וְגַם־ אָהֳלֵי מִקְנֶה הִכּוּ וַיִּשְׁבּוּ צֹאן לָרֹב וּגְמַלִּים וַיָּשֻׁבוּ יְרוּשָׁלָ͏ִם: ס

טו וַעֲזַרְיָהוּ בֶּן־עוֹדֵד הָיְתָה עָלָיו רוּחַ אֱלֹהִים: ² וַיֵּצֵא לִפְנֵי אָסָא וַיֹּאמֶר לוֹ שְׁמָעוּנִי אָסָא וְכָל־יְהוּדָה וּבִנְיָמִן יְהוָה עִמָּכֶם בִּהְיוֹתְכֶם עִמּוֹ וְאִם־תִּדְרְשֻׁהוּ יִמָּצֵא לָכֶם וְאִם־תַּעַזְבֻהוּ יַעֲזֹב אֶתְכֶם: ס ³ וְיָמִים רַבִּים לְיִשְׂרָאֵל לְלֹא אֱלֹהֵי אֱמֶת וּלְלֹא כֹּהֵן מוֹרֶה וּלְלֹא תוֹרָה: ⁴ וַיָּשָׁב בַּצַּר־לוֹ עַל־יְהוָה אֱלֹהֵי יִשְׂרָאֵל וַיְבַקְשֻׁהוּ וַיִּמָּצֵא לָהֶם: ⁵ וּבָעִתִּים הָהֵם אֵין שָׁלוֹם לַיּוֹצֵא וְלַבָּא כִּי מְהוּמֹת רַבּוֹת עַל כָּל־יוֹשְׁבֵי הָאֲרָצוֹת: ⁶ וְכֻתְּתוּ גוֹי־בְּגוֹי וְעִיר בְּעִיר כִּי־אֱלֹהִים הֲמָמָם בְּכָל־צָרָה: ⁷ וְאַתֶּם חִזְקוּ וְאַל־יִרְפּוּ יְדֵיכֶם כִּי יֵשׁ שָׂכָר לִפְעֻלַּתְכֶם: ס ⁸ וְכִשְׁמֹעַ אָסָא הַדְּבָרִים הָאֵלֶּה וְהַנְּבוּאָה עֹדֵד הַנָּבִיא הִתְחַזַּק וַיַּעֲבֵר הַשִּׁקּוּצִים מִכָּל־אֶרֶץ יְהוּדָה וּבִנְיָמִן וּמִן־הֶעָרִים אֲשֶׁר לָכַד מֵהַר אֶפְרָיִם וַיְחַדֵּשׁ אֶת־מִזְבַּח יְהוָה אֲשֶׁר לִפְנֵי אוּלָם יְהוָה: ⁹ וַיִּקְבֹּץ אֶת־כָּל־יְהוּדָה וּבִנְיָמִן וְהַגָּרִים עִמָּהֶם מֵאֶפְרַיִם וּמְנַשֶּׁה וּמִשִּׁמְעוֹן כִּי־נָפְלוּ עָלָיו מִיִּשְׂרָאֵל לָרֹב בִּרְאֹתָם כִּי־יְהוָה אֱלֹהָיו עִמּוֹ: פ ¹⁰ וַיִּקָּבְצוּ יְרוּשָׁלַ͏ִם בַּחֹדֶשׁ הַשְּׁלִשִׁי לִשְׁנַת חֲמֵשׁ־ עֶשְׂרֵה לְמַלְכוּת אָסָא: ¹¹ וַיִּזְבְּחוּ לַיהוָה בַּיּוֹם

seven hundred bulls and seven thousand sheep from the spoil they had brought. ¹²Then they entered into a covenant to seek the LORD God of their fathers with all their heart and with all their soul; ¹³and whoever would not seek the LORD God of Israel was to be put to death, whether small or great, whether man or woman. ¹⁴Then they took an oath before the LORD with a loud voice, with shouting and trumpets and rams' horns. ¹⁵And all Judah rejoiced at the oath, for they had sworn with all their heart and sought Him with all their soul; and He was found by them, and the LORD gave them rest all around.

¹⁶Also he removed Maachah, the mother of Asa the king, from *being* queen mother, because she had made an obscene image of Asherah; and Asa cut down her obscene image, then crushed and burned *it* by the Brook Kidron. ¹⁷But the high places were not removed from Israel. Nevertheless the heart of Asa was loyal all his days.

¹⁸He also brought into the house of God the things that his father had dedicated and that he himself had dedicated: silver and gold and utensils. ¹⁹And there was no war until the thirty-fifth year of the reign of Asa.

16 In the thirty-sixth year of the reign of Asa, Baasha king of Israel came up against Judah and built Ramah, that he might let none go out or come in to Asa king of Judah. ²Then Asa brought silver and gold from the treasuries of the house of the LORD and of the king's house, and sent to Ben-Hadad king of Syria, who dwelt in Damascus, saying, ³"*Let there be* a treaty between you and me, as there was between my father and your father. See, I have sent you silver and gold; come, break your treaty with Baasha king of Israel, so that he will withdraw from me."

⁴So Ben-Hadad heeded King Asa, and sent the captains of his armies against the cities of Israel. They attacked Ijon, Dan, Abel Maim, and all the storage cities of Naphtali. ⁵Now it happened, when Baasha heard *it*, that he stopped building Ramah and ceased his work. ⁶Then King Asa took all Judah, and they carried away the stones and timber of Ramah, which Baasha had used for building; and with them he built Geba and Mizpah.

⁷And at that time Hanani the seer came to Asa king of Judah, and said to him: "Because you have relied on the king of Syria, and have not relied on the LORD your God, therefore the army of the king of Syria has escaped from your hand. ⁸Were the Ethiopians and the Lubim not a huge army with very many chariots and horsemen? Yet, because

הַהוּא מִן־הַשָּׁלָל הֵבִיאוּ בָּקָר שְׁבַע מֵאוֹת וְצֹאן שִׁבְעַת אֲלָפִים: ¹²וַיָּבֹאוּ בַבְּרִית לִדְרוֹשׁ אֶת־יְהוָה אֱלֹהֵי אֲבוֹתֵיהֶם בְּכָל־לְבָבָם וּבְכָל־נַפְשָׁם: ¹³וְכֹל אֲשֶׁר לֹא־יִדְרֹשׁ לַיהוָה אֱלֹהֵי־יִשְׂרָאֵל יוּמָת לְמִן־קָטֹן וְעַד־גָּדוֹל לְמֵאִישׁ וְעַד־אִשָּׁה: ¹⁴וַיִּשָּׁבְעוּ לַיהוָה בְּקוֹל גָּדוֹל וּבִתְרוּעָה וּבַחֲצֹצְרוֹת וּבְשׁוֹפָרוֹת: ¹⁵וַיִּשְׂמְחוּ כָל־יְהוּדָה עַל־הַשְּׁבוּעָה כִּי בְכָל־לְבָבָם נִשְׁבָּעוּ וּבְכָל־רְצוֹנָם בִּקְשֻׁהוּ וַיִּמָּצֵא לָהֶם וַיָּנַח יְהוָה לָהֶם מִסָּבִיב: ¹⁶ וְגַם־מַעֲכָה אֵם אָסָא הַמֶּלֶךְ הֱסִירָהּ מִגְּבִירָה אֲשֶׁר־עָשְׂתָה לָאֲשֵׁרָה מִפְלָצֶת וַיִּכְרֹת אָסָא אֶת־מִפְלַצְתָּהּ וַיָּדֶק וַיִּשְׂרֹף בְּנַחַל קִדְרוֹן: ¹⁷וְהַבָּמוֹת לֹא־סָרוּ מִיִּשְׂרָאֵל רַק לְבַב־אָסָא הָיָה שָׁלֵם כָּל־יָמָיו: ¹⁸וַיָּבֵא אֶת־קָדְשֵׁי אָבִיו וְקָדָשָׁיו בֵּית הָאֱלֹהִים כֶּסֶף וְזָהָב וְכֵלִים: ¹⁹וּמִלְחָמָה לֹא הָיָתָה עַד שְׁנַת־שְׁלֹשִׁים וְחָמֵשׁ לְמַלְכוּת אָסָא: ס

טז בִּשְׁנַת שְׁלֹשִׁים וָשֵׁשׁ לְמַלְכוּת אָסָא עָלָה בַּעְשָׁא מֶלֶךְ־יִשְׂרָאֵל עַל־יְהוּדָה וַיִּבֶן אֶת־הָרָמָה לְבִלְתִּי תֵּת יוֹצֵא וָבָא לְאָסָא מֶלֶךְ יְהוּדָה: ²וַיֹּצֵא אָסָא כֶּסֶף וְזָהָב מֵאֹצְרוֹת בֵּית יְהוָה וּבֵית הַמֶּלֶךְ וַיִּשְׁלַח אֶל־בֶּן־הֲדַד מֶלֶךְ אֲרָם הַיּוֹשֵׁב בְּדַרְמֶשֶׂק לֵאמֹר: ³בְּרִית בֵּינִי וּבֵינֶךָ וּבֵין אָבִי וּבֵין אָבִיךָ הִנֵּה שָׁלַחְתִּי לְךָ כֶּסֶף וְזָהָב לֵךְ הָפֵר בְּרִיתְךָ אֶת־בַּעְשָׁא מֶלֶךְ יִשְׂרָאֵל וְיַעֲלֶה מֵעָלָי: ⁴וַיִּשְׁמַע בֶּן־הֲדַד אֶל־הַמֶּלֶךְ אָסָא וַיִּשְׁלַח אֶת־שָׂרֵי הַחֲיָלִים אֲשֶׁר־לוֹ אֶל־עָרֵי יִשְׂרָאֵל וַיַּכּוּ אֶת־עִיּוֹן וְאֶת־דָּן וְאֵת אָבֵל מָיִם וְאֵת כָּל־מִסְכְּנוֹת עָרֵי נַפְתָּלִי: ⁵וַיְהִי כִּשְׁמֹעַ בַּעְשָׁא וַיֶּחְדַּל מִבְּנוֹת אֶת־הָרָמָה וַיַּשְׁבֵּת אֶת־מְלַאכְתּוֹ: ס ⁶וְאָסָא הַמֶּלֶךְ לָקַח אֶת־כָּל־יְהוּדָה וַיִּשְׂאוּ אֶת־אַבְנֵי הָרָמָה וְאֶת־עֵצֶיהָ אֲשֶׁר בָּנָה בַּעְשָׁא וַיִּבֶן בָּהֶם אֶת־גֶּבַע וְאֶת־הַמִּצְפָּה: ס ⁷וּבָעֵת הַהִיא בָּא חֲנָנִי הָרֹאֶה אֶל־אָסָא מֶלֶךְ יְהוּדָה וַיֹּאמֶר אֵלָיו בְּהִשָּׁעֶנְךָ עַל־מֶלֶךְ אֲרָם וְלֹא נִשְׁעַנְתָּ עַל־יְהוָה אֱלֹהֶיךָ עַל־כֵּן נִמְלַט חֵיל מֶלֶךְ־אֲרָם מִיָּדֶךָ: ⁸הֲלֹא הַכּוּשִׁים וְהַלּוּבִים הָיוּ לְחַיִל ׀ לָרֹב לְרֶכֶב וּלְפָרָשִׁים

you relied on the LORD, He delivered them into your hand. ⁹For the eyes of the LORD run to and fro throughout the whole earth, to show Himself strong on behalf of *those* whose heart *is* loyal to Him. In this you have done foolishly; therefore from now on you shall have wars." ¹⁰Then Asa was angry with the seer, and put him in prison, for *he was* enraged at him because of this. And Asa oppressed *some* of the people at that time.

¹¹Note that the acts of Asa, first and last, are indeed written in the book of the kings of Judah and Israel. ¹²And in the thirty-ninth year of his reign, Asa became diseased in his feet, and his malady was severe; yet in his disease he did not seek the LORD, but the physicians.

¹³So Asa rested with his fathers; he died in the forty-first year of his reign. ¹⁴They buried him in his own tomb, which he had made for himself in the City of David; and they laid him in the bed which was filled with spices and various ingredients prepared in a mixture of ointments. They made a very great burning for him.

17 Then Jehoshaphat his son reigned in his place, and strengthened himself against Israel. ²And he placed troops in all the fortified cities of Judah, and set garrisons in the land of Judah and in the cities of Ephraim which Asa his father had taken. ³Now the LORD was with Jehoshaphat, because he walked in the former ways of his father David; he did not seek the Baals, ⁴but sought the God of his father, and walked in His commandments and not according to the acts of Israel. ⁵Therefore the LORD established the kingdom in his hand; and all Judah gave presents to Jehoshaphat, and he had riches and honor in abundance. ⁶And his heart took delight in the ways of the LORD; moreover he removed the high places and wooden images from Judah.

⁷Also in the third year of his reign he sent his leaders, Ben-Hail, Obadiah, Zechariah, Nethanel, and Michaiah, to teach in the cities of Judah. ⁸And with them *he sent* Levites: Shemaiah, Nethaniah, Zebadiah, Asahel, Shemiramoth, Jehonathan, Adonijah, Tobijah, and Tobadonijah—the Levites; and with them Elishama and Jehoram, the priests. ⁹So they taught in Judah, and *had* the Book of the Law of the LORD with them; they went throughout all the cities of Judah and taught the people.

¹⁰And the fear of the LORD fell on all the kingdoms of the lands that *were* around Judah, so that they did not make war against Jehoshaphat. ¹¹Also *some* of the Philistines brought Jehoshaphat presents and silver as tribute; and the Arabians

לְהַרְבֵּ֤ה מְאֹד֙ וּבְהִשָּֽׁעֶנְךָ֣ עַל־יְהוָ֔ה נְתָנָ֖ם בְּיָדֶֽךָ׃ 9 כִּ֣י יְהוָ֗ה עֵינָ֞יו מְשֹׁטְט֤וֹת בְּכָל־הָאָ֙רֶץ֙ לְ֠הִתְחַזֵּ֞ק עִם־לְבָבָ֤ם שָׁלֵם֙ אֵלָ֔יו נִסְכַּ֖לְתָּ עַל־זֹ֑את כִּ֣י מֵעַ֔תָּה יֵ֥שׁ עִמְּךָ֖ מִלְחָמֽוֹת׃ 10 וַיִּכְעַ֨ס אָסָ֜א אֶל־הָ֣רֹאֶ֗ה וַֽיִּתְּנֵ֙הוּ֙ בֵּ֣ית הַמַּהְפֶּ֔כֶת כִּֽי־בְזַ֥עַף עִמּ֖וֹ עַל־זֹ֑את וַיְרַצֵּ֥ץ אָסָ֛א מִן־הָעָ֖ם בָּעֵ֥ת הַהִֽיא׃ 11 וְהִנֵּ֞ה דִּבְרֵ֣י אָסָ֗א הָרִֽאשׁוֹנִים֙ וְהָאַ֣חֲרוֹנִ֔ים הִנָּ֤ם כְּתוּבִים֙ עַל־סֵ֣פֶר הַמְּלָכִ֔ים לִיהוּדָ֖ה וְיִשְׂרָאֵֽל׃ 12 וַיֶּחֱלֶ֣א אָסָ֡א בִּשְׁנַת֩ שְׁלוֹשִׁ֨ים וָתֵ֤שַׁע לְמַלְכוּתוֹ֙ בְּרַגְלָ֔יו עַד־לְמַ֖עְלָה חָלְי֑וֹ וְגַם־בְּחָלְיוֹ֙ לֹא־דָרַ֣שׁ אֶת־יְהוָ֔ה כִּ֖י בָּרֹפְאִֽים׃ 13 וַיִּשְׁכַּ֥ב אָסָ֖א עִם־אֲבֹתָ֑יו וַיָּ֕מָת בִּשְׁנַ֥ת אַרְבָּעִ֛ים וְאַחַ֖ת לְמָלְכֽוֹ׃ 14 וַיִּקְבְּרֻ֣הוּ בְקִבְרֹתָ֗יו אֲשֶׁ֨ר כָּֽרָה־לוֹ֜ בְּעִ֣יר דָּוִ֗יד וַיַּשְׁכִּיבֻ֙הוּ֙ בַּמִּשְׁכָּ֔ב אֲשֶׁ֣ר מִלֵּ֗א בְּשָׂמִ֤ים וּזְנִים֙ מְרֻקָּחִ֔ים בְּמִרְקַ֖חַת מַעֲשֶׂ֑ה וַיִּשְׂרְפוּ־ל֥וֹ שְׂרֵפָ֖ה גְּדוֹלָ֥ה עַד־לִמְאֹֽד׃ פ

17 וַיִּמְלֹ֛ךְ יְהוֹשָׁפָ֥ט בְּנ֖וֹ תַּחְתָּ֑יו וַיִּתְחַזֵּ֖ק עַל־יִשְׂרָאֵֽל׃ 2 וַיִּ֨תֶּן־חַ֔יִל בְּכָל־עָרֵ֥י יְהוּדָ֖ה הַבְּצֻר֑וֹת וַיִּתֵּ֤ן נְצִיבִים֙ בְּאֶ֣רֶץ יְהוּדָ֔ה וּבְעָרֵ֣י אֶפְרַ֔יִם אֲשֶׁ֥ר לָכַ֖ד אָסָ֥א אָבִֽיו׃ 3 וַיְהִ֥י יְהוָ֖ה עִם־יְהוֹשָׁפָ֑ט כִּ֣י הָלַ֗ךְ בְּדַרְכֵ֞י דָּוִ֤יד אָבִיו֙ הָרִ֣אשֹׁנִ֔ים וְלֹ֥א דָרַ֖שׁ לַבְּעָלִֽים׃ 4 כִּ֠י לֵֽאלֹהֵ֤י אָבִיו֙ דָּרָ֔שׁ וּבְמִצְוֺתָ֖יו הָלָ֑ךְ וְלֹ֖א כְּמַעֲשֵׂ֥ה יִשְׂרָאֵֽל׃ 5 וַיָּ֨כֶן יְהוָ֤ה אֶת־הַמַּמְלָכָה֙ בְּיָד֔וֹ וַיִּתְּנ֧וּ כָל־יְהוּדָ֛ה מִנְחָ֖ה לִיהוֹשָׁפָ֑ט וַֽיְהִי־ל֥וֹ עֹֽשֶׁר־וְכָב֖וֹד לָרֹֽב׃ 6 וַיִּגְבַּ֥הּ לִבּ֖וֹ בְּדַרְכֵ֣י יְהוָ֑ה וְע֗וֹד הֵסִ֛יר אֶת־הַבָּמ֥וֹת וְאֶת־הָאֲשֵׁרִ֖ים מִיהוּדָֽה׃ פ 7 וּבִשְׁנַ֨ת שָׁל֜וֹשׁ לְמָלְכ֗וֹ שָׁלַ֤ח לְשָׂרָיו֙ לְבֶן־חַ֙יִל֙ וּלְעֹבַדְיָ֣ה וְלִזְכַרְיָ֔ה וְלִנְתַנְאֵ֖ל וּלְמִיכָ֑יָהוּ לְלַמֵּ֖ד בְּעָרֵ֥י יְהוּדָֽה׃ 8 וְעִמָּהֶ֣ם הַלְוִיִּ֗ם שְֽׁמַֽעְיָ֡הוּ וּנְתַנְיָ֡הוּ וּזְבַדְיָ֡הוּ וַעֲשָׂהאֵ֡ל וּֽשְׁמִֽרִימ֩וֹת וִיהוֹנָתָ֨ן וַאֲדֹ֥נִיָּ֙הוּ֙ וְטֽוֹבִיָּ֔הוּ וְט֖וֹב אֲדוֹנִיָּ֣ה הַלְוִיִּ֑ם וְעִמָּהֶ֛ם אֱלִישָׁמָ֥ע וִֽיהוֹרָ֖ם הַכֹּהֲנִֽים׃ 9 וַֽיְלַמְּד֖וּ בִּֽיהוּדָ֑ה וְעִ֨מָּהֶ֔ם סֵ֖פֶר תּוֹרַ֣ת יְהוָ֑ה וַיָּסֹ֙בּוּ֙ בְּכָל־עָרֵ֣י יְהוּדָ֔ה וַֽיְלַמְּד֖וּ בָּעָֽם׃ 10 וַיְהִ֣י ׀ פַּ֣חַד יְהוָ֗ה עַ֚ל כָּל־מַמְלְכ֣וֹת הָֽאֲרָצ֔וֹת אֲשֶׁ֖ר סְבִיב֣וֹת יְהוּדָ֑ה וְלֹ֥א נִלְחֲמ֖וּ עִם־יְהוֹשָׁפָֽט׃ 11 וּמִן־פְּלִשְׁתִּ֗ים מְבִיאִ֤ים לִֽיהוֹשָׁפָט֙ מִנְחָ֔ה וְכֶ֖סֶף

ת 8 וּֽשְׁמִֽרִימֽוֹת

brought him flocks, seven thousand seven hundred rams and seven thousand seven hundred male goats.

12 So Jehoshaphat became increasingly powerful, and he built fortresses and storage cities in Judah. 13 He had much property in the cities of Judah; and the men of war, mighty men of valor, *were* in Jerusalem.

14 These *are* their numbers, according to their fathers' houses. Of Judah, the captains of thousands: Adnah the captain, and with him three hundred thousand mighty men of valor; 15 and next to him *was* Jehohanan the captain, and with him two hundred and eighty thousand; 16 and next to him *was* Amasiah the son of Zichri, who willingly offered himself to the LORD, and with him two hundred thousand mighty men of valor. 17 Of Benjamin: Eliada a mighty man of valor, and with him two hundred thousand men armed with bow and shield; 18 and next to him *was* Jehozabad, and with him one hundred and eighty thousand prepared for war. 19 These served the king, besides those the king put in the fortified cities throughout all Judah.

18 Jehoshaphat had riches and honor in abundance; and by marriage he allied himself with Ahab. 2 After some years he went down to *visit* Ahab in Samaria; and Ahab killed sheep and oxen in abundance for him and the people who were with him, and persuaded him to go up *with him* to Ramoth Gilead. 3 So Ahab king of Israel said to Jehoshaphat king of Judah, "Will you go with me *against* Ramoth Gilead?"

And he answered him, "I *am* as you *are,* and my people as your people; *we will be* with you in the war."

4 Also Jehoshaphat said to the king of Israel, "Please inquire for the word of the LORD today."

5 Then the king of Israel gathered the prophets together, four hundred men, and said to them, "Shall we go to war against Ramoth Gilead, or shall I refrain?"

So they said, "Go up, for God will deliver it into the king's hand."

6 But Jehoshaphat said, "*Is there* not still a prophet of the LORD here, that we may inquire of Him?"

7 So the king of Israel said to Jehoshaphat, "*There is* still one man by whom we may inquire of the LORD; but I hate him, because he never prophesies good concerning me, but always evil. He *is* Micaiah the son of Imla."

מַשָּׂא גַּם־הָעַרְבִיאִים מְבִיאִים לוֹ צֹאן אֵילִים שִׁבְעַת אֲלָפִים וּשְׁבַע מֵאוֹת וּתְיָשִׁים שִׁבְעַת אֲלָפִים וּשְׁבַע מֵאוֹת: פ

12 וַיְהִי יְהוֹשָׁפָט הֹלֵךְ וְגָדֵל עַד־לְמָעְלָה וַיִּבֶן בִּיהוּדָה בִּירָנִיּוֹת וְעָרֵי מִסְכְּנוֹת: 13 וּמְלָאכָה רַבָּה הָיָה לוֹ בְּעָרֵי יְהוּדָה וְאַנְשֵׁי מִלְחָמָה גִּבּוֹרֵי חַיִל בִּירוּשָׁלָ͏ִם: 14 וְאֵלֶּה פְקֻדָּתָם לְבֵית אֲבוֹתֵיהֶם לִיהוּדָה שָׂרֵי אֲלָפִים עַדְנָה הַשָּׂר וְעִמּוֹ גִּבּוֹרֵי חַיִל שְׁלֹשׁ מֵאוֹת אָלֶף: ס 15 וְעַל־יָדוֹ יְהוֹחָנָן הַשָּׂר וְעִמּוֹ מָאתַיִם וּשְׁמוֹנִים אָלֶף: ס 16 וְעַל־יָדוֹ עֲמַסְיָה בֶן־זִכְרִי הַמִּתְנַדֵּב לַיהוָה וְעִמּוֹ מָאתַיִם אֶלֶף גִּבּוֹר חָיִל: ס 17 וּמִן־בִּנְיָמִן גִּבּוֹר חַיִל אֶלְיָדָע וְעִמּוֹ נֹשְׁקֵי־קֶשֶׁת וּמָגֵן מָאתַיִם אָלֶף: ס 18 וְעַל־יָדוֹ יְהוֹזָבָד וְעִמּוֹ מֵאָה־ וּשְׁמוֹנִים אֶלֶף חֲלוּצֵי צָבָא: ס 19 אֵלֶּה הַמְשָׁרְתִים אֶת־הַמֶּלֶךְ מִלְּבַד אֲשֶׁר־נָתַן הַמֶּלֶךְ בְּעָרֵי הַמִּבְצָר בְּכָל־יְהוּדָה: פ

יח וַיְהִי לִיהוֹשָׁפָט עֹשֶׁר וְכָבוֹד לָרֹב וַיִּתְחַתֵּן לְאַחְאָב: 2 וַיֵּרֶד לְקֵץ שָׁנִים אֶל־אַחְאָב לְשֹׁמְרוֹן וַיִּזְבַּח־לוֹ אַחְאָב צֹאן וּבָקָר לָרֹב וְלָעָם אֲשֶׁר עִמּוֹ וַיְסִיתֵהוּ לַעֲלוֹת אֶל־רָמוֹת גִּלְעָד: 3 וַיֹּאמֶר אַחְאָב מֶלֶךְ־יִשְׂרָאֵל אֶל־יְהוֹשָׁפָט מֶלֶךְ יְהוּדָה הֲתֵלֵךְ עִמִּי רָמֹת גִּלְעָד וַיֹּאמֶר לוֹ כָּמוֹנִי כָמוֹךָ וּכְעַמְּךָ עַמִּי וְעִמְּךָ בַּמִּלְחָמָה: 4 וַיֹּאמֶר יְהוֹשָׁפָט אֶל־מֶלֶךְ יִשְׂרָאֵל דְּרָשׁ־נָא כַיּוֹם אֶת־דְּבַר יְהוָה: 5 וַיִּקְבֹּץ מֶלֶךְ־יִשְׂרָאֵל אֶת־הַנְּבִאִים אַרְבַּע מֵאוֹת אִישׁ וַיֹּאמֶר אֲלֵהֶם הֲנֵלֵךְ אֶל־רָמֹת גִּלְעָד לַמִּלְחָמָה אִם־אֶחְדָּל וַיֹּאמְרוּ עֲלֵה וְיִתֵּן הָאֱלֹהִים בְּיַד הַמֶּלֶךְ: 6 וַיֹּאמֶר יְהוֹשָׁפָט הַאֵין פֹּה נָבִיא לַיהוָה עוֹד וְנִדְרְשָׁה מֵאֹתוֹ: 7 וַיֹּאמֶר מֶלֶךְ־יִשְׂרָאֵל | אֶל־יְהוֹשָׁפָט עוֹד אִישׁ־אֶחָד לִדְרוֹשׁ אֶת־יְהוָה מֵאֹתוֹ וַאֲנִי שְׂנֵאתִיהוּ כִּי־אֵינֶנּוּ מִתְנַבֵּא עָלַי לְטוֹבָה כִּי כָל־יָמָיו לְרָעָה הוּא מִיכָיְהוּ בֶן־ יִמְלָא וַיֹּאמֶר יְהוֹשָׁפָט אַל־יֹאמַר הַמֶּלֶךְ כֵּן:

And Jehoshaphat said, "Let not the king say such things!"

⁸ Then the king of Israel called one *of his* officers and said, "Bring Micaiah the son of Imla quickly!"

⁹ The king of Israel and Jehoshaphat king of Judah, clothed in *their* robes, sat each on his throne; and they sat at a threshing floor at the entrance of the gate of Samaria; and all the prophets prophesied before them. ¹⁰ Now Zedekiah the son of Chenaanah had made horns of iron for himself; and he said, "Thus says the LORD: 'With these you shall gore the Syrians until they are destroyed.' "

¹¹ And all the prophets prophesied so, saying, "Go up to Ramoth Gilead and prosper, for the LORD will deliver *it* into the king's hand."

¹² Then the messenger who had gone to call Micaiah spoke to him, saying, "Now listen, the words of the prophets with one accord encourage the king. Therefore please let your word be like *the word of* one of them, and speak encouragement."

¹³ And Micaiah said, "*As* the LORD lives, whatever my God says, that I will speak."

¹⁴ Then he came to the king; and the king said to him, "Micaiah, shall we go to war against Ramoth Gilead, or shall I refrain?"

And he said, "Go and prosper, and they shall be delivered into your hand!"

¹⁵ So the king said to him, "How many times shall I make you swear that you tell me nothing but the truth in the name of the LORD?"

¹⁶ Then he said, "I saw all Israel scattered on the mountains, as sheep that have no shepherd. And the LORD said, 'These have no master. Let each return to his house in peace.' "

¹⁷ And the king of Israel said to Jehoshaphat, "Did I not tell you he would not prophesy good concerning me, but evil?"

¹⁸ Then *Micaiah* said, "Therefore hear the word of the LORD: I saw the LORD sitting on His throne, and all the host of heaven standing on His right hand and His left. ¹⁹ And the LORD said, 'Who will persuade Ahab king of Israel to go up, that he may fall at Ramoth Gilead?' So one spoke in this manner, and another spoke in that manner. ²⁰ Then a spirit came forward and stood before the LORD, and said, 'I will persuade him.' The LORD said to him, 'In what way?' ²¹ So he said, 'I will go out and be a lying spirit in the mouth of all his prophets.' And *the* LORD said, 'You shall persuade *him* and also prevail; go out and do so.' ²² Therefore look! The LORD has put a lying spirit in the mouth of these prophets of yours, and the LORD has declared disaster against you."

8 וַיִּקְרָא מֶלֶךְ יִשְׂרָאֵל אֶל־סָרִיס אֶחָד וַיֹּאמֶר מַהֵר מִיכָיְהוּ בֶן־יִמְלָא: 9 וּמֶלֶךְ יִשְׂרָאֵל וִיהוֹשָׁפָט מֶלֶךְ־יְהוּדָה יוֹשְׁבִים אִישׁ עַל־כִּסְאוֹ מְלֻבָּשִׁים בְּגָדִים וְיֹשְׁבִים בְּגֹרֶן פֶּתַח שַׁעַר שֹׁמְרוֹן וְכָל־הַנְּבִאִים מִתְנַבְּאִים לִפְנֵיהֶם: 10 וַיַּעַשׂ לוֹ צִדְקִיָּהוּ בֶן־כְּנַעֲנָה קַרְנֵי בַרְזֶל וַיֹּאמֶר כֹּה־אָמַר יְהוָה בְּאֵלֶּה תְּנַגַּח אֶת־אֲרָם עַד־כַּלּוֹתָם: 11 וְכָל־הַנְּבִאִים נִבְּאִים כֵּן לֵאמֹר עֲלֵה רָמֹת גִּלְעָד וְהַצְלַח וְנָתַן יְהוָה בְּיַד הַמֶּלֶךְ: 12 וְהַמַּלְאָךְ אֲשֶׁר־הָלַךְ ׀ לִקְרֹא לְמִיכָיְהוּ דִּבֶּר אֵלָיו לֵאמֹר הִנֵּה דִּבְרֵי הַנְּבִאִים פֶּה־אֶחָד טוֹב אֶל־הַמֶּלֶךְ וִיהִי־נָא דְבָרְךָ כְּאַחַד מֵהֶם וְדִבַּרְתָּ טּוֹב: 13 וַיֹּאמֶר מִיכָיְהוּ חַי־יְהוָה כִּי אֶת־אֲשֶׁר־יֹאמַר אֱלֹהַי אֹתוֹ אֲדַבֵּר: 14 וַיָּבֹא אֶל־הַמֶּלֶךְ וַיֹּאמֶר הַמֶּלֶךְ אֵלָיו מִיכָה הֲנֵלֵךְ אֶל־רָמֹת גִּלְעָד לַמִּלְחָמָה אִם־אֶחְדָּל וַיֹּאמֶר עֲלוּ וְהַצְלִיחוּ וְיִנָּתְנוּ בְּיֶדְכֶם: 15 וַיֹּאמֶר אֵלָיו הַמֶּלֶךְ עַד־כַּמֶּה פְעָמִים אֲנִי מַשְׁבִּיעֶךָ אֲשֶׁר לֹא־תְדַבֵּר אֵלַי רַק־אֱמֶת בְּשֵׁם יְהוָה: 16 וַיֹּאמֶר רָאִיתִי אֶת־כָּל־יִשְׂרָאֵל נְפוֹצִים עַל־הֶהָרִים כַּצֹּאן אֲשֶׁר אֵין־לָהֶן רֹעֶה וַיֹּאמֶר יְהוָה לֹא־אֲדֹנִים לָאֵלֶּה יָשׁוּבוּ אִישׁ־לְבֵיתוֹ בְּשָׁלוֹם: 17 וַיֹּאמֶר מֶלֶךְ־יִשְׂרָאֵל אֶל־יְהוֹשָׁפָט הֲלֹא אָמַרְתִּי אֵלֶיךָ לֹא־יִתְנַבֵּא עָלַי טוֹב כִּי אִם־לְרָע: ס 18 וַיֹּאמֶר לָכֵן שִׁמְעוּ דְבַר־יְהוָה רָאִיתִי אֶת־יְהוָה יוֹשֵׁב עַל־כִּסְאוֹ וְכָל־צְבָא הַשָּׁמַיִם עֹמְדִים עַל־יְמִינוֹ וּשְׂמֹאלוֹ: 19 וַיֹּאמֶר יְהוָה מִי יְפַתֶּה אֶת־אַחְאָב מֶלֶךְ־יִשְׂרָאֵל וְיַעַל וְיִפֹּל בְּרָמוֹת גִּלְעָד וַיֹּאמֶר זֶה אֹמֵר כָּכָה וְזֶה אֹמֵר כָּכָה: 20 וַיֵּצֵא הָרוּחַ וַיַּעֲמֹד לִפְנֵי יְהוָה וַיֹּאמֶר אֲנִי אֲפַתֶּנּוּ וַיֹּאמֶר יְהוָה אֵלָיו בַּמֶּה: 21 וַיֹּאמֶר אֵצֵא וְהָיִיתִי לְרוּחַ שֶׁקֶר בְּפִי כָּל־נְבִיאָיו וַיֹּאמֶר תְּפַתֶּה וְגַם־תּוּכָל צֵא וַעֲשֵׂה־כֵן: 22 וְעַתָּה הִנֵּה נָתַן יְהוָה רוּחַ שֶׁקֶר בְּפִי נְבִיאֶיךָ אֵלֶּה וַיהוָה

23 Then Zedekiah the son of Chenaanah went near and struck Micaiah on the cheek, and said, "Which way did the spirit from the LORD go from me to speak to you?"

24 And Micaiah said, "Indeed you shall see on that day when you go into an inner chamber to hide!"

25 Then the king of Israel said, "Take Micaiah, and return him to Amon the governor of the city and to Joash the king's son; 26 and say, 'Thus says the king: "Put this *fellow* in prison, and feed him with bread of affliction and water of affliction, until I return in peace." ' "

27 But Micaiah said, "If you ever return in peace, the LORD has not spoken by me." And he said, "Take heed, all you people!"

28 So the king of Israel and Jehoshaphat the king of Judah went up to Ramoth Gilead. 29 And the king of Israel said to Jehoshaphat, "I will disguise myself and go into battle; but you put on your robes." So the king of Israel disguised himself, and they went into battle.

30 Now the king of Syria had commanded the captains of the chariots who *were* with him, saying, "Fight with no one small or great, but only with the king of Israel."

31 So it was, when the captains of the chariots saw Jehoshaphat, that they said, "It *is* the king of Israel!" Therefore they surrounded him to attack; but Jehoshaphat cried out, and the LORD helped him, and God diverted them from him. 32 For so it was, when the captains of the chariots saw that it was not the king of Israel, that they turned back from pursuing him. 33 Now a certain man drew a bow at random, and struck the king of Israel between the joints of his armor. So he said to the driver of his chariot, "Turn around and take me out of the battle, for I am wounded." 34 The battle increased that day, and the king of Israel propped *himself* up in *his* chariot facing the Syrians until evening; and about the time of sunset he died.

19 Then Jehoshaphat the king of Judah returned safely to his house in Jerusalem. 2 And Jehu the son of Hanani the seer went out to meet him, and said to King Jehoshaphat, "Should you help the wicked and love those who hate the LORD? Therefore the wrath of the LORD *is* upon you. 3 Nevertheless good things are found in you, in that you have removed the wooden images from the land, and have prepared your heart to seek God."

4 So Jehoshaphat dwelt at Jerusalem; and he went out again among the people from Beersheba to the mountains of Ephraim, and brought them back to

דִּבֶּר עָלֶיךָ רָעָה: ס 23 וַיִּגַּשׁ צִדְקִיָּהוּ בֶן־
כְּנַעֲנָה וַיַּךְ אֶת־מִיכָיְהוּ עַל־הַלֶּחִי וַיֹּאמֶר אֵי זֶה
הַדֶּרֶךְ עָבַר רוּחַ־יְהֹוָה מֵאִתִּי לְדַבֵּר אֹתָךְ: 24 וַיֹּאמֶר
מִיכָיְהוּ הִנְּךָ רֹאֶה בַּיּוֹם הַהוּא אֲשֶׁר תָּבוֹא חֶדֶר
בְּחֶדֶר לְהֵחָבֵא: 25 וַיֹּאמֶר מֶלֶךְ יִשְׂרָאֵל קְחוּ אֶת־
מִיכָיְהוּ וַהֲשִׁיבֻהוּ אֶל־אָמוֹן שַׂר־הָעִיר וְאֶל־יוֹאָשׁ
בֶּן־הַמֶּלֶךְ: 26 וַאֲמַרְתֶּם כֹּה אָמַר הַמֶּלֶךְ שִׂימוּ זֶה
בֵּית הַכֶּלֶא וְהַאֲכִלֻהוּ לֶחֶם לַחַץ וּמַיִם לַחַץ עַד
שׁוּבִי בְשָׁלוֹם: 27 וַיֹּאמֶר מִיכָיְהוּ אִם־שׁוֹב תָּשׁוּב
בְּשָׁלוֹם לֹא־דִבֶּר יְהֹוָה בִּי וַיֹּאמֶר שִׁמְעוּ עַמִּים
כֻּלָּם:
פ
28 וַיַּעַל מֶלֶךְ־יִשְׂרָאֵל וִיהוֹשָׁפָט מֶלֶךְ־יְהוּדָה אֶל־
רָמֹת גִּלְעָד: 29 וַיֹּאמֶר מֶלֶךְ יִשְׂרָאֵל אֶל־יְהוֹשָׁפָט
הִתְחַפֵּשׂ וָבוֹא בַמִּלְחָמָה וְאַתָּה לְבַשׁ בְּגָדֶיךָ
וַיִּתְחַפֵּשׂ מֶלֶךְ יִשְׂרָאֵל וַיָּבֹאוּ בַּמִּלְחָמָה: 30 וּמֶלֶךְ
אֲרָם צִוָּה אֶת־שָׂרֵי הָרֶכֶב אֲשֶׁר־לוֹ לֵאמֹר לֹא
תִּלָּחֲמוּ אֶת־הַקָּטֹן אֶת־הַגָּדוֹל כִּי אִם־אֶת־מֶלֶךְ
יִשְׂרָאֵל לְבַדּוֹ: 31 וַיְהִי כִּרְאוֹת שָׂרֵי הָרֶכֶב אֶת־
יְהוֹשָׁפָט וְהֵמָּה אָמְרוּ מֶלֶךְ יִשְׂרָאֵל הוּא וַיָּסֹבּוּ
עָלָיו לְהִלָּחֵם וַיִּזְעַק יְהוֹשָׁפָט וַיהֹוָה עֲזָרוֹ וַיְסִיתֵם
אֱלֹהִים מִמֶּנּוּ: 32 וַיְהִי כִּרְאוֹת שָׂרֵי הָרֶכֶב כִּי לֹא־
הָיָה מֶלֶךְ יִשְׂרָאֵל וַיָּשֻׁבוּ מֵאַחֲרָיו: 33 וְאִישׁ מָשַׁךְ
בַּקֶּשֶׁת לְתֻמּוֹ וַיַּךְ אֶת־מֶלֶךְ יִשְׂרָאֵל בֵּין הַדְּבָקִים
וּבֵין הַשִּׁרְיָן וַיֹּאמֶר לָרַכָּב הֲפֹךְ יָדֶךָ וְהוֹצֵאתַנִי
מִן־הַמַּחֲנֶה כִּי הָחֳלֵיתִי: 34 וַתַּעַל הַמִּלְחָמָה בַּיּוֹם
הַהוּא וּמֶלֶךְ יִשְׂרָאֵל הָיָה מַעֲמִיד בַּמֶּרְכָּבָה נֹכַח
אֲרָם עַד־הָעֶרֶב וַיָּמָת לְעֵת בּוֹא הַשָּׁמֶשׁ:

יט וַיָּשָׁב יְהוֹשָׁפָט מֶלֶךְ־יְהוּדָה אֶל־בֵּיתוֹ בְּשָׁלוֹם
לִירוּשָׁלִָם: 2 וַיֵּצֵא אֶל־פָּנָיו יֵהוּא בֶן־חֲנָנִי הַחֹזֶה
וַיֹּאמֶר אֶל־הַמֶּלֶךְ יְהוֹשָׁפָט הֲלָרָשָׁע לַעְזֹר וּלְשֹׂנְאֵי
יְהֹוָה תֶּאֱהָב וּבָזֹאת עָלֶיךָ קֶּצֶף מִלִּפְנֵי יְהֹוָה: 3 אֲבָל
דְּבָרִים טוֹבִים נִמְצְאוּ עִמָּךְ כִּי־בִעַרְתָּ הָאֲשֵׁרוֹת
מִן־הָאָרֶץ וַהֲכִינוֹתָ לְבָבְךָ לִדְרֹשׁ הָאֱלֹהִים: 4 וַיֵּשֶׁב
יְהוֹשָׁפָט בִּירוּשָׁלִָם ס וַיָּשָׁב וַיֵּצֵא בָעָם
מִבְּאֵר שֶׁבַע עַד־הַר אֶפְרַיִם וַיְשִׁיבֵם אֶל־יְהֹוָה

the LORD God of their fathers. ⁵Then he set judges in the land throughout all the fortified cities of Judah, city by city, ⁶and said to the judges, "Take heed to what you are doing, for you do not judge for man but for the LORD, who *is* with you in the judgment. ⁷Now therefore, let the fear of the LORD be upon you; take care and do *it,* for *there is* no iniquity with the LORD our God, no partiality, nor taking of bribes."

⁸Moreover in Jerusalem, for the judgment of the LORD and for controversies, Jehoshaphat appointed some of the Levites and priests, and some of the chief fathers of Israel, when they returned to Jerusalem. ⁹And he commanded them, saying, "Thus you shall act in the fear of the LORD, faithfully and with a loyal heart: ¹⁰Whatever case comes to you from your brethren who dwell in their cities, whether of bloodshed or offenses against law or commandment, against statutes or ordinances, you shall warn them, lest they trespass against the LORD and wrath come upon you and your brethren. Do this, and you will not be guilty. ¹¹And take notice: Amariah the chief priest *is* over you in all matters of the LORD; and Zebadiah the son of Ishmael, the ruler of the house of Judah, for all the king's matters; also the Levites *will be* officials before you. Behave courageously, and the LORD will be with the good."

20 It happened after this *that* the people of Moab with the people of Ammon, and *others* with them besides the Ammonites, came to battle against Jehoshaphat. ²Then some came and told Jehoshaphat, saying, "A great multitude is coming against you from beyond the sea, from Syria; and they are in Hazazon Tamar" (which *is* En Gedi). ³And Jehoshaphat feared, and set himself to seek the LORD, and proclaimed a fast throughout all Judah. ⁴So Judah gathered together to ask *help* from the LORD; and from all the cities of Judah they came to seek the LORD.

⁵Then Jehoshaphat stood in the assembly of Judah and Jerusalem, in the house of the LORD, before the new court, ⁶and said: "O LORD God of our fathers, *are* You not God in heaven, and do You *not* rule over all the kingdoms of the nations, and in Your hand *is there not* power and might, so that no one is able to withstand You? ⁷*Are* You not our God, *who* drove out the inhabitants of this land before Your people Israel, and gave it to the descendants of Abraham Your friend forever? ⁸And they dwell in it, and have built You a sanctuary in it for Your name, saying, ⁹'If disaster comes upon us—sword, judgment, pestilence, or

אֱלֹהֵ֖י אֲבוֹתֵיהֶֽם: 5 וַיַּעֲמֵ֨ד שֹׁפְטִים֙ בָּאָ֔רֶץ בְּכָל־עָרֵ֥י יְהוּדָ֖ה הַבְּצֻר֑וֹת לְעִ֥יר וָעִֽיר: 6 וַיֹּ֙אמֶר֙ אֶל־הַשֹּׁ֣פְטִ֔ים רְאוּ֙ מָֽה־אַתֶּ֣ם עֹשִׂ֔ים כִּ֣י לֹ֧א לְאָדָ֛ם תִּשְׁפְּט֖וּ כִּ֣י לַיהוָ֑ה וְעִמָּכֶ֖ם בִּדְבַ֥ר מִשְׁפָּֽט: 7 וְעַתָּ֕ה יְהִ֥י פַֽחַד־יְהוָ֖ה עֲלֵיכֶ֑ם שִׁמְר֣וּ וַעֲשׂ֔וּ כִּֽי־אֵ֞ין עִם־יְהוָ֣ה אֱלֹהֵ֗ינוּ עַוְלָ֛ה וּמַשֹּׂ֥א פָנִ֖ים וּמִקַּח־שֹֽׁחַד: 8 וְגַ֣ם בִּירֽוּשָׁלִַ֡ם הֶעֱמִ֣יד יְהוֹשָׁפָ֣ט מִן־הַלְוִיִּ֣ם וְהַכֹּהֲנִ֡ים וּמֵרָאשֵׁ֣י הָאָבוֹת֩ לְיִשְׂרָאֵ֨ל לְמִשְׁפַּ֧ט יְהוָ֛ה וְלָרִ֖יב וַיָּשֻׁ֥בוּ יְרוּשָׁלָֽ͏ִם: 9 וַיְצַ֣ו עֲלֵיהֶ֗ם לֵאמֹ֑ר כֹּ֤ה תַעֲשׂוּן֙ בְּיִרְאַ֣ת יְהוָ֔ה בֶּאֱמוּנָ֖ה וּבְלֵבָ֥ב שָׁלֵֽם: 10 וְכָל־רִ֣יב אֲשֶׁר־יָב֣וֹא עֲלֵיכֶ֣ם מֵאֲחֵיכֶ֣ם ׀ הַיֹּשְׁבִים֮ בְּעָרֵיהֶם֒ בֵּֽין־דָּ֣ם ׀ לְדָ֡ם בֵּֽין־תּוֹרָ֣ה לְמִצְוָ֣ה לְחֻקִּים֮ וּלְמִשְׁפָּטִים֒ וְהִזְהַרְתֶּ֣ם אֹתָ֔ם וְלֹ֤א יֶאְשְׁמוּ֙ לַֽיהוָ֔ה וְהָֽיָה־קֶ֣צֶף עֲלֵיכֶ֖ם וְעַל־אֲחֵיכֶ֑ם כֹּ֥ה תַעֲשׂ֖וּן וְלֹ֥א תֶאְשָֽׁמוּ: 11 וְהִנֵּ֡ה אֲמַרְיָ֣הוּ כֹהֵן֩ הָרֹ֨אשׁ עֲלֵיכֶ֜ם לְכֹ֣ל דְּבַר־יְהוָ֗ה וּזְבַדְיָ֨הוּ בֶן־יִשְׁמָעֵ֤אל הַנָּגִיד֙ לְבֵית־יְהוּדָ֔ה לְכֹ֖ל דְּבַר־הַמֶּ֑לֶךְ וְשֹׁטְרִ֤ים הַלְוִיִּם֙ לִפְנֵיכֶ֔ם חִזְק֣וּ וַעֲשׂ֔וּ וִיהִ֥י יְהוָ֖ה עִם־הַטּֽוֹב: פ

כ וַיְהִ֣י אַֽחֲרֵי־כֵ֗ן בָּ֣אוּ בְנֵי־מוֹאָ֤ב וּבְנֵ֣י עַמּ֔וֹן וְעִמָּהֶ֧ם ׀ מֵהָעַמּוֹנִ֛ים עַל־יְהוֹשָׁפָ֖ט לַמִּלְחָמָֽה: 2 וַיָּבֹ֗אוּ וַיַּגִּ֤ידוּ לִיהוֹשָׁפָט֙ לֵאמֹ֔ר בָּ֣א עָלֶ֜יךָ הָמ֥וֹן רָב֙ מֵעֵ֣בֶר לַיָּ֔ם מֵאֲרָ֑ם וְהִנָּ֣ם בְּחַֽצְצ֣וֹן תָּמָ֔ר הִ֖יא עֵ֥ין גֶּֽדִי: 3 וַיִּרָ֕א וַיִּתֵּ֧ן יְהוֹשָׁפָ֛ט אֶת־פָּנָ֖יו לִדְר֣וֹשׁ לַיהוָ֑ה וַיִּקְרָא־צ֖וֹם עַל־כָּל־יְהוּדָֽה: 4 וַיִּקָּבְצ֣וּ יְהוּדָ֔ה לְבַקֵּ֖שׁ מֵֽיהוָ֑ה גַּ֚ם מִכָּל־עָרֵ֣י יְהוּדָ֔ה בָּ֖אוּ לְבַקֵּ֥שׁ אֶת־יְהוָֽה: 5 וַיַּעֲמֹ֣ד יְהוֹשָׁפָ֗ט בִּקְהַ֧ל יְהוּדָ֛ה וִירֽוּשָׁלַ֖͏ִם בְּבֵ֣ית יְהוָ֑ה לִפְנֵ֖י הֶחָצֵ֥ר הַחֲדָשָֽׁה: 6 וַיֹּאמַ֗ר יְהוָ֞ה אֱלֹהֵ֤י אֲבֹתֵ֙ינוּ֙ הֲלֹ֨א אַתָּֽה־ה֤וּא אֱלֹהִים֙ בַּשָּׁמַ֔יִם וְאַתָּ֣ה מוֹשֵׁ֔ל בְּכֹ֖ל מַמְלְכ֣וֹת הַגּוֹיִ֑ם וּבְיָדְךָ֙ כֹּ֣חַ וּגְבוּרָ֔ה וְאֵ֥ין עִמְּךָ֖ לְהִתְיַצֵּֽב: 7 הֲלֹ֣א ׀ אַתָּ֣ה אֱלֹהֵ֗ינוּ הוֹרַ֙שְׁתָּ֙ אֶת־יֹשְׁבֵי֙ הָאָ֣רֶץ הַזֹּ֔את מִלִּפְנֵ֖י עַמְּךָ֣ יִשְׂרָאֵ֑ל וַֽתִּתְּנָ֗הּ לְזֶ֛רַע אַבְרָהָ֥ם אֹֽהַבְךָ֖ לְעוֹלָֽם: 8 וַיֵּ֣שְׁבוּ־בָ֑הּ וַיִּבְנ֣וּ לְךָ֧ ׀ בָּ֣הּ מִקְדָּ֛שׁ לְשִׁמְךָ֖ לֵאמֹֽר: 9 אִם־תָּב֨וֹא עָלֵ֜ינוּ רָעָ֗ה חֶ֣רֶב שְׁפוֹט֮ וְדֶ֣בֶר וְרָעָב֒ נַֽעַמְדָ֞ה לִפְנֵ֨י הַבַּ֤יִת הַזֶּה֙ וּלְפָנֶ֔יךָ כִּ֥י שִׁמְךָ֖ בַּבַּ֣יִת הַזֶּ֑ה וְנִזְעַ֥ק אֵלֶ֖יךָ

famine—we will stand before this temple and in Your presence (for Your name *is* in this temple), and cry out to You in our affliction, and You will hear and save.' ¹⁰And now, here are the people of Ammon, Moab, and Mount Seir—whom You would not let Israel invade when they came out of the land of Egypt, but they turned from them and did not destroy them— ¹¹here they are, rewarding us by coming to throw us out of Your possession which You have given us to inherit. ¹²O our God, will You not judge them? For we have no power against this great multitude that is coming against us; nor do we know what to do, but our eyes *are* upon You."

¹³Now all Judah, with their little ones, their wives, and their children, stood before the Lord.

¹⁴Then the Spirit of the Lord came upon Jahaziel the son of Zechariah, the son of Benaiah, the son of Jeiel, the son of Mattaniah, a Levite of the sons of Asaph, in the midst of the assembly. ¹⁵And he said, "Listen, all you of Judah and you inhabitants of Jerusalem, and you, King Jehoshaphat! Thus says the Lord to you: 'Do not be afraid nor dismayed because of this great multitude, for the battle *is* not yours, but God's. ¹⁶Tomorrow go down against them. They will surely come up by the Ascent of Ziz, and you will find them at the end of the brook before the Wilderness of Jeruel. ¹⁷You will not *need* to fight in this *battle*. Position yourselves, stand still and see the salvation of the Lord, who is with you, O Judah and Jerusalem!' Do not fear or be dismayed; tomorrow go out against them, for the Lord *is* with you."

¹⁸And Jehoshaphat bowed his head with *his* face to the ground, and all Judah and the inhabitants of Jerusalem bowed before the Lord, worshiping the Lord. ¹⁹Then the Levites of the children of the Kohathites and of the children of the Korahites stood up to praise the Lord God of Israel with voices loud and high.

²⁰So they rose early in the morning and went out into the Wilderness of Tekoa; and as they went out, Jehoshaphat stood and said, "Hear me, O Judah and you inhabitants of Jerusalem: Believe in the Lord your God, and you shall be established; believe His prophets, and you shall prosper." ²¹And when he had consulted with the people, he appointed those who should sing to the Lord, and who should praise the beauty of holiness, as they went out before the army and were saying:

"Praise the Lord,
  For His mercy *endures* forever."

מִצָּרָתֵנוּ וְתִשְׁמַע וְתוֹשִׁיעַ: 10 וְעַתָּה הִנֵּה בְנֵי־
עַמּוֹן וּמוֹאָב וְהַר־שֵׂעִיר אֲשֶׁר לֹא־נָתַתָּה לְיִשְׂרָאֵל
לָבוֹא בָהֶם בְּבֹאָם מֵאֶרֶץ מִצְרָיִם כִּי סָרוּ מֵעֲלֵיהֶם
וְלֹא הִשְׁמִידוּם: 11 וְהִנֵּה־הֵם גֹּמְלִים עָלֵינוּ לָבוֹא
לְגָרְשֵׁנוּ מִירֻשָּׁתְךָ אֲשֶׁר הוֹרַשְׁתָּנוּ: 12 אֱלֹהֵינוּ הֲלֹא
תִשְׁפָּט־בָּם כִּי אֵין בָּנוּ כֹּחַ לִפְנֵי הֶהָמוֹן הָרָב הַזֶּה
הַבָּא עָלֵינוּ וַאֲנַחְנוּ לֹא נֵדַע מַה־נַּעֲשֶׂה כִּי עָלֶיךָ
עֵינֵינוּ: 13 וְכָל־יְהוּדָה עֹמְדִים לִפְנֵי יְהוָה גַּם־טַפָּם
נְשֵׁיהֶם וּבְנֵיהֶם:
                                              פ

14 וַיַחֲזִיאֵל בֶּן־זְכַרְיָהוּ בֶּן־בְּנָיָה בֶּן־יְעִיאֵל בֶּן־
מַתַּנְיָה הַלֵּוִי מִן־בְּנֵי אָסָף הָיְתָה עָלָיו רוּחַ
יְהוָה בְּתוֹךְ הַקָּהָל: 15 וַיֹּאמֶר הַקְשִׁיבוּ כָל־יְהוּדָה
וְיֹשְׁבֵי יְרוּשָׁלַ͏ִם וְהַמֶּלֶךְ יְהוֹשָׁפָט כֹּה־אָמַר יְהוָה
לָכֶם אַתֶּם אַל־תִּירְאוּ וְאַל־תֵּחַתּוּ מִפְּנֵי הֶהָמוֹן
הָרָב הַזֶּה כִּי לֹא לָכֶם הַמִּלְחָמָה כִּי לֵאלֹהִים:
16 מָחָר רְדוּ עֲלֵיהֶם הִנָּם עֹלִים בְּמַעֲלֵה הַצִּיץ
וּמְצָאתֶם אֹתָם בְּסוֹף הַנַּחַל פְּנֵי מִדְבַּר יְרוּאֵל:
17 לֹא לָכֶם לְהִלָּחֵם בָּזֹאת הִתְיַצְּבוּ עִמְדוּ וּרְאוּ
אֶת־יְשׁוּעַת יְהוָה עִמָּכֶם יְהוּדָה וִירוּשָׁלַ͏ִם אַל־
תִּירְאוּ וְאַל־תֵּחַתּוּ מָחָר צְאוּ לִפְנֵיהֶם וַיהוָה
עִמָּכֶם: 18 וַיִּקֹּד יְהוֹשָׁפָט אַפַּיִם אַרְצָה וְכָל־
יְהוּדָה וְיֹשְׁבֵי יְרוּשָׁלַ͏ִם נָפְלוּ לִפְנֵי יְהוָה לְהִשְׁתַּחֲוֹת
לַיהוָה: 19 וַיָּקֻמוּ הַלְוִיִּם מִן־בְּנֵי הַקְּהָתִים וּמִן־
בְּנֵי הַקָּרְחִים לְהַלֵּל לַיהוָה אֱלֹהֵי יִשְׂרָאֵל בְּקוֹל
גָּדוֹל לְמָעְלָה: 20 וַיַּשְׁכִּימוּ בַבֹּקֶר וַיֵּצְאוּ לְמִדְבַּר
תְּקוֹעַ וּבְצֵאתָם עָמַד יְהוֹשָׁפָט וַיֹּאמֶר שְׁמָעוּנִי
יְהוּדָה וְיֹשְׁבֵי יְרוּשָׁלַ͏ִם הַאֲמִינוּ בַּיהוָה אֱלֹהֵיכֶם
וְתֵאָמֵנוּ הַאֲמִינוּ בִנְבִיאָיו וְהַצְלִיחוּ: 21 וַיִּוָּעַץ אֶל־
הָעָם וַיַּעֲמֵד מְשֹׁרְרִים לַיהוָה וּמְהַלְלִים לְהַדְרַת־
קֹדֶשׁ בְּצֵאת לִפְנֵי הֶחָלוּץ וְאֹמְרִים הוֹדוּ לַיהוָה

²² Now when they began to sing and to praise, the LORD set ambushes against the people of Ammon, Moab, and Mount Seir, who had come against Judah; and they were defeated. ²³ For the people of Ammon and Moab stood up against the inhabitants of Mount Seir to utterly kill and destroy *them*. And when they had made an end of the inhabitants of Seir, they helped to destroy one another.

²⁴ So when Judah came to a place overlooking the wilderness, they looked toward the multitude; and there *were* their dead bodies, fallen on the earth. No one had escaped.

²⁵ When Jehoshaphat and his people came to take away their spoil, they found among them an abundance of valuables on the dead bodies, and precious jewelry, which they stripped off for themselves, more than they could carry away; and they were three days gathering the spoil because there was so much. ²⁶ And on the fourth day they assembled in the Valley of Berachah, for there they blessed the LORD; therefore the name of that place was called The Valley of Berachah until this day. ²⁷ Then they returned, every man of Judah and Jerusalem, with Jehoshaphat in front of them, to go back to Jerusalem with joy, for the LORD had made them rejoice over their enemies. ²⁸ So they came to Jerusalem, with stringed instruments and harps and trumpets, to the house of the LORD. ²⁹ And the fear of God was on all the kingdoms of *those* countries when they heard that the LORD had fought against the enemies of Israel. ³⁰ Then the realm of Jehoshaphat was quiet, for his God gave him rest all around.

³¹ So Jehoshaphat was king over Judah. *He was* thirty-five years old when he became king, and he reigned twenty-five years in Jerusalem. His mother's name *was* Azubah the daughter of Shilhi. ³² And he walked in the way of his father Asa, and did not turn aside from it, doing *what was* right in the sight of the LORD. ³³ Nevertheless the high places were not taken away, for as yet the people had not directed their hearts to the God of their fathers.

³⁴ Now the rest of the acts of Jehoshaphat, first and last, indeed they *are* written in the book of Jehu the son of Hanani, which *is* mentioned in the book of the kings of Israel.

³⁵ After this Jehoshaphat king of Judah allied himself with Ahaziah king of Israel, who acted very wickedly. ³⁶ And he allied himself with him to make ships to go to Tarshish, and they made the ships in Ezion Geber. ³⁷ But Eliezer the son of Dodavah of Mareshah prophesied against Jehoshaphat, saying, "Because you have allied yourself with Ahaziah, the

22 כִּי לְעוֹלָם חַסְדּֽוֹ: וּבְעֵת הֵחֵלּוּ בְרִנָּה וּתְהִלָּה נָתַן יְהוָה ׀ מְאָֽרְבִים עַל־בְּנֵי עַמּוֹן מוֹאָב וְהַר־שֵׂעִיר הַבָּאִים לִֽיהוּדָה וַיִּנָּגֵֽפוּ: 23 וַיַּעַמְדוּ בְּנֵי עַמּוֹן וּמוֹאָב עַל־יֹשְׁבֵי הַר־שֵׂעִיר לְהַחֲרִים וּלְהַשְׁמִיד וּכְכַלּוֹתָם בְּיוֹשְׁבֵי שֵׂעִיר עָזְרוּ אִישׁ־בְּרֵעֵהוּ לְמַשְׁחִֽית: 24 וִֽיהוּדָה בָּא עַל־הַמִּצְפֶּה לַמִּדְבָּר וַיִּפְנוּ אֶל־הֶהָמוֹן וְהִנָּם פְּגָרִים נֹפְלִים אַרְצָה וְאֵין פְּלֵיטָֽה: 25 וַיָּבֹא יְהוֹשָׁפָט וְעַמּוֹ לָבֹז אֶת־שְׁלָלָם וַיִּמְצְאוּ בָהֶם לָרֹב וּרְכוּשׁ וּפְגָרִים וּכְלֵי חֲמֻדוֹת וַיְנַצְּלוּ לָהֶם לְאֵין מַשָּׂא וַיִּֽהְיוּ יָמִים שְׁלוֹשָׁה בֹּזְזִים אֶת־הַשָּׁלָל כִּי רַב־הֽוּא: 26 וּבַיּוֹם הָרְבִעִי נִקְהֲלוּ לְעֵמֶק בְּרָכָה כִּי־שָׁם בֵּרְכוּ אֶת־יְהוָה עַל־כֵּן קָרְאוּ אֶת־שֵׁם הַמָּקוֹם הַהוּא עֵמֶק בְּרָכָה עַד־הַיּֽוֹם: 27 וַיָּשֻׁבוּ כָּל־אִישׁ יְהוּדָה וִירוּשָׁלַ͏ִם וִיהוֹשָׁפָט בְּרֹאשָׁם לָשׁוּב אֶל־יְרוּשָׁלַ͏ִם בְּשִׂמְחָה כִּי־שִׂמְּחָם יְהוָה מֵאוֹיְבֵיהֶֽם: 28 וַיָּבֹאוּ יְרוּשָׁלַ͏ִם בִּנְבָלִים וּבְכִנֹּרוֹת וּבַחֲצֹצְרוֹת אֶל־בֵּית יְהוָֽה: 29 וַיְהִי פַּחַד אֱלֹהִים עַל כָּל־מַמְלְכוֹת הָאֲרָצוֹת בְּשָׁמְעָם כִּי נִלְחַם יְהוָה עִם אוֹיְבֵי יִשְׂרָאֵֽל: 30 וַתִּשְׁקֹט מַלְכוּת יְהוֹשָׁפָט וַיָּנַח לוֹ אֱלֹהָיו מִסָּבִֽיב: פ

31 וַיִּמְלֹךְ יְהוֹשָׁפָט עַל־יְהוּדָה בֶּן־שְׁלֹשִׁים וְחָמֵשׁ שָׁנָה בְּמָלְכוֹ וְעֶשְׂרִים וְחָמֵשׁ שָׁנָה מָלַךְ בִּירוּשָׁלָ͏ִם וְשֵׁם אִמּוֹ עֲזוּבָה בַּת־שִׁלְחִֽי: 32 וַיֵּלֶךְ בְּדֶרֶךְ אָבִיו אָסָא וְלֹא־סָר מִמֶּנָּה לַעֲשׂוֹת הַיָּשָׁר בְּעֵינֵי יְהוָֽה: 33 אַךְ הַבָּמוֹת לֹא־סָרוּ וְעוֹד הָעָם לֹא־הֵכִינוּ לְבָבָם לֵאלֹהֵי אֲבֹתֵיהֶֽם: 34 וְיֶתֶר דִּבְרֵי יְהוֹשָׁפָט הָרִאשֹׁנִים וְהָאַחֲרֹנִים הִנָּם כְּתוּבִים בְּדִבְרֵי יֵהוּא בֶן־חֲנָנִי אֲשֶׁר הֹעֲלָה עַל־סֵפֶר מַלְכֵי יִשְׂרָאֵֽל: 35 וְאַחֲרֵיכֵן אֶתְחַבַּר יְהוֹשָׁפָט מֶֽלֶךְ־יְהוּדָה עִם אֲחַזְיָה מֶֽלֶךְ־יִשְׂרָאֵל הוּא הִרְשִׁיעַ לַעֲשֽׂוֹת: 36 וַיְחַבְּרֵהוּ עִמּוֹ לַעֲשׂוֹת אֳנִיּוֹת לָלֶכֶת תַּרְשִׁישׁ וַיַּעֲשׂוּ אֳנִיּוֹת בְּעֶצְיוֹן גָּֽבֶר: 37 וַיִּתְנַבֵּא אֱלִיעֶזֶר בֶּן־דֹּדָוָהוּ מִמָּרֵשָׁה עַל־יְהוֹשָׁפָט לֵאמֹר כְּהִֽתְחַבֶּרְךָ

LORD has destroyed your works." Then the ships were wrecked, so that they were not able to go to Tarshish.

21 And Jehoshaphat rested with his fathers, and was buried with his fathers in the City of David. Then Jehoram his son reigned in his place. 2 He had brothers, the sons of Jehoshaphat: Azariah, Jehiel, Zechariah, Azaryahu, Michael, and Shephatiah; all these *were* the sons of Jehoshaphat king of Israel. 3 Their father gave them great gifts of silver and gold and precious things, with fortified cities in Judah; but he gave the kingdom to Jehoram, because he *was* the firstborn.

4 Now when Jehoram was established over the kingdom of his father, he strengthened himself and killed all his brothers with the sword, and also *others* of the princes of Israel.

5 Jehoram *was* thirty-two years old when he became king, and he reigned eight years in Jerusalem. 6 And he walked in the way of the kings of Israel, just as the house of Ahab had done, for he had the daughter of Ahab as a wife; and he did evil in the sight of the LORD. 7 Yet the LORD would not destroy the house of David, because of the covenant that He had made with David, and since He had promised to give a lamp to him and to his sons forever.

8 In his days Edom revolted against Judah's authority, and made a king over themselves. 9 So Jehoram went out with his officers, and all his chariots with him. And he rose by night and attacked the Edomites who had surrounded him and the captains of the chariots. 10 Thus Edom has been in revolt against Judah's authority to this day. At that time Libnah revolted against his rule, because he had forsaken the LORD God of his fathers. 11 Moreover he made high places in the mountains of Judah, and caused the inhabitants of Jerusalem to commit harlotry, and led Judah astray.

12 And a letter came to him from Elijah the prophet, saying,

Thus says the LORD God of your father David:

Because you have not walked in the ways of Jehoshaphat your father, or in the ways of Asa king of Judah, 13 but have walked in the way of the kings of Israel, and have made Judah and the inhabitants of Jerusalem to play the harlot like the harlotry of the house of Ahab, and also have killed your brothers, those of your father's household, *who were*

עִם־אֲחַזְיָהוּ פָּרַץ יְהֹוָה אֶת־מַעֲשֶׂיךָ וַיִּשָּׁבְרוּ אֳנִיּוֹת וְלֹא עָצְרוּ לָלֶכֶת אֶל־תַּרְשִׁישׁ:

כא וַיִּשְׁכַּב יְהוֹשָׁפָט עִם־אֲבֹתָיו וַיִּקָּבֵר עִם־ אֲבֹתָיו בְּעִיר דָּוִיד וַיִּמְלֹךְ יְהוֹרָם בְּנוֹ תַּחְתָּיו: 2 וְלוֹ־אַחִים בְּנֵי יְהוֹשָׁפָט עֲזַרְיָה וִיחִיאֵל וּזְכַרְיָהוּ וַעֲזַרְיָהוּ וּמִיכָאֵל וּשְׁפַטְיָהוּ כָּל־אֵלֶּה בְּנֵי יְהוֹשָׁפָט מֶלֶךְ־יִשְׂרָאֵל: 3 וַיִּתֵּן לָהֶם ׀ אֲבִיהֶם מַתָּנוֹת רַבּוֹת לְכֶסֶף וּלְזָהָב וּלְמִגְדָּנוֹת עִם־עָרֵי מְצֻרוֹת בִּיהוּדָה וְאֶת־הַמַּמְלָכָה נָתַן לִיהוֹרָם כִּי־הוּא הַבְּכוֹר: פ 4 וַיָּקָם יְהוֹרָם עַל־מַמְלֶכֶת אָבִיו וַיִּתְחַזַּק וַיַּהֲרֹג אֶת־כָּל־אֶחָיו בֶּחָרֶב וְגַם מִשָּׂרֵי יִשְׂרָאֵל: 5 בֶּן־ שְׁלֹשִׁים וּשְׁתַּיִם שָׁנָה יְהוֹרָם בְּמָלְכוֹ וּשְׁמוֹנֶה שָׁנִים מָלַךְ בִּירוּשָׁלִָם: 6 וַיֵּלֶךְ בְּדֶרֶךְ ׀ מַלְכֵי יִשְׂרָאֵל כַּאֲשֶׁר עָשׂוּ בֵּית אַחְאָב כִּי בַּת־אַחְאָב הָיְתָה לּוֹ אִשָּׁה וַיַּעַשׂ הָרַע בְּעֵינֵי יְהֹוָה: 7 וְלֹא־אָבָה יְהֹוָה לְהַשְׁחִית אֶת־בֵּית דָּוִיד לְמַעַן הַבְּרִית אֲשֶׁר כָּרַת לְדָוִיד וְכַאֲשֶׁר אָמַר לָתֵת לוֹ נִיר וּלְבָנָיו כָּל־הַיָּמִים: 8 בְּיָמָיו פָּשַׁע אֱדוֹם מִתַּחַת יַד־יְהוּדָה וַיַּמְלִיכוּ עֲלֵיהֶם מֶלֶךְ: 9 וַיַּעֲבֹר יְהוֹרָם עִם־שָׂרָיו וְכָל־הָרֶכֶב עִמּוֹ וַיְהִי קָם לַיְלָה וַיַּךְ אֶת־אֱדוֹם הַסּוֹבֵב אֵלָיו וְאֵת שָׂרֵי הָרָכֶב: 10 וַיִּפְשַׁע אֱדוֹם מִתַּחַת יַד־יְהוּדָה עַד הַיּוֹם הַזֶּה אָז תִּפְשַׁע לִבְנָה בָּעֵת הַהִיא מִתַּחַת יָדוֹ כִּי עָזַב אֶת־יְהֹוָה אֱלֹהֵי אֲבֹתָיו: 11 גַּם־הוּא עָשָׂה־בָמוֹת בְּהָרֵי יְהוּדָה וַיֶּזֶן אֶת־יֹשְׁבֵי יְרוּשָׁלִַם וַיַּדַּח אֶת־יְהוּדָה: פ 12 וַיָּבֹא אֵלָיו מִכְתָּב מֵאֵלִיָּהוּ הַנָּבִיא לֵאמֹר ׀ כֹּה אָמַר יְהֹוָה אֱלֹהֵי דָּוִיד אָבִיךָ תַּחַת אֲשֶׁר לֹא־ הָלַכְתָּ בְּדַרְכֵי יְהוֹשָׁפָט אָבִיךָ וּבְדַרְכֵי אָסָא מֶלֶךְ־ יְהוּדָה: 13 וַתֵּלֶךְ בְּדֶרֶךְ מַלְכֵי יִשְׂרָאֵל וַתַּזְנֶה אֶת־ יְהוּדָה וְאֶת־יֹשְׁבֵי יְרוּשָׁלִַם כְּהַזְנוֹת בֵּית אַחְאָב וְגַם אֶת־אַחֶיךָ בֵית־אָבִיךָ הַטּוֹבִים מִמְּךָ הָרָגְתָּ:

better than yourself, ¹⁴behold, the LORD will strike your people with a serious affliction—your children, your wives, and all your possessions; ¹⁵and you *will become* very sick with a disease of your intestines, until your intestines come out by reason of the sickness, day by day.

¹⁶Moreover the LORD stirred up against Jehoram the spirit of the Philistines and the Arabians who *were* near the Ethiopians. ¹⁷And they came up into Judah and invaded it, and carried away all the possessions that were found in the king's house, and also his sons and his wives, so that there was not a son left to him except Jehoahaz, the youngest of his sons.

¹⁸After all this the LORD struck him in his intestines with an incurable disease. ¹⁹Then it happened in the course of time, after the end of two years, that his intestines came out because of his sickness; so he died in severe pain. And his people made no burning for him, like the burning for his fathers.

²⁰He was thirty-two years old when he became king. He reigned in Jerusalem eight years and, to no one's sorrow, departed. However they buried him in the City of David, but not in the tombs of the kings.

22 Then the inhabitants of Jerusalem made Ahaziah his youngest son king in his place, for the raiders who came with the Arabians into the camp had killed all the older *sons*. So Ahaziah the son of Jehoram, king of Judah, reigned. ²Ahaziah *was* forty-two years old when he became king, and he reigned one year in Jerusalem. His mother's name *was* Athaliah the granddaughter of Omri. ³He also walked in the ways of the house of Ahab, for his mother advised him to do wickedly. ⁴Therefore he did evil in the sight of the LORD, like the house of Ahab; for they were his counselors after the death of his father, to his destruction. ⁵He also followed their advice, and went with Jehoram the son of Ahab king of Israel to war against Hazael king of Syria at Ramoth Gilead; and the Syrians wounded Joram. ⁶Then he returned to Jezreel to recover from the wounds which he had received at Ramah, when he fought against Hazael king of Syria. And Azariah the son of Jehoram, king of Judah, went down to see Jehoram the son of Ahab in Jezreel, because he was sick.

⁷His going to Joram was God's occasion for Ahaziah's downfall; for when he arrived, he went out with Jehoram against Jehu the son of Nimshi, whom the LORD had anointed to cut off the house

14 הִנֵּה יְהוָה נֹגֵף מַגֵּפָה גְדוֹלָה בְּעַמֶּךָ וּבְבָנֶיךָ וּבְנָשֶׁיךָ וּבְכָל־רְכוּשֶׁךָ: 15 וְאַתָּה בָּחֳלָיִים רַבִּים בְּמַחֲלֵה מֵעֶיךָ עַד־יֵצְאוּ מֵעֶיךָ מִן־הַחֹלִי יָמִים עַל־יָמִים: 16 וַיָּעַר יְהוָה עַל־יְהוֹרָם אֵת רוּחַ הַפְּלִשְׁתִּים וְהָעַרְבִים אֲשֶׁר עַל־יַד כּוּשִׁים: 17 וַיַּעֲלוּ בִיהוּדָה וַיִּבְקָעוּהָ וַיִּשְׁבּוּ אֵת כָּל־הָרְכוּשׁ הַנִּמְצָא לְבֵית־הַמֶּלֶךְ וְגַם־בָּנָיו וְנָשָׁיו וְלֹא נִשְׁאַר־לוֹ בֵּן כִּי אִם־יְהוֹאָחָז קְטֹן בָּנָיו: 18 וְאַחֲרֵי כָּל־זֹאת נְגָפוֹ יְהוָה בְּמֵעָיו לָחֳלִי לְאֵין מַרְפֵּא: 19 וַיְהִי לְיָמִים מִיָּמִים וּכְעֵת צֵאת הַקֵּץ לְיָמִים שְׁנַיִם יָצְאוּ מֵעָיו עִם־חָלְיוֹ וַיָּמָת בְּתַחֲלֻאִים רָעִים וְלֹא־עָשׂוּ לוֹ עַמּוֹ שְׂרֵפָה כִּשְׂרֵפַת אֲבֹתָיו: 20 בֶּן־שְׁלֹשִׁים וּשְׁתַּיִם הָיָה בְמָלְכוֹ וּשְׁמוֹנֶה שָׁנִים מָלַךְ בִּירוּשָׁלִָם וַיֵּלֶךְ בְּלֹא חֶמְדָּה וַיִּקְבְּרֻהוּ בְּעִיר דָּוִיד וְלֹא בְּקִבְרוֹת הַמְּלָכִים:

כב וַיַּמְלִיכוּ יוֹשְׁבֵי יְרוּשָׁלִַם אֶת־אֲחַזְיָהוּ בְנוֹ הַקָּטֹן תַּחְתָּיו כִּי כָל־הָרִאשֹׁנִים הָרַג הַגְּדוּד הַבָּא בָעַרְבִים לַמַּחֲנֶה וַיִּמְלֹךְ אֲחַזְיָהוּ בֶן־יְהוֹרָם מֶלֶךְ יְהוּדָה: פ

2 בֶּן־אַרְבָּעִים וּשְׁתַּיִם שָׁנָה אֲחַזְיָהוּ בְמָלְכוֹ וְשָׁנָה אַחַת מָלַךְ בִּירוּשָׁלִָם וְשֵׁם אִמּוֹ עֲתַלְיָהוּ בַּת־עָמְרִי: 3 גַּם־הוּא הָלַךְ בְּדַרְכֵי בֵּית אַחְאָב כִּי אִמּוֹ הָיְתָה יוֹעַצְתּוֹ לְהַרְשִׁיעַ: 4 וַיַּעַשׂ הָרַע בְּעֵינֵי יְהוָה כְּבֵית אַחְאָב כִּי־הֵמָּה הָיוּ־לוֹ יוֹעֲצִים אַחֲרֵי מוֹת אָבִיו לְמַשְׁחִית לוֹ: 5 גַּם בַּעֲצָתָם הָלַךְ וַיֵּלֶךְ אֶת־יְהוֹרָם בֶּן־אַחְאָב מֶלֶךְ יִשְׂרָאֵל לַמִּלְחָמָה עַל־חֲזָאֵל מֶלֶךְ־אֲרָם בְּרָמֹת גִּלְעָד וַיַּכּוּ הָרַמִּים אֶת־יוֹרָם: 6 וַיָּשָׁב לְהִתְרַפֵּא בְיִזְרְעֶאל כִּי הַמַּכִּים אֲשֶׁר הִכֻּהוּ בְרָמָה בְּהִלָּחֲמוֹ אֶת־חֲזָהאֵל מֶלֶךְ אֲרָם וַעֲזַרְיָהוּ בֶן־יְהוֹרָם מֶלֶךְ יְהוּדָה יָרַד לִרְאוֹת אֶת־יְהוֹרָם בֶּן־אַחְאָב בְּיִזְרְעֶאל כִּי־חֹלֶה הוּא: 7 וּמֵאֱלֹהִים הָיְתָה תְּבוּסַת אֲחַזְיָהוּ לָבוֹא אֶל־יוֹרָם וּבְבֹאוֹ יָצָא עִם־יְהוֹרָם אֶל־

of Ahab. ⁸And it happened, when Jehu was executing judgment on the house of Ahab, and found the princes of Judah and the sons of Ahaziah's brothers who served Ahaziah, that he killed them. ⁹Then he searched for Ahaziah; and they caught him (he was hiding in Samaria), and brought him to Jehu. When they had killed him, they buried him, "because," they said, "he is the son of Jehoshaphat, who sought the LORD with all his heart."

So the house of Ahaziah had no one to assume power over the kingdom.

¹⁰Now when Athaliah the mother of Ahaziah saw that her son was dead, she arose and destroyed all the royal heirs of the house of Judah. ¹¹But Jehoshabeath, the daughter of the king, took Joash the son of Ahaziah, and stole him away from among the king's sons who were being murdered, and put him and his nurse in a bedroom. So Jehoshabeath, the daughter of King Jehoram, the wife of Jehoiada the priest (for she was the sister of Ahaziah), hid him from Athaliah so that she did not kill him. ¹²And he was hidden with them in the house of God for six years, while Athaliah reigned over the land.

23 In the seventh year Jehoiada strengthened himself, *and made a* covenant with the captains of hundreds: Azariah the son of Jeroham, Ishmael the son of Jehohanan, Azariah the son of Obed, Maaseiah the son of Adaiah, and Elishaphat the son of Zichri. ²And they went throughout Judah and gathered the Levites from all the cities of Judah, and the chief fathers of Israel, and they came to Jerusalem.

³Then all the assembly made a covenant with the king in the house of God. And he said to them, "Behold, the king's son shall reign, as the LORD has said of the sons of David. ⁴This *is* what you shall do: One-third of you entering on the Sabbath, of the priests and the Levites, *shall be* keeping watch over the doors; ⁵one-third *shall be* at the king's house; and one-third at the Gate of the Foundation. All the people *shall be* in the courts of the house of the LORD. ⁶But let no one come into the house of the LORD except the priests and those of the Levites who serve. They may go in, for they *are* holy; but all the people shall keep the watch of the LORD. ⁷And the Levites shall surround the king on all sides, every man with his weapons in his hand; and whoever comes into the house, let him be put to death. You are to be with the king when he comes in and when he goes out."

יֵה֣וּא בֶן־נִמְשִׁ֔י אֲשֶׁ֥ר מְשָׁח֖וֹ יְהוָ֑ה לְהַכְרִ֖ית אֶת־
בֵּ֣ית אַחְאָֽב: ⁸ וַיְהִ֗י כְּהִשָּׁפֵ֤ט יֵהוּא֙ עִם־בֵּ֣ית אַחְאָ֔ב
וַיִּמְצָ֞א אֶת־שָׂרֵ֤י יְהוּדָה֙ וּבְנֵי֙ אֲחֵ֣י אֲחַזְיָ֔הוּ מְשָׁרְתִ֖ים
לַאֲחַזְיָ֑הוּ וַיַּהַרְגֵֽם: ⁹ וַיְבַקֵּשׁ֙ אֶת־אֲחַזְיָ֔הוּ וַיִּלְכְּדֻ֗הוּ
וְה֤וּא מִתְחַבֵּא֙ בְשֹֽׁמְר֔וֹן וַיְבִאֻ֥הוּ אֶל־יֵה֖וּא וַיְמִתֻ֑הוּ
וַֽיִּקְבְּרֻ֗הוּ כִּ֤י אָֽמְרוּ֙ בֶּן־יְהוֹשָׁפָ֣ט ה֔וּא אֲשֶׁר־דָּרַ֥שׁ
אֶת־יְהוָ֖ה בְּכָל־לְבָב֑וֹ וְאֵין֙ לְבֵ֣ית אֲחַזְיָ֔הוּ לַעְצֹ֥ר כֹּ֖חַ
לְמַמְלָכָֽה: ¹⁰ וַעֲתַלְיָ֙הוּ֙ אֵ֣ם אֲחַזְיָ֔הוּ רָאֲתָ֖ה כִּ֣י מֵ֣ת
בְּנָ֑הּ וַתָּ֗קָם וַתְּדַבֵּ֛ר אֶת־כָּל־זֶ֥רַע הַמַּמְלָכָ֖ה לְבֵ֥ית
יְהוּדָֽה: ¹¹ וַתִּקַּ֣ח יְהוֹשַׁבְעַ֣ת בַּת־הַמֶּ֡לֶךְ אֶת־יוֹאָ֣שׁ
בֶּן־אֲחַזְיָ֡הוּ וַתִּגְנֹ֣ב אֹתוֹ֩ מִתּ֨וֹךְ בְּנֵֽי־הַמֶּ֜לֶךְ הַמּֽוּמָתִ֗ים
וַתִּתֵּ֥ן אֹתוֹ֙ וְאֶת־מֵינִקְתּ֔וֹ בַּחֲדַ֣ר הַמִּטּ֑וֹת וַתַּסְתִּירֵ֡הוּ
יְהוֹשַׁבְעַ֣ת בַּת־הַמֶּ֣לֶךְ יְהוֹרָ֡ם אֵשֶׁת֩ יְהוֹיָדָ֨ע הַכֹּהֵ֜ן
כִּ֣י הִ֧יא הָֽיְתָ֣ה אֲח֣וֹת אֲחַזְיָ֗הוּ מִפְּנֵ֧י עֲתַלְיָ֛הוּ וְלֹ֥א
הֱמִיתָֽתְהוּ: ¹² וַיְהִ֣י אִתָּ֗ם בְּבֵ֧ית הָאֱלֹהִ֛ים מִתְחַבֵּ֖א
שֵׁ֣שׁ שָׁנִ֑ים וַעֲתַלְיָ֖ה מֹלֶ֥כֶת עַל־הָאָֽרֶץ: פ

כג וּבַשָּׁנָ֨ה הַשְּׁבִעִ֜ית הִתְחַזַּ֣ק יְהוֹיָדָ֗ע וַיִּקַּ֣ח
אֶת־שָׂרֵ֪י הַמֵּא֟וֹת לַֽעֲזַרְיָ֣הוּ בֶן־יְרֹחָ֡ם וּֽלְיִשְׁמָעֵ֣אל
בֶּן־יְהֽוֹחָנָ֡ן וְלַעֲזַרְיָ֣הוּ בֶן־עוֹבֵ֣ד וְאֶת־מַעֲשֵׂיָ֣הוּ בֶן־
עֲדָיָ֗הוּ וְאֶת־אֱלִישָׁפָ֛ט בֶּן־זִכְרִ֖י עִמּ֣וֹ בַבְּרִֽית: ² וַיָּסֹ֙בּוּ֙
בִּֽיהוּדָ֔ה וַיִּקְבְּצ֤וּ אֶת־הַֽלְוִיִּם֙ מִכָּל־עָרֵ֣י יְהוּדָ֔ה
וְרָאשֵׁ֥י הָאָב֖וֹת לְיִשְׂרָאֵ֑ל וַיָּבֹ֖אוּ אֶל־יְרוּשָׁלִָֽם:
³ וַיִּכְרֹ֨ת כָּל־הַקָּהָ֜ל בְּרִ֗ית בְּבֵ֤ית הָֽאֱלֹהִים֙ עִם־
הַמֶּ֔לֶךְ וַיֹּ֣אמֶר לָהֶ֔ם הִנֵּ֥ה בֶן־הַמֶּ֖לֶךְ יִמְלֹ֑ךְ כַּאֲשֶׁ֛ר
דִּבֶּ֥ר יְהוָ֖ה עַל־בְּנֵ֥י דָוִֽיד: ⁴ זֶ֥ה הַדָּבָ֖ר אֲשֶׁ֣ר
תַּעֲשׂ֑וּ הַשְּׁלִשִׁ֨ית מִכֶּ֜ם בָּאֵ֣י הַשַּׁבָּ֗ת לַכֹּֽהֲנִים֙
וְלַלְוִיִּ֔ם לְשֹֽׁעֲרֵ֖י הַסִּפִּֽים: ⁵ וְהַשְּׁלִשִׁית֙ בְּבֵ֣ית הַמֶּ֔לֶךְ
וְהַשְּׁלִשִׁ֖ית בְּשַׁ֣עַר הַיְס֑וֹד וְכָל־הָעָ֔ם בְּחַצְר֖וֹת בֵּ֥ית
יְהוָֽה: ⁶ וְאַל־יָב֣וֹא בֵית־יְהוָ֗ה כִּ֤י אִם־הַכֹּֽהֲנִים֙
וְהַמְשָׁרְתִ֣ים לַלְוִיִּ֔ם הֵ֥מָּה יָבֹ֖אוּ כִּי־קֹ֣דֶשׁ הֵ֑מָּה
וְכָל־הָעָ֔ם יִשְׁמְר֖וּ מִשְׁמֶ֥רֶת יְהוָֽה: ⁷ וְהִקִּיפוּ֩ הַלְוִיִּ֨ם
אֶת־הַמֶּ֜לֶךְ סָבִ֗יב אִ֚ישׁ וְכֵלָ֣יו בְּיָד֔וֹ וְהַבָּ֥א אֶל־הַבַּ֖יִת

8 So the Levites and all Judah did according to all that Jehoiada the priest commanded. And each man took his men who were to be on duty on the Sabbath, with those who were going *off duty* on the Sabbath; for Jehoiada the priest had not dismissed the divisions. 9 And Jehoiada the priest gave to the captains of hundreds the spears and the large and small shields which *had belonged* to King David, that *were* in the temple of God. 10 Then he set all the people, every man with his weapon in his hand, from the right side of the temple to the left side of the temple, along by the altar and by the temple, all around the king. 11 And they brought out the king's son, put the crown on him, *gave him* the Testimony, and made him king. Then Jehoiada and his sons anointed him, and said, "*Long* live the king!"

12 Now when Athaliah heard the noise of the people running and praising the king, she came to the people *in* the temple of the LORD. 13 *When* she looked, there was the king standing by his pillar at the entrance; and the leaders and the trumpeters *were* by the king. All the people of the land were rejoicing and blowing trumpets, also the singers with musical instruments, and those who led in praise. So Athaliah tore her clothes and said, "Treason! Treason!"

14 And Jehoiada the priest brought out the captains of hundreds who were set over the army, and said to them, "Take her outside under guard, and slay with the sword whoever follows her." For the priest had said, "Do not kill her in the house of the LORD."

15 So they seized her; and she went by way of the entrance of the Horse Gate *into* the king's house, and they killed her there.

16 Then Jehoiada made a covenant between himself, the people, and the king, that they should be the LORD's people. 17 And all the people went to the temple of Baal, and tore it down. They broke in pieces its altars and images, and killed Mattan the priest of Baal before the altars. 18 Also Jehoiada appointed the oversight of the house of the LORD to the hand of the priests, the Levites, whom David had assigned in the house of the LORD, to offer the burnt offerings of the LORD, as *it is* written in the Law of Moses, with rejoicing and with singing, *as it was established* by David. 19 And he set the gatekeepers at the gates of the house of the LORD, so that no one *who was* in any way unclean should enter.

20 Then he took the captains of hundreds, the nobles, the governors of the people, and all the people of the land, and brought the king down from the house of the LORD; and they went through the

8 וַיַּעֲשׂוּ הַלְוִיִּם וְכָל־יְהוּדָה כְּכֹל אֲשֶׁר־צִוָּה יְהוֹיָדָע הַכֹּהֵן וַיִּקְחוּ אִישׁ אֶת־אֲנָשָׁיו בָּאֵי הַשַּׁבָּת עִם יוֹצְאֵי הַשַּׁבָּת כִּי לֹא פָטַר יְהוֹיָדָע הַכֹּהֵן אֶת־הַמַּחְלְקוֹת: 9 וַיִּתֵּן יְהוֹיָדָע הַכֹּהֵן לְשָׂרֵי הַמֵּאוֹת אֶת־הַחֲנִיתִים וְאֶת־הַמָּגִנּוֹת וְאֶת־הַשְּׁלָטִים אֲשֶׁר לַמֶּלֶךְ דָּוִיד אֲשֶׁר בֵּית הָאֱלֹהִים: 10 וַיַּעֲמֵד אֶת־כָּל־הָעָם וְאִישׁ ׀ שִׁלְחוֹ בְיָדוֹ מִכֶּתֶף הַבַּיִת הַיְמָנִית עַד־כֶּתֶף הַבַּיִת הַשְּׂמָאלִית לַמִּזְבֵּחַ וְלַבָּיִת עַל־הַמֶּלֶךְ סָבִיב: 11 וַיּוֹצִיאוּ אֶת־בֶּן־הַמֶּלֶךְ וַיִּתְּנוּ עָלָיו אֶת־הַנֵּזֶר וְאֶת־הָעֵדוּת וַיַּמְלִיכוּ אֹתוֹ וַיִּמְשָׁחֻהוּ יְהוֹיָדָע וּבָנָיו וַיֹּאמְרוּ יְחִי הַמֶּלֶךְ: ס 12 וַתִּשְׁמַע עֲתַלְיָהוּ אֶת־קוֹל הָעָם הָרָצִים וְהַמְהַלְלִים אֶת־הַמֶּלֶךְ וַתָּבוֹא אֶל־הָעָם בֵּית יְהוָה: 13 וַתֵּרֶא וְהִנֵּה הַמֶּלֶךְ עוֹמֵד עַל־עַמּוּדוֹ בַּמָּבוֹא וְהַשָּׂרִים וְהַחֲצֹצְרוֹת עַל־הַמֶּלֶךְ וְכָל־עַם הָאָרֶץ שָׂמֵחַ וְתוֹקֵעַ בַּחֲצֹצְרוֹת וְהַמְשׁוֹרֲרִים בִּכְלֵי הַשִּׁיר וּמוֹדִיעִים לְהַלֵּל וַתִּקְרַע עֲתַלְיָהוּ אֶת־בְּגָדֶיהָ וַתֹּאמֶר קֶשֶׁר קָשֶׁר: ס 14 וַיּוֹצֵא יְהוֹיָדָע הַכֹּהֵן אֶת־שָׂרֵי הַמֵּאוֹת ׀ פְּקוּדֵי הַחַיִל וַיֹּאמֶר אֲלֵהֶם הוֹצִיאוּהָ אֶל־מִבֵּית הַשְּׂדֵרוֹת וְהַבָּא אַחֲרֶיהָ יוּמַת בֶּחָרֶב כִּי אָמַר הַכֹּהֵן לֹא תְמִיתוּהָ בֵּית יְהוָה: 15 וַיָּשִׂימוּ לָהּ יָדַיִם וַתָּבוֹא אֶל־מְבוֹא שַׁעַר־הַסּוּסִים בֵּית הַמֶּלֶךְ וַיְמִיתוּהָ שָׁם: פ

16 וַיִּכְרֹת יְהוֹיָדָע בְּרִית בֵּינוֹ וּבֵין כָּל־הָעָם וּבֵין הַמֶּלֶךְ לִהְיוֹת לְעָם לַיהוָה: 17 וַיָּבֹאוּ כָל־הָעָם בֵּית־הַבַּעַל וַיִּתְּצֻהוּ וְאֶת־מִזְבְּחֹתָיו וְאֶת־צְלָמָיו שִׁבֵּרוּ וְאֵת מַתָּן כֹּהֵן הַבַּעַל הָרְגוּ לִפְנֵי הַמִּזְבְּחוֹת: 18 וַיָּשֶׂם יְהוֹיָדָע פְּקֻדֹּת בֵּית יְהוָה בְּיַד הַכֹּהֲנִים הַלְוִיִּם אֲשֶׁר חָלַק דָּוִיד עַל־בֵּית יְהוָה לְהַעֲלוֹת עֹלוֹת יְהוָה כַּכָּתוּב בְּתוֹרַת מֹשֶׁה בְּשִׂמְחָה וּבְשִׁיר עַל יְדֵי דָוִיד: 19 וַיַּעֲמֵד הַשּׁוֹעֲרִים עַל־שַׁעֲרֵי בֵּית יְהוָה וְלֹא־יָבֹא טָמֵא לְכָל־דָּבָר: 20 וַיִּקַּח אֶת־שָׂרֵי הַמֵּאוֹת וְאֶת־הָאַדִּירִים וְאֶת־הַמּוֹשְׁלִים בָּעָם וְאֵת ׀ כָּל־עַם הָאָרֶץ וַיּוֹרֶד אֶת־הַמֶּלֶךְ מִבֵּית יְהוָה וַיָּבֹאוּ בְּתוֹךְ־שַׁעַר הָעֶלְיוֹן בֵּית הַמֶּלֶךְ וַיּוֹשִׁיבוּ

Upper Gate to the king's house, and set the king on the throne of the kingdom. ²¹ So all the people of the land rejoiced; and the city was quiet, for they had slain Athaliah with the sword.

24 Joash *was* seven years old when he became king, and he reigned forty years in Jerusalem. His mother's name *was* Zibiah of Beersheba. ² Joash did *what was* right in the sight of the LORD all the days of Jehoiada the priest. ³ And Jehoiada took two wives for him, and he had sons and daughters.

⁴ Now it happened after this *that* Joash set his heart on repairing the house of the LORD. ⁵ Then he gathered the priests and the Levites, and said to them, "Go out to the cities of Judah, and gather from all Israel money to repair the house of your God from year to year, and see that you do it quickly."

However the Levites did not do it quickly. ⁶ So the king called Jehoiada the chief *priest,* and said to him, "Why have you not required the Levites to bring in from Judah and from Jerusalem the collection, *according to the commandment* of Moses the servant of the LORD and of the assembly of Israel, for the tabernacle of witness?" ⁷ For the sons of Athaliah, that wicked woman, had broken into the house of God, and had also presented all the dedicated things of the house of the LORD to the Baals.

⁸ Then at the king's command they made a chest, and set it outside at the gate of the house of the LORD. ⁹ And they made a proclamation throughout Judah and Jerusalem to bring to the LORD the collection *that* Moses the servant of God *had imposed* on Israel in the wilderness. ¹⁰ Then all the leaders and all the people rejoiced, brought their contributions, and put *them* into the chest until all had given. ¹¹ So it was, at that time, when the chest was brought to the king's official by the hand of the Levites, and when they saw that *there was* much money, that the king's scribe and the high priest's officer came and emptied the chest, and took it and returned it to its place. Thus they did day by day, and gathered money in abundance.

¹² The king and Jehoiada gave it to those who did the work of the service of the house of the LORD; and they hired masons and carpenters to repair the house of the LORD, and also those who worked in iron and bronze to restore the house of the LORD. ¹³ So the workmen labored, and the work was completed by them; they restored the house of God to its original condition and reinforced it. ¹⁴ When they had finished, they brought the rest of the money before the king and Jehoiada; they made

אֶת־הַמֶּלֶךְ עַל כִּסֵּא הַמַּמְלָכָה: 21 וַיִּשְׂמְחוּ כָל־
עַם־הָאָרֶץ וְהָעִיר שָׁקָטָה וְאֶת־עֲתַלְיָהוּ הֵמִיתוּ
בֶחָרֶב: ס

כד בֶּן־שֶׁבַע שָׁנִים יֹאָשׁ בְּמָלְכוֹ וְאַרְבָּעִים שָׁנָה
מָלַךְ בִּירוּשָׁלָ͏ִם וְשֵׁם אִמּוֹ צִבְיָה מִבְּאֵר שָׁבַע:
2 וַיַּעַשׂ יוֹאָשׁ הַיָּשָׁר בְּעֵינֵי יְהוָה כָּל־יְמֵי יְהוֹיָדָע
הַכֹּהֵן: 3 וַיִּשָּׂא־לוֹ יְהוֹיָדָע נָשִׁים שְׁתָּיִם וַיּוֹלֶד בָּנִים
וּבָנוֹת: 4 וַיְהִי אַחֲרֵיכֵן הָיָה עִם־לֵב יוֹאָשׁ לְחַדֵּשׁ
אֶת־בֵּית יְהוָה: 5 וַיִּקְבֹּץ אֶת־הַכֹּהֲנִים וְהַלְוִיִּם
וַיֹּאמֶר לָהֶם צְאוּ לְעָרֵי יְהוּדָה וְקִבְצוּ מִכָּל־יִשְׂרָאֵל
כֶּסֶף לְחַזֵּק ׀ אֶת־בֵּית אֱלֹהֵיכֶם מִדֵּי שָׁנָה בְּשָׁנָה
וְאַתֶּם תְּמַהֲרוּ לַדָּבָר וְלֹא מִהֲרוּ הַלְוִיִּם: 6 וַיִּקְרָא
הַמֶּלֶךְ לִיהוֹיָדָע הָרֹאשׁ וַיֹּאמֶר לוֹ מַדּוּעַ לֹא־דָרַשְׁתָּ
עַל־הַלְוִיִּם לְהָבִיא מִיהוּדָה וּמִירוּשָׁלַ͏ִם אֶת־מַשְׂאַת
מֹשֶׁה עֶבֶד־יְהוָה וְהַקָּהָל לְיִשְׂרָאֵל לְאֹהֶל הָעֵדוּת:
7 כִּי־עֲתַלְיָהוּ הַמִּרְשַׁעַת בָּנֶיהָ פָרְצוּ אֶת־בֵּית
הָאֱלֹהִים וְגַם כָּל־קָדְשֵׁי בֵית־יְהוָה עָשׂוּ לַבְּעָלִים:
8 וַיֹּאמֶר הַמֶּלֶךְ וַיַּעֲשׂוּ אֲרוֹן אֶחָד וַיִּתְּנֻהוּ בְּשַׁעַר
בֵּית־יְהוָה חוּצָה: 9 וַיִּתְּנוּ־קוֹל בִּיהוּדָה וּבִירוּשָׁלַ͏ִם
לְהָבִיא לַיהוָה מַשְׂאַת מֹשֶׁה עֶבֶד־הָאֱלֹהִים עַל־
יִשְׂרָאֵל בַּמִּדְבָּר: 10 וַיִּשְׂמְחוּ כָל־הַשָּׂרִים וְכָל־הָעָם
וַיָּבִיאוּ וַיַּשְׁלִיכוּ לָאָרוֹן עַד־לְכַלֵּה: 11 וַיְהִי בְּעֵת
יָבִיא אֶת־הָאָרוֹן אֶל־פְּקֻדַּת הַמֶּלֶךְ בְּיַד הַלְוִיִּם
וְכִרְאוֹתָם כִּי־רַב הַכֶּסֶף וּבָא סוֹפֵר הַמֶּלֶךְ וּפְקִיד
כֹּהֵן הָרֹאשׁ וִיעָרוּ אֶת־הָאָרוֹן וְיִשָּׂאֻהוּ וִישִׁיבֻהוּ
אֶל־מְקֹמוֹ כֹּה עָשׂוּ לְיוֹם ׀ בְּיוֹם וַיַּאַסְפוּ־כֶסֶף
לָרֹב: 12 וַיִּתְּנֵהוּ הַמֶּלֶךְ וִיהוֹיָדָע אֶל־עוֹשֵׂה מְלֶאכֶת
עֲבוֹדַת בֵּית־יְהוָה וַיִּהְיוּ שֹׂכְרִים חֹצְבִים וְחָרָשִׁים
לְחַדֵּשׁ בֵּית יְהוָה וְגַם לְחָרָשֵׁי בַרְזֶל וּנְחֹשֶׁת לְחַזֵּק
אֶת־בֵּית יְהוָה: 13 וַיַּעֲשׂוּ עֹשֵׂי הַמְּלָאכָה וַתַּעַל
אֲרוּכָה לַמְּלָאכָה בְּיָדָם וַיַּעֲמִידוּ אֶת־בֵּית הָאֱלֹהִים
עַל־מַתְכֻּנְתּוֹ וַיְאַמְּצֻהוּ: 14 וּכְכַלּוֹתָם הֵבִיאוּ לִפְנֵי
הַמֶּלֶךְ וִיהוֹיָדָע אֶת־שְׁאָר הַכֶּסֶף וַיַּעֲשֵׂהוּ כֵלִים
לְבֵית־יְהוָה כְּלֵי שָׁרֵת וְהַעֲלוֹת וְכַפּוֹת וּכְלֵי זָהָב

from it articles for the house of the LORD, articles for serving and offering, spoons and vessels of gold and silver. And they offered burnt offerings in the house of the LORD continually all the days of Jehoiada.

15 But Jehoiada grew old and was full of days, and he died; *he was* one hundred and thirty years old when he died. 16 And they buried him in the City of David among the kings, because he had done good in Israel, both toward God and His house.

17 Now after the death of Jehoiada the leaders of Judah came and bowed down to the king. And the king listened to them. 18 Therefore they left the house of the LORD God of their fathers, and served wooden images and idols; and wrath came upon Judah and Jerusalem because of their trespass. 19 Yet He sent prophets to them, to bring them back to the LORD; and they testified against them, but they would not listen.

20 Then the Spirit of God came upon Zechariah the son of Jehoiada the priest, who stood above the people, and said to them, "Thus says God: 'Why do you transgress the commandments of the LORD, so that you cannot prosper? Because you have forsaken the LORD, He also has forsaken you.'" 21 So they conspired against him, and at the command of the king they stoned him with stones in the court of the house of the LORD. 22 Thus Joash the king did not remember the kindness which Jehoiada his father had done to him, but killed his son; and as he died, he said, "The LORD look on *it*, and repay!"

23 So it happened in the spring of the year *that* the army of Syria came up against him; and they came to Judah and Jerusalem, and destroyed all the leaders of the people from among the people, and sent all their spoil to the king of Damascus. 24 For the army of the Syrians came with a small company of men; but the LORD delivered a very great army into their hand, because they had forsaken the LORD God of their fathers. So they executed judgment against Joash. 25 And when they had withdrawn from him (for they left him severely wounded), his own servants conspired against him because of the blood of the sons of Jehoiada the priest, and killed him on his bed. So he died. And they buried him in the City of David, but they did not bury him in the tombs of the kings.

26 These are the ones who conspired against him: Zabad the son of Shimeath the Ammonitess, and Jehozabad the son of Shimrith the Moabitess. 27 Now *concerning* his sons, and the many oracles about him, and the repairing of the house of God,

וָכֶ֫סֶף וַיִּהְי֣וּ מַעֲלִ֗ים עֹל֤וֹת בְּבֵית־יְהוָה֙ תָּמִ֔יד כֹּ֖ל יְמֵ֥י יְהוֹיָדָֽע׃ פ

15 וַיִּזְקַ֧ן יְהוֹיָדָ֛ע וַיִּשְׂבַּ֥ע יָמִ֖ים וַיָּמֹ֑ת בֶּן־מֵאָ֧ה וּשְׁלֹשִׁ֛ים שָׁנָ֖ה בְּמוֹתֽוֹ׃ 16 וַיִּקְבְּרֻ֤הוּ בְעִיר־דָּוִיד֙ עִם־הַמְּלָכִ֔ים כִּי־עָשָׂ֥ה טוֹבָ֖ה בְּיִשְׂרָאֵ֑ל וְעִ֥ם הָאֱלֹהִ֖ים וּבֵיתֽוֹ׃ ס 17 וְאַחֲרֵ֞י מ֣וֹת יְהוֹיָדָ֗ע בָּ֚אוּ שָׂרֵ֣י יְהוּדָ֔ה וַיִּֽשְׁתַּחֲו֖וּ לַמֶּ֑לֶךְ אָ֛ז שָׁמַ֥ע הַמֶּ֖לֶךְ אֲלֵיהֶֽם׃ 18 וַיַּֽעַזְב֗וּ אֶת־בֵּ֤ית יְהוָה֙ אֱלֹהֵ֣י אֲבוֹתֵיהֶ֔ם וַיַּֽעַבְד֥וּ אֶת־הָאֲשֵׁרִ֖ים וְאֶת־הָֽעֲצַבִּ֑ים וַיְהִי־קֶ֗צֶף עַל־יְהוּדָ֙ה וִיר֣וּשָׁלִַ֔ם בְּאַשְׁמָתָ֖ם זֹֽאת׃ 19 וַיִּשְׁלַ֙ח בָּהֶ֤ם נְבִאִים֙ לַהֲשִׁיבָ֣ם אֶל־יְהוָ֔ה וַיָּעִ֥ידוּ בָ֖ם וְלֹ֥א הֶאֱזִֽינוּ׃ ס 20 וְר֣וּחַ אֱלֹהִ֗ים לָֽבְשָׁה֙ אֶת־זְכַרְיָה֙ בֶּן־יְהוֹיָדָ֣ע הַכֹּהֵ֔ן וַֽיַּעֲמֹ֖ד מֵעַ֣ל לָעָ֑ם וַיֹּ֨אמֶר לָהֶ֜ם כֹּ֣ה ׀ אָמַ֣ר הָאֱלֹהִ֗ים לָ֤מָה אַתֶּם֙ עֹֽבְרִים֙ אֶת־מִצְוֺ֣ת יְהוָ֔ה וְלֹ֖א תַצְלִ֑יחוּ כִּֽי־עֲזַבְתֶּ֥ם אֶת־יְהוָ֖ה וַיַּֽעֲזֹ֥ב אֶתְכֶֽם׃ 21 וַיִּקְשְׁר֣וּ עָלָ֔יו וַיִּרְגְּמֻ֥הוּ אֶ֖בֶן בְּמִצְוַ֣ת הַמֶּ֑לֶךְ בַּחֲצַ֖ר בֵּ֥ית יְהוָֽה׃ 22 וְלֹא־זָכַ֞ר יוֹאָ֣שׁ הַמֶּ֗לֶךְ הַחֶ֙סֶד֙ אֲשֶׁ֨ר עָשָׂ֜ה יְהוֹיָדָ֤ע אָבִיו֙ עִמּ֔וֹ וַֽיַּהֲרֹ֖ג אֶת־בְּנ֑וֹ וּכְמוֹת֣וֹ אָמַ֔ר יֵ֥רֶא יְהוָ֖ה וְיִדְרֹֽשׁ׃ פ

23 וַיְהִ֣י ׀ לִתְקוּפַ֣ת הַשָּׁנָ֗ה עָלָ֤ה עָלָיו֙ חֵ֣יל אֲרָ֔ם וַיָּבֹ֗אוּ אֶל־יְהוּדָה֙ וִיר֣וּשָׁלִַ֔ם וַיַּשְׁחִ֥יתוּ אֶת־כָּל־שָׂרֵ֥י הָעָ֖ם מֵעָ֑ם וְכָל־שְׁלָלָ֥ם שִׁלְּח֖וּ לְמֶ֥לֶךְ דַּרְמָֽשֶׂק׃ 24 כִּי֩ בְמִצְעַ֨ר אֲנָשִׁ֜ים בָּ֣אוּ ׀ חֵ֣יל אֲרָ֗ם וַֽיהוָ֞ה נָתַ֧ן בְּיָדָ֛ם חַ֖יִל לָרֹ֣ב מְאֹ֑ד כִּ֣י עָֽזְב֔וּ אֶת־יְהוָ֖ה אֱלֹהֵ֣י אֲבוֹתֵיהֶ֑ם וְאֶת־יוֹאָ֖שׁ עָשׂ֥וּ שְׁפָטִֽים׃ 25 וּבְלֶכְתָּ֣ם מִמֶּ֗נּוּ כִּֽי־עָזְב֣וּ אֹתוֹ֮ בְּמַחֲלוּיִ֣ם רַבִּים֒ הִתְקַשְּׁר֤וּ עָלָיו֙ עֲבָדָ֗יו בִּדְמֵי֙ בְּנֵי֙ יְהוֹיָדָ֣ע הַכֹּהֵ֔ן וַיַּֽהַרְגֻ֥הוּ עַל־מִטָּת֖וֹ וַיָּמֹ֑ת וַֽיִּקְבְּרֻ֙הוּ֙ בְּעִ֣יר דָּוִ֔יד וְלֹ֥א קְבָרֻ֖הוּ בְּקִבְר֥וֹת הַמְּלָכִֽים׃ ס 26 וְאֵ֖לֶּה הַמִּתְקַשְּׁרִ֣ים עָלָ֑יו זָבָ֗ד בֶּן־שִׁמְעָת֙ הָֽעַמּוֹנִ֔ית וִיה֣וֹזָבָ֔ד בֶּן־שִׁמְרִ֖ית הַמּוֹאָבִֽית׃ 27 וּבָנָ֞יו וְרֹ֤ב הַמַּשָּׂא֙ עָלָ֔יו וִיס֖וֹד בֵּ֥ית

כד 25 בְּמַחֲלֻיִּ֑ים 27 יֶֽרֶב

indeed they *are* written in the annals of the book of the kings. Then Amaziah his son reigned in his place.

25 Amaziah *was* twenty-five years old *when he* became king, and he reigned twenty-nine years in Jerusalem. His mother's name *was* Jehoaddan of Jerusalem. ² And he did *what was* right in the sight of the LORD, but not with a loyal heart.

³ Now it happened, as soon as the kingdom was established for him, that he executed his servants who had murdered his father the king. ⁴ However he did not execute their children, but *did* as *it is* written in the Law in the Book of Moses, where the LORD commanded, saying, "The fathers shall not be put to death for their children, nor shall the children be put to death for their fathers; but a person shall die for his own sin."

⁵ Moreover Amaziah gathered Judah together and set over them captains of thousands and captains of hundreds, according to *their* fathers' houses, throughout all Judah and Benjamin; and he numbered them from twenty years old and above, and found them to be three hundred thousand choice *men, able* to go to war, who could handle spear and shield. ⁶ He also hired one hundred thousand mighty men of valor from Israel for one hundred talents of silver. ⁷ But a man of God came to him, saying, "O king, do not let the army of Israel go with you, for the LORD *is* not with Israel— *not with* any of the children of Ephraim. ⁸ But if you go, be gone! Be strong in battle! *Even so,* God shall make you fall before the enemy; for God has power to help and to overthrow."

⁹ Then Amaziah said to the man of God, "But what *shall we* do about the hundred talents which I have given to the troops of Israel?"

And the man of God answered, "The LORD is able to give you much more than this." ¹⁰ So Amaziah discharged the troops that had come to him from Ephraim, to go back home. Therefore their anger was greatly aroused against Judah, and they returned home in great anger.

¹¹ Then Amaziah strengthened himself, and leading his people, he went to the Valley of Salt and killed ten thousand of the people of Seir. ¹² Also the children of Judah took captive ten thousand alive, brought them to the top of the rock, and cast them down from the top of the rock, so that they all were dashed in pieces.

הָאֱלֹהִים הִנָּם כְּתוּבִים עַל־מִדְרַשׁ סֵפֶר הַמְּלָכִים
וַיִּמְלֹךְ אֲמַצְיָהוּ בְנוֹ תַּחְתָּיו: פ

כה בֶּן־עֶשְׂרִים וְחָמֵשׁ שָׁנָה מָלַךְ אֲמַצְיָהוּ
וְעֶשְׂרִים וָתֵשַׁע שָׁנָה מָלַךְ בִּירוּשָׁלִָם וְשֵׁם אִמּוֹ
יְהוֹעַדָּן מִירוּשָׁלָיִם: 2 וַיַּעַשׂ הַיָּשָׁר בְּעֵינֵי יְהוָה רַק
לֹא בְּלֵבָב שָׁלֵם: 3 וַיְהִי כַּאֲשֶׁר חָזְקָה הַמַּמְלָכָה
עָלָיו וַיַּהֲרֹג אֶת־עֲבָדָיו הַמַּכִּים אֶת־הַמֶּלֶךְ אָבִיו:
4 וְאֶת־בְּנֵיהֶם לֹא הֵמִית כִּי כַכָּתוּב בַּתּוֹרָה בְּסֵפֶר
מֹשֶׁה אֲשֶׁר־צִוָּה יְהוָה לֵאמֹר לֹא־יָמוּתוּ אָבוֹת עַל־
בָּנִים וּבָנִים לֹא־יָמוּתוּ עַל־אָבוֹת כִּי אִישׁ בְּחֶטְאוֹ
יָמוּתוּ: פ

5 וַיִּקְבֹּץ אֲמַצְיָהוּ אֶת־יְהוּדָה וַיַּעֲמִידֵם לְבֵית־אָבוֹת
לְשָׂרֵי הָאֲלָפִים וּלְשָׂרֵי הַמֵּאוֹת לְכָל־יְהוּדָה וּבִנְיָמִן
וַיִּפְקְדֵם לְמִבֶּן עֶשְׂרִים שָׁנָה וָמַעְלָה וַיִּמְצָאֵם שְׁלֹשׁ־
מֵאוֹת אֶלֶף בָּחוּר יוֹצֵא צָבָא אֹחֵז רֹמַח וְצִנָּה:
6 וַיִּשְׂכֹּר מִיִּשְׂרָאֵל מֵאָה אֶלֶף גִּבּוֹר חָיִל בְּמֵאָה
כִכַּר־כָּסֶף: 7 וְאִישׁ הָאֱלֹהִים בָּא אֵלָיו לֵאמֹר הַמֶּלֶךְ
אַל־יָבֹא עִמְּךָ צְבָא יִשְׂרָאֵל כִּי אֵין יְהוָה עִם־
יִשְׂרָאֵל כֹּל בְּנֵי אֶפְרָיִם: 8 כִּי אִם־בֹּא אַתָּה עֲשֵׂה
חֲזַק לַמִּלְחָמָה יַכְשִׁילְךָ הָאֱלֹהִים לִפְנֵי אוֹיֵב כִּי יֶשׁ־
כֹּחַ בֵּאלֹהִים לַעְזוֹר וּלְהַכְשִׁיל: 9 וַיֹּאמֶר אֲמַצְיָהוּ
לְאִישׁ הָאֱלֹהִים וּמַה־לַּעֲשׂוֹת לִמְאַת הַכִּכָּר אֲשֶׁר
נָתַתִּי לִגְדוּד יִשְׂרָאֵל וַיֹּאמֶר אִישׁ הָאֱלֹהִים יֵשׁ
לַיהוָה לָתֶת לְךָ הַרְבֵּה מִזֶּה: 10 וַיַּבְדִּילֵם אֲמַצְיָהוּ
לְהַגְּדוּד אֲשֶׁר־בָּא אֵלָיו מֵאֶפְרַיִם לָלֶכֶת לִמְקוֹמָם
וַיִּחַר אַפָּם מְאֹד בִּיהוּדָה וַיָּשׁוּבוּ לִמְקוֹמָם בָּחֳרִי־
אָף: פ

11 וַאֲמַצְיָהוּ הִתְחַזַּק וַיִּנְהַג אֶת־עַמּוֹ וַיֵּלֶךְ גֵּיא
הַמֶּלַח וַיַּךְ אֶת־בְּנֵי־שֵׂעִיר עֲשֶׂרֶת אֲלָפִים: 12 וַעֲשֶׂרֶת אֲלָפִים חַיִּים שָׁבוּ בְּנֵי יְהוּדָה וַיְבִיאוּם
לְרֹאשׁ הַסָּלַע וַיַּשְׁלִיכוּם מֵרֹאשׁ־הַסֶּלַע וְכֻלָּם

13 But as for the soldiers of the army which Amaziah had discharged, so that they would not go with him to battle, they raided the cities of Judah from Samaria to Beth Horon, killed three thousand in them, and took much spoil.

14 Now it was so, after Amaziah came from the slaughter of the Edomites, that he brought the gods of the people of Seir, set them up to be his gods, and bowed down before them and burned incense to them. 15 Therefore the anger of the LORD was aroused against Amaziah, and He sent him a prophet who said to him, "Why have you sought the gods of the people, which could not rescue their own people from your hand?"

16 So it was, as he talked with him, that the king said to him, "Have we made you the king's counselor? Cease! Why should you be killed?"

Then the prophet ceased, and said, "I know that God has determined to destroy you, because you have done this and have not heeded my advice."

17 Now Amaziah king of Judah asked advice and sent to Joash the son of Jehoahaz, the son of Jehu, king of Israel, saying, "Come, let us face one another in battle."

18 And Joash king of Israel sent to Amaziah king of Judah, saying, "The thistle that was in Lebanon sent to the cedar that was in Lebanon, saying, 'Give your daughter to my son as wife'; and a wild beast that was in Lebanon passed by and trampled the thistle. 19 Indeed you say that you have defeated the Edomites, and your heart is lifted up to boast. Stay at home now; why should you meddle with trouble, that you should fall you and Judah with you?"

20 But Amaziah would not heed, for it came from God, that He might give them into the hand of their enemies, because they sought the gods of Edom. 21 So Joash king of Israel went out; and he and Amaziah king of Judah faced one another at Beth Shemesh, which belongs to Judah. 22 And Judah was defeated by Israel, and every man fled to his tent. 23 Then Joash the king of Israel captured Amaziah king of Judah, the son of Joash, the son of Jehoahaz, at Beth Shemesh; and he brought him to Jerusalem, and broke down the wall of Jerusalem from the Gate of Ephraim to the Corner Gate— four hundred cubits. 24 And he took all the gold and silver, all the articles that were found in the house of God with Obed-Edom, the treasures of the king's house, and hostages, and returned to Samaria.

25 Amaziah the son of Joash, king of Judah, lived fifteen years after the death of Joash the son of Jehoahaz, king of Israel. 26 Now the rest of the acts of Amaziah, from first to last, indeed are they not written in the book of the kings of Judah and

13 וּבְנֵי הַגְּדוּד אֲשֶׁר הֵשִׁיב ס
אֲמַצְיָהוּ מִלֶּכֶת עִמּוֹ לַמִּלְחָמָה וַיִּפְשְׁטוּ בְּעָרֵי
יְהוּדָה מִשֹּׁמְרוֹן וְעַד־בֵּית חוֹרוֹן וַיַּכּוּ מֵהֶם שְׁלֹשֶׁת
אֲלָפִים וַיָּבֹזּוּ בִּזָּה רַבָּה: ס 14 וַיְהִי אַחֲרֵי
בוֹא אֲמַצְיָהוּ מֵהַכּוֹת אֶת־אֲדוֹמִים וַיָּבֵא אֶת־אֱלֹהֵי
בְּנֵי שֵׂעִיר וַיַּעֲמִידֵם לוֹ לֵאלֹהִים וְלִפְנֵיהֶם יִשְׁתַּחֲוֶה
וְלָהֶם יְקַטֵּר: 15 וַיִּחַר־אַף יְהוָה בַּאֲמַצְיָהוּ וַיִּשְׁלַח
אֵלָיו נָבִיא וַיֹּאמֶר לוֹ לָמָה דָרַשְׁתָּ אֶת־אֱלֹהֵי הָעָם
אֲשֶׁר לֹא־הִצִּילוּ אֶת־עַמָּם מִיָּדֶךָ: 16 וַיְהִי | בְּדַבְּרוֹ
אֵלָיו וַיֹּאמֶר לוֹ הַלְיוֹעֵץ לַמֶּלֶךְ נְתַנּוּךָ חֲדַל־לְךָ
לָמָה יַכּוּךָ וַיֶּחְדַּל הַנָּבִיא וַיֹּאמֶר יָדַעְתִּי כִּי־יָעַץ
אֱלֹהִים לְהַשְׁחִיתֶךָ כִּי־עָשִׂיתָ זֹּאת וְלֹא שָׁמַעְתָּ
לַעֲצָתִי: פ

17 וַיִּוָּעַץ אֲמַצְיָהוּ מֶלֶךְ יְהוּדָה וַיִּשְׁלַח אֶל־יוֹאָשׁ בֶּן־
יְהוֹאָחָז בֶּן־יֵהוּא מֶלֶךְ יִשְׂרָאֵל לֵאמֹר לְךָ נִתְרָאֶה
פָנִים: 18 וַיִּשְׁלַח יוֹאָשׁ מֶלֶךְ־יִשְׂרָאֵל אֶל־אֲמַצְיָהוּ
מֶלֶךְ־יְהוּדָה לֵאמֹר הַחוֹחַ אֲשֶׁר בַּלְּבָנוֹן שָׁלַח
אֶל־הָאֶרֶז אֲשֶׁר בַּלְּבָנוֹן לֵאמֹר תְּנָה־אֶת־בִּתְּךָ
לִבְנִי לְאִשָּׁה וַתַּעֲבֹר חַיַּת הַשָּׂדֶה אֲשֶׁר בַּלְּבָנוֹן
וַתִּרְמֹס אֶת־הַחוֹחַ: 19 אָמַרְתָּ הִנֵּה הִכִּיתָ אֶת־
אֱדוֹם וּנְשָׂאֲךָ לִבְּךָ לְהַכְבִּיד עַתָּה שְׁבָה בְּבֵיתֶךָ
לָמָּה תִתְגָּרֶה בְּרָעָה וְנָפַלְתָּ אַתָּה וִיהוּדָה עִמָּךְ:
20 וְלֹא־שָׁמַע אֲמַצְיָהוּ כִּי מֵהָאֱלֹהִים הִיא לְמַעַן
תִּתָּם בְּיָד כִּי דָרְשׁוּ אֵת אֱלֹהֵי אֱדוֹם: 21 וַיַּעַל
יוֹאָשׁ מֶלֶךְ־יִשְׂרָאֵל וַיִּתְרָאוּ פָנִים הוּא וַאֲמַצְיָהוּ
מֶלֶךְ־יְהוּדָה בְּבֵית שֶׁמֶשׁ אֲשֶׁר לִיהוּדָה: 22 וַיִּנָּגֶף
יְהוּדָה לִפְנֵי יִשְׂרָאֵל וַיָּנֻסוּ אִישׁ לְאֹהָלָיו: 23 וְאֵת
אֲמַצְיָהוּ מֶלֶךְ־יְהוּדָה בֶּן־יוֹאָשׁ בֶּן־יְהוֹאָחָז תָּפַשׂ
יוֹאָשׁ מֶלֶךְ־יִשְׂרָאֵל בְּבֵית שֶׁמֶשׁ וַיְבִיאֵהוּ יְרוּשָׁלִַם
וַיִּפְרֹץ בְּחוֹמַת יְרוּשָׁלִַם מִשַּׁעַר אֶפְרַיִם עַד־שַׁעַר
הַפּוֹנֶה אַרְבַּע מֵאוֹת אַמָּה: 24 וְכָל־הַזָּהָב וְהַכֶּסֶף
וְאֵת כָּל־הַכֵּלִים הַנִּמְצְאִים בְּבֵית־הָאֱלֹהִים עִם־
עֹבֵד אֱדוֹם וְאֶת־אֹצְרוֹת בֵּית הַמֶּלֶךְ וְאֵת בְּנֵי
הַתַּעֲרֻבוֹת וַיָּשָׁב שֹׁמְרוֹן: פ

25 וַיְחִי אֲמַצְיָהוּ בֶן־יוֹאָשׁ מֶלֶךְ יְהוּדָה אַחֲרֵי מוֹת
יוֹאָשׁ בֶּן־יְהוֹאָחָז מֶלֶךְ יִשְׂרָאֵל חֲמֵשׁ עֶשְׂרֵה שָׁנָה:
26 וְיֶתֶר דִּבְרֵי אֲמַצְיָהוּ הָרִאשֹׁנִים וְהָאַחֲרוֹנִים הֲלֹא
הִנָּם כְּתוּבִים עַל־סֵפֶר מַלְכֵי־יְהוּדָה וְיִשְׂרָאֵל:

Israel? ²⁷ After the time that Amaziah turned away from following the LORD, they made a conspiracy against him in Jerusalem, and he fled to Lachish; but they sent after him to Lachish and killed him there. ²⁸ Then they brought him on horses and buried him with his fathers in the City of Judah.

26 Now all the people of Judah took Uzziah, who *was* sixteen years old, and made him king instead of his father Amaziah. ² He built Elath and restored it to Judah, after the king rested with his fathers.

³ Uzziah *was* sixteen years old when he became king, and he reigned fifty-two years in Jerusalem. His mother's name was Jecholiah of Jerusalem. ⁴ And he did *what was* right in the sight of the LORD, according to all that his father Amaziah had done. ⁵ He sought God in the days of Zechariah, who had understanding in the visions of God; and as long as he sought the LORD, God made him prosper.

⁶ Now he went out and made war against the Philistines, and broke down the wall of Gath, the wall of Jabneh, and the wall of Ashdod; and he built cities *around* Ashdod and among the Philistines. ⁷ God helped him against the Philistines, against the Arabians who lived in Gur Baal, and against the Meunites. ⁸ Also the Ammonites brought tribute to Uzziah. His fame spread as far as the entrance of Egypt, for he became exceedingly strong.

⁹ And Uzziah built towers in Jerusalem at the Corner Gate, at the Valley Gate, and at the corner buttress of the wall; then he fortified them. ¹⁰ Also he built towers in the desert. He dug many wells, for he had much livestock, both in the lowlands and in the plains; *he also had* farmers and vinedressers in the mountains and in Carmel, for he loved the soil.

¹¹ Moreover Uzziah had an army of fighting men who went out to war by companies, according to the number on their roll as prepared by Jeiel the scribe and Maaseiah the officer, under the hand of Hananiah, *one* of the king's captains. ¹² The total number of chief officers of the mighty men of valor *was* two thousand six hundred. ¹³ And under their authority *was* an army of three hundred and seven thousand five hundred, that made war with mighty power, to help the king against the enemy. ¹⁴ Then Uzziah prepared for them, for the entire army, shields, spears, helmets, body armor, bows, and slings *to cast* stones. ¹⁵ And he made devices in Jerusalem, invented by skillful men, to be on the towers and the corners, to shoot arrows and large stones. So his fame spread far and wide, for he was marvelously helped till he became strong.

27 וּמֵעֵת אֲשֶׁר־סָר אֲמַצְיָהוּ מֵאַחֲרֵי יְהֹוָה וַיִּקְשְׁרוּ
עָלָיו קֶשֶׁר בִּירוּשָׁלַ͏ִם וַיָּ֫נָס לָכִ֫ישָׁה וַיִּשְׁלְחוּ אַחֲרָיו
לָכִישָׁה וַיְמִיתֻ֫הוּ שָׁם: 28 וַיִּשָּׂאֻ֫הוּ עַל־הַסּוּסִים
וַיִּקְבְּר֫וּ אֹתוֹ עִם־אֲבֹתָיו בְּעִיר יְהוּדָה:

כו וַיִּקְחוּ כָּל־עַם יְהוּדָה אֶת־עֻזִּיָּהוּ וְהוּא בֶּן־שֵׁשׁ
עֶשְׂרֵה שָׁנָה וַיַּמְלִיכוּ אֹתוֹ תַּחַת אָבִיו אֲמַצְיָהוּ:
2 הוּא בָּנָה אֶת־אֵילוֹת וַיְשִׁבֶ֫הָ לִיהוּדָה אַחֲרֵי
שְׁכַב־הַמֶּלֶךְ עִם־אֲבֹתָיו: פ

3 בֶּן־שֵׁשׁ עֶשְׂרֵה שָׁנָה עֻזִּיָּהוּ בְמָלְכוֹ וַחֲמִשִּׁים
וּשְׁתַּיִם שָׁנָה מָלַךְ בִּירוּשָׁלָ͏ִם וְשֵׁם אִמּוֹ יְכָ֫לְיָהֿ מִן־
יְרוּשָׁלָ͏ִם: 4 וַיַּ֫עַשׂ הַיָּשָׁר בְּעֵינֵי יְהֹוָה כְּכֹל אֲשֶׁר־
עָשָׂה אֲמַצְיָהוּ אָבִיו: 5 וַיְהִי לִדְרֹשׁ אֱלֹהִים בִּימֵי
זְכַרְיָהוּ הַמֵּבִין בִּרְאֹת הָאֱלֹהִים וּבִימֵי דָּרְשׁוֹ אֶת־
יְהֹוָה הִצְלִיח֫וֹ הָאֱלֹהִים: ס 6 וַיֵּצֵא וַיִּלָּחֶם
בַּפְּלִשְׁתִּים וַיִּפְרֹץ אֶת־חוֹמַת גַּת וְאֵת חוֹמַת
יַבְנֵה וְאֵת חוֹמַת אַשְׁדּוֹד וַיִּבְנֶה עָרִים בְּאַשְׁדּוֹד
וּבַפְּלִשְׁתִּים: 7 וַיַּעְזְרֵ֫הוּ הָאֱלֹהִים עַל־פְּלִשְׁתִּים וְעַל־
הָעַרְבִיים הַיּשְׁבִים בְּגוּר־בָּעַל וְהַמְּעוּנִים: 8 וַיִּתְּנוּ
הָעַמּוֹנִים מִנְחָה לְעֻזִּיָּהוּ וַיֵּלֶךְ שְׁמוֹ עַד־לְבוֹא
מִצְרַיִם כִּי הֶחֱזִיק עַד־לְמָעְלָה: 9 וַיִּ֫בֶן עֻזִּיָּהוּ
מִגְדָּלִים בִּירוּשָׁלַ͏ִם עַל־שַׁעַר הַפִּנָּה וְעַל־שַׁעַר הַגַּיְא
וְעַל־הַמִּקְצוֹעַ וַיְחַזְּקֵם: 10 וַיִּ֫בֶן מִגְדָּלִים בַּמִּדְבָּר
וַיַּחְצֹב בֹּרוֹת רַבִּים כִּי מִקְנֶה־רַּב הָיָה לוֹ וּבַשְּׁפֵלָה
וּבַמִּישׁוֹר אִכָּרִים וְכֹרְמִים בֶּהָרִים וּבַכַּרְמֶל כִּי־
אֹהֵב אֲדָמָה הָיָה: ס 11 וַיְהִי לְעֻזִּיָּהוּ
חַיִל עֹשֵׂה מִלְחָמָה יוֹצְאֵי צָבָא לִגְדוּד בְּמִסְפַּר
פְּקֻדָּתָם בְּיַד יְעִיאֵלֿ הַסּוֹפֵר וּמַעֲשֵׂיָ֫הוּ הַשּׁוֹטֵר
עַל יַד־חֲנַנְיָהוּ מִשָּׂרֵי הַמֶּלֶךְ: 12 כֹּל מִסְפַּר רָאשֵׁי
הָאָבוֹת לְגִבּוֹרֵי חָיִל אַלְפַּיִם וְשֵׁשׁ מֵאוֹת: 13 וְעַל־
יָדָם חֵיל צָבָא שְׁלֹשׁ מֵאוֹת אֶלֶף וְשִׁבְעַת אֲלָפִים
וַחֲמֵשׁ מֵאוֹת עוֹשֵׂי מִלְחָמָה בְּכֹחַ חָיִל לַעְזֹר
לַמֶּלֶךְ עַל־הָאוֹיֵב: 14 וַיָּכֶן לָהֶם עֻזִּיָּהוּ לְכָל־הַצָּבָא
מָגִנִּים וּרְמָחִים וְכוֹבָעִים וְשִׁרְיֹנוֹת וּקְשָׁתוֹת וּלְאַבְנֵי
קְלָעִים: 15 וַיַּעַשׂ ׀ בִּירוּשָׁלַ͏ִם חִשְּׁבֹנוֹת מַחֲשֶׁבֶת
חוֹשֵׁב לִהְיוֹת עַל־הַמִּגְדָּלִים וְעַל־הַפִּנּוֹת לִירוֹא

16 But when he was strong his heart was lifted up, to *his* destruction, for he transgressed against the LORD his God by entering the temple of the LORD to burn incense on the altar of incense. 17 So Azariah the priest went in after him, and with him were eighty priests of the LORD—valiant men. 18 And they withstood King Uzziah, and said to him, "*It is* not for you, Uzziah, to burn incense to the LORD, but for the priests, the sons of Aaron, who are consecrated to burn incense. Get out of the sanctuary, for you have trespassed! You *shall have* no honor from the LORD God."

19 Then Uzziah became furious; and he *had* a censer in his hand to burn incense. And while he was angry with the priests, leprosy broke out on his forehead, before the priests in the house of the LORD, beside the incense altar. 20 And Azariah the chief priest and all the priests looked at him, and there, on his forehead, he *was* leprous; so they thrust him out of that place. Indeed he also hurried to get out, because the LORD had struck him.

21 King Uzziah was a leper until the day of his death. He dwelt in an isolated house, because he was a leper; for he was cut off from the house of the LORD. Then Jotham his son *was* over the king's house, judging the people of the land.

22 Now the rest of the acts of Uzziah, from first to last, the prophet Isaiah the son of Amoz wrote. 23 So Uzziah rested with his fathers, and they buried him with his fathers in the field of burial which *belonged* to the kings, for they said, "He is a leper." Then Jotham his son reigned in his place.

27

Jotham *was* twenty-five years old when he became king, and he reigned sixteen years in Jerusalem. His mother's name *was* Jerushah the daughter of Zadok. 2 And he did *what was* right in the sight of the LORD, according to all that his father Uzziah had done (although he did not enter the temple of the LORD). But still the people acted corruptly.

3 He built the Upper Gate of the house of the LORD, and he built extensively on the wall of Ophel. 4 Moreover he built cities in the mountains of Judah, and in the forests he built fortresses and towers. 5 He also fought with the king of the Ammonites and defeated them. And the people of Ammon gave him in that year one hundred talents of silver, ten thousand kors of wheat, and ten thousand of barley. The people of Ammon paid this to him in the second and third years also. 6 So Jotham became mighty, because he prepared his ways before the LORD his God.

בְּחֵצִים וּבָאֲבָנִים גְּדֹלוֹת וַיֵּצֵא שְׁמוֹ עַד־לְמֵרָחוֹק 16 וּכְחֶזְקָתוֹ גָּבַהּ כִּי־הִפְלִיא לְהֵעָזֵר עַד כִּי־חָזָק לִבּוֹ עַד־לְהַשְׁחִית וַיִּמְעַל בַּיהֹוָה אֱלֹהָיו וַיָּבֹא אֶל־הֵיכַל יְהֹוָה לְהַקְטִיר עַל־מִזְבַּח הַקְּטֹרֶת: 17 וַיָּבֹא אַחֲרָיו עֲזַרְיָהוּ הַכֹּהֵן וְעִמּוֹ כֹּהֲנִים לַיהֹוָה שְׁמוֹנִים בְּנֵי־חָיִל: 18 וַיַּעַמְדוּ עַל־עֻזִּיָּהוּ הַמֶּלֶךְ וַיֹּאמְרוּ לוֹ לֹא־לְךָ עֻזִּיָּהוּ לְהַקְטִיר לַיהֹוָה כִּי לַכֹּהֲנִים בְּנֵי־אַהֲרֹן הַמְקֻדָּשִׁים לְהַקְטִיר צֵא מִן־הַמִּקְדָּשׁ כִּי מָעַלְתָּ וְלֹא־לְךָ לְכָבוֹד מֵיְהֹוָה אֱלֹהִים: 19 וַיִּזְעַף עֻזִּיָּהוּ וּבְיָדוֹ מִקְטֶרֶת לְהַקְטִיר וּבְזַעְפּוֹ עִם־הַכֹּהֲנִים וְהַצָּרַעַת זָרְחָה בְמִצְחוֹ לִפְנֵי הַכֹּהֲנִים בְּבֵית יְהֹוָה מֵעַל לְמִזְבַּח הַקְּטֹרֶת: 20 וַיִּפֶן אֵלָיו עֲזַרְיָהוּ כֹהֵן הָרֹאשׁ וְכָל־הַכֹּהֲנִים וְהִנֵּה־הוּא מְצֹרָע בְּמִצְחוֹ וַיַּבְהִלוּהוּ מִשָּׁם וְגַם־הוּא נִדְחַף לָצֵאת כִּי נִגְּעוֹ יְהֹוָה: 21 וַיְהִי עֻזִּיָּהוּ הַמֶּלֶךְ מְצֹרָע עַד־יוֹם מוֹתוֹ וַיֵּשֶׁב בֵּית הַחׇפְשִׁיתᵖ מְצֹרָע כִּי נִגְזַר מִבֵּית יְהֹוָה וְיוֹתָם בְּנוֹ עַל־בֵּית הַמֶּלֶךְ שׁוֹפֵט אֶת־עַם הָאָרֶץ: 22 וְיֶתֶר דִּבְרֵי עֻזִּיָּהוּ הָרִאשֹׁנִים וְהָאַחֲרֹנִים כָּתַב יְשַׁעְיָהוּ בֶן־אָמוֹץ הַנָּבִיא: 23 וַיִּשְׁכַּב עֻזִּיָּהוּ עִם־אֲבֹתָיו וַיִּקְבְּרוּ אֹתוֹ עִם־אֲבֹתָיו בִּשְׂדֵה הַקְּבוּרָה אֲשֶׁר לַמְּלָכִים כִּי אָמְרוּ מְצוֹרָע הוּא וַיִּמְלֹךְ יוֹתָם בְּנוֹ תַּחְתָּיו: פ

כז בֶּן־עֶשְׂרִים וְחָמֵשׁ שָׁנָה יוֹתָם בְּמׇלְכוֹ וְשֵׁשׁ־עֶשְׂרֵה שָׁנָה מָלַךְ בִּירוּשָׁלָ͏ִם וְשֵׁם אִמּוֹ יְרוּשָׁה בַּת־צָדוֹק: 2 וַיַּעַשׂ הַיָּשָׁר בְּעֵינֵי יְהֹוָה כְּכֹל אֲשֶׁר־עָשָׂה עֻזִּיָּהוּ אָבִיו רַק לֹא־בָא אֶל־הֵיכַל יְהֹוָה וְעוֹד הָעָם מַשְׁחִיתִים: 3 הוּא בָּנָה אֶת־שַׁעַר בֵּית־יְהֹוָה הָעֶלְיוֹן וּבְחוֹמַת הָעֹפֶל בָּנָה לָרֹב: 4 וְעָרִים בָּנָה בְּהַר־יְהוּדָה וּבֶחֳרָשִׁים בָּנָה בִּירָנִיּוֹת וּמִגְדָּלִים: 5 וְהוּא נִלְחַם עִם־מֶלֶךְ בְּנֵי־עַמּוֹן וַיֶּחֱזַק עֲלֵיהֶם וַיִּתְּנוּ־לוֹ בְנֵי־עַמּוֹן בַּשָּׁנָה הַהִיא מֵאָה כִּכַּר־כֶּסֶף וַעֲשֶׂרֶת אֲלָפִים כֹּרִים חִטִּים וּשְׂעוֹרִים עֲשֶׂרֶת אֲלָפִים זֹאת הֵשִׁיבוּ לוֹ בְּנֵי עַמּוֹן ס וּבַשָּׁנָה הַשֵּׁנִית וְהַשְּׁלִשִׁית: 6 וַיִּתְחַזֵּק יוֹתָם כִּי הֵכִין דְּרָכָיו

כו 21 הַחׇפְשִׁית

7 Now the rest of the acts of Jotham, and all his wars and his ways, indeed they *are* written in the book of the kings of Israel and Judah. 8 He was twenty-five years old when he became king, and he reigned sixteen years in Jerusalem. 9 So Jotham rested with his fathers, and they buried him in the City of David. Then Ahaz his son reigned in his place.

28 Ahaz *was* twenty years old when he became king, and he reigned sixteen years in Jerusalem; and he did not do *what was* right in the sight of the LORD, as his father David *had done*. 2 For he walked in the ways of the kings of Israel, and made molded images for the Baals. 3 He burned incense in the Valley of the Son of Hinnom, and burned his children in the fire, according to the abominations of the nations whom the LORD had cast out before the children of Israel. 4 And he sacrificed and burned incense on the high places, on the hills, and under every green tree.

5 Therefore the LORD his God delivered him into the hand of the king of Syria. They defeated him, and carried away a great multitude of them as captives, and brought *them* to Damascus. Then he was also delivered into the hand of the king of Israel, who defeated him with a great slaughter. 6 For Pekah the son of Remaliah killed one hundred and twenty thousand in Judah in one day, all valiant men, because they had forsaken the LORD God of their fathers. 7 Zichri, a mighty man of Ephraim, killed Maaseiah the king's son, Azrikam the officer over the house, and Elkanah *who was* second to the king. 8 And the children of Israel carried away captive of their brethren two hundred thousand women, sons, and daughters; and they also took away much spoil from them, and brought the spoil to Samaria.

9 But a prophet of the LORD was there, whose name *was* Oded; and he went out before the army that came to Samaria, and said to them: "Look, because the LORD God of your fathers was angry with Judah, He has delivered them into your hand; but you have killed them in a rage *that* reaches up to heaven. 10 And now you propose to force the children of Judah and Jerusalem to be your male and female slaves; *but are* you not also guilty before the LORD your God? 11 Now hear me, therefore, and return the captives, whom you have taken captive from your brethren, for the fierce wrath of the LORD *is* upon you."

12 Then some of the heads of the children of Ephraim, Azariah the son of Johanan, Berechiah the son of Meshillemoth, Jehizkiah the son of

לִפְנֵי יְהֹוָה אֱלֹהָיו: 7 וְיֶתֶר דִּבְרֵי יוֹתָם וְכָל־ מִלְחֲמֹתָיו וּדְרָכָיו הִנָּם כְּתוּבִים עַל־סֵפֶר מַלְכֵי־ יִשְׂרָאֵל וִיהוּדָה: 8 בֶּן־עֶשְׂרִים וְחָמֵשׁ שָׁנָה הָיָה בְמָלְכוֹ וְשֵׁשׁ־עֶשְׂרֵה שָׁנָה מָלַךְ בִּירוּשָׁלִָם: 9 וַיִּשְׁכַּב יוֹתָם עִם־אֲבֹתָיו וַיִּקְבְּרוּ אֹתוֹ בְּעִיר דָּוִיד וַיִּמְלֹךְ אָחָז בְּנוֹ תַּחְתָּיו: פ

כה בֶּן־עֶשְׂרִים שָׁנָה אָחָז בְּמָלְכוֹ וְשֵׁשׁ־עֶשְׂרֵה שָׁנָה מָלַךְ בִּירוּשָׁלִָם וְלֹא־עָשָׂה הַיָּשָׁר בְּעֵינֵי יְהֹוָה כְּדָוִיד אָבִיו: 2 וַיֵּלֶךְ בְּדַרְכֵי מַלְכֵי יִשְׂרָאֵל וְגַם מַסֵּכוֹת עָשָׂה לַבְּעָלִים: 3 וְהוּא הִקְטִיר בְּגֵיא בֶן־ הִנֹּם וַיַּבְעֵר אֶת־בָּנָיו בָּאֵשׁ כְּתֹעֲבוֹת הַגּוֹיִם אֲשֶׁר הֹרִישׁ יְהֹוָה מִפְּנֵי בְּנֵי יִשְׂרָאֵל: 4 וַיְזַבֵּחַ וַיְקַטֵּר בַּבָּמוֹת וְעַל־הַגְּבָעוֹת וְתַחַת כָּל־עֵץ רַעֲנָן: 5 וַיִּתְּנֵהוּ יְהֹוָה אֱלֹהָיו בְּיַד מֶלֶךְ אֲרָם וַיַּכּוּ־בוֹ וַיִּשְׁבּוּ מִמֶּנּוּ שִׁבְיָה גְדוֹלָה וַיָּבִיאוּ דַּרְמָשֶׂק וְגַם בְּיַד־מֶלֶךְ יִשְׂרָאֵל נִתָּן וַיַּךְ־בּוֹ מַכָּה גְדוֹלָה: ס 6 וַיַּהֲרֹג פֶּקַח בֶּן־רְמַלְיָהוּ בִּיהוּדָה מֵאָה וְעֶשְׂרִים אֶלֶף בְּיוֹם אֶחָד הַכֹּל בְּנֵי־חָיִל בְּעָזְבָם אֶת־יְהֹוָה אֱלֹהֵי אֲבוֹתָם: 7 וַיַּהֲרֹג זִכְרִי ׀ גִּבּוֹר אֶפְרַיִם אֶת־מַעֲשֵׂיָהוּ בֶּן־הַמֶּלֶךְ וְאֶת־עַזְרִיקָם נְגִיד הַבָּיִת וְאֶת־אֶלְקָנָה מִשְׁנֵה הַמֶּלֶךְ: ס 8 וַיִּשְׁבּוּ בְנֵי־יִשְׂרָאֵל מֵאֲחֵיהֶם מָאתַיִם אֶלֶף נָשִׁים בָּנִים וּבָנוֹת וְגַם־שָׁלָל רָב בָּזְזוּ מֵהֶם וַיָּבִיאוּ אֶת־הַשָּׁלָל לְשֹׁמְרוֹן: ס 9 וְשָׁם הָיָה נָבִיא לַיהֹוָה עֹדֵד שְׁמוֹ וַיֵּצֵא לִפְנֵי הַצָּבָא הַבָּא לְשֹׁמְרוֹן וַיֹּאמֶר לָהֶם הִנֵּה בַּחֲמַת יְהֹוָה אֱלֹהֵי־אֲבוֹתֵיכֶם עַל־יְהוּדָה נְתָנָם בְּיֶדְכֶם וַתַּהַרְגוּ־בָם בְּזַעַף עַד לַשָּׁמַיִם הִגִּיעַ: 10 וְעַתָּה בְּנֵי־יְהוּדָה וִירוּשָׁלִַם אַתֶּם אֹמְרִים לִכְבֹּשׁ לַעֲבָדִים וְלִשְׁפָחוֹת לָכֶם הֲלֹא רַק־ אַתֶּם עִמָּכֶם אֲשָׁמוֹת לַיהֹוָה אֱלֹהֵיכֶם: 11 וְעַתָּה שְׁמָעוּנִי וְהָשִׁיבוּ הַשִּׁבְיָה אֲשֶׁר שְׁבִיתֶם מֵאֲחֵיכֶם כִּי חֲרוֹן אַף־יְהֹוָה עֲלֵיכֶם: ס 12 וַיָּקֻמוּ אֲנָשִׁים מֵרָאשֵׁי בְנֵי־אֶפְרַיִם עֲזַרְיָהוּ בֶן־יְהוֹחָנָן בֶּרֶכְיָהוּ בֶן־מְשִׁלֵּמוֹת וִיחִזְקִיָּהוּ בֶּן־שַׁלֻּם וַעֲמָשָׂא

Shallum, and Amasa the son of Hadlai, stood up
against those who came from the war, 13 and said to
them, "You shall not bring the captives here, for we
already have offended the LORD. You intend to add
to our sins and to our guilt; for our guilt is great,
and *there is* fierce wrath against Israel." 14 So the
armed men left the captives and the spoil before the
leaders and all the assembly. 15 Then the men who
were designated by name rose up and took the
captives, and from the spoil they clothed all who
were naked among them, dressed them and gave
them sandals, gave them food and drink, and
anointed them; and they let all the feeble ones ride
on donkeys. So they brought them to their brethren
at Jericho, the city of palm trees. Then they
returned to Samaria.

16 At the same time King Ahaz sent to the kings
of Assyria to help him. 17 For again the Edomites
had come, attacked Judah, and carried away
captives. 18 The Philistines also had invaded the
cities of the lowland and of the South of Judah, and
had taken Beth Shemesh, Aijalon, Gederoth,
Sochoh with its villages, Timnah with its villages,
and Gimzo with its villages; and they dwelt there.
19 For the LORD brought Judah low because of
Ahaz king of Israel, for he had encouraged moral
decline in Judah and had been continually unfaithful to the LORD. 20 Also Tiglath-Pileser king of
Assyria came to him and distressed him, and did
not assist him. 21 For Ahaz took part *of the
treasures* from the house of the LORD, from the
house of the king, and from the leaders, and he gave
it to the king of Assyria; but he did not help him.

22 Now in the time of his distress King Ahaz
became increasingly unfaithful to the LORD. This *is
that* King Ahaz. 23 For he sacrificed to the gods of
Damascus which had defeated him, saying, "Because the gods of the kings of Syria help them, I will
sacrifice to them that they may help me." But they
were the ruin of him and of all Israel. 24 So Ahaz
gathered the articles of the house of God, cut in
pieces the articles of the house of God, shut up the
doors of the house of the LORD, and made for
himself altars in every corner of Jerusalem. 25 And
in every single city of Judah he made high places to
burn incense to other gods, and provoked to anger
the LORD God of his fathers.

26 Now the rest of his acts and all his ways, from
first to last, indeed they *are* written in the book of
the kings of Judah and Israel. 27 So Ahaz rested
with his fathers, and they buried him in the city, in
Jerusalem; but they did not bring him into the
tombs of the kings of Israel. Then Hezekiah his son
reigned in his place.

בֶּן־חֲדְלַי עַל־הַבָּאִים מִן־הַצָּבָא: 13 וַיֹּאמְרוּ לָהֶם
לֹא־תָבִיאוּ אֶת־הַשִּׁבְיָה הֵנָּה כִּי לְאַשְׁמַת יְהוָה
עָלֵינוּ אַתֶּם אֹמְרִים לְהֹסִיף עַל־חַטֹּאתֵינוּ וְעַל־
אַשְׁמָתֵינוּ כִּי־רַבָּה אַשְׁמָה לָנוּ וַחֲרוֹן אַף עַל־
יִשְׂרָאֵל: ס 14 וַיַּעֲזֹב הֶחָלוּץ אֶת־הַשִּׁבְיָה
וְאֶת־הַבִּזָּה לִפְנֵי הַשָּׂרִים וְכָל־הַקָּהָל: 15 וַיָּקֻמוּ
הָאֲנָשִׁים אֲשֶׁר־נִקְּבוּ בְשֵׁמוֹת וַיַּחֲזִיקוּ בַשִּׁבְיָה וְכָל־
מַעֲרֻמֵּיהֶם הִלְבִּישׁוּ מִן־הַשָּׁלָל וַיַּלְבִּשׁוּם וַיַּנְעִלוּם
וַיַּאֲכִלוּם וַיַּשְׁקוּם וַיְסֻכוּם וַיְנַהֲלוּם בַּחֲמֹרִים לְכָל־
כּוֹשֵׁל וַיְבִיאוּם יְרֵחוֹ עִיר־הַתְּמָרִים אֵצֶל אֲחֵיהֶם
וַיָּשׁוּבוּ שֹׁמְרוֹן: פ

16 בָּעֵת הַהִיא שָׁלַח הַמֶּלֶךְ אָחָז עַל־מַלְכֵי אַשּׁוּר
לַעְזֹר לוֹ: 17 וְעוֹד אֲדוֹמִים בָּאוּ וַיַּכּוּ בִיהוּדָה
וַיִּשְׁבּוּ־שֶׁבִי: 18 וּפְלִשְׁתִּים פָּשְׁטוּ בְּעָרֵי הַשְּׁפֵלָה
וְהַנֶּגֶב לִיהוּדָה וַיִּלְכְּדוּ אֶת־בֵּית־שֶׁמֶשׁ וְאֶת־אַיָּלוֹן
וְאֶת־הַגְּדֵרוֹת וְאֶת־שׂוֹכוֹ וּבְנוֹתֶיהָ וְאֶת־תִּמְנָה
וּבְנוֹתֶיהָ וְאֶת־גִּמְזוֹ וְאֶת־בְּנֹתֶיהָ וַיֵּשְׁבוּ שָׁם: 19 כִּי־
הִכְנִיעַ יְהוָה אֶת־יְהוּדָה בַּעֲבוּר אָחָז מֶלֶךְ־יִשְׂרָאֵל
כִּי הִפְרִיעַ בִּיהוּדָה וּמָעוֹל מַעַל בַּיהוָה: 20 וַיָּבֹא
עָלָיו תִּלְּגַת פִּלְנְאֶסֶר מֶלֶךְ אַשּׁוּר וַיָּצַר לוֹ וְלֹא
חֲזָקוֹ: 21 כִּי־חָלַק אָחָז אֶת־בֵּית יְהוָה וְאֶת־בֵּית
הַמֶּלֶךְ וְהַשָּׂרִים וַיִּתֵּן לְמֶלֶךְ אַשּׁוּר וְלֹא לְעֶזְרָה לוֹ:
22 וּבְעֵת הָצֵר לוֹ וַיּוֹסֶף לִמְעוֹל בַּיהוָה הוּא הַמֶּלֶךְ
אָחָז: 23 וַיִּזְבַּח לֵאלֹהֵי דַרְמֶשֶׂק הַמַּכִּים בּוֹ וַיֹּאמֶר
כִּי אֱלֹהֵי מַלְכֵי־אֲרָם הֵם מַעְזְרִים אוֹתָם לָהֶם
אֲזַבֵּחַ וְיַעְזְרוּנִי וְהֵם הָיוּ־לוֹ לְהַכְשִׁילוֹ וּלְכָל־יִשְׂרָאֵל:
24 וַיֶּאֱסֹף אָחָז אֶת־כְּלֵי בֵית־הָאֱלֹהִים וַיְקַצֵּץ אֶת־
כְּלֵי בֵית־הָאֱלֹהִים וַיִּסְגֹּר אֶת־דַּלְתוֹת בֵּית־יְהוָה
וַיַּעַשׂ לוֹ מִזְבְּחוֹת בְּכָל־פִּנָּה בִּירוּשָׁלָ͏ִם: 25 וּבְכָל־
עִיר וָעִיר לִיהוּדָה עָשָׂה בָמוֹת לְקַטֵּר לֵאלֹהִים
אֲחֵרִים וַיַּכְעֵס אֶת־יְהוָה אֱלֹהֵי אֲבֹתָיו: 26 וְיֶתֶר
דְּבָרָיו וְכָל־דְּרָכָיו הָרִאשֹׁנִים וְהָאַחֲרוֹנִים הִנָּם
כְּתוּבִים עַל־סֵפֶר מַלְכֵי־יְהוּדָה וְיִשְׂרָאֵל: 27 וַיִּשְׁכַּב
אָחָז עִם־אֲבֹתָיו וַיִּקְבְּרֻהוּ בָעִיר בִּירוּשָׁלַ͏ִם כִּי לֹא
הֱבִיאֻהוּ לְקִבְרֵי מַלְכֵי יִשְׂרָאֵל וַיִּמְלֹךְ יְחִזְקִיָּהוּ בְנוֹ
תַּחְתָּיו: פ

29 Hezekiah became king *when he was* twenty-five years old, and he reigned twenty-nine years in Jerusalem. His mother's name *was* Abijah the daughter of Zechariah. ² And he did *what was* right in the sight of the LORD, according to all that his father David had done.

³ In the first year of his reign, in the first month, he opened the doors of the house of the LORD and repaired them. ⁴ Then he brought in the priests and the Levites, and gathered them in the East Square, ⁵ and said to them: "Hear me, Levites! Now sanctify yourselves, sanctify the house of the LORD God of your fathers, and carry out the rubbish from the holy *place*. ⁶ For our fathers have trespassed and done evil in the eyes of the LORD our God; they have forsaken Him, have turned their faces away from the dwelling place of the LORD, and turned *their* backs *on Him*. ⁷ They have also shut up the doors of the vestibule, put out the lamps, and have not burned incense or offered burnt offerings in the holy *place* to the God of Israel. ⁸ Therefore the wrath of the LORD fell upon Judah and Jerusalem, and He has given them up to trouble, to desolation, and to jeering, as you see with your eyes. ⁹ For indeed, because of this our fathers have fallen by the sword; and our sons, our daughters, and our wives *are* in captivity.

¹⁰ "Now *it is* in my heart to make a covenant with the LORD God of Israel, that His fierce wrath may turn away from us. ¹¹ My sons, do not be negligent now, for the LORD has chosen you to stand before Him, to serve Him, and that you should minister to Him and burn incense."

¹² Then these Levites arose: Mahath the son of Amasai and Joel the son of Azariah, of the sons of the Kohathites; of the sons of Merari, Kish the son of Abdi and Azariah the son of Jehallelel; of the Gershonites, Joah the son of Zimmah and Eden the son of Joah; ¹³ of the sons of Elizaphan, Shimri and Jeiel; of the sons of Asaph, Zechariah and Mattaniah; ¹⁴ of the sons of Heman, Jehiel and Shimei; and of the sons of Jeduthun, Shemaiah and Uzziel.

¹⁵ And they gathered their brethren, sanctified themselves, and went according to the commandment of the king, at the words of the LORD, to cleanse the house of the LORD. ¹⁶ Then the priests went into the inner part of the house of the LORD to cleanse *it,* and brought out all the debris that they found in the temple of the LORD to the court of the house of the LORD. And the Levites took *it* out and carried *it* to the Brook Kidron.

כט **יְחִזְקִיָּהוּ** מָלַךְ בֶּן־עֶשְׂרִים וְחָמֵשׁ שָׁנָה וְעֶשְׂרִים וָתֵשַׁע שָׁנָה מָלַךְ בִּירוּשָׁלִָם וְשֵׁם אִמּוֹ אֲבִיָּה בַּת־זְכַרְיָהוּ: ² וַיַּעַשׂ הַיָּשָׁר בְּעֵינֵי יְהֹוָה כְּכֹל אֲשֶׁר־עָשָׂה דָּוִיד אָבִיו: ³ הוּא בַשָּׁנָה הָרִאשׁוֹנָה לְמָלְכוֹ בַּחֹדֶשׁ הָרִאשׁוֹן פָּתַח אֶת־דַּלְתוֹת בֵּית־יְהֹוָה וַיְחַזְּקֵם: ⁴ וַיָּבֵא אֶת־הַכֹּהֲנִים וְאֶת־הַלְוִיִּם וַיַּאַסְפֵם לִרְחוֹב הַמִּזְרָח: ⁵ וַיֹּאמֶר לָהֶם שְׁמָעוּנִי הַלְוִיִּם עַתָּה הִתְקַדְּשׁוּ וְקַדְּשׁוּ אֶת־בֵּית יְהֹוָה אֱלֹהֵי אֲבֹתֵיכֶם וְהוֹצִיאוּ אֶת־הַנִּדָּה מִן־הַקֹּדֶשׁ: ⁶ כִּי־מָעֲלוּ אֲבֹתֵינוּ וְעָשׂוּ הָרַע בְּעֵינֵי יְהֹוָה־אֱלֹהֵינוּ וַיַּעַזְבֻהוּ וַיַּסֵּבּוּ פְנֵיהֶם מִמִּשְׁכַּן יְהֹוָה וַיִּתְּנוּ־עֹרֶף: ⁷ גַּם סָגְרוּ דַּלְתוֹת הָאוּלָם וַיְכַבּוּ אֶת־הַנֵּרוֹת וּקְטֹרֶת לֹא הִקְטִירוּ וְעֹלָה לֹא־הֶעֱלוּ בַקֹּדֶשׁ לֵאלֹהֵי יִשְׂרָאֵל: ⁸ וַיְהִי קֶצֶף יְהֹוָה עַל־יְהוּדָה וִירוּשָׁלִָם וַיִּתְּנֵם לְזַעֲוָה⁵ לְשַׁמָּה וְלִשְׁרֵקָה כַּאֲשֶׁר אַתֶּם רֹאִים בְּעֵינֵיכֶם: ⁹ וְהִנֵּה נָפְלוּ אֲבוֹתֵינוּ בֶּחָרֶב וּבָנֵינוּ וּבְנוֹתֵינוּ וְנָשֵׁינוּ בַּשְּׁבִי עַל־זֹאת: ¹⁰ עַתָּה עִם־לְבָבִי לִכְרוֹת בְּרִית לַיהֹוָה אֱלֹהֵי יִשְׂרָאֵל וְיָשֹׁב מִמֶּנּוּ חֲרוֹן אַפּוֹ: ¹¹ בָּנַי עַתָּה אַל־תִּשָּׁלוּ כִּי־בָכֶם בָּחַר יְהֹוָה לַעֲמֹד לְפָנָיו לְשָׁרְתוֹ וְלִהְיוֹת לוֹ מְשָׁרְתִים וּמַקְטִרִים: ס ¹² וַיָּקֻמוּ הַלְוִיִּם מַחַת בֶּן־עֲמָשַׂי וְיוֹאֵל בֶּן־עֲזַרְיָהוּ מִן־בְּנֵי הַקְּהָתִי וּמִן־בְּנֵי מְרָרִי קִישׁ בֶּן־עַבְדִּי וַעֲזַרְיָהוּ בֶּן־יְהַלֶּלְאֵל וּמִן־הַגֵּרְשֻׁנִּי יוֹאָח בֶּן־זִמָּה וְעֵדֶן בֶּן־יוֹאָח: ¹³ וּמִן־בְּנֵי אֱלִיצָפָן שִׁמְרִי וִיעוּאֵל⁵ וּמִן־בְּנֵי אָסָף זְכַרְיָהוּ וּמַתַּנְיָהוּ: ס ¹⁴ וּמִן־בְּנֵי הֵימָן יְחוּאֵל⁵ וְשִׁמְעִי ס וּמִן־בְּנֵי יְדוּתוּן שְׁמַעְיָה וְעֻזִּיאֵל: ¹⁵ וַיַּאַסְפוּ אֶת־אֲחֵיהֶם וַיִּתְקַדְּשׁוּ וַיָּבֹאוּ כְמִצְוַת־הַמֶּלֶךְ בְּדִבְרֵי יְהֹוָה לְטַהֵר בֵּית יְהֹוָה: ¹⁶ וַיָּבֹאוּ הַכֹּהֲנִים לִפְנִימָה בֵית־יְהֹוָה לְטַהֵר וַיּוֹצִיאוּ אֵת כָּל־הַטֻּמְאָה אֲשֶׁר מָצְאוּ בְּהֵיכַל יְהֹוָה לַחֲצַר בֵּית יְהֹוָה וַיְקַבְּלוּ הַלְוִיִּם לְהוֹצִיא לְנַחַל־

17 Now they began to sanctify on the first *day* of the first month, and on the eighth day of the month they came to the vestibule of the LORD. So they sanctified the house of the LORD in eight days, and on the sixteenth day of the first month they finished.

18 Then they went in to King Hezekiah and said, "We have cleansed all the house of the LORD, the altar of burnt offerings with all its articles, and the table of the showbread with all its articles. 19 Moreover all the articles which King Ahaz in his reign had cast aside in his transgression we have prepared and sanctified; and there they *are,* before the altar of the LORD."

20 Then King Hezekiah rose early, gathered the rulers of the city, and went up to the house of the LORD. 21 And they brought seven bulls, seven rams, seven lambs, and seven male goats for a sin offering for the kingdom, for the sanctuary, and for Judah. Then he commanded the priests, the sons of Aaron, to offer *them* on the altar of the LORD. 22 So they killed the bulls, and the priests received the blood and sprinkled *it* on the altar. Likewise they killed the rams and sprinkled the blood on the altar. They also killed the lambs and sprinkled the blood on the altar. 23 Then they brought out the male goats *for* the sin offering before the king and the assembly, and they laid their hands on them. 24 And the priests killed them; and they presented their blood on the altar as a sin offering to make an atonement for all Israel, for the king commanded *that* the burnt offering and the sin offering *be made* for all Israel.

25 And he stationed the Levites in the house of the LORD with cymbals, with stringed instruments, and with harps, according to the commandment of David, of Gad the king's seer, and of Nathan the prophet; for thus *was* the commandment of the LORD by his prophets. 26 The Levites stood with the instruments of David, and the priests with the trumpets. 27 Then Hezekiah commanded *them* to offer the burnt offering on the altar. And when the burnt offering began, the song of the LORD *also* began, with the trumpets and with the instruments of David king of Israel. 28 So all the assembly worshiped, the singers sang, and the trumpeters sounded; all *this* continued until the burnt offering was finished. 29 And when they had finished offering, the king and all who were present with him bowed and worshiped. 30 Moreover King Hezekiah and the leaders commanded the Levites to sing praise to the LORD with the words of David and of Asaph the seer. So they sang praises with gladness, and they bowed their heads and worshiped.

קָדְרוֹן חוּצָה: 17 וַיָּחֵלּוּ בְּאֶחָד לַחֹדֶשׁ הָרִאשׁוֹן לְקַדֵּשׁ וּבְיוֹם שְׁמוֹנָה לַחֹדֶשׁ בָּאוּ לְאוּלָם יְהוָה וַיְקַדְּשׁוּ אֶת־בֵּית־יְהוָה לְיָמִים שְׁמוֹנָה וּבְיוֹם שִׁשָּׁה עָשָׂר לַחֹדֶשׁ הָרִאשׁוֹן כִּלּוּ: ס 18 וַיָּבוֹאוּ פְנִימָה אֶל־חִזְקִיָּהוּ הַמֶּלֶךְ וַיֹּאמְרוּ טִהַרְנוּ אֶת־כָּל־בֵּית יְהוָה אֶת־מִזְבַּח הָעוֹלָה וְאֶת־כָּל־כֵּלָיו וְאֶת־שֻׁלְחַן הַמַּעֲרֶכֶת וְאֶת־כָּל־כֵּלָיו: 19 וְאֵת כָּל־הַכֵּלִים אֲשֶׁר הִזְנִיחַ הַמֶּלֶךְ אָחָז בְּמַלְכוּתוֹ בְּמַעֲלוֹ הֵכַנּוּ וְהִקְדָּשְׁנוּ וְהִנָּם לִפְנֵי מִזְבַּח יְהוָה: ס 20 וַיַּשְׁכֵּם יְחִזְקִיָּהוּ הַמֶּלֶךְ וַיֶּאֱסֹף אֵת שָׂרֵי הָעִיר וַיַּעַל בֵּית יְהוָה:

21 וַיָּבִיאוּ פָרִים־שִׁבְעָה וְאֵילִים שִׁבְעָה וּכְבָשִׂים שִׁבְעָה וּצְפִירֵי עִזִּים שִׁבְעָה לְחַטָּאת עַל־הַמַּמְלָכָה וְעַל־הַמִּקְדָּשׁ וְעַל־יְהוּדָה וַיֹּאמֶר לִבְנֵי אַהֲרֹן הַכֹּהֲנִים לְהַעֲלוֹת עַל־מִזְבַּח יְהוָה: 22 וַיִּשְׁחֲטוּ הַבָּקָר וַיְקַבְּלוּ הַכֹּהֲנִים אֶת־הַדָּם וַיִּזְרְקוּ הַמִּזְבֵּחָה וַיִּשְׁחֲטוּ הָאֵילִם וַיִּזְרְקוּ הַדָּם הַמִּזְבֵּחָה וַיִּשְׁחֲטוּ הַכְּבָשִׂים וַיִּזְרְקוּ הַדָּם הַמִּזְבֵּחָה: 23 וַיַּגִּישׁוּ אֶת־שְׂעִירֵי הַחַטָּאת לִפְנֵי הַמֶּלֶךְ וְהַקָּהָל וַיִּסְמְכוּ יְדֵיהֶם עֲלֵיהֶם: 24 וַיִּשְׁחָטוּם הַכֹּהֲנִים וַיְחַטְּאוּ אֶת־דָּמָם הַמִּזְבֵּחָה לְכַפֵּר עַל־כָּל־יִשְׂרָאֵל כִּי לְכָל־יִשְׂרָאֵל אָמַר הַמֶּלֶךְ הָעוֹלָה וְהַחַטָּאת: 25 וַיַּעֲמֵד אֶת־הַלְוִיִּם בֵּית יְהוָה בִּמְצִלְתַּיִם בִּנְבָלִים וּבְכִנֹּרוֹת בְּמִצְוַת דָּוִיד וְגָד חֹזֵה־הַמֶּלֶךְ וְנָתָן הַנָּבִיא כִּי בְיַד־יְהוָה הַמִּצְוָה בְּיַד־נְבִיאָיו: ס 26 וַיַּעַמְדוּ הַלְוִיִּם בִּכְלֵי דָוִיד וְהַכֹּהֲנִים בַּחֲצֹצְרוֹת: ס 27 וַיֹּאמֶר חִזְקִיָּהוּ לְהַעֲלוֹת הָעֹלָה לְהַמִּזְבֵּחַ וּבְעֵת הֵחֵל הָעוֹלָה הֵחֵל שִׁיר־יְהוָה וְהַחֲצֹצְרוֹת וְעַל־יְדֵי כְּלֵי דָּוִיד מֶלֶךְ־יִשְׂרָאֵל: 28 וְכָל־הַקָּהָל מִשְׁתַּחֲוִים וְהַשִּׁיר מְשׁוֹרֵר וְהַחֲצֹצְרוֹת מַחְצְרִים הַכֹּל עַד לִכְלוֹת הָעֹלָה: 29 וּכְכַלּוֹת לְהַעֲלוֹת כָּרְעוּ הַמֶּלֶךְ וְכָל־הַנִּמְצְאִים אִתּוֹ וַיִּשְׁתַּחֲווּ: 30 וַיֹּאמֶר יְחִזְקִיָּהוּ הַמֶּלֶךְ וְהַשָּׂרִים לַלְוִיִּם לְהַלֵּל לַיהוָה בְּדִבְרֵי דָוִיד וְאָסָף הַחֹזֶה וַיְהַלְלוּ עַד־לְשִׂמְחָה וַיִּקְּדוּ וַיִּשְׁתַּחֲווּ: ס

³¹ Then Hezekiah answered and said, "Now *that* you have consecrated yourselves to the LORD, come near, and bring sacrifices and thank offerings into the house of the LORD." So the assembly brought in sacrifices and thank offerings, and as many as were of a willing heart *brought* burnt offerings. ³² And the number of the burnt offerings which the assembly brought was seventy bulls, one hundred rams, *and* two hundred lambs; all these *were* for a burnt offering to the LORD. ³³ The consecrated things *were* six hundred bulls and three thousand sheep. ³⁴ But the priests were too few, so that they could not skin all the burnt offerings; therefore their brethren the Levites helped them until the work was ended and until the *other* priests had sanctified themselves, for the Levites were more diligent in sanctifying themselves than the priests. ³⁵ Also the burnt offerings *were* in abundance, with the fat of the peace offerings and *with* the drink offerings for *every* burnt offering.

So the service of the house of the LORD was set in order. ³⁶ Then Hezekiah and all the people rejoiced that God had prepared the people, since the events took place so suddenly.

30 And Hezekiah sent to all Israel and Judah, and also wrote letters to Ephraim and Manasseh, that they should come to the house of the LORD at Jerusalem, to keep the Passover to the LORD God of Israel. ² For the king and his leaders and all the assembly in Jerusalem had agreed to keep the Passover in the second month. ³ For they could not keep it at the regular time, because a sufficient number of priests had not consecrated themselves, nor had the people gathered together at Jerusalem. ⁴ And the matter pleased the king and all the assembly. ⁵ So they resolved to make a proclamation throughout all Israel, from Beersheba to Dan, that they should come to keep the Passover to the LORD God of Israel at Jerusalem, since they had not done *it* for a long *time* in the *prescribed* manner.

⁶ Then the runners went throughout all Israel and Judah with the letters from the king and his leaders, and spoke according to the command of the king: "Children of Israel, return to the LORD God of Abraham, Isaac, and Israel; then He will return to the remnant of you who have escaped from the hand of the kings of Assyria. ⁷ And do not be like your fathers and your brethren, who trespassed against the LORD God of their fathers, so that He gave them up to desolation, as you see. ⁸ Now do not be stiff-necked, as your fathers *were,* but yield yourselves to the LORD; and enter His sanctuary, which He has sanctified forever, and serve the LORD

31 וַיַּעַן יְחִזְקִיָּהוּ וַיֹּאמֶר עַתָּה מִלֵּאתֶם יֶדְכֶם
לַיהוָה גֹּשׁוּ וְהָבִיאוּ זְבָחִים וְתוֹדוֹת לְבֵית יְהוָה
וַיָּבִיאוּ הַקָּהָל זְבָחִים וְתוֹדוֹת וְכָל־נְדִיב לֵב
עֹלוֹת: 32 וַיְהִי מִסְפַּר הָעֹלָה אֲשֶׁר הֵבִיאוּ הַקָּהָל
בָּקָר שִׁבְעִים אֵילִים מֵאָה כְּבָשִׂים מָאתַיִם לְעֹלָה
לַיהוָה כָּל־אֵלֶּה: 33 וְהַקֳּדָשִׁים בָּקָר שֵׁשׁ מֵאוֹת
וְצֹאן שְׁלֹשֶׁת אֲלָפִים: 34 רַק הַכֹּהֲנִים הָיוּ לִמְעָט
וְלֹא יָכְלוּ לְהַפְשִׁיט אֶת־כָּל־הָעֹלוֹת וַיְחַזְּקוּם
אֲחֵיהֶם הַלְוִיִּם עַד־כְּלוֹת הַמְּלָאכָה וְעַד יִתְקַדְּשׁוּ
הַכֹּהֲנִים כִּי הַלְוִיִּם יִשְׁרֵי לֵבָב לְהִתְקַדֵּשׁ מֵהַכֹּהֲנִים:

35 וְגַם־עֹלָה לָרֹב בְּחֶלְבֵי הַשְּׁלָמִים וּבַנְּסָכִים לָעֹלָה
וַתִּכּוֹן עֲבוֹדַת בֵּית־יְהוָה: 36 וַיִּשְׂמַח יְחִזְקִיָּהוּ וְכָל־
הָעָם עַל הַהֵכִין הָאֱלֹהִים לָעָם כִּי בְּפִתְאֹם הָיָה
הַדָּבָר: פ

ל וַיִּשְׁלַח יְחִזְקִיָּהוּ עַל־כָּל־יִשְׂרָאֵל וִיהוּדָה וְגַם־
אִגְּרוֹת כָּתַב עַל־אֶפְרַיִם וּמְנַשֶּׁה לָבוֹא לְבֵית־יְהוָה
בִּירוּשָׁלִָם לַעֲשׂוֹת פֶּסַח לַיהוָה אֱלֹהֵי יִשְׂרָאֵל:

2 וַיִּוָּעַץ הַמֶּלֶךְ וְשָׂרָיו וְכָל־הַקָּהָל בִּירוּשָׁלִַם לַעֲשׂוֹת
הַפֶּסַח בַּחֹדֶשׁ הַשֵּׁנִי: 3 כִּי לֹא יָכְלוּ לַעֲשֹׂתוֹ בָּעֵת
הַהִיא כִּי הַכֹּהֲנִים לֹא־הִתְקַדְּשׁוּ לְמַדַּי וְהָעָם לֹא־
נֶאֶסְפוּ לִירוּשָׁלִָם: 4 וַיִּישַׁר הַדָּבָר בְּעֵינֵי הַמֶּלֶךְ
וּבְעֵינֵי כָּל־הַקָּהָל: 5 וַיַּעֲמִידוּ דָבָר לְהַעֲבִיר קוֹל
בְּכָל־יִשְׂרָאֵל מִבְּאֵר־שֶׁבַע וְעַד־דָּן לָבוֹא לַעֲשׂוֹת
פֶּסַח לַיהוָה אֱלֹהֵי־יִשְׂרָאֵל בִּירוּשָׁלִָם כִּי לֹא לָרֹב
עָשׂוּ כַּכָּתוּב: 6 וַיֵּלְכוּ הָרָצִים בָּאִגְּרוֹת מִיַּד הַמֶּלֶךְ
וְשָׂרָיו בְּכָל־יִשְׂרָאֵל וִיהוּדָה וּכְמִצְוַת הַמֶּלֶךְ לֵאמֹר
בְּנֵי יִשְׂרָאֵל שׁוּבוּ אֶל־יְהוָה אֱלֹהֵי אַבְרָהָם יִצְחָק
וְיִשְׂרָאֵל וְיָשֹׁב אֶל־הַפְּלֵיטָה הַנִּשְׁאֶרֶת לָכֶם מִכַּף
מַלְכֵי אַשּׁוּר: 7 וְאַל־תִּהְיוּ כַּאֲבוֹתֵיכֶם וְכַאֲחֵיכֶם
אֲשֶׁר מָעֲלוּ בַּיהוָה אֱלֹהֵי אֲבוֹתֵיהֶם וַיִּתְּנֵם לְשַׁמָּה
כַּאֲשֶׁר אַתֶּם רֹאִים: 8 עַתָּה אַל־תַּקְשׁוּ עָרְפְּכֶם
כַּאֲבוֹתֵיכֶם תְּנוּ־יָד לַיהוָה וּבֹאוּ לְמִקְדָּשׁוֹ אֲשֶׁר
הִקְדִּישׁ לְעוֹלָם וְעִבְדוּ אֶת־יְהוָה אֱלֹהֵיכֶם וְיָשֹׁב

your God, that the fierceness of His wrath may turn away from you. ⁹For if you return to the Lord, your brethren and your children *will be treated* with compassion by those who lead them captive, so that they may come back to this land; for the Lord your God *is* gracious and merciful, and will not turn *His* face from you if you return to Him."

¹⁰So the runners passed from city to city through the country of Ephraim and Manasseh, as far as Zebulun; but they laughed at them and mocked them. ¹¹Nevertheless some from Asher, Manasseh, and Zebulun humbled themselves and came to Jerusalem. ¹²Also the hand of God was on Judah to give them singleness of heart to obey the command of the king and the leaders, at the word of the Lord.

¹³Now many people, a very great assembly, gathered at Jerusalem to keep the Feast of Unleavened Bread in the second month. ¹⁴They arose and took away the altars that *were* in Jerusalem, and they took away all the incense altars and cast *them* into the Brook Kidron. ¹⁵Then they slaughtered the Passover *lambs* on the fourteenth *day* of the second month. The priests and the Levites were ashamed, and sanctified themselves, and brought the burnt offerings to the house of the Lord. ¹⁶They stood in their place according to their custom, according to the Law of Moses the man of God; the priests sprinkled the blood *received* from the hand of the Levites. ¹⁷For *there were* many in the assembly who had not sanctified themselves; therefore the Levites had charge of the slaughter of the Passover *lambs* for everyone *who was* not clean, to sanctify *them* to the Lord. ¹⁸For a multitude of the people, many from Ephraim, Manasseh, Issachar, and Zebulun, had not cleansed themselves, yet they ate the Passover contrary to what was written. But Hezekiah prayed for them, saying, "May the good Lord provide atonement for everyone ¹⁹*who* prepares his heart to seek God, the Lord God of his fathers, though *he is* not *cleansed* according to the purification of the sanctuary." ²⁰And the Lord listened to Hezekiah and healed the people.

²¹So the children of Israel who were present at Jerusalem kept the Feast of Unleavened Bread seven days with great gladness; and the Levites and the priests praised the Lord day by day, *singing* to the Lord, accompanied by loud instruments. ²²And Hezekiah gave encouragement to all the Levites who taught the good knowledge of the Lord; and they ate throughout the feast seven days, offering peace offerings and making confession to the Lord God of their fathers.

מִכֶּם חֲרוֹן אַפּוֹ: ⁹ כִּי בְשׁוּבְכֶם עַל־יְהוָה אֲחֵיכֶם
וּבְנֵיכֶם לְרַחֲמִים לִפְנֵי שׁוֹבֵיהֶם וְלָשׁוּב לָאָרֶץ
הַזֹּאת כִּי־חַנּוּן וְרַחוּם יְהוָה אֱלֹהֵיכֶם וְלֹא־יָסִיר
פָּנִים מִכֶּם אִם־תָּשׁוּבוּ אֵלָיו: פ

¹⁰ וַיִּהְיוּ הָרָצִים עֹבְרִים מֵעִיר ׀ לָעִיר בְּאֶרֶץ־
אֶפְרַיִם וּמְנַשֶּׁה וְעַד־זְבֻלוּן וַיִּהְיוּ מַשְׂחִיקִים
עֲלֵיהֶם וּמַלְעִגִים בָּם: ¹¹ אַךְ־אֲנָשִׁים מֵאָשֵׁר
וּמְנַשֶּׁה וּמִזְּבֻלוּן נִכְנְעוּ וַיָּבֹאוּ לִירוּשָׁלָ͏ִם: ¹² גַּם
בִּיהוּדָה הָיְתָה יַד הָאֱלֹהִים לָתֵת לָהֶם לֵב
אֶחָד לַעֲשׂוֹת מִצְוַת הַמֶּלֶךְ וְהַשָּׂרִים בִּדְבַר
יְהוָה: ¹³ וַיֵּאָסְפוּ יְרוּשָׁלַ͏ִם עַם־רָב לַעֲשׂוֹת אֶת־
חַג הַמַּצּוֹת בַּחֹדֶשׁ הַשֵּׁנִי קָהָל לָרֹב מְאֹד:
¹⁴ וַיָּקֻמוּ וַיָּסִירוּ אֶת־הַמִּזְבְּחוֹת אֲשֶׁר בִּירוּשָׁלָ͏ִם
וְאֵת כָּל־הַמְקַטְּרוֹת הֵסִירוּ וַיַּשְׁלִיכוּ לְנַחַל קִדְרוֹן:
¹⁵ וַיִּשְׁחֲטוּ הַפֶּסַח בְּאַרְבָּעָה עָשָׂר לַחֹדֶשׁ הַשֵּׁנִי
וְהַכֹּהֲנִים וְהַלְוִיִּם נִכְלְמוּ וַיִּתְקַדְּשׁוּ וַיָּבִיאוּ עֹלוֹת
בֵּית יְהוָה: ¹⁶ וַיַּעַמְדוּ עַל־עָמְדָם כְּמִשְׁפָּטָם
כְּתוֹרַת מֹשֶׁה אִישׁ־הָאֱלֹהִים הַכֹּהֲנִים זֹרְקִים אֶת־
הַדָּם מִיַּד הַלְוִיִּם: ¹⁷ כִּי־רַבַּת בַּקָּהָל אֲשֶׁר לֹא־
הִתְקַדָּשׁוּ וְהַלְוִיִּם עַל־שְׁחִיטַת הַפְּסָחִים לְכֹל
לֹא טָהוֹר לְהַקְדִּישׁ לַיהוָה: ¹⁸ כִּי מַרְבִּית
הָעָם רַבַּת מֵאֶפְרַיִם וּמְנַשֶּׁה יִשָּׂשכָר וּזְבֻלוּן
לֹא הִטֶּהָרוּ כִּי־אָכְלוּ אֶת־הַפֶּסַח בְּלֹא כַכָּתוּב
כִּי הִתְפַּלֵּל יְחִזְקִיָּהוּ עֲלֵיהֶם לֵאמֹר יְהוָה
הַטּוֹב יְכַפֵּר בְּעַד: ¹⁹ כָּל־לְבָבוֹ הֵכִין לִדְרוֹשׁ
הָאֱלֹהִים ׀ יְהוָה אֱלֹהֵי אֲבוֹתָיו וְלֹא כְּטָהֳרַת
הַקֹּדֶשׁ: ס ²⁰ וַיִּשְׁמַע יְהוָה אֶל־יְחִזְקִיָּהוּ וַיִּרְפָּא
אֶת־הָעָם: ס ²¹ וַיַּעֲשׂוּ בְנֵי־יִשְׂרָאֵל הַנִּמְצָאִים
בִּירוּשָׁלַ͏ִם אֶת־חַג הַמַּצּוֹת שִׁבְעַת יָמִים בְּשִׂמְחָה
גְדוֹלָה וּמְהַלְלִים לַיהוָה יוֹם ׀ בְּיוֹם הַלְוִיִּם
וְהַכֹּהֲנִים בִּכְלֵי־עֹז לַיהוָה: ס ²² וַיְדַבֵּר יְחִזְקִיָּהוּ
עַל־לֵב כָּל־הַלְוִיִּם הַמַּשְׂכִּילִים שֵׂכֶל־טוֹב לַיהוָה
וַיֹּאכְלוּ אֶת־הַמּוֹעֵד שִׁבְעַת הַיָּמִים מְזַבְּחִים
זִבְחֵי שְׁלָמִים וּמִתְוַדִּים לַיהוָה אֱלֹהֵי

²³Then the whole assembly agreed to keep *the feast* another seven days, and they kept it *another* seven days with gladness. ²⁴For Hezekiah king of Judah gave to the assembly a thousand bulls and seven thousand sheep, and the leaders gave to the assembly a thousand bulls and ten thousand sheep; and a great number of priests sanctified themselves. ²⁵The whole assembly of Judah rejoiced, also the priests and Levites, all the assembly that came from Israel, the sojourners who came from the land of Israel, and those who dwelt in Judah. ²⁶So there was great joy in Jerusalem, for since the time of Solomon the son of David, king of Israel, *there had* been nothing like this in Jerusalem. ²⁷Then the priests, the Levites, arose and blessed the people, and their voice was heard; and their prayer came *up* to His holy dwelling place, to heaven.

31 Now when all this was finished, all Israel who were present went out to the cities of Judah and broke the sacred pillars in pieces, cut down the wooden images, and threw down the high places and the altars—from all Judah, Benjamin, Ephraim, and Manasseh—until they had utterly destroyed them all. Then all the children of Israel returned to their own cities, every man to his possession.

²And Hezekiah appointed the divisions of the priests and the Levites according to their divisions, each man according to his service, the priests and Levites for burnt offerings and peace offerings, to serve, to give thanks, and to praise in the gates of the camp of the LORD. ³The king also *appointed* a portion of his possessions for the burnt offerings: for the morning and evening burnt offerings, the burnt offerings for the Sabbaths and the New Moons and the set feasts, as *it is* written in the Law of the LORD.

⁴Moreover he commanded the people who dwelt in Jerusalem to contribute support for the priests and the Levites, that they might devote themselves to the Law of the LORD.

⁵As soon as the commandment was circulated, the children of Israel brought in abundance the firstfruits of grain and wine, oil and honey, and of all the produce of the field; and they brought in abundantly the tithe of everything. ⁶And the children of Israel and Judah, who dwelt in the cities of Judah, brought the tithe of oxen and sheep; also the tithe of holy things which were consecrated to the LORD their God they laid in heaps.

⁷In the third month they began laying them in heaps, and they finished in the seventh month. ⁸And when Hezekiah and the leaders came and saw

אֲבוֹתֵיהֶם: ס ²³ וַיִּוָּעֲצוּ כָּל־הַקָּהָל לַעֲשׂוֹת שִׁבְעַת יָמִים אֲחֵרִים וַיַּעֲשׂוּ שִׁבְעַת־יָמִים שִׂמְחָה: ²⁴ כִּי חִזְקִיָּהוּ מֶלֶךְ־יְהוּדָה הֵרִים לַקָּהָל אֶלֶף פָּרִים וְשִׁבְעַת אֲלָפִים צֹאן ס וְהַשָּׂרִים הֵרִימוּ לַקָּהָל פָּרִים אֶלֶף וְצֹאן עֲשֶׂרֶת אֲלָפִים וַיִּתְקַדְּשׁוּ כֹהֲנִים לָרֹב: ²⁵ וַיִּשְׂמְחוּ ׀ כָּל־קְהַל יְהוּדָה וְהַכֹּהֲנִים וְהַלְוִיִּם וְכָל־הַקָּהָל הַבָּאִים מִיִּשְׂרָאֵל וְהַגֵּרִים הַבָּאִים מֵאֶרֶץ יִשְׂרָאֵל וְהַיּוֹשְׁבִים בִּיהוּדָה: ²⁶ וַתְּהִי שִׂמְחָה־גְדוֹלָה בִּירוּשָׁלָ͏ִם כִּי מִימֵי שְׁלֹמֹה בֶן־דָּוִיד מֶלֶךְ יִשְׂרָאֵל לֹא כָזֹאת בִּירוּשָׁלָ͏ִם: ס ²⁷ וַיָּקֻמוּ הַכֹּהֲנִים הַלְוִיִּם וַיְבָרֲכוּ אֶת־הָעָם וַיִּשָּׁמַע בְּקוֹלָם וַתָּבוֹא תְפִלָּתָם לִמְעוֹן קָדְשׁוֹ לַשָּׁמָיִם: פ

לא וּכְכַלּוֹת כָּל־זֹאת יָצְאוּ כָל־יִשְׂרָאֵל הַנִּמְצְאִים לְעָרֵי יְהוּדָה וַיְשַׁבְּרוּ הַמַּצֵּבוֹת וַיְגַדְּעוּ הָאֲשֵׁרִים וַיְנַתְּצוּ אֶת־הַבָּמוֹת וְאֶת־הַמִּזְבְּחֹת מִכָּל־יְהוּדָה וּבִנְיָמִן וּבְאֶפְרַיִם וּמְנַשֶּׁה עַד־לְכַלֵּה וַיָּשׁוּבוּ כָּל־בְּנֵי יִשְׂרָאֵל אִישׁ לַאֲחֻזָּתוֹ לְעָרֵיהֶם: ס ² וַיַּעֲמֵד יְחִזְקִיָּהוּ אֶת־מַחְלְקוֹת הַכֹּהֲנִים וְהַלְוִיִּם עַל־מַחְלְקוֹתָם אִישׁ ׀ כְּפִי עֲבֹדָתוֹ לַכֹּהֲנִים וְלַלְוִיִּם לְעֹלָה וְלִשְׁלָמִים לְשָׁרֵת וּלְהֹדוֹת וּלְהַלֵּל בְּשַׁעֲרֵי מַחֲנוֹת יְהוָה: ס ³ וּמְנָת הַמֶּלֶךְ מִן־רְכוּשׁוֹ לָעֹלוֹת לְעֹלוֹת הַבֹּקֶר וְהָעֶרֶב וְהָעֹלוֹת לַשַּׁבָּתוֹת וְלֶחֳדָשִׁים וְלַמֹּעֲדִים כַּכָּתוּב בְּתוֹרַת יְהוָה: ⁴ וַיֹּאמֶר לָעָם לְיוֹשְׁבֵי יְרוּשָׁלַ͏ִם לָתֵת מְנָת הַכֹּהֲנִים וְהַלְוִיִּם לְמַעַן יֶחֶזְקוּ בְּתוֹרַת יְהוָה: ⁵ וְכִפְרֹץ הַדָּבָר הִרְבּוּ בְנֵי־יִשְׂרָאֵל רֵאשִׁית דָּגָן תִּירוֹשׁ וְיִצְהָר וּדְבַשׁ וְכֹל תְּבוּאַת שָׂדֶה וּמַעֲשַׂר הַכֹּל לָרֹב הֵבִיאוּ: ⁶ וּבְנֵי יִשְׂרָאֵל וִיהוּדָה הַיּוֹשְׁבִים בְּעָרֵי יְהוּדָה גַּם־הֵם מַעְשַׂר בָּקָר וָצֹאן וּמַעְשַׂר קָדָשִׁים הַמְקֻדָּשִׁים לַיהוָה אֱלֹהֵיהֶם הֵבִיאוּ וַיִּתְּנוּ עֲרֵמוֹת עֲרֵמוֹת: ס ⁷ בַּחֹדֶשׁ הַשְּׁלִשִׁי הֵחֵלּוּ הָעֲרֵמוֹת לְיִסּוֹד וּבַחֹדֶשׁ הַשְּׁבִיעִי כִּלּוּ: ס ⁸ וַיָּבֹאוּ יְחִזְקִיָּהוּ וְהַשָּׂרִים וַיִּרְאוּ

the heaps, they blessed the LORD and His people Israel. ⁹ Then Hezekiah questioned the priests and the Levites concerning the heaps. ¹⁰ And Azariah the chief priest, from the house of Zadok, answered him and said, "Since *the people* began to bring the offerings into the house of the LORD, we have had enough to eat and have plenty left, for the LORD has blessed His people; and what is left *is* this great abundance."

¹¹ Now Hezekiah commanded *them* to prepare rooms in the house of the LORD, and they prepared them. ¹² Then they faithfully brought in the offerings, the tithes, and the dedicated things; Cononiah the Levite had charge of them, and Shimei his brother *was* the next. ¹³ Jehiel, Azaziah, Nahath, Asahel, Jerimoth, Jozabad, Eliel, Ismachiah, Mahath, and Benaiah *were* overseers under the hand of Cononiah and Shimei his brother, at the commandment of Hezekiah the king and Azariah the ruler of the house of God. ¹⁴ Kore the son of Imnah the Levite, the keeper of the East Gate, *was* over the freewill offerings to God, to distribute the offerings of the LORD and the most holy things. ¹⁵ And under him *were* Eden, Miniamin, Jeshua, Shemaiah, Amariah, and Shecaniah, *his* faithful assistants in the cities of the priests, to distribute allotments to their brethren by divisions, to the great as well as the small.

¹⁶ Besides those males from three years old and up who were written in the genealogy, they distributed to everyone who entered the house of the LORD his daily portion for the work of his service, by his division, ¹⁷ and to the priests who were written in the genealogy according to their father's house, and to the Levites from twenty years old and up according to their work, by their divisions, ¹⁸ and to all who were written in the genealogy—their little ones and their wives, their sons and daughters, the whole company of them—for in their faithfulness they sanctified themselves in holiness.

¹⁹ Also for the sons of Aaron the priests, *who were* in the fields of the common-lands of their cities, in every single city, *there were* men who were designated by name to distribute portions to all the males among the priests and to all who were listed by genealogies among the Levites.

²⁰ Thus Hezekiah did throughout all Judah, and he did what *was* good and right and true before the LORD his God. ²¹ And in every work that he began in the service of the house of God, in the law and in the commandment, to seek his God, he did *it* with all his heart. So he prospered.

אֶת־הָעֲרֵמֹות וַיְבָרְכוּ אֶת־יְהוָה וְאֵת עַמֹּו יִשְׂרָאֵל: פ

9 וַיִּדְרֹשׁ יְחִזְקִיָּהוּ עַל־הַכֹּהֲנִים וְהַלְוִיִּם עַל־ הָעֲרֵמֹות: 10 וַיֹּאמֶר אֵלָיו עֲזַרְיָהוּ הַכֹּהֵן הָרֹאשׁ לְבֵית צָדֹוק וַיֹּאמֶר מֵהָחֵל הַתְּרוּמָה לָבִיא בֵית־יְהוָה אָכֹול וְשָׂבֹועַ וְהֹותֵר עַד־לָרֹוב כִּי יְהוָה בֵּרַךְ אֶת־עַמֹּו וְהַנֹּותָר אֶת־הֶהָמֹון הַזֶּה: ס

11 וַיֹּאמֶר יְחִזְקִיָּהוּ לְהָכִין לְשָׁכֹות בְּבֵית יְהוָה וַיָּכִינוּ: 12 וַיָּבִיאוּ אֶת־ הַתְּרוּמָה וְהַמַּעֲשֵׂר וְהַקֳּדָשִׁים בֶּאֱמוּנָה וַעֲלֵיהֶם נָגִיד כוּנַנְיָהוּ הַלֵּוִי וְשִׁמְעִי אָחִיהוּ מִשְׁנֶה: 13 וִיחִיאֵל וַעֲזַזְיָהוּ וְנַחַת וַעֲשָׂהאֵל וִירִימֹות וְיֹוזָבָד וֶאֱלִיאֵל וְיִסְמַכְיָהוּ וּמַחַת וּבְנָיָהוּ פְּקִידִים מִיַּד כוּנַנְיָהוּ וְשִׁמְעִי אָחִיו בְּמִפְקַד יְחִזְקִיָּהוּ הַמֶּלֶךְ וַעֲזַרְיָהוּ נְגִיד בֵּית־הָאֱלֹהִים: 14 וְקֹורֵא בֶן־יִמְנָה הַלֵּוִי הַשֹּׁועֵר לַמִּזְרָחָה עַל נִדְבֹות הָאֱלֹהִים לָתֵת תְּרוּמַת יְהוָה וְקָדְשֵׁי הַקֳּדָשִׁים: 15 וְעַל־יָדֹו עֵדֶן וּמִנְיָמִן וְיֵשׁוּעַ וּשְׁמַעְיָהוּ אֲמַרְיָהוּ וּשְׁכַנְיָהוּ בְּעָרֵי הַכֹּהֲנִים בֶּאֱמוּנָה לָתֵת לַאֲחֵיהֶם בְּמַחְלְקֹות כַּגָּדֹול כַּקָּטָן: 16 מִלְּבַד הִתְיַחְשָׂם לִזְכָרִים מִבֶּן שָׁלֹושׁ שָׁנִים וּלְמַעְלָה לְכָל־הַבָּא לְבֵית־ יְהוָה לִדְבַר־יֹום בְּיֹומֹו לַעֲבֹודָתָם בְּמִשְׁמְרֹותָם כְּמַחְלְקֹותֵיהֶם: 17 וְאֵת הִתְיַחֵשׂ הַכֹּהֲנִים לְבֵית אֲבֹותֵיהֶם וְהַלְוִיִּם מִבֶּן עֶשְׂרִים שָׁנָה וּלְמָעְלָה בְּמִשְׁמְרֹותֵיהֶם בְּמַחְלְקֹותֵיהֶם: 18 וּלְהִתְיַחֵשׂ בְּכָל־ טַפָּם נְשֵׁיהֶם וּבְנֵיהֶם וּבְנֹותֵיהֶם לְכָל־קָהָל כִּי בֶאֱמוּנָתָם יִתְקַדְּשׁוּ־קֹדֶשׁ: 19 וְלִבְנֵי אַהֲרֹן הַכֹּהֲנִים בִּשְׂדֵי מִגְרַשׁ עָרֵיהֶם בְּכָל־עִיר וָעִיר אֲנָשִׁים אֲשֶׁר נִקְּבוּ בְּשֵׁמֹות לָתֵת מָנֹות לְכָל־זָכָר בַּכֹּהֲנִים וּלְכָל־ הִתְיַחֵשׂ בַּלְוִיִּם: 20 וַיַּעַשׂ כָּזֹאת יְחִזְקִיָּהוּ בְּכָל־ יְהוּדָה וַיַּעַשׂ הַטֹּוב וְהַיָּשָׁר וְהָאֱמֶת לִפְנֵי יְהוָה אֱלֹהָיו: 21 וּבְכָל־מַעֲשֶׂה אֲשֶׁר־הֵחֵל | בַּעֲבֹודַת בֵּית־הָאֱלֹהִים וּבַתֹּורָה וּבַמִּצְוָה לִדְרֹשׁ לֵאלֹהָיו בְּכָל־לְבָבֹו עָשָׂה וְהִצְלִיחַ: פ

לא 12 כְּנַנְיָהוּ   13 כְּנַנְיָהוּ

32 After these deeds of faithfulness, Sennacherib king of Assyria came and entered Judah; he encamped against the fortified cities, thinking to win them over to himself. 2 And when Hezekiah saw that Sennacherib had come, and that his purpose was to make war against Jerusalem, 3 he consulted with his leaders and commanders to stop the water from the springs which *were* outside the city; and they helped him. 4 Thus many people gathered together who stopped all the springs and the brook that ran through the land, saying, "Why should the kings of Assyria come and find much water?" 5 And he strengthened himself, built up all the wall that was broken, raised *it* up to the towers, and *built* another wall outside; also he repaired the Millo *in* the City of David, and made weapons and shields in abundance. 6 Then he set military captains over the people, gathered them together to him in the open square of the city gate, and gave them encouragement, saying, 7 "Be strong and courageous; do not be afraid nor dismayed before the king of Assyria, nor before all the multitude that *is* with him; for *there are* more with us than with him. 8 With him *is* an arm of flesh; but with us *is* the LORD our God, to help us and to fight our battles." And the people were strengthened by the words of Hezekiah king of Judah.

9 After this Sennacherib king of Assyria sent his servants to Jerusalem (but he and all the forces with him *laid siege* against Lachish), to Hezekiah king of Judah, and to all Judah who *were* in Jerusalem, saying, 10 "Thus says Sennacherib king of Assyria: 'In what do you trust, that you remain under siege in Jerusalem? 11 Does not Hezekiah persuade you to give yourselves over to die by famine and by thirst, saying, "The LORD our God will deliver us from the hand of the king of Assyria"? 12 Has not the same Hezekiah taken away His high places and His altars, and commanded Judah and Jerusalem, saying, "You shall worship before one altar and burn incense on it"? 13 Do you not know what I and my fathers have done to all the peoples of *other* lands? Were the gods of the nations of those lands in any way able to deliver their lands out of my hand? 14 Who *was there* among all the gods of those nations that my fathers utterly destroyed that could deliver his people from my hand, that your God should be able to deliver you from my hand? 15 Now therefore, do not let Hezekiah deceive you or persuade you like this, and do not believe him; for no god of any nation or kingdom was able to deliver his people from my hand or the hand of my fathers. How much less will your God deliver you from my hand?' "

לב אַחֲרֵי הַדְּבָרִים וְהָאֱמֶת הָאֵלֶּה בָּא
סַנְחֵרִיב מֶלֶךְ־אַשּׁוּר וַיָּבֹא בִיהוּדָה וַיִּחַן עַל־הֶעָרִים
הַבְּצֻרוֹת וַיֹּאמֶר לְבִקְעָם אֵלָיו: 2 וַיַּרְא יְחִזְקִיָּהוּ כִּי־
בָא סַנְחֵרִיב וּפָנָיו לַמִּלְחָמָה עַל־יְרוּשָׁלִָם: 3 וַיִּוָּעַץ
עִם־שָׂרָיו וְגִבֹּרָיו לִסְתּוֹם אֶת־מֵימֵי הָעֲיָנוֹת אֲשֶׁר
מִחוּץ לָעִיר וַיַּעְזְרוּהוּ: 4 וַיִּקָּבְצוּ עַם־רָב וַיִּסְתְּמוּ
אֶת־כָּל־הַמַּעְיָנוֹת וְאֶת־הַנַּחַל הַשּׁוֹטֵף בְּתוֹךְ־הָאָרֶץ
לֵאמֹר לָמָּה יָבוֹאוּ מַלְכֵי אַשּׁוּר וּמָצְאוּ מַיִם רַבִּים:
5 וַיִּתְחַזַּק וַיִּבֶן אֶת־כָּל־הַחוֹמָה הַפְּרוּצָה וַיַּעַל עַל־
הַמִּגְדָּלוֹת וְלַחוּצָה הַחוֹמָה אַחֶרֶת וַיְחַזֵּק אֶת־
הַמִּלּוֹא עִיר דָּוִיד וַיַּעַשׂ שֶׁלַח לָרֹב וּמָגִנִּים: 6 וַיִּתֵּן
שָׂרֵי מִלְחָמוֹת עַל־הָעָם וַיִּקְבְּצֵם אֵלָיו אֶל־רְחוֹב
שַׁעַר הָעִיר וַיְדַבֵּר עַל־לְבָבָם לֵאמֹר: 7 חִזְקוּ וְאִמְצוּ
אַל־תִּירְאוּ וְאַל־תֵּחַתּוּ מִפְּנֵי מֶלֶךְ אַשּׁוּר וּמִלִּפְנֵי
כָּל־הֶהָמוֹן אֲשֶׁר־עִמּוֹ כִּי־עִמָּנוּ רַב מֵעִמּוֹ: 8 עִמּוֹ
זְרוֹעַ בָּשָׂר וְעִמָּנוּ יְהוָה אֱלֹהֵינוּ לְעָזְרֵנוּ וּלְהִלָּחֵם
מִלְחֲמֹתֵנוּ וַיִּסָּמְכוּ הָעָם עַל־דִּבְרֵי יְחִזְקִיָּהוּ מֶלֶךְ־
יְהוּדָה:
פ

9 אַחַר זֶה שָׁלַח סַנְחֵרִיב מֶלֶךְ־אַשּׁוּר עֲבָדָיו
יְרוּשָׁלַיְמָה וְהוּא עַל־לָכִישׁ וְכָל־מֶמְשַׁלְתּוֹ עִמּוֹ
עַל־יְחִזְקִיָּהוּ מֶלֶךְ יְהוּדָה וְעַל־כָּל־יְהוּדָה אֲשֶׁר
בִּירוּשָׁלִַם לֵאמֹר: 10 כֹּה אָמַר סַנְחֵרִיב מֶלֶךְ
אַשּׁוּר עַל־מָה אַתֶּם בֹּטְחִים וְיֹשְׁבִים בְּמָצוֹר
בִּירוּשָׁלִָם: 11 הֲלֹא יְחִזְקִיָּהוּ מַסִּית אֶתְכֶם לָתֵת
אֶתְכֶם לָמוּת בְּרָעָב וּבְצָמָא לֵאמֹר יְהוָה אֱלֹהֵינוּ
יַצִּילֵנוּ מִכַּף מֶלֶךְ אַשּׁוּר: 12 הֲלֹא־הוּא יְחִזְקִיָּהוּ
הֵסִיר אֶת־בָּמֹתָיו וְאֶת־מִזְבְּחֹתָיו וַיֹּאמֶר לִיהוּדָה
וְלִירוּשָׁלַם לֵאמֹר לִפְנֵי מִזְבֵּחַ אֶחָד תִּשְׁתַּחֲווּ
וְעָלָיו תַּקְטִירוּ: 13 הֲלֹא תֵדְעוּ מֶה עָשִׂיתִי אֲנִי
וַאֲבוֹתַי לְכֹל עַמֵּי הָאֲרָצוֹת הֲיָכוֹל יָכְלוּ אֱלֹהֵי
גּוֹיֵ הָאֲרָצוֹת לְהַצִּיל אֶת־אַרְצָם מִיָּדִי: 14 מִי בְּכָל־
אֱלֹהֵי הַגּוֹיִם הָאֵלֶּה אֲשֶׁר הֶחֱרִימוּ אֲבוֹתַי אֲשֶׁר
יָכוֹל לְהַצִּיל אֶת־עַמּוֹ מִיָּדִי כִּי יוּכַל אֱלֹהֵיכֶם
לְהַצִּיל אֶתְכֶם מִיָּדִי: 15 וְעַתָּה אַל־יַשִּׁיא אֶתְכֶם
חִזְקִיָּהוּ וְאַל־יַסִּית אֶתְכֶם כָּזֹאת וְאַל־תַּאֲמִינוּ לוֹ
כִּי־לֹא יוּכַל כָּל־אֱלוֹהַ כָּל־גּוֹי וּמַמְלָכָה לְהַצִּיל

16 Furthermore, his servants spoke against the LORD God and against His servant Hezekiah.

17 He also wrote letters to revile the LORD God of Israel, and to speak against Him, saying, "As the gods of the nations of *other* lands have not delivered their people from my hand, so the God of Hezekiah will not deliver His people from my hand." 18 Then they called out with a loud voice in Hebrew to the people of Jerusalem who *were* on the wall, to frighten them and trouble them, that they might take the city. 19 And they spoke against the God of Jerusalem, as against the gods of the people of the earth—the work of men's hands.

20 Now because of this King Hezekiah and the prophet Isaiah, the son of Amoz, prayed and cried out to heaven. 21 Then the LORD sent an angel who cut down every mighty man of valor, leader, and captain in the camp of the king of Assyria. So he returned shamefaced to his own land. And when he had gone into the temple of his god, some of his own offspring struck him down with the sword there.

22 Thus the LORD saved Hezekiah and the inhabitants of Jerusalem from the hand of Sennacherib the king of Assyria, and from the hand of all *others,* and guided them on every side. 23 And many brought gifts to the LORD at Jerusalem, and presents to Hezekiah king of Judah, so that he was exalted in the sight of all nations thereafter.

24 In those days Hezekiah was sick and near death, and he prayed to the LORD; and He spoke to him and gave him a sign. 25 But Hezekiah did not repay according to the favor *shown* him, for his heart was lifted up; therefore wrath was looming over him and over Judah and Jerusalem. 26 Then Hezekiah humbled himself for the pride of his heart, he and the inhabitants of Jerusalem, so that the wrath of the LORD did not come upon them in the days of Hezekiah.

27 Hezekiah had very great riches and honor. And he made himself treasuries for silver, for gold, for precious stones, for spices, for shields, and for all kinds of desirable items; 28 storehouses for the harvest of grain, wine, and oil; and stalls for all kinds of livestock, and folds for flocks. 29 Moreover he provided cities for himself, and possessions of flocks and herds in abundance; for God had given him very much property. 30 This same Hezekiah also stopped the water outlet of Upper Gihon, and brought the water by tunnel to the west side of the City of David. Hezekiah prospered in all his works.

עַמּוֹ מִיָּדִי וּמִיַּד אֲבוֹתַי אַף כִּי אֱלֹהֵיכֶם לֹא־
יַצִּילוּ אֶתְכֶם מִיָּדִי: 16 וְעוֹד דִּבְּרוּ עֲבָדָיו עַל־יְהוָה
הָאֱלֹהִים וְעַל יְחִזְקִיָּהוּ עַבְדּוֹ: 17 וּסְפָרִים כָּתַב
לְחָרֵף לַיהוָה אֱלֹהֵי יִשְׂרָאֵל וְלֵאמֹר עָלָיו לֵאמֹר
כֵּאלֹהֵי גּוֹיֵ הָאֲרָצוֹת אֲשֶׁר לֹא־הִצִּילוּ עַמָּם מִיָּדִי
כֵּן לֹא־יַצִּיל אֱלֹהֵי יְחִזְקִיָּהוּ עַמּוֹ מִיָּדִי: 18 וַיִּקְרְאוּ
בְקוֹל־גָּדוֹל יְהוּדִית עַל־עַם יְרוּשָׁלִַם אֲשֶׁר עַל־
הַחוֹמָה לְיָרְאָם וּלְבַהֲלָם לְמַעַן יִלְכְּדוּ אֶת־הָעִיר:
19 וַיְדַבְּרוּ אֶל־אֱלֹהֵי יְרוּשָׁלִָם כְּעַל אֱלֹהֵי עַמֵּי
הָאָרֶץ מַעֲשֵׂה יְדֵי הָאָדָם: ס 20 וַיִּתְפַּלֵּל
יְחִזְקִיָּהוּ הַמֶּלֶךְ וִישַׁעְיָהוּ בֶן־אָמוֹץ הַנָּבִיא עַל־זֹאת
וַיִּזְעֲקוּ הַשָּׁמָיִם: פ

21 וַיִּשְׁלַח יְהוָה מַלְאָךְ וַיַּכְחֵד כָּל־גִּבּוֹר חַיִל וְנָגִיד
וְשָׂר בְּמַחֲנֵה מֶלֶךְ אַשּׁוּר וַיָּשָׁב בְּבֹשֶׁת פָּנִים לְאַרְצוֹ
וַיָּבֹא בֵּית אֱלֹהָיו וּמִיצִיאֵו° מֵעָיו שָׁם הִפִּילֻהוּ
בֶחָרֶב: 22 וַיּוֹשַׁע יְהוָה אֶת־יְחִזְקִיָּהוּ וְאֵת | יֹשְׁבֵי
יְרוּשָׁלִַם מִיַּד סַנְחֵרִיב מֶלֶךְ־אַשּׁוּר וּמִיַּד־כֹּל וַיְנַהֲלֵם
מִסָּבִיב: 23 וְרַבִּים מְבִיאִים מִנְחָה לַיהוָה לִירוּשָׁלִָם
וּמִגְדָּנוֹת לִיחִזְקִיָּהוּ מֶלֶךְ יְהוּדָה וַיִּנַּשֵּׂא לְעֵינֵי
כָל־הַגּוֹיִם מֵאַחֲרֵי־כֵן: ס 24 בַּיָּמִים הָהֵם
חָלָה יְחִזְקִיָּהוּ עַד־לָמוּת וַיִּתְפַּלֵּל אֶל־יְהוָה וַיֹּאמֶר
לוֹ וּמוֹפֵת נָתַן לוֹ: 25 וְלֹא־כִגְמֻל עָלָיו הֵשִׁיב
יְחִזְקִיָּהוּ כִּי גָבַהּ לִבּוֹ וַיְהִי עָלָיו קֶצֶף וְעַל־יְהוּדָה
וִירוּשָׁלִָם: 26 וַיִּכָּנַע יְחִזְקִיָּהוּ בְּגֹבַהּ לִבּוֹ הוּא וְיֹשְׁבֵי
יְרוּשָׁלִָם וְלֹא־בָא עֲלֵיהֶם קֶצֶף יְהוָה בִּימֵי יְחִזְקִיָּהוּ:

27 וַיְהִי לִיחִזְקִיָּהוּ עֹשֶׁר וְכָבוֹד הַרְבֵּה מְאֹד וְאֹצָרוֹת
עָשָׂה־לוֹ לְכֶסֶף וּלְזָהָב וּלְאֶבֶן יְקָרָה וְלִבְשָׂמִים
וּלְמָגִנִּים וּלְכֹל כְּלֵי חֶמְדָּה: 28 וּמִסְכְּנוֹת לִתְבוּאַת
דָּגָן וְתִירוֹשׁ וְיִצְהָר וְאֻרָוֹת לְכָל־בְּהֵמָה וּבְהֵמָה
וַעֲדָרִים לָאֲוֵרוֹת: 29 וְעָרִים עָשָׂה לוֹ וּמִקְנֵה־צֹאן
וּבָקָר לָרֹב כִּי נָתַן־לוֹ אֱלֹהִים רְכוּשׁ רַב מְאֹד:
30 וְהוּא יְחִזְקִיָּהוּ סָתַם אֶת־מוֹצָא מֵימֵי גִיחוֹן
הָעֶלְיוֹן וַיַּישְׁרֵם לְמַטָּה־מַּעְרָבָה לְעִיר דָּוִיד וַיַּצְלַח

³¹ However, *regarding* the ambassadors of the princes of Babylon, whom they sent to him to inquire about the wonder that was *done* in the land, God withdrew from him, in order to test him, that He might know all *that was* in his heart.

³² Now the rest of the acts of Hezekiah, and his goodness, indeed they *are* written in the vision of Isaiah the prophet, the son of Amoz, *and* in the book of the kings of Judah and Israel. ³³ So Hezekiah rested with his fathers, and they buried him in the upper tombs of the sons of David; and all Judah and the inhabitants of Jerusalem honored him at his death. Then Manasseh his son reigned in his place.

33 Manasseh *was* twelve years old when he became king, and he reigned fifty-five years in Jerusalem. ² But he did evil in the sight of the LORD, according to the abominations of the nations whom the LORD had cast out before the children of Israel. ³ For he rebuilt the high places which Hezekiah his father had broken down; he raised up altars for the Baals, and made wooden images; and he worshiped all the host of heaven and served them. ⁴ He also built altars in the house of the LORD, of which the LORD had said, "In Jerusalem shall My name be forever." ⁵ And he built altars for all the host of heaven in the two courts of the house of the LORD. ⁶ Also he caused his sons to pass through the fire in the Valley of the Son of Hinnom; he practiced soothsaying, used witchcraft and sorcery, and consulted mediums and spiritists. He did much evil in the sight of the LORD, to provoke Him to anger. ⁷ He even set a carved image, the idol which he had made, in the house of God, of which God had said to David and to Solomon his son, "In this house and in Jerusalem, which I have chosen out of all the tribes of Israel, I will put My name forever; ⁸ and I will not again remove the foot of Israel from the land which I have appointed for your fathers—only if they are careful to do all that I have commanded them, according to the whole law and the statutes and the ordinances by the hand of Moses." ⁹ So Manasseh seduced Judah and the inhabitants of Jerusalem to do more evil than the nations whom the LORD had destroyed before the children of Israel.

¹⁰ And the LORD spoke to Manasseh and his people, but they would not listen. ¹¹ Therefore the LORD brought upon them the captains of the army of the king of Assyria, who took Manasseh with hooks, bound him with bronze *fetters,* and carried him off to Babylon. ¹² Now when he was in affliction, he implored the LORD his God, and

יְחִזְקִיָּהוּ בְּכָל־מַעֲשֵׂהוּ: 31 וְכֵן בִּמְלִיצֵי ׀ שָׂרֵי בָּבֶל הַמְשַׁלְּחִים עָלָיו לִדְרֹשׁ הַמּוֹפֵת אֲשֶׁר הָיָה בָאָרֶץ עֲזָבוֹ הָאֱלֹהִים לְנַסּוֹתוֹ לָדַעַת כָּל־בִּלְבָבוֹ: 32 וְיֶתֶר דִּבְרֵי יְחִזְקִיָּהוּ וַחֲסָדָיו הִנָּם כְּתוּבִים בַּחֲזוֹן יְשַׁעְיָהוּ בֶן־אָמוֹץ הַנָּבִיא עַל־סֵפֶר מַלְכֵי־יְהוּדָה וְיִשְׂרָאֵל:

33 וַיִּשְׁכַּב יְחִזְקִיָּהוּ עִם־אֲבֹתָיו וַיִּקְבְּרֻהוּ בְּמַעֲלֵה קִבְרֵי בְנֵי־דָוִיד וְכָבוֹד עָשׂוּ־לוֹ בְמוֹתוֹ כָּל־יְהוּדָה וְיֹשְׁבֵי יְרוּשָׁלַ͏ִם וַיִּמְלֹךְ מְנַשֶּׁה בְנוֹ תַּחְתָּיו: פ

לג בֶּן־שְׁתֵּים עֶשְׂרֵה שָׁנָה מְנַשֶּׁה בְמָלְכוֹ וַחֲמִשִּׁים וְחָמֵשׁ שָׁנָה מָלַךְ בִּירוּשָׁלָ͏ִם: 2 וַיַּעַשׂ הָרַע בְּעֵינֵי יְהוָה כְּתוֹעֲבוֹת הַגּוֹיִם אֲשֶׁר הוֹרִישׁ יְהוָה מִפְּנֵי בְּנֵי יִשְׂרָאֵל: 3 וַיָּשָׁב וַיִּבֶן אֶת־הַבָּמוֹת אֲשֶׁר נִתַּץ יְחִזְקִיָּהוּ אָבִיו וַיָּקֶם מִזְבְּחוֹת לַבְּעָלִים וַיַּעַשׂ אֲשֵׁרוֹת וַיִּשְׁתַּחוּ לְכָל־צְבָא הַשָּׁמַיִם וַיַּעֲבֹד אֹתָם: 4 וּבָנָה מִזְבְּחוֹת בְּבֵית יְהוָה אֲשֶׁר אָמַר יְהוָה בִּירוּשָׁלַ͏ִם יִהְיֶה־שְּׁמִי לְעוֹלָם: 5 וַיִּבֶן מִזְבְּחוֹת לְכָל־צְבָא הַשָּׁמָיִם בִּשְׁתֵּי חַצְרוֹת בֵּית־יְהוָה: 6 וְהוּא הֶעֱבִיר אֶת־בָּנָיו בָּאֵשׁ בְּגֵי בֶן־הִנֹּם וְעוֹנֵן וְנִחֵשׁ וְכִשֵּׁף וְעָשָׂה אוֹב וְיִדְּעוֹנִי הִרְבָּה לַעֲשׂוֹת הָרַע בְּעֵינֵי יְהוָה לְהַכְעִיסוֹ: 7 וַיָּשֶׂם אֶת־פֶּסֶל הַסֶּמֶל אֲשֶׁר עָשָׂה בְּבֵית הָאֱלֹהִים אֲשֶׁר אָמַר אֱלֹהִים אֶל־דָּוִיד וְאֶל־שְׁלֹמֹה בְנוֹ בַּבַּיִת הַזֶּה וּבִירוּשָׁלַ͏ִם אֲשֶׁר בָּחַרְתִּי מִכֹּל שִׁבְטֵי יִשְׂרָאֵל אָשִׂים אֶת־שְׁמִי לְעֵילוֹם: 8 וְלֹא אוֹסִיף לְהָסִיר אֶת־רֶגֶל יִשְׂרָאֵל מֵעַל הָאֲדָמָה אֲשֶׁר הֶעֱמַדְתִּי לַאֲבֹתֵיכֶם רַק ׀ אִם־יִשְׁמְרוּ לַעֲשׂוֹת אֵת כָּל־אֲשֶׁר צִוִּיתִים לְכָל־הַתּוֹרָה וְהַחֻקִּים וְהַמִּשְׁפָּטִים בְּיַד־מֹשֶׁה: 9 וַיֶּתַע מְנַשֶּׁה אֶת־יְהוּדָה וְיֹשְׁבֵי יְרוּשָׁלָ͏ִם לַעֲשׂוֹת רָע מִן־הַגּוֹיִם אֲשֶׁר הִשְׁמִיד יְהוָה מִפְּנֵי בְּנֵי יִשְׂרָאֵל: פ

10 וַיְדַבֵּר יְהוָה אֶל־מְנַשֶּׁה וְאֶל־עַמּוֹ וְלֹא הִקְשִׁיבוּ: 11 וַיָּבֵא יְהוָה עֲלֵיהֶם אֶת־שָׂרֵי הַצָּבָא אֲשֶׁר לְמֶלֶךְ אַשּׁוּר וַיִּלְכְּדוּ אֶת־מְנַשֶּׁה בַּחֹחִים וַיַּאַסְרֻהוּ בַּנְחֻשְׁתַּיִם וַיּוֹלִיכֻהוּ בָּבֶלָה: 12 וּכְהָצֵר לוֹ חִלָּה אֶת־פְּנֵי יְהוָה אֱלֹהָיו וַיִּכָּנַע מְאֹד מִלִּפְנֵי אֱלֹהֵי

humbled himself greatly before the God of his fathers, 13 and prayed to Him; and He received his entreaty, heard his supplication, and brought him back to Jerusalem into his kingdom. Then Manasseh knew that the LORD *was* God.

14 After this he built a wall outside the City of David on the west side of Gihon, in the valley, as far as the entrance of the Fish Gate; and *it* enclosed Ophel, and he raised it to a very great height. Then he put military captains in all the fortified cities of Judah. 15 He took away the foreign gods and the idol from the house of the LORD, and all the altars that he had built in the mount of the house of the LORD and in Jerusalem; and he cast *them* out of the city. 16 He also repaired the altar of the LORD, sacrificed peace offerings and thank offerings on it, and commanded Judah to serve the LORD God of Israel. 17 Nevertheless the people still sacrificed on the high places, *but* only to the LORD their God.

18 Now the rest of the acts of Manasseh, his prayer to his God, and the words of the seers who spoke to him in the name of the LORD God of Israel, indeed they *are written* in the book of the kings of Israel. 19 Also his prayer and *how God* received his entreaty, and all his sin and trespass, and the sites where he built high places and set up wooden images and carved images, before he was humbled, indeed they *are* written among the sayings of Hozai. 20 So Manasseh rested with his fathers, and they buried him in his own house. Then his son Amon reigned in his place.

21 Amon *was* twenty-two years old when he became king, and he reigned two years in Jerusalem. 22 But he did evil in the sight of the LORD, as his father Manasseh had done; for Amon sacrificed to all the carved images which his father Manasseh had made, and served them. 23 And he did not humble himself before the LORD, as his father Manasseh had humbled himself; but Amon trespassed more and more.

24 Then his servants conspired against him, and killed him in his own house. 25 But the people of the land executed all those who had conspired against King Amon. Then the people of the land made his son Josiah king in his place.

34 Josiah *was* eight years old when he became king, and he reigned thirty-one years in Jerusalem. 2 And he did *what was* right in the sight of the LORD, and walked in the ways of his father David; *he did not* turn aside to the right hand or to the left.

3 For in the eighth year of his reign, while he was still young, he began to seek the God of his father David; and in the twelfth year he began to purge

אֲבֹתָ֑יו: 13 וַיִּתְפַּלֵּ֣ל אֵלָ֗יו וַיֵּעָ֤תֶר לוֹ֙ וַיִּשְׁמַ֣ע תְּחִנָּת֔וֹ וַיְשִׁיבֵ֧הוּ יְרוּשָׁלַ֛͏ִם לְמַלְכוּת֖וֹ וַיֵּ֣דַע מְנַשֶּׁ֑ה כִּ֥י יְהוָ֖ה ה֥וּא הָאֱלֹהִֽים: 14 וְאַחֲרֵי־כֵ֡ן בָּנָ֣ה חוֹמָ֣ה חִֽיצוֹנָ֣ה ׀ לְעִיר־דָּוִ֡יד מַעְרָ֣בָה לְגִיחוֹן֩ בַּנַּ֨חַל וְלָב֜וֹא בְשַׁ֣עַר הַדָּגִ֗ים וְסָבַ֤ב לָעֹ֨פֶל֙ וַיַּגְבִּיהֶ֣הָ מְאֹ֔ד וַיָּ֧שֶׂם שָֽׂרֵי־חַ֛יִל בְּכָל־הֶעָרִ֥ים הַבְּצֻר֖וֹת בִּֽיהוּדָֽה: 15 וַיָּ֠סַר אֶת־אֱלֹהֵ֨י הַנֵּכָ֜ר וְאֶת־הַסֶּ֗מֶל מִבֵּ֣ית יְהוָ֔ה וְכָל־הַֽמִּזְבְּח֗וֹת אֲשֶׁ֨ר בָּנָ֜ה בְּהַ֤ר בֵּית־יְהוָה֙ וּבִיר֣וּשָׁלַ֔͏ִם וַיַּשְׁלֵ֖ךְ ח֥וּצָה לָעִֽיר: 16 וַיִּ֙כֶן֙ אֶת־מִזְבַּ֣ח יְהוָ֔ה וַיִּזְבַּ֣ח עָלָ֔יו זִבְחֵ֥י שְׁלָמִ֖ים וְתוֹדָ֑ה וַיֹּ֙אמֶר֙ לִֽיהוּדָ֔ה לַעֲב֕וֹד אֶת־ יְהוָ֖ה אֱלֹהֵ֥י יִשְׂרָאֵֽל: 17 אֲבָ֕ל ע֥וֹד הָעָ֖ם זֹבְחִ֣ים בַּבָּמ֑וֹת רַ֖ק לַיהוָ֥ה אֱלֹהֵיהֶֽם: 18 וְיֶ֨תֶר דִּבְרֵ֣י מְנַשֶּׁ֗ה וּתְפִלָּתוֹ֙ אֶל־אֱלֹהָ֔יו וְדִבְרֵי֙ הַֽחֹזִ֔ים הַֽמְדַבְּרִ֣ים אֵלָ֔יו בְּשֵׁ֥ם יְהוָ֖ה אֱלֹהֵ֣י יִשְׂרָאֵ֑ל הִנָּ֕ם עַל־דִּבְרֵ֖י מַלְכֵ֥י יִשְׂרָאֵֽל: 19 וּתְפִלָּת֣וֹ וְהֵעָֽתֶר־לוֹ֮ וְכָל־חַטָּאת֣וֹ וּמַעְלוֹ֒ וְהַמְּקֹמ֗וֹת אֲשֶׁר֩ בָּנָ֨ה בָהֶ֤ם בָּמוֹת֙ וְהֶעֱמִ֤יד הָֽאֲשֵׁרִים֙ וְהַפְּסִלִ֔ים לִפְנֵ֖י הִכָּֽנְע֑וֹ הִנָּ֣ם כְּתוּבִ֔ים עַ֖ל דִּבְרֵ֥י חוֹזָֽי: 20 וַיִּשְׁכַּ֤ב מְנַשֶּׁה֙ עִם־אֲבֹתָ֔יו וַֽיִּקְבְּרֻ֖הוּ בֵּית֑וֹ וַיִּמְלֹ֛ךְ אָמ֥וֹן בְּנ֖וֹ תַּחְתָּֽיו: פ

21 בֶּן־עֶשְׂרִ֤ים וּשְׁתַּ֨יִם֙ שָׁנָ֣ה אָמ֣וֹן בְּמָלְכ֔וֹ וּשְׁתַּ֣יִם שָׁנִ֔ים מָלַ֖ךְ בִּירֽוּשָׁלָֽ͏ִם: 22 וַיַּ֤עַשׂ הָרַע֙ בְּעֵינֵ֣י יְהוָ֔ה כַּאֲשֶׁ֥ר עָשָׂ֖ה מְנַשֶּׁ֣ה אָבִ֑יו וּלְכָל־הַפְּסִילִ֗ים אֲשֶׁ֤ר עָשָׂה֙ מְנַשֶּׁ֣ה אָבִ֔יו זִבַּ֥ח אָמ֖וֹן וַיַּֽעַבְדֵֽם: 23 וְלֹ֤א נִכְנַע֙ מִלִּפְנֵ֣י יְהוָ֔ה כְּהִכָּנַ֖ע מְנַשֶּׁ֣ה אָבִ֑יו כִּ֣י ה֤וּא אָמוֹן֙ הִרְבָּ֣ה אַשְׁמָֽה: 24 וַיִּקְשְׁר֤וּ עָלָיו֙ עֲבָדָ֔יו וַיְמִיתֻ֖הוּ בְּבֵית֑וֹ: 25 וַיַּכּוּ֙ עַם־הָאָ֔רֶץ אֵ֥ת כָּל־הַקֹּֽשְׁרִ֖ים עַל־ הַמֶּ֣לֶךְ אָמ֑וֹן וַיַּמְלִ֧יכוּ עַם־הָאָ֛רֶץ אֶת־יֹאשִׁיָּ֥הוּ בְנ֖וֹ תַּחְתָּֽיו: פ

לד בֶּן־שְׁמוֹנֶ֤ה שָׁנִים֙ יֹאשִׁיָּ֣הוּ בְמָלְכ֔וֹ וּשְׁלֹשִׁ֤ים וְאַחַת֙ שָׁנָ֔ה מָלַ֖ךְ בִּירֽוּשָׁלָֽ͏ִם: 2 וַיַּ֥עַשׂ הַיָּשָׁ֖ר בְּעֵינֵ֣י יְהוָ֑ה וַיֵּ֗לֶךְ בְּדַרְכֵי֙ דָּוִ֣יד אָבִ֔יו וְלֹא־ סָ֖ר יָמִ֥ין וּשְׂמֹֽאול: 3 וּבִשְׁמוֹנֶ֨ה שָׁנִ֜ים לְמָלְכ֗וֹ וְהוּא֙ עוֹדֶ֣נּוּ נַ֔עַר הֵחֵ֕ל לִדְרֹ֕ושׁ לֵאלֹהֵ֖י דָּוִ֣יד אָבִ֑יו וּבִשְׁתֵּ֧ים עֶשְׂרֵ֣ה שָׁנָ֗ה הֵחֵל֙ לְטַהֵ֣ר אֶת־ יְהוּדָה֙ וִיר֣וּשָׁלַ֔͏ִם מִן־הַבָּמוֹת֙ וְהָ֣אֲשֵׁרִ֔ים וְהַפְּסִלִ֖ים

לד 16 וַיִּ֙כֶן֙

Judah and Jerusalem of the high places, the wooden images, the carved images, and the molded images. ⁴ They broke down the altars of the Baals in his presence, and the incense altars which *were* above them he cut down; and the wooden images, the carved images, and the molded images he broke in pieces, and made dust of them and scattered *it* on the graves of those who had sacrificed to them. ⁵ He also burned the bones of the priests on their altars, and cleansed Judah and Jerusalem. ⁶ And *so he did* in the cities of Manasseh, Ephraim, and Simeon, as far as Naphtali and all around, with axes. ⁷ When he had broken down the altars and the wooden images, had beaten the carved images into powder, and cut down all the incense altars throughout all the land of Israel, he returned to Jerusalem.

⁸ In the eighteenth year of his reign, when he had purged the land and the temple, he sent Shaphan the son of Azaliah, Maaseiah the governor of the city, and Joah the son of Joahaz the recorder, to repair the house of the LORD his God. ⁹ When they came to Hilkiah the high priest, they delivered the money that was brought into the house of God, which the Levites who kept the doors had gathered from the hand of Manasseh and Ephraim, from all the remnant of Israel, from all Judah and Benjamin, and *which* they had brought back to Jerusalem. ¹⁰ Then they put *it* in the hand of the foremen who had the oversight of the house of the LORD; and they gave it to the workmen who worked in the house of the LORD, to repair and restore the house. ¹¹ They gave *it* to the craftsmen and builders to buy hewn stone and timber for beams, and to floor the houses which the kings of Judah had destroyed. ¹² And the men did the work faithfully. Their overseers *were* Jahath and Obadiah the Levites, of the sons of Merari, and Zechariah and Meshullam, of the sons of the Kohathites, to supervise. *Others of* the Levites, all of whom were skillful with instruments of music, ¹³ *were* over the burden bearers and *were* overseers of all who did work in any kind of service. And *some* of the Levites *were* scribes, officers, and gatekeepers.

¹⁴ Now when they brought out the money that was brought into the house of the LORD, Hilkiah the priest found the Book of the Law of the LORD *given* by Moses. ¹⁵ Then Hilkiah answered and said to Shaphan the scribe, "I have found the Book of the Law in the house of the LORD." And Hilkiah gave the book to Shaphan. ¹⁶ So Shaphan carried the book to the king, bringing the king word, saying, "All that was committed to your servants they are doing. ¹⁷ And they have gathered the money that was found in the house of the LORD,

וְהַמַּסֵּכוֹת: ⁴ וַיְנַתְּצוּ לְפָנָיו אֵת מִזְבְּחוֹת הַבְּעָלִים וְהַחַמָּנִים אֲשֶׁר־לְמַעְלָה מֵעֲלֵיהֶם גִּדֵּעַ וְהָאֲשֵׁרִים וְהַפְּסִלִים וְהַמַּסֵּכוֹת שִׁבַּר וְהֵדַק וַיִּזְרֹק עַל־פְּנֵי הַקְּבָרִים הַזֹּבְחִים לָהֶם: ⁵ וְעַצְמוֹת כֹּהֲנִים שָׂרַף עַל־מִזְבְּחוֹתָם וַיְטַהֵר אֶת־יְהוּדָה וְאֶת־יְרוּשָׁלָ͏ִם: ⁶ וּבְעָרֵי מְנַשֶּׁה וְאֶפְרַיִם וְשִׁמְעוֹן וְעַד־נַפְתָּלִי בְּהַר בָּתֵּיהֶם סָבִיב: ⁷ וַיְנַתֵּץ אֶת־הַמִּזְבְּחוֹת וְאֶת־הָאֲשֵׁרִים וְהַפְּסִלִים כִּתַּת לְהֵדַק וְכָל־הַחַמָּנִים גִּדַּע בְּכָל־אֶרֶץ יִשְׂרָאֵל וַיָּשָׁב לִירוּשָׁלָ͏ִם: ס ⁸ וּבִשְׁנַת שְׁמוֹנֶה עֶשְׂרֵה לְמָלְכוֹ לְטַהֵר הָאָרֶץ וְהַבָּיִת שָׁלַח אֶת־שָׁפָן בֶּן־אֲצַלְיָהוּ וְאֶת־מַעֲשֵׂיָהוּ שַׂר־הָעִיר וְאֵת יוֹאָח בֶּן־יוֹאָחָז הַמַּזְכִּיר לְחַזֵּק אֶת־בֵּית יְהוָה אֱלֹהָיו: ⁹ וַיָּבֹאוּ אֶל־חִלְקִיָּהוּ הַכֹּהֵן הַגָּדוֹל וַיִּתְּנוּ אֶת־הַכֶּסֶף הַמּוּבָא בֵית־אֱלֹהִים אֲשֶׁר אָסְפוּ־הַלְוִיִּם שֹׁמְרֵי הַסַּף מִיַּד מְנַשֶּׁה וְאֶפְרַיִם וּמִכֹּל שְׁאֵרִית יִשְׂרָאֵל וּמִכָּל־יְהוּדָה וּבִנְיָמִן וַיָּשֻׁבִי יְרוּשָׁלָ͏ִם: ¹⁰ וַיִּתְּנוּ עַל־יַד עֹשֵׂה הַמְּלָאכָה הַמֻּפְקָדִים בְּבֵית יְהוָה וַיִּתְּנוּ אֹתוֹ עוֹשֵׂי הַמְּלָאכָה אֲשֶׁר עֹשִׂים בְּבֵית יְהוָה לִבְדּוֹק וּלְחַזֵּק הַבָּיִת: ¹¹ וַיִּתְּנוּ לֶחָרָשִׁים וְלַבֹּנִים לִקְנוֹת אַבְנֵי מַחְצֵב וְעֵצִים לַמְחַבְּרוֹת וּלְקָרוֹת אֶת־הַבָּתִּים אֲשֶׁר הִשְׁחִיתוּ מַלְכֵי יְהוּדָה: ¹² וְהָאֲנָשִׁים עֹשִׂים בֶּאֱמוּנָה בַּמְּלָאכָה וַעֲלֵיהֶם מֻפְקָדִים יַחַת וְעֹבַדְיָהוּ הַלְוִיִּם מִן־בְּנֵי מְרָרִי וּזְכַרְיָה וּמְשֻׁלָּם מִן־בְּנֵי הַקְּהָתִים לְנַצֵּחַ וְהַלְוִיִּם כָּל־מֵבִין בִּכְלֵי־שִׁיר: ¹³ וְעַל הַסַּבָּלִים וּמְנַצְּחִים לְכֹל עֹשֵׂה מְלָאכָה לַעֲבוֹדָה וַעֲבוֹדָה וּמֵהַלְוִיִּם סוֹפְרִים וְשֹׁטְרִים וְשׁוֹעֲרִים: ¹⁴ וּבְהוֹצִיאָם אֶת־הַכֶּסֶף הַמּוּבָא בֵּית יְהוָה מָצָא חִלְקִיָּהוּ הַכֹּהֵן אֶת־סֵפֶר תּוֹרַת־יְהוָה בְּיַד־מֹשֶׁה: ¹⁵ וַיַּעַן חִלְקִיָּהוּ וַיֹּאמֶר אֶל־שָׁפָן הַסּוֹפֵר סֵפֶר הַתּוֹרָה מָצָאתִי בְּבֵית יְהוָה וַיִּתֵּן חִלְקִיָּהוּ אֶת־הַסֵּפֶר אֶל־שָׁפָן: ¹⁶ וַיָּבֵא שָׁפָן אֶת־הַסֵּפֶר אֶל־הַמֶּלֶךְ וַיָּשֶׁב עוֹד אֶת־הַמֶּלֶךְ דָּבָר לֵאמֹר כֹּל אֲשֶׁר־נִתַּן בְּיַד־עֲבָדֶיךָ הֵם עֹשִׂים: ¹⁷ וַיַּתִּיכוּ אֶת־הַכֶּסֶף הַנִּמְצָא בְּבֵית־יְהוָה וַיִּתְּנוּהוּ

and have delivered it into the hand of the overseers and the workmen." ¹⁸ Then Shaphan the scribe told the king, saying, "Hilkiah the priest has given me a book." And Shaphan read it before the king.

¹⁹ Thus it happened, when the king heard the words of the Law, that he tore his clothes. ²⁰ Then the king commanded Hilkiah, Ahikam the son of Shaphan, Abdon the son of Micah, Shaphan the scribe, and Asaiah a servant of the king, saying, ²¹ "Go, inquire of the LORD for me, and for those who are left in Israel and Judah, concerning the words of the book that is found; for great *is* the wrath of the LORD that is poured out on us, because our fathers have not kept the word of the LORD, to do according to all that is written in this book."

²² So Hilkiah and those the king *had appointed* went to Huldah the prophetess, the wife of Shallum the son of Tokhath, the son of Hasrah, keeper of the wardrobe. (She dwelt in Jerusalem in the Second Quarter.) And they spoke to her to that *effect.*

²³ Then she answered them, "Thus says the LORD God of Israel, 'Tell the man who sent you to Me, ²⁴ "Thus says the LORD: 'Behold, I will bring calamity on this place and on its inhabitants, all the curses that are written in the book which they have read before the king of Judah, ²⁵ because they have forsaken Me and burned incense to other gods, that they might provoke Me to anger with all the works of their hands. Therefore My wrath will be poured out on this place, and not be quenched.' " ' ²⁶ But as for the king of Judah, who sent you to inquire of the LORD, in this manner you shall speak to him, 'Thus says the LORD God of Israel: "*Concerning* the words which you have heard— ²⁷ because your heart was tender, and you humbled yourself before God when you heard His words against this place and against its inhabitants, and you humbled yourself before Me, and you tore your clothes and wept before Me, I also have heard *you,*" says the LORD. ²⁸ "Surely I will gather you to your fathers, and you shall be gathered to your grave in peace; and your eyes shall not see all the calamity which I will bring on this place and its inhabitants." ' " So they brought back word to the king.

²⁹ Then the king sent and gathered all the elders of Judah and Jerusalem. ³⁰ The king went up to the house of the LORD, with all the men of Judah and the inhabitants of Jerusalem—the priests and the Levites, and all the people, great and small. And he read in their hearing all the words of the Book of the Covenant which had been found in the house of the LORD. ³¹ Then the king stood in his place and made a covenant before the LORD, to follow the

עַל־יַד הַמֻּפְקָדִים וְעַל־יַד עֹשֵׂי הַמְּלָאכָה: 18 וַיַּגֵּד שָׁפָן הַסּוֹפֵר לַמֶּלֶךְ לֵאמֹר סֵפֶר נָתַן לִי חִלְקִיָּהוּ הַכֹּהֵן וַיִּקְרָא־בוֹ שָׁפָן לִפְנֵי הַמֶּלֶךְ: 19 וַיְהִי כִּשְׁמֹעַ הַמֶּלֶךְ אֵת דִּבְרֵי הַתּוֹרָה וַיִּקְרַע אֶת־בְּגָדָיו: 20 וַיְצַו הַמֶּלֶךְ אֶת־חִלְקִיָּהוּ וְאֶת־אֲחִיקָם בֶּן־שָׁפָן וְאֶת־עַבְדּוֹן בֶּן־מִיכָה וְאֵת שָׁפָן הַסּוֹפֵר וְאֵת עֲשָׂיָה עֶבֶד־הַמֶּלֶךְ לֵאמֹר: 21 לְכוּ דִרְשׁוּ אֶת־יְהוָה בַּעֲדִי וּבְעַד הַנִּשְׁאָר בְּיִשְׂרָאֵל וּבִיהוּדָה עַל־דִּבְרֵי הַסֵּפֶר אֲשֶׁר נִמְצָא כִּי־גְדוֹלָה חֲמַת־יְהוָה אֲשֶׁר נִתְּכָה בָנוּ עַל אֲשֶׁר לֹא־שָׁמְרוּ אֲבוֹתֵינוּ אֶת־דְּבַר יְהוָה לַעֲשׂוֹת כְּכָל־הַכָּתוּב עַל־הַסֵּפֶר הַזֶּה: פ

22 וַיֵּלֶךְ חִלְקִיָּהוּ וַאֲשֶׁר הַמֶּלֶךְ אֶל־חֻלְדָּה הַנְּבִיאָה אֵשֶׁת שַׁלֻּם בֶּן־תָּוְקְהַת בֶּן־חַסְרָה שׁוֹמֵר הַבְּגָדִים וְהִיא יוֹשֶׁבֶת בִּירוּשָׁלִַם בַּמִּשְׁנֶה וַיְדַבְּרוּ אֵלֶיהָ כָּזֹאת: ס 23 וַתֹּאמֶר לָהֶם כֹּה־אָמַר יְהוָה אֱלֹהֵי יִשְׂרָאֵל אִמְרוּ לָאִישׁ אֲשֶׁר־שָׁלַח אֶתְכֶם אֵלָי: ס 24 כֹּה אָמַר יְהוָה הִנְנִי מֵבִיא רָעָה עַל־הַמָּקוֹם הַזֶּה וְעַל־יוֹשְׁבָיו אֵת כָּל־הָאָלוֹת הַכְּתוּבוֹת עַל־הַסֵּפֶר אֲשֶׁר קָרְאוּ לִפְנֵי מֶלֶךְ יְהוּדָה: 25 תַּחַת אֲשֶׁר עֲזָבוּנִי וַיְקַטִּירוּ לֵאלֹהִים אֲחֵרִים לְמַעַן הַכְעִיסֵנִי בְּכֹל מַעֲשֵׂי יְדֵיהֶם וְתִתַּךְ חֲמָתִי בַּמָּקוֹם הַזֶּה וְלֹא תִכְבֶּה: 26 וְאֶל־מֶלֶךְ יְהוּדָה הַשֹּׁלֵחַ אֶתְכֶם לִדְרוֹשׁ בַּיהוָה כֹּה תֹאמְרוּ אֵלָיו ס כֹּה־אָמַר יְהוָה אֱלֹהֵי יִשְׂרָאֵל הַדְּבָרִים אֲשֶׁר שָׁמָעְתָּ: 27 יַעַן רַךְ־לְבָבְךָ וַתִּכָּנַע מִלִּפְנֵי אֱלֹהִים בְּשָׁמְעֲךָ אֶת־דְּבָרָיו עַל־הַמָּקוֹם הַזֶּה וְעַל־יוֹשְׁבָיו וַתִּכָּנַע לְפָנַי וַתִּקְרַע אֶת־בְּגָדֶיךָ וַתֵּבְךְּ לְפָנָי וְגַם־אֲנִי שָׁמַעְתִּי נְאֻם־יְהוָה: 28 הִנְנִי אֹסִפְךָ אֶל־אֲבֹתֶיךָ וְנֶאֱסַפְתָּ אֶל־קִבְרֹתֶיךָ בְּשָׁלוֹם וְלֹא־תִרְאֶינָה עֵינֶיךָ בְּכֹל הָרָעָה אֲשֶׁר אֲנִי מֵבִיא עַל־הַמָּקוֹם הַזֶּה וְעַל־יֹשְׁבָיו וַיָּשִׁיבוּ אֶת־הַמֶּלֶךְ דָּבָר: פ

30 וַיִּשְׁלַח הַמֶּלֶךְ וַיֶּאֱסֹף אֶת־כָּל־זִקְנֵי יְהוּדָה וִירוּשָׁלִָם: 30 וַיַּעַל הַמֶּלֶךְ בֵּית־יְהוָה וְכָל־אִישׁ יְהוּדָה וְיֹשְׁבֵי יְרוּשָׁלִַם וְהַכֹּהֲנִים וְהַלְוִיִּם וְכָל־הָעָם מִגָּדוֹל וְעַד־קָטָן וַיִּקְרָא בְאָזְנֵיהֶם אֶת־כָּל־דִּבְרֵי סֵפֶר הַבְּרִית הַנִּמְצָא בֵּית יְהוָה: 31 וַיַּעֲמֹד הַמֶּלֶךְ עַל־עָמְדוֹ וַיִּכְרֹת אֶת־הַבְּרִית לִפְנֵי יְהוָה

לד 22 תָּקְהַת   25 וַיְקַטְּרוּ

LORD, and to keep His commandments and His testimonies and His statutes with all his heart and all his soul, to perform the words of the covenant that were written in this book. ³² And he made all who were present in Jerusalem and Benjamin take a stand. So the inhabitants of Jerusalem did according to the covenant of God, the God of their fathers. ³³ Thus Josiah removed all the abominations from all the country that *belonged* to the children of Israel, and made all who were present in Israel diligently serve the LORD their God. All his days they did not depart from following the LORD God of their fathers.

35 Now Josiah kept a Passover to the LORD in Jerusalem, and they slaughtered the Passover *lambs* on the fourteenth *day* of the first month. ² And he set the priests in their duties and encouraged them for the service of the house of the LORD. ³ Then he said to the Levites who taught all Israel, who were holy to the LORD: "Put the holy ark in the house which Solomon the son of David, king of Israel, built. *It shall* no longer *be* a burden on *your* shoulders. Now serve the LORD your God and His people Israel. ⁴ Prepare *yourselves* according to your fathers' houses, according to your divisions, following the written instruction of David king of Israel and the written instruction of Solomon his son. ⁵ And stand in the holy *place* according to the divisions of the fathers' houses of your brethren the *lay* people, and *according to* the division of the father's house of the Levites. ⁶ So slaughter the Passover *offerings,* consecrate yourselves, and prepare *them* for your brethren, that *they* may do according to the word of the LORD by the hand of Moses."

⁷ Then Josiah gave the *lay* people lambs and young goats from the flock, all for Passover *offerings* for all who were present, to the number of thirty thousand, as well as three thousand cattle; these *were* from the king's possessions. ⁸ And his leaders gave willingly to the people, to the priests, and to the Levites. Hilkiah, Zechariah, and Jehiel, rulers of the house of God, gave to the priests for the Passover *offerings* two thousand six hundred *from the flock,* and three hundred cattle. ⁹ Also Conaniah, his brothers Shemaiah and Nethanel, and Hashabiah and Jeiel and Jozabad, chief of the Levites, gave to the Levites for Passover *offerings* five thousand *from the flock* and five hundred cattle.

¹⁰ So the service was prepared, and the priests stood in their places, and the Levites in their divisions, according to the king's command. ¹¹ And

לָלֶ֣כֶת אַחֲרֵ֣י יְהֹוָ֡ה וְלִשְׁמ֣וֹר אֶת־מִצְוֺתָ֣יו וְעֵדְוֺתָ֣יו וְחֻקָּ֑יו בְּכׇל־לְבָב֣וֹ וּבְכׇל־נַפְשׁ֔וֹ לַעֲשׂ֕וֹת אֶת־דִּבְרֵ֣י הַבְּרִ֔ית הַכְּתוּבִ֖ים עַל־הַסֵּ֥פֶר הַזֶּֽה: 32 וַיַּעֲמֵ֕ד אֵ֣ת כׇּל־הַנִּמְצָ֣א בִירוּשָׁלַ֖͏ִם וּבִנְיָמִ֑ן וַיַּֽעֲשׂוּ֙ יֹשְׁבֵ֣י יְרוּשָׁלַ֔͏ִם כִּבְרִ֥ית אֱלֹהִ֖ים אֱלֹהֵ֥י אֲבוֹתֵיהֶֽם: 33 וַיָּ֨סַר יֹאשִׁיָּ֜הוּ אֶֽת־כׇּל־הַתּֽוֹעֵב֗וֹת מִכׇּל־הָאֲרָצוֹת֮ אֲשֶׁ֣ר לִבְנֵ֣י יִשְׂרָאֵל֒ וַֽיַּעֲבֵ֗ד אֵ֤ת כׇּל־הַנִּמְצָא֙ בְּיִשְׂרָאֵ֔ל לַעֲב֖וֹד אֶת־יְהֹוָ֣ה אֱלֹהֵיהֶ֑ם כׇּל־יָמָ֕יו לֹ֣א סָ֔רוּ מֵֽאַחֲרֵ֕י יְהֹוָ֖ה אֱלֹהֵ֥י אֲבוֹתֵיהֶֽם: פ

לה וַיַּ֨עַשׂ יֹאשִׁיָּ֧הוּ בִֽירוּשָׁלַ֛͏ִם פֶּ֖סַח לַֽיהֹוָ֑ה וַיִּשְׁחֲט֣וּ הַפֶּ֔סַח בְּאַרְבָּעָ֥ה עָשָׂ֖ר לַחֹ֥דֶשׁ הָרִאשֽׁוֹן: 2 וַיַּעֲמֵ֧ד הַכֹּהֲנִ֛ים עַל־מִשְׁמְרוֹתָ֖ם וַֽיְחַזְּקֵ֑ם לַעֲבוֹדַ֖ת בֵּ֥ית יְהֹוָֽה: 3 וַיֹּ֣אמֶר לַלְוִיִּ֣ם הַמְּבִינִ֣ים֮ לְכׇל־יִשְׂרָאֵל֒ הַקְּדוֹשִׁ֣ים לַיהֹוָ֔ה תְּנ֤וּ אֶת־אֲרוֹן־הַקֹּ֙דֶשׁ֙ בַּבַּ֗יִת אֲשֶׁ֥ר בָּנָ֛ה שְׁלֹמֹ֥ה בֶן־דָּוִ֖יד מֶ֣לֶךְ יִשְׂרָאֵ֑ל אֵֽין־לָכֶ֥ם מַשָּׂ֖א בַּכָּתֵ֑ף עַתָּ֗ה עִבְדוּ֙ אֶת־יְהֹוָ֣ה אֱלֹהֵיכֶ֔ם וְאֵ֖ת עַמּ֥וֹ יִשְׂרָאֵֽל: 4 וְהָכִ֥ינֽוּ לְבֵית־אֲבוֹתֵיכֶ֖ם כְּמַחְלְקוֹתֵיכֶ֑ם בִּכְתָ֗ב דָּוִיד֙ מֶ֣לֶךְ יִשְׂרָאֵ֔ל וּבְמִכְתַּ֖ב שְׁלֹמֹ֥ה בְנֽוֹ: 5 וְעִמְד֣וּ בַקֹּ֗דֶשׁ לִפְלֻגּוֹת֙ בֵּ֣ית הָֽאָב֔וֹת לַאֲחֵיכֶ֖ם בְּנֵ֣י הָעָ֑ם וַחֲלֻקַּ֥ת בֵּֽית־אָ֖ב לַלְוִיִּֽם: 6 וְשַׁחֲט֖וּ הַפָּ֑סַח וְהִתְקַדְּשׁ֗וּ וְהָכִ֙ינוּ֙ לַאֲחֵיכֶ֔ם לַעֲשׂ֥וֹת כִּדְבַר־יְהֹוָ֖ה בְּיַד־מֹשֶֽׁה: פ

7 וַיָּ֣רֶם יֹאשִׁיָּ֣הוּ לִבְנֵ֣י הָעָם֩ צֹ֨אן כְּבָשִׂ֤ים וּבְנֵֽי־עִזִּים֙ הַכֹּ֣ל לַפְּסָחִ֔ים לְכׇל־הַנִּמְצָ֖א לְמִסְפַּ֣ר שְׁלֹשִׁ֣ים אֶ֑לֶף וּבָקָ֖ר שְׁלֹ֣שֶׁת אֲלָפִ֑ים אֵ֖לֶּה מֵרְכ֥וּשׁ הַמֶּֽלֶךְ: ס 8 וְשָׂרָ֞יו לִנְדָבָ֣ה לָעָ֣ם לַכֹּהֲנִ֣ים וְלַלְוִיִּם֮ הֵרִ֒ימוּ֒ חִלְקִיָּ֨ה וּזְכַרְיָ֜הוּ וִיחִיאֵ֗ל נְגִידֵי֙ בֵּ֣ית הָֽאֱלֹהִ֔ים לַכֹּהֲנִ֛ים נָתְנ֥וּ לַפְּסָחִ֖ים אַלְפַּ֣יִם וְשֵׁ֣שׁ מֵא֑וֹת וּבָקָ֖ר שְׁלֹ֥שׁ מֵאֽוֹת: 9 וְכׇנַנְיָ֡הֽוּ וּשְׁמַעְיָ֡הֽוּ וּנְתַנְאֵ֣ל אֶחָ֡יו וַחֲשַׁבְיָ֡הֽוּ וִֽיעִיאֵ֣ל וְיוֹזָבָד֙ שָׂרֵ֣י הַלְוִיִּ֔ם הֵרִ֥ימוּ לַלְוִיִּ֖ם לַפְּסָחִ֑ים חֲמֵ֣שֶׁת אֲלָפִ֔ים וּבָקָ֖ר חֲמֵ֥שׁ מֵאֽוֹת: 10 וַתִּכּ֖וֹן הָעֲבוֹדָ֑ה וַיַּעַמְד֤וּ הַכֹּהֲנִים֙ עַל־עׇמְדָ֔ם וְהַלְוִיִּ֥ם עַל־מַחְלְקוֹתָ֖ם כְּמִצְוַ֥ת הַמֶּֽלֶךְ: 11 וַֽיִּשְׁחֲט֖וּ הַפָּ֑סַח וַיִּזְרְק֤וּ הַכֹּהֲנִים֙ מִיָּדָ֔ם

they slaughtered the Passover *offerings;* and the priests sprinkled *the blood* with their hands, while the Levites skinned *the animals.* 12 Then they removed the burnt offerings that *they* might give them to the divisions of the fathers' houses of the *lay* people, to offer to the LORD, as *it is* written in the Book of Moses. And so *they did* with the cattle. 13 Also they roasted the Passover *offerings* with fire according to the ordinance; but the *other* holy *offerings* they boiled in pots, in caldrons, and in pans, and divided *them* quickly among all the *lay* people. 14 Then afterward they prepared portions for themselves and for the priests, because the priests, the sons of Aaron, *were busy* in offering burnt offerings and fat until night; therefore the Levites prepared portions for themselves and for the priests, the sons of Aaron. 15 And the singers, the sons of Asaph, *were* in their places, according to the command of David, Asaph, Heman, and Jeduthun the king's seer. Also the gatekeepers were at each gate; they did not have to leave their position, because their brethren the Levites prepared portions for them.

16 So all the service of the LORD was prepared the same day, to keep the Passover and to offer burnt offerings on the altar of the LORD, according to the command of King Josiah. 17 And the children of Israel who were present kept the Passover at that time, and the Feast of Unleavened Bread for seven days. 18 There had been no Passover kept in Israel like that since the days of Samuel the prophet; and none of the kings of Israel had kept such a Passover as Josiah kept, with the priests and the Levites, all Judah and Israel who were present, and the inhabitants of Jerusalem. 19 In the eighteenth year of the reign of Josiah this Passover was kept.

20 After all this, when Josiah had prepared the temple, Necho king of Egypt came up to fight against Carchemish by the Euphrates; and Josiah went out against him. 21 But he sent messengers to him, saying, "What have I to do with you, king of Judah? *I have* not *come* against you this day, but against the house with which I have war; for God commanded me to make haste. Refrain *from meddling with* God, who *is* with me, lest He destroy you." 22 Nevertheless Josiah would not turn his face from him, but disguised himself so that he might fight with him, and did not heed the words of Necho from the mouth of God. So he came to fight in the Valley of Megiddo.

23 And the archers shot King Josiah; and the king said to his servants, "Take me away, for I am severely wounded." 24 His servants therefore took him out of that chariot and put him in the second

וְהַלְוִיִּם מַפְשִׁיטִים: 12 וַיָּסִירוּ הָעֹלָה לְתִתָּם לְמִפְלַגּוֹת לְבֵית־אָבוֹת לִבְנֵי הָעָם לְהַקְרִיב לַיהוָה כַּכָּתוּב בְּסֵפֶר מֹשֶׁה וְכֵן לַבָּקָר: 13 וַיְבַשְּׁלוּ הַפֶּסַח בָּאֵשׁ כַּמִּשְׁפָּט וְהַקֳּדָשִׁים בִּשְּׁלוּ בַּסִּירוֹת וּבַדְּוָדִים וּבַצֵּלָחוֹת וַיָּרִיצוּ לְכָל־בְּנֵי הָעָם: 14 וְאַחַר הֵכִינוּ לָהֶם וְלַכֹּהֲנִים כִּי הַכֹּהֲנִים בְּנֵי אַהֲרֹן בְּהַעֲלוֹת הָעוֹלָה וְהַחֲלָבִים עַד־לָיְלָה וְהַלְוִיִּם הֵכִינוּ לָהֶם וְלַכֹּהֲנִים בְּנֵי אַהֲרֹן: 15 וְהַמְשֹׁרְרִים בְּנֵי־אָסָף עַל־מַעֲמָדָם כְּמִצְוַת דָּוִיד וְאָסָף וְהֵימָן וִידֻתוּן חוֹזֵה הַמֶּלֶךְ וְהַשֹּׁעֲרִים לְשַׁעַר וָשָׁעַר אֵין לָהֶם לָסוּר מֵעַל עֲבֹדָתָם כִּי־אֲחֵיהֶם הַלְוִיִּם הֵכִינוּ לָהֶם: 16 וַתִּכּוֹן כָּל־עֲבוֹדַת יְהוָה בַּיּוֹם הַהוּא לַעֲשׂוֹת הַפֶּסַח וְהַעֲלוֹת עֹלוֹת עַל מִזְבַּח יְהוָה כְּמִצְוַת הַמֶּלֶךְ יֹאשִׁיָּהוּ: 17 וַיַּעֲשׂוּ בְנֵי־ יִשְׂרָאֵל הַנִּמְצְאִים אֶת־הַפֶּסַח בָּעֵת הַהִיא וְאֶת־ חַג הַמַּצּוֹת שִׁבְעַת יָמִים: 18 וְלֹא־נַעֲשָׂה פֶסַח כָּמֹהוּ בְּיִשְׂרָאֵל מִימֵי שְׁמוּאֵל הַנָּבִיא וְכָל־מַלְכֵי יִשְׂרָאֵל לֹא־עָשׂוּ כַּפֶּסַח אֲשֶׁר־עָשָׂה יֹאשִׁיָּהוּ וְהַכֹּהֲנִים וְהַלְוִיִּם וְכָל־יְהוּדָה וְיִשְׂרָאֵל הַנִּמְצָא וְיוֹשְׁבֵי יְרוּשָׁלִָם: ס 19 בִּשְׁמוֹנֶה עֶשְׂרֵה שָׁנָה לְמַלְכוּת יֹאשִׁיָּהוּ נַעֲשָׂה הַפֶּסַח הַזֶּה:

20 אַחֲרֵי כָל־זֹאת אֲשֶׁר הֵכִין יֹאשִׁיָּהוּ אֶת־הַבַּיִת עָלָה נְכוֹ מֶלֶךְ־מִצְרַיִם לְהִלָּחֵם בְּכַרְכְּמִישׁ עַל־ פְּרָת וַיֵּצֵא לִקְרָאתוֹ יֹאשִׁיָּהוּ: 21 וַיִּשְׁלַח אֵלָיו מַלְאָכִים לֵאמֹר מַה־לִּי וָלָךְ מֶלֶךְ יְהוּדָה לֹא־ עָלֶיךָ אַתָּה הַיּוֹם כִּי אֶל־בֵּית מִלְחַמְתִּי וֵאלֹהִים אָמַר לְבַהֲלֵנִי חֲדַל־לְךָ מֵאֱלֹהִים אֲשֶׁר־עִמִּי וְאַל־ יַשְׁחִיתֶךָ: 22 וְלֹא־הֵסֵב יֹאשִׁיָּהוּ פָּנָיו מִמֶּנּוּ כִּי לְהִלָּחֶם־בּוֹ הִתְחַפֵּשׂ וְלֹא שָׁמַע אֶל־דִּבְרֵי נְכוֹ מִפִּי אֱלֹהִים וַיָּבֹא לְהִלָּחֵם בְּבִקְעַת מְגִדּוֹ: 23 וַיֹּרוּ הַיֹּרִים לַמֶּלֶךְ יֹאשִׁיָּהוּ וַיֹּאמֶר הַמֶּלֶךְ לַעֲבָדָיו הַעֲבִירוּנִי כִּי הָחֳלֵיתִי מְאֹד: 24 וַיַּעֲבִירֻהוּ עֲבָדָיו מִן־הַמֶּרְכָּבָה וַיַּרְכִּיבֻהוּ עַל רֶכֶב הַמִּשְׁנֶה אֲשֶׁר־לוֹ וַיּוֹלִיכֻהוּ יְרוּשָׁלִַם וַיָּמָת וַיִּקָּבֵר בְּקִבְרוֹת אֲבֹתָיו וְכָל־יְהוּדָה וִירוּשָׁלִַם מִתְאַבְּלִים עַל־יֹאשִׁיָּהוּ: פ

chariot that he had, and they brought him to Jerusalem. So he died, and was buried in *one of* the tombs of his fathers. And all Judah and Jerusalem mourned for Josiah.

25 Jeremiah also lamented for Josiah. And to this day all the singing men and the singing women speak of Josiah in their lamentations. They made it a custom in Israel; and indeed they *are* written in the Laments.

26 Now the rest of the acts of Josiah and his goodness, according to *what was* written in the Law of the LORD, 27 and his deeds from first to last, indeed they *are* written in the book of the kings of Israel and Judah.

36 Then the people of the land took Jehoahaz the son of Josiah, and made him king in his father's place in Jerusalem. 2 Jehoahaz *was* twenty-three years old when he became king, and he reigned three months in Jerusalem. 3 Now the king of Egypt deposed him at Jerusalem; and he imposed on the land a tribute of one hundred talents of silver and a talent of gold. 4 Then the king of Egypt made *Jehoahaz's* brother Eliakim king over Judah and Jerusalem, and changed his name to Jehoiakim. And Necho took Jehoahaz his brother and carried him off to Egypt.

5 Jehoiakim *was* twenty-five years old when he became king, and he reigned eleven years in Jerusalem. And he did evil in the sight of the LORD his God. 6 Nebuchadnezzar king of Babylon came up against him, and bound him in bronze *fetters* to carry him off to Babylon. 7 Nebuchadnezzar also carried off *some* of the articles from the house of the LORD to Babylon, and put them in his temple at Babylon. 8 Now the rest of the acts of Jehoiakim, the abominations which he did, and what was found against him, indeed they *are* written in the book of the kings of Israel and Judah. Then Jehoiachin his son reigned in his place.

9 Jehoiachin *was* eight years old when he became king, and he reigned in Jerusalem three months and ten days. And he did evil in the sight of the LORD. 10 At the turn of the year King Nebuchadnezzar summoned *him* and took him to Babylon, with the costly articles from the house of the LORD, and made Zedekiah, *Jehoiakim's* brother, king over Judah and Jerusalem.

11 Zedekiah *was* twenty-one years old when he became king, and he reigned eleven years in Jerusalem. 12 He did evil in the sight of the LORD his God, *and* did not humble himself before Jeremiah the prophet, *who spoke* from the mouth of the LORD. 13 And he also rebelled against King

25 וַיְקוֹנֵן יִרְמְיָהוּ֮ עַל־יֹאשִׁיָּהוּ֒ וַיֹּאמְר֨וּ כָל־הַשָּׁרִ֣ים ׀ וְֽהַשָּׁר֡וֹת בְּקִינ֨וֹתֵיהֶ֤ם עַל־יֹאשִׁיָּ֙הוּ֙ עַד־הַיּ֔וֹם וַיִּתְּנ֥וּם לְחֹ֖ק עַל־יִשְׂרָאֵ֑ל וְהִנָּ֥ם כְּתוּבִ֖ים עַל־הַקִּינֽוֹת׃

26 וְיֶ֛תֶר דִּבְרֵ֥י יֹאשִׁיָּ֖הוּ וַחֲסָדָ֑יו כַּכָּת֖וּב בְּתוֹרַ֥ת יְהוָֽה׃ 27 וּדְבָרָ֖יו הָרִאשֹׁנִ֣ים וְהָאַחֲרֹנִ֑ים הִנָּ֣ם כְּתוּבִ֔ים עַל־סֵ֥פֶר מַלְכֵֽי־יִשְׂרָאֵ֖ל וִיהוּדָֽה׃

לו וַיִּקְחוּ֙ עַם־הָאָ֔רֶץ אֶת־יְהֽוֹאָחָ֖ז בֶּן־יֹאשִׁיָּ֑הוּ וַיַּמְלִיכֻ֥הוּ תַֽחַת־אָבִ֖יו בִּירוּשָׁלָֽ͏ִם׃ 2 בֶּן־שָׁל֧וֹשׁ וְעֶשְׂרִ֛ים שָׁנָ֖ה יוֹאָחָ֣ז בְּמָלְכ֑וֹ וּשְׁלֹשָׁ֣ה חֳדָשִׁ֔ים מָלַ֖ךְ בִּירוּשָׁלָֽ͏ִם׃ 3 וַיְסִירֵ֥הוּ מֶֽלֶךְ־מִצְרַ֖יִם בִּירֽוּשָׁלָ֑͏ִם וַֽיַּעֲנֹשׁ֙ אֶת־הָאָ֔רֶץ מֵאָ֥ה כִכַּר־כֶּ֖סֶף וְכִכַּ֥ר זָהָֽב׃

4 וַיַּמְלֵ֣ךְ מֶֽלֶךְ־מִצְרַֹיִם אֶת־אֶלְיָקִ֤ים אָחִיו֙ עַל־יְהוּדָ֣ה וִירֽוּשָׁלַ֔͏ִם וַיַּסֵּ֥ב אֶת־שְׁמ֖וֹ יְהֽוֹיָקִ֑ים וְאֶת־יוֹאָחָ֤ז אָחִיו֙ לָקַ֣ח נְכ֔וֹ וַיְבִיאֵ֖הוּ מִצְרָֽיְמָה׃ פ

5 בֶּן־עֶשְׂרִ֨ים וְחָמֵ֤שׁ שָׁנָה֙ יְהוֹיָקִ֣ים בְּמָלְכ֔וֹ וְאַחַ֤ת עֶשְׂרֵה֙ שָׁנָ֔ה מָלַ֖ךְ בִּירֽוּשָׁלָ֑͏ִם וַיַּ֣עַשׂ הָרַ֔ע בְּעֵינֵ֖י יְהוָ֥ה אֱלֹהָֽיו׃ 6 עָלָ֣יו עָלָ֔ה נְבוּכַדְנֶאצַּ֖ר מֶ֣לֶךְ בָּבֶ֑ל וַיַּֽאַסְרֵ֙הוּ֙ בַּֽנְחֻשְׁתַּ֔יִם לְהֹלִיכ֖וֹ בָּבֶֽלָה׃ 7 וּמִכְּלֵי֙ בֵּ֣ית יְהוָ֔ה הֵבִ֥יא נְבֽוּכַדְנֶאצַּ֖ר לְבָבֶ֑ל וַיִּתְּנֵ֥ם בְּהֵיכָל֖וֹ בְּבָבֶֽל׃ 8 וְיֶ֩תֶר֩ דִּבְרֵ֨י יְהוֹיָקִ֜ים וְתֹֽעֲבֹתָ֣יו אֲשֶׁר־עָשָׂ֗ה וְהַנִּמְצָ֣א עָלָ֔יו הִנָּ֣ם כְּתוּבִ֔ים עַל־סֵ֕פֶר מַלְכֵ֥י יִשְׂרָאֵ֖ל וִיהוּדָ֑ה וַיִּמְלֹ֛ךְ יְהוֹיָכִ֥ין בְּנ֖וֹ תַּחְתָּֽיו׃ פ

9 בֶּן־שְׁמוֹנֶ֤ה שָׁנִים֙ יְהוֹיָכִ֣ין בְּמָלְכ֔וֹ וּשְׁלֹשָׁ֤ה חֳדָשִׁים֙ וַעֲשֶׂ֣רֶת יָמִ֔ים מָלַ֖ךְ בִּירֽוּשָׁלָ֑͏ִם וַיַּ֥עַשׂ הָרַ֖ע בְּעֵינֵ֥י יְהוָֽה׃ 10 וְלִתְשׁוּבַ֣ת הַשָּׁנָ֗ה שָׁלַח֙ הַמֶּ֣לֶךְ נְבֽוּכַדְנֶאצַּ֔ר וַיְבִאֵ֣הוּ בָבֶ֔לָה עִם־כְּלֵ֖י חֶמְדַּ֣ת בֵּית־יְהוָ֑ה וַיַּמְלֵךְ֙ אֶת־צִדְקִיָּ֣הוּ אָחִ֔יו עַל־יְהוּדָ֖ה וִירוּשָׁלָֽ͏ִם׃ פ

11 בֶּן־עֶשְׂרִ֧ים וְאַחַ֛ת שָׁנָ֖ה צִדְקִיָּ֣הוּ בְמָלְכ֑וֹ וְאַחַ֤ת עֶשְׂרֵה֙ שָׁנָ֔ה מָלַ֖ךְ בִּירֽוּשָׁלָֽ͏ִם׃ 12 וַיַּ֣עַשׂ הָרַ֔ע בְּעֵינֵ֖י יְהוָ֣ה אֱלֹהָ֑יו לֹ֣א נִכְנַ֗ע מִלִּפְנֵ֛י יִרְמְיָ֥הוּ הַנָּבִ֖יא מִפִּ֥י יְהוָֽה׃ 13 וְ֠גַם בַּמֶּ֤לֶךְ נְבֽוּכַדְנֶאצַּר֙ מָרָ֔ד אֲשֶׁ֣ר

Nebuchadnezzar, who had made him swear *an oath* by God; but he stiffened his neck and hardened his heart against turning to the LORD God of Israel. ¹⁴ Moreover all the leaders of the priests and the people transgressed more and more, *according* to all the abominations of the nations, and defiled the house of the LORD which He had consecrated in Jerusalem.

¹⁵ And the LORD God of their fathers sent *warnings* to them by His messengers, rising up early and sending *them,* because He had compassion on His people and on His dwelling place. ¹⁶ But they mocked the messengers of God, despised His words, and scoffed at His prophets, until the wrath of the LORD arose against His people, till *there was* no remedy.

¹⁷ Therefore He brought against them the king of the Chaldeans, who killed their young men with the sword in the house of their sanctuary, and had no compassion on young man or virgin, on the aged or the weak; He gave *them* all into his hand. ¹⁸ And all the articles from the house of God, great and small, the treasures of the house of the LORD, and the treasures of the king and of his leaders, all *these* he took to Babylon. ¹⁹ Then they burned the house of God, broke down the wall of Jerusalem, burned all its palaces with fire, and destroyed all its precious possessions. ²⁰ And those who escaped from the sword he carried away to Babylon, where they became servants to him and his sons until the rule of the kingdom of Persia, ²¹ to fulfill the word of the LORD by the mouth of Jeremiah, until the land had enjoyed her Sabbaths. As long as she lay desolate she kept Sabbath, to fulfill seventy years.

²² Now in the first year of Cyrus king of Persia, that the word of the LORD by the mouth of Jeremiah might be fulfilled, the LORD stirred up the spirit of Cyrus king of Persia, so that he made a proclamation throughout all his kingdom, and also *put it* in writing, saying,

23 Thus says Cyrus king of Persia:
    All the kingdoms of the earth the LORD God of heaven has given me. And He has commanded me to build Him a house at Jerusalem which is in Judah. Who *is* among you of all His people? May the LORD his God *be* with him, and let him go up!

הִשְׁבִּיעוֹ בֵּאלֹהִים וַיֶּקֶשׁ אֶת־עָרְפּוֹ וַיְאַמֵּץ אֶת־
לְבָבוֹ מִשּׁוּב אֶל־יְהֹוָה אֱלֹהֵי יִשְׂרָאֵל: ¹⁴ גַּם כָּל־
שָׂרֵי הַכֹּהֲנִים וְהָעָם הִרְבּוּ לִמְעָול־ᴾ מַעַל כְּכֹל
תֹּעֲבוֹת הַגּוֹיִם וַיְטַמְּאוּ אֶת־בֵּית יְהֹוָה אֲשֶׁר הִקְדִּישׁ
בִּירוּשָׁלָ͏ִם: ¹⁵ וַיִּשְׁלַח יְהֹוָה אֱלֹהֵי אֲבוֹתֵיהֶם עֲלֵיהֶם
בְּיַד מַלְאָכָיו הַשְׁכֵּם וְשָׁלוֹחַ כִּי־חָמַל עַל־עַמּוֹ וְעַל־
מְעוֹנוֹ: ¹⁶ וַיִּהְיוּ מַלְעִבִים בְּמַלְאֲכֵי הָאֱלֹהִים וּבוֹזִים
דְּבָרָיו וּמִתַּעְתְּעִים בִּנְבִאָיו עַד עֲלוֹת חֲמַת־יְהֹוָה
בְּעַמּוֹ עַד־לְאֵין מַרְפֵּא: ¹⁷ וַיַּעַל עֲלֵיהֶם אֶת־מֶלֶךְ
כַּשְׂדִּייםᴾ וַיַּהֲרֹג בַּחוּרֵיהֶם בַּחֶרֶב בְּבֵית מִקְדָּשָׁם
וְלֹא חָמַל עַל־בָּחוּר וּבְתוּלָה זָקֵן וְיָשֵׁשׁ הַכֹּל נָתַן
בְּיָדוֹ: ¹⁸ וְכֹל כְּלֵי בֵּית הָאֱלֹהִים הַגְּדֹלִים וְהַקְּטַנִּים
וְאֹצְרוֹת בֵּית יְהֹוָה וְאֹצְרוֹת הַמֶּלֶךְ וְשָׂרָיו הַכֹּל
הֵבִיא בָבֶל: ¹⁹ וַיִּשְׂרְפוּ אֶת־בֵּית הָאֱלֹהִים וַיְנַתְּצוּ
אֵת חוֹמַת יְרוּשָׁלָ͏ִם וְכָל־אַרְמְנוֹתֶיהָ שָׂרְפוּ בָאֵשׁ
וְכָל־כְּלֵי מַחֲמַדֶּיהָ לְהַשְׁחִית: ס ²⁰ וַיֶּגֶל
הַשְּׁאֵרִית מִן־הַחֶרֶב אֶל־בָּבֶל וַיִּהְיוּ־לוֹ וּלְבָנָיו
לַעֲבָדִים עַד־מְלֹךְ מַלְכוּת פָּרָס: ²¹ לְמַלֹּאות דְּבַר־
יְהֹוָה בְּפִי יִרְמְיָהוּ עַד־רָצְתָה הָאָרֶץ אֶת־שַׁבְּתוֹתֶיהָ
כָּל־יְמֵי הָשַּׁמָּה שָׁבָתָה לְמַלֹּאות שִׁבְעִים שָׁנָה: פ

²² וּבִשְׁנַת אַחַת לְכוֹרֶשׁ מֶלֶךְ פָּרַס לִכְלוֹת דְּבַר־
יְהֹוָה בְּפִי יִרְמְיָהוּ הֵעִיר יְהֹוָה אֶת־רוּחַ כּוֹרֶשׁ
מֶלֶךְ־פָּרַס וַיַּעֲבֶר־קוֹל בְּכָל־מַלְכוּתוֹ וְגַם־בְּמִכְתָּב
לֵאמֹר: ס ²³ כֹּה־אָמַר כּוֹרֶשׁ ׀ מֶלֶךְ פָּרַס
כָּל־מַמְלְכוֹת הָאָרֶץ נָתַן לִי יְהֹוָה אֱלֹהֵי הַשָּׁמַיִם
וְהוּא־פָקַד עָלַי לִבְנוֹת־לוֹ בַיִת בִּירוּשָׁלַ͏ִם אֲשֶׁר
בִּיהוּדָה מִי־בָכֶם מִכָּל־עַמּוֹ יְהֹוָה אֱלֹהָיו עִמּוֹ וְיָעַל:

לוֹ 14 לִמְעָל־ · 17 כַּשְׂדִּים

הברית החדשה

THE
NEW TESTAMENT

MATTHEW

1 The book of the genealogy of Jesus Christ, the Son of David, the Son of Abraham:

² Abraham begot Isaac, Isaac begot Jacob, and Jacob begot Judah and his brothers. ³ Judah begot Perez and Zerah by Tamar, Perez begot Hezron, and Hezron begot Ram. ⁴ Ram begot Amminadab, Amminadab begot Nahshon, and Nahshon begot Salmon. ⁵ Salmon begot Boaz by Rahab, Boaz begot Obed by Ruth, Obed begot Jesse, ⁶ and Jesse begot David the king.

David the king begot Solomon by her *who had been the wife* of Uriah. ⁷ Solomon begot Rehoboam, Rehoboam begot Abijah, and Abijah begot Asa. ⁸ Asa begot Jehoshaphat, Jehoshaphat begot Joram, and Joram begot Uzziah. ⁹ Uzziah begot Jotham, Jotham begot Ahaz, and Ahaz begot Hezekiah. ¹⁰ Hezekiah begot Manasseh, Manasseh begot Amon, and Amon begot Josiah. ¹¹ Josiah begot Jeconiah and his brothers about the time they were carried away to Babylon.

¹² And after they were brought to Babylon, Jeconiah begot Shealtiel, and Shealtiel begot Zerubbabel. ¹³ Zerubbabel begot Abiud, Abiud begot Eliakim, and Eliakim begot Azor. ¹⁴ Azor begot Zadok, Zadok begot Achim, and Achim begot Eliud. ¹⁵ Eliud begot Eleazar, Eleazar begot Matthan, and Matthan begot Jacob. ¹⁶ And Jacob begot Joseph the husband of Mary, of whom was born Jesus who is called Christ.

¹⁷ So all the generations from Abraham to David *are* fourteen generations, from David until the captivity in Babylon *are* fourteen generations, and from the captivity in Babylon until the Christ *are* fourteen generations.

¹⁸ Now the birth of Jesus Christ was as follows: After His mother Mary was betrothed to Joseph, before they came together, she was found with child of the Holy Spirit. ¹⁹ Then Joseph her husband, being a just *man,* and not wanting to make her a public example, was minded to put her away secretly. ²⁰ But while he thought about these things, behold, an angel of the Lord appeared to him in a dream, saying, "Joseph, son of David, do not be afraid to take to you Mary your wife, for that which is conceived in her is of the Holy Spirit. ²¹ And she will bring forth a Son, and you shall call His name JESUS, for He will save His people from their sins."

הַבְּשׂוֹרָה עַל־פִּי מַתַּי

א סֵפֶר הַיֻּחֲסִין שֶׁל יֵשׁוּעַ הַמָּשִׁיחַ בֶּן־דָּוִד בֶּן־אַבְרָהָם: ² אַבְרָהָם הוֹלִיד אֶת יִצְחָק, יִצְחָק הוֹלִיד אֶת יַעֲקֹב וְיַעֲקֹב הוֹלִיד אֶת יְהוּדָה וְאֶת אֶחָיו. ³ יְהוּדָה הוֹלִיד אֶת פֶּרֶץ וְאֶת זֶרַח מִתָּמָר, פֶּרֶץ הוֹלִיד אֶת חֶצְרוֹן וְחֶצְרוֹן הוֹלִיד אֶת רָם. ⁴ רָם הוֹלִיד אֶת עַמִּינָדָב, עַמִּינָדָב הוֹלִיד אֶת נַחְשׁוֹן וְנַחְשׁוֹן הוֹלִיד אֶת שַׂלְמוֹן. ⁵ שַׂלְמוֹן הוֹלִיד אֶת בֹּעַז מֵרָחָב, בֹּעַז הוֹלִיד אֶת עוֹבֵד מֵרוּת וְעוֹבֵד הוֹלִיד אֶת יִשַׁי. ⁶ יִשַׁי הוֹלִיד אֶת דָּוִד הַמֶּלֶךְ, דָּוִד הוֹלִיד אֶת שְׁלֹמֹה מִזּוֹ שֶׁהָיְתָה אֵשֶׁת אוּרִיָּה. ⁷ שְׁלֹמֹה הוֹלִיד אֶת רְחַבְעָם, רְחַבְעָם הוֹלִיד אֶת אֲבִיָּה וַאֲבִיָּה הוֹלִיד אֶת אָסָא. ⁸ אָסָא הוֹלִיד אֶת יְהוֹשָׁפָט, יְהוֹשָׁפָט הוֹלִיד אֶת יוֹרָם וְיוֹרָם הוֹלִיד אֶת עֻזִּיָּהוּ. ⁹ עֻזִּיָּהוּ הוֹלִיד אֶת יוֹתָם, יוֹתָם הוֹלִיד אֶת אָחָז וְאָחָז הוֹלִיד אֶת חִזְקִיָּהוּ. ¹⁰ חִזְקִיָּהוּ הוֹלִיד אֶת מְנַשֶּׁה, מְנַשֶּׁה הוֹלִיד אֶת אָמוֹן וְאָמוֹן הוֹלִיד אֶת יֹאשִׁיָּהוּ. ¹¹ יֹאשִׁיָּהוּ הוֹלִיד אֶת יְכָנְיָהוּ וְאֶת אֶחָיו בִּימֵי גָּלוּת בָּבֶל. ¹² לְאַחַר שֶׁהָגְלוּ בָּבֶלָה הוֹלִיד יְכָנְיָהוּ אֶת שְׁאַלְתִּיאֵל וּשְׁאַלְתִּיאֵל הוֹלִיד אֶת זְרֻבָּבֶל. ¹³ זְרֻבָּבֶל הוֹלִיד אֶת אֲבִיהוּד, אֲבִיהוּד הוֹלִיד אֶת אֶלְיָקִים וֶאֱלְיָקִים הוֹלִיד אֶת עַזּוּר. ¹⁴ עַזּוּר הוֹלִיד אֶת צָדוֹק, צָדוֹק הוֹלִיד אֶת יָכִין וְיָכִין הוֹלִיד אֶת אֱלִיהוּד. ¹⁵ אֱלִיהוּד הוֹלִיד אֶת אֶלְעָזָר, אֶלְעָזָר הוֹלִיד אֶת מַתָּן וּמַתָּן הוֹלִיד אֶת יַעֲקֹב. ¹⁶ יַעֲקֹב הוֹלִיד אֶת יוֹסֵף בַּעַל מִרְיָם אֲשֶׁר מִמֶּנָּה נוֹלַד יֵשׁוּעַ הַנִּקְרָא מָשִׁיחַ.

¹⁷ וּבְכֵן כָּל הַדּוֹרוֹת מֵאַבְרָהָם עַד דָּוִד אַרְבָּעָה־עָשָׂר דּוֹרוֹת, וּמִדָּוִד עַד גָּלוּת בָּבֶל אַרְבָּעָה־עָשָׂר דּוֹרוֹת, וּמִגָּלוּת בָּבֶל עַד הַמָּשִׁיחַ אַרְבָּעָה־עָשָׂר דּוֹרוֹת.

¹⁸ כָּךְ הָיְתָה הֻלֶּדֶת יֵשׁוּעַ הַמָּשִׁיחַ: מִרְיָם אִמּוֹ הָיְתָה מְאֹרֶסֶת לְיוֹסֵף וּבְטֶרֶם הִתְאַחֲדוּ נִמְצְאָה הָרָה לְרוּחַ הַקֹּדֶשׁ. ¹⁹ יוֹסֵף בַּעְלָהּ, שֶׁהָיָה צַדִּיק וְלֹא רָצָה לְהָצִיג אוֹתָהּ לְחֶרְפָּה, הֶחְלִיט לְשַׁלַּח אוֹתָהּ בַּסֵּתֶר. ²⁰ בְּעוֹד שֶׁהָיָה מְהַרְהֵר בָּזֶה נִרְאָה אֵלָיו מַלְאַךְ יהוה בַּחֲלוֹם וְאָמַר: "יוֹסֵף בֶּן דָּוִד, אַל תְּחֲשֹׁשׁ לָקַחַת אֵלֶיךָ אֶת מִרְיָם אִשְׁתְּךָ, כִּי אֲשֶׁר הוֹרָה בָּהּ מֵרוּחַ הַקֹּדֶשׁ הוּא. ²¹ הִיא יוֹלֶדֶת בֵּן וְאַתָּה תִּקְרָא

²²So all this was done that it might be fulfilled which was spoken by the Lord through the prophet, saying: ²³"*Behold, the virgin shall be with child, and bear a Son, and they shall call His name Immanuel,*" which is translated, "God with us."

²⁴Then Joseph, being aroused from sleep, did as the angel of the Lord commanded him and took to him his wife, ²⁵and did not know her till she had brought forth her firstborn Son. And he called His name Jesus.

2 Now after Jesus was born in Bethlehem of Judea in the days of Herod the king, behold, wise men from the East came to Jerusalem, ²saying, "Where is He who has been born King of the Jews? For we have seen His star in the East and have come to worship Him."

³When Herod the king heard *this,* he was troubled, and all Jerusalem with him. ⁴And when he had gathered all the chief priests and scribes of the people together, he inquired of them where the Christ was to be born.

⁵So they said to him, "In Bethlehem of Judea, for thus it is written by the prophet:

⁶ 'But you, Bethlehem, *in the land of Judah,*
     Are not the least among the rulers of Judah;
     For out of you shall come a Ruler
     Who will shepherd My people Israel.'"

⁷Then Herod, when he had secretly called the wise men, determined from them what time the star appeared. ⁸And he sent them to Bethlehem and said, "Go and search carefully for the young Child, and when you have found *Him,* bring back word to me, that I may come and worship Him also."

⁹When they heard the king, they departed; and behold, the star which they had seen in the East went before them, till it came and stood over where the young Child was. ¹⁰When they saw the star, they rejoiced with exceedingly great joy. ¹¹And when they had come into the house, they saw the young Child with Mary His mother, and fell down and worshiped Him. And when they had opened their treasures, they presented gifts to Him: gold, frankincense, and myrrh.

¹²Then, being divinely warned in a dream that they should not return to Herod, they departed for their own country another way.

¹³Now when they had departed, behold, an angel of the Lord appeared to Joseph in a dream, saying, "Arise, take the young Child and His mother, flee to Egypt, and stay there until I bring you word; for Herod will seek the young Child to destroy Him."

שְׁמוֹ יֵשׁוּעַ, כִּי הוּא יוֹשִׁיעַ אֶת עַמּוֹ מֵחַטֹּאתֵיהֶם." ²²כָּל זֶה אֵרַע לְמַעַן יִתְקַיֵּם מַה שֶּׁדִּבֶּר אֲדֹנָי בְּפִי הַנָּבִיא: ²³"הִנֵּה הָעַלְמָה הָרָה וְיֹלֶדֶת בֵּן וְקָרֵאת שְׁמוֹ עִמָּנוּ אֵל." ²⁴לְאַחַר מִכֵּן הֵקִיץ יוֹסֵף מִשְּׁנָתוֹ וְעָשָׂה כְּפִי שֶׁצִּוָּהוּ מַלְאַךְ יהוה. הוּא לָקַח אֵלָיו אֶת אִשְׁתּוֹ ²⁵מִבְּלִי שֶׁיָּדַע אוֹתָהּ עַד אֲשֶׁר יָלְדָה בֵּן, וְקָרָא אֶת שְׁמוֹ יֵשׁוּעַ.

ב בְּעֵת שֶׁנּוֹלַד יֵשׁוּעַ בְּבֵית לֶחֶם יְהוּדָה, בִּימֵי הוֹרְדוֹס הַמֶּלֶךְ, בָּאוּ לִירוּשָׁלַיִם חֲכָמִים מִן הַמִּזְרָח. ²שָׁאֲלוּ: "הֵיכָן מֶלֶךְ הַיְּהוּדִים אֲשֶׁר נוֹלַד? כִּי רָאִינוּ אֶת כּוֹכָבוֹ בַּמִּזְרָח וּבָאנוּ לְהִשְׁתַּחֲווֹת לוֹ." ³כַּאֲשֶׁר שָׁמַע זֹאת הוֹרְדוֹס הַמֶּלֶךְ נִדְהַם הוּא וְכָל יְרוּשָׁלַיִם עִמּוֹ. ⁴הוּא כִּנֵּס אֶת כָּל רָאשֵׁי הַכֹּהֲנִים וְסוֹפְרֵי הָעָם וְשָׁאַל אוֹתָם אֵיפֹה יִוָּלֵד הַמָּשִׁיחַ. ⁵אָמְרוּ לוֹ: "בְּבֵית לֶחֶם יְהוּדָה, כִּי כֵן נִכְתַּב עַל-יְדֵי הַנָּבִיא: ⁶'וְאַתָּה בֵּית לֶחֶם אֶרֶץ יְהוּדָה, אֵינְךָ צָעִיר בְּאַלּוּפֵי יְהוּדָה, כִּי מִמְּךָ יֵצֵא מוֹשֵׁל אֲשֶׁר יִרְעֶה אֶת עַמִּי יִשְׂרָאֵל'." ⁷אָז קָרָא הוֹרְדוֹס בַּחֲשַׁאי לְחַכְמֵי הַמִּזְרָח וּבֵרֵר אֶצְלָם מָתַי הוֹפִיעַ הַכּוֹכָב. ⁸אַחֲרֵי כֵן שָׁלַח אוֹתָם לְבֵית לֶחֶם בְּאָמְרוֹ: "לְכוּ חִקְרוּ הֵיטֵב עַל-אוֹדוֹת הַיֶּלֶד וְכַאֲשֶׁר תִּמְצְאוּ אוֹתוֹ הוֹדִיעוּ לִי כְּדֵי שֶׁאָבוֹא וְאֶשְׁתַּחֲוֶה לוֹ גַּם אֲנִי."

⁹הֵם שָׁמְעוּ אֶת דִּבְרֵי הַמֶּלֶךְ וְהָלְכוּ, וְהִנֵּה הַכּוֹכָב שֶׁרָאוּ בַּמִּזְרָח הִתְקַדֵּם לִפְנֵיהֶם עַד אֲשֶׁר בָּא וְנֶעֱמַד מֵעַל לַמָּקוֹם שֶׁהָיָה שָׁם הַיֶּלֶד. ¹⁰כִּרְאוֹתָם אֶת הַכּוֹכָב שָׂמְחוּ שִׂמְחָה גְּדוֹלָה עַד מְאֹד. ¹¹הֵם נִכְנְסוּ לַבַּיִת וְרָאוּ אֶת הַיֶּלֶד עִם מִרְיָם אִמּוֹ. נָפְלוּ עַל פְּנֵיהֶם וְהִשְׁתַּחֲווּ לוֹ, וּפָתְחוּ אֶת צְרוֹרוֹתֵיהֶם וְהִגִּישׁוּ לוֹ מַתָּנוֹת: זָהָב וּלְבוֹנָה וָמוֹר. ¹²לְאַחַר שֶׁהֻזְהֲרוּ בַּחֲלוֹם שֶׁלֹּא לַחֲזֹר אֶל הוֹרְדוֹס יָצְאוּ לְאַרְצָם בְּדֶרֶךְ אַחֶרֶת.

¹³הֵם הָלְכוּ מִשָּׁם וּמַלְאַךְ יהוה נִרְאָה אֶל יוֹסֵף בַּחֲלוֹם וְאָמַר: "קוּם, קַח אֶת הַיֶּלֶד וְאֶת אִמּוֹ וּבְרַח לְמִצְרַיִם וֶהֱיֵה שָׁם עַד אֲשֶׁר אֹמַר לְךָ, כִּי הוֹרְדוֹס יְחַפֵּשׂ אֶת הַיֶּלֶד כְּדֵי לְהַשְׁמִיד אוֹתוֹ."

14 When he arose, he took the young Child and His mother by night and departed for Egypt, 15 and was there until the death of Herod, that it might be fulfilled which was spoken by the Lord through the prophet, saying, *"Out of Egypt I called My Son."*

16 Then Herod, when he saw that he was deceived by the wise men, was exceedingly angry; and he sent forth and put to death all the male children who were in Bethlehem and in all its districts, from two years old and under, according to the time which he had determined from the wise men. 17 Then was fulfilled what was spoken by Jeremiah the prophet, saying:

18 *"A voice was heard in Ramah,*
Lamentation, weeping, and great mourning,
Rachel weeping for her children,
Refusing to be comforted,
Because they are no more."

19 Now when Herod was dead, behold, an angel of the Lord appeared in a dream to Joseph in Egypt, 20 saying, "Arise, take the young Child and His mother, and go to the land of Israel, for those who sought the young Child's life are dead." 21 Then he arose, took the young Child and His mother, and came into the land of Israel.

22 But when he heard that Archelaus was reigning over Judea instead of his father Herod, he was afraid to go there. And being warned by God in a dream, he turned aside into the region of Galilee. 23 And he came and dwelt in a city called Nazareth, that it might be fulfilled which was spoken by the prophets, "He shall be called a Nazarene."

3 In those days John the Baptist came preaching in the wilderness of Judea, 2 and saying, "Repent, for the kingdom of heaven is at hand!" 3 For this is he who was spoken of by the prophet Isaiah, saying:

"*The voice of one crying in the wilderness:*
'*Prepare the way of the LORD;*
Make His paths straight.'"

4 Now John himself was clothed in camel's hair, with a leather belt around his waist; and his food was locusts and wild honey. 5 Then Jerusalem, all Judea, and all the region around the Jordan went out to him 6 and were baptized by him in the Jordan, confessing their sins.

7 But when he saw many of the Pharisees and Sadducees coming to his baptism, he said to them, "Brood of vipers! Who warned you to flee from the wrath to come? 8 Therefore bear fruits worthy of repentance, 9 and do not think to say to yourselves, 'We have Abraham as *our* father.' For I say to you that God is able to raise up children to Abraham

14 הוּא קָם וְלָקַח אֶת הַיֶּלֶד וְאֶת אִמּוֹ בַּלַּיְלָה וְיָצָא לְמִצְרָיִם. 15 שָׁם נִשְׁאַר עַד מוֹת הוֹרְדוֹס, לְקַיֵּם אֶת אֲשֶׁר דִּבֶּר אֲדֹנָי בְּפִי הַנָּבִיא: "מִמִּצְרַיִם קָרָאתִי לִבְנִי."

16 כַּאֲשֶׁר רָאָה הוֹרְדוֹס כִּי הִתְלוּ בּוֹ הַחֲכָמִים רָגַז עַד מְאֹד, וְשָׁלַח לַהֲרֹג אֶת כָּל הַיְלָדִים שֶׁבְּבֵית לֶחֶם וּבְכָל סְבִיבוֹתֶיהָ, מִבְּנֵי שְׁנָתַיִם וָמַטָּה, לְפִי הָעֵת אֲשֶׁר קָבַע מִפִּי הַחֲכָמִים. 17 אָז נִתְקַיֵּם הַנֶּאֱמַר בְּפִי יִרְמְיָהוּ הַנָּבִיא: 18 "קוֹל בְּרָמָה נִשְׁמָע, נְהִי בְּכִי תַמְרוּרִים, רָחֵל מְבַכָּה עַל־בָּנֶיהָ, מֵאֲנָה לְהִנָּחֵם כִּי אֵינָם."

19 אַחֲרֵי מוֹת הוֹרְדוֹס נִרְאָה מַלְאַךְ יהוה אֶל יוֹסֵף בַּחֲלוֹם בְּאֶרֶץ מִצְרַיִם 20 וְאָמַר: "קוּם, קַח אֶת הַיֶּלֶד וְאֶת אִמּוֹ וְלֵךְ לְאֶרֶץ יִשְׂרָאֵל, כִּי מֵתוּ הַמְבַקְשִׁים אֶת נֶפֶשׁ הַיֶּלֶד." 21 הוּא קָם וְלָקַח אֶת הַיֶּלֶד וְאֶת אִמּוֹ וּבָא לְאֶרֶץ יִשְׂרָאֵל. 22 אֲבָל בְּשָׁמְעוֹ כִּי אַרְכֶלָאוֹס מוֹלֵךְ בִּיהוּדָה בִּמְקוֹם הוֹרְדוֹס אָבִיו, פָּחַד לָלֶכֶת לְשָׁם. לְאַחַר שֶׁהֻזְהַר בַּחֲלוֹם יָצָא אֶל סְבִיבוֹת הַגָּלִיל. 23 הוּא בָּא וְיָשַׁב בָּעִיר הַנִּקְרֵאת נָצְרַת, לְמַעַן יִתְקַיֵּם הַנֶּאֱמַר עַל־פִּי הַנְּבִיאִים כִּי נָצְרִי יִקָּרֵא לוֹ.

3 בַּיָּמִים הָהֵם הוֹפִיעַ יוֹחָנָן הַמַּטְבִּיל כְּשֶׁהוּא קוֹרֵא בְּמִדְבַּר יְהוּדָה לֵאמֹר: 2 "שׁוּבוּ בִּתְשׁוּבָה, כִּי קָרְבָה מַלְכוּת שָׁמַיִם." 3 הוּא הָיָה זֶה שֶׁנֶּאֱמַר עָלָיו בְּפִי יְשַׁעְיָהוּ הַנָּבִיא: "קוֹל קוֹרֵא בַּמִּדְבָּר פַּנּוּ דֶרֶךְ יהוה, יַשְּׁרוּ מְסִלּוֹתָיו."

4 אוֹתוֹ יוֹחָנָן לְבוּשׁוֹ הָיָה מִשְּׂעַר גְּמַלִּים וַחֲגוֹרַת עוֹר עַל מָתְנָיו, וּמַאֲכָלוֹ חֲגָבִים וּדְבַשׁ הַיַּעַר. 5 אָז יָצְאוּ אֵלָיו יְרוּשָׁלַיִם וְכָל יְהוּדָה וְכָל כִּכַּר הַיַּרְדֵּן 6 וְהִטְבְּלוּ עַל־יָדָיו בַּיַּרְדֵּן כְּשֶׁהֵם מִתְוַדִּים עַל חַטֹּאתֵיהֶם.

7 כְּשֶׁרָאָה רַבִּים מִן הַפְּרוּשִׁים וְהַצְּדוֹקִים בָּאִים לְהִטָּבֵל אָמַר לָהֶם: "יַלְדֵי צִפְעוֹנִים, מִי הוֹרָה אֶתְכֶם לְהִמָּלֵט מִן הֶחָרוֹן הַבָּא? 8 לָכֵן עֲשׂוּ פְרִי רָאוּי לִתְשׁוּבָה 9 וְאַל תַּחְשְׁבוּ בִּלְבַבְכֶם לֵאמֹר, 'אַבְרָהָם הוּא אָבִינוּ, כִּי אֲנִי אוֹמֵר לָכֶם שֶׁמִּן הָאֲבָנִים הָאֵלֶּה

18 נ"ב: קוֹל בְּרָמָה נִשְׁמָע, נְהִי בְּכִי תַמְרוּרִים, רָחֵל מְבַכָּה עַל בָּנֶיהָ,
מֵאֲנָה לְהִנָּחֵם כִּי אֵינָם. (ירמיה ל"א: 14)

from these stones. ¹⁰ And even now the ax is laid to the root of the trees. Therefore every tree which does not bear good fruit is cut down and thrown into the fire. ¹¹ I indeed baptize you with water unto repentance, but He who is coming after me is mightier than I, whose sandals I am not worthy to carry. He will baptize you with the Holy Spirit and fire. ¹² His winnowing fan *is* in His hand, and He will thoroughly clean out His threshing floor, and gather His wheat into the barn; but He will burn up the chaff with unquenchable fire."

¹³ Then Jesus came from Galilee to John at the Jordan to be baptized by him. ¹⁴ And John *tried to* prevent Him, saying, "I need to be baptized by You, and are You coming to me?"

¹⁵ But Jesus answered and said to him, "Permit *it to be so* now, for thus it is fitting for us to fulfill all righteousness." Then he allowed Him.

¹⁶ When He had been baptized, Jesus came up immediately from the water; and behold, the heavens were opened to Him, and He saw the Spirit of God descending like a dove and alighting upon Him. ¹⁷ And suddenly a voice *came* from heaven, saying, "This is My beloved Son, in whom I am well pleased."

4 Then Jesus was led up by the Spirit into the wilderness to be tempted by the devil. ² And when He had fasted forty days and forty nights, afterward He was hungry. ³ Now when the tempter came to Him, he said, "If You are the Son of God, command that these stones become bread."

⁴ But He answered and said, "It is written, *'Man shall not live by bread alone, but by every word that proceeds from the mouth of God.'*"

⁵ Then the devil took Him up into the holy city, set Him on the pinnacle of the temple, ⁶ and said to Him, "If You are the Son of God, throw Yourself down. For it is written:

'He shall give His angels charge over you,'

and,

'In their hands they shall bear you up,
Lest you dash your foot against a stone.'"

⁷ Jesus said to him, "It is written again, *'You shall not tempt the LORD your God.'"*

⁸ Again, the devil took Him up on an exceedingly high mountain, and showed Him all the kingdoms of the world and their glory. ⁹ And he said to Him, "All these things I will give You if You will fall down and worship me."

¹⁰ Then Jesus said to him, "Away with you, Satan! For it is written, *'You shall worship the LORD your God, and Him only you shall serve.'"*

יָכוֹל אֱלֹהִים לְהָקִים בָּנִים לְאַבְרָהָם. ¹⁰ וּכְבָר מֻנָּח הַגַּרְזֶן עַל שֹׁרֶשׁ הָעֵצִים. עַל כֵּן כָּל עֵץ אֲשֶׁר אֵינֶנּוּ עוֹשֶׂה פְּרִי טוֹב יִגָּדַע וְיֻשְׁלַךְ לְתוֹךְ הָאֵשׁ. ¹¹ אֲנִי אָמְנָם מַטְבִּיל אֶתְכֶם בְּמַיִם לִתְשׁוּבָה, אַךְ הַבָּא אַחֲרַי חָזָק מִמֶּנִּי וְאֵינֶנִּי רָאוּי לָשֵׂאת אֶת נְעָלָיו. הוּא יַטְבִּיל אֶתְכֶם בְּרוּחַ הַקֹּדֶשׁ וּבָאֵשׁ. ¹² בְּיָדוֹ קִלְשׁוֹן הַמִּזְרֶה לְנַקּוֹת אֶת גָּרְנוֹ וְהוּא יֶאֱסֹף אֶת דְּגָנוֹ אֶל הָאָסָם, אַךְ אֶת הַמֹּץ יִשְׂרֹף בְּאֵשׁ בִּלְתִּי נִכְבֵּית."

¹³ אָז הִגִּיעַ יֵשׁוּעַ מִן הַגָּלִיל לַיַּרְדֵּן וּבָא אֶל יוֹחָנָן לְהִטָּבֵל אֶצְלוֹ, ¹⁴ אֶלָּא שֶׁיּוֹחָנָן נִסָּה לַהֲנִיאוֹ מִכָּךְ בְּאָמְרוֹ: "אֲנִי צָרִיךְ לְהִטָּבֵל אֶצְלְךָ, וְאַתָּה בָּא אֵלַי?"

¹⁵ הֵשִׁיב לוֹ יֵשׁוּעַ וְאָמַר: "הַנַּח כָּעֵת, כִּי מִן הָרָאוּי שֶׁנְּקַיֵּם אֶת הַצֶּדֶק כֻּלּוֹ." וְיוֹחָנָן הִנִּיחַ לוֹ. ¹⁶ יֵשׁוּעַ נִטְבַּל וְעָלָה מִיַּד מִן הַמַּיִם. אוֹתָהּ עֵת נִפְתְּחוּ הַשָּׁמַיִם וְהוּא רָאָה אֶת רוּחַ אֱלֹהִים יוֹרֶדֶת כְּיוֹנָה וּבָאָה עָלָיו. ¹⁷ וְהִנֵּה קוֹל מִן הַשָּׁמַיִם אוֹמֵר: "זֶה בְּנִי אֲהוּבִי אֲשֶׁר בּוֹ חָפַצְתִּי."

ד אָז הוֹבִילָה הָרוּחַ אֶת יֵשׁוּעַ אֶל הַמִּדְבָּר לְהִתְנַסּוֹת עַל־יְדֵי הַשָּׂטָן, ² וּלְאַחַר שֶׁצָּם אַרְבָּעִים יוֹם וְאַרְבָּעִים לַיְלָה הָיָה רָעֵב. ³ נִגַּשׁ אֵלָיו הַמְנַסֶּה וְאָמַר: "אִם בֶּן־הָאֱלֹהִים אַתָּה, צַוֵּה שֶׁהָאֲבָנִים הָאֵלֶּה יִהְיוּ לְלֶחֶם." ⁴ הֵשִׁיב יֵשׁוּעַ וְאָמַר: "כָּתוּב, 'לֹא עַל־הַלֶּחֶם לְבַדּוֹ יִחְיֶה הָאָדָם, כִּי עַל־כָּל־מוֹצָא פִי־יהוה'."

⁵ לָקַח אוֹתוֹ הַשָּׂטָן אֶל עִיר הַקֹּדֶשׁ וְהֶעֱמִידוֹ עַל פִּנַּת גַּג בֵּית הַמִּקְדָּשׁ. ⁶ אָמַר לוֹ: "אִם בֶּן־הָאֱלֹהִים אַתָּה, הַשְׁלֵךְ עַצְמְךָ לְמַטָּה, שֶׁהֲרֵי כָּתוּב, 'כִּי מַלְאָכָיו יְצַוֶּה־לָּךְ, עַל־כַּפַּיִם יִשָּׂאוּנְךָ, פֶּן־תִּגֹּף בָּאֶבֶן רַגְלֶךָ'."

⁷ אָמַר לוֹ יֵשׁוּעַ: "עוֹד כָּתוּב, 'לֹא תְנַסֶּה אֶת־יהוה אֱלֹהֶיךָ'."

⁸ לָקַח אוֹתוֹ הַשָּׂטָן לְהַר גָּבֹהַּ מְאֹד וְהֶרְאָה לוֹ אֶת כָּל מַמְלְכוֹת תֵּבֵל וּכְבוֹדָן. ⁹ אָמַר אֵלָיו: "אֶת כָּל אֵלֶּה אֶתֵּן לְךָ אִם תִּפֹּל עַל פָּנֶיךָ וְתִשְׁתַּחֲוֶה לִי."

¹⁰ הֵשִׁיב לוֹ יֵשׁוּעַ: "הִסְתַּלֵּק, הַשָּׂטָן, הֵן כָּתוּב, 'לַיהוה אֱלֹהֶיךָ תִּשְׁתַּחֲוֶה וְאוֹתוֹ לְבַדּוֹ תַּעֲבֹד'."

11 Then the devil left Him, and behold, angels came and ministered to Him.

12 Now when Jesus heard that John had been put in prison, He departed to Galilee. 13 And leaving Nazareth, He came and dwelt in Capernaum, which is by the sea, in the regions of Zebulun and Naphtali, 14 that it might be fulfilled which was spoken by Isaiah the prophet, saying:

15 "The land of Zebulun and the land of Naphtali,
    By the way of the sea, beyond the Jordan,
    Galilee of the Gentiles:
16 The people who sat in darkness have seen a great
        light,
    And upon those who sat in the region and
        shadow of death
    Light has dawned."

17 From that time Jesus began to preach and to say, "Repent, for the kingdom of heaven is at hand."

18 And Jesus, walking by the Sea of Galilee, saw two brothers, Simon called Peter, and Andrew his brother, casting a net into the sea; for they were fishermen. 19 Then He said to them, "Follow Me, and I will make you fishers of men." 20 They immediately left *their* nets and followed Him.

21 Going on from there, He saw two other brothers, James *the son* of Zebedee, and John his brother, in the boat with Zebedee their father, mending their nets. He called them, 22 and immediately they left the boat and their father, and followed Him.

23 And Jesus went about all Galilee, teaching in their synagogues, preaching the gospel of the kingdom, and healing all kinds of sickness and all kinds of disease among the people. 24 Then His fame went throughout all Syria; and they brought to Him all sick people who were afflicted with various diseases and torments, and those who were demon-possessed, epileptics, and paralytics; and He healed them. 25 Great multitudes followed Him—from Galilee, and *from* Decapolis, Jerusalem, Judea, and beyond the Jordan.

5 And seeing the multitudes, He went up on a mountain, and when He was seated His disciples came to Him. 2 Then He opened His mouth and taught them, saying:

3 "Blessed *are* the poor in spirit,
      For theirs is the kingdom of heaven.
4   Blessed *are* those who mourn,
      For they shall be comforted.
5   Blessed *are* the meek,
      For they shall inherit the earth.
6   Blessed *are* those who hunger and thirst for
        righteousness,

11 לְאַחַר מִכֵּן עָזַב אוֹתוֹ הַשָּׂטָן וּמַלְאָכִים נִגְּשׁוּ לְשָׁרְתוֹ.

12 כַּאֲשֶׁר שָׁמַע יֵשׁוּעַ כִּי הִסְגִּירוּ אֶת יוֹחָנָן יָצָא אֶל הַגָּלִיל. 13 הוּא עָזַב אֶת נָצְרַת וּבָא לָגוּר בִּכְפַר נַחוּם לְיַד הַיָּם, בְּחֶבֶל זְבוּלוּן וְנַפְתָּלִי, 14 לְמַעַן יִתְקַיֵּם הַנֶּאֱמַר בְּפִי יְשַׁעְיָהוּ הַנָּבִיא: 15 "אַרְצָה זְבוּלוּן וְאַרְצָה נַפְתָּלִי, דֶּרֶךְ הַיָּם, עֵבֶר הַיַּרְדֵּן, גְּלִיל הַגּוֹיִם. 16 הָעָם הַהֹלְכִים בַּחֹשֶׁךְ רָאוּ אוֹר גָּדוֹל, יֹשְׁבֵי בְּאֶרֶץ צַלְמָוֶת אוֹר נָגַהּ עֲלֵיהֶם."

17 מִן הָעֵת הַהִיא הֵחֵל יֵשׁוּעַ לְהַכְרִיז וְלוֹמַר: "חִזְרוּ בִתְשׁוּבָה, כִּי קָרְבָה מַלְכוּת שָׁמַיִם."

18 כְּשֶׁהָלַךְ לְיַד יָם הַגָּלִיל רָאָה שְׁנֵי אַחִים, אֶת שִׁמְעוֹן הַנִּקְרָא כֵּיפָא וְאֶת אַנְדְּרֵי אָחִיו, מַשְׁלִיכִים רֶשֶׁת לְתוֹךְ הַיָּם, כִּי דַיָּגִים הָיוּ. 19 אָמַר לָהֶם: "בּוֹאוּ אַחֲרַי וְאֶעֱשֶׂה אֶתְכֶם דַּיָּגֵי אָדָם." 20 מִיָּד עָזְבוּ אֶת הָרְשָׁתוֹת וְהָלְכוּ אַחֲרָיו.

21 בְּלֶכְתּוֹ הָלְאָה רָאָה שְׁנֵי אַחִים אֲחֵרִים, אֶת יַעֲקֹב בֶּן זַבְדַּי וְאֶת יוֹחָנָן אָחִיו, בַּסְּפִינָה עִם זַבְדַּי אֲבִיהֶם וְהֵם מְתַקְּנִים אֶת רִשְׁתוֹתֵיהֶם. קָרָא לָהֶם 22 וּמִיָּד עָזְבוּ אֶת הַסְּפִינָה וְאֶת אֲבִיהֶם וְהָלְכוּ אַחֲרָיו.

23 הוּא סָבַב בְּכָל הַגָּלִיל כְּשֶׁהוּא מְלַמֵּד בְּבָתֵּי הַכְּנֶסֶת וּמַכְרִיז אֶת בְּשׂוֹרַת הַמַּלְכוּת וּמְרַפֵּא כָּל מַחֲלָה וְכָל מַדְוֶה בָּעָם. 24 שִׁמְעוֹ יָצָא בְּכָל סוּרְיָה וְהֵבִיאוּ אֵלָיו אֶת כָּל הַחוֹלִים הַסּוֹבְלִים מִמַּחֲלוֹת וּמַכְאוֹבִים לְמִינֵיהֶם, וְגַם אֲנָשִׁים אֲחוּזֵי שֵׁדִים, מְכֵּי יֶרַח וּמְשֻׁתָּקִים, וְהוּא רִפֵּא אוֹתָם. 25 הֲמוֹנִים הֲמוֹנִים הָלְכוּ אַחֲרָיו מֵהַגָּלִיל וּמִדֶּקַפּוֹלִיס, מִירוּשָׁלַיִם וִיהוּדָה וּמֵעֵבֶר הַיַּרְדֵּן.

ה כִּרְאוֹתוֹ אֶת הֲמוֹן הָעָם עָלָה בְּמַעֲלֵה הָהָר וְיָשַׁב, וְתַלְמִידָיו נִגְּשׁוּ אֵלָיו. 2 פָּתַח פִּיו וְלִמֵּד אוֹתָם בְּאָמְרוֹ:

3 "אַשְׁרֵי עֲנִיֵּי הָרוּחַ, כִּי לָהֶם מַלְכוּת הַשָּׁמַיִם. 4 אַשְׁרֵי הָאֲבֵלִים, כִּי הֵם יְנֻחָמוּ. 5 אַשְׁרֵי הָעֲנָוִים, כִּי הֵם יִירְשׁוּ אֶת הָאָרֶץ. 6 אַשְׁרֵי הָרְעֵבִים וְהַצְּמֵאִים

For they shall be filled.

7 Blessed *are* the merciful,
   For they shall obtain mercy.

8 Blessed *are* the pure in heart,
   For they shall see God.

9 Blessed *are* the peacemakers,
   For they shall be called sons of God.

10 Blessed are those who are persecuted for
    righteousness' sake,
    For theirs is the kingdom of heaven.

11 "Blessed are you when they revile and persecute you, and say all kinds of evil against you
falsely for My sake. 12 Rejoice and be exceedingly
glad, for great *is* your reward in heaven, for so they
persecuted the prophets who were before you.

13 "You are the salt of the earth; but if the salt
loses its flavor, how shall it be seasoned? It is then
good for nothing but to be thrown out and
trampled underfoot by men.

14 "You are the light of the world. A city that is
set on a hill cannot be hidden. 15 Nor do they light a
lamp and put it under a basket, but on a lampstand,
and it gives light to all *who are* in the house. 16 Let
your light so shine before men, that they may see
your good works and glorify your Father in heaven.

17 "Do not think that I came to destroy the Law
or the Prophets. I did not come to destroy but to
fulfill. 18 For assuredly, I say to you, till heaven and
earth pass away, one jot or one tittle will by no
means pass from the law till all is fulfilled. 19 Whoever therefore breaks one of the least of these
commandments, and teaches men so, shall be called
least in the kingdom of heaven; but whoever does
and teaches *them,* he shall be called great in the
kingdom of heaven. 20 For I say to you, that unless
your righteousness exceeds *the righteousness* of the
scribes and Pharisees, you will by no means enter
the kingdom of heaven.

21 "You have heard that it was said to those of
old, 'You *shall not murder,* and whoever murders
will be in danger of the judgment.' 22 But I say to
you that whoever is angry with his brother without
a cause shall be in danger of the judgment. And
whoever says to his brother, 'Raca!' shall be in
danger of the council. But whoever says, 'You fool!'
shall be in danger of hell fire. 23 Therefore if you
bring your gift to the altar, and there remember that
your brother has something against you, 24 leave
your gift there before the altar, and go your way.
First be reconciled to your brother, and then come
and offer your gift. 25 Agree with your adversary
quickly, while you are on the way with him, lest
your adversary deliver you to the judge, the judge
hand you over to the officer, and you be thrown

לְצֶדֶק, כִּי הֵם יִשְׂבָּעוּ. 7 אַשְׁרֵי הָרַחֲמָנִים, כִּי הֵם
יְרֻחָמוּ. 8 אַשְׁרֵי בָּרֵי לֵבָב, כִּי הֵם יִרְאוּ אֶת אֱלֹהִים.
9 אַשְׁרֵי רוֹדְפֵי שָׁלוֹם, כִּי בְנֵי אֱלֹהִים יִקָּרְאוּ. 10 אַשְׁרֵי
הַנִּרְדָּפִים בִּגְלַל הַצֶּדֶק, כִּי לָהֶם מַלְכוּת הַשָּׁמַיִם.
11 אַשְׁרֵיכֶם אִם יְחָרְפוּ וְיִרְדְּפוּ אֶתְכֶם וְיַעֲלִילוּ עֲלֵיכֶם
בִּגְלָלִי. 12 שִׂמְחוּ וְגִילוּ, כִּי שְׂכַרְכֶם רַב בַּשָּׁמַיִם; הֲרֵי
כָּךְ רָדְפוּ אֶת הַנְּבִיאִים שֶׁהָיוּ לִפְנֵיכֶם."

13 "אַתֶּם מֶלַח הָאָרֶץ, וְאִם תֹּאבַד לַמֶּלַח מְלִיחוּתוֹ,
כֵּיצַד תַּחֲזֹר לוֹ? הֵן לֹא יִצְלַח עוֹד לְשׁוּם דָּבָר כִּי אִם
לְהַשְׁלִיכוֹ הַחוּצָה לִהְיוֹת מִרְמָס לְרַגְלֵי הַבְּרִיּוֹת.
14 אַתֶּם אוֹר הָעוֹלָם. עִיר שׁוֹכֶנֶת עַל הַר אֵינָה
יְכוֹלָה לְהִסָּתֵר. 15 גַּם אֵין מַדְלִיקִים מְנוֹרָה וְשָׂמִים
אוֹתָהּ תַּחַת כְּלִי, אֶלָּא עַל כֵּן שָׁמִים אוֹתָהּ וְאָז
תָּאִיר לְכָל בָּאֵי הַבַּיִת. 16 כָּךְ יָאֵר נָא אוֹרְכֶם לִפְנֵי
בְּנֵי אָדָם, לְמַעַן יִרְאוּ אֶת מַעֲשֵׂיכֶם הַטּוֹבִים וִיכַבְּדוּ
אֶת אֲבִיכֶם שֶׁבַּשָּׁמַיִם."

17 "אַל תַּחְשְׁבוּ שֶׁבָּאתִי לְבַטֵּל אֶת הַתּוֹרָה אוֹ אֶת
הַנְּבִיאִים; לֹא בָּאתִי לְבַטֵּל כִּי אִם לְקַיֵּם. 18 אָמֵן.
אוֹמֵר אֲנִי לָכֶם, עַד אֲשֶׁר יַעַבְרוּ הַשָּׁמַיִם וְהָאָרֶץ אַף
יוֹד אַחַת אוֹ תָּג אֶחָד לֹא יַעַבְרוּ מִן הַתּוֹרָה בְּטֶרֶם
יִתְקַיֵּם הַכֹּל. 19 לָכֵן כָּל הַמֵּפֵר אַחַת מִן הַמִּצְווֹת
הַקְּטַנּוֹת הָאֵלֶּה וּמְלַמֵּד כָּךְ אֶת הַבְּרִיּוֹת, קָטוֹן יִקָּרֵא
בְּמַלְכוּת הַשָּׁמַיִם. אֲבָל כָּל הָעוֹשֶׂה וּמְלַמֵּד, הוּא
גָּדוֹל יִקָּרֵא בְּמַלְכוּת הַשָּׁמַיִם. 20 אוֹמֵר אֲנִי לָכֶם, אִם
לֹא תִהְיֶה צִדְקַתְכֶם מְרֻבָּה מִצִּדְקַת הַסּוֹפְרִים
וְהַפְּרוּשִׁים לֹא תִכָּנְסוּ לְמַלְכוּת הַשָּׁמַיִם."

21 "שְׁמַעְתֶּם כִּי נֶאֱמַר לָרִאשׁוֹנִים 'לֹא תִרְצַח', וְכָל
רוֹצֵחַ חַיָּב לַעֲמֹד לְדִין'. 22 וַאֲנִי אוֹמֵר לָכֶם: כָּל
הַכּוֹעֵס עַל אָחִיו חַיָּב לַעֲמֹד לְדִין; הָאוֹמֵר לְאָחִיו
'רֵיק' חַיָּב לַעֲמֹד לְמִשְׁפַּט הַסַּנְהֶדְרִין; וְהָאוֹמֵר 'אֱוִיל'
דִּינוֹ אֵשׁ גֵּיהִנּוֹם. 23 לָכֵן אִם תָּבִיא אֶת קָרְבָּנְךָ אֶל
הַמִּזְבֵּחַ וְשָׁם תִּזְכֹּר כִּי לְאָחִיךָ דָּבָר נֶגְדְּךָ, 24 עֲזֹב אֶת
קָרְבָּנְךָ שָׁם לִפְנֵי הַמִּזְבֵּחַ וְלֵךְ תְּחִלָּה לְהִתְרַצּוֹת
לְאָחִיךָ וְאַחַר כָּךְ בּוֹא וְהַקְרֵב אֶת קָרְבָּנְךָ. 25 מַהֵר
לְהִתְפַּיֵּס עִם אִישׁ רִיבְךָ בְּעוֹדְךָ בַּדֶּרֶךְ אִתּוֹ, פֶּן יִמְסֹר
אוֹתְךָ לַשּׁוֹפֵט וְהַשּׁוֹפֵט יִמְסֹר אוֹתְךָ לַשּׁוֹטֵר וְתֻשְׁלַךְ

into prison. 26 Assuredly, I say to you, you will by no means get out of there till you have paid the last penny.

27 "You have heard that it was said to those of old, 'You shall not commit adultery.' 28 But I say to you that whoever looks at a woman to lust for her has already committed adultery with her in his heart. 29 If your right eye causes you to sin, pluck it out and cast it from you; for it is more profitable for you that one of your members perish, than for your whole body to be cast into hell. 30 And if your right hand causes you to sin, cut it off and cast it from you; for it is more profitable for you that one of your members perish, than for your whole body to be cast into hell.

31 "Furthermore it has been said, 'Whoever divorces his wife, let him give her a certificate of divorce.' 32 But I say to you that whoever divorces his wife for any reason except sexual immorality causes her to commit adultery; and whoever marries a woman who is divorced commits adultery.

33 "Again you have heard that it was said to those of old, 'You shall not swear falsely, but shall perform your oaths to the Lord.' 34 But I say to you, do not swear at all: neither by heaven, for it is God's throne; 35 nor by the earth, for it is His footstool; nor by Jerusalem, for it is the city of the great King. 36 Nor shall you swear by your head, because you cannot make one hair white or black. 37 But let your 'Yes' be 'Yes,' and your 'No,' 'No.' For whatever is more than these is from the evil one.

38 "You have heard that it was said, 'An eye for an eye and a tooth for a tooth.' 39 But I tell you not to resist an evil person. But whoever slaps you on your right cheek, turn the other to him also. 40 If anyone wants to sue you and take away your tunic, let him have your cloak also. 41 And whoever compels you to go one mile, go with him two. 42 Give to him who asks you, and from him who wants to borrow from you do not turn away.

43 "You have heard that it was said, 'You shall love your neighbor and hate your enemy.' 44 But I say to you, love your enemies, bless those who curse you, do good to those who hate you, and pray for those who spitefully use you and persecute you, 45 that you may be sons of your Father in heaven; for He makes His sun rise on the evil and on the good, and sends rain on the just and on the unjust. 46 For if you love those who love you, what reward have you? Do not even the tax collectors do the same? 47 And if you greet your brethren only, what

לְבֵית הַסֹּהַר. 26 אָמֵן אוֹמֵר אֲנִי לְךָ, לֹא תֵצֵא מִשָּׁם עַד אֲשֶׁר תְּשַׁלֵּם אֶת הַפְּרוּטָה הָאַחֲרוֹנָה."

27 "שְׁמַעְתֶּם כִּי נֶאֱמַר 'לֹא תִנְאָף'. 28 וַאֲנִי אוֹמֵר לָכֶם שֶׁכָּל הַמַּבִּיט בְּאִשָּׁה מִתּוֹךְ תַּאֲוָה אֵלֶיהָ כְּבָר נָאַף אוֹתָהּ בְּלִבּוֹ. 29 אִם עֵינְךָ הַיְמָנִית תַּכְשִׁיל אוֹתְךָ, נַקֵּר אוֹתָהּ וְהַשְׁלֵךְ אוֹתָהּ מִמְּךָ, כִּי מוּטָב לְךָ שֶׁיֹּאבַד אֶחָד מֵאֵבָרֶיךָ מִשֶּׁיֻּשְׁלַךְ כָּל גּוּפְךָ לְגֵיהִנֹּם. 30 וְאִם יָדְךָ הַיְמָנִית תַּכְשִׁיל אוֹתְךָ, קַצֵּץ אוֹתָהּ וְהַשְׁלֵךְ אוֹתָהּ מִמְּךָ, כִּי מוּטָב לְךָ שֶׁיֹּאבַד אֶחָד מֵאֵבָרֶיךָ מֵרֶדֶת כָּל גּוּפְךָ לְגֵיהִנֹּם."

31 "נֶאֱמַר, 'אִישׁ כִּי יְשַׁלַּח אֶת אִשְׁתּוֹ יִתֶּן לָהּ סֵפֶר כְּרִיתוּת'. 32 וַאֲנִי אוֹמֵר לָכֶם: כָּל הַמְגָרֵשׁ אֶת אִשְׁתּוֹ חוּץ מֵאֲשֶׁר עַל-דְּבַר זְנוּת, עוֹשֶׂה אוֹתָהּ לְנוֹאֶפֶת, וְהַלּוֹקֵחַ אֶת הַגְּרוּשָׁה לְאִשָּׁה נוֹאֵף הוּא."

33 "עוֹד שְׁמַעְתֶּם כִּי נֶאֱמַר לָרִאשׁוֹנִים 'לֹא תִשָּׁבַע לַשֶּׁקֶר וְשַׁלֵּם לַאדֹנָי נְדָרֶיךָ'. 34 וַאֲנִי אוֹמֵר לָכֶם שֶׁלֹּא לְהִשָּׁבַע בִּכְלָל: לֹא בַּשָּׁמַיִם, כִּי כִּסֵּא אֱלֹהִים הֵם; 35 אַף לֹא בָאָרֶץ, כִּי הֲדֹם רַגְלָיו הִיא; וְלֹא בִּירוּשָׁלַיִם, שֶׁהֲרֵי קִרְיַת מֶלֶךְ רָב הִיא. 36 גַּם בְּרֹאשְׁךָ אַל תִּשָּׁבַע, כִּי אֵינְךָ יָכוֹל לַהֲפֹךְ שַׂעֲרָה אַחַת לְלָבָן אוֹ לִשְׁחוֹרָה. 37 אַךְ תְּהֵא מִלַּתְכֶם 'כֵּן' כֵּן, 'לֹא' לֹא. יוֹתֵר מִזֶּה מִן הָרָע הוּא."

38 "שְׁמַעְתֶּם כִּי נֶאֱמַר 'עַיִן תַּחַת עַיִן, שֵׁן תַּחַת שֵׁן'. 39 וַאֲנִי אוֹמֵר לָכֶם שֶׁלֹּא לְהִתְקוֹמֵם עַל עוֹשֶׂה הָרָע. אַדְּרַבָּא, הַסּוֹטֵר לְךָ עַל הַלְּחִי הַיְמָנִית, הַפְנֵה אֵלָיו גַּם אֶת הָאַחֶרֶת. 40 מִי שֶׁרוֹצֶה לִתְבֹּעַ אוֹתְךָ לַדִּין כְּדֵי לָקַחַת אֶת כֻּתָּנְתְּךָ, הַנַּח לוֹ גַּם אֶת מְעִילְךָ. 41 וּמִי שֶׁמְּאַלֵּץ אוֹתְךָ לָלֶכֶת אִתּוֹ מֶרְחָק שֶׁל מִיל אֶחָד, לֵךְ אִתּוֹ שְׁנַיִם. 42 תֵּן לַמְבַקֵּשׁ מִמְּךָ וְאַל תִּפְנֶה מִן הָרוֹצֶה לִלְווֹת מִמְּךָ."

43 "שְׁמַעְתֶּם כִּי נֶאֱמַר 'אֱהַב אֶת רֵעֲךָ וְשִׂנְא אֶת אוֹיִבְךָ'. 44 וַאֲנִי אוֹמֵר לָכֶם, אֶהֱבוּ אֶת אוֹיְבֵיכֶם וְהִתְפַּלְלוּ בְּעַד רוֹדְפֵיכֶם, 45 לְמַעַן תִּהְיוּ בָנִים לַאֲבִיכֶם שֶׁבַּשָּׁמַיִם, כִּי הוּא מַזְרִיחַ שִׁמְשׁוֹ עַל רָעִים וְעַל טוֹבִים וּמַמְטִיר גֶּשֶׁם עַל צַדִּיקִים וְעַל רְשָׁעִים. 46 הֵן אִם תֹּאהֲבוּ אֶת אוֹהֲבֵיכֶם מַה שְּׂכַרְכֶם? הֲלֹא גַּם הַמּוֹכְסִים עוֹשִׂים זֹאת. 47 וְאִם תִּשְׁאֲלוּ בִּשְׁלוֹם אֲחֵיכֶם בִּלְבַד, מַהוּ הַמְיֻחָד שֶׁאַתֶּם עוֹשִׂים? הֲלֹא

do you do more *than others?* Do not even the tax collectors do so? ⁴⁸Therefore you shall be perfect, just as your Father in heaven is perfect.

6 "Take heed that you do not do your charitable deeds before men, to be seen by them. Otherwise you have no reward from your Father in heaven. ²Therefore, when you do a charitable deed, do not sound a trumpet before you as the hypocrites do in the synagogues and in the streets, that they may have glory from men. Assuredly, I say to you, they have their reward. ³But when you do a charitable deed, do not let your left hand know what your right hand is doing, ⁴that your charitable deed may be in secret; and your Father who sees in secret will Himself reward you openly.

⁵"And when you pray, you shall not be like the hypocrites. For they love to pray standing in the synagogues and on the corners of the streets, that they may be seen by men. Assuredly, I say to you, they have their reward. ⁶But you, when you pray, go into your room, and when you have shut your door, pray to your Father who *is* in the secret *place;* and your Father who sees in secret will reward you openly. ⁷And when you pray, do not use vain repetitions as the heathen *do.* For they think that they will be heard for their many words.

⁸"Therefore do not be like them. For your Father knows the things you have need of before you ask Him. ⁹In this manner, therefore, pray:

Our Father in heaven,
Hallowed be Your name.
¹⁰ Your kingdom come.
Your will be done
On earth as *it is* in heaven.
¹¹ Give us this day our daily bread.
¹² And forgive us our debts,
As we forgive our debtors.
¹³ And do not lead us into temptation,
But deliver us from the evil one.
For Yours is the kingdom and the power and the glory forever. Amen.

¹⁴"For if you forgive men their trespasses, your heavenly Father will also forgive you. ¹⁵But if you do not forgive men their trespasses, neither will your Father forgive your trespasses.

¹⁶"Moreover, when you fast, do not be like the hypocrites, with a sad countenance. For they disfigure their faces that they may appear to men to be fasting. Assuredly, I say to you, they have their reward. ¹⁷But you, when you fast, anoint your head and wash your face, ¹⁸so that you do not

גַּם הַגּוֹיִים עוֹשִׂים זֹאת. 48לָכֵן הֱיוּ שְׁלֵמִים, כְּמוֹ שֶׁאֲבִיכֶם שֶׁבַּשָּׁמַיִם שָׁלֵם הוּא."

ו 1"הִשָּׁמְרוּ מִלַּעֲשׂוֹת אֶת צִדְקַתְכֶם לִפְנֵי בְּנֵי אָדָם מִתּוֹךְ כַּוָּנָה שֶׁיִּרְאוּ אֶתְכֶם; אִם תַּעֲשׂוּ כֵן, אֵין לָכֶם שָׂכָר אֵצֶל אֲבִיכֶם שֶׁבַּשָּׁמַיִם. 2לָכֵן בַּעֲשׂוֹתְךָ מַעֲשֵׂי חֶסֶד אַל תַּשְׁמִיעַ קוֹל תְּרוּעָה לְפָנֶיךָ כְּמוֹ שֶׁעוֹשִׂים הַצְּבוּעִים בְּבָתֵּי הַכְּנֶסֶת וּבָרְחוֹבוֹת כְּדֵי שֶׁיְּכַבְּדוּ אוֹתָם הַבְּרִיּוֹת. אָמֵן אוֹמֵר אֲנִי לָכֶם, שְׂכָרָם אִתָּם. 3וְאַתָּה בַּעֲשׂוֹתְךָ מַעֲשֵׂה חֶסֶד אַל תֵּדַע שְׂמֹאלְךָ אֶת אֲשֶׁר עוֹשָׂה יְמִינֶךָ, 4לְמַעַן יִהְיוּ חֲסָדֶיךָ בַּסֵּתֶר וְאָבִיךָ הָרוֹאֶה בַּמִּסְתָּרִים יִגְמֹל לָךְ."

5"כַּאֲשֶׁר אַתֶּם מִתְפַּלְּלִים אַל תִּהְיוּ כַּצְּבוּעִים, הָאוֹהֲבִים לְהִתְפַּלֵּל בְּעָמְדָם בְּבָתֵּי כְּנֶסֶת וּבְפִנּוֹת שֶׁל רְחוֹבוֹת לְמַעַן יֵרָאוּ לִבְנֵי אָדָם. אָמֵן אוֹמֵר אֲנִי לָכֶם, שְׂכָרָם אִתָּם. 6וְאַתָּה כַּאֲשֶׁר תִּתְפַּלֵּל הִכָּנֵס לַחֲדָרְךָ, סְגֹר אֶת הַדֶּלֶת וְהִתְפַּלֵּל לְאָבִיךָ אֲשֶׁר בַּסֵּתֶר, וְאָבִיךָ הָרוֹאֶה בַּמִּסְתָּרִים יִגְמֹל לָךְ. 7כַּאֲשֶׁר אַתֶּם מִתְפַּלְּלִים הִמָּנְעוּ מִלְּהַגֵּב מִלִּים פְּגוּיִים, הַחוֹשְׁבִים שֶׁבְּרֹב דִּבּוּרִים יִשָּׁמְעוּ. 8אַל תִּהְיוּ דוֹמִים לָהֶם, כִּי יוֹדֵעַ אֲבִיכֶם אֶת צָרְכֵיכֶם בְּטֶרֶם תְּבַקְשׁוּ מִמֶּנּוּ. 9לָכֵן כָּךְ הִתְפַּלְּלוּ אַתֶּם:
'אָבִינוּ שֶׁבַּשָּׁמַיִם, יִתְקַדַּשׁ שְׁמֶךָ,
10תָּבוֹא מַלְכוּתְךָ, יֵעָשֶׂה רְצוֹנְךָ כְּבַשָּׁמַיִם כֵּן בָּאָרֶץ.
11אֶת לֶחֶם חֻקֵּנוּ תֶּן לָנוּ הַיּוֹם,
12וּסְלַח לָנוּ עַל חֲטָאֵינוּ כְּפִי שֶׁסּוֹלְחִים גַּם אֲנַחְנוּ לַחוֹטְאִים לָנוּ.
13וְאַל תְּבִיאֵנוּ לִידֵי נִסָּיוֹן, כִּי אִם חַלְּצֵנוּ מִן הָרַע.' 14כִּי אִם תִּסְלְחוּ לִבְנֵי אָדָם עַל חַטֹּאתֵיהֶם, גַּם אֲבִיכֶם שֶׁבַּשָּׁמַיִם יִסְלַח לָכֶם. 15וְאִם לֹא תִּסְלְחוּ לִבְנֵי אָדָם, גַּם אֲבִיכֶם לֹא יִסְלַח לָכֶם עַל חַטֹּאתֵיכֶם."

16"כַּאֲשֶׁר אַתֶּם צָמִים אַל תְּהַלְכוּ קוֹדְרִים כְּמוֹ הַצְּבוּעִים, הַמְשַׁנִּים אֶת פְּנֵיהֶם כְּדֵי לְהֵרָאוֹת צָמִים לִבְנֵי אָדָם. אָמֵן אוֹמֵר אֲנִי לָכֶם, שְׂכָרָם אִתָּם. 17וְאַתָּה כַּאֲשֶׁר תָּצוּם מְשַׁח אֶת רֹאשְׁךָ בְּשֶׁמֶן וּרְחַץ אֶת פָּנֶיךָ, 18כְּדֵי שֶׁלֹּא תֵּרָאֶה צָם לִבְנֵי אָדָם כִּי אִם

appear to men to be fasting, but to your Father who *is* in the secret *place;* and your Father who sees in secret will reward you openly.

[19] "Do not lay up for yourselves treasures on earth, where moth and rust destroy and where thieves break in and steal; [20] but lay up for yourselves treasures in heaven, where neither moth nor rust destroys and where thieves do not break in and steal. [21] For where your treasure is, there your heart will be also.

[22] "The lamp of the body is the eye. If therefore your eye is good, your whole body will be full of light. [23] But if your eye is bad, your whole body will be full of darkness. If therefore the light that is in you is darkness, how great *is* that darkness!

[24] "No one can serve two masters; for either he will hate the one and love the other, or else he will be loyal to the one and despise the other. You cannot serve God and mammon.

[25] "Therefore I say to you, do not worry about your life, what you will eat or what you will drink; nor about your body, what you will put on. Is not life more than food and the body more than clothing? [26] Look at the birds of the air, for they neither sow nor reap nor gather into barns; yet your heavenly Father feeds them. Are you not of more value than they? [27] Which of you by worrying can add one cubit to his stature?

[28] "So why do you worry about clothing? Consider the lilies of the field, how they grow: they neither toil nor spin; [29] and yet I say to you that even Solomon in all his glory was not arrayed like one of these. [30] Now if God so clothes the grass of the field, which today is, and tomorrow is thrown into the oven, *will He* not much more *clothe* you, O you of little faith?

[31] "Therefore do not worry, saying, 'What shall we eat?' or 'What shall we drink?' or 'What shall we wear?' [32] For after all these things the Gentiles seek. For your heavenly Father knows that you need all these things. [33] But seek first the kingdom of God and His righteousness, and all these things shall be added to you. [34] Therefore do not worry about tomorrow, for tomorrow will worry about its own things. Sufficient for the day *is* its own trouble.

7 "Judge not, that you be not judged. [2] For with what judgment you judge, you will be judged; and with the measure you use, it will be measured back to you. [3] And why do you look at the speck in your brother's eye, but do not consider the plank in your own eye? [4] Or how can you say to your brother, 'Let me remove the speck from your eye'; and look, a

לְאָבִיךָ אֲשֶׁר בַּסֵּתֶר, וְאָבִיךָ הָרוֹאֶה בַּמִּסְתָּרִים הוּא יִגְמֹל לָךְ."

[19] "אַל תַּאַצְרוּ לָכֶם אוֹצָרוֹת עֲלֵי אֲדָמוֹת, בְּמָקוֹם שֶׁהָעָשׁ וְהֶחָלוּדָה מַשְׁחִיתִים וְהַגַּנָּבִים חוֹפְרִים וְגוֹנְבִים. [20] אִצְרוּ לָכֶם אוֹצָרוֹת בַּשָּׁמַיִם, בְּמָקוֹם אֲשֶׁר עָשׁ וַחֲלוּדָה לֹא יַשְׁחִיתוּ וְגַנָּבִים לֹא יַחְפְּרוּ וְלֹא יִגְנֹבוּ; [21] כִּי בַּמָּקוֹם שֶׁאוֹצָרְךָ נִמְצָא, שָׁם יִהְיֶה גַּם לְבָבְךָ.

[22] "מְנוֹרַת הַגּוּף הִיא הָעָיִן. לְפִיכָךְ אִם עֵינְךָ טוֹבָה כָּל גּוּפְךָ יָאוֹר. [23] אַךְ אִם עֵינְךָ רָעָה כָּל גּוּפְךָ יֶחְשַׁךְ; וְאִם יֶחְשַׁךְ הָאוֹר אֲשֶׁר בְּקִרְבְּךָ, מָה רַב הַחֹשֶׁךְ!

[24] "אֵין אִישׁ יָכוֹל לַעֲבֹד שְׁנֵי אֲדוֹנִים, שֶׁכֵּן אוֹ יִשְׂנָא אֶחָד וְיֹאהַב אֶת הַשֵּׁנִי, אוֹ יִהְיֶה מָסוּר לְאֶחָד וְיִלְזַל בַּשֵּׁנִי. אֵינְכֶם יְכוֹלִים לַעֲבֹד אֶת הָאֱלֹהִים וְאֶת הַמָּמוֹן."

[25] "לָכֵן אוֹמֵר אֲנִי לָכֶם: אַל תִּדְאֲגוּ לְנַפְשְׁכֶם – מַה תֹּאכְלוּ אוֹ מַה תִּשְׁתּוּ, וּלְגוּפְכֶם – מַה תִּלְבָּשׁוּ. הֲלֹא הַנֶּפֶשׁ חֲשׁוּבָה מִן הַמָּזוֹן, וְהַגּוּף חָשׁוּב מִן הַלְּבוּשׁ. [26] הַבִּיטוּ אֶל עוֹף הַשָּׁמַיִם: אֵינָם זוֹרְעִים וְאֵינָם קוֹצְרִים, אַף אֵינָם אוֹסְפִים אֶל אֲסָמִים, וַאֲבִיכֶם שֶׁבַּשָּׁמַיִם מְכַלְכֵּל אוֹתָם. הֲלֹא אַתֶּם חֲשׁוּבִים יוֹתֵר מֵהֶם. [27] וּמִי מִכֶּם בְּדַאֲגָתוֹ יָכוֹל לְהוֹסִיף טֶפַח אֶחָד עַל שְׁנוֹת חַיָּיו? [28] וְלָמָּה אַתֶּם דּוֹאֲגִים לַלְּבוּשׁ? הִתְבּוֹנְנוּ אֶל שׁוֹשַׁנֵּי הַשָּׂדֶה וּרְאוּ אֵיךְ הֵם גְּדֵלִים: אֵינָם עֲמֵלִים וְאֵינָם טוֹוִים. [29] אוֹמֵר אֲנִי לָכֶם שֶׁגַּם שְׁלֹמֹה בְּכָל הֲדָרוֹ לֹא הָיָה לָבוּשׁ כְּאֶחָד מֵהֶם. [30] וְאִם כָּכָה מַלְבִּישׁ אֱלֹהִים אֶת חֲצִיר הַשָּׂדֶה אֲשֶׁר הַיּוֹם יֶשְׁנוֹ וּמָחָר יֻשְׁלַךְ לְתוֹךְ הַתַּנּוּר, עַל אַחַת כַּמָּה וְכַמָּה אֶתְכֶם, קְטַנֵּי אֱמוּנָה! [31] לָכֵן אַל תִּדְאֲגוּ לֵאמֹר: מַה נֹּאכַל? מַה נִּשְׁתֶּה? וּמַה נִּלְבָּשׁ? [32] הֵן אֶת כָּל אֵלֶּה מְבַקְשִׁים הַגּוֹיִים, וַהֲרֵי אֲבִיכֶם שֶׁבַּשָּׁמַיִם יוֹדֵעַ שֶׁצְּרִיכִים אַתֶּם לְכָל אֵלֶּה. [33] אַתֶּם בַּקְּשׁוּ תְּחִלָּה אֶת מַלְכוּתוֹ וְאֶת צִדְקָתוֹ, וְכָל אֵלֶּה יִוָּסְפוּ לָכֶם. [34] לָכֵן אַל תִּדְאֲגוּ לְיוֹם מָחָר, כִּי הַמָּחָר יִדְאַג לְעַצְמוֹ; דַּי לוֹ לַיּוֹם צָרָתוֹ."

ז "אַל תִּשְׁפְּטוּ לְמַעַן לֹא תִּשָּׁפְטוּ, [2] כִּי בַּמִּשְׁפָּט אֲשֶׁר אַתֶּם שׁוֹפְטִים תִּשָּׁפְטוּ וּבַמִּדָּה אֲשֶׁר אַתֶּם מוֹדְדִים יִמַּד לָכֶם.

[3] מַדּוּעַ אַתָּה רוֹאֶה אֶת הַקֵּיסָם אֲשֶׁר בְּעֵין אָחִיךָ וְאֵינְךָ שָׂם לֵב לַקּוֹרָה אֲשֶׁר בְּעֵינֶךָ? [4] אֵיךְ תֹּאמַר לְאָחִיךָ: 'הַנַּח לִי לְהוֹצִיא אֶת הַקֵּיסָם מֵעֵינֶךָ', וְהִנֵּה

27 אוֹ: ...לְהוֹסִיף אַמָּה אַחַת עַל קוֹמָתוֹ?

plank *is* in your own eye? [5] Hypocrite! First remove the plank from your own eye, and then you will see clearly to remove the speck from your brother's eye.

[6] "Do not give what is holy to the dogs; nor cast your pearls before swine, lest they trample them under their feet, and turn and tear you in pieces."

[7] "Ask, and it will be given to you; seek, and you will find; knock, and it will be opened to you. [8] For everyone who asks receives, and he who seeks finds, and to him who knocks it will be opened. [9] Or what man is there among you who, if his son asks for bread, will give him a stone? [10] Or if he asks for a fish, will he give him a serpent? [11] If you then, being evil, know how to give good gifts to your children, how much more will your Father who is in heaven give good things to those who ask Him! [12] Therefore, whatever you want men to do to you, do also to them, for this is the Law and the Prophets.

[13] "Enter by the narrow gate; for wide *is* the gate and broad *is* the way that leads to destruction, and there are many who go in by it. [14] Because narrow *is* the gate and difficult *is* the way which leads to life, and there are few who find it.

[15] "Beware of false prophets, who come to you in sheep's clothing, but inwardly they are ravenous wolves. [16] You will know them by their fruits. Do men gather grapes from thornbushes or figs from thistles? [17] Even so, every good tree bears good fruit, but a bad tree bears bad fruit. [18] A good tree cannot bear bad fruit, nor *can* a bad tree bear good fruit. [19] Every tree that does not bear good fruit is cut down and thrown into the fire. [20] Therefore by their fruits you will know them.

[21] "Not everyone who says to Me, 'Lord, Lord,' shall enter the kingdom of heaven, but he who does the will of My Father in heaven. [22] Many will say to Me in that day, 'Lord, Lord, have we not prophesied in Your name, cast out demons in Your name, and done many wonders in Your name?' [23] And then I will declare to them, 'I never knew you; depart from Me, you who practice lawlessness!'

[24] "Therefore whoever hears these sayings of Mine, and does them, I will liken him to a wise man who built his house on the rock: [25] and the rain descended, the floods came, and the winds blew and beat on that house; and it did not fall, for it was founded on the rock.

[26] "But everyone who hears these sayings of Mine, and does not do them, will be like a foolish man who built his house on the sand: [27] and the rain descended, the floods came, and the winds blew and beat on that house; and it fell. And great was its fall."

הַקּוֹרָה בְּעֵינֶךָ? [5] צָבוּעַ! הוֹצֵא תְחִלָּה אֶת הַקּוֹרָה מֵעֵינֶךָ; אַחֲרֵי כֵן תִּרְאֶה הֵיטֵב וְתוּכַל לְהוֹצִיא אֶת הַקֵּיסָם מֵעֵינוֹ שֶׁל אָחִיךָ. [6] אַל תִּתְּנוּ אֶת הַקֹּדֶשׁ לַכְּלָבִים וְאַל תַּשְׁלִיכוּ פְּנִינֵיכֶם לִפְנֵי הַחֲזִירִים, פֶּן יִרְמְסוּ אוֹתָם בְּרַגְלֵיהֶם וְיִפְנוּ וְיִטְרְפוּ אֶתְכֶם."

[7] "בַּקְּשׁוּ וְיִנָּתֵן לָכֶם. חַפְּשׂוּ וְתִמְצָאוּ. דִּפְקוּ וְיִפָּתַח לָכֶם. [8] כִּי כָּל הַמְבַקֵּשׁ מְקַבֵּל, וְהַמְחַפֵּשׂ מוֹצֵא, וְהַמִּתְדַּפֵּק יִפָּתַח לוֹ. [9] מִי מִכֶּם הָאִישׁ אֲשֶׁר בְּנוֹ יְבַקֵּשׁ לֶחֶם וְהוּא יִתֵּן לוֹ אֶבֶן? [10] אוֹ אִם יְבַקֵּשׁ דָּג הֲיִתֵּן לוֹ נָחָשׁ? [11] הֵן אִם אַתֶּם הָרָעִים יוֹדְעִים לָתֵת מַתָּנוֹת טוֹבוֹת לִבְנֵיכֶם, כָּל שֶׁכֵּן אֲבִיכֶם שֶׁבַּשָּׁמַיִם יִתֵּן אַךְ טוֹב לַמְבַקְשִׁים מִמֶּנּוּ. [12] לָכֵן כָּל מַה שֶּׁתִּרְצוּ שֶׁיַּעֲשׂוּ לָכֶם בְּנֵי הָאָדָם, כֵּן גַּם אַתֶּם עֲשׂוּ לָהֶם, כִּי זֹאת הַתּוֹרָה וְהַנְּבִיאִים."

[13] "הִכָּנְסוּ דֶּרֶךְ הַפֶּתַח הַצַּר, כִּי רָחָב הַפֶּתַח וּמְרֻוַּחַת הַדֶּרֶךְ הַמּוֹלִיכָה לַאֲבַדּוֹן וְרַבִּים הַהוֹלְכִים בָּהּ. [14] אַךְ צַר הַפֶּתַח וְצָרָה הַדֶּרֶךְ הַמּוֹלִיכָה לַחַיִּים וּמְעַטִּים הַמּוֹצְאִים אוֹתָהּ."

[15] "הִזָּהֲרוּ מִנְּבִיאֵי הַשֶּׁקֶר הַבָּאִים אֲלֵיכֶם בִּלְבוּשׁ כְּבָשִׂים וּבְתוֹךְ תּוֹכָם זְאֵבִים טוֹרְפִים הֵם. [16] בְּפֵרוֹתֵיהֶם תַּכִּירוּ אוֹתָם. הַאִם אוֹסְפִים עֲנָבִים מִן הַקּוֹצִים אוֹ תְּאֵנִים מִן הַבַּרְקָנִים? [17] כֵּן כָּל עֵץ טוֹב עוֹשֶׂה פְּרִי טוֹב, וְהָעֵץ הַנִּשְׁחָת עוֹשֶׂה פְּרִי רַע. [18] עֵץ טוֹב אֵינֶנּוּ יָכוֹל לַעֲשׂוֹת פְּרִי רַע וְעֵץ נִשְׁחָת אֵינֶנּוּ יָכוֹל לַעֲשׂוֹת פְּרִי טוֹב. [19] כָּל עֵץ שֶׁאֵינוֹ עוֹשֶׂה פְּרִי טוֹב כּוֹרְתִים אוֹתוֹ וּמַשְׁלִיכִים אוֹתוֹ לְתוֹךְ הָאֵשׁ. [20] לָכֵן בְּפֵרוֹתֵיהֶם תַּכִּירוּ אוֹתָם."

[21] "לֹא כָּל הָאוֹמֵר לִי 'אֲדוֹנִי, אֲדוֹנִי' יָבֹא לְמַלְכוּת הַשָּׁמַיִם, אֶלָּא הָעוֹשֶׂה אֶת רְצוֹן אָבִי שֶׁבַּשָּׁמַיִם. [22] רַבִּים יֹאמְרוּ אֵלַי בַּיּוֹם הַהוּא: 'אֲדוֹנִי, אֲדוֹנִי', הֲלֹא בְּשִׁמְךָ נִבֵּאנוּ וּבְשִׁמְךָ גֵּרַשְׁנוּ שֵׁדִים וּבְשִׁמְךָ עָשִׂינוּ נִפְלָאוֹת רַבּוֹת.' [23] אָז אוֹדִיעַ לָהֶם: 'מֵעוֹלָם לֹא הִכַּרְתִּי אֶתְכֶם, סוּרוּ מִמֶּנִּי עוֹשֵׂי רֶשַׁע.'"

[24] "לָכֵן כָּל הַשּׁוֹמֵעַ אֶת דְּבָרַי אֵלֶּה וְעוֹשֶׂה אוֹתָם יִהְיֶה דּוֹמֶה לְאִישׁ נָבוֹן אֲשֶׁר בָּנָה אֶת בֵּיתוֹ עַל הַסֶּלַע. [25] הַגֶּשֶׁם יָרַד, בָּאוּ הַשְּׁטָפוֹנוֹת וְנָשְׁבוּ הָרוּחוֹת וְהִתְלַמּוּ בַּבַּיִת הַהוּא, אַךְ הוּא לֹא נָפַל, כִּי יֻסַּד עַל הַסֶּלַע. [26] וְכָל הַשּׁוֹמֵעַ אֶת דְּבָרַי אֵלֶּה וְאֵינוֹ עוֹשֶׂה אוֹתָם יִדְמֶה לֶאֱוִיל אֲשֶׁר בָּנָה אֶת בֵּיתוֹ עַל חוֹל. [27] הַגֶּשֶׁם יָרַד, בָּאוּ הַשְּׁטָפוֹנוֹת וְנָשְׁבוּ הָרוּחוֹת וְהִתְלַמּוּ בַּבַּיִת הַהוּא; נָפַל הַבַּיִת וּגְדוֹלָה הָיְתָה מַפַּלְתּוֹ."

28 And so it was, when Jesus had ended these sayings, that the people were astonished at His teaching, 29 for He taught them as one having authority, and not as the scribes.

8 When He had come down from the mountain, great multitudes followed Him. 2 And behold, a leper came and worshiped Him, saying, "Lord, if You are willing, You can make me clean."

3 Then Jesus put out *His* hand and touched him, saying, "I am willing; be cleansed." Immediately his leprosy was cleansed.

4 And Jesus said to him, "See that you tell no one; but go your way, show yourself to the priest, and offer the gift that Moses commanded, as a testimony to them."

5 Now when Jesus had entered Capernaum, a centurion came to Him, pleading with Him, 6 saying, "Lord, my servant is lying at home paralyzed, dreadfully tormented."

7 And Jesus said to him, "I will come and heal him."

8 The centurion answered and said, "Lord, I am not worthy that You should come under my roof. But only speak a word, and my servant will be healed. 9 For I also am a man under authority, having soldiers under me. And I say to this *one,* 'Go,' and he goes; and to another, 'Come,' and he comes; and to my servant, 'Do this,' and he does *it.*"

10 When Jesus heard *it,* He marveled, and said to those who followed, "Assuredly, I say to you, I have not found such great faith, not even in Israel! 11 And I say to you that many will come from east and west, and sit down with Abraham, Isaac, and Jacob in the kingdom of heaven. 12 But the sons of the kingdom will be cast out into outer darkness. There will be weeping and gnashing of teeth." 13 Then Jesus said to the centurion, "Go your way; and as you have believed, *so* let it be done for you." And his servant was healed that same hour.

14 Now when Jesus had come into Peter's house, He saw his wife's mother lying sick with a fever. 15 So He touched her hand, and the fever left her. And she arose and served them.

16 When evening had come, they brought to Him many who were demon-possessed. And He cast out the spirits with a word, and healed all who were sick, 17 that it might be fulfilled which was spoken by Isaiah the prophet, saying:

"*He Himself took our infirmities*
And bore our sicknesses."

28 כְּשֶׁגָּמַר יֵשׁוּעַ אֶת דְּבָרָיו אֵלֶּה הִשְׁתּוֹמֲמוּ הֲמוֹן הָעָם עַל תּוֹרָתוֹ, 29 כִּי לִמַּד אוֹתָם כְּבַעַל סַמְכוּת וְלֹא כְּדֶרֶךְ שֶׁלִּמְּדוּ סוֹפְרֵיהֶם.

ח הוּא יָרַד מִן הָהָר וַהֲמוֹן עַם רַב הָלְכוּ אַחֲרָיו. 2 אָז הִתְקָרֵב אִישׁ מְצֹרָע, הִשְׁתַּחֲוָה לוֹ וְאָמַר: "אֲדוֹנִי, אִם תִּרְצֶה תּוּכַל לְטַהֵר אוֹתִי." 3 הוֹשִׁיט יֵשׁוּעַ אֶת יָדוֹ, נָגַע בּוֹ וְאָמַר: "רוֹצֶה אֲנִי! הִטָּהֵר!" וּמִיָּד נִרְפְּאָה צָרַעְתּוֹ. 4 אָמַר לוֹ יֵשׁוּעַ: "רְאֵה, אַל תְּסַפֵּר לְאִישׁ, אֲבָל לֵךְ הֵרָאֵה אֶל הַכֹּהֵן וְהַקְרֵב אֶת הַקָּרְבָּן אֲשֶׁר צִוָּה מֹשֶׁה לְעֵדוּת לָהֶם."

5 כַּאֲשֶׁר נִכְנַס לִכְפַר נַחוּם נִגַּשׁ אֵלָיו שַׂר-מֵאָה אֶחָד וְהִתְחַנֵּן לְפָנָיו: 6 "אֲדוֹנִי, נַעֲרִי שׁוֹכֵב בַּבַּיִת וְהוּא מְשֻׁתָּק וְסוֹבֵל מְאֹד."

7 אָמַר לוֹ יֵשׁוּעַ: "אֲנִי אָבוֹא וַאֲרַפֵּא אוֹתוֹ."

8 הֵשִׁיב שַׂר-הַמֵּאָה וְאָמַר: "אֲדוֹנִי, אֵינֶנִּי רָאוּי לְכָךְ שֶׁתָּבוֹא בְּצֵל קוֹרָתִי. רַק דַּבֵּר דָּבָר וְיֵרָפֵא נַעֲרִי. 9 גַּם אֲנִי אִישׁ כָּפוּף לְמָרוּת וּכְפוּפִים לִי אַנְשֵׁי צָבָא, וְכַאֲשֶׁר אֲנִי אוֹמֵר לָזֶה, 'לֵךְ!', הוּא הוֹלֵךְ; וּלְאַחֵר 'בּוֹא!', הוּא בָּא; וּלְעַבְדִּי, 'עֲשֵׂה זֹאת!', הוּא עוֹשֶׂה."

10 שָׁמַע יֵשׁוּעַ וְהִתְפַּלֵּא. אָמַר אֶל הַהוֹלְכִים אַחֲרָיו: "אָמֵן אוֹמֵר אֲנִי לָכֶם, אֵצֶל שׁוּם אִישׁ בְּיִשְׂרָאֵל לֹא מָצָאתִי אֱמוּנָה כָּזֹאת. 11 וַאֲנִי אוֹמֵר לָכֶם, רַבִּים יָבוֹאוּ מִמִּזְרָח וּמִמַּעֲרָב וְיֵשְׁבוּ עִם אַבְרָהָם וְיִצְחָק וְיַעֲקֹב בְּמַלְכוּת הַשָּׁמַיִם, 12 אֲבָל בְּנֵי הַמַּלְכוּת יְגֹרְשׁוּ אֶל הַחֹשֶׁךְ הַחִיצוֹן; שָׁם יִהְיוּ הַיְלָלָה וַחֲרוֹק הַשִּׁנַּיִם." 13 וּלְשַׂר-הַמֵּאָה אָמַר יֵשׁוּעַ: "לֵךְ וּכְאֱמוּנָתְךָ כֵּן יִהְיֶה לָךְ." אוֹתָהּ שָׁעָה נִרְפָּא נַעֲרוֹ.

14 כְּשֶׁנִּכְנַס יֵשׁוּעַ לְבֵיתוֹ שֶׁל כֵּיפָא רָאָה אֶת חֲמוֹתוֹ שׁוֹכֶבֶת וְהִיא סוֹבֶלֶת מֵחֹם. 15 הוּא נָגַע בְּיָדָהּ וְהַחֹם סָר מִמֶּנָּה. אָז קָמָה וְשֵׁרְתָה אוֹתָם. 16 לְעֵת עֶרֶב הֵבִיאוּ אֵלָיו רַבִּים שֶׁהָיוּ אֲחוּזֵי שֵׁדִים וְהוּא גֵּרֵשׁ אֶת הָרוּחוֹת בִּדְבַר פִּיו וְרִפֵּא אֶת כָּל הַחוֹלִים, 17 לְקַיֵּם אֶת אֲשֶׁר נֶאֱמַר בְּפִי יְשַׁעְיָהוּ הַנָּבִיא: "חֳלָיֵנוּ הוּא נָשָׂא וּמַכְאוֹבֵינוּ סְבָלָם."

18 And when Jesus saw great multitudes about Him, He gave a command to depart to the other side. 19 Then a certain scribe came and said to Him, "Teacher, I will follow You wherever You go."

20 And Jesus said to him, "Foxes have holes and birds of the air *have* nests, but the Son of Man has nowhere to lay *His* head."

21 Then another of His disciples said to Him, "Lord, let me first go and bury my father."

22 But Jesus said to him, "Follow Me, and let the dead bury their own dead."

23 Now when He got into a boat, His disciples followed Him. 24 And suddenly a great tempest arose on the sea, so that the boat was covered with the waves. But He was asleep. 25 Then His disciples came to *Him* and awoke Him, saying, "Lord, save us! We are perishing!"

26 But He said to them, "Why are you fearful, O you of little faith?" Then He arose and rebuked the winds and the sea, and there was a great calm. 27 So the men marveled, saying, "Who can this be, that even the winds and the sea obey Him?"

28 When He had come to the other side, to the country of the Gergesenes, there met Him two demon-possessed *men,* coming out of the tombs, exceedingly fierce, so that no one could pass that way. 29 And suddenly they cried out, saying, "What have we to do with You, Jesus, You Son of God? Have You come here to torment us before the time?"

30 Now a good way off from them there was a herd of many swine feeding. 31 So the demons begged Him, saying, "If You cast us out, permit us to go away into the herd of swine."

32 And He said to them, "Go." So when they had come out, they went into the herd of swine. And suddenly the whole herd of swine ran violently down the steep place into the sea, and perished in the water.

33 Then those who kept *them* fled; and they went away into the city and told everything, including what *had happened* to the demon-possessed *men.* 34 And behold, the whole city came out to meet Jesus. And when they saw Him, they begged *Him* to depart from their region.

9 So He got into a boat, crossed over, and came to His own city. 2 Then behold, they brought to Him a paralytic lying on a bed. When Jesus saw their faith, He said to the paralytic, "Son, be of good cheer; your sins are forgiven you."

3 And at once some of the scribes said within themselves, "This Man blasphemes!"

18 כְּשֶׁרָאָה יֵשׁוּעַ הֲמוֹן עָם רַב מִסְּבִיבוֹ צִוָּה לַעֲבֹר אֶל עֵבֶר הַיָּם. 19 נִגַּשׁ אֵלָיו אַחַד הַסּוֹפְרִים וְאָמַר לוֹ: "רַבִּי, אֵלֵךְ אַחֲרֶיךָ אֶל כָּל מָקוֹם שֶׁתֵּלֵךְ."

20 עָנָה לוֹ יֵשׁוּעַ: "לַשׁוּעָלִים יֵשׁ מְאוּרוֹת וּלְעוֹף הַשָּׁמַיִם קִנִּים, אַךְ בֶּן־הָאָדָם אֵין לוֹ מָקוֹם לְהָנִיחַ אֶת רֹאשׁוֹ."

21 אִישׁ אַחֵר מִן הַתַּלְמִידִים אָמַר אֵלָיו: "אֲדוֹנִי, הַרְשֵׁה לִי תְּחִלָּה לָלֶכֶת לִקְבֹּר אֶת אָבִי."

22 אָמַר לוֹ יֵשׁוּעַ: "לֵךְ אַחֲרַי וְהַנַּח לַמֵּתִים לִקְבֹּר אֶת מֵתֵיהֶם."

23 הוּא נִכְנַס לַסִּירָה וְתַלְמִידָיו נִכְנְסוּ אַחֲרָיו. 24 וְהִנֵּה סְעָרָה גְדוֹלָה הִתְחוֹלְלָה בַּיָּם עַד אֲשֶׁר כִּסּוּ הַגַּלִּים אֶת הַסִּירָה, אַךְ הוּא הָיָה יָשֵׁן. 25 נִגְּשׁוּ אֵלָיו וְהֵעִירוּ אוֹתוֹ בְּאָמְרָם: "אֲדוֹנֵנוּ, הַצֵּל אוֹתָנוּ, אֲנַחְנוּ טוֹבְעִים!" 26 אָמַר לָהֶם: "לָמָּה אַתֶּם פּוֹחֲדִים, קְטַנֵּי אֱמוּנָה?!" הוּא קָם וְגָעַר בָּרוּחוֹת וּבַיָּם וְנִשְׁתַּרְרָה דְמָמָה עֲמֻקָּה. 27 תָּמְהוּ הָאֲנָשִׁים וְאָמְרוּ: "מִי הוּא זֶה שֶׁגַּם הָרוּחוֹת וְהַיָּם נִשְׁמָעִים לוֹ?"

28 כַּאֲשֶׁר בָּא אֶל עֵבֶר הַיָּם, אֶל אֶרֶץ הַגַּדְרִיִּים, פְּגָשׁוּהוּ שְׁנֵי אֲנָשִׁים אֲחוּזֵי שֵׁדִים בְּצֵאתָם מִמְּעָרוֹת הַקְּבָרִים. הֵם הָיוּ תוֹקְפָנִיִּים כָּל כָּךְ, שֶׁאִישׁ לֹא הָיָה יָכוֹל לַעֲבֹר בְּאוֹתָהּ דֶּרֶךְ. 29 אָז הֵחֵלּוּ צוֹעֲקִים: "מַה לָּנוּ וָלָךְ בֶּן־הָאֱלֹהִים – בָּאתָ הֵנָּה לְעַנּוֹת אוֹתָנוּ בְּטֶרֶם עֵת?"

30 בְּמֶרְחָק מֵהֶם רָעָה עֵדֶר חֲזִירִים גָּדוֹל. 31 הִפְצִירוּ בּוֹ הַשֵּׁדִים וְאָמְרוּ: "אִם תְּגָרֵשׁ אוֹתָנוּ, שְׁלַח אוֹתָנוּ לְתוֹךְ עֵדֶר הַחֲזִירִים."

32 אָמַר לָהֶם: "לְכוּ!" הֵם יָצְאוּ וְנִכְנְסוּ לְתוֹךְ הַחֲזִירִים, וְהִנֵּה כָּל הָעֵדֶר הִסְתָּעֵר בַּמּוֹרָד אֶל הַיָּם וּמֵת בַּמַּיִם. 33 בָּרְחוּ הָרוֹעִים וּבָאוּ הָעִירָה. שָׁם סִפְּרוּ אֶת הַכֹּל וְאֶת מַה שֶּׁקָּרָה לַאֲחוּזֵי הַשֵּׁדִים, 34 וְכָל הָעִיר יָצְאָה לִקְרַאת יֵשׁוּעַ. כְּשֶׁרָאוּ אוֹתוֹ הַתּוֹשָׁבִים בִּקְשׁוּ מִמֶּנּוּ שֶׁיֵּלֵךְ מֵאֵזוֹרָם.

ט הוּא יָרַד לַסִּירָה, עָבַר אֶת הַיָּם וּבָא אֶל עִירוֹ. 2 וְהִנֵּה הֵבִיאוּ אֵלָיו אִישׁ מְשֻׁתָּק שׁוֹכֵב עַל אֲלוּנְקָה. כְּשֶׁרָאָה יֵשׁוּעַ אֶת אֱמוּנָתָם אָמַר אֶל הַמְשֻׁתָּק: "הִתְחַזֵּק, בְּנִי, נִסְלְחוּ לְךָ חֲטָאֶיךָ."

3 אֲחָדִים מִן הַסּוֹפְרִים אָמְרוּ בְּלִבָּם: "זֶה מְגַדֵּף שֵׁם שָׁמַיִם!"

4 But Jesus, knowing their thoughts, said, "Why do you think evil in your hearts? 5 For which is easier, to say, 'Your sins are forgiven you,' or to say, 'Arise and walk'? 6 But that you may know that the Son of Man has power on earth to forgive sins"— then He said to the paralytic, "Arise, take up your bed, and go to your house." 7 And he arose and departed to his house.

8 Now when the multitudes saw *it*, they marveled and glorified God, who had given such power to men.

9 As Jesus passed on from there, He saw a man named Matthew sitting at the tax office. And He said to him, "Follow Me." So he arose and followed Him.

10 Now it happened, as Jesus sat at the table in the house, *that* behold, many tax collectors and sinners came and sat down with Him and His disciples. 11 And when the Pharisees saw *it*, they said to His disciples, "Why does your Teacher eat with tax collectors and sinners?"

12 When Jesus heard *that*, He said to them, "Those who are well have no need of a physician, but those who are sick. 13 But go and learn what *this* means: 'I desire mercy and not sacrifice.' For I did not come to call the righteous, but sinners, to repentance."

14 Then the disciples of John came to Him, saying, "Why do we and the Pharisees fast often, but Your disciples do not fast?"

15 And Jesus said to them, "Can the friends of the bridegroom mourn as long as the bridegroom is with them? But the days will come when the bridegroom will be taken away from them, and then they will fast. 16 No one puts a piece of unshrunk cloth on an old garment; for the patch pulls away from the garment, and the tear is made worse. 17 Nor do they put new wine into old wineskins, or else the wineskins break, the wine is spilled, and the wineskins are ruined. But they put new wine into new wineskins, and both are preserved."

18 While He spoke these things to them, behold, a ruler came and worshiped Him, saying, "My daughter has just died, but come and lay Your hand on her and she will live." 19 So Jesus arose and followed him, and so *did* His disciples.

20 And suddenly, a woman who had a flow of blood for twelve years came from behind and touched the hem of His garment. 21 For she said to herself, "If only I may touch His garment, I shall be made well." 22 But Jesus turned around, and when

4 יֵשׁוּעַ הֵבִין בְּמַחְשְׁבוֹתֵיהֶם וְאָמַר: "לָמָּה אַתֶּם חוֹשְׁבִים רָעוֹת בִּלְבַבְכֶם? 5 מַה יוֹתֵר קַל: לוֹמַר 'נִסְלְחוּ לְךָ חֲטָאֶיךָ', אוֹ לוֹמַר 'קוּם וְהִתְהַלֵּךְ'? 6 אַךְ לְמַעַן תֵּדְעוּ כִּי לְבֶן־הָאָדָם הַסַּמְכוּת עֲלֵי אַדְמוֹת לִסְלֹחַ עַל חֲטָאִים", – וְאָז פָּנָה וְאָמַר לַמְשֻׁתָּק – "קוּם, קַח אֶת הָאֲלוּנְקָה וְלֵךְ לְבֵיתְךָ!"

7 הוּא קָם וְהָלַךְ לְבֵיתוֹ. 8 כְּשֶׁרָאוּ זֹאת הֲמוֹן הָעָם נִתְמַלְּאוּ יִרְאָה וְשִׁבְּחוּ אֶת הָאֱלֹהִים שֶׁנָּתַן סַמְכוּת כָּזֹאת לִבְנֵי אָדָם.

9 כַּאֲשֶׁר עָבַר מִשָּׁם רָאָה יֵשׁוּעַ אִישׁ יוֹשֵׁב בְּבֵית הַמֶּכֶס וּשְׁמוֹ מַתַּי. אָמַר אֵלָיו: "לֵךְ אַחֲרַי." הוּא קָם וְהָלַךְ אַחֲרָיו. 10 כְּשֶׁהֵסֵב בַּבַּיִת בָּאוּ מוֹכְסִים וְחוֹטְאִים רַבִּים וְהֵסֵבּוּ עִם יֵשׁוּעַ וְתַלְמִידָיו. 11 רָאוּ הַפְּרוּשִׁים וְאָמְרוּ לְתַלְמִידָיו: "מַדּוּעַ אוֹכֵל רַבְּכֶם עִם הַמּוֹכְסִים וְהַחוֹטְאִים?"

12 שָׁמַע יֵשׁוּעַ וְאָמַר לָהֶם: "לֹא הַבְּרִיאִים צְרִיכִים לְרוֹפֵא, אֶלָּא הַחוֹלִים. 13 וְאַתֶּם צְאוּ וְלִמְדוּ מַה מַּשְׁמָע 'חֶסֶד חָפַצְתִּי וְלֹא־זֶבַח', כִּי לֹא בָּאתִי לִקְרֹא לַצַּדִּיקִים כִּי אִם לַחוֹטְאִים."

14 אָז נִגְּשׁוּ אֵלָיו תַּלְמִידֵי יוֹחָנָן וְשָׁאֲלוּ: "מַדּוּעַ אֲנַחְנוּ וְהַפְּרוּשִׁים צָמִים הַרְבֵּה וְתַלְמִידֶיךָ אֵינָם צָמִים?" 15 הֵשִׁיב לָהֶם יֵשׁוּעַ: "הַאִם יְכוֹלִים בְּנֵי הַחֻפָּה לְהִתְאַבֵּל בְּעוֹד הֶחָתָן אִתָּם? אַךְ יָמִים יָבוֹאוּ שֶׁהֶחָתָן יֻלְקַח מֵהֶם וְאָז יָצוּמוּ. 16 אֵין אִישׁ שָׂם פִּסָּה שֶׁל בַּד חָדָשׁ עַל בֶּגֶד יָשָׁן, שֶׁכֵּן הַטְּלַאי יִתָּלֵשׁ מִן הַבֶּגֶד וְהַקֶּרַע יִגְדַּל. 17 וְאֵין שָׂמִים יַיִן חָדָשׁ בְּנֹאדוֹת יְשָׁנִים; אִם יַעֲשׂוּ כֵּן, יִתְבַּקְּעוּ הַנֹּאדוֹת וְהַיַּיִן יִשָּׁפֵךְ וְהַנֹּאדוֹת לֹא יִצְלְחוּ עוֹד. אֲבָל שָׂמִים אֶת הַיַּיִן הֶחָדָשׁ בְּנֹאדוֹת חֲדָשִׁים וּשְׁנֵיהֶם יַחְדָּיו יִשָּׁמְרוּ."

18 כַּאֲשֶׁר דִּבֶּר אֲלֵיהֶם אֶת הַדְּבָרִים הָאֵלֶּה בָּא אֶחָד הַנִּכְבָּדִים, הִשְׁתַּחֲוָה לוֹ וְאָמַר: "זֶה עַתָּה מֵתָה בִּתִּי. בּוֹא נָא וּסְמֹךְ אֶת יָדְךָ עָלֶיהָ וְתִחְיֶה."

19 יֵשׁוּעַ קָם וְהָלַךְ אַחֲרָיו הוּא וְתַלְמִידָיו. 20 וְהִנֵּה אִשָּׁה שֶׁהָיְתָה זָבַת דָּם שְׁתֵּים־עֶשְׂרֵה שָׁנָה הִתְקָרְבָה מֵאָחוֹר וְנָגְעָה בִּכְנַף בִּגְדוֹ, 21 כִּי אָמְרָה בְּלִבָּהּ 'אִם רַק אֶגַּע בְּבִגְדוֹ אֶתְרַפֵּא'.

22 פָּנָה יֵשׁוּעַ וְרָאָה אוֹתָהּ. אָמַר לָהּ: "חִזְקִי, בִּתִּי, אֱמוּנָתֵךְ הוֹשִׁיעָה אוֹתָךְ." מֵאוֹתָהּ שָׁעָה נִרְפְּאָה

He saw her He said, "Be of good cheer, daughter; your faith has made you well." And the woman was made well from that hour.

23 When Jesus came into the ruler's house, and saw the flute players and the noisy crowd wailing, 24 He said to them, "Make room, for the girl is not dead, but sleeping." And they ridiculed Him. 25 But when the crowd was put outside, He went in and took her by the hand, and the girl arose. 26 And the report of this went out into all that land.

27 When Jesus departed from there, two blind men followed Him, crying out and saying, "Son of David, have mercy on us!"

28 And when He had come into the house, the blind men came to Him. And Jesus said to them, "Do you believe that I am able to do this?"

They said to Him, "Yes, Lord."

29 Then He touched their eyes, saying, "According to your faith let it be to you." 30 And their eyes were opened. And Jesus sternly warned them, saying, "See that no one knows it." 31 But when they had departed, they spread the news about Him in all that country.

32 As they went out, behold, they brought to Him a man, mute and demon-possessed. 33 And when the demon was cast out, the mute spoke. And the multitudes marveled, saying, "It was never seen like this in Israel!"

34 But the Pharisees said, "He casts out demons by the ruler of the demons."

35 Then Jesus went about all the cities and villages, teaching in their synagogues, preaching the gospel of the kingdom, and healing every sickness and every disease among the people. 36 But when He saw the multitudes, He was moved with compassion for them, because they were weary and scattered, like sheep having no shepherd. 37 Then He said to His disciples, "The harvest truly is plentiful, but the laborers are few. 38 Therefore pray the Lord of the harvest to send out laborers into His harvest."

10 And when He had called His twelve disciples to Him, He gave them power over unclean spirits, to cast them out, and to heal all kinds of sickness and all kinds of disease. 2 Now the names of the twelve apostles are these: first, Simon, who is called Peter, and Andrew his brother; James the son of Zebedee, and John his brother; 3 Philip and Bartholomew; Thomas and Matthew the tax collector; James the son of Alphaeus, and Lebbaeus, whose surname was Thaddaeus; 4 Simon the Cananite, and Judas Iscariot, who also betrayed Him.

הָאִשָּׁה. 23 כְּשֶׁבָּא יֵשׁוּעַ אֶל בֵּית הַנִּכְבָּד וְרָאָה אֶת הַמְחַלְלִים בַּחֲלִילִים וְאֶת הָעָם הָרוֹגֵשׁ, אָמַר: 24 "צְאוּ, כִּי הַיַּלְדָּה לֹא מֵתָה. הִיא רַק יְשֵׁנָה." אַךְ הֵם צָחֲקוּ לוֹ. 25 לְאַחַר שֶׁהוּצְאוּ הָאֲנָשִׁים נִכְנַס, אָחַז בְּיָדָהּ וְהַנַּעֲרָה קָמָה. 26 שֵׁמַע הַדָּבָר הַזֶּה יָצָא בְּכָל אוֹתוֹ הָאֵזוֹר.

27 כַּאֲשֶׁר יָצָא מִשָּׁם יֵשׁוּעַ הָלְכוּ אַחֲרָיו שְׁנֵי אֲנָשִׁים עִוְרִים כְּשֶׁהֵם צוֹעֲקִים: "בֶּן־דָּוִד, רַחֵם עָלֵינוּ!" 28 בְּהִכָּנְסוֹ הַבַּיְתָה נִגְּשׁוּ אֵלָיו הָעִוְרִים. אָמַר לָהֶם יֵשׁוּעַ: "הַאִם מַאֲמִינִים אַתֶּם שֶׁאֲנִי יָכוֹל לַעֲשׂוֹת זֹאת?"

"כֵּן, אֲדוֹנֵנוּ!" הֵשִׁיבוּ.

29 נָגַע בְּעֵינֵיהֶם וְאָמַר: "יְהֵא לָכֶם כֶּאֱמוּנַתְכֶם!" 30 אָז נִפְקְחוּ עֵינֵיהֶם וְיֵשׁוּעַ הִזְהִיר אוֹתָם בְּאָמְרוֹ: "שִׂימוּ לֵב שֶׁלֹּא יֵדַע לְאִישׁ!" 31 אַךְ הֵם יָצְאוּ וְהִשְׁמִיעוּ אֶת שִׁמְעוֹ בְּכָל הָאֵזוֹר הַהוּא.

32 לְאַחַר שֶׁיָּצְאוּ הֵבִיאוּ אֵלָיו אִישׁ אִלֵּם אֲחוּז שֵׁד. 33 הוּא גֵּרֵשׁ אֶת הַשֵּׁד, וְהָאִלֵּם הֵחֵל לְדַבֵּר. הִתְפַּלְאוּ הַהֲמוֹנִים וְאָמְרוּ: "מֵעוֹלָם לֹא נִרְאָה כַּדָּבָר הַזֶּה בְּיִשְׂרָאֵל." 34 אַךְ הַפְּרוּשִׁים אָמְרוּ: "בְּעֶזְרַת שַׂר הַשֵּׁדִים הוּא מְגָרֵשׁ אֶת הַשֵּׁדִים."

35 יֵשׁוּעַ עָבַר בְּכָל הֶעָרִים וְהַכְּפָרִים כְּשֶׁהוּא מְלַמֵּד בְּבָתֵּי הַכְּנֶסֶת, מְבַשֵּׂר אֶת בְּשׂוֹרַת הַמַּלְכוּת וּמְרַפֵּא כָּל מַחֲלָה וְכָל מַדְוֶה בָּעָם. 36 כִּרְאוֹתוֹ אֶת הַהֲמוֹנִים נִתְמַלֵּא רַחֲמִים עֲלֵיהֶם, שֶׁכֵּן הָיוּ יְגֵעִים וְנִדָּחִים כַּצֹּאן אֲשֶׁר אֵין לָהֶם רוֹעֶה. 37 אָמַר אֶל תַּלְמִידָיו: "הַקָּצִיר רַב, אֲבָל הַפּוֹעֲלִים מְעַטִּים. 38 לָכֵן הִתְפַּלְּלוּ אֶל אֲדוֹן הַקָּצִיר שֶׁיִּשְׁלַח פּוֹעֲלִים לִקְצִירוֹ."

י הוּא קָרָא אֵלָיו אֶת שְׁנֵים־עָשָׂר תַּלְמִידָיו וְנָתַן לָהֶם סַמְכוּת עַל רוּחוֹת הַטֻּמְאָה, לְגָרֵשׁ אוֹתָן וּלְרַפֵּא כָּל מַחֲלָה וְכָל מַדְוֶה. 2 וְאֵלֶּה שְׁמוֹת שְׁנֵים־עָשָׂר הַשְּׁלִיחִים: הָרִאשׁוֹן שִׁמְעוֹן הַמְכֻנֶּה כֵּיפָא, אַנְדְּרֵי אָחִיו, יַעֲקֹב בֶּן זַבְדַּי וְיוֹחָנָן אָחִיו, 3 פִילִיפּוֹס וּבַר־תַּלְמַי, תֹּאמָא וּמַתִּי הַמּוֹכֵס, יַעֲקֹב בֶּן חַלְפַי וְתַדַּי, 4 שִׁמְעוֹן הַקַּנַּאי וִיהוּדָה אִישׁ קְרִיּוֹת – הָאִישׁ שֶׁמָּסַר אוֹתוֹ.

5 These twelve Jesus sent out and commanded them, saying: "Do not go into the way of the Gentiles, and do not enter a city of the Samaritans. 6 But go rather to the lost sheep of the house of Israel. 7 And as you go, preach, saying, 'The kingdom of heaven is at hand.' 8 Heal the sick, cleanse the lepers, raise the dead, cast out demons. Freely you have received, freely give. 9 Provide neither gold nor silver nor copper in your money belts, 10 nor bag for *your* journey, nor two tunics, nor sandals, nor staffs; for a worker is worthy of his food.

11 "Now whatever city or town you enter, inquire who in it is worthy, and stay there till you go out. 12 And when you go into a household, greet it. 13 If the household is worthy, let your peace come upon it. But if it is not worthy, let your peace return to you. 14 And whoever will not receive you nor hear your words, when you depart from that house or city, shake off the dust from your feet. 15 Assuredly, I say to you, it will be more tolerable for the land of Sodom and Gomorrah in the day of judgment than for that city!

16 "Behold, I send you out as sheep in the midst of wolves. Therefore be wise as serpents and harmless as doves. 17 But beware of men, for they will deliver you up to councils and scourge you in their synagogues. 18 You will be brought before governors and kings for My sake, as a testimony to them and to the Gentiles. 19 But when they deliver you up, do not worry about how or what you should speak. For it will be given to you in that hour what you should speak; 20 for it is not you who speak, but the Spirit of your Father who speaks in you.

21 "Now brother will deliver up brother to death, and a father *his* child; and children will rise up against parents and cause them to be put to death. 22 And you will be hated by all for My name's sake. But he who endures to the end will be saved. 23 When they persecute you in this city, flee to another. For assuredly, I say to you, you will not have gone through the cities of Israel before the Son of Man comes.

24 "A disciple is not above *his* teacher, nor a servant above his master. 25 It is enough for a disciple that he be like his teacher, and a servant like his master. If they have called the master of the house Beelzebub, how much more *will they call* those of his household! 26 Therefore do not fear them. For there is nothing covered that will not be revealed, and hidden that will not be known.

5 אֶת שְׁנֵים־עָשָׂר אֵלֶּה שָׁלַח יֵשׁוּעַ בְּצַוּוֹתוֹ עֲלֵיהֶם אֶת הַדָּבָר הַזֶּה: "אַל תֵּלְכוּ לְדֶרֶךְ הַגּוֹיִים וְאֶל תִּכָּנְסוּ לְעִיר שֶׁל שׁוֹמְרוֹנִים, 6 אֶלָּא לְכוּ אֶל הַצֹּאן הָאוֹבְדוֹת אֲשֶׁר לְבֵית יִשְׂרָאֵל. 7 וּבְלֶכְתְּכֶם הַכְרִיזוּ: 'קָרְבָה מַלְכוּת שָׁמַיִם!' 8 רַפְּאוּ חוֹלִים, הָקִימוּ מֵתִים, טַהֲרוּ מְצֹרָעִים, גָּרְשׁוּ שֵׁדִים; חִנָּם קִבַּלְתֶּם, חִנָּם תִּתְּנוּ. 9 לֹא תִקְחוּ זָהָב וְלֹא כֶסֶף וְלֹא נְחֹשֶׁת בְּכִיסֵי חֲגוֹרוֹתֵיכֶם; 10 לֹא תַרְמִיל לַדֶּרֶךְ, לֹא שְׁתֵּי כֻתָּנוֹת, לֹא נַעֲלַיִם וְלֹא מַקֵּל, כִּי רָאוּי הַפּוֹעֵל לְלַחְמוֹ. 11 וּבְכָל עִיר וּכְפָר שֶׁתִּכָּנְסוּ אֲלֵיהֶם בָּרְרוּ מִי רָאוּי בְּתוֹכָם וּשְׁבוּ שָׁם עַד צֵאתְכֶם. 12 כְּשֶׁאַתֶּם נִכְנָסִים לְבַיִת בָּרְכוּהוּ בְּשָׁלוֹם. 13 אִם רָאוּי הַבַּיִת יָבוֹא עָלָיו הַשָּׁלוֹם שֶׁלָּכֶם, אַךְ אִם אֵינֶנּוּ רָאוּי יָשׁוּב הַשָּׁלוֹם שֶׁלָּכֶם אֲלֵיכֶם. 14 כָּל מִי שֶׁלֹּא יְקַבֵּל אֶתְכֶם וְלֹא יִשְׁמַע לְדִבְרֵיכֶם, צְאוּ מִן הַבַּיִת הַהוּא וּמִן הָעִיר הַהִיא וְנַעֲרוּ אֶת הָאָבָק מֵעַל רַגְלֵיכֶם. 15 אָמֵן אוֹמֵר אֲנִי לָכֶם, קַל יוֹתֵר יִהְיֶה בְּיוֹם הַדִּין לְאֶרֶץ סְדוֹם וַעֲמוֹרָה מֵאֲשֶׁר לָאוֹתָהּ עִיר."

16 "הִנֵּה אָנֹכִי שׁוֹלֵחַ אֶתְכֶם כִּכְבָשִׂים בֵּין זְאֵבִים. לָכֵן הֱיוּ עֲרוּמִים כַּנְּחָשִׁים וּתְמִימִים כַּיּוֹנִים. 17 הִזָּהֲרוּ מִבְּנֵי אָדָם, כִּי יִמְסְרוּ אֶתְכֶם לַסַּנְהֶדְרִיּוֹת וְיַלְקוּ אֶתְכֶם בְּבָתֵּי הַכְּנֶסֶת שֶׁלָּהֶם. 18 לִפְנֵי מוֹשְׁלִים וּמְלָכִים תּוּבְאוּ בִּגְלָלִי, לְעֵדוּת לָהֶם וְלַגּוֹיִים. 19 אֲבָל כַּאֲשֶׁר יִמְסְרוּ אֶתְכֶם אַל תִּדְאֲגוּ אֵיךְ וּמַה תְּדַבְּרוּ, כִּי בְּאוֹתָהּ שָׁעָה יִנָּתֵן לָכֶם מַה לּוֹמַר; 20 שֶׁכֵּן לֹא אַתֶּם תְּדַבְּרוּ, אֶלָּא רוּחַ אֲבִיכֶם הִיא אֲשֶׁר תְּדַבֵּר בָּכֶם. 21 זֹאת וְעוֹד, אָח יִמְסֹר אֶת אָחִיו לַמָּוֶת וְאָב יִמְסֹר אֶת בְּנוֹ. בָּנִים יָקוּמוּ עַל הוֹרֵיהֶם וְיָמִיתוּ אוֹתָם. 22 וְתִהְיוּ שְׂנוּאִים עַל הַכֹּל לְמַעַן שְׁמִי, אַךְ הַמַּחֲזִיק מַעֲמָד עַד קֵץ הוּא יִוָּשַׁע. 23 כַּאֲשֶׁר יִרְדְּפוּ אֶתְכֶם בְּעִיר אַחַת נוּסוּ לְעִיר אַחֶרֶת. אָמֵן אוֹמֵר אֲנִי לָכֶם, לֹא תַסְפִּיקוּ לַעֲבֹר אֶת עָרֵי יִשְׂרָאֵל עַד שֶׁיָּבוֹא בֶּן־הָאָדָם. 24 תַּלְמִיד אֵינֶנּוּ גָּדוֹל מִן הַמּוֹרֶה אַף לֹא הָעֶבֶד גָּדוֹל מֵאֲדוֹנָיו. 25 דַּי לוֹ לַתַּלְמִיד שֶׁיִּהְיֶה כְּרַבּוֹ וְהָעֶבֶד כַּאֲדוֹנָיו. אִם לְבַעַל הַבַּיִת קָרְאוּ בַּעַל־זְבוּל, כָּל שֶׁכֵּן לְאַנְשֵׁי בֵּיתוֹ."

26 "לָכֵן אַל תִּפְחֲדוּ מִפְּנֵיהֶם, כִּי אֵין דָּבָר מְכֻסֶּה

27 "Whatever I tell you in the dark, speak in the light; and what you hear in the ear, preach on the housetops. 28 And do not fear those who kill the body but cannot kill the soul. But rather fear Him who is able to destroy both soul and body in hell. 29 Are not two sparrows sold for a copper coin? And not one of them falls to the ground apart from your Father's will. 30 But the very hairs of your head are all numbered. 31 Do not fear therefore; you are of more value than many sparrows.

32 "Therefore whoever confesses Me before men, him I will also confess before My Father who is in heaven. 33 But whoever denies Me before men, him I will also deny before My Father who is in heaven.

34 "Do not think that I came to bring peace on earth. I did not come to bring peace but a sword. 35 For I have come to *set a man against his father, a daughter against her mother, and a daughter-in-law against her mother-in-law';* 36 and *'a man's enemies will be those of his own household.'* 37 He who loves father or mother more than Me is not worthy of Me. And he who loves son or daughter more than Me is not worthy of Me. 38 And he who does not take his cross and follow after Me is not worthy of Me. 39 He who finds his life will lose it, and he who loses his life for My sake will find it.

40 "He who receives you receives Me, and he who receives Me receives Him who sent Me. 41 He who receives a prophet in the name of a prophet shall receive a prophet's reward. And he who receives a righteous man in the name of a righteous man shall receive a righteous man's reward. 42 And whoever gives one of these little ones only a cup of cold *water* in the name of a disciple, assuredly, I say to you, he shall by no means lose his reward."

11 Now it came to pass, when Jesus finished commanding His twelve disciples, that He departed from there to teach and to preach in their cities.

2 And when John had heard in prison about the works of Christ, he sent two of his disciples 3 and said to Him, "Are You the Coming One, or do we look for another?"

4 Jesus answered and said to them, "Go and tell John the things which you hear and see: 5 *The* blind see and *the* lame walk; *the* lepers are cleansed and *the* deaf hear; *the* dead are raised up and *the* poor have the gospel preached to them. 6 And blessed is he who is not offended because of Me."

7 As they departed, Jesus began to say to the multitudes concerning John: "What did you go out into the wilderness to see? A reed shaken by the wind? 8 But what did you go out to see? A man clothed in soft garments? Indeed, those who wear

27 אֶת מַה שֶׁאֲנִי אוֹמֵר לָכֶם בַּחֹשֶׁךְ אִמְרוּ בָּאוֹר, וּמַה שֶׁנִּלְחַשׁ לְאָזְנֵיכֶם הַכְרִיזוּ מֵעַל הַגַּגּוֹת. 28 אַל תִּפְחֲדוּ מִן הַהוֹרְגִים אֶת הַגּוּף שֶׁאֵין בִּיכָלְתָּם לַהֲרֹג אֶת הַנֶּפֶשׁ, אֶלָּא יְראוּ מִזֶּה אֲשֶׁר יָכוֹל לְגָרֵם הֵן לְאָבְדַן הַנֶּפֶשׁ וְהֵן לְאָבְדַן הַגּוּף בְּגֵיהִנּוֹם. 29 הַאִם לֹא נִמְכָּרוֹת שְׁתֵּי צִפֳּרִים בְּאִסָּר אֶחָד? גַּם אַחַת מֵהֶן לֹא תִּפֹּל אַרְצָה מִבְּלִי הַשְׁגָּחַת אֲבִיכֶם. 30 אַךְ אַתֶּם, אֲפִלּוּ שַׂעֲרוֹת רֹאשְׁכֶם נִמְנוּ כֻּלָּן. 31 לָכֵן אַל תִּפְחֲדוּ; יְקָרִים אַתֶּם מִצִּפֳּרִים רַבּוֹת."

32 "כָּל מִי שֶׁיּוֹדֶה בִּי לִפְנֵי בְּנֵי אָדָם גַּם אֲנִי אוֹדֶה בּוֹ לִפְנֵי אָבִי שֶׁבַּשָּׁמַיִם. 33 וְכָל הַמְכַחֵשׁ בִּי לִפְנֵי בְּנֵי אָדָם גַּם אֲנִי אֲכַחֵשׁ בּוֹ לִפְנֵי אָבִי שֶׁבַּשָּׁמַיִם. 34 אַל תַּחְשְׁבוּ שֶׁבָּאתִי לְהָטִיל שָׁלוֹם עַל הָאָרֶץ. לֹא בָּאתִי לְהָטִיל שָׁלוֹם אֶלָּא חֶרֶב, 35 שֶׁהֲרֵי בָּאתִי לְגָרֵם פִּלּוּג בֵּין אִישׁ לְאָבִיו, בֵּין בַּת לְאִמָּהּ וּבֵין כַּלָּה לַחֲמוֹתָהּ, 36 וְיִהְיוּ אֹיְבֵי אִישׁ אַנְשֵׁי בֵיתוֹ. 37 הָאוֹהֵב אֶת אָבִיו אוֹ אֶת אִמּוֹ יוֹתֵר מִמֶּנִּי אֵינוֹ כְדַאי לִי, וְהָאוֹהֵב אֶת בְּנוֹ אוֹ אֶת בִּתּוֹ יוֹתֵר מִמֶּנִּי אֵינוֹ כְדַאי לִי. 38 וּמִי שֶׁאֵינוֹ לוֹקֵחַ אֶת צְלָבוֹ וְהוֹלֵךְ אַחֲרַי אֵינוֹ כְדַאי לִי. 39 הַמּוֹצֵא אֶת נַפְשׁוֹ יְאַבֵּד אוֹתָהּ, וְהַמְאַבֵּד אֶת נַפְשׁוֹ לְמַעֲנִי יִמְצָא אוֹתָהּ."

40 "הַמְקַבֵּל אֶתְכֶם מְקַבֵּל אוֹתִי, וְהַמְקַבֵּל אוֹתִי מְקַבֵּל אֶת אֲשֶׁר שְׁלָחַנִי. 41 הַמְקַבֵּל נָבִיא מִשּׁוּם הֱיוֹתוֹ נָבִיא שְׂכַר נָבִיא יְקַבֵּל, וְהַמְקַבֵּל צַדִּיק מִשּׁוּם הֱיוֹתוֹ צַדִּיק שְׂכַר צַדִּיק יְקַבֵּל. 42 וְכָל הַמַּשְׁקֶה אֶת אַחַד הַקְּטַנִּים הָאֵלֶּה רַק כּוֹס מַיִם קָרִים מִשּׁוּם הֱיוֹתוֹ תַּלְמִיד, אָמֵן אוֹמֵר אֲנִי לָכֶם, לֹא יֹאבַד שְׂכָרוֹ."

יא יֵשׁוּעַ סִיֵּם אֶת הוֹרָאוֹתָיו לִשְׁנֵים-עָשָׂר תַּלְמִידָיו וְהָלַךְ מִשָּׁם לְלַמֵּד וּלְהַטִּיף בְּעָרֵיהֶם. 2 כַּאֲשֶׁר שָׁמַע יוֹחָנָן בְּבֵית הַסֹּהַר עַל מַעֲשֵׂי הַמָּשִׁיחַ שָׁלַח בְּיַד תַּלְמִידָיו לִשְׁאָל אוֹתוֹ: 3 "אַתָּה הוּא אֲשֶׁר נוֹעַד לָבוֹא, אוֹ נְחַכֶּה לְאַחֵר?" 4 הֵשִׁיב יֵשׁוּעַ וְאָמַר לָהֶם: "לְכוּ הַגִּידוּ לְיוֹחָנָן אֶת אֲשֶׁר אַתֶּם שׁוֹמְעִים וְרוֹאִים: 5 עִוְרִים רוֹאִים, פִּסְחִים מְהַלְּכִים, מְצֹרָעִים מְטֹהָרִים, חֵרְשִׁים שׁוֹמְעִים, מֵתִים קָמִים, עֲנִיִּים מִתְבַּשְּׂרִים, 6 וְאַשְׁרֵי מִי שֶׁלֹּא אֶהְיֶה לּוֹ לְמִכְשׁוֹל." 7 הֵם הָלְכוּ וְיֵשׁוּעַ הֵחֵל לְדַבֵּר אֶל הֶהָמוֹן הָעָם עַל-אוֹדוֹת יוֹחָנָן: "מַה יְצָאתֶם לַמִּדְבָּר לִרְאוֹת? קָנֶה מִתְנוֹעֵעַ בָּרוּחַ? 8 וּבְכֵן מַה יְצָאתֶם לִרְאוֹת? אִישׁ

soft *clothing* are in kings' houses. [9] But what did you go out to see? A prophet? Yes, I say to you, and more than a prophet. [10] For this is *he* of whom it is written:

> 'Behold, I send My messenger before Your face,
> Who will prepare Your way before You.'

[11] "Assuredly, I say to you, among those born of women there has not risen one greater than John the Baptist; but he who is least in the kingdom of heaven is greater than he. [12] And from the days of John the Baptist until now the kingdom of heaven suffers violence, and the violent take it by force. [13] For all the prophets and the law prophesied until John. [14] And if you are willing to receive *it,* he is Elijah who is to come. [15] He who has ears to hear, let him hear!

[16] "But to what shall I liken this generation? It is like children sitting in the marketplaces and calling to their companions, [17] and saying:

> 'We played the flute for you,
> And you did not dance;
> We mourned to you,
> And you did not lament.'

[18] For John came neither eating nor drinking, and they say, 'He has a demon.' [19] The Son of Man came eating and drinking, and they say, 'Look, a glutton and a winebibber, a friend of tax collectors and sinners!' But wisdom is justified by her children."

[20] Then He began to rebuke the cities in which most of His mighty works had been done, because they did not repent: [21] "Woe to you, Chorazin! Woe to you, Bethsaida! For if the mighty works which were done in you had been done in Tyre and Sidon, they would have repented long ago in sackcloth and ashes. [22] But I say to you, it will be more tolerable for Tyre and Sidon in the day of judgment than for you. [23] And you, Capernaum, who are exalted to heaven, will be brought down to Hades; for if the mighty works which were done in you had been done in Sodom, it would have remained until this day. [24] But I say to you that it shall be more tolerable for the land of Sodom in the day of judgment than for you."

[25] At that time Jesus answered and said, "I thank You, Father, Lord of heaven and earth, that You have hidden these things from *the* wise and prudent and have revealed them to babes. [26] Even so, Father, for so it seemed good in Your sight. [27] All things have been delivered to Me by My Father, and no one knows the Son except the Father. Nor does anyone know the Father except the Son, and *the one* to whom the Son wills to reveal *Him.*

לָבֻשׁ בְּגָדִים מְעֻדָּנִים? הֲרֵי הַלּוֹבְשִׁים לְבוּשׁ מְעֻדָּן בְּבָתֵּי מְלָכִים הֵם. 9 מַה בְּכָל זֹאת יְצָאתֶם לִרְאוֹת? נָבִיא? כֵּן, אֲנִי אוֹמֵר לָכֶם, אַף יוֹתֵר מִנָּבִיא. 10 זֶה הוּא אֲשֶׁר כָּתוּב עָלָיו, 'הִנְנִי שׁוֹלֵחַ מַלְאָכִי לְפָנֶיךָ וּפִנָּה דַּרְכְּךָ לְפָנֶיךָ'. 11 אָמֵן. אוֹמֵר אֲנִי לָכֶם, לֹא קָם בִּילוּדֵי אִשָּׁה גָּדוֹל מִיּוֹחָנָן הַמַּטְבִּיל, אַךְ הַקָּטֹן בְּמַלְכוּת הַשָּׁמַיִם גָּדוֹל מִמֶּנּוּ. 12 וּמִימֵי יוֹחָנָן הַמַּטְבִּיל וְעַד עַתָּה מַלְכוּת הַשָּׁמַיִם פּוֹרֶצֶת וְהַפּוֹרְצִים אוֹחֲזִים בָּהּ. 13 הֵן כָּל הַנְּבִיאִים וְהַתּוֹרָה עַד יוֹחָנָן נִבְּאוּ. 14 וְאִם תִּרְצוּ לְקַבֵּל הֲרֵי הוּא אֵלִיָּהוּ הֶעָתִיד לָבוֹא. 15 מִי שֶׁאָזְנַיִם לוֹ, שֶׁיִּשְׁמַע!

16 לְמִי אֲשַׁוֶּה אֶת הַדּוֹר הַזֶּה? דּוֹמֶה הוּא לִילָדִים הַיּוֹשְׁבִים בְּחַצְרוֹת הַשְּׁוָקִים וְקוֹרְאִים אֶל חַבְרֵיהֶם בְּקוֹל: 17 'חִלַּלְנוּ לָכֶם בַּחֲלִילִים וְלֹא רְקַדְתֶּם, קוֹנַנּוּ לָכֶם קִינָה וְלֹא בְּכִיתֶם'. 18 כִּי בָּא יוֹחָנָן, לֹא אָכַל וְלֹא שָׁתָה, וְאוֹמְרִים עָלָיו 'שֵׁד בּוֹ'. 19 בָּא בֶּן־הָאָדָם וְהוּא אוֹכֵל וְשׁוֹתֶה, וְאוֹמְרִים 'הִנֵּה אִישׁ זוֹלֵל וְסוֹבֵא, יְדִיד הַמּוֹכְסִים וְהַחוֹטְאִים'. אָכֵן, צִדְקָתָהּ שֶׁל הַחָכְמָה הוּכְחָה בְּמַעֲשֶׂיהָ."

20 אָז הֵחֵל לִגְעֹר בֶּעָרִים שֶׁהִתְחוֹלְלוּ בָּהֶן נִסָּיו הָרַבִּים וְלֹא חָזְרוּ בִּתְשׁוּבָה: 21 "אוֹי לָךְ כּוֹרָזִין! אוֹי לָךְ בֵּית צַיְדָה! כִּי אִלּוּ נַעֲשׂוּ בְּצוֹר וּבְצִידוֹן הַפְּלָאוֹת שֶׁנַּעֲשׂוּ בְּתוֹכְכֶן, הֲרֵי מִכְּבָר הָיוּ חוֹזְרוֹת בִּתְשׁוּבָה בְּשַׂק וָאֵפֶר. 22 בְּרַם אוֹמֵר אֲנִי לָכֶן, קַל יוֹתֵר יִהְיֶה בְּיוֹם הַדִּין לְצוֹר וּלְצִידוֹן מֵאֲשֶׁר לָכֶן. 23 וְאַתְּ, כְּפַר נַחוּם, הַאִם לַשָּׁמַיִם תַּעֲלִי? אֶל שְׁאוֹל תֵּרְדִי! כִּי אִלּוּ בִּסְדוֹם נַעֲשׂוּ הַנִּסִּים שֶׁהָיוּ בְּתוֹכֵךְ, עוֹמֶדֶת הָיְתָה עַל תִּלָּהּ עַד הַיּוֹם. 24 וְאוּלָם אֲנִי אוֹמֵר לָךְ, קַל יוֹתֵר יִהְיֶה בְּיוֹם הַדִּין לְאֶרֶץ סְדוֹם מֵאֲשֶׁר לָךְ."

25 בָּעֵת הַהִיא אָמַר יֵשׁוּעַ: "מוֹדֶה אֲנִי לְךָ, אָבִי, אֲדוֹן הַשָּׁמַיִם וְהָאָרֶץ, כִּי הִסְתַּרְתָּ אֶת הַדְּבָרִים הָאֵלֶּה מִן הַחֲכָמִים וְהַנְּבוֹנִים וְגִלִּיתָם לְעוֹלָלִים. 26 כֵּן, אָבִי, שֶׁהֲרֵי כָּךְ הָיָה רָצוֹן מִלְּפָנֶיךָ. 27 הַכֹּל נִמְסַר לִי מֵאֵת אָבִי וְאֵין אִישׁ מַכִּיר אֶת הַבֵּן, זוּלָתִי

12 או: "...מַלְכוּת הַשָּׁמַיִם נִלְקַחַת בְּחָזְקָה וְתַקִּיפִים תּוֹפְסִים אוֹתָהּ."

28 Come to Me, all *you* who labor and are heavy laden, and I will give you rest. 29 Take My yoke upon you and learn from Me, for I am gentle and lowly in heart, and you will find rest for your souls. 30 For My yoke *is* easy and My burden is light."

12 At that time Jesus went through the grainfields on the Sabbath. And His disciples were hungry, and began to pluck heads of grain and to eat. 2 And when the Pharisees saw *it*, they said to Him, "Look, Your disciples are doing what is not lawful to do on the Sabbath!"

3 But He said to them, "Have you not read what David did when he was hungry, he and those who were with him: 4 how he entered the house of God and ate the showbread which was not lawful for him to eat, nor for those who were with him, but only for the priests? 5 Or have you not read in the law that on the Sabbath the priests in the temple profane the Sabbath, and are blameless? 6 Yet I say to you that in this place there is *One* greater than the temple. 7 But if you had known what *this* means, '*I desire mercy and not sacrifice,*' you would not have condemned the guiltless. 8 For the Son of Man is Lord even of the Sabbath."

9 Now when He had departed from there, He went into their synagogue. 10 And behold, there was a man who had a withered hand. And they asked Him, saying, "Is it lawful to heal on the Sabbath?"—that they might accuse Him.

11 Then He said to them, "What man is there among you who has one sheep, and if it falls into a pit on the Sabbath, will not lay hold of it and lift *it* out? 12 Of how much more value then is a man than a sheep? Therefore it is lawful to do good on the Sabbath." 13 Then He said to the man, "Stretch out your hand." And he stretched *it* out, and it was restored as whole as the other. 14 Then the Pharisees went out and plotted against Him, how they might destroy Him.

15 But when Jesus knew *it*, He withdrew from there. And great multitudes followed Him, and He healed them all. 16 Yet He warned them not to make Him known, 17 that it might be fulfilled which was spoken by Isaiah the prophet, saying:

18   "*Behold! My Servant whom I have chosen,*
    My Beloved in whom My soul is well pleased!
    I will put My Spirit upon Him,
    And He will declare justice to the Gentiles.
19   *He will not quarrel nor cry out,*
    Nor will anyone hear His voice in the streets.
20   *A bruised reed He will not break,*
    And smoking flax He will not quench,
    Till He sends forth justice to victory;
21   *And in His name Gentiles will trust.*"

הָאָב; אַף אֵין אִישׁ מַכִּיר אֶת הָאָב, זוּלָתִי הַבֵּן וְכָל מִי שֶׁהַבֵּן רוֹצֶה לְגַלּוֹת לוֹ. 28 בּוֹאוּ אֵלַי כָּל הָעֲמֵלִים וְהָעֲמוּסִים וַאֲנִי אַמְצִיא לָכֶם מְנוּחָה. 29 קְחוּ עֲלֵיכֶם אֶת עֻלִּי וְלִמְדוּ מִמֶּנִּי, כִּי עָנָו אֲנִי וּנְמוּךְ רוּחַ; תִּמְצְאוּ מַרְגּוֹעַ לְנַפְשׁוֹתֵיכֶם, 30 כִּי עֻלִּי נָעִים וְקַל מַשָּׂאִי."

יב בְּאוֹתָהּ הָעֵת עָבַר יֵשׁוּעַ בְּשַׁבָּת בִּשְׂדֵה קָמָה; תַּלְמִידָיו הָיוּ רְעֵבִים וְהֵחֵלּוּ לִקְטֹף שִׁבֳּלִים וְלֶאֱכֹל. 2 רָאוּ זֹאת הַפְּרוּשִׁים וְאָמְרוּ לוֹ: "הִנֵּה תַּלְמִידֶיךָ עוֹשִׂים מַה שֶּׁאָסוּר לַעֲשׂוֹת בְּשַׁבָּת."

3 הֵשִׁיב לָהֶם: "הַאִם לֹא קְרָאתֶם מַה שֶּׁעָשָׂה דָּוִד כַּאֲשֶׁר רָעֵב הוּא וְהָאֲנָשִׁים אֲשֶׁר אִתּוֹ? 4 הֲרֵי נִכְנַס לְבֵית הָאֱלֹהִים וְאָכַל אֶת לֶחֶם הַפָּנִים שֶׁלֹּא הָיָה מֻתָּר לוֹ וְלַאֲנָשָׁיו לֶאֱכֹל כִּי אִם לַכֹּהֲנִים בִּלְבָד. 5 הַאִם לֹא קְרָאתֶם בַּתּוֹרָה כִּי בְּשַׁבָּתוֹת מְחַלְּלִים הַכֹּהֲנִים אֶת הַשַּׁבָּת בַּמִּקְדָּשׁ וְאֵין עֲלֵיהֶם אַשְׁמָה? 6 וַאֲנִי אוֹמֵר לָכֶם שֶׁגָּדוֹל מִן הַמִּקְדָּשׁ נִמְצָא כָּאן. 7 אַךְ אִלּוּ יְדַעְתֶּם מַה מַּשְׁמָע 'חֶסֶד חָפַצְתִּי וְלֹא־זֶבַח', לֹא הֱיִיתֶם מַרְשִׁיעִים אֶת הַנְּקִיִּים, 8 שֶׁהֲרֵי בֶּן־הָאָדָם הוּא אֲדוֹן הַשַּׁבָּת."

9 הוּא הָלַךְ מִשָּׁם וְנִכְנַס לְבֵית הַכְּנֶסֶת. 10 הָיָה שָׁם אִישׁ שֶׁיָּדוֹ יְבֵשָׁה וְהֵם פָּנוּ אֵלָיו בִּשְׁאֵלָה: "הַאִם מֻתָּר לְרַפֵּא בְּשַׁבָּת?" וְזֹאת כְּדֵי שֶׁיּוּכְלוּ לְהַאֲשִׁים אוֹתוֹ.

11 אָמַר לָהֶם: "מִי מִכֶּם שֶׁכֶּבֶשׂ אֶחָד לוֹ וְאִם יִפֹּל בְּשַׁבָּת לְתוֹךְ בּוֹר לֹא יַחֲזִיק בּוֹ וְיָרִים אוֹתוֹ? 12 וְכַמָּה חָשׁוּב הָאָדָם יוֹתֵר מִן הַכֶּבֶשׂ! לָכֵן מֻתָּר לַעֲשׂוֹת אֶת הַטּוֹב בְּשַׁבָּת."

13 אָז אָמַר אֶל הָאִישׁ: "הוֹשֵׁט יָדְךָ!" הוּא הוֹשִׁיט אֶת יָדוֹ וְאָמְנָם שָׁבָה לְאֵיתָנָהּ וְהָיְתָה בְּרִיאָה כְּמוֹ הַשְּׁנִיָּה. 14 יָצְאוּ הַפְּרוּשִׁים וְטִכְּסוּ עֵצָה לְהַכְחִיד אֶת יֵשׁוּעַ.

15 יֵשׁוּעַ יָדַע אֶת זֹאת וְהִתְרַחֵק מִשָּׁם, אַךְ רַבִּים הָלְכוּ אַחֲרָיו. הוּא רִפֵּא אֶת כֻּלָּם 16 וְהִזְהִיר אוֹתָם שֶׁלֹּא יְגַלּוּ אוֹתוֹ, 17 לְמַעַן יִתְקַיֵּם מַה שֶּׁנֶּאֱמַר בְּפִי יְשַׁעְיָהוּ הַנָּבִיא: 18 "הֵן עַבְדִּי אֶתְמָךְ־בּוֹ, בְּחִירִי רָצְתָה נַפְשִׁי. נָתַתִּי רוּחִי עָלָיו, מִשְׁפָּט לַגּוֹיִם יוֹצִיא; 19 לֹא יִצְעַק וְלֹא יִשָּׂא וְלֹא־יַשְׁמִיעַ בַּחוּץ קוֹלוֹ. 20 קָנֶה רָצוּץ לֹא יִשְׁבּוֹר וּפִשְׁתָּה כֵהָה לֹא יְכַבֶּנָּה, 21 עַד יוֹצִיא לָנֶצַח מִשְׁפָּט; וְלִשְׁמוֹ גּוֹיִם יְיַחֵלוּ."

21 נ"מ: לאמת יוציא משפט... ולתורתו איים יְיַחֵלוּ (ישעיה מב:3-4).

22 Then one was brought to Him who was demon-possessed, blind and mute; and He healed him, so that the blind and mute man both spoke and saw. 23 And all the multitudes were amazed and said, "Could this be the Son of David?"

24 Now when the Pharisees heard *it* they said, "This *fellow* does not cast out demons except by Beelzebub, the ruler of the demons."

25 But Jesus knew their thoughts, and said to them: "Every kingdom divided against itself is brought to desolation, and every city or house divided against itself will not stand. 26 If Satan casts out Satan, he is divided against himself. How then will his kingdom stand? 27 And if I cast out demons by Beelzebub, by whom do your sons cast *them* out? Therefore they shall be your judges. 28 But if I cast out demons by the Spirit of God, surely the kingdom of God has come upon you. 29 Or how can one enter a strong man's house and plunder his goods, unless he first binds the strong man? And then he will plunder his house. 30 He who is not with Me is against Me, and he who does not gather with Me scatters abroad.

31 "Therefore I say to you, every sin and blasphemy will be forgiven men, but the blasphemy *against* the Spirit will not be forgiven men. 32 Anyone who speaks a word against the Son of Man, it will be forgiven him; but whoever speaks against the Holy Spirit, it will not be forgiven him, either in this age or in the *age* to come.

33 "Either make the tree good and its fruit good, or else make the tree bad and its fruit bad; for a tree is known by *its* fruit. 34 Brood of vipers! How can you, being evil, speak good things? For out of the abundance of the heart the mouth speaks. 35 A good man out of the good treasure of his heart brings forth good things, and an evil man out of the evil treasure brings forth evil things. 36 But I say to you that for every idle word men may speak, they will give account of it in the day of judgment. 37 For by your words you will be justified, and by your words you will be condemned."

38 Then some of the scribes and Pharisees answered, saying, "Teacher, we want to see a sign from You."

39 But He answered and said to them, "An evil and adulterous generation seeks after a sign, and no sign will be given to it except the sign of the prophet Jonah. 40 For as Jonah was three days and three nights in the belly of the great fish, so will the Son of Man be three days and three nights in the heart of the earth. 41 The men of Nineveh will rise up in the judgment with this generation and condemn it, because they repented at the preaching of Jonah;

22 אָז הוּבָא אֵלָיו אִישׁ אֶחָד שֵׁד וְהוּא עִוֵּר וְאִלֵּם. יֵשׁוּעַ רִפֵּא אוֹתוֹ וְהָאִלֵּם דִּבֵּר וְגַם רָאָה. 23 הִשְׁתּוֹמְמוּ כָּל הֲמוֹנֵי הָעָם וְאָמְרוּ: "הַאִם לֹא זֶה בֶּן־דָּוִד?"

24 כְּשֶׁשָּׁמְעוּ זֹאת הַפְּרוּשִׁים אָמְרוּ: "זֶה אֵינֶנּוּ מְגָרֵשׁ אֶת הַשֵּׁדִים אֶלָּא בְּעֶזְרַת בַּעַל־זְבוּל שַׂר הַשֵּׁדִים." 25 הוֹאִיל וְיָדַע אֶת מַחְשְׁבוֹתֵיהֶם אָמַר לָהֶם: "כָּל מַמְלָכָה הַמְפֻלֶּגֶת בְּתוֹךְ עַצְמָהּ סוֹפָהּ שֶׁהִיא נֶחְרֶבֶת, וְכָל עִיר אוֹ בַּיִת הַמְפֻלָּגִים בְּתוֹךְ עַצְמָם לֹא יַחֲזִיקוּ מַעֲמָד. 26 אִם הַשָּׂטָן מְגָרֵשׁ אֶת הַשָּׂטָן, כִּי אָז הִתְפַּלֵּג בְּתוֹךְ עַצְמוֹ וְאֵיךְ תַּעֲמֹד מַמְלַכְתּוֹ? 27 וְאִם אֲנִי מְגָרֵשׁ אֶת הַשֵּׁדִים בְּעֶזְרַת בַּעַל־זְבוּל, בְּעֶזְרַת מִי מְגָרְשִׁים אוֹתָם בְּנֵיכֶם? לָכֵן הֵם יִהְיוּ שׁוֹפְטֵיכֶם. 28 אַךְ אִם עַל־יְדֵי רוּחַ אֱלֹהִים אֲנִי מְגָרֵשׁ אֶת הַשֵּׁדִים, כִּי אָז הִגִּיעָה אֲלֵיכֶם מַלְכוּת הָאֱלֹהִים. 29 אוֹ אֵיךְ יוּכַל אִישׁ לְהִכָּנֵס לְבֵיתוֹ שֶׁל גִּבּוֹר וְלִטֹּל אֶת כֵּלָיו אִם לֹא יִכְפֹּת תְּחִלָּה אֶת הַגִּבּוֹר? רַק אַחֲרֵי כֵן יָבֹז אֶת בֵּיתוֹ. 30 מִי שֶׁאֵינֶנּוּ אִתִּי נֶגְדִּי הוּא, וּמִי שֶׁאֵינֶנּוּ אוֹסֵף אִתִּי – מְפַזֵּר. 31 עַל כֵּן אֲנִי אוֹמֵר לָכֶם, כָּל חֵטְא וְגִדּוּף יִסָּלַח לִבְנֵי אָדָם, אַךְ גִּדּוּף כְּלַפֵּי הָרוּחַ לֹא יִסָּלַח. 32 כָּל הַמְדַבֵּר דָּבָר נֶגֶד בֶּן־הָאָדָם יִסָּלַח לוֹ, אֲבָל כָּל הַמְדַבֵּר נֶגֶד רוּחַ הַקֹּדֶשׁ לֹא יִסָּלַח לוֹ לֹא בָּעוֹלָם הַזֶּה וְלֹא בָּעוֹלָם הַבָּא."

33 "אוֹ שֶׁהָעֵץ טוֹב וּפִרְיוֹ טוֹב, אוֹ שֶׁהָעֵץ רַע וּפִרְיוֹ רַע; שֶׁהֲרֵי בְּפִרְיוֹ נִכָּר הָעֵץ. 34 יַלְדֵי צִפְעוֹנִים, אֵיךְ תּוּכְלוּ לְדַבֵּר טוֹבוֹת וְאַתֶּם רָעִים? הֵן מִתּוֹךְ הַשּׁוֹפֵעַ בַּלֵּב מְדַבֵּר הַפֶּה. 35 אִישׁ טוֹב מֵפִיק דְּבָרִים טוֹבִים מֵאוֹצָרוֹ הַטּוֹב; אִישׁ רַע מֵפִיק דְּבָרִים רָעִים מֵאוֹצָרוֹ הָרַע. 36 וַאֲנִי אוֹמֵר לָכֶם, כָּל מִלָּה בְּטֵלָה שֶׁיְּדַבְּרוּ בְּנֵי אָדָם יִתְּנוּ עָלֶיהָ דִּין וְחֶשְׁבּוֹן בְּיוֹם הַדִּין. 37 מִדְּבָרֶיךָ תִּצְדַּק וּמִדְּבָרֶיךָ תְּחֻיַּב."

38 אֲחָדִים מִן הַסּוֹפְרִים וְהַפְּרוּשִׁים פָּנוּ אֵלָיו וְאָמְרוּ: "רַבִּי, רוֹצִים אָנוּ לִרְאוֹת מִמְּךָ אוֹת."

39 הֵשִׁיב וְאָמַר לָהֶם: "דּוֹר רַע וּמְנָאֵף מְבַקֵּשׁ אוֹת, וְאוֹת לֹא יִנָּתֵן לוֹ מִלְּבַד אוֹת יוֹנָה הַנָּבִיא. 40 כְּמוֹ שֶׁהָיָה יוֹנָה בִּמְעֵי הַדָּג שְׁלֹשָׁה יָמִים וּשְׁלֹשָׁה לֵילוֹת, כָּךְ יִהְיֶה בֶּן־הָאָדָם בְּלֵב הָאֲדָמָה שְׁלֹשָׁה יָמִים וּשְׁלֹשָׁה לֵילוֹת. 41 אַנְשֵׁי נִינְוֵה יָקוּמוּ בַּמִּשְׁפָּט עִם הַדּוֹר הַזֶּה וְיַרְשִׁיעוּהוּ, כִּי חָזְרוּ בִּתְשׁוּבָה

and indeed a greater than Jonah *is* here. ⁴²The queen of the South will rise up in the judgment with this generation and condemn it, for she came from the ends of the earth to hear the wisdom of Solomon; and indeed a greater than Solomon *is* here.

⁴³ "When an unclean spirit goes out of a man, he goes through dry places, seeking rest, and finds none. ⁴⁴Then he says, 'I will return to my house from which I came.' And when he comes, he finds *it* empty, swept, and put in order. ⁴⁵Then he goes and takes with him seven other spirits more wicked than himself, and they enter and dwell there; and the last *state* of that man is worse than the first. So shall it also be with this wicked generation."

⁴⁶While He was still talking to the multitudes, behold, His mother and brothers stood outside, seeking to speak with Him. ⁴⁷Then one said to Him, "Look, Your mother and Your brothers are standing outside, seeking to speak with You."

⁴⁸But He answered and said to the one who told Him, "Who is My mother and who are My brothers?" ⁴⁹And He stretched out His hand toward His disciples and said, "Here are My mother and My brothers! ⁵⁰For whoever does the will of My Father in heaven is My brother and sister and mother."

13 On the same day Jesus went out of the house and sat by the sea. ²And great multitudes were gathered together to Him, so that He got into a boat and sat; and the whole multitude stood on the shore.

³Then He spoke many things to them in parables, saying: "Behold, a sower went out to sow. ⁴And as he sowed, some *seed* fell by the wayside; and the birds came and devoured them. ⁵Some fell on stony places, where they did not have much earth; and they immediately sprang up because they had no depth of earth. ⁶But when the sun was up they were scorched, and because they had no root they withered away. ⁷And some fell among thorns, and the thorns sprang up and choked them. ⁸But others fell on good ground and yielded a crop: some a hundredfold, some sixty, some thirty. ⁹He who has ears to hear, let him hear!"

¹⁰And the disciples came and said to Him, "Why do You speak to them in parables?"

¹¹He answered and said to them, "Because it has been given to you to know the mysteries of the kingdom of heaven, but to them it has not been given. ¹²For whoever has, to him more will be given, and he will have abundance; but whoever

בִּקְרִיאַת יוֹנָה; וְהִנֵּה גָּדוֹל מִיּוֹנָה כָּאן. ⁴²מַלְכַּת תֵּימָן תָּקוּם בַּמִּשְׁפָּט עִם הַדּוֹר הַזֶּה וְתַרְשִׁיעַ אוֹתוֹ, כִּי בָּאָה מִקְצֵה הָאָרֶץ לִשְׁמֹעַ אֶת חָכְמַת שְׁלֹמֹה; וְהִנֵּה גָּדוֹל מִשְּׁלֹמֹה כָּאן."

⁴³הָרוּחַ הַטְּמֵאָה הַיּוֹצֵאת מִן הָאָדָם מְשׁוֹטֶטֶת בִּמְקוֹמוֹת צִיָּה וּמְבַקֶּשֶׁת לָהּ מָנוֹחַ וְאֵינָה מוֹצֵאת. ⁴⁴אָז תֹּאמַר: 'אָשׁוּבָה אֶל בֵּיתִי שֶׁיָּצָאתִי מִמֶּנּוּ.' הִיא בָּאָה וּמוֹצֵאת אוֹתוֹ מְפֻנֶּה, מְטֻאטָא וּמְהֻדָּר. ⁴⁵מִיָּד הִיא הוֹלֶכֶת וְלוֹקַחַת אִתָּהּ שֶׁבַע רוּחוֹת אֲחֵרוֹת רָעוֹת מִמֶּנָּה וְכֻלָּן נִכְנָסוֹת לִשְׁכֹּן שָׁם. אָכֵן גְּרוּעָה אַחֲרִיתוֹ שֶׁל הָאִישׁ הַהוּא מֵרֵאשִׁיתוֹ. כֵּן גַּם יִהְיֶה לַדּוֹר הָרַע הַזֶּה."

⁴⁶בְּשָׁעָה שֶׁדִּבֵּר אֶל הֲמוֹן הָעָם בָּאוּ אִמּוֹ וְאֶחָיו. הֵם עָמְדוּ בַּחוּץ וְרָצוּ לְדַבֵּר אִתּוֹ. ⁴⁷אָמַר לוֹ מִישֶׁהוּ: "הִנֵּה אִמְּךָ וְאַחֶיךָ עוֹמְדִים בַּחוּץ וּמְבַקְשִׁים לְדַבֵּר אִתְּךָ." ⁴⁸הֵשִׁיב וְאָמַר לָאִישׁ אֲשֶׁר הוֹדִיעַ לוֹ: "מִי הִיא אִמִּי וּמִי הֵם אַחַי?" ⁴⁹וּבְהוֹשִׁיטוֹ אֶת יָדוֹ אֶל תַּלְמִידָיו אָמַר: "הִנֵּה אִמִּי וְאַחַי, ⁵⁰כִּי כָּל הָעוֹשֶׂה אֶת רְצוֹן אָבִי שֶׁבַּשָּׁמַיִם הוּא אָחִי וַאֲחוֹתִי וְאִמִּי."

יג בַּיּוֹם הַהוּא יָצָא יֵשׁוּעַ מִן הַבַּיִת וְיָשַׁב עַל-יַד הַיָּם. ²כֵּיוָן שֶׁנִּקְהֲלוּ אֵלָיו הֲמוֹן עַם רַב יָרַד לַסִּירָה לָשֶׁבֶת בָּהּ, וְכָל הֶהָמוֹן עָמַד עַל הַחוֹף. ³אָז דִּבֵּר אֲלֵיהֶם רַבּוֹת בִּמְשָׁלִים וְאָמַר: "הִנֵּה הַזּוֹרֵעַ יָצָא לִזְרֹעַ. ⁴כַּאֲשֶׁר זָרַע נָפְלוּ כַּמָּה זְרָעִים בְּשׁוּלֵי הַדֶּרֶךְ וּבָאוּ צִפֳּרִים וְאָכְלוּ אוֹתָם. ⁵אֲחֵרִים נָפְלוּ עַל אַדְמַת טְרָשִׁים, בִּמְקוֹם שֶׁלֹּא הָיְתָה לָהֶם הַרְבֵּה אֲדָמָה, וּמִהֲרוּ לִצְמֹחַ מִפְּנֵי שֶׁלֹּא הָיְתָה לָהֶם אֲדָמָה עֲמֻקָּה. ⁶אוּלָם כְּשֶׁזָּרְחָה הַשֶּׁמֶשׁ נִצְרְבוּ וּבְאֵין שֹׁרֶשׁ הִתְיַבְּשׁוּ. ⁷אֲחֵרִים נָפְלוּ בֵּין קוֹצִים, אַךְ הַקּוֹצִים צָמְחוּ וְהֶחֱנִיקוּ אוֹתָם. ⁸וַאֲחֵרִים נָפְלוּ עַל אֲדָמָה טוֹבָה וְעָשׂוּ פְּרִי – זֶה פִּי מֵאָה, זֶה פִּי שִׁשִּׁים וְזֶה פִּי שְׁלוֹשִׁים. ⁹מִי שֶׁאָזְנַיִם לוֹ, שֶׁיִּשְׁמַע!"

¹⁰נִגְּשׁוּ הַתַּלְמִידִים וְשָׁאֲלוּ: "מַדּוּעַ אַתָּה מְדַבֵּר אֲלֵיהֶם בִּמְשָׁלִים?" ¹¹הֵשִׁיב וְאָמַר: "מִפְּנֵי שֶׁלָּכֶם נִתַּן לָדַעַת אֶת סוֹדוֹת מַלְכוּת הַשָּׁמַיִם, אַךְ לָהֶם לֹא נִתָּן. ¹²כִּי מִי שֶׁיֵּשׁ לוֹ נָתוֹן יִנָּתֵן לוֹ וְשֶׁפַע יִהְיֶה לוֹ,

does not have, even what he has will be taken away from him. 13 Therefore I speak to them in parables, because seeing they do not see, and hearing they do not hear, nor do they understand. 14 And in them the prophecy of Isaiah is fulfilled, which says:

'Hearing you will hear and shall not understand,
And seeing you will see and not perceive;
15 For the hearts of this people have grown dull.
    Their ears are hard of hearing,
    And their eyes they have closed,
    Lest they should see with *their* eyes and hear with
        their ears,
    Lest they should understand with *their* hearts and
        turn,
    So that I should heal them.'

16 But blessed *are* your eyes for they see, and your ears for they hear; 17 for assuredly, I say to you that many prophets and righteous *men* desired to see what you see, and did not see *it,* and to hear what you hear, and did not hear *it.*

18 "Therefore hear the parable of the sower: 19 When anyone hears the word of the kingdom, and does not understand *it,* then the wicked *one* comes and snatches away what was sown in his heart. This is he who received seed by the wayside. 20 But he who received the seed on stony places, this is he who hears the word and immediately receives it with joy; 21 yet he has no root in himself, but endures only for a while. For when tribulation or persecution arises because of the word, immediately he stumbles. 22 Now he who received seed among the thorns is he who hears the word, and the cares of this world and the deceitfulness of riches choke the word, and he becomes unfruitful. 23 But he who received seed on the good ground is he who hears the word and understands *it,* who indeed bears fruit and produces: some a hundredfold, some sixty, some thirty."

24 Another parable He put forth to them, saying: "The kingdom of heaven is like a man who sowed good seed in his field; 25 but while men slept, his enemy came and sowed tares among the wheat and went his way. 26 But when the grain had sprouted and produced a crop, then the tares also appeared. 27 So the servants of the owner came and said to him, 'Sir, did you not sow good seed in your field? How then does it have tares?' 28 He said to them, 'An enemy has done this.' The servants said to him, 'Do you want us then to go and gather them up?' 29 But he said, 'No, lest while you gather up the tares you also uproot the wheat with them. 30 Let both grow together until the harvest, and at the time of harvest I will say to the reapers, "First

אַךְ מִי שֶׁאֵין לוֹ, גַּם מַה שֶּׁיֵּשׁ לוֹ יֻלָּקַח מִמֶּנּוּ. 13 לָכֵן בִּמְשָׁלִים אֲנִי מְדַבֵּר אֲלֵיהֶם, כִּי בִּרְאוֹתָם אֵינָם רוֹאִים וּבְשָׁמְעָם אֵינָם שׁוֹמְעִים אַף אֵינָם מְבִינִים. 14 וּמִתְקַיֶּמֶת בָּהֶם נְבוּאַת יְשַׁעְיָהוּ לֵאמֹר: ״שָׁמוֹעַ תִּשְׁמְעוּ וְאַל־תָּבִינוּ וּרְאוֹ רָאוֹ וְאַל־תֵּדָעוּ. 15 הַשְׁמֵן לֵב־הָעָם הַזֶּה וְאָזְנָיו הַכְבֵּד וְעֵינָיו הָשַׁע, פֶּן־יִרְאֶה בְעֵינָיו וּבְאָזְנָיו יִשְׁמַע וּלְבָבוֹ יָבִין, וָשָׁב וְרָפָא לוֹ. 16 אַשְׁרֵי עֵינֵיכֶם הָרוֹאוֹת וְאָזְנֵיכֶם הַשּׁוֹמְעוֹת. 17 אָמֵן. אוֹמֵר אֲנִי לָכֶם, נְבִיאִים וְצַדִּיקִים רַבִּים נִכְסְפוּ לִרְאוֹת אֶת אֲשֶׁר אַתֶּם רוֹאִים וְלֹא רָאוּ, וְלִשְׁמֹעַ אֶת אֲשֶׁר אַתֶּם שׁוֹמְעִים וְלֹא שָׁמֵעוּ.״

18 ״וּבְכֵן שִׁמְעוּ אַתֶּם אֶת פֵּשֶׁר מְשַׁל הַזּוֹרֵעַ. 19 כָּל הַשּׁוֹמֵעַ אֶת דְּבַר הַמַּלְכוּת וְאֵינֶנּוּ מֵבִין, בָּא הָרָע וְחוֹטֵף אֶת מַה שֶּׁנִּזְרַע בִּלְבָבוֹ; זֶהוּ הַנִּזְרָע בְּשׁוּלֵי הַדֶּרֶךְ. 20 הַנִּזְרָע עַל אַדְמַת טְרָשִׁים הוּא הַשּׁוֹמֵעַ אֶת הַדָּבָר וּמִיָּד מְקַבֵּל אוֹתוֹ בְּשִׂמְחָה, 21 אַךְ אֵין לוֹ שֹׁרֶשׁ בְּתוֹכוֹ וְרַק לְשָׁעָה יַעֲמֹד, וּבִהְיוֹת צָרָה אוֹ רְדִיפָה בִּגְלַל הַדָּבָר הוּא נִכְשָׁל מִיָּד. 22 הַנִּזְרָע בֵּין הַקּוֹצִים הוּא הַשּׁוֹמֵעַ אֶת הַדָּבָר, אֶלָּא שֶׁדַּאֲגוֹת הָעוֹלָם הַזֶּה וּמַדּוּחֵי הָעֹשֶׁר מַחֲנִיקִים אֶת הַדָּבָר וְלֹא יַעֲשֶׂה פְּרִי. 23 הַנִּזְרָע עַל הָאֲדָמָה הַטּוֹבָה הוּא הַשּׁוֹמֵעַ אֶת הַדָּבָר וּמֵבִין וְגַם עוֹשֶׂה פְּרִי – זֶה עוֹשֶׂה פִּי מֵאָה, זֶה פִּי שִׁשִּׁים וְזֶה פִּי שְׁלֹשִׁים.״

24 הַמָּשִׁיחַ וְסִפֵּר לָהֶם מְשָׁל אַחֵר: ״מַלְכוּת הַשָּׁמַיִם דּוֹמָה לְאִישׁ הַזּוֹרֵעַ זֶרַע טוֹב בְּשָׂדֵהוּ. 25 וְהִנֵּה כְּשֶׁיָּשְׁנוּ הָאֲנָשִׁים בָּא אוֹיֵב, זָרַע עֲשָׂבִים רָעִים בֵּין הַחִטִּים וְהָלַךְ לוֹ. 26 כַּאֲשֶׁר צָמְחוּ הַגִּבְעוֹלִים וְעָשׂוּ תְּבוּאָה נִרְאוּ גַּם הָעֲשָׂבִים הָרָעִים. 27 אָז נִגְּשׁוּ עַבְדֵי בַּעַל־הַבַּיִת וְאָמְרוּ אֵלָיו, 'אֲדוֹנֵנוּ, הֲלֹא זֶרַע טוֹב זָרַעְתָּ בְּשָׂדֶךָ; מִנַּיִן יֵשׁ בּוֹ עֲשָׂבִים רָעִים?' 28 אָמַר לָהֶם, 'אִישׁ אוֹיֵב עָשָׂה זֹאת'. שָׁאֲלוּ הָעֲבָדִים, 'הַאִם אַתָּה רוֹצֶה שֶׁנֵּלֵךְ וּנְלַקֵּט אוֹתָם?' 29 הֵשִׁיב בַּעַל־הַבַּיִת, 'לֹא, שֶׁמָּא בְּלַקֶּטְכֶם אֶת הָעֲשָׂבִים הָרָעִים תַּעַקְרוּ אִתָּם גַּם אֶת הַחִטִּים. 30 הַנִּיחוּ לִשְׁנֵיהֶם לִגְדֹּל יַחַד עַד הַקָּצִיר. בְּעֵת הַקָּצִיר אֹמַר לַקּוֹצְרִים: לַקְּטוּ בָּרִאשׁוֹנָה אֶת הָעֲשָׂבִים הָרָעִים וְאַגְדוּ אוֹתָם לַאֲלֻמּוֹת כְּדֵי לְשָׂרְפָם, וְאֶת הַחִטִּים אִסְפוּ לַאֲסָם שֶׁלִּי'.״

gather together the tares and bind them in bundles to burn them, but gather the wheat into my barn." ' "

31 Another parable He put forth to them, saying: "The kingdom of heaven is like a mustard seed, which a man took and sowed in his field, 32 which indeed is the least of all the seeds; but when it is grown it is greater than the herbs and becomes a tree, so that the birds of the air come and nest in its branches."

33 Another parable He spoke to them: "The kingdom of heaven is like leaven, which a woman took and hid in three measures of meal till it was all leavened."

34 All these things Jesus spoke to the multitude in parables; and without a parable He did not speak to them, 35 that it might be fulfilled which was spoken by the prophet, saying:

"I will open My mouth in parables;
I will utter things kept secret from the foundation of the world."

36 Then Jesus sent the multitude away and went into the house. And His disciples came to Him, saying, "Explain to us the parable of the tares of the field."

37 He answered and said to them: "He who sows the good seed is the Son of Man. 38 The field is the world, the good seeds are the sons of the kingdom, but the tares are the sons of the wicked *one*. 39 The enemy who sowed them is the devil, the harvest is the end of the age, and the reapers are the angels. 40 Therefore as the tares are gathered and burned in the fire, so it will be at the end of this age. 41 The Son of Man will send out His angels, and they will gather out of His kingdom all things that offend, and those who practice lawlessness, 42 and will cast them into the furnace of fire. There will be wailing and gnashing of teeth. 43 Then the righteous will shine forth as the sun in the kingdom of their Father. He who has ears to hear, let him hear!

44 "Again, the kingdom of heaven is like treasure hidden in a field, which a man found and hid; and for joy over it he goes and sells all that he has and buys that field.

45 "Again, the kingdom of heaven is like a merchant seeking beautiful pearls, 46 who, when he had found one pearl of great price, went and sold all that he had and bought it.

47 "Again, the kingdom of heaven is like a dragnet that was cast into the sea and gathered some of every kind, 48 which, when it was full, they drew to shore; and they sat down and gathered the good into vessels, but threw the bad away. 49 So it

31 הוֹסִיף וְסִפֵּר מָשָׁל אַחֵר: "מַלְכוּת הַשָּׁמַיִם דּוֹמָה לְגַרְגִּיר חַרְדָּל אֲשֶׁר לָקְחוֹ אִישׁ וְזָרַע אוֹתוֹ בְּשָׂדֵהוּ. 32 אָמְנָם קָטֹן הוּא מִכָּל הַזְּרָעִים, אַךְ לְאַחַר צְמִיחָתוֹ גָּדוֹל הוּא מִן הַיְרָקוֹת וְהוֹפֵךְ לְעֵץ, כָּךְ שֶׁעוֹפוֹת הַשָּׁמַיִם בָּאִים וּמְקַנְּנִים בֵּין עֲנָפָיו."

33 עוֹד מָשָׁל סִפֵּר לָהֶם: "מַלְכוּת הַשָּׁמַיִם דּוֹמָה לִשְׂאוֹר אֲשֶׁר לָקְחָה אִשָּׁה וְטָמְנָה אוֹתוֹ בִּשְׁלוֹשׁ סְאִים קֶמַח עַד שֶׁהֶחְמִיץ כֻּלּוֹ."

34 אֶת כָּל אֵלֶּה דִּבֵּר יֵשׁוּעַ לַהֲמוֹן הָעָם בִּמְשָׁלִים, וּבְלִי מָשָׁל לֹא דִּבֵּר אֲלֵיהֶם; 35 לְמַעַן יִתְקַיֵּם מַה שֶּׁנֶּאֱמַר בְּפִי הַנָּבִיא: "אֶפְתְּחָה בְמָשָׁל פִּי, אַבִּיעָה חִידוֹת מִנִּי-קֶדֶם."

36 אַחֲרֵי כֵן שִׁלַּח יֵשׁוּעַ אֶת הֲמוֹן הָעָם וְנִכְנַס הַבַּיְתָה. נִגְּשׁוּ אֵלָיו תַּלְמִידָיו וְאָמְרוּ: "הַסְבֵּר נָא לָנוּ אֶת מְשַׁל הָעֲשָׂבִים הָרָעִים."

37 הֵשִׁיב וְאָמַר: "הַזּוֹרֵעַ אֶת הַזֶּרַע הַטּוֹב הוּא בֶּן-הָאָדָם. 38 הַשָּׂדֶה הוּא הַתֵּבֵל. הַזֶּרַע הַטּוֹב הוּא בְּנֵי הַמַּלְכוּת, וְהָעֲשָׂבִים הָרָעִים הֵם בְּנֵי רָע, 39 הָאוֹיֵב הַזּוֹרֵעַ אוֹתָם הוּא הַשָּׂטָן. הַקָּצִיר הוּא קֵץ הָעוֹלָם, וְהַקּוֹצְרִים הֵם הַמַּלְאָכִים. 40 וּכְמוֹ שֶׁאוֹסְפִים אֶת הָעֲשָׂבִים הָרָעִים וְשׂוֹרְפִים אוֹתָם בָּאֵשׁ כָּךְ יִהְיֶה בְּקֵץ הָעוֹלָם. 41 בֶּן-הָאָדָם יִשְׁלַח אֶת מַלְאָכָיו וְיִלְקְטוּ מִמַּמְלַכְתּוֹ אֶת כָּל הַמִּכְשׁוֹלוֹת וְאֶת כָּל עוֹשֵׂי הָרֶשַׁע, 42 וְיַשְׁלִיכוּ אוֹתָם אֶל תַּנּוּר הָאֵשׁ; שָׁם יִהְיוּ הַיְלָלָה וַחֲרוֹק הַשִּׁנַּיִם. 43 אָז יַזְהִירוּ הַצַּדִּיקִים כַּשֶּׁמֶשׁ בְּמַמְלֶכֶת אֲבִיהֶם. מִי שֶׁאָזְנַיִם לוֹ, שֶׁיִּשְׁמַע!"

44 "דּוֹמָה מַלְכוּת הַשָּׁמַיִם לְאוֹצָר טָמוּן בַּשָּׂדֶה, וְהִנֵּה מְצָאוֹ אִישׁ. הוּא טוֹמֵן אוֹתוֹ שׁוּב וּבְשִׂמְחָתוֹ הוּא הוֹלֵךְ וּמוֹכֵר אֶת כָּל אֲשֶׁר לוֹ וְקוֹנֶה אֶת הַשָּׂדֶה הַהוּא. 45 עוֹד דּוֹמָה מַלְכוּת הַשָּׁמַיִם לְסוֹחֵר הַמְחַפֵּשׂ מַרְגָּלִיּוֹת יָפוֹת. 46 כַּאֲשֶׁר מָצָא מַרְגָּלִית אַחַת יְקָרַת עֵרֶךְ הָלַךְ וּמָכַר אֶת כָּל אֲשֶׁר לוֹ וְקָנָה אוֹתָהּ.

47 וְעוֹד דּוֹמָה מַלְכוּת הַשָּׁמַיִם לְרֶשֶׁת שֶׁהֻשְׁלְכָה לַיָּם וְאָסְפָה מִכָּל מִין. 48 כַּאֲשֶׁר נִתְמַלְאָה הֶעֱלוּ אוֹתָהּ לַחוֹף וְיָשְׁבוּ וְלִקְּטוּ אֶת הַטּוֹבִים לְתוֹךְ הַכֵּלִים וְאֶת הָרָעִים הִשְׁלִיכוּ. 49 כָּךְ יִהְיֶה בְּקֵץ הָעוֹלָם. הַמַּלְאָכִים

will be at the end of the age. The angels will come forth, separate the wicked from among the just, 50 and cast them into the furnace of fire. There will be wailing and gnashing of teeth."

51 Jesus said to them, "Have you understood all these things?"

They said to Him, "Yes, Lord."

52 Then He said to them, "Therefore every scribe instructed concerning the kingdom of heaven is like a householder who brings out of his treasure *things* new and old."

53 Now it came to pass, when Jesus had finished these parables, that He departed from there. 54 When He had come to His own country, He taught them in their synagogue, so that they were astonished and said, "Where did this *Man* get this wisdom and *these* mighty works? 55 Is this not the carpenter's son? Is not His mother called Mary? And His brothers James, Joses, Simon, and Judas? 56 And His sisters, are they not all with us? Where then did this *Man* get all these things?" 57 So they were offended at Him.

But Jesus said to them, "A prophet is not without honor except in his own country and in his own house." 58 Now He did not do many mighty works there because of their unbelief.

14 At that time Herod the tetrarch heard the report about Jesus 2 and said to his servants, "This is John the Baptist; he is risen from the dead, and therefore these powers are at work in him." 3 For Herod had laid hold of John and bound him, and put *him* in prison for the sake of Herodias, his brother Philip's wife. 4 Because John had said to him, "It is not lawful for you to have her." 5 And although he wanted to put him to death, he feared the multitude, because they counted him as a prophet.

6 But when Herod's birthday was celebrated, the daughter of Herodias danced before them and pleased Herod. 7 Therefore he promised with an oath to give her whatever she might ask.

8 So she, having been prompted by her mother, said, "Give me John the Baptist's head here on a platter."

9 And the king was sorry; nevertheless, because of the oaths and because of those who sat with him, he commanded *it* to be given *to her.* 10 So he sent and had John beheaded in prison. 11 And his head was brought on a platter and given to the girl, and she brought *it* to her mother. 12 Then his disciples came and took away the body and buried it, and went and told Jesus.

יֵצְאוּ וְיַבְדִּילוּ אֶת הָרְשָׁעִים מִבֵּין הַצַּדִּיקִים 50 וְיַשְׁלִיכוּ אוֹתָם אֶל תַּנּוּר הָאֵשׁ; שָׁם יִהְיוּ הַיְלָלָה וַחֲרוֹק הַשִּׁנַּיִם. 51 הַאִם הֲבִינוֹתֶם אֶת כָּל זֶה?" הֵשִׁיבוּ לוֹ: "כֵּן".

52 אָמַר לָהֶם: "לָכֵן כָּל סוֹפֵר לָמוּד מַלְכוּת שָׁמַיִם דּוֹמֶה לְבַעַל־בַּיִת הַמּוֹצִיא מֵאוֹצָרוֹ חֲדָשׁוֹת וְגַם יְשָׁנוֹת."

53 כַּאֲשֶׁר סִיֵּם יֵשׁוּעַ אֶת הַמְּשָׁלִים הָאֵלֶּה הָלַךְ מִשָּׁם. 54 הוּא בָּא אֶל עִירוֹ וְלִמֵּד אוֹתָם בְּבֵית הַכְּנֶסֶת עַד כִּי הִשְׁתּוֹמְמוּ וְאָמְרוּ: "מִנַּיִן לוֹ הַחָכְמָה הַזֹּאת וּמַעֲשֵׂי הַנִּסִּים? 55 הֲרֵי זֶה בְּנוֹ שֶׁל הַנַּגָּר. הֲלֹא שֵׁם אִמּוֹ מִרְיָם וְאֶחָיו יַעֲקֹב וְיוֹסֵף וְשִׁמְעוֹן וִיהוּדָה. 56 וַאֲחִיוֹתָיו הֲרֵי כֻּלָּן פֹּה אִתָּנוּ. אִם כֵּן מִנַּיִן לוֹ כָּל הַדְּבָרִים הָאֵלֶּה?" 57 הוּא הָיָה לָהֶם לְמִכְשׁוֹל. אָמַר לָהֶם יֵשׁוּעַ: "אֵין נָבִיא בְּעִירוֹ וּבְבֵיתוֹ", 58 וְלֹא עָשָׂה שָׁם נִסִּים רַבִּים בִּגְלַל חֹסֶר אֱמוּנָתָם.

יד בָּעֵת הַהִיא שָׁמַע הוֹרְדוֹס שַׂר־רֹבַע הַמְּדִינָה אֶת שֵׁמַע יֵשׁוּעַ. 2 אָמַר אֶל מְשָׁרְתָיו: "זֶהוּ יוֹחָנָן הַמַּטְבִּיל. הוּא קָם מִן הַמֵּתִים וְלָכֵן פּוֹעֲלִים בּוֹ מַעֲשֵׂי הַנִּסִּים"; 3 שֶׁכֵּן הוֹרְדוֹס תָּפַס אֶת יוֹחָנָן, כָּבַל אוֹתוֹ וְשָׂם אוֹתוֹ בְּבֵית הַסֹּהַר בִּגְלַל הוֹרוֹדְיָה אֵשֶׁת פִילִיפּוֹס אָחִיו, 4 לְאַחַר שֶׁיּוֹחָנָן אָמַר לוֹ, "אָסוּר לְךָ לָקַחַת אוֹתָהּ." 5 הוֹרְדוֹס רָצָה לַהֲרֹג אוֹתוֹ, אוּלָם חָשַׁשׁ מִן הֶהָמוֹן מִפְּנֵי שֶׁחֲשָׁבוּהוּ לְנָבִיא. 6 כְּשֶׁהוּחַג יוֹם הֻלַּדְתּוֹ שֶׁל הוֹרְדוֹס רָקְדָה בַּת־הוֹרוֹדְיָה בֵּין הַנּוֹכְחִים וּמָצְאָה חֵן בְּעֵינֵי הוֹרְדוֹס. 7 לְפִיכָךְ הִבְטִיחַ לָהּ בִּשְׁבוּעָה לָתֵת לָהּ כָּל מַה שֶׁתְּבַקֵּשׁ. 8 עַל־פִּי הוֹרָאַת אִמָּהּ – אָמְרָה: "תֵּן לִי פֹּה בִּקְעָרָה אֶת רֹאשׁ יוֹחָנָן הַמַּטְבִּיל." 9 הִתְעַצֵּב הַמֶּלֶךְ, אֶלָּא שֶׁבִּגְלַל הַשְּׁבוּעָה וְהַמְּסֻבִּים אִתּוֹ צִוָּה לָתֵת לָהּ. 10 הוּא שָׁלַח לִכְרֹת אֶת רֹאשׁ יוֹחָנָן בְּבֵית הַסֹּהַר, 11 וְכַאֲשֶׁר הוּבָא רֹאשׁוֹ בַּקְּעָרָה נִתְּנוֹהוּ לַנַּעֲרָה וְהִיא הֵבִיאָה אוֹתוֹ לְאִמָּהּ. 12 בָּאוּ תַּלְמִידָיו, לָקְחוּ אֶת גּוּפָתוֹ וְקָבְרוּ אוֹתָהּ, וְהָלְכוּ וְהוֹדִיעוּ לְיֵשׁוּעַ.

13 When Jesus heard *it,* He departed from there by boat to a deserted place by Himself. But when the multitudes heard it, they followed Him on foot from the cities. 14 And when Jesus went out He saw a great multitude; and He was moved with compassion for them, and healed their sick. 15 When it was evening, His disciples came to Him, saying, "This is a deserted place, and the hour is already late. Send the multitudes away, that they may go into the villages and buy themselves food."

16 But Jesus said to them, "They do not need to go away. You give them something to eat."

17 And they said to Him, "We have here only five loaves and two fish."

18 He said, "Bring them here to Me." 19 Then He commanded the multitudes to sit down on the grass. And He took the five loaves and the two fish, and looking up to heaven, He blessed and broke and gave the loaves to the disciples; and the disciples gave to the multitudes. 20 So they all ate and were filled, and they took up twelve baskets full of the fragments that remained. 21 Now those who had eaten were about five thousand men, besides women and children.

22 Immediately Jesus made His disciples get into the boat and go before Him to the other side, while He sent the multitudes away. 23 And when He had sent the multitudes away, He went up on the mountain by Himself to pray. Now when evening came, He was alone there. 24 But the boat was now in the middle of the sea, tossed by the waves, for the wind was contrary.

25 Now in the fourth watch of the night Jesus went to them, walking on the sea. 26 And when the disciples saw Him walking on the sea, they were troubled, saying, "It is a ghost!" And they cried out for fear.

27 But immediately Jesus spoke to them, saying, "Be of good cheer! It is I; do not be afraid."

28 And Peter answered Him and said, "Lord, if it is You, command me to come to You on the water."

29 So He said, "Come." And when Peter had come down out of the boat, he walked on the water to go to Jesus. 30 But when he saw that the wind *was* boisterous, he was afraid; and beginning to sink he cried out, saying, "Lord, save me!"

31 And immediately Jesus stretched out *His* hand and caught him, and said to him, "O you of little faith, why did you doubt?" 32 And when they got into the boat, the wind ceased.

13 יֵשׁוּעַ שָׁמַע וְנָסַע מִשָּׁם בִּסְיִרָה אֶל מָקוֹם שׁוֹמֵם, הוּא לְבַדּוֹ. כֵּיוָן שֶׁשָּׁמְעוּ הֲהֲמוֹנִים הָלְכוּ אַחֲרָיו בָּרֶגֶל מִן הֶעָרִים. 14 כְּשֶׁיָּצָא רָאָה הֲמוֹן עַם רַב. הוּא נִתְמַלֵּא רַחֲמִים עֲלֵיהֶם וְרִפֵּא אֶת הַחוֹלִים שֶׁבֵּינֵיהֶם. 15 לְעֵת עֶרֶב נִגְּשׁוּ אֵלָיו תַּלְמִידָיו וְאָמְרוּ: "הַמָּקוֹם שׁוֹמֵם וְהַשָּׁעָה כְּבָר מְאֻחֶרֶת; שְׁלַח אֶת הֲמוֹן הָעָם וְיֵלְכוּ אֶל הַכְּפָרִים לִקְנוֹת לָהֶם אֹכֶל."

16 אָמַר לָהֶם יֵשׁוּעַ: "אֵין הֵם צְרִיכִים לָלֶכֶת. תְּנוּ לָהֶם אַתֶּם לֶאֱכֹל."

17 הֵשִׁיבוּ לוֹ: "אֵין לָנוּ פֹּה אֶלָּא חָמֵשׁ כִּכְּרוֹת לֶחֶם וּשְׁנֵי דָגִים."

18 אָמַר: "הָבִיאוּ אוֹתָם אֵלַי הֵנָּה." 19 הוּא צִוָּה אֶת הָעָם לָשֶׁבֶת עַל הַדֶּשֶׁא, לָקַח אֶת חֲמֵשׁ כִּכְּרוֹת הַלֶּחֶם וְאֶת שְׁנֵי הַדָּגִים, נָשָׂא עֵינָיו הַשָּׁמַיְמָה וּבֵרֵךְ. לְאַחַר מִכֵּן בָּצַע אֶת הַלֶּחֶם וְנָתַן לַתַּלְמִידִים וְהַתַּלְמִידִים נָתְנוּ לָעָם. 20 הַכֹּל אָכְלוּ וְשָׂבְעוּ, וּמִמַּה שֶּׁנּוֹתַר אָסְפוּ שְׁנֵים־עָשָׂר סַלִּים מְלֵאִים. 21 מִסְפַּר הָאוֹכְלִים הָיָה כַּחֲמֵשֶׁת אֲלָפִים אִישׁ מִלְּבַד הַנָּשִׁים וְהַטַּף.

22 מִיַּד הֵאִיץ בְּתַלְמִידָיו לְהִכָּנֵס לַסְּיִרָה וּלְהַקְדִּים אוֹתוֹ בַּנְּסִיעָה אֶל עֵבֶר הַיָּם עַד שֶׁהוּא יְשַׁלַּח אֶת הֲמוֹן הָעָם. 23 הוּא שָׁלַח אֶת הָעָם וְעָלָה לָהָר לְבַדּוֹ כְּדֵי לְהִתְפַּלֵּל. לְעֵת עֶרֶב הָיָה שָׁם לְבַדּוֹ. 24 בֵּינְתַיִם הִגִּיעָה הַסְּיִרָה לְמֶרְחָק כַּמָּה מִילִין מִן הַחוֹף כְּשֶׁהִיא מְטֻלְטֶלֶת עַל הַגַּלִּים וְהָרוּחַ נוֹשֶׁבֶת נֶגְדָּהּ. 25 וְהִנֵּה בְּאַשְׁמֹרֶת הַלַּיְלָה הָרְבִיעִית בָּא אֲלֵיהֶם יֵשׁוּעַ וְהוּא מְהַלֵּךְ עַל פְּנֵי הַיָּם. 26 כְּשֶׁרָאוּהוּ הַתַּלְמִידִים מְהַלֵּךְ עַל פְּנֵי הַיָּם נִבְהֲלוּ. אָמְרוּ: "רוּחַ רְפָאִים הִיא", וְהֵחֵלּוּ לִצְעֹק מִפַּחַד.

27 מִיַּד דִּבֵּר אֲלֵיהֶם יֵשׁוּעַ וְאָמַר: "חִזְקוּ, אֲנִי הוּא. אַל תִּפְחֲדוּ."

28 הֵשִׁיב כֵּיפָא וְאָמַר אֵלָיו: "אֲדוֹנִי, אִם אַתָּה הוּא, צַוֵּנִי לָבוֹא אֵלֶיךָ עַל פְּנֵי הַמַּיִם."

29 אָמַר יֵשׁוּעַ: "בּוֹא!"

כֵּיפָא יָרַד מִן הַסְּיִרָה וְהָלַךְ עַל פְּנֵי הַמַּיִם לִקְרַאת יֵשׁוּעַ. 30 אוּלָם כְּשֶׁרָאָה אֶת הָרוּחַ הַסּוֹעֶרֶת פָּחַד וְהֵחֵל לִשְׁקֹעַ. הוּא צָעַק: "אֲדוֹנִי, הַצֵּל אוֹתִי!"

31 מִיַּד הוֹשִׁיט יֵשׁוּעַ אֶת יָדוֹ, הֶחֱזִיק בּוֹ וְאָמַר לוֹ: "קְטַן אֱמוּנָה, מַדּוּעַ עָלָה סָפֵק בְּלִבְּךָ?"

32 בַּעֲלוֹתָם לַסְּיִרָה פָּסְקָה הָרוּחַ, 33 וְהָאֲנָשִׁים שֶׁהָיוּ

33 Then those who were in the boat came and worshiped Him, saying, "Truly You are the Son of God."

34 When they had crossed over, they came to the land of Gennesaret. 35 And when the men of that place recognized Him, they sent out into all that surrounding region, brought to Him all who were sick, 36 and begged Him that they might only touch the hem of His garment. And as many as touched *it* were made perfectly well.

15 Then the scribes and Pharisees who were from Jerusalem came to Jesus, saying, 2 "Why do Your disciples transgress the tradition of the elders? For they do not wash their hands when they eat bread."

3 He answered and said to them, "Why do you also transgress the commandment of God because of your tradition? 4 For God commanded, saying, 'Honor your father and your mother'; and, 'He who curses father or mother, let him be put to death.' 5 But you say, 'Whoever says to his father or mother, "Whatever profit you might have received from me *is* a gift *to God*"— 6 then he need not honor his father or mother.' Thus you have made the commandment of God of no effect by your tradition. 7 Hypocrites! Well did Isaiah prophesy about you, saying:

8   'These people draw near to Me with their mouth,
          And honor Me with *their* lips,
          But their heart is far from Me.
9   And in vain they worship Me,
          Teaching *as* doctrines the commandments of men.'"

10 When He had called the multitude to *Himself*, He said to them, "Hear and understand: 11 Not what goes into the mouth defiles a man; but what comes out of the mouth, this defiles a man."

12 Then His disciples came and said to Him, "Do You know that the Pharisees were offended when they heard this saying?"

13 But He answered and said, "Every plant which My heavenly Father has not planted will be uprooted. 14 Let them alone. They are blind leaders of the blind. And if the blind leads the blind, both will fall into a ditch."

15 Then Peter answered and said to Him, "Explain this parable to us."

16 So Jesus said, "Are you also still without understanding? 17 Do you not yet understand that whatever enters the mouth goes into the stomach and is eliminated? 18 But those things which proceed out of the mouth come from the heart, and they defile a man. 19 For out of the heart proceed evil thoughts, murders, adulteries, fornications, thefts,

בַּסְּפִינָה הִשְׁתַּחֲווּ לוֹ בְּאָמְרָם: "בֶּאֱמֶת בֶּן־הָאֱלֹהִים אָתָּה."

34 הֵם עָבְרוּ אֶת הַיָּם וּבָאוּ לְחוֹף גְּנוֹסַר. 35 אַנְשֵׁי הַמָּקוֹם הִכִּירוּ אוֹתוֹ וְשָׁלְחוּ לְהוֹדִיעַ לְכָל הַסְּבִיבָה. הֵבִיאוּ אֵלָיו אֶת כָּל הַחוֹלִים 36 וּבִקְשׁוּ מִמֶּנּוּ רַק לִנְגֹּעַ בִּכְנַף בִּגְדוֹ; וְכָל הַנּוֹגְעִים נִרְפָּאוּ.

טו אַחֲרֵי כֵן נִגְּשׁוּ אֶל יֵשׁוּעַ סוֹפְרִים וּפְרוּשִׁים מִירוּשָׁלַיִם 2 וְשָׁאֲלוּ אוֹתוֹ: "מַדּוּעַ עוֹבְרִים תַּלְמִידֶיךָ עַל מָסֹרֶת הַזְּקֵנִים, שֶׁאֵין הֵם נוֹטְלִים יָדַיִם לִסְעוּדָה?"

3 הֵשִׁיב וְאָמַר לָהֶם: "מַדּוּעַ גַּם אַתֶּם עוֹבְרִים עַל מִצְוַת אֱלֹהִים לְמַעַן הַמָּסֹרֶת שֶׁלָּכֶם? 4 הֵן הָאֱלֹהִים צִוָּה, 'כַּבֵּד אֶת־אָבִיךָ וְאֶת־אִמֶּךָ' וּ'מְקַלֵּל אָבִיו וְאִמּוֹ מוֹת יוּמָת', 5 אֲבָל אַתֶּם אוֹמְרִים, 'כָּל הָאוֹמֵר לְאָבִיו אוֹ לְאִמּוֹ, "כָּל דָּבָר מִשֶּׁלִּי שֶׁאַתָּה יָכוֹל לֵהָנוֹת מִמֶּנּוּ הֲרֵי הוּא הֶקְדֵּשׁ", 6 אֵינוֹ חַיָּב לְכַבֵּד אֶת אָבִיו וְאִמּוֹ'; וַהֲפַרְתֶּם אֶת דְּבַר אֱלֹהִים לְמַעַן הַמָּסֹרֶת שֶׁלָּכֶם. 7 צְבוּעִים! הֵיטֵב נִבָּא עֲלֵיכֶם יְשַׁעְיָהוּ בְּאָמְרוֹ: 8 'הָעָם הַזֶּה בִּשְׂפָתָיו כִּבְּדוּנִי וְלִבּוֹ רִחַק מִמֶּנִּי. 9 וַתְּהִי יִרְאָתָם אֹתִי מִצְוַת אֲנָשִׁים מְלֻמָּדָה'."

10 הוּא קָרָא לָעָם וְאָמַר לָהֶם: "שִׁמְעוּ וְהָבִינוּ! 11 לֹא הַנִּכְנָס אֶל הַפֶּה מְטַמֵּא אֶת הָאָדָם, אֶלָּא הַיּוֹצֵא מִן הַפֶּה – זֶה מְטַמֵּא אֶת הָאָדָם."

12 נִגְּשׁוּ תַּלְמִידָיו וְאָמְרוּ לוֹ: "הַאִם אַתָּה יוֹדֵעַ שֶׁהַפְּרוּשִׁים בְּשָׁמְעָם אֶת הַדָּבָר הִזְדַּעְזְעוּ?"

13 הֵשִׁיב וְאָמַר: "כָּל נֶטַע אֲשֶׁר לֹא נָטַע אָבִי שֶׁבַּשָּׁמַיִם עָקוֹר יֵעָקֵר. 14 הַנִּיחוּ לָהֶם. מוֹרֵי־דֶרֶךְ עִוְרִים הֵם לְעִוְרִים; וְאִם עִוֵּר מַדְרִיךְ אֶת הָעִוֵּר הֲרֵי שְׁנֵיהֶם יִפְּלוּ לָבוֹר."

15 הֵגִיב כֵּיפָא וְאָמַר לוֹ: "בָּאֵר נָא לָנוּ אֶת הַמָּשָׁל."

16 הֵשִׁיב יֵשׁוּעַ: "גַּם אַתֶּם עוֹד חַסְרֵי בִּינָה? 17 הַאֵינְכֶם מְבִינִים שֶׁכָּל מַה שֶּׁנִּכְנָס לַפֶּה יוֹרֵד אֶל הַבֶּטֶן וּמוּטָל לַמּוֹצָאוֹת? 18 אֲבָל הַדְּבָרִים הַיּוֹצְאִים מִן הַפֶּה נוֹבְעִים מִן הַלֵּב וְאֵלֶּה מְטַמְּאִים אֶת הָאָדָם. 19 כִּי מִן הַלֵּב נוֹבְעוֹת מַחְשְׁבוֹת רֶשַׁע, רְצִיחוֹת, נִאוּפִים, זְנוּנִים, גְּנֵבוֹת, עֵדֻיּוֹת שֶׁקֶר וְגִדּוּפִים.

false witness, blasphemies. ²⁰ These are *the things* which defile a man, but to eat with unwashed hands does not defile a man."

²¹ Then Jesus went out from there and departed to the region of Tyre and Sidon. ²² And behold, a woman of Canaan came from that region and cried out to Him, saying, "Have mercy on me, O Lord, Son of David! My daughter is severely demon-possessed."

²³ But He answered her not a word.

And His disciples came and urged Him, saying, "Send her away, for she cries out after us."

²⁴ But He answered and said, "I was not sent except to the lost sheep of the house of Israel."

²⁵ Then she came and worshiped Him, saying, "Lord, help me!"

²⁶ But He answered and said, "It is not good to take the children's bread and throw *it* to the little dogs."

²⁷ And she said, "Yes, Lord, yet even the little dogs eat the crumbs which fall from their masters' table."

²⁸ Then Jesus answered and said to her, "O woman, great *is* your faith! Let it be to you as you desire." And her daughter was healed from that very hour.

²⁹ Jesus departed from there, skirted the Sea of Galilee, and went up on the mountain and sat down there. ³⁰ Then great multitudes came to Him, having with them *the* lame, blind, mute, maimed, and many others; and they laid them down at Jesus' feet, and He healed them. ³¹ So the multitude marveled when they saw *the* mute speaking, *the* maimed made whole, *the* lame walking, and *the* blind seeing; and they glorified the God of Israel.

³² Now Jesus called His disciples to *Himself* and said, "I have compassion on the multitude, because they have now continued with Me three days and have nothing to eat. And I do not want to send them away hungry, lest they faint on the way."

³³ Then His disciples said to Him, "Where could we get enough bread in the wilderness to fill such a great multitude?"

³⁴ Jesus said to them, "How many loaves do you have?"

And they said, "Seven, and a few little fish."

³⁵ So He commanded the multitude to sit down on the ground. ³⁶ And He took the seven loaves and the fish and gave thanks, broke *them* and gave *them* to His disciples; and the disciples *gave* to the multitude. ³⁷ So they all ate and were filled, and they took up seven large baskets full of the fragments that were left. ³⁸ Now those who ate

²⁰ אֵלֶּה הֵם הַמְטַמְּאִים אֶת הָאָדָם, אֲבָל אֲכִילָה בְּלֹא נְטִילַת יָדַיִם אֵינֶנָּה מְטַמֵּאת אֶת הָאָדָם."

²¹ יֵשׁוּעַ יָצָא מִשָּׁם וּפָרַשׁ אֶל סְבִיבוֹת צוֹר וְצִידוֹן. ²² וְהִנֵּה יָצְאָה מֵאוֹתוֹ הָאֵזוֹר אִשָּׁה כְּנַעֲנִית וְצָעֲקָה אֵלָיו: "רַחֵם עָלַי, אֲדוֹנִי, בֶּן־דָּוִד. בִּתִּי מְעֻנָּה מְאֹד עַל־יְדֵי שֵׁד." ²³ אַךְ הוּא לֹא הֵשִׁיב לָהּ דָּבָר. נִגְּשׁוּ תַּלְמִידָיו וּבִקְשׁוּ מִמֶּנּוּ: "שַׁלַּח אוֹתָהּ, כִּי הִיא צוֹעֶקֶת אַחֲרֵינוּ."

²⁴ עָנָה יֵשׁוּעַ וְאָמַר: "לֹא נִשְׁלַחְתִּי אֶלָּא אֶל הַצֹּאן הָאוֹבְדוֹת אֲשֶׁר לְבֵית יִשְׂרָאֵל."

²⁵ הִיא הִתְקָרְבָה, הִשְׁתַּחַוְתָה לוֹ וְאָמְרָה: "אֲדוֹנִי, עֲזָר לִי."

²⁶ הֵשִׁיב לָהּ בְּאָמְרוֹ: "לֹא נָאֶה לָקַחַת אֶת הַלֶּחֶם שֶׁל הַבָּנִים וְלִזְרֹק אוֹתוֹ לַכְּלָבִים."

²⁷ אָמְרָה לוֹ: "כֵּן, אֲדוֹנִי, אֲבָל אֲפִלּוּ הַכְּלָבִים אוֹכְלִים מִן הַפֵּרוּרִים הַנּוֹפְלִים מִשֻּׁלְחַן אֲדוֹנֵיהֶם."

²⁸ אָמַר לָהּ יֵשׁוּעַ: "אִשָּׁה, גְּדוֹלָה אֱמוּנָתֵךְ. יְהִי לָךְ כִּרְצוֹנֵךְ", וּבְאוֹתָהּ שָׁעָה נִרְפְּאָה בִּתָּהּ.

²⁹ יֵשׁוּעַ עָזַב אֶת הַמָּקוֹם, וּלְאַחַר שֶׁעָבַר לְיַד יָם הַגָּלִיל עָלָה לָהָר וְיָשַׁב שָׁם. ³⁰ בָּאוּ אֵלָיו הֲמוֹן עַם רַב וְאִתָּם פִּסְּחִים, נָכִים, עִוְרִים, אִלְּמִים וְרַבִּים אֲחֵרִים שֶׁהִנִּיחוּ לְרַגְלָיו, וְהוּא רִפֵּא אוֹתָם. ³¹ כִּרְאוֹת הָעָם אִלְּמִים מְדַבְּרִים, נָכִים בְּרִיאִים, פִּסְּחִים מְהַלְּכִים וְעִוְרִים רוֹאִים, נִתְמַלְאוּ פְּלִיאָה וְשִׁבְּחוּ אֶת אֱלֹהֵי יִשְׂרָאֵל.

³² קָרָא יֵשׁוּעַ לְתַלְמִידָיו וְאָמַר: "נִכְמְרוּ רַחֲמַי עַל הָעָם. זֶה שְׁלֹשָׁה יָמִים הֵם נִמְצָאִים אִתִּי וְאֵין לָהֶם מַה לֶּאֱכֹל. אֵינֶנִּי חָפֵץ לְשַׁלַּח אוֹתָם רְעֵבִים פֶּן יִתְעַלְּפוּ בַּדֶּרֶךְ."

³³ אָמְרוּ לוֹ תַּלְמִידָיו: "מֵאַיִן לָנוּ בַּמִּדְבָּר דֵּי לֶחֶם לְהַשְׂבִּיעַ הָמוֹן רַב כָּזֶה?"

³⁴ אָמַר יֵשׁוּעַ: "כַּמָּה כִּכְּרוֹת לֶחֶם יֵשׁ לָכֶם?" הֵשִׁיבוּ: "שֶׁבַע, וּמְעַט דָּגִים קְטַנִּים."

³⁵ אָז צִוָּה אֶת הָעָם לָשֶׁבֶת עַל הָאָרֶץ; ³⁶ לָקַח אֶת שֶׁבַע כִּכְּרוֹת הַלֶּחֶם וְאֶת הַדָּגִים וּלְאַחַר שֶׁבֵּרֵךְ, פָּרַס וְנָתַן לַתַּלְמִידִים וְהַתַּלְמִידִים נָתְנוּ לָעָם. ³⁷ הַכֹּל אָכְלוּ וְשָׂבְעוּ, וּמִמַּה שֶּׁנּוֹתַר אָסְפוּ שִׁבְעָה סַלִּים מְלֵאִים. ³⁸ מִסְפַּר הָאוֹכְלִים הָיָה אַרְבַּעַת אֲלָפִים

were four thousand men, besides women and children. ³⁹ And He sent away the multitude, got into the boat, and came to the region of Magdala.

16 Then the Pharisees and Sadducees came, and testing Him asked that He would show them a sign from heaven. ² He answered and said to them, "When it is evening you say, *'It will be* fair weather, for the sky is red'; ³ and in the morning, *'It will be* foul weather today, for the sky is red and threatening.' Hypocrites! You know how to discern the face of the sky, but you cannot *discern* the signs of the times. ⁴ A wicked and adulterous generation seeks after a sign, and no sign shall be given to it except the sign of the prophet Jonah." And He left them and departed.

⁵ Now when His disciples had come to the other side, they had forgotten to take bread. ⁶ Then Jesus said to them, "Take heed and beware of the leaven of the Pharisees and the Sadducees."

⁷ And they reasoned among themselves, saying, *"It is* because we have taken no bread."

⁸ But Jesus, being aware of *it,* said to them, "O you of little faith, why do you reason among yourselves because you have brought no bread? ⁹ Do you not yet understand, or remember the five loaves of the five thousand and how many baskets you took up? ¹⁰ Nor the seven loaves of the four thousand and how many large baskets you took up? ¹¹ How is it you do not understand that I did not speak to you concerning bread?—*but* to beware of the leaven of the Pharisees and Sadducees." ¹² Then they understood that He did not tell *them* to beware of the leaven of bread, but of the doctrine of the Pharisees and Sadducees.

¹³ When Jesus came into the region of Caesarea Philippi, He asked His disciples, saying, "Who do men say that I, the Son of Man, am?"

¹⁴ So they said, "Some *say* John the Baptist, some Elijah, and others Jeremiah or one of the prophets."

¹⁵ He said to them, "But who do you say that I am?"

¹⁶ Simon Peter answered and said, "You are the Christ, the Son of the living God."

¹⁷ Jesus answered and said to him, "Blessed are you, Simon Bar-Jonah, for flesh and blood has not revealed *this* to you, but My Father who is in heaven. ¹⁸ And I also say to you that you are Peter, and on this rock I will build My church, and the gates of Hades shall not prevail against it. ¹⁹ And I will give you the keys of the kingdom of heaven, and whatever you bind on earth will be bound in heaven, and whatever you loose on earth will be loosed in heaven."

אִישׁ מִלְּבַד הַנָּשִׁים וְהַטָּף. 39 לְאַחַר מִכֵּן שָׁלַח אֶת הָעָם, יָרַד לַסִּירָה וְהִגִּיעַ אֶל אֵזוֹר מַגְדָּן.

טז הַפְּרוּשִׁים וְהַצְּדוֹקִים נִגְּשׁוּ לְנַסּוֹת אוֹתוֹ וּבִקְּשׁוּ מִמֶּנּוּ לְהַרְאוֹת לָהֶם אוֹת מִן הַשָּׁמַיִם. 2 הֵשִׁיב וְאָמַר לָהֶם: "לְעֵת עֶרֶב אַתֶּם אוֹמְרִים, 'מֶזֶג אֲוִיר נָאֶה, כִּי הַשָּׁמַיִם אֲדֻמִּים'; 3 וּבַבֹּקֶר, 'סַגְרִיר הַיּוֹם, כִּי אֲדֻמִּים וְקוֹדְרִים הַשָּׁמַיִם'. אֶת פְּנֵי הַשָּׁמַיִם אַתֶּם יוֹדְעִים לְפָרֵשׁ, אַךְ אֶת אוֹתוֹת הַזְּמַנִּים אֵינְכֶם יְכוֹלִים? 4 דּוֹר רַע וּמְנָאֵף מְבַקֵּשׁ לוֹ אוֹת, וְאוֹת לֹא יִנָּתֵן לוֹ מִלְּבַד אוֹת יוֹנָה הַנָּבִיא". הוּא עָזַב אוֹתָם וְהָלַךְ. 5 כְּשֶׁעָבְרוּ הַתַּלְמִידִים אֶל הַצַּד הַשֵּׁנִי שָׁכְחוּ לָקַחַת לָהֶם. אָמַר לָהֶם יֵשׁוּעַ: 6 "שִׂימוּ לְבַבְכֶם וְהִזָּהֲרוּ מִשְּׂאוֹר הַפְּרוּשִׁים וְהַצְּדוֹקִים". 7 אַךְ הֵם אָמְרוּ בְּלִבָּם, "לֶחֶם לֹא לָקַחְנוּ."

8 יֵשׁוּעַ הִבְחִין בְּזֶה וְאָמַר: "קְטַנֵּי אֱמוּנָה, מַדּוּעַ אַתֶּם אוֹמְרִים בִּלְבַבְכֶם שֶׁאֵין לָכֶם לֶחֶם? 9 עֲדַיִן אֵינְכֶם מְבִינִים אַף לֹא זוֹכְרִים אֶת חֲמֵשׁ כִּכְּרוֹת הַלֶּחֶם לַחֲמֵשֶׁת אֲלָפִים אִישׁ וְכַמָּה סַלִּים לְקַחְתֶּם? 10 גַּם לֹא אֶת שֶׁבַע כִּכְּרוֹת הַלֶּחֶם לְאַרְבַּעַת אֲלָפִים אִישׁ וְכַמָּה סַלִּים לְקַחְתֶּם? 11 אֵיךְ זֶה אֵינְכֶם מְבִינִים שֶׁלֹּא עַל כִּכְּרוֹת הַלֶּחֶם דִּבַּרְתִּי אֲלֵיכֶם? הִזָּהֲרוּ מִשְּׂאוֹר הַפְּרוּשִׁים וְהַצְּדוֹקִים!" 12 אָז הֵבִינוּ כִּי לֹא אָמַר לָהֶם לְהִזָּהֵר מִשְּׂאוֹר הַלֶּחֶם אֶלָּא מִתּוֹרַת הַפְּרוּשִׁים וְהַצְּדוֹקִים.

13 וּכְשֶׁבָּא יֵשׁוּעַ אֶל סְבִיבוֹת קֵיסַרְיָה שֶׁל פִילִיפּוֹס שָׁאַל אֶת תַּלְמִידָיו: "מָה אוֹמְרִים הָאֲנָשִׁים עַל בֶּן הָאָדָם, מִי הוּא?"

14 הֵשִׁיבוּ: "יֵשׁ אוֹמְרִים, 'יוֹחָנָן הַמַּטְבִּיל'; אֲחֵרִים אוֹמְרִים, 'אֵלִיָּהוּ'; וַאֲחֵרִים – 'יִרְמְיָהוּ אוֹ אֶחָד מֵהַנְּבִיאִים'."

15 שָׁאַל אוֹתָם: "וְאַתֶּם מָה אוֹמְרִים, מִי אֲנִי?"

16 עָנָה שִׁמְעוֹן כֵּיפָא וְאָמַר: "אַתָּה הַמָּשִׁיחַ, בֶּן אֱלֹהִים חַיִּים!"

17 אָמַר לוֹ יֵשׁוּעַ: "אַשְׁרֶיךָ שִׁמְעוֹן בַּר־יוֹנָה, כִּי לֹא בָּשָׂר וָדָם גִּלָּה לְךָ, אֶלָּא אָבִי שֶׁבַּשָּׁמַיִם. 18 וְגַם אֲנִי אוֹמֵר לְךָ כִּי אַתָּה כֵּיפָא וְעַל הַצּוּר הַזֶּה אֶבְנֶה אֶת קְהִלָּתִי וְשַׁעֲרֵי שְׁאוֹל לֹא יִגְבְּרוּ עָלֶיהָ. 19 אֶתֵּן לְךָ אֶת מַפְתְּחוֹת מַלְכוּת הַשָּׁמַיִם וְכָל מַה שֶּׁתֶּאֱסֹר עַל הָאָרֶץ יִהְיֶה אָסוּר בַּשָּׁמַיִם, וְכָל מַה שֶּׁתַּתִּיר עַל

18 כֵּיפָא הִיא אֲרַמִּית שֶׁמַּשְׁמָעָהּ סֶלַע אוֹ צוּר.

20 Then He commanded His disciples that they should tell no one that He was Jesus the Christ.

21 From that time Jesus began to show to His disciples that He must go to Jerusalem, and suffer many things from the elders and chief priests and scribes, and be killed, and be raised the third day.

22 Then Peter took Him aside and began to rebuke Him, saying, "Far be it from You, Lord; this shall not happen to You!"

23 But He turned and said to Peter, "Get behind Me, Satan! You are an offense to Me, for you are not mindful of the things of God, but the things of men."

24 Then Jesus said to His disciples, "If anyone desires to come after Me, let him deny himself, and take up his cross, and follow Me. 25 For whoever desires to save his life will lose it, but whoever loses his life for My sake will find it. 26 For what profit is it to a man if he gains the whole world, and loses his own soul? Or what will a man give in exchange for his soul? 27 For the Son of Man will come in the glory of His Father with His angels, and then He will reward each according to his works. 28 Assuredly, I say to you, there are some standing here who shall not taste death till they see the Son of Man coming in His kingdom."

17 Now after six days Jesus took Peter, James, and John his brother, led them up on a high mountain by themselves; 2 and He was transfigured before them. His face shone like the sun, and His clothes became as white as the light. 3 And behold, Moses and Elijah appeared to them, talking with Him. 4 Then Peter answered and said to Jesus, "Lord, it is good for us to be here; if You wish, let us make here three tabernacles: one for You, one for Moses, and one for Elijah."

5 While he was still speaking, behold, a bright cloud overshadowed them; and suddenly a voice came out of the cloud, saying, "This is My beloved Son, in whom I am well pleased. Hear Him!" 6 And when the disciples heard it, they fell on their faces and were greatly afraid. 7 But Jesus came and touched them and said, "Arise, and do not be afraid." 8 When they had lifted up their eyes, they saw no one but Jesus only.

9 Now as they came down from the mountain, Jesus commanded them, saying, "Tell the vision to no one until the Son of Man is risen from the dead."

10 And His disciples asked Him, saying, "Why then do the scribes say that Elijah must come first?"

הָאָרֶץ יִהְיֶה מֻתָּר בַּשָּׁמָיִם." 20 אָז הִזְהִיר אֶת תַּלְמִידָיו שֶׁלֹּא יְסַפְּרוּ לְאִישׁ כִּי הוּא הַמָּשִׁיחַ.

21 מֵאוֹתָהּ עֵת הֵחֵל יֵשׁוּעַ לְהַבְהִיר לְתַלְמִידָיו כִּי עָלָיו לָלֶכֶת לִירוּשָׁלַיִם וְלִסְבֹּל הַרְבֵּה מִידֵי הַזְּקֵנִים וְרָאשֵׁי הַכֹּהֲנִים וְהַסּוֹפְרִים, וּלְהֵהָרֵג וּבַיּוֹם הַשְּׁלִישִׁי לָקוּם. 22 לָקַח אוֹתוֹ כֵּיפָא לַצַּד וְהֵחֵל לִגְעֹר בּוֹ בְּאָמְרוֹ: "חָלִילָה לְךָ, אֲדוֹנִי. אַל יִהְיֶה הַדָּבָר הַזֶּה לְךָ!"

23 פָּנָה יֵשׁוּעַ וְאָמַר לְכֵיפָא: "סוּר מִלְּפָנַי, שָׂטָן. מִכְשׁוֹל אַתָּה לִי, כִּי אֵין לִבְּךָ לְדִבְרֵי אֱלֹהִים אֶלָּא לְדִבְרֵי בְּנֵי אָדָם."

24 אָז אָמַר יֵשׁוּעַ לְתַלְמִידָיו: "מִי שֶׁרוֹצֶה לָבוֹא אַחֲרַי, שֶׁיִּתְכַּחֵשׁ לְעַצְמוֹ וְיִקַּח אֶת צְלָבוֹ וְיֵלֵךְ אַחֲרַי; 25 כִּי הֶחָפֵץ לְהַצִּיל אֶת נַפְשׁוֹ יְאַבֵּד אוֹתָהּ, אֲבָל הַמְאַבֵּד אֶת נַפְשׁוֹ לְמַעֲנִי יִמְצָאֶנָּה. 26 מַה תּוֹעֶלֶת תִּצְמַח לְאָדָם אִם יָרוִיחַ אֶת כָּל הָעוֹלָם וְיַפְסִיד אֶת נַפְשׁוֹ, אוֹ מַה יִּתֵּן אָדָם כִּתְמוּרָה בְּעַד נַפְשׁוֹ? 27 הֵן עָתִיד בֶּן־הָאָדָם לָבוֹא בִּכְבוֹד אָבִיו עִם מַלְאָכָיו וְאָז יְשַׁלֵּם לְכָל אִישׁ כְּמַעֲשֵׂהוּ. 28 אָמֵן, אוֹמֵר אֲנִי לָכֶם, יֵשׁ מִן הָעוֹמְדִים פֹּה שֶׁלֹּא יִטְעֲמוּ מָוֶת עַד כִּי יִרְאוּ אֶת בֶּן־הָאָדָם בָּא בְּמַלְכוּתוֹ."

יז לְאַחַר שִׁשָּׁה יָמִים לָקַח יֵשׁוּעַ אֶת כֵּיפָא וְאֶת יַעֲקֹב וְאֶת יוֹחָנָן אָחִיו. הוּא הֶעֱלָה אוֹתָם לְהַר גָּבוֹהַּ לְבַדָּם 2 וְהִשְׁתַּנָּה לְעֵינֵיהֶם; פָּנָיו זָהֲרוּ כַּשֶּׁמֶשׁ וּבְגָדָיו הִלְבִּינוּ כָּאוֹר. 3 לְפֶתַע נִרְאוּ אֲלֵיהֶם מֹשֶׁה וְאֵלִיָּהוּ כְּשֶׁהֵם מְדַבְּרִים אִתּוֹ. 4 הֵגִיב כֵּיפָא וְאָמַר אֶל יֵשׁוּעַ: "אֲדוֹנִי, טוֹב שֶׁאֲנַחְנוּ כָּאן. אִם תִּרְצֶה אֶעֱשֶׂה פֹּה שָׁלוֹשׁ סֻכּוֹת, לְךָ אַחַת, לְמֹשֶׁה אַחַת וּלְאֵלִיָּהוּ אַחַת." 5 עוֹדוֹ מְדַבֵּר וְעָנָן בָּהִיר סָכַךְ עֲלֵיהֶם וְהִנֵּה קוֹל אוֹמֵר מִתּוֹךְ הֶעָנָן: "זֶה בְּנִי אֲהוּבִי אֲשֶׁר חָפַצְתִּי בּוֹ; אֵלָיו תִּשְׁמָעוּן."

6 כְּשֶׁשָּׁמְעוּ זֹאת נָפְלוּ הַתַּלְמִידִים עַל פְּנֵיהֶם וּפָחֲדוּ עַד מְאֹד. 7 יֵשׁוּעַ נִגַּשׁ, נָגַע בָּהֶם וְאָמַר: "קוּמוּ וְאַל תִּפְחֲדוּ!" 8 הֵם נָשְׂאוּ עֵינֵיהֶם וְלֹא רָאוּ אִישׁ זוּלָתִי יֵשׁוּעַ לְבַדּוֹ. 9 כְּשֶׁיָּרְדוּ מִן הָהָר צִוָּה עֲלֵיהֶם יֵשׁוּעַ: "אַל תְּסַפְּרוּ אֶת הַמַּרְאֶה לְאִישׁ עַד אֲשֶׁר יָקוּם בֶּן־ הָאָדָם מִן הַמֵּתִים." 10 שְׁאָלוּהוּ הַתַּלְמִידִים: "מַדּוּעַ זֶה אוֹמְרִים הַסּוֹפְרִים כִּי אֵלִיָּהוּ צָרִיךְ לָבוֹא תְּחִלָּה?"

¹¹Jesus answered and said to them, "Indeed, Elijah is coming first and will restore all things. ¹²But I say to you that Elijah has come already, and they did not know him but did to him whatever they wished. Likewise the Son of Man is also about to suffer at their hands." ¹³Then the disciples understood that He spoke to them of John the Baptist.

¹⁴And when they had come to the multitude, a man came to Him, kneeling down to Him and saying, ¹⁵"Lord, have mercy on my son, for he is an epileptic and suffers severely; for he often falls into the fire and often into the water. ¹⁶So I brought him to Your disciples, but they could not cure him."

¹⁷Then Jesus answered and said, "O faithless and perverse generation, how long shall I be with you? How long shall I bear with you? Bring him here to Me." ¹⁸And Jesus rebuked the demon, and it came out of him; and the child was cured from that very hour.

¹⁹Then the disciples came to Jesus privately and said, "Why could we not cast it out?"

²⁰So Jesus said to them, "Because of your unbelief; for assuredly, I say to you, if you have faith as a mustard seed, you will say to this mountain, 'Move from here to there,' and it will move; and nothing will be impossible for you. ²¹However, this kind does not go out except by prayer and fasting."

²²Now while they were staying in Galilee, Jesus said to them, "The Son of Man is about to be betrayed into the hands of men, ²³and they will kill Him, and the third day He will be raised up." And they were exceedingly sorrowful.

²⁴When they had come to Capernaum, those who received the *temple* tax came to Peter and said, "Does your Teacher not pay the *temple* tax?"

²⁵He said, "Yes."

And when he had come into the house, Jesus anticipated him, saying, "What do you think, Simon? From whom do the kings of the earth take customs or taxes, from their sons or from strangers?"

²⁶Peter said to Him, "From strangers."

Jesus said to him, "Then the sons are free. ²⁷Nevertheless, lest we offend them, go to the sea, cast in a hook, and take the fish that comes up first. And when you have opened its mouth, you will find a piece of money; take that and give it to them for Me and you."

¹¹ הֵשִׁיב יֵשׁוּעַ וְאָמַר: "אֵלִיָּהוּ אָמְנָם יָבוֹא וְיָשִׁיב אֶת הַכֹּל, ¹² אֲבָל אוֹמֵר אֲנִי לָכֶם שֶׁאֵלִיָּהוּ כְּבָר בָּא וְלֹא הִכִּירוּהוּ אֶלָּא עָשׂוּ בּוֹ כִּרְצוֹנָם; כָּךְ גַּם בֶּן־הָאָדָם עָתִיד לִסְבֹּל מִיָּדָם."

¹³ אָז הֵבִינוּ הַתַּלְמִידִים כִּי עַל יוֹחָנָן הַמַּטְבִּיל דִּבֵּר אֲלֵיהֶם.

¹⁴ כַּאֲשֶׁר בָּאוּ אֶל הֶהָמוֹן הָעָם נִגַּשׁ אֵלָיו אִישׁ וְכָרַע עַל בִּרְכָּיו לְפָנָיו. ¹⁵ אָמַר הָאִישׁ: "אֲדוֹנִי, רַחֵם נָא עַל בְּנִי. הוּא מֻכֵּה יָרֵחַ וּמַחֲלָתוֹ קָשָׁה, כִּי לְעִתִּים קְרוֹבוֹת הוּא נוֹפֵל לָאֵשׁ וּלְעִתִּים קְרוֹבוֹת לַמַּיִם. ¹⁶ הֲבֵאתִי אוֹתוֹ אֶל תַּלְמִידֶיךָ וְהֵם לֹא יָכְלוּ לְרַפְּאוֹ."

¹⁷ הֵשִׁיב יֵשׁוּעַ וְאָמַר: "הוֹי דּוֹר חֲסַר אֱמוּנָה וּמְעֻוַּת דֶּרֶךְ, עַד מָתַי אֶהְיֶה עִמָּכֶם? עַד מָתַי אֶסְבֹּל אֶתְכֶם? הָבִיאוּ אוֹתוֹ הֵנָּה אֵלַי!"

¹⁸ גָּעַר יֵשׁוּעַ בַּשֵּׁד וְהַשֵּׁד יָצָא מִמֶּנּוּ. מֵאוֹתָהּ שָׁעָה נִרְפָּא הַנַּעַר. ¹⁹ לְאַחַר מִכֵּן נִגְּשׁוּ הַתַּלְמִידִים אֶל יֵשׁוּעַ לְבַדָּם וְשָׁאֲלוּ: "מַדּוּעַ לֹא יָכֹלְנוּ אֲנַחְנוּ לְגָרֵשׁ אוֹתוֹ?"

²⁰ הֵשִׁיב לָהֶם: "בִּגְלַל מְעוּט אֱמוּנַתְכֶם. אָמֵן אוֹמֵר אֲנִי לָכֶם, אִם יֵשׁ לָכֶם אֱמוּנָה כְּגַרְגִּיר הַחַרְדָּל וְתֹאמְרוּ לָהָר הַזֶּה 'זוּז מִפֹּה לְשָׁם' – הוּא יָזוּז, וְשׁוּם דָּבָר לֹא יִבָּצֵר מִכֶּם.

²² כַּאֲשֶׁר הִתְהַלְּכוּ בַּגָּלִיל אָמַר לָהֶם יֵשׁוּעַ: "עָתִיד בֶּן־הָאָדָם לְהִמָּסֵר לִידֵי אֲנָשִׁים ²³ וְיַהַרְגוּהוּ וּבַיּוֹם הַשְּׁלִישִׁי יָקוּם". אָז הִתְעַצְּבוּ עֶצֶב רַב.

²⁴ כְּבוֹאָם אֶל כְּפַר נַחוּם נִגְּשׁוּ אֶל כֵּיפָא גּוֹבֵי מַחֲצִית הַשֶּׁקֶל וְשָׁאֲלוּ: "הַאִם רַבְּכֶם אֵינוֹ מְשַׁלֵּם אֶת מַחֲצִית הַשֶּׁקֶל?"

הֵשִׁיב לָהֶם: ²⁵ "כֵּן".

כַּאֲשֶׁר נִכְנַס הַבַּיְתָה הִקְדִּים יֵשׁוּעַ לִשְׁאֹל אוֹתוֹ: "מָה דַעְתְּךָ, שִׁמְעוֹן, מַלְכֵי הָאָרֶץ מִמִּי הֵם לוֹקְחִים מֶכֶס וּמַס, מִבְּנֵיהֶם אוֹ מִן הַזָּרִים?"

²⁶ כְּשֶׁהֵשִׁיב "מִן הַזָּרִים", אָמַר לוֹ יֵשׁוּעַ: "אִם כֵּן, הַבָּנִים פְּטוּרִים. ²⁷ אֲבָל כְּדֵי שֶׁלֹּא נִהְיֶה לָהֶם לְמִכְשׁוֹל, לֵךְ אֶל הַיָּם, הַשְׁלֵךְ חַכָּה וְקַח אֶת הַדָּג שֶׁיַּעֲלֶה רִאשׁוֹנָה. כְּשֶׁתִּפְתַּח אֶת פִּיו תִּמְצָא מַטְבֵּעַ; קַח אוֹתוֹ וְתֵן לָהֶם בַּעֲדִי וּבַעֲדְךָ."

18 At that time the disciples came to Jesus, saying, "Who then is greatest in the kingdom of heaven?"

2 Then Jesus called a little child to Him, set him in the midst of them, 3 and said, "Assuredly, I say to you, unless you are converted and become as little children, you will by no means enter the kingdom of heaven. 4 Therefore whoever humbles himself as this little child is the greatest in the kingdom of heaven. 5 Whoever receives one little child like this in My name receives Me.

6 "Whoever causes one of these little ones who believe in Me to sin, it would be better for him if a millstone were hung around his neck, and he were drowned in the depth of the sea. 7 Woe to the world because of offenses! For offenses must come, but woe to that man by whom the offense comes!

8 "If your hand or foot causes you to sin, cut it off and cast *it* from you. It is better for you to enter into life lame or maimed, rather than having two hands or two feet, to be cast into the everlasting fire. 9 And if your eye causes you to sin, pluck it out and cast *it* from you. It is better for you to enter into life with one eye, rather than having two eyes, to be cast into hell fire.

10 "Take heed that you do not despise one of these little ones, for I say to you that in heaven their angels always see the face of My Father who is in heaven. 11 For the Son of Man has come to save that which was lost.

12 "What do you think? If a man has a hundred sheep, and one of them goes astray, does he not leave the ninety-nine and go to the mountains to seek the one that is straying? 13 And if he should find it, assuredly, I say to you, he rejoices more over that *sheep* than over the ninety-nine that did not go astray. 14 Even so it is not the will of your Father who is in heaven that one of these little ones should perish.

15 "Moreover if your brother sins against you, go and tell him his fault between you and him alone. If he hears you, you have gained your brother. 16 But if he will not hear, take with you one or two more, that 'by the mouth of two or three witnesses every word may be established.' 17 And if he refuses to hear them, tell *it* to the church. But if he refuses even to hear the church, let him be to you like a heathen and a tax collector.

18 "Assuredly, I say to you, whatever you bind on earth will be bound in heaven, and whatever you loose on earth will be loosed in heaven.

יח אוֹתָהּ שָׁעָה נִגְּשׁוּ הַתַּלְמִידִים אֶל יֵשׁוּעַ וְשָׁאֲלוּ: "מִי הוּא הַגָּדוֹל בְּמַלְכוּת הַשָּׁמַיִם?"
2 יֵשׁוּעַ קָרָא אֵלָיו יֶלֶד, הֶעֱמִידוֹ בֵּינֵיהֶם 3 וְאָמַר: "אָמֵן אוֹמֵר אֲנִי לָכֶם, אִם לֹא תָּשׁוּבוּ וְתִהְיוּ כִּילָדִים לֹא תִּכָּנְסוּ לְמַלְכוּת הַשָּׁמַיִם. 4 לָכֵן מִי שֶׁיַּשְׁפִּיל אֶת עַצְמוֹ לִהְיוֹת כַּיֶּלֶד הַזֶּה הוּא הַגָּדוֹל בְּמַלְכוּת הַשָּׁמַיִם. 5 כָּל הַמְקַבֵּל יֶלֶד כָּזֶה אֶחָד בִּשְׁמִי, אוֹתִי הוּא מְקַבֵּל."

6 "אַךְ כָּל הַמַּכְשִׁיל אֶחָד מִן הַקְּטַנִּים הָאֵלֶּה הַמַּאֲמִינִים בִּי, מוּטָב לוֹ שֶׁתִּתָּלֶה אֶבֶן רֵחַיִם עַל צַוָּארוֹ וְיִטָּבַע בִּמְצוּלוֹת יָם. 7 אוֹי לָעוֹלָם מִן הַמִּכְשׁוֹלִים, כִּי מִן הַהֶכְרֵחַ שֶׁיָּבוֹאוּ מִכְשׁוֹלִים, אֲבָל אוֹי לָאִישׁ שֶׁהַמִּכְשׁוֹל יָבוֹא דַּרְכּוֹ.

8 אִם יָדְךָ אוֹ רַגְלְךָ תַּכְשִׁיל אוֹתְךָ, קַצֵּץ אוֹתָהּ וְהַשְׁלֵךְ אוֹתָהּ מִמְּךָ. מוּטָב לְךָ לָבוֹא לַחַיִּים גִּדֵּם אוֹ קִטֵּעַ מֵהְיוֹתְךָ מֻשְׁלָךְ לְאֵשׁ עוֹלָם עִם שְׁתֵּי יָדַיִם אוֹ שְׁתֵּי רַגְלַיִם. 9 וְאִם עֵינְךָ תַּכְשִׁיל אוֹתְךָ, נַקֵּר אוֹתָהּ וְהַשְׁלֵךְ אוֹתָהּ מִמְּךָ. מוּטָב לְךָ לָבוֹא לַחַיִּים עִם עַיִן אַחַת מֵהְיוֹתְךָ מֻשְׁלָךְ לְגֵיהִנֹּם הָאֵשׁ עִם שְׁתֵּי עֵינַיִם."

10 "הִזָּהֲרוּ שֶׁלֹּא תָּבוּזוּ לְאַחַד הַקְּטַנִּים הָאֵלֶּה. הֲרֵינִי אוֹמֵר לָכֶם כִּי הַמַּלְאָכִים שֶׁלָּהֶם בַּשָּׁמַיִם רוֹאִים תָּמִיד אֶת פְּנֵי אָבִי שֶׁבַּשָּׁמַיִם. 12 מַה דַּעְתְּכֶם? אִם יֵשׁ לְאִישׁ מֵאָה כְּבָשִׂים וְאָבַד אֶחָד מֵהֶם, הַאִם לֹא יַעֲזֹב אֶת הַתִּשְׁעִים וְתִשְׁעָה עַל הֶהָרִים וְיֵלֵךְ לְחַפֵּשׂ אֶת הָאוֹבֵד? 13 וְכַאֲשֶׁר יִמְצָא אוֹתוֹ, אָמֵן אוֹמֵר אֲנִי לָכֶם, יִשְׂמַח עָלָיו יוֹתֵר מֵאֲשֶׁר עַל הַתִּשְׁעִים וְתִשְׁעָה שֶׁלֹּא אָבָדוּ. 14 כָּךְ אֵין רָצוֹן מִלִּפְנֵי אֲבִיכֶם שֶׁבַּשָּׁמַיִם שֶׁיֹּאבַד אֶחָד מִן הַקְּטַנִּים הָאֵלֶּה."

15 "אִם יֶחֱטָא לְךָ אָחִיךָ, לֵךְ וְהוֹכַח אוֹתוֹ בֵּינְךָ וּבֵינוֹ לְבַד. אִם יִשְׁמַע לְךָ, קָנִיתָ לְךָ אֶת אָחִיךָ. 16 וְאִם לֹא יִשְׁמַע, קַח אִתְּךָ עוֹד אֶחָד אוֹ שְׁנַיִם, כְּדֵי שֶׁעַל־פִּי שְׁנַיִם אוֹ שְׁלוֹשָׁה עֵדִים יָקוּם כָּל דָּבָר. 17 אִם לֹא יִשְׁמַע לָהֶם, הַגֵּד לַקְּהִלָּה; וְאִם לֹא יִשְׁמַע גַּם לַקְּהִלָּה, שֶׁיִּהְיֶה לְךָ כַּגּוֹי וְכַמּוֹכֵס.

18 אָמֵן אֲנִי אוֹמֵר לָכֶם, כָּל מַה שֶׁתַּאַסְרוּ עַל הָאָרֶץ אָסוּר יִהְיֶה בַּשָּׁמַיִם וְכָל מַה שֶׁתַּתִּירוּ עַל הָאָרֶץ

19 "Again I say to you that if two of you agree on earth concerning anything that they ask, it will be done for them by My Father in heaven. 20 For where two or three are gathered together in My name, I am there in the midst of them."

21 Then Peter came to Him and said, "Lord, how often shall my brother sin against me, and I forgive him? Up to seven times?"

22 Jesus said to him, "I do not say to you, up to seven times, but up to seventy times seven. 23 Therefore the kingdom of heaven is like a certain king who wanted to settle accounts with his servants. 24 And when he had begun to settle accounts, one was brought to him who owed him ten thousand talents. 25 But as he was not able to pay, his master commanded that he be sold, with his wife and children and all that he had, and that payment be made. 26 The servant therefore fell down before him, saying, 'Master, have patience with me, and I will pay you all.' 27 Then the master of that servant was moved with compassion, released him, and forgave him the debt.

28 "But that servant went out and found one of his fellow servants who owed him a hundred denarii; and he laid hands on him and took *him* by the throat, saying, 'Pay me what you owe!' 29 So his fellow servant fell down at his feet and begged him, saying, 'Have patience with me, and I will pay you all.' 30 And he would not, but went and threw him into prison till he should pay the debt. 31 So when his fellow servants saw what had been done, they were very grieved, and came and told their master all that had been done. 32 Then his master, after he had called him, said to him, 'You wicked servant! I forgave you all that debt because you begged me. 33 Should you not also have had compassion on your fellow servant, just as I had pity on you?' 34 And his master was angry, and delivered him to the torturers until he should pay all that was due to him.

35 "So My heavenly Father also will do to you if each of you, from his heart, does not forgive his brother his trespasses."

19 Now it came to pass, when Jesus had finished these sayings, *that* He departed from Galilee and came to the region of Judea beyond the Jordan. 2 And great multitudes followed Him, and He healed them there.

3 The Pharisees also came to Him, testing Him, and saying to Him, "Is it lawful for a man to divorce his wife for *just* any reason?"

19 עוֹד אוֹמֵר אֲנִי לָכֶם, אִם יִהְיֶה מֶתָּר בַּשָּׁמַיִם. שְׁנַיִם מִכֶּם יַסְכִּימוּ עֲלֵי אֲדָמוֹת בְּכָל דָּבָר אֲשֶׁר יְבַקְּשׁוּ, הָיֹה יִהְיֶה לָהֶם מֵאֵת אָבִי שֶׁבַּשָּׁמַיִם; 20 כִּי בְּמָקוֹם אֲשֶׁר שְׁנַיִם אוֹ שְׁלוֹשָׁה נֶאֱסָפִים לִשְׁמִי שָׁם אֲנִי בְּתוֹכָם."

21 כֵּיפָא נִגַּשׁ וְשָׁאַל אוֹתוֹ: "אֲדוֹנִי, כַּמָּה פְּעָמִים יֶחֱטָא לִי אָחִי וְאֶסְלַח לוֹ? הַאִם עַד שֶׁבַע פְּעָמִים?" 22 הֵשִׁיב לוֹ יֵשׁוּעַ: "אֵינֶנִּי אוֹמֵר לְךָ עַד שֶׁבַע פְּעָמִים אֶלָּא עַד שִׁבְעִים וָשֶׁבַע. 23 עַל כֵּן דּוֹמָה מַלְכוּת הַשָּׁמַיִם לְמֶלֶךְ בָּשָׂר וָדָם שֶׁרָצָה לַעֲרֹךְ חֶשְׁבּוֹן עִם עֲבָדָיו. 24 כַּאֲשֶׁר הֵחֵל לְחַשֵּׁב הוּבָא לְפָנָיו אִישׁ שֶׁהָיָה חַיָּב לוֹ עֲשֶׂרֶת אֲלָפִים כִּכְּרֵי כֶסֶף. 25 כֵּיוָן שֶׁלֹּא הָיָה לוֹ לְשַׁלֵּם צִוָּה אֲדוֹנָיו לִמְכֹּר אוֹתוֹ וְאֶת אִשְׁתּוֹ וְאֶת בָּנָיו וְאֶת כָּל אֲשֶׁר לוֹ כְּדֵי שֶׁיְּשַׁלֵּם הַחוֹב. 26 כָּרַע הָעֶבֶד וְהִשְׁתַּחֲוָה לוֹ בְּאָמְרוֹ, 'אָנָּא, הֱיֵה סַבְלָן כְּלַפַּי וַאֲשַׁלֵּם לְךָ אֶת הַכֹּל.' 27 נִכְמְרוּ רַחֲמֵי הָאָדוֹן עַל הָעֶבֶד הַהוּא, פָּטַר אוֹתוֹ וְוִתֵּר לוֹ עַל הַחוֹב. 28 כְּשֶׁיָּצָא הָעֶבֶד הַהוּא מָצָא אֶת אֶחָד מֵחֲבֵרָיו הָעֲבָדִים שֶׁהָיָה חַיָּב לוֹ מֵאָה דִּינָרִים. תָּפַס אוֹתוֹ בִּגְרוֹנוֹ וְאָמַר, 'שַׁלֵּם מַה שֶּׁאַתָּה חַיָּב!' 29 נָפַל חֲבֵרוֹ לְרַגְלָיו וּבִקֵּשׁ מֵאִתּוֹ, 'אָנָּא, הֱיֵה סַבְלָן כְּלַפַּי וַאֲשַׁלֵּם לְךָ.' 30 אֶלָּא שֶׁהוּא לֹא הִסְכִּים וְעוֹד הָלַךְ וְהִשְׁלִיךְ אוֹתוֹ לַכֶּלֶא עַד אֲשֶׁר יְשַׁלֵּם אֶת הַחוֹב. 31 כְּשֶׁרָאוּ חֲבֵרָיו הָעֲבָדִים אֶת הַנַּעֲשֶׂה הִתְעַצְּבוּ מְאֹד וּבָאוּ וְסִפְּרוּ לַאֲדוֹנָם אֶת כָּל אֲשֶׁר הָיָה. 32 אָז קָרָא לוֹ אֲדוֹנָיו וְאָמַר לוֹ, 'עֶבֶד רָשָׁע, אֶת כָּל הַחוֹב הַהוּא מָחַלְתִּי לְךָ מִשּׁוּם שֶׁבִּקַּשְׁתָּ מִמֶּנִּי. 33 הַאִם לֹא הָיִיתָ צָרִיךְ גַּם אַתָּה לְרַחֵם עַל חֲבֵרְךָ הָעֶבֶד כְּשֵׁם שֶׁאֲנִי רִחַמְתִּי עָלֶיךָ?' 34 וּבְכַעְסוֹ מָסַר אוֹתוֹ אֲדוֹנָיו לַנּוֹגְשִׂים עַד אֲשֶׁר יְשַׁלֵּם אֶת הַחוֹב כֻּלּוֹ. 35 כָּכָה גַם אָבִי שֶׁבַּשָּׁמַיִם יַעֲשֶׂה לָכֶם אִם לֹא תִּמְחֲלוּ אִישׁ לְאָחִיו בְּכָל לְבַבְכֶם."

יט כְּשֶׁגָּמַר יֵשׁוּעַ לְדַבֵּר אֶת הַדְּבָרִים הָאֵלֶּה יָצָא מִן הַגָּלִיל וּבָא לְאֵזוֹר יְהוּדָה שֶׁבְּעֵבֶר הַיַּרְדֵּן. 2 הֲמוֹן עַם רַב הָלְכוּ אַחֲרָיו וְהוּא רִפֵּא אוֹתָם שָׁם. 3 נִגְּשׁוּ אֵלָיו כַּמָּה פְּרוּשִׁים לִנְסוֹת אוֹתוֹ וְאָמְרוּ: "הַאִם מֻתָּר לְאִישׁ לְגָרֵשׁ אֶת אִשְׁתּוֹ עַל כָּל דָּבָר?"

⁴ And He answered and said to them, "Have you not read that He who made *them* at the beginning 'made *them* male and female,' ⁵ and said, 'For this reason a man shall leave his father and mother and be joined to his wife, and the two shall become one flesh'? ⁶ So then, they are no longer two but one flesh. Therefore what God has joined together, let not man separate."

⁷ They said to Him, "Why then did Moses command to give a certificate of divorce, and to put her away?"

⁸ He said to them, "Moses, because of the hardness of your hearts, permitted you to divorce your wives, but from the beginning it was not so. ⁹ And I say to you, whoever divorces his wife, except for sexual immorality, and marries another, commits adultery; and whoever marries her who is divorced commits adultery."

¹⁰ His disciples said to Him, "If such is the case of the man with *his* wife, it is better not to marry."

¹¹ But He said to them, "All cannot accept this saying, but only *those* to whom it has been given: ¹² For there are eunuchs who were born thus from *their* mother's womb, and there are eunuchs who were made eunuchs by men, and there are eunuchs who have made themselves eunuchs for the kingdom of heaven's sake. He who is able to accept *it*, let him accept *it.*"

¹³ Then little children were brought to Him that He might put *His* hands on them and pray, but the disciples rebuked them. ¹⁴ But Jesus said, "Let the little children come to Me, and do not forbid them; for of such is the kingdom of heaven." ¹⁵ And He laid *His* hands on them and departed from there.

¹⁶ Now behold, one came and said to Him, "Good Teacher, what good thing shall I do that I may have eternal life?"

¹⁷ So He said to him, "Why do you call Me good? No one *is* good but One, *that is,* God. But if you want to enter into life, keep the commandments."

¹⁸ He said to Him, "Which ones?"

Jesus said, "'*You shall not murder,*' '*You shall not commit adultery,*' '*You shall not steal,*' '*You shall not bear false witness,*' ¹⁹ '*Honor your father and your mother,*' and, '*You shall love your neighbor as yourself.*'"

²⁰ The young man said to Him, "All these things I have kept from my youth. What do I still lack?"

²¹ Jesus said to him, "If you want to be perfect, go, sell what you have and give to the poor, and you will have treasure in heaven; and come, follow Me."

²² But when the young man heard that saying, he went away sorrowful, for he had great possessions.

⁴ הֵשִׁיב לָהֶם וְאָמַר: "הַאִם לֹא קְרָאתֶם שֶׁהַבּוֹרֵא עָשָׂה אוֹתָם זָכָר וּנְקֵבָה מִבְּרֵאשִׁית ⁵ וְגַם אָמַר, 'עַל־ כֵּן יַעֲזָב־אִישׁ אֶת־אָבִיו וְאֶת־אִמּוֹ וְדָבַק בְּאִשְׁתּוֹ וְהָיוּ לְבָשָׂר אֶחָד'? ⁶ אֵין הֵם עוֹד שְׁנַיִם אֶלָּא בָּשָׂר אֶחָד. לָכֵן מַה שֶּׁחִבֵּר הָאֱלֹהִים אַל יַפְרִיד הָאָדָם."

⁷ שָׁאֲלוּ אוֹתוֹ: "אִם כֵּן לָמָּה צִוָּה מֹשֶׁה לָתֵת לָהּ סֵפֶר כְּרִיתוּת וּלְשַׁלְּחָהּ?"

⁸ הֵשִׁיב לָהֶם: "בִּגְלַל קְשִׁי לְבַבְכֶם הִתִּיר לָכֶם מֹשֶׁה לְשַׁלֵּחַ אֶת נְשֵׁיכֶם, אַךְ מֵרֵאשִׁית לֹא הָיָה כָּךְ. ⁹ וַאֲנִי אוֹמֵר לָכֶם, הַמְגָרֵשׁ אֶת אִשְׁתּוֹ שֶׁלֹּא עַל־דְּבַר זְנוּת וְנוֹשֵׂא אַחֶרֶת נוֹאֵף הוּא."

¹⁰ אָמְרוּ לוֹ הַתַּלְמִידִים: "אִם כָּךְ הוּא דִּין הָאִישׁ וְהָאִשָּׁה לֹא כְּדַאי לְהִתְחַתֵּן."

¹¹ אָמַר לָהֶם: "לֹא הַכֹּל מְבִינִים אֶת הַדָּבָר הַזֶּה, רַק אֵלֶּה שֶׁנִּתַּן לָהֶם. ¹² יֵשׁ סָרִיסִים שֶׁנּוֹלְדוּ כָּךְ מִבֶּטֶן אִמָּם, יֵשׁ סָרִיסִים שֶׁנַּעֲשׂוּ סָרִיסִים עַל־יְדֵי בְּנֵי אָדָם, יֵשׁ סָרִיסִים אֲשֶׁר עָשׂוּ עַצְמָם לְסָרִיסִים לְמַעַן מַלְכוּת שָׁמַיִם. מִי שֶׁבִּיכָלְתּוֹ לְקַבֵּל, שֶׁיְּקַבֵּל."

¹³ אָז הֵבִיאוּ אֵלָיו יְלָדִים כְּדֵי שֶׁיִּסְמֹךְ יָדָיו עֲלֵיהֶם וְיִתְפַּלֵּל בַּעֲדָם, אֶלָּא שֶׁהַתַּלְמִידִים גָּעֲרוּ בָּהֶם. ¹⁴ אַךְ יֵשׁוּעַ אָמַר: "הַנִּיחוּ לַיְלָדִים לָבוֹא אֵלַי וְאַל תִּמְנְעוּ בַּעֲדָם, כִּי לְכָאֵלֶּה מַלְכוּת הַשָּׁמַיִם." ¹⁵ הוּא סָמַךְ יָדָיו עֲלֵיהֶם וְאַחֲרֵי כֵן הָלַךְ מִשָּׁם.

¹⁶ נִגַּשׁ אֵלָיו אִישׁ אֶחָד וְשָׁאַל: "רַבִּי, אֵיזֶה טוֹב עָלַי לַעֲשׂוֹת כְּדֵי לְהַשִּׂיג חַיֵּי עוֹלָם?"

¹⁷ אָמַר אֵלָיו: "מַדּוּעַ אַתָּה שׁוֹאֵל אוֹתִי בְּנוֹגֵעַ לַטּוֹב? אֶחָד הוּא הַטּוֹב, אֲבָל אִם רְצוֹנְךָ לָבוֹא לַחַיִּים, שְׁמֹר אֶת הַמִּצְווֹת."

¹⁸ שָׁאַל הָאִישׁ: "אֵיזֶה?" הֵשִׁיב יֵשׁוּעַ: "לֹא תִּרְצַח, לֹא תִּנְאָף, לֹא תִּגְנֹב, לֹא־תַעֲנֶה בְרֵעֲךָ עֵד שָׁקֶר, ¹⁹ כַּבֵּד אֶת־אָבִיךָ וְאֶת־אִמֶּךָ, וְאָהַבְתָּ לְרֵעֲךָ כָּמוֹךָ'."

²⁰ אָמַר הַבָּחוּר: "אֶת כָּל אֵלֶּה שָׁמַרְתִּי, מַה עוֹד חָסֵר לִי?"

²¹ אָמַר לוֹ יֵשׁוּעַ: "אִם רְצוֹנְךָ לִהְיוֹת שָׁלֵם, לֵךְ מְכֹר אֶת רְכוּשְׁךָ וְתֵן לָעֲנִיִּים וְיִהְיֶה לְךָ אוֹצָר בַּשָּׁמַיִם; אַחַר כָּךְ בּוֹא וְלֵךְ אַחֲרַי."

²² כְּשֶׁשָּׁמַע הַבָּחוּר אֶת הַדָּבָר הַזֶּה הָלַךְ מִשָּׁם

23 Then Jesus said to His disciples, "Assuredly, I say to you that it is hard for a rich man to enter the kingdom of heaven. 24 And again I say to you, it is easier for a camel to go through the eye of a needle than for a rich man to enter the kingdom of God."

25 When His disciples heard *it,* they were greatly astonished, saying, "Who then can be saved?"

26 But Jesus looked at *them* and said to them, "With men this is impossible, but with God all things are possible."

27 Then Peter answered and said to Him, "See, we have left all and followed You. Therefore what shall we have?"

28 So Jesus said to them, "Assuredly I say to you, that in the regeneration, when the Son of Man sits on the throne of His glory, you who have followed Me will also sit on twelve thrones, judging the twelve tribes of Israel. 29 And everyone who has left houses or brothers or sisters or father or mother or wife or children or lands, for My name's sake, shall receive a hundredfold, and inherit eternal life. 30 But many *who are* first will be last, and the last first.

20 "For the kingdom of heaven is like a landowner who went out early in the morning to hire laborers for his vineyard. 2 Now when he had agreed with the laborers for a denarius a day, he sent them into his vineyard. 3 And he went out about the third hour and saw others standing idle in the marketplace, 4 and said to them, 'You also go into the vineyard, and whatever is right I will give you.' So they went. 5 Again he went out about the sixth and the ninth hour, and did likewise. 6 And about the eleventh hour he went out and found others standing idle, and said to them, 'Why have you been standing here idle all day?' 7 They said to him, 'Because no one hired us.' He said to them, 'You also go into the vineyard, and whatever is right you will receive.'

8 "So when evening had come, the owner of the vineyard said to his steward, 'Call the laborers and give them *their* wages, beginning with the last to the first.' 9 And when those came who *were hired* about the eleventh hour, they each received a denarius. 10 But when the first came, they supposed that they would receive more; and they likewise received each a denarius. 11 And when they had received *it,* they complained against the landowner, 12 saying, 'These last *men* have worked *only* one hour, and you made them equal to us who have borne the burden and the heat of the day.' 13 But he answered one of them and said, 'Friend, I am doing you no wrong. Did you not agree with me for a denarius? 14 Take *what is* yours and go your way. I wish to give to this last

23 אָמַר יֵשׁוּעַ לְתַלְמִידָיו: "אָמֵן אוֹמֵר אֲנִי לָכֶם, בְּקֹשִׁי יִכָּנֵס עָשִׁיר לְמַלְכוּת הַשָּׁמַיִם. 24 וְעוֹד אֲנִי אוֹמֵר לָכֶם, נָקֵל לַגָּמָל לַעֲבֹר דֶּרֶךְ נֶקֶב מַחַט מֵהִכָּנֵס עָשִׁיר אֶל מַלְכוּת הָאֱלֹהִים."

25 שָׁמְעוּ הַתַּלְמִידִים וְתָמְהוּ מְאֹד. שְׁאָלוּהוּ: "אִם כֵּן, מִי יָכוֹל לְהִוָּשַׁע?"

26 הִבִּיט בָּהֶם יֵשׁוּעַ וְאָמַר: "מִבְּנֵי אָדָם נִבְצָר הַדָּבָר, אֲבָל הָאֱלֹהִים כָּל יָכוֹל."

27 הֵגִיב כֵּיפָא וְאָמַר אֵלָיו: "הִנֵּה אֲנַחְנוּ עָזַבְנוּ הַכֹּל וְהָלַכְנוּ אַחֲרֶיךָ, אִם כֵּן מַה יִּהְיֶה לָנוּ?"

28 אָמַר לָהֶם יֵשׁוּעַ: "אָמֵן אוֹמֵר אֲנִי לָכֶם, אַתֶּם הַהוֹלְכִים אַחֲרַי, כַּאֲשֶׁר תִּתְחַדֵּשׁ הַבְּרִיאָה וּבֶן הָאָדָם יֵשֵׁב עַל כִּסֵּא כְבוֹדוֹ, תֵּשְׁבוּ גַם אַתֶּם עַל שְׁנֵים-עָשָׂר כִּסְאוֹת לִשְׁפֹּט אֶת שְׁנֵים-עָשָׂר שִׁבְטֵי יִשְׂרָאֵל. 29 וְכָל מִי שֶׁעָזַב בָּתִּים אוֹ אַחִים וַאֲחָיוֹת אוֹ אָב וְאֵם אוֹ אִשָּׁה אוֹ בָּנִים אוֹ שָׂדוֹת לְמַעַן שְׁמִי – יְקַבֵּל פִּי מֵאָה וְיִירַשׁ חַיֵּי עוֹלָם. 30 אֲבָל רַבִּים מִן הָרִאשׁוֹנִים יִהְיוּ אַחֲרוֹנִים וּמֵהָאַחֲרוֹנִים – רִאשׁוֹנִים."

כ "כִּי דּוֹמָה מַלְכוּת הַשָּׁמַיִם לְאִישׁ בַּעַל אֲחֻזָּה שֶׁיָּצָא הַשְׁכֵּם בַּבֹּקֶר לִשְׂכֹּר פּוֹעֲלִים לְכַרְמוֹ, 2 וּלְאַחַר שֶׁהִסְכִּים עִם הַפּוֹעֲלִים עַל שְׂכַר דִּינָר לַיּוֹם שָׁלַח אוֹתָם אֶל כַּרְמוֹ. 3 כְּשֶׁיָּצָא בְּשָׁעָה תֵּשַׁע רָאָה אֲחֵרִים עוֹמְדִים בְּטֵלִים בַּשּׁוּק. 4 אָמַר לָהֶם, 'לְכוּ גַם אַתֶּם אֶל כַּרְמִי וְאֶתֵּן לָכֶם אֶת הַמַּגִּיעַ לָכֶם'. הֵם הָלְכוּ. 5 יָצָא גַם בְּשָׁעָה שְׁתֵּים-עֶשְׂרֵה וְגַם בְּשָׁעָה שָׁלֹשׁ וְעָשָׂה כַּדָּבָר הַזֶּה. 6 אַחֲרֵי כֵן יָצָא בְּשָׁעָה חָמֵשׁ לִפְנוֹת עֶרֶב וּמָצָא אֲחֵרִים עוֹמְדִים. שָׁאַל אוֹתָם, 'לָמָּה אַתֶּם עוֹמְדִים פֹּה בְּטֵלִים כָּל הַיּוֹם?' 7 הֵשִׁיבוּ לוֹ, 'מִפְּנֵי שֶׁלֹּא שָׂכַר אוֹתָנוּ אִישׁ'. אָמַר לָהֶם, 'לְכוּ גַם אַתֶּם אֶל הַכֶּרֶם'. 8 לְעֵת עֶרֶב אָמַר בַּעַל הַכֶּרֶם אֶל פְּקִידוֹ, 'קְרָא אֶת הַפּוֹעֲלִים וְשַׁלֵּם לָהֶם אֶת שְׂכָרָם, הָחֵל בָּאַחֲרוֹנִים וְכַלֵּה בָּרִאשׁוֹנִים.' 9 בָּאוּ אֵלֶּה שֶׁנִּשְׂכְּרוּ בְּשָׁעָה חָמֵשׁ לִפְנוֹת עֶרֶב וְקִבְּלוּ אִישׁ אִישׁ דִּינָר אֶחָד. 10 כְּשֶׁבָּאוּ הָרִאשׁוֹנִים דִּמּוּ בְּנַפְשָׁם שֶׁיְּקַבְּלוּ יוֹתֵר, אַךְ גַּם הֵם קִבְּלוּ אִישׁ אִישׁ דִּינָר אֶחָד. 11 לְאַחַר שֶׁקִּבְּלוּ הִתְלוֹנְנוּ לִפְנֵי בַּעַל הַבַּיִת בְּאָמְרָם, 12 'אֵלֶּה הָאַחֲרוֹנִים עָבְדוּ שָׁעָה אַחַת וְאַתָּה הִשְׁוֵיתָ אוֹתָם אֵלֵינוּ – אֲנַחְנוּ שֶׁסָּבַלְנוּ אֶת כֹּבֶד הַיּוֹם וְאֶת הַחֹם!' 13 הֵשִׁיב וְאָמַר אֶל אֶחָד מֵהֶם, 'חָבֵר, אֵינֶנִּי עוֹשֵׁק אוֹתְךָ. הֲרֵי עַל שְׂכַר דִּינָר הִסְכַּמְתָּ אִתִּי. 14 קַח אֶת שֶׁלְּךָ וָלֵךְ, וְאוּלָם רְצוֹנִי

man *the same* as to you. ¹⁵Is it not lawful for me to do what I wish with my own things? Or is your eye evil because I am good?' ¹⁶So the last will be first, and the first last. For many are called, but few chosen."

¹⁷Now Jesus, going up to Jerusalem, took the twelve disciples aside on the road and said to them, ¹⁸"Behold, we are going up to Jerusalem, and the Son of Man will be betrayed to the chief priests and to the scribes; and they will condemn Him to death, ¹⁹and deliver Him to the Gentiles to mock and to scourge and to crucify. And the third day He will rise again."

²⁰Then the mother of Zebedee's sons came to Him with her sons, kneeling down and asking something from Him.

²¹And He said to her, "What do you wish?"

She said to Him, "Grant that these two sons of mine may sit, one on Your right hand and the other on the left, in Your kingdom."

²²But Jesus answered and said, "You do not know what you ask. Are you able to drink the cup that I am about to drink, and be baptized with the baptism that I am baptized with?"

They said to Him, "We are able."

²³So He said to them, "You will indeed drink My cup, and be baptized with the baptism that I am baptized with; but to sit on My right hand and on My left is not Mine to give, but *it is for those* for whom it is prepared by My Father."

²⁴And when the ten heard *it,* they were greatly displeased with the two brothers. ²⁵But Jesus called them to *Himself* and said, "You know that the rulers of the Gentiles lord it over them, and those who are great exercise authority over them. ²⁶Yet it shall not be so among you; but whoever desires to become great among you, let him be your servant. ²⁷And whoever desires to be first among you, let him be your slave— ²⁸just as the Son of Man did not come to be served, but to serve, and to give His life a ransom for many."

²⁹Now as they went out of Jericho, a great multitude followed Him. ³⁰And behold, two blind men sitting by the road, when they heard that Jesus was passing by, cried out, saying, "Have mercy on us, O Lord, Son of David!"

³¹Then the multitude warned them that they should be quiet; but they cried out all the more, saying, "Have mercy on us, O Lord, Son of David!"

³²So Jesus stood still and called them, and said, "What do you want Me to do for you?"

לָתֵת לָאַחֲרוֹן הַזֶּה כְּמוֹ לְךָ. ¹⁵הַאִם אָסוּר לִי לַעֲשׂוֹת בְּשֶׁלִּי כִּרְצוֹנִי? אוֹ שֶׁמָּא עֵינְךָ צָרָה עַל שֶׁטּוֹב אֲנִי?' ¹⁶כָּכָה יִהְיוּ הָאַחֲרוֹנִים רִאשׁוֹנִים וְהָרִאשׁוֹנִים אַחֲרוֹנִים."

¹⁷כְּשֶׁהָיָה יֵשׁוּעַ קָרוֹב לַעֲלוֹת לִירוּשָׁלַיִם לָקַח אֶת הַשְּׁנֵים־עָשָׂר לְבַדָּם וּבַדֶּרֶךְ אָמַר לָהֶם: ¹⁸"הִנֵּה אֲנַחְנוּ עוֹלִים לִירוּשָׁלַיִם וּבֶן־הָאָדָם יִמָּסֵר לְרָאשֵׁי הַכֹּהֲנִים וְלַסּוֹפְרִים. הֵם יַחֲרִצוּ אֶת דִּינוֹ לְמָוֶת ¹⁹וְיִמְסְרוּ אוֹתוֹ לַגּוֹיִים לְהָתֵל בּוֹ וּלְהַלְקוֹתוֹ וְלִצְלֹב אוֹתוֹ, וּבַיּוֹם הַשְּׁלִישִׁי יָקוּם."

²⁰אַחֲרֵי כֵן נִגְּשָׁה אֵלָיו הָאֵם שֶׁל בְּנֵי זַבְדַּי עִם בָּנֶיהָ וְהִשְׁתַּחֲוָתָה לוֹ לְבַקֵּשׁ מִמֶּנּוּ דָּבָר.

²¹שָׁאַל אוֹתָהּ: "מַה בַּקָּשָׁתֵךְ?" הֵשִׁיבָה לוֹ: "אֱמֹר נָא שֶׁיֵּשְׁבוּ שְׁנֵי בָּנַי אֵלֶּה אֶחָד לִימִינְךָ וְאֶחָד לִשְׂמֹאלְךָ בְּמַלְכוּתֶךָ."

²²עָנָה יֵשׁוּעַ וְאָמַר: "אֵינְכֶם יוֹדְעִים מַה שֶּׁאַתֶּם מְבַקְּשִׁים. הַאִם יְכוֹלִים אַתֶּם לִשְׁתּוֹת אֶת הַכּוֹס אֲשֶׁר אֲנִי עָתִיד לִשְׁתּוֹת?" הֵשִׁיבוּ לוֹ: "יְכוֹלִים אָנוּ."

²³אָמַר לָהֶם: "אָמְנָם אֶת כּוֹסִי תִּשְׁתּוּ, אַךְ לָשֶׁבֶת לִימִינִי וְלִשְׂמֹאלִי אֵין בְּיָדִי לָתֵת אֶלָּא לַאֲשֶׁר הוּכַן לָהֶם מֵאֵת אָבִי."

²⁴כַּאֲשֶׁר שָׁמְעוּ זֹאת הָעֲשָׂרָה נִתְמַלְּאוּ כַּעַס עַל שְׁנֵי הָאַחִים. ²⁵קָרָא לָהֶם יֵשׁוּעַ וְאָמַר: "אַתֶּם יוֹדְעִים שֶׁהַמּוֹשְׁלִים בַּגּוֹיִים רוֹדִים בָּהֶם וְהַגְּדוֹלִים שׁוֹלְטִים בָּהֶם. ²⁶אַל יְהִי כֵן בֵּינֵיכֶם. אַדְּרַבָּא, הֶחָפֵץ לִהְיוֹת גָּדוֹל בָּכֶם יְהֵא מְשָׁרֵת שֶׁלָּכֶם, ²⁷וְהֶחָפֵץ לִהְיוֹת רִאשׁוֹן בֵּינֵיכֶם יְהֵא עֶבֶד לָכֶם, ²⁸כְּשֵׁם שֶׁבֶּן־הָאָדָם לֹא בָּא כְּדֵי שֶׁיְּשָׁרְתוּהוּ אֶלָּא כְּדֵי לְשָׁרֵת וְלָתֵת אֶת נַפְשׁוֹ כֹּפֶר בְּעַד רַבִּים."

²⁹בְּצֵאתָם מִירִיחוֹ הָלְכוּ אַחֲרָיו הֲמוֹן עַם רַב. ³⁰וְהִנֵּה שְׁנֵי עִוְרִים, שֶׁיָּשְׁבוּ בְּצַד הַדֶּרֶךְ וְשָׁמְעוּ כִּי יֵשׁוּעַ עוֹבֵר, הֵחֵלּוּ לִצְעֹק: "אֲדוֹנֵנוּ בֶּן־דָּוִד, רַחֵם עָלֵינוּ!" ³¹הָעָם גָּעַר בָּהֶם לְהַשְׁתִּיקָם, אַךְ הֵם צָעֲקוּ בְּיֶתֶר שְׂאֵת: "אֲדוֹנֵנוּ בֶּן־דָּוִד, רַחֵם עָלֵינוּ!" ³²יֵשׁוּעַ נֶעֱצַר, קָרָא לָהֶם וְשָׁאַל: "מַה רְצוֹנְכֶם שֶׁאֶעֱשֶׂה

33 They said to Him, "Lord, that our eyes may be opened." 34 So Jesus had compassion and touched their eyes. And immediately their eyes received sight, and they followed Him.

21 Now when they drew near Jerusalem, and came to Bethphage, at the Mount of Olives, then Jesus sent two disciples, 2 saying to them, "Go into the village opposite you, and immediately you will find a donkey tied, and a colt with her. Loose *them* and bring *them* to Me. 3 And if anyone says anything to you, you shall say, 'The Lord has need of them,' and immediately he will send them."

4 All this was done that it might be fulfilled which was spoken by the prophet, saying:

5   "Tell the daughter of Zion,
      'Behold, your King is coming to you,
      Lowly, and sitting on a donkey,
      A colt, the foal of a donkey.' "

6 So the disciples went and did as Jesus commanded them. 7 They brought the donkey and the colt, laid their clothes on them, and set *Him* on them. 8 And a very great multitude spread their clothes on the road; others cut down branches from the trees and spread *them* on the road. 9 Then the multitudes who went before and those who followed cried out, saying:

     "Hosanna to the Son of David!
     'Blessed is He who comes in the name of the
      LORD!'
     Hosanna in the highest!"

10 And when He had come into Jerusalem, all the city was moved, saying, "Who is this?"

11 So the multitudes said, "This is Jesus, the prophet from Nazareth of Galilee."

12 Then Jesus went into the temple of God and drove out all those who bought and sold in the temple, and overturned the tables of the money changers and the seats of those who sold doves. 13 And He said to them, "It is written, 'My house shall be called a house of prayer,' but you have made it a 'den of thieves.' "

14 Then *the* blind and *the* lame came to Him in the temple, and He healed them. 15 But when the chief priests and scribes saw the wonderful things that He did, and the children crying out in the temple and saying, "Hosanna to the Son of David!" they were indignant 16 and said to Him, "Do You hear what these are saying?"

And Jesus said to them, "Yes. Have you never read,

     'Out of the mouth of babes and nursing infants
      You have perfected praise'? "

לָכֶם?" 33 הֵשִׁיבוּ לוֹ: "אָדוֹן – שֶׁתִּפָּקַחְנָה עֵינֵינוּ!" 34 נִתְמַלֵּא יֵשׁוּעַ רַחֲמִים וְנָגַע בְּעֵינֵיהֶם. מִיָּד רָאוּ וְהָלְכוּ אַחֲרָיו.

כא כַּאֲשֶׁר הִתְקָרְבוּ לִירוּשָׁלַיִם וּבָאוּ אֶל בֵּית-פַּגֵּי, אֶל הַר הַזֵּיתִים, שָׁלַח יֵשׁוּעַ שְׁנֵי תַלְמִידִים 2 בְּאָמְרוֹ לָהֶם: "לְכוּ אֶל הַכְּפָר אֲשֶׁר מִמּוּלְכֶם וּמִיָּד תִּמְצְאוּ אָתוֹן קְשׁוּרָה וְעַיִר אִתָּהּ. הַתִּירוּ אוֹתָם וְהָבִיאוּ אֵלַי. 3 וְאִם מִישֶׁהוּ יֹאמַר לָכֶם דָּבָר, תֹּאמְרוּ 'הָאָדוֹן זָקוּק לָהֶם' וּמִיָּד יִשְׁלַח אוֹתָם."

4 כָּל זֶה קָרָה כְּדֵי שֶׁיִּתְקַיֵּם דְּבַר הַנָּבִיא: 5 "אִמְרוּ לְבַת-צִיּוֹן: הִנֵּה מַלְכֵּךְ יָבוֹא לָךְ, עָנִי וְרֹכֵב עַל-חֲמוֹר וְעַל-עַיִר בֶּן-אֲתוֹנוֹת."

6 הַתַּלְמִידִים הָלְכוּ וְעָשׂוּ כְּמִצְוַת יֵשׁוּעַ. 7 הֵם הֵבִיאוּ אֶת הָאָתוֹן וְאֶת הָעַיִר וּלְאַחַר שֶׁשָּׂמוּ עֲלֵיהֶם אֶת בִּגְדֵיהֶם הוּא יָשַׁב עֲלֵיהֶם. 8 רַבִּים מִן הֶהָמוֹן פָּרְשׂוּ אֶת בִּגְדֵיהֶם עַל הַדֶּרֶךְ וַאֲחֵרִים כָּרְתוּ עֲנָפִים מִן הָעֵצִים וְשָׁטְחוּ אוֹתָם עַל הַדֶּרֶךְ. 9 וַהֲמוֹן הָעָם שֶׁהָלְכוּ לְפָנָיו וְאַחֲרָיו קָרְאוּ: "הוֹשַׁע-נָא לְבֶן-דָּוִד! בָּרוּךְ הַבָּא בְּשֵׁם יהוה! הוֹשַׁע-נָא בַּמְּרוֹמִים!"

10 בְּהִכָּנְסוֹ לִירוּשָׁלַיִם הָמְתָה כָּל הָעִיר וְהַכֹּל שָׁאֲלוּ: "מִי הוּא זֶה?"

11 הֵשִׁיבוּ הֲמוֹנֵי הָעָם: "זֶה הַנָּבִיא יֵשׁוּעַ מִנְּצֶרֶת אֲשֶׁר בַּגָּלִיל."

12 יֵשׁוּעַ נִכְנַס לְבֵית הַמִּקְדָּשׁ וְגֵרֵשׁ אֶת כָּל הַמּוֹכְרִים וְהַקּוֹנִים בְּבֵית הַמִּקְדָּשׁ וְהָפַךְ אֶת שֻׁלְחָנוֹת הַחַלְפָנִים וְאֶת כִּסְאוֹת מוֹכְרֵי הַיּוֹנִים.

13 אָמַר לָהֶם: "הֵן כָּתוּב, 'בֵּיתִי בֵּית-תְּפִלָּה יִקָּרֵא', אַךְ אַתֶּם חוֹפְכִים אוֹתוֹ לִמְעָרַת פָּרִיצִים."

14 נִגְּשׁוּ אֵלָיו עִוְרִים וּפִסְחִים בְּבֵית הַמִּקְדָּשׁ וְהוּא רִפֵּא אוֹתָם. 15 כִּרְאוֹת רָאשֵׁי הַכֹּהֲנִים וְהַסּוֹפְרִים אֶת הַנִּפְלָאוֹת אֲשֶׁר עָשָׂה וְאֶת הַיְלָדִים הַצּוֹעֲקִים בַּמִּקְדָּשׁ, "הוֹשַׁע-נָא לְבֶן-דָּוִד!", נִתְמַלְּאוּ כַּעַס 16 וְאָמְרוּ לוֹ: "אַתָּה שׁוֹמֵעַ מַה שֶּׁאֵלֶּה אוֹמְרִים?" הֵשִׁיב לָהֶם יֵשׁוּעַ: "כֵּן, הַאִם מֵעוֹדְכֶם לֹא קְרָאתֶם,

¹⁷ Then He left them and went out of the city to Bethany, and He lodged there.

¹⁸ Now in the morning, as He returned to the city, He was hungry. ¹⁹ And seeing a fig tree by the road, He came to it and found nothing on it but leaves, and said to it, "Let no fruit grow on you ever again." Immediately the fig tree withered away.

²⁰ And when the disciples saw *it,* they marveled, saying, "How did the fig tree wither away so soon?"

²¹ So Jesus answered and said to them, "Assuredly, I say to you, if you have faith and do not doubt, you will not only do what was done to the fig tree, but also if you say to this mountain, 'Be removed and be cast into the sea,' it will be done. ²² And whatever things you ask in prayer, believing, you will receive."

²³ Now when He came into the temple, the chief priests and the elders of the people confronted Him as He was teaching, and said, "By what authority are You doing these things? And who gave You this authority?"

²⁴ But Jesus answered and said to them, "I also will ask you one thing, which if you tell Me, I likewise will tell you by what authority I do these things: ²⁵ The baptism of John—where was it from? From heaven or from men?"

And they reasoned among themselves, saying, "If we say, 'From heaven,' He will say to us, 'Why then did you not believe him?' ²⁶ But if we say, 'From men,' we fear the multitude, for all count John as a prophet." ²⁷ So they answered Jesus and said, "We do not know."

And He said to them, "Neither will I tell you by what authority I do these things.

²⁸ "But what do you think? A man had two sons, and he came to the first and said, 'Son, go, work today in my vineyard.' ²⁹ He answered and said, 'I will not,' but afterward he regretted it and went. ³⁰ Then he came to the second and said likewise. And he answered and said, 'I *go,* sir,' but he did not go. ³¹ Which of the two did the will of *his* father?"

They said to Him, "The first."

Jesus said to them, "Assuredly, I say to you that tax collectors and harlots enter the kingdom of God before you. ³² For John came to you in the way of righteousness, and you did not believe him; but tax collectors and harlots believed him; and when you saw *it,* you did not afterward relent and believe him.

³³ "Hear another parable: There was a certain landowner who planted a vineyard and set a hedge around it, dug a winepress in it and built a tower. And he leased it to vinedressers and went into a far country. ³⁴ Now when vintage-time drew near, he sent his servants to the vinedressers, that they might

¹⁷ לְאַחַר מִכֵּן 'מְפִי עוֹלְלִים וְיוֹנְקִים יִסַּדְתָּ עֹז'?" עָזַב אוֹתָם וְיָצָא אֶל מִחוּץ לָעִיר, אֶל בֵּית עַנְיָה, וְלָן שָׁם.

¹⁸ בַּבֹּקֶר שָׁב אֶל הָעִיר וְהוּא רָעֵב. ¹⁹ כְּשֶׁרָאָה עֵץ תְּאֵנָה אֶחָד בְּדֶרֶךְ הִתְקָרֵב אֵלָיו וְלֹא מָצָא בּוֹ מְאוּמָה מִלְּבַד עָלִים. אָמַר אֵלָיו: "מֵעַתָּה לֹא יִהְיֶה מִמְּךָ פְּרִי לְעוֹלָם!" וּבוֹ בָּרֶגַע הִתְיַבֵּשׁ עֵץ הַתְּאֵנָה. ²⁰ כִּרְאוֹתָם זֹאת תָּמְהוּ הַתַּלְמִידִים וְאָמְרוּ: "אֵיךְ יָבֵשׁ עֵץ הַתְּאֵנָה פִּתְאֹם?"

²¹ הֵשִׁיב לָהֶם יֵשׁוּעַ: "אָמֵן אוֹמֵר אֲנִי לָכֶם, אִם יֵשׁ לָכֶם אֱמוּנָה וְאֵינְכֶם מְפַקְפְּקִים, לֹא רַק כְּמַעֲשֶׂה הַתְּאֵנָה הַזֹּאת תַּעֲשׂוּ, אֶלָּא גַּם אִם תַּגִּידוּ לָהָר הַזֶּה 'הֵעָקֵר וְהִזָּרֵק לְתוֹךְ הַיָּם', יִתְקַיֵּם הַדָּבָר. ²² וְכָל מַה שֶּׁתְּבַקְשׁוּ בִּתְפִלָּה וְאַתֶּם מַאֲמִינִים תְּקַבְּלוּהוּ."

²³ כְּשֶׁנִּכְנַס לְבֵית הַמִּקְדָּשׁ וְלִמֵּד שָׁם נִגְּשׁוּ אֵלָיו רָאשֵׁי הַכֹּהֲנִים וְזִקְנֵי הָעָם וְשָׁאֲלוּ: "בְּאֵיזוֹ סַמְכוּת אַתָּה עוֹשֶׂה אֶת הַדְּבָרִים הָאֵלֶּה וּמִי נָתַן לְךָ אֶת הַסַּמְכוּת הַזֹּאת?" ²⁴ הֵשִׁיב יֵשׁוּעַ וְאָמַר לָהֶם: "גַּם אֲנִי אֶשְׁאַל אֶתְכֶם דָּבָר אֶחָד אֲשֶׁר אִם תַּגִּידוּ לִי אוֹתוֹ, גַּם אֲנִי אַגִּיד לָכֶם בְּאֵיזוֹ סַמְכוּת אֲנִי עוֹשֶׂה אֶת הַדְּבָרִים הָאֵלֶּה. ²⁵ טְבִילַת יוֹחָנָן מֵאַיִן הָיְתָה, מִן הַשָּׁמַיִם אוֹ מִבְּנֵי אָדָם?"

²⁶ אָז חָשְׁבוּ בִּלְבָבָם: "אִם נֹאמַר 'מִן הַשָּׁמַיִם', יֹאמַר לָנוּ 'אִם כֵּן מַדּוּעַ לֹא הֶאֱמַנְתֶּם לוֹ?' וְאִם נֹאמַר 'מִבְּנֵי אָדָם', חוֹשְׁשִׁים אָנוּ מִן הָעָם, כִּי כֻּלָּם חוֹשְׁבִים אֶת יוֹחָנָן לְנָבִיא."

²⁷ הֵשִׁיבוּ וְאָמְרוּ לְיֵשׁוּעַ: "אֵין אָנוּ יוֹדְעִים." אָמַר לָהֶם: "גַּם אֲנִי לֹא אֹמַר לָכֶם בְּאֵיזוֹ סַמְכוּת אֲנִי עוֹשֶׂה אֶת הַדְּבָרִים הָאֵלֶּה."

²⁸ "אֲבָל מַה דַּעְתְּכֶם: לְאִישׁ הָיוּ שְׁנֵי בָּנִים. הוּא נִגַּשׁ אֶל הָרִאשׁוֹן וְאָמַר, 'בְּנִי, לֵךְ לַעֲבֹד הַיּוֹם בַּכֶּרֶם'. ²⁹ הֵשִׁיב הָרִאשׁוֹן, 'אֵינֶנִּי רוֹצֶה', אֲבָל לְאַחַר מִכֵּן הִתְחָרֵט וְהָלַךְ. ³⁰ נִגַּשׁ אֶל הַשֵּׁנִי וְאָמַר לוֹ אוֹתוֹ דָּבָר. הֵשִׁיב הַשֵּׁנִי, 'כֵּן, אֲדוֹנִי' וְלֹא הָלַךְ. ³¹ מִי מִשְּׁנֵיהֶם עָשָׂה אֶת רְצוֹן הָאָב?" הֵשִׁיבוּ: "הָרִאשׁוֹן." אָמַר לָהֶם יֵשׁוּעַ: "אָמֵן, אוֹמֵר אֲנִי לָכֶם, הַמּוֹכְסִים וְהַזּוֹנוֹת יָבוֹאוּ לִפְנֵיכֶם לְמַלְכוּת הָאֱלֹהִים, ³² כִּי יוֹחָנָן בָּא אֲלֵיכֶם בְּדֶרֶךְ צְדָקָה וְלֹא הֶאֱמַנְתֶּם לוֹ, אֲבָל הַמּוֹכְסִים וְהַזּוֹנוֹת הֶאֱמִינוּ לוֹ. אַתֶּם לְעֻמַּת זֹאת רְאִיתֶם וְלֹא חֲזַרְתֶּם בָּכֶם אַחֲרֵי כֵן לְהַאֲמִין לוֹ."

³³ "שִׁמְעוּ מָשָׁל אַחֵר: אִישׁ בַּעַל אֲחֻזָּה נָטַע כֶּרֶם.

receive its fruit. [35] And the vinedressers took his servants, beat one, killed one, and stoned another. [36] Again he sent other servants, more than the first, and they did likewise to them. [37] Then last of all he sent his son to them, saying, 'They will respect my son.' [38] But when the vinedressers saw the son, they said among themselves, 'This is the heir. Come, let us kill him and seize his inheritance.' [39] So they took him and cast *him* out of the vineyard and killed *him*.

[40] "Therefore, when the owner of the vineyard comes, what will he do to those vinedressers?"

[41] They said to Him, "He will destroy those wicked men miserably, and lease *his* vineyard to other vinedressers who will render to him the fruits in their seasons."

[42] Jesus said to them, "Have you never read in the Scriptures:

> 'The stone which the builders rejected
> Has become the chief cornerstone.
> This was the LORD's doing,
> And it is marvelous in our eyes'?

[43] "Therefore I say to you, the kingdom of God will be taken from you and given to a nation bearing the fruits of it. [44] And whoever falls on this stone will be broken; but on whomever it falls, it will grind him to powder."

[45] Now when the chief priests and Pharisees heard His parables, they perceived that He was speaking of them. [46] But when they sought to lay hands on Him, they feared the multitudes, because they took Him for a prophet.

22 And Jesus answered and spoke to them again by parables and said: [2] "The kingdom of heaven is like a certain king who arranged a marriage for his son, [3] and sent out his servants to call those who were invited to the wedding; and they were not willing to come. [4] Again, he sent out other servants, saying, 'Tell those who are invited, "See, I have prepared my dinner; my oxen and fatted cattle *are* killed, and all things are ready. Come to the wedding."' [5] But they made light of it and went their ways, one to his own farm, another to his business. [6] And the rest seized his servants, treated *them* spitefully, and killed *them*. [7] But when the king heard *about it*, he was furious. And he sent out his armies, destroyed those murderers, and burned up their city. [8] Then he said to his servants, 'The wedding is ready, but those who were invited were not worthy. [9] Therefore go into the highways, and as many as you find, invite to the wedding.' [10] So those servants went out into the highways and

הוּא גָּדֵר אוֹתוֹ מִסָּבִיב, חָצַב בּוֹ יֶקֶב וּבָנָה מִגְדָּל, וּלְאַחַר שֶׁהֶחְכִּיר אוֹתוֹ לְכוֹרְמִים נָסַע. 34 בְּהַגִּיעַ עֵת הַבָּצִיר שָׁלַח אֶת עֲבָדָיו אֶל הַכּוֹרְמִים לְקַבֵּל אֶת הַפְּרִי שֶׁלּוֹ. 35 תָּפְסוּ הַכּוֹרְמִים אֶת עֲבָדָיו, אֶת זֶה הִלְקוּ, אֶת זֶה הָרְגוּ וְאֶת זֶה סָקְלוּ. 36 הוֹסִיף וְשָׁלַח עֲבָדִים אֲחֵרִים, רַבִּים מִן הָרִאשׁוֹנִים, וְגַם לָהֶם עָשׂוּ כָּךְ. 37 לְבַסּוֹף שָׁלַח אֲלֵיהֶם אֶת בְּנוֹ בְּאָמְרוֹ, 'אֶת בְּנִי יְכַבְּדוּ'. 38 כְּשֶׁרָאוּ הַכּוֹרְמִים אֶת הַבֵּן אָמְרוּ אִישׁ אֶל רֵעֵהוּ, 'זֶה הַיּוֹרֵשׁ, בּוֹאוּ נַהֲרֹג אוֹתוֹ וְנִקַּח לָנוּ אֶת נַחֲלָתוֹ'. 39 הֵם תָּפְסוּ אוֹתוֹ, גֵּרְשׁוּהוּ אֶל מִחוּץ לַכֶּרֶם וַהֲרָגוּהוּ. 40 וּבְכֵן, כְּשֶׁיָּבוֹא בַּעַל הַכֶּרֶם מַה יַּעֲשֶׂה לַכּוֹרְמִים הָהֵם?"

41 הֵשִׁיבוּ לוֹ: "הַשְׁמֵד יַשְׁמִיד אֶת הָרְשָׁעִים הָהֵם, וְאֶת הַכֶּרֶם יַחְכִּיר לְכוֹרְמִים אֲחֵרִים אֲשֶׁר יָשִׁיבוּ לוֹ אֶת הַפְּרִי בְּעִתּוֹ." 42 אָמַר לָהֶם יֵשׁוּעַ: "הַאִם לֹא קְרָאתֶם בַּכְּתוּבִים, 'אֶבֶן מָאֲסוּ הַבּוֹנִים הָיְתָה לְרֹאשׁ פִּנָּה; מֵאֵת יְהוָה הָיְתָה זֹּאת, הִיא נִפְלָאת בְּעֵינֵינוּ'? 43 עַל כֵּן אֲנִי אוֹמֵר לָכֶם כִּי תֻּלָּקַח מִכֶּם מַלְכוּת הָאֱלֹהִים וְתִנָּתֵן לְגוֹי אֲשֶׁר יָפִיק אֶת פִּרְיָהּ. 44 וְהַנּוֹפֵל עַל הָאֶבֶן הַזֹּאת יִשָּׁבֵר לִרְסִיסִים, וְכָל מִי שֶׁתִּפֹּל עָלָיו תִּכְתְּשׁ אוֹתוֹ."

45 כַּאֲשֶׁר שָׁמְעוּ רָאשֵׁי הַכֹּהֲנִים וְהַפְּרוּשִׁים אֶת מְשָׁלָיו הֵבִינוּ כִּי עֲלֵיהֶם הוּא מְדַבֵּר. 46 הֵם בִּקְשׁוּ לִתְפֹּס אוֹתוֹ, אֲבָל חָשְׁשׁוּ מִפְּנֵי הֲמוֹנֵי הָעָם, שֶׁכֵּן אֵלֶּה חֲשָׁבוּהוּ לְנָבִיא.

כב יֵשׁוּעַ הוֹסִיף לְדַבֵּר אֲלֵיהֶם בִּמְשָׁלִים וְאָמַר: 2 "דּוֹמָה מַלְכוּת הַשָּׁמַיִם לְמֶלֶךְ בָּשָׂר וָדָם שֶׁעָשָׂה חֲתֻנָּה לִבְנוֹ. 3 שָׁלַח אֶת עֲבָדָיו לִקְרֹא אֶת הַמְּזֻמָּנִים אֶל הַחֲתֻנָּה וְלֹא רָצוּ לָבוֹא. 4 הוֹסִיף לִשְׁלֹחַ עֲבָדִים אֲחֵרִים שֶׁיֹּאמְרוּ לַמְּזֻמָּנִים, 'הִנֵּה עָרַכְתִּי אֶת סְעוּדָתִי, הַשְּׁוָרִים וְהַבָּקָר הַמְּפֻטָּם טְבוּחִים וְהַכֹּל מוּכָן. בּוֹאוּ לַחֲתֻנָּה'. 5 אַךְ הֵם לֹא שָׂמוּ לֵב וְהָלְכוּ לָהֶם זֶה אֶל שָׂדֵהוּ וְזֶה אֶל מִסְחָרוֹ; 6 וְהַנּוֹתָרִים תָּפְסוּ אֶת עֲבָדָיו, הִתְעַלְּלוּ בָּהֶם וַהֲרָגוּם. 7 הַמֶּלֶךְ נִתְמַלֵּא חֵמָה; שָׁלַח אֶת חֵילָיו וְהִשְׁמִיד אֶת הַמְּרַצְּחִים הָהֵם וְשָׂרַף אֶת עִירָם בָּאֵשׁ. 8 אָז אָמַר אֶל עֲבָדָיו, 'הִנֵּה הַחֲתֻנָּה מוּכָנָה, אַךְ אֵלֶּה שֶׁהֻזְמְנוּ לֹא הָיוּ רְאוּיִים. 9 לָכֵן לְכוּ אֶל פָּרָשׁוֹת הַדְּרָכִים וְכָל מִי שֶׁתִּמְצְאוּ קִרְאוּ אוֹתוֹ לַחֲתֻנָּה.' 10 יָצְאוּ הָעֲבָדִים הָהֵם אֶל הַדְּרָכִים וְאָסְפוּ אֶת כָּל מִי שֶׁמָּצְאוּ, גַּם

gathered together all whom they found, both bad and good. And the wedding *hall* was filled with guests.

11 "But when the king came in to see the guests, he saw a man there who did not have on a wedding garment. 12 So he said to him, 'Friend, how did you come in here without a wedding garment?' And he was speechless. 13 Then the king said to the servants, 'Bind him hand and foot, take him away, and cast *him* into outer darkness; there will be weeping and gnashing of teeth.'

14 "For many are called, but few *are* chosen."

15 Then the Pharisees went and plotted how they might entangle Him in *His* talk. 16 And they sent to Him their disciples with the Herodians, saying, "Teacher, we know that You are true, and teach the way of God in truth; nor do You care about anyone, for You do not regard the person of men. 17 Tell us, therefore, what do You think? Is it lawful to pay taxes to Caesar, or not?"

18 But Jesus perceived their wickedness, and said, "Why do you test Me, *you* hypocrites? 19 Show Me the tax money."

So they brought Him a denarius.

20 And He said to them, "Whose image and inscription *is* this?"

21 They said to Him, "Caesar's."

And He said to them, "Render therefore to Caesar the things that are Caesar's, and to God the things that are God's." 22 When they had heard *these words,* they marveled, and left Him and went their way.

23 The same day the Sadducees, who say there is no resurrection, came to Him and asked Him, 24 saying: "Teacher, Moses said that if a man dies, having no children, his brother shall marry his wife and raise up offspring for his brother. 25 Now there were with us seven brothers. The first died after he had married, and having no offspring, left his wife to his brother. 26 Likewise the second also, and the third, even to the seventh. 27 Last of all the woman died also. 28 Therefore, in the resurrection, whose wife of the seven will she be? For they all had her."

29 Jesus answered and said to them, "You are mistaken, not knowing the Scriptures nor the power of God. 30 For in the resurrection they neither marry nor are given in marriage, but are like angels of God in heaven. 31 But concerning the resurrection of the dead, have you not read what was spoken to you by God, saying, 32 'I am the God of Abraham, the God of Isaac, and the God of Jacob'? God is not the God of the dead, but of the living." 33 And when the multitudes heard *this,* they were astonished at His teaching.

רָעִים וְגַם טוֹבִים, וְנִתְמַלֵּא אוּלָם הַחֲתֻנָּה מְסֻבִּים. 11 כְּשֶׁבָּא הַמֶּלֶךְ לִרְאוֹת אֶת הַמְסֻבִּים רָאָה שָׁם אִישׁ שֶׁאֵינֶנּוּ לָבוּשׁ בִּגְדֵי חֲתֻנָּה. 12 אָמַר אֵלָיו, 'חָבֵר, אֵיךְ בָּאתָ לְכָאן בְּלִי בִּגְדֵי חֲתֻנָּה?' הַלָּה הֶחֱרִישׁ. 13 אָמַר הַמֶּלֶךְ לַמְשָׁרְתִים, 'קִשְׁרוּ אֶת יָדָיו וְרַגְלָיו וְהַשְׁלִיכוּהוּ אֶל הַחֹשֶׁךְ הַחִיצוֹן; שָׁם יִהְיוּ הַיְלָלָה וַחֲרוֹק הַשִּׁנַּיִם'. 14 הֵן רַבִּים הַקְּרוּאִים וּמְעַטִּים הַנִּבְחָרִים."

15 הָלְכוּ הַפְּרוּשִׁים וְהִתְיָעֲצוּ לְהַכְשִׁיל אוֹתוֹ בִּדְבָרָיו. 16 שָׁלְחוּ אֵלָיו אֶת תַּלְמִידֵיהֶם יַחַד עִם חֲסִידֵי בֵּית הוֹרְדוֹס וְהַלָּלוּ אָמְרוּ: "רַבִּי, אֲנַחְנוּ יוֹדְעִים שֶׁאַתָּה אִישׁ אֱמֶת וְאֶת דֶּרֶךְ אֱלֹהִים אַתָּה מוֹרֶה עַל-פִּי הָאֱמֶת. גַּם אֵינְךָ חוֹשֵׁשׁ מֵאִישׁ, כִּי אֵינְךָ נוֹשֵׂא פָּנִים לָאֲנָשִׁים. 17 עַל כֵּן אֱמֹר נָא לָנוּ, מַה דַּעְתְּךָ: הַאִם מֻתָּר לָתֵת מַס לַקֵּיסָר אוֹ לֹא?"

18 הִבְחִין יֵשׁוּעַ בְּרִשְׁעָתָם וְאָמַר: "לָמָּה אַתֶּם מְנַסִּים אוֹתִי? צְבוּעִים! 19 הַרְאוּ לִי אֶת מַטְבֵּעַ הַמַּס." הִגִּישׁוּ לוֹ דִּינָר. 20 שָׁאַל אוֹתָם: "שֶׁל מִי הַדְּמוּת הַזֹּאת וְהַכְּתֹבֶת?"

21 הֵשִׁיבוּ: "שֶׁל הַקֵּיסָר."

אָמַר לָהֶם: "אִם כֵּן, תְּנוּ לַקֵּיסָר אֶת אֲשֶׁר לַקֵּיסָר וְלֵאלֹהִים אֶת אֲשֶׁר לֵאלֹהִים."

22 כְּשָׁמְעָם זֹאת הִשְׁתּוֹמְמוּ, הִנִּיחוּ לוֹ וְהָלְכוּ. 23 בְּאוֹתוֹ יוֹם נִגְּשׁוּ אֵלָיו צְדוֹקִים, הָאוֹמְרִים שֶׁאֵין תְּחִיַּת מֵתִים, וְשָׁאֲלוּ אוֹתוֹ: 24 "רַבִּי, מֹשֶׁה אָמַר: 'אִישׁ אִם יָמוּת וּבָנִים אֵין לוֹ, יִקַּח אָחִיו אֶת אִשְׁתּוֹ וְיָקִים זֶרַע לְאָחִיו.' 25 וּבְכֵן הָיוּ עִמָּנוּ שִׁבְעָה אַחִים. הָרִאשׁוֹן הִתְחַתֵּן וּמֵת, וְכֵיוָן שֶׁלֹּא הָיוּ לוֹ יְלָדִים הִשְׁאִיר אֶת אִשְׁתּוֹ לְאָחִיו. 26 כָּךְ גַּם הַשֵּׁנִי וְהַשְּׁלִישִׁי עַד הַשְּׁבִיעִי, 27 וְאַחֲרֵי כֻּלָּם מֵתָה הָאִשָּׁה. 28 אִם כֵּן לְמִי מֵהַשִּׁבְעָה תִּהְיֶה לְאִשָּׁה בִּתְחִיַּת הַמֵּתִים, שֶׁהֲרֵי הָיְתָה שַׁיֶּכֶת לְכֻלָּם?"

29 הֵשִׁיב לָהֶם יֵשׁוּעַ וְאָמַר: "אַתֶּם טוֹעִים מִשּׁוּם שֶׁאֵינְכֶם יוֹדְעִים אֶת הַכְּתוּבִים, אַף לֹא אֶת גְּבוּרַת הָאֱלֹהִים: 30 בַּתְּחִיָּה אֵין הָאֲנָשִׁים מִתְחַתְּנִים, אֶלָּא שֶׁהֵם כְּמַלְאֲכֵי שָׁמַיִם. 31 וַאֲשֶׁר לִתְחִיַּת הַמֵּתִים, הַאִם לֹא קְרָאתֶם מַה שֶּׁנֶּאֱמַר לָכֶם מִפִּי אֱלֹהִים, 32 'אָנֹכִי אֱלֹהֵי אַבְרָהָם, אֱלֹהֵי יִצְחָק וֵאלֹהֵי יַעֲקֹב'? אֵין הוּא אֱלֹהֵי הַמֵּתִים כִּי אִם אֱלֹהֵי הַחַיִּים."

33 שָׁמְעוּ זֹאת הַהֲמוֹנִים וְהִשְׁתּוֹמְמוּ עַל תּוֹרָתוֹ.

34 But when the Pharisees heard that He had silenced the Sadducees, they gathered together. 35 Then one of them, a lawyer, asked *Him a question,* testing Him, and saying, 36 "Teacher, which *is* the great commandment in the law?"

37 Jesus said to him, " 'You *shall love the* LORD *your God with all your heart, with all your soul, and with all your mind.'* 38 This is *the* first and great commandment. 39 And *the* second *is* like it: '*You shall love your neighbor as yourself.'* 40 On these two commandments hang all the Law and the Prophets."

41 While the Pharisees were gathered together, Jesus asked them, 42 saying, "What do you think about the Christ? Whose Son is He?"

They said to Him, *"The Son* of David."

43 He said to them, "How then does David in the Spirit call Him 'Lord,' saying:

44 '*The* LORD *said to my Lord,*
"*Sit at My right hand,*
Till I make Your enemies Your footstool" '?

45 If David then calls Him 'Lord,' how is He his Son?" 46 And no one was able to answer Him a word, nor from that day on did anyone dare question Him anymore.

23 Then Jesus spoke to the multitudes and to His disciples, 2 saying: "The scribes and the Pharisees sit in Moses' seat. 3 Therefore whatever they tell you to observe, *that* observe and do, but do not do according to their works; for they say, and do not do. 4 For they bind heavy burdens, hard to bear, and lay *them* on men's shoulders; but they *themselves* will not move them with one of their fingers. 5 But all their works they do to be seen by men. They make their phylacteries broad and enlarge the borders of their garments. 6 They love the best places at feasts, the best seats in the synagogues, 7 greetings in the marketplaces, and to be called by men, 'Rabbi, Rabbi.' 8 But you, do not be called 'Rabbi'; for One is your Teacher, the Christ, and you are all brethren. 9 Do not call anyone on earth your father; for One is your Father, He who is in heaven. 10 And do not be called teachers; for One is your Teacher, the Christ. 11 But he who is greatest among you shall be your servant. 12 And whoever exalts himself will be humbled, and he who humbles himself will be exalted.

13 "But woe to you, scribes and Pharisees, hypocrites! For you shut up the kingdom of heaven against men; for you neither go in *yourselves,* nor do you allow those who are entering to go in.

34 כַּאֲשֶׁר שָׁמְעוּ הַפְּרוּשִׁים כִּי הִשְׁתִּיק אֶת הַצַּדּוֹקִים, נֶאֶסְפוּ יַחְדָּיו 35 וְאֶחָד מִבַּעֲלֵי הַתּוֹרָה שֶׁבֵּינֵיהֶם שָׁאַל אוֹתוֹ כְּדֵי לְנַסּוֹתוֹ: 36 "רַבִּי, אֵיזוֹהִי הַמִּצְוָה הַגְּדוֹלָה שֶׁבַּתּוֹרָה?"

37 הֵשִׁיב לוֹ יֵשׁוּעַ: "'וְאָהַבְתָּ אֶת יהוה אֱלֹהֶיךָ בְּכָל-לְבָבְךָ וּבְכָל-נַפְשְׁךָ וּבְכָל מְאֹדֶךָ. 38 זֹאת הַמִּצְוָה הַגְּדוֹלָה וְהָרִאשׁוֹנָה. 39 הַשְּׁנִיָּה דּוֹמָה לָהּ: 'וְאָהַבְתָּ לְרֵעֲךָ כָּמוֹךָ. 40 בִּשְׁתֵּי מִצְווֹת אֵלֶּה תְּלוּיָה כָּל הַתּוֹרָה וְהַנְּבִיאִים."

41 כְּשֶׁנִּקְהֲלוּ הַפְּרוּשִׁים שָׁאַל אוֹתָם יֵשׁוּעַ: 42 "מַה דַּעְתְּכֶם עַל הַמָּשִׁיחַ? בֶּן מִי הוּא?" הֵשִׁיבוּ לוֹ: "בֶּן דָּוִד." 43 אָמַר לָהֶם: "אִם כֵּן כֵּיצַד, בְּהַשְׁרָאַת הָרוּחַ, קוֹרֵא לוֹ דָּוִד 'אָדוֹן' בְּאָמְרוֹ: 44 'נְאֻם יהוה לַאדֹנִי: שֵׁב לִימִינִי עַד-אָשִׁית אֹיְבֶיךָ הֲדֹם לְרַגְלֶיךָ'? 45 וּבְכֵן אִם דָּוִד קוֹרֵא לוֹ 'אָדוֹן' כֵּיצַד הוּא בְּנוֹ?" 46 אַף אֶחָד לֹא הָיָה יָכוֹל לַעֲנוֹת לוֹ דָּבָר, וּמֵאוֹתוֹ יוֹם גַּם לֹא הֵעֵז אִישׁ לְהוֹסִיף לִשְׁאָל אוֹתוֹ.

כג אָז דִּבֶּר יֵשׁוּעַ אֶל הֲמוֹן הָעָם וְאֶל תַּלְמִידָיו. 2 אָמַר לָהֶם: "הַסּוֹפְרִים וְהַפְּרוּשִׁים יוֹשְׁבִים עַל כִּסֵּא מֹשֶׁה. 3 לָכֵן כָּל אֲשֶׁר יֹאמְרוּ לָכֶם עֲשׂוּ וְשִׁמְרוּ, אַךְ כְּמַעֲשֵׂיהֶם אַל תַּעֲשׂוּ, כִּי אוֹמְרִים הֵם וְאֵינָם עוֹשִׂים. 4 הֵם קוֹשְׁרִים מַשָּׂאוֹת כְּבֵדִים וּמַעֲמִיסִים אוֹתָם עַל שִׁכְמֵי הָאֲנָשִׁים, אַךְ אֵינָם רוֹצִים לְהָנִיעַ אוֹתָם אַף בְּאֶצְבָּעָם; 5 וְעוֹשִׂים אֶת כָּל מַעֲשֵׂיהֶם כְּדֵי לְהֵרָאוֹת לִבְנֵי אָדָם, בְּהַרְחִיבָם אֶת תְּפִלֵּיהֶם וּבְהַאֲרִיכָם אֶת צִיצִיּוֹתֵיהֶם. 6 אוֹהֲבִים הֵם אֶת מוֹשַׁב הָרֹאשׁ בַּסְּעוּדוֹת וְאֶת הַמּוֹשָׁבִים הָרִאשׁוֹנִים בְּבָתֵּי הַכְּנֶסֶת 7 וּבִרְכוֹת שָׁלוֹם בַּשְּׁוָקִים וּלְהִקָּרֵא 'רַבִּי' עַל-יְדֵי אֲנָשִׁים. 8 אַךְ אַתֶּם אַל יִקָּרֵא לָכֶם 'רַבִּי', כִּי אֶחָד הוּא רַבְּכֶם וְאַתֶּם אַחִים כֻּלְּכֶם. 9 וְאַל תִּקְרְאוּ 'אָב' לְאִישׁ מִכֶּם בָּאָרֶץ, כִּי אֶחָד הוּא אֲבִיכֶם שֶׁבַּשָּׁמַיִם. 10 גַּם אַל תִּקָּרְאוּ 'מוֹרֵי תוֹרָה', כִּי אֶחָד הוּא הַמּוֹרֶה שֶׁלָּכֶם – הַמָּשִׁיחַ. 11 הַגָּדוֹל בָּכֶם יִהְיֶה מְשָׁרֶתְכֶם. 12 הַמְרוֹמֵם אֶת עַצְמוֹ יֻשְׁפַּל וְהַמַּשְׁפִּיל אֶת עַצְמוֹ יְרוֹמָם.

13 אוֹי לָכֶם סוֹפְרִים וּפְרוּשִׁים צְבוּעִים, כִּי סוֹגְרִים אַתֶּם אֶת מַלְכוּת הַשָּׁמַיִם בִּפְנֵי בְּנֵי אָדָם; הֵן אַתֶּם

14 Woe to you, scribes and Pharisees, hypocrites! For you devour widows' houses, and for a pretense make long prayers. Therefore you will receive greater condemnation.

15 "Woe to you, scribes and Pharisees, hypocrites! For you travel land and sea to win one proselyte, and when he is won, you make him twice as much a son of hell as yourselves.

16 "Woe to you, blind guides, who say, 'Whoever swears by the temple, it is nothing; but whoever swears by the gold of the temple, he is obliged *to perform it.*' 17 Fools and blind! For which is greater, the gold or the temple that sanctifies the gold? 18 And, 'Whoever swears by the altar, it is nothing; but whoever swears by the gift that is on it, he is obliged *to perform it.*' 19 Fools and blind! For which is greater, the gift or the altar that sanctifies the gift? 20 Therefore he who swears by the altar, swears by it and by all things on it. 21 He who swears by the temple, swears by it and by Him who dwells in it. 22 And he who swears by heaven, swears by the throne of God and by Him who sits on it.

23 "Woe to you, scribes and Pharisees, hypocrites! For you pay tithe of mint and anise and cummin, and have neglected the weightier *matters* of the law: justice and mercy and faith. These you ought to have done, without leaving the others undone. 24 Blind guides, who strain out a gnat and swallow a camel!

25 "Woe to you, scribes and Pharisees, hypocrites! For you cleanse the outside of the cup and dish, but inside they are full of extortion and self-indulgence. 26 Blind Pharisee, first cleanse the inside of the cup and dish, that the outside of them may be clean also.

27 "Woe to you, scribes and Pharisees, hypocrites! For you are like whitewashed tombs which indeed appear beautiful outwardly, but inside are full of dead *men's* bones and all uncleanness. 28 Even so you also outwardly appear righteous to men, but inside you are full of hypocrisy and lawlessness.

29 "Woe to you, scribes and Pharisees, hypocrites! Because you build the tombs of the prophets and adorn the monuments of the righteous, 30 and say, 'If we had lived in the days of our fathers, we would not have been partakers with them in the blood of the prophets.'

31 "Therefore you are witnesses against yourselves that you are sons of those who murdered the prophets. 32 Fill up, then, the measure of your fathers' *guilt.* 33 Serpents, brood of vipers! How can you escape the condemnation of hell? 34 Therefore, indeed, I send you prophets, wise men, and scribes: *some* of them you will kill and crucify, and *some* of

אֵינְכֶם נִכְנָסִים לְתוֹכָהּ וְגַם לַבָּאִים אֵינְכֶם מַנִּיחִים לְהִכָּנֵס.

15 אוֹי לָכֶם סוֹפְרִים וּפְרוּשִׁים צְבוּעִים, כִּי סוֹבְבִים אַתֶּם בַּיָּם וּבַיַּבָּשָׁה כְּדֵי לְגַיֵּר אִישׁ אֶחָד, וְכַאֲשֶׁר יִתְגַּיֵּר אַתֶּם עוֹשִׂים אוֹתוֹ לְבֶן גֵּיהִנּוֹם כִּפְלַיִם מִכֶּם.

16 אוֹי לָכֶם מוֹרֵי דֶּרֶךְ עִוְרִים הָאוֹמְרִים: 'הַנִּשְׁבָּע בַּהֵיכָל אֵין בְּכָךְ כְּלוּם, אֲבָל הַנִּשְׁבָּע בִּזְהַב הַהֵיכָל חַיָּב.' 17 כְּסִילִים וְעִוְרִים! מַה גָּדוֹל יוֹתֵר, הַזָּהָב אוֹ הַהֵיכָל הַמְּקַדֵּשׁ אֶת הַזָּהָב? 18 וְכֵן גַּם אוֹמְרִים אַתֶּם, 'הַנִּשְׁבָּע בַּמִּזְבֵּחַ אֵין בְּכָךְ כְּלוּם, אֲבָל הַנִּשְׁבָּע בַּקָּרְבָּן שֶׁעָלָיו – חַיָּב.' 19 עִוְרִים! מַה גָּדוֹל יוֹתֵר, הַקָּרְבָּן אוֹ הַמִּזְבֵּחַ הַמְּקַדֵּשׁ אֶת הַקָּרְבָּן? 20 לָכֵן הַנִּשְׁבָּע בַּמִּזְבֵּחַ נִשְׁבַּע בּוֹ וּבְכָל אֲשֶׁר עָלָיו, 21 וְהַנִּשְׁבָּע בַּהֵיכָל נִשְׁבַּע בּוֹ וּבְשׁוֹכֵן בּוֹ, 22 וְהַנִּשְׁבָּע בַּשָּׁמַיִם נִשְׁבַּע בְּכִסֵּא אֱלֹהִים וּבַיּוֹשֵׁב עָלָיו. 23 אוֹי לָכֶם סוֹפְרִים וּפְרוּשִׁים צְבוּעִים, כִּי נוֹתְנִים אַתֶּם מַעַשְׂרוֹת מִמִּנְתָּה וְשֶׁבֶת וְכַמּוֹן, וּמַזְנִיחִים אֶת הַדְּבָרִים הַחֲשׁוּבִים יוֹתֵר שֶׁבַּתּוֹרָה – אֶת הַמִּשְׁפָּט, אֶת הַחֶסֶד וְאֶת הָאֱמוּנָה. צָרִיךְ הָיָה לַעֲשׂוֹת אֶת אֵלֶּה הָאַחֲרוֹנִים וְאֵין לַעֲזֹב אֶת הַדְּבָרִים הָאֲחֵרִים. 24 מוֹרֵי דֶּרֶךְ עִוְרִים הָעוֹצְרִים אֶת הַיַּתּוּשׁ בְּמִסְנֶנֶת וּבוֹלְעִים אֶת הַגָּמָל.

25 אוֹי לָכֶם סוֹפְרִים וּפְרוּשִׁים צְבוּעִים, כִּי מְטַהֲרִים אַתֶּם אֶת הַכּוֹס וְאֶת הַקְּעָרָה מִבַּחוּץ וְתוֹכָן מָלֵא גֵּזֶל וְתַאַוְתָנוּת. 26 פָּרוּשׁ עִוֵּר, טַהֵר תְּחִלָּה אֶת תּוֹךְ הַכּוֹס כְּדֵי שֶׁתִּהְיֶה טְהוֹרָה גַּם מִבַּחוּץ.

27 אוֹי לָכֶם סוֹפְרִים וּפְרוּשִׁים צְבוּעִים, כִּי דוֹמִים אַתֶּם לִקְבָרִים מְסֻיָּדִים הַנִּרְאִים יָפִים מִבַּחוּץ וְאִלּוּ תוֹכָם מָלֵא עַצְמוֹת מֵתִים וְכָל טֻמְאָה. 28 כָּךְ גַּם אַתֶּם: מִבַּחוּץ אַתֶּם נִרְאִים צַדִּיקִים לְעֵינֵי הַבְּרִיּוֹת, אֲבָל בִּפְנִים מְלֵאֵי צְבִיעוּת וְעָוֶל.

29 אוֹי לָכֶם סוֹפְרִים וּפְרוּשִׁים צְבוּעִים, כִּי בּוֹנִים אַתֶּם אֶת קִבְרֵי הַנְּבִיאִים וּמְיַפִּים אֶת מַצְבוֹת הַצַּדִּיקִים. 30 אוֹמְרִים אַתֶּם: 'אִלּוּ חָיִינוּ בִּימֵי אֲבוֹתֵינוּ לֹא הָיִינוּ שֻׁתָּפִים עִמָּהֶם לִשְׁפֹּךְ אֶת דַּם הַנְּבִיאִים.' 31 כָּךְ אַתֶּם מְעִידִים עַל עַצְמְכֶם שֶׁבָּנִים אַתֶּם לְרוֹצְחֵי הַנְּבִיאִים. 32 אַף אַתֶּם מַלְאוּ אֶת סְאַת אֲבוֹתֵיכֶם! 33 נְחָשִׁים בְּנֵי צִפְעוֹנִים, אֵיךְ תִּמָּלְטוּ מִדִּין גֵּיהִנּוֹם? 34 לָכֵן הִנְנִי שׁוֹלֵחַ לָכֶם נְבִיאִים וַחֲכָמִים וְסוֹפְרִים וּמֵהֶם תַּהַרְגוּ וְתִצְלְבוּ וּמֵהֶם תַּלְקוּ

them you will scourge in your synagogues and persecute from city to city, ³⁵that on you may come all the righteous blood shed on the earth, from the blood of righteous Abel to the blood of Zechariah, son of Berechiah, whom you murdered between the temple and the altar. ³⁶Assuredly, I say to you, all these things will come upon this generation.

³⁷"O Jerusalem, Jerusalem, the one who kills the prophets and stones those who are sent to her! How often I wanted to gather your children together, as a hen gathers her chicks under *her* wings, but you were not willing! ³⁸See! Your house is left to you desolate; ³⁹for I say to you, you shall see Me no more till you say, 'Blessed *is* He who comes in the name of the LORD!'"

24 Then Jesus went out and departed from the temple, and His disciples came up to show Him the buildings of the temple. ²And Jesus said to them, "Do you not see all these things? Assuredly, I say to you, not *one* stone shall be left here upon another, that shall not be thrown down."

³Now as He sat on the Mount of Olives, the disciples came to Him privately, saying, "Tell us, when will these things be? And what *will be* the sign of Your coming, and of the end of the age?"

⁴And Jesus answered and said to them: "Take heed that no one deceives you. ⁵For many will come in My name, saying, 'I am the Christ,' and will deceive many. ⁶And you will hear of wars and rumors of wars. See that you are not troubled; for all *these things* must come to pass, but the end is not yet. ⁷For nation will rise against nation, and kingdom against kingdom. And there will be famines, pestilences, and earthquakes in various places. ⁸All these *are* the beginning of sorrows.

⁹"Then they will deliver you up to tribulation and kill you, and you will be hated by all nations for My name's sake. ¹⁰And then many will be offended, will betray one another, and will hate one another. ¹¹Then many false prophets will rise up and deceive many. ¹²And because lawlessness will abound, the love of many will grow cold. ¹³But he who endures to the end shall be saved. ¹⁴And this gospel of the kingdom will be preached in all the world as a witness to all the nations, and then the end will come.

¹⁵"Therefore when you see the 'abomination of desolation,' spoken of by Daniel the prophet, standing in the holy place" (whoever reads, let him understand), ¹⁶"then let those who are in Judea flee to the mountains. ¹⁷Let him who is on the housetop not go down to take anything out of his house. ¹⁸And let him who is in the field not go back

בְּבָתֵּי הַכְּנֶסֶת שֶׁלָּכֶם וְתִרְדְּפוּם מֵעִיר לָעִיר. 35 לְמַעַן יָבוֹא עֲלֵיכֶם כָּל דָּם נָקִי שֶׁנִּשְׁפַּךְ עַל הָאָרֶץ מִדַּם הֶבֶל הַצַּדִּיק עַד דַּם זְכַרְיָה בֶּן בֶּרֶכְיָה אֲשֶׁר רְצַחְתֶּם אוֹתוֹ בֵּין הַהֵיכָל לַמִּזְבֵּחַ. 36 אָמֵן אוֹמֵר אֲנִי לָכֶם, בּוֹא יָבוֹא כָּל זֶה עַל הַדּוֹר הַזֶּה."

37 "יְרוּשָׁלַיִם, יְרוּשָׁלַיִם, הַהוֹרֶגֶת אֶת הַנְּבִיאִים וְסוֹקֶלֶת אֶת הַשְּׁלוּחִים אֵלֶיהָ, כַּמָּה פְּעָמִים חָפַצְתִּי לְקַבֵּץ אֶת בָּנַיִךְ כְּתַרְנְגֹלֶת הַמְקַבֶּצֶת אֶת אֶפְרוֹחֶיהָ תַּחַת כְּנָפֶיהָ וְלֹא רְצִיתֶם. 38 הִנֵּה בֵּיתְכֶם יֻטַּשׁ לָכֶם, 39 וַאֲנִי אוֹמֵר לָכֶם: מֵעַתָּה לֹא תִרְאוּנִי עַד אֲשֶׁר תֹּאמְרוּ 'בָּרוּךְ הַבָּא בְּשֵׁם יהוה!'"

כד בְּצֵאתוֹ מִבֵּית הַמִּקְדָּשׁ לָלֶכֶת לְדַרְכּוֹ נִגְּשׁוּ תַּלְמִידָיו לְהַרְאוֹת לוֹ אֶת בִּנְיְנֵי הַמִּקְדָּשׁ. 2 הֵגִיב יֵשׁוּעַ וְאָמַר לָהֶם: "רוֹאִים אַתֶּם אֶת כָּל אֵלֶּה? אָמֵן אוֹמֵר אֲנִי לָכֶם, לֹא תִשָּׁאֵר פֹּה אֶבֶן עַל אֶבֶן אֲשֶׁר לֹא תִפֹּל אַרְצָה." 3 כַּאֲשֶׁר יָשַׁב עַל הַר הַזֵּיתִים נִגְּשׁוּ אֵלָיו הַתַּלְמִידִים לְבַדָּם וְאָמְרוּ: "הַגֶּד נָא לָנוּ מָתַי יִהְיֶה הַדָּבָר הַזֶּה וּמָה הוּא אוֹת בּוֹאֲךָ וְקֵץ הָעוֹלָם?" 4 הֵשִׁיב יֵשׁוּעַ וְאָמַר לָהֶם: "הִזָּהֲרוּ שֶׁלֹּא יַתְעֶה אֶתְכֶם אִישׁ, 5 כִּי רַבִּים יָבוֹאוּ בִּשְׁמִי וְיֹאמְרוּ 'אֲנִי הַמָּשִׁיחַ' וְיַתְעוּ רַבִּים. 6 וְאַתֶּם עֲתִידִים לִשְׁמֹעַ מִלְחָמוֹת וּשְׁמוּעוֹת מִלְחָמָה. שִׂימוּ לֵב, אַל תִּבָּהֲלוּ; כִּי צָרִיךְ לִהְיוֹת הַדָּבָר הַזֶּה, וּבְכָל זֹאת עוֹד לֹא בָּא הַקֵּץ. 7 גּוֹי יָקוּם עַל גּוֹי וּמַמְלָכָה עַל מַמְלָכָה וְיִהְיוּ רָעָב וּרְעִידוֹת אֲדָמָה בִּמְקוֹמוֹת רַבִּים, 8 אַךְ כָּל אֵלֶּה רֵאשִׁית הַצָּרוֹת. 9 אָז יִמְסְרוּ אֶתְכֶם לָרוֹדְפִים וְיַהַרְגוּ אֶתְכֶם וְתִהְיוּ שְׂנוּאִים עַל כָּל הַגּוֹיִים בִּגְלַל שְׁמִי. 10 רַבִּים יִכָּשְׁלוּ בְּאוֹתָהּ עֵת וְיַסְגִּירוּ זֶה אֶת זֶה וְיִשְׂנְאוּ זֶה אֶת זֶה. 11 נְבִיאֵי שֶׁקֶר יָקוּמוּ וְיַתְעוּ רַבִּים, 12 וּמֵאַחַר שֶׁתִּרְבֶּה הַהֶפְקֵרוּת תִּתְקָרֵר אַהֲבַת רַבִּים. 13 אֲבָל הַמַּחֲזִיק מַעֲמָד עַד קֵץ הוּא יִוָּשֵׁעַ. 14 וּבְשׂוֹרָה זוֹ שֶׁל הַמַּלְכוּת תֻּכְרַז בְּכָל הָעוֹלָם לְעֵדוּת לְכָל הַגּוֹיִים וְאַחֲרֵי כֵן יָבוֹא הַקֵּץ."

15 "לָכֵן כַּאֲשֶׁר תִּרְאוּ אֶת הַשִּׁקּוּץ הַמְשֹׁמֵם, כַּנֶּאֱמַר בְּפִי דָּנִיֵּאל הַנָּבִיא, עוֹמֵד בְּמָקוֹם קָדוֹשׁ – עַל הַקּוֹרֵא לְהָבִין – 16 אֲזַי הַנִּמְצָאִים בִּיהוּדָה, שֶׁיָּנוּסוּ אֶל הֶהָרִים; 17 מִי שֶׁעַל הַגַּג אַל יֵרֵד לָקַחַת חֲפָצִים מִבֵּיתוֹ, 18 וּמִי שֶׁבַּשָּׂדֶה אַל יַחֲזֹר לָקַחַת אֶת בִּגְדוֹ.

35 אֶפְשָׁר שֶׁהַמְדֻבָּר בְּזְכַרְיָה בֶּן יְהוֹיָדָע. הַשְׁוֵה דִּבְרֵי הַיָּמִים ב' כד:20–22.

to get his clothes. 19 But woe to those who are pregnant and to those who are nursing babies in those days! 20 And pray that your flight may not be in winter or on the Sabbath. 21 For then there will be great tribulation, such as has not been since the beginning of the world until this time, no, nor ever shall be. 22 And unless those days were shortened, no flesh would be saved; but for the elect's sake those days will be shortened.

23 "Then if anyone says to you, 'Look, here *is* the Christ!' or 'There!' do not believe *it*. 24 For false christs and false prophets will rise and show great signs and wonders to deceive, if possible, even the elect. 25 See, I have told you beforehand.

26 "Therefore if they say to you, 'Look, He is in the desert!' do not go out; *or* 'Look, *He is* in the inner rooms!' do not believe *it*. 27 For as the lightning comes from the east and flashes to the west, so also will the coming of the Son of Man be. 28 For wherever the carcass is, there the eagles will be gathered together.

29 "Immediately after the tribulation of those days the sun will be darkened, and the moon will not give its light; the stars will fall from heaven, and the powers of the heavens will be shaken. 30 Then the sign of the Son of Man will appear in heaven, and then all the tribes of the earth will mourn, and they will see the Son of Man coming on the clouds of heaven with power and great glory. 31 And He will send His angels with a great sound of a trumpet, and they will gather together His elect from the four winds, from one end of heaven to the other.

32 "Now learn this parable from the fig tree: When its branch has already become tender and puts forth leaves, you know that summer *is* near. 33 So you also, when you see all these things, know that it is near—at the doors! 34 Assuredly, I say to you, this generation will by no means pass away till all these things take place. 35 Heaven and earth will pass away, but My words will by no means pass away.

36 "But of that day and hour no one knows, not even the angels of heaven, but My Father only. 37 But as the days of Noah *were*, so also will the coming of the Son of Man be. 38 For as in the days before the flood, they were eating and drinking, marrying and giving in marriage, until the day that Noah entered the ark, 39 and did not know until the flood came and took them all away, so also will the coming of the Son of Man be. 40 Then two *men* will be in the field: one will be taken and the other left. 41 Two *women will be* grinding at the mill: one will be taken and the other left. 42 Watch therefore, for

19 וְאוֹי לֶהָרוֹת וְלַמֵּינִיקוֹת בַּיָּמִים הָהֵם. 20 בְּרַם הִתְפַּלְּלוּ שֶׁלֹּא תִהְיֶה מְנוּסַתְכֶם בַּחֹרֶף אַף לֹא בְּשַׁבָּת, 21 כִּי אָז תִּהְיֶה צָרָה גְדוֹלָה אֲשֶׁר לֹא הָיְתָה כָּמוֹהָ מֵרֵאשִׁית הָעוֹלָם וְעַד עַתָּה, אַף לֹא תִהְיֶה כָּמוֹהָ. 22 וְאִלּוּלֵא קֻצְּרוּ הַיָּמִים הָהֵם לֹא הָיָה נִצָּל כָּל בָּשָׂר, אַךְ לְמַעַן הַבְּחִירִים יְקֻצְּרוּ הַיָּמִים הָהֵם. 23 אִם יֹאמַר לָכֶם אִישׁ בָּעֵת הַהִיא, 'הִנֵּה פֹה הַמָּשִׁיחַ' אוֹ 'הִנֵּהוּ שָׁם', אַל תַּאֲמִינוּ, 24 כִּי יָקוּמוּ מְשִׁיחֵי שֶׁקֶר וּנְבִיאֵי שֶׁקֶר וְיִתְּנוּ אוֹתוֹת גְּדוֹלִים וּמוֹפְתִים כְּדֵי לְהַתְעוֹת, אִם אֶפְשָׁר, גַּם אֶת הַבְּחִירִים. 25 הִנֵּה מֵרֹאשׁ אָמַרְתִּי לָכֶם. 26 לָכֵן אִם יֹאמְרוּ לָכֶם 'הִנֵּהוּ בַּמִּדְבָּר', אַל תֵּצְאוּ, 'הִנֵּהוּ בְּחַדְרֵי חֲדָרִים', אַל תַּאֲמִינוּ; 27 כִּי כַּבָּרָק הַיּוֹצֵא מִמִּזְרָח וּמֵאִיר עַד מַעֲרָב כֵּן יִהְיֶה בּוֹאוֹ שֶׁל בֶּן־הָאָדָם. 28 בַּמָּקוֹם שֶׁהַגְּוִיָּה נִמְצֵאת, שָׁם יִקָּבְצוּ הַנְּשָׁרִים."

29 "מִיָּד אַחֲרֵי צָרַת הַיָּמִים הָהֵם תֶּחְשַׁךְ הַשֶּׁמֶשׁ וְהַיָּרֵחַ לֹא יַגִּיהַּ אוֹרוֹ, הַכּוֹכָבִים יִפְּלוּ מִן הַשָּׁמַיִם וְכֹחוֹת הַשָּׁמַיִם יִזְדַּעְזְעוּ. 30 אָז יֵרָאֶה אוֹת בֶּן־הָאָדָם בַּשָּׁמַיִם וְאָז יִסְפְּדוּ כָּל מִשְׁפְּחוֹת הָאָרֶץ וְיִרְאוּ אֶת בֶּן־הָאָדָם בָּא עִם עַנְנֵי הַשָּׁמַיִם בִּגְבוּרָה וּבְכָבוֹד רַב. 31 וְהוּא יִשְׁלַח אֶת מַלְאָכָיו בְּשׁוֹפָר גָּדוֹל וִיקַבְּצוּ אֶת בְּחִירָיו מֵאַרְבַּע הָרוּחוֹת, מִקְצוֹת הַשָּׁמַיִם עַד קְצוֹתָם.

32 לִמְדוּ אֶת הַמָּשָׁל מִן הַתְּאֵנָה: כַּאֲשֶׁר עֲנָפֶיהָ מִתְרַכְּכִים וְהֶעָלִים צָצִים יוֹדְעִים אַתֶּם שֶׁהַקַּיִץ קָרוֹב. 33 כֵּן גַּם אַתֶּם, כִּרְאוֹתְכֶם אֶת כָּל אֵלֶּה דְּעוּ כִּי קָרוֹב הוּא בַּפֶּתַח. 34 אָמֵן. אוֹמֵר אֲנִי לָכֶם שֶׁלֹּא יַעֲבֹר הַדּוֹר הַזֶּה עַד אֲשֶׁר יִהְיוּ כָל אֵלֶּה. 35 הַשָּׁמַיִם וְהָאָרֶץ יַעַבְרוּ וּדְבָרַי לֹא יַעַבְרוּ. 36 אֲבָל אֶת הַיּוֹם הַהוּא וְהַשָּׁעָה אֵין אִישׁ יוֹדֵעַ, גַּם לֹא מַלְאֲכֵי הַשָּׁמַיִם וְגַם לֹא הַבֵּן, אֶלָּא הָאָב לְבַדּוֹ. 37 כִּימֵי נֹחַ כֵּן יִהְיֶה בּוֹאוֹ שֶׁל בֶּן־הָאָדָם. 38 כְּמוֹ שֶׁבַּיָּמִים קֹדֶם לַמַּבּוּל הָיוּ אוֹכְלִים וְשׁוֹתִים וּמִתְחַתְּנִים עַד הַיּוֹם שֶׁנִּכְנַס נֹחַ לַתֵּבָה 39 וְלֹא יָדְעוּ עַד שֶׁבָּא הַמַּבּוּל וְסָחַף אֶת הַכֹּל, כָּךְ יִהְיֶה גַם בּוֹאוֹ שֶׁל בֶּן־הָאָדָם. 40 אוֹתָהּ עֵת יִהְיוּ שְׁנַיִם בַּשָּׂדֶה, אֶחָד יִלָּקַח וְאֶחָד יֵעָזֵב; 41 שְׁתַּיִם טוֹחֲנוֹת בָּרֵחַיִם – אַחַת תִּלָּקַח וְאַחַת תֵּעָזֵב. 42 עַל כֵּן עִמְדוּ עַל הַמִּשְׁמָר, כִּי אֵינְכֶם יוֹדְעִים בְּאֵיזֶה יוֹם יָבוֹא

you do not know what hour your Lord is coming. ⁴³ But know this, that if the master of the house had known what hour the thief would come, he would have watched and not allowed his house to be broken into. ⁴⁴ Therefore you also be ready, for the Son of Man is coming at an hour you do not expect.

⁴⁵ "Who then is a faithful and wise servant, whom his master made ruler over his household, to give them food in due season? ⁴⁶ Blessed *is* that servant whom his master, when he comes, will find so doing. ⁴⁷ Assuredly, I say to you that he will make him ruler over all his goods. ⁴⁸ But if that evil servant says in his heart, 'My master is delaying his coming,' ⁴⁹ and begins to beat *his* fellow servants, and to eat and drink with the drunkards, ⁵⁰ the master of that servant will come on a day when he is not looking for *him* and at an hour that he is not aware of, ⁵¹ and will cut him in two and appoint *him* his portion with the hypocrites. There shall be weeping and gnashing of teeth.

25 "Then the kingdom of heaven shall be likened to ten virgins who took their lamps and went out to meet the bridegroom. ² Now five of them were wise, and five *were* foolish. ³ Those who *were* foolish took their lamps and took no oil with them, ⁴ but the wise took oil in their vessels with their lamps. ⁵ But while the bridegroom was delayed, they all slumbered and slept.

⁶ "And at midnight a cry was *heard:* 'Behold, the bridegroom is coming; go out to meet him!' ⁷ Then all those virgins arose and trimmed their lamps. ⁸ And the foolish said to the wise, 'Give us *some* of your oil, for our lamps are going out.' ⁹ But the wise answered, saying, 'No, lest there should not be enough for us and you; but go rather to those who sell, and buy for yourselves.' ¹⁰ And while they went to buy, the bridegroom came, and those who were ready went in with him to the wedding; and the door was shut.

¹¹ "Afterward the other virgins came also, saying, 'Lord, Lord, open to us!' ¹² But he answered and said, 'Assuredly, I say to you, I do not know you.'

¹³ "Watch therefore, for you know neither the day nor the hour in which the Son of Man is coming.

¹⁴ "For *the kingdom of heaven is* like a man traveling to a far country, *who* called his own servants and delivered his goods to them. ¹⁵ And to one he gave five talents, to another two, and to another one, to each according to his own ability; and immediately he went on a journey. ¹⁶ Then he who had received the five talents went and traded with them, and made another five talents. ¹⁷ And

אֲדוֹנְכֶם. ⁴³ וְזֹאת דְּעוּ: אִלּוּ יָדַע בַּעַל הַבַּיִת בְּאֵיזוֹ אַשְׁמוּרָה יָבוֹא הַגַּנָּב, הָיָה שׁוֹקֵד וְלֹא מַנִּיחַ לוֹ לַחְדֹּר לְבֵיתוֹ. ⁴⁴ לָכֵן הֱיוּ מוּכָנִים גַּם אַתֶּם, כִּי בְּשָׁעָה שֶׁלֹּא תַעֲלֶה עַל דַּעְתְּכֶם יָבוֹא בֶּן־הָאָדָם."

⁴⁵ "מִי הוּא אֵפוֹא הָעֶבֶד הַנֶּאֱמָן שֶׁהִפְקִידוֹ הָאָדוֹן עַל בְּנֵי בֵיתוֹ לָתֵת לָהֶם אֶת אָכְלָם בְּעִתּוֹ? ⁴⁶ אַשְׁרֵי הָעֶבֶד שֶׁיָּבוֹא אֲדוֹנָיו וְיִמְצָא אוֹתוֹ עוֹשֶׂה כֵן. ⁴⁷ אָמֵן אוֹמֵר אֲנִי לָכֶם, הוּא יַפְקִיד אוֹתוֹ עַל כָּל אֲשֶׁר לוֹ. ⁴⁸ אֲבָל אִם הָעֶבֶד הָרָע יֹאמַר בְּלִבּוֹ 'אֲדֹנִי מִתְמַהְמֵהַּ' ⁴⁹ וְיַתְחִיל לְהַכּוֹת אֶת חֲבֵרָיו הָעֲבָדִים וְיֹאכַל וְיִשְׁתֶּה עִם הַשִּׁכּוֹרִים, ⁵⁰ בּוֹא יָבוֹא אֲדוֹנָיו שֶׁל הָעֶבֶד הַהוּא בְּיוֹם שֶׁאֵינוֹ מְצַפֶּה לוֹ וּבְשָׁעָה שֶׁאֵינוֹ יוֹדֵעַ, ⁵¹ יְשַׁסַּף אוֹתוֹ וְיָשִׂים חֶלְקוֹ עִם הַצְּבוּעִים; שָׁם יִהְיוּ הַיְלָלָה וַחֲרוֹק הַשִּׁנַּיִם."

כה "אָז תִּדְמֶה מַלְכוּת הַשָּׁמַיִם לְעֶשֶׂר עֲלָמוֹת אֲשֶׁר לָקְחוּ אֶת מְנוֹרוֹתֵיהֶן וְיָצְאוּ לִקְרַאת הֶחָתָן. ² חָמֵשׁ מֵהֶן הָיוּ כְּסִילוֹת וְחָמֵשׁ הָיוּ נְבוֹנוֹת, ³ שֶׁכֵּן הַכְּסִילוֹת לָקְחוּ אֶת הַמְּנוֹרוֹת וְלֹא לָקְחוּ אִתָּן שֶׁמֶן, ⁴ אֲבָל הַנְּבוֹנוֹת לָקְחוּ שֶׁמֶן בִּכְלֵיהֶן יַחַד עִם מְנוֹרוֹתֵיהֶן. ⁵ כֵּיוָן שֶׁהִתְמַהְמַהּ הֶחָתָן נִמְנְמוּ כֻּלָּן וְנִרְדְּמוּ. ⁶ בַּחֲצוֹת הַלַּיְלָה נִשְׁמְעָה קְרִיאָה, 'הִנֵּה הֶחָתָן, צְאֶינָה לִקְרָאתוֹ!' ⁷ אָז הִתְעוֹרְרוּ הָעֲלָמוֹת הָהֵן וְהֵכִינוּ אֶת מְנוֹרוֹתֵיהֶן. ⁸ אָמְרוּ הַכְּסִילוֹת לַנְּבוֹנוֹת, 'תֵּנָּה לָנוּ מִן הַשֶּׁמֶן שֶׁלָּכֶן, כִּי מְנוֹרוֹתֵינוּ דּוֹעֲכוֹת'. ⁹ עָנוּ הַנְּבוֹנוֹת וְאָמְרוּ, "שֶׁמָּא לֹא יַסְפִּיק לָנוּ וְלָכֶן. לֵכְנָה אֶל הַמּוֹכְרִים וּקְנֶינָה בִּשְׁבִילְכֶן'. ¹⁰ בְּשָׁעָה שֶׁהָלְכוּ לִקְנוֹת בָּא הֶחָתָן; הָעֲלָמוֹת הַמּוּכָנוֹת נִכְנְסוּ אִתּוֹ לַחֲתֻנָּה וְהַדֶּלֶת נִסְגְּרָה. ¹¹ לְאַחַר מִכֵּן בָּאוּ גַּם שְׁאָר הָעֲלָמוֹת וְאָמְרוּ, 'אֲדוֹנֵנוּ אֲדוֹנֵנוּ, פְּתַח לָנוּ'. ¹² אַךְ הוּא הֵשִׁיב, 'אָמֵן אוֹמֵר אֲנִי לָכֶן, אֵינֶנִּי מַכִּיר אֶתְכֶן'. ¹³ לָכֵן עִמְדוּ עַל הַמִּשְׁמָר, כִּי אֵינְכֶם יוֹדְעִים אֶת הַיּוֹם אַף לֹא אֶת הַשָּׁעָה."

¹⁴ "דּוֹמֶה הַדָּבָר לְאִישׁ הַיּוֹצֵא לְמַסָּע. קֹדֶם לָכֵן קָרָא לַעֲבָדָיו וְהִפְקִיד בְּיָדָם אֶת הוֹנוֹ; ¹⁵ לְאֶחָד נָתַן חָמֵשׁ כִּכְּרֵי כֶסֶף, לְאַחֵר שְׁתַּיִם וּלְאַחֵר אַחַת, לְכָל אִישׁ לְפִי כִּשְׁרוֹנוֹ, וְנָסַע. ¹⁶ זֶה שֶׁקִּבֵּל חָמֵשׁ כִּכָּרִים הָלַךְ מִיָּד, סָחַר בָּהֶן וְהִרְוִיחַ חָמֵשׁ אֲחֵרוֹת. ¹⁷ כְּמוֹ כֵן זֶה

likewise he who *had received* two gained two more also. ¹⁸But he who had received one went and dug in the ground, and hid his lord's money. ¹⁹After a long time the lord of those servants came and settled accounts with them.

²⁰"So he who had received five talents came and brought five other talents, saying, 'Lord, you delivered to me five talents; look, I have gained five more talents besides them.' ²¹His lord said to him, 'Well *done,* good and faithful servant; you were faithful over a few things, I will make you ruler over many things. Enter into the joy of your lord.' ²²He also who had received two talents came and said, 'Lord, you delivered to me two talents; look, I have gained two more talents besides them.' ²³His lord said to him, 'Well *done,* good and faithful servant; you have been faithful over a few things, I will make you ruler over many things. Enter into the joy of your lord.'

²⁴"Then he who had received the one talent came and said, 'Lord, I knew you to be a hard man, reaping where you have not sown, and gathering where you have not scattered seed. ²⁵And I was afraid, and went and hid your talent in the ground. Look, *there* you have *what is* yours.'

²⁶"But his lord answered and said to him, 'You wicked and lazy servant, you knew that I reap where I have not sown, and gather where I have not scattered seed. ²⁷So you ought to have deposited my money with the bankers, and at my coming I would have received back my own with interest. ²⁸So take the talent from him, and give *it* to him who has ten talents.

²⁹'For to everyone who has, more will be given, and he will have abundance; but from him who does not have, even what he has will be taken away. ³⁰And cast the unprofitable servant into the outer darkness. There will be weeping and gnashing of teeth.'

³¹"When the Son of Man comes in His glory, and all the holy angels with Him, then He will sit on the throne of His glory. ³²All the nations will be gathered before Him, and He will separate them one from another, as a shepherd divides *his* sheep from the goats. ³³And He will set the sheep on His right hand, but the goats on the left. ³⁴Then the King will say to those on His right hand, 'Come, you blessed of My Father, inherit the kingdom prepared for you from the foundation of the world: ³⁵for I was hungry and you gave Me food; I was thirsty and you gave Me drink; I was a stranger and you took Me in; ³⁶I *was* naked and you clothed Me; I was sick and you visited Me; I was in prison and you came to Me.'

שֶׁקִּבֵּל שְׁתַּיִם הִרְוִיחַ שְׁתַּיִם אֲחֵרוֹת. ¹⁸ אַךְ זֶה שֶׁקִּבֵּל אַחַת הָלַךְ וְחָפַר בָּאֲדָמָה וְהִטְמִין אֶת כֶּסֶף אֲדוֹנָיו. ¹⁹ אַחֲרֵי זְמַן רַב בָּא הָאָדוֹן שֶׁל הָעֲבָדִים הָהֵם וְעָרַךְ עִמָּהֶם חֶשְׁבּוֹן. ²⁰ כַּאֲשֶׁר נִגַּשׁ זֶה שֶׁקִּבֵּל חָמֵשׁ כִּכָּרִים הֵבִיא חָמֵשׁ כִּכָּרִים נוֹסָפוֹת וְאָמַר, 'אֲדוֹנִי, חָמֵשׁ כִּכָּרִים הִפְקַדְתָּ בְּיָדִי, הִנֵּה הִרְוַחְתִּי חָמֵשׁ כִּכָּרִים נוֹסָפוֹת'. ²¹ הֵשִׁיב לוֹ אֲדוֹנָיו, 'יָפֶה, עֶבֶד טוֹב וְנֶאֱמָן! הָיִיתָ נֶאֱמָן בִּמְעַט, אַפְקִיד אוֹתְךָ עַל הַרְבֵּה. בּוֹא אֶל שִׂמְחַת אֲדוֹנְךָ'. ²² נִגַּשׁ גַּם זֶה שֶׁקִּבֵּל שְׁתֵּי כִּכָּרִים וְאָמַר, 'שְׁתֵּי כִּכָּרִים הִפְקַדְתָּ בְּיָדִי, הִנֵּה הִרְוַחְתִּי שְׁתֵּי כִּכָּרִים נוֹסָפוֹת'. ²³ הֵשִׁיב לוֹ אֲדוֹנָיו, 'יָפֶה, עֶבֶד טוֹב וְנֶאֱמָן! הָיִיתָ נֶאֱמָן בִּמְעַט, אַפְקִיד אוֹתְךָ עַל הַרְבֵּה. בּוֹא אֶל שִׂמְחַת אֲדוֹנְךָ'. ²⁴ נִגַּשׁ גַּם זֶה שֶׁקִּבֵּל כִּכָּר אַחַת וְאָמַר, 'אֲדוֹנִי, יָדַעְתִּי שֶׁאַתָּה אִישׁ קָשֶׁה, הַקּוֹצֵר בְּמָקוֹם שֶׁלֹּא זָרַעְתָּ וְאוֹסֵף בְּמָקוֹם שֶׁלֹּא פִּזַּרְתָּ, ²⁵ וּמֵאַחַר שֶׁפָּחַדְתִּי הָלַכְתִּי וְהִטְמַנְתִּי אֶת כִּכָּרְךָ בָּאֲדָמָה. הֲרֵי אֲשֶׁר לְךָ!' ²⁶ הֵשִׁיב אֲדוֹנָיו וְאָמַר אֵלָיו, 'עֶבֶד רַע וְעָצֵל! יָדַעְתָּ שֶׁאֲנִי קוֹצֵר בְּמָקוֹם שֶׁלֹּא זָרַעְתִּי וְאוֹסֵף בְּמָקוֹם שֶׁלֹּא פִּזַּרְתִּי, ²⁷ לָכֵן הָיִיתָ צָרִיךְ לְהַפְקִיד אֶת כַּסְפִּי אֵצֶל הַשֻּׁלְחָנִים וַאֲנִי בְּבוֹאִי הָיִיתִי מְקַבֵּל אֶת שֶׁלִּי עִם הָרִבִּית. ²⁸ עַל כֵּן קְחוּ אֶת הַכִּכָּר וּתְנוּ לָאִישׁ אֲשֶׁר לוֹ עֶשֶׂר הַכִּכָּרִים; ²⁹ כִּי כָּל מִי שֶׁיֵּשׁ לוֹ נָתוֹן יִנָּתֶן לוֹ וְשֶׁפַע יִהְיֶה לוֹ, אַךְ מִי שֶׁאֵין לוֹ גַּם מַה שֶּׁיֵּשׁ לוֹ יִלָּקַח מִמֶּנּוּ. ³⁰ וְאֶת הָעֶבֶד הַבִּלְתִּי מוֹעִיל הַשְׁלִיכוּ אֶל הַחֹשֶׁךְ הַחִיצוֹן; שָׁם יִהְיוּ הַיְלָלָה וַחֲרוֹק הַשִּׁנַּיִם'".

³¹ "כַּאֲשֶׁר יָבוֹא בֶּן־הָאָדָם בִּכְבוֹדוֹ וְכָל הַמַּלְאָכִים אִתּוֹ, יֵשֵׁב עַל כִּסֵּא כְבוֹדוֹ וְיֵאָסְפוּ לְפָנָיו כָּל הַגּוֹיִים.³² אָז יַפְרִידֵם זֶה מִזֶּה כִּרוֹעֶה הַמַּפְרִיד אֶת הַכְּבָשִׂים מִן הָעִזִּים ³³ וְיַצִּיב אֶת הַכְּבָשִׂים לִימִינוֹ וְאֶת הָעִזִּים לִשְׂמֹאלוֹ. ³⁴ יֹאמַר הַמֶּלֶךְ אֶל הַנִּצָּבִים לִימִינוֹ, 'בּוֹאוּ בְּרוּכֵי אָבִי וּרְשׁוּ אֶת הַמַּלְכוּת הַמּוּכָנָה לָכֶם מֵאָז הִוָּסֵד תֵּבֵל, ³⁵ כִּי רָעֵב הָיִיתִי וּנְתַתֶּם לִי לֶאֱכֹל, צָמֵא הָיִיתִי וְהִשְׁקֵיתֶם אוֹתִי, עוֹבֵר אֹרַח הָיִיתִי וַאֲסַפְתֶּם אוֹתִי, ³⁶ עָרוֹם – וְהִלְבַּשְׁתֶּם אוֹתִי, חוֹלֶה הָיִיתִי וּבִקַּרְתֶּם אוֹתִי, בְּמַאֲסָר הָיִיתִי

37 "Then the righteous will answer Him, saying, 'Lord, when did we see You hungry and feed *You,* or thirsty and give *You* drink? 38 When did we see You a stranger and take *You* in, or naked and clothe *You?* 39 Or when did we see You sick, or in prison, and come to You?' 40 And the King will answer and say to them, 'Assuredly, I say to you, inasmuch as you did *it* to one of the least of these My brethren, you did *it* to Me.'

41 "Then He will also say to those on the left hand, 'Depart from Me, you cursed, into the everlasting fire prepared for the devil and his angels: 42 for I was hungry and you gave Me no food; I was thirsty and you gave Me no drink; 43 I was a stranger and you did not take Me in, naked and you did not clothe Me, sick and in prison and you did not visit Me.'

44 "Then they also will answer Him, saying, 'Lord, when did we see You hungry or thirsty or a stranger or naked or sick or in prison, and did not minister to You?' 45 Then He will answer them, saying, 'Assuredly, I say to you, inasmuch as you did not do *it* to one of the least of these, you did not do *it* to Me.' 46 And these will go away into everlasting punishment, but the righteous into eternal life."

26 Now it came to pass, when Jesus had finished all these sayings, *that* He said to His disciples, 2 "You know that after two days is the Passover, and the Son of Man will be delivered up to be crucified."

3 Then the chief priests, the scribes, and the elders of the people assembled at the palace of the high priest, who was called Caiaphas, 4 and plotted to take Jesus by trickery and kill *Him.* 5 But they said, "Not during the feast, lest there be an uproar among the people."

6 And when Jesus was in Bethany at the house of Simon the leper, 7 a woman came to Him having an alabaster flask of very costly fragrant oil, and she poured *it* on His head as He sat *at the table.* 8 But when His disciples saw *it,* they were indignant, saying, "Why this waste? 9 For this fragrant oil might have been sold for much and given to *the* poor."

10 But when Jesus was aware of *it,* He said to them, "Why do you trouble the woman? For she has done a good work for Me. 11 For you have the poor with you always, but Me you do not have always. 12 For in pouring this fragrant oil on My body, she did *it* for My burial. 13 Assuredly, I say to

37 יַעֲנוּ הַצַּדִּיקִים וְיֹאמְרוּ אֵלָיו, וּבָאתֶם אֵלָי'. 'אֲדוֹנֵנוּ, מָתַי רָאִינוּ אוֹתְךָ רָעֵב וְהֶאֱכַלְנוּ אוֹתְךָ, אוֹ צָמֵא וְהִשְׁקִינוּ אוֹתְךָ? 38 מָתַי רְאִינוּךָ עוֹבֵר אֹרַח וְאָסַפְנוּ אוֹתְךָ, אוֹ עָרוֹם וְהִלְבַּשְׁנוּ אוֹתְךָ? 39 וּמָתַי רָאִינוּ אוֹתְךָ חוֹלֶה אוֹ בְּמַאֲסָר וּבָאנוּ אֵלֶיךָ?' 40 יָשִׁיב הַמֶּלֶךְ וְיֹאמַר לָהֶם, 'אָמֵן, אוֹמֵר אֲנִי לָכֶם, מַה שֶּׁעֲשִׂיתֶם לְאֶחָד מֵאַחַי הַקְּטַנִּים הָאֵלֶּה לִי עֲשִׂיתֶם'.

41 אַחֲרֵי כֵן יֹאמַר אֶל הַנִּצָּבִים לִשְׂמֹאלוֹ, 'לְכוּ מִמֶּנִּי, אֲרוּרִים, אֶל אֵשׁ עוֹלָם הַמּוּכָנָה לַשָּׂטָן וּלְמַלְאָכָיו, 42 כִּי רָעֵב הָיִיתִי וְלֹא נְתַתֶּם לִי לֶאֱכֹל, צָמֵא הָיִיתִי וְלֹא הִשְׁקִיתֶם אוֹתִי, 43 עוֹבֵר אֹרַח הָיִיתִי וְלֹא אֲסַפְתֶּם אוֹתִי, עָרוֹם – וְלֹא הִלְבַּשְׁתֶּם אוֹתִי, חוֹלֶה וּבְמַאֲסָר – וְלֹא בִּקַּרְתֶּם אוֹתִי'. 44 יָשִׁיבוּ גַּם הֵם וְיֹאמְרוּ, 'אֲדוֹנֵנוּ, מָתַי רָאִינוּ אוֹתְךָ רָעֵב אוֹ צָמֵא אוֹ עוֹבֵר אֹרַח אוֹ עָרוֹם אוֹ חוֹלֶה אוֹ בְּמַאֲסָר וְלֹא שֵׁרַתְנוּ אוֹתְךָ?' 45 אָז יַעֲנֶה לָהֶם וְיֹאמַר, 'אָמֵן, אוֹמֵר אֲנִי לָכֶם, מַה שֶּׁלֹּא עֲשִׂיתֶם לְאֶחָד מִן הַקְּטַנִּים הָאֵלֶּה גַּם לִי לֹא עֲשִׂיתֶם'. 46 וּבְכֵן אֵלֶּה יֵלְכוּ לְעֹנֶשׁ עוֹלָם וְהַצַּדִּיקִים לְחַיֵּי עוֹלָם."

כו לְאַחַר שֶׁדִּבֵּר יֵשׁוּעַ אֶת כָּל הַדְּבָרִים הָאֵלֶּה אָמַר לְתַלְמִידָיו: 2 "אַתֶּם יוֹדְעִים כִּי בְּעוֹד יוֹמַיִם הַפֶּסַח בָּא וּבֶן־הָאָדָם יִמָּסֵר לְהִצָּלֵב." 3 בְּאוֹתָהּ עֵת נִקְהֲלוּ רָאשֵׁי הַכֹּהֲנִים וְזִקְנֵי הָעָם אֶל חֲצַר הַכֹּהֵן הַגָּדוֹל, קַיָּפָא שְׁמוֹ, 4 וְהֶחְלִיטוּ לִתְפֹּס אֶת יֵשׁוּעַ בְּעָרְמָה וּלְהָמִית אוֹתוֹ, 5 אַךְ אָמְרוּ: "לֹא בֶּחָג, שֶׁמָּא תִּהְיֶה מְהוּמָה בָּעָם."

6 כְּשֶׁהָיָה יֵשׁוּעַ בְּבֵית עַנְיָה בְּבֵיתוֹ שֶׁל שִׁמְעוֹן הַמְצֹרָע, 7 נִגְּשָׁה אֵלָיו אִשָּׁה שֶׁהֶחֱזִיקָה פַּךְ שֶׁמֶן וּבוֹ בֹּשֶׂם יָקָר מְאֹד וְיָצְקָה אוֹתוֹ עַל רֹאשׁוֹ בַּהֲיוֹתוֹ מֵסֵב לְיַד הַשֻּׁלְחָן. 8 כִּרְאוֹתָם זֹאת כָּעֲסוּ הַתַּלְמִידִים וְאָמְרוּ: "לָמָּה הַבִּזְבּוּז הַזֶּה? 9 הֲלֹא אֶפְשָׁר הָיָה לִמְכֹּר אֶת זֶה בִּמְחִיר רַב וְלָתֵת לָעֲנִיִּים."

10 כְּשֶׁהִבְחִין בְּזֶה בָּזֶה יֵשׁוּעַ, אָמַר לָהֶם: "מַדּוּעַ תָּצִיקוּ לָאִשָּׁה? הֲרֵי מַעֲשֶׂה טוֹב עָשְׂתָה לִי. 11 הָעֲנִיִּים אִתְּכֶם תָּמִיד, אֲבָל אֲנִי, לֹא תָּמִיד אֲנִי אִתְּכֶם. 12 וְהִיא כְּשֶׁיָּצְקָה אֶת שֶׁמֶן הַבֹּשֶׂם הַזֶּה עַל גּוּפִי עָשְׂתָה זֹאת בִּשְׁבִיל קְבוּרָתִי. 13 אָמֵן. אוֹמֵר אֲנִי

you, wherever this gospel is preached in the whole world, what this woman has done will also be told as a memorial to her."

14 Then one of the twelve, called Judas Iscariot, went to the chief priests 15 and said, "What are you willing to give me if I deliver Him to you?" And they counted out to him thirty pieces of silver. 16 So from that time he sought opportunity to betray Him.

17 Now on the first *day of the Feast* of the Unleavened Bread the disciples came to Jesus, saying to Him, "Where do You want us to prepare for You to eat the Passover?"

18 And He said, "Go into the city to a certain man, and say to him, 'The Teacher says, "My time is at hand; I will keep the Passover at your house with My disciples." ' "

19 So the disciples did as Jesus had directed them; and they prepared the Passover.

20 When evening had come, He sat down with the twelve. 21 Now as they were eating, He said, "Assuredly, I say to you, one of you will betray Me."

22 And they were exceedingly sorrowful, and each of them began to say to Him, "Lord, is it I?"

23 He answered and said, "He who dipped *his* hand with Me in the dish will betray Me. 24 The Son of Man indeed goes just as it is written of Him, but woe to that man by whom the Son of Man is betrayed! It would have been good for that man if he had not been born."

25 Then Judas, who was betraying Him, answered and said, "Rabbi, is it I?"

He said to him, "You have said it."

26 And as they were eating, Jesus took bread, blessed and broke *it,* and gave *it* to the disciples and said, "Take, eat; this is My body."

27 Then He took the cup, and gave thanks, and gave *it* to them, saying, "Drink from it, all of you. 28 For this is My blood of the new covenant, which is shed for many for the remission of sins. 29 But I say to you, I will not drink of this fruit of the vine from now on until that day when I drink it new with you in My Father's kingdom."

30 And when they had sung a hymn, they went out to the Mount of Olives.

31 Then Jesus said to them, "All of you will be made to stumble because of Me this night, for it is written:

'I will strike the Shepherd,
     And the sheep of the flock will be scattered.'

32 But after I have been raised, I will go before you to Galilee."

לָכֶם, בְּכָל מָקוֹם שֶׁתְּכְרַז הַבְּשׂוֹרָה הַזֹּאת, בְּכָל הָעוֹלָם, יְסֻפַּר גַּם מַה שֶׁעֲשְׂתָה הִיא, וְזֶה לְזִכְרָה."

14 לְאַחַר מִכֵּן הָלַךְ אֶחָד מִן הַשְּׁנֵים־עָשָׂר, יְהוּדָה אִישׁ קְרִיּוֹת שְׁמוֹ, אֶל רָאשֵׁי הַכֹּהֲנִים 15 וְאָמַר: "מָה אַתֶּם רוֹצִים לָתֵת לִי וַאֲנִי אֶמְסֹר אוֹתוֹ לָכֶם?" נָתְנוּ לוֹ שְׁלוֹשִׁים שִׁקְלֵי כֶּסֶף, 16 וּמֵאוֹתָהּ עֵת חִפֵּשׂ הַזְדַּמְּנוּת לְהַסְגִּיר אוֹתוֹ.

17 בָּרִאשׁוֹן לְחַג הַמַּצּוֹת נִגְּשׁוּ הַתַּלְמִידִים אֶל יֵשׁוּעַ וְשָׁאֲלוּ: "הֵיכָן אַתָּה רוֹצֶה שֶׁנָּכִין לְךָ לֶאֱכֹל אֶת הַפֶּסַח?"

18 הֵשִׁיב לָהֶם: "לְכוּ הָעִירָה, אֶל פְּלוֹנִי וְאִמְרוּ לוֹ, 'כֹּה אָמַר רַבֵּנוּ, עִתִּי קְרוֹבָה. אֶצְלְךָ אֶעֱשֶׂה אֶת הַפֶּסַח עִם תַּלְמִידַי'."

19 הַתַּלְמִידִים עָשׂוּ כְּמִצְוַת יֵשׁוּעַ וְהֵכִינוּ אֶת הַפֶּסַח.

20 בָּעֶרֶב הֵסֵב עִם הַשְּׁנֵים־עָשָׂר, 21 וְכַאֲשֶׁר אָכְלוּ אָמַר: "אָמֵן אוֹמֵר אֲנִי לָכֶם, אֶחָד מִכֶּם יַסְגִּירֵנִי."

22 הֵם הִתְעַצְּבוּ מְאֹד וְהֵחֵלּוּ אִישׁ אִישׁ לִשְׁאֹל אוֹתוֹ: "זֶה אֲנִי, אֲדוֹנִי?"

23 הֵשִׁיב וְאָמַר: "הַטּוֹבֵל אִתִּי אֶת יָדוֹ בַּקְּעָרָה הוּא יַסְגִּירֵנִי. 24 בֶּן־הָאָדָם אָמְנָם הוֹלֵךְ כַּכָּתוּב עָלָיו, אַךְ אוֹי לָאִישׁ אֲשֶׁר יַסְגִּיר אֶת בֶּן־הָאָדָם. הָאִישׁ הַהוּא, מוּטָב הָיָה לוֹ אִלּוּלָא נוֹלָד."

25 הֵגִיב יְהוּדָה שֶׁהָיָה עָתִיד לְהַסְגִּירוֹ – וְשָׁאַל: "זֶה אֲנִי, רַבִּי?"

הֵשִׁיב לוֹ: "אַתָּה אָמַרְתָּ."

26 כַּאֲשֶׁר אָכְלוּ לָקַח יֵשׁוּעַ לֶחֶם, בֵּרַךְ וּבָצַע וְנָתַן לַתַּלְמִידִים בְּאָמְרוֹ: "קְחוּ וְאִכְלוּ, זֶה גּוּפִי."

27 לָקַח אֶת הַכּוֹס, בֵּרַךְ וְנָתַן לָהֶם בְּאָמְרוֹ: "שְׁתוּ מִמֶּנָּה כֻּלְּכֶם, 28 כִּי זֶה דָמִי, דַּם הַבְּרִית [הַחֲדָשָׁה] הַנִּשְׁפָּךְ בְּעַד רַבִּים לִסְלִיחַת חֲטָאִים. 29 וַאֲנִי אוֹמֵר לָכֶם, מֵעַתָּה לֹא אֶשְׁתֶּה מִפְּרִי הַגֶּפֶן הַזֶּה עַד אוֹתוֹ הַיּוֹם אֲשֶׁר אֶשְׁתֶּהוּ חָדָשׁ עִמָּכֶם בְּמַלְכוּת אָבִי."

30 לְאַחַר שֶׁשָּׁרוּ אֶת הַהַלֵּל יָצְאוּ אֶל הַר הַזֵּיתִים.

31 אָמַר לָהֶם יֵשׁוּעַ: "אַתֶּם כֻּלְּכֶם תִּכָּשְׁלוּ בִּגְלָלִי הַלַּיְלָה, שֶׁהֲרֵי כָּתוּב, 'אַכֶּה אֶת־הָרֹעֶה וּתְפוּצֶיןָ הַצֹּאן'.

32 אֲבָל אַחֲרֵי שֶׁאָקוּם אֵלֵךְ לִפְנֵיכֶם לַגָּלִיל."

33 Peter answered and said to Him, "Even if all are made to stumble because of You, I will never be made to stumble."

34 Jesus said to him, "Assuredly, I say to you that this night, before the rooster crows, you will deny Me three times."

35 Peter said to Him, "Even if I have to die with You, I will not deny You!"

And so said all the disciples.

36 Then Jesus came with them to a place called Gethsemane, and said to the disciples, "Sit here while I go and pray over there." 37 And He took with Him Peter and the two sons of Zebedee, and He began to be sorrowful and deeply distressed. 38 Then He said to them, "My soul is exceedingly sorrowful, even to death. Stay here and watch with Me."

39 He went a little farther and fell on His face, and prayed, saying, "O My Father, if it is possible, let this cup pass from Me; nevertheless, not as I will, but as You *will*."

40 Then He came to the disciples and found them sleeping, and said to Peter, "What! Could you not watch with Me one hour? 41 Watch and pray, lest you enter into temptation. The spirit indeed *is* willing, but the flesh *is* weak."

42 Again, a second time, He went away and prayed, saying, "O My Father, if this cup cannot pass away from Me unless I drink it, Your will be done." 43 And He came and found them asleep again, for their eyes were heavy.

44 So He left them, went away again, and prayed the third time, saying the same words. 45 Then He came to His disciples and said to them, "Are *you* still sleeping and resting? Behold, the hour is at hand, and the Son of Man is being betrayed into the hands of sinners. 46 Rise, let us be going. See, My betrayer is at hand."

47 And while He was still speaking, behold, Judas, one of the twelve, with a great multitude with swords and clubs, came from the chief priests and elders of the people. 48 Now His betrayer had given them a sign, saying, "Whomever I kiss, He is the One; seize Him." 49 Immediately he went up to Jesus and said, "Greetings, Rabbi!" and kissed Him.

50 But Jesus said to him, "Friend, why have you come?"

Then they came and laid hands on Jesus and took Him. 51 And suddenly, one of those *who were* with Jesus stretched out *his* hand and drew his sword, struck the servant of the high priest, and cut off his ear.

33 הֵשִׁיב לוֹ כֵּיפָא וְאָמַר: "אִם הַכֹּל יִכָּשְׁלוּ בִּגְלָלְךָ, אֲנִי לְעוֹלָם לֹא אֶכָּשֵׁל!"

34 אָמַר לוֹ יֵשׁוּעַ: "אָמֵן אוֹמֵר אֲנִי לְךָ כִּי בַּלַּיְלָה הַזֶּה, בְּטֶרֶם יִקְרָא הַתַּרְנְגוֹל, שָׁלֹשׁ פְּעָמִים תִּתְכַּחֵשׁ לִי."

35 אָמַר כֵּיפָא: "גַּם אִם עָלַי לָמוּת אִתְּךָ לֹא אֶתְכַּחֵשׁ לְךָ!" וְכֵן אָמְרוּ כָּל הַתַּלְמִידִים.

36 אַחֲרֵי כֵן בָּא אִתָּם יֵשׁוּעַ אֶל מָקוֹם הַנִּקְרָא גַת שְׁמָנִים וְאָמַר אֶל הַתַּלְמִידִים: "שְׁבוּ לָכֶם פֹּה עַד שֶׁאֵלֵךְ לְשָׁם וְאֶתְפַּלֵּל." 37 הוּא לָקַח אִתּוֹ אֶת כֵּיפָא וְאֶת שְׁנֵי בְּנֵי זַבְדַּי וְהֵחֵל מִתְמַלֵּא עֶצֶב וּמוּעָקָה. 38 אָמַר לָהֶם: "נַפְשִׁי מָרָה עָלַי עַד מָוֶת, הִשָּׁאֲרוּ פֹה וְהֱיוּ עֵרִים אִתִּי." 39 אָז הָלַךְ מְעַט הָלְאָה, נָפַל עַל פָּנָיו וְהִתְפַּלֵּל בְּאָמְרוֹ: "אָבִי, אִם אֶפְשָׁר הַדָּבָר, הַעֲבֵר נָא מִמֶּנִּי אֶת הַכּוֹס הַזֹּאת, אַךְ לֹא כִרְצוֹנִי אֲנִי כִּי אִם כִּרְצוֹנְךָ אַתָּה."

40 לְאַחַר מִכֵּן בָּא אֶל הַתַּלְמִידִים וּמְצָאָם יְשֵׁנִים. אָמַר אֶל כֵּיפָא: "וּבְכֵן לֹא יְכָלְתֶּם לְהִשָּׁאֵר עֵרִים אִתִּי שָׁעָה אַחַת? 41 הֱיוּ עֵרִים וְהִתְפַּלְלוּ כְּדֵי שֶׁלֹּא תָבוֹאוּ לִידֵי נִסָּיוֹן. אָמְנָם הָרוּחַ חֲפֵצָה, אֲבָל הַבָּשָׂר חַלָּשׁ." 42 הָלַךְ שֵׁנִית וְהִתְפַּלֵּל בְּאָמְרוֹ: "אָבִי, אִם אִי אֶפְשָׁר שֶׁהַכּוֹס תַּעֲבֹר מִבְּלִי שֶׁאֶשְׁתֶּה אוֹתָהּ, יְהִי נָא כִּרְצוֹנְךָ." 43 הוּא חָזַר וְשׁוּב מָצָא אוֹתָם יְשֵׁנִים, כִּי עֵינֵיהֶם הָיוּ כְּבֵדוֹת. 44 עוֹד פַּעַם עָזַב אוֹתָם וְהָלַךְ לְהִתְפַּלֵּל בַּשְּׁלִישִׁית בְּאָמְרוֹ שׁוּב אֶת אוֹתָן הַמִּלִּים. 45 אַחֲרֵי כֵן בָּא אֶל הַתַּלְמִידִים וְאָמַר לָהֶם: "עוֹדְכֶם יְשֵׁנִים וְנָחִים? הִנֵּה בָּאָה הַשָּׁעָה וּבֶן־הָאָדָם יִמָּסֵר לִידֵי אֲנָשִׁים חוֹטְאִים. 46 קוּמוּ וְנֵלֵךְ. הִנֵּה מִתְקָרֵב הַמַּסְגִּיר אוֹתִי!"

47 עוֹדֶנּוּ מְדַבֵּר וְהִנֵּה בָּא יְהוּדָה, אֶחָד מִן הַשְּׁנֵים־עָשָׂר, וְאִתּוֹ הָמוֹן רַב, מֵאֵת רָאשֵׁי הַכֹּהֲנִים וְזִקְנֵי הָעָם, בַּחֲרָבוֹת וּבְמַקְלוֹת. 48 הַמַּסְגִּיר אוֹתוֹ הִקְדִּים לָתֵת סִימָן בְּאָמְרוֹ: "מִי שֶׁאֶתֵּן לוֹ נְשִׁיקָה זֶה הוּא; תִּפְסוּ אוֹתוֹ." 49 מִיָּד נִגַּשׁ אֶל יֵשׁוּעַ וְאָמַר: "שָׁלוֹם, רַבִּי", וְנָשַׁק אוֹתוֹ. 50 אָמַר לוֹ יֵשׁוּעַ: "חָבֵר, לְשֵׁם מָה אַתָּה כָּאן?" אָז נִגְּשׁוּ אֶל יֵשׁוּעַ, אָחֲזוּ בּוֹ בִּידֵיהֶם וְעָצְרוּ אוֹתוֹ.

51 אֶחָד מֵהָאֲנָשִׁים שֶׁהָיוּ עִם יֵשׁוּעַ שָׁלַח יָדוֹ וְשָׁלַף אֶת חַרְבּוֹ, וּבְהַכּוֹתוֹ אֶת עֶבֶד הַכֹּהֵן הַגָּדוֹל קָצַץ אֶת

52 But Jesus said to him, "Put your sword in its place, for all who take the sword will perish by the sword. 53 Or do you think that I cannot now pray to My Father, and He will provide Me with more than twelve legions of angels? 54 How then could the Scriptures be fulfilled, that it must happen thus?"

55 In that hour Jesus said to the multitudes, "Have you come out, as against a robber, with swords and clubs to take Me? I sat daily with you, teaching in the temple, and you did not seize Me. 56 But all this was done that the Scriptures of the prophets might be fulfilled."

Then all the disciples forsook Him and fled.

57 And those who had laid hold of Jesus led *Him* away to Caiaphas the high priest, where the scribes and the elders were assembled. 58 But Peter followed Him at a distance to the high priest's courtyard. And he went in and sat with the servants to see the end.

59 Now the chief priests, the elders, and all the council sought false testimony against Jesus to put Him to death, 60 but found none. Even though many false witnesses came forward, they found none. But at last two false witnesses came forward 61 and said, "This *fellow* said, 'I am able to destroy the temple of God and to build it in three days.' "

62 And the high priest arose and said to Him, "Do You answer nothing? What *is it* these men testify against You?" 63 But Jesus kept silent. And the high priest answered and said to Him, "I put You under oath by the living God: Tell us if You are the Christ, the Son of God!"

64 Jesus said to him, "*It is as* you said. Nevertheless, I say to you, hereafter you will see the Son of Man sitting at the right hand of the Power, and coming on the clouds of heaven."

65 Then the high priest tore his clothes, saying, "He has spoken blasphemy! What further need do we have of witnesses? Look, now you have heard His blasphemy! 66 What do you think?"

They answered and said, "He is deserving of death."

67 Then they spat in His face and beat Him; and others struck *Him* with the palms of their hands, 68 saying, "Prophesy to us, Christ! Who is the one who struck You?"

69 Now Peter sat outside in the courtyard. And a servant girl came to him, saying, "You also were with Jesus of Galilee."

70 But he denied it before *them* all, saying, "I do not know what you are saying."

אָזְנוֹ. 52 אָמַר אֵלָיו יֵשׁוּעַ: "הָשֵׁב אֶת חַרְבְּךָ אֶל מְקוֹמָהּ, כִּי כָּל הָאוֹחֲזִים בַּחֶרֶב, בַּחֶרֶב יֹאבֵדוּ. 53 שֶׁמָּא חוֹשֵׁב אַתָּה שֶׁאֵינֶנִּי יָכוֹל לְבַקֵּשׁ מֵאָבִי וּמִיָּד יַמְצִיא לִי יוֹתֵר מִשְּׁנֵים-עָשָׂר לִגְיוֹנוֹת מַלְאָכִים? 54 אֲבָל כֵּיצַד יִתְקַיְּמוּ דִּבְרֵי הַכְּתוּבִים שֶׁכָּךְ צָרִיךְ לִהְיוֹת?"

55 אוֹתָהּ שָׁעָה אָמַר יֵשׁוּעַ אֶל הֶהָמוֹן: "כְּמוֹ עַל שׁוֹדֵד יְצָאתֶם בַּחֲרָבוֹת וּבְמַקְלוֹת לְתָפְסֵם אוֹתִי. הֲרֵי יוֹם יוֹם יָשַׁבְתִּי בַּמִּקְדָּשׁ וְלִמַּדְתִּי וְלֹא שְׁלַחְתֶּם יָד לְתָפְסֵם אוֹתִי. 56 אַךְ כָּל זֶה קָרָה לְמַעַן יִתְקַיְּמוּ כִּתְבֵי הַנְּבִיאִים." אָז עֲזָבוּהוּ כָּל תַּלְמִידָיו וּבָרְחוּ.

57 הָאֲנָשִׁים אֲשֶׁר עָצְרוּ אֶת יֵשׁוּעַ הוֹלִיכוּהוּ אֶל קַיָּפָא הַכֹּהֵן הַגָּדוֹל וְשָׁם נִקְהֲלוּ הַסּוֹפְרִים וְהַזְּקֵנִים. 58 כֵּיפָא הָלַךְ אַחֲרָיו בְּמֶרְחָק מָה וּכְשֶׁהִגִּיעַ לַחֲצַר הַכֹּהֵן הַגָּדוֹל נִכְנַס פְּנִימָה וְיָשַׁב עִם הַמְשָׁרְתִים לִרְאוֹת מַה יִּהְיֶה הַסּוֹף. 59 אָז חִפְּשׂוּ רָאשֵׁי הַכֹּהֲנִים וְכָל הַסַּנְהֶדְרִין עֵדוּת שֶׁקֶר עַל יֵשׁוּעַ כְּדֵי לְהָמִית אוֹתוֹ, 60 אַךְ לֹא מָצְאוּ, אַף שֶׁבָּאוּ לְשָׁם עֵדֵי שֶׁקֶר רַבִּים. אַחֲרֵי כֵן נִגְּשׁוּ שְׁנֵי עֵדֵי שֶׁקֶר וְאָמְרוּ, 61 "זֶה אָמַר, 'אֲנִי יָכוֹל לַהֲרֹם אֶת הֵיכַל הָאֱלֹהִים וּבִשְׁלוֹשָׁה יָמִים לִבְנוֹת אוֹתוֹ'." 62 קָם הַכֹּהֵן הַגָּדוֹל וְשָׁאַל אוֹתוֹ: "אֵינְךָ מֵשִׁיב דָּבָר עַל מַה שֶּׁאֵלֶּה מְעִידִים נֶגְדְּךָ?" 63 אוּלָם יֵשׁוּעַ שָׁתַק. אָמַר אֵלָיו הַכֹּהֵן הַגָּדוֹל: "אֲנִי מַשְׁבִּיעַ אוֹתְךָ בֵּאלֹהִים חַיִּים שֶׁתֹּאמַר לָנוּ אִם אַתָּה הַמָּשִׁיחַ בֶּן-הָאֱלֹהִים?"

64 הֵשִׁיב לוֹ יֵשׁוּעַ: "אַתָּה אָמַרְתָּ, אַךְ אוֹמֵר אֲנִי לָכֶם, מֵעַתָּה תִּרְאוּ אֶת בֶּן-הָאָדָם יוֹשֵׁב לִימִין הַגְּבוּרָה וּבָא עִם עַנְנֵי הַשָּׁמַיִם."

65 מִיָּד קָרַע הַכֹּהֵן הַגָּדוֹל אֶת בְּגָדָיו וְאָמַר: "מְגַדֵּף הוּא. מַה לָּנוּ עוֹד צֹרֶךְ בְּעֵדִים? הִנֵּה כָּעֵת שְׁמַעְתֶּם אֶת הַגִּדּוּף. 66 מַה דַּעְתְּכֶם?" הֵשִׁיבוּ: "בֶּן-מָוֶת הוּא."

67 אָז יָרְקוּ בְּפָנָיו וְהִכּוּהוּ בְּאֶגְרוֹף; גַּם סָטְרוּ לוֹ 68 וְאָמְרוּ: "נַבֵּא לָנוּ, הַמָּשִׁיחַ, מִיהוּ הַמַּכֶּה אוֹתְךָ?" 69 אוֹתָהּ שָׁעָה יָשַׁב כֵּיפָא מִחוּץ לַבַּיִת, בֶּחָצֵר. נִגְּשָׁה אֵלָיו שִׁפְחָה אַחַת וְאָמְרָה: "גַּם אַתָּה הָיִיתָ עִם יֵשׁוּעַ הַגְּלִילִי." 70 אַךְ הוּא הִכְחִישׁ בִּפְנֵי הַכֹּל

71 And when he had gone out to the gateway, another *girl* saw him and said to those *who were* there, "This *fellow* also was with Jesus of Nazareth."

72 But again he denied with an oath, "I do not know the Man!"

73 And a little later those who stood by came up and said to Peter, "Surely you also are *one* of them, for your speech betrays you."

74 Then he began to curse and swear, *saying*, "I do not know the Man!"

Immediately a rooster crowed. 75 And Peter remembered the word of Jesus who had said to him, "Before the rooster crows, you will deny Me three times." So he went out and wept bitterly.

27 When morning came, all the chief priests and elders of the people plotted against Jesus to put Him to death. 2 And when they had bound Him, they led Him away and delivered Him to Pontius Pilate the governor.

3 Then Judas, His betrayer, seeing that He had been condemned, was remorseful and brought back the thirty pieces of silver to the chief priests and elders, 4 saying, "I have sinned by betraying innocent blood."

And they said, "What *is that* to us? You see *to it!*"

5 Then he threw down the pieces of silver in the temple and departed, and went and hanged himself.

6 But the chief priests took the silver pieces and said, "It is not lawful to put them into the treasury, because they are the price of blood." 7 And they consulted together and bought with them the potter's field, to bury strangers in. 8 Therefore that field has been called the Field of Blood to this day.

9 Then was fulfilled what was spoken by Jeremiah the prophet, saying, *"And they took the thirty pieces of silver, the value of Him who was priced, whom they of the children of Israel priced,* 10 *and gave them for the potter's field, as the* LORD *directed me."*

11 Now Jesus stood before the governor. And the governor asked Him, saying, "Are You the King of the Jews?"

Jesus said to him, *"It is as* you say." 12 And while He was being accused by the chief priests and elders, He answered nothing.

13 Then Pilate said to Him, "Do You not hear how many things they testify against You?" 14 But He answered him not one word, so that the governor marveled greatly.

בְּאָמְרוֹ: "אֵינֶנִּי יוֹדֵעַ מָה אַתְּ אוֹמֶרֶת." 71 כְּשֶׁיָּצָא אֶל מְבוֹא הֶחָצֵר רָאֲתָה אוֹתוֹ אַחֶרֶת וְאָמְרָה לַנִּמְצָאִים שָׁם: "זֶה הָיָה עִם יֵשׁוּעַ מִנָּצְרַת." 72 שׁוּב הִכְחִישׁ בִּשְׁבוּעָה וְאָמַר: "אֵינֶנִּי מַכִּיר אֶת הָאִישׁ." 73 לְאַחַר שָׁעָה קַלָּה נִגְּשׁוּ הָעוֹמְדִים שָׁם וְאָמְרוּ אֶל כֵּיפָא: "בֶּאֱמֶת גַּם אַתָּה מֵהֶם, כִּי הַמִּבְטָא שֶׁלְּךָ מְגַלֶּה אוֹתְךָ." 74 אָז הֵחֵל לְקַלֵּל וּלְהִשָּׁבַע שֶׁאֵינֶנּוּ מַכִּיר אֶת הָאִישׁ וּמִיָּד קָרָא הַתַּרְנְגוֹל. 75 נִזְכַּר כֵּיפָא בַּדָּבָר שֶׁאָמַר לוֹ יֵשׁוּעַ – "בְּטֶרֶם יִקְרָא הַתַּרְנְגוֹל, שָׁלֹשׁ פְּעָמִים תִּתְכַּחֵשׁ לִי", יָצָא הַחוּצָה וּבָכָה בְּכִי מַר.

כז עִם בֹּקֶר נוֹעֲצוּ כָּל רָאשֵׁי הַכֹּהֲנִים וְזִקְנֵי הָעָם עַל יֵשׁוּעַ כְּדֵי לַהֲמִית אוֹתוֹ. 2 הֵם קָשְׁרוּ אוֹתוֹ, הוֹלִיכוּהוּ מִשָּׁם וּמְסָרוּהוּ לְפִילָטוֹס הַנָּצִיב. 3 יְהוּדָה שֶׁהִסְגִּירוֹ, כְּשֶׁרָאָה שֶׁהִרְשִׁיעוּ אוֹתוֹ, הִתְחָרֵט וְהֶחֱזִיר לְרָאשֵׁי הַכֹּהֲנִים וְלַזְּקֵנִים אֶת שְׁלֹשִׁים שִׁקְלֵי הַכֶּסֶף בְּאָמְרוֹ: 4 "חָטָאתִי, כִּי דָם נָקִי הִסְגַּרְתִּי." אַךְ הֵם אָמְרוּ: "מָה אִכְפַּת לָנוּ? זֶה עִנְיָנְךָ שֶׁלְּךָ!" 5 הוּא הִשְׁלִיךְ אֶת הַכֶּסֶף לְתוֹךְ בֵּית אוֹצַר הַמִּקְדָּשׁ, הָלַךְ מִשָּׁם וְתָלָה אֶת עַצְמוֹ. 6 לָקְחוּ רָאשֵׁי הַכֹּהֲנִים אֶת הַכֶּסֶף וְאָמְרוּ: "אָסוּר לְהָכְנִיס אֶת הַכֶּסֶף לְאוֹצַר הַמִּקְדָּשׁ, כִּי מְחִיר דָּמִים הוּא." 7 הִתְיָעֲצוּ וְקָנוּ בּוֹ אֶת שְׂדֵה הַיּוֹצֵר לִקְבוּרַת הַזָּרִים. 8 עַל כֵּן נִקְרָא הַשָּׂדֶה הַהוּא "שְׂדֵה הַדָּם" עַד הַיּוֹם הַזֶּה. 9 אָז נִתְקַיֵּם מַה שֶּׁנֶּאֱמַר בְּפִי יִרְמְיָהוּ הַנָּבִיא: "וַיִּקְחוּ שְׁלוֹשִׁים הַכֶּסֶף, אֶדֶר הַיְקָר אֲשֶׁר יָקָר מֵעַל בְּנֵי יִשְׂרָאֵל, 10 וַיִּתְּנוּ אוֹתָם בְּעַד שְׂדֵה הַיּוֹצֵר כַּאֲשֶׁר צִוַּנִי יהוה."

11 יֵשׁוּעַ עָמַד לִפְנֵי הַנָּצִיב. שָׁאַל אוֹתוֹ הַנָּצִיב: "אַתָּה מֶלֶךְ הַיְּהוּדִים?"

הֵשִׁיב יֵשׁוּעַ: "אַתָּה אוֹמֵר", 12 וְלֹא עָנָה דָבָר כַּאֲשֶׁר הֶאֱשִׁימוּהוּ רָאשֵׁי הַכֹּהֲנִים וְהַזְּקֵנִים.

13 אָמַר אֵלָיו פִּילָטוֹס: "אֵינְךָ שׁוֹמֵעַ כַּמָּה הֵם מְעִידִים נֶגְדְּךָ?" 14 אַךְ הוּא לֹא הֵשִׁיב לוֹ גַּם לֹא עַל טַעֲנָה אַחַת, לְתִמְהוֹנוֹ הָרַב שֶׁל הַנָּצִיב.

15 Now at the feast the governor was accustomed to releasing to the multitude one prisoner whom they wished. 16 And at that time they had a notorious prisoner called Barabbas. 17 Therefore, when they had gathered together, Pilate said to them, "Whom do you want me to release to you? Barabbas, or Jesus who is called Christ?" 18 For he knew that they had handed Him over because of envy.

19 While he was sitting on the judgment seat, his wife sent to him, saying, "Have nothing to do with that just Man, for I have suffered many things today in a dream because of Him."

20 But the chief priests and elders persuaded the multitudes that they should ask for Barabbas and destroy Jesus. 21 The governor answered and said to them, "Which of the two do you want me to release to you?"

They said, "Barabbas!"

22 Pilate said to them, "What then shall I do with Jesus who is called Christ?"

They all said to him, "Let Him be crucified!"

23 Then the governor said, "Why, what evil has He done?"

But they cried out all the more, saying, "Let Him be crucified!"

24 When Pilate saw that he could not prevail at all, but rather *that* a tumult was rising, he took water and washed *his* hands before the multitude, saying, "I am innocent of the blood of this just Person. You see *to it.*"

25 And all the people answered and said, "His blood *be* on us and on our children."

26 Then he released Barabbas to them; and when he had scourged Jesus, he delivered *Him* to be crucified.

27 Then the soldiers of the governor took Jesus into the Praetorium and gathered the whole garrison around Him. 28 And they stripped Him and put a scarlet robe on Him. 29 When they had twisted a crown of thorns, they put *it* on His head, and a reed in His right hand. And they bowed the knee before Him and mocked Him, saying, "Hail, King of the Jews!" 30 Then they spat on Him, and took the reed and struck Him on the head. 31 And when they had mocked Him, they took the robe off Him, put His *own* clothes on Him, and led Him away to be crucified.

32 Now as they came out, they found a man of Cyrene, Simon by name. Him they compelled to bear His cross. 33 And when they had come to a place called Golgotha, that is to say, Place of a

15 בְּחַג הָיָה הַנָּצִיב נוֹהֵג לְשַׁחְרֵר לָעָם אָסִיר אֶחָד עַל־פִּי בְחִירָתָם. 16 אוֹתָהּ עֵת הָיָה לָהֶם אָסִיר מְפֻרְסָם, יֵשׁוּעַ בַּר־אַבָּא שְׁמוֹ. 17 לָכֵן כַּאֲשֶׁר נִקְהֲלוּ שָׁאַל אוֹתָם פִּילָטוֹס: "אֶת מִי אַתֶּם רוֹצִים שֶׁאֲשַׁחְרֵר לָכֶם, אֶת יֵשׁוּעַ בַּר־אַבָּא אוֹ אֶת יֵשׁוּעַ הַנִּקְרָא מָשִׁיחַ?" 18 כִּי יָדַע שֶׁמִּקִּנְאָה מָסְרוּ אוֹתוֹ.

19 כַּאֲשֶׁר יָשַׁב עַל כֵּס הַמִּשְׁפָּט שָׁלְחָה אֵלָיו אִשְׁתּוֹ לֵאמֹר: "אַל יִהְיֶה לְךָ דָּבָר עִם אוֹתוֹ צַדִּיק, כִּי רַבּוֹת סָבַלְתִּי הַיּוֹם בַּחֲלוֹם בִּגְלָלוֹ."

20 וְאוּלָם רָאשֵׁי הַכֹּהֲנִים וְהַזְּקֵנִים שִׁכְנְעוּ אֶת הֲמוֹן הָעָם לְבַקֵּשׁ אֶת בַּר־אַבָּא וּלְהַכְחִיד אֶת יֵשׁוּעַ. 21 פָּנָה אֲלֵיהֶם הַנָּצִיב וְשָׁאַל: "אֶת מִי מִשְּׁנֵיהֶם תִּרְצוּ שֶׁאֲשַׁחְרֵר לָכֶם?"

אָמְרוּ: "אֶת בַּר־אַבָּא."

22 שָׁאַל אוֹתָם פִּילָטוֹס: "אִם כֵּן, מַה אֶעֱשֶׂה לְיֵשׁוּעַ הַנִּקְרָא מָשִׁיחַ?" אָמְרוּ כֻּלָּם: "שֶׁיִּצָּלֵב!"

23 שָׁאַל: "אֲבָל מַה רָעָה עָשָׂה?" אַךְ הֵם צָעֲקוּ בְּיֶתֶר שְׂאֵת: "שֶׁיִּצָּלֵב!"

24 כְּשֶׁרָאָה פִּילָטוֹס כִּי אֵינוֹ מוֹעִיל דָּבָר וּמַה גַּם שֶׁמִּתְרַגֶּשֶׁת מְהוּמָה, לָקַח מַיִם וְרָחַץ אֶת יָדָיו לִפְנֵי הֶהָמוֹן בְּאָמְרוֹ: "נָקִי אָנֹכִי מִדָּמוֹ שֶׁל זֶה. זֶהוּ עִנְיַנְכֶם!"

25 עָנוּ וְאָמְרוּ כָּל הָעָם: "דָּמוֹ עָלֵינוּ וְעַל בָּנֵינוּ."

26 אָז שִׁחְרֵר לָהֶם אֶת בַּר־אַבָּא, וְאֶת יֵשׁוּעַ הִלְקָה וּמָסַר לִצְלִיבָה. 27 לָקְחוּ חַיָּלֵי הַנָּצִיב אֶת יֵשׁוּעַ לְבֵית הַמִּמְשָׁל וְהִקְהִילוּ אֵלָיו אֶת כָּל הַגְּדוּד. 28 הִפְשִׁיטוּהוּ וְהֶעֱטוּ עָלָיו מְעִיל שָׁנִי, 29 וּלְאַחַר שֶׁשָּׂרְגוּ עֲטֶרֶת קוֹצִים שָׂמוּ אוֹתָהּ עַל רֹאשׁוֹ, נָתְנוּ קָנֶה בְּיַד יְמִינוֹ וְכָרְעוּ לְפָנָיו כְּשֶׁהֵם מִתְלוֹצְצִים בּוֹ וְאוֹמְרִים: "שָׁלוֹם לְךָ, מֶלֶךְ הַיְּהוּדִים!" 30 הֵם יָרְקוּ בּוֹ, לָקְחוּ אֶת הַקָּנֶה וְהִכּוּהוּ עַל רֹאשׁוֹ. 31 לְאַחַר שֶׁהִתְלוֹצְצוּ בּוֹ הֵסִירוּ מֵעָלָיו אֶת הַמְּעִיל, הִלְבִּישׁוּהוּ אֶת בְּגָדָיו וְהוֹבִילוּהוּ לְהַצָּלֵב.

32 בְּצֵאתָם מָצְאוּ אִישׁ מֵאֶרֶץ קִירֶנְיָה, שִׁמְעוֹן שְׁמוֹ, וְהִכְרִיחוּ אוֹתוֹ לָשֵׂאת אֶת צְלָבוֹ. 33 הֵם בָּאוּ אֶל מָקוֹם הַנִּקְרָא גָּלְגְּתָא, כְּלוֹמַר מְקוֹם הַגֻּלְגֹּלֶת,

Skull, ³⁴they gave Him sour wine mingled with gall to drink. But when He had tasted *it,* He would not drink.

³⁵Then they crucified Him, and divided His garments, casting lots, that it might be fulfilled which was spoken by the prophet:

"*They divided My garments among them,*
And for My clothing they cast lots."

³⁶Sitting down, they kept watch over Him there. ³⁷And they put up over His head the accusation written against Him:

THIS IS JESUS THE KING OF THE JEWS.

³⁸Then two robbers were crucified with Him, one on the right and another on the left.

³⁹And those who passed by blasphemed Him, wagging their heads ⁴⁰and saying, "You who destroy the temple and build *it* in three days, save Yourself! If You are the Son of God, come down from the cross."

⁴¹Likewise the chief priests also, mocking with the scribes and elders, said, ⁴²"He saved others; Himself He cannot save. If He is the King of Israel, let Him now come down from the cross, and we will believe Him. ⁴³He trusted in God; let Him deliver Him now if He will have Him; for He said, 'I am the Son of God.'"

⁴⁴Even the robbers who were crucified with Him reviled Him with the same thing.

⁴⁵Now from the sixth hour until the ninth hour there was darkness over all the land. ⁴⁶And about the ninth hour Jesus cried out with a loud voice, saying, "Eli, Eli, lama sabachthani?" that is, "*My God, My God, why have You forsaken Me?*"

⁴⁷Some of those who stood there, when they heard *that,* said, "This Man is calling for Elijah!" ⁴⁸Immediately one of them ran and took a sponge, filled *it* with sour wine and put *it* on a reed, and offered it to Him to drink.

⁴⁹The rest said, "Let Him alone; let us see if Elijah will come to save Him."

⁵⁰And Jesus cried out again with a loud voice, and yielded up His spirit.

⁵¹Then, behold, the veil of the temple was torn in two from top to bottom; and the earth quaked, and the rocks were split, ⁵²and the graves were opened; and many bodies of the saints who had fallen asleep were raised; ⁵³and coming out of the graves after His resurrection, they went into the holy city and appeared to many.

⁵⁴So when the centurion and those with him, who were guarding Jesus, saw the earthquake and the things that had happened, they feared greatly, saying, "Truly this was the Son of God!"

34 וְנָתְנוּ לוֹ לִשְׁתּוֹת יַיִן מָהוּל בִּמְרוֹרַת צֶמַח הָרֹאשׁ. הוּא טָעַם, אַךְ לֹא רָצָה לִשְׁתּוֹת. 35 אַחֲרֵי שֶׁצָּלְבוּ אוֹתוֹ חִלְּקוּ אֶת בְּגָדָיו בְּהַפִּילָם גּוֹרָל, 36 וַיֵּשְׁבוּ לִשְׁמֹר עָלָיו שָׁם. 37 מֵעַל לְרֹאשׁוֹ שָׂמוּ אֶת כְּתַב אַשְׁמָתוֹ: "זֶה הוּא יֵשׁוּעַ מֶלֶךְ הַיְּהוּדִים."

38 אוֹתָהּ שָׁעָה נִצְלְבוּ אִתּוֹ שְׁנֵי שׁוֹדְדִים, אֶחָד מִימִינוֹ וְאֶחָד מִשְּׂמֹאלוֹ. 39 וְהָעוֹבְרִים שָׁם גִּדְּפוּ אוֹתוֹ, הֵנִיעוּ רֹאשָׁם 40 וְאָמְרוּ: "הַהוֹרֵס אֶת בֵּית הַמִּקְדָּשׁ וּבוֹנֶה אוֹתוֹ בִּשְׁלֹשָׁה יָמִים! הוֹשַׁע אֶת עַצְמְךָ, אִם בֶּן־הָאֱלֹהִים אַתָּה, וְרֵד מִן הַצְּלָב!" 41 כָּךְ גַּם הִתְלוֹצְצוּ רָאשֵׁי הַכֹּהֲנִים עִם הַסּוֹפְרִים וְהַזְּקֵנִים בְּאָמְרָם: 42 "אֲחֵרִים הוֹשִׁיעַ; אֶת עַצְמוֹ אֵינֶנּוּ יָכוֹל לְהוֹשִׁיעַ?! מֶלֶךְ יִשְׂרָאֵל הוּא! שֶׁיֵּרֵד עַכְשָׁו מִן הַצְּלָב וְנַאֲמִין בּוֹ! 43 בָּטַח בֵּאלֹהִים, עַתָּה יְפַלְּטֵהוּ אִם חָפֵץ בּוֹ, כִּי אָמַר 'בֶּן אֱלֹהִים אָנִי'." 44 כָּךְ חֵרְפוּהוּ גַּם הַשּׁוֹדְדִים שֶׁנִּצְלְבוּ אִתּוֹ.

45 מִשָּׁעָה שְׁתֵּים־עֶשְׂרֵה בַּצָּהֳרַיִם הִשְׂתָּרֵר חֹשֶׁךְ עַל כָּל הָאָרֶץ עַד הַשָּׁעָה שָׁלוֹשׁ, 46 וּבְעֶרֶךְ בְּשָׁעָה שָׁלוֹשׁ צָעַק יֵשׁוּעַ בְּקוֹל גָּדוֹל: "אֵלִי, אֵלִי, לְמָה שְׁבַקְתַּנִי?" כְּלוֹמַר, "אֵלִי, אֵלִי, לָמָה עֲזַבְתָּנִי?" 47 כַּמָּה מִן הָעוֹמְדִים שָׁם שָׁמְעוּ זֹאת וְאָמְרוּ: "לְאֵלִיָּהוּ הוּא קוֹרֵא." 48 מִיָּד רָץ אֶחָד מֵהֶם, לָקַח סְפוֹג וּמִלֵּא אוֹתוֹ חֹמֶץ, הִצְמִיד אוֹתוֹ אֶל קָנֶה וְהִגִּישׁ לוֹ לִשְׁתּוֹת. 49 אַךְ יֶתֶר הָאֲנָשִׁים אָמְרוּ: "הָבָה נִרְאֶה אִם יָבוֹא אֵלִיָּהוּ לְהַצִּיל אוֹתוֹ."

50 יֵשׁוּעַ צָעַק שׁוּב בְּקוֹל גָּדוֹל וְנָפַח אֶת רוּחוֹ. 51 וְהִנֵּה נִקְרְעָה פָּרֹכֶת הַמִּקְדָּשׁ לִשְׁתַּיִם, מִלְמַעְלָה עַד לְמַטָּה; הָאָרֶץ רָעֲדָה, הַסְּלָעִים נִבְקְעוּ, 52 הַקְּבָרִים נִפְתְּחוּ וְגוּפוֹת רַבּוֹת שֶׁל קְדוֹשִׁים יְשֵׁנֵי עָפָר נֵעוֹרוּ. 53 הֵם יָצְאוּ מִן הַקְּבָרִים אַחֲרֵי שֶׁהוּא קָם, נִכְנְסוּ לָעִיר הַקֹּדֶשׁ וְנִרְאוּ לָרַבִּים.

54 שַׂר הַמֵּאָה וְהָאֲנָשִׁים אֲשֶׁר אִתּוֹ, הַשּׁוֹמְרִים אֶת יֵשׁוּעַ, כִּרְאוֹתָם אֶת רְעִידַת הָאֲדָמָה וְאֵת כָּל

⁵⁵ And many women who followed Jesus from Galilee, ministering to Him, were there looking on from afar, ⁵⁶ among whom were Mary Magdalene, Mary the mother of James and Joses, and the mother of Zebedee's sons.

⁵⁷ Now when evening had come, there came a rich man from Arimathea, named Joseph, who himself had also become a disciple of Jesus. ⁵⁸ This man went to Pilate and asked for the body of Jesus. Then Pilate commanded the body to be given to him. ⁵⁹ When Joseph had taken the body, he wrapped it in a clean linen cloth, ⁶⁰ and laid it in his new tomb which he had hewn out of the rock; and he rolled a large stone against the door of the tomb, and departed. ⁶¹ And Mary Magdalene was there, and the other Mary, sitting opposite the tomb.

⁶² On the next day, which followed the Day of Preparation, the chief priests and Pharisees gathered together to Pilate, ⁶³ saying, "Sir, we remember, while He was still alive, how that deceiver said, 'After three days I will rise.' ⁶⁴ Therefore command that the tomb be made secure until the third day, lest His disciples come by night and steal Him *away*, and say to the people, 'He has risen from the dead.' So the last deception will be worse than the first."

⁶⁵ Pilate said to them, "You have a guard; go your way, make *it* as secure as you know how." ⁶⁶ So they went and made the tomb secure, sealing the stone and setting the guard.

28 Now after the Sabbath, as the first *day* of the week began to dawn, Mary Magdalene and the other Mary came to see the tomb. ² And behold, there was a great earthquake; for an angel of the Lord descended from heaven, and came and rolled back the stone from the door, and sat on it. ³ His countenance was like lightning, and his clothing as white as snow. ⁴ And the guards shook for fear of him, and became like dead *men*.

⁵ But the angel answered and said to the women, "Do not be afraid, for I know that you seek Jesus who was crucified. ⁶ He is not here; for He is risen, as He said. Come, see the place where the Lord lay. ⁷ And go quickly and tell His disciples that He is risen from the dead, and indeed He is going before you into Galilee; there you will see Him. Behold, I have told you."

⁸ So they went out quickly from the tomb with fear and great joy, and ran to bring His disciples word.

⁹ And as they went to tell His disciples, behold, Jesus met them, saying, "Rejoice!" So they came and held Him by the feet and worshiped Him.

הַנַּעֲשָׂה, נִתְמַלְאוּ פַּחַד רַב וְאָמְרוּ: "בֶּאֱמֶת בֶּן־אֱלֹהִים הָיָה זֶה!" ⁵⁵ גַּם נָשִׁים רַבּוֹת שֶׁהָלְכוּ אַחֲרֵי יֵשׁוּעַ מִן הַגָּלִיל וְשֵׁרְתוּ אוֹתוֹ הָיוּ שָׁם וְהִתְבּוֹנְנוּ מֵרָחוֹק. ⁵⁶ בֵּינֵיהֶן הָיוּ מִרְיָם הַמַּגְדָּלִית, מִרְיָם אֵם יַעֲקֹב וְיוֹסֵף, וְאֵם שֶׁל בְּנֵי זַבְדַּי.

⁵⁷ לְעֵת עֶרֶב בָּא אִישׁ עָשִׁיר תּוֹשַׁב רָמָתַיִם, יוֹסֵף שְׁמוֹ, שֶׁגַּם הוּא נַעֲשָׂה לְתַלְמִיד שֶׁל יֵשׁוּעַ. ⁵⁸ הוּא בָּא אֶל פִּילָטוֹס וּבִקֵּשׁ אֶת גוּפַת יֵשׁוּעַ. אָז צִוָּה פִּילָטוֹס לִמְסֹר אוֹתָהּ. ⁵⁹ יוֹסֵף לָקַח אֶת הַגּוּפָה, עָטַף אוֹתָהּ בְּסָדִין נָקִי ⁶⁰ וְהִנִּיחַ אוֹתָהּ בְּקִבְרוֹ הֶחָדָשׁ שֶׁלּוֹ אֲשֶׁר חָצַב בַּסֶּלַע. לְאַחַר שֶׁגִּלֵּל אֶבֶן גְּדוֹלָה עַל פֶּתַח הַקֶּבֶר הָלַךְ לְדַרְכּוֹ. ⁶¹ וּמִרְיָם הַמַּגְדָּלִית וּמִרְיָם הָאַחֶרֶת הָיוּ שָׁם, יוֹשְׁבוֹת מוּל הַקֶּבֶר.

⁶² לְמָחֳרַת עֶרֶב הַשַּׁבָּת נִקְהֲלוּ רָאשֵׁי הַכֹּהֲנִים וְהַפְּרוּשִׁים אֶל פִּילָטוֹס. ⁶³ אָמְרוּ לוֹ: "אֲדוֹנֵנוּ, נִזְכַּרְנוּ כִּי בְּעֵת שֶׁהָיָה חַי אָמַר הַמַּתְעֶה הַהוּא, 'אַחֲרֵי שְׁלוֹשָׁה יָמִים קוּם אָקוּם.' ⁶⁴ לָכֵן צַוֵּה נָא שֶׁיִּשָּׁמֵר הַקֶּבֶר עַד הַיּוֹם הַשְּׁלִישִׁי, שֶׁמָּא יָבוֹאוּ תַלְמִידָיו וְיִגְנְבוּ אוֹתוֹ. לְאַחַר מִכֵּן יֹאמְרוּ לָעָם 'הוּא קָם מִן הַמֵּתִים', וְתִהְיֶה הַתַּרְמִית הָאַחֲרוֹנָה גְּרוּעָה מִן הָרִאשׁוֹנָה."

⁶⁵ אָמַר לָהֶם פִּילָטוֹס: "הִנֵּה לָכֶם מִשְׁמָר, לְכוּ וְשִׁמְרוּ כְּמוֹ שֶׁאַתֶּם יוֹדְעִים."

⁶⁶ הֵם הָלְכוּ וְהִבְטִיחוּ אֶת הַקֶּבֶר בְּכָךְ שֶׁשָּׂמוּ חוֹתָם עַל הָאֶבֶן וְהִצִּיבוּ מִשְׁמָר.

כח אַחֲרֵי הַשַּׁבָּת, עִם עֲלוֹת הַשַּׁחַר שֶׁל יוֹם רִאשׁוֹן, בָּאוּ מִרְיָם הַמַּגְדָּלִית וּמִרְיָם הָאַחֶרֶת לִרְאוֹת אֶת הַקֶּבֶר. ² לְפֶתַע הָיְתָה רְעִידַת אֲדָמָה חֲזָקָה, כִּי מַלְאַךְ יהוה יָרַד מִן הַשָּׁמַיִם, נִגַּשׁ וְגָלַל אֶת הָאֶבֶן מִן הַפֶּתַח וְיָשַׁב עָלֶיהָ. ³ מַרְאֵהוּ הָיָה כַּבָּרָק וּלְבוּשׁוֹ לָבָן כַּשֶּׁלֶג, ⁴ וּמִפַּחְדּוֹ נִבְהֲלוּ הַשּׁוֹמְרִים וְהָיוּ כְּמֵתִים.

⁵ אָמַר הַמַּלְאָךְ אֶל הַנָּשִׁים: "אַל תִּפְחַדְנָה אַתֶּן. אֲנִי יוֹדֵעַ כִּי אֶת יֵשׁוּעַ שֶׁנִּצְלַב אַתֶּן מְחַפְּשׂוֹת. ⁶ הוּא אֵינֶנּוּ כָּאן, שֶׁהֲרֵי קָם לִתְחִיָּה כְּפִי שֶׁאָמַר. בֹּאנָה וּרְאֶינָה אֶת הַמָּקוֹם שֶׁשָּׁכַב בּוֹ. ⁷ לֵכְנָה מַהֵר וְהַגֵּדְנָה לְתַלְמִידָיו: 'הוּא קָם מִן הַמֵּתִים וְהִנֵּה הוּא הוֹלֵךְ לִפְנֵיכֶם לַגָּלִיל. שָׁם תִּרְאוּ אוֹתוֹ.' הִנֵּה אָמַרְתִּי לָכֶן."

⁸ הֵן עָזְבוּ מַהֵר אֶת הַקֶּבֶר בְּיִרְאָה וּבְשִׂמְחָה גְּדוֹלָה, וְרָצוּ לְהוֹדִיעַ לְתַלְמִידָיו. ⁹ פִּתְאוֹם פָּגַשׁ אוֹתָן יֵשׁוּעַ וְאָמַר: "שָׁלוֹם לָכֶן." הֵן נִגְּשׁוּ אֵלָיו, אָחֲזוּ בְּרַגְלָיו

10 Then Jesus said to them, "Do not be afraid. Go *and* tell My brethren to go to Galilee, and there they will see Me."

11 Now while they were going, behold, some of the guard came into the city and reported to the chief priests all the things that had happened. 12 When they had assembled with the elders and consulted together, they gave a large sum of money to the soldiers, 13 saying, "Tell them, 'His disciples came at night and stole Him *away* while we slept.' 14 And if this comes to the governor's ears, we will appease him and make you secure." 15 So they took the money and did as they were instructed; and this saying is commonly reported among the Jews until this day.

16 Then the eleven disciples went away into Galilee, to the mountain which Jesus had appointed for them. 17 When they saw Him, they worshiped Him; but some doubted.

18 And Jesus came and spoke to them, saying, "All authority has been given to Me in heaven and on earth. 19 Go therefore and make disciples of all the nations, baptizing them in the name of the Father and of the Son and of the Holy Spirit, 20 teaching them to observe all things that I have commanded you; and lo, I am with you always, *even* to the end of the age." Amen.

וְהִשְׁתַּחֲווּ לוֹ. 10 אָמַר לָהֶן יֵשׁוּעַ: "אַל תִּפְחַדְנָה, לֵכְנָה וְהַגֵּדְנָה לְאַחַי שֶׁיֵּלְכוּ לַגָּלִיל וְשָׁם יִרְאוּנִי."

11 בְּשָׁעָה שֶׁהָלְכוּ בָּאוּ הָעִירָה כַּמָּה מִן הַשּׁוֹמְרִים וְהוֹדִיעוּ לְרָאשֵׁי הַכֹּהֲנִים אֶת כָּל אֲשֶׁר קָרָה. 12 רָאשֵׁי הַכֹּהֲנִים הִתְכַּנְּסוּ עִם הַזְּקֵנִים וּלְאַחַר הִתְיָעֲצוּת נָתְנוּ לַחַיָּלִים סְכוּם כֶּסֶף נִכָּר 13 בְּאָמְרָם: "הַגִּידוּ כָּךְ: 'בָּאוּ תַלְמִידָיו בַּלַּיְלָה וְגָנְבוּ אוֹתוֹ כַּאֲשֶׁר יָשַׁנּוּ'. 14 וְאִם זֶה יִוָּדַע לַנָּצִיב, אֲנַחְנוּ נְשַׁכְנֵעַ אוֹתוֹ וְנִפְטֹר אֶתְכֶם מִדְּאָגָה." 15 הֵם לָקְחוּ אֶת הַכֶּסֶף וְעָשׂוּ כְּמוֹ שֶׁהוֹרוּ לָהֶם. וְאָמְנָם שֵׁמַע הַדָּבָר הַזֶּה נָפוֹץ בְּקֶרֶב הָעָם עַד הַיּוֹם הַזֶּה.

16 בֵּינְתַיִם הָלְכוּ אַחַד־עָשָׂר הַתַּלְמִידִים לַגָּלִיל, אֶל הָהָר אֲשֶׁר אָמַר לָהֶם יֵשׁוּעַ. 17 כְּשֶׁרָאוּ אוֹתוֹ הִשְׁתַּחֲווּ לוֹ, אֲבָל הָיוּ כַּמָּה שֶׁהַסָּפֵק קִנֵּן בְּלִבָּם. 18 נִגַּשׁ יֵשׁוּעַ לְדַבֵּר אִתָּם וְאָמַר: "נִתְּנָה לִי כָּל סַמְכוּת בַּשָּׁמַיִם וּבָאָרֶץ. 19 עַל כֵּן לְכוּ וַעֲשׂוּ אֶת כָּל הַגּוֹיִים לְתַלְמִידִים, הַטְבִּילוּ אוֹתָם לְשֵׁם הָאָב וְהַבֵּן וְרוּחַ הַקֹּדֶשׁ 20 וְלַמְּדוּ אוֹתָם לִשְׁמֹר אֶת כָּל מַה שֶּׁצִּוִּיתִי אֶתְכֶם. הִנֵּה אִתְּכֶם אֲנִי כָּל הַיָּמִים עַד קֵץ הָעוֹלָם."

The Gospel According to

MARK

1 The beginning of the gospel of Jesus Christ, the Son of God. ² As it is written in the Prophets:

> "Behold, I send My messenger before Your face,
> Who will prepare Your way before You."
> ³ "The voice of one crying in the wilderness:
> 'Prepare the way of the LORD;
> Make His paths straight.'"

⁴ John came baptizing in the wilderness and preaching a baptism of repentance for the remission of sins. ⁵ Then all the land of Judea, and those from Jerusalem, went out to him and were all baptized by him in the Jordan River, confessing their sins.

⁶ Now John was clothed with camel's hair and with a leather belt around his waist, and he ate locusts and wild honey. ⁷ And he preached, saying, "There comes One after me who is mightier than I, whose sandal strap I am not worthy to stoop down and loose. ⁸ I indeed baptized you with water, but He will baptize you with the Holy Spirit."

⁹ It came to pass in those days that Jesus came from Nazareth of Galilee, and was baptized by John in the Jordan. ¹⁰ And immediately, coming up from the water, He saw the heavens parting and the Spirit descending upon Him like a dove. ¹¹ Then a voice came from heaven, "You are My beloved Son, in whom I am well pleased."

¹² Immediately the Spirit drove Him into the wilderness. ¹³ And He was there in the wilderness forty days, tempted by Satan, and was with the wild beasts; and the angels ministered to Him.

¹⁴ Now after John was put in prison, Jesus came to Galilee, preaching the gospel of the kingdom of God, ¹⁵ and saying, "The time is fulfilled, and the kingdom of God is at hand. Repent, and believe in the gospel."

¹⁶ And as He walked by the Sea of Galilee, He saw Simon and Andrew his brother casting a net into the sea; for they were fishermen. ¹⁷ Then Jesus said to them, "Follow Me, and I will make you become fishers of men." ¹⁸ They immediately left their nets and followed Him.

¹⁹ When He had gone a little farther from there, He saw James the son of Zebedee, and John his brother, who also were in the boat mending their

---

הַבְּשׂוֹרָה עַל־פִּי מַרְקוֹס

א תְּחִלַּת בְּשׂוֹרַת יֵשׁוּעַ הַמָּשִׁיחַ בֶּן־אֱלֹהִים. ² כַּכָּתוּב בִּישַׁעְיָהוּ הַנָּבִיא:

"הִנְנִי שֹׁלֵחַ מַלְאָכִי לְפָנֶיךָ וּפִנָּה דַרְכֶּךָ. ³ קוֹל קוֹרֵא בַּמִּדְבָּר פַּנּוּ דֶּרֶךְ יהוה, יַשְּׁרוּ מְסִלּוֹתָיו."

⁴ יוֹחָנָן הַמַּטְבִּיל הוֹפִיעַ בַּמִּדְבָּר כְּשֶׁהוּא מַכְרִיז עַל טְבִילָה שֶׁל תְּשׁוּבָה לְשֵׁם סְלִיחַת חֲטָאִים. ⁵ יָצְאוּ אֵלָיו כָּל אֶרֶץ יְהוּדָה וְכָל אַנְשֵׁי יְרוּשָׁלַיִם וְהוּא הִטְבִּיל אוֹתָם בִּנְהַר הַיַּרְדֵּן בִּהְיוֹתָם מִתְוַדִּים עַל חֲטָאֵיהֶם.

⁶ יוֹחָנָן הָיָה לָבוּשׁ שְׂעַר גְּמַלִּים וְחָגוּר חֲגוֹרַת עוֹר בְּמָתְנָיו, וּמַאֲכָלוֹ חֲגָבִים וּדְבַשׁ הַיַּעַר. ⁷ הִכְרִיז יוֹחָנָן וְאָמַר: "הִנֵּה חָזָק מִמֶּנִּי בָּא אַחֲרַי, אֲשֶׁר אֵינֶנִּי רָאוּי לְהִתְכּוֹפֵף וּלְהַתִּיר אֶת שְׂרוֹךְ נְעָלָיו. ⁸ אֲנִי הִטְבַּלְתִּי אֶתְכֶם בְּמַיִם, אַךְ הוּא יַטְבִּיל אֶתְכֶם בְּרוּחַ הַקֹּדֶשׁ."

⁹ בַּיָּמִים הָהֵם בָּא יֵשׁוּעַ מִנְּצֶרֶת אֲשֶׁר בַּגָּלִיל וְיוֹחָנָן הִטְבִּילוֹ בַּיַּרְדֵּן. ¹⁰ בְּרֶגַע שֶׁעָלָה מִן הַמַּיִם רָאָה אֶת הַשָּׁמַיִם נִפְתָּחִים וְאֶת הָרוּחַ יוֹרֶדֶת עָלָיו בִּדְמוּת יוֹנָה. ¹¹ יָצָא קוֹל מִן הַשָּׁמַיִם: "אַתָּה בְּנִי אֲהוּבִי, בְּךָ חָפַצְתִּי." ¹² מִיָּד הוֹצִיאָה אוֹתוֹ הָרוּחַ אֶל הַמִּדְבָּר, ¹³ וּבַמִּדְבָּר שָׁהָה אַרְבָּעִים יוֹם כְּשֶׁהַשָּׂטָן מְנַסֶּה אוֹתוֹ. הוּא הָיָה שָׁם עִם הַחַיּוֹת, וְהַמַּלְאָכִים שֵׁרְתוּהוּ.

¹⁴ אַחֲרֵי שֶׁהֻסְגַּר יוֹחָנָן בָּא יֵשׁוּעַ לַגָּלִיל וְהִכְרִיז אֶת בְּשׂוֹרַת הָאֱלֹהִים בְּאָמְרוֹ: ¹⁵ "מָלְאָה הָעֵת וְקָרְבָה מַלְכוּת אֱלֹהִים! שׁוּבוּ בִּתְשׁוּבָה וְהַאֲמִינוּ בַּבְּשׂוֹרָה!" ¹⁶ כַּאֲשֶׁר הָלַךְ עַל שְׂפַת יָם הַגָּלִיל רָאָה אֶת שִׁמְעוֹן וְאֶת אַנְדְּרֵי אֲחִי שִׁמְעוֹן פּוֹרְשִׂים רְשָׁתוֹת בַּיָּם, כִּי דַּיָּגִים הָיוּ. ¹⁷ אָמַר לָהֶם יֵשׁוּעַ: "לְכוּ אַחֲרַי וְאֶעֱשֶׂה אֶתְכֶם לְדַיָּגֵי אֲנָשִׁים." ¹⁸ מִיָּד עָזְבוּ אֶת הָרְשָׁתוֹת וְהָלְכוּ אַחֲרָיו. ¹⁹ הוּא הָלַךְ קְצָת הָלְאָה וְרָאָה אֶת יַעֲקֹב בֶּן־זַבְדַּי וְאֶת יוֹחָנָן אָחִיו וְהֵם בַּסְּפִינָה מְתַקְּנִים

nets. ²⁰ And immediately He called them, and they
left their father Zebedee in the boat with the hired
servants, and went after Him.

²¹ Then they went into Capernaum, and immedi-
ately on the Sabbath He entered the synagogue and
taught. ²² And they were astonished at His teaching,
for He taught them as one having authority, and
not as the scribes.

²³ Now there was a man in their synagogue with
an unclean spirit. And he cried out, ²⁴ saying, "Let
us alone! What have we to do with You, Jesus of
Nazareth? Did You come to destroy us? I know
who You are—the Holy One of God!"

²⁵ But Jesus rebuked him, saying, "Be quiet, and
come out of him!" ²⁶ And when the unclean spirit
had convulsed him and cried out with a loud voice,
he came out of him. ²⁷ Then they were all amazed,
so that they questioned among themselves, saying,
"What is this? What new doctrine is this? For with
authority He commands even the unclean spirits,
and they obey Him." ²⁸ And immediately His fame
spread throughout all the region around Galilee.

²⁹ Now as soon as they had come out of the
synagogue, they entered the house of Simon and
Andrew, with James and John. ³⁰ But Simon's wife's
mother lay sick with a fever, and they told Him
about her at once. ³¹ So He came and took her by
the hand and lifted her up, and immediately the
fever left her. And she served them.

³² At evening, when the sun had set, they brought
to Him all who were sick and those who were
demon-possessed. ³³ And the whole city was gathered together at the door. ³⁴ Then He healed many
who were sick with various diseases, and cast out
many demons; and He did not allow the demons to
speak, because they knew Him.

³⁵ Now in the morning, having risen a long while
before daylight, He went out and departed to a
solitary place; and there He prayed. ³⁶ And Simon
and those who were with Him searched for Him.
³⁷ When they found Him, they said to Him,
"Everyone is looking for You."

³⁸ But He said to them, "Let us go into the next
towns, that I may preach there also, because for this
purpose I have come forth."

³⁹ And He was preaching in their synagogues
throughout all Galilee, and casting out demons.

⁴⁰ Now a leper came to Him, imploring Him,
kneeling down to Him and saying to Him, "If You
are willing, You can make me clean."

⁴¹ Then Jesus, moved with compassion, stretched
out His hand and touched him, and said to him, "I
am willing; be cleansed." ⁴² As soon as He had
spoken, immediately the leprosy left him, and he

אֶת הָרְשָׁתוֹת. ²⁰ מִיָּד קָרָא לָהֶם. הֵם עָזְבוּ אֶת זַבְדִּי
אֲבִיהֶם בַּסִּירָה עִם הַשְּׂכִירִים וְהָלְכוּ אַחֲרָיו.

²¹ אַחֲרֵי בּוֹאָם אֶל כְּפַר נַחוּם מִהֵר לְהִכָּנֵס בְּשַׁבָּת
לְבֵית הַכְּנֶסֶת וְלִמֵּד שָׁם. ²² הִשְׁתּוֹמְמוּ הָאֲנָשִׁים עַל
הוֹרָאָתוֹ, כִּי הָיָה מְלַמֵּד אוֹתָם כְּבַעַל סַמְכוּת וְלֹא
כַּסּוֹפְרִים. ²³ אוֹתָה עֵת נִמְצָא בְּבֵית הַכְּנֶסֶת אִישׁ
וּבוֹ רוּחַ טְמֵאָה. צָעַק הָאִישׁ וְאָמַר: ²⁴ "מַה לָּנוּ וּלְךָ
יֵשׁוּעַ מִנָּצֶרֶת? בָּאתָ לְהַשְׁמִיד אוֹתָנוּ! אֲנִי יוֹדֵעַ מִי
אַתָּה – קְדוֹשׁ הָאֱלֹהִים!"

²⁵ יֵשׁוּעַ גָּעַר בָּרוּחַ וְאָמַר: "שְׁתֹק וְצֵא מִמֶּנּוּ!"
²⁶ וְעָוְעָה הָרוּחַ הַטְּמֵאָה אֶת הָאִישׁ, צָעֲקָה בְּקוֹל
גָּדוֹל וְיָצְאָה מִמֶּנּוּ.

²⁷ הַכֹּל הִשְׁתּוֹמְמוּ וְשָׁאֲלוּ זֶה אֶת זֶה: "מַה זֶּה? מַה
הַתּוֹרָה הַחֲדָשָׁה הַזֹּאת? גַּם עַל הָרוּחוֹת הַטְּמֵאוֹת
הוּא מְצַוֶּה בְּסַמְכוּת וְהֵן נִשְׁמָעוֹת לוֹ!"

²⁸ עַד מְהֵרָה יָצָא שָׁמְעוֹ בְּכָל אֵזוֹר הַגָּלִיל.

²⁹ הֵם יָצְאוּ מִבֵּית הַכְּנֶסֶת וְנִכְנְסוּ מִיָּד לְבֵיתָם שֶׁל
שִׁמְעוֹן וְאַנְדְּרֵי. גַּם יַעֲקֹב וְיוֹחָנָן בָּאוּ אִתָּם. ³⁰ הוֹאִיל
וַחֲמוֹתוֹ שֶׁל שִׁמְעוֹן שָׁכְבָה קוֹדַחַת מֵהֶם דִּבְּרוּ אֵלָיו
בְּנוֹגֵעַ אֵלֶיהָ. ³¹ הוּא נִגַּשׁ, הֶחֱזִיק בְּיָדָהּ וְהֵקִים
אוֹתָהּ. הַחֹם סָר מִמֶּנָּה וְהִיא שֵׁרְתָה אוֹתָם.

³² בָּעֶרֶב, עִם שְׁקִיעַת הַשֶּׁמֶשׁ, הֵבִיאוּ אֵלָיו אֶת כָּל
הַחוֹלִים וַאֲחוּזֵי הַשֵּׁדִים. ³³ כָּל הָעִיר נֶאֶסְפָה אֶל
פֶּתַח הַבַּיִת ³⁴ וְהוּא רִפֵּא רַבִּים שֶׁהָיוּ חוֹלִים
בְּמַחֲלוֹת לְמִינֵיהֶן; גַּם שֵׁדִים רַבִּים גֵּרַשׁ וְלֹא הִנִּיחַ
לַשֵּׁדִים לְדַבֵּר מִפְּנֵי שֶׁהִכִּירוּהוּ.

³⁵ בַּבֹּקֶר הַשְׁכֵּם, בְּעוֹד חֹשֶׁךְ, קָם וְיָצָא אֶל מָקוֹם
שׁוֹמֵם וְהִתְפַּלֵּל שָׁם. ³⁶ שִׁמְעוֹן וְהָאֲנָשִׁים אֲשֶׁר אִתּוֹ
יָצְאוּ בְּעִקְבוֹתָיו ³⁷ וּמְצָאוּ אוֹתוֹ. אָמְרוּ לוֹ: "הַכֹּל
מְחַפְּשִׂים אוֹתְךָ!"

³⁸ אָמַר לָהֶם: "בּוֹאוּ נֵלֵךְ אֶל הֶעָרוֹת הַקְּרוֹבוֹת
וַאֲבַשֵּׂר גַּם שָׁם, כִּי לְשֵׁם כָּךְ יָצָאתִי." ³⁹ הָלַךְ וּבִשֵּׂר
בְּבָתֵּי הַכְּנֶסֶת בְּכָל הַגָּלִיל וְגֵרַשׁ אֶת הַשֵּׁדִים.

⁴⁰ בָּא אֵלָיו אִישׁ מְצֹרָע וְהִתְחַנֵּן לְפָנָיו. הוּא כָּרַע עַל
בִּרְכָּיו וְאָמַר לוֹ: "אִם תִּרְצֶה תּוּכַל לְטַהֵר אוֹתִי."
⁴¹ בְּרֹב רַחֲמָיו הוֹשִׁיט יֵשׁוּעַ אֶת יָדוֹ, נָגַע בּוֹ וְאָמַר
אֵלָיו: "רוֹצֶה אֲנִי! הִטַּהֵר!" ⁴² בְּאוֹתוֹ רֶגַע סָרָה

was cleansed. 43 And He strictly warned him and sent him away at once, 44 and said to him, "See that you say nothing to anyone; but go your way, show yourself to the priest, and offer for your cleansing those things which Moses commanded, as a testimony to them."

45 However, he went out and began to proclaim *it* freely, and to spread the matter, so that Jesus could no longer openly enter the city, but was outside in deserted places; and they came to Him from every direction.

2 And again He entered Capernaum after *some* days, and it was heard that He was in the house. 2 Immediately many gathered together, so that there was no longer room to receive *them,* not even near the door. And He preached the word to them. 3 Then they came to Him, bringing a paralytic who was carried by four *men.* 4 And when they could not come near Him because of the crowd, they uncovered the roof where He was. So when they had broken through, they let down the bed on which the paralytic was lying.

5 When Jesus saw their faith, He said to the paralytic, "Son, your sins are forgiven you."

6 And some of the scribes were sitting there and reasoning in their hearts, 7 "Why does this *Man* speak blasphemies like this? Who can forgive sins but God alone?"

8 But immediately, when Jesus perceived in His spirit that they reasoned thus within themselves, He said to them, "Why do you reason about these things in your hearts? 9 Which is easier, to say to the paralytic, '*Your* sins are forgiven you,' or to say, 'Arise, take up your bed and walk'? 10 But that you may know that the Son of Man has power on earth to forgive sins"—He said to the paralytic, 11 "I say to you, arise, take up your bed, and go to your house." 12 Immediately he arose, took up the bed, and went out in the presence of them all, so that all were amazed and glorified God, saying, "We never saw *anything* like this!"

13 Then He went out again by the sea; and all the multitude came to Him, and He taught them. 14 As He passed by, He saw Levi the *son* of Alphaeus sitting at the tax office. And He said to him, "Follow Me." So he arose and followed Him.

15 Now it happened, as He was dining in *Levi's* house, that many tax collectors and sinners also sat together with Jesus and His disciples; for there were many, and they followed Him. 16 And when the scribes and Pharisees saw Him eating with the tax

מִמֶּנּוּ הַצָּרַעַת וְהוּא נִטְהָר. 43 יֵשׁוּעַ הִזְהִיר אוֹתוֹ וּמִהֵר לְשַׁלֵּחַ אוֹתוֹ. 44 אָמַר אֵלָיו: "רְאֵה, אַל תַּגִּיד דָּבָר לְאִישׁ. בְּרַם לֵךְ הֵרָאֵה אֶל הַכֹּהֵן וְהַקְרֵב לְטָהֳרָתְךָ אֶת אֲשֶׁר צִוָּה מֹשֶׁה לְעֵדוּת לָהֶם." 45 אַךְ הוּא יָצָא וְהִרְבָּה לְהַכְרִיז וּלְהָפִיץ בָּרַבִּים אֶת הַדָּבָר, עַד אֲשֶׁר יֵשׁוּעַ לֹא הָיָה יָכוֹל עוֹד לָבוֹא אֶל עִיר בְּגָלוּי אֶלָּא הָיָה נִשְׁאָר מִחוּץ לָעִיר בִּמְקוֹמוֹת שׁוֹמֵמִים; וּמִכָּל מָקוֹם בָּאוּ אֵלָיו.

ב אַחֲרֵי יָמִים אֲחָדִים בָּא שֵׁנִית אֶל כְּפַר נַחוּם. כְּשֶׁנּוֹדַע כִּי הוּא בַּבַּיִת 2 נֶאֶסְפוּ רַבִּים עַד אֲשֶׁר לֹא הָיָה עוֹד מָקוֹם גַּם לִפְנֵי פֶּתַח הַבַּיִת, וְהוּא דִּבֵּר אֲלֵיהֶם אֶת דְּבָרוֹ. 3 אָז הֵבִיאוּ אֵלָיו אִישׁ מְשֻׁתָּק וְאַרְבָּעָה אֲנָשִׁים נוֹשְׂאִים אוֹתוֹ. 4 בִּגְלַל הֶהָמוֹן לֹא יָכְלוּ לְהַכְנִיסוֹ אֵלָיו וְלָכֵן פֵּרְקוּ אֶת הַגַּג מֵעַל הַמָּקוֹם שֶׁהָיָה בּוֹ יֵשׁוּעַ, וְדֶרֶךְ הַפֶּתַח שֶׁעָשׂוּ הוֹרִידוּ אֶת הָאֲלוּנְקָה עִם הַמְשֻׁתָּק הַשּׁוֹכֵב עָלֶיהָ. 5 רָאָה יֵשׁוּעַ אֶת אֱמוּנָתָם וְאָמַר אֶל הַמְשֻׁתָּק: "בְּנִי, נִסְלְחוּ לְךָ חֲטָאֶיךָ."

6 אֲחָדִים מִן הַסּוֹפְרִים אֲשֶׁר יָשְׁבוּ שָׁם אָמְרוּ בְּלִבָּם: 7 "מַדּוּעַ הוּא מְדַבֵּר כָּךְ? מְגַדֵּף הוּא. מִי יָכוֹל לִסְלֹחַ עַל חֲטָאִים זוּלָתִי הָאֱלֹהִים לְבַדּוֹ?!" 8 בְּאוֹתוֹ רֶגַע הִבְחִין יֵשׁוּעַ בְּרוּחוֹ שֶׁכָּכָה חָשְׁבוּ בְּלִבָּבָם. אָמַר לָהֶם: "לָמָּה אַתֶּם אוֹמְרִים אֶת הַדְּבָרִים הָאֵלֶּה בִּלְבַבְכֶם? 9 מַה קַּל יוֹתֵר: לְהַגִּיד לַמְשֻׁתָּק 'נִסְלְחוּ לְךָ חֲטָאֶיךָ', אוֹ לוֹמַר 'קוּם, קַח אֶת הָאֲלוּנְקָה וְהִתְהַלֵּךְ'? 10 אַךְ לְמַעַן תֵּדְעוּ כִּי לְבֶן הָאָדָם הַסַּמְכוּת לִסְלֹחַ עַל חֲטָאִים עֲלֵי אֲדָמוֹת" – אָמַר לַמְשֻׁתָּק – 11 "אֵלֶיךָ אֲנִי אוֹמֵר: קוּם, קַח אֶת הָאֲלוּנְקָה וְלֵךְ לְבֵיתְךָ!" 12 הוּא קָם וּמִיָּד לָקַח אֶת הָאֲלוּנְקָה וְיָצָא לְעֵינֵי כֻּלָּם. הַכֹּל הִשְׁתּוֹמְמוּ וְשִׁבְּחוּ אֶת אֱלֹהִים בְּאָמְרָם: "מֵעוֹלָם לֹא רָאִינוּ כַּדָּבָר הַזֶּה!" 13 יֵשׁוּעַ יָצָא שׁוּב אֶל שְׂפַת הַיָּם. בָּא אֵלָיו כָּל הֶהָמוֹן וְהוּא לִמֵּד אוֹתָם. 14 כַּאֲשֶׁר עָבַר בַּדֶּרֶךְ וְרָאָה אֶת לֵוִי בֶּן חַלְפַי יוֹשֵׁב בְּבֵית הַמֶּכֶס, אָמַר אֵלָיו: "לֵךְ אַחֲרַי!" הוּא קָם וְהָלַךְ אַחֲרָיו. 15 אַחֲרֵי כֵן הֵסֵב יֵשׁוּעַ בְּבֵיתוֹ וּמוֹכְסִים וְחוֹטְאִים רַבִּים הֵסֵבּוּ עִמּוֹ וְעִם תַּלְמִידָיו, כִּי רַבִּים הָיוּ וְהֵם הָלְכוּ אַחֲרָיו. 16 רָאוּ הַסּוֹפְרִים וְהַפְּרוּשִׁים שֶׁהוּא אוֹכֵל עִם הַחוֹטְאִים וְהַמּוֹכְסִים, אָמְרוּ אֶל תַּלְמִידָיו: "עִם הַמּוֹכְסִים וְהַחוֹטְאִים הוּא אוֹכֵל?!"

collectors and sinners, they said to His disciples, "How *is it* that He eats and drinks with tax collectors and sinners?"

[17] When Jesus heard *it,* He said to them, "Those who are well have no need of a physician, but those who are sick. I did not come to call *the* righteous, but sinners, to repentance."

[18] The disciples of John and of the Pharisees were fasting. Then they came and said to Him, "Why do the disciples of John and of the Pharisees fast, but Your disciples do not fast?"

[19] And Jesus said to them, "Can the friends of the bridegroom fast while the bridegroom is with them? As long as they have the bridegroom with them they cannot fast. [20] But the days will come when the bridegroom will be taken away from them, and then they will fast in those days. [21] No one sews a piece of unshrunk cloth on an old garment; or else the new piece pulls away from the old, and the tear is made worse. [22] And no one puts new wine into old wineskins; or else the new wine bursts the wineskins, the wine is spilled, and the wineskins are ruined. But new wine must be put into new wineskins."

[23] Now it happened that He went through the grainfields on the Sabbath; and as they went His disciples began to pluck the heads of grain. [24] And the Pharisees said to Him, "Look, why do they do what is not lawful on the Sabbath?"

[25] But He said to them, "Have you never read what David did when he was in need and hungry, he and those with him: [26] how he went into the house of God *in the days* of Abiathar the high priest, and ate the showbread, which is not lawful to eat except for the priests, and also gave some to those who were with him?"

[27] And He said to them, "The Sabbath was made for man, and not man for the Sabbath. [28] Therefore the Son of Man is also Lord of the Sabbath."

3 And He entered the synagogue again, and a man was there who had a withered hand. [2] So they watched Him closely, whether He would heal him on the Sabbath, so that they might accuse Him. [3] And He said to the man who had the withered hand, "Step forward." [4] Then He said to them, "Is it lawful on the Sabbath to do good or to do evil, to save life or to kill?" But they kept silent. [5] And when He had looked around at them with anger, being grieved by the hardness of their hearts, He said to the man, "Stretch out your hand." And he stretched *it* out, and his hand was restored as whole as the

[17] שָׁמַע יֵשׁוּעַ וְאָמַר לָהֶם: "לֹא הַבְּרִיאִים צְרִיכִים לְרוֹפֵא, אֶלָּא הַחוֹלִים. לֹא בָּאתִי לִקְרֹא לַצַּדִּיקִים אֶלָּא לַחוֹטְאִים."

[18] תַּלְמִידֵי יוֹחָנָן וְתַלְמִידֵי הַפְּרוּשִׁים צָמוּ. בָּאוּ וְשָׁאֲלוּ אוֹתוֹ: "מַדּוּעַ תַּלְמִידֵי יוֹחָנָן וְתַלְמִידֵי הַפְּרוּשִׁים צָמִים וְתַלְמִידֶיךָ אֵינָם צָמִים?"

[19] הֵשִׁיב לָהֶם יֵשׁוּעַ: "הַאִם יְכוֹלִים בְּנֵי הַחֻפָּה לָצוּם בְּעוֹד הֶחָתָן אִתָּם? כָּל עוֹד הֶחָתָן עִמָּהֶם אֵין הֵם יְכוֹלִים לָצוּם. [20] אַךְ יוֹם יָבוֹא וְהֶחָתָן יֻלַּקַח מֵהֶם, וּבַיּוֹם הַהוּא יָצוּמוּ.

[21] אֵין אִישׁ תּוֹפֵר פִּסַּת בַּד חָדָשׁ עַל בֶּגֶד יָשָׁן; אִם יַעֲשֶׂה כֵּן, יִתָּלֵשׁ הַטְּלַאי מִן הַיָּשָׁן וְהַקֶּרַע יִהְיֶה גָּרוּעַ יוֹתֵר. [22] וְאֵין אִישׁ שָׂם יַיִן חָדָשׁ בְּנֹאדוֹת יְשָׁנִים; אִם יַעֲשֶׂה כֵּן, יְבַקַּע הַיַּיִן אֶת הַנֹּאדוֹת וְיֹאבַד הַיַּיִן וְכֵן גַּם הַנֹּאדוֹת. הֵן יַיִן חָדָשׁ יוֹצְקִים לְנֹאדוֹת חֲדָשִׁים."

[23] בְּשַׁבָּת עָבַר בִּשְׂדוֹת הַקָּמָה וְתַלְמִידָיו הֵחֵלּוּ לִקְטֹף שִׁבֳּלִים בְּדַרְכָּם. [24] אָמְרוּ לוֹ הַפְּרוּשִׁים: "רְאֵה, מַדּוּעַ הֵם עוֹשִׂים בְּשַׁבָּת דָּבָר שֶׁאָסוּר לַעֲשׂוֹתוֹ?" [25] הֵשִׁיב לָהֶם: "הַאִם מֵעוֹדְכֶם לֹא קְרָאתֶם מַה שֶּׁעָשָׂה דָּוִד בִּהְיוֹתוֹ בְּמַחְסוֹר וּבְרָעָב הוּא וַאֲנָשָׁיו? [26] הֲרֵי נִכְנַס לְבֵית הָאֱלֹהִים בִּימֵי אֶבְיָתָר הַכֹּהֵן הַגָּדוֹל וְאָכַל אֶת לֶחֶם הַפָּנִים אֲשֶׁר אֵינוֹ מֻתָּר לַאֲכִילָה אֶלָּא לַכֹּהֲנִים, וְנָתַן גַּם לָאֲנָשִׁים אֲשֶׁר אִתּוֹ." [27] הוֹסִיף וְאָמַר לָהֶם: "הַשַּׁבָּת נֶעֶשְׂתָה לְמַעַן הָאָדָם וְלֹא הָאָדָם לְמַעַן הַשַּׁבָּת. [28] לָכֵן בֶּן־הָאָדָם אָדוֹן גַּם לַשַּׁבָּת."

ג הוּא נִכְנַס שׁוּב לְבֵית הַכְּנֶסֶת. הָיָה שָׁם אִישׁ שֶׁיָּדוֹ יְבֵשָׁה, [2] וְהֵם הִתְבּוֹנְנוּ בְּיֵשׁוּעַ לִרְאוֹת אִם יְרַפֵּא אוֹתוֹ בְּשַׁבָּת, כְּדֵי שֶׁיּוּכְלוּ לְהַאֲשִׁים אוֹתוֹ. [3] אָמַר אֶל הָאִישׁ אֲשֶׁר יָדוֹ יְבֵשָׁה: "עֲמֹד בָּאֶמְצַע!" [4] פָּנָה אֲלֵיהֶם וְשָׁאַל: "הַאִם מֻתָּר לְהֵיטִיב בְּשַׁבָּת אוֹ לַעֲשׂוֹת רָעָה? לְהַצִּיל נֶפֶשׁ אוֹ לַהֲרֹג?" אַךְ הֵם שָׁתְקוּ. [5] הִבִּיט בָּהֶם כֹּה וָכֹה בְּזַעַם, כְּרֻב עֶצֶב עַל קְשִׁי לְבָבָם, וְאָמַר לָאִישׁ: "הוֹשֵׁט אֶת הַיָּד!" הוּא

other. ⁶ Then the Pharisees went out and immediately plotted with the Herodians against Him, how they might destroy Him.

⁷ But Jesus withdrew with His disciples to the sea. And a great multitude from Galilee followed Him, and from Judea ⁸ and Jerusalem and Idumea and beyond the Jordan; and those from Tyre and Sidon, a great multitude, when they heard how many things He was doing, came to Him. ⁹ So He told His disciples that a small boat should be kept ready for Him because of the multitude, lest they should crush Him. ¹⁰ For He healed many, so that as many as had afflictions pressed about Him to touch Him. ¹¹ And the unclean spirits, whenever they saw Him, fell down before Him and cried out, saying, "You are the Son of God." ¹² But He sternly warned them that they should not make Him known.

¹³ And He went up on the mountain and called to *Him* those He Himself wanted. And they came to Him. ¹⁴ Then He appointed twelve, that they might be with Him and that He might send them out to preach, ¹⁵ and to have power to heal sicknesses and to cast out demons: ¹⁶ Simon, to whom He gave the name Peter; ¹⁷ James the *son* of Zebedee and John the brother of James, to whom He gave the name Boanerges, that is, "Sons of Thunder"; ¹⁸ Andrew, Philip, Bartholomew, Matthew, Thomas, James the *son* of Alphaeus, Thaddaeus, Simon the Cananite; ¹⁹ and Judas Iscariot, who also betrayed Him. And they went into a house.

²⁰ Then the multitude came together again, so that they could not so much as eat bread. ²¹ But when His own people heard *about this,* they went out to lay hold of Him, for they said, "He is out of His mind."

²² And the scribes who came down from Jerusalem said, "He has Beelzebub," and, "By the ruler of the demons He casts out demons."

²³ So He called them to *Himself* and said to them in parables: "How can Satan cast out Satan? ²⁴ If a kingdom is divided against itself, that kingdom cannot stand. ²⁵ And if a house is divided against itself, that house cannot stand. ²⁶ And if Satan has risen up against himself, and is divided, he cannot stand, but has an end. ²⁷ No one can enter a strong man's house and plunder his goods, unless he first binds the strong man. And then he will plunder his house.

²⁸ "Assuredly, I say to you, all sins will be forgiven the sons of men, and whatever blasphemies they may utter; ²⁹ but he who blasphemes against the Holy Spirit never has forgiveness, but is subject to eternal condemnation"— ³⁰ because they said, "He has an unclean spirit."

הוֹשִׁיט אוֹתָהּ וַיָּדוֹ שָׁבָה לְאֵיתָנָהּ. ⁶ יָצְאוּ הַפְּרוּשִׁים וּמִיָּד טִכְּסוּ עָלָיו עֵצָה עִם חֲסִידֵי בֵּית הוֹרְדוֹס – כֵּיצַד לְהַכְחִיד אוֹתוֹ.

⁷ יֵשׁוּעַ הָלַךְ מִשָּׁם עִם תַּלְמִידָיו אֶל שְׂפַת הַיָּם וְהָמוֹן רַב מִן הַגָּלִיל הָלְכוּ אַחֲרָיו. ⁸ גַּם מִיהוּדָה, מִירוּשָׁלַיִם, מֵאֱדוֹם, מֵעֵבֶר הַיַּרְדֵּן וּמִסְּבִיבוֹת צוֹר וְצִידוֹן בָּאוּ אֵלָיו הָמוֹן רַב, כִּי שָׁמְעוּ אֶת כָּל אֲשֶׁר עָשָׂה. ⁹ הוּא אָמַר לְתַלְמִידָיו שֶׁיָּכִינוּ לוֹ סִירָה פֶּן יִלְחָצֻהוּ הֶהָמוֹן, ¹⁰ כִּי רִפֵּא רַבִּים, וְלָכֵן נִדְחֲקוּ אֵלָיו כָּל הַחוֹלִים כְּדֵי לָגַעַת בּוֹ. ¹¹ וְהָרוּחוֹת הַטְּמֵאוֹת כִּרְאוֹתָן אוֹתוֹ נָפְלוּ לְפָנָיו וְצָעֲקוּ: "אַתָּה הוּא בֶּן־הָאֱלֹהִים!" ¹² אַךְ הוּא גָּעַר בָּהֶן בְּחָזְקָה שֶׁלֹּא תְּגַלֶּינָה מִי הוּא.

¹³ יֵשׁוּעַ עָלָה לָהָר וְקָרָא לָאֲנָשִׁים שֶׁרָצָה בָּהֶם. הֵם בָּאוּ אֵלָיו ¹⁴ וְהוּא קָבַע שְׁנֵים־עָשָׂר אִישׁ שֶׁיִּהְיוּ אִתּוֹ, שֶׁיִּשְׁלַח אוֹתָם לְבַשֵּׂר ¹⁵ וְשֶׁתִּהְיֶה לָהֶם סַמְכוּת לְגָרֵשׁ אֶת הַשֵּׁדִים. ¹⁶ הוּא מִנָּה אֶת הַשְּׁנֵים־עָשָׂר: שִׁמְעוֹן, אֲשֶׁר לוֹ הוּא נָתַן אֶת הַשֵּׁם כֵּיפָא; ¹⁷ יַעֲקֹב בֶּן זַבְדַּי וְיוֹחָנָן אֲחִי יַעֲקֹב, אֲשֶׁר לָהֶם נָתַן אֶת הַשֵּׁם בְּנֵי רָגֶשׁ, שֶׁפֵּרוּשׁוֹ בְּנֵי רַעַם; ¹⁸ אַנְדְּרֵי, פִילִיפּוֹס, בַּר־תַּלְמַי, מַתַּי, תֹּאמָא, יַעֲקֹב בֶּן חַלְפַי, תַּדַּי, שִׁמְעוֹן הַקַּנַּאי ¹⁹ וִיהוּדָה אִישׁ קְרִיּוֹת אֲשֶׁר גַּם הִסְגִּיר אוֹתוֹ.

²⁰ הֵם בָּאוּ הַבַּיְתָה, וְשׁוּב הִתְאַסֵּף הָמוֹן עַם, עַד כִּי לֹא יָכְלוּ אֲפִלּוּ לֶאֱכֹל אֶת אֲרוּחָתָם. ²¹ שָׁמְעוּ זֹאת קְרוֹבָיו וַיֵּצְאוּ לְתָפְסָם אוֹתוֹ, כִּי אָמְרוּ: "יָצָא מִדַּעְתּוֹ!" ²² וְהַסּוֹפְרִים אֲשֶׁר יָרְדוּ מִירוּשָׁלַיִם אָמְרוּ: "בַּעַל־זְבוּל בּוֹ וּבְעֶזְרַת שַׂר הַשֵּׁדִים הוּא מְגָרֵשׁ אֶת הַשֵּׁדִים."

²³ קָרָא אוֹתָם אֵלָיו וְדִבֵּר אֲלֵיהֶם בִּמְשָׁלִים: "אֵיךְ יָכוֹל הַשָּׂטָן לְגָרֵשׁ אֶת הַשָּׂטָן? ²⁴ אִם מַמְלָכָה מֻפְלֶגֶת בְּתוֹךְ עַצְמָהּ, אוֹתָהּ מַמְלָכָה אֵינָהּ יְכוֹלָה לַעֲמֹד. ²⁵ וּבַיִת אִם מֻפְלָג הוּא בְּתוֹךְ עַצְמוֹ, לֹא יוּכַל לַעֲמֹד הַבַּיִת הַהוּא. ²⁶ וְאִם הַשָּׂטָן הִתְקוֹמֵם נֶגֶד עַצְמוֹ וְהִתְפַּלֵּג, כִּי אָז אֵינוֹ יָכוֹל לַעֲמֹד וְהִגִּיעַ אֶל קִצּוֹ. ²⁷ לֹא יוּכַל אִישׁ לְהִכָּנֵס לְבֵיתוֹ שֶׁל גִּבּוֹר וְלָבֹז אֶת כֵּלָיו אִם לֹא יִכְפֹּת תְּחִלָּה אֶת הַגִּבּוֹר; אַחַר כָּךְ יָבֹז אֶת בֵּיתוֹ. ²⁸ אָמֵן אוֹמֵר אֲנִי לָכֶם, כָּל הַחֲטָאִים יִסָּלְחוּ לִבְנֵי הָאָדָם, וְכֵן גַּם כָּל הַגִּדּוּפִים אֲשֶׁר יְגַדֵּפוּ, ²⁹ אַךְ הַמְגַדֵּף אֶת רוּחַ הַקֹּדֶשׁ אֵין לוֹ סְלִיחָה

31 Then His brothers and His mother came, and standing outside they sent to Him, calling Him. 32 And a multitude was sitting around Him; and they said to Him, "Look, Your mother and Your brothers are outside seeking You."

33 But He answered them, saying, "Who is My mother, or My brothers?" 34 And He looked around in a circle at those who sat about Him, and said, "Here are My mother and My brothers! 35 For whoever does the will of God is My brother and My sister and mother."

4 And again He began to teach by the sea. And a great multitude was gathered to Him, so that He got into a boat and sat *in it* on the sea; and the whole multitude was on the land facing the sea. 2 Then He taught them many things by parables, and said to them in His teaching:

3 "Listen! Behold, a sower went out to sow. 4 And it happened, as he sowed, *that* some *seed* fell by the wayside; and the birds of the air came and devoured it. 5 Some fell on stony ground, where it did not have much earth; and immediately it sprang up because it had no depth of earth. 6 But when the sun was up it was scorched, and because it had no root it withered away. 7 And some *seed* fell among thorns; and the thorns grew up and choked it, and it yielded no crop. 8 But other *seed* fell on good ground and yielded a crop that sprang up, increased and produced: some thirtyfold, some sixty, and some a hundred."

9 And He said to them, "He who has ears to hear, let him hear!"

10 But when He was alone, those around Him with the twelve asked Him about the parable. 11 And He said to them, "To you it has been given to know the mystery of the kingdom of God; but to those who are outside, all things come in parables, 12 so that

'Seeing they may see and not perceive,
And hearing they may hear and not understand;
Lest they should turn,
And their sins be forgiven them.'"

13 And He said to them, "Do you not understand this parable? How then will you understand all the parables? 14 The sower sows the word. 15 And these are the ones by the wayside where the word is sown. When they hear, Satan comes immediately and takes away the word that was sown in their hearts. 16 These likewise are the ones sown on stony ground who, when they hear the word, immediately receive

לְעוֹלָם כִּי אָשֵׁם הוּא בְּחֵטְא עוֹלָם", 30 זֹאת מִפְּנֵי שֶׁאָמְרוּ "רוּחַ טְמֵאָה בּוֹ."

31 אִמּוֹ וְאֶחָיו בָּאוּ. הֵם עָמְדוּ בַּחוּץ וְשָׁלְחוּ לִקְרֹא לוֹ. 32 אוֹתָהּ שָׁעָה יָשְׁבוּ סְבִיבוֹ הֲמוֹן עַם וְהֵם אָמְרוּ לוֹ: "הִנֵּה אִמְּךָ וְאַחֶיךָ וְאַחְיוֹתֶיךָ בַּחוּץ. הֵם מְבַקְשִׁים אוֹתְךָ."

33 עָנָה וְאָמַר לָהֶם: "מִי הֵם אִמִּי וְאַחַי?" 34 הוּא הִבִּיט כֹּה וָכֹה אֶל הַיּוֹשְׁבִים סְבִיבוֹ בַּמַּעְגָּל וְאָמַר: "הִנֵּה אִמִּי וְאַחַי! 35 כָּל הָעוֹשֶׂה אֶת רְצוֹן אֱלֹהִים הוּא אָחִי וַאֲחוֹתִי וְאִמִּי."

ד שׁוּב הֵחֵל לְלַמֵּד עַל שְׂפַת הַיָּם וְהָמוֹן רַב נֶאֶסְפוּ אֵלָיו. עַל כֵּן יָרַד וְיָשַׁב בִּסְפִינָה בַּיָּם וְכָל הֶהָמוֹן הָיוּ עַל הַחוֹף לְיַד הַיָּם. 2 הוּא לִמֵּד אוֹתָם דְּבָרִים רַבִּים בִּמְשָׁלִים וּבְלַמְּדוֹ אוֹתָם אָמַר לָהֶם:

3 "שִׁמְעוּ! הִנֵּה יָצָא הַזּוֹרֵעַ לִזְרֹעַ. 4 וְכַאֲשֶׁר זֶרַע נָפְלוּ כַּמָּה זְרָעִים בְּשׁוּלֵי הַדֶּרֶךְ וּבָאוּ צִפֳּרִים וְאָכְלוּ אוֹתָם. 5 אֲחֵרִים נָפְלוּ עַל אַדְמַת טְרָשִׁים, בְּמָקוֹם שֶׁלֹּא הָיְתָה לָהֶם הַרְבֵּה אֲדָמָה, וּמִהֲרוּ לִצְמֹחַ מִפְּנֵי שֶׁלֹּא הָיְתָה לָהֶם אֲדָמָה עֲמֻקָּה. 6 כְּשֶׁזָּרְחָה הַשֶּׁמֶשׁ נִצְרְבוּ וּבְאֵין שֹׁרֶשׁ הִתְיַבְּשׁוּ. 7 אֲחֵרִים נָפְלוּ בֵּין הַקּוֹצִים, אַךְ הַקּוֹצִים צָמְחוּ וְהֶחֱנִיקוּ אוֹתָם וְלֹא נָתְנוּ פְּרִי. 8 אֲחֵרִים נָפְלוּ עַל אֲדָמָה טוֹבָה וְנָתְנוּ פְּרִי עוֹלֶה וְגָדֵל – זֶה פִּי שְׁלוֹשִׁים, זֶה פִּי שִׁשִּׁים וְזֶה פִּי מֵאָה." 9 אָמַר לָהֶם: "מִי שֶׁאָזְנַיִם לוֹ לִשְׁמֹעַ, שֶׁיִּשְׁמַע!"

10 בִּהְיוֹתוֹ לְבַדּוֹ שְׁאָלוּהוּ הָאֲנָשִׁים אֲשֶׁר סְבִיבוֹ, יַחַד עִם הַשְּׁנֵים-עָשָׂר, עַל דְּבַר הַמְּשָׁלִים. 11 אָמַר לָהֶם: "לָכֶם נִתַּן סוֹד מַלְכוּת הָאֱלֹהִים, אַךְ לְאוֹתָם אֲשֶׁר בַּחוּץ הַכֹּל יִהְיֶה בִּמְשָׁלִים, 12 לְמַעַן יִרְאוּ רָאֹה וְלֹא יֵדְעוּ וְשָׁמוֹעַ יִשְׁמְעוּ וְלֹא יָבִינוּ, פֶּן יָשׁוּבוּ וְיִסָּלַח לָהֶם."

13 הוֹסִיף וְאָמַר לָהֶם: "אֵינְכֶם מְבִינִים אֶת הַמָּשָׁל הַזֶּה וְאֵיךְ תָּבִינוּ אֶת כָּל הַמְּשָׁלִים? 14 הַזּוֹרֵעַ זוֹרֵעַ אֶת הַדָּבָר. 15 וַאֲשֶׁר בְּשׁוּלֵי הַדֶּרֶךְ, בְּמָקוֹם שֶׁנִּזְרַע הַדָּבָר, אֵלֶּה הֵם אֲשֶׁר בְּשָׁמְעָם בָּא הַשָּׂטָן מִיָּד וְלוֹקֵחַ אֶת הַדָּבָר שֶׁנִּזְרַע בָּהֶם. 16 וְכֵן הַנִּזְרָעִים עַל אַדְמַת טְרָשִׁים אֵלֶּה הֵם אֲשֶׁר בְּשָׁמְעָם אֶת הַדָּבָר

it with gladness; ¹⁷and they have no root in themselves, and so endure only for a time. Afterward, when tribulation or persecution arises for the word's sake, immediately they stumble. ¹⁸Now these are the ones sown among thorns; *they are* the ones who hear the word, ¹⁹and the cares of this world, the deceitfulness of riches, and the desires for other things entering in choke the word, and it becomes unfruitful. ²⁰But these are the ones sown on good ground, those who hear the word, accept *it,* and bear fruit: some thirtyfold, some sixty, and some a hundred."

²¹Also He said to them, "Is a lamp brought to be put under a basket or under a bed? Is it not to be set on a lampstand? ²²For there is nothing hidden which will not be revealed, nor has anything been kept secret but that it should come to light. ²³If anyone has ears to hear, let him hear."

²⁴Then He said to them, "Take heed what you hear. With the same measure you use, it will be measured to you; and to you who hear, more will be given. ²⁵For whoever has, to him more will be given; but whoever does not have, even what he has will be taken away from him."

²⁶And He said, "The kingdom of God is as if a man should scatter seed on the ground, ²⁷and should sleep by night and rise by day, and the seed should sprout and grow, he himself does not know how. ²⁸For the earth yields crops by itself: first the blade, then the head, after that the full grain in the head. ²⁹But when the grain ripens, immediately he puts in the sickle, because the harvest has come."

³⁰Then He said, "To what shall we liken the kingdom of God? Or with what parable shall we picture it? ³¹*It is* like a mustard seed which, when it is sown on the ground, is smaller than all the seeds on earth; ³²but when it is sown, it grows up and becomes greater than all herbs, and shoots out large branches, so that the birds of the air may nest under its shade."

³³And with many such parables He spoke the word to them as they were able to hear *it.* ³⁴But without a parable He did not speak to them. And when they were alone, He explained all things to His disciples.

³⁵On the same day, when evening had come, He said to them, "Let us cross over to the other side." ³⁶Now when they had left the multitude, they took Him along in the boat as He was. And other little boats were also with Him. ³⁷And a great windstorm arose, and the waves beat into the boat, so that it

מְקַבְּלִים אוֹתוֹ מִיָּד בְּשִׂמְחָה, ¹⁷אַךְ אֵין לָהֶם שֹׁרֶשׁ בְּקִרְבָּם וְרַק לְשָׁעָה יַחֲזִיקוּ מַעֲמָד; לְאַחַר מִכֵּן, בְּבוֹא צָרָה אוֹ רְדִיפָה בִּגְלַל הַדָּבָר, יִכָּשְׁלוּ מִיָּד. ¹⁸וְהָאֲחֵרִים הֵם הַנִּזְרָעִים בֵּין הַקּוֹצִים; אֵלֶּה הֵם הַשּׁוֹמְעִים אֶת הַדָּבָר, ¹⁹אֶלָּא שֶׁדַּאֲגוֹת הָעוֹלָם הַזֶּה וּמִדּוּחֵי הָעֹשֶׁר וְתַאֲווֹת לִשְׁאָר דְּבָרִים בָּאִים וּמַחֲנִיקִים אֶת הַדָּבָר וְלֹא יַעֲשֶׂה פְּרִי. ²⁰הַנִּזְרָעִים עַל הָאֲדָמָה הַטּוֹבָה הֵם הַשּׁוֹמְעִים אֶת הַדָּבָר וּמְקַבְּלִים אוֹתוֹ וְעוֹשִׂים פְּרִי – זֶה פִּי שְׁלוֹשִׁים, זֶה פִּי שִׁשִּׁים וְזֶה פִּי מֵאָה."

²¹אָמַר לָהֶם: "הַאִם הַמְּנוֹרָה קַיֶּמֶת כְּדֵי שֶׁיְּשִׂימוּ אוֹתָהּ תַּחַת כְּלִי אוֹ תַּחַת הַמִּטָּה? הַאִם לֹא יַעֲמִידוּ אוֹתָהּ עַל כֵּן? ²²כִּי אֵין נִסְתָּר אֲשֶׁר לֹא יִגָּלֶה, וְלֹא נִגְנַז דָּבָר אֶלָּא כְּדֵי שֶׁיֵּצֵא לָאוֹר. ²³מִי שֶׁאָזְנַיִם לוֹ לִשְׁמֹעַ, שֶׁיִּשְׁמָע." ²⁴עוֹד אָמַר לָהֶם: "שִׂימוּ לְבַבְכֶם אֶל מַה שֶּׁאַתֶּם שׁוֹמְעִים. בַּמִּדָּה שֶׁאַתֶּם מוֹדְדִים יִמָּדֵד לָכֶם וְגַם יֻסַּף לָכֶם, ²⁵כִּי מִי שֶׁיֵּשׁ לוֹ יִנָּתֵן לוֹ, וּמִי שֶׁאֵין לוֹ, גַּם מַה שֶּׁיֵּשׁ לוֹ יֻלַּקַח מִמֶּנּוּ."

²⁶עוֹד אָמַר: "כָּךְ הִיא מַלְכוּת הָאֱלֹהִים, כְּאִישׁ הַזּוֹרֵעַ זֶרַע בָּאֲדָמָה; ²⁷וְיָשַׁן הוּא וְקָם, לַיְלָה וָיוֹם, וְהַזֶּרַע נוֹבֵט וְגָדֵל וְהָאִישׁ אֵינֶנּוּ יוֹדֵעַ כֵּיצַד. ²⁸מֵאֵלֶיהָ מוֹצִיאָה הָאֲדָמָה פְּרִי: בָּרִאשׁוֹנָה אֶת הַקָּנֶה, אַחֲרָיו אֶת הַשִּׁבֹּלֶת וְאַחַר כָּךְ אֶת הַחִטָּה מְלוֹא הַשִּׁבֹּלֶת. ²⁹וְכַאֲשֶׁר בָּשֵׁל הַפְּרִי יְמַהֵר הָאִישׁ לִשְׁלֹחַ מַגָּל, כִּי הִגִּיעַ הַקָּצִיר."

³⁰הוֹסִיף וְאָמַר: "אֵיךְ נְדַמֶּה אֶת מַלְכוּת הָאֱלֹהִים אוֹ בְּאֵיזֶה מָשָׁל נַמְשִׁיל אוֹתָהּ? ³¹כְּגַרְגִּיר חַרְדָּל הִיא. כַּאֲשֶׁר זוֹרְעִים אוֹתוֹ בָּאֲדָמָה הוּא קָטָן מִכָּל הַזְּרָעִים עֲלֵי אֲדָמוֹת, ³²אֲבָל לְאַחַר שֶׁנִּזְרַע הוּא צוֹמֵחַ וְנַעֲשֶׂה גָּדוֹל מִכָּל הַשִּׂיחִים וּמוֹצִיא עֲנָפִים גְּדוֹלִים עַד אֲשֶׁר עוֹף הַשָּׁמַיִם יְכוֹלִים לִשְׁכֹּן בְּצִלּוֹ."

³³בִּמְשָׁלִים רַבִּים כָּאֵלֶּה דִּבֵּר אֲלֵיהֶם אֶת הַדָּבָר, כְּכָל אֲשֶׁר יָכְלוּ לִשְׁמֹעַ, ³⁴וּבִלְּי מָשָׁל לֹא דִּבֵּר אֲלֵיהֶם; אֲבָל בִּיחִידוּת הִסְבִּיר לְתַלְמִידָיו אֶת הַכֹּל. ³⁵בְּאוֹתוֹ הַיּוֹם, לְעֵת עֶרֶב, אָמַר לָהֶם: "בּוֹאוּ נַעֲבֹר לַצַּד הַשֵּׁנִי. ³⁶הֵם עָזְבוּ אֶת הֶהָמוֹן וְלָקְחוּ אֶת יֵשׁוּעַ בִּסְפִינָה אֲשֶׁר יָשַׁב בָּהּ. גַּם סִירוֹת אֲחֵרוֹת הָיוּ אִתּוֹ. ³⁷וְהִנֵּה הִתְחוֹלְלָה רוּחַ-סְעָרָה גְּדוֹלָה וְהַגַּלִּים שָׁטְפוּ

was already filling. ³⁸ But He was in the stern, asleep on a pillow. And they awoke Him and said to Him, "Teacher, do You not care that we are perishing?"

³⁹ Then He arose and rebuked the wind, and said to the sea, "Peace, be still!" And the wind ceased and there was a great calm. ⁴⁰ But He said to them, "Why are you so fearful? How *is it* that you have no faith?" ⁴¹ And they feared exceedingly, and said to one another, "Who can this be, that even the wind and the sea obey Him!"

5 Then they came to the other side of the sea, to the country of the Gadarenes. ² And when He had come out of the boat, immediately there met Him out of the tombs a man with an unclean spirit, ³ who had *his* dwelling among the tombs; and no one could bind him, not even with chains, ⁴ because he had often been bound with shackles and chains. And the chains had been pulled apart by him, and the shackles broken in pieces; neither could anyone tame him. ⁵ And always, night and day, he was in the mountains and in the tombs, crying out and cutting himself with stones.

⁶ When he saw Jesus from afar, he ran and worshiped Him. ⁷ And he cried out with a loud voice and said, "What have I to do with You, Jesus, Son of the Most High God? I implore You by God that You do not torment me."

⁸ For He said to him, "Come out of the man, unclean spirit!" ⁹ Then He asked him, "What *is* your name?"

And he answered, saying, "My name *is* Legion; for we are many." ¹⁰ Also he begged Him earnestly that He would not send them out of the country.

¹¹ Now a large herd of swine was feeding there near the mountains. ¹² So all the demons begged Him, saying, "Send us to the swine, that we may enter them." ¹³ And at once Jesus gave them permission. Then the unclean spirits went out and entered the swine (there were about two thousand); and the herd ran violently down the steep place into the sea, and drowned in the sea.

¹⁴ So those who fed the swine fled, and they told *it* in the city and in the country. And they went out to see what it was that had happened. ¹⁵ Then they came to Jesus, and saw the one *who had been* demon-possessed and had the legion, sitting and clothed and in his right mind. And they were afraid. ¹⁶ And those who saw it told them how it happened to him *who had been* demon-possessed, and about the swine. ¹⁷ Then they began to plead with Him to depart from their region.

³⁸ אוֹתָהּ שָׁעָה הָיָה אֶת הַסְּפִינָה עַד שֶׁנִּתְמַלְּאָה. יֵשׁוּעַ יָשֵׁן עַל כַּר בְּיַרְכְּתֵי הַסְּפִינָה. הֵעִירוּ אוֹתוֹ וְאָמְרוּ לוֹ: "רַבִּי, הַאִם לֹא אִכְפַּת לְךָ שֶׁאֲנַחְנוּ טוֹבְעִים?"

³⁹ הוּא הִתְעוֹרֵר, גָּעַר בָּרוּחַ וְאָמַר אֶל הַיָּם: "דֹּם! הֵרָגַע!" אָז פָּסְקָה הָרוּחַ וְנִשְׁתָּרְרָה דְּמָמָה עֲמֻקָּה. ⁴⁰ אָמַר לָהֶם: "מַדּוּעַ אַתֶּם פּוֹחֲדִים כָּל כָּךְ? אֵיךְ זֶה שֶׁאֵין לָכֶם אֱמוּנָה?" ⁴¹ הֵם יָרְאוּ יִרְאָה גְּדוֹלָה וְאָמְרוּ זֶה אֶל זֶה: "אִם כֵּן מִי הוּא זֶה שֶׁגַּם הָרוּחַ וְהַיָּם נִשְׁמָעִים לוֹ?"

ה הֵם בָּאוּ אֶל עֵבֶר הַיָּם, אֶל אֶרֶץ הַגֵּרְשִׁיִּים. ² אַךְ יָצָא מִן הַסְּפִינָה וְהִנֵּה בָּא לִקְרָאתוֹ אִישׁ מִבֵּין הַקְּבָרִים וְרוּחַ טְמֵאָה בּוֹ. ³ הוּא הָיָה גָּר בִּמְעָרוֹת הַקְּבָרִים וְאִישׁ לֹא יָכֹל עוֹד לִכְבֹּל אוֹתוֹ, גַּם לֹא בָּאֲזִקִּים, ⁴ כִּי פְּעָמִים רַבּוֹת כָּבְלוּ אוֹתוֹ בִּכְבָלִים וּבַאֲזִקִּים וְהוּא נִתֵּק אֶת הָאֲזִקִּים וְקָרַע אֶת הַכְּבָלִים וְאִישׁ לֹא הָיָה יָכֹל לְהַכְנִיעַ אוֹתוֹ. ⁵ תָּמִיד, יוֹמָם וָלַיְלָה, בַּקְּבָרוֹת וּבֶהָרִים הָיָה צוֹעֵק וּפוֹצֵעַ אֶת עַצְמוֹ בָּאֲבָנִים. ⁶ כִּרְאוֹתוֹ אֶת יֵשׁוּעַ מֵרָחוֹק, רָץ וְהִשְׁתַּחֲוָה לוֹ, ⁷ וְצָעַק בְּקוֹל גָּדוֹל: "מַה לִּי וּלְךָ, יֵשׁוּעַ בֶּן אֶל עֶלְיוֹן? אֲנִי מַשְׁבִּיעַ אוֹתְךָ בֵּאלֹהִים, אַל תְּעַנֶּה אוֹתִי!" (⁸ כִּי יֵשׁוּעַ הָיָה אוֹמֵר לוֹ, "צֵא מִן הָאִישׁ, הָרוּחַ הַטְּמֵאָה!")

⁹ שָׁאַל אוֹתוֹ יֵשׁוּעַ: "מַה שְּׁמְךָ?" הֵשִׁיב לוֹ: "שְׁמִי לִגְיוֹן, כִּי רַבִּים אֲנַחְנוּ." ¹⁰ הֵן הִפְצִירוּ בּוֹ מְאֹד שֶׁלֹּא יִשְׁלַח אוֹתָן אֶל מִחוּץ לָאֵזוֹר. ¹¹ עֵדֶר גָּדוֹל שֶׁל חֲזִירִים הָיָה רוֹעֶה שָׁם סָמוּךְ לָהָר, ¹² וְהֵן בִּקְשׁוּ מִיֵּשׁוּעַ: "שְׁלַח אוֹתָנוּ אֶל הַחֲזִירִים וְנִכָּנֵס לְתוֹכָם." ¹³ הוּא הִרְשָׁה לָהֶן. יָצְאוּ הָרוּחוֹת הַטְּמֵאוֹת וְנִכְנְסוּ בַּחֲזִירִים, וְהָעֵדֶר הִסְתָּעֵר מִמּוֹרַד הָהָר אֶל הַיָּם. כְּאַלְפַּיִם רֹאשׁ טָבְעוּ בַּיָּם. ¹⁴ בָּרְחוּ הָרוֹעִים וְסִפְּרוּ אֶת הַמַּעֲשֶׂה בָּעִיר וּבַכְּפָרִים, וַאֲנָשִׁים בָּאוּ לִרְאוֹת מַה שֶּׁקָּרָה. ¹⁵ הֵם בָּאוּ אֶל יֵשׁוּעַ וְרָאוּ אֶת אַחוּז הַשֵּׁדִים אֲשֶׁר דָּבַק בּוֹ הַלִּגְיוֹן, וְהוּא יוֹשֵׁב לָבוּשׁ, שָׁפוּי בְּדַעְתּוֹ. פַּחַד נָפַל עֲלֵיהֶם. ¹⁶ הָאֲנָשִׁים שֶׁרָאוּ אֶת הַמַּעֲשֶׂה סִפְּרוּ לָהֶם אֶת שֶׁקָּרָה לַאֲחוּז הַשֵּׁדִים, וְגַם אֶת עִנְיַן הַחֲזִירִים. ¹⁷ אָז הֵחֵלּוּ מְבַקְשִׁים מִמֶּנּוּ

18 And when He got into the boat, he who had been demon-possessed begged Him that he might be with Him. 19 However, Jesus did not permit him, but said to him, "Go home to your friends, and tell them what great things the Lord has done for you, and how He has had compassion on you." 20 And he departed and began to proclaim in Decapolis all that Jesus had done for him; and all marveled.

21 Now when Jesus had crossed over again by boat to the other side, a great multitude gathered to Him; and He was by the sea. 22 And behold, one of the rulers of the synagogue came, Jairus by name. And when he saw Him, he fell at His feet 23 and begged Him earnestly, saying, "My little daughter lies at the point of death. Come and lay Your hands on her, that she may be healed, and she will live." 24 So *Jesus* went with him, and a great multitude followed Him and thronged Him.

25 Now a certain woman had a flow of blood for twelve years, 26 and had suffered many things from many physicians. She had spent all that she had and was no better, but rather grew worse. 27 When she heard about Jesus, she came behind *Him* in the crowd and touched His garment. 28 For she said, "If only I may touch His clothes, I shall be made well."

29 Immediately the fountain of her blood was dried up, and she felt in *her* body that she was healed of the affliction. 30 And Jesus, immediately knowing in Himself that power had gone out of Him, turned around in the crowd and said, "Who touched My clothes?"

31 But His disciples said to Him, "You see the multitude thronging You, and You say, 'Who touched Me?'"

32 And He looked around to see her who had done this thing. 33 But the woman, fearing and trembling, knowing what had happened to her, came and fell down before Him and told Him the whole truth. 34 And He said to her, "Daughter, your faith has made you well. Go in peace, and be healed of your affliction."

35 While He was still speaking, *some* came from the ruler of the synagogue's *house* who said, "Your daughter is dead. Why trouble the Teacher any further?"

36 As soon as Jesus heard the word that was spoken, He said to the ruler of the synagogue, "Do not be afraid; only believe." 37 And He permitted no one to follow Him except Peter, James, and John the brother of James. 38 Then He came to the house of the ruler of the synagogue, and saw a tumult and those who wept and wailed loudly. 39 When He

שֶׁיֵּלֵךְ מֵאֵזוֹרָם. 18 כְּשֶׁנִּכְנַס לַסִּירָה בִּקֵּשׁ מִמֶּנּוּ אֲחוּז הַשֵּׁדִים לְהִשָּׁאֵר אִתּוֹ, 19 אַךְ יֵשׁוּעַ לֹא הִרְשָׁה לוֹ כִּי אִם אָמַר אֵלָיו: "לֵךְ לְבֵיתְךָ אֶל מִשְׁפַּחְתְּךָ וְהַגֵּד לָהֶם מַה שֶּׁעָשָׂה לְךָ אֱלֹהִים בְּרַחֲמָיו עָלֶיךָ." 20 הוּא הָלַךְ וְהֵחֵל לְהַכְרִיז בְּעֶשֶׂר הֶעָרִים אֶת אֲשֶׁר עָשָׂה לוֹ יֵשׁוּעַ, וְהַכֹּל תָּמְהוּ.

21 יֵשׁוּעַ חָזַר בַּסִּירָה אֶל הַצַּד הַשֵּׁנִי וְהָמוֹן רַב נֶאֱסַף אֵלָיו בִּהְיוֹתוֹ עַל שְׂפַת הַיָּם. 22 בָּא אֶחָד מֵרָאשֵׁי בֵּית הַכְּנֶסֶת, יָאִיר שְׁמוֹ, וּכְשֶׁרָאָה אֶת יֵשׁוּעַ נָפַל לְרַגְלָיו. 23 הִתְחַנֵּן אֵלָיו מְאֹד וְאָמַר: "בִּתִּי נוֹטָה לָמוּת. אָנָּא, בּוֹא וְסָמֹךְ יָדֶיךָ עָלֶיהָ כְּדֵי שֶׁהִיא תִּתְרַפֵּא וְתִחְיֶה." 24 יֵשׁוּעַ הָלַךְ אִתּוֹ, וְאַחֲרָיו הוֹלְכִים הָמוֹן רַב וְדוֹחֲקִים אוֹתוֹ. 25 וְאִשָּׁה זָבַת דָּם זֶה שְׁתֵּים-עֶשְׂרֵה שָׁנָה – 26 שֶׁסָּבְלָה רַבּוֹת בִּידֵי רוֹפְאִים רַבִּים וְהוֹצִיאָה אֶת כָּל רְכוּשָׁהּ, וְלֹא הוּטַב לָהּ אֶלָּא שֶׁעוֹד הוּרַע לָהּ – 27 כְּשֶׁשָּׁמְעָה עַל-אוֹדוֹת יֵשׁוּעַ, בָּאָה מֵאָחוֹר בְּתוֹךְ הֶהָמוֹן וְנָגְעָה בְּבִגְדוֹ, 28 כִּי אָמְרָה "אִם אֶגַּע אַפִלּוּ בִּבְגָדָיו אֶתְרַפֵּא." 29 בּוֹ בָּרֶגַע הִתְיַבֵּשׁ מְקוֹר דָּמָהּ וְהִיא חָשָׁה בְּגוּפָהּ שֶׁנִּרְפְּאָה מִן הַמַּחֲלָה. 30 מִיָּד הִבְחִין יֵשׁוּעַ בְּתוֹכוֹ הוּא שֶׁיָּצְאָה מִמֶּנּוּ גְּבוּרָה. פָּנָה אֶל הֶהָמוֹן וְאָמַר: "מִי נָגַע בִּבְגָדַי?"

31 אָמְרוּ לוֹ תַּלְמִידָיו: "אַתָּה רוֹאֶה אֶת הֶהָמוֹן דּוֹחֵק אוֹתְךָ וְאַתָּה שׁוֹאֵל 'מִי נָגַע בִּי'?" 32 הוּא הִבִּיט סְבִיבוֹ לִרְאוֹת מִי עָשָׂה זֹאת. 33 פָּחֲדָה הָאִשָּׁה וְרָעֲדָה, כִּי יָדְעָה מַה שֶּׁקָּרָה לָהּ. הִיא נִגְּשָׁה וְנָפְלָה לְפָנָיו וְאָמְרָה לוֹ אֶת כָּל הָאֱמֶת. 34 אָמַר לָהּ: "בִּתִּי, אֱמוּנָתֵךְ הוֹשִׁיעָה אוֹתָךְ. לְכִי לְשָׁלוֹם וְהֵרָפְאִי מִמַּחֲלָתֵךְ." 35 עוֹדֶנּוּ מְדַבֵּר וְהִנֵּה בָּאוּ אֲנָשִׁים מִבֵּיתוֹ שֶׁל רֹאשׁ בֵּית הַכְּנֶסֶת וְאָמְרוּ: "בִּתְּךָ מֵתָה, לָמָּה תַּטְרִיחַ עוֹד אֶת הָרַב?" 36 שָׁמַע יֵשׁוּעַ אֶת מַה שֶּׁדֻּבְּרוּ וְאָמַר לְרֹאשׁ בֵּית הַכְּנֶסֶת: "אַל תִּפְחַד; רַק הַאֲמֵן." 37 יֵשׁוּעַ לֹא הִנִּיחַ לְאִישׁ לְהִלָּווֹת אֵלָיו, חוּץ מִכֵּיפָא וְיַעֲקֹב וְיוֹחָנָן אֲחִי יַעֲקֹב. 38 כַּאֲשֶׁר בָּאוּ אֶל בֵּיתוֹ שֶׁל רֹאשׁ בֵּית הַכְּנֶסֶת, רָאָה הֲמֻלָּה וַאֲנָשִׁים בּוֹכִים וּמְיַלְלִים הַרְבֵּה. 39 נִכְנַס וְאָמַר לָהֶם: "מָה אַתֶּם הוֹמִים וּבוֹכִים? הַיַּלְדָּה לֹא מֵתָה. הִיא רַק יְשֵׁנָה."

came in, He said to them, "Why make this commotion and weep? The child is not dead, but sleeping."

40 And they ridiculed Him. But when He had put them all outside, He took the father and the mother of the child, and those *who were* with Him, and entered where the child was lying. 41 Then He took the child by the hand, and said to her, "Talitha, cumi," which is translated, "Little girl, I say to you, arise." 42 Immediately the girl arose and walked, for she was twelve years *of age.* And they were overcome with great amazement. 43 But He commanded them strictly that no one should know it, and said that *something* should be given her to eat.

6 Then He went out from there and came to His own country, and His disciples followed Him. 2 And when the Sabbath had come, He began to teach in the synagogue. And many hearing *Him* were astonished, saying, "Where *did* this Man *get* these things? And what wisdom *is* this which is given to Him, that such mighty works are performed by His hands! 3 Is this not the carpenter, the Son of Mary, and brother of James, Joses, Judas, and Simon? And are not His sisters here with us?" So they were offended at Him.

4 But Jesus said to them, "A prophet is not without honor except in his own country, among his own relatives, and in his own house." 5 Now He could do no mighty work there, except that He laid His hands on a few sick people and healed *them.* 6 And He marveled because of their unbelief. Then He went about the villages in a circuit, teaching.

7 And He called the twelve to *Himself,* and began to send them out two *by* two, and gave them power over unclean spirits. 8 He commanded them to take nothing for the journey except a staff—no bag, no bread, no copper in *their* money belts— 9 but to wear sandals, and not to put on two tunics.

10 Also He said to them, "In whatever place you enter a house, stay there till you depart from that place. 11 And whoever will not receive you nor hear you, when you depart from there, shake off the dust under your feet as a testimony against them. Assuredly, I say to you, it will be more tolerable for Sodom and Gomorrah in the day of judgment than for that city!"

12 So they went out and preached that *people* should repent. 13 And they cast out many demons, and anointed with oil many who were sick, and healed *them.*

40 הֵם צָחֲקוּ לוֹ, אַךְ הוּא הוֹצִיא אֶת כֻּלָּם, לָקַח אֶת אֲבִי הַיַּלְדָּה וְאֶת אִמָּהּ, עִם הָאֲנָשִׁים אֲשֶׁר אִתּוֹ, וְנִכְנַס לַמָּקוֹם שֶׁשָּׁכְבָה בּוֹ הַיַּלְדָּה. 41 הוּא אָחַז בְּיָדָהּ שֶׁל הַיַּלְדָּה וְאָמַר אֵלֶיהָ: "טַלְיְתָא, קוּמִי!" שֶׁתַּרְגּוּמוֹ, "נַעֲרָה, קוּמִי – אֲנִי אוֹמֵר לָךְ." 42 מִיָּד קָמָה הַנַּעֲרָה וְהִתְהַלְּכָה; וְהִיא בַּת שְׁתֵּים-עֶשְׂרֵה שָׁנָה. הֵם נִתְמַלְּאוּ תִּמָּהוֹן גָּדוֹל. 43 אָז צִוָּה עֲלֵיהֶם בְּתֹקֶף שֶׁלֹּא יֵדַע הַדָּבָר לְאִישׁ וְאָמַר לָתֵת לָהּ לֶאֱכֹל.

6 אַחֲרֵי צֵאתוֹ מִשָּׁם הָלַךְ לְעִירוֹ וְתַלְמִידָיו הָלְכוּ אַחֲרָיו. 2 בְּיוֹם הַשַּׁבָּת הֵחֵל לְלַמֵּד בְּבֵית הַכְּנֶסֶת. תָּמְהוּ הַשּׁוֹמְעִים הָרַבִּים וְאָמְרוּ: "מִנַּיִן לוֹ הַדְּבָרִים הָאֵלֶּה וּמַה הִיא הַחָכְמָה שֶׁנִּתְּנָה לוֹ וְהַגְּבוּרוֹת הָאֵלֶּה הַנַּעֲשׂוֹת בְּיָדוֹ? 3 הֲלֹא זֶה הַנַּגָּר בֶּן מִרְיָם וַאֲחֵי יַעֲקֹב וְיוֹסֵי וִיהוּדָה וְשִׁמְעוֹן, וַהֲרֵי אֲחִיוֹתָיו פֹּה אִתָּנוּ!" הוּא הָיָה לָהֶם לְמִכְשׁוֹל.

4 אָמַר לָהֶם יֵשׁוּעַ: "אֵין נָבִיא נִקְלֶה אֶלָּא בְּעִירוֹ, בֵּין קְרוֹבָיו וּבְבֵיתוֹ."

5 וְלֹא הָיָה יָכוֹל לַעֲשׂוֹת שָׁם שׁוּם נֵס; רַק עַל חוֹלִים אֲחָדִים סָמַךְ אֶת יָדָיו וְרִפֵּא אוֹתָם. 6 תָּמַהּ הָיָה עַל חֹסֶר אֱמוּנָתָם.

הוּא עָבַר בַּכְּפָרִים מִסָּבִיב וְלִמֵּד. 7 קָרָא לַשְּׁנֵים-עָשָׂר וְהֵחֵל לִשְׁלֹחַ אוֹתָם שְׁנַיִם שְׁנַיִם וְנָתַן לָהֶם סַמְכוּת עַל הָרוּחוֹת הַטְּמֵאוֹת. 8 גַּם צִוָּה עֲלֵיהֶם שֶׁלֹּא יִקְחוּ מְאוּמָה לַדֶּרֶךְ מִלְּבַד מַקֵּל; לֹא לֶחֶם, לֹא תַרְמִיל וְלֹא כֶּסֶף בַּחֲגוֹרָתָם; 9 שֶׁיִּנְעֲלוּ סַנְדָּלִים וְלֹא יִלְבְּשׁוּ שְׁתֵּי כֻּתֳּנוֹת. 10 אָמַר לָהֶם: "בְּכָל מָקוֹם שֶׁתִּכָּנְסוּ לְבַיִת, שָׁם תֵּשְׁבוּ עַד צֵאתְכֶם מִשָּׁם. 11 וּבְכָל מָקוֹם אֲשֶׁר לֹא יְקַבְּלוּ אֶתְכֶם וְלֹא יִשְׁמְעוּ לָכֶם, צְאוּ מִשָּׁם וְנַעֲרוּ אֶת הֶעָפָר אֲשֶׁר תַּחַת רַגְלֵיכֶם לְעֵדוּת לָהֶם." 12 הֵם יָצְאוּ וְקָרְאוּ לַבְּרִיּוֹת לַחֲזֹר בִּתְשׁוּבָה, 13 גַּם גֵּרְשׁוּ שֵׁדִים רַבִּים וּמָשְׁחוּ בְּשֶׁמֶן חוֹלִים רַבִּים וְרִפְּאוּ אוֹתָם.

14 Now King Herod heard *of Him,* for His name had become well known. And he said, "John the Baptist is risen from the dead, and therefore these powers are at work in him."

15 Others said, "It is Elijah."

And others said, "It is the Prophet, or like one of the prophets."

16 But when Herod heard, he said, "This is John, whom I beheaded; he has been raised from the dead!" 17 For Herod himself had sent and laid hold of John, and bound him in prison for the sake of Herodias, his brother Philip's wife; for he had married her. 18 Because John had said to Herod, "It is not lawful for you to have your brother's wife."

19 Therefore Herodias held it against him and wanted to kill him, but she could not; 20 for Herod feared John, knowing that he *was* a just and holy man, and he protected him. And when he heard him, he did many things, and heard him gladly.

21 Then an opportune day came when Herod on his birthday gave a feast for his nobles, the high officers, and the chief *men* of Galilee. 22 And when Herodias' daughter herself came in and danced, and pleased Herod and those who sat with him, the king said to the girl, "Ask me whatever you want, and I will give *it* to you." 23 He also swore to her, "Whatever you ask me, I will give you, up to half my kingdom."

24 So she went out and said to her mother, "What shall I ask?"

And she said, "The head of John the Baptist!"

25 Immediately she came in with haste to the king and asked, saying, "I want you to give me at once the head of John the Baptist on a platter."

26 And the king was exceedingly sorry; *yet,* because of the oaths and because of those who sat with him, he did not want to refuse her. 27 Immediately the king sent an executioner and commanded his head to be brought. And he went and beheaded him in prison, 28 brought his head on a platter, and gave it to the girl; and the girl gave it to her mother. 29 When his disciples heard *of it,* they came and took away his corpse and laid it in a tomb.

30 Then the apostles gathered to Jesus and told Him all things, both what they had done and what they had taught. 31 And He said to them, "Come aside by yourselves to a deserted place and rest a while." For there were many coming and going, and they did not even have time to eat. 32 So they departed to a deserted place in the boat by themselves.

14 הַמֶּלֶךְ הוֹרְדוֹס שָׁמַע עַל כָּךְ, שֶׁכֵּן שְׁמוֹ שֶׁל יֵשׁוּעַ נוֹדַע בְּרַבִּים וְיֵשׁ שֶׁאָמְרוּ: "יוֹחָנָן הַמַּטְבִּיל קָם מִן הַמֵּתִים וְלָכֵן פּוֹעֲלוֹת בּוֹ הַגְּבוּרוֹת." 15 אֲחֵרִים אָמְרוּ: "זֶה אֵלִיָּהוּ", וַאֲחֵרִים אָמְרוּ: "נָבִיא כְּאַחַד הַנְּבִיאִים." 16 כְּשֶׁשָּׁמַע הוֹרְדוֹס, אָמַר: "זֶהוּ יוֹחָנָן. הוּא אֲשֶׁר אֲנִי עָרַפְתִּי אֶת רֹאשׁוֹ קָם לִתְחִיָּה", 17 שֶׁהֲרֵי הוֹרְדוֹס עַצְמוֹ שָׁלַח לִתְפֹּס אֶת יוֹחָנָן וְכָלָא אוֹתוֹ בַּכֶּלֶא עַל־דְּבַר הוֹרוֹדְיָה, אֵשֶׁת פִילִיפּוֹס אָחִיו, אֲשֶׁר הוּא נָשָׂא לְאִשָּׁה; 18 כִּי יוֹחָנָן אָמַר לְהוֹרְדוֹס: "אֵשֶׁת אָחִיךָ אֵינָה מֻתֶּרֶת לְךָ." 19 עַל כֵּן שָׂנְאָה אוֹתוֹ הוֹרוֹדְיָה וְרָצְתָה לַהֲרֹג אוֹתוֹ, אַךְ לֹא יָכְלָה 20 מִשּׁוּם שֶׁהוֹרְדוֹס פָּחַד מִיּוֹחָנָן וְשָׁמַר עָלָיו בְּיָדְעוֹ שֶׁיּוֹחָנָן אִישׁ צַדִּיק וְקָדוֹשׁ; הוּא הָיָה שׁוֹמֵעַ אֶת דְּבָרָיו בְּרָצוֹן אַף כִּי בָּא בִּמְבוּכָה רַבָּה בְּשָׁמְעוֹ אוֹתָם.

21 שְׁעַת הַכֹּשֶׁר הִגִּיעָה כַּאֲשֶׁר בְּיוֹם הֻלַּדְתּוֹ עָרַךְ הוֹרְדוֹס מִשְׁתֶּה לִגְדוֹלָיו וּלְשָׂרֵי הָאֲלָפִים וּלְרָאשֵׁי הַגָּלִיל. 22 אָז נִכְנְסָה בִּתָּהּ שֶׁל הוֹרוֹדְיָה וְרָקְדָה וּמָצְאָה חֵן בְּעֵינֵי הוֹרְדוֹס וְהַמְסֻבִּים אִתּוֹ. אָמַר הַמֶּלֶךְ אֶל הַנַּעֲרָה: "בַּקְּשִׁי מִמֶּנִּי מַה שֶּׁתִּרְצִי וְאֶתֵּן לָךְ." 23 הוּא גַּם נִשְׁבַּע לָהּ: "מַה שֶּׁתִּתְבַּקְשִׁי מִמֶּנִּי אֶתֵּן לָךְ עַד חֲצִי הַמַּלְכוּת!"

24 יָצְאָה וְאָמְרָה לְאִמָּהּ: "מָה אֲבַקֵּשׁ?" הֵשִׁיבָה אִמָּהּ: "אֶת רֹאשׁ יוֹחָנָן הַמַּטְבִּיל!"

25 הִיא נִכְנְסָה מִיָּד אֶל הַמֶּלֶךְ וּבִקְּשָׁה: "אֲנִי רוֹצָה שֶׁתִּתֵּן לִי עַכְשָׁו בִּקְעָרָה אֶת רֹאשׁ יוֹחָנָן הַמַּטְבִּיל!" 26 הִתְעַצֵּב הַמֶּלֶךְ מְאֹד, אַךְ בִּגְלַל הַשְּׁבוּעָה וּבִגְלַל הַמְסֻבִּים לֹא רָצָה לְהָשִׁיב אֶת פָּנֶיהָ רֵיקָם. 27 מִיָּד שָׁלַח הַמֶּלֶךְ אֶחָד מִן הַשּׁוֹמְרִים וְצִוָּה לְהָבִיא אֶת רֹאשׁוֹ. הָלַךְ הַשּׁוֹמֵר וְכָרַת אֶת רֹאשׁוֹ בַּכֶּלֶא. 28 לְאַחַר מִכֵּן הֵבִיא אֶת רֹאשׁוֹ בִּקְעָרָה וְנָתַן אוֹתוֹ לַנַּעֲרָה, וְהַנַּעֲרָה נָתְנָה אוֹתוֹ לְאִמָּהּ. 29 כַּאֲשֶׁר שָׁמְעוּ תַּלְמִידָיו, בָּאוּ וְלָקְחוּ אֶת גּוּפָתוֹ וְהִנִּיחוּ אוֹתָהּ בְּקֶבֶר.

30 נֶאֶסְפוּ הַשְּׁלִיחִים אֶל יֵשׁוּעַ וְסִפְּרוּ לוֹ אֶת כָּל אֲשֶׁר עָשׂוּ וְכָל אֲשֶׁר לִמְּדוּ. 31 אָמַר לָהֶם: "בּוֹאוּ אַתֶּם לְבַדְּכֶם לְמָקוֹם שׁוֹמֵם וְנוּחוּ מְעַט", שֶׁכֵּן רַבִּים הָיוּ הַבָּאִים וְהַיּוֹצְאִים, עַד כְּדֵי כָּךְ שֶׁלֹּא הָיָה לָהֶם פְּנַאי לֶאֱכֹל. 32 הֵם הִפְלִיגוּ מִשָּׁם בַּסִּירָה אֶל מָקוֹם שׁוֹמֵם לְבַדָּם.

33 But the multitudes saw them departing, and many knew Him and ran there on foot from all the cities. They arrived before them and came together to Him. 34 And Jesus, when He came out, saw a great multitude and was moved with compassion for them, because they were like sheep not having a shepherd. So He began to teach them many things. 35 When the day was now far spent, His disciples came to Him and said, "This is a deserted place, and already the hour is late. 36 Send them away, that they may go into the surrounding country and villages and buy themselves bread; for they have nothing to eat."

37 But He answered and said to them, "You give them something to eat."

And they said to Him, "Shall we go and buy two hundred denarii worth of bread and give them something to eat?"

38 But He said to them, "How many loaves do you have? Go and see."

And when they found out they said, "Five, and two fish."

39 Then He commanded them to make them all sit down in groups on the green grass. 40 So they sat down in ranks, in hundreds and in fifties. 41 And when He had taken the five loaves and the two fish, He looked up to heaven, blessed and broke the loaves, and gave them to His disciples to set before them; and the two fish He divided among them all. 42 So they all ate and were filled. 43 And they took up twelve baskets full of fragments and of the fish. 44 Now those who had eaten the loaves were about five thousand men.

45 Immediately He made His disciples get into the boat and go before Him to the other side, to Bethsaida, while He sent the multitude away. 46 And when He had sent them away, He departed to the mountain to pray. 47 Now when evening came, the boat was in the middle of the sea; and He was alone on the land. 48 Then He saw them straining at rowing, for the wind was against them. Now about the fourth watch of the night He came to them, walking on the sea, and would have passed them by. 49 And when they saw Him walking on the sea, they supposed it was a ghost, and cried out; 50 for they all saw Him and were troubled. But immediately He talked with them and said to them, "Be of good cheer! It is I; do not be afraid." 51 Then He went up into the boat to them, and the wind ceased. And they were greatly amazed in themselves beyond measure, and marveled. 52 For they had not understood about the loaves, because their heart was hardened.

33 רַבִּים רָאוּ אֶת יֵשׁוּעַ וְהַשְּׁלִיחִים יוֹצְאִים וְהִכִּירוּ אוֹתָם, וּמִכָּל הֶעָרִים רָצוּ לְשָׁם בָּרֶגֶל וְהִקְדִּימוּ אוֹתָם. 34 כְּשֶׁיָּצָא יֵשׁוּעַ וְרָאָה הָמוֹן רַב נִכְמְרוּ רַחֲמָיו עֲלֵיהֶם, כִּי הָיוּ כַּצֹּאן אֲשֶׁר אֵין לָהֶם רוֹעֶה. הוּא הֵחֵל לְלַמֵּד אוֹתָם דְּבָרִים רַבִּים. 35 כְּשֶׁנָּטָה הַיּוֹם לַעֲרֹב נִגְּשׁוּ אֵלָיו תַּלְמִידָיו וְאָמְרוּ: "הַמָּקוֹם שׁוֹמֵם וְהַשָּׁעָה כְּבָר מְאֻחֶרֶת. 36 שְׁלַח אוֹתָם שֶׁיֵּלְכוּ אֶל הֶעֲיָרוֹת וְהַכְּפָרִים מִסָּבִיב וְיִקְנוּ לָהֶם לֶאֱכֹל."

37 הֵשִׁיב וְאָמַר לָהֶם: "תְּנוּ לָהֶם אַתֶּם לֶאֱכֹל." שָׁאֲלוּ אוֹתוֹ: "הַאִם נֵלֵךְ וְנִקְנֶה לֶחֶם בְּמָאתַיִם דִּינָר וְנִתֵּן לָהֶם לֶאֱכֹל?"

38 אָמַר לָהֶם: "כַּמָּה כִּכְּרוֹת לֶחֶם יֵשׁ לָכֶם? לְכוּ וּרְאוּ." אַחֲרֵי שֶׁבֵּרְרוּ הֵשִׁיבוּ: "חָמֵשׁ, וּשְׁנֵי דָגִים."

39 הוּא צִוָּה עֲלֵיהֶם לְהוֹשִׁיב אֶת כֻּלָּם חֲבוּרָה חֲבוּרָה עַל הַדֶּשֶׁא הַיָּרֹק, 40 וְהֵם יָשְׁבוּ בִּקְבוּצוֹת שֶׁל מֵאָה וְשֶׁל חֲמִשִּׁים. 41 לָקַח אֶת חֲמֵשׁ כִּכְּרוֹת הַלֶּחֶם וְאֶת שְׁנֵי הַדָּגִים וּלְאַחַר שֶׁנָּשָׂא עֵינָיו הַשָּׁמַיְמָה וּבֵרַךְ, בָּצַע אֶת הַלֶּחֶם וְנָתַן לְתַלְמִידָיו לְהַגִּישׁ לָהֶם, וְגַם אֶת שְׁנֵי הַדָּגִים חִלֵּק לְכֻלָּם. 42 הַכֹּל אָכְלוּ וְשָׂבְעוּ, 43 וּמִמַּה שֶׁנּוֹתַר אָסְפוּ שְׁנֵים־עָשָׂר סַלִּים מְלֵאִים, בִּכְלָל זֶה גַם דָּגִים. 44 מִסְפַּר הָאוֹכְלִים הָיָה חֲמֵשֶׁת אֲלָפִים אִישׁ.

45 מִיָּד אַחֲרֵי כֵן הֵאִיץ בְּתַלְמִידָיו לְהִכָּנֵס לַסִּירָה וּלְהַפְלִיג אֶל הַצַּד הַשֵּׁנִי, לְבֵית צַיְדָא, בְּעוֹד שֶׁהוּא יְשַׁלֵּחַ אֶת הֶהָמוֹן. 46 אַחֲרֵי שֶׁנִּפְרַד מֵהֶם עָלָה לָהָר לְהִתְפַּלֵּל. 47 לְעֵת עֶרֶב הָיְתָה הַסִּירָה בְּאֶמְצַע הַיָּם וְהוּא לְבַדּוֹ עַל הַיַּבָּשָׁה. 48 רָאָה אוֹתָם מִתְיַגְּעִים בַּחֲתִירָה, כִּי הָרוּחַ נָשְׁבָה נֶגְדָּם, וּבָא אֲלֵיהֶם בְּעֵרֶךְ בְּאַשְׁמֹרֶת הָרְבִיעִית שֶׁל הַלַּיְלָה כְּשֶׁהוּא הוֹלֵךְ עַל פְּנֵי הַיָּם וְכַוָּנָתוֹ לַעֲבֹר לְיָדָם. 49 כְּשֶׁרָאוּהוּ הוֹלֵךְ עַל פְּנֵי הַיָּם חָשְׁבוּ שֶׁהוּא רוּחַ רְפָאִים וְהֵחֵלּוּ לִצְעֹק, 50 כִּי כֻּלָּם רָאוּ אוֹתוֹ וְנִבְהֲלוּ, אַךְ הוּא דִּבֵּר אִתָּם מִיָּד וְאָמַר לָהֶם: "חִזְקוּ, זֶה אֲנִי, אַל תִּפְחֲדוּ!" 51 הוּא בָּא אֲלֵיהֶם לְתוֹךְ הַסִּירָה וְהָרוּחַ פָּסְקָה. הֵם הִשְׁתּוֹמְמוּ עַד מְאֹד, 52 כִּי לֹא לָמְדוּ דָבָר מֵעִנְיַן כִּכְּרוֹת הַלֶּחֶם בִּגְלַל קְהוּת לְבָבָם.

53 When they had crossed over, they came to the land of Gennesaret and anchored there. 54 And when they came out of the boat, immediately the people recognized Him, 55 ran through that whole surrounding region, and began to carry about on beds those who were sick to wherever they heard He was. 56 Wherever He entered, into villages, cities, or the country, they laid the sick in the marketplaces, and begged Him that they might just touch the hem of His garment. And as many as touched Him were made well.

7 Then the Pharisees and some of the scribes came together to Him, having come from Jerusalem. 2 Now when they saw some of His disciples eat bread with defiled, that is, with unwashed hands, they found fault. 3 For the Pharisees and all the Jews do not eat unless they wash *their* hands in a special way, holding the tradition of the elders. 4 *When they come* from the marketplace, they do not eat unless they wash. And there are many other things which they have received and hold, *like* the washing of cups, pitchers, copper vessels, and couches.

5 Then the Pharisees and scribes asked Him, "Why do Your disciples not walk according to the tradition of the elders, but eat bread with unwashed hands?"

6 He answered and said to them, "Well did Isaiah prophesy of you hypocrites, as it is written:

'This people honors Me with *their* lips,
But their heart is far from Me.
7   And in vain they worship Me,
Teaching as doctrines the commandments of men.'

8 For laying aside the commandment of God, you hold the tradition of men—the washing of pitchers and cups, and many other such things you do."

9 He said to them, "*All too* well you reject the commandment of God, that you may keep your tradition. 10 For Moses said, 'Honor your father and your mother'; and, 'He who curses father or mother, let him be put to death.' 11 But you say, 'If a man says to his father or mother, "Whatever profit you might have received from me *is* Corban"—' (that is, a gift *to God*), 12 then you no longer let him do anything for his father or his mother, 13 making the word of God of no effect through your tradition which you have handed down. And many such things you do."

14 When He had called all the multitude to *Himself*, He said to them, "Hear Me, everyone, and understand: 15 There is nothing that enters a

53 עָבְרוּ אֶת הַיָּם וְהִגִּיעוּ אֶל חוֹף גִּנּוֹסַר וְעָגְנוּ שָׁם. 54 בְּצֵאתָם מִן הַסִּירָה הִכִּירוּ אוֹתוֹ מִיָּד, 55 וּבְכָל הָאֵזוֹר הַהוּא רָצוּ וְהֵחֵלּוּ לְהָבִיא אֶת הַחוֹלִים עַל אֲלוּנְקוֹת לְכָל מָקוֹם שֶׁשָּׁמְעוּ כִּי הוּא שָׁם. 56 בְּכָל מָקוֹם שֶׁבָּא אֵלָיו, בַּכְּפָרִים אוֹ בֶּעָרִים אוֹ בָּעֲיָרוֹת, שָׂמוּ אֶת הַחוֹלִים בַּחוּצוֹת וּבִקְשׁוּ מִמֶּנּוּ שֶׁיַּנִּיחַ לָהֶם לִנְגֹּעַ וְלוּ רַק בִּכְנַף בִּגְדוֹ, וְכָל הַנּוֹגְעִים בּוֹ נִרְפְּאוּ.

ז נִקְהֲלוּ אֵלָיו הַפְּרוּשִׁים וְכַמָּה מִן הַסּוֹפְרִים אֲשֶׁר בָּאוּ מִירוּשָׁלַיִם. 2 כִּרְאוֹתָם שֶׁאֲחָדִים מִתַּלְמִידָיו אוֹכְלִים לֶחֶם בְּיָדַיִם טְמֵאוֹת (כְּלוֹמַר, בְּלֹא נְטִילַת יָדַיִם, 3 שֶׁכֵּן הַפְּרוּשִׁים וְכָל הַיְּהוּדִים מַחֲזִיקִים בְּמָסֹרֶת הַזְּקֵנִים וְאֵינָם אוֹכְלִים לְלֹא נְטִילַת יָדַיִם כַּהֲלָכָה, 4 וּבְשׁוּבָם מִן הַשּׁוּק אֵינָם אוֹכְלִים לְלֹא רְחִיצָה. וְעוֹד דְּבָרִים רַבִּים קִבְּלוּ לִשְׁמֹר, כְּגוֹן טְבִילַת כּוֹסוֹת וְכַדִּים וּכְלֵי נְחֹשֶׁת) 5 שָׁאֲלוּ אוֹתוֹ הַפְּרוּשִׁים וְהַסּוֹפְרִים: "מַדּוּעַ אֵין תַּלְמִידֶיךָ נוֹהֲגִים לְפִי מָסֹרֶת הַזְּקֵנִים אֶלָּא אוֹכְלִים אֶת הַלֶּחֶם בְּיָדַיִם טְמֵאוֹת?" 6 אָמַר לָהֶם: "הֵיטֵב נִבָּא יְשַׁעְיָהוּ עֲלֵיכֶם הַצְּבוּעִים, כַּכָּתוּב: 'הָעָם הַזֶּה בִּשְׂפָתָיו כִּבְּדוּנִי וְלִבּוֹ רָחַק מִמֶּנִּי 7 וַתְּהִי יִרְאָתָם אֹתִי מִצְוַת אֲנָשִׁים מְלֻמָּדָה'; 8 כִּי עוֹזְבִים אַתֶּם אֶת מִצְוַת אֱלֹהִים בְּמָסֹרֶת בְּנֵי אָדָם."

9 עוֹד אָמַר לָהֶם: "יָפֶה, בְּטַלְתֶּם אֶת מִצְוַת אֱלֹהִים כְּדֵי לִשְׁמֹר אֶת הַמָּסֹרֶת שֶׁלָּכֶם! 10 הֵן מֹשֶׁה אָמַר, 'כַּבֵּד אֶת אָבִיךָ וְאֶת אִמֶּךָ' וּ'מְקַלֵּל אָבִיו וְאִמּוֹ מוֹת יוּמָת'; 11 וְאַתֶּם אוֹמְרִים, 'אִישׁ אִם יֹאמַר לְאָבִיו אוֹ לְאִמּוֹ: כָּל דָּבָר מִשֶּׁלִּי שֶׁאַתָּה יָכוֹל לַהֲנוֹת מִמֶּנּוּ – קָרְבָּן!' 12 הֲרֵי שֶׁאֵינְכֶם מַנִּיחִים לוֹ עוֹד לַעֲשׂוֹת מְאוּמָה לְמַעַן אָבִיו אוֹ אִמּוֹ, 13 וּמְפִירִים אַתֶּם אֶת דְּבַר אֱלֹהִים עַל־יְדֵי הַמָּסֹרֶת שֶׁלָּכֶם אֲשֶׁר מְסַרְתֶּם. וּדְבָרִים רַבִּים דּוֹמִים לָזֶה אַתֶּם עוֹשִׂים." 14 הוּא קָרָא אֶת הֶהָמוֹן שֵׁנִית וְאָמַר לָהֶם: "הַקְשִׁיבוּ אֵלַי כֻּלְּכֶם וְהָבִינוּ. 15 אֵין דָּבָר הַנִּמְצָא מִחוּץ לָאָדָם

11 המקור היווני מביא כאן את המלה העברית "קרבן" ומוסיף שפירושה מתנה. הכוונה: מתנה המוקדשת לבית המקדש.

man from outside which can defile him; but the things which come out of him, those are the things that defile a man. 16 If anyone has ears to hear, let him hear!"

17 When He had entered a house away from the crowd, His disciples asked Him concerning the parable. 18 So He said to them, "Are you thus without understanding also? Do you not perceive that whatever enters a man from outside cannot defile him, 19 because it does not enter his heart but his stomach, and is eliminated, *thus* purifying all foods?" 20 And He said, "What comes out of a man, that defiles a man. 21 For from within, out of the heart of men, proceed evil thoughts, adulteries, fornications, murders, 22 thefts, covetousness, wickedness, deceit, lewdness, an evil eye, blasphemy, pride, foolishness. 23 All these evil things come from within and defile a man."

24 From there He arose and went to the region of Tyre and Sidon. And He entered a house and wanted no one to know *it,* but He could not be hidden. 25 For a woman whose young daughter had an unclean spirit heard about Him, and she came and fell at His feet. 26 The woman was a Greek, a Syro-Phoenician by birth, and she kept asking Him to cast the demon out of her daughter. 27 But Jesus said to her, "Let the children be filled first, for it is not good to take the children's bread and throw *it* to the little dogs."

28 And she answered and said to Him, "Yes, Lord, yet even the little dogs under the table eat from the children's crumbs."

29 Then He said to her, "For this saying go your way; the demon has gone out of your daughter."

30 And when she had come to her house, she found the demon gone out, and her daughter lying on the bed.

31 Again, departing from the region of Tyre and Sidon, He came through the midst of the region of Decapolis to the Sea of Galilee. 32 Then they brought to Him one who was deaf and had an impediment in his speech, and they begged Him to put His hand on him. 33 And He took him aside from the multitude, and put His fingers in his ears, and He spat and touched his tongue. 34 Then, looking up to heaven, He sighed, and said to him, "Ephphatha," that is, "Be opened."

35 Immediately his ears were opened, and the impediment of his tongue was loosed, and he spoke plainly. 36 Then He commanded them that they should tell no one; but the more He commanded them, the more widely they proclaimed *it.* 37 And

יָכוֹל לְטַמֵּא אוֹתוֹ בְּהִכָּנְסוֹ לְתוֹכוֹ, אֶלָּא הַדְּבָרִים הַיּוֹצְאִים מִתּוֹךְ הָאָדָם הֵם הַמְטַמְּאִים אֶת הָאָדָם." 17 כַּאֲשֶׁר בָּא הַבַּיְתָה מִן הֶהָמוֹן, שְׁאָלוּהוּ תַּלְמִידָיו עַל הַמָּשָׁל. 18 אָמַר לָהֶם: "גַּם אַתֶּם חַסְרֵי הֲבָנָה כָּל כָּךְ? הַאִם אֵינְכֶם מְבִינִים שֶׁכָּל הַנִּכְנָס לְתוֹךְ הָאָדָם מִן הַחוּץ אֵינוֹ יָכוֹל לְטַמֵּא אוֹתוֹ, 19 כִּי אֵינוֹ נִכְנָס אֶל לִבּוֹ אֶלָּא לְבִטְנוֹ וְיוֹצֵא אֶל הַמּוֹצָאוֹת?" – בְּכָךְ טִהַר אֶת כָּל הַמַּאֲכָלִים.

20 הוֹסִיף וְאָמַר: "הַיּוֹצֵא מִן הָאָדָם – זֶה מְטַמֵּא אֶת הָאָדָם, 21 כִּי מִבִּפְנִים, מִלֵּב בְּנֵי הָאָדָם, יוֹצְאוֹת מַחֲשָׁבוֹת רָעוֹת, זְנוּנִים, גְּנֵבוֹת, רְצִיחוֹת, 22 נִאוּפִים, חַמְדָנוּת, רִשְׁעָה, רְמִיָּה, זִמָּה, עַיִן רָעָה, גִּדּוּף, גַּאֲוָה, אֱוִילוּת. 23 כָּל הָרָעוֹת הָאֵלֶּה יוֹצְאוֹת מִבִּפְנִים וּמְטַמְּאוֹת אֶת הָאָדָם."

24 הוּא קָם וְהָלַךְ מִשָּׁם אֶל אֵזוֹר צוֹר וְצִידוֹן. נִכְנַס לְבַיִת וְלֹא רָצָה שֶׁיִּוָּדַע לְאִישׁ, אַךְ לֹא הָיָה יָכוֹל לְהֵחָבֵא. 25 אִשָּׁה, שֶׁרוּחַ טְמֵאָה אָחֲזָה בְּבִתָּהּ הַקְּטַנָּה, שָׁמְעָה עָלָיו וּמִיָּד בָּאָה וְנָפְלָה לְרַגְלָיו, 26 וְהָאִשָּׁה נָכְרִיָּה מְמוֹצָא פֵנִיקִי סוּרִי. הִיא בִּקְשָׁה מִמֶּנּוּ לְגָרֵשׁ אֶת הַשֵּׁד מִבִּתָּהּ. 27 אָמַר לָהּ יֵשׁוּעַ: "הַנִּיחִי קֹדֶם לַבָּנִים לִשְׂבֹּעַ, כִּי לֹא נָאֶה לָקַחַת אֶת לֶחֶם הַבָּנִים וּלְהַשְׁלִיךְ אוֹתוֹ לַכְּלָבִים." 28 הֵשִׁיבָה וְאָמְרָה אֵלָיו: "כֵּן, אֲדוֹנִי, אֲבָל גַּם הַכְּלָבִים תַּחַת הַשֻּׁלְחָן אוֹכְלִים מִפְּרוּרֵי הַלֶּחֶם שֶׁל הַבָּנִים!" 29 אָמַר לָהּ: "בִּגְלַל דְּבָרֵךְ זֶה לְכִי לְדַרְכֵּךְ; יָצָא הַשֵּׁד מִבִּתֵּךְ."

30 הִיא הָלְכָה לְבֵיתָהּ וּמָצְאָה אֶת הַיַּלְדָּה שׁוֹכֶבֶת בַּמִּטָּה וְהַשֵּׁד כְּבָר יָצָא מִמֶּנָּה.

31 יֵשׁוּעַ יָצָא מֵאֵזוֹר צוֹר וְחָזַר דֶּרֶךְ צִידוֹן אֶל יָם הַגָּלִיל, דֶּרֶךְ אֵזוֹר עֶשֶׂר הֶעָרִים. 32 הֵבִיאוּ אֵלָיו אִישׁ חֵרֵשׁ וּמִתְקַשֶּׁה בְּדִבּוּר וּבִקְשׁוּ מִמֶּנּוּ שֶׁיִּסְמֹךְ אֶת יָדוֹ עָלָיו. 33 לָקַח אוֹתוֹ יֵשׁוּעַ אֶל מִחוּץ לֶהָמוֹן בִּיחִידוּת, שָׂם אֶת אֶצְבְּעוֹתָיו בְּאָזְנָיו וּלְאַחַר שֶׁיָּרַק נָגַע בִּלְשׁוֹנוֹ, 34 וּבְהַבִּיטוֹ הַשָּׁמַיְמָה נֶאֱנַח וְאָמַר אֵלָיו: "הִפָּתַח!" 35 אָזְנָיו נִפְתְּחוּ וּמִיָּד הֻתַּר קֶשֶׁר לְשׁוֹנוֹ וְהוּא דִּבֵּר בְּבֵרוּר. 36 אָז צִוָּה עֲלֵיהֶם שֶׁלֹּא יְסַפְּרוּ לְאִישׁ, אַךְ כְּכָל שֶׁצִּוָּה זֹאת עֲלֵיהֶם כֵּן הִרְבּוּ לְהַכְרִיז עַל כָּךְ. 37 הֵם הִשְׁתּוֹמְמוּ עַד מְאֹד וְאָמְרוּ: "הַכֹּל

they were astonished beyond measure, saying, "He has done all things well. He makes both the deaf to hear and the mute to speak."

8 In those days, the multitude being very great and having nothing to eat, Jesus called His disciples *to Him* and said to them, 2 "I have compassion on the multitude, because they have now continued with Me three days and have nothing to eat. 3 And if I send them away hungry to their own houses, they will faint on the way; for some of them have come from afar."

4 Then His disciples answered Him, "How can one satisfy these people with bread here in the wilderness?"

5 He asked them, "How many loaves do you have?"

And they said, "Seven."

6 So He commanded the multitude to sit down on the ground. And He took the seven loaves and gave thanks, broke *them* and gave *them* to His disciples to set before *them;* and they set *them* before the multitude. 7 They also had a few small fish; and having blessed them, He said to set them also before *them.* 8 So they ate and were filled, and they took up seven large baskets of leftover fragments. 9 Now those who had eaten were about four thousand. And He sent them away, 10 immediately got into the boat with His disciples, and came to the region of Dalmanutha.

11 Then the Pharisees came out and began to dispute with Him, seeking from Him a sign from heaven, testing Him. 12 But He sighed deeply in His spirit, and said, "Why does this generation seek a sign? Assuredly, I say to you, no sign shall be given to this generation."

13 And He left them, and getting into the boat again, departed to the other side. 14 Now the disciples had forgotten to take bread, and they did not have more than one loaf with them in the boat. 15 Then He charged them, saying, "Take heed, beware of the leaven of the Pharisees and the leaven of Herod."

16 And they reasoned among themselves, saying, "It is because we have no bread."

17 But Jesus, being aware of *it,* said to them, "Why do you reason because you have no bread? Do you not yet perceive nor understand? Is your heart still hardened? 18 Having eyes, do you not see? And having ears, do you not hear? And do you not remember? 19 When I broke the five loaves for the five thousand, how many baskets full of fragments did you take up?"

They said to Him, "Twelve."

עָשָׂה יָפֶה! אֶת הַחֵרְשִׁים הוּא עוֹשֶׂה לְשׁוֹמְעִים וְאֶת הָאִלְּמִים לְמְדַבְּרִים!"

ח בְּאֶחָד הַיָּמִים שׁוּב נֶאֱסַף עַם רַב וְלֹא הָיָה לָהֶם מַה לֶאֱכֹל. קָרָא יֵשׁוּעַ לְתַלְמִידָיו וְאָמַר לָהֶם: 2 "נִכְמְרוּ רַחֲמַי עַל הֶהָמוֹן, כִּי כְּבָר שְׁלוֹשָׁה יָמִים הֵם אִתִּי וְאֵין לָהֶם מַה לֶאֱכֹל. 3 אִם אֲשַׁלַּח אוֹתָם לְבָתֵּיהֶם רְעֵבִים, יִתְעַלְּפוּ בַּדֶּרֶךְ וְיֵשׁ מֵהֶם שֶׁבָּאוּ מֵרָחוֹק."

4 הֵשִׁיבוּ לוֹ תַלְמִידָיו: "מֵאַיִן יוּכַל אִישׁ לְהַשְׂבִּיעַ אוֹתָם בְּלֶחֶם פֹּה בַּמִּדְבָּר?"

5 שָׁאַל אוֹתָם: "כַּמָּה כִּכְּרוֹת לֶחֶם יֵשׁ לָכֶם?" עָנוּ לוֹ: "שֶׁבַע".

6 הוּא צִוָּה אֶת הָעָם לָשֶׁבֶת עַל הָאָרֶץ; לָקַח אֶת שֶׁבַע כִּכְּרוֹת הַלֶּחֶם וּלְאַחַר שֶׁבֵּרֵךְ וּבָצַע, נָתַן לְתַלְמִידָיו לְהַגִּישׁ, וְהֵם הִגִּישׁוּ לָעָם. 7 גַּם כַּמָּה דָגִים קְטַנִּים הָיוּ לָהֶם. בֵּרַךְ עֲלֵיהֶם וְאָמַר לְהַגִּישׁ גַּם אֶת אֵלֶּה. 8 הֵם אָכְלוּ וְשָׂבְעוּ. אַחֲרֵי כֵן אָסְפוּ שִׁבְעָה סַלִּים מְלֵאִים מְנוֹת נוֹתָרוֹת. 9 מִסְפַּר הָאוֹכְלִים הָיָה כְּאַרְבַּעַת אֲלָפִים. הוּא שִׁלַּח אוֹתָם 10 וּמִיָּד נִכְנַס לַסִּירָה עִם תַּלְמִידָיו וְעָבַר אֶל אֵזוֹר דַּלְמָנוּתָא.

11 יָצְאוּ הַפְּרוּשִׁים וְהֵחֵלּוּ לְהִתְוַכֵּחַ אִתּוֹ, וּכְדֵי לְנַסּוֹת אוֹתוֹ בִּקְשׁוּ מִמֶּנּוּ אוֹת מִן הַשָּׁמַיִם. 12 נֶאֱנַח יֵשׁוּעַ בְּרוּחוֹ וְאָמַר: לָמָּה הַדּוֹר הַזֶּה מְבַקֵּשׁ אוֹת? אָמֵן אוֹמֵר אֲנִי לָכֶם, אִם יִנָּתֵן אוֹת לַדּוֹר הַזֶּה! 13 עָזַב אוֹתָם, חָזַר לַסִּירָה וְהִפְלִיג לַצַּד הַשֵּׁנִי.

14 הַתַּלְמִידִים שָׁכְחוּ לָקַחַת לֶחֶם וּבַסִּירָה הָיְתָה לָהֶם רַק כִּכַּר לֶחֶם אַחַת. 15 הִזְהִיר אוֹתָם בְּאָמְרוֹ: "שִׂימוּ לְבַבְכֶם, הִשָּׁמְרוּ מִשְּׂאוֹר הַפְּרוּשִׁים וּמִשְּׂאוֹר הוֹרְדוֹם."

16 הֵם דִּבְּרוּ זֶה עִם זֶה עַל כָּךְ שֶׁאֵין לָהֶם לֶחֶם. 17 הִבְחִין בְּזֶה וְאָמַר לָהֶם: "מַדּוּעַ אַתֶּם מְדַבְּרִים עַל כָּךְ שֶׁאֵין לָכֶם לֶחֶם? עֲדַיִן אֵינְכֶם מְבִינִים אַף לֹא תוֹפְסִים? הַאִם קָהָה לְבַבְכֶם? 18 עֵינַיִם לָכֶם וְלֹא תִרְאוּ וְאָזְנַיִם לָכֶם וְלֹא תִשְׁמָעוּ? גַּם אֵינְכֶם זוֹכְרִים 19 כַּאֲשֶׁר בָּצַעְתִּי אֶת חֲמֵשׁ כִּכְּרוֹת הַלֶּחֶם לַחֲמֵשֶׁת הָאֲלָפִים, כַּמָּה סַלִּים מְלֵאֵי מְנוֹת נוֹתָרוֹת לְקַחְתֶּם?" הֵשִׁיבוּ לוֹ: "שְׁנֵים-עָשָׂר".

²⁰"Also, when I broke the seven for the four thousand, how many large baskets full of fragments did you take up?"

And they said, "Seven."

²¹So He said to them, "How *is it* you do not understand?"

²²Then He came to Bethsaida; and they brought a blind man to Him, and begged Him to touch him. ²³So He took the blind man by the hand and led him out of the town. And when He had spit on his eyes and put His hands on him, He asked him if he saw anything.

²⁴And he looked up and said, "I see men like trees, walking."

²⁵Then He put *His* hands on his eyes again and made him look up. And he was restored and saw everyone clearly. ²⁶Then He sent him away to his house, saying, "Neither go into the town, nor tell anyone in the town."

²⁷Now Jesus and His disciples went out to the towns of Caesarea Philippi; and on the road He asked His disciples, saying to them, "Who do men say that I am?"

²⁸So they answered, "John the Baptist; but some *say,* Elijah; and others, one of the prophets."

²⁹He said to them, "But who do you say that I am?"

Peter answered and said to Him, "You are the Christ."

³⁰Then He strictly warned them that they should tell no one about Him.

³¹And He began to teach them that the Son of Man must suffer many things, and be rejected by the elders and chief priests and scribes, and be killed, and after three days rise again. ³²He spoke this word openly. Then Peter took Him aside and began to rebuke Him. ³³But when He had turned around and looked at His disciples, He rebuked Peter, saying, "Get behind Me, Satan! For you are not mindful of the things of God, but the things of men."

³⁴When He had called the people to *Himself,* with His disciples also, He said to them, "Whoever desires to come after Me, let him deny himself, and take up his cross, and follow Me. ³⁵For whoever desires to save his life will lose it, but whoever loses his life for My sake and the gospel's will save it. ³⁶For what will it profit a man if he gains the whole world, and loses his own soul? ³⁷Or what will a man give in exchange for his soul? ³⁸For whoever is ashamed of Me and My words in this adulterous and sinful generation, of him the Son of Man also will be ashamed when He comes in the glory of His Father with the holy angels."

²⁰"וְהַשֶּׁבַע לְאַרְבַּעַת הָאֲלָפִים, כַּמָּה סַלִּים מְלֵאֵי מְנוֹת נוֹתָרוֹת לְקַחְתֶּם?" אָמְרוּ לוֹ: "שִׁבְעָה."

²¹אָמַר לָהֶם: "עֲדַיִן אֵינְכֶם תּוֹפְסִים?"

²²כַּאֲשֶׁר בָּאוּ לְבֵית צַיְדָא הֵבִיאוּ אֵלָיו עִוֵּר וּבִקְּשׁוּ מִמֶּנּוּ לִגְעֹת בָּעִוֵּר. ²³הֶחֱזִיק יֵשׁוּעַ אֶת הָעִוֵּר וְהוֹלִיכוֹ אֶל מִחוּץ לַכְּפָר. הוּא יָרַק בְּעֵינָיו וְסָמַךְ יָדָיו עָלָיו. שָׁאַל אוֹתוֹ: "הַאִם אַתָּה רוֹאֶה מַשֶּׁהוּ?"

²⁴הִבִּיט וְאָמַר: "אֲנִי רוֹאֶה אֲנָשִׁים; כְּמוֹ עֵצִים אֲנִי רוֹאֶה אוֹתָם מִתְהַלְּכִים." ²⁵סָמַךְ אֶת יָדָיו עַל עֵינָיו שֵׁנִית וְהָאִישׁ רָאָה הֵיטֵב; הוּא נִרְפָּא וְרָאָה אֶת הַכֹּל בְּאֹפֶן בָּרוּר. ²⁶שָׁלַח אוֹתוֹ יֵשׁוּעַ לְבֵיתוֹ בְּאָמְרוֹ: "אַל תִּכָּנֵס לַכְּפָר."

²⁷יֵשׁוּעַ יָצָא עִם תַּלְמִידָיו אֶל הַכְּפָרִים שֶׁבְּאֵזוֹר קֵיסַרְיָה פִילִיפִּי. בַּדֶּרֶךְ שָׁאַל אֶת תַּלְמִידָיו: "מָה אוֹמְרִים הָאֲנָשִׁים עָלַי, מִי אֲנִי?"

²⁸הֵשִׁיבוּ לוֹ וְאָמְרוּ: "יוֹחָנָן הַמַּטְבִּיל'; וְיֵשׁ אוֹמְרִים 'אֵלִיָּהוּ' וַאֲחֵרִים אוֹמְרִים, 'אַחַד הַנְּבִיאִים'."

²⁹שָׁאַל אוֹתָם: "וְאַתֶּם, מָה אַתֶּם אוֹמְרִים – מִי אֲנִי?"

הֵשִׁיב כֵּיפָא וְאָמַר לוֹ: "אַתָּה הַמָּשִׁיחַ."

³⁰הִזְהִיר אוֹתָם יֵשׁוּעַ שֶׁלֹּא יַגִּידוּ עָלָיו לְאִישׁ.

³¹הוּא הֵחֵל לְלַמֵּד אוֹתָם שֶׁבֶּן־הָאָדָם צָרִיךְ לִסְבֹּל הַרְבֵּה, שֶׁהַזְּקֵנִים וְרָאשֵׁי הַכֹּהֲנִים וְהַסּוֹפְרִים יְדָחוּהוּ, שֶׁיֵּהָרֵג וּלְאַחַר שְׁלוֹשָׁה יָמִים יָקוּם. ³²אֶת הַדָּבָר הַזֶּה אָמַר בְּגָלוּי. לָקַח אוֹתוֹ כֵּיפָא הַצִּדָּה וְהֵחֵל לִגְעֹר בּוֹ. ³³אַךְ יֵשׁוּעַ פָּנָה וְהִבִּיט בְּתַלְמִידָיו, גָּעַר בְּכֵיפָא וְאָמַר: "סוּר מִלְּפָנַי, שָׂטָן, כִּי אֵין לִבְּךָ לְדִבְרֵי אֱלֹהִים אֶלָּא לְדִבְרֵי בְּנֵי אָדָם."

³⁴קָרָא אֵלָיו אֶת הֶהָמוֹן עִם תַּלְמִידָיו וְאָמַר לָהֶם: "מִי שֶׁרוֹצֶה לָבוֹא אַחֲרַי, שֶׁיִּתְכַּחֵשׁ לְעַצְמוֹ וְיִקַּח אֶת צְלָבוֹ וְיֵלֵךְ אַחֲרַי; ³⁵כִּי הֶחָפֵץ לְהַצִּיל אֶת נַפְשׁוֹ יְאַבֵּד אוֹתָהּ, אֲבָל הַמְאַבֵּד אֶת נַפְשׁוֹ לְמַעֲנִי וּלְמַעַן הַבְּשׂוֹרָה – יַצִּילֶנָּה. ³⁶מַה תּוֹעֶלֶת תִּצְמַח לְאָדָם אִם יָרְוִיחַ אֶת כָּל הָעוֹלָם וְיַפְסִיד אֶת נַפְשׁוֹ? ³⁷שֶׁכֵּן מַה יִּתֵּן אָדָם כִּתְמוּרָה בְּעַד נַפְשׁוֹ? ³⁸כִּי אִישׁ אֲשֶׁר אֲנִי וּדְבָרַי הָיִינוּ לוֹ לְחֶרְפָּה בַּדּוֹר הַנּוֹאֵף וְהַחוֹטֵא הַזֶּה, גַּם הוּא יִהְיֶה לְחֶרְפָּה לְבֶן־הָאָדָם כַּאֲשֶׁר יָבוֹא בִּכְבוֹד אָבִיו עִם הַמַּלְאָכִים הַקְּדוֹשִׁים."

9 And He said to them, "Assuredly, I say to you that there are some standing here who will not taste death till they see the kingdom of God present with power."

2 Now after six days Jesus took Peter, James, and John, and led them up on a high mountain apart by themselves; and He was transfigured before them. 3 His clothes became shining, exceedingly white, like snow, such as no launderer on earth can whiten them. 4 And Elijah appeared to them with Moses, and they were talking with Jesus. 5 Then Peter answered and said to Jesus, "Rabbi, it is good for us to be here; and let us make three tabernacles: one for You, one for Moses, and one for Elijah"— 6 because he did not know what to say, for they were greatly afraid.

7 And a cloud came and overshadowed them; and a voice came out of the cloud, saying, "This is My beloved Son. Hear Him!" 8 Suddenly, when they had looked around, they saw no one anymore, but only Jesus with themselves.

9 Now as they came down from the mountain, He commanded them that they should tell no one the things they had seen, till the Son of Man had risen from the dead. 10 So they kept this word to themselves, questioning what the rising from the dead meant.

11 And they asked Him, saying, "Why do the scribes say that Elijah must come first?"

12 Then He answered and told them, "Indeed, Elijah is coming first and restores all things. And how is it written concerning the Son of Man, that He must suffer many things and be treated with contempt? 13 But I say to you that Elijah has also come, and they did to him whatever they wished, as it is written of him."

14 And when He came to the disciples, He saw a great multitude around them, and scribes disputing with them. 15 Immediately, when they saw Him, all the people were greatly amazed, and running to *Him,* greeted Him. 16 And He asked the scribes, "What are you discussing with them?"

17 Then one of the crowd answered and said, "Teacher, I brought You my son, who has a mute spirit. 18 And wherever it seizes him, it throws him down; he foams at the mouth, gnashes his teeth, and becomes rigid. So I spoke to Your disciples, that they should cast it out, but they could not."

19 He answered him and said, "O faithless generation, how long shall I be with you? How long shall I bear with you? Bring him to Me." 20 Then they brought him to Him. And when he saw

ט הוֹסִיף וְאָמַר לָהֶם: "אָמֵן אֲנִי אֹמֵר אֲנִי לָכֶם שֶׁיֵּשׁ מִן הָעוֹמְדִים פֹּה אֲשֶׁר לֹא יִטְעֲמוּ מָוֶת עַד כִּי יִרְאוּ אֶת מַלְכוּת הָאֱלֹהִים בָּאָה בִּגְבוּרָה."

2 אַחֲרֵי שֵׁשָׁה יָמִים לָקַח אִתּוֹ יֵשׁוּעַ אֶת כֵּיפָא וְאֶת יַעֲקֹב וְאֶת יוֹחָנָן. הוּא הֶעֱלָה אֹתָם לְהַר גָּבֹהַּ לְבַדָּם וְהִשְׁתַּנָּה לְעֵינֵיהֶם. 3 בְּגָדָיו הִבְרִיקוּ וְהִלְבִּינוּ עַד מְאֹד, עַד כְּדֵי כָּךְ אֵין כּוֹבֵס עֲלֵי אֲדָמוֹת יָכֹל לְהַלְבִּין בְּגָדִים. 4 אָז נִרְאוּ אֲלֵיהֶם אֵלִיָּהוּ וּמֹשֶׁה וְהֵם מְדַבְּרִים עִם יֵשׁוּעַ. 5 הֵגִיב כֵּיפָא וְאָמַר אֶל יֵשׁוּעַ: "רַבִּי, טוֹב שֶׁאָנוּ כָּאן. נַעֲשֶׂה נָא שָׁלוֹשׁ סֻכּוֹת: לְךָ אַחַת, לְמֹשֶׁה אַחַת וּלְאֵלִיָּהוּ אַחַת." 6 הוּא לֹא יָדַע מַה לוֹמַר, שֶׁכֵּן הוּא וַחֲבֵרָיו פָּחֲדוּ מְאֹד. 7 וְהִנֵּה הוֹפִיעַ עָנָן וְסָכַךְ עֲלֵיהֶם. יָצָא קוֹל מִתּוֹךְ הֶעָנָן: "זֶה בְּנִי אֲהוּבִי; אֵלָיו תִּשְׁמָעוּן!" 8 וּפִתְאֹם, בְּהִסְתַּכְּלָם סָבִיב, לֹא רָאוּ עוֹד אִישׁ אִתָּם מִלְּבַד יֵשׁוּעַ.

9 כְּשֶׁיָּרְדוּ מִן הָהָר צִוָּה עֲלֵיהֶם שֶׁלֹּא יַגִּידוּ לְאִישׁ מַה שֶׁרָאוּ עַד אֲשֶׁר יָקוּם בֶּן־הָאָדָם מִן הַמֵּתִים. 10 הֵם שָׁמְרוּ לָהֶם אֶת הַדָּבָר וְחָקְרוּ בֵּינָם לְבֵין עַצְמָם מַה פֵּרוּשׁ "לָקוּם מִן הַמֵּתִים." 11 שָׁאֲלוּ אוֹתוֹ: "מַדּוּעַ אוֹמְרִים הַסּוֹפְרִים כִּי אֵלִיָּהוּ צָרִיךְ לָבוֹא תְּחִלָּה?"

12 הֵשִׁיב לָהֶם: "אֵלִיָּהוּ אָמְנָם יָבוֹא רִאשׁוֹנָה וְיָשִׁיב אֶת הַכֹּל; וְאֵיךְ כָּתוּב עַל בֶּן־הָאָדָם שֶׁיִּסְבֹּל הַרְבֵּה וְיִמְאֲסוּ בּוֹ? 13 בְּרַם אוֹמֵר אֲנִי לָכֶם כִּי אָכֵן בָּא אֵלִיָּהוּ וְעָשׂוּ בּוֹ כִּרְצוֹנָם, כַּכָּתוּב עָלָיו."

14 כַּאֲשֶׁר הֵם בָּאוּ אֶל הַתַּלְמִידִים רָאוּ עַם רַב סָבִיב לָהֶם וְסוֹפְרִים מִתְוַכְּחִים אִתָּם. 15 כָּל הֶהָמוֹן, בְּרֶגַע שֶׁרָאוּ אוֹתוֹ, תָּמְהוּ מְאֹד וְרָצוּ אֵלָיו וּבֵרְכוּהוּ בְּבִרְכַּת שָׁלוֹם. 16 שָׁאַל אוֹתָם: "עַל מָה אַתֶּם מִתְוַכְּחִים אִתָּם?"

17 הֵשִׁיב לוֹ אֶחָד מִן הֶהָמוֹן: "רַבִּי, הֵבֵאתִי אֵלֶיךָ אֶת בְּנִי אֲשֶׁר רוּחַ אִלֶּמֶת בְּקִרְבּוֹ. 18 בְּכָל מָקוֹם הָרוּחַ אוֹחֶזֶת בּוֹ וּמַפִּילָה אוֹתוֹ, וְהוּא מַעֲלֶה קֶצֶף, חוֹרֵק שִׁנָּיו וְגוּפוֹ מִתְקַשֶּׁה. אָמַרְתִּי לְתַלְמִידֶיךָ שֶׁיְּגָרְשׁוּ אוֹתָהּ, אַךְ הֵם לֹא יָכְלוּ."

19 הֵשִׁיב וְאָמַר לָהֶם: "הוֹי דּוֹר חֲסַר אֱמוּנָה, עַד מָתַי אֶהְיֶה עִמָּכֶם? עַד מָתַי אֶסְבֹּל אֶתְכֶם? הָבִיאוּ אוֹתוֹ אֵלַי." 20 הֵבִיאוּ אוֹתוֹ אֵלָיו. רָאֲתָה הָרוּחַ אֶת יֵשׁוּעַ וּמִיָּד זִעְזְעָה אֶת הַיֶּלֶד. הוּא נָפַל אַרְצָה

Him, immediately the spirit convulsed him, and he fell on the ground and wallowed, foaming at the mouth.

21 So He asked his father, "How long has this been happening to him?"

And he said, "From childhood. 22 And often he has thrown him both into the fire and into the water to destroy him. But if You can do anything, have compassion on us and help us."

23 Jesus said to him, "If you can believe, all things *are* possible to him who believes."

24 Immediately the father of the child cried out and said with tears, "Lord, I believe; help my unbelief!"

25 When Jesus saw that the people came running together, He rebuked the unclean spirit, saying to it, "Deaf and dumb spirit, I command you, come out of him and enter him no more!" 26 Then *the spirit* cried out, convulsed him greatly, and came out of him. And he became as one dead, so that many said, "He is dead." 27 But Jesus took him by the hand and lifted him up, and he arose.

28 And when He had come into the house, His disciples asked Him privately, "Why could we not cast it out?"

29 So He said to them, "This kind can come out by nothing but prayer and fasting."

30 Then they departed from there and passed through Galilee, and He did not want anyone to know *it*. 31 For He taught His disciples and said to them, "The Son of Man is being betrayed into the hands of men, and they will kill Him. And after He is killed, He will rise the third day." 32 But they did not understand this saying, and were afraid to ask Him.

33 Then He came to Capernaum. And when He was in the house He asked them, "What was it you disputed among yourselves on the road?" 34 But they kept silent, for on the road they had disputed among themselves who *would be the* greatest. 35 And He sat down, called the twelve, and said to them, "If anyone desires to be first, he shall be last of all and servant of all." 36 Then He took a little child and set him in the midst of them. And when He had taken him in His arms, He said to them, 37 "Whoever receives one of these little children in My name receives Me; and whoever receives Me, receives not Me but Him who sent Me."

38 Now John answered Him, saying, "Teacher, we saw someone who does not follow us casting out demons in Your name, and we forbade him because he does not follow us."

---

21 שָׁאַל יֵשׁוּעַ אֶת אָבִיו: מִתְגּוֹלֵל וּמַעֲלֶה קֶצֶף. "מִמָּתַי זֶה קוֹרֶה לוֹ?"

הֵשִׁיב: "מִקַּטְנוּתוֹ, 22 וּפְעָמִים רַבּוֹת גַּם הִפִּילָה אוֹתוֹ עַל אֵשׁ וּלְתוֹךְ מַיִם כְּדֵי לְהָמִית אוֹתוֹ. אֲבָל אִם אַתָּה יָכוֹל לַעֲשׂוֹת מַשֶּׁהוּ, רַחֵם עָלֵינוּ וַעֲזֹר לָנוּ."

23 אָמַר לוֹ יֵשׁוּעַ: "אִם אַתָּה יָכוֹל'?! הַכֹּל אֶפְשָׁרִי לַמַּאֲמִין!"

24 מִיָּד צָעַק אֲבִי הַיֶּלֶד וְאָמַר: "אֲנִי מַאֲמִין, עֲזֹר נָא לִי בְּחֶסְרוֹן אֱמוּנָתִי!"

25 כְּשֶׁרָאָה יֵשׁוּעַ הָמוֹן עַם רָצִים וּמִתְקַבְּצִים, גָּעַר בְּרוּחַ הַטֻּמְאָה וְאָמַר לָהּ: "רוּחַ אִלֶּמֶת וְחֵרֶשֶׁת, אֲנִי מְצַוֶּךְ, צְאִי מִמֶּנּוּ וְאַל תִּכָּנְסִי בּוֹ עוֹד!"

26 הִיא צָעֲקָה, וְזִעְזְעָה אוֹתוֹ מְאֹד וְיָצְאָה. הוּא הָיָה כְּמֵת וְרַבִּים אָמְרוּ שֶׁהוּא מֵת. 27 אָחַז יֵשׁוּעַ בְּיָדוֹ, הֵקִים אוֹתוֹ וְהוּא קָם. 28 כְּשֶׁנִּכְנַס יֵשׁוּעַ הַבַּיְתָה שָׁאֲלוּהוּ תַּלְמִידָיו בִּיחִידוּת: "מַדּוּעַ לֹא יָכֹלְנוּ אֲנַחְנוּ לְגָרֵשׁ אוֹתָהּ?"

29 הֵשִׁיב לָהֶם: "הַמִּין הַזֶּה אֵינוֹ יָכוֹל לָצֵאת אֶלָּא בִּתְפִלָּה."

30 יָצְאוּ מִשָּׁם וְעָבְרוּ דֶּרֶךְ הַגָּלִיל. הוּא לֹא רָצָה שֶׁזֶּה יֵדַע לְאִישׁ, 31 שֶׁכֵּן לִמֵּד אֶת תַּלְמִידָיו וְאָמַר לָהֶם: "בֶּן-הָאָדָם יִמָּסֵר לִידֵי אֲנָשִׁים, וְיַהַרְגוּהוּ, וּשְׁלוֹשָׁה יָמִים אַחֲרֵי שֶׁיַּהַרְגוּהוּ יָקוּם." 32 אַךְ הֵם לֹא הֵבִינוּ אֶת הַדָּבָר וּפָחֲדוּ לִשְׁאָל אוֹתוֹ.

33 הֵם בָּאוּ לִכְפַר נַחוּם, וּכְשֶׁהָיוּ בַּבַּיִת שָׁאַל אוֹתָם: "עַל מַה הִתְוַכַּחְתֶּם בַּדֶּרֶךְ?"

34 שָׁתְקוּ וְלֹא עָנוּ, שֶׁכֵּן הִתְוַכְּחוּ זֶה עִם זֶה – מִי הַגָּדוֹל שֶׁבָּהֶם. 35 יָשַׁב וְקָרָא לִשְׁנֵים-עָשָׂר וְאָמַר לָהֶם: "מִי שֶׁרוֹצֶה לִהְיוֹת רִאשׁוֹן יְהֵא אַחֲרוֹן לַכֹּל וּמְשָׁרֵת לַכֹּל."

36 לָקַח יֶלֶד וְהֶעֱמִיד אוֹתוֹ בֵּינֵיהֶם, חִבֵּק אוֹתוֹ וְאָמַר לָהֶם: 37 "כָּל הַמְקַבֵּל יֶלֶד אֶחָד כָּזֶה בִּשְׁמִי, אוֹתִי הוּא מְקַבֵּל; וְהַמְקַבֵּל אוֹתִי אֵינוֹ מְקַבֵּל אוֹתִי אֶלָּא אֶת אֲשֶׁר שְׁלָחַנִי."

38 אָמַר לוֹ יוֹחָנָן: "רַבִּי, רָאִינוּ אִישׁ מְגָרֵשׁ שֵׁדִים בִּשְׁמְךָ שֶׁאֵינֶנּוּ הוֹלֵךְ אַחֲרֵינוּ וּמְנַעֲנוּ בַּעֲדוֹ, כִּי אֵינוֹ הוֹלֵךְ אַחֲרֵינוּ."

39 But Jesus said, "Do not forbid him, for no one who works a miracle in My name can soon afterward speak evil of Me. 40 For he who is not against us is on our side. 41 For whoever gives you a cup of water to drink in My name, because you belong to Christ, assuredly, I say to you, he will by no means lose his reward.

42 "But whoever causes one of these little ones who believe in Me to stumble, it would be better for him if a millstone were hung around his neck, and he were thrown into the sea. 43 If your hand causes you to sin, cut it off. It is better for you to enter into life maimed, rather than having two hands, to go to hell, into the fire that shall never be quenched— 44 where

> 'Their worm does not die
> And the fire is not quenched.'

45 And if your foot causes you to sin, cut it off. It is better for you to enter life lame, rather than having two feet, to be cast into hell, into the fire that shall never be quenched— 46 where

> 'Their worm does not die
> And the fire is not quenched.'

47 And if your eye causes you to sin, pluck it out. It is better for you to enter the kingdom of God with one eye, rather than having two eyes, to be cast into hell fire— 48 where

> 'Their worm does not die
> And the fire is not quenched.'

49 "For everyone will be seasoned with fire, and every sacrifice will be seasoned with salt. 50 Salt *is* good, but if the salt loses its flavor, how will you season it? Have salt in yourselves, and have peace with one another."

10 Then He arose from there and came to the region of Judea by the other side of the Jordan. And multitudes gathered to Him again, and as He was accustomed, He taught them again.

2 The Pharisees came and asked Him, "Is it lawful for a man to divorce *his* wife?" testing Him.

3 And He answered and said to them, "What did Moses command you?"

4 They said, "Moses permitted *a man* to write a certificate of divorce, and to dismiss *her*."

5 And Jesus answered and said to them, "Because of the hardness of your heart he wrote you this precept. 6 But from the beginning of the creation, God 'made them male and female.' 7 'For this reason a man shall leave his father and mother and be joined to his wife, 8 and the two shall become one

39 אָמַר יֵשׁוּעַ: "אַל תִּמְנָעוּ בַּעֲדוֹ, כִּי אֵין אִישׁ אֲשֶׁר יַעֲשֶׂה גְּבוּרָה בִּשְׁמִי וּמִיָּד יוּכַל לְדַבֵּר עָלַי רָעוֹת; 40 כִּי מִי שֶׁאֵינוֹ נֶגְדֵּנוּ, אִתָּנוּ הוּא. 41 כָּל הַמַּשְׁקֶה אֶתְכֶם כּוֹס מַיִם מִשּׁוּם הֱיוֹתְכֶם שֶׁל הַמָּשִׁיחַ, אָמֵן אֲנִי אוֹמֵר לָכֶם שֶׁלֹּא יֹאבַד שְׂכָרוֹ."

42 "וְכָל הַמַּכְשִׁיל אֶחָד מִן הַקְּטַנִּים הָאֵלֶּה הַמַּאֲמִינִים, מוּטָב לוֹ שֶׁתֻּנַּח אֶבֶן רֵחַיִם עַל צַוָּארוֹ וְיֻשְׁלַךְ לַיָּם. 43 אִם יָדְךָ תַּכְשִׁיל אוֹתְךָ, קַצֵּץ אוֹתָהּ. מוּטָב לְךָ לָבוֹא לַחַיִּים גִּדֵּם מֵאֲשֶׁר לָבוֹא עִם שְׁתֵּי יָדַיִם לְגֵיהִנּוֹם, אֶל הָאֵשׁ אֲשֶׁר לֹא תִכְבֶּה. 45 וְאִם רַגְלְךָ תַּכְשִׁיל אוֹתְךָ, קַצֵּץ אוֹתָהּ. מוּטָב לְךָ לָבוֹא לַחַיִּים קִטֵּעַ מֵאֲשֶׁר לִהְיוֹת מֻשְׁלָךְ לְגֵיהִנּוֹם עִם שְׁתֵּי רַגְלַיִם. 47 אִם עֵינְךָ תַּכְשִׁיל אוֹתְךָ, עֲקֹר אוֹתָהּ. מוּטָב לְךָ לָבוֹא לְמַלְכוּת אֱלֹהִים עִם עַיִן אַחַת מֵאֲשֶׁר לִהְיוֹת מֻשְׁלָךְ לְגֵיהִנּוֹם עִם שְׁתֵּי עֵינַיִם, 48 בְּמָקוֹם אֲשֶׁר תּוֹלַעְתָּם לֹא תָמוּת וְאִשָּׁם לֹא תִכְבֶּה. 49 הֵן כָּל אֶחָד יְמֻלַּח בָּאֵשׁ. 50 הַמֶּלַח טוֹב הוּא, אַךְ אִם תֹּאבַד לוֹ מְלִיחוּתוֹ, כֵּיצַד תָּשִׁיבוּ לוֹ אֶת טַעֲמוֹ? יְהָא מֶלַח בְּקִרְבְּכֶם וִהְיוּ בְּשָׁלוֹם זֶה עִם זֶה."

י הוּא קָם וְהָלַךְ מִשָּׁם אֶל אֵזוֹר יְהוּדָה וְאֶל עֵבֶר הַיַּרְדֵּן. שׁוּב נִקְבְּצוּ אֵלָיו הֲמוֹנִים וּכְמִנְהָגוֹ שׁוּב לִמֵּד אוֹתָם. 2 נִגְּשׁוּ הַפְּרוּשִׁים לְנַסּוֹתוֹ וְשָׁאֲלוּ אוֹתוֹ: "הַאִם מֻתָּר לְאִישׁ לְגָרֵשׁ אֶת אִשְׁתּוֹ?"

3 עָנָה וְאָמַר לָהֶם: "מַה צִוָּה אֶתְכֶם מֹשֶׁה?" 4 הֵשִׁיבוּ: "מֹשֶׁה הִתִּיר לִכְתֹּב סֵפֶר כְּרִיתוּת וּלְגָרֵשׁ." 5 אָמַר לָהֶם יֵשׁוּעַ: "בִּגְלַל קְשִׁי לְבַבְכֶם כָּתַב לָכֶם אֶת הַמִּצְוָה הַזֹּאת, 6 אֲבָל מֵרֵאשִׁית הַבְּרִיאָה 'זָכָר וּנְקֵבָה בָּרָא אֹתָם. 7 עַל־כֵּן יַעֲזָב אִישׁ אֶת־אָבִיו וְאֶת־אִמּוֹ [וְדָבַק בְּאִשְׁתּוֹ] 8 וְהָיוּ שְׁנֵיהֶם לְבָשָׂר אֶחָד.' וּבְכֵן אֵינָם עוֹד שְׁנַיִם אֶלָּא בָּשָׂר אֶחָד.

flesh'; so then they are no longer two, but one flesh.
⁹Therefore what God has joined together, let not man separate."

¹⁰In the house His disciples also asked Him again about the same *matter*. ¹¹So He said to them, "Whoever divorces his wife and marries another commits adultery against her. ¹²And if a woman divorces her husband and marries another, she commits adultery."

¹³Then they brought little children to Him, that He might touch them; but the disciples rebuked those who brought *them*. ¹⁴But when Jesus saw *it*, He was greatly displeased and said to them, "Let the little children come to Me, and do not forbid them; for of such is the kingdom of God. ¹⁵Assuredly, I say to you, whoever does not receive the kingdom of God as a little child will by no means enter it." ¹⁶And He took them up in His arms, laid *His* hands on them, and blessed them.

¹⁷Now as He was going out on the road, one came running, knelt before Him, and asked Him, "Good Teacher, what shall I do that I may inherit eternal life?"

¹⁸So Jesus said to him, "Why do you call Me good? No one *is* good but One, *that is,* God. ¹⁹You know the commandments: 'Do not commit adultery,' 'Do not murder,' 'Do not steal,' 'Do not bear false witness,' 'Do not defraud,' 'Honor your father and your mother.'"

²⁰And he answered and said to Him, "Teacher, all these things I have kept from my youth."

²¹Then Jesus, looking at him, loved him, and said to him, "One thing you lack: Go your way, sell whatever you have and give to the poor, and you will have treasure in heaven; and come, take up the cross, and follow Me."

²²But he was sad at this word, and went away sorrowful, for he had great possessions.

²³Then Jesus looked around and said to His disciples, "How hard it is for those who have riches to enter the kingdom of God!" ²⁴And the disciples were astonished at His words. But Jesus answered again and said to them, "Children, how hard it is for those who trust in riches to enter the kingdom of God! ²⁵It is easier for a camel to go through the eye of a needle than for a rich man to enter the kingdom of God."

²⁶And they were greatly astonished, saying among themselves, "Who then can be saved?"

²⁷But Jesus looked at them and said, "With men *it is* impossible, but not with God; for with God all things are possible."

²⁸Then Peter began to say to Him, "See, we have left all and followed You."

⁹ לְפִיכָךְ מַה שֶּׁחִבֵּר אֱלֹהִים אַל יַפְרִיד אָדָם."

¹⁰ כְּשֶׁהָיוּ בַּבַּיִת שָׁאֲלוּ אוֹתוֹ גַּם הַתַּלְמִידִים עַל זֹאת.

¹¹ אָמַר לָהֶם: "כָּל הַמְגָרֵשׁ אֶת אִשְׁתּוֹ וְנוֹשֵׂא אַחֶרֶת נוֹאֵף הוּא. ¹² וְאִם הִיא תְּגָרֵשׁ אֶת בַּעְלָהּ וְתִנָּשֵׂא לְאַחֵר נוֹאֶפֶת הִיא."

¹³ הֵבִיאוּ אֵלָיו יְלָדִים כְּדֵי שֶׁיִּגַּע בָּהֶם, אַךְ הַתַּלְמִידִים גָּעֲרוּ בָּהֶם. ¹⁴ רָאָה יֵשׁוּעַ וְהִתְכַּעֵס. אָמַר לָהֶם: "הַנִּיחוּ לַיְלָדִים לָבוֹא אֵלַי, אַל תִּמְנְעוּ בַּעֲדָם, כִּי לְכָאֵלֶּה מַלְכוּת הָאֱלֹהִים. ¹⁵ אָמֵן אוֹמֵר אֲנִי לָכֶם, כָּל מִי שֶׁאֵינֶנּוּ מְקַבֵּל אֶת מַלְכוּת הָאֱלֹהִים כְּיֶלֶד לֹא יִכָּנֵס לְתוֹכָהּ." ¹⁶ הוּא חִבֵּק אוֹתָם וּבֵרְכָם בְּשִׂימוֹ אֶת יָדָיו עֲלֵיהֶם.

¹⁷ בְּצֵאתוֹ לַדֶּרֶךְ רָץ אֵלָיו אִישׁ אֶחָד, כָּרַע לְפָנָיו וְשָׁאַל אוֹתוֹ: "רַבִּי הַטּוֹב, מֶה עָלַי לַעֲשׂוֹת כְּדֵי לָרֶשֶׁת חַיֵּי עוֹלָם?"

¹⁸ אָמַר לוֹ יֵשׁוּעַ: "מַדּוּעַ אַתָּה קוֹרֵא לִי 'טוֹב'? אֵין טוֹב כִּי אִם אֶחָד וְהוּא הָאֱלֹהִים. ¹⁹ אֶת הַמִּצְווֹת אַתָּה יוֹדֵעַ: לֹא תִרְצַח, לֹא תִנְאָף, לֹא תִגְנֹב, לֹא תַעֲנֶה בְרֵעֲךָ עֵד שָׁקֶר, לֹא תַעֲשֹׁק, כַּבֵּד אֶת־אָבִיךָ וְאֶת־אִמֶּךָ."

²⁰ הֵשִׁיב לוֹ: "רַבִּי, אֶת כָּל אֵלֶּה שָׁמַרְתִּי מִנְּעוּרַי."

²¹ הִבִּיט בּוֹ יֵשׁוּעַ וְרָחַשׁ לוֹ אַהֲבָה. אָמַר אֵלָיו: "דָּבָר אֶחָד חָסֵר לְךָ. לֵךְ מְכֹר מַה שֶּׁיֵּשׁ לְךָ וְתֵן לָעֲנִיִּים, וְיִהְיֶה לְךָ אוֹצָר בַּשָּׁמַיִם; אַחַר כָּךְ בּוֹא וְלֵךְ אַחֲרַי." ²² לְשֵׁמַע הַדָּבָר נָפְלוּ פָּנָיו וְהוּא הָלַךְ מִשָּׁם עָצוּב, שֶׁכֵּן הָיוּ לוֹ נְכָסִים רַבִּים. ²³ הִבִּיט יֵשׁוּעַ סָבִיב וְאָמַר לְתַלְמִידָיו: "בְּאֵיזֶה קֹשִׁי יִכָּנְסוּ הָעֲשִׁירִים לְמַלְכוּת הָאֱלֹהִים!"

²⁴ נִדְהֲמוּ הַתַּלְמִידִים בִּגְלַל דְּבָרָיו, אַךְ יֵשׁוּעַ הֵגִיב בְּאָמְרוֹ לָהֶם שֵׁנִית: "בָּנַי, כַּמָּה קָשֶׁה לַבּוֹטְחִים בָּעֹשֶׁר לְהִכָּנֵס לְמַלְכוּת הָאֱלֹהִים! ²⁵ נָקֵל לְגָמָל לַעֲבֹר דֶּרֶךְ נֶקֶב מַחַט מֵהִכָּנֵס עָשִׁיר אֶל מַלְכוּת הָאֱלֹהִים."

²⁶ הֵם הִשְׁתּוֹמְמוּ עַד מְאֹד וְאָמְרוּ זֶה אֶל זֶה: "וּמִי יָכוֹל לְהִוָּשַׁע?"

²⁷ הִבִּיט בָּהֶם יֵשׁוּעַ וְאָמַר: "מִבְּנֵי אָדָם נִבְצָר הַדָּבָר, אַךְ לֹא מֵאֱלֹהִים; כִּי הָאֱלֹהִים כֹּל יָכוֹל."

²⁸ הֵחֵל כֵּיפָא לוֹמַר לוֹ: "הִנֵּה אֲנַחְנוּ עָזַבְנוּ הַכֹּל וְהָלַכְנוּ אַחֲרֶיךָ."

²⁹ So Jesus answered and said, "Assuredly, I say to you, there is no one who has left house or brothers or sisters or father or mother or wife or children or lands, for My sake and the gospel's, ³⁰ who shall not receive a hundredfold now in this time—houses and brothers and sisters and mothers and children and lands, with persecutions—and in the age to come, eternal life. ³¹ But many *who are* first will be last, and the last first."

³² Now they were on the road, going up to Jerusalem, and Jesus was going before them; and they were amazed. And as they followed they were afraid. Then He took the twelve aside again and began to tell them the things that would happen to Him: ³³ "Behold, we are going up to Jerusalem, and the Son of Man will be betrayed to the chief priests and to the scribes; and they will condemn Him to death and deliver Him to the Gentiles; ³⁴ and they will mock Him, and scourge Him, and spit on Him, and kill Him. And the third day He will rise again."

³⁵ Then James and John, the sons of Zebedee, came to Him, saying, "Teacher, we want You to do for us whatever we ask."

³⁶ And He said to them, "What do you want Me to do for you?"

³⁷ They said to Him, "Grant us that we may sit, one on Your right hand and the other on Your left, in Your glory."

³⁸ But Jesus said to them, "You do not know what you ask. Are you able to drink the cup that I drink, and be baptized with the baptism that I am baptized with?"

³⁹ They said to Him, "We are able."

So Jesus said to them, "You will indeed drink the cup that I drink, and with the baptism I am baptized with you will be baptized; ⁴⁰ but to sit on My right hand and on My left is not Mine to give, but *it is for those* for whom it is prepared."

⁴¹ And when the ten heard *it,* they began to be greatly displeased with James and John. ⁴² But Jesus called them to *Himself* and said to them, "You know that those who are considered rulers over the Gentiles lord it over them, and their great ones exercise authority over them. ⁴³ Yet it shall not be so among you; but whoever desires to become great among you shall be your servant. ⁴⁴ And whoever of you desires to be first shall be slave of all. ⁴⁵ For even the Son of Man did not come to be served, but to serve, and to give His life a ransom for many."

⁴⁶ Now they came to Jericho. As He went out of Jericho with His disciples and a great multitude, blind Bartimaeus, the son of Timaeus, sat by the

²⁹ אָמַר יֵשׁוּעַ: "אָמֵן, אוֹמֵר אֲנִי לָכֶם, אֵין אִישׁ אֲשֶׁר עָזַב בַּיִת אוֹ אַחִים אוֹ אֲחָיוֹת אוֹ אֵם אוֹ אָב אוֹ בָּנִים אוֹ שָׂדוֹת לְמַעֲנִי וּלְמַעַן הַבְּשׂוֹרָה, ³⁰ שֶׁלֹּא יְקַבֵּל כָּעֵת, בַּזְּמַן הַזֶּה, פִּי מֵאָה: בָּתִּים וְאַחִים וַאֲחָיוֹת וְאִמָּהוֹת וּבָנִים וְשָׂדוֹת, עִם רְדִיפוֹת, וּבָעוֹלָם הַבָּא – חַיֵּי עוֹלָם. ³¹ אֲבָל רִאשׁוֹנִים הַרְבֵּה יִהְיוּ אַחֲרוֹנִים וְאַחֲרוֹנִים הַרְבֵּה – רִאשׁוֹנִים."

³² הֵם הָיוּ בַּדֶּרֶךְ, עוֹלִים לִירוּשָׁלַיִם, וְיֵשׁוּעַ הוֹלֵךְ לִפְנֵיהֶם. חֲרָדָה קָנְנָה בְּלִבָּם וְהַהוֹלְכִים אַחֲרֵיהֶם פָּחֲדוּ. לָקַח שׁוּב אֶת הַשְּׁנֵים-עָשָׂר וְהֵחֵל לְהַגִּיד לָהֶם מַה שֶּׁעָתִיד לִקְרוֹת לוֹ: ³³ "הִנֵּה אֲנַחְנוּ עוֹלִים לִירוּשָׁלַיִם וּבֶן-הָאָדָם יִמָּסֵר לְרָאשֵׁי הַכֹּהֲנִים וְלַסּוֹפְרִים. הֵם יַחְרְצוּ אֶת דִּינוֹ לַמָּוֶת וְיִמְסְרוּ אוֹתוֹ לַגּוֹיִים. ³⁴ הַלָּלוּ יְהָתְלוּ בּוֹ וְיִירְקוּ בּוֹ, יַלְקוּ אוֹתוֹ וְיַהַרְגוּהוּ, וְאַחֲרֵי שְׁלוֹשָׁה יָמִים יָקוּם."

³⁵ נִגְּשׁוּ אֵלָיו יַעֲקֹב וְיוֹחָנָן בְּנֵי זַבְדַּי וְאָמְרוּ לוֹ: "רַבִּי, חֲפֵצִים אָנוּ שֶׁתַּעֲשֶׂה לְמַעֲנֵנוּ מַה שֶּׁנְּבַקֵּשׁ מִמְּךָ."

³⁶ שָׁאַל אוֹתָם: "מָה אַתֶּם רוֹצִים שֶׁאֶעֱשֶׂה לְמַעַנְכֶם?"

³⁷ הֵשִׁיבוּ לוֹ: "תֵּן לָנוּ לָשֶׁבֶת אֶחָד לִימִינְךָ וְאֶחָד לִשְׂמֹאלְךָ בְּתִפְאֶרֶת כְּבוֹדֶךָ."

³⁸ אָמַר לָהֶם יֵשׁוּעַ: "אֵינְכֶם יוֹדְעִים מַה שֶּׁאַתֶּם מְבַקְשִׁים. הַאִם יְכוֹלִים אַתֶּם לִשְׁתּוֹת אֶת הַכּוֹס שֶׁאֲנִי שׁוֹתֶה אוֹ לְהִטָּבֵל בַּטְּבִילָה שֶׁאֲנִי נִטְבָּל?"

³⁹ אָמְרוּ לוֹ: "אֲנַחְנוּ יְכוֹלִים." הֵשִׁיב לָהֶם יֵשׁוּעַ: "אֶת הַכּוֹס שֶׁאֲנִי שׁוֹתֶה תִּשְׁתּוּ וּבַטְּבִילָה שֶׁאֲנִי נִטְבָּל תִּטָּבְלוּ, ⁴⁰ אַךְ לָשֶׁבֶת לִימִינִי אוֹ לִשְׂמֹאלִי אֵין בְּיָדִי לָתֵת אֶלָּא לַאֲשֶׁר הוּכַן לָהֶם."

⁴¹ שָׁמְעוּ הָעֲשָׂרָה וְהֵחֵלּוּ לִכְעֹס עַל יַעֲקֹב וְיוֹחָנָן. ⁴² קָרָא לָהֶם יֵשׁוּעַ וְאָמַר לָהֶם: "אַתֶּם יוֹדְעִים שֶׁאֵלֶּה הַנֶּחְשָׁבִים לְמוֹשְׁלִים בַּגּוֹיִים רוֹדִים בָּהֶם וְהַגְּדוֹלִים שֶׁבָּהֶם שׁוֹלְטִים בָּהֶם. ⁴³ אַל יְהִי כֵן בֵּינֵיכֶם. אַדְּרַבָּא, הֶחָפֵץ לִהְיוֹת גָּדוֹל בָּכֶם יְהֵא מְשָׁרֵת שֶׁלָּכֶם, ⁴⁴ וְהֶחָפֵץ לִהְיוֹת רִאשׁוֹן בֵּינֵיכֶם יְהֵא עֶבֶד לַכֹּל; ⁴⁵ כִּי גַם בֶּן-הָאָדָם לֹא בָּא כְּדֵי שֶׁיְּשָׁרְתוּהוּ אֶלָּא כְּדֵי לְשָׁרֵת וְלָתֵת אֶת נַפְשׁוֹ כֹּפֶר בְּעַד רַבִּים."

⁴⁶ הֵם בָּאוּ לִירִיחוֹ. כַּאֲשֶׁר יָצָא מִירִיחוֹ הוּא וְתַלְמִידָיו וַהֲמוֹן עַם רַב, יָשַׁב עַל-יַד הַדֶּרֶךְ עִוֵּר

road begging. ⁴⁷ And when he heard that it was
Jesus of Nazareth, he began to cry out and say,
"Jesus, Son of David, have mercy on me!"

⁴⁸ Then many warned him to be quiet; but he
cried out all the more, "Son of David, have mercy
on me!"

⁴⁹ So Jesus stood still and commanded him to be
called.

Then they called the blind man, saying to him,
"Be of good cheer. Rise, He is calling you."

⁵⁰ And throwing aside his garment, he rose and
came to Jesus.

⁵¹ So Jesus answered and said to him, "What do
you want Me to do for you?"

The blind man said to Him, "Rabboni, that I
may receive my sight."

⁵² Then Jesus said to him, "Go your way; your
faith has made you well." And immediately he
received his sight and followed Jesus on the road.

11 Now when they drew near Jerusalem, to
Bethphage and Bethany, at the Mount of Olives, He
sent two of His disciples; ² and He said to them,
"Go into the village opposite you; and as soon as
you have entered it you will find a colt tied, on
which no one has sat. Loose it and bring it. ³ And if
anyone says to you, 'Why are you doing this?' say,
'The Lord has need of it,' and immediately he will
send it here."

⁴ So they went their way, and found the colt tied
by the door outside on the street, and they loosed it.
⁵ But some of those who stood there said to them,
"What are you doing, loosing the colt?"

⁶ And they spoke to them just as Jesus had
commanded. So they let them go. ⁷ Then they
brought the colt to Jesus and threw their clothes on
it, and He sat on it. ⁸ And many spread their clothes
on the road, and others cut down leafy branches
from the trees and spread them on the road. ⁹ Then
those who went before and those who followed
cried out, saying:

"Hosanna!
'Blessed is He who comes in the name of the
LORD!'
¹⁰   Blessed is the kingdom of our father David
That comes in the name of the Lord!
Hosanna in the highest!"

¹¹ And Jesus went into Jerusalem and into the
temple. So when He had looked around at all
things, as the hour was already late, He went out to
Bethany with the twelve.

קַבְּצָן, בַּרְטִימַי בְּנוֹ שֶׁל טִימַי. ⁴⁷ שָׁמַע בַּרְטִימַי כִּי
יֵשׁוּעַ מִנָּצְרַת הוּא וְהֵחֵל לִצְעֹק: "בֶּן־דָּוִד, יֵשׁוּעַ,
רַחֵם עָלַי!" ⁴⁸ אָז גָּעֲרוּ בּוֹ רַבִּים לְהַשְׁתִּיקוֹ, אַךְ הוּא
הִרְבָּה עוֹד יוֹתֵר לִצְעֹק: "בֶּן־דָּוִד, רַחֵם עָלַי!"
⁴⁹ נֶעֱצַר יֵשׁוּעַ וְאָמַר: "קִרְאוּ לוֹ." קָרְאוּ לָעִוֵּר וְאָמְרוּ
לוֹ: "הִתְעוֹדֵד, קוּם. הוּא קוֹרֵא לָךְ." ⁵⁰ הִשְׁלִיךְ
מֵעָלָיו אֶת מְעִילוֹ, קָם מִיָּד וּבָא אֶל יֵשׁוּעַ. ⁵¹ הֵשִׁיב
לוֹ יֵשׁוּעַ וְאָמַר: "מָה אַתָּה רוֹצֶה שֶׁאֶעֱשֶׂה לְּךָ?"
אָמַר לוֹ הָעִוֵּר: "רַבִּי, שֶׁאֶרְאֶה!"
⁵² אָמַר לוֹ יֵשׁוּעַ: "לֵךְ, אֱמוּנָתְךָ הוֹשִׁיעָה אוֹתְךָ."
בּוֹ בָּרֶגַע רָאָה וְהָלַךְ אַחֲרָיו בַּדֶּרֶךְ.

יא כַּאֲשֶׁר הִתְקָרְבוּ לִירוּשָׁלַיִם אֶל בֵּית פַּגֵּי וּבֵית
עַנְיָה שֶׁבְּהַר הַזֵּיתִים, שָׁלַח שְׁנַיִם מִתַּלְמִידָיו. ² אָמַר
לָהֶם: "לְכוּ אֶל הַכְּפָר אֲשֶׁר מִמּוּלְכֶם; בְּרֶגַע
שֶׁתִּכָּנְסוּ אֵלָיו תִּמְצְאוּ עַיִר קָשׁוּר אֲשֶׁר לֹא יָשַׁב
עָלָיו אָדָם מֵעוֹלָם. הַתִּירוּ אוֹתוֹ וַהֲבִיאוּהוּ. ³ וְאִם
מִישֶׁהוּ יֹאמַר לָכֶם 'לָמָּה אַתֶּם עוֹשִׂים זֹאת?' אִמְרוּ,
'הָאָדוֹן זָקוּק לוֹ וּמִיָּד יִשְׁלַח אוֹתוֹ הֵנָּה בַּחֲזָרָה.'"
⁴ הֵם הָלְכוּ וּמָצְאוּ עַיִר קָשׁוּר אֶל שַׁעַר מִבַּחוּץ,
בָּרְחוֹב. ⁵ כַּמָּה מִן הָעוֹמְדִים שָׁם אָמְרוּ לָהֶם: "מָה
אַתֶּם עוֹשִׂים? לָמָּה אַתֶּם מַתִּירִים אֶת הָעַיִר?"
⁶ הֵשִׁיבוּ לָהֶם כְּפִי שֶׁאָמַר יֵשׁוּעַ וְהַלָּלוּ הִנִּיחוּ לָהֶם.
⁷ הֵבִיאוּ אֶת הָעַיִר אֶל יֵשׁוּעַ, שָׂמוּ עַל הָעַיִר אֶת
בִּגְדֵיהֶם וְיֵשׁוּעַ יָשַׁב עָלָיו. ⁸ רַבִּים פָּרְשׂוּ אֶת בִּגְדֵיהֶם
עַל הַדֶּרֶךְ וַאֲחֵרִים פָּרְשׂוּ עֲנָפִים שֶׁכָּרְתוּ בַּשָּׂדוֹת.
⁹ וְהַהוֹלְכִים לְפָנָיו וְאַחֲרָיו קָרְאוּ:

"הוֹשַׁע־נָא! בָּרוּךְ הַבָּא בְּשֵׁם יהוה!
¹⁰ תְּבֹרַךְ מַלְכוּת דָּוִד אָבִינוּ הַבָּאָה עָלֵינוּ!
הוֹשַׁע־נָא בַּמְּרוֹמִים!"

¹¹ הוּא נִכְנַס לִירוּשָׁלַיִם אֶל בֵּית הַמִּקְדָּשׁ וְהִתְבּוֹנֵן
סָבִיב בַּכֹּל. כֵּיוָן שֶׁהַשָּׁעָה כְּבָר הָיְתָה מְאֻחֶרֶת יָצָא
אֶל בֵּית עַנְיָה עִם הַשְּׁנֵים־עָשָׂר.

¹² Now the next day, when they had come out from Bethany, He was hungry. ¹³ And seeing from afar a fig tree having leaves, He went to see if perhaps He would find something on it. When He came to it, He found nothing but leaves, for it was not the season for figs. ¹⁴ In response Jesus said to it, "Let no one eat fruit from you ever again."

And His disciples heard *it*.

¹⁵ So they came to Jerusalem. Then Jesus went into the temple and began to drive out those who bought and sold in the temple, and overturned the tables of the money changers and the seats of those who sold doves. ¹⁶ And He would not allow anyone to carry wares through the temple. ¹⁷ Then He taught, saying to them, "Is it not written, '*My house shall be called a house of prayer for all nations*'? But you have made it a '*den of thieves.*'"

¹⁸ And the scribes and chief priests heard it and sought how they might destroy Him; for they feared Him, because all the people were astonished at His teaching. ¹⁹ When evening had come, He went out of the city.

²⁰ Now in the morning, as they passed by, they saw the fig tree dried up from the roots. ²¹ And Peter, remembering, said to Him, "Rabbi, look! The fig tree which You cursed has withered away."

²² So Jesus answered and said to them, "Have faith in God. ²³ For assuredly, I say to you, whoever says to this mountain, 'Be removed and be cast into the sea,' and does not doubt in his heart, but believes that those things he says will be done, he will have whatever he says. ²⁴ Therefore I say to you, whatever things you ask when you pray, believe that you receive *them*, and you will have *them*.

²⁵ "And whenever you stand praying, if you have anything against anyone, forgive him, that your Father in heaven may also forgive you your trespasses. ²⁶ But if you do not forgive, neither will your Father in heaven forgive your trespasses."

²⁷ Then they came again to Jerusalem. And as He was walking in the temple, the chief priests, the scribes, and the elders came to Him. ²⁸ And they said to Him, "By what authority are You doing these things? And who gave You this authority to do these things?"

²⁹ But Jesus answered and said to them, "I also will ask you one question; then answer Me, and I will tell you by what authority I do these things: ³⁰ The baptism of John—was it from heaven or from men? Answer Me."

³¹ And they reasoned among themselves, saying, "If we say, 'From heaven,' He will say, 'Why then did you not believe him?' ³² But if we say, 'From

¹² לְמָחֳרָת, אַחֲרֵי צֵאתָם מִבֵּית עַנְיָה, הָיָה רָעֵב. ¹³ הוּא רָאָה מֵרָחוֹק עֵץ תְּאֵנָה שֶׁיֵּשׁ בּוֹ עָלִים וְהִתְקָרֵב אֵלָיו – אוּלַי יִמְצָא בּוֹ מַשֶּׁהוּ. נִגַּשׁ אֶל הָעֵץ וְלֹא מָצָא מְאוּמָה מִלְּבַד עָלִים, כִּי טֶרֶם הִגִּיעָה עוֹנַת הַתְּאֵנִים. ¹⁴ הֵגִיב וְאָמַר אֶל הָעֵץ: "מֵעַתָּה אִישׁ לֹא יֹאכַל מִמְּךָ פְּרִי לְעוֹלָם!" וְתַלְמִידָיו שָׁמְעוּ.

¹⁵ הֵם בָּאוּ לִירוּשָׁלַיִם. כְּשֶׁנִּכְנַס לְבֵית הַמִּקְדָּשׁ הֵחֵל לְגָרֵשׁ אֶת הַמּוֹכְרִים וְהַקּוֹנִים בְּבֵית הַמִּקְדָּשׁ, הָפַךְ אֶת שֻׁלְחֲנוֹת הַחַלְפָנִים וְאֶת כִּסְאוֹת מוֹכְרֵי הַיּוֹנִים. ¹⁶ וְלֹא הִנִּיחַ לְאִישׁ לְהַעֲבִיר כְּלִי דֶּרֶךְ בֵּית הַמִּקְדָּשׁ. ¹⁷ לִמֵּד אוֹתָם וְאָמַר לָהֶם: "הֲלֹא כָתוּב, 'בֵּיתִי בֵּית־תְּפִלָּה יִקָּרֵא לְכָל־הָעַמִּים', אַךְ אַתֶּם עֲשִׂיתֶם אוֹתוֹ לִמְעָרַת פָּרִיצִים."

¹⁸ שָׁמְעוּ רָאשֵׁי הַכֹּהֲנִים וְהַסּוֹפְרִים וְחִפְּשׂוּ דֶּרֶךְ לְהַכְחִיד אוֹתוֹ, כִּי פָּחֲדוּ מִמֶּנּוּ, שֶׁכֵּן כָּל הֶהָמוֹן הִתְפַּעֵל מִתּוֹרָתוֹ. ¹⁹ לְעֵת עֶרֶב יָצָא אֶל מִחוּץ לָעִיר.

²⁰ בַּבֹּקֶר עָבְרוּ וְרָאוּ אֶת עֵץ הַתְּאֵנָה יָבֵשׁ מִשָּׁרָשָׁיו. ²¹ נִזְכַּר כֵּיפָא וְאָמַר אֵלָיו: "רַבִּי, רְאֵה, עֵץ הַתְּאֵנָה שֶׁקִּלַּלְתָּ יָבֵשׁ!"

²² הֵשִׁיב יֵשׁוּעַ וְאָמַר לָהֶם: "תְּהֵא נָא בָּכֶם אֱמוּנַת אֱלֹהִים. ²³ אָמֵן אוֹמֵר אֲנִי לָכֶם, כָּל הָאוֹמֵר לָהָר הַזֶּה 'הֵעָקֵר וְהִזָּרֵק לְתוֹךְ הַיָּם' וְאֵינוֹ מְפַקְפֵּק בְּלִבּוֹ אֶלָּא מַאֲמִין שֶׁיִּתְקַיֵּם דְּבָרוֹ, כֵּן יִהְיֶה לוֹ. ²⁴ לָכֵן אוֹמֵר אֲנִי לָכֶם, כָּל מַה שֶּׁתְּבַקְשׁוּ בִּתְפִלָּה – הַאֲמִינוּ שֶׁקִּבַּלְתֶּם אוֹתוֹ, וְיִהְיֶה לָכֶם. ²⁵ וְכַאֲשֶׁר אַתֶּם עוֹמְדִים בִּתְפִלָּה וְיֵשׁ לָכֶם דָּבָר נֶגֶד מִישֶׁהוּ – סִלְחוּ, כְּדֵי שֶׁגַּם אֲבִיכֶם שֶׁבַּשָּׁמַיִם יִסְלַח לָכֶם עַל חֲטָאֵיכֶם."

²⁷ הֵם חָזְרוּ לִירוּשָׁלַיִם. כַּאֲשֶׁר הִתְהַלֵּךְ בְּבֵית הַמִּקְדָּשׁ בָּאוּ אֵלָיו רָאשֵׁי הַכֹּהֲנִים וְהַסּוֹפְרִים וְהַזְּקֵנִים. ²⁸ שָׁאֲלוּ אוֹתוֹ: "בְּאֵיזוֹ סַמְכוּת אַתָּה עוֹשֶׂה אֶת הַדְּבָרִים הָאֵלֶּה; מִי נָתַן לְךָ אֶת הַסַּמְכוּת הַזֹּאת לַעֲשׂוֹת אוֹתָם?"

²⁹ הֵשִׁיב לָהֶם יֵשׁוּעַ: "אֶשְׁאַל אֶתְכֶם דָּבָר אֶחָד וְהָשִׁיבוּ לִי, וְאֹמַר לָכֶם בְּאֵיזוֹ סַמְכוּת אֲנִי עוֹשֶׂה אֶת אֵלֶּה. ³⁰ טְבִילַת יוֹחָנָן הַאִם מִן הַשָּׁמַיִם הָיְתָה אוֹ מִבְּנֵי אָדָם? הָשִׁיבוּ לִי!"

³¹ אָמְרוּ זֶה אֶל זֶה: "אִם נֹאמַר 'מִן הַשָּׁמַיִם', יֹאמַר 'אִם כֵּן מַדּוּעַ לֹא הֶאֱמַנְתֶּם לוֹ?' ³² אַךְ אִם נֹאמַר

men'"—they feared the people, for all counted
John to have been a prophet indeed. [33] So they
answered and said to Jesus, "We do not know."

And Jesus answered and said to them, "Neither
will I tell you by what authority I do these things."

12 Then He began to speak to them in parables:
"A man planted a vineyard and set a hedge around
it, dug *a place for* the wine vat and built a tower.
And he leased it to vinedressers and went into a far
country. [2] Now at vintage-time he sent a servant to
the vinedressers, that he might receive some of the
fruit of the vineyard from the vinedressers. [3] And
they took *him* and beat him and sent *him* away
empty-handed. [4] Again he sent them another
servant, and at him they threw stones, wounded
him in the head, and sent *him* away shamefully
treated. [5] And again he sent another, and him they
killed; and many others, beating some and killing
some. [6] Therefore still having one son, his beloved,
he also sent him to them last, saying, 'They will
respect my son.' [7] But those vinedressers said
among themselves, 'This is the heir. Come, let us
kill him, and the inheritance will be ours.' [8] So they
took him and killed *him* and cast *him* out of the
vineyard.

[9] "Therefore what will the owner of the vineyard
do? He will come and destroy the vinedressers, and
give the vineyard to others. [10] Have you not even
read this Scripture:

'The stone which the builders rejected
    Has become the chief cornerstone.
[11]   This was the LORD's doing,
    And it is marvelous in our eyes'?"

[12] And they sought to lay hands on Him, but
feared the multitude, for they knew He had spoken
the parable against them. So they left Him and went
away.

[13] Then they sent to Him some of the Pharisees
and the Herodians, to catch Him in *His* words.
[14] When they had come, they said to Him,
"Teacher, we know that You are true, and care
about no one; for You do not regard the person of
men, but teach the way of God in truth. Is it lawful
to pay taxes to Caesar, or not? [15] Shall we pay, or
shall we not pay?"

But He, knowing their hypocrisy, said to them,
"Why do you test Me? Bring Me a denarius that I
may see *it.*" [16] So they brought *it.*

And He said to them, "Whose image and
inscription *is* this?" They said to Him, "Caesar's."

'מִבְּנֵי אָדָם' ..." הֵם פָּחֲדוּ מִן הָעָם, כִּי הַכֹּל חָשְׁבוּ
שֶׁיּוֹחָנָן אָכֵן נָבִיא. [33] הֵשִׁיבוּ וְאָמְרוּ לְיֵשׁוּעַ: "אֵין אָנוּ
יוֹדְעִים."

אָמַר לָהֶם יֵשׁוּעַ: "גַּם אֲנִי לֹא אֹמַר לָכֶם בְּאֵיזוֹ
סַמְכוּת אֲנִי עוֹשֶׂה אֶת הַדְּבָרִים הָאֵלֶּה."

יב הוּא הֵחֵל לְדַבֵּר אֲלֵיהֶם בִּמְשָׁלִים: "אִישׁ אֶחָד
נָטַע כֶּרֶם. הוּא הֵקִים גָּדֵר סָבִיב, גַּם חָצַב יֶקֶב וּבָנָה
מִגְדָּל, וּלְאַחַר שֶׁהֶחְכִּירוֹ לְכוֹרְמִים נָסַע. [2] בְּבוֹא
הָעֵת שָׁלַח עֶבֶד אֶל הַכּוֹרְמִים לְקַבֵּל מִיְּדֵיהֶם מִפְּרִי
הַכֶּרֶם. [3] תָּפְסוּ אוֹתוֹ וְהִכּוּהוּ וְשִׁלְּחוּ אוֹתוֹ רֵיקָם.
[4] הוֹסִיף וְשָׁלַח אֲלֵיהֶם עֶבֶד אַחֵר. פָּצְעוּ אוֹתוֹ
בְּרֹאשׁוֹ וְהִתְעַלְּלוּ בּוֹ. [5] שָׁלַח אַחֵר וְהָרְגוּ אוֹתוֹ; וְכֵן גַּם
רַבִּים אֲחֵרִים, אֶת אֵלֶּה הִכּוּ וְאֶת אֵלֶּה הָרְגוּ. [6] נוֹתַר
לוֹ אֶחָד – בְּנוֹ אֲהוּבוֹ. לַבַּסּוֹף שָׁלַח אוֹתוֹ אֲלֵיהֶם,
בְּאָמְרוֹ 'אֶת בְּנִי יְכַבְּדוּ', [7] אֶלָּא שֶׁהַכּוֹרְמִים הָהֵם
אָמְרוּ זֶה אֶל זֶה, 'הוּא הַיּוֹרֵשׁ; בּוֹאוּ נַהֲרֹג אוֹתוֹ
וְתִהְיֶה לָנוּ הַיְרֻשָּׁה.' [8] לָקְחוּ אוֹתוֹ וַהֲרָגוּהוּ
וְהִשְׁלִיכוּהוּ אֶל מִחוּץ לַכֶּרֶם. [9] מַה יַּעֲשֶׂה בַּעַל
הַכֶּרֶם? יָבוֹא וְיַשְׁמִיד אֶת הַכּוֹרְמִים וְיִתֵּן אֶת הַכֶּרֶם
לַאֲחֵרִים. [10] הַאִם לֹא קְרָאתֶם אֶת הַכָּתוּב הַזֶּה,
'אֶבֶן מָאֲסוּ הַבּוֹנִים הָיְתָה לְרֹאשׁ פִּנָּה;
[11] מֵאֵת יהוה הָיְתָה זֹּאת, הִיא נִפְלָאת
בְּעֵינֵינוּ'?"

[12] הֵם בִּקְשׁוּ לִתְפֹּס אוֹתוֹ, כִּי יָדְעוּ שֶׁדִּבֵּר אֶת
הַמָּשָׁל עֲלֵיהֶם, אֲבָל חָשְׁשׁוּ מִפְּנֵי הָעָם. עָזְבוּ אוֹתוֹ
וְהָלְכוּ מִשָּׁם.

[13] שָׁלְחוּ אֵלָיו מֵאַנְשֵׁי הַפְּרוּשִׁים וּמֵחֲסִידֵי בֵּית
הוֹרְדוֹס לִלְכֹּד אוֹתוֹ בְּדִבְרוֹ. [14] בָּאוּ וְאָמְרוּ לוֹ: "רַבִּי,
אֲנַחְנוּ יוֹדְעִים שֶׁאַתָּה אִישׁ אֱמֶת וְאֵינְךָ חוֹשֵׁשׁ
מֵאִישׁ, שֶׁכֵּן אֵינְךָ נוֹשֵׂא פָּנִים לַאֲנָשִׁים אֶלָּא מוֹרֶה
אַתָּה אֶת דֶּרֶךְ הָאֱלֹהִים עַל־פִּי הָאֱמֶת. הַאִם מֻתָּר
לָתֵת מַס לַקֵּיסָר אוֹ לֹא? הַאִם עָלֵינוּ לָתֵת אוֹ לֹא
לָתֵת?"

[15] הוֹאִיל וְהִכִּיר אֶת צְבִיעוּתָם אָמַר לָהֶם: "לָמָּה
אַתֶּם מְנַסִּים אוֹתִי? הָבִיאוּ לִי דִּינָר וְאֶרְאֶה."
[16] הֵבִיאוּ לוֹ וְהוּא שָׁאַל אוֹתָם: "שֶׁל מִי הַדְּמוּת
הַזֹּאת וְהַכְּתֹבֶת?"

17 And Jesus answered and said to them, "Render to Caesar the things that are Caesar's, and to God the things that are God's."

And they marveled at Him.

18 Then *some* Sadducees, who say there is no resurrection, came to Him; and they asked Him, saying: 19 "Teacher, Moses wrote to us that if a man's brother dies, and leaves *his* wife behind, and leaves no children, his brother should take his wife and raise up offspring for his brother. 20 Now there were seven brothers. The first took a wife; and dying, he left no offspring. 21 And the second took her, and he died; nor did he leave any offspring. And the third likewise. 22 So the seven had her and left no offspring. Last of all the woman died also. 23 Therefore, in the resurrection, when they rise, whose wife will she be? For all seven had her as wife."

24 Jesus answered and said to them, "Are you not therefore mistaken, because you do not know the Scriptures nor the power of God? 25 For when they rise from the dead, they neither marry nor are given in marriage, but are like angels in heaven. 26 But concerning the dead, that they rise, have you not read in the book of Moses, in the *burning* bush *passage,* how God spoke to him, saying, '*I am the God of Abraham, the God of Isaac, and the God of Jacob*'? 27 He is not the God of the dead, but the God of the living. You are therefore greatly mistaken."

28 Then one of the scribes came, and having heard them reasoning together, perceiving that He had answered them well, asked Him, "Which is the first commandment of all?"

29 Jesus answered him, "The first of all the commandments *is:* '*Hear, O Israel, the* LORD *our God, the* LORD *is one.* 30 *And you shall love the* LORD *your God with all your heart, with all your soul, and with all your mind, and with all your strength.*' This *is* the first commandment. 31 And the second, like *it, is* this: '*You shall love your neighbor as yourself.*' There is no other commandment greater than these."

32 So the scribe said to Him, "Well *said,* Teacher. You have spoken the truth, for there is one God, and there is no other but He. 33 And to love Him with all the heart, with all the understanding, with all the soul, and with all the strength, and to love one's neighbor as oneself, is more than all the whole burnt offerings and sacrifices."

34 Now when Jesus saw that he answered wisely, He said to him, "You are not far from the kingdom of God."

But after that no one dared question Him.

הֵשִׁיבוּ לוֹ: "שֶׁל הַקֵּיסָר." 17 אָמַר לָהֶם יֵשׁוּעַ: "אֶת אֲשֶׁר לַקֵּיסָר תְּנוּ לַקֵּיסָר וְאֶת אֲשֶׁר לֵאלֹהִים – לֵאלֹהִים." הֵם הִשְׁתּוֹמְמוּ עָלָיו.

18 בָּאוּ אֵלָיו צְדוֹקִים, הָאוֹמְרִים שֶׁאֵין תְּחִיַּת מֵתִים, וְשָׁאֲלוּ אוֹתוֹ: 19 "רַבִּי, מֹשֶׁה כָּתַב לָנוּ שֶׁאִם יָמוּת אִישׁ וְהִנִּיחַ אִשָּׁה וְלֹא הִשְׁאִיר בָּנִים, יִקַּח אָחִיו אֶת אִשְׁתּוֹ וְיָקִים זֶרַע לְאָחִיו. 20 הָיוּ שִׁבְעָה אַחִים. הָרִאשׁוֹן נָשָׂא אִשָּׁה וּמֵת וְלֹא הִשְׁאִיר צֶאֱצָאִים. 21 לָקַח אוֹתָהּ הַשֵּׁנִי וּמֵת וְלֹא הִשְׁאִיר צֶאֱצָאִים, וְכֵן גַּם הַשְּׁלִישִׁי. 22 כָּכָה כָּל הַשִּׁבְעָה לֹא הִשְׁאִירוּ צֶאֱצָאִים. אַחֲרֵי כֻּלָּם מֵתָה גַּם הָאִשָּׁה. 23 בַּתְּחִיָּה, כַּאֲשֶׁר יָקוּמוּ, לְמִי מֵהֶם תִּהְיֶה לְאִשָּׁה, שֶׁהֲרֵי הָיְתָה אִשָּׁה לְכָל הַשִּׁבְעָה?"

24 הֵשִׁיב לָהֶם יֵשׁוּעַ: "כְּלוּם אֵינְכֶם טוֹעִים מִשּׁוּם שֶׁאֵינְכֶם יוֹדְעִים אֶת הַכְּתוּבִים, אַף לֹא אֶת גְּבוּרַת אֱלֹהִים? 25 כַּאֲשֶׁר הַמֵּתִים קָמִים אֵין הֵם מִתְחַתְּנִים, אֶלָּא שֶׁהֵם כְּמַלְאָכִים בַּשָּׁמַיִם. 26 וַאֲשֶׁר לְכָךְ שֶׁהַמֵּתִים קָמִים, הַאִם לֹא קְרָאתֶם בְּסֵפֶר מֹשֶׁה, בְּמַעֲשֵׂה הַסְּנֶה, שֶׁהָאֱלֹהִים אָמַר לוֹ, 'אָנֹכִי אֱלֹהֵי אַבְרָהָם, אֱלֹהֵי יִצְחָק וֵאלֹהֵי יַעֲקֹב'? 27 אֵין הוּא אֱלֹהֵי הַמֵּתִים כִּי אִם אֱלֹהֵי הַחַיִּים. אַתֶּם טוֹעִים מְאֹד."

28 אַחַד הַסּוֹפְרִים הִתְקָרֵב וְשָׁמַע אוֹתָם מִתְוַכְּחִים. כִּרְאוֹתוֹ שֶׁיֵּשׁוּעַ הֵשִׁיב לָהֶם הֵיטֵב, שָׁאַל אוֹתוֹ: "אֵיזוֹהִי הַמִּצְוָה הָרִאשׁוֹנָה מִכֹּל?"

29 עָנָה יֵשׁוּעַ: "הָרִאשׁוֹנָה הִיא 'שְׁמַע יִשְׂרָאֵל יהוה אֱלֹהֵינוּ יהוה אֶחָד, 30 וְאָהַבְתָּ אֵת יהוה אֱלֹהֶיךָ בְּכָל לְבָבְךָ וּבְכָל־נַפְשְׁךָ וּבְכָל שִׂכְלְךָ וּבְכָל־מְאֹדֶךָ.' 31 וְהַשְּׁנִיָּה הִיא 'וְאָהַבְתָּ לְרֵעֲךָ כָּמוֹךָ.' אֵין מִצְוָה אַחֶרֶת גְּדוֹלָה מֵאֵלֶּה."

32 אָמַר אֵלָיו הַסּוֹפֵר: "יָפֶה, רַבִּי, אֱמֶת אָמַרְתָּ שֶׁאֶחָד הוּא וְאֵין עוֹד מִלְּבַדּוֹ. 33 וְלֶאֱהֹב אוֹתוֹ בְּכָל לְבָבְךָ וּבְכָל בִּינָתְךָ וּבְכָל־מְאֹדֶךָ', וְלֶאֱהֹב 'לְרֵעֲךָ כָּמוֹךָ', הֲרֵי זֶה גָּדוֹל מִכָּל עוֹלָה וָזֶבַח."

34 רָאָה יֵשׁוּעַ כִּי הֵשִׁיב בְּחָכְמָה וְאָמַר לוֹ: "אֵינְךָ רָחוֹק מִמַּלְכוּת הָאֱלֹהִים." וְאִישׁ לֹא הֵעֵז עוֹד לִשְׁאֹל אוֹתוֹ שׁוּם דָּבָר.

³⁵Then Jesus answered and said, while He taught in the temple, "How *is it* that the scribes say that the Christ is the Son of David? ³⁶For David himself said by the Holy Spirit:

'The LORD said to my Lord,
"Sit at My right hand,
Till I make Your enemies Your footstool."'

³⁷Therefore David himself calls Him 'Lord'; how is He *then* his Son?"

And the common people heard Him gladly.

³⁸Then He said to them in His teaching, "Beware of the scribes, who desire to go around in long robes, *love* greetings in the marketplaces, ³⁹the best seats in the synagogues, and the best places at feasts, ⁴⁰who devour widows' houses, and for a pretense make long prayers. These will receive greater condemnation."

⁴¹Now Jesus sat opposite the treasury and saw how the people put money into the treasury. And many *who were* rich put in much. ⁴²Then one poor widow came and threw in two mites, which make a quadrans. ⁴³So He called His disciples to *Himself* and said to them, "Assuredly, I say to you that this poor widow has put in more than all those who have given to the treasury; ⁴⁴for they all put in out of their abundance, but she out of her poverty put in all that she had, her whole livelihood."

13 Then as He went out of the temple, one of His disciples said to Him, "Teacher, see what manner of stones and what buildings *are here!*"

²And Jesus answered and said to him, "Do you see these great buildings? Not *one* stone shall be left upon another, that shall not be thrown down."

³Now as He sat on the Mount of Olives opposite the temple, Peter, James, John, and Andrew asked Him privately, ⁴"Tell us, when will these things be? And what *will be* the sign when all these things will be fulfilled?"

⁵And Jesus, answering them, began to say: "Take heed that no one deceives you. ⁶For many will come in My name, saying, 'I am *He*,' and will deceive many. ⁷But when you hear of wars and rumors of wars, do not be troubled; for *such things* must happen, but the end *is* not yet. ⁸For nation will rise against nation, and kingdom against kingdom. And there will be earthquakes in various places, and there will be famines and troubles. These *are* the beginnings of sorrows.

⁹"But watch out for yourselves, for they will deliver you up to councils, and you will be beaten in the synagogues. You will be brought before rulers and kings for My sake, for a testimony to them.

35 כְּשֶׁלִּמֵּד יֵשׁוּעַ בְּבֵית הַמִּקְדָּשׁ, אָמַר: "כֵּיצַד זֶה אוֹמְרִים הַסּוֹפְרִים שֶׁהַמָּשִׁיחַ הוּא בֶּן דָּוִד? 36 הֲלֹא דָוִד עַצְמוֹ אָמַר בְּהַשְׁרָאַת רוּחַ הַקֹּדֶשׁ,

'נְאֻם יהוה לַאדֹנִי: שֵׁב לִימִינִי עַד־אָשִׁית אֹיְבֶיךָ הֲדֹם לְרַגְלֶיךָ.'

37 דָּוִד עַצְמוֹ קוֹרֵא לוֹ 'אָדוֹן', וְאֵיךְ הוּא בְּנוֹ?" הֶהָמוֹן הָרַב שָׁמַע אוֹתוֹ בְּרָצוֹן. 38 וּבְלַמְּדוֹ אוֹתָם אָמַר: "הִזָּהֲרוּ מִן הַסּוֹפְרִים הָאוֹהֲבִים לְהִתְהַלֵּךְ לְבוּשֵׁי גְלִימוֹת וְאוֹהֲבִים בְּרְכוֹת שָׁלוֹם בַּשְּׁוָקִים 39 וּמוֹשָׁבִים רִאשׁוֹנִים בְּבָתֵּי הַכְּנֶסֶת וּמְקוֹמוֹת נִכְבָּדִים בַּסְּעוּדוֹת; 40 הַבּוֹלְעִים אֶת בָּתֵּי הָאַלְמָנוֹת וּמַאֲרִיכִים לְהִתְפַּלֵּל לְמַרְאִית עַיִן. דִּינָם שֶׁל אֵלֶּה יִהְיֶה חָמוּר יוֹתֵר."

41 הוּא יָשַׁב מוּל תֵּבַת הָאוֹצָר וְרָאָה אֶת הָעָם שָׂמִים מַטְבְּעוֹת בְּתֵבַת הָאוֹצָר וַעֲשִׁירִים רַבִּים שָׂמוּ הַרְבֵּה. 42 בָּאָה אַלְמָנָה עֲנִיָּה וְשָׂמָה שְׁתֵּי פְּרוּטוֹת, שֶׁהֵן חֲצִי אִסָּר. 43 קָרָא לְתַלְמִידָיו וְאָמַר לָהֶם: "אָמֵן אוֹמֵר אֲנִי לָכֶם, הָאַלְמָנָה הָעֲנִיָּה הַזֹּאת שָׂמָה יוֹתֵר מִכָּל אֵלֶּה שֶׁשָּׂמוּ בְּתֵבַת הָאוֹצָר; 44 כִּי הַכֹּל נָתְנוּ מִן הָעֹדֶף שֶׁלָּהֶם, אַךְ הִיא מִמַּחְסוֹרָהּ נָתְנָה אֶת כָּל אֲשֶׁר הָיָה לָהּ, אֶת כָּל מִחְיָתָהּ."

יג בְּצֵאתוֹ מִבֵּית הַמִּקְדָּשׁ אָמַר אֵלָיו אֶחָד מִתַּלְמִידָיו: "רַבִּי, רְאֵה אֵיזֶה אֲבָנִים וְאֵיזֶה בִּנְיָנִים!" 2 אָמַר לוֹ יֵשׁוּעַ: "אַתָּה רוֹאֶה אֶת הַבִּנְיָנִים הַגְּדוֹלִים הָאֵלֶּה? לֹא תִּשָּׁאֵר אֶבֶן עַל אֶבֶן אֲשֶׁר לֹא תֻּפַּל אָרְצָה." 3 כְּשֶׁיָּשַׁב עַל הַר הַזֵּיתִים, מוּל בֵּית הַמִּקְדָּשׁ, שְׁאָלוּהוּ כֵּיפָא וְיַעֲקֹב וְיוֹחָנָן וְאַנְדְּרֵי בִּהְיוֹתָם לְבַדָּם אִתּוֹ: 4 "אֱמֹר נָא לָנוּ, מָתַי יִהְיֶה הַדָּבָר הַזֶּה וּמַהוּ הָאוֹת לִפְנֵי שֶׁכָּל זֶה יִתְגַּשֵּׁם?" 5 אָמַר לָהֶם יֵשׁוּעַ: "הִזָּהֲרוּ שֶׁלֹּא יַתְעֶה אֶתְכֶם אִישׁ. 6 רַבִּים יָבוֹאוּ בִּשְׁמִי וְיֹאמְרוּ 'אֲנִי הוּא' וְיַתְעוּ רַבִּים. 7 וּכְשֶׁתִּשְׁמְעוּ מִלְחָמוֹת וּשְׁמוּעוֹת מִלְחָמָה אַל תִּבָּהֵלוּ; זֶה מַה שֶּׁצָּרִיךְ לִהְיוֹת, וּבְכָל זֹאת עוֹד לֹא בָּא הַקֵּץ. 8 גּוֹי יָקוּם עַל גּוֹי וּמַמְלָכָה עַל מַמְלָכָה וְתִהְיֶינָה רְעִידוֹת אֲדָמָה בִּמְקוֹמוֹת רַבִּים וְיִהְיֶה רָעָב. אֵלֶּה רֵאשִׁית הַצָּרוֹת. 9 וְאַתֶּם הִזָּהֲרוּ; יִמְסְרוּ אֶתְכֶם לַסַּנְהֶדְרִיּוֹת, יַכּוּ אֶתְכֶם בְּבָתֵּי כְנֶסֶת, וְלִפְנֵי מוֹשְׁלִים

¹⁰And the gospel must first be preached to all the nations. ¹¹But when they arrest *you* and deliver you up, do not worry beforehand, or premeditate what you will speak. But whatever is given you in that hour, speak that; for it is not you who speak, but the Holy Spirit. ¹²Now brother will betray brother to death, and a father *his* child; and children will rise up against parents and cause them to be put to death. ¹³And you will be hated by all for My name's sake. But he who endures to the end shall be saved.

¹⁴"So when you see the *'abomination of desolation,'* spoken of by Daniel the prophet, standing where it ought not" (let the reader understand), "then let those who are in Judea flee to the mountains. ¹⁵Let him who is on the housetop not go down into the house, nor enter to take anything out of his house. ¹⁶And let him who is in the field not go back to get his clothes. ¹⁷But woe to those who are pregnant and to those who are nursing babies in those days! ¹⁸And pray that your flight may not be in winter. ¹⁹For *in* those days there will be tribulation, such as has not been since the beginning of the creation which God created until this time, nor ever shall be. ²⁰And unless the Lord had shortened those days, no flesh would be saved; but for the elect's sake, whom He chose, He shortened the days.

²¹"Then if anyone says to you, 'Look, here *is* the Christ!' or, 'Look, *He is* there!' do not believe it. ²²For false christs and false prophets will rise and show signs and wonders to deceive, if possible, even the elect. ²³But take heed; see, I have told you all things beforehand.

²⁴"But in those days, after that tribulation, the sun will be darkened, and the moon will not give its light; ²⁵the stars of heaven will fall, and the powers in the heavens will be shaken. ²⁶Then they will see the Son of Man coming in the clouds with great power and glory. ²⁷And then He will send His angels, and gather together His elect from the four winds, from the farthest part of earth to the farthest part of heaven.

²⁸"Now learn this parable from the fig tree: When its branch has already become tender, and puts forth leaves, you know that summer is near. ²⁹So you also, when you see these things happening, know that it is near—at the doors! ³⁰Assuredly, I say to you, this generation will by no means pass away till all these things take place. ³¹Heaven and earth will pass away, but My words will by no means pass away.

וּמְלָכִים יַעֲמִדוּ אֶתְכֶם בִּגְלָלִי, לְעֵדוּת לָהֶם. ¹⁰ אֲבָל תְּחִלָּה צָרִיךְ שֶׁהַבְּשׂוֹרָה תְּכֹרַז לְכָל הַגּוֹיִם. ¹¹ כַּאֲשֶׁר יוֹלִיכוּ אֶתְכֶם כְּדֵי לְהַסְגִּירְכֶם, אַל תִּדְאֲגוּ לָמָה שֶׁתְּדַבְּרוּ, כִּי מַה שֶׁיִּנָּתֵן לָכֶם בְּאוֹתָהּ שָׁעָה אֶת זֶה דַּבְּרוּ; שֶׁכֵּן לֹא אַתֶּם תְּדַבְּרוּ אֶלָּא רוּחַ הַקֹּדֶשׁ. ¹² אָז יַסְגִּיר אָח אֶת אָחִיו לַמָּוֶת וְאָב יַסְגִּיר אֶת בְּנוֹ. בָּנִים יָקוּמוּ עַל הוֹרֵיהֶם וְיָמִיתוּ אוֹתָם. ¹³ וְתִהְיוּ שְׂנוּאִים עַל הַכֹּל בִּגְלַל שְׁמִי, אַךְ הַמַּחֲזִיק מַעֲמָד עַד קֵץ הוּא יִוָּשֵׁעַ."

¹⁴ "וּכְשֶׁתִּרְאוּ אֶת הַשִּׁקּוּץ הַמְשׁוֹמֵם עוֹמֵד בְּמָקוֹם שֶׁאֵינוֹ מְקוֹמוֹ – עַל הַקּוֹרֵא לְהָבִין – אֲזַי הַנִּמְצָאִים בִּיהוּדָה, שֶׁיָּנוּסוּ אֶל הֶהָרִים; ¹⁵ מִי שֶׁעַל הַגַּג אַל יֵרֵד וְאַל יִכָּנֵס לָקַחַת דָּבָר מִבֵּיתוֹ; ¹⁶ וּמִי שֶׁבַּשָּׂדֶה אַל יַחֲזֹר לָקַחַת אֶת בִּגְדוֹ. ¹⁷ וְאוֹי לֶהָרוֹת וְלַמֵּינִיקוֹת בַּיָּמִים הָהֵם! ¹⁸ הִתְפַּלְלוּ שֶׁלֹּא יִהְיֶה זֶה בַּחֹרֶף, ¹⁹ כִּי הַיָּמִים הָהֵם יִהְיוּ צָרָה אֲשֶׁר לֹא הָיְתָה כָּמוֹהָ מֵרֵאשִׁית הַבְּרִיאָה שֶׁבָּרָא אֱלֹהִים וְעַד עַתָּה; אַף לֹא תִהְיֶה כָּמוֹהָ. ²⁰ וְלוּלֵא קִצֵּר אֲדֹנָי אֶת הַיָּמִים לֹא הָיָה נִצָּל כָּל בָּשָׂר, אַךְ לְמַעַן הַבְּחִירִים אֲשֶׁר בָּחַר בָּהֶם קִצֵּר אֶת הַיָּמִים. ²¹ וְאָז אִם יֹאמַר לָכֶם אִישׁ, 'הִנֵּה פֹּה הַמָּשִׁיחַ, הִנֵּה שָׁם,' אַל תַּאֲמִינוּ לוֹ; ²² כִּי יָקוּמוּ מְשִׁיחֵי שֶׁקֶר וּנְבִיאֵי שֶׁקֶר וְיַעֲשׂוּ אוֹתוֹת וּמוֹפְתִים לְהַתְעוֹת, אִם אֶפְשָׁר, אֶת הַבְּחִירִים. ²³ וְאַתֶּם הִזָּהֲרוּ; אָמַרְתִּי לָכֶם אֶת הַכֹּל מֵרֹאשׁ."

²⁴ "בַּיָּמִים הָהֵם, אַחֲרֵי הַצָּרָה הַהִיא, תֶּחְשַׁךְ הַשֶּׁמֶשׁ וְהַיָּרֵחַ לֹא יַגִּיהַּ אוֹרוֹ, ²⁵ הַכּוֹכָבִים יִפְּלוּ מִן הַשָּׁמַיִם וְכֹחוֹת הַשָּׁמַיִם יִזְדַּעְזְעוּ. ²⁶ אָז יִרְאוּ אֶת בֶּן־הָאָדָם בָּא בַּעֲנָנִים בִּגְבוּרָה רַבָּה וּבְכָבוֹד. ²⁷ וְאָז יִשְׁלַח אֶת הַמַּלְאָכִים וִיקַבֵּץ אֶת בְּחִירָיו מֵאַרְבַּע הָרוּחוֹת, מִקְצֵה הָאָרֶץ עַד קְצֵה הַשָּׁמַיִם.

²⁸ לִמְדוּ אֶת הַמָּשָׁל מִן הַתְּאֵנָה: כַּאֲשֶׁר עֲנָפֶיהָ מִתְרַכְּכִים וְהֶעָלִים צָצִים יוֹדְעִים אַתֶּם שֶׁהַקַּיִץ קָרוֹב. ²⁹ כֵּן גַּם אַתֶּם, כְּשֶׁתִּרְאוּ אֶת הַדְּבָרִים הָאֵלֶּה מִתְקַיְּמִים דְּעוּ כִּי קָרוֹב הוּא בַּפֶּתַח. ³⁰ אָמֵן אֲנִי לָכֶם, לֹא יַעֲבֹר הַדּוֹר הַזֶּה עַד אֲשֶׁר יִהְיוּ כָל אֵלֶּה. ³¹ הַשָּׁמַיִם וְהָאָרֶץ יַעֲבֹרוּ וּדְבָרַי לֹא יַעֲבֹרוּ.

³²"But of that day and hour no one knows, not even the angels in heaven, nor the Son, but only the Father. ³³Take heed, watch and pray; for you do not know when the time is. ³⁴It is like a man going to a far country, who left his house and gave authority to his servants, and to each his work, and commanded the doorkeeper to watch. ³⁵Watch therefore, for you do not know when the master of the house is coming—in the evening, at midnight, at the crowing of the rooster, or in the morning—³⁶lest, coming suddenly, he find you sleeping. ³⁷And what I say to you, I say to all: Watch!"

14 After two days it was the Passover and the Feast of Unleavened Bread. And the chief priests and the scribes sought how they might take Him by trickery and put Him to death. ²But they said, "Not during the feast, lest there be an uproar of the people."

³And being in Bethany at the house of Simon the leper, as He sat at the table, a woman came having an alabaster flask of very costly oil of spikenard. Then she broke the flask and poured it on His head. ⁴But there were some who were indignant among themselves, and said, "Why was this fragrant oil wasted? ⁵For it might have been sold for more than three hundred denarii and given to the poor." And they criticized her sharply.

⁶But Jesus said, "Let her alone. Why do you trouble her? She has done a good work for Me. ⁷For you have the poor with you always, and whenever you wish you may do them good; but Me you do not have always. ⁸She has done what she could. She has come beforehand to anoint My body for burial. ⁹Assuredly, I say to you, wherever this gospel is preached in the whole world, what this woman has done will also be told as a memorial to her."

¹⁰Then Judas Iscariot, one of the twelve, went to the chief priests to betray Him to them. ¹¹And when they heard it, they were glad, and promised to give him money. So he sought how he might conveniently betray Him.

¹²Now on the first day of Unleavened Bread, when they killed the Passover lamb, His disciples said to Him, "Where do You want us to go and prepare, that You may eat the Passover?"

¹³And He sent out two of His disciples and said to them, "Go into the city, and a man will meet you carrying a pitcher of water; follow him. ¹⁴Wherever he goes in, say to the master of the house, 'The Teacher says, "Where is the guest room in which I

³²אֲבָל אֶת הַיּוֹם הַהוּא אוֹ הַשָּׁעָה אֵין אִישׁ יוֹדֵעַ, גַּם לֹא הַמַּלְאָכִים בַּשָּׁמַיִם וְגַם לֹא הַבֵּן, אֶלָּא הָאָב. ³³הִזָּהֲרוּ, הֱיוּ עֵרִים, כִּי אֵינְכֶם יוֹדְעִים מָתַי הָעֵת. ³⁴דּוֹמֶה הַדָּבָר לְאִישׁ הַיּוֹצֵא לְמַסָּע. כְּשֶׁעָזַב אֶת בֵּיתוֹ נָתַן סַמְכוּת לַעֲבָדָיו, לְכָל אֶחָד אֶת מְלַאכְתּוֹ, וְעַל הַשּׁוֹעֵר צִוָּה לַעֲמֹד עַל הַמִּשְׁמָר. ³⁵לָכֵן עִמְדוּ עַל הַמִּשְׁמָר, כִּי אֵינְכֶם יוֹדְעִים מָתַי יָבוֹא בַּעַל הַבַּיִת, אִם בָּעֶרֶב אוֹ בַּחֲצוֹת הַלַּיְלָה, אִם בְּעֵת קְרִיאַת הַתַּרְנְגוֹל אוֹ בַּבֹּקֶר, ³⁶פֶּן יָבוֹא פִּתְאוֹם וְיִמְצָא אֶתְכֶם יְשֵׁנִים. ³⁷אֶת אֲשֶׁר אֲנִי אוֹמֵר לָכֶם אוֹמֵר אֲנִי לַכֹּל: עִמְדוּ עַל הַמִּשְׁמָר!"

יד נוֹתְרוּ יוֹמַיִם עַד חַג הַפֶּסַח וְהַמַּצּוֹת. רָאשֵׁי הַכֹּהֲנִים וְהַסּוֹפְרִים חִפְּשׂוּ דֶּרֶךְ לִתְפֹּס אוֹתוֹ בְּעָרְמָה כְּדֵי לַהֲמִית אוֹתוֹ; ²כִּי אָמְרוּ, "לֹא בֶּחָג, פֶּן תִּהְיֶה מְהוּמָה בָּעָם."

³כַּאֲשֶׁר הָיָה בְּבֵית עַנְיָה, בְּבֵיתוֹ שֶׁל שִׁמְעוֹן הַמְּצֹרָע, הֵסֵב אֶל הַשֻּׁלְחָן. בָּאָה אִשָּׁה שֶׁהֶחֱזִיקָה פַּךְ וּבוֹ שֶׁמֶן נֵרְדְּ טָהוֹר וְיָקָר מְאֹד, שָׁבְרָה אֶת פִּי הַפַּךְ וְיָצְקָה אֶת הַנֵּרְדְּ עַל רֹאשׁוֹ. ⁴הָיוּ אֲחָדִים שֶׁכָּעֲסוּ וְאָמְרוּ זֶה אֶל זֶה: "לָמָּה הַבִּזְבּוּז הַזֶּה שֶׁל הַשֶּׁמֶן? ⁵הֲלֹא הָיָה אֶפְשָׁר לִמְכֹּר אֶת הַשֶּׁמֶן הַזֶּה בִּשְׁלוֹשׁ מֵאוֹת דִּינָר וְיוֹתֵר וְלָתֵת לָעֲנִיִּים!" וְהֵם גָּעֲרוּ בָּהּ. ⁶אָמַר יֵשׁוּעַ: "הַנִּיחוּ לָהּ, מַדּוּעַ תָּצִיקוּ לָהּ? מַעֲשֶׂה טוֹב עָשְׂתָה לִי. ⁷הָעֲנִיִּים אִתְּכֶם תָּמִיד וּבְכָל עֵת שֶׁתִּרְצוּ תּוּכְלוּ לְהֵיטִיב עִמָּהֶם, אֲבָל אֲנִי, לֹא תָּמִיד אֲנִי אִתְּכֶם. ⁸מַה שֶּׁהָיָה בִּיכָלְתָּהּ עָשְׂתָה; הִיא הִקְדִּימָה לִמְשֹׁחַ אֶת גּוּפִי בִּשְׁבִיל הַקְּבוּרָה. ⁹אָמֵן אוֹמֵר אֲנִי לָכֶם, בְּכָל מָקוֹם שֶׁתְּבֻשַּׂר הַבְּשׂוֹרָה, בְּכָל הָעוֹלָם, יְסֻפַּר גַּם מַה שֶּׁעָשְׂתָה הִיא, וְזֶה לְזִכְרָהּ."

¹⁰הָלַךְ יְהוּדָה אִישׁ קְרִיּוֹת, אֶחָד מִן הַשְּׁנֵים־עָשָׂר, אֶל רָאשֵׁי הַכֹּהֲנִים כְּדֵי לְהַסְגִּיר לָהֶם אֶת יֵשׁוּעַ. ¹¹כְּשָׁמְעָם זֹאת שָׂמְחוּ וְהִבְטִיחוּ לָתֵת לוֹ כֶּסֶף, וְהוּא חִפֵּשׂ הִזְדַּמְּנוּת לְהַסְגִּיר אוֹתוֹ.

¹²בָּרִאשׁוֹן לְחַג הַמַּצּוֹת, בַּיּוֹם שֶׁנִּשְׁחֲגוּ לִזְבֹּחַ אֶת קָרְבַּן הַפֶּסַח, שָׁאֲלוּ אוֹתוֹ תַּלְמִידָיו: "לְאָן אַתָּה רוֹצֶה שֶׁנֵּלֵךְ וְנָכִין לְךָ לֶאֱכֹל אֶת הַפֶּסַח?" ¹³הוּא שָׁלַח שְׁנַיִם מִתַּלְמִידָיו בְּאָמְרוֹ לָהֶם: "לְכוּ הָעִירָה וְיִפְגֹּשׁ אֶתְכֶם אִישׁ נוֹשֵׂא כַּד מַיִם. לְכוּ אַחֲרָיו, ¹⁴וּבַמָּקוֹם אֲשֶׁר יִכָּנֵס אֵלָיו אִמְרוּ לְבַעַל הַבַּיִת, 'כֹּה אָמַר רַבֵּנוּ: אֵיפֹה חַדְרִי אֲשֶׁר אֹכַל בּוֹ

may eat the Passover with My disciples?" ' ¹⁵ Then he will show you a large upper room, furnished *and* prepared; there make ready for us."

¹⁶ So His disciples went out, and came into the city, and found it just as He had said to them; and they prepared the Passover.

¹⁷ In the evening He came with the twelve. ¹⁸ Now as they sat and ate, Jesus said, "Assuredly, I say to you, one of you who eats with Me will betray Me."

¹⁹ And they began to be sorrowful, and to say to Him one by one, "*Is it I?*" And another *said,* "*Is it I?*"

²⁰ He answered and said to them, "*It is* one of the twelve, who dips with Me in the dish. ²¹ The Son of Man indeed goes just as it is written of Him, but woe to that man by whom the Son of Man is betrayed! It would have been good for that man if he had never been born."

²² And as they were eating, Jesus took bread, blessed and broke *it,* and gave *it* to them and said, "Take, eat; this is My body."

²³ Then He took the cup, and when He had given thanks He gave *it* to them, and they all drank from it. ²⁴ And He said to them, "This is My blood of the new covenant, which is shed for many. ²⁵ Assuredly, I say to you, I will no longer drink of the fruit of the vine until that day when I drink it new in the kingdom of God."

²⁶ And when they had sung a hymn, they went out to the Mount of Olives.

²⁷ Then Jesus said to them, "All of you will be made to stumble because of Me this night, for it is written:

> 'I will strike the Shepherd,
> And the sheep will be scattered.'

²⁸ "But after I have been raised, I will go before you to Galilee."

²⁹ Peter said to Him, "Even if all are made to stumble, yet I *will* not *be.*"

³⁰ Jesus said to him, "Assuredly, I say to you that today, *even* this night, before the rooster crows twice, you will deny Me three times."

³¹ But he spoke more vehemently, "If I have to die with You, I will not deny You!"

And they all said likewise.

³² Then they came to a place which was named Gethsemane; and He said to His disciples, "Sit here while I pray." ³³ And He took Peter, James, and John with Him, and He began to be troubled and deeply distressed. ³⁴ Then He said to them, "My soul is exceedingly sorrowful, *even* to death. Stay here and watch."

אֶת הַפֶּסַח עִם תַּלְמִידָי?' ¹⁵ אוֹתוֹ אִישׁ יַרְאֶה לָכֶם עֲלִיָּה גְדוֹלָה מֻצַּעַת וּמְסֻדֶּרֶת; שָׁם תָּכִינוּ לָנוּ."

¹⁶ יָצְאוּ תַּלְמִידָיו וּבָאוּ הָעִירָה. הֵם מָצְאוּ הַכֹּל כְּפִי שֶׁאָמַר לָהֶם וְהֵכִינוּ אֶת הַפֶּסַח. ¹⁷ בָּעֶרֶב בָּא יֵשׁוּעַ עִם הַשְּׁנֵים-עָשָׂר, ¹⁸ וְכַאֲשֶׁר הֵסֵבּוּ וְאָכְלוּ אָמַר יֵשׁוּעַ: "אָמֵן אוֹמֵר אֲנִי לָכֶם, אֶחָד מִכֶּם יַסְגִּירֵנִי – אֶחָד שֶׁאוֹכֵל אִתִּי." ¹⁹ הֵם הֵחֵלּוּ לְהִתְעַצֵּב וְשָׁאֲלוּהוּ אִישׁ אִישׁ: "זֶה אֲנִי?" ²⁰ אָמַר לָהֶם: "אֶחָד מִן הַשְּׁנֵים-עָשָׂר, הַטּוֹבֵל אִתִּי בַּקְּעָרָה. ²¹ בֶּן-הָאָדָם אָמְנָם הוֹלֵךְ כַּכָּתוּב עָלָיו, אַךְ אוֹי לָאִישׁ אֲשֶׁר יַסְגִּיר אֶת בֶּן-הָאָדָם. טוֹב הָיָה לוֹ אִלּוּלֵא נוֹלַד הָאִישׁ הַהוּא."

²² כַּאֲשֶׁר אָכְלוּ לָקַח יֵשׁוּעַ אֶת הַלֶּחֶם, בֵּרַךְ וּבָצַע וְנָתַן לָהֶם בְּאָמְרוֹ: "קְחוּ, זֶה גּוּפִי." ²³ לָקַח אֶת הַכּוֹס, בֵּרַךְ וְנָתַן לָהֶם וְכֻלָּם שָׁתוּ מִמֶּנָּה. ²⁴ אָמַר לָהֶם: "זֶה דָמִי, דַּם הַבְּרִית הַנִּשְׁפָּךְ בְּעַד רַבִּים. ²⁵ אָמֵן אוֹמֵר אֲנִי לָכֶם, לֹא אֶשְׁתֶּה עוֹד מִפְּרִי הַגֶּפֶן עַד אוֹתוֹ הַיּוֹם אֲשֶׁר אֶשְׁתֵּהוּ חָדָשׁ בְּמַלְכוּת הָאֱלֹהִים."

²⁶ לְאַחַר שֶׁשָּׁרוּ אֶת הַהַלֵּל יָצְאוּ אֶל הַר הַזֵּיתִים. ²⁷ אָמַר לָהֶם יֵשׁוּעַ: "כֻּלְּכֶם תִּכָּשְׁלוּ, שֶׁהֲרֵי כָּתוּב, 'אַכֶּה אֶת-הָרֹעֶה וּתְפוּצֶיןָ הַצֹּאן,' ²⁸ אֲבָל אַחֲרֵי שֶׁאָקוּם אֵלֵךְ לִפְנֵיכֶם לַגָּלִיל."

²⁹ אָמַר לוֹ כֵּיפָא: "גַּם אִם הַכֹּל יִכָּשְׁלוּ, אֲנִי לֹא אֶכָּשֵׁל!" ³⁰ הֵשִׁיב לוֹ יֵשׁוּעַ: "אָמֵן אוֹמֵר אֲנִי לְךָ כִּי הַיּוֹם בְּעֶצֶם הַלַּיְלָה הַזֶּה, בְּטֶרֶם יִקְרָא הַתַּרְנְגוֹל פַּעֲמַיִם, שָׁלֹשׁ פְּעָמִים תִּתְכַּחֵשׁ לִי." ³¹ אַךְ כֵּיפָא אָמַר בְּיֶתֶר תֹּקֶף: "אִם עָלַי לָמוּת אִתְּךָ, בְּשׁוּם פָּנִים לֹא אֶתְכַּחֵשׁ לְךָ!" וְכֵן אָמְרוּ כֻּלָּם.

³² הֵם בָּאוּ אֶל מָקוֹם הַנִּקְרָא גַּת שְׁמָנִים. אָמַר לְתַלְמִידָיו: "שְׁבוּ פֹּה עַד שֶׁאֶתְפַּלֵּל." ³³ לָקַח אִתּוֹ אֶת כֵּיפָא וְאֶת יַעֲקֹב וְאֶת יוֹחָנָן וְהֵחֵל מִתְמַלֵּא חֲרָדָה וּמוּעָקָה. ³⁴ אָמַר לָהֶם: "נַפְשִׁי מָרָה עָלַי עַד

35 He went a little farther, and fell on the ground, and prayed that if it were possible, the hour might pass from Him. 36 And He said, "Abba, Father, all things *are* possible for You. Take this cup away from Me; nevertheless, not what I will, but what You *will*."

37 Then He came and found them sleeping, and said to Peter, "Simon, are you sleeping? Could you not watch one hour? 38 Watch and pray, lest you enter into temptation. The spirit indeed *is* willing, but the flesh *is* weak."

39 Again He went away and prayed, and spoke the same words. 40 And when He returned, He found them asleep again, for their eyes were heavy; and they did not know what to answer Him.

41 Then He came the third time and said to them, "Are you still sleeping and resting? It is enough! The hour has come; behold, the Son of Man is being betrayed into the hands of sinners. 42 Rise, let us be going. See, My betrayer is at hand."

43 And immediately, while He was still speaking, Judas, one of the twelve, with a great multitude with swords and clubs, came from the chief priests and the scribes and the elders. 44 Now His betrayer had given them a signal, saying, "Whomever I kiss, He is the One; seize Him and lead *Him* away safely."

45 As soon as he had come, immediately he went up to Him and said to Him, "Rabbi, Rabbi!" and kissed Him.

46 Then they laid their hands on Him and took Him. 47 And one of those who stood by drew his sword and struck the servant of the high priest, and cut off his ear.

48 Then Jesus answered and said to them, "Have you come out, as against a robber, with swords and clubs to take Me? 49 I was daily with you in the temple teaching, and you did not seize Me. But the Scriptures must be fulfilled."

50 Then they all forsook Him and fled.

51 Now a certain young man followed Him, having a linen cloth thrown around *his* naked *body*. And the young men laid hold of him, 52 and he left the linen cloth and fled from them naked.

53 And they led Jesus away to the high priest; and with him were assembled all the chief priests, the elders, and the scribes. 54 But Peter followed Him at a distance, right into the courtyard of the high priest. And he sat with the servants and warmed himself at the fire.

55 Now the chief priests and all the council sought testimony against Jesus to put Him to death, but found none. 56 For many bore false witness against Him, but their testimonies did not agree.

מֵת. הִשְׁאִירוּ פֹּה וְהִיוּ עֵרִים." 35 הוּא הָלַךְ מְעַט הָלְאָה, נָפַל אַרְצָה וְהִתְפַּלֵּל שֶׁתַּעֲבֹר מִמֶּנּוּ הַשָּׁעָה, אִם אֶפְשָׁר. 36 אָמַר יֵשׁוּעַ: "אַבָּא, אָבִי אַתָּה כֹּל יָכוֹל, הַעֲבֵר נָא מִמֶּנִּי אֶת הַכּוֹס הַזֹּאת, אַךְ לֹא כִּרְצוֹנִי אֲנִי כִּי אִם כִּרְצוֹנְךָ אַתָּה."

37 לְאַחַר מִכֵּן בָּא וּמָצָא אוֹתָם יְשֵׁנִים. אָמַר אֶל כֵּיפָא: "שִׁמְעוֹן, אַתָּה יָשֵׁן? הַאִם לֹא יָכֹלְתָּ לִהְיוֹת עֵר שָׁעָה אַחַת? 38 הֱיוּ עֵרִים וְהִתְפַּלְּלוּ כְּדֵי שֶׁלֹּא תָּבוֹאוּ לִידֵי נִסָּיוֹן. אָמְנָם הָרוּחַ חֲפֵצָה, אֲבָל הַבָּשָׂר חַלָּשׁ. 39 שׁוּב הָלַךְ וְהִתְפַּלֵּל בְּאָמְרוֹ אוֹתָם דְּבָרִים.

40 וְשׁוּב בָּא וּמָצָא אוֹתָם יְשֵׁנִים, כִּי עֵינֵיהֶם הָיוּ כְּבֵדוֹת, וְלֹא יָדְעוּ מַה לַעֲנוֹת לוֹ. 41 הוּא בָּא פַעַם שְׁלִישִׁית וְאָמַר לָהֶם: "עוֹדְכֶם יְשֵׁנִים וְנָחִים? דַּי! הִגִּיעָה הַשָּׁעָה, הִנֵּה בֶּן-הָאָדָם נִמְסָר לִידֵי אֲנָשִׁים חוֹטְאִים. 42 קוּמוּ וְנֵלֵךְ. הִנֵּה הַמַּסְגִּיר אוֹתִי מִתְקָרֵב!"

43 עוֹדֶנּוּ מְדַבֵּר וְהִנֵּה בָּא יְהוּדָה, אֶחָד מִן הַשְּׁנֵים-עָשָׂר, וְאִתּוֹ הָמוֹן, בַּחֲרָבוֹת וּבְמַקְלוֹת, בָּאִים מִטַּעַם רָאשֵׁי הַכֹּהֲנִים וְהַסּוֹפְרִים וְהַזְּקֵנִים. 44 הַמַּסְגִּיר אוֹתוֹ הִקְדִּים לָתֵת לָהֶם סִימָן בְּאָמְרוֹ: "מִי שֶׁאֶתֵּן לוֹ נְשִׁיקָה זֶה הוּא; תִּפְשׂוּ אוֹתוֹ וְהוֹלִיכוּהוּ בִּלְוָיַת מִשְׁמָר." 45 כַּאֲשֶׁר הִגִּיעַ נִגַּשׁ אֵלָיו מִיָּד וְאָמַר: "רַבִּי", וְנָשַׁק לוֹ. 46 הֵם שָׁלְחוּ יְדֵיהֶם וְתָפְסוּ אוֹתוֹ.

47 אֲבָל אֶחָד הָעוֹמְדִים שָׁם שָׁלַף חֶרֶב וּבְהַכּוֹתוֹ אֶת עֶבֶד הַכֹּהֵן הַגָּדוֹל קִצֵּץ אֶת אָזְנוֹ. 48 אָמַר לָהֶם יֵשׁוּעַ: "כְּמוֹ עַל שׁוֹדֵד יְצָאתֶם בַּחֲרָבוֹת וּבְמַקְלוֹת לִתְפֹּשׂ אוֹתִי. 49 יוֹם יוֹם הָיִיתִי אִתְּכֶם בַּמִּקְדָּשׁ וְלִמַּדְתִּי וְלֹא תְּפַסְתֶּם אוֹתִי, אַךְ זֹאת כְּדֵי שֶׁיִּתְמַלְּאוּ הַכְּתוּבִים." 50 אָז עֲזָבוּהוּ כֻּלָּם וּבָרְחוּ.

51 בָּחוּר אֶחָד שֶׁהָיָה עָטוּף סָדִין לְכַסּוֹ גּוּפוֹ נִתְלַוָּה אֵלָיו. תָּפְסוּ אוֹתוֹ, 52 אַךְ הוּא עָזַב אֶת הַסָּדִין בְּיָדָם וּבָרַח עָרוֹם.

53 הוֹלִיכוּ אֶת יֵשׁוּעַ אֶל הַכֹּהֵן הַגָּדוֹל וְשָׁם נִקְהֲלוּ כָּל רָאשֵׁי הַכֹּהֲנִים וְהַזְּקֵנִים וְהַסּוֹפְרִים. 54 כֵּיפָא הָלַךְ אַחֲרָיו בְּמֶרְחָק מָה עַד לְתוֹךְ חֲצַר הַכֹּהֵן הַגָּדוֹל, וְשָׁם יָשַׁב עִם הַמְשָׁרְתִים וְהִתְחַמֵּם לְיַד הָאֵשׁ. 55 אוֹתָהּ שָׁעָה חִפְּשׂוּ רָאשֵׁי הַכֹּהֲנִים וְכָל הַסַּנְהֶדְרִין עֵדוּת נֶגֶד יֵשׁוּעַ כְּדֵי לַהֲמִית אוֹתוֹ וְלֹא מָצְאוּ, 56 כִּי רַבִּים הֵעִידוּ עֵדוּת שֶׁקֶר נֶגְדּוֹ וְהָעֵדֻיּוֹת לֹא הָיוּ

⁵⁷Then some rose up and bore false witness against Him, saying, ⁵⁸"We heard Him say, 'I will destroy this temple made with hands, and within three days I will build another made without hands.'" ⁵⁹But not even then did their testimony agree.

⁶⁰And the high priest stood up in the midst and asked Jesus, saying, "Do You answer nothing? What *is it* these men testify against You?" ⁶¹But He kept silent and answered nothing.

Again the high priest asked Him, saying to Him, "Are You the Christ, the Son of the Blessed?"

⁶²Jesus said, "I am. And you will see the Son of Man sitting at the right hand of the Power, and coming with the clouds of heaven."

⁶³Then the high priest tore his clothes and said, "What further need do we have of witnesses? ⁶⁴You have heard the blasphemy! What do you think?"

And they all condemned Him to be deserving of death.

⁶⁵Then some began to spit on Him, and to blindfold Him, and to beat Him, and to say to Him, "Prophesy!" And the officers struck Him with the palms of their hands.

⁶⁶Now as Peter was below in the courtyard, one of the servant girls of the high priest came. ⁶⁷And when she saw Peter warming himself, she looked at him and said, "You also were with Jesus of Nazareth."

⁶⁸But he denied it, saying, "I neither know nor understand what you are saying." And he went out on the porch, and a rooster crowed.

⁶⁹And the servant girl saw him again, and began to say to those who stood by, "This is one of them." ⁷⁰But he denied it again.

And a little later those who stood by said to Peter again, "Surely you are *one* of them; for you are a Galilean, and your speech shows *it*."

⁷¹Then he began to curse and swear, "I do not know this Man of whom you speak!"

⁷²A second time *the* rooster crowed. Then Peter called to mind the word that Jesus had said to him, "Before the rooster crows twice, you will deny Me three times." And when he thought about it, he wept.

15 Immediately, in the morning, the chief priests held a consultation with the elders and scribes and the whole council; and they bound Jesus, led *Him* away, and delivered *Him* to Pilate. ²Then Pilate asked Him, "Are You the King of the Jews?"

He answered and said to him, "*It is as* you say."

תּוֹאַמוֹת. ⁵⁷קָמוּ אֲחָדִים וְהֵעִידוּ נֶגְדּוֹ דְּבַר שֶׁקֶר בְּאָמְרָם: ⁵⁸"אֲנַחְנוּ שְׁמַעֲנוּ אוֹתוֹ אוֹמֵר 'אֲנִי אֶהֱרֹס אֶת הַהֵיכָל הַזֶּה שֶׁנַּעֲשָׂה בִּידֵי אָדָם וּבִשְׁלוֹשָׁה יָמִים אֶבְנֶה אַחֵר שֶׁאֵינֶנּוּ מַעֲשֵׂה יְדֵי אָדָם'." ⁵⁹וְגַם בָּזֹאת לֹא תָּאֲמוּ דִּבְרֵי עֵדוּתָם. ⁶⁰קָם הַכֹּהֵן הַגָּדוֹל, עָמַד בָּאֶמְצַע וְשָׁאַל אֶת יֵשׁוּעַ: "אֵינְךָ מֵשִׁיב דָּבָר עַל מַה שֶּׁאֵלֶּה מְעִידִים נֶגְדְּךָ?" ⁶¹אַךְ הוּא שָׁתַק וְלֹא הֵשִׁיב דָּבָר. הוֹסִיף הַכֹּהֵן הַגָּדוֹל וְשָׁאַל אוֹתוֹ: "הַאִם אַתָּה הַמָּשִׁיחַ בֶּן־הַמְבֹרָךְ?"

⁶²אָמַר יֵשׁוּעַ: "אֲנִי הוּא. וְאַתֶּם תִּרְאוּ אֶת בֶּן־הָאָדָם יוֹשֵׁב לִימִין הַגְּבוּרָה וּבָא עִם עַנְנֵי הַשָּׁמַיִם."

⁶³קָרַע הַכֹּהֵן הַגָּדוֹל אֶת בְּגָדָיו וְאָמַר: "מַה לָּנוּ עוֹד צֹרֶךְ בְּעֵדִים? ⁶⁴שְׁמַעְתֶּם אֶת הַגִּדּוּף. מַה דַּעְתְּכֶם?"

הַכֹּל הִרְשִׁיעוּ אוֹתוֹ וּפָסְקוּ שֶׁהוּא בֶּן מָוֶת. ⁶⁵אֲחָדִים הֵחֵלּוּ לִירֹק בּוֹ; גַּם כִּסּוּ אֶת פָּנָיו, הִכּוּהוּ בְּאֶגְרוֹף וְאָמְרוּ לוֹ: "הִתְנַבֵּא!" וְהַמְשָׁרְתִים קִדְּמוּ אוֹתוֹ בְּמַכּוֹת.

⁶⁶כְּשֶׁהָיָה כֵּיפָא בֶּחָצֵר לְמַטָּה בָּאָה אַחַת מִשִּׁפְחוֹת הַכֹּהֵן הַגָּדוֹל ⁶⁷וְרָאֲתָה אֶת כֵּיפָא מִתְחַמֵּם. הִבִּיטָה בּוֹ וְאָמְרָה: "גַּם אַתָּה הָיִיתָ עִם יֵשׁוּעַ מִנָּצְרַת."

⁶⁸אַךְ הוּא הִכְחִישׁ בְּאָמְרוֹ: "אֵינֶנִּי מֵבִין מָה אַתְּ אוֹמֶרֶת", וְיָצָא הַחוּצָה אֶל מְבוֹא הֶחָצֵר. ⁶⁹רָאֲתָה אוֹתוֹ הַשִּׁפְחָה וְאָמְרָה שֵׁנִית אֶל הָעוֹמְדִים שָׁם: "זֶה אֶחָד מֵהֶם." ⁷⁰שׁוּב הִכְחִישׁ. לְאַחַר שָׁעָה קַלָּה גַּם הָעוֹמְדִים שָׁם אָמְרוּ לְכֵיפָא: "בֶּאֱמֶת אַתָּה מֵהֶם, כִּי גַּם אַתָּה גְּלִילִי." ⁷¹הוּא הֵחֵל לְקַלֵּל וּלְהִשָּׁבַע. אָמַר: "אֵינֶנִּי מַכִּיר אֶת הָאִישׁ הַזֶּה שֶׁאַתֶּם מְדַבְּרִים עָלָיו", ⁷²וּמִיָּד קָרָא הַתַּרְנְגוֹל שֵׁנִית. נִזְכַּר כֵּיפָא בַּדָּבָר שֶׁאָמַר לוֹ יֵשׁוּעַ "בְּטֶרֶם יִקְרָא הַתַּרְנְגוֹל פַּעֲמַיִם, שָׁלוֹשׁ פְּעָמִים תִּתְכַּחֵשׁ לִי" – וְהִתְיַפַּח בִּבְכִי.

טו בַּבֹּקֶר מִהֲרוּ רָאשֵׁי הַכֹּהֲנִים לְקַיֵּם הִתְיַעֲצוּת עִם הַזְּקֵנִים וְהַסּוֹפְרִים וְכָל הַסַּנְהֶדְרִין. הֵם כָּבְלוּ אֶת יֵשׁוּעַ וְהוֹלִיכוּהוּ וּמְסָרוּהוּ לְפִילָטוֹס. ²שָׁאַל אוֹתוֹ פִּילָטוֹס: "אַתָּה מֶלֶךְ הַיְּהוּדִים?"

³And the chief priests accused Him of many things, but He answered nothing. ⁴Then Pilate asked Him again, saying, "Do You answer nothing? See how many things they testify against You!" ⁵But Jesus still answered nothing, so that Pilate marveled.

⁶Now at the feast he was accustomed to releasing one prisoner to them, whomever they requested. ⁷And there was one named Barabbas, *who was* chained with his fellow rebels; they had committed murder in the rebellion. ⁸Then the multitude, crying aloud, began to ask *him to do* just as he had always done for them. ⁹But Pilate answered them, saying, "Do you want me to release to you the King of the Jews?" ¹⁰For he knew that the chief priests had handed Him over because of envy.

¹¹But the chief priests stirred up the crowd, so that he should rather release Barabbas to them. ¹²Pilate answered and said to them again, "What then do you want me to do *with Him* whom you call the King of the Jews?"

¹³So they cried out again, "Crucify Him!"

¹⁴Then Pilate said to them, "Why, what evil has He done?"

But they cried out all the more, "Crucify Him!"

¹⁵So Pilate, wanting to gratify the crowd, released Barabbas to them; and he delivered Jesus, after he had scourged *Him,* to be crucified.

¹⁶Then the soldiers led Him away into the hall called Praetorium, and they called together the whole garrison. ¹⁷And they clothed Him with purple; and they twisted a crown of thorns, put it on His *head,* ¹⁸and began to salute Him, "Hail, King of the Jews!" ¹⁹Then they struck Him on the head with a reed and spat on Him; and bowing the knee, they worshiped Him. ²⁰And when they had mocked Him, they took the purple off Him, put His own clothes on Him, and led Him out to crucify Him.

²¹Then they compelled a certain man, Simon a Cyrenian, the father of Alexander and Rufus, as he was coming out of the country and passing by, to bear His cross. ²²And they brought Him to the place Golgotha, which is translated, Place of a Skull. ²³Then they gave Him wine mingled with myrrh to drink, but He did not take *it.* ²⁴And when they crucified Him, they divided His garments, casting lots for them to determine what every man should take.

²⁵Now it was the third hour, and they crucified Him. ²⁶And the inscription of His accusation was written above:

THE KING OF THE JEWS.

³ וְרָאשֵׁי הַכֹּהֲנִים הִשְׁמִיעוּ נֶגְדּוֹ הָאֲשָׁמוֹת רַבּוֹת. הֵשִׁיב וְאָמַר אֵלָיו: "אַתָּה אוֹמֵר."

⁴ הוֹסִיף פִּילָטוֹס וְשָׁאַל אוֹתוֹ: "אֵינְךָ מֵשִׁיב דָּבָר; רְאֵה כַּמָּה הֵם מַאֲשִׁימִים אוֹתְךָ!" ⁵ אוּלָם יֵשׁוּעַ לֹא הֵשִׁיב עוֹד דָּבָר, לִתְמָהוֹנוֹ שֶׁל פִּילָטוֹס.

⁶ בֶּחָג הָיָה מְשַׁחְרֵר לָהֶם אָסִיר אֶחָד עַל-פִּי בַּקָּשָׁתָם. ⁷ אִישׁ אֶחָד, בַּר-אַבָּא שְׁמוֹ, יָשַׁב אָז בַּכֶּלֶא עִם הַמּוֹרְדִים שֶׁבִּצְּעוּ מַעֲשֵׂה רֶצַח בְּעֵת הַמֶּרֶד. ⁸ בָּא הֶהָמוֹן וְהֵחֵל לְבַקֵּשׁ שֶׁיַּעֲשֶׂה לְמַעֲנָם כְּמִנְהָגוֹ. ⁹ הֵשִׁיב לָהֶם פִּילָטוֹס: "הַאִם רוֹצִים אַתֶּם שֶׁאֲשַׁחְרֵר לָכֶם אֶת מֶלֶךְ הַיְּהוּדִים?" ¹⁰ כִּי יָדַע שֶׁמִּקִּנְאָה מָסְרוּ אוֹתוֹ רָאשֵׁי הַכֹּהֲנִים. ¹¹ אַךְ רָאשֵׁי הַכֹּהֲנִים הֵסִיתוּ אֶת הֶהָמוֹן לְהַעֲדִיף שֶׁיְּשַׁחְרֵר לָהֶם אֶת בַּר-אַבָּא. ¹² הוֹסִיף פִּילָטוֹס וְאָמַר לָהֶם: "אִם כֵּן מַה אֶעֱשֶׂה לָזֶה שֶׁאַתֶּם קוֹרְאִים לוֹ] מֶלֶךְ הַיְּהוּדִים?"

¹³ "צְלֹב אוֹתוֹ!" צָעֲקוּ.

¹⁴ "אֲבָל מַה רָעָה עָשָׂה?" אָמַר לָהֶם פִּילָטוֹס. אַךְ הֵם צָעֲקוּ בְּיֶתֶר שְׂאֵת: "צְלֹב אוֹתוֹ!"

¹⁵ כֵּיוָן שֶׁרָצָה פִּילָטוֹס לְהַשְׂבִּיעַ אֶת רְצוֹן הֶהָמוֹן, שִׁחְרֵר לָהֶם אֶת בַּר-אַבָּא, וְאֶת יֵשׁוּעַ הִלְקָה וּמָסַר אוֹתוֹ לִצְלִיבָה. ¹⁶ הַחַיָּלִים הוֹלִיכוּ אוֹתוֹ לִפְנִים הֶחָצֵר שֶׁבְּבֵית הַמִּמְשָׁל וְקָרְאוּ לְכָל הַגְּדוּד. ¹⁷ הֵם הִלְבִּישׁוּהוּ אַרְגָּמָן, שָׂמוּ עָלָיו עֲטֶרֶת שֶׁקָּלְעוּ מִקּוֹצִים ¹⁸ וְהֵחֵלּוּ לְבָרֵךְ אוֹתוֹ: "שָׁלוֹם לְךָ, מֶלֶךְ הַיְּהוּדִים!" ¹⁹ הִכּוּהוּ עַל רֹאשׁוֹ בְּקָנֶה וְיָרְקוּ בּוֹ; גַּם כָּרְעוּ עַל בִּרְכֵּיהֶם וְהִשְׁתַּחֲווּ לוֹ. ²⁰ אַחֲרֵי שֶׁהִתְלוֹצְצוּ בּוֹ הֵסִירוּ מֵעָלָיו אֶת הָאַרְגָּמָן, הִלְבִּישׁוּהוּ אֶת בְּגָדָיו וְהוֹצִיאוּהוּ לִצְלִיבָה.

²¹ אוֹתָהּ שָׁעָה עָבַר שָׁם שִׁמְעוֹן מִקִּירֶנְיָה, אֲבִיהֶם שֶׁל אֲלֶכְּסַנְדֶּר וְרוּפוֹס, כַּאֲשֶׁר בָּא מִן הַשָּׂדֶה. חָם הִכְרִיחוּ אוֹתוֹ לָשֵׂאת אֶת צְלָבוֹ שֶׁל יֵשׁוּעַ ²² וְהוֹלִיכוּ אֶת יֵשׁוּעַ אֶל מְקוֹם גָּלְגָּתָּא, שֶׁפֵּרוּשׁוֹ מְקוֹם הַגֻּלְגֹּלֶת. ²³ נָתְנוּ לְיֵשׁוּעַ יַיִן מָהוּל בְּמֹר וְלֹא לָקַח אוֹתוֹ. ²⁴ אָז צָלְבוּ אוֹתוֹ וְחִלְּקוּ אֶת בְּגָדָיו בְּהַפִּילָם עֲלֵיהֶם גּוֹרָל, לִקְבֹּעַ מַה יִּקַּח כָּל אֶחָד. ²⁵ הַשָּׁעָה הָיְתָה תֵּשַׁע בַּבֹּקֶר כַּאֲשֶׁר צָלְבוּ אוֹתוֹ. ²⁶ מֵעָלָיו הָיָה

27 With Him they also crucified two robbers, one on His right and the other on His left. 28 So the Scripture was fulfilled which says, "*And He was numbered with the transgressors.*"

29 And those who passed by blasphemed Him, wagging their heads and saying, "Aha! *You* who destroy the temple and build *it* in three days, 30 save Yourself, and come down from the cross!"

31 Likewise the chief priests also, mocking among themselves with the scribes, said, "He saved others; Himself He cannot save. 32 Let the Christ, the King of Israel, descend now from the cross, that we may see and believe."

Even those who were crucified with Him reviled Him.

33 Now when the sixth hour had come, there was darkness over the whole land until the ninth hour. 34 And at the ninth hour Jesus cried out with a loud voice, saying, "Eloi, Eloi, lama sabachthani?" which is translated, "*My God, My God, why have You forsaken Me?*"

35 Some of those who stood by, when they heard *that,* said, "Look, He is calling for Elijah!" 36 Then someone ran and filled a sponge full of sour wine, put *it* on a reed, and offered *it* to Him to drink, saying, "Let Him alone; let us see if Elijah will come to take Him down."

37 And Jesus cried out with a loud voice, and breathed His last.

38 Then the veil of the temple was torn in two from top to bottom. 39 So when the centurion, who stood opposite Him, saw that He cried out like this and breathed His last, he said, "Truly this Man was the Son of God!"

40 There were also women looking on from afar, among whom were Mary Magdalene, Mary the mother of James the Less and of Joses, and Salome, 41 who also followed Him and ministered to Him when He was in Galilee, and many other women who came up with Him to Jerusalem.

42 Now when evening had come, because it was the Preparation Day, that is, the day before the Sabbath, 43 Joseph of Arimathea, a prominent council member, who was himself waiting for the kingdom of God, coming and taking courage, went in to Pilate and asked for the body of Jesus. 44 Pilate marveled that He was already dead; and summoning the centurion, he asked him if He had been dead for some time. 45 So when he found out from the centurion, he granted the body to Joseph. 46 Then he bought fine linen, took Him down, and wrapped Him in the linen. And he laid Him in a tomb which had been hewn out of the rock, and rolled a stone

27 וְיַחַד אִתּוֹ קָבְעוּ כְּתַב אַשְׁמָתוֹ, "מֶלֶךְ הַיְּהוּדִים." צָלְבוּ שְׁנֵי שׁוֹדְדִים, אֶחָד מִימִינוֹ וְאֶחָד מִשְּׂמֹאלוֹ. 28 [כָּזֶה הִתְקַיֵּם הַכָּתוּב "וְאֶת פּוֹשְׁעִים נִמְנָה."] 29 וְהָעוֹבְרִים שָׁם גִּדְּפוּ אוֹתוֹ, הֵנִיעוּ רֹאשָׁם וְאָמְרוּ: "אֲהָהּ! הַהוֹרֵס אֶת בֵּית הַמִּקְדָּשׁ וּבוֹנֶה אוֹתוֹ בִּשְׁלוֹשָׁה יָמִים, 30 הוֹשַׁע אֶת עַצְמְךָ וְרֵד מִן הַצְּלָב!" 31 כָּךְ גַּם הִתְלוֹצְצוּ רָאשֵׁי הַכֹּהֲנִים וְהַסּוֹפְרִים בְּאָמְרָם זֶה אֶל זֶה: "אֲחֵרִים הוֹשִׁיעַ; אֶת עַצְמוֹ אֵינֶנּוּ יָכוֹל לְהוֹשִׁיעַ?! 32 הַמָּשִׁיחַ מֶלֶךְ יִשְׂרָאֵל, שֶׁיֵּרֵד עַכְשָׁו מִן הַצְּלָב וְנִרְאֶה וְנַאֲמִין!" גַּם הַנִּצְלָבִים אִתּוֹ חֵרְפוּ אוֹתוֹ.

33 בְּשָׁעָה שְׁתֵּים-עֶשְׂרֵה בַּצָּהֳרַיִם הִשְׂתָּרֵר חֹשֶׁךְ עַל כָּל הָאָרֶץ עַד הַשָּׁעָה שָׁלוֹשׁ, 34 וּבְשָׁעָה שָׁלוֹשׁ צָעַק יֵשׁוּעַ בְּקוֹל גָּדוֹל: "אֱלֹהִי, אֱלֹהִי, לְמָה שְׁבַקְתָּנִי?" שֶׁתַּרְגּוּמוֹ "אֵלִי, אֵלִי, לָמָה עֲזַבְתָּנִי?" 35 כַּמָּה מִן הָעוֹמְדִים שָׁם שָׁמְעוּ זֹאת וְאָמְרוּ: "הִנֵּה לְאֵלִיָּהוּ הוּא קוֹרֵא." 36 מִישֶׁהוּ רָץ וּמִלֵּא סְפוֹג בְּחֹמֶץ, הִצְמִיד אוֹתוֹ אֶל קָנֶה וְהִגִּישׁ לוֹ לִשְׁתּוֹת בְּאָמְרוֹ: "הָבָה נִרְאֶה אִם יָבוֹא אֵלִיָּהוּ לְהוֹרִיד אוֹתוֹ."

37 יֵשׁוּעַ צָעַק בְּקוֹל גָּדוֹל וְנָפַח אֶת רוּחוֹ. 38 וּפָרֹכֶת הַמִּקְדָּשׁ נִקְרְעָה לִשְׁנַיִם, מִלְמַעְלָה עַד לְמַטָּה. 39 כְּשֶׁרָאָה שַׂר הַמֵּאָה הָעוֹמֵד מוּלוֹ כִּי כָּךְ נָפַח אֶת רוּחוֹ, אָמַר: "בֶּאֱמֶת, הָאִישׁ הַזֶּה הָיָה בֶּן-אֱלֹהִים!"

40 גַּם הָיוּ נָשִׁים שֶׁהִסְתַּכְּלוּ מֵרָחוֹק וּבֵינֵיהֶן מִרְיָם הַמַּגְדָּלִית, מִרְיָם אִמּוֹ שֶׁל יַעֲקֹב הַצָּעִיר וְשֶׁל יוֹסֵי וּשְׁלוֹמִית, 41 אֲשֶׁר הָלְכוּ אַחֲרָיו בִּהְיוֹתוֹ בַּגָּלִיל וְשֵׁרְתוּהוּ, וְרַבּוֹת אֲחֵרוֹת שֶׁעָלוּ אִתּוֹ לִירוּשָׁלַיִם.

42 לְעֵת עֶרֶב – וּמֵאַחַר שֶׁהָיָה עֶרֶב שַׁבָּת – 43 בָּא יוֹסֵף אִישׁ רָמָתַיִם, חֲבֵר סַנְהֶדְרִין נִכְבָּד שֶׁהָיָה גַּם הוּא מְחַכֶּה לְמַלְכוּת הָאֱלֹהִים. הֵעֵז וּבָא אֶל פִּילָטוֹס וּבִקֵּשׁ מִמֶּנּוּ אֶת גּוּפַת יֵשׁוּעַ. 44 פִּילָטוֹס הִתְפַּלֵּא שֶׁהוּא כְּבָר מֵת. קָרָא לְשַׂר הַמֵּאָה וְשָׁאַל אוֹתוֹ אִם יֵשׁוּעַ כְּבָר מֵת. 45 כְּשֶׁנִּתְבָּרֵר לוֹ הַדָּבָר מִפִּי שַׂר הַמֵּאָה, נָתַן לְיוֹסֵף אֶת הַגּוּפָה. 46 יוֹסֵף קָנָה סָדִין. הוּא הוֹרִיד אוֹתוֹ וְעָטַף אוֹתוֹ בַּסָּדִין, הִנִּיחוֹ בְּקֶבֶר

against the door of the tomb. ⁴⁷And Mary
Magdalene and Mary *the mother* of Joses observed
where He was laid.

16 Now when the Sabbath was past, Mary
Magdalene, Mary *the mother* of James, and Salome
bought spices, that they might come and anoint
Him. ²Very early in the morning, on the first *day* of
the week, they came to the tomb when the sun had
risen. ³And they said among themselves, "Who will
roll away the stone from the door of the tomb for
us?" ⁴But when they looked up, they saw that the
stone had been rolled away—for it was very large.
⁵And entering the tomb, they saw a young man
clothed in a long white robe sitting on the right side;
and they were alarmed.

⁶But he said to them, "Do not be alarmed. You
seek Jesus of Nazareth, who was crucified. He is
risen! He is not here. See the place where they laid
Him. ⁷But go, tell His disciples—and Peter—that
He is going before you into Galilee; there you will
see Him, as He said to you."

⁸So they went out quickly and fled from the
tomb, for they trembled and were amazed. And
they said nothing to anyone, for they were afraid.

⁹Now when *He* rose early on the first *day* of the
week, He appeared first to Mary Magdalene, out of
whom He had cast seven demons. ¹⁰She went and
told those who had been with Him, as they
mourned and wept. ¹¹And when they heard that He
was alive and had been seen by her, they did not
believe.

¹²After that, He appeared in another form to two
of them as they walked and went into the country.
¹³And they went and told *it* to the rest, *but* they did
not believe them either.

¹⁴Later He appeared to the eleven as they sat at
the table; and He rebuked their unbelief and
hardness of heart, because they did not believe
those who had seen Him after He had risen. ¹⁵And
He said to them, "Go into all the world and preach
the gospel to every creature. ¹⁶He who believes and
is baptized will be saved; but he who does not
believe will be condemned. ¹⁷And these signs will
follow those who believe: In My name they will cast
out demons; they will speak with new tongues;
¹⁸they will take up serpents; and if they drink
anything deadly, it will by no means hurt them; they
will lay hands on the sick, and they will recover."

¹⁹So then, after the Lord had spoken to them, He
was received up into heaven, and sat down at the
right hand of God. ²⁰And they went out and

⁴⁷וּמִרְיָם חָצוּב בְּסֶלַע וְגָלַל אֶבֶן עַל פִּי הַקֶּבֶר.
הַמַּגְדָּלִית וּמִרְיָם אֵם יוֹסֵי רָאוּ הֵיכָן הֻנַּח אוֹתוֹ.

טז כְּשֶׁעָבַר יוֹם הַשַּׁבָּת, מִרְיָם הַמַּגְדָּלִית וּמִרְיָם
אֵם יַעֲקֹב וּשְׁלוֹמִית קָנוּ בְּשָׂמִים, כִּי הִתְכַּוְּנוּ לָבוֹא
וְלִמְשֹׁחַ אוֹתוֹ. ²בָּרִאשׁוֹן בַּשָּׁבוּעַ, בַּבֹּקֶר הַשְׁכֵּם, בָּאוּ
אֶל הַקֶּבֶר עִם זְרִיחַת הַשֶּׁמֶשׁ. ³אָמְרוּ זוֹ אֶל זוֹ: "מִי
יָגֹל לָנוּ אֶת הָאֶבֶן מֵעַל פֶּתַח הַקֶּבֶר?" ⁴כַּאֲשֶׁר
הִבִּיטוּ רָאוּ כִּי הָאֶבֶן כְּבָר נָגֹלָה, וְהִיא גְדוֹלָה מְאֹד.
⁵נִכְנְסוּ לְתוֹךְ הַקֶּבֶר וְרָאוּ בָּחוּר אֶחָד יוֹשֵׁב מִיָּמִין
וְהוּא לָבוּשׁ גְּלִימָה לְבָנָה. הֵן נִדְהֲמוּ. ⁶אָמַר לָהֶן:
"אַל תִּבָּהֲלְנָה. אֶת יֵשׁוּעַ מִנָּצְרַת אֲשֶׁר נִצְלַב אַתֶּן
מְחַפְּשׂוֹת? הוּא קָם לִתְחִיָּה וְאֵינֶנּוּ פֹּה עוֹד. הִנֵּה
הַמָּקוֹם שֶׁהִנִּיחוּהוּ בּוֹ. ⁷וְעַתָּה לֵכְנָה וְהַגֵּדְנָה
לְתַלְמִידָיו וּלְכֵיפָא, 'הוּא הוֹלֵךְ לִפְנֵיכֶם לַגָּלִיל. שָׁם
תִּרְאוּ אוֹתוֹ כְּפִי שֶׁאָמַר לָכֶם.'"

⁸הֵן יָצְאוּ וּבָרְחוּ מִן הַקֶּבֶר, כִּי רְעָדָה וְתַדְהֵמָה אָחֲזוּ
בָּהֶן, וְלֹא סִפְּרוּ דָּבָר לְאִישׁ מִפְּנֵי שֶׁפָּחֲדוּ.

[⁹כַּאֲשֶׁר קָם בַּבֹּקֶר בָּרִאשׁוֹן בַּשָּׁבוּעַ, נִרְאָה
בָּרִאשׁוֹנָה לְמִרְיָם הַמַּגְדָּלִית אֲשֶׁר מִמֶּנָּה גֵּרַשׁ
שִׁבְעָה שֵׁדִים. ¹⁰הִיא הָלְכָה וְסִפְּרָה לַאֲנָשִׁים שֶׁהָיוּ
אִתּוֹ לִפְנֵי כֵן וְהֵם מִתְאַבְּלִים וּבוֹכִים. ¹¹כַּאֲשֶׁר
שָׁמְעוּ שֶׁהוּא חַי וְנִרְאָה אֵלֶיהָ לֹא הֶאֱמִינוּ. ¹²אַחֲרֵי
כֵן נִרְאָה בִּדְמוּת אַחֶרֶת לִשְׁנַיִם מֵהֶם בְּעֵת שֶׁהָלְכוּ
בְּדַרְכָּם לְאַחַד הַכְּפָרִים. ¹³הַלָּלוּ הָלְכוּ וְסִפְּרוּ
לַאֲחֵרִים וְגַם לָהֶם לֹא הֶאֱמִינוּ. ¹⁴אַחַר כָּךְ נִרְאָה
אֶל הָאַחַד־עָשָׂר בִּהְיוֹתָם מְסֻבִּים לֶאֱכֹל. הוּא גָּעַר
בָּהֶם עַל חֹסֶר אֱמוּנָתָם וּקְשִׁיחוּת לְבָבָם, מִפְּנֵי שֶׁלֹּא
הֶאֱמִינוּ לְאֵלֶּה שֶׁרָאוּ אוֹתוֹ אַחֲרֵי קוּמוֹ לִתְחִיָּה.
¹⁵אָמַר לָהֶם: "לְכוּ אֶל כָּל הָעוֹלָם וְהַכְרִיזוּ אֶת
הַבְּשׂוֹרָה לְכָל הַבְּרִיאָה. ¹⁶הַמַּאֲמִין וְנִטְבָּל יִוָּשַׁע,
וּמִי שֶׁלֹּא יַאֲמִין יֻאֲשָׁם. ¹⁷וְאֵלֶּה הָאוֹתוֹת אֲשֶׁר יִלְווּ
אֶל הַמַּאֲמִינִים: יְגָרְשׁוּ שֵׁדִים בִּשְׁמִי; בִּלְשׁוֹנוֹת
חֲדָשׁוֹת יְדַבְּרוּ; ¹⁸יָרִימוּ נְחָשִׁים, וְאִם יִשְׁתּוּ רַעַל
מֵמִית לֹא יַנִּיקֵם; יְדֵיהֶם יִסְמְכוּ עַל חוֹלִים וְיֵיטַב
לָהֶם."

¹⁹לְאַחַר שֶׁדִּבֵּר אֲלֵיהֶם נִשָּׂא הָאָדוֹן הַשָּׁמַיְמָה וְיָשַׁב
לִימִין אֱלֹהִים. ²⁰הֵם יָצְאוּ וְהִכְרִיזוּ אֶת הַבְּשׂוֹרָה

preached everywhere, the Lord working with *them* and confirming the word through the accompanying signs. Amen.

בְּכָל מָקוֹם, וְהָאָדוֹן פָּעַל עִמָּהֶם וְאִשֵּׁר אֶת הַדָּבָר בָּאוֹתוֹת שֶׁנִּלְווּ אֲלֵיהֶם.]

The Gospel According to

LUKE

1 Inasmuch as many have taken in hand to set in order a narrative of those things which have been fulfilled among us, ²just as those who from the beginning were eyewitnesses and ministers of the word delivered them to us, ³it seemed good to me also, having had perfect understanding of all things from the very first, to write to you an orderly account, most excellent Theophilus, ⁴that you may know the certainty of those things in which you were instructed.

⁵There was in the days of Herod, the king of Judea, a certain priest named Zacharias, of the division of Abijah. His wife *was* of the daughters of Aaron, and her name *was* Elizabeth. ⁶And they were both righteous before God, walking in all the commandments and ordinances of the Lord blameless. ⁷But they had no child, because Elizabeth was barren, and they were both well advanced in years.

⁸So it was, that while he was serving as priest before God in the order of his division, ⁹according to the custom of the priesthood, his lot fell to burn incense when he went into the temple of the Lord. ¹⁰And the whole multitude of the people was praying outside at the hour of incense. ¹¹Then an angel of the Lord appeared to him, standing on the right side of the altar of incense. ¹²And when Zacharias saw *him,* he was troubled, and fear fell upon him.

¹³But the angel said to him, "Do not be afraid, Zacharias, for your prayer is heard; and your wife Elizabeth will bear you a son, and you shall call his name John. ¹⁴And you will have joy and gladness, and many will rejoice at his birth. ¹⁵For he will be great in the sight of the Lord, and shall drink neither wine nor strong drink. He will also be filled with the Holy Spirit, even from his mother's womb. ¹⁶And he will turn many of the children of Israel to the Lord their God. ¹⁷He will also go before Him in the spirit and power of Elijah, '*to turn the hearts of the fathers to the children,*' and the disobedient to the wisdom of the just, to make ready a people prepared for the Lord."

¹⁸And Zacharias said to the angel, "How shall I know this? For I am an old man, and my wife is well advanced in years."

הַבְּשׂוֹרָה עַל־פִּי לוּקָם

א רַבִּים שָׁלְחוּ יָדָם לְחַבֵּר אֶת סִפּוּר הַדְּבָרִים אֲשֶׁר הִתְקַיְמוּ בְּקִרְבֵּנוּ, ²כְּפִי שֶׁמָּסְרוּם לָנוּ אֵלֶּה אֲשֶׁר מִתְּחִלָּה הָיוּ עֵדֵי רְאִיָּה וּמְשָׁרְתֵי דְּבַר יהוה. ³לְפִיכָךְ, לְאַחַר שֶׁהִתְחַקֵּיתִי הֵיטֵב עַל כָּל הַדְּבָרִים מֵרֵאשִׁיתָם, חָשַׁבְתִּי גַּם אֲנִי לָנָכוֹן לְכָתְבָם לְךָ כְּסִדְרָם, תֵּאוֹפִילוֹס הַנִּכְבָּד, ⁴לְמַעַן תֵּדַע בַּאֲמִתּוּת הַדְּבָרִים שֶׁלֻּמַּדְתָּ.

⁵בִּימֵי הוֹרְדוֹס מֶלֶךְ אֶרֶץ יְהוּדָה הָיָה כֹּהֵן מִמִּשְׁמֶרֶת אֲבִיָּה וּשְׁמוֹ זְכַרְיָה, וְלוֹ אִשָּׁה מִבְּנוֹת אַהֲרֹן וּשְׁמָהּ אֱלִישֶׁבַע. ⁶שְׁנֵיהֶם הָיוּ צַדִּיקִים לִפְנֵי אֱלֹהִים, הוֹלְכֵי תָּמִים בְּכָל מִצְווֹתָיו וְחֻקּוֹתָיו. ⁷וּבֵן לֹא הָיָה לָהֶם, כִּי אֱלִישֶׁבַע עֲקָרָה וּשְׁנֵיהֶם בָּאִים בַּיָּמִים. ⁸בְּאַחַד הַיָּמִים, כַּאֲשֶׁר כִּהֵן לִפְנֵי הָאֱלֹהִים בְּסֵדֶר מִשְׁמַרְתּוֹ ⁹עַל־פִּי מִנְהַג הַכְּהֻנָּה, יָצָא גוֹרָלוֹ לְהִכָּנֵס אֶל הֵיכַל יהוה לְהַקְטִיר קְטֹרֶת. ¹⁰וְכָל קְהַל הָעָם הָיָה מִתְפַּלֵּל בַּחוּץ בִּשְׁעַת הַקְּטֹרֶת. ¹¹לְפֶתַע נִרְאָה אֵלָיו מַלְאַךְ יהוה נִצָּב לִימִין מִזְבַּח הַקְּטֹרֶת. ¹²כִּרְאוֹתוֹ זֹאת נִבְהַל זְכַרְיָה וּפַחַד נָפַל עָלָיו.

¹³אָמַר אֵלָיו הַמַּלְאָךְ: "אַל תִּירָא, זְכַרְיָה, כִּי נִשְׁמְעָה תְּפִלָּתְךָ. אֱלִישֶׁבַע אִשְׁתְּךָ תֵּלֵד לְךָ בֵּן וְאַתָּה תִּקְרָא שְׁמוֹ יוֹחָנָן. ¹⁴כִּי שִׂמְחָה וְשָׂשׂוֹן יִהְיוּ לְךָ וְרַבִּים יִשְׂמְחוּ בְּהִוָּלְדוֹ; ¹⁵כִּי גָּדוֹל יִהְיֶה לִפְנֵי יהוה, יַיִן וְשֵׁכָר לֹא יִשְׁתֶּה, וְיִמָּלֵא רוּחַ הַקֹּדֶשׁ מֵרֶחֶם אִמּוֹ. ¹⁶רַבִּים מִבְּנֵי יִשְׂרָאֵל יָשִׁיב אֶל יהוה אֱלֹהֵיהֶם, ¹⁷וְיֵלֵךְ לְפָנָיו בְּרוּחַ אֵלִיָּהוּ וּגְבוּרָתוֹ, לְהָשִׁיב לֵב אָבוֹת עַל בָּנִים, וְסוֹרְרִים אֶל תְּבוּנַת הַצַּדִּיקִים, לְהַכְשִׁיר עַם מוּכָן לַיהוה."

¹⁸אָמַר זְכַרְיָה אֶל הַמַּלְאָךְ: "לְפִי מָה אֵדַע זֹאת? הֲרֵי אֲנִי זָקֵן וְאִשְׁתִּי בָּאָה בַּיָּמִים."

¹⁹ And the angel answered and said to him, "I am Gabriel, who stands in the presence of God, and was sent to speak to you and bring you these glad tidings. ²⁰ But behold, you will be mute and not able to speak until the day these things take place, because you did not believe my words which will be fulfilled in their own time."

²¹ And the people waited for Zacharias, and marveled that he lingered so long in the temple. ²² But when he came out, he could not speak to them; and they perceived that he had seen a vision in the temple, for he beckoned to them and remained speechless.

²³ So it was, as soon as the days of his service were completed, that he departed to his own house. ²⁴ Now after those days his wife Elizabeth conceived; and she hid herself five months, saying, ²⁵ "Thus the Lord has dealt with me, in the days when He looked on *me,* to take away my reproach among people."

²⁶ Now in the sixth month the angel Gabriel was sent by God to a city of Galilee named Nazareth, ²⁷ to a virgin betrothed to a man whose name was Joseph, of the house of David. The virgin's name *was* Mary. ²⁸ And having come in, the angel said to her, "Rejoice, highly favored *one,* the Lord *is* with you; blessed *are* you among women!"

²⁹ But when she saw *him,* she was troubled at his saying, and considered what manner of greeting this was. ³⁰ Then the angel said to her, "Do not be afraid, Mary, for you have found favor with God. ³¹ And behold, you will conceive in your womb and bring forth a Son, and shall call His name Jesus. ³² He will be great, and will be called the Son of the Highest; and the Lord God will give Him the throne of His father David. ³³ And He will reign over the house of Jacob forever, and of His kingdom there will be no end."

³⁴ Then Mary said to the angel, "How can this be, since I do not know a man?"

³⁵ And the angel answered and said to her, "*The* Holy Spirit will come upon you, and the power of the Highest will overshadow you; therefore, also, that Holy One who is to be born will be called the Son of God. ³⁶ Now indeed, Elizabeth your relative has also conceived a son in her old age; and this is now the sixth month for her who was called barren. ³⁷ For with God nothing will be impossible."

³⁸ Then Mary said, "Behold the maidservant of the Lord! Let it be to me according to your word." And the angel departed from her.

³⁹ Now Mary arose in those days and went into the hill country with haste, to a city of Judah, ⁴⁰ and entered the house of Zacharias and greeted

¹⁹ הֵשִׁיב לוֹ הַמַּלְאָךְ: "אֲנִי גַּבְרִיאֵל הַנִּצָּב לִפְנֵי אֱלֹהִים. נִשְׁלַחְתִּי לְדַבֵּר אֵלֶיךָ וּלְבַשֵּׂר לְךָ זֹאת. ²⁰ וְהִנֵּה תֵּאָלֵם וְלֹא תוּכַל לְדַבֵּר עַד אֲשֶׁר יָקֻרוּ הַדְּבָרִים הָאֵלֶּה, עַל שֶׁלֹּא הֶאֱמַנְתָּ לִדְבָרַי אֲשֶׁר יִתְקַיְּמוּ בְּעִתָּם."

²¹ הָעָם חִכָּה לִזְכַרְיָה וְתָמַהּ עַל שֶׁהִתְעַכֵּב בַּהֵיכָל. ²² וְהִנֵּה בְּצֵאתוֹ מִשָּׁם לֹא הָיָה יָכוֹל לְדַבֵּר אֲלֵיהֶם, וְהֵם הֵבִינוּ שֶׁרָאָה מַרְאָה בַּהֵיכָל; הוּא עַצְמוֹ הָיָה רוֹמֵז לָהֶם וְעוֹדֶנּוּ אִלֵּם. ²³ כְּתֹם יְמֵי שֵׁרוּתוֹ חָזַר לְבֵיתוֹ, ²⁴ וּלְאַחַר הַיָּמִים הָאֵלֶּה הָרְתָה אֱלִישֶׁבַע אִשְׁתּוֹ. בְּמֶשֶׁךְ חֲמִשָּׁה חֳדָשִׁים הִסְתַּתְּרָה, וְזֹאת אָמְרָה: ²⁵ "כָּךְ עָשָׂה לִי אֱלֹהִים כַּאֲשֶׁר רָאָה לְהָסִיר אֶת חֶרְפָּתִי בְּקֶרֶב בְּנֵי אָדָם."

²⁶ בַּחֹדֶשׁ הַשִּׁשִּׁי נִשְׁלַח הַמַּלְאָךְ גַּבְרִיאֵל מֵאֵת הָאֱלֹהִים לְעִיר בַּגָּלִיל, אֲשֶׁר שְׁמָהּ נָצְרַת, ²⁷ אֶל בְּתוּלָה מְאֹרֶסֶת לְאִישׁ מִבֵּית דָּוִד וּשְׁמוֹ יוֹסֵף, וְשֵׁם הַבְּתוּלָה מִרְיָם.

²⁸ בְּהִכָּנְסוֹ לַחֲדָרָהּ אָמַר הַמַּלְאָךְ: "שִׂמְחִי, בְּרוּכַת הַחֶסֶד. יהוה עִמָּךְ". ²⁹ הִיא נִרְהֲמָה לְשֵׁמַע הַדָּבָר וְחָשְׁבָה בְּלִבָּהּ מַה טִּיבָהּ שֶׁל הַבְּרָכָה הַזֹּאת. ³⁰ אָמַר לָהּ הַמַּלְאָךְ: "אַל תִּפְחֲדִי, מִרְיָם, כִּי מָצָאת חֵן לִפְנֵי אֱלֹהִים. ³¹ הִנֵּה תַּהֲרִי וְתֵלְדִי בֵּן, וְתִקְרְאִי שְׁמוֹ יֵשׁוּעַ. ³² הוּא גָּדוֹל יִהְיֶה וּבֶן־עֶלְיוֹן יִקָּרֵא, וַיהוה אֱלֹהִים יִתֵּן לוֹ אֶת כִּסֵּא דָּוִד אָבִיו; ³³ וְיִמְלֹךְ עַל בֵּית יַעֲקֹב לְעוֹלָם וְאֵין קֵץ לְמַלְכוּתוֹ."

³⁴ אָמְרָה מִרְיָם אֶל הַמַּלְאָךְ: "אֵיךְ יִהְיֶה הַדָּבָר הַזֶּה, הֲרֵי אֵינֶנִּי יוֹדַעַת אִישׁ?" ³⁵ הֵשִׁיב הַמַּלְאָךְ וְאָמַר: "רוּחַ הַקֹּדֶשׁ תָּבוֹא עָלַיִךְ וּגְבוּרַת עֶלְיוֹן תָּצֵל עָלָיִךְ. לָכֵן קָדוֹשׁ יִקָּרֵא הַיִּלּוֹד, בֶּן־אֱלֹהִים. ³⁶ וְהִנֵּה אֱלִישֶׁבַע קְרוֹבָתֵךְ גַּם הִיא הָרְתָה בֵּן בְּזִקְנָתָהּ, וְזֹאת שֶׁקָּרְאוּ לָהּ עֲקָרָה הָרָה זֶה הַחֹדֶשׁ הַשִּׁשִּׁי, ³⁷ כִּי לֹא יִפָּלֵא מֵאֱלֹהִים כָּל דָּבָר."

³⁸ אָמְרָה מִרְיָם: "הִנְנִי שִׁפְחַת אֲדֹנָי, יְהִי לִי כִּדְבָרֶךָ". וְהַמַּלְאָךְ הָלַךְ לוֹ.

³⁹ בַּיָּמִים הָהֵם קָמָה מִרְיָם וּמִהֲרָה לָלֶכֶת אֶל אֵזוֹר הָהָר, אֶל אַחַת מֵעָרֵי יְהוּדָה. ⁴⁰ הִיא נִכְנְסָה לְבֵית

Elizabeth. ⁴¹And it happened, when Elizabeth heard the greeting of Mary, that the babe leaped in her womb; and Elizabeth was filled with the Holy Spirit. ⁴²Then she spoke out with a loud voice and said, "Blessed *are* you among women, and blessed *is* the fruit of your womb! ⁴³But why *is* this *granted* to me, that the mother of my Lord should come to me? ⁴⁴For indeed, as soon as the voice of your greeting sounded in my ears, the babe leaped in my womb for joy. ⁴⁵Blessed *is* she who believed, for there will be a fulfillment of those things which were told her from the Lord."

⁴⁶And Mary said:

"My soul magnifies the Lord,
⁴⁷ And my spirit has rejoiced in God my Savior.
⁴⁸ For He has regarded the lowly state of His
maidservant;
For behold, henceforth all generations will
call me blessed.
⁴⁹ For He who is mighty has done great things
for me,
And holy *is* His name.
⁵⁰ And His mercy *is* on those who fear Him
From generation to generation.
⁵¹ He has shown strength with His arm;
He has scattered *the* proud in the imagina-
tion of their hearts.
⁵² He has put down the mighty from *their*
thrones,
And exalted *the* lowly.
⁵³ He has filled *the* hungry with good things,
And *the* rich He has sent away empty.
⁵⁴ He has helped His servant Israel,
In remembrance of *His* mercy,
⁵⁵ As He spoke to our fathers,
To Abraham and to his seed forever."

⁵⁶And Mary remained with her about three months, and returned to her house.

⁵⁷Now Elizabeth's full time came for her to be delivered, and she brought forth a son. ⁵⁸When her neighbors and relatives heard how the Lord had shown great mercy to her, they rejoiced with her.

⁵⁹So it was, on the eighth day, that they came to circumcise the child; and they would have called him by the name of his father, Zacharias. ⁶⁰His mother answered and said, "No; he shall be called John."

⁶¹But they said to her, "There is no one among your relatives who is called by this name." ⁶²So they made signs to his father—what he would have him called.

זְכַרְיָה וּבֵרְכָה אֶת אֱלִישֶׁבַע. ⁴¹וְהִנֵּה כַּאֲשֶׁר שָׁמְעָה אֱלִישֶׁבַע אֶת בִּרְכַּת מִרְיָם, רָקַד הַיֶּלֶד בְּבִטְנָהּ; אֱלִישֶׁבַע נִתְמַלְאָה רוּחַ הַקֹּדֶשׁ ⁴²וְקָרְאָה בְּקוֹל גָּדוֹל: "בְּרוּכָה אַתְּ בַּנָּשִׁים וּבָרוּךְ פְּרִי בִטְנֵךְ. ⁴³וּמֵאַיִן לִי זֹאת, שֶׁאֵם אֲדֹנִי בָּאָה אֵלָי? ⁴⁴כִּי הִנֵּה, כַּאֲשֶׁר קוֹל בִּרְכָתֵךְ בָּא בְּאָזְנַי, רָקַד הַיֶּלֶד מִשִּׂמְחָה בְּבִטְנִי. ⁴⁵אַשְׁרֵי זוֹ שֶׁהֶאֱמִינָה כִּי יִתְקַיְּמוּ הַדְּבָרִים אֲשֶׁר נֶאֶמְרוּ לָהּ מֵאֵת אֱלֹהִים."

⁴⁶אָז אָמְרָה מִרְיָם:

"תְּרוֹמֵם נַפְשִׁי אֶת אֲדֹנָי
⁴⁷וְתָגֵל רוּחִי בֵּאלֹהֵי יִשְׁעִי
⁴⁸כִּי רָאָה בָּעֳנִי אֲמָתוֹ.
הִנֵּה 'אַשְׁרֶיהָ' יֹאמְרוּ מֵעַתָּה וּלְדוֹר דּוֹרִים.
⁴⁹כִּי גְדוֹלוֹת עָשָׂה בִּי שַׁדַּי, קָדוֹשׁ שְׁמוֹ
⁵⁰וְחֶסֶד יהוה מֵעוֹלָם וְעַד עוֹלָם עַל יְרֵאָיו.
⁵¹עָשָׂה חַיִל בִּזְרוֹעוֹ
פִּזֵּר אֶת אֲשֶׁר מַחְשְׁבוֹת גַּאֲוָה בְּלִבָּם.
⁵²שַׁלִּיטִים הוֹרִיד מֵעַל כִּסְאוֹתָם
וּשְׁפָלִים שָׂם לְמָרוֹם.
⁵³נַפְשׁוֹת רְעֵבִים מִלֵּא טוֹב
וַעֲשִׁירִים שִׁלַּח רֵיקָם.
⁵⁴תָּמַךְ בְּיִשְׂרָאֵל עַבְדוֹ
זֵכֶר יהוה רַחֲמָיו
⁵⁵כַּאֲשֶׁר דִּבֶּר אֶל אֲבוֹתֵינוּ –
אֶת אַבְרָהָם וְאֶת זַרְעוֹ עַד עוֹלָם."

⁵⁶וּמִרְיָם נִשְׁאֲרָה אֵצֶל אֱלִישֶׁבַע כִּשְׁלוֹשָׁה חֳדָשִׁים וְאַחֲרֵי כֵן חָזְרָה לְבֵיתָהּ.

⁵⁷עַתָּה מָלְאוּ יְמֵי אֱלִישֶׁבַע לָלֶדֶת וְהִיא יָלְדָה בֵּן. ⁵⁸כַּאֲשֶׁר שָׁמְעוּ שְׁכֵנֶיהָ וּקְרוֹבֶיהָ כִּי הִגְדִּיל אֱלֹהִים חַסְדּוֹ עִמָּהּ, שָׂמְחוּ אִתָּהּ. ⁵⁹בַּיּוֹם הַשְּׁמִינִי בָּאוּ לָמוּל אֶת הַיֶּלֶד וְקָרְאוּ לוֹ זְכַרְיָה, כְּשֵׁם אָבִיו. ⁶⁰אַךְ אִמּוֹ הֵגִיבָה וְאָמְרָה: "לֹא! יוֹחָנָן הוּא יִקָּרֵא." ⁶¹אָמְרוּ לָהּ: "אֵין אִישׁ בְּמִשְׁפַּחְתֵּךְ אֲשֶׁר נִקְרָא בַּשֵּׁם הַזֶּה", ⁶²וְרָמְזוּ לְאָבִיו כְּדֵי לָדַעַת אֵיזֶה שֵׁם יִרְצֶה כִּי יִקָּרֵא.

63 And he asked for a writing tablet, and wrote, saying, "His name is John." So they all marveled. 64 Immediately his mouth was opened and his tongue *loosed,* and he spoke, praising God. 65 Then fear came on all who dwelt around them; and all these sayings were discussed throughout all the hill country of Judea. 66 And all those who heard *them* kept *them* in their hearts, saying, "What kind of child will this be?" And the hand of the Lord was with him.

67 Now his father Zacharias was filled with the Holy Spirit, and prophesied, saying:

68 "Blessed *is* the Lord God of Israel,
　　For He has visited and redeemed His people,
69 And has raised up a horn of salvation for us
　　In the house of His servant David,
70 As He spoke by the mouth of His holy
　　　prophets,
　　Who *have been* since the world began,
71 That we should be saved from our enemies
　　And from the hand of all who hate us,
72 To perform the mercy *promised* to our
　　　fathers
　　And to remember His holy covenant,
73 The oath which He swore to our father
　　　Abraham:
74 To grant us that we,
　　Being delivered from the hand of our
　　　enemies,
　　Might serve Him without fear,
75 In holiness and righteousness before Him all
　　the days of our life.
76 "And you, child, will be called the prophet of
　　the Highest;
　　For you will go before the face of the Lord to
　　prepare His ways,
77 To give knowledge of salvation to His people
　　By the remission of their sins,
78 Through the tender mercy of our God,
　　With which the Dayspring from on high has
　　visited us;
79 To give light to those who sit in darkness and
　　the shadow of death,
　　To guide our feet into the way of peace."

80 So the child grew and became strong in spirit, and was in the deserts till the day of his manifestation to Israel.

2 And it came to pass in those days *that* a decree went out from Caesar Augustus that all the world should be registered. 2 This census first took place while Quirinius was governing Syria. 3 So all went to be registered, everyone to his own city.

63 זְכַרְיָה בִּקֵּשׁ לוּחַ וְכָתַב עָלָיו "יוֹחָנָן שְׁמוֹ". כֻּלָּם תָּמְהוּ. 64 בְּאוֹתוֹ רֶגַע נִפְתַּח פִּיו וְהֻתְּרָה לְשׁוֹנוֹ, וְהוּא דִבֶּר וּבֵרַךְ אֶת אֱלֹהִים. 65 יִרְאָה הָיְתָה עַל כָּל שְׁכֵנֵיהֶם, וְכָל הַדְּבָרִים הָאֵלֶּה סֻפְּרוּ בְּכָל חֶבֶל הָרֵי יְהוּדָה. 66 כָּל הַשּׁוֹמְעִים שָׁמְרוּ זֹאת בְּלִבָּם וְאָמְרוּ "מָה אֵפוֹא יִהְיֶה הַיֶּלֶד הַזֶּה?" וְאָמְנָם יַד יהוה הָיְתָה עִמּוֹ.

67 אָז נִתְמַלֵּא זְכַרְיָה אָבִיו רוּחַ הַקֹּדֶשׁ וְנִבָּא לֵאמֹר:

68 "בָּרוּךְ אֲדֹנָי אֱלֹהֵי יִשְׂרָאֵל
אֲשֶׁר פָּקַד אֶת עַמּוֹ וּפְדוּת שָׁלַח לוֹ
69 וְהִצְמִיחַ לָנוּ קֶרֶן יְשׁוּעָה בְּבֵית דָּוִד עַבְדּוֹ
70 כְּדַבֵּר אֲדֹנָי מֵעוֹלָם בְּיַד נְבִיאָיו הַקְּדוֹשִׁים
71 לְהוֹשִׁיעֵנוּ מִיַּד אוֹיֵב וּמִיַּד כָּל שׂוֹנֵא
72 לַעֲשׂוֹת חֶסֶד עִם אֲבוֹתֵינוּ
וְלִזְכֹּר לְעוֹלָם בְּרִיתוֹ
73 אֲשֶׁר נִשְׁבַּע לְאַבְרָהָם אָבִינוּ
74 לְהַצִּילֵנוּ מִיַּד אוֹיֵב
לְתִתֵּנוּ לְעָבְדוֹ בְּאֵין מוֹרָא
75 בִּקְדֻשָּׁה וָצֶדֶק לְפָנָיו כָּל יָמֵינוּ.
76 וְלְךָ, הַיֶּלֶד, נְבִיא אֵל עֶלְיוֹן יִקָּרֵא
כִּי לְפָנָיו תֵּלֵךְ לְפַנּוֹת דֶּרֶךְ יהוה
77 לְהוֹדִיעַ יְשׁוּעַת יהוה לְעַמּוֹ
כִּי יִסְלַח לְחַטֹּאתָם
78 בְּרֹב רַחֲמָיו עִמָּנוּ
וְדָרַךְ כּוֹכַב מִשָּׁמַיִם, פָּקֹד יִפְקְדֵנוּ
79 לְהָאִיר לְיוֹשְׁבֵי חֹשֶׁךְ וְצַלְמָוֶת
וְלָשִׂים פְּעָמֵינוּ לְדֶרֶךְ שָׁלוֹם."

80 וְהַיֶּלֶד גָּדֵל וְהִתְחַזֵּק בְּרוּחַ בִּהְיוֹתוֹ בַּמִּדְבָּר עַד יוֹם הֵרָאוֹתוֹ אֶל יִשְׂרָאֵל.

ב בַּיָּמִים הָהֵם יָצָא צַו מֵאֵת הַקֵּיסָר אוֹגוּסְטוֹס לַעֲרֹךְ רִשׁוּם תּוֹשָׁבִים בְּכָל הָאֲרָצוֹת. 2 הַמִּפְקָד הַזֶּה, הָרִאשׁוֹן, נֶעֱרַךְ בִּהְיוֹת קִירִנְיוֹס נְצִיב סוּרְיָה. 3 הַכֹּל

4 Joseph also went up from Galilee, out of the city of Nazareth, into Judea, to the city of David, which is called Bethlehem, because he was of the house and lineage of David, 5 to be registered with Mary, his betrothed wife, who was with child. 6 So it was, that while they were there, the days were completed for her to be delivered. 7 And she brought forth her firstborn Son, and wrapped Him in swaddling cloths, and laid Him in a manger, because there was no room for them in the inn.

8 Now there were in the same country shepherds living out in the fields, keeping watch over their flock by night. 9 And behold, an angel of the Lord stood before them, and the glory of the Lord shone around them, and they were greatly afraid. 10 Then the angel said to them, "Do not be afraid, for behold, I bring you good tidings of great joy which will be to all people. 11 For there is born to you this day in the city of David a Savior, who is Christ the Lord. 12 And this *will be* the sign to you: You will find a Babe wrapped in swaddling cloths, lying in a manger."

13 And suddenly there was with the angel a multitude of the heavenly host praising God and saying:

14 "Glory to God in the highest,
   And on earth peace, goodwill toward men!"

15 So it was, when the angels had gone away from them into heaven, that the shepherds said to one another, "Let us now go to Bethlehem and see this thing that has come to pass, which the Lord has made known to us." 16 And they came with haste and found Mary and Joseph, and the Babe lying in a manger. 17 Now when they had seen *Him*, they made widely known the saying which was told them concerning this Child. 18 And all those who heard *it* marveled at those things which were told them by the shepherds. 19 But Mary kept all these things and pondered *them* in her heart. 20 Then the shepherds returned, glorifying and praising God for all the things that they had heard and seen, as it was told them.

21 And when eight days were completed for the circumcision of the Child, His name was called JESUS, the name given by the angel before He was conceived in the womb.

22 Now when the days of her purification according to the law of Moses were completed, they brought Him to Jerusalem to present *Him* to the Lord 23 (as it is written in the law of the Lord, *"Every male who opens the womb shall be called*

הָלְכוּ לְהִתְפַּקֵּד, אִישׁ אִישׁ לְעִירוֹ. 4 וְגַם יוֹסֵף, שֶׁהָיָה מִבֵּית דָּוִד וּמִמִּשְׁפַּחְתּוֹ, עָלָה מִן הַגָּלִיל אֶל יְהוּדָה, מֵהָעִיר נָצְרַת לְעִיר דָּוִד הַנִּקְרֵאת בֵּית לֶחֶם, 5 לְהִתְפַּקֵּד עִם מִרְיָם אֲרוּסָתוֹ וְהִיא הָרָה. 6 כַּאֲשֶׁר הָיוּ שָׁם מָלְאוּ יָמֶיהָ לָלֶדֶת 7 וְהִיא יָלְדָה אֶת בְּנָהּ הַבְּכוֹר. לְאַחַר שֶׁחִתְּלָה אוֹתוֹ הִשְׁכִּיבָה אוֹתוֹ בָּאֵבוּס, כִּי לֹא הָיָה לָהֶם מָקוֹם בַּמָּלוֹן. 8 וּבְאוֹתוֹ חֶבֶל אֶרֶץ הָיוּ רוֹעִים שֶׁנֶּהֱגוּ לָגוּר בַּשָּׂדֶה וְלִשְׁמֹר עַל עֶדְרָם בְּאַשְׁמוּרוֹת הַלַּיְלָה. 9 לְפֶתַע נִצַּב עֲלֵיהֶם מַלְאַךְ יהוה וּכְבוֹד יהוה נָגַהּ סְבִיבָם. הֵם נִבְהֲלוּ עַד מְאֹד, 10 אוּלָם הַמַּלְאָךְ אָמַר לָהֶם: "אַל תִּפְחֲדוּ, כִּי הִנְנִי מְבַשֵּׂר לָכֶם שִׂמְחָה גְּדוֹלָה אֲשֶׁר תִּהְיֶה לְכָל הָעָם. 11 הַיּוֹם נוֹלַד לָכֶם מוֹשִׁיעַ בְּעִיר דָּוִד, הוּא הַמָּשִׁיחַ הָאָדוֹן. 12 וְזֶה לָכֶם הָאוֹת: תִּמְצְאוּ תִּינוֹק מְחֻתָּל שׁוֹכֵב בְּאֵבוּס."

13 פִּתְאוֹם הָיוּ לְיַד הַמַּלְאָךְ הֲמוֹן צְבָא הַשָּׁמַיִם וְהֵמָּה מְהַלְלִים אֶת הָאֱלֹהִים וְאוֹמְרִים:

14 "כָּבוֹד לֵאלֹהִים בַּמְּרוֹמִים,
   וּבָאָרֶץ שָׁלוֹם עַל בְּנֵי אָדָם רְצוֹנוֹ."

15 לְאַחַר שֶׁעָלוּ הַמַּלְאָכִים מֵעֲלֵיהֶם הַשָּׁמַיְמָה, אָמְרוּ הָרוֹעִים אִישׁ אֶל רֵעֵהוּ: "בּוֹאוּ נֵלֵךְ עַד בֵּית לֶחֶם וְנִרְאֶה אֶת הַדָּבָר הַזֶּה אֲשֶׁר קָרָה, מַה שֶּׁאֱלֹהִים הוֹדִיעַ לָנוּ." 16 הֵם הָלְכוּ מַהֵר וּמָצְאוּ אֶת מִרְיָם וְיוֹסֵף וְאֶת הַתִּינוֹק הַשּׁוֹכֵב בָּאֵבוּס. 17 כַּאֲשֶׁר רָאוּ אוֹתוֹ הִשְׁמִיעוּ אֶת הַדָּבָר שֶׁנֶּאֱמַר לָהֶם עַל־אוֹדוֹת הַיֶּלֶד הַזֶּה. 18 כָּל הַשּׁוֹמְעִים תָּמְהוּ עַל הַדְּבָרִים שֶׁאָמְרוּ לָהֶם הָרוֹעִים, 19 אַךְ מִרְיָם שָׁמְרָה אֶת הַדְּבָרִים הָאֵלֶּה וְשָׁקְלָה אוֹתָם בְּלִבָּהּ. 20 לְאַחַר מִכֵּן חָזְרוּ הָרוֹעִים כְּשֶׁהֵם מְהַלְלִים וּמְשַׁבְּחִים אֶת הָאֱלֹהִים עַל כָּל אֲשֶׁר שָׁמְעוּ וְרָאוּ כְּפִי שֶׁנֶּאֱמַר לָהֶם.

21 כְּשֶׁמָּלְאוּ שְׁמוֹנָה יָמִים וְהִגִּיעַ הַזְּמַן לָמוּל אוֹתוֹ קָרְאוּ אֶת שְׁמוֹ יֵשׁוּעַ, כַּשֵּׁם שֶׁקָּרָא לוֹ הַמַּלְאָךְ לִפְנֵי שֶׁהוֹרָה בַּבֶּטֶן.

22 כַּאֲשֶׁר מָלְאוּ יְמֵי טָהֳרָתָם לְפִי תּוֹרַת מֹשֶׁה, הֶעֱלוּהוּ לִירוּשָׁלַיִם לְהַצִּיגוֹ לִפְנֵי אֱלֹהִים 23 כַּכָּתוּב בְּתוֹרַת יהוה, שֶׁכָּל בְּכוֹר פֶּטֶר רֶחֶם קָדוֹשׁ לַיהוה

holy to the LORD"), ²⁴and to offer a sacrifice according to what is said in the law of the Lord, "A pair of turtledoves or two young pigeons."

²⁵And behold, there was a man in Jerusalem whose name was Simeon, and this man was just and devout, waiting for the Consolation of Israel, and the Holy Spirit was upon him. ²⁶And it had been revealed to him by the Holy Spirit that he would not see death before he had seen the Lord's Christ. ²⁷So he came by the Spirit into the temple. And when the parents brought in the Child Jesus, to do for Him according to the custom of the law, ²⁸he took Him up in his arms and blessed God and said:

²⁹ "Lord, now You are letting Your servant
    depart in peace,
    According to Your word;
³⁰ For my eyes have seen Your salvation
³¹ Which You have prepared before the face of
    all peoples,
³² A light to *bring* revelation to the Gentiles,
    And the glory of Your people Israel."

³³And Joseph and His mother marveled at those things which were spoken of Him. ³⁴Then Simeon blessed them, and said to Mary His mother, "Behold, this *Child* is destined for the fall and rising of many in Israel, and for a sign which will be spoken against ³⁵(yes, a sword will pierce through your own soul also), that the thoughts of many hearts may be revealed."

³⁶Now there was one, Anna, a prophetess, the daughter of Phanuel, of the tribe of Asher. She was of a great age, and had lived with a husband seven years from her virginity; ³⁷and this woman *was* a widow of about eighty-four years, who did not depart from the temple, but served *God* with fastings and prayers night and day. ³⁸And coming in that instant she gave thanks to the Lord, and spoke of Him to all those who looked for redemption in Jerusalem.

³⁹So when they had performed all things according to the law of the Lord, they returned to Galilee, to their *own* city, Nazareth. ⁴⁰And the Child grew and became strong in spirit, filled with wisdom; and the grace of God was upon Him.

⁴¹His parents went to Jerusalem every year at the Feast of the Passover. ⁴²And when He was twelve years old, they went up to Jerusalem according to the custom of the feast. ⁴³When they had finished the days, as they returned, the Boy Jesus lingered behind in Jerusalem. And Joseph and His mother did not know *it;* ⁴⁴but supposing Him to have been in the company, they went a day's journey, and sought Him among *their* relatives and

יִקָּרֵא; ²⁴ וּלְהַקְרִיב קָרְבָּן כָּאָמוּר בְּתוֹרַת יהוה, שְׁתֵּי־ תֹרִים אוֹ שְׁנֵי בְּנֵי יוֹנָה. ²⁵ אִישׁ הָיָה בִּירוּשָׁלַיִם בְּאוֹתָהּ עֵת, שִׁמְעוֹן שְׁמוֹ; וְהָאִישׁ צַדִּיק וְחָסִיד וּמְחַכֶּה לְנֶחָמַת יִשְׂרָאֵל, וְרוּחַ הַקֹּדֶשׁ הָיְתָה עָלָיו. ²⁶ וּבְרוּחַ הַקֹּדֶשׁ נִגְלָה לוֹ שֶׁלֹּא יִרְאֶה מְוֶת בְּטֶרֶם יִרְאֶה אֶת מְשִׁיחַ יהוה. ²⁷ וּבְהַדְרָכַת הָרוּחַ הוּא נִכְנַס אֶל הַמִּקְדָּשׁ. כַּאֲשֶׁר הֵבִיאוּ הַהוֹרִים אֶת הַיֶּלֶד יֵשׁוּעַ, לַעֲשׂוֹת בּוֹ כַּנָּהוּג עַל־פִּי הַתּוֹרָה, ²⁸ לָקַח אוֹתוֹ בִּזְרוֹעוֹתָיו וּבֵרַךְ אֶת אֱלֹהִים וְאָמַר:

²⁹ "וְעַתָּה, אֲדֹנָי, פְּטֹר נָא
אֶת עַבְדְּךָ בְּשָׁלוֹם, כַּאֲשֶׁר דִּבַּרְתָּ,
³⁰ כִּי רָאוּ עֵינַי אֶת יְשׁוּעָתְךָ
³¹ אֲשֶׁר הֲכִינוֹתָ לְעֵינֵי כָּל הָעַמִּים:
³² אוֹר לְהָאִיר לַגּוֹיִים
וְתִפְאֶרֶת יִשְׂרָאֵל עַמֶּךָ."

³³ אָבִיו וְאִמּוֹ תָּמְהוּ עַל הַדְּבָרִים שֶׁנֶּאֶמְרוּ עָלָיו. ³⁴ בֵּרְכָם שִׁמְעוֹן וְאָמַר אֶל מִרְיָם אִמּוֹ: "הִנֵּה זֶה נוֹסָד לְמִכְשׁוֹל וּלְתְקוּמָה לְרַבִּים בְּיִשְׂרָאֵל וּלְאוֹת אֲשֶׁר יִתְנַגְּדוּ לוֹ – ³⁵ וְגַם בִּלְבָבֵךְ אַת תַּעֲבֹר חֶרֶב – לְמַעַן תִּגָּלֶינָה מַחְשְׁבוֹת לֵב רַבִּים."

³⁶ גַּם אִשָּׁה נְבִיאָה הָיְתָה שָׁם, חַנָּה בַּת פְּנוּאֵל מִשֵּׁבֶט אָשֵׁר, וְהִיא בָּאָה בַּיָּמִים. שֶׁבַע שָׁנִים חָיְתָה עִם בַּעֲלָהּ מֵעֵת בְּתוּלֶיהָ; ³⁷ וְהִיא אַלְמָנָה בַּת שְׁמוֹנִים וְאַרְבַּע שָׁנִים וְלֹא עָזְבָה אֶת הַמִּקְדָּשׁ בְּעָבְדָהּ אֶת אֱלֹהִים בְּצוֹם וְתַחֲנוּנִים יוֹמָם וָלַיְלָה. ³⁸ בְּאוֹתָהּ שָׁעָה בָּאָה וְהוֹדְתָה לֵאלֹהִים וְדִבְּרָה עַל הַיֶּלֶד בְּאָזְנֵי כָּל הַמְחַכִּים לַגְּאֻלָּה בִּירוּשָׁלָיִם. ³⁹ לְאַחַר שֶׁהִשְׁלִימוּ אֶת הַכֹּל עַל־פִּי תּוֹרַת יהוה, חָזְרוּ לַגָּלִיל, לְנָצְרַת עִירָם. ⁴⁰ וְהַיֶּלֶד גָּדַל וְהִתְחַזֵּק, מָלֵא חָכְמָה, וְחֶסֶד אֱלֹהִים הָיָה עָלָיו.

⁴¹ מִדֵּי שָׁנָה בְּשָׁנָה עָלוּ הוֹרָיו לִירוּשָׁלַיִם בְּחַג הַפֶּסַח. ⁴² וּבִמְלֹאת לוֹ שְׁתֵּים־עֶשְׂרֵה שָׁנִים עָלוּ לִירוּשָׁלַיִם כְּמִנְהַג הֶחָג. ⁴³ כְּשֶׁמָּלְאוּ הַיָּמִים שָׁבוּ, אַךְ הַנַּעַר יֵשׁוּעַ נִשְׁאַר בִּירוּשָׁלַיִם וְהוֹרָיו לֹא יָדְעוּ. ⁴⁴ הוֹאִיל וְחָשְׁבוּ שֶׁהוּא נִמְצָא בַּשַּׁיָּרָה הָלְכוּ כִּבְרַת דֶּרֶךְ יוֹם אֶחָד וְחִפְּשׂוּהוּ בֵּין הַקְּרוֹבִים וְהַמַּכָּרִים,

acquaintances. ⁴⁵ So when they did not find Him, they returned to Jerusalem, seeking Him. ⁴⁶ Now so it was *that* after three days they found Him in the temple, sitting in the midst of the teachers, both listening to them and asking them questions. ⁴⁷ And all who heard Him were astonished at His understanding and answers. ⁴⁸ So when they saw Him, they were amazed; and His mother said to Him, "Son, why have You done this to us? Look, Your father and I have sought You anxiously."

⁴⁹ And He said to them, "Why did you seek Me? Did you not know that I must be about My Father's business?" ⁵⁰ But they did not understand the statement which He spoke to them.

⁵¹ Then He went down with them and came to Nazareth, and was subject to them, but His mother kept all these things in her heart. ⁵² And Jesus increased in wisdom and stature, and in favor with God and men.

3 Now in the fifteenth year of the reign of Tiberius Caesar, Pontius Pilate being governor of Judea, Herod being tetrarch of Galilee, his brother Philip tetrarch of Iturea and the region of Trachonitis, and Lysanias tetrarch of Abilene, ² while Annas and Caiaphas were high priests, the word of God came to John the son of Zacharias in the wilderness. ³ And he went into all the region around the Jordan, preaching a baptism of repentance for the remission of sins, ⁴ as it is written in the book of the words of Isaiah the prophet, saying:

"The voice of one crying in the wilderness:
'Prepare the way of the LORD;
Make His paths straight.
⁵ Every valley shall be filled
And every mountain and hill brought low;
The crooked places shall be made straight
And the rough ways smooth;
⁶ And all flesh shall see the salvation of God.' "

⁷ Then he said to the multitudes that came out to be baptized by him, "Brood of vipers! Who warned you to flee from the wrath to come? ⁸ Therefore bear fruits worthy of repentance, and do not begin to say to yourselves, 'We have Abraham as *our* father.' For I say to you that God is able to raise up children to Abraham from these stones. ⁹ And even now the ax is laid to the root of the trees. Therefore every tree which does not bear good fruit is cut down and thrown into the fire."

¹⁰ So the people asked him, saying, "What shall we do then?"

⁴⁵ אַךְ כֵּיוָן שֶׁלֹּא מְצָאוּהוּ חָזְרוּ לִירוּשָׁלַיִם לְחַפֵּשׂ אוֹתוֹ. ⁴⁶ לְאַחַר שְׁלֹשָׁה יָמִים מְצָאוּהוּ בַּמִּקְדָּשׁ וְהוּא יוֹשֵׁב בֵּין הַמּוֹרִים, שׁוֹמֵעַ אוֹתָם וְשׁוֹאֵל אוֹתָם; ⁴⁷ וְכָל שׁוֹמְעָיו הִתְפַּלְאוּ עַל שִׂכְלוֹ וְעַל תְּשׁוּבוֹתָיו. ⁴⁸ כַּאֲשֶׁר רָאוּ אוֹתוֹ הוֹרָיו הִשְׁתּוֹמְמוּ. אָמְרָה לוֹ אִמּוֹ: "בְּנִי, לָמָּה עָשִׂיתָ לָנוּ כָּכָה? הִנֵּה אָבִיךָ וַאֲנִי חִפַּשְׂנוּ אוֹתְךָ בִּדְאָגָה רַבָּה."

⁴⁹ הֵשִׁיב לָהֶם: "לָמָּה חִפַּשְׂתֶּם אוֹתִי? הַאִם לֹא יְדַעְתֶּם כִּי עָלַי לִהְיוֹת בַּאֲשֶׁר לְאָבִי?" ⁵⁰ אַךְ הֵם לֹא הֵבִינוּ אֶת הַדָּבָר שֶׁדִּבֵּר אֲלֵיהֶם.

⁵¹ הוּא יָרַד אִתָּם וּבָא לְנָצְרַת וְהָיָה נִכְנָע לְמָרוּתָם. אֶת כָּל הַדְּבָרִים הָאֵלֶּה שָׁמְרָה אִמּוֹ בְּלִבָּה. ⁵² וְיֵשׁוּעַ הוֹסִיף לִגְדֹּל בְּחָכְמָה וּבְקוֹמָה וּבְחֵן לִפְנֵי אֱלֹהִים וּבְנֵי אָדָם.

ג בִּשְׁנַת חֲמֵשׁ־עֶשְׂרֵה לְשִׁלְטוֹן הַקֵּיסָר טִיבֶּרְיוֹס, פּוֹנְטְיוֹס פִּילָטוֹס הָיָה נְצִיב יְהוּדָה, הוֹרְדוֹס שַׂר רֶבַע עַל הַגָּלִיל, אָחִיו פִילִיפּוֹס שַׂר רֶבַע עַל מְדִינוֹת יִטּוּר וְטְרַכוֹנָה, וְלִיסַנְיַס שַׂר רֶבַע עַל אֲבִילִין. ² אוֹתָהּ עֵת, בִּימֵי הַכֹּהֲנִים הַגְּדוֹלִים חָנָן וְקַיָּפָא, הָיָה דְבַר אֱלֹהִים אֶל יוֹחָנָן בֶּן זְכַרְיָה בַּמִּדְבָּר. ³ הָלַךְ יוֹחָנָן בְּכָל כִּכַּר הַיַּרְדֵּן וְהִכְרִיז אֶת טְבִילַת הַתְּשׁוּבָה לִסְלִיחַת חֲטָאִים, ⁴ כַּכָּתוּב בְּסֵפֶר דִּבְרֵי יְשַׁעְיָהוּ הַנָּבִיא:

"קוֹל קוֹרֵא
בַּמִּדְבָּר פַּנּוּ דֶּרֶךְ יהוה,
יַשְּׁרוּ מְסִלּוֹתָיו.
⁵ כָּל־גֵּיא יִנָּשֵׂא, וְכָל־הַר וְגִבְעָה יִשְׁפְּלוּ;
וְהָיָה הֶעָקֹב לְמִישׁוֹר, וְהָרְכָסִים לְבִקְעָה;
⁶ וְרָאוּ כָל־בָּשָׂר אֵת יְשׁוּעַת אֱלֹהֵינוּ."

⁷ אָז אָמַר אֶל הֲמוֹן הָעָם שֶׁיָּצְאוּ לְהִטָּבֵל אֶצְלוֹ: "יַלְדֵי צִפְעוֹנִים, מִי הוֹרָה אֶתְכֶם לְהִמָּלֵט מִן הֶחָרוֹן הַבָּא. ⁸ לָכֵן עֲשׂוּ פְּרִי רָאוּי לִתְשׁוּבָה וְאַל תֹּאמְרוּ בִּלְבַבְכֶם 'אַבְרָהָם הוּא אָבִינוּ', כִּי אֲנִי אוֹמֵר לָכֶם שֶׁמִּן הָאֲבָנִים הָאֵלֶּה יָכוֹל אֱלֹהִים לְהָקִים בָּנִים לְאַבְרָהָם. ⁹ וּכְבָר מֻנָּח הַגַּרְזֶן עַל שֹׁרֶשׁ הָעֵצִים. עַל כֵּן כָּל עֵץ אֲשֶׁר אֵינֶנּוּ עוֹשֶׂה פְּרִי טוֹב, יִגָּדַע וְיֻשְׁלַךְ לְתוֹךְ הָאֵשׁ."

¹⁰ שָׁאֲלוּ הֲמוֹן הָעָם: "אִם כֵּן, מֶה עָלֵינוּ לַעֲשׂוֹת?"

11 He answered and said to them, "He who has two tunics, let him give to him who has none; and he who has food, let him do likewise."

12 Then tax collectors also came to be baptized, and said to him, "Teacher, what shall we do?"

13 And he said to them, "Collect no more than what is appointed for you."

14 Likewise the soldiers asked him, saying, "And what shall we do?"

So he said to them, "Do not intimidate anyone or accuse falsely, and be content with your wages."

15 Now as the people were in expectation, and all reasoned in their hearts about John, whether he was the Christ or not, 16 John answered, saying to all, "I indeed baptize you with water; but One mightier than I is coming, whose sandal strap I am not worthy to loose. He will baptize you with the Holy Spirit and fire. 17 His winnowing fan is in His hand, and He will thoroughly clean out His threshing floor, and gather the wheat into His barn; but the chaff He will burn with unquenchable fire."

18 And with many other exhortations he preached to the people. 19 But Herod the tetrarch, being rebuked by him concerning Herodias, his brother Philip's wife, and for all the evils which Herod had done, 20 also added this, above all, that he shut John up in prison.

21 When all the people were baptized, it came to pass that Jesus also was baptized; and while He prayed, the heaven was opened. 22 And the Holy Spirit descended in bodily form like a dove upon Him, and a voice came from heaven which said, "You are My beloved Son; in You I am well pleased."

23 Now Jesus Himself began His ministry at about thirty years of age, being (as was supposed) the son of Joseph, the son of Heli, 24 the son of Matthat, the son of Levi, the son of Melchi, the son of Janna, the son of Joseph, 25 the son of Mattathiah, the son of Amos, the son of Nahum, the son of Esli, the son of Naggai, 26 the son of Maath, the son of Mattathiah, the son of Semei, the son of Joseph, the son of Judah, 27 the son of Joannas, the son of Rhesa, the son of Zerubbabel, the son of Shealtiel, the son of Neri, 28 the son of Melchi, the son of Addi, the son of Cosam, the son of Elmodam, the son of Er, 29 the son of Jose, the son of Eliezer, the son of Jorim, the son of Matthat, the son of Levi, 30 the son of Simeon, the son of Judah, the son of Joseph, the son of Jonan, the son of Eliakim, 31 the son of Melea, the son of Menan, the son of Mattathah, the son of Nathan, the son of David, 32 the son of Jesse, the son of Obed, the son of Boaz, the son of Salmon, the son of Nahshon, 33 the son of Amminadab, the son of Ram,

11 הֵשִׁיב לָהֶם: "מִי שֶׁיֵּשׁ לוֹ שְׁתֵּי כֻתֳּנוֹת יַחֲלֹק עִם מִי שֶׁאֵין לוֹ, וּמִי שֶׁיֵּשׁ לוֹ מָזוֹן יַעֲשֶׂה כֵּן גַּם הוּא."

12 גַּם מוֹכְסִים בָּאוּ לְהִטָּבֵל. שָׁאֲלוּ: "רַבִּי, מֶה עָלֵינוּ לַעֲשׂוֹת?"

13 הֵשִׁיב לָהֶם: "אַל תִּגְבּוּ יוֹתֵר מִמַּה שֶׁנִּקְבַּע לָכֶם."

14 גַּם אַנְשֵׁי צָבָא שָׁאֲלוּ אוֹתוֹ: "וַאֲנַחְנוּ, מַה נַּעֲשֶׂה?"

אָמַר לָהֶם: "אַל תַּעַשְׁקוּ אִישׁ וְאַל תִּגְזְלוּ, וְהִסְתַּפְּקוּ בְּמַשְׂכֻּרְתְּכֶם."

15 כֵּיוָן שֶׁהָעָם הָיָה שָׁרוּי בְּצִפִּיָּה וְהַכֹּל מְהַרְהֲרִים בְּלִבָּם עַל יוֹחָנָן שֶׁמָּא הוּא הַמָּשִׁיחַ, 16 פָּנָה יוֹחָנָן וְאָמַר אֶל כֻּלָּם: "אֲנִי אָמְנָם מַטְבִּיל אֶתְכֶם בְּמַיִם, אֲבָל בּוֹא יָבוֹא הֶחָזָק מִמֶּנִּי אֲשֶׁר אֵינֶנִּי רָאוּי לְהַתִּיר אֶת שְׂרוֹךְ נְעָלָיו. הוּא יַטְבִּיל אֶתְכֶם בְּרוּחַ הַקֹּדֶשׁ וּבָאֵשׁ. 17 בְּיָדוֹ קִלְשׁוֹן הַמִּזְרֶה לְנַקּוֹת אֶת גָּרְנוֹ וְלֶאֱסֹף אֶת הַחִטָּה אֶל הָאָסָם שֶׁלּוֹ, אַךְ אֶת הַמֹּץ יִשְׂרֹף בְּאֵשׁ בִּלְתִּי נִכְבֵּית."

18 גַּם בִּדְבָרִים רַבִּים אֲחֵרִים הֵאִיץ בָּעָם בְּהַטִּיפוֹ לָהֶם אֶת הַבְּשׂוֹרָה. 19 אֲבָל הוֹרְדוֹס שַׂר הָרֶבַע, אֲשֶׁר יוֹחָנָן הוֹכִיחוֹ עַל־דְּבַר אֵשֶׁת אָחִיו פִילִיפּוֹס וְעַל כָּל מַעֲשָׂיו הָרָעִים, 20 הוֹסִיף עַל הַכֹּל גַּם אֶת זֹאת: הוּא כָּלָא אֶת יוֹחָנָן בְּבֵית סֹהַר.

21 כַּאֲשֶׁר נִטְבַּל כָּל הָעָם נִטְבַּל גַּם יֵשׁוּעַ; וּבְעוֹדוֹ מִתְפַּלֵּל נִפְתְּחוּ הַשָּׁמַיִם 22 וְרוּחַ הַקֹּדֶשׁ יָרְדָה עָלָיו בִּדְמוּת גַּשְׁמִית כְּיוֹנָה, וְקוֹל הָיָה מִן הַשָּׁמַיִם: "אַתָּה בְּנִי אֲהוּבִי, בְּךָ חָפַצְתִּי."

23 כְּבֶן שְׁלוֹשִׁים שָׁנָה הָיָה יֵשׁוּעַ כַּאֲשֶׁר הֵחֵל בְּפָעֳלוֹ, וּלְפִי מַה שֶׁנֶּחְשַׁב הָיָה בֶּן יוֹסֵף, בֶּן עֵלִי, 24 בֶּן מַתָּת, בֶּן לֵוִי, בֶּן מַלְכִּי, בֶּן יַנַּי, בֶּן יוֹסֵף, 25 בֶּן מַתִּתְיָה, בֶּן אָמוֹץ, בֶּן נַחוּם, בֶּן חֶסְלִי, בֶּן נַגַּי, 26 בֶּן מַחַת, בֶּן מַתִּתְיָה, בֶּן שִׁמְעִי, בֶּן יוֹסֵף, בֶּן יוֹדָה, 27 בֶּן יוֹחָנָן, בֶּן רֵישָׁא, בֶּן זְרֻבָּבֶל, בֶּן שְׁאַלְתִּיאֵל, בֶּן נֵרִי, 28 בֶּן מַלְכִּי, בֶּן אַדִּי, בֶּן קוֹסָם, בֶּן אֶלְמָדָן, בֶּן עֵר, 29 בֶּן יֵשׁוּעַ, בֶּן אֱלִיעֶזֶר, בֶּן יוֹרִים, בֶּן מַתָּת, בֶּן לֵוִי, 30 בֶּן שִׁמְעוֹן, בֶּן יְהוּדָה, בֶּן יוֹסֵף, בֶּן יוֹנָם, בֶּן אֶלְיָקִים, 31 בֶּן מַלְאָה, בֶּן מַנָּא, בֶּן מַתַּתָּה, בֶּן נָתָן, בֶּן דָּוִד, 32 בֶּן יִשַׁי, בֶּן עוֹבֵד, בֶּן בֹּעַז, בֶּן שַׂלְמוֹן, בֶּן נַחְשׁוֹן, 33 בֶּן עַמִּינָדָב, בֶּן אַדְמִין, בֶּן אַרְנִי, בֶּן חֶצְרוֹן, בֶּן פֶּרֶץ, בֶּן יְהוּדָה,

the son of Hezron, *the son* of Perez, *the son* of Judah, ³⁴ *the son* of Jacob, *the son* of Isaac, *the son* of Abraham, *the son* of Terah, *the son* of Nahor, ³⁵ *the son* of Serug, *the son* of Reu, *the son* of Peleg, *the son* of Eber, *the son* of Shelah, ³⁶ *the son* of Cainan, *the son* of Arphaxad, *the son* of Shem, *the son* of Noah, *the son* of Lamech, ³⁷ *the son* of Methuselah, *the son* of Enoch, *the son* of Jared, *the son* of Mahalalel, *the son* of Cainan, ³⁸ *the son* of Enosh, *the son* of Seth, *the son* of Adam, *the son* of God.

4 Then Jesus, being filled with the Holy Spirit, returned from the Jordan and was led by the Spirit into the wilderness, ² being tempted for forty days by the devil. And in those days He ate nothing, and afterward, when they had ended, He was hungry.

³ And the devil said to Him, "If You are the Son of God, command this stone to become bread."

⁴ But Jesus answered him, saying, "It is written, *'Man shall not live by bread alone, but by every word of God.'"*

⁵ Then the devil, taking Him up on a high mountain, showed Him all the kingdoms of the world in a moment of time. ⁶ And the devil said to Him, "All this authority I will give You, and their glory; for *this* has been delivered to me, and I give it to whomever I wish. ⁷ Therefore, if You will worship before me, all will be Yours."

⁸ And Jesus answered and said to him, "Get behind Me, Satan! For it is written, *'You shall worship the* LORD *your God, and Him only you shall serve.'"*

⁹ Then he brought Him to Jerusalem, set Him on the pinnacle of the temple, and said to Him, "If You are the Son of God, throw Yourself down from here. ¹⁰ For it is written:

    'He shall give His angels charge over you,
     To keep you,'

¹¹ and,

    'In their hands they shall bear you up,
     Lest you dash your foot against a stone.'"

¹² And Jesus answered and said to him, "It has been said, *'You shall not tempt the* LORD *your God.'"*

¹³ Now when the devil had ended every temptation, he departed from Him until an opportune time.

¹⁴ Then Jesus returned in the power of the Spirit to Galilee, and news of Him went out through all the surrounding region. ¹⁵ And He taught in their synagogues, being glorified by all.

‫34 בֶּן יַעֲקֹב, בֶּן יִצְחָק, בֶּן אַבְרָהָם, בֶּן תֶּרַח, בֶּן נָחוֹר,‬
‫35 בֶּן שְׂרוּג, בֶּן רְעוּ, בֶּן פֶּלֶג, בֶּן עֵבֶר, בֶּן שֶׁלַח, 36 בֶּן‬
‫קֵינָן, בֶּן אַרְפַּכְשָׁד, בֶּן שֵׁם, בֶּן נֹחַ, בֶּן לֶמֶךְ, 37 בֶּן‬
‫מְתוּשֶׁלַח, בֶּן חֲנוֹךְ, בֶּן יֶרֶד, בֶּן מַהֲלַלְאֵל, בֶּן קֵינָן,‬
‫38 בֶּן אֱנוֹשׁ, בֶּן שֵׁת, בֶּן אָדָם, בֶּן אֱלֹהִים.‬

ד בִּהְיוֹתוֹ מָלֵא רוּחַ הַקֹּדֶשׁ שָׁב יֵשׁוּעַ מִן הַיַּרְדֵּן, וְהָרוּחַ הוֹבִילָה אוֹתוֹ בַּמִּדְבָּר 2 בְּמֶשֶׁךְ אַרְבָּעִים יוֹם כְּשֶׁהַשָּׂטָן מְנַסֶּה אוֹתוֹ. בְּאוֹתָם יָמִים לֹא אָכַל מְאוּמָה, וְכַאֲשֶׁר הִגִּיעוּ לְקִצָּם הָיָה רָעֵב. 3 אָמַר לוֹ הַשָּׂטָן: "אִם בֶּן־הָאֱלֹהִים אַתָּה, צַוֵּה עַל הָאֶבֶן הַזֹּאת שֶׁתְּהֵא לְלֶחֶם." 4 הֵשִׁיב לוֹ יֵשׁוּעַ: "הֵן כָּתוּב, 'כִּי לֹא עַל־הַלֶּחֶם לְבַדּוֹ יִחְיֶה הָאָדָם'."

5 הֶעֱלָה אוֹתוֹ הַשָּׂטָן אֶל מָקוֹם גָּבוֹהַּ וְהֶרְאָה לוֹ בְּרֶגַע אֶחָד אֶת כָּל מַמְלְכוֹת תֵּבֵל. 6 אָמַר לוֹ הַשָּׂטָן: "לְךָ אֶתֵּן אֶת כָּל הַשִּׁלְטוֹן הַזֶּה וְגַם אֶת כְּבוֹד הַמַּמְלָכוֹת הָאֵלֶּה; כִּי לִי נִמְסַר הַשִּׁלְטוֹן, וַאֲנִי נוֹתֵן אוֹתוֹ לְכָל מִי שֶׁאֲנִי רוֹצֶה. 7 לָכֵן אִם תִּשְׁתַּחֲוֶה לְפָנַי, לְךָ יִהְיֶה הַכֹּל."

8 הֵשִׁיב לוֹ יֵשׁוּעַ: "כָּתוּב, 'לַיהוה אֱלֹהֶיךָ תִּשְׁתַּחֲוֶה וְאֹתוֹ לְבַדּוֹ תַּעֲבֹד'."

9 הֵבִיא אוֹתוֹ לִירוּשָׁלַיִם, הֶעֱמִידוֹ עַל פִּנַּת גַּג בֵּית הַמִּקְדָּשׁ וְאָמַר לוֹ: "אִם בֶּן־הָאֱלֹהִים אַתָּה, הַשְׁלֵךְ עַצְמְךָ מִכָּאן לְמַטָּה, 10 שֶׁהֲרֵי כָּתוּב, כִּי מַלְאָכָיו יְצַוֶּה־לָךְ לִשְׁמָרְךָ 11 עַל־כַּפַּיִם יִשָּׂאוּנְךָ פֶּן־תִּגֹּף בָּאֶבֶן רַגְלֶךָ'."

12 הֵשִׁיב לוֹ יֵשׁוּעַ: "הֲלֹא נֶאֱמַר 'לֹא תְנַסֶּה אֶת־יהוה אֱלֹהֶיךָ'."

13 לְאַחַר שֶׁגָּמַר הַשָּׂטָן אֶת כָּל נִסְיוֹנוֹתָיו סָר מֵעָלָיו עַד לְעֵת מוֹעֵד. 14 וְיֵשׁוּעַ חָזַר בִּגְבוּרַת הָרוּחַ אֶל הַגָּלִיל וְשִׁמְעוֹ יָצָא בְּכָל הָאֵזוֹר. 15 הוּא לִמֵּד בְּבָתֵּי הַכְּנֶסֶת וְהַכֹּל שִׁבְּחוּ אוֹתוֹ.

³³ יֵשׁ שֶׁמְּבִיאִים בֶּן אֶרָם בִּמְקוֹם שְׁנֵי הַשֵּׁמוֹת בֶּן אַדְמִין וּבֶן אַרְנִי

16 So He came to Nazareth, where He had been brought up. And as His custom was, He went into the synagogue on the Sabbath day, and stood up to read. 17 And He was handed the book of the prophet Isaiah. And when He had opened the book, He found the place where it was written:

18 "The Spirit of the LORD is upon Me,
   Because He has anointed Me
   To preach the gospel to the poor;
   He has sent Me to heal the brokenhearted,
   To proclaim liberty to the captives
   And recovery of sight to the blind,
   To set at liberty those who are oppressed;
19 To proclaim the acceptable year of the LORD."

20 Then He closed the book, and gave it back to the attendant and sat down. And the eyes of all who were in the synagogue were fixed on Him. 21 And He began to say to them, "Today this Scripture is fulfilled in your hearing." 22 So all bore witness to Him, and marveled at the gracious words which proceeded out of His mouth. And they said, "Is this not Joseph's son?"

23 He said to them, "You will surely say this proverb to Me, 'Physician, heal yourself! Whatever we have heard done in Capernaum, do also here in Your country.'" 24 Then He said, "Assuredly, I say to you, no prophet is accepted in his own country. 25 But I tell you truly, many widows were in Israel in the days of Elijah, when the heaven was shut up three years and six months, and there was a great famine throughout all the land; 26 but to none of them was Elijah sent except to Zarephath, in the region of Sidon, to a woman who was a widow. 27 And many lepers were in Israel in the time of Elisha the prophet, and none of them was cleansed except Naaman the Syrian."

28 So all those in the synagogue, when they heard these things, were filled with wrath, 29 and rose up and thrust Him out of the city; and they led Him to the brow of the hill on which their city was built, that they might throw Him down over the cliff. 30 Then passing through the midst of them, He went His way.

31 Then He went down to Capernaum, a city of Galilee, and was teaching them on the Sabbaths. 32 And they were astonished at His teaching, for His word was with authority. 33 Now in the synagogue there was a man who had a spirit of an unclean demon. And he cried out with a loud voice, 34 saying, "Let us alone! What have we to do with You, Jesus of Nazareth? Did You come to destroy us? I know who You are—the Holy One of God!"

16 הוּא בָּא אֶל הָעִיר נָצְרַת, הָעִיר אֲשֶׁר גֻּדַּל בָּהּ, וּבְיוֹם הַשַּׁבָּת הָלַךְ כְּמִנְהָגוֹ לְבֵית הַכְּנֶסֶת וְקָם לִקְרֹא. 17 כַּאֲשֶׁר נָתְנוּ לוֹ אֶת מְגִלַּת סֵפֶר יְשַׁעְיָהוּ הַנָּבִיא, פָּתַח אֶת הַמְּגִלָּה וּמָצָא אֶת הַמָּקוֹם שֶׁכָּתוּב בּוֹ:

18 "רוּחַ אֲדֹנָי עָלַי,
יַעַן מָשַׁח אֹתִי לְבַשֵּׂר עֲנָוִים.
שְׁלָחַנִי לִקְרֹא לִשְׁבוּיִים דְּרוֹר,
וּלְעִוְרִים פְּקַח-קוֹחַ;
לְשַׁלֵּחַ רְצוּצִים חָפְשִׁים,
19 לִקְרֹא שְׁנַת רָצוֹן לַיהוה."

20 לְאַחַר שֶׁגָּלַל אֶת הַמְּגִלָּה, הֶחֱזִירָהּ לַגַּבַּאי וְהִתְיַשֵּׁב. עֵינֵי כָּל הַנּוֹכְחִים הָיוּ נְשׂוּאוֹת אֵלָיו 21 וְהוּא הֵחֵל לְדַבֵּר אֲלֵיהֶם וְאָמַר: "הַיּוֹם נִתְמַלֵּא הַכָּתוּב הַזֶּה בְּאָזְנֵיכֶם." 22 כֻּלָּם דִּבְּרוּ טוֹבוֹת עָלָיו וְהִתְפַּלְּאוּ עַל דִּבְרֵי הַחֵן שֶׁיָּצְאוּ מִפִּיו. אָמְרוּ: "הַאִם הוּא לֹא בֶּן יוֹסֵף?"

23 אָמַר לָהֶם: "אֵין סָפֵק שֶׁתֹּאמְרוּ לִי אֶת הַפִּתְגָּם הַזֶּה, 'רוֹפֵא, רַפֵּא אֶת עַצְמְךָ!' כָּל הַדְּבָרִים שֶׁשָּׁמַעְנוּ כִּי נַעֲשׂוּ בִּכְפַר נַחוּם עֲשֵׂה גַם פֹּה, בְּעִירְךָ." 24 הוֹסִיף וְאָמַר: "אָמֵן אוֹמֵר אֲנִי לָכֶם, אֵין נָבִיא בְּעִירוֹ. 25 וֶאֱמֶת אֲנִי אוֹמֵר לָכֶם: אַלְמָנוֹת רַבּוֹת הָיוּ בְּיִשְׂרָאֵל בִּימֵי אֵלִיָּהוּ, בְּעֵת שֶׁנֶּעֶצְרוּ הַשָּׁמַיִם שָׁלֹשׁ שָׁנִים וְשִׁשָּׁה חֳדָשִׁים וְרָעָב גָּדוֹל הָיָה בְּכָל הָאָרֶץ, 26 אַךְ אֵלֶיהָ לֹא נִשְׁלַח אֶל אַחַת מֵהֶן כִּי אִם אֶל אִשָּׁה אַלְמָנָה בְּצָרְפַת שֶׁבְּחֶבֶל צִידוֹן. 27 מְצֹרָעִים רַבִּים הָיוּ בְּיִשְׂרָאֵל בִּימֵי אֱלִישָׁע הַנָּבִיא וְלֹא טֹהַר מֵהֶם מִלְּבַד נַעֲמָן הָאֲרַמִּי."

28 כָּל הַנּוֹכְחִים בְּבֵית הַכְּנֶסֶת נִתְמַלְּאוּ כַּעַס בְּשָׁמְעָם אֶת הַדְּבָרִים הָאֵלֶּה. 29 הֵם קָמוּ וְהוֹצִיאוּ אוֹתוֹ אֶל מִחוּץ לָעִיר, וֶהֱבִילוּהוּ אֶל הָהָר אֲשֶׁר עִירָם בְּנוּיָה עָלָיו, כְּדֵי לְהַשְׁלִיכוֹ לְמַטָּה. 30 אַךְ הוּא עָבַר בֵּינֵיהֶם וְהָלַךְ לוֹ.

31 הוּא יָרַד אֶל הָעִיר הַגְּלִילִית כְּפַר נַחוּם וְלִמֵּד בַּשַּׁבָּתוֹת. 32 שׁוֹמְעָיו הִשְׁתּוֹמְמוּ עַל תּוֹרָתוֹ, כִּי בְּסַמְכוּת דִּבֵּר אֶת דְּבָרוֹ. 33 אוֹתָהּ שָׁעָה הָיָה בְּבֵית הַכְּנֶסֶת אִישׁ וּבוֹ רוּחַ שֵׁד טָמֵא, וְהָאִישׁ צָעַק בְּקוֹל גָּדוֹל: 34 "אֲהָהּ, מַה לָּנוּ וּלְךָ, יֵשׁוּעַ מִנָּצְרַת? הַאִם בָּאתָ לְהַשְׁמִידֵנוּ? אֲנִי יוֹדֵעַ מִי אַתָּה – קְדוֹשׁ הָאֱלֹהִים!"

35 But Jesus rebuked him, saying, "Be quiet, and come out of him!" And when the demon had thrown him in *their* midst, it came out of him and did not hurt him. 36 Then they were all amazed and spoke among themselves, saying, "What a word this *is*! For with authority and power He commands the unclean spirits, and they come out." 37 And the report about Him went out into every place in the surrounding region.

38 Now He arose from the synagogue and entered Simon's house. But Simon's wife's mother was sick with a high fever, and they made request of Him concerning her. 39 So He stood over her and rebuked the fever, and it left her. And immediately she arose and served them.

40 When the sun was setting, all those who had any that were sick with various diseases brought them to Him; and He laid His hands on every one of them and healed them. 41 And demons also came out of many, crying out and saying, "You are the Christ, the Son of God!"

And He, rebuking *them,* did not allow them to speak, for they knew that He was the Christ.

42 Now when it was day, He departed and went into a deserted place. And the crowd sought Him and came to Him, and tried to keep Him from leaving them; 43 but He said to them, "I must preach the kingdom of God to the other cities also, because for this purpose I have been sent." 44 And He was preaching in the synagogues of Galilee.

5 So it was, as the multitude pressed about Him to hear the word of God, that He stood by the Lake of Gennesaret, 2 and saw two boats standing by the lake; but the fishermen had gone from them and were washing *their* nets. 3 Then He got into one of the boats, which was Simon's, and asked him to put out a little from the land. And He sat down and taught the multitudes from the boat.

4 When He had stopped speaking, He said to Simon, "Launch out into the deep and let down your nets for a catch."

5 But Simon answered and said to Him, "Master, we have toiled all night and caught nothing; nevertheless at Your word I will let down the net." 6 And when they had done this, they caught a great number of fish, and their net was breaking. 7 So they signaled to *their* partners in the other boat to come and help them. And they came and filled both the boats, so that they began to sink. 8 When Simon Peter saw *it,* he fell down at Jesus' knees, saying, "Depart from me, for I am a sinful man, O Lord!"

35 גָּעַר בּוֹ יֵשׁוּעַ וְאָמַר: "שְׁתֹק וְצֵא מִמֶּנּוּ!" הַשֵּׁד הִפִּיל אוֹתוֹ אַרְצָה בֵּין הַנּוֹכְחִים וְיָצָא מִמֶּנּוּ מִבְּלִי לְהַזִּיק לוֹ. 36 הַכֹּל נִדְהֲמוּ וְאָמְרוּ זֶה אֶל זֶה: "מָה הַדָּבָר הַזֶּה? בְּסַמְכוּת וּבְכֹחַ הוּא מְצַוֶּה עַל הָרוּחוֹת הַטְּמֵאוֹת וְהֵן יוֹצְאוֹת!" 37 הַשְּׁמוּעָה עָלָיו יָצְאָה בְּכָל הָאֵזוֹר מִסָּבִיב.

38 אַחֲרֵי צֵאתוֹ מִבֵּית הַכְּנֶסֶת נִכְנַס לְבֵיתוֹ שֶׁל שִׁמְעוֹן. חוֹתֶנֶת שִׁמְעוֹן סָבְלָה מֵחֹם גָּבֹהַּ וְהֵם בִּקְשׁוּ מִמֶּנּוּ לְמַעֲנָהּ. 39 הוּא נֶעֱמַד לְיָדָהּ, גָּעַר בָּהּ וְהַחֹם הִרְפָּה מִמֶּנָּה. מִיָּד קָמָה וְשֵׁרְתָה אוֹתָם. 40 עִם שְׁקִיעַת הַשֶּׁמֶשׁ, כָּל הָאֲנָשִׁים אֲשֶׁר הָיוּ לָהֶם חוֹלִים בְּמַחֲלוֹת לְמִינֵיהֶן הֵבִיאוּ אוֹתָם אֵלָיו. הוּא סָמַךְ אֶת יָדָיו עַל כָּל אֶחָד מֵהֶם וְרִפֵּא אוֹתָם. 41 מֵרַבִּים יָצְאוּ שֵׁדִים כְּשֶׁהֵם קוֹרְאִים "אַתָּה הוּא בֶּן־הָאֱלֹהִים!" אַךְ הוּא גָּעַר בָּהֶם וְלֹא הִנִּיחַ לָהֶם לְדַבֵּר, כִּי יָדְעוּ שֶׁהוּא הַמָּשִׁיחַ.

42 עִם אוֹר הַבֹּקֶר יָצָא וְהָלַךְ לְמָקוֹם בּוֹדֵד וַהֲמוֹנֵי הָעָם חִפְּשׂוּ אוֹתוֹ. הֵם בָּאוּ אֵלָיו וְנִסּוּ לְעַכְּבוֹ כְּדֵי שֶׁלֹּא יֵלֵךְ מֵאִתָּם, 43 אַךְ הוּא אָמַר לָהֶם: "גַּם לְעָרִים אֲחֵרוֹת עָלַי לְבַשֵּׂר אֶת מַלְכוּת הָאֱלֹהִים, כִּי לְכָךְ נִשְׁלַחְתִּי." 44 וְהוּא הָיָה מְבַשֵּׂר בְּבָתֵּי הַכְּנֶסֶת אֲשֶׁר בַּגָּלִיל.

ה כַּאֲשֶׁר עָמַד לְיַד יַם כִּנֶּרֶת וְהֶהָמוֹן נִדְחַק אֵלָיו כְּדֵי לִשְׁמֹעַ אֶת דְּבַר אֱלֹהִים, 2 רָאָה שְׁתֵּי סִירוֹת עַל שְׂפַת הָאֲגַם; הַדַּיָּגִים שֶׁיָּצְאוּ מֵהֶן הָיוּ עֲסוּקִים בִּרְחִיצַת הָרְשָׁתוֹת. 3 הוּא נִכְנַס אֶל אַחַת הַסִּירוֹת, אֶל זוֹ שֶׁל שִׁמְעוֹן, וּבִקֵּשׁ מִמֶּנּוּ לָשׁוּט מְעַט מִן הַחוֹף. אַחֲרֵי כֵן יָשַׁב וְלִמֵּד אֶת הָעָם מִתּוֹךְ הַסִּירָה. 4 כְּשֶׁגָּמַר לְדַבֵּר אָמַר אֶל שִׁמְעוֹן: "שׁוּט אֶל הָעֹמֶק וְהַטִּילוּ אֶת רִשְׁתוֹתֵיכֶם לָדוּג."

5 הֵשִׁיב שִׁמְעוֹן: "אֲדוֹנִי, כָּל הַלַּיְלָה יָגַעְנוּ וְלֹא לָכַדְנוּ כְּלוּם, אַךְ עַל־פִּי דְבָרְךָ אָטִיל אֶת הָרְשָׁתוֹת." 6 הֵם עָשׂוּ כֵן וְלָכְדוּ דָּגִים רַבִּים מְאֹד, עַד שֶׁכִּמְעַט נִקְרְעוּ הָרְשָׁתוֹת. 7 אוֹתְתוּ אֶל חַבְרֵיהֶם אֲשֶׁר בַּסִּירָה הַשְּׁנִיָּה לָבוֹא לַעֲזוֹר לָהֶם, וְהַלָּלוּ בָּאוּ. אָז מִלְּאוּ אֶת שְׁתֵּי הַסִּירוֹת עַד שֶׁהֶחֵלּוּ שׁוֹקְעוֹת. 8 כִּרְאוֹתוֹ זֹאת כָּרַע שִׁמְעוֹן כֵּיפָא לְרַגְלֵי יֵשׁוּעַ וְאָמַר: "אֲדוֹנִי, לֵךְ

9 For he and all who were with him were astonished at the catch of fish which they had taken; 10 and so also *were* James and John, the sons of Zebedee, who were partners with Simon. And Jesus said to Simon, "Do not be afraid. From now on you will catch men." 11 So when they had brought their boats to land, they forsook all and followed Him.

12 And it happened when He was in a certain city, that behold, a man who was full of leprosy saw Jesus; and he fell on *his* face and implored Him, saying, "Lord, if You are willing, You can make me clean."

13 Then He put out *His* hand and touched him, saying, "I am willing; be cleansed." Immediately the leprosy left him. 14 And He charged him to tell no one, "But go and show yourself to the priest, and make an offering for your cleansing, as a testimony to them, just as Moses commanded."

15 However, the report went around concerning Him all the more; and great multitudes came together to hear, and to be healed by Him of their infirmities. 16 So He Himself *often* withdrew into the wilderness and prayed.

17 Now it happened on a certain day, as He was teaching, that there were Pharisees and teachers of the law sitting by, who had come out of every town of Galilee, Judea, and Jerusalem. And the power of the Lord was *present* to heal them. 18 Then behold, men brought on a bed a man who was paralyzed, whom they sought to bring in and lay before Him. 19 And when they could not find how they might bring him in, because of the crowd, they went up on the housetop and let him down with *his* bed through the tiling into the midst before Jesus.

20 When He saw their faith, He said to him, "Man, your sins are forgiven you."

21 And the scribes and the Pharisees began to reason, saying, "Who is this who speaks blasphemies? Who can forgive sins but God alone?"

22 But when Jesus perceived their thoughts, He answered and said to them, "Why are you reasoning in your hearts? 23 Which is easier, to say, 'Your sins are forgiven you,' or to say, 'Rise up and walk'? 24 But that you may know that the Son of Man has power on earth to forgive sins"—He said to the man who was paralyzed, "I say to you, arise, take up your bed, and go to your house."

25 Immediately he rose up before them, took up what he had been lying on, and departed to his own house, glorifying God. 26 And they were all amazed, and they glorified God and were filled with fear, saying, "We have seen strange things today!"

נָא מִמֶּנִּי, כִּי אִישׁ חוֹטֵא אָנִי"; 9 שֶׁכֵּן תַּרְדֵּמָה אָחֲזָה אוֹתוֹ וְאֶת כָּל אֲשֶׁר הָיוּ אִתּוֹ עַל צֵיד הַדָּגִים אֲשֶׁר צָדוּ; 10 וְכֵן גַּם אֶת יַעֲקֹב וְאֶת יוֹחָנָן בְּנֵי זַבְדַּי אֲשֶׁר הָיוּ שֻׁתָּפִים לְשִׁמְעוֹן. אָמַר יֵשׁוּעַ אֶל שִׁמְעוֹן: "אַל תִּירָא, מֵעַתָּה תָּדוּג בְּנֵי אָדָם."

11 לְאַחַר שֶׁהֵבִיאוּ אֶת הַסִּירוֹת אֶל הַיַּבָּשָׁה עָזְבוּ אֶת הַכֹּל וְהָלְכוּ אַחֲרָיו.

12 בִּהְיוֹתוֹ בְּאַחַת הֶעָרִים בָּא אִישׁ נָגוּעַ כֻּלּוֹ בְּצָרַעַת. כַּאֲשֶׁר רָאָה אֶת יֵשׁוּעַ, נָפַל עַל פָּנָיו וְהִתְחַנֵּן אֵלָיו: "אֲדוֹנִי, אִם תִּרְצֶה תּוּכַל לְטַהֵר אוֹתִי."

13 יֵשׁוּעַ הוֹשִׁיט אֶת יָדוֹ וּבְנָגְעוֹ בּוֹ אָמַר: "רוֹצֶה אֲנִי! הִטָּהֵר!" וּמִיָּד נֶעֶלְמָה הַצָּרַעַת. 14 צִוָּה עָלָיו יֵשׁוּעַ: "אַל תְּסַפֵּר לְאִישׁ, כִּי אִם לֵךְ הֵרָאֵה אֶל הַכֹּהֵן וְהַקְרֵב קָרְבָּן עַל טָהֳרָתְךָ, כְּמוֹ שֶׁצִּוָּה מֹשֶׁה לְעֵדוּת לָהֶם." 15 אוּלָם הַשְּׁמוּעָה עַל־אוֹדוֹתָיו הָלְכָה וְהִתְפַּשְּׁטָה וַהֲמוֹנִים רַבִּים נִקְבְּצוּ לִשְׁמֹעַ וּלְהֵרָפֵא מִתַּחֲלוּאֵיהֶם, 16 אַךְ הוּא הָיָה פּוֹרֵשׁ אֶל מְקוֹמוֹת שׁוֹמְמִים וּמִתְפַּלֵּל.

17 בְּאַחַד הַיָּמִים, כַּאֲשֶׁר לִמֵּד וּלְיָדוֹ יָשְׁבוּ פְּרוּשִׁים וּמוֹרֵי תוֹרָה שֶׁבָּאוּ מִכָּל כְּפָרֵי הַגָּלִיל וּמִיהוּדָה וִירוּשָׁלַיִם, הָיְתָה בּוֹ גְּבוּרַת יהוה לְרַפֵּא. 18 וְהִנֵּה אֲנָשִׁים נוֹשְׂאִים אִישׁ מְשֻׁתָּק עַל אֲלֻנְקָה וְהֵם מְנַסִּים לְהַכְנִיסוֹ לְתוֹךְ הַבַּיִת כְּדֵי לְהַנִּיחוֹ לְפָנָיו. 19 אַךְ כֵּיוָן שֶׁלֹּא מָצְאוּ דֶּרֶךְ לְהַכְנִיסוֹ בִּגְלַל הֶהָמוֹן, עָלוּ עַל הַגַּג וְהוֹרִידוּהוּ עִם הָאֲלֻנְקָה דֶּרֶךְ הָרְעָפִים לְתוֹךְ הַבַּיִת, לִפְנֵי יֵשׁוּעַ. 20 כִּרְאוֹתוֹ אֶת אֱמוּנָתָם אָמַר אֵלָיו: "בֶּן אָדָם, נִסְלְחוּ לְךָ חֲטָאֶיךָ." 21 הֵחֵלּוּ הַסּוֹפְרִים וְהַפְּרוּשִׁים לְהַרְהֵר וְאָמְרוּ: "מִי הוּא זֶה הַמְדַבֵּר דִּבְרֵי נְאָצָה? מִי יָכוֹל לִסְלֹחַ עַל חֲטָאִים זוּלָתִי אֱלֹהִים לְבַדּוֹ?"

22 אוּלָם יֵשׁוּעַ יָדַע אֶת מַחְשְׁבוֹתֵיהֶם וְהֵשִׁיב לָהֶם: "מָה אַתֶּם מְהַרְהֲרִים בִּלְבַבְכֶם? 23 מַה יּוֹתֵר קַל: לוֹמַר 'נִסְלְחוּ לְךָ חֲטָאֶיךָ', אוֹ לוֹמַר 'קוּם וְהִתְהַלֵּךְ'? 24 אַךְ לְמַעַן תֵּדְעוּ כִּי לְבֶן־הָאָדָם הַסַּמְכוּת עֲלֵי אֲדָמוֹת לִסְלֹחַ עַל חֲטָאִים, הֲרֵינִי אוֹמֵר לְךָ – פְּנָה אֶל הַמְשֻׁתָּק – "קוּם, קַח אֶת הָאֲלֻנְקָה וְלֵךְ לְבֵיתְךָ!"

25 הוּא קָם מִיָּד לְנֶגֶד עֵינֵיהֶם, הֵרִים אֶת הָאֲלֻנְקָה וְהָלַךְ לְבֵיתוֹ כְּשֶׁהוּא מְהַלֵּל אֶת אֱלֹהִים. 26 תַּרְדֵּמָה אָחֲזָה אֶת כֻּלָּם, וּבְלֵב מָלֵא יִרְאָה הִלְּלוּ אֶת אֱלֹהִים וְאָמְרוּ: "נִפְלָאוֹת רָאִינוּ הַיּוֹם!"

27 After these things He went out and saw a tax collector named Levi, sitting at the tax office. And He said to him, "Follow Me." 28 So he left all, rose up, and followed Him.

29 Then Levi gave Him a great feast in his own house. And there were a great number of tax collectors and others who sat down with them. 30 And their scribes and the Pharisees complained against His disciples, saying, "Why do You eat and drink with tax collectors and sinners?"

31 Jesus answered and said to them, "Those who are well have no need of a physician, but those who are sick. 32 I have not come to call the righteous, but sinners, to repentance."

33 Then they said to Him, "Why do the disciples of John fast often and make prayers, and likewise those of the Pharisees, but Yours eat and drink?"

34 And He said to them, "Can you make the friends of the bridegroom fast while the bridegroom is with them? 35 But the days will come when the bridegroom will be taken away from them; then they will fast in those days."

36 Then He spoke a parable to them: "No one puts a piece from a new garment on an old one; otherwise the new makes a tear, and also the piece that was taken out of the new does not match the old. 37 And no one puts new wine into old wineskins; or else the new wine will burst the wineskins and be spilled, and the wineskins will be ruined. 38 But new wine must be put into new wineskins, and both are preserved. 39 And no one, having drunk old wine, immediately desires new; for he says, 'The old is better.'"

6 Now it happened on the second Sabbath after the first that He went through the grainfields. And His disciples plucked the heads of grain and ate them, rubbing them in their hands. 2 And some of the Pharisees said to them, "Why are you doing what is not lawful to do on the Sabbath?"

3 But Jesus answering them said, "Have you not even read this, what David did when he was hungry, he and those who were with him: 4 how he went into the house of God, took and ate the showbread, and also gave some to those with him, which is not lawful for any but the priests to eat?" 5 And He said to them, "The Son of Man is also Lord of the Sabbath."

6 Now it happened on another Sabbath, also, that He entered the synagogue and taught. And a man was there whose right hand was withered. 7 So the scribes and Pharisees watched Him closely, whether He would heal on the Sabbath, that they might find an accusation against Him. 8 But He knew their

27 בְּצֵאתוֹ אַחֲרֵי כֵן רָאָה מוֹכֵס יוֹשֵׁב בְּבֵית הַמֶּכֶס וּשְׁמוֹ לֵוִי. אָמַר לוֹ יֵשׁוּעַ: "לֵךְ אַחֲרַי". 28 הוּא קָם, עָזַב אֶת הַכֹּל וְהָלַךְ אַחֲרָיו. 29 בְּבֵיתוֹ עָרַךְ לֵוִי מִשְׁתֶּה גָּדוֹל, וְקָהָל רַב שֶׁל מוֹכְסִים וַאֲנָשִׁים אֲחֵרִים הָיוּ מְסֻבִּים עִמָּהֶם. 30 אַךְ הַפְּרוּשִׁים וְסוֹפְרֵיהֶם רָטְנוּ וְאָמְרוּ לְתַלְמִידָיו: "מַדּוּעַ אַתֶּם אוֹכְלִים וְשׁוֹתִים עִם הַמּוֹכְסִים וְהַחוֹטְאִים?"

31 הֵשִׁיב לָהֶם יֵשׁוּעַ וְאָמַר: "לֹא הַבְּרִיאִים צְרִיכִים לְרוֹפֵא, אֶלָּא הַחוֹלִים. 32 לֹא בָּאתִי לִקְרֹא אֶת הַצַּדִּיקִים לִתְשׁוּבָה, כִּי אִם אֶת הַחוֹטְאִים."

33 אָמְרוּ לוֹ: "תַּלְמִידֵי יוֹחָנָן מַרְבִּים לָצוּם וּמַקְמִים תְּפִלּוֹת, וְכֵן גַּם תַּלְמִידֵי הַפְּרוּשִׁים, אַךְ תַּלְמִידֶיךָ אוֹכְלִים וְשׁוֹתִים."

34 הֵשִׁיב לָהֶם יֵשׁוּעַ: "וְכִי יְכוֹלִים אַתֶּם לְהָנִיעַ אֶת בְּנֵי הַחֻפָּה לָצוּם בְּעוֹד הֶחָתָן עִמָּהֶם? 35 הִנֵּה יָמִים בָּאִים וְהֶחָתָן יֻלְקַח מֵהֶם; בַּיָּמִים הָהֵם יָצוּמוּ." 36 גַּם מָשָׁל סִפֵּר לָהֶם: "אֵין אִישׁ קוֹרֵעַ פֶּסֶת בַּד מִבֶּגֶד חָדָשׁ וְתוֹפֵר אוֹתָהּ עַל בֶּגֶד יָשָׁן; אִם יַעֲשֶׂה כֵן, יִקְרַע אֶת הֶחָדָשׁ וְגַם פֶּסַת הַבַּד שֶׁנִּלְקְחָה מִן הֶחָדָשׁ לֹא תִּשְׁתַּלֵּב בַּיָּשָׁן. 37 וְאֵין אִישׁ שָׂם יַיִן חָדָשׁ בְּנֹאדוֹת יְשָׁנִים; אִם יַעֲשֶׂה כֵן, יִבְקַע הַיַּיִן הֶחָדָשׁ אֶת הַנֹּאדוֹת וְיִשָּׁפֵךְ, וְהַנֹּאדוֹת לֹא יִצְלְחוּ עוֹד. 38 כִּי יַיִן חָדָשׁ יֵשׁ לָצֶקֶת לְנֹאדוֹת חֲדָשִׁים וּשְׁנֵיהֶם יִשָּׁמְרוּ. 39 וּמִי שֶׁשָּׁתָה יַיִן יָשָׁן אֵינוֹ רוֹצֶה בֶּחָדָשׁ שֶׁכֵּן יֹאמַר 'הַיָּשָׁן טוֹב יוֹתֵר'."

ו בְּשַׁבָּת הַשְּׁנִיָּה לִסְפִירַת הָעֹמֶר בְּעָבְרוֹ בִּשְׂדוֹת קָמָה קָטְפוּ תַּלְמִידָיו שִׁבֳּלִים וְלְאַחַר שֶׁמִּלְּלוּ אוֹתָן בִּידֵיהֶם אָכְלוּ. 2 אָמְרוּ אֲחָדִים מִן הַפְּרוּשִׁים: "מַדּוּעַ אַתֶּם עוֹשִׂים מַה שֶּׁאָסוּר בְּשַׁבָּת?"

3 הֵשִׁיב לָהֶם יֵשׁוּעַ וְאָמַר: "הַאִם לֹא קְרָאתֶם מַה שֶּׁעָשָׂה דָּוִד כַּאֲשֶׁר רָעֵב הוּא וְהָאֲנָשִׁים אֲשֶׁר אִתּוֹ? 4 הֲרֵי נִכְנַס אֶל בֵּית הָאֱלֹהִים וְלָקַח אֶת לֶחֶם הַפָּנִים, שֶׁאֵינוֹ מֻתָּר לַאֲכִילָה אֶלָּא לַכֹּהֲנִים בִּלְבַד, אָכַל וְגַם נָתַן לַאֲשֶׁר אִתּוֹ." 5 הוֹסִיף וְאָמַר לָהֶם: "בֶּן הָאָדָם הוּא אֲדוֹן הַשַּׁבָּת."

6 בְּשַׁבָּת אַחֶרֶת נִכְנַס לְבֵית הַכְּנֶסֶת וְהֵחֵל לְלַמֵּד, וְשָׁם הָיָה אִישׁ אֲשֶׁר יָדוֹ הַיְמָנִית יְבֵשָׁה. 7 הַסּוֹפְרִים וְהַפְּרוּשִׁים הִתְבּוֹנְנוּ בּוֹ לִרְאוֹת אִם יְרַפֵּא בְּשַׁבָּת, כְּדֵי לִמְצֹא עִלָּה לְהַאֲשִׁים אוֹתוֹ. 8 אַךְ הוּא יָדַע אֶת הַרְהוּרֵי לִבָּם וְאָמַר אֶל הָאִישׁ אֲשֶׁר יָדוֹ יְבֵשָׁה:

thoughts, and said to the man who had the withered hand, "Arise and stand here." And he arose and stood. 9 Then Jesus said to them, "I will ask you one thing: Is it lawful on the Sabbath to do good or to do evil, to save life or to destroy?" 10 And when He had looked around at them all, He said to the man, "Stretch out your hand." And he did so, and his hand was restored as whole as the other. 11 But they were filled with rage, and discussed with one another what they might do to Jesus.

12 Now it came to pass in those days that He went out to the mountain to pray, and continued all night in prayer to God. 13 And when it was day, He called His disciples to *Himself;* and from them He chose twelve whom He also named apostles: 14 Simon, whom He also named Peter, and Andrew his brother; James and John; Philip and Bartholomew; 15 Matthew and Thomas; James the *son of* Alphaeus, and Simon called the Zealot; 16 Judas *the son* of James, and Judas Iscariot who also became a traitor.

17 And He came down with them and stood on a level place with a crowd of His disciples and a great multitude of people from all Judea and Jerusalem, and from the seacoast of Tyre and Sidon, who came to hear Him and be healed of their diseases, 18 as well as those who were tormented with unclean spirits. And they were healed. 19 And the whole multitude sought to touch Him, for power went out from Him and healed *them* all.

20 Then He lifted up His eyes toward His disciples, and said:

"Blessed *are you* poor,
 For yours is the kingdom of God.
21 Blessed *are you* who hunger now,
 For you shall be filled.
 Blessed *are you* who weep now,
 For you shall laugh.
22 Blessed are you when men hate you,
 And when they exclude you,
 And revile *you,* and cast out your name as evil,
 For the Son of Man's sake.
23 Rejoice in that day and leap for joy!
 For indeed your reward *is* great in heaven,
 For in like manner their fathers did to the prophets.
24 "But woe to you who are rich,
 For you have received your consolation.
25 Woe to you who are full,
 For you shall hunger.
 Woe to you who laugh now,
 For you shall mourn and weep.

"קוּם וַעֲמֹד בָּאֶמְצַע!" הַלָּה קָם וְעָמַד. 9 אָמַר לָהֶם יֵשׁוּעַ: "אֶשְׁאַל אֶתְכֶם דָּבָר. הַאִם מֻתָּר לְהֵיטִיב בְּשַׁבָּת אוֹ לַעֲשׂוֹת רָעָה, לְהַצִּיל נֶפֶשׁ אוֹ לְקַפְּחָהּ?" 10 הִבִּיט סָבִיב אֶל כֻּלָּם וְאָמַר לָאִישׁ: "הוֹשֵׁט אֶת יָדְךָ!" הוּא עָשָׂה כָּךְ וְיָדוֹ שָׁבָה לְאֵיתָנָהּ. 11 אוּלָם הֵם נִתְמַלְּאוּ חֵמָה וְהִתְיָעֲצוּ בֵּינֵיהֶם מַה לַעֲשׂוֹת לְיֵשׁוּעַ.

12 בְּאוֹתָם יָמִים יָצָא אֶל הָהָר לְהִתְפַּלֵּל. לַיְלָה שָׁלֵם הִתְמִיד בִּתְפִלָּה לָאלֹהִים, 13 וְעִם אוֹר הַבֹּקֶר קָרָא אֵלָיו אֶת תַּלְמִידָיו וּבָחַר מֵהֶם שְׁנֵים־עָשָׂר בְּכַנּוֹתוֹ אוֹתָם שְׁלִיחִים: 14 אֶת שִׁמְעוֹן, אֲשֶׁר גַּם קָרָא לוֹ כֵּיפָא, וְאֶת אַנְדְּרֵי אָחִיו, אֶת יַעֲקֹב וְאֶת יוֹחָנָן, אֶת פִילִיפּוֹס וְאֶת בַּר תַּלְמַי, 15 אֶת מַתַּי וְאֶת תֹּאמָא, אֶת יַעֲקֹב בֶּן חַלְפַי וְאֶת שִׁמְעוֹן הַמְּכֻנֶּה הַקַּנָּאי, 16 אֶת יְהוּדָה בֶּן יַעֲקֹב וְאֶת יְהוּדָה אִישׁ קְרִיּוֹת אֲשֶׁר נִהְיָה לִמְסַגִּירוֹ.

17 הוּא יָרַד אִתָּם וְעָמַד בְּמִישׁוֹר בְּקֶרֶב קָהָל גָּדוֹל מִתַּלְמִידָיו וְעַם רַב מִכָּל יְהוּדָה וִירוּשָׁלַיִם וּמֵחוֹף צוֹר וְצִידוֹן, אֲשֶׁר בָּאוּ לִשְׁמֹעַ וּלְהֵרָפֵא מֵחָלְיֵיהֶם. 18 וְהָאֲנָשִׁים שֶׁהָיוּ מְעֻנִּים עַל־יְדֵי רוּחוֹת טְמֵאוֹת נִרְפְּאוּ גַם הֵם. 19 כָּל הֶהָמוֹן בִּקְּשׁוּ לָגַעַת בּוֹ, כִּי גְבוּרָה יָצְאָה מִמֶּנּוּ וְרִפְּאָה אֶת הַכֹּל.

20 נָשָׂא אֶת עֵינָיו אֶל תַּלְמִידָיו וְאָמַר:
"אַשְׁרֵיכֶם הָעֲנִיִּים, כִּי לָכֶם מַלְכוּת הָאֱלֹהִים.
21 אַשְׁרֵיכֶם הָרְעֵבִים כָּעֵת, כִּי אַתֶּם תִּשְׂבָּעוּ.
אַשְׁרֵיכֶם הַבּוֹכִים כָּעֵת, כִּי אַתֶּם תִּשְׂחָקוּ.
22 אַשְׁרֵיכֶם אִם בְּנֵי אָדָם יִשְׂנְאוּ אֶתְכֶם וְיָנֻדּוּ וִיחָרְפוּ אֶתְכֶם וְיוֹצִיאוּ שֵׁם רַע עֲלֵיכֶם בִּגְלַל בֶּן־הָאָדָם. 23 שִׂמְחוּ בַּיּוֹם הַהוּא וְרִקְדוּ, כִּי הִנֵּה שְׂכַרְכֶם רַב בַּשָּׁמַיִם; הֲרֵי כַּדָּבָר הַזֶּה עָשׂוּ אֲבוֹתֵיהֶם לַנְּבִיאִים.
24 אַךְ אוֹי לָכֶם הָעֲשִׁירִים, כִּי כְּבָר קִבַּלְתֶּם אֶת נֶחָמַתְכֶם.
25 אוֹי לָכֶם הַשְּׂבֵעִים כָּעֵת, כִּי אַתֶּם תִּרְעָבוּ.
אוֹי לָכֶם הַשׂוֹחֲקִים כָּעֵת, כִּי אַתֶּם תִּתְאַבְּלוּ וְתִבְכּוּ.

26 Woe to you when all men speak well of you,
For so did their fathers to the false
prophets.

27 "But I say to you who hear: Love your
enemies, do good to those who hate you, 28 bless
those who curse you, and pray for those who
spitefully use you. 29 To him who strikes you on the
one cheek, offer the other also. And from him who
takes away your cloak, do not withhold *your* tunic
either. 30 Give to everyone who asks of you. And
from him who takes away your goods do not ask
them back. 31 And just as you want men to do to
you, you also do to them likewise.

32 "But if you love those who love you, what
credit is that to you? For even sinners love those
who love them. 33 And if you do good to those who
do good to you, what credit is that to you? For even
sinners do the same. 34 And if you lend *to those* from
whom you hope to receive back, what credit is that
to you? For even sinners lend to sinners to receive
as much back. 35 But love your enemies, do good,
and lend, hoping for nothing in return; and your
reward will be great, and you will be sons of the
Most High. For He is kind to the unthankful and
evil. 36 Therefore be merciful, just as your Father
also is merciful.

37 "Judge not, and you shall not be judged.
Condemn not, and you shall not be condemned.
Forgive, and you will be forgiven. 38 Give, and it
will be given to you: good measure, pressed down,
shaken together, and running over will be put into
your bosom. For with the same measure that you
use, it will be measured back to you."

39 And He spoke a parable to them: "Can the
blind lead the blind? Will they not both fall into the
ditch? 40 A disciple is not above his teacher, but
everyone who is perfectly trained will be like his
teacher. 41 And why do you look at the speck in
your brother's eye, but do not perceive the plank in
your own eye? 42 Or how can you say to your
brother, 'Brother, let me remove the speck that *is* in
your eye,' when you yourself do not see the plank
that *is* in your own eye? Hypocrite! First remove the
plank from your own eye, and then you will see
clearly to remove the speck that is in your brother's
eye.

43 "For a good tree does not bear bad fruit, nor
does a bad tree bear good fruit. 44 For every tree is
known by its own fruit. For *men* do not gather figs
from thorns, nor do they gather grapes from a
bramble bush. 45 A good man out of the good
treasure of his heart brings forth good; and an evil

26 אוֹי לָכֶם אִם כָּל הָאֲנָשִׁים מְשַׁבְּחִים אֶתְכֶם, כִּי כֵן
עָשׂוּ אֲבוֹתֵיהֶם לִנְבִיאֵי הַשֶּׁקֶר."

27 "אֲבָל אֲלֵיכֶם, הַשּׁוֹמְעִים, אוֹמֵר אֲנִי: אֶהֱבוּ אֶת
אוֹיְבֵיכֶם, הֵיטִיבוּ עִם שׂוֹנְאֵיכֶם. 28 בָּרְכוּ אֶת
מְקַלְלֵיכֶם וְהִתְפַּלְלוּ בְּעַד הַפּוֹגְעִים בָּכֶם. 29 הַמַּכֶּה
אוֹתְךָ עַל הַלֶּחִי, הַטֵּה לוֹ גַּם אֶת הַשְּׁנִיָּה. הַלּוֹקֵחַ
אֶת מְעִילְךָ, אַל תִּמְנַע מִמֶּנּוּ גַּם אֶת כֻּתָּנְתְּךָ. 30 הֱיֵה
נוֹתֵן לְכָל הַמְבַקֵּשׁ מִמְּךָ; וְהַלּוֹקֵחַ אֶת אֲשֶׁר לְךָ, אַל
תִּתְבַּע מִמֶּנּוּ. 31 מַה שֶׁתִּרְצוּ שֶׁיַּעֲשׂוּ לָכֶם בְּנֵי אָדָם,
כֵּן תַּעֲשׂוּ לָהֶם גַּם אַתֶּם. 32 וְאִם תֹּאהֲבוּ אֶת
אוֹהֲבֵיכֶם, אֵיזוֹ זְכוּת תַּעֲמֹד לָכֶם? הֲלֹא גַּם
הַחוֹטְאִים אוֹהֲבִים אֶת אוֹהֲבֵיהֶם. 33 אִם תֵּיטִיבוּ
לַמֵּיטִיבִים עִמָּכֶם, אֵיזוֹ זְכוּת תַּעֲמֹד לָכֶם? הֲלֹא גַּם
הַחוֹטְאִים עוֹשִׂים זֹאת. 34 וְאִם תַּלְווּ לַאֲנָשִׁים
שֶׁאַתֶּם מְקַוִּים לְקַבֵּל מֵהֶם, אֵיזוֹ זְכוּת תַּעֲמֹד לָכֶם?
גַּם הַחוֹטְאִים מַלְוִים לְחוֹטְאִים כְּדֵי שֶׁיַּחֲזַר לָהֶם
הָעֵרֶךְ הַשָּׁוֶה. 35 אַדְּרַבָּא, אֶהֱבוּ אֶת אוֹיְבֵיכֶם
וְהֵיטִיבוּ וְהַלְווּ מִבְּלִי לְצַפּוֹת לִגְמוּל, וְרַב יִהְיֶה
שְׂכַרְכֶם וּבְנֵי עֶלְיוֹן תִּהְיוּ, כִּי טוֹב הוּא גַּם לִכְפוּיֵי
טוֹבָה וְגַם לָרָעִים. 36 הֱיוּ רַחֲמָנִים כְּשֵׁם שֶׁאֲבִיכֶם
רַחֲמָן הוּא."

37 "אַל תִּשְׁפְּטוּ וְלֹא תִשָּׁפְטוּ. אַל תַּרְשִׁיעוּ וְלֹא
תֻרְשְׁעוּ. סִלְחוּ וְיִסָּלַח לָכֶם. 38 תְּנוּ וְיִנָּתֵן לָכֶם; מִדָּה
יָפָה, דְּחוּסָה, גְּדוּשָׁה וְשׁוֹפַעַת יִתְּנוּ בְּחֵיקְכֶם, כִּי
בַּמִּדָּה שֶׁאַתֶּם מוֹדְדִים יִמָּדֵד לָכֶם."

39 גַּם מָשָׁל סִפֵּר לָהֶם: "הֲיוּכַל עִוֵּר לְהַדְרִיךְ עִוֵּר?
הֲלֹא שְׁנֵיהֶם יִפְּלוּ לְתוֹךְ בּוֹר. 40 תַּלְמִיד אֵינֶנּוּ גָּדוֹל
מִן הַמּוֹרֶה, אֲבָל כָּל מִי שֶׁהֻשְׁלַם לִמּוּדוֹ יִהְיֶה
כְּמוֹרֵהוּ.

41 מַדּוּעַ אַתָּה רוֹאֶה אֶת הַקִּיסָם אֲשֶׁר בְּעֵין אָחִיךָ
וְאֵינְךָ שָׂם לֵב לַקּוֹרָה אֲשֶׁר בְּעֵינְךָ שֶׁלְּךָ? 42 אֵיךְ
תוּכַל לוֹמַר לְאָחִיךָ: 'אָחִי, הַנַּח לִי לְהוֹצִיא אֶת
הַקִּיסָם אֲשֶׁר בְּעֵינֶךָ', כְּשֶׁאַתָּה בְּעַצְמְךָ אֵינְךָ רוֹאֶה
אֶת הַקּוֹרָה אֲשֶׁר בְּעֵינְךָ? צָבוּעַ! רֵאשִׁית, טֹל קוֹרָה
מֵעֵינְךָ; אַחַר כָּךְ תֵּיטִיב לִרְאוֹת אֶת הַקִּיסָם אֲשֶׁר
בְּעֵין אָחִיךָ וְתוּכַל לְהוֹצִיאוֹ."

43 "עֵץ טוֹב אֵינֶנּוּ עוֹשֶׂה פְּרִי מָשְׁחָת וְעֵץ מָשְׁחָת
אֵינֶנּוּ עוֹשֶׂה פְּרִי טוֹב. 44 כָּל עֵץ נִכָּר בְּפִרְיוֹ, שֶׁהֲרֵי
לֹא מִן הַקּוֹצִים אוֹסְפִים תְּאֵנִים וְלֹא מִשִּׂיחַ קוֹצָנִי
בּוֹצְרִים עֲנָבִים. 45 הָאִישׁ הַטּוֹב, מֵאוֹצַר לִבּוֹ הַטּוֹב
מֵפִיק אֶת הַטּוֹב, וְהָאִישׁ הָרָע, מֵאוֹצַר לִבּוֹ הָרָע
מֵפִיק אֶת הָרָע; כִּי מִתּוֹךְ הַשֶּׁפַע בַּלֵּב מְדַבֵּר פִּיו."

man out of the evil treasure of his heart brings forth evil. For out of the abundance of the heart his mouth speaks.

⁴⁶ "But why do you call Me 'Lord, Lord,' and not do the things which I say? ⁴⁷ Whoever comes to Me, and hears My sayings and does them, I will show you whom he is like: ⁴⁸ He is like a man building a house, who dug deep and laid the foundation on the rock. And when the flood arose, the stream beat vehemently against that house, and could not shake it, for it was founded on the rock. ⁴⁹ But he who heard and did nothing is like a man who built a house on the earth without a foundation, against which the stream beat vehemently; and immediately it fell. And the ruin of that house was great."

7 Now when He concluded all His sayings in the hearing of the people, He entered Capernaum. ² And a certain centurion's servant, who was dear to him, was sick and ready to die. ³ So when he heard about Jesus, he sent elders of the Jews to Him, pleading with Him to come and heal his servant. ⁴ And when they came to Jesus, they begged Him earnestly, saying that the one for whom He should do this was deserving, ⁵ "for he loves our nation, and has built us a synagogue."

⁶ Then Jesus went with them. And when He was already not far from the house, the centurion sent friends to Him, saying to Him, "Lord, do not trouble Yourself, for I am not worthy that You should enter under my roof. ⁷ Therefore I did not even think myself worthy to come to You. But say the word, and my servant will be healed. ⁸ For I also am a man placed under authority, having soldiers under me. And I say to one, 'Go,' and he goes; and to another, 'Come,' and he comes; and to my servant, 'Do this,' and he does *it*."

⁹ When Jesus heard these things, He marveled at him, and turned around and said to the crowd that followed Him, "I say to you, I have not found such great faith, not even in Israel!" ¹⁰ And those who were sent, returning to the house, found the servant well who had been sick.

¹¹ Now it happened, the day after, *that* He went into a city called Nain; and many of His disciples went with Him, and a large crowd. ¹² And when He came near the gate of the city, behold, a dead man was being carried out, the only son of his mother; and she was a widow. And a large crowd from the city was with her. ¹³ When the Lord saw her, He had compassion on her and said to her, "Do not weep." ¹⁴ Then He came and touched the open coffin, and those who carried *him* stood still. And He said,

⁴⁶ "וְלָמָּה אַתֶּם קוֹרְאִים לִי 'אֲדוֹנִי, אֲדוֹנִי', וְאֵינְכֶם עוֹשִׂים אֶת אֲשֶׁר אֲנִי אוֹמֵר? ⁴⁷ כָּל הַבָּא אֵלַי וְשׁוֹמֵעַ אֶת דְּבָרַי וְעוֹשֶׂה אוֹתָם, אַגִּיד לָכֶם לְמִי הוּא דּוֹמֶה: ⁴⁸ דּוֹמֶה הוּא לְאִישׁ בּוֹנֶה בַּיִת, אֲשֶׁר הֶעֱמִיק לַחְפֹּר וְהִנִּיחַ אֶת יְסוֹדוֹ עַל הַסֶּלַע; כַּאֲשֶׁר בָּא שִׁטָּפוֹן הִכָּה הַזֶּרֶם בַּבַּיִת הַהוּא, אַךְ לֹא הָיָה יָכוֹל לְמוֹטְטוֹ מִשּׁוּם שֶׁנִּבְנָה הֵיטֵב. ⁴⁹ אֲבָל הַשּׁוֹמֵעַ וְאֵינוֹ עוֹשֶׂה דּוֹמֶה לְאִישׁ אֲשֶׁר בָּנָה בַּיִת עַל הַקַּרְקַע בְּלִי יְסוֹד; כַּאֲשֶׁר הַזֶּרֶם נָגַח בּוֹ הִתְמוֹטֵט מִיָּד וְגָדוֹל הָיָה חֻרְבַּן הַבַּיִת הַהוּא."

ז לְאַחַר שֶׁהִשְׁמִיעַ אֶת כָּל דְּבָרָיו אֵלֶּה בְּאָזְנֵי הָעָם, נִכְנַס אֶל כְּפַר נַחוּם. ² אוֹתָהּ עֵת הָיָה עַבְדּוֹ שֶׁל שַׂר מֵאָה אֶחָד חוֹלֶה וְנוֹטֶה לָמוּת, וְהָעֶבֶד הָיָה יָקָר לוֹ מְאֹד. ³ כֵּיוָן שֶׁשָּׁמַע עַל־אוֹדוֹת יֵשׁוּעַ, שָׁלַח אֵלָיו אֲנָשִׁים מִזִּקְנֵי הַיְּהוּדִים וּבִקֵּשׁ מִמֶּנּוּ לָבוֹא לְהַצִּיל אֶת עַבְדּוֹ. ⁴ כְּבוֹאָם אֶל יֵשׁוּעַ הִפְצִירוּ בּוֹ מְאֹד וְאָמְרוּ: "רָאוּי הוּא שֶׁתַּעֲשֶׂה לּוֹ זֹאת, ⁵ מִשּׁוּם שֶׁהוּא אוֹהֵב אֶת עַמֵּנוּ וְהוּא בָּנָה לָנוּ אֶת בֵּית הַכְּנֶסֶת."

⁶ יֵשׁוּעַ הָלַךְ אִתָּם, אַךְ כְּשֶׁהָיָה לֹא הַרְחֵק מִן הַבַּיִת שָׁלַח אֵלָיו שַׂר הַמֵּאָה אֶת יְדִידָיו לוֹמַר לוֹ, "אֲדוֹנִי, אַל תַּטְרִיחַ אֶת עַצְמְךָ, כִּי אֵינֶנִּי רָאוּי שֶׁתָּבוֹא בְּצֵל קוֹרָתִי. ⁷ מִשּׁוּם כָּךְ אַף לֹא חָשַׁבְתִּי עַצְמִי רָאוּי לָבוֹא אֵלֶיךָ. אֲבָל אֱמֹר נָא מִלָּה וְנַעֲרִי יֵרָפֵא. ⁸ הֲרֵי גַם אֲנִי אִישׁ כָּפוּף לְמָרוּת וּכְפוּפִים לִי אַנְשֵׁי צָבָא, וְכַאֲשֶׁר אֲנִי אוֹמֵר לָזֶה, 'עֲשֵׂה זֹאת', הוּא עוֹשֶׂה."

⁹ כַּאֲשֶׁר שָׁמַע יֵשׁוּעַ אֶת הַדְּבָרִים הָאֵלֶּה הִתְפַּלֵּא עָלָיו. הוּא פָּנָה וְאָמַר אֶל הֶהָמוֹן הַהוֹלֵךְ אַחֲרָיו: "אוֹמֵר אֲנִי לָכֶם, אֲפִלּוּ בְּיִשְׂרָאֵל לֹא מָצָאתִי אֱמוּנָה כָּזֹאת." ¹⁰ הַשְּׁלוּחִים שָׁבוּ אֶל הַבַּיִת וּמָצְאוּ אֶת הָעֶבֶד בָּרִיא.

¹¹ לְמָחֳרָת הָלַךְ אֶל עִיר אֲשֶׁר שְׁמָהּ נַעִים, וְאִתּוֹ הָלְכוּ תַּלְמִידָיו וְהָמוֹן רַב. ¹² הוּא הִתְקָרֵב אֶל שַׁעַר הָעִיר וְהִנֵּה מוֹצִיאִים מֵת אֲשֶׁר בֵּן יָחִיד הוּא לְאִמּוֹ הָאַלְמָנָה, וְקָהָל רַב מִן הָעִיר הוֹלֵךְ עִמָּהּ. ¹³ כְּשֶׁרָאָה אוֹתָהּ הָאָדוֹן נִכְמְרוּ רַחֲמָיו עָלֶיהָ וְאָמַר: "אַל תִּבְכִּי." ¹⁴ הוּא נִגַּשׁ, נָגַע בַּמִּטָּה וְנוֹשְׂאֵי הַמִּטָּה נֶעֶמְדוּ. אָז אָמַר: "בָּחוּר, הֲרֵינִי אוֹמֵר לְךָ, קוּם!"

"Young man, I say to you, arise." [15] So he who was dead sat up and began to speak. And He presented him to his mother.

[16] Then fear came upon all, and they glorified God, saying, "A great prophet has risen up among us"; and, "God has visited His people." [17] And this report about Him went throughout all Judea and all the surrounding region.

[18] Then the disciples of John reported to him concerning all these things. [19] And John, calling two of his disciples to *him,* sent *them* to Jesus, saying, "Are You the Coming One, or do we look for another?"

[20] When the men had come to Him, they said, "John the Baptist has sent us to You, saying, 'Are You the Coming One, or do we look for another?'" [21] And that very hour He cured many of infirmities, afflictions, and evil spirits; and to many blind He gave sight.

[22] Jesus answered and said to them, "Go and tell John the things you have seen and heard: that *the* blind see, *the* lame walk, *the* lepers are cleansed, *the* deaf hear, *the* dead are raised, *the* poor have the gospel preached to them. [23] And blessed is *he* who is not offended because of Me."

[24] When the messengers of John had departed, He began to speak to the multitudes concerning John: "What did you go out into the wilderness to see? A reed shaken by the wind? [25] But what did you go out to see? A man clothed in soft garments? Indeed those who are gorgeously apparelled and live in luxury are in kings' courts. [26] But what did you go out to see? A prophet? Yes, I say to you, and more than a prophet. [27] This is *he* of whom it is written:

'Behold, I send My messenger before Your face,
Who will prepare Your way before You.'

[28] For I say to you, among those born of women there is not a greater prophet than John the Baptist; but he who is least in the kingdom of God is greater than he."

[29] And when all the people heard *Him,* even the tax collectors justified God, having been baptized with the baptism of John. [30] But the Pharisees and lawyers rejected the will of God for themselves, not having been baptized by him.

[31] And the Lord said, "To what then shall I liken the men of this generation, and what are they like? [32] They are like children sitting in the marketplace and calling to one another, saying:

'We played the flute for you,
And you did not dance;
We mourned to you,

[15] הַמֵּת יָשַׁב וְהֵחֵל לְדַבֵּר, וְיֵשׁוּעַ נָתַן אוֹתוֹ לְאִמּוֹ.
[16] הַכֹּל נִתְמַלְאוּ יִרְאָה וְהִלְלוּ אֶת אֱלֹהִים בְּאָמְרָם: "נָבִיא גָּדוֹל קָם בְּקִרְבֵּנוּ, אֱלֹהִים פָּקַד אֶת עַמּוֹ."
[17] הַדָּבָר הַזֶּה עַל־אוֹדוֹתָיו הִתְפַּשֵּׁט בְּכָל יְהוּדָה וּבְכָל הָאֵזוֹר אֲשֶׁר מִסָּבִיב.
[18] תַּלְמִידֵי יוֹחָנָן הוֹדִיעוּ לוֹ אֶת כָּל הַדְּבָרִים הָאֵלֶּה.
[19] יוֹחָנָן קָרָא אֵלָיו שְׁנַיִם מִתַּלְמִידָיו וְשָׁלַח אוֹתָם אֶל הָאָדוֹן לִשְׁאֹל: "הַאִם אַתָּה הוּא אֲשֶׁר נוֹעַד לָבוֹא, אוֹ נְחַכֶּה לְאַחֵר?"

[20] בְּבוֹאָם אֵלָיו אָמְרוּ הָאֲנָשִׁים: "יוֹחָנָן הַמַּטְבִּיל שָׁלַח אוֹתָנוּ אֵלֶיךָ לִשְׁאֹל הַאִם אַתָּה הוּא אֲשֶׁר נוֹעַד לָבוֹא, אוֹ נְחַכֶּה לְאַחֵר?" [21] בְּאוֹתָה עֵת רִפֵּא רַבִּים מִמַּחֲלוֹת, מִנְּגָעִים וּמֵרוּחוֹת רָעוֹת, וּלְעִוְרִים רַבִּים הֶעֱנִיק מְאוֹר עֵינַיִם.

[22] הֵשִׁיב לָהֶם: "לְכוּ, וְהַגִּידוּ לְיוֹחָנָן אֶת אֲשֶׁר רְאִיתֶם וּשְׁמַעְתֶּם: עִוְרִים רוֹאִים, פִּסְחִים מְהַלְּכִים, מְצֹרָעִים מְטֹהָרִים, חֵרְשִׁים שׁוֹמְעִים, מֵתִים קָמִים, וַעֲנִיִּים מְתְבַּשְּׂרִים. [23] וְאַשְׁרֵי מִי שֶׁלֹּא אֶהְיֶה לוֹ לְמִכְשׁוֹל."

[24] לְאַחַר שֶׁהָלְכוּ שְׁלִיחֵי יוֹחָנָן הֵחֵל יֵשׁוּעַ לְדַבֵּר אֶל הֲמוֹן הָעָם עַל־אוֹדוֹת יוֹחָנָן: "מַה יְּצָאתֶם לַמִּדְבָּר לִרְאוֹת? קָנֶה מִתְנוֹעֵעַ בָּרוּחַ? [25] וּבְכֵן מַה יְּצָאתֶם לִרְאוֹת? אִישׁ לָבוּשׁ בְּגָדִים מְעֻדָּנִים? הֲרֵי הַלּוֹבְשִׁים בְּגָדִים מְהֻדָּרִים וְחַיִּים בְּמוֹתָרוֹת, בְּאַרְמְנוֹת מְלָכִים הֵם נִמְצָאִים! [26] מַה בְּכָל זֹאת יְצָאתֶם לִרְאוֹת? נָבִיא? כֵּן, אוֹמֵר אֲנִי לָכֶם, אַף יוֹתֵר מִנָּבִיא. [27] זֶה הוּא אֲשֶׁר כָּתוּב עָלָיו, 'הִנְנִי שֹׁלֵחַ מַלְאָכִי לְפָנֶיךָ וּפִנָּה דַּרְכְּךָ לְפָנֶיךָ'. [28] אוֹמֵר אֲנִי לָכֶם, אֵין אִישׁ בִּילוּדֵי אִשָּׁה גָּדוֹל מִיּוֹחָנָן, אַךְ הַקָּטֹן בְּמַלְכוּת הָאֱלֹהִים גָּדוֹל מִמֶּנּוּ."

[29] כָּל הָעָם אֲשֶׁר שָׁמְעוּ, וְגַם הַמּוֹכְסִים, הִכִּירוּ בְּצִדְקַת אֱלֹהִים וְנִטְבְּלוּ בִּטְבִילַת יוֹחָנָן. [30] אוּלָם הַפְּרוּשִׁים וּבַעֲלֵי הַתּוֹרָה לֹא נִטְבְּלוּ אֶצְלוֹ וּבְכָךְ שָׂמוּ לְאַל אֶת תָּכְנִית הָאֱלֹהִים בַּעֲדָם.

[31] "אִם כֵּן לְמִי אֲשַׁוֶּה אֶת אַנְשֵׁי הַדּוֹר הַזֶּה, וּלְמִי הֵם דּוֹמִים? [32] דּוֹמִים הֵם לִילָדִים הַיּוֹשְׁבִים בַּחֲצַר הַשּׁוּק וְקוֹרְאִים אֶל חַבְרֵיהֶם בְּקוֹל: 'חִלַּלְנוּ לָכֶם בַּחֲלִילִים וְלֹא רְקַדְתֶּם, קוֹנַנּוּ לָכֶם קִינָה וְלֹא

And you did not weep.'

³³ For John the Baptist came neither eating bread nor drinking wine, and you say, 'He has a demon.' ³⁴ The Son of Man has come eating and drinking, and you say, 'Look, a glutton and a winebibber, a friend of tax collectors and sinners!' ³⁵ But wisdom is justified by all her children."

³⁶ Then one of the Pharisees asked Him to eat with him. And He went to the Pharisee's house, and sat down to eat. ³⁷ And behold, a woman in the city who was a sinner, when she knew that *Jesus* sat at the table in the Pharisee's house, brought an alabaster flask of fragrant oil, ³⁸ and stood at His feet behind *Him* weeping; and she began to wash His feet with her tears, and wiped *them* with the hair of her head; and she kissed His feet and anointed *them* with the fragrant oil. ³⁹ Now when the Pharisee who had invited Him saw *this,* he spoke to himself, saying, "This Man, if He were a prophet, would know who and what manner of woman *this is* who is touching Him, for she is a sinner."

⁴⁰ And Jesus answered and said to him, "Simon, I have something to say to you."

So he said, "Teacher, say it."

⁴¹ "There was a certain creditor who had two debtors. One owed five hundred denarii, and the other fifty. ⁴² And when they had nothing with which to repay, he freely forgave them both. Tell Me, therefore, which of them will love him more?"

⁴³ Simon answered and said, "I suppose the *one* whom he forgave more."

And He said to him, "You have rightly judged." ⁴⁴ Then He turned to the woman and said to Simon, "Do you see this woman? I entered your house; you gave Me no water for My feet, but she has washed My feet with her tears and wiped *them* with the hair of her head. ⁴⁵ You gave Me no kiss, but this woman has not ceased to kiss My feet since the time I came in. ⁴⁶ You did not anoint My head with oil, but this woman has anointed My feet with fragrant oil. ⁴⁷ Therefore I say to you, her sins, *which are* many, are forgiven, for she loved much. But to whom little is forgiven, *the same* loves little."

⁴⁸ Then He said to her, "Your sins are forgiven."

⁴⁹ And those who sat at the table with Him began to say to themselves, "Who is this who even forgives sins?"

⁵⁰ Then He said to the woman, "Your faith has saved you. Go in peace."

בְּכִיתֶם'. ³³ כִּי בָא יוֹחָנָן הַמַּטְבִּיל, לֶחֶם לֹא אָכַל וְיַיִן לֹא שָׁתָה, וְאַתֶּם אוֹמְרִים 'שֵׁד בּוֹ'. ³⁴ בָּא בֶּן־הָאָדָם וְהוּא אוֹכֵל וְשׁוֹתֶה, וְאַתֶּם אוֹמְרִים 'הִנֵּה אִישׁ זוֹלֵל וְסוֹבֵא, יְדִיד הַמּוֹכְסִים וְהַחוֹטְאִים'. ³⁵ אָכֵן, צִדְקָתָהּ שֶׁל הַחָכְמָה הוּכְחָה בְּכָל בָּנֶיהָ."

³⁶ אַחַד הַפְּרוּשִׁים בִּקֵּשׁ מֵיֵשׁוּעַ כִּי יִסְעַד אִתּוֹ. הוּא נִכְנַס לְבֵית הַפָּרוּשׁ וְהֵסֵב שָׁם. ³⁷ וְהִנֵּה אִשָּׁה חוֹטֵאת מִן הָעִיר, שֶׁיָּדְעָה כִּי הוּא מֵסֵב בְּבֵית הַפָּרוּשׁ, הֵבִיאָה פַּךְ שֶׁמֶן בְּשָׂם. ³⁸ הִיא הִתְקָרְבָה מֵאָחוֹר וְרָכְנָה לְרַגְלָיו כְּשֶׁהִיא בּוֹכָה, וּבְדִמְעוֹתֶיהָ הֵחֵלָּה לְהַרְטִיב אֶת רַגְלָיו. אַחֲרֵי כֵן נִגְּבָה אוֹתָן בְּשַׂעֲרוֹת רֹאשָׁהּ, נִשְּׁקָה אֶת רַגְלָיו וּמָשְׁחָה אוֹתָן בְּשֶׁמֶן בְּשָׂם. ³⁹ הַפָּרוּשׁ שֶׁהִזְמִינוֹ, כִּרְאוֹתוֹ אֶת הַנַּעֲשֶׂה, אָמַר בְּלִבּוֹ: "אִלּוּ הָיָה זֶה נָבִיא, הָיָה יוֹדֵעַ מִי הִיא וּמַה טִּיבָהּ שֶׁל הָאִשָּׁה הַנּוֹגַעַת בּוֹ – שֶׁהִיא אִשָּׁה חוֹטֵאת."

⁴⁰ פָּנָה אֵלָיו יֵשׁוּעַ וְאָמַר: "שִׁמְעוֹן, יֵשׁ לִי דָּבָר לוֹמַר לְךָ."

אָמַר שִׁמְעוֹן: "דַּבֵּר, רַבִּי."

⁴¹ "לְנוֹשֶׁה מְסַיֵּם הָיוּ שְׁנֵי בַּעֲלֵי חוֹב. הָאֶחָד הָיָה חַיָּב לוֹ חֲמֵשׁ מֵאוֹת דִּינָרִים, וְהַשֵּׁנִי חֲמִשִּׁים דִּינָרִים. ⁴² כֵּיוָן שֶׁלֹּא הִשִּׂיגָה יָדָם לְשַׁלֵּם וִתֵּר לִשְׁנֵיהֶם. וְעַכְשָׁו, אֱמֹר נָא, מִי מִשְּׁנֵיהֶם יֹאהַב אוֹתוֹ יוֹתֵר?"

⁴³ הֵשִׁיב שִׁמְעוֹן: "לְפִי דַּעְתִּי, זֶה שֶׁהַנּוֹשֶׁה וִתֵּר לוֹ יוֹתֵר."

אָמַר יֵשׁוּעַ: "יָפֶה פָּסַקְתָּ."

⁴⁴ וּבְפָנוֹתוֹ אֶל הָאִשָּׁה אָמַר אֶל שִׁמְעוֹן: "אַתָּה רוֹאֶה אֶת הָאִשָּׁה הַזֹּאת? אֲנִי נִכְנַסְתִּי לְבֵיתְךָ וּמַיִם בִּשְׁבִיל רַגְלַי לֹא נָתַתָּ, אַךְ הִיא בְּדִמְעוֹתֶיהָ הִרְטִיבָה אֶת רַגְלַי וּבְשַׂעֲרוֹתֶיהָ נִגְּבָה אוֹתָן. ⁴⁵ אַתָּה נְשִׁיקָה לֹא נָתַתָּ לִי, אַךְ הִיא מֵאָז שֶׁנִּכְנַסְתִּי לֹא חָדְלָה לְנַשֵּׁק אֶת רַגְלַי. ⁴⁶ בְּשֶׁמֶן אֶת רֹאשִׁי לֹא מָשַׁחְתָּ, אַךְ הִיא בְּשֶׁמֶן בְּשָׂם מָשְׁחָה אֶת רַגְלַי. ⁴⁷ עַל כֵּן אוֹמֵר אֲנִי לְךָ: נִסְלְחוּ לָהּ חֲטָאֶיהָ הָרַבִּים, כִּי רַבָּה אַהֲבָתָהּ. אֲבָל מִי שֶׁנִּסְלַח לוֹ מְעַט אוֹהֵב מְעַט."

⁴⁸ וְאֵלֶיהָ אָמַר: "נִסְלְחוּ לָךְ חֲטָאַיִךְ."

⁴⁹ הַמְסֻבִּים עִמּוֹ הֵחֵלּוּ לוֹמַר בְּלִבָּם: "מִי הוּא זֶה שֶׁגַּם סוֹלֵחַ עַל חֲטָאִים?" ⁵⁰ הוֹסִיף וְאָמַר אֶל הָאִשָּׁה: "אֱמוּנָתֵךְ הוֹשִׁיעָה אוֹתָךְ, לְכִי לְשָׁלוֹם."

8 Now it came to pass, afterward, that He went through every city and village, preaching and bringing the glad tidings of the kingdom of God. And the twelve *were* with Him, ²and certain women who had been healed of evil spirits and infirmities—Mary called Magdalene, out of whom had come seven demons, ³and Joanna the wife of Chuza, Herod's steward, and Susanna, and many others who provided for Him from their substance.

⁴And when a great multitude had gathered, and they had come to Him from every city, He spoke by a parable: ⁵"A sower went out to sow his seed. And as he sowed, some fell by the wayside; and it was trampled down, and the birds of the air devoured it. ⁶Some fell on rock; and as soon as it sprang up, it withered away because it lacked moisture. ⁷And some fell among thorns, and the thorns sprang up with it and choked it. ⁸But others fell on good ground, sprang up, and yielded a crop a hundredfold." When He had said these things He cried, "He who has ears to hear, let him hear!"

⁹Then His disciples asked Him, saying, "What does this parable mean?"

¹⁰And He said, "To you it has been given to know the mysteries of the kingdom of God, but to the rest *it is given* in parables, that

'Seeing they may not see,
And hearing they may not understand.'

¹¹"Now the parable is this: The seed is the word of God. ¹²Those by the wayside are the ones who hear; then the devil comes and takes away the word out of their hearts, lest they should believe and be saved. ¹³But the ones on the rock *are those* who, when they hear, receive the word with joy; and these have no root, who believe for a while and in time of temptation fall away. ¹⁴Now the ones *that* fell among thorns are those who, when they have heard, go out and are choked with cares, riches, and pleasures of life, and bring no fruit to maturity. ¹⁵But the ones *that* fell on the good ground are those who, having heard the word with a noble and good heart, keep *it* and bear fruit with patience.

¹⁶"No one, when he has lit a lamp, covers it with a vessel or puts *it* under a bed, but sets *it* on a lampstand, that those who enter may see the light. ¹⁷For nothing is secret that will not be revealed, nor *anything* hidden that will not be known and come to light. ¹⁸Therefore take heed how you hear. For whoever has, to him *more* will be given; and whoever does not have, even what he seems to have will be taken from him."

ח אַחֲרֵי כֵן עָבַר מֵעִיר לְעִיר וּמִכְּפָר לִכְפָר כְּשֶׁהוּא מַכְרִיז וּמְבַשֵּׂר אֶת מַלְכוּת הָאֱלֹהִים. הַשְּׁנֵים־עָשָׂר הָיוּ אִתּוֹ ² וְגַם כַּמָּה נָשִׁים שֶׁנִּרְפְּאוּ מֵרוּחוֹת רָעוֹת וּמֵחֳלָאִים: מִרְיָם הַנִּקְרֵאת מַגְדָּלִית, אֲשֶׁר שִׁבְעָה שֵׁדִים יָצְאוּ מִמֶּנָּה, ³ וְיוֹחָנָה, אֵשֶׁת כּוּזָא מְנַהֵל מֶשֶׁק בֵּיתוֹ שֶׁל הוֹרְדוֹס, וְשׁוֹשַׁנָּה וְרַבּוֹת אֲחֵרוֹת אֲשֶׁר כִּלְכְּלוּ אוֹתוֹ מִנִּכְסֵיהֶן.

⁴ כַּאֲשֶׁר הִתְאַסְּפוּ הֲמוֹנֵי אֲנָשִׁים שֶׁבָּאוּ אֵלָיו מִכָּל עִיר, דִּבֵּר בְּמָשָׁל: ⁵ "הַזּוֹרֵעַ יָצָא לִזְרֹעַ אֶת זַרְעוֹ; כַּאֲשֶׁר זָרַע נָפְלוּ כַּמָּה זְרָעִים בְּשׁוּלֵי הַדֶּרֶךְ וְנִרְמְסוּ, וְעוֹף הַשָּׁמַיִם אָכַל אוֹתָם. ⁶ אֲחֵרִים נָפְלוּ עַל סֶלַע, אַךְ עִם צְמִיחָתָם הִתְיַבְּשׁוּ בִּגְלַל חֹסֶר לַחוּת. ⁷ אֲחֵרִים נָפְלוּ בֵּין קוֹצִים, אַךְ הַקּוֹצִים שֶׁצָּמְחוּ יַחַד עִמָּם הֶחֱנִיקוּ אוֹתָם. ⁸ וַאֲחֵרִים נָפְלוּ עַל אֲדָמָה טוֹבָה, צָמְחוּ וְעָשׂוּ פְּרִי פִּי מֵאָה." לְאַחַר שֶׁאָמַר זֹאת קָרָא: "מִי שֶׁאָזְנַיִם לוֹ, שֶׁיִּשְׁמַע!"

⁹ שְׁאָלוּהוּ תַּלְמִידָיו: "מַה פֵּשֶׁר הַמָּשָׁל הַזֶּה?" ¹⁰ הֵשִׁיב: "לָכֶם נִתַּן לָדַעַת אֶת סוֹדוֹת מַלְכוּת הָאֱלֹהִים, אֲבָל לָאֲחֵרִים – בִּמְשָׁלִים, לְמַעַן רְאֹה לֹא יִרְאוּ וּבְשָׁמְעָם לֹא יָבִינוּ. ¹¹ זֶהוּ פֵּשֶׁר הַמָּשָׁל: הַזֶּרַע הוּא דְּבַר אֱלֹהִים. ¹² אֵלֶּה אֲשֶׁר בְּשׁוּלֵי הַדֶּרֶךְ הֵם הַשּׁוֹמְעִים. אַחַר כָּךְ בָּא הַשָּׂטָן וְלוֹקֵחַ אֶת הַדָּבָר מִלִּבָּם, לְמֹנֵעַ אוֹתָם מִלְּהַאֲמִין וּלְהִוָּשַׁע. ¹³ אֵלֶּה אֲשֶׁר עַל הַסֶּלַע הֵם הַשּׁוֹמְעִים אֶת הַדָּבָר וּמְקַבְּלִים אוֹתוֹ בְּשִׂמְחָה, אַךְ שֹׁרֶשׁ אֵין לָהֶם; זְמַן־מָה יַאֲמִינוּ וּבְעֵת נִסָּיוֹן יִסֹּגוּ. ¹⁴ הַנּוֹפְלִים בֵּין הַקּוֹצִים הֵם הַשּׁוֹמְעִים אֲשֶׁר בְּלֶכְתָּם נֶחֱנָקִים בִּדְאָגוֹת וּבְעֹשֶׁר וּבְתַעֲנוּגוֹת הַחַיִּים, וְאֵינָם עוֹשִׂים פְּרִי רָאוּי לַאֲכִילָה. ¹⁵ וְאֵלֶּה אֲשֶׁר בָּאֲדָמָה הַטּוֹבָה הֵם שׁוֹמְעֵי הַדָּבָר הַמַּחֲזִיקִים בּוֹ בְּלֵב יָשָׁר וְטוֹב וְעוֹשִׂים פְּרִי בְּסַבְלָנוּת."

¹⁶ "אֵין אִישׁ מַדְלִיק מְנוֹרָה וּמְכַסֶּה אוֹתָהּ בִּכְלִי, אַף לֹא יָשִׂים אוֹתָהּ תַּחַת הַמִּטָּה, אֶלָּא עַל כֵּן יָשִׂים אוֹתָהּ כְּדֵי שֶׁבָּאֵי הַבַּיִת יִרְאוּ אֶת הָאוֹר; ¹⁷ כִּי אֵין נִסְתָּר אֲשֶׁר לֹא יִגָּלֶה וְאֵין נֶעְלָם אֲשֶׁר לֹא יִוָּדַע וְיֵצֵא לָאוֹר. ¹⁸ לָכֵן שִׂימוּ לִבְּכֶם בְּאֵיזֶה אֹפֶן אַתֶּם שׁוֹמְעִים, כִּי מִי שֶׁיֵּשׁ לוֹ יִנָּתֵן לוֹ; וּמִי שֶׁאֵין לוֹ, גַּם מַה שֶּׁחוֹשֵׁב שֶׁיֵּשׁ לוֹ יִלָּקַח מִמֶּנּוּ."

19 Then His mother and brothers came to Him, and could not approach Him because of the crowd. 20 And it was told Him *by some,* who said, "Your mother and Your brothers are standing outside, desiring to see You."

21 But He answered and said to them, "My mother and My brothers are these who hear the word of God and do it."

22 Now it happened, on a certain day, that He got into a boat with His disciples. And He said to them, "Let us cross over to the other side of the lake." And they launched out. 23 But as they sailed He fell asleep. And a windstorm came down on the lake, and they were filling *with water,* and were in jeopardy. 24 And they came to Him and awoke Him, saying, "Master, Master, we are perishing!"

Then He arose and rebuked the wind and the raging of the water. And they ceased, and there was a calm. 25 But He said to them, "Where is your faith?"

And they were afraid, and marveled, saying to one another, "Who can this be? For He commands even the winds and water, and they obey Him!"

26 Then they sailed to the country of the Gadarenes, which is opposite Galilee. 27 And when He stepped out on the land, there met Him a certain man from the city who had demons for a long time. And he wore no clothes, nor did he live in a house but in the tombs. 28 When he saw Jesus, he cried out, fell down before Him, and with a loud voice said, "What have I to do with You, Jesus, Son of the Most High God? I beg You, do not torment me!" 29 For He had commanded the unclean spirit to come out of the man. For it had often seized him, and he was kept under guard, bound with chains and shackles; and he broke the bonds and was driven by the demon into the wilderness.

30 Jesus asked him, saying, "What is your name?" And he said, "Legion," because many demons had entered him. 31 And they begged Him that He would not command them to go out into the abyss.

32 Now a herd of many swine was feeding there on the mountain. So they begged Him that He would permit them to enter them. And He permitted them. 33 Then the demons went out of the man and entered the swine, and the herd ran violently down the steep place into the lake and drowned.

34 When those who fed *them* saw what had happened, they fled and told *it* in the city and in the country. 35 Then they went out to see what had happened, and came to Jesus, and found the man from whom the demons had departed, sitting at the feet of Jesus, clothed and in his right mind. And

19 אָז בָּאוּ אֵלָיו אִמּוֹ וְאֶחָיו, וְלֹא יָכְלוּ לָגֶשֶׁת אֵלָיו בִּגְלַל הֶהָמוֹן. 20 הוֹדִיעוּ לוֹ: "אִמְּךָ וְאַחֶיךָ עוֹמְדִים בַּחוּץ וְהֵם חֲפֵצִים לִרְאוֹתְךָ", 21 אַךְ הוּא הֵשִׁיב וְאָמַר לָהֶם: "אֵלֶּה אִמִּי וְאַחַי – הַשּׁוֹמְעִים אֶת דְּבַר אֱלֹהִים וְעוֹשִׂים."

22 בְּאַחַד הַיָּמִים יָרַד לְסִירָה יַחַד עִם תַּלְמִידָיו. אָמַר לָהֶם: "בּוֹאוּ נַעֲבֹר לְצִדּוֹ הַשֵּׁנִי שֶׁל הָאֲגַם." אָז הִפְלִיגוּ מִשָּׁם. 23 כַּאֲשֶׁר שָׁטוּ הוּא נִרְדַּם, וְהִנֵּה רוּחַ סְעָרָה יָרְדָה עַל הָאֲגַם וְהַסִּירָה נִתְמַלְּאָה מַיִם עַד כְּדֵי כָךְ שֶׁהָיוּ בְּסַכָּנָה. 24 הֵם נִגְּשׁוּ אֵלָיו וֶהֱעִירוּהוּ בְּאָמְרָם, "אֲדוֹנֵנוּ, אֲדוֹנֵנוּ, אֲנַחְנוּ טוֹבְעִים!" הוּא הִתְעוֹרֵר וְגָעַר בָּרוּחַ וּבַגַּלִּים הַזּוֹעֲפִים. הַלָּלוּ שָׁכְכוּ וְנִשְׁתָּרְרָה דְּמָמָה.

25 שָׁאַל אוֹתָם: "אֵיפֹה אֱמוּנַתְכֶם?" בִּהְיוֹתָם אֲחוּזֵי יִרְאָה וּפְלִיאָה אָמְרוּ זֶה לָזֶה: "וּבְכֵן מִי הוּא זֶה אֲשֶׁר מְצַוֶּה עַל הָרוּחַ וְעַל הַמַּיִם וְהֵם נִשְׁמָעִים לוֹ!"

26 הֵם שָׁטוּ אֶל חֶבֶל אֶרֶץ הַגִּרְגְּשִׁיִּים אֲשֶׁר מִמּוּל הַגָּלִיל. 27 כַּאֲשֶׁר עָלָה לַיַּבָּשָׁה, פָּגַשׁ אוֹתוֹ אִישׁ מִן הָעִיר וְהָאִישׁ אֲחוּז שֵׁדִים; זְמַן רַב לֹא לָבַשׁ בְּגָדִים וְלֹא גָּר בְּבַיִת כִּי אִם בִּמְעָרוֹת הַקְּבָרִים. 28 כִּרְאוֹתוֹ אֶת יֵשׁוּעַ צָעַק וְנָפַל אַרְצָה לְפָנָיו וְקָרָא בְּקוֹל גָּדוֹל: "מַה לִּי וּלְךָ יֵשׁוּעַ, בֶּן אֵל עֶלְיוֹן? אֲנִי מִתְחַנֵּן אֵלֶיךָ, אַל תְּעַנֶּה אוֹתִי"; 29 שֶׁכֵּן יֵשׁוּעַ צִוָּה עַל הָרוּחַ הַטְּמֵאָה לָצֵאת מִן הָאִישׁ. פְּעָמִים רַבּוֹת הִתְקִיפָה אוֹתוֹ, וְהָיוּ שׁוֹמְרִים אוֹתוֹ כָּבוּל בְּיָדַיִם וּבְרַגְלַיִם, אֶלָּא שֶׁהָיָה מְנַתֵּק אֶת הַכְּבָלִים וְנִדְחַף עַל-יְדֵי הַשֵּׁד אֶל מְקוֹמוֹת שׁוֹמֵמִים.

30 שָׁאַל אוֹתוֹ יֵשׁוּעַ: "מַה שִּׁמְךָ?" הֵשִׁיב הָאִישׁ: "שְׁמִי לִגְיוֹן", שֶׁכֵּן שֵׁדִים רַבִּים נִכְנְסוּ בּוֹ. 31 הַשֵּׁדִים בִּקְשׁוּ מִיֵּשׁוּעַ שֶׁלֹּא יְצַוֶּה עֲלֵיהֶם לָרֶדֶת אֶל הַתְּהוֹם, 32 וְכֵיוָן שֶׁעֵדֶר גָּדוֹל שֶׁל חֲזִירִים הָיָה רוֹעֶה שָׁם בָּהָר, הִתְחַנְּנוּ אֶל יֵשׁוּעַ שֶׁיַּנִּיחַ לָהֶם לְהִכָּנֵס לְתוֹכָם. הוּא הִרְשָׁה לָהֶם. 33 לְאַחַר צֵאתָם מִן הָאִישׁ נִכְנְסוּ הַשֵּׁדִים בַּחֲזִירִים, וְהָעֵדֶר הִסְתָּעֵר מִמּוֹרָד הָהָר אֶל הַיָּם וְטָבַע. 34 כִּרְאוֹתָם אֶת הַנַּעֲשֶׂה בָּרְחוּ הָרוֹעִים וְסִפְּרוּ אֶת הַדָּבָר בָּעִיר וּבַכְּפָרִים.

35 הַתּוֹשָׁבִים יָצְאוּ לִרְאוֹת מַה קָּרָה. בְּבוֹאָם אֶל יֵשׁוּעַ מָצְאוּ אֶת הָאִישׁ שֶׁהַשֵּׁדִים יָצְאוּ מִתּוֹכוֹ, וְהוּא יוֹשֵׁב לְרַגְלֵי יֵשׁוּעַ לָבוּשׁ וְשָׁפוּי בְּדַעְתּוֹ. פַּחַד מִלֵּא

they were afraid. 36They also who had seen *it* told them by what means he who had been demon-possessed was healed. 37Then the whole multitude of the surrounding region of the Gadarenes asked Him to depart from them, for they were seized with great fear. And He got into the boat and returned.

38Now the man from whom the demons had departed begged Him that he might be with Him. But Jesus sent him away, saying, 39"Return to your own house, and tell what great things God has done for you." And he went his way and proclaimed throughout the whole city what great things Jesus had done for him.

40So it was, when Jesus returned, that the multitude welcomed Him, for they were all waiting for Him. 41And behold, there came a man named Jairus, and he was a ruler of the synagogue. And he fell down at Jesus' feet and begged Him to come to his house, 42for he had an only daughter about twelve years of age, and she was dying.

But as He went, the multitudes thronged Him. 43Now a woman, having a flow of blood for twelve years, who had spent all her livelihood on physicians and could not be healed by any, 44came from behind and touched the border of His garment. And immediately her flow of blood stopped.

45And Jesus said, "Who touched Me?"

When all denied it, Peter and those with him said, "Master, the multitudes throng and press You, and You say, 'Who touched Me?' "

46But Jesus said, "Somebody touched Me, for I perceived power going out from Me." 47Now when the woman saw that she was not hidden, she came trembling; and falling down before Him, she declared to Him in the presence of all the people the reason she had touched Him and how she was healed immediately.

48And He said to her, "Daughter, be of good cheer; your faith has made you well. Go in peace."

49While He was still speaking, someone came from the ruler of the synagogue's *house,* saying to him, "Your daughter is dead. Do not trouble the Teacher."

50But when Jesus heard *it,* He answered him, saying, "Do not be afraid; only believe, and she will be made well." 51When He came into the house, He permitted no one to go in except Peter, James, and John, and the father and mother of the girl. 52Now all wept and mourned for her; but He said, "Do not weep; she is not dead, but sleeping." 53And they ridiculed Him, knowing that she was dead.

אֶת לְבָּם. 36 הָאֲנָשִׁים שֶׁרָאוּ אֶת הַמַּעֲשֶׂה סִפְּרוּ לָהֶם כֵּיצַד נִרְפָּא אֲחוּז הַשֵּׁדִים. 37 וְכָל הֶהָמוֹן שֶׁבָּא מֵאֵזוֹר הַגַּרְגְּשִׁיִּים בִּקֵּשׁ מִיֵּשׁוּעַ שֶׁיֵּלֵךְ מֵאִתָּם, כִּי פַּחַד גָּדוֹל נָפַל עֲלֵיהֶם. לְפִיכָךְ יָרַד לַסִּירָה וְחָזַר. 38 אַךְ הָאִישׁ שֶׁיָּצְאוּ מִתּוֹכוֹ הַשֵּׁדִים בִּקֵּשׁ מִיֵּשׁוּעַ שֶׁיַּנִּיחַ לוֹ לְהִשָּׁאֵר אִתּוֹ, 39 אֶלָּא שֶׁיֵּשׁוּעַ שִׁלַּח אוֹתוֹ בְּאָמְרוֹ: "שׁוּב לְבֵיתְךָ וְסַפֵּר אֶת כָּל אֲשֶׁר עָשָׂה לְךָ אֱלֹהִים." הוּא הָלַךְ וְהִשְׁמִיעַ בְּכָל הָעִיר אֶת כָּל אֲשֶׁר עָשָׂה לוֹ יֵשׁוּעַ.

40 כַּאֲשֶׁר חָזַר יֵשׁוּעַ קִבֵּל הָעָם אֶת פָּנָיו, שֶׁכֵּן הַכֹּל חִכּוּ לוֹ. 41 וְהִנֵּה בָּא אִישׁ, יָאִיר שְׁמוֹ, וְהוּא רֹאשׁ בֵּית כְּנֶסֶת. הוּא נָפַל לְרַגְלֵי יֵשׁוּעַ וּבִקֵּשׁ מִמֶּנּוּ שֶׁיָּבוֹא אֶל בֵּיתוֹ, 42 כִּי בַּת יְחִידָה הָיְתָה לוֹ, כְּבַת שְׁתֵּים־עֶשְׂרֵה שָׁנָה, וְהִיא נְטֻיָּה לָמוּת. אָז הָלַךְ לְשָׁם כְּשֶׁהֲמוֹן הָעָם נִדְחָק סְבִיבוֹ. 43 וְאִשָּׁה זָבַת דָּם זֶה שְׁתֵּים־עֶשְׂרֵה שָׁנָה – שֶׁהוֹצִיאָה אֶת כָּל מִחְיָתָהּ עַל רוֹפְאִים וְאִישׁ לֹא הִצְלִיחַ לְרַפְּאָהּ – 44 הִתְקָרְבָה מֵאֲחוֹרָיו וְנָגְעָה בִּכְנַף בִּגְדוֹ. מִיָּד נֶעֱצַר זוֹב דָּמָהּ. 45 שָׁאַל יֵשׁוּעַ: "מִי זֶה שֶׁנָּגַע בִּי?" כֵּיוָן שֶׁהַכֹּל הִכְחִישׁוּ, אָמַר כֵּיפָא: "אֲדוֹנִי, הֲמוֹן הָעָם דּוֹחֵק וְלוֹחֵץ אוֹתְךָ!" 46 אַךְ יֵשׁוּעַ אָמַר: "מִישֶׁהוּ נָגַע בִּי, כִּי הִבְחַנְתִּי שֶׁיָּצְאָה מִמֶּנִּי גְּבוּרָה."

47 הָאִשָּׁה, כִּרְאוֹתָהּ שֶׁאֵין הִיא נִסְתֶּרֶת מִמֶּנּוּ, נִגְּשָׁה בִּרְעָדָה וְנָפְלָה לְפָנָיו, וּבְאָזְנֵי כָּל הָעָם סִפְּרָה מַדּוּעַ נָגְעָה בּוֹ, וְכִי נִרְפְּאָה מִיָּד. 48 אָמַר לָהּ יֵשׁוּעַ: "אֱמוּנָתֵךְ הוֹשִׁיעָה אוֹתָךְ, בִּתִּי, לְכִי לְשָׁלוֹם."

49 בְּשָׁעָה שֶׁדִּבֵּר בָּא אִישׁ מִבֵּיתוֹ שֶׁל רֹאשׁ בֵּית הַכְּנֶסֶת וְאָמַר: "בִּתְּךָ מֵתָה, אַל תַּטְרִיחַ עוֹד אֶת הַמּוֹרֶה." 50 אַךְ יֵשׁוּעַ בְּשָׁמְעוֹ זֹאת אָמַר: "אַל תִּירָא, רַק הַאֲמֵן וְהִיא תֵּרָפֵא."

51 כַּאֲשֶׁר בָּא אֶל הַבַּיִת לֹא הִנִּיחַ לְאִישׁ לְהִכָּנֵס אִתּוֹ, חוּץ מִכֵּיפָא, יוֹחָנָן, יַעֲקֹב, אֲבִי הַיַּלְדָּה וְאִמָּהּ. 52 הַכֹּל בָּכוּ וְקוֹנְנוּ עָלֶיהָ, אַךְ הוּא אָמַר: "אַל תִּבְכּוּ, הִיא לֹא מֵתָה. הִיא רַק יְשֵׁנָה." 53 הֵם צָחֲקוּ לוֹ, כִּי יָדְעוּ שֶׁהִיא מֵתָה. 54 אוּלָם הוּא

54 But He put them all outside, took her by the hand and called, saying, "Little girl, arise." 55 Then her spirit returned, and she arose immediately. And He commanded that she be given *something* to eat. 56 And her parents were astonished, but He charged them to tell no one what had happened.

9 Then He called His twelve disciples together and gave them power and authority over all demons, and to cure diseases. 2 He sent them to preach the kingdom of God and to heal the sick. 3 And He said to them, "Take nothing for the journey, neither staffs nor bag nor bread nor money; and do not have two tunics apiece.

4 "Whatever house you enter, stay there, and from there depart. 5 And whoever will not receive you, when you go out of that city, shake off the very dust from your feet as a testimony against them."

6 So they departed and went through the towns, preaching the gospel and healing everywhere.

7 Now Herod the tetrarch heard of all that was done by Him; and he was perplexed, because it was said by some that John had risen from the dead, 8 and by some that Elijah had appeared, and by others that one of the old prophets had risen again. 9 Herod said, "John I have beheaded, but who is this of whom I hear such things?" So he sought to see Him.

10 And the apostles, when they had returned, told Him all that they had done. Then He took them and went aside privately into a deserted place belonging to the city called Bethsaida. 11 But when the multitudes knew *it*, they followed Him; and He received them and spoke to them about the kingdom of God, and healed those who had need of healing. 12 When the day began to wear away, the twelve came and said to Him, "Send the multitude away, that they may go into the surrounding towns and country, and lodge and get provisions; for we are in a deserted place here."

13 But He said to them, "You give them something to eat."

And they said, "We have no more than five loaves and two fish, unless we go and buy food for all these people." 14 For there were about five thousand men.

Then He said to His disciples, "Make them sit down in groups of fifty." 15 And they did so, and made them all sit down.

16 Then He took the five loaves and the two fish, and looking up to heaven, He blessed and broke *them*, and gave *them* to the disciples to set before

אָחַז בְּיָדָהּ וְקָרָא: "יַלְדָּה, קוּמִי!" 55 אָז שָׁבָה רוּחָהּ וְהִיא קָמָה מִיָּד. צִוָּה יֵשׁוּעַ: "תְּנוּ לָהּ לֶאֱכֹל!" 56 הוֹרֶיהָ הִשְׁתּוֹמְמוּ, אַךְ הוּא צִוָּה עֲלֵיהֶם שֶׁלֹּא יַגִּידוּ לְאִישׁ אֶת אֲשֶׁר נַעֲשָׂה.

ט לְאַחַר שֶׁכִּנֵּס אֶת הַשְּׁנֵים-עָשָׂר וְנָתַן לָהֶם כֹּחַ וְסַמְכוּת עַל כָּל הַשֵּׁדִים, וְגַם לְרַפֵּא מַחֲלוֹת, 2 שָׁלַח אוֹתָם לְהַכְרִיז עַל מַלְכוּת הָאֱלֹהִים וּלְרַפֵּא אֶת הַחוֹלִים. 3 אָמַר לָהֶם: "אַל תִּקְחוּ מְאוּמָה לַדֶּרֶךְ, לֹא מַקֵּל וְלֹא תַּרְמִיל, לֹא לֶחֶם וְלֹא כֶּסֶף, וְלֹא שְׁתֵּי כֻּתֳּנוֹת לְאִישׁ. 4 כָּל בַּיִת שֶׁתִּכָּנְסוּ אֵלָיו, שָׁם תֵּשְׁבוּ וּמִשָּׁם תֵּצְאוּ לַדֶּרֶךְ. 5 וְכָל אֲשֶׁר לֹא יְקַבְּלוּ אֶתְכֶם, צְאוּ מִן הָעִיר הַהִיא וְנַעֲרוּ אֶת הָאָבָק מֵעַל רַגְלֵיכֶם לְעֵדוּת נֶגְדָּם."

6 הֵם יָצְאוּ וְעָבְרוּ בַּכְּפָרִים כְּשֶׁהֵם מְבַשְּׂרִים אֶת הַבְּשׂוֹרָה וּמְרַפְּאִים בְּכָל מָקוֹם.

7 הוֹרְדוֹס שַׂר הָרֶבַע שָׁמַע עַל כָּל מַה שֶּׁקָּרָה וְנִתְמַלֵּא מְבוּכָה, מִשּׁוּם שֶׁכַּמָּה אֲנָשִׁים אָמְרוּ: "יוֹחָנָן קָם מִבֵּין הַמֵּתִים." 8 אֲחֵרִים אָמְרוּ: "אֵלִיָּהוּ הוֹפִיעַ", וַאֲחֵרִים אָמְרוּ שֶׁאֶחָד הַנְּבִיאִים הַקַּדְמוֹנִים קָם לִתְחִיָּה. 9 אַךְ הוֹרְדוֹס אָמַר: "אֶת יוֹחָנָן הֲרֵי אֲנִי עֲרַפְתִּי, וּמִי זֶה שֶׁאֲנִי שׁוֹמֵעַ עָלָיו כַּדְּבָרִים הָאֵלֶּה?" הוּא הִשְׁתַּדֵּל לִרְאוֹת אוֹתוֹ.

10 כַּאֲשֶׁר חָזְרוּ הַשְּׁלִיחִים סִפְּרוּ לְיֵשׁוּעַ אֶת כָּל אֲשֶׁר עָשׂוּ. הוּא לָקַח אוֹתָם וְיָצָא אִתָּם לְבַד לְכִוּוּן עִיר הַנִּקְרֵאת בֵּית צַיְדָא. 11 כְּשֶׁנּוֹדַע הַדָּבָר לַהֲמוֹן הָעָם הָלְכוּ אַחֲרָיו. הוּא קִבֵּל אוֹתָם, דִּבֵּר אֲלֵיהֶם עַל מַלְכוּת הָאֱלֹהִים וְרִפֵּא אֶת הַזְּקוּקִים לְרִפּוּי.

12 הַיּוֹם נָטָה לָעֶרֶב וְהַשְּׁנֵים-עָשָׂר נִגְּשׁוּ וְאָמְרוּ אֵלָיו: "שְׁלַח נָא אֶת הָעָם וְיֵלְכוּ אֶל הַיְּשׁוּבִים וְהַכְּפָרִים שֶׁמִּסָּבִיב כְּדֵי לָלוּן וּלְהַשִּׂיג אֹכֶל, כִּי פֹּה נִמְצָאִים אָנוּ בִּמְקוֹם שׁוֹמֵם." 13 אָמַר לָהֶם: "תְּנוּ לָהֶם אַתֶּם לֶאֱכֹל", אַךְ הֵם אָמְרוּ: "אֵין לָנוּ יוֹתֵר מֵחֲמֵשׁ כִּכְּרוֹת לֶחֶם וּשְׁנֵי דָּגִים, אֶלָּא אִם כֵּן נֵלֵךְ אֲנַחְנוּ וְנִקְנֶה אֹכֶל לְכָל הָעָם הַזֶּה"; 14 כִּי הָיוּ שָׁם כַּחֲמֵשֶׁת אֲלָפִים אֲנָשִׁים.

עָנָה וְאָמַר לְתַלְמִידָיו: "הוֹשִׁיבוּ אוֹתָם בִּקְבוּצוֹת, כַּחֲמִשִּׁים אִישׁ בְּכָל קְבוּצָה."

15 כָּךְ עָשׂוּ וְהוֹשִׁיבוּ אֶת כֻּלָּם. 16 לָקַח יֵשׁוּעַ אֶת חֲמֵשׁ כִּכְּרוֹת הַלֶּחֶם וְאֶת שְׁנֵי הַדָּגִים, וּלְאַחַר שֶׁנָּשָׂא

the multitude. ¹⁷So they all ate and were filled, and twelve baskets of the leftover fragments were taken up by them.

¹⁸And it happened, as He was alone praying, *that* His disciples joined Him, and He asked them, saying, "Who do the crowds say that I am?"

¹⁹So they answered and said, "John the Baptist, but some *say* Elijah; and others *say* that one of the old prophets has risen again."

²⁰He said to them, "But who do you say that I am?"

Peter answered and said, "The Christ of God."

²¹And He strictly warned and commanded them to tell this to no one, ²²saying, "The Son of Man must suffer many things, and be rejected by the elders and chief priests and scribes, and be killed, and be raised the third day."

²³Then He said to *them* all, "If anyone desires to come after Me, let him deny himself, and take up his cross daily, and follow Me. ²⁴For whoever desires to save his life will lose it, but whoever loses his life for My sake will save it. ²⁵For what profit is it to a man if he gains the whole world, and is himself destroyed or lost? ²⁶For whoever is ashamed of Me and My words, of him the Son of Man will be ashamed when He comes in His *own* glory, and *in His* Father's, and of the holy angels.

²⁷But I tell you truly, there are some standing here who shall not taste death till they see the kingdom of God."

²⁸Now it came to pass, about eight days after these sayings, that He took Peter, John, and James and went up on the mountain to pray. ²⁹As He prayed, the appearance of His face was altered, and His robe *became* white *and* glistening. ³⁰And behold, two men talked with Him, who were Moses and Elijah, ³¹who appeared in glory and spoke of His decease which He was about to accomplish at Jerusalem. ³²But Peter and those with him were heavy with sleep; and when they were fully awake, they saw His glory and the two men who stood with Him. ³³Then it happened, as they were parting from Him, *that* Peter said to Jesus, "Master, it is good for us to be here; and let us make three tabernacles: one for You, one for Moses, and one for Elijah"—not knowing what he said.

³⁴While he was saying this, a cloud came and overshadowed them; and they were fearful as they entered the cloud. ³⁵And a voice came out of the cloud, saying, "This is My beloved Son. Hear Him!" ³⁶When the voice had ceased, Jesus was found alone. But they kept quiet, and told no one in those days any of the things they had seen.

עֵינָיו הַשָּׁמַיְמָה וּבֵרַךְ עֲלֵיהֶם, בָּצַע אוֹתָם וּנְתָנָם לְתַלְמִידָיו לְהַגִּישׁ לָעָם. ¹⁷הַכֹּל אָכְלוּ וְשָׂבְעוּ, וּמִמַּה שֶּׁנּוֹתַר לָהֶם נֶאֶסְפוּ שְׁנֵים־עָשָׂר סַלִּים.

¹⁸פַּעַם אַחַת כְּשֶׁהִתְפַּלֵּל בְּמָקוֹם בּוֹדֵד וְתַלְמִידָיו הָיוּ עִמּוֹ שָׁאַל אוֹתָם: "מָה אוֹמֵר עָלַי הָעָם, מִי אֲנִי?"

¹⁹הֵשִׁיבוּ: "יֵשׁ אוֹמְרִים, 'יוֹחָנָן הַמַּטְבִּיל', יֵשׁ אוֹמְרִים, 'אֵלִיָּהוּ', וַאֲחֵרִים אוֹמְרִים שֶׁאַחַד הַנְּבִיאִים הַקַּדְמוֹנִים קָם לִתְחִיָּה."

²⁰שָׁאַל יֵשׁוּעַ: "וְאַתֶּם מָה אוֹמְרִים, מִי אֲנִי?" הֵשִׁיב כֵּיפָא: "מְשִׁיחַ הָאֱלֹהִים."

²¹אָז הִזְהִיר אוֹתָם בְּצַוּוֹתוֹ עֲלֵיהֶם שֶׁלֹּא יַגִּידוּ זֹאת לְאִישׁ; ²²כְּמוֹ כֵן אָמַר: "צָרִיךְ שֶׁבֶּן־הָאָדָם יִסְבֹּל הַרְבֵּה, שֶׁהַזְּקֵנִים וְרָאשֵׁי הַכֹּהֲנִים וְהַסּוֹפְרִים יִדְחוּהוּ, שֶׁיֵּהָרֵג וּבַיּוֹם הַשְּׁלִישִׁי יָקוּם."

²³אָמַר אֶל הַכֹּל: "מִי שֶׁרוֹצֶה לָבוֹא אַחֲרַי, שֶׁיִּתְכַּחֵשׁ לְעַצְמוֹ וְיִשָּׂא אֶת צְלָבוֹ יוֹם יוֹם וְיֵלֵךְ אַחֲרַי, ²⁴כִּי הֶחָפֵץ לְהַצִּיל אֶת נַפְשׁוֹ יְאַבֵּד אוֹתָהּ. אֲבָל הַמְאַבֵּד אֶת נַפְשׁוֹ לְמַעֲנִי, יַצִּילֶנָּה. ²⁵מַה תּוֹעֶלֶת תִּצְמַח לְאָדָם אִם יַרְוִיחַ אֶת כָּל הָעוֹלָם וְהוּא עַצְמוֹ יֹאבַד אוֹ יֻזַּק? ²⁶כִּי הָאִישׁ אֲשֶׁר אֲנִי וּדְבָרַי הָיִינוּ לוֹ לְחֶרְפָּה, הוּא יִהְיֶה לְחֶרְפָּה לְבֶן־הָאָדָם כַּאֲשֶׁר יָבוֹא בִּכְבוֹדוֹ וּבִכְבוֹד הָאָב וְהַמַּלְאָכִים הַקְּדוֹשִׁים. ²⁷וּבֶאֱמֶת אֲנִי אוֹמֵר לָכֶם, יֵשׁ מִן הָעוֹמְדִים פֹּה אֲשֶׁר לֹא יִטְעֲמוּ מָוֶת עַד כִּי יִרְאוּ אֶת מַלְכוּת הָאֱלֹהִים."

²⁸כִּשְׁמוֹנָה יָמִים אַחֲרֵי שֶׁאָמַר אֶת הַדְּבָרִים הָאֵלֶּה לָקַח אֶת כֵּיפָא וְאֶת יוֹחָנָן וְאֶת יַעֲקֹב וְעָלָה לָהָר לְהִתְפַּלֵּל. ²⁹בְּעוֹד הוּא מִתְפַּלֵּל הִשְׁתַּנָּה מַרְאֵה פָּנָיו, וּלְבוּשׁוֹ נַעֲשָׂה לָבָן מַבְהִיק. ³⁰וְהִנֵּה שְׁנֵי אֲנָשִׁים מְשׂוֹחֲחִים אִתּוֹ, מֹשֶׁה וְאֵלִיָּהוּ ³¹שֶׁהוֹפִיעוּ בֶּהָדָר כָּבוֹד וְדִבְּרוּ עַל הִסְתַּלְּקוּתוֹ אֲשֶׁר הָיָה עָתִיד לְהַגְשִׁים בִּירוּשָׁלַיִם. ³²כֵּיפָא וַחֲבֵרָיו הָיוּ רְדוּמִים. הֵם הִתְעוֹרְרוּ וְאָז רָאוּ אֶת כְּבוֹדוֹ וְאֶת שְׁנֵי הָאֲנָשִׁים הָעוֹמְדִים לְיָדוֹ. ³³כְּשֶׁנִּפְרְדוּ מִמֶּנּוּ אָמַר כֵּיפָא אֶל יֵשׁוּעַ: "אֲדוֹנִי, טוֹב שֶׁאֲנַחְנוּ כָּאן. נַעֲשֶׂה נָא שָׁלוֹשׁ סֻכּוֹת; לְךָ אַחַת, לְמֹשֶׁה אַחַת וּלְאֵלִיָּהוּ אַחַת", וְלֹא יָדַע מַה שֶּׁאָמַר. ³⁴בְּדַבְּרוֹ אֶת הַדְּבָרִים הָאֵלֶּה הוֹפִיעַ עָנָן וְסָכַךְ עֲלֵיהֶם, וּפַחַד נָפַל עֲלֵיהֶם בְּהִוָּתְם בְּתוֹךְ הֶעָנָן. ³⁵יָצָא קוֹל מִתּוֹךְ הֶעָנָן לֵאמֹר: "זֶה בְּנִי בְּחִירִי, אֵלָיו תִּשְׁמָעוּן!" ³⁶כַּאֲשֶׁר נִשְׁמַע הַקּוֹל נִמְצָא יֵשׁוּעַ לְבַדּוֹ. הֵם שָׁתְקוּ וּבְאוֹתָם יָמִים לֹא סִפְּרוּ לְאִישׁ מִכָּל מַה שֶּׁרָאוּ.

³⁷Now it happened on the next day, when they had come down from the mountain, that a great multitude met Him. ³⁸Suddenly a man from the multitude cried out, saying, "Teacher, I implore You, look on my son, for he is my only child. ³⁹And behold, a spirit seizes him, and he suddenly cries out; it convulses him so that he foams *at the mouth;* and it departs from him with great difficulty, bruising him. ⁴⁰So I implored Your disciples to cast it out, but they could not."

⁴¹Then Jesus answered and said, "O faithless and perverse generation, how long shall I be with you and bear with you? Bring your son here." ⁴²And as he was still coming, the demon threw him down and convulsed *him.* Then Jesus rebuked the unclean spirit, healed the child, and gave him back to his father.

⁴³And they were all amazed at the majesty of God.

But while everyone marveled at all the things which Jesus did, He said to His disciples, ⁴⁴"Let these words sink down into your ears, for the Son of Man is about to be betrayed into the hands of men." ⁴⁵But they did not understand this saying, and it was hidden from them so that they did not perceive it; and they were afraid to ask Him about this saying.

⁴⁶Then a dispute arose among them as to which of them would be greatest. ⁴⁷And Jesus, perceiving the thought of their heart, took a little child and set him by Him, ⁴⁸and said to them, "Whoever receives this little child in My name receives Me; and whoever receives Me receives Him who sent Me. For he who is least among you all will be great."

⁴⁹Now John answered and said, "Master, we saw someone casting out demons in Your name, and we forbade him because he does not follow with us."

⁵⁰But Jesus said to him, "Do not forbid *him,* for he who is not against us is on our side."

⁵¹Now it came to pass, when the time had come for Him to be received up, that He steadfastly set His face to go to Jerusalem, ⁵²and sent messengers before His face. And as they went, they entered a village of the Samaritans, to prepare for Him. ⁵³But they did not receive Him, because His face was *set* for the journey to Jerusalem. ⁵⁴And when His disciples James and John saw *this,* they said, "Lord, do You want us to command fire to come down from heaven and consume them, just as Elijah did?"

⁵⁵But He turned and rebuked them, and said, "You do not know what manner of spirit you are of. ⁵⁶For the Son of Man did not come to destroy men's lives but to save *them.*" And they went to another village.

³⁷ כַּאֲשֶׁר יָרְדוּ מִן הָהָר בְּיוֹם הַמָּחֳרָת, בָּאוּ עַם רַב לִקְרָאתוֹ. ³⁸ צָעַק אִישׁ מִן הֶהָמוֹן: "רַבִּי, אֲנִי מִתְחַנֵּן אֵלֶיךָ, הַבֶּט נָא אֶל בְּנִי, כִּי בֵּן יָחִיד הוּא לִי. ³⁹ רוּחַ אוֹחֶזֶת בּוֹ וְהוּא צוֹעֵק פִּתְאוֹם; הִיא מְזַעְזַעַת אוֹתוֹ עַד שֶׁהַקֶּצֶף יוֹרֵד מִפִּיו, מִתְעַלֶּלֶת בּוֹ וּבְקֹשִׁי מַרְפָּה מִמֶּנּוּ. ⁴⁰ בִּקַּשְׁתִּי מִתַּלְמִידֶיךָ לְגָרֵשׁ אוֹתָהּ וְלֹא יָכְלוּ."

⁴¹ הֵשִׁיב יֵשׁוּעַ: "הוֹי דּוֹר חֲסַר אֱמוּנָה וּמְעֻוָּת דֶּרֶךְ, עַד מָתַי אֶהְיֶה עִמָּכֶם וְאֶסְבֹּל אֶתְכֶם? הָבֵא אֶת בִּנְךָ הֵנָּה!"

⁴² בְּעוֹד הוּא מִתְקָרֵב אֶל יֵשׁוּעַ הִפִּילוֹ הַשֵּׁד וְזִעְזֵעַ אֶת גּוּפוֹ. אַךְ יֵשׁוּעַ גָּעַר בָּרוּחַ הַטְּמֵאָה וְרִפֵּא אֶת הַיֶּלֶד. לְאַחַר מִכֵּן הֶחֱזִירוֹ לְאָבִיו, ⁴³ וְהַכֹּל הִשְׁתּוֹמְמוּ עַל גְּדֻלַּת הָאֱלֹהִים.

כַּאֲשֶׁר הַכֹּל הָיוּ תְּמֵהִים עַל מַה שֶׁעָשָׂה, אָמַר לְתַלְמִידָיו: ⁴⁴ "הַטּוּ אָזְנְכֶם לַמִּלִּים הָאֵלֶּה: הִנֵּה עָתִיד בֶּן־הָאָדָם לְהִמָּסֵר לִידֵי אֲנָשִׁים." ⁴⁵ אַךְ הֵם לֹא הֵבִינוּ אֶת אֲשֶׁר אָמַר, כִּי מַשְׁמָעוֹ הֻסְתַּר מֵהֶם שֶׁלֹּא יָבִינוּ – וְגַם פָּחֲדוּ לִשְׁאֹל אוֹתוֹ עַל הַדָּבָר הַזֶּה.

⁴⁶ נֶעוֹרָה בָּהֶם הַשְּׁאֵלָה – מִי הַגָּדוֹל בָּהֶם. ⁴⁷ יֵשׁוּעַ, שֶׁיָּדַע אֶת מַחְשֶׁבֶת לִבָּם, לָקַח יֶלֶד, הֶעֱמִיד אוֹתוֹ לְיָדוֹ ⁴⁸ וְאָמַר לָהֶם: "כָּל הַמְקַבֵּל אֶת הַיֶּלֶד הַזֶּה בִּשְׁמִי, אוֹתִי הוּא מְקַבֵּל; וְהַמְקַבֵּל אוֹתִי מְקַבֵּל אֶת אֲשֶׁר שְׁלָחַנִי. הַקָּטֹן שֶׁבְּכֻלְּכֶם הוּא הַגָּדוֹל."

⁴⁹ יוֹחָנָן פָּנָה אֵלָיו וְאָמַר: "אֲדוֹנִי, רָאִינוּ אִישׁ מְגָרֵשׁ שֵׁדִים בְּשִׁמְךָ וּמְנַעֲנוּ בַּעֲדוֹ, כִּי אֵינֶנּוּ הוֹלֵךְ עִמָּנוּ."

⁵⁰ אָמַר לוֹ יֵשׁוּעַ: "אַל תִּמְנָעוּ בַּעֲדוֹ, כִּי מִי שֶׁאֵינֶנּוּ נֶגְדְּכֶם, אִתְּכֶם הוּא."

⁵¹ כַּאֲשֶׁר מָלְאוּ יָמָיו לְהִלָּקַח הַשָּׁמַיְמָה שָׂם פָּנָיו לָלֶכֶת לִירוּשָׁלַיִם ⁵² וְשָׁלַח שְׁלִיחִים לְפָנָיו. הֵם הָלְכוּ וּבָאוּ אֶל אֶחָד מִכַּפְרֵי הַשּׁוֹמְרוֹנִים לְהָכִין מַה שֶּׁנָּחוּץ בִּשְׁבִילוֹ, ⁵³ אַךְ לֹא קִבְּלוּהוּ מִשּׁוּם שֶׁפָּנָיו הָיוּ מוּעָדוֹת לִירוּשָׁלַיִם. ⁵⁴ כְּשֶׁרָאוּ זֹאת יַעֲקֹב וְיוֹחָנָן תַּלְמִידָיו, אָמְרוּ: "אֲדוֹנֵנוּ, רְצוֹנְךָ כִּי נְצַוֶּה שֶׁתֵּרֵד אֵשׁ מִן הַשָּׁמַיִם וְתֹאכַל אוֹתָם?" ⁵⁵ אַךְ הוּא פָּנָה אֲלֵיהֶם וְגָעַר בָּהֶם [וְאָמְרוּ: "אֵינְכֶם יוֹדְעִים בְּנֵי אֵיזוֹ רוּחַ אַתֶּם! ⁵⁶ כִּי בֶּן־הָאָדָם לֹא בָּא לְגָרֹם לְאָבְדַן נַפְשׁוֹת בְּנֵי אָדָם, אֶלָּא לְהוֹשִׁיעָן."] הֵם הָלְכוּ לִכְפָר אַחֵר.

57 Now it happened as they journeyed on the road, *that* someone said to Him, "Lord, I will follow You wherever You go."

58 And Jesus said to him, "Foxes have holes and birds of the air *have* nests, but the Son of Man has nowhere to lay *His* head."

59 Then He said to another, "Follow Me."

But he said, "Lord, let me first go and bury my father."

60 Jesus said to him, "Let the dead bury their own dead, but you go and preach the kingdom of God."

61 And another also said, "Lord, I will follow You, but let me first go *and* bid them farewell who are at my house."

62 But Jesus said to him, "No one, having put his hand to the plow, and looking back, is fit for the kingdom of God."

10 After these things the Lord appointed seventy others also, and sent them two by two before His face into every city and place where He Himself was about to go. 2 Then He said to them, "The harvest truly *is* great, but the laborers *are* few; therefore pray the Lord of the harvest to send out laborers into His harvest. 3 Go your way; behold, I send you out as lambs among wolves. 4 Carry neither money bag, knapsack, nor sandals; and greet no one along the road. 5 But whatever house you enter, first say, 'Peace to this house.' 6 And if a son of peace is there, your peace will rest on it; if not, it will return to you. 7 And remain in the same house, eating and drinking such things as they give, for the laborer is worthy of his wages. Do not go from house to house. 8 Whatever city you enter, and they receive you, eat such things as are set before you. 9 And heal the sick there, and say to them, 'The kingdom of God has come near to you.' 10 But whatever city you enter, and they do not receive you, go out into its streets and say, 11 'The very dust of your city which clings to us we wipe off against you. Nevertheless know this, that the kingdom of God has come near you.' 12 But I say to you that it will be more tolerable in that Day for Sodom than for that city.

13 "Woe to you, Chorazin! Woe to you, Bethsaida! For if the mighty works which were done in you had been done in Tyre and Sidon, they would have repented long ago, sitting in sackcloth and ashes. 14 But it will be more tolerable for Tyre and Sidon at the judgment than for you. 15 And you, Capernaum, who are exalted to heaven, will be brought down to Hades. 16 He who hears you hears Me, he who rejects you rejects Me, and he who rejects Me rejects Him who sent Me."

57 בְּעֵת שֶׁהָלְכוּ בַּדֶּרֶךְ פָּנָה אֵלָיו מִישֶׁהוּ וְאָמַר: "אֲדוֹנִי, אֵלֵךְ אַחֲרֶיךָ לְכָל מָקוֹם שֶׁתֵּלֵךְ."

58 אָמַר לוֹ יֵשׁוּעַ: "לַשּׁוּעָלִים יֵשׁ מְאוּרוֹת וּלְעוֹף הַשָּׁמַיִם קִנִּים, אֲבָל בֶּן־הָאָדָם אֵין לוֹ מָקוֹם לְהָנִיחַ אֶת רֹאשׁוֹ."

59 וְאֶל אִישׁ אַחֵר אָמַר: "לֵךְ אַחֲרַי!" אַךְ הַלָּה הֵשִׁיב: "אֲדוֹנִי, תֶּן לִי תְחִלָּה לָלֶכֶת לִקְבֹּר אֶת אָבִי."

60 אָמַר לוֹ יֵשׁוּעַ: "הַנַּח לַמֵּתִים לִקְבֹּר אֶת מֵתֵיהֶם וְאַתָּה לֵךְ הַכְרֵז אֶת מַלְכוּת הָאֱלֹהִים."

61 אִישׁ שְׁלִישִׁי פָּנָה אֵלָיו וְאָמַר: "אֵלֵךְ אַחֲרֶיךָ, אֲדוֹנִי, אֲבָל קֹדֶם הַנִּיחָה לִי לְהִפָּרֵד מִבְּנֵי בֵיתִי."

62 הֵשִׁיב לוֹ יֵשׁוּעַ: "מִי שֶׁשָּׂם אֶת יָדוֹ עַל הַמַּחֲרֵשָׁה וּמַבִּיט אֲחוֹרַנִּית לֹא יִכְשַׁר לְמַלְכוּת הָאֱלֹהִים."

י אַחֲרֵי הַדְּבָרִים הָאֵלֶּה מִנָּה הָאָדוֹן עוֹד שִׁבְעִים וּשְׁנַיִם וְשָׁלַח אוֹתָם לְפָנָיו, שְׁנַיִם שְׁנַיִם, אֶל כָּל עִיר וּמָקוֹם אֲשֶׁר הִתְכַּוֵּן לָבוֹא לְשָׁם. 2 אָמַר לָהֶם: "הַקָּצִיר רַב, וְאוּלֵי הַפּוֹעֲלִים מְעַטִּים, לָכֵן הִתְפַּלְלוּ לַאֲדוֹן הַקָּצִיר שֶׁיִּשְׁלַח פּוֹעֲלִים אֶל קְצִירוֹ. 3 לְכוּ! הִנְנִי שׁוֹלֵחַ אֶתְכֶם כִּכְבָשִׂים בֵּין זְאֵבִים. 4 אַל תִּקְחוּ עִמָּכֶם לֹא אַרְנָק וְלֹא תַּרְמִיל וְלֹא נַעֲלַיִם, וְאַל תִּשְׁאֲלוּ לִשְׁלוֹם אִישׁ בַּדֶּרֶךְ. 5 לְכָל בַּיִת שֶׁתִּכָּנְסוּ אִמְרוּ תְּחִלָּה 'שָׁלוֹם לַבַּיִת הַזֶּה'. 6 וְאִם יִהְיֶה שָׁם אִישׁ שָׁלוֹם, הַשָּׁלוֹם שֶׁלָּכֶם יִשְׁרֶה עָלָיו; אִם לֹא – אֲלֵיכֶם יָשׁוּב. 7 בְּאוֹתוֹ הַבַּיִת הִשָּׁאֲרוּ, וְאִכְלוּ וּשְׁתוּ מִמַּה שֶּׁיֵּשׁ אֶצְלָם, כִּי רָאוּי הַפּוֹעֵל לִשְׂכָרוֹ. אַל תַּעַבְרוּ מִבַּיִת לְבַיִת. 8 בְּכָל עִיר שֶׁתִּכָּנְסוּ אֵלֶיהָ וִיקַבְּלוּ אֶתְכֶם, אִכְלוּ אֶת אֲשֶׁר יֻגְּשׁוּ לָכֶם, 9 רִפְאוּ אֶת הַחוֹלִים אֲשֶׁר בָּהּ וְאִמְרוּ לָהֶם, 'קָרְבָה אֲלֵיכֶם מַלְכוּת הָאֱלֹהִים'. 10 וּבְכָל עִיר שֶׁתִּכָּנְסוּ אֵלֶיהָ וְלֹא יְקַבְּלוּ אֶתְכֶם, צְאוּ אֶל רְחוֹבוֹתֶיהָ וְאִמְרוּ, 11 'גַּם אֶת אֲבַק עִירְכֶם שֶׁנִּדְבַּק לְרַגְלֵינוּ אֲנַחְנוּ מְנַעֲרִים עֲלֵיכֶם; אַךְ דְּעוּ לָכֶם: קָרְבָה מַלְכוּת הָאֱלֹהִים. 12 אוֹמֵר אֲנִי לָכֶם, קַל יוֹתֵר יִהְיֶה לִסְדוֹם בַּיּוֹם הַהוּא מֵאֲשֶׁר לָאוֹתָהּ עִיר. 13 אוֹי לָךְ פּוֹרִין! אוֹי לָךְ בֵּית צַיְדָא! כִּי אִלּוּ נַעֲשׂוּ בְּצוֹר וְצִידוֹן הַפְּלָאוֹת שֶׁנַּעֲשׂוּ בְּתוֹכְכֶן, הֲרֵי מִכְּבָר הָיוּ חוֹזְרִים בִּתְשׁוּבָה וְיוֹשְׁבִים בְּשַׂק וָאֵפֶר. 14 וּבְכָל זֹאת לְצוֹר וְצִידוֹן יֵקַל בַּדִּין מִכֶּם. 15 וְאַתְּ כְּפַר נַחוּם, הַאִם לַשָּׁמַיִם תַּעֲלִי? שְׁאוֹלָה תֵּרְדִי!

16 הַשּׁוֹמֵעַ אֲלֵיכֶם, אֵלַי הוּא שׁוֹמֵעַ. הַדּוֹחֶה אֶתְכֶם, אוֹתִי הוּא דּוֹחֶה. וְהַדּוֹחֶה אוֹתִי דּוֹחֶה אֶת אֲשֶׁר שְׁלָחַנִי."

17Then the seventy returned with joy, saying, "Lord, even the demons are subject to us in Your name."

18And He said to them, "I saw Satan fall like lightning from heaven. 19Behold, I give you the authority to trample on serpents and scorpions, and over all the power of the enemy, and nothing shall by any means hurt you. 20Nevertheless do not rejoice in this, that the spirits are subject to you, but rather rejoice because your names are written in heaven."

21In that hour Jesus rejoiced in the Spirit and said, "I thank You, Father, Lord of heaven and earth, that You have hidden these things from *the* wise and prudent and revealed them to babes. Even so, Father, for so it seemed good in Your sight. 22All things have been delivered to Me by My Father, and no one knows who the Son is except the Father, and who the Father is except the Son, and *the one* to whom the Son wills to reveal *Him*."

23Then He turned to *His* disciples and said privately, "Blessed *are* the eyes which see the things you see; 24for I tell you that many prophets and kings have desired to see what you see, and have not seen *it,* and to hear what you hear, and have not heard *it.*"

25And behold, a certain lawyer stood up and tested Him, saying, "Teacher, what shall I do to inherit eternal life?"

26He said to him, "What is written in the law? What is your reading *of it?*"

27So he answered and said, "'You shall love the LORD your God with all your heart, with all your soul, with all your strength, and with all your mind,' and 'your neighbor as yourself.'"

28And He said to him, "You have answered rightly; do this and you will live."

29But he, wanting to justify himself, said to Jesus, "And who is my neighbor?"

30Then Jesus answered and said: "A certain *man* went down from Jerusalem to Jericho, and fell among thieves, who stripped him of his clothing, wounded *him,* and departed, leaving *him* half dead. 31Now by chance a certain priest came down that road. And when he saw him, he passed by on the other side. 32Likewise a Levite, when he arrived at the place, came and looked, and passed by on the other side. 33But a certain Samaritan, as he journeyed, came where he was. And when he saw him, he had compassion. 34So he went to *him* and bandaged his wounds, pouring on oil and wine; and he set him on his own animal, brought him to an inn, and took care of him. 35On the next day, when he departed, he took out two denarii, gave *them* to

17הַשִּׁבְעִים וּשְׁנַיִם חָזְרוּ בְּשִׂמְחָה וְאָמְרוּ: "אֲדוֹנֵנוּ, אֲפִלּוּ הַשֵּׁדִים נִכְנָעִים לָנוּ בְּשִׁמְךָ."

18אָמַר לָהֶם: "רָאִיתִי אֶת הַשָּׂטָן נוֹפֵל כְּבָרָק מִן הַשָּׁמַיִם. 19הִנֵּה נָתַתִּי לָכֶם אֶת הַכֹּחַ לִרְמֹס נְחָשִׁים וְעַקְרַבִּים וְאֶת כָּל כֹּחַ הָאוֹיֵב, וּמְאוּמָה לֹא יִפְגַּע בָּכֶם. 20וּבְכָל זֹאת אַל תִּשְׂמְחוּ עַל שֶׁהָרוּחוֹת נִכְנָעוֹת לָכֶם; שִׂמְחוּ עַל כָּךְ שֶׁשְּׁמוֹתֵיכֶם נִכְתְּבוּ בַּשָּׁמַיִם."

21אוֹתָהּ שָׁעָה נִתְמַלֵּא בְּשִׂמְחַת רוּחַ הַקֹּדֶשׁ וְאָמַר: "מוֹדֶה אֲנִי לְךָ, אָבִי, אֲדוֹן הַשָּׁמַיִם וְהָאָרֶץ, כִּי הִסְתַּרְתָּ אֶת הַדְּבָרִים הָאֵלֶּה מִן הַחֲכָמִים וְהַנְּבוֹנִים וְגִלִּיתָם לָעוֹלָלִים. כֵּן, אָבִי, שֶׁהֲרֵי כָּךְ הָיָה רָצוֹן מִלְּפָנֶיךָ. 22הַכֹּל נִמְסַר לִי מֵאֵת אָבִי וְאֵין אִישׁ יוֹדֵעַ מִי הוּא הַבֵּן, זוּלָתִי הָאָב; אַף לֹא מִי הוּא הָאָב, זוּלָתִי הַבֵּן וְכָל מִי שֶׁהַבֵּן רוֹצֶה לְגַלּוֹת לוֹ."

23הוּא פָּנָה אֶל הַתַּלְמִידִים לְבַדָּם וְאָמַר: "אַשְׁרֵי הָעֵינַיִם הָרוֹאוֹת אֶת מַה שֶּׁאַתֶּם רוֹאִים. 24אוֹמֵר אֲנִי לָכֶם, נְבִיאִים וּמְלָכִים רַבִּים חָפְצוּ לִרְאוֹת אֶת אֲשֶׁר אַתֶּם רוֹאִים וְלֹא רָאוּ; וְלִשְׁמֹעַ אֶת אֲשֶׁר אַתֶּם שׁוֹמְעִים וְלֹא שָׁמְעוּ."

25אִישׁ אֶחָד, בַּעַל תּוֹרָה, קָם לִבְחֹן אוֹתוֹ וְאָמַר: "רַבִּי, מֶה עָלַי לַעֲשׂוֹת כְּדֵי לָרֶשֶׁת חַיֵּי עוֹלָם?"

26שָׁאַל יֵשׁוּעַ: "מַה כָּתוּב בַּתּוֹרָה? מָה אַתָּה קוֹרֵא?"

27הֵשִׁיב בַּעַל הַתּוֹרָה: "וְאָהַבְתָּ אֵת יהוה אֱלֹהֶיךָ בְּכָל־לְבָבְךָ וּבְכָל־נַפְשְׁךָ וּבְכָל־מְאֹדְךָ וּבְכָל שִׂכְלְךָ, וְאָהַבְתָּ לְרֵעֲךָ כָּמוֹךָ."

28אָמַר לוֹ יֵשׁוּעַ: "יָפֶה עָנִיתָ, עֲשֵׂה זֹאת וְתִחְיֶה."

29אֲבָל מֵאַחַר שֶׁרָצָה לְהַמְצִיא הַצְדֵּק לְעַצְמוֹ, שָׁאַל אֶת יֵשׁוּעַ: "וּמִי הוּא רֵעִי?"

30הֵשִׁיב יֵשׁוּעַ וְאָמַר: "אִישׁ אֶחָד יָרַד מִירוּשָׁלַיִם לִירִיחוֹ וְנָפַל בִּידֵי שׁוֹדְדִים. הַלָּלוּ הִפְשִׁיטוּ אוֹתוֹ וְהִכּוּהוּ, וְהָלְכוּ לָהֶם בְּעָזְבָם אוֹתוֹ מֻטָּל בֵּין מָוֶת לְחַיִּים. 31וְהִנֵּה כֹּהֵן אֶחָד יָרַד בְּאוֹתָהּ הַדֶּרֶךְ, אַךְ כְּרָאוֹתוֹ אֶת הָאִישׁ, עָבַר לַצַּד הַשֵּׁנִי שֶׁל הַדֶּרֶךְ. 32כֵּן גַּם אִישׁ לֵוִי, כַּאֲשֶׁר בָּא לַמָּקוֹם וְרָאָה אוֹתוֹ, עָבַר לַצַּד הַשֵּׁנִי שֶׁל הַדֶּרֶךְ. 33וְהִנֵּה שׁוֹמְרוֹנִי אֶחָד, שֶׁעָבַר בַּדֶּרֶךְ, הִגִּיעַ אֵלָיו, וּכְשֶׁרָאָה אוֹתוֹ נִתְמַלֵּא רַחֲמִים. 34נִגַּשׁ אֵלָיו, יָצַק שֶׁמֶן וָיַיִן עַל פְּצָעָיו וְחָבַשׁ אוֹתָם. אַחֲרֵי כֵן הוֹשִׁיבוֹ עַל בְּהֶמְתּוֹ וְהוֹבִיל אוֹתוֹ

the innkeeper, and said to him, 'Take care of him; and whatever more you spend, when I come again, I will repay you.' 36 So which of these three do you think was neighbor to him who fell among the thieves?"

37 And he said, "He who showed mercy on him." Then Jesus said to him, "Go and do likewise."

38 Now it happened as they went that He entered a certain village; and a certain woman named Martha welcomed Him into her house. 39 And she had a sister called Mary, who also sat at Jesus' feet and heard His word. 40 But Martha was distracted with much serving, and she approached Him and said, "Lord, do You not care that my sister has left me to serve alone? Therefore tell her to help me."

41 And Jesus answered and said to her, "Martha, Martha, you are worried and troubled about many things. 42 But one thing is needed, and Mary has chosen that good part, which will not be taken away from her."

11 Now it came to pass, as He was praying in a certain place, when He ceased, *that* one of His disciples said to Him, "Lord, teach us to pray, as John also taught his disciples."

2 So He said to them, "When you pray, say:

Our Father in heaven,
Hallowed be Your name.
Your kingdom come.
Your will be done
On earth as *it is* in heaven.
3   Give us day by day our daily bread.
4   And forgive us our sins,
     For we also forgive everyone who is indebted
        to us.
     And do not lead us into temptation,
     But deliver us from the evil one."

5 And He said to them, "Which of you shall have a friend, and go to him at midnight and say to him, 'Friend, lend me three loaves; 6 for a friend of mine has come to me on his journey, and I have nothing to set before him'; 7 and he will answer from within and say, 'Do not trouble me; the door is now shut, and my children are with me in bed; I cannot rise and give to you'? 8 I say to you, though he will not rise and give to him because he is his friend, yet because of his persistence he will rise and give him as many as he needs.

9 "So I say to you, ask, and it will be given to you; seek, and you will find; knock, and it will be opened to you. 10 For everyone who asks receives, and he who seeks finds, and to him who knocks it will be opened. 11 If a son asks for bread from any

אֶל פֻּנְדָּק וְשָׁם דָּאַג לְצָרְכָיו. 35 לְמָחֳרָת הוֹצִיא שְׁנֵי דִּינָרִים, נְתָנָם לְבַעַל הַפֻּנְדָּק וְאָמַר: 'דְּאַג לוֹ אַתָּה, וְכָל מַה שֶּׁתּוֹסִיף אַחֲזִיר לְךָ בְּשׁוּבִי.' 36 וּבְכֵן מַה דַּעְתְּךָ, מִי מִן הַשְּׁלוֹשָׁה הָיָה רֵעַ לַנּוֹפֵל בִּידֵי הַשּׁוֹדְדִים?"

37 הֵשִׁיב בַּעַל הַתּוֹרָה: "זֶה שֶׁעָשָׂה עִמּוֹ חֶסֶד." אָמַר לוֹ יֵשׁוּעַ: "לֵךְ וַעֲשֵׂה כֵּן גַּם אַתָּה."

38 בְּעֵת מַסָּעָם נִכְנַס לִכְפָר אֶחָד, וְאִשָּׁה אַחַת אֲשֶׁר שְׁמָהּ מַרְתָּא קִבְּלָה אוֹתוֹ אֶל בֵּיתָהּ. 39 הָיְתָה לָהּ אָחוֹת, מִרְיָם שְׁמָהּ, שֶׁיָּשְׁבָה לְרַגְלֵי הָאָדוֹן וְשָׁמְעָה אֶת דְּבָרוֹ, 40 וְאִלּוּ מַרְתָּא הָיְתָה טְרוּדָה בְּרֹב שֵׁרוּתָהּ. הִיא נִגְּשָׁה אֵלָיו וְאָמְרָה: "אֲדוֹנִי, הַאִם לֹא אִכְפַּת לְךָ שֶׁאֲחוֹתִי הִשְׁאִירָה אוֹתִי לְשָׁרֵת לְבַדִּי? אֱמֹר נָא לָהּ שֶׁתַּעֲזֹר לִי."

41 הֵשִׁיב לָהּ הָאָדוֹן: "מַרְתָּא, מַרְתָּא, אַתְּ דּוֹאֶגֶת וּמִתְרַגֶּשֶׁת עַל דְּבָרִים רַבִּים, 42 וְרַק דָּבָר אֶחָד צָרִיךְ; וּמִרְיָם בָּחֲרָה בַּחֵלֶק הַטּוֹב אֲשֶׁר לֹא יִלָּקַח מִמֶּנָּה."

יא הוּא הָיָה בְּאֵיזֶה מָקוֹם וְהִתְפַּלֵּל. כְּשֶׁסִּיֵּם אָמַר לוֹ אֶחָד מִתַּלְמִידָיו: "אֲדוֹנִי, לַמְּדֵנוּ לְהִתְפַּלֵּל, כְּשֵׁם שֶׁגַּם יוֹחָנָן לִמֵּד אֶת תַּלְמִידָיו."

2 אָמַר לָהֶם יֵשׁוּעַ: "כַּאֲשֶׁר אַתֶּם מִתְפַּלְּלִים אִמְרוּ: אָבִינוּ, יִתְקַדַּשׁ שְׁמֶךָ, תָּבוֹא מַלְכוּתְךָ.

3 אֶת לֶחֶם חֻקֵּנוּ תֶּן לָנוּ יוֹם יוֹם;

4 וּסְלַח לָנוּ עַל חֲטָאֵינוּ, כִּי גַּם אֲנַחְנוּ סוֹלְחִים לְכָל הַחוֹטְאִים לָנוּ; וְאַל תְּבִיאֵנוּ לִידֵי נִסָּיוֹן."

5 הוֹסִיף וְאָמַר לָהֶם: "אִם אֶחָד מִכֶּם יֵלֵךְ אֶל יְדִידוֹ בַּחֲצוֹת הַלַּיְלָה וְיֹאמַר לוֹ, 'יְדִידִי, הַלְוֵה לִי שָׁלוֹשׁ כִּכְּרוֹת לֶחֶם, 6 כִּי חֲבֵרִי הִגִּיעַ אֵלַי מִן הַדֶּרֶךְ וְאֵין לִי מַה לְהַגִּישׁ לוֹ.' 7 וְזֶה שֶׁבְּתוֹךְ הַבַּיִת יָשִׁיב וְיֹאמַר, 'אַל תַּטְרִיד אוֹתִי, הַדֶּלֶת כְּבָר נְעוּלָה וִילָדַי אִתִּי בַּמִּטָּה. אֵינֶנִּי יָכוֹל לָקוּם וְלָתֵת לְךָ' – 8 אוֹמֵר אֲנִי לָכֶם, גַּם אִם לֹא יָקוּם לָתֵת לוֹ עַל הֱיוֹתוֹ יְדִידוֹ, יָקוּם בִּגְלַל הֶעָנָתוֹ וְיִתֵּן לוֹ כְּכָל צָרְכּוֹ. 9 וַאֲנִי אוֹמֵר לָכֶם, בַּקְּשׁוּ וְיִנָּתֵן לָכֶם, חַפְּשׂוּ וְתִמְצָאוּ, דִּפְקוּ וְיִפָּתַח לָכֶם. 10 כִּי כָּל הַמְבַקֵּשׁ מְקַבֵּל, וְהַמְחַפֵּשׂ מוֹצֵא, וְהַמִּתְדַּפֵּק יִפָּתַח לוֹ. 11 וּמִי מִכֶּם הָאָב שֶׁבְּנוֹ

father among you, will he give him a stone? Or if *he asks* for a fish, will he give him a serpent instead of a fish? 12 Or if he asks for an egg, will he offer him a scorpion? 13 If you then, being evil, know how to give good gifts to your children, how much more will *your* heavenly Father give the Holy Spirit to those who ask Him!"

14 And He was casting out a demon, and it was mute. So it was, when the demon had gone out, that the mute spoke; and the multitudes marveled. 15 But some of them said, "He casts out demons by Beelzebub, the ruler of the demons."

16 Others, testing *Him,* sought from Him a sign from heaven. 17 But He, knowing their thoughts, said to them: "Every kingdom divided against itself is brought to desolation, and a house *divided* against a house falls. 18 If Satan also is divided against himself, how will his kingdom stand? Because you say I cast out demons by Beelzebub. 19 And if I cast out demons by Beelzebub, by whom do your sons cast *them* out? Therefore they will be your judges. 20 But if I cast out demons with the finger of God, surely the kingdom of God has come upon you. 21 When a strong man, fully armed, guards his own palace, his goods are in peace. 22 But when a stronger than he comes upon him and overcomes him, he takes from him all his armor in which he trusted, and divides his spoils. 23 He who is not with Me is against Me, and he who does not gather with Me scatters.

24 "When an unclean spirit goes out of a man, he goes through dry places, seeking rest; and finding none, he says, 'I will return to my house from which I came.' 25 And when he comes, he finds *it* swept and put in order. 26 Then he goes and takes with *him* seven other spirits more wicked than himself, and they enter and dwell there; and the last *state* of that man is worse than the first."

27 And it happened, as He spoke these things, that a certain woman from the crowd raised her voice and said to Him, "Blessed *is* the womb that bore You, and *the* breasts which nursed You!"

28 But He said, "More than that, blessed *are* those who hear the word of God and keep it!"

29 And while the crowds were thickly gathered together, He began to say, "This is an evil generation. It seeks a sign, and no sign will be given to it except the sign of Jonah the prophet. 30 For as Jonah became a sign to the Ninevites, so also the Son of Man will be to this generation. 31 The queen of the South will rise up in the judgment with the men of this generation and condemn them, for she came from the ends of the earth to hear the wisdom of Solomon; and indeed a

יְבַקֵּשׁ מִמֶּנּוּ דָּג וְהוּא יִתֵּן לוֹ נָחָשׁ בִּמְקוֹם דָּג? 12 אוֹ אִם יְבַקֵּשׁ בֵּיצָה יִתֵּן לוֹ עַקְרָב? 13 הֵן אַתֶּם הָרָעִים יוֹדְעִים לָתֵת מַתָּנוֹת טוֹבוֹת לִבְנֵיכֶם, כָּל שֶׁכֵּן הָאָב שֶׁבַּשָּׁמַיִם יִתֵּן אֶת רוּחַ הַקֹּדֶשׁ לַמְבַקְשִׁים מִמֶּנּוּ!" 14 בְּאַחַד הַיָּמִים גֵּרַשׁ שֵׁד שֶׁגָּרַם לְאִלְּמוּת. כַּאֲשֶׁר יָצָא הַשֵּׁד הֵחֵל הָאִלֵּם לְדַבֵּר וְהֶהָמוֹן הִשְׁתּוֹמֵם. 15 אֶלָּא שֶׁכַּמָּה מֵהֶם אָמְרוּ: "בְּעֶזְרַת בַּעַל־זְבוּל שַׂר הַשֵּׁדִים הוּא מְגָרֵשׁ אֶת הַשֵּׁדִים."

16 וַאֲחֵרִים שֶׁהִתְכַּוְּנוּ לְנַסּוֹתוֹ בִּקְשׁוּ מִמֶּנּוּ אוֹת מִן הַשָּׁמַיִם. 17 אַךְ הוּא יָדַע אֶת מַחְשְׁבוֹתֵיהֶם וְאָמַר לָהֶם: "כָּל מַמְלָכָה הַמְּפֻלֶּגֶת בְּתוֹךְ עַצְמָהּ – תֶּחֱרַב, וּבַיִת עַל בַּיִת יִפֹּל בָּהּ. 18 וְאִם גַּם הַשָּׂטָן הִתְפַּלֵּג בְּתוֹךְ עַצְמוֹ, כֵּיצַד תַּעֲמֹד מַמְלַכְתּוֹ? שֶׁכֵּן אוֹמְרִים אַתֶּם כִּי בְּעֶזְרַת בַּעַל־זְבוּל אֲנִי מְגָרֵשׁ אֶת הַשֵּׁדִים. 19 אַךְ אִם אֲנִי מְגָרֵשׁ אֶת הַשֵּׁדִים בְּעֶזְרַת בַּעַל־זְבוּל, בְּעֶזְרַת מִי מְגָרְשִׁים אוֹתָם בְּנֵיכֶם? לָכֵן הֵם יִהְיוּ שׁוֹפְטֵיכֶם. 20 וְאִם בְּאֶצְבַּע אֱלֹהִים מְגָרֵשׁ אֲנִי אֶת הַשֵּׁדִים, כִּי אָז הִגִּיעָה אֲלֵיכֶם מַלְכוּת הָאֱלֹהִים. 21 כַּאֲשֶׁר הָאִישׁ הֶחָזָק הֶחָמוּשׁ הֵיטֵב שׁוֹמֵר אֶת בֵּיתוֹ שֶׁלּוֹ, הֲרֵי שָׁלוֹם לִרְכוּשׁוֹ. 22 אַךְ כְּשֶׁתֹּקֵף אוֹתוֹ אִישׁ חָזָק מִמֶּנּוּ וּמִתְגַּבֵּר עָלָיו, הוּא לוֹקֵחַ מִמֶּנּוּ אֶת נִשְׁקוֹ שֶׁבָּטַח בּוֹ וּמְחַלֵּק אֶת הַשָּׁלָל. 23 מִי שֶׁאֵינֶנּוּ אִתִּי – נֶגְדִּי הוּא, וּמִי שֶׁאֵינֶנּוּ אוֹסֵף אִתִּי – מְפַזֵּר."

24 "הָרוּחַ הַטְּמֵאָה הַיּוֹצֵאת מִן הָאָדָם מְשׁוֹטֶטֶת בִּמְקוֹמוֹת צִיָּה וּמְבַקֶּשֶׁת לָהּ מָנוֹחַ, וּכְשֶׁאֵינָהּ מוֹצֵאת הִיא אוֹמֶרֶת, 'אָשׁוּבָה אֶל בֵּיתִי שֶׁיָּצָאתִי מִמֶּנּוּ'. 25 הִיא בָּאָה וּמוֹצֵאת אוֹתוֹ מְטֻאטָא וּמְהֻדָּר. 26 אָז הִיא הוֹלֶכֶת וְלוֹקַחַת אִתָּהּ שֶׁבַע רוּחוֹת אֲחֵרוֹת רָעוֹת מִמֶּנָּה וְכֻלָּן נִכְנָסוֹת לִשְׁכֹּן שָׁם. אָכֵן גְּרוּעָה אַחֲרִיתוֹ שֶׁל הָאִישׁ הַהוּא מֵרֵאשִׁיתוֹ."

27 כַּאֲשֶׁר דִּבֵּר אֶת הַדְּבָרִים הָאֵלֶּה קָרְאָה אִשָּׁה אַחַת מִן הֶהָמוֹן וְאָמְרָה לוֹ: "אַשְׁרֵי הַבֶּטֶן אֲשֶׁר נָשְׂאָה אוֹתְךָ וְאַשְׁרֵי הַשָּׁדַיִם שֶׁיָּנַקְתָּ מֵהֶם!" 28 עַל כָּךְ הֵגִיב בְּאָמְרוֹ: "וְיוֹתֵר נָכוֹן, אַשְׁרֵי הַשּׁוֹמְעִים אֶת דְּבַר אֱלֹהִים וְשׁוֹמְרִים אוֹתוֹ."

29 בְּהִתְקַהֵל עַם רַב סְבִיבוֹ פָּתַח פִּיו וְאָמַר: "הַדּוֹר הַזֶּה דּוֹר רַע הוּא. אוֹת הוּא מְבַקֵּשׁ, אַךְ אוֹת לֹא יִנָּתֵן לוֹ מִלְּבַד אוֹת יוֹנָה הַנָּבִיא. 30 וּכְמוֹ שֶׁיּוֹנָה הָיָה לְאוֹת לְאַנְשֵׁי נִינְוֵה כֵּן גַּם יִהְיֶה בֶּן־הָאָדָם לַדּוֹר הַזֶּה. 31 מַלְכַּת תֵּימָן תָּקוּם בַּמִּשְׁפָּט עִם אַנְשֵׁי הַדּוֹר הַזֶּה וְתַרְשִׁיעַ אוֹתָם, שֶׁכֵּן הִיא בָּאָה מִקְצֵה הָאָרֶץ לִשְׁמֹעַ אֶת חָכְמַת שְׁלֹמֹה; וְהִנֵּה גָּדוֹל מִשְּׁלֹמֹה כָּאן!

greater than Solomon *is* here. [32] The men of Nineveh will rise up in the judgment with this generation and condemn it, for they repented at the preaching of Jonah; and indeed a greater than Jonah *is* here.

[33] "No one, when he has lit a lamp, puts *it* in a secret place or under a basket, but on a lampstand, that those who come in may see the light. [34] The lamp of the body is the eye. Therefore, when your eye is good, your whole body also is full of light. But when *your eye* is bad, your body also *is* full of darkness. [35] Therefore take heed that the light which is in you is not darkness. [36] If then your whole body *is* full of light, having no part dark, *the* whole *body* will be full of light, as when the bright shining of a lamp gives you light."

[37] And as He spoke, a certain Pharisee asked Him to dine with him. So He went in and sat down to eat. [38] When the Pharisee saw *it,* he marveled that He had not first washed before dinner.

[39] Then the Lord said to him, "Now you Pharisees make the outside of the cup and dish clean, but your inward part is full of greed and wickedness. [40] Foolish ones! Did not He who made the outside make the inside also? [41] But rather give alms of such things as you have; then indeed all things are clean to you.

[42] "But woe to you Pharisees! For you tithe mint and rue and all manner of herbs, and pass by justice and the love of God. These you ought to have done, without leaving the others undone. [43] Woe to you Pharisees! For you love the best seats in the synagogues and greetings in the marketplaces. [44] Woe to you, scribes and Pharisees, hypocrites! For you are like graves which are not seen, and the men who walk over *them* are not aware *of them.*"

[45] Then one of the lawyers answered and said to Him, "Teacher, by saying these things You reproach us also."

[46] And He said, "Woe to you also, lawyers! For you load men with burdens hard to bear, and you yourselves do not touch the burdens with one of your fingers. [47] Woe to you! For you build the tombs of the prophets, and your fathers killed them. [48] In fact, you bear witness that you approve the deeds of your fathers; for they indeed killed them, and you build their tombs. [49] Therefore the wisdom of God also said, 'I will send them prophets and apostles, and *some* of them they will kill and persecute,' [50] that the blood of all the prophets which was shed from the foundation of the world may be required of this generation, [51] from the

32 אַנְשֵׁי נִינְוֵה יָקוּמוּ בַּמִּשְׁפָּט עִם הַדּוֹר הַזֶּה וְיַרְשִׁיעוּהוּ, שֶׁכֵּן הֵם חָזְרוּ בִּתְשׁוּבָה בִּקְרִיאַת יוֹנָה, וְהִנֵּה גָּדוֹל מִיּוֹנָה כָּאן!"

33 "אֵין אִישׁ מַדְלִיק מְנוֹרָה וְשָׂם אוֹתָהּ בְּמָקוֹם נִסְתָּר אוֹ תַּחַת כַּד, אֶלָּא עַל כֵּן יָשִׂים אוֹתָהּ כְּדֵי שֶׁבָּאֵי הַבַּיִת יִרְאוּ אֶת הָאוֹר. 34 מְנוֹרַת הַגּוּף הִיא הָעַיִן. כַּאֲשֶׁר עֵינְךָ טוֹבָה, גַּם כָּל גּוּפְךָ מֵאָר. אַךְ בִּהְיוֹתָהּ רָעָה, גַּם גּוּפְךָ חָשׁוּךְ. 35 עַל כֵּן הִזָּהֵר פֶּן יֶחְשַׁךְ הָאוֹר אֲשֶׁר בְּקִרְבְּךָ. 36 לְפִיכָךְ אִם כָּל גּוּפְךָ אוֹר הוּא וְאֵין בּוֹ שׁוּם חֹשֶׁךְ, אֲזַי כֻּלּוֹ יָאִיר כְּמוֹ בְּהָאִיר לְךָ הַמְּנוֹרָה בְּזָהֳרָהּ."

37 בְּשָׁעָה שֶׁדִּבֵּר בִּקֵּשׁ מִמֶּנּוּ פָּרוּשׁ אֶחָד כִּי יִסְעַד אִתּוֹ, וְאָמְנָם הוּא נִכְנַס וְהֵסֵב אֶל הַשֻּׁלְחָן. 38 רָאָה זֹאת הַפָּרוּשׁ וְתָמַהּ עַל שֶׁלֹּא טָבַל לִפְנֵי הַסְּעוּדָה. 39 אָמַר אֵלָיו הָאָדוֹן: "הִנֵּה אַתֶּם הַפְּרוּשִׁים מְטַהֲרִים אֶת הַכּוֹס וְאֶת הַקְּעָרָה מִבַּחוּץ, אֶלָּא שֶׁתּוֹכְכֶם מָלֵא גֶּזֶל וָרֶשַׁע. 40 כְּסִילִים! הֲיוֹצֵר אֶת הַחוּץ הַאִם לֹא יָצַר גַּם אֶת הַפְּנִים? 41 וְאַתֶּם, תְּנוּ לִצְדָקָה אֶת מַה שֶּׁבִּפְנִים וְאָז הַכֹּל טָהוֹר לָכֶם. 42 אוֹי לָכֶם הַפְּרוּשִׁים, כִּי נוֹתְנִים אַתֶּם מַעֲשֵׂר מִמִּנְתָּה וּפִיגָם וּמִכָּל יָרָק, וּמַזְנִיחִים אֶת הַמִּשְׁפָּט וְאֶת אַהֲבַת אֱלֹהִים. אֶת אֵלֶּה הָיָה צָרִיךְ לַעֲשׂוֹת וְאַף אֶת הָאֲחֵרִים לֹא לְהַזְנִיחַ. 43 אוֹי לָכֶם הַפְּרוּשִׁים, כִּי אוֹהֲבִים אַתֶּם אֶת מוֹשַׁב הַכָּבוֹד בְּבָתֵּי הַכְּנֶסֶת וּבִרְכוֹת שָׁלוֹם בַּשְּׁוָקִים. 44 אוֹי לָכֶם, כִּי דּוֹמִים אַתֶּם לִקְבָרִים שֶׁאֵינָם נִכָּרִים וּבְנֵי אָדָם מִתְהַלְּכִים עֲלֵיהֶם מִבְּלִי לָדַעַת זֹאת."

45 אֶחָד מִבַּעֲלֵי הַתּוֹרָה הֵגִיב וְאָמַר: "רַבִּי, בְּדַבֶּרְךָ אֵלֶּה אַתָּה פּוֹגֵעַ גַּם בָּנוּ."

46 הֵשִׁיב יֵשׁוּעַ: "אוֹי גַּם לָכֶם בַּעֲלֵי הַתּוֹרָה, כִּי מַעֲמִיסִים אַתֶּם עַל בְּנֵי אָדָם מַשָּׂאוֹת כְּבֵדִים מִנְּשֹׂא, וְאַתֶּם בְּעַצְמְכֶם אֵינְכֶם נוֹגְעִים בַּמַּשָּׂאוֹת גַּם בְּאַחַת מֵאֶצְבְּעוֹתֵיכֶם. 47 אוֹי לָכֶם, כִּי בּוֹנִים אַתֶּם אֶת קִבְרוֹת הַנְּבִיאִים וַהֲרֵי אֲבוֹתֵיכֶם הֲרָגוּם. 48 עַל כֵּן עֵדִים אַתֶּם הַמַּסְכִּימִים לְמַעֲשֵׂי אֲבוֹתֵיכֶם, שֶׁכֵּן הֵמָּה הָרְגוּ אוֹתָם וְאַתֶּם בּוֹנִים אֶת קִבְרֵיהֶם. 49 מִשּׁוּם כָּךְ גַּם אָמְרָה חָכְמַת הָאֱלֹהִים: 'אֶשְׁלַח אֲלֵיהֶם נְבִיאִים וּשְׁלִיחִים וּמֵהֶם יַהַרְגוּ וְיִרְדְּפוּ', 50 לְמַעַן יִדָּרֵשׁ מִן הַדּוֹר הַזֶּה דַּם כָּל הַנְּבִיאִים אֲשֶׁר נִשְׁפַּךְ מֵאָז הִוָּסֵד תֵּבֵל, 51 מִדַּם הֶבֶל עַד דַּם זְכַרְיָהוּ

blood of Abel to the blood of Zechariah who perished between the altar and the temple. Yes, I say to you, it shall be required of this generation.

52 "Woe to you lawyers! For you have taken away the key of knowledge. You did not enter in yourselves, and those who were entering in you hindered."

53 And as He said these things to them, the scribes and the Pharisees began to assail *Him* vehemently, and to cross-examine Him about many things, 54 lying in wait for Him, and seeking to catch Him in something He might say, that they might accuse Him.

12 In the meantime, when an innumerable multitude of people had gathered together, so that they trampled one another, He began to say to His disciples first *of all,* "Beware of the leaven of the Pharisees, which is hypocrisy. 2 For there is nothing covered that will not be revealed, nor hidden that will not be known. 3 Therefore whatever you have spoken in the dark will be heard in the light, and what you have spoken in the ear in inner rooms will be proclaimed on the housetops.

4 "And I say to you, My friends, do not be afraid of those who kill the body, and after that have no more that they can do. 5 But I will show you whom you should fear: Fear Him who, after He has killed, has power to cast into hell; yes, I say to you, fear Him!

6 "Are not five sparrows sold for two copper coins? And not one of them is forgotten before God. 7 But the very hairs of your head are all numbered. Do not fear therefore; you are of more value than many sparrows.

8 "Also I say to you, whoever confesses Me before men, him the Son of Man also will confess before the angels of God. 9 But he who denies Me before men will be denied before the angels of God.

10 "And anyone who speaks a word against the Son of Man, it will be forgiven him; but to him who blasphemes against the Holy Spirit, it will not be forgiven.

11 "Now when they bring you to the synagogues and magistrates and authorities, do not worry about how or what you should answer, or what you should say. 12 For the Holy Spirit will teach you in that very hour what you ought to say."

13 Then one from the crowd said to Him, "Teacher, tell my brother to divide the inheritance with me."

אֲשֶׁר נֶהֱרַג בֵּין הַמִּזְבֵּחַ וְהַבָּיִת. כֵּן, אוֹמֵר אֲנִי לָכֶם: דָּרוֹשׁ יִדָּרֵשׁ מִן הַדּוֹר הַזֶּה.

52 אוֹי לָכֶם בַּעֲלֵי הַתּוֹרָה! כִּי הֲסִירוֹתֶם אֶת מַפְתֵּחַ הַדַּעַת; אַתֶּם עַצְמְכֶם לֹא נִכְנַסְתֶּם וּמִן הַבָּאִים מְנַעְתֶּם לְהִכָּנֵס."

53 כַּאֲשֶׁר יָצָא מִשָּׁם הֵחֵלּוּ הַסּוֹפְרִים וְהַפְּרוּשִׁים לְהִתְרַחֵם אֵלָיו בְּעֶנְיָנוּת עֲמֻקָּה וְלַחֲקֹר אוֹתוֹ בְּעִנְיָנִים רַבִּים, 54 בְּצַפִּיָּה לְלָכְדוֹ בִּדְבַר פִּיו.

יב בְּזֹמַן שֶׁהִתְאַסְּפוּ רִבְבוֹת אֲנָשִׁים עַד כִּי דָּרְכוּ זֶה עַל רַגְלוֹ שֶׁל זֶה, הֵחֵל לְדַבֵּר אֶל תַּלְמִידָיו תְּחִלָּה: "הִזָּהֲרוּ מִשְּׂאוֹר הַפְּרוּשִׁים, שֶׁהוּא הַצְּבִיעוּת. 2 אֵין דָּבָר מְכֻסֶּה שֶׁלֹּא יִגָּלֶה וְאֵין נִסְתָּר שֶׁלֹּא יִוָּדַע. 3 לְפִיכָךְ כָּל מַה שֶּׁאֲמַרְתֶּם בַּחֹשֶׁךְ יִשָּׁמַע בָּאוֹר, וּמַה שֶּׁלְּחַשְׁתֶּם בַּחַדְרֵי חֲדָרִים יִכְרַז מֵעַל הַגַּגּוֹת. 4 וַאֲנִי אוֹמֵר לָכֶם, יְדִידַי, אַל תִּפְחֲדוּ מִן הַהוֹרְגִים אֶת הַגּוּף שֶׁאַחֲרֵי כֵן לֹא נוֹתָר לָהֶם לַעֲשׂוֹת דָּבָר. 5 אֲבָל אַזְהִיר אֶתְכֶם מִפְּנֵי מִי לִירֹא: יִרְאוּ מִמִּי שֶׁסַּמְכוּת בְּיָדוֹ לַהֲרֹג וְאַחֲרֵי כֵן לְהַשְׁלִיךְ לַגֵּיהִנּוֹם. כֵּן, אוֹמֵר אֲנִי לָכֶם, מִפָּנָיו יִרְאוּ. 6 הַאִם לֹא נִמְכָּרוֹת חָמֵשׁ צִפֳּרִים בִּשְׁנֵי אִסָּרִים? גַּם אַחַת מֵהֶן אֵינָהּ נִשְׁכַּחַת מִלִּפְנֵי אֱלֹהִים. 7 וְאוּלָם אֲפִלּוּ שַׂעֲרוֹת רֹאשְׁכֶם נִמְנוּ כֻּלָּן. אַל תִּפְחֲדוּ; יְקָרִים אַתֶּם מִצִּפֳּרִים רַבּוֹת. 8 וַאֲנִי אוֹמֵר לָכֶם, כָּל הַמּוֹדֶה בִּי לִפְנֵי בְּנֵי אָדָם גַּם בֶּן־ הָאָדָם יוֹדֶה בּוֹ לִפְנֵי מַלְאֲכֵי אֱלֹהִים. 9 וְהַמְכַחֵשׁ בִּי לִפְנֵי בְּנֵי אָדָם יְכֻחַשׁ בּוֹ לִפְנֵי מַלְאֲכֵי אֱלֹהִים. 10 כָּל מִי שֶׁיֹּאמַר דָּבָר נֶגֶד בֶּן־הָאָדָם יִסָּלַח לוֹ, אַךְ הַמְנָאֵץ אֶת רוּחַ הַקֹּדֶשׁ לֹא יִסָּלַח לוֹ. 11 וְכַאֲשֶׁר יָבִיאוּ אֶתְכֶם אֶל בָּתֵּי כְנֶסֶת וְלִפְנֵי שַׁלִּיטִים וְרָשֻׁיּוֹת, אַל תִּדְאֲגוּ אֵיךְ וּמַה תָּשִׁיבוּ אוֹ מַה תֹּאמְרוּ; 12 כִּי רוּחַ הַקֹּדֶשׁ תּוֹרֶה לָכֶם בְּאוֹתָהּ שָׁעָה אֶת מַה שֶּׁצָּרִיךְ לוֹמַר."

13 מִישֶׁהוּ מִן הֶהָמוֹן אָמַר אֵלָיו: "רַבִּי, הַגֵּד נָא לְאָחִי

14 But He said to him, "Man, who made Me a judge or an arbitrator over you?" 15 And He said to them, "Take heed and beware of covetousness, for one's life does not consist in the abundance of the things he possesses."

16 Then He spoke a parable to them, saying: "The ground of a certain rich man yielded plentifully. 17 And he thought within himself, saying, 'What shall I do, since I have no room to store my crops?' 18 So he said, 'I will do this: I will pull down my barns and build greater, and there I will store all my crops and my goods. 19 And I will say to my soul, "Soul, you have many goods laid up for many years; take your ease; eat, drink, *and* be merry." ' 20 But God said to him, 'Fool! This night your soul will be required of you; then whose will those things be which you have provided?'

21 "So *is* he who lays up treasure for himself, and is not rich toward God."

22 Then He said to His disciples, "Therefore I say to you, do not worry about your life, what you will eat; nor about the body, what you will put on. 23 Life is more than food, and the body *is more* than clothing. 24 Consider the ravens, for they neither sow nor reap, which have neither storehouse nor barn; and God feeds them. Of how much more value are you than the birds? 25 And which of you by worrying can add one cubit to his stature? 26 If you then are not able to do *the* least, why are you anxious for the rest? 27 Consider the lilies, how they grow: they neither toil nor spin; and yet I say to you, even Solomon in all his glory was not arrayed like one of these. 28 If then God so clothes the grass, which today is in the field and tomorrow is thrown into the oven, how much more *will He clothe* you, O *you* of little faith?

29 "And do not seek what you should eat or what you should drink, nor have an anxious mind. 30 For all these things the nations of the world seek after, and your Father knows that you need these things. 31 But seek the kingdom of God, and all these things shall be added to you.

32 "Do not fear, little flock, for it is your Father's good pleasure to give you the kingdom. 33 Sell what you have and give alms; provide yourselves money bags which do not grow old, a treasure in the heavens that does not fail, where no thief approaches nor moth destroys. 34 For where your treasure is, there your heart will be also.

35 "Let your waist be girded and *your* lamps burning; 36 and you yourselves be like men who wait for their master, when he will return from the wedding, that when he comes and knocks they may open to him immediately. 37 Blessed *are* those

שֶׁיַּחֲלֹק אִתִּי אֶת הַיְרֻשָּׁה." 14 אַךְ הוּא הֵשִׁיב לוֹ: "בֶּן־אָדָם, מִי שָׂם אוֹתִי לְשׁוֹפֵט עֲלֵיכֶם אוֹ לִמְחַלֵּק?" 15 הוֹסִיף וְאָמַר לָהֶם: "שִׂימוּ לֵב וְהִזָּהֲרוּ מִכָּל חַמְדָנוּת, כִּי חַיֵּי הָאָדָם אֵינָם תְּלוּיִים בְּשֶׁפַע נְכָסָיו."

16 סִפֵּר לָהֶם מָשָׁל: "שָׂדֵהוּ שֶׁל אִישׁ עָשִׁיר אֶחָד הֵנִיב יְבוּל רַב. 17 חָשַׁב הָאִישׁ בְּלִבּוֹ, 'מָה אֶעֱשֶׂה, אֵין לִי מָקוֹם לֶאֱסֹף אֶת יְבוּלִי.' 18 אָמַר, 'זֹאת אֶעֱשֶׂה, אֶהֱרֹס אֶת אֲסָמַי וְאֶבְנֶה גְּדוֹלִים מֵהֶם, וּבָהֶם אֲכַנֵּס אֶת כָּל תְּבוּאָתִי וּרְכוּשִׁי. 19 וְאֹמַר לְנַפְשִׁי: נַפְשִׁי, יֵשׁ לָךְ הַרְבֵּה דְּבָרִים טוֹבִים שֶׁנֶּאֶגְרוּ לְשָׁנִים רַבּוֹת. הִנָּפְשִׁי, אִכְלִי, שְׁתִי וְשִׂמְחִי.' 20 אֶלָּא שֶׁאֱלֹהִים אָמַר לוֹ: 'כְּסִיל! בְּעֶצֶם הַלַּיְלָה הַזֶּה יִדְרְשׁוּ מִמְּךָ אֶת נַפְשְׁךָ, וְהַדְּבָרִים שֶׁהֵכַנְתָּ לְמִי יִהְיוּ?' 21 כָּכָה הוּא מִי שֶׁאוֹצֵר בִּשְׁבִיל עַצְמוֹ וְאֵינוֹ מַעֲשִׁיר לְמַעַן אֱלֹהִים."

22 אָמַר לְתַלְמִידָיו: "לָכֵן אוֹמֵר אֲנִי לָכֶם: אַל תִּדְאֲגוּ לְנַפְשְׁכֶם מַה תֹּאכְלוּ; וּלְגוּפְכֶם – מַה תִּלְבְּשׁוּ. 23 הֲלֹא הַנֶּפֶשׁ חֲשׁוּבָה מִן הַמָּזוֹן, וְהַגּוּף חָשׁוּב מִן הַלְּבוּשׁ. 24 הִתְבּוֹנְנוּ אֶל הָעוֹרְבִים: אֵינָם זוֹרְעִים וְאֵינָם קוֹצְרִים. גַּם אָסָם אוֹ מַחְסָן אֵין לָהֶם, וֵאלֹהִים מְכַלְכֵּל אוֹתָם. עַל אַחַת כַּמָּה וְכַמָּה חֲשׁוּבִים אַתֶּם מִן הַצִּפֳּרִים! 25 וּמִי מִכֶּם בִּדְאָגָתוֹ יָכוֹל לְהוֹסִיף טֶפַח עַל שְׁנוֹת חַיָּיו? 26 וְכֵיוָן שֶׁאֵינְכֶם יְכוֹלִים לַעֲשׂוֹת דְּבָרִים פְּעוּטִים, לָמָּה תִּדְאֲגוּ לִשְׁאָר הַדְּבָרִים? 27 הִתְבּוֹנְנוּ אֶל הַשּׁוֹשַׁנִּים, אֵיךְ הֵם גְּדֵלִים; אֵינָם טוֹוִים אַף אֵינָם אוֹרְגִים. אַךְ אוֹמֵר אֲנִי לָכֶם, גַּם שְׁלֹמֹה בְּכָל הֲדָרוֹ לֹא הָיָה לָבוּשׁ כְּאַחַד מֵהֶם. 28 וְאִם כָּכָה מַלְבִּישׁ אֱלֹהִים אֶת חֲצִיר הַשָּׂדֶה, אֲשֶׁר הַיּוֹם יֶשְׁנוֹ וּמָחָר יֻשְׁלַךְ לְתוֹךְ הַתַּנּוּר, עַל אַחַת כַּמָּה וְכַמָּה אֶתְכֶם, קְצַוֵּי אֱמוּנָה! 29 גַּם אַתֶּם, אַל תִּהְיוּ שׁוֹאֲלִים מַה תֹּאכְלוּ וּמַה תִּשְׁתּוּ, וְאַל תִּהְיוּ דוֹאֲגִים. 30 כִּי אֻמּוֹת הָעוֹלָם מְבַקְשִׁים אֶת כָּל הַדְּבָרִים הָאֵלֶּה, וְאַתֶּם, אֲבִיכֶם יוֹדֵעַ שֶׁאַתֶּם צְרִיכִים לָהֶם. 31 לָכֵן בַּקְּשׁוּ אֶת מַלְכוּתוֹ, וְכָל אֵלֶּה יוֹסְפוּ לָכֶם. 32 אַל תִּירָא עֵדֶר קָטָן, כִּי לְרָצוֹן הָיָה מִלִּפְנֵי אֲבִיכֶם לָתֵת לָכֶם אֶת הַמַּלְכוּת. 33 מִכְרוּ אֶת נִכְסֵיכֶם וּתְנוּ לִצְדָקָה. עֲשׂוּ לָכֶם אַרְנָקִים שֶׁאֵינָם מִתְבַּלִּים, אוֹצָר לֹא מִתְכַּלֶּה בַּשָּׁמַיִם – בַּמָּקוֹם שֶׁאֵין גַּנָּב מִתְקָרֵב לְשָׁם וְאֵין הָעָשׁ עוֹשֶׂה מַשְׁחִית; 34 כִּי בַּמָּקוֹם שֶׁמְּנַח אוֹצַרְכֶם, שָׁם יִהְיֶה גַּם לְבַבְכֶם."

35 "יִהְיוּ מָתְנֵיכֶם חֲגוּרִים וּמְנוֹרוֹתֵיכֶם דּוֹלְקוֹת. 36 וְאַתֶּם הֱיוּ דּוֹמִים לַאֲנָשִׁים הַמְחַכִּים לַאֲדוֹנָם בְּצֵאתוֹ לָבוֹא מִן הַחֲתֻנָּה, בְּאֹפֶן שֶׁבְּבוֹאוֹ וּבְדָפְקוֹ יִפְתְּחוּ לוֹ מִיָּד. 37 אַשְׁרֵי אוֹתָם הָעֲבָדִים אֲשֶׁר

servants whom the master, when he comes, will find watching. Assuredly, I say to you that he will gird himself and have them sit down *to eat,* and will come and serve them. 38 And if he should come in the second watch, or come in the third watch, and find *them* so, blessed are those servants. 39 But know this, that if the master of the house had known what hour the thief would come, he would have watched and not allowed his house to be broken into. 40 Therefore you also be ready, for the Son of Man is coming at an hour you do not expect."

41 Then Peter said to Him, "Lord, do You speak this parable *only* to us, or to all *people?*"

42 And the Lord said, "Who then is that faithful and wise steward, whom *his* master will make ruler over his household, to give *them their* portion of food in due season? 43 Blessed *is* that servant whom his master will find so doing when he comes. 44 Truly, I say to you that he will make him ruler over all that he has. 45 But if that servant says in his heart, 'My master is delaying his coming,' and begins to beat the male and female servants, and to eat and drink and be drunk, 46 the master of that servant will come on a day when he is not looking for *him,* and at an hour when he is not aware, and will cut him in two and appoint *him* his portion with the unbelievers. 47 And that servant who knew his master's will, and did not prepare *himself* or do according to his will, shall be beaten with many *stripes.* 48 But he who did not know, yet committed things deserving of stripes, shall be beaten with few. For everyone to whom much is given, from him much will be required; and to whom much has been committed, of him they will ask the more.

49 "I came to send fire on the earth, and how I wish it were already kindled! 50 But I have a baptism to be baptized with, and how distressed I am till it is accomplished! 51 Do *you* suppose that I came to give peace on earth? I tell you, not at all, but rather division. 52 For from now on five in one house will be divided: three against two, and two against three. 53 Father will be divided against son and son against father, mother against daughter and daughter against mother, mother-in-law against her daughter-in-law and daughter-in-law against her mother-in-law."

54 Then He also said to the multitudes, "Whenever *you see* a cloud rising out of the west, immediately you say, 'A shower is coming'; and so it is. 55 And when you see the south wind blow, you say, 'There will be hot weather'; and there is. 56 Hypocrites! You can discern the face of the sky and of the earth, but how *is it* you do not discern this time?

הָאָדוֹן בְּבוֹאוֹ יִמְצָאֵם עוֹמְדִים עַל הַמִּשְׁמָר. אָמֵן אוֹמֵר אֲנִי לָכֶם, הוּא יֶאֱזֹר אֶת מָתְנָיו, יוֹשִׁיבֵם, וְיִגַּשׁ לְשָׁרֵת אוֹתָם. 38 וְאִם יָבוֹא בָּאַשְׁמֹרֶת הַשְּׁנִיָּה אוֹ בָּאַשְׁמֹרֶת הַשְּׁלִישִׁית וְיִמְצָאֵם כָּךְ, אַשְׁרֵי הָעֲבָדִים הָהֵם. 39 וְאַת דְּעוּ: אִלּוּ יָדַע בַּעַל הַבַּיִת בְּאֵיזוֹ שָׁעָה יָבוֹא הַגַּנָּב, לֹא הָיָה מַנִּיחַ לַחְדֹּר אֶל בֵּיתוֹ. 40 גַּם אַתֶּם הֱיוּ מוּכָנִים, כִּי בְּשָׁעָה שֶׁלֹּא תַעֲלֶה עַל דַּעְתְּכֶם יָבוֹא בֶּן-הָאָדָם."

41 שָׁאַל כֵּיפָא: "אֲדוֹנֵנוּ, הֲרַק לָנוּ אַתָּה אוֹמֵר אֶת הַמָּשָׁל הַזֶּה אוֹ לַכֹּל?"

42 הֵשִׁיב הָאָדוֹן: "מִי הוּא אֵפוֹא הַסּוֹכֵן הַנֶּאֱמָן וְהַנָּבוֹן אֲשֶׁר הָאָדוֹן יַפְקִידֵהוּ עַל מְשָׁרְתָיו לָתֵת לָהֶם אֶת אֲרוּחָתָם בַּזְּמַן? 43 אַשְׁרֵי הָעֶבֶד הַהוּא אֲשֶׁר אֲדוֹנָיו יָבוֹא וְיִמְצָאֵהוּ עוֹשֶׂה כֵּן. 44 אֱמֶת אֲנִי אוֹמֵר לָכֶם, עַל כָּל נְכָסָיו יַפְקִיד אוֹתוֹ. 45 אַךְ הָעֶבֶד הַהוּא אִם יֹאמַר בְּלִבּוֹ, 'מְאַחֵר אֲדוֹנִי לָבוֹא', וְיַתְחִיל לְהַכּוֹת אֶת הָעֲבָדִים וְהַשְּׁפָחוֹת וְלֶאֱכֹל וְלִשְׁתּוֹת וּלְהִשְׁתַּכֵּר, 46 בּוֹא יָבוֹא הָאָדוֹן שֶׁל אוֹתוֹ עֶבֶד בְּיוֹם שֶׁאֵינֶנּוּ מְצַפֶּה לוֹ וּבְשָׁעָה שֶׁאֵינוֹ יוֹדֵעַ, וִישַׁסֵּף אוֹתוֹ וְיָשִׂים חֶלְקוֹ עִם הַבִּלְתִּי-מַאֲמִינִים. 47 וְהָעֶבֶד הַהוּא אֲשֶׁר יָדַע אֶת רְצוֹן אֲדוֹנָיו וְלֹא הֵכִין וְלֹא עָשָׂה כִּרְצוֹנוֹ יֻכֶּה מַכּוֹת רַבּוֹת. 48 אֲבָל זֶה שֶׁלֹּא יָדַע וְעָשָׂה דְּבָרִים שֶׁהוּא חַיָּב עֲלֵיהֶם מַכּוֹת, יֻכֶּה מְעָט. כָּל מִי שֶׁנִּתַּן לוֹ הַרְבֵּה, יִדָּרֵשׁ מִמֶּנּוּ הַרְבֵּה; וּמִי שֶׁהָפְקַד בְּיָדוֹ הַרְבֵּה, יִדְרְשׁוּ מִמֶּנּוּ עוֹד יוֹתֵר."

49 "אֵשׁ בָּאתִי לִשְׁלֹחַ עַל פְּנֵי הָאָרֶץ וּמֶה חָפַצְתִּי שֶׁכְּבָר תִּבְעַר! 50 אֶלָּא שֶׁעָלַי לְהִטָּבֵל טְבִילָה וּמַה כְּבֵדָה עָלַי הַמּוּעָקָה עַד אֲשֶׁר תֻּשְׁלַם! 51 הַסְּבוּרִים אַתֶּם שֶׁבָּאתִי לָשִׂים שָׁלוֹם בָּאָרֶץ? לֹא, אוֹמֵר אֲנִי לָכֶם, אֶלָּא מַחֲלֹקֶת. 52 מֵעַתָּה חֲמִשָּׁה בְּבַיִת אֶחָד יִהְיוּ שְׁרוּיִים בְּמַחֲלֹקֶת, שְׁלוֹשָׁה נֶגֶד שְׁנַיִם וּשְׁנַיִם נֶגֶד שְׁלוֹשָׁה. 53 הָאָב נֶגֶד הַבֵּן וְהַבֵּן נֶגֶד הָאָב; הָאֵם נֶגֶד הַבַּת וְהַבַּת נֶגֶד הָאֵם; הֶחָמוֹת נֶגֶד כַּלָּתָהּ וְהַכַּלָּה נֶגֶד חֲמוֹתָהּ." 54 אָמַר גַּם אֶל הֶהָמוֹן: "כַּאֲשֶׁר אַתֶּם רוֹאִים עָנָן עוֹלֶה מִמַּעֲרָב, מִיָּד אַתֶּם אוֹמְרִים 'גֶּשֶׁם בָּא'; וְאָכֵן הַגֶּשֶׁם בָּא. 55 וְכַאֲשֶׁר נוֹשֶׁבֶת רוּחַ דְּרוֹמִית אַתֶּם אוֹמְרִים 'יִהְיֶה חַם', וְאָכֵן הַחֹם בָּא. 56 צְבוּעִים! אֶת פְּנֵי הָאָרֶץ וּפְנֵי הַשָּׁמַיִם יוֹדְעִים אַתֶּם לְפָרֵשׁ, הֲכֵיצַד אֵינְכֶם יוֹדְעִים לְפָרֵשׁ אֶת הַזְּמַן הַזֶּה?"

57 "Yes, and why, even of yourselves, do you not judge what is right? 58 When you go with your adversary to the magistrate, make every effort along the way to settle with him, lest he drag you to the judge, the judge deliver you to the officer, and the officer throw you into prison. 59 I tell you, you shall not depart from there till you have paid the very last mite."

13 There were present at that season some who told Him about the Galileans whose blood Pilate had mingled with their sacrifices. 2 And Jesus answered and said to them, "Do you suppose that these Galileans were worse sinners than all *other* Galileans, because they suffered such things? 3 I tell you, no; but unless you repent you will all likewise perish. 4 Or those eighteen on whom the tower in Siloam fell and killed them, do you think that they were worse sinners than all *other* men who dwelt in Jerusalem? 5 I tell you, no; but unless you repent you will all likewise perish."

6 He also spoke this parable: "A certain *man* had a fig tree planted in his vineyard, and he came seeking fruit on it and found none. 7 Then he said to the keeper of his vineyard, 'Look, for three years I have come seeking fruit on this fig tree and find none. Cut it down; why does it use up the ground?' 8 But he answered and said to him, 'Sir, let it alone this year also, until I dig around it and fertilize *it*. 9 And if it bears fruit, *well*. But if not, after that you can cut it down.' "

10 Now He was teaching in one of the synagogues on the Sabbath. 11 And behold, there was a woman who had a spirit of infirmity eighteen years, and was bent over and could in no way raise *herself* up. 12 But when Jesus saw her, He called *her* to Him and said to her, "Woman, you are loosed from your infirmity." 13 And He laid *His* hands on her, and immediately she was made straight, and glorified God.

14 But the ruler of the synagogue answered with indignation, because Jesus had healed on the Sabbath; and he said to the crowd, "There are six days on which men ought to work; therefore come and be healed on them, and not on the Sabbath day."

15 The Lord then answered him and said, "Hypocrite! Does not each one of you on the Sabbath loose his ox or donkey from the stall, and lead *it* away to water it? 16 So ought not this woman, being a daughter of Abraham, whom Satan has bound—think of it—for eighteen years, be loosed from this bond on the Sabbath?" 17 And

57 "וּמַדּוּעַ אַתֶּם בְּעַצְמְכֶם אֵינְכֶם שׁוֹפְטִים נְכוֹנָה? 58 כַּאֲשֶׁר אַתָּה הוֹלֵךְ עִם אִישׁ רִיבְךָ אֶל הַשַּׁלִּיט, הִשְׁתַּדֵּל לְהַשְׁלִים עִמּוֹ בְּעוֹדְךָ בַּדָּרֶךְ; שֶׁאִם לֹא כֵן יִסְחַב אוֹתְךָ אֶל הַשּׁוֹפֵט, וְהַשּׁוֹפֵט יִמְסֹר אוֹתְךָ לַשּׁוֹטֵר, וְהַשּׁוֹטֵר יַשְׁלִיךְ אוֹתְךָ לַכֶּלֶא. 59 אוֹמֵר אֲנִי לְךָ, לֹא תֵצֵא מִשָּׁם עַד אֲשֶׁר תְּשַׁלֵּם אֶת הַפְּרוּטָה הָאַחֲרוֹנָה."

יג בָּאוֹתָהּ עֵת הָיוּ שָׁם אֲנָשִׁים שֶׁסִּפְּרוּ לוֹ עַל הַגְּלִילִיִּים אֲשֶׁר פִּילָטוֹס עֵרַב אֶת דָּמָם בְּזִבְחֵיהֶם. 2 הֵשִׁיב לָהֶם יֵשׁוּעַ: "הַאִם מִפְּנֵי שֶׁהַגְּלִילִיִּים הָאֵלֶּה סָבְלוּ זֹאת סְבוּרִים אַתֶּם שֶׁהֵם הָיוּ חוֹטְאִים גְּדוֹלִים יוֹתֵר מִכָּל אַנְשֵׁי הַגָּלִיל? 3 לֹא! אוֹמֵר אֲנִי לָכֶם. אַךְ אִם לֹא תָּחֻזְרוּ בִּתְשׁוּבָה, כֻּלְּכֶם תֹּאבְדוּ כְּמוֹתָם. 4 אוֹ אוֹתָם הַשְּׁמוֹנָה-עָשָׂר אֲשֶׁר נָפַל עֲלֵיהֶם הַמִּגְדָּל בְּשִׁלּוֹחַ וַהֲרָגָם, הַסְבוּרִים אַתֶּם שֶׁהֵם הָיוּ אֲשֵׁמִים יוֹתֵר מִכָּל הָאֲנָשִׁים הַגָּרִים בִּירוּשָׁלַיִם? 5 אֲנִי אוֹמֵר לָכֶם שֶׁלֹּא; אַךְ אִם לֹא תָּחֻזְרוּ בִּתְשׁוּבָה, כֻּלְּכֶם תֹּאבְדוּ כְּמוֹתָם."

6 סִפֵּר אֶת הַמָּשָׁל הַזֶּה: "לְאִישׁ אֶחָד הָיְתָה תְּאֵנָה נְטוּעָה בְּכַרְמוֹ; פַּעַם בָּא לְחַפֵּשׂ בָּהּ פְּרִי וְלֹא מָצָא. 7 אָמַר אֶל הַכּוֹרֵם: 'הִנֵּה זֶה שָׁלוֹשׁ שָׁנִים אֲנִי בָּא לְחַפֵּשׂ פְּרִי בַּתְּאֵנָה הַזֹּאת וְלֹא מָצָאתִי. כְּרֹת אוֹתָהּ. לָמָּה לְהָנִיחַ לָהּ גַּם לְדַלְדֵּל אֶת הַקַּרְקַע?' 8 הֵשִׁיב לוֹ הַכּוֹרֵם: 'אֲדוֹנִי, הַשְׁאֵר נָא אוֹתָהּ עוֹד הַשָּׁנָה הַזֹּאת עַד שֶׁאֶעֱדֹר מִסָּבִיב וְאָשִׂים זֶבֶל; 9 אוּלַי תִּתֵּן פְּרִי בַּשָּׁנָה הַבָּאָה וְאִם לֹא, תִּכְרֹת אוֹתָהּ.' "

10 בְּיוֹם הַשַּׁבָּת לִמֵּד בְּאֶחָד מִבָּתֵּי הַכְּנֶסֶת. 11 וְהִנֵּה הָיְתָה שָׁם אִשָּׁה נְגוּעָה בְּרוּחַ-חֳלִי זֶה שְׁמוֹנֶה-עֶשְׂרֵה שָׁנָה; כְּפוּפָה הָיְתָה וְלֹא יָכְלָה לִזְקֹף קוֹמָתָהּ. 12 כִּרְאוֹתוֹ אוֹתָהּ קָרָא לָהּ יֵשׁוּעַ וְאָמַר: "אִשָּׁה, שְׁחַרְרְתְּ מֵחָלְיֵךְ!" 13 הוּא סָמַךְ אֶת יָדָיו עָלֶיהָ וּמִיָּד זָקְפָה קוֹמָתָהּ וְשִׁבְּחָה אֶת הָאֱלֹהִים. 14 אֲבָל רֹאשׁ בֵּית הַכְּנֶסֶת נִתְמַלֵּא כַּעַס עַל שֶׁיֵּשׁוּעַ רִפֵּא בְּשַׁבָּת. הוּא פָּנָה אֶל הַקָּהָל וְאָמַר: "יֵשׁ שִׁשָּׁה יָמִים שֶׁמָּן הַדִּין לַעֲבֹד בָּהֶם. עַל כֵּן בּוֹאוּ וְהֵרָפְאוּ בַּיָּמִים הָאֵלֶּה וְלֹא בְּיוֹם הַשַּׁבָּת."

15 אָמַר לוֹ הָאָדוֹן: "צְבוּעִים! הַאִם כָּל אֶחָד וְאֶחָד מִכֶּם אֵינֶנּוּ מַתִּיר בְּשַׁבָּת אֶת שׁוֹרוֹ אוֹ חֲמוֹרוֹ מִן הָאֵבוּס וּמוֹלִיךְ אוֹתוֹ לִשְׁתּוֹת מַיִם? 16 וְאִשָּׁה זֹאת, בַּת אַבְרָהָם, אֲשֶׁר הַשָּׂטָן כָּבַל אוֹתָהּ בְּמֶשֶׁךְ שְׁמוֹנֶה-עֶשְׂרֵה שָׁנָה, הַאִם לֹא הָיָה צָרִיךְ לְהַתִּיר אוֹתָהּ מִן הַכֶּבֶל הַזֶּה בְּיוֹם הַשַּׁבָּת?" 17 כְּשֶׁאָמַר אֶת הַדְּבָרִים הָאֵלֶּה הִתְבַּיְּשׁוּ כָּל

when He said these things, all His adversaries were put to shame; and all the multitude rejoiced for all the glorious things that were done by Him.

18 Then He said, "What is the kingdom of God like? And to what shall I compare it? 19 It is like a mustard seed, which a man took and put in his garden; and it grew and became a large tree, and the birds of the air nested in its branches."

20 And again He said, "To what shall I liken the kingdom of God? 21 It is like leaven, which a woman took and hid in three measures of meal till it was all leavened."

22 And He went through the cities and villages, teaching, and journeying toward Jerusalem. 23 Then one said to Him, "Lord, are there few who are saved?"

And He said to them, 24 "Strive to enter through the narrow gate, for many, I say to you, will seek to enter and will not be able. 25 When once the Master of the house has risen up and shut the door, and you begin to stand outside and knock at the door, saying, 'Lord, Lord, open for us,' and He will answer and say to you, 'I do not know you, where you are from,' 26 then you will begin to say, 'We ate and drank in Your presence, and You taught in our streets.' 27 But He will say, 'I tell you I do not know you, where you are from. Depart from Me, all you workers of iniquity.' 28 There will be weeping and gnashing of teeth, when you see Abraham and Isaac and Jacob and all the prophets in the kingdom of God, and yourselves thrust out. 29 They will come from the east and the west, from the north and the south, and sit down in the kingdom of God. 30 And indeed there are last who will be first, and there are first who will be last."

31 On that very day some Pharisees came, saying to Him, "Get out and depart from here, for Herod wants to kill You."

32 And He said to them, "Go, tell that fox, 'Behold, I cast out demons and perform cures today and tomorrow, and the third *day* I shall be perfected.' 33 Nevertheless I must journey today, tomorrow, and the *day* following; for it cannot be that a prophet should perish outside of Jerusalem.

34 "O Jerusalem, Jerusalem, the one who kills the prophets and stones those who are sent to her! How often I wanted to gather your children together, as a hen *gathers* her brood under *her* wings, but you were not willing! 35 See! Your house is left to you desolate; and assuredly, I say to you, you shall not see Me until *the time* comes when you say, '*Blessed is He who comes in the name of the LORD!*'"

הַמִּתְנַגְּדִים לוֹ, וְכָל הַקָּהָל שָׂמַח עַל הַנִּפְלָאוֹת שֶׁעָשָׂה.

18 אָז אָמַר: "לְמָה דּוֹמָה מַלְכוּת הָאֱלֹהִים וְאֶל מָה אֲדַמֶּה אוֹתָהּ? 19 דּוֹמָה הִיא לְגַרְגִּיר שֶׁל חַרְדָּל אֲשֶׁר לְקָחוֹ אִישׁ וְזָרַע אוֹתוֹ בְּגַנּוֹ. הַגַּרְגִּיר צָמַח וְהָיָה לְעֵץ וְעוֹפוֹת הַשָּׁמַיִם קִנְּנוּ בַּעֲנָפָיו." 20 וְעוֹד אָמַר: "אֶל מָה אֲדַמֶּה אֶת מַלְכוּת הָאֱלֹהִים? 21 דּוֹמָה הִיא לִשְׂאוֹר אֲשֶׁר לָקְחָה אִשָּׁה וְטָמְנָה אוֹתוֹ בִּשְׁלוֹשׁ סְאִים קֶמַח עַד שֶׁהֶחְמִיץ כֻּלּוֹ."

22 הוּא עָבַר בְּעָרִים וּבִכְפָרִים וְלִמֵּד כְּשֶׁהוּא עוֹשֶׂה אֶת דַּרְכּוֹ לִירוּשָׁלַיִם. 23 וְהִנֵּה מִישֶׁהוּ שָׁאַל אוֹתוֹ: "אֲדוֹנִי, הַאִם מְעַטִּים הַנּוֹשָׁעִים?"

24 הֵשִׁיב לָהֶם: "הִתְאַמְּצוּ לְהִכָּנֵס דֶּרֶךְ הַפֶּתַח הַצַּר כִּי רַבִּים, אוֹמֵר אֲנִי לָכֶם, יִרְצוּ לְהִכָּנֵס וְלֹא יוּכְלוּ. 25 לְאַחַר שֶׁיָּקוּם בַּעַל הַבַּיִת וְיִסְגֹּר אֶת הַדֶּלֶת תַּתְחִילוּ לַעֲמֹד בַּחוּץ וְלִדְפֹּק עַל הַדֶּלֶת וְתֹאמְרוּ, 'אֲדוֹנֵנוּ, פְּתַח לָנוּ!' אַךְ הוּא יַעֲנֶה וְיֹאמַר לָכֶם, 'אֵינֶנִּי מַכִּיר אֶתְכֶם, מֵאַיִן אַתֶּם?' 26 אָז תַּתְחִילוּ לוֹמַר, 'אָכַלְנוּ וְשָׁתִינוּ לְפָנֶיךָ וּבִרְחוֹבוֹתֵינוּ לִמַּדְתָּ!' 27 וְהוּא יֹאמַר לָכֶם, 'אֵינֶנִּי יוֹדֵעַ מֵאַיִן אַתֶּם, סוּרוּ מִמֶּנִּי כָּל עוֹשֵׂי רֶשַׁע!' 28 שָׁם יִהְיֶה הַיְלָלָה וַחֲרוֹק הַשִּׁנַּיִם, כַּאֲשֶׁר תִּרְאוּ אֶת אַבְרָהָם וְיִצְחָק וְיַעֲקֹב וְאֶת כָּל הַנְּבִיאִים בְּמַלְכוּת הָאֱלֹהִים וְאַתֶּם מְגֹרָשִׁים הַחוּצָה. 29 וְיָבוֹאוּ מִמִּזְרָח וּמִמַּעֲרָב, מִצָּפוֹן וּמִדָּרוֹם, וְיֵשְׁבוּ בְּמַלְכוּת הָאֱלֹהִים. 30 וְהִנֵּה יֵשׁ אַחֲרוֹנִים שֶׁיִּהְיוּ רִאשׁוֹנִים וְרִאשׁוֹנִים שֶׁיִּהְיוּ אַחֲרוֹנִים."

31 אוֹתָהּ שָׁעָה נִגְּשׁוּ כַּמָּה פְּרוּשִׁים וְאָמְרוּ לוֹ: "צֵא וְלֵךְ מִכָּאן, כִּי הוֹרְדוֹס רוֹצֶה לְהָרְגְךָ." 32 הֵשִׁיב לָהֶם יֵשׁוּעַ: "לְכוּ וְאִמְרוּ לַשּׁוּעָל הַזֶּה: 'הִנְנִי מְגָרֵשׁ שֵׁדִים וּפוֹעֵל רְפוּאוֹת הַיּוֹם וּמָחָר, וּבַיּוֹם הַשְּׁלִישִׁי אַגִּיעַ עַד תַּכְלִית.' 33 וְאוּלָם עָלַי לְהַמְשִׁיךְ וְלָלֶכֶת הַיּוֹם וּמָחָר וּבַיּוֹם שֶׁלְּאַחַר מִכֵּן, כִּי לֹא יִתָּכֵן שֶׁיִּסָּפֶה נָבִיא מִחוּץ לִירוּשָׁלַיִם. 34 יְרוּשָׁלַיִם, יְרוּשָׁלַיִם, הַהוֹרֶגֶת אֶת הַנְּבִיאִים וְסוֹקֶלֶת אֶת הַשְּׁלוּחִים אֵלֶיהָ, כַּמָּה פְּעָמִים חָפַצְתִּי לְקַבֵּץ אֶת בָּנַיִךְ כְּתַרְנְגֹלֶת הַמְקַבֶּצֶת אֶת אֶפְרוֹחֶיהָ תַּחַת כְּנָפֶיהָ וְלֹא רְצִיתֶם, 35 הִנֵּה בֵּיתְכֶם יִנָּטֵשׁ לָכֶם, וַאֲנִי אוֹמֵר לָכֶם: רָאֹה לֹא תִרְאוּנִי עַד כִּי תָבוֹא הָעֵת שֶׁתֹּאמְרוּ 'בָּרוּךְ הַבָּא בְּשֵׁם יהוה!'"

21 שָׁלוֹשׁ סְאִים – כְּעֶשְׂרִים קִילוֹגְרָם.

14 Now it happened, as He went into the house of one of the rulers of the Pharisees to eat bread on the Sabbath, that they watched Him closely. ² And behold, there was a certain man before Him who had dropsy. ³ And Jesus, answering, spoke to the lawyers and Pharisees, saying, "Is it lawful to heal on the Sabbath?"

⁴ But they kept silent. And He took *him* and healed him, and let him go. ⁵ Then He answered them, saying, "Which of you, having a donkey or an ox that has fallen into a pit, will not immediately pull him out on the Sabbath day?" ⁶ And they could not answer Him regarding these things.

⁷ So He told a parable to those who were invited, when He noted how they chose the best places, saying to them: ⁸ "When you are invited by anyone to a wedding feast, do not sit down in the best place, lest one more honorable than you be invited by him; ⁹ and he who invited you and him come and say to you, 'Give place to this man,' and then you begin with shame to take the lowest place. ¹⁰ But when you are invited, go and sit down in the lowest place, so that when he who invited you comes he may say to you, 'Friend, go up higher.' Then you will have glory in the presence of those who sit at the table with you. ¹¹ For whoever exalts himself will be humbled, and he who humbles himself will be exalted."

¹² Then He also said to him who invited Him, "When you give a dinner or a supper, do not ask your friends, your brothers, your relatives, nor rich neighbors, lest they also invite you back, and you be repaid. ¹³ But when you give a feast, invite *the* poor, *the* maimed, *the* lame, *the* blind. ¹⁴ And you will be blessed, because they cannot repay you; for you shall be repaid at the resurrection of the just."

¹⁵ Now when one of those who sat at the table with Him heard these things, he said to Him, "Blessed *is* he who shall eat bread in the kingdom of God!"

¹⁶ Then He said to him, "A certain man gave a great supper and invited many, ¹⁷ and sent his servant at supper time to say to those who were invited, 'Come, for all things are now ready.' ¹⁸ But they all with one *accord* began to make excuses. The first said to him, 'I have bought a piece of ground, and I must go and see it. I ask you to have me excused.' ¹⁹ And another said, 'I have bought five yoke of oxen, and I am going to test them. I ask you to have me excused.' ²⁰ Still another said, 'I have married a wife, and therefore I cannot come.' ²¹ So that servant came and reported these things to his master. Then the master of the house, being angry, said to his servant, 'Go out quickly into the streets

יד בְּשַׁבָּת אַחַת נִכְנַס לֶאֱכֹל לֶחֶם בְּבֵיתוֹ שֶׁל אֶחָד מֵרָאשֵׁי הַפְּרוּשִׁים, וְהֵם הִתְבּוֹנְנוּ בּוֹ בִּדְרִיכוּת. ² וְהִנֵּה לְפָנָיו אִישׁ שֶׁגּוּפוֹ תָּפוּחַ מִמַּיִם. ³ פָּנָה יֵשׁוּעַ לְבַעֲלֵי הַתּוֹרָה וְהַפְּרוּשִׁים וְשָׁאַל: "הַמֻתָּר לְרַפֵּא בְּשַׁבָּת אוֹ לֹא?" ⁴ אַךְ הַלָּלוּ שָׁתְקוּ. אָז הֶחֱזִיק בּוֹ, רִפֵּא אוֹתוֹ וְשִׁלַּח אוֹתוֹ. ⁵ הוֹסִיף וְאָמַר לָהֶם: "מִי מִכֶּם, שֶׁחֲמוֹרוֹ אוֹ שׁוֹרוֹ יִפֹּל לְתוֹךְ בְּאֵר, לֹא יְמַהֵר לְהַעֲלוֹתוֹ בְּיוֹם הַשַּׁבָּת?" ⁶ עַל זֹאת לֹא יָכְלוּ לַעֲנוֹת.

⁷ כִּרְאוֹתוֹ כֵּיצַד בּוֹחֲרִים לָהֶם הַמֻזְמָנִים אֶת הַמְּקוֹמוֹת הַמְכֻבָּדִים, אָמַר לָהֶם מָשָׁל: ⁸ "כַּאֲשֶׁר מִישֶׁהוּ מַזְמִין אוֹתְךָ לַחֲתֻנָּה אַל תֵּשֵׁב בַּמָּקוֹם הַמְכֻבָּד בְּיוֹתֵר, שֶׁמָּא הִזְמִין אִישׁ נִכְבָּד מִמְּךָ; ⁹ וּמִי שֶׁהִזְמִין אוֹתְךָ וְאוֹתוֹ יָבוֹא וְיֹאמַר לְךָ 'תֵּן מָקוֹם לָאִישׁ הַזֶּה', וְאָז תֵּלֵךְ בְּבֹשֶׁת פָּנִים לִתְפֹּס אֶת הַמָּקוֹם הָאַחֲרוֹן. ¹⁰ אַדְּרַבָּא, כְּשֶׁאַתָּה מְזֻמָּן לֵךְ וְהֵסֵב בַּמָּקוֹם הָאַחֲרוֹן; וְכַאֲשֶׁר זֶה שֶׁהִזְמִין אוֹתְךָ וְיֹאמַר לְךָ 'עֲלֵה יְדִידִי', יִהְיֶה לְךָ כָּבוֹד לְעֵינֵי כָּל הַמְסֻבִּים עִמְּךָ. ¹¹ כִּי כָּל הַמְרוֹמֵם אֶת עַצְמוֹ יֻשְׁפַּל וְהַמַּשְׁפִּיל אֶת עַצְמוֹ יְרוֹמַם." ¹² וְגַם לָאִישׁ שֶׁהִזְמִין אוֹתוֹ אָמַר: "כַּאֲשֶׁר אַתָּה עוֹרֵךְ סְעוּדַת צָהֳרַיִם אוֹ סְעוּדַת עֶרֶב, אַל תִּקְרָא לִידִידֶיךָ, אַף לֹא לְאַחֶיךָ וּקְרוֹבֶיךָ וְלֹא לִשְׁכֵנֶיךָ הָעֲשִׁירִים, שֶׁמָּא יַזְמִינוּךְ גַּם הֵם וְזֶה יִהְיֶה גְּמוּלְךָ. ¹³ כְּשֶׁאַתָּה עוֹרֵךְ מִשְׁתֶּה הַזְמֵן אֶת הָעֲנִיִּים, אֶת בַּעֲלֵי הַמּוּם, אֶת הַפִּסְחִים וְהָעִוְרִים. ¹⁴ וְאַשְׁרֶיךָ שֶׁאֵין לָהֶם לִגְמֹל לְךָ, כִּי בִּתְחִיַּת הַצַּדִּיקִים יְשֻׁלַּם לְךָ."

¹⁵ אֶחָד מִן הַמְסֻבִּים שֶׁשָּׁמַע אֶת הַדְּבָרִים הָאֵלֶּה אָמַר אֵלָיו: "אַשְׁרֵי הָאוֹכֵל לֶחֶם בְּמַלְכוּת הָאֱלֹהִים." ¹⁶ הֵשִׁיב לוֹ יֵשׁוּעַ: "אִישׁ אֶחָד עָרַךְ סְעוּדָּה גְּדוֹלָה וְהִזְמִין אֲנָשִׁים רַבִּים. ¹⁷ סָמוּךְ לִשְׁעַת הַסְּעוּדָה שָׁלַח אֶת עַבְדּוֹ לוֹמַר לַמֻזְמָנִים 'בּוֹאוּ, כִּי הַכֹּל כְּבָר מוּכָן.' ¹⁸ אַךְ כֻּלָּם הֵחֵלּוּ לְהִתְנַצֵּל פֶּה אֶחָד. הָרִאשׁוֹן אָמַר: 'קָנִיתִי שָׂדֶה וַאֲנִי חַיָּב לָצֵאת לִרְאוֹתוֹ. אֲנִי מְבַקֵּשׁ מִמְּךָ, קַבֵּל אֶת הִתְנַצְּלוּתִי.' ¹⁹ אַחֵר אָמַר 'קָנִיתִי חֲמִשָּׁה צִמְדֵי שְׁוָרִים וַאֲנִי הוֹלֵךְ לִבְחֹן אוֹתָם. אֲנִי מְבַקֵּשׁ מִמְּךָ, קַבֵּל אֶת הִתְנַצְּלוּתִי.' ²⁰ וְאַחֵר אָמַר 'נָשָׂאתִי אִשָּׁה וְלָכֵן אֵינֶנִּי יָכוֹל לָבוֹא.' ²¹ כְּשֶׁחָזַר הָעֶבֶד וְסִפֵּר לַאֲדוֹנָיו אֶת הַדְּבָרִים הָאֵלֶּה, הִתְכַּעֵס בַּעַל הַבַּיִת וְאָמַר לְעַבְדּוֹ, 'צֵא מַהֵר אֶל רְחוֹבוֹת הָעִיר וְאֶל סִמְטָאוֹתֶיהָ וְהָבֵא הֵנָּה אֶת הָעֲנִיִּים, אֶת

and lanes of the city, and bring in here *the* poor and *the* maimed and *the* lame and *the* blind.' 22 And the servant said, 'Master, it is done as you commanded, and still there is room.' 23 Then the master said to the servant, 'Go out into the highways and hedges, and compel *them* to come in, that my house may be filled. 24 For I say to you that none of those men who were invited shall taste my supper.' "

25 Now great multitudes went with Him. And He turned and said to them, 26 "If anyone comes to Me and does not hate his father and mother, wife and children, brothers and sisters, yes, and his own life also, he cannot be My disciple. 27 And whoever does not bear his cross and come after Me cannot be My disciple. 28 For which of you, intending to build a tower, does not sit down first and count the cost, whether he has *enough* to finish *it*— 29 lest, after he has laid the foundation, and is not able to finish, all who see *it* begin to mock him, 30 saying, 'This man began to build and was not able to finish.' 31 Or what king, going to make war against another king, does not sit down first and consider whether he is able with ten thousand to meet him who comes against him with twenty thousand? 32 Or else, while the other is still a great way off, he sends a delegation and asks conditions of peace. 33 So likewise, whoever of you does not forsake all that he has cannot be My disciple.

34 "Salt *is* good; but if the salt has lost its flavor, how shall it be seasoned? 35 It is neither fit for the land nor for the dunghill, *but* men throw it out. He who has ears to hear, let him hear!"

15 Then all the tax collectors and the sinners drew near to Him to hear Him. 2 And the Pharisees and scribes complained, saying, "This Man receives sinners and eats with them." 3 So He spoke this parable to them, saying:

4 "What man of you, having a hundred sheep, if he loses one of them, does not leave the ninety-nine in the wilderness, and go after the one which is lost until he finds it? 5 And when he has found *it,* he lays *it* on his shoulders, rejoicing. 6 And when he comes home, he calls together *his* friends and neighbors, saying to them, 'Rejoice with me, for I have found my sheep which was lost!' 7 I say to you that likewise there will be more joy in heaven over one sinner who repents than over ninety-nine just persons who need no repentance.

8 "Or what woman, having ten silver coins, if she loses one coin, does not light a lamp, sweep the house, and search carefully until she finds *it?* 9 And when she has found *it,* she calls *her* friends and neighbors together, saying, 'Rejoice with me, for I

בַּעֲלֵי הַמּוּם, אֶת הָעִוְרִים וְהַפִּסְחִים.' 22 אָמַר הָעֶבֶד, 'אֲדוֹנִי, מַה שֶּׁצִּוִּיתָ נַעֲשָׂה וַעֲדַיִן יֵשׁ מָקוֹם.' 23 אָמַר הָאָדוֹן אֶל הָעֶבֶד, 'צֵא אֶל הַדְּרָכִים וְאֶל הַמִּשְׁעוֹלִים וְאַלֵּץ אֲנָשִׁים לְהִכָּנֵס כְּדֵי שֶׁיִּמָּלֵא בֵּיתִי.' 24 אוֹמֵר אֲנִי לָכֶם, אִישׁ מֵאוֹתָם הָאֲנָשִׁים שֶׁהֻזְמְנוּ לֹא יִטְעַם אֶת סְעֻדָּתִי."

25 הֲמוֹן עַם רַב הָלְכוּ אִתּוֹ; פָּנָה אֲלֵיהֶם וְאָמַר: 26 "מִי שֶׁבָּא אֵלַי וְאֵינֶנּוּ שׂוֹנֵא אֶת אָבִיו וְאֶת אִמּוֹ, אֶת אִשְׁתּוֹ וְאֶת בָּנָיו, אֶת אֶחָיו וְאֶת אַחְיוֹתָיו וְאַף אֶת נַפְשׁוֹ שֶׁלּוֹ, אֵינוֹ יָכוֹל לִהְיוֹת תַּלְמִידִי. 27 מִי שֶׁאֵינוֹ נוֹשֵׂא אֶת צְלָבוֹ וְאֵינוֹ בָּא אַחֲרַי אֵינֶנּוּ יָכוֹל לִהְיוֹת תַּלְמִידִי. 28 מִי מִכֶּם, הֶחָפֵץ לִבְנוֹת מִגְדָּל, לֹא יֵשֵׁב תְּחִלָּה וִיחַשֵּׁב אֶת הַהוֹצָאוֹת, לִבְרֹר אִם יֵשׁ לְאֵל יָדוֹ לְהַשְׁלִים אוֹתוֹ? 29 שֶׁהֲרֵי אִם אַחֲרֵי שֶׁהִנִּיחַ יְסוֹד לֹא יוּכַל לְסַיֵּם, כָּל רוֹאָיו יַתְחִילוּ לִלְעֹג לוֹ וְיֹאמְרוּ: 30 'הָאִישׁ הַזֶּה הִתְחִיל לִבְנוֹת וְלֹא הָיָה יָכוֹל לִגְמֹר!' 31 אוֹ אֵיזֶה מֶלֶךְ, הַיּוֹצֵא לַעֲרֹךְ מִלְחָמָה נֶגֶד מֶלֶךְ אַחֵר, לֹא יֵשֵׁב תְּחִלָּה וְיִשְׁקֹל אִם יֵשׁ בִּיכָלְתּוֹ לָצֵאת בַּעֲשֶׂרֶת אֲלָפִים לִקְרַאת הַבָּא עָלָיו בְּעֶשְׂרִים אֶלֶף? 32 אִם לֹא יוּכַל, יִשְׁלַח אֵלָיו מִשְׁלַחַת בְּעוֹדֶנּוּ רָחוֹק וְיִשְׁאַל לִתְנָאֵי שָׁלוֹם. 33 לְפִיכָךְ כָּל אִישׁ מִכֶּם שֶׁאֵינֶנּוּ מְוַתֵּר עַל כָּל רְכוּשׁוֹ אֵינוֹ יָכוֹל לִהְיוֹת תַּלְמִידִי.

34 הַמֶּלַח הוּא טוֹב; אַךְ אִם גַּם לַמֶּלַח תֹּאבַד מְלִיחוּתוֹ, כֵּיצַד תֻּחְזַר לוֹ? 35 אֵין הוּא מוֹעִיל לֹא לָאֲדָמָה וְלֹא לַדֹּמֶן; הַחוּצָה מַשְׁלִיכִים אוֹתוֹ. מִי שֶׁאָזְנַיִם לוֹ לִשְׁמֹעַ, שֶׁיִּשְׁמַע!"

טו כֵּיוָן שֶׁכָּל הַמּוֹכְסִים וְהָאֲנָשִׁים הַחַטָּאִים הִתְקָרְבוּ לִשְׁמֹעַ אוֹתוֹ, 2 הִתְלוֹנְנוּ הַפְּרוּשִׁים וְהַסּוֹפְרִים לֵאמֹר: "הִנֵּה זֶה מְקַבֵּל אֶת הַחוֹטְאִים וְאוֹכֵל בְּחֶבְרָתָם." 3 הִשְׁמִיעַ לָהֶם אֶת הַמָּשָׁל הַזֶּה: 4 "מִי מִכֶּם הָאִישׁ שֶׁיֵּשׁ לוֹ מֵאָה כְּבָשִׂים וּכְשֶׁאוֹבֵד לוֹ אֶחָד מֵהֶם לֹא יַעֲזֹב אֶת הַתִּשְׁעִים וְתִשְׁעָה בַּמִּדְבָּר וְיֵלֵךְ אַחֲרֵי הָאוֹבֵד עַד שֶׁיִּמְצָאֵהוּ? 5 וְכַאֲשֶׁר יִמְצָאֵהוּ יָשִׂים אוֹתוֹ עַל כְּתֵפָיו בְּשִׂמְחָה, 6 וּכְשֶׁיָּבוֹא הַבַּיְתָה יִקְרָא לִידִידָיו וְלִשְׁכֵנָיו וְיֹאמַר, 'שִׂמְחוּ אִתִּי, כִּי מָצָאתִי אֶת הַכֶּבֶשׂ שֶׁלִּי שֶׁאָבַד.' 7 אוֹמֵר אֲנִי לָכֶם, כָּךְ תִּהְיֶה שִׂמְחָה בַּשָּׁמַיִם עַל חוֹטֵא אֶחָד שֶׁחוֹזֵר בִּתְשׁוּבָה, יוֹתֵר מֵאֲשֶׁר עַל תִּשְׁעִים וְתִשְׁעָה צַדִּיקִים שֶׁאֵינָם צְרִיכִים לִתְשׁוּבָה."

8 אוֹ אֵיזוֹ אִשָּׁה, שֶׁיֵּשׁ לָהּ עֲשָׂרָה מַטְבְּעוֹת כֶּסֶף וְאָבַד לָהּ מַטְבֵּעַ אֶחָד, לֹא תַּדְלִיק מְנוֹרָה וּתְטַאטֵא אֶת הַבַּיִת וּתְחַפֵּשׂ הֵיטֵב עַד אֲשֶׁר תִּמְצָאֵהוּ? 9 וְכַאֲשֶׁר תִּמְצָא אוֹתוֹ תִּקְרָא לַחֲבֵרוֹתֶיהָ וְשִׁכְנוֹתֶיהָ

have found the piece which I lost!' ¹⁰Likewise, I say to you, there is joy in the presence of the angels of God over one sinner who repents.''

¹¹Then He said: ''A certain man had two sons. ¹²And the younger of them said to *his* father, 'Father, give me the portion of goods that falls *to me.*' So he divided to them *his* livelihood. ¹³And not many days after, the younger son gathered all together, journeyed to a far country, and there wasted his possessions with prodigal living. ¹⁴But when he had spent all, there arose a severe famine in that land, and he began to be in want. ¹⁵Then he went and joined himself to a citizen of that country, and he sent him into his fields to feed swine. ¹⁶And he would gladly have filled his stomach with the pods that the swine ate, and no one gave him *anything.*

¹⁷''But when he came to himself, he said, 'How many of my father's hired servants have bread enough and to spare, and I perish with hunger! ¹⁸I will arise and go to my father, and will say to him, ''Father, I have sinned against heaven and before you, ¹⁹and I am no longer worthy to be called your son. Make me like one of your hired servants.'' '

²⁰''And he arose and came to his father. But when he was still a great way off, his father saw him and had compassion, and ran and fell on his neck and kissed him. ²¹And the son said to him, 'Father, I have sinned against heaven and in your sight, and am no longer worthy to be called your son.'

²²''But the father said to his servants, 'Bring out the best robe and put *it* on him, and put a ring on his hand and sandals on *his* feet. ²³And bring the fatted calf here and kill *it,* and let us eat and be merry; ²⁴for this my son was dead and is alive again; he was lost and is found.' And they began to be merry.

²⁵''Now his older son was in the field. And as he came and drew near to the house, he heard music and dancing. ²⁶So he called one of the servants and asked what these things meant. ²⁷And he said to him, 'Your brother has come, and because he has received him safe and sound, your father has killed the fatted calf.'

²⁸''But he was angry and would not go in. Therefore his father came out and pleaded with him. ²⁹So he answered and said to *his* father, 'Lo, these many years I have been serving you; I never transgressed your commandment at any time; and yet you never gave me a young goat, that I might make merry with my friends. ³⁰But as soon as this son of yours came, who has devoured your livelihood with harlots, you killed the fatted calf for him.'

וַתֹּאמַר, 'שִׂמְחוּ אִתִּי, כִּי מָצָאתִי אֶת הַמַּטְבֵּעַ שֶׁאָבַד לִי.' ¹⁰אוֹמֵר אֲנִי לָכֶם, כָּךְ יֵשׁ שִׂמְחָה לִפְנֵי מַלְאֲכֵי אֱלֹהִים עַל חוֹטֵא אֶחָד שֶׁחוֹזֵר בִּתְשׁוּבָה.''

¹¹וְעוֹד אָמַר: ''לְאִישׁ אֶחָד הָיוּ שְׁנֵי בָנִים. ¹²אָמַר הַצָּעִיר אֶל אָבִיו: 'אַבָּא, תֵּן לִי אֶת חֵלֶק הָרְכוּשׁ הַמַּגִּיעַ לִי.' וְאָמְנָם חִלֵּק לָהֶם אֲבִיהֶם אֶת הַנְּכָסִים. ¹³לְאַחַר יָמִים לֹא רַבִּים אָסַף הַבֵּן הַצָּעִיר אֶת כָּל אֲשֶׁר לוֹ וְיָצָא אֶל אֶרֶץ רְחוֹקָה וְשָׁם בִּזְבֵּז אֶת רְכוּשׁוֹ בְּחַיֵּי הוֹלְלוּת. ¹⁴אַחֲרֵי שֶׁבִּזְבֵּז אֶת הַכֹּל בָּא רָעָב חָזָק עַל אוֹתָהּ אֶרֶץ וְהוּא הֵחֵל לִסְבֹּל מַחְסוֹר. ¹⁵הָלַךְ לְהִסְתַּפֵּחַ אֶל אֶחָד מִתּוֹשָׁבֵי הָאָרֶץ הַהִיא וְהַלָּה שָׁלַח אוֹתוֹ לִרְעוֹת חֲזִירִים בִּשְׂדוֹתָיו. ¹⁶שָׁם הִשְׁתּוֹקֵק לְמַלֵּא אֶת בִּטְנוֹ בֶּחָרוּבִים שֶׁאָכְלוּ הַחֲזִירִים, אֶלָּא שֶׁאִישׁ לֹא נָתַן לוֹ. ¹⁷כְּשֶׁעָשָׂה חֶשְׁבּוֹן נֶפֶשׁ אָמַר, 'כַּמָּה מְשָׁרְתִים שְׂכִירִים שֶׁל אָבִי יֵשׁ לָהֶם לֶחֶם בְּשֶׁפַע וַאֲנִי גּוֹוֵעַ כָּאן בְּרָעָב! ¹⁸אָקוּם וְאֵלֵךְ אֶל אָבִי וְאֹמַר לוֹ: אַבָּא, חָטָאתִי לַשָּׁמַיִם וּלְךָ. ¹⁹אֵינֶנִּי רָאוּי עוֹד לְהִקָּרֵא בִּנְךָ. שִׂים אוֹתִי כְּאַחַד מִשְׂכִּירֶיךָ.' ²⁰הוּא קָם וְהָלַךְ אֶל אָבִיו. בִּהְיוֹתוֹ עוֹד רָחוֹק רָאָהוּ אָבִיו וְנִכְמְרוּ רַחֲמָיו עָלָיו. הוּא רָץ אֵלָיו וְנָפַל עַל צַוָּארָיו וְנָשַׁק לוֹ. ²¹אָמַר לוֹ הַבֵּן, 'אַבָּא, חָטָאתִי לַשָּׁמַיִם וּלְךָ וְאֵינֶנִּי רָאוּי עוֹד לְהִקָּרֵא בִּנְךָ.' ²²אַךְ הָאָב אָמַר לַעֲבָדָיו, 'הָבִיאוּ מַהֵר אֶת הַגְּלִימָה הַנָּאָה בְּיוֹתֵר וְהַלְבִּישׁוּהוּ, שִׂימוּ טַבַּעַת עַל יָדוֹ וְנַעֲלַיִם לְרַגְלָיו, ²³הָבִיאוּ אֶת הָעֵגֶל הַמְפֻטָּם וְשַׁחֲטוּ אוֹתוֹ וְנֹאכַל וְנִשְׂמַח, ²⁴כִּי בְּנִי זֶה הָיָה מֵת וְהִנֵּה חָזַר לַחַיִּים, אָבַד וְהִנֵּה נִמְצָא.' וְהֵם הֵחֵלּוּ לִשְׂמֹחַ. ²⁵אוֹתָהּ שָׁעָה הָיָה בְּנוֹ הַגָּדוֹל בַּשָּׂדֶה. כְּשֶׁחָזַר וְהִתְקָרֵב הַבַּיְתָה שָׁמַע קוֹל נְגִינוֹת וְרִקּוּדִים. ²⁶הוּא קָרָא לְאַחַד הַנְּעָרִים וְשָׁאַל לָדַעַת מַה הַדָּבָר. ²⁷הֵשִׁיב לוֹ הַנַּעַר, 'אָחִיךָ בָּא, וְאָבִיךָ שָׁחַט אֶת הָעֵגֶל הַמְפֻטָּם מִפְּנֵי שֶׁחָזַר אֵלָיו בָּרִיא וְשָׁלֵם.' ²⁸כָּעַס הַבֵּן הַגָּדוֹל וְלֹא רָצָה לְהִכָּנֵס. אָז יָצָא אָבִיו לְדַבֵּר עַל לִבּוֹ. ²⁹אָמַר הַבֵּן לְאָבִיו, 'הִנֵּה זֶה שָׁנִים רַבּוֹת אֲנִי עוֹבֵד אֶצְלְךָ וּמֵעוֹלָם לֹא עָבַרְתִּי עַל מִצְוָתְךָ, וְאַתָּה מֵעוֹלָם לֹא נָתַתָּ לִי גְּדִי כְּדֵי שֶׁאֶשְׂמַח עִם יְדִידַי. ³⁰אֲבָל כְּשֶׁבָּא בִּנְךָ זֶה אֲשֶׁר בִּזְבֵּז אֶת רְכוּשְׁךָ עִם זוֹנוֹת, שָׁחַטְתָּ בִּשְׁבִילוֹ אֶת הָעֵגֶל

31 "And he said to him, 'Son, you are always with me, and all that I have is yours. 32 It was right that we should make merry and be glad, for your brother was dead and is alive again, and was lost and is found.' "

31 אָמַר הָאָב, 'בְּנִי, אַתָּה תָּמִיד אִתִּי, וְכָל אֲשֶׁר לִי שֶׁלְּךָ הוּא. 32 אֲבָל מִן הָרָאוּי לָשׂוּשׂ וְלִשְׂמֹחַ, כִּי אָחִיךָ זֶה הָיָה מֵת וְהִנֵּה חָזַר לַחַיִּים, אָבַד וְהִנֵּה נִמְצָא.' "

16 He also said to His disciples: "There was a certain rich man who had a steward, and an accusation was brought to him that this man was wasting his goods. 2 So he called him and said to him, 'What is this I hear about you? Give an account of your stewardship, for you can no longer be steward.'

3 "Then the steward said within himself, 'What shall I do? For my master is taking the stewardship away from me. I cannot dig; I am ashamed to beg. 4 I have resolved what to do, that when I am put out of the stewardship, they may receive me into their houses.'

5 "So he called every one of his master's debtors to *him,* and said to the first, 'How much do you owe my master?' 6 And he said, 'A hundred measures of oil.' So he said to him, 'Take your bill, and sit down quickly and write fifty.' 7 Then he said to another, 'And how much do you owe?' So he said, 'A hundred measures of wheat.' And he said to him, 'Take your bill, and write eighty.' 8 So the master commended the unjust steward because he had dealt shrewdly. For the sons of this world are more shrewd in their generation than the sons of light.

9 "And I say to you, make friends for yourselves by unrighteous mammon, that when you fail, they may receive you into an everlasting home. 10 He who *is* faithful in *what is* least is faithful also in much; and he who is unjust in *what is* least is unjust also in much. 11 Therefore if you have not been faithful in the unrighteous mammon, who will commit to your trust the true *riches?* 12 And if you have not been faithful in what is another man's, who will give you what is your own?

13 "No servant can serve two masters; for either he will hate the one and love the other, or else he will be loyal to the one and despise the other. You cannot serve God and mammon."

14 Now the Pharisees, who were lovers of money, also heard all these things, and they derided Him. 15 And He said to them, "You are those who justify yourselves before men, but God knows your hearts. For what is highly esteemed among men is an abomination in the sight of God.

טז הוֹסִיף וְאָמַר גַּם לְתַלְמִידָיו: "לְאִישׁ עָשִׁיר אֶחָד הָיָה סוֹכֵן בַּיִת, וְהִלְשִׁינוּ בְּאָזְנָיו עַל הַסּוֹכֵן שֶׁהוּא מְבַזְבֵּז אֶת נִכְסֵי הָאִישׁ. 2 קָרָא לוֹ וְאָמַר, 'מַה זֶּה שֶׁאֲנִי שׁוֹמֵעַ עָלֶיךָ? מְסֹר דִּין וְחֶשְׁבּוֹן עַל עֲסָקֶיךָ, כִּי לֹא תּוּכַל עוֹד לִהְיוֹת הַסּוֹכֵן שֶׁלִּי.' 3 אָמַר הַסּוֹכֵן בְּלִבּוֹ, 'מָה אֶעֱשֶׂה, שֶׁהֲרֵי אֲדֹנִי לוֹקֵחַ מִמֶּנִּי אֶת מִשְׂרַת הַסּוֹכֵן? אֵין בִּי כֹּחַ לַחְפֹּר, וְלִקְבֹּץ נְדָבוֹת אֲנִי מִתְבַּיֵּשׁ. 4 כֵּן, יוֹדֵעַ אֲנִי מַה לַעֲשׂוֹת כְּדֵי שֶׁאֲנָשִׁים יְקַבְּלוּ אוֹתִי בְּבָתֵּיהֶם כַּאֲשֶׁר אֶפֻּטַּר מִמִּשְׂרָתִי.' 5 הוּא קָרָא אֵלָיו בְּזֶה אַחַר זֶה אֶת בַּעֲלֵי-הַחוֹב שֶׁל אֲדֹנָיו. שָׁאַל אֶת הָרִאשׁוֹן, 'כַּמָּה אַתָּה חַיָּב לַאֲדוֹנִי?' 6 אָמַר הָאִישׁ, 'מֵאָה כַּדֵּים שֶׁמֶן.' אָמַר לוֹ הַסּוֹכֵן, 'קַח אֶת הַשְּׁטָר שֶׁלְּךָ וּמַהֵר וּכְתֹב חֲמִשִּׁים.' 7 לְאַחַר מִכֵּן אָמַר לְאַחֵר, 'כַּמָּה אַתָּה חַיָּב?' הֵשִׁיב בַּעַל-הַחוֹב, 'מֵאָה שַׂקִּים חִטָּה.' אָמַר לוֹ הַסּוֹכֵן, 'קַח אֶת שְׁטָרְךָ וּכְתֹב שְׁמוֹנִים.' 8 שִׁבַּח בַּעַל הַבַּיִת אֶת הַסּוֹכֵן הָרַמַּאי עַל שֶׁפָּעַל בְּפִקְחוּת, שֶׁכֵּן בְּנֵי הָעוֹלָם הַזֶּה פִּקְחִים בְּדוֹרָם יוֹתֵר מִבְּנֵי הָאוֹר."

9 "וְאָנֹכִי אוֹמֵר לָכֶם, הַשִּׂיגוּ לָכֶם יְדִידִים בְּמָמוֹן הַמִּרְמָה כְּדֵי שֶׁכַּאֲשֶׁר הוּא יִכְלֶה הֵם יְקַבְּלוּ אֶתְכֶם לְמִשְׁכְּנוֹת עוֹלָם. 10 מִי שֶׁנֶּאֱמָן בִּמְעַט מִזְעָר נֶאֱמָן גַּם בְּהַרְבֵּה, וּמִי שֶׁאֵינֶנּוּ יָשָׁר בִּמְעַט מִזְעָר גַּם בְּהַרְבֵּה אֵינֶנּוּ יָשָׁר. 11 לָכֵן אִם בְּמָמוֹן הַמִּרְמָה לֹא הֱיִיתֶם נֶאֱמָנִים, מִי יַפְקִיד בְּיֶדְכֶם אֶת הָאֲמִתִּי? 12 וְאִם בְּמַה שֶּׁשַּׁיָּךְ לַזּוּלַת לֹא הֱיִיתֶם נֶאֱמָנִים, מִי יִתֵּן לָכֶם אֶת אֲשֶׁר שַׁיָּךְ לָכֶם? 13 אֵין עֶבֶד יָכוֹל לַעֲבֹד שְׁנֵי אֲדוֹנִים, שֶׁכֵּן אוֹ יִשְׂנָא אֶחָד וְיֹאהַב אֶת הַשֵּׁנִי אוֹ יִהְיֶה מָסוּר לְאֶחָד וְיָזֵל בַּשֵּׁנִי. אֵינְכֶם יְכוֹלִים לַעֲבֹד גַּם אֶת הָאֱלֹהִים וְגַם אֶת הַמָּמוֹן."

14 הַפְּרוּשִׁים שֶׁהָיוּ אוֹהֲבֵי כֶּסֶף שָׁמְעוּ אֶת כָּל הַדְּבָרִים הָאֵלֶּה וְלָעֲגוּ לוֹ. 15 אָמַר לָהֶם: "אַתֶּם – אַתֶּם הָעוֹשִׂים אֶת עַצְמְכֶם צַדִּיקִים לְעֵינֵי הָאֲנָשִׁים! אֲבָל אֱלֹהִים מַכִּיר אֶת לְבַבְכֶם. הֲרֵי מַה שֶּׁמְּרוֹמָם אֵצֶל בְּנֵי אָדָם תּוֹעֵבָה הוּא לִפְנֵי אֱלֹהִים.

16 "The law and the prophets *were* until John. Since that time the kingdom of God has been preached, and everyone is pressing into it. 17 And it is easier for heaven and earth to pass away than for one tittle of the law to fail.

18 "Whoever divorces his wife and marries another commits adultery; and whoever marries her who is divorced from *her* husband commits adultery.

19 "There was a certain rich man who was clothed in purple and fine linen and fared sumptuously every day. 20 But there was a certain beggar named Lazarus, full of sores, who was laid at his gate, 21 desiring to be fed with the crumbs which fell from the rich man's table. Moreover the dogs came and licked his sores. 22 So it was that the beggar died, and was carried by the angels to Abraham's bosom. The rich man also died and was buried. 23 And being in torments in Hades, he lifted up his eyes and saw Abraham afar off, and Lazarus in his bosom.

24 "Then he cried and said, 'Father Abraham, have mercy on me, and send Lazarus that he may dip the tip of his finger in water and cool my tongue; for I am tormented in this flame.' 25 But Abraham said, 'Son, remember that in your lifetime you received your good things, and likewise Lazarus evil things; but now he is comforted and you are tormented. 26 And besides all this, between us and you there is a great gulf fixed, so that those who want to pass from here to you cannot, nor can those from there pass to us.'

27 "Then he said, 'I beg you therefore, father, that you would send him to my father's house, 28 for I have five brothers, that he may testify to them, lest they also come to this place of torment.' 29 Abraham said to him, 'They have Moses and the prophets; let them hear them.' 30 And he said, 'No, father Abraham; but if one goes to them from the dead, they will repent.' 31 But he said to him, 'If they do not hear Moses and the prophets, neither will they be persuaded though one rise from the dead.'"

17 Then He said to the disciples, "It is impossible that no offenses should come, but woe *to him* through whom they do come! 2 It would be better for him if a millstone were hung around his neck, and he were thrown into the sea, than that he should offend one of these little ones. 3 Take heed to yourselves. If your brother sins against you, rebuke him; and if he repents, forgive him. 4 And if he sins against you seven times in a day, and seven times in a day returns to you, saying, 'I repent,' you shall forgive him."

16 עַד יְמֵי יוֹחָנָן – הַתּוֹרָה וְהַנְּבִיאִים; מֵאָז וָהָלְאָה מַלְכוּת הָאֱלֹהִים מִתְבַּשֶּׂרֶת לַבְּרִיּוֹת, וְכָל אֶחָד פּוֹרֵץ אֵלֶיהָ. 17 אֲבָל נָקֵל לַשָּׁמַיִם וְלָאָרֶץ לַחֲלֹף מֵאֲשֶׁר יִפֹּל תָּג אֶחָד מִן הַתּוֹרָה.

18 כָּל הַמְגָרֵשׁ אֶת אִשְׁתּוֹ וְנוֹשֵׂא אַחֶרֶת נוֹאֵף הוּא. וְהַנּוֹשֵׂא אֶת הַמְגֹרֶשֶׁת מִבַּעֲלָהּ נוֹאֵף הוּא."

19 "הָיֹה הָיָה אִישׁ עָשִׁיר שֶׁנָּהַג לִלְבֹּשׁ אַרְגָּמָן וָשֵׁשׁ וְיוֹם יוֹם הִתְעַנֵּג בְּמוֹתָרוֹת. 20 לְיַד שַׁעַר בֵּיתוֹ הֻשְׁכַּב אִישׁ עָנִי אֶחָד, אֶלְעָזָר שְׁמוֹ, שֶׁהָיָה מָלֵא פְּצָעִים 21 וְהִשְׁתּוֹקֵק לִשְׂבֹּעַ מִן הַפֵּרוּרִים הַנּוֹפְלִים מֵעַל שֻׁלְחַן הֶעָשִׁיר, וְהִנֵּה בָּאוּ הַכְּלָבִים וְלִקְקוּ אֶת פְּצָעָיו. 22 הֶעָנִי מֵת וְהַמַּלְאָכִים נְשָׂאוּהוּ אֶל חֵיק אַבְרָהָם, וְגַם הֶעָשִׁיר מֵת וְנִקְבָּר. 23 בַּשְּׁאוֹל, כְּשֶׁהָיָה בְּיִסּוּרִים, נָשָׂא אֶת עֵינָיו וְרָאָה אֶת אַבְרָהָם מֵרָחוֹק וְאֶת אֶלְעָזָר בְּחֵיקוֹ. 24 קָרָא וְאָמַר, 'אָבִי אַבְרָהָם, רַחֵם עָלַי וּשְׁלַח נָא אֶת אֶלְעָזָר שֶׁיִּטְבֹּל אֶת קְצֵה אֶצְבָּעוֹ בְּמַיִם וִיקָרֵר אֶת לְשׁוֹנִי, כִּי סוֹבֵל אֲנִי בִּיקוֹד הַזֶּה.' 25 הֵשִׁיב לוֹ אַבְרָהָם, 'בְּנִי, זְכֹר שֶׁאַתָּה קִבַּלְתָּ אֶת טוּבְךָ בְּחַיֶּיךָ וְאֶלְעָזָר קִבֵּל אֶת הָרָעוֹת. עַכְשָׁו הוּא מְנֻחָם כָּאן וְאַתָּה סוֹבֵל. 26 נוֹסָף עַל כָּל זֶה, תְּהוֹם גְּדוֹלָה נִקְבְּעָה בֵּינֵינוּ לְבֵינֵיכֶם כְּדֵי שֶׁהֶחֲפֵצִים בְּכָךְ לֹא יוּכְלוּ לַעֲבֹר מִפֹּה אֲלֵיכֶם, וּכְדֵי שֶׁלֹּא יַעַבְרוּ מִשָּׁם אֵלֵינוּ.' 27 אָמַר הָאִישׁ, 'אִם כֵּן, אָבִי, אֲנִי מְבַקֵּשׁ מִמְּךָ לִשְׁלֹחַ אוֹתוֹ אֶל בֵּית אָבִי, 28 כִּי חֲמִשָּׁה אַחִים לִי; שֶׁיַּזְהִיר אוֹתָם פֶּן יָבוֹאוּ גַּם הֵם אֶל מְקוֹם הַיִּסּוּרִים הַזֶּה.' 29 הֵשִׁיב לוֹ אַבְרָהָם, 'יֵשׁ לָהֶם מֹשֶׁה וְהַנְּבִיאִים, שֶׁיִּשְׁמְעוּ בְּקוֹלָם.' 30 אָמַר הָאִישׁ, 'לֹא, אָבִי אַבְרָהָם; אִם יֵלֵךְ אֲלֵיהֶם אֶחָד מִן הַמֵּתִים, יַחְזְרוּ בִּתְשׁוּבָה.' 31 אָמַר לוֹ אַבְרָהָם, 'אִם אֵינָם שׁוֹמְעִים אֶל מֹשֶׁה וְאֶל הַנְּבִיאִים, לֹא יִשְׁתַּכְנְעוּ גַּם אִם יָקוּם אֶחָד מֵעִם הַמֵּתִים'."

יז בְּדַבְּרוֹ אֶל תַּלְמִידָיו אָמַר: "אִי אֶפְשָׁר שֶׁלֹּא יָבוֹאוּ הַמִּכְשׁוֹלִים, אֲבָל אוֹי לָאִישׁ אֲשֶׁר דַּרְכּוֹ יָבוֹאוּ. 2 מוּטָב לוֹ שֶׁתִּתָּלֶה אֶבֶן רֵחַיִם עַל צַוָּארוֹ וְיֻשְׁלַךְ לְתוֹךְ הַיָּם מֵאֲשֶׁר יַכְשִׁיל אֶחָד מֵהַקְּטַנִּים הָאֵלֶּה. 3 הִשָּׁמְרוּ לָכֶם. אִם יֶחֱטָא אָחִיךָ הוֹכֵחַ אוֹתוֹ, וְאִם יִתְחָרֵט סְלַח לוֹ. 4 וְגַם אִם שֶׁבַע פְּעָמִים בַּיּוֹם יֶחֱטָא לְךָ וְשֶׁבַע פְּעָמִים יִפְנֶה אֵלֶיךָ לֵאמֹר, 'אֲנִי מִתְחָרֵט' – סְלַח לוֹ."

⁵And the apostles said to the Lord, "Increase our faith."

⁶So the Lord said, "If you have faith as a mustard seed, you can say to this mulberry tree, 'Be pulled up by the roots and be planted in the sea,' and it would obey you. ⁷And which of you, having a servant plowing or tending sheep, will say to him when he has come in from the field, 'Come at once and sit down to eat'? ⁸But will he not rather say to him, 'Prepare something for my supper, and gird yourself and serve me till I have eaten and drunk, and afterward you will eat and drink'? ⁹Does he thank that servant because he did the things that were commanded him? I think not. ¹⁰So likewise you, when you have done all those things which you are commanded, say, 'We are unprofitable servants. We have done what was our duty to do.'"

¹¹Now it happened as He went to Jerusalem that He passed through the midst of Samaria and Galilee. ¹²Then as He entered a certain village, there met Him ten men who were lepers, who stood afar off. ¹³And they lifted up *their* voices and said, "Jesus, Master, have mercy on us!"

¹⁴So when He saw *them*, He said to them, "Go, show yourselves to the priests." And so it was that as they went, they were cleansed.

¹⁵And one of them, when he saw that he was healed, returned, and with a loud voice glorified God, ¹⁶and fell down on *his* face at His feet, giving Him thanks. And he was a Samaritan.

¹⁷So Jesus answered and said, "Were there not ten cleansed? But where *are* the nine? ¹⁸Were there not any found who returned to give glory to God except this foreigner?" ¹⁹And He said to him, "Arise, go your way. Your faith has made you well."

²⁰Now when He was asked by the Pharisees when the kingdom of God would come, He answered them and said, "The kingdom of God does not come with observation; ²¹nor will they say, 'See here!' or 'See there!' For indeed, the kingdom of God is within you."

²²Then He said to the disciples, "The days will come when you will desire to see one of the days of the Son of Man, and you will not see *it*. ²³And they will say to you, 'Look here!' or 'Look there!' Do not go after *them* or follow *them*. ²⁴For as the lightning that flashes out of one *part* under heaven shines to the other *part* under heaven, so also the Son of Man will be in His day. ²⁵But first He must suffer many things and be rejected by this generation. ²⁶And as it was in the days of Noah, so it will be also in the days of the Son of Man: ²⁷They ate, they drank, they married wives, they were given in marriage,

⁵אָמְרוּ הַשְּׁלִיחִים לָאָדוֹן: "הוֹסֵף לָנוּ אֱמוּנָה." ⁶הֵשִׁיב הָאָדוֹן: "לוּ הָיְתָה לָכֶם אֱמוּנָה כְּגַרְגִּיר הַחַרְדָּל וַאֲמַרְתֶּם אֶל הַשִּׁקְמָה הַזֹּאת 'הֵעָקְרִי וְהִנָּטְעִי בַּיָּם!' – הִיא הָיְתָה נִשְׁמַעַת לָכֶם." ⁷"מִי מִכֶּם, שֶׁיֵּשׁ לוֹ עֶבֶד חוֹרֵשׁ אוֹ רוֹעֶה, יֹאמַר לָעֶבֶד לְאַחַר שׁוּבוֹ מִן הַשָּׂדֶה, 'בּוֹא הִנֵּה מִיָּד וְהָסֵב אֶל הַשֻּׁלְחָן'? ⁸הַאִם לֹא יֹאמַר לוֹ, 'הָכֵן לִי אֲרוּחַת עֶרֶב, חֲגֹר מָתְנֶיךָ וְשָׁרְתֵנִי עַד שֶׁאֶגְמֹר לֶאֱכֹל וְלִשְׁתּוֹת. אַחֲרֵי כֵן תֹּאכַל וְתִשְׁתֶּה אַתָּה'? ⁹הַאִם יִהְיֶה אָסִיר תּוֹדָה לָעֶבֶד עַל שֶׁעָשָׂה אֶת אֲשֶׁר צֻוָּה? ¹⁰כֵּן גַּם אַתֶּם, לְאַחַר עֲשׂוֹתְכֶם אֶת כָּל שֶׁצֻּוֵּיתֶם, אָמְרוּ: 'עֲבָדִים אֲנַחְנוּ וְתוּ לֹא, עָשִׂינוּ מַה שֶּׁמְּחוּבָתֵנוּ לַעֲשׂוֹת'." ¹¹בְּלֶכְתּוֹ לִירוּשָׁלַיִם עָבַר בְּשׁוֹמְרוֹן וּבַגָּלִיל. ¹²כְּשֶׁנִּכְנַס לִכְפָר אֶחָד בָּאוּ לִקְרָאתוֹ עֲשָׂרָה אֲנָשִׁים מְצֹרָעִים. הֵם נֶעֶמְדוּ מֵרָחוֹק ¹³וְקָרְאוּ בְּקוֹל רָם: "יֵשׁוּעַ אֲדוֹנֵנוּ, רַחֵם נָא עָלֵינוּ!" ¹⁴כִּרְאוֹתוֹ אוֹתָם אָמַר לָהֶם: "לְכוּ וְהֵרָאוּ אֶל הַכֹּהֲנִים." הֵם הָלְכוּ וּבִהְיוֹתָם בַּדֶּרֶךְ נִטְהָרוּ. ¹⁵אֶחָד מֵהֶם, כַּאֲשֶׁר רָאָה כִּי נִרְפָּא, חָזַר כְּשֶׁהוּא מְהַלֵּל אֶת אֱלֹהִים בְּקוֹל גָּדוֹל, ¹⁶נָפַל עַל פָּנָיו לְרַגְלֵי יֵשׁוּעַ וְהוֹדָה לוֹ. אוֹתוֹ הָאִישׁ הָיָה שׁוֹמְרוֹנִי. ¹⁷הֵשִׁיב יֵשׁוּעַ וְאָמַר: "הֲלֹא טֹהֲרוּ הָעֲשָׂרָה, וְהֵיכָן הַתִּשְׁעָה? ¹⁸כְּלוּם לֹא נִמְצָא מִי שֶׁיָּשׁוּב לָתֵת כָּבוֹד לֵאלֹהִים זוּלָתִי בֶּן־נֵכָר זֶה?" ¹⁹וְאֵלָיו אָמַר: "קוּם וְלֵךְ. אֱמוּנָתְךָ הוֹשִׁיעָה אוֹתְךָ." ²⁰כַּאֲשֶׁר שְׁאָלוּהוּ הַפְּרוּשִׁים מָתַי תָּבוֹא מַלְכוּת אֱלֹהִים הֵשִׁיב לָהֶם: "מַלְכוּת אֱלֹהִים אֵינֶנָּה בָּאָה בְּנִגְלוֹת. ²¹אַף לֹא יֹאמְרוּ 'הִנֵּה פֹּה' אוֹ 'הִנֵּה שָׁם הִיא', כִּי הִנֵּה מַלְכוּת אֱלֹהִים בְּקִרְבְּכֶם הִיא." ²²אָמַר לְתַלְמִידָיו: "יָבוֹאוּ יָמִים וְתִשְׁתּוֹקְקוּ לִרְאוֹת יוֹם אֶחָד מִימוֹת בֶּן־הָאָדָם וְלֹא תִּרְאוּ. ²³וְיֹאמְרוּ לָכֶם 'הִנֵּה שָׁם' אוֹ 'הִנֵּה פֹּה'! אַל תֵּלְכוּ וְאַל תָּרוּצוּ אַחֲרֵיהֶם. ²⁴כִּי כְּבָרָק הַמַּבְרִיק תַּחַת הַשָּׁמַיִם וּמֵאִיר עַד קְצֵה הַשָּׁמַיִם, כֵּן יִהְיֶה בֶּן־הָאָדָם בְּיוֹמוֹ. ²⁵אַךְ תְּחִלָּה עָלָיו לִסְבֹּל רַבּוֹת וּלְהִדָּחוֹת עַל־יְדֵי הַדּוֹר הַזֶּה. ²⁶וּכְמוֹ שֶׁהָיָה בִּימֵי נֹחַ כֵּן יִהְיֶה גַּם בִּימֵי בֶּן־הָאָדָם: ²⁷אָכְלוּ, שָׁתוּ, הִתְחַתְּנוּ, עַד הַיּוֹם שֶׁנִּכְנַס

until the day that Noah entered the ark, and the flood came and destroyed them all. 28 Likewise as it was also in the days of Lot: They ate, they drank, they bought, they sold, they planted, they built; 29 but on the day that Lot went out of Sodom it rained fire and brimstone from heaven and destroyed *them* all. 30 Even so will it be in the day when the Son of Man is revealed.

31 "In that day, he who is on the housetop, and his goods *are* in the house, let him not come down to take them away. And likewise the one who is in the field, let him not turn back. 32 Remember Lot's wife. 33 Whoever seeks to save his life will lose it, and whoever loses his life will preserve it. 34 I tell you, in that night there will be two *men* in one bed: the one will be taken and the other will be left. 35 Two *women* will be grinding together: the one will be taken and the other left. 36 Two *men* will be in the field: the one will be taken and the other left."

37 And they answered and said to Him, "Where, Lord?"

So He said to them, "Wherever the body is, there the eagles will be gathered together."

18 Then He spoke a parable to them, that men always ought to pray and not lose heart, 2 saying: "There was in a certain city a judge who did not fear God nor regard man. 3 Now there was a widow in that city; and she came to him, saying, 'Get justice for me from my adversary.' 4 And he would not for a while; but afterward he said within himself, 'Though I do not fear God nor regard man, 5 yet because this widow troubles me I will avenge her, lest by her continual coming she weary me.' "

6 Then the Lord said, "Hear what the unjust judge said. 7 And shall God not avenge His own elect who cry out day and night to Him, though He bears long with them? 8 I tell you that He will avenge them speedily. Nevertheless, when the Son of Man comes, will He really find faith on the earth?"

9 Also He spoke this parable to some who trusted in themselves that they were righteous, and despised others: 10 "Two men went up to the temple to pray, one a Pharisee and the other a tax collector. 11 The Pharisee stood and prayed thus with himself, 'God, I thank You that I am not like other men—extortioners, unjust, adulterers, or even as this tax collector. 12 I fast twice a week; I give tithes of all that I possess.' 13 And the tax collector, standing afar off, would not so much as raise *his* eyes to heaven, but beat his breast, saying, 'God, be merciful to me a sinner!' 14 I tell you, this man went

נֹחַ לַתֵּבָה וּבָא הַמַּבּוּל וְהִשְׁמִיד אֶת הַכֹּל. 28 וּכְמוֹ שֶׁהָיָה בִּימֵי לוֹט – אָכְלוּ וְשָׁתוּ, קָנוּ וּמָכְרוּ, נָטְעוּ וּבָנוּ, 29 אַךְ בַּיּוֹם שֶׁיָּצָא לוֹט מִסְּדוֹם הִמְטִירוּ אֵשׁ וְגָפְרִית מִן הַשָּׁמַיִם וְהִשְׁמִידוּ אֶת הַכֹּל. 30 כָּךְ יִהְיֶה בַּיּוֹם שֶׁיִּתְגַּלֶּה בֶּן־הָאָדָם. 31 מִי שֶׁיִּהְיֶה בַּיּוֹם הַהוּא עַל הַגַּג וַחֲפָצָיו בַּבַּיִת אַל יֵרֵד לָקַחַת אוֹתָם; כְּמוֹ כֵן מִי שֶׁבַּשָּׂדֶה אַל יִפְנֶה לְאָחוֹר. 32 זִכְרוּ אֶת אֵשֶׁת לוֹט. 33 הַמְבַקֵּשׁ לְהַצִּיל אֶת נַפְשׁוֹ יְאַבְּדֶנָּה, וּמִי שֶׁיְּאַבֵּד אוֹתָהּ יַצִּילֶנָּה. 34 אוֹמֵר אֲנִי לָכֶם, בַּלַּיְלָה הַהוּא יִהְיוּ שְׁנַיִם בְּמִטָּה אַחַת; אֶחָד יִלָּקַח וְהַשֵּׁנִי יֵעָזֵב. 35 שְׁתֵּי נָשִׁים תִּהְיֶינָה טוֹחֲנוֹת יַחְדָּיו; אַחַת תִּלָּקַח וְהַשְּׁנִיָּה תֵּעָזֵב.

37 הֵם הֵגִיבוּ וְשָׁאֲלוּ אוֹתוֹ: "אֵיפֹה, אֲדוֹנֵנוּ?" הֵשִׁיב לָהֶם: "הֵיכָן שֶׁהַגּוּף, שָׁם גַּם יִתְקַבְּצוּ הַנְּשָׁרִים."

יח הוּא סִפֵּר לָהֶם מָשָׁל, לְהַרְאוֹת כִּי עֲלֵיהֶם לְהִתְפַּלֵּל תָּמִיד וְלֹא לִרְפּוֹת." 2 שׁוֹפֵט הָיָה בְּעִיר אַחַת; אֶת אֱלֹהִים לֹא יָרֵא וּבְאָדָם לֹא הִתְחַשֵּׁב. 3 וּבְאוֹתָהּ עִיר הָיְתָה אַלְמָנָה שֶׁבָּאָה לָבוֹא אֵלָיו וְלוֹמַר, "שְׁפָטְנִי נָא מֵאִישׁ רִיבִי.' 4 זְמַן מָה סֵרֵב, אֲבָל אַחֲרֵי כֵן אָמַר בְּלִבּוֹ, 'אַף שֶׁאֵינֶנִּי יָרֵא אֶת אֱלֹהִים וּבְאָדָם אֵינֶנִּי מִתְחַשֵּׁב, 5 הֲרֵי מִפְּנֵי שֶׁהָאַלְמָנָה הַזֹּאת מְצִיקָה לִי אֶעֱשֶׂה אֶת מִשְׁפָּטָהּ, שֶׁאִם לֹא כֵן תָּבוֹא תָּמִיד וּתְיַגֵּעַ אוֹתִי."

6 הוֹסִיף הָאָדוֹן וְאָמַר: "שִׁמְעוּ מַה שֶּׁאוֹמֵר הַשּׁוֹפֵט הָרָשָׁע. 7 וְהָאֱלֹהִים, הַאִם לֹא יַעֲשֶׂה אֶת מִשְׁפַּט בְּחִירָיו הַקּוֹרְאִים אֵלָיו יוֹמָם וָלַיְלָה? הַאִם יִתְמַהְמֵהַּ בְּעִנְיָנָם? 8 אֲנִי אוֹמֵר לָכֶם שֶׁיַּעֲשֶׂה אֶת מִשְׁפָּטָם מַהֵר. אַךְ כַּאֲשֶׁר יָבוֹא בֶּן־הָאָדָם, הֲיִמְצָא אֶת הָאֱמוּנָה עֲלֵי אֲדָמוֹת?"

9 וּלְכַמָּה אֲנָשִׁים, שֶׁבָּטְחוּ בְּעַצְמָם כִּי צַדִּיקִים הֵם וּבָזוּ לָאֲחֵרִים, סִפֵּר אֶת הַמָּשָׁל הַזֶּה: 10 "שְׁנֵי אֲנָשִׁים עָלוּ אֶל בֵּית הַמִּקְדָּשׁ לְהִתְפַּלֵּל; אֶחָד פָּרוּשׁ וְהַשֵּׁנִי מוֹכֵס. 11 עָמַד הַפָּרוּשׁ לְבַדּוֹ וְהִתְפַּלֵּל, 'אֱלֹהִים, אֲנִי מוֹדֶה לְךָ שֶׁאֵינֶנִּי כִּשְׁאָר הָאֲנָשִׁים – גַּזְלָנִים, רְשָׁעִים, נוֹאֲפִים, וְאַף לֹא כַּמּוֹכֵס הַזֶּה. 12 אֲנִי צָם פַּעֲמַיִם בַּשָּׁבוּעַ, אֲנִי נוֹתֵן מַעֲשֵׂר מִכָּל מַה שֶּׁאֲנִי מַרְוִיחַ.' 13 וְאִלּוּ הַמּוֹכֵס, שֶׁעָמַד מֵרָחוֹק, אַף לֹא רָצָה לָשֵׂאת אֶת עֵינָיו לַשָּׁמַיִם, אֶלָּא טָפַח עַל לִבּוֹ וְאָמַר, 'אֱלֹהִים, רַחֵם נָא עָלַי, עַל אִישׁ חוֹטֵא.' 14 אוֹמֵר אֲנִי לָכֶם, הָאִישׁ הַזֶּה יָרַד אֶל בֵּיתוֹ נִצְדָּק

down to his house justified *rather* than the other; for everyone who exalts himself will be humbled, and he who humbles himself will be exalted."

15 Then they also brought infants to Him that He might touch them; but when the disciples saw *it*, they rebuked them. 16 But Jesus called them to *Him* and said, "Let the little children come to Me, and do not forbid them; for of such is the kingdom of God. 17 Assuredly, I say to you, whoever does not receive the kingdom of God as a little child will by no means enter it."

18 Now a certain ruler asked Him, saying, "Good Teacher, what shall I do to inherit eternal life?"

19 So Jesus said to him, "Why do you call Me good? No one *is* good but One, *that is,* God. 20 You know the commandments: 'Do not commit adultery,' 'Do not murder,' 'Do not steal,' 'Do not bear false witness,' 'Honor your father and your mother.'"

21 And he said, "All these things I have kept from my youth."

22 So when Jesus heard these things, He said to him, "You still lack one thing. Sell all that you have and distribute to the poor, and you will have treasure in heaven; and come, follow Me."

23 But when he heard this, he became very sorrowful, for he was very rich.

24 And when Jesus saw that he became very sorrowful, He said, "How hard it is for those who have riches to enter the kingdom of God! 25 For it is easier for a camel to go through the eye of a needle than for a rich man to enter the kingdom of God."

26 And those who heard it said, "Who then can be saved?"

27 But He said, "The things which are impossible with men are possible with God."

28 Then Peter said, "See, we have left all and followed You."

29 So He said to them, "Assuredly, I say to you, there is no one who has left house or parents or brothers or wife or children, for the sake of the kingdom of God, 30 who shall not receive many times more in this present time, and in the age to come eternal life."

31 Then He took the twelve aside and said to them, "Behold, we are going up to Jerusalem, and all things that are written by the prophets concerning the Son of Man will be accomplished. 32 For He will be delivered to the Gentiles and will be mocked and insulted and spit upon. 33 They will scourge *Him* and kill Him. And the third day He will rise again."

יוֹתֵר מֵהָאִישׁ הַהוּא; כִּי כָּל הַמְרוֹמֵם אֶת עַצְמוֹ יִשָּׁפֵל, וְהַמַּשְׁפִּיל אֶת עַצְמוֹ יְרוֹמַם." 15 הֵבִיאוּ אֵלָיו גַּם אֶת הַיְלָדִים הַקְּטַנִּים כְּדֵי שֶׁיִּגַּע בָּהֶם. כְּשֶׁרָאוּ זֹאת הַתַּלְמִידִים גָּעֲרוּ בָהֶם. 16 אוּלָם יֵשׁוּעַ קָרָא אֵלָיו אֶת הַיְלָדִים וְאָמַר: "הַנִּיחוּ לַיְלָדִים לָבוֹא אֵלַי וְאַל תִּמְנָעוּ בַּעֲדָם, כִּי לְכָאֵלֶּה מַלְכוּת הָאֱלֹהִים. 17 אָמֵן. אוֹמֵר אֲנִי לָכֶם, כָּל מִי שֶׁאֵינֶנּוּ מְקַבֵּל אֶת מַלְכוּת הָאֱלֹהִים כְּיֶלֶד לֹא יָבֹא לְתוֹכָהּ."

18 נִכְבָּד אֶחָד פָּנָה אֵלָיו וְשָׁאַל: "רַבִּי הַטּוֹב, מֶה עָלַי לַעֲשׂוֹת כְּדֵי לָרֶשֶׁת חַיֵּי עוֹלָם?"

19 אָמַר לוֹ יֵשׁוּעַ: "מַדּוּעַ אַתָּה אוֹמֵר לִי 'טוֹב'? אֵין טוֹב כִּי אִם אֶחָד וְהוּא הָאֱלֹהִים. 20 אֶת הַמִּצְווֹת אַתָּה יוֹדֵעַ: 'לֹא תִנְאַף, לֹא תִרְצַח, לֹא תִגְנֹב, לֹא תַעֲנֶה בְרֵעֲךָ עֵד שָׁקֶר, כַּבֵּד אֶת אָבִיךָ וְאֶת אִמֶּךָ'."

21 הֵשִׁיב הָאִישׁ: "אֶת כָּל אֵלֶּה שָׁמַרְתִּי מִנְּעוּרָי."

22 שָׁמַע יֵשׁוּעַ וְאָמַר: "עוֹד דָּבָר אֶחָד חָסֵר לְךָ. מְכֹר אֶת כָּל אֲשֶׁר לְךָ וְחַלֵּק לָעֲנִיִּים, וְיִהְיֶה לְךָ אוֹצָר בַּשָּׁמַיִם; אַחַר כָּךְ בּוֹא וְלֵךְ אַחֲרַי." 23 אַךְ כְּשָׁמְעוֹ זֹאת הִתְעַצֵּב עֶצֶב רַב, כִּי עָשִׁיר הָיָה עַד מְאֹד.

24 כְּשֶׁרָאָה יֵשׁוּעַ כִּי הִתְעַצֵּב, אָמַר: "בְּאֵיזֶה קֹשִׁי נִכְנָסִים בַּעֲלֵי נְכָסִים לְמַלְכוּת הָאֱלֹהִים! 25 נָקֵל לְגָמָל לַעֲבֹר דֶּרֶךְ נֶקֶב מַחַט מֵהִכָּנֵס עָשִׁיר אֶל מַלְכוּת הָאֱלֹהִים."

26 שָׁאֲלוּ הַשּׁוֹמְעִים: "וּמִי יָכוֹל לְהִוָּשַׁע?" 27 עָנָה יֵשׁוּעַ וְאָמַר: "מַה שֶּׁנִּבְצָר מִבְּנֵי אָדָם הוּא בִּיכָלְתּוֹ שֶׁל אֱלֹהִים."

28 אָמַר כֵּיפָא: "הֵן אֲנַחְנוּ עָזַבְנוּ אֶת אֲשֶׁר לָנוּ וְהָלַכְנוּ אַחֲרֶיךָ."

29 הֵשִׁיב לָהֶם יֵשׁוּעַ: "אָמֵן. אוֹמֵר אֲנִי לָכֶם, אֵין אִישׁ אֲשֶׁר עָזַב בַּיִת אוֹ אִשָּׁה אוֹ אַחִים אוֹ הוֹרִים אוֹ יְלָדִים לְמַעַן מַלְכוּת הָאֱלֹהִים – 30 שֶׁלֹּא יְקַבֵּל כֶּפֶל כִּפְלַיִם בַּזְּמַן הַזֶּה, וְחַיֵּי עוֹלָם בָּעוֹלָם הַבָּא."

31 הוּא לָקַח אִתּוֹ אֶת הַשְּׁנֵים־עָשָׂר וְאָמַר לָהֶם: "הִנֵּה אֲנַחְנוּ עוֹלִים לִירוּשָׁלַיִם וְכָל מַה שֶּׁנִּכְתַּב בִּידֵי הַנְּבִיאִים עַל בֶּן־הָאָדָם יִתָּקְנַים; 32 הוּא יִמָּסֵר לַגּוֹיִים וְהֵם יִתְהַתְּלוּ בּוֹ, גַּם יִתְעַלְּלוּ בוֹ וְיִרְקוּ עָלָיו, 33 וּלְאַחַר

34 But they understood none of these things; this saying was hidden from them, and they did not know the things which were spoken.

35 Then it happened, as He was coming near Jericho, that a certain blind man sat by the road begging. 36 And hearing a multitude passing by, he asked what it meant. 37 So they told him that Jesus of Nazareth was passing by. 38 And he cried out, saying, "Jesus, Son of David, have mercy on me!"

39 Then those who went before warned him that he should be quiet; but he cried out all the more, "Son of David, have mercy on me!"

40 So Jesus stood still and commanded him to be brought to Him. And when he had come near, He asked him, 41 saying, "What do you want Me to do for you?"

He said, "Lord, that I may receive my sight."

42 Then Jesus said to him, "Receive your sight; your faith has made you well." 43 And immediately he received his sight, and followed Him, glorifying God. And all the people, when they saw it, gave praise to God.

19 Then Jesus entered and passed through Jericho. 2 Now behold, there was a man named Zacchaeus who was a chief tax collector, and he was rich. 3 And he sought to see who Jesus was, but could not because of the crowd, for he was of short stature. 4 So he ran ahead and climbed up into a sycamore tree to see Him, for He was going to pass that way. 5 And when Jesus came to the place, He looked up and saw him, and said to him, "Zacchaeus, make haste and come down, for today I must stay at your house." 6 So he made haste and came down, and received Him joyfully. 7 But when they saw it, they all complained, saying, "He has gone to be a guest with a man who is a sinner."

8 Then Zacchaeus stood and said to the Lord, "Look, Lord, I give half of my goods to the poor; and if I have taken anything from anyone by false accusation, I restore fourfold."

9 And Jesus said to him, "Today salvation has come to this house, because he also is a son of Abraham; 10 for the Son of Man has come to seek and to save that which was lost."

11 Now as they heard these things, He spoke another parable, because He was near Jerusalem and because they thought the kingdom of God would appear immediately. 12 Therefore He said: "A certain nobleman went into a far country to receive for himself a kingdom and to return. 13 So he called ten of his servants, delivered to them ten minas, and said to them, 'Do business till I come.'

34 אֲבָל הֵם לֹא הֵבִינוּ דָּבָר מִן הַדְּבָרִים הָאֵלֶּה; הַמִּלִּים הָאֵלֶּה נִסְתְּרוּ מֵהֶם וְהֵם לֹא יָדְעוּ בַּמֶּה מְדֻבָּר. 35 הוּא הִתְקָרֵב אֶל יְרִיחוֹ, וּבְאוֹתָהּ עֵת הָיָה אִישׁ עִוֵּר יוֹשֵׁב עַל־יַד הַדֶּרֶךְ וּמְבַקֵּשׁ נְדָבוֹת. 36 כְּשֶׁשָּׁמַע הָעִוֵּר אֶת הָעָם עוֹבְרִים שָׁאַל לָדַעַת מָה הַדָּבָר. 37 הֵשִׁיבוּ לוֹ: "יֵשׁוּעַ מִנָּצְרַת עוֹבֵר." 38 אָז הֵחֵל לִצְעֹק: "יֵשׁוּעַ בֶּן־דָּוִד, רַחֵם עָלַי!" 39 הַהוֹלְכִים לְפָנָיו גָּעֲרוּ בּוֹ לְהַשְׁתִּיקוֹ, אַךְ הוּא הִרְבָּה עוֹד יוֹתֵר לִצְעֹק, "בֶּן־דָּוִד, רַחֵם עָלַי!" 40 יֵשׁוּעַ נֶעֱצַר וְצִוָּה לַהֲבִיאוֹ אֵלָיו. כַּאֲשֶׁר הִתְקָרֵב שָׁאַל אוֹתוֹ: 41 "מָה אַתָּה רוֹצֶה שֶׁאֶעֱשֶׂה לְּךָ?" הֵשִׁיב: "אֲדוֹנִי, שֶׁאֶרְאֶה". 42 אָמַר לוֹ יֵשׁוּעַ: "רְאֵה! אֱמוּנָתְךָ הוֹשִׁיעָה אוֹתְךָ." 43 מִיָּד רָאָה וְהָלַךְ אַחֲרָיו כְּשֶׁהוּא מְשַׁבֵּחַ אֶת אֱלֹהִים, וְכָל הָעָם כִּרְאוֹתָם זֹאת הוֹדוּ לֵאלֹהִים.

יט הוּא נִכְנַס לִירִיחוֹ וְעָבַר בָּהּ. 2 וְאִישׁ אֶחָד, זַכַּי שְׁמוֹ, שֶׁהָיָה מוֹכֵס רָאשִׁי וְאִישׁ עָשִׁיר, 3 הִשְׁתַּדֵּל לִרְאוֹת מִי הוּא יֵשׁוּעַ וְלֹא יָכוֹל בִּגְלַל הֶהָמוֹן, שֶׁכֵּן הָיָה נְמוּךְ קוֹמָה. 4 הוּא רָץ הָלְאָה לְפָנִים וְעָלָה עַל עֵץ שִׁקְמָה כְּדֵי לִרְאוֹת אוֹתוֹ, כִּי בְּאוֹתָהּ דֶּרֶךְ עָמַד יֵשׁוּעַ לַעֲבֹר. 5 כַּאֲשֶׁר הִגִּיעַ יֵשׁוּעַ לַמָּקוֹם, הִבִּיט לְמַעְלָה וְאָמַר לוֹ: "זַכַּי, רֵד מַהֵר, כִּי הַיּוֹם עָלַי לָשֶׁבֶת בְּבֵיתְךָ." 6 הוּא יָרַד מַהֵר וְקִבֵּל אוֹתוֹ לְבֵיתוֹ בְּשִׂמְחָה.

7 כְּשֶׁרָאוּ זֹאת הִתְלוֹנְנוּ הַכֹּל וְאָמְרוּ: "אֵצֶל אִישׁ חוֹטֵא הוּא בָּא לְהִתְאָרֵחַ!" 8 עָמַד זַכַּי וְאָמַר אֶל הָאָדוֹן: "אֲדוֹנִי, הֲרֵינִי נוֹתֵן אֶת מַחֲצִית נְכָסַי לָעֲנִיִּים, וְאִם עָשַׁקְתִּי אִישׁ אַחֲזִיר לוֹ אַרְבַּעְתַּיִם." 9 אָמַר לוֹ יֵשׁוּעַ: "הַיּוֹם הָיְתָה תְּשׁוּעָה לַבַּיִת הַזֶּה, כִּי הָאִישׁ גַּם הוּא בֶּן־אַבְרָהָם. 10 הֵן בֶּן־הָאָדָם בָּא לְבַקֵּשׁ אֶת הָאוֹבֵד וּלְהוֹשִׁיעוֹ."

11 לְאַחַר שֶׁשָּׁמְעוּ אֶת זֹאת הוֹסִיף וְסִפֵּר מָשָׁל, מִשּׁוּם שֶׁהָיָה קָרוֹב לִירוּשָׁלַיִם וְהֵם חָשְׁבוּ כִּי מִיָּד תִּגָּלֶה מַלְכוּת הָאֱלֹהִים. 12 לְפִיכָךְ אָמַר: "אִישׁ אָצִיל אֶחָד הָלַךְ אֶל אֶרֶץ רְחוֹקָה לְקַבֵּל סַמְכוּת לִמְלוּכָה וְלָשׁוּב לְאַרְצוֹ. 13 קָדַם לָכֵן קָרָא לַעֲשֶׂרֶת עֲבָדָיו, נָתַן לָהֶם עֲשָׂרָה מָנִים וְאָמַר לָהֶם, 'סַחֲרוּ עַד בּוֹאִי'.

14 But his citizens hated him, and sent a delegation after him, saying, 'We will not have this *man* to reign over us.'

15 "And so it was that when he returned, having received the kingdom, he then commanded these servants, to whom he had given the money, to be called to him, that he might know how much every man had gained by trading. 16 Then came the first, saying, 'Master, your mina has earned ten minas.' 17 And he said to him, 'Well *done*, good servant; because you were faithful in a very little, have authority over ten cities.' 18 And the second came, saying, 'Master, your mina has earned five minas.' 19 Likewise he said to him, 'You also be over five cities.'

20 "Then another came, saying, 'Master, here is your mina, which I have kept put away in a handkerchief. 21 For I feared you, because you are an austere man. You collect what you did not deposit, and reap what you did not sow.' 22 And he said to him, 'Out of your own mouth I will judge you, *you* wicked servant. You knew that I was an austere man, collecting what I did not deposit and reaping what I did not sow. 23 Why then did you not put my money in the bank, that at my coming I might have collected it with interest?'

24 "And he said to those who stood by, 'Take the mina from him, and give *it* to him who has ten minas.' 25 (But they said to him, 'Master, he has ten minas.') 26 'For I say to you, that to everyone who has will be given; and from him who does not have, even what he has will be taken away from him. 27 But bring here those enemies of mine, who did not want me to reign over them, and slay *them* before me.'"

28 When He had said this, He went on ahead, going up to Jerusalem. 29 And it came to pass, when He drew near to Bethphage and Bethany, at the mountain called Olivet, *that* He sent two of His disciples, 30 saying, "Go into the village opposite *you*, where as you enter you will find a colt tied, on which no one has ever sat. Loose it and bring *it* here. 31 And if anyone asks you, 'Why are you loosing *it?*' thus you shall say to him, 'Because the Lord has need of it.'"

32 So those who were sent went their way and found *it* just as He had said to them. 33 But as they were loosing the colt, the owners of it said to them, "Why are you loosing the colt?"

34 And they said, "The Lord has need of him." 35 Then they brought him to Jesus. And they threw their own clothes on the colt, and they set Jesus on him. 36 And as He went, *many* spread their clothes on the road.

14 אוּלָם בְּנֵי אַרְצוֹ שָׂנְאוּ אוֹתוֹ וְשָׁלְחוּ מִשְׁלַחַת אַחֲרָיו, לוֹמַר: 'אֵינֶנּוּ רוֹצִים שֶׁזֶּה יִמְלֹךְ עָלֵינוּ.' 15 אַחֲרֵי שֶׁקִּבֵּל אֶת הַמְּלוּכָה חָזַר וְצִוָּה לִקְרֹא אֵלָיו אֶת הָעֲבָדִים אֲשֶׁר נָתַן לָהֶם אֶת הַכֶּסֶף, כְּדֵי לָדַעַת מַה הִרְוִיחַ כָּל אֶחָד בְּמִסְחָרוֹ. 16 נִגַּשׁ הָרִאשׁוֹן וְאָמַר, 'אֲדוֹנִי, הַמָּנֶה שֶׁלְּךָ הֵכִין עֲשָׂרָה מָנִים.' 17 הֵשִׁיב וְאָמַר לוֹ, 'יָפֶה, עֶבֶד טוֹב! הוֹאִיל וְהָיִיתָ נֶאֱמָן בִּמְעַט מִזְעָר, הֱיֵה שַׁלִּיט עַל עֶשֶׂר עָרִים.' 18 בָּא הַשֵּׁנִי וְאָמַר, 'אֲדוֹנִי, הַמָּנֶה שֶׁלְּךָ עָשָׂה חֲמִשָּׁה מָנִים.' 19 הֵשִׁיב וְאָמַר גַּם לָזֶה, 'אַתָּה הֱיֵה עַל חָמֵשׁ עָרִים.' 20 וְאַחֵר בָּא וְאָמַר, 'אֲדוֹנִי, הִנֵּה הַמָּנֶה שֶׁלְּךָ שֶׁהָיָה צָרוּר אֶצְלִי בְּמִטְפַּחַת, 21 שֶׁכֵּן פָּחַדְתִּי מִמְּךָ מִפְּנֵי שֶׁאִישׁ קָשֶׁה אַתָּה: לוֹקֵחַ אֶת אֲשֶׁר לֹא הִנַּחְתָּ וְקוֹצֵר אֶת אֲשֶׁר לֹא זָרַעְתָּ.' 22 הֵשִׁיב וְאָמַר לוֹ, 'עַל־פִּי דְּבָרְךָ אֶשְׁפֹּט אוֹתְךָ, עֶבֶד רָשָׁע! אַתָּה יָדַעְתָּ כִּי אִישׁ קָשֶׁה אֲנִי, לוֹקֵחַ אֶת אֲשֶׁר לֹא הִנַּחְתִּי וְקוֹצֵר אֶת אֲשֶׁר לֹא זָרַעְתִּי. 23 מַדּוּעַ לֹא הִפְקַדְתָּ אֶת כַּסְפִּי אֵצֶל הַשֻּׁלְחָנִי, וַאֲנִי בְּבוֹאִי הָיִיתִי תּוֹבֵעַ אוֹתוֹ עִם הָרִבִּית?' 24 וְלָעוֹמְדִים לְיָדוֹ אָמַר, 'קְחוּ מִמֶּנּוּ אֶת הַמָּנֶה וּתְנוּ לָזֶה אֲשֶׁר לוֹ עֲשָׂרָה מָנִים.' 25 הֵשִׁיבוּ לוֹ, 'אֲדוֹנֵנוּ, יֵשׁ לוֹ עֲשָׂרָה מָנִים!' 26 אוֹמֵר אֲנִי לָכֶם, כָּל מִי שֶׁיֵּשׁ לוֹ יֻתַּן לוֹ; וּמִי שֶׁאֵין לוֹ, גַּם מַה שֶּׁיֵּשׁ לוֹ יִלָּקַח מִמֶּנּוּ. 27 אֲבָל אֶת אוֹיְבַי אֵלֶּה, אֲשֶׁר אֵינָם רוֹצִים כִּי אֶמְלֹךְ עֲלֵיהֶם, הָבִיאוּ אוֹתָם הֵנָּה וְהִרְגוּ אוֹתָם לְפָנַי.'"

28 לְאַחַר שֶׁאָמַר אֶת הַדְּבָרִים הָאֵלֶּה הָלַךְ הָלְאָה בְּדַרְכּוֹ לַעֲלוֹת לִירוּשָׁלַיִם. 29 כַּאֲשֶׁר הִתְקָרֵב אֶל בֵּית פַּגֵּי וּבֵית עַנְיָה, אֶל הָהָר הַנִּקְרָא הַר הַזֵּיתִים, שָׁלַח שְׁנַיִם מִתַּלְמִידָיו בְּאָמְרוֹ: 30 "לְכוּ אֶל הַכְּפָר אֲשֶׁר מִמּוּל; כְּשֶׁתִּכָּנְסוּ לְתוֹכוֹ תִּמְצְאוּ עַיִר קָשׁוּר אֲשֶׁר לֹא יָשַׁב עָלָיו אָדָם מֵעוֹלָם. הַתִּירוּ אוֹתוֹ וַהֲבִיאוּהוּ. 31 וְאִם מִישֶׁהוּ יִשְׁאַל אֶתְכֶם, 'לָמָּה אַתֶּם מַתִּירִים אוֹתוֹ?', כֹּה תֹּאמְרוּ לוֹ: 'מִפְּנֵי שֶׁהָאָדוֹן זָקוּק לוֹ.'" 32 הַשְּׁלוּחִים הָלְכוּ וּמָצְאוּ כְּפִי שֶׁאָמַר לָהֶם. 33 כְּשֶׁהִתִּירוּ אֶת הָעַיִר שָׁאֲלוּ אוֹתָם בַּעֲלֵי הָעַיִר: "לָמָה אַתֶּם מַתִּירִים אֶת הָעַיִר?" 34 הֵשִׁיבוּ: "מִפְּנֵי שֶׁהָאָדוֹן זָקוּק לוֹ." 35 הֵם הֵבִיאוּ אוֹתוֹ אֶל יֵשׁוּעַ וּלְאַחַר שֶׁשָּׂמוּ אֶת בִּגְדֵיהֶם עַל הָעַיִר הִרְכִּיבוּ עָלָיו אֶת יֵשׁוּעַ. 36 כַּאֲשֶׁר הִמְשִׁיךְ בְּדַרְכּוֹ פָּרְשׂוּ אֲנָשִׁים אֶת בִּגְדֵיהֶם עַל

37 Then, as He was now drawing near the descent of the Mount of Olives, the whole multitude of the disciples began to rejoice and praise God with a loud voice for all the mighty works they had seen, 38 saying:

" 'Blessed is the King who comes in the name of
the LORD!'
Peace in heaven and glory in the highest!"

39 And some of the Pharisees called to Him from the crowd, "Teacher, rebuke Your disciples."

40 But He answered and said to them, "I tell you that if these should keep silent, the stones would immediately cry out."

41 Now as He drew near, He saw the city and wept over it, 42 saying, "If you had known, even you, especially in this your day, the things that make for your peace! But now they are hidden from your eyes. 43 For days will come upon you when your enemies will build an embankment around you, surround you and close you in on every side, 44 and level you, and your children within you, to the ground; and they will not leave in you one stone upon another, because you did not know the time of your visitation."

45 Then He went into the temple and began to drive out those who bought and sold in it, 46 saying to them, "It is written, 'My house is a house of prayer,' but you have made it a 'den of thieves.'"

47 And He was teaching daily in the temple. But the chief priests, the scribes, and the leaders of the people sought to destroy Him, 48 and were unable to do anything; for all the people were very attentive to hear Him.

20 Now it happened on one of those days, as He taught the people in the temple and preached the gospel, that the chief priests and the scribes, together with the elders, confronted Him 2 and spoke to Him, saying, "Tell us, by what authority are You doing these things? Or who is he who gave You this authority?"

3 But He answered and said to them, "I also will ask you one thing, and answer Me: 4 The baptism of John—was it from heaven or from men?"

5 And they reasoned among themselves, saying, "If we say, 'From heaven,' He will say, 'Why then did you not believe him?' 6 But if we say, 'From men,' all the people will stone us, for they are persuaded that John was a prophet." 7 So they answered that they did not know where it was from.

8 And Jesus said to them, "Neither will I tell you by what authority I do these things."

הַדֶּרֶךְ. 37 הוּא הִתְקָרֵב אֶל מוֹרַד הַר הַזֵּיתִים וְכָל קְהַל הַתַּלְמִידִים הֵחֵל לְשַׁבֵּחַ אֶת אֱלֹהִים בְּשִׂמְחָה וּבְקוֹל גָּדוֹל עַל כָּל הַנִּפְלָאוֹת אֲשֶׁר רָאוּ, בְּאָמְרָם: 38 "בָּרוּךְ הַבָּא בְּשֵׁם יהוה! שָׁלוֹם בַּשָּׁמַיִם וְכָבוֹד בַּמְּרוֹמִים!"

39 כַּמָּה מִן הַפְּרוּשִׁים שֶׁהָיוּ בְּקֶרֶב הֶהָמוֹן אָמְרוּ אֵלָיו: "רַבִּי, גְּעַר בְּתַלְמִידֶיךָ."

40 הֵשִׁיב וְאָמַר: "אוֹמֵר אֲנִי לָכֶם, אִם אֵלֶּה יִשְׁתְּקוּ, הָאֲבָנִים תִּזְעַקְנָה."

41 כַּאֲשֶׁר הִתְקָרֵב וְרָאָה אֶת הָעִיר, בָּכָה עָלֶיהָ וְאָמַר: 42 "לוּ יָדַעְתָּ הַיּוֹם גַּם אַתְּ אֶת אֲשֶׁר אֵלַי שָׁלוֹם! אֶלָּא שֶׁעַתָּה נִסְתָּר הוּא מֵעֵינַיִךְ. 43 הִנֵּה יָמִים בָּאִים עָלַיִךְ וְאוֹיְבַיִךְ יָקִימוּ סוֹלְלָה סְבִיבֵךְ, וְיַקִּיפוּךְ וְיָצוּרוּ עָלַיִךְ מִכָּל עֵבֶר. 44 וַיְמַגְּרוּ אוֹתָךְ וְאֶת בָּנַיִךְ אֲשֶׁר בְּקִרְבֵּךְ, וְלֹא יַשְׁאִירוּ בָּךְ אֶבֶן עַל אֶבֶן עֵקֶב אֲשֶׁר לֹא יָדַעְתְּ אֶת מוֹעֵד פְּקֻדָּתֵךְ."

45 בְּהִכָּנְסוֹ אֶל בֵּית הַמִּקְדָּשׁ הֵחֵל לְגָרֵשׁ מִשָּׁם אֶת הַמּוֹכְרִים. 46 אָמַר לָהֶם: "הֵן כָּתוּב, 'בֵּיתִי בֵּית-תְּפִלָּה יִהְיֶה', אַךְ אַתֶּם עֲשִׂיתֶם אוֹתוֹ מְעָרַת פָּרִיצִים."

47 יוֹם יוֹם הָיָה מְלַמֵּד בְּבֵית הַמִּקְדָּשׁ, וְרָאשֵׁי הַכֹּהֲנִים וְהַסּוֹפְרִים וְגַם רָאשֵׁי הָעָם בִּקְשׁוּ לְהַכְחִיד אוֹתוֹ, 48 אַךְ לֹא מָצְאוּ מַה לַּעֲשׂוֹת, כִּי כָּל הָעָם נִצְמְדוּ אֵלָיו לִשְׁמֹעַ אוֹתוֹ.

20 בְּאַחַד הַיָּמִים, כְּשֶׁהָיָה מְלַמֵּד אֶת הָעָם בְּבֵית הַמִּקְדָּשׁ וּמַטִּיף אֶת הַבְּשׂוֹרָה, נִגְּשׁוּ רָאשֵׁי הַכֹּהֲנִים וְהַסּוֹפְרִים עִם הַזְּקֵנִים 2 וְאָמְרוּ לוֹ: "אֱמָר נָא לָנוּ, בְּאֵיזוֹ סַמְכוּת אַתָּה עוֹשֶׂה דְּבָרִים אֵלֶּה, אוֹ מִיהוּ שֶׁנָּתַן לְךָ אֶת הַסַּמְכוּת הַזֹּאת?"

3 הֵשִׁיב לָהֶם: "גַּם אֲנִי אֶשְׁאַל אֶתְכֶם דָּבָר וְהָשִׁיבוּ לִי. 4 טְבִילַת יוֹחָנָן, הַאִם מִשָּׁמַיִם הָיְתָה אוֹ מִבְּנֵי אָדָם?"

5 הִתְוַעֲצוּ זֶה עִם זֶה בְּאָמְרָם: "אִם נֹאמַר 'מִן הַשָּׁמַיִם', יֹאמַר, 'מַדּוּעַ לֹא הֶאֱמַנְתֶּם לוֹ?' 6 וְאִם נֹאמַר 'מִבְּנֵי אָדָם', כָּל הָעָם יִסְקְלוּ אוֹתָנוּ, כִּי בְּטוּחִים הֵם שֶׁיּוֹחָנָן הָיָה נָבִיא." 7 הֵשִׁיבוּ וְאָמְרוּ שֶׁאֵינָם יוֹדְעִים מֵאַיִן.

8 אָמַר לָהֶם יֵשׁוּעַ: "גַּם אֲנִי לֹא אֹמַר לָכֶם בְּאֵיזוֹ סַמְכוּת אֲנִי עוֹשֶׂה אֶת אֵלֶּה."

9 Then He began to tell the people this parable: "A certain man planted a vineyard, leased it to vinedressers, and went into a far country for a long time. 10 Now at vintage-time he sent a servant to the vinedressers, that they might give him some of the fruit of the vineyard. But the vinedressers beat him and sent *him* away empty-handed. 11 Again he sent another servant; and they beat him also, treated *him* shamefully, and sent *him* away empty-handed. 12 And again he sent a third; and they wounded him also and cast *him* out.

13 "Then the owner of the vineyard said, 'What shall I do? I will send my beloved son. Probably they will respect *him* when they see him.' 14 But when the vinedressers saw him, they reasoned among themselves, saying, 'This is the heir. Come, let us kill him, that the inheritance may be ours.' 15 So they cast him out of the vineyard and killed *him*. Therefore what will the owner of the vineyard do to them? 16 He will come and destroy those vinedressers and give the vineyard to others."

And when they heard *it* they said, "Certainly not!"

17 Then He looked at them and said, "What then is this that is written:

'The stone which the builders rejected
Has become the chief cornerstone'?

18 Whoever falls on that stone will be broken; but on whomever it falls, it will grind him to powder."

19 And the chief priests and the scribes that very hour sought to lay hands on Him, but they feared the people—for they knew He had spoken this parable against them.

20 So they watched *Him,* and sent spies who pretended to be righteous, that they might seize on His words, in order to deliver Him to the power and the authority of the governor. 21 Then they asked Him, saying, "Teacher, we know that You say and teach rightly, and You do not show personal favoritism, but teach the way of God in truth: 22 Is it lawful for us to pay taxes to Caesar or not?"

23 But He perceived their craftiness, and said to them, "Why do you test Me? 24 Show Me a denarius. Whose image and inscription does it have?"

They answered and said, "Caesar's."

25 And He said to them, "Render therefore to Caesar the things that are Caesar's, and to God the things that are God's."

26 But they could not catch Him in His words in the presence of the people. And they marveled at His answer and kept silent.

9 הוּא סִפֵּר לָעָם אֶת הַמָּשָׁל הַזֶּה: "אִישׁ אֶחָד נָטַע כֶּרֶם וְהֶחְכִּירוֹ לְכוֹרְמִים. לְאַחַר מִכֵּן נָסַע לִתְקוּפָה אֲרֻכָּה. 10 בְּבוֹא הָעֵת שָׁלַח עֶבֶד אֶל הַכּוֹרְמִים כְּדֵי שֶׁיִּתְּנוּ לוֹ מִפְּרִי הַכֶּרֶם, אֶלָּא שֶׁהַכּוֹרְמִים הִכּוּהוּ וְשִׁלְּחוּ אוֹתוֹ רֵיקָם. 11 הוֹסִיף וְשָׁלַח עֶבֶד אַחֵר, אַךְ גַּם אוֹתוֹ הִכּוּ וּבִזּוּ וְשִׁלְּחוּהוּ רֵיקָם. 12 הוֹסִיף וְשָׁלַח שְׁלִישִׁי, וְאוּלָם גַּם אוֹתוֹ פָּצְעוּ וְהִשְׁלִיכוּהוּ הַחוּצָה. 13 אָמַר בַּעַל הַכֶּרֶם, 'מָה אֶעֱשֶׂה? אֶשְׁלַח אֶת בְּנִי אֲהוּבִי, אוּלַי אוֹתוֹ יְכַבְּדוּ'. 14 כְּשֶׁרָאוּ אוֹתוֹ הַכּוֹרְמִים נוֹעֲצוּ יַחְדָּיו לֵאמֹר, 'זֶהוּ הַיּוֹרֵשׁ; בּוֹאוּ וְנַהַרְגֵ אוֹתוֹ וְהַיְרֻשָּׁה תִּהְיֶה לָנוּ'. 15 הֵם גֵּרְשׁוּהוּ אֶל מִחוּץ לַכֶּרֶם וַהֲרָגוּהוּ. וְעַתָּה מַה יַּעֲשֶׂה לָהֶם בַּעַל הַכֶּרֶם? 16 יָבוֹא וְיַשְׁמִיד אֶת הַכּוֹרְמִים הָהֵם, וְאֶת הַכֶּרֶם יִתֵּן לַאֲחֵרִים."

כְּשֶׁמְעָם זֹאת אָמְרוּ: "חַס וְחָלִילָה!" 17 הוּא נָעַץ בָּהֶם מַבָּטוֹ וְאָמַר: "וּמַהוּ הַכָּתוּב הַזֶּה, 'אֶבֶן מָאֲסוּ הַבּוֹנִים הָיְתָה לְרֹאשׁ פִּנָּה'? 18 כָּל הַנּוֹפֵל עַל אוֹתָהּ אֶבֶן יִשָּׁבֵר לִרְסִיסִים, וּמִי שֶׁהָאֶבֶן תִּפֹּל עָלָיו – תִּכְתֹּשׁ הִיא אוֹתוֹ." 19 אוֹתָהּ שָׁעָה בִּקְשׁוּ הַסּוֹפְרִים וְרָאשֵׁי הַכֹּהֲנִים לִשְׁלֹחַ אֶת יָדָם בּוֹ, כִּי הֵבִינוּ שֶׁעֲלֵיהֶם הִמְשִׁיל אֶת הַמָּשָׁל הַזֶּה, אֶלָּא שֶׁפָּחֲדוּ מִן הָעָם.

20 הֵם הִתְחַקּוּ אַחֲרָיו וְשָׁלְחוּ מְרַגְּלִים שֶׁהֶעֱמִידוּ פְּנֵי צַדִּיקִים כְּדֵי לְהֵאָחֵז בִּדְבַר מִדְּבָרָיו, בְּמִטְרָה לִמְסֹר אוֹתוֹ לְסַמְכוּת הַנָּצִיב וּלְשִׁפּוּטוֹ. 21 הַלָּלוּ פָּנוּ אֵלָיו בִּשְׁאֵלָה: "רַבִּי, אֲנַחְנוּ יוֹדְעִים שֶׁאַתָּה מְדַבֵּר וּמְלַמֵּד נְכוֹנָה וְאֵינְךָ נוֹשֵׂא פָנִים אֶלָּא מוֹרֶה אֶת דֶּרֶךְ אֱלֹהִים עַל-פִּי הָאֱמֶת. 22 הַאִם מֻתָּר לָנוּ לָתֵת מַס לַקֵּיסָר אוֹ לֹא?"

23 הוֹאִיל וְרָאָה אֶת עָרְמָתָם אָמַר לָהֶם: 24 "הַרְאוּ לִי דִּינָר. שֶׁל מִי הַדְּמוּת וְהַכְּתֹבֶת אֲשֶׁר עָלָיו?" הֵשִׁיבוּ: "שֶׁל הַקֵּיסָר."

25 אָמַר לָהֶם: "אִם כֵּן, תְּנוּ לַקֵּיסָר אֶת אֲשֶׁר לַקֵּיסָר וְלֵאלֹהִים אֶת אֲשֶׁר לֵאלֹהִים."

26 הֵם לֹא יָכְלוּ לְהֵאָחֵז בִּדְבַר מִדְּבָרָיו בְּנוֹכְחוּת הָעָם, וּבִתְמִיהָתָם עַל תְּשׁוּבָתוֹ שָׁתְקוּ.

27 Then some of the Sadducees, who deny that there is a resurrection, came to *Him* and asked Him, 28 saying: "Teacher, Moses wrote to us *that* if a man's brother dies, having a wife, and he dies without children, his brother should take his wife and raise up offspring for his brother. 29 Now there were seven brothers. And the first took a wife, and died without children. 30 And the second took her as wife, and he died childless. 31 Then the third took her, and in like manner the seven also; and they left no children, and died. 32 Last of all the woman died also. 33 Therefore, in the resurrection, whose wife does she become? For all seven had her as wife."

34 Jesus answered and said to them, "The sons of this age marry and are given in marriage. 35 But those who are counted worthy to attain that age, and the resurrection from the dead, neither marry nor are given in marriage; 36 nor can they die anymore, for they are equal to the angels and are sons of God, being sons of the resurrection. 37 But even Moses showed in the *burning* bush *passage* that the dead are raised, when he called the Lord 'the *God of Abraham, the God of Isaac, and the God of Jacob.*' 38 For He is not the God of the dead but of the living, for all live to Him."

39 Then some of the scribes answered and said, "Teacher, You have spoken well." 40 But after that they dared not question Him anymore.

41 And He said to them, "How can they say that the Christ is the Son of David? 42 Now David himself said in the Book of Psalms:

'The LORD said to my Lord,
"Sit at My right hand,
43　　Till I make Your enemies Your footstool." '

44 Therefore David calls Him 'Lord'; how is He then his Son?"

45 Then, in the hearing of all the people, He said to His disciples, 46 "Beware of the scribes, who desire to go around in long robes, love greetings in the marketplaces, the best seats in the synagogues, and the best places at feasts, 47 who devour widows' houses, and for a pretense make long prayers. These will receive greater condemnation."

21 And He looked up and saw the rich putting their gifts into the treasury, 2 and He saw also a certain poor widow putting in two mites. 3 So He said, "Truly I say to you that this poor widow has put in more than all; 4 for all these out of their abundance have put in offerings for God, but she out of her poverty put in all the livelihood that she had."

27 נִגְּשׁוּ כַּמָּה מִן הַצְּדוֹקִים, הָאוֹמְרִים שֶׁאֵין תְּחִיַּת מֵתִים, וְשָׁאֲלוּ אוֹתוֹ: 28 "רַבִּי, מֹשֶׁה כָּתַב לָנוּ שֶׁאִם יָמוּת אִישׁ שֶׁיֵּשׁ לוֹ אִשָּׁה וְאֵין לוֹ בָּנִים, יִקַּח אָחִיו אֶת אִשְׁתּוֹ וְיָקִים זֶרַע לְאָחִיו. 29 וּבְכֵן הָיוּ שִׁבְעָה אַחִים. הָרִאשׁוֹן נָשָׂא אִשָּׁה וּמֵת בְּלִי בָּנִים. 30 לָקַח אוֹתָהּ הַשֵּׁנִי 31 וְאַחֲרֵי כֵן הַשְּׁלִישִׁי; וְכָךְ כָּל הַשִּׁבְעָה לֹא הִנִּיחוּ בָנִים וּמֵתוּ. 32 לַבַּסּוֹף מֵתָה גַם הָאִשָּׁה. 33 אִם כֵּן לְמִי מֵהֶם תִּהְיֶה לְאִשָּׁה בִּתְחִיַּת הַמֵּתִים, שֶׁהֲרֵי הָיְתָה אִשָּׁה לְכָל הַשִּׁבְעָה?"

34 הֵשִׁיב לָהֶם יֵשׁוּעַ: "בְּנֵי הָעוֹלָם הַזֶּה מִתְחַתְּנִים, 35 אַךְ הַזּוֹכִּים לִנְחֹל אֶת הָעוֹלָם הַבָּא וְאֶת הַתְּחִיָּה מִן הַמֵּתִים אֵינָם מִתְחַתְּנִים, 36 כִּי גַם אֵינָם יְכוֹלִים לָמוּת עוֹד, שֶׁהֲרֵי שָׁוִים הֵם לַמַּלְאָכִים וּבְנֵי אֱלֹהִים הֵם בִּהְיוֹתָם בְּנֵי הַתְּחִיָּה. 37 וְשֶׁהַמֵּתִים קָמִים לִתְחִיָּה גַּם מֹשֶׁה רָמַז בְּפָרָשַׁת הַסְּנֶה שֶׁנֶּאֱמַר 'יהוה אֱלֹהֵי אַבְרָהָם, אֱלֹהֵי יִצְחָק וֵאלֹהֵי יַעֲקֹב.' 38 וְהָאֱלֹהִים לֹא אֱלֹהֵי הַמֵּתִים כִּי אִם אֱלֹהֵי הַחַיִּים, שֶׁהֲרֵי הַכֹּל חַיִּים לוֹ."

39 כַּמָּה מִן הַסּוֹפְרִים אָמְרוּ בִּתְגוּבָה: "רַבִּי, יָפֶה דִּבַּרְתָּ!"

40 וְלֹא הֵעֵזּוּ עוֹד לִשְׁאֹל אוֹתוֹ שׁוּם דָּבָר.

41 שָׁאַל הוּא אוֹתָם: "כֵּיצַד זֶה אוֹמְרִים עַל הַמָּשִׁיחַ שֶׁבֶּן דָּוִד הוּא? 42 הֵן דָּוִד עַצְמוֹ אוֹמֵר בְּסֵפֶר תְּהִלִּים, 'נְאֻם יהוה לַאדֹנִי, שֵׁב לִימִינִי 43 עַד־ אָשִׁית אוֹיְבֶיךָ הֲדֹם לְרַגְלֶיךָ.' 44 הִנֵּה דָּוִד קוֹרֵא לוֹ 'אָדוֹן', וְאֵיךְ הוּא בְּנוֹ?"

45 וּבְאָזְנֵי כָּל הָעָם אָמַר לְתַלְמִידָיו: 46 "הִזָּהֲרוּ מִן הַסּוֹפְרִים הָאוֹהֲבִים לְהִתְהַלֵּךְ לְבוּשֵׁי גְּלִימוֹת וְאוֹהֲבִים בִּרְכוֹת שָׁלוֹם בַּשְּׁוָקִים וּמוֹשָׁבִים רִאשׁוֹנִים בְּבָתֵּי הַכְּנֶסֶת וּמְקוֹמוֹת נִכְבָּדִים בַּסְּעוּדוֹת; 47 הַבּוֹלְעִים אֶת בָּתֵּי הָאַלְמָנוֹת וּמַאֲרִיכִים לְהִתְפַּלֵּל לְמַרְאִית עַיִן. דִּינָם שֶׁל אֵלֶּה יִהְיֶה חָמוּר יוֹתֵר."

כא הוּא הִתְבּוֹנֵן וְרָאָה אֶת הָעֲשִׁירִים שָׂמִים נִדְבוֹתֵיהֶם בְּתֵבַת הָאוֹצָר. 2 כִּרְאוֹתוֹ אַלְמָנָה עֲנִיָּה שָׂמָה בּוֹ שְׁתֵּי פְרוּטוֹת, 3 אָמַר: "אֱמֶת אוֹמֵר אֲנִי לָכֶם, הָאַלְמָנָה הָעֲנִיָּה הַזֹּאת נָתְנָה יוֹתֵר מִכֻּלָּם. 4 כִּי כָּל אֵלֶּה נָתְנוּ אֶת נִדְבוֹתֵיהֶם מִן הָעֹדֶף שֶׁלָּהֶם, אַךְ הִיא מִמַּחְסוֹרָהּ נָתְנָה אֶת כָּל אֲשֶׁר הָיָה לָהּ לְמִחְיָה."

⁵ Then, as some spoke of the temple, how it was adorned with beautiful stones and donations, He said, ⁶ "These things which you see—the days will come in which not *one* stone shall be left upon another that shall not be thrown down."

⁷ So they asked Him, saying, "Teacher, but when will these things be? And what sign *will there be* when these things are about to take place?"

⁸ And He said: "Take heed that you not be deceived. For many will come in My name, saying, 'I am *He*,' and, 'The time has drawn near.' Therefore do not go after them. ⁹ But when you hear of wars and commotions, do not be terrified; for these things must come to pass first, but the end *will not come* immediately."

¹⁰ Then He said to them, "Nation will rise against nation, and kingdom against kingdom. ¹¹ And there will be great earthquakes in various places, and famines and pestilences; and there will be fearful sights and great signs from heaven. ¹² But before all these things, they will lay their hands on you and persecute *you*, delivering *you* up to the synagogues and prisons. You will be brought before kings and rulers for My name's sake. ¹³ But it will turn out for you as an occasion for testimony. ¹⁴ Therefore settle *it* in your hearts not to meditate beforehand on what you will answer; ¹⁵ for I will give you a mouth and wisdom which all your adversaries will not be able to contradict or resist. ¹⁶ You will be betrayed even by parents and brothers, relatives and friends; and they will put *some* of you to death. ¹⁷ And you will be hated by all for My name's sake. ¹⁸ But not a hair of your head shall be lost. ¹⁹ By your patience possess your souls.

²⁰ "But when you see Jerusalem surrounded by armies, then know that its desolation is near. ²¹ Then let those who are in Judea flee to the mountains, let those who are in the midst of her depart, and let not those who are in the country enter her. ²² For these are the days of vengeance, that all things which are written may be fulfilled. ²³ But woe to those who are pregnant and to those who are nursing babies in those days! For there will be great distress in the land and wrath upon this people. ²⁴ And they will fall by the edge of the sword, and be led away captive into all nations. And Jerusalem will be trampled by Gentiles until the times of the Gentiles are fulfilled.

²⁵ "And there will be signs in the sun, in the moon, and in the stars; and on the earth distress of nations, with perplexity, the sea and the waves roaring; ²⁶ men's hearts failing them from fear and the expectation of those things which are coming on the earth, for the powers of the heavens will be

shaken. 27 Then they will see the Son of Man coming in a cloud with power and great glory. 28 Now when these things begin to happen, look up and lift up your heads, because your redemption draws near."

29 Then He spoke to them a parable: "Look at the fig tree, and all the trees. 30 When they are already budding, you see and know for yourselves that summer is now near. 31 So you also, when you see these things happening, know that the kingdom of God is near. 32 Assuredly, I say to you, this generation will by no means pass away till all things take place. 33 Heaven and earth will pass away, but My words will by no means pass away.

34 "But take heed to yourselves, lest your hearts be weighed down with carousing, drunkenness, and cares of this life, and that Day come on you unexpectedly. 35 For it will come as a snare on all those who dwell on the face of the whole earth. 36 Watch therefore, and pray always that you may be counted worthy to escape all these things that will come to pass, and to stand before the Son of Man."

37 And in the daytime He was teaching in the temple, but at night He went out and stayed on the mountain called Olivet. 38 Then early in the morning all the people came to Him in the temple to hear Him.

22 Now the Feast of Unleavened Bread drew near, which is called Passover. 2 And the chief priests and the scribes sought how they might kill Him, for they feared the people.

3 Then Satan entered Judas, surnamed Iscariot, who was numbered among the twelve. 4 So he went his way and conferred with the chief priests and captains, how he might betray Him to them. 5 And they were glad, and agreed to give him money. 6 So he promised and sought opportunity to betray Him to them in the absence of the multitude.

7 Then came the Day of Unleavened Bread, when the Passover must be killed. 8 And He sent Peter and John, saying, "Go and prepare the Passover for us, that we may eat."

9 So they said to Him, "Where do You want us to prepare?"

10 And He said to them, "Behold, when you have entered the city, a man will meet you carrying a pitcher of water; follow him into the house which he enters. 11 Then you shall say to the master of the house, 'The Teacher says to you, "Where is the guest room where I may eat the Passover with My disciples?"' 12 Then he will show you a large, furnished upper room; there make ready."

הָעוֹלָם, כִּי כֹּחוֹת הַשָּׁמַיִם יִזְדַּעְזָעוּ. 27 אָז יִרְאוּ אֶת בֶּן־הָאָדָם בָּא בְּעָנָן בִּגְבוּרָה וּבְכָבוֹד רַב. 28 כַּאֲשֶׁר יָתֵחִלּוּ לִקְרוֹת הַדְּבָרִים הָאֵלֶּה הִתְעוֹדְדוּ וְהָרִימוּ רָאשֵׁיכֶם, כִּי קְרֵבָה גְּאֻלַּתְכֶם." 29 הוּא סִפֵּר לָהֶם מָשָׁל: "רְאוּ אֶת הַתְּאֵנָה וְאֶת כָּל הָעֵצִים. 30 כְּשֶׁאַתֶּם רוֹאִים אוֹתָם מְלַבְלְבִים, יוֹדְעִים אַתֶּם בְּעַצְמְכֶם כִּי קָרוֹב הַקַּיִץ. 31 כֵּן גַּם כְּשֶׁתִּרְאוּ אֶת הַדְּבָרִים הָאֵלֶּה מִתְקַיְּמִים, דְּעוּ כִּי קְרוֹבָה מַלְכוּת הָאֱלֹהִים. 32 אָמֵן, אוֹמֵר אֲנִי לָכֶם, לֹא יַעֲבֹר הַדּוֹר הַזֶּה עַד אֲשֶׁר יִהְיוּ כָּל אֵלֶּה. 33 הַשָּׁמַיִם וְהָאָרֶץ יַעַבְרוּ וּדְבָרַי לֹא יַעֲבֹרוּ.

34 הִשָּׁמְרוּ לָכֶם שֶׁלֹּא יִכְבַּד לְבַבְכֶם בִּשְׁתִיָּה וּבְשִׁכָּרוֹן וּבְדַאֲגוֹת הַחַיִּים וְהַיּוֹם הַהוּא יָבוֹא עֲלֵיכֶם פִּתְאֹם; 35 כִּי כְּמוֹ פַּח יָבוֹא עַל כָּל הַיּוֹשְׁבִים עַל פְּנֵי כָל הָאָרֶץ. 36 לָכֵן עִמְדוּ עַל הַמִּשְׁמָר בְּכָל עֵת וְהִתְפַּלְּלוּ שֶׁיִּהְיֶה בְּכֹחֲכֶם לְהִמָּלֵט מִכָּל הָעֲתִידוֹת הָאֵלֶּה וּלְהִתְיַצֵּב לִפְנֵי בֶן־הָאָדָם."

37 בִּשְׁעוֹת הַיּוֹם הָיָה מְלַמֵּד בְּבֵית הַמִּקְדָּשׁ וּבַלֵּילוֹת הָיָה יוֹצֵא לָלוּן בָּהָר הַנִּקְרָא הַר הַזֵּיתִים. 38 וְכָל הָעָם הִשְׁכִּימוּ לָבוֹא אֵלָיו לְבֵית הַמִּקְדָּשׁ לִשְׁמֹעַ אוֹתוֹ.

כב פֶּסַח, חַג הַמַּצּוֹת, הִתְקָרֵב. 2 וְרָאשֵׁי הַכֹּהֲנִים וְהַסּוֹפְרִים חִפְּשׂוּ דֶּרֶךְ לְהַכְחִיד אוֹתוֹ, כִּי חָשְׁשׁוּ מִפְּנֵי הָעָם. 3 אָז נִכְנַס הַשָּׂטָן בִּיהוּדָה הַנִּקְרָא אִישׁ קְרִיּוֹת, שֶׁנִּמְנָה עִם הַשְּׁנֵים־עָשָׂר. 4 הָלַךְ יְהוּדָה וְדִבֵּר עִם רָאשֵׁי הַכֹּהֲנִים וְהַקְּצִינִים לִקְבֹּעַ אֵיךְ יַסְגִּיר אוֹתוֹ בְּיָדָם. 5 הֵם שָׂמְחוּ וְהִסְכִּימוּ לָתֵת לוֹ כֶּסֶף, 6 וְהוּא הִסְכִּים לְכָךְ וְחִפֵּשׂ הִזְדַּמְּנוּת לְהַסְגִּירוֹ בְּיָדָם שֶׁלֹּא בִּפְנֵי הֶהָמוֹן.

7 כְּשֶׁהִגִּיעַ הַיּוֹם שֶׁצָּרִיךְ לִזְבֹּחַ בּוֹ אֶת הַפֶּסַח, 8 שָׁלַח יֵשׁוּעַ אֶת כֵּיפָא וְאֶת יוֹחָנָן בְּאָמְרוֹ: "לְכוּ וְהָכִינוּ לָנוּ אֶת הַפֶּסַח כְּדֵי שֶׁנֹּאכַל."

9 אָמְרוּ: "אֵיפֹה אַתָּה רוֹצֶה שֶׁנָּכִין אוֹתוֹ?"

10 הֵשִׁיב לָהֶם: "הִנֵּה כַּאֲשֶׁר תִּכָּנְסוּ הָעִירָה יִפְגֹּשׁ אֶתְכֶם אִישׁ נוֹשֵׂא כַּד מַיִם. לְכוּ אַחֲרָיו אֶל הַבַּיִת שֶׁיִּכָּנֵס לְתוֹכוֹ 11 וְאִמְרוּ לְבַעַל הַבַּיִת: 'כֹּה אוֹמֵר לְךָ רַבֵּנוּ, הֵיכָן הַחֶדֶר אֲשֶׁר אֹכַל שָׁם אֶת הַפֶּסַח עִם תַּלְמִידַי?' 12 הוּא יַרְאֶה לָכֶם עֲלִיָּה גְּדוֹלָה מְצַעַת וּמְסֻדֶּרֶת; שָׁם תָּכִינוּ אֶת הַפֶּסַח."

13 So they went and found it just as He had said to them, and they prepared the Passover.

14 When the hour had come, He sat down, and the twelve apostles with Him. 15 Then He said to them, "With *fervent* desire I have desired to eat this Passover with you before I suffer; 16 for I say to you, I will no longer eat of it until it is fulfilled in the kingdom of God."

17 Then He took the cup, and gave thanks, and said, "Take this and divide *it* among yourselves; 18 for I say to you, I will not drink of the fruit of the vine until the kingdom of God comes."

19 And He took bread, gave thanks and broke *it*, and gave *it* to them, saying, "This is My body which is given for you; do this in remembrance of Me."

20 Likewise He also *took* the cup after supper, saying, "This cup *is* the new covenant in My blood, which is shed for you. 21 But behold, the hand of My betrayer *is* with Me on the table. 22 And truly the Son of Man goes as it has been determined, but woe to that man by whom He is betrayed!"

23 Then they began to question among themselves, which of them it was who would do this thing.

24 Now there was also a dispute among them, as to which of them should be considered the greatest. 25 And He said to them, "The kings of the Gentiles exercise lordship over them, and those who exercise authority over them are called 'benefactors.' 26 But not so *among* you; on the contrary, he who is greatest among you, let him be as the younger, and he who governs as he who serves. 27 For who *is* greater, he who sits at the table, or he who serves? *Is* it not he who sits at the table? Yet I am among you as the One who serves.

28 "But you are those who have continued with Me in My trials. 29 And I bestow upon you a kingdom, just as My Father bestowed *one* upon Me, 30 that you may eat and drink at My table in My kingdom, and sit on thrones judging the twelve tribes of Israel."

31 And the Lord said, "Simon, Simon! Indeed, Satan has asked for you, that he may sift *you* as wheat. 32 But I have prayed for you, that your faith should not fail; and when you have returned to *Me*, strengthen your brethren."

33 But he said to Him, "Lord, I am ready to go with You, both to prison and to death."

34 Then He said, "I tell you, Peter, the rooster shall not crow this day before you will deny three times that you know Me."

35 And He said to them, "When I sent you without money bag, knapsack, and sandals, did you lack anything?"

---

13 הֵם הָלְכוּ וּמָצְאוּ הַכֹּל כְּפִי שֶׁאָמַר לָהֶם, וְהֵכִינוּ אֶת הַפֶּסַח.

14 כַּאֲשֶׁר הִגִּיעָה הַשָּׁעָה הֵסֵב הוּא וְהַשְּׁלִיחִים עִמּוֹ. 15 אָמַר לָהֶם: "נִכְסֹף נִכְסַפְתִּי לֶאֱכֹל אִתְּכֶם אֶת הַפֶּסַח הַזֶּה לִפְנֵי עֱנוּתִי, 16 כִּי אוֹמֵר אֲנִי לָכֶם, לֹא אֹכַל אוֹתוֹ עוֹד עַד כִּי יִתְקַיַּם בְּמַלְכוּת הָאֱלֹהִים."

17 הוּא לָקַח אֶת הַכּוֹס, בֵּרַךְ, וְאָמַר: "קְחוּ אוֹתָהּ וְחַלְּקוּ בֵּינֵיכֶם; 18 כִּי אוֹמֵר אֲנִי לָכֶם, מֵעַתָּה שָׁתֹה לֹא אֶשְׁתֶּה מִפְּרִי הַגֶּפֶן עַד אֲשֶׁר תָּבוֹא מַלְכוּת הָאֱלֹהִים." 19 לָקַח אֶת הַלֶּחֶם, בֵּרַךְ וּבָצַע וְנָתַן לָהֶם בְּאָמְרוֹ: "זֶה גּוּפִי הַנִּתָּן בַּעַדְכֶם, זֹאת עֲשׂוּ לְזִכְרִי."

20 כֵּן גַּם אֶת הַכּוֹס אַחַר הַסְּעוּדָה, וְאָמַר: "הַכּוֹס הַזֹּאת הִיא הַבְּרִית הַחֲדָשָׁה בְּדָמִי הַנִּשְׁפָּךְ בַּעַדְכֶם. 21 אַךְ הִנֵּה יַד הַמַּסְגִּיר אוֹתִי אִתִּי עַל הַשֻּׁלְחָן. 22 בֶּן־הָאָדָם אָמְנָם הוֹלֵךְ כְּפִי שֶׁנִּגְזַר, אֲבָל אוֹי לְאוֹתוֹ אִישׁ שֶׁמַּסְגִּיר אוֹתוֹ."

23 הֵם הֵחֵלּוּ לְבָרֵר בֵּינֵיהֶם מִי מֵהֶם הוּא הָעוֹמֵד לַעֲשׂוֹת זֹאת. 24 גַּם מְרִיבָה הָיְתָה בֵּינֵיהֶם בַּשְּׁאֵלָה מִי מֵהֶם נֶחְשָׁב לַגָּדוֹל בְּיוֹתֵר. 25 אָמַר לָהֶם: "מַלְכֵי הַגּוֹיִים רוֹדִים בָּהֶם, וְהָאֲנָשִׁים הַשּׁוֹלְטִים עֲלֵיהֶם 'עוֹשֵׂי־חֶסֶד' נִקְרָאִים. 26 אַךְ אַתֶּם לֹא כֵן; אַדְּרַבָּא, הַגָּדוֹל בָּכֶם שֶׁיְּהֵא כַּצָּעִיר, וְהַמַּנְהִיג כַּמְשָׁרֵת. 27 וּמִי הַגָּדוֹל, הַמֵּסֵב אֶל הַשֻּׁלְחָן אוֹ הַמְשָׁרֵת? הֲלֹא הַמֵּסֵב! וַאֲנִי בְּתוֹכְכֶם כְּמוֹ הַמְשָׁרֵת. 28 אַתֶּם עֲמַדְתֶּם אִתִּי בְּנִסְיוֹנוֹתַי, 29 וַאֲנִי מַנְחִיל לָכֶם מַלְכוּת כְּמוֹ שֶׁהִנְחִילַנִי אָבִי, 30 לְמַעַן תֹּאכְלוּ וְתִשְׁתּוּ עַל שֻׁלְחָנִי בְּמַלְכוּתִי וְתֵשְׁבוּ עַל כִּסְאוֹת לִשְׁפֹּט אֶת שְׁנֵים־עָשָׂר שִׁבְטֵי יִשְׂרָאֵל."

31 "שִׁמְעוֹן, שִׁמְעוֹן, הִנֵּה דָּרַשׁ הַשָּׂטָן לְטַלְטֵל אֶתְכֶם כְּחִטִּים בַּכְּבָרָה. 32 אֲבָל אֲנִי הִתְפַּלַּלְתִּי בַּעַדְךָ שֶׁלֹּא תִכְלֶה אֱמוּנָתְךָ, וְאַתָּה לְאַחַר שֶׁתָּשׁוּב, חַזֵּק אֶת אַחֶיךָ."

33 אָמַר כֵּיפָא: "אֲדוֹנִי! אִתְּךָ אֲנִי מוּכָן לָלֶכֶת גַּם לְבֵית הָאֲסוּרִים גַּם לַמָּוֶת."

34 הֵשִׁיב יֵשׁוּעַ: "אֲנִי אוֹמֵר לְךָ, כֵּיפָא, תַּרְנְגוֹל לֹא יִקְרָא הַיּוֹם עַד אֲשֶׁר שָׁלוֹשׁ פְּעָמִים תִּתְכַּחֵשׁ לִי כְּאִלּוּ שֶׁאֵינְךָ מַכִּיר אוֹתִי."

35 הוֹסִיף וְשָׁאַל אוֹתָם: "כַּאֲשֶׁר שָׁלַחְתִּי אֶתְכֶם בְּלִי אַרְנָק וְתַרְמִיל וְנַעֲלַיִם, הַאִם חֲסַרְתֶּם דָּבָר?" הֵשִׁיבוּ: "לֹא חָסַרְנוּ כְּלוּם."

So they said, "Nothing."

36 Then He said to them, "But now, he who has a money bag, let him take *it,* and likewise a knapsack; and he who has no sword, let him sell his garment and buy one. 37 For I say to you that this which is written must still be accomplished in Me: *'And He was numbered with the transgressors.'* For the things concerning Me have an end."

38 So they said, "Lord, look, here *are* two swords."

And He said to them, "It is enough."

39 Coming out, He went to the Mount of Olives, as He was accustomed, and His disciples also followed Him. 40 When He came to the place, He said to them, "Pray that you may not enter into temptation."

41 And He was withdrawn from them about a stone's throw, and He knelt down and prayed, 42 saying, "Father, if it is Your will, take this cup away from Me; nevertheless not My will, but Yours, be done." 43 Then an angel appeared to Him from heaven, strengthening Him. 44 And being in agony, He prayed more earnestly. Then His sweat became like great drops of blood falling down to the ground.

45 When He rose up from prayer, and had come to His disciples, He found them sleeping from sorrow. 46 Then He said to them, "Why do you sleep? Rise and pray, lest you enter into temptation."

47 And while He was still speaking, behold, a multitude; and he who was called Judas, one of the twelve, went before them and drew near to Jesus to kiss Him. 48 But Jesus said to him, "Judas, are you betraying the Son of Man with a kiss?"

49 When those around Him saw what was going to happen, they said to Him, "Lord, shall we strike with the sword?" 50 And one of them struck the servant of the high priest and cut off his right ear.

51 But Jesus answered and said, "Permit even this." And He touched his ear and healed him.

52 Then Jesus said to the chief priests, captains of the temple, and the elders who had come to Him, "Have you come out, as against a robber, with swords and clubs? 53 When I was with you daily in the temple, you did not try to seize Me. But this is your hour, and the power of darkness."

54 Having arrested Him, they led *Him* and brought Him into the high priest's house. But Peter followed at a distance. 55 Now when they had kindled a fire in the midst of the courtyard and sat down together, Peter sat among them. 56 And a

36 אָמַר לָהֶם: "אֲבָל כָּעֵת מִי שֶׁיֵּשׁ לוֹ אַרְנָק יִקַּח נָא אוֹתוֹ, וְכֵן גַּם אֶת הַתַּרְמִיל; וּמִי שֶׁאֵין לוֹ חֶרֶב, שֶׁיִּמְכֹּר אֶת בִּגְדוֹ וְיִקְנֶה. 37 אוֹמֵר אֲנִי לָכֶם, צָרִיךְ שֶׁיִּמָּלֵא בִּי הַכָּתוּב הַזֶּה: 'וְאֶת־פּוֹשְׁעִים נִמְנָה.' וְאָמְנָם מַה שֶּׁמְּכֻוָּן אֵלַי הוֹלֵךְ וְנִשְׁלָם."

38 אָמְרוּ הַתַּלְמִידִים: "אֲדוֹנֵנוּ, הִנֵּה שְׁתֵּי חֲרָבוֹת פֹּה!" אָמַר לָהֶם: "דַּי!"

39 כַּאֲשֶׁר יָצָא הָלַךְ כְּמִנְהָגוֹ אֶל הַר הַזֵּיתִים וְגַם תַּלְמִידָיו הָלְכוּ אַחֲרָיו. 40 בְּהַגִּיעוֹ לַמָּקוֹם אָמַר לָהֶם: "הִתְפַּלְּלוּ שֶׁלֹּא תָּבוֹאוּ לִידֵי נִסָּיוֹן." 41 הוּא פָּרַשׁ מֵהֶם כְּמֶרְחָק שֶׁל יִדּוּי אֶבֶן, כָּרַע עַל בִּרְכָּיו וְהִתְפַּלֵּל לֵאמֹר: 42 "אָבִי, אִם תִּרְצֶה, הַעֲבֵר נָא מֵעָלַי אֶת הַכּוֹס הַזֹּאת. אַךְ אַל יְהֵא כִּרְצוֹנִי כִּי אִם כִּרְצוֹנְךָ." [43 אָז נִרְאָה אֵלָיו מַלְאָךְ מִן הַשָּׁמַיִם וְחִזֵּק אוֹתוֹ. 44 וּכְבוֹא עָלָיו חֶבְלֵי מָוֶת הִתְפַּלֵּל בְּיֶתֶר חָזְקָה וְזֵעָתוֹ הָיְתָה כְּנִטְפֵי דָם יוֹרְדִים עַל הָאָרֶץ.] 45 לְאַחַר שֶׁקָּם מִן הַתְּפִלָּה נִגַּשׁ אֶל הַתַּלְמִידִים וּמָצָא אוֹתָם יְשֵׁנִים מִיָּגוֹן. 46 שָׁאַל אוֹתָם: "לָמָּה אַתֶּם יְשֵׁנִים? קוּמוּ וְהִתְפַּלְּלוּ כְּדֵי שֶׁלֹּא תָּבוֹאוּ לִידֵי נִסָּיוֹן."

47 עוֹדֶנּוּ מְדַבֵּר וְהִנֵּה קְהַל אֲנָשִׁים, וְאֶחָד מִן הַשְּׁנֵים־עָשָׂר הַנִּקְרָא יְהוּדָה הוֹלֵךְ לִפְנֵיהֶם וּמִתְקָרֵב אֶל יֵשׁוּעַ לְנַשְּׁקוֹ. 48 אָמַר לוֹ יֵשׁוּעַ: "יְהוּדָה, בִּנְשִׁיקָה אַתָּה מוֹסֵר אֶת בֶּן־הָאָדָם?"

49 הָאֲנָשִׁים אֲשֶׁר סְבִיבוֹ, כִּרְאוֹתָם מַה עוֹמֵד לִקְרוֹת, אָמְרוּ: "אֲדוֹנֵנוּ, הַאִם לְהַכּוֹת בֶּחָרֶב?" 50 וְאֶחָד מֵהֶם הִכָּה וְקִצֵּץ אֶת אָזְנוֹ הַיְמָנִית שֶׁל עֶבֶד הַכֹּהֵן הַגָּדוֹל. 51 אַךְ יֵשׁוּעַ הֵשִׁיב: "הַרְפּוּ! עַד כָּאן!", נָגַע בְּאָזְנוֹ וְרִפֵּא אוֹתוֹ. 52 פָּנָה יֵשׁוּעַ אֶל רָאשֵׁי הַכֹּהֲנִים וְקָצִינֵי הַמִּקְדָּשׁ וְהַזְּקֵנִים אֲשֶׁר בָּאוּ עָלָיו, וְאָמַר: "כְּמוֹ עַל שׁוֹדֵד יְצָאתֶם בַּחֲרָבוֹת וּבְמַקְלוֹת! 53 יוֹם יוֹם הָיִיתִי עִמָּכֶם בַּמִּקְדָּשׁ וְלֹא שְׁלַחְתֶּם בִּי יָד, אֶלָּא שֶׁזֹּאת שְׁעַתְכֶם וּשְׁעַת שִׁלְטוֹן הַחֹשֶׁךְ."

54 הֵם תָּפְסוּ אוֹתוֹ. הוֹלִיכוּהוּ וְהִכְנִיסוּ אוֹתוֹ לְבֵית הַכֹּהֵן הַגָּדוֹל וְכֵיפָא הָלַךְ אַחֲרָיו מֵרָחוֹק. 55 כַּאֲשֶׁר הִדְלִיקוּ אֵשׁ בְּמֶרְכַּז הֶחָצֵר וְיָשְׁבוּ יַחְדָּיו, יָשַׁב גַּם כֵּיפָא בֵּינֵיהֶם. 56 רָאֲתָה אוֹתוֹ שִׁפְחָה אַחַת יוֹשֵׁב לְיַד הָאֵשׁ, הִתְבּוֹנְנָה בּוֹ וְאָמְרָה: "גַּם זֶה הָיָה אִתּוֹ."

certain servant girl, seeing him as he sat by the fire, looked intently at him and said, "This man was also with Him."

⁵⁷ But he denied Him, saying, "Woman, I do not know Him."

⁵⁸ And after a little while another saw him and said, "You also are of them."

But Peter said, "Man, I am not!"

⁵⁹ Then after about an hour had passed, another confidently affirmed, saying, "Surely this *fellow* also was with Him, for he is a Galilean."

⁶⁰ But Peter said, "Man, I do not know what you are saying!"

Immediately, while he was still speaking, the rooster crowed. ⁶¹ And the Lord turned and looked at Peter. Then Peter remembered the word of the Lord, how He had said to him, "Before the rooster crows, you will deny Me three times." ⁶² So Peter went out and wept bitterly.

⁶³ Now the men who held Jesus mocked Him and beat Him. ⁶⁴ And having blindfolded Him, they struck Him on the face and asked Him, saying, "Prophesy! Who is the one who struck You?" ⁶⁵ And many other things they blasphemously spoke against Him.

⁶⁶ As soon as it was day, the elders of the people, both chief priests and scribes, came together and led Him into their council, saying, ⁶⁷ "If You are the Christ, tell us."

But He said to them, "If I tell you, you will by no means believe. ⁶⁸ And if I also ask *you,* you will by no means answer Me or let *Me* go. ⁶⁹ Hereafter the Son of Man will sit on the right hand of the power of God."

⁷⁰ Then they all said, "Are You then the Son of God?"

So He said to them, "You *rightly* say that I am."

⁷¹ And they said, "What further testimony do we need? For we have heard it ourselves from His own mouth."

23 Then the whole multitude of them arose and led Him to Pilate. ²And they began to accuse Him, saying, "We found this *fellow* perverting the nation, and forbidding to pay taxes to Caesar, saying that He Himself is Christ, a King."

³ Then Pilate asked Him, saying, "Are You the King of the Jews?"

He answered him and said, "*It is as* you say."

⁴ So Pilate said to the chief priests and the crowd, "I find no fault in this Man."

⁵ But they were the more fierce, saying, "He stirs up the people, teaching throughout all Judea, beginning from Galilee to this place."

⁵⁷ אַךְ הוּא הִתְכַּחֵשׁ וְאָמַר: "אִשָּׁה, אֵינֶנִּי מַכִּיר אוֹתוֹ."

⁵⁸ שָׁעָה קַלָּה לְאַחַר מִכֵּן רָאָהוּ אִישׁ אַחֵר וְאָמַר: "גַּם אַתָּה מֵהֶם." אַךְ כֵּיפָא הֵשִׁיב: "בֶּן־אָדָם, אֵינֶנִּי מֵהֶם." ⁵⁹ כַּעֲבֹר שָׁעָה בְּעֵרֶךְ אָמַר אִישׁ אַחֵר בְּהֶחְלֵטִיּוּת: "בֶּאֱמֶת גַּם זֶה הָיָה אִתּוֹ, וַהֲרֵי גְּלִילִי הוּא." ⁶⁰ הֵשִׁיב כֵּיפָא: "בֶּן־אָדָם, אֵינֶנִּי מֵבִין מַה שָּׁאַתָּה אוֹמֵר." וּמִיָּד, בְּעוֹדוֹ מְדַבֵּר, קָרָא הַתַּרְנְגוֹל. ⁶¹ אָז פָּנָה הָאָדוֹן וְהִבִּיט אֶל כֵּיפָא. נִזְכַּר כֵּיפָא בַּדָּבָר שֶׁהָאָדוֹן אָמַר לוֹ – "בְּטֶרֶם יִקְרָא הַיּוֹם הַתַּרְנְגוֹל תִּתְכַּחֵשׁ לִי שָׁלוֹשׁ פְּעָמִים" –, ⁶² יָצָא הַחוּצָה וּמֵרַר בְּבֶכִי.

⁶³ וְהָאֲנָשִׁים שֶׁעָצְרוּ אֶת יֵשׁוּעַ הִתְלוּ בּוֹ וְהִכּוּהוּ. ⁶⁴ הֵם כִּסּוּ אֶת עֵינָיו וְאָמְרוּ: "הִנָּבֵא! מִי הוּא הַמַּכֶּה אוֹתְךָ?" ⁶⁵ וְעוֹד דִּבְרֵי גִּדּוּף רַבִּים הֵטִיחוּ כְּלַפָּיו.

⁶⁶ עִם אוֹר הַיּוֹם נִקְהֲלוּ זִקְנֵי הָעָם, הֵן כֹּהֲנִים גְּדוֹלִים וְהֵן סוֹפְרִים, וְהוֹלִיכוּהוּ אֶל הַסַּנְהֶדְרִין שֶׁלָּהֶם. ⁶⁷ אָמְרוּ לוֹ: "אִם אַתָּה הַמָּשִׁיחַ, אֱמֹר לָנוּ." הֵשִׁיב לָהֶם: "אִם אַגִּיד לָכֶם לֹא תַּאֲמִינוּ, ⁶⁸ וְאִם אֶשְׁאַל לֹא תַּעֲנוּ לִי וְלֹא תְּשַׁחְרְרוּ אוֹתִי. ⁶⁹ אֲבָל מֵעַתָּה יִהְיֶה בֶּן־הָאָדָם יוֹשֵׁב לִימִין גְּבוּרַת הָאֱלֹהִים." ⁷⁰ אָמְרוּ כֻּלָּם: "אִם כֵּן, אַתָּה הוּא בֶּן־הָאֱלֹהִים?" הֵשִׁיב לָהֶם: "אַתֶּם אוֹמְרִים כִּי אֲנִי הוּא." ⁷¹ אָמְרוּ: "מַה לָּנוּ עוֹד צֹרֶךְ בְּעֵדוּת? הֲרֵי בְּעַצְמֵנוּ שָׁמַעְנוּ מִפִּיו."

כג כָּל הַנֶּאֱסָפִים קָמוּ וְהוֹלִיכוּהוּ אֶל פִּילָטוֹס. ²שָׁם הֵחֵלּוּ לְהַאֲשִׁים אוֹתוֹ בְּאָמְרָם: "אֶת זֶה מָצָאנוּ מַדִּיחַ אֶת עַמֵּנוּ, אוֹסֵר לָתֵת מַס לַקֵּיסָר, וְאוֹמֵר עַל עַצְמוֹ שֶׁהוּא מָשִׁיחַ, כְּלוֹמַר מֶלֶךְ." ³שָׁאַל אוֹתוֹ פִּילָטוֹס: "אַתָּה מֶלֶךְ הַיְּהוּדִים?" הֵשִׁיב לוֹ יֵשׁוּעַ: "אַתָּה אוֹמֵר." ⁴אָמַר פִּילָטוֹס אֶל רָאשֵׁי הַכֹּהֲנִים וְאֶל הֲמוֹן הָעָם: "אֵינֶנִּי מוֹצֵא שׁוּם אַשְׁמָה בָּאִישׁ הַזֶּה." ⁵אַךְ הֵם טָעֲנוּ בְּיֶתֶר שְׂאֵת: "הוּא מֵסִית אֶת הָעָם בְּלַמְּדוֹ בְּכָל יְהוּדָה, הָחֵל מִן הַגָּלִיל וְעַד כָּאן."

⁶When Pilate heard of Galilee, he asked if the Man were a Galilean. ⁷And as soon as he knew that He belonged to Herod's jurisdiction, he sent Him to Herod, who was also in Jerusalem at that time. ⁸Now when Herod saw Jesus, he was exceedingly glad; for he had desired for a long *time* to see Him, because he had heard many things about Him, and he hoped to see some miracle done by Him. ⁹Then he questioned Him with many words, but He answered him nothing. ¹⁰And the chief priests and scribes stood and vehemently accused Him. ¹¹Then Herod, with his men of war, treated Him with contempt and mocked *Him,* arrayed Him in a gorgeous robe, and sent Him back to Pilate. ¹²That very day Pilate and Herod became friends with each other, for previously they had been at enmity with each other.

¹³Then Pilate, when he had called together the chief priests, the rulers, and the people, ¹⁴said to them, "You have brought this Man to me, as one who misleads the people. And indeed, having examined *Him* in your presence, I have found no fault in this Man concerning those things of which you accuse Him; ¹⁵no, neither did Herod, for I sent you back to him; and indeed nothing deserving of death has been done by Him. ¹⁶I will therefore chastise Him and release *Him*" ¹⁷(for it was necessary for him to release one to them at the feast).

¹⁸And they all cried out at once, saying, "Away with this *Man,* and release to us Barabbas"— ¹⁹who had been thrown into prison for a certain rebellion made in the city, and for murder.

²⁰Pilate, therefore, wishing to release Jesus, again called out to them. ²¹But they shouted, saying, "Crucify *Him,* crucify Him!"

²²Then he said to them the third time, "Why, what evil has He done? I have found no reason for death in Him. I will therefore chastise Him and let *Him* go."

²³But they were insistent, demanding with loud voices that He be crucified. And the voices of these men and of the chief priests prevailed. ²⁴So Pilate gave sentence that it should be as they requested. ²⁵And he released to them the one they requested, who for rebellion and murder had been thrown into prison; but he delivered Jesus to their will.

²⁶Now as they led Him away, they laid hold of a certain man, Simon a Cyrenian, who was coming from the country, and on him they laid the cross that he might bear *it* after Jesus.

²⁷And a great multitude of the people followed Him, and women who also mourned and lamented Him. ²⁸But Jesus, turning to them, said, "Daugh-

⁶ כַּאֲשֶׁר שָׁמַע זֹאת פִּילָטוֹס חָקַר אִם הָאִישׁ גְּלִילִי. ⁷ מִשֶּׁנּוֹכַח כִּי מִתְּחוּם שִׁלְטוֹנוֹ שֶׁל הוֹרְדוֹס הוּא, שָׁלַח אוֹתוֹ אֶל הוֹרְדוֹס, שֶׁהָיָה גַם הוּא בִּירוּשָׁלַיִם בְּאוֹתָם יָמִים. ⁸ הוֹרְדוֹס שָׂמַח מְאֹד כִּרְאוֹתוֹ אֶת יֵשׁוּעַ, שֶׁכֵּן מִיָּמִים רַבִּים הִשְׁתּוֹקֵק לִרְאוֹת אוֹתוֹ מִפְּנֵי שֶׁשָּׁמַע עַל אוֹדוֹתָיו וְקִוָּה לִרְאוֹת גַם נַעֲשָׂה עַל־יָדָיו. ⁹ הוּא שָׁאַל אוֹתוֹ עַל דְּבָרִים רַבִּים, אַךְ יֵשׁוּעַ לֹא הֵשִׁיב לוֹ דָּבָר. ¹⁰ עָמְדוּ רָאשֵׁי הַכֹּהֲנִים וְהַסּוֹפְרִים וְהֶאֱשִׁימוּהוּ נִמְרָצוֹת. ¹¹ הִתְחִילוּ הוֹרְדוֹס וַחֲיָלָיו לְבַזּוֹתוֹ וְהֵתֵלּוּ בּוֹ. הֵם הִלְבִּישׁוּהוּ גְּלִימָה מַבְהִיקָה וּשְׁלָחוּהוּ אֶל פִּילָטוֹס. ¹² אוֹתוֹ יוֹם נַעֲשׂוּ פִּילָטוֹס וְהוֹרְדוֹס יְדִידִים זֶה לָזֶה, כִּי קֹדֶם לָכֵן שָׂרְרָה אֵיבָה בֵּינֵיהֶם.

¹³ פִּילָטוֹס קָרָא אֵלָיו אֶת רָאשֵׁי הַכֹּהֲנִים וְהַשָּׂרִים וְהָעָם, ¹⁴ וְאָמַר לָהֶם: "הֲבֵאתֶם אֵלַי אֶת הָאִישׁ הַזֶּה כְּמַדִּיחַ אֶת הָעָם, וְהִנֵּה אֲנִי חֲקַרְתִּי אוֹתוֹ לְעֵינֵיכֶם וְלֹא מָצָאתִי בָּאִישׁ הַזֶּה כָּל אַשְׁמָה מִן הַדְּבָרִים שֶׁאַתֶּם מַאֲשִׁימִים אוֹתוֹ. ¹⁵ גַּם הוֹרְדוֹס לֹא מָצָא כְּלוּם, שֶׁהֲרֵי שָׁלַח אוֹתוֹ בַּחֲזָרָה אֵלֵינוּ. רְאוּ, הָאִישׁ אַף לֹא עָשָׂה דָּבָר אֶחָד הַמְחַיֵּב מָוֶת. ¹⁶ לָכֵן אֲעַנִּישׁ אוֹתוֹ בְּמַלְקוֹת וַאֲשַׁחְרֵר אוֹתוֹ." ¹⁸ אֶלָּא שֶׁכֻּלָּם יַחְדָּיו צָעֲקוּ: "קַח אוֹתוֹ וְשַׁחְרֵר לָנוּ אֶת בַּר־אַבָּא!" — ¹⁹ אִישׁ שֶׁהֻשְׁלַךְ לְבֵית כֶּלֶא בִּגְלַל אֵיזֶה מֶרֶד שֶׁהָיָה בָּעִיר וּבִגְלַל רֶצַח.

²⁰ פִּילָטוֹס הוֹסִיף לְדַבֵּר אֲלֵיהֶם, כִּי רָצָה לְשַׁחְרֵר אֶת יֵשׁוּעַ. ²¹ אַךְ הֵם צָעֲקוּ: "צְלֹב, צְלֹב אוֹתוֹ!" ²² אָמַר לָהֶם פַּעַם שְׁלִישִׁית: "אֲבָל מֶה רָעָה עָשָׂה זֶה? לֹא מָצָאתִי בּוֹ כָּל אַשְׁמָה מְחַיֶּבֶת מָוֶת. עַל כֵּן אֲעַנִּישׁ אוֹתוֹ בְּמַלְקוֹת וַאֲשַׁחְרֵר אוֹתוֹ." ²³ אַךְ הֵם הִגְבִּירוּ לַחֲצָם וּבְקוֹל גָּדוֹל דָּרְשׁוּ שֶׁיִּצָּלֵב. וְאָכֵן הִכְרִיעוּ קוֹלוֹתֵיהֶם אֶת הַכַּף. ²⁴ פִּילָטוֹס פָּסַק שֶׁתִּתְמַלֵּא דְּרִישָׁתָם ²⁵ וְשִׁחְרֵר אֶת הָאִישׁ אֲשֶׁר בִּקְּשׁוּ, זֶה שֶׁהֻשְׁלַךְ לְבֵית כֶּלֶא בִּגְלַל מֶרֶד וָרֶצַח, וְאֶת יֵשׁוּעַ הִפְקִיד לִרְצוֹנָם. ²⁶ כַּאֲשֶׁר הוֹלִיכוּהוּ מִשָּׁם עָצְרוּ אִישׁ אֶחָד שֶׁבָּא מִן הַשָּׂדֶה, אֶת שִׁמְעוֹן מִקִּירֶנְיָה, וְשָׂמוּ עָלָיו אֶת הַצְּלָב כְּדֵי שֶׁיִּשָּׂא אוֹתוֹ אַחֲרֵי יֵשׁוּעַ. ²⁷ אַחֲרָיו הָלְכוּ הָמוֹן רַב מִן הָעָם, וְגַם נָשִׁים שֶׁסָּפְדוּ וְקוֹנְנוּ עָלָיו. ²⁸ פָּנָה אֲלֵיהֶן יֵשׁוּעַ

ters of Jerusalem, do not weep for Me, but weep for yourselves and for your children. ²⁹ For indeed the days are coming in which they will say, 'Blessed *are* the barren, wombs that never bore, and breasts which never nursed!' ³⁰ Then they will begin *'to say to the mountains, "Fall on us!" and to the hills, "Cover us!"'* ³¹ For if they do these things in the green wood, what will be done in the dry?"

³² There were also two others, criminals, led with Him to be put to death. ³³ And when they had come to the place called Calvary, there they crucified Him, and the criminals, one on the right hand and the other on the left. ³⁴ Then Jesus said, "Father, forgive them, for they do not know what they do."

And they divided His garments and cast lots. ³⁵ And the people stood looking on. But even the rulers with them sneered, saying, "He saved others; let Him save Himself if He is the Christ, the chosen of God."

³⁶ The soldiers also mocked Him, coming and offering Him sour wine, ³⁷ and saying, "If You are the King of the Jews, save Yourself."

³⁸ And an inscription also was written over Him in letters of Greek, Latin, and Hebrew:

THIS IS THE KING OF THE JEWS.

³⁹ Then one of the criminals who were hanged blasphemed Him, saying, "If You are the Christ, save Yourself and us."

⁴⁰ But the other, answering, rebuked him, saying, "Do you not even fear God, seeing you are under the same condemnation? ⁴¹ And we indeed justly, for we receive the due reward of our deeds; but this Man has done nothing wrong." ⁴² Then he said to Jesus, "Lord, remember me when You come into Your kingdom."

⁴³ And Jesus said to him, "Assuredly, I say to you, today you will be with Me in Paradise."

⁴⁴ Now it was about the sixth hour, and there was darkness over all the earth until the ninth hour. ⁴⁵ Then the sun was darkened, and the veil of the temple was torn in two. ⁴⁶ And when Jesus had cried out with a loud voice, He said, "Father, *'into Your hands I commit My spirit.'*" Having said this, He breathed His last.

⁴⁷ So when the centurion saw what had happened, he glorified God, saying, "Certainly this was a righteous Man!"

⁴⁸ And the whole crowd who came together to that sight, seeing what had been done, beat their breasts and returned. ⁴⁹ But all His acquaintances, and the women who followed Him from Galilee, stood at a distance, watching these things.

וְאָמַר: "בְּנוֹת יְרוּשָׁלַיִם, אַל תִּבְכֶּינָה עָלַי, אֶלָּא עַל עַצְמְכֶן בְּכֶינָה וְעַל יַלְדֵיכֶן, ²⁹ כִּי הִנֵּה יָמִים בָּאִים וְיֹאמְרוּ, 'אַשְׁרֵי הָעֲקָרוֹת, אַשְׁרֵי כָּל בֶּטֶן שֶׁלֹּא יָלְדָה וְאַשְׁרֵי הַשָּׁדַיִם שֶׁלֹּא הֵינִיקוּ'. ³⁰ אָז יֹאמְרוּ אֶל הֶהָרִים, 'נִפְלוּ עָלֵינוּ', וְאֶל הַגְּבָעוֹת, 'כַּסּוּנוּ'; ³¹ שֶׁהֲרֵי אִם כָּכָה עוֹשִׂים בָּעֵץ הַלַּח, מַה יְּקָרֶה לַיָּבֵשׁ?"

³² גַּם שְׁנַיִם אֲחֵרִים, פּוֹשְׁעִים, הוּבְלוּ כְּדֵי שֶׁיּוּמְתוּ אִתּוֹ. ³³ כְּשֶׁבָּאוּ אֶל הַמָּקוֹם הַנִּקְרָא גָּלְגָּתָא צָלְבוּ אוֹתוֹ שָׁם עִם הַפּוֹשְׁעִים, אֶחָד מִימִינוֹ וְאֶחָד מִשְׂמֹאלוֹ. ³⁴ אָמַר יֵשׁוּעַ: "אָבִי, סְלַח לָהֶם, כִּי אֵינָם יוֹדְעִים מַה שֶּׁהֵם עוֹשִׂים." וְהֵם חִלְּקוּ אֶת בְּגָדָיו לְאַחַר שֶׁהִפִּילוּ גּוֹרָלוֹת.

³⁵ אוֹתָהּ שָׁעָה עָמַד הָעָם וְהִתְבּוֹנֵן, וְהַמַּנְהִיגִים גַּם הֵם לָעֲגוּ לוֹ בְּאָמְרָם: "אֲחֵרִים הוּא הוֹשִׁיעַ; שֶׁיּוֹשִׁיעַ אֶת עַצְמוֹ אִם הוּא הַמָּשִׁיחַ בְּחִיר הָאֱלֹהִים!" ³⁶ גַּם אַנְשֵׁי הַצָּבָא הֵתֵלּוּ בּוֹ. הֵם הִתְקָרְבוּ וְהִגִּישׁוּ לוֹ חֹמֶץ, ³⁷ וְאָמְרוּ: "אִם אַתָּה מֶלֶךְ הַיְּהוּדִים, הוֹשַׁע אֶת עַצְמְךָ!" ³⁸ וְגַם כְּתֹבֶת הָיְתָה מֵעָלָיו: "זֶהוּ מֶלֶךְ הַיְּהוּדִים."

³⁹ אַחַד הַפּוֹשְׁעִים הַמּוּקָעִים הֵטִיחַ כְּלַפָּיו: "הֲלֹא אַתָּה הַמָּשִׁיחַ! הַצֵּל אֶת עַצְמְךָ וְאוֹתָנוּ!" ⁴⁰ הֵשִׁיב הַשֵּׁנִי כְּשֶׁהוּא גּוֹעֵר בּוֹ: "אֵינְךָ יָרֵא מֵאֱלֹהִים? הֲרֵי אַתָּה נָתוּן בְּאוֹתוֹ גְּזַר דִּין! ⁴¹ אֲנַחְנוּ לְפִי הַצֶּדֶק, כִּי אָנוּ מְקַבְּלִים גְּמוּל רָאוּי עַל מַה שֶּׁעָשִׂינוּ, אֲבָל הָאִישׁ הַזֶּה לֹא עָשָׂה שׁוּם רַע." ⁴² וְעוֹד אָמַר: "יֵשׁוּעַ, אָנָּא זְכֹר אוֹתִי כַּאֲשֶׁר תָּבֹּא לְמַלְכוּתְךָ." ⁴³ הֵשִׁיב לוֹ יֵשׁוּעַ: "אָמֵן. אוֹמֵר אֲנִי לְךָ, הַיּוֹם תִּהְיֶה אַתָּה אִתִּי בְּגַן־עֵדֶן."

⁴⁴ בְּעֵרֶךְ בְּשָׁעָה שְׁתֵּים־עֶשְׂרֵה בַּצָּהֳרַיִם הִשְׁתָּרַר חֹשֶׁךְ עַל כָּל הָאָרֶץ עַד הַשָּׁעָה שָׁלֹשׁ. ⁴⁵ הַשֶּׁמֶשׁ חָשְׁכָה וּפָרֹכֶת הַהֵיכָל נִקְרְעָה לִשְׁנַיִם. ⁴⁶ וְיֵשׁוּעַ קָרָא בְּקוֹל גָּדוֹל: "אָבִי, בְּיָדְךָ אַפְקִיד רוּחִי", וְנָפַח אֶת רוּחוֹ. ⁴⁷ כְּשֶׁרָאָה שַׂר הַמֵּאָה אֶת הַמִּתְרַחֵשׁ נָתַן כָּבוֹד לֵאלֹהִים בְּאָמְרוֹ: "בֶּאֱמֶת, הָאִישׁ הַזֶּה הָיָה צַדִּיק!" ⁴⁸ כָּל הֶהָמוֹן אֲשֶׁר נִקְהֲלוּ אֶל הַמַּרְאֶה הַזֶּה, כִּרְאוֹתָם אֶת הַמִּתְרַחֵשׁ הִכּוּ עַל חֲזוֹתֵיהֶם. הֵם חָזְרוּ לְבָתֵּיהֶם, ⁴⁹ אַךְ כָּל מַכָּרָיו, גַּם הַנָּשִׁים אֲשֶׁר הָלְכוּ אִתּוֹ מִן הַגָּלִיל, עָמְדוּ מֵרָחוֹק וְרָאוּ אֶת הַנַּעֲשָׂה.

⁵⁰ Now behold, *there was* a man named Joseph, a council member, a good and just man. ⁵¹ He had not consented to their decision and deed. *He was* from Arimathea, a city of the Jews, who himself was also waiting for the kingdom of God. ⁵² This man went to Pilate and asked for the body of Jesus. ⁵³ Then he took it down, wrapped it in linen, and laid it in a tomb *that was* hewn out of the rock, where no one had ever lain before. ⁵⁴ That day was the Preparation, and the Sabbath drew near.

⁵⁵ And the women who had come with Him from Galilee followed after, and they observed the tomb and how His body was laid. ⁵⁶ Then they returned and prepared spices and fragrant oils. And they rested on the Sabbath according to the commandment.

24 Now on the first *day* of the week, very early in the morning, they, and certain *other women* with them, came to the tomb bringing the spices which they had prepared. ² But they found the stone rolled away from the tomb. ³ Then they went in and did not find the body of the Lord Jesus. ⁴ And it happened, as they were greatly perplexed about this, that behold, two men stood by them in shining garments. ⁵ Then, as they were afraid and bowed *their* faces to the earth, they said to them, "Why do you seek the living among the dead? ⁶ He is not here, but is risen! Remember how He spoke to you when He was still in Galilee, ⁷ saying, 'The Son of Man must be delivered into the hands of sinful men, and be crucified, and the third day rise again.'"

⁸ And they remembered His words. ⁹ Then they returned from the tomb and told all these things to the eleven and to all the rest. ¹⁰ It was Mary Magdalene, Joanna, Mary *the mother* of James, and the other *women* with them, who told these things to the apostles. ¹¹ And their words seemed to them like idle tales, and they did not believe them. ¹² But Peter arose and ran to the tomb; and stooping down, he saw the linen cloths lying by themselves; and he departed, marveling to himself at what had happened.

¹³ Now behold, two of them were traveling that same day to a village called Emmaus, which was seven miles from Jerusalem. ¹⁴ And they talked together of all these things which had happened. ¹⁵ So it was, while they conversed and reasoned, that Jesus Himself drew near and went with them. ¹⁶ But their eyes were restrained, so that they did not know Him.

¹⁷ And He said to them, "What kind of conversation *is* this that you have with one another as you walk and are sad?"

⁵⁰ וְאִישׁ אֶחָד, יוֹסֵף שְׁמוֹ, שֶׁהָיָה חֲבֵר הַסַּנְהֶדְרִין וְתוֹשָׁב הָעִיר הַיְהוּדִית רָמָתַיִם, אִישׁ טוֹב וְצַדִּיק וּמְחַכֶּה לְמַלְכוּת אֱלֹהִים, ⁵¹ לֹא הִסְכִּים לִתְכָנִיתָם וּלְפָעֳלָם. ⁵² הוּא בָּא אֶל פִּילָטוֹס וּבִקֵּשׁ מִמֶּנּוּ אֶת גוּפַת יֵשׁוּעַ. ⁵³ אַחֲרֵי שֶׁהוֹרִידָהּ עָטַף אוֹתָהּ בְּסָדִין וְהִנִּיחָהּ בְּקֶבֶר חָצוּב בְּסֶלַע, שַׁעַר אָז לֹא הֻנַּח בּוֹ אִישׁ. ⁵⁴ אוֹתוֹ יוֹם הָיָה עֶרֶב שַׁבָּת וְהַשַּׁבָּת קְרֵבָה. ⁵⁵ הַנָּשִׁים שֶׁבָּאוּ עִם יֵשׁוּעַ מִן הַגָּלִיל הָלְכוּ אַחֲרֵי יוֹסֵף. הֵן רָאוּ אֶת הַקֶּבֶר וְרָאוּ כֵּיצַד הֻנְּחָה גוּפָתוֹ. ⁵⁶ אַחֲרֵי שֶׁחָזְרוּ הֵכִינוּ בְּשָׂמִים וּמִרְקָחוֹת וּבַשַּׁבָּת שָׁבְתוּ עַל־פִּי הַמִּצְוָה.

כד בָּרִאשׁוֹן בַּשָּׁבוּעַ, לִפְנֵי עֲלוֹת הַשַּׁחַר, נָשְׂאוּ אֶת הַבְּשָׂמִים אֲשֶׁר הֵכִינוּ וּבָאוּ אֶל הַקֶּבֶר. ² הֵן רָאוּ שֶׁהָאֶבֶן כְּבָר נָגֹלָּה מִן הַקֶּבֶר ³ וְנִכְנְסוּ לְתוֹכוֹ, אַךְ לֹא מָצְאוּ אֶת גוּפַת הָאָדוֹן יֵשׁוּעַ. ⁴ עוֹדָן נְבוּכוֹת עַל הַדָּבָר הַזֶּה וְהִנֵּה שְׁנֵי אֲנָשִׁים מַבְרִיקִים נִצְּבוּ עַל־יָדָן. ⁵ הֵן נִתְמַלְּאוּ פַחַד וְהִרְכִּינוּ פְּנֵיהֶן אַרְצָה. "לָמָּה אַתֶּן מְחַפְּשׂוֹת אֶת הַחַי בֵּין הַמֵּתִים?" שָׁאֲלוּ הַשְּׁנַיִם. ⁶ "הוּא אֵינֶנּוּ פֹּה, הוּא קָם לִתְחִיָּה. זִכְרֹנָה מַה שֶּׁאָמַר לָכֶן עוֹד בִּהְיוֹתוֹ בַּגָּלִיל. ⁷ הוּא אָמַר כִּי 'בֶּן־הָאָדָם צָרִיךְ לְהִמָּסֵר לִידֵי אֲנָשִׁים חוֹטְאִים וּלְהִצָּלֵב, וּבַיּוֹם הַשְּׁלִישִׁי לָקוּם'." ⁸ וְאָמְנָם הֵן נִזְכְּרוּ בִּדְבָרָיו. ⁹ לְאַחַר מִכֵּן חָזְרוּ מִן הַקֶּבֶר וְסִפְּרוּ אֶת כָּל הַדְּבָרִים הָאֵלֶּה לְאַחַד־עָשָׂר וּלְכָל הַשְּׁאָר. ¹⁰ הַנָּשִׁים שֶׁסִּפְּרוּ זֹאת לַשְּׁלִיחִים הָיוּ מִרְיָם הַמַּגְדָּלִית, יוֹחָנָה, מִרְיָם אֵם יַעֲקֹב, וַאֲחֵרוֹת שֶׁהָיוּ אִתָּן, ¹¹ אֶלָּא שֶׁדִּבְרֵיהֶן נִרְאוּ בְּעֵינֵיהֶם כְּדִבְרֵי הֶבֶל וְלֹא הֶאֱמִינוּ לָהֶן. ¹² אוּלָם כֵּיפָא קָם וְרָץ אֶל הַקֶּבֶר. כְּשֶׁהִתְכּוֹפֵף רָאָה אֶת הַתַּכְרִיכִים לְבַדָּם, וְחָזַר הַבַּיְתָה תָּמֵהַּ עַל מַה שֶּׁקָּרָה.

¹³ אוֹתוֹ יוֹם הָיוּ שְׁנַיִם מֵהֶם הוֹלְכִים אֶל הַכְּפָר הַנִּקְרָא עַמָּאוּס, שֶׁמֶּרְחָקוֹ מִירוּשָׁלַיִם כְּשִׁבְעָה מִילִין, ¹⁴ וּמְשׂוֹחֲחִים בֵּינֵיהֶם עַל כָּל מַה שֶׁקָּרָה. ¹⁵ וְהִנֵּה בְּשָׁעָה שֶׁשּׂוֹחֲחוּ וְהִתְוַכְּחוּ הִתְקָרֵב יֵשׁוּעַ עַצְמוֹ וְהָלַךְ עִמָּהֶם, ¹⁶ אֶלָּא שֶׁעֵינֵיהֶם הָיוּ אֲחוּזוֹת וְלֹא הִכִּירוּהוּ. ¹⁷ אָמַר לָהֶם: "מָה הַדְּבָרִים הָאֵלֶּה

13 כְּשִׁבְעָה מִילִין – כְּאַחַד־עָשָׂר קִילוֹמֶטֶר.

18 Then the one whose name was Cleopas answered and said to Him, "Are You the only stranger in Jerusalem, and have You not known the things which happened there in these days?"

19 And He said to them, "What things?"

So they said to Him, "The things concerning Jesus of Nazareth, who was a Prophet mighty in deed and word before God and all the people, 20 and how the chief priests and our rulers delivered Him to be condemned to death, and crucified Him. 21 But we were hoping that it was He who was going to redeem Israel. Indeed, besides all this, today is the third day since these things happened. 22 Yes, and certain women of our company, who arrived at the tomb early, astonished us. 23 When they did not find His body, they came saying that they had also seen a vision of angels who said He was alive. 24 And certain of those *who were* with us went to the tomb and found *it* just as the women had said; but Him they did not see."

25 Then He said to them, "O foolish ones, and slow of heart to believe in all that the prophets have spoken! 26 Ought not the Christ to have suffered these things and to enter into His glory?" 27 And beginning at Moses and all the Prophets, He expounded to them in all the Scriptures the things concerning Himself.

28 Then they drew near to the village where they were going, and He indicated that He would have gone farther. 29 But they constrained Him, saying, "Abide with us, for it is toward evening, and the day is far spent." And He went in to stay with them.

30 Now it came to pass, as He sat at the table with them, that He took bread, blessed and broke *it*, and gave it to them. 31 Then their eyes were opened and they knew Him; and He vanished from their sight.

32 And they said to one another, "Did not our heart burn within us while He talked with us on the road, and while He opened the Scriptures to us?" 33 So they rose up that very hour and returned to Jerusalem, and found the eleven and those *who were* with them gathered together, 34 saying, "The Lord is risen indeed, and has appeared to Simon!" 35 And they told about the things *that had happened* on the road, and how He was known to them in the breaking of bread.

36 Now as they said these things, Jesus Himself stood in the midst of them, and said to them, "Peace to you." 37 But they were terrified and frightened, and supposed they had seen a spirit. 38 And He said to them, "Why are you troubled? And why do doubts arise in your hearts? 39 Behold

שֶׁאַתֶּם מִתְדַּיְּנִים בָּהֶם בַּדֶּרֶךְ?" הַשָּׁנַיִם נֶעֶצְרוּ וְעֶצֶב נָסוּךְ עַל פְּנֵיהֶם. 18 אֶחָד מֵהֶם, קְלֵיוֹפָס שְׁמוֹ, הֵשִׁיב וְאָמַר אֵלָיו: "הַאָם אַתָּה רַק אוֹרֵחַ בִּירוּשָׁלַיִם וְאֵינְךָ יוֹדֵעַ מַה נַּעֲשָׂה בְּתוֹכָה בַּיָּמִים אֵלֶּה?" 19 שָׁאַל אוֹתָם: "מַה הַדָּבָר?" אָמְרוּ לוֹ: "מַה שֶׁקָּרָה לְיֵשׁוּעַ מִנָּצְרַת שֶׁהָיָה אִישׁ נָבִיא, גִּבּוֹר בְּמַעֲשֶׂה וּבְאֹמֶר לִפְנֵי אֱלֹהִים וְלִפְנֵי כָּל הָעָם. 20 כֹּהֲנֵינוּ הַגְּדוֹלִים וּמַנְהִיגֵינוּ הִסְגִּירוּהוּ לְמִשְׁפַּט מָוֶת וְצָלְבוּ אוֹתוֹ, 21 וַאֲנַחְנוּ קִוִּינוּ כִּי הוּא זֶה אֲשֶׁר עָתִיד לִגְאֹל אֶת יִשְׂרָאֵל. אֲבָל נוֹסָף עַל כָּל זֹאת, כְּעֵת הַיּוֹם הַשְּׁלִישִׁי מֵאָז קָרוּ הַדְּבָרִים הָאֵלֶּה. 22 וּמַה גַּם שֶׁכַּמָּה נָשִׁים מִקְּרְבֵּנוּ הֶדְהִימוּ אוֹתָנוּ: בַּבֹּקֶר הַשְׁכֵּם הָיוּ בַּקֶּבֶר 23 וְלֹא מָצְאוּ אֶת גּוּפָתוֹ, וּבָאוּ וְסִפְּרוּ שֶׁאַף רָאוּ בְּחֶזְיוֹן מַלְאָכִים אֲשֶׁר אָמְרוּ כִּי הוּא חַי. 24 אֲחָדִים מֵאִתָּנוּ הָלְכוּ אֶל הַקֶּבֶר וּמְצָאוּהוּ בְּדִיּוּק כְּפִי שֶׁהַנָּשִׁים סִפְּרוּ, אַךְ אוֹתוֹ לֹא רָאוּ."

25 הֵשִׁיב וְאָמַר לָהֶם: "הוֹי חַסְרֵי דַעַת וְכִבְדֵי לֵב מֵהַאֲמִין בְּכָל אֲשֶׁר דִּבְּרוּ הַנְּבִיאִים! 26 הֲרֵי עַל הַמָּשִׁיחַ הָיָה לִסְבֹּל אֶת כָּל זֹאת וּלְהִכָּנֵס אֶל תִּפְאֶרֶת כְּבוֹדוֹ!" 27 הוּא הֵחֵל מִמֹּשֶׁה וּמִכָּל הַנְּבִיאִים וּבֵאֵר לָהֶם אֶת הַדְּבָרִים הַמְּכֻוָּנִים אֵלָיו בְּכָל הַכְּתוּבִים.

28 כַּאֲשֶׁר הִתְקָרְבוּ אֶל הַכְּפָר שֶׁהָיָה מְגַמַּת פְּנֵיהֶם הוּא הֶעֱמִיד פָּנִים כְּהוֹלֵךְ לוֹ לְדַרְכּוֹ. 29 אַךְ הֵם הִפְצִירוּ בּוֹ בְּאָמְרָם: "הִשָּׁאֵר אִתָּנוּ, כִּי הָעֶרֶב קָרֵב וּכְבָר פָּנָה הַיּוֹם." לְפִיכָךְ נִכְנַס וְנִשְׁאַר אִתָּם. 30 כַּאֲשֶׁר הֵסֵב עִמָּהֶם לָקַח אֶת הַלֶּחֶם, בֵּרַךְ וּבָצַע אוֹתוֹ וְנָתַן לָהֶם. 31 אָז נִפְקְחוּ עֵינֵיהֶם וְהִכִּירוּהוּ, וְהוּא נֶעֱלַם מֵהֶם. 32 אָמְרוּ זֶה לָזֶה: "הֲרֵי לִבֵּנוּ הָיָה בּוֹעֵר בְּקִרְבֵּנוּ כְּשֶׁדִּבֶּר אֵלֵינוּ בַּדֶּרֶךְ וּפָתַר לָנוּ אֶת הַכְּתוּבִים!" 33 אוֹתָהּ שָׁעָה קָמוּ וְחָזְרוּ לִירוּשָׁלַיִם. הֵם מָצְאוּ אֶת הָאַחַד-עָשָׂר מְכֻנָּסִים עִם חַבְרֵיהֶם, 34 וְהַכֹּל אוֹמְרִים כִּי הָאָדוֹן אָכֵן קָם וְנִרְאָה אֶל שִׁמְעוֹן. 35 הֵם סִפְּרוּ מַה שֶּׁקָּרָה בַּדֶּרֶךְ וְכִי הִכִּירוּהוּ כַּאֲשֶׁר בָּצַע אֶת הַלֶּחֶם.

36 עוֹדָם מְדַבְּרִים כָּזֹאת וְהוּא עָמַד בְּתוֹכָם. אָמַר לָהֶם: "שָׁלוֹם לָכֶם", 37 אַךְ הֵם נִבְהֲלוּ וְנִתְמַלְאוּ פַחַד, וְחָשְׁבוּ כִּי רוּחַ הֵם רוֹאִים. 38 אָמַר לָהֶם: "מַדּוּעַ נֶחֱרַדְתֶּם וּמַדּוּעַ עוֹלִים סְפֵקוֹת בִּלְבַבְכֶם? 39 רְאוּ אֶת יָדַי וְאֶת רַגְלַי – שֶׁאֲנִי הוּא. מַשְׁשׁוּנִי

My hands and My feet, that it is I Myself. Handle Me and see, for a spirit does not have flesh and bones as you see I have."

40 When He had said this, He showed them His hands and His feet. 41 But while they still did not believe for joy, and marveled, He said to them, "Have you any food here?" 42 So they gave Him a piece of a broiled fish and some honeycomb. 43 And He took *it* and ate in their presence.

44 Then He said to them, "These *are* the words which I spoke to you while I was still with you, that all things must be fulfilled which were written in the Law of Moses and *the* Prophets and *the* Psalms concerning Me." 45 And He opened their understanding, that they might comprehend the Scriptures.

46 Then He said to them, "Thus it is written, and thus it was necessary for the Christ to suffer and to rise from the dead the third day, 47 and that repentance and remission of sins should be preached in His name to all nations, beginning at Jerusalem. 48 And you are witnesses of these things. 49 Behold, I send the Promise of My Father upon you; but tarry in the city of Jerusalem until you are endued with power from on high."

50 And He led them out as far as Bethany, and He lifted up His hands and blessed them. 51 Now it came to pass, while He blessed them, that He was parted from them and carried up into heaven. 52 And they worshiped Him, and returned to Jerusalem with great joy, 53 and were continually in the temple praising and blessing God. Amen.

וּרְאוּ, הֲרֵי לְרוּחַ אֵין בָּשָׂר וַעֲצָמוֹת כְּמוֹ שֶׁאַתֶּם רוֹאִים בִּי." 40 וּבְאָמְרוֹ זֹאת הֶרְאָה לָהֶם אֶת יָדָיו וְאֶת רַגְלָיו. 41 מֵאַחַר שֶׁעוֹד לֹא הֶאֱמִינוּ מֵרֹב שִׂמְחָה וְהָיוּ מְלֵאֵי פְּלִיאָה, אָמַר לָהֶם: "הַאִם יֵשׁ לָכֶם פֹּה אֵיזֶה אֹכֶל?" 42 הֵם נָתְנוּ לוֹ חֲתִיכַת דָּג צָלוּי, 43 וְהוּא לָקַח וְאָכַל לְעֵינֵיהֶם.

44 הוֹסִיף וְאָמַר לָהֶם: "אֵלֶּה דְּבָרַי אֲשֶׁר דִּבַּרְתִּי אֲלֵיכֶם בְּעוֹד שֶׁהָיִיתִי עִמָּכֶם: צָרִיךְ שֶׁיִּתְקַיֵּם כָּל הַכָּתוּב עָלַי בְּתוֹרַת מֹשֶׁה וּבַנְּבִיאִים וּבַתְּהִלִּים." 45 אָז פָּתַח אֶת לְבָבָם לְהָבִין אֶת הַכְּתוּבִים 46 וְאָמַר לָהֶם: "כָּךְ כָּתוּב, שֶׁהַמָּשִׁיחַ יִסְבֹּל וְיָקוּם מִן הַמֵּתִים בַּיּוֹם הַשְּׁלִישִׁי, 47 וּבִשְׁמוֹ תֻּכְרַז תְּשׁוּבָה וּסְלִיחַת חֲטָאִים לְכָל הַגּוֹיִים הָחֵל מִירוּשָׁלַיִם. 48 אַתֶּם עֵדִים לַדְּבָרִים הָאֵלֶּה. 49 הִנְנִי שׁוֹלֵחַ לָכֶם אֶת אֲשֶׁר הִבְטִיחַ אָבִי, וְאַתֶּם שְׁבוּ בָּעִיר עַד שֶׁתִּלְבְּשׁוּ עֹז מִמָּרוֹם."

50 הוּא הוֹצִיא אוֹתָם עַד בֵּית עַנְיָה, נָשָׂא אֶת יָדָיו וּבֵרְכָם. 51 בְּשָׁעָה שֶׁבֵּרֵךְ אוֹתָם נִפְרַד מֵהֶם וְנִשָּׂא הַשָּׁמַיְמָה. 52 הֵם הִשְׁתַּחֲווּ לוֹ וְחָזְרוּ לִירוּשָׁלַיִם בְּשִׂמְחָה גְּדוֹלָה, 53 וְהִתְמִידוּ לִהְיוֹת בַּמִּקְדָּשׁ כְּשֶׁהֵם מְבָרְכִים אֶת הָאֱלֹהִים.

הַבְּשׂוֹרָה עַל־פִּי יוֹחָנָן

1 In the beginning was the Word, and the Word was with God, and the Word was God. ²He was in the beginning with God. ³All things were made through Him, and without Him nothing was made that was made. ⁴In Him was life, and the life was the light of men. ⁵And the light shines in the darkness, and the darkness did not comprehend it.

⁶There was a man sent from God, whose name *was* John. ⁷This man came for a witness, to bear witness of the Light, that all through him might believe. ⁸He was not that Light, but *was sent* to bear witness of that Light. ⁹That was the true Light which gives light to every man coming into the world.

¹⁰He was in the world, and the world was made through Him, and the world did not know Him. ¹¹He came to His own, and His own did not receive Him. ¹²But as many as received Him, to them He gave the right to become children of God, to those who believe in His name: ¹³who were born, not of blood, nor of the will of the flesh, nor of the will of man, but of God.

¹⁴And the Word became flesh and dwelt among us, and we beheld His glory, the glory as of the only begotten of the Father, full of grace and truth.

¹⁵John bore witness of Him and cried out, saying, "This was He of whom I said, 'He who comes after me is preferred before me, for He was before me.'"

¹⁶And of His fullness we have all received, and grace for grace. ¹⁷For the law was given through Moses, *but* grace and truth came through Jesus Christ. ¹⁸No one has seen God at any time. The only begotten Son, who is in the bosom of the Father, He has declared *Him*.

¹⁹Now this is the testimony of John, when the Jews sent priests and Levites from Jerusalem to ask him, "Who are you?"

²⁰He confessed, and did not deny, but confessed, "I am not the Christ."

²¹And they asked him, "What then? Are you Elijah?"

He said, "I am not."

"Are you the Prophet?"

And he answered, "No."

א בְּרֵאשִׁית הָיָה הַדָּבָר, וְהַדָּבָר הָיָה עִם הָאֱלֹהִים, וֵאלֹהִים הָיָה הַדָּבָר. ²הוּא הָיָה בְּרֵאשִׁית עִם הָאֱלֹהִים. ³הַכֹּל נִהְיָה עַל־יָדָיו, וּמִבַּלְעָדָיו לֹא נִהְיָה כָּל אֲשֶׁר נִהְיָה. ⁴בּוֹ הָיוּ חַיִּים וְהַחַיִּים הָיוּ הָאוֹר לִבְנֵי הָאָדָם. ⁵וְהָאוֹר מֵאִיר בַּחֹשֶׁךְ וְהַחֹשֶׁךְ לֹא הִשִּׂיגוֹ.

⁶אִישׁ הָיָה שָׁלוּחַ מֵאֵת אֱלֹהִים וּשְׁמוֹ יוֹחָנָן. ⁷הוּא בָּא לְעֵדוּת, לְהָעִיד עַל הָאוֹר כְּדֵי שֶׁעַל־פִּיו יַאֲמִינוּ הַכֹּל. ⁸הוּא לֹא הָיָה הָאוֹר; הוּא בָּא לְהָעִיד עַל הָאוֹר. ⁹הָאוֹר הָאֲמִתִּי, הַמֵּאִיר לְכָל אָדָם, בָּא אֶל הָעוֹלָם. ¹⁰בָּעוֹלָם הָיָה וְעַל־יָדָיו נִהְיָה הָעוֹלָם, וְהָעוֹלָם לֹא הִכִּירוֹ. ¹¹הוּא בָּא אֶל שֶׁלּוֹ וְאֵלֶּה אֲשֶׁר לוֹ לֹא קִבְּלוּ אוֹתוֹ. ¹²אֲבָל לְאֵלֶּה אֲשֶׁר קִבְּלוּ אוֹתוֹ, הַמַּאֲמִינִים בִּשְׁמוֹ, נָתַן תֹּקֶף לִהְיוֹת בָּנִים לֵאלֹהִים. ¹³לֹא מִדָּם וְלֹא מֵחֵפֶץ הַבָּשָׂר נוֹלְדוּ, אַף לֹא מֵחֵפֶץ גֶּבֶר, כִּי אִם מֵאֱלֹהִים.

¹⁴הַדָּבָר נִהְיָה בָּשָׂר וְשָׁכַן בְּתוֹכֵנוּ; וַאֲנַחְנוּ רָאִינוּ אֶת כְּבוֹדוֹ, כְּבוֹד בֵּן יָחִיד מִלִּפְנֵי אָבִיו, מָלֵא חֶסֶד וֶאֱמֶת. ¹⁵יוֹחָנָן הֵעִיד עָלָיו וְקָרָא בְּאָמְרוֹ: "זֶה הוּא שֶׁאָמַרְתִּי עָלָיו, 'הַבָּא אַחֲרַי הוּא כְּבָר לְפָנַי, כִּי קֹדֶם לִי הָיָה'." ¹⁶הֵן מִמְּלוֹאוֹ כֻּלָּנוּ קִבַּלְנוּ, וְחֶסֶד עַל חָסֶד, ¹⁷כִּי הַתּוֹרָה נִתְּנָה עַל־יְדֵי מֹשֶׁה, וְהַחֶסֶד וְהָאֱמֶת בָּאוּ דֶּרֶךְ יֵשׁוּעַ הַמָּשִׁיחַ. ¹⁸אֶת הָאֱלֹהִים לֹא רָאָה אִישׁ מֵעוֹלָם; הַבֵּן הַיָּחִיד, הַנִּמְצָא בְּחֵיק הָאָב, הוּא אֲשֶׁר הוֹדִיעוֹ.

¹⁹וְזֹאת עֵדוּתוֹ שֶׁל יוֹחָנָן כַּאֲשֶׁר רָאשֵׁי הַיְּהוּדִים שָׁלְחוּ אֵלָיו כֹּהֲנִים וּלְוִיִּם מִירוּשָׁלַיִם לִשְׁאֹל אוֹתוֹ "מִי אַתָּה?". ²⁰הוּא לֹא כִּחֵשׁ אֶלָּא הוֹדָה וְאָמַר: "אֵינֶנִּי הַמָּשִׁיחַ."

²¹שָׁאֲלוּ אוֹתוֹ: "אִם כֵּן, מִי אַתָּה? הַאִם אַתָּה אֵלִיָּהוּ?"

הֵשִׁיב: "לֹא."

"הַאִם אַתָּה הַנָּבִיא?"

הֵשִׁיב לָהֶם: "לֹא."

22 שָׁאֲלוּ אוֹתוֹ: "אָז מִי אַתָּה? – כְּדֵי שֶׁנִּתֵּן תְּשׁוּבָה לְשׁוֹלְחֵנוּ. מָה אַתָּה אוֹמֵר עַל עַצְמְךָ?"

23 הֵשִׁיב וְאָמַר: "אֲנִי קוֹל קוֹרֵא בַּמִּדְבָּר פַּנּוּ דֶרֶךְ יהוה, כְּמוֹ שֶׁאָמַר יְשַׁעְיָהוּ הַנָּבִיא."

24 הַשְּׁלוּחִים הָיוּ מִן הַפְּרוּשִׁים 25 וְהֵם הוֹסִיפוּ וְשָׁאֲלוּ אוֹתוֹ: "אִם כֵּן מַדּוּעַ אַתָּה מַטְבִּיל אִם אֵינְךָ הַמָּשִׁיחַ וְלֹא אֵלִיָּהוּ וְלֹא הַנָּבִיא?"

26 הֵשִׁיב לָהֶם יוֹחָנָן וְאָמַר: "אֲנִי מַטְבִּיל בְּמַיִם, אֲבָל בֵּינֵיכֶם עוֹמֵד אֶחָד שֶׁאֵינְכֶם מַכִּירִים אוֹתוֹ. 27 הוּא הַבָּא אַחֲרַי וַאֲנִי אֵינֶנִּי רָאוּי לְהַתִּיר אֶת שְׂרוֹךְ נַעֲלָיו." 28 כָּל זֶה קָרָה בְּבֵית עֲנָיָה מֵעֵבֶר לַיַּרְדֵּן, בַּמָּקוֹם שֶׁהָיָה יוֹחָנָן מַטְבִּיל.

29 לְמָחֳרָת רָאָה יוֹחָנָן אֶת יֵשׁוּעַ בָּא לִקְרָאתוֹ. אָמַר יוֹחָנָן: "הִנֵּה שֵׂה הָאֱלֹהִים הַנּוֹשֵׂא חַטַּאת הָעוֹלָם. 30 זֶה שֶׁאָמַרְתִּי עָלָיו, 'אַחֲרַי בָּא אִישׁ אֲשֶׁר הוּא כְּבָר לְפָנַי, כִּי קֹדֶם לִי הָיָה'. 31 וַאֲנִי לֹא הִכַּרְתִּיו, אֲבָל לְמַעַן יִגָּלֶה לְיִשְׂרָאֵל בָּאתִי אֲנִי לְהַטְבִּיל בְּמַיִם."

32 הֵעִיד יוֹחָנָן וְאָמַר: "רָאִיתִי אֶת הָרוּחַ יוֹרֶדֶת מִשָּׁמַיִם כְּיוֹנָה וְנָחָה עָלָיו. 33 אֲנִי לֹא הִכַּרְתִּיו, אֶלָּא שֶׁהַשּׁוֹלֵחַ אוֹתִי לְהַטְבִּיל בְּמַיִם הוּא אָמַר אֵלַי, 'זֶה שֶׁתִּרְאֶה אֶת הָרוּחַ יוֹרֶדֶת וְנָחָה עָלָיו, הוּא הַמַּטְבִּיל בְּרוּחַ הַקֹּדֶשׁ'. 34 וַאֲנִי רָאִיתִי וְהֵעַדְתִּי שֶׁזֶּה הוּא בֶּן־הָאֱלֹהִים."

35 לְמָחֳרָת שׁוּב עָמַד יוֹחָנָן וְאִתּוֹ שְׁנַיִם מִתַּלְמִידָיו. 36 כִּרְאוֹתוֹ אֶת יֵשׁוּעַ מִתְהַלֵּךְ אָמַר: "הִנֵּה שֵׂה הָאֱלֹהִים!" 37 שָׁמְעוּ שְׁנֵי תַּלְמִידָיו אֶת דְּבָרוֹ וְהָלְכוּ אַחֲרֵי יֵשׁוּעַ. 38 כַּאֲשֶׁר פָּנָה יֵשׁוּעַ וְרָאָה אוֹתָם הוֹלְכִים אַחֲרָיו, שָׁאַל אוֹתָם: "מָה אַתֶּם מְחַפְּשִׂים?" אָמְרוּ לוֹ: "רַבִּי, אֵיפֹה אַתָּה גָּר?"

39 הֵשִׁיב לָהֶם: "בּוֹאוּ וְתִרְאוּ."

הָלְכוּ וְרָאוּ הֵיכָן הוּא גָּר וְשָׁהוּ אִתּוֹ בְּאוֹתוֹ יוֹם. הַשָּׁעָה הָיְתָה אַרְבַּע אַחֲרֵי הַצָּהֳרַיִם בְּעֶרֶךְ.

40 אַנְדְּרֵי, אָחִיו שֶׁל שִׁמְעוֹן כֵּיפָא, הָיָה אֶחָד מִן הַשְּׁנַיִם אֲשֶׁר שָׁמְעוּ מִפִּי יוֹחָנָן וְהָלְכוּ אַחֲרָיו. 41 תְּחִלָּה מָצָא אֶת אָחִיו שִׁמְעוֹן וְאָמַר לוֹ: "מָצָאנוּ אֶת הַמָּשִׁיחַ." 42 הוּא הֵבִיא אוֹתוֹ אֶל יֵשׁוּעַ. הִבִּיט בּוֹ יֵשׁוּעַ וְאָמַר: "אַתָּה שִׁמְעוֹן בֶּן יוֹחָנָן,

22 Then they said to him, "Who are you, that we may give an answer to those who sent us? What do you say about yourself?"

23 He said: "I *am*

'The voice of one crying in the wilderness:
"Make straight the way of the LORD," '

as the prophet Isaiah said."

24 Now those who were sent were from the Pharisees. 25 And they asked him, saying, "Why then do you baptize if you are not the Christ, nor Elijah, nor the Prophet?"

26 John answered them, saying, "I baptize with water, but there stands One among you whom you do not know. 27 It is He who, coming after me, is preferred before me, whose sandal strap I am not worthy to loose."

28 These things were done in Bethabara beyond the Jordan, where John was baptizing.

29 The next day John saw Jesus coming toward him, and said, "Behold! The Lamb of God who takes away the sin of the world! 30 This is He of whom I said, 'After me comes a Man who is preferred before me, for He was before me.' 31 I did not know Him; but that He should be revealed to Israel, therefore I came baptizing with water."

32 And John bore witness, saying, "I saw the Spirit descending from heaven like a dove, and He remained upon Him. 33 I did not know Him, but He who sent me to baptize with water said to me, 'Upon whom you see the Spirit descending, and remaining on Him, this is He who baptizes with the Holy Spirit.' 34 And I have seen and testified that this is the Son of God."

35 Again, the next day, John stood with two of his disciples. 36 And looking at Jesus as He walked, he said, "Behold the Lamb of God!"

37 The two disciples heard him speak, and they followed Jesus. 38 Then Jesus turned, and seeing them following, said to them, "What do you seek?"

They said to Him, "Rabbi" (which is to say, when translated, Teacher), "where are You staying?"

39 He said to them, "Come and see." They came and saw where He was staying, and remained with Him that day (now it was about the tenth hour).

40 One of the two who heard John *speak,* and followed Him, was Andrew, Simon Peter's brother. 41 He first found his own brother Simon, and said to him, "We have found the Messiah" (which is translated, the Christ). 42 And he brought him to Jesus.

Now when Jesus looked at him, He said, "You are Simon the son of Jonah. You shall be called Cephas" (which is translated, A Stone).

43 The following day Jesus wanted to go to Galilee, and He found Philip and said to him, "Follow Me." 44 Now Philip was from Bethsaida, the city of Andrew and Peter. 45 Philip found Nathanael and said to him, "We have found Him of whom Moses in the law, and also the prophets, wrote—Jesus of Nazareth, the son of Joseph."

46 And Nathanael said to him, "Can anything good come out of Nazareth?"

Philip said to him, "Come and see."

47 Jesus saw Nathanael coming toward Him, and said of him, "Behold, an Israelite indeed, in whom is no deceit!"

48 Nathanael said to Him, "How do You know me?"

Jesus answered and said to him, "Before Philip called you, when you were under the fig tree, I saw you."

49 Nathanael answered and said to Him, "Rabbi, You are the Son of God! You are the King of Israel!"

50 Jesus answered and said to him, "Because I said to you, 'I saw you under the fig tree,' do you believe? You will see greater things than these."

51 And He said to him, "Most assuredly, I say to you, hereafter you shall see heaven open, and the angels of God ascending and descending upon the Son of Man."

2 On the third day there was a wedding in Cana of Galilee, and the mother of Jesus was there. 2 Now both Jesus and His disciples were invited to the wedding. 3 And when they ran out of wine, the mother of Jesus said to Him, "They have no wine."

4 Jesus said to her, "Woman, what does your concern have to do with Me? My hour has not yet come."

5 His mother said to the servants, "Whatever He says to you, do it."

6 Now there were set there six waterpots of stone, according to the manner of purification of the Jews, containing twenty or thirty gallons apiece. 7 Jesus said to them, "Fill the waterpots with water." And they filled them up to the brim. 8 And He said to them, "Draw some out now, and take it to the master of the feast." And they took it. 9 When the master of the feast had tasted the water that was made wine, and did not know where it came from (but the servants who had drawn the water knew), the master of the feast called the bridegroom. 10 And he said to him, "Every man at the beginning

---

אַתָּה תִּקָּרֵא כֵּיפָא" (שֶׁמַּשְׁמָעוֹ סֶלַע). 43 לְמָחֳרָת רָצָה יֵשׁוּעַ לָלֶכֶת לַגָּלִיל. הוּא מָצָא אֶת פִילִיפּוֹס וְאָמַר לוֹ: "לֵךְ אַחֲרַי!" 44 פִילִיפּוֹס הָיָה מִבֵּית צַיְדָא, מֵעִירָם שֶׁל אַנְדְּרֵי וְכֵיפָא. 45 פִילִיפּוֹס פָּגַשׁ אֶת נְתַנְאֵל וְאָמַר לוֹ: "מָצָאנוּ אֶת זֶה שֶׁכָּתַב עָלָיו מֹשֶׁה בַּתּוֹרָה, וְכֵן גַּם הַנְּבִיאִים, אֶת יֵשׁוּעַ בֶּן יוֹסֵף מִנְּצֶרֶת."

46 אָמַר לוֹ נְתַנְאֵל: "מִנְּצֶרֶת יָכוֹל לָבוֹא מַשֶּׁהוּ טוֹב?"

אָמַר לוֹ פִילִיפּוֹס: "בּוֹא וּרְאֵה."

47 כְּשֶׁרָאָה יֵשׁוּעַ אֶת נְתַנְאֵל בָּא לִקְרָאתוֹ, אָמַר עָלָיו: "הִנֵּה בֶּאֱמֶת בֶּן יִשְׂרָאֵל שֶׁאֵין בּוֹ מִרְמָה."

48 שָׁאַל אוֹתוֹ נְתַנְאֵל: "מִנַּיִן אַתָּה מַכִּיר אוֹתִי?" עָנָה לוֹ יֵשׁוּעַ: "לִפְנֵי שֶׁקָּרָא לְךָ פִילִיפּוֹס, כַּאֲשֶׁר הָיִיתָ תַּחַת עֵץ הַתְּאֵנָה, רְאִיתִי אוֹתְךָ."

49 הֵשִׁיב לוֹ נְתַנְאֵל: "רַבִּי, אַתָּה בֶּן־הָאֱלֹהִים, אַתָּה מֶלֶךְ יִשְׂרָאֵל!"

50 אָמַר לוֹ יֵשׁוּעַ: "מִפְּנֵי שֶׁאָמַרְתִּי לְךָ כִּי רְאִיתִיךָ תַּחַת עֵץ הַתְּאֵנָה הֶאֱמַנְתָּ? גְּדוֹלוֹת מֵאֵלֶּה תִּרְאֶה!" 51 וְעוֹד אָמַר לוֹ: "אָמֵן אָמֵן אֲנִי אוֹמֵר לָכֶם, אַתֶּם תִּרְאוּ אֶת הַשָּׁמַיִם פְּתוּחִים וּמַלְאֲכֵי אֱלֹהִים עוֹלִים וְיוֹרְדִים עַל בֶּן־הָאָדָם."

ב בַּיּוֹם הַשְּׁלִישִׁי הָיְתָה חֲתֻנָּה בְּקָנָה אֲשֶׁר בַּגָּלִיל. אִמּוֹ שֶׁל יֵשׁוּעַ הָיְתָה שָׁם, 2 וְגַם יֵשׁוּעַ וְתַלְמִידָיו הֻזְמְנוּ לַחֲתֻנָּה. 3 כְּשֶׁחָסַר לָהֶם יַיִן אָמְרָה אֵם יֵשׁוּעַ אֵלָיו: "אֵין לָהֶם יַיִן."

4 אָמַר לָהּ יֵשׁוּעַ: "מַה לִי וָלָךְ, אִשָּׁה? עוֹד לֹא הִגִּיעָה שְׁעָתִי."

5 אָמְרָה אִמּוֹ לַמְשָׁרְתִים: "כָּל מַה שֶּׁיֹּאמַר לָכֶם עֲשׂוּ."

6 שִׁשָּׁה כַּדֵּי אֶבֶן הָיוּ עֲרוּכִים שָׁם, כְּמִנְהַג הַיְּהוּדִים לְטָהֳרָתָם, וְכָל אֶחָד מֵכִיל שְׁנַיִם אוֹ שְׁלוֹשָׁה בַּתִּים. 7 אָמַר לָהֶם יֵשׁוּעַ: "מַלְּאוּ אֶת הַכַּדִּים מַיִם", וְהֵם מִלְּאוּ אוֹתָם עַד לְמַעְלָה. 8 אָמַר לָהֶם: "שַׁאֲבוּ עַכְשָׁו וְהָבִיאוּ אֶל רֹאשׁ הַמְּסִבָּה." הֵם שָׁאֲבוּ וְהֵבִיאוּ אֵלָיו. 9 טָעַם רֹאשׁ הַמְּסִבָּה אֶת הַמַּיִם שֶׁנֶּהֶפְכוּ לְיַיִן וְלֹא יָדַע מֵאַיִן הוּא, אֶלָּא שֶׁהַמְשָׁרְתִים אֲשֶׁר שָׁאֲבוּ אֶת הַמַּיִם יָדְעוּ. קָרָא רֹאשׁ הַמְּסִבָּה אֶת הֶחָתָן 10 וְאָמַר לוֹ: "כָּל אָדָם מַגִּישׁ תְּחִלָּה אֶת הַיַּיִן הַטּוֹב וְכַאֲשֶׁר הָאֲנָשִׁים מְבֻסָּמִים יַגִּישׁ אֶת הַטּוֹב־פָּחוֹת, אֲבָל אַתָּה שָׁמַרְתָּ אֶת הַיַּיִן הַטּוֹב עַד עַכְשָׁו."

6 שְׁנַיִם אוֹ שְׁלוֹשָׁה בַּתִּים – כִּשְׁמוֹנִים עַד מֵאָה וְעֶשְׂרִים לִיטֶר.

sets out the good wine, and when the *guests* have well drunk, then the inferior. You have kept the good wine until now!"

[11] This beginning of signs Jesus did in Cana of Galilee, and manifested His glory; and His disciples believed in Him.

[12] After this He went down to Capernaum, He, His mother, His brothers, and His disciples; and they did not stay there many days.

[13] Now the Passover of the Jews was at hand, and Jesus went up to Jerusalem. [14] And He found in the temple those who sold oxen and sheep and doves, and the money changers doing business. [15] When He had made a whip of cords, He drove them all out of the temple, with the sheep and the oxen, and poured out the changers' money and overturned the tables. [16] And He said to those who sold doves, "Take these things away! Do not make My Father's house a house of merchandise!" [17] Then His disciples remembered that it was written, *Zeal for Your house has eaten Me up.*

[18] So the Jews answered and said to Him, "What sign do You show to us, since You do these things?"

[19] Jesus answered and said to them, "Destroy this temple, and in three days I will raise it up."

[20] Then the Jews said, "It has taken forty-six years to build this temple, and will You raise it up in three days?"

[21] But He was speaking of the temple of His body. [22] Therefore, when He had risen from the dead, His disciples remembered that He had said this to them; and they believed the Scripture and the word which Jesus had said.

[23] Now when He was in Jerusalem at the Passover, during the feast, many believed in His name when they saw the signs which He did. [24] But Jesus did not commit Himself to them, because He knew all *men*, [25] and had no need that anyone should testify of man, for He knew what was in man.

3 There was a man of the Pharisees named Nicodemus, a ruler of the Jews. [2] This man came to Jesus by night and said to Him, "Rabbi, we know that You are a teacher come from God; for no one can do these signs that You do unless God is with him."

[3] Jesus answered and said to him, "Most assuredly, I say to you, unless one is born again, he cannot see the kingdom of God."

[4] Nicodemus said to Him, "How can a man be born when he is old? Can he enter a second time into his mother's womb and be born?"

11 זֹאת תְּחִלַּת הָאוֹתוֹת שֶׁל יֵשׁוּעַ. הוּא עָשָׂה זֹאת בְּקָנָה שֶׁבַּגָּלִיל. אָז הֶרְאָה אֶת כְּבוֹדוֹ וְתַלְמִידָיו הֶאֱמִינוּ בּוֹ. 12 אַחֲרֵי כֵן יָרַד אֶל כְּפַר נַחוּם הוּא וְאִמּוֹ עִם אֶחָיו וְתַלְמִידָיו, וְשָׁם שָׁהוּ יָמִים לֹא רַבִּים.

13 עִם הִתְקָרֵב הַפֶּסַח, חַג הַיְּהוּדִים, עָלָה יֵשׁוּעַ לִירוּשָׁלַיִם 14 וּמָצָא בְּבֵית הַמִּקְדָּשׁ מוֹכְרֵי בָּקָר וְצֹאן וְיוֹנִים וְחַלְפָנִים יוֹשְׁבִים שָׁם. 15 הוּא הֵכִין שׁוֹט מֵחֲבָלִים וְגֵרַשׁ אֶת כֻּלָּם מִבֵּית הַמִּקְדָּשׁ יַחַד עִם הַצֹּאן וְהַבָּקָר, כֵּן גַּם פִּזֵּר אֶת מַטְבְּעוֹת הַחַלְפָנִים וְהָפַךְ אֶת הַשֻּׁלְחָנוֹת, 16 וּלְמוֹכְרֵי הַיּוֹנִים אָמַר: " קְחוּ אֶת אֵלֶּה מִכָּאן. אַל תַּעֲשׂוּ אֶת בֵּית אָבִי לְבֵית מִסְחָר." 17 אָז נִזְכְּרוּ תַלְמִידָיו בַּכָּתוּב: "קִנְאַת בֵּיתְךָ אֲכָלָתְנִי."

18 הֵגִיבוּ רָאשֵׁי הַיְּהוּדִים וְאָמְרוּ אֵלָיו: "אֵיזֶה אוֹת אַתָּה מַרְאֶה לָנוּ בַּעֲשׂוֹתְךָ אֶת הַדְּבָרִים הָאֵלֶּה?" 19 הֵשִׁיב יֵשׁוּעַ וְאָמַר לָהֶם: "הִרְסוּ אֶת הַהֵיכָל הַזֶּה וּבִשְׁלוֹשָׁה יָמִים אָקִים אוֹתוֹ."

20 הֵם אָמְרוּ: "אַרְבָּעִים וְשֵׁשׁ שָׁנִים נִבְנָה הַהֵיכָל הַזֶּה וְאַתָּה בִּשְׁלוֹשָׁה יָמִים תָּקִים אוֹתוֹ?" 21 אַךְ הוּא דִּבֵּר עַל הֵיכַל גּוּפוֹ. 22 לָכֵן, כַּאֲשֶׁר קָם מִן הַמֵּתִים, נִזְכְּרוּ תַלְמִידָיו כִּי אָמַר לָהֶם אֶת זֹאת, וְהֶאֱמִינוּ בַּכָּתוּב וּבַדָּבָר שֶׁאָמַר יֵשׁוּעַ.

23 כְּשֶׁהָיָה בִּירוּשָׁלַיִם בְּחַג הַפֶּסַח, הֶאֱמִינוּ רַבִּים בִּשְׁמוֹ כִּרְאוֹתָם אֶת הָאוֹתוֹת שֶׁעָשָׂה, 24 אֶלָּא שֶׁיֵּשׁוּעַ לֹא סָמַךְ עֲלֵיהֶם, שֶׁכֵּן הִכִּיר אֶת כֻּלָּם 25 וְלֹא הָיָה צָרִיךְ כְּלָל שֶׁמִּישֶׁהוּ יָעִיד עַל הָאָדָם, כִּי יָדַע מַה שֶּׁבָּאָדָם.

ג אַחַד הַפְּרוּשִׁים מִמַּנְהִיגֵי הַיְּהוּדִים, נַקְדִּימוֹן שְׁמוֹ, 2 בָּא אֶל יֵשׁוּעַ בַּלַּיְלָה וְאָמַר אֵלָיו: "רַבִּי, אֲנַחְנוּ יוֹדְעִים כִּי מֵאֵת אֱלֹהִים בָּאתָ לִהְיוֹת מוֹרֶה, שֶׁהֲרֵי אֵין אִישׁ יָכוֹל לַעֲשׂוֹת אֶת הָאוֹתוֹת שֶׁאַתָּה עוֹשֶׂה אֶלָּא אִם כֵּן אֱלֹהִים אִתּוֹ."

3 הֵשִׁיב יֵשׁוּעַ וְאָמַר אֵלָיו: "אָמֵן אָמֵן אֲנִי אוֹמֵר לְךָ, אִם לֹא יִוָּלֵד אָדָם מִלְמַעְלָה, לֹא יוּכַל לִרְאוֹת אֶת מַלְכוּת הָאֱלֹהִים."

4 שָׁאַל נַקְדִּימוֹן: "אֵיךְ יָכוֹל אָדָם לְהִוָּלֵד בִּהְיוֹתוֹ זָקֵן? הַאִם הוּא יָכוֹל לְהִכָּנֵס שֵׁנִית לְרֶחֶם אִמּוֹ וּלְהִוָּלֵד?"

⁵ Jesus answered, "Most assuredly, I say to you, unless one is born of water and the Spirit, he cannot enter the kingdom of God. ⁶ That which is born of the flesh is flesh, and that which is born of the Spirit is spirit. ⁷ Do not marvel that I said to you, 'You must be born again.' ⁸ The wind blows where it wishes, and you hear the sound of it, but cannot tell where it comes from and where it goes. So is everyone who is born of the Spirit."

⁹ Nicodemus answered and said to Him, "How can these things be?"

¹⁰ Jesus answered and said to him, "Are you the teacher of Israel, and do not know these things? ¹¹ Most assuredly, I say to you, We speak what We know and testify what We have seen, and you do not receive Our witness. ¹² If I have told you earthly things and you do not believe, how will you believe if I tell you heavenly things? ¹³ No one has ascended to heaven but He who came down from heaven, *that is,* the Son of Man who is in heaven. ¹⁴ And as Moses lifted up the serpent in the wilderness, even so must the Son of Man be lifted up, ¹⁵ that whoever believes in Him should not perish but have eternal life. ¹⁶ For God so loved the world that He gave His only begotten Son, that whoever believes in Him should not perish but have everlasting life. ¹⁷ For God did not send His Son into the world to condemn the world, but that the world through Him might be saved.

¹⁸ "He who believes in Him is not condemned; but he who does not believe is condemned already, because he has not believed in the name of the only begotten Son of God. ¹⁹ And this is the condemnation, that the light has come into the world, and men loved darkness rather than light, because their deeds were evil. ²⁰ For everyone practicing evil hates the light and does not come to the light, lest his deeds should be exposed. ²¹ But he who does the truth comes to the light, that his deeds may be clearly seen, that they have been done in God."

²² After these things Jesus and His disciples came into the land of Judea, and there He remained with them and baptized. ²³ Now John also was baptizing in Aenon near Salim, because there was much water there. And they came and were baptized. ²⁴ For John had not yet been thrown into prison.

²⁵ Then there arose a dispute between *some* of John's disciples and the Jews about purification. ²⁶ And they came to John and said to him, "Rabbi, He who was with you beyond the Jordan, to whom you have testified—behold, He is baptizing, and all are coming to Him!"

⁵ הֵשִׁיב יֵשׁוּעַ: "אָמֵן אָמֵן אֲנִי אוֹמֵר לְךָ, אִם לֹא יִוָּלֵד אִישׁ מִן הַמַּיִם וְהָרוּחַ לֹא יוּכַל לְהִכָּנֵס לְמַלְכוּת הָאֱלֹהִים. ⁶ הַנּוֹלָד מִן הַבָּשָׂר בָּשָׂר הוּא וְהַנּוֹלָד מִן הָרוּחַ רוּחַ הוּא. ⁷ אַל תִּתְמַהּ עַל שֶׁאוֹמֵר אֲנִי לְךָ כִּי עֲלֵיכֶם לְהִוָּלֵד מִלְמַעְלָה. ⁸ הָרוּחַ נוֹשֶׁבֶת הֵיכָן שֶׁהִיא רוֹצָה וְאֶת קוֹלָהּ אַתָּה שׁוֹמֵעַ, אַךְ אֵינְךָ יוֹדֵעַ מֵאַיִן הִיא בָּאָה וּלְאָן הִיא הוֹלֶכֶת. כָּךְ כָּל מִי שֶׁנּוֹלָד מִן הָרוּחַ."

⁹ הֵשִׁיב נַקְדִּימוֹן וְאָמַר לוֹ: "כֵּיצַד יִתָּכְנוּ הַדְּבָרִים הָאֵלֶּה?"

¹⁰ עָנָה יֵשׁוּעַ וְאָמַר אֵלָיו: "אַתָּה מוֹרֶה בְּיִשְׂרָאֵל וְאֵינְךָ יוֹדֵעַ אֶת זֹאת? ¹¹ אָמֵן אָמֵן אֲנִי אוֹמֵר לְךָ, אֶת אֲשֶׁר אָנוּ יוֹדְעִים מְדַבְּרִים אֲנַחְנוּ וְאֶת אֲשֶׁר רָאִינוּ עַל זֶה אֲנַחְנוּ מְעִידִים, וְאֶת עֵדוּתֵנוּ אֵינְכֶם מְקַבְּלִים. ¹² אִם בְּאָמְרִי לָכֶם דְּבָרִים מֵעִנְיְנֵי הָאָרֶץ אֵינְכֶם מַאֲמִינִים, אֵיךְ תַּאֲמִינוּ אִם אֹמַר לָכֶם דְּבָרִים מֵעִנְיְנֵי הַשָּׁמַיִם? ¹³ אִישׁ לֹא עָלָה הַשָּׁמַיְמָה מִלְּבַד זֶה שֶׁיָּרַד מִן הַשָּׁמַיִם – בֶּן־הָאָדָם. ¹⁴ וּכְמוֹ שֶׁהִגְבִּיהַּ מֹשֶׁה אֶת הַנָּחָשׁ בַּמִּדְבָּר, כָּךְ צָרִיךְ שֶׁיּוּרַם בֶּן־הָאָדָם ¹⁵ לְמַעַן יִהְיוּ חַיֵּי עוֹלָם לְכָל הַמַּאֲמִין בּוֹ; ¹⁶ כִּי כֹּה אָהַב אֱלֹהִים אֶת הָעוֹלָם עַד כִּי נָתַן אֶת בְּנוֹ יְחִידוֹ לְמַעַן לֹא יֹאבַד כָּל הַמַּאֲמִין בּוֹ, אֶלָּא יִנְחַל חַיֵּי עוֹלָם. ¹⁷ הֵן הָאֱלֹהִים לֹא שָׁלַח אֶת בְּנוֹ אֶל הָעוֹלָם לִשְׁפֹּט אֶת הָעוֹלָם, אֶלָּא כְּדֵי שֶׁיִּוָּשַׁע הָעוֹלָם עַל־יָדָיו. ¹⁸ הַמַּאֲמִין בּוֹ אֵינֶנּוּ נָדוֹן. מִי שֶׁאֵינֶנּוּ מַאֲמִין כְּבָר נָדוֹן, מִפְּנֵי שֶׁלֹּא הֶאֱמִין בְּשֵׁם בֶּן־הָאֱלֹהִים הַיָּחִיד. ¹⁹ וְזֶהוּ הַדִּין: הָאוֹר בָּא אֶל הָעוֹלָם וּבְנֵי הָאָדָם אָהֲבוּ אֶת הַחֹשֶׁךְ יוֹתֵר מִן הָאוֹר, כִּי רָעִים הָיוּ מַעֲשֵׂיהֶם. ²⁰ כָּל עוֹשֵׂה עַוְלָה שׂוֹנֵא אֶת הָאוֹר וְאֵינוֹ בָּא אֶל הָאוֹר פֶּן יוּכְחוּ מַעֲשָׂיו. ²¹ אוּלָם עוֹשֵׂה הָאֱמֶת בָּא אֶל הָאוֹר לְמַעַן יִגָּלוּ מַעֲשָׂיו כִּי נַעֲשׂוּ בֵּאלֹהִים."

²² אַחֲרֵי הַדְּבָרִים הָאֵלֶּה בָּא יֵשׁוּעַ עִם תַּלְמִידָיו לְאֶרֶץ יְהוּדָה וְשָׁם שָׁהָה עִמָּהֶם וְהִטְבִּיל. ²³ גַּם יוֹחָנָן הָיָה מַטְבִּיל בְּעֵינוֹן עַל־יַד שָׁלֵם, שֶׁכֵּן מַיִם רַבִּים הָיוּ שָׁם וְהָאֲנָשִׁים בָּאוּ וְנִטְבְּלוּ; ²⁴ זֹאת עוֹד לִפְנֵי שֶׁהֻשְׁלַךְ יוֹחָנָן לַכֶּלֶא.

²⁵ וַכּוּחַ הֻחַל בֵּין תַּלְמִידֵי יוֹחָנָן לְבֵין פָּרוּשׁ אֶחָד בְּנוֹגֵעַ לַטָּהֳרָה. ²⁶ בָּאוּ אֶל יוֹחָנָן וְאָמְרוּ לוֹ: "רַבִּי, הָאִישׁ אֲשֶׁר הָיָה אִתְּךָ בְּעֵבֶר הַיַּרְדֵּן וַאֲשֶׁר הֵעַדְתָּ עָלָיו, הִנֵּהוּ מַטְבִּיל וְהַכֹּל בָּאִים אֵלָיו."

27 John answered and said, "A man can receive
nothing unless it has been given to him from
heaven. 28 You yourselves bear me witness, that I
said, 'I am not the Christ,' but, 'I have been sent
before Him.' 29 He who has the bride is the
bridegroom; but the friend of the bridegroom,
who stands and hears him, rejoices greatly because
of the bridegroom's voice. Therefore this joy of
mine is fulfilled. 30 He must increase, but I *must*
decrease. 31 He who comes from above is above all;
he who is of the earth is earthly and speaks of the
earth. He who comes from heaven is above all.
32 And what He has seen and heard, that He
testifies; and no one receives His testimony. 33 He
who has received His testimony has certified that
God is true. 34 For He whom God has sent speaks
the words of God, for God does not give the Spirit
by measure. 35 The Father loves the Son, and has
given all things into His hand. 36 He who believes in
the Son has everlasting life; and he who does not
believe the Son shall not see life, but the wrath of
God abides on him."

4 Therefore, when the Lord knew that the
Pharisees had heard that Jesus made and baptized
more disciples than John 2 (though Jesus Himself
did not baptize, but His disciples), 3 He left Judea
and departed again to Galilee. 4 But He needed to
go through Samaria.
5 So He came to a city of Samaria which is called
Sychar, near the plot of ground that Jacob gave to
his son Joseph. 6 Now Jacob's well was there. Jesus
therefore, being wearied from *His* journey, sat thus
by the well. It was about the sixth hour.
7 A woman of Samaria came to draw water. Jesus
said to her, "Give Me a drink." 8 For His disciples
had gone away into the city to buy food.
9 Then the woman of Samaria said to Him, "How
is it that You, being a Jew, ask a drink from me, a
Samaritan woman?" For Jews have no dealings
with Samaritans.
10 Jesus answered and said to her, "If you knew
the gift of God, and who it is who says to you, 'Give
Me a drink,' you would have asked Him, and He
would have given you living water."
11 The woman said to Him, "Sir, You have
nothing to draw with, and the well is deep. Where
then do You get that living water? 12 Are You
greater than our father Jacob, who gave us the well,
and drank from it himself, as well as his sons and
his livestock?"
13 Jesus answered and said to her, "Whoever
drinks of this water will thirst again, 14 but whoever
drinks of the water that I shall give him will never

27 הֵשִׁיב יוֹחָנָן וְאָמַר: "אֵין אִישׁ יָכוֹל לָקַחַת דָּבָר
אֶלָּא אִם כֵּן נִתַּן לוֹ מִן הַשָּׁמַיִם. 28 אַתֶּם עַצְמְכֶם
עֵדִים לִי שֶׁאָמַרְתִּי, 'אֵינֶנִּי הַמָּשִׁיחַ, אֶלָּא שָׁלוּחַ אֲנִי
לְפָנָיו'. 29 זֶה אֲשֶׁר לוֹ הַכַּלָּה הוּא הֶחָתָן, אֲבָל יְדִיד
הֶחָתָן הָעוֹמֵד וְשׁוֹמֵעַ אוֹתוֹ שָׂמוֹחַ יִשְׂמַח לְקוֹל
הֶחָתָן. זֹאת שִׂמְחָתִי וְכָעֵת הִיא שְׁלֵמָה. 30 מִן
הַהֶכְרֵחַ שֶׁהוּא יֵלֵךְ וְיִגְדַּל וַאֲנִי אֶקְטָן.
31 הַבָּא מִלְמַעְלָה הוּא מֵעַל הַכֹּל. זֶה שֶׁמְּן הָאָרֶץ מִן
הָאָרֶץ הוּא וּמֵעִנְיְנֵי הָאָרֶץ יְדַבֵּר. הַבָּא מִן הַשָּׁמַיִם
הוּא מֵעַל הַכֹּל. 32 אֶת מַה שֶּׁרָאָה וְשָׁמַע הוּא מֵעִיד,
וְאֵין מְקַבְּלִים אֶת עֵדוּתוֹ. 33 הַמְּקַבֵּל אֶת עֵדוּתוֹ
חָתַם שֶׁהָאֱלֹהִים אֱמֶת, 34 כִּי מִי שֶׁשְּׁלָחוֹ הָאֱלֹהִים
מְדַבֵּר אֶת דִּבְרֵי אֱלֹהִים, וַהֲרֵי לֹא בְּמִדָּה הוּא נוֹתֵן
אֶת הָרוּחַ. 35 הָאָב אוֹהֵב אֶת בְּנוֹ וְאֶת הַכֹּל נָתַן
בְּיָדוֹ. 36 הַמַּאֲמִין בַּבֵּן יֵשׁ לוֹ חַיֵּי עוֹלָם, אַךְ הַמְסָרֵב
לְהַאֲמִין בַּבֵּן לֹא יִרְאֶה חַיִּים, אֶלָּא חֲרוֹן אֱלֹהִים חָל
עָלָיו."

ד כְּשֶׁנּוֹדַע לָאָדוֹן כִּי שָׁמְעוּ הַפְּרוּשִׁים שֶׁיֵּשׁוּעַ
מַרְבֶּה יוֹתֵר מִיּוֹחָנָן לַעֲשׂוֹת תַּלְמִידִים וּלְהַטְבִּילָם –
2 – אִם כִּי יֵשׁוּעַ עַצְמוֹ לֹא הִטְבִּיל, אֶלָּא תַּלְמִידָיו –
3 עָזַב אֶת יְהוּדָה וְיָצָא לָשׁוּב לַגָּלִיל. 4 כֵּיוָן שֶׁהָיָה
צָרִיךְ לַעֲבֹר דֶּרֶךְ שׁוֹמְרוֹן, 5 הוּא בָּא לְעִיר בְּשׁוֹמְרוֹן,
שְׁכֶם שְׁמָהּ, עַל-יַד חֶלְקַת הַשָּׂדֶה שֶׁנָּתַן יַעֲקֹב לְיוֹסֵף
בְּנוֹ, 6 וְשָׁם הָיְתָה בְּאֵר יַעֲקֹב. יֵשׁוּעַ, שֶׁהָיָה עָיֵף
מִמַּסָּעוֹ, יָשַׁב לוֹ לְיַד הַבְּאֵר. הַשָּׁעָה הָיְתָה הַשָּׁעָה
הַשִּׁשִּׁית בְּעֵרֶךְ. 7 וְהִנֵּה בָּאָה אִשָּׁה מִשּׁוֹמְרוֹן לִשְׁאֹב
מַיִם. אָמַר לָהּ יֵשׁוּעַ: "תְּנִי לִי לִשְׁתּוֹת", 8 שֶׁכֵּן
תַּלְמִידָיו הָלְכוּ הָעִירָה לִקְנוֹת אֹכֶל.
9 אָמְרָה לוֹ הָאִשָּׁה הַשּׁוֹמְרוֹנִית: "אֵיךְ אַתָּה, שֶׁיְּהוּדִי
אַתָּה, מְבַקֵּשׁ מִמֶּנִּי לִשְׁתּוֹת וַאֲנִי אִשָּׁה שׁוֹמְרוֹנִית?"
– כִּי הַיְּהוּדִים אֵינָם מִתְעָרְבִים עִם שׁוֹמְרוֹנִים.
10 הֵשִׁיב יֵשׁוּעַ וְאָמַר לָהּ: "לוּ יָדַעַתְּ אֶת מַתְּנַת
הָאֱלֹהִים וּמִי הוּא הָאוֹמֵר לָךְ 'תְּנִי לִי לִשְׁתּוֹת', הָיִית
אַתְּ מְבַקֶּשֶׁת מִמֶּנּוּ וְהוּא הָיָה נוֹתֵן לָךְ מַיִם חַיִּים."
11 אָמְרָה לוֹ הָאִשָּׁה: "אֲדוֹנִי, אֲפִלּוּ דְּלִי אֵין לְךָ
וְהַבְּאֵר עֲמֻקָּה, אִם כֵּן מֵאַיִן לְךָ מַיִם חַיִּים? 12 הַאִם
גָּדוֹל אַתָּה מִיַּעֲקֹב אָבִינוּ שֶׁנָּתַן לָנוּ אֶת הַבְּאֵר
וְשָׁתָה מִמֶּנָּה הוּא וּבָנָיו וּמִקְנֵהוּ?"
13 עָנָה יֵשׁוּעַ וְאָמַר לָהּ: "כָּל הַשּׁוֹתֶה מִן הַמַּיִם
הָאֵלֶּה יִצְמָא שׁוּב, 14 אֲבָל הַשּׁוֹתֶה מִן הַמַּיִם אֲשֶׁר

thirst. But the water that I shall give him will become in him a fountain of water springing up into everlasting life."

15 The woman said to Him, "Sir, give me this water, that I may not thirst, nor come here to draw."

16 Jesus said to her, "Go, call your husband, and come here."

17 The woman answered and said, "I have no husband."

Jesus said to her, "You have well said, 'I have no husband,' 18 for you have had five husbands, and the one whom you now have is not your husband; in that you spoke truly."

19 The woman said to Him, "Sir, I perceive that You are a prophet. 20 Our fathers worshiped on this mountain, and you *Jews* say that in Jerusalem is the place where one ought to worship."

21 Jesus said to her, "Woman, believe Me, the hour is coming when you will neither on this mountain, nor in Jerusalem, worship the Father. 22 You worship what you do not know; we know what we worship, for salvation is of the Jews. 23 But the hour is coming, and now is, when the true worshipers will worship the Father in spirit and truth; for the Father is seeking such to worship Him. 24 God *is* Spirit, and those who worship Him must worship in spirit and truth."

25 The woman said to Him, "I know that Messiah is coming (who is called Christ). "When He comes, He will tell us all things."

26 Jesus said to her, "I who speak to you am *He.*"

27 And at this *point* His disciples came, and they marveled that He talked with a woman; yet no one said, "What do You seek?" or, "Why are You talking with her?"

28 The woman then left her waterpot, went her way into the city, and said to the men, 29 "Come, see a Man who told me all things that I ever did. Could this be the Christ?" 30 Then they went out of the city and came to Him.

31 In the meantime His disciples urged Him, saying, "Rabbi, eat."

32 But He said to them, "I have food to eat of which you do not know."

33 Therefore the disciples said to one another, "Has anyone brought Him *anything* to eat?"

34 Jesus said to them, "My food is to do the will of Him who sent Me, and to finish His work. 35 Do you not say, 'There are still four months and *then* comes the harvest'? Behold, I say to you, lift up your eyes and look at the fields, for they are already white for harvest! 36 And he who reaps receives wages, and gathers fruit for eternal life, that both he

אֲנִי אֶתֶּן לוֹ לֹא יִצְמָא לְעוֹלָם; הַמַּיִם שֶׁאֶתֵּן לוֹ יִהְיוּ בוֹ לִמְקוֹר מַיִם נוֹבְעִים לְחַיֵּי עוֹלָם."

15 אָמְרָה לוֹ הָאִשָּׁה: "אֲדוֹנִי, תֶּן לִי אֶת הַמַּיִם הָהֵם כְּדֵי שֶׁלֹּא אֶצְמָא וְלֹא אָבוֹא הֵנָּה לִשְׁאֹב."

16 אָמַר לָהּ: "לְכִי וְקִרְאִי לְבַעְלֵךְ וּבוֹאִי לְכָאן."

17 הֵשִׁיבָה הָאִשָּׁה: "אֵין לִי בַּעַל."

אָמַר לָהּ יֵשׁוּעַ: "צָדַקְתְּ בְּאָמְרֵךְ 'אֵין לִי בַּעַל', 18 כִּי חֲמִשָּׁה בְּעָלִים הָיוּ לָךְ וְזֶה שֶׁיֵּשׁ לָךְ כָּעֵת אֵינֶנּוּ בַּעְלֵךְ. בָּזֶה אֱמֶת דִּבַּרְתְּ."

19 אָמְרָה לוֹ הָאִשָּׁה: "אֲדוֹנִי, אֲנִי רוֹאָה שֶׁאַתָּה נָבִיא.

20 אֲבוֹתֵינוּ הִשְׁתַּחֲווּ בָּהָר הַזֶּה, וְאַתֶּם אוֹמְרִים כִּי בִּירוּשָׁלַיִם הַמָּקוֹם שֶׁצָּרִיךְ לְהִשְׁתַּחֲווֹת שָׁם."

21 אָמַר לָהּ יֵשׁוּעַ: "הַאֲמִינִי לִי, אִשָּׁה, כִּי תָּבוֹא שָׁעָה שֶׁלֹּא בָּהָר הַזֶּה וְלֹא בִּירוּשָׁלַיִם תִּשְׁתַּחֲווּ לָאָב. 22 אַתֶּם מִשְׁתַּחֲוִים לְמָה שֶׁאֵינְכֶם מַכִּירִים, אֲנַחְנוּ מִשְׁתַּחֲוִים לְמָה שֶׁאָנוּ מַכִּירִים, שֶׁהֲרֵי הַיְשׁוּעָה מֵאֵת הַיְּהוּדִים הִיא. 23 אוּלָם תָּבוֹא שָׁעָה, וְעַתָּה הִיא, שֶׁעוֹבְדֵי הָאֵל הָאֲמִתִּיִּים יִשְׁתַּחֲווּ לָאָב בְּרוּחַ וּבֶאֱמֶת, כִּי עוֹבְדֵי אֵל כָּאֵלֶּה מְחַפֵּשׂ לוֹ הָאָב. 24 הָאֱלֹהִים הוּא רוּחַ וְהָעוֹבְדִים אוֹתוֹ צְרִיכִים לְעָבְדוֹ בְּרוּחַ וּבֶאֱמֶת."

25 אָמְרָה לוֹ הָאִשָּׁה: "אֲנִי יוֹדַעַת שֶׁיָּבוֹא מָשִׁיחַ. כְּשֶׁהוּא יָבוֹא, הוּא יַגִּיד לָנוּ אֶת הַכֹּל."

26 אָמַר לָהּ יֵשׁוּעַ: "אֲנִי הַמְדַבֵּר אֵלַיִךְ, אֲנִי הוּא." 27 בְּאוֹתוֹ רֶגַע בָּאוּ תַּלְמִידָיו וְתָמְהוּ עַל שֶׁהוּא מְדַבֵּר עִם אִשָּׁה, אַךְ אִישׁ לֹא אָמַר: "מָה אַתָּה מְבַקֵּשׁ?" אוֹ "לָמָּה אַתָּה מְדַבֵּר אִתָּהּ?"

28 עָזְבָה הָאִשָּׁה אֶת כַּדָּהּ, הָלְכָה הָעִירָה וְאָמְרָה לָאֲנָשִׁים: 29 "בּוֹאוּ וּרְאוּ אִישׁ שֶׁאָמַר לִי כָּל מַה שֶּׁעָשִׂיתִי; הַאִם לֹא זֶהוּ הַמָּשִׁיחַ?"

30 הֵם יָצְאוּ מֵהָעִיר וּבָאוּ אֵלָיו. 31 בֵּינְתַיִם בִּקְשׁוּ מִמֶּנּוּ תַּלְמִידָיו שֶׁיֹּאכַל. אָמְרוּ: "רַבִּי, אֱכֹל." 32 אָמַר לָהֶם: "יֵשׁ לִי אֹכֶל לֶאֱכֹל שֶׁאֵינְכֶם יוֹדְעִים."

33 אָמְרוּ הַתַּלְמִידִים זֶה אֶל זֶה: "הַאִם מִישֶׁהוּ הֵבִיא לוֹ לֶאֱכֹל?"

34 אָמַר לָהֶם יֵשׁוּעַ: "מַאֲכָלִי הוּא לַעֲשׂוֹת אֶת רְצוֹן שׁוֹלְחִי וּלְהַשְׁלִים אֶת פָּעֳלוֹ. 35 הֲלֹא אַתֶּם אוֹמְרִים שֶׁעוֹד אַרְבָּעָה חֳדָשִׁים וְהַקָּצִיר בָּא. הִנֵּה, אוֹמֵר אֲנִי לָכֶם, שְׂאוּ עֵינֵיכֶם וּרְאוּ אֶת הַשָּׂדוֹת, כִּי לְבָנִים הֵם וּבְשֵׁלִים לַקָּצִיר. 36 הַקּוֹצֵר מְקַבֵּל כְּבָר שָׂכָר וְאוֹסֵף

who sows and he who reaps may rejoice together.
[37] For in this the saying is true: 'One sows and
another reaps.' [38] I sent you to reap that for which
you have not labored; others have labored, and you
have entered into their labors."

[39] And many of the Samaritans of that city
believed in Him because of the word of the woman
who testified, "He told me all that I *ever* did." [40] So
when the Samaritans had come to Him, they urged
Him to stay with them; and He stayed there two
days. [41] And many more believed because of His
own word.

[42] Then they said to the woman, "Now we
believe, not because of what you said, for we
ourselves have heard *Him* and we know that this is
indeed the Christ, the Savior of the world."

[43] Now after the two days He departed from
there and went to Galilee. [44] For Jesus Himself
testified that a prophet has no honor in his own
country. [45] So when He came to Galilee, the
Galileans received Him, having seen all the things
He did in Jerusalem at the feast; for they also had
gone to the feast.

[46] So Jesus came again to Cana of Galilee where
He had made the water wine. And there was a
certain nobleman whose son was sick at
Capernaum. [47] When he heard that Jesus had come
out of Judea into Galilee, he went to Him and
implored Him to come down and heal his son, for
he was at the point of death. [48] Then Jesus said to
him, "Unless you *people* see signs and wonders, you
will by no means believe."

[49] The nobleman said to Him, "Sir, come down
before my child dies!"

[50] Jesus said to him, "Go your way; your son
lives." So the man believed the word that Jesus
spoke to him, and he went his way. [51] And as he was
now going down, his servants met him and told *him,*
saying, "Your son lives!"

[52] Then he inquired of them the hour when he got
better. And they said to him, "Yesterday at the
seventh hour the fever left him." [53] So the father
knew that *it was* at the same hour in which Jesus
said to him, "Your son lives." And he himself
believed, and his whole household.

[54] This again *is* the second sign Jesus did when He
had come out of Judea into Galilee.

5 After this there was a feast of the Jews, and Jesus
went up to Jerusalem. [2] Now there is in Jerusalem
by the Sheep *Gate* a pool, which is called in
Hebrew, Bethesda, having five porches. [3] In these
lay a great multitude of sick people, blind, lame,
paralyzed, waiting for the moving of the water.

פְּרִי לְחַיֵּי עוֹלָם, כְּדֵי שֶׁיִּשְׂמְחוּ יַחְדָּו הַזּוֹרֵעַ וְהַקּוֹצֵר.
[37] בָּזֶה מִתְאַמֶּתֶת הָאִמְרָה – "זֶה זוֹרֵעַ וְזֶה קוֹצֵר".
[38] אֲנִי שָׁלַחְתִּי אֶתְכֶם לִקְצֹר אֶת אֲשֶׁר לֹא עֲמַלְתֶּם
בּוֹ; אֲחֵרִים עָמְלוּ וְאַתֶּם הִגַּעְתֶּם אֶל פְּרִי עֲמָלָם."

[39] שׁוֹמְרוֹנִים רַבִּים מִן הָעִיר הַהִיא הֶאֱמִינוּ בּוֹ עַל־
סְמַךְ הַדָּבָר שֶׁהֵעִידָה הָאִשָּׁה, "הוּא אָמַר לִי כָּל מַה
שֶׁעָשִׂיתִי." [40] כְּשֶׁבָּאוּ הַשּׁוֹמְרוֹנִים בִּקְשׁוּ מִמֶּנּוּ
לִשְׁהוֹת אִתָּם וְהוּא שָׁהָה שָׁם יוֹמָיִם. [41] רַבִּים
יוֹתֵר הֶאֱמִינוּ בִּגְלַל דְּבָרוֹ, [42] וְאֶל הָאִשָּׁה אָמְרוּ: "לֹא
עוֹד בִּגְלַל דְּבָרֵךְ אֲנַחְנוּ מַאֲמִינִים, כִּי בְּעַצְמֵנוּ
שָׁמַעְנוּ וְיוֹדְעִים אָנוּ שֶׁזֶּהוּ בֶּאֱמֶת מוֹשִׁיעַ הָעוֹלָם."

[43] לְאַחַר שְׁנֵי הַיָּמִים יָצָא מִשָּׁם אֶל הַגָּלִיל. [44] אָמְנָם
הוּא עַצְמוֹ הֵעִיד כִּי אֵין כָּבוֹד לְנָבִיא בְּעִירוֹ. [45] בְּרַם
כַּאֲשֶׁר בָּא לַגָּלִיל קִבְּלוּהוּ אַנְשֵׁי הַגָּלִיל, שֶׁכֵּן רָאוּ
אֶת כָּל אֲשֶׁר עָשָׂה בִּירוּשָׁלַיִם בִּימֵי הֶחָג, כִּי גַם הֵם
עָלוּ לָחֹג אֶת הֶחָג. [46] הוּא בָּא שׁוּב אֶל קָנָה
שֶׁבַּגָּלִיל, אֲשֶׁר שָׁם הָפַךְ אֶת הַמַּיִם לְיַיִן. וְאֶחָד
מֵאַנְשֵׁי הַמֶּלֶךְ, שֶׁבְּנוֹ הָיָה חוֹלֶה בִּכְפַר נַחוּם,
[47] שָׁמַע כִּי יֵשׁוּעַ בָּא מִיהוּדָה לַגָּלִיל. הָלַךְ אֵלָיו
וּבִקֵּשׁ מִמֶּנּוּ שֶׁיֵּרֵד וִירַפֵּא אֶת בְּנוֹ, כִּי נָטָה לָמוּת.
[48] אָמַר לוֹ יֵשׁוּעַ: "אִם אֵינְכֶם רוֹאִים אוֹתוֹת
וּמוֹפְתִים, בְּשׁוּם פָּנִים לֹא תַּאֲמִינוּ."

[49] אָמַר אֵלָיו הָאִישׁ: "אֲדוֹנִי, רֵד נָא בְּטֶרֶם יָמוּת
בְּנִי."

[50] הֵשִׁיב לוֹ יֵשׁוּעַ: "לֵךְ, בִּנְךָ חַי."
הֶאֱמִין הָאִישׁ לַדָּבָר שֶׁאָמַר לוֹ יֵשׁוּעַ וְהָלַךְ. [51] כַּאֲשֶׁר
יָרַד בָּאוּ עֲבָדָיו לִקְרָאתוֹ וְאָמְרוּ לוֹ שֶׁבְּנוֹ חַי. [52] שָׁאַל
אוֹתָם בְּאֵיזוֹ שָׁעָה הוּטַב לוֹ, וְאָמְרוּ לוֹ: "אֶתְמוֹל
בְּשָׁעָה אַחַת אַחֲרֵי הַצָּהֳרַיִם הִרְפָּה מִמֶּנּוּ הַחֹם."
[53] אָז נוֹכַח הָאָב כִּי זֶה הָיָה בְּאוֹתָהּ שָׁעָה שֶׁאָמַר לוֹ
יֵשׁוּעַ 'בִּנְךָ חַי', וְהֶאֱמִין הוּא וְכָל בֵּיתוֹ. [54] זֹאת
הַפַּעַם הַשְּׁנִיָּה שֶׁיֵּשׁוּעַ עָשָׂה אוֹת עִם בּוֹאוֹ מִיהוּדָה
לַגָּלִיל.

ה אַחֲרֵי כֵן הָיָה חַג לַיְּהוּדִים וְיֵשׁוּעַ עָלָה
לִירוּשָׁלַיִם. [2] בִּירוּשָׁלַיִם, עַל־יַד שַׁעַר הַצֹּאן הָיְתָה
בְּרֵכָה, שֶׁנִּקְרְאָה בֵּית חַסְדָּא, וּסְבִיבָהּ חָמֵשׁ
אַכְסַדְרָאוֹת בַּעֲלוֹת עַמּוּדִים. [3] בָּאַכְסַדְרָאוֹת
הָאֵלֶּה שָׁכְבוּ הַרְבֵּה חוֹלִים וְעִוְרִים וּפִסְחִים וִיבֵשֵׁי

3‑4 אֵיבָרִים—כַּמָּה כִּתְבֵי יָד מוֹסִיפִים אֶת הַקֶּטַע הַבָּא: בְּצִפִּיָּה
לִתְנוּעַת הַמַּיִם, 4 שֶׁכֵּן מַלְאַךְ יהוה הָיָה יוֹרֵד לְעִתִּים מְזֻמָּנוֹת אֶל
הַבְּרֵכָה וּמֵנִיעַ אֶת הַמַּיִם, וּמִי שֶׁיָּרַד לַתּוֹכָהּ רִאשׁוֹן לְאַחַר תְּנוּעַת
הַמַּיִם נִרְפָּא מִכָּל מַחֲלָה שֶׁהָיְתָה לוֹ.

⁴For an angel went down at a certain time into the pool and stirred up the water; then whoever stepped in first, after the stirring of the water, was made well of whatever disease he had. ⁵Now a certain man was there who had an infirmity thirty-eight years. ⁶When Jesus saw him lying there, and knew that he already had been *in that condition* a long time, He said to him, "Do you want to be made well?"

⁷The sick man answered Him, "Sir, I have no man to put me into the pool when the water is stirred up; but while I am coming, another steps down before me."

⁸Jesus said to him, "Rise, take up your bed and walk." ⁹And immediately the man was made well, took up his bed, and walked.

And that day was the Sabbath. ¹⁰The Jews therefore said to him who was cured, "It is the Sabbath; it is not lawful for you to carry your bed."

¹¹He answered them, "He who made me well said to me, 'Take up your bed and walk.' "

¹²Then they asked him, "Who is the Man who said to you, 'Take up your bed and walk'?" ¹³But the one who was healed did not know who it was, for Jesus had withdrawn, a multitude being in *that* place. ¹⁴Afterward Jesus found him in the temple, and said to him, "See, you have been made well. Sin no more, lest a worse thing come upon you."

¹⁵The man departed and told the Jews that it was Jesus who had made him well.

¹⁶For this reason the Jews persecuted Jesus, and sought to kill Him, because He had done these things on the Sabbath. ¹⁷But Jesus answered them, "My Father has been working until now, and I have been working."

¹⁸Therefore the Jews sought all the more to kill Him, because He not only broke the Sabbath, but also said that God was His Father, making Himself equal with God. ¹⁹Then Jesus answered and said to them, "Most assuredly, I say to you, the Son can do nothing of Himself, but what He sees the Father do; for whatever He does, the Son also does in like manner. ²⁰For the Father loves the Son, and shows Him all things that He Himself does; and He will show Him greater works than these, that you may marvel. ²¹For as the Father raises the dead and gives life to *them,* even so the Son gives life to whom He will. ²²For the Father judges no one, but has committed all judgment to the Son, ²³that all should honor the Son just as they honor the Father. He who does not honor the Son does not honor the Father who sent Him.

²⁴"Most assuredly, I say to you, he who hears My word and believes in Him who sent Me has everlasting life, and shall not come into judgment,

אֵבָרִים. ⁵הָיָה שָׁם אִישׁ אֶחָד וְהוּא בְּחָלְיוֹ שְׁלוֹשִׁים וּשְׁמוֹנֶה שָׁנִים. ⁶יֵשׁוּעַ רָאָה אוֹתוֹ שׁוֹכֵב וְיָדַע כִּי זְמַן רַב הוּא חוֹלֶה. שָׁאַל אוֹתוֹ: "אַתָּה רוֹצֶה לִהְיוֹת בָּרִיא?"

⁷הֵשִׁיב לוֹ הַחוֹלֶה: "אֲדוֹנִי, אֵין אִתִּי אִישׁ שֶׁיָּטִיל אוֹתִי לַבְּרֵכָה בְּעֵת תְּנוּעַת הַמַּיִם. עַד שֶׁאֲנִי בָּא, אַחֵר יוֹרֵד לְפָנַי."

⁸אָמַר לוֹ יֵשׁוּעַ: "קוּם, קַח אֶת מִשְׁכָּבְךָ וְהִתְהַלֵּךְ." ⁹מִיָּד נִרְפָּא, לָקַח אֶת מִשְׁכָּבוֹ וְהִתְהַלֵּךְ. אוֹתוֹ יוֹם הָיָה יוֹם שַׁבָּת.

¹⁰אָמְרוּ רָאשֵׁי הַיְּהוּדִים לָאִישׁ שֶׁנִּרְפָּא: "שַׁבָּת הַיּוֹם; אָסוּר לְךָ לָשֵׂאת אֶת מִשְׁכָּבְךָ."

¹¹הֵשִׁיב לָהֶם: "זֶה שֶׁרִפֵּא אוֹתִי, הוּא אָמַר לִי, 'קַח אֶת מִשְׁכָּבְךָ וְהִתְהַלֵּךְ'."

¹²שָׁאֲלוּ אוֹתוֹ: "מִיהוּ הָאִישׁ שֶׁאָמַר לְךָ 'קַח וְהִתְהַלֵּךְ'?" ¹³אֶלָּא שֶׁהַנִּרְפָּא לֹא יָדַע מִיהוּ, כִּי יֵשׁוּעַ חָמַק בִּהְיוֹת הָמוֹן רַב בַּמָּקוֹם.

¹⁴לְאַחַר מִכֵּן פָּגַשׁ אוֹתוֹ יֵשׁוּעַ בְּבֵית הַמִּקְדָּשׁ וְאָמַר לוֹ: "הִנֵּה נִרְפֵּאתָ. אַל תּוֹסִיף לַחֲטֹא פֶּן תְּאֻנֶּה לְךָ רָעָה גְדוֹלָה מִזֹּאת."

¹⁵הָלַךְ הָאִישׁ וְסִפֵּר לְרָאשֵׁי הַיְּהוּדִים כִּי יֵשׁוּעַ הוּא שֶׁרִפֵּא אוֹתוֹ. ¹⁶לָכֵן הֵם רָדְפוּ אֶת יֵשׁוּעַ, כִּי עָשָׂה זֹאת בְּשַׁבָּת. ¹⁷הֵשִׁיב לָהֶם יֵשׁוּעַ: "אָבִי פּוֹעֵל עַד עַתָּה וְגַם אֲנִי פּוֹעֵל." ¹⁸מִשּׁוּם כָּךְ עוֹד יוֹתֵר הִשְׁתַּדְּלוּ לַהֲרֹג אוֹתוֹ, כִּי לֹא רַק שֶׁהֵפֵר אֶת הַשַּׁבָּת אֶלָּא גַּם אָמַר שֶׁהָאֱלֹהִים הוּא אָבִיו וְעָשָׂה עַצְמוֹ שָׁוֶה לֵאלֹהִים.

¹⁹עָנָה יֵשׁוּעַ וְאָמַר לָהֶם: "אָמֵן אָמֵן אֲנִי אוֹמֵר לָכֶם, הַבֵּן אֵינֶנּוּ יָכוֹל לַעֲשׂוֹת דָּבָר מִלְּבוֹ זוּלָתִי מַה שֶׁהוּא רוֹאֶה אֶת הָאָב עוֹשֶׂה. כָּל מַה שֶׁעוֹשֶׂה הָאָב –זֹאת גַּם הַבֵּן עוֹשֶׂה כָּמוֹהוּ. ²⁰כִּי הָאָב אוֹהֵב אֶת הַבֵּן וּמַרְאֶה לוֹ אֶת כָּל אֲשֶׁר הוּא עוֹשֶׂה. וּמַעֲשִׂים גְּדוֹלִים מֵאֵלֶּה יַרְאֶה לוֹ, עַד כִּי תִּתְפַּלְאוּ; ²¹כִּי כְּשֵׁם שֶׁהָאָב מֵעִיר וּמְחַיֶּה אֶת הַמֵּתִים, כֵּן גַּם הַבֵּן מְחַיֶּה אֶת מִי שֶׁהוּא רוֹצֶה. ²²הָאָב אֵינֶנּוּ שׁוֹפֵט אִישׁ, אֶלָּא נָתַן אֶת כָּל הַמִּשְׁפָּט בְּיַד הַבֵּן ²³כְּדֵי שֶׁהַכֹּל יְכַבְּדוּ אֶת הַבֵּן כְּמוֹ שֶׁמְּכַבְּדִים אֶת הָאָב. מִי שֶׁאֵינוֹ מְכַבֵּד אֶת הַבֵּן, אֵינוֹ מְכַבֵּד אֶת הָאָב אֲשֶׁר שָׁלַח אוֹתוֹ. ²⁴אָמֵן אָמֵן אֲנִי אוֹמֵר לָכֶם, הַשּׁוֹמֵעַ

but has passed from death into life. ²⁵ Most assuredly, I say to you, the hour is coming, and now is, when the dead will hear the voice of the Son of God; and those who hear will live. ²⁶ For as the Father has life in Himself, so He has granted the Son to have life in Himself, ²⁷ and has given Him authority to execute judgment also, because He is the Son of Man. ²⁸ Do not marvel at this; for the hour is coming in which all who are in the graves will hear His voice ²⁹ and come forth—those who have done good, to the resurrection of life, and those who have done evil, to the resurrection of condemnation. ³⁰ I can of Myself do nothing. As I hear, I judge; and My judgment is righteous, because I do not seek My own will but the will of the Father who sent Me.

³¹ "If I bear witness of Myself, My witness is not true. ³² There is another who bears witness of Me, and I know that the witness which He witnesses of Me is true. ³³ You have sent to John, and he has borne witness to the truth. ³⁴ Yet I do not receive testimony from man, but I say these things that you may be saved. ³⁵ He was the burning and shining lamp, and you were willing for a time to rejoice in his light. ³⁶ But I have a greater witness than John's; for the works which the Father has given Me to finish—the very works that I do—bear witness of Me, that the Father has sent Me. ³⁷ And the Father Himself, who sent Me, has testified of Me. You have neither heard His voice at any time, nor seen His form. ³⁸ But you do not have His word abiding in you, because whom He sent, Him you do not believe. ³⁹ You search the Scriptures, for in them you think you have eternal life; and these are they which testify of Me. ⁴⁰ But you are not willing to come to Me that you may have life.

⁴¹ "I do not receive honor from men. ⁴² But I know you, that you do not have the love of God in you. ⁴³ I have come in My Father's name, and you do not receive Me; if another comes in his own name, him you will receive. ⁴⁴ How can you believe, who receive honor from one another, and do not seek the honor that *comes* from the only God? ⁴⁵ Do not think that I shall accuse you to the Father; there is *one* who accuses you—Moses, in whom you trust. ⁴⁶ For if you believed Moses, you would believe Me; for he wrote about Me. ⁴⁷ But if you do not believe his writings, how will you believe My words?"

6 After these things Jesus went over the Sea of Galilee, which is *the Sea* of Tiberias. ² Then a great multitude followed Him, because they saw His signs

אֶת דְּבָרִי וּמַאֲמִין לְשׁוֹלְחִי יֶשׁ לוֹ חַיֵּי עוֹלָם וְאֵינוֹ בָּא בְּמִשְׁפָּט כִּי אִם עָבַר מִמָּוֶת לְחַיִּים. ²⁵ אָמֵן אָמֵן אֲנִי אוֹמֵר לָכֶם, תָּבוֹא שָׁעָה, וְכָעֵת הִיא, שֶׁהַמֵּתִים יִשְׁמְעוּ אֶת קוֹל בֶּן־הָאֱלֹהִים וְהַשּׁוֹמְעִים יִחְיוּ. ²⁶ כִּי כְּשֵׁם שֶׁלָּאָב יֵשׁ חַיִּים בְּעַצְמוֹ, כָּךְ גַּם נָתַן לַבֵּן שֶׁיִּהְיוּ לוֹ חַיִּים בְּעַצְמוֹ. ²⁷ גַּם סַמְכוּת נָתַן לוֹ לַעֲשׂוֹת מִשְׁפָּט, כִּי בֶּן־הָאָדָם הוּא. ²⁸ אַל תִּתְמְהוּ עַל זֹאת, כִּי תָּבוֹא שָׁעָה שֶׁכָּל שׁוֹכְנֵי קֶבֶר יִשְׁמְעוּ אֶת קוֹלוֹ, ²⁹ וְיֵצְאוּ עוֹשֵׂי הַטּוֹב לִתְקוּמָה שֶׁל חַיִּים וְעוֹשֵׂי הָרַע לִתְקוּמָה שֶׁל מִשְׁפָּט."

³⁰ "אֵין אֲנִי יָכוֹל לַעֲשׂוֹת דָּבָר מִלִּבִּי. לְפִי מַה שֶּׁאֲנִי שׁוֹמֵעַ אֲנִי שׁוֹפֵט. וּמִשְׁפָּטִי צוֹדֵק, מִפְּנֵי שֶׁאֵינֶנִּי מְבַקֵּשׁ אֶת רְצוֹנִי אֶלָּא אֶת רְצוֹן שׁוֹלְחִי. ³¹ אִם אָנֹכִי מֵעִיד עַל עַצְמִי, עֵדוּתִי אֵינֶנָּה אֱמֶת. ³² יֵשׁ אַחֵר הַמֵּעִיד עָלַי, וְיוֹדֵעַ אֲנִי כִּי עֵדוּת אֱמֶת הוּא מֵעִיד עָלַי. ³³ אַתֶּם שְׁלַחְתֶּם אֶל יוֹחָנָן וְהוּא הֵעִיד עַל הָאֱמֶת. ³⁴ אַךְ אֲנִי לֹא מֵאָדָם מְקַבֵּל אֶת הָעֵדוּת. אוּלָם אוֹמֵר אֲנִי אֶת הַדְּבָרִים הָאֵלֶּה כְּדֵי שֶׁאַתֶּם תִּוָּשֵׁעוּ. ³⁵ הוּא הָיָה הַנֵּר הַדּוֹלֵק וּמֵאִיר וְאַתֶּם חֲפַצְתֶּם לִשְׂמֹחַ לְשָׁעָה בְּאוֹרוֹ, ³⁶ אַךְ אֲנִי יֶשׁ לִי עֵדוּת גְּדוֹלָה מֵעֵדוּת יוֹחָנָן, שֶׁכֵּן הַמַּעֲשִׂים שֶׁנָּתַן לִי הָאָב לְהַשְׁלִימָם - אוֹתָם הַמַּעֲשִׂים אֲשֶׁר אֲנִי עוֹשֶׂה - מְעִידִים עָלַי שֶׁהָאָב שְׁלָחַנִי. ³⁷ וְהָאָב אֲשֶׁר שְׁלָחַנִי הוּא הֵעִיד עָלַי. אֶת קוֹלוֹ מֵעוֹלָם לֹא שְׁמַעְתֶּם וְאֶת מַרְאֵהוּ לֹא רְאִיתֶם. ³⁸ דְּבָרוֹ אֵינוֹ שׁוֹכֵן בָּכֶם, כִּי אֵין אַתֶּם מַאֲמִינִים לָזֶה אֲשֶׁר הָאָב שְׁלָחוֹ. ³⁹ אַתֶּם חוֹקְרִים אֶת הַכְּתוּבִים, כִּי חוֹשְׁבִים אַתֶּם שֶׁיֵּשׁ לָכֶם חַיֵּי עוֹלָם בָּהֶם; וְהֵם הַמְּעִידִים עָלַי. ⁴⁰ וְאִלּוּ אַתֶּם אֵינְכֶם רוֹצִים לָבוֹא אֵלַי כְּדֵי שֶׁיִּהְיוּ לָכֶם חַיִּים. ⁴¹ אֵין אֲנִי לוֹקֵחַ לִי כָּבוֹד מִבְּנֵי אָדָם. ⁴² וְאוּלָם אֲנִי מַכִּיר אֶתְכֶם: אֵין לָכֶם אַהֲבַת אֱלֹהִים בְּקִרְבְּכֶם. ⁴³ אֲנִי בָּאתִי בְּשֵׁם אָבִי וְלֹא קִבַּלְתֶּם אוֹתִי; אִם יָבוֹא אַחֵר בְּשֵׁם עַצְמוֹ - אוֹתוֹ תְּקַבְּלוּ. ⁴⁴ כֵּיצַד תּוּכְלוּ לְהַאֲמִין בְּשָׁעָה שֶׁאַתֶּם מְקַבְּלִים כָּבוֹד אִישׁ מֵרֵעֵהוּ וְאֶת הַכָּבוֹד מֵאֱלֹהִים הָאֶחָד אֵינְכֶם מְבַקְשִׁים? ⁴⁵ אַל תַּחְשְׁבוּ שֶׁאֲנִי אֶטְעַן עֲלֵיכֶם לִפְנֵי אָבִי. מֹשֶׁה אֲשֶׁר שַׂמְתֶּם בּוֹ בִּטְחוֹנְכֶם הוּא הַטּוֹעֵן עֲלֵיכֶם. ⁴⁶ אִלּוּ הֶאֱמַנְתֶּם לְמֹשֶׁה, הֱיִיתֶם מַאֲמִינִים לִי, כִּי עָלַי כָּתַב. ⁴⁷ אֲבָל אִם לִכְתָבָיו אֵינְכֶם מַאֲמִינִים, אֵיךְ תַּאֲמִינוּ לִדְבָרַי?"

ו אַחֲרֵי הַדְּבָרִים הָאֵלֶּה עָבַר יֵשׁוּעַ לַצַּד הַשֵּׁנִי שֶׁל יָם כִּנֶּרֶת. ² הֲמוֹן עַם רַב בָּאוּ אַחֲרָיו, כִּי רָאוּ אֶת

which He performed on those who were diseased.
3 And Jesus went up on the mountain, and there He sat with His disciples.

4 Now the Passover, a feast of the Jews, was near. 5 Then Jesus lifted up *His* eyes, and seeing a great multitude coming toward Him, He said to Philip, "Where shall we buy bread, that these may eat?" 6 But this He said to test him, for He Himself knew what He would do.

7 Philip answered Him, "Two hundred denarii worth of bread is not sufficient for them, that every one of them may have a little."

8 One of His disciples, Andrew, Simon Peter's brother, said to Him, 9 "There is a lad here who has five barley loaves and two small fish, but what are they among so many?"

10 Then Jesus said, "Make the people sit down." Now there was much grass in the place. So the men sat down, in number about five thousand. 11 And Jesus took the loaves, and when He had given thanks He distributed *them* to the disciples, and the disciples to those sitting down; and likewise of the fish, as much as they wanted. 12 So when they were filled, He said to His disciples, "Gather up the fragments that remain, so that nothing is lost." 13 Therefore they gathered *them* up, and filled twelve baskets with the fragments of the five barley loaves which were left over by those who had eaten. 14 Then those men, when they had seen the sign that Jesus did, said, "This is truly the Prophet who is to come into the world."

15 Therefore when Jesus perceived that they were about to come and take Him by force to make Him king, He departed again to the mountain by Himself alone.

16 Now when evening came, His disciples went down to the sea, 17 got into the boat, and went over the sea toward Capernaum. And it was already dark, and Jesus had not come to them. 18 Then the sea arose because a great wind was blowing. 19 So when they had rowed about three or four miles, they saw Jesus walking on the sea and drawing near the boat; and they were afraid. 20 But He said to them, "It is I; do not be afraid." 21 Then they willingly received Him into the boat, and immediately the boat was at the land where they were going.

22 On the following day, when the people who were standing on the other side of the sea saw that there was no other boat there, except that one which His disciples had entered, and that Jesus had not entered the boat with His disciples, but His disciples had gone away alone— 23 however, other boats came from Tiberias, near the place where they

הַנִּסִּים שֶׁעָשָׂה בַחוֹלִים. 3 הוּא עָלָה עַל הָהָר וַיֵּשֶׁב שָׁם עִם תַּלְמִידָיו. 4 הָיָה זֶה סָמוּךְ לְפֶסַח, חַג הַיְּהוּדִים. 5 כְּשֶׁנָּשָׂא יֵשׁוּעַ אֶת עֵינָיו וְרָאָה עַם רַב בָּאִים אֵלָיו, אָמַר לְפִילִיפּוֹס: "אֵיפֹה נִקְנֶה לֶחֶם כְּדֵי שֶׁיֹּאכְלוּ אֵלֶּה?" 6 וְזֹאת אָמַר כְּשֶׁהוּא מְנַסֶּה אוֹתוֹ, שֶׁהֲרֵי יָדַע מַה הִתְכַּוֵּן לַעֲשׂוֹת.

7 הֵשִׁיב לוֹ פִילִיפּוֹס: "כְּדֵי שֶׁכָּל אֶחָד יְקַבֵּל קְצָת לֹא יַסְפִּיקוּ לָהֶם כִּכְּרוֹת לֶחֶם בְּמָאתַיִם דִּינָר."

8 אֶחָד מִתַּלְמִידָיו, וְהוּא אַנְדְּרֵי אָחִיו שֶׁל שִׁמְעוֹן כֵּיפָא, אָמַר לוֹ: 9 "יֵשׁ פֹּה נַעַר וְלוֹ חָמֵשׁ כִּכְּרוֹת לֶחֶם שְׂעוֹרִים וּשְׁנֵי דָגִים, אַךְ מָה אֵלֶּה בִּשְׁבִיל עַם רַב כָּזֶה?"

10 אָמַר יֵשׁוּעַ: "הוֹשִׁיבוּ אֶת הָאֲנָשִׁים!" הַרְבֵּה עֵשֶׂב הָיָה בְּאוֹתוֹ מָקוֹם וְהָאֲנָשִׁים יָשְׁבוּ. מִסְפָּרָם הָיָה כַּחֲמֵשֶׁת אֲלָפִים. 11 לָקַח יֵשׁוּעַ אֶת כִּכְּרוֹת הַלֶּחֶם, בֵּרַךְ וְחִלֵּק לָהֶם כְּאַוַּת נַפְשָׁם, וְכֵן גַּם עָשָׂה בַּדָּגִים. 12 כַּאֲשֶׁר שָׂבְעוּ אָמַר לְתַלְמִידָיו: "אִסְפוּ אֶת מַה שֶׁנּוֹתַר כְּדֵי שֶׁלֹּא יֹאבַד מְאוּמָה." 13 וְהֵם אָסְפוּ, וּמִלְאוּ שְׁנֵים־עָשָׂר סַלִּים בִּשְׁיָרֵי חֲמֵשׁ כִּכְּרוֹת לֶחֶם הַשְּׂעוֹרִים שֶׁהוֹתִירוּ הָאוֹכְלִים. 14 רָאוּ הָאֲנָשִׁים אֶת הָאוֹת שֶׁעָשָׂה וְאָמְרוּ: "זֶהוּ בֶּאֱמֶת הַנָּבִיא שֶׁבָּא אֶל הָעוֹלָם." 15 כְּשֶׁהִבְחִין יֵשׁוּעַ שֶׁהֵם עוֹמְדִים לָבוֹא וְלִתְפֹּס אוֹתוֹ כְּדֵי לְהַמְלִיכוֹ, יָצָא שׁוּב אֶל הָהָר הוּא לְבַדּוֹ.

16 לְעֵת עֶרֶב יָרְדוּ תַּלְמִידָיו אֶל הַיָּם 17 וְנִכְנְסוּ לְסִירָה כְּדֵי לַעֲבֹר אֶת הַיָּם אֶל כְּפַר נַחוּם. הַחֹשֶׁךְ כְּבָר יָרַד וְיֵשׁוּעַ עוֹד לֹא בָּא אֲלֵיהֶם. 18 אוֹתָהּ שָׁעָה נָשְׁבָה רוּחַ חֲזָקָה וְהַיָּם הֵחֵל לִסְעֹר. 19 לְאַחַר שֶׁחָתְרוּ כִּשְׁנַיִם אוֹ שְׁלוֹשָׁה מִילִין, רָאוּ אֶת יֵשׁוּעַ הוֹלֵךְ עַל הַיָּם וּמִתְקָרֵב אֶל הַסִּירָה. פַּחַד נָפַל עֲלֵיהֶם, 20 אַךְ הוּא אָמַר לָהֶם: "אֲנִי הוּא, אַל תִּפְחָדוּ." 21 אָז חָפְצוּ לְקַבֵּל אוֹתוֹ לַסִּירָה וּלְפֶתַע הָיְתָה הַסִּירָה בַּחוֹף אֲשֶׁר הִפְלִיגוּ אֵלָיו.

22 לְמָחֳרָת רָאָה הֶהָמוֹן אֲשֶׁר עָמַד מֵעֵבֶר לַיָּם כִּי קֹדֶם לָכֵן לֹא הָיְתָה שָׁם אֶלָּא סִירָה אַחַת, וְכִי יֵשׁוּעַ לֹא נִכְנַס לַסִּירָה עִם תַּלְמִידָיו אֶלָּא שֶׁתַּלְמִידָיו נָסְעוּ לְבַדָּם. 23 סִירוֹת אֲחֵרוֹת בָּאוּ מִטְּבֶרְיָה אֶל קִרְבַת הַמָּקוֹם שֶׁאָכְלוּ שָׁם אֶת הַלֶּחֶם לְאַחַר שֶׁבֵּרַךְ עָלָיו

ate bread after the Lord had given thanks— ²⁴when the people therefore saw that Jesus was not there, nor His disciples, they also got into boats and came to Capernaum, seeking Jesus. ²⁵And when they found Him on the other side of the sea, they said to Him, "Rabbi, when did You come here?"

²⁶Jesus answered them and said, "Most assuredly, I say to you, you seek Me, not because you saw the signs, but because you ate of the loaves and were filled. ²⁷Do not labor for the food which perishes, but for the food which endures to everlasting life, which the Son of Man will give you, because God the Father has set His seal on Him."

²⁸Then they said to Him, "What shall we do, that we may work the works of God?"

²⁹Jesus answered and said to them, "This is the work of God, that you believe in Him whom He sent."

³⁰Therefore they said to Him, "What sign will You perform then, that we may see it and believe You? What work will You do? ³¹Our fathers ate the manna in the desert; as it is written, 'He gave them bread from heaven to eat.'"

³²Then Jesus said to them, "Most assuredly, I say to you, Moses did not give you the bread from heaven, but My Father gives you the true bread from heaven. ³³For the bread of God is He who comes down from heaven and gives life to the world."

³⁴Then they said to Him, "Lord, give us this bread always."

³⁵And Jesus said to them, "I am the bread of life. He who comes to Me shall never hunger, and he who believes in Me shall never thirst. ³⁶But I said to you that you have seen Me and yet do not believe. ³⁷All that the Father gives Me will come to Me, and the one who comes to Me I will by no means cast out. ³⁸For I have come down from heaven, not to do My own will, but the will of Him who sent Me. ³⁹This is the will of the Father who sent Me, that of all He has given Me I should lose nothing, but should raise it up at the last day. ⁴⁰And this is the will of Him who sent Me, that everyone who sees the Son and believes in Him may have everlasting life; and I will raise him up at the last day."

⁴¹The Jews then complained about Him, because He said, "I am the bread which came down from heaven." ⁴²And they said, "Is not this Jesus, the son of Joseph, whose father and mother we know? How is it then that He says, 'I have come down from heaven'?"

הָאָדוֹן. ²⁴כִּרְאוֹת הֲמוֹן הָעָם שֶׁיֵּשׁוּעַ אֵינֶנּוּ שָׁם וְגַם לֹא תַּלְמִידָיו, נִכְנְסוּ לַסִּירוֹת וּבָאוּ לִכְפַר נַחוּם לְחַפֵּשׂ אֶת יֵשׁוּעַ. ²⁵כַּאֲשֶׁר מָצְאוּ אוֹתוֹ מֵעֵבֶר לַיָּם, שָׁאֲלוּ אוֹתוֹ: "רַבִּי, מָתַי בָּאתָ לְכָאן?"

²⁶עָנָה לָהֶם יֵשׁוּעַ וְאָמַר: "אָמֵן אָמֵן אֲנִי אוֹמֵר לָכֶם, אַתֶּם מְחַפְּשִׂים אוֹתִי, לֹא מִשּׁוּם שֶׁרְאִיתֶם אוֹתוֹת, אֶלָּא מִשּׁוּם שֶׁאֲכַלְתֶּם מִכִּכְּרוֹת הַלֶּחֶם וּשְׂבַעְתֶּם. ²⁷אַל תַּעַמְלוּ בְּעַד הָאֹכֶל הַכָּלֶה וְאוֹבֵד, אֶלָּא בְּעַד הָאֹכֶל הַקַּיָּם לְחַיֵּי עוֹלָם, אֲשֶׁר בֶּן־הָאָדָם יִתְּנֶהוּ לָכֶם, כִּי אוֹתוֹ חָתַם הָאֱלֹהִים הָאָב בְּחוֹתָמוֹ."

²⁸שָׁאֲלוּ אוֹתוֹ: "מַה עָלֵינוּ לַעֲשׂוֹת כְּדֵי שֶׁנִּפְעַל אֶת פָּעֳלֵי אֱלֹהִים?"

²⁹הֵשִׁיב יֵשׁוּעַ וְאָמַר לָהֶם: "זֶהוּ פֹּעַל הָאֱלֹהִים – שֶׁתַּאֲמִינוּ בְּזֶה אֲשֶׁר הוּא שָׁלַח."

³⁰אָמְרוּ לוֹ: "אִם כֵּן, מָה הָאוֹת שֶׁאַתָּה עוֹשֶׂה לְמַעַן נִרְאֶה וְנַאֲמִין בְּךָ? מָה אַתָּה פּוֹעֵל? ³¹אֲבוֹתֵינוּ אָכְלוּ אֶת הַמָּן בַּמִּדְבָּר, כְּמוֹ שֶׁכָּתוּב: 'לֶחֶם מִן הַשָּׁמַיִם נָתַן לָמוֹ לֶאֱכֹל'."

³²הֵשִׁיב לָהֶם יֵשׁוּעַ: "אָמֵן אָמֵן אֲנִי אוֹמֵר לָכֶם, לֹא מֹשֶׁה נָתַן לָכֶם אֶת הַלֶּחֶם מִן הַשָּׁמַיִם אֶלָּא אָבִי נוֹתֵן לָכֶם אֶת הַלֶּחֶם הָאֲמִתִּי מִן הַשָּׁמַיִם, ³³כִּי לֶחֶם הָאֱלֹהִים הוּא הַיּוֹרֵד מִן הַשָּׁמַיִם וְנוֹתֵן חַיִּים לָעוֹלָם."

³⁴אָמְרוּ אֵלָיו: "אָדוֹן, תֵּן נָא לָנוּ תָּמִיד אֶת הַלֶּחֶם הַזֶּה."

³⁵אָמַר לָהֶם יֵשׁוּעַ: "אֲנִי הוּא לֶחֶם הַחַיִּים. כָּל הַבָּא אֵלַי לֹא יִרְעַב, וְהַמַּאֲמִין בִּי לֹא יִצְמָא עוֹד. ³⁶אֲבָל אָמַרְתִּי לָכֶם כִּי רְאִיתֶם אוֹתִי וּבְכָל זֹאת אֵינְכֶם מַאֲמִינִים. ³⁷כָּל מִי שֶׁהָאָב נוֹתֵן אוֹתוֹ לִי יָבוֹא אֵלַי, וְאֶת הַבָּא אֵלַי לֹא אַשְׁלִיךְ הַחוּצָה, ³⁸כִּי יָרַדְתִּי מִן הַשָּׁמַיִם לֹא לַעֲשׂוֹת אֶת רְצוֹנִי שֶׁלִּי אֶלָּא אֶת רְצוֹן שׁוֹלְחִי. ³⁹וְזֶה רְצוֹן שׁוֹלְחִי: שֶׁלֹּא יֹאבַד לִי אִישׁ מִכָּל אֲשֶׁר נָתַן לִי, אֶלָּא שֶׁאָקִים אוֹתוֹ בַּיּוֹם הָאַחֲרוֹן. ⁴⁰הֵן זֶהוּ רְצוֹן אָבִי: שֶׁכָּל הָרוֹאֶה אֶת הַבֵּן וּמַאֲמִין בּוֹ יִהְיוּ לוֹ חַיֵּי עוֹלָם וַאֲנִי אָקִים אוֹתוֹ בַּיּוֹם הָאַחֲרוֹן."

⁴¹הָיוּ שֶׁרָטְנוּ עָלָיו מִשּׁוּם שֶׁאָמַר "אֲנִי הַלֶּחֶם הַיּוֹרֵד מִן הַשָּׁמַיִם", ⁴²וְאָמְרוּ: "הֲלֹא זֶהוּ יֵשׁוּעַ בֶּן יוֹסֵף אֲשֶׁר אֲנַחְנוּ מַכִּירִים אֶת אָבִיו וְאֶת אִמּוֹ! אֵיךְ כָּעֵת הוּא אוֹמֵר 'מִן הַשָּׁמַיִם יָרַדְתִּי'?"

43 Jesus therefore answered and said to them, "Do not murmur among yourselves. 44 No one can come to Me unless the Father who sent Me draws him; and I will raise him up at the last day. 45 It is written in the prophets, 'And they shall all be taught by God.' Therefore everyone who has heard and learned from the Father comes to Me. 46 Not that anyone has seen the Father, except He who is from God; He has seen the Father. 47 Most assuredly, I say to you, he who believes in Me has everlasting life. 48 I am the bread of life. 49 Your fathers ate the manna in the wilderness, and are dead. 50 This is the bread which comes down from heaven, that one may eat of it and not die. 51 I am the living bread which came down from heaven. If anyone eats of this bread, he will live forever; and the bread that I shall give is My flesh, which I shall give for the life of the world."

52 The Jews therefore quarreled among themselves, saying, "How can this Man give us His flesh to eat?"

53 Then Jesus said to them, "Most assuredly, I say to you, unless you eat the flesh of the Son of Man and drink His blood, you have no life in you. 54 Whoever eats My flesh and drinks My blood has eternal life, and I will raise him up at the last day. 55 For My flesh is food indeed, and My blood is drink indeed. 56 He who eats My flesh and drinks My blood abides in Me, and I in him. 57 As the living Father sent Me, and I live because of the Father, so he who feeds on Me will live because of Me. 58 This is the bread which came down from heaven—not as your fathers ate the manna, and are dead. He who eats this bread will live forever."

59 These things He said in the synagogue as He taught in Capernaum.

60 Therefore many of His disciples, when they heard this, said, "This is a hard saying; who can understand it?"

61 When Jesus knew in Himself that His disciples complained about this, He said to them, "Does this offend you? 62 What then if you should see the Son of Man ascend where He was before? 63 It is the Spirit who gives life; the flesh profits nothing. The words that I speak to you are spirit, and they are life. 64 But there are some of you who do not believe." For Jesus knew from the beginning who they were who did not believe, and who would betray Him. 65 And He said, "Therefore I have said to you that no one can come to Me unless it has been granted to him by My Father."

66 From that time many of His disciples went back and walked with Him no more. 67 Then Jesus said to the twelve, "Do you also want to go away?"

43 הֵשִׁיב יֵשׁוּעַ וְאָמַר לָהֶם: "אַל תִּרְגְּנוּ בֵּינֵיכֶם. 44 אֵין אִישׁ יָכוֹל לָבוֹא אֵלַי אֶלָּא אִם כֵּן יִמְשֹׁךְ אוֹתוֹ הָאָב אֲשֶׁר שְׁלָחַנִי, וַאֲנִי אָקִים אוֹתוֹ בַּיּוֹם הָאַחֲרוֹן. 45 הֵן כָּתוּב בַּנְּבִיאִים, 'וְכָל-בָּנַיִךְ לִמּוּדֵי יְהוָה'. כָּל הַשּׁוֹמֵעַ מִן הָאָב וְלוֹמֵד יָבוֹא אֵלַי. 46 לֹא שֶׁאֵיזֶה אִישׁ רָאָה אֶת הָאָב, כִּי אִם זֶה שֶׁהוּא מֵאֵת הָאֱלֹהִים– הוּא רָאָה אֶת הָאָב. 47 אָמֵן אָמֵן אֲנִי אוֹמֵר לָכֶם, הַמַּאֲמִין יֵשׁ לוֹ חַיֵּי עוֹלָם. 48 אֲנִי הוּא לֶחֶם הַחַיִּים. 49 אֲבוֹתֵיכֶם אָכְלוּ אֶת הַמָּן בַּמִּדְבָּר וָמֵתוּ. 50 זֶה הוּא הַלֶּחֶם הַיּוֹרֵד מִן הַשָּׁמַיִם כְּדֵי שֶׁיֹּאכְלוּ מִמֶּנּוּ וְלֹא יָמוּתוּ. 51 אֲנִי הַלֶּחֶם הַחַי הַיּוֹרֵד מִן הַשָּׁמַיִם. אִם יֹאכַל אִישׁ מִן הַלֶּחֶם הַזֶּה יִחְיֶה לְעוֹלָם. וְהַלֶּחֶם אֲשֶׁר אֶתֵּן הֲרֵיהוּ בְּשָׂרִי בְּעַד חַיָּיו שֶׁל הָעוֹלָם."

52 הִתְוַכְּחוּ הַשּׁוֹמְעִים זֶה עִם זֶה וְאָמְרוּ: "אֵיךְ יָכוֹל זֶה לָתֵת לָנוּ אֶת בְּשָׂרוֹ לֶאֱכֹל?"

53 אָמַר לָהֶם יֵשׁוּעַ: "אָמֵן אָמֵן אֲנִי אוֹמֵר לָכֶם, אִם לֹא תֹּאכְלוּ אֶת בְּשַׂר בֶּן-הָאָדָם וְלֹא תִּשְׁתּוּ אֶת דָּמוֹ, אֵין לָכֶם חַיִּים בְּקִרְבְּכֶם. 54 הָאוֹכֵל אֶת בְּשָׂרִי וְשׁוֹתֶה אֶת דָּמִי יֵשׁ לוֹ חַיֵּי עוֹלָם וַאֲנִי אָקִים אוֹתוֹ בַּיּוֹם הָאַחֲרוֹן. 55 כִּי בְּשָׂרִי הוּא מַאֲכָל אֲמִתִּי וְדָמִי הוּא מַשְׁקֶה אֲמִתִּי. 56 הָאוֹכֵל אֶת בְּשָׂרִי וְשׁוֹתֶה אֶת דָּמִי שׁוֹכֵן בִּי וַאֲנִי בּוֹ. 57 כְּמוֹ שֶׁהָאָב הַחַי שָׁלַח אוֹתִי וַאֲנִי חַי בִּגְלַל הָאָב, גַּם הָאוֹכֵל אוֹתִי אַף הוּא יִחְיֶה בִּגְלָלִי. 58 זֶהוּ הַלֶּחֶם אֲשֶׁר יָרַד מִן הַשָּׁמַיִם: לֹא כְּמוֹ שֶׁאָכְלוּ הָאָבוֹת וָמֵתוּ. הָאוֹכֵל אֶת הַלֶּחֶם הַזֶּה יִחְיֶה לְעוֹלָם."

59 אֶת הַדְּבָרִים הָאֵלֶּה אָמַר בְּבֵית הַכְּנֶסֶת כַּאֲשֶׁר לִמֵּד בִּכְפַר נַחוּם.

60 רַבִּים מִתַּלְמִידָיו שֶׁשָּׁמְעוּ זֹאת אָמְרוּ: "קָשֶׁה הַדָּבָר הַזֶּה; מִי יָכוֹל לִשְׁמֹעַ אוֹתוֹ?"

61 יֵשׁוּעַ יָדַע בְּלִבּוֹ שֶׁתַּלְמִידָיו רוֹטְנִים עַל זֹאת וּלְפִיכָךְ אָמַר לָהֶם: "הַאִם זֶה מַכְשִׁיל אֶתְכֶם? 62 וּמָה אִם תִּרְאוּ אֶת בֶּן-הָאָדָם עוֹלֶה אֶל אֲשֶׁר הָיָה שָׁם בָּרִאשׁוֹנָה? 63 הָרוּחַ הִיא הַמְחַיָּה; הַבָּשָׂר אֵינוֹ מוֹעִיל כְּלוּם. הַדְּבָרִים שֶׁדִּבַּרְתִּי אֲלֵיכֶם רוּחַ הֵם וְחַיִּים. 64 אַךְ יֵשׁ אֲנָשִׁים מִכֶּם שֶׁאֵינָם מַאֲמִינִים"; שֶׁכֵּן יֵשׁוּעַ יָדַע מֵרֹאשׁ מִי הֵם שֶׁאֵינָם מַאֲמִינִים וּמִי יַסְגִּיר אוֹתוֹ. 65 הוֹסִיף וְאָמַר: "עַל-כֵּן אָמַרְתִּי לָכֶם שֶׁאֵין אִישׁ יָכוֹל לָבוֹא אֵלַי אֶלָּא אִם כֵּן נִתַּן לוֹ מֵאֵת הָאָב."

66 בְּשֶׁל הַדָּבָר הַזֶּה נָסוֹגוּ רַבִּים מִתַּלְמִידָיו וְלֹא הוֹסִיפוּ לְהִתְהַלֵּךְ אִתּוֹ. 67 אָמַר יֵשׁוּעַ אֶל הַשְּׁנֵים-עָשָׂר: "שֶׁמָּא גַּם אַתֶּם רוֹצִים לָלֶכֶת?"

68 But Simon Peter answered Him, "Lord, to whom shall we go? You have the words of eternal life. 69 Also we have come to believe and know that You are the Christ, the Son of the living God."

70 Jesus answered them, "Did I not choose you, the twelve, and one of you is a devil?" 71 He spoke of Judas Iscariot, *the son* of Simon, for it was he who would betray Him, being one of the twelve.

7 After these things Jesus walked in Galilee; for He did not want to walk in Judea, because the Jews sought to kill Him. 2 Now the Jews' Feast of Tabernacles was at hand. 3 His brothers therefore said to Him, "Depart from here and go into Judea, that Your disciples also may see the works that You are doing. 4 For no one does anything in secret while he himself seeks to be known openly. If You do these things, show Yourself to the world." 5 For even His brothers did not believe in Him.

6 Then Jesus said to them, "My time has not yet come, but your time is always ready. 7 The world cannot hate you, but it hates Me because I testify of it that its works are evil. 8 You go up to this feast. I am not yet going up to this feast, for My time has not yet fully come." 9 When He had said these things to them, He remained in Galilee.

10 But when His brothers had gone up, then He also went up to the feast, not openly, but as it were in secret. 11 Then the Jews sought Him at the feast, and said, "Where is He?" 12 And there was much complaining among the people concerning Him. Some said, "He is good"; others said, "No, on the contrary, He deceives the people." 13 However, no one spoke openly of Him for fear of the Jews.

14 Now about the middle of the feast Jesus went up into the temple and taught. 15 And the Jews marveled, saying, "How does this Man know letters, having never studied?"

16 Jesus answered them and said, "My doctrine is not Mine, but His who sent Me. 17 If anyone wills to do His will, he shall know concerning the doctrine, whether it is from God or *whether* I speak on My own *authority*. 18 He who speaks from himself seeks his own glory; but He who seeks the glory of the One who sent Him is true, and no unrighteousness is in Him. 19 Did not Moses give you the law, yet none of you keeps the law? Why do you seek to kill Me?"

20 The people answered and said, "You have a demon. Who is seeking to kill You?"

21 Jesus answered and said to them, "I did one work, and you all marvel. 22 Moses therefore gave you circumcision (not that it is from Moses, but from the fathers), and you circumcise a man on the

68 הֵשִׁיב לוֹ שִׁמְעוֹן כֵּיפָא: "אֲדוֹנֵנוּ, אֶל מִי נֵלֵךְ? דִּבְרֵי חַיֵּי עוֹלָם עִמָּךְ. 69 וַאֲנַחְנוּ הֶאֱמַנּוּ וְיָדַעְנוּ שֶׁאַתָּה קְדוֹשׁ הָאֱלֹהִים."

70 אָמַר לָהֶם יֵשׁוּעַ: "הֲרֵי אֲנִי בָּחַרְתִּי אֶתְכֶם, הַשְּׁנֵים־עָשָׂר, וְאֶחָד מִכֶּם שָׂטָן." 71 יֵשׁוּעַ דִּבֶּר עַל יְהוּדָה בֶּן שִׁמְעוֹן אִישׁ קְרִיּוֹת, כִּי הוּא הָיָה עָתִיד לְהַסְגִּיר אוֹתוֹ וְהוּא אֶחָד מִן הַשְּׁנֵים־עָשָׂר.

ז 1 אַחֲרֵי כֵן הִתְהַלֵּךְ יֵשׁוּעַ בַּגָּלִיל; הוּא לֹא רָצָה לְהִתְהַלֵּךְ בִּיהוּדָה מִפְּנֵי שֶׁרָאשֵׁי הַיְּהוּדִים שָׁם בִּקְשׁוּ לְהָמִית אוֹתוֹ. 2 כֵּיוָן שֶׁסֻּכּוֹת, חַג הַיְּהוּדִים, הָיָה קָרוֹב, 3 אָמְרוּ לוֹ אֶחָיו: "צֵא מִכָּאן וְלֵךְ לִיהוּדָה כְּדֵי שֶׁיִּרְאוּ גַּם תַּלְמִידֶיךָ אֶת הַמַּעֲשִׂים שֶׁאַתָּה עוֹשֶׂה, 4 כִּי אֵין אִישׁ עוֹשֶׂה דָבָר בַּסֵּתֶר וְעִם זֹאת מְבַקֵּשׁ לִהְיוֹת יָדוּעַ בָּרַבִּים. אִם אַתָּה עוֹשֶׂה אֶת הַמַּעֲשִׂים הָאֵלֶּה, גַּלֵּה עַצְמְךָ לָעוֹלָם"; 5 כִּי גַּם אֶחָיו לֹא הֶאֱמִינוּ בוֹ.

6 אָמַר לָהֶם יֵשׁוּעַ: "זְמַנִּי טֶרֶם הִגִּיעַ, אֲבָל זְמַנְכֶם תָּמִיד בַּמְּצֻיָּא. 7 הָעוֹלָם אֵינֶנּוּ יָכוֹל לִשְׂנֹא אֶתְכֶם, וְאִלּוּ אוֹתִי הוּא שׂוֹנֵא, כִּי אֲנִי מֵעִיד עָלָיו שֶׁרָעִים מַעֲשָׂיו. 8 עֲלוּ אַתֶּם לֶחָג. אֲנִי אֵינֶנִּי עוֹלֶה לֶחָג הַנּוֹכְחִי, כִּי זְמַנִּי עוֹד לֹא נִשְׁלַם." 9 אֶת זֹאת אָמַר לָהֶם וְנִשְׁאַר בַּגָּלִיל.

10 בְּרַם אַחֲרֵי שֶׁעָלוּ אֶחָיו לֶחָג עָלָה גַם הוּא, לֹא בְּגָלוּי אֶלָּא כְּמוֹ בַּחֲשַׁאי. 11 לָכֵן חִפְּשׂוּהוּ רָאשֵׁי הַיְּהוּדִים בֶּחָג וְאָמְרוּ: "אֵיפֹה הוּא?" 12 הִתְלַחֲשׁוּת רַבָּה הָיְתָה עַל־אוֹדוֹתָיו בְּקֶרֶב הֲמוֹן הָעָם. אֵלֶּה אָמְרוּ שֶׁהוּא טוֹב, וְאֵלֶּה אָמְרוּ: "לֹא, הוּא מַתְעֶה אֶת הָעָם." 13 אַךְ אִישׁ לֹא דִּבֶּר עָלָיו בְּגָלוּי, וְזֹאת בְּשֶׁל הַפַּחַד מִפְּנֵי רָאשֵׁי הַיְּהוּדִים.

14 בַּחֲצִי יְמֵי הֶחָג עָלָה יֵשׁוּעַ לְבֵית הַמִּקְדָּשׁ וְלִמֵּד. 15 תָּמְהוּ הַיְּהוּדִים וְאָמְרוּ: "הֵיאַךְ זֶה יוֹדֵעַ סֵפֶר בְּלִי שֶׁלָּמַד?"

16 הֵשִׁיב לָהֶם יֵשׁוּעַ וְאָמַר: "תּוֹרָתִי אֵינָהּ שֶׁלִּי כִּי אִם שֶׁל שׁוֹלְחִי. 17 הָרוֹצֶה לַעֲשׂוֹת אֶת רְצוֹנוֹ יֵדַע אִם תּוֹרָתִי מֵאֱלֹהִים הִיא אוֹ אִם מֵעַצְמִי אֲנִי מְדַבֵּר. 18 הַמְדַבֵּר מִתּוֹךְ עַצְמוֹ מְבַקֵּשׁ אֶת כְּבוֹד עַצְמוֹ, אֲבָל הַמְבַקֵּשׁ אֶת כְּבוֹד שׁוֹלְחוֹ נֶאֱמָן הוּא וְאֵין עַוְלָה בּוֹ. 19 הֲלֹא מֹשֶׁה נָתַן לָכֶם אֶת הַתּוֹרָה וְאֵין אִישׁ מִכֶּם מְקַיֵּם אֶת הַתּוֹרָה. מַדּוּעַ אַתֶּם מְבַקְשִׁים לַהֲרֹג אוֹתִי?"

20 הֵשִׁיב הֶהָמוֹן: "שֵׁד בְּךָ, מִי מְבַקֵּשׁ לַהֲרֹג אוֹתְךָ?"

21 עָנָה יֵשׁוּעַ וְאָמַר לָהֶם: "מַעֲשֶׂה אֶחָד עָשִׂיתִי וְכֻלְּכֶם תְּמֵהִים. 22 מֹשֶׁה נָתַן לָכֶם אֶת הַמִּילָה אֶלָּא שֶׁלֹּא מִמֹּשֶׁה הִיא כִּי אִם מִן הָאָבוֹת – וְגַם בְּשַׁבָּת

Sabbath. ²³ If a man receives circumcision on the Sabbath, so that the law of Moses should not be broken, are you angry with Me because I made a man completely well on the Sabbath? ²⁴ Do not judge according to appearance, but judge with righteous judgment."

²⁵ Now some of them from Jerusalem said, "Is this not He whom they seek to kill? ²⁶ But look! He speaks boldly, and they say nothing to Him. Do the rulers know indeed that this is truly the Christ? ²⁷ However, we know where this Man is from; but when the Christ comes, no one knows where He is from."

²⁸ Then Jesus cried out, as He taught in the temple, saying, "You both know Me, and you know where I am from; and I have not come of Myself, but He who sent Me is true, whom you do not know. ²⁹ But I know Him, for I am from Him, and He sent Me."

³⁰ Therefore they sought to take Him; but no one laid a hand on Him, because His hour had not yet come. ³¹ And many of the people believed in Him, and said, "When the Christ comes, will He do more signs than these which this *Man* has done?"

³² The Pharisees heard the crowd murmuring these things concerning Him, and the Pharisees and the chief priests sent officers to take Him. ³³ Then Jesus said to them, "I shall be with you a little while longer, and *then* I go to Him who sent Me. ³⁴ You will seek Me and not find *Me,* and where I am you cannot come."

³⁵ Then the Jews said among themselves, "Where does He intend to go that we shall not find Him? Does He intend to go to the Dispersion among the Greeks and teach the Greeks? ³⁶ What is this thing that He said, 'You will seek Me and not find Me, and where I am you cannot come'?"

³⁷ On the last day, that great *day* of the feast, Jesus stood and cried out, saying, "If anyone thirsts, let him come to Me and drink. ³⁸ He who believes in Me, as the Scripture has said, out of his heart will flow rivers of living water." ³⁹ But this He spoke concerning the Spirit, whom those believing in Him would receive; for the Holy Spirit was not yet *given,* because Jesus was not yet glorified.

⁴⁰ Therefore many from the crowd, when they heard this saying, said, "Truly this is the Prophet." ⁴¹ Others said, "This is the Christ."

But some said, "Will the Christ come out of Galilee? ⁴² Has not the Scripture said that the Christ comes from the seed of David and from the town of Bethlehem, where David was?" ⁴³ So there was a

אַתֶּם מְקַיְּמִים אֶת הַמִּילָה. ²³ וּבְכֵן, אִם נִמּוֹל אָדָם בְּשַׁבָּת כְּדֵי שֶׁלֹּא תּוּפַר תּוֹרַת מֹשֶׁה, עָלַי כּוֹעֲסִים אַתֶּם מִפְּנֵי שֶׁרִפֵּאתִי כָּלִיל אִישׁ בְּשַׁבָּת?! ²⁴ אַל תִּשְׁפְּטוּ עַל-פִּי מַרְאֵה עֵינַיִם; מִשְׁפַּט צֶדֶק שְׁפֹטוּ."

²⁵ הֵגִיבוּ וְאָמְרוּ כַּמָּה אֲנָשִׁים מִיּוֹשְׁבֵי יְרוּשָׁלַיִם: "הֲלֹא זֶהוּ הָאִישׁ שֶׁרוֹצִים לַהֲרֹג אוֹתוֹ! ²⁶ הִנֵּהוּ מְדַבֵּר בְּגָלוּי וְהֵם אֵינָם אוֹמְרִים לוֹ דָבָר. הַאֻמְנָם הִכִּירוּ הַמַּנְהִיגִים שֶׁהוּא הַמָּשִׁיחַ? ²⁷ אֶלָּא שֶׁיּוֹדְעִים אָנוּ מֵאַיִן הָאִישׁ הַזֶּה, אַךְ כְּשֶׁיָּבוֹא הַמָּשִׁיחַ לֹא יֵדַע אִישׁ מֵאַיִן הוּא."

²⁸ בְּלַמְּדוֹ בְּבֵית הַמִּקְדָּשׁ הִכְרִיז יֵשׁוּעַ וְאָמַר: "אַתֶּם מַכִּירִים אוֹתִי וְגַם יוֹדְעִים מֵאַיִן אֲנִי, עִם זֹאת לֹא מֵעַצְמִי עַצְמִי בָּאתִי, אֶלָּא שֶׁשּׁוֹלְחִי הוּא אֱמֶת וְאוֹתוֹ אֵינְכֶם מַכִּירִים. ²⁹ אֲנִי מַכִּיר אוֹתוֹ מִפְּנֵי שֶׁמֵּאִתּוֹ אֲנִי, וְהוּא שָׁלַח אוֹתִי."

³⁰ אָז בִּקְשׁוּ לִתְפֹּס אוֹתוֹ, אַךְ אִישׁ לֹא שָׁלַח בּוֹ יָד, כִּי עוֹד לֹא הִגִּיעָה שְׁעָתוֹ.

³¹ רַבִּים מִן הָעָם הֶאֱמִינוּ בּוֹ וְאָמְרוּ: "כַּאֲשֶׁר יָבוֹא הַמָּשִׁיחַ, הַאִם יַעֲשֶׂה נִסִּים יוֹתֵר מֵאֲשֶׁר עָשָׂה זֶה?"

³² כַּאֲשֶׁר שָׁמְעוּ הַפְּרוּשִׁים אֶת הָעָם מִתְלַחֲשִׁים עָלָיו כָּךְ, שָׁלְחוּ רָאשֵׁי הַכֹּהֲנִים וְהַפְּרוּשִׁים מְשָׁרְתִים לְתָפְסוֹ אוֹתוֹ.

³³ אָמַר יֵשׁוּעַ: "עוֹד זְמַן מְעַט אֲנִי אִתְּכֶם וְהוֹלֵךְ אֲנִי אֶל מִי שֶׁשְּׁלָחַנִי. ³⁴ תְּחַפְּשׂוּנִי וְלֹא תִמְצָאוּ; וּבַאֲשֶׁר אֲנִי אֶהְיֶה, לְשָׁם אֵינְכֶם יְכוֹלִים לָבוֹא."

³⁵ אָמְרוּ אִישׁ אֶל רֵעֵהוּ: "לְאָן הוּא מִתְעַתֵּד לָלֶכֶת שֶׁלֹּא נִמְצָא אוֹתוֹ? הַאִם יֵלֵךְ אֶל הַתְּפוּצוֹת שֶׁל הַיְּוָנִים וִילַמֵּד אֶת הַיְּוָנִים? ³⁶ מָה הַדָּבָר הַזֶּה שֶׁאָמַר, 'תְּחַפְּשׂוּנִי וְלֹא תִמְצָאוּ; וּבַאֲשֶׁר אֲנִי אֶהְיֶה, לְשָׁם אֵינְכֶם יְכוֹלִים לָבוֹא'?"

³⁷ בַּיּוֹם הָאַחֲרוֹן, בַּיּוֹם הַגָּדוֹל שֶׁל הֶחָג, עָמַד יֵשׁוּעַ וְהִכְרִיז: "מִי שֶׁצָּמֵא יָבוֹא נָא אֵלַי וְיִשְׁתֶּה! ³⁸ הַמַּאֲמִין בִּי כְּדִבְרֵי הַכָּתוּב, נַהֲרוֹת שֶׁל מַיִם חַיִּים יִזְרְמוּ מִקִּרְבּוֹ." ³⁹ זֹאת אָמַר עַל הָרוּחַ שֶׁהָיוּ עֲתִידִים לְקַבֵּל הַמַּאֲמִינִים בּוֹ, שֶׁהֲרֵי עוֹד לֹא נִשְׁלְחָה רוּחַ הַקֹּדֶשׁ, כִּי יֵשׁוּעַ טֶרֶם נִתְפָּאֵר בְּכָבוֹד.

⁴⁰ אֲנָשִׁים מֵהֲמוֹן הָעָם, שֶׁשָּׁמְעוּ אֶת הַדְּבָרִים הָאֵלֶּה, אָמְרוּ: "זֶהוּ בֶּאֱמֶת הַנָּבִיא." ⁴¹ אֲחֵרִים אָמְרוּ: "זֶהוּ הַמָּשִׁיחַ", וַאֲחֵרִים אָמְרוּ: "מָה – מֵהַגָּלִיל יָבוֹא הַמָּשִׁיחַ? ⁴² הֲרֵי הַכָּתוּב אוֹמֵר שֶׁמִּזֶּרַע דָּוִד וּמִבֵּית לֶחֶם עִיר דָּוִד יָבוֹא הַמָּשִׁיחַ." ⁴³ מִשּׁוּם

division among the people because of Him. 44 Now some of them wanted to take Him, but no one laid hands on Him.

45 Then the officers came to the chief priests and Pharisees, who said to them, "Why have you not brought Him?"

46 The officers answered, "No man ever spoke like this Man!"

47 Then the Pharisees answered them, "Are you also deceived? 48 Have any of the rulers or the Pharisees believed in Him? 49 But this crowd that does not know the law is accursed."

50 Nicodemus (he who came to Jesus by night, being one of them) said to them, 51 "Does our law judge a man before it hears him and knows what he is doing?"

52 They answered and said to him, "Are you also from Galilee? Search and look, for no prophet has arisen out of Galilee."

53 And everyone went to his *own* house.

8 But Jesus went to the Mount of Olives.

2 Now early in the morning He came again into the temple, and all the people came to Him; and He sat down and taught them. 3 Then the scribes and Pharisees brought to Him a woman caught in adultery. And when they had set her in the midst, 4 they said to Him, "Teacher, this woman was caught in adultery, in the very act. 5 Now Moses, in the law, commanded us that such should be stoned. But what do You say?" 6 This they said, testing Him, that they might have *something* of which to accuse Him. But Jesus stooped down and wrote on the ground with *His* finger, as though He did not hear.

7 So when they continued asking Him, He raised Himself up and said to them, "He who is without sin among you, let him throw a stone at her first." 8 And again He stooped down and wrote on the ground. 9 Then those who heard *it*, being convicted by *their* conscience, went out one by one, beginning with the oldest *even* to the last. And Jesus was left alone, and the woman standing in the midst. 10 When Jesus had raised Himself up and saw no one but the woman, He said to her, "Woman, where are those accusers of yours? Has no one condemned you?"

11 She said, "No one, Lord."

And Jesus said to her, "Neither do I condemn you; go and sin no more."

12 Then Jesus spoke to them again, saying, "I am the light of the world. He who follows Me shall not walk in darkness, but have the light of life."

כָּךְ נָפְלָה מַחֲלֹקֶת בֵּין הֲמוֹן הָעָם עַל־אוֹדוֹתָיו. 44 כַּמָּה מֵהֶם רָצוּ לְתָפְסֹ אוֹתוֹ, אַךְ אִישׁ לֹא שָׁלַח בּוֹ יָד.

45 אַחֲרֵי כֵן חָזְרוּ הַמְשָׁרְתִים אֶל רָאשֵׁי הַכֹּהֲנִים וְהַפְּרוּשִׁים וְאֵלֶּה שָׁאֲלוּ אוֹתָם: "מַדּוּעַ לֹא הֲבֵאתֶם אוֹתוֹ?"

46 הֵשִׁיבוּ הַמְשָׁרְתִים: "מֵעוֹלָם לֹא דִּבֶּר אִישׁ כְּמוֹ שֶׁמְּדַבֵּר הָאִישׁ הַזֶּה."

47 אָמְרוּ הַפְּרוּשִׁים: "הַאִם גַּם אַתֶּם הֻתְעֵיתֶם? 48 כְּלוּם הֶאֱמִין בּוֹ מִישֶׁהוּ מֵהַמַּנְהִיגִים אוֹ מֵהַפְּרוּשִׁים? 49 אַךְ הֲמוֹן הַזֶּה, שֶׁאֵינָם יוֹדְעִים אֶת הַתּוֹרָה, אֲרוּרִים הֵם!"

50 אָמַר לָהֶם נַקְדִּימוֹן, אֲשֶׁר בָּא אֵלָיו קֹדֶם לָכֵן, וְהוּא אֶחָד מֵהֶם: 51 "הַאִם תִּשְׁפֹּט תּוֹרָתֵנוּ אֶת הָאָדָם בְּלֹא שֶׁתִּשְׁמַע אוֹתוֹ תְּחִלָּה וְתֵדַע מַה שֶּׁעָשָׂה?"

52 עָנוּ וְאָמְרוּ לוֹ: "הַאִם גַּם אַתָּה מִן הַגָּלִיל? חֲקֹר וּרְאֵה שֶׁלֹּא יָקוּם נָבִיא מֵהַגָּלִיל."

[53 אַחֲרֵי כֵן הָלְכוּ אִישׁ אִישׁ לְבֵיתוֹ.

ח וְיֵשׁוּעַ הָלַךְ אֶל הַר הַזֵּיתִים. 2 בַּבֹּקֶר הַשְׁכֵּם חָזַר לְבֵית הַמִּקְדָּשׁ וְכָל הָעָם בָּאוּ אֵלָיו. הוּא יָשַׁב וְלִמֵּד אוֹתָם. 3 אָז הֵבִיאוּ הַסּוֹפְרִים וְהַפְּרוּשִׁים אִשָּׁה שֶׁנִּתְפְּסָה בְּנִאוּף, הֶעֱמִידוּ אוֹתָהּ בָּאֶמְצַע 4 וְאָמְרוּ לוֹ: "רַבִּי, הָאִשָּׁה הַזֹּאת נִתְפְּסָה בְּנִאוּף, בִּשְׁעַת מַעֲשֶׂה. 5 מֹשֶׁה צִוָּנוּ בַּתּוֹרָה לִסְקֹל נָשִׁים כָּאֵלֶּה, וּמָה אַתָּה אוֹמֵר?" 6 זֹאת אָמְרוּ כְּדֵי לְנַסּוֹת אוֹתוֹ, שֶׁיִּהְיֶה לָהֶם בַּמֶּה לְהַאֲשִׁימוֹ. אוּלָם יֵשׁוּעַ הִתְכּוֹפֵף וּבְאֶצְבָּעוֹ כָּתַב עַל הָאָרֶץ. 7 כְּשֶׁהוֹסִיפוּ לִשְׁאֹל אוֹתוֹ, זָקַף קוֹמָתוֹ וְאָמַר: "מִי מִכֶּם נָקִי מֵחֵטְא, שֶׁיְּהֵא הוּא רִאשׁוֹן לְהַשְׁלִיךְ עָלֶיהָ אָבֶן!" 8 וְשׁוּב הִתְכּוֹפֵף וְכָתַב עַל הָאָרֶץ. 9 כְּשֶׁשָּׁמְעוּ זֹאת יָצְאוּ אֶחָד אֶחָד, הָחֵל מֵהַזְּקֵנִים. הוּא נוֹתַר לְבַדּוֹ וְהָאִשָּׁה עוֹדֶנָּה בִּמְקוֹמָהּ. 10 הִזְדַּקֵּף יֵשׁוּעַ וְאָמַר לָהּ: "אִשָּׁה, אֵיפֹה הֵם? הַאִם לֹא הִרְשִׁיעַ אוֹתָךְ אִישׁ?"

11 הֵשִׁיבָה וְאָמְרָה: "אַף לֹא אֶחָד, אֲדוֹנִי." אָמַר לָהּ: "גַּם אֲנִי אֵינֶנִּי מַרְשִׁיעַ אוֹתָךְ; לְכִי וְאַל תּוֹסִיפִי לַחֲטֹא עוֹד."]

12 יֵשׁוּעַ הוֹסִיף לְדַבֵּר אֲלֵיהֶם וְאָמַר: "אֲנִי אוֹר הָעוֹלָם. אִישׁ הַהוֹלֵךְ אַחֲרַי לֹא יִתְהַלֵּךְ בַּחֹשֶׁךְ, אֶלָּא אוֹר הַחַיִּים יִהְיֶה לוֹ."

13 The Pharisees therefore said to Him, "You bear witness of Yourself; Your witness is not true."

14 Jesus answered and said to them, "Even if I bear witness of Myself, My witness is true, for I know where I came from and where I am going; but you do not know where I come from and where I am going. 15 You judge according to the flesh; I judge no one. 16 And yet if I do judge, My judgment is true; for I am not alone, but I *am* with the Father who sent Me. 17 It is also written in your law that the testimony of two men is true. 18 I am One who bears witness of Myself, and the Father who sent Me bears witness of Me."

19 Then they said to Him, "Where is Your Father?"

Jesus answered, "You know neither Me nor My Father. If you had known Me, you would have known My Father also."

20 These words Jesus spoke in the treasury, as He taught in the temple; and no one laid hands on Him, for His hour had not yet come.

21 Then Jesus said to them again, "I am going away, and you will seek Me, and will die in your sin. Where I go you cannot come."

22 So the Jews said, "Will He kill Himself, because He says, 'Where I go you cannot come'?"

23 And He said to them, "You are from beneath; I am from above. You are of this world; I am not of this world. 24 Therefore I said to you that you will die in your sins; for if you do not believe that I am *He,* you will die in your sins."

25 Then they said to Him, "Who are You?"

And Jesus said to them, "Just what I have been saying to you from the beginning. 26 I have many things to say and to judge concerning you, but He who sent Me is true; and I speak to the world those things which I heard from Him."

27 They did not understand that He spoke to them of the Father.

28 Then Jesus said to them, "When you lift up the Son of Man, then you will know that I am *He,* and *that* I do nothing of Myself; but as My Father taught Me, I speak these things. 29 And He who sent Me is with Me. The Father has not left Me alone, for I always do those things that please Him." 30 As He spoke these words, many believed in Him.

31 Then Jesus said to those Jews who believed Him, "If you abide in My word, you are My disciples indeed. 32 And you shall know the truth, and the truth shall make you free."

33 They answered Him, "We are Abraham's descendants, and have never been in bondage to anyone. How *can* You say, 'You will be made free'?"

---

13 אָמְרוּ לוֹ הַפְּרוּשִׁים: "אַתָּה מֵעִיד עַל עַצְמְךָ; עֵדוּתְךָ אֵינֶנָּה נֶאֱמָנָה."

14 הֵשִׁיב יֵשׁוּעַ וְאָמַר לָהֶם: "גַּם אִם אֲנִי מֵעִיד עַל עַצְמִי עֵדוּתִי נֶאֱמָנָה, כִּי יוֹדֵעַ אֲנִי מֵאַיִן בָּאתִי וּלְאָן אֲנִי הוֹלֵךְ. אֲבָל אַתֶּם אֵינְכֶם יוֹדְעִים מֵאַיִן אֲנִי בָּא אוֹ לְאָן אֲנִי הוֹלֵךְ. 15 אַתֶּם שׁוֹפְטִים כְּדֶרֶךְ הַבָּשָׂר; אֲנִי אֵינֶנִּי שׁוֹפֵט אִישׁ. 16 וְגַם אִם אֲנִי שׁוֹפֵט, מִשְׁפָּטִי אֱמֶת, שֶׁכֵּן אֵינֶנִּי לְבַדִּי, אֶלָּא אֲנִי וְהָאָב אֲשֶׁר שְׁלָחַנִי. 17 אַף בְּתוֹרַתְכֶם כָּתוּב שֶׁעֵדוּת שְׁנֵי אֲנָשִׁים מְהֵימָנָה הִיא. 18 אֲנִי הוּא הַמֵּעִיד עַל עַצְמִי וְגַם הָאָב אֲשֶׁר שְׁלָחַנִי מֵעִיד עָלָי."

19 שָׁאֲלוּ אוֹתוֹ: "אֵיפֹה אָבִיךָ?"

הֵשִׁיב יֵשׁוּעַ: "גַּם אוֹתִי גַם אֶת אָבִי אֵינְכֶם מַכִּירִים. אִלּוּ הִכַּרְתֶּם אוֹתִי, גַּם אֶת אָבִי הֱיִיתֶם מַכִּירִים."

20 אֶת הַדְּבָרִים הָאֵלֶּה דִּבֵּר בְּלִשְׁכַּת הָאוֹצָר, כַּאֲשֶׁר לִמֵּד בְּבֵית הַמִּקְדָּשׁ, וְלֹא תָּפַס אוֹתוֹ אִישׁ מִפְּנֵי שֶׁטֶּרֶם הִגִּיעָה שְׁעָתוֹ.

21 הוֹסִיף יֵשׁוּעַ וְאָמַר לָהֶם: "אֲנִי הוֹלֵךְ וְאַתֶּם תְּחַפְּשׂוּ אוֹתִי, בְּרַם בְּחַטַּאתְכֶם תָּמוּתוּ. אֶל אֲשֶׁר אֲנִי הוֹלֵךְ אֵינְכֶם יְכוֹלִים לָבוֹא."

22 הֵם אָמְרוּ: "הַאִם יַהֲרֹג אֶת עַצְמוֹ, שֶׁהֲרֵי הוּא אוֹמֵר 'אֶל אֲשֶׁר אֲנִי הוֹלֵךְ אֵינְכֶם יְכוֹלִים לָבוֹא'?"

23 אָמַר לָהֶם: "אַתֶּם מִלְּמַטָּה; אֲנִי מִלְמַעְלָה. אַתֶּם מִן הָעוֹלָם הַזֶּה; אֲנִי אֵינֶנִּי מִן הָעוֹלָם הַזֶּה. 24 לָכֵן אָמַרְתִּי לָכֶם שֶׁתָּמוּתוּ בַּחֲטָאֵיכֶם; שֶׁכֵּן אִם אֵינְכֶם מַאֲמִינִים כִּי אֲנִי הוּא, מוֹת תָּמוּתוּ בַּחֲטָאֵיכֶם."

25 שָׁאֲלוּ אוֹתוֹ: "מִי אַתָּה?"

הֵשִׁיב לָהֶם יֵשׁוּעַ: "מַה שֶּׁאֲנִי מְדַבֵּר אֲלֵיכֶם גַּם מֵרֵאשִׁית. 26 רַבּוֹת יֵשׁ לִי לְדַבֵּר עֲלֵיכֶם וְלִשְׁפֹּט, אֲבָל שׁוֹלְחִי אֱמֶת וַאֲנִי אֶת אֲשֶׁר שָׁמַעְתִּי מִמֶּנּוּ, זֹאת אֲנִי מְדַבֵּר אֶל הָעוֹלָם."

27 הֵם לֹא הֵבִינוּ שֶׁדִּבֵּר אֲלֵיהֶם עַל הָאָב. 28 אָמַר לָהֶם יֵשׁוּעַ: "כַּאֲשֶׁר תָּרִימוּ אֶת בֶּן-הָאָדָם אָז תֵּדְעוּ כִּי אֲנִי הוּא וְכִי אֵינֶנִּי עוֹשֶׂה דָבָר מִתּוֹךְ עַצְמִי, אֶלָּא עַל-פִּי מַה שֶּׁלִּמְּדַנִי אָבִי – אֶת זֹאת אֲנִי מְדַבֵּר. 29 וְשׁוֹלְחִי הֲרֵיהוּ אִתִּי. הוּא לֹא עֲזָבַנִי לְבַדִּי, כִּי אֶת הַטּוֹב בְּעֵינָיו אֲנִי עוֹשֶׂה תָּמִיד." 30 כְּשֶׁאָמַר אֶת הַדְּבָרִים הָאֵלֶּה הֶאֱמִינוּ בּוֹ רַבִּים.

31 אָמַר יֵשׁוּעַ אֶל הַפְּרוּשִׁים שֶׁהֶאֱמִינוּ לוֹ: "אִם תַּעַמְדוּ בִּדְבָרִי, תַּלְמִידַי אַתֶּם בֶּאֱמֶת; 32 וְתֵדְעוּ אֶת הָאֱמֶת וְהָאֱמֶת תְּשַׁחְרֵר אֶתְכֶם."

33 הֵשִׁיבוּ לוֹ: "זֶרַע אַבְרָהָם אֲנַחְנוּ וּמֵעוֹלָם לֹא הָיִינוּ מְשֻׁעְבָּדִים לְאִישׁ. מַדּוּעַ אַתָּה אוֹמֵר 'בְּנֵי חוֹרִין תִּהְיוּ'?"

34 Jesus answered them, "Most assuredly, I say to you, whoever commits sin is a slave of sin. 35 And a slave does not abide in the house forever, *but* a son abides forever. 36 Therefore if the Son makes you free, you shall be free indeed.

37 "I know that you are Abraham's descendants, but you seek to kill Me, because My word has no place in you. 38 I speak what I have seen with My Father, and you do what you have seen with your father."

39 They answered and said to Him, "Abraham is our father."

Jesus said to them, "If you were Abraham's children, you would do the works of Abraham. 40 But now you seek to kill Me, a Man who has told you the truth which I heard from God. Abraham did not do this. 41 You do the deeds of your father."

Then they said to Him, "We were not born of fornication; we have one Father—God."

42 Jesus said to them, "If God were your Father, you would love Me, for I proceeded forth and came from God; nor have I come of Myself, but He sent Me. 43 Why do you not understand My speech? Because you are not able to listen to My word. 44 You are of *your* father the devil, and the desires of your father you want to do. He was a murderer from the beginning, and does not stand in the truth, because there is no truth in him. When he speaks a lie, he speaks from his own *resources,* for he is a liar and the father of it. 45 But because I tell the truth, you do not believe Me. 46 Which of you convicts Me of sin? And if I tell the truth, why do you not believe Me? 47 He who is of God hears God's words; therefore you do not hear, because you are not of God."

48 Then the Jews answered and said to Him, "Do we not say rightly that You are a Samaritan and have a demon?"

49 Jesus answered, "I do not have a demon; but I honor My Father, and you dishonor Me. 50 And I do not seek My *own* glory; there is One who seeks and judges. 51 Most assuredly, I say to you, if anyone keeps My word he shall never see death."

52 Then the Jews said to Him, "Now we know that You have a demon! Abraham is dead, and the prophets; and You say, 'If anyone keeps My word he shall never taste death.' 53 Are You greater than our father Abraham, who is dead? And the prophets are dead. Who do You make Yourself out to be?"

54 Jesus answered, "If I honor Myself, My honor is nothing. It is My Father who honors Me, of whom you say that He is your God. 55 Yet you have not known Him, but I know Him. And if I say, 'I

34 עָנָה לָהֶם יֵשׁוּעַ: "אָמֵן אָמֵן אֲנִי אוֹמֵר לָכֶם, כָּל עוֹשֵׂה חֵטְא עֶבֶד הוּא לַחֵטְא. 35 וְאֵין הָעֶבֶד שׁוֹכֵן בַּבַּיִת לְעוֹלָם; הַבֵּן שׁוֹכֵן לְעוֹלָם. 36 לָכֵן אִם הַבֵּן מְשַׁחְרֵר אֶתְכֶם, בֶּאֱמֶת בְּנֵי חוֹרִין תִּהְיוּ. 37 אֲנִי יוֹדֵעַ שֶׁזֶּרַע אַבְרָהָם אַתֶּם. וְאוּלָם מְבַקְשִׁים אַתֶּם לַהֲרֹג אוֹתִי, כִּי אֵין לִדְבָרַי מָקוֹם בְּקִרְבְּכֶם. 38 אֲנִי מְדַבֵּר אֵת אֲשֶׁר רָאִיתִי אֵצֶל הָאָב; אַתֶּם עוֹשִׂים מַה שֶּׁשְּׁמַעְתֶּם אֵצֶל אֲבִיכֶם."

39 הֵשִׁיבוּ וְאָמְרוּ לוֹ: "אַבְרָהָם הוּא אָבִינוּ." אָמַר לָהֶם יֵשׁוּעַ: "אִם בְּנֵי אַבְרָהָם אַתֶּם, עֲשׂוּ כְּמַעֲשֵׂי אַבְרָהָם; 40 אֶלָּא שֶׁעַתָּה אַתֶּם רוֹצִים לַהֲרֹג אוֹתִי, אִישׁ שֶׁדִּבֵּר אֲלֵיכֶם אֶת הָאֱמֶת אֲשֶׁר שָׁמַעְתִּי אֵצֶל הָאָב. זֹאת לֹא עָשָׂה אַבְרָהָם. 41 אַתֶּם עוֹשִׂים אֶת מַעֲשֵׂי אֲבִיכֶם." אָמְרוּ לוֹ: "לֹא יַלְדֵי זְנוּנִים אֲנַחְנוּ. יֵשׁ לָנוּ אָב אֶחָד – הָאֱלֹהִים."

42 הֵשִׁיב לָהֶם יֵשׁוּעַ: "אִלּוּ אֱלֹהִים הָיָה אֲבִיכֶם, הֱיִיתֶם אוֹהֲבִים אוֹתִי, שֶׁכֵּן אֲנִי מֵאֵת הָאֱלֹהִים יָצָאתִי וּבָאתִי. הֵן לֹא מֵעַצְמִי בָּאתִי, הוּא שְׁלָחַנִי. 43 מַדּוּעַ אֵינְכֶם מְבִינִים אֶת דִּבּוּרִי? מִפְּנֵי שֶׁאֵינְכֶם יְכוֹלִים לִשְׁמֹעַ אֶת דְּבָרִי. 44 אַתֶּם מֵאֲבִיכֶם הַשָּׂטָן וְאֶת מַאֲוַיֵּי אֲבִיכֶם חֲפֵצִים אַתֶּם לַעֲשׂוֹת. הוּא רוֹצֵחַ הָיָה מֵרֵאשִׁית וּבָאֱמֶת לֹא עָמַד, כִּי אֵין אֱמֶת בּוֹ. מִדֵּי דַבְּרוֹ שֶׁקֶר, מִתּוֹךְ יְשׁוּתוֹ שֶׁלּוֹ יְדַבֵּר, כִּי שַׁקְרָן הוּא וַאֲבִי הַשֶּׁקֶר. 45 וַאֲנִי, כִּי אוֹמֵר אֲנִי אֶת הָאֱמֶת, אֵין אַתֶּם מַאֲמִינִים לִי. 46 מִי מִכֶּם עַל עָוֹן יוֹכִיחֵנִי? וְאִם דּוֹבֵר אֱמֶת אֲנִי, לָמָּה אֵין אַתֶּם מַאֲמִינִים לִי? 47 זֶה אֲשֶׁר מֵאֵת הָאֱלֹהִים שׁוֹמֵעַ אֶת דִּבְרֵי אֱלֹהִים. אַתֶּם אֵינְכֶם שׁוֹמְעִים, כִּי אֵינְכֶם מֵאֵת הָאֱלֹהִים."

48 הֵשִׁיבוּ וְאָמְרוּ אֵלָיו: "הַאִם לֹא צָדַקְנוּ בְּאָמְרֵנוּ שֶׁשּׁוֹמְרוֹנִי אַתָּה וְשֵׁד בְּךָ?"

49 עָנָה יֵשׁוּעַ: "אֲנִי אֵין בִּי שֵׁד, אֶלָּא שֶׁמְּכַבֵּד אֲנִי אֶת אָבִי וְאַתֶּם בְּזִים לִי. 50 אֲנִי אֵינֶנִּי מְבַקֵּשׁ אֶת כְּבוֹדִי; יֵשׁ אֶחָד הַמְבַקֵּשׁ וְשׁוֹפֵט. 51 אָמֵן אָמֵן אֲנִי אוֹמֵר לָכֶם, אִם יִשְׁמֹר אִישׁ אֶת דְּבָרִי לֹא יִרְאֶה מָוֶת לְעוֹלָם."

52 אָמְרוּ לוֹ: "כָּעֵת נוֹכַחְנוּ לָדַעַת שֶׁיֵּשׁ בְּךָ שֵׁד. אַבְרָהָם מֵת, וְכֵן גַּם הַנְּבִיאִים, וְאַתָּה אוֹמֵר 'אִם יִשְׁמֹר אִישׁ אֶת דְּבָרַי לֹא יִטְעַם מָוֶת לְעוֹלָם'. 53 הַאִם אַתָּה גָּדוֹל מֵאַבְרָהָם אָבִינוּ שֶׁמֵּת? גַּם הַנְּבִיאִים מֵתוּ. מָה אַתָּה עוֹשֶׂה אֶת עַצְמְךָ?"

54 עָנָה יֵשׁוּעַ: "אִם אֲנִי נוֹתֵן כָּבוֹד לְעַצְמִי, כְּבוֹדִי אֵין בּוֹ כְּלוּם. אָבִי, אֲשֶׁר אַתֶּם אוֹמְרִים עָלָיו 'הוּא אֱלֹהֵינוּ', הוּא הַמְכַבֵּד אוֹתִי. 55 וְאַתֶּם אֵינְכֶם

do not know Him,' I shall be a liar like you; but I do know Him and keep His word. 56 Your father Abraham rejoiced to see My day, and he saw *it* and was glad."

57 Then the Jews said to Him, "You are not yet fifty years old, and have You seen Abraham?"

58 Jesus said to them, "Most assuredly, I say to you, before Abraham was, I AM."

59 Then they took up stones to throw at Him; but Jesus hid Himself and went out of the temple, going through the midst of them, and so passed by.

9 Now as *Jesus* passed by, He saw a man who was blind from birth. 2 And His disciples asked Him, saying, "Rabbi, who sinned, this man or his parents, that he was born blind?"

3 Jesus answered, "Neither this man nor his parents sinned, but that the works of God should be revealed in him. 4 I must work the works of Him who sent Me while it is day; *the* night is coming when no one can work. 5 As long as I am in the world, I am the light of the world."

6 When He had said these things, He spat on the ground and made clay with the saliva; and He anointed the eyes of the blind man with the clay. 7 And He said to him, "Go, wash in the pool of Siloam" (which is translated, Sent). So he went and washed, and came back seeing.

8 Therefore the neighbors and those who previously had seen that he was blind said, "Is not this he who sat and begged?"

9 Some said, "This is he." Others *said,* "He is like him."

He said, "I am *he.*"

10 Therefore they said to him, "How were your eyes opened?"

11 He answered and said, "A Man called Jesus made clay and anointed my eyes and said to me, 'Go to the pool of Siloam and wash.' So I went and washed, and I received sight."

12 Then they said to him, "Where is He?"

He said, "I do not know."

13 They brought him who formerly was blind to the Pharisees. 14 Now it was a Sabbath when Jesus made the clay and opened his eyes. 15 Then the Pharisees also asked him again how he had received his sight. He said to them, "He put clay on my eyes, and I washed, and I see."

16 Therefore some of the Pharisees said, "This Man is not from God, because He does not keep the Sabbath."

Others said, "How can a man who is a sinner do such signs?" And there was a division among them.

מַכִּירִים אוֹתוֹ, אֲבָל אֲנִי מַכִּיר אוֹתוֹ. אִם אמַר שֶׁאֵינֶנִּי מַכִּיר אוֹתוֹ אֶהְיֶה שַׁקְרָן כְּמוֹכֶם. בְּרַם אֲנִי מַכִּיר אוֹתוֹ וְשׁוֹמֵר אֶת דְּבָרוֹ. 56 אַבְרָהָם אֲבִיכֶם שָׂשׂ לִרְאוֹת אֶת יוֹמִי, וְאָכֵן רָאָה וְשָׂמַח."

57 אָמְרוּ לוֹ: "עֲדַיִן אֵינְךָ בֶּן חֲמִשִּׁים שָׁנָה וְאֶת אַבְרָהָם רָאִיתָ?"

58 הֵשִׁיב לָהֶם יֵשׁוּעַ: "אָמֵן אָמֵן אֲנִי אוֹמֵר לָכֶם, בְּטֶרֶם הֱיוֹת אַבְרָהָם, אֲנִי הוּא." 59 מִשּׁוּם כָּךְ הֵרִימוּ אֲבָנִים לְהַשְׁלִיךְ עָלָיו, אֶלָּא שֶׁיֵּשׁוּעַ הִסְתַּתֵּר וְיָצָא מִבֵּית הַמִּקְדָּשׁ.

ט כַּאֲשֶׁר עָבַר בְּדַרְכּוֹ רָאָה אִישׁ עִוֵּר מִיּוֹם הִוָּלְדוֹ. 2 שָׁאֲלוּ אוֹתוֹ תַּלְמִידָיו: "רַבִּי, מִי חָטָא שֶׁהוּא נוֹלָד עִוֵּר? הוּא אוֹ הוֹרָיו?"

3 עָנָה יֵשׁוּעַ: "לֹא הוּא חָטָא וְלֹא הוֹרָיו; אֵין זֶה אֶלָּא כְּדֵי שֶׁיִּגָּלוּ בּוֹ פַּעֲלֵי אֱלֹהִים. 4 עָלֵינוּ לִפְעֹל אֶת פַּעֲלֵי שׁוֹלְחִי כָּל עוֹד יוֹם. יָבוֹא לַיְלָה, וְאָז לֹא יוּכַל אִישׁ לִפְעֹל. 5 בְּעוֹדֶנִּי בָּעוֹלָם אֲנִי אוֹר הָעוֹלָם."

6 אַחֲרֵי אָמְרוֹ זֹאת יָרַק עַל הָאֲדָמָה וְעָשָׂה טִיט מִן הָרוֹק, מָרַח אֶת הַטִּיט עַל עֵינֵי הָעִוֵּר 7 וְאָמַר אֵלָיו: "לֵךְ וּרְחַץ בִּבְרֵכַת הַשִּׁלּוֹחַ" [שֶׁפֵּרוּשׁוֹ שָׁלוּחַ]. הָלַךְ וְרָחַץ, וּבָא כְּשֶׁהוּא רוֹאֶה.

8 אָמְרוּ הַשְּׁכֵנִים וְאוֹתָם הָאֲנָשִׁים שֶׁרָאוּהוּ קֹדֶם לָכֵן בִּהְיוֹתוֹ קַבְּצָן: "הֲלֹא זֶהוּ שֶׁיָּשַׁב וְקִבֵּץ נְדָבוֹת!"

9 אֵלֶּה אָמְרוּ: "זֶה הוּא", וְאֵלֶּה אָמְרוּ: "לֹא, הוּא רַק דּוֹמֶה לוֹ." הוּא עַצְמוֹ אָמַר: "אֲנִי הוּא." 10 לְפִיכָךְ שָׁאֲלוּ אוֹתוֹ: "אֵיךְ נִפְקְחוּ עֵינֶיךָ?"

11 הֵשִׁיב לָהֶם וְאָמַר: "אִישׁ אֲשֶׁר שְׁמוֹ יֵשׁוּעַ עָשָׂה טִיט, מָרַח עַל עֵינַי וְאָמַר לִי, 'לֵךְ וּרְחַץ בִּבְרֵכַת הַשִּׁלּוֹחַ'. הָלַכְתִּי וּלְאַחַר שֶׁרָחַצְתִּי רָאִיתִי."

12 שָׁאֲלוּ אוֹתוֹ: "אֵיפֹה הוּא?"

הֵשִׁיב: "אֵינֶנִּי יוֹדֵעַ."

13 הֵבִיאוּ אוֹתוֹ אֶל הַפְּרוּשִׁים, אֶת הָאִישׁ שֶׁהָיָה עִוֵּר קֹדֶם לָכֵן. 14 וְהַיּוֹם שֶׁעָשָׂה יֵשׁוּעַ אֶת הַטִּיט וּפָקַח אֶת עֵינָיו הָיָה יוֹם שַׁבָּת. 15 שְׁאָלוּהוּ גַּם הַפְּרוּשִׁים אֵיךְ נִפְקְחוּ עֵינָיו. אָמַר לָהֶם: "טִיט מָרַח עַל עֵינַי וְרָחַצְתִּי, וַהֲרֵינִי רוֹאֶה."

16 אָמְרוּ כַּמָּה מִן הַפְּרוּשִׁים: "הָאִישׁ הַזֶּה אֵינֶנּוּ מֵאֵת אֱלֹהִים, כִּי אֵינוֹ שׁוֹמֵר אֶת הַשַּׁבָּת." אֲחֵרִים אָמְרוּ: "אֵיךְ יָכוֹל אִישׁ חוֹטֵא לַעֲשׂוֹת אוֹתוֹת

17 They said to the blind man again, "What do you say about Him because He opened your eyes?"

He said, "He is a prophet."

18 But the Jews did not believe concerning him, that he had been blind and received his sight, until they called the parents of him who had received his sight. 19 And they asked them, saying, "Is this your son, who you say was born blind? How then does he now see?"

20 His parents answered them and said, "We know that this is our son, and that he was born blind; 21 but by what means he now sees we do not know, or who opened his eyes we do not know. He is of age; ask him. He will speak for himself." 22 His parents said these *things* because they feared the Jews, for the Jews had agreed already that if anyone confessed *that* He *was* Christ, he would be put out of the synagogue. 23 Therefore his parents said, "He is of age; ask him."

24 So they again called the man who was blind, and said to him, "Give God the glory! We know that this Man is a sinner."

25 He answered and said, "Whether He is a sinner *or not* I do not know. One thing I know: that though I was blind, now I see."

26 Then they said to him again, "What did He do to you? How did He open your eyes?"

27 He answered them, "I told you already, and you did not listen. Why do you want to hear *it* again? Do you also want to become His disciples?"

28 Then they reviled him and said, "You are His disciple, but we are Moses' disciples. 29 We know that God spoke to Moses; *as for* this *fellow*, we do not know where He is from."

30 The man answered and said to them, "Why, this is a marvelous thing, that you do not know where He is from; yet He has opened my eyes! 31 Now we know that God does not hear sinners; but if anyone is a worshiper of God and does His will, He hears him. 32 Since the world began it has been unheard of that anyone opened the eyes of one who was born blind. 33 If this Man were not from God, He could do nothing."

34 They answered and said to him, "You were completely born in sins, and are you teaching us?" And they cast him out.

35 Jesus heard that they had cast him out; and when He had found him, He said to him, "Do you believe in the Son of God?"

36 He answered and said, "Who is He, Lord, that I may believe in Him?"

37 And Jesus said to him, "You have both seen Him and it is He who is talking with you."

כְּאֵלֶּה?" מַחֲלֹקֶת נָפְלָה בֵּינֵיהֶם. 17 עַל כֵּן הוֹסִיפוּ וְשָׁאֲלוּ אֶת הָאִישׁ שֶׁהָיָה עִוֵּר: "מָה אַתָּה אוֹמֵר עָלָיו עַל שֶׁפָּקַח אֶת עֵינֶיךָ?" הֵשִׁיב וְאָמַר: "נָבִיא הוּא." 18 בְּכָל זֹאת לֹא הֶאֱמִינוּ שֶׁהָיָה עִוֵּר וְנִפְקְחוּ עֵינָיו. לְבַסּוֹף קָרְאוּ לְהוֹרָיו שֶׁל הַנִּרְפָּא 19 וְשָׁאֲלוּ אוֹתָם: "הַאִם זֶהוּ בִּנְכֶם שֶׁאַתֶּם אוֹמְרִים כִּי נוֹלַד עִוֵּר? אִם כֵּן, אֵיךְ זֶה שֶׁהוּא רוֹאֶה עַכְשָׁו?"

20 הֵשִׁיבוּ הוֹרָיו וְאָמְרוּ: "אֲנַחְנוּ יוֹדְעִים כִּי זֶה בְּנֵנוּ וְכִי נוֹלַד עִוֵּר, 21 אֲבָל אֵינֶנּוּ יוֹדְעִים אֵיךְ זֶה שֶׁהוּא רוֹאֶה עַכְשָׁו אוֹ מִי פָּקַח אֶת עֵינָיו; אֵינֶנּוּ יוֹדְעִים. שַׁאֲלוּ נָא אוֹתוֹ! הוּא מְבֻגָּר וִידַבֵּר בְּעַד עַצְמוֹ." 22 אֶת זֹאת אָמְרוּ הוֹרָיו מִשּׁוּם שֶׁפָּחֲדוּ מֵרָאשֵׁי הַיְּהוּדִים, אֲשֶׁר כְּבָר הֶחְלִיטוּ לְנַדּוֹת אֶת כָּל מִי שֶׁיּוֹדֶה כִּי הוּא הַמָּשִׁיחַ. 23 לָכֵן אָמְרוּ הוֹרָיו: "הוּא מְבֻגָּר; שַׁאֲלוּ נָא אוֹתוֹ."

24 קָרְאוּ שֵׁנִית אֶת הָאִישׁ שֶׁהָיָה עִוֵּר וְאָמְרוּ: "תֵּן כָּבוֹד לֵאלֹהִים. אֲנַחְנוּ יוֹדְעִים שֶׁהָאִישׁ הַזֶּה אִישׁ חוֹטֵא הוּא."

25 הֵשִׁיב לָהֶם הַנִּרְפָּא: "אִם חוֹטֵא הוּא אֵינֶנִּי יוֹדֵעַ. דָּבָר אֶחָד אֲנִי יוֹדֵעַ: הָיִיתִי עִוֵּר וְעַכְשָׁו אֲנִי רוֹאֶה." 26 הוֹסִיפוּ וְשָׁאֲלוּ אוֹתוֹ: "מֶה עָשָׂה לְךָ? אֵיךְ פָּקַח אֶת עֵינֶיךָ?"

27 עָנָה לָהֶם: "כְּבָר אָמַרְתִּי לָכֶם וְלֹא שְׁמַעְתֶּם. לָמָּה תִּרְצוּ לִשְׁמֹעַ עוֹד פַּעַם? גַּם אַתֶּם רוֹצִים לִהְיוֹת תַּלְמִידָיו?"

28 חֵרְפוּ אוֹתוֹ וְאָמְרוּ: "אַתָּה תַּלְמִידוֹ! אֲנַחְנוּ תַּלְמִידָיו שֶׁל מֹשֶׁה! 29 אֲנַחְנוּ יוֹדְעִים שֶׁאֱלֹהִים דִּבֶּר אֶל מֹשֶׁה, אֲבָל זֶה – אֵין אָנוּ יוֹדְעִים מֵאַיִן הוּא." 30 הֵשִׁיב הָאִישׁ וְאָמַר לָהֶם: "אָכֵן הַפֶּלֶא וָפֶלֶא שֶׁאֵינְכֶם יוֹדְעִים מֵאַיִן הוּא, וַהֲרֵי הוּא פָּקַח אֶת עֵינַי! 31 אֲנַחְנוּ יוֹדְעִים שֶׁאֱלֹהִים אֵינוֹ שׁוֹמֵעַ לְחוֹטְאִים, אֲבָל לְאָדָם יְרֵא אֱלֹהִים וְעוֹשֶׂה רְצוֹנוֹ הוּא שׁוֹמֵעַ. 32 מֵעוֹלָם לֹא נִשְׁמַע שֶׁמִּישֶׁהוּ פָּקַח עֵינֵי עִוֵּר מִלֵּדָה. 33 לוּלֵא הָיָה הוּא מֵאֵת אֱלֹהִים, לֹא הָיָה יָכוֹל לַעֲשׂוֹת מְאוּמָה."

34 הֵשִׁיבוּ וְאָמְרוּ לוֹ: "אַתָּה בְּכָל בַּחֵטְא נוֹלַדְתָּ וְאַתָּה מְלַמֵּד אוֹתָנוּ?!" וּדְחָפוּהוּ הַחוּצָה. 35 יֵשׁוּעַ שָׁמַע כִּי דְחָפוּהוּ הַחוּצָה, וּכְשֶׁפָּגַשׁ אוֹתוֹ שָׁאַל: "הַאִם אַתָּה מַאֲמִין בְּבֶן־הָאָדָם?" 36 הֵשִׁיב הָאִישׁ: "וּמִי הוּא, אֲדוֹנִי? – לְמַעַן אַאֲמִין בּוֹ." 37 אָמַר לוֹ יֵשׁוּעַ: "גַּם רָאִיתָ אוֹתוֹ וְגַם הַמְדַבֵּר אִתְּךָ זֶה הוּא!"

38 Then he said, "Lord, I believe!" And he worshiped Him.

39 And Jesus said, "For judgment I have come into this world, that those who do not see may see, and that those who see may be made blind."

40 Then *some* of the Pharisees who were with Him heard these words, and said to Him, "Are we blind also?"

41 Jesus said to them, "If you were blind, you would have no sin; but now you say, 'We see.' Therefore your sin remains.

10 "Most assuredly, I say to you, he who does not enter the sheepfold by the door, but climbs up some other way, the same is a thief and a robber. 2 But he who enters by the door is the shepherd of the sheep. 3 To him the doorkeeper opens, and the sheep hear his voice; and he calls his own sheep by name and leads them out. 4 And when he brings out his own sheep, he goes before them; and the sheep follow him, for they know his voice. 5 Yet they will by no means follow a stranger, but will flee from him, for they do not know the voice of strangers." 6 Jesus used this illustration, but they did not understand the things which He spoke to them.

7 Then Jesus said to them again, "Most assuredly, I say to you, I am the door of the sheep. 8 All who *ever* came before Me are thieves and robbers, but the sheep did not hear them. 9 I am the door. If anyone enters by Me, he will be saved, and will go in and out and find pasture. 10 The thief does not come except to steal, and to kill, and to destroy. I have come that they may have life, and that they may have *it* more abundantly.

11 "I am the good shepherd. The good shepherd gives His life for the sheep. 12 But a hireling, *he who is* not the shepherd, one who does not own the sheep, sees the wolf coming and leaves the sheep and flees; and the wolf catches the sheep and scatters them. 13 The hireling flees because he is a hireling and does not care about the sheep. 14 I am the good shepherd; and I know My *sheep,* and am known by My own. 15 As the Father knows Me, even so I know the Father; and I lay down My life for the sheep. 16 And other sheep I have which are not of this fold; them also I must bring, and they will hear My voice; and there will be one flock *and* one shepherd.

17 "Therefore My Father loves Me, because I lay down My life that I may take it again. 18 No one takes it from Me, but I lay it down of Myself. I have power to lay it down, and I have power to take it again. This command I have received from My Father."

38 עָנָה הָאִישׁ: "אֲנִי מַאֲמִין, אֲדוֹנִי", וְהִשְׁתַּחֲוָה לוֹ.
39 אָמַר יֵשׁוּעַ: "אֲנִי בָּאתִי לָעוֹלָם הַזֶּה לְשֵׁם מִשְׁפָּט, כְּדֵי שֶׁהַלֹּא־רוֹאִים יִרְאוּ, וְהָרוֹאִים יִהְיוּ לְעִוְרִים."
40 שָׁמְעוּ זֹאת כַּמָּה מִן הַפְּרוּשִׁים שֶׁהָיוּ אִתּוֹ. שָׁאֲלוּ אוֹתוֹ: "הַאִם גַּם אָנוּ עִוְרִים?"
41 אָמַר לָהֶם יֵשׁוּעַ: "אִלּוּ הֱיִיתֶם עִוְרִים לֹא הָיָה בָּכֶם חֵטְא. אֲבָל כָּעֵת, בְּאָמְרְכֶם 'אֲנַחְנוּ רוֹאִים', עוֹמֶדֶת חַטַּאתְכֶם."

י "אָמֵן אָמֵן אֲנִי אוֹמֵר לָכֶם, מִי שֶׁאֵינוֹ נִכְנָס אֶל מִכְלָא הַצֹּאן דֶּרֶךְ הַשַּׁעַר, אֶלָּא מְטַפֵּס בְּדֶרֶךְ אַחֶרֶת, גַּנָּב הוּא וְשׁוֹדֵד. 2 הַנִּכְנָס דֶּרֶךְ הַשַּׁעַר הוּא רוֹעֵה הַצֹּאן. 3 לוֹ יִפְתַּח שׁוֹמֵר הַשַּׁעַר, וְהַצֹּאן שׁוֹמְעוֹת בְּקוֹלוֹ. הוּא קוֹרֵא לְצֹאנוֹ בְּשֵׁם וּמוֹצִיא אוֹתָן. 4 לְאַחַר שֶׁהוֹצִיא אֶת כָּל אֲשֶׁר לוֹ הוּא הוֹלֵךְ לִפְנֵיהֶן וְהַצֹּאן הוֹלְכוֹת אַחֲרָיו, כִּי מַכִּירוֹת הֵן אֶת קוֹלוֹ. 5 אַחֲרֵי זָר לֹא תֵּלַכְנָה כִּי אִם תִּבְרַחְנָה מִמֶּנּוּ, מִפְּנֵי שֶׁאֵינָן מַכִּירוֹת אֶת קוֹלָם שֶׁל זָרִים." 6 אֶת הַמָּשָׁל הַזֶּה אָמַר לָהֶם יֵשׁוּעַ, אַךְ הֵם לֹא הֵבִינוּ אֶת פֵּשֶׁר הַדְּבָרִים שֶׁדִּבֵּר אֲלֵיהֶם.

7 הוֹסִיף יֵשׁוּעַ וְאָמַר: "אָמֵן אָמֵן אֲנִי אוֹמֵר לָכֶם, אֲנִי הוּא שַׁעַר הַצֹּאן. 8 כָּל אֲשֶׁר בָּאוּ לְפָנַי גַּנָּבִים הֵם וְשׁוֹדְדִים, וְהַצֹּאן לֹא שָׁמְעוּ לָהֶם. 9 אֲנִי הַשַּׁעַר. אִישׁ אִם יִכָּנֵס דַּרְכִּי – יִוָּשַׁע; הוּא יִכָּנֵס וְיֵצֵא וְיִמְצָא מִרְעֶה. 10 אֵין הַגַּנָּב בָּא אֶלָּא לִגְנֹב וְלַהֲרֹג וּלְהַשְׁמִיד. אֲנִי בָּאתִי כְּדֵי שֶׁיִּהְיוּ לָהֶם חַיִּים וּבְשֶׁפַע שֶׁיִּהְיוּ לָהֶם.

11 אֲנִי הָרוֹעֶה הַטּוֹב. הָרוֹעֶה הַטּוֹב נוֹתֵן אֶת נַפְשׁוֹ בְּעַד הַצֹּאן. 12 הַשָּׂכִיר, שֶׁאֵינֶנּוּ רוֹעֶה וְהַצֹּאן אֵינָן צֹאנוֹ, כִּרְאוֹתוֹ אֶת הַזְּאֵב בָּא, עוֹזֵב אֶת הַצֹּאן וּבוֹרֵחַ וְהַזְּאֵב חוֹטֵף וּמְפַזֵּר אוֹתָן, 13 שֶׁכֵּן הַבּוֹרֵחַ אֵינוֹ אֶלָּא שָׂכִיר וְאֵין הוּא דוֹאֵג לַצֹּאן. 14 אֲנִי הָרוֹעֶה הַטּוֹב. אֲנִי מַכִּיר אֶת שֶׁלִּי וְשֶׁלִּי מַכִּירִים אוֹתִי, 15 כְּשֵׁם שֶׁהָאָב מַכִּיר אוֹתִי וַאֲנִי מַכִּיר אֶת הָאָב; וְאֶת נַפְשִׁי נוֹתֵן אֲנִי בְּעַד הַצֹּאן. 16 גַּם צֹאן אֲחֵרוֹת יֵשׁ לִי, אֲשֶׁר אֵינָן מִן הַמִּכְלָא הַזֶּה. עָלַי לְהַנְהִיג גַּם אוֹתָן. הֵן אֶת קוֹלִי תִּשְׁמַעְנָה וְיִהְיֶה עֵדֶר אֶחָד וְרוֹעֶה אֶחָד.

17 מִשּׁוּם כָּךְ אוֹהֵב אוֹתִי הָאָב: מִשּׁוּם שֶׁאֲנִי נוֹתֵן אֶת נַפְשִׁי וְאֶקַּח אוֹתָהּ שׁוּב. 18 אִישׁ לֹא נָטַל אוֹתָהּ מִמֶּנִּי, אֶלָּא שֶׁאֲנִי נוֹתֵן אוֹתָהּ מֵעַצְמִי. יֵשׁ לִי סַמְכוּת לָתֵת אוֹתָהּ וְיֵשׁ לִי סַמְכוּת לָקַחַת אוֹתָהּ שׁוּב. אֶת הַמִּצְוָה הַזֹּאת קִבַּלְתִּי מֵאֵת אָבִי."

¹⁹ Therefore there was a division again among the Jews because of these sayings. ²⁰ And many of them said, "He has a demon and is mad. Why do you listen to Him?"

²¹ Others said, "These are not the words of one who has a demon. Can a demon open the eyes of the blind?"

²² Now it was the Feast of Dedication in Jerusalem, and it was winter. ²³ And Jesus walked in the temple, in Solomon's porch. ²⁴ Then the Jews surrounded Him and said to Him, "How long do You keep us in doubt? If You are the Christ, tell us plainly."

²⁵ Jesus answered them, "I told you, and you do not believe. The works that I do in My Father's name, they bear witness of Me. ²⁶ But you do not believe, because you are not of My sheep, as I said to you. ²⁷ My sheep hear My voice, and I know them, and they follow Me. ²⁸ And I give them eternal life, and they shall never perish; neither shall anyone snatch them out of My hand. ²⁹ My Father, who has given *them* to Me, is greater than all; and no one is able to snatch *them* out of My Father's hand. ³⁰ I and *My* Father are one."

³¹ Then the Jews took up stones again to stone Him. ³² Jesus answered them, "Many good works I have shown you from My Father. For which of those works do you stone Me?"

³³ The Jews answered Him, saying, "For a good work we do not stone You, but for blasphemy, and because You, being a Man, make Yourself God."

³⁴ Jesus answered them, "Is it not written in your law, 'I said, "You are gods"'? ³⁵ If He called them gods, to whom the word of God came (and the Scripture cannot be broken), ³⁶ do you say of Him whom the Father sanctified and sent into the world, 'You are blaspheming,' because I said, 'I am the Son of God'? ³⁷ If I do not do the works of My Father, do not believe Me; ³⁸ but if I do, though you do not believe Me, believe the works, that you may know and believe that the Father *is* in Me, and I in Him." ³⁹ Therefore they sought again to seize Him, but He escaped out of their hand.

⁴⁰ And He went away again beyond the Jordan to the place where John was baptizing at first, and there He stayed. ⁴¹ Then many came to Him and said, "John performed no sign, but all the things that John spoke about this Man were true." ⁴² And many believed in Him there.

11 Now a certain *man* was sick, Lazarus of Bethany, the town of Mary and her sister Martha. ² It was *that* Mary who anointed the Lord with fragrant oil and wiped His feet with her hair, whose

¹⁹ שׁוּב נָפְלָה מַחֲלֹקֶת בֵּינֵיהֶם בִּגְלַל דְּבָרָיו אֵלֶּה. ²⁰ אָמְרוּ רַבִּים מֵהֶם: "שֵׁד בּוֹ; הוּא מְשֻׁגָּע. לָמָּה אַתֶּם מַקְשִׁיבִים אֵלָיו?" ²¹ אֲחֵרִים אָמְרוּ: "אֵלֶּה אֵינָן מִלִּים שֶׁל אֲחוּז שֵׁד. הַאִם יָכוֹל שֵׁד לִפְקֹחַ עֵינֵי עִוְרִים?"

²² אוֹתָהּ עֵת חָגְגוּ בִּירוּשָׁלַיִם אֶת חַג הַחֲנֻכָּה. חֹרֶף הָיָה. ²³ כַּאֲשֶׁר הִתְהַלֵּךְ יֵשׁוּעַ בְּבֵית הַמִּקְדָּשׁ בְּאוּלָם שְׁלֹמֹה, ²⁴ הִקִּיפוּהוּ וְאָמְרוּ לוֹ: "עַד מָתַי תַּחֲזִיק אֶת נַפְשֵׁנוּ בְּמֶתַח? אִם אַתָּה הַמָּשִׁיחַ, אֱמָר לָנוּ בְּבֵרוּר."

²⁵ הֵשִׁיב לָהֶם יֵשׁוּעַ: "אָמַרְתִּי לָכֶם וְאֵינְכֶם מַאֲמִינִים. הַמַּעֲשִׂים שֶׁאֲנִי עוֹשֶׂה בְּשֵׁם אָבִי – אֵלֶּה מְעִידִים עָלַי, ²⁶ אַךְ אַתֶּם אֵינְכֶם מַאֲמִינִים מִשּׁוּם שֶׁאֵינְכֶם מִצֹּאנִי. ²⁷ צֹאנִי שׁוֹמְעוֹת אֶת קוֹלִי וַאֲנִי מַכִּיר אוֹתָן; הֵן הוֹלְכוֹת אַחֲרַי ²⁸ וַאֲנִי נוֹתֵן לָהֶן חַיֵּי עוֹלָם; וְלֹא תֹּאבַדְנָה לְעוֹלָם, אַף לֹא יַחֲטֹף אוֹתָן אִישׁ מִיָּדִי. ²⁹ אָבִי שֶׁנָּתַן אוֹתָן לִי גָּדוֹל מִכֹּל וְאֵין אִישׁ יָכוֹל לַחֲטֹף אוֹתָן מִיַּד הָאָב. ³⁰ אֲנִי וְהָאָב אֶחָד אֲנַחְנוּ."

³¹ שׁוּב הֵרִימוּ אֲבָנִים כְּדֵי לִרְגֹּם אוֹתוֹ. ³² הֵשִׁיב לָהֶם יֵשׁוּעַ: "מַעֲשִׂים טוֹבִים רַבִּים הֶרְאֵיתִי לָכֶם מֵאֵת הָאָב; עַל אֵיזֶה מַעֲשֶׂה מֵהֶם תִּרְגְּמוּנִי?"

³³ עָנוּ לוֹ: "לֹא עַל מַעֲשֶׂה טוֹב נִרְגֹּם אוֹתְךָ, אֶלָּא עַל חִלּוּל שֵׁם שָׁמַיִם וְעַל שֶׁבִּהְיוֹתְךָ אָדָם אַתָּה עוֹשֶׂה אֶת עַצְמְךָ אֱלֹהִים."

³⁴ הֵשִׁיב לָהֶם יֵשׁוּעַ: "כְּלוּם לֹא כָּתוּב בְּתוֹרַתְכֶם, 'אֲנִי-אָמַרְתִּי אֱלֹהִים אַתֶּם'? ³⁵ אִם הוּא אָמַר 'אֱלֹהִים' לְאֵלֶּה אֲשֶׁר דְּבַר אֱלֹהִים הָיָה אֲלֵיהֶם – וְאֶת הַכָּתוּב אִי אֶפְשָׁר לְהָפֵר – ³⁶ הַאִם תֹּאמְרוּ אַתֶּם לָזֶה אֲשֶׁר הָאָב קִדְּשׁוֹ וְשָׁלַח אוֹתוֹ אֶל הָעוֹלָם, 'מְגַדֵּף אַתָּה', מִשּׁוּם שֶׁאָמַרְתִּי 'בֶּן-אֱלֹהִים אֲנִי'? ³⁷ אִם אֵינֶנִּי עוֹשֶׂה אֶת מַעֲשֵׂי אָבִי, אַל תַּאֲמִינוּ לִי. ³⁸ אֲבָל אִם אֲנִי עוֹשֶׂה, אַף אִם אֵינְכֶם מַאֲמִינִים לִי, הַאֲמִינוּ לַמַּעֲשִׂים, לְמַעַן תַּכִּירוּ וְתֵדְעוּ שֶׁהָאָב בִּי וַאֲנִי בָּאָב."

³⁹ אָז נִסּוּ שׁוּב לִתְפֹּס אוֹתוֹ וְהוּא חָמַק מִיָּדָם. ⁴⁰ הוּא הָלַךְ וְשָׁב אֶל עֵבֶר הַיַּרְדֵּן, אֶל הַמָּקוֹם אֲשֶׁר שָׁם הִטְבִּיל יוֹחָנָן בָּרִאשׁוֹנָה, וְנִשְׁאַר שָׁם. ⁴¹ רַבִּים בָּאוּ אֵלָיו. אָמְרוּ: "יוֹחָנָן לֹא עָשָׂה שׁוּם נֵס, אַךְ כָּל מַה שֶּׁאָמַר יוֹחָנָן עַל הָאִישׁ הַזֶּה הָיָה אֱמֶת." ⁴² וְרַבִּים הֶאֱמִינוּ בּוֹ שָׁם.

יא מַעֲשֶׂה בְּחוֹלֶה אֶחָד, אֶלְעָזָר מִבֵּית עַנְיָה, מִן הַכְּפָר שֶׁגָּרוּ בּוֹ מִרְיָם וּמָרְתָא אֲחוֹתָהּ. ² מִרְיָם הִיא אֲשֶׁר מָשְׁחָה אֶת הָאָדוֹן בְּשֶׁמֶן בֹּשֶׂם וְנִגְּבָה אֶת

brother Lazarus was sick. ³ Therefore the sisters sent to Him, saying, "Lord, behold, he whom You love is sick."

⁴ When Jesus heard *that,* He said, "This sickness is not unto death, but for the glory of God, that the Son of God may be glorified through it."

⁵ Now Jesus loved Martha and her sister and Lazarus. ⁶ So, when He heard that he was sick, He stayed two more days in the place where He was. ⁷ Then after this He said to *the* disciples, "Let us go to Judea again."

⁸ *The* disciples said to Him, "Rabbi, lately the Jews sought to stone You, and are You going there again?"

⁹ Jesus answered, "Are there not twelve hours in the day? If anyone walks in the day, he does not stumble, because he sees the light of this world. ¹⁰ But if one walks in the night, he stumbles, because the light is not in him." ¹¹ These things He said, and after that He said to them, "Our friend Lazarus sleeps, but I go that I may wake him up."

¹² Then His disciples said, "Lord, if he sleeps he will get well." ¹³ However, Jesus spoke of his death, but they thought that He was speaking about taking rest in sleep.

¹⁴ Then Jesus said to them plainly, "Lazarus is dead. ¹⁵ And I am glad for your sakes that I was not there, that you may believe. Nevertheless let us go to him."

¹⁶ Then Thomas, who is called the Twin, said to his fellow disciples, "Let us also go, that we may die with Him."

¹⁷ So when Jesus came, He found that he had already been in the tomb four days. ¹⁸ Now Bethany was near Jerusalem, about two miles away. ¹⁹ And many of the Jews had joined the women around Martha and Mary, to comfort them concerning their brother.

²⁰ Now Martha, as soon as she heard that Jesus was coming, went and met Him, but Mary was sitting in the house. ²¹ Now Martha said to Jesus, "Lord, if You had been here, my brother would not have died. ²² But even now I know that whatever You ask of God, God will give You."

²³ Jesus said to her, "Your brother will rise again."

²⁴ Martha said to Him, "I know that he will rise again in the resurrection at the last day."

²⁵ Jesus said to her, "I am the resurrection and the life. He who believes in Me, though he may die, he shall live. ²⁶ And whoever lives and believes in Me shall never die. Do you believe this?"

רַגְלָיו בְּשַׂעֲרוֹתֶיהָ. אָחִיהָ אֶלְעָזָר הוּא שָׁחֲלָה. ³ שָׁלְחוּ הָאֲחָיוֹת לְהַגִּיד לְיֵשׁוּעַ: "אֲדוֹנֵנוּ, רְאֵה נָא, זֶה שֶׁאָהוּב עָלֶיךָ חוֹלֶה."

⁴ שָׁמַע יֵשׁוּעַ וְאָמַר: "הַמַּחֲלָה הַזֹּאת אֵינֶנָּה לְמָוֶת, אֶלָּא לִכְבוֹד אֱלֹהִים, כְּדֵי שֶׁיְּכֻבַּד בָּהּ בֶּן־הָאֱלֹהִים."

⁵ יֵשׁוּעַ אָהַב אֶת מַרְתָּא וְאֶת אֲחוֹתָהּ וְאֶת אֶלְעָזָר. ⁶ כַּאֲשֶׁר שָׁמַע כִּי חָלָה, שָׁהָה עוֹד יוֹמַיִם בְּאוֹתוֹ מָקוֹם. ⁷ אַחֲרֵי כֵן אָמַר לְתַלְמִידָיו: "בּוֹאוּ נַחֲזֹר לְאֶרֶץ יְהוּדָה."

⁸ אָמְרוּ לוֹ הַתַּלְמִידִים: "רַבִּי, לֹא מִכְּבָר בִּקְּשׁוּ לִרְגֹם אוֹתְךָ וְאַתָּה חוֹזֵר לְשָׁם?"

⁹ הֵשִׁיב יֵשׁוּעַ: "הֲרֵי שְׁתֵּים־עֶשְׂרֵה שָׁעוֹת לַיּוֹם. הַמִּתְהַלֵּךְ בַּיּוֹם אֵינֶנּוּ נִכְשָׁל, כִּי רוֹאֶה הוּא אֶת אוֹר הָעוֹלָם הַזֶּה. ¹⁰ אֲבָל הַמִּתְהַלֵּךְ בַּלַּיְלָה נִכְשָׁל, כִּי הָאוֹר אֵינֶנּוּ בּוֹ." ¹¹ אַחֲרֵי שֶׁאָמַר זֹאת הוֹסִיף: "אֶלְעָזָר יְדִידֵנוּ נִרְדָּם, אַךְ אֲנִי הוֹלֵךְ לְהָעִיר אוֹתוֹ."

¹² אָמְרוּ לוֹ הַתַּלְמִידִים: "אִם נִרְדָּם, אֲזַי יֵרָפֵא."

¹³ יֵשׁוּעַ דִּבֶּר עַל מוֹתוֹ, אֶלָּא שֶׁהֵם חָשְׁבוּ כִּי דִבֶּר עַל תַּרְדֵּמַת הַשֵּׁנָה. ¹⁴ אָז אָמַר לָהֶם יֵשׁוּעַ בִּמְפֹרָשׁ: "אֶלְעָזָר מֵת. ¹⁵ וַאֲשֶׁר לָכֶם, אֲנִי שָׂמֵחַ שֶׁלֹּא הָיִיתִי שָׁם – לְמַעַן תַּאֲמִינוּ. אַךְ בּוֹאוּ נֵלֵךְ אֵלָיו."

¹⁶ תְּאוֹמָא, הַנִּקְרָא דִּידִימוֹס, אָמַר לַחֲבֵרָיו הַתַּלְמִידִים: "נֵלֵךְ נָא גַם אֲנַחְנוּ כְּדֵי שֶׁנָּמוּת אִתּוֹ."

¹⁷ כַּאֲשֶׁר בָּא יֵשׁוּעַ, מָצָא שֶׁכְּבָר אַרְבָּעָה יָמִים הוּא בַּקֶּבֶר. ¹⁸ בֵּית עַנְיָה הָיְתָה מְרֻחֶקֶת מִירוּשָׁלַיִם כִּשְׁנֵי מִילִין, ¹⁹ וְרַבִּים בָּאוּ אֶל מַרְתָּא וּמִרְיָם לְנַחֵם אוֹתָן עַל אֲחִיהֶן. ²⁰ כְּשָׁמְעָ מַרְתָּא שֶׁיֵּשׁוּעַ בָּא הָלְכָה לִקְרָאתוֹ, וְאִלּוּ מִרְיָם יָשְׁבָה בַּבַּיִת. ²¹ אָמְרָה מַרְתָּא לְיֵשׁוּעַ: "אֲדוֹנִי, לוּ הָיִיתָ פֹּה, לֹא הָיָה אָחִי מֵת. ²² אֲבָל גַּם עַכְשָׁו יוֹדַעַת אֲנִי שֶׁכָּל מַה שֶׁתְּבַקֵּשׁ מֵאֱלֹהִים, אֱלֹהִים יִתֵּן לְךָ."

²³ אָמַר לָהּ יֵשׁוּעַ: "אָחִיךְ יָקוּם."

²⁴ הֵשִׁיבָה לוֹ מַרְתָּא: "אֲנִי יוֹדַעַת שֶׁהוּא יָקוּם בַּתְּחִיָּה בַּיּוֹם הָאַחֲרוֹן."

²⁵ אָמַר לָהּ יֵשׁוּעַ: "אֲנִי הַתְּחִיָּה וְהַחַיִּים. הַמַּאֲמִין בִּי יִחְיֶה גַּם אִם יָמוּת. ²⁶ וְכָל מִי שֶׁחַי וּמַאֲמִין בִּי לֹא יָמוּת לְעוֹלָם. הַאִם מַאֲמִינָה אַתְּ בָּזֶה?"

18 כִּשְׁנֵי מִילִין – כִּשְׁלוֹשָׁה קִילוֹמֶטְרִים.

27 She said to Him, "Yes, Lord, I believe that You are the Christ, the Son of God, who is to come into the world."

28 And when she had said these things, she went her way and secretly called Mary her sister, saying, "The Teacher has come and is calling for you." 29 As soon as she heard *that,* she arose quickly and came to Him. 30 Now Jesus had not yet come into the town, but was in the place where Martha met Him. 31 Then the Jews who were with her in the house, and comforting her, when they saw that Mary rose up quickly and went out, followed her, saying, "She is going to the tomb to weep there."

32 Then, when Mary came where Jesus was, and saw Him, she fell down at His feet, saying to Him, "Lord, if You had been here, my brother would not have died."

33 Therefore, when Jesus saw her weeping, and the Jews who came with her weeping, He groaned in the spirit and was troubled. 34 And He said, "Where have you laid him?"

They said to Him, "Lord, come and see."

35 Jesus wept. 36 Then the Jews said, "See how He loved him!"

37 And some of them said, "Could not this Man, who opened the eyes of the blind, also have kept this man from dying?"

38 Then Jesus, again groaning in Himself, came to the tomb. It was a cave, and a stone lay against it. 39 Jesus said, "Take away the stone."

Martha, the sister of him who was dead, said to Him, "Lord, by this time there is a stench, for he has been *dead* four days."

40 Jesus said to her, "Did I not say to you that if you would believe you would see the glory of God?" 41 Then they took away the stone *from the place* where the dead man was lying. And Jesus lifted up *His* eyes and said, "Father, I thank You that You have heard Me. 42 And I know that You always hear Me, but because of the people who are standing by I said *this,* that they may believe that You sent Me." 43 Now when He had said these things, He cried with a loud voice, "Lazarus, come forth!" 44 And he who had died came out bound hand and foot with graveclothes, and his face was wrapped with a cloth. Jesus said to them, "Loose him, and let him go."

45 Then many of the Jews who had come to Mary, and had seen the things Jesus did, believed in Him. 46 But some of them went away to the Pharisees and told them the things Jesus did. 47 Then the chief priests and the Pharisees gathered a council and said, "What shall we do? For this Man works many signs. 48 If we let Him alone like

27 אָמְרָה לוֹ: "כֵּן, אֲדוֹנִי, אֲנִי מַאֲמִינָה שֶׁאַתָּה הַמָּשִׁיחַ בֶּן־הָאֱלֹהִים שֶׁבָּא אֶל הָעוֹלָם." 28 אַחֲרֵי שֶׁאָמְרָה זֹאת הָלְכָה וְקָרְאָה לְמִרְיָם אֲחוֹתָהּ בַּסֵּתֶר. אָמְרָה לָהּ: "רַבֵּנוּ הִגִּיעַ, הוּא קוֹרֵא לָךְ." 29 הִיא שָׁמְעָה, מִהֲרָה לָקוּם וּבָאָה אֵלָיו.

30 יֵשׁוּעַ טֶרֶם נִכְנַס לַכְּפָר, כִּי הָיָה עוֹד בַּמָּקוֹם שֶׁפָּגְשָׁה אוֹתוֹ מָרְתָא. 31 אֵלֶּה שֶׁהָיוּ אֵצֶל מִרְיָם בַּבַּיִת וְנִחֲמוּ אוֹתָהּ, כְּשֶׁרָאוּ כִּי מִהֲרָה לָקוּם וְלָצֵאת, הָלְכוּ אַחֲרֶיהָ בְּחָשְׁבָם שֶׁהִיא הוֹלֶכֶת לַקֶּבֶר לִבְכּוֹת שָׁם. 32 בְּהַגִּיעָהּ אֶל הַמָּקוֹם שֶׁהָיָה בּוֹ יֵשׁוּעַ, נָפְלָה מִרְיָם לְרַגְלָיו וְאָמְרָה לוֹ: "אֲדוֹנִי, לוּ הָיִיתָ פֹּה, לֹא הָיָה אָחִי מֵת."

33 כִּרְאוֹתוֹ אוֹתָהּ בּוֹכִיָּה, וְהָאֲנָשִׁים שֶׁבָּאוּ אִתָּהּ בּוֹכִים גַּם הֵם, נִסְעֲרָה רוּחוֹ שֶׁל יֵשׁוּעַ וְהוּא הִזְדַּעְזַע. 34 הוּא שָׁאַל: "אֵיפֹה הִנַּחְתֶּם אוֹתוֹ?" הֵשִׁיבוּ לוֹ: "אָדוֹן, בּוֹא וּרְאֵה."

35 בָּכָה יֵשׁוּעַ. 36 הִגִּיבוּ וְאָמְרוּ: "רְאוּ עַד כַּמָּה אָהַב אוֹתוֹ!" 37 אַךְ כַּמָּה מֵהֶם אָמְרוּ: "הַפּוֹקֵחַ עֵינֵי עִוֵּר הַאִם לֹא הָיָה יָכוֹל גַּם לִמְנֹעַ אֶת מוֹתוֹ שֶׁל הָאִישׁ הַזֶּה?" 38 וְאָז יֵשׁוּעַ, נַפְשׁוֹ שׁוּב סוֹעֶרֶת בְּקִרְבּוֹ, נִגַּשׁ אֶל מְעָרַת הַקֶּבֶר הַמְכֻסָּה אֶבֶן. 39 אָמַר יֵשׁוּעַ: "הָסִירוּ אֶת הָאֶבֶן!"

אָמְרָה לוֹ מָרְתָא אֲחוֹתוֹ שֶׁל הַמֵּת: "אֲדוֹנִי, הֲרֵיהוּ כְּבָר מַעֲלֶה רֵיחַ, כִּי עָבְרוּ אַרְבָּעָה יָמִים."

40 הֵשִׁיב לָהּ יֵשׁוּעַ: "הֲלֹא אָמַרְתִּי לָךְ שֶׁאִם תַּאֲמִינִי תִּרְאִי אֶת כְּבוֹד הָאֱלֹהִים." 41 הֵם הֵסִירוּ אֶת הָאֶבֶן וְיֵשׁוּעַ נָשָׂא אֶת עֵינָיו לַמָּרוֹם וְאָמַר: "אָבִי, אוֹדְךָ כִּי שְׁמַעְתָּנִי. 42 יָדַעְתִּי כִּי תָמִיד שׁוֹמֵעַ אַתָּה אוֹתִי, וְרַק לְמַעַן הָעָם הָעוֹמֵד מִסָּבִיב אָמַרְתִּי זֹאת, שֶׁיַּאֲמִינוּ כִּי אַתָּה שְׁלַחְתָּנִי." 43 לְאַחַר שֶׁאָמַר אֶת הַדָּבָר הַזֶּה, קָרָא בְּקוֹל גָּדוֹל: "אֶלְעָזָר, צֵא הַחוּצָה!" 44 יָצָא הַמֵּת כְּשֶׁרַגְלָיו וְיָדָיו כְּרוּכוֹת בְּתַכְרִיכִים וּפָנָיו עֲטוּפוֹת בְּמִטְפַּחַת. אָמַר לָהֶם יֵשׁוּעַ: "הַתִּירוּ אוֹתוֹ וְהַנִּיחוּ לוֹ לָלֶכֶת."

45 רַבִּים מֵאֵלֶּה שֶׁבָּאוּ אֶל מִרְיָם הֶאֱמִינוּ בּוֹ כִּרְאוֹתָם אֶת אֲשֶׁר עָשָׂה. 46 אַךְ מִקְצָתָם הָלְכוּ אֶל הַפְּרוּשִׁים וְסִפְּרוּ לָהֶם מַה שֶּׁעָשָׂה יֵשׁוּעַ. 47 כִּנְּסוּ רָאשֵׁי הַכֹּהֲנִים וְהַפְּרוּשִׁים אֶת הַסַּנְהֶדְרִין. אָמְרוּ: "מַה נַּעֲשֶׂה? הֲרֵי הָאִישׁ הַזֶּה עוֹשֶׂה אוֹתוֹת רַבִּים! 48 אִם נַנִּיחַ לוֹ כָּךְ, הַכֹּל יַאֲמִינוּ בּוֹ וְהָרוֹמָאִים יָבוֹאוּ וְיַחֲרִיבוּ אֶת מְקוֹמֵנוּ וְאֶת אֻמָּתֵנוּ."

this, everyone will believe in Him, and the Romans will come and take away both our place and nation."

[49] And one of them, Caiaphas, being high priest that year, said to them, "You know nothing at all, [50] nor do you consider that it is expedient for us that one man should die for the people, and not that the whole nation should perish." [51] Now this he did not say on his own *authority;* but being high priest that year he prophesied that Jesus would die for the nation, [52] and not for that nation only, but also that He would gather together in one the children of God who were scattered abroad.

[53] Then, from that day on, they plotted to put Him to death. [54] Therefore Jesus no longer walked openly among the Jews, but went from there into the country near the wilderness, to a city called Ephraim, and there remained with His disciples.

[55] And the Passover of the Jews was near, and many went from the country up to Jerusalem before the Passover, to purify themselves. [56] Then they sought Jesus, and spoke among themselves as they stood in the temple, "What do you think—that He will not come to the feast?" [57] Now both the chief priests and the Pharisees had given a command, that if anyone knew where He was, he should report *it,* that they might seize Him.

12 Then, six days before the Passover, Jesus came to Bethany, where Lazarus was who had been dead, whom He had raised from the dead. [2] There they made Him a supper; and Martha served, but Lazarus was one of those who sat at the table with Him. [3] Then Mary took a pound of very costly oil of spikenard, anointed the feet of Jesus, and wiped His feet with her hair. And the house was filled with the fragrance of the oil.

[4] But one of His disciples, Judas Iscariot, Simon's *son,* who would betray Him, said, [5] "Why was this fragrant oil not sold for three hundred denarii and given to the poor?" [6] This he said, not that he cared for the poor, but because he was a thief, and had the money box; and he used to take what was put in it.

[7] But Jesus said, "Let her alone; she has kept this for the day of My burial. [8] For the poor you have with you always, but Me you do not have always."

[9] Now a great many of the Jews knew that He was there; and they came, not for Jesus' sake only, but that they might also see Lazarus, whom He had raised from the dead. [10] But the chief priests plotted to put Lazarus to death also, [11] because on account of him many of the Jews went away and believed in Jesus.

[49] קַיָּפָא, שֶׁהָיָה אֶחָד מֵהֶם וְהוּא הַכֹּהֵן הַגָּדוֹל בְּאוֹתָהּ שָׁנָה, אָמַר לָהֶם: "אֵין אַתֶּם יוֹדְעִים כְּלוּם, [50] אַף אֵינְכֶם מְבִינִים שֶׁכְּדַאי לָנוּ כִּי אִישׁ אֶחָד יָמוּת בְּעַד הָעָם וְלֹא תֹּאבַד כָּל הָאֻמָּה כֻּלָּהּ." [51] לֹא מִלִּבּוֹ אָמַר זֹאת, אֶלָּא שֶׁבִּהְיוֹתוֹ כֹּהֵן גָּדוֹל בְּאוֹתָהּ שָׁנָה הִתְנַבֵּא כִּי יֵשׁוּעַ עָתִיד לָמוּת בְּעַד הָאֻמָּה; [52] וְלֹא רַק בְּעַד הָאֻמָּה, אֶלָּא גַּם כְּדֵי שֶׁיְּקַבֵּץ לְאֶחָד אֶת נְפוּצוֹת בְּנֵי־הָאֱלֹהִים.

[53] מֵאוֹתוֹ יוֹם גָּמְרוּ אֹמֶר לַהֲמִית אוֹתוֹ. [54] לָכֵן לֹא הוֹסִיף יֵשׁוּעַ לְהִתְהַלֵּךְ בְּגָלוּי בִּיהוּדָה. הוּא הָלַךְ מִשָּׁם אֶל אֵזוֹר קָרוֹב לַמִּדְבָּר, לָעִיר הַנִּקְרֵאת אֶפְרַיִם, וְגָר שָׁם עִם תַּלְמִידָיו.

[55] יְמֵי הַפֶּסַח קָרְבוּ וְרַבִּים מִתּוֹשָׁבֵי הָאָרֶץ עָלוּ לִירוּשָׁלַיִם לִפְנֵי הַפֶּסַח כְּדֵי לְהִטַּהֵר. [56] הֵם חִפְּשׂוּ אֶת יֵשׁוּעַ, וּבִהְיוֹתָם בְּבֵית הַמִּקְדָּשׁ שָׁאֲלוּ אִישׁ אֶת רֵעֵהוּ: "מַה דַּעְתְּךָ, הַאִם יָבוֹא לֶחָג אוֹ לֹא?" [57] וְרָאשֵׁי הַכֹּהֲנִים וְהַפְּרוּשִׁים גָּזְרוּ שֶׁאִם יֵדַע אִישׁ אֶת מְקוֹם הִמָּצְאוֹ יוֹדִיעַ עַל כָּךְ כְּדֵי שֶׁיִּתְפְּשׂוּהוּ.

יב שִׁשָּׁה יָמִים לִפְנֵי הַפֶּסַח בָּא יֵשׁוּעַ לְבֵית עַנְיָה, מְקוֹם מְגוּרָיו שֶׁל אֶלְעָזָר אֲשֶׁר יֵשׁוּעַ הֱקִימוֹ מִן הַמֵּתִים. [2] עָרְכוּ לוֹ שָׁם סְעֻדָּה וּמָרְתָא שֵׁרְתָה אוֹתָם, וְאִלּוּ אֶלְעָזָר הָיָה אֶחָד מִן הַמְסֻבִּים אִתּוֹ. [3] אָז לָקְחָה מִרְיָם בְּשֶׂם נֵרְדְּ זַךְ וְיָקָר, לִיטְרָה אַחַת מִשְׁקָלוֹ, מָשְׁחָה אֶת רַגְלֵי יֵשׁוּעַ וְנִגְּבָה אוֹתָן בְּשַׂעֲרוֹתֶיהָ, וְהַבַּיִת נִתְמַלֵּא רֵיחַ הַבֹּשֶׂם. [4] אָמַר יְהוּדָה אִישׁ קְרִיּוֹת, אֶחָד מִתַּלְמִידָיו שֶׁהָיָה עָתִיד לְהַסְגִּיר אוֹתוֹ: [5] "מַדּוּעַ לֹא נִמְכַּר הַבֹּשֶׂם בִּשְׁלֹשׁ מֵאוֹת דִּינָר וְנִתַּן לָעֲנִיִּים?" [6] אַךְ הוּא אָמַר זֹאת לֹא מִדַּאֲגָתוֹ לָעֲנִיִּים, אֶלָּא מִפְּנֵי שֶׁהָיָה גַּנָּב, הַקֻּפָּה הָיְתָה בְּיָדָיו וְהוּא הָיָה נוֹטֵל מִמַּה שֶּׁשָּׂמוּ בָּהּ. [7] אָמַר יֵשׁוּעַ: "הַנַּח לָהּ; הִיא שָׁמְרָה זֹאת לְיוֹם קְבוּרָתִי. [8] הֲרֵי הָעֲנִיִּים אִתְּכֶם תָּמִיד, אֲבָל אֲנִי לֹא תָּמִיד אֲנִי אִתְּכֶם."

[9] רַבִּים שָׁמְעוּ שֶׁהוּא שָׁם וּבָאוּ לֹא רַק בִּגְלַל יֵשׁוּעַ, אֶלָּא גַּם כְּדֵי לִרְאוֹת אֶת אֶלְעָזָר אֲשֶׁר יֵשׁוּעַ הֱקִימוֹ מִן הַמֵּתִים. [10] נוֹעֲצוּ רָאשֵׁי הַכֹּהֲנִים לַהֲרֹג גַּם אֶת אֶלְעָזָר, [11] כִּי בִּגְלָלוֹ הָלְכוּ רַבִּים וְהֶאֱמִינוּ בְּיֵשׁוּעַ.

[3] לִיטְרָה אַחַת – כִּשְׁלוֹשׁ מֵאוֹת גְּרָם.

12 The next day a great multitude that had come to the feast, when they heard that Jesus was coming to Jerusalem, 13 took branches of palm trees and went out to meet Him, and cried out:

"Hosanna!
'Blessed is He who comes in the name of the LORD!'
The King of Israel!"

14 Then Jesus, when He had found a young donkey, sat on it; as it is written:

15 "Fear not, daughter of Zion;
Behold, your King is coming,
Sitting on a donkey's colt."

16 His disciples did not understand these things at first; but when Jesus was glorified, then they remembered that these things were written about Him and that they had done these things to Him.

17 Therefore the people, who were with Him when He called Lazarus out of his tomb and raised him from the dead, bore witness. 18 For this reason the people also met Him, because they heard that He had done this sign. 19 The Pharisees therefore said among themselves, "You see that you are accomplishing nothing. Look, the world has gone after Him!"

20 Now there were certain Greeks among those who came up to worship at the feast. 21 Then they came to Philip, who was from Bethsaida of Galilee, and asked him, saying, "Sir, we wish to see Jesus."

22 Philip came and told Andrew, and in turn Andrew and Philip told Jesus.

23 But Jesus answered them, saying, "The hour has come that the Son of Man should be glorified. 24 Most assuredly, I say to you, unless a grain of wheat falls into the ground and dies, it remains alone; but if it dies, it produces much grain. 25 He who loves his life will lose it, and he who hates his life in this world will keep it for eternal life. 26 If anyone serves Me, let him follow Me; and where I am, there My servant will be also. If anyone serves Me, him My Father will honor.

27 "Now My soul is troubled, and what shall I say? 'Father, save Me from this hour'? But for this purpose I came to this hour. 28 Father, glorify Your name."

Then a voice came from heaven, saying, "I have both glorified it and will glorify it again."

29 Therefore the people who stood by and heard it said that it had thundered. Others said, "An angel has spoken to Him."

30 Jesus answered and said, "This voice did not come because of Me, but for your sake. 31 Now is the judgment of this world; now the ruler of this

12 לְמָחֳרַת שָׁמְעוּ הֲמוֹנֵי הָעָם שֶׁבָּאוּ לֶחַג כִּי יֵשׁוּעַ עוֹמֵד לָבוֹא לִירוּשָׁלַיִם. 13 לָקְחוּ כַּפּוֹת תְּמָרִים וַיֵּצְאוּ לִקְרָאתוֹ כְּשֶׁהֵם קוֹרְאִים: "הוֹשַׁע נָא! בָּרוּךְ הַבָּא בְּשֵׁם יהוה! מֶלֶךְ יִשְׂרָאֵל!" 14 יֵשׁוּעַ מָצָא קְדַם לָכֵן עַיִר וַיֵּשֶׁב עָלָיו, לְפִי הַכָּתוּב: 15 "אַל תִּירְאִי בַּת־צִיּוֹן, הִנֵּה מַלְכֵּךְ יָבוֹא לָךְ רֹכֵב עַל־עַיִר בֶּן־אֲתוֹנוֹת."

16 בַּתְּחִלָּה לֹא הֵבִינוּ תַלְמִידָיו אֶת הַדְּבָרִים הָאֵלֶּה, אֲבָל כְּשֶׁנִּתְפָּאֵר יֵשׁוּעַ בִּכְבוֹדוֹ זָכְרוּ שֶׁכָּךְ הָיָה כָתוּב עָלָיו וְשֶׁכָּךְ עָשׂוּ לוֹ. 17 הָאֲנָשִׁים הָרַבִּים, שֶׁהָיוּ אִתּוֹ כַּאֲשֶׁר קָרָא לְאֶלְעָזָר מִן הַקֶּבֶר וְהֵקִימוֹ מִן הַמֵּתִים, הֵעִידוּ עַל זֹאת. 18 לָכֵן גַּם יָצָא הֲמוֹן הָעָם לִקְרָאתוֹ, כִּי שָׁמְעוּ שֶׁהוּא עָשָׂה אֶת הַנֵּס הַזֶּה. 19 הִגִּיבוּ הַפְּרוּשִׁים וְאָמְרוּ זֶה אֶל זֶה: "אַתֶּם רוֹאִים, אֵין מַה לַעֲשׂוֹת. הִנֵּה הָעוֹלָם נוֹהֶה אַחֲרָיו."

20 בֵּין הָעוֹלִים לְהִשְׁתַּחֲווֹת בֶּחָג הָיוּ אֲנָשִׁים יְוָנִים. 21 הַלָּלוּ נִגְּשׁוּ אֶל פִילִיפּוֹס אִישׁ בֵּית צַיְדָא שֶׁבַּגָּלִיל וּבִקְשָׁה בְּפִיהֶם: "אָדוֹן, רוֹצִים אָנוּ לִרְאוֹת אֶת יֵשׁוּעַ." 22 הָלַךְ פִילִיפּוֹס וְאָמַר לְאַנְדְּרֵי, וְאַנְדְּרֵי וּפִילִיפּוֹס הָלְכוּ וְאָמְרוּ לְיֵשׁוּעַ. 23 הֵשִׁיב לָהֶם יֵשׁוּעַ וְאָמַר: "הִגִּיעָה הַשָּׁעָה שֶׁיִּפְאַר בֶּן־הָאָדָם בִּכְבוֹד. 24 אָמֵן אָמֵן אֲנִי אוֹמֵר לָכֶם, אִם לֹא יָמוּת גַּרְגִּיר הַחִטָּה הַנּוֹפֵל לְתוֹךְ הָאֲדָמָה, הוּא יִשָּׁאֵר לְבַדּוֹ. אֲבָל אִם יָמוּת, יַעֲשֶׂה פְּרִי הַרְבֵּה. 25 הָאוֹהֵב אֶת נַפְשׁוֹ מְאַבֵּד אוֹתָהּ, וְהַשּׂוֹנֵא אֶת נַפְשׁוֹ בָּעוֹלָם הַזֶּה יִשְׁמְרֶנָּה לְחַיֵּי עוֹלָם. 26 אִם מִישֶׁהוּ מְשָׁרֵת אוֹתִי, שֶׁיֵּלֵךְ אַחֲרַי, הֵיכָן שֶׁאֶהְיֶה אֲנִי, שָׁם יִהְיֶה גַּם מְשָׁרְתִי. אִישׁ אִם יְשָׁרֵת אוֹתִי, הָאָב יְכַבֵּד אוֹתוֹ.

27 וְעַתָּה נִבְהֲלָה נַפְשִׁי, וַאֲנִי מַה אֹמַר: 'אָבִי, הַצִּילֵנִי מִן הַשָּׁעָה הַזֹּאת'? אַדְּרַבָּא, הֲרֵי לְשֵׁם כָּךְ בָּאתִי לַשָּׁעָה הַזֹּאת. 28 אָבִי, פָּאֵר אֶת שִׁמְךָ!" אָז יָצָא קוֹל מִן הַשָּׁמַיִם וְאָמַר: "כְּבָר פֵּאַרְתִּי וְשׁוּב אֲפָאֵר."

29 אֲנָשִׁים מִן הֶהָמוֹן, שֶׁעָמְדוּ שָׁם וְשָׁמְעוּ, אָמְרוּ: "רַעַם הָיָה." אֲחֵרִים אָמְרוּ: "מַלְאָךְ דִּבֵּר אֵלָיו." 30 הֵשִׁיב יֵשׁוּעַ וְאָמַר: "לֹא לְמַעֲנִי הָיָה הַקּוֹל הַזֶּה, אֶלָּא לְמַעַנְכֶם. 31 כָּעֵת הַמִּשְׁפָּט שֶׁל הָעוֹלָם הַזֶּה;

world will be cast out. ³² And I, if I am lifted up from the earth, will draw all *peoples* to Myself." ³³ This He said, signifying by what death He would die.

³⁴ The people answered Him, "We have heard from the law that the Christ remains forever; and how *can* You say, 'The Son of Man must be lifted up'? Who is this Son of Man?"

³⁵ Then Jesus said to them, "A little while longer the light is with you. Walk while you have the light, lest darkness overtake you; he who walks in darkness does not know where he is going. ³⁶ While you have the light, believe in the light, that you may become sons of light." These things Jesus spoke, and departed, and was hidden from them.

³⁷ But although He had done so many signs before them, they did not believe in Him, ³⁸ that the word of Isaiah the prophet might be fulfilled, which he spoke:

> "Lord, who has believed our report?
> And to whom has the arm of the LORD been revealed?"

³⁹ Therefore they could not believe, because Isaiah said again:

> ⁴⁰ "He has blinded their eyes and hardened their hearts,
> Lest they should see with *their* eyes,
> Lest they should understand with *their* hearts and turn,
> So that I should heal them."

⁴¹ These things Isaiah said when he saw His glory and spoke of Him.

⁴² Nevertheless even among the rulers many believed in Him, but because of the Pharisees they did not confess *Him,* lest they should be put out of the synagogue; ⁴³ for they loved the praise of men more than the praise of God.

⁴⁴ Then Jesus cried out and said, "He who believes in Me, believes not in Me but in Him who sent Me. ⁴⁵ And he who sees Me sees Him who sent Me. ⁴⁶ I have come *as* a light into the world, that whoever believes in Me should not abide in darkness. ⁴⁷ And if anyone hears My words and does not believe, I do not judge him; for I did not come to judge the world but to save the world. ⁴⁸ He who rejects Me, and does not receive My words, has that which judges him—the word that I have spoken will judge him in the last day. ⁴⁹ For I have not spoken on My own *authority;* but the Father who sent Me gave Me a command, what I should say and what I should speak. ⁵⁰ And I know that

---

³² כָּעֵת יֻשְׁלַךְ הַחוּצָה שַׂר הָעוֹלָם הַזֶּה. וַאֲנִי בְּהִנָּשְׂאִי מִן הָאָרֶץ אֶמְשֹׁךְ אֶת הַכֹּל אֵלָי." ³³ וְזֹאת אָמַר בְּרָמְזוֹ עַל אֹפֶן הַמָּוֶת שֶׁהָיָה עָתִיד לָמוּת.

³⁴ הֵשִׁיבוּ לוֹ הָאֲנָשִׁים: "אֲנַחְנוּ קִבַּלְנוּ מִן הַתּוֹרָה כִּי הַמָּשִׁיחַ יִשָּׁאֵר לְעוֹלָם, וְאֵיךְ זֶה אַתָּה אוֹמֵר שֶׁבֶּן־הָאָדָם צָרִיךְ לְהִנָּשֵׂא מִן הָאָרֶץ? מִי בֶּן־הָאָדָם הַזֶּה?"

³⁵ אָמַר לָהֶם יֵשׁוּעַ: "רַק עוֹד מְעַט־קַט הָאוֹר בְּקִרְבְּכֶם. הֱיוּ מִתְהַלְּכִים בְּעוֹד הָאוֹר מֵאִיר לָכֶם, פֶּן יַשִּׂיגְכֶם הַחֹשֶׁךְ. הַמִּתְהַלֵּךְ בַּחֹשֶׁךְ אֵינוֹ יוֹדֵעַ אָנָה הוּא בָּא. ³⁶ בְּעוֹד הָאוֹר נִשְׁאָר עִמָּכֶם הַאֲמִינוּ בָּאוֹר, לְמַעַן תִּהְיוּ לִבְנֵי הָאוֹר."

לְאַחַר שֶׁדִּבֵּר יֵשׁוּעַ אֶת הַדְּבָרִים הָאֵלֶּה הָלַךְ וְהִסְתַּתֵּר מֵהֶם. ³⁷ אַף כִּי עָשָׂה אוֹתוֹת רַבִּים לְנֶגֶד עֵינֵיהֶם, לֹא הֶאֱמִינוּ בּוֹ. ³⁸ וְזֹאת לְקַיֵּם אֶת דְּבַר יְשַׁעְיָהוּ הַנָּבִיא: "יהוה, מִי הֶאֱמִין לִשְׁמֻעָתֵנוּ וּזְרוֹעַ יהוה עַל־מִי נִגְלָתָה?" ³⁹ לָכֵן לֹא יָכְלוּ לְהַאֲמִין, כִּי עוֹד אָמַר יְשַׁעְיָהוּ: ⁴⁰ "הֵשַׁע עֵינֵיהֶם וְהִשְׁמִן לְבָבָם, פֶּן יִרְאוּ בְעֵינֵיהֶם וּלְבָבָם יָבִין וָשָׁבוּ וְרָפָא לָהֶם." ⁴¹ אֶת הַדְּבָרִים הָאֵלֶּה אָמַר יְשַׁעְיָהוּ בִּרְאוֹתוֹ אֶת כְּבוֹדוֹ, וְעָלָיו דִּבֵּר. ⁴² אַף־עַל־פִּי־כֵן הֶאֱמִינוּ בּוֹ גַּם רַבִּים מֵהַמַּנְהִיגִים, אַךְ לֹא הוֹדוּ בָזֶה בִּגְלַל הַפְּרוּשִׁים, כְּדֵי שֶׁלֹּא יְנֻדּוּ מִן הַקָּהָל, ⁴³ שֶׁכֵּן אָהֲבוּ כְּבוֹד בְּנֵי אָדָם יוֹתֵר מִכְּבוֹד אֱלֹהִים.

⁴⁴ קָרָא יֵשׁוּעַ וְאָמַר: "הַמַּאֲמִין בִּי, לֹא בִּי הוּא מַאֲמִין אֶלָּא בְּשׁוֹלְחִי. ⁴⁵ הָרוֹאֶה אוֹתִי רוֹאֶה אֶת שׁוֹלְחִי. ⁴⁶ אֲנִי אוֹר. אֶל הָעוֹלָם בָּאתִי כְּדֵי שֶׁכָּל הַמַּאֲמִין בִּי לֹא יֵשֵׁב בַּחֹשֶׁךְ. ⁴⁷ אִישׁ הַשּׁוֹמֵעַ אֶת דְּבָרַי וְאֵינוֹ שׁוֹמֵר אוֹתָם, אֵינֶנִּי שׁוֹפֵט אוֹתוֹ; כִּי לֹא בָּאתִי לִשְׁפֹּט אֶת הָעוֹלָם, אֶלָּא לְהוֹשִׁיעַ אֶת הָעוֹלָם. ⁴⁸ מִי שֶׁדּוֹחֶה אוֹתִי וְאֵינוֹ מְקַבֵּל אֶת דְּבָרַי, יֵשׁ הַשּׁוֹפֵט אוֹתוֹ. הַדָּבָר אֲשֶׁר דִּבַּרְתִּי הוּא יִשְׁפֹּט אוֹתוֹ בַּיּוֹם הָאַחֲרוֹן, ⁴⁹ כִּי לֹא מֵעַצְמִי דִּבַּרְתִּי, אֶלָּא הָאָב אֲשֶׁר שְׁלָחַנִי הוּא צִוַּנִי מַה שֶּׁאֹמַר וּמַה שֶּׁאֲדַבֵּר. ⁵⁰ וַאֲנִי יוֹדֵעַ שֶׁמִּצְוָתוֹ חַיֵּי עוֹלָם. לָכֵן אֶת אֲשֶׁר אֲנִי

His command is everlasting life. Therefore, whatever I speak, just as the Father has told Me, so I speak."

13 Now before the Feast of the Passover, when Jesus knew that His hour had come that He should depart from this world to the Father, having loved His own who were in the world, He loved them to the end.

²And supper being ended, the devil having already put it into the heart of Judas Iscariot, Simon's *son,* to betray Him, ³Jesus, knowing that the Father had given all things into His hands, and that He had come from God and was going to God, ⁴rose from supper and laid aside His garments, took a towel and girded Himself. ⁵After that, He poured water into a basin and began to wash the disciples' feet, and to wipe *them* with the towel with which He was girded. ⁶Then He came to Simon Peter. And *Peter* said to Him, "Lord, are You washing my feet?"

⁷Jesus answered and said to him, "What I am doing you do not understand now, but you will know after this."

⁸Peter said to Him, "You shall never wash my feet!"

Jesus answered him, "If I do not wash you, you have no part with Me."

⁹Simon Peter said to Him, "Lord, not my feet only, but also *my* hands and *my* head!"

¹⁰Jesus said to him, "He who is bathed needs only to wash *his* feet, but is completely clean; and you are clean, but not all of you." ¹¹For He knew who would betray Him; therefore He said, "You are not all clean."

¹²So when He had washed their feet, taken His garments, and sat down again, He said to them, "Do you know what I have done to you? ¹³You call Me Teacher and Lord, and you say well, for *so* I am. ¹⁴If I then, *your* Lord and Teacher, have washed your feet, you also ought to wash one another's feet. ¹⁵For I have given you an example, that you should do as I have done to you. ¹⁶Most assuredly, I say to you, a servant is not greater than his master; nor is he who is sent greater than he who sent him. ¹⁷If you know these things, blessed are you if you do them.

¹⁸"I do not speak concerning all of you. I know whom I have chosen; but that the Scripture may be fulfilled, '*He who eats bread with Me has lifted up his heel against Me.*' ¹⁹Now I tell you before it comes, that when it does come to pass, you may believe that I am *He.* ²⁰Most assuredly, I say to

מְדַבֵּר, כְּפִי שֶׁאָמַר לִי הָאָב כָּךְ אֲנִי מְדַבֵּר."

יג הָיָה זֶה לִפְנֵי חַג הַפֶּסַח: יֵשׁוּעַ יָדַע כִּי הִגִּיעָה שְׁעָתוֹ לְהִסְתַּלֵּק מִן הָעוֹלָם הַזֶּה אֶל הָאָב; וּבְאַהֲבָתוֹ אֶת הַשַּׁיָּכִים לוֹ בָּעוֹלָם, אָהַב אוֹתָם עַד תֹּם. ²לְעֵת סְעוּדַת עֶרֶב, הַשָּׂטָן כְּבָר שָׂם בְּלֵב יְהוּדָה בֶּן שִׁמְעוֹן אִישׁ קְרִיּוֹת לְהַסְגִּיר אוֹתוֹ. ³יֵשׁוּעַ, שֶׁיָּדַע כִּי הָאָב נָתַן אֶת הַכֹּל בְּיָדָיו וְכִי מֵאֵת אֱלֹהִים יָצָא וְאֶל אֱלֹהִים הוּא הוֹלֵךְ, ⁴קָם מִן הַסְּעוּדָה וּפָשַׁט אֶת בְּגָדָיו, לָקַח מַגֶּבֶת וְחָגַר אֶת עַצְמוֹ; ⁵אַחַר כָּךְ יָצַק מַיִם בַּקְּעָרָה וְהֵחֵל לִרְחֹץ אֶת רַגְלֵי הַתַּלְמִידִים וּלְנַגֵּב בַּמַּגֶּבֶת שֶׁהָיָה חָגוּר בָּהּ. ⁶וּכְשֶׁקָּרַב אֶל שִׁמְעוֹן כֵּיפָא, אָמַר לוֹ זֶה: "אֲדוֹנִי, אַתָּה תִּרְחַץ אֶת רַגְלַי?!"

⁷הֵשִׁיב יֵשׁוּעַ וְאָמַר אֵלָיו: "מַה שֶּׁאֲנִי עוֹשֶׂה אֵינְךָ יוֹדֵעַ כָּעֵת, אֲבָל אַחֲרֵי כֵן תָּבִין."

⁸אָמַר לוֹ כֵּיפָא: "לְעוֹלָם לֹא תִרְחַץ אֶת רַגְלַי!" הֵשִׁיב לוֹ יֵשׁוּעַ: "אִם לֹא אֶרְחַץ אוֹתְךָ אֵין לְךָ חֵלֶק אִתִּי."

⁹אָמַר לוֹ שִׁמְעוֹן כֵּיפָא: "אֲדוֹנִי, לֹא רַק אֶת רַגְלַי, אֶלָּא גַּם אֶת יָדַי וְאֶת רֹאשִׁי."

¹⁰הֵשִׁיב לוֹ יֵשׁוּעַ: "מִי שֶׁרָחוּץ טָהוֹר הוּא לַחֲלוּטִין וְאֵינוֹ זָקוּק אֶלָּא לִרְחִיצַת הָרַגְלַיִם. וְאַתֶּם טְהוֹרִים, אַךְ לֹא כֻּלְּכֶם"; ¹¹שֶׁהֲרֵי הִכִּיר אֶת מִי שֶׁיַּסְגִּיר אוֹתוֹ וְלָכֵן אָמַר: "לֹא כֻּלְּכֶם טְהוֹרִים."

¹²לְאַחַר שֶׁרָחַץ אֶת רַגְלֵיהֶם וְלָבַשׁ אֶת בְּגָדָיו, חָזַר וְהֵסֵב אִתָּם. אָמַר לָהֶם: "יוֹדְעִים אַתֶּם מָה עָשִׂיתִי לָכֶם? ¹³אַתֶּם קוֹרְאִים לִי רַבִּי וְאָדוֹן; יָפֶה אַתֶּם עוֹשִׂים, שֶׁכֵּן אֲנִי הוּא. ¹⁴לָכֵן אִם אֲנִי, הָאָדוֹן וְהַמּוֹרֶה, רָחַצְתִּי אֶת רַגְלֵיכֶם, גַּם אַתֶּם חַיָּבִים לִרְחֹץ זֶה אֶת רַגְלֵי זֶה, ¹⁵כִּי מוֹפֵת נָתַתִּי לָכֶם כְּדֵי שֶׁתַּעֲשׂוּ גַּם אַתֶּם כְּמוֹ שֶׁעָשִׂיתִי לָכֶם. ¹⁶אָמֵן אָמֵן אֲנִי אוֹמֵר לָכֶם, עֶבֶד אֵינֶנּוּ גָּדוֹל מֵאֲדוֹנָיו וְשָׁלִיחַ אֵינֶנּוּ גָּדוֹל מִשּׁוֹלְחוֹ. ¹⁷אִם יוֹדְעִים אַתֶּם אֶת זֹאת, אַשְׁרֵיכֶם בַּעֲשׂוֹתְכֶם כֵּן. ¹⁸לֹא עַל כֻּלְּכֶם דִּבַּרְתִּי – אֲנִי יוֹדֵעַ מִי אֵלֶּה שֶׁבָּחַרְתִּי אוֹתָם – אַךְ לְמַעַן יִמָּלֵא הַכָּתוּב, 'אוֹכֵל לַחְמִי הִגְדִּיל עָלַי עָקֵב'. ¹⁹מֵעַתָּה אֲנִי אוֹמֵר לָכֶם בְּטֶרֶם יִקְרֶה הַדָּבָר, לְמַעַן תַּאֲמִינוּ כַּאֲשֶׁר יִקְרֶה כִּי אֲנִי הוּא. ²⁰אָמֵן אָמֵן אֲנִי אוֹמֵר לָכֶם, הַמְקַבֵּל אֶת מִי שֶׁאֶשְׁלַח מְקַבֵּל אוֹתִי, וְהַמְקַבֵּל אוֹתִי מְקַבֵּל אֶת שׁוֹלְחִי."

you, he who receives whomever I send receives Me; and he who receives Me receives Him who sent Me."

21 When Jesus had said these things, He was troubled in spirit, and testified and said, "Most assuredly, I say to you, one of you will betray Me." 22 Then the disciples looked at one another, perplexed about whom He spoke.

23 Now there was leaning on Jesus' bosom one of His disciples, whom Jesus loved. 24 Simon Peter therefore motioned to him to ask who it was of whom He spoke.

25 Then, leaning back on Jesus' breast, he said to Him, "Lord, who is it?"

26 Jesus answered, "It is he to whom I shall give a piece of bread when I have dipped it." And having dipped the bread, He gave it to Judas Iscariot, the son of Simon. 27 Now after the piece of bread, Satan entered him. Then Jesus said to him, "What you do, do quickly." 28 But no one at the table knew for what reason He said this to him. 29 For some thought, because Judas had the money box, that Jesus had said to him, "Buy those things we need for the feast," or that he should give something to the poor.

30 Having received the piece of bread, he then went out immediately. And it was night.

31 So, when he had gone out, Jesus said, "Now the Son of Man is glorified, and God is glorified in Him. 32 If God is glorified in Him, God will also glorify Him in Himself, and glorify Him immediately. 33 Little children, I shall be with you a little while longer. You will seek Me; and as I said to the Jews, 'Where I am going, you cannot come,' so now I say to you. 34 A new commandment I give to you, that you love one another; as I have loved you, that you also love one another. 35 By this all will know that you are My disciples, if you have love for one another."

36 Simon Peter said to Him, "Lord, where are You going?"

Jesus answered him, "Where I am going you cannot follow Me now, but you shall follow Me afterward."

37 Peter said to Him, "Lord, why can I not follow You now? I will lay down my life for Your sake."

38 Jesus answered him, "Will you lay down your life for My sake? Most assuredly, I say to you, the rooster shall not crow till you have denied Me three times.

14 "Let not your heart be troubled; you believe in God, believe also in Me. 2 In My Father's house are many mansions; if it were not so, I would have told

21 לְאַחַר שֶׁאָמַר זֹאת נִפְעַם יֵשׁוּעַ בְּרוּחוֹ וְהֵעִיד בְּאָמְרוֹ: "אָמֵן אָמֵן אֲנִי אוֹמֵר לָכֶם, אֶחָד מִכֶּם יַסְגִּירֵנִי."

22 הִבִּיטוּ הַתַּלְמִידִים זֶה בָּזֶה, תּוֹהִים הָיוּ עַל מִי דִּבֵּר. 23 אוֹתָהּ שָׁעָה הָיָה אַחַד הַתַּלְמִידִים סָמוּךְ אֶל חֵיק יֵשׁוּעַ. אוֹתוֹ תַּלְמִיד הָיָה אָהוּב עַל יֵשׁוּעַ. 24 רָמַז לוֹ שִׁמְעוֹן כֵּיפָא לִשְׁאֹל עַל מִי הוּא מְדַבֵּר. 25 נִשְׁעַן אוֹתוֹ תַּלְמִיד עַל לִבּוֹ שֶׁל יֵשׁוּעַ וְשָׁאַל אוֹתוֹ: "אֲדוֹנִי, מִי הוּא?"

26 עָנָה יֵשׁוּעַ: "זֶה שֶׁבִּשְׁבִילוֹ אֶטְבֹּל אֶת הַפְּרוּסָה וְאֶתֵּן לוֹ". טָבַל אֶת הַפְּרוּסָה וְנָתַן אוֹתָהּ לִיהוּדָה בֶּן שִׁמְעוֹן אִישׁ קְרִיּוֹת. 27 לְאַחַר שֶׁנִּתְּנָה לוֹ הַפְּרוּסָה נִכְנַס בּוֹ הַשָּׂטָן. אָמַר לוֹ יֵשׁוּעַ: "אֶת אֲשֶׁר תַּעֲשֶׂה עֲשֵׂה מַהֵר." 28 וְאִישׁ מִן הַמְּסֻבִּים לֹא יָדַע לְשֵׁם מַה אָמַר לוֹ זֹאת. 29 הוֹאִיל וְהַקֻּפָּה הָיְתָה אֵצֶל יְהוּדָה, חָשְׁבוּ אֲחָדִים שֶׁיֵּשׁוּעַ אָמַר לוֹ, "קְנֵה מַה שֶּׁנָּחוּץ לָנוּ לֶחָג", אוֹ שֶׁיִּתֵּן מַשֶּׁהוּ לַעֲנִיִּים. 30 וְהוּא, אַחֲרֵי שֶׁלָּקַח אֶת הַפְּרוּסָה, יָצָא מִיָּד. הָיָה אָז לַיְלָה.

31 עִם צֵאתוֹ אָמַר יֵשׁוּעַ: "עַתָּה נִתְפָּאֵר בֶּן־הָאָדָם בְּכָבוֹד וְהָאֱלֹהִים נִתְפָּאֵר בּוֹ. 32 אִם אֱלֹהִים נִתְפָּאֵר בּוֹ, אֱלֹהִים יְפָאֲרֵהוּ בּוֹ וּבִמְהֵרָה יְפָאֲרֵהוּ. 33 בָּנַי, אַךְ זְמַן מוּעָט אֶהְיֶה עִמָּכֶם. אַתֶּם תְּחַפְּשׂוּנִי, וּכְשֵׁם שֶׁכְּבָר אָמַרְתִּי, 'אֶל אֲשֶׁר אֲנִי הוֹלֵךְ אֵינְכֶם יְכוֹלִים לָבוֹא', כָּךְ אֲנִי אוֹמֵר לָכֶם עַכְשָׁו. 34 מִצְוָה חֲדָשָׁה אֲנִי נוֹתֵן לָכֶם: אֶהֱבוּ זֶה אֶת זֶה; כְּמוֹ שֶׁאָהַבְתִּי אֶתְכֶם כָּךְ גַּם אַתֶּם אֶהֱבוּ זֶה אֶת זֶה. 35 בְּזֹאת יֵדְעוּ הַכֹּל שֶׁתַּלְמִידַי אַתֶּם: אִם תִּהְיֶה אַהֲבָה בֵּינֵיכֶם."

36 שָׁאַל אוֹתוֹ שִׁמְעוֹן כֵּיפָא: "אֲדוֹנִי, לְאָן אַתָּה הוֹלֵךְ?" הֵשִׁיב יֵשׁוּעַ: "אֶל אֲשֶׁר אֲנִי הוֹלֵךְ אֵינְךָ יָכוֹל לָלֶכֶת אַחֲרַי עַכְשָׁו, אֲבָל אַחֲרֵי כֵן תֵּלֵךְ."

37 אָמַר לוֹ כֵּיפָא: "מַדּוּעַ לֹא אוּכַל לָלֶכֶת אַחֲרֶיךָ עַכְשָׁו? אֶת נַפְשִׁי אֶתֵּן בַּעֲדְךָ."

38 הֵשִׁיב יֵשׁוּעַ: "אֶת נַפְשְׁךָ תִּתֵּן בַּעֲדִי? אָמֵן אָמֵן אֲנִי אוֹמֵר לְךָ, תַּרְנְגוֹל לֹא יִקְרָא עַד אֲשֶׁר תִּתְכַּחֵשׁ לִי שָׁלוֹשׁ פְּעָמִים."

יד "אַל יִבָּהֵל לְבַבְכֶם. הַאֲמִינוּ בֵּאלֹהִים; הַאֲמִינוּ גַּם בִּי. 2 בְּבֵית אָבִי מְעוֹנוֹת רַבִּים. לוּלֵא כֵן, כְּלוּם הָיִיתִי אוֹמֵר לָכֶם שֶׁאֲנִי הוֹלֵךְ לְהָכִין לָכֶם מָקוֹם?

you. I go to prepare a place for you. ³ And if I go
and prepare a place for you, I will come again and
receive you to Myself; that where I am, *there* you
may be also. ⁴ And where I go you know, and the
way you know."

⁵ Thomas said to Him, "Lord, we do not know
where You are going, and how can we know the
way?"

⁶ Jesus said to him, "I am the way, the truth, and
the life. No one comes to the Father except through
Me.

⁷ "If you had known Me, you would have known
My Father also; and from now on you know Him
and have seen Him."

⁸ Philip said to Him, "Lord, show us the Father,
and it is sufficient for us."

⁹ Jesus said to him, "Have I been with you so
long, and yet you have not known Me, Philip? He
who has seen Me has seen the Father; so how can
you say, 'Show us the Father'? ¹⁰ Do you not believe
that I am in the Father, and the Father in Me? The
words that I speak to you I do not speak on My
own *authority;* but the Father who dwells in Me
does the works. ¹¹ Believe Me that I *am* in the
Father and the Father in Me, or else believe Me for
the sake of the works themselves.

¹² "Most assuredly, I say to you, he who believes
in Me, the works that I do he will do also; and
greater *works* than these he will do, because I go to
My Father. ¹³ And whatever you ask in My name,
that I will do, that the Father may be glorified in
the Son. ¹⁴ If you ask anything in My name, I will
do *it.*

¹⁵ "If you love Me, keep My commandments.
¹⁶ And I will pray the Father, and He will give you
another Helper, that He may abide with you
forever— ¹⁷ the Spirit of truth, whom the world
cannot receive, because it neither sees Him nor
knows Him; but you know Him, for He dwells with
you and will be in you. ¹⁸ I will not leave you
orphans; I will come to you.

¹⁹ "A little while longer and the world will see Me
no more, but you will see Me. Because I live, you
will live also. ²⁰ At that day you will know that I *am*
in My Father, and you in Me, and I in you. ²¹ He
who has My commandments and keeps them, it is
he who loves Me. And he who loves Me will be
loved by My Father, and I will love him and
manifest Myself to him."

²² Judas (not Iscariot) said to Him, "Lord, how is
it that You will manifest Yourself to us, and not to
the world?"

³ וְאִם אֵלֵךְ וְאָכִין לָכֶם מָקוֹם, אָשׁוּב וְאֶקַּח אֶתְכֶם
אֵלַי לְמַעַן תִּהְיוּ גַּם אַתֶּם בַּאֲשֶׁר אֲנִי שָׁם. ⁴ וּלְאָן אֲנִי
הוֹלֵךְ, יוֹדְעִים אַתֶּם אֶת הַדֶּרֶךְ."

⁵ אָמַר לוֹ תֹּאמָא: "אֲדוֹנִי, אֵינֶנּוּ יוֹדְעִים לְאָן אַתָּה
הוֹלֵךְ; אֵיךְ נֵדַע אֶת הַדֶּרֶךְ?"

⁶ אָמַר לוֹ יֵשׁוּעַ: "אֲנִי הַדֶּרֶךְ וְהָאֱמֶת וְהַחַיִּים. אֵין
אִישׁ בָּא אֶל הָאָב אֶלָּא דַּרְכִּי. ⁷ אִלּוּ הִכַּרְתֶּם אוֹתִי
גַּם אֶת אָבִי הֱיִיתֶם מַכִּירִים. מֵעַתָּה אַתֶּם מַכִּירִים
אוֹתוֹ אַף רְאִיתֶם אוֹתוֹ!"

⁸ אָמַר לוֹ פִילִיפּוֹס: "אֲדוֹנִי, הַרְאֵה לָנוּ אֶת הָאָב וְדַי
לָנוּ."

⁹ אָמַר לוֹ יֵשׁוּעַ: "יָמִים רַבִּים כָּל כָּךְ אֲנִי עִמָּכֶם
וְאֵינְךָ מַכִּיר אוֹתִי, פִילִיפּוֹס? הָרוֹאֶה אוֹתִי רָאָה אֶת
הָאָב, וּמַדּוּעַ אַתָּה אוֹמֵר 'הַרְאֵה לָנוּ אֶת הָאָב'?
¹⁰ הַאֵינְךָ מַאֲמִין שֶׁאֲנִי בָּאָב וְהָאָב בִּי? הַדְּבָרִים
שֶׁאֲנִי אוֹמֵר לָכֶם אֵינֶנִּי אוֹמֵר אוֹתָם מֵעַצְמִי; הָאָב
הַשּׁוֹכֵן בִּי, הוּא עוֹשֶׂה אֶת מַעֲשָׂיו. ¹¹ הַאֲמִינוּ לִי
שֶׁאֲנִי בָּאָב וְהָאָב בִּי. וְאִם לֹא, הַאֲמִינוּ בִּגְלַל
הַמַּעֲשִׂים עַצְמָם. ¹² אָמֵן אָמֵן אֲנִי אוֹמֵר לָכֶם,
הַמַּאֲמִין בִּי יַעֲשֶׂה גַּם הוּא אֶת הַמַּעֲשִׂים שֶׁאֲנִי
עוֹשֶׂה; וּגְדוֹלִים מֵאֵלֶּה יַעֲשֶׂה, כִּי הוֹלֵךְ אֲנִי אֶל
הָאָב. ¹³ וְכָל מַה שֶׁתְּבַקְשׁוּ בִּשְׁמִי אֶעֱשֶׂה, לְמַעַן
יְכֻבַּד הָאָב בַּבֵּן. ¹⁴ אִם תְּבַקְשׁוּ מִמֶּנִּי דָּבָר בִּשְׁמִי,
אֲנִי אֶעֱשֶׂה."

¹⁵ "אִם אַתֶּם אוֹהֲבִים אוֹתִי, הֲרֵי שֶׁתִּשְׁמְרוּ אֶת
מִצְווֹתַי. ¹⁶ וַאֲנִי אֲבַקֵּשׁ מֵהָאָב וְיִתֵּן לָכֶם מְנַחֵם אַחֵר
שֶׁיִּהְיֶה עִמָּכֶם לְעוֹלָם: ¹⁷ אֶת רוּחַ הָאֱמֶת אֲשֶׁר
הָעוֹלָם אֵינוֹ יָכוֹל לְקַבֵּל מִשּׁוּם שֶׁאֵינוֹ רוֹאֶה אוֹתָהּ,
אַף אֵינוֹ מַכִּיר אוֹתָהּ. אַתֶּם מַכִּירִים אוֹתָהּ, כִּי הִיא
שׁוֹכֶנֶת עִמָּכֶם וְתִהְיֶה בָּכֶם. ¹⁸ לֹא אֶעֱזֹב אֶתְכֶם
יְתוֹמִים; אָבוֹא אֲלֵיכֶם. ¹⁹ עוֹד מְעַט וְהָעוֹלָם לֹא
יוֹסִיף לִרְאוֹתֵנִי, אֲבָל אַתֶּם תִּרְאוּנִי, שֶׁכֵּן אֲנִי חַי וְגַם
אַתֶּם תִּחְיוּ. ²⁰ בַּיּוֹם הַהוּא תֵּדְעוּ שֶׁאֲנִי בְּאָבִי וְאַתֶּם
בִּי וַאֲנִי בָּכֶם. ²¹ הַמַּחֲזִיק בְּמִצְווֹתַי וְשׁוֹמֵר אוֹתָן הוּא
הָאוֹהֵב אוֹתִי, וְהָאוֹהֵב אוֹתִי אָבִי יֹאהַב אוֹתוֹ; גַּם
אֲנִי אֹהַב אוֹתוֹ וַאֲגַלֶּה לוֹ אֶת עַצְמִי."

²² שָׁאַל אוֹתוֹ יְהוּדָה, לֹא אִישׁ קְרִיּוֹת: "אֲדוֹנִי, וְלָמָּה
עָתִיד אַתָּה לְהִתְגַּלּוֹת לָנוּ וְלֹא לָעוֹלָם?"

23 Jesus answered and said to him, "If anyone loves Me, he will keep My word; and My Father will love him, and We will come to him and make Our home with him. 24 He who does not love Me does not keep My words; and the word which you hear is not Mine but the Father's who sent Me.

25 "These things I have spoken to you while being present with you. 26 But the Helper, the Holy Spirit, whom the Father will send in My name, He will teach you all things, and bring to your remembrance all things that I said to you. 27 Peace I leave with you, My peace I give to you; not as the world gives do I give to you. Let not your heart be troubled, neither let it be afraid. 28 You have heard Me say to you, 'I am going away and coming *back* to you.' If you loved Me, you would rejoice because I said, 'I am going to the Father,' for My Father is greater than I.

29 "And now I have told you before it comes, that when it does come to pass, you may believe. 30 I will no longer talk much with you, for the ruler of this world is coming, and he has nothing in Me. 31 But that the world may know that I love the Father, and as the Father gave Me commandment, so I do. Arise, let us go from here.

15 "I am the true vine, and My Father is the vinedresser. 2 Every branch in Me that does not bear fruit He takes away; and every *branch* that bears fruit He prunes, that it may bear more fruit. 3 You are already clean because of the word which I have spoken to you. 4 Abide in Me, and I in you. As the branch cannot bear fruit of itself, unless it abides in the vine, neither can you, unless you abide in Me.

5 "I am the vine, you *are* the branches. He who abides in Me, and I in him, bears much fruit; for without Me you can do nothing. 6 If anyone does not abide in Me, he is cast out as a branch and is withered; and they gather them and throw *them* into the fire, and they are burned. 7 If you abide in Me, and My words abide in you, you will ask what you desire, and it shall be done for you. 8 By this My Father is glorified, that you bear much fruit; so you will be My disciples.

9 "As the Father loved Me, I also have loved you; abide in My love. 10 If you keep My commandments, you will abide in My love, just as I have kept My Father's commandments and abide in His love.

11 "These things I have spoken to you, that My joy may remain in you, and *that* your joy may be full. 12 This is My commandment, that you love one another as I have loved you. 13 Greater love has no one than this, than to lay down one's life for his

23 הֵשִׁיב לוֹ יֵשׁוּעַ: "מִי שֶׁאוֹהֵב אוֹתִי יִשְׁמֹר אֶת דְּבָרִי וְאָבִי יֶאֱהַב אוֹתוֹ; גַּם נָבוֹא אֵלָיו וְנִשְׁכֹּן אֶצְלוֹ. 24 מִי שֶׁאֵינוֹ אוֹהֵב אוֹתִי אֵינוֹ שׁוֹמֵר אֶת דְּבָרַי, וְהַדָּבָר אֲשֶׁר אַתֶּם שׁוֹמְעִים אֵינוֹ שֶׁלִּי כִּי אִם שֶׁל הָאָב אֲשֶׁר שְׁלָחַנִי. 25 אֶת אֵלֶּה דִּבַּרְתִּי אֲלֵיכֶם בְּעוֹדִי עִמָּכֶם. 26 אֲבָל הַמְּנַחֵם, רוּחַ הַקֹּדֶשׁ שֶׁהָאָב יִשְׁלַח לָכֶם בִּשְׁמִי, הוּא יְלַמֵּד אֶתְכֶם הַכֹּל וְיַזְכִּיר לָכֶם כָּל מַה שֶּׁאֲנִי אָמַרְתִּי לָכֶם. 27 שָׁלוֹם אֲנִי מַשְׁאִיר לָכֶם, אֶת שְׁלוֹמִי אֲנִי נוֹתֵן לָכֶם; לֹא כְּדֶרֶךְ שֶׁהָעוֹלָם נוֹתֵן אֲנִי נוֹתֵן לָכֶם. אַל נָא יֵחַת לְבַבְכֶם וְאַל יִירָא. 28 שְׁמַעְתֶּם שֶׁאָמַרְתִּי לָכֶם 'אֲנִי הוֹלֵךְ וְאָבוֹא אֲלֵיכֶם'. אִם אַתֶּם אוֹהֲבִים אוֹתִי, אֲזַי תִּשְׂמְחוּ שֶׁאֲנִי הוֹלֵךְ אֶל הָאָב, כִּי הָאָב גָּדוֹל מִמֶּנִּי. 29 כָּעֵת אָמַרְתִּי לָכֶם, בְּטֶרֶם יִתְרַחֵשׁ הַדָּבָר, כְּדֵי שֶׁתַּאֲמִינוּ כַּאֲשֶׁר הוּא יִתְרַחֵשׁ. 30 לֹא אַרְבֶּה עוֹד לְדַבֵּר אִתְּכֶם, כִּי שַׂר הָעוֹלָם הַזֶּה הִנֵּה הוּא בָּא וּבִי אֵין לוֹ מְאוּמָה, 31 אֶלָּא שֶׁיֵּדַע הָעוֹלָם כִּי אוֹהֵב אֲנִי אֶת הָאָב וּכְפִי שֶׁצִּוַּנִי הָאָב כֵּן אֲנִי עוֹשֶׂה. קוּמוּ, נֵלֵךְ מִכָּאן."

טו "אֲנִי הַגֶּפֶן הָאֲמִתִּית וְאָבִי הַכּוֹרֵם. 2 כָּל שָׂרִיג בִּי שֶׁאֵינוֹ עוֹשֶׂה פְּרִי, הוּא מֵסִיר אוֹתוֹ; וְכָל אֲשֶׁר עוֹשֶׂה פְּרִי, הוּא מְטַהֵר אוֹתוֹ כְּדֵי שֶׁיַּרְבֶּה פִּרְיוֹ. 3 אַתֶּם כְּבָר מְטֹהָרִים עַל־יְדֵי הַדָּבָר שֶׁדִּבַּרְתִּי אֲלֵיכֶם. 4 עִמְדוּ בִּי וַאֲנִי בָּכֶם. כְּמוֹ שֶׁהַשָּׂרִיג אֵינוֹ יָכוֹל לַעֲשׂוֹת פְּרִי מֵאֵלָיו אִם לֹא יַעֲמֹד בַּגֶּפֶן, כָּךְ גַּם אַתֶּם אִם לֹא תַּעַמְדוּ בִּי. 5 אֲנִי הַגֶּפֶן; אַתֶּם הַשָּׂרִיגִים. הָעוֹמֵד בִּי וַאֲנִי בּוֹ עוֹשֶׂה פְּרִי לָרֹב, שֶׁכֵּן בִּלְעָדַי אֵינְכֶם יְכוֹלִים לַעֲשׂוֹת דָּבָר. 6 מִי שֶׁאֵינוֹ עוֹמֵד בִּי מֻשְׁלָךְ הַחוּצָה, כְּשָׂרִיג, וּמִתְיַבֵּשׁ. לְאַחַר שֶׁמְּלַקְּטִים אוֹתָם מַשְׁלִיכִים אוֹתָם לָאֵשׁ וְשָׁם הֵם נִשְׂרָפִים. 7 אִם עוֹמְדִים אַתֶּם בִּי וּדְבָרַי עוֹמְדִים בָּכֶם, בַּקְּשׁוּ מַה שֶּׁתִּרְצוּ, וְיִהְיֶה לָכֶם. 8 בְּזֹאת יְפֹאַר אָבִי: שֶׁתַּעֲשׂוּ פְּרִי לָרֹב וְתִהְיוּ לִי לְתַלְמִידִים. 9 כְּשֵׁם שֶׁהָאָב אוֹהֵב אוֹתִי כֵּן גַּם אֲנִי אוֹהֵב אֶתְכֶם. עִמְדוּ בְּאַהֲבָתִי. 10 אִם תִּשְׁמְרוּ אֶת מִצְווֹתַי תַּעַמְדוּ בְּאַהֲבָתִי, כְּשֵׁם שֶׁאֲנִי שָׁמַרְתִּי אֶת מִצְווֹת אָבִי וַהֲרֵינִי עוֹמֵד בְּאַהֲבָתוֹ. 11 אֶת הַדְּבָרִים הָאֵלֶּה דִּבַּרְתִּי אֲלֵיכֶם כְּדֵי שֶׁשִּׂמְחָתִי תִּהְיֶה בְּקִרְבְּכֶם וְשִׂמְחַתְכֶם תִּהְיֶה שְׁלֵמָה. 12 זֹאת מִצְוָתִי: אֶהֱבוּ זֶה אֶת זֶה כְּמוֹ שֶׁאֲנִי אֲהַבְתִּי אֶתְכֶם. 13 אֵין אַהֲבָה גְּדוֹלָה מֵאַהֲבָתוֹ שֶׁל הַנּוֹתֵן אֶת נַפְשׁוֹ

friends. 14 You are My friends if you do whatever I command you. 15 No longer do I call you servants, for a servant does not know what his master is doing; but I have called you friends, for all things that I heard from My Father I have made known to you. 16 You did not choose Me, but I chose you and appointed you that you should go and bear fruit, and *that* your fruit should remain, that whatever you ask the Father in My name He may give you. 17 These things I command you, that you love one another.

18 "If the world hates you, you know that it hated Me before *it hated* you. 19 If you were of the world, the world would love its own. Yet because you are not of the world, but I chose you out of the world, therefore the world hates you. 20 Remember the word that I said to you, 'A servant is not greater than his master.' If they persecuted Me, they will also persecute you. If they kept My word, they will keep yours also. 21 But all these things they will do to you for My name's sake, because they do not know Him who sent Me. 22 If I had not come and spoken to them, they would have no sin, but now they have no excuse for their sin. 23 He who hates Me hates My Father also. 24 If I had not done among them the works which no one else did, they would have no sin; but now they have seen and also hated both Me and My Father. 25 But *this happened* that the word might be fulfilled which is written in their law, '*They hated Me without a cause.*'

26 "But when the Helper comes, whom I shall send to you from the Father, the Spirit of truth who proceeds from the Father, He will testify of Me. 27 And you also will bear witness, because you have been with Me from the beginning.

16 "These things I have spoken to you, that you should not be made to stumble. 2 They will put you out of the synagogues; yes, the time is coming that whoever kills you will think that he offers God service. 3 And these things they will do to you because they have not known the Father nor Me. 4 But these things I have told you, that when the time comes, you may remember that I told you of them.

"And these things I did not say to you at the beginning, because I was with you.

5 "But now I go away to Him who sent Me, and none of you asks Me, 'Where are You going?' 6 But because I have said these things to you, sorrow has filled your heart. 7 Nevertheless I tell you the truth. It is to your advantage that I go away; for if I do not go away, the Helper will not come to you; but if I depart, I will send Him to you. 8 And when He has

בְּעַד יְדִידָיו. 14 יְדִידַי אַתֶּם – אִם תַּעֲשׂוּ אֶת אֲשֶׁר אֲנִי מְצַוֶּה אֶתְכֶם. 15 לֹא אוֹסִיף לִקְרֹא לָכֶם עֲבָדִים, כִּי הָעֶבֶד אֵינוֹ יוֹדֵעַ אֶת אֲשֶׁר יַעֲשֶׂה אֲדוֹנָיו. קָרָאתִי לָכֶם 'יְדִידִים', מִפְּנֵי שֶׁהוֹדַעְתִּי לָכֶם אֶת כָּל אֲשֶׁר שָׁמַעְתִּי מֵאֵת אָבִי. 16 לֹא אַתֶּם בְּחַרְתֶּם בִּי, כִּי אִם אֲנִי בָּחַרְתִּי בָּכֶם וְהִפְקַדְתִּי אֶתְכֶם לָלֶכֶת וְלַעֲשׂוֹת פְּרִי, שֶׁפֶּרְיְכֶם יִתְקַיָּם וְכָל אֲשֶׁר תְּבַקְשׁוּ מֵהָאָב בִּשְׁמִי הוּא יִתֵּן לָכֶם. 17 אֶת זֹאת אֲנִי מְצַוֶּה עֲלֵיכֶם: אֶהֱבוּ זֶה אֶת זֶה."

18 "אִם הָעוֹלָם שׂוֹנֵא אֶתְכֶם, דְּעוּ כִּי אוֹתִי שָׂנֵא רִאשׁוֹנָה. 19 אִלּוּ הֱיִיתֶם מִן הָעוֹלָם, הָעוֹלָם הָיָה אוֹהֵב אֶת שֶׁלּוֹ. אֵינְכֶם מִן הָעוֹלָם, כִּי אֲנִי בָּחַרְתִּי אֶתְכֶם מִן הָעוֹלָם. מִשּׁוּם כָּךְ הָעוֹלָם שׂוֹנֵא אֶתְכֶם. 20 זִכְרוּ אֶת הַדָּבָר אֲשֶׁר אָמַרְתִּי לָכֶם: 'עֶבֶד אֵינוֹ גָּדוֹל מֵאֲדוֹנָיו.' אִם אוֹתִי רָדְפוּ, גַּם אֶתְכֶם יִרְדְּפוּ; אִם אֶת דְּבָרִי שָׁמְרוּ, גַּם אֶת דִּבְרֵכֶם יִשְׁמְרוּ. 21 וְאֶת כָּל הַדְּבָרִים הָאֵלֶּה יַעֲשׂוּ לָכֶם בַּעֲבוּר שְׁמִי, כִּי אֵין הֵם יוֹדְעִים אֶת שׁוֹלְחִי. 22 לוּלֵא בָּאתִי וְדִבַּרְתִּי אֲלֵיהֶם לֹא הָיָה בָּהֶם חֵטְא, אֲבָל כָּעֵת אֵין לָהֶם תֵּרוּץ עַל חֲטָאָם. 23 הַשּׂוֹנֵא אוֹתִי שׂוֹנֵא גַּם אֶת אָבִי. 24 לוּלֵא עָשִׂיתִי בְּתוֹכָם אֶת הַמַּעֲשִׂים אֲשֶׁר אִישׁ זוּלָתִי לֹא עָשָׂה, לֹא הָיָה בָּהֶם חֵטְא; אֶלָּא שֶׁעַתָּה הֵם רָאוּ וְגַם שָׂנְאוּ, גַּם אוֹתִי וְגַם אֶת אָבִי; 25 לְקַיֵּם אֶת הַכָּתוּב בְּתוֹרָתָם 'שָׂנְאַת חִנָּם שְׂנֵאוּנִי.' 26 בְּבוֹא הַמְנַחֵם אֲשֶׁר אֶשְׁלַח לָכֶם מֵאֵת הָאָב – רוּחַ הָאֱמֶת הַיּוֹצֵאת מֵאֵת הָאָב – הוּא יָעִיד עָלַי. 27 וְגַם אַתֶּם תָּעִידוּ, מִפְּנֵי שֶׁמִּתְּחִלָּה אַתֶּם אִתִּי.

טז אֶת אֵלֶּה דִּבַּרְתִּי אֲלֵיכֶם כְּדֵי שֶׁלֹּא תִּכָּשְׁלוּ. 2 הִנֵּה יְנַדּוּ אֶתְכֶם וְאַף תָּבוֹא שָׁעָה שֶׁכָּל הַהוֹרֵג אֶתְכֶם יַחְשֹׁב זֹאת לַעֲבוֹדַת אֱלֹהִים. 3 אֶת הַדְּבָרִים הָאֵלֶּה יַעֲשׂוּ לָכֶם כִּי אֵין הֵם יוֹדְעִים אֶת אָבִי, אַף לֹא אוֹתִי. 4 וַאֲנִי הִגַּדְתִּי לָכֶם אֶת הַדְּבָרִים הָאֵלֶּה כְּדֵי שֶׁבְּבוֹא הַשָּׁעָה תִּזְכְּרוּ, שֶׁאֲנִי אָמַרְתִּי לָכֶם. לֹא אָמַרְתִּי לָכֶם אוֹתָם בַּתְּחִלָּה מִשּׁוּם שֶׁהָיִיתִי עִמָּכֶם."

5 "עַכְשָׁו הוֹלֵךְ אֲנִי אֶל שׁוֹלְחִי וְאִישׁ מִכֶּם אֵינוֹ שׁוֹאֵל אוֹתִי 'לְאָן אַתָּה הוֹלֵךְ?'; 6 וּמִפְּנֵי שֶׁדִּבַּרְתִּי אֲלֵיכֶם אֶת הַדְּבָרִים הָאֵלֶּה נִתְמַלֵּא לְבַבְכֶם עֶצֶב. 7 אֲבָל אֲנִי, אֶת הָאֱמֶת אֲנִי אוֹמֵר לָכֶם: מוּטָב לָכֶם שֶׁאֵלֵךְ. אִם לֹא אֵלֵךְ, הַמְנַחֵם לֹא יָבוֹא אֲלֵיכֶם; וְאִם אֵלֵךְ, אֶשְׁלַח אוֹתוֹ אֲלֵיכֶם. 8 כַּאֲשֶׁר יָבוֹא יוֹכִיחַ אֶת

come, He will convict the world of sin, and of righteousness, and of judgment: [9]of sin, because they do not believe in Me; [10]of righteousness, because I go to My Father and you see Me no more; [11]of judgment, because the ruler of this world is judged.

[12]"I still have many things to say to you, but you cannot bear *them* now. [13]However, when He, the Spirit of truth, has come, He will guide you into all truth; for He will not speak on His own *authority,* but whatever He hears He will speak; and He will tell you things to come. [14]He will glorify Me, for He will take of what is Mine and declare *it* to you. [15]All things that the Father has are Mine. Therefore I said that He will take of Mine and declare *it* to you.

[16]"A little while, and you will not see Me; and again a little while, and you will see Me, because I go to the Father."

[17]Then *some* of His disciples said among themselves, "What is this that He says to us, 'A little while, and you will not see Me; and again a little while, and you will see Me'; and, 'because I go to the Father'?" [18]They said therefore, "What is this that He says, 'A little while'? We do not know what He is saying."

[19]Now Jesus knew that they desired to ask Him, and He said to them, "Are you inquiring among yourselves about what I said, 'A little while, and you will not see Me; and again a little while, and you will see Me'? [20]Most assuredly, I say to you that you will weep and lament, but the world will rejoice; and you will be sorrowful, but your sorrow will be turned into joy. [21]A woman, when she is in labor, has sorrow because her hour has come; but as soon as she has given birth to the child, she no longer remembers the anguish, for joy that a human being has been born into the world. [22]Therefore you now have sorrow; but I will see you again and your heart will rejoice, and your joy no one will take from you.

[23]"And in that day you will ask Me nothing. Most assuredly, I say to you, whatever you ask the Father in My name He will give you. [24]Until now you have asked nothing in My name. Ask, and you will receive, that your joy may be full.

[25]"These things I have spoken to you in figurative language; but the time is coming when I will no longer speak to you in figurative language, but I will tell you plainly about the Father. [26]In that day you will ask in My name, and I do not say to you that I shall pray the Father for you; [27]for the Father Himself loves you, because you have loved Me, and have believed that I came forth from God.

הָעוֹלָם עַל חֵטְא וְעַל צֶדֶק וְעַל מִשְׁפָּט; [9]עַל חֵטְא, מִפְּנֵי שֶׁאֵינָם מַאֲמִינִים בִּי; [10]עַל צֶדֶק, כִּי אֵלֵךְ אֶל אָבִי וְלֹא תוֹסִיפוּ לִרְאוֹת אוֹתִי; [11]עַל מִשְׁפָּט, כִּי נִשְׁפַּט שַׂר הָעוֹלָם הַזֶּה.

[12]עוֹד רַבּוֹת יֵשׁ לִי לְהַגִּיד לָכֶם, אֶלָּא שֶׁאַתֶּם אֵינְכֶם יְכוֹלִים לָשֵׂאת זֹאת עַכְשָׁו. [13]אֲבָל הוּא, אֲשֶׁר הוּא רוּחַ הָאֱמֶת, כְּשֶׁיָּבוֹא יַדְרִיךְ אֶתְכֶם אֶל כָּל הָאֱמֶת, כִּי לֹא יְדַבֵּר מֵעַצְמוֹ, אֶלָּא אֶת אֲשֶׁר הוּא שׁוֹמֵעַ יְדַבֵּר וְאֶת הַבָּאוֹת יוֹדִיעַ לָכֶם. [14]הוּא יְכַבְּדֵנִי כִּי מִשֶּׁלִּי יִקַּח וְיוֹדִיעַ לָכֶם. [15]כָּל אֲשֶׁר לְאָבִי שֶׁךְ לִי, עַל כֵּן אָמַרְתִּי כִּי מִשֶּׁלִּי יִקַּח וְיוֹדִיעַ לָכֶם."

[16]"עוֹד מְעַט וְלֹא תוֹסִיפוּ לִרְאוֹתֵנִי וְעוֹד מְעַט וְשׁוּב תִּרְאוּנִי."

[17]כַּמָּה מִתַּלְמִידָיו אָמְרוּ זֶה אֶל זֶה: "מָה הַדָּבָר שֶׁהוּא אוֹמֵר לָנוּ, 'עוֹד מְעַט וְלֹא תִּרְאוּנִי וְעוֹד מְעַט וְשׁוּב תִּרְאוּנִי' וְגַם 'מִשּׁוּם שֶׁאֲנִי הוֹלֵךְ אֶל הָאָב'? [18]הֵם אָמְרוּ: "מַהוּ הָ'עוֹד מְעַט' הַזֶּה שֶׁהוּא אוֹמֵר? אֵינֶנּוּ מְבִינִים מַה הוּא מְדַבֵּר!"

[19]יֵשׁוּעַ יָדַע שֶׁהֵם רוֹצִים לִשְׁאֹל אוֹתוֹ, וּלְפִיכָךְ אָמַר לָהֶם: "עַל עִנְיָן זֶה שׁוֹאֲלִים אַתֶּם אִישׁ אֶת רֵעֵהוּ, עַל שֶׁאָמַרְתִּי 'עוֹד מְעַט וְלֹא תוֹסִיפוּ לִרְאוֹתֵנִי וְעוֹד מְעַט וְשׁוּב תִּרְאוּנִי'? [20]אָמֵן אָמֵן אֲנִי אוֹמֵר לָכֶם, אַתֶּם תִּבְכּוּ וּתְקוֹנְנוּ וְהָעוֹלָם יִשְׂמַח. אַתֶּם תֵּעָצְבוּ, אֲבָל עַצְבוֹנְכֶם יֵהָפֵךְ לְשָׂשׂוֹן. [21]הָאִשָּׁה הַיּוֹלֶדֶת שְׁרוּיָה בְּעֶצֶב, כִּי הִגִּיעָה שְׁעָתָהּ. אֲבָל לְאַחַר שֶׁיָּלְדָה אֶת הַיֶּלֶד אֵין הִיא זוֹכֶרֶת עוֹד אֶת הַהֶבֶל, בְּשֶׁל הַשִּׂמְחָה כִּי נוֹלַד אָדָם לָעוֹלָם. [22]וּבְכֵן גַּם אַתֶּם עֲצוּבִים כָּעֵת, אַךְ שׁוּב אֶרְאֶה אֶתְכֶם וְיָגִיל לְבַבְכֶם, וְאִישׁ לֹא יִקַּח מִכֶּם אֶת שִׂמְחַתְכֶם. [23]בַּיּוֹם הַהוּא לֹא תִשְׁאָלוּנִי דָּבָר. אָמֵן אָמֵן אֲנִי אוֹמֵר לָכֶם, כָּל מַה שֶּׁתְּבַקְשׁוּ מֵאֵת הָאָב בִּשְׁמִי יִתֵּן לָכֶם. [24]עַד כֹּה לֹא בִּקַּשְׁתֶּם דָּבָר בִּשְׁמִי; בַּקְּשׁוּ וּתְקַבְּלוּ לְמַעַן תִּמָּלֵא שִׂמְחַתְכֶם.

[25]אֶת אֵלֶּה דִּבַּרְתִּי אֲלֵיכֶם בִּמְשָׁלִים. תָּבוֹא שָׁעָה שֶׁלֹּא אוֹסִיף לְדַבֵּר אֲלֵיכֶם בִּמְשָׁלִים, אֶלָּא בָּרוּר אֲדַבֵּר אֲלֵיכֶם עַל אָבִי. [26]בַּיּוֹם הַהוּא תְּבַקְשׁוּ בִּשְׁמִי וְאֵינֶנִּי אוֹמֵר לָכֶם שֶׁאֲנִי אַעְתִּיר לָאָב בַּעֲדְכֶם, [27]שֶׁכֵּן הָאָב עַצְמוֹ אוֹהֵב אֶתְכֶם מִפְּנֵי שֶׁאֲהַבְתֶּם אוֹתִי וְהֶאֱמַנְתֶּם כִּי אֲנִי מֵאֵת הָאֱלֹהִים יָצָאתִי.

²⁸ I came forth from the Father and have come into the world. Again, I leave the world and go to the Father."

²⁹ His disciples said to Him, "See, now You are speaking plainly, and using no figure of speech! ³⁰ Now we are sure that You know all things, and have no need that anyone should question You. By this we believe that You came forth from God."

³¹ Jesus answered them, "Do you now believe? ³² Indeed the hour is coming, yes, has now come, that you will be scattered, each to his own, and will leave Me alone. And yet I am not alone, because the Father is with Me. ³³ These things I have spoken to you, that in Me you may have peace. In the world you will have tribulation; but be of good cheer, I have overcome the world."

17 Jesus spoke these words, lifted up His eyes to heaven, and said: "Father, the hour has come. Glorify Your Son, that Your Son also may glorify You, ² as You have given Him authority over all flesh, that He should give eternal life to as many as You have given Him. ³ And this is eternal life, that they may know You, the only true God, and Jesus Christ whom You have sent. ⁴ I have glorified You on the earth. I have finished the work which You have given Me to do. ⁵ And now, O Father, glorify Me together with Yourself, with the glory which I had with You before the world was.

⁶ "I have manifested Your name to the men whom You have given Me out of the world. They were Yours, You gave them to Me, and they have kept Your word. ⁷ Now they have known that all things which You have given Me are from You. ⁸ For I have given to them the words which You have given Me; and they have received *them,* and have known surely that I came forth from You; and they have believed that You sent Me.

⁹ "I pray for them. I do not pray for the world but for those whom You have given Me, for they are Yours. ¹⁰ And all Mine are Yours, and Yours are Mine, and I am glorified in them. ¹¹ Now I am no longer in the world, but these are in the world, and I come to You. Holy Father, keep through Your name those whom You have given Me, that they may be one as We *are.* ¹² While I was with them in the world, I kept them in Your name. Those whom You gave Me I have kept; and none of them is lost except the son of perdition, that the Scripture might be fulfilled. ¹³ But now I come to You, and these things I speak in the world, that they may have My joy fulfilled in themselves. ¹⁴ I have given them Your word; and the world has hated them because they are not of the world, just

²⁸ יָצָאתִי מֵאֵת הָאָב וּבָאתִי אֶל הָעוֹלָם; שׁוּב, עוֹזֵב אֲנִי אֶת הָעוֹלָם וְהוֹלֵךְ אֶל הָאָב."

²⁹ אָמְרוּ תַּלְמִידָיו: "הִנֵּה כָּעֵת אַתָּה מְדַבֵּר בְּרוּרוֹת וְאֵינְךָ אוֹמֵר שׁוּם מָשָׁל. ³⁰ כָּעֵת אָנוּ יוֹדְעִים שֶׁאַתָּה יוֹדֵעַ הַכֹּל וְאֵינְךָ צָרִיךְ שֶׁיִּשְׁאֲלוּ אוֹתְךָ. מִסִּבָּה זֹאת אֲנַחְנוּ מַאֲמִינִים שֶׁיָּצָאתָ מֵאֵת אֱלֹהִים."

³¹ הֵשִׁיב לָהֶם יֵשׁוּעַ: "עַכְשָׁו אַתֶּם מַאֲמִינִים?! ³² הִנֵּה תָּבוֹא שָׁעָה, וְהִיא כְּבָר בָּאָה, שֶׁתִּתְפַּזְּרוּ אִישׁ אִישׁ לִמְקוֹמוֹ וְאוֹתִי תַּעַזְבוּ לְבַדִּי, אֲבָל אֵינֶנִּי לְבַדִּי מִשּׁוּם שֶׁהָאָב אִתִּי. ³³ אָמַרְתִּי לָכֶם אֶת הַדְּבָרִים הָאֵלֶּה כְּדֵי שֶׁבִּי יִהְיֶה לָכֶם שָׁלוֹם. בָּעוֹלָם – צָרָה לָכֶם, אַךְ הִתְעוֹדְדוּ: אֲנִי נִצַּחְתִּי אֶת הָעוֹלָם."

יז זֹאת דִּבֶּר יֵשׁוּעַ. לְאַחַר מִכֵּן נָשָׂא אֶת עֵינָיו הַשָּׁמַיְמָה וְאָמַר: "אָבִי, בָּאָה הַשָּׁעָה. פָּאֵר נָא אֶת בִּנְךָ בְּכָבוֹד לְמַעַן יְפָאֵר הַבֵּן אוֹתְךָ; ² לְמַעַן יִתֵּן חַיֵּי עוֹלָם לְכָל מִי שֶׁנָּתַתָּ לוֹ, כְּפִי הַסַּמְכוּת שֶׁנָּתַתָּ לּוֹ עַל כָּל בָּשָׂר. ³ וְאֵלֶּה הֵם חַיֵּי עוֹלָם: שֶׁיַּכִּירוּ אוֹתְךָ, אֱלֹהֵי הָאֱמֶת לְבַדּוֹ, וְאֶת אֲשֶׁר שָׁלַחְתָּ – אֶת יֵשׁוּעַ הַמָּשִׁיחַ. ⁴ אֲנִי פֵּאַרְתִּיךָ עֲלֵי אֲדָמוֹת, הִשְׁלַמְתִּי אֶת הַמַּעֲשֶׂה שֶׁנָּתַתָּ לִי לַעֲשׂוֹת. ⁵ כָּעֵת אַתָּה, פָּאֲרֵנִי לְיָדְךָ בְּכָבוֹד שֶׁהָיָה לִי לְיָדְךָ בְּטֶרֶם הֱיוֹת הָעוֹלָם.

⁶ גִּלִּיתִי אֶת שִׁמְךָ לָאֲנָשִׁים אֲשֶׁר נָתַתָּ לִי מִן הָעוֹלָם. שֶׁלְּךָ הָיוּ וְלִי נְתַתָּם וְאֶת דְּבָרְךָ שָׁמָרוּ. ⁷ כָּעֵת הֵם יוֹדְעִים שֶׁכָּל אֲשֶׁר נָתַתָּ לִי מִמְּךָ הוּא, ⁸ כִּי דְּבָרֶיךָ אֲשֶׁר נָתַתָּ לִי נָתַתִּי לָהֶם וְהֵם קִבְּלוּ אוֹתָם, וְאָכֵן הִכִּירוּ שֶׁמִּמְּךָ יָצָאתִי וְהֶאֱמִינוּ שֶׁאַתָּה שְׁלַחְתָּנִי.

⁹ אֲנִי מַעְתִּיר בַּעֲדָם; אֵינֶנִּי מַעְתִּיר בְּעַד הָעוֹלָם, אֶלָּא בְּעַד אֵלֶּה שֶׁנָּתַתָּ לִי, כִּי שֶׁלְּךָ הֵם. ¹⁰ כָּל אֲשֶׁר לִי שֶׁלְּךָ הוּא וְשֶׁלְּךָ שֶׁלִּי, וַאֲנִי נִתְפָּאַרְתִּי בָּהֶם. ¹¹ אֲנִי אֵינֶנִּי עוֹד בָּעוֹלָם; הֵם בָּעוֹלָם, וַאֲנִי בָּא אֵלֶיךָ. אָבִי הַקָּדוֹשׁ, שְׁמֹר אוֹתָם בְּשִׁמְךָ אֲשֶׁר נָתַתָּ לִי, לְמַעַן יִהְיוּ אֶחָד כָּמוֹנוּ. ¹² כְּשֶׁהָיִיתִי עִמָּהֶם שָׁמַרְתִּי אוֹתָם בְּשִׁמְךָ אֲשֶׁר נָתַתָּ לִי; שְׁמַרְתִּי וְלֹא אָבַד מֵהֶם אִישׁ זוּלָתִי בֶּן הָאֲבַדּוֹן, וְזֹאת לְקַיֵּם אֶת הַכָּתוּב. ¹³ אֲבָל כָּעֵת אֲנִי בָּא אֵלֶיךָ וּדְבָרִים אֵלֶּה אֲנִי אוֹמֵר בָּעוֹלָם כְּדֵי שֶׁתִּשְׁלַם שִׂמְחָתִי בְּקִרְבָּם. ¹⁴ אֲנִי נָתַתִּי לָהֶם אֶת דְּבָרְךָ וְהָעוֹלָם שָׂנֵא אוֹתָם, כִּי אֵינָם מִן

as I am not of the world. 15 I do not pray that You should take them out of the world, but that You should keep them from the evil one. 16 They are not of the world, just as I am not of the world. 17 Sanctify them by Your truth. Your word is truth. 18 As You sent Me into the world, I also have sent them into the world. 19 And for their sakes I sanctify Myself, that they also may be sanctified by the truth.

20 "I do not pray for these alone, but also for those who will believe in Me through their word; 21 that they all may be one, as You, Father, *are* in Me, and I in You; that they also may be one in Us, that the world may believe that You sent Me. 22 And the glory which You gave Me I have given them, that they may be one just as We are one: 23 I in them, and You in Me; that they may be made perfect in one, and that the world may know that You have sent Me, and have loved them as You have loved Me.

24 "Father, I desire that they also whom You gave Me may be with Me where I am, that they may behold My glory which You have given Me; for You loved Me before the foundation of the world. 25 O righteous Father! The world has not known You, but I have known You; and these have known that You sent Me. 26 And I have declared to them Your name, and will declare *it,* that the love with which You loved Me may be in them, and I in them."

18 When Jesus had spoken these words, He went out with His disciples over the Brook Kidron, where there was a garden, which He and His disciples entered. 2 And Judas, who betrayed Him, also knew the place; for Jesus often met there with His disciples. 3 Then Judas, having received a detachment *of troops,* and officers from the chief priests and Pharisees, came there with lanterns, torches, and weapons. 4 Jesus therefore, knowing all things that would come upon Him, went forward and said to them, "Whom are you seeking?"

5 They answered Him, "Jesus of Nazareth."

Jesus said to them, "I am *He.*" And Judas, who betrayed Him, also stood with them. 6 Now when He said to them, "I am *He,*" they drew back and fell to the ground.

7 Then He asked them again, "Whom are you seeking?"

And they said, "Jesus of Nazareth."

8 Jesus answered, "I have told you that I am *He.* Therefore, if you seek Me, let these go their way," 9 that the saying might be fulfilled which He spoke, "Of those whom You gave Me I have lost none."

הָעוֹלָם, כְּשֵׁם שֶׁאֲנִי אֵינֶנִּי מִן הָעוֹלָם. 15 אֵינֶנִּי מְבַקֵּשׁ שֶׁתִּקָּחֵם מִן הָעוֹלָם, אֶלָּא שֶׁתִּשְׁמְרֵם מִן הָרָע. 16 אֵין הֵם מִן הָעוֹלָם, כְּשֵׁם שֶׁאֲנִי אֵינֶנִּי מִן הָעוֹלָם. 17 קַדֵּשׁ אוֹתָם בָּאֱמֶת: דְּבָרְךָ אֱמֶת. 18 כְּמוֹ שֶׁשְּׁלַחְתָּ אוֹתִי אֶל הָעוֹלָם כֵּן גַּם אֲנִי שָׁלַחְתִּי אוֹתָם אֶל הָעוֹלָם; 19 וּלְמַעֲנָם אֲנִי מַקְדִּישׁ אֶת עַצְמִי, כְּדֵי שֶׁיִּהְיוּ גַם הֵם מְקֻדָּשִׁים בָּאֱמֶת.

20 לֹא רַק בַּעֲדָם אֲנִי מְבַקֵּשׁ, אֶלָּא גַּם בְּעַד הַמַּאֲמִינִים בִּי עַל־יְסוֹד דְּבָרָם. 21 יִהְיוּ נָא כֻלָּם אֶחָד; כְּמוֹ שֶׁאַתָּה, אָבִי, בִּי וַאֲנִי בְּךָ, שֶׁיִּהְיוּ גַם הֵם בָּנוּ, כְּדֵי שֶׁיַּאֲמִין הָעוֹלָם כִּי אַתָּה שְׁלַחְתָּנִי. 22 אֲנִי נָתַתִּי לָהֶם אֶת הַכָּבוֹד שֶׁנָּתַתָּ לִי, לְמַעַן יִהְיוּ אֶחָד כְּמוֹ שֶׁאֲנַחְנוּ אֶחָד. 23 אֲנִי בָּהֶם וְאַתָּה בִּי כְּדֵי שֶׁיֻּשְׁלְמוּ לִהְיוֹתָם אֶחָד, לְמַעַן יֵדַע הָעוֹלָם כִּי אַתָּה שְׁלַחְתָּנִי וַאֲהַבְתָּ אוֹתָם כְּמוֹ שֶׁאֲהַבְתָּ אוֹתִי. 24 אָבִי, אֵלֶּה שֶׁנָּתַתָּם לִי רְצוֹנִי שֶׁיִּהְיוּ גַם הֵם אִתִּי בַּאֲשֶׁר אֲנִי, לְמַעַן יֶחֱזוּ בִּכְבוֹדִי אֲשֶׁר נָתַתָּ לִי, כִּי אֲהַבְתָּ אוֹתִי מִלִּפְנֵי הִוָּסֵד תֵּבֵל. 25 אָבִי הַצַּדִּיק, הָעוֹלָם לֹא הִכִּירְךָ, אֲבָל אֲנִי הִכַּרְתִּיךָ, וְאֵלֶּה הִכִּירוּ שֶׁאַתָּה שְׁלַחְתָּנִי. 26 הוֹדַעְתִּי לָהֶם אֶת שִׁמְךָ וְאוֹסִיף לְהוֹדִיעַ, כְּדֵי שֶׁתִּהְיֶה בָּהֶם הָאַהֲבָה אֲשֶׁר אֲהַבְתַּנִי וַאֲנִי אֶהְיֶה בָּהֶם."

יח אַחֲרֵי שֶׁאָמַר אֶת הַדְּבָרִים הָאֵלֶּה יָצָא יֵשׁוּעַ עִם תַּלְמִידָיו אֶל מֵעֵבֶר לְנַחַל קִדְרוֹן וְנִכְנַס עִם תַּלְמִידָיו אֶל גַּן אֲשֶׁר הָיָה שָׁם. 2 גַּם יְהוּדָה הַמַּסְגִּיר אוֹתוֹ הִכִּיר אֶת הַמָּקוֹם, שֶׁכֵּן פְּעָמִים רַבּוֹת נוֹעַד שָׁם יֵשׁוּעַ עִם תַּלְמִידָיו. 3 לָקַח יְהוּדָה קְבוּצַת חַיָּלִים וְגַם מְשָׁרְתִים מֵאֵת רָאשֵׁי הַכֹּהֲנִים וְהַפְּרוּשִׁים, וּבָא לְשָׁם בְּלַפִּידִים וּבִמְנוֹרוֹת וּבִכְלֵי נֶשֶׁק. 4 יֵשׁוּעַ, שֶׁיָּדַע כָּל מַה שֶּׁיָּבוֹא עָלָיו, יָצָא וְאָמַר לָהֶם: "אֶת מִי אַתֶּם מְחַפְּשִׂים?"

5 הֵשִׁיבוּ לוֹ: "אֶת יֵשׁוּעַ מִנָּצְרַת."

אָמַר לָהֶם: "אֲנִי הוּא". גַּם יְהוּדָה הַמַּסְגִּיר אוֹתוֹ הָיָה שָׁם. 6 כַּאֲשֶׁר אָמַר לָהֶם יֵשׁוּעַ "אֲנִי הוּא", נָסוֹגוּ לְאָחוֹר וְנָפְלוּ אַרְצָה.

7 שׁוּב שָׁאַל אוֹתָם: "אֶת מִי אַתֶּם מְחַפְּשִׂים?" הֵשִׁיבוּ: "אֶת יֵשׁוּעַ מִנָּצְרַת."

8 עָנָה יֵשׁוּעַ: "אָמַרְתִּי לָכֶם שֶׁאֲנִי הוּא. לָכֵן אִם אוֹתִי אַתֶּם מְחַפְּשִׂים, הַנִּיחוּ לָאֵלֶּה לָלֶכֶת" – 9 לְקַיֵּם אֶת הַדָּבָר שֶׁאָמַר, "מֵאֵלֶּה אֲשֶׁר נָתַתָּ לִי לֹא אָבַד לִי אִישׁ".

10 Then Simon Peter, having a sword, drew it and struck the high priest's servant, and cut off his right ear. The servant's name was Malchus.

11 So Jesus said to Peter, "Put your sword into the sheath. Shall I not drink the cup which My Father has given Me?"

12 Then the detachment *of troops* and the captain and the officers of the Jews arrested Jesus and bound Him. 13 And they led Him away to Annas first, for he was the father-in-law of Caiaphas who was high priest that year. 14 Now it was Caiaphas who advised the Jews that it was expedient that one man should die for the people.

15 And Simon Peter followed Jesus, and so *did* another disciple. Now that disciple was known to the high priest, and went with Jesus into the courtyard of the high priest. 16 But Peter stood at the door outside. Then the other disciple, who was known to the high priest, went out and spoke to her who kept the door, and brought Peter in. 17 Then the servant girl who kept the door said to Peter, "You are not also *one* of this Man's disciples, are you?"

He said, "I am not."

18 Now the servants and officers who had made a fire of coals stood there, for it was cold, and they warmed themselves. And Peter stood with them and warmed himself.

19 The high priest then asked Jesus about His disciples and His doctrine.

20 Jesus answered him, "I spoke openly to the world. I always taught in synagogues and in the temple, where the Jews always meet, and in secret I have said nothing. 21 Why do you ask Me? Ask those who have heard Me what I said to them. Indeed they know what I said."

22 And when He had said these things, one of the officers who stood by struck Jesus with the palm of his hand, saying, "Do You answer the high priest like that?"

23 Jesus answered him, "If I have spoken evil, bear witness of the evil; but if well, why do you strike Me?"

24 Then Annas sent Him bound to Caiaphas the high priest.

25 Now Simon Peter stood and warmed himself. Therefore they said to him, "You are not also *one* of His disciples, are you?"

He denied *it* and said, "I am not!"

26 One of the servants of the high priest, a relative *of him* whose ear Peter cut off, said, "Did I not see you in the garden with Him?" 27 Peter then denied again; and immediately a rooster crowed.

10 אָז שָׁלַף שִׁמְעוֹן כֵּיפָא חֶרֶב שֶׁהָיְתָה אֶצְלוֹ, הִכָּה בְּעַבְדּוֹ שֶׁל הַכֹּהֵן הַגָּדוֹל וְקִצֵּץ אֶת אָזְנוֹ הַיְמָנִית. שֵׁם הָעֶבֶד הָיָה מֶלֶךְ. 11 אָמַר יֵשׁוּעַ אֶל כֵּיפָא: "הָשֵׁב אֶת הַחֶרֶב אֶל נְדָנָהּ. הַאִם לֹא אֶשְׁתֶּה אֶת הַכּוֹס שֶׁנָּתַן לִי הָאָב?"

12 הַחַיָּלִים וּמְפַקְּדָם עִם הַמְשָׁרְתִים מִטַּעַם רָאשֵׁי הַיְּהוּדִים אָחֲזוּ בְּיֵשׁוּעַ וְקָשְׁרוּ אוֹתוֹ. 13 הֵם הוֹלִיכוּהוּ תְּחִלָּה אֶל חָנָן, שֶׁהָיָה חוֹתְנוֹ שֶׁל קַיָּפָא הַכֹּהֵן הַגָּדוֹל בְּאוֹתָה שָׁנָה. 14 קַיָּפָא הוּא שֶׁיָּעַץ לְרָאשֵׁי הַכֹּהֲנִים וְלַפְּרוּשִׁים כִּי מוּטָב שֶׁיָּמוּת אִישׁ אֶחָד בְּעַד הָעָם.

15 שִׁמְעוֹן כֵּיפָא וְתַלְמִיד אַחֵר הָלְכוּ אַחֲרֵי יֵשׁוּעַ. אוֹתוֹ תַּלְמִיד הָיָה מֻכָּר לַכֹּהֵן הַגָּדוֹל וְהוּא נִכְנַס עִם יֵשׁוּעַ לַחֲצַר הַכֹּהֵן הַגָּדוֹל, 16 אֲבָל כֵּיפָא עָמַד בַּחוּץ עַל־יַד הַשַּׁעַר. יָצָא הַתַּלְמִיד הָאַחֵר, הַמֻּכָּר לַכֹּהֵן הַגָּדוֹל, דִּבֵּר עִם הַשּׁוֹעֶרֶת וְהִכְנִיס אֶת כֵּיפָא.

17 אָמְרָה הַמְשָׁרֶתֶת הַשּׁוֹעֶרֶת אֶל כֵּיפָא: "הֲרֵי גַּם אַתָּה מִתַּלְמִידֵי הָאִישׁ הַזֶּה!"

הוּא הֵשִׁיב: "לֹא, אֵינֶנִּי".

18 אוֹתָהּ שָׁעָה עָמְדוּ הָעֲבָדִים וְהַמְשָׁרְתִים לְיַד הַמְּדוּרָה שֶׁהִדְלִיקוּ בִּגְלַל הַקֹּר, וְהִתְחַמְּמוּ. גַּם כֵּיפָא עָמַד אִתָּם וְהִתְחַמֵּם.

19 שָׁאַל הַכֹּהֵן הַגָּדוֹל אֶת יֵשׁוּעַ עַל־אוֹדוֹת תַּלְמִידָיו וְתוֹרָתוֹ. 20 הֵשִׁיב לוֹ יֵשׁוּעַ: "אֲנִי בְּגָלוּי דִּבַּרְתִּי אֶל הָעוֹלָם. תָּמִיד לִמַּדְתִּי בְּבֵית כְּנֶסֶת וּבְבֵית הַמִּקְדָּשׁ, בַּמָּקוֹם שֶׁנִּקְהָלִים כָּל הַיְּהוּדִים, וְלֹא דִבַּרְתִּי דָבָר בַּסֵּתֶר. 21 מַדּוּעַ אַתָּה שׁוֹאֵל אוֹתִי? שְׁאַל נָא אֶת הָאֲנָשִׁים שֶׁשָּׁמְעוּ, מַה דִּבַּרְתִּי אֲלֵיהֶם. הֵם יוֹדְעִים מַה שֶּׁאֲנִי אָמַרְתִּי."

22 לְאַחַר שֶׁאָמַר זֹאת, סָטַר אֶחָד הַמְשָׁרְתִים הָעוֹמְדִים שָׁם עַל לֶחְיוֹ שֶׁל יֵשׁוּעַ וְאָמַר: "כָּכָה אַתָּה עוֹנֶה לַכֹּהֵן הַגָּדוֹל?"

23 הֵשִׁיב לוֹ יֵשׁוּעַ: "אִם דִּבַּרְתִּי רָעָה, הָעֵד עַל הָרָעָה. אַךְ אִם נְכוֹנָה, מַדּוּעַ תַּכֵּנִי?"

24 אָז שָׁלַח אוֹתוֹ חָנָן אָסוּר בַּאֲזִקִּים אֶל קַיָּפָא הַכֹּהֵן הַגָּדוֹל.

25 כַּאֲשֶׁר שִׁמְעוֹן כֵּיפָא הָיָה עוֹמֵד וּמִתְחַמֵּם, אָמְרוּ לוֹ: "הֲלֹא גַּם אַתָּה מִתַּלְמִידָיו?" הַכְחִישׁ וְאָמַר: "לֹא, אֵינֶנִּי".

26 אֶחָד מֵעַבְדֵי הַכֹּהֵן הַגָּדוֹל, קָרוֹב מִשְׁפַּחְתָּה לְזֶה אֲשֶׁר כֵּיפָא קִצֵּץ אֶת אָזְנוֹ, אָמַר: "הֲרֵי רְאִיתִיךָ בַּגַּן אִתּוֹ!" 27 שׁוּב הִכְחִישׁ כֵּיפָא וּמִיָּד קָרָא הַתַּרְנְגוֹל.

²⁸Then they led Jesus from Caiaphas to the Praetorium, and it was early morning. But they themselves did not go into the Praetorium, lest they should be defiled, but that they might eat the Passover. ²⁹Pilate then went out to them and said, "What accusation do you bring against this Man?"

³⁰They answered and said to him, "If He were not an evildoer, we would not have delivered Him up to you."

³¹Then Pilate said to them, "You take Him and judge Him according to your law."

Therefore the Jews said to him, "It is not lawful for us to put anyone to death," ³²that the saying of Jesus might be fulfilled which He spoke, signifying by what death He would die.

³³Then Pilate entered the Praetorium again, called Jesus, and said to Him, "Are You the King of the Jews?"

³⁴Jesus answered him, "Are you speaking for yourself about this, or did others tell you this concerning Me?"

³⁵Pilate answered, "Am I a Jew? Your own nation and the chief priests have delivered You to me. What have You done?"

³⁶Jesus answered, "My kingdom is not of this world. If My kingdom were of this world, My servants would fight, so that I should not be delivered to the Jews; but now My kingdom is not from here."

³⁷Pilate therefore said to Him, "Are You a king then?"

Jesus answered, "You say *rightly* that I am a king. For this cause I was born, and for this cause I have come into the world, that I should bear witness to the truth. Everyone who is of the truth hears My voice."

³⁸Pilate said to Him, "What is truth?" And when he had said this, he went out again to the Jews, and said to them, "I find no fault in Him at all.

³⁹"But you have a custom that I should release someone to you at the Passover. Do you therefore want me to release to you the King of the Jews?"

⁴⁰Then they all cried again, saying, "Not this Man, but Barabbas!" Now Barabbas was a robber.

19 So then Pilate took Jesus and scourged *Him*. ²And the soldiers twisted a crown of thorns and put *it* on His head, and they put on Him a purple robe. ³Then they said, "Hail, King of the Jews!" And they struck Him with their hands.

⁴Pilate then went out again, and said to them, "Behold, I am bringing Him out to you, that you may know that I find no fault in Him."

---

²⁸ בַּבֹּקֶר הִשְׁכֵּם הוֹלִיכוּ אֶת יֵשׁוּעַ מִבֵּית קַיָּפָא אֶל בֵּית הַמִּמְשָׁל. הֵם לֹא נִכְנְסוּ לְבֵית הַמִּמְשָׁל, פֶּן יִטָּמְאוּ וְלֹא יוּכְלוּ לֶאֱכֹל אֶת הַפֶּסַח. ²⁹ עַל כֵּן יָצָא פִּילָטוֹס אֲלֵיהֶם וְשָׁאַל: "בַּמֶּה אַתֶּם מַאֲשִׁימִים אֶת הָאִישׁ הַזֶּה?"

³⁰ עָנוּ וְאָמְרוּ לוֹ: "לוּלֵא הָיָה זֶה עוֹשֶׂה רָעָה, לֹא הָיִינוּ מוֹסְרִים אוֹתוֹ אֵלֶיךָ."

³¹ אָמַר לָהֶם פִּילָטוֹס: "קְחוּ אוֹתוֹ וְשִׁפְטוּהוּ עַל־פִּי תּוֹרַתְכֶם." אָמְרוּ לוֹ רָאשֵׁי הַכֹּהֲנִים: "אֵין לָנוּ רְשׁוּת לְהָמִית אִישׁ." – ³² זֹאת לְמַעַן יִתְקַיֵּם הַדָּבָר שֶׁאָמַר יֵשׁוּעַ בְּרָמְזוֹ אֵיזֶה מָוֶת הָיָה עָתִיד לָמוּת.

³³ פִּילָטוֹס נִכְנַס בַּחֲזָרָה לְבֵית הַמִּמְשָׁל, קָרָא לְיֵשׁוּעַ וְשָׁאַל אוֹתוֹ: "אַתָּה מֶלֶךְ הַיְּהוּדִים?"

³⁴ הֵשִׁיב יֵשׁוּעַ: "הַאִם מִלְּבָד אַתָּה אוֹמֵר זֹאת אוֹ שֶׁאֲחֵרִים אָמְרוּ לְךָ עַל־אוֹדוֹתַי?"

³⁵ עָנָה פִּילָטוֹס: "וְכִי יְהוּדִי אֲנִי? הֲרֵי עַמְּךָ וְרָאשֵׁי הַכֹּהֲנִים מָסְרוּ אוֹתְךָ אֵלַי. מֶה עָשִׂיתָ?"

³⁶ הֵשִׁיב יֵשׁוּעַ: "מַלְכוּתִי אֵינֶנָּה מִן הָעוֹלָם הַזֶּה. אִלּוּ הָיְתָה מַלְכוּתִי מִן הָעוֹלָם הַזֶּה, הָיוּ מְשָׁרְתַי נִלְחָמִים שֶׁלֹּא אֶמָּסֵר לְרָאשֵׁי הַיְּהוּדִים; אֶלָּא שֶׁכָּעֵת מַלְכוּתִי אֵינֶנָּה מִפֹּה."

³⁷ אָמַר לוֹ פִּילָטוֹס: "אִם כֵּן, אַתָּה מֶלֶךְ?" עָנָה יֵשׁוּעַ: "אַתָּה אוֹמֵר שֶׁאֲנִי מֶלֶךְ; לְכָךְ אֲנִי נוֹלַדְתִּי וּלְשֵׁם כָּךְ בָּאתִי לָעוֹלָם, כְּדֵי שֶׁאָעִיד עַל הָאֱמֶת. כָּל אֲשֶׁר הוּא מִן הָאֱמֶת שׁוֹמֵעַ לְקוֹלִי."

³⁸ אָמַר לוֹ פִּילָטוֹס: "מַהִי אֱמֶת?" לְאַחַר שֶׁאָמַר זֹאת יָצָא שֵׁנִית אֶל רָאשֵׁי הַכֹּהֲנִים וְאָמַר לָהֶם: "אֵינֶנִּי מוֹצֵא בּוֹ שׁוּם אַשְׁמָה. ³⁹ אֲבָל מִנְהָג הוּא אֶצְלְכֶם שֶׁאֲשַׁחְרֵר לָכֶם אֶחָד בְּפֶסַח. רְצוֹנְכֶם שֶׁאֲשַׁחְרֵר לָכֶם אֶת מֶלֶךְ הַיְּהוּדִים?"

⁴⁰ הֵשִׁיבוּ וְצָעֲקוּ: "לֹא אֶת זֶה אֶלָּא אֶת בַּר־אַבָּא!" וּבַר־אַבָּא הָיָה שׁוֹדֵד.

יט אָז לָקַח פִּילָטוֹס אֶת יֵשׁוּעַ וְהִלְקָה אוֹתוֹ. ² הַחַיָּלִים שָׂמוּ עַל רֹאשׁוֹ עֲטֶרֶת שֶׁקָּלְעוּ מִקּוֹצִים וְהִלְבִּישׁוּהוּ גְּלִימַת אַרְגָּמָן. ³ נִגְּשׁוּ אֵלָיו וְאָמְרוּ: "שָׁלוֹם לְךָ מֶלֶךְ הַיְּהוּדִים!" וְסָטְרוּ עַל פָּנָיו.

⁴ שׁוּב יָצָא פִּילָטוֹס וְאָמַר לָהֶם: "רְאוּ! אֲנִי מוֹצִיא אוֹתוֹ אֲלֵיכֶם לְמַעַן תֵּדְעוּ שֶׁאֵינֶנִּי מוֹצֵא בּוֹ שׁוּם אַשְׁמָה."

⁵Then Jesus came out, wearing the crown of thorns and the purple robe. And *Pilate* said to them, "Behold the Man!"

⁶Therefore, when the chief priests and officers saw Him, they cried out, saying, "Crucify *Him*, crucify *Him!*"

Pilate said to them, "You take Him and crucify *Him*, for I find no fault in Him."

⁷The Jews answered him, "We have a law, and according to our law He ought to die, because He made Himself the Son of God."

⁸Therefore, when Pilate heard that saying, he was the more afraid, ⁹and went again into the Praetorium, and said to Jesus, "Where are You from?" But Jesus gave him no answer.

¹⁰Then Pilate said to Him, "Are You not speaking to me? Do You not know that I have power to crucify You, and power to release You?"

¹¹Jesus answered, "You could have no power at all against Me unless it had been given you from above. Therefore the one who delivered Me to you has the greater sin."

¹²From then on Pilate sought to release Him, but the Jews cried out, saying, "If you let this Man go, you are not Caesar's friend. Whoever makes himself a king speaks against Caesar."

¹³When Pilate therefore heard that saying, he brought Jesus out and sat down in the judgment seat in a place that is called *The* Pavement, but in Hebrew, Gabbatha. ¹⁴Now it was the Preparation Day of the Passover, and about the sixth hour. And he said to the Jews, "Behold your King!"

¹⁵But they cried out, "Away with *Him*, away with *Him!* Crucify Him!"

Pilate said to them, "Shall I crucify your King?"

The chief priests answered, "We have no king but Caesar!"

¹⁶Then he delivered Him to them to be crucified. Then they took Jesus and led *Him* away.

¹⁷And He, bearing His cross, went out to a place called *the Place* of a Skull, which is called in Hebrew, Golgotha, ¹⁸where they crucified Him, and two others with Him, one on either side, and Jesus in the center. ¹⁹Now Pilate wrote a title and put *it* on the cross. And the writing was:

JESUS OF NAZARETH,
THE KING OF THE JEWS.

²⁰Then many of the Jews read this title, for the place where Jesus was crucified was near the city; and it was written in Hebrew, Greek, *and* Latin.

²¹Therefore the chief priests of the Jews said to Pilate, "Do not write, 'The King of the Jews,' but, 'He said, "I am the King of the Jews."'"

⁵יָצָא יֵשׁוּעַ לָבוּשׁ גְּלִימַת הָאַרְגָּמָן וְעַל רֹאשׁוֹ עֲטֶרֶת הַקּוֹצִים. "הִנֵּה הָאִישׁ!" אָמַר לָהֶם פִּילָטוֹס. ⁶כְּשֶׁרָאוּ אוֹתוֹ רָאשֵׁי הַכֹּהֲנִים וְהַמְשָׁרְתִים, הֵחֵלּוּ צוֹעֲקִים: "צְלֹב! צְלֹב!" ⁷אָמַר לָהֶם פִּילָטוֹס: "קְחוּהוּ אַתֶּם וְצִלְבוּ אוֹתוֹ, כִּי אֲנִי אֵינֶנִּי מוֹצֵא בּוֹ אַשְׁמָה." ⁷הֵשִׁיבוּ לוֹ: "תּוֹרָה יֵשׁ לָנוּ וְעַל־פִּי הַתּוֹרָה הוּא חַיָּב מִיתָה, כִּי עָשָׂה עַצְמוֹ בֶּן־אֱלֹהִים." ⁸כְּשֶׁשָּׁמַע פִּילָטוֹס אֶת הַדָּבָר הַזֶּה גָּבַר פַּחְדּוֹ. ⁹הוּא נִכְנַס שׁוּב לְבֵית הַמִּמְשָׁל וְשָׁאַל אֶת יֵשׁוּעַ: "מֵאַיִן אַתָּה?" אַךְ יֵשׁוּעַ לֹא עָנָה לוֹ. ¹⁰אָמַר לוֹ פִּילָטוֹס: "אֵלַי לֹא תְדַבֵּר? הַאֵינְךָ יוֹדֵעַ שֶׁיֵּשׁ לִי סַמְכוּת לְשַׁחְרֵר אוֹתְךָ וְיֵשׁ לִי סַמְכוּת לִצְלֹב אוֹתְךָ?" ¹¹הֵשִׁיב לוֹ יֵשׁוּעַ: "לֹא הָיְתָה לְךָ שׁוּם סַמְכוּת עָלַי לוּלֵא נִתַּן לְךָ מִלְמַעְלָה. לָכֵן גָּדוֹל יוֹתֵר עֲוֹנוֹ שֶׁל הַמּוֹסֵר אוֹתִי אֵלֶיךָ." ¹²מֵרֶגַע זֶה נִסָּה פִּילָטוֹס לְשַׁחְרֵר אוֹתוֹ, אֶלָּא שֶׁהַיְּהוּדִים צָעֲקוּ בְּאָמְרָם: "אִם תְּשַׁחְרֵר אֶת זֶה אֵינְךָ יְדִיד הַקֵּיסָר! כָּל הָעוֹשֶׂה עַצְמוֹ מֶלֶךְ מִתְקוֹמֵם נֶגֶד הַקֵּיסָר!" ¹³כַּאֲשֶׁר שָׁמַע פִּילָטוֹס אֶת הַמִּלִּים הָאֵלֶּה, הוֹצִיא אֶת יֵשׁוּעַ וְיָשַׁב עַל כֵּס הַמִּשְׁפָּט בְּמָקוֹם מְרֻצָּף אֲבָנִים הַנִּקְרָא "גַּבְּתָא". ¹⁴אוֹתוֹ יוֹם הָיָה עֶרֶב פֶּסַח וְהַשָּׁעָה הַשִּׁשִּׁית בְּעֶרֶךְ. אָמַר לָהֶם: "הִנֵּה מַלְכְּכֶם!" ¹⁵אַךְ הַלָּלוּ צָעֲקוּ: "קַח, קַח וּצְלֹב אוֹתוֹ!" אָמַר לָהֶם פִּילָטוֹס: "הַאֶצְלֹב אֶת מַלְכְּכֶם?" הֵשִׁיבוּ רָאשֵׁי הַכֹּהֲנִים: "אֵין לָנוּ מֶלֶךְ זוּלָתִי הַקֵּיסָר!" ¹⁶אָז מָסַר אוֹתוֹ לָהֶם לְצָלְבוֹ. לָקְחוּ אֶת יֵשׁוּעַ, ¹⁷וּכְשֶׁהוּא נוֹשֵׂא אֶת צְלָבוֹ יָצָא אֶל הַמָּקוֹם הַנִּקְרָא נָלְגָּתָא, כְּלוֹמַר מְקוֹם הַגֻּלְגֹּלֶת. ¹⁸שָׁם צָלְבוּ אוֹתוֹ עִם שְׁנַיִם אֲחֵרִים, הָאֶחָד מִזֶּה וְהַשֵּׁנִי מִזֶּה וְיֵשׁוּעַ בֵּינֵיהֶם. ¹⁹פִּילָטוֹס כָּתַב שֶׁלֶט וְקָבַע אוֹתוֹ עַל הַצְּלָב, וְזֶה לְשׁוֹן הַכָּתוּב: "יֵשׁוּעַ מִנָּצְרַת, מֶלֶךְ הַיְּהוּדִים." ²⁰אֶת הַכְּתֹבֶת הַזֹּאת קָרְאוּ יְהוּדִים רַבִּים, כִּי מְקוֹם צְלִיבָתוֹ שֶׁל יֵשׁוּעַ הָיָה קָרוֹב לָעִיר, וּכְתוּבָה הָיְתָה בְּעִבְרִית, בְּרוֹמִית וּבְיָוָנִית. ²¹אָמְרוּ רָאשֵׁי הַכֹּהֲנִים אֶל פִּילָטוֹס: "אַל נָא תִּכְתֹּב 'מֶלֶךְ הַיְּהוּדִים', אֶלָּא 'זֶה אָמַר: אֲנִי מֶלֶךְ הַיְּהוּדִים'."

²²Pilate answered, "What I have written, I have written."

²³Then the soldiers, when they had crucified Jesus, took His garments and made four parts, to each soldier a part, and also the tunic. Now the tunic was without seam, woven from the top in one piece. ²⁴They said therefore among themselves, "Let us not tear it, but cast lots for it, whose it shall be," that the Scripture might be fulfilled which says:

"They divided My garments among them,
And for My clothing they cast lots."

Therefore the soldiers did these things.

²⁵Now there stood by the cross of Jesus His mother, and His mother's sister, Mary the *wife of* Clopas, and Mary Magdalene. ²⁶When Jesus therefore saw His mother, and the disciple whom He loved standing by, He said to His mother, "Woman, behold your son!" ²⁷Then He said to the disciple, "Behold your mother!" And from that hour that disciple took her to his own *home.*

²⁸After this, Jesus, knowing that all things were now accomplished, that the Scripture might be fulfilled, said, "I thirst!" ²⁹Now a vessel full of sour wine was sitting there; and they filled a sponge with sour wine, put *it* on hyssop, and put *it* to His mouth. ³⁰So when Jesus had received the sour wine, He said, "It is finished!" And bowing His head, He gave up His spirit.

³¹Therefore, because it was the Preparation *Day,* that the bodies should not remain on the cross on the Sabbath (for that Sabbath was a high day), the Jews asked Pilate that their legs might be broken, and *that* they might be taken away. ³²Then the soldiers came and broke the legs of the first and of the other who was crucified with Him. ³³But when they came to Jesus and saw that He was already dead, they did not break His legs. ³⁴But one of the soldiers pierced His side with a spear, and immediately blood and water came out. ³⁵And he who has seen has testified, and his testimony is true; and he knows that he is telling the truth, so that you may believe. ³⁶For these things were done that the Scripture should be fulfilled, "Not one of His bones shall be broken." ³⁷And again another Scripture says, "They shall look on Him whom they pierced."

³⁸After this, Joseph of Arimathea, being a disciple of Jesus, but secretly, for fear of the Jews, asked Pilate that he might take away the body of Jesus; and Pilate gave *him* permission. So he came and took the body of Jesus. ³⁹And Nicodemus, who at first came to Jesus by night, also came, bringing a mixture of myrrh and aloes, about a hundred pounds. ⁴⁰Then they took the body of Jesus, and

²²הֵשִׁיב פִּילָטוֹס: "מַה שֶּׁכָּתַבְתִּי כָּתַבְתִּי."
²³הַחַיָּלִים שֶׁצָּלְבוּ אֶת יֵשׁוּעַ לָקְחוּ אֶת בְּגָדָיו וְחִלְּקוּם לְאַרְבָּעָה חֲלָקִים, חֵלֶק אֶחָד לְכָל חַיָּל. הֵם לָקְחוּ גַּם אֶת הַכֻּתֹּנֶת, אֶלָּא שֶׁהִיא הָיְתָה לְלֹא תֶּפֶר, אֲרִיגָה רְצוּפָה מִלְמַעְלָה לְמַטָּה. ²⁴אָמְרוּ זֶה אֶל זֶה: "אַל נָא נִקְרַע אוֹתָהּ, אֶלָּא נַפִּיל עָלֶיהָ גּוֹרָל לְמִי תִּהְיֶה." זֶה הָיָה כְּדֵי שֶׁיִּתְקַיֵּם הַכָּתוּב: "יְחַלְּקוּ בְּגָדַי לָהֶם וְעַל־לְבוּשִׁי יַפִּילוּ גוֹרָל", וְאָמְנָם כָּךְ עָשׂוּ הַחַיָּלִים.
²⁵עַל־יַד צְלָב יֵשׁוּעַ עָמְדוּ אִמּוֹ וַאֲחוֹת אִמּוֹ, מִרְיָם אֵשֶׁת קְלוֹפָה וּמִרְיָם הַמַּגְדָּלִית. ²⁶כְּשֶׁרָאָה יֵשׁוּעַ אֶת אִמּוֹ וְאֶת הַתַּלְמִיד הָאָהוּב עָלָיו עוֹמֵד לְיָדָהּ, אָמַר לְאִמּוֹ: "אִשָּׁה, הִנֵּה בְּנֵךְ." ²⁷לְאַחַר מִכֵּן אָמַר לַתַּלְמִיד: "הִנֵּה אִמֶּךָ." מֵאוֹתָהּ שָׁעָה אָסַף אוֹתָהּ הַתַּלְמִיד לְבֵיתוֹ.
²⁸יֵשׁוּעַ יָדַע כִּי עַתָּה כְּבָר נִשְׁלַם הַכֹּל, וּכְדֵי שֶׁיִּתְקַיֵּם הַכָּתוּב אָמַר: "אֲנִי צָמֵא."
²⁹כְּלִי מָלֵא חֹמֶץ הָיָה מֻנָּח שָׁם. שָׁמוּ סְפוֹג רָוּוּי חֹמֶץ עַל אֵזוֹב, וְהִגִּישׁוּ אוֹתוֹ אֶל פִּיו. ³⁰אַחֲרֵי שֶׁקִּבֵּל אֶת הַחֹמֶץ אָמַר יֵשׁוּעַ: "נִשְׁלַם", וּבְהַרְכִּינוֹ רֹאשׁוֹ מָסַר אֶת רוּחוֹ.
³¹מִכֵּיוָן שֶׁאוֹתוֹ יוֹם הָיָה עֶרֶב שַׁבָּת, בִּקְשׁוּ רָאשֵׁי הַיְּהוּדִים מִפִּילָטוֹס לְצַוּוֹת לִשְׁבֹּר אֶת שׁוֹקֵיהֶם שֶׁל הַנִּצְלָבִים וּלְהָסִיר אֶת הַגּוּפוֹת, כְּדֵי שֶׁלֹּא תִּשָּׁאַרְנָה עַל הַצְּלָב בְּשַׁבָּת, כִּי גָּדוֹל הָיָה אוֹתוֹ יוֹם שַׁבָּת. ³²לְפִיכָךְ בָּאוּ הַחַיָּלִים וְשָׁבְרוּ אֶת הַשּׁוֹקַיִם שֶׁל הָרִאשׁוֹן וְגַם שֶׁל הַשֵּׁנִי שֶׁנִּצְלַב אִתּוֹ. ³³כְּשֶׁבָּאוּ אֶל יֵשׁוּעַ וְרָאוּ שֶׁהוּא כְּבָר מֵת, לֹא שָׁבְרוּ אֶת שׁוֹקָיו. ³⁴אוּלָם אַחַד הַחַיָּלִים דָּקַר אֶת צִדּוֹ בְּרֹמַח וּמִיָּד יָצְאוּ דָּם וּמַיִם. ³⁵זֶה שֶׁרָאָה הֵעִיד – וְעֵדוּתוֹ נֶאֱמָנָה וְהוּא יוֹדֵעַ שֶׁהוּא מְדַבֵּר אֱמֶת – לְמַעַן תַּאֲמִינוּ גַּם אַתֶּם. ³⁶הַדְּבָרִים הָאֵלֶּה אֵרְעוּ כְּדֵי שֶׁיִּתְקַיֵּם הַכָּתוּב: "וְעֶצֶם לֹא־תִשְׁבְּרוּ בוֹ." ³⁷וְעוֹד כָּתוּב אַחֵר אוֹמֵר: "וְהִבִּיטוּ אֵלָיו אֵת אֲשֶׁר־דָּקָרוּ."
³⁸אַחֲרֵי כֵן בָּא יוֹסֵף אִישׁ רָמָתַיִם – שֶׁהָיָה תַּלְמִידוֹ שֶׁל יֵשׁוּעַ בַּסֵּתֶר, מִפַּחַד רָאשֵׁי הַיְּהוּדִים – וּבִקֵּשׁ מִפִּילָטוֹס שֶׁיַּנִּיחַ לוֹ לָקַחַת אֶת גּוּפַת יֵשׁוּעַ. פִּילָטוֹס הִרְשָׁה לוֹ וְהוּא הָלַךְ וְלָקַח אֶת גּוּפָתוֹ. ³⁹בָּא גַּם נַקְדִּימוֹן, זֶה שֶׁבָּרִאשׁוֹנָה בָּא אֶל יֵשׁוּעַ בַּלַּיְלָה, וְהוּא נוֹשֵׂא תַּעֲרֹבֶת מוֹר וַאֲהָלוֹת, כְּמֵאָה לִיטְרָאוֹת. ⁴⁰הֵם לָקְחוּ אֶת גּוּפַת יֵשׁוּעַ וַעֲטָפוּ אוֹתָהּ

³⁹ כְּמֵאָה לִיטְרָאוֹת – כִּשְׁלוֹשִׁים קִילוֹגְרַם.

bound it in strips of linen with the spices, as the custom of the Jews is to bury. ⁴¹ Now in the place where He was crucified there was a garden, and in the garden a new tomb in which no one had yet been laid. ⁴² So there they laid Jesus, because of the Jews' Preparation *Day,* for the tomb was nearby.

20 Now the first *day* of the week Mary Magdalene went to the tomb early, while it was still dark, and saw *that* the stone had been taken away from the tomb. ² Then she ran and came to Simon Peter, and to the other disciple, whom Jesus loved, and said to them, "They have taken away the Lord out of the tomb, and we do not know where they have laid Him."

³ Peter therefore went out, and the other disciple, and were going to the tomb. ⁴ So they both ran together, and the other disciple outran Peter and came to the tomb first. ⁵ And he, stooping down and looking in, saw the linen cloths lying *there;* yet he did not go in. ⁶ Then Simon Peter came, following him, and went into the tomb; and he saw the linen cloths lying *there,* ⁷ and the hand-kerchief that had been around His head, not lying with the linen cloths, but folded together in a place by itself. ⁸ Then the other disciple, who came to the tomb first, went in also; and he saw and believed. ⁹ For as yet they did not know the Scripture, that He must rise again from the dead. ¹⁰ Then the disciples went away again to their own homes.

¹¹ But Mary stood outside by the tomb weeping, and as she wept she stooped down *and looked* into the tomb. ¹² And she saw two angels in white sitting, one at the head and the other at the feet, where the body of Jesus had lain. ¹³ Then they said to her, "Woman, why are you weeping?"

She said to them, "Because they have taken away my Lord, and I do not know where they have laid Him."

¹⁴ Now when she had said this, she turned around and saw Jesus standing *there,* and did not know that it was Jesus. ¹⁵ Jesus said to her, "Woman, why are you weeping? Whom are you seeking?"

She, supposing Him to be the gardener, said to Him, "Sir, if You have carried Him away, tell me where You have laid Him, and I will take Him away."

¹⁶ Jesus said to her, "Mary!"

She turned and said to Him, "Rabboni!" (which is to say, Teacher).

בְּתַכְרִיכִים עִם הַבְּשָׂמִים כְּמִנְהַג הַקְּבוּרָה אֵצֶל הַיְּהוּדִים. ⁴¹ בַּמָּקוֹם שֶׁנִּצְלַב יֵשׁוּעַ הָיָה גַּן וּבַגַּן קֶבֶר חָדָשׁ שֶׁעוֹד לֹא הֻנַּח בּוֹ אִישׁ. ⁴² שָׁם הִנִּיחוּ אֶת יֵשׁוּעַ, כִּי עֶרֶב שַׁבָּת הָיָה לַיְּהוּדִים וְהַקֶּבֶר קָרוֹב.

כ בָּרִאשׁוֹן בַּשָּׁבוּעַ, לִפְנוֹת בֹּקֶר בְּעוֹד חֹשֶׁךְ, בָּאָה מִרְיָם הַמַּגְדָּלִית אֶל הַקֶּבֶר וְרָאֲתָה שֶׁהָאֶבֶן הוּסָרָה מִן הַקֶּבֶר. ² הִיא רָצָה וּבָאָה אֶל שִׁמְעוֹן כֵּיפָא וְאֶל הַתַּלְמִיד הַשֵּׁנִי, זֶה שֶׁהָיָה אָהוּב עַל יֵשׁוּעַ. אָמְרָה לָהֶם: "לָקְחוּ אֶת הָאָדוֹן מִן הַקֶּבֶר וְלֹא יָדוּעַ לָנוּ אֵיפֹה הִנִּיחוּ אוֹתוֹ."

³ יָצְאוּ כֵּיפָא וְהַתַּלְמִיד הַשֵּׁנִי לָבוֹא אֶל הַקֶּבֶר. ⁴ שְׁנֵיהֶם רָצוּ יַחְדָּיו, אֶלָּא שֶׁהַתַּלְמִיד הַשֵּׁנִי רָץ מַהֵר יוֹתֵר מִכֵּיפָא וְהִגִּיעַ רִאשׁוֹן לַקֶּבֶר. ⁵ הוּא הִתְכּוֹפֵף וְרָאָה אֶת הַתַּכְרִיכִים מֻנָּחִים, אַךְ לֹא נִכְנַס פְּנִימָה. ⁶ אַחֲרָיו בָּא גַם שִׁמְעוֹן כֵּיפָא. הוּא נִכְנַס אֶל הַקֶּבֶר וְרָאָה אֶת הַתַּכְרִיכִים מֻנָּחִים, ⁷ וְהַמִּטְפַּחַת שֶׁהָיְתָה עַל רֹאשׁוֹ אֵינֶנָּה מֻנַּחַת עִם הַתַּכְרִיכִים, אֶלָּא מְקֻפֶּלֶת לְבַדָּהּ בְּמָקוֹם אֶחָד. ⁸ אָז נִכְנַס גַם הַתַּלְמִיד הַשֵּׁנִי שֶׁבָּא רִאשׁוֹן אֶל הַקֶּבֶר. הוּא רָאָה וְהֶאֱמִין, ⁹ הֲרֵי עוֹד לֹא יָדְעוּ אֶת הַכָּתוּב שֶׁעָלָיו לָקוּם מִן הַמֵּתִים. ¹⁰ אַחֲרֵי כֵן חָזְרוּ הַתַּלְמִידִים לְבֵיתָם.

¹¹ וּמִרְיָם עָמְדָה בּוֹכִיָּה מִחוּץ לַקֶּבֶר. בְּשָׁעָה שֶׁבָּכְתָה הִתְכּוֹפְפָה אֶל תּוֹךְ הַקֶּבֶר ¹² וְרָאֲתָה שְׁנֵי מַלְאָכִים עוֹטֵי לָבָן יוֹשְׁבִים בַּמָּקוֹם שֶׁקֹּדֶם לָכֵן נָחָה גּוּפַת יֵשׁוּעַ, אֶחָד לְמַרְאֲשׁוֹתָיו וְאֶחָד לְמַרְגְּלוֹתָיו. ¹³ אָמְרוּ לָהּ: "אִשָּׁה, לָמָּה אַתְּ בּוֹכָה?"

הֵשִׁיבָה לָהֶם: "לָקְחוּ אֶת אֲדוֹנִי וְאֵינֶנִּי יוֹדַעַת אֵיפֹה הִנִּיחוּ אוֹתוֹ."

¹⁴ אַחֲרֵי שֶׁאָמְרָה זֹאת פָּנְתָה לְאָחוֹר וְרָאֲתָה אֶת יֵשׁוּעַ עוֹמֵד, אַךְ לֹא יָדְעָה כִּי הוּא יֵשׁוּעַ. ¹⁵ שָׁאַל אוֹתָהּ יֵשׁוּעַ: "אִשָּׁה, לָמָּה אַתְּ בּוֹכָה? אֶת מִי אַתְּ מְחַפֶּשֶׂת?"

הוֹאִיל וְחָשְׁבָה שֶׁהוּא שׁוֹמֵר הַגַּן אָמְרָה לוֹ: "אָדוֹן, אִם אַתָּה הֶעֱבַרְתָּ אוֹתוֹ, אֱמֹר נָא לִי אֵיפֹה הִנַּחְתָּ אוֹתוֹ וַאֲנִי אֶקַּח אוֹתוֹ."

¹⁶ אָמַר לָהּ יֵשׁוּעַ: "מִרְיָם!"

אָז פָּנְתָה וְאָמְרָה לוֹ: "רַבִּי!"

¹⁷ Jesus said to her, "Do not cling to Me, for I have not yet ascended to My Father; but go to My brethren and say to them, 'I am ascending to My Father and your Father, and *to* My God and your God.'"

¹⁸ Mary Magdalene came and told the disciples that she had seen the Lord, and *that* He had spoken these things to her.

¹⁹ Then, the same day at evening, being the first *day* of the week, when the doors were shut where the disciples were assembled, for fear of the Jews, Jesus came and stood in the midst, and said to them, "Peace *be* with you." ²⁰ When He had said this, He showed them *His* hands and His side. Then the disciples were glad when they saw the Lord.

²¹ So Jesus said to them again, "Peace to you! As the Father has sent Me, I also send you." ²² And when He had said this, He breathed on *them,* and said to them, "Receive the Holy Spirit. ²³ If you forgive the sins of any, they are forgiven them; if you retain the *sins* of any, they are retained."

²⁴ Now Thomas, called the Twin, one of the twelve, was not with them when Jesus came. ²⁵ The other disciples therefore said to him, "We have seen the Lord."

So he said to them, "Unless I see in His hands the print of the nails, and put my finger into the print of the nails, and put my hand into His side, I will not believe."

²⁶ And after eight days His disciples were again inside, and Thomas with them. Jesus came, the doors being shut, and stood in the midst, and said, "Peace to you!" ²⁷ Then He said to Thomas, "Reach your finger here, and look at My hands; and reach your hand *here,* and put *it* into My side. Do not be unbelieving, but believing."

²⁸ And Thomas answered and said to Him, "My Lord and my God!"

²⁹ Jesus said to him, "Thomas, because you have seen Me, you have believed. Blessed *are* those who have not seen and *yet* have believed."

³⁰ And truly Jesus did many other signs in the presence of His disciples, which are not written in this book; ³¹ but these are written that you may believe that Jesus is the Christ, the Son of God, and that believing you may have life in His name.

21 After these things Jesus showed Himself again to the disciples at the Sea of Tiberias, and in this way He showed *Himself:* ² Simon Peter, Thomas called the Twin, Nathanael of Cana in Galilee, the *sons* of Zebedee, and two others of His disciples were together. ³ Simon Peter said to them, "I am going fishing."

---

¹⁷ אָמַר לָהּ יֵשׁוּעַ: "אַל תִּגְּעִי בִּי, כִּי עֲדַיִן לֹא עָלִיתִי אֶל הָאָב, אֶלָּא לְכִי אֶל אַחַי וְהַגִּידִי לָהֶם: 'אֲנִי עוֹלֶה אֶל אָבִי וַאֲבִיכֶם, אֶל אֱלֹהַי וֵאלֹהֵיכֶם'."

¹⁸ הָלְכָה מִרְיָם הַמַּגְדָּלִית וְהוֹדִיעָה לַתַּלְמִידִים כִּי רָאֲתָה אֶת הָאָדוֹן וְכִי אָמַר לָהּ אֶת הַדְּבָרִים הַלָּלוּ.

¹⁹ לְעֵת עֶרֶב, בְּאוֹתוֹ יוֹם רִאשׁוֹן בַּשָּׁבוּעַ, כַּאֲשֶׁר דַּלְתוֹת הַמָּקוֹם שֶׁנֶּאֶסְפוּ בּוֹ הַתַּלְמִידִים הָיוּ סְגוּרוֹת מִפַּחַד רָאשֵׁי הַיְּהוּדִים, בָּא יֵשׁוּעַ וְעָמַד בֵּינֵיהֶם. אָמַר לָהֶם: "שָׁלוֹם לָכֶם." ²⁰ לְאַחַר מִכֵּן הֶרְאָה לָהֶם אֶת יָדָיו וְאֶת צִדּוֹ, וְהַתַּלְמִידִים נִתְמַלְּאוּ שִׂמְחָה כִּרְאוֹתָם אֶת הָאָדוֹן. ²¹ הוֹסִיף יֵשׁוּעַ וְאָמַר לָהֶם: "שָׁלוֹם לָכֶם. כְּשֵׁם שֶׁהָאָב שָׁלַח אוֹתִי, כֵּן גַּם אֲנִי שׁוֹלֵחַ אֶתְכֶם." ²² אַחֲרֵי אָמְרוֹ זֹאת נָפַח עֲלֵיהֶם וְאָמַר לָהֶם: "קַבְּלוּ אֶת רוּחַ הַקֹּדֶשׁ. ²³ כָּל מִי שֶׁתִּסְלְחוּ לוֹ עַל חֲטָאָיו, הֵם יִסָּלְחוּ לוֹ; לְכָל מִי שֶׁתַּחֲזִיקוּ אוֹתָם, יָחְזְקוּ לוֹ."

²⁴ תֹּאמָא, אֶחָד מֵהַשְּׁנֵים-עָשָׂר הַנִּקְרָא דִּידִימוֹס, לֹא הָיָה אִתָּם כַּאֲשֶׁר בָּא יֵשׁוּעַ. ²⁵ אָמְרוּ לוֹ יֶתֶר הַתַּלְמִידִים: "רָאִינוּ אֶת הָאָדוֹן."

הֵשִׁיב לָהֶם: "אִם לֹא אֶרְאֶה אֶת סִימָן הַמַּסְמְרִים בְּיָדָיו וְלֹא אָשִׂים אֶת אֶצְבָּעִי בַּמָּקוֹם שֶׁהָיוּ הַמַּסְמְרִים וְלֹא אָשִׂים אֶת יָדִי בְּצִדּוֹ, לֹא אַאֲמִין."

²⁶ אַחֲרֵי שְׁמוֹנָה יָמִים שׁוּב הָיוּ הַתַּלְמִידִים בַּבַּיִת וְתֹאמָא אִתָּם. כַּאֲשֶׁר הָיוּ הַדְּלָתוֹת סְגוּרוֹת בָּא יֵשׁוּעַ, עָמַד בֵּינֵיהֶם וְאָמַר: "שָׁלוֹם לָכֶם." ²⁷ אָז אָמַר לְתֹאמָא: "הָבֵא אֶת אֶצְבָּעֲךָ הֵנָּה וּרְאֵה אֶת יָדַי; הוֹשֵׁט אֶת יָדְךָ וְשִׂים אוֹתָהּ בְּצִדִּי, וְאַל תְּהֵא חֲסַר אֱמוּנָה, אֶלָּא מַאֲמִין."

²⁸ הֵשִׁיב תֹּאמָא וְאָמַר לוֹ: "אֲדֹנִי וֵאלֹהָי!"

²⁹ אָמַר לוֹ יֵשׁוּעַ: "מִפְּנֵי שֶׁרָאִיתָ אוֹתִי הֶאֱמַנְתָּ. אַשְׁרֵי אֵלֶּה שֶׁאֵינָם רוֹאִים וְעִם זֹאת מַאֲמִינִים."

³⁰ גַּם אוֹתוֹת רַבִּים אֲחֵרִים עָשָׂה יֵשׁוּעַ לְעֵינֵי תַּלְמִידָיו, אֲשֶׁר לֹא נִכְתְּבוּ בַּסֵּפֶר הַזֶּה. ³¹ אֲבָל אֵלֶּה נִכְתְּבוּ כְּדֵי שֶׁתַּאֲמִינוּ כִּי יֵשׁוּעַ הוּא הַמָּשִׁיחַ בֶּן הָאֱלֹהִים, וּכְדֵי שֶׁבְּהַאֲמִינְכֶם יִהְיוּ לָכֶם חַיִּים בִּשְׁמוֹ.

כא אַחֲרֵי כֵן הוֹסִיף יֵשׁוּעַ לְהֵרָאוֹת אֶל תַּלְמִידָיו לְיַד יָם טְבֶרְיָה. הוּא הוֹפִיעַ בְּדֶרֶךְ זֹאת: ² שִׁמְעוֹן כֵּיפָא וְתֹאמָא הַנִּקְרָא דִּידִימוֹס הָיוּ יַחַד עִם נְתַנְאֵל מִקָּנָה שֶׁבַּגָּלִיל וְעִם בְּנֵי זַבְדַּי וּשְׁנַיִם אֲחֵרִים מִתַּלְמִידָיו. ³ אָמַר לָהֶם שִׁמְעוֹן כֵּיפָא: "אֲנִי הוֹלֵךְ לָדוּג."

They said to him, "We are going with you also."
They went out and immediately got into the boat,
and that night they caught nothing. 4 But when the
morning had now come, Jesus stood on the shore;
yet the disciples did not know that it was Jesus.
5 Then Jesus said to them, "Children, have you any
food?"

They answered Him, "No."

6 And He said to them, "Cast the net on the right
side of the boat, and you will find *some*." So they
cast, and now they were not able to draw it in
because of the multitude of fish.

7 Therefore that disciple whom Jesus loved said
to Peter, "It is the Lord!" Now when Simon Peter
heard that it was the Lord, he put on *his* outer
garment (for he had removed it), and plunged into
the sea. 8 But the other disciples came in the little
boat (for they were not far from land, but about
two hundred cubits), dragging the net with fish.
9 Then, as soon as they had come to land, they saw a
fire of coals there, and fish laid on it, and bread.
10 Jesus said to them, "Bring some of the fish which
you have just caught."

11 Simon Peter went up and dragged the net to
land, full of large fish, one hundred and fifty-three;
and although there were so many, the net was not
broken. 12 Jesus said to them, "Come *and* eat
breakfast." Yet none of the disciples dared ask
Him, "Who are You?"—knowing that it was the
Lord. 13 Jesus then came and took the bread and
gave it to them, and likewise the fish.

14 This *is* now the third time Jesus showed
Himself to His disciples after He was raised from
the dead.

15 So when they had eaten breakfast, Jesus said to
Simon Peter, "Simon, *son* of Jonah, do you love Me
more than these?"

He said to Him, "Yes, Lord; You know that I
love You."

He said to him, "Feed My lambs."

16 He said to him again a second time, "Simon,
son of Jonah, do you love Me?"

He said to Him, "Yes, Lord; You know that I
love You."

He said to him, "Tend My sheep."

17 He said to him the third time, "Simon, *son* of
Jonah, do you love Me?" Peter was grieved because
He said to him the third time, "Do you love Me?"

And he said to Him, "Lord, You know all things;
You know that I love You."

Jesus said to him, "Feed My sheep. 18 Most
assuredly, I say to you, when you were younger,
you girded yourself and walked where you wished;
but when you are old, you will stretch out your

אָמְרוּ לוֹ: "גַּם אֲנַחְנוּ בָּאִים אִתְּךָ." הָלְכוּ וְנִכְנְסוּ
לַסִּירָה וְלֹא לָכְדוּ מְאוּמָה בְּאוֹתוֹ לַיְלָה. 4 עִם בֹּקֶר
עָמַד יֵשׁוּעַ עַל הַחוֹף, אַךְ הַתַּלְמִידִים לֹא הִכִּירוּ
שֶׁזֶּה יֵשׁוּעַ. 5 אָמַר לָהֶם יֵשׁוּעַ: "בָּנַי, אֵין לָכֶם
דָּגִים?"

הֵשִׁיבוּ לוֹ: "אֵין."

6 אָמַר לָהֶם: "הַשְׁלִיכוּ אֶת הָרֶשֶׁת בְּצִדָּהּ הַיְמָנִי שֶׁל
הַסִּירָה וְתִמְצְאוּ." הֵם הִשְׁלִיכוּ וְלֹא יָכְלוּ עוֹד לִמְשֹׁךְ
אוֹתָהּ מֵרֹב דָּגִים.

7 הֵגִיב הַתַּלְמִיד הָאָהוּב עַל יֵשׁוּעַ וְאָמַר לְכֵיפָא: "זֶה
הָאָדוֹן!" כַּאֲשֶׁר שָׁמַע שִׁמְעוֹן כֵּיפָא שֶׁזֶּה הָאָדוֹן,
לָבַשׁ אֶת בִּגְדוֹ הַחִיצוֹן, כִּי גּוּף הָיָה חָשׂוּף, וְהֵטִיל
עַצְמוֹ לַיָּם. 8 אַךְ יֶתֶר הַתַּלְמִידִים בָּאוּ בַּסִּירָה
הַקְּטַנָּה כְּשֶׁהֵם גּוֹרְרִים אֶת הָרֶשֶׁת עִם הַדָּגִים, כִּי
לֹא הָיוּ רְחוֹקִים מִן הַחוֹף אֶלָּא כְּמָאתַיִם אַמָּה.
9 כַּאֲשֶׁר עָלוּ לַחוֹף רָאוּ גֶּחָלִים עֲרוּכוֹת וְדָגִים
מֻנָּחִים עֲלֵיהֶן, וְלֶחֶם. 10 אָמַר לָהֶם יֵשׁוּעַ: "הָבִיאוּ
מִן הַדָּגִים אֲשֶׁר לְכַדְתֶּם כָּעֵת." 11 עָלָה שִׁמְעוֹן
כֵּיפָא וּמָשַׁךְ אֶת הָרֶשֶׁת אֶל הַחוֹף וְהִיא מְלֵאָה דָּגִים
גְּדוֹלִים, מֵאָה וַחֲמִשִּׁים וּשְׁלוֹשָׁה, וְאַף שֶׁהָיוּ רַבִּים
כָּל כָּךְ לֹא נִקְרְעָה הָרֶשֶׁת. 12 אָמַר לָהֶם יֵשׁוּעַ:
"בּוֹאוּ, אִכְלוּ!" אַף אֶחָד מֵהַתַּלְמִידִים לֹא הֵעֵז
לִשְׁאֹל אוֹתוֹ "מִי אַתָּה?", כִּי יָדְעוּ שֶׁהוּא הָאָדוֹן.
13 נִגַּשׁ יֵשׁוּעַ, לָקַח אֶת הַלֶּחֶם וְנָתַן לָהֶם וְכֵן גַּם אֶת
הַדָּגִים. 14 זֹאת הָיְתָה הַפַּעַם הַשְּׁלִישִׁית שֶׁיֵּשׁוּעַ
הִתְגַּלָּה לַתַּלְמִידִים אַחֲרֵי קוּמוֹ מִן הַמֵּתִים.
15 לְאַחַר שֶׁאָכְלוּ אָמַר יֵשׁוּעַ לְשִׁמְעוֹן כֵּיפָא: "שִׁמְעוֹן
בֶּן יוֹחָנָן, הַאִם אַתָּה אוֹהֵב אוֹתִי יוֹתֵר מֵאֵלֶּה?"
הֵשִׁיב לוֹ: "כֵּן, אֲדוֹנִי, אַתָּה יוֹדֵעַ שֶׁאֲנִי אוֹהֵב
אוֹתְךָ."

אָמַר לוֹ יֵשׁוּעַ: "רְעֵה אֶת טְלָאַי."

16 שָׁאַל אוֹתוֹ פַּעַם שְׁנִיָּה: "שִׁמְעוֹן בֶּן יוֹחָנָן, הַאִם
אַתָּה אוֹהֵב אוֹתִי?"

הֵשִׁיב לוֹ: "כֵּן, אֲדוֹנִי, אַתָּה יוֹדֵעַ שֶׁאֲנִי אוֹהֵב
אוֹתְךָ."

אָמַר לוֹ יֵשׁוּעַ: "נְהַג אֶת צֹאנִי."

17 שָׁאַל אוֹתוֹ פַּעַם שְׁלִישִׁית: "שִׁמְעוֹן בֶּן יוֹחָנָן,
הַאִם אַתָּה אוֹהֵב אוֹתִי?"

הִתְעַצֵּב כֵּיפָא עַל שֶׁשָּׁאַל אוֹתוֹ בַּשְּׁלִישִׁית "הַאִם
אַתָּה אוֹהֵב אוֹתִי?" וְאָמַר אֵלָיו: "אֲדוֹנִי, הַכֹּל אַתָּה
יוֹדֵעַ; אַתָּה יוֹדֵעַ שֶׁאֲנִי אוֹהֵב אוֹתְךָ."

אָמַר לוֹ יֵשׁוּעַ: "רְעֵה אֶת צֹאנִי. 18 אָמֵן אָמֵן אֲנִי

8 כמאתיים אמה – כמה מטרים.

hands, and another will gird you and carry *you* where you do not wish." ¹⁹This He spoke, signifying by what death he would glorify God. And when He had spoken this, He said to him, "Follow Me."

²⁰Then Peter, turning around, saw the disciple whom Jesus loved following, who also had leaned on His breast at the supper, and said, "Lord, who is the one who betrays You?" ²¹Peter, seeing him, said to Jesus, "But Lord, what *about* this man?"

²²Jesus said to him, "If I will that he remain till I come, what *is that* to you? You follow Me."

²³Then this saying went out among the brethren that this disciple would not die. Yet Jesus did not say to him that he would not die, but, "If I will that he remain till I come, what *is that* to you?"

²⁴This is the disciple who testifies of these things, and wrote these things; and we know that his testimony is true.

²⁵And there are also many other things that Jesus did, which if they were written one by one, I suppose that even the world itself could not contain the books that would be written. Amen

אוֹמֵר לְךָ, כְּשֶׁהָיִיתָ יוֹתֵר צָעִיר חָגַרְתָּ אֶת עַצְמְךָ וְהָלַכְתָּ לְאָן שֶׁרָצִיתָ, אֲבָל כַּאֲשֶׁר תִּזְקַן תִּפְרֹשׂ אֶת יָדֶיךָ וְאַחֵר יַחְגָּרְךָ וְיוֹבִיל אוֹתְךָ אֶל אֲשֶׁר אֵינְךָ רוֹצֶה." ¹⁹ זֹאת אָמַר בְּרָמְזוֹ עַל אֹפֶן הַמָּוֶת שֶׁיְּכַבֵּד בּוֹ אֶת הָאֱלֹהִים. לְאַחַר אָמְרוֹ זֹאת אָמַר אֵלָיו: "לֵךְ אַחֲרַי!"

²⁰ כֵּיפָא פָּנָה וְרָאָה אֶת הַתַּלְמִיד הָאָהוּב עַל יֵשׁוּעַ הוֹלֵךְ אַחֲרֵיהֶם – זֶה שֶׁגַּם נִשְׁעַן עַל לִבּוֹ בְּעֵת הַסְּעוּדָה וְשָׁאַל "אֲדוֹנִי, מִי הוּא הַמַּסְגִּיר אוֹתְךָ?". ²¹ כְּשֶׁרָאָה אוֹתוֹ כֵּיפָא, אָמַר אֶל יֵשׁוּעַ: "אֲדוֹנִי, וְהוּא מַה?"

²² הֵשִׁיב לוֹ יֵשׁוּעַ: "אִם רְצוֹנִי שֶׁהוּא יִשָּׁאֵר עַד בּוֹאִי, מַה אִכְפַּת לְךָ? אַתָּה לֵךְ אַחֲרַי!" ²³ לָכֵן נִתְפַּרְסֵם הַדָּבָר הַזֶּה בְּקֶרֶב הָאַחִים שֶׁהַתַּלְמִיד הַהוּא לֹא יָמוּת. אוּלָם יֵשׁוּעַ לֹא אָמַר לוֹ שֶׁאֵינוֹ עָתִיד לָמוּת, אֶלָּא "אִם רְצוֹנִי שֶׁהוּא יִשָּׁאֵר עַד בּוֹאִי, מַה אִכְפַּת לְךָ?"

²⁴ זֶהוּ הַתַּלְמִיד אֲשֶׁר מֵעִיד עַל הַדְּבָרִים הָאֵלֶּה וַאֲשֶׁר כָּתַב אוֹתָם, וַאֲנַחְנוּ יוֹדְעִים שֶׁעֵדוּתוֹ אֱמֶת. ²⁵ יֵשׁ עוֹד מַעֲשִׂים רַבִּים אֲחֵרִים שֶׁעָשָׂה יֵשׁוּעַ, וְאִלּוּ נִכְתְּבוּ בִּמְפֹרָט חוֹשְׁבְנִי שֶׁהָעוֹלָם עַצְמוֹ לֹא הָיָה יָכוֹל לְהָכִיל אֶת הַסְּפָרִים הַנִּכְתָּבִים.

ACTS
of the Apostles

1 The former account I made, O Theophilus, of all that Jesus began both to do and teach, ²until the day in which He was taken up, after He through the Holy Spirit had given commandments to the apostles whom He had chosen, ³to whom He also presented Himself alive after His suffering by many infallible proofs, being seen by them during forty days and speaking of the things pertaining to the kingdom of God.

⁴And being assembled together with *them*, He commanded them not to depart from Jerusalem, but to wait for the Promise of the Father, "which," *He said*, "you have heard from Me; ⁵for John truly baptized with water, but you shall be baptized with the Holy Spirit not many days from now." ⁶Therefore, when they had come together, they asked Him, saying, "Lord, will You at this time restore the kingdom to Israel?" ⁷And He said to them, "It is not for you to know times or seasons which the Father has put in His own authority. ⁸But you shall receive power when the Holy Spirit has come upon you; and you shall be witnesses to Me in Jerusalem, and in all Judea and Samaria, and to the end of the earth."

⁹Now when He had spoken these things, while they watched, He was taken up, and a cloud received Him out of their sight. ¹⁰And while they looked steadfastly toward heaven as He went up, behold, two men stood by them in white apparel, ¹¹who also said, "Men of Galilee, why do you stand gazing up into heaven? This *same* Jesus, who was taken up from you into heaven, will so come in like manner as you saw Him go into heaven."

¹²Then they returned to Jerusalem from the mount called Olivet, which is near Jerusalem, a Sabbath day's journey. ¹³And when they had entered, they went up into the upper room where they were staying: Peter, James, John, and Andrew; Philip and Thomas; Bartholomew and Matthew; James *the son* of Alphaeus and Simon the Zealot; and Judas *the son* of James. ¹⁴These all continued with one accord in prayer and supplication, with the women and Mary the mother of Jesus, and with His brothers.

¹⁵And in those days Peter stood up in the midst of the disciples (altogether the number of names was about a hundred and twenty), and said,

מַעֲשֵׂי הַשְּׁלִיחִים

א תֵּאוֹפִילוֹס, בַּחִבּוּר הָרִאשׁוֹן כָּתַבְתִּי עַל כָּל מַה שֶּׁיֵּשׁוּעַ עָשָׂה וְלִמֵּד מִתְּחִלָּה ²וְעַד יוֹם הִלָּקְחוֹ לַמָּרוֹם לְאַחַר שֶׁמָּסַר הוֹרָאוֹת, לְפִי רוּחַ הַקֹּדֶשׁ, לַשְּׁלִיחִים אֲשֶׁר בָּחַר בָּהֶם; ³לִפְנֵיהֶם הוּא הוֹפִיעַ חַי בְּהוֹכָחוֹת רַבּוֹת, אַחֲרֵי עִנּוּתוֹ, וּבְמֶשֶׁךְ אַרְבָּעִים יוֹם נִרְאָה אֲלֵיהֶם וְדִבֵּר אִתָּם עַל מַלְכוּת הָאֱלֹהִים. ⁴כַּאֲשֶׁר הָיָה בְּחֶבְרָתָם צִוָּה עֲלֵיהֶם: "אַל תַּעַזְבוּ אֶת יְרוּשָׁלַיִם, כִּי אִם חַכּוּ לְקִיּוּם הַבְטָחַת הָאָב אֲשֶׁר שְׁמַעְתֶּם אוֹתָהּ מִפִּי; ⁵כִּי יוֹחָנָן הִטְבִּיל בְּמַיִם, אֲבָל אַתֶּם תִּטָּבְלוּ בְּרוּחַ הַקֹּדֶשׁ בְּעוֹד יָמִים לֹא רַבִּים."

⁶שָׁאֲלוּ אוֹתוֹ הַנֶּאֱסָפִים: "אֲדוֹנֵנוּ, הַאִם בַּזְּמַן הַזֶּה תָּשִׁיב אֶת הַמַּלְכוּת לְיִשְׂרָאֵל?"

⁷עָנָה לָהֶם: "לֹא לָכֶם לָדַעַת עִתִּים וּזְמַנִּים שֶׁקָּבַע הָאָב בְּסַמְכוּתוֹ שֶׁלּוֹ. ⁸אֲבָל בְּבוֹא עֲלֵיכֶם רוּחַ הַקֹּדֶשׁ תְּקַבְּלוּ כֹּחַ וְתִהְיוּ עֵדַי הֵן בִּירוּשָׁלַיִם וְהֵן בְּכָל יְהוּדָה וְשׁוֹמְרוֹן, עַד קְצֵה הָאָרֶץ."

⁹אַחֲרֵי שֶׁאָמַר אֶת הַדְּבָרִים הָאֵלֶּה נִשָּׂא מֵעֲלֵיהֶם בְּעוֹדָם מִסְתַּכְּלִים, וְעָנָן נָטַל אוֹתוֹ מִנֶּגֶד עֵינֵיהֶם. ¹⁰עוֹדָם מַבִּיטִים הַשָּׁמַיְמָה בַּעֲלִיָּתוֹ, וְהִנֵּה שְׁנֵי אֲנָשִׁים לְבוּשֵׁי לָבָן נִצְּבוּ לְיָדָם ¹¹וְאָמְרוּ: "אַנְשֵׁי הַגָּלִיל, לָמָה אַתֶּם עוֹמְדִים וּמִסְתַּכְּלִים אֶל הַשָּׁמַיִם? יֵשׁוּעַ זֶה אֲשֶׁר נִשָּׂא מֵעֲלֵיכֶם הַשָּׁמַיְמָה – בּוֹא יָבוֹא בְּאוֹתוֹ אֹפֶן שֶׁרְאִיתֶם אוֹתוֹ עוֹלֶה לַשָּׁמַיִם."

¹²אַחֲרֵי כֵן שָׁבוּ לִירוּשָׁלַיִם מֵהַר הַזֵּיתִים, הַקָּרוֹב לִירוּשָׁלַיִם כְּדֶרֶךְ תְּחוּם שַׁבָּת. ¹³בָּאוּ כֵּיפָא וְיוֹחָנָן וְיַעֲקֹב, אַנְדְּרֵי וּפִילִיפּוֹס וְתָאוֹמָא, בַּר־תַּלְמַי וּמַתַּי וְיַעֲקֹב בֶּן־חַלְפַי, שִׁמְעוֹן הַקַּנַּאי וִיהוּדָה בֶּן־יַעֲקֹב, וְעָלוּ אֶל הָעֲלִיָּה – הַמָּקוֹם שֶׁנָּהֲגוּ לִשְׁהוֹת בּוֹ. ¹⁴כָּל אֵלֶּה הִתְמִידוּ בְּלֵב אֶחָד בִּתְפִלָּה, הֵם וְהַנָּשִׁים וּמִרְיָם אֵם יֵשׁוּעַ וְאֶחָיו.

¹⁵בְּאוֹתָם יָמִים קָם כֵּיפָא בֵּין הָאַחִים – מִסְפַּר הָאֲנָשִׁים שֶׁנִּקְהֲלוּ יַחַד הָיָה כְּמֵאָה וְעֶשְׂרִים –

16"Men *and* brethren, this Scripture had to be fulfilled, which the Holy Spirit spoke before by the mouth of David concerning Judas, who became a guide to those who arrested Jesus; 17for he was numbered with us and obtained a part in this ministry."

18(Now this man purchased a field with the wages of iniquity; and falling headlong, he burst open in the middle and all his entrails gushed out. 19And it became known to all those dwelling in Jerusalem; so that field is called in their own language, Akel Dama, that is, Field of Blood.)

20"For it is written in the Book of Psalms:

'Let his dwelling place be desolate,
And let no one live in it';

and,

'Let another take his office.'

21"Therefore, of these men who have accompanied us all the time that the Lord Jesus went in and out among us, 22beginning from the baptism of John to that day when He was taken up from us, one of these must become a witness with us of His resurrection."

23And they proposed two: Joseph called Barsabas, who was surnamed Justus, and Matthias. 24And they prayed and said, "You, O Lord, who know the hearts of all, show which of these two You have chosen 25to take part in this ministry and apostleship from which Judas by transgression fell, that he might go to his own place." 26And they cast their lots, and the lot fell on Matthias. And he was numbered with the eleven apostles.

2 When the Day of Pentecost had fully come, they were all with one accord in one place. 2And suddenly there came a sound from heaven, as of a rushing mighty wind, and it filled the whole house where they were sitting. 3Then there appeared to them divided tongues, as of fire, and *one* sat upon each of them. 4And they were all filled with the Holy Spirit and began to speak with other tongues, as the Spirit gave them utterance.

5And there were dwelling in Jerusalem Jews, devout men, from every nation under heaven. 6And when this sound occurred, the multitude came together, and were confused, because everyone heard them speak in his own language. 7Then they were all amazed and marveled, saying to one another, "Look, are not all these who speak Galileans? 8And how *is it that* we hear, each in our own language in which we were born? 9Parthians and Medes and Elamites, those dwelling

וַאֲמַר: 16 "אֲנָשִׁים אַחִים, צָרִיךְ הָיָה שֶׁיִּתְקַיַּם הַכָּתוּב אֲשֶׁר רוּחַ הַקֹּדֶשׁ דִּבְּרָה מִקֶּדֶם בְּפִי דָוִד עַל יְהוּדָה, זֶה שֶׁנִּהְיָה הַמּוֹבִיל שֶׁל תּוֹפְסֵי יֵשׁוּעַ. 17 הוּא נִמְנָה אִתָּנוּ וְקִבֵּל חֵלֶק בַּשֵּׁרוּת הַזֶּה. 18 וְהִנֵּה קָנָה לוֹ שָׂדֶה בִּשְׂכַר הָרֶשַׁע וּבְנָפְלוֹ נִבְקְעָה בִּטְנוֹ וְכָל מֵעָיו נִשְׁפְּכוּ הַחוּצָה 19 – הַדָּבָר הַזֶּה נוֹדַע לְכָל יוֹשְׁבֵי יְרוּשָׁלַיִם וּלְפִיכָךְ נִקְרָא אוֹתוֹ שָׂדֶה בִּלְשׁוֹנָם 'חֲקַל דְּמָא', שֶׁפֵּרוּשׁוֹ שָׂדֶה הַדָּם – 20 שֶׁהֲרֵי כָּתוּב בְּסֵפֶר תְּהִלִּים, 'תְּהִי-טִירָתוֹ נְשַׁמָּה וְאַל-יְהִי בָהּ יוֹשֵׁב', וְגַם 'פְּקֻדָּתוֹ יִקַּח אַחֵר'. 21 עַל כֵּן צָרִיךְ שֶׁאֶחָד מִן הָאֲנָשִׁים אֲשֶׁר נִלְווּ אֵלֵינוּ בְּכָל הָעֵת אֲשֶׁר הָאָדוֹן יֵשׁוּעַ בָּא וְיָצָא בְּתוֹכֵנוּ, 22 הָחֵל מִטְּבִילַת יוֹחָנָן עַד יוֹם הִנָּשְׂאוֹ מֵאִתָּנוּ, יִהְיֶה עַד אִתָּנוּ עַל תְּחִיָּתוֹ."

23 הֵם הֶעֱמִידוּ שְׁנַיִם, אֶת יוֹסֵף הַנִּקְרָא בַּר-שַׁבָּא וְהַמְכֻנֶּה גַּם יוּסְטוֹס, וְאֶת מַתִּתְיָה. 24 הִתְפַּלְלוּ וַאֲמָרוּ: "אַתָּה אֲדֹנָי הַיּוֹדֵעַ כָּל הַלְּבָבוֹת, הַרְאֵה נָא מִי הוּא הָאֶחָד מִן הַשְּׁנַיִם שֶׁבָּחַרְתָּ בּוֹ 25 לָקַחַת אֶת מְקוֹם הַשֵּׁרוּת הַזֶּה וְהַשְּׁלִיחוּת אֲשֶׁר סָטָה מִמֶּנּוּ יְהוּדָה בְּלֶכְתּוֹ אֶל מְקוֹמוֹ שֶׁלּוֹ." 26 נָתְנוּ לָהֶם גּוֹרָלוֹת; הַגּוֹרָל נָפַל עַל מַתִּתְיָה וְהוּא נִסְפַּח אֶל אַחַד-עָשָׂר הַשְּׁלִיחִים.

ב בְּיוֹם מְלֹאת שִׁבְעַת הַשָּׁבוּעוֹת הָיוּ כֻלָּם יַחְדָּיו. 2 פִּתְאוֹם הָיָה קוֹל מִן הַשָּׁמַיִם, כְּקוֹל מַשַּׁב רוּחַ עַזָּה, וְהוּא מִלֵּא אֶת כָּל הַבַּיִת אֲשֶׁר יָשְׁבוּ בּוֹ. 3 אָז הוֹפִיעוּ לְנֶגֶד עֵינֵיהֶם לְשׁוֹנוֹת כְּלַהֲבוֹת אֵשׁ, שֶׁהִתְפַּזְּרוּ וְנָחוּ אַחַת אַחַת עַל כָּל אֶחָד מֵהֶם. 4 וְכֻלָּם נִמְלְאוּ רוּחַ הַקֹּדֶשׁ וְהֵחֵלּוּ לְדַבֵּר בִּלְשׁוֹנוֹת אֲחֵרוֹת כְּפִי שֶׁנָּתְנָה לָהֶם הָרוּחַ לְדַבֵּר.

5 בִּירוּשָׁלַיִם הִתְגּוֹרְרוּ יְהוּדִים יִרְאֵי אֱלֹהִים מִכָּל עַם וְעַם אֲשֶׁר תַּחַת הַשָּׁמַיִם. 6 כַּאֲשֶׁר נִשְׁמַע הַקּוֹל הַזֶּה הִתְקַהֲלוּ עַם רַב וְכֻלָּם נְבוֹכוּ, שֶׁכֵּן כָּל אִישׁ שָׁמַע אוֹתָם מְדַבְּרִים בִּשְׂפָתוֹ שֶׁלּוֹ. 7 הֵם נִתְמַלְּאוּ תְּמָהוֹן וּפְלִיאָה וַאֲמָרוּ: "הֲרֵי כָּל הַמְדַבְּרִים הָאֵלֶּה גְּלִילִיִּים, 8 וְאֵיךְ כָּל אֶחָד מֵאִתָּנוּ שׁוֹמֵעַ בִּשְׂפַת מוֹלַדְתּוֹ?

in Mesopotamia, Judea and Cappadocia, Pontus and Asia, [10] Phrygia and Pamphylia, Egypt and the parts of Libya adjoining Cyrene, visitors from Rome, both Jews and proselytes, [11] Cretans and Arabs—we hear them speaking in our own tongues the wonderful works of God." [12] So they were all amazed and perplexed, saying to one another, "Whatever could this mean?"

[13] Others mocking said, "They are full of new wine."

[14] But Peter, standing up with the eleven, raised his voice and said to them, "Men of Judea and all who dwell in Jerusalem, let this be known to you, and heed my words. [15] For these are not drunk, as you suppose, since it is *only* the third hour of the day. [16] But this is what was spoken by the prophet Joel:

[17]   'And it shall come to pass in the last days,
          says God,
        That I will pour out of My Spirit on all flesh;
        Your sons and your daughters shall pro-
          phesy,
        Your young men shall see visions,
        Your old men shall dream dreams.
[18]   And on My menservants and on My
          maidservants
        I will pour out My Spirit in those days;
        And they shall prophesy.
[19]   I will show wonders in heaven above
        And signs in the earth beneath:
        Blood and fire and vapor of smoke.
[20]   The sun shall be turned into darkness,
        And the moon into blood,
        Before the coming of the great and awesome
          day of the LORD.
[21]   And it shall come to pass
        That whoever calls on the name of the LORD
        Shall be saved.'

[22] "Men of Israel, hear these words: Jesus of Nazareth, a Man attested by God to you by miracles, wonders, and signs which God did through Him in your midst, as you yourselves also know— [23] Him, being delivered by the determined purpose and foreknowledge of God, you have taken by lawless hands, have crucified, and put to death; [24] whom God raised up, having loosed the pains of death, because it was not possible that He should be held by it. [25] For David says concerning Him:

        'I foresaw the LORD always before my face,
        For He is at my right hand, that I may not be
          shaken.
[26]   Therefore my heart rejoiced, and my tongue
          was glad;

9 פַּרְתִּים אֲנַחְנוּ וּמָדִים, עֵילָמִים וְתוֹשְׁבֵי אֲרַם נַהֲרַיִם, תּוֹשְׁבֵי יְהוּדָה וְקַפַּדוֹקְיָה וּפוֹנְטוֹס וְאַסְיָה, 10 פְרִיגְיָה וּפַמְפִּילְיָה, מִצְרַיִם וּמְחוֹזוֹת לוּב הַסְּמוּכִים לְקִירֵנְיָה, תּוֹשְׁבֵי רוֹמָא הַמִּתְגּוֹרְרִים כָּאן, 11 יְהוּדִים וְגֵרִים, כְּרֵתִים וַעֲרָבִים – וְהִנֵּה אֲנַחְנוּ שׁוֹמְעִים אוֹתָם מְסַפְּרִים בִּלְשׁוֹנוֹתֵינוּ אֶת גְּדֻלּוֹת הָאֱלֹהִים!" 12 הַכֹּל הִשְׁתּוֹמְמוּ וְנָבוֹכוּ, אָמְרוּ זֶה אֶל זֶה: "מַה זֶּה צָרִיךְ לִהְיוֹת?"

13 אֲבָל אֲחֵרִים לָעֲגוּ וְאָמְרוּ: "מְלֵאֵי יַיִן הֵם."

14 עָמַד כֵּיפָא עִם הָאַחַד-עָשָׂר, נָשָׂא קוֹלוֹ וְדִבֵּר אֲלֵיהֶם: "אֲנָשִׁים יְהוּדִים, וְכָל יוֹשְׁבֵי יְרוּשָׁלַיִם. זֹאת דְּעוּ לָכֶם וְהַקְשִׁיבוּ לִדְבָרַי; 15 הָאֲנָשִׁים הָאֵלֶּה אֵינָם שִׁכּוֹרִים, כְּמוֹ שֶׁאַתֶּם סְבוּרִים, שֶׁכֵּן הַשָּׁעָה תֵּשַׁע בַּבֹּקֶר; 16 אֶלָּא שֶׁזֶּה הַדָּבָר שֶׁנֶּאֱמַר בְּפִי יוֹאֵל הַנָּבִיא:

17 וְהָיָה בְּאַחֲרִית הַיָּמִים, נְאֻם אֲדֹנָי,
    אֶשְׁפּוֹךְ אֶת-רוּחִי עַל-כָּל-בָּשָׂר
    וְנִבְּאוּ בְּנֵיכֶם וּבְנוֹתֵיכֶם;
    בַּחוּרֵיכֶם חֶזְיוֹנוֹת יִרְאוּ
    וְזִקְנֵיכֶם חֲלֹמוֹת יַחֲלֹמוּן.
18 וְגַם עַל עֲבָדַי וְעַל שִׁפְחוֹתַי בַּיָּמִים הָהֵמָּה
    אֶשְׁפּוֹךְ אֶת-רוּחִי וְנִבָּאוּ.
19 וְנָתַתִּי מוֹפְתִים בַּשָּׁמַיִם מִמַּעַל
    וְאוֹתוֹת בָּאָרֶץ מִתָּחַת,
    דָּם וָאֵשׁ וְתִמְרוֹת עָשָׁן.
20 הַשֶּׁמֶשׁ יֵהָפֵךְ לְחֹשֶׁךְ וְהַיָּרֵחַ לְדָם
    לִפְנֵי בּוֹא יוֹם יהוה הַגָּדוֹל וְהַנּוֹרָא.'
21 וְהָיָה כֹּל אֲשֶׁר-יִקְרָא בְּשֵׁם יהוה יִמָּלֵט.'

22 אַנְשֵׁי יִשְׂרָאֵל, שִׁמְעוּ אֶת הַדְּבָרִים הָאֵלֶּה: יֵשׁוּעַ מִנְּצֶרֶת, אִישׁ שֶׁנִּתְאַשֵּׁר לָכֶם מִטַּעַם אֱלֹהִים בִּגְבוּרוֹת וּבְנִסִּים וּבְאוֹתוֹת אֲשֶׁר הָאֱלֹהִים עָשָׂה עַל-יָדָיו בְּתוֹכְכֶם, כְּפִי שֶׁאַתֶּם עַצְמְכֶם יוֹדְעִים; 23 הוּא שֶׁהֻסְגַּר עַל-פִּי עֲצַת אֱלֹהִים הַנֶּחֱרָצָה וִידִיעָתוֹ-מֵרֹאשׁ – אוֹתוֹ לְקַחְתֶּם וּבִידֵי רְשָׁעִים צְלַבְתֶּם וַהֲרַגְתֶּם. 24 וֵאלֹהִים הֵקִימוֹ לִתְחִיָּה בְּהַתִּירוֹ אֶת חֶבְלֵי הַמָּוֶת, שֶׁכֵּן הַמָּוֶת לֹא הָיָה יָכוֹל לַעֲצֹר אוֹתוֹ. 25 הֵן דָּוִד אוֹמֵר עָלָיו:
'שִׁוִּיתִי יהוה לְנֶגְדִּי תָמִיד,
    כִּי מִימִינִי בַּל-אֶמּוֹט.
26 לָכֵן שָׂמַח לִבִּי וַיָּגֶל כְּבוֹדִי,
    אַף-בְּשָׂרִי יִשְׁכֹּן לָבֶטַח;

23 רשעים מילולית: שאין להם חוק, שאין להם תורה; רמז לגויים, קור"א מו:21. ראה גם מרקום טו:28.

Moreover my flesh also will rest in hope.

27 For You will not leave my soul in Hades,
Nor will You allow Your Holy One to see
corruption.

28 You have made known to me the ways of
life;
You will make me full of joy in Your
presence.'

29 "Men *and* brethren, let *me* speak freely to you
of the patriarch David, that he is both dead and
buried, and his tomb is with us to this day.
30 Therefore, being a prophet, and knowing that
God had sworn with an oath to him that of the fruit
of his body, according to the flesh, He would raise
up the Christ to sit on his throne, 31 he, foreseeing
this, spoke concerning the resurrection of the
Christ, that His soul was not left in Hades, nor
did His flesh see corruption. 32 This Jesus God has
raised up, of which we are all witnesses. 33 Therefore
being exalted to the right hand of God, and having
received from the Father the promise of the Holy
Spirit, He poured out this which you now see and
hear.

34 "For David did not ascend into the heavens,
but he says himself:

'The LORD said to my Lord,
"Sit at My right hand,
35 Till I make Your enemies Your footstool."'

36 "Therefore let all the house of Israel know
assuredly that God has made this Jesus, whom you
crucified, both Lord and Christ."

37 Now when they heard *this,* they were cut to the
heart, and said to Peter and the rest of the apostles,
"Men *and* brethren, what shall we do?"

38 Then Peter said to them, "Repent, and let
every one of you be baptized in the name of Jesus
Christ for the remission of sins; and you shall
receive the gift of the Holy Spirit. 39 For the promise
is to you and to your children, and to all who are
afar off, as many as the Lord our God will call."

40 And with many other words he testified and
exhorted them, saying, "Be saved from this perverse
generation." 41 Then those who gladly received his
word were baptized; and that day about three
thousand souls were added *to them.* 42 And they
continued steadfastly in the apostles' doctrine and
fellowship, in the breaking of bread, and in prayers.
43 Then fear came upon every soul, and many
wonders and signs were done through the apostles.
44 Now all who believed were together, and had all
things in common, 45 and sold their possessions and
goods, and divided them among all, as anyone had
need.

27 כִּי לֹא־תַעֲזֹב נַפְשִׁי לִשְׁאוֹל,
לֹא־תִתֵּן חֲסִידְךָ לִרְאוֹת שָׁחַת.
28 תּוֹדִיעֵנִי אֹרַח חַיִּים,
שֹׂבַע שְׂמָחוֹת אֶת־פָּנֶיךָ.'

29 אֲנָשִׁים אַחִים, אֶפְשָׁר לוֹמַר לָכֶם בְּבִטָּחוֹן עַל דָּוִד
אָבִינוּ, שֶׁהוּא מֵת וְגַם נִקְבַּר וְקִבְרוֹ נִמְצָא עִמָּנוּ עַד
הַיּוֹם הַזֶּה. 30 מִכֵּיוָן שֶׁהָיָה נָבִיא וְיָדַע כִּי אֱלֹהִים
נִשְׁבַּע לוֹ שְׁבוּעָה לְהוֹשִׁיב מִפְּרִי חֲלָצָיו עַל כִּסְאוֹ,
31 בַּחֲזוֹתוֹ מֵרֹאשׁ דִּבֶּר עַל תְּחִיַּת הַמָּשִׁיחַ – שֶׁלֹּא
נֶעֶזְבָה לִשְׁאוֹל נַפְשׁוֹ וּבְשָׂרוֹ לֹא רָאָה שָׁחַת. 32 אֶת
יֵשׁוּעַ זֶה הֵקִים אֱלֹהִים לִתְחִיָּה וְעַל זֹאת אֲנַחְנוּ כֻּלָּנוּ
עֵדִים. 33 וּלְאַחַר שֶׁנִּשָּׂא אֶל יְמִין הָאֱלֹהִים וְקִבֵּל
מֵאֵת הָאָב אֶת רוּחַ הַקֹּדֶשׁ הַמֻּבְטַחַת, שָׁפַךְ אוֹתָהּ
כְּפִי שֶׁאַתֶּם רוֹאִים וְגַם שׁוֹמְעִים. 34 הֲרֵי דָּוִד לֹא
עָלָה הַשָּׁמַיְמָה, אֶלָּא שֶׁהוּא אוֹמֵר:
35 'נְאֻם יהוה לַאדֹנִי, שֵׁב לִימִינִי
עַד אָשִׁית אוֹיְבֶיךָ הֲדֹם לְרַגְלֶיךָ.'

36 לָכֵן יֵדַע נָא כָּל בֵּית יִשְׂרָאֵל בְּבֵרוּר, שֶׁאֱלֹהִים שָׂם
לְאָדוֹן וּלְמָשִׁיחַ אֶת יֵשׁוּעַ זֶה אֲשֶׁר אַתֶּם צְלַבְתֶּם."
37 כְּשָׁמְעָם הִתְעַצְּבוּ מְאֹד בִּלְבָבָם וְאָמְרוּ לְכֵיפָא
וְלִשְׁאָר הַשְּׁלִיחִים: "אֲנָשִׁים אַחִים, מַה עָלֵינוּ
לַעֲשׂוֹת?"
38 אָמַר לָהֶם כֵּיפָא: "שׁוּבוּ בִּתְשׁוּבָה וְהִטָּבְלוּ אִישׁ
אִישׁ מִכֶּם בְּשֵׁם יֵשׁוּעַ הַמָּשִׁיחַ לִסְלִיחַת חֲטָאֵיכֶם,
וּתְקַבְּלוּ אֶת מַתְּנַת רוּחַ הַקֹּדֶשׁ; 39 כִּי לָכֶם
הַהַבְטָחָה וְלִבְנֵיכֶם וּלְכָל הָרְחוֹקִים, לְכָל אֲשֶׁר
יִקְרָא לָהֶם אֲדֹנָי אֱלֹהֵינוּ."
40 גַּם בְּמִלִּים רַבּוֹת אֲחֵרוֹת הֵעִיד בָּהֶם וְהֵאִיץ בָּהֶם
בְּאָמְרוֹ: "הִמָּלְטוּ מִן הַדּוֹר הַסּוֹרֵר הַזֶּה!" 41 אֵלֶּה
שֶׁקִּבְּלוּ בְּרָצוֹן אֶת דְּבָרוֹ נִטְבְּלוּ, וּבְאוֹתוֹ יוֹם נוֹסְפוּ
כִּשְׁלֹשֶׁת אֲלָפִים נְפָשׁוֹת. 42 הֵם הָיוּ שׁוֹקְדִים עַל
תּוֹרַת הַשְּׁלִיחִים, עַל הַהִתְחַבְּרוּת, עַל בְּצִיעַת
הַלֶּחֶם וְעַל הַתְּפִלּוֹת.
43 כָּל נֶפֶשׁ נִתְמַלְּאָה יִרְאָה וּמוֹפְתִים וְאוֹתוֹת רַבִּים
עָשׂוּ הַשְּׁלִיחִים. 44 כָּל הַמַּאֲמִינִים הָיוּ יַחְדָּו וּבְכָל
אֲשֶׁר הָיָה לָהֶם הָיוּ שֻׁתָּפִים. 45 הֵם מָכְרוּ אֶת
אֲחֻזּוֹתֵיהֶם וְאֶת רְכוּשָׁם וְחִלְּקוּ אוֹתָם לַכֹּל, לְכָל

46 So continuing daily with one accord in the temple, and breaking bread from house to house, they ate their food with gladness and simplicity of heart, 47 praising God and having favor with all the people. And the Lord added to the church daily those who were being saved.

3 Now Peter and John went up together to the temple at the hour of prayer, the ninth *hour*. 2 And a certain man lame from his mother's womb was carried, whom they laid daily at the gate of the temple which is called Beautiful, to ask alms from those who entered the temple; 3 who, seeing Peter and John about to go into the temple, asked for alms. 4 And fixing his eyes on him, with John, Peter said, "Look at us." 5 So he gave them his attention, expecting to receive something from them. 6 Then Peter said, "Silver and gold I do not have, but what I do have I give you: In the name of Jesus Christ of Nazareth, rise up and walk." 7 And he took him by the right hand and lifted *him* up, and immediately his feet and ankle bones received strength. 8 So he, leaping up, stood and walked and entered the temple with them—walking, leaping, and praising God. 9 And all the people saw him walking and praising God. 10 Then they knew that it was he who sat begging alms at the Beautiful Gate of the temple; and they were filled with wonder and amazement at what had happened to him.

11 Now as the lame man who was healed held on to Peter and John, all the people ran together to them in the porch which is called Solomon's, greatly amazed. 12 So when Peter saw *it*, he responded to the people: "Men of Israel, why do you marvel at this? Or why look so intently at us, as though by our own power or godliness we had made this man walk? 13 The God of Abraham, Isaac, and Jacob, the God of our fathers, glorified His Servant Jesus, whom you delivered up and denied in the presence of Pilate, when he was determined to let *Him* go. 14 But you denied the Holy One and the Just, and asked for a murderer to be granted to you, 15 and killed the Prince of life, whom God raised from the dead, of which we are witnesses. 16 And His name, through faith in His name, has made this man strong, whom you see and know. Yes, the faith which *comes* through Him has given him this perfect soundness in the presence of you all.

17 "Yet now, brethren, I know that you did *it* in ignorance, as *did* also your rulers. 18 But those things which God foretold by the mouth of all His prophets, that the Christ would suffer, He has thus fulfilled. 19 Repent therefore and be converted, that your sins may be blotted out, so that times of

אִישׁ כְּפִי צָרְכּוֹ. 46 יוֹם יוֹם הִתְמִידוּ לִהְיוֹת לֵב אֶחָד בְּבֵית הַמִּקְדָּשׁ וְהָיוּ בּוֹצְעִים אֶת הַלֶּחֶם בְּבָתֵּיהֶם, אוֹכְלִים אֶת מְזוֹנָם בְּשִׂמְחָה וּבְתֹם לֵב 47 וּמְשַׁבְּחִים אֶת אֱלֹהִים. הֵם מָצְאוּ חֵן בְּעֵינֵי כָּל הָעָם, וְהָאָדוֹן הוֹסִיף עֲלֵיהֶם יוֹם יוֹם אֶת הַנּוֹשָׁעִים.

ג כֵּיפָא וְיוֹחָנָן הָיוּ בְּדַרְכָּם אֶל בֵּית הַמִּקְדָּשׁ בְּעֵת תְּפִלַּת מִנְחָה, בְּשָׁעָה שָׁלוֹשׁ אַחֲרֵי הַצָּהֳרַיִם. 2 וְאִישׁ אֶחָד, פִּסֵּחַ מִבֶּטֶן אִמּוֹ, נִשָּׂא לְשָׁם; מִדֵּי יוֹם בְּיוֹמוֹ הָיוּ מַנִּיחִים אוֹתוֹ לְיַד שַׁעַר בֵּית הַמִּקְדָּשׁ, הַשַּׁעַר הַמְכֻנֶּה "מְהֻדָּר", לְבַקֵּשׁ נְדָבוֹת מִן הַבָּאִים אֶל בֵּית הַמִּקְדָּשׁ. 3 כִּרְאוֹתוֹ אֶת כֵּיפָא וְאֶת יוֹחָנָן עוֹמְדִים לְהִכָּנֵס לְבֵית הַמִּקְדָּשׁ, בִּקֵּשׁ מֵהֶם נְדָבָה. 4 נָעַץ בּוֹ כֵּיפָא אֶת עֵינָיו, וְכֵן עָשָׂה גַּם יוֹחָנָן, וְאָמַר: "הַבֵּט אֵלֵינוּ!" 5 הוּא הִסְתַּכֵּל אֲלֵיהֶם בְּקַוּוֹתוֹ לְקַבֵּל מֵהֶם מַשֶּׁהוּ, 6 אֶלָּא שֶׁכֵּיפָא אָמַר: "כֶּסֶף וְזָהָב אֵין לִי, אֲבָל אֶת מַה שֶּׁיֵּשׁ לִי, אֶת זֶה אֶתֵּן לְךָ: בְּשֵׁם יֵשׁוּעַ הַמָּשִׁיחַ מִנָּצְרַת – הִתְהַלֵּךְ!" 7 הוּא הֶחֱזִיק בְּיָדוֹ הַיְמָנִית וְהֵקִים אוֹתוֹ, וּפִתְאוֹם הִתְחַזְּקוּ רַגְלָיו וְקַרְסֻלָּיו. 8 קָפַץ הָאִישׁ וְעָמַד עַל רַגְלָיו. מִיָּד הָלַךְ וְנִכְנַס אִתָּם לְבֵית הַמִּקְדָּשׁ כְּשֶׁהוּא מְהַלֵּךְ וּמְקַפֵּץ וּמְהַלֵּל אֶת אֱלֹהִים. 9 רָאוּהוּ כָּל הָאֲנָשִׁים מִתְהַלֵּךְ וּמְשַׁבֵּחַ אֶת אֱלֹהִים, 10 וְהִכִּירוּ שֶׁזֶּה הוּא אֲשֶׁר הָיָה יוֹשֵׁב לְבַקֵּשׁ נְדָבוֹת בַּשַּׁעַר הַמְהֻדָּר שֶׁל בֵּית הַמִּקְדָּשׁ; נִתְמַלְּאוּ תִּמָּהוֹן וְתַדְהֵמָה עַל מַה שֶּׁקָּרָה לוֹ.

11 הָאִישׁ לֹא הִרְפָּה מִכֵּיפָא וְיוֹחָנָן, וְאָז רָצוּ אֲלֵיהֶם כָּל הָאֲנָשִׁים, מְלֵאֵי הִשְׁתּוֹמְמוּת, בָּאוּלָם הַנִּקְרָא "אוּלָם שְׁלֹמֹה". 12 רָאָה זֹאת כֵּיפָא וְאָמַר אֶל הָעָם: "אַנְשֵׁי יִשְׂרָאֵל, לָמָּה אַתֶּם תְּמֵהִים עַל הַדָּבָר הַזֶּה? וּמַדּוּעַ אַתֶּם מִסְתַּכְּלִים בָּנוּ כְּאִלּוּ בְּכֹחֵנוּ אוֹ בַּחֲסִידוּתֵנוּ עָשִׂינוּ שֶׁהוּא יִתְהַלֵּךְ? 13 אֱלֹהֵי אַבְרָהָם וְיִצְחָק וְיַעֲקֹב, אֱלֹהֵי אֲבוֹתֵינוּ, פֵּאַר בִּכְבוֹד אֶת עַבְדּוֹ יֵשׁוּעַ אֲשֶׁר מְסַרְתֶּם אוֹתוֹ וּכְפַרְתֶּם בּוֹ לִפְנֵי פִּילָטוֹס כַּאֲשֶׁר הֶחֱלִיט לְשַׁלְּחוֹ לַחָפְשִׁי. 14 אַתֶּם כְּפַרְתֶּם בַּקָּדוֹשׁ וּבַצַּדִּיק וּבִקַּשְׁתֶּם שֶׁיְּשֻׁחְרַר לָכֶם אִישׁ רוֹצֵחַ, 15 וְאֶת שַׂר חַיִּים הֲרַגְתֶּם – הוּא אֲשֶׁר אֱלֹהִים הֱקִימוֹ מִן הַמֵּתִים וְעַל זֹאת אֲנַחְנוּ עֵדִים. 16 עַל-סְמַךְ הָאֱמוּנָה בִּשְׁמוֹ חִזֵּק שְׁמוֹ אֶת הָאִישׁ הַזֶּה אֲשֶׁר אַתֶּם רוֹאִים וּמַכִּירִים, וְהָאֱמוּנָה בּוֹ נָתְנָה לָאִישׁ אֶת הָרְפוּאָה הַשְּׁלֵמָה הַזֹּאת לְעֵינֵי כֻּלְּכֶם. 17 וְעַתָּה, אַחַי, אֲנִי יוֹדֵעַ שֶׁבִּבְלִי דַעַת פְּעַלְתֶּם, כְּמוֹ שֶׁפָּעֲלוּ מַנְהִיגֵיכֶם. 18 אַךְ אֱלֹהִים קִיֵּם בְּדֶרֶךְ זֹאת אֶת אֲשֶׁר הוֹדִיעַ מִקֶּדֶם בְּפִי כָּל הַנְּבִיאִים – שֶׁמְּשִׁיחוֹ יִסְבֹּל. 19 לָכֵן הִתְחָרְטוּ וְשׁוּבוּ בִּתְשׁוּבָה כְּדֵי שֶׁיִּמָּחוּ

refreshing may come from the presence of the Lord, ²⁰ and that He may send Jesus Christ, who was preached to you before, ²¹ whom heaven must receive until the times of restoration of all things, which God has spoken by the mouth of all His holy prophets since the world began. ²² For Moses truly said to the fathers, *'The LORD your God will raise up for you a Prophet like me from your brethren. Him you shall hear in all things, whatever He says to you. ²³ And it shall be that every soul who will not hear that Prophet shall be utterly destroyed from among the people.'* ²⁴ Yes, and all the prophets, from Samuel and those who follow, as many as have spoken, have also foretold these days. ²⁵ You are sons of the prophets, and of the covenant which God made with our fathers, saying to Abraham, *'And in your seed all the families of the earth shall be blessed.'* ²⁶ To you first, God, having raised up His Servant Jesus, sent Him to bless you, in turning away every one *of you* from your iniquities."

4 Now as they spoke to the people, the priests, the captain of the temple, and the Sadducees came upon them, ² being greatly disturbed that they taught the people and preached in Jesus the resurrection from the dead. ³ And they laid hands on them, and put *them* in custody until the next day, for it was already evening. ⁴ However, many of those who heard the word believed; and the number of the men came to be about five thousand.

⁵ And it came to pass, on the next day, that their rulers, elders, and scribes, ⁶ as well as Annas the high priest, Caiaphas, John, and Alexander, and as many as were of the family of the high priest, were gathered together at Jerusalem. ⁷ And when they had set them in the midst, they asked, "By what power or by what name have you done this?"

⁸ Then Peter, filled with the Holy Spirit, said to them, "Rulers of the people and elders of Israel: ⁹ If we this day are judged for a good deed *done* to a helpless man, by what means he has been made well, ¹⁰ let it be known to you all, and to all the people of Israel, that by the name of Jesus Christ of Nazareth, whom you crucified, whom God raised from the dead, by Him this man stands here before you whole. ¹¹ This is the *'stone which was rejected by you builders, which has become the chief cornerstone.'* ¹² Nor is there salvation in any other, for there is no other name under heaven given among men by which we must be saved."

¹³ Now when they saw the boldness of Peter and John, and perceived that they were uneducated and untrained men, they marveled. And they realized

חֲטָאֵיכֶם, ²⁰ לְמַעַן יָבוֹאוּ יְמֵי רְוָחָה מִלִּפְנֵי אֲדֹנָי וְהוּא יִשְׁלַח אֶת אֲשֶׁר יָעַד לָכֶם מִקֶּדֶם, אֶת הַמָּשִׁיחַ יֵשׁוּעַ, ²¹ אֲשֶׁר צָרִיךְ שֶׁיְּקַבְּלוּ אוֹתוֹ הַשָּׁמַיִם עַד עֵת הָשֵׁבַת הַכֹּל לְתִקּוּנוֹ, דָּבָר שֶׁאֱלֹהִים דִּבֶּר מֵעוֹלָם בְּפִי נְבִיאָיו הַקְּדוֹשִׁים. ²² הֵן מֹשֶׁה אָמַר אֶל אֲבוֹתֵינוּ: 'נָבִיא יָקִים לָכֶם יהוה אֱלֹהֵיכֶם מִקֶּרֶב אֲחֵיכֶם, כָּמוֹנִי; אֵלָיו תִּשְׁמָעוּן כְּכֹל אֲשֶׁר יְדַבֵּר אֲלֵיכֶם. ²³ וְהָיָה כָּל הַנֶּפֶשׁ אֲשֶׁר לֹא תִשְׁמַע אֶל הַנָּבִיא הַהוּא וְנִכְרְתָה מֵעַמֶּיהָ.' ²⁴ וְכָל הַנְּבִיאִים מִשְּׁמוּאֵל וָאֵילָךְ, כֻּלָּם דִּבְּרוּ וְהוֹדִיעוּ עַל־אוֹדוֹת הַיָּמִים הָאֵלֶּה. ²⁵ אַתֶּם בְּנֵי הַנְּבִיאִים וּבְנֵי הַבְּרִית אֲשֶׁר כָּרַת אֱלֹהִים עִם אֲבוֹתֵינוּ כְּאָמְרוֹ אֶל אַבְרָהָם: 'וְנִבְרְכוּ בְזַרְעֲךָ כָּל מִשְׁפְּחוֹת הָאֲדָמָה.' ²⁶ לָכֶם רִאשׁוֹנָה הֵקִים אֱלֹהִים אֶת עַבְדּוֹ וְשָׁלַח אוֹתוֹ לְבָרֵךְ אֶתְכֶם, בְּשׁוּבְכֶם אִישׁ אִישׁ מִדַּרְכּוֹ הָרָעָה."

ד כַּאֲשֶׁר דִּבְּרוּ אֶל הָעָם בָּאוּ אֲלֵיהֶם הַכֹּהֲנִים וּנְגִיד בֵּית הַמִּקְדָּשׁ וְהַצְּדוֹקִים; ² כּוֹעֲסִים הָיוּ עַל שֶׁלִּמְּדוּ אֶת הָעָם וּבִשְּׂרוּ בְּיֵשׁוּעַ אֶת הַתְּחִיָּה מִן הַמֵּתִים. ³ הֵם תָּפְסוּ אוֹתָם וְכֵיוָן שֶׁהָיָה כְּבָר עֶרֶב כָּלְאוּ אוֹתָם עַד לְמָחֳרָת. ⁴ אוּלָם רַבִּים מֵהַשּׁוֹמְעִים אֶת הַדָּבָר הֶאֱמִינוּ, וּמִסְפָּרָם הָיָה כַּחֲמֵשֶׁת אַלְפִים אִישׁ. ⁵ לְמָחֳרָת נֶאֶסְפוּ שָׂרֵיהֶם וְזִקְנֵיהֶם וְסוֹפְרֵיהֶם בִּירוּשָׁלַיִם, ⁶ גַּם חָנָן הַכֹּהֵן הַגָּדוֹל וְקַיָּפָא וְיוֹחָנָן וַאֲלֶכְּסַנְדֶּר וּבְנֵי מִשְׁפְּחוֹת הַכֹּהֲנִים הַגְּדוֹלִים. ⁷ הֵם הֶעֱמִידוּ אוֹתָם בַּתָּוֶךְ וְשָׁאֲלוּ: "בְּאֵיזֶה כֹּחַ אוֹ בְּאֵיזֶה שֵׁם עֲשִׂיתֶם אֶת זֹאת?"

⁸ כֵּיפָא נִתְמַלֵּא רוּחַ הַקֹּדֶשׁ וְאָמַר לָהֶם: "שָׂרֵי הָעָם וְזִקְנֵי יִשְׂרָאֵל, ⁹ אִם אֲנַחְנוּ נֶחְקָרִים הַיּוֹם עַל מַעֲשֶׂה טוֹב שֶׁנַּעֲשָׂה לְאִישׁ חוֹלֶה – כֵּיצַד נִרְפָּא הָאִישׁ הַזֶּה – ¹⁰ שֶׁיְּהֵא יָדוּעַ לְכֻלְּכֶם וּלְכָל עַם יִשְׂרָאֵל כִּי בְּשֵׁם יֵשׁוּעַ הַמָּשִׁיחַ מִנָּצְרַת, אֲשֶׁר אַתֶּם צְלַבְתֶּם וַאֲשֶׁר אֱלֹהִים הֵקִימוֹ מִן הַמֵּתִים, בַּשֵּׁם הַזֶּה הוּא עוֹמֵד בָּרִיא לִפְנֵיכֶם. ¹¹ הוּא הָאֶבֶן שֶׁמְּאַסְתֶּם, אַתֶּם הַבּוֹנִים, אֲשֶׁר הָיְתָה לְרֹאשׁ פִּנָּה. ¹² וְאֵין יְשׁוּעָה בְּאַחֵר, כִּי אֵין שֵׁם אַחֵר נָתוּן לִבְנֵי אָדָם תַּחַת הַשָּׁמַיִם, וּבוֹ עָלֵינוּ לְהִוָּשַׁע."

¹³ כְּשֶׁרָאוּ אֶת בִּטְחוֹנָם שֶׁל כֵּיפָא וְיוֹחָנָן וְהִבְחִינוּ שֶׁהֵם אֲנָשִׁים פְּשׁוּטִים וּבִלְתִּי מְלֻמָּדִים – תָּמְהוּ. הֵם

that they had been with Jesus. 14 And seeing the man who had been healed standing with them, they could say nothing against it. 15 But when they had commanded them to go aside out of the council, they conferred among themselves, 16 saying, "What shall we do to these men? For, indeed, that a notable miracle has been done through them *is* evident to all who dwell in Jerusalem, and we cannot deny *it.* 17 But so that it spreads no further among the people, let us severely threaten them, that from now on they speak to no man in this name."

18 So they called them and commanded them not to speak at all nor teach in the name of Jesus. 19 But Peter and John answered and said to them, "Whether it is right in the sight of God to listen to you more than to God, you judge. 20 For we cannot but speak the things which we have seen and heard." 21 So when they had further threatened them, they let them go, finding no way of punishing them, because of the people, since they all glorified God for what had been done. 22 For the man was over forty years old on whom this miracle of healing had been performed.

23 And being let go, they went to their own *companions* and reported all that the chief priests and elders had said to them. 24 So when they heard that, they raised their voice to God with one accord and said: "Lord, You *are* God, who made heaven and earth and the sea, and all that is in them, 25 who by the mouth of Your servant David have said:

'Why did the nations rage,
    And the people plot vain things?
26   The kings of the earth took their stand,
    And the rulers were gathered together
    Against the LORD and against His Christ.'

27 "For truly against Your holy Servant Jesus, whom You anointed, both Herod and Pontius Pilate, with the Gentiles and the people of Israel, were gathered together 28 to do whatever Your hand and Your purpose determined before to be done. 29 Now, Lord, look on their threats, and grant to Your servants that with all boldness they may speak Your word, 30 by stretching out Your hand to heal, and that signs and wonders may be done through the name of Your holy Servant Jesus."

31 And when they had prayed, the place where they were assembled together was shaken; and they were all filled with the Holy Spirit, and they spoke the word of God with boldness.

32 Now the multitude of those who believed were of one heart and one soul; neither did anyone say that any of the things he possessed was his own, but

זֶהוּ אוֹתָם, שֶׁבְּעָבָר הָיוּ יַחַד עִם יֵשׁוּעַ. 14 אַךְ בִּרְאוֹתָם אֶת הָאִישׁ שֶׁנִּרְפָּא עוֹמֵד עִמָּהֶם, לֹא הָיָה לָהֶם מַה לִטְעוֹן. 15 לְאַחַר שֶׁצִּוּוּ עֲלֵיהֶם לָצֵאת מִן הַסַּנְהֶדְרִין הִתְיָעֲצוּ יַחְדָּיו. 16 אָמְרוּ: "מַה נַּעֲשֶׂה לָאֲנָשִׁים הָאֵלֶּה? הֲרֵי אוֹת בָּרוּר נַעֲשָׂה עַל־יָדָם, גָּלוּי הוּא לְכָל יוֹשְׁבֵי יְרוּשָׁלַיִם וְאֵין אָנוּ יְכוֹלִים לְהַכְחִישׁ אוֹתוֹ. 17 אֲבָל כְּדֵי שֶׁלֹּא יוֹסִיף הַדָּבָר לְהִתְפַּרְסֵם בָּעָם, נָאֵים עֲלֵיהֶם שֶׁלֹּא יְדַבְּרוּ עוֹד בַּשֵּׁם הַזֶּה אֶל שׁוּם אָדָם." 18 הֵם קָרְאוּ לָהֶם וְצִוּוּ אוֹתָם שֶׁלֹּא לְדַבֵּר וְלֹא לְלַמֵּד דָּבָר בְּשֵׁם יֵשׁוּעַ.

19 הֵשִׁיבוּ כֵּיפָא וְיוֹחָנָן וְאָמְרוּ לָהֶם: "הַאִם מֻצְדָּק לִפְנֵי אֱלֹהִים לִשְׁמוֹעַ לָכֶם יוֹתֵר מֵאֲשֶׁר לֵאלֹהִים? שִׁפְטוּ אַתֶּם! 20 הֲרֵי אֵינֶנּוּ יְכוֹלִים שֶׁלֹּא לְהַגִּיד אֶת אֲשֶׁר רָאִינוּ וְשָׁמַעְנוּ!"

21 אַחֲרֵי אִיּוּמִים נוֹסָפִים שִׁחְרְרוּ אוֹתָם, כִּי לֹא מָצְאוּ דֶּרֶךְ לְהַעֲנִישׁ אוֹתָם בִּגְלַל הָעָם, שֶׁכֵּן הַכֹּל שִׁבְּחוּ אֶת אֱלֹהִים עַל מַה שֶּׁנַּעֲשָׂה; 22 כִּי בֶּן אַרְבָּעִים שָׁנָה וָמַעְלָה הָיָה הָאִישׁ אֲשֶׁר נַעֲשָׂה בּוֹ נֵס הָרִפּוּי הַזֶּה. 23 לְאַחַר שֶׁשֻּׁחְרְרוּ הָלְכוּ אֶל חַבְרֵיהֶם וְסִפְּרוּ מַה שֶּׁאָמְרוּ לָהֶם רָאשֵׁי הַכֹּהֲנִים וְהַזְּקֵנִים. 24 הֵם שָׁמְעוּ זֹאת וּבְלֵב אֶחָד נָשְׂאוּ קוֹלָם לֵאלֹהִים וְאָמְרוּ: "אֲדֹנָי, אַתָּה אֲשֶׁר עָשִׂיתָ אֶת־הַשָּׁמַיִם וְאֶת־הָאָרֶץ אֶת־הַיָּם וְאֶת־כָּל־אֲשֶׁר־בָּם, 25 בְּפִי דָוִד עַבְדְּךָ אָבִינוּ אָמַרְתָּ בְּרוּחַ הַקֹּדֶשׁ:

'לָמָּה רָגְשׁוּ גוֹיִם
וּלְאֻמִּים יֶהְגּוּ־רִיק?
26 יִתְיַצְּבוּ מַלְכֵי־אֶרֶץ
וְרוֹזְנִים נוֹסְדוּ־יָחַד
עַל־יהוה וְעַל־מְשִׁיחוֹ.'

27 כִּי אָמְנָם נֶאֶסְפוּ בָּעִיר הַזֹּאת הוֹרְדוֹס וּפּוֹנְטְיוֹס פִּילָטוֹס עִם גּוֹיִם וּלְאֻמֵּי יִשְׂרָאֵל עַל עַבְדְּךָ הַקָּדוֹשׁ יֵשׁוּעַ אֲשֶׁר מָשַׁחְתָּ – 28 לַעֲשׂוֹת אֶת מַה שֶּׁיָּדְךָ וַעֲצָתְךָ כְּבָר מִקֶּדֶם גָּזְרוּ שֶׁיִּהְיֶה. 29 וְכָעֵת, אֲדֹנָי, רְאֵה אֶת אִיּוּמֵיהֶם וְתֵן לַעֲבָדֶיךָ לוֹמַר אֶת דְּבָרְךָ בְּכָל אֹמֶץ הַלֵּב, 30 בִּנְטוֹתְךָ אֶת יָדְךָ לְמַרְפֵּא וְלַעֲשׂוֹת אוֹתוֹת וּמוֹפְתִים עַל־יְדֵי שֵׁם יֵשׁוּעַ עַבְדְּךָ הַקָּדוֹשׁ."

31 כְּשֶׁסִּיְּמוּ אֶת תְּפִלָּתָם הִזְדַּעְזַע הַמָּקוֹם שֶׁהִתְאַסְּפוּ בּוֹ וְכֻלָּם נִתְמַלְּאוּ רוּחַ הַקֹּדֶשׁ וְדִבְּרוּ אֶת דְּבַר אֱלֹהִים בְּאֹמֶץ לֵב. 32 קְהַל הַמַּאֲמִינִים הָיָה לֵב אֶחָד וְנֶפֶשׁ אַחַת. אִישׁ מֵהֶם לֹא אָמַר עַל דָּבָר מִקִּנְיָנָיו כִּי שֶׁלּוֹ הוּא, אֶלָּא

they had all things in common. ³³ And with great power the apostles gave witness to the resurrection of the Lord Jesus. And great grace was upon them all. ³⁴ Nor was there anyone among them who lacked; for all who were possessors of lands or houses sold them, and brought the proceeds of the things that were sold, ³⁵ and laid *them* at the apostles' feet; and they distributed to each as anyone had need.

³⁶ And Joses, who was also named Barnabas by the apostles (which is translated Son of Encouragement), a Levite of the country of Cyprus, ³⁷ having land, sold *it,* and brought the money and laid *it* at the apostles' feet.

5 But a certain man named Ananias, with Sapphira his wife, sold a possession. ² And he kept back *part* of the proceeds, his wife also being aware *of it,* and brought a certain part and laid *it* at the apostles' feet. ³ But Peter said, "Ananias, why has Satan filled your heart to lie to the Holy Spirit and keep back *part* of the price of the land for yourself? ⁴ While it remained, was it not your own? And after it was sold, was it not in your own control? Why have you conceived this thing in your heart? You have not lied to men but to God."

⁵ Then Ananias, hearing these words, fell down and breathed his last. So great fear came upon all those who heard these things. ⁶ And the young men arose and wrapped him up, carried *him* out, and buried *him.*

⁷ Now it was about three hours later when his wife came in, not knowing what had happened. ⁸ And Peter answered her, "Tell me whether you sold the land for so much?"

She said, "Yes, for so much."

⁹ Then Peter said to her, "How is it that you have agreed together to test the Spirit of the Lord? Look, the feet of those who have buried your husband *are* at the door, and they will carry you out." ¹⁰ Then immediately she fell down at his feet and breathed her last. And the young men came in and found her dead, and carrying *her* out, buried *her* by her husband. ¹¹ So great fear came upon all the church and upon all who heard these things.

¹² And through the hands of the apostles many signs and wonders were done among the people. And they were all with one accord in Solomon's Porch. ¹³ Yet none of the rest dared join them, but the people esteemed them highly. ¹⁴ And believers were increasingly added to the Lord, multitudes of both men and women, ¹⁵ so that they brought the sick out into the streets and laid *them* on beds and couches, that at least the shadow of Peter passing

שֻׁתָּפִים הָיוּ בַּכֹּל. 33 הַשְּׁלִיחִים הֵעִידוּ בְּכֹחַ רַב עַל תְּחִיַּת הָאָדוֹן יֵשׁוּעַ וְחֶסֶד רַב הָיָה עַל כֻּלָּם. 34 גַּם לֹא הָיָה בָּהֶם אִישׁ שָׁרוּי בְּמַחְסוֹר, כִּי כָּל בַּעֲלֵי הַשָּׂדוֹת וּבַעֲלֵי הַבָּתִּים מָכְרוּ אֶת נִכְסֵיהֶם וְהֵבִיאוּ אֶת כֶּסֶף מְחִירָם. 35 הֵם הִנִּיחוּהוּ לְרַגְלֵי הַשְּׁלִיחִים וּלְכָל אִישׁ נִתַּן כְּפִי צָרְכּוֹ. 36 וְיוֹסֵף, אֲשֶׁר הַשְּׁלִיחִים כִּנּוּהוּ בַּר־נַבָּא, כְּלוֹמַר בֶּן הַנֶּחָמָה, אִישׁ לֵוִי יְלִיד קַפְרִיסִין, 37 מָכַר אֶת שָׂדֵהוּ וְגַם הוּא הֵבִיא אֶת הַכֶּסֶף וְהִנִּיחוֹ לְרַגְלֵי הַשְּׁלִיחִים.

ה אִישׁ אֶחָד, חֲנַנְיָה שְׁמוֹ, וְאִשְׁתּוֹ שַׁפִּירָה מָכְרוּ שָׂדֶה. 2 בִּידִיעַת אִשְׁתּוֹ הוּא נָטַל לְעַצְמוֹ חֵלֶק מִן הַכֶּסֶף וְאַחֲרֵי כֵן הֵבִיא חֵלֶק מְסֻיָּם וְהִנִּיחוֹ לְרַגְלֵי הַשְּׁלִיחִים. 3 אָמַר לוֹ כֵּיפָא: "חֲנַנְיָה, לָמָּה זֶה מִלֵּא הַשָּׂטָן אֶת לִבְּךָ לְשַׁקֵּר לְרוּחַ הַקֹּדֶשׁ וְלִטֹּל לְעַצְמְךָ מִמְּחִיר הַשָּׂדֶה? 4 הֲרֵי כְּשֶׁעָמַד בִּרְשׁוּתְךָ – שֶׁלְּךָ הָיָה, וְאַחֲרֵי שֶׁנִּמְכַּר עָמְדָה תְמוּרָתוֹ בִּרְשׁוּתְךָ. לָמָּה עָלָה עַל לִבְּךָ מַעֲשֶׂה זֶה? לֹא לִבְנֵי אָדָם שִׁקַּרְתָּ כִּי אִם לֵאלֹהִים!" 5 כְּשֶׁשָּׁמַע חֲנַנְיָה אֶת הַדְּבָרִים הָאֵלֶּה נָפַל וְנָפַח אֶת רוּחוֹ, וּפַחַד גָּדוֹל נָפַל עַל כָּל הַשּׁוֹמְעִים. 6 קָמוּ הַצְּעִירִים, עָטְפוּ אוֹתוֹ, נְשָׂאוּהוּ הַחוּצָה וְקָבְרוּ אוֹתוֹ.

7 כְּשָׁלֹשׁ שָׁעוֹת לְאַחַר מִכֵּן נִכְנְסָה אִשְׁתּוֹ וְהִיא אֵינֶנָּה יוֹדַעַת מַה שֶּׁאֵרַע. 8 פָּנָה אֵלֶיהָ כֵּיפָא וְאָמַר: "הַגִּידִי לִי, הַאִם בַּמְּחִיר הַזֶּה מְכַרְתֶּם אֶת הַשָּׂדֶה?" אָמְרָה: "כֵּן, בַּמְּחִיר הַזֶּה".

9 אָמַר לָהּ כֵּיפָא: "לָמָּה הִתְאַחַדְתֶּם שְׁנֵיכֶם לְנַסּוֹת אֶת רוּחַ אֱלֹהִים? הִנֵּה בַּפֶּתַח רַגְלֵי הַקּוֹבְרִים אֶת בַּעֲלֵךְ וְהֵם יִשְׂאוּ אוֹתָךְ הַחוּצָה." 10 מִיָּד נָפְלָה לְרַגְלָיו וְנָפְחָה אֶת רוּחָהּ. כְּשֶׁנִּכְנְסוּ הַבַּחוּרִים מְצָאוּהָ מֵתָה. הֵם נָשְׂאוּ אוֹתָהּ הַחוּצָה וְקָבְרוּ אוֹתָהּ עַל־יַד בַּעֲלָהּ. 11 פַּחַד גָּדוֹל נָפַל עַל כָּל הַקְּהִלָּה וְעַל כָּל הַשּׁוֹמְעִים אֶת הַדְּבָרִים הָאֵלֶּה.

12 אוֹתוֹת וּמוֹפְתִים רַבִּים עָשׂוּ הַשְּׁלִיחִים בְּקֶרֶב הָעָם, וְהַכֹּל נֶאֶסְפוּ לֵב אֶחָד בְּאוּלָם שְׁלֹמֹה. 13 מִן הָאֲחֵרִים לֹא הֵעֵז אִישׁ לְהִצְטָרֵף אֲלֵיהֶם, אַךְ הָעָם הוֹקִיר אוֹתָם. 14 וְאָמְנָם נִסְפְּחוּ אֶל הָאָדוֹן עוֹד מַאֲמִינִים, גְּבָרִים וְנָשִׁים רַבִּים מְאֹד, 15 עַד כִּי נָשְׂאוּ אֶת הַחוֹלִים אֶל הָרְחוֹבוֹת וְשָׂמוּ אוֹתָם עַל מִטּוֹת וּמַצָּעִים כְּדֵי שֶׁבְּבוֹא כֵּיפָא אֲפִלּוּ רַק צִלּוֹ יֵצֵל עַל

by might fall on some of them. 16 Also a multitude gathered from the surrounding cities to Jerusalem, bringing sick people and those who were tormented by unclean spirits, and they were all healed.

17 Then the high priest rose up, and all those who *were* with him (which is the sect of the Sadducees), and they were filled with indignation, 18 and laid their hands on the apostles and put them in the common prison. 19 But at night an angel of the Lord opened the prison doors and brought them out, and said, 20 "Go, stand in the temple and speak to the people all the words of this life."

21 And when they heard *that,* they entered the temple early in the morning and taught. But the high priest and those with him came and called the council together, with all the elders of the children of Israel, and sent to the prison to have them brought.

22 But when the officers came and did not find them in the prison, they returned and reported, 23 saying, "Indeed we found the prison shut securely, and the guards standing outside before the doors; but when we opened them, we found no one inside!" 24 Now when the high priest, the captain of the temple, and the chief priests heard these things, they wondered what the outcome would be. 25 So one came and told them, saying, "Look, the men whom you put in prison are standing in the temple and teaching the people!"

26 Then the captain went with the officers and brought them without violence, for they feared the people, lest they should be stoned. 27 And when they had brought them, they set *them* before the council. And the high priest asked them, 28 saying, "Did we not strictly command you not to teach in this name? And look, you have filled Jerusalem with your doctrine, and intend to bring this Man's blood on us!"

29 But Peter and the *other* apostles answered and said: "We ought to obey God rather than men. 30 The God of our fathers raised up Jesus whom you murdered by hanging on a tree. 31 Him God has exalted to His right hand *to be* Prince and Savior, to give repentance to Israel and forgiveness of sins. 32 And we are His witnesses to these things, and *so* also *is* the Holy Spirit whom God has given to those who obey Him."

33 When they heard *this,* they were furious and plotted to kill them. 34 Then one in the council stood up, a Pharisee named Gamaliel, a teacher of the law held in respect by all the people, and commanded them to put the apostles outside for a little while. 35 And he said to them: "Men of Israel, take heed to yourselves what you intend to do

16 גַּם הֲמוֹן הָעָם מִן הֶעָרִים הַסְּמוּכוֹת לִירוּשָׁלַיִם נִקְבְּצוּ כְּשֶׁהֵם נוֹשְׂאִים חוֹלִים וּמְעֻנִּים עַל־יְדֵי רוּחוֹת טְמֵאוֹת, וְכֻלָּם נִרְפְּאוּ.

17 הַכֹּהֵן הַגָּדוֹל וְכָל אֲנָשָׁיו, אַנְשֵׁי כַּת הַצְּדוֹקִים, נִתְמַלְּאוּ קִנְאָה. הֵם קָמוּ, 18 תָּפְסוּ אֶת הַשְּׁלִיחִים וְשָׂמוּ אוֹתָם בַּכֶּלֶא הָעִירוֹנִי. 19 אֶלָּא שֶׁמַּלְאַךְ יהוה פָּתַח בַּלַּיְלָה אֶת דַּלְתוֹת בֵּית הַכֶּלֶא וְהוֹצִיאָם בְּאָמְרוֹ: 20 "לְכוּ וְהִתְיַצְּבוּ בַּמִּקְדָּשׁ וְדַבְּרוּ אֶל הָעָם אֶת כָּל דִּבְרֵי הַחַיִּים הָאֵלֶּה."

21 הֵם שָׁמְעוּ וְעִם שַׁחַר נִכְנְסוּ לְבֵית הַמִּקְדָּשׁ וְהֵחֵלּוּ לְלַמֵּד. בָּא הַכֹּהֵן הַגָּדוֹל וַאֲנָשָׁיו וְכִנְּסוּ אֶת הַסַּנְהֶדְרִין וְכָל מוֹעֶצֶת זִקְנֵי בְּנֵי יִשְׂרָאֵל. הֵם שָׁלְחוּ אֶל הַכֶּלֶא לְהָבִיא אוֹתָם, 22 אַךְ כְּשֶׁבָּאוּ הַמְשָׁרְתִים לֹא מָצְאוּ אוֹתָם בַּכֶּלֶא. חָזְרוּ וְהוֹדִיעוּ: 23 "מָצָאנוּ אֶת בֵּית הַסֹּהַר סָגוּר בְּאֹפֶן בָּטוּחַ לַחֲלוּטִין וְהַשּׁוֹמְרִים נִצָּבִים לְיַד הַדְּלָתוֹת. אֲבָל כְּשֶׁפְּתַחְנוּ לֹא מָצָאנוּ אִישׁ בִּפְנִים." 24 לְשֵׁמַע הַדְּבָרִים הָאֵלֶּה נָבוֹכוּ נְגִיד בֵּית הַמִּקְדָּשׁ וְרָאשֵׁי הַכֹּהֲנִים; תְּמֵהִים הָיוּ עַל פֵּשֶׁר הַדָּבָר. 25 אָז בָּא מִישֶׁהוּ וְהוֹדִיעַ לָהֶם: "הִנֵּה הָאֲנָשִׁים אֲשֶׁר שַׂמְתֶּם בַּמַּאֲסָר עוֹמְדִים בְּבֵית הַמִּקְדָּשׁ וּמְלַמְּדִים אֶת הָעָם!" 26 הָלַךְ הַנָּגִיד עִם הַמְשָׁרְתִים וֶהֱבִיאָם אוֹתָם, אַךְ לֹא בְּכֹחַ, כִּי פָחֲדוּ מִן הָעָם פֶּן יִרְגְּמוּ אוֹתָם. 27 הֵבִיאוּ אוֹתָם וְהֶעֱמִידוּם לִפְנֵי הַסַּנְהֶדְרִין. שָׁאַל אוֹתָם הַכֹּהֵן הַגָּדוֹל: 28 "הַאִם לֹא צִוִּינוּ עֲלֵיכֶם בְּתֹקֶף שֶׁלֹּא לְלַמֵּד בַּשֵּׁם הַזֶּה? וְהִנֵּה מִלֵּאתֶם אֶת יְרוּשָׁלַיִם בְּתוֹרַתְכֶם וְאַתֶּם מִתְכַּוְּנִים לְהָבִיא עָלֵינוּ אֶת דַּם הָאִישׁ הַזֶּה!"

29 הֵשִׁיב כֵּיפָא עִם הַשְּׁלִיחִים וְאָמַר: "לֵאלֹהִים צָרִיךְ לְהִשָּׁמַע יוֹתֵר מֵאֲשֶׁר לִבְנֵי אָדָם. 30 אֱלֹהֵי אֲבוֹתֵינוּ הֵקִים אֶת יֵשׁוּעַ אֲשֶׁר הֲרַגְתֶּם בְּהוֹקָעָה עַל עֵץ. 31 אֶת זֶה הֵרִים אֱלֹהִים בִּימִינוֹ לִהְיוֹת שַׂר וּמוֹשִׁיעַ, לָתֵת לְיִשְׂרָאֵל תְּשׁוּבָה וּסְלִיחַת חֲטָאִים. 32 אֲנַחְנוּ עֵדֵי הַדְּבָרִים הָאֵלֶּה, וְגַם רוּחַ הַקֹּדֶשׁ אֲשֶׁר נָתַן הָאֱלֹהִים לַשּׁוֹמְעִים בְּקוֹלוֹ." 33 כְּשֶׁשָּׁמְעוּ אֶת זֹאת הִתְרַתְּחוּ וְהֶחֱלִיטוּ לַהֲרֹג אוֹתָם. 34 אֲבָל אֶחָד מִן הַפְּרוּשִׁים בַּסַּנְהֶדְרִין, גַּמְלִיאֵל שְׁמוֹ, מוֹרֵה־תּוֹרָה מְכֻבָּד בְּעֵינֵי כָּל הָעָם, קָם וְצִוָּה לְהוֹצִיא אֶת הַשְּׁלִיחִים הַחוּצָה לִזְמַן־מָה. 35 אָמַר לָהֶם: "אַנְשֵׁי יִשְׂרָאֵל, הִזָּהֲרוּ לָכֶם בַּמֶּה שֶׁאַתֶּם מִתְכַּוְּנִים לַעֲשׂוֹת

regarding these men. 36 For some time ago Theudas rose up, claiming to be somebody. A number of men, about four hundred, joined him. He was slain, and all who obeyed him were scattered and came to nothing. 37 After this man, Judas of Galilee rose up in the days of the census, and drew away many people after him. He also perished, and all who obeyed him were dispersed. 38 And now I say to you, keep away from these men and let them alone; for if this plan or this work is of men, it will come to nothing; 39 but if it is of God, you cannot overthrow it—lest you even be found to fight against God."

40 And they agreed with him, and when they had called for the apostles and beaten *them,* they commanded that they should not speak in the name of Jesus, and let them go. 41 So they departed from the presence of the council, rejoicing that they were counted worthy to suffer shame for His name. 42 And daily in the temple, and in every house, they did not cease teaching and preaching Jesus *as* the Christ.

6 Now in those days, when *the number of* the disciples was multiplying, there arose a complaint against the Hebrews by the Hellenists, because their widows were neglected in the daily distribution. 2 Then the twelve summoned the multitude of the disciples and said, "It is not desirable that we should leave the word of God and serve tables. 3 Therefore, brethren, seek out from among you seven men of *good* reputation, full of the Holy Spirit and wisdom, whom we may appoint over this business; 4 but we will give ourselves continually to prayer and to the ministry of the word."

5 And the saying pleased the whole multitude. And they chose Stephen, a man full of faith and the Holy Spirit, and Philip, Prochorus, Nicanor, Timon, Parmenas, and Nicolas, a proselyte from Antioch, 6 whom they set before the apostles; and when they had prayed, they laid hands on them.

7 Then the word of God spread, and the number of the disciples multiplied greatly in Jerusalem, and a great many of the priests were obedient to the faith.

8 And Stephen, full of faith and power, did great wonders and signs among the people. 9 Then there arose some from what is called the Synagogue of the Freedmen (Cyrenians, Alexandrians, and those from Cilicia and Asia), disputing with Stephen. 10 And they were not able to resist the wisdom and the Spirit by which he spoke. 11 Then they secretly induced men to say, "We have heard him speak blasphemous words against Moses and God." 12 And they stirred up the people, the elders, and

לָאֲנָשִׁים הָאֵלֶּה; 36 כִּי לִפְנֵי הַיָּמִים הָאֵלֶּה קָם תּוֹדָס, שֶׁהִתְחַמֵּר לִהְיוֹת מִישֶׁהוּ, וְנִסְפְּחוּ אֵלָיו כְּאַרְבַּע מֵאוֹת אִישׁ. הוּא נֶהֱרַג וְכָל אֲשֶׁר שָׁמְעוּ בְּקוֹלוֹ נָפוֹצוּ וְהָיוּ לְאָיִן. 37 אַחֲרָיו קָם יְהוּדָה הַגְּלִילִי בִּימֵי מִפְקַד הַתּוֹשָׁבִים, וּמָשַׁךְ אַחֲרָיו אֲנָשִׁים. הַלָּה נֶהֱרַג וְכָל הַמַּצִיתִים לוֹ נִתְפַּזְּרוּ. 38 וְעַתָּה אֲנִי אוֹמֵר לָכֶם, חִדְלוּ מִן הָאֲנָשִׁים הָאֵלֶּה וְהַנִּיחוּ לָהֶם, כִּי הָעֵצָה אוֹ הַפְּעֻלָּה הַזֹּאת תּוּפַר – אִם מֵאֵת בְּנֵי אָדָם הִיא. 39 אֲבָל אִם מֵאֵת אֱלֹהִים הִיא, לֹא תּוּכְלוּ לְהָפֵר אוֹתָהּ פֶּן תִּמָּצְאוּ נִלְחָמִים בֵּאלֹהִים!" 40 הֵם שָׁמְעוּ בְּקוֹלוֹ וְקָרְאוּ לַשְּׁלִיחִים. לְאַחַר שֶׁהִלְקוּ אוֹתָם וְצִוּוּ עֲלֵיהֶם שֶׁלֹּא יְדַבְּרוּ בְּשֵׁם יֵשׁוּעַ, שִׁחְרְרוּ אוֹתָם. 41 יָצְאוּ הַשְּׁלִיחִים מִלִּפְנֵי הַסַּנְהֶדְרִין שְׂמֵחִים עַל שֶׁזָּכוּ לִסְבֹּל חֶרְפָּה לְמַעַן הַשֵּׁם. 42 וְיוֹם יוֹם, בְּבֵית הַמִּקְדָּשׁ וּבַבָּתִּים, לֹא חָדְלוּ לְלַמֵּד וּלְבַשֵּׂר עַל הַמָּשִׁיחַ יֵשׁוּעַ.

ו בַּיָּמִים הָהֵם, כְּשֶׁגָּדַל מִסְפַּר הַתַּלְמִידִים, הֵחֵלּוּ הַיְּהוּדִים דּוֹבְרֵי הַיְּוָנִית לְהִתְלוֹנֵן עַל דּוֹבְרֵי הָעִבְרִית עַל שֶׁהֶזְנִיחוּ אֶת אַלְמְנוֹתֵיהֶם בַּחֲלֻקַּת הַסַּעַד הַיּוֹמִית. 2 קָרְאוּ שְׁנֵים-עָשָׂר הַשְּׁלִיחִים אֶת הֲמוֹן הַתַּלְמִידִים וְאָמְרוּ: "לֹא רָצוּי שֶׁאֲנַחְנוּ נַעֲזֹב אֶת דְּבַר אֱלֹהִים וּנְשָׁרֵת בַּשֻּׁלְחָנוֹת. 3 לָכֵן, אַחִים, בַּחֲרוּ מִבֵּינֵיכֶם שִׁבְעָה אֲנָשִׁים בַּעֲלֵי שֵׁם טוֹב, מְלֵאֵי רוּחַ וְחָכְמָה, וְנַפְקִיד אוֹתָם עַל הָעִנְיָן הַזֶּה. 4 וַאֲנַחְנוּ נַתְמִיד בַּתְּפִלָּה וּבְשֵׁרוּת דְּבַר אֱלֹהִים." 5 נִתְקַבֵּל הַדָּבָר בְּעֵינֵי כָּל הַקָּהָל וּבָחֲרוּ אֶת סְטֶפָנוֹס, אִישׁ מָלֵא אֱמוּנָה וְרוּחַ הַקֹּדֶשׁ, וְאֶת פִילִיפּוֹס, אֶת פְּרוֹכוֹרוֹס וְאֶת נִיקָנוֹר, אֶת טִימוֹן וְאֶת פַּרְמְנָס וְאֶת נִיקוֹלָאוֹס, שֶׁהָיָה גֵּר מֵאַנְטְיוֹכְיָה. 6 הֶעֱמִידוּ אוֹתָם לִפְנֵי הַשְּׁלִיחִים, הִתְפַּלְּלוּ וְסָמְכוּ יָדַיִם עֲלֵיהֶם. 7 דְּבַר אֱלֹהִים שָׂגְשֵׂג וּמִסְפַּר הַתַּלְמִידִים בִּירוּשָׁלַיִם גָּדַל מְאֹד וְגַם הֲמוֹן רַב מִן הַכֹּהֲנִים נִשְׁמְעוּ לָאֱמוּנָה. 8 סְטֶפָנוֹס, שֶׁהָיָה מָלֵא חֶסֶד וּגְבוּרָה, עָשָׂה אוֹתוֹת וּמוֹפְתִים גְּדוֹלִים בְּקֶרֶב הָעָם. 9 קָמוּ אֲנָשִׁים מִבֵּית הַכְּנֶסֶת שֶׁל הַמְשֻׁחְרָרִים – כָּךְ הָיָה מְכֻנֶּה – וְגַם אֲנָשִׁים מִקִּירֶנְיָה וְאָלֶכְּסַנְדְּרִיָּה וּמִקִּילִיקְיָה וְאָסְיָה, וְהִתְוַכְּחוּ עִם סְטֶפָנוֹס. 10 אַךְ לֹא יָכְלוּ לַעֲמֹד נֶגֶד הַחָכְמָה וְהָרוּחַ אֲשֶׁר בְּעֶזְרָתָן דִּבֵּר. 11 הֵם הֵדִיחוּ אֲנָשִׁים לוֹמַר, "שָׁמַעְנוּ אוֹתוֹ מְדַבֵּר דִּבְרֵי נְאָצָה עַל מֹשֶׁה וְעַל אֱלֹהִים", 12 וְהֵסִיתוּ אֶת הָעָם וְאֶת

the scribes; and they came upon *him,* seized him, and brought *him* to the council. [13] They also set up false witnesses who said, "This man does not cease to speak blasphemous words against this holy place and the law; [14] for we have heard him say that this Jesus of Nazareth will destroy this place and change the customs which Moses delivered to us." [15] And all who sat in the council, looking steadfastly at him, saw his face as the face of an angel.

7 Then the high priest said, "Are these things so?"

[2] And he said, "Brethren and fathers, listen: The God of glory appeared to our father Abraham when he was in Mesopotamia, before he dwelt in Haran, [3] and said to him, *'Get out of your country and from your relatives, and come to a land that I will show you.'* [4] Then he came out of the land of the Chaldeans and dwelt in Haran. And from there, when his father was dead, He moved him to this land in which you now dwell. [5] And *God* gave him no inheritance in it, not even *enough* to set his foot on. But even when *Abraham* had no child, He promised to give it to him for a possession, and to his descendants after him. [6] But God spoke in this way: that his descendants would dwell in a foreign land, and that they would bring them into bondage and oppress *them* four hundred years. [7] *'And the nation to whom they will be in bondage I will judge,'* said God, *'and after that they shall come out and serve Me in this place.'* [8] Then He gave him the covenant of circumcision; and so *Abraham* begot Isaac and circumcised him on the eighth day; and Isaac *begot* Jacob, and Jacob *begot* the twelve patriarchs.

[9] "And the patriarchs, becoming envious, sold Joseph into Egypt. But God was with him [10] and delivered him out of all his troubles, and gave him favor and wisdom in the presence of Pharaoh, king of Egypt; and he made him governor over Egypt and all his house. [11] Now a famine and great trouble came over all the land of Egypt and Canaan, and our fathers found no sustenance. [12] But when Jacob heard that there was grain in Egypt, he sent out our fathers first. [13] And the second *time* Joseph was made known to his brothers, and Joseph's family became known to the Pharaoh. [14] Then Joseph sent and called his father Jacob and all his relatives to *him,* seventy-five people. [15] So Jacob went down to Egypt; and he died, he and our fathers. [16] And they were carried back to Shechem and laid in the tomb that Abraham bought for a sum of money from the sons of Hamor, *the father* of Shechem.

הַזְּקֵנִים וְהַסּוֹפְרִים. קָמוּ עָלָיו וְתָפְסוּ אוֹתוֹ וֶהֱבִיאוּהוּ אֶל הַסַּנְהֶדְרִין. 13 שָׁם הֶעֱמִידוּ עֵדֵי שֶׁקֶר וְהַלָּלוּ אָמְרוּ: "הָאִישׁ הַזֶּה אֵינֶנּוּ חָדֵל לְדַבֵּר דְּבָרִים נֶגֶד הַמָּקוֹם הַקָּדוֹשׁ הַזֶּה וְנֶגֶד הַתּוֹרָה, 14 כִּי שָׁמַעְנוּ אוֹתוֹ אוֹמֵר שֶׁיֵּשׁוּעַ מִנְּצֶרֶת הַזֶּה יַהֲרֹם אֶת הַמָּקוֹם הַזֶּה וִישַׁנֶּה אֶת הַחֻקִּים שֶׁמָּסַר לָנוּ מֹשֶׁה." 15 הִבִּיטוּ בּוֹ כָּל הַיּוֹשְׁבִים בַּסַּנְהֶדְרִין וְרָאוּ אֶת פָּנָיו כִּפְנֵי מַלְאָךְ.

7 שָׁאַל הַכֹּהֵן הַגָּדוֹל: "הַאִם נְכוֹנִים הַדְּבָרִים הָאֵלֶּה?" 2 הֵשִׁיב סְטֶפָנוֹס וְאָמַר: "אֲנָשִׁים, אַחִים וְאָבוֹת, שִׁמְעוּ נָא. אֱלֹהֵי הַכָּבוֹד נִרְאָה אֶל אַבְרָהָם אָבִינוּ בִּהְיוֹתוֹ בַּאֲרַם נַהֲרַיִם, לִפְנֵי שֶׁגָּר בְּחָרָן, 3 וְאָמַר אֵלָיו, 'לֶךְ־לְךָ מֵאַרְצְךָ וּמִמּוֹלַדְתְּךָ וּבֹא אֶל־הָאָרֶץ אֲשֶׁר אַרְאֶךָּ.' 4 אָז יָצָא מֵאֶרֶץ כַּשְׂדִּים וְגָר בְּחָרָן, וְאַחֲרֵי מוֹת אָבִיו הֶעֱבִיר אוֹתוֹ אֱלֹהִים מִשָּׁם אֶל הָאָרֶץ הַזֹּאת אֲשֶׁר אַתֶּם גָּרִים בָּהּ כָּעֵת. 5 וְלֹא נָתַן לוֹ בָּהּ נַחֲלָה, אַף לֹא מִדְרַךְ כַּף רֶגֶל. הוּא הִבְטִיחַ לָתֵת אוֹתָהּ לַאֲחֻזָּה לוֹ וּלְזַרְעוֹ אַחֲרָיו בְּטֶרֶם הָיָה לוֹ בֵּן. 6 כְּמוֹ כֵן אָמַר לוֹ הָאֱלֹהִים כִּי גֵר יִהְיֶה זַרְעוֹ בְּאֶרֶץ נָכְרִיָּה וְיַעַבְדוּ אוֹתוֹ וְיִעֲנּוּהוּ אַרְבַּע מֵאוֹת שָׁנָה. 7 'וְגַם אֶת־הַגּוֹי אֲשֶׁר יַעַבְדוּ דָן אָנֹכִי,' אָמַר אֱלֹהִים, 'וְאַחֲרֵי־כֵן יֵצְאוּ וְיַעַבְדוּנִי בַּמָּקוֹם הַזֶּה.' 8 גַּם נָתַן לוֹ אֶת בְּרִית הַמִּילָה וּכְשֶׁהוֹלִיד אֶת יִצְחָק מָל אוֹתוֹ בַּיּוֹם הַשְּׁמִינִי; וְיִצְחָק אֶת יַעֲקֹב, וְיַעֲקֹב אֶת שְׁנֵים־עָשָׂר הָאָבוֹת.

9 הָאָבוֹת קִנְאוּ בְּיוֹסֵף וּמְכָרוּ אוֹתוֹ מִצְרַיְמָה, אַךְ אֱלֹהִים הָיָה אִתּוֹ 10 וְהִצִּיל אוֹתוֹ מִכָּל צָרוֹתָיו; גַּם נָתַן לוֹ חֵן וְחָכְמָה לִפְנֵי פַּרְעֹה מֶלֶךְ מִצְרַיִם, וְהַלָּה מִנָּה אוֹתוֹ עַל מִצְרַיִם וְעַל כָּל בֵּיתוֹ. 11 אֲבָל רָעָב בָּא עַל כָּל אֶרֶץ מִצְרַיִם וְאֶרֶץ כְּנַעַן וְגַם צָרָה גְדוֹלָה, וַאֲבוֹתֵינוּ לֹא מָצְאוּ אֹכֶל. 12 כַּאֲשֶׁר שָׁמַע יַעֲקֹב כִּי יֵשׁ חִטָּה בְּמִצְרַיִם, שָׁלַח אֶת אֲבוֹתֵינוּ בַּפַּעַם הָרִאשׁוֹנָה. 13 בַּפַּעַם הַשְּׁנִיָּה הִתְוַדַּע יוֹסֵף אֶל אֶחָיו, וּמוֹצָאוֹ שֶׁל יוֹסֵף נִתְגַּלָּה לְפַרְעֹה. 14 שָׁלַח יוֹסֵף וְקָרָא לְיַעֲקֹב אָבִיו וּלְכָל מִשְׁפַּחְתּוֹ, שִׁבְעִים וְחָמֵשׁ נְפָשׁוֹת. 15 יַעֲקֹב יָרַד מִצְרַיְמָה וְשָׁם מֵת הוּא וַאֲבוֹתֵינוּ. 16 הֵם הוּבְאוּ לִשְׁכֶם וְנִטְמְנוּ בַּקֶּבֶר שֶׁקָּנָה אַבְרָהָם בִּמְחִיר כֶּסֶף מִבְּנֵי חֲמוֹר אֲשֶׁר בִּשְׁכֶם.

17 "But when the time of the promise drew near which God had sworn to Abraham, the people grew and multiplied in Egypt 18 till another king arose who did not know Joseph. 19 This man dealt treacherously with our people, and oppressed our forefathers, making them expose their babies, so that they might not live. 20 At this time Moses was born, and was well pleasing to God; and he was brought up in his father's house for three months. 21 But when he was set out, Pharaoh's daughter took him away and brought him up as her own son. 22 And Moses was learned in all the wisdom of the Egyptians, and was mighty in words and deeds.

23 "Now when he was forty years old, it came into his heart to visit his brethren, the children of Israel. 24 And seeing one of *them* suffer wrong, he defended and avenged him who was oppressed, and struck down the Egyptian. 25 For he supposed that his brethren would have understood that God would deliver them by his hand, but they did not understand. 26 And the next day he appeared to two of them as they were fighting, and *tried to* reconcile them, saying, 'Men, you are brethren; why do you wrong one another?' 27 But he who did his neighbor wrong pushed him away, saying, '*Who made you a ruler and a judge over us? 28 Do you want to kill me as you did the Egyptian yesterday?*' 29 Then, at this saying, Moses fled and became a dweller in the land of Midian, where he had two sons.

30 "And when forty years had passed, an Angel of the Lord appeared to him in a flame of fire in a bush, in the wilderness of Mount Sinai. 31 When Moses saw *it,* he marveled at the sight; and as he drew near to observe, the voice of the Lord came to him, 32 saying, '*I am the God of your fathers—the God of Abraham, the God of Isaac, and the God of Jacob.*' And Moses trembled and dared not look. 33 'Then the LORD said to him, "*Take your sandals off your feet, for the place where you stand is holy ground. 34 I have surely seen the oppression of My people who are in Egypt; I have heard their groaning and have come down to deliver them. And now come, I will send you to Egypt.*" '

35 "This Moses whom they rejected, saying, '*Who made you a ruler and a judge?*' is the one God sent *to be* a ruler and a deliverer by the hand of the Angel who appeared to him in the bush. 36 He brought them out, after he had shown wonders and signs in the land of Egypt, and in the Red Sea, and in the wilderness forty years.

17 כְּשֶׁקָּרַב מוֹעֵד קִיּוּם הַהַבְטָחָה שֶׁנִּשְׁבַּע אֱלֹהִים לְאַבְרָהָם, גָּדַל הָעָם וְהִתְרַבָּה בְּמִצְרַיִם, 18 עַד שֶׁקָּם מֶלֶךְ־חָדָשׁ אֲשֶׁר לֹא־יָדַע אֶת־יוֹסֵף. 19 זֶה הִתְחַכֵּם לְעַמֵּנוּ וְהֵרַע לַאֲבוֹתֵינוּ בְּהַכְרִיחוֹ אוֹתָם לְהַפְקִיר אֶת עוֹלְלֵיהֶם כְּדֵי שֶׁלֹּא יִחְיוּ. 20 בָּעֵת הַהִיא נוֹלַד מֹשֶׁה, שֶׁהָיָה טוֹב בְּעֵינֵי אֱלֹהִים. שְׁלוֹשָׁה חֳדָשִׁים גֻּדַּל בְּבֵית אָבִיו 21 וְכַאֲשֶׁר הֻפְקַר אָסְפָה אוֹתוֹ בַּת פַּרְעֹה וְגִדְּלָה אוֹתוֹ לָהּ לְבֵן. 22 מֹשֶׁה לֻמַּד בְּכָל חָכְמַת הַמִּצְרִים וְהָיָה בֶּן־חַיִל בִּדְבָרָיו וּבְמַעֲשָׂיו.

23 כְּשֶׁמָּלְאוּ לוֹ אַרְבָּעִים שָׁנָה עָלָה עַל לִבּוֹ לִפְקֹד אֶת אֶחָיו בְּנֵי יִשְׂרָאֵל. 24 כִּרְאוֹתוֹ אִישׁ אֶחָד מֻכֶּה הֵגֵן עָלָיו וְנָקַם אֶת נִקְמָתוֹ שֶׁל הַנִּפְגָּע בַּהֲמִיתוֹ אֶת הַמִּצְרִי. 25 הוּא חָשַׁב שֶׁאֶחָיו יָבִינוּ כִּי עַל־יָדָיו יִתֵּן לָהֶם אֱלֹהִים תְּשׁוּעָה, אֶלָּא שֶׁהֵם לֹא הֵבִינוּ. 26 בַּיּוֹם הַשֵּׁנִי הוֹפִיעַ בֵּינֵיהֶם כַּאֲשֶׁר רָבוּ, וּבִקֵּשׁ לְפַיֵּס אוֹתָם לְשָׁלוֹם בְּאָמְרוֹ, 'אֲנָשִׁים אַחִים אַתֶּם, לָמָּה תָרֵעוּ זֶה לָזֶה?' 27 אֲבָל הַפּוֹגֵעַ בְּרֵעֵהוּ הֲדָפוֹ אוֹתוֹ וְאָמַר, 'מִי שָׂמְךָ לְשַׂר וְשֹׁפֵט עָלֵינוּ? 28 הַלְהָרְגֵנִי אַתָּה אֹמֵר כַּאֲשֶׁר הָרַגְתָּ אֶתְמוֹל אֶת־הַמִּצְרִי?' 29 בִּגְלַל הַדָּבָר הַזֶּה בָּרַח מֹשֶׁה וְהָיָה לְגֵר בְּאֶרֶץ מִדְיָן וְשָׁם הוֹלִיד שְׁנֵי בָנִים.

30 כַּעֲבֹר אַרְבָּעִים שָׁנָה נִרְאָה אֵלָיו מַלְאָךְ בְּמִדְבַּר הַר סִינַי, בְּלַבַּת אֵשׁ מִתּוֹךְ הַסְּנֶה. 31 רָאָה מֹשֶׁה וְתָמַהּ עַל הַמַּרְאֶה, אַךְ כְּשֶׁנִּגַּשׁ לְהַבִּיט הָיָה אֵלָיו קוֹל אֲדֹנָי: 32 'אָנֹכִי אֱלֹהֵי אֲבוֹתֶיךָ, אֱלֹהֵי אַבְרָהָם, יִצְחָק וְיַעֲקֹב.' מֹשֶׁה נֶחֱרַד וְלֹא הֵעֵז לְהַבִּיט. 33 אָמַר אֵלָיו אֱלֹהִים, 'שַׁל־נְעָלֶיךָ מֵעַל רַגְלֶיךָ, כִּי הַמָּקוֹם אֲשֶׁר אַתָּה עוֹמֵד עָלָיו אַדְמַת־קֹדֶשׁ הוּא. 34 רָאֹה רָאִיתִי אֶת־עֳנִי עַמִּי אֲשֶׁר בְּמִצְרַיִם וְאֶת נַאֲקָתָם שָׁמַעְתִּי וָאֵרֵד לְהַצִּילָם; וְעַתָּה לְכָה וְאֶשְׁלָחֲךָ מִצְרָיְמָה.' 35 מֹשֶׁה זֶה, אֲשֶׁר כָּפְרוּ בּוֹ בְּאָמְרָם 'מִי שָׂמְךָ לְשַׂר וְשֹׁפֵט' – אוֹתוֹ שָׁלַח אֱלֹהִים בְּיַד הַמַּלְאָךְ הַנִּרְאָה אֵלָיו בַּסְּנֶה, לִהְיוֹת לְשַׂר וְגוֹאֵל. 36 הוּא הוֹצִיאָם בַּעֲשׂוֹתוֹ אוֹתוֹת וּמוֹפְתִים בְּאֶרֶץ מִצְרַיִם וּבְיַם סוּף, וְכֵן גַּם בַּמִּדְבָּר בְּמֶשֶׁךְ אַרְבָּעִים

37 "This is that Moses who said to the children of Israel, 'The LORD your God will raise up for you a Prophet like me from your brethren. Him you shall hear.'

38 "This is he who was in the congregation in the wilderness with the Angel who spoke to him on Mount Sinai, and *with* our fathers, the one who received the living oracles to give to us, 39 whom our fathers would not obey, but rejected. And in their hearts they turned back to Egypt, 40 saying to Aaron, 'Make us gods to go before us; *as for this Moses who brought us out of the land of Egypt, we do not know what has become of him.'* 41 And they made a calf in those days, offered sacrifices to the idol, and rejoiced in the works of their own hands. 42 Then God turned and gave them up to worship the host of heaven, as it is written in the book of the Prophets:

'Did you offer Me slaughtered animals and sacrifices *during forty years in the wilderness, O house of Israel?*
43 You also took up the tabernacle of Moloch, And the star of your god Remphan, Images which you made to worship; And I will carry you away beyond Babylon.'

44 "Our fathers had the tabernacle of witness in the wilderness, as He appointed, instructing Moses to make it according to the pattern that he had seen, 45 which our fathers, having received it in turn, also brought with Joshua into the land possessed by the Gentiles, whom God drove out before the face of our fathers until the days of David, 46 who found favor before God and asked to find a dwelling for the God of Jacob. 47 But Solomon built Him a house.

48 "However, the Most High does not dwell in temples made with hands, as the prophet says:

49 'Heaven is My throne, And earth is My footstool. What house will you build for Me? says the LORD, Or what is the place of My rest?
50 Has My hand not made all these things?'

51 "*You* stiff-necked and uncircumcised in heart and ears! You always resist the Holy Spirit; as your fathers *did*, so *do* you. 52 Which of the prophets did your fathers not persecute? And they killed those who foretold the coming of the Just One, of whom you now have become the betrayers and murderers, 53 who have received the law by the direction of angels and have not kept *it*."

54 When they heard these things they were cut to the heart, and they gnashed at him with *their* teeth. 55 But he, being full of the Holy Spirit, gazed into

שָׁנָה. 37 זֶהוּ אוֹתוֹ מֹשֶׁה אֲשֶׁר אָמַר לִבְנֵי יִשְׂרָאֵל, 'נָבִיא מִקֶּרֶב אֲחֵיכֶם, כָּמוֹנִי, יָקִים לָכֶם אֱלֹהִים.' 38 הוּא הָאִישׁ שֶׁהָיָה בַּקָּהָל בַּמִּדְבָּר עִם הַמַּלְאָךְ הַדּוֹבֵר אֵלָיו בְּהַר סִינַי וְעִם אֲבוֹתֵינוּ, הָאִישׁ שֶׁקִּבֵּל דִּבְרֵי חַיִּים לָתֵת לָנוּ. 39 וַאֲבוֹתֵינוּ לֹא רָצוּ לִשְׁמֹעַ בְּקוֹלוֹ כִּי אִם דָּחוּ אוֹתוֹ וּבִלְבָבָם שָׁבוּ מִצְרַיְמָה, 40 בְּאָמְרָם אֶל אַהֲרֹן 'עֲשֵׂה לָנוּ אֱלֹהִים אֲשֶׁר יֵלְכוּ לְפָנֵינוּ, כִּי זֶה מֹשֶׁה אֲשֶׁר הֶעֱלָנוּ מֵאֶרֶץ מִצְרַיִם לֹא יָדַעְנוּ מֶה הָיָה לוֹ.' 41 וְאָכֵן עָשׂוּ עֵגֶל בָּאוֹתָם יָמִים וְהִקְרִיבוּ זֶבַח לָאֱלִיל, וְשָׂמְחוּ בְּמַעֲשֵׂי יְדֵיהֶם. 42 אָז פָּנָה הָאֱלֹהִים וּמָסַר אוֹתָם לְפֻלְחַן צְבָא הַשָּׁמַיִם כַּכָּתוּב בְּסֵפֶר הַנְּבִיאִים, 'הַזְּבָחִים וּמִנְחָה הִגַּשְׁתֶּם לִי בַּמִּדְבָּר אַרְבָּעִים שָׁנָה, בֵּית יִשְׂרָאֵל? 43 וּנְשָׂאתֶם אֶת סֻכַּת מֹלֶךְ וְאֵת כּוֹכַב אֱלֹהֵיכֶם רֵיפָן, הַצְּלָמִים אֲשֶׁר עֲשִׂיתֶם לְהִשְׁתַּחֲווֹת לָהֶם. וְהִגְלֵיתִי אֶתְכֶם מֵהָלְאָה לְבָבֶל.'

44 מִשְׁכַּן הָעֵדוּת הָיָה לַאֲבוֹתֵינוּ בַּמִּדְבָּר, כְּמוֹ שֶׁצִּוָּה הַמְדַבֵּר אֶל מֹשֶׁה לַעֲשׂוֹתוֹ עַל פִּי הַתַּבְנִית שֶׁרָאָה. 45 אֲבוֹתֵינוּ קִבְּלוּ אוֹתוֹ וּבְהַנְהָגַת יְהוֹשֻׁעַ הֱבִיאוּהוּ לַאֲחֻזַּת הַגּוֹיִם אֲשֶׁר גֵּרְשָׁם אֱלֹהִים מִפְּנֵי אֲבוֹתֵינוּ, עַד שֶׁהִגִּיעוּ יְמֵי דָוִד. 46 הוּא מָצָא חֵן בְּעֵינֵי אֱלֹהִים וּבִקֵּשׁ לִמְצֹא מִשְׁכָּן לֵאלֹהֵי יַעֲקֹב. 47 אָמְנָם שְׁלֹמֹה בָּנָה לוֹ בַּיִת, 48 אַךְ הָעֶלְיוֹן אֵינֶנּוּ שׁוֹכֵן בְּהֵיכָלוֹת מַעֲשֵׂי יָדַיִם, כְּמוֹ שֶׁאוֹמֵר הַנָּבִיא, 49 'הַשָּׁמַיִם כִּסְאִי וְהָאָרֶץ הֲדֹם רַגְלָי. אֵי זֶה בַּיִת אֲשֶׁר תִּבְנוּ לִי, נְאֻם יהוה, וְאֵי זֶה מָקוֹם מְנוּחָתִי? 50 הֲלֹא אֶת כָּל אֵלֶּה יָדִי עָשָׂתָה.'

51 קְשֵׁי עֹרֶף וְעַרְלֵי לֵב וְאָזְנַיִם, תָּמִיד מִתְנַגְּדִים אַתֶּם לְרוּחַ הַקֹּדֶשׁ, כַּאֲבוֹתֵיכֶם כֵּן גַּם אַתֶּם. 52 אֶת מִי מֵהַנְּבִיאִים לֹא רָדְפוּ אֲבוֹתֵיכֶם? גַּם הָרְגוּ אֶת אֵלֶּה שֶׁהִגִּידוּ מֵרֹאשׁ אֶת דְּבַר בּוֹא הַצַּדִּיק אֲשֶׁר כָּעֵת אַתֶּם הֱיִיתֶם מַסְגִּירָיו וְהוֹרְגָיו; 53 אַתֶּם שֶׁקִּבַּלְתֶּם אֶת הַתּוֹרָה בְּאֶמְצָעוּת מַלְאָכִים וְלֹא שְׁמַרְתֶּם אוֹתָהּ."

54 כְּשָׁמְעָם אֶת הַדְּבָרִים הָאֵלֶּה כָּעֲסוּ עַד עֹמֶק לִבָּם וְחָרְקוּ עָלָיו שִׁנֵּיהֶם; 55 וְהוּא מָלֵא רוּחַ הַקֹּדֶשׁ וּמַבִּיט הַשָּׁמַיְמָה. רָאָה אֶת כְּבוֹד אֱלֹהִים וְאֶת יֵשׁוּעַ

heaven and saw the glory of God, and Jesus standing at the right hand of God, 56 and said, "Look! I see the heavens opened and the Son of Man standing at the right hand of God!"

57 Then they cried out with a loud voice, stopped their ears, and ran at him with one accord; 58 and they cast *him* out of the city and stoned *him*. And the witnesses laid down their clothes at the feet of a young man named Saul. 59 And they stoned Stephen as he was calling on *God* and saying, "Lord Jesus, receive my spirit." 60 Then he knelt down and cried out with a loud voice, "Lord, do not charge them with this sin." And when he had said this, he fell asleep.

8 Now Saul was consenting to his death.

At that time a great persecution arose against the church which was at Jerusalem; and they were all scattered throughout the regions of Judea and Samaria, except the apostles. 2 And devout men carried Stephen *to his burial*, and made great lamentation over him.

3 As for Saul, he made havoc of the church, entering every house, and dragging off men and women, committing *them* to prison.

4 Therefore those who were scattered went everywhere preaching the word. 5 Then Philip went down to the city of Samaria and preached Christ to them. 6 And the multitudes with one accord heeded the things spoken by Philip, hearing and seeing the miracles which he did. 7 For unclean spirits, crying with a loud voice, came out of many who were possessed; and many who were paralyzed and lame were healed. 8 And there was great joy in that city.

9 But there was a certain man called Simon, who previously practiced sorcery in the city and astonished the people of Samaria, claiming that he was someone great, 10 to whom they all gave heed, from the least to the greatest, saying, "This man is the great power of God." 11 And they heeded him because he had astonished them with his sorceries for a long time. 12 But when they believed Philip as he preached the things concerning the kingdom of God and the name of Jesus Christ, both men and women were baptized. 13 Then Simon himself also believed; and when he was baptized he continued with Philip, and was amazed, seeing the miracles and signs which were done.

14 Now when the apostles who were at Jerusalem heard that Samaria had received the word of God, they sent Peter and John to them, 15 who, when they had come down, prayed for them that they might receive the Holy Spirit. 16 For as yet He had fallen

עוֹמֵד לִימִין הָאֱלֹהִים 56 וַיֹּאמַר: "הִנְנִי רוֹאֶה אֶת הַשָּׁמַיִם פְּתוּחִים וְאֶת בֶּן־הָאָדָם עוֹמֵד לִימִין הָאֱלֹהִים." 57 אַךְ הֵם צָעֲקוּ בְּקוֹל גָּדוֹל, בְּאָטְמָם אֶת אָזְנֵיהֶם, וּכְאִישׁ אֶחָד הִסְתָּעֲרוּ עָלָיו, 58 הֲדָפוּהוּ אֶל מִחוּץ לָעִיר וְסָקְלוּ אוֹתוֹ בַּאֲבָנִים. הָעֵדִים הִנִּיחוּ אֶת בִּגְדֵיהֶם לְרַגְלֵי בָּחוּר אֶחָד, שָׁאוּל שְׁמוֹ, 59 וּסְקָפֿנוּם נִסְקַל כְּשֶׁהוּא זוֹעֵק וְאוֹמֵר: "אֲדֹנִי יֵשׁוּעַ, קַבֵּל אֶת רוּחִי!" 60 כְּמוֹ כֵן כָּרַע עַל בִּרְכָּיו וְצָעַק בְּקוֹל גָּדוֹל: "אֲדֹנָי, אַל תִּפְקֹד עֲלֵיהֶם אֶת הַחֵטְא הַזֶּה!" אָמַר זֹאת וָמֵת.

ח גַּם שָׁאוּל הִסְכִּים לַהֲרִיגָתוֹ.

בַּיּוֹם הַהוּא הֵחֵלָּה רְדִיפָה גְדוֹלָה נֶגֶד הַקְּהִלָּה בִּירוּשָׁלַיִם, וְכֻלָּם נָפוֹצוּ בְּאַזוֹרֵי יְהוּדָה וְשׁוֹמְרוֹן, חוּץ מִן הַשְּׁלִיחִים. 2 אָז אָסְפוּ אֲנָשִׁים יִרְאֵי שָׁמַיִם אֶת סְטֶפָנוֹס וְסָפְדוּ עָלָיו מִסְפֵּד גָּדוֹל. 3 וְשָׁאוּל עָשָׂה שַׁמּוֹת בַּקְּהִלָּה; הוּא עָבַר מִבַּיִת לְבַיִת וְגֵרֵר גְּבָרִים וְנָשִׁים וְהִסְגִּירָם לַכֶּלֶא.

4 הָאֲנָשִׁים שֶׁנָּפוֹצוּ עָבְרוּ בָּאָרֶץ וּבִשְּׂרוּ אֶת דְּבַר אֱלֹהִים. 5 אָז יָרַד פִילִפּוֹס אֶל עִיר בְּשׁוֹמְרוֹן וְהִכְרִיז לָהֶם אֶת הַמָּשִׁיחַ. 6 הֶהָמוֹן הָעָם הִקְשִׁיב בְּלֵב אֶחָד לְדִבְרֵי פִילִפּוֹס, כְּשָׁמְעָם וְכִרְאוֹתָם אֶת הָאוֹתוֹת שֶׁעָשָׂה; 7 כִּי רַבִּים אֲשֶׁר הָיוּ אֲחוּזֵי רוּחוֹת טְמֵאָה, הָרוּחוֹת יָצְאוּ מֵהֶם וְהֵן צוֹעֲקוֹת בְּקוֹל גָּדוֹל. גַּם מְשֻׁתָּקִים וּפִסְחִים רַבִּים נִרְפְּאוּ 8 וְשִׂמְחָה גְדוֹלָה הָיְתָה בָּעִיר הַהִיא.

9 אִישׁ אֶחָד, שִׁמְעוֹן שְׁמוֹ, הָיָה עוֹסֵק זֶה מִכְּבָר בִּכְשׁוּף בְּשׁוֹמְרוֹן וּמַדְהִים אֶת תּוֹשָׁבֵי הָעִיר בְּאָמְרוֹ עַל עַצְמוֹ שֶׁהוּא אָדָם גָּדוֹל. 10 הַכֹּל הִקְשִׁיבוּ אֵלָיו, מִקָּטֹן וְעַד גָּדוֹל. אָמְרוּ: "הָאִישׁ הַזֶּה הוּא כֹּחַ הָאֱלֹהִים הַנִּקְרָא הַכֹּחַ הַגָּדוֹל." 11 הֵם הִקְשִׁיבוּ אֵלָיו מִפְּנֵי שֶׁזְּמַן רַב הִדְהִים אוֹתָם בִּכְשָׁפָיו. 12 אֲבָל כַּאֲשֶׁר הֶאֱמִינוּ לְפִילִפּוֹס בְּבַשְּׂרוֹ עַל מַלְכוּת הָאֱלֹהִים וְשֵׁם יֵשׁוּעַ הַמָּשִׁיחַ, נִטְבְּלוּ גְּבָרִים וְנָשִׁים, 13 וְגַם שִׁמְעוֹן עַצְמוֹ הֶאֱמִין. הוּא נִטְבַּל וְנִסְפַּח אֶל פִילִפּוֹס; וְכִרְאוֹתוֹ אֶת הָאוֹתוֹת וְהַמּוֹפְתִים הַגְּדוֹלִים שֶׁנַּעֲשׂוּ, נִתְמַלֵּא תִּמָּהוֹן.

14 הַשְּׁלִיחִים אֲשֶׁר בִּירוּשָׁלַיִם שָׁמְעוּ שֶׁשּׁוֹמְרוֹן קִבְּלָה אֶת דְּבַר אֱלֹהִים וְשָׁלְחוּ אֲלֵיהֶם אֶת כֵּיפָא וְאֶת יוֹחָנָן. 15 הַלָּלוּ יָרְדוּ לְשָׁם וְהִתְפַּלְלוּ בַּעֲדָם שֶׁיְּקַבְּלוּ אֶת רוּחַ הַקֹּדֶשׁ, 16 כִּי עוֹד לֹא צָלְחָה הָרוּחַ עַל אִישׁ

upon none of them. They had only been baptized in the name of the Lord Jesus. [17] Then they laid hands on them, and they received the Holy Spirit.

[18] And when Simon saw that through the laying on of the apostles' hands the Holy Spirit was given, he offered them money, [19] saying, "Give me this power also, that anyone on whom I lay hands may receive the Holy Spirit."

[20] But Peter said to him, "Your money perish with you, because you thought that the gift of God could be purchased with money! [21] You have neither part nor portion in this matter, for your heart is not right in the sight of God. [22] Repent therefore of this your wickedness, and pray God if perhaps the thought of your heart may be forgiven you. [23] For I see that you are poisoned by bitterness and bound by iniquity."

[24] Then Simon answered and said, "Pray to the Lord for me, that none of the things which you have spoken may come upon me."

[25] So when they had testified and preached the word of the Lord, they returned to Jerusalem, preaching the gospel in many villages of the Samaritans.

[26] Now an angel of the Lord spoke to Philip, saying, "Arise and go toward the south along the road which goes down from Jerusalem to Gaza." This is desert. [27] So he arose and went. And behold, a man of Ethiopia, a eunuch of great authority under Candace the queen of the Ethiopians, who had charge of all her treasury, and had come to Jerusalem to worship, [28] was returning. And sitting in his chariot, he was reading Isaiah the prophet. [29] Then the Spirit said to Philip, "Go near and overtake this chariot."

[30] So Philip ran to him, and heard him reading the prophet Isaiah, and said, "Do you understand what you are reading?"

[31] And he said, "How can I, unless someone guides me?" And he asked Philip to come up and sit with him. [32] The place in the Scripture which he read was this:

"He was led as a sheep to the slaughter;
And as a lamb before its shearer is silent,
So He opened not His mouth.
[33] In His humiliation His justice was taken away,
And who will declare His generation?
For His life is taken from the earth."

[34] So the eunuch answered Philip and said, "I ask you, of whom does the prophet say this, of himself or of some other man?" [35] Then Philip opened his mouth, and beginning at this Scripture, preached

מֵהֶם; הֵם רַק נִטְבְּלוּ בְּשֵׁם הָאָדוֹן יֵשׁוּעַ. [17] אָז סָמְכוּ יָדַיִם עֲלֵיהֶם וְהֵם קִבְּלוּ אֶת רוּחַ הַקֹּדֶשׁ. [18] כְּשֶׁרָאָה שִׁמְעוֹן כִּי בִּסְמִיכַת יְדֵי הַשְּׁלִיחִים נִתְּנָה רוּחַ הַקֹּדֶשׁ, הִגִּישׁ לָהֶם כֶּסֶף בְּאָמְרוֹ: [19] "תְּנוּ גַם לִי אֶת הַסַּמְכוּת הַזֹּאת, שֶׁכָּל מִי שֶׁאֶסְמֹךְ אֶת יָדַי עָלָיו יְקַבֵּל אֶת רוּחַ הַקֹּדֶשׁ."

[20] אָמַר לוֹ כֵּיפָא: "כַּסְפְּךָ יְהֵא אִתְּךָ לַאֲבַדּוֹן, מִפְּנֵי שֶׁחָשַׁבְתָּ לִקְנוֹת אֶת מַתְּנַת אֱלֹהִים. [21] אֵין לְךָ חֵלֶק וְנַחֲלָה בַּדָּבָר הַזֶּה, כִּי לְבָבְךָ אֵינֶנּוּ יָשָׁר לִפְנֵי הָאֱלֹהִים. [22] עַל כֵּן שׁוּב מֵרִשְׁעָתְךָ זוֹ וְהִתְחַנֵּן אֶל הָאָדוֹן, אוּלַי תִּסָּלַח לְךָ מְזִמַּת לִבְּךָ; [23] כִּי אֲנִי רוֹאֶה אוֹתְךָ נָתוּן בִּמְרוֹרַת לַעֲנָה וּבְכַבְלֵי רֶשַׁע."

[24] הֵשִׁיב שִׁמְעוֹן וְאָמַר: "הִתְחַנְּנוּ אַתֶּם בַּעֲדִי אֶל הָאָדוֹן שֶׁלֹּא יָבוֹא עָלַי דָּבָר מִמַּה שֶּׁאֲמַרְתֶּם."

[25] לְאַחַר שֶׁהֵעִידוּ אֶת עֵדוּתָם וְדִבְּרוּ אֶת דְּבַר הָאָדוֹן חָזְרוּ לִירוּשָׁלַיִם וּבְדַרְכָּם בִּשְּׂרוּ אֶת הַבְּשׂוֹרָה בִּכְפָרִים רַבִּים שֶׁל שׁוֹמְרוֹנִים.

[26] מַלְאַךְ יְהוה דִּבֶּר אֶל פִילִיפּוֹס וְאָמַר: "קוּם וְלֵךְ דָּרוֹמָה בַּדֶּרֶךְ הַיּוֹרֶדֶת מִירוּשָׁלַיִם לְעַזָּה, בַּדֶּרֶךְ הַמִּדְבָּרִית." [27] הוּא קָם וְהָלַךְ. וְהִנֵּה אִישׁ אֶתְיוֹפִי, סָרִיס וְשַׂר בַּחֲצַר קַנְדָּק מַלְכַּת הָאֶתְיוֹפִים וּמְמֻנֶּה עַל כָּל אוֹצְרוֹתֶיהָ, חָזַר לְאַרְצוֹ לְאַחַר שֶׁבָּא לְהִשְׁתַּחֲווֹת בִּירוּשָׁלַיִם, [28] וְהוּא יוֹשֵׁב בְּמֶרְכַּבְתּוֹ וְקוֹרֵא בְּסֵפֶר יְשַׁעְיָהוּ הַנָּבִיא. [29] אָמְרָה הָרוּחַ לְפִילִיפּוֹס: "הִתְקָרֵב וְהִלָּוֵה אֶל הַמֶּרְכָּבָה הַזֹּאת." [30] פִילִיפּוֹס רָץ אֶל הַמֶּרְכָּבָה וְשָׁמַע אוֹתוֹ קוֹרֵא בִּישַׁעְיָהוּ הַנָּבִיא. שָׁאַל אוֹתוֹ: "הַאִם אַתָּה מֵבִין מַה שֶּׁאַתָּה קוֹרֵא?" [31] הֵשִׁיב וְאָמַר: "וְאֵיךְ אוּכַל אִם לֹא יַדְרִיךְ אוֹתִי אִישׁ?" הוּא בִּקֵּשׁ מִפִּילִיפּוֹס שֶׁיַּעֲלֶה וְיֵשֵׁב אִתּוֹ. [32] קֶטַע הַכָּתוּב שֶׁקָּרָא הָיָה:

"כְּשֶׂה לַטֶּבַח יוּבָל וּכְרָחֵל לִפְנֵי גּוֹזְזֶיהָ נֶאֱלָמָה, וְלֹא יִפְתַּח פִּיו.
[33] מֵעֹצֶר וּמִמִּשְׁפָּט לֻקָּח וְאֶת־דּוֹרוֹ מִי יְשׂוֹחֵחַ, כִּי נִגְזַר מֵאֶרֶץ חַיִּים."

[34] אָמַר הַסָּרִיס אֶל פִילִיפּוֹס: "אֶשְׁאַל אוֹתְךָ, עַל מִי הַנָּבִיא אוֹמֵר זֹאת, עַל עַצְמוֹ אוֹ עַל מִישֶׁהוּ אַחֵר?" [35] פָּתַח פִילִיפּוֹס בְּדַבְּרוֹ וּבְהַתְחִילוֹ מִן הַכָּתוּב הַזֶּה

Jesus to him. ³⁶ Now as they went down the road, they came to some water. And the eunuch said, "See, *here is* water. What hinders me from being baptized?"

³⁷ Then Philip said, "If you believe with all your heart, you may."

And he answered and said, "I believe that Jesus Christ is the Son of God."

³⁸ So he commanded the chariot to stand still. And both Philip and the eunuch went down into the water, and he baptized him. ³⁹ Now when they came up out of the water, the Spirit of the Lord caught Philip away, so that the eunuch saw him no more; and he went on his way rejoicing. ⁴⁰ But Philip was found at Azotus. And passing through, he preached in all the cities till he came to Caesarea.

9 Then Saul, still breathing threats and murder against the disciples of the Lord, went to the high priest ² and asked letters from him to the synagogues of Damascus, so that if he found any who were of the Way, whether men or women, he might bring them bound to Jerusalem.

³ As he journeyed he came near Damascus, and suddenly a light shone around him from heaven. ⁴ Then he fell to the ground, and heard a voice saying to him, "Saul, Saul, why are you persecuting Me?"

⁵ And he said, "Who are You, Lord?"

Then the Lord said, "I am Jesus, whom you are persecuting. It *is* hard for you to kick against the goads."

⁶ So he, trembling and astonished, said, "Lord, what do You want me to do?"

Then the Lord *said* to him, "Arise and go into the city, and you will be told what you must do."

⁷ And the men who journeyed with him stood speechless, hearing a voice but seeing no one. ⁸ Then Saul arose from the ground, and when his eyes were opened he saw no one. But they led him by the hand and brought *him* into Damascus. ⁹ And he was three days without sight, and neither ate nor drank.

¹⁰ Now there was a certain disciple at Damascus named Ananias; and to him the Lord said in a vision, "Ananias."

And he said, "Here I am, Lord."

¹¹ So the Lord *said* to him, "Arise and go to the street called Straight, and inquire at the house of Judas for *one* called Saul of Tarsus, for behold, he is praying. ¹² And in a vision he has seen a man named Ananias coming in and putting *his* hand on him, so that he might receive his sight."

בִּשֵּׂר לוֹ אֶת יֵשׁוּעַ. ³⁶ כַּאֲשֶׁר נָסְעוּ בַּדֶּרֶךְ בָּאוּ אֶל מְקוֹם מַיִם. אָמַר הַסָּרִיס: "הִנֵּה מַיִם. מַה יִּמְנַע אוֹתִי מֵהִטָּבֵל?"

³⁸ הוּא צִוָּה לַעֲצֹר אֶת הַמֶּרְכָּבָה וּשְׁנֵיהֶם יָרְדוּ אֶל הַמַּיִם, הֵן פִילִיפּוֹס וְהֵן הַסָּרִיס, וּפִילִיפּוֹס הִטְבִּילוֹ. ³⁹ כְּשֶׁעָלוּ מִתּוֹךְ הַמַּיִם חֲטָפָה רוּחַ יהוה אֶת פִילִיפּוֹס, וְהַסָּרִיס לֹא רָאָה אוֹתוֹ עוֹד. אָז נָסַע לְדַרְכּוֹ שָׂמֵחַ. ⁴⁰ וּפִילִיפּוֹס נִרְאָה בְּאַשְׁדוֹד. הוּא עָבַר וּבִשֵּׂר בְּכָל הֶעָרִים עַד בּוֹאוֹ לְקֵיסַרְיָה.

ט וְשָׁאוּל עוֹדֶנּוּ מֵפִיחַ אִיּוּמִים וָרֶצַח נֶגֶד תַּלְמִידֵי הָאָדוֹן. הוּא בָּא אֶל הַכֹּהֵן הַגָּדוֹל ² וּבִקֵּשׁ מִמֶּנּוּ אִגְּרוֹת לְבָתֵּי הַכְּנֶסֶת בְּדַמֶּשֶׂק, כְּדֵי שֶׁיֶּאֱסֹר בִּכְבָלִים אֶת מִי שֶׁיִּמָּצֵא מִן הַמַּחֲזִיקִים בַּדֶּרֶךְ הַהִיא, הֵן גְּבָרִים וְהֵן נָשִׁים, וְיָבִיא אוֹתָם לִירוּשָׁלַיִם. ³ בְּעֵת שֶׁהָלַךְ וְהִתְקָרֵב לְדַמֶּשֶׂק, פִּתְאוֹם נֹגַהּ סְבִיבוֹ אוֹר מִן הַשָּׁמַיִם. ⁴ הוּא נָפַל אַרְצָה וְשָׁמַע קוֹל אוֹמֵר אֵלָיו: "שָׁאוּל, שָׁאוּל, לָמָּה תִּרְדְּפֵנִי?"

⁵ שָׁאַל שָׁאוּל: "מִי אַתָּה, אֲדוֹנִי?"

"אָנֹכִי יֵשׁוּעַ אֲשֶׁר אַתָּה רוֹדֵף. ⁶ אֲבָל קוּם לֵךְ הָעִירָה וְיֵאָמֵר לְךָ מַה שֶּׁעָלֶיךָ לַעֲשׂוֹת."

⁷ הָאֲנָשִׁים הַנּוֹסְעִים אִתּוֹ עָמְדוּ אִלְּמִים. הֵם שָׁמְעוּ אֶת הַקּוֹל, אַךְ לֹא רָאוּ אִישׁ. ⁸ שָׁאוּל קָם מִן הָאָרֶץ וּכְשֶׁפָּקַח אֶת עֵינָיו לֹא רָאָה דָּבָר. הֶחֱזִיקוּ בְּיָדוֹ וְהוֹלִיכוּהוּ לְדַמֶּשֶׂק. ⁹ בְּמֶשֶׁךְ שְׁלוֹשָׁה יָמִים לֹא רָאָה בְּעֵינָיו וְלֹא אָכַל וְלֹא שָׁתָה.

¹⁰ בְּדַמֶּשֶׂק הָיָה תַּלְמִיד אֶחָד, חֲנַנְיָה שְׁמוֹ, וְהָאָדוֹן אָמַר אֵלָיו בְּמַרְאֵה חָזוֹן: "חֲנַנְיָה!"

הוּא הֵשִׁיב: "הִנְנִי, אֲדוֹנִי." ¹¹ אָמַר אֵלָיו הָאָדוֹן: "קוּם לֵךְ אֶל הָרְחוֹב הַנִּקְרָא יָשָׁר וּבַקֵּשׁ בְּבֵית יְהוּדָה אִישׁ טַרְסִי, שָׁאוּל שְׁמוֹ. הִנֵּהוּ מִתְפַּלֵּל ¹² וּבְחָזוֹן רָאָה אִישׁ, חֲנַנְיָה שְׁמוֹ, נִכְנָס וְסוֹמֵךְ אֶת יָדָיו עָלָיו כְּדֵי שֶׁיִּרְאֶה שׁוּב."

13 Then Ananias answered, "Lord, I have heard from many about this man, how much harm he has done to Your saints in Jerusalem. 14 And here he has authority from the chief priests to bind all who call on Your name."

15 But the Lord said to him, "Go, for he is a chosen vessel of Mine to bear My name before Gentiles, kings, and the children of Israel. 16 For I will show him how many things he must suffer for My name's sake."

17 And Ananias went his way and entered the house; and laying his hands on him he said, "Brother Saul, the Lord Jesus, who appeared to you on the road as you came, has sent me that you may receive your sight and be filled with the Holy Spirit." 18 Immediately there fell from his eyes *something* like scales, and he received his sight at once; and he arose and was baptized.

19 So when he had received food, he was strengthened. Then Saul spent some days with the disciples at Damascus.

20 Immediately he preached the Christ in the synagogues, that He is the Son of God.

21 Then all who heard were amazed, and said, "Is this not he who destroyed those who called on this name in Jerusalem, and has come here for that purpose, so that he might bring them bound to the chief priests?"

22 But Saul increased all the more in strength, and confounded the Jews who dwelt in Damascus, proving that this *Jesus* is the Christ.

23 Now after many days were past, the Jews plotted to kill him. 24 But their plot became known to Saul. And they watched the gates day and night, to kill him. 25 Then the disciples took him by night and let *him* down through the wall in a large basket.

26 And when Saul had come to Jerusalem, he tried to join the disciples; but they were all afraid of him, and did not believe that he was a disciple. 27 But Barnabas took him and brought *him* to the apostles. And he declared to them how he had seen the Lord on the road, and that He had spoken to him, and how he had preached boldly at Damascus in the name of Jesus. 28 So he was with them at Jerusalem, coming in and going out. 29 And he spoke boldly in the name of the Lord Jesus and disputed against the Hellenists, but they attempted to kill him. 30 When the brethren found out, they brought him down to Caesarea and sent him out to Tarsus.

31 Then the churches throughout all Judea, Galilee, and Samaria had peace and were edified. And walking in the fear of the Lord and in the comfort of the Holy Spirit, they were multiplied.

13 הֵשִׁיב חֲנַנְיָה: "אֲדוֹנִי, שָׁמַעְתִּי מִפִּי רַבִּים עַל הָאִישׁ הַזֶּה, כַּמָּה רָעוֹת עָשָׂה לִקְדוֹשֶׁיךָ בִּירוּשָׁלַיִם. 14 וְגַם פֹּה יֶשׁ לוֹ סַמְכוּת מֵאֵת רָאשֵׁי הַכֹּהֲנִים לֶאֱסֹר אֶת כָּל הַקּוֹרְאִים בִּשְׁמֶךָ."

15 אָמַר לוֹ הָאָדוֹן: "לֵךְ, כִּי כְּלִי נִבְחָר הוּא לִי לָשֵׂאת אֶת שְׁמִי לִפְנֵי גּוֹיִם וּמְלָכִים וְלִפְנֵי בְּנֵי יִשְׂרָאֵל. 16 וַאֲנִי אַרְאֶה לוֹ כַּמָּה עָלָיו לִסְבֹּל לְמַעַן שְׁמִי."

17 הָלַךְ חֲנַנְיָה וְנִכְנַס לַבַּיִת; הוּא סָמַךְ אֶת יָדָיו עָלָיו וְאָמַר: "שָׁאוּל, אָחִי. הָאָדוֹן יֵשׁוּעַ שֶׁנִּרְאָה אֵלֶיךָ בַּדֶּרֶךְ בּוֹאֲךָ שְׁלָחַנִי כְּדֵי שֶׁתִּרְאֶה שׁוּב וְתִמָּלֵא רוּחַ הַקֹּדֶשׁ." 18 מִיָּד נָפְלוּ מֵעֵינָיו כְּמוֹ קַשְׂקַשִּׂים וְנִפְקְחוּ עֵינָיו. הוּא קָם וְנִטְבַּל, 19 וּלְאַחַר שֶׁאָכַל הִתְחַזֵּק.

כַּמָּה יָמִים שָׁהָה בְּדַמֶּשֶׂק עִם הַתַּלְמִידִים 20 וּבְלִי לְהִתְמַהְמֵהַּ הִכְרִיז עַל יֵשׁוּעַ בְּבָתֵּי הַכְּנֶסֶת, שֶׁהוּא בֶּן־הָאֱלֹהִים. 21 נִדְהֲמוּ כָּל הַשּׁוֹמְעִים וְאָמְרוּ: "הֲרֵי זֶהוּ הָאִישׁ שֶׁבִּירוּשָׁלַיִם עָשָׂה שַׁמּוֹת בְּקֶרֶב הַקּוֹרְאִים בַּשֵּׁם הַזֶּה וּלְמַטָּרָה זֹאת בָּא הֵנָּה, לַהֲבִיאָם בִּכְבָלִים אֶל הַכֹּהֲנִים הַגְּדוֹלִים." 22 בְּרַם שָׁאוּל נִתְמַלֵּא בְּיֶתֶר כֹּחַ וְהֵבִיךְ אֶת הַיְּהוּדִים הַגָּרִים בְּדַמֶּשֶׂק בְּהוֹכִיחוֹ כִּי זֶהוּ הַמָּשִׁיחַ.

23 כַּעֲבֹר זְמַן גִּבֵּר נוֹעֲצוּ יְהוּדִים אֵלֶּה לַהֲמִיתוֹ, 24 אַךְ מְזִמָּתָם נוֹדְעָה לְשָׁאוּל. מֵאַחַר שֶׁשָּׁמְרוּ אֶת הַשְּׁעָרִים יוֹמָם וָלַיְלָה כְּדֵי לְהָרְגוֹ, 25 לָקְחוּ אוֹתוֹ הַתַּלְמִידִים בַּלַּיְלָה וְהוֹרִידוּהוּ בְּסַל מִן הַחוֹמָה.

26 כַּאֲשֶׁר בָּא שָׁאוּל לִירוּשָׁלַיִם וְנִסָּה לְהִלָּווֹת אֶל הַתַּלְמִידִים פָּחֲדוּ מִמֶּנּוּ כֻּלָּם, כִּי לֹא הֶאֱמִינוּ שֶׁהוּא תַּלְמִיד. 27 לָקַח אוֹתוֹ בַּר־נַבָּא וֶהֱבִיאוֹ אֶל הַשְּׁלִיחִים. הוּא סִפֵּר לָהֶם כֵּיצַד רָאָה שָׁאוּל בַּדֶּרֶךְ אֶת הָאָדוֹן, שֶׁגַּם דִּבֵּר אֵלָיו, וְכֵיצַד בְּדַמֶּשֶׂק דִּבֵּר בְּבִטָּחוֹן בְּשֵׁם יֵשׁוּעַ. 28 אַחֲרֵי כֵן הָיָה שָׁאוּל אִתָּם, יוֹצֵא וּבָא בִּירוּשָׁלַיִם וּמְדַבֵּר בְּבִטָּחוֹן בְּשֵׁם הָאָדוֹן. 29 הוּא דִּבֵּר וְגַם הִתְוַכֵּחַ עִם הַיְּהוּדִים הַיְּוָנִים וְהֵם נִסּוּ לַהֲמִיתוֹ. 30 כְּשֶׁנּוֹדַע הַדָּבָר לָאַחִים הוֹרִידוּהוּ לְקֵיסַרְיָה וְשִׁלְחוּ אוֹתוֹ אֶל טַרְסוֹס. 31 בְּאוֹתָהּ עֵת הָיָה שָׁלוֹם לַקְּהִלָּה בְּכָל יְהוּדָה וְהַגָּלִיל וּבְשׁוֹמְרוֹן; הִיא נִבְנְתָה וְהִתְהַלְּכָה בְּיִרְאַת יהוה, וְגָדְלָה בְּמִסְפָּר בְּעִדּוּד רוּחַ הַקֹּדֶשׁ.

³² Now it came to pass, as Peter went through all *parts of the country,* that he also came down to the saints who dwelt in Lydda. ³³ There he found a certain man named Aeneas, who had been bedridden eight years and was paralyzed. ³⁴ And Peter said to him, "Aeneas, Jesus the Christ heals you. Arise and make your bed." Then he arose immediately. ³⁵ So all who dwelt at Lydda and Sharon saw him and turned to the Lord.

³⁶ At Joppa there was a certain disciple named Tabitha, which is translated Dorcas. This woman was full of good works and charitable deeds which she did. ³⁷ But it happened in those days that she became sick and died. When they had washed her, they laid *her* in an upper room. ³⁸ And since Lydda was near Joppa, and the disciples had heard that Peter was there, they sent two men to him, imploring *him* not to delay in coming to them. ³⁹ Then Peter arose and went with them. When he had come, they brought *him* to the upper room. And all the widows stood by him weeping, showing the tunics and garments which Dorcas had made while she was with them. ⁴⁰ But Peter put them all out, and knelt down and prayed. And turning to the body he said, "Tabitha, arise." And she opened her eyes, and when she saw Peter she sat up. ⁴¹ Then he gave her *his* hand and lifted her up; and when he had called the saints and widows, he presented her alive. ⁴² And it became known throughout all Joppa, and many believed on the Lord. ⁴³ So it was that he stayed many days in Joppa with Simon, a tanner.

10 There was a certain man in Caesarea called Cornelius, a centurion of what was called the Italian Regiment, ² a devout *man* and one who feared God with all his household, who gave alms generously to the people, and prayed to God always. ³ About the ninth hour of the day he saw clearly in a vision an angel of God coming in and saying to him, "Cornelius!"

⁴ And when he observed him, he was afraid, and said, "What is it, lord?"

So he said to him, "Your prayers and your alms have come up for a memorial before God. ⁵ Now send men to Joppa, and send for Simon whose surname is Peter. ⁶ He is lodging with Simon, a tanner, whose house is by the sea. He will tell you what you must do." ⁷ And when the angel who spoke to him had departed, Cornelius called two of his household servants and a devout soldier from among those who waited on him continually. ⁸ So when he had explained all *these* things to them, he sent them to Joppa.

³² וַיְהִי כַּאֲשֶׁר סָבַב כֵּיפָא בְּכָל הַמְּקוֹמוֹת יָרַד גַּם אֶל הַקְּדוֹשִׁים שֶׁגָּרוּ בְלוֹד. ³³ שָׁם מָצָא אִישׁ, אֶנְאָס שְׁמוֹ, וְהוּא מְשֻׁתָּק וְשׁוֹכֵב בַּמִּטָּה זֶה שְׁמוֹנֶה שָׁנִים. ³⁴ אָמַר אֵלָיו כֵּיפָא: "אֶנְאָס, יֵשׁוּעַ הַמָּשִׁיחַ מְרַפֵּא אוֹתְךָ! קוּם וְסַדֵּר אֶת מִטָּתְךָ!" הוּא קָם מִיָּד. ³⁵ רָאוּ אוֹתוֹ כָּל תּוֹשָׁבֵי לוֹד וְהַשָּׁרוֹן וּפָנוּ אֶל הָאָדוֹן. ³⁶ בְּיָפוֹ הָיְתָה תַּלְמִידָה וּשְׁמָהּ טָבִיתָא, כְּלוֹמַר צְבִיָּה, וְהִיא רַבַּת מַעֲשִׂים טוֹבִים וּמַרְבָּה בִּגְמִילוּת חֲסָדִים. ³⁷ בַּיָּמִים הָהֵם חָלְתָה וָמֵתָה, וּלְאַחַר שֶׁרָחֲצוּהָ שָׂמוּ אוֹתָהּ בַּחֲדַר הָעֲלִיָּה. ³⁸ כֵּיוָן שֶׁלּוֹד קְרוֹבָה לְיָפוֹ וְהַתַּלְמִידִים שָׁמְעוּ כִּי כֵיפָא שָׁם, שָׁלְחוּ אֵלָיו שְׁנֵי אֲנָשִׁים לְהַפְצִיר בּוֹ שֶׁיְּמַהֵר לָבוֹא אֲלֵיהֶם. ³⁹ כֵּיפָא קָם וְהָלַךְ אִתָּם. כְּשֶׁהִגִּיעַ הִכְנִיסוּהוּ אֶל הָעֲלִיָּה, וְכָל הָאַלְמָנוֹת עָמְדוּ לְיָדוֹ בּוֹכִיּוֹת וְהֶרְאוּ לוֹ כֻּתֳּנוֹת וּבְגָדִים שֶׁעָשְׂתָה צְבִיָּה בְּעוֹדָהּ עִמָּהֶן. ⁴⁰ הוֹצִיא כֵּיפָא אֶת כֻּלָּם הַחוּצָה, כָּרַע עַל בִּרְכָּיו וְהִתְפַּלֵּל, וּבְפָנוֹתוֹ אֶל הַגּוּפָה אָמַר: "טָבִיתָא, קוּמִי!" הִיא פָּקְחָה אֶת עֵינֶיהָ וּכְשֶׁרָאֲתָה אֶת כֵּיפָא יָשְׁבָה. ⁴¹ הוּא הוֹשִׁיט אֵלֶיהָ אֶת יָדוֹ וְהֵקִים אוֹתָהּ. אָז קָרָא לַקְּדוֹשִׁים וְלָאַלְמָנוֹת וְהִצִּיג אוֹתָהּ חַיָּה לִפְנֵיהֶם. ⁴² הַדָּבָר נוֹדַע בְּכָל יָפוֹ וְרַבִּים הֶאֱמִינוּ בָּאָדוֹן. ⁴³ אַחֲרֵי כֵן נִשְׁאַר כֵּיפָא בְּיָפוֹ יָמִים רַבִּים אֵצֶל אִישׁ אֶחָד שֶׁהִתְפַּרְנֵס מֵעִבּוּד עוֹרוֹת, שִׁמְעוֹן שְׁמוֹ.

י אִישׁ הָיָה בְּקֵיסַרְיָה, קוֹרְנֵלְיוֹס שְׁמוֹ, שַׂר מֵאָה מִן הַגְּדוּד הַנִּקְרָא הָאִיטַלְקִי; ² חָסִיד הָיָה וִירֵא אֱלֹהִים הוּא וְכָל בֵּיתוֹ, וְגוֹמֵל חֲסָדִים רַבִּים לָעָם וּמִתְפַּלֵּל בְּכָל עֵת. ³ בְּאַחַד הַיָּמִים, סָמוּךְ לְשָׁעָה שָׁלוֹשׁ אַחֲרֵי הַצָּהֳרַיִם, רָאָה מַרְאֵה בָּרוּר: מַלְאַךְ אֱלֹהִים בָּא אֵלָיו וְאוֹמֵר לוֹ, "קוֹרְנֵלְיוֹס!" ⁴ כְּשֶׁהִבִּיט בּוֹ נִתְמַלֵּא פַּחַד וְאָמַר: "מַה זֶּה, אֲדוֹנִי?" הֵשִׁיב לוֹ הַמַּלְאָךְ: "תְּפִלּוֹתֶיךָ וְצִדְקוֹתֶיךָ עָלוּ לְזִכָּרוֹן לִפְנֵי הָאֱלֹהִים. ⁵ וְעַכְשָׁו שְׁלַח אֲנָשִׁים לְיָפוֹ וּקְרָא לְשִׁמְעוֹן הַמְכֻנֶּה כֵּיפָא. ⁶ הוּא מִתְאָרֵחַ אֵצֶל בֻּרְסִי אֶחָד, שִׁמְעוֹן שְׁמוֹ, אֲשֶׁר בֵּיתוֹ עַל־יַד הַיָּם." ⁷ אַחֲרֵי שֶׁהָלַךְ הַמַּלְאָךְ הַמְדַבֵּר אֵלָיו, קָרָא קוֹרְנֵלְיוֹס לִשְׁנַיִם מֵעֲבָדָיו וּלְחַיָּל יְרֵא שָׁמַיִם שֶׁהָיָה מִמְּשָׁרְתָיו הַמְקֹרָבִים. ⁸ הוּא סִפֵּר לָהֶם אֶת הַכֹּל וְשָׁלַח אוֹתָם לְיָפוֹ.

9 The next day, as they went on their journey and drew near the city, Peter went up on the housetop to pray, about the sixth hour. 10 Then he became very hungry and wanted to eat; but while they made ready, he fell into a trance 11 and saw heaven opened and an object like a great sheet bound at the four corners, descending to him and let down to the earth. 12 In it were all kinds of four-footed animals of the earth, wild beasts, creeping things, and birds of the air. 13 And a voice came to him, "Rise, Peter; kill and eat."

14 But Peter said, "Not so, Lord! For I have never eaten anything common or unclean."

15 And a voice *spoke* to him again the second time, "What God has cleansed you must not call common." 16 This was done three times. And the object was taken up into heaven again.

17 Now while Peter wondered within himself what this vision which he had seen meant, behold, the men who had been sent from Cornelius had made inquiry for Simon's house, and stood before the gate. 18 And they called and asked whether Simon, whose surname was Peter, was lodging there.

19 While Peter thought about the vision, the Spirit said to him, "Behold, three men are seeking you. 20 Arise therefore, go down and go with them, doubting nothing; for I have sent them."

21 Then Peter went down to the men who had been sent to him from Cornelius, and said, "Yes, I am he whom you seek. For what reason have you come?"

22 And they said, "Cornelius *the* centurion, a just man, one who fears God and has a good reputation among all the nation of the Jews, was divinely instructed by a holy angel to summon you to his house, and to hear words from you." 23 Then he invited them in and lodged *them*.

On the next day Peter went away with them, and some brethren from Joppa accompanied him.

24 And the following day they entered Caesarea. Now Cornelius was waiting for them, and had called together his relatives and close friends. 25 As Peter was coming in, Cornelius met him and fell down at his feet and worshiped *him*. 26 But Peter lifted him up, saying, "Stand up; I myself am also a man." 27 And as he talked with him, he went in and found many who had come together. 28 Then he said to them, "You know how unlawful it is for a Jewish man to keep company with or go to one of another nation. But God has shown me that I should not call any man common or unclean. 29 Therefore I came without objection as soon as I was sent for. I ask, then, for what reason have you sent for me?"

9 לְמָחֳרָת, כַּאֲשֶׁר נָסְעוּ בַּדֶּרֶךְ וְהִתְקָרְבוּ אֶל הָעִיר, עָלָה כֵיפָא אֶל הַגַּג לְהִתְפַּלֵּל; זֶה הָיָה בְּעֵרֶךְ בִּשְׁעַת הַצָּהֳרָיִם. 10 הוּא הָיָה רָעֵב וְרָצָה לֶאֱכֹל. אֲבָל בְּעֵת שֶׁהֵכִינוּ אֶת הָאֹכֶל הָיְתָה עָלָיו הָרוּחַ 11 וְהִנֵּה הוּא רוֹאֶה אֶת הַשָּׁמַיִם נִפְתָּחִים וְיוֹרֵד אֵיזֶה כְּלִי דּוֹמֶה לְמִפְרָשׂ גָּדוֹל, מוּרָד בְּאַרְבַּע קְצוֹתָיו אֶל הָאָרֶץ, 12 וּבוֹ מִכָּל חַיּוֹת הָאָרֶץ וְהָרְמָשִׂים וּמִכָּל עוֹף הַשָּׁמַיִם. 13 וְקוֹל הָיָה אֵלָיו: "קוּם, כֵּיפָא, שְׁחַט וֶאֱכֹל!"

14 אָמַר כֵּיפָא: "בְּשׁוּם פָּנִים לֹא, אֲדוֹנִי, כִּי מֵעוֹלָם לֹא אָכַלְתִּי שׁוּם פִּגּוּל וְטָמֵא."

15 שֵׁנִית הָיָה הַקּוֹל אֵלָיו: "לַאֲשֶׁר טִהַר אֱלֹהִים, אַתָּה אַל תִּקְרָא 'טָמֵא.'" 16 כָּךְ הָיָה שָׁלֹשׁ פְּעָמִים וּמִיָּד נִלְקַח הַכְּלִי הַשָּׁמַיְמָה.

17 כֵּיפָא הָיָה עוֹדֶנּוּ חוֹכֵךְ בְּדַעְתּוֹ מַה כַּוָּנַת הַמַּרְאֶה שֶׁרָאָה, וְהִנֵּה הָאֲנָשִׁים, שֶׁנִּשְׁלְחוּ מֵאֵת קוֹרְנֶלְיוֹס וְחִפְּשׂוּ אֶת בֵּיתוֹ שֶׁל שִׁמְעוֹן, עָמְדוּ בַּשַּׁעַר. 18 הֵם קָרְאוּ וְשָׁאֲלוּ אִם שִׁמְעוֹן הַמְכֻנֶּה כֵּיפָא מִתְאָרֵחַ שָׁם. 19 כְּשֶׁהִרְהֵר כֵּיפָא עַל הַמַּרְאֶה אָמְרָה לוֹ הָרוּחַ: "הִנֵּה כַּמָּה אֲנָשִׁים מְבַקְשִׁים אוֹתְךָ. 20 קוּם, רֵד וְלֵךְ אִתָּם, אַל תְּהַסֵּס, כִּי אֲנִי שְׁלַחְתִּים."

21 יָרַד כֵּיפָא אֶל הָאֲנָשִׁים וְאָמַר: "הִנֵּה אֲנִי הָאִישׁ שֶׁאַתֶּם מְבַקְשִׁים. לְשֵׁם מָה בָּאתֶם?" 22 הֵשִׁיבוּ וְאָמְרוּ: "שַׂר הַמֵּאָה קוֹרְנֶלְיוֹס, אִישׁ צַדִּיק וִירֵא אֱלֹהִים אֲשֶׁר שֵׁם טוֹב לוֹ בְּקֶרֶב כָּל הָעָם הַיְּהוּדִי, צֻוָּה עַל-יְדֵי מַלְאָךְ קָדוֹשׁ לִקְרֹא לְךָ אֶל בֵּיתוֹ וְלִשְׁמֹעַ דְּבָרִים מִפִּיךָ." 23 כֵּיפָא הִזְמִינָם לְהִכָּנֵס וְאֵרַח אוֹתָם.

לְמָחֳרָת קָם וְיָצָא אִתָּם, וְכַמָּה מִן הָאַחִים שֶׁבְּיָפוֹ נִלְווּ אֵלָיו. 24 יוֹם לְאַחַר מִכֵּן בָּאוּ לְקֵיסַרְיָה, וְקוֹרְנֶלְיוֹס חִכָּה לָהֶם עִם בְּנֵי מִשְׁפַּחְתּוֹ וִידִידָיו הַמְקֹרָבִים שֶׁכִּנֵּס אֶצְלוֹ. 25 כַּאֲשֶׁר הִגִּיעַ כֵּיפָא נִגַּשׁ אֵלָיו קוֹרְנֶלְיוֹס, נָפַל לְרַגְלָיו וְהִשְׁתַּחֲוָה. 26 הֵקִים אוֹתוֹ כֵּיפָא בְּאָמְרוֹ: "קוּם! גַּם אֲנִי עַצְמִי בֶּן אֱנוֹשׁ." 27 כְּשֶׁהוּא מְשׂוֹחֵחַ אִתּוֹ נִכְנַס הַבַּיְתָה וּמָצָא נֶאֱסָפִים רַבִּים. 28 אָמַר לָהֶם: "אַתֶּם יוֹדְעִים שֶׁאָסוּר לְאִישׁ יְהוּדִי לִהְיוֹת חָבֵר לְנָכְרִי אוֹ לָבוֹא אֵלָיו, אַךְ לִי הֶרְאָה אֱלֹהִים שֶׁלֹּא לִקְרֹא לְשׁוּם אָדָם 'שִׁקּוּץ' אוֹ 'טָמֵא.' 29 לָכֵן גַּם בָּאתִי לְלֹא הִתְנַגְּדוּת כְּשֶׁנִּקְרֵאתִי. כָּעֵת אֲנִי שׁוֹאֵל לְשֵׁם מָה קְרָאתֶם לִי?"

³⁰So Cornelius said, "Four days ago I was fasting until this hour; and at the ninth hour I prayed in my house, and behold, a man stood before me in bright clothing, ³¹and said, 'Cornelius, your prayer has been heard, and your alms are remembered in the sight of God. ³²Send therefore to Joppa and call Simon here, whose surname is Peter. He is lodging in the house of Simon, a tanner, by the sea. When he comes, he will speak to you.' ³³So I sent to you immediately, and you have done well to come. Now therefore, we are all present before God, to hear all the things commanded you by God."

³⁴Then Peter opened *his* mouth and said: "In truth I perceive that God shows no partiality. ³⁵But in every nation whoever fears Him and works righteousness is accepted by Him. ³⁶The word which *God* sent to the children of Israel, preaching peace through Jesus Christ—He is Lord of all— ³⁷that word you know, which was proclaimed throughout all Judea, and began from Galilee after the baptism which John preached: ³⁸how God anointed Jesus of Nazareth with the Holy Spirit and with power, who went about doing good and healing all who were oppressed by the devil, for God was with Him. ³⁹And we are witnesses of all things which He did both in the land of the Jews and in Jerusalem, whom they killed by hanging on a tree. ⁴⁰Him God raised up on the third day, and showed Him openly, ⁴¹not to all the people, but to witnesses chosen before by God, *even* to us who ate and drank with Him after He arose from the dead. ⁴²And He commanded us to preach to the people, and to testify that it is He who was ordained by God *to be* Judge of the living and the dead. ⁴³To Him all the prophets witness that, through His name, whoever believes in Him will receive remission of sins."

⁴⁴While Peter was still speaking these words, the Holy Spirit fell upon all those who heard the word. ⁴⁵And those of the circumcision who believed were astonished, as many as came with Peter, because the gift of the Holy Spirit had been poured out on the Gentiles also. ⁴⁶For they heard them speak with tongues and magnify God.

Then Peter answered, ⁴⁷"Can anyone forbid water, that these should not be baptized who have received the Holy Spirit just as we *have?*" ⁴⁸And he commanded them to be baptized in the name of the Lord. Then they asked him to stay a few days.

11 Now the apostles and brethren who were in Judea heard that the Gentiles had also received the word of God. ²And when Peter came up to

³⁰הֵשִׁיב קוֹרְנֵלְיוֹס: "לִפְנֵי שְׁלוֹשָׁה יָמִים הִתְפַּלַּלְתִּי בְּבֵיתִי בְּדִיּוּק בַּשָּׁעָה הַזֹּאת, בִּשְׁלוֹשׁ אַחֲרֵי הַצָּהֳרַיִם, וְהִנֵּה עָמַד לְפָנַי אִישׁ בִּלְבוּשׁ מַבְהִיק ³¹וְאָמַר, 'קוֹרְנֵלְיוֹס, תְּפִלָּתְךָ נִשְׁמְעָה וְצִדְקוֹתֶיךָ עָלוּ לְזִכָּרוֹן לִפְנֵי אֱלֹהִים. ³²שְׁלַח לְיָפוֹ וּקְרָא לְשִׁמְעוֹן הַמְכֻנֶּה כֵּיפָא. הוּא מִתְאָרֵחַ בְּבֵיתוֹ שֶׁל שִׁמְעוֹן הַבֻּרְסִי עַל־יַד הַיָּם.' ³³לְפִיכָךְ שָׁלַחְתִּי אֵלֶיךָ מִיָּד וְאָכֵן טוֹב עָשִׂיתָ שֶׁבָּאתָ. כָּעֵת אֲנַחְנוּ כֻּלָּנוּ נִמְצָאִים לִפְנֵי הָאֱלֹהִים לִשְׁמֹעַ אֶת כָּל מַה שֶׁאֲדֹנָי צִוָּה עָלֶיךָ."

³⁴פָּתַח כֵּיפָא אֶת פִּיו וְאָמַר: "בֶּאֱמֶת רוֹאֶה אֲנִי שֶׁאֱלֹהִים אֵינֶנּוּ נוֹשֵׂא פָּנִים, ³⁵אֶלָּא בְּכָל עַם וְעַם מִי שֶׁיָּרֵא אוֹתוֹ וְעוֹשֶׂה צֶדֶק רָצוּי לְפָנָיו. ³⁶אַתֶּם יוֹדְעִים אֶת הַדָּבָר שֶׁשָּׁלַח לִבְנֵי יִשְׂרָאֵל, בְּבַשְּׂרוֹ שָׁלוֹם עַל־יְדֵי יֵשׁוּעַ הַמָּשִׁיחַ אֲדוֹן הַכֹּל, ³⁷דָּבָר שֶׁהָיָה בְּכָל יְהוּדָה וְהֵחֵל בַּגָּלִיל לְאַחַר הַטְּבִילָה שֶׁהִכְרִיז יוֹחָנָן: ³⁸יֵשׁוּעַ מִנְּצֶרֶת, אֲשֶׁר מָשַׁח אוֹתוֹ בְּרוּחַ הַקֹּדֶשׁ וּבִגְבוּרָה, הִתְהַלֵּךְ בָּאָרֶץ כְּשֶׁהוּא עוֹשֶׂה חֶסֶד וּמְרַפֵּא אֶת כָּל הַנִּדְכָּאִים תַּחַת יַד הַשָּׂטָן, כִּי אֱלֹהִים הָיָה אִתּוֹ. ³⁹וַאֲנוּ עֵדִים עַל כָּל מַה שֶּׁעָשָׂה בְּאֶרֶץ הַיְּהוּדִים וּבִירוּשָׁלַיִם; הוּא אֲשֶׁר גַּם הֲרָגוּהוּ בְּהוֹקָעָה עַל עֵץ. ⁴⁰אוֹתוֹ הֵקִים הָאֱלֹהִים בַּיּוֹם הַשְּׁלִישִׁי וְנָתַן לוֹ לְהֵרָאוֹת, ⁴¹לֹא לְכָל הָעָם, אֶלָּא לְעֵדִים שֶׁאֱלֹהִים קָבַע אוֹתָם מֵרֹאשׁ, לָנוּ אֲשֶׁר אָכַלְנוּ וְשָׁתִינוּ אִתּוֹ אַחֲרֵי קוּמוֹ מִן הַמֵּתִים. ⁴²הוּא צִוָּה עָלֵינוּ לְהַכְרִיז לָעָם וּלְהָעִיד כִּי אוֹתוֹ שָׂם הָאֱלֹהִים לְשׁוֹפֵט הַחַיִּים וְהַמֵּתִים. ⁴³עָלָיו כָּל הַנְּבִיאִים מְעִידִים כִּי כָּל הַמַּאֲמִין בּוֹ יְקַבֵּל בִּשְׁמוֹ סְלִיחַת חֲטָאִים."

⁴⁴בְּשָׁעָה שֶׁדִּבֵּר כֵּיפָא אֶת הַדְּבָרִים הָאֵלֶּה צָלְחָה רוּחַ הַקֹּדֶשׁ עַל כָּל הַשּׁוֹמְעִים אֶת הַדָּבָר. ⁴⁵הַמַּאֲמִינִים בְּנֵי הַמִּילָה אֲשֶׁר נִלְווּ אֶל כֵּיפָא הִשְׁתּוֹמְמוּ עַל שֶׁמַּתְּנַת רוּחַ הַקֹּדֶשׁ נִשְׁפְּכָה גַּם עַל הַגּוֹיִים, ⁴⁶שֶׁכֵּן שָׁמְעוּ אוֹתָם מְדַבְּרִים בִּלְשׁוֹנוֹת וְנוֹתְנִים גְּדֻלָּה לֵאלֹהִים. ⁴⁷הֵגִיב כֵּיפָא וְאָמַר: "הַאִם יָכוֹל מִישֶׁהוּ לִמְנֹעַ אֶת הַטְּבִילָה בַּמַּיִם מֵאֵלֶּה שֶׁקִּבְּלוּ אֶת רוּחַ הַקֹּדֶשׁ כָּמוֹנוּ?" ⁴⁸הוּא צִוָּה עֲלֵיהֶם לְהִטָּבֵל בְּשֵׁם יֵשׁוּעַ הַמָּשִׁיחַ. אַחֲרֵי כֵן בִּקְשׁוּ מִמֶּנּוּ לְהִשָּׁאֵר אֶצְלָם כַּמָּה יָמִים.

יא הַשְּׁלִיחִים וְהָאַחִים אֲשֶׁר בִּיהוּדָה שָׁמְעוּ שֶׁגַּם הַגּוֹיִים קִבְּלוּ אֶת דְּבַר אֱלֹהִים. ²אֲבָל כַּאֲשֶׁר עָלָה

Jerusalem, those of the circumcision contended with him, ³ saying, "You went in to uncircumcised men and ate with them!"

⁴ But Peter explained *it* to them in order from the beginning, saying: ⁵ "I was in the city of Joppa praying; and in a trance I saw a vision, an object descending like a great sheet, let down from heaven by four corners; and it came to me. ⁶ When I observed it intently and considered, I saw four-footed animals of the earth, wild beasts, creeping things, and birds of the air. ⁷ And I heard a voice saying to me, 'Rise, Peter; kill and eat.' ⁸ But I said, 'Not so, Lord! For nothing common or unclean has at any time entered my mouth.' ⁹ But the voice answered me again from heaven, 'What God has cleansed you must not call common.' ¹⁰ Now this was done three times, and all were drawn up again into heaven. ¹¹ At that very moment, three men stood before the house where I was, having been sent to me from Caesarea. ¹² Then the Spirit told me to go with them, doubting nothing. Moreover these six brethren accompanied me, and we entered the man's house. ¹³ And he told us how he had seen an angel standing in his house, who said to him, 'Send men to Joppa, and call for Simon whose surname is Peter, ¹⁴ who will tell you words by which you and all your household will be saved.' ¹⁵ And as I began to speak, the Holy Spirit fell upon them, as upon us at the beginning. ¹⁶ Then I remembered the word of the Lord, how He said, 'John indeed baptized with water, but you shall be baptized with the Holy Spirit.' ¹⁷ If therefore God gave them the same gift as *He gave* us when we believed on the Lord Jesus Christ, who was I that I could withstand God?"

¹⁸ When they heard these things they became silent; and they glorified God, saying, "Then God has also granted to the Gentiles repentance to life."

¹⁹ Now those who were scattered after the persecution that arose over Stephen traveled as far as Phoenicia, Cyprus, and Antioch, preaching the word to no one but the Jews only. ²⁰ But some of them were men from Cyprus and Cyrene, who, when they had come to Antioch, spoke to the Hellenists, preaching the Lord Jesus. ²¹ And the hand of the Lord was with them, and a great number believed and turned to the Lord.

²² Then news of these things came to the ears of the church in Jerusalem, and they sent out Barnabas to go as far as Antioch. ²³ When he came and had seen the grace of God, he was glad, and encouraged them all that with purpose of heart they should continue with the Lord. ²⁴ For he was a good man, full of the Holy Spirit and of faith. And a great many people were added to the Lord.

כֵּיפָא לִירוּשָׁלַיִם הִתְוַכְּחוּ אִתּוֹ בְּנֵי הַמִּילָה בְּאָמְרָם: ³ "נִכְנַסְתָּ אֶל אֲנָשִׁים עֲרֵלִים וְאָכַלְתָּ אִתָּם?!" ⁴ הִתְחִיל כֵּיפָא לְסַפֵּר לָהֶם אֶת הָעִנְיָן לְפִי הַסֵּדֶר: ⁵ "מִתְפַּלֵּל הָיִיתִי בָּעִיר יָפוֹ וּבִהְיוֹתִי בְּהִתְעַלּוּת רָאִיתִי מַרְאֶה: אֵיזֶה כְּלִי דוֹמֶה לְמִפְרָשׂ גָּדוֹל מוּרָד בְּאַרְבַּע קְצוֹתָיו מִן הַשָּׁמַיִם וּמַגִּיעַ עַד אֵלָי. ⁶ כְּשֶׁהִתְבּוֹנַנְתִּי בּוֹ רָאִיתִי אֶת בֶּהֱמַת הָאָרֶץ, אֶת חַיּוֹת הַיַּעַר וְהָרְמָשִׂים וְאֶת עוֹף הַשָּׁמַיִם. ⁷ גַּם שָׁמַעְתִּי קוֹל אוֹמֵר אֵלַי, 'קוּם, כֵּיפָא, שְׁחַט וֶאֱכֹל.' ⁸ אֶלָּא שֶׁאָמַרְתִּי, 'בְּשׁוּם פָּנִים לֹא, אֲדוֹנִי, כִּי מֵעוֹלָם לֹא נִכְנַס לְתוֹךְ פִּי פִּגּוּל אוֹ טָמֵא.' ⁹ שֵׁנִית הֵשִׁיב קוֹל מִן הַשָּׁמַיִם, 'לַאֲשֶׁר טִהֵר אֱלֹהִים, אַתָּה אַל תִּקְרָא "טָמֵא".' ¹⁰ זֶה הָיָה שָׁלֹשׁ פְּעָמִים וְהַכֹּל שָׁב וְהָעֲלָה לַשָּׁמַיִם. ¹¹ וְהִנֵּה בְּדִיּוּק אָז עָמְדוּ שְׁלֹשָׁה אֲנָשִׁים לְיַד הַבַּיִת אֲשֶׁר הָיִיתִי בּוֹ וְהֵם נִשְׁלְחוּ אֵלַי מִקֵּיסַרְיָה. ¹² הָרוּחַ אָמְרָה לִי לָלֶכֶת אִתָּם וְלֹא לְהַסֵּס. גַּם שֵׁשֶׁת הָאַחִים הָאֵלֶּה בָּאוּ אִתִּי וְנִכְנַסְנוּ לְבֵיתוֹ שֶׁל הָאִישׁ. ¹³ הוּא סִפֵּר לָנוּ שֶׁרָאָה אֶת הַמַּלְאָךְ בְּבֵיתוֹ, עוֹמֵד וְאוֹמֵר: 'שְׁלַח אֶל יָפוֹ וּקְרָא לְשִׁמְעוֹן הַמְכֻנֶּה כֵּיפָא. ¹⁴ הוּא יְדַבֵּר אֵלֶיךָ דְּבָרִים אֲשֶׁר תִּוָּשַׁע בָּהֶם אַתָּה וְכָל בֵּיתְךָ.' ¹⁵ כַּאֲשֶׁר הִתְחַלְתִּי לְדַבֵּר צָלְחָה עֲלֵיהֶם רוּחַ הַקֹּדֶשׁ כְּמוֹ שֶׁצָּלְחָה עָלֵינוּ בַּתְּחִלָּה. ¹⁶ וְנִזְכַּרְתִּי בַּדָּבָר שֶׁאָמַר הָאָדוֹן, 'יוֹחָנָן הִטְבִּיל אֶתְכֶם בְּמַיִם, אַךְ אַתֶּם תִּטָּבְלוּ בְּרוּחַ הַקֹּדֶשׁ.' ¹⁷ וּבְכֵן, אִם אֱלֹהִים נָתַן לָהֶם אֶת אוֹתָהּ הַמַּתָּנָה כְּמוֹ שֶׁנָּתַן לָנוּ, הַמַּאֲמִינִים בָּאָדוֹן יֵשׁוּעַ הַמָּשִׁיחַ, מִי אֲנִי שֶׁאוּכַל לַעֲצֹר בְּעַד אֱלֹהִים?" ¹⁸ כְּשָׁמְעָם זֹאת לֹא הֵשִׁיבוּ דָבָר, אֶלָּא נָתְנוּ כָּבוֹד לֵאלֹהִים בְּאָמְרָם: אָכֵן גַּם לַגּוֹיִים נָתַן אֱלֹהִים לַחֲזֹר בִּתְשׁוּבָה אֱלֵי חַיִּים."

¹⁹ הָאֲנָשִׁים שֶׁנָּפוֹצוּ מִפְּנֵי הַצָּרָה אֲשֶׁר נִגְרְמָה עַל-אוֹדוֹת סְטֶפָנוֹס הִגִּיעוּ עַד פֵּינִיקְיָה וְקַפְרִיסִין וְאַנְטְיוֹכְיָה וְלֹא הִשְׁמִיעוּ אֶת דְּבַר אֱלֹהִים אֶלָּא לַיְּהוּדִים בִּלְבַד. ²⁰ אֲבָל הָיוּ בֵּינֵיהֶם כַּמָּה אֲנָשִׁים קַפְרִיסָאִים וְקִירֵנִיִּים אֲשֶׁר בְּבוֹאָם לְאַנְטְיוֹכְיָה דִּבְּרוּ גַּם אֶל הַיְּוָנִים וּבִשְּׂרוּ עַל הָאָדוֹן יֵשׁוּעַ. ²¹ יַד-יהוה הָיְתָה עִמָּהֶם וַאֲנָשִׁים רַבִּים הֶאֱמִינוּ וּפָנוּ אֶל הָאָדוֹן. ²² נִשְׁמַע הַדָּבָר בְּאָזְנֵי הַקְּהִלָּה אֲשֶׁר בִּירוּשָׁלַיִם וְשָׁלְחוּ אֶת בַּר-נַבָּא אֶל אַנְטְיוֹכְיָה. ²³ כַּאֲשֶׁר הִגִּיעַ לְשָׁם וְרָאָה אֶת חֶסֶד אֱלֹהִים, שָׂמַח וְהֵאִיץ בְּכֻלָּם לִהְיוֹת דְּבֵקִים בָּאָדוֹן בְּלֵב שָׁלֵם – ²⁴ כִּי הָיָה אִישׁ טוֹב, מָלֵא רוּחַ הַקֹּדֶשׁ וֶאֱמוּנָה – וְקָהָל רַב נִסְפַּח

25 Then Barnabas departed for Tarsus to seek Saul. 26 And when he had found him, he brought him to Antioch. So it was that for a whole year they assembled with the church and taught a great many people. And the disciples were first called Christians in Antioch.

27 And in these days prophets came from Jerusalem to Antioch. 28 Then one of them, named Agabus, stood up and showed by the Spirit that there was going to be a great famine throughout all the world, which also happened in the days of Claudius Caesar. 29 Then the disciples, each according to his ability, determined to send relief to the brethren dwelling in Judea. 30 This they also did, and sent it to the elders by the hands of Barnabas and Saul.

12 Now about that time Herod the king stretched out *his* hand to harass some from the church. 2 Then he killed James the brother of John with the sword. 3 And because he saw that it pleased the Jews, he proceeded further to seize Peter also. Now it was *during* the Days of Unleavened Bread. 4 So when he had arrested him, he put *him* in prison, and delivered *him* to four squads of soldiers to keep him, intending to bring him before the people after Passover.

5 Peter was therefore kept in prison, but constant prayer was offered to God for him by the church. 6 And when Herod was about to bring him out, that night Peter was sleeping, bound with two chains between two soldiers; and the guards before the door were keeping the prison. 7 Now behold, an angel of the Lord stood by *him,* and a light shone in the prison; and he struck Peter on the side and raised him up, saying, "Arise quickly!" And his chains fell off *his* hands. 8 Then the angel said to him, "Gird yourself and tie on your sandals"; and so he did. And he said to him, "Put on your garment and follow me." 9 So he went out and followed him, and did not know that what was done by the angel was real, but thought he was seeing a vision. 10 When they were past the first and the second guard posts, they came to the iron gate that leads to the city, which opened to them of its own accord; and they went out and went down one street, and immediately the angel departed from him.

11 And when Peter had come to himself, he said, "Now I know for certain that the Lord has sent His angel, and has delivered me from the hand of Herod and *from* all the expectation of the Jewish people."

אֶל הָאָדוֹן. 25 אַחֲרֵי כֵן יָצָא אֶל טַרְסוֹס לְחַפֵּשׂ אֶת שָׁאוּל, 26 וּכְשֶׁמְּצָא אוֹתוֹ הֱבִיאוֹ לְאַנְטִיוֹכְיָה. שָׁנָה תְּמִימָה הִתְאָרְחוּ אֵצֶל הַקְּהִלָּה וְלִמְּדוּ קָהָל רַב. וּבְאַנְטִיוֹכְיָה לָרִאשׁוֹנָה כֻּנּוּ אֶת הַתַּלְמִידִים "מְשִׁיחִיִּים".

27 בַּיָּמִים הָהֵם יָרְדוּ נְבִיאִים מִירוּשָׁלַיִם אֶל אַנְטִיוֹכְיָה. 28 קָם אֶחָד מֵהֶם, אֲגָבוֹם שְׁמוֹ, וְהוֹדִיעַ עַל־פִּי הָרוּחַ כִּי רָעָב גָּדוֹל עָתִיד לָבוֹא עַל כָּל הָעוֹלָם, דָּבָר שֶׁהִתְגַּשֵּׁם בִּזְמַן קְלוֹדְיוֹס. 29 הֶחֱלִיטוּ הַתַּלְמִידִים לִשְׁלֹחַ, אִישׁ אִישׁ כְּפִי שֶׁיָּדוֹ מַשֶּׂגֶת, לְעֶזְרַת הָאַחִים הַגָּרִים בִּיהוּדָה. 30 הֵם עָשׂוּ כֵן וְשָׁלְחוּ אֶל הַזְּקֵנִים בִּידֵי בַּר־נַבָּא וְשָׁאוּל.

יב בָּעֵת הַהִיא שָׁלַח הוֹרְדוֹס הַמֶּלֶךְ אֶת יָדוֹ לִפְגֹּעַ בַּאֲנָשִׁים מִן הַקְּהִלָּה, 2 וְהֵמִית בַּחֶרֶב אֶת יַעֲקֹב אֲחִי יוֹחָנָן. 3 כִּרְאוֹתוֹ שֶׁהָעָם מְרֻצֶּה מִזֶּה הוֹסִיף וְתָפַשׂ גַּם אֶת כֵּיפָא. אוֹתָם יָמִים הָיוּ יְמֵי חַג הַמַּצּוֹת. 4 לְאַחַר שֶׁעָצַר אֶת כֵּיפָא כָּלָא אוֹתוֹ בְּבֵית הַסֹּהַר וְהִפְקִיד אַרְבַּע מִשְׁמָרוֹת שֶׁל אַרְבָּעָה חַיָּלִים לִשְׁמֹר עָלָיו. הוּא הִתְכַּוֵּן לְהַעֲמִיד אוֹתוֹ לִפְנֵי הָעָם אַחֲרֵי הַפֶּסַח. 5 וְאוּלָם בְּעֵת שֶׁנִּשְׁמַר כֵּיפָא בְּבֵית הַסֹּהַר הִתְפַּלְּלָה הַקְּהִלָּה בַּעֲדוֹ בְּחָזְקָה אֶל הָאֱלֹהִים.

6 בַּלַּיְלָה, קֹדֶם שֶׁעָמַד הוֹרְדוֹס לַהֲבִיאוֹ לְפָנָיו, יָשֵׁן כֵּיפָא בֵּין שְׁנֵי חַיָּלִים כְּשֶׁהוּא כָּבוּל בִּשְׁתֵּי שַׁרְשְׁרוֹת, וְהַשּׁוֹמְרִים אֲשֶׁר לִפְנֵי הַדֶּלֶת שָׁמְרוּ עַל בֵּית הַסֹּהַר. 7 וְהִנֵּה מַלְאַךְ יהוה הוֹפִיעַ וְאוֹר נָגַהּ בַּחֶדֶר. הוּא טָפַח עַל צִדּוֹ שֶׁל כֵּיפָא, הֵעִיר אוֹתוֹ וְאָמַר: "קוּם מַהֵר!" אָז נָפְלוּ הַשַּׁרְשְׁרוֹת מֵעַל יָדָיו. 8 אָמַר לוֹ הַמַּלְאָךְ: "חֲגֹר מָתְנֶיךָ וּנְעַל נְעָלֶיךָ." כֵּיפָא עָשָׂה כֵן. אָמַר לוֹ: "הִתְעַטֵּף בְּמְעִילְךָ וּבוֹא אַחֲרַי." 9 יָצָא כֵּיפָא וְהָלַךְ אַחֲרָיו וְלֹא יָדַע כִּי מַה שֶּׁנַּעֲשָׂה עַל־יְדֵי הַמַּלְאָךְ הוּא דָּבָר מַמָּשׁ, אֶלָּא חָשַׁב שֶׁהוּא רוֹאֶה חָזוֹן. 10 הֵם עָבְרוּ דֶּרֶךְ הַמִּשְׁמֶרֶת הָרִאשׁוֹנָה וְהַשְּׁנִיָּה וּבָאוּ עַד שַׁעַר הַבַּרְזֶל הַפּוֹנֶה אֶל הָעִיר. הַשַּׁעַר נִפְתַּח לִפְנֵיהֶם מֵאֵלָיו וְהֵם יָצְאוּ הַחוּצָה וְעָבְרוּ בִּרְחוֹב אֶחָד. פִּתְאֹם עָזַב אוֹתוֹ הַמַּלְאָךְ. 11 כַּאֲשֶׁר שָׁבָה אֵלָיו דַּעְתּוֹ אָמַר כֵּיפָא: "עַכְשָׁו אֲנִי יוֹדֵעַ בֶּאֱמֶת כִּי אֲדֹנָי שָׁלַח אֶת מַלְאָכוֹ וְהִצִּילַנִי מִיַּד הוֹרְדוֹס וּמִכָּל צִפִּיּוֹתֵיהֶם שֶׁל קְהַל הַיְּהוּדִים."

¹² So, when he had considered *this,* he came to the house of Mary, the mother of John whose surname was Mark, where many were gathered together praying. ¹³ And as Peter knocked at the door of the gate, a girl named Rhoda came to answer. ¹⁴ When she recognized Peter's voice, because of *her* gladness she did not open the gate, but ran in and announced that Peter stood before the gate. ¹⁵ But they said to her, "You are beside yourself!" Yet she kept insisting that it was so. So they said, "It is his angel."

¹⁶ Now Peter continued knocking; and when they opened *the door* and saw him, they were astonished. ¹⁷ But motioning to them with his hand to keep silent, he declared to them how the Lord had brought him out of the prison. And he said, "Go, tell these things to James and to the brethren." And he departed and went to another place.

¹⁸ Then, as soon as it was day, there was no small stir among the soldiers about what had become of Peter. ¹⁹ But when Herod had searched for him and not found him, he examined the guards and commanded that *they* should be put to death.

And he went down from Judea to Caesarea, and stayed *there.*

²⁰ Now Herod had been very angry with the people of Tyre and Sidon; but they came to him with one accord, and having made Blastus the king's personal aide their friend, they asked for peace, because their country was supplied with food by the king's *country.*

²¹ So on a set day Herod, arrayed in royal apparel, sat on his throne and gave an oration to them. ²² And the people kept shouting, "The voice of a god and not of a man!" ²³ Then immediately an angel of the Lord struck him, because he did not give glory to God. And he was eaten by worms and died.

²⁴ But the word of God grew and multiplied.

²⁵ And Barnabas and Saul returned from Jerusalem when they had fulfilled *their* ministry, and they also took with them John whose surname was Mark.

13 Now in the church that was at Antioch there were certain prophets and teachers: Barnabas, Simeon who was called Niger, Lucius of Cyrene, Manaen who had been brought up with Herod the tetrarch, and Saul. ² As they ministered to the Lord and fasted, the Holy Spirit said, "Now separate to Me Barnabas and Saul for the work to which I have called them." ³ Then, having fasted and prayed, and laid hands on them, they sent *them* away.

---

¹² כְּשֶׁהִכִּיר בַּמְּצִיאוּת הָלַךְ לְבֵית מִרְיָם אֵם יוֹחָנָן הַמְכֻנֶּה מַרְקוֹס; בְּאוֹתוֹ מָקוֹם נֶאֶסְפוּ רַבִּים וְהִתְפַּלְּלוּ. ¹³ הוּא דָּפַק עַל דֶּלֶת הַשַּׁעַר וְנַעֲרָה אַחַת, רוֹדָה שְׁמָהּ, נִגְּשָׁה לַעֲנוֹת. ¹⁴ הִיא הִכִּירָה אֶת קוֹלוֹ שֶׁל כֵּיפָא, אַךְ מִשִּׂמְחָתָהּ לֹא פָּתְחָה אֶת הַשַּׁעַר וְרָצָה פְּנִימָה לְהוֹדִיעַ שֶׁכֵּיפָא עוֹמֵד לִפְנֵי הַשַּׁעַר. ¹⁵ אָמְרוּ לָהּ: "מְשֻׁגַּעַת", אַךְ הִיא טָעֲנָה בְּתֹקֶף כִּי כֵן הַדָּבָר. אָז אָמְרוּ: "זֶה הַמַּלְאָךְ שֶׁלּוֹ."

¹⁶ בֵּינְתַיִם הוֹסִיף כֵּיפָא לִדְפֹּק עַל הַשַּׁעַר, וּכְשֶׁפָּתְחוּ רָאוּ אוֹתוֹ וְהִשְׁתּוֹמְמוּ. ¹⁷ הוּא רָמַז לָהֶם בְּיָדוֹ לִשְׁתֹּק וְסִפֵּר לָהֶם כֵּיצַד הוֹצִיאוֹ הָאָדוֹן מִבֵּית הַסֹּהַר. אָמַר: "הַגִּידוּ זֹאת לְיַעֲקֹב וְלָאַחִים." לְאַחַר מִכֵּן יָצָא וְהָלַךְ לְמָקוֹם אַחֵר.

¹⁸ עִם אוֹר הַבֹּקֶר הָיְתָה מְבוּכָה גְדוֹלָה בֵּין הַחַיָּלִים עַל־אוֹדוֹת כֵּיפָא. תָּמְהוּ: "מַה קָּרָה לוֹ?" ¹⁹ כְּשֶׁבִּקֵּשׁ אוֹתוֹ הוֹרְדוֹס וְלֹא מָצָא, חָקַר אֶת הַשּׁוֹמְרִים וְצִוָּה לְהוֹצִיאָם לַהוֹרֵג. אַחֲרֵי כֵן יָרַד מִיהוּדָה אֶל קֵיסַרְיָה וְשָׁהָה שָׁם.

²⁰ סִכְסוּךְ חָרִיף הָיָה בֵּין הוֹרְדוֹס לְבֵין אַנְשֵׁי צוֹר וְצִידוֹן. הֵם בָּאוּ אֵלָיו בְּיַחַד וְאַחֲרֵי שֶׁהִתְרַצּוּ אֶל בְּלַסְטוֹס, הַמְמֻנֶּה עַל חֲצַר הַמֶּלֶךְ, בִּקְשׁוּ שָׁלוֹם, שֶׁכֵּן פַּרְנָסַת אַרְצָם הָיְתָה תְּלוּיָה בְּאֶרֶץ הַמֶּלֶךְ. ²¹ בַּיּוֹם הַמְיֹעָד לָבַשׁ הוֹרְדוֹס לְבוּשׁ מַלְכוּת, יָשַׁב עַל כֵּס הַמִּשְׁפָּט וְנָשָׂא לִפְנֵיהֶם נְאוּם. ²² "זֶה קוֹל אֱלֹהִים וְלֹא קוֹל שֶׁל אָדָם!" הֵרַע הַקָּהָל. ²³ מִיָּד הִכָּהוּ מַלְאַךְ יהוה מִשּׁוּם שֶׁלֹּא נָתַן אֶת הַכָּבוֹד לֵאלֹהִים; הוּא נָפַח אֶת נַפְשׁוֹ כְּשֶׁהוּא אֲכוּל תּוֹלָעִים. ²⁴ דְּבַר אֱלֹהִים שִׂגְשֵׂג וְנָפֹץ, ²⁵ וּבַר־נַבָּא וְשָׁאוּל הִשְׁלִימוּ אֶת שֵׁרוּתָם וְחָזְרוּ מִירוּשָׁלַיִם בַּהֲבִיאָם אִתָּם אֶת יוֹחָנָן הַמְכֻנֶּה מַרְקוֹס.

יג נְבִיאִים וּמוֹרִים הָיוּ בַּקְּהִלָּה אֲשֶׁר בְּאַנְטִיּוֹכְיָה: בַּר־נַבָּא, שִׁמְעוֹן הַנִּקְרָא נִיגֶר, לוּקְיוֹס הַקּוּרֵינִי, מְנַחֵם אֲשֶׁר גֻּדַּל עִם הוֹרְדוֹס שַׂר הָרֶבַע, וְשָׁאוּל. ² בְּעֵת שֵׁרוּתוֹ בַּקֹּדֶשׁ אֶת הָאָדוֹן וְצוֹמוֹ אָמְרָה רוּחַ הַקֹּדֶשׁ: "הַבְדִּילוּ לִי אֶת בַּר־נַבָּא וְאֶת שָׁאוּל לָעֲבוֹדָה אֲשֶׁר קָרָאתִי אוֹתָם אֵלֶיהָ." ³ לְאַחַר שֶׁצָּמוּ וְהִתְפַּלְּלוּ

4 So, being sent out by the Holy Spirit, they went down to Seleucia, and from there they sailed to Cyprus. 5 And when they arrived in Salamis, they preached the word of God in the synagogues of the Jews. They also had John as *their* assistant.

6 Now when they had gone through the island to Paphos, they found a certain sorcerer, a false prophet, a Jew whose name *was* Bar-Jesus, 7 who was with the proconsul, Sergius Paulus, an intelligent man. This man called for Barnabas and Saul and sought to hear the word of God. 8 But Elymas the sorcerer (for so his name is translated) withstood them, seeking to turn the proconsul away from the faith. 9 Then Saul, who also *is called* Paul, filled with the Holy Spirit, looked intently at him 10 and said, "O full of all deceit and all fraud, *you* son of the devil, *you* enemy of all righteousness, will you not cease perverting the straight ways of the Lord? 11 And now, indeed, the hand of the Lord *is* upon you, and you shall be blind, not seeing the sun for a time."

And immediately a dark mist fell on him, and he went around seeking someone to lead him by the hand. 12 Then the proconsul believed, when he saw what had been done, being astonished at the teaching of the Lord.

13 Now when Paul and his party set sail from Paphos, they came to Perga in Pamphylia; and John, departing from them, returned to Jerusalem. 14 But when they departed from Perga, they came to Antioch in Pisidia, and went into the synagogue on the Sabbath day and sat down. 15 And after the reading of the Law and the Prophets, the rulers of the synagogue sent to them, saying, "Men *and* brethren, if you have any word of exhortation for the people, say on."

16 Then Paul stood up, and motioning with *his* hand said, "Men of Israel, and you who fear God, listen: 17 The God of this people Israel chose our fathers, and exalted the people when they dwelt as strangers in the land of Egypt, and with an uplifted arm He brought them out of it. 18 Now for a time of about forty years He put up with their ways in the wilderness. 19 And when He had destroyed seven nations in the land of Canaan, He distributed their land to them by allotment.

20 "After that He gave *them* judges for about four hundred and fifty years, until Samuel the prophet. 21 And afterward they asked for a king; so God gave them Saul the son of Kish, a man of the tribe of Benjamin, for forty years. 22 And when He had removed him, He raised up for them David as king, to whom also He gave testimony and said, 'I have found David the *son* of Jesse, a man after My own

סָמְכוּ אֶת יְדֵיהֶם עֲלֵיהֶם וְשִׁלְּחוּ אוֹתָם. 4 הַשְּׁלוּחִים מִטַּעַם רוּחַ הַקֹּדֶשׁ יָרְדוּ אֶל סֶלֶבְקְיָה וּמִשָּׁם הִפְלִיגוּ אֶל קַפְרִיסִין. 5 הֵם בָּאוּ אֶל סָלָמִיס וְהִשְׁמִיעוּ אֶת דְּבַר אֱלֹהִים בְּבָתֵּי הַכְּנֶסֶת; גַּם יוֹחָנָן הָיָה עוֹזֵר עַל יָדָם. 6 אַחֲרֵי שֶׁעָבְרוּ בְּכָל הָאִי וְהִגִּיעוּ עַד פָּפוֹס מָצְאוּ אִישׁ מְכַשֵּׁף וּנְבִיא שֶׁקֶר, יְהוּדִי אֲשֶׁר שְׁמוֹ בַּר־יֵשׁוּעַ, 7 וְהוּא מְקֹרָב לַמּוֹשֵׁל סֶרְגִּיּוֹס פּוֹלוֹס. הַמּוֹשֵׁל, שֶׁהָיָה אָדָם נָבוֹן, קָרָא לְבַּר־נַבָּא וּלְשָׁאוּל וּבִקֵּשׁ לִשְׁמֹעַ אֶת דְּבַר אֱלֹהִים. 8 אֶלָּא שֶׁאֱלִימָס הַמְכַשֵּׁף – זֶה תַּרְגּוּם שְׁמוֹ – הִתְנַגֵּד לָהֶם בְּנַסּוֹתוֹ לְהַטּוֹת אֶת הַמּוֹשֵׁל מִן הָאֱמוּנָה. 9 שָׁאוּל, הַנִּקְרָא גַּם פּוֹלוֹס, בִּהְיוֹתוֹ מָלֵא רוּחַ הַקֹּדֶשׁ, הִבִּיט בּוֹ וְאָמַר: 10 "אַתָּה הַמָּלֵא כָּל מִרְמָה וְכָל רֶשַׁע, בֶּן הַשָּׂטָן, שׂוֹנֵא כָּל צֶדֶק, הַאִם לֹא תֶּחְדַּל לְסַלֵּף אֶת דַּרְכֵי אֱלֹהִים הַיְשָׁרִים? 11 וְעַתָּה הִנֵּה יַד־יהוה בָּךְ; עִוֵּר תִּהְיֶה וְלֹא תִרְאֶה אֶת אוֹר הַשֶּׁמֶשׁ עַד בּוֹא מוֹעֵד."

בּוֹ בַּמָּקוֹם נָפְלָה עָלָיו אֲפֵלָה וַחֲשֵׁכָה. הוּא הָלַךְ הֵנֶּה וְהֵנָּה בְּחַפְּשׂוֹ מִישֶׁהוּ שֶׁיּוֹלִיכוֹ בְּיָד. 12 כְּשֶׁרָאָה הַמּוֹשֵׁל אֶת הַנַּעֲשֶׂה הֶאֱמִין וְהִשְׁתּוֹמֵם עַל תּוֹרַת הָאָדוֹן.

13 שָׁאוּל וַחֲבֵרָיו הִפְלִיגוּ מִפָּפוֹס וּבָאוּ אֶל פֶּרְגִּי שֶׁבְּפַּמְפִילְיָה, אַךְ יוֹחָנָן עָזַב אוֹתָם וְחָזַר לִירוּשָׁלַיִם. 14 מִפֶּרְגִּי הִמְשִׁיכוּ בְּדַרְכָּם וְהִגִּיעוּ אֶל אַנְטִיוֹכְיָה אֲשֶׁר בְּפִיסִידְיָה, וּבְשַׁבָּת נִכְנְסוּ לְבֵית הַכְּנֶסֶת וְיָשְׁבוּ. 15 אַחֲרֵי קְרִיאַת הַתּוֹרָה וְהַנְּבִיאִים, שָׁלְחוּ אֲלֵיהֶם רָאשֵׁי בֵּית הַכְּנֶסֶת לֵאמֹר: "אֲנָשִׁים אַחִים, אִם יֵשׁ לָכֶם דְּבַר מוּסָר אֶל הָעָם, דַּבֵּרוּ." 16 קָם שָׁאוּל, הֵנִיף אֶת יָדוֹ וְאָמַר:

"אַנְשֵׁי יִשְׂרָאֵל וְיִרְאֵי הָאֱלֹהִים שִׁמְעוּ. 17 אֱלֹהֵי הָעָם הַזֶּה, אֱלֹהֵי יִשְׂרָאֵל, בָּחַר בַּאֲבוֹתֵינוּ וְרוֹמֵם אֶת הָעָם בִּהְיוֹתָם גֵּרִים בְּאֶרֶץ מִצְרַיִם וּבְיָד רָמָה הוֹצִיאָם מִשָּׁם. 18 בְּמֶשֶׁךְ כְּאַרְבָּעִים שָׁנָה נָשָׂא אוֹתָם בַּמִּדְבָּר 19 וּלְאַחַר שֶׁהִשְׁמִיד שִׁבְעָה גּוֹיִים בְּאֶרֶץ כְּנַעַן חִלֵּק לָהֶם אֶת אַרְצָם לְנַחֲלָה. 20 כָּל זֶה אָרַךְ כְּאַרְבַּע מֵאוֹת וַחֲמִשִּׁים שָׁנָה וְאַחֲרֵי כֵן נָתַן לָהֶם שׁוֹפְטִים עַד שְׁמוּאֵל הַנָּבִיא. 21 לְאַחַר מִכֵּן בִּקְּשׁוּ מֶלֶךְ וֵאלֹהִים נָתַן לָהֶם אֶת שָׁאוּל בֶּן־קִישׁ, אִישׁ מִשֵּׁבֶט בִּנְיָמִין, לְמֶשֶׁךְ אַרְבָּעִים שָׁנָה. 22 כַּאֲשֶׁר הֵסִיר אוֹתוֹ הֵקִים לָהֶם אֶת דָּוִד לְמֶלֶךְ וְעָלָיו הֵעִיד בְּאָמְרוֹ: 'מָצָאתִי דָוִד בֶּן־יִשַׁי, אִישׁ כִּלְבָבִי, וְהוּא יַעֲשֶׂה אֶת

heart, who will do all My will.' ²³ From this man's seed, according to *the* promise, God raised up for Israel a Savior—Jesus— ²⁴ after John had first preached, before His coming, the baptism of repentance to all the people of Israel. ²⁵ And as John was finishing his course, he said, 'Who do you think I am? I am not *He*. But behold, there comes One after me, the sandals of whose feet I am not worthy to loose.'

²⁶ "Men *and* brethren, sons of the family of Abraham, and those among you who fear God, to you the word of this salvation has been sent. ²⁷ For those who dwell in Jerusalem, and their rulers, because they did not know Him, nor even the voices of the Prophets which are read every Sabbath, have fulfilled *them* in condemning *Him*. ²⁸ And though they found no cause for death *in Him,* they asked Pilate that He should be put to death. ²⁹ Now when they had fulfilled all that was written concerning Him, they took *Him* down from the tree and laid *Him* in a tomb. ³⁰ But God raised Him from the dead. ³¹ He was seen for many days by those who came up with Him from Galilee to Jerusalem, who are His witnesses to the people. ³² And we declare to you glad tidings—that promise which was made to the fathers. ³³ God has fulfilled this for us their children, in that He has raised up Jesus. As it is also written in the second Psalm:

'You are My Son,
Today I have begotten You.'

³⁴ And that He raised Him from the dead, no more to return to corruption, He has spoken thus:

'I will give you the sure mercies of David.'

³⁵ Therefore He also says in another *Psalm:*

'You will not allow Your Holy One to see corruption.'

³⁶ "For David, after he had served his own generation by the will of God, fell asleep, was buried with his fathers, and saw corruption; ³⁷ but He whom God raised up saw no corruption. ³⁸ Therefore let it be known to you, brethren, that through this Man is preached to you the forgiveness of sins; ³⁹ and by Him everyone who believes is justified from all things from which you could not be justified by the law of Moses. ⁴⁰ Beware therefore, lest what has been spoken in the prophets come upon you:

⁴¹ 'Behold, you despisers,
Marvel and perish!
For I work a work in your days,
A work which you will by no means believe,

כָּל חֶפְצִי.' ²³ מִזַּרְעוֹ הֵבִיא אֱלֹהִים, כְּפִי הַהַבְטָחָה, מוֹשִׁיעַ לְיִשְׂרָאֵל – אֶת יֵשׁוּעַ, ²⁴ אֲשֶׁר לִפְנֵי בּוֹאוֹ הִכְרִיז יוֹחָנָן אֶת טְבִילַת הַתְּשׁוּבָה אֶל כָּל עַם יִשְׂרָאֵל. ²⁵ כְּשֶׁהִשְׁלִים יוֹחָנָן אֶת מְרוּצָתוֹ אָמַר, 'לְמִי אַתֶּם חוֹשְׁבִים אוֹתִי? לֹא אֲנִי הוּא. אַךְ הִנֵּה הוּא בָּא אַחֲרַי וַאֲנִי אֵינֶנִּי רָאוּי לְהַתִּיר אֶת נְעָלָיו.'

²⁶ אֲנָשִׁים אַחִים, בְּנֵי מִשְׁפַּחַת אַבְרָהָם, וִירְאֵי אֱלֹהִים אֲשֶׁר בְּקִרְבְּכֶם; אֵלֵינוּ נִשְׁלַח דְּבַר הַיְשׁוּעָה הַזֹּאת. ²⁷ כִּי יוֹשְׁבֵי יְרוּשָׁלַיִם וְהָעוֹמְדִים בְּרֹאשָׁם לֹא הִכִּירוּהוּ וּבְשָׁפְטָם אוֹתוֹ מִלְּאוּ אֶת דִּבְרֵי הַנְּבִיאִים הַנִּקְרָאִים בְּכָל שַׁבָּת, ²⁸ וְאַף כִּי לֹא מָצְאוּ שׁוּם עִלָּה לְמִשְׁפַּט מָוֶת בִּקְשׁוּ מִפִּילָטוֹס לַהֲמִיתוֹ. ²⁹ כַּאֲשֶׁר הִשְׁלִימוּ אֶת כָּל הַדְּבָרִים הַכְּתוּבִים עָלָיו הוֹרִידוּהוּ מִן הָעֵץ וְהִנִּיחוּהוּ בַּקֶּבֶר, ³⁰ אַךְ אֱלֹהִים הֵקִימוֹ מִן הַמֵּתִים. ³¹ יָמִים רַבִּים נִרְאָה אֶל הָאֲנָשִׁים שֶׁעָלוּ אִתּוֹ מִן הַגָּלִיל לִירוּשָׁלַיִם, וְעַתָּה הֵם עֵדָיו לִפְנֵי הָעָם. ³² וַאֲנַחְנוּ מְבַשְּׂרִים לָכֶם כִּי הַהַבְטָחָה אֲשֶׁר הֻבְטְחָה לַאֲבוֹתֵינוּ, ³³ אֱלֹהִים קִיֵּם אוֹתָהּ לָנוּ, הַבָּנִים, בַּהֲקִימוֹ אֶת יֵשׁוּעַ, כְּמוֹ שֶׁכָּתוּב בַּמִּזְמוֹר הַשֵּׁנִי:

'בְּנִי אַתָּה, אֲנִי הַיּוֹם יְלִדְתִּיךָ.'

³⁴ וְעַל הֲקִימוֹ אוֹתוֹ מִן הַמֵּתִים לְבִלְתִּי שׁוּב עוֹד אֶל שַׁחַת, כֹּה אָמַר:

'אֶתֵּן לָכֶם חַסְדֵי דָוִד הַנֶּאֱמָנִים.'

³⁵ לָכֵן נֶאֱמַר גַּם בְּמָקוֹם אַחֵר:

'לֹא־תִתֵּן חֲסִידְךָ לִרְאוֹת שָׁחַת.'

³⁶ הֵן דָּוִד, לְאַחַר שֶׁשֵּׁרֵת בְּדוֹרוֹ לְפִי תָכְנִית אֱלֹהִים, שָׁכַב וְנֶאֱסַף אֶל אֲבוֹתָיו וְרָאָה שָׁחַת. ³⁷ אֲבָל זֶה שֶׁאֱלֹהִים הֱקִימוֹ לֹא רָאָה שָׁחַת. ³⁸ עַל כֵּן, אֲנָשִׁים אַחִים, שֶׁיְּהֵא יָדוּעַ לָכֶם כִּי הוֹדוֹת לוֹ מֻכְרֶזֶת לָכֶם סְלִיחַת חֲטָאִים; ³⁹ וּבְכָל הַדְּבָרִים שֶׁלֹּא יְכָלְתֶּם לְהִצָּדֵק בָּהֶם בְּתוֹרַת מֹשֶׁה, הֲרֵי שָׁבּוֹ נִצְדָּק כָּל מִי שֶׁמַּאֲמִין. ⁴⁰ לָכֵן הִזָּהֲרוּ שֶׁלֹּא יָבוֹא עֲלֵיכֶם הַנֶּאֱמָר בַּנְּבִיאִים:

⁴¹ 'רְאוּ בַּגּוֹיִם וְהַבִּיטוּ וְהִתַּמְּהוּ תְּמָהוּ. כִּי־פֹעַל פֹּעֵל בִּימֵיכֶם לֹא תַאֲמִינוּ כִּי יְסֻפָּר."

Though one were to declare it to you.'"

42 So when the Jews went out of the synagogue, the Gentiles begged that these words might be preached to them the next Sabbath. 43 Now when the congregation had broken up, many of the Jews and devout proselytes followed Paul and Barnabas, who, speaking to them, persuaded them to continue in the grace of God.

44 On the next Sabbath almost the whole city came together to hear the word of God. 45 But when the Jews saw the multitudes, they were filled with envy; and contradicting and blaspheming, they opposed the things spoken by Paul. 46 Then Paul and Barnabas grew bold and said, "It was necessary that the word of God should be spoken to you first; but since you reject it, and judge yourselves unworthy of everlasting life, behold, we turn to the Gentiles. 47 For so the Lord has commanded us:

'I have set you as a light to the Gentiles,
That you should be for salvation to the ends of the earth.'"

48 Now when the Gentiles heard this, they were glad and glorified the word of the Lord. And as many as had been appointed to eternal life believed.

49 And the word of the Lord was being spread throughout all the region. 50 But the Jews stirred up the devout and prominent women and the chief men of the city, raised up persecution against Paul and Barnabas, and expelled them from their region. 51 But they shook off the dust from their feet against them, and came to Iconium. 52 And the disciples were filled with joy and with the Holy Spirit.

14 Now it happened in Iconium that they went together to the synagogue of the Jews, and so spoke that a great multitude both of the Jews and of the Greeks believed. 2 But the unbelieving Jews stirred up the Gentiles and poisoned their minds against the brethren. 3 Therefore they stayed there a long time, speaking boldly in the Lord, who was bearing witness to the word of His grace, granting signs and wonders to be done by their hands.

4 But the multitude of the city was divided: part sided with the Jews, and part with the apostles. 5 And when a violent attempt was made by both the Gentiles and Jews, with their rulers, to abuse and stone them, 6 they became aware of it and fled to Lystra and Derbe, cities of Lycaonia, and to the surrounding region. 7 And they were preaching the gospel there.

8 And in Lystra a certain man without strength in his feet was sitting, a cripple from his mother's womb, who had never walked. 9 *This* man heard

42 כְּשֶׁיָּצְאוּ בִּקְּשׁוּ מִשָּׁאוּל וּבַר־נַבָּא לְדַבֵּר אֲלֵיהֶם אֶת הַדְּבָרִים הָאֵלֶּה בַּשַּׁבָּת הַבָּאָה. 43 לְאַחַר שֶׁהִתְפַּזְּרוּ בָּאֵי בֵּית הַכְּנֶסֶת הָלְכוּ אַחֲרֵי שָׁאוּל וּבַר־נַבָּא רַבִּים מִן הַיְּהוּדִים וּמִן הַגֵּרִים יִרְאֵי הָאֱלֹהִים. הַשְּׁנַיִם דִּבְּרוּ אֲלֵיהֶם וְהֶאִיצוּ בָּהֶם לְהַמְשִׁיךְ בַּעֲמִידָתָם בְּחֶסֶד הָאֱלֹהִים.

44 בַּשַּׁבָּת הַשְּׁנִיָּה הִתְאַסְּפָה כִּמְעַט כָּל הָעִיר לִשְׁמֹעַ אֶת דְּבַר הָאָדוֹן. 45 אֲבָל כִּרְאוֹת יְהוּדֵי הַמָּקוֹם אֶת הֲמוֹן הָעָם, נִתְמַלְּאוּ קִנְאָה וְהֵחֵלּוּ לְגַדֵּף וּלְדַבֵּר נֶגֶד דִּבְרֵי שָׁאוּל. 46 הֵשִׁיבוּ שָׁאוּל וּבַר־נַבָּא בְּאֹמֶץ לֵב וְאָמְרוּ: "מִן הַהֶכְרֵחַ הָיָה כִּי לָכֶם רִאשׁוֹנָה יֵשָּׁמַע אֶת דְּבַר אֱלֹהִים, אַךְ מִכֵּיוָן שֶׁאַתֶּם דּוֹחִים אוֹתוֹ וְדָנִים אֶת עַצְמְכֶם לְבִלְתִּי רְאוּיִים לְחַיֵּי עוֹלָם, הִנֵּה אָנוּ פּוֹנִים אֶל הַגּוֹיִים. 47 הֵן כֹּה צִוָּנוּ אֲדֹנָי:

'וּנְתַתִּיךָ לְאוֹר גּוֹיִם, לִהְיוֹת יְשׁוּעָתִי עַד־קְצֵה הָאָרֶץ.'

48 הַגּוֹיִים כְּשָׁמְעָם שָׂמְחוּ וְהִלְּלוּ אֶת דְּבַר הָאָדוֹן, וְכָל אֲשֶׁר הָיוּ מְיֹעָדִים לְחַיֵּי עוֹלָם הֶאֱמִינוּ.

49 דְּבַר הָאָדוֹן הָלַךְ וְנָפוֹץ בְּכָל הָאֵזוֹר. 50 אֲבָל רָאשֵׁי הַיְּהוּדִים הֵסִיתוּ אֶת הַנָּשִׁים הַנִּכְבָּדוֹת הַיִּרְאוֹת אֶת אֱלֹהִים וְאֶת נִכְבַּדֵּי הָעִיר, וְעוֹרְרוּ רְדִיפָה נֶגֶד שָׁאוּל וּבַר־נַבָּא וְגֵרְשׁוּ אוֹתָם מֵאֱזוֹרָם. 51 הַשְּׁנַיִם נָעֲרוּ לְעֶבְרָם אֶת אֲבַק רַגְלֵיהֶם וְהָלְכוּ לְאִיקוֹנְיוֹן; 52 וְאוּלָם הַתַּלְמִידִים מָלְאוּ שִׂמְחָה וְרוּחַ הַקֹּדֶשׁ.

יד בְּאִיקוֹנְיוֹן נִכְנְסוּ יַחְדָּיו לְבֵית הַכְּנֶסֶת וְדִבְּרוּ בְּאֹפֶן כָּזֶה שֶׁעַם רַב מִן הַיְּהוּדִים וּמִן הַיְּוָנִים הֶאֱמִינוּ. 2 אֲבָל אֵלֶּה מִן הַיְּהוּדִים שֶׁסֵּרְבוּ לְהַאֲמִין עוֹרְרוּ שִׂנְאָה בְּלֵב הַגּוֹיִים נֶגֶד הָאַחִים. 3 הַשְּׁנַיִם יָשְׁבוּ שָׁם זְמַן רַב וְדִבְּרוּ בְּאֹמֶץ לֵב עַל הָאָדוֹן, וְהָאָדוֹן הֵעִיד לַאֲשׁוּר דְּבַר חַסְדּוֹ בַּעֲשׂוֹתוֹ אוֹתוֹת וּמוֹפְתִים דַּרְכָּם. 4 אָז הִתְפַּלְּגוּ תּוֹשְׁבֵי הָעִיר; אֵלֶּה אַחֲרֵי קְבוּצַת הַיְּהוּדִים וְאֵלֶּה אַחֲרֵי הַשְּׁלִיחִים. 5 גּוֹיִים וִיהוּדִים, יַחַד עִם הָעוֹמְדִים בְּרֹאשָׁם, קָמוּ עֲלֵיהֶם לְהִתְעַלֵּל בָּהֶם וְלִסְקֹל אוֹתָם, 6 אַךְ הֵם הִבְחִינוּ בָּזֶה וְנִמְלְטוּ אֶל עָרֵי לִיקָאוֹנְיָה, לִיסְטְרָה וְדַרְבִּי וְהַסְּבִיבָה, 7 וּבִשְּׂרוּ שָׁם אֶת הַבְּשׂוֹרָה. 8 בְּלִיסְטְרָה יָשַׁב אִישׁ אֶחָד רְפֵה רַגְלַיִם, פִּסֵּחַ מִבֶּטֶן אִמּוֹ שֶׁלֹּא הָלַךְ מִיָּמָיו. 9 הוּא שָׁמַע אֶת שָׁאוּל מְדַבֵּר. כְּשֶׁהִבִּיט בּוֹ שָׁאוּל

Paul speaking. Paul, observing him intently and seeing that he had faith to be healed, [10] said with a loud voice, "Stand up straight on your feet!" And he leaped and walked. [11] Now when the people saw what Paul had done, they raised their voices, saying in the Lycaonian *language,* "The gods have come down to us in the likeness of men!" [12] And Barnabas they called Zeus, and Paul, Hermes, because he was the chief speaker. [13] Then the priest of Zeus, whose temple was in front of their city, brought oxen and garlands to the gates, intending to sacrifice with the multitudes.

[14] But when the apostles Barnabas and Paul heard this, they tore their clothes and ran in among the multitude, crying out [15] and saying, "Men, why are you doing these things? We also are men with the same nature as you, and preach to you that you should turn from these useless things to the living God, who made the heaven, the earth, the sea, and all things that are in them, [16] who in bygone generations allowed all nations to walk in their own ways. [17] Nevertheless He did not leave Himself without witness, in that He did good, gave us rain from heaven and fruitful seasons, filling our hearts with food and gladness." [18] And with these sayings they could scarcely restrain the multitudes from sacrificing to them.

[19] Then Jews from Antioch and Iconium came there; and having persuaded the multitudes, they stoned Paul *and* dragged *him* out of the city, supposing him to be dead. [20] However, when the disciples gathered around him, he rose up and went into the city. And the next day he departed with Barnabas to Derbe.

[21] And when they had preached the gospel to that city and made many disciples, they returned to Lystra, Iconium, and Antioch, [22] strengthening the souls of the disciples, exhorting *them* to continue in the faith, and *saying,* "We must through many tribulations enter the kingdom of God." [23] So when they had appointed elders in every church, and prayed with fasting, they commended them to the Lord in whom they had believed. [24] And after they had passed through Pisidia, they came to Pamphylia. [25] Now when they had preached the word in Perga, they went down to Attalia. [26] From there they sailed to Antioch, where they had been commended to the grace of God for the work which they had completed.

[27] Now when they had come and gathered the church together, they reported all that God had done with them, and that He had opened the door of faith to the Gentiles. [28] So they stayed there a long time with the disciples.

וְרָאָה שֶׁיֵּשׁ לוֹ אֱמוּנָה לְהֵרָפֵא, [10] אָמַר בְּקוֹל גָּדוֹל: "קוּם עַל רַגְלֶיךָ וְהִזְדַּקֵּף!" הוּא זָנֵק וְהִתְהַלֵּךְ. [11] כִּרְאוֹת הֲמוֹן הָעָם אֶת הַמַּעֲשֶׂה שֶׁל שָׁאוּל נָשְׂאוּ קוֹלָם וְאָמְרוּ בַּלָּשׁוֹן הַלִּיקָאוֹנִית: "הָאֵלִים יָרְדוּ אֵלֵינוּ בִּדְמוּת אֲנָשִׁים", [12] וּלְבַר-נַבָּא קָרְאוּ זֵאוּס וּלְשָׁאוּל קָרְאוּ הֶרְמֶס, כִּי הָיָה רֹאשׁ הַמְדַבְּרִים. [13] הַכֹּהֵן שֶׁל זֵאוּס, שֶׁהֵיכָלוֹ לִפְנֵי הָעִיר, הֵבִיא פָּרִים וַעֲטָרוֹת אֶל הַשְּׁעָרִים וְרָצָה לְהַקְרִיב קָרְבָּנוֹת הוּא וַהֲמוֹן הָעָם. [14] כַּאֲשֶׁר שָׁמְעוּ זֹאת שָׁאוּל וּבַר-נַבָּא הַשְּׁלִיחִים, קָרְעוּ אֶת בִּגְדֵיהֶם. הֵם רָצוּ אֶל תּוֹךְ הֶהָמוֹן וְצָעֲקוּ: [15] "אֲנָשִׁים, לָמָה אַתֶּם עוֹשִׂים זֹאת? גַּם אֲנַחְנוּ בְּנֵי אֱנוֹשׁ כְּמוֹכֶם, וּמְבַשְּׂרִים לָכֶם אֶת הַבְּשׂוֹרָה כְּדֵי שֶׁתִּפְנוּ מִן הַהֲבָלִים הָאֵלֶּה לֵאלֹהִים חַיִּים אֲשֶׁר עָשָׂה אֶת הַשָּׁמַיִם וְאֶת הָאָרֶץ וְאֶת הַיָּם וְאֶת כָּל אֲשֶׁר בָּם, [16] וַאֲשֶׁר בַּדּוֹרוֹת הַקּוֹדְמִים הִנִּיחַ לְכָל הַגּוֹיִים לָלֶכֶת בְּדַרְכֵיהֶם. [17] וּבְכָל זֹאת לֹא חָדַל לְהָעִיד עַל עַצְמוֹ בְּמַעֲשָׂיו הַטּוֹבִים, בְּתִתּוֹ לָנוּ גֶּשֶׁם מִן הַשָּׁמַיִם וְעוֹנוֹת פּוֹרִיּוֹת, וּבְמַלְּאוֹ אֶת לְבָבֵינוּ מָזוֹן וְשִׂמְחָה." [18] וְגַם בְּאָמְרָם אֶת הַדְּבָרִים הָאֵלֶּה, בְּקֹשִׁי מָנְעוּ מֵהֲמוֹן הָעָם לְהַקְרִיב לָהֶם קָרְבָּן.

[19] יְהוּדִים מֵאַנְטְיוֹכְיָה וּמֵאִיקוֹנְיוֹן בָּאוּ לְשָׁם. הֵם הֵסִיתוּ אֶת הֲמוֹן הָעָם וְרָגְמוּ אֶת שָׁאוּל בַּאֲבָנִים. לְאַחַר מִכֵּן גָּרְרוּ אוֹתוֹ אֶל מִחוּץ לָעִיר בְּחָשְׁבָם אוֹתוֹ לְמֵת. [20] אֲבָל כַּאֲשֶׁר הִקִּיפוּהוּ הַתַּלְמִידִים קָם וְהָלַךְ הָעִירָה. לְמָחֳרָת יָצָא עִם בַּר-נַבָּא אֶל דֶּרְבִּי. [21] הֵם בִּשְּׂרוּ אֶת הַבְּשׂוֹרָה בָּעִיר הַהִיא וְאַחֲרֵי שֶׁהֶעֱמִידוּ תַּלְמִידִים רַבִּים חָזְרוּ אֶל לִיסְטְרָה וְאִיקוֹנְיוֹן וְאַנְטְיוֹכְיָה; [22] שָׁם חִזְּקוּ אֶת לֵב הַתַּלְמִידִים וְהֵאִיצוּ בָּהֶם לְהוֹסִיף לַעֲמֹד בָּאֱמוּנָה, כִּי "דֶּרֶךְ צָרוֹת רַבּוֹת עָלֵינוּ לְהִכָּנֵס לְמַלְכוּת אֱלֹהִים." [23] בְּכָל קְהִלָּה מִנּוּ לָהֶם זְקֵנִים וּלְאַחַר שֶׁהִתְפַּלְּלוּ וְצָמוּ הִפְקִידוּ אוֹתָם בְּיַד הָאָדוֹן אֲשֶׁר הֶאֱמִינוּ בּוֹ. [24] הֵם עָבְרוּ דֶּרֶךְ פִּיסִידְיָה וּבָאוּ אֶל פַּמְפִילְיָה, [25] וְאַחֲרֵי שֶׁהִשְׁמִיעוּ אֶת הַדָּבָר בְּפֶרְגֵּי יָרְדוּ אֶל אַטַּלְיָה. [26] מִשָּׁם הִפְלִיגוּ לְאַנְטְיוֹכְיָה, אֶל הַמָּקוֹם שֶׁבּוֹ הִפְקְדוּ בְּעֶבֶר לְחֶסֶד אֱלֹהִים לְשֵׁם הָעֲבוֹדָה אֲשֶׁר הִשְׁלִימוּ. [27] כְּשֶׁהִגִּיעוּ כִּנְּסוּ אֶת הַקְּהִלָּה וְסִפְּרוּ אֶת כָּל מַה שֶּׁעָשָׂה אֱלֹהִים עִמָּהֶם וְכִי פָּתַח לַגּוֹיִים אֶת שַׁעַר הָאֱמוּנָה. [28] וְשָׁם שָׁהוּ יָמִים לֹא מְעַטִּים עִם הַתַּלְמִידִים.

15 And certain *men* came down from Judea and taught the brethren, "Unless you are circumcised according to the custom of Moses, you cannot be saved." ²Therefore, when Paul and Barnabas had no small dissension and dispute with them, they determined that Paul and Barnabas and certain others of them should go up to Jerusalem, to the apostles and elders, about this question.

³So, being sent on their way by the church, they passed through Phoenicia and Samaria, describing the conversion of the Gentiles; and they caused great joy to all the brethren. ⁴And when they had come to Jerusalem, they were received by the church and the apostles and the elders; and they reported all things that God had done with them. ⁵But some of the sect of the Pharisees who believed rose up, saying, "It is necessary to circumcise them, and to command *them* to keep the law of Moses."

⁶Now the apostles and elders came together to consider this matter. ⁷And when there had been much dispute, Peter rose up and said to them: "Men and brethren, you know that a good while ago God chose among us, that by my mouth the Gentiles should hear the word of the gospel and believe. ⁸So God, who knows the heart, acknowledged them by giving them the Holy Spirit, just as *He did* to us, ⁹and made no distinction between us and them, purifying their hearts by faith. ¹⁰Now therefore, why do you test God by putting a yoke on the neck of the disciples which neither our fathers nor we were able to bear? ¹¹But we believe that through the grace of the Lord Jesus Christ we shall be saved in the same manner as they."

¹²Then all the multitude kept silent and listened to Barnabas and Paul declaring how many miracles and wonders God had worked through them among the Gentiles. ¹³And after they had become silent, James answered, saying, "Men *and* brethren, listen to me: ¹⁴Simon has declared how God at the first visited the Gentiles to take out of them a people for His name. ¹⁵And with this the words of the prophets agree, just as it is written:

¹⁶ 'After this I will return
   And will rebuild the tabernacle of David,
     which has fallen down;
   I will rebuild its ruins,
   And I will set it up;
¹⁷ So that the rest of mankind may seek the
    LORD,
   Even all the Gentiles who are called by My
    name,
   Says the LORD who does all these things.'

טו כַּמָּה אֲנָשִׁים יָרְדוּ מִיהוּדָה וְלִמְּדוּ אֶת הָאַחִים שֶׁאִם לֹא יִמּוֹלוּ כְּדַת מֹשֶׁה לֹא יוּכְלוּ לְהִוָּשֵׁעַ. ²לְשָׁאוּל וּלְבַר־נַבָּא הָיוּ דִּין וּדְבָרִים לֹא מְעַטִּים עִמָּהֶם, לָכֵן הֶחְלַט שֶׁשָּׁאוּל וּבַר־נַבָּא וְעוֹד כַּמָּה מֵהֶם יַעֲלוּ לִירוּשָׁלַיִם אֶל הַשְּׁלִיחִים וְהַזְּקֵנִים בְּנוֹגֵעַ לַשְּׁאֵלָה הַזֹּאת.

³הֵם שֻׁלְּחוּ לְדַרְכָּם עַל־יְדֵי הַקְּהִלָּה וּכְשֶׁעָבְרוּ בִּפְנִיקְיָה וּבְשׁוֹמְרוֹן סִפְּרוּ עַל תְּשׁוּבַת הַגּוֹיִים וְגָרְמוּ שִׂמְחָה גְדוֹלָה לְכָל הָאַחִים. ⁴בְּהַגִּיעָם לִירוּשָׁלַיִם נִתְקַבְּלוּ עַל־יְדֵי הַקְּהִלָּה וְהַשְּׁלִיחִים וְהַזְּקֵנִים, וְסִפְּרוּ אֶת כָּל מַה שֶּׁעָשָׂה אֱלֹהִים עִמָּהֶם. ⁵אַךְ מַאֲמִינִים אֲחָדִים מִכַּת הַפְּרוּשִׁים קָמוּ וְאָמְרוּ שֶׁצָּרִיךְ לָמוּל אוֹתָם וּלְצַוּוֹתָם לִשְׁמֹר אֶת תּוֹרַת מֹשֶׁה.

⁶הִתְכַּנְּסוּ הַשְּׁלִיחִים וְהַזְּקֵנִים לָעַיֵּן בַּדָּבָר הַזֶּה. ⁷אַחֲרֵי וִכּוּחַ מְמֻשָּׁךְ קָם כֵּיפָא וְאָמַר לָהֶם: "אֲנָשִׁים אַחִים, אַתֶּם יוֹדְעִים כִּי מִיָּמִים רִאשׁוֹנִים בָּחֲרַנִי אֱלֹהִים מִבֵּינֵיכֶם כְּדֵי שֶׁמִּפִּי יִשְׁמְעוּ הַגּוֹיִים אֶת דְּבַר הַבְּשׂוֹרָה וְיַאֲמִינוּ. ⁸וֵאלֹהִים הַיּוֹדֵעַ אֶת הַלְּבָבוֹת הֵעִיד עֲלֵיהֶם בְּתִתּוֹ לָהֶם אֶת רוּחַ הַקֹּדֶשׁ כְּשֵׁם שֶׁנְּתָנָהּ גַּם לָנוּ. ⁹הוּא לֹא הִבְדִּיל כְּלָל בֵּינֵינוּ לְבֵינָם, כִּי עַל־יְדֵי הָאֱמוּנָה טִהַר אֶת לְבָבָם. ¹⁰וְעַתָּה מַדּוּעַ תְּנַסּוּ אֶת אֱלֹהִים לָשִׂים עֹל עַל צַוְּארֵי הַתַּלְמִידִים, עֹל אֲשֶׁר גַּם אֲבוֹתֵינוּ וְגַם אֲנַחְנוּ לֹא יָכֹלְנוּ לָשֵׂאת? ¹¹אַדְרַבָּא, אָנוּ מַאֲמִינִים שֶׁבְּחֶסֶד הָאָדוֹן יֵשׁוּעַ הַמָּשִׁיחַ נוֹשָׁעֵנוּ, כָּמוֹנוּ כְּמוֹהֶם."

¹²כָּל הַנֶּאֱסָפִים שָׁתְקוּ וְהִטּוּ אֹזֶן לְבַר־נַבָּא וּלְשָׁאוּל אֲשֶׁר סִפְּרוּ אֵלּוּ אוֹתוֹת וּמוֹפְתִים עָשָׂה אֱלֹהִים עַל־יָדָם בְּקֶרֶב הַגּוֹיִים. ¹³כְּשֶׁגָּמְרוּ לְסַפֵּר הֵגִיב יַעֲקֹב וְאָמַר: "אֲנָשִׁים אַחִים, שִׁמְעוּ אֵלַי. ¹⁴שִׁמְעוֹן סִפֵּר כֵּיצַד לָרִאשׁוֹנָה פָּקַד אֱלֹהִים אֶת הַגּוֹיִים לָקַחַת מִקִּרְבָּם עַם לִשְׁמוֹ. ¹⁵וְלָזֹאת מַסְכִּימִים דִּבְרֵי הַנְּבִיאִים, כַּכָּתוּב:

¹⁶'אַחֲרֵי כֵן אָשׁוּב וְאָקִים אֶת־סֻכַּת דָּוִיד הַנֹּפֶלֶת
וַהֲרִיסוֹתָיו אָקִים וּבְנִיתִיהָ,
¹⁷לְמַעַן יִדְרְשׁוּ אֶת יְהוָה שְׁאֵרִית אָדָם
וְכָל הַגּוֹיִם אֲשֶׁר נִקְרָא שְׁמִי עֲלֵיהֶם.
נְאֻם יְהוָה עֹשֶׂה כָּל אֵלֶּה.

¹⁸"Known to God from eternity are all His works. ¹⁹Therefore I judge that we should not trouble those from among the Gentiles who are turning to God, ²⁰but that we write to them to abstain from things polluted by idols, *from* sexual immorality, *from* things strangled, and *from* blood. ²¹For Moses has had throughout many generations those who preach him in every city, being read in the synagogues every Sabbath."

²²Then it pleased the apostles and elders, with the whole church, to send chosen men of their own company to Antioch with Paul and Barnabas, *namely,* Judas who was also named Barsabas, and Silas, leading men among the breathren.

²³They wrote this *letter* by them:

The apostles, the elders, and the brethren,

To the brethren who are of the Gentiles in Antioch, Syria, and Cilicia:

Greetings.

24 Since we have heard that some who went out from us have troubled you with words, unsettling your souls, saying, "*You must* be circumcised and keep the law"—to whom we gave no *such* commandment—²⁵it seemed good to us, being assembled with one accord, to send chosen men to you with our beloved Barnabas and Paul, ²⁶men who have risked their lives for the name of our Lord Jesus Christ. ²⁷We have therefore sent Judas and Silas, who will also report the same things by word of mouth. ²⁸For it seemed good to the Holy Spirit, and to us, to lay upon you no greater burden than these necessary things: ²⁹that you abstain from things offered to idols, from blood, from things strangled, and from sexual immorality. If you keep your-selves from these, you will do well.

Farewell.

³⁰So when they were sent off, they came to Antioch; and when they had gathered the multitude together, they delivered the letter. ³¹When they had read it, they rejoiced over its encouragement. ³²Now Judas and Silas, themselves being prophets also, exhorted and strengthened the brethren with many words. ³³And after they had stayed *there* for a time, they were sent back with greetings from the brethren to the apostles.

³⁴However, it seemed good to Silas to remain there. ³⁵Paul and Barnabas also remained in Antioch, teaching and preaching the word of the Lord, with many others also.

¹⁸ הַנּוֹדָעִים מֵעוֹלָם.'

¹⁹ עַל כֵּן אֲנִי פוֹסֵק שֶׁלֹּא לְהַקְשׁוֹת עַל אוֹתָם אֲנָשִׁים מִן הַגּוֹיִים אֲשֶׁר שָׁבִים אֶל אֱלֹהִים, ²⁰ אֶלָּא לִכְתֹּב אֲלֵיהֶם לְהִמָּנַע מִטֻּמְאוֹת אֱלִילִים וּמִזְּנוּת, מִבְּשַׂר הַנֶּחֱנָק וּמִן הַדָּם. ²¹ הֲרֵי לְמֹשֶׁה יֵשׁ מְדוֹרוֹת קְדוּמִים אֲנָשִׁים הַמַּכְרִיזִים אוֹתוֹ בְּכָל עִיר וָעִיר, וּמְדֵי שַׁבָּת הוּא נִקְרָא בְּבָתֵּי הַכְּנֶסֶת."

²² נִתְקַבֵּל עַל דַּעַת הַשְּׁלִיחִים וְהַזְּקֵנִים וְכָל הַקְּהִלָּה לִשְׁלֹחַ אֲנָשִׁים שֶׁנִּבְחֲרוּ מִקִּרְבָּם אֶל אַנְטִיוֹכְיָה, יַחַד עִם שָׁאוּל וּבַר־נַבָּא – אֶת יְהוּדָה, הַמְכֻנֶּה בַּר־שַׁבָּא, וְאֶת סִילָא אֲשֶׁר הָיוּ מִן הַמַּנְהִיגִים בְּקֶרֶב הָאַחִים. ²³ אֶת הַמִּכְתָּב הַזֶּה מָסְרוּ בְּיָדָם:

"הַשְּׁלִיחִים וְזִקְנֵי הָאַחִים דּוֹרְשִׁים בִּשְׁלוֹם הָאַחִים שֶׁמִּקֶּרֶב הַגּוֹיִים בְּאַנְטִיוֹכְיָה וּבְסוּרְיָה וּבְקִילִיקְיָה. ²⁴ הוֹאִיל וְשָׁמַעְנוּ כִּי אֲחָדִים מֵאִתָּנוּ פָּעֲלוּ מִבְּלִי שֶׁצִּוִּינוּ אוֹתָם וּבִלְבְּלוּ אֶתְכֶם בְּדִבְרֵיהֶם וְהֵבִיכוּ אֶת נַפְשׁוֹתֵיכֶם, ²⁵ נִתְקַבֵּל עַל דַּעְתֵּנוּ פֶּה אֶחָד לִשְׁלֹחַ אֲלֵיכֶם אֲנָשִׁים נִבְחָרִים יַחַד עִם חֲבִיבֵינוּ בַּר־נַבָּא וְשָׁאוּל, ²⁶ אֲנָשִׁים אֲשֶׁר מָסְרוּ אֶת נַפְשָׁם לְמַעַן שֵׁם אֲדוֹנֵנוּ יֵשׁוּעַ הַמָּשִׁיחַ. ²⁷ לָכֵן שָׁלַחְנוּ אֶת יְהוּדָה וְאֶת סִילָא וְהֵם יַגִּידוּ בְּמוֹ פִּיהֶם אֶת אוֹתָם הַדְּבָרִים. ²⁸ נִרְאָה לְרוּחַ הַקֹּדֶשׁ וְלָנוּ שֶׁלֹּא לְהָטִיל עֲלֵיכֶם שׁוּם מַעֲמָסָה נוֹסֶפֶת מִלְּבַד הַדְּבָרִים הַנְּחוּצִים הָאֵלֶּה: ²⁹ לְהִמָּנַע מִזִּבְחֵי אֱלִילִים וּמִדָּם, מִבְּשַׂר הַנֶּחֱנָק וּמִן הַזְּנוּת. אִם תִּשָּׁמְרוּ מֵאֵלֶּה תֵּיטִיבוּ לַעֲשׂוֹת. שָׁלוֹם לָכֶם."

³⁰ הָאֲנָשִׁים שֻׁלְּחוּ לְדַרְכָּם. הֵם יָרְדוּ אֶל אַנְטִיוֹכְיָה, כִּנְּסוּ אֶת הָעָם וּמָסְרוּ אֶת הָאִגֶּרֶת. ³¹ כְּשֶׁקָּרְאוּ הָאַחִים אֶת הָאִגֶּרֶת נִתְמַלְּאוּ שִׂמְחָה עַל הָעִדּוּד. ³² וִיהוּדָה וְסִילָא, שֶׁהָיוּ גַם נְבִיאִים, עוֹדְדוּ אוֹתָם בְּמִלִּים רַבּוֹת וְחִזְּקוּ אוֹתָם. ³³ הֵם שָׁהוּ שָׁם זְמַן מְסֻיָּם, וְאַחֲרֵי כֵן שֻׁלְּחוּ אוֹתָם הָאַחִים בְּשָׁלוֹם אֶל שׁוֹלְחֵיהֶם. ³⁵ שָׁאוּל וּבַר־נַבָּא נִשְׁאֲרוּ בְּאַנְטִיוֹכְיָה, וְיַחַד עִם רַבִּים אֲחֵרִים לִמְּדוּ וּבִשְּׂרוּ אֶת דְּבַר אֱלֹהִים.

36 Then after some days Paul said to Barnabas, "Let us now go back and visit our brethren in every city where we have preached the word of the Lord, *and see* how they are doing." 37 Now Barnabas was determined to take with them John called Mark. 38 But Paul insisted that they should not take with them the one who had departed from them in Pamphylia, and had not gone with them to the work. 39 Then the contention became so sharp that they parted from one another. And so Barnabas took Mark and sailed to Cyprus; 40 but Paul chose Silas and departed, being commended by the brethren to the grace of God. 41 And he went through Syria and Cilicia, strengthening the churches.

16 Then he came to Derbe and Lystra. And behold, a certain disciple was there, named Timothy, *the* son of a certain Jewish woman who believed, but his father *was* Greek. 2 He was well spoken of by the brethren who were at Lystra and Iconium. 3 Paul wanted to have him go on with him. And he took *him* and circumcised him because of the Jews who were in that region, for they all knew that his father was Greek. 4 And as they went through the cities, they delivered to them the decrees to keep, which were determined by the apostles and elders at Jerusalem. 5 So the churches were strengthened in the faith, and increased in number daily.

6 Now when they had gone through Phrygia and the region of Galatia, they were forbidden by the Holy Spirit to preach the word in Asia. 7 After they had come to Mysia, they tried to go into Bithynia, but the Spirit did not permit them. 8 So passing by Mysia, they came down to Troas. 9 And a vision appeared to Paul in the night. A man of Macedonia stood and pleaded with him, saying, "Come over to Macedonia and help us." 10 Now after he had seen the vision, immediately we sought to go to Macedonia, concluding that the Lord had called us to preach the gospel to them.

11 Therefore, sailing from Troas, we ran a straight course to Samothrace, and the next *day* came to Neapolis, 12 and from there to Philippi, which is the foremost city of that part of Macedonia, a colony. And we were staying in that city for some days. 13 And on the Sabbath day we went out of the city to the riverside, where prayer was customarily made; and we sat down and spoke to the women who met *there*. 14 Now a certain woman named Lydia heard *us*. She was a seller of purple from the city of Thyatira, who worshiped God. The Lord opened her heart to heed the things spoken by Paul.

36 לְאַחַר כַּמָּה יָמִים אָמַר שָׁאוּל לְבַר־נַבָּא: "בּוֹא נַחֲזוֹר וּנְבַקֵּר אֶת הָאַחִים בְּכָל עִיר וָעִיר שֶׁהִשְׁמַעְנוּ בָּהּ אֶת דְּבַר אֱלֹהִים, וְנִרְאֶה מַה מַּצָּבָם." 37 בַּר־נַבָּא רָצָה לָקַחַת אִתָּם גַּם אֶת יוֹחָנָן הַמְכֻנֶּה מַרְקוֹס, 38 אַךְ שָׁאוּל חָשַׁב שֶׁלֹּא רָצוּי לָקַחַת אִתָּם אֶת זֶה שֶׁפָּרַשׁ מֵהֶם בְּפַמְפִילְיָה וְלֹא נִתְלַוָּה אֲלֵיהֶם לַעֲבוֹדָה. 39 הָרִיב הָיָה חָרִיף עַד כְּדֵי כָּךְ שֶׁנִּפְרְדוּ זֶה מִזֶּה. לָקַח בַּר־נַבָּא אֶת מַרְקוֹס וְהִפְלִיג לְקַפְרִיסִין, 40 וְשָׁאוּל בָּחַר אֶת סִילָא וְיָצָא לְדַרְכּוֹ לְאַחַר שֶׁהָאַחִים הִפְקִידוּהוּ לְחֶסֶד הָאָדוֹן. 41 הוּא עָבַר בְּסוּרְיָה וּבְקִילִיקְיָה וְחִזֵּק אֶת הַקְּהִלּוֹת.

טז הוּא בָּא אֶל דַּרְבִּי וְאֶל לִיסְטְרָה. הָיָה שָׁם תַּלְמִיד אֶחָד, טִימוֹתֵאוֹס שְׁמוֹ, בֶּן לְאִשָּׁה יְהוּדִיָּה מַאֲמִינָה וּלְאָב יְוָנִי, 2 וְשֵׁם טוֹב לוֹ בֵּין הָאַחִים אֲשֶׁר בְּלִיסְטְרָה וּבְאִיקוֹנְיוֹן. 3 אִתּוֹ רָצָה שָׁאוּל לָצֵאת לַדֶּרֶךְ. הוּא לָקַח אוֹתוֹ וּבִגְלַל הַיְּהוּדִים שֶׁהָיוּ בִּמְקוֹמוֹת הָהֵם מָל אוֹתוֹ, שֶׁכֵּן הַכֹּל יָדְעוּ שֶׁאָבִיו יְוָנִי. 4 הֵם עָבְרוּ בֶּעָרִים וּמָסְרוּ לָהֶם שֶׁיֵּשׁ לִשְׁמֹר אֶת הַהֲלָכוֹת שֶׁפָּסְקוּ הַשְּׁלִיחִים וְהַזְּקֵנִים בִּירוּשָׁלַיִם. 5 אָז הִתְחַזְּקוּ הַקְּהִלּוֹת בָּאֱמוּנָה וּמִסְפָּר הַמַּאֲמִינִים גָּדֵל מִיּוֹם לְיוֹם.

6 הֵם עָבְרוּ בְּאֵזוֹר פְרִיגְיָה וְגָלַטְיָה, כִּי רוּחַ הַקֹּדֶשׁ מָנְעָה אוֹתָם מִלְהַשְׁמִיעַ אֶת דְּבַר אֱלֹהִים בְּאַסְיָה. 7 כְּשֶׁבָּאוּ אֶל מִיסְיָה נִסּוּ לָלֶכֶת אֶל בִּיתִינְיָה, אַךְ רוּחַ יֵשׁוּעַ לֹא הִנִּיחָה לָהֶם. 8 לְפִיכָךְ עָבְרוּ לְיַד מִיסְיָה וְיָרְדוּ אֶל טְרוֹאַס. 9 בַּלַּיְלָה נִרְאָה חָזוֹן אֶל שָׁאוּל: אִישׁ מָקֶדוֹנִי אֶחָד נִרְאָה עוֹמֵד וּמְבַקֵּשׁ מִמֶּנּוּ, 'עֲבֹר אֶל מָקֶדוֹנְיָה וַעֲזֹר לָנוּ.' 10 מִיָּד לְאַחַר שֶׁרָאָה אֶת הֶחָזוֹן הִשְׁתַּדַּלְנוּ לָצֵאת אֶל מָקֶדוֹנְיָה, כִּי הֵבַנּוּ שֶׁאֱלֹהִים קוֹרֵא לָנוּ לְבַשֵּׂר לָהֶם אֶת הַבְּשׂוֹרָה.

11 הִפְלַגְנוּ מִטְּרוֹאַס וְשַׁטְנוּ בִּנְתִיב יָשָׁר אֶל סָמוֹתְרַקְיָה, וּלְמָחֳרָת אֶל נֵאפוֹלִים; 12 מִשָּׁם אֶל פִילִיפִּי, עִיר בַּחֵבֶל הָרִאשׁוֹן שֶׁל מָקֶדוֹנְיָה וּמוֹשָׁבָה רוֹמִית. בָּעִיר הַזֹּאת הָיִינוּ כַּמָּה יָמִים. 13 בְּיוֹם הַשַּׁבָּת יָצָאנוּ דֶּרֶךְ שַׁעַר הָעִיר אֶל שְׂפַת נָהָר, אֶל מָקוֹם שֶׁחֲשַׁבְנוּהוּ לִמְקוֹם תְּפִלָּה, וְיָשַׁבְנוּ וְדִבַּרְנוּ אֶל הַנָּשִׁים הַנֶּאֱסָפוֹת. 14 הָיְתָה שָׁם אִשָּׁה אַחַת יְרֵאת אֱלֹהִים, לִידְיָה שְׁמָהּ, מוֹכֶרֶת אַרְגָּמָן מִן הָעִיר תִּיאָטִירָה. הִיא שָׁמְעָה וְהָאָדוֹן פָּתַח אֶת לִבָּהּ

¹⁵ And when she and her household were baptized, she begged *us,* saying, "If you have judged me to be faithful to the Lord, come to my house and stay." So she persuaded us.

¹⁶ Now it happened, as we went to prayer, that a certain slave girl possessed with a spirit of divination met us, who brought her masters much profit by fortune-telling. ¹⁷ This girl followed Paul and us, and cried out, saying, "These men are the servants of the Most High God, who proclaim to us the way of salvation." ¹⁸ And this she did for many days.

But Paul, greatly annoyed, turned and said to the spirit, "I command you in the name of Jesus Christ to come out of her." And he came out that very hour. ¹⁹ But when her masters saw that their hope of profit was gone, they seized Paul and Silas and dragged *them* into the marketplace to the authorities.

²⁰ And they brought them to the magistrates, and said, "These men, being Jews, exceedingly trouble our city; ²¹ and they teach customs which are not lawful for us, being Romans, to receive or observe." ²² Then the multitude rose up together against them; and the magistrates tore off their clothes and commanded *them* to be beaten with rods. ²³ And when they had laid many stripes on them, they threw *them* into prison, commanding the jailer to keep them securely. ²⁴ Having received such a charge, he put them into the inner prison and fastened their feet in the stocks.

²⁵ But at midnight Paul and Silas were praying and singing hymns to God, and the prisoners were listening to them. ²⁶ Suddenly there was a great earthquake, so that the foundations of the prison were shaken; and immediately all the doors were opened and everyone's chains were loosed. ²⁷ And the keeper of the prison, awaking from sleep and seeing the prison doors open, supposing the prisoners had fled, drew his sword and was about to kill himself. ²⁸ But Paul called with a loud voice, saying, "Do yourself no harm, for we are all here."

²⁹ Then he called for a light, ran in, and fell down trembling before Paul and Silas. ³⁰ And he brought them out and said, "Sirs, what must I do to be saved?"

³¹ So they said, "Believe on the Lord Jesus Christ, and you will be saved, you and your household." ³² Then they spoke the word of the Lord to him and to all who were in his house. ³³ And he took them the same hour of the night and washed *their* stripes. And immediately he and all his family were baptized. ³⁴ Now when he had brought them into his house, he set food before them; and he rejoiced, having believed in God with all his household.

לְהַקְשִׁיב אֶל דִּבְרֵי שָׁאוּל. ‏¹⁵ אַחֲרֵי שֶׁנִּטְבְּלָה הִיא וּבְנֵי בֵיתָהּ, פָּנְתָה בְּבַקָּשָׁה: "אִם רְאִיתֶם אוֹתִי נֶאֱמָנָה לָאָדוֹן, בּוֹאוּ נָא לְבֵיתִי לְהִתְאַכְסֵן בּוֹ." וְהִיא שִׁכְנְעָה אוֹתָנוּ.

‏¹⁶ כְּשֶׁהָלַכְנוּ פַּעַם לִמְקוֹם הַתְּפִלָּה פָּגְשׁוּ נַעֲרָה אַחַת אֲחוּזַת רוּחַ נִחוּשׁ, שֶׁעֲשָׂתָה הוֹן רַב לַאֲדוֹנֶיהָ בְּנִחוּשׁ הֶעָתִיד. ‏¹⁷ אוֹתָהּ נַעֲרָה הָלְכָה אַחֲרֵי שָׁאוּל וְאַחֲרֵינוּ וְקָרְאָה: "הָאֲנָשִׁים הָאֵלֶּה עַבְדֵי אֵל עֶלְיוֹן וְהֵם מַכְרִיזִים לָכֶם דֶּרֶךְ יְשׁוּעָה!" ‏¹⁸ כָּךְ עָשְׂתָה יָמִים רַבִּים. מֵאַחַר שֶׁזֶּה הִטְרִיד מְאֹד אֶת שָׁאוּל, פָּנָה אֶל הָרוּחַ וְאָמַר: "אֲנִי מְצַוֶּה עָלֶיךָ בְּשֵׁם יֵשׁוּעַ הַמָּשִׁיחַ, צְאִי מִמֶּנָּה!" בְּאוֹתָהּ שָׁעָה יָצְאָה הָרוּחַ.

‏¹⁹ רָאוּ אֲדוֹנֵי הַנַּעֲרָה כִּי אָבְדָה תִּקְוָתָם לַעֲשׂוֹת רְוָחִים, תָּפְסוּ אֶת שָׁאוּל וְאֶת סִילָא וְסָחֲבוּ אוֹתָם אֶל כִּכַּר הָעִיר לְהַעֲמִידָם לִפְנֵי הַשִּׁלְטוֹנוֹת.

‏²⁰ כְּשֶׁהֵבִיאוּ אוֹתָם אֶל הַשָּׂרִים אָמְרוּ: "הָאֲנָשִׁים הָאֵלֶּה מְעוֹרְרִים אַנְדְּרָלָמוּסְיָה בְּעִירֵנוּ. יְהוּדִים הֵם, ‏²¹ וּמְלַמְּדִים מִנְהָגִים שֶׁאָסוּר לָנוּ לְקַבְּלָם וְאָסוּר לָנוּ לַעֲשׂוֹתָם, שֶׁכֵּן רוֹמִים אֲנַחְנוּ." ‏²² אָז קָם עֲלֵיהֶם הֶהָמוֹן כְּאִישׁ אֶחָד וְהַשָּׂרִים קָרְעוּ אֶת בִּגְדֵיהֶם מֵעֲלֵיהֶם וְצִוּוּ לְהַלְקוֹתָם. ‏²³ אַחֲרֵי שֶׁהִלְקוּ אוֹתָם מַלְקוֹת רַבּוֹת הִשְׁלִיכוּ אוֹתָם לַכֶּלֶא וְצִוּוּ עַל הַסּוֹהֵר לְשָׁמְרָם הֵיטֵב. ‏²⁴ עִם קַבָּלַת הַפְּקֻדָּה הִשְׁלִיךְ אוֹתָם אֶל הַכֶּלֶא הַפְּנִימִי וְאֶת רַגְלֵיהֶם סָגַר בַּסַּד.

‏²⁵ בַּחֲצוֹת הַלַּיְלָה, בְּשָׁעָה שֶׁשָּׁאוּל וְסִילָא הִתְפַּלְלוּ וְשָׁרוּ שִׁירֵי הַלֵּל לֵאלֹהִים וְהָאֲסִירִים מַקְשִׁיבִים לָהֶם, ‏²⁶ הָיְתָה פִּתְאֹם רְעִידַת אֲדָמָה חֲזָקָה עַד כְּדֵי כָּךְ שֶׁיְּסוֹדוֹת בֵּית הַסֹּהַר הִזְדַּעְזְעוּ, וּבְבַת אַחַת נִפְתְּחוּ כָּל הַדְּלָתוֹת וְכָל הַשַּׁרְשָׁרוֹת נִתְּקוּ. ‏²⁷ הַסּוֹהֵר הִתְעוֹרֵר מִשְּׁנָתוֹ וּכְשֶׁרָאָה כִּי דַּלְתוֹת הַכֶּלֶא פְּתוּחוֹת שָׁלַף אֶת חַרְבּוֹ וְעָמַד לַהֲרֹג אֶת עַצְמוֹ, בְּחָשְׁבוֹ שֶׁהָאֲסִירִים בָּרְחוּ. ‏²⁸ אַךְ שָׁאוּל קָרָא בְּקוֹל גָּדוֹל וְאָמַר: "אַל תַּעֲשֶׂה שׁוּם רַע לְעַצְמְךָ; כֻּלָּנוּ פֹּה!"

‏²⁹ הַסּוֹהֵר בִּקֵּשׁ שֶׁיַּעֲלוּ אוֹר וּמִהֵר פְּנִימָה, וּבְרָעֲדָה נָפַל לְרַגְלֵי שָׁאוּל וְסִילָא. ‏³⁰ כַּאֲשֶׁר הוֹצִיא אוֹתָם אָמַר: "רַבּוֹתַי, מֶה עָלַי לַעֲשׂוֹת כְּדֵי לְהִוָּשַׁע?"

‏³¹ הֵשִׁיבוּ וְאָמְרוּ: "הַאֲמֵן בָּאָדוֹן יֵשׁוּעַ וְתִוָּשַׁע אַתָּה וּבְנֵי בֵיתְךָ." ‏³² הֵם הִשְׁמִיעוּ לוֹ אֶת דְּבַר הָאָדוֹן, וּלְכָל אֲשֶׁר הָיוּ אִתּוֹ בְּבֵיתוֹ. ‏³³ בְּאוֹתָהּ שְׁעַת לַיְלָה לָקַח אוֹתָם וְרָחַץ אֶת חַבּוּרוֹתֵיהֶם, וּמִיָּד נִטְבַּל הוּא וְכָל בְּנֵי בֵיתוֹ. ‏³⁴ הוּא הֶעֱלָה אוֹתָם אֶל בֵּיתוֹ, עָרַךְ שֻׁלְחָן לִפְנֵיהֶם וְשָׂמַח מְאֹד עִם כָּל בְּנֵי בֵיתוֹ כִּי הֶאֱמִין בֵּאלֹהִים.

³⁵ And when it was day, the magistrates sent the officers, saying, "Let those men go."

³⁶ So the keeper of the prison reported these words to Paul, saying, "The magistrates have sent to let you go. Now therefore depart, and go in peace."

³⁷ But Paul said to them, "They have beaten us openly, uncondemned Romans, *and* have thrown *us* into prison. And now do they put us out secretly? No indeed! Let them come themselves and get us out."

³⁸ And the officers told these words to the magistrates, and they were afraid when they heard that they were Romans. ³⁹ Then they came and pleaded with them and brought *them* out, and asked *them* to depart from the city. ⁴⁰ So they went out of the prison and entered *the house of* Lydia; and when they had seen the brethren, they encouraged them and departed.

17 Now when they had passed through Amphipolis and Apollonia, they came to Thessalonica, where there was a synagogue of the Jews. ² Then Paul, as his custom was, went in to them, and for three Sabbaths reasoned with them from the Scriptures, ³ explaining and demonstrating that the Christ had to suffer and rise again from the dead, and *saying,* "This Jesus whom I preach to you is the Christ." ⁴ And some of them were persuaded; and a great multitude of the devout Greeks, and not a few of the leading women, joined Paul and Silas.

⁵ But the Jews who were not persuaded, becoming envious, took some of the evil men from the marketplace, and gathering a mob, set all the city in an uproar and attacked the house of Jason, and sought to bring them out to the people. ⁶ But when they did not find them, they dragged Jason and some brethren to the rulers of the city, crying out, "These who have turned the world upside down have come here too. ⁷ Jason has harbored them, and these are all acting contrary to the decrees of Caesar, saying there is another king—Jesus." ⁸ And they troubled the crowd and the rulers of the city when they heard these things. ⁹ So when they had taken security from Jason and the rest, they let them go.

¹⁰ Then the brethren immediately sent Paul and Silas away by night to Berea. When they arrived, they went into the synagogue of the Jews. ¹¹ These were more fair-minded than those in Thessalonica, in that they received the word with all readiness, and searched the Scriptures daily *to find out* whether these things were so. ¹² Therefore many of them believed, and also not a few of the Greeks,

³⁵ בַּבֹּקֶר שָׁלְחוּ הַשָּׂרִים אֶת הַשּׁוֹטְרִים לוֹמַר לַסּוֹהַר: "שַׁחְרֵר אֶת הָאֲנָשִׁים הָהֵם". ³⁶ אָמַר הַסּוֹהַר אֶת הַדְּבָרִים הָאֵלֶּה לְשָׁאוּל: "הַשָּׂרִים שָׁלְחוּ לְשַׁחְרֵר אֶתְכֶם. עַל כֵּן צְאוּ עַכְשָׁו וּלְכוּ לְשָׁלוֹם." ³⁷ אַךְ שָׁאוּל אָמַר לָהֶם: "הִלְקוּ אוֹתָנוּ בְּפֻמְבֵּי בְּלֹא מִשְׁפָּט, אַף כִּי אֶזְרָחִים רוֹמִיִּים אֲנַחְנוּ; הִשְׁלִיכוּ אוֹתָנוּ לַכֶּלֶא וְעַכְשָׁו הֵם רוֹצִים לְגָרֵשׁ אוֹתָנוּ בַּחֲשַׁאי?! לֹא וָלֹא! שֶׁיָּבוֹאוּ בְּעַצְמָם וְיוֹצִיאוּ אוֹתָנוּ!"

³⁸ מָסְרוּ הַשּׁוֹטְרִים אֶת הַדְּבָרִים הָאֵלֶּה לַשָּׂרִים, וְכַאֲשֶׁר הַלָּלוּ שָׁמְעוּ שֶׁהֵם אֶזְרָחִים רוֹמִיִּים הֶחֱלוּ לְפַחֵד. ³⁹ בָּאוּ הַשָּׂרִים וְדִבְּרוּ עַל לִבָּם; אַחֲרֵי כֵן הוֹצִיאוּ אוֹתָם וּבִקְשׁוּ מֵהֶם לָצֵאת מִן הָעִיר. ⁴⁰ הֵם יָצְאוּ מִן הַכֶּלֶא וּבָאוּ לְבֵיתָהּ שֶׁל לִידְיָה, וּלְאַחַר שֶׁרָאוּ אֶת הָאַחִים וְעוֹדְדוּ אוֹתָם הָלְכוּ לְדַרְכָּם.

יז הֵם עָבְרוּ דֶּרֶךְ אַמְפִיפּוֹלִיס וְאַפּוֹלוֹנְיָה וְהִגִּיעוּ אֶל תֶּסָלוֹנִיקִי, מָקוֹם שֶׁהָיָה בּוֹ בֵּית כְּנֶסֶת. ² כְּמִנְהָגוֹ נִכְנַס שָׁאוּל אֲלֵיהֶם וְשָׁלוֹשׁ שַׁבָּתוֹת דָּרַשׁ לִפְנֵיהֶם מִתּוֹךְ הַכְּתוּבִים ³ כְּשֶׁהוּא מַסְבִּיר וּמוֹכִיחַ כִּי הַמָּשִׁיחַ הָיָה צָרִיךְ לִסְבֹּל וְלָקוּם מִן הַמֵּתִים, וְכִי "יֵשׁוּעַ זֶה שֶׁאֲנִי מַכְרִיז לָכֶם – הוּא הַמָּשִׁיחַ."

⁴ מִקְצָתָם הֶאֱמִינוּ וְנִסְפְּחוּ אֶל שָׁאוּל וְסִילָא, וְכֵן גַּם הַרְבֵּה יְוָנִים יִרְאֵי אֱלֹהִים וְנָשִׁים נִכְבָּדוֹת לֹא מְעָט. ⁵ אֲבָל הָיוּ יְהוּדִים שֶׁהִתְמַלְּאוּ קִנְאָה. הֵם לִקְטוּ כַּמָּה אַנְשֵׁי בְּלִיַּעַל מִן הַשּׁוּק, וּלְאַחַר שֶׁהִקְהִילוּ אֲסַפְסוּף עוֹרְרוּ מְהוּמָה בָּעִיר וְהִתְקִיפוּ אֶת בֵּיתוֹ שֶׁל יָסוֹן לְחַפֵּשׂ אֶת הַשְּׁנַיִם וְלַהֲבִיאָם לִפְנֵי הָעָם. ⁶ כֵּיוָן שֶׁלֹּא מָצְאוּ אוֹתָם סָחֲבוּ אֶת יָסוֹן עִם כַּמָּה אַחִים אֶל רָאשֵׁי הָעִיר וְצָעֲקוּ: "הָאֲנָשִׁים שֶׁהָפְכוּ אֶת כָּל הָעוֹלָם בָּאוּ גַּם לְכָאן ⁷ וְיָסוֹן אֵרַח אוֹתָם בְּבֵיתוֹ. כָּל אֵלֶּה פּוֹעֲלִים נֶגֶד חֻקֵּי הַקֵּיסָר בְּאָמְרָם שֶׁיֵּשׁ מֶלֶךְ אַחֵר – יֵשׁוּעַ."

⁸ כָּךְ הִסְעִירוּ אֶת הָעָם וְאֶת רָאשֵׁי הָעִיר אֲשֶׁר שָׁמְעוּ זֹאת, ⁹ וְהֵלָּלוּ לָקְחוּ עַרְבוּת מִיָּסוֹן וּמֵהַשְּׁאָר וְשִׁחְרְרוּ אוֹתָם.

¹⁰ בַּלַּיְלָה מִהֲרוּ הָאַחִים לְשַׁלַּח אֶת שָׁאוּל וְאֶת סִילָא לְבֶרֵאָה, וּכְשֶׁאֵלֶּה הִגִּיעוּ לְשָׁם נִכְנְסוּ לְבֵית הַכְּנֶסֶת. ¹¹ יְהוּדֵי בֶּרֵאָה הָיוּ אֲצִילֵי־רוּחַ יוֹתֵר מִן הַיְּהוּדִים שֶׁבְּתֶסָלוֹנִיקִי וְקִבְּלוּ אֶת הַדָּבָר בְּכָל לֵב כְּשֶׁהֵם בּוֹדְקִים יוֹם יוֹם בַּכְּתוּבִים אִם הַדְּבָרִים הָאֵלֶּה אָכֵן כָּךְ. ¹² אָז הֶאֱמִינוּ רַבִּים מֵהֶם וְכֵן גַּם

prominent women as well as men. ¹³But when the Jews from Thessalonica learned that the word of God was preached by Paul at Berea, they came there also and stirred up the crowds. ¹⁴Then immediately the brethren sent Paul away, to go to the sea; but both Silas and Timothy remained there. ¹⁵So those who conducted Paul brought him to Athens; and receiving a command for Silas and Timothy to come to him with all speed, they departed.

¹⁶Now while Paul waited for them at Athens, his spirit was provoked within him when he saw that the city was given over to idols. ¹⁷Therefore he reasoned in the synagogue with the Jews and with the *Gentile* worshipers, and in the marketplace daily with those who happened to be there. ¹⁸Then certain Epicurean and Stoic philosophers encountered him. And some said, "What does this babbler want to say?"

Others said, "He seems to be a proclaimer of foreign gods," because he preached to them Jesus and the resurrection.

¹⁹And they took him and brought him to the Areopagus, saying, "May we know what this new doctrine *is* of which you speak? ²⁰For you are bringing some strange things to our ears. Therefore we want to know what these things mean." ²¹For all the Athenians and the foreigners who were there spent their time in nothing else but either to tell or to hear some new thing.

²²Then Paul stood in the midst of the Areopagus and said, "Men of Athens, I perceive that in all things you are very religious; ²³for as I was passing through and considering the objects of your worship, I even found an altar with this inscription:

TO THE UNKNOWN GOD.

Therefore, the One whom you worship without knowing, Him I proclaim to you: ²⁴God, who made the world and everything in it, since He is Lord of heaven and earth, does not dwell in temples made with hands. ²⁵Nor is He worshiped with men's hands, as though He needed anything, since He gives to all life, breath, and all things. ²⁶And He has made from one blood every nation of men to dwell on all the face of the earth, and has determined their preappointed times and the boundaries of their dwellings, ²⁷so that they should seek the Lord, in the hope that they might grope for Him and find Him, though He is not far from each one of us; ²⁸for in Him we live and move and have our being, as also some of your own poets have said, 'For we are also His offspring.' ²⁹Therefore, since we are the offspring of God, we ought not to think that the

יָוָנִים לֹא מְעַטִּים, הֵן נָשִׁים נִכְבָּדוֹת וְהֵן גְּבָרִים. ¹³ כְּשֶׁנּוֹדַע לָאוֹתָם יְהוּדִים אֲשֶׁר בִּתְסַלוֹנִיקִי כִּי גַּם בִּבְרֵאָה מַשְׁמִיעַ שָׁאוּל אֶת דְּבַר אֱלֹהִים, בָּאוּ גַּם לְשָׁם וְעוֹרְרוּ וְהֵסִיתוּ אֶת הֲמוֹן הָעָם. ¹⁴ מִיָּד שָׁלְחוּ הָאַחִים אֶת שָׁאוּל כְּדֵי שֶׁיֵּלֵךְ עַד הַיָּם, אַךְ סִילָא וְטִימוֹתִיאוֹס נִשְׁאֲרוּ שָׁם. ¹⁵ מְלַוָּיו שֶׁל שָׁאוּל הוֹבִילוּ אוֹתוֹ עַד אַתּוּנָה וּמִשָּׁם הָלְכוּ לְדַרְכָּם לְאַחַר שֶׁמָּסַר לָהֶם הוֹרָאָה בִּשְׁבִיל סִילָא וְטִימוֹתִיאוֹס – שֶׁיָּבוֹאוּ אֵלָיו בִּמְהֵרָה.

¹⁶ כַּאֲשֶׁר שָׁאוּל חִכָּה לָהֶם בְּאַתּוּנָה רָאָה אֶת הָעִיר מְלֵאָה אֱלִילִים וְרוּחוֹ נִסְעֲרָה בְּקִרְבּוֹ. ¹⁷ הוּא דִּבֵּר בְּבֵית הַכְּנֶסֶת עִם הַיְהוּדִים וְעִם יִרְאֵי הָאֱלֹהִים, וּמִדֵּי יוֹם בְּיוֹם דִּבֵּר בְּכִכַּר הָעִיר עִם הַמִּזְדַּמְּנִים לְשָׁם. ¹⁸ גַּם כַּמָּה פִילוֹסוֹפִים מִן הָאַסְכּוֹלָה הָאֶפִּיקוּרְסִית וּמִן הָאַסְכּוֹלָה הַסְּטוֹאִית הִתְוַכְּחוּ אִתּוֹ. יֵשׁ שֶׁאָמְרוּ: "מָה רוֹצֶה הַפַּטְפְּטָן הַזֶּה לוֹמַר?" וַאֲחֵרִים אָמְרוּ: "נִרְאֶה שֶׁהוּא מַכְרִיז עַל אֵלִים זָרִים", שֶׁכֵּן בִּשֵּׂר עַל יֵשׁוּעַ וְעַל הַתְּחִיָּה. ¹⁹ הֵם לָקְחוּ אוֹתוֹ וֶהֱבִיאוּהוּ אֶל גִּבְעַת הַמּוֹעֵצָה, הָאֲרֵיוֹפָּגוֹס, וְאָמְרוּ: "אֶפְשָׁר לָדַעַת מָה הַתּוֹרָה הַחֲדָשָׁה הַזֹּאת שֶׁאַתָּה מַטִּיף? ²⁰ כִּי דְּבָרִים מוּזָרִים אַתָּה מַשְׁמִיעַ בְּאָזְנֵינוּ. לָכֵן רְצוֹנֵנוּ לָדַעַת מַה כַּוָּנַת הַדְּבָרִים הָאֵלֶּה." ²¹ בָּעֵת הַהִיא כָּל אַנְשֵׁי אַתּוּנָה וְהַזָּרִים הַגָּרִים בָּהּ לֹא בִּלּוּ אֶת זְמַנָּם הַפָּנוּי אֶלָּא בְּסִפּוּר דְּבָרִים חֲדָשִׁים אוֹ בִּשְׁמִיעָתָם.

²² עָמַד שָׁאוּל בְּאֶמְצַע הָאֲרֵיוֹפָּגוֹס וְאָמַר: "אַנְשֵׁי אַתּוּנָה, בְּכָל דָּבָר רוֹאֶה אֲנִי שֶׁיִּרְאֵי אֱלֹהוּת אַתֶּם מְאֹד, ²³ כִּי כַּאֲשֶׁר עָבַרְתִּי וְהִתְבּוֹנַנְתִּי בְּקָדְשֵׁיכֶם מָצָאתִי גַּם מִזְבֵּחַ שֶׁכָּתוּב עָלָיו, 'לָאֵל בִּלְתִּי נוֹדָע'. וּבְכֵן, אֶת זֶה שֶׁאַתֶּם עוֹבְדִים מִבְּלִי לָדַעַת אוֹתוֹ, אוֹתוֹ אֲנִי מַכְרִיז לָכֶם: ²⁴ הָאֵל אֲשֶׁר עָשָׂה אֶת הָעוֹלָם וְכָל אֲשֶׁר בּוֹ. הוּא אֲדוֹן הַשָּׁמַיִם וְהָאָרֶץ וְאֵין הוּא שׁוֹכֵן בְּהֵיכָלוֹת מַעֲשֵׂה יָדַיִם; ²⁵ גַּם אֵין יְדֵי אָדָם מְשָׁרְתוֹת אוֹתוֹ כְּאִלּוּ הוּא זָקוּק לְאֵיזֶה דָּבָר, שֶׁהֲרֵי לַכֹּל הוּא נוֹתֵן חַיִּים וּנְשָׁמָה וְכָל דָּבָר. ²⁶ מֵאָדָם אֶחָד הוּא יָצַר אֶת כָּל עַמְמֵי בְּנֵי אָדָם לְהוֹשִׁיבָם עַל פְּנֵי כָל הָאָרֶץ, וְעַד זְמַנִּים קְבוּעִים וְקָבַע אֶת גְּבוּלוֹת מוֹשָׁבָם – ²⁷ לְמַעַן יְחַפְּשׂוּ אֶת הָאֱלֹהִים; אוּלַי יְגַשְׁשׁוּ אַחֲרָיו וְיִמְצְאוּ אוֹתוֹ, אַף שֶׁאֵינוֹ רָחוֹק מִכָּל אֶחָד מֵאִתָּנוּ. ²⁸ הֵן בּוֹ אֲנַחְנוּ חַיִּים וּמִתְנוֹעֲעִים וְקַיָּמִים, כְּמוֹ שֶׁגַּם אֲחָדִים מִמְּשׁוֹרְרֵיכֶם אָמְרוּ שֶׁגַּם אֲנַחְנוּ צֶאֱצָאָיו. ²⁹ לָכֵן בִּהְיוֹתֵנוּ צֶאֱצָאֵי

Divine Nature is like gold or silver or stone, something shaped by art and man's devising. ³⁰ Truly, these times of ignorance God overlooked, but now commands all men everywhere to repent, ³¹ because He has appointed a day on which He will judge the world in righteousness by the Man whom He has ordained. He has given assurance of this to all by raising Him from the dead."

³² And when they heard of the resurrection of the dead, some mocked, while others said, "We will hear you again on this *matter*." ³³ So Paul departed from among them. ³⁴ However, some men joined him and believed, among them Dionysius the Areopagite, a woman named Damaris, and others with them.

18 After these things Paul departed from Athens and went to Corinth. ² And he found a certain Jew named Aquila, born in Pontus, who had recently come from Italy with his wife Priscilla (because Claudius had commanded all the Jews to depart from Rome); and he came to them. ³ So, because he was of the same trade, he stayed with them and worked; for by occupation they were tentmakers. ⁴ And he reasoned in the synagogue every Sabbath, and persuaded both Jews and Greeks.

⁵ When Silas and Timothy had come from Macedonia, Paul was compelled by the Spirit, and testified to the Jews *that* Jesus *is* the Christ. ⁶ But when they opposed him and blasphemed, he shook *his* garments and said to them, "Your blood *be* upon your *own* heads; I *am* clean. From now on I will go to the Gentiles." ⁷ And he departed from there and entered the house of a certain *man* named Justus, *one* who worshiped God, whose house was next door to the synagogue. ⁸ Then Crispus, the ruler of the synagogue, believed on the Lord with all his household. And many of the Corinthians, hearing, believed and were baptized.

⁹ Now the Lord spoke to Paul in the night by a vision, "Do not be afraid, but speak, and do not keep silent; ¹⁰ for I am with you, and no one will attack you to hurt you; for I have many people in this city." ¹¹ And he continued *there* a year and six months, teaching the word of God among them.

¹² When Gallio was proconsul of Achaia, the Jews with one accord rose up against Paul and brought him to the judgment seat, ¹³ saying, "This *fellow* persuades men to worship God contrary to the law."

¹⁴ And when Paul was about to open *his* mouth, Gallio said to the Jews, "If it were a matter of wrongdoing or wicked crimes, O Jews, there would be reason why I should bear with you. ¹⁵ But if it is

אֱלֹהִים אֵין אָנוּ צְרִיכִים לַחֲשֹׁב שֶׁהָאֱלֹהוּת דּוֹמָה לְזָהָב אוֹ לְכֶסֶף אוֹ לְאֶבֶן, פְּסִילֵי אֻמָּנוּת וּפְרִי מַחֲשֶׁבֶת אָדָם. ³⁰ אֱלֹהִים אָמְנָם הִתְעַלֵּם מֵעִתּוֹת הַבַּעֲרוּת, אַךְ כָּעֵת הוּא מְצַוֶּה עַל כָּל בְּנֵי אָדָם בְּכָל מָקוֹם לַחֲזֹר בִּתְשׁוּבָה, ³¹ שֶׁכֵּן יָעַד יוֹם לִשְׁפֹּט תֵּבֵל בְּצֶדֶק עַל־יְדֵי אִישׁ אֲשֶׁר מִנָּה, וְהִמְצִיא הוֹכָחָה לַכֹּל בַּהֲקִימוֹ אוֹתוֹ מִן הַמֵּתִים."

³² כַּאֲשֶׁר שָׁמְעוּ עַל תְּחִיַּת מֵתִים, אֲחָדִים לִגְלְגוּ וַאֲחֵרִים אָמְרוּ: "נִשְׁמַע אוֹתְךָ בְּעִנְיָן זֶה עוֹד פַּעַם." ³³ אָז יָצָא שָׁאוּל מִתּוֹכָם. ³⁴ אֲבָל כַּמָּה אֲנָשִׁים הִצְטָרְפוּ אֵלָיו וְהֶאֱמִינוּ; בִּכְלָלָם דִּיּוֹנִיסִיוֹס, מִן הַשּׁוֹפְטִים שֶׁל הָאַרְיוֹפָּגוֹס, וְאִשָּׁה אַחַת, דָּמָרִיס שְׁמָהּ, וַאֲחֵרִים עִמָּהֶם.

יח אַחֲרֵי כֵן יָצָא שָׁאוּל מֵאַתּוּנָה וּבָא אֶל קוֹרִינְתּוֹס. ² שָׁם מָצָא יְהוּדִי אֶחָד יְלִיד פּוֹנְטוֹס, עֲקִילַס שְׁמוֹ, שֶׁלֹּא מִכְּבָר בָּא מֵאִיטַלְיָה עִם פְּרִיסְקִילָה אִשְׁתּוֹ, מִשּׁוּם שֶׁקְּלוֹדְיוֹס צִוָּה עַל כָּל הַיְּהוּדִים לַעֲזֹב אֶת רוֹמָא. ³ הוּא בָּא אֲלֵיהֶם וּמֵאַחַר שֶׁהָיָה לוֹ אוֹתוֹ מִקְצוֹעַ, עֲשִׂיַּת אֹהָלִים, הִתְגּוֹרֵר אֶצְלָם וְעָבַד אִתָּם. ⁴ וּמִדֵּי שַׁבָּת דִּבֵּר בְּבֵית הַכְּנֶסֶת וְשִׁכְנֵעַ הֵן יְהוּדִים וְהֵן יְוָנִים.

⁵ כְּשֶׁבָּאוּ סִילָא וְטִימוֹתִיאוֹס מִמַּקֶּדוֹנְיָה, שָׁאוּל הִתְמַסֵּר לְגַמְרֵי לִדְבַר הַבְּשׂוֹרָה וְהֵעִיד לַיְּהוּדִים שֶׁהַמָּשִׁיחַ הוּא יֵשׁוּעַ. ⁶ כֵּיוָן שֶׁהִתְנַגְּדוּ וְגִדְּפוּ נִעֵר אֶת בְּגָדָיו וְאָמַר לָהֶם: "דְּמְכֶם בְּרֹאשְׁכֶם. אֲנִי נָקִי. מֵעַתָּה אֵלֵךְ לַגּוֹיִים." ⁷ הָלַךְ מִשָּׁם וְנִכְנַס לְבֵיתוֹ שֶׁל אִישׁ יְרֵא אֱלֹהִים, טִיטוֹס יוּסְטוֹס שְׁמוֹ, וּבֵיתוֹ סָמוּךְ לְבֵית הַכְּנֶסֶת. ⁸ קְרִיסְפּוֹס, רֹאשׁ בֵּית הַכְּנֶסֶת, הֶאֱמִין בָּאָדוֹן הוּא וְכָל בְּנֵי בֵּיתוֹ, וְגַם קוֹרִינְתִים רַבִּים כְּשָׁמְעָם אֶת הַדְּבָרִים הֶאֱמִינוּ וְנִטְבְּלוּ. ⁹ בְּלַיְלָה אֶחָד אָמַר הָאָדוֹן אֶל שָׁאוּל בְּחָזוֹן: "אַל תִּירָא. דַּבֵּר, אַל תֶּחֱשֶׁה, ¹⁰ כִּי אִתְּךָ אָנִי. אִישׁ לֹא יִפְגַּע בְּךָ וְלֹא יָרַע לְךָ, כִּי עַם רַב לִי בָּעִיר הַזֹּאת." ¹¹ וְשָׁאוּל יָשַׁב שָׁם שָׁנָה וְשִׁשָּׁה חֳדָשִׁים וְהָיָה מְלַמֵּד אֶת דְּבַר אֱלֹהִים.

¹² כַּאֲשֶׁר גַּלְיוֹן הָיָה נְצִיב מְדִינַת אֲכַיָה, חָבְרוּ הַיְּהוּדִים יַחְדָּיו עַל שָׁאוּל וֶהֱבִיאוּהוּ לִפְנֵי כֵּס הַמִּשְׁפָּט. ¹³ אָמְרוּ: "הָאִישׁ הַזֶּה מֵסִית בְּנֵי אָדָם לַעֲבֹד אֶת אֱלֹהִים שֶׁלֹּא כַּחֹק." ¹⁴ כְּשֶׁהִתְכּוֹנֵן שָׁאוּל לְהַתְחִיל לְדַבֵּר אָמַר גַּלְיוֹן אֶל הַיְּהוּדִים: "יְהוּדִים, אִלּוּ הָיָה כָּאן אֵיזֶה פֶּשַׁע אוֹ מַעֲשֵׂה נְבָלָה, אֲזַי, לְפִי שׁוּרַת הַהִגָּיוֹן, הָיִיתִי מְקַבֵּל אֶתְכֶם בְּסַבְלָנוּת. ¹⁵ אֲבָל אִם אֵלֶּה שְׁאֵלוֹת עַל מִלִּים וְעַל שֵׁמוֹת

a question of words and names and your own law, look *to it* yourselves; for I do not want to be a judge of such *matters.*" ¹⁶ And he drove them from the judgment seat. ¹⁷ Then all the Greeks took Sosthenes, the ruler of the synagogue, and beat *him* before the judgment seat. But Gallio took no notice of these things.

¹⁸ So Paul still remained a good while. Then he took leave of the brethren and sailed for Syria, and Priscilla and Aquila *were* with him. He had *his* hair cut off at Cenchrea, for he had taken a vow. ¹⁹ And he came to Ephesus, and left them there; but he himself entered the synagogue and reasoned with the Jews. ²⁰ When they asked *him* to stay a longer time with them, he did not consent, ²¹ but took leave of them, saying, "I must by all means keep this coming feast in Jerusalem; but I will return again to you, God willing." And he sailed from Ephesus.

²² And when he had landed at Caesarea, and gone up and greeted the church, he went down to Antioch. ²³ After he had spent some time *there*, he departed and went over the region of Galatia and Phrygia in order, strengthening all the disciples.

²⁴ Now a certain Jew named Apollos, born at Alexandria, an eloquent man *and* mighty in the Scriptures, came to Ephesus. ²⁵ This man had been instructed in the way of the Lord; and being fervent in spirit, he spoke and taught accurately the things of the Lord, though he knew only the baptism of John. ²⁶ So he began to speak boldly in the synagogue. When Aquila and Priscilla heard him, they took him aside and explained to him the way of God more accurately. ²⁷ And when he desired to cross to Achaia, the brethren wrote, exhorting the disciples to receive him; and when he arrived, he greatly helped those who had believed through grace; ²⁸ for he vigorously refuted the Jews publicly, showing from the Scriptures that Jesus is the Christ.

19 And it happened, while Apollos was at Corinth, that Paul, having passed through the upper regions, came to Ephesus. And finding some disciples ² he said to them, "Did you receive the Holy Spirit when you believed?"

So they said to him, "We have not so much as heard whether there is a Holy Spirit."

³ And he said to them, "Into what then were you baptized?"

So they said, "Into John's baptism."

⁴ Then Paul said, "John indeed baptized with a baptism of repentance, saying to the people that they should believe on Him who would come after him, that is, on Christ Jesus."

וְעַל הַתּוֹרָה שֶׁלָּכֶם – זֶה עִנְיַנְכֶם. אֲנִי אֵינֶנִּי רוֹצֶה לִהְיוֹת שׁוֹפֵט בְּעִנְיָנִים כָּאֵלֶּה." ¹⁶ אָז שִׁלַּח אוֹתָם מִלְּפָנֵי כֵּס הַמִּשְׁפָּט. ¹⁷ תָּפְסוּ כֻּלָּם אֶת סוֹסְתֶּנִים, רֹאשׁ בֵּית הַכְּנֶסֶת, וְהִכּוּהוּ לִפְנֵי כֵּס הַמִּשְׁפָּט, אַךְ לְגַלְיוֹן לֹא הָיָה אִכְפַּת.

¹⁸ שָׁאוּל שָׁהָה שָׁם עוֹד יָמִים רַבִּים. אַחֲרֵי כֵן נִפְרַד מֵהָאַחִים וְהִפְלִיג בִּדְרָכּוֹ לְסוּרְיָה יַחַד עִם פְּרִיסְקִילָה וַעֲקִילָס, לְאַחַר שֶׁגַּזַּז אֶת שְׂעַר רֹאשׁוֹ בְּקֶנְכְּרָאָה בִּגְלַל נֶדֶר שֶׁנָּדַר. ¹⁹ הֵם בָּאוּ לְאֶפְסוֹס וְשָׁם עָזַב אֶת פְּרִיסְקִילָה וַעֲקִילָס. הוּא נִכְנַס לְבֵית הַכְּנֶסֶת וְדִבֵּר עִם הַיְּהוּדִים. ²⁰ כְּשֶׁבִּקְשׁוּ מִמֶּנּוּ לְהִשָּׁאֵר זְמַן רַב יוֹתֵר לֹא הִסְכִּים, ²¹ אֶלָּא נִפְרַד מֵהֶם וְאָמַר: "עוֹד אָשׁוּב אֲלֵיכֶם, אִם יִרְצֶה אֱלֹהִים." הוּא הִפְלִיג מֵאֶפְסוֹס ²² וּלְאַחַר שֶׁהִגִּיעַ לְקֵיסַרְיָה עָלָה לִירוּשָׁלַיִם וְשָׁאַל לִשְׁלוֹם הַקְּהִלָּה. אַחֲרֵי כֵן יָרַד לְאַנְטִיוֹכְיָה, ²³ שָׁהָה שָׁם זְמַן מָה וְיָצָא וְעָבַר מִמָּקוֹם לְמָקוֹם בְּאֵזוֹר גָּלַטְיָה וּבְאֵזוֹר פְרִיגְיָה כְּשֶׁהוּא מְחַזֵּק אֶת הַתַּלְמִידִים.

²⁴ אֶל אֶפְסוֹס הִגִּיעַ יְהוּדִי אֶחָד יְלִיד אֲלֶכְּסַנְדְּרִיָה וּשְׁמוֹ אַפּוֹלוֹס, אִישׁ־דְּבָרִים וְגָדוֹל בַּמִּקְרָא. ²⁵ מְלֻמָּד הָיָה בְּדֶרֶךְ הָאָדוֹן, וּבְרוּחוֹ נִלְהֶבֶת דִּבֵּר וְלִמֵּד הֵיטֵב עַל־אוֹדוֹת יֵשׁוּעַ, אַךְ יָדַע רַק עַל טְבִילַת יוֹחָנָן. ²⁶ הוּא הֵחֵל לְדַבֵּר בְּאֹמֶץ לֵב בְּבֵית הַכְּנֶסֶת. כַּאֲשֶׁר שָׁמְעוּ אוֹתוֹ פְּרִיסְקִילָה וַעֲקִילָס לָקְחוּ אוֹתוֹ אֲלֵיהֶם וְהִסְבִּירוּ לוֹ אֶת דֶּרֶךְ אֱלֹהִים בְּיֶתֶר דִּיּוּק. ²⁷ כַּאֲשֶׁר רָצָה לָלֶכֶת לַאֲכָיָה עוֹדְדוּהוּ הָאַחִים וְכָתְבוּ לַתַּלְמִידִים לְקַבֵּל אוֹתוֹ. הוּא הִגִּיעַ לְשָׁם וְהוֹדוֹת לַחֶסֶד עָזַר הַרְבֵּה לַמַּאֲמִינִים, ²⁸ כִּי בְּפֻמְבֵּי וּבְתֹקֶף הוֹכִיחַ לַיְּהוּדִים וְהֶרְאָה עַל־יְדֵי הַכְּתוּבִים שֶׁהַמָּשִׁיחַ הוּא יֵשׁוּעַ.

יט בְּעֵת שֶׁאַפּוֹלוֹס הָיָה בְּקוֹרִינְתּוֹס עָבַר שָׁאוּל בָּאֵזוֹרִים הָעֶלְיוֹנִים וְהִגִּיעַ אֶל אֶפְסוֹס. הוּא מָצָא כַּמָּה תַּלְמִידִים ² וְשָׁאַל אוֹתָם: "הַאִם קִבַּלְתֶּם אֶת רוּחַ הַקֹּדֶשׁ כַּאֲשֶׁר הֶאֱמַנְתֶּם?"

הֵשִׁיבוּ לוֹ: "אַף לֹא שָׁמַעְנוּ שֶׁיֵּשׁ רוּחַ הַקֹּדֶשׁ."

³ שָׁאַל: "אִם כֵּן, אֵיזוֹ טְבִילָה נִטְבַּלְתֶּם?"

אָמְרוּ: "טְבִילַת יוֹחָנָן."

⁴ אָמַר שָׁאוּל: "יוֹחָנָן הִטְבִּיל טְבִילָה שֶׁל תְּשׁוּבָה, בְּאָמְרוֹ לָעָם שֶׁיַּאֲמִינוּ בְּזֶה שֶׁיָּבוֹא אַחֲרָיו, כְּלוֹמַר, בְּיֵשׁוּעַ."

⁵ When they heard *this,* they were baptized in the name of the Lord Jesus. ⁶ And when Paul had laid hands on them, the Holy Spirit came upon them, and they spoke with tongues and prophesied. ⁷ Now the men were about twelve in all.

⁸ And he went into the synagogue and spoke boldly for three months, reasoning and persuading concerning the things of the kingdom of God. ⁹ But when some were hardened and did not believe, but spoke evil of the Way before the multitude, he departed from them and withdrew the disciples, reasoning daily in the school of Tyrannus. ¹⁰ And this continued for two years, so that all who dwelt in Asia heard the word of the Lord Jesus, both Jews and Greeks.

¹¹ Now God worked unusual miracles by the hands of Paul, ¹² so that even handkerchiefs or aprons were brought from his body to the sick, and the diseases left them and the evil spirits went out of them. ¹³ Then some of the itinerant Jewish exorcists took it upon themselves to call the name of the Lord Jesus over those who had evil spirits, saying, "We exorcise you by the Jesus whom Paul preaches." ¹⁴ Also there were seven sons of Sceva, a Jewish chief priest, who did so.

¹⁵ And the evil spirit answered and said, "Jesus I know, and Paul I know; but who are you?"

¹⁶ Then the man in whom the evil spirit was leaped on them, overpowered them, and prevailed against them, so that they fled out of that house naked and wounded. ¹⁷ This became known both to all Jews and Greeks dwelling in Ephesus; and fear fell on them all, and the name of the Lord Jesus was magnified. ¹⁸ And many who had believed came confessing and telling their deeds. ¹⁹ Also, many of those who had practiced magic brought their books together and burned *them* in the sight of all. And they counted up the value of them, and *it* totaled fifty thousand *pieces* of silver. ²⁰ So the word of the Lord grew mightily and prevailed.

²¹ When these things were accomplished, Paul purposed in the Spirit, when he had passed through Macedonia and Achaia, to go to Jerusalem, saying, "After I have been there, I must also see Rome." ²² So he sent into Macedonia two of those who ministered to him, Timothy and Erastus, but he himself stayed in Asia for a time.

²³ And about that time there arose a great commotion about the Way. ²⁴ For a certain man named Demetrius, a silversmith, who made silver shrines of Diana, brought no small profit to the craftsmen. ²⁵ He called them together with the workers of similar occupation, and said: "Men, you know that we have our prosperity by this trade.

⁵ הֵם שָׁמְעוּ וְנִטְבְּלוּ לְשֵׁם הָאָדוֹן יֵשׁוּעַ. ⁶ כְּשֶׁסָּמַךְ שָׁאוּל אֶת יָדָיו עֲלֵיהֶם, בָּאָה רוּחַ הַקֹּדֶשׁ עֲלֵיהֶם וְאָז דִּבְּרוּ בִּלְשׁוֹנוֹת וְהִתְנַבְּאוּ. ⁷ כֻּלָּם הָיוּ כִּשְׁנֵים-עָשָׂר אִישׁ.

⁸ הוּא נִכְנַס לְבֵית הַכְּנֶסֶת וְדִבֵּר בְּאֹמֶץ לֵב. בְּמֶשֶׁךְ שְׁלוֹשָׁה חֳדָשִׁים טָעַן וְשִׁכְנֵעַ בְּעִנְיַן מַלְכוּת אֱלֹהִים. ⁹ יֵשׁ שֶׁהִקְשׁוּ לְבָבָם וְסֵרְבוּ לְהַאֲמִין, וְדִבְּרוּ רָעוֹת עַל הַדֶּרֶךְ הַהִיא בְּאָזְנֵי הַקָּהָל. לָכֵן פָּרַשׁ מֵהֶם בְּהַבְדִּילוֹ מִתּוֹכָם אֶת הַתַּלְמִידִים, וְיוֹם יוֹם דִּבֵּר בְּאוּלַם הַמִּדְרָשׁ שֶׁל טִירָנוֹס. ¹⁰ כָּךְ זֶה הָיָה בְּמֶשֶׁךְ שְׁנָתַיִם עַד שֶׁכָּל תּוֹשָׁבֵי אַסְיָה הַיְּהוּדִים וְהַיְּוָנִים שָׁמְעוּ אֶת דְּבַר הָאָדוֹן.

¹¹ וֵאלֹהִים עָשָׂה גְּבוּרוֹת בִּלְתִּי רְגִילוֹת עַל-יְדֵי שָׁאוּל, ¹² עַד כְּדֵי כָּךְ שֶׁחוֹלִים נִרְפְּאוּ מִמַּחֲלוֹתֵיהֶם וְהָרוּחוֹת הָרָעוֹת יָצְאוּ מֵהֶם כַּאֲשֶׁר הוּבְאוּ אֲלֵיהֶם מִטְפָּחוֹת אוֹ סִנָּרִים שֶׁנָּגְעוּ בְּעוֹר גּוּפוֹ. ¹³ גַּם כַּמָּה יְהוּדִים מְשׁוֹטְטִים שֶׁעָסְקוּ בְּגֵרוּשׁ שֵׁדִים נִסּוּ לְבַטֵּא אֶת שֵׁם הָאָדוֹן יֵשׁוּעַ עַל אֲחוּזֵי רוּחוֹת רָעוֹת בְּאָמְרָם: "אֲנִי מַשְׁבִּיעַ אֶתְכֶן בְּיֵשׁוּעַ אֲשֶׁר שָׁאוּל מַכְרִיז עָלָיו!" ¹⁴ הָעוֹשִׂים זֹאת הָיוּ שִׁבְעַת בָּנָיו שֶׁל סְקֵוָה, כֹּהֵן גָּדוֹל יְהוּדִי. ¹⁵ הֵשִׁיבָה הָרוּחַ הָרָעָה וְאָמְרָה לָהֶם: "אֶת יֵשׁוּעַ אֲנִי מַכִּירָה וּמִיהוּ שָׁאוּל אֲנִי יוֹדַעַת, אַךְ מִי אַתֶּם?" ¹⁶ הִתְנַפֵּל עֲלֵיהֶם הָאִישׁ בַּעַל הָרוּחַ הָרָעָה וּבְחָזְקָה רַבָּה גָּבַר עֲלֵיהֶם, עַד כִּי בָּרְחוּ מִן הַבַּיִת הַהוּא עֲרֻמִּים וּפְצוּעִים. ¹⁷ כַּאֲשֶׁר נוֹדַע הַדָּבָר לְכָל הַיְּהוּדִים וְהַיְּוָנִים תּוֹשָׁבֵי אֶפְסוֹס, נָפַל פַּחַד עַל כֻּלָּם וְנִתְגַּדֵּל שֵׁם הָאָדוֹן יֵשׁוּעַ. ¹⁸ רַבִּים מֵאוֹתָם הָאֲנָשִׁים שֶׁקִּבְּלוּ אֶת הָאֱמוּנָה בָּאוּ לְהִתְוַדּוֹת וְסִפְּרוּ אֶת מַעֲשֵׂיהֶם. ¹⁹ רַבִּים שֶׁעָסְקוּ בְּכִשּׁוּף אָסְפוּ אֶת סִפְרֵיהֶם וְשָׂרְפוּ אוֹתָם לְעֵינֵי כֹּל. חָשְׁבוּ וּמָצְאוּ שֶׁמְּחִירָם חֲמִשִּׁים אֶלֶף מַטְבְּעוֹת כֶּסֶף. ²⁰ בִּגְבוּרָה כָּזֹאת שָׂגְשֵׂג וְגָבַר דְּבַר הָאָדוֹן.

²¹ כַּאֲשֶׁר כָּל זֶה נִגְמַר, עָלָה בְּדַעְתּוֹ שֶׁל שָׁאוּל לַעֲבֹר דֶּרֶךְ מָקֵדוֹנְיָה וְאָכַיָּה וּלְהַמְשִׁיךְ בְּדַרְכּוֹ אֶל יְרוּשָׁלַיִם. אָמַר: "אַחֲרֵי שֶׁאֶהְיֶה שָׁם עָלַי לִרְאוֹת גַּם אֶת רוֹמָא." ²² הוּא שָׁלַח אֶל מָקֵדוֹנְיָה שְׁנַיִם מִן הַמְשָׁרְתִים אוֹתוֹ, אֶת טִימוֹתֵיאוֹס וְאֶת אֵרַסְטוֹס, וְהוּא עַצְמוֹ שָׁהָה זְמַן מָסֻיָּם בְּאַסְיָה.

²³ בָּעֵת הַהִיא הָיְתָה מְהוּמָה לֹא קְטַנָּה עַל-אוֹדוֹת דֶּרֶךְ הָאָדוֹן, ²⁴ בִּגְלַל צוֹרֵף אֶחָד, דֶּמֶטְרִיּוֹס שְׁמוֹ, שֶׁהָיָה עוֹשֶׂה תַּבְנִיּוֹת כֶּסֶף שֶׁל הֵיכָל אַרְטֶמִיס וּמַמְצִיא רֶוַח לֹא מְבֻטָּל לַפּוֹעֲלִים. ²⁵ הוּא כִּנֵּס אוֹתָם עִם בַּעֲלֵי הַמִּקְצוֹעַ הָעוֹבְדִים בְּאוֹתָהּ מְלָאכָה

26 Moreover you see and hear that not only at
Ephesus, but throughout almost all Asia, this Paul
has persuaded and turned away many people,
saying that they are not gods which are made with
hands. 27 So not only is this trade of ours in danger
of falling into disrepute, but also the temple of the
great goddess Diana may be despised and her
magnificence destroyed, whom all Asia and the
world worship."

28 Now when they heard *this*, they were full of
wrath and cried out, saying, "Great *is* Diana of the
Ephesians!" 29 So the whole city was filled with
confusion, and rushed into the theater with one
accord, having seized Gaius and Aristarchus,
Macedonians, Paul's travel companions. 30 And
when Paul wanted to go in to the people, the
disciples would not allow him. 31 Then some of the
officials of Asia, who were his friends, sent to him
pleading that he would not venture into the theater.
32 Some therefore cried one thing and some another,
for the assembly was confused, and most of them
did not know why they had come together. 33 And
they drew Alexander out of the multitude, the Jews
putting him forward. And Alexander motioned
with his hand, and wanted to make his defense to
the people. 34 But when they found out that he was
a Jew, all with one voice cried out for about two
hours, "Great *is* Diana of the Ephesians!"

35 And when the city clerk had quieted the crowd,
he said: "Men of Ephesus, what man is there who
does not know that the city of the Ephesians is
temple guardian of the great goddess Diana, and of
the *image* which fell down from Zeus? 36 Therefore,
since these things cannot be denied, you ought to be
quiet and do nothing rashly. 37 For you have
brought these men here who are neither robbers
of temples nor blasphemers of your goddess.
38 Therefore, if Demetrius and his fellow craftsmen
have a case against anyone, the courts are open and
there are proconsuls. Let them bring charges
against one another. 39 But if you have any other
inquiry to make, it shall be determined in the lawful
assembly. 40 For we are in danger of being called in
question for today's uproar, there being no reason
which we may give to account for this disorderly
gathering." 41 And when he had said these things, he
dismissed the assembly.

20 After the uproar had ceased, Paul called the
disciples to *himself*, embraced *them*, and departed to
go to Macedonia. 2 Now when he had gone over
that region and encouraged them with many words,
he came to Greece 3 and stayed three months. And
when the Jews plotted against him as he was about

וְאָמַר: "חֲבֵרִים, אַתֶּם יוֹדְעִים כִּי מֵהַמְּלָאכָה הַזֹּאת
יֵשׁ לָנוּ רֶוַח. 26 וְאַתֶּם רוֹאִים וְשׁוֹמְעִים שֶׁלֹּא רַק
בְּאֶפֶסוֹס אֶלָּא כִּמְעַט בְּכָל אַסְיָה שָׁאוּל הַזֶּה שִׁכְנֵעַ
וְהֵדִיחַ הָמוֹן רַב בְּאָמְרוֹ שֶׁאֵלִים מַעֲשֵׂי יָדַיִם אֵינָם
אֵלִים. 27 אֲבָל לֹא רַק מְלַאכְתֵּנוּ זֹאת עֲלוּלָה לִהְיוֹת
לְבוּז, אֶלָּא גַּם הַהֵיכָל שֶׁל הָאֵלָה הַגְּדוֹלָה אַרְטֶמִיס
עָלוּל לְהֵחָשֵׁב לְאֶפֶס, וְהִיא אֲשֶׁר כָּל אַסְיָה וְכָל
הָעוֹלָם עוֹבְדִים אוֹתָהּ גַּם תַּפְסִיד אֶת גְּדֻלָּתָהּ."
28 כְּשָׁמְעָם אֶת דְּבָרָיו נִתְמַלְּאוּ זַעַם וְצָעֲקוּ: "גְּדוֹלָה
אַרְטֶמִיס שֶׁל הָאֶפֶסִים!" 29 מְהוּמָה הִתְפַּשְּׁטָה בְּכָל
הָעִיר וְהַתּוֹשָׁבִים רָצוּ כְּאִישׁ אֶחָד אֶל
הָאַמְפִיתֵיאַטְרוֹן כְּשֶׁהֵם סוֹחֲבִים אֶת גָּיוֹס וְאֶת
אֲרִיסְטַרְכוֹס, שְׁנֵי הַמַּקְדוֹנִים חֲבֵרָיו שֶׁל שָׁאוּל
לַמַּסָּע. 30 שָׁאוּל רָצָה לְהִכָּנֵס אֶל תּוֹךְ הֶהָמוֹן, אַךְ
הַתַּלְמִידִים לֹא הִנִּיחוּ לוֹ. 31 גַּם כַּמָּה מֵרָאשֵׁי אַסְיָה
שֶׁהָיוּ חֲבֵרָיו שָׁלְחוּ אֵלָיו לְבַקֵּשׁ מִמֶּנּוּ שֶׁלֹּא יִכָּנֵס
לָאַמְפִיתֵיאַטְרוֹן. 32 בֵּינְתַיִם צָעֲקוּ אֵלֶּה דָּבָר אֶחָד
וְאֵלֶּה דָּבָר אַחֵר, כִּי הַקָּהָל הָיָה נָבוֹךְ וְרֻבָּם לֹא יָדְעוּ
לָמָּה הִתְאַסְּפוּ. 33 אֲנָשִׁים מִן הֶהָמוֹן הִסְבִּירוּ מַשֶּׁהוּ
לַאֲלֶכְּסַנְדֶּר לְאַחַר שֶׁבְּנֵי עַמּוֹ הַיְּהוּדִים דְּחָקוּהוּ
קָדִימָה. הֵנִיף אֲלֶכְּסַנְדֶּר אֶת יָדוֹ וְרָצָה לְהַשְׁמִיעַ
לֶהָמוֹן דְּבַר הֲגַנָּה. 34 אַךְ כְּשֶׁהִבְחִינוּ שֶׁהוּא יְהוּדִי
רָעֲמוּ כֻּלָּם בְּקוֹל אֶחָד וּבְמֶשֶׁךְ שְׁעָתַיִם צָעֲקוּ:
"גְּדוֹלָה אַרְטֶמִיס שֶׁל הָאֶפֶסִים!" 35 הִשְׁקִיט מַזְכִּיר
הָעִיר אֶת הָעָם וְאָמַר: "אַנְשֵׁי אֶפֶסוֹס, מִי מִבְּנֵי אָדָם
אֵינוֹ יוֹדֵעַ שֶׁהָעִיר אֶפֶסוֹס מְפַקֶּדֶת עַל הֵיכַל
אַרְטֶמִיס הַגְּדוֹלָה וְעַל צַלְמָהּ שֶׁנָּפַל מִן הַשָּׁמַיִם?
36 מֵאַחַר שֶׁאֵין לְהַכְחִישׁ זֹאת, עֲלֵיכֶם לְהֵרָגַע וְלֹא
לַעֲשׂוֹת שׁוּם דָּבָר נִמְהָר. 37 הִנֵּה הֲבֵאתֶם אֶת
הָאֲנָשִׁים הָאֵלֶּה, שֶׁאֵינָם שׁוֹדְדֵי מִקְדָּשִׁים אַף לֹא
מְחַלְּלִים אֶת שֵׁם הָאֵלָה שֶׁלָּכֶם. 38 לָכֵן, אִם יֵשׁ
לִדְמֶטְרִיוֹס וְלָאֻמָּנִים אֲשֶׁר אִתּוֹ דָּבָר נֶגֶד מִישֶׁהוּ, יֵשׁ
בָּתֵּי מִשְׁפָּט וְיֵשׁ שׁוֹפְטִים; שֶׁיִּטְעֲנוּ זֶה נֶגֶד זֶה.
39 אֲבָל אִם רוֹצִים אַתֶּם מַשֶּׁהוּ נוֹסָף, אֲזַי שֶׁיֵּחָרֵץ
בַּאֲסֵפָה חֻקִּית. 40 הֲרֵי עֲלוּלִים אָנוּ לִהְיוֹת מֶאֱשָׁמִים
בַּמְּהוּמַת חַיּוֹם הַזֶּה, מְהוּמָה לְלֹא שׁוּם סִבָּה, וְלֹא
נוּכַל לָתֵת נִמּוּק עַל הַהִתְקַהֲלוּת הַזֹּאת." 41 הוּא
אָמַר אֶת הַדְּבָרִים הָאֵלֶּה וְשִׁלַּח אֶת הַקָּהָל.

כ אַחֲרֵי שֶׁפָּסְקָה הַמְּהוּמָה קָרָא שָׁאוּל לַתַּלְמִידִים
וְעוֹדֵד אוֹתָם. הוּא נִפְרַד מֵהֶם וְיָצָא לָדֶרֶךְ אֶל
מַקְדוֹנְיָה. 2 לְאַחַר שֶׁעָבַר בָּאֲזוֹרִים הָהֵם וְעוֹדֵד אֶת
הַתַּלְמִידִים בְּדִבְרֵי עִדּוּד רַבִּים, בָּא לְיָוָן 3 וַיֵּשֶׁב שָׁם

to sail to Syria, he decided to return through
Macedonia. ⁴And Sopater of Berea accompanied
him to Asia—also Aristarchus and Secundus of the
Thessalonians, and Gaius of Derbe, and Timothy,
and Tychicus and Trophimus of Asia. ⁵These men,
going ahead, waited for us at Troas. ⁶But we sailed
away from Philippi after the Days of Unleavened
Bread, and in five days joined them at Troas, where
we stayed seven days.

⁷Now on the first *day* of the week, when the
disciples came together to break bread, Paul, ready
to depart the next day, spoke to them and
continued his message until midnight. ⁸There were
many lamps in the upper room where they were
gathered together. ⁹And in a window sat a certain
young man named Eutychus, who was sinking into
a deep sleep. He was overcome by sleep; and as Paul
continued speaking, he fell down from the third
story and was taken up dead. ¹⁰But Paul went
down, fell on him, and embracing *him* said, "Do
not trouble yourselves, for his life is in him." ¹¹Now
when he had come up, had broken bread and eaten,
and talked a long while, even till daybreak, he
departed. ¹²And they brought the young man in
alive, and they were not a little comforted.

¹³Then we went ahead to the ship and sailed to
Assos, there intending to take Paul on board; for so
he had given orders, intending himself to go on
foot. ¹⁴And when he met us at Assos, we took him
on board and came to Mitylene. ¹⁵We sailed from
there, and the next *day* came opposite Chios. The
following *day* we arrived at Samos and stayed at
Trogyllium. The next *day* we came to Miletus.
¹⁶For Paul had decided to sail past Ephesus, so that
he would not have to spend time in Asia; for he was
hurrying to be at Jerusalem, if possible, on the Day
of Pentecost.

¹⁷From Miletus he sent to Ephesus and called for
the elders of the church. ¹⁸And when they had come
to him, he said to them: "You know, from the first
day that I came to Asia, in what manner I always
lived among you, ¹⁹serving the Lord with all
humility, with many tears and trials which happened to me by the plotting of the Jews; ²⁰how I
kept back nothing that was helpful, but proclaimed
it to you, and taught you publicly and from house
to house, ²¹testifying to Jews, and also to Greeks,
repentance toward God and faith toward our Lord
Jesus Christ. ²²And see, now I go bound in the
spirit to Jerusalem, not knowing the things that will
happen to me there, ²³except that the Holy Spirit
testifies in every city, saying that chains and
tribulations await me. ²⁴But none of these things
move me; nor do I count my life dear to myself, so

שְׁלוֹשָׁה חֳדָשִׁים. כְּשֶׁעָמַד לְהַפְלִיג לְסוּרְיָה הִתְנַכְּלוּ
יְהוּדֵי הַמָּקוֹם לְהָרַע לוֹ, לְפִיכָךְ הֶחֱלִיט לָשׁוּב דֶּרֶךְ
מָקֶדוֹנְיָה. ⁴נִלְווּ אֵלָיו סוֹפַּטְרוֹס בֶּן־פִּירוֹס אִישׁ
בֶּרְאָה, אֲרִיסְטַרְכוֹס וְסֶקוּנְדוֹס הַתֶּסָלוֹנִיקִים, גָּיוֹס
הַדַּרְבִּי, טִימוֹתִיאוֹס, וְטִיכִיקוֹס וּטְרוֹפִימוֹס אַנְשֵׁי
אַסְיָה. ⁵הַלָּלוּ הָלְכוּ לְפָנֵינוּ וְחִכּוּ לָנוּ בִּטְרוֹאָס.
⁶אֲנַחְנוּ הִפְלַגְנוּ מִפִילִיפִּי אַחֲרֵי יְמֵי חַג הַמַּצּוֹת וּבָאנוּ
אֲלֵיהֶם לִטְרוֹאָס כַּעֲבוֹר חֲמִשָּׁה יָמִים. שָׁם נִשְׁאַרְנוּ
שִׁבְעָה יָמִים.

⁷בָּרִאשׁוֹן בַּשָּׁבוּעַ נֶאֱסַפְנוּ לִבְצֹעַ לֶחֶם. שָׁאוּל,
שֶׁעָמַד לָצֵאת לְמָחֳרָת, דִּבֶּר אֲלֵיהֶם וְהֶאֱרִיךְ אֶת
דְּבָרוֹ עַד חֲצוֹת. ⁸מְנוֹרוֹת רַבּוֹת הָיוּ בָּעֲלִיָּה
שֶׁנֶּאֱסַפְנוּ בָּהּ. ⁹וּבַחוּר אֶחָד, אוּטִיכוֹס שְׁמוֹ, יָשַׁב
עַל אֶרֶן הַחַלּוֹן כְּשֶׁהוּא שׁוֹקֵעַ בְּתַרְדֵּמָה עֲמֻקָּה.
כְּשֶׁהֶאֱרִיךְ שָׁאוּל אֶת דְּבָרוֹ גָּבְרָה עָלָיו הַתַּרְדֵּמָה
וְנָפַל מִן הַקּוֹמָה הַשְּׁלִישִׁית לְמַטָּה. הֵם הֵרִימוּ אוֹתוֹ
מֵת. ¹⁰אֲבָל שָׁאוּל יָרַד, גָּהַר עָלָיו וּבְחַבְּקוֹ אוֹתוֹ
אָמַר: "אַל תִּבָּהֲלוּ, נִשְׁמָתוֹ בּוֹ." ¹¹הוּא עָלָה, בָּצַע
אֶת הַלֶּחֶם וְאָכַל. לְאַחַר שֶׁשּׂוֹחַח אִתָּם שָׁעָה אֲרֻכָּה,
עַד אוֹר הַבֹּקֶר, יָצָא לְדַרְכּוֹ. ¹²וְהֵם הֵבִיאוּ אֶת
הַצָּעִיר חַי וְהִתְנַחֲמוּ מְאֹד.

¹³אֲנַחְנוּ הִקְדַּמְנוּ לַעֲלוֹת לָאֳנִיָּה וְהִפְלַגְנוּ אֶל אַסּוֹס
כְּדֵי לָקַחַת שָׁם אֶת שָׁאוּל; כָּךְ קָבַע, מִשּׁוּם
שֶׁהִתְכַּוֵּן לְהַגִּיעַ לְשָׁם בְּדֶרֶךְ הַיַּבָּשָׁה. ¹⁴כַּאֲשֶׁר פָּגַשׁ
אוֹתָנוּ בְּאַסּוֹס לָקַחְנוּ אוֹתוֹ וּבָאנוּ אֶל מִיטוֹלִינִי.
¹⁵מִשָּׁם הִפְלַגְנוּ וְהִגַּעְנוּ לְמָחֳרָת אֶל מוּל כִּיּוֹם. יוֹם
אַחֲרֵי כֵן עָבַרְנוּ אֶל סָמוֹס וּלְמָחֳרָת בָּאנוּ אֶל
מִילֵיטוֹם. ¹⁶כִּי שָׁאוּל הֶחֱלִיט לַעֲבֹר בַּיָּם עַל־פְּנֵי
אֶפְסוֹס כְּדֵי שֶׁלֹּא יִצְטָרֵךְ לִשְׁהוֹת בְּאַסְיָה; זֹאת מִפְּנֵי
שֶׁמִּהֵר בְּדַרְכּוֹ – אוּלַי יוּכַל לִהְיוֹת בִּירוּשָׁלַיִם בְּחַג
הַשָּׁבוּעוֹת.

¹⁷מִמִּילֵיטוֹם שָׁלַח אֶל אֶפְסוֹס וְקָרָא אֶת זִקְנֵי
הַקְּהִלָּה. ¹⁸כַּאֲשֶׁר בָּאוּ אֵלָיו אָמַר לָהֶם: "אַתֶּם
יוֹדְעִים כֵּיצַד הָיִיתִי אִתְּכֶם בְּכָל עֵת לְמִן הַיּוֹם
הָרִאשׁוֹן שֶׁרַגְלִי דָּרְכָה בְּאַסְיָה. ¹⁹עָבַדְתִּי אֶת הָאָדוֹן
בְּכָל עֲנָוָה וּבִדְמָעוֹת וּבְמַסּוֹת אֲשֶׁר בָּאוּ עָלַי בְּגִלַּל
נוֹכְלִים מִבֵּין הַיְּהוּדִים. ²⁰לֹא נִרְתַּעְתִּי מִלְּהוֹדִיעַ
לָכֶם כָּל דָּבָר מוֹעִיל וּמִלְּלַמֵּד אֶתְכֶם בָּרַבִּים וּבְכָל
בַּיִת וּבַיִת, ²¹בְּהַעִידִי גַּם בִּיהוּדִים וְגַם בְּיָוָנִים לַחֲזֹר
בִּתְשׁוּבָה אֶל אֱלֹהִים וּלְהַאֲמִין בַּאֲדוֹנֵנוּ יֵשׁוּעַ.
²²וְעַכְשָׁו הִנְנִי הוֹלֵךְ לִירוּשָׁלַיִם כָּבוּל בָּרוּחַ וְאֵינִי
יוֹדֵעַ מַה יִּקְרֶה לִי שָׁם, ²³לְבַד מִזֶּה שֶׁרוּחַ הַקֹּדֶשׁ
מְצַהִירָה לִי בְּכָל עִיר וָעִיר וְאוֹמֶרֶת שֶׁכְּבָלִים וְצָרוֹת
מְצַפִּים לִי. ²⁴אוּלָם חַיַּי אֵינָם יְקָרִים לִי כָּל עִקָּר

that I may finish my race with joy, and the ministry which I received from the Lord Jesus, to testify to the gospel of the grace of God.

25 "And indeed, now I know that you all, among whom I have gone preaching the kingdom of God, will see my face no more. 26 Therefore I testify to you this day that I *am* innocent of the blood of all *men*. 27 For I have not shunned to declare to you the whole counsel of God. 28 Therefore take heed to yourselves and to all the flock, among which the Holy Spirit has made you overseers, to shepherd the church of God which He purchased with His own blood. 29 For I know this, that after my departure savage wolves will come in among you, not sparing the flock. 30 Also from among yourselves men will rise up, speaking perverse things, to draw away the disciples after themselves. 31 Therefore watch, and remember that for three years I did not cease to warn everyone night and day with tears.

32 "So now, brethren, I commend you to God and to the word of His grace, which is able to build you up and give you an inheritance among all those who are sanctified. 33 I have coveted no one's silver or gold or apparel. 34 Yes, you yourselves know that these hands have provided for my necessities, and for those who were with me. 35 I have shown you in every way, by laboring like this, that you must support the weak. And remember the words of the Lord Jesus, that He said, 'It is more blessed to give than to receive.' "

36 And when he had said these things, he knelt down and prayed with them all. 37 Then they all wept freely, and fell on Paul's neck and kissed him, 38 sorrowing most of all for the words which he spoke, that they would see his face no more. And they accompanied him to the ship.

21 Now it came to pass, that when we had departed from them and set sail, running a straight course we came to Cos, the following *day* to Rhodes, and from there to Patara. 2 And finding a ship sailing over to Phoenicia, we went aboard and set sail. 3 When we had sighted Cyprus, we passed it on the left, sailed to Syria, and landed at Tyre; for there the ship was to unload her cargo. 4 And finding disciples, we stayed there seven days. They told Paul through the Spirit not to go up to Jerusalem. 5 When we had come to the end of those days, we departed and went on our way; and they all accompanied us, with wives and children, till *we were* out of the city. And we knelt down on the shore and prayed. 6 When we had taken our leave of one another, we boarded the ship, and they returned home.

וּבִלְבַד שֶׁאַשְׁלִים אֶת מְרוּצָתִי וְאֶת הַשֵּׁרוּת אֲשֶׁר קִבַּלְתִּי מֵאֵת הָאָדוֹן יֵשׁוּעַ – לְהָעִיד עַל בְּשׂוֹרַת חֶסֶד אֱלֹהִים.

25 וְעַתָּה אֲנִי יוֹדֵעַ כִּי אַתֶּם כֻּלְּכֶם, אֲשֶׁר בֵּינֵיכֶם הִתְהַלַּכְתִּי וְהִכְרַזְתִּי אֶת הַמַּלְכוּת, לֹא תּוֹסִיפוּ עוֹד לִרְאוֹת אֶת פָּנַי. 26 לָכֵן אֲנִי מֵעִיד בָּכֶם הַיּוֹם הַזֶּה שֶׁנָּקִי אֲנִי מִדַּם כֻּלְּכֶם, 27 כִּי לֹא נִרְתַּעְתִּי מִלְּהוֹדִיעַ לָכֶם אֶת עֲצַת אֱלֹהִים כֻּלָּהּ. 28 הִשָּׁגְיחוּ עַל עַצְמְכֶם וְעַל כָּל הָעֵדֶר אֲשֶׁר רוּחַ הַקֹּדֶשׁ שָׂמָה אֶתְכֶם לִמְנַהֲגִים בְּתוֹכוֹ, לִרְעוֹת אֶת קְהִלַּת אֱלֹהִים אֲשֶׁר קָנָה בְּדָמוֹ שֶׁלּוֹ. 29 אֲנִי יוֹדֵעַ שֶׁאַחֲרֵי צֵאתִי יָבוֹאוּ בְּתוֹכְכֶם זְאֵבִים עַזִּים אֲשֶׁר לֹא יָחוּסוּ עַל הָעֵדֶר, 30 וּמִקִּרְבְּכֶם יָקוּמוּ אֲנָשִׁים דּוֹבְרֵי תַהְפּוּכוֹת לְהַטּוֹת אַחֲרֵיהֶם אֶת הַתַּלְמִידִים. 31 עַל כֵּן עִמְדוּ עַל הַמִּשְׁמָר. זִכְרוּ כִּי שָׁלוֹשׁ שָׁנִים, יוֹמָם וָלַיְלָה, לֹא חָדַלְתִּי לְהוֹכִיחַ כָּל אֶחָד וְאֶחָד בְּדִמְעוֹת. 32 וְעַכְשָׁו אֲנִי מַפְקִיד אֶתְכֶם בִּידֵי אֱלֹהִים וּדְבַר חַסְדּוֹ; לוֹ הַכֹּחַ לִבְנוֹת אֶתְכֶם וְלָתֵת לָכֶם נַחֲלָה בְּקֶרֶב כָּל הַמְקֻדָּשִׁים. 33 לֹא חָמַדְתִּי אֶת כַּסְפּוֹ שֶׁל אִישׁ, גַּם לֹא אֶת זְהָבוֹ אוֹ לְבוּשׁוֹ. 34 אַתֶּם עַצְמְכֶם יוֹדְעִים שֶׁיָּדַי אֵלֶּה שֵׁרְתוּ בְּעַד צָרְכַי וּבְעַד צָרְכֵי הָאֲנָשִׁים אֲשֶׁר אִתִּי. 35 בַּכֹּל הֶרְאֵיתִי לָכֶם כִּי בְּהִיּוֹתְנוּ עֲמֵלִים כָּךְ יֵשׁ לִתְמֹךְ בַּחַלָּשִׁים וְלִזְכֹּר אֶת דִּבְרֵי הָאָדוֹן יֵשׁוּעַ, שֶׁהֲרֵי הוּא אָמַר 'טוֹב לָתֵת מֵאֲשֶׁר לְקַבֵּל'." 36 אַחֲרֵי שֶׁאָמַר אֶת הַדְּבָרִים הָאֵלֶּה כָּרַע עַל בִּרְכָּיו וְהִתְפַּלֵּל עִם כֻּלָּם. 37 הַכֹּל בָּכוּ בְּכִי רַב, נָפְלוּ עַל צַוְּארֵי שָׁאוּל וְנִשְּׁקוּ לוֹ, 38 וּבְיוֹתֵר הִתְעַצְּבוּ עַל הַדָּבָר שֶׁאָמַר – שֶׁלֹּא יוֹסִיפוּ עוֹד לִרְאוֹת אֶת פָּנָיו. אַחֲרֵי כֵן לִוּוּהוּ אֶל הָאֳנִיָּה.

כא לְאַחַר שֶׁנִּפְרַדְנוּ מֵהֶם הִפְלַגְנוּ וּבְנָתִיב יָשָׁר בָּאנוּ אֶל קוֹם. לְמָחֳרָת בָּאנוּ אֶל רוֹדוֹם וּמִשָּׁם אֶל פָּטָרָה. 2 שָׁם מָצָאנוּ אֳנִיָּה שֶׁמִּמַּגְמָתָהּ פֵּנִיקְיָה. נִכְנַסְנוּ לָאֳנִיָּה וְהִפְלַגְנוּ. 3 בַּדֶּרֶךְ רָאִינוּ אֶת קַפְרִיסִין וְעָבַרְנוּ עַל פָּנֶיהָ כְּשֶׁהִיא מִשְּׂמֹאלֵנוּ. הִמְשַׁכְנוּ בַּמַּסָּע אֶל סוּרְיָה וְהִגַּעְנוּ אֶל צוֹר, כִּי שָׁם פֵּרְקוּ אֶת מִטְעַן הָאֳנִיָּה. 4 מָצָאנוּ תַּלְמִידִים וְיָשַׁבְנוּ שָׁם שִׁבְעָה יָמִים. הַלָּלוּ אָמְרוּ לְשָׁאוּל עַל-פִּי הָרוּחַ שֶׁלֹּא יַעֲלֶה לִירוּשָׁלַיִם. 5 כַּאֲשֶׁר תַּמּוּ הַיָּמִים יָצְאוּ לְדַרְכֵּנוּ וְהֵם כֻּלָּם לִוּוּ אוֹתָנוּ עִם נְשֵׁיהֶם וְיַלְדֵיהֶם עַד מְחוּץ לָעִיר. בְּחוֹף כָּרַעְנוּ עַל בִּרְכֵּינוּ וְהִתְפַּלַּלְנוּ. 6 אַחֲרֵי שֶׁבֵּרַכְנוּ זֶה אֶת זֶה לְשָׁלוֹם וְנִכְנַסְנוּ לָאֳנִיָּה, הֵם שָׁבוּ אִישׁ אִישׁ לְבֵיתוֹ.

7 And when we had finished *our* voyage from Tyre, we came to Ptolemais, greeted the brethren, and stayed with them one day. 8 On the next *day* we who were Paul's companions departed and came to Caesarea, and entered the house of Philip the evangelist, who was *one* of the seven, and stayed with him. 9 Now this man had four virgin daughters who prophesied. 10 And as we stayed many days, a certain prophet named Agabus came down from Judea. 11 When he had come to us, he took Paul's belt, bound his *own* hands and feet, and said, "Thus says the Holy Spirit, 'So shall the Jews at Jerusalem bind the man who owns this belt, and deliver *him* into the hands of the Gentiles.' "

12 Now when we heard these things, both we and those from that place pleaded with him not to go up to Jerusalem. 13 Then Paul answered, "What do you mean by weeping and breaking my heart? For I am ready not only to be bound, but also to die at Jerusalem for the name of the Lord Jesus."

14 So when he would not be persuaded, we ceased, saying, "The will of the Lord be done."

15 And after those days we packed and went up to Jerusalem. 16 Also some of the disciples from Caesarea went with us and brought with them a certain Mnason of Cyprus, an early disciple, with whom we were to lodge.

17 And when we had come to Jerusalem, the brethren received us gladly. 18 On the following *day* Paul went in with us to James, and all the elders were present. 19 When he had greeted them, he told in detail those things which God had done among the Gentiles through his ministry. 20 And when they heard *it,* they glorified the Lord. And they said to him, "You see, brother, how many myriads of Jews there are who have believed, and they are all zealous for the law; 21 but they have been informed about you that you teach all the Jews who are among the Gentiles to forsake Moses, saying that they ought not to circumcise *their* children nor to walk according to the customs. 22 What then? The assembly must certainly meet, for they will hear that you have come. 23 Therefore do what we tell you: We have four men who have taken a vow. 24 Take them and be purified with them, and pay their expenses so that they may shave *their* heads, and that all may know that those things of which they were informed concerning you are nothing, but *that* you yourself also walk orderly and keep the law. 25 But concerning the Gentiles who believe, we have written *and* decided that they should observe no such thing, except that they should keep

7 כְּשֶׁסִּיַּמְנוּ אֶת הַמַּסָּע מִצּוֹר הִגַּעְנוּ לְעַכּוֹ. שָׁאַלְנוּ אֶת הָאַחִים לִשְׁלוֹמָם וְיָשַׁבְנוּ אֶצְלָם יוֹם אֶחָד. 8 לְמָחֳרָת יָצָאנוּ לַדֶּרֶךְ וּבָאנוּ לְקֵיסַרְיָה. שָׁם נִכְנַסְנוּ לְבֵיתוֹ שֶׁל פִילִיפּוֹס הַמְבַשֵּׂר, שֶׁהָיָה אֶחָד מִן הַשִּׁבְעָה, וְגַרְנוּ אֶצְלוֹ. 9 הָיוּ לוֹ אַרְבַּע בָּנוֹת בְּתוּלוֹת שֶׁהָיוּ מִתְנַבְּאוֹת. 10 כְּשֶׁהָיִינוּ שָׁם יָמִים רַבִּים יָרַד נָבִיא אֶחָד מִיהוּדָה, אֲגָבוֹס שְׁמוֹ. 11 הוּא נִכְנַס אֵלֵינוּ, לָקַח אֶת חֲגוֹרָתוֹ שֶׁל שָׁאוּל וּלְאַחַר שֶׁקָּשַׁר אֶת רַגְלָיו וְיָדָיו שֶׁלוֹ אָמַר: "כֹּה אוֹמֶרֶת רוּחַ הַקֹּדֶשׁ: הָאִישׁ אֲשֶׁר לוֹ הַחֲגוֹרָה הַזֹּאת, כָּכָה יִקְשְׁרוּ אוֹתוֹ הַיְּהוּדִים בִּירוּשָׁלַיִם וְיַסְגִּירוּהוּ בִּידֵי הַגּוֹיִים."

12 כַּאֲשֶׁר שָׁמַעְנוּ זֹאת הִפְצַרְנוּ בּוֹ, אֲנַחְנוּ וְגַם אַנְשֵׁי הַמָּקוֹם, שֶׁלֹּא יַעֲלֶה לִירוּשָׁלַיִם. 13 אַךְ שָׁאוּל הֵשִׁיב: "מָה אַתֶּם עוֹשִׂים? לָמָּה אַתֶּם בּוֹכִים וּמְמַסְמְסִים אֶת לִבִּי? הֲרֵינִי מוּכָן לֹא רַק לְהֵאָסֵר אֶלָּא גַּם לָמוּת בִּירוּשָׁלַיִם עַל שֵׁם הָאָדוֹן יֵשׁוּעַ."

14 הוֹאִיל וְלֹא שָׁמַע לָנוּ חָדַלְנוּ לְהַפְצִיר בּוֹ וְאָמַרְנוּ: "רְצוֹן אֲדֹנָי יֵעָשֶׂה."

15 אַחֲרֵי הַיָּמִים הָהֵם אָרַזְנוּ אֶת חֲפָצֵינוּ וְעָלִינוּ לִירוּשָׁלַיִם. 16 הָלְכוּ אִתָּנוּ גַּם תַּלְמִידִים אֲחָדִים מִקֵּיסַרְיָה. הֵם הֵבִיאוּ אוֹתָנוּ אֶל קַפְרִיסַאי אֶחָד, תַּלְמִיד וָתִיק וּשְׁמוֹ מְנָסוֹן, כְּדֵי לְהִתְאַכְסֵן אֶצְלוֹ. 17 כְּשֶׁבָּאנוּ לִירוּשָׁלַיִם קִבְּלוּ אוֹתָנוּ הָאַחִים בְּשִׂמְחָה. 18 שָׁאוּל נִכְנַס אִתָּנוּ לְמָחֳרָת אֶל יַעֲקֹב, וְכָל הַזְּקֵנִים נִכְחוּ שָׁם. 19 הוּא שָׁאַל לִשְׁלוֹמָם וְסִפֵּר בִּפְרוֹט מַה שֶּׁעָשָׂה אֱלֹהִים בְּקֶרֶב הַגּוֹיִים דַּרְכּוֹ. 20 הֵם שָׁמְעוּ וְשִׁבְּחוּ אֶת אֱלֹהִים. לְאַחַר מִכֵּן אָמְרוּ: "אַתָּה רוֹאֶה, אָחִינוּ, כַּמָּה רִבְבוֹת יְהוּדִים נִהְיוּ מַאֲמִינִים וְכֻלָּם קַנָּאִים לַתּוֹרָה! 21 וְהֵם שָׁמְעוּ עָלֶיךָ שֶׁאַתָּה מְלַמֵּד אֶת כָּל הַיְּהוּדִים אֲשֶׁר בְּקֶרֶב הַגּוֹיִים לַעֲזֹב אֶת מֹשֶׁה, בְּאָמְרְךָ לָהֶם שֶׁלֹּא לָמוּל אֶת הַיְּלָדִים וְלֹא לִנְהֹג עַל־פִּי הַמִּנְהָגִים. 22 וּבְכֵן מַה לַּעֲשׂוֹת? לְלֹא סָפֵק יִשְׁמְעוּ שֶׁבָּאתָ. 23 לָכֵן עֲשֵׂה אֶת מַה שֶּׁאֲנַחְנוּ אוֹמְרִים לְךָ: יֵשׁ לָנוּ אַרְבָּעָה אֲנָשִׁים אֲשֶׁר נֶדֶר עֲלֵיהֶם. 24 קַח אוֹתָם, הִטָּהֵר אִתָּם וְשַׁלֵּם בַּעֲדָם כְּדֵי שֶׁיְּגַלְּחוּ אֶת רֹאשָׁם וְהַכֹּל יֵדְעוּ שֶׁהַדְּבָרִים אֲשֶׁר שָׁמְעוּ עָלֶיךָ אֵינָם נְכוֹנִים, כִּי גַּם אַתָּה בְּעַצְמְךָ שׁוֹמֵר אֶת הַתּוֹרָה. 25 וּבְנוֹגֵעַ לַגּוֹיִים אֲשֶׁר נִהְיוּ

themselves from *things* offered to idols, from blood, from things strangled, and from sexual immorality."

26 Then Paul took the men, and the next day, having been purified with them, entered the temple to announce the expiration of the days of purification, at which time an offering should be made for each one of them.

27 Now when the seven days were almost ended, the Jews from Asia, seeing him in the temple, stirred up the whole crowd and laid hands on him, 28 crying out, "Men of Israel, help! This is the man who teaches all *men* everywhere against the people, the law, and this place; and furthermore he also brought Greeks into the temple and has defiled this holy place." 29 (For they had previously seen Trophimus the Ephesian with him in the city, whom they supposed that Paul had brought into the temple.)

30 And all the city was disturbed; and the people ran together, seized Paul, and dragged him out of the temple; and immediately the doors were shut. 31 Now as they were seeking to kill him, news came to the commander of the garrison that all Jerusalem was in an uproar. 32 He immediately took soldiers and centurions, and ran down to them. And when they saw the commander and the soldiers, they stopped beating Paul. 33 Then the commander came near and took him, and commanded *him* to be bound with two chains; and he asked who he was and what he had done. 34 And some among the multitude cried one thing and some another.

So when he could not ascertain the truth because of the tumult, he commanded him to be taken into the barracks. 35 When he reached the stairs, he had to be carried by the soldiers because of the violence of the mob. 36 For the multitude of the people followed after, crying out, "Away with him!"

37 Then as Paul was about to be led into the barracks, he said to the commander, "May I speak to you?"

He replied, "Can you speak Greek? 38 Are you not the Egyptian who some time ago stirred up a rebellion and led the four thousand assassins out into the wilderness?"

39 But Paul said, "I am a Jew from Tarsus, in Cilicia, a citizen of no mean city; and I implore you, permit me to speak to the people."

40 So when he had given him permission, Paul stood on the stairs and motioned with his hand to the people. And when there was a great silence, he spoke to *them* in the Hebrew language, saying,

מַאֲמִינִים כָּתַבְנוּ וּפָסַקְנוּ שֶׁעֲלֵיהֶם לְהִשָּׁמֵר מִזִּבְחֵי אֱלִילִים, מִדָּם, מִבְּשַׂר הַנֶּחֱנָק וּמִזְּנוּת."

26 לְמָחֳרָת לָקַח שָׁאוּל אֶת הָאֲנָשִׁים וְנִטְהַר אִתָּם. הוּא נִכְנַס לְבֵית הַמִּקְדָּשׁ לְהוֹדִיעַ מָתַי יִשְׁלְמוּ יְמֵי הַטָּהֳרָה וְיִקְרַב קָרְבָּן בְּעַד כָּל אֶחָד מֵהֶם.

27 סָמוּךְ לִמְלֹאת שִׁבְעַת הַיָּמִים רָאוּהוּ יְהוּדִים מֵאַסְיָה בְּבֵית הַמִּקְדָּשׁ. הֵם הֵסִיתוּ אֶת כָּל הֶהָמוֹן, תָּפְסוּ אוֹתוֹ 28 וְצָעֲקוּ: "אַנְשֵׁי יִשְׂרָאֵל, עִזְרוּ! זֶהוּ הָאִישׁ הַמְלַמֵּד אֶת כָּל הָאֲנָשִׁים בְּכָל מָקוֹם נֶגֶד הָעָם הַזֶּה וְנֶגֶד הַתּוֹרָה וְהַמָּקוֹם הַזֶּה, וַאֲפִלּוּ יְוָנִים הֵבִיא אֶל הַמִּקְדָּשׁ וְחִלֵּל אֶת הַמָּקוֹם הַקָּדוֹשׁ הַזֶּה."

29 זֹאת מִשּׁוּם שֶׁקֹּדֶם לָכֵן רָאוּ אֶת טְרוֹפִימוֹס הָאֶפֶסִי אִתּוֹ בָּעִיר, וְחָשְׁבוּ שֶׁשָּׁאוּל אוֹתוֹ אֶל הַמִּקְדָּשׁ.

30 כָּל הָעִיר רָגְשָׁה. הָאֲנָשִׁים רָצוּ יַחַד, אָחֲזוּ אֶת שָׁאוּל וְסָחֲבוּ אוֹתוֹ אֶל מִחוּץ לַמִּקְדָּשׁ וּמִיָּד נִסְגְּרוּ הַדְּלָתוֹת. 31 הֵם נִסּוּ לַהֲרֹג אוֹתוֹ, וְהִנֵּה הִגִּיעָה יְדִיעָה אֶל מְפַקֵּד הַגְּדוּד שֶׁכָּל יְרוּשָׁלַיִם אֲחוּזַת מְהוּמָה. 32 מִיָּד לָקַח אִתּוֹ חַיָּלִים וְשָׂרֵי מֵאוֹת וְרָץ אֲלֵיהֶם. כִּרְאוֹתָם אֶת שַׂר הָאֶלֶף וְאֶת הַחַיָּלִים חָדְלוּ לְהַכּוֹת אֶת שָׁאוּל. 33 נִגַּשׁ שַׂר הָאֶלֶף וְהֶחֱזִיק בּוֹ. הוּא צִוָּה לְכַבֵּל אוֹתוֹ בִּשְׁתֵּי שַׁרְשְׁרוֹת וְשָׁאַל מִיהוּ וּמֶה עָשָׂה. 34 כַּמָּה אֲנָשִׁים מִן הֶהָמוֹן צָעֲקוּ דָּבָר אֶחָד וַאֲחֵרִים צָעֲקוּ דָּבָר אַחֵר. בִּגְלַל הַמְּהוּמָה לֹא הָיָה יָכוֹל לְבָרֵר בְּוַדָּאוּת מֶה הָעִנְיָן, לָכֵן צִוָּה לַהֲבִיאוֹ אֶל הַמְּצוּדָה. 35 כַּאֲשֶׁר הִגִּיעַ שָׁאוּל אֶל הַמַּדְרֵגוֹת נָשְׂאוּ אוֹתוֹ הַחַיָּלִים בִּגְלַל לַחַץ הֶהָמוֹן, 36 כִּי הֲמוֹן הָעָם הָלַךְ אַחֲרָיו וְצָעַק: "חַסֵּל אוֹתוֹ!"

37 כְּשֶׁעָמְדוּ לְהַכְנִיס אֶת שָׁאוּל לַמְּצוּדָה, אָמַר אֶל שַׂר הָאֶלֶף: "הַאִם מֻתָּר לִי לוֹמַר לְךָ מַשֶּׁהוּ?" הֵגִיב הַמְפַקֵּד: "אַתָּה יוֹדֵעַ יְוָנִית? 38 הַאִם לֹא אַתָּה הַמִּצְרִי אֲשֶׁר לִפְנֵי זְמַן מָה חִפִּיחַ מֶרֶד וְהִנְהִיג אֶת אַרְבַּעַת אַלְפֵי הַסִּיקָרִים אֶל הַמִּדְבָּר?" 39 הֵשִׁיב שָׁאוּל וְאָמַר: "אִישׁ יְהוּדִי אֲנִי מִטַּרְסוֹס אֲשֶׁר בְּקִילִיקְיָה, אֶזְרָח שֶׁל עִיר לֹא נְחוּתָה. אֲנִי מְבַקֵּשׁ מִמְּךָ, תֵּן לִי לְדַבֵּר אֶל הָעָם."

40 הוּא הִרְשָׁה לוֹ. עָמַד שָׁאוּל עַל הַמַּדְרֵגוֹת וְהֵנִיף אֶת יָדוֹ אֶל הָעָם. כַּאֲשֶׁר הִשְׁתָּרֵר שֶׁקֶט מֻחְלָט נָשָׂא דְּבָרוֹ בַּשָּׂפָה הָעִבְרִית וְאָמַר:

22 "Brethren and fathers, hear my defense before you now." ²And when they heard that he spoke to them in the Hebrew language, they kept all the more silent.

Then he said: ³"I am indeed a Jew, born in Tarsus of Cilicia, but brought up in this city at the feet of Gamaliel, taught according to the strictness of our fathers' law, and was zealous toward God as you all are today. ⁴I persecuted this Way to the death, binding and delivering into prisons both men and women, ⁵as also the high priest bears me witness, and all the council of the elders, from whom I also received letters to the brethren, and went to Damascus to bring in chains even those who were there to Jerusalem to be punished.

⁶"Now it happened, as I journeyed and came near Damascus at about noon, suddenly a great light from heaven shone around me. ⁷And I fell to the ground and heard a voice saying to me, 'Saul, Saul, why are you persecuting Me?' ⁸So I answered, 'Who are You, Lord?' And He said to me, 'I am Jesus of Nazareth, whom you are persecuting.'

⁹"And those who were with me indeed saw the light and were afraid, but they did not hear the voice of Him who spoke to me. ¹⁰So I said, 'What shall I do, Lord?' And the Lord said to me, 'Arise and go into Damascus, and there you will be told all things which are appointed for you to do.' ¹¹And since I could not see for the glory of that light, being led by the hand of those who were with me, I came into Damascus.

¹²"Then a certain Ananias, a devout man according to the law, having a good testimony with all the Jews who dwelt there, ¹³came to me; and he stood and said to me, 'Brother Saul, receive your sight.' And at that same hour I looked up at him. ¹⁴Then he said, 'The God of our fathers has chosen you that you should know His will, and see the Just One, and hear the voice of His mouth. ¹⁵For you will be His witness to all men of what you have seen and heard. ¹⁶And now why are you waiting? Arise and be baptized, and wash away your sins, calling on the name of the Lord.'

¹⁷"Now it happened, when I returned to Jerusalem and was praying in the temple, that I was in a trance ¹⁸and saw Him saying to me, 'Make haste and get out of Jerusalem quickly, for they will not receive your testimony concerning Me.' ¹⁹So I said, 'Lord, they know that in every synagogue I imprisoned and beat those who believe on You. ²⁰And when the blood of Your martyr Stephen was shed, I also was standing by consenting to his death,

כב "אֲנָשִׁים אַחִים וְאָבוֹת, שִׁמְעוּ נָא כָּעֵת אֶת דְּבַר הִצְטַדְּקוּתִי לִפְנֵיכֶם" – ²כַּאֲשֶׁר שָׁמְעוּ אוֹתוֹ מְדַבֵּר אֲלֵיהֶם בַּשָּׂפָה הָעִבְרִית הָיְתָה שְׁתִיקָתָם עֲמֻקָּה יוֹתֵר, וְהוּא הִמְשִׁיךְ – ³"אִישׁ יְהוּדִי אָנִי, יְלִיד טַרְסוֹס אֲשֶׁר בְּקִילִיקְיָה, אֲבָל גֻּדַּלְתִּי בָּעִיר הַזֹּאת לְרַגְלֵי גַּמְלִיאֵל. חֻנַּכְתִּי עַל-פִּי דִקְדּוּקֵי תּוֹרַת אֲבוֹתֵינוּ וְהָיִיתִי קַנַּאי לֵאלֹהִים כְּמוֹ כֻּלְּכֶם הַיּוֹם. ⁴רָדַפְתִּי אֶת הַדֶּרֶךְ הַזֹּאת עַד מָוֶת. כָּבַלְתִּי אֲנָשִׁים וְנָשִׁים וְהִסְגַּרְתִּי אוֹתָם לְבָתֵּי כֶלֶא, ⁵דָּבָר שֶׁגַּם הַכֹּהֵן הַגָּדוֹל יָעִיד עָלַי וְכָל הַסַּנְהֶדְרִין; מֵהֶם גַּם קִבַּלְתִּי אִגְּרוֹת אֶל אַחֵינוּ, וְהָלַכְתִּי לְדַמֶּשֶׂק לַעֲצֹר אֶת הַנִּמְצָאִים שָׁם וְלַהֲבִיאָם בִּכְבָלִים לִירוּשָׁלַיִם כְּדֵי שֶׁיֵּעָנְשׁוּ. ⁶וְהִנֵּה כְּשֶׁהָלַכְתִּי וְהִתְקָרַבְתִּי לְדַמֶּשֶׂק, בִּשְׁעַת הַצָּהֳרַיִם בְּעֵרֶךְ, לְפֶתַע פִּתְאֹם נָגַהּ סְבִיבִי אוֹר גָּדוֹל מִן הַשָּׁמַיִם. ⁷נָפַלְתִּי אַרְצָה וְשָׁמַעְתִּי קוֹל אוֹמֵר אֵלַי, 'שָׁאוּל, שָׁאוּל, לָמָּה אַתָּה רוֹדֵף אוֹתִי?' ⁸שָׁאַלְתִּי, 'מִי אַתָּה, אֲדוֹנִי?' הֵשִׁיב וְאָמַר אֵלַי, 'אֲנִי יֵשׁוּעַ מִנָּצְרַת אֲשֶׁר אַתָּה רוֹדֵף.' ⁹הָאֲנָשִׁים שֶׁהָיוּ אִתִּי אָמְנָם רָאוּ אֶת הָאוֹר, אַךְ לֹא שָׁמְעוּ אֶת קוֹלוֹ שֶׁל הַמְדַבֵּר אֵלָי. ¹⁰אָמַרְתִּי, 'מֶה עָלַי לַעֲשׂוֹת, אֲדוֹנִי?' וְהָאָדוֹן אָמַר אֵלַי, 'קוּם, לֵךְ אֶל דַּמֶּשֶׂק וְשָׁם יֵאָמֵר לְךָ כָּל אֲשֶׁר יֹעַד לְךָ לַעֲשׂוֹת.' ¹¹מֵאַחַר שֶׁלֹּא יָכֹלְתִּי לִרְאוֹת מִפְּנֵי הַזֹּהַר שֶׁל אוֹתוֹ הָאוֹר, בָּאתִי לְדַמֶּשֶׂק כְּשֶׁמְּלַוַּי מוֹבִילִים אוֹתִי בְּיָד. ¹²אִישׁ אֶחָד, חֲנַנְיָה שְׁמוֹ, אִישׁ חָסִיד עַל-פִּי הַתּוֹרָה וְשֵׁם טוֹב לוֹ בְּקֶרֶב כָּל הַתּוֹשָׁבִים הַיְּהוּדִים, ¹³בָּא אֵלַי וְעָמַד לְיָדִי. אָמַר אֵלַי, 'שָׁאוּל אָחִי, רְאֵה שׁוּב!' בְּאוֹתָהּ שָׁעָה רָאִיתִי אוֹתוֹ. ¹⁴הוֹסִיף וְאָמַר, 'אֱלֹהֵי אֲבוֹתֵינוּ בָּחַר בְּךָ לָדַעַת אֶת רְצוֹנוֹ וְלִרְאוֹת אֶת הַצַּדִּיק וְלִשְׁמֹעַ קוֹל מִפִּיו, ¹⁵כִּי תִהְיֶה לּוֹ לְעֵד אֶל כָּל בְּנֵי אָדָם עַל הַדְּבָרִים אֲשֶׁר רָאִיתָ וְשָׁמַעְתָּ. ¹⁶וְעַכְשָׁו לָמָּה אַתָּה מִתְמַהְמֵהַּ? קוּם, הִטָּבֵל וְהִתְרַחֵץ מֵחֲטָאֶיךָ בְּקָרְאֲךָ בִּשְׁמוֹ.' ¹⁷כַּאֲשֶׁר חָזַרְתִּי לִירוּשָׁלַיִם וְהִתְפַּלַּלְתִּי בַּמִּקְדָּשׁ הָיְתָה עָלַי יַד-יהוה ¹⁸וְרָאִיתִי אוֹתוֹ אוֹמֵר אֵלַי, 'הִזְדָּרֵז וְצֵא מַהֵר מִירוּשָׁלַיִם, כִּי לֹא יְקַבְּלוּ אֶת עֵדוּתְךָ עָלַי.' ¹⁹וַאֲנִי אָמַרְתִּי, 'אֲדוֹנִי, הֲרֵי הֵם יוֹדְעִים שֶׁאֲנִי הִשְׁלַכְתִּי אֶת הַמַּאֲמִינִים בְּךָ לַכֶּלֶא וְהִלְקֵיתִים בְּבָתֵּי הַכְּנֶסֶת; ²⁰וְכַאֲשֶׁר נִשְׁפַּךְ דַּם

and guarding the clothes of those who were killing
him.' 21 Then He said to me, 'Depart, for I will send
you far from here to the Gentiles.' "

22 And they listened to him until this word, and
then they raised their voices and said, "Away with
such a *fellow* from the earth, for he is not fit to
live!" 23 Then, as they cried out and tore off *their*
clothes and threw dust into the air, 24 the commander ordered him to be brought into the barracks,
and said that he should be examined under
scourging, so that he might know why they shouted
so against him. 25 And as they bound him with
thongs, Paul said to the centurion who stood by, "Is
it lawful for you to scourge a man who is a Roman,
and uncondemned?"

26 When the centurion heard *that,* he went and
told the commander, saying, "Take care what you
do, for this man is a Roman."

27 Then the commander came and said to him,
"Tell me, are you a Roman?"

He said, "Yes."

28 The commander answered, "With a large sum I
obtained this citizenship."

And Paul said, "But I was born *a citizen.*"

29 Then immediately those who were about to
examine him withdrew from him; and the commander was also afraid after he found out that he was a
Roman, and because he had bound him.

30 The next day, because he wanted to know for
certain why he was accused by the Jews, he released
him from *his* bonds, and commanded the chief
priests and all their council to appear, and brought
Paul down and set him before them.

23 Then Paul, looking earnestly at the council,
said, "Men *and* brethren, I have lived in all good
conscience before God until this day." 2 And the
high priest Ananias commanded those who stood
by him to strike him on the mouth. 3 Then Paul said
to him, "God will strike you, *you* whitewashed wall!
For you sit to judge me according to the law, and
do you command me to be struck contrary to the
law?"

4 And those who stood by said, "Do you revile
God's high priest?"

5 Then Paul said, "I did not know, brethren, that
he was the high priest; for it is written, '*You shall
not speak evil of a ruler of your people.*'"

6 But when Paul perceived that one part were
Sadducees and the other Pharisees, he cried out in
the council, "Men *and* brethren, I am a Pharisee,
the son of a Pharisee; concerning the hope and
resurrection of the dead I am being judged!"

סְטֶפָנוֹס עָדֶךְ – אַף אֲנִי עָמַדְתִּי שָׁם בְּהַסְכָּמָה
לְמַעֲשֶׂה וְשָׁמַרְתִּי אֶת הַבְּגָדִים שֶׁל הוֹרְגָיו.' 21 אַךְ
הוּא אָמַר אֵלַי, 'לֵךְ, כִּי אֲנִי אֶשְׁלַח אוֹתְךָ הַרְחֵק –
אֶל הַגּוֹיִים.'"

22 עַד לַדָּבָר הַזֶּה הִקְשִׁיבוּ אֵלָיו וְאָז הֵרִימוּ קוֹלָם
וְקָרְאוּ: "הָסֵר מֵעַל הָאֲדָמָה אֶחָד שֶׁכָּזֶה! הוּא לֹא
רָאוּי לִחְיוֹת!" 23 הֵם צָעֲקוּ, הִשְׁלִיכוּ אֶת בִּגְדֵיהֶם
וְהֵטִילוּ עָפָר בָּאֲוִיר. 24 כִּתְגוּבָה צִוָּה שַׂר הָאֶלֶף
לְהָבִיא אֶל תּוֹךְ הַמְּצוּדָה וְהוֹרָה לַחֲקֹר אוֹתוֹ
בְּמַלְקוֹת כְּדֵי לְבָרֵר מַדּוּעַ צָעֲקוּ עָלָיו כָּךְ. 25 אֲבָל
בְּעֵת שֶׁקָּשְׁרוּ אוֹתוֹ בִּרְצוּעוֹת אָמַר שָׁאוּל אֶל שַׂר
הַמֵּאָה הָעוֹמֵד לְיָדוֹ: "הַאִם מֻתָּר לָכֶם לְהַלְקוֹת
אֶזְרָח רוֹמִי בְּלֹא מִשְׁפָּט?" 26 שָׁמַע שַׂר הַמֵּאָה, הָלַךְ
אֶל שַׂר הָאֶלֶף וְאָמַר לוֹ: "מָה אַתָּה עוֹמֵד לַעֲשׂוֹת?
הֲרֵי הָאִישׁ הַזֶּה רוֹמִי!" 27 בָּא שַׂר הָאֶלֶף וְאָמַר
אֵלָיו: "הַגֵּד לִי, הַאִם אַתָּה רוֹמִי?"
הֵשִׁיב שָׁאוּל: "כֵּן."

28 אָמַר שַׂר הָאֶלֶף: "אֲנִי בְּכֶסֶף רַב קָנִיתִי אֶת
הָאֶזְרָחוּת הַזֹּאת."

אָמַר שָׁאוּל: "אֲבָל אֲנִי נוֹלַדְתִּי בָּהּ." 29 כָּאוֹתוֹ רֶגַע
הִרְפּוּ מִמֶּנּוּ הָאֲנָשִׁים שֶׁעָמְדוּ לַחֲקֹר אוֹתוֹ; אֲפִלּוּ שַׂר
הָאֶלֶף פָּחַד כְּשֶׁנּוֹכַח כִּי הוּא רוֹמִי וְכִי כָּבַל אוֹתוֹ.
30 לְמָחֳרָת, כֵּיוָן שֶׁרָצָה לָדַעַת נְכוֹנָה מַדּוּעַ
הֶאֱשִׁימוּהוּ בְּנֵי עַמּוֹ, הִתִּיר אֶת כְּבָלָיו וְצִוָּה עַל
רָאשֵׁי הַכֹּהֲנִים וְכָל הַסַּנְהֶדְרִין לְהִתְאַסֵּף. הוּא הֵבִיא
אֶת שָׁאוּל וְהֶעֱמִידוֹ לִפְנֵיהֶם.

כג הִבִּיט שָׁאוּל בַּסַּנְהֶדְרִין וְאָמַר: "אֲנָשִׁים אַחִים,
אֲנִי בְּמַצְפּוּן נָקִי לְגַמְרֵי הִתְהַלַּכְתִּי לִפְנֵי הָאֱלֹהִים עַד
הַיּוֹם הַזֶּה." 2 אָז צִוָּה חֲנַנְיָה הַכֹּהֵן הַגָּדוֹל עַל
הָעוֹמְדִים לְיָדוֹ לְהַכּוֹתוֹ עַל פִּיו. 3 אָמַר לוֹ שָׁאוּל:
"עָתִיד אֱלֹהִים לְהַכּוֹת אוֹתְךָ, קִיר מְטֻיָּח שֶׁכְּמוֹתְךָ!
אַתָּה יוֹשֵׁב לִשְׁפֹּט אוֹתִי עַל-פִּי הַתּוֹרָה וּמְצַוֶּה
לְהַכּוֹתֵנִי שֶׁלֹּא כַּתּוֹרָה?"

4 אָמְרוּ הָעוֹמְדִים לְיָדוֹ: "אֶת הַכֹּהֵן הַגָּדוֹל לֵאלֹהִים
אַתָּה מְחָרֵף?"

5 הֵשִׁיב שָׁאוּל: "אַחַי, לֹא יָדַעְתִּי שֶׁהוּא הַכֹּהֵן
הַגָּדוֹל; הֵן כָּתוּב 'נָשִׂיא בְעַמְּךָ לֹא תָאֹר.'"

6 הוֹאִיל וְשָׁאוּל יָדַע כִּי חֵלֶק מֵהֶם צְדוֹקִים וְחֵלֶק
פְּרוּשִׁים הִכְרִיז לִפְנֵי הַסַּנְהֶדְרִין: "אֲנָשִׁים אַחִים,
פָּרוּשׁ בֶּן-פָּרוּשׁ אָנֹכִי וְעַל הַתִּקְוָה לִתְחִיַּת הַמֵּתִים

7 And when he had said this, a dissension arose between the Pharisees and the Sadducees; and the assembly was divided. 8 For Sadducees say that there is no resurrection—and no angel or spirit; but the Pharisees confess both. 9 Then there arose a loud outcry. And the scribes of the Pharisees' party arose and protested, saying, "We find no evil in this man; but if a spirit or an angel has spoken to him, let us not fight against God."

10 Now when there arose a great dissension, the commander, fearing lest Paul might be pulled to pieces by them, commanded the soldiers to go down and take him by force from among them, and bring *him* into the barracks.

11 But the following night the Lord stood by him and said, "Be of good cheer, Paul; for as you have testified for Me in Jerusalem, so you must also bear witness at Rome."

12 And when it was day, some of the Jews banded together and bound themselves under an oath, saying that they would neither eat nor drink till they had killed Paul. 13 Now there were more than forty who had formed this conspiracy. 14 They came to the chief priests and elders, and said, "We have bound ourselves under a great oath that we will eat nothing until we have killed Paul. 15 Now you, therefore, together with the council, suggest to the commander that he be brought down to you tomorrow, as though you were going to make further inquiries concerning him; but we are ready to kill him before he comes near."

16 So when Paul's sister's son heard of their ambush, he went and entered the barracks and told Paul. 17 Then Paul called one of the centurions to *him* and said, "Take this young man to the commander, for he has something to tell him." 18 So he took him and brought *him* to the commander and said, "Paul the prisoner called me to *him* and asked *me* to bring this young man to you. He has something to say to you."

19 Then the commander took him by the hand, went aside, and asked privately, "What is it that you have to tell me?"

20 And he said, "The Jews have agreed to ask that you bring Paul down to the council tomorrow, as though they were going to inquire more fully about him. 21 But do not yield to them, for more than forty of them lie in wait for him, men who have bound themselves by an oath that they will neither eat nor drink till they have killed him; and now they are ready, waiting for the promise from you."

22 So the commander let the young man depart, and commanded *him*, "Tell no one that you have revealed these things to me."

אֲנִי נִשְׁפָּט!" 7 כַּאֲשֶׁר אָמַר זֹאת הֶחֱלָה הַתִּנְצְחוּת בֵּין הַפְּרוּשִׁים לַצְּדוֹקִים וְהַקָּהָל נִתְפַּלֵּג לִשְׁנַיִם, 8 כִּי הַצְּדוֹקִים אוֹמְרִים שֶׁאֵין תְּחִיָּה וְאֵין מַלְאָךְ וְאֵין רוּחַ, אַךְ הַפְּרוּשִׁים מוֹדִים בְּכָל אֵלֶּה. 9 הָיְתָה הַמִּלָּה גְדוֹלָה וְאָז קָמוּ סוֹפְרִים אֲחָדִים מִכַּת הַפְּרוּשִׁים וְטָעֲנוּ בְּתֹקֶף: אֵין אָנוּ מוֹצְאִים שׁוּם רַע בָּאִישׁ הַזֶּה. וְאִם רוּחַ דִּבְּרָה אֵלָיו אוֹ מַלְאָךְ [אַל נִלָּחֵם בֵּאלֹהִים]." 10 הַהִתְנַצְחוּת גָּבְרָה מְאֹד וְשַׂר הָאֶלֶף חָשַׁשׁ שֶׁמָּא יְשַׁסְּעוּ אֶת שָׁאוּל. לְפִיכָךְ צִוָּה עַל הַחַיָּלִים לָרֶדֶת וְלַחֲטֹף אוֹתוֹ מִתּוֹכָם וְלַהֲבִיאוֹ אֶל הַמְּצוּדָה.

11 בַּלַּיְלָה נִצַּב הָאָדוֹן עַל שָׁאוּל וְאָמַר: "הִתְחַזֵּק! כְּמוֹ שֶׁהֵעִידוֹתָ עָלַי בִּירוּשָׁלַיִם כָּךְ עָלֶיךָ לְהָעִיד גַּם בְּרוֹמָא."

12 בַּבֹּקֶר חָבְרוּ יְהוּדִים יַחַד וְקִבְּלוּ עֲלֵיהֶם בִּשְׁבוּעָה שֶׁלֹּא יֹאכְלוּ וְלֹא יִשְׁתּוּ עַד אֲשֶׁר יַהַרְגוּ אֶת שָׁאוּל. 13 מִסְפַּר הַמִּשְׁתַּתְּפִים בַּמְּזִמָּה הַזֹּאת עָלָה עַל אַרְבָּעִים. 14 הֵם בָּאוּ אֶל רָאשֵׁי הַכֹּהֲנִים וְאֶל הַזְּקֵנִים וְאָמְרוּ: "קִבַּלְנוּ עָלֵינוּ שְׁבוּעָה שֶׁלֹּא לִטְעֹם מְאוּמָה עַד שֶׁנַּהֲרֹג אֶת שָׁאוּל. 15 וְעַכְשָׁו אַתֶּם וְהַסַּנְהֶדְרִין הַגִּידוּ לְשַׂר הָאֶלֶף שֶׁיּוֹרִיד אוֹתוֹ אֲלֵיכֶם, כְּאִלּוּ שֶׁכַּוָּנַתְכֶם לְבָרֵר בְּיֶתֶר דִּיּוּק אֶת עִנְיָנוֹ, וַאֲנַחְנוּ מוּכָנִים לַהֲרֹג אוֹתוֹ לִפְנֵי שֶׁיַּגִּיעַ."

16 כַּאֲשֶׁר שָׁמַע בֶּן אֲחוֹתוֹ שֶׁל שָׁאוּל עַל־דְּבַר הַמַּאֲרָב הָלַךְ וְנִכְנַס לַמְּצוּדָה וְהוֹדִיעַ לְשָׁאוּל. 17 קָרָא שָׁאוּל לְאֶחָד מִשָּׂרֵי הַמֵּאוֹת וְאָמַר: "הָבֵא נָא אֶת הַבָּחוּר הַזֶּה אֶל שַׂר הָאֶלֶף, כִּי יֶשׁ לוֹ דָּבָר לְהוֹדִיעוֹ." 18 הוּא הֵבִיא אוֹתוֹ אֶל שַׂר הָאֶלֶף וְאָמַר: "הָאָסִיר שָׁאוּל קָרָא לִי וּבִקֵּשׁ מִמֶּנִּי לְהָבִיא אֵלֶיךָ אֶת הַבָּחוּר הַזֶּה, כִּי יֶשׁ לוֹ אֵיזֶה דָּבָר לוֹמַר לָךְ."

19 הֶחֱזִיק שַׂר הָאֶלֶף בְּיָדוֹ, הוֹבִיל אוֹתוֹ הַצִּדָּה וְשָׁאַל: "מַה יֶּשׁ לְךָ לְהוֹדִיעַ לִי?" 20 הֵשִׁיב הַבָּחוּר: "רָאשֵׁי הַיְּהוּדִים נוֹעֲצוּ יַחְדָּיו לְבַקֵּשׁ מִמְּךָ לְהוֹרִיד מָחָר אֶת שָׁאוּל אֶל הַסַּנְהֶדְרִין כְּאִלּוּ הֵם מִתְכַּוְּנִים לַחֲקֹר אֶת עִנְיָנוֹ בְּיֶתֶר דִּיּוּק. 21 לָכֵן אַל נָא תִשְׁמַע לָהֶם, כִּי יוֹתֵר מֵאַרְבָּעִים אִישׁ מֵהֶם אוֹרְבִים לוֹ. הַלָּלוּ קִבְּלוּ עֲלֵיהֶם בִּשְׁבוּעָה שֶׁלֹּא לֶאֱכֹל וְלֹא לִשְׁתּוֹת עַד שֶׁיַּהַרְגוּ אוֹתוֹ וְכָעֵת הֵם מוּכָנִים בְּצִפִּיָּה לְהַבְטָחָה מִמְּךָ."

22 שִׁלַּח שַׂר הָאֶלֶף אֶת הַבָּחוּר בְּצַוּוֹתוֹ עָלָיו: "אַל תַּגִּיד לְאִישׁ שֶׁהוֹדַעְתָּ לִי אֶת הַדָּבָר הַזֶּה!"

23 And he called for two centurions, saying, "Prepare two hundred soldiers, seventy horsemen, and two hundred spearmen to go to Caesarea at the third hour of the night; 24 and provide mounts to set Paul on, and bring *him* safely to Felix the governor." 25 He wrote a letter in the following manner:

26   Claudius Lysias,

     To the most excellent governor Felix:

     Greetings.

27   This man was seized by the Jews and was about to be killed by them. Coming with the troops I rescued him, having learned that he was a Roman. 28 And when I wanted to know the reason they accused him, I brought him before their council. 29 I found out that he was accused concerning questions of their law, but had nothing charged against him deserving of death or chains. 30 And when it was told me that the Jews lay in wait for the man, I sent him immediately to you, and also commanded his accusers to state before you the charges against him.

     Farewell.

31 Then the soldiers, as they were commanded, took Paul and brought *him* by night to Antipatris. 32 The next day they left the horsemen to go on with him, and returned to the barracks. 33 When they came to Caesarea and had delivered the letter to the governor, they also presented Paul to him. 34 And when the governor had read *it,* he asked what province he was from. And when he understood that *he was* from Cilicia, 35 he said, "I will hear you when your accusers also have come." And he commanded him to be kept in Herod's Praetorium.

24 Now after five days Ananias the high priest came down with the elders and a certain orator *named* Tertullus. These gave evidence to the governor against Paul.

2 And when he was called upon, Tertullus began his accusation, saying: "Seeing that through you we enjoy great peace, and prosperity is being brought to this nation by your foresight, 3 we accept *it* always and in all places, most noble Felix, with all thankfulness. 4 Nevertheless, not to be tedious to you any further, I beg you to hear, by your courtesy, a few words from us. 5 For we have found this man a plague, a creator of dissension among all the Jews throughout the world, and a ringleader of the sect of the Nazarenes. 6 He even tried to profane

the temple, and we seized him, and wanted to judge him according to our law. [7] But the commander Lysias came by and with great violence took *him* out of our hands, [8] commanding his accusers to come to you. By examining him yourself you may ascertain all these things of which we accuse him." [9] And the Jews also assented, maintaining that these things were so.

[10] Then Paul, after the governor had nodded to him to speak, answered: "Inasmuch as I know that you have been for many years a judge of this nation, I do the more cheerfully answer for myself, [11] because you may ascertain that it is no more than twelve days since I went up to Jerusalem to worship. [12] And they neither found me in the temple disputing with anyone nor inciting the crowd, either in the synagogues or in the city. [13] Nor can they prove the things of which they now accuse me. [14] But this I confess to you, that according to the Way which they call a sect, so I worship the God of my fathers, believing all things which are written in the Law and in the Prophets. [15] I have hope in God, which they themselves also accept, that there will be a resurrection of *the* dead, both of *the* just and *the* unjust. [16] This *being* so, I myself always strive to have a conscience without offense toward God and men.

[17] "Now after many years I came to bring alms and offerings to my nation, [18] in the midst of which some Jews from Asia found me purified in the temple, neither with a mob nor with tumult. [19] They ought to have been here before you to object if they had anything against me. [20] Or else let those who are *here* themselves say if they found any wrongdoing in me while I stood before the council, [21] unless *it is* for this one statement which I cried out, standing among them, 'Concerning the resurrection of the dead I am being judged by you this day.'"

[22] But when Felix heard these things, having more accurate knowledge of *the* Way, he adjourned the proceedings and said, "When Lysias the commander comes down, I will make a decision on your case." [23] So he commanded the centurion to keep Paul and to let *him* have liberty, and told him not to forbid any of his friends to provide for or visit him.

[24] And after some days, when Felix came with his wife Drusilla, who was Jewish, he sent for Paul and heard him concerning the faith in Christ. [25] Now as he reasoned about righteousness, self-control, and the judgment to come, Felix was afraid and answered, "Go away for now; when I have a convenient time I will call for you." [26] Meanwhile he

אֶת הַמִּקְדָּשׁ, אַךְ תְּפַסְנוּ אוֹתוֹ. [8] אִם תַּחְקֹר אוֹתוֹ תּוּכַל לָדַעַת בְּעַצְמְךָ מַה כָּל הַדְּבָרִים שֶׁבָּהֶם אֲנַחְנוּ מַאֲשִׁימִים אוֹתוֹ." [9] גַּם הַיְּהוּדִים הָעוֹמְדִים שָׁם הִסְכִּימוּ אִתּוֹ, בְּאָמְרָם שֶׁכָּךְ הֵם הַדְּבָרִים.

[10] רָמַז הַנָּצִיב לְשָׁאוּל לְדַבֵּר וְשָׁאוּל הֵשִׁיב: "אֲנִי יוֹדֵעַ כִּי שָׁנִים רַבּוֹת אַתָּה הַשּׁוֹפֵט שֶׁל הָאֻמָּה הַזֹּאת, לָכֵן בְּבִטָּחוֹן אֲנִי מֵגֵן עַל עַצְמִי בְּכָל מַה שֶּׁנּוֹגֵעַ לְעִנְיָנִי. [11] יָכוֹל אַתָּה לְהִוָּכַח שֶׁלֹּא עָבְרוּ יוֹתֵר מִשְּׁנֵים־עָשָׂר יוֹם מֵאָז שֶׁעָלִיתִי לִירוּשָׁלַיִם לְהִשְׁתַּחֲווֹת לַאֲדֹנָי, [12] וְלֹא בְּבֵית הַמִּקְדָּשׁ מְצָאוּנִי מִתְוַכֵּחַ עִם אִישׁ אוֹ גּוֹרֵם לְהִתְפָּרְעוּת הָמוֹן, אַף לֹא בְּבָתֵּי כְנֶסֶת וְלֹא בָעִיר. [13] גַּם אֵינָם יְכוֹלִים לְהָבִיא לְךָ רְאָיָה לַדְּבָרִים שֶׁהֵם טוֹעֲנִים נֶגְדִּי כָּעֵת. [14] אֲבָל אֶת זֶה אֲנִי מוֹדֶה לְפָנֶיךָ: בַּדֶּרֶךְ הַנִּקְרֵאת בְּפִיהֶם 'כַּת' עוֹבֵד אֲנִי אֶת אֱלֹהֵי אֲבוֹתֵינוּ, וּמַאֲמִין בְּכָל הַכָּתוּב בַּתּוֹרָה וּבַנְּבִיאִים; [15] וְיֵשׁ לִי תִּקְוָה בֵּאלֹהִים שֶׁתִּהְיֶה תְּחִיָּה הֵן שֶׁל הַצַּדִּיקִים וְהֵן שֶׁל הָרְשָׁעִים, דָּבָר שֶׁגַּם הֵם מְחַכִּים לוֹ. [16] לָכֵן אֲנִי גַּם מִתְאַמֵּץ שֶׁתִּהְיֶה לִי מַצְפּוּן נָקִי לִפְנֵי אֱלֹהִים וּבְנֵי אָדָם בְּכָל עֵת. [17] וְהִנֵּה אַחֲרֵי שָׁנִים רַבּוֹת בָּאתִי לְהָבִיא נְדָבוֹת לְעַמִּי וְכֵן גַּם קָרְבָּנוֹת, [18] וּבַהֲבִיאִי אֶת אֵלֶּה מְצָאוּנִי בַּמִּקְדָּשׁ לְאַחַר שֶׁנִּטְהַרְתִּי; לֹא הָיִיתִי כָּרוּךְ לֹא בֶּהָמוֹן וְלֹא בִּמְהוּמָה. [19] אֲבָל הָיוּ כַּמָּה יְהוּדִים מֵאַסְיָה וְהַלָּלוּ הָיוּ צְרִיכִים לַעֲמֹד לְפָנֶיךָ וּלְהַאֲשִׁימֵנִי אִם יֵשׁ לָהֶם מַשֶּׁהוּ נֶגְדִּי. [20] אוֹ שֶׁיַּגִּידוּ אֵלֶּה אֲשֶׁר כָּאן, אֵיזֶה עָוֶל מָצְאוּ בִּי כַּאֲשֶׁר עָמַדְתִּי לִפְנֵי הַסַּנְהֶדְרִין – [21] מִלְּבַד הַהַכְרָזָה הָאַחַת הַזֹּאת שֶׁהִכְרַזְתִּי בְּעָמְדִי בֵּינֵיהֶם: 'עַל תְּחִיַּת הַמֵּתִים אֲנִי נִשְׁפָּט הַיּוֹם לִפְנֵיכֶם.'" [22] פֶלִיקְס, שֶׁהָיְתָה לוֹ יְדִיעָה בְּרוּרָה עַל אוֹתָהּ דֶּרֶךְ, דָּחָה אֶת הַדִּיּוּן בְּעִנְיָנָם בְּאָמְרוֹ: "כַּאֲשֶׁר יֵרֵד אֵלַי לִיסִיאַס שַׂר הָאֶלֶף אַחֲלִיט בְּנוֹגֵעַ לְעִנְיַנְכֶם." [23] הוּא צִוָּה עַל שַׂר הַמֵּאָה לָשִׂים עַל שָׁאוּל מִשְׁמָר, אַךְ לְהָקֵל עָלָיו וְלֹא לִמְנֹעַ אִישׁ מֵאֲנָשָׁיו מִלְּשָׁרֵת אוֹתוֹ.

[24] אַחֲרֵי כַּמָּה יָמִים בָּא פֶלִיקְס עִם דְּרוּסִילָה אִשְׁתּוֹ, שֶׁהָיְתָה יְהוּדִיָּה. הוּא שָׁלַח לִקְרֹא לְשָׁאוּל וְשָׁמַע אוֹתוֹ עַל־דְּבַר הָאֱמוּנָה בַּמָּשִׁיחַ יֵשׁוּעַ. [25] כְּשֶׁדִּבֵּר עַל הַצֶּדֶק וְעַל כִּבּוּשׁ הַיֵּצֶר וְעַל הַדִּין הֶעָתִיד לָבוֹא, פָּחַד פֶלִיקְס וְאָמַר: "לֵךְ לְעֵת עַתָּה, אֲבָל כְּשֶׁאֶמְצָא לִי פְּנַאי אֶקְרָא לְךָ." [26] בְּאָמְרוֹ זֹאת גַּם קִוָּה שֶׁשָּׁאוּל

also hoped that money would be given him by Paul, that he might release him. Therefore he sent for him more often and conversed with him.

27 But after two years Porcius Festus succeeded Felix; and Felix, wanting to do the Jews a favor, left Paul bound.

25 Now when Festus had come to the province, after three days he went up from Caesarea to Jerusalem. 2 Then the high priest and the chief men of the Jews informed him against Paul; and they petitioned him, 3 asking a favor against him, that he would summon him to Jerusalem—while *they* lay in ambush along the road to kill him. 4 But Festus answered that Paul should be kept at Caesarea, and that he himself was going *there* shortly. 5 "Therefore," he said, "let those who have authority among you go down with *me* and accuse this man, to see if there is any fault in him."

6 And when he had remained among them more than ten days, he went down to Caesarea. And the next day, sitting on the judgment seat, he commanded Paul to be brought. 7 When he had come, the Jews who had come down from Jerusalem stood about and laid many serious complaints against Paul, which they could not prove, 8 while he answered for himself, "Neither against the law of the Jews, nor against the temple, nor against Caesar have I offended in anything at all."

9 But Festus, wanting to do the Jews a favor, answered Paul and said, "Are you willing to go up to Jerusalem and there be judged before me concerning these things?"

10 So Paul said, "I stand at Caesar's judgment seat, where I ought to be judged. To the Jews I have done no wrong, as you very well know. 11 For if I am an offender, or have committed anything deserving of death, I do not object to dying; but if there is nothing in these things of which these men accuse me, no one can deliver me to them. I appeal to Caesar."

12 Then Festus, when he had conferred with the council, answered, "You have appealed to Caesar? To Caesar you shall go!"

13 And after some days King Agrippa and Bernice came to Caesarea to greet Festus. 14 When they had been there many days, Festus laid Paul's case before the king, saying: "There is a certain man left a prisoner by Felix, 15 about whom the chief priests and the elders of the Jews informed *me*, when I was in Jerusalem, asking for a judgment against him. 16 To them I answered, 'It is not the custom of the Romans to deliver any man to

יִתֶּן לוֹ כֶּסֶף; לָכֵן קָרָא לוֹ פְּעָמִים רַבּוֹת וְשׂוֹחֵחַ אִתּוֹ. 27 אַחֲרֵי שְׁנָתַיִם יָרַשׁ פּוֹרְקִיּוֹס פֶסְטוּס אֶת מְקוֹמוֹ שֶׁל פֵלִיקָס. רָצָה פֵלִיקָס לְהַרְאוֹת חֶסֶד לְרָאשֵׁי הַיְּהוּדִים וְעָזַב אֶת שָׁאוּל בַּמַּאֲסָר.

כה פֶסְטוּס הִגִּיעַ לַמְּדִינָה וּלְאַחַר שְׁלוֹשָׁה יָמִים עָלָה מִקֵּיסַרְיָה לִירוּשָׁלַיִם. 2 שָׁם הוֹדִיעוּ לוֹ רָאשֵׁי הַכֹּהֲנִים וְרָאשֵׁי הַיְּהוּדִים אֶת עִנְיָנָם נֶגֶד שָׁאוּל. 3 הֵם הִפְצִירוּ בּוֹ וּבִקְשׁוּ מִמֶּנּוּ שֶׁיַּעֲשֶׂה עִמָּהֶם חֶסֶד וְיִשְׁלַח לַהֲבִיאוֹ לִירוּשָׁלַיִם, שֶׁכֵּן הֵם הִתְנַכְּלוּ לוֹ לְהָרְגוֹ בַּדֶּרֶךְ. 4 הֵשִׁיב פֶסְטוּס וְאָמַר: "שָׁאוּל עָצוּר בְּקֵיסַרְיָה וַאֲנִי עוֹמֵד לָצֵאת לְשָׁם בְּקָרוֹב. 5 לָכֵן יֵרְדוּ נָא אִתִּי בַּעֲלֵי הַסַּמְכוּת שֶׁבָּכֶם; וְאִם יֵשׁ עָוֹן בָּאִישׁ, שִׁיטְעֲנוּ נֶגְדּוֹ."

6 הוּא שָׁהָה שָׁם לֹא יוֹתֵר מִשְּׁמוֹנָה אוֹ עֲשָׂרָה יָמִים. לְאַחַר מִכֵּן יָרַד לְקֵיסַרְיָה וּלְמָחֳרַת יָשַׁב עַל כֵּס הַמִּשְׁפָּט וְצִוָּה לְהָבִיא אֶת שָׁאוּל. 7 כַּאֲשֶׁר בָּא נִצְּבוּ סְבִיבוֹ הַיְּהוּדִים שֶׁיָּרְדוּ מִירוּשָׁלַיִם, וְהֶאֱשִׁימוּ אוֹתוֹ בַּאֲשָׁמוֹת רַבּוֹת וְקָשׁוֹת אֲשֶׁר לֹא יָכְלוּ לְהוֹכִיחַ אוֹתָן. 8 הֵגֵן שָׁאוּל עַל עַצְמוֹ וְאָמַר: "לֹא חָטָאתִי בִּמְאוּמָה לְחֻקֵּי הַיְּהוּדִים, אַף לֹא לַמִּקְדָּשׁ וְלֹא לַקֵּיסָר." 9 אַךְ פֶסְטוּס, בְּחָפְצוֹ לְהַרְאוֹת חֶסֶד לְרָאשֵׁי הַיְּהוּדִים, פָּנָה אֶל שָׁאוּל וְשָׁאַל: "הַאִם אַתָּה רוֹצֶה לַעֲלוֹת לִירוּשָׁלַיִם וּלְהִשָּׁפֵט שָׁם לְפָנַי עַל הַדְּבָרִים הָאֵלֶּה?"

10 עָנָה שָׁאוּל: "לִפְנֵי כֵּס הַמִּשְׁפָּט שֶׁל הַקֵּיסָר אֲנִי עוֹמֵד וְשָׁם עָלַי לְהִשָּׁפֵט. לֹא עָשִׂיתִי עָוֶל לְאַף יְהוּדִי, וְזֹאת גַּם אַתָּה יוֹדֵעַ הֵיטֵב. 11 אִם אָמְנָם גָּרַמְתִּי עָוֶל וְעָשִׂיתִי דָּבָר הַמְחַיֵּב מָוֶת אֵינֶנִּי מְסָרֵב לָמוּת. אֲבָל אִם אֵין מְאוּמָה בְּמַה שֶׁאֵלֶּה מַאֲשִׁימִים אוֹתִי, אִישׁ לֹא יוּכַל לְהַסְגִּירֵנִי בְּיָדָם. אֶל הַקֵּיסָר אֲנִי פּוֹנֶה!" 12 נוֹעַץ פֶסְטוּס עִם הַיּוֹעֲצִים וְהֵשִׁיב: "פָּנִיתָ אֶל הַקֵּיסָר, אֶל הַקֵּיסָר תֵּלֵךְ."

13 יָמִים מִסְפָּר אַחֲרֵי כֵן בָּאוּ אַגְרִיפַּס הַמֶּלֶךְ וּבֶרְנִיקָה לְקֵיסַרְיָה לְבָרֵךְ אֶת פֶסְטוּס. 14 כְּרֹבוֹת יְמֵי שְׁהִיָּתָם שָׁם סִפֵּר פֶסְטוּס לַמֶּלֶךְ עַל-אוֹדוֹת שָׁאוּל וְאָמַר: "יֵשׁ אִישׁ אֶחָד אֲשֶׁר פֵלִיקָס הִשְׁאִיר אוֹתוֹ בַּמַּאֲסָר. 15 כַּאֲשֶׁר הָיִיתִי בִּירוּשָׁלַיִם הוֹדִיעוּ לִי רָאשֵׁי הַכֹּהֲנִים וְזִקְנֵי הַיְּהוּדִים עַל-אוֹדוֹתָיו וּבִקְשׁוּ אֶת הַרְשָׁעָתוֹ. 16 אָמַרְתִּי לָהֶם שֶׁאֵין הָרוֹמִים נוֹהֲגִים

destruction before the accused meets the accusers face to face, and has opportunity to answer for himself concerning the charge against him.' ¹⁷ Therefore when they had come together, without any delay, the next day I sat on the judgment seat and commanded the man to be brought in. ¹⁸ When the accusers stood up, they brought no accusation against him of such things as I supposed, ¹⁹ but had some questions against him about their own religion and about a certain Jesus, who had died, whom Paul affirmed to be alive. ²⁰ And because I was uncertain of such questions, I asked whether he was willing to go to Jerusalem and there be judged concerning these matters. ²¹ But when Paul appealed to be reserved for the decision of Augustus, I commanded him to be kept till I could send him to Caesar."

²² Then Agrippa said to Festus, "I also would like to hear the man myself."

"Tomorrow," he said, "you shall hear him."

²³ So the next day, when Agrippa and Bernice had come with great pomp, and had entered the auditorium with the commanders and the prominent men of the city, at Festus' command Paul was brought in. ²⁴ And Festus said: "King Agrippa and all the men who are here present with us, you see this man about whom the whole assembly of the Jews petitioned me, both at Jerusalem and here, crying out that he was not fit to live any longer. ²⁵ But when I found that he had committed nothing deserving of death, and that he himself had appealed to Augustus, I decided to send him. ²⁶ I have nothing certain to write to my lord concerning him. Therefore I have brought him out before you, and especially before you, King Agrippa, so that after the examination has taken place I may have something to write. ²⁷ For it seems to me unreasonable to send a prisoner and not to specify the charges against him."

26

Then Agrippa said to Paul, "You are permitted to speak for yourself."

So Paul stretched out his hand and answered for himself: ² "I think myself happy, King Agrippa, because today I shall answer for myself before you concerning all the things of which I am accused by the Jews, ³ especially because you are expert in all customs and questions which have to do with the Jews. Therefore I beg you to hear me patiently.

⁴ "My manner of life from my youth, which was spent from the beginning among my own nation at Jerusalem, all the Jews know. ⁵ They knew me from the first, if they were willing to testify, that according to the strictest sect of our religion I lived

---

לְהַסְגִּיר אָדָם נֶאֱשָׁם בְּטֶרֶם יַעֲמֹד מוּל הַמַּאֲשִׁימִים וְתִנָּתֵן לוֹ אֶפְשָׁרוּת לְהָגֵן עַל עַצְמוֹ מִפְּנֵי הָהַאֲשָׁמָה. ¹⁷ לָכֵן כְּשֶׁבָּאוּ יַחַד הֵנָּה לֹא הִתְמַהְמַהְתִּי, וּלְמָחֳרָת יָשַׁבְתִּי עַל כֵּס הַמִּשְׁפָּט וְצִוִּיתִי לְהָבִיא אֶת הָאִישׁ. ¹⁸ אָז עָמְדוּ מַאֲשִׁימָיו וְלֹא הֵבִיאוּ נֶגְדּוֹ דָּבָר מִן הַדְּבָרִים הָרָעִים שֶׁחָשַׁדְתִּי. ¹⁹ אַךְ הָיוּ לָהֶם כַּמָּה חִלּוּקֵי דֵעוֹת אִתּוֹ עַל הֲדַת שֶׁלָּהֶם וְעַל אֵיזֶה יֵשׁוּעַ שֶׁמֵּת, אֲשֶׁר שָׁאוּל טָעַן שֶׁהוּא חַי. ²⁰ אֲנִי לֹא הִתְמַצֵּאתִי בַּחֲקִירַת הָעִנְיָנִים הָאֵלֶּה וְשָׁאַלְתִּי אִם הוּא רוֹצֶה לַעֲלוֹת לִירוּשָׁלַיִם וּלְהִשָּׁפֵט שָׁם עַל הַדְּבָרִים הָאֵלֶּה. ²¹ אַךְ הוֹאִיל וְשָׁאוּל עִרְעֵר כְּדֵי שֶׁיִּשְׁמְרוּהוּ עַד לְהַחְלָטַת הַקֵּיסָר, צִוִּיתִי לִשְׁמֹר אוֹתוֹ עַד אֲשֶׁר אֶשְׁלַח אוֹתוֹ אֶל הוֹד מַלְכוּתוֹ."

²² אָמַר אַגְרִיפַּס אֶל פֶסְטוּס: "גַּם אֲנִי חָפַצְתִּי לִשְׁמֹעַ אֶת הָאִישׁ."

הֵשִׁיב פֶסְטוּס: "מָחָר תִּשְׁמַע אוֹתוֹ." ²³ לְמָחֳרָת בָּאוּ אַגְרִיפַּס וּבֶרְנִיקָה בְּרֹב הָדָר וְנִכְנְסוּ לָאוּלָם עִם שָׂרֵי הָאֶלֶף וְנִכְבַּדֵּי הָעִיר, וּפֶסְטוּס צִוָּה לְהָבִיא אֶת שָׁאוּל. ²⁴ אָמַר פֶסְטוּס: "אַגְרִיפַּס הַמֶּלֶךְ וְכָל הָאֲנָשִׁים הַנִּמְצָאִים אִתָּנוּ, אַתֶּם רוֹאִים אֶת הָאִישׁ הַזֶּה אֲשֶׁר בִּגְלָלוֹ פָּנוּ אֵלַי כָּל קְהַל הַיְּהוּדִים, גַּם בִּירוּשָׁלַיִם וְגַם פֹּה, וְצָעֲקוּ שֶׁאֵינוֹ רָאוּי לִחְיוֹת עוֹד. ²⁵ אֲנִי נוֹכַחְתִּי כִּי לֹא עָשָׂה שׁוּם דָּבָר הַמְחַיֵּב מָוֶת, אַךְ מִכֵּיוָן שֶׁבִּקֵּשׁ לְהִשָּׁפֵט לִפְנֵי הַקֵּיסָר הֶחְלַטְתִּי לְשַׁלֵּחַ אוֹתוֹ. ²⁶ אֲבָל אֵין לִי שׁוּם דָּבָר בָּרוּר לִכְתֹּב עָלָיו לַאֲדוֹנֵנוּ. לָכֵן הֵבֵאתִי אוֹתוֹ לִפְנֵיכֶם וּבְיִחוּד לְפָנֶיךָ, הַמֶּלֶךְ אַגְרִיפַּס, כְּדֵי שֶׁיֵּחָקֵר וְיִהְיֶה לִי מַה לִּכְתֹּב, ²⁷ שֶׁהֲרֵי לֹא מִתְקַבֵּל עַל דַּעְתִּי לִשְׁלֹחַ אָסִיר בְּלִי לְהוֹדִיעַ גַּם אֶת הָאַשְׁמוֹת הַמְיֻחָסוֹת לוֹ."

כו אָמַר אַגְרִיפַּס אֶל שָׁאוּל: "נִתָּן לְךָ לְלַמֵּד זְכוּת עַל עַצְמְךָ." הוֹשִׁיט שָׁאוּל אֶת יָדוֹ וְהֵחֵל לְהָגֵן עַל עַצְמוֹ: ² "הַמֶּלֶךְ אַגְרִיפַּס, חוֹשֵׁב אֲנִי אֶת עַצְמִי לִמְאֻשָּׁר עַל שֶׁאֲנִי מֵגֵן עַל עַצְמִי לְפָנֶיךָ הַיּוֹם בְּעִנְיַן כָּל מַה שֶּׁיְּהוּדִים אֲחֵרִים מַאֲשִׁימִים אוֹתִי, ³ בְּיִחוּד מִשּׁוּם שֶׁאַתָּה בָּקִי בְּכָל הַמִּנְהָגִים וְהַשְּׁאֵלוֹת שֶׁבְּקֶרֶב הַיְּהוּדִים. לְפִיכָךְ מְבַקֵּשׁ אֲנִי מִמְּךָ לִשְׁמֹעַ אוֹתִי בְּאֹרֶךְ-רוּחַ. ⁴ וּבְכֵן, כָּל הַיְּהוּדִים יוֹדְעִים אֶת דַּרְכֵי חַיַּי מִתְּקוּפַת נְעוּרַי, מֵרֵאשִׁית יְמֵי מְגוּרַי בְּקֶרֶב עַמִּי בִּירוּשָׁלַיִם. ⁵ הֵם הִכִּירוּנִי מִתְּחִלָּה – אִם יֹאוּתוּ

a Pharisee. ⁶ And now I stand and am judged for the hope of the promise made by God to our fathers. ⁷ To this *promise* our twelve tribes, earnestly serving *God* night and day, hope to attain. For this hope's sake, King Agrippa, I am accused by the Jews. ⁸ Why should it be thought incredible by you that God raises the dead?

⁹ "Indeed, I myself thought I must do many things contrary to the name of Jesus of Nazareth. ¹⁰ This I also did in Jerusalem, and many of the saints I shut up in prison, having received authority from the chief priests; and when they were put to death, I cast my vote against *them*. ¹¹ And I punished them often in every synagogue and compelled *them* to blaspheme; and being exceedingly enraged against them, I persecuted *them* even to foreign cities.

¹² "While thus occupied, as I journeyed to Damascus with authority and commission from the chief priests, ¹³ at midday, O king, along the road I saw a light from heaven, brighter than the sun, shining around me and those who journeyed with me. ¹⁴ And when we all had fallen to the ground, I heard a voice speaking to me and saying in the Hebrew language, 'Saul, Saul, why are you persecuting Me? *It is* hard for you to kick against the goads.' ¹⁵ So I said, 'Who are You, Lord?' And He said, 'I am Jesus, whom you are persecuting. ¹⁶ But rise and stand on your feet; for I have appeared to you for this purpose, to make you a minister and a witness both of the things which you have seen and of the things which I will yet reveal to you. ¹⁷ I will deliver you from the *Jewish* people, as well as *from* the Gentiles, to whom I now send you, ¹⁸ to open their eyes, *in order* to turn *them* from darkness to light, and *from* the power of Satan to God, that they may receive forgiveness of sins and an inheritance among those who are sanctified by faith in Me.'

¹⁹ "Therefore, King Agrippa, I was not disobedient to the heavenly vision, ²⁰ but declared first to those in Damascus and in Jerusalem, and throughout all the region of Judea, and *then* to the Gentiles, that they should repent, turn to God, and do works befitting repentance. ²¹ For these reasons the Jews seized me in the temple and tried to kill *me*. ²² Therefore, having obtained help from God, to this day I stand, witnessing both to small and great, saying no other things than those which the prophets and Moses said would come— ²³ that the Christ would suffer, that He would be the first to rise from the dead, and would proclaim light to the *Jewish* people and to the Gentiles."

לְהָעִיד – וְיוֹדְעִים שֶׁחָיִיתִי כְּפָרוּשׁ עַל־פִּי הַכַּת הָאֲדוּקָה בְּיוֹתֵר שֶׁל דָּתֵנוּ. ⁶ וְעַכְשָׁו אֲנִי עוֹמֵד לְמִשְׁפָּט עַל תִּקְוַת הַהַבְטָחָה שֶׁהִבְטִיחַ אֱלֹהִים לַאֲבוֹתֵינוּ, ⁷ הַבְטָחָה אֲשֶׁר שְׁנֵים־עָשָׂר שְׁבָטֵינוּ מְקַוִּים לְהַגִּיעַ לְהַגְשָׁמָתָהּ בְּעָבְדָם אֶת אֱלֹהִים בִּדְבֵקוּת יוֹמָם וָלַיְלָה. עַל־דְּבַר הַתִּקְוָה הַזֹּאת, הַמֶּלֶךְ אַגְרִיפַּס, יֵשׁ יְהוּדִים הַמַּאֲשִׁימִים אוֹתִי. ⁸ מַדּוּעַ תֵּחָשְׁבוּ לְדָבָר לֹא יֵאָמֵן שֶׁאֱלֹהִים מְחַיֶּה מֵתִים? ⁹ אָכֵן אֲנִי עַצְמִי חָשַׁבְתִּי כִּי מְחוֹבָתִי לַעֲשׂוֹת דְּבָרִים רַבִּים נֶגֶד שֵׁם יֵשׁוּעַ מִנָּצְרַת, ¹⁰ מַה שֶׁגַּם עָשִׂיתִי בִּירוּשָׁלַיִם. קְדוֹשִׁים רַבִּים כָּלָאתִי בְּבָתֵּי כֶּלֶא, עַל־פִּי הַסַּמְכוּת שֶׁקִּבַּלְתִּי מֵאֵת רָאשֵׁי הַכֹּהֲנִים, וְכַאֲשֶׁר הוּצְאוּ לַהוֹרֵג הִצְבַּעְתִּי עִם הַמְּחַיְּבִים. ¹¹ פְּעָמִים רַבּוֹת, בְּכָל בָּתֵּי הַכְּנֶסֶת, הֶעֱנַשְׁתִּי אוֹתָם וְדָחַקְתִּי בָּהֶם לְגַדֵּף אֶת שְׁמוֹ, וּבְשֶׁצֶף זַעַם עֲלֵיהֶם רָדַפְתִּי אוֹתָם אֲפִלּוּ עַד עָרִים מִחוּץ לָאָרֶץ.

¹² הָלַכְתִּי לְשֵׁם כָּךְ לְדַמֶּשֶׂק עִם סַמְכוּת וּרְשׁוּת מִטַּעַם רָאשֵׁי הַכֹּהֲנִים. ¹³ וְהִנֵּה, אֲדוֹנִי הַמֶּלֶךְ, בִּהְיוֹתִי בַּדֶּרֶךְ, בַּצָּהֳרַיִם, רָאִיתִי אוֹר מִן הַשָּׁמַיִם, מַבְרִיק יוֹתֵר מִזֹּהַר הַשֶּׁמֶשׁ, נוֹגֵהַּ סָבִיב לִי וְלַהוֹלְכִים אִתִּי. ¹⁴ כֻּלָּנוּ נָפַלְנוּ אַרְצָה וַאֲנִי שָׁמַעְתִּי קוֹל אוֹמֵר אֵלַי בַּלָּשׁוֹן הָעִבְרִית, "שָׁאוּל, שָׁאוּל, לָמָּה אַתָּה רוֹדֵף אוֹתִי? קָשֶׁה לְךָ לִבְעֹט עַל רַגְלֶיךָ." ¹⁵ שָׁאַלְתִּי, 'מִי אַתָּה, אֲדוֹנִי?' וְהָאָדוֹן הֵשִׁיב, 'אֲנִי יֵשׁוּעַ שֶׁאַתָּה רוֹדֵף. ¹⁶ אֲבָל קוּם וַעֲמֹד עַל רַגְלֶיךָ, כִּי לְשֵׁם כָּךְ נִרְאֵיתִי אֵלֶיךָ – לְמַנּוֹת אוֹתְךָ לִמְשָׁרֵת וּלְעֵד עַל דְּבַר זֶה שֶׁרָאִיתָ אוֹתִי וְעַל הַדְּבָרִים שֶׁלְּשָׁמָּם אֵרָאֶה אֵלֶיךָ, ¹⁷ בְּהַצִּילִי אוֹתְךָ מִן הָעָם וּמִן הַגּוֹיִים אֲשֶׁר אֲנִי שׁוֹלֵחַ אוֹתְךָ אֲלֵיהֶם ¹⁸ לִפְקֹחַ אֶת עֵינֵיהֶם, לְהָשִׁיב אוֹתָם מֵחֹשֶׁךְ לָאוֹר וּמִשִּׁלְטוֹן הַשָּׂטָן לֵאלֹהִים כְּדֵי שֶׁיְּקַבְּלוּ עַל־יְדֵי אֱמוּנָה בִּי סְלִיחַת חֲטָאִים וְנַחֲלָה בְּקֶרֶב הַמְּקֻדָּשִׁים.' ¹⁹ עַל כֵּן, הַמֶּלֶךְ אַגְרִיפַּס, לֹא הִתְנַגַּדְתִּי לַצֵּאת לַמַּרְאֶה מִן הַשָּׁמַיִם, ²⁰ כִּי אִם הִגַּדְתִּי תְּחִלָּה לְאַנְשֵׁי דַמֶּשֶׂק, וְכֵן גַּם בִּירוּשָׁלַיִם וּבְכָל אֶרֶץ יְהוּדָה וְגַם לַגּוֹיִים – לַחֲזֹר בִּתְשׁוּבָה וְלִפְנוֹת אֶל אֱלֹהִים בַּעֲשׂוֹתָם מַעֲשִׂים רְאוּיִים לִתְשׁוּבָה. ²¹ בִּגְלַל זֶה תְּפָסוּנִי יְהוּדִים בַּמִּקְדָּשׁ וְנִסּוּ לַהֲרֹג אוֹתִי. ²² וּבִהְיוֹת הָאֱלֹהִים בְּעֶזְרִי עַד הַיּוֹם הַזֶּה, הֲרֵינִי עוֹמֵד וּמֵעִיד לִפְנֵי קְטַנִּים וּגְדוֹלִים וְאֵינֶנִּי אוֹמֵר דָּבָר מִלְּבַד הַדְּבָרִים שֶׁהַנְּבִיאִים וּמֹשֶׁה אָמְרוּ כִּי עֲתִידִים הֵם לִקְרוֹת: ²³ שֶׁהַמָּשִׁיחַ יִסְבֹּל, יִהְיֶה רִאשׁוֹן לִתְחִיַּת הַמֵּתִים וִיבַשֵּׂר אוֹר לָעָם וְלַגּוֹיִים."

24 Now as he thus made his defense, Festus said with a loud voice, "Paul, you are beside yourself! Much learning is driving you mad!"

25 But he said, "I am not mad, most noble Festus, but speak the words of truth and reason. 26 For the king, before whom I also speak freely, knows these things; for I am convinced that none of these things escapes his attention, since this thing was not done in a corner. 27 King Agrippa, do you believe the prophets? I know that you do believe."

28 Then Agrippa said to Paul, "You almost persuade me to become a Christian."

29 And Paul said, "I would to God that not only you, but also all who hear me today, might become both almost and altogether such as I am, except for these chains."

30 When he had said these things, the king stood up, as well as the governor and Bernice and those who sat with them; 31 and when they had gone aside, they talked among themselves, saying, "This man is doing nothing deserving of death or chains."

32 Then Agrippa said to Festus, "This man might have been set free if he had not appealed to Caesar."

27 And when it was decided that we should sail to Italy, they delivered Paul and some other prisoners to *one* named Julius, a centurion of the Augustan Regiment. 2 So, entering a ship of Adramyttium, we put to sea, meaning to sail along the coasts of Asia. Aristarchus, a Macedonian of Thessalonica, was with us. 3 And the next *day* we landed at Sidon. And Julius treated Paul kindly and gave *him* liberty to go to his friends and receive care. 4 When we had put to sea from there, we sailed under *the shelter of* Cyprus, because the winds were contrary. 5 And when we had sailed over the sea which is off Cilicia and Pamphylia, we came to Myra, *a city* of Lycia. 6 There the centurion found an Alexandrian ship sailing to Italy, and he put us on board.

7 When we had sailed slowly many days, and arrived with difficulty off Cnidus, the wind not permitting us to proceed, we sailed under *the shelter of* Crete off Salmone. 8 Passing it with difficulty, we came to a place called Fair Havens, near the city *of* Lasea.

9 Now when much time had been spent, and sailing was now dangerous because the Fast was already over, Paul advised them, 10 saying, "Men, I perceive that this voyage will end with disaster and much loss, not only of the cargo and ship, but also our lives." 11 Nevertheless the centurion was more persuaded by the helmsman and the owner of the

24 כְּשֶׁאָמַר אֶת הַדְּבָרִים הָאֵלֶּה לַהֲגָנָתוֹ, אָמַר פֶסְטוֹס בְּקוֹל רָם: "אַתָּה מִשְׁתַּגֵּעַ, שָׁאוּל! הַלִּמּוּד הָרַב מֵבִיא אוֹתְךָ לִידֵי שִׁגָּעוֹן."

25 הֵשִׁיב שָׁאוּל: "אֵינֶנִּי מִשְׁתַּגֵּעַ, הוֹד מַעֲלָתוֹ פֶסְטוֹס, אֶלָּא דְּבָרִים שֶׁל אֱמֶת וְשֶׁל טַעַם אֲנִי מַשְׁמִיעַ. 26 הֲרֵי הַמֶּלֶךְ יוֹדֵעַ אֶת הָעִנְיָנִים הָאֵלֶּה וַאֲנִי מְדַבֵּר אֵלָיו בְּבִטָּחוֹן, שֶׁכֵּן אֲנִי בָּטוּחַ שֶׁלֹּא נֶעְלָם מִמֶּנּוּ דָּבָר מִן הַדְּבָרִים הָאֵלֶּה, כִּי לֹא בְּקֶרֶן זָוִית נֶעֶשְׂתָה זֹאת. 27 הַמֶּלֶךְ אַגְרִיפַס, הֲמַאֲמִין אַתָּה בַּנְּבִיאִים? אֲנִי יוֹדֵעַ שֶׁאַתָּה מַאֲמִין!"

28 עָנָה אַגְרִיפַס לְשָׁאוּל: "עוֹד מְעַט וְאַתָּה מְשַׁכְנֵעַ אוֹתִי לִהְיוֹת מְשִׁיחִי!"

29 אָמַר שָׁאוּל: "אִם עוֹד מְעַט וְאִם עוֹד הַרְבֵּה, תְּפִלָּתִי לֵאלֹהִים שֶׁלֹּא רַק אַתָּה אֶלָּא גַּם כָּל הַשּׁוֹמְעִים אוֹתִי הַיּוֹם, יִהְיוּ כָּמוֹנִי – רַק בְּלִי הַכְּבָלִים הָאֵלֶּה." 30 הַמֶּלֶךְ וְהַנָּצִיב קָמוּ וְכֵן גַּם בֶּרְנִיקֶה וְהַיּוֹשְׁבִים אִתָּם. 31 אַחֲרֵי צֵאתָם דִּבְּרוּ זֶה אֶל זֶה וְאָמְרוּ: "הָאִישׁ הַזֶּה לֹא עָשָׂה שׁוּם דָּבָר הַמְחַיֵּב מָוֶת אוֹ מַאֲסָר." 32 אָמַר אַגְרִיפַס לְפֶסְטוֹס: "הָאִישׁ הַזֶּה הָיָה יָכוֹל לְהִשְׁתַּחְרֵר לוּלֵא פָנָה אֶל הַקֵּיסָר."

כז כַּאֲשֶׁר הֻחְלַט שֶׁנַּפְלִיג לְאִיטַלְיָה מָסְרוּ אֶת שָׁאוּל עִם כַּמָּה אֲסִירִים אֲחֵרִים לִידֵי שַׂר מֵאָה מִן הַגְּדוּד הַקֵּיסָרִי, יוּלְיוֹם שְׁמוֹ. 2 נִכְנַסְנוּ לָאֳנִיָּה אַדְרָמִיטִּית, שֶׁעָמְדָה לִנְסֹעַ לַמְּקוֹמוֹת אֲשֶׁר לְאֹרֶךְ חוֹף אַסְיָה, וְהִפְלַגְנוּ. אִתָּנוּ הָיָה אֲרִיסְטַרְכוֹס, מָקֵדוֹנִי מִתֶּסָלוֹנִיקִי. 3 לְמָחֳרָת הִגַּעְנוּ לְצִידוֹן. יוּלְיוֹם נָהַג בְּנִדִיבוּת עִם שָׁאוּל וְהִרְשָׁה לוֹ לָלֶכֶת אֶל חֲבֵרָיו וְלֵהָנוֹת מֵעֶזְרָתָם. 4 מִשָּׁם הִפְלַגְנוּ וְשַׁטְנוּ עַל יַד קַפְרִיסִין בִּגְלַל הָרוּחוֹת הַנֶּגְדִּיּוֹת. 5 עָבַרְנוּ בַּיָּם שֶׁמִּמּוּל לְקִילִיקְיָה וּפַמְפִילְיָה וּבָאנוּ אֶל מִירָה אֲשֶׁר בְּלִיקְיָה. 6 שַׂר הַמֵּאָה מָצָא שָׁם אֳנִיָּה מֵאֲלֶכְּסַנְדְּרִיָּה שֶׁמְּגַמַּת פָּנֶיהָ לְאִיטַלְיָה וְהֶעֱבִיר אוֹתָנוּ אֵלֶיהָ. 7 שַׁטְנוּ כַּמָּה יָמִים בְּאִטִּיּוּת וְהִגַּעְנוּ בְּקֹשִׁי רַב אֶל מוּל קְנִידוֹם. מֵאַחַר שֶׁהָרוּחַ הַנּוֹשֶׁבֶת הִפְרִיעָה לָנוּ, שַׁטְנוּ עַל יַד כְּרֵתִים וְעָבַרְנוּ עַל פְּנֵי כֵּף סַלְמוֹנִי. 8 שַׁטְנוּ סָמוּךְ לָאִי בְּקֹשִׁי רַב וְהִגַּעְנוּ לְמָקוֹם אֶחָד שֶׁנִּקְרָא הַמְּעַגָּנִים הַטּוֹבִים, קָרוֹב לָעִיר לָסַיָה. 9 מִכֵּיוָן שֶׁעָבַר זְמַן נִכָּר וְהַשַּׁיִט כְּבָר הָיָה מְסֻכָּן, שֶׁכֵּן אֲפִלּוּ יוֹם הַכִּפּוּרִים כְּבָר עָבַר, הִזְהִיר אוֹתָם שָׁאוּל 10 בְּאָמְרוֹ: "אֲנָשִׁים, אֲנִי רוֹאֶה שֶׁלַּמַּסָּע צָפוּי נֶזֶק עִם אָבְדָן רַב לֹא רַק לַמִּטְעָן וְלָאֳנִיָּה, אֶלָּא גַּם לְחַיֵּינוּ." 11 אַךְ שַׂר הַמֵּאָה הֶאֱמִין יוֹתֵר לְרַב הַחוֹבֵל וּלְבַעַל

ship than by the things spoken by Paul. 12 And because the harbor was not suitable to winter in, the majority advised to set sail from there also, if by any means they could reach Phoenix, a harbor of Crete opening toward the southwest and northwest, *and* winter *there.*

13 When the south wind blew softly, supposing that they had obtained *their* desire, putting out to sea, they sailed close by Crete. 14 But not long after, a tempestuous head wind arose, called Euroclydon. 15 So when the ship was caught, and could not head into the wind, we let *her* drive. 16 And running under *the shelter of* an island called Clauda, we secured the skiff with difficulty. 17 When they had taken it on board, they used cables to undergird the ship; and fearing lest they should run aground on the Syrtis *Sands*, they struck sail and so were driven. 18 And because we were exceedingly tempest-tossed, the next *day* they lightened the ship. 19 On the third *day* we threw the ship's tackle overboard with our own hands. 20 Now when neither sun nor stars appeared for many days, and no small tempest beat on *us*, all hope that we would be saved was finally given up.

21 But after long abstinence from food, then Paul stood in the midst of them and said, "Men, you should have listened to me, and not have sailed from Crete and incurred this disaster and loss. 22 And now I urge you to take heart, for there will be no loss of life among you, but only of the ship. 23 For there stood by me this night an angel of the God to whom I belong and whom I serve, 24 saying, 'Do not be afraid, Paul; you must be brought before Caesar; and indeed God has granted you all those who sail with you.' 25 Therefore take heart, men, for I believe God that it will be just as it was told me. 26 However, we must run aground on a certain island."

27 Now when the fourteenth night had come, as we were driven up and down in the Adriatic *Sea*, about midnight the sailors sensed that they were drawing near some land. 28 And they took soundings and found *it* to be twenty fathoms; and when they had gone a little farther, they took soundings again and found *it* to be fifteen fathoms. 29 Then, fearing lest we should run aground on the rocks, they dropped four anchors from the stern, and prayed for day to come. 30 And as the sailors were seeking to escape from the ship, when they had let down the skiff into the sea, under pretense of putting out anchors from the prow, 31 Paul said to the centurion and the soldiers, "Unless these men

הָאֳנִיָּה מֵאֲשֶׁר לְדִבְרֵי שָׁאוּל. 12 הוֹאִיל וְהַנָּמֵל לֹא הִתְאִים לַעֲגִינַת חֹרֶף הִצִּיעַ הָרֹב לְהַפְלִיג מִשָּׁם, בְּתִקְוָה שֶׁיּוּכְלוּ לְהַגִּיעַ לְפֵנִיקָס – נָמֵל כְּרֵתִי הַפּוֹנֶה לְדָרוֹם מַעֲרָב וְלִצְפוֹן מַעֲרָב – וְלִשְׁהוֹת שָׁם בַּחֹרֶף. 13 רוּחַ אַטִּית נָשְׁבָה מִן הַדָּרוֹם וְהֵם חָשְׁבוּ שֶׁיָּשִׂיגוּ אֶת מַטָּרָתָם; לָכֵן הֵרִימוּ עֹגֶן וְשָׁטוּ סָמוּךְ לַיַּבָּשָׁה לְאֹרֶךְ חוֹף כְּרֵתִים. 14 לְאַחַר זְמַן קָצָר נָשְׁבָה מִן הָאִי רוּחַ סוּפָה צְפוֹנִית מִזְרָחִית הַנִּקְרֵאת אֵירָקִלוֹן. 15 כֵּיוָן שֶׁהָאֳנִיָּה נִלְכְּדָה וְלֹא יָכְלָה לָשׁוּט נֶגֶד הָרוּחַ, נִכְנַעְנוּ וְנִסְחַפְנוּ. 16 כַּאֲשֶׁר עָבַרְנוּ עַל־יַד אִי אֶחָד, קוֹדָה שְׁמוֹ, הִצְלַחְנוּ בְּמַאֲמָץ רַב לְהִשְׁתַּלֵּט עַל הַסִּירָה הַנִּגְרֶרֶת. 17 הֵם הֶעֱלוּ אוֹתָהּ לַסִּפּוּן וְהִשְׁתַּמְּשׁוּ בַּחֲבָלִים לַחֲגִירַת דְּפָנוֹת הָאֳנִיָּה; וּמֵאַחַר שֶׁפָּחֲדוּ שֶׁמָּא יִסָּחֲפוּ אֶל חוֹלוֹת סִירְטִים, הִנְמִיכוּ אֶת הַמִּפְרָשׂ וְנִסְחֲפוּ בְּאֹפֶן זֶה. 18 לְמָחֳרָת, בִּהְיוֹתֵנוּ מְטֻלְטָלִים בְּחָזְקָה עַל־יְדֵי הַסְּעָרָה, הֵקֵלוּ מִמַּשָּׂא הָאֳנִיָּה. 19 אַחֲרֵי יוֹם נוֹסָף הִשְׁלִיכוּ בְּמוֹ יְדֵיהֶם אֶת צִיּוּד הָאֳנִיָּה. 20 הוֹאִיל וְיָמִים רַבִּים לֹא הוֹפִיעוּ הַשֶּׁמֶשׁ וְהַכּוֹכָבִים וְהִתְחוֹלְלָה סְעָרָה חֲזָקָה, אָפְסָה כָּל תִּקְוָה שֶׁנִּנָּצֵל.

21 אַחֲרֵי שֶׁנִּמְנַעְנוּ זְמַן רַב מֵאֹכֶל, עָמַד שָׁאוּל בֵּינֵיהֶם וְאָמַר: "וּבְכֵן, חֲבֵרִים, הָיָה צָרִיךְ לִשְׁמֹעַ בְּקוֹלִי וְלֹא לְהַפְלִיג מִכְּרֵתִים וּלְהַגִּיעַ לִידֵי הַנֶּזֶק וְהָאָבְדָן הַזֶּה. 22 וְעַכְשָׁו אֲנִי מַצִּיעַ לָכֶם לְהִתְעוֹדֵד, כִּי לֹא תֹאבַד שׁוּם נֶפֶשׁ מִכֶּם; רַק הָאֳנִיָּה תֹּאבַד; 23 כִּי בַּלַּיְלָה נִצָּב עָלַי מַלְאָךְ שֶׁל אֱלֹהִים אֲשֶׁר לוֹ אֲנִי שַׁיָּךְ וְאוֹתוֹ אֲנִי עוֹבֵד – 24 וְאָמַר, 'אַל תִּפְחַד, שָׁאוּל, אַתָּה צָרִיךְ לַעֲמֹד לִפְנֵי הַקֵּיסָר, וְהִנֵּה הָאֱלֹהִים בְּחַסְדּוֹ חָנַן לְךָ אֶת כָּל הַמַּפְלִיגִים אִתְּךָ.' 25 וּבְכֵן, חֲבֵרִים, הִתְעוֹדְדוּ! אֲנִי בּוֹטֵחַ בֵּאלֹהִים שֶׁכְּמוֹ שֶׁנֶּאֱמַר לִי כֵּן יִהְיֶה. 26 אֲבָל עָלֵינוּ לְהִסָּחֵף אֶל אֵיזֶה אִי."

27 בַּחֲצוֹת הַלַּיְלָה הָאַרְבָּעָה־עָשָׂר, כְּשֶׁנִּסְחַפְנוּ הֵנֵּה וְהֵנָּה בַּיָּם הָאַדְרִיָּתִי, סָבְרוּ הַמַּלָּחִים שֶׁאָנוּ מִתְקָרְבִים לְאֵיזוֹ אֶרֶץ. 28 הֵם הוֹרִידוּ אֲנָךְ וּמָצְאוּ שֶׁהָעֹמֶק שְׁלֹשִׁים וְשִׁבְעָה מֶטְרִים. אַחֲרֵי מֶרְחָק מְעַט מָדְדוּ שֵׁנִית וּמָצְאוּ עֶשְׂרִים וְשִׁבְעָה מֶטְרִים. 29 הוֹאִיל וְחָשְׁשׁוּ שֶׁמָּא נִפְּחַח אֶל אַזוֹרֵי סְלָעִים, הִטִּילוּ אַרְבָּעָה עֳגָנִים מִן הַצַּד הָאֲחוֹרִי שֶׁל הָאֳנִיָּה וְהִתְפַּלְלוּ שֶׁיָּאִיר הַיּוֹם. 30 כְּשֶׁנִּסּוּ הַמַּלָּחִים לִבְרֹחַ מִן הָאֳנִיָּה וְהִתְחִילוּ לְהוֹרִיד אֶת הַסִּירָה אֶל הַיָּם בְּאֲמַתְלָה שֶׁהֵם מִתְכַּוְּנִים לִמְשֹׁךְ עֳגָנִים מֵחַרְטוֹם הָאֳנִיָּה, 31 אָמַר שָׁאוּל לְשַׂר הַמֵּאָה וְלַחַיָּלִים: "אִם

stay in the ship, you cannot be saved." ³² Then the soldiers cut away the ropes of the skiff and let it fall off.

³³ And as day was about to dawn, Paul implored *them* all to take food, saying, "Today is the fourteenth day you have waited and continued without food, and eaten nothing. ³⁴ Therefore I urge you to take nourishment, for this is for your survival, since not a hair will fall from the head of any of you." ³⁵ And when he had said these things, he took bread and gave thanks to God in the presence of them all; and when he had broken *it* he began to eat. ³⁶ Then they were all encouraged, and also took food themselves. ³⁷ And in all we were two hundred and seventy-six persons on the ship. ³⁸ So when they had eaten enough, they lightened the ship and threw out the wheat into the sea.

³⁹ When it was day, they did not recognize the land; but they observed a bay with a beach, onto which they planned to run the ship if possible. ⁴⁰ And they let go the anchors and left *them* in the sea, meanwhile loosing the rudder ropes; and they hoisted the mainsail to the wind and made for shore. ⁴¹ But striking a place where two seas met, they ran the ship aground; and the prow stuck fast and remained immovable, but the stern was being broken up by the violence of the waves.

⁴² And the soldiers' plan was to kill the prisoners, lest any of them should swim away and escape. ⁴³ But the centurion, wanting to save Paul, kept them from *their* purpose, and commanded that those who could swim should jump *overboard* first and get to land, ⁴⁴ and the rest, some on boards and some on *parts* of the ship. And so it was that they all escaped safely to land.

28 Now when they had escaped, they then found out that the island was called Malta. ² And the natives showed us unusual kindness; for they kindled a fire and made us all welcome, because of the rain that was falling and because of the cold. ³ But when Paul had gathered a bundle of sticks and laid *them* on the fire, a viper came out because of the heat, and fastened on his hand. ⁴ So when the natives saw the creature hanging from his hand, they said to one another, "No doubt this man is a murderer, whom, though he has escaped the sea, yet justice does not allow to live." ⁵ But he shook off the creature into the fire and suffered no harm. ⁶ However, they were expecting that he would swell up or suddenly fall down dead. But after they had looked for a long time and saw no harm come to him, they changed their minds and said that he was a god.

אֵלֶּה לֹא יִשָּׁאֲרוּ בָאֳנִיָּה לֹא תוּכְלוּ אַתֶּם לְהִנָּצֵל." ³² אָז חָתְכוּ הַחַיָּלִים אֶת חַבְלֵי הַסִּירָה וְהִנִּיחוּ לָהּ לִפֹּל.

³³ עוֹד לִפְנֵי אוֹר הַבֹּקֶר בִּקֵּשׁ שָׁאוּל מִכָּל הָאֲנָשִׁים שֶׁיֹּאכְלוּ, בְּאָמְרוֹ: "הַיּוֹם כְּבָר הַיּוֹם הָאַרְבָּעָה-עָשָׂר שֶׁאַתֶּם מַמְשִׁיכִים וּמְחַכִּים בְּלֹא לֶאֱכֹל כְּלוּם. ³⁴ לָכֵן אֲנִי מְבַקֵּשׁ מִכֶּם לֶאֱכֹל, כִּי זֶה נָחוּץ לְהַצָּלַתְכֶם, שֶׁכֵּן לֹא תֹאבַד שַׂעֲרָה מֵרֹאשׁוֹ שֶׁל אִישׁ מִכֶּם." ³⁵ לְאַחַר שֶׁאָמַר זֹאת לָקַח לֶחֶם, הוֹדָה לֵאלֹהִים לְעֵינֵי כֻלָּם, בָּצַע וְהֵחֵל לֶאֱכֹל. ³⁶ הַכֹּל הִתְעוֹדְדוּ וְגַם הֵם אָכְלוּ. ³⁷ בְּסַךְ הַכֹּל הָיִינוּ מָאתַיִם וְשִׁבְעִים וְשֵׁשׁ נְפָשׁוֹת בָּאֳנִיָּה. ³⁸ אַחֲרֵי שֶׁאָכְלוּ לְשָׂבְעָה הֵקֵלּוּ מֵעַל הָאֳנִיָּה בְּהַטִּילָם אֶת הַחִטָּה לַיָּם.

³⁹ כְּשֶׁהֵאִיר הַיּוֹם לֹא הִכִּירוּ אֶת הָאָרֶץ, אַךְ הִבְחִינוּ בְּמִפְרָץ עִם חוֹף חוֹלִי וְהֶחֱלִיטוּ לְהַסִּיעַ אֶת הָאֳנִיָּה לְשָׁם, אִם אֶפְשָׁר. ⁴⁰ הֵם נָתְקוּ אֶת קִשְׁרֵי הָעֳגָנִים וְעָזְבוּ אוֹתָם בַּיָּם. יַחַד עִם זֹאת הִתִּירוּ אֶת הַחֲבָלִים שֶׁל הַהֶגָּאִים, פָּרְשׂוּ אֶת הַמִּפְרָשׂ הַקִּדְמִי אֶל הָרוּחַ וְכִוְּנוּ אֶת הָאֳנִיָּה אֶל הַחוֹף. ⁴¹ אָז הִגִּיעוּ לְמָקוֹם בֵּין זְרָמִים וְהֶעֱלוּ אֶת הָאֳנִיָּה עַל שִׂרְטוֹן. הַחַרְטוֹם נִתְקַע וְנִשְׁאַר קָבוּעַ בִּמְקוֹמוֹ, אֲבָל הַיַּרְכָתַיִם נִשְׁבְּרוּ מֵעָצְמַת הַגַּלִּים.

⁴² כַּוָּנַת הַחַיָּלִים הָיְתָה לַהֲרֹג אֶת הָאֲסִירִים, כְּדֵי שֶׁלֹּא יִשְׂחֶה אִישׁ מֵהֶם וְיִמָּלֵט. ⁴³ אַךְ שַׂר הַמֵּאָה רָצָה לְהַצִּיל אֶת שָׁאוּל וְהֵנִיא אוֹתָם מִכַּוָּנָתָם. הוּא צִוָּה שֶׁהַיּוֹדְעִים לִשְׂחוֹת יִקְפְּצוּ רִאשׁוֹנִים וְיַגִּיעוּ אֶל הַיַּבָּשָׁה, ⁴⁴ וְהַיֶּתֶר, שֶׁיַּעֲשׂוּ זֹאת חֶלְקָם עַל קְרָשִׁים וְחֶלְקָם עַל חֲפָצִים מִן הָאֳנִיָּה. בְּדֶרֶךְ זֹאת נֶחְלְצוּ כֻּלָּם אֶל הַיַּבָּשָׁה.

כח אַחֲרֵי שֶׁנִּצַּלְנוּ הִתְבָּרֵר לָנוּ כִּי שֵׁם הָאִי מַלְטָה. ² הַתּוֹשָׁבִים, שֶׁלֹּא הָיוּ יְוָנִים, נָהֲגוּ בָּנוּ בִּנְדִיבוּת בִּלְתִּי רְגִילָה, כִּי הִדְלִיקוּ אֵשׁ בִּגְלַל הַגֶּשֶׁם הַיּוֹרֵד וְהַקֹּר וְקִבְּלוּ אֶת כֻּלָּנוּ. ³ שָׁאוּל אָסַף מְלֹא יָדָיו שִׂבְרֵי עֲנָפִים וּכְשֶׁשָּׂם אוֹתָם עַל הָאֵשׁ יָצָא מִתּוֹכָם צֶפַע, בִּגְלַל הַחֹם, וְנִצְמַד אֶל יָדוֹ. ⁴ רָאוּ הַתּוֹשָׁבִים אֶת הַחַיָּה תְּלוּיָה עַל יָדוֹ וְאָמְרוּ זֶה אֶל זֶה: "אֵין סָפֵק שֶׁהָאִישׁ הַזֶּה רוֹצֵחַ. נִצַּל מִן הַיָּם, אַךְ הַצֶּדֶק לֹא הִנִּיחַ לוֹ לִחְיוֹת." ⁵ אֲבָל שָׁאוּל נִעֵר אֶת הַחַיָּה אֶל תּוֹךְ הָאֵשׁ וְלֹא נִזַּק כְּלָל. ⁶ הֵם צִפּוּ שֶׁגּוּפוֹ יִתְנַפֵּחַ אוֹ שֶׁיִּפֹּל מֵת פִּתְאוֹם. חִכּוּ שָׁעָה אֲרֻכָּה וְרָאוּ שֶׁלֹּא קָרָה לוֹ שׁוּם רַע; שִׁנּוּ דַעְתָּם וְאָמְרוּ שֶׁהוּא אֵל.

7 In that region there was an estate of the leading citizen of the island, whose name was Publius, who received us and entertained us courteously for three days. 8 And it happened that the father of Publius lay sick of a fever and dysentery. Paul went in to him and prayed, and he laid his hands on him and healed him. 9 So when this was done, the rest of those on the island who had diseases also came and were healed. 10 They also honored us in many ways; and when we departed, they provided such things as were necessary.

11 After three months we sailed in an Alexandrian ship whose figurehead was the Twin Brothers, which had wintered at the island. 12 And landing at Syracuse, we stayed three days. 13 From there we circled round and reached Rhegium. And after one day the south wind blew; and the next day we came to Puteoli, 14 where we found brethren, and were invited to stay with them seven days. And so we went toward Rome. 15 And from there, when the brethren heard about us, they came to meet us as far as Appii Forum and Three Inns. When Paul saw them, he thanked God and took courage.

16 Now when we came to Rome, the centurion delivered the prisoners to the captain of the guard; but Paul was permitted to dwell by himself with the soldier who guarded him.

17 And it came to pass after three days that Paul called the leaders of the Jews together. So when they had come together, he said to them: "Men *and* brethren, though I have done nothing against our people or the customs of our fathers, yet I was delivered as a prisoner from Jerusalem into the hands of the Romans, 18 who, when they had examined me, wanted to let *me* go, because there was no cause for putting me to death. 19 But when the Jews spoke against *it*, I was compelled to appeal to Caesar, not that I had anything of which to accuse my nation. 20 For this reason therefore I have called for you, to see *you* and speak with *you,* because for the hope of Israel I am bound with this chain."

21 Then they said to him, "We neither received letters from Judea concerning you, nor have any of the brethren who came reported or spoken any evil of you. 22 But we desire to hear from you what you think; for concerning this sect, we know that it is spoken against everywhere."

23 So when they had appointed him a day, many came to him at *his* lodging, to whom he explained and solemnly testified of the kingdom of God, persuading them concerning Jesus from both the Law of Moses and the Prophets, from morning till evening. 24 And some were persuaded by the things

7 סָמוּךְ לְאוֹתוֹ מָקוֹם הָיוּ שְׂדוֹתָיו שֶׁל רֹאשׁ הָאִי, פּוּבְּלִיּוֹס שְׁמוֹ. הוּא קִבֵּל אוֹתָנוּ וְאֵרַח אוֹתָנוּ בִּידִידוּת שְׁלוֹשָׁה יָמִים. 8 אוֹתָה עֵת שָׁכַב אָבִיו שֶׁל פּוּבְּלִיּוֹס כְּשֶׁהוּא סוֹבֵל מֵחֹם וְדִיזֶנְטֶרְיָה. שָׁאוּל נִכְנַס אֵלָיו, הִתְפַּלֵּל וְסָמַךְ יָדָיו עָלָיו וְרִפֵּא אוֹתוֹ. 9 אַחֲרֵי כֵן בָּאוּ גַּם יֶתֶר הַחוֹלִים אֲשֶׁר בָּאִי וְנִרְפְּאוּ. 10 הֵם כִּבְּדוּ אוֹתָנוּ בִּמְחֹוֹת כָּבוֹד רַבּוֹת וּכְשֶׁעָמַדְנוּ לְהַפְלִיג נָתְנוּ לָנוּ אֶת הָאַסְפָּקָה הַנְּחוּצָה.

11 אַחֲרֵי שְׁלוֹשָׁה חֳדָשִׁים עָלִינוּ עַל אֳנִיָּה אֲלֶכְּסַנְדְּרִית נוֹשֵׂאת סֵמֶל הָאֵלִים הַתְּאוֹמִים, שֶׁהִמְתִּינָה כָּל הַחֹרֶף בָּאִי. 12 יָרַדְנוּ בְּסִירָקוּ וְנִשְׁאַרְנוּ שָׁם שְׁלוֹשָׁה יָמִים. 13 מִשָּׁם שַׁטְנוּ הָלְאָה וְהִגַּעֲנוּ לְרֶגְיוּם. יוֹם אֶחָד אַחֲרֵי כֵן נָשְׁבָה רוּחַ דְּרוֹמִית וּלְמָחֳרָת בָּאנוּ אֶל פּוֹטִיוֹלִי. 14 מָצָאנוּ שָׁם אַחִים וְנִתְבַּקַּשְׁנוּ לְהִשָּׁאֵר אֶצְלָם שִׁבְעָה יָמִים. כָּךְ בָּאנוּ לְרוֹמָא. 15 הָאַחִים אֲשֶׁר שָׁם שָׁמְעוּ עָלֵינוּ וְיָצְאוּ לִקְרָאתֵנוּ עַד לְכִכַּר אַפִּיּוֹם וּשְׁלֹשֶׁת הַפֻּנְדָּקִים. כְּשֶׁרָאָה אוֹתָם שָׁאוּל, הוֹדָה לָאֱלֹהִים וְהִתְעוֹדֵד.

16 בָּאנוּ לְרוֹמָא וְשָׁם הֻתַּר לְשָׁאוּל לְהִתְגּוֹרֵר לְבַדּוֹ עִם חַיָּל שֶׁשָּׁמַר עָלָיו. 17 אַחֲרֵי שְׁלוֹשָׁה יָמִים הַזְּמִין שָׁאוּל אֶת רָאשֵׁי הַיְּהוּדִים. כַּאֲשֶׁר הִתְכַּנְּסוּ יַחַד אָמַר לָהֶם: "אֲנָשִׁים אַחִים, אֲנִי לֹא עָשִׂיתִי דָבָר נֶגֶד הָעָם אוֹ נֶגֶד מִנְהֲגֵי אֲבוֹתֵינוּ וּבְכָל זֹאת נִמְסַרְתִּי כְּאָסִיר מִירוּשָׁלַיִם לִידֵי הָרוֹמָאִים. 18 הַלָּלוּ חָקְרוּ אוֹתִי וּכְשֶׁלֹּא מָצְאוּ בִּי שׁוּם אַשְׁמַת מָוֶת הִתְכַּוְּנוּ לְשַׁחְרְרֵנִי. 19 אֲבָל רָאשֵׁי הַיְּהוּדִים הִתְנַגְּדוּ וְלָכֵן נֶאֱלַצְתִּי לִפְנוֹת אֶל הַקֵּיסַר – לֹא שֶׁיֵּשׁ לִי אֵיזֶה דָבָר לְהַאֲשִׁים בּוֹ אֶת עַמִּי. 20 מִשּׁוּם כָּךְ בִּקַּשְׁתִּי לִרְאוֹת אֶתְכֶם וּלְדַבֵּר עִמָּכֶם, כִּי בִּגְלַל תִּקְוַת יִשְׂרָאֵל אֲנִי אָסוּר בַּכֶּבֶל הַזֶּה."

21 הֵשִׁיבוּ וְאָמְרוּ לוֹ: "לֹא קִבַּלְנוּ אִגְּרוֹת עַל־אוֹדוֹתֶיךָ מֵאֶרֶץ יְהוּדָה, אַף לֹא הִגִּיעַ אִישׁ מִן הָאַחִים וְהוֹדִיעַ אוֹ דִבֵּר מַשֶּׁהוּ רַע עָלֶיךָ. 22 אֲבָל מִן הָרָאוּי שֶׁנִּשְׁמַע מִפִּיךָ מַה דֵּעוֹתֶיךָ, כִּי יָדוּעַ לָנוּ שֶׁבְּכָל מָקוֹם מִתְנַגְּדִים לַכַּת הַזֹּאת."

23 הֵם קָבְעוּ אִתּוֹ מוֹעֵד וּבַיּוֹם שֶׁנִּקְבַּע בָּאוּ רַבִּים עוֹד יוֹתֵר אֶל מְקוֹם מְגוּרָיו. הוּא הֵעִיד מֵהַבֹּקֶר עַד הָעֶרֶב וְהִסְבִּיר לָהֶם אֶת מַלְכוּת הָאֱלֹהִים, וְהוֹכִיחַ לָהֶם עַל־אוֹדוֹת יֵשׁוּעַ מִתּוֹרַת מֹשֶׁה וּמִן הַנְּבִיאִים. 24 יֵשׁ שֶׁהִשְׁתַּכְנְעוּ מִדְּבָרָיו וְיֵשׁ שֶׁלֹּא הֶאֱמִינוּ. 25 הֵם

which were spoken, and some disbelieved. ²⁵So
when they did not agree among themselves, they
departed after Paul had said one word: "The Holy
Spirit spoke rightly through Isaiah the prophet to
our fathers, ²⁶saying,

> 'Go to this people and say:
> "Hearing you will hear, and shall not under-
>   stand;
> And seeing you will see, and not perceive;
> ²⁷ For the hearts of this people have grown
>   dull.
> Their ears are hard of hearing,
> And their eyes they have closed,
> Lest they should see with their eyes and hear
>   with their ears,
> Lest they should understand with their hearts
>   and turn,
> So that I should heal them."'

²⁸"Therefore let it be known to you that the
salvation of God has been sent to the Gentiles, and
they will hear it!" ²⁹And when he had said these
words, the Jews departed and had a great dispute
among themselves.

³⁰Then Paul dwelt two whole years in his own
rented house, and received all who came to him,
³¹preaching the kingdom of God and teaching the
things which concern the Lord Jesus Christ with all
confidence, no one forbidding him.

לֹא הִסְכִּימוּ אִישׁ עִם רֵעֵהוּ וְהָלְכוּ לְדַרְכָּם לְאַחַר

שֶׁשָּׁאוּל אָמַר לָהֶם: "הֵיטֵב דִּבְּרָה רוּחַ הַקֹּדֶשׁ

לַאֲבוֹתֵיכֶם בְּפִי יְשַׁעְיָהוּ הַנָּבִיא לֵאמֹר:

26 לֵךְ וְאָמַרְתָּ לָעָם הַזֶּה:

שִׁמְעוּ שָׁמוֹעַ וְאַל־תָּבִינוּ

וּרְאוּ רָאוֹ וְאַל־תֵּדָעוּ;

27 הַשְׁמֵן לֵב־הָעָם הַזֶּה

וְאָזְנָיו הַכְבֵּד וְעֵינָיו הָשַׁע;

פֶּן־יִרְאֶה בְעֵינָיו וּבְאָזְנָיו יִשְׁמָע

וּלְבָבוֹ יָבִין וָשָׁב וְרָפָא לוֹ.'

28 לָכֵן שֶׁיְּהֵא יָדוּעַ לָכֶם כִּי אֶל הַגּוֹיִים נִשְׁלְחָה

תְּשׁוּעַת אֱלֹהִים וְהֵם יִשְׁמָעוּ."

30 שָׁאוּל יָשַׁב שְׁנָתַיִם תְּמִימוֹת בְּדִירָה שֶׁשָּׂכַר לוֹ,

וְקִבֵּל אֶת כָּל הַבָּאִים אֵלָיו. 31 הוּא הִכְרִיז אֶת

מַלְכוּת הָאֱלֹהִים וְלִמֵּד עַל־אוֹדוֹת הָאָדוֹן יֵשׁוּעַ בְּלִי

כָּל פַּחַד וּבְאֵין מַפְרִיעַ.

The Epistle of Paul to the

ROMANS

1 Paul, a bondservant of Jesus Christ, called *to be* an apostle, separated to the gospel of God [2]which He promised before through His prophets in the Holy Scriptures, [3]concerning His Son Jesus Christ our Lord, who was born of the seed of David according to the flesh, [4]*and* declared *to be* the Son of God with power according to the Spirit of holiness, by the resurrection from the dead. [5]Through Him we have received grace and apostleship for obedience to the faith among all nations for His name, [6]among whom you also are the called of Jesus Christ;

[7]To all who are in Rome, beloved of God, called *to be* saints:

Grace to you and peace from God our Father and the Lord Jesus Christ.

[8]First, I thank my God through Jesus Christ for you all, that your faith is spoken of throughout the whole world. [9]For God is my witness, whom I serve with my spirit in the gospel of His Son, that without ceasing I make mention of you always in my prayers, [10]making request if, by some means, now at last I may find a way in the will of God to come to you. [11]For I long to see you, that I may impart to you some spiritual gift, so that you may be established— [12]that is, that I may be encouraged together with you by the mutual faith both of you and me.

[13]Now I do not want you to be unaware, brethren, that I often planned to come to you (but was hindered until now), that I might have some fruit among you also, just as among the other Gentiles. [14]I am a debtor both to Greeks and to barbarians, both to wise and to unwise. [15]So, as much as is in me, *I am* ready to preach the gospel to you who are in Rome also.

[16]For I am not ashamed of the gospel of Christ, for it is the power of God to salvation for everyone who believes, for the Jew first and also for the Greek. [17]For in it the righteousness of God is revealed from faith to faith; as it is written, *"The just shall live by faith."*

[18]For the wrath of God is revealed from heaven against all ungodliness and unrighteousness of men, who suppress the truth in unrighteousness, [19]because what may be known of God is manifest in them, for God has shown *it* to them. [20]For since the

אִגֶּרֶת שָׁאוּל אֶל הָרוֹמִיִּם

א מֵאֵת שָׁאוּל, עֶבֶד הַמָּשִׁיחַ יֵשׁוּעַ, אֲשֶׁר נִקְרָא לִהְיוֹת שָׁלִיחַ וְיֻחַד לִבְשׂוֹרַת אֱלֹהִים, [2]בִּשׂוֹרָה שֶׁאֱלֹהִים הִבְטִיחַ מִקֶּדֶם בְּפִי נְבִיאָיו בְּכִתְבֵי הַקֹּדֶשׁ, [3]עַל־אוֹדוֹת בְּנוֹ, יֵשׁוּעַ הַמָּשִׁיחַ אֲדוֹנֵנוּ, שֶׁלְּפִי הַבָּשָׂר מוֹצָאוֹ מִזֶּרַע דָּוִד [4]וּלְפִי רוּחַ הַקֹּדֶשׁ הֻפַן שֶׁהוּא בֶּן־ אֱלֹהִים בִּגְבוּרָה בִּתְחִיָּתוֹ מִן הַמֵּתִים. [5]דַּרְכּוֹ קִבַּלְנוּ חֶסֶד וּשְׁלִיחוּת לְהָבִיא לִידֵי צִיּוּת שֶׁבָּאֱמוּנָה בְּכָל הָאֻמּוֹת לְמַעַן שְׁמוֹ; [6]בֵּינֵיהֶם גַּם אַתֶּם קְרוּאֵי יֵשׁוּעַ הַמָּשִׁיחַ.

[7]וּבְכֵן, אֶל כָּל אֲהוּבֵי אֱלֹהִים בְּרוֹמָא הַנִּקְרָאִים לִהְיוֹת קְדוֹשִׁים: חֶסֶד וְשָׁלוֹם לָכֶם מֵאֵת הָאֱלֹהִים אָבִינוּ וְהָאָדוֹן יֵשׁוּעַ הַמָּשִׁיחַ.

[8]רֵאשִׁית, אֲנִי מוֹדֶה לֵאלֹהַי עַל כֻּלְּכֶם בְּאֶמְצָעוּת יֵשׁוּעַ הַמָּשִׁיחַ, מִשּׁוּם שֶׁדְּבַר אֱמוּנַתְכֶם נִשְׁמַע בְּכָל הָעוֹלָם. [9]וְהָאֱלֹהִים אֲשֶׁר אֲנִי עוֹבֵד אוֹתוֹ בְּרוּחִי בְּהַכְרִיזִי אֶת בְּשׂוֹרַת בְּנוֹ, הוּא עֵדִי לְכָךְ שֶׁאֲנִי מַזְכִּיר אֶתְכֶם לְלֹא הֶרֶף בִּתְפִלּוֹתַי, [10]וּמְבַקֵּשׁ אֲנִי תָּמִיד כִּי אַצְלִיחַ פַּעַם בְּאֵיזֶה אֹפֶן שֶׁהוּא לָבוֹא אֲלֵיכֶם, אִם יִרְצֶה אֱלֹהִים, [11]שֶׁכֵּן אֲנִי נִכְסָף לִרְאוֹתְכֶם כְּדֵי לַחֲלֹק עִמָּכֶם מַתָּנָה רוּחָנִית לְחִזּוּקְכֶם; [12]כְּלוֹמַר, שֶׁנִּתְעוֹדֵד יַחְדָּיו בָּאֱמוּנָה הַמְשֻׁתֶּפֶת לָכֶם וְגַם לִי. [13]אֵינֶנִּי רוֹצֶה שֶׁיֵּעָלֵם מִכֶּם, אַחַי, שֶׁפְּעָמִים רַבּוֹת הִתְכַּוַּנְתִּי לָבוֹא אֲלֵיכֶם, כְּדֵי שֶׁגַּם בְּקִרְבְּכֶם אוּכַל לַעֲשׂוֹת פְּרִי כְּבִקְרֶב יֶתֶר הַגּוֹיִים, אַךְ עַד כֹּה נִמְנַע מִמֶּנִּי לָבוֹא. [14]חַיָּב אֲנִי לַיְּוָנִים וְגַם לִבְנֵי עַמִּים אֲחֵרִים, לִבְנֵי תַּרְבּוּת וְגַם לַחַסְרֵי תַּרְבּוּת. [15]מִשּׁוּם כָּךְ בִּרְצוֹנִי לְבַשֵּׂר אֶת הַבְּשׂוֹרָה גַּם לָכֶם הַנִּמְצָאִים בְּרוֹמָא.

[16]אֵינֶנִּי בּוֹשׁ בִּבְשׂוֹרַת הַמָּשִׁיחַ, שֶׁהֲרֵי הִיא כֹּחַ הָאֱלֹהִים לְהוֹשִׁיעַ אֶת כָּל מִי שֶׁמַּאֲמִין, אֶת הַיְּהוּדִי בָּרִאשׁוֹנָה וְגַם אֶת הַלֹּא־יְהוּדִי; [17]כִּי בָּהּ צִדְקַת הָאֱלֹהִים מִתְגַּלָּה מִתּוֹךְ אֱמוּנָה לְתַכְלִית אֱמוּנָה, כַּכָּתוּב: "וְצַדִּיק בֶּאֱמוּנָתוֹ יִחְיֶה."

[18]וְאָמְנָם זַעַם אֱלֹהִים נִגְלָה מִן הַשָּׁמַיִם עַל כָּל עַוְלָתָם וְרִשְׁעָתָם שֶׁל בְּנֵי אָדָם הַמְעַכְּבִים בְּרִשְׁעָתָם אֶת הָאֱמֶת; [19]כִּי מַה שֶּׁנּוֹדַע עַל אֱלֹהִים גָּלוּי בְּקִרְבָּם, שֶׁהֲרֵי אֱלֹהִים גִּלָּה לָהֶם. [20]הֲלֹא עַצְמוּתוֹ

creation of the world His invisible *attributes* are clearly seen, being understood by the things that are made, *even* His eternal power and Godhead, so that they are without excuse, 21 because, although they knew God, they did not glorify *Him* as God, nor were thankful, but became futile in their thoughts, and their foolish hearts were darkened. 22 Professing to be wise, they became fools, 23 and changed the glory of the incorruptible God into an image made like corruptible man—and birds and four-footed animals and creeping things.

24 Therefore God also gave them up to uncleanness, in the lusts of their hearts, to dishonor their bodies among themselves, 25 who exchanged the truth of God for the lie, and worshiped and served the creature rather than the Creator, who is blessed forever. Amen.

26 For this reason God gave them up to vile passions. For even their women exchanged the natural use for what is against nature. 27 Likewise also the men, leaving the natural use of the woman, burned in their lust for one another, men with men committing what is shameful, and receiving in themselves the penalty of their error which was due.

28 And even as they did not like to retain God in *their* knowledge, God gave them over to a debased mind, to do those things which are not fitting; 29 being filled with all unrighteousness, sexual immorality, wickedness, covetousness, maliciousness; full of envy, murder, strife, deceit, evilmindedness; *they are* whisperers, 30 backbiters, haters of God, violent, proud, boasters, inventors of evil things, disobedient to parents, 31 undiscerning, untrustworthy, unloving, unforgiving, unmerciful; 32 who, knowing the righteous judgment of God, that those who practice such things are deserving of death, not only do the same but also approve of those who practice them.

2 Therefore you are inexcusable, O man, whoever you are who judge, for in whatever you judge another you condemn yourself; for you who judge practice the same things. 2 But we know that the judgment of God is according to truth against those who practice such things. 3 And do you think this, O man, you who judge those practicing such things, and doing the same, that you will escape the judgment of God? 4 Or do you despise the riches of His goodness, forbearance, and longsuffering, not knowing that the goodness of God leads you to repentance? 5 But in accordance with your hardness and your impenitent heart you are treasuring up for yourself wrath in the day of wrath and revelation of the righteous judgment of God, 6 who *"will render*

הַנֶּעְלָמֶת, הִיא כֹחוֹ הַנִּצְחִי וֵאלֹהוּתוֹ, נִרְאֵית בְּבֵרוּר מֵאָז בְּרִיאַת הָעוֹלָם בִּהְיוֹתָה נִתְפֶּסֶת בַּשֵּׂכֶל בְּאֶמְצָעוּת הַדְּבָרִים שֶׁנִּבְרָאוּ. לָכֵן אֵין לָהֶם בַּמֶּה לְהִצְטַדֵּק, 21 שֶׁהֲרֵי לַמְרוֹת שֶׁיּוֹדְעִים הֵם אֶת אֱלֹהִים לֹא כִּבְּדוּ אוֹתוֹ כָּרָאוּי לֵאלֹהִים, אַף לֹא הוֹדוּ לוֹ, אֶלָּא נִתְפְּסוּ לְמַחֲשֶׁבֶת הֶבֶל וְנִטַּמְטַם לִבָּם הָאֱוִילִי. 22 הֵם הִתְיַמְּרוּ לִהְיוֹת חֲכָמִים, אַךְ נִהְיוּ לִכְסִילִים 23 וְהֵמִירוּ אֶת כְּבוֹדוֹ שֶׁל אֱלֹהִים בִּלְתִּי חוֹלֵף בִּדְמוּת צַלְמוֹ שֶׁל אָדָם בֶּן־חֲלוֹף וּבִדְמוּת צַלְמֵי עוֹפוֹת, חַיּוֹת וּרְמָשִׂים. 24 לָכֵן מְסָרָם אֱלֹהִים לְטֻמְאָה בִּידֵי תַאֲוֹת לִבָּם, לְחַלֵּל אֶת גּוּפָם בֵּינָם לְבֵין עַצְמָם – 25 אֲנָשִׁים שֶׁהֵמִירוּ אֶת אֱמֶת הָאֱלֹהִים בַּשֶּׁקֶר וְכִבְּדוּ וְעָבְדוּ אֶת הַנִּבְרָא בִּמְקוֹם אֶת הַבּוֹרֵא הַמְבֹרָךְ לְעוֹלָמִים. אָמֵן. 26 מִשּׁוּם כָּךְ הִסְגִּירָם אֱלֹהִים לִתְשׁוּקוֹת בִּזְוִיּוֹת, עַד כִּי אֲפִלּוּ נְשֵׁיהֶם הֶחֱלִיפוּ יְחָסִים טִבְעִיִּים בְּבִלְתִּי טִבְעִיִּים. 27 וְכֵן גַּם הַגְּבָרִים נָטְשׁוּ אֶת הַיְחָסִים הַטִּבְעִיִּים עִם הַנָּשִׁים וּבָעֲרוּ בְּתַאֲוָה זֶה אֶל זֶה, גְּבָרִים עָשׂוּ תּוֹעֵבָה בִּגְבָרִים וְקִבְּלוּ בְּגוּפָם הֵם אֶת הַגְּמוּל הָרָאוּי לִסְטִיָּה שֶׁלָּהֶם. 28 וְכֵיוָן שֶׁלֹּא חָשְׁבוּ לְנָכוֹן לְהַכִּיר בֵּאלֹהִים, הִסְגִּירָם אֱלֹהִים לַהֲלָךְ־רוּחַ מֻגְנֶה, לַעֲשׂוֹת אֶת הַדְּבָרִים שֶׁאֵינָם הֲגוּנִים. 29 אָכֵן מְלֵאִים הֵם בְּכָל עַוְלָה, רֶשַׁע, חַמְדָנוּת, רֹעַ; מְלֵאֵי קִנְאָה, רֶצַח, מְרִיבָה, מִרְמָה, מִזִּמָּה. 30 הוֹלְכֵי רָכִיל הֵם, מוֹצִיאֵי דִבָּה, שׂוֹנְאֵי אֱלֹהִים, חֲצוּפִים, גֵּאִים, רַבְרְבָנִים, חוֹרְשֵׁי רָעָה, מַמְרִים פִּי הוֹרִים, 31 חַסְרֵי הֲבָנָה, בִּלְתִּי נֶאֱמָנִים, קְשׁוּחֵי לֵב, אַכְזָרִים. 32 הֵם יוֹדְעִים אֶת חֻקַּת אֱלֹהִים, אֲשֶׁר לְפִיהָ עוֹשֵׂי מַעֲשִׂים כָּאֵלֶּה רְאוּיִים לְמִיתָה, אַךְ לֹא זֹאת בִּלְבַד שֶׁהֵם עוֹשִׂים אוֹתָם, הֵם גַּם תּוֹמְכִים בְּעוֹשֵׂיהֶם.

ב עַל כֵּן אַתָּה, בֶּן־אָדָם, בֶּן־אָדָם הַחוֹרֵץ מִשְׁפָּט, אֵין לְךָ בַּמֶּה לְהִצְטַדֵּק, וְתִהְיֶה מִי שֶׁתִּהְיֶה, כִּי בְּשָׁפְטְךָ אֶת הַזּוּלַת אַתָּה מַרְשִׁיעַ אֶת עַצְמְךָ, שֶׁכֵּן אַתָּה הַחוֹרֵץ מִשְׁפָּט עוֹשֶׂה אוֹתָם דְּבָרִים. 2 אֲנַחְנוּ יוֹדְעִים שֶׁאֱלֹהִים שׁוֹפֵט עַל־פִּי הָאֱמֶת אֶת הָעוֹשִׂים דְּבָרִים כָּאֵלֶּה. 3 וְאַתָּה, בֶּן־אָדָם, הַחוֹרֵץ מִשְׁפָּט עַל הָעוֹשִׂים דְּבָרִים כָּאֵלֶּה וּבְעַצְמְךָ עוֹשֶׂה אוֹתָם, הֲחוֹשֵׁב אַתָּה כִּי תִמָּלֵט מִמִּשְׁפַּט אֱלֹהִים? 4 אוֹ שֶׁמָּא אַתָּה מְזַלְזֵל בְּשֶׁפַע טוּבוֹ וְאֶרֶךְ רוּחוֹ וְסַבְלָנוּתוֹ, וְאֵינְךָ מֵבִין כִּי טוּבוֹ זֶה שֶׁל אֱלֹהִים מַדְרִיךְ אוֹתְךָ לִתְשׁוּבָה? 5 בְּעַקְשָׁנוּתְךָ וּבְסֵרוּב לְבָבְךָ לַחֲזֹר בִּתְשׁוּבָה אַתָּה צוֹבֵר לְךָ זַעַם לְיוֹם זַעַם, בַּיּוֹם שֶׁיִּתְגַּלֶּה מִשְׁפַּט־הַצֶּדֶק שֶׁל אֱלֹהִים, 6 אֲשֶׁר

to each one according to his deeds": [7] eternal life to those who by patient continuance in doing good seek for glory, honor, and immortality; [8] but to those who are self-seeking and do not obey the truth, but obey unrighteousness—indignation and wrath, [9] tribulation and anguish, on every soul of man who does evil, of the Jew first and also of the Greek; [10] but glory, honor, and peace to everyone who works what is good, to the Jew first and also to the Greek. [11] For there is no partiality with God.

[12] For as many as have sinned without law will also perish without law, and as many as have sinned in the law will be judged by the law [13] (for not the hearers of the law *are* just in the sight of God, but the doers of the law will be justified; [14] for when Gentiles, who do not have the law, by nature do the things in the law, these, although not having the law, are a law to themselves, [15] who show the work of the law written in their hearts, their conscience also bearing witness, and between themselves *their* thoughts accusing or else excusing *them*) [16] in the day when God will judge the secrets of men by Jesus Christ, according to my gospel.

[17] Indeed you are called a Jew, and rest on the law, and make your boast in God, [18] and know *His* will, and approve the things that are excellent, being instructed out of the law, [19] and are confident that you yourself are a guide to the blind, a light to those who are in darkness, [20] an instructor of the foolish, a teacher of babes, having the form of knowledge and truth in the law. [21] You, therefore, who teach another, do you not teach yourself? You who preach that a man should not steal, do you steal? [22] You who say, "Do not commit adultery," do you commit adultery? You who abhor idols, do you rob temples? [23] You who make your boast in the law, do you dishonor God through breaking the law? [24] For *"the name of God is blasphemed among the Gentiles because of you,"* as it is written.

[25] For circumcision is indeed profitable if you keep the law; but if you are a breaker of the law, your circumcision has become uncircumcision. [26] Therefore, if an uncircumcised man keeps the righteous requirements of the law, will not his uncircumcision be counted as circumcision? [27] And will not the physically uncircumcised, if he fulfills the law, judge you who, *even with your written code* and circumcision, *are* a transgressor of the law? [28] For he is not a Jew who *is one* outwardly, nor *is* circumcision that which *is* outward in the flesh; [29] but *he is* a Jew who *is one* inwardly; and circumcision *is that* of the heart, in the Spirit, not in the letter; whose praise *is* not from men but from God.

יְשַׁלֵּם לְכָל אִישׁ כְּמַעֲשָׂיו: 7 חַיֵּי עוֹלָם לָאֲנָשִׁים הַמַּתְמִידִים לַעֲשׂוֹת אֶת הַטּוֹב וּמְבַקְּשִׁים אֶת הַתִּפְאֶרֶת וְהַכָּבוֹד וְהָאַלְמָוֶת, 8 אַךְ חֵמָה וָזַעַם לַסּוֹרְרִים אֲשֶׁר אֵינָם נִשְׁמָעִים לָאֱמֶת אֶלָּא לָעַוְלָה; 9 צָרָה וּמְצוּקָה עַל נֶפֶשׁ כָּל אָדָם הָעוֹשֶׂה רָע, עַל הַיְּהוּדִי בָּרִאשׁוֹנָה וְגַם עַל הַלֹּא־יְהוּדִי; 10 אַךְ תִּפְאֶרֶת וְכָבוֹד וְשָׁלוֹם לְכָל הָעוֹשֶׂה אֶת הַטּוֹב, לַיְּהוּדִי בָּרִאשׁוֹנָה וְגַם לְמִי שֶׁאֵינוֹ יְהוּדִי; 11 כִּי אֵין מַשּׂוֹא פָנִים עִם הָאֱלֹהִים, 12 שֶׁכֵּן כָּל אֲשֶׁר חָטְאוּ בְּלִי תוֹרָה גַּם יֹאבְדוּ בְּלִי תוֹרָה, וְכָל אֲשֶׁר חָטְאוּ וְיֵשׁ לָהֶם תּוֹרָה, עַל־פִּי הַתּוֹרָה יִשָּׁפְטוּ. 13 הֲרֵי לֹא שׁוֹמְעֵי הַתּוֹרָה צַדִּיקִים לִפְנֵי אֱלֹהִים, אֶלָּא הַמְקַמְּמִים אֶת הַתּוֹרָה הֵם אֲשֶׁר יִצְדְּקוּ – 14 גּוֹיִים שֶׁאֵין לָהֶם תּוֹרָה וְהֵם מְקַיְּמִים אֶת דִּבְרֵי הַתּוֹרָה כְּדָבָר מוּבָן מֵאֵלָיו, הֵם תּוֹרָה לְעַצְמָם אַף שֶׁאֵין לָהֶם תּוֹרָה. 15 הֵם מַרְאִים שֶׁפֹּעַל הַתּוֹרָה כָּתוּב בְּלִבָּם, שֶׁכֵּן מַצְפּוּנָם מֵעִיד בָּהֶם וּמַחְשְׁבוֹתֵיהֶם מְחַיְּבוֹת אוֹ מְזַכּוֹת אוֹתָם – 16 בַּיּוֹם שֶׁיִּשְׁפֹּט אֱלֹהִים אֶת תַּעֲלוּמוֹת בְּנֵי אָדָם עַל־יְדֵי יֵשׁוּעַ הַמָּשִׁיחַ, כְּדָבָר בְּשׂוֹרָתִי.

17 אֲבָל אִם אַתָּה נִקְרָא יְהוּדִי וְאַתָּה נִשְׁעָן עַל הַתּוֹרָה וּמִתְהַלֵּל בֵּאלֹהִים, 18 וְאַתָּה יוֹדֵעַ אֶת רְצוֹנוֹ וּמַבְחִין בַּדְּבָרִים הַטּוֹבִים, מֵהְיוֹתְךָ מְחֻנָּךְ בַּתּוֹרָה, 19 וְאַתָּה סָמוּךְ וּבָטוּחַ כִּי אַתָּה מוֹרֵה דֶרֶךְ לָעִוְרִים, אוֹר לַשְּׁרוּיִים בַּחֹשֶׁךְ, 20 מַדְרִיךְ לַפְּתָאִים וּמְלַמֵּד לָעוֹלְלִים, וּלְךָ בִּטּוּי הַדַּעַת וְהָאֱמֶת שֶׁבַּתּוֹרָה – 21 הַאִם לֹא תְלַמֵּד אֶת עַצְמְךָ, אַתָּה הַמְלַמֵּד אֲחֵרִים? אַתָּה הַמַּכְרִיז לֹא תִגְנֹב, הֲתִגְנֹב אַתָּה? 22 אַתָּה הָאוֹמֵר לֹא תִנְאַף, הֲתִנְאַף אַתָּה? אַתָּה הַמְתַעֵב אֶת הָאֱלִילִים, הֲתָבֹז אֶת מִקְדָּשֵׁיהֶם? 23 אַתָּה הַמִּתְגָּאֶה בַּתּוֹרָה, הֲתְחַלֵּל אֶת שֵׁם אֱלֹהִים בְּהַפְרְךָ אֶת הַתּוֹרָה? 24 הֲרֵי, כְּפִי שֶׁכָּתוּב, שֵׁם אֱלֹהִים מְחֻלָּל בַּגּוֹיִים בִּגְלַלְכֶם. 25 אָמְנָם יֵשׁ עֵרֶךְ לַמִּילָה אִם אַתָּה מְקַיֵּם אֶת הַתּוֹרָה, אַךְ אִם אַתָּה מֵפֵר אֶת הַתּוֹרָה, מִילָתְךָ נֶהֶיְתָה לְעָרְלָה. 26 לָכֵן אִם יִשְׁמֹר עָרֵל אֶת דִּינֵי הַתּוֹרָה, הַאִם לֹא תֵחָשֵׁב לוֹ עָרְלָתוֹ לְמִילָה? 27 וְהֶעָרֵל מִבְּחִינָה גּוּפָנִית, הַמְקַיֵּם אֶת הַתּוֹרָה, יָחֲרֹץ עָלֶיךָ מִשְׁפָּט, שֶׁהֲרֵי לְךָ הַכְּתוּבִים וְהַמִּילָה וְאַתָּה מֵפֵר אֶת הַתּוֹרָה. 28 הֵן לֹא עַל־פִּי מַרְאִית עַיִן יְהוּדִי הוּא יְהוּדִי, וְלֹא מַה שֶּׁרוּאִים בַּגּוּף הוּא מִילָה. 29 יְהוּדִי הוּא זֶה שֶׁבְּתוֹךְ תּוֹכוֹ הוּא יְהוּדִי וּמִילָה הִיא זוֹ שֶׁבַּלֵּב, לְפִי הָרוּחַ וְלֹא לְפִי אוֹת כְּתוּבָה; שֶׁבְּחוֹ אֵינוֹ בָּא מִבְּנֵי אָדָם, כִּי אִם מֵאֱלֹהִים.

3 What advantage then has the Jew, or what *is* the profit of circumcision? ² Much in every way! Chiefly because to them were committed the oracles of God. ³ For what if some did not believe? Will their unbelief make the faithfulness of God without effect? ⁴ Certainly not! Indeed, let God be true but every man a liar. As it is written:

"That You may be justified in Your words,
And may overcome when You are judged."

⁵ But if our unrighteousness demonstrates the righteousness of God, what shall we say? *Is God unjust who inflicts wrath?* (I speak as a man.) ⁶ Certainly not! For then how will God judge the world?

⁷ For if the truth of God has increased through my lie to His glory, why am I also still judged as a sinner? ⁸ And *why* not *say*, "Let us do evil that good may come"?—as we are slanderously reported and as some affirm that we say. Their condemnation is just.

⁹ What then? Are we better *than they?* Not at all. For we have previously charged both Jews and Greeks that they are all under sin.

¹⁰ As it is written:

"There is none righteous, no, not one;
11   There is none who understands;
There is none who seeks after God.
12   They have all turned aside;
They have together become unprofitable;
There is none who does good, no, not one."
13   "Their throat *is* an open tomb;
With their tongues they have practiced deceit";
"The poison of asps *is* under their lips";
14   "Whose mouth *is* full of cursing and bitterness."
15   "Their feet *are* swift to shed blood;
16   Destruction and misery *are* in their ways;
17   And the way of peace they have not known."
18   "There is no fear of God before their eyes."

¹⁹ Now we know that whatever the law says, it says to those who are under the law, that every mouth may be stopped, and all the world may become guilty before God. ²⁰ Therefore by the deeds of the law no flesh will be justified in His sight, for by the law *is* the knowledge of sin.

²¹ But now the righteousness of God apart from the law is revealed, being witnessed by the Law and the Prophets, ²² even the righteousness of God, through faith in Jesus Christ, to all and on all who believe. For there is no difference; ²³ for all have

---

א אִם כֵּן, מַהוּ יִתְרוֹנוֹ שֶׁל הַיְּהוּדִי אוֹ מָה הַתּוֹעֶלֶת אֲשֶׁר בַּמִּילָה? ² הַרְבֵּה, מִכָּל הַבְּחִינוֹת; רֵאשִׁית כֹּל, בִּידֵיהֶם הֻפְקְדוּ דִּבְרֵי אֱלֹהִים. ³ וְאִם יֵשׁ שֶׁלֹּא הֶאֱמִינוּ, אֲזַי מָה? הַאִם יְבַטֵּל חֹסֶר אֱמוּנָתָם אֶת נֶאֱמָנוּתוֹ שֶׁל אֱלֹהִים? ⁴ חָלִילָה! צָרִיךְ שֶׁיֵּכֵר כִּי הָאֱלֹהִים נֶאֱמָן וְכָל אָדָם כּוֹזֵב, כַּכָּתוּב: "לְמַעַן תִּצְדַּק בְּדַבְרֶךָ, תִּזְכֶּה בְשָׁפְטֶךָ." ⁵ אֲבָל אִם רִשְׁעָתֵנוּ מַפְגִּינָה אֶת הַצֶּדֶק שֶׁל אֱלֹהִים, מַה נֹּאמַר? הַאִם יֵשׁ עָוֶל בֵּאלֹהִים הַשּׁוֹפֵךְ אֶת זַעֲמוֹ – וַאֲנִי מְדַבֵּר מִנְּקֻדַּת מַבָּטוֹ שֶׁל הָאָדָם – ⁶ חַס וְחָלִילָה! שֶׁאִם כֵּן, אֵיךְ יִשְׁפֹּט אֱלֹהִים אֶת הָעוֹלָם? ⁷ אַךְ אִם בִּגְלַל מִרְמָתִי מִשְׂגַּשֶׂגֶת אֱמֶת הָאֱלֹהִים לְתִהְלָתוֹ, מַדּוּעַ עוֹד אֲשָׁפֵט כְּחוֹטֵא? ⁸ וּמַדּוּעַ לֹא "נַעֲשֶׂה אֶת הָרַע כְּדֵי שֶׁיֵּצֵא טוֹב", כְּפִי שֶׁמַּעֲלִילִים עָלֵינוּ וְטוֹעֲנִים כִּי כָךְ אָנוּ אוֹמְרִים? אָכֵן מִשְׁפָּט צֶדֶק נֶחֱרַץ עֲלֵיהֶם.

⁹ וּבְכֵן, הֲטוֹבִים אָנוּ מֵאֲחֵרִים? לֹא, כְּלָל וּכְלָל לֹא; שֶׁהֲרֵי כְּבָר הוֹכַחְנוּ לְעֵיל כִּי הַיְּהוּדִים וְהַגּוֹיִים כְּאֶחָד מְשֻׁעְבָּדִים כֻּלָּם לַחֵטְא, ¹⁰ כַּכָּתוּב:

"אֵין צַדִּיק, אֵין גַּם אֶחָד.
¹¹ אֵין מַשְׂכִּיל, אֵין דֹּרֵשׁ אֶת־אֱלֹהִים.
¹² הַכֹּל סָר, יַחְדָּו נֶאֱלָחוּ;
אֵין עֹשֵׂה־טוֹב, אֵין גַּם־אֶחָד.
¹³ קֶבֶר־פָּתוּחַ גְּרֹנָם, לְשׁוֹנָם יַחֲלִיקוּן,
חֲמַת עַכְשׁוּב תַּחַת שְׂפָתֵימוֹ;
¹⁴ אֲשֶׁר אָלָה פִּיהֶם מָלֵא וּמְרֹרוֹת.
¹⁵ רַגְלֵיהֶם יְמַהֲרוּ לִשְׁפָּךְ דָּם.
¹⁶ שֹׁד וָשֶׁבֶר בִּמְסִלּוֹתָם,
¹⁷ וְדֶרֶךְ שָׁלוֹם לֹא יָדָעוּ.
¹⁸ אֵין־פַּחַד אֱלֹהִים לְנֶגֶד עֵינֵיהֶם."

¹⁹ אָנוּ יוֹדְעִים כִּי כָּל מַה שֶּׁהַתּוֹרָה אוֹמֶרֶת, הִיא אוֹמֶרֶת לָאֲנָשִׁים הַכְּפוּפִים לַתּוֹרָה, כְּדֵי שֶׁלֹּא יִהְיֶה פִּתְחוֹן פֶּה לְאִישׁ וְכָל הָעוֹלָם יִמָּצֵא אָשֵׁם לִפְנֵי אֱלֹהִים. ²⁰ זֹאת מִפְּנֵי שֶׁבְּמַעֲשֵׂי הַתּוֹרָה לֹא יִצְדַּק לְפָנָיו כָּל בָּשָׂר, כִּי הַתּוֹרָה רַק מְבִיאָה לִידֵי הַכָּרַת חֵטְא.

²¹ אַךְ כָּעֵת נִגְלְתָה צִדְקַת הָאֱלֹהִים בְּלִי תּוֹרָה, צְדָקָה שֶׁהַתּוֹרָה וְהַנְּבִיאִים מְעִידִים עָלֶיהָ. ²² וְהִיא צְדָקָה שֶׁל הָאֱלֹהִים, בְּאֶמְצָעוּת אֱמוּנַת יֵשׁוּעַ הַמָּשִׁיחַ, אֶל כָּל וְעַל כָּל הַמַּאֲמִינִים; שֶׁהֲרֵי אֵין הֶבְדֵּל, ²³ כִּי הַכֹּל חָטְאוּ וּמְחֻסְּרֵי כְּבוֹד אֱלֹהִים

sinned and fall short of the glory of God, 24 being justified freely by His grace through the redemption that is in Christ Jesus, 25 whom God set forth *as a* propitiation by His blood, through faith, to demonstrate His righteousness, because in His forbearance God had passed over the sins that were previously committed, 26 to demonstrate at the present time His righteousness, that He might be just and the justifier of the one who has faith in Jesus.

27 Where *is* boasting then? It is excluded. By what law? Of works? No, but by the law of faith. 28 Therefore we conclude that a man is justified by faith apart from the deeds of the law. 29 Or *is He* the God of the Jews only? *Is He* not also the God of the Gentiles? Yes, of the Gentiles also, 30 since *there is* one God who will justify the circumcised by faith and the uncircumcised through faith. 31 Do we then make void the law through faith? Certainly not! On the contrary, we establish the law.

4 What then shall we say that Abraham our father has found according to the flesh? 2 For if Abraham was justified by works, he has *something* to boast about, but not before God. 3 For what does the Scripture say? *"Abraham believed God, and it was accounted to him for righteousness."* 4 Now to him who works, the wages are not counted as grace but as debt.

5 But to him who does not work but believes on Him who justifies the ungodly, his faith is accounted for righteousness, 6 just as David also describes the blessedness of the man to whom God imputes righteousness apart from works:

7 *"Blessed are those whose lawless deeds are forgiven,*
And whose sins are covered;
8 *Blessed is the man to whom the* LORD *shall not impute sin."*

9 *Does* this blessedness then *come* upon the circumcised *only,* or upon the uncircumcised also? For we say that faith was accounted to Abraham for righteousness. 10 How then was it accounted? While he was circumcised, or uncircumcised? Not while circumcised, but while uncircumcised. 11 And he received the sign of circumcision, a seal of the righteousness of the faith which *he had while still* uncircumcised, that he might be the father of all those who believe, though they are uncircumcised, that righteousness might be imputed to them also, 12 and the father of circumcision to those who not

הֵמָּה. 24 אַךְ הֵם מֻצְדָּקִים בְּחַסְדּוֹ, בְּחִנָּם, הוֹדוֹת לַפְּדוּת שֶׁבַּמָּשִׁיחַ יֵשׁוּעַ, 25 אֲשֶׁר הָאֱלֹהִים שָׂם אוֹתוֹ לְכַפָּרָה בְּדָמוֹ, כַּפָּרָה עַל־יְסוֹד אֱמוּנָה. כָּל זֶה כְּדֵי לְהַרְאוֹת אֶת הַצְּדָקָה שֶׁל אֱלֹהִים בְּכָךְ שֶׁבְּאֹרֶךְ רוּחוֹ פָּסַח עַל חֲטָאֵי הֶעָבָר, 26 וּלְהַרְאוֹת אֶת צִדְקָתוֹ בַּזְּמָן הַזֶּה: שֶׁהוּא צַדִּיק וּמַצְדִּיק אֶת בֶּן אֱמוּנַת יֵשׁוּעַ.

27 אִם כֵּן, הֲיֵשׁ מָקוֹם לְגַאֲוָה? לֹא, אֵין לָהּ מָקוֹם. הוֹדוֹת לְאֵיזוֹ תּוֹרָה? שֶׁל הַמַּעֲשִׂים? לֹא, הוֹדוֹת לְתוֹרָה שֶׁל אֱמוּנָה. 28 וְאָמְנָם אָנוּ קוֹבְעִים שֶׁהָאָדָם מֻצְדָּק עַל־יְדֵי אֱמוּנָה לְלֹא תְּלוּת בְּמַעֲשֵׂי הַתּוֹרָה. 29 אוֹ שֶׁמָּא הוּא אֱלֹהֵי הַיְּהוּדִים בִּלְבָד? הַאֵין הוּא גַּם אֱלֹהֵי הַגּוֹיִים? כֵּן, גַּם אֱלֹהֵי הַגּוֹיִים הוּא, 30 שֶׁכֵּן אֱלֹהִים אֶחָד הוּא הַמַּצְדִּיק אֶת הַנִּמּוֹלִים עַל־יְסוֹד אֱמוּנָה, וְאֶת הָעֲרֵלִים עַל־יְדֵי הָאֱמוּנָה. 31 הַאִם אָנוּ מְבַטְּלִים אֵפוֹא אֶת הַתּוֹרָה עַל־יְדֵי הָאֱמוּנָה? חַס וְחָלִילָה! אַדְּרַבָּא, אָנוּ נוֹתְנִים תֹּקֶף לַתּוֹרָה.

ד וּבְכֵן, מַה נֹּאמַר עַל אַבְרָהָם אָבִינוּ, מַה הִשִּׂיג בִּזְכוּת מַעֲשָׂיו הוּא? 2 אִם אָמְנָם הֻצְדַּק אַבְרָהָם בִּגְלַל מַעֲשִׂים, כִּי אָז יֵשׁ לוֹ בַּמֶּה לְהִתְפָּאֵר, אַךְ לֹא לִפְנֵי אֱלֹהִים. 3 מַה אוֹמֵר הַכָּתוּב? "וְהֶאֱמִן אַבְרָהָם בַּיהוה וַיַּחְשְׁבֶהָ לּוֹ צְדָקָה." 4 וַהֲרֵי שְׂכָרוֹ שֶׁל עוֹבֵד אֵינוֹ נֶחְשָׁב לוֹ כְּחֶסֶד, אֶלָּא כְּחוֹב הַמַּגִּיעַ לוֹ. 5 אֲבָל זֶה שֶׁאֵינוֹ עוֹבֵד, אֶלָּא מַאֲמִין בַּמַּצְדִּיק אֶת הַחוֹטֵא, אֱמוּנָתוֹ נֶחְשֶׁבֶת לוֹ לִצְדָקָה. 6 כָּךְ גַּם גַּם דָּוִד מַבִּיעַ אֶת אָשְׁרוֹ שֶׁל הָאִישׁ אֲשֶׁר אֱלֹהִים יַחְשֹׁב לוֹ צְדָקָה בְּלִי תְּלוּת בְּמַעֲשִׂים:

7 "אַשְׁרֵי נְשׂוּי־פֶּשַׁע, כְּסוּי חֲטָאָה.

8 אַשְׁרֵי־אָדָם לֹא יַחְשֹׁב יהוה לוֹ עָוֹן."

9 הַאִם הָאֹשֶׁר הַזֶּה רַק לַנִּמּוֹלִים, אוֹ גַּם לָעֲרֵלִים? וַהֲרֵי אָנוּ אוֹמְרִים כִּי אֱמוּנָתוֹ שֶׁל אַבְרָהָם נֶחְשְׁבָה לוֹ צְדָקָה. 10 מָתַי נֶחְשְׁבָה לוֹ? כַּאֲשֶׁר הָיָה נִמּוֹל אוֹ כְּשֶׁהָיָה עָרֵל? – לֹא בִּהְיוֹתוֹ נִמּוֹל, כִּי אִם בִּהְיוֹתוֹ עָרֵל. 11 הוּא קִבֵּל אֶת אוֹת הַמִּילָה לְצַדֵּקָה שֶׁזָּכָה בָּהּ בִּגְלַל הָאֱמוּנָה בְּעוֹדֶנּוּ עָרֵל, כְּדֵי שֶׁיִּהְיֶה אָב לְכָל הַמַּאֲמִינִים הַבִּלְתִּי נִמּוֹלִים, לְמַעַן תֵּחָשֵׁב גַּם לָהֶם צְדָקָה, 12 וְאָב לַנִּמּוֹלִים, לְאוֹתָם שֶׁאֵינָם

only *are* of the circumcision, but who also walk in the steps of the faith which our father Abraham *had while still* uncircumcised.

[13] For the promise that he would be the heir of the world *was* not to Abraham or to his seed through the law, but through the righteousness of faith. [14] For if those who are of the law *are* heirs, faith is made void and the promise made of no effect, [15] because the law brings about wrath; for where there is no law *there is* no transgression.

[16] Therefore *it is* of faith that *it might be* according to grace, so that the promise might be sure to all the seed, not only to those who are of the law, but also to those who are of the faith of Abraham, who is the father of us all [17] (as it is written, "I have made you a father of many nations") in the presence of Him whom he believed—God, who gives life to the dead and calls those things which do not exist as though they did; [18] who, contrary to hope, in hope believed, so that he became the father of many nations, according to what was spoken, "So shall your descendants be." [19] And not being weak in faith, he did not consider his own body, already dead (since he was about a hundred years old), and the deadness of Sarah's womb. [20] He did not waver at the promise of God through unbelief, but was strengthened in faith, giving glory to God, [21] and being fully convinced that what He had promised He was also able to perform. [22] And therefore "it was accounted to him for righteousness."

[23] Now it was not written for his sake alone that it was imputed to him, [24] but also for us. It shall be imputed to us who believe in Him who raised up Jesus our Lord from the dead, [25] who was delivered up because of our offenses, and was raised because of our justification.

5 Therefore, having been justified by faith, we have peace with God through our Lord Jesus Christ, [2] through whom also we have access by faith into this grace in which we stand, and rejoice in hope of the glory of God. [3] And not only *that*, but we also glory in tribulations, knowing that tribulation produces perseverance; [4] and perseverance, character; and character, hope. [5] Now hope does not disappoint, because the love of God has been poured out in our hearts by the Holy Spirit who was given to us.

[6] For when we were still without strength, in due time Christ died for the ungodly. [7] For scarcely for a righteous man will one die; yet perhaps for a good man someone would even dare to die. [8] But God demonstrates His own love toward us, in that while

נְמוֹלִים בִּלְבַד אֶלָּא גַּם הוֹלְכִים בְּעִקְּבוֹת הָאֱמוּנָה שֶׁהָיְתָה לְאַבְרָהָם אָבִינוּ בְּטֶרֶם נִמּוֹל. [13] הֲרֵי הַהַבְטָחָה כִּי יִירַשׁ אֶת הָעוֹלָם לֹא נִתְּנָה לְאַבְרָהָם אוֹ לְזַרְעוֹ עַל־סְמַךְ תּוֹרָה, אֶלָּא עַל־סְמַךְ צְדָקָה שֶׁהֻשַּׂג בָּאֱמוּנָה, [14] שֶׁכֵּן אִם מַחֲזִיקֵי הַתּוֹרָה הֵם הַיּוֹרְשִׁים, אֲזַי הָאֱמוּנָה הִיא לַשָּׁוְא וְהַהַבְטָחָה חֲסַרַת תֹּקֶף. [15] הַתּוֹרָה מְבִיאָה זַעַם, וּבְמָקוֹם שֶׁאֵין תּוֹרָה אֵין עֲבֵרָה עַל הַתּוֹרָה. [16] לָכֵן עַל־יְדֵי אֱמוּנָה, כְּדֵי שֶׁכָּל זֶה יִהְיֶה בְּחֶסֶד וְהַהַבְטָחָה תָּחוּל עַל כָּל הַצֶּאֱצָאִים, לֹא רַק עַל בְּנֵי הַתּוֹרָה, אֶלָּא גַּם עַל בְּנֵי אֱמוּנַת אַבְרָהָם, שֶׁהוּא אָב לְכֻלָּנוּ – [17] כְּפִי שֶׁכָּתוּב: "כִּי אַב־הֲמוֹן גּוֹיִם נְתַתִּיךָ" – לְעֵינֵי אֱלֹהִים אֲשֶׁר בּוֹ הֶאֱמִין, הָאֱלֹהִים הַמְחַיֶּה אֶת הַמֵּתִים וְהַקּוֹרֵא בְּשֵׁם דְּבָרִים בְּעוֹד אֵינָם בְּנִמְצָא. [18] וּבְאֵין סִבָּה לְתִקְוָה הוּא הֶאֱמִין וְקִוָּה כִּי יִהְיֶה לְאַב־הֲמוֹן גּוֹיִם, כְּפִי שֶׁנֶּאֱמַר: "כֹּה יִהְיֶה זַרְעֶךָ." [19] אֱמוּנָתוֹ לֹא נִתְרוֹפְפָה גַּם כַּאֲשֶׁר בְּהִיּוֹתוֹ כְּבֶן מֵאָה שָׁנִים חָשַׁב עַל תְּשִׁישׁוּת גּוּפוֹ וְעַל עֲקָרוּת שָׂרָה. [20] הוּא לֹא חָדַל מֵאֱמוּנָה וְלֹא פִּקְפֵּק בְּהַבְטָחַת אֱלֹהִים, אֶלָּא הִתְחַזֵּק בֶּאֱמוּנָתוֹ וְנָתַן כָּבוֹד לֵאלֹהִים, [21] בְּהִיּוֹתוֹ בָּטוּחַ לַחֲלוּטִין כִּי אֶת אֲשֶׁר הִבְטִיחַ יוּכַל גַּם לָקֵם. [22] לָכֵן נֶחְשְׁבָה לוֹ זֹאת לִצְדָקָה. [23] וְלֹא לְמַעֲנוֹ בִּלְבַד נִכְתַּב שֶׁנֶּחְשְׁבָה לוֹ, [24] כִּי אִם גַּם לְמַעֲנֵנוּ; וְהִיא עֲתִידָה לְהֵחָשֵׁב לָנוּ – הַמַּאֲמִינִים בְּמִי שֶׁהֵקִים אֶת יֵשׁוּעַ אֲדוֹנֵנוּ מִן הַמֵּתִים, [25] הוּא אֲשֶׁר נִמְסַר לַמָּוֶת מִפְּנֵי חֲטָאֵינוּ וְהוּקַם לִתְחִיָּה מִפְּנֵי שֶׁהִצְדִּיקָנוּ.

ה עַל כֵּן לְאַחַר שֶׁהִצְדִּיקָנוּ עַל־סְמַךְ אֱמוּנָה יֵשׁ לָנוּ שָׁלוֹם עִם אֱלֹהִים הוֹדוֹת לַאֲדוֹנֵנוּ יֵשׁוּעַ הַמָּשִׁיחַ. [2] דַּרְכּוֹ יֵשׁ לָנוּ גַּם גִּישָׁה, בָּאֶמְצָעוּת אֱמוּנָה, לַחֶסֶד הַזֶּה שֶׁאָנוּ עוֹמְדִים בּוֹ, וְאָנוּ מִתְהַלְּלִים בַּתִּקְוָה אֶל כְּבוֹד אֱלֹהִים. [3] אַךְ לֹא זֹאת בִּלְבַד; אֲנַחְנוּ מִתְהַלְּלִים גַּם בַּצָּרוֹת, שֶׁכֵּן יוֹדְעִים אָנוּ כִּי הַצָּרָה מְבִיאָה לִידֵי סַבְלָנוּת, [4] וְהַסַּבְלָנוּת לִידֵי עֲמִידָה בַּנִּסָּיוֹן, וַעֲמִידָה בַּנִּסָּיוֹן לִידֵי תִקְוָה. [5] וְהַתִּקְוָה אֵינָה מַכְזִיבָה, כִּי אַהֲבַת אֱלֹהִים הוּצְקָה לְתוֹךְ לִבֵּנוּ עַל־יְדֵי רוּחַ הַקֹּדֶשׁ שֶׁנִּתְּנָה לָנוּ.

[6] הִנֵּה בְּעוֹד שֶׁהָיִינוּ חַסְרֵי אוֹנִים, בְּהַגִּיעַ הַשָּׁעָה מֵת הַמָּשִׁיחַ בְּעַד הָרְשָׁעִים. [7] וַהֲרֵי לֹא בִּמְהֵרָה יָמוּת מִישֶׁהוּ בְּעַד אָדָם צַדִּיק, אִם כִּי בְּעַד הָאִישׁ הַטּוֹב אוּלַי יָעֵז מִישֶׁהוּ לָמוּת. [8] אוּלָם אֱלֹהִים מְגַלֶּה אֶת

we were still sinners, Christ died for us. ⁹ Much more then, having now been justified by His blood, we shall be saved from wrath through Him. ¹⁰ For if when we were enemies we were reconciled to God through the death of His Son, much more, having been reconciled, we shall be saved by His life. ¹¹ And not only *that,* but we also rejoice in God through our Lord Jesus Christ, through whom we have now received the reconciliation.

¹² Therefore, just as through one man sin entered the world, and death through sin, and thus death spread to all men, because all sinned— ¹³ (For until the law sin was in the world, but sin is not imputed when there is no law. ¹⁴ Nevertheless death reigned from Adam to Moses, even over those who had not sinned according to the likeness of the transgression of Adam, who is a type of Him who was to come. ¹⁵ But the free gift *is* not like the offense. For if by the one man's offense many died, much more the grace of God and the gift by the grace of the one Man, Jesus Christ, abounded to many. ¹⁶ And the gift *is* not like *that which came* through the one who sinned. For the judgment *which came* from one *offense resulted* in condemnation, but the free gift *which came* from many offenses *resulted* in justification. ¹⁷ For if by the one man's offense death reigned through the one, much more those who receive abundance of grace and of the gift of righteousness will reign in life through the One, Jesus Christ.)

¹⁸ Therefore, as through one man's offense *judgment* came to all men, resulting in condemnation, even so through one Man's righteous act *the free gift came* to all men, resulting in justification of life. ¹⁹ For as by one man's disobedience many were made sinners, so also by one Man's obedience many will be made righteous.

²⁰ Moreover the law entered that the offense might abound. But where sin abounded, grace abounded much more, ²¹ so that as sin reigned in death, even so grace might reign through righteousness to eternal life through Jesus Christ our Lord.

6 What shall we say then? Shall we continue in sin that grace may abound? ² Certainly not! How shall we who died to sin live any longer in it? ³ Or do you not know that as many of us as were baptized into Christ Jesus were baptized into His death? ⁴ Therefore we were buried with Him through baptism into death, that just as Christ was raised from the dead by the glory of the Father, even so we also should walk in newness of life.

אֲהֵבָתוֹ אֵלֵינוּ בְּכָךְ שֶׁהַמָּשִׁיחַ מֵת בַּעֲדֵנוּ כַּאֲשֶׁר עוֹד הָיִינוּ אֲנָשִׁים חוֹטְאִים. ⁹ וְכָעֵת, לְאַחַר שֶׁכְּבָר הֻצְדַּקְנוּ בְּדָמוֹ, בְּוַדַּאי וּבְוַדַּאי שֶׁנִּוָּשַׁע עַל-יָדוֹ מִן הַזַּעַם; ¹⁰ שֶׁכֵּן אִם בִּזְמַן שֶׁהָיִינוּ אוֹיְבִים נִרְצֵינוּ לֵאלֹהִים בְּמוֹת בְּנוֹ, עַל אַחַת כַּמָּה וְכַמָּה נִוָּשַׁע בְּחַיֵּי בְּנוֹ לְאַחַר שֶׁכְּבָר נִרְצֵינוּ. ¹¹ וְלֹא זֹאת בִּלְבַד, אֶנַחְנוּ גַּם מִתְהַלְּלִים בֵּאלֹהִים הוֹדוֹת לַאֲדוֹנֵנוּ יֵשׁוּעַ הַמָּשִׁיחַ שֶׁבְּאֶמְצָעוּתוֹ קִבַּלְנוּ עַתָּה אֶת הָרָצוּי.

¹² לְפִיכָךְ, כְּשֵׁם שֶׁעַל-יְדֵי אָדָם אֶחָד בָּא הַחֵטְא לָעוֹלָם, וְעֵקֶב הַחֵטְא בָּא הַמָּוֶת, כָּךְ עָבַר הַמָּוֶת לְכָל בְּנֵי אָדָם מִשּׁוּם שֶׁכֻּלָּם חָטְאוּ. ¹³ הֲרֵי עוֹד לִפְנֵי הַתּוֹרָה הָיָה הַחֵטְא בָּעוֹלָם, אֶלָּא שֶׁאֵין הוּא נֶחְשָׁב בְּאֵין תּוֹרָה. ¹⁴ בְּכָל זֹאת שָׁלַט הַמָּוֶת מֵאָדָם וְעַד מֹשֶׁה גַּם עַל אֵלֶּה שֶׁלֹּא חָטְאוּ בַּעֲבֵרָה דּוֹמָה לַעֲבֵרָה שֶׁל אָדָם, אֲשֶׁר הוּא דְּמוּת מַקְבִּילָה לְאֶחָד שֶׁהָיָה עָתִיד לָבוֹא.

¹⁵ אוּלָם לֹא הֲרֵי הָעֲבֵרָה כַּהֲרֵי מַתְּנַת הַחֶסֶד; שֶׁכֵּן אִם בִּגְלַל הָעֲבֵרָה שֶׁל אֶחָד מֵתוּ הָרַבִּים, עַל אַחַת כַּמָּה וְכַמָּה, בְּחֶסֶד הָאָדָם הָאֶחָד יֵשׁוּעַ הַמָּשִׁיחַ, שָׁפְעוּ לָרַבִּים חֶסֶד אֱלֹהִים וּמַתְּנָתוֹ. ¹⁶ וְאֵין הַמַּתָּנָה כְּמַעֲשֵׂה הָאֶחָד שֶׁחָטָא; כִּי הַמִּשְׁפָּט עֵקֶב עֲבֵרָה אַחַת יָצָא לְהַרְשָׁעָה, אֲבָל לְאַחַר עֲבֵרוֹת רַבּוֹת מַתְּנַת הַחֶסֶד הִיא זִכּוּי; ¹⁷ שֶׁהֲרֵי אִם עַל-יְדֵי עֲבֵרָה שֶׁל אָדָם אֶחָד מָלַךְ הַמָּוֶת, כָּל שֶׁכֵּן הַמְּקַבְּלִים אֶת שֶׁפַע הַחֶסֶד וְאֶת מַתְּנַת הַצְּדָקָה יִמְלְכוּ בַּחַיִּים בִּגְלַל הָאֶחָד יֵשׁוּעַ הַמָּשִׁיחַ. ¹⁸ וּבְכֵן, כְּשֵׁם שֶׁעֲבֵרָה אַחַת הִיא הַרְשָׁעָה לְכָל בְּנֵי אָדָם, כֵּן גַּם מַעֲשֵׂה צְדָקָה אֶחָד הוּא זִכּוּי שֶׁל חַיִּים לְכָל בְּנֵי אָדָם; ¹⁹ כִּי כְּשֵׁם שֶׁבִּגְלַל אִי-צִיּוּתוֹ שֶׁל אָדָם אֶחָד נַעֲשׂוּ הָרַבִּים לְחוֹטְאִים, כֵּן גַּם בִּגְלַל צִיּוּתוֹ שֶׁל הָאֶחָד יֵעָשׂוּ הָרַבִּים לְצַדִּיקִים. ²⁰ הַתּוֹרָה בָּאָה וּבְכָךְ רַבּוּ הָעֲבֵרוֹת. אֲבָל הֵיכָן שֶׁהִתְרַבָּה הַחֵטְא, הַחֶסֶד שָׁפַע עוֹד יוֹתֵר. ²¹ וְכָךְ כְּשֵׁם שֶׁהַחֵטְא מָשַׁל בַּמָּוֶת, כֵּן גַּם יִמְשֹׁל הַחֶסֶד בְּאֶמְצָעוּת צְדָקָה, וְהַתּוֹצָאָה – חַיֵּי עוֹלָם עַל-יְדֵי יֵשׁוּעַ הַמָּשִׁיחַ אֲדוֹנֵנוּ.

ו אִם כֵּן, מַה נֹּאמַר? הֲנַמְשִׁיךְ בַּחֵטְא כְּדֵי שֶׁיִּרְבֶּה הַחֶסֶד? ² חַס וְחָלִילָה! אָנוּ שֶׁמַּתְנוּ לְגַבֵּי הַחֵטְא, אֵיךְ נַמְשִׁיךְ וְנִחְיֶה בּוֹ? ³ הַאֵינְכֶם יוֹדְעִים כִּי כֻּלָּנוּ אֲשֶׁר נִטְבַּלְנוּ לַמָּשִׁיחַ יֵשׁוּעַ, לְמוֹתוֹ נִטְבַּלְנוּ? ⁴ נִקְבַּרְנוּ אִתּוֹ בַּטְּבִילָה לַמָּוֶת כְּדֵי שֶׁנִּתְהַלֵּךְ גַּם אֲנַחְנוּ בְּחַיִּים חֲדָשִׁים, כְּשֵׁם שֶׁהַמָּשִׁיחַ הוּקַם מִן

⁵For if we have been united together in the likeness of His death, certainly we also shall be *in the likeness* of *His* resurrection, ⁶knowing this, that our old man was crucified with *Him,* that the body of sin might be done away with, that we should no longer be slaves of sin. ⁷For he who has died has been freed from sin. ⁸Now if we died with Christ, we believe that we shall also live with Him, ⁹knowing that Christ, having been raised from the dead, dies no more. Death no longer has dominion over Him. ¹⁰For *the death* that He died, He died to sin once for all; but *the life* that He lives, He lives to God. ¹¹Likewise you also, reckon yourselves to be dead indeed to sin, but alive to God in Christ Jesus our Lord.

¹²Therefore do not let sin reign in your mortal body, that you should obey it in its lusts. ¹³And do not present your members *as* instruments of unrighteousness to sin, but present yourselves to God as being alive from the dead, and your members *as* instruments of righteousness to God. ¹⁴For sin shall not have dominion over you, for you are not under law but under grace.

¹⁵What then? Shall we sin because we are not under law but under grace? Certainly not! ¹⁶Do you not know that to whom you present yourselves slaves to obey, you are that one's slaves whom you obey, whether of sin *leading* to death, or of obedience *leading* to righteousness? ¹⁷But God be thanked that *though* you were slaves of sin, yet you obeyed from the heart that form of doctrine to which you were delivered. ¹⁸And having been set free from sin, you became slaves of righteousness. ¹⁹I speak in human *terms* because of the weakness of your flesh. For just as you presented your members *as* slaves of uncleanness, and of lawlessness *leading* to *more* lawlessness, so now present your members *as* slaves *of* righteousness for holiness.

²⁰For when you were slaves of sin, you were free in regard to righteousness. ²¹What fruit did you have then in the things of which you are now ashamed? For the end of those things *is* death. ²²But now having been set free from sin, and having become slaves of God, you have your fruit to holiness, and the end, everlasting life. ²³For the wages of sin *is* death, but the gift of God *is* eternal life in Christ Jesus our Lord.

7 Or do you not know, brethren (for I speak to those who know the law), that the law has dominion over a man as long as he lives? ²For the woman who has a husband is bound by the law to *her* husband as long as he lives. But if the

הַמֵּתִים עַל־יְדֵי כְּבוֹדוֹ שֶׁל הָאָב; ⁵שֶׁכֵּן אִם הִתְאַחַדְנוּ אִתּוֹ בִּמְוֹת דּוֹמֶה לְמוֹתוֹ, כָּךְ גַּם נִתְאַחֵד אִתּוֹ בִּתְחִיָּתוֹ. ⁶וְזֹאת אָנוּ יוֹדְעִים: הָאָדָם הַיָּשָׁן אֲשֶׁר בָּנוּ נִצְלַב אִתּוֹ כְּדֵי שֶׁיֵּהָרֵס גּוּף הַחֵטְא וְלֹא נִהְיֶה עוֹד עֲבָדִים לַחֵטְא; ⁷שֶׁהֲרֵי הַמֵּת מְשֻׁחְרָר מִן הַחֵטְא. ⁸אֲבָל אִם מַתְנוּ עִם הַמָּשִׁיחַ, מַאֲמִינִים אָנוּ כִּי גַם נִחְיֶה עִמּוֹ. ⁹אֲנַחְנוּ יוֹדְעִים כִּי הַמָּשִׁיחַ, לְאַחַר שֶׁקָּם מִן הַמֵּתִים, לֹא יָמוּת עוֹד; הַמָּוֶת לֹא יוֹסִיף לִשְׁלֹט בּוֹ. ¹⁰הֲרֵי בְּמוֹתוֹ מֵת אַחַת וּלְתָמִיד לְגַבֵּי הַחֵטְא, אַךְ בְּחַיּוֹתוֹ הוּא חַי לֵאלֹהִים. ¹¹בְּדֶרֶךְ זֹאת גַּם אַתֶּם חִשְׁבוּ אֶת עַצְמְכֶם מֵתִים לְגַבֵּי הַחֵטְא, אַךְ חַיִּים לֵאלֹהִים בַּמָּשִׁיחַ יֵשׁוּעַ.

¹²לָכֵן, אַל יִמְשֹׁל הַחֵטְא בְּגוּפְכֶם בֶּן הַתְּמוּתָה וְאַל יַכְנִיעַ אֶתְכֶם לְתַאֲוֹותָיו. ¹³וְאַל תִּמְסְרוּ אֶת אֵיבְרֵיכֶם לַחֵטְא כִּכְלִים שֶׁל רֶשַׁע, אֶלָּא מִסְרוּ אֶת עַצְמְכֶם לֵאלֹהִים כַּאֲנָשִׁים חַיִּים שֶׁהוּקְמוּ מִן הַמֵּתִים, וְאֶת אֵיבְרֵיכֶם תִּמְסְרוּ לֵאלֹהִים כְּכֵלִים שֶׁל צֶדֶק. ¹⁴הַחֵטְא לֹא יִשְׁלֹט בָּכֶם, כִּי אֵינְכֶם תַּחַת יַד הַתּוֹרָה אֶלָּא תַּחַת יַד הַחֶסֶד.

¹⁵וּבְכֵן מָה? הַאִם נֶחֱטָא מִפְּנֵי שֶׁאֵין אָנוּ תַּחַת יַד הַתּוֹרָה אֶלָּא תַּחַת יַד הַחֶסֶד? חַס וְחָלִילָה! ¹⁶הַאֵינְכֶם יוֹדְעִים שֶׁכַּאֲשֶׁר אַתֶּם מוֹסִרִים אֶת עַצְמְכֶם כַּעֲבָדִים לְמִישֶׁהוּ כְּדֵי לָצֵית לוֹ, עֲבָדִים אַתֶּם לְמִי שֶׁאַתֶּם מְצַיְּתִים לוֹ – אוֹ לַחֵטְא הַמּוֹלִיךְ אֶל מָוֶת, אוֹ לַצַּיְּתָנוּת הַמּוֹלִיךְ אֱלֵי צְדָקָה. ¹⁷אַךְ תּוֹדָה לֵאלֹהִים עַל שֶׁאַתֶּם, אֲשֶׁר קֹדֶם לָכֵן הֱיִיתֶם עֲבָדִים לַחֵטְא, נִשְׁמַעְתֶּם בְּכָל לֵב לְדֶרֶךְ הַתּוֹרָה אֲשֶׁר חֻנַּכְתֶּם בָּהּ. ¹⁸וּלְאַחַר שֶׁשֻּׁחְרַרְתֶּם מִן הַחֵטְא נַעֲשֵׂיתֶם עֲבָדִים לַצְּדָקָה. ¹⁹אֲנִי מְדַבֵּר בִּדְרָמָאוֹת אֱנוֹשִׁיּוֹת בִּגְלַל חֻלְשַׁתְכֶם, חֻלְשַׁת בָּשָׂר וָדָם. כְּמוֹ שֶׁכִּעֲבָדִים לַטֻּמְאָה וְרֶשַׁע מְסַרְתֶּם אֶת אֵיבְרֵיכֶם לַתַּכְלִית שֶׁל רֶשַׁע, כֵּן עַתָּה כַּעֲבָדִים לַצְּדָקָה מִסְרוּ אֶת אֵיבְרֵיכֶם לַתַּכְלִית שֶׁל קְדֻשָּׁה. ²⁰הֲרֵי בְּעֵת שֶׁהֱיִיתֶם עֲבָדִים לַחֵטְא חָפְשִׁים הֱיִיתֶם מִן הַצְּדָקָה. ²¹וְאוּלָם אֵיזֶה פְּרִי הָיָה לָכֶם אָז מֵאוֹתָם דְּבָרִים שֶׁאַתֶּם מִתְבַּיְּשִׁים בָּהֶם עַכְשָׁו? הֲלֹא הַמָּוֶת הוּא תּוֹצָאָתָם. ²²אֲבָל כָּעֵת, כְּשֶׁאַתֶּם מְשֻׁחְרָרִים מֵהַחֵטְא וּמְשֻׁעְבָּדִים לֵאלֹהִים, יֵשׁ לָכֶם פְּרִי הַמֵּבִיא לִידֵי קְדֻשָּׁה, וְהַתּוֹצָאָה הִיא חַיֵּי עוֹלָם; ²³כִּי שְׂכַר הַחֵטְא הוּא מָוֶת, אֲבָל מַתְּנָתוֹ שֶׁל אֱלֹהִים הִיא חַיֵּי עוֹלָם בַּמָּשִׁיחַ יֵשׁוּעַ אֲדוֹנֵנוּ.

ז ¹אַחַי, הַאִם אֵינְכֶם יוֹדְעִים – וַהֲרֵי אֲנִי מְדַבֵּר אֶל יוֹדְעֵי תוֹרָה – כִּי לַתּוֹרָה יֵשׁ מָרוּת עַל הָאָדָם כָּל זְמַן שֶׁהוּא חַי? ²הָאִשָּׁה הַנְּשׂוּאָה קְשׁוּרָה לְבַעְלָהּ עַל־יְדֵי הַתּוֹרָה כָּל עוֹד הוּא חַי, אַךְ אִם יָמוּת בַּעְלָהּ פְּטוּרָה הִיא מֵחֹק הַתּוֹרָה הַקּוֹשֵׁר אוֹתָהּ

husband dies, she is released from the law of *her* husband. ³So then if, while *her* husband lives, she marries another man, she will be called an adulteress; but if her husband dies, she is free from that law, so that she is no adulteress, though she has married another man. ⁴Therefore, my brethren, you also have become dead to the law through the body of Christ, that you may be married to another—to Him who was raised from the dead, that we should bear fruit to God. ⁵For when we were in the flesh, the sinful passions which were aroused by the law were at work in our members to bear fruit to death. ⁶But now we have been delivered from the law, having died to what we were held by, so that we should serve in the newness of the Spirit and not *in* the oldness of the letter.

⁷What shall we say then? *Is* the law sin? Certainly not! On the contrary, I would not have known sin except through the law. For I would not have known covetousness unless the law had said, "*You shall not covet.*" ⁸But sin, taking opportunity by the commandment, produced in me all *manner of* evil desire. For apart from the law sin *was* dead. ⁹I was alive once without the law, but when the commandment came, sin revived and I died. ¹⁰And the commandment, which *was* to *bring* life, I found to *bring* death. ¹¹For sin, taking occasion by the commandment, deceived me, and by it killed *me*. ¹²Therefore the law *is* holy, and the commandment holy and just and good.

¹³Has then what is good become death to me? Certainly not! But sin, that it might appear sin, was producing death in me through what is good, so that sin through the commandment might become exceedingly sinful. ¹⁴For we know that the law is spiritual, but I am carnal, sold under sin. ¹⁵For what I am doing, I do not understand. For what I will to do, that I do not practice; but what I hate, that I do. ¹⁶If, then, I do what I will not to do, I agree with the law that *it is* good. ¹⁷But now, *it is* no longer I who do it, but sin that dwells in me. ¹⁸For I know that in me (that is, in my flesh) nothing good dwells; for to will is present with me, but *how* to perform what is good I do not find. ¹⁹For the good that I will *to do,* I do not do; but the evil I will not *to do,* that I practice. ²⁰Now if I do what I will not *to do,* it is no longer I who do it, but sin that dwells in me.

²¹I find then a law, that evil is present with me, the one who wills to do good. ²²For I delight in the law of God according to the inward man. ²³But I see another law in my members, warring against the law of my mind, and bringing me into captivity to the law of sin which is in my members. ²⁴O

לְבַעֲלָהּ. ³לָכֵן אִם תִּנָּשֵׂא לְאִישׁ אַחֵר בְּעוֹד בַּעֲלָהּ חַי, הִיא תִּקָּרֵא נוֹאָפֶת. אַךְ אִם יָמוּת בַּעֲלָהּ, פְּטוּרָה הִיא מֵאוֹתוֹ חֹק וּבְהִנָּשְׂאָהּ לְאִישׁ אַחֵר אֵין הִיא נוֹאָפֶת. ⁴כֵּן גַּם אַתֶּם, אַחַי, מַתֶּם לְגַבֵּי הַתּוֹרָה בְּגוּפוֹ שֶׁל הַמָּשִׁיחַ, בְּאֹפֶן שֶׁנַּעֲשִׂיתֶם שַׁיָּכִים לְאַחֵר, לָזֶה שֶׁהוּקַם מִן הַמֵּתִים, כְּדֵי שֶׁנַּעֲשֶׂה פְּרִי לֵאלֹהִים. ⁵הֲרֵי כַּאֲשֶׁר הָיִינוּ מְשֻׁעְבָּדִים לַבָּשָׂר, תַּאֲווֹת הַחֵטְא שֶׁעוֹרְרוּ עַל-יְדֵי הַתּוֹרָה פָּעֲלוּ בְּאֵבָרֵינוּ לַעֲשׂוֹת פְּרִי הַגּוֹרֵם לְמָוֶת. ⁶אֲבָל כָּעֵת, לְאַחַר שֶׁמַּתְנוּ לְגַבֵּי מַה שֶׁכָּבַל אוֹתָנוּ, שֻׁחְרַרְנוּ מִן הַתּוֹרָה כְּדֵי לַעֲבֹד אֶת אֱלֹהִים בְּחַדְשׁוּת הָרוּחַ וְלֹא בְּיֹשֶׁן שֶׁל אוֹת כְּתוּבָה.

⁷אִם כֵּן, מַה נֹּאמַר? הַאִם הַתּוֹרָה הִיא בְּחֶזְקַת חֵטְא? חַס וְחָלִילָה! אַךְ לֹא הָיִיתִי יוֹדֵעַ מַהוּ חֵטְא אִלּוּלֵי הַתּוֹרָה; הֲרֵי לֹא הָיִיתִי מַכִּיר אֶת הַתַּאֲוָה אִלּוּ לֹא אָמְרָה הַתּוֹרָה "לֹא-תַחְמֹד". ⁸הַחֵטְא נִצֵּל אֶת הָאִסּוּר שֶׁבַּדִּבּוּר כְּדֵי לְעוֹרֵר בְּקִרְבִּי כָּל מִינֵי תַּאֲווֹת, שֶׁכֵּן בְּלִי תּוֹרָה הַחֵטְא מֵת. ⁹וּבְעָבַר אֲנִי הָיִיתִי חַי בְּלִי תּוֹרָה, אַךְ כְּשֶׁהוֹפִיעַ הַדִּבּוּר נֵעוֹר הַחֵטְא לְחַיִּים וַאֲנִי מַתִּי. ¹⁰וּמָצָאתִי כִּי הַדִּבּוּר, שֶׁהָיָה דַּרְכּוֹ לְחַיִּים, גּוֹרֵם מָוֶת; ¹¹שֶׁכֵּן הַחֵטְא, בְּנַצְּלוֹ אֶת הַדִּבּוּר, הִתְעָה אוֹתִי וּבְאֶמְצָעוּתוֹ הֵמִית אוֹתִי. ¹²וּבְכֵן הַתּוֹרָה קְדוֹשָׁה, וְהַדִּבּוּר הוּא קָדוֹשׁ וְיָשָׁר וְטוֹב. ¹³הֲיִתָּכֵן, מִכָּאן, שֶׁדָּבָר טוֹב גָּרַם לִי מָוֶת? בְּשׁוּם פָּנִים לֹא! אוּלָם הַחֵטְא, לְמַעַן יֵרָאֶה שֶׁהוּא חֵטְא, גָּרַם לִי מָוֶת בְּאֶמְצָעוּת מַשֶּׁהוּ טוֹב כְּדֵי שֶׁעַל-יְדֵי הַדִּבּוּר יָבֹלֶת הַחֵטְא בִּמְלֹא חֻמְרָתוֹ.

¹⁴אָנוּ יוֹדְעִים שֶׁהַתּוֹרָה הִיא רוּחָנִית, אַךְ אֲנִי הִנְנִי בְּשַׂר דָּם וּמָכוּר לַחֵטְא. ¹⁵אָכֵן אֵינֶנִּי מֵבִין אֶת מַעֲשַׂי, כִּי לֹא אֶת מַה שֶּׁאֲנִי חָפֵץ אֲנִי עוֹשֶׂה, אֶלָּא דַּוְקָא אֶת מַה שֶּׁשָּׂנוּא עָלַי אֲנִי עוֹשֶׂה. ¹⁶וְאִם אֶת מַה שֶּׁאֵינֶנִּי חָפֵץ לַעֲשׂוֹת, אֲנִי מוֹדֶה שֶׁהַתּוֹרָה טוֹבָה. ¹⁷מִכָּאן שֶׁלֹּא עוֹד אֲנִי עוֹשֶׂה אֶת הַמַּעֲשֶׂה, אֶלָּא הַחֵטְא הַשּׁוֹכֵן בִּי. ¹⁸שֶׁהֲרֵי אֲנִי יוֹדֵעַ כִּי בִּי, כְּלוֹמַר בִּבְשָׂרִי, לֹא שׁוֹכֵן הַטּוֹב. אָמְנָם לִרְצוֹת אֲנִי יָכוֹל, אַךְ לַעֲשׂוֹת אֶת הַטּוֹב אֵינֶנִּי יָכוֹל; ¹⁹כִּי אֵינֶנִּי עוֹשֶׂה אֶת הַטּוֹב שֶׁאֲנִי חָפֵץ בּוֹ, אֶלָּא אֶת הָרַע שֶׁאֵינֶנִּי חָפֵץ בּוֹ – אוֹתוֹ אֲנִי עוֹשֶׂה. ²⁰וְאִם אֲנִי עוֹשֶׂה אֶת מַה שֶּׁבְּנִגּוּד לִרְצוֹנִי, הֲרֵי שֶׁלֹּא עוֹד אֲנִי עוֹשֶׂה אוֹתוֹ, אֶלָּא הַחֵטְא הַשּׁוֹכֵן בִּי. ²¹לְפִיכָךְ אֲנִי מוֹצֵא אֶת הַחֹק הַזֶּה: רְצוֹנִי לַעֲשׂוֹת אֶת הַטּוֹב, אֶלָּא שֶׁהָרַע עוֹמֵד לְפָנָי. ²²בְּאָדָם הַפְּנִימִי שֶׁבִּי אֲנִי שָׂמֵחַ בְּתוֹרַת אֱלֹהִים, ²³אַךְ בְּאֵבָרַי אֲנִי רוֹאֶה חֹק אַחֵר, וְהוּא נִלְחָם נֶגֶד הַחֹק שֶׁבְּשִׂכְלִי וּמְשַׁעְבֵּד אוֹתִי לְחֹק הַחֵטְא הַשּׁוֹרֵר בְּאֵבָרַי. ²⁴אוֹי לִי, אָדָם אֻמְלָל

wretched man that I am! Who will deliver me from this body of death? 25 I thank God—through Jesus Christ our Lord!

So then, with the mind I myself serve the law of God, but with the flesh the law of sin.

8 There is therefore now no condemnation to those who are in Christ Jesus, who do not walk according to the flesh, but according to the Spirit. 2 For the law of the Spirit of life in Christ Jesus has made me free from the law of sin and death. 3 For what the law could not do in that it was weak through the flesh, God did by sending His own Son in the likeness of sinful flesh, on account of sin: He condemned sin in the flesh, 4 that the righteous requirement of the law might be fulfilled in us who do not walk according to the flesh but according to the Spirit. 5 For those who live according to the flesh set their minds on the things of the flesh, but those who live according to the Spirit, the things of the Spirit. 6 For to be carnally minded is death, but to be spiritually minded is life and peace. 7 Because the carnal mind is enmity against God; for it is not subject to the law of God, nor indeed can be. 8 So then, those who are in the flesh cannot please God.

9 But you are not in the flesh but in the Spirit, if indeed the Spirit of God dwells in you. Now if anyone does not have the Spirit of Christ, he is not His. 10 And if Christ is in you, the body is dead because of sin, but the Spirit is life because of righteousness. 11 But if the Spirit of Him who raised Jesus from the dead dwells in you, He who raised Christ from the dead will also give life to your mortal bodies through His Spirit who dwells in you.

12 Therefore, brethren, we are debtors—not to the flesh, to live according to the flesh. 13 For if you live according to the flesh you will die; but if by the Spirit you put to death the deeds of the body, you will live. 14 For as many as are led by the Spirit of God, these are sons of God. 15 For you did not receive the spirit of bondage again to fear, but you received the Spirit of adoption by whom we cry out, "Abba, Father." 16 The Spirit Himself bears witness with our spirit that we are children of God, 17 and if children, then heirs—heirs of God and joint heirs with Christ, if indeed we suffer with Him, that we may also be glorified together.

18 For I consider that the sufferings of this present time are not worthy to be compared with the glory which shall be revealed in us. 19 For the earnest expectation of the creation eagerly waits for the revealing of the sons of God. 20 For the creation was subjected to futility, not willingly, but because of Him who subjected it in hope; 21 because the

שֶׁכְּמוֹתִי, מִי יַצִּילֵנִי מִגּוּף זֶה שֶׁהַמָּוֶת בּוֹ? 25 תּוֹדָה לֵאלֹהִים עַל יֵשׁוּעַ הַמָּשִׁיחַ אֲדוֹנֵנוּ! וּבְכֵן, בְּשִׂכְלִי אֲנִי עֶבֶד לְתוֹרַת אֱלֹהִים, אַךְ בִּבְשָׂרִי אֲנִי מְשֻׁעְבָּד לְחֹק הַחֵטְא.

ח לָכֵן אֵין עַכְשָׁו שׁוּם הַרְשָׁעָה עַל אֵלֶּה שֶׁנִּמְצָאִים בַּמָּשִׁיחַ יֵשׁוּעַ, 2 כִּי חֹק רוּחַ הַחַיִּים שֶׁבַּמָּשִׁיחַ יֵשׁוּעַ שִׁחְרֵר אוֹתִי מֵחֹק הַחֵטְא וְהַמָּוֶת; 3 שֶׁכֵּן מַה שֶּׁלֹּא יָכְלָה הַתּוֹרָה לַעֲשׂוֹת, מִפְּנֵי שֶׁלֹּא יָכְלָה לְהִתְגַּבֵּר עַל הַבָּשָׂר, זֹאת עָשָׂה אֱלֹהִים: הוּא שָׁלַח אֶת בְּנוֹ לָבוּשׁ בָּשָׂר בִּדְמוּת בְּשַׂר הַחֵטְא, לִהְיוֹת קָרְבָּן עַל חֵטְא, וְחָרַץ אֶת דִּינוֹ שֶׁל הַחֵטְא בַּבָּשָׂר, 4 כְּדֵי שֶׁחֶקַּת הַתּוֹרָה תִּתְקַיֵּם בָּנוּ, הַמִּתְהַלְּכִים לֹא לְפִי הַבָּשָׂר אֶלָּא לְפִי הָרוּחַ. 5 אֲנָשִׁים שֶׁחַיִּים לְפִי הַבָּשָׂר הוֹגִים בַּמֶּה שֶׁשַּׁיָּךְ לַבָּשָׂר, אַךְ אֲנָשִׁים שֶׁחַיִּים לְפִי הָרוּחַ הוֹגִים בַּמֶּה שֶׁשַּׁיָּךְ לָרוּחַ. 6 מַחְשְׁבוֹת הַבָּשָׂר מָוֶת הֵן, אֲבָל מַחְשְׁבוֹת הָרוּחַ הֵן חַיִּים וְשָׁלוֹם; 7 שֶׁהֲרֵי מַחְשְׁבוֹת הַבָּשָׂר עוֹיְנוֹת אֶת אֱלֹהִים מִפְּנֵי שֶׁאֵינָן נִכְנָעוֹת לְתוֹרַת אֱלֹהִים, אַף אֵינָן יְכוֹלוֹת לְהִכָּנַע. 8 וְהַכְּפוּפִים לַבָּשָׂר אֵינָם יְכוֹלִים לִהְיוֹת רְצוּיִים לֵאלֹהִים. 9 אַךְ אַתֶּם אֵינְכֶם כְּפוּפִים לַבָּשָׂר, כִּי אִם לָרוּחַ, אִם אָמְנָם רוּחַ אֱלֹהִים שׁוֹכֶנֶת בָּכֶם. וּמִי שֶׁאֵין לוֹ רוּחַ הַמָּשִׁיחַ אֵינוֹ שַׁיָּךְ לַמָּשִׁיחַ. 10 אֲבָל אִם הַמָּשִׁיחַ בְּקִרְבְּכֶם, אֲזַי הַגּוּף אָמְנָם מֵת עֵקֶב הַחֵטְא, אַךְ הָרוּחַ הִיא חַיִּים מִפְּנֵי שֶׁהַצְּדָקְתָּה. 11 וְאִם רוּחוֹ שֶׁל הַמֵּקִים אֶת יֵשׁוּעַ מִן הַמֵּתִים שׁוֹכֶנֶת בְּקִרְבְּכֶם, זֶה שֶׁהֵקִים אֶת הַמָּשִׁיחַ מִן הַמֵּתִים יְחַיֶּה גַּם אֶת גּוּפְכֶם בֶּן הַתְּמוּתָה עַל־יְדֵי רוּחוֹ הַשּׁוֹכֶנֶת בְּקִרְבְּכֶם. 12 לָכֵן, אַחַי, חַיָּבִים אֲנַחְנוּ, אַךְ לֹא לַבָּשָׂר חַיָּבִים אָנוּ שֶׁנִּחְיֶה עַל־פִּיו. 13 אִם תִּחְיוּ לְפִי הַבָּשָׂר, תָּמוּתוּ. אַךְ אִם עַל־יְדֵי הָרוּחַ תָּמִיתוּ אֶת מַעֲלָלֵי הַגּוּף, תִּחְיוּ. 14 כָּל אֲשֶׁר רוּחַ אֱלֹהִים מַדְרִיכָה אוֹתָם, בָּנִים הֵם לֵאלֹהִים. 15 הֲרֵי לֹא קִבַּלְתֶּם רוּחַ שֶׁל עַבְדוּת לַחֲזֹר אֶל הַפַּחַד, אֶלָּא קִבַּלְתֶּם רוּחַ הַמְּקֻנָּה מַעֲמָד שֶׁל בָּנִים, וּבְרוּחַ זֹאת אָנוּ קוֹרְאִים "אַבָּא, אָבִינוּ". 16 הָרוּחַ עַצְמָהּ מְעִידָה יַחַד עִם רוּחֵנוּ שֶׁבָּנִים לֵאלֹהִים אָנוּ. 17 וְאִם בָּנִים, אֲזַי יוֹרְשִׁים: יוֹרְשֵׁי נַחֲלַת אֱלֹהִים וְגַם יוֹרְשִׁים הַשֻּׁתָּפִים לַמָּשִׁיחַ, שֶׁכֵּן סוֹבְלִים אָנוּ עִמּוֹ כְּדֵי שֶׁגַּם נִזְכֶּה לִכְבוֹד עִמּוֹ. 18 אֲנִי סָבוּר שֶׁסִּבְלוֹת הַזְּמַן הַזֶּה אֵינָם שְׁקוּלִים כְּנֶגֶד הַכָּבוֹד הֶעָתִיד לְהִגָּלוֹת בָּנוּ. 19 כָּל הַבְּרִיאָה מְצַפָּה בְּכִסּוּפִים לְהִתְגַּלּוּת הַבָּנִים לֵאלֹהִים. 20 הֵן הַבְּרִיאָה – לֹא מֵרְצוֹנָהּ אֶלָּא עַל־יְדֵי הַמַּכְנִיעַ אוֹתָהּ – הֻכְנְעָה לַהֶבֶל בְּתִקְוָה 21 שֶׁגַּם הַבְּרִיאָה עַצְמָהּ

creation itself also will be delivered from the bondage of corruption into the glorious liberty of the children of God. 22 For we know that the whole creation groans and labors with birth pangs together until now. 23 Not only *that,* but we also who have the firstfruits of the Spirit, even we ourselves groan within ourselves, eagerly waiting for the adoption, the redemption of our body. 24 For we were saved in this hope, but hope that is seen is not hope; for why does one still hope for what he sees? 25 But if we hope for what we do not see, we eagerly wait for *it* with perseverance.

26 Likewise the Spirit also helps in our weaknesses. For we do not know what we should pray for as we ought, but the Spirit Himself makes intercession for us with groanings which cannot be uttered. 27 Now He who searches the hearts knows what the mind of the Spirit *is,* because He makes intercession for the saints according to *the will of* God.

28 And we know that all things work together for good to those who love God, to those who are the called according to *His* purpose. 29 For whom He foreknew, He also predestined *to be* conformed to the image of His Son, that He might be the firstborn among many brethren. 30 Moreover whom He predestined, these He also called; whom He called, these He also justified; and whom He justified, these He also glorified.

31 What then shall we say to these things? If God *is* for us, who *can be* against us? 32 He who did not spare His own Son, but delivered Him up for us all, how shall He not with Him also freely give us all things? 33 Who shall bring a charge against God's elect? *It is* God who justifies. 34 Who *is* he who condemns? *It is* Christ who died, and furthermore is also risen, who is even at the right hand of God, who also makes intercession for us. 35 Who shall separate us from the love of Christ? *Shall* tribulation, or distress, or persecution, or famine, or nakedness, or peril, or sword? 36 As it is written:

"For Your sake we are killed all day long;
  We are accounted as sheep for the slaughter."

37 Yet in all these things we are more than conquerors through Him who loved us. 38 For I am persuaded that neither death nor life, nor angels nor principalities nor powers, nor things present nor things to come, 39 nor height nor depth, nor any other created thing, shall be able to separate us from the love of God which is in Christ Jesus our Lord.

תְּשֻׁחְרַר מִשִּׁעְבּוּד הַכִּלָּיוֹן אֶל הַחֵרוּת וְהַכָּבוֹד שֶׁל הַבָּנִים־לֵאלֹהִים. 22 אָנוּ יוֹדְעִים שֶׁכָּל הַבְּרִיאָה נֶאֱנַחַת וְסוֹבֶלֶת כְּבַצִּירֵי לֵדָה עַד הַיּוֹם הַזֶּה. 23 וְלֹא זֹאת בִּלְבַד, אֶלָּא גַּם אֲנַחְנוּ, שֶׁיֵּשׁ לָנוּ בִּכּוּרֵי הָרוּחַ, נֶאֱנָחִים בְּנַפְשֵׁנוּ וּמְצַפִּים לְמִמּוּשׁ אִמּוּצֵנוּ לְבָנִים – לִפְדוּת גּוּפֵנוּ, 24 שֶׁכֵּן בַּתִּקְוָה נוֹשַׁעְנוּ. אַךְ תִּקְוָה לְדָבָר שֶׁנִּרְאָה לָעֵינַיִם אֵינָהּ תִּקְוָה, כִּי מַדּוּעַ יְקַוֶּה אָדָם לְמַה שֶׁהוּא רוֹאֶה? 25 אֲבָל אִם אָנוּ מְקַוִּים לְדָבָר שֶׁאֵינֶנּוּ רוֹאִים, מְצַפִּים אָנוּ לוֹ בְּסַבְלָנוּת.

26 וְכֵן גַּם הָרוּחַ עוֹזֶרֶת לָנוּ בְּחֻלְשׁוֹתֵינוּ, כִּי אֵין אָנוּ יוֹדְעִים לְהִתְפַּלֵּל כָּרָאוּי. וְאוּלָם הָרוּחַ עַצְמָהּ מַפְגִּיעָה בַּעֲדֵנוּ בַּאֲנָחוֹת עֲמֻקּוֹת מִמִּלִּים. 27 וְהַבּוֹחֵן לְבָבוֹת יוֹדֵעַ אֶת מַחְשְׁבוֹת הָרוּחַ, מִפְּנֵי שֶׁהִיא מַפְגִּיעָה בְּעַד הַקְּדוֹשִׁים בְּהֶתְאֵם לִרְצוֹן אֱלֹהִים. 28 אָנוּ יוֹדְעִים כִּי אֱלֹהִים גּוֹרֵם לְכָךְ שֶׁכָּל הַדְּבָרִים חוֹבְרִים יַחַד לְטוֹבַת אוֹהֲבָיו, הַקְּרוּאִים עַל־פִּי תָכְנִיתוֹ; 29 שֶׁכֵּן אֶת אֵלֶּה שֶׁהִכִּיר מִקֶּדֶם, אוֹתָם גַּם יָעַד לְהִדָּמוּת לְצֶלֶם בְּנוֹ, כְּדֵי שֶׁיִּהְיֶה הַבְּכוֹר בֵּין אַחִים רַבִּים. 30 וְאֶת אֵלֶּה שֶׁיָּעַד, לָהֶם גַּם קָרָא; וְאֶת הַקְּרוּאִים גַּם הִצְדִּיק; וְאֶת הַמֻּצְדָּקִים אַף פֵּאַר בִּכְבוֹדוֹ.

31 אִם כֵּן מַה נֹּאמַר עַל הַדְּבָרִים הָאֵלֶּה? אִם אֱלֹהִים אִתָּנוּ, מִי יַעֲמֹד נֶגְדֵּנוּ? 32 הוּא אֲשֶׁר לֹא חָשַׂךְ אֶת בְּנוֹ שֶׁלּוֹ, אֶלָּא מָסַר אוֹתוֹ בְּעַד כֻּלָּנוּ, הַאִם לֹא יַעֲנִיק לָנוּ אִתּוֹ אֶת הַכֹּל? 33 מִי יִטְעַן נֶגֶד בְּחִירֵי אֱלֹהִים? הֲרֵי אֱלֹהִים הוּא הַמַּצְדִּיק! 34 מִי הַמַּרְשִׁיעַ? הַאִם הַמָּשִׁיחַ יֵשׁוּעַ אֲשֶׁר מֵת, וְלֹא זוֹ בִּלְבַד כִּי אִם קָם לִתְחִיָּה, וְהוּא נִמְצָא לִימִין אֱלֹהִים וּמַפְגִּיעַ בַּעֲדֵנוּ? 35 מִי יַפְרִידֵנוּ מֵאַהֲבַת הַמָּשִׁיחַ? הַאִם צָרָה אוֹ מְצוּקָה, רְדִיפוֹת אוֹ רָעָב, הַאִם עֵירֹם אוֹ סַכָּנָה אוֹ חֶרֶב? 36 כַּכָּתוּב: "כִּי־עָלֶיךָ הֹרַגְנוּ כָל־הַיּוֹם, נֶחְשַׁבְנוּ כְּצֹאן טִבְחָה."

37 בְּרַם בְּכָל אֵלֶּה, בְּעֶזְרַת הָאוֹהֵב אוֹתָנוּ, אֲנַחְנוּ יוֹתֵר מִמְּנַצְּחִים. 38 וַאֲנִי בָּטוּחַ כִּי לֹא הַמָּוֶת וְלֹא הַחַיִּים, לֹא מַלְאָכִים וְלֹא שַׁלִּיטִים, לֹא דְּבָרִים שֶׁבַּהֹוֶה וְלֹא דְּבָרִים שֶׁעֲתִידִים לָבוֹא, לֹא כֹחוֹת, 39 לֹא גְּבָהִים וְלֹא מַעֲמַקִּים וְלֹא שׁוּם יְצוּר אַחֵר לֹא יוּכְלוּ לְהַפְרִידֵנוּ מֵאַהֲבַת אֱלֹהִים שֶׁבַּמָּשִׁיחַ יֵשׁוּעַ אֲדוֹנֵנוּ.

9 I tell the truth in Christ, I am not lying, my conscience also bearing me witness in the Holy Spirit, ²that I have great sorrow and continual grief in my heart. ³For I could wish that I myself were accursed from Christ for my brethren, my countrymen according to the flesh, ⁴who are Israelites, to whom *pertain* the adoption, the glory, the covenants, the giving of the law, the service *of God,* and the promises; ⁵of whom *are* the fathers and from whom, according to the flesh, Christ *came,* who is over all, *the* eternally blessed God. Amen.

⁶But it is not that the word of God has taken no effect. For they *are* not all Israel who *are* of Israel, ⁷nor *are they* all children because they are the seed of Abraham; but, "In Isaac your seed shall be called." ⁸That is, those who *are* the children of the flesh, these *are* not the children of God; but the children of the promise are counted as the seed. ⁹For this *is* the word of promise: "At this time I will come and Sarah shall have a son."

¹⁰And not only *this,* but when Rebecca also had conceived by one man, *even* by our father Isaac ¹¹(for *the children* not yet being born, nor having done any good or evil, that the purpose of God according to election might stand, not of works but of Him who calls), ¹²it was said to her, "The older shall serve the younger." ¹³As it is written, "Jacob I have loved, but Esau I have hated."

¹⁴What shall we say then? *Is there* unrighteousness with God? Certainly not! ¹⁵For He says to Moses, "I will have mercy on whomever I will have mercy, and I will have compassion on whomever I will have compassion." ¹⁶So then *it is* not of him who wills, nor of him who runs, but of God who shows mercy. ¹⁷For the Scripture says to the Pharaoh, "For this very purpose I have raised you up, that I may show My power in you, and that My name may be declared in all the earth." ¹⁸Therefore He has mercy on whom He wills, and whom He wills He hardens.

¹⁹You will say to me then, "Why does He still find fault? For who has resisted His will?" ²⁰But indeed, O man, who are you to reply against God? Will the thing formed say to him who formed *it,* "Why have you made me like this?" ²¹Does not the potter have power over the clay, from the same lump to make one vessel for honor and another for dishonor?

²²*What* if God, wanting to show *His* wrath and to make His power known, endured with much longsuffering the vessels of wrath prepared for destruction, ²³and that He might make known the riches of His glory on the vessels of mercy, which

ט אֱמֶת אֲנִי מְדַבֵּר, בַּמָּשִׁיחַ, אֵינֶנִּי מְשַׁקֵּר; מַצְפּוּנִי מֵעִיד עָמָּדִי בְּרוּחַ הַקֹּדֶשׁ: ²גָּדוֹל צַעֲרִי וְלִבִּי דּוֹאֵב תָּמִיד, ³עַד כִּי הָיִיתִי מוּכָן לִהְיוֹת מְנֻדֶּה מִן הַמָּשִׁיחַ לְמַעַן אַחַי, שֶׁהֵם בְּנֵי עַמִּי, עַצְמִי וּבְשָׂרִי, ⁴בְּנֵי יִשְׂרָאֵל; אֲשֶׁר לָהֶם מַעֲמַד הַבָּנִים, הַכָּבוֹד, הַבְּרִיתוֹת, מַתַּן הַתּוֹרָה, עֲבוֹדַת הַקֹּדֶשׁ וְהַהַבְטָחוֹת; ⁵לָהֶם הָאָבוֹת, וּמֵהֶם, מִצַּד יִחוּסוֹ הָאֱנוֹשִׁי, הַמָּשִׁיחַ שֶׁהוּא מֵעַל כֹּל, אֵל מְבֹרָךְ לְעוֹלָמִים. אָמֵן. ⁶לֹא כְּאִלּוּ דְּבַר אֱלֹהִים שָׁב רֵיקָם. הֲרֵי לֹא כָל אֲשֶׁר מִיִּשְׂרָאֵל יִשְׂרָאֵל הֵם. ⁷גַּם לֹא מִשּׁוּם הֱיוֹתָם צֶאֱצָאֵי אַבְרָהָם הַכֹּל בָּנִים, אֶלָּא – "בְּיִצְחָק יִקָּרֵא לְךָ זָרַע." ⁸כְּלוֹמַר, לֹא בְּנֵי הַבָּשָׂר הֵם בָּנִים לֵאלֹהִים, אֶלָּא בְּנֵי הַהַבְטָחָה נֶחְשָׁבִים לַזָּרַע. ⁹הֵן זֶה דְּבַר הַהַבְטָחָה: "לַמּוֹעֵד אָשׁוּב אֵלֶיךָ בְּעֵת חַיָּה וּלְשָׂרָה בֵן." ¹⁰וְלֹא זוֹ בִּלְבַד, אֶלָּא גַּם רִבְקָה בִּהְיוֹתָהּ הָרָה לְאִישׁ אֶחָד, לְיִצְחָק אָבִינוּ, ¹¹⁻¹²בְּטֶרֶם נוֹלְדוּ בָּנֶיהָ וּבְטֶרֶם עָשׂוּ טוֹב אוֹ רַע נֶאֱמַר לָהּ "וְרַב יַעֲבֹד צָעִיר", כְּדֵי שֶׁתִּכּוֹן תָּכְנִית אֱלֹהִים הַמִּשְׁתַּתֶּתֶת עַל בְּחִירָה, לֹא מִתּוֹךְ מַעֲשִׂים אֶלָּא לְפִי קְרִיאָתוֹ שֶׁל הַקּוֹרֵא – ¹³כַּכָּתוּב: "וָאֹהַב אֶת-יַעֲקֹב, וְאֶת-עֵשָׂו שָׂנֵאתִי."

¹⁴אִם כֵּן מַה נֹּאמַר? הֲיֵשׁ אִי-צֶדֶק אֵצֶל אֱלֹהִים? חַם וְחָלִילָה! ¹⁵הֲרֵי לְמֹשֶׁה הוּא אוֹמֵר: "וְחַנֹּתִי אֶת-אֲשֶׁר אָחֹן, וְרִחַמְתִּי אֶת-אֲשֶׁר אֲרַחֵם." ¹⁶לְפִיכָךְ אֵין זֶה בְּיָדָיו שֶׁל הָאָדָם הָרוֹצֶה אוֹ הַמִּתְאַמֵּץ, כִּי אִם בִּידֵי אֱלֹהִים הַמְרַחֵם. ¹⁷וְאָכֵן אוֹמֵר הַכָּתוּב לְפַרְעֹה: "בַּעֲבוּר זֹאת הֶעֱמַדְתִּיךָ, בַּעֲבוּר הַרְאֹתְךָ אֶת כֹּחִי, וּלְמַעַן סַפֵּר שְׁמִי בְּכָל-הָאָרֶץ." ¹⁸וּבְכֵן הוּא מְרַחֵם עַל מִי שֶׁהוּא רוֹצֶה, וּמַקְשֶׁה אֶת לֵב מִי שֶׁהוּא רוֹצֶה.

¹⁹אַז אַתָּה תֹּאמַר לִי: "מַדּוּעַ הוּא עוֹד מַאֲשִׁים, שֶׁהֲרֵי מִי יַעֲמֹד נֶגֶד רְצוֹנוֹ?" ²⁰אַךְ מִי אַתָּה, בֶּן אָדָם, כִּי תִּתְוַכֵּחַ עִם אֱלֹהִים? הַאִם יֹאמַר מַעֲשֶׂה לְעוֹשֵׂהוּ "מַדּוּעַ כָּכָה עֲשִׂיתָנִי?" ²¹הַאִם מֵאוֹתוֹ חֹמֶר אֵין יוֹצֵר רַשַּׁאי לִיצֹר כְּלִי אֶחָד לְכָבוֹד, וּכְלִי אַחֵר לְשִׁמּוּשׁ שֶׁאֵין בּוֹ כָּבוֹד? ²²וּמָה אִם אֱלֹהִים, אַף כִּי חָפֵץ לְהַרְאוֹת אֶת זַעְמוֹ וּלְגַלּוֹת אֶת כֹּחוֹ, סָבַל בְּאֹרֶךְ רוּחַ רַב כְּלֵי זַעַם מוּכָנִים לְהֶרֶס, ²³כְּדֵי לְגַלּוֹת אֶת עֹשֶׁר כְּבוֹדוֹ בִּכְלֵי חֲנִינָה שֶׁמֵּרֹאשׁ הֵכִין

He had prepared beforehand for glory, [24] *even us* whom He called, not of the Jews only, but also of the Gentiles?

[25] As He says also in Hosea:

"I will call them My people, who were not My people,
And her beloved, who was not beloved."

[26] "And it shall come to pass in the place where it was said to them,
'You are not My people,'
There they shall be called sons of the living God."

[27] Isaiah also cries out concerning Israel:

"Though the number of the children of Israel be as the sand of the sea,
The remnant will be saved.
[28] For He will finish the work and cut *it* short in righteousness,
Because the LORD will make a short work upon the earth."

[29] And as Isaiah said before:

"Unless the LORD of Sabaoth had left us a seed,
We would have become like Sodom,
And we would have been made like Gomorrah."

[30] What shall we say then? That Gentiles, who did not pursue righteousness, have attained to righteousness, even the righteousness of faith; [31] but Israel, pursuing the law of righteousness, has not attained to the law of righteousness. [32] Why? Because *they did* not seek *it* by faith, but as it were, by the works of the law. For they stumbled at that stumbling stone. [33] As it is written:

"Behold, I lay in Zion a stumbling stone and rock of offense,
And whoever believes on Him will not be put to shame."

10 Brethren, my heart's desire and prayer to God for Israel is that they may be saved. [2] For I bear them witness that they have a zeal for God, but not according to knowledge. [3] For they being ignorant of God's righteousness, and seeking to establish their own righteousness, have not submitted to the righteousness of God. [4] For Christ *is* the end of the law for righteousness to everyone who believes.

[5] For Moses writes about the righteousness which is of the law, "The man who does those things shall live by them." [6] But the righteousness of faith speaks in this way, "Do not say in your heart, 'Who

אוֹתָם לְכָבוֹד? – 24 כְּלוֹמַר, אוֹתָנוּ אֲשֶׁר גַּם קָרָא לֹא רַק מִקֶּרֶב הַיְהוּדִים אֶלָּא גַּם מִקֶּרֶב הַגּוֹיִים,

25 כְּמוֹ שֶׁהוּא אוֹמֵר גַּם בְּהוֹשֵׁעַ:

"אֶקְרָא לְלֹא־עַמִּי עַמִּי, וּלְלֹא־רֻחָמָה רֻחָמָה.

26 וְהָיָה בִּמְקוֹם אֲשֶׁר־יֵאָמֵר לָהֶם לֹא־עַמִּי אַתֶּם,

יֵאָמֵר לָהֶם בְּנֵי אֵל־חָי."

27 וִישַׁעְיָהוּ מַכְרִיז עַל יִשְׂרָאֵל:

"כִּי אִם־יִהְיֶה מִסְפַּר בְּנֵי יִשְׂרָאֵל כְּחוֹל הַיָּם, שְׁאָר יָשׁוּב בּוֹ.

28 כִּי־כָלָה וְנֶחֱרָצָה אֲדֹנָי עֹשֶׂה בְּקֶרֶב הָאָרֶץ."

29 וְכֵן אָמַר יְשַׁעְיָהוּ קֹדֶם לָכֵן:

"לוּלֵי יהוה צְבָאוֹת הוֹתִיר לָנוּ שָׂרִיד כִּמְעַט כִּסְדֹם הָיִינוּ לַעֲמֹרָה דָּמִינוּ."

30 אִם כֵּן מַה נֹּאמַר? גּוֹיִים שֶׁלֹּא רָדְפוּ צְדָקָה הִשִּׂיגוּ צְדָקָה, אֲבָל צְדָקָה שֶׁעַל־יְסוֹד אֱמוּנָה. 31 יִשְׂרָאֵל, לְעֻמַּת זֹאת, חָתְרוּ לְתוֹרָה שֶׁל צְדָקָה, אַךְ לְתוֹרָה זוֹ לֹא הִגִּיעוּ. 32 מַדּוּעַ? מִפְּנֵי שֶׁלֹּא בִּקְשׁוּהָ מִתּוֹךְ אֱמוּנָה, אֶלָּא מִתּוֹךְ מַעֲשִׂים. הֵם נִכְשְׁלוּ בְּאֶבֶן הַנֶּגֶף, 33 כַּכָּתוּב: "הִנְנִי יִסַּד בְּצִיּוֹן אֶבֶן נֶגֶף וְצוּר מִכְשׁוֹל, וְהַמַּאֲמִין בּוֹ לֹא יֵבוֹשׁ."

י אַחַי, מִשְׁאֶלֶת לִבִּי וּתְפִלָּתִי לֵאלֹהִים – שֶׁיִּוָּשֵׁעוּ. 2 אֲנִי מֵעִיד עֲלֵיהֶם שֶׁיֵּשׁ לָהֶם קִנְאָה לֵאלֹהִים, אֲבָל קִנְאָה שֶׁאֵין עִמָּהּ דַּעַת; 3 כִּי מֵאַחַר שֶׁלֹּא יָדְעוּ אֶת צִדְקַת הָאֱלֹהִים וְנִסּוּ לְהָקִים צִדְקָה מִשֶּׁלָּהֶם, לֹא נִכְנְעוּ לַצְּדָקָה שֶׁל אֱלֹהִים. 4 הֲרֵי הַמָּשִׁיחַ הוּא תַּכְלִית הַתּוֹרָה, כְּדֵי שֶׁיִּצְדַּק כָּל מִי שֶׁמַּאֲמִין.

5 מֹשֶׁה אָמְנָם כָּתַב עַל הַצְּדָקָה שֶׁמִּתּוֹךְ הַתּוֹרָה "אֲשֶׁר יַעֲשֶׂה אֹתָם הָאָדָם וָחַי בָּהֶם." 6 אַךְ כָּךְ אוֹמֶרֶת הַצְּדָקָה שֶׁמִּתּוֹךְ אֱמוּנָה: "אַל־תֹּאמַר בִּלְבָבְךָ מִי יַעֲלֶה הַשָּׁמַיְמָה?" זֹאת, כְּדֵי לְהוֹרִיד

will ascend into heaven?'" (that is, to bring Christ down *from above*) [7] or, "'Who will descend into the abyss?'" (that is, to bring Christ up from the dead). [8] But what does it say? *"The word is near you, in your mouth and in your heart"* (that is, the word of faith which we preach): [9] that if you confess with your mouth the Lord Jesus and believe in your heart that God has raised Him from the dead, you will be saved. [10] For with the heart one believes unto righteousness, and with the mouth confession is made unto salvation. [11] For the Scripture says, *"Whoever believes on Him will not be put to shame."* [12] For there is no distinction between Jew and Greek, for the same Lord over all is rich to all who call upon Him. [13] For *"whoever calls on the name of the LORD shall be saved."*

[14] How then shall they call on Him in whom they have not believed? And how shall they believe in Him of whom they have not heard? And how shall they hear without a preacher? [15] And how shall they preach unless they are sent? As it is written:

> *"How beautiful are the feet of those who preach the gospel of peace,*
> *Who bring glad tidings of good things!"*

[16] But they have not all obeyed the gospel. For Isaiah says, *"LORD, who has believed our report?"* [17] So then faith *comes* by hearing, and hearing by the word of God.

[18] But I say, have they not heard? Yes indeed:

> *"Their sound has gone out to all the earth,*
> *And their words to the ends of the world."*

[19] But I say, did Israel not know? First Moses says:

> *"I will provoke you to jealousy by those who are not a nation,*
> *I will move you to anger by a foolish nation."*

[20] But Isaiah is very bold and says:

> *"I was found by those who did not seek Me;*
> *I was made manifest to those who did not ask for Me."*

[21] But to Israel he says:

> *"All day long I have stretched out My hands*
> *To a disobedient and contrary people."*

11 I say then, has God cast away His people? Certainly not! For I also am an Israelite, of the seed of Abraham, *of* the tribe of Benjamin. [2] God has not cast away His people whom He foreknew. Or do you not know what the Scripture says of Elijah, how he pleads with God against Israel, saying, [3] "LORD, they have killed Your prophets and torn down Your altars, and I alone am left, and they

אֶת הַמָּשִׁיחַ. [7] אוֹ "מִי יֵרֵד לַתְּהוֹם?" זֹאת, כְּדֵי לְהַעֲלוֹת אֶת הַמָּשִׁיחַ מִן הַמֵּתִים. [8] אֲבָל מַה הִיא אוֹמֶרֶת? "כִּי-קָרוֹב אֵלֶיךָ הַדָּבָר, בְּפִיךָ וּבִלְבָבְךָ." זֶהוּ דְּבַר הָאֱמוּנָה שֶׁאָנוּ מְבַשְּׂרִים. [9] וְאִם אַתָּה מוֹדֶה בְּפִיךָ שֶׁיֵּשׁוּעַ הוּא הָאָדוֹן וּמַאֲמִין בִּלְבָבְךָ שֶׁאֱלֹהִים הֵקִים אוֹתוֹ מִן הַמֵּתִים – תִּוָּשַׁע, [10] הֲרֵי בְּלִבּוֹ מַאֲמִין אִישׁ וְיִצְדַּק, וּבְפִיו יוֹדֶה וְיִוָּשַׁע, [11] וְהַכָּתוּב אוֹמֵר: "כָּל הַמַּאֲמִין בּוֹ לֹא יֵבוֹשׁ." [12] אֵין הֶבְדֵּל בָּזֶה בֵּין יְהוּדִי לְלֹא-יְהוּדִי, כִּי אָדוֹן אֶחָד לְכֻלָּם וְרַב חֶסֶד הוּא לְכָל הַקּוֹרְאִים אֵלָיו, [13] שֶׁכֵּן "כֹּל אֲשֶׁר-יִקְרָא בְּשֵׁם יהוה יִמָּלֵט."

[14] אַךְ כֵּיצַד יִקְרְאוּ אֶל מִי שֶׁלֹּא הֶאֱמִינוּ בּוֹ? וְכֵיצַד יַאֲמִינוּ בָּזֶה אֲשֶׁר לֹא שָׁמְעוּ אוֹתוֹ? וְכֵיצַד יִשְׁמְעוּ בְּאֵין מְבַשֵּׂר? [15] כֵּיצַד יְבַשְּׂרוּ אִם לֹא יִשָּׁלְחוּ? הֵן כָּתוּב: "מַה-נָּאווּ רַגְלֵי מְבַשְּׂרֵי טוֹב!" [16] אֲבָל לֹא הַכֹּל צִיְּתוּ לַבְּשׂוֹרָה, שֶׁכֵּן יְשַׁעְיָהוּ אוֹמֵר: "אֲדֹנָי, מִי הֶאֱמִין לִשְׁמֻעָתֵנוּ?" [17] לְפִיכָךְ הָאֱמוּנָה בָּאָה בִּשְׁמִיעָה וְהַשְּׁמִיעָה – בְּהַכְרָזַת דְּבַר הַמָּשִׁיחַ. [18] שׁוֹאֵל אֲנִי, הַאִם לֹא שָׁמְעוּ? בְּוַדַּאי שֶׁכֵּן, הֲלֹא "בְּכָל-הָאָרֶץ יָצָא קַוָּם, וּבִקְצֵה תֵבֵל מִלֵּיהֶם!" [19] וְעוֹד שׁוֹאֵל אֲנִי, הַאִם יִשְׂרָאֵל לֹא יָדַע? הֲרֵי מֹשֶׁה כְּבָר אָמַר: "אֲנִי אַקְנִיאֲכֶם בְּלֹא עָם, בְּגוֹי נָבָל אַכְעִיסְכֶם". [20] וִישַׁעְיָהוּ מֵעֵז לוֹמַר: "נִדְרַשְׁתִּי לְלוֹא שָׁאָלוּ נִמְצֵאתִי לְלֹא בִקְשֻׁנִי." [21] וְהוּא אוֹמֵר לְיִשְׂרָאֵל: "פֵּרַשְׂתִּי יָדַי כָּל-הַיּוֹם אֶל-עַם סוֹרֵר וּמוֹרֶה."

יא אִם כֵּן, אֲנִי שׁוֹאֵל, הַאִם נָטַשׁ אֱלֹהִים אֶת עַמּוֹ? בְּשׁוּם פָּנִים לֹא! הֲרֵי גַּם אֲנִי בֶּן עַם יִשְׂרָאֵל, מִזֶּרַע אַבְרָהָם וּמִשֵּׁבֶט בִּנְיָמִין. [2] אֱלֹהִים לֹא נָטַשׁ אֶת עַמּוֹ, הָעָם שֶׁהוּא יָדַע מִקֶּדֶם. וְכִי אֵינְכֶם יוֹדְעִים מַה אוֹמֵר הַכָּתוּב עַל אֵלִיָּהוּ, כֵּיצַד הִתְלוֹנֵן עַל יִשְׂרָאֵל לִפְנֵי אֱלֹהִים? [3] "אֲדֹנָי, אֶת-נְבִיאֶיךָ הָרְגוּ

seek my life"? [4] But what does the divine response say to him? *"I have reserved for Myself seven thousand men who have not bowed the knee to Baal."* [5] Even so then, at this present time there is a remnant according to the election of grace. [6] And if by grace, then *it is* no longer of works; otherwise grace is no longer grace. But if *it is* of works, it is no longer grace; otherwise work is no longer work.

[7] What then? Israel has not obtained what it seeks; but the elect have obtained it, and the rest were blinded. [8] Just as it is written:

"God has given them a spirit of stupor,
Eyes that they should not see
And ears that they should not hear,
To this very day."

[9] And David says:

"Let their table become a snare and a trap,
A stumbling block and a recompense to them.
[10] *Let their eyes be darkened, so that they do not see,*
And bow down their back always."

[11] I say then, have they stumbled that they should fall? Certainly not! But through their fall, to provoke them to jealousy, salvation *has come* to the Gentiles. [12] Now if their fall *is* riches for the world, and their failure riches for the Gentiles, how much more their fullness!

[13] For I speak to you Gentiles; inasmuch as I am an apostle to the Gentiles, I magnify my ministry, [14] if by any means I may provoke to jealousy *those who are* my flesh and save some of them. [15] For if their being cast away *is* the reconciling of the world, what *will* their acceptance *be* but life from the dead?

[16] For if the firstfruit *is* holy, the lump *is* also holy; and if the root *is* holy, so *are* the branches. [17] And if some of the branches were broken off, and you, being a wild olive tree, were grafted in among them, and with them became a partaker of the root and fatness of the olive tree, [18] do not boast against the branches. But if you do boast, *remember that* you do not support the root, but the root supports you.

[19] You will say then, "Branches were broken off that I might be grafted in." [20] Well *said.* Because of unbelief they were broken off, and you stand by faith. Do not be haughty, but fear. [21] For if God did not spare the natural branches, He may not spare you either. [22] Therefore consider the goodness and severity of God: on those who fell, severity; but toward you, goodness, if you continue in *His* goodness. Otherwise you also will be cut off. [23] And they also, if they do not continue in unbelief, will be grafted in, for God is able to graft them in

וְאֶת־מִזְבְּחֹתֶיךָ הָרָסוּ, וָאִוָּתֵר אֲנִי לְבַדִּי, וַיְבַקְשׁוּ אֶת־נַפְשִׁי לְקַחְתָּהּ." [4] אַךְ מַה אוֹמֵר לוֹ דְּבַר אֱלֹהִים? "הִשְׁאַרְתִּי לִי בְיִשְׂרָאֵל שִׁבְעַת אֲלָפִים אֲשֶׁר לֹא־כָרְעוּ לַבַּעַל." [5] כֵּן גַּם בַּיָּמִים נִשְׁאֲרָה שְׁאֵרִית עַל־פִּי בְּחִירָה שֶׁל חֶסֶד. [6] וְאִם בְּחֶסֶד, הֲרֵי שֶׁלֹּא עוֹד מִתּוֹךְ מַעֲשִׂים; אַחֶרֶת הַחֶסֶד חָדֵל לִהְיוֹת חֶסֶד.

[7] וּבְכֵן מָה? יִשְׂרָאֵל לֹא הִשִּׂיג אֶת מְבַקְשׁוֹ, אֲבָל הַנִּבְחָרִים הִשִּׂיגוּ; וְהַשְּׁאָר הֻקְשׁוּ לְבָבָם, [8] כַּכָּתוּב: "נָתַן לָהֶם הָאֱלֹהִים רוּחַ תַּרְדֵּמָה, עֵינַיִם לֹא לִרְאוֹת וְאָזְנַיִם לֹא לִשְׁמֹעַ עַד הַיּוֹם הַזֶּה." [9] וְדָוִד אוֹמֵר: "יְהִי־שֻׁלְחָנָם לִפְנֵיהֶם לְפָח וּלְרֶשֶׁת וְלַשִּׁלּוּמִים לְמוֹקֵשׁ. [10] תֶּחְשַׁכְנָה עֵינֵיהֶם מֵרְאוֹת, וּמָתְנֵיהֶם תָּמִיד הַמְעַד."

[11] עַל כֵּן שׁוֹאֵל אֲנִי, הַאִם מָעֲדוּ כְּדֵי שֶׁיִּפְּלוּ לְלֹא קוּם? חַס וְחָלִילָה! אֶלָּא שֶׁבִּמְעִידָתָם הַיְשׁוּעָה לַגּוֹיִים, לְהַקְנִיא אוֹתָם. [12] וְאִם מְעִידָתָם הִיא עֹשֶׁר לָעוֹלָם וְהֶפְסֵדָם הוּא עֹשֶׁר לַגּוֹיִים, שְׁלֵמוּתָם – עַל אַחַת כַּמָּה וְכַמָּה!

[13] אֲלֵיכֶם הַגּוֹיִים אֲנִי מְדַבֵּר; בִּהְיוֹתִי אֲנִי שְׁלִיחַ לַגּוֹיִים מְכַבֵּד אֲנִי אֶת שֵׁרוּתִי, [14] בְּתִקְוָה לְעוֹרֵר קִנְאָה בִּבְנֵי עַמִּי וּלְהוֹשִׁיעַ כַּמָּה מֵהֶם. [15] הֲרֵי אִם הַדָּחְתָם הִיא רָצוּי בִּשְׁבִיל הָעוֹלָם, מַה תִּהְיֶה הֲשָׁבָתָם אִם לֹא תְּקוּמָה מִמָּוֶת אֱלֵי חַיִּים? [16] אִם תְּרוּמַת הָעִסָּה קֹדֶשׁ, כֵּן גַּם כָּל הַבָּצֵק! וְאִם הַשֹּׁרֶשׁ קֹדֶשׁ, כֵּן גַּם הָעֲנָפִים.

[17] וְאִם נִכְרְתוּ כַּמָּה עֲנָפִים מֵעֵץ הַזַּיִת, וְאַתָּה, זֵית־בָּר, הֻרְכַּבְתָּ בִּמְקוֹמָם וְשֻׁתַּפְתָּ בְּשֹׁרֶשׁ הָעֵץ וּבְלִשְׁדּוֹ, [18] אֲזַי אַל תִּתְנַשֵּׂא עַל הָעֲנָפִים. אִם תִּתְנַשֵּׂא, דַּע לְךָ שֶׁלֹּא אַתָּה נוֹשֵׂא אֶת הַשֹּׁרֶשׁ, אֶלָּא הַשֹּׁרֶשׁ נוֹשֵׂא אוֹתְךָ. [19] אַתָּה תֹּאמַר: "הָעֲנָפִים נִכְרְתוּ כְּדֵי שֶׁאֻרְכַּב אָנִי." [20] יָפֶה! בִּגְלַל אִי־אֱמוּנָה נִכְרְתוּ, אַךְ אַתָּה עַל־יְדֵי אֱמוּנָה מַחֲזִיק מַעֲמָד. אַל תִּתְגָּאֶה אֶלָּא הִמָּלֵא יִרְאָה, [21] שֶׁהֲרֵי אִם לֹא חָס אֱלֹהִים עַל הָעֲנָפִים הַמְּקוֹרִיִּים, גַּם עָלֶיךָ לֹא יָחוּס. [22] לָכֵן שִׂים לֵב לְטוּבוֹ שֶׁל אֱלֹהִים וּלְחָמְרָתוֹ: מְחַד גִּיסָא חָמְרָה כְּלַפֵּי הַנּוֹפְלִים; מֵאִידָךְ גִּיסָא, טוּבוֹ שֶׁל אֱלֹהִים עָלֶיךָ אִם תַּעֲמֹד בְּטוּבוֹ, וְלֹא – גַּם אַתָּה תִּכָּרֵת. [23] וְאִם לֹא יַמְשִׁיכוּ בְחֹסֶר אֱמוּנָתָם יֻרְכְּבוּ גַּם הֵם,

again. ²⁴ For if you were cut out of the olive tree which is wild by nature, and were grafted contrary to nature into a cultivated olive tree, how much more will these, who *are* natural *branches,* be grafted into their own olive tree?

²⁵ For I do not desire, brethren, that you should be ignorant of this mystery, lest you should be wise in your own opinion, that blindness in part has happened to Israel until the fullness of the Gentiles has come in. ²⁶ And so all Israel will be saved, as it is written:

> "The Deliverer will come out of Zion,
> And He will turn away ungodliness from Jacob;
> ²⁷ For this is My covenant with them,
> When I take away their sins."

²⁸ Concerning the gospel *they are* enemies for your sake, but concerning the election *they are* beloved for the sake of the fathers. ²⁹ For the gifts and the calling of God *are* irrevocable. ³⁰ For as you were once disobedient to God, yet have now obtained mercy through their disobedience, ³¹ even so these also have now been disobedient, that through the mercy shown you they also may obtain mercy. ³² For God has committed them all to disobedience, that He might have mercy on all.

³³ Oh, the depth of the riches both of the wisdom and knowledge of God! How unsearchable *are* His judgments and His ways past finding out!

> ³⁴ "For who has known the mind of the LORD?
> Or who has become His counselor?"
> ³⁵ "Or who has first given to Him
> And it shall be repaid to him?"

³⁶ For of Him and through Him and to Him *are* all things, to whom *be* glory forever. Amen.

12 I beseech you therefore, brethren, by the mercies of God, that you present your bodies a living sacrifice, holy, acceptable to God, *which is* your reasonable service. ² And do not be conformed to this world, but be transformed by the renewing of your mind, that you may prove what *is* that good and acceptable and perfect will of God.

³ For I say, through the grace given to me, to everyone who is among you, not to think *of himself* more highly than he ought to think, but to think soberly, as God has dealt to each one a measure of faith. ⁴ For as we have many members in one body, but all the members do not have the same function, ⁵ so we, *being* many, are one body in Christ, and individually members of one another. ⁶ Having then gifts differing according to the grace that is given to us, *let us use them:* if prophecy, *let us prophesy* in proportion to our faith; ⁷ or ministry, *let us use it* in

שֶׁכֵּן אֱלֹהִים יָכוֹל לְהַחֲזִירָם וּלְהַרְכִּיבָם. ²⁴ הֲרֵי אִם אַתָּה נִכְרַתָּ מֵעֵץ זַיִת בַּר מִטִּבְעוֹ, וּבְנִגּוּד לַטֶּבַע הֻרְכַּבְתָּ עַל עֵץ זַיִת טוֹב, כָּל שֶׁכֵּן אֵלֶּה, הַמְּקוֹרִיִּים, יֻרְכְּבוּ עַל עֵץ הַזַּיִת שֶׁלָּהֶם! ²⁵ הֵן, אַחַי, אֵינֶנִּי רוֹצֶה שֶׁיַּעֲלַם מִכֶּם הָרָז הַזֶּה, פֶּן תִּהְיוּ חֲכָמִים בְּעֵינֵיכֶם: קְהוּת לֵב אָחֲזָה בְּמִדַּת מָה אֶת יִשְׂרָאֵל, עַד אֲשֶׁר יִכָּנֵס מְלוֹא הַגּוֹיִים. ²⁶ וְכָךְ כָּל יִשְׂרָאֵל יִוָּשַׁע, כְּמוֹ שֶׁכָּתוּב:

"וּבָא מִצִּיּוֹן גּוֹאֵל וְיָשִׁיב פֶּשַׁע בְּיַעֲקֹב, ²⁷ וַאֲנִי זֹאת בְּרִיתִי אוֹתָם, כִּי אֶסְלַח לַעֲוֹנָם."

²⁸ אָמְנָם בְּמַה שֶּׁנּוֹגֵעַ לַבְּשׂוֹרָה הֵם אוֹיְבִים בִּגְלַלְכֶם, אֲבָל בְּמַה שֶּׁנּוֹגֵעַ לַבְּחִירָה אֲהוּבִים הֵם בִּגְלַל הָאָבוֹת, ²⁹ שֶׁהֲרֵי אֵין הָאֱלֹהִים מִתְחָרֵט עַל מַתְּנוֹתָיו וְעַל בְּחִירָתוֹ. ³⁰ וּכְשֵׁם שֶׁאַתֶּם בְּעָבָר לֹא צִיַּתֶּם לֵאלֹהִים, אַךְ כָּעֵת רֻחַמְתֶּם אַגַּב אִי־צִיּוּתָם, ³¹ כֵּן גַּם אֵלֶּה לֹא צִיְּתוּ כָּעֵת, וְכָךְ בָּרַחֲמִים אֲשֶׁר הֻשְׁפְּעוּ עֲלֵיכֶם יְרֻחֲמוּ גַּם הֵם כָּעֵת; ³² כִּי אֱלֹהִים כָּלָא אֶת הַכֹּל בְּאִי־צִיּוּת כְּדֵי שֶׁיְּרַחֵם עַל הַכֹּל.

³³ מָה עֹמֶק עֹשֶׁר הָאֱלֹהִים, מָה עֹמֶק חָכְמָתוֹ וְדַעְתּוֹ! אֵין חֵקֶר לְמִשְׁפָּטָיו וְאֵין מַשִּׂיג אֶת דְּרָכָיו, ³⁴ כִּי "מִי־תִכֵּן אֶת־רוּחַ יהוה וְאִישׁ עֲצָתוֹ יוֹדִיעֶנּוּ?" ³⁵ וּמִי הִקְדִּים לָתֵת לוֹ דָבָר וִישֻׁלַּם לוֹ? ³⁶ הֲרֵי הַכֹּל מִמֶּנּוּ, הַכֹּל דַּרְכּוֹ, וְהַכֹּל אֵלָיו. לוֹ הַכָּבוֹד לְעוֹלָמִים! אָמֵן.

יב וּבְכֵן, אַחַי, בִּגְלַל רַחֲמֵי אֱלֹהִים אֲנִי מְבַקֵּשׁ מִכֶּם שֶׁתִּמְסְרוּ אֶת גּוּפְכֶם קָרְבָּן חַי, קָדוֹשׁ וְרָצוּי לֵאלֹהִים; כָּךְ תַּעַבְדוּהוּ עֲבוֹדָה שֶׁבַּלֵּב. ² וְאַל תִּדַּמּוּ לָעוֹלָם הַזֶּה, כִּי אִם הִשְׁתַּנּוּ עַל־יְדֵי הִתְחַדְּשׁוּת הַדַּעַת כְּדֵי שֶׁתַּבְחִינוּ מַהוּ רְצוֹן אֱלֹהִים, מַהוּ הַטּוֹב וְהָרָצוּי וְהַמֻּשְׁלָם בְּעֵינָיו. ³ עַל־סְמַךְ הַחֶסֶד אֲשֶׁר נִתַּן לִי, הֲרֵינִי אוֹמֵר לְכָל אֶחָד מִכֶּם: אִישׁ אַל יַחְשֹׁב אֶת עַצְמוֹ לְיוֹתֵר מִשֶּׁרָאוּי לוֹ לַחְשֹׁב, אֶלָּא יְהֵא צָנוּעַ בְּהַעֲרָכָתוֹ, כְּמִדַּת הָאֱמוּנָה שֶׁהֶעֱנִיק לוֹ אֱלֹהִים. ⁴ כְּשֵׁם שֶׁבְּגוּף אֶחָד יֵשׁ לָנוּ אֵיבָרִים רַבִּים וְלֹא לְכָל הָאֵיבָרִים אוֹתוֹ תַּפְקִיד, ⁵ כָּךְ אֲנַחְנוּ הָרַבִּים מְהַוִּים גּוּף אֶחָד בַּמָּשִׁיחַ וְכָל אֶחָד אֵיבָר לַחֲבֵרוֹ. ⁶ וְיֵשׁ לָנוּ מַתָּנוֹת שׁוֹנוֹת, לְפִי הַחֶסֶד הַנִּתָּן לָנוּ: אִם נְבוּאָה הֲרֵיהִי כְּמִדַּת הָאֱמוּנָה; ⁷ אִם לְאִישׁ שֵׁרוּת, יְשָׁרֵת; אִם הוּא מוֹרֶה, יְלַמֵּד; ⁸ מִי

our ministering; he who teaches, in teaching; [8] he who exhorts, in exhortation; he who gives, with liberality; he who leads, with diligence; he who shows mercy, with cheerfulness.

[9] *Let* love *be* without hypocrisy. Abhor what is evil. Cling to what is good. [10] *Be* kindly affectionate to one another with brotherly love, in honor giving preference to one another; [11] not lagging in diligence, fervent in spirit, serving the Lord; [12] rejoicing in hope, patient in tribulation, continuing steadfastly in prayer; [13] distributing to the needs of the saints, given to hospitality.

[14] Bless those who persecute you; bless and do not curse. [15] Rejoice with those who rejoice, and weep with those who weep. [16] Be of the same mind toward one another. Do not set your mind on high things, but associate with the humble. Do not be wise in your own opinion.

[17] Repay no one evil for evil. Have regard for good things in the sight of all men. [18] If it is possible, as much as depends on you, live peaceably with all men. [19] Beloved, do not avenge yourselves, but *rather* give place to wrath; for it is written, "Vengeance *is* Mine, I will repay," says the Lord. [20] Therefore

> "If your enemy is hungry, feed him;
> If he is thirsty, give him a drink;
> For in so doing you will heap coals of fire on his head."

[21] Do not be overcome by evil, but overcome evil with good.

13 Let every soul be subject to the governing authorities. For there is no authority except from God, and the authorities that exist are appointed by God. [2] Therefore whoever resists the authority resists the ordinance of God, and those who resist will bring judgment on themselves. [3] For rulers are not a terror to good works, but to evil. Do you want to be unafraid of the authority? Do what is good, and you will have praise from the same. [4] For he is God's minister to you for good. But if you do evil, be afraid; for he does not bear the sword in vain; for he is God's minister, an avenger to *execute* wrath on him who practices evil. [5] Therefore *you* must be subject, not only because of wrath but also for conscience' sake. [6] For because of this you also pay taxes, for they are God's ministers attending continually to this very thing. [7] Render therefore to all their due: taxes to whom taxes *are* due, customs to whom customs, fear to whom fear, honor to whom honor.

שְׁמַחְתֵּנוּ הָעֲדוּד, יְעוֹדֵד; הַנּוֹתֵן יִתֵּן בְּתֹם לֵב; הַמַּנְהִיג יְמַלֵּא אֶת תַּפְקִידוֹ בִּשְׁקִידָה; וְהַגּוֹמֵל חֶסֶד יַעֲשֶׂה זֹאת בְּמְאוֹר פָּנִים.

[9] תְּהֵא אַהֲבַתְכֶם לְלֹא הַעֲמָדַת פָּנִים. שִׂנְאוּ אֶת הָרַע וְדִבְקוּ בַּטּוֹב. [10] אֶהֱבוּ אִישׁ אֶת רֵעֵהוּ בְּאַהֲבַת אַחִים כֵּנָה. הַקְדִּימוּ לִנְהֹג כָּבוֹד אִישׁ בְּרֵעֵהוּ. [11] שָׁקְדוּ וְאַל תִּתְעַצְּלוּ. הֱיוּ נִלְהָבֵי רוּחַ וְשָׁרְתוּ אֶת הָאָדוֹן. [12] גִּילוּ בַּתִּקְוָה. הֱיוּ סַבְלָנִים בַּצָּרָה. הַתְמִידוּ בַּתְּפִלָּה. [13] תְּנוּ אֶת חֶלְקְכֶם לְצָרְכֵי הַקְּדוֹשִׁים וְשָׁאֲפוּ לְהַכְנִיס אוֹרְחִים. [14] בָּרְכוּ אֶת רוֹדְפֵיכֶם, בָּרְכוּ וְאַל תְּקַלְּלוּ. [15] שִׂמְחוּ עִם הַשְּׂמֵחִים וּבְכוּ עִם הַבּוֹכִים. [16] הֱיוּ תְּמִימֵי דֵעִים זֶה עִם זֶה. אַל תְּהַלְּכוּ בִּגְדוֹלוֹת וְאַל תַּבְדְּלוּ מֵאֲנָשִׁים פְּשׁוּטִים. אַל תִּהְיוּ חֲכָמִים בְּעֵינֵיכֶם. [17] אַל תְּשַׁלְּמוּ לְאִישׁ רָעָה תַּחַת רָעָה. בַּקְּשׁוּ אֶת הַטּוֹב בְּעֵינֵי כָּל בְּנֵי אָדָם. [18] עַד כַּמָּה שֶׁהַדָּבָר בְּיֶדְכֶם חֲיוּ בְשָׁלוֹם עִם כָּל אָדָם. [19] יַקִּירַי, אַל תִּתְנַקְּמוּ אֶלָּא הַנִּיחוּ לַזַּעַם, כִּי כָתוּב "לִי נָקָם וְשִׁלֵּם אָמַר יהוה". [20] אֲבָל "אִם־ רָעֵב שֹׂנַאֲךָ הַאֲכִילֵהוּ לָחֶם, וְאִם־צָמֵא הַשְׁקֵהוּ מָיִם; כִּי גֶחָלִים אַתָּה חֹתֶה עַל־רֹאשׁוֹ." [21] אַל תִּנִּיחַ לָרַע לְהִתְגַּבֵּר עָלֶיךָ, אֶלָּא הִתְגַּבֵּר עַל הָרַע בַּטּוֹב.

יג כָּל אָדָם יִכָּנַע לְרָשׁוּיוֹת הַשִּׁלְטוֹן, שֶׁהֲרֵי אֵין שִׁלְטוֹן אֶלָּא מִטַּעַם אֱלֹהִים, וְהַשִּׁלְטוֹנוֹת הַנּוֹכְחִיִּים נִקְבְּעוּ מִטַּעַם אֱלֹהִים. [2] לְפִיכָךְ כָּל הַמִּתְקוֹמֵם נֶגֶד הַשִּׁלְטוֹן מִתְנַגֵּד לְצַו אֱלֹהִים, וְהַמִּתְנַגְּדִים יָבִיאוּ עַל עַצְמָם מִשְׁפָּט. [3] הֲרֵי אֵין פַּחַד הַשַּׁלִּיטִים עַל עוֹשֵׂה הַטּוֹב, אֶלָּא עַל עוֹשֵׂה הָרַע. הַאִם אַתָּה רוֹצֶה שֶׁלֹּא לִפְחֹד מִן הַשִּׁלְטוֹנוֹת? עֲשֵׂה אֶת הַטּוֹב וְתִזְכֶּה לְשֶׁבַח מֵהֶם. [4] הַשִּׁלְטוֹנוֹת הֵם מְשָׁרְתֵי אֱלֹהִים לְטוֹבָתְךָ. אַךְ אִם תַּעֲשֶׂה אֶת הָרַע, עָלֶיךָ לִפְחֹד; שֶׁהֲרֵי לֹא לְחִנָּם הֵם מַחֲזִיקִים בַּחֶרֶב, כִּי מְשָׁרְתֵי אֱלֹהִים הֵם לִנְקֹם וְלִשְׁפֹּךְ זַעַם עַל עוֹשֵׂי הָרַע. [5] לָכֵן עָלֶיךָ לְהִכָּנַע לֹא רַק בִּגְלַל הַזַּעַם, אֶלָּא גַם בִּגְלַל הַמַּצְפּוּן. [6] וְלָכֵן אַתֶּם גַּם מְשַׁלְּמִים מִסִּים, כִּי מְשָׁרְתֵי אֱלֹהִים הֵם הַשּׁוֹקְדִים עַל מִלּוּי תַּפְקִידָה זֶה. [7] תְּנוּ לְכָל אָדָם מַה שֶּׁמַּגִּיעַ לוֹ: מַס לְמִי שֶׁעַל הַמַּס; מֶכֶס לְמִי שֶׁעַל הַמֶּכֶס; יִרְאָה לְמִי שֶׁרָאוּי לְיִרְאָה מִמֶּנּוּ; כָּבוֹד לְמִי שֶׁמַּגִּיעַ לוֹ כָּבוֹד.

⁸ Owe no one anything except to love one another, for he who loves another has fulfilled the law. ⁹ For the commandments, "You shall not commit adultery," "You shall not murder," "You shall not steal," "You shall not bear false witness," "You shall not covet," and if there is any other commandment, are all summed up in this saying, namely, "You shall love your neighbor as yourself." ¹⁰ Love does no harm to a neighbor; therefore love is the fulfillment of the law.

¹¹ And do this, knowing the time, that now it is high time to awake out of sleep; for now our salvation is nearer than when we first believed. ¹² The night is far spent, the day is at hand. Therefore let us cast off the works of darkness, and let us put on the armor of light. ¹³ Let us walk properly, as in the day, not in revelry and drunkenness, not in lewdness and lust, not in strife and envy. ¹⁴ But put on the Lord Jesus Christ, and make no provision for the flesh, to fulfill its lusts.

14 Receive one who is weak in the faith, but not to disputes over doubtful things. ² For one believes he may eat all things, but he who is weak eats only vegetables. ³ Let not him who eats despise him who does not eat, and let not him who does not eat judge him who eats; for God has received him. ⁴ Who are you to judge another's servant? To his own master he stands or falls. Indeed, he will be made to stand, for God is able to make him stand.

⁵ One person esteems one day above another; another esteems every day alike. Let each be fully convinced in his own mind. ⁶ He who observes the day, observes it to the Lord; and he who does not observe the day, to the Lord he does not observe it. He who eats, eats to the Lord, for he gives God thanks; and he who does not eat, to the Lord he does not eat, and gives God thanks. ⁷ For none of us lives to himself, and no one dies to himself. ⁸ For if we live, we live to the Lord; and if we die, we die to the Lord. Therefore, whether we live or die, we are the Lord's. ⁹ For to this end Christ died and rose and lived again, that He might be Lord of both the dead and the living. ¹⁰ But why do you judge your brother? Or why do you show contempt for your brother? For we shall all stand before the judgment seat of Christ. ¹¹ For it is written:

"As I live, says the LORD,
  Every knee shall bow to Me,
  And every tongue shall confess to God."

⁸ אַל תִּהְיוּ חַיָּבִים דָּבָר לְאִישׁ מִלְּבַד אַהֲבַת הַגּוֹמֵל, כִּי הָאוֹהֵב אֶת הַזּוּלַת קִיֵּם אֶת הַתּוֹרָה. ⁹ הֵן הַמִּצְווֹת "לֹא תִנְאָף", "לֹא תִרְצַח", "לֹא תִגְנֹב", "לֹא תַחְמֹד", וְכָל מִצְוָה אַחֶרֶת, כְּלוּלוֹת בַּמַּאֲמָר "וְאָהַבְתָּ לְרֵעֲךָ כָּמוֹךָ". ¹⁰ הָאַהֲבָה אֵינָהּ גּוֹרֶמֶת רָעָה לַזּוּלַת, לָכֵן הָאַהֲבָה הִיא קִיּוּם הַתּוֹרָה בִּמְלוֹאָהּ.

¹¹ נוֹסָף עַל כָּךְ, יְדוּעִים לָכֶם הַזְּמַנִּים, הִגִּיעַ שְׁעַת הַשָּׁעָה לְהִתְעוֹרֵר מִן הַשֵּׁנָה, כִּי יְשׁוּעָתֵנוּ קְרוֹבָה עַכְשָׁו יוֹתֵר מִשֶּׁהָיְתָה בַּיּוֹם שֶׁהִתְחַלְנוּ לְהַאֲמִין. ¹² הַלַּיְלָה חוֹלֵף וְהַיּוֹם קָרֵב. עַל כֵּן נָסִירָה מֵעָלֵינוּ אֶת מַעֲשֵׂי הַחֹשֶׁךְ וְנִלְבַּשׁ אֶת שִׁרְיוֹן הָאוֹר. ¹³ וּכְמוֹ בַּיּוֹם נִתְנַהֵג נָא כַּיָּאוּת, לֹא בַּהוֹלְלוּת וּבְשִׁכְרוּת, לֹא בְּזִמָּה וּפְרִיצוּת, לֹא בְּרִיב וְקִנְאָה, ¹⁴ כִּי אִם לִבְשׁוּ אֶת הָאָדוֹן יֵשׁוּעַ הַמָּשִׁיחַ, וְאַל תִּדְאֲגוּ לַגּוּף בְּמִגַּמָּה לְהַשְׂבִּיעַ אֶת הַתַּאֲווֹת.

יד קַבְּלוּ אֶת הֶחָלָשׁ בָּאֱמוּנָה, אַךְ לֹא לְשֵׁם וִכּוּחִים עַל דֵּעוֹת. ² אֶחָד מַאֲמִין שֶׁמֻּתָּר לֶאֱכֹל הַכֹּל; אַחֵר, שֶׁהוּא חַלָּשׁ, אוֹכֵל מַאֲכָלִים צִמְחִיִּים. ³ אַל יָבוּז הָאוֹכֵל לְזֶה שֶׁאֵינוֹ אוֹכֵל, וְזֶה שֶׁאֵינוֹ אוֹכֵל אַל יַחֲרֹץ מִשְׁפָּט עַל הָאוֹכֵל, שֶׁכֵּן אֱלֹהִים קִבֵּל אוֹתוֹ בְּרָצוֹן. ⁴ מִי אַתָּה כִּי תִשְׁפֹּט אֶת עַבְדּוֹ שֶׁל אַחֵר? הֲרֵי בְּעֵינֵי אֲדוֹנָיו הוּא עוֹמֵד אוֹ נוֹפֵל. אַךְ הוּא יַעֲמֹד, כִּי הָאָדוֹן יָכוֹל לַעֲזֹר לוֹ לַעֲמֹד. ⁵ יֵשׁ אָדָם הַמַּחֲשִׁיב יוֹם אֶחָד יוֹתֵר מִיּוֹם אַחֵר, וְיֵשׁ שֶׁמַּחֲשִׁיב כָּל יוֹם וָיוֹם. יְהֵא כָּל אָדָם בָּטוּחַ בְּדַעְתּוֹ. ⁶ מִי שֶׁמַּחֲשִׁיב אֶת הַיּוֹם מַחֲשִׁיב אוֹתוֹ לְשֵׁם הָאָדוֹן. הָאוֹכֵל אוֹכֵל לְשֵׁם הָאָדוֹן, שֶׁכֵּן הוּא מוֹדֶה לֵאלֹהִים. וְזֶה שֶׁאֵינוֹ אוֹכֵל, לְשֵׁם הָאָדוֹן אֵינוֹ אוֹכֵל וְגַם הוּא מוֹדֶה לֵאלֹהִים. ⁷ אִישׁ מֵאִתָּנוּ אֵינוֹ חַי אֶת חַיָּיו לְשֵׁם עַצְמוֹ וְאִישׁ אֵינוֹ מֵת לְשֵׁם עַצְמוֹ. ⁸ כְּשֶׁאָנוּ חַיִּים, לְשֵׁם הָאָדוֹן אָנוּ חַיִּים. כְּשֶׁאָנוּ מֵתִים, לְשֵׁם הָאָדוֹן אָנוּ מֵתִים. לְפִיכָךְ, בֵּין שֶׁחַיִּים בֵּין שֶׁמֵּתִים, לָאָדוֹן אָנוּ שַׁיָּכִים; ⁹ שֶׁהֲרֵי הַמָּשִׁיחַ מֵת וְקָם שׁוּב לַחַיִּים כְּדֵי שֶׁיִּהְיֶה אָדוֹן גַּם לַמֵּתִים גַּם לַחַיִּים. ¹⁰ וּמַדּוּעַ אַתָּה חוֹרֵץ מִשְׁפָּט עַל אָחִיךָ? מַדּוּעַ אַתָּה בָּז לְאָחִיךָ? הֲרֵי כֻּלָּנוּ נַעֲמֹד לִפְנֵי כֵּס הַמִּשְׁפָּט שֶׁל אֱלֹהִים; ¹¹ הֲלֹא כָּתוּב: "חַי אָנִי, נְאֻם יהוה, כִּי לִי תִּכְרַע כָּל בֶּרֶךְ וְכָל לָשׁוֹן

¹²So then each of us shall give account of himself to God. ¹³Therefore let us not judge one another anymore, but rather resolve this, not to put a stumbling block or a cause to fall in *our* brother's way.

¹⁴I know and am convinced by the Lord Jesus that *there is* nothing unclean of itself; but to him who considers anything to be unclean, to him *it is* unclean. ¹⁵Yet if your brother is grieved because of *your* food, you are no longer walking in love. Do not destroy with your food the one for whom Christ died. ¹⁶Therefore do not let your good be spoken of as evil; ¹⁷for the kingdom of God is not eating and drinking, but righteousness and peace and joy in the Holy Spirit. ¹⁸For he who serves Christ in these things *is* acceptable to God and approved by men.

¹⁹Therefore let us pursue the things *which make* for peace and the things by which one may edify another. ²⁰Do not destroy the work of God for the sake of food. All things indeed *are* pure, but *it is* evil for the man who eats with offense. ²¹*It is* good neither to eat meat nor drink wine nor *do anything* by which your brother stumbles or is offended or is made weak. ²²Do you have faith? Have *it* to yourself before God. Happy *is* he who does not condemn himself in what he approves. ²³But he who doubts is condemned if he eats, because *he does* not *eat* from faith; for whatever *is* not from faith is sin.

15 We then who are strong ought to bear with the scruples of the weak, and not to please ourselves. ²Let each of us please *his* neighbor for *his* good, leading to edification. ³For even Christ did not please Himself; but as it is written, *"The reproaches of those who reproached You fell on Me."* ⁴For whatever things were written before were written for our learning, that we through the patience and comfort of the Scriptures might have hope. ⁵Now may the God of patience and comfort grant you to be like-minded toward one another, according to Christ Jesus, ⁶that you may with one mind *and* one mouth glorify the God and Father of our Lord Jesus Christ.

⁷Therefore receive one another, just as Christ also received us, to the glory of God. ⁸Now I say that Jesus Christ has become a servant to the circumcision for the truth of God, to confirm the promises *made* to the fathers, ⁹and that the Gentiles might glorify God for *His* mercy, as it is written:

"For this reason I will confess to You among the Gentiles,
And sing to Your name."

¹² וּבְכֵן כָּל אֶחָד מֵאִתָּנוּ יִתֵּן דִּין וְחֶשְׁבּוֹן עַל עַצְמוֹ לִפְנֵי אֱלֹהִים. ¹³ לָכֵן אַל נִשְׁפֹּט עוֹד אִישׁ אֶת רֵעֵהוּ, אֶלָּא שֶׁזֶּה יִהְיֶה שְׁפּוּטְכֶם: שֶׁלֹּא יִתֵּן אִישׁ אֶבֶן נֶגֶף אוֹ מִכְשׁוֹל לִפְנֵי אָחִיו. ¹⁴ יוֹדֵעַ אֲנִי, וְגַם בָּטוּחַ אֲנִי בָּאָדוֹן יֵשׁוּעַ, שֶׁשּׁוּם דָּבָר אֵינוֹ טָמֵא בִּפְנֵי עַצְמוֹ, אֶלָּא טָמֵא הוּא לְמִי שֶׁחוֹשֵׁב אוֹתוֹ לְטָמֵא. ¹⁵ אִם בִּגְלַל הַמַּאֲכָל שֶׁלְּךָ נִגְרָם צַעַר לְאָחִיךָ, הֲרֵי שֶׁאֵינְךָ מִתְהַלֵּךְ עוֹד בְּדֶרֶךְ שֶׁל אַהֲבָה. אַל נָא תַהֲרֹס בְּמַאֲכָלְךָ אָדָם שֶׁהַמָּשִׁיחַ מֵת בַּעֲדוֹ. ¹⁶ וּבְכֵן, שֶׁלֹּא יֵצֵא שֵׁם רַע לְמָה שֶׁטּוֹב בְּעֵינֵיכֶם; ¹⁷ כִּי מַלְכוּת אֱלֹהִים אֵינָהּ אֲכִילָה וּשְׁתִיָּה, אֶלָּא צֶדֶק וְשָׁלוֹם וְשִׂמְחָה בְּרוּחַ הַקֹּדֶשׁ. ¹⁸ מִי שֶׁמְּשָׁרֵת אֶת הַמָּשִׁיחַ בְּדֶרֶךְ זוֹ, רָצוּי הוּא לֵאלֹהִים וּמְקֻבָּל עַל הַבְּרִיּוֹת. ¹⁹ לָכֵן נֵחָתֹר נָא אֶל דְּבָרִים שֶׁמְּבִיאִים לִידֵי שָׁלוֹם, וְאֶל דְּבָרִים שֶׁבְּאֶמְצָעוּתָם יְבַנֶּה אִישׁ אֶת רֵעֵהוּ. ²⁰ אַל תַּהֲרֹס אֶת מְלֶאכֶת אֱלֹהִים בִּגְלַל מַאֲכָל. אָמְנָם הַכֹּל טָהוֹר, אַךְ רַע הַמַּעֲשֶׂה כְּשֶׁאָדָם אוֹכֵל וְהָאֲכִילָה הִיא לְמִכְשׁוֹל. ²¹ מוּטָב שֶׁלֹּא לֶאֱכֹל בָּשָׂר וְלֹא לִשְׁתּוֹת יַיִן וּלְהִמָּנַע מִכָּל מַה שֶׁיֵּשׁ בּוֹ כְּדֵי לְהַכְשִׁיל אֶת אָחִיךָ. ²² יֵשׁ לְךָ אֱמוּנָה, חֲיֵה בָּהּ בְּעַצְמְךָ לִפְנֵי אֱלֹהִים. אַשְׁרֵי הָאָדָם שֶׁאֵינוֹ מַרְשִׁיעַ אֶת עַצְמוֹ בַּמֶּה שֶׁהוּא בּוֹרֵר לוֹ. ²³ אַךְ הָאוֹכֵל וּבְלִבּוֹ סָפֵק – אָשֵׁם, כִּי לֹא מִתּוֹךְ אֱמוּנָה פָּעַל. וְכָל מַה שֶׁאֵינוֹ מִתּוֹךְ אֱמוּנָה חֵטְא הוּא.

טו אֲנַחְנוּ הַחֲזָקִים חַיָּבִים לָשֵׂאת אֶת חֻלְשׁוֹת הַחַלָּשִׁים וְלֹא לְבַקֵּשׁ הֲנָאָה לְעַצְמֵנוּ. ² כָּל אֶחָד מֵאִתָּנוּ יִדְאַג לְטוֹבַת רֵעֵהוּ כְּדֵי שֶׁרֵעֵהוּ יִבָּנֶה, ³ שֶׁכֵּן גַּם הַמָּשִׁיחַ לֹא בִּקֵּשׁ הֲנָאָה לְעַצְמוֹ, אֶלָּא כַּכָּתוּב: "וְחֶרְפּוֹת חוֹרְפֶיךָ נָפְלוּ עָלָי." ⁴ וַהֲרֵי כָּל מַה שֶׁנִּכְתַּב מִקֹּדֶם, נִכְתַּב לְהַדְרָכָתֵנוּ, כְּדֵי שֶׁתִּהְיֶה לָנוּ תִּקְוָה מִתּוֹךְ הַסַּבְלָנוּת וְהַנֶּחָמָה שֶׁבַּכְּתוּבִים. ⁵ וֵאלֹהֵי הַסַּבְלָנוּת וְהַנֶּחָמָה יִתֵּן וְתִהְיוּ תְּמִימֵי דֵעִים זֶה עִם זֶה כִּרְצוֹן הַמָּשִׁיחַ יֵשׁוּעַ, ⁶ כְּדֵי שֶׁבְּלֵב אֶחָד וּבְפֶה אֶחָד תְּהַלְלוּ אֶת אֱלֹהִים, אֲבִי אֲדוֹנֵנוּ יֵשׁוּעַ הַמָּשִׁיחַ.

⁷ עַל כֵּן קַבְּלוּ אִישׁ אֶת רֵעֵהוּ, כְּשֵׁם שֶׁגַּם הַמָּשִׁיחַ קִבֵּל אוֹתָנוּ לִכְבוֹד אֱלֹהִים. ⁸ וַאֲנִי אוֹמֵר שֶׁהַמָּשִׁיחַ הָיָה לִמְשָׁרֵת הַנִּמּוֹלִים בִּגְלַל נֶאֱמָנוּת אֱלֹהִים, כְּדֵי לְקַיֵּם אֶת הַהַבְטָחוֹת שֶׁנִּתְּנוּ לָאָבוֹת, ⁹ וּכְדֵי שֶׁהַגּוֹיִים יְהַלְלוּ אֶת אֱלֹהִים עַל רַחֲמָיו, כַּכָּתוּב: "עַל־כֵּן אוֹדְךָ יהוה בַּגּוֹיִם וּלְשִׁמְךָ אֲזַמֵּר."

[10] And again he says:

"Rejoice, O Gentiles, with His people!"

[11] And again:

"Praise the LORD, all you Gentiles!
Laud Him, all you peoples!"

[12] And again, Isaiah says:

"There shall be a root of Jesse;
And He who shall rise to reign over the
Gentiles,
In Him the Gentiles shall hope."

[13] Now may the God of hope fill you with all joy and peace in believing, that you may abound in hope by the power of the Holy Spirit.

[14] Now I myself am confident concerning you, my brethren, that you also are full of goodness, filled with all knowledge, able also to admonish one another. [15] Nevertheless, brethren, I have written more boldly to you on *some* points, as reminding you, because of the grace given to me by God, [16] that I might be a minister of Jesus Christ to the Gentiles, ministering the gospel of God, that the offering of the Gentiles might be acceptable, sanctified by the Holy Spirit. [17] Therefore I have reason to glory in Christ Jesus in the things *which* pertain to God. [18] For I will not dare to speak of any of those things which Christ has not accomplished through me, in word and deed, to make the Gentiles obedient— [19] in mighty signs and wonders, by the power of the Spirit of God, so that from Jerusalem and round about to Illyricum I have fully preached the gospel of Christ. [20] And so I have made it my aim to preach the gospel, not where Christ was named, lest I should build on another man's foundation, [21] but as it is written:

"To whom He was not announced, they shall
see;
And those who have not heard shall understand."

[22] For this reason I also have been much hindered from coming to you. [23] But now no longer having a place in these parts, and having a great desire these many years to come to you, [24] whenever I journey to Spain, I shall come to you. For I hope to see you on my journey, and to be helped on my way there by you, if first I may enjoy your *company* for a while. [25] But now I am going to Jerusalem to minister to the saints. [26] For it pleased those from Macedonia and Achaia to make a certain contribution for the poor among the saints who are in Jerusalem. [27] It pleased them indeed, and they are their debtors. For if the Gentiles have been partakers of their

[10] וְעוֹד הוּא אוֹמֵר:

"הַרְנִינוּ גוֹיִם עַמּוֹ",

[11] וְעוֹד:

"הַלְלוּ־אֶת יהוה כָּל־גּוֹיִם, שַׁבְּחוּהוּ כָּל־
הָאֻמִּים."

[12] וִישַׁעְיָהוּ אוֹמֵר:

"וְהָיָה שֹׁרֶשׁ יִשַׁי אֲשֶׁר עֹמֵד לְנֵס עַמִּים, אֵלָיו
גּוֹיִם יִדְרֹשׁוּ."

[13] וֵאלֹהֵי הַתִּקְוָה יְמַלֵּא אֶתְכֶם כָּל שִׂמְחָה וְשָׁלוֹם בֶּאֱמוּנַתְכֶם, כְּדֵי שֶׁתִּגְאֶה בָכֶם הַתִּקְוָה בְּכֹחַ רוּחַ הַקֹּדֶשׁ.

[14] אֲנִי בָּטוּחַ, אַחַי, שֶׁאַתֶּם שׁוֹפְעִים טוֹב, מְלֵאִים כָּל דַּעַת וְיוֹדְעִים גַּם לְהוֹכִיחַ אִישׁ אֶת רֵעֵהוּ. [15] בְּכָל זֹאת כָּתַבְתִּי לָכֶם פֹּה וְשָׁם בְּהֶעָזָה רַבָּה לְמַדַּי, כְּמִי שֶׁמְּעוֹרֵר אֶת זִכְרוֹנְכֶם, וְזֹאת עַל־סְמַךְ הַחֶסֶד הַנָּתוּן לִי מֵאֵת אֱלֹהִים [16] לִהְיוֹת מְשָׁרֵת־קֹדֶשׁ שֶׁל הַמָּשִׁיחַ יֵשׁוּעַ בִּשְׁבִיל הַגּוֹיִם וּלְכַהֵן בִּבְשׂוֹרַת אֱלֹהִים, כְּדֵי שֶׁהַגּוֹיִם יִהְיוּ לְמִנְחָה רְצוּיָה, מְקֻדֶּשֶׁת בְּרוּחַ הַקֹּדֶשׁ. [17] לָכֵן, הוֹדוֹת לַמָּשִׁיחַ יֵשׁוּעַ יָכוֹל אֲנִי לְהִתְגָּאוֹת בַּדְּבָרִים הַשַּׁיָּכִים לֵאלֹהִים. [18] וְלֹא אָעֵז לְדַבֵּר בִּלְתִּי אִם עַל הַדְּבָרִים שֶׁהַמָּשִׁיחַ עָשָׂה דַּרְכִּי כְּדֵי לְהָבִיא אֶת הַגּוֹיִם לִידֵי צִיּוּת, וְזֹאת עַל־יְדֵי דִּבּוּר וּמַעֲשֶׂה, [19] בְּכֹחַ אוֹתוֹת וּמוֹפְתִים, וּבְכֹחַ רוּחַ הַקֹּדֶשׁ, בְּאֹפֶן שֶׁהִסְפַּקְתִּי לְבַשֵּׂר אֶת בְּשׂוֹרַת הַמָּשִׁיחַ מִירוּשָׁלַיִם וּסְבִיבוֹתֶיהָ עַד אִלּוּרִיקוֹן. [20] וְאָמְנָם הִשְׁתַּדַּלְתִּי לְבַשֵּׂר בִּמְקוֹמוֹת שֶׁטֶּרֶם הִשְׁמִיעוּ בָּהֶם אֶת שֵׁם הַמָּשִׁיחַ, כְּדֵי שֶׁלֹּא אֶבְנֶה עַל יְסוֹד שֶׁל אֲחֵרִים, [21] אֶלָּא כַּכָּתוּב:

"אֲשֶׁר לֹא־סֻפַּר לָהֶם רָאוּ,
וַאֲשֶׁר לֹא־שָׁמְעוּ הִתְבּוֹנָנוּ."

[22] לָכֵן גַּם פְּעָמִים רַבּוֹת נִמְנַע מִמֶּנִּי לָבוֹא אֲלֵיכֶם. [23] אֲבָל כָּעֵת, הוֹאִיל וְאֵין לִי עוֹד מָקוֹם לִפְעֻלָּה בָּאֵזוֹרִים הָאֵלֶּה, וְשָׁנִים רַבּוֹת מִשְׁתּוֹקֵק אֲנִי לָבוֹא אֲלֵיכֶם, [24] אֲנִי מְקַוֶּה שֶׁבְּדַרְכִּי לִסְפָרַד אָסוּר לִרְאוֹתְכֶם, וּלְאַחַר שֶׁאֶהֱנֶה קִמְעָה אֶצְלְכֶם תְּשַׁלְּחוּנִי לְהֶמְשֵׁךְ דַּרְכִּי. [25] אוּלָם כָּעֵת אֲנִי עוֹלֶה לִירוּשָׁלַיִם לַעֲזֹר לַקְּדוֹשִׁים, [26] כִּי מֵקֶדוֹנְיָה וְאַכַיָּה רָאוּ לְנָכוֹן לִתְרֹם תְּרוּמָה לַעֲנִיֵּי הַקְּדוֹשִׁים. [27] הֵם רָאוּ זֹאת לְנָכוֹן וְזוֹהִי חוֹבָתָם כְּלַפֵּיהֶם; שֶׁכֵּן אִם הַגּוֹיִם שֻׁתְּפוּ בַּדְּבָרִים הָרוּחָנִיִּים שֶׁלָּהֶם, עֲלֵיהֶם גַּם

spiritual things, their duty is also to minister to them in material things. 28 Therefore, when I have performed this and have sealed to them this fruit, I shall go by way of you to Spain. 29 But I know that when I come to you, I shall come in the fullness of the blessing of the gospel of Christ.

30 Now I beg you, brethren, through the Lord Jesus Christ, and through the love of the Spirit, that you strive together with me in prayers to God for me, 31 that I may be delivered from those in Judea who do not believe, and that my service for Jerusalem may be acceptable to the saints, 32 that I may come to you with joy by the will of God, and may be refreshed together with you. 33 Now the God of peace be with you all. Amen.

16 I commend to you Phoebe our sister, who is a servant of the church in Cenchrea, 2 that you may receive her in the Lord in a manner worthy of the saints, and assist her in whatever business she has need of you; for indeed she has been a helper of many and of myself also.

3 Greet Priscilla and Aquila, my fellow workers in Christ Jesus, 4 who risked their own necks for my life, to whom not only I give thanks, but also all the churches of the Gentiles. 5 Likewise greet the church that is in their house.

Greet my beloved Epaenetus, who is the first-fruits of Achaia to Christ. 6 Greet Mary, who labored much for us. 7 Greet Andronicus and Junia, my countrymen and my fellow prisoners, who are of note among the apostles, who also were in Christ before me.

8 Greet Amplias, my beloved in the Lord. 9 Greet Urbanus, our fellow worker in Christ, and Stachys, my beloved. 10 Greet Apelles, approved in Christ. Greet those who are of the household of Aristobulus. 11 Greet Herodion, my countryman. Greet those who are of the household of Narcissus who are in the Lord.

12 Greet Tryphena and Tryphosa, who have labored in the Lord. Greet the beloved Persis, who labored much in the Lord. 13 Greet Rufus, chosen in the Lord, and his mother and mine. 14 Greet Asyncritus, Phlegon, Hermas, Patrobas, Hermes, and the brethren who are with them. 15 Greet Philologus and Julia, Nereus and his sister, and Olympas, and all the saints who are with them.

16 Greet one another with a holy kiss. The churches of Christ greet you.

17 Now I urge you, brethren, note those who cause divisions and offenses, contrary to the doctrine which you learned, and avoid them. 18 For those who are such do not serve our Lord

לִסְעַ לָהֶם בְּדִבְרִים חָמְרִיִּים. 28 לָכֵן לְאַחַר שֶׁאֲשַׁלֵּים זֹאת וְאֶמְסֹר לָהֶם בַּחֲתִימָתִי אֶת הַתְּרוּמָה הַזֹּאת, אָסוּר אֲלֵיכֶם בְּדַרְכִּי לִסְפָרַד. 29 אֲנִי בָּטוּחַ כִּי כַּאֲשֶׁר אָבוֹא אֲלֵיכֶם, אָבוֹא בִּמְלוֹא בִּרְכַּת הַמָּשִׁיחַ.

30 וַאֲנִי מְבַקֵּשׁ מִכֶּם, אַחַי, לְמַעַן אֲדוֹנֵנוּ יֵשׁוּעַ הַמָּשִׁיחַ וּלְמַעַן אַהֲבַת הָרוּחַ, לְהֵאָבֵק יַחַד אִתִּי בִּתְפִלּוֹת לֵאלֹהִים בַּעֲדִי, 31 כְּדֵי שֶׁאֶנָּצֵל מִידֵי הַסּוֹרְרִים בְּאֶרֶץ יְהוּדָה וְשֵׁרוּתִי לְמַעַן יְרוּשָׁלַיִם יִהְיֶה לְרָצוֹן בְּעֵינֵי הַקְּדוֹשִׁים, 32 וּכְדֵי שֶׁאָבוֹא אֲלֵיכֶם בְּשִׂמְחָה, כִּרְצוֹן אֱלֹהִים, וְאָנוּחַ בְּחֶבְרַתְכֶם. 33 אֱלֹהֵי הַשָּׁלוֹם עִם כֻּלְּכֶם. אָמֵן.

טז אֲנִי מַמְלִיץ לִפְנֵיכֶם עַל אֲחוֹתֵנוּ פֶבִּי, שַׁמָּשִׁית הַקְּהִלָּה בְּקֶנְכְרָאָה. 2 קַבְּלוּ נָא אוֹתָהּ בָּאָדוֹן, כַּיָּאֶה לַקְּדוֹשִׁים, וְעִזְרוּ לָהּ בְּכָל דָּבָר שֶׁתִּזְדָּקֵק לָכֶם; כִּי אָכֵן הָיְתָה עֵזֶר לְרַבִּים וְגַם לִי. 3 דִּרְשׁוּ בִּשְׁלוֹם פְּרִיסְקִילָה וַעֲקִילַס חֲבֵרַי לָעֲבוֹדָה בַּמָּשִׁיחַ יֵשׁוּעַ, 4 אֲשֶׁר סִכְּנוּ אֶת רֹאשָׁם בְּעַד נַפְשִׁי, וְלֹא רַק אֲנִי מַכִּיר לָהֶם טוֹבָה, אֶלָּא גַּם כָּל קְהִלּוֹת הַגּוֹיִים. 5 וְדִרְשַׁת שָׁלוֹם לַקְּהִלָּה שֶׁבְּבֵיתָם. דִּרְשׁוּ בִּשְׁלוֹם אֶפֶּנְטוֹס יַקִּירִי, שֶׁהָיָה פְּרִי רִאשׁוֹן לַמָּשִׁיחַ בְּמְחוֹז אַסְיָה. 6 דִּרְשׁוּ בִּשְׁלוֹם מִרְיָם, שֶׁעָמְלָה רַבּוֹת בִּשְׁבִילְכֶם. 7 דִּרְשׁוּ בִּשְׁלוֹם אַנְדְּרוֹנִיקוֹס וְיוּנְיַס, בְּנֵי־עַמִּי שֶׁהָיוּ אִתִּי בַּמַּאֲסָר; נִכְבָּדִים הֵם בְּקֶרֶב הַשְּׁלִיחִים וְגַם הָיוּ בַּמָּשִׁיחַ לְפָנַי. 8 דִּרְשַׁת שָׁלוֹם לְאַמְפְּלִיאָטוֹס יַקִּירִי בָּאָדוֹן. 9 דִּרְשַׁת שָׁלוֹם לְאוּרְבָּנוֹס חֲבֵרֵנוּ לָעֲבוֹדָה בַּמָּשִׁיחַ, וּלְאִסְטָכִים יַקִּירִי. 10 דִּרְשַׁת שָׁלוֹם לְאַפֵּלִּים הַבָּחוּן בַּמָּשִׁיחַ וְלִבְנֵי בֵּיתוֹ שֶׁל אֲרִיסְטוֹבּוּלוֹם. 11 דִּרְשַׁת שָׁלוֹם לְהוֹרוֹדְיוֹן בֶּן־עַמִּי וְלִבְנֵי בֵּיתוֹ שֶׁל נַרְקִיסוֹם אֲשֶׁר בָּאָדוֹן. 12 דִּרְשַׁת שָׁלוֹם לְטְרִיפֵינָה וּטְרִיפוֹסָה הָעֲמֵלוֹת בָּאָדוֹן, וּלְפֶרְסִים הַחֲבִיבָה שֶׁעָמְלָה רַבּוֹת בָּאָדוֹן. 13 דִּרְשַׁת שָׁלוֹם לְרוּפוֹם הַנִּבְחָר בָּאָדוֹן, וּלְאִמּוֹ שֶׁהִיא כְּאֵם גַּם לִי. 14 דִּרְשַׁת שָׁלוֹם לְאַסִינְקְרִיטוֹם, לִפְלֵיגוֹן, לְהֶרְמֶס, לְפַטְרוֹבָּא וְהֶרְמַס וְלָאַחִים אֲשֶׁר אִתָּם. 15 דִּרְשַׁת שָׁלוֹם לְפִילוֹלוֹגוֹם וְיוּלְיָה, לְנֵרֵאַס וַאֲחוֹתוֹ, לְאוֹלִימְפָּם וְכָל הַקְּדוֹשִׁים אֲשֶׁר אִתָּם. 16 בָּרְכוּ לְשָׁלוֹם אִישׁ אֶת רֵעֵהוּ בִּנְשִׁיקָה קְדוֹשָׁה. כָּל קְהִלּוֹת הַמָּשִׁיחַ דּוֹרְשׁוֹת בִּשְׁלוֹמְכֶם.

17 וַאֲנִי מְבַקֵּשׁ מִכֶּם, אַחַי: הִשָּׁמְרוּ מִן הַמְעוֹרְרִים מַחֲלֹקוֹת וּמִן הַמַּכְשִׁילִים, הַפּוֹעֲלִים בְּנִגּוּד לַלִּמּוּד שֶׁלֻּמַּדְתֶּם, וְהִתְרַחֲקוּ מֵהֶם. 18 אֲנָשִׁים כָּאֵלֶּה אֵינָם

Jesus Christ, but their own belly, and by smooth words and flattering speech deceive the hearts of the simple. 19 For your obedience has become known to all. Therefore I am glad on your behalf; but I want you to be wise in what is good, and simple concerning evil. 20 And the God of peace will crush Satan under your feet shortly.

The grace of our Lord Jesus Christ *be* with you. Amen.

21 Timothy, my fellow worker, and Lucius, Jason, and Sosipater, my countrymen, greet you.

22 I, Tertius, who wrote *this* epistle, greet you in the Lord.

23 Gaius, my host and *the host* of the whole church, greets you. Erastus, the treasurer of the city, greets you, and Quartus, a brother. 24 The grace of our Lord Jesus Christ *be* with you all. Amen.

25 Now to Him who is able to establish you according to my gospel and the preaching of Jesus Christ, according to the revelation of the mystery kept secret since the world began 26 but now made manifest, and by the prophetic Scriptures made known to all nations, according to the commandment of the everlasting God, for obedience to the faith— 27 to God, alone wise, *be* glory through Jesus Christ forever. Amen.

מְשָׁרְתִים אֶת אֲדוֹנֵנוּ הַמָּשִׁיחַ, אֶלָּא אֶת כִּרְסָם שֶׁלָּהֶם, וּבְאִמְרֵי נֹעַם וּבְדִבּוּרִים יָפִים הֵם מוֹלִיכִים שׁוֹלָל אֶת לֵב הַתְּמִימִים. 19 שָׂמֵחַ אֲנִי עֲלֵיכֶם, כִּי צִיּוּתְכֶם נוֹדַע לַכֹּל, אֲבָל רְצוֹנִי שֶׁתִּהְיוּ חֲכָמִים לַטּוֹב וּתְמִימִים לְגַבֵּי הָרָע. 20 וֵאלֹהֵי הַשָּׁלוֹם יָכְרִיעַ בִּמְהֵרָה אֶת הַשָּׂטָן תַּחַת רַגְלֵיכֶם. חֶסֶד אֲדוֹנֵנוּ יֵשׁוּעַ הַמָּשִׁיחַ עִמָּכֶם.

21 טִימוֹתִיאוֹס, חֲבֵרִי לַעֲבוֹדָה, וְגַם לוּקִיּוֹס וְיָסוֹן וְסוֹסִיפַּטְרוֹס בְּנֵי־עַמִּי דּוֹרְשִׁים בִּשְׁלוֹמְכֶם. 22 אֲנִי טֶרְטִיּוֹס, הַכּוֹתֵב אֶת הָאִגֶּרֶת הַזֹּאת, שׁוֹאֵל בִּשְׁלוֹמְכֶם בָּאָדוֹן. 23 גָּיוֹס הַמְאָרֵחַ אוֹתִי וְאֶת כָּל הַקְּהִלָּה דּוֹרֵשׁ בִּשְׁלוֹמְכֶם. אֶרַסְטוֹס גִּזְבַּר הָעִיר וּקְוַרְטוֹס אָחִינוּ דּוֹרְשִׁים בִּשְׁלוֹמְכֶם.

25 וְהוּא אֲשֶׁר יָכוֹל לְחַזֵּק אֶתְכֶם לְפִי בְּשׂוֹרָתִי וְהַכְרָזַת יֵשׁוּעַ הַמָּשִׁיחַ – לְפִי הִתְגַּלּוּת הָרָז שֶׁהָיָה כָּמוּס בְּעִתּוֹת עוֹלָם, 26 אַךְ כָּעֵת, בִּפְקֻדַּת אֱלֹהֵי עוֹלָם, נִתְגַּלָּה עַל־יְדֵי כְּתוּבִים נְבוּאִיִּים וּפֻרְסַם לְכָל הַגּוֹיִים כְּדֵי לַהֲבִיאָם לִידֵי צִיּוּת שֶׁבֶּאֱמוּנָה – 27 הָאֱלֹהִים אֲשֶׁר לוֹ לְבַדּוֹ הַחָכְמָה, לוֹ הַכָּבוֹד בְּיֵשׁוּעַ הַמָּשִׁיחַ לְעוֹלְמֵי עוֹלָמִים. אָמֵן.

CORINTHIANS

1 Paul, called *to be* an apostle of Jesus Christ through the will of God, and Sosthenes *our* brother,

2 To the church of God which is at Corinth, to those who are sanctified in Christ Jesus, called *to be* saints, with all who in every place call on the name of Jesus Christ our Lord, both theirs and ours:

3 Grace to you and peace from God our Father and the Lord Jesus Christ.

4 I thank my God always concerning you for the grace of God which was given to you by Christ Jesus, 5 that you were enriched in everything by Him in all utterance and all knowledge, 6 even as the testimony of Christ was confirmed in you, 7 so that you come short in no gift, eagerly waiting for the revelation of our Lord Jesus Christ, 8 who will also confirm you to the end, *that you may be* blameless in the day of our Lord Jesus Christ. 9 God *is* faithful, by whom you were called into the fellowship of His Son, Jesus Christ our Lord.

10 Now I plead with you, brethren, by the name of our Lord Jesus Christ, that you all speak the same thing, and *that* there be no divisions among you, but *that* you be perfectly joined together in the same mind and in the same judgment. 11 For it has been declared to me concerning you, my brethren, by those of Chloe's *household,* that there are contentions among you. 12 Now I say this, that each of you says, "I am of Paul," or "I am of Apollos," or "I am of Cephas," or "I am of Christ." 13 Is Christ divided? Was Paul crucified for you? Or were you baptized in the name of Paul?

14 I thank God that I baptized none of you except Crispus and Gaius, 15 lest anyone should say that I had baptized in my own name. 16 Yes, I also baptized the household of Stephanas. Besides, I do not know whether I baptized any other. 17 For Christ did not send me to baptize, but to preach the gospel, not with wisdom of words, lest the cross of Christ should be made of no effect.

18 For the message of the cross is foolishness to those who are perishing, but to us who are being saved it is the power of God. 19 For it is written:

> "I will destroy the wisdom of the wise,
> And bring to nothing the understanding of the prudent."

אִגֶּרֶת שָׁאוּל הָרִאשׁוֹנָה אֶל הַקּוֹרִינְתִים

א מֵאֵת שָׁאוּל, שֶׁנִּקְרָא לִהְיוֹת שְׁלִיחַ הַמָּשִׁיחַ יֵשׁוּעַ בִּרְצוֹן אֱלֹהִים, וּמֵאֵת סוֹסְתְנִים אָחִינוּ, 2 אֶל קְהִלַּת אֱלֹהִים שֶׁבְּקוֹרִינְתוֹס, לָאֵלֶּה אֲשֶׁר קֻדְּשׁוּ בַּמָּשִׁיחַ יֵשׁוּעַ וְנִקְרְאוּ לִהְיוֹת קְדוֹשִׁים יַחַד עִם כָּל הַקּוֹרְאִים בְּכָל מָקוֹם וּמָקוֹם בְּשֵׁם אֲדוֹנֵנוּ יֵשׁוּעַ הַמָּשִׁיחַ – אֲדוֹנֵנוּ כַּאֲדוֹנָם: 3 חֶסֶד וְשָׁלוֹם לָכֶם מֵאֵת הָאֱלֹהִים אָבִינוּ וְהָאָדוֹן יֵשׁוּעַ הַמָּשִׁיחַ.

4 אֲנִי מוֹדֶה לֵאלֹהַי בְּכָל עֵת בַּעֲבוּרְכֶם עַל חֶסֶד אֱלֹהִים שֶׁנִּתַּן לָכֶם בַּמָּשִׁיחַ יֵשׁוּעַ, 5 כִּי בּוֹ נַעֲשֵׂיתֶם עֲשִׁירִים בַּכֹּל, בְּכָל אֹמֶר וּבְכָל דַּעַת; 6 וְעֵדוּת הַמָּשִׁיחַ קֻבְּלָה תֹּקֶף בְּקִרְבְּכֶם, 7 בְּאֹפֶן שֶׁאֵינְכֶם חֲסֵרִים שׁוּם מַתָּנָה רוּחָנִית בְּצִפִּיָּתְכֶם לְהִתְגַּלּוּת אֲדוֹנֵנוּ יֵשׁוּעַ הַמָּשִׁיחַ, 8 אֲשֶׁר גַּם יְחַזֵּק אֶתְכֶם עַד קֵץ לְמַעַן תִּהְיוּ נְקִיִּים מִכָּל אַשְׁמָה בְּיוֹם אֲדוֹנֵנוּ יֵשׁוּעַ הַמָּשִׁיחַ. 9 נֶאֱמָן הוּא הָאֱלֹהִים אֲשֶׁר קָרָא אֶתְכֶם לְחֶבְרַת בְּנוֹ יֵשׁוּעַ הַמָּשִׁיחַ אֲדוֹנֵנוּ.

10 אַחַי, אֲנִי מַפְצִיר בָּכֶם בְּשֵׁם אֲדוֹנֵנוּ יֵשׁוּעַ הַמָּשִׁיחַ שֶׁתִּהְיוּ כֻּלְּכֶם תְּמִימֵי דֵעִים בְּמוֹצָא פִּיכֶם וְשֶׁלֹּא יִהְיוּ פִּלּוּגִים בֵּינֵיכֶם, אֶלָּא עִמְדוּ מְאֻחָדִים לְגַמְרֵי בְּאוֹתָהּ מַחֲשָׁבָה וּבְאוֹתָהּ דֵּעָה. 11 אַחַי, נִמְסַר לִי מֵאֵת בְּנֵי מִשְׁפַּחַת כְּלוֹאָה שֶׁיֵּשׁ מְרִיבוֹת בֵּינֵיכֶם. 12 אֲנִי מִתְכַּוֵּן לְכָךְ שֶׁכָּל אֶחָד מִכֶּם אוֹמֵר: "אֲנִי שַׁיָּךְ לְשָׁאוּל", אוֹ "אֲנִי לְאַפּוֹלוֹס", "אֲנִי שֶׁל כֵּיפָא", "וַאֲנִי שֶׁל הַמָּשִׁיחַ". 13 וּבְכֵן, הַאִם הַמָּשִׁיחַ הִתְפַּלֵּג? הַאִם שָׁאוּל נִצְלַב בַּעֲדְכֶם? אוֹ לְשֵׁם שָׁאוּל נִטְבַּלְתֶּם? 14 תּוֹדָה לָאֵל שֶׁלֹּא הִטְבַּלְתִּי אִישׁ מִכֶּם זוּלַת קְרִיסְפּוֹס וְגָיוֹס, 15 פֶּן יֹאמַר מִישֶׁהוּ כִּי לִשְׁמִי נִטְבַּלְתֶּם. 16 אָמְנָם הִטְבַּלְתִּי גַם אֶת בְּנֵי בֵיתוֹ שֶׁל סְטֶפָנַס. מִלְּבַד אֵלֶּה, אֵינֶנִּי יוֹדֵעַ אִם הִטְבַּלְתִּי אִישׁ; 17 כִּי הַמָּשִׁיחַ לֹא שְׁלָחַנִי לְהַטְבִּיל, אֶלָּא לְבַשֵּׂר אֶת הַבְּשׂוֹרָה – לֹא בְּחָכְמַת מִלִּים, פֶּן יִהְיֶה לָרִיק צְלָב הַמָּשִׁיחַ.

18 הֵן דְּבַר הַצְּלָב הוּא סִכְלוּת בְּעֵינֵי הָאוֹבְדִים, אַךְ לָנוּ הַנּוֹשָׁעִים הוּא גְּבוּרַת אֱלֹהִים, 19 שֶׁהֲרֵי כָּתוּב: "אֲאַבֵּד חָכְמַת חֲכָמִים וּבִינַת נְבוֹנִים אַסְתִּיר".

²⁰Where *is* the wise? Where *is* the scribe? Where *is* the disputer of this age? Has not God made foolish the wisdom of this world? ²¹For since, in the wisdom of God, the world through wisdom did not know God, it pleased God through the foolishness of the message preached to save those who believe. ²²For Jews request a sign, and Greeks seek after wisdom; ²³but we preach Christ crucified, to the Jews a stumbling block and to the Greeks foolishness, ²⁴but to those who are called, both Jews and Greeks, Christ the power of God and the wisdom of God. ²⁵Because the foolishness of God is wiser than men, and the weakness of God is stronger than men.

²⁶For you see your calling, brethren, that not many wise according to the flesh, not many mighty, not many noble, *are called.* ²⁷But God has chosen the foolish things of the world to put to shame the wise, and God has chosen the weak things of the world to put to shame the things which are mighty; ²⁸and the base things of the world and the things which are despised God has chosen, and the things which are not, to bring to nothing the things that are, ²⁹that no flesh should glory in His presence. ³⁰But of Him you are in Christ Jesus, who became for us wisdom from God—and righteousness and sanctification and redemption— ³¹that, as it is written, *"He who glories, let him glory in the* Lord.*"*

2 And I, brethren, when I came to you, did not come with excellence of speech or of wisdom declaring to you the testimony of God. ²For I determined not to know anything among you except Jesus Christ and Him crucified. ³I was with you in weakness, in fear, and in much trembling. ⁴And my speech and my preaching *were* not with persuasive words of human wisdom, but in demonstration of the Spirit and of power, ⁵that your faith should not be in the wisdom of men but in the power of God.

⁶However, we speak wisdom among those who are mature, yet not the wisdom of this age, nor of the rulers of this age, who are coming to nothing. ⁷But we speak the wisdom of God in a mystery, the hidden *wisdom* which God ordained before the ages for our glory, ⁸which none of the rulers of this age knew; for had they known, they would not have crucified the Lord of glory.

⁹But as it is written:

"Eye has not seen, nor ear heard,
Nor have entered into the heart of man

²⁰ אַיֵּה הֶחָכָם? אַיֵּה הַסֹּפֵר? אַיֵּה הַמִּתְפַּלְמֵם שֶׁל הָעוֹלָם הַזֶּה? הַאִם לֹא שָׂם הָאֱלֹהִים אֶת חָכְמַת הָעוֹלָם לְאִוֶּלֶת? ²¹ וּמֵאַחַר שֶׁבְּחָכְמַת הָאֱלֹהִים לֹא הִשְׂכִּיל הָעוֹלָם לָדַעַת אֶת אֱלֹהִים בְּאֶמְצָעוּת חָכְמָה, רָאָה אֱלֹהִים לְנָכוֹן לְהוֹשִׁיעַ אֶת הַמַּאֲמִינִים עַל־יְדֵי הַכְּרָזָה שֶׁנֶּחְשֶׁבֶת לְסִכְלוּת. ²² הִנֵּה הַיְּהוּדִים מְבַקְּשִׁים אוֹתוֹת וְהַיְּוָנִים מְחַפְּשִׂים חָכְמָה, ²³ אֲבָל אֲנַחְנוּ מַכְרִיזִים מָשִׁיחַ צָלוּב, אֶבֶן נֶגֶף לַיְּהוּדִים וְסִכְלוּת בְּעֵינֵי הַיְּוָנִים. ²⁴ אוּלָם לַנִּקְרָאִים הֵן מִקֶּרֶב הַיְּהוּדִים הֵן מִקֶּרֶב הַיְּוָנִים – מָשִׁיחַ שֶׁהוּא גְּבוּרַת אֱלֹהִים וְחָכְמַת אֱלֹהִים. ²⁵ הֵן "סִכְלוּת" אֱלֹהִים חֲכָמָה מִבְּנֵי אָדָם, וְ"חֻלְשַׁת" אֱלֹהִים חֲזָקָה מִבְּנֵי אָדָם.

²⁶ אַחַי, רְאוּ מִי אַתֶּם שֶׁנִּקְרֵאתֶם: לֹא רַבִּים מִכֶּם חֲכָמִים מִבְּחִינַת הָעוֹלָם הַזֶּה, לֹא רַבִּים חֲזָקִים וְלֹא רַבִּים רָמֵי יַחַשׂ. ²⁷ אֲבָל אֱלֹהִים בָּחַר בְּכְּסִילִים אֲשֶׁר בָּעוֹלָם כְּדֵי לְבַיֵּשׁ אֶת הַחֲכָמִים, וּבְחַלָּשִׁים אֲשֶׁר בָּעוֹלָם כְּדֵי לְבַיֵּשׁ אֶת הַחֲזָקִים; ²⁸ בַּנִּחוּתִים אֲשֶׁר בָּעוֹלָם וּבַנֶּחְשָׁבִים לְפְחוּתֵי עֵרֶךְ בָּחַר אֱלֹהִים, בַּדְּבָרִים שֶׁהֵם כְּאַפַס, כְּדֵי לְהַשְׁפִּיל עַד לְאֶפֶס אֶת הַדְּבָרִים הַקַּיָּמִים, ²⁹ לְמַעַן לֹא יִתְהַלֵּל אִישׁ לִפְנֵי הָאֱלֹהִים. ³⁰ אֲבָל מִמֶּנּוּ קַיָּמִים אַתֶּם בַּמָּשִׁיחַ יֵשׁוּעַ אֲשֶׁר הָיָה לָנוּ לְחָכְמָה מֵאֵת אֱלֹהִים, לִצְדָקָה, לִקְדֻשָּׁה וְלִפְדוּת, ³¹ כְּדֵי שֶׁהַמִּתְהַלֵּל יִתְהַלֵּל בַּיהוה, כְּמוֹ שֶׁגַּם כָּתוּב.

ב וַאֲנִי, אַחַי, כְּשֶׁבָּאתִי לְהוֹדִיעַ לָכֶם אֶת רָז אֱלֹהִים, לֹא בָּאתִי אֲלֵיכֶם בְּמִלִּים רָמוֹת אוֹ בְּרוֹמְמוּת חָכְמָה. ² הֶחְלַטְתִּי אָז שֶׁלֹּא לָדַעַת דָּבָר בְּקִרְבְּכֶם זוּלַת יֵשׁוּעַ הַמָּשִׁיחַ וְהוּא – צָלוּב. ³ וַאֲנִי בְּחֻלְשָׁה וּבְפַחַד וּבְרֶעָדָה רַבָּה הָיִיתִי אֶצְלְכֶם. ⁴ דִּבּוּרִי וְהַטָּפָתִי לֹא לָווּ בְּפִתּוּיֵי מִלִּים שֶׁל חָכְמָה אֱנוֹשִׁית, אֶלָּא בְּהוֹכָחָה שֶׁל רוּחַ וּגְבוּרָה, ⁵ כְּדֵי שֶׁלֹּא תִּסָּמֵךְ אֱמוּנַתְכֶם עַל חָכְמַת בְּנֵי אָדָם אֶלָּא עַל גְּבוּרַת אֱלֹהִים.

⁶ אֲנַחְנוּ דּוֹבְרִים חָכְמָה בֵּין הַמְבֻגָּרִים, אַךְ לֹא חָכְמַת הָעוֹלָם הַזֶּה, גַּם לֹא חָכְמַת שַׁלִּיטֵי הָעוֹלָם הַזֶּה הַבָּאִים אֶל קִצָּם. ⁷ אֲנַחְנוּ דּוֹבְרִים אֶת חָכְמַת אֱלֹהִים הַנִּסְתֶּרֶת, הַחָכְמָה שֶׁהָיְתָה גְּנוּזָה וַאֲשֶׁר לִפְנֵי הָעוֹלָמִים יְעָדָה אֱלֹהִים לְתִפְאַרְתֵּנוּ, – ⁸ וְאִישׁ מִשַּׁלִּיטֵי הָעוֹלָם הַזֶּה לֹא יְדָעָהּ, שֶׁכֵּן אִלּוּ יְדָעוּהָ לֹא הָיוּ צוֹלְבִים אֶת אֲדוֹן הַכָּבוֹד. ⁹ כְּמוֹ שֶׁכָּתוּב:

"אֲשֶׁר עַיִן לֹא רָאָתָה
וְאֹזֶן לֹא שָׁמְעָה
וְלֹא עָלָה עַל לֵב אִישׁ
כֹּל אֲשֶׁר הֵכִין הָאֱלֹהִים לְאוֹהֲבָיו."

The things which God has prepared for those who love Him."

10 But God has revealed *them* to us through His Spirit. For the Spirit searches all things, yes, the deep things of God. 11 For what man knows the things of a man except the spirit of the man which is in him? Even so no one knows the things of God except the Spirit of God. 12 Now we have received, not the spirit of the world, but the Spirit who is from God, that we might know the things that have been freely given to us by God.

13 These things we also speak, not in words which man's wisdom teaches but which the Holy Spirit teaches, comparing spiritual things with spiritual. 14 But the natural man does not receive the things of the Spirit of God, for they are foolishness to him; nor can he know *them,* because they are spiritually discerned. 15 But he who is spiritual judges all things, yet he himself is *rightly* judged by no one. 16 For *"who has known the mind of the LORD that he may instruct Him?"* But we have the mind of Christ.

3 And I, brethren, could not speak to you as to spiritual *people* but as to carnal, as to babes in Christ. 2 I fed you with milk and not with solid food; for until now you were not able *to receive it,* and even now you are still not able; 3 for you are still carnal. For where *there are* envy, strife, and divisions among you, are you not carnal and behaving like *mere* men? 4 For when one says, "I am of Paul," and another, "I *am* of Apollos," are you not carnal?

5 Who then is Paul, and who *is* Apollos, but ministers through whom you believed, as the Lord gave to each one? 6 I planted, Apollos watered, but God gave the increase. 7 So then neither he who plants is anything, nor he who waters, but God who gives the increase. 8 Now he who plants and he who waters are one, and each one will receive his own reward according to his own labor.

9 For we are God's fellow workers; you are God's field, *you are* God's building. 10 According to the grace of God which was given to me, as a wise master builder I have laid the foundation, and another builds on it. But let each one take heed how he builds on it. 11 For no other foundation can anyone lay than that which is laid, which is Jesus Christ. 12 Now if anyone builds on this foundation *with* gold, silver, precious stones, wood, hay, straw, 13 each one's work will become clear; for the Day will declare it, because it will be revealed by fire; and the fire will test each one's work, of what sort it is. 14 If anyone's work which he has built on *it*

10 אַךְ לָנוּ גִּלָּה אֱלֹהִים עַל־יְדֵי רוּחוֹ אֲפִלּוּ אֶת עֲמֻקּוֹת הָאֱלֹהִים, מִשּׁוּם שֶׁהָרוּחַ חוֹקֶרֶת הַכֹּל. 11 מִי מִבְּנֵי אָדָם יוֹדֵעַ אֶת אֲשֶׁר בָּאָדָם, זוּלָתִי רוּחַ הָאָדָם אֲשֶׁר בְּקִרְבּוֹ? כֵּן גַּם אֶת אֲשֶׁר בֵּאלֹהִים אֵין יוֹדֵעַ זוּלָתִי רוּחַ הָאֱלֹהִים. 12 וַאֲנַחְנוּ לֹא קִבַּלְנוּ אֶת רוּחַ הָעוֹלָם, אֶלָּא אֶת הָרוּחַ אֲשֶׁר מֵאֵת הָאֱלֹהִים, כְּדֵי שֶׁנֵּדַע אֶת הַדְּבָרִים שֶׁאֱלֹהִים נוֹתֵן לָנוּ בְּחַסְדּוֹ.

13 וְאוֹתָם אֲנַחְנוּ מַבִּיעִים לֹא בְּמִלִּים שֶׁחָכְמַת אֱנוֹשׁ מְלַמֶּדֶת, אֶלָּא בְּמִלִּים שֶׁהָרוּחַ מְלַמֶּדֶת, כְּשֶׁאָנוּ מְפָרְשִׁים דְּבָרִים רוּחָנִיִּים בְּהַגְדָּרוֹת רוּחָנִיּוֹת. 14 אַךְ הָאָדָם הַנַּפְשִׁי אֵינוֹ מְקַבֵּל אֶת דִּבְרֵי רוּחַ אֱלֹהִים, שֶׁכֵּן סִכְלוּת הֵם בְּעֵינָיו; גַּם אֵין הוּא יָכוֹל לָדַעַת אוֹתָם, מִשּׁוּם שֶׁהֵם נִבְחָנִים בְּאֹפֶן רוּחָנִי. 15 לְעֻמַּת זֹאת הָאָדָם הָרוּחָנִי בּוֹחֵן אֶת הַכֹּל וְאִישׁ לֹא יִבְחַן אוֹתוֹ; 16 כִּי "מִי־תִכֵּן אֶת־רוּחַ יהוה וְאִישׁ עֲצָתוֹ יוֹדִיעֶנּוּ?", אַךְ אֲנַחְנוּ יֵשׁ לָנוּ רוּחַ הַמָּשִׁיחַ.

ג וַאֲנִי, אַחַי, לֹא יָכֹלְתִּי לְדַבֵּר אֲלֵיכֶם כְּאֶל אֲנָשִׁים רוּחָנִיִּים, אֶלָּא כְּאֶל בִּלְתִּי־רוּחָנִיִּים, כְּאֶל תִּינוֹקוֹת בַּמָּשִׁיחַ. 2 בְּחָלָב הֵנַקְתִּי אֶתְכֶם, לֹא בְּמַאֲכָל, כִּי עוֹד לֹא יְכָלְתֶּם לֶאֱכֹל. אֲבָל גַּם כָּעֵת אֵינְכֶם יְכוֹלִים, 3 כִּי עוֹדְכֶם בִּלְתִּי־רוּחָנִיִּים. וּמֵאַחַר שֶׁיֵּשׁ בְּקִרְבְּכֶם קִנְאָה וּמְרִיבָה, הַאֵין אַתֶּם בִּלְתִּי־רוּחָנִיִּים וּמִתְנַהֲגִים כְּמוֹ הָאֲנָשִׁים? 4 הֲלֹא כַּאֲשֶׁר מִישֶׁהוּ אוֹמֵר "אֲנִי שַׁיָּךְ לְשָׁאוּל" וְאַחֵר אוֹמֵר "אֲנִי לְאַפּוֹלוֹס", הַאֵין אַתֶּם כְּבָל הָאָדָם? 5 מִי הוּא אֵפוֹא אַפּוֹלוֹס? וּמִי הוּא שָׁאוּל? מְשָׁרְתִים אֲשֶׁר בְּאֶמְצָעוּתָם בָּאתֶם לָאֱמוּנָה! וְאִישׁ אִישׁ כְּפִי שֶׁחָלַק לוֹ הָאָדוֹן: 6 אֲנִי נָטַעְתִּי, אַפּוֹלוֹס הִשְׁקָה, אֲבָל הָאֱלֹהִים הִצְמִיחַ. 7 לְפִיכָךְ לֹא הַנּוֹטֵעַ חָשׁוּב, אַף לֹא הַמַּשְׁקֶה, אֶלָּא הָאֱלֹהִים – הַמַּצְמִיחַ. 8 הַנּוֹטֵעַ וְהַמַּשְׁקֶה הֵם הֵינוּ הַךְ, וְכָל אֶחָד יְקַבֵּל אֶת שְׂכָרוֹ כְּפִי עֲמָלוֹ; 9 שֶׁכֵּן אֲנַחְנוּ עוֹבְדִים יַחַד עִם אֱלֹהִים וְאַתֶּם שְׂדֵה אֱלֹהִים, בִּנְיַן אֱלֹהִים.

10 כְּפִי חֶסֶד אֱלֹהִים שֶׁנִּתַּן לִי הִנַּחְתִּי יְסוֹד כְּבַנַּאי חָכָם וְאַחֵר בּוֹנֶה עָלָיו. אֲבָל יַשְׁגִּיחַ כָּל אֶחָד כֵּיצַד הוּא בּוֹנֶה, 11 כִּי אִישׁ לֹא יוּכַל לְהַנִּיחַ יְסוֹד אַחֵר זוּלָתִי הַיְסוֹד שֶׁהֻנַּח, וְהוּא יֵשׁוּעַ הַמָּשִׁיחַ. 12 וְכָל אִישׁ, אִם יִבְנֶה עַל הַיְסוֹד הַזֶּה זָהָב אוֹ כֶּסֶף אוֹ אֲבָנִים יְקָרוֹת אוֹ עֵץ אוֹ חָצִיר אוֹ קַשׁ – 13 מַעֲשֵׂהוּ יִתְבָּרֵר, שֶׁכֵּן הַיּוֹם יוֹצִיאוֹ לָאוֹר, מִפְּנֵי שֶׁבָּאֵשׁ יִתְגַּלֶּה; וְהָאֵשׁ תִּבְחַן אֶת מַעֲשֵׂהוּ שֶׁל כָּל אִישׁ וְאִישׁ. 14 אִם יַעֲמֹד הַמַּעֲשֶׂה שֶׁבָּנָה, יְקַבֵּל הָאִישׁ אֶת

endures, he will receive a reward. ¹⁵If anyone's work is burned, he will suffer loss; but he himself will be saved, yet so as through fire.

¹⁶Do you not know that you are the temple of God and *that* the Spirit of God dwells in you? ¹⁷If anyone defiles the temple of God, God will destroy him. For the temple of God is holy, which *temple* you are.

¹⁸Let no one deceive himself. If anyone among you seems to be wise in this age, let him become a fool that he may become wise. ¹⁹For the wisdom of this world is foolishness with God. For it is written, *"He catches the wise in their own craftiness"*; ²⁰and again, *"The LORD knows the thoughts of the wise, that they are futile."* ²¹Therefore let no one boast in men. For all things are yours: ²²whether Paul or Apollos or Cephas, or the world or life or death, or things present or things to come—all are yours. ²³And you *are* Christ's, and Christ *is* God's.

4 Let a man so consider us, as servants of Christ and stewards of the mysteries of God. ²Moreover it is required in stewards that one be found faithful. ³But with me it is a very small thing that I should be judged by you or by a human court. In fact, I do not even judge myself. ⁴For I know of nothing against myself, yet I am not justified by this; but He who judges me is the Lord. ⁵Therefore judge nothing before the time, until the Lord comes, who will both bring to light the hidden things of darkness and reveal the counsels of the hearts. Then each one's praise will come from God.

⁶Now these things, brethren, I have figuratively transferred to myself and Apollos for your sakes, that you may learn in us not to think beyond what is written, that none of you may be puffed up on behalf of one against the other. ⁷For who makes you differ *from another?* And what do you have that you did not receive? Now if you did indeed receive *it,* why do you boast as if you had not received *it?*

⁸You are already full! You are already rich! You have reigned as kings without us—and indeed I could wish you did reign, that we also might reign with you! ⁹For I think that God has displayed us, the apostles, last, as men condemned to death; for we have been made a spectacle to the world, both to angels and to men. ¹⁰We *are* fools for Christ's sake, but you *are* wise in Christ! We *are* weak, but you *are* strong! You *are* distinguished, but we *are* dishonored! ¹¹To the present hour we both hunger and thirst, and we are poorly clothed, and beaten, and homeless. ¹²And we labor, working with our own hands. Being reviled, we bless; being perse-

שְׂכָרוֹ. ¹⁵אִם יִשָּׂרֵף מַעֲשֵׂהוּ – יַפְסִיד; הוּא עַצְמוֹ יִוָּשַׁע, אַךְ זֹאת כְּאוּד מֻצָּל מֵאֵשׁ.

¹⁶הַאִם אֵינְכֶם יוֹדְעִים כִּי הֵיכַל אֱלֹהִים אַתֶּם וְכִי רוּחַ אֱלֹהִים שׁוֹכֶנֶת בְּקִרְבְּכֶם? ¹⁷אִם יַשְׁחִית אִישׁ אֶת הֵיכַל אֱלֹהִים, אֱלֹהִים יַשְׁחִית אוֹתוֹ; כִּי הֵיכַל הָאֱלֹהִים קָדוֹשׁ, וְאַתֶּם הֵיכָלוֹ.

¹⁸אִישׁ אַל יַטְעֶה אֶת עַצְמוֹ. אִם מִישֶׁהוּ מִכֶּם סָבוּר שֶׁהוּא חָכָם בָּעוֹלָם הַזֶּה, יְהֵא נָא לִכְסִיל לְמַעַן יֶחְכַּם; ¹⁹כִּי חָכְמַת הָעוֹלָם הַזֶּה הִיא סִכְלוּת בְּעֵינֵי אֱלֹהִים, שֶׁהֲרֵי כָּתוּב: "לֹכֵד חֲכָמִים בְּעָרְמָם." ²⁰וְעוֹד: "יהוה יֹדֵעַ מַחְשְׁבוֹת אָדָם, כִּי-הֵמָּה הָבֶל." ²¹עַל כֵּן, אַל יִתְהַלֵּל אִישׁ בִּבְנֵי אָדָם. הֲרֵי הַכֹּל שֶׁלָּכֶם: ²²שָׁאוּל, אַפּוֹלוֹס, כֵּיפָא, הָעוֹלָם, הַחַיִּים, הַמָּוֶת, דְּבָרִים שֶׁבַּהֹוֶה, דְּבָרִים שֶׁבֶּעָתִיד – הַכֹּל שֶׁלָּכֶם; ²³וְאַתֶּם שֶׁל הַמָּשִׁיחַ, וְהַמָּשִׁיחַ הוּא שֶׁל אֱלֹהִים.

ד וּבְכֵן צָרִיךְ שֶׁהַבְּרִיּוֹת יִרְאוּ אוֹתָנוּ כִּמְשָׁרְתֵי הַמָּשִׁיחַ וּכְמֻפְקָדִים עַל סוֹדוֹת אֱלֹהִים. ²וְאוּלָם מִן הַמֻּפְקָדִים נִדְרָשׁ לְהִמָּצֵא נֶאֱמָנִים. ³לְגַבֵּי דִּידִי דָּבָר פָּחוֹת עֵרֶךְ הוּא לְהִשָּׁפֵט עַל-יְדֵיכֶם אוֹ לְהִשָּׁפֵט בְּיוֹם דִּין אֱנוֹשִׁי. אֲנִי אַף לֹא דָן אֶת עַצְמִי, ⁴כִּי אֵינֶנִּי יוֹדֵעַ דָּבָר נֶגֶד עַצְמִי. אֲבָל לֹא בְּכָךְ אֲנִי יוֹצֵא זַכַּאי; הָאָדוֹן הוּא הַשּׁוֹפֵט אוֹתִי. ⁵לָכֵן אַל תִּשְׁפְּטוּ דָּבָר בְּטֶרֶם עֵת, עַד כִּי יָבוֹא הָאָדוֹן אֲשֶׁר גַּם יוֹצִיא לָאוֹר אֶת תַּעֲלוּמוֹת הַחֹשֶׁךְ וְגַם יְגַלֶּה אֶת מַחְשְׁבוֹת הַלֵּב. אָז תִּנָּתֵן הַתְּהִלָּה לְכָל אִישׁ מֵאֵת הָאֱלֹהִים.

⁶אַחַי, הִסַּבּוֹתִי אֶת הַדְּבָרִים הָאֵלֶּה עַל עַצְמִי וְעַל אַפּוֹלוֹס בִּשְׁבִילְכֶם, לְמַעַן תִּלְמְדוּ מֵהַדֻּגְמָה הַנּוֹגַעַת לָנוּ שֶׁלֹּא לַחֲרֹג מִן הַכָּתוּב, כְּדֵי שֶׁלֹּא יִתְנַשֵּׂא אִישׁ עַל רֵעֵהוּ בִּשְׁמוֹ שֶׁל אַחֵר; ⁷שֶׁכֵּן מִי מַקְנֶה לְךָ יְחוּד? וּמַה יֵּשׁ לְךָ שֶׁלֹּא קִבַּלְתָּ? וְאִם אָמְנָם קִבַּלְתָּ, מַדּוּעַ תִּתְגָּאֶה כְּאִלּוּ שֶׁלֹּא קִבַּלְתָּ? ⁸אַתֶּם כְּבָר שְׂבֵעִים! אַתֶּם כְּבָר עֲשִׁירִים! בִּלְעָדֵינוּ אַתֶּם מוֹלְכִים! הַלְוַאי שֶׁמְּלַכְתֶּם בֶּאֱמֶת כְּדֵי שֶׁגַּם אֲנַחְנוּ נִמְלֹךְ אִתְּכֶם. ⁹אֲשֶׁר לָנוּ הַשְּׁלִיחִים, אֲנִי סָבוּר שֶׁאֱלֹהִים הִצִּיג אוֹתָנוּ אַחֲרוֹנִים, כִּנְדּוֹנִים לָמָוֶת; כִּי הָיִינוּ לְמַחֲזֶה לָעוֹלָם, הֵן לַמַּלְאָכִים הֵן לִבְנֵי אָדָם. ¹⁰אָנוּ כְּסִילִים בִּגְלַל הַמָּשִׁיחַ, אַךְ אַתֶּם חֲכָמִים בַּמָּשִׁיחַ! אֲנַחְנוּ חַלָּשִׁים, אַךְ אַתֶּם חֲזָקִים! אַתֶּם נִכְבָּדִים, אַךְ אֲנַחְנוּ נִקְלִים! ¹¹עַד עֶצֶם הַשָּׁעָה הַזֹּאת אֲנַחְנוּ רְעֵבִים וּצְמֵאִים, עֲרֻמִּים וּמֻכִּים וְנָדִים מִמָּקוֹם לְמָקוֹם, ¹²וִיגֵעִים בַּעֲמַל יָדֵינוּ. מְגֻדָּפִים

cuted, we endure; 13 being defamed, we entreat. We
have been made as the filth of the world, the
offscouring of all things until now.

14 I do not write these things to shame you, but as
my beloved children I warn *you*. 15 For though you
might have ten thousand instructors in Christ, yet
you do not *have* many fathers; for in Christ Jesus I
have begotten you through the gospel. 16 Therefore
I urge you, imitate me. 17 For this reason I have sent
Timothy to you, who is my beloved and faithful son
in the Lord, who will remind you of my ways in
Christ, as I teach everywhere in every church.

18 Now some are puffed up, as though I were not
coming to you. 19 But I will come to you shortly, if
the Lord wills, and I will know, not the word of
those who are puffed up, but the power. 20 For the
kingdom of God *is* not in word but in power.
21 What do you want? Shall I come to you with a
rod, or in love and a spirit of gentleness?

5 It is actually reported *that there is* sexual
immorality among you, and such sexual immorality
as is not even named among the Gentiles—that a
man has his father's wife! 2 And you are puffed up,
and have not rather mourned, that he who has done
this deed might be taken away from among you.
3 For I indeed, as absent in body but present in
spirit, have already judged (as though I were
present) him who has so done this deed. 4 In the
name of our Lord Jesus Christ, when you are
gathered together, along with my spirit, with the
power of our Lord Jesus Christ, 5 deliver such a one
to Satan for the destruction of the flesh, that his
spirit may be saved in the day of the Lord Jesus.

6 Your glorying *is* not good. Do you not know
that a little leaven leavens the whole lump?
7 Therefore purge out the old leaven, that you
may be a new lump, since you truly are unleavened.
For indeed Christ, our Passover, was sacrificed for
us. 8 Therefore let us keep the feast, not with old
leaven, nor with the leaven of malice and wickedness, but with the unleavened *bread* of sincerity and
truth.

9 I wrote to you in my epistle not to keep
company with sexually immoral people. 10 Yet *I*
certainly *did* not *mean* with the sexually immoral
people of this world, or with the covetous, or
extortioners, or idolaters, since then you would
need to go out of the world. 11 But now I have
written to you not to keep company with anyone
named a brother, who is sexually immoral, or
covetous, or an idolater, or a reviler, or a drunkard,
or an extortioner—not even to eat with such a
person.

אוֹתָנוּ – אֲנַחְנוּ מְבָרְכִים; רוֹדְפִים אוֹתָנוּ – אֲנַחְנוּ
נוֹשְׂאִים זֹאת; 13 מְחָרְפִים אוֹתָנוּ, אַךְ בְּפִינוּ מִלּוֹת
עֵדוּד; כִּסְחִי הָעוֹלָם הָיִינוּ, מְאוּסִים לַכֹּל עַד הַיּוֹם
הַזֶּה.
14 לֹא כְּדֵי לְבַיֵּשׁ אֶתְכֶם אֲנִי כּוֹתֵב אֶת הַדְּבָרִים
הָאֵלֶּה, אֶלָּא לְהַזְהִיר אֶתְכֶם כִּילָדַי הָאֲהוּבִים.
15 הֲלֹא גַם אִם יֵשׁ לָכֶם עֲשֶׂרֶת אֲלָפִים מְחַנְּכִים
בַּמָּשִׁיחַ, אֵין לָכֶם אָבוֹת רַבִּים; כִּי אֲנִי, עַל־יְדֵי
הַבְּשׂוֹרָה, הוֹלַדְתִּי אֶתְכֶם בַּמָּשִׁיחַ יֵשׁוּעַ. 16 לָכֵן אֲנִי
מְבַקֵּשׁ מִכֶּם לְהִתְנַהֵג כָּמוֹנִי. 17 מִשּׁוּם כָּךְ שָׁלַחְתִּי
אֲלֵיכֶם אֶת טִימוֹתִיאוֹס בְּנִי הָאָהוּב וְהַנֶּאֱמָן בָּאָדוֹן.
הוּא יַזְכִּיר לָכֶם אֶת דְּרָכַי בַּמָּשִׁיחַ, כְּפִי שֶׁאֲנִי מְלַמֵּד
בְּכָל קְהִלָּה וּקְהִלָּה בְּכָל מָקוֹם.
18 יֵשׁ אֲשֶׁר הֵחֵלּוּ לְהִתְנַשֵּׂא וּלְהִתְנַהֵג כְּאִלּוּ לֹא
אָבוֹא אֲלֵיכֶם. 19 אוּלָם אֲנִי אָבוֹא אֲלֵיכֶם בְּקָרוֹב,
אִם יִרְצֶה הָאָדוֹן, וְאֶרְאֶה לֹא אֶת דִּבּוּרָם שֶׁל
הַמִּתְנַשְּׂאִים, אֶלָּא אֶת כֹּחָם; 20 שֶׁכֵּן מַלְכוּת
הָאֱלֹהִים אֵינָהּ בְּדִבּוּר כִּי אִם בְּכֹחַ הַפֹּעַל. 21 מָה
אַתֶּם רוֹצִים? שֶׁאָבוֹא אֲלֵיכֶם בְּשֵׁבֶט מוּסָר, אוֹ
בְּאַהֲבָה וַעֲנָוַת רוּחַ?

ה בְּאָזְנֵי כֹּל נִשְׁמַע שֶׁיֵּשׁ זְנוּת בְּקִרְבְּכֶם, וּזְנוּת אֲשֶׁר
אֵין כָּמוֹהָ אֲפִלּוּ בֵּין הַגּוֹיִים: אִישׁ לָקַח לוֹ אֶת אֵשֶׁת
אָבִיו. 2 וְאַתֶּם עוֹד מִתְגָּאִים בִּמְקוֹם לְהִתְאַבֵּל כְּדֵי
שֶׁעוֹשֵׂה הַמַּעֲשֶׂה הַזֶּה יְרֻחַק מִקִּרְבְּכֶם! 3 וַאֲנִי, אַף
כִּי אֲנִי נֶעְדָּר מִבֵּינֵיכֶם בְּגוּפִי (אַךְ נוֹכֵחַ בְּרוּחִי), כְּבָר
שָׁפַטְתִּי אֶת עוֹשֵׂה הַמַּעֲשֶׂה הַזֶּה כְּאִלּוּ הָיִיתִי
אִתְּכֶם: 4 בְּשֵׁם הָאָדוֹן יֵשׁוּעַ, כַּאֲשֶׁר תִּתְאַסְּפוּ וְרוּחִי
בֵּינֵיכֶם עִם גְּבוּרַת אֲדוֹנֵנוּ יֵשׁוּעַ, 5 תִּמְסְרוּ אֶת הָאִישׁ
הַהוּא לַשָּׂטָן לְאָבְדָן הַגּוּף כְּדֵי שֶׁרוּחוֹ תִּוָּשַׁע בְּיוֹם
הָאָדוֹן.
6 הִתְפָּאֲרוּתְכֶם אֵינֶנָּה הוֹלֶמֶת. הַאִם אֵינְכֶם יוֹדְעִים
שֶׁמְּעַט שְׂאוֹר מַחְמִיץ אֶת כָּל הָעִסָּה? 7 בַּעֲרוּ אֶת
הַשְּׂאוֹר הַיָּשָׁן לְמַעַן תִּהְיוּ עִסָּה חֲדָשָׁה. הֲלֹא אַתֶּם
כְּמַצּוֹת, שֶׁהֲרֵי נִזְבַּח שֵׂה הַפֶּסַח שֶׁלָּנוּ – הַמָּשִׁיחַ.
8 לָכֵן נָחֹגָּה לֹא בִּשְׂאוֹר יָשָׁן וְלֹא בִּשְׂאוֹר הָרַע
וְהָרֶשַׁע, אֶלָּא בְּמַצּוֹת הַתֹּם וְהָאֱמֶת.
9 כָּתַבְתִּי לָכֶם בָּאִגֶּרֶת שֶׁלֹּא לְהִתְעָרֵב עִם זוֹנִים.
10 אֵינֶנִּי מִתְכַּוֵּן לַזּוֹנִים בְּנֵי הָעוֹלָם הַזֶּה, אוֹ
לַחֲמָדָנִים, לַחוֹמְסִים וְעוֹבְדֵי אֱלִילִים, שֶׁכֵּן אָז
הֱיִיתֶם חַיָּבִים לָצֵאת מִן הָעוֹלָם. 11 אֲבָל כָּתַבְתִּי
לָכֶם שֶׁלֹּא לְהִתְעָרֵב עִם מִי שֶׁנִּקְרָא "אָח" וְהוּא זוֹנֶה

¹²For what *have* I *to do* with judging those also who are outside? Do you not judge those who are inside? ¹³But those who are outside God judges. Therefore *"put away from yourselves the evil person."*

6 Dare any of you, having a matter against another, go to law before the unrighteous, and not before the saints? ²Do you not know that the saints will judge the world? And if the world will be judged by you, are you unworthy to judge the smallest matters? ³Do you not know that we shall judge angels? How much more, things that pertain to this life? ⁴If then you have judgments concerning things pertaining to this life, do you appoint those who are least esteemed by the church to judge? ⁵I say this to your shame. Is it so, that there is not a wise man among you, not even one, who will be able to judge between his brethren? ⁶But brother goes to law against brother, and that before unbelievers!

⁷Now therefore, it is already an utter failure for you that you go to law against one another. Why do you not rather accept wrong? Why do you not rather *let yourselves* be cheated? ⁸No, you yourselves do wrong and cheat, and *you do* these things *to your* brethren! ⁹Do you not know that the unrighteous will not inherit the kingdom of God? Do not be deceived. Neither fornicators, nor idolaters, nor adulterers, nor homosexuals, nor sodomites, ¹⁰nor thieves, nor covetous, nor drunkards, nor revilers, nor extortioners will inherit the kingdom of God. ¹¹And such were some of you. But you were washed, but you were sanctified, but you were justified in the name of the Lord Jesus and by the Spirit of our God.

¹²All things are lawful for me, but all things are not helpful. All things are lawful for me, but I will not be brought under the power of any. ¹³Foods for the stomach and the stomach for foods, but God will destroy both it and them. Now the body *is* not for sexual immorality but for the Lord, and the Lord for the body. ¹⁴And God both raised up the Lord and will also raise us up by His power.

¹⁵Do you not know that your bodies are members of Christ? Shall I then take the members of Christ and make *them* members of a harlot? Certainly not! ¹⁶Or do you not know that he who is joined to a harlot is one body *with her?* For *"the two,"* He says, *"shall become one flesh."* ¹⁷But he who is joined to the Lord is one spirit *with Him.*

¹⁸Flee sexual immorality. Every sin that a man does is outside the body, but he who commits sexual immorality sins against his own body. ¹⁹Or

---

אוֹ חוֹמֵד אֶת אֲשֶׁר לַזּוּלַת, אוֹ עוֹבֵד אֱלִילִים אוֹ מְגַדֵּף אוֹ סוֹבֵא אוֹ חוֹמֵס; אַף אַל תִּסְבּוּ לֶאֱכֹל עִם אִישׁ כָּזֶה; ¹²כִּי מַה לִּי לִשְׁפֹּט אֶת אֵלֶּה אֲשֶׁר בַּחוּץ? הֲאִם אֵינְכֶם שׁוֹפְטִים אֶת אֵלֶּה שֶׁבְּקִרְבְּכֶם? ¹³אֵלֶּה אֲשֶׁר בַּחוּץ אֱלֹהִים יִשְׁפְּטֵם. אַתֶּם בַּעֲרוּ אֶת הָרָע מִקִּרְבְּכֶם.

ו הֲאִם מֵעֵז אִישׁ מִכֶּם, שֶׁיֵּשׁ לוֹ דָּבָר נֶגֶד רֵעֵהוּ, לְהָבִיא אֶת מִשְׁפָּטוֹ לִפְנֵי הָרְשָׁעִים וְלֹא לִפְנֵי הַקְּדוֹשִׁים? ²הֲאִם אֵינְכֶם יוֹדְעִים שֶׁהַקְּדוֹשִׁים יִשְׁפְּטוּ אֶת הָעוֹלָם? וְאִם אֶת הָעוֹלָם תִּשְׁפְּטוּ, כֵּיצַד אֵינְכֶם מְסֻגָּלִים לִשְׁפֹּט בָּעִנְיָנִים הַפְּעוּטִים בְּיוֹתֵר? ³הֲאִם אֵינְכֶם יוֹדְעִים שֶׁאָנַחְנוּ נִשְׁפֹּט מַלְאָכִים? כָּל שֶׁכֵּן דְּבָרִים הַשַּׁיָּכִים לְחַיֵּי יוֹם יוֹם! ⁴וְהִנֵּה כְּשֶׁיֵּשׁ בֵּינֵיכֶם עִנְיָנִים שֶׁל חַיֵּי יוֹם יוֹם, דַּוְקָא אֶת הַנְּקֻלִּים בְּעֵינֵי הַקְּהִלָּה אַתֶּם מוֹשִׁיבִים לְשׁוֹפְטִים. ⁵אֲנִי אוֹמֵר זֹאת לְבָשְׁתְּכֶם. וְכִי אֵין בָּכֶם שׁוּם חָכָם שֶׁיָּכוֹל לִשְׁפֹּט בֵּין אִישׁ לְאָחִיו? ⁶בִּמְקוֹם זֹאת אָח נִשְׁפָּט עִם אָחִיו, וְזֹאת לִפְנֵי בִּלְתִּי מַאֲמִינִים! ⁷בִּכְלָל, בְּעֶצֶם הָעֻבְדָּה שֶׁאַתֶּם תּוֹבְעִים זֶה אֶת זֶה לַמִּשְׁפָּט, כְּבָר הִפְסַדְתֶּם. מַדּוּעַ לֹא תְּבַכְּרוּ לִהְיוֹת מְקֻפָּחִים? מַדּוּעַ לֹא תְּבַכְּרוּ לִהְיוֹת נֶעֱשָׁקִים? ⁸וְאוּלָם אַתֶּם בְּעַצְמְכֶם עוֹשִׂים עָוֶל וְעוֹשְׁקִים, וְלָאֲחֵיכֶם אַתֶּם עוֹשִׂים זֹאת! ⁹אוֹ שֶׁמָּא אֵינְכֶם יוֹדְעִים כִּי עוֹשֵׂי עָוֶל לֹא יִירְשׁוּ אֶת מַלְכוּת הָאֱלֹהִים? אַל תִּטְעוּ; לֹא זוֹנִים וְלֹא עוֹבְדֵי אֱלִילִים, לֹא מְנָאֲפִים וְלֹא עוֹשֵׂי זִמָּה וְלֹא יוֹדְעֵי מִשְׁכַּב זָכָר, ¹⁰לֹא גַּנָּבִים וְלֹא חַמְדָנִים, לֹא סוֹבְאִים וְלֹא מְגַדְּפִים וְלֹא חוֹמְסִים יִירְשׁוּ אֶת מַלְכוּת הָאֱלֹהִים. ¹¹וְכָאֵלֶּה הָיוּ כַּמָּה מִכֶּם, אֲבָל אַתֶּם רֻחַצְתֶּם, אַתֶּם קֻדַּשְׁתֶּם, אַתֶּם הֻצְדַּקְתֶּם בְּשֵׁם הָאָדוֹן יֵשׁוּעַ הַמָּשִׁיחַ וּבְרוּחַ אֱלֹהֵינוּ.

¹²הַכֹּל מֻתָּר לִי, אֲבָל לֹא הַכֹּל מוֹעִיל. הַכֹּל מֻתָּר לִי, אַךְ לֹא אֶשְׁתַּעְבֵּד לְשׁוּם דָּבָר. ¹³הַמַּאֲכָל הוּא בִּשְׁבִיל הַכֶּרֶס וְהַכֶּרֶס בִּשְׁבִיל הַמַּאֲכָל, וֵאלֹהִים יְכַלֶּה גַּם אֶת זֶה וְגַם אֶת זֶה. אֲבָל הַגּוּף אֵינוֹ בִּשְׁבִיל הַזְּנוּת, אֶלָּא בִּשְׁבִיל הָאָדוֹן, וְהָאָדוֹן בִּשְׁבִיל הַגּוּף. ¹⁴וֵאלֹהִים הֵקִים לִתְחִיָּה אֶת אֲדוֹנֵנוּ וּבִגְבוּרָתוֹ יָקִים גַּם אוֹתָנוּ.

¹⁵הַאִם אֵינְכֶם יוֹדְעִים שֶׁגּוּפֵיכֶם הֵם אֵיבְרֵי הַמָּשִׁיחַ? לְפִיכָךְ, הַאִם אֶקַּח אֶת אֵיבְרֵי הַמָּשִׁיחַ וְאֶעֱשֶׂה אוֹתָם לְאֵיבְרֵי זוֹנָה? חַס וְחָלִילָה! ¹⁶הַאֵינְכֶם יוֹדְעִים כִּי הַדָּבֵק בְּזוֹנָה נִהְיֶה עִמָּהּ לְגוּף אֶחָד? שֶׁהֲרֵי נֶאֱמַר: "וְהָיוּ שְׁנֵיהֶם לְבָשָׂר אֶחָד." ¹⁷אֲבָל הַדָּבֵק בָּאָדוֹן, רוּחַ אַחַת הוּא אִתּוֹ. ¹⁸הִתְרַחֲקוּ מִן הַזְּנוּת. כָּל חֵטְא שֶׁאָדָם עוֹשֶׂה הוּא מִחוּץ לְגוּפוֹ, אֲבָל הַזּוֹנֶה חוֹטֵא לְגוּפוֹ שֶׁלּוֹ. ¹⁹הַאִם

do you not know that your body is the temple of the Holy Spirit *who is* in you, whom you have from God, and you are not your own? [20] For you were bought at a price; therefore glorify God in your body and in your spirit, which are God's.

7 Now concerning the things of which you wrote to me:

It is good for a man not to touch a woman. [2] Nevertheless, because of sexual immorality, let each man have his own wife, and let each woman have her own husband. [3] Let the husband render to his wife the affection due her, and likewise also the wife to her husband. [4] The wife does not have authority over her own body, but the husband *does*. And likewise the husband does not have authority over his own body, but the wife *does*. [5] Do not deprive one another except with consent for a time, that you may give yourselves to fasting and prayer; and come together again so that Satan does not tempt you because of your lack of self-control. [6] But I say this as a concession, not as a commandment. [7] For I wish that all men were even as I myself. But each one has his own gift from God, one in this manner and another in that.

[8] But I say to the unmarried and to the widows: It is good for them if they remain even as I am; [9] but if they cannot exercise self-control, let them marry. For it is better to marry than to burn *with passion*.

[10] Now to the married I command, *yet* not I but the Lord: A wife is not to depart from *her* husband. [11] But even if she does depart, let her remain unmarried or be reconciled to *her* husband. And a husband is not to divorce *his* wife.

[12] But to the rest I, not the Lord, say: If any brother has a wife who does not believe, and she is willing to live with him, let him not divorce her. [13] And a woman who has a husband who does not believe, if he is willing to live with her, let her not divorce him. [14] For the unbelieving husband is sanctified by the wife, and the unbelieving wife is sanctified by the husband; otherwise your children would be unclean, but now they are holy. [15] But if the unbeliever departs, let him depart; a brother or a sister is not under bondage in such *cases*. But God has called us to peace. [16] For how do you know, O wife, whether you will save *your* husband? Or how do you know, O husband, whether you will save *your* wife?

[17] But as God has distributed to each one, as the Lord has called each one, so let him walk. And so I ordain in all the churches. [18] Was anyone called while circumcised? Let him not become uncircumcised. Was anyone called while uncircumcised? Let

אֵינְכֶם יוֹדְעִים כִּי גוּפְכֶם הוּא הֵיכַל שֶׁל רוּחַ הַקֹּדֶשׁ הַשּׁוֹכֶנֶת בְּתוֹכֲכֶם, אֲשֶׁר קִבַּלְתֶּם אוֹתָהּ מֵאֵת אֱלֹהִים, וְכִי אֵינְכֶם שַׁיָּכִים לְעַצְמְכֶם? [20] הֲלֹא בִּמְחִיר נִקְנֵיתֶם, לָכֵן כַּבְּדוּ אֶת אֱלֹהִים בְּגוּפְכֶם.

ז לְעִנְיַן מַה שֶׁכְּתַבְתֶּם אֵלַי: 'טוֹב לוֹ לְאִישׁ לְהִמָּנַע מֵאִשָּׁה', [2] אַךְ מִשּׁוּם הַזְּנוּת – כָּל אִישׁ יִשָּׂא לוֹ אִשָּׁה וְכָל אִשָּׁה יִהְיֶה לָהּ בַּעַל. [3] הָאִישׁ יָקִים אֶת חוֹבָתוֹ לְאִשְׁתּוֹ, וְכֵן גַּם הָאִשָּׁה תָּקִים אֶת חוֹבָתָהּ לְבַעֲלָהּ. [4] הָאִשָּׁה אֵין גוּפָהּ בִּרְשׁוּתָהּ אֶלָּא בִּרְשׁוּת בַּעֲלָהּ; כֵּן גַּם הָאִישׁ, אֵין גוּפוֹ בִּרְשׁוּתוֹ אֶלָּא בִּרְשׁוּת אִשְׁתּוֹ. [5] אַל תִּמְנְעוּ אֶת עַצְמְכֶם זֶה מִזֶּה בִּלְתִּי אִם מִתּוֹךְ הַסְכָּמָה לִזְמַן מְסֻיָּם כְּדֵי לְהִתְפַּנּוֹת לִתְפִלָּה. אַחֲרֵי כֵן שׁוּבוּ וְהִתְאַחֲדוּ, פֶּן יְנַסֶּה אֶתְכֶם הַשָּׂטָן בִּגְלַל אִי יְכָלְתְּכֶם לִרְסֵן אֶת הַיֵּצֶר. [6] וְזֹאת אֲנִי אוֹמֵר בְּדֶרֶךְ שֶׁל רְשׁוּת וְלֹא בְּדֶרֶךְ שֶׁל פְּקֻדָּה. [7] מִי יִתֵּן וְכָל הָאֲנָשִׁים יִהְיוּ כָּמוֹנִי, אֶלָּא שֶׁלְּכָל אֶחָד מַתָּנָתוֹ שֶׁלּוֹ מֵאֵת הָאֱלֹהִים, זֶה בְּכֹה וְזֶה בְּכֹה.

[8] וְאֶל הַפְּנוּיִים וְהָאַלְמָנוֹת אֲנִי אוֹמֵר: כְּדַאי לָהֶם לְהִשָּׁאֵר כָּמוֹנִי. [9] אֲבָל אִם אֵינָם יְכוֹלִים לִכְבֹּשׁ אֶת יִצְרָם – שֶׁיִּתְחַתְּנוּ; מוּטָב לָשֵׂאת אִשָּׁה מִלְּבְעֹר בְּתַאֲוָה. [10] וְעַל הַנְּשׂוּאִים אֲנִי מְצַוֶּה, וְלֹא אֲנִי כִּי אִם הָאָדוֹן, שֶׁלֹּא תִּפָּרֵד אִשָּׁה מִבַּעֲלָהּ – [11] אַךְ אִם נִפְרְדָה, שֶׁתִּשָּׁאֵר פְּנוּיָה אוֹ תִתְפַּיֵּס עִם בַּעֲלָהּ – וְאַל יַעֲזֹב אִישׁ אֶת אִשְׁתּוֹ. [12] אֶל הַשְּׁאָר אֲנִי אוֹמֵר, וְלֹא הָאָדוֹן: אִם לְאִישׁ מַאֲמִין יֵשׁ אִשָּׁה בִּלְתִּי מַאֲמִינָה וְהִיא רוֹצָה לְהִשָּׁאֵר אִתּוֹ, אַל יַעֲזֹב אוֹתָהּ. [13] וְאִשָּׁה שֶׁיֵּשׁ לָהּ בַּעַל בִּלְתִּי מַאֲמִין וְהוּא חָפֵץ לְהִשָּׁאֵר אִתָּהּ, אַל תַּעֲזֹב הִיא אוֹתוֹ, [14] כִּי הַבַּעַל שֶׁאֵינֶנּוּ מַאֲמִין מְקֻדָּשׁ בְּאִשְׁתּוֹ, וְהָאִשָּׁה שֶׁאֵינֶנָה מַאֲמִינָה מְקֻדֶּשֶׁת בְּבַעֲלָהּ; אִם לֹא כֵן, בְּנֵיכֶם טְמֵאִים, וְאִלּוּ עַתָּה קְדוֹשִׁים הֵם. [15] אֲבָל אִם זֶה שֶׁאֵינֶנּוּ מַאֲמִין נִפְרָד, שֶׁיִּפָּרֵד לוֹ. גַּם הַמַּאֲמִין גַּם הַמַּאֲמִינָה אֵינָם מְשֻׁעְבָּדִים בְּמִקְרִים כָּאֵלֶּה; הֲרֵי לְשָׁלוֹם קָרָא אוֹתָנוּ הָאֱלֹהִים. [16] כְּלוּם יוֹדַעַת אַתְּ, אִשָּׁה, אִם תּוֹשִׁיעִי אֶת בַּעֲלֵךְ? אוֹ כְּלוּם יוֹדֵעַ אַתָּה, הַבַּעַל, אִם תּוֹשִׁיעַ אֶת אִשְׁתְּךָ?

[17] כָּל אִישׁ יִחְיֶה אֶת חַיָּיו לְפִי מַה שֶׁחָלַק לוֹ הָאָדוֹן, לְפִי מַצְּבוֹ כַּאֲשֶׁר קָרָא לוֹ הָאֱלֹהִים. כָּךְ אֲנִי מְצַוֶּה בְּכָל הַקְּהִלּוֹת. [18] אִם נִקְרָא הָאִישׁ בְּעֵת הֱיוֹתוֹ נִמּוֹל, אַל יִמְשֹׁךְ לוֹ עָרְלָה. אִם נִקְרָא כְּשֶׁהוּא עָרֵל, אַל

him not be circumcised. ¹⁹Circumcision is nothing and uncircumcision is nothing, but keeping the commandments of God *is what matters.* ²⁰Let each one remain in the same calling in which he was called. ²¹Were you called *while* a slave? Do not be concerned about it; but if you can be made free, rather use *it.* ²²For he who is called in the Lord *while* a slave is the Lord's freedman. Likewise he who is called *while* free is Christ's slave. ²³You were bought at a price; do not become slaves of men. ²⁴Brethren, let each one remain with God in that *state* in which he was called.

²⁵Now concerning virgins: I have no commandment from the Lord; yet I give judgment as one whom the Lord in His mercy *has made* trustworthy. ²⁶I suppose therefore that this is good because of the present distress—that *it is* good for a man to remain as he is: ²⁷Are you bound to a wife? Do not seek to be loosed. Are you loosed from a wife? Do not seek a wife. ²⁸But even if you do marry, you have not sinned; and if a virgin marries, she has not sinned. Nevertheless such will have trouble in the flesh, but I would spare you.

²⁹But this I say, brethren, the time *is* short, so that from now on even those who have wives should be as though they had none, ³⁰those who weep as though they did not weep, those who rejoice as though they did not rejoice, those who buy as though they did not possess, ³¹and those who use this world as not misusing *it.* For the form of this world is passing away.

³²But I want you to be without care. He who is unmarried cares for the things of the Lord—how he may please the Lord. ³³But he who is married cares about the things of the world—how he may please *his* wife. ³⁴There is a difference between a wife and a virgin. The unmarried woman cares about the things of the Lord, that she may be holy both in body and in spirit. But she who is married cares about the things of the world—how she may please *her* husband. ³⁵And this I say for your own profit, not that I may put a leash on you, but for what is proper, and that you may serve the Lord without distraction.

³⁶But if any man thinks he is behaving improperly toward his virgin, if she is past the flower of youth, and thus it must be, let him do what he wishes. He does not sin; let them marry. ³⁷Nevertheless he who stands steadfast in his heart, having no necessity, but has power over his own will, and has so determined in his heart that he will keep his virgin, does well. ³⁸So then he who gives *her* in marriage does well, but he who does not give *her* in marriage does better.

¹⁹יִמּוֹל. לֹא הַמִּילָה חֲשׁוּבָה, אַף לֹא הָעָרְלָה, אֶלָּא שְׁמִירַת מִצְווֹת הָאֱלֹהִים. ²⁰יִשָּׁאֵר כָּל אִישׁ בְּמַעֲמָד שֶׁבּוֹ נִקְרָא. ²¹אִם נִקְרֵאתָ בְּעֵת הֱיוֹתְךָ עֶבֶד, אַל תִּדְאַג. אֲבָל אִם בִּיכָלְתְּךָ לָצֵאת לַחָפְשִׁי, אַדְרַבָּא, נַצֵּל זֹאת. ²²הֲרֵי עֶבֶד שֶׁנִּקְרָא מִטַּעַם הָאָדוֹן, בֶּן־חוֹרִין הוּא לָאָדוֹן; כֵּן מִי שֶׁנִּקְרָא בִּהְיוֹתוֹ בֶּן־חוֹרִין, עֶבֶד הוּא לַמָּשִׁיחַ. ²³בִּמְחִיר נִקְנֵיתֶם; אַל תִּשְׁתַּעַבְּדוּ לִבְנֵי אָדָם. ²⁴אַחַי, אִישׁ אִישׁ בְּמַעֲמָד שֶׁנִּקְרָא בּוֹ, בּוֹ יַעֲמֹד לִפְנֵי אֱלֹהִים.

²⁵עַל־אוֹדוֹת הַבְּתוּלוֹת אֵין לִי מִצְוָה מֵאֵת הָאָדוֹן, אֲבָל אֲחַוֶּה דַעְתִּי בְּתוֹר מִי שֶׁזָּכָה, בְּרַחֲמֵי הָאָדוֹן, לִהְיוֹת נֶאֱמָן. ²⁶אֲנִי סָבוּר שֶׁמִּפְּנֵי הַמְּצוּקָה הַנּוֹכַחַת מוּטָב לְאִישׁ לְהִשָּׁאֵר כָּךְ: ²⁷אִם אַתָּה קָשׁוּר לְאִשָּׁה, אַל תְּבַקֵּשׁ לְהַתִּיר אֶת הַקֶּשֶׁר; אִם אֵינְךָ קָשׁוּר לְאִשָּׁה, אַל תְּבַקֵּשׁ לְךָ אִשָּׁה. ²⁸אַךְ אִם תִּקַּח לְךָ אִשָּׁה אֵינְךָ חוֹטֵא. וְהַבְּתוּלָה אִם תִּנָּשֵׂא אֵינֶנָּה חוֹטֵאת, אֶלָּא שֶׁיִּהְיוּ לָהֶם צָרוֹת בַּבָּשָׂר וַאֲנִי חָס עֲלֵיכֶם. ²⁹וְזֹאת אֹמַר לָכֶם, אַחַי: הַזְּמַן דּוֹחֵק. עַל כֵּן יִהְיוּ אֵלֶּה שֶׁיֵּשׁ לָהֶם נָשִׁים כְּאִלּוּ אֵין לָהֶם; ³⁰יִהְיוּ הַבּוֹכִים כְּאִלּוּ אֵינָם בּוֹכִים; הַשְּׂמֵחִים כְּאִלּוּ אֵינָם שְׂמֵחִים; הַקּוֹנִים כְּאִלּוּ אֵינָם בַּעֲלֵי קִנְיָן; ³¹וְהַנֶּהֱנִים מִן הָעוֹלָם הַזֶּה כְּאִלּוּ אֵינָם נֶהֱנִים מִמֶּנּוּ, כִּי חָלוֹף תַּחֲלֹף צוּרַת הָעוֹלָם הַזֶּה. ³²רְצוֹנִי לִמְנֹעַ דְּאָגָה מִכֶּם. מִי שֶׁאֵינוֹ נָשׂוּי דּוֹאֵג לַדְּבָרִים אֲשֶׁר לָאָדוֹן, אֵיךְ יִיטַב בְּעֵינֵי הָאָדוֹן. ³³אֲבָל מִי שֶׁנָּשׂוּי דּוֹאֵג לַדְּבָרִים הָאַרְצִיִּים, אֵיךְ יִיטַב בְּעֵינֵי הָאִשָּׁה, ³⁴וּתְשׂוּמַת לִבּוֹ מְפֻלֶּגֶת. וְהָאִשָּׁה שֶׁאֵינָה נְשׂוּאָה, אוֹ הַבְּתוּלָה, דּוֹאֶגֶת לַדְּבָרִים אֲשֶׁר לָאָדוֹן כְּדֵי שֶׁתִּהְיֶה קְדוֹשָׁה הֵן בַּגּוּף וְהֵן בָּרוּחַ. אֲבָל הַנְּשׂוּאָה דּוֹאֶגֶת לַדְּבָרִים הָאַרְצִיִּים, כֵּיצַד תִּיטַב בְּעֵינֵי בַּעְלָהּ. ³⁵וְזֹאת אֲנִי אוֹמֵר לְטוֹבַתְכֶם, לֹא כְּדֵי לְהַכְבִּיד עֲלֵיכֶם, אֶלָּא כְּדֵי שֶׁתִּתְנַהֲגוּ כַּיָּאוּת וְתִתְמַסְּרוּ לָאָדוֹן בְּאֵין מַפְרִיעַ.

³⁶מִי שֶׁסָּבוּר כִּי אֵינוֹ נוֹהֵג כַּשּׁוּרָה בִּבְתוּלָתוֹ אִם יַעַבְרוּ עָלֶיהָ יְמֵי נְעוּרֶיהָ, וְשֶׁהַדָּבָר הוּא בִּלְתִּי נִמְנָע, יַעֲשֶׂה כִּרְצוֹנוֹ. שֶׁיִּתְחַתְּנוּ; אֵין הוּא חוֹטֵא. ³⁷אֲבָל אִישׁ אֵיתָן בְּדַעְתּוֹ, שֶׁאֵינוֹ שָׁרוּי בְּצֹרֶךְ וְהוּא שׁוֹלֵט עַל רְצוֹנוֹ, אִם הֶחְלִיט בְּלִבּוֹ לִשְׁמֹר אֶת בְּתוּלָתוֹ – טוֹב יַעֲשֶׂה. ³⁸לְפִיכָךְ, הַנּוֹשֵׂא אֶת בְּתוּלָתוֹ טוֹב הוּא עוֹשֶׂה; וְזֶה שֶׁאֵינוֹ נוֹשֵׂא אוֹתָהּ יֵיטִיב עוֹד יוֹתֵר

39 A wife is bound by law as long as her husband lives; but if her husband dies, she is at liberty to be married to whom she wishes, only in the Lord. **40** But she is happier if she remains as she is, according to my judgment—and I think I also have the Spirit of God.

8 Now concerning things offered to idols: We know that we all have knowledge. Knowledge puffs up, but love edifies. **2** And if anyone thinks that he knows anything, he knows nothing yet as he ought to know. **3** But if anyone loves God, this one is known by Him.

4 Therefore concerning the eating of things offered to idols, we know that an idol *is* nothing in the world, and that *there is* no other God but one. **5** For even if there are so-called gods, whether in heaven or on earth (as there are many gods and many lords), **6** yet for us *there is* one God, the Father, of whom *are* all things, and we for Him; and one Lord Jesus Christ, through whom *are* all things, and through whom we *live*.

7 However, *there is* not in everyone that knowledge; for some, with consciousness of the idol, until now eat *it* as a thing offered to an idol; and their conscience, being weak, is defiled. **8** But food does not commend us to God; for neither if we eat are we the better, nor if we do not eat are we the worse.

9 But beware lest somehow this liberty of yours become a stumbling block to those who are weak. **10** For if anyone sees you who have knowledge eating in an idol's temple, will not the conscience of him who is weak be emboldened to eat those things offered to idols? **11** And because of your knowledge shall the weak brother perish, for whom Christ died? **12** But when you thus sin against the brethren, and wound their weak conscience, you sin against Christ. **13** Therefore, if food makes my brother stumble, I will never again eat meat, lest I make my brother stumble.

9 Am I not an apostle? Am I not free? Have I not seen Jesus Christ our Lord? Are you not my work in the Lord? **2** If I am not an apostle to others, yet doubtless I am to you. For you are the seal of my apostleship in the Lord.

3 My defense to those who examine me is this: **4** Do we have no right to eat and drink? **5** Do we have no right to take along a believing wife, as *do* also the other apostles, the brothers of the Lord, and Cephas? **6** Or *is it* only Barnabas and I *who* have no right to refrain from working? **7** Who ever goes

לַעֲשׂוֹת. 39 הָאִשָּׁה קְשׁוּרָה לְבַעֲלָהּ כָּל זְמַן שֶׁהוּא חַי. וְאִם יָמוּת הַבַּעַל, רַשָּׁאִית הִיא לְהִנָּשֵׂא לְמִי שֶׁתִּרְצֶה וּבִלְבַד שֶׁזֶּה יִהְיֶה בָּאָדוֹן. 40 וְאוּלָם הִיא תִּהְיֶה מְאֻשֶּׁרֶת יוֹתֵר אִם תִּשָּׁאֵר פְּנוּיָה; זוֹ דַעְתִּי, וַחֲשׁוּבַנִי שֶׁגַּם בִּי רוּחַ אֱלֹהִים.

ח בְּעִנְיַן זִבְחֵי אֱלִילִים, אָנוּ יוֹדְעִים שֶׁכֻּלָּנוּ דַעַת. דַעַת מְבִיאָה לִידֵי גַּאֲוָה, אַךְ הָאַהֲבָה בּוֹנָה. 2 מִי שֶׁסָּבוּר כִּי הוּא יוֹדֵעַ דְּבַר מָה, עֲדַיִן אֵינוֹ יוֹדֵעַ כְּפִי שֶׁצָּרִיךְ לָדַעַת. 3 אֲבָל מִי שֶׁאוֹהֵב אֶת אֱלֹהִים, הוּא יָדוּעַ לֵאלֹהִים. 4 וּבְכֵן בְּנוֹגֵעַ לַאֲכִילַת זִבְחֵי אֱלִילִים, אֲנַחְנוּ יוֹדְעִים כִּי אֵין מַמָּשׁוּת לָאֱלִיל בָּעוֹלָם וְכִי אֵין אֱלֹהִים אֶלָּא אֶחָד. 5 וְגַם אִם יֵשׁ הַקְּרוּיִים "אֵלִים", אִם בַּשָּׁמַיִם וְאִם בָּאָרֶץ, – כְּשֵׁם שֶׁיֵּשׁ אֵלִים רַבִּים וַאֲדוֹנִים רַבִּים – 6 הֲרֵי לָנוּ יֵשׁ אֱלֹהִים אֶחָד, הָאָב אֲשֶׁר הַכֹּל מִמֶּנּוּ וַאֲנַחְנוּ לְמַעֲנוֹ; וְאָדוֹן אֶחָד, יֵשׁוּעַ הַמָּשִׁיחַ, אֲשֶׁר הַכֹּל דַּרְכּוֹ וְדַרְכּוֹ אֲנַחְנוּ מִתְקַיְּמִים. 7 אַךְ לֹא הַכֹּל יוֹדְעִים זֹאת. יֵשׁ אֲנָשִׁים שֶׁעֲדַיִן רְגִילִים לָאֱלִיל וְאוֹכְלִים אֶת הַמַּאֲכָל כְּאִלּוּ הוּא זֶבַח לָאֱלִיל, וּמֵאַחַר שֶׁמַּצְפּוּנָם חַלָּשׁ הֲרֵי שֶׁהוּא נִטְמָא. 8 אוּלָם הַמַּאֲכָל לֹא יְקָרֵב אוֹתָנוּ לֵאלֹהִים. אִם לֹא נֹאכַל לֹא נִפְסִיד, וְאִם נֹאכַל לֹא נַשִּׂיג יִתְרוֹן. 9 אֲבָל הִזָּהֲרוּ שֶׁלֹּא תִּהְיֶה רְשׁוּתְכֶם זוֹ מִכְשׁוֹל לַחַלָּשִׁים; 10 שֶׁכֵּן אִם יִרְאוּ אוֹתְךָ, אַתָּה אֲשֶׁר לְךָ הַדַּעַת, מֵסֵב בְּבֵית אֱלִילִים, כְּלוּם לֹא יְעוֹדַד הַדָּבָר אֶת בַּעַל הַמַּצְפּוּן הַחַלָּשׁ לֶאֱכֹל זִבְחֵי אֱלִילִים? 11 וּבִגְלַל הַדַּעַת שֶׁלְּךָ יֵהָרֵס הָאָח הַחַלָּשׁ שֶׁלְּמַעֲנוֹ מֵת הַמָּשִׁיחַ. 12 אִם כָּךְ תֶּחְטְאוּ לַאֲחֵיכֶם וְתִפְגְּעוּ בְּמַצְפּוּנָם הַחַלָּשׁ – לַמָּשִׁיחַ אַתֶּם חוֹטְאִים. 13 לָכֵן אִם מַאֲכָל הוּא מִכְשׁוֹל לְאָחִי, לֹא אֹכַל בָּשָׂר לְעוֹלָם לְמַעַן לֹא אַכְשִׁיל אֶת אָחִי.

ט הַאִם אֵינֶנִּי חָפְשִׁי? הַאִם אֵינֶנִּי שָׁלִיחַ? הַאִם לֹא רָאִיתִי אֶת יֵשׁוּעַ אֲדוֹנֵנוּ? הַאִם אַתֶּם אֵינְכֶם פָּעֳלִי בָּאָדוֹן? 2 אִם לַאֲחֵרִים אֵינֶנִּי שָׁלִיחַ, לָכֶם בְּוַדַּאי שֶׁאֲנִי שָׁלִיחַ, שֶׁהֲרֵי חוֹתַם שְׁלִיחוּתִי אַתֶּם בָּאָדוֹן. 3 תְּשׁוּבָתִי לַמּוֹתְחִים עָלַי בִּקֹּרֶת הִיא זֹאת: 4 הַאֵין לָנוּ רְשׁוּת לֶאֱכֹל וְלִשְׁתּוֹת? 5 הַאֵין לָנוּ רְשׁוּת לְהוֹבִיל אִתָּנוּ אִשָּׁה מַאֲמִינָה, כְּמוֹ יֶתֶר הַשְּׁלִיחִים, לַאֲחֵי הָאָדוֹן וּלְכֵיפָא? 6 אוֹ רַק אֲנִי וּבַר־נַבָּא אֵין לָנוּ רְשׁוּת לִהְיוֹת פְּטוּרִים מֵעֲבוֹדָה? 7 מִי מְשָׁרֵת בַּצָּבָא

to war at his own expense? Who plants a vineyard and does not eat of its fruit? Or who tends a flock and does not drink of the milk of the flock?

8 Do I say these things as a *mere* man? Or does not the law say the same also? 9 For it is written in the law of Moses, "You shall not muzzle an ox *while it treads out the grain.*" Is it oxen God is concerned about? 10 Or does He say *it* altogether for our sakes? For our sakes, no doubt, *this* is written, that he who plows should plow in hope, and he who threshes in hope should be partaker of his hope. 11 If we have sown spiritual things for you, *is it* a great thing if we reap your material things? 12 If others are partakers of *this* right over you, *are we* not even more?

Nevertheless we have not used this right, but endure all things lest we hinder the gospel of Christ. 13 Do you not know that those who minister the holy things eat *of the things* of the temple, and those who serve at the altar partake of *the offerings of* the altar? 14 Even so the Lord has commanded that those who preach the gospel should live from the gospel.

15 But I have used none of these things, nor have I written these things that it should be done so to me; for it *would be* better for me to die than that anyone should make my boasting void. 16 For if I preach the gospel, I have nothing to boast of, for necessity is laid upon me; yes, woe is me if I do not preach the gospel! 17 For if I do this willingly, I have a reward; but if against my will, I have been entrusted with a stewardship. 18 What is my reward then? That when I preach the gospel, I may present the gospel of Christ without charge, that I may not abuse my authority in the gospel.

19 For though I am free from all *men,* I have made myself a servant to all, that I might win the more; 20 and to the Jews I became as a Jew, that I might win Jews; to those *who are* under the law, as under the law, that I might win those *who are* under the law; 21 to those *who are* without law, as without law (not being without law toward God, but under law toward Christ), that I might win those *who are* without law; 22 to the weak I became as weak, that I might win the weak. I have become all things to all *men,* that I might by all means save some. 23 Now this I do for the gospel's sake, that I may be partaker of it with *you.*

24 Do you not know that those who run in a race all run, but one receives the prize? Run in such a way that you may obtain *it.* 25 And everyone who competes *for the prize* is temperate in all things. Now they *do it* to obtain a perishable crown, but we *for* an imperishable *crown.* 26 Therefore I run thus:

וּמְשַׁלֵּם אֶת כַּלְכָּלָתוֹ שֶׁלּוֹ? מִי נוֹטֵעַ כֶּרֶם וְאֵינוֹ אוֹכֵל מִפִּרְיוֹ? מִי רוֹעֶה עֵדֶר וְאֵינוֹ שׁוֹתֶה מִן הֶחָלָב שֶׁל הָעֵדֶר? 8 וְכִי אֲנִי אוֹמֵר אֶת הַדְּבָרִים הָאֵלֶּה עַל-פִּי בְּנֵי אָדָם? הַאִין גַּם הַתּוֹרָה אוֹמֶרֶת זֹאת? 9 הֲרֵי בְּתוֹרַת מֹשֶׁה כָּתוּב: "לֹא-תַחְסֹם שׁוֹר בְּדִישׁוֹ." הַאִם לַשְּׁוָרִים דּוֹאֵג אֱלֹהִים? 10 אוֹ שֶׁבִּכְלָל לְמַעֲנֵנוּ הוּא אוֹמֵר זֹאת? אָכֵן לְמַעֲנֵנוּ זֶה נִכְתַּב, כְּדֵי שֶׁהַחוֹרֵשׁ יַחֲרֹשׁ בְּתִקְוָה וְהַדָּשׁ יָדוּשׁ בְּתִקְוָה לְהִשְׁתַּתֵּף בִּיבוּל. 11 אִם זָרַעְנוּ לָכֶם דְּבָרִים רוּחָנִיִּים, מַה רַבּוּתָא בְּכָךְ אִם נִקְצֹר דְּבָרִים חָמְרִיִּים מִכֶּם? 12 וְאִם לַאֲחֵרִים יֵשׁ חֵלֶק בִּזְכוּת עֲלֵיכֶם, הֲלֹא כָּל שֶׁכֵּן לָנוּ?

אֲבָל לֹא נִצַּלְנוּ אֶת הַזְּכוּת הַזֹּאת, אֶלָּא סוֹבְלִים אָנוּ הַכֹּל לְמַעַן לֹא נָשִׂים שׁוּם מִכְשׁוֹל לִבְשׂוֹרַת הַמָּשִׁיחַ. 13 הַאֵינְכֶם יוֹדְעִים כִּי הָעוֹבְדִים בַּקֹּדֶשׁ פַּרְנָסָתָם מִבֵּית הַמִּקְדָּשׁ וּמְשָׁרְתֵי הַמִּזְבֵּחַ נוֹטְלִים אֶת חֶלְקָם מִן הַמִּזְבֵּחַ? 14 כָּךְ גַּם תִּקֵּן תִּקֵּן הָאָדוֹן, שֶׁהַמְּבַשְּׂרִים אֶת הַבְּשׂוֹרָה יִחְיוּ מִן הַבְּשׂוֹרָה. 15 בְּרַם אֲנִי לֹא נִצַּלְתִּי דָּבָר מִן הַדְּבָרִים הָאֵלֶּה, אַף לֹא כָּתַבְתִּי זֹאת כְּדֵי שֶׁלִּי יִהְיֶה כָּךְ. מוּטָב לִי לָמוּת וְשֶׁלֹּא יָשִׂים אִישׁ אֶת תְּהִלָּתִי זוֹ לָרִיק; 16 כִּי כַּאֲשֶׁר אֲנִי מְבַשֵּׂר אֶת הַבְּשׂוֹרָה אֵין לִי מַה לְהִתְהַלֵּל, שֶׁכֵּן חוֹבָה מֻטֶּלֶת עָלַי וְאוֹי לִי אִם לֹא אֲבַשֵּׂר. 17 אִם מֵרְצוֹנִי אֲנִי עוֹשֶׂה זֹאת, מַגִּיעַ לִי שָׂכָר. אֲבָל אִם לֹא מֵרְצוֹנִי, הֲרֵי שֶׁתַּפְקִיד הֻפְקַד בְּיָדִי; 18 מָה אֵפוֹא שְׂכָרִי? – בָּזֶה שֶׁאֲנִי מְבַשֵּׂר אֶת הַבְּשׂוֹרָה וּמַצִּיעַ אוֹתָהּ בְּלֹא מְחִיר מִבְּלִי לְנַצֵּל אֶת הַזְּכוּת שֶׁיֵּשׁ לִי בַּבְּשׂוֹרָה!

19 אַף כִּי אֵינֶנִּי מְשֻׁעְבָּד לְאִישׁ שִׁעְבַּדְתִּי אֶת עַצְמִי לַכֹּל כְּדֵי לִרְכֹּשׁ אֶת הָרַבִּים. 20 לְמַעַן הַיְּהוּדִים אֲנִי כִּיהוּדִי כְּדֵי לְהַשִּׂיג יְהוּדִים; לְמַעַן הַכְּפוּפִים לַתּוֹרָה אֲנִי כְּמוֹ כָּפוּף לַתּוֹרָה – הֲגַם שֶׁאֵינֶנִּי כָּפוּף לַתּוֹרָה – כְּדֵי לְהַשִּׂיג אֶת הַכְּפוּפִים לַתּוֹרָה; 21 לְמַעַן אֵלֶּה שֶׁאֵין לָהֶם תּוֹרָה אֲנִי כְּמוֹ בְּלִי תּוֹרָה – אַף שֶׁאֵינֶנִּי עוֹמֵד בְּלֹא תּוֹרַת אֱלֹהִים בִּהְיוֹתִי כָּפוּף לְתוֹרַת הַמָּשִׁיחַ – כְּדֵי לְהַשִּׂיג אֶת אֵלֶּה שֶׁאֵין לָהֶם תּוֹרָה; 22 לְמַעַן הַחַלָּשִׁים אֲנִי חַלָּשׁ כְּדֵי לְהַשִּׂיג אֶת הַחַלָּשִׁים; אֲנִי הַכֹּל לְמַעַן הַכֹּל כְּדֵי שֶׁאוֹשִׁיעַ לְפָחוֹת כַּמָּה מֵהֶם. 23 אַךְ אֶת הַכֹּל אֲנִי עוֹשֶׂה בַּעֲבוּר הַבְּשׂוֹרָה כְּדֵי שֶׁיִּהְיֶה לִי חֵלֶק בָּהּ.

24 הַאִם אֵינְכֶם יוֹדְעִים שֶׁהָרָצִים בָּאִצְטַדְיוֹן אָמְנָם רָצִים כֻּלָּם, אֲבָל אֶחָד מְקַבֵּל אֶת הַפְּרָס? בְּדוֹמֶה לְכָךְ, רוּצוּ לְמַעַן תַּשִּׂיגוּהוּ. 25 כָּל מִתְחָרֶה נוֹהֵג לְהִזָּהֵר בְּכָל הַתְּחוּמִים; הַלָּלוּ – כְּדֵי לְהַשִּׂיג זֵר נוֹבֵל, אֲבָל אֲנַחְנוּ כְּדֵי לְהַשִּׂיג זֵר שֶׁלֹּא יִבֹּל. 26 לָכֵן אֲנִי רָץ

not with uncertainty. Thus I fight: not as *one who* beats the air. 27 But I discipline my body and bring *it* into subjection, lest, when I have preached to others, I myself should become disqualified.

10 Moreover, brethren, I do not want you to be unaware that all our fathers were under the cloud, all passed through the sea, 2 all were baptized into Moses in the cloud and in the sea, 3 all ate the same spiritual food, 4 and all drank the same spiritual drink. For they drank of that spiritual Rock that followed them, and that Rock was Christ. 5 But with most of them God was not well pleased, for *their bodies* were scattered in the wilderness.

6 Now these things became our examples, to the intent that we should not lust after evil things as they also lusted. 7 And do not become idolaters as *were* some of them. As it is written, *"The people sat down to eat and drink, and rose up to play."* 8 Nor let us commit sexual immorality, as some of them did, and in one day twenty-three thousand fell; 9 nor let us tempt Christ, as some of them also tempted, and were destroyed by serpents; 10 nor complain, as some of them also complained, and were destroyed by the destroyer. 11 Now all these things happened to them as examples, and they were written for our admonition, upon whom the ends of the ages have come.

12 Therefore let him who thinks he stands take heed lest he fall. 13 No temptation has overtaken you except such as is common to man; but God *is* faithful, who will not allow you to be tempted beyond what you are able, but with the temptation will also make the way of escape, that you may be able to bear *it*.

14 Therefore, my beloved, flee from idolatry. 15 I speak as to wise men; judge for yourselves what I say. 16 The cup of blessing which we bless, is it not the communion of the blood of Christ? The bread which we break, is it not the communion of the body of Christ? 17 For we, *though* many, are one bread *and* one body; for we all partake of that one bread.

18 Observe Israel after the flesh: Are not those who eat of the sacrifices partakers of the altar? 19 What am I saying then? That an idol is anything, or what is offered to idols is anything? 20 Rather, that the things which the Gentiles sacrifice they sacrifice to demons and not to God, and I do not want you to have fellowship with demons. 21 You cannot drink the cup of the Lord and the cup of demons; you cannot partake of the Lord's table and of the table of demons. 22 Or do we provoke the Lord to jealousy? Are we stronger than He?

לֹא כְּמִי שֶׁמְּנַשֵּׁשׁ בַּאֲפֵלָה, וַאֲנִי נֶאֱבָק לֹא כְּמִי שֶׁמַּכֶּה בָּאֲוִיר, 27 אֶלָּא נוֹהֵג אֲנִי בְּקַשְׁיוּת עִם גּוּפִי וּמְשַׁעְבְּדוֹ, שֶׁמָּא לְאַחַר שֶׁאַטִּיף לַאֲחֵרִים, אֲנִי עַצְמִי אֶמָּצֵא פָּסוּל.

1 אַחַי, אֵינֶנִּי רוֹצֶה שֶׁיַּעֲלֵם מִכֶּם שֶׁאֲבוֹתֵינוּ כֻּלָּם הָיוּ תַּחַת הֶעָנָן, וְכֻלָּם עָבְרוּ בְּתוֹךְ הַיָּם, 2 וְכֻלָּם נִטְבְּלוּ לְמֹשֶׁה בֶּעָנָן וּבַיָּם. 3 כֻּלָּם אָכְלוּ אוֹתוֹ מַאֲכָל רוּחָנִי, 4 וְכֻלָּם שָׁתוּ אוֹתוֹ מַשְׁקֶה רוּחָנִי, כִּי שָׁתוּ מִן הַצּוּר הָרוּחָנִי הַהוֹלֵךְ עִמָּהֶם וְהַצּוּר הוּא הַמָּשִׁיחַ. 5 אֲבָל בְּרֻבָּם לֹא רָצָה אֱלֹהִים וְהֵם הוּמְתוּ בַּמִּדְבָּר. 6 כָּל זֶה הָיָה דֻּגְמָה לָנוּ, לְמַעַן לֹא נִתְאַוֶּה לְרָעוֹת כְּשֵׁם שֶׁהִתְאַווּ הֵם. 7 אַל תִּהְיוּ עוֹבְדֵי אֱלִילִים כְּשֵׁם שֶׁהָיוּ כַּמָּה מֵהֶם, כַּכָּתוּב: "וַיֵּשֶׁב הָעָם לֶאֱכֹל וְשָׁתוֹ וַיָּקֻמוּ לְצַחֵק." 8 גַּם אַל נִזְנֶה כְּשֵׁם שֶׁזָּנוּ כַּמָּה מֵהֶם וּבְיוֹם אֶחָד נָפְלוּ עֶשְׂרִים וּשְׁלֹשָׁה אֶלֶף. 9 וְאַל נְנַסֶּה אֶת יהוה כְּשֵׁם שֶׁנִּסּוּהוּ אֲנָשִׁים מֵהֶם וְהוּמְתוּ עַל-יְדֵי הַנְּחָשִׁים. 10 אַף אַל תִּתְלוֹנְנוּ כְּשֵׁם שֶׁהִתְלוֹנְנוּ כַּמָּה מֵהֶם וּמֵתוּ בִּידֵי הַמַּלְאָךְ הַמַּשְׁחִית. 11 מַה שֶּׁקָּרָה לָהֶם הָיָה לָקַח לְדֻגְמָה וְזֶה נִכְתַּב כְּדֵי לְהַזְהִיר אוֹתָנוּ, אֲנַחְנוּ אֲשֶׁר קְצֵי הָעוֹלָמִים הִגִּיעוּ אֵלֵינוּ. 12 לָכֵן מִי שֶׁחוֹשֵׁב כִּי עֲמִידָתוֹ אֵיתָנָה, יִזָּהֵר פֶּן יִפֹּל. 13 שׁוּם נִסָּיוֹן לֹא בָּא עֲלֵיכֶם מִלְּבַד נִסָּיוֹן אֱנוֹשִׁי רָגִיל. נֶאֱמָן הוּא הָאֱלֹהִים וְלֹא יַנִּיחַ לָכֶם לְהִתְנַסּוֹת לְמַעְלָה מִיְּכָלְתְּכֶם, אֶלָּא עִם הַנִּסָּיוֹן יָכִין גַּם אֶת דֶּרֶךְ הַמּוֹצָא כְּדֵי שֶׁתּוּכְלוּ לַעֲמֹד בּוֹ.

14 עַל כֵּן, חֲבִיבַי, תִּבְרְחוּ מֵעֲבוֹדַת אֱלִילִים. 15 כְּאֶל אֲנָשִׁים נְבוֹנִים אֲנִי מְדַבֵּר; שִׁפְטוּ אַתֶּם מַה שֶּׁאֲנִי אוֹמֵר: 16 כּוֹס הַבְּרָכָה שֶׁאָנוּ מְבָרְכִים עָלֶיהָ, הַאֵין הִיא הִתְחַבְּרוּת לְדַם הַמָּשִׁיחַ? הַלֶּחֶם שֶׁאָנוּ בּוֹצְעִים, הַאֵין הוּא הִתְחַבְּרוּת לְגוּף הַמָּשִׁיחַ? 17 מִשּׁוּם שֶׁהַלֶּחֶם אֶחָד, אֲנַחְנוּ הָרַבִּים גּוּף אֶחָד; שֵׁכֵן כֻּלָּנוּ מִשְׁתַּתְּפִים בַּלֶּחֶם הָאֶחָד. 18 רְאוּ נָא אֶת עַם יִשְׂרָאֵל. הַאִם אֵין הָאוֹכְלִים מִן הַקָּרְבָּנוֹת שֻׁתָּפִים בַּמִּזְבֵּחַ? 19 וּבְכֵן מָה אֲנִי אוֹמֵר – שֶׁיֵּשׁ מַמָּשׁ בְּזִבְחֵי אֱלִילִים? שֶׁיֵּשׁ מַמָּשׁ בָּאֱלִיל? 20 לֹא! אֶלָּא מַה שֶׁהַגּוֹיִים מַקְרִיבִים, לַשֵּׁדִים הֵם מַקְרִיבִים וְלֹא לֵאלֹהִים; וְאֵינֶנִּי רוֹצֶה שֶׁתִּהְיוּ שֻׁתָּפִים לַשֵּׁדִים. 21 אֵינְכֶם יְכוֹלִים לִשְׁתּוֹת מִכּוֹס הָאָדוֹן וּמִכּוֹס הַשֵּׁדִים; אֵינְכֶם יְכוֹלִים לְהִשְׁתַּתֵּף בְּשֻׁלְחַן הָאָדוֹן וּבְשֻׁלְחַן הַשֵּׁדִים. 22 הַאִם נֵעוֹר לְעוֹרֵר אֶת קִנְאַת הָאָדוֹן? כְּלוּם חֲזָקִים אֲנַחְנוּ מִמֶּנּוּ?

23 All things are lawful for me, but not all things are helpful; all things are lawful for me, but not all things edify. 24 Let no one seek his own, but each one the other's *well-being.*

25 Eat whatever is sold in the meat market, asking no questions for conscience' sake; 26 for *"the earth is the LORD's, and all its fullness."*

27 If any of those who do not believe invites you *to dinner,* and you desire to go, eat whatever is set before you, asking no question for conscience' sake. 28 But if anyone says to you, "This was offered to idols," do not eat it for the sake of the one who told you, and for conscience' sake; for *"the earth is the LORD's, and all its fullness."* 29 "Conscience," I say, not your own, but that of the other. For why is my liberty judged by another *man's* conscience? 30 But if I partake with thanks, why am I evil spoken of for *the food* over which I give thanks?

31 Therefore, whether you eat or drink, or whatever you do, do all to the glory of God. 32 Give no offense, either to the Jews or to the Greeks or to the church of God, 33 just as I also please all *men* in all *things,* not seeking my own profit, but the *profit* of many, that they may be saved.

11 Imitate me, just as I also *imitate* Christ.

2 Now I praise you, brethren, that you remember me in all things and keep the traditions just as I delivered *them* to you. 3 But I want you to know that the head of every man is Christ, the head of woman *is* man, and the head of Christ *is* God. 4 Every man praying or prophesying, having *his* head covered, dishonors his head. 5 But every woman who prays or prophesies with *her* head uncovered dishonors her head, for that is one and the same as if her head were shaved. 6 For if a woman is not covered, let her also be shorn. But if it is shameful for a woman to be shorn or shaved, let her be covered. 7 For a man indeed ought not to cover *his* head, since he is the image and glory of God; but woman is the glory of man. 8 For man is not from woman, but woman from man. 9 Nor was man created for the woman, but woman for the man. 10 For this reason the woman ought to have *a symbol of* authority on *her* head, because of the angels. 11 Nevertheless, neither *is* man independent of woman, nor woman independent of man, in the Lord. 12 For as woman *came* from man, even so man also *comes* through woman; but all things are from God.

13 Judge among yourselves. Is it proper for a woman to pray to God with her head uncovered? 14 Does not even nature itself teach you that if a man has long hair, it is a dishonor to him? 15 But if a

23 הַכֹּל מֻתָּר, אַךְ לֹא הַכֹּל מוֹעִיל; הַכֹּל מֻתָּר, אַךְ לֹא הַכֹּל בּוֹנֶה. 24 אִישׁ אַל יְבַקֵּשׁ אֶת טוֹבַת עַצְמוֹ אֶלָּא אֶת טוֹבַת זוּלָתוֹ. 25 אִכְלוּ כָּל מַה שֶּׁנִּמְכָּר בַּשּׁוּק וְאַל תִּשְׁאֲלוּ שׁוּם שְׁאֵלָה שֶׁל מַצְפּוּן, 26 כִּי לַיהוה הָאָרֶץ וּמְלוֹאָהּ. 27 אִם יַזְמִינְכֶם אִישׁ בִּלְתִּי מַאֲמִין וּרְצוֹנְכֶם לָלֶכֶת אֵלָיו, אִכְלוּ כָּל מַה שֶּׁיֻּגַּשׁ לָכֶם וְאַל תִּשְׁאֲלוּ שׁוּם שְׁאֵלָה שֶׁל מַצְפּוּן. 28 אֲבָל אִם מִישֶׁהוּ יֹאמַר לָכֶם: "זֶה נִזְבַּח לָאֱלִיל", אַל תֹּאכְלוּ לְמַעַן הָאִישׁ שֶׁהוֹדִיעַ לָכֶם וּלְמַעַן הַמַּצְפּוּן. 29 מַצְפּוּן, אֲנִי אוֹמֵר – לֹא זֶה שֶׁלְּךָ אֶלָּא שֶׁל הָאַחֵר, שֶׁכֵּן לָמָּה שֶׁתִּשָּׁפֵט חֵרוּתִי עַל-יְדֵי מַצְפּוּנוֹ שֶׁל אַחֵר? 30 אִם אֲנִי מְבָרֵךְ וְאוֹכֵל לָמָּה שֶׁיְּדֻבַּר בִּי רָעוֹת בִּגְלַל מַה שֶׁאֲנִי מְבָרֵךְ עָלָיו? 31 וּבְכֵן אִם תֹּאכְלוּ אוֹ תִשְׁתּוּ, אוֹ כָּל מַה שֶׁתַּעֲשׂוּ – עֲשׂוּ אֶת הַכֹּל לְמַעַן כְּבוֹד אֱלֹהִים. 32 אַל תִּהְיוּ מִכְשׁוֹל לֹא לַיְּהוּדִים וְלֹא לַגּוֹיִם וְלֹא לִקְהִלַּת אֱלֹהִים, 33 כְּדֶרֶךְ שֶׁגַּם אֲנִי מִשְׁתַּדֵּל לִהְיוֹת רָצוּי לְכֻלָּם בְּכָל דָּבָר וְאֵינֶנִּי מְבַקֵּשׁ אֶת טוֹבָתִי אֲנִי, אֶלָּא אֶת טוֹבַת הָרַבִּים לְמַעַן יִוָּשֵׁעוּ.

יא לְכוּ בְּעִקְבוֹתַי, כְּשֵׁם שֶׁגַּם אֲנִי הוֹלֵךְ בְּעִקְבוֹת הַמָּשִׁיחַ. 2 אַחַי, מְשַׁבֵּחַ אֲנִי אֶתְכֶם עַל שֶׁאַתֶּם זוֹכְרִים אוֹתִי בְּכָל דָּבָר וּמַחֲזִיקִים בַּמָּסֹרֶת שֶׁמָּסַרְתִּי לָכֶם. 3 רְצוֹנִי שֶׁתֵּדְעוּ כִּי רֹאשׁ כָּל אִישׁ הוּא הַמָּשִׁיחַ, וְרֹאשׁ הָאִשָּׁה הוּא הָאִישׁ, וְרֹאשׁ הַמָּשִׁיחַ הוּא אֱלֹהִים. 4 כָּל אִישׁ הַמִּתְפַּלֵּל אוֹ מִתְנַבֵּא וְרֹאשׁוֹ מְכֻסֶּה, מְבַזֶּה הוּא אֶת רֹאשׁוֹ. 5 וְכָל אִשָּׁה הַמִּתְפַּלֶּלֶת אוֹ מִתְנַבֵּאת בְּגִלּוּי רֹאשׁ, מְבַזָּה אֶת רֹאשָׁהּ; שֶׁכֵּן כָּמוֹהָ כְּמִי שֶׁגֻּלַּח שְׂעַר רֹאשָׁהּ. 6 אִם רֹאשׁ הָאִשָּׁה אֵינוֹ מְכֻסֶּה, אֲזַי גַּם רָאוּי שֶׁיְּגֻזַּז שְׂעַר רֹאשָׁהּ. אֲבָל אִם בּוּשָׁה הִיא לְאִשָּׁה לָגֹז אוֹ לְגַלֵּחַ אֶת שְׂעָרָהּ, שֶׁתִּתְכַּסֶּה. 7 הָאִישׁ אָמְנָם אֵינוֹ חַיָּב לְכַסּוֹת אֶת רֹאשׁוֹ, מִהְיוֹתוֹ צֶלֶם אֱלֹהִים וּכְבוֹדוֹ, אַךְ הָאִשָּׁה הִיא כְּבוֹד הָאִישׁ; 8 כִּי אֵין הָאִישׁ מִן הָאִשָּׁה, אֶלָּא הָאִשָּׁה מִן הָאִישׁ; 9 גַּם, הָאִישׁ לֹא נִבְרָא לְמַעַן הָאִשָּׁה, כִּי אִם הָאִשָּׁה לְמַעַן הָאִישׁ. 10 מִשּׁוּם כָּךְ חוֹבָה שֶׁתִּהְיֶה מָרוּת עַל רֹאשׁ הָאִשָּׁה מִפְּנֵי הַמַּלְאָכִים. 11 וְאוּלָם בְּאָדוֹן אֵין הָאִשָּׁה בְּלִי תְלוּת בָּאִישׁ וְאֵין הָאִישׁ בְּלִי תְלוּת בָּאִשָּׁה, 12 כִּי כְּשֵׁם שֶׁהָאִשָּׁה מִן הָאִישׁ כֵּן גַּם הָאִישׁ נוֹלָד מִן הָאִשָּׁה, וְהַכֹּל מֵאֱלֹהִים. 13 שִׁפְטוּ אַתֶּם בְּעַצְמְכֶם: הֲיָאֶה לְאִשָּׁה לְהִתְפַּלֵּל לֵאלֹהִים בְּגִלּוּי רֹאשׁ? 14 כְּלוּם הַטֶּבַע עַצְמוֹ אֵינוֹ מְלַמֵּד אֶתְכֶם שֶׁאִם לְאִישׁ שֵׂעָר אָרֹךְ הֲרֵי זֶה לִבְזוּתוֹ? 15 אֲבָל הָאִשָּׁה אִם יֵשׁ לָהּ

woman has long hair, it is a glory to her; for *her* hair is given to her for a covering. ¹⁶ But if anyone seems to be contentious, we have no such custom, nor *do* the churches of God.

¹⁷ Now in giving these instructions I do not praise *you,* since you come together not for the better but for the worse. ¹⁸ For first of all, when you come together as a church, I hear that there are divisions among you, and in part I believe it. ¹⁹ For there must also be factions among you, that those who are approved may be recognized among you. ²⁰ Therefore when you come together in one place, it is not to eat the Lord's Supper. ²¹ For in eating, each one takes his own supper ahead of *others;* and one is hungry and another is drunk. ²² What! Do you not have houses to eat and drink in? Or do you despise the church of God and shame those who have nothing? What shall I say to you? Shall I praise you in this? I do not praise *you.*

²³ For I received from the Lord that which I also delivered to you: that the Lord Jesus on the *same* night in which He was betrayed took bread; ²⁴ and when He had given thanks, He broke *it* and said, "Take, eat; this is My body which is broken for you; do this in remembrance of Me." ²⁵ In the same manner *He* also *took* the cup after supper, saying, "This cup is the new covenant in My blood. This do, as often as you drink *it,* in remembrance of Me."

²⁶ For as often as you eat this bread and drink this cup, you proclaim the Lord's death till He comes.

²⁷ Therefore whoever eats this bread or drinks *this* cup of the Lord in an unworthy manner will be guilty of the body and blood of the Lord. ²⁸ But let a man examine himself, and so let him eat of the bread and drink of the cup. ²⁹ For he who eats and drinks in an unworthy manner eats and drinks judgment to himself, not discerning the Lord's body. ³⁰ For this reason many *are* weak and sick among you, and many sleep. ³¹ For if we would judge ourselves, we would not be judged. ³² But when we are judged, we are chastened by the Lord, that we may not be condemned with the world.

³³ Therefore, my brethren, when you come together to eat, wait for one another. ³⁴ But if anyone is hungry, let him eat at home, lest you come together for judgment. And the rest I will set in order when I come.

12 Now concerning spiritual *gifts,* brethren, I do not want you to be ignorant: ² You know that you were Gentiles, carried away to these dumb idols, however you were led. ³ Therefore I make known to

שֵׂעָר אָרֹךְ הֲרֵי זֶה לְכָבוֹד לָהּ, כִּי נִתַּן לָהּ הַשֵּׂעָר לִכְסוּת. ¹⁶ וְאִם מִישֶׁהוּ מִתְכַּוֵּן לְהִתְוַכֵּחַ, לָנוּ אֵין מִנְהָג כָּזֶה, אַף לֹא לִקְהִלּוֹת אֱלֹהִים.

¹⁷ בְּמָסְרִי אֶת הַהוֹרָאוֹת הָאֵלֶּה אֵינֶנִּי מְשַׁבֵּחַ אֶתְכֶם, שֶׁכֵּן אֵינְכֶם נֶאֱסָפִים יַחַד לְטוֹבָה אֶלָּא לְרָעָה. ¹⁸ רֵאשִׁית כֹּל, שָׁמַעְתִּי כִּי בְּעֵת שֶׁאַתֶּם מִתְאַסְּפִים בִּקְהִלָּה מִתְגַּלְעוֹת מַחֲלוֹקוֹת בֵּינֵיכֶם. בְּמִדַּת מָה אֲנִי מַאֲמִין בָּזֶה, ¹⁹ שֶׁכֵּן צָרִיךְ שֶׁיִּהְיוּ פִּלּוּגִים בֵּינֵיכֶם לְמַעַן יִוָּדַע מִי הֵם הַנֶּאֱמָנִים בֵּינֵיכֶם. ²⁰ וְהִנֵּה כַּאֲשֶׁר אַתֶּם נֶאֱסָפִים יַחַד לְמָקוֹם אֶחָד, אֵין זֹאת כְּדֵי לֶאֱכֹל אֶת סְעוּדַת הָאָדוֹן, ²¹ כִּי כָּל אֶחָד מַקְדִּים לֶאֱכֹל אֶת אֲרוּחָתוֹ, וְהַתּוֹצָאָה – זֶה רָעֵב וְזֶה שִׁכּוֹר. ²² הַאָמְנָם אֵין לָכֶם בָּתִּים לֶאֱכֹל וְלִשְׁתּוֹת בָּהֶם? אוֹ שֶׁמָּא בָּזִים אַתֶּם לִקְהִלַּת אֱלֹהִים וּמְבִיְּשִׁים אֶת מִי שֶׁאֵין לוֹ? מָה אֹמַר לָכֶם? אֲשַׁבֵּחַ אֶתְכֶם? עַל זֹאת לֹא אֲשַׁבֵּחַ. ²³ אָכֵן אֲנִי קִבַּלְתִּי מֵאֵת הָאָדוֹן אֶת אֲשֶׁר גַּם מָסַרְתִּי לָכֶם: שֶׁהָאָדוֹן יֵשׁוּעַ, בַּלַּיְלָה שֶׁהֻסְגַּר בּוֹ, לָקַח אֶת הַלֶּחֶם, ²⁴ בֵּרֵךְ, בָּצַע אוֹתוֹ וְאָמַר: "זֶה גּוּפִי הַנִּבְצָע בַּעֲדְכֶם, זֹאת עֲשׂוּ לְזִכְרִי." ²⁵ כֵּן גַּם לָקַח אֶת הַכּוֹס לְאַחַר הַסְּעוּדָה וְאָמַר: "הַכּוֹס הַזֹּאת הִיא הַבְּרִית הַחֲדָשָׁה בְּדָמִי, זֹאת עֲשׂוּ לְזִכְרִי בְּכָל עֵת שֶׁתִּשְׁתּוּ." ²⁶ הֵן בְּכָל עֵת שֶׁאַתֶּם אוֹכְלִים אֶת הַלֶּחֶם הַזֶּה וְשׁוֹתִים מִן הַכּוֹס הַזֹּאת, אַתֶּם מַזְכִּירִים אֶת מוֹת אֲדוֹנֵנוּ, עַד שֶׁיָּבוֹא.

²⁷ לָכֵן מִי שֶׁאוֹכֵל מֵהַלֶּחֶם הַזֶּה אוֹ שׁוֹתֶה מִכּוֹס הָאָדוֹן שֶׁלֹּא כָרָאוּי, יִהְיֶה אָשֵׁם לְגַבֵּי גּוּף הָאָדוֹן וְדָמוֹ. ²⁸ יִבְחַן נָא אִישׁ אֶת עַצְמוֹ וְכָךְ יֹאכַל מִן הַלֶּחֶם וְיִשְׁתֶּה מִן הַכּוֹס; ²⁹ כִּי הָאוֹכֵל וְהַשּׁוֹתֶה מִבְּלִי לִנְהֹג הַבְחָנָה בְּגוּף הָאָדוֹן, אוֹכֵל וְשׁוֹתֶה דִּין לְעַצְמוֹ. ³⁰ מִסִּבָּה זֹאת רַבִּים מִכֶּם חַלָּשִׁים וְחוֹלִים וְיֵשׁ אֲשֶׁר מֵתוּ. ³¹ אִם נִבְחַן אֶת עַצְמֵנוּ לֹא נִשָּׁפֵט. ³² אֲבָל כַּאֲשֶׁר הָאָדוֹן שׁוֹפֵט אוֹתָנוּ הוּא מְיַסֵּר אוֹתָנוּ כְּדֵי שֶׁלֹּא נֵרָשַׁע עִם הָעוֹלָם. ³³ עַל כֵּן, אַחַי, הַמִּתְּנוּ זֶה לָזֶה כְּשֶׁאַתֶּם נֶאֱסָפִים לֶאֱכֹל. ³⁴ מִי שֶׁרָעֵב יֹאכַל בַּבַּיִת, לְמַעַן לֹא תֵּאָסְפוּ לְמִשְׁפָּט. וְאֶת יֶתֶר הַדְּבָרִים אֲסַדֵּר בְּבוֹאִי.

יב בְּעִנְיַן הַמַּתָּנוֹת הָרוּחָנִיּוֹת, אַחַי, אֵינֶנִּי רוֹצֶה שֶׁיֵּעָלֵם מִכֶּם דָּבָר. ² אַתֶּם יוֹדְעִים כִּי בְּעֵת הֱיוֹתְכֶם עוֹבְדֵי אֱלִילִים נִדְחַתֶּם וְנִמְשַׁכְתֶּם אֶל אֱלִילִים אִלְּמִים. ³ וּבְכֵן אֲנִי מוֹדִיעַ לָכֶם: אֵין אִישׁ מְדַבֵּר

you that no one speaking by the Spirit of God calls Jesus accursed, and no one can say that Jesus is Lord except by the Holy Spirit.

⁴ There are diversities of gifts, but the same Spirit. ⁵ There are differences of ministries, but the same Lord. ⁶ And there are diversities of activities, but it is the same God who works all in all. ⁷ But the manifestation of the Spirit is given to each one for the profit *of all:* ⁸ for to one is given the word of wisdom through the Spirit, to another the word of knowledge through the same Spirit, ⁹ to another faith by the same Spirit, to another gifts of healings by the same Spirit, ¹⁰ to another the working of miracles, to another prophecy, to another discerning of spirits, to another *different* kinds of tongues, to another the interpretation of tongues. ¹¹ But one and the same Spirit works all these things, distributing to each one individually as He wills.

¹² For as the body is one and has many members, but all the members of that one body, being many, are one body, so also *is* Christ. ¹³ For by one Spirit we were all baptized into one body—whether Jews or Greeks, whether slaves or free—and have all been made to drink into one Spirit. ¹⁴ For in fact the body is not one member but many.

¹⁵ If the foot should say, "Because I am not a hand, I am not of the body," is it therefore not of the body? ¹⁶ And if the ear should say, "Because I am not an eye, I am not of the body," is it therefore not of the body? ¹⁷ If the whole body *were* an eye, where *would be* the hearing? If the whole *were* hearing, where *would be* the smelling? ¹⁸ But now God has set the members, each one of them, in the body just as He pleased. ¹⁹ And if they *were* all one member, where *would* the body *be?*

²⁰ But now indeed *there are* many members, yet one body. ²¹ And the eye cannot say to the hand, "I have no need of you"; nor again the head to the feet, "I have no need of you." ²² No, much rather, those members of the body which seem to be weaker are necessary. ²³ And those *members* of the body which we think to be less honorable, on these we bestow greater honor; and our unpresentable *parts* have greater modesty, ²⁴ but our presentable *parts* have no need. But God composed the body, having given greater honor to that *part* which lacks it, ²⁵ that there should be no schism in the body, but *that* the members should have the same care for one another. ²⁶ And if one member suffers, all the members suffer with *it;* or if one member is honored, all the members rejoice with *it.*

²⁷ Now you are the body of Christ, and members individually. ²⁸ And God has appointed these in the church: first apostles, second prophets, third

teachers, after that miracles, then gifts of healings, helps, administrations, varieties of tongues. [29] *Are* all apostles? *Are* all prophets? *Are* all teachers? *Are* all workers of miracles? [30] Do all have gifts of healings? Do all speak with tongues? Do all interpret? [31] But earnestly desire the best gifts. And yet I show you a more excellent way.

13 Though I speak with the tongues of men and of angels, but have not love, I have become sounding brass or a clanging cymbal. [2] And though I have *the gift of* prophecy, and understand all mysteries and all knowledge, and though I have all faith, so that I could remove mountains, but have not love, I am nothing. [3] And though I bestow all my goods to feed *the poor,* and though I give my body to be burned, but have not love, it profits me nothing.

[4] Love suffers long *and* is kind; love does not envy; love does not parade itself, is not puffed up; [5] does not behave rudely, does not seek its own, is not provoked, thinks no evil; [6] does not rejoice in iniquity, but rejoices in the truth; [7] bears all things, believes all things, hopes all things, endures all things.

[8] Love never fails. But whether *there are* prophecies, they will fail; whether *there are* tongues, they will cease; whether *there is* knowledge, it will vanish away. [9] For we know in part and we prophesy in part. [10] But when that which is perfect has come, then that which is in part will be done away.

[11] When I was a child, I spoke as a child, I understood as a child, I thought as a child; but when I became a man, I put away childish things. [12] For now we see in a mirror, dimly, but then face to face. Now I know in part, but then I shall know just as I also am known.

[13] And now abide faith, hope, love, these three; but the greatest of these *is* love.

14 Pursue love, and desire spiritual *gifts,* but especially that you may prophesy. [2] For he who speaks in a tongue does not speak to men but to God, for no one understands *him;* however, in the spirit he speaks mysteries. [3] But he who prophesies speaks edification and exhortation and comfort to men. [4] He who speaks in a tongue edifies himself, but he who prophesies edifies the church. [5] I wish you all spoke with tongues, but even more that you prophesied; for he who prophesies *is* greater than he who speaks with tongues, unless indeed he interprets, that the church may receive edification.

שֵׁנִית נְבִיאִים, שְׁלִישִׁית מוֹרִים, אַחֲרֵי כֵן עוֹשֵׂי נִסִּים, אַחֲרֵי כֵן מַתְּנוֹת הָרִפּוּי, עֶזְרָה לַזּוּלַת, הַנְהָגָה, וּמִינֵי לְשׁוֹנוֹת. 29 הַאִם כֻּלָּם שְׁלִיחִים? הַאִם כֻּלָּם נְבִיאִים? הַאִם כֻּלָּם מוֹרִים? כֻּלָּם עוֹשֵׂי נִסִּים? 30 הַאִם לְכֻלָּם מַתְּנוֹת הָרִפּוּי? הַאִם כֻּלָּם מְדַבְּרִים בִּלְשׁוֹנוֹת? כֻּלָּם מְבָאֲרֵי לְשׁוֹנוֹת? 31 וּבְכֵן הִשְׁתּוֹקְקוּ לַמַּתָּנוֹת הַחֲשׁוּבוֹת יוֹתֵר; עִם זֹאת אַרְאֶה לָכֶם דֶּרֶךְ נַעֲלָה בְּיוֹתֵר:

יג אִם בִּלְשׁוֹנוֹת בְּנֵי אָדָם וּמַלְאָכִים אֲדַבֵּר וְאֵין בִּי אַהֲבָה, הֲרֵינִי כִּנְחֹשֶׁת הוֹמָה אוֹ כִּמְצִלְתַּיִם רוֹעֲשִׁים. 2 אִם תִּהְיֶה לִי מַתַּת הַנְּבוּאָה וְאֵדַע כָּל הַסּוֹדוֹת וְאַשִּׂיג כָּל הַדַּעַת, וְאִם תִּהְיֶה בִּי כָּל הָאֱמוּנָה עַד לְהַעֲתִיק הָרִים מִמְּקוֹמָם, וְאֵין בִּי אַהֲבָה, הֲרֵינִי כְּאַיִן וּכְאָפֶס. 3 אִם אֲחַלֵּק אֶת כָּל רְכוּשִׁי לִצְדָקָה וְגַם אֶתֵּן אֶת גּוּפִי לִשְׂרֵפָה וְאֵין בִּי אַהֲבָה – לֹא יוֹעִיל לִי דָּבָר. 4 הָאַהֲבָה סַבְלָנִית וּגְדִיבָה; הָאַהֲבָה אֵינָהּ מְקַנֵּאת; הָאַהֲבָה לֹא תִתְפָּאֵר וְלֹא תִתְנַשֵּׂא; 5 הִיא לֹא תִנְהַג בִּנְפוּת, לֹא תִדְרֹשׁ טוֹבַת עַצְמָהּ, לֹא תִרְגַּז וְלֹא תַחֲשֹׁב רָעָה. 6 הָאַהֲבָה לֹא תִשְׂמַח בָּעַוְלָה, כִּי בֶּאֱמֶת שִׂמְחָתָהּ. 7 הִיא תְכַסֶּה עַל הַכֹּל, תַּאֲמִין בַּכֹּל, תְּקַוֶּה לַכֹּל וְתִסְבֹּל אֶת הַכֹּל. 8 הָאַהֲבָה לֹא תִמּוֹט לְעוֹלָם, אַךְ נְבוּאוֹת תִּבָּטֶלְנָה, לְשׁוֹנוֹת תֶּחְדַּלְנָה, דַּעַת תִּבָּטֵל; 9 כִּי חֶלְקִית הִיא יְדִיעָתֵנוּ וּבְאֹרַח חֶלְקִי מִתְנַבְּאִים אָנוּ, 10 אַךְ בְּבוֹא הַמֻּשְׁלָם יְבֻטַּל הַחֶלְקִי. 11 בִּהְיוֹתִי יֶלֶד דִּבַּרְתִּי כְּיֶלֶד, הִבַּנְתִּי כְּיֶלֶד, חָשַׁבְתִּי כְּיֶלֶד. כְּשֶׁהָיִיתִי לְאִישׁ שַׂמְתִּי קֵץ לְדִבְרֵי הַיַּלְדוּת. 12 עַכְשָׁו רוֹאִים אָנוּ בְּמַרְאָה, בִּמְעֻרְפָּל, אֲבָל אָז – פָּנִים אֶל פָּנִים. עַכְשָׁו יְדִיעָתִי חֶלְקִית, אֲבָל אָז אַכִּיר אָז כְּדֶרֶךְ שֶׁגַּם אֲנִי מֻכָּר. 13 אַךְ כָּעֵת עוֹמְדוֹת שָׁלוֹשׁ אֵלֶּה: אֱמוּנָה, תִּקְוָה, אַהֲבָה; וְהַגְּדוֹלָה שֶׁבָּהֶן – אַהֲבָה.

יד רִדְפוּ אַהֲבָה וְהִשְׁתּוֹקְקוּ לַמַּתָּנוֹת רוּחָנִיּוֹת, וּבְעִקָּר שֶׁתִּתְנַבְּאוּ. 2 הַמְדַבֵּר בְּלָשׁוֹן אֵינוֹ מְדַבֵּר לַאֲנָשִׁים אֶלָּא לֵאלֹהִים; אִישׁ אֵינֶנּוּ מֵבִין אוֹתוֹ, כִּי בְרוּחַ הוּא מְבַטֵּא סוֹדוֹת. 3 אֲבָל הַמִּתְנַבֵּא מַשְׁמִיעַ לַאֲנָשִׁים דְּבָרִים שֶׁתַּכְלִיתָם לִבְנוֹת, לְעוֹדֵד וּלְנַחֵם. 4 הַמְדַבֵּר בְּלָשׁוֹן בּוֹנֶה אֶת עַצְמוֹ; הַמִּתְנַבֵּא בּוֹנֶה אֶת הַקְּהִלָּה. 5 רְצוֹנִי שֶׁכֻּלְּכֶם תְּדַבְּרוּ בִּלְשׁוֹנוֹת, אַךְ עָדִיף שֶׁתִּתְנַבְּאוּ. הַמִּתְנַבֵּא גָּדוֹל מִן הַמְדַבֵּר בִּלְשׁוֹנוֹת, זוּלָתִי אִם יְפָרֵשׁ הָאַחֲרוֹן אֶת דְּבָרָיו כְּדֵי שֶׁהַקְּהִלָּה תִּבָּנֶה.

⁶But now, brethren, if I come to you speaking with tongues, what shall I profit you unless I speak to you either by revelation, by knowledge, by prophesying, or by teaching? ⁷Even things without life, whether flute or harp, when they make a sound, unless they make a distinction in the sounds, how will it be known what is piped or played? ⁸For if the trumpet makes an uncertain sound, who will prepare for battle? ⁹So likewise you, unless you utter by the tongue words easy to understand, how will it be known what is spoken? For you will be speaking into the air. ¹⁰There are, it may be, so many kinds of languages in the world, and none of them *is* without significance. ¹¹Therefore, if I do not know the meaning of the language, I shall be a foreigner to him who speaks, and he who speaks *will be* a foreigner to me. ¹²Even so you, since you are zealous for spiritual *gifts, let it be* for the edification of the church *that* you seek to excel.

¹³Therefore let him who speaks in a tongue pray that he may interpret. ¹⁴For if I pray in a tongue, my spirit prays, but my understanding is unfruitful. ¹⁵What is *the conclusion* then? I will pray with the spirit, and I will also pray with the understanding. I will sing with the spirit, and I will also sing with the understanding. ¹⁶Otherwise, if you bless with the spirit, how will he who occupies the place of the uninformed say "Amen" at your giving of thanks, since he does not understand what you say? ¹⁷For you indeed give thanks well, but the other is not edified.

¹⁸I thank my God I speak with tongues more than you all; ¹⁹yet in the church I would rather speak five words with my understanding, that I may teach others also, than ten thousand words in a tongue.

²⁰Brethren, do not be children in understanding; however, in malice be babes, but in understanding be mature.

²¹In the law it is written:

"With *men of other tongues and other lips*
I will speak to this people;
And yet, for all that, they will not hear Me,"

says the Lord.

²²Therefore tongues are for a sign, not to those who believe but to unbelievers; but prophesying is not for unbelievers but for those who believe. ²³Therefore if the whole church comes together in one place, and all speak with tongues, and there come in *those who are* uninformed or unbelievers, will they not say that you are out of your mind? ²⁴But if all prophesy, and an unbeliever or an uninformed person comes in, he is convinced by all,

⁶וְעַתָּה, אַחַי, אִם אָבוֹא אֲלֵיכֶם וַאֲדַבֵּר בִּלְשׁוֹנוֹת, מָה אוֹעִיל לָכֶם אִם לֹא אַגִּיד לָכֶם דְּבַר הִתְגַּלּוּת אוֹ דְבַר דַּעַת, דְּבַר נְבוּאָה אוֹ דְבַר הַהוֹרָאָה? ⁷אֲפִלּוּ כֵּלִים דּוֹמְמִים הַמַּשְׁמִיעִים קוֹל, כְּגוֹן חָלִיל אוֹ כִּנּוֹר, אִם לֹא יָפִיקוּ צְלִיל בָּרוּר, אֵיךְ יֻכַּירוּ אֶת מַה שֶּׁנִּגֵּן הֶחָלִיל אוֹ הַכִּנּוֹר? ⁸וְאִם הַחֲצוֹצְרָה תַּשְׁמִיעַ קוֹל בִּלְתִּי בָּרוּר, מִי יִתְכּוֹנֵן לַקְּרָב? ⁹כֵּן גַּם אַתֶּם, אִם לֹא תַּשְׁמִיעוּ דְּבָרִים בְּרוּרִים בַּלָּשׁוֹן, כֵּיצַד יוּבַן מַה שֶּׁנֶּאֱמַר? הֲרֵי תִּהְיוּ מְדַבְּרִים אֶל הָאֲוִיר! ¹⁰רַבִּים הֵם מִינֵי הַקּוֹלוֹת בָּעוֹלָם וְאֵין אֶחָד מֵהֶם שֶׁאֵינוֹ מַבִּיעַ מַשֶּׁהוּ. ¹¹לְפִיכָךְ אִם אֵינֶנִּי מֵבִין אֶת הַתֹּכֶן שֶׁל הַקּוֹל, אֶהְיֶה לוֹעֵז בְּעֵינֵי הַמְדַבֵּר וְהַמְדַבֵּר יִהְיֶה לוֹעֵז בְּעֵינַי. ¹²כֵּן גַּם אַתֶּם, הֱיוֹת שֶׁאַתֶּם לְהוּטִים אַחֲרֵי מַתָּנוֹת רוּחָנִיּוֹת, בַּקְּשׁוּ לְהַעֲשִׁיר בְּמַה שֶּׁבּוֹנֶה אֶת הַקְּהִלָּה.

¹³לָכֵן הַמְדַבֵּר בְּלָשׁוֹן יִתְפַּלֵּל שֶׁיּוּכַל לְפָרֵשׁ אֶת דְּבָרָיו. ¹⁴אִם אֲנִי מִתְפַּלֵּל בְּלָשׁוֹן רוּחִי מִתְפַּלֶּלֶת, אֲבָל שִׂכְלִי אֵינוֹ עוֹשֶׂה פְּרִי. ¹⁵אִם כֵּן מַה לַעֲשׂוֹת? אֶתְפַּלֵּל בְּאֶמְצָעוּת הָרוּחַ וְאֶתְפַּלֵּל גַּם בְּאֶמְצָעוּת הַשֵּׂכֶל, אָשִׁיר בְּאֶמְצָעוּת הָרוּחַ וְאָשִׁיר גַּם בְּאֶמְצָעוּת הַשֵּׂכֶל; ¹⁶שֶׁכֵּן אִם תְּבָרֵךְ בְּרוּחַ, כֵּיצַד יֹאמַר "אָמֵן" עַל הוֹדָיָתְךָ מִי שֶׁנִּמְנֶה עִם הַבִּלְתִּי מְבִינִים? הֲרֵי אֵין הוּא יוֹדֵעַ מָה אַתָּה אוֹמֵר! ¹⁷אַתָּה אָמְנָם מַשְׁמִיעַ תּוֹדָה כָּרָאוּי, אַךְ רֵעֲךָ אֵינֶנּוּ נִבְנֶה. ¹⁸אֲנִי מוֹדֶה לֵאלֹהִים שֶׁאֲנִי מְדַבֵּר בִּלְשׁוֹנוֹת יוֹתֵר מִכֻּלְּכֶם. ¹⁹בְּרַם בַּקְּהִלָּה אֲנִי מַעֲדִיף לוֹמַר חָמֵשׁ מִלִּים בְּעֶזְרַת שִׂכְלִי כְּדֵי לְלַמֵּד גַּם אֲחֵרִים – מֵאֲשֶׁר לְהַשְׁמִיעַ רִבְבוֹת מִלִּים בְּלָשׁוֹן.

²⁰אַחַי, אַל תִּהְיוּ יְלָדִים בַּחֲשִׁיבָה; הֱיוּ יְלָדִים בְּעִנְיְנֵי רִשְׁעוּת, אַךְ בַּחֲשִׁיבָה הֱיוּ מְבֻגָּרִים. ²¹בַּתּוֹרָה כָּתוּב: "כִּי בְּלַעֲגֵי שָׂפָה וּבְלָשׁוֹן אַחֶרֶת יְדַבֵּר אֶל־הָעָם הַזֶּה וְלֹא אָבוּא שְׁמוֹעַ." ²²לְפִיכָךְ הַלְּשׁוֹנוֹת אֵינָן אוֹת לַמַּאֲמִינִים, אֶלָּא לַבִּלְתִּי מַאֲמִינִים. וְהַנְּבוּאָה אֵינֶנָּה לַבִּלְתִּי מַאֲמִינִים, אֶלָּא לַמַּאֲמִינִים. ²³וְהִנֵּה אִם תִּתְכַּנֵּס כָּל הַקְּהִלָּה וְכֻלָּם יְדַבְּרוּ בִּלְשׁוֹנוֹת, וְיִכָּנְסוּ אֲנָשִׁים שֶׁאֵין לָהֶם מֻשָּׂג בָּעִנְיָן, אוֹ אֲנָשִׁים בִּלְתִּי מַאֲמִינִים, כְּלוּם לֹא יֹאמְרוּ שֶׁאַתֶּם מְשֻׁגָּעִים? ²⁴אֲבָל אִם הַכֹּל מִתְנַבְּאִים וְיִכָּנֵס אִישׁ בִּלְתִּי מַאֲמִין, אוֹ מִי שֶׁאֵין לוֹ מֻשָּׂג בָּעִנְיָן, אֲזֵי יוּכַח

he is convicted by all. 25 And thus the secrets of his heart are revealed; and so, falling down on *his* face, he will worship God and report that God is truly among you.

26 How is it then, brethren? Whenever you come together, each of you has a psalm, has a teaching, has a tongue, has a revelation, has an interpretation. Let all things be done for edification. 27 If anyone speaks in a tongue, *let there be* two or at the most three, *each* in turn, and let one interpret. 28 But if there is no interpreter, let him keep silent in church, and let him speak to himself and to God. 29 Let two or three prophets speak, and let the others judge. 30 But if *anything* is revealed to another who sits by, let the first keep silent. 31 For you can all prophesy one by one, that all may learn and all may be encouraged. 32 And the spirits of the prophets are subject to the prophets. 33 For God is not *the author* of confusion but of peace, as in all the churches of the saints.

34 Let your women keep silent in the churches, for they are not permitted to speak; but *they are* to be submissive, as the law also says. 35 And if they want to learn something, let them ask their own husbands at home; for it is shameful for women to speak in church.

36 Or did the word of God come *originally* from you? Or *was it* you only that it reached? 37 If anyone thinks himself to be a prophet or spiritual, let him acknowledge that the things which I write to you are the commandments of the Lord. 38 But if anyone is ignorant, let him be ignorant.

39 Therefore, brethren, desire earnestly to prophesy, and do not forbid to speak with tongues. 40 Let all things be done decently and in order.

15 Moreover, brethren, I declare to you the gospel which I preached to you, which also you received and in which you stand, 2 by which also you are saved, if you hold fast that word which I preached to you—unless you believed in vain.

3 For I delivered to you first of all that which I also received: that Christ died for our sins according to the Scriptures, 4 and that He was buried, and that He rose again the third day according to the Scriptures, 5 and that He was seen by Cephas, then by the twelve. 6 After that He was seen by over five hundred brethren at once, of whom the greater part remain to the present, but some have fallen asleep. 7 After that He was seen by James, then by all the apostles. 8 Then last of all He was seen by me also, as by one born out of due time.

עַל־יְדֵי כֻלָּם וְיִדּוֹן עַל־יְדֵי כֻלָּם: 25 סִתְרֵי לִבּוֹ יִגָּלוּ וְהוּא יִפֹּל עַל פָּנָיו בְּהִשְׁתַּחֲוָיָה לֵאלֹהִים וְיַכְרִיז כִּי אָכֵן יֵשׁ אֱלֹהִים בְּקִרְבְּכֶם.

26 וּבְכֵן מַה תַּעֲשׂוּ, אַחַי? כַּאֲשֶׁר אַתֶּם נִקְהָלִים יַחְדָּיו, לְאֶחָד יֵשׁ מִזְמוֹר, לְאַחֵר יֵשׁ דְּבַר־הוֹרָאָה, לָזֶה הִתְגַּלּוּת, לָזֶה לָשׁוֹן וְלָזֶה פֵּרוּשׁ: יְהֵא נָא הַכֹּל לְמַעַן תִּבָּנוּ. 27 אִם מְדַבְּרִים בְּלָשׁוֹן, יְדַבְּרוּ שְׁנַיִם אוֹ שְׁלוֹשָׁה, לֹא יוֹתֵר; זֶה אַחַר זֶה יְדַבְּרוּ וְאֶחָד יְפָרֵשׁ. 28 אַךְ אִם אֵין מְפָרֵשׁ, יַחֲרִישׁ בַּקְּהִלָּה וִידַבֵּר לְעַצְמוֹ וְלֵאלֹהִים. 29 אֲשֶׁר לַנְּבִיאִים, שְׁנַיִם אוֹ שְׁלוֹשָׁה יְדַבְּרוּ וְהַשְּׁאָר יְבַחֲנוּ אֶת דִּבְרֵיהֶם. 30 אִם יִגָּלֶה דָּבָר לְאַחַד הַיּוֹשְׁבִים שָׁם יַחֲרִישׁ הָרִאשׁוֹן, 31 כִּי כֻלְּכֶם יְכוֹלִים לְהִתְנַבֵּא זֶה אַחַר זֶה בְּאֹפֶן שֶׁהַכֹּל יִלְמְדוּ וְהַכֹּל יִתְעוֹדְדוּ. 32 וְרוּחוֹת הַנְּבִיאִים כְּפוּפוֹת לַנְּבִיאִים, 33 שֶׁהֲרֵי אֱלֹהִים אֵינוֹ אֱלֹהֵי מְהוּמָה אֶלָּא אֱלֹהֵי הַשָּׁלוֹם.

כַּנָּהוּג בְּכָל קְהִלּוֹת הַקְּדוֹשִׁים, 34 הַנָּשִׁים תֶּחֱשֶׁינָה בַּקְּהִלּוֹת; אֵין לָהֶן רְשׁוּת לְדַבֵּר, אֶלָּא תִּכָּנַעְנָה לְמֹרוּת, כְּמוֹ שֶׁגַּם הַתּוֹרָה אוֹמֶרֶת. 35 וְאִם רְצוֹנָן לִלְמֹד דָּבָר, תִּשְׁאַלְנָה אֶת בַּעֲלֵיהֶן בַּבַּיִת, כִּי לֹא יָאֶה שֶׁאִשָּׁה תְּדַבֵּר בַּקְּהִלָּה.

36 הַאִם מִכֶּם יָצָא דְּבַר אֱלֹהִים? וְכִי רַק אֲלֵיכֶם הִגִּיעַ? 37 כָּל הַחוֹשֵׁב שֶׁהוּא עַצְמוֹ נָבִיא אוֹ אִישׁ רוּחָנִי, שֶׁיַּכִּיר כִּי הַדְּבָרִים אֲשֶׁר כָּתַבְתִּי אֲלֵיכֶם מִצְווֹת הָאָדוֹן הֵם. 38 וְאִם מִישֶׁהוּ אֵינוֹ מַכִּיר, לֹא יֻכַּר בּוֹ. 39 וּבְכֵן, אַחַי, הִשְׁתַּדְּלוּ לְהִתְנַבֵּא וְאַל תִּמְנְעוּ דִּבּוּר בִּלְשׁוֹנוֹת, 40 אֲבָל יֵעָשֶׂה נָא הַכֹּל בְּאֹפֶן רָאוּי וּבְסֵדֶר.

טו אַחַי, אֲנִי מַזְכִּיר לָכֶם אֶת הַבְּשׂוֹרָה שֶׁהִשְׁמַעְתִּי לָכֶם, בְּשׂוֹרָה אֲשֶׁר גַּם קִבַּלְתֶּם אוֹתָהּ וְגַם עוֹמְדִים אַתֶּם בָּהּ; 2 בְּאֶמְצָעוּתָהּ אַתֶּם גַּם נוֹשָׁעִים, אִם מַחֲזִיקִים אַתֶּם בַּדָּבָר שֶׁבִּשַּׂרְתִּי לָכֶם – שֶׁאִם לֹא כֵן, לַשָּׁוְא הָיְתָה אֱמוּנַתְכֶם. 3 מָסַרְתִּי לָכֶם בָּרֹאשׁ וּבָרִאשׁוֹנָה מַה שֶּׁגַּם קִבַּלְתִּי, שֶׁהַמָּשִׁיחַ מֵת בְּעַד חֲטָאֵינוּ, לְפִי הַכְּתוּבִים, 4 נִקְבַּר וְקָם לִתְחִיָּה בַּיּוֹם הַשְּׁלִישִׁי, לְפִי הַכְּתוּבִים; 5 וְנִרְאָה אֶל כֵּיפָא וְאַחַר כָּךְ אֶל הַשְּׁנֵים־עָשָׂר. 6 אַחֲרֵי כֵן נִרְאָה בְּבַת אַחַת אֶל יוֹתֵר מֵחֲמֵשׁ מֵאוֹת אַחִים, אֲשֶׁר רֻבָּם עוֹדָם בַּחַיִּים וּמִקְצָתָם מֵתִים. 7 אַחַר כָּךְ נִרְאָה אֶל יַעֲקֹב וּלְאַחַר מִכֵּן אֶל כָּל הַשְּׁלִיחִים. 8 אַחֲרֵי כֻלָּם נִרְאָה

9 For I am the least of the apostles, who am not worthy to be called an apostle, because I persecuted the church of God. 10 But by the grace of God I am what I am, and His grace toward me was not in vain; but I labored more abundantly than they all, yet not I, but the grace of God *which was* with me. 11 Therefore, whether *it was* I or they, so we preach and so you believed.

12 Now if Christ is preached that He has been raised from the dead, how do some among you say that there is no resurrection of the dead? 13 But if there is no resurrection of the dead, then Christ is not risen. 14 And if Christ is not risen, then our preaching *is* empty and your faith *is* also empty. 15 Yes, and we are found false witnesses of God, because we have testified of God that He raised up Christ, whom He did not raise up—if in fact the dead do not rise. 16 For if *the* dead do not rise, then Christ is not risen. 17 And if Christ is not risen, your faith *is* futile; you are still in your sins! 18 Then also those who have fallen asleep in Christ have perished. 19 If in this life only we have hope in Christ, we are of all men the most pitiable.

20 But now Christ is risen from the dead, *and* has become the firstfruits of those who have fallen asleep. 21 For since by man *came* death, by Man also *came* the resurrection of the dead. 22 For as in Adam all die, even so in Christ all shall be made alive. 23 But each one in his own order: Christ the firstfruits, afterward those *who are* Christ's at His coming. 24 Then *comes* the end, when He delivers the kingdom to God the Father, when He puts an end to all rule and all authority and power. 25 For He must reign till He has put all enemies under His feet. 26 The last enemy *that* will be destroyed *is* death. 27 For *"He has put all things under His feet."* But when He says "all things are put under *Him*," it *is* evident that He who put all things under Him is excepted. 28 Now when all things are made subject to Him, then the Son Himself will also be subject to Him who put all things under Him, that God may be all in all.

29 Otherwise, what will they do who are baptized for the dead, if the dead do not rise at all? Why then are they baptized for the dead? 30 And why do we stand in jeopardy every hour? 31 I affirm, by the boasting in you which I have in Christ Jesus our Lord, I die daily. 32 If, in the manner of men, I have fought with beasts at Ephesus, what advantage *is it* to me? If *the* dead do not rise, *"Let us eat and drink, for tomorrow we die!"*

גַּם אֵלַי, אֲנִי, הָאַחֲרוֹן, אֲשֶׁר כְּנֵפֶל אָנִי; 9 שֶׁכֵּן אֲנִי הַפָּחוּת בַּשְּׁלִיחִים וְאֵינֶנִּי רָאוּי לְהִקָּרֵא שָׁלִיחַ מִשּׁוּם שֶׁרָדַפְתִּי אֶת קְהִלַּת אֱלֹהִים. 10 אֲבָל בְּחֶסֶד אֱלֹהִים הֲרֵינִי מַה שֶּׁאֲנִי וְחַסְדּוֹ עָלַי לֹא הָיָה לָרִיק. אַדְּרַבָּא, עָמַלְתִּי יוֹתֵר מִכֻּלָּם, אַךְ לֹא אֲנִי אֶלָּא חֶסֶד אֱלֹהִים אֲשֶׁר אִתִּי. 11 עַל כָּל פָּנִים, בֵּין שֶׁאֲנִי בֵּין שֶׁהֵם, כָּךְ אָנוּ מְבַשְּׂרִים וְכָךְ הֶאֱמַנְתֶּם.

12 וּבְכֵן אִם מֻכְרָז כִּי הַמָּשִׁיחַ קָם מִן הַמֵּתִים, אֵיךְ אוֹמְרִים כַּמָּה מִכֶּם שֶׁאֵין תְּחִיַּת מֵתִים? 13 אִם אֵין תְּחִיַּת מֵתִים, גַּם הַמָּשִׁיחַ לֹא קָם. 14 וְאִם הַמָּשִׁיחַ לֹא קָם, הַכְרָזָתֵנוּ הֶבֶל וְגַם אֱמוּנַתְכֶם הֶבֶל. 15 וְאָז גַּם נִמְצָא עֵדֵי שֶׁקֶר לֵאלֹהִים, שֶׁכֵּן הֵעִידוֹנוּ עַל אֱלֹהִים כִּי הֵקִים אֶת הַמָּשִׁיחַ לִתְחִיָּה – וְהוּא לֹא הֵקִימוֹ אִם אָמְנָם אֵין הַמֵּתִים קָמִים לִתְחִיָּה; 16 וְאִם אֵין הַמֵּתִים קָמִים לִתְחִיָּה, גַּם הַמָּשִׁיחַ לֹא קָם לִתְחִיָּה. 17 וְאִם הַמָּשִׁיחַ לֹא קָם לִתְחִיָּה, לַשָּׁוְא אֱמוּנַתְכֶם וַעֲדַיִן שְׁרוּיִים אַתֶּם בַּחֲטָאֵיכֶם. 18 וְאָז גַּם הָאֲנָשִׁים אֲשֶׁר מֵתוּ בִּהְיוֹתָם שָׁיָּכִים לַמָּשִׁיחַ – אֲבוּדִים הֵם. 19 אִם אֲנַחְנוּ תּוֹלִים תִּקְוָה בַּמָּשִׁיחַ אַךְ וְרַק לְמַעַן חַיִּים אֵלֶּה, אֲזַי אֻמְלָלִים אָנוּ מִכָּל אָדָם.

20 אֲבָל כָּעֵת הַמָּשִׁיחַ קָם מִן הַמֵּתִים, בִּכּוּרֵי כָּל יְשֵׁנֵי עָפָר. 21 וּמֵאַחַר שֶׁהַמָּוֶת בָּא עַל־יְדֵי אָדָם, גַּם תְּחִיַּת הַמֵּתִים הִיא עַל־יְדֵי אָדָם; 22 שֶׁכֵּן כְּמוֹ שֶׁבְּאָדָם הַכֹּל מֵתִים, כָּךְ גַּם בַּמָּשִׁיחַ הַכֹּל יִחְיוּ. 23 אַךְ כָּל אֶחָד כְּסִדְרוֹ: הָרִאשׁוֹן הוּא הַמָּשִׁיחַ; אַחֲרֵי כֵן, בְּבוֹאוֹ, הַשַּׁיָּכִים לַמָּשִׁיחַ. 24 אַחֲרֵי כֵן הַקֵּץ, כַּאֲשֶׁר יִמְסֹר לֵאלֹהִים הָאָב אֶת הַמַּלְכוּת לְאַחַר שֶׁיְּבַטֵּל כָּל מִמְשָׁל וְכָל סַמְכוּת וְשִׁלְטוֹן; 25 כִּי עָלָיו לִמְלֹךְ עַד כִּי יָשִׁית אֶת כָּל אוֹיְבָיו תַּחַת רַגְלָיו. 26 הָאוֹיֵב הָאַחֲרוֹן שֶׁיְּמֻגַּר הוּא הַמָּוֶת, 27 שֶׁכֵּן הָאֱלֹהִים שָׁת הַכֹּל תַּחַת רַגְלָיו. וּבְאָמְרוֹ שֶׁהַכֹּל הוּשַׁת תַּחְתָּיו, בָּרוּר כִּי הַשָּׁת אֶת הַכֹּל תַּחְתָּיו אֵינֶנּוּ בִּכְלָל הַזֶּה. 28 וְכַאֲשֶׁר הַכֹּל יוּשַׁת תַּחְתָּיו, אָז גַּם הַבֵּן עַצְמוֹ יִהְיֶה כָּפוּף לְמִי שֶׁשָּׁת תַּחְתָּיו אֶת הַכֹּל, לְמַעַן יִהְיֶה הָאֱלֹהִים הַכֹּל בַּכֹּל.

29 אִם לֹא כֵן, מַה יַּעֲשׂוּ הָאֲנָשִׁים שֶׁנִּטְבָּלִים בְּעַד הַמֵּתִים? אִם אָמְנָם אֵין הַמֵּתִים קָמִים לִתְחִיָּה, לָמָּה הֵם נִטְבָּלִים בַּעֲדָם? 30 וְלָמָּה אֲנַחְנוּ נְתוּנִים בְּסַכָּנָה שָׁעָה שָׁעָה? 31 אָחִי, אֲנִי נִשְׁבָּע בַּגַּאֲוָה שֶׁיֵּשׁ לִי בָּכֶם בַּמָּשִׁיחַ יֵשׁוּעַ אֲדוֹנֵנוּ, כִּי יוֹם יוֹם אֲנִי מֵת. 32 אִם כְּדֶרֶךְ בְּנֵי אָדָם נֶאֱבַקְתִּי בְּאֶפְסוֹס עִם חַיּוֹת רָעוֹת, מַה הַתּוֹעֶלֶת שֶׁתִּצְמַח לִי מִזֶּה? אִם אֵין תְּקוּמַת מֵתִים, הָבָה נֹאכַל וְנִשְׁתֶּה, כִּי מָחָר נָמוּת!

33 Do not be deceived: "Evil company corrupts good habits." 34 Awake to righteousness, and do not sin; for some do not have the knowledge of God. I speak *this* to your shame.

35 But someone will say, "How are the dead raised up? And with what body do they come?" 36 Foolish one, what you sow is not made alive unless it dies. 37 And what you sow, you do not sow that body that shall be, but mere grain—perhaps wheat or some other *grain*. 38 But God gives it a body as He pleases, and to each seed its own body.

39 All flesh *is* not the same flesh, but *there is one kind of* flesh of men, another flesh of animals, another of fish, *and* another of birds.

40 *There are* also celestial bodies and terrestrial bodies; but the glory of the celestial *is* one, and the *glory* of the terrestrial *is* another. 41 *There is* one glory of the sun, another glory of the moon, and another glory of the stars; for *one* star differs from *another* star in glory.

42 So also *is* the resurrection of the dead. *The body* is sown in corruption, it is raised in incorruption. 43 It is sown in dishonor, it is raised in glory. It is sown in weakness, it is raised in power. 44 It is sown a natural body, it is raised a spiritual body. There is a natural body, and there is a spiritual body. 45 And so it is written, *"The first man Adam became a living being."* The last Adam *became* a life-giving spirit.

46 However, the spiritual is not first, but the natural, and afterward the spiritual. 47 The first man *was* of the earth, *made* of dust; the second Man *is* the Lord from heaven. 48 As *was* the *man* of dust, so also *are* those *who are made* of dust; and as *is* the heavenly *Man,* so also *are* those *who are* heavenly. 49 And as we have borne the image of the *man* of dust, we shall also bear the image of the heavenly *Man.*

50 Now this I say, brethren, that flesh and blood cannot inherit the kingdom of God; nor does corruption inherit incorruption. 51 Behold, I tell you a mystery: We shall not all sleep, but we shall all be changed— 52 in a moment, in the twinkling of an eye, at the last trumpet. For the trumpet will sound, and the dead will be raised incorruptible, and we shall be changed. 53 For this corruptible must put on incorruption, and this mortal *must* put on immortality. 54 So when this corruptible has put on incorruption, and this mortal has put on immortality, then shall be brought to pass the saying that is written: *"Death is swallowed up in victory."*

55 *"O Death, where is your sting?*
   O Hades, where is your victory?"

33 אַל תִּטְעוּ: חֶבְרַת אֲנָשִׁים רָעִים תַּשְׁחִית מִדּוֹת טוֹבוֹת. 34 הִתְפַּכְּחוּ לַצֶּדֶק וְאַל תֶּחֱטָאוּ, כִּי יֵשׁ כַּמָּה שֶׁאֵין בָּהֶם דַּעַת אֱלֹהִים; לְבָשְׁתְּכֶם אֲנִי אוֹמֵר זֹאת. 35 "אֲבָל אֵיךְ יָקוּמוּ הַמֵּתִים?" יִשְׁאַל אָחָד, "בְּאֵיזֶה גּוּף הֵם יָבוֹאוּ?" 36 אַתָּה הַסָּכָל, הֵן מַה שֶּׁתִּזְרַע לֹא יִחְיֶה אֶלָּא אִם יָמוּת. 37 כַּאֲשֶׁר אַתָּה זוֹרֵעַ אֵינְךָ זוֹרֵעַ אֶת הַגּוּף שֶׁיִּהְיֶה, אֶלָּא גַּרְגִּיר עֵרוֹם שֶׁל חִטָּה, אוֹ זֶרַע אַחֵר. 38 וֵאלֹהִים נוֹתֵן לוֹ גּוּף כִּרְצוֹן אֱלֹהִים, וּלְכָל זֶרַע אֶת גּוּפוֹ הוּא. 39 לֹא כָּל בָּשָׂר הוּא אוֹתוֹ הַבָּשָׂר; לָאָדָם בָּשָׂר מִשֶּׁלּוֹ, לַחַיּוֹת בָּשָׂר אַחֵר, לָעוֹפוֹת בָּשָׂר אַחֵר וְלַדָּגִים אַחֵר. 40 יֵשׁ גּוּפִים שְׁמֵימִיִּים וְגוּפִים אַרְצִיִּים, אַךְ שׁוֹנֶה הוּא הֲדַר הַגּוּפִים הַשְּׁמֵימִיִּים מֵהֲדַר הַגּוּפִים הָאַרְצִיִּים. 41 לַשֶּׁמֶשׁ הֲדַר מִשֶּׁלָּה, אֲבָל אַחֵר הוּא הֲדַר הַיָּרֵחַ וְאַחֵר הוּא הֲדַר הַכּוֹכָבִים, שֶׁהֲרֵי כּוֹכָב מִכּוֹכָב שׁוֹנֶה בַּהֲדָרוֹ. 42 כֵּן גַּם תְּחִיַּת הַמֵּתִים: מַה שֶּׁנִּזְרַע בְּמַצָּב שֶׁל כִּלָּיוֹן יָקוּם בְּאִי כִּלָּיוֹן; 43 נִזְרַע בְּקָלוֹן וְיָקוּם בְּכָבוֹד; נִזְרַע בַּחֲלָשָׁה וְיָקוּם בִּגְבוּרָה; 44 נִזְרַע גּוּף נַפְשִׁי וְיָקוּם גּוּף רוּחָנִי. אִם יֵשׁ גּוּף נַפְשִׁי יֵשׁ גַּם גּוּף רוּחָנִי. 45 וְכֵן כָּתוּב עַל אָדָם הָרִאשׁוֹן: "וַיְהִי הָאָדָם לְנֶפֶשׁ חַיָּה", אֲבָל אָדָם הָאַחֲרוֹן – לְרוּחַ מְחַיָּה. 46 לֹא הָרוּחָנִי הוּא הָרִאשׁוֹן, אֶלָּא הַנַּפְשִׁי, וְאַחֲרֵי כֵן הָרוּחָנִי. 47 הָאָדָם הָרִאשׁוֹן הוּא עָפָר מִן הָאֲדָמָה; הָאָדָם הַשֵּׁנִי מִן הַשָּׁמַיִם הוּא. 48 כְּאָחָד שֶׁהוּא עָפָר כֵּן גַּם אֵלֶּה אֲשֶׁר עָפָר הֵם; כְּאָחָד שֶׁהוּא שְׁמֵימִי כֵּן גַּם אֵלֶּה אֲשֶׁר שְׁמֵימִיִּים הֵם. 49 וּכְמוֹ שֶׁלָּבַשְׁנוּ אֶת צַלְמוֹ שֶׁל הָאַרְצִי נִלְבַּשׁ גַּם אֶת צֶלֶם הַשְּׁמֵימִי. 50 אוֹמֵר זֹאת, אַחַי: בָּשָׂר וָדָם אֵינוֹ יָכוֹל לָרֶשֶׁת אֶת מַלְכוּת הָאֱלֹהִים; גַּם אֵין הַכִּלָּיוֹן יוֹרֵשׁ אַל-כִּלָּיוֹן. 51 הִנֵּה רָז אַגִּיד לָכֶם: לֹא כֻּלָּנוּ נָמוּת, אֲבָל כֻּלָּנוּ נִשְׁתַּנֶּה 52 בֶּן רֶגַע וּכְהֶרֶף עַיִן בַּשּׁוֹפָר הָאַחֲרוֹן, שֶׁכֵּן יִתָּקַע בַּשּׁוֹפָר וְהַמֵּתִים יָקוּמוּ בְּלִי כִּלָּיוֹן וַאֲנַחְנוּ נִשְׁתַּנֶּה. 53 כִּי מִן הָרָאוּי שֶׁזֶּה הַכָּפוּף לְכִלָּיוֹן יִלְבַּשׁ אַל-כִּלָּיוֹן וְזֶה הַכָּפוּף לָמוּת יִלְבַּשׁ אַלְמָוֶת. 54 וְכַאֲשֶׁר הַכָּפוּף לְכִלָּיוֹן יִלְבַּשׁ אַל-כִּלָּיוֹן וְהַכָּפוּף לָמוּת יִלְבַּשׁ אַלְמָוֶת, אָז יִתְקַיֵּם דְּבַר הַכָּתוּב: "בֻּלַּע הַמָּוֶת לָנֶצַח." 55 "אַיֵּה עָקְצְךָ מָוֶת? אַיֵּה נִצְחוֹנְךָ

56 The sting of death *is* sin, and the strength of sin *is* the law. 57 But thanks *be* to God, who gives us the victory through our Lord Jesus Christ.

58 Therefore, my beloved brethren, be steadfast, immovable, always abounding in the work of the Lord, knowing that your labor is not in vain in the Lord.

16 Now concerning the collection for the saints, as I have given orders to the churches of Galatia, so you must do also: 2 On the first *day* of the week let each one of you lay something aside, storing up as he may prosper, that there be no collections when I come. 3 And when I come, whomever you approve by *your* letters I will send to bear your gift to Jerusalem. 4 But if it is fitting that I go also, they will go with me.

5 Now I will come to you when I pass through Macedonia (for I am passing through Macedonia). 6 And it may be that I will remain, or even spend the winter with you, that you may send me on my journey, wherever I go. 7 For I do not wish to see you now on the way; but I hope to stay a while with you, if the Lord permits.

8 But I will tarry in Ephesus until Pentecost. 9 For a great and effective door has opened to me, and *there are* many adversaries.

10 And if Timothy comes, see that he may be with you without fear; for he does the work of the Lord, as I also *do*. 11 Therefore let no one despise him. But send him on his journey in peace, that he may come to me; for I am waiting for him with the brethren.

12 Now concerning *our* brother Apollos, I strongly urged him to come to you with the brethren, but he was quite unwilling to come at this time; however, he will come when he has a convenient time.

13 Watch, stand fast in the faith, be brave, be strong. 14 Let all *that* you *do* be done with love.

15 I urge you, brethren—you know the household of Stephanas, that it is the firstfruits of Achaia, and *that* they have devoted themselves to the ministry of the saints— 16 that you also submit to such, and to everyone who works and labors with *us*.

17 I am glad about the coming of Stephanas, Fortunatus, and Achaicus, for what was lacking on your part they supplied. 18 For they refreshed my spirit and yours. Therefore acknowledge such men.

19 The churches of Asia greet you. Aquila and Priscilla greet you heartily in the Lord, with the church that is in their house. 20 All the brethren greet you.

Greet one another with a holy kiss.

מָוֶת?" 56 עֹקֶץ הַמָּוֶת הוּא הַחֵטְא, וְהַחֵטְא תָּקְפּוֹ בָּא מִן הַתּוֹרָה. 57 אֲבָל תּוֹדָה לֵאלֹהִים הַנּוֹתֵן לָנוּ אֶת הַנִּצָּחוֹן עַל־יְדֵי אֲדוֹנֵנוּ יֵשׁוּעַ הַמָּשִׁיחַ. 58 עַל כֵּן, אַחַי הָאֲהוּבִים, עִמְדוּ הֵיטֵב וְהִיוּ צַיָּבִים; הֱיוּ תָמִיד עַתִּירֵי פֹעַל בַּעֲבוֹדָתוֹ שֶׁל הָאָדוֹן, בִּידִיעָה שֶׁעֲמָלְכֶם אֵינֶנּוּ לָרִיק בָּאָדוֹן.

טז בְּעִנְיַן אֹסוּף הַתְּרוּמוֹת לְעֶזְרַת הַקְּדוֹשִׁים, כְּפִי שֶׁהוֹרֵיתִי לַקְּהִלּוֹת בְּגָלַטְיָה כֵּן עֲשׂוּ גַם אַתֶּם. 2 מִדֵּי רִאשׁוֹן בַּשָּׁבוּעַ יַנִּיחַ כָּל אֶחָד מִכֶּם תְּרוּמָה כְּפִי שֶׁיָּדוֹ מַשֶּׂגֶת וְיִשְׁמְרֶה אֶצְלוֹ, כְּדֵי שֶׁלֹּא יִתְחִילוּ בְּאֹסוּף הַתְּרוּמוֹת בְּעֵת בּוֹאִי. 3 וְכַאֲשֶׁר אָבוֹא אֶשְׁלַח אֶת הָאֲנָשִׁים הַטּוֹבִים בְּעֵינֵיכֶם עִם אִגְּרוֹת בְּיָדָם לְהָבִיא אֶת תְּרוּמַתְכֶם לִירוּשָׁלַיִם. 4 אִם יִמָּצֵא לָנָכוֹן שֶׁגַם אֲנִי אֵלֵךְ, יֵלְכוּ אִתִּי.

5 אָבוֹא אֲלֵיכֶם אַחֲרֵי שֶׁאֶעֱבֹר בְּמָקֶדוֹנְיָה, כִּי אֲנִי עוֹבֵר דֶּרֶךְ מָקֶדוֹנְיָה. 6 אוּלַי אֶשְׁהֶה אֶצְלְכֶם, אוּלַי אֲפִלּוּ בְּמֶשֶׁךְ כָּל הַחֹרֶף, וּלְאַחַר מִכֵּן תְּשַׁלְּחוּנִי לְהֵיכָן שֶׁעָלַי לָלֶכֶת. 7 אֵינֶנִּי חָפֵץ לִרְאוֹת אֶתְכֶם כָּעֵת כְּעוֹבֵר אֹרַח; אֲנִי מְקַוֶּה לִהְיוֹת זְמַן מָה אֶצְלְכֶם, אִם יִרְצֶה הָאָדוֹן. 8 אֲבָל אֶתְעַכֵּב בְּאֶפֶסוֹס עַד חַג הַשָּׁבוּעוֹת, 9 כִּי נִפְתַּח לִי פֶּתַח רָחָב לִפְעֻלָּה פּוֹרִיָּה, וְרַבִּים הַמִּתְנַגְּדִים.

10 אִם טִימוֹתֵאוֹס יָבוֹא, דַּאֲגוּ לְכָךְ שֶׁיֵּשֵׁב עִמָּכֶם בְּלֹא חֲשָׁשׁוֹת, שֶׁכֵּן הוּא עָסוּק בַּעֲבוֹדָתוֹ שֶׁל הָאָדוֹן כָּמוֹנִי. 11 אִישׁ אַל יָקֵל רֹאשׁ כְּנֶגְדּוֹ, אֶלָּא שַׁלְּחוּ אוֹתוֹ בְּשָׁלוֹם לָבוֹא אֵלַי, כִּי אֲנִי מְחַכֶּה לוֹ וְלָאַחִים אֲשֶׁר אִתּוֹ.

12 בְּנוֹגֵעַ לְאָחִינוּ אַפּוֹלוֹס, הִפְצַרְתִּי בּוֹ הַרְבֵּה שֶׁיָּבוֹא אֲלֵיכֶם עִם הָאַחִים, אַךְ בְּשׁוּם פָּנִים לֹא רָצָה לָבוֹא עַתָּה. הוּא יָבוֹא כַּאֲשֶׁר תִּהְיֶה לוֹ הַזְדַּמְּנוּת.

13 שִׁקְדוּ, עִמְדוּ בָּאֱמוּנָה, חִזְקוּ וְאִמְצוּ. 14 אֶת כָּל מַעֲשֵׂיכֶם עֲשׂוּ בְּאַהֲבָה.

15 וַאֲנִי מְבַקֵּשׁ מִכֶּם, אַחַי: אַתֶּם מַכִּירִים אֶת מִשְׁפַּחַת סְטֶפָנָס; הֲרֵי הֵם רִאשׁוֹנֵי הַמַּאֲמִינִים בְּאָכָיָה וְאַף קִבְּלוּ עַל עַצְמָם לְשָׁרֵת אֶת הַקְּדוֹשִׁים. 16 לָכֵן גַּם אַתֶּם הִשָּׁמְעוּ לַאֲנָשִׁים כָּאֵלֶּה וּלְכָל מִי שֶׁעוֹבֵד וְעָמֵל עִמָּהֶם. 17 שָׂמֵחַ אֲנִי עַל בּוֹאָם שֶׁל סְטֶפָנָס וּפוֹרְטוּנָטוֹס וַאֲכָיְקוֹס, כִּי הֵם הָיוּ לִי לְפִצּוּי עַל חֶסְרוֹנְכֶם 18 וְהִרְגִּיעוּ אֶת רוּחִי וְאֶת רוּחֲכֶם. לָכֵן הֱיוּ מוֹקִירִים אֲנָשִׁים כָּאֵלֶּה.

19 הַקְּהִלּוֹת אֲשֶׁר בְּאַסְיָה דּוֹרְשׁוֹת בִּשְׁלוֹמְכֶם. עֲקִילָס וּפְרִיסְקִלָּה עִם הַקָּהִלָּה אֲשֶׁר בְּבֵיתָם מוֹסְרִים לָכֶם בִּרְכַּת שָׁלוֹם רַב בָּאָדוֹן. 20 הָאַחִים כֻּלָּם דּוֹרְשִׁים בִּשְׁלוֹמְכֶם. בִּרְכוּ לְשָׁלוֹם אִישׁ אֶת רֵעֵהוּ בִּנְשִׁיקָה קְדוֹשָׁה.

²¹ The salutation with my own hand—Paul's.

²² If anyone does not love the Lord Jesus Christ, let him be accursed. O Lord, come!

²³ The grace of our Lord Jesus Christ *be* with you. ²⁴ My love *be* with you all in Christ Jesus. Amen.

²¹ אֲנִי שָׁאוּל שׁוֹלֵחַ לָכֶם בִּרְכַּת שָׁלוֹם בִּכְתָב יָדִי. ²² מִי שֶׁאֵינֶנּוּ אוֹהֵב אֶת הָאָדוֹן, חֵרֶם יִהְיֶה! מָרָנָא תָא! ²³ חֶסֶד הָאָדוֹן יֵשׁוּעַ עִמָּכֶם. ²⁴ אַהֲבָתִי אֶל כֻּלְּכֶם בַּמָּשִׁיחַ יֵשׁוּעַ.

CORINTHIANS

1 Paul, an apostle of Jesus Christ by the will of God, and Timothy *our* brother,

To the church of God which is at Corinth, with all the saints who are in all Achaia:

2 Grace to you and peace from God our Father and the Lord Jesus Christ.

3 Blessed *be* the God and Father of our Lord Jesus Christ, the Father of mercies and God of all comfort, 4 who comforts us in all our tribulation, that we may be able to comfort those who are in any trouble, with the comfort with which we ourselves are comforted by God. 5 For as the sufferings of Christ abound in us, so our consolation also abounds through Christ. 6 Now if we are afflicted, *it is* for your consolation and salvation, which is effective for enduring the same sufferings which we also suffer. Or if we are comforted, *it is* for your consolation and salvation. 7 And our hope for you *is* steadfast, because we know that as you are partakers of the sufferings, so also *you will partake* of the consolation.

8 For we do not want you to be ignorant, brethren, of our trouble which came to us in Asia: that we were burdened beyond measure, above strength, so that we despaired even of life. 9 Yes, we had the sentence of death in ourselves, that we should not trust in ourselves but in God who raises the dead, 10 who delivered us from so great a death, and does deliver us; in whom we trust that He will still deliver *us*, 11 you also helping together in prayer for us, that thanks may be given by many persons on our behalf for the gift *granted* to us through many.

12 For our boasting is this: the testimony of our conscience that we conducted ourselves in the world in simplicity and godly sincerity, not with fleshly wisdom but by the grace of God, and more abundantly toward you. 13 For we are not writing any other things to you than what you read or understand. Now I trust you will understand, even to the end 14 (as also you have understood us in part), that we are your boast as you also *are* ours, in the day of the Lord Jesus.

15 And in this confidence I intended to come to you before, that you might have a second benefit—16 to pass by way of you to Macedonia, to come again from Macedonia to you, and be helped by

אִגֶּרֶת שָׁאוּל הַשְּׁנִיָּה אֶל הַקּוֹרִינְתִים

א מֵאֵת שָׁאוּל, שְׁלִיחַ הַמָּשִׁיחַ יֵשׁוּעַ עַל-פִּי רְצוֹן אֱלֹהִים, וּמֵאֵת הָאָח טִימוֹתִיאוֹם, אֶל קְהִלַּת אֱלֹהִים אֲשֶׁר בְּקוֹרִינְתּוֹס וּלְכָל הַקְּדוֹשִׁים אֲשֶׁר בְּאָכְיָה: 2 חֶסֶד וְשָׁלוֹם לָכֶם מֵאֵת הָאֱלֹהִים אָבִינוּ וְהָאָדוֹן יֵשׁוּעַ הַמָּשִׁיחַ.

3 בָּרוּךְ הָאֱלֹהִים אֲבִי אֲדוֹנֵנוּ יֵשׁוּעַ הַמָּשִׁיחַ, אַב הָרַחֲמִים וֵאלֹהֵי כָּל נֶחָמָה, 4 הַמְנַחֵם אוֹתָנוּ בְּכָל צָרוֹתֵינוּ בְּאֹפֶן שֶׁנּוּכַל לְנַחֵם אֶת הַלְּחוּצִים בְּכָל צָרָה שֶׁהִיא – בַּנֶּחָמָה שֶׁנְּחַמְנוּ אָנוּ מֵאֵת אֱלֹהִים; 5 כִּי כְּשֵׁם שֶׁשּׁוֹפְעִים בָּנוּ סִבְלוֹת הַמָּשִׁיחַ, כֵּן גַּם שׁוֹפַעַת נֶחָמָתֵנוּ עַל-יְדֵי הַמָּשִׁיחַ. 6 וְאִם אֲנַחְנוּ סוֹבְלִים, הֲרֵי זֶה לְמַעַן נֶחָמַתְכֶם וִישׁוּעַתְכֶם; אִם אֲנַחְנוּ מְנֻחָמִים, הֲרֵי זֶה לְמַעַן נֶחָמַתְכֶם, כְּדֵי שֶׁתּוּכְלוּ לְהַחֲזִיק מַעֲמָד בְּאוֹתָן הַצָּרוֹת שֶׁגַּם אֲנַחְנוּ סוֹבְלִים. 7 וְתִקְוָתֵנוּ עַל-אוֹדוֹתֵיכֶם אֵיתָנָה הִיא, בְּיָדְעֵנוּ כִּי כְּשֵׁם שֶׁאַתֶּם שֻׁתָּפִים לַצָּרוֹת, כֵּן גַּם שֻׁתָּפִים אַתֶּם לַנֶּחָמָה.

8 אַחִים, אֵינֶנּוּ רוֹצִים שֶׁיֵּעָלֵם מִכֶּם דְּבַר הַצָּרָה שֶׁעָבְרָה עָלֵינוּ בְּאַסְיָה; נִלְחַצְנוּ לְלֹא נְשׂוֹא, עַד כְּדֵי כָּךְ שֶׁנּוֹאַשְׁנוּ אֲפִלּוּ מֵחַיֵּינוּ. 9 פְּסַק דִּין מָוֶת קָנֵן בְּתוֹכֵנוּ, וְזֹאת כְּדֵי שֶׁלֹּא נִבְטַח בְּעַצְמֵנוּ, אֶלָּא בֵּאלֹהִים הַמְחַיֶּה אֶת הַמֵּתִים; 10 הוּא הִצִּילָנוּ מִמָּוֶת חָמוּר כָּל כָּךְ וְעוֹד יָשׁוּב וְיַצִּילֵנוּ; בּוֹ אָנוּ תוֹלִים תִּקְוָתֵנוּ כִּי יוֹסִיף לְהַצִּילֵנוּ. 11 גַּם אַתֶּם הִשְׁתַּתְּפוּ בִּתְפִלָּה בַּעֲדֵנוּ, כְּדֵי שֶׁרַבִּים יוֹדוּ בִּגְלָלֵנוּ עַל מַתְּנַת הַחֶסֶד שֶׁנִּתְּנָה לָנוּ בִּזְכוּת רַבִּים.

12 זֹאת הִיא גַאֲוָתֵנוּ: עֵדוּת מַצְפּוּנֵנוּ כִּי הִתְנַהַגְנוּ בָּעוֹלָם, וּבְעִקָּר כְּלַפֵּיכֶם, בִּקְדֻשָּׁה וּבְיֹשֶׁר אֱלֹהִים – לֹא בְּחָכְמַת בָּשָׂר-וָדָם, אֶלָּא בְּחֶסֶד אֱלֹהִים. 13 אֵינֶנּוּ כּוֹתְבִים לָכֶם דְּבָרִים שׁוֹנִים מִמַּה שֶׁאַתֶּם קוֹרְאִים וְגַם מַכִּירִים. וַאֲנִי מְקַוֶּה שֶׁתַּכִּירוּ בָּנוּ לַחֲלוּטִין, 14 כְּמוֹ שֶׁגַּם הִכַּרְתֶּם בְּאֹפֶן חֶלְקִי, שֶׁאֲנַחְנוּ תְּהִלַּתְכֶם כְּשֵׁם שֶׁגַּם אַתֶּם תְּהִלָּתֵנוּ בְּיוֹם אֲדוֹנֵנוּ יֵשׁוּעַ.

15 מִתּוֹךְ בִּטָּחוֹן זֶה רָצִיתִי לָבוֹא קֹדֶם כֹּל אֲלֵיכֶם, לְמַעַן תִּהְיֶה עֲלֵיכֶם בִּרְכַּת חֶסֶד פַּעַם שְׁנִיָּה, 16 וּמִכֶּם לְהַמְשִׁיךְ אֶת דַּרְכִּי אֶל מָקֵדוֹנְיָה,

you on my way to Judea. [17] Therefore, when I was planning this, did I do it lightly? Or the things I plan, do I plan according to the flesh, that with me there should be Yes, Yes, and No, No? [18] But *as* God *is* faithful, our word to you was not Yes and No. [19] For the Son of God, Jesus Christ, who was preached among you by us—by me, Silvanus, and Timothy—was not Yes and No, but in Him was Yes. [20] For all the promises of God in Him *are* Yes, and in Him Amen, to the glory of God through us. [21] Now He who establishes us with you in Christ and has anointed us *is* God, [22] who also has sealed us and given us the Spirit in our hearts as a guarantee.

[23] Moreover I call God as witness against my soul, that to spare you I came no more to Corinth. [24] Not that we have dominion over your faith, but are fellow workers for your joy; for by faith you stand.

2 But I determined this within myself, that I would not come again to you in sorrow. [2] For if I make you sorrowful, then who is he who makes me glad but the one who is made sorrowful by me?

[3] And I wrote this very thing to you, lest, when I came, I should have sorrow over those from whom I ought to have joy, having confidence in you all that my joy is *the* joy of you all. [4] For out of much affliction and anguish of heart I wrote to you, with many tears, not that you should be grieved, but that you might know the love which I have so abundantly for you.

[5] But if anyone has caused grief, he has not grieved me, but all of you to some extent—not to be too severe. [6] This punishment which *was inflicted* by the majority *is* sufficient for such a man, [7] so that, on the contrary, you *ought* rather to forgive and comfort *him*, lest perhaps such a one be swallowed up with too much sorrow. [8] Therefore I urge you to reaffirm *your* love to him. [9] For to this end I also wrote, that I might put you to the test, whether you are obedient in all things. [10] Now whom you forgive anything, I also *forgive*. For if indeed I have forgiven anything, I have forgiven that one for your sakes in the presence of Christ, [11] lest Satan should take advantage of us; for we are not ignorant of his devices.

[12] Furthermore, when I came to Troas to *preach* Christ's gospel, and a door was opened to me by the Lord, [13] I had no rest in my spirit, because I did not find Titus my brother; but taking my leave of them, I departed for Macedonia.

וּמִמָּקֶדוֹנְיָה לַחֲזֹר אֲלֵיכֶם, וְאַחֲרֵי כֵן שֶׁתְּשַׁלְּחוּנִי לְאֶרֶץ יְהוּדָה. [17] כְּשֶׁהִתְחַלַּטְתִּי כָּךְ, כְּלוּם נָהַגְתִּי בְּקַלּוּת דַּעַת? וּמַה שֶּׁאֲנִי מַחְלִיט, הַאִם עַל־פִּי מַחְשֶׁבֶת בָּשָׂר־וָדָם אֲנִי מַחְלִיט, בְּאֹפֶן שֶׁאוּכַל לְהַחֲזִיק בְּ"כֵּן כֵּן" וְ"לֹא לֹא", בְּבַת אַחַת? [18] נֶאֱמָן הָאֱלֹהִים שֶׁדְּבָרֵנוּ אֲלֵיכֶם אֵינֶנּוּ "כֵּן וְלֹא", [19] שֶׁהֲרֵי בֶּן־הָאֱלֹהִים הַמָּשִׁיחַ יֵשׁוּעַ, שֶׁאֲנִי וְסִילְוָנוֹס וְטִימוֹתִיאוֹס הִכְרַזְנוּ עָלָיו בְּקִרְבְּכֶם, לֹא הָיָה "כֵּן וְלֹא", אֶלָּא "כֵּן" הָיָה בּוֹ; [20] כִּי כָּל הַבְטָחוֹת אֱלֹהִים "כֵּן" הֵן בּוֹ. לָכֵן הָ"אָמֵן" שֶׁאָנוּ נוֹתְנִים בּוֹ כָּבוֹד לֵאלֹהִים גַּם הוּא בְּאֶמְצָעוּתוֹ. [21] וֵאלֹהִים הוּא הַמְכוֹנֵן אוֹתָנוּ עִמָּכֶם בַּמָּשִׁיחַ. הוּא מָשַׁח אוֹתָנוּ, [22] וְהוּא אֲשֶׁר גַּם חָתַם אוֹתָנוּ בְּחוֹתָמוֹ וְשָׂם בְּלִבֵּנוּ אֶת הָעֵרָבוֹן שֶׁל הָרוּחַ.

[23] אֲנִי קוֹרֵא לֵאלֹהִים לְהָעִיד עָלַי, שֶׁחַסְתִּי עֲלֵיכֶם וְלָכֵן לֹא בָּאתִי עוֹד פַּעַם לְקוֹרִינְתּוֹס. [24] לֹא שֶׁאֲדוֹנִים אָנוּ עַל אֱמוּנַתְכֶם, אֶלָּא פּוֹעֲלִים אָנוּ אִתְּכֶם לְמַעַן שִׂמְחַתְכֶם, שֶׁכֵּן בָּאֱמוּנָה אַתֶּם יַצִּיבִים.

ב גָּמַרְתִּי אֹמֶר בְּלִבִּי שֶׁלֹּא אָבוֹא עוֹד לְצַעֵר אֶתְכֶם; [2] שֶׁהֲרֵי אִם אֲצַעֵר אֶתְכֶם, מִי יְשַׂמַּח אוֹתִי מִלְּבַד מִי שֶׁעֲצָרַמְתִּי לוֹ צַעַר? [3] כָּתַבְתִּי אֶת הַדָּבָר הַזֶּה כְּדֵי שֶׁבְּבוֹאִי לֹא יְצַעֲרוּנִי אֵלֶּה אֲשֶׁר צָרִיךְ הָיִיתִי לִשְׂמֹחַ בָּהֶם, וּבוֹטֵחַ אֲנִי בְּכֻלְּכֶם שֶׁשִּׂמְחָתִי הִיא שִׂמְחַת כֻּלְּכֶם. [4] כָּתַבְתִּי לָכֶם מִתּוֹךְ מְצוּקָה רַבָּה וְעָגְמַת לֵב וּבְדִמְעוֹת רַבּוֹת, לֹא כְּדֵי לְצַעֵר אֶתְכֶם, אֶלָּא כְּדֵי שֶׁתֵּדְעוּ מָה רַבָּה אַהֲבָתִי אֲלֵיכֶם. [5] וְאִם מִישֶׁהוּ גָּרַם צַעַר, הֲרֵי לֹא אוֹתִי צִעֵר, אֶלָּא אֶת כֻּלְּכֶם – לְפָחוֹת בְּמִדַּת מָה, כְּדֵי שֶׁלֹּא לְהַגְזִים. [6] דַּי לוֹ לָאִישׁ כֹּה הַתּוֹכֵחָה הַזֹּאת מֵאֵת הָרַבִּים. [7] וּבְכֵן, לְהֶפֶךְ, עָדִיף שֶׁתִּסְלְחוּ לוֹ וּתְנַחֲמוּהוּ, לְמַעַן לֹא יִתְמוֹטֵט הָאִישׁ מֵרֹב צַעַר. [8] עַל כֵּן אֲנִי מְבַקֵּשׁ מִכֶּם שֶׁתּוֹכִיחוּ לוֹ אֶת אַהֲבַתְכֶם. [9] לְשֵׁם כָּךְ גַּם כָּתַבְתִּי, לְהִוָּכַח אִם מְצַיְּתִים אַתֶּם בְּכָל הַדְּבָרִים. [10] וְאִישׁ אֲשֶׁר תִּסְלְחוּ לוֹ עַל אֵיזֶה דָּבָר, גַּם אֲנִי אֶסְלַח לוֹ; כִּי גַּם מַה שֶּׁאֲנִי סָלַחְתִּי, אִם סָלַחְתִּי עַל דְּבַר מָה, הֲרֵי סָלַחְתִּי לְמַעַנְכֶם לְנֹכַח הַמָּשִׁיחַ, [11] כְּדֵי שֶׁלֹּא יַעֲרִים עָלֵינוּ הַשָּׂטָן, שֶׁכֵּן מְזִמּוֹתָיו לֹא נֶעְלְמוּ מֵאִתָּנוּ.

[12] כַּאֲשֶׁר בָּאתִי לִטְרוֹאָס לְבַשֵּׂר אֶת בְּשׂוֹרַת הַמָּשִׁיחַ גַּם נִפְתַּח לִי פֶּתַח מִטַּעַם הָאָדוֹן, [13] אַךְ לֹא הָיָה מָנוֹחַ לְרוּחִי מִפְּנֵי שֶׁלֹּא מָצָאתִי אֶת טִיטוֹס אָחִי. אָז

14 Now thanks *be* to God who always leads us in triumph in Christ, and through us diffuses the fragrance of His knowledge in every place. 15 For we are to God the fragrance of Christ among those who are being saved and among those who are perishing. 16 To the one *we are* the aroma of death *leading* to death, and to the other the aroma of life *leading* to life. And who *is* sufficient for these things? 17 For we are not, as so many, peddling the word of God; but as of sincerity, but as from God, we speak in the sight of God in Christ.

3 Do we begin again to commend ourselves? Or do we need, as some *others,* epistles of commendation to you or *letters* of commendation from you? 2 You are our epistle written in our hearts, known and read by all men; 3 clearly *you are* an epistle of Christ, ministered by us, written not with ink but by the Spirit of the living God, not on tablets of stone but on tablets of flesh, *that is,* of the heart.

4 And we have such trust through Christ toward God. 5 Not that we are sufficient of ourselves to think of anything as *being* from ourselves, but our sufficiency *is* from God, 6 who also made us sufficient as ministers of the new covenant, not of the letter but of the Spirit; for the letter kills, but the Spirit gives life.

7 But if the ministry of death, written *and* engraved on stones, was glorious, so that the children of Israel could not look steadily at the face of Moses because of the glory of his countenance, which *glory* was passing away, 8 how will the ministry of the Spirit not be more glorious? 9 For if the ministry of condemnation *had* glory, the ministry of righteousness exceeds much more in glory. 10 For even what was made glorious had no glory in this respect, because of the glory that excels. 11 For if what is passing away *was* glorious, what remains *is* much more glorious.

12 Therefore, since we have such hope, we use great boldness of speech— 13 unlike Moses, *who* put a veil over his face so that the children of Israel could not look steadily at the end of what was passing away. 14 But their minds were blinded. For until this day the same veil remains unlifted in the reading of the Old Testament, because the *veil* is taken away in Christ. 15 But even to this day, when Moses is read, a veil lies on their heart. 16 Nevertheless when one turns to the Lord, the veil is taken away. 17 Now the Lord is the Spirit; and where the Spirit of the Lord *is,* there *is* liberty. 18 But we all, with unveiled face, beholding as in a mirror the

נִפְרַדְתִּי מֵהֶם וְיָצָאתִי אֶל מַקְדּוֹנְיָה. 14 אֲבָל תּוֹדָה לָאלֹהִים הַמּוֹבִיל אוֹתָנוּ בְּמַסַּע נִצָּחוֹן בַּמָּשִׁיחַ וּמֵפִיץ עַל-יָדֵינוּ אֶת נִיחוֹחַ דַּעַת אֱלֹהִים בְּכָל מָקוֹם. 15 הֲלֹא נִיחוֹחַ הַמָּשִׁיחַ אֲנַחְנוּ לֵאלֹהִים, בְּקֶרֶב הַנּוֹשָׁעִים וּבְקֶרֶב הָאוֹבְדִים; 16 לָאַחֲרוֹנִים רֵיחַ שֶׁל מָוֶת אֱלֵי מָוֶת, לָרִאשׁוֹנִים רֵיחַ שֶׁל חַיִּים אֱלֵי חַיִּים. וּמִי הָרָאוּי לְכָךְ? 17 הֲרֵי אֵין אָנוּ כְּמוֹ הָרַבִּים הָעוֹשִׂים מִסְחָר בִּדְבַר אֱלֹהִים, אֶלָּא לְנֶגֶד עֵינֵי אֱלֹהִים, בְּיֹשֶׁר לֵב וּמִטַּעַם אֱלֹהִים, בַּמָּשִׁיחַ אָנוּ מְדַבְּרִים.

ג הַאִם נַתְחִיל שׁוּב לְשַׁבֵּחַ אֶת עַצְמֵנוּ? אוֹ שֶׁמָּא זְקוּקִים אָנוּ, כַּאֲחֵרִים, לְאִגְּרוֹת שֶׁבַח אֲלֵיכֶם אוֹ מִכֶּם? 2 הֲרֵי אַתֶּם אִגַּרְתֵּנוּ הַכְּתוּבָה בְּלִבֵּנוּ, וְכָל אָדָם מַכִּיר אוֹתָהּ וְקוֹרֵא אוֹתָהּ. 3 רוֹאִים בְּבֵרוּר שֶׁאַתֶּם אִגֶּרֶת הַמָּשִׁיחַ הַנֶּעֱרֶכֶת עַל-יָדֵינוּ – כְּתוּבָה לֹא בִּדְיוֹ, אֶלָּא בְּרוּחַ אֱלֹהִים חַיִּים, לֹא עַל לוּחוֹת אֶבֶן, אֶלָּא עַל לוּחוֹת שֶׁל לֵב בָּשָׂר.

4 וּבִגְלַל הַמָּשִׁיחַ יֵשׁ לָנוּ בִּטָּחוֹן כָּזֶה בֵּאלֹהִים. 5 לֹא שֶׁאֲנַחְנוּ בְּעַצְמֵנוּ מֻכְשָׁרִים בְּאֹפֶן שֶׁנַּחֲשֹׁב כְּאִלּוּ מַשֶּׁהוּ נוֹבֵעַ מֵעַצְמֵנוּ, אֶלָּא שֶׁכִּשְׁרוֹנֵנוּ בָּא מֵאֵת אֱלֹהִים. 6 הוּא הִכְשִׁיר אוֹתָנוּ לִהְיוֹת מְשָׁרְתִים שֶׁל בְּרִית חֲדָשָׁה, לֹא שֶׁל אוֹת כְּתוּבָה, אֶלָּא שֶׁל הָרוּחַ; שֶׁכֵּן הָאוֹת מְמִיתָה, אֲבָל הָרוּחַ מְחַיָּה.

7 וְאִם שֵׁרוּת שֶׁל מִשְׁטַר הַמָּוֶת, הֶחָקוּק אוֹתִיּוֹת בָּאֶבֶן, נִמְלָא כָּבוֹד עַד כְּדֵי כָּךְ שֶׁבְּנֵי יִשְׂרָאֵל לֹא יָכְלוּ לְהַבִּיט אֶל פְּנֵי מֹשֶׁה בִּגְלַל זִיו פָּנָיו הַחוֹלֵף, 8 הַאִם שֵׁרוּת שֶׁל מִשְׁטַר הָרוּחַ לֹא יִמָּלֵא כָּבוֹד עַל אַחַת כַּמָּה וְכַמָּה? 9 הֲרֵי אִם שֵׁרוּת הָרִשְׁעָה לוֹבֵשׁ כָּבוֹד, כָּל שֶׁכֵּן מַרְבֶּה לְהִתְעַלּוֹת בִּכְבוֹד שֵׁרוּת הַצְּדָקָה! 10 הֵן אֲפִלּוּ מַה שֶּׁלָּבַשׁ כָּבוֹד, כְּבוֹדוֹ הָיָה לְאַיִן בִּגְלַל הַכָּבוֹד הַנַּעֲלֶה יוֹתֵר. 11 וְאִם מַה שֶּׁבָּטֵל לָבַשׁ כָּבוֹד, הַבִּלְתִּי חוֹלֵף נִכְבָּד עַל אַחַת כַּמָּה וְכַמָּה!

12 וּבְכֵן בִּהְיוֹת לָנוּ תִּקְוָה כָּזֹאת, יֶתֶר עֹז לָנוּ. 13 וְאֵין אָנוּ כְּמֹשֶׁה שֶׁשָּׂם מַסְוֶה עַל פָּנָיו כְּדֵי שֶׁבְּנֵי יִשְׂרָאֵל לֹא יִתְבּוֹנְנוּ אֶל קֵץ הַדָּבָר הַמִּתְבַּטֵּל. 14 בְּרַם לְבוֹתֵיהֶם קָהוּ, כִּי עַד הַיּוֹם הַזֶּה בְּקָרְאָם בַּבְּרִית הַיְשָׁנָה נִשְׁאָר אוֹתוֹ הַמַּסְוֶה בִּלְתִּי מֻסְלָק, שֶׁכֵּן בַּמָּשִׁיחַ הוּא מִתְבַּטֵּל. 15 עַד הַיּוֹם הַזֶּה, כַּאֲשֶׁר הֵם קוֹרְאִים אֶת דִּבְרֵי מֹשֶׁה, הַמַּסְוֶה מֻנָּח עַל לִבָּם. 16 אַךְ כַּאֲשֶׁר יִפְנֶה לִבָּם אֶל הָאָדוֹן יוּסַר הַמַּסְוֶה. 17 הָאָדוֹן הוּא הָרוּחַ וּבַאֲשֶׁר רוּחַ הָאָדוֹן שָׁם הַחֵרוּת. 18 אֲבָל אֲנַחְנוּ כֻּלָּנוּ בְּפָנִים מְגֻלִּים רוֹאִים

glory of the Lord, are being transformed into the same image from glory to glory, just as by the Spirit of the Lord.

4 Therefore, since we have this ministry, as we have received mercy, we do not lose heart. [2] But we have renounced the hidden things of shame, not walking in craftiness nor handling the word of God deceitfully, but by manifestation of the truth commending ourselves to every man's conscience in the sight of God. [3] But even if our gospel is veiled, it is veiled to those who are perishing, [4] whose minds the god of this age has blinded, who do not believe, lest the light of the gospel of the glory of Christ, who is the image of God, should shine on them. [5] For we do not preach ourselves, but Christ Jesus the Lord, and ourselves your bondservants for Jesus' sake. [6] For it is the God who commanded light to shine out of darkness, who has shone in our hearts to *give* the light of the knowledge of the glory of God in the face of Jesus Christ.

[7] But we have this treasure in earthen vessels, that the excellence of the power may be of God and not of us. [8] *We are* hard-pressed on every side, yet not crushed; *we are* perplexed, but not in despair; [9] persecuted, but not forsaken; struck down, but not destroyed— [10] always carrying about in the body the dying of the Lord Jesus, that the life of Jesus also may be manifested in our body. [11] For we who live are always delivered to death for Jesus' sake, that the life of Jesus also may be manifested in our mortal flesh. [12] So then death is working in us, but life in you.

[13] And since we have the same spirit of faith, according to what is written, *"I believed and therefore I spoke,"* we also believe and therefore speak, [14] knowing that He who raised up the Lord Jesus will also raise us up with Jesus, and will present *us* with you. [15] For all things *are* for your sakes, that grace, having spread through the many, may cause thanksgiving to abound to the glory of God.

[16] Therefore we do not lose heart. Even though our outward man is perishing, yet the inward *man* is being renewed day by day. [17] For our light affliction, which is but for a moment, is working for us a far more exceeding *and* eternal weight of glory, [18] while we do not look at the things which are seen, but at the things which are not seen. For the things which are seen *are* temporary, but the things which are not seen *are* eternal.

בְּמַרְאָה אֶת כְּבוֹד הָאָדוֹן וְנֶהְפָּכִים לְאוֹתוֹ צֶלֶם, מְכָבוֹד אֶל כָּבוֹד, כְּמוֹ מִיַּד הָאָדוֹן – הָרוּחַ.

ד הַשֵּׁרוּת הַזֶּה הָפְקַד בְּיָדֵינוּ כְּפִי שֶׁגַּם רֻחַמְנוּ. לָכֵן אֵין אָנוּ מִתְיָאֲשִׁים. [2] סִלַּקְנוּ יָדֵינוּ מִמַּעֲשֵׂי הַסֵּתֶר הַמְּבִישִׁים; אֵין אָנוּ הוֹלְכִים בְּדַרְכֵי מִרְמָה וְאֵינֶנּוּ מְסַלְּפִים אֶת דְּבַר אֱלֹהִים, אֶלָּא מְגַלִּים אָנוּ אֶת הָאֱמֶת וּבְכָךְ אָנוּ מַמְלִיצִים עַל עַצְמֵנוּ לִפְנֵי מַצְפּוּנוֹ שֶׁל כָּל אָדָם לְנֶגֶד עֵינֵי אֱלֹהִים. [3] אַךְ אִם אִם נִסְתֶּרֶת בְּשׂוֹרָתֵנוּ, נִסְתֶּרֶת הִיא לָאוֹבְדִים. [4] אֵל הָעוֹלָם הַזֶּה עִוֵּר אֶת שִׂכְלָם שֶׁל הַבִּלְתִּי מַאֲמִינִים לְבַל יִזְרַח עֲלֵיהֶם אוֹר הַבְּשׂוֹרָה שֶׁל כְּבוֹד הַמָּשִׁיחַ אֲשֶׁר הוּא צֶלֶם הָאֱלֹהִים. [5] הֲרֵי לֹא עַל עַצְמֵנוּ אָנוּ מַכְרִיזִים, אֶלָּא עַל הַמָּשִׁיחַ יֵשׁוּעַ כְּאָדוֹן, וְאִלּוּ עַל עַצְמֵנוּ כְּעַל עַבְדֵיכֶם לְמַעַן יֵשׁוּעַ. [6] הָאֱלֹהִים הָאוֹמֵר ״וֹפַע אוֹר מֵחֹשֶׁךְ״ הוּא הִגִּיהַּ אוֹר בְּלִבֵּנוּ לְהָאִיר דַּעַת עַל־ אוֹדוֹת כְּבוֹד אֱלֹהִים אֲשֶׁר בִּפְנֵי שֶׁל הַמָּשִׁיחַ.

[7] בְּרַם הָאוֹצָר הַזֶּה נָתוּן לָנוּ בִּכְלֵי חֶרֶס, כְּדֵי שֶׁיִּהְיֶה הַכֹּחַ הַנִּשְׂגָּב מֵאֵת אֱלֹהִים וְלֹא מִיָּדֵינוּ אָנוּ. [8] נִלְחָצִים אֲנַחְנוּ מִכָּל עֵבֶר, אַךְ אֵינֶנּוּ רְצוּצִים; נְבוֹכִים, אַךְ לֹא נוֹאָשִׁים; [9] נִרְדָּפִים, אַךְ לֹא נְטוּשִׁים; מֻשְׁלָכִים אַרְצָה, אַךְ לֹא נִשְׁמָדִים. [10] וְתָמִיד נוֹשְׂאִים אָנוּ בַּגּוּף אֶת מוֹת יֵשׁוּעַ, כְּדֵי שֶׁגַּם חַיֵּי יֵשׁוּעַ יִתְגַּלּוּ בְּגוּפֵנוּ; [11] כִּי אֲנַחְנוּ הַחַיִּים נִמְסָרִים תָּמִיד לַמָּוֶת בַּעֲבוּר יֵשׁוּעַ, כְּדֵי שֶׁגַּם חַיֵּי יֵשׁוּעַ יִתְגַּלּוּ בִּבְשָׂרֵנוּ בֶּן־ הַתְּמוּתָה. [12] לְפִיכָךְ בָּנוּ פּוֹעֵל הַמָּוֶת, וּבָכֶם – הַחַיִּים.

[13] מִכֵּיוָן שֶׁיֵּשׁ לָנוּ אוֹתָהּ רוּחַ שֶׁל אֱמוּנָה, כַּכָּתוּב ״הֶאֱמַנְתִּי כִּי אֲדַבֵּר״, גַּם אֲנַחְנוּ מַאֲמִינִים וְלָכֵן גַּם מְדַבְּרִים; [14] בְּיָדְעֵנוּ כִּי הוּא אֲשֶׁר הֵקִים לִתְחִיָּה אֶת הָאָדוֹן יֵשׁוּעַ, יָקִים גַּם אוֹתָנוּ עִם יֵשׁוּעַ וְיַצִּיגֵנוּ עִמָּכֶם. [15] אָכֵן הַכֹּל לְמַעַנְכֶם, וְכָךְ בְּשֶׁל הַחֶסֶד שֶׁשָּׁפַע בִּגְלַל הָרַבִּים תִּרְבֶּה הַהוֹדָיָה לִכְבוֹד אֱלֹהִים.

[16] לָכֵן אֵין אָנוּ מִתְיָאֲשִׁים, וְאַף עַל פִּי שֶׁהָאָדָם הַחִיצוֹנִי שֶׁלָּנוּ הוֹלֵךְ וּבָלֶה, הָאָדָם הַפְּנִימִי שֶׁלָּנוּ מִתְחַדֵּשׁ יוֹם יוֹם. [17] הֵן צָרָתֵנוּ הַקַּלָּה שֶׁל הָרֶגַע מְכִינָה לָנוּ כְּבוֹד עוֹלָמִים גָּדוֹל וְרַב עַד מְאֹד. [18] וְאֵין אָנוּ צוֹפִים אֶל הַדְּבָרִים הַנִּרְאִים, אֶלָּא אֶל אֲשֶׁר אֵינָם נִרְאִים; כִּי הַדְּבָרִים הַנִּרְאִים לְשָׁעָה הֵם, אֲבָל הַבִּלְתִּי נִרְאִים – לְעוֹלָמִים.

5 For we know that if our earthly house, *this* tent, is destroyed, we have a building from God, a house not made with hands, eternal in the heavens. ²For in this we groan, earnestly desiring to be clothed with our habitation which is from heaven, ³if indeed, having been clothed, we shall not be found naked. ⁴For we who are in *this* tent groan, being burdened, not because we want to be unclothed, but further clothed, that mortality may be swallowed up by life. ⁵Now He who has prepared us for this very thing *is* God, who also has given us the Spirit as a guarantee.

⁶So *we are* always confident, knowing that while we are at home in the body we are absent from the Lord. ⁷For we walk by faith, not by sight. ⁸We are confident, yes, well pleased rather to be absent from the body and to be present with the Lord.

⁹Therefore we make it our aim, whether present or absent, to be well pleasing to Him. ¹⁰For we must all appear before the judgment seat of Christ, that each one may receive the things *done* in the body, according to what he has done, whether good or bad. ¹¹Knowing, therefore, the terror of the Lord, we persuade men; but we are well known to God, and I also trust are well known in your consciences.

¹²For we do not commend ourselves again to you, but give you opportunity to boast on our behalf, that you may have *an answer* for those who boast in appearance and not in heart. ¹³For if we are beside ourselves, *it is* for God; or if we are of sound mind, *it is* for you. ¹⁴For the love of Christ compels us, because we judge thus: that if One died for all, then all died; ¹⁵and He died for all, that those who live should live no longer for themselves, but for Him who died for them and rose again.

¹⁶Therefore, from now on, we regard no one according to the flesh. Even though we have known Christ according to the flesh, yet now we know *Him thus* no longer. ¹⁷Therefore, if anyone *is* in Christ, *he is* a new creation; old things have passed away; behold, all things have become new. ¹⁸Now all things *are* of God, who has reconciled us to Himself through Jesus Christ, and has given us the ministry of reconciliation, ¹⁹that is, that God was in Christ reconciling the world to Himself, not imputing their trespasses to them, and has committed to us the word of reconciliation.

²⁰Now then, we are ambassadors for Christ, as though God were pleading through us: we implore *you* on Christ's behalf, be reconciled to God. ²¹For He made Him who knew no sin *to be* sin for us, that we might become the righteousness of God in Him.

ה כִּי אָנוּ יוֹדְעִים שֶׁאִם יֵהָרֵס בֵּית מִשְׁכָּנֵנוּ הָאָרְצִי, יֵשׁ לָנוּ בִּנְיָן מֵאֵת אֱלֹהִים, בֵּית שֶׁאֵינוֹ מַעֲשֵׂה יָדַיִם וְהוּא בַּשָּׁמַיִם לְעוֹלָמִים. ² הֵן בָּזֶה, בְּמִשְׁכָּנֵנוּ הָאָרְצִי, נֶאֱנָחִים אָנוּ וְעַזִּים כִּסּוּפֵינוּ לִלְבּשׁ גַּם אֶת בֵּיתֵנוּ אֲשֶׁר מִן הַשָּׁמַיִם – ³ אִם אָמְנָם נִמָּצֵא עוֹד לְבוּשִׁים וְלֹא עֲרֻמִּים – ⁴ כִּי גַם בִּהְיוֹתֵנוּ בְּמִשְׁכָּנֵנוּ כָּעֵת, נֶאֱנָחִים אָנוּ מְכֻבָּד הַמַּשָּׂא; שֶׁהֲרֵי אֵינֶנּוּ חֲפֵצִים לְהִתְפַּשֵּׁט, אֶלָּא לְהוֹסִיף לִבְשׁ בְּאֹפֶן שֶׁהַכָּפוּף לַמָּוֶת יְבֻלַּע עַל-יְדֵי הַחַיִּים. ⁵ וֵאלֹהִים הוּא אֲשֶׁר הֵכִין אוֹתָנוּ לְכָךְ וְנָתַן לָנוּ אֶת עֵרְבוֹן הָרוּחַ.

⁶ עַל כֵּן מְלֵאֵי בִּטָּחוֹן אָנוּ בְּכָל עֵת וְיוֹדְעִים כִּי בְּהִמָּצְאֵנוּ בַּגּוּף רְחוֹקִים אָנוּ מִן הָאָדוֹן, ⁷ שֶׁכֵּן עַל-פִּי אֱמוּנָה אֲנַחְנוּ מִתְהַלְּכִים וְלֹא עַל-פִּי מַרְאֵה עֵינָיִם. ⁸ וְאוּלָם מְלֵאֵי בִּטָּחוֹן אָנוּ וּמַעֲדִיפִים לָצֵאת מִמִּשְׁכַּן הַגּוּף וְלָבוֹא הַבַּיְתָה אֶל הָאָדוֹן. ⁹ לָכֵן גַּם שׁוֹאֲפִים אָנוּ לִהְיוֹת רְצוּיִים לְפָנָיו, בֵּין שֶׁאָנוּ בְּמִשְׁכָּנֵנוּ בֵּין שֶׁאָנוּ מְחוּצָה לוֹ, ¹⁰ כִּי כֻּלָּנוּ חַיָּבִים לְהֵרָאוֹת לִפְנֵי כֵּס הַמִּשְׁפָּט שֶׁל הַמָּשִׁיחַ, לְמַעַן יְקַבֵּל כָּל אֶחָד כְּפִי הַמַּעֲשִׂים שֶׁעָשָׂה בְּעֵת הֱיוֹתוֹ בַּגּוּף, אִם טוֹב וְאִם רַע.

¹¹ מִתּוֹךְ הַכָּרַת יִרְאַת אֲדֹנָי אֲנַחְנוּ מְדַבְּרִים עַל לֵב בְּנֵי אָדָם כְּדֵי לְשַׁכְנְעָם. גְּלוּיִים אָנוּ לֵאלֹהִים, וַאֲנִי מְקַוֶּה שֶׁאֲנַחְנוּ גְּלוּיִים גַּם לְעֵינֵי מַצְפּוּנְכֶם. ¹² אֵין אָנוּ שׁוּב מְשַׁבְּחִים אֶת עַצְמֵנוּ לִפְנֵיכֶם, אֶלָּא נוֹתְנִים בְּיֶדְכֶם סִבָּה לְהִתְגָּאוֹת בָּנוּ, כְּדֵי שֶׁיִּהְיֶה לָכֶם מַה לְהָצִיב נֶגֶד הָאֲנָשִׁים הַמִּתְגָּאִים בְּמַרְאֵה פָּנִים וְלֹא בְּמַה שֶׁבַּלֵּב. ¹³ וְאִם יָצָאנוּ מִדַּעְתֵּנוּ, הֲרֵי זֶה לְמַעַן אֱלֹהִים; וְאִם מְפֻכָּחִים אָנוּ, הֲרֵי זֶה לְמַעַנְכֶם; ¹⁴ שֶׁכֵּן אַהֲבַת הַמָּשִׁיחַ דּוֹחֶקֶת בָּנוּ, בְּהַכִּירֵנוּ שֶׁאֶחָד מֵת בְּעַד הַכֹּל, לָכֵן הַכֹּל מֵתוּ. ¹⁵ וּבְעַד הַכֹּל הוּא מֵת, כְּדֵי שֶׁאֵלֶּה הַחַיִּים לֹא יִחְיוּ עוֹד לְמַעַן עַצְמָם, אֶלָּא לְמַעַן זֶה אֲשֶׁר מֵת וְקָם בַּעֲדָם. ¹⁶ עַל כֵּן מֵעַתָּה אֵין אָנוּ מַכִּירִים אִישׁ עַל-פִּי רְאוּת אֱנוֹשִׁית; וְגַם אִם הִכַּרְנוּ אֶת הַמָּשִׁיחַ עַל-פִּי רְאוּת אֱנוֹשִׁית, הֲרֵי כָּעֵת אֵינֶנּוּ מַכִּירִים אוֹתוֹ עוֹד בְּאֹפֶן כָּזֶה. ¹⁷ עַל כֵּן מִי שֶׁנִּמְצָא בַּמָּשִׁיחַ הוּא בְּרִיאָה חֲדָשָׁה. הַיְשָׁנוֹת עָבְרוּ; הִנֵּה נִהְיוּ חֲדָשׁוֹת. ¹⁸ וְהַכֹּל מֵאֵת הָאֱלֹהִים שֶׁרִצָּה אוֹתָנוּ אֵלָיו עַל-יְדֵי הַמָּשִׁיחַ, וּמָסַר לָנוּ אֶת שֵׁרוּת הָרִצּוּי. ¹⁹ כְּלוֹמַר: אֱלֹהִים הָיָה בַּמָּשִׁיחַ מְרַצֶּה אֶת הָעוֹלָם אֶל עַצְמוֹ מִבְּלִי לַחְשֹׁב לָהֶם אֶת עֲווֹנוֹתֵיהֶם, וְהוּא שָׂם בָּנוּ אֶת דְּבַר הָרִצּוּי. ²⁰ לָכֵן שְׁגִרִירֵי הַמָּשִׁיחַ אָנוּ וֵאלֹהִים כְּמוֹ מַפְצִיר בְּאֶמְצָעוּתֵנוּ. וּבְכֵן מַפְצִירִים אָנוּ בְּשֵׁם הַמָּשִׁיחַ: הִתְרַצּוּ נָא לֵאלֹהִים! ²¹ אֶת זֶה אֲשֶׁר לֹא יָדַע חַטָּא עָשָׂה לַחֵטְא בַּעֲדֵנוּ, כְּדֵי שֶׁאָנוּ נִלְבַּשׁ אֶת הַצְּדָקָה שֶׁל אֱלֹהִים בּוֹ.

6 We then, *as* workers together *with Him* also plead with *you* not to receive the grace of God in vain. [2] For He says:

"In an acceptable time I have heard you,
And in the day of salvation I have helped you."

Behold, now *is* the accepted time; behold, now *is* the day of salvation.

[3] We give no offense in anything, that our ministry may not be blamed. [4] But in all *things* we commend ourselves as ministers of God: in much patience, in tribulations, in needs, in distresses, [5] in stripes, in imprisonments, in tumults, in labors, in sleeplessness, in fastings; [6] by purity, by knowledge, by longsuffering, by kindness, by the Holy Spirit, by sincere love, [7] by the word of truth, by the power of God, by the armor of righteousness on the right hand and on the left, [8] by honor and dishonor, by evil report and good report; as deceivers, and *yet* true; [9] as unknown, and *yet* well known; as dying, and behold we live; as chastened, and *yet* not killed; [10] as sorrowful, yet always rejoicing; as poor, yet making many rich; as having nothing, and *yet* possessing all things.

[11] O Corinthians! We have spoken openly to you, our heart is wide open. [12] You are not restricted by us, but you are restricted by your *own* affections. [13] Now in return for the same (I speak as to children), you also be open.

[14] Do not be unequally yoked together with unbelievers. For what fellowship has righteousness with lawlessness? And what communion has light with darkness? [15] And what accord has Christ with Belial? Or what part has a believer with an unbeliever? [16] And what agreement has the temple of God with idols? For you are the temple of the living God. As God has said:

"I will dwell in them
And walk among *them.*
I will be their God,
And they shall be My people."

[17] Therefore

"Come out from among them
And be separate, says the Lord.
Do not touch what is unclean,
And I will receive you."

[18] "I will be a Father to you,
And you shall be My sons and daughters,
Says the LORD Almighty."

7 Therefore, having these promises, beloved, let us cleanse ourselves from all filthiness of the flesh and spirit, perfecting holiness in the fear of God.

ו כֵּיוָן שֶׁאֲנַחְנוּ שֻׁתָּפִים לְפׇעֳלוֹ, אָנוּ גַּם מְבַקְשִׁים מִכֶּם: אַל נָא תְקַבְּלוּ לָרִיק אֶת חֶסֶד אֱלֹהִים. [2] הֵן הוּא אוֹמֵר: "בְּעֵת רָצוֹן עֲנִיתִיךָ וּבְיוֹם יְשׁוּעָה עֲזַרְתִּיךָ." הִנֵּה עַתָּה עֵת רָצוֹן, הִנֵּה עַתָּה יוֹם יְשׁוּעָה. [3] אֵין אָנוּ שָׂמִים מִכְשׁוֹל בְּשׁוּם דָּבָר, פֶּן יִהְיֶה שֵׁרוּתֵנוּ לִשְׁמְצָה. [4] אַדְּרַבָּא, בְּכָל דָּבָר אֲנַחְנוּ מַצִּיגִים אֶת עַצְמֵנוּ כִּמְשׇׁרְתֵי אֱלֹהִים: בְּרֹב סַבְלָנוּת, בְּצָרוֹת, בְּמַחְסוֹר, בִּמְצוּקוֹת, [5] בְּמַכּוֹת, בְּבָתֵּי כֶּלֶא, בִּמְהוּמוֹת, בְּעָמָל, בְּלֵילוֹת לְלֹא שֵׁנָה, בְּצוֹמוֹת, [6] בְּטׇהֳרָה, בְּדַעַת, בְּאֹרֶךְ רוּחַ, בִּנְדִיבוּת לֵב, בְּרוּחַ הַקֹּדֶשׁ, בְּאַהֲבָה אֲמִתִּית, [7] בִּדְבּוּר אֱמֶת, בִּגְבוּרַת אֱלֹהִים, בְּנֶשֶׁק הַצֶּדֶק שֶׁבִּימִינֵנוּ וּבִשְׂמֹאלֵנוּ, [8] בְּכָבוֹד וּבְקָלוֹן, בְּשֵׁם רַע וּבְשֵׁם טוֹב; כְּאִלּוּ מַתְעִים, אַךְ אָנוּ נֶאֱמָנִים; [9] כְּאִלּוּ בִּלְתִּי מֻכָּרִים, אַךְ אָנוּ מֻכָּרִים; כְּמֵתִים וְהִנֵּה אָנוּ חַיִּים; כְּנֶעֱנָשִׁים וְלֹא מוּמָתִים; [10] כְּנֶעֱצָבִים, אַךְ שְׂמֵחִים תָּמִיד; כַּעֲנִיִּים, אַךְ מַעֲשִׁירִים אֶת הָרַבִּים; כְּחַסְרֵי כֹּל וְעִם זֹאת יֵשׁ לָנוּ הַכֹּל.

[11] קוֹרִינְתִים, דִּבַּרְנוּ אֲלֵיכֶם בְּכֵנוּת וְנִהֲגְנוּ בְּרַחַב לֵב. [12] לֹא צַר לָכֶם הַמָּקוֹם בְּלִבֵּנוּ; בְּלִבַּבְכֶם צַר הַמָּקוֹם. [13] הָשִׁיבוּ אֶת אוֹתוֹ הַגְּמוּל – כְּאֶל בָּנַי אֲנִי מְדַבֵּר – וְהִתְנַהֲגוּ בְּרַחַב לֵב גַּם אַתֶּם.

[14] אַל תֵּרָתְמוּ לְעֹל אֶחָד עִם הַבִּלְתִּי מַאֲמִינִים; כִּי אֵיזוֹ שֻׁתָּפוּת לִצְדָקָה עִם עַוְלָה? וּמָה רֵעוּת יֵשׁ לָאוֹר עִם חֹשֶׁךְ? [15] מַה הַסְכָּמָה יֵשׁ לַמָּשִׁיחַ עִם בְּלִיַּעַל? אוֹ מַה חֵלֶק לַמַּאֲמִין עִם מִי שֶׁאֵינוֹ מַאֲמִין? [16] וּמַה קֶּשֶׁר יֵשׁ לְהֵיכַל אֱלֹהִים עִם אֱלִילִים? הֵן אֲנַחְנוּ הֵיכַל אֱלֹהִים חַיִּים, כְּפִי שֶׁאָמַר אֱלֹהִים: "וְשָׁכַנְתִּי בְּתוֹכָם"; "וְהִתְהַלַּכְתִּי בְּתוֹכְכֶם"; "וְהָיִיתִי לָהֶם לֵאלֹהִים וְהֵמָּה יִהְיוּ לִי לְעָם." [17] עַל כֵּן "צְאוּ מִתּוֹכָם וְהִבָּרוּ, נְאֻם יהוה, וְטָמֵא אַל־תִּגָּעוּ"; וַאֲנִי אֲקַבֵּל אֶתְכֶם. [18] וְהָיִיתִי לָכֶם לְאָב וְאַתֶּם תִּהְיוּ לִי לְבָנִים וּלְבָנוֹת, נְאֻם יהוה צְבָאוֹת.

ז לָכֵן, חֲבִיבַי, בִּהְיוֹת לָנוּ הַהַבְטָחוֹת הָאֵלֶּה, נִטַּהֵר אֶת עַצְמֵנוּ מִכָּל טֻמְאַת גּוּף וְרוּחַ וְנַשְׁלִים קְדֻשָּׁתֵנוּ בְּיִרְאַת אֱלֹהִים.

² Open *your hearts* to us. We have wronged no one, we have corrupted no one, we have cheated no one. ³ I do not say *this* to condemn; for I have said before that you are in our hearts, to die together and to live together. ⁴ Great *is* my boldness of speech toward you, great *is* my boasting on your behalf. I am filled with comfort. I am exceedingly joyful in all our tribulation.

⁵ For indeed, when we came to Macedonia, our bodies had no rest, but we were troubled on every side. Outside *were* conflicts, inside *were* fears. ⁶ Nevertheless God, who comforts the downcast, comforted us by the coming of Titus, ⁷ and not only by his coming, but also by the consolation with which he was comforted in you, when he told us of your earnest desire, your mourning, your zeal for me, so that I rejoiced even more.

⁸ For even if I made you sorry with my letter, I do not regret it; though I did regret it. For I perceive that the same epistle made you sorry, though only for a while. ⁹ Now I rejoice, not that you were made sorry, but that your sorrow led to repentance. For you were made sorry in a godly manner, that you might suffer loss from us in nothing. ¹⁰ For godly sorrow produces repentance *leading* to salvation, not to be regretted; but the sorrow of the world produces death. ¹¹ For observe this very thing, that you sorrowed in a godly manner: What diligence it produced in you, *what* clearing *of yourselves, what* indignation, *what* fear, *what* vehement desire, *what* zeal, *what* vindication! In all *things* you proved yourselves to be clear in this matter. ¹² Therefore, although I wrote to you, *I did* not *do it* for the sake of him who had done the wrong, nor for the sake of him who suffered wrong, but that our care for you in the sight of God might appear to you.

¹³ Therefore we have been comforted in your comfort. And we rejoiced exceedingly more for the joy of Titus, because his spirit has been refreshed by you all. ¹⁴ For if in anything I have boasted to him about you, I am not ashamed. But as we spoke all things to you in truth, even so our boasting to Titus was found true. ¹⁵ And his affections are greater for you as he remembers the obedience of you all, how with fear and trembling you received him. ¹⁶ Therefore I rejoice that I have confidence in you in everything.

8 Moreover, brethren, we make known to you the grace of God bestowed on the churches of Macedonia: ² that in a great trial of affliction the abundance of their joy and their deep poverty abounded in the riches of their liberality. ³ For I bear witness that according to *their* ability, yes, and

² הַרְחִיבוּ לָנוּ לְבַבְכֶם; לֹא עָשִׂינוּ עָוֶל לְאִישׁ, לֹא גֵרַמְנוּ נֶזֶק לְאִישׁ, לֹא רִמִּינוּ אִישׁ. ³ אֵינֶנִּי מְדַבֵּר מִתּוֹךְ כַּוָּנָה לְהַרְשִׁיעַ, שֶׁהֲרֵי כְּבָר אָמַרְתִּי שֶׁאַתֶּם בְּלִבֵּנוּ, גַּם לַחַיִּים גַּם לָמָוֶת. ⁴ רַב בִּטְחוֹנִי בָּכֶם. גְּדוֹלָה גַּאֲוָתִי בָכֶם. מָלֵאתִי נֶחָמָה וַאֲנִי שׁוֹפֵעַ שִׂמְחָה בְּכָל צָרָתֵנוּ.

⁵ הֵן גַּם כַּאֲשֶׁר בָּאנוּ לְמָקֶדוֹנְיָה לֹא הָיָה מָנוֹחַ לְגוּפֵנוּ, אֶלָּא צָרוֹת מִכָּל עֵבֶר, מַאֲבָקִים מִחוּץ וַחֲשָׁשׁוֹת מִבַּיִת. ⁶ אֲבָל אֱלֹהִים, הַמְנַחֵם אֶת הַנִּדְכָּאִים, נִחַם אוֹתָנוּ בְּבוֹאוֹ שֶׁל טִיטוֹס. ⁷ וְלֹא בְּבוֹאוֹ בִּלְבַד, אֶלָּא גַם בַּנֶּחָמָה שֶׁהוּא נִחַם בָּכֶם; שֶׁכֵּן סִפֵּר לָנוּ עַל כִּסּוּפֵיכֶם, עַל רֹב צַעֲרְכֶם, עַל הַקִּנְאָה שֶׁאַתֶּם מְקַנְּאִים לִי, וְלָכֵן שָׂמַחְתִּי עוֹד יוֹתֵר.

⁸ הֵן גַּם אִם הֶעֱצַבְתִּי אֶתְכֶם בְּאִגַּרְתִּי, אֵינֶנִּי מִתְחָרֵט. גַּם אִם הִתְחָרַטְתִּי – אֲנִי רוֹאֶה שֶׁהָאִגֶּרֶת הַהִיא הֶעֱצִיבָה אֶתְכֶם, אַף כִּי רַק לְזְמַן מָה – ⁹ כָּעֵת אֲנִי שָׂמֵחַ לֹא עַל שֶׁנֶּעֱצַבְתֶּם, אֶלָּא עַל שֶׁהָעֶצֶב הַזֶּה הֵבִיא אֶתְכֶם לִידֵי תְּשׁוּבָה; כִּי נֶעֱצַבְתֶּם כִּרְצוֹן אֱלֹהִים, בְּאֹפֶן שֶׁלֹּא נִגְרַם לָכֶם שׁוּם נֶזֶק עַל-יָדֵינוּ. ¹⁰ הֵן הָעֶצֶב שֶׁהוּא כִּרְצוֹן אֱלֹהִים מְעוֹרֵר לִתְשׁוּבָה אֲשֶׁר תּוֹצָאָתָהּ יְשׁוּעָה, וְעַל עֶצֶב כָּזֶה אֵין לְהִצְטַעֵר. אֲבָל הָעֶצֶב כְּדֶרֶךְ הָעוֹלָם גּוֹרֵם מָוֶת. ¹¹ רְאוּ מָה עוֹרֵר בָּכֶם הָעֶצֶב הַזֶּה אֲשֶׁר כִּרְצוֹן אֱלֹהִים! הוּא עוֹרֵר בָּכֶם חֲרִיצוּת, הִתְנַצְּלוּת, הִתְלַהֲטוּת, יִרְאָה, כִּסּוּפִים, קִנְאָה, נְכוֹנוּת לַעֲשִׂיַּת דִּין. מִכָּל הַבְּחִינוֹת הוֹכַחְתֶּם שֶׁאֵין בָּכֶם דֹּפִי בָּעִנְיָן הַהוּא. ¹² וּבְכֵן, גַּם כְּשֶׁכָּתַבְתִּי אֲלֵיכֶם, לֹא כָּתַבְתִּי לְמַעַן זֶה שֶׁעָשָׂה אֶת הָרָעָה וְלֹא לְמַעַן זֶה שֶׁסֻּבַּל אֶת הָרָעָה, אֶלָּא לְמַעַן תִּוָּכְחוּ לָדַעַת לְנֹכַח הָאֱלֹהִים מַהִי מְסִירוּתְכֶם לָנוּ. ¹³ לָכֵן נֶחָמְנוּ. אֲבָל הַרְבֵּה יוֹתֵר מִשֶּׁנִּחַמְנוּ שָׂמַחְנוּ בְּשִׂמְחַת טִיטוֹס, שֶׁכֵּן כֻּלְּכֶם גְּרַמְתֶּם לוֹ נַחַת רוּחַ. ¹⁴ אִם בְּמִדַּת מָה הִתְגָּאֵיתִי בָּכֶם לְפָנָיו, לֹא הִתְאַכְזַבְתִּי – אֶלָּא כְּשֵׁם שֶׁתָּמִיד דִּבַּרְנוּ אֲלֵיכֶם אֱמֶת, כֵּן גַּם דִּבְרֵי הִתְגָּאוּתֵנוּ לִפְנֵי טִיטוֹס הוּכְחוּ כֶּאֱמֶת. ¹⁵ הוּא רוֹחֵשׁ לָכֶם אַהֲבָה רַבָּה עַד מְאֹד, כִּי זוֹכֵר הוּא אֶת הַצִּיּוּת שֶׁל כֻּלְּכֶם כְּשֶׁקִּבַּלְתֶּם אוֹתוֹ בְּיִרְאָה וּבַחֲרָדָה. ¹⁶ אֲנִי שָׂמֵחַ שֶׁבְּכָל דָּבָר אֲנִי בָּטוּחַ בָּכֶם.

ח וְעַתָּה, אַחַי, נְסַפֵּר לָכֶם עַל חֶסֶד אֱלֹהִים שֶׁהָאֱצַל בִּקְהִלּוֹת מָקֶדוֹנְיָה: ² פְּעָמִים רַבּוֹת עָמְדוּ בְּמִבְחַן הַצָּרוֹת, וּמִתּוֹךְ שִׁפְעַת שִׂמְחָתָם וְעֹמֶק עֲנִיּוּתָם גָּאָה עֹשֶׁר נְדִיבוּתָם. ³ הֲרֵינִי מֵעִיד כִּי נָדְבוּ

beyond *their* ability, *they were* freely willing, [4] imploring us with much urgency that we would receive the gift and the fellowship of the ministering to the saints. [5] And not *only* as we had hoped, but they first gave themselves to the Lord, and *then* to us by the will of God. [6] So we urged Titus, that as he had begun, so he would also complete this grace in you as well. [7] But as you abound in everything—in faith, in speech, in knowledge, in all diligence, and in your love for us—*see* that you abound in this grace also.

[8] I speak not by commandment, but I am testing the sincerity of your love by the diligence of others. [9] For you know the grace of our Lord Jesus Christ, that though He was rich, yet for your sakes He became poor, that you through His poverty might become rich.

[10] And in this I give advice: It is to your advantage not only to be doing what you began and were desiring to do a year ago; [11] but now you also must complete the doing *of it;* that as *there was* a readiness to desire *it,* so *there* also *may be* a completion out of what *you* have. [12] For if there is first a willing mind, *it is* accepted according to what one has, *and* not according to what he does not have.

[13] For *I do* not *mean* that others should be eased and you burdened; [14] but by an equality, *that* now at this time your abundance *may supply* their lack, that their abundance also may supply your lack—that there may be equality. [15] As it is written, "*He who gathered* much had *nothing left over, and he who gathered* little had *no lack.*"

[16] But thanks *be* to God who puts the same earnest care for you into the heart of Titus. [17] For he not only accepted the exhortation, but being more diligent, he went to you of his own accord. [18] And we have sent with him the brother whose praise *is* in the gospel throughout all the churches, [19] and not only *that,* but who was also chosen by the churches to travel with us with this gift, which is administered by us to the glory of the Lord Himself and *to show* your ready mind, [20] avoiding this: that anyone should blame us in this lavish gift which is administered by us— [21] providing honorable things, not only in the sight of the Lord, but also in the sight of men.

[22] And we have sent with them our brother whom we have often proved diligent in many things, but now much more diligent, because of the great confidence which *we have* in you. [23] If *anyone inquires* about Titus, *he is* my partner and fellow worker concerning you. Or if our brethren *are inquired about, they are* messengers of the churches,

כְּפִי יְכָלְתָּם, וְיוֹתֵר מִכְּפִי יְכָלְתָּם, 4 וּבְהַפְצָרוֹת רַבּוֹת בִּקְשׁוּ מֵאִתָּנוּ אֶת הַזְּכוּת לְהִשְׁתַּתֵּף בַּעֲזוּרָה לַקְּדוֹשִׁים. 5 וְלֹא כְּפִי שֶׁצִּפִּינוּ, אֶלָּא קֹדֶם הִקְדִּישׁוּ אֶת עַצְמָם לָאָדוֹן וְאַחַר כָּךְ לָנוּ, כִּרְצוֹן אֱלֹהִים. 6 עַל כֵּן בִּקַּשְׁנוּ מִטִּיטוֹס, כִּי כְּשֵׁם שֶׁהֶחְדִּים וְהִתְחִיל, כֵּן גַּם יַשְׁלִים בְּקִרְבְּכֶם אֶת מַעֲשֵׂה הַחֶסֶד הַזֶּה. 7 וּכְשֵׁם שֶׁאַתֶּם שׁוֹפְעִים בַּכֹּל – בָּאֱמוּנָה, בַּהַטָּפָה, בְּדַעַת, בְּכָל שְׁקִידָה, וּבָאַהֲבָה אֲשֶׁר עוֹרַרְנוּ בָּכֶם – שִׁפְעוּ גַּם בַּחֶסֶד הַזֶּה.

8 אֵינֶנִּי מְדַבֵּר בְּדֶרֶךְ שֶׁל פְּקֻדָּה, אֶלָּא שֶׁעַל-יְדֵי חֲרִיצוּתָם שֶׁל אֲחֵרִים אֲנִי בּוֹחֵן גַּם אֶת אֲמִתּוּת אַהֲבַתְכֶם. 9 הֵן יוֹדְעִים אַתֶּם אֶת מַעֲשֵׂה הַחֶסֶד שֶׁל אֲדוֹנֵנוּ יֵשׁוּעַ הַמָּשִׁיחַ, שֶׁבִּהְיוֹתוֹ עָשִׁיר נַעֲשָׂה עָנִי לְמַעַנְכֶם, כְּדֵי שֶׁתַּעַשִׁירוּ אַתֶּם עַל-יְדֵי עֲנִיּוּתוֹ. 10 מְחַוֶּה אֲנִי אֶת דַּעְתִּי בְּעִנְיָן זֶה, שֶׁכֵּן הַדָּבָר יוֹעִיל לָכֶם, אַתֶּם אֲשֶׁר לִפְנֵי שָׁנָה הִקְדַּמְתֶּם וְהִתְחַלְתֶּם לֹא רַק לַעֲשׂוֹת אֶלָּא גַּם לִרְצוֹת. 11 אֲבָל כָּעֵת הַשְׁלִימוּ גַּם אֶת הַמַּעֲשֶׂה, כְּדֵי שֶׁתִּהְיֶה הַשְׁלָמַת הַמַּעֲשֶׂה מִתּוֹךְ מַה שֶׁמַּשִּׂגֶת יֶדְכֶם, כְּפִי שֶׁהָיְתָה הַנְּכוֹנוּת לִרְצוֹת; 12 שֶׁהֲרֵי אִם קַיֶּמֶת הַנְּכוֹנוּת, רְצוּיָה הִיא לְפִי מַה שֶׁיֵּשׁ בְּיַד אִישׁ, לֹא לְפִי מַה שֶׁאֵין בְּיָדוֹ. 13 אֵין זֶה כְּדֵי שֶׁתִּהְיֶה לַאֲחֵרִים רְוָחָה וְלָכֶם מַחְסוֹר, אֶלָּא לְשֵׁם הַשִּׁוְיוֹן. 14 כָּעֵת הַשֶּׁפַע שֶׁלָּכֶם יְמַלֵּא אֶת מַחְסוֹרָם, כְּדֵי שֶׁבְּעֵת הַצֹּרֶךְ יְמַלֵּא הַשֶּׁפַע שֶׁלָּהֶם אֶת מַחְסוֹרְכֶם אַתֶּם, וְכָךְ יָקוּם הַשִּׁוְיוֹן, 15 כְּפִי שֶׁכָּתוּב: "וְלֹא הֶעְדִּיף הַמַּרְבֶּה וְהַמַּמְעִיט לֹא הֶחְסִיר."

16 תּוֹדָה לֵאלֹהִים הַנּוֹתֵן בְּלֵב טִיטוֹס אֶת אוֹתָהּ חֲרִיצוּת לְמַעַנְכֶם; 17 כִּי אָכֵן שָׁמַע לַבַּקָּשָׁה וּמִתּוֹךְ חֲרִיצוּתוֹ הַיְתֵרָה הָלַךְ אֲלֵיכֶם מֵרָצוֹן. 18 יַחַד אִתּוֹ שָׁלַחְנוּ אֶת הָאָח אֲשֶׁר שֵׁם טוֹב לוֹ בְּכָל הַקְּהִלּוֹת עַל חֶלְקוֹ בְּהַכְרָזַת הַבְּשׂוֹרָה. 19 וְלֹא עוֹד אֶלָּא שֶׁהַקְּהִלּוֹת בָּחֲרוּ בּוֹ לִהְיוֹת חֲבֵרֵנוּ לַמַּסָּע בַּהֲבָאַת הַתְּרוּמָה הַזֹּאת, שֵׁרוּת שֶׁאָנוּ עוֹשִׂים לִכְבוֹד הָאָדוֹן מִתּוֹךְ וְכוֹנוּתֵנוּ אָנוּ. 20 וַאֲנַחְנוּ נִשְׁמָרִים מִלָּתֵת לְאִישׁ פִּתְחוֹן פֶּה נֶגְדֵּנוּ עַל-דְּבַר הַתְּרוּמוֹת הָרַבּוֹת שֶׁאָנוּ מְפַקְּדִים עֲלֵיהֶן; 21 שֶׁכֵּן נוֹתְנִים אָנוּ דַּעְתֵּנוּ לִנְהֹג בְּיֹשֶׁר לֹא רַק לִפְנֵי הָאָדוֹן, אֶלָּא גַּם לִפְנֵי בְּנֵי אָדָם. 22 שָׁלַחְנוּ אַתָּם אֶת אָחִינוּ אֲשֶׁר פְּעָמִים רַבּוֹת וּבִדְבָרִים רַבִּים הוֹכַחְנוּ לָנוּ חֲרִיצוּתוֹ, וְעַתָּה חֲרִיצוּתוֹ רַבָּה עוֹד יוֹתֵר בִּגְלַל הָאֵמוּן הָרַב שֶׁהוּא נוֹתֵן בָּכֶם. 23 אֲשֶׁר לְטִיטוֹס, שֻׁתָּפִי הוּא וְעוֹבֵד אִתִּי

the glory of Christ. 24 Therefore show to them, and before the churches the proof of your love and of our boasting on your behalf.

9 Now concerning the ministering to the saints, it is superfluous for me to write to you; 2 for I know your willingness, about which I boast of you to the Macedonians, that Achaia was ready a year ago; and your zeal has stirred up the majority. 3 Yet I have sent the brethren, lest our boasting of you should be in vain in this respect, that, as I said, you may be ready; 4 lest if *some* Macedonians come with me and find you unprepared, we (not to mention you!) should be ashamed of this confident boasting. 5 Therefore I thought it necessary to exhort the brethren to go to you ahead of time, and prepare your generous gift beforehand, which *you had* previously promised, that it may be ready as *a matter of* generosity and not as a grudging obligation.

6 But this I *say:* He who sows sparingly will also reap sparingly, and he who sows bountifully will also reap bountifully. 7 *So let* each one *give* as he purposes in his heart, not grudgingly or of necessity; for God loves a cheerful giver. 8 And God *is* able to make all grace abound toward you, that you, always having all sufficiency in all *things,* may have an abundance for every good work. 9 As it is written:

   "He has dispersed abroad,
    He has given to the poor;
    His righteousness endures forever."

10 Now may He who supplies seed to the sower, and bread for food, supply and multiply the seed you have *sown* and increase the fruits of your righteousness, 11 while *you are* enriched in everything for all liberality, which causes thanksgiving through us to God. 12 For the administration of this service not only supplies the needs of the saints, but also is abounding through many thanksgivings to God, 13 while, through the proof of this ministry, they glorify God for the obedience of your confession to the gospel of Christ, and for *your* liberal sharing with them and all *men,* 14 and by their prayer for you, who long for you because of the exceeding grace of God in you. 15 Thanks *be* to God for His indescribable gift!

10 Now I, Paul, myself am pleading with you by the meekness and gentleness of Christ—who in presence *am* lowly among you, but being absent am bold toward you. 2 But I beg *you* that when I am present I may not be bold with that confidence by

לְמַעַנְכֶם. אֲשֶׁר לְאַחֵינוּ, שְׁלִיחֵי הַקְּהִלּוֹת הֵם לְתִפְאֶרֶת הַמָּשִׁיחַ. 24 עַל כֵּן, לְעֵינֵי הַקְּהִלּוֹת, הַרְאוּ לָהֶם אֶת אַהֲבַתְכֶם וְהוֹכִיחוּ אֶת צִדְקַת גַּאֲוָתֵנוּ בָּכֶם.

ט בְּנוֹגֵעַ לַשֵּׁרוּת לְמַעַן הַקְּדוֹשִׁים אֵינֶנִּי צָרִיךְ לִכְתֹּב אֲלֵיכֶם; 2 כִּי יוֹדֵעַ אֲנִי אֶת נְכוֹנוּתְכֶם, אֲשֶׁר בִּגְלָלָהּ אֲנִי מִתְגָּאֶה בָּכֶם לִפְנֵי אַנְשֵׁי מָקֶדוֹנְיָה, בְּאָמְרִי שֶׁאֲכַיָּה הָיְתָה נְכוֹנָה כְּבָר לִפְנֵי שָׁנָה; וְאָמְנָם הַלַּהַט שֶׁלָּכֶם עוֹרֵר אֶת רֻבָּם. 3 אֲבָל שָׁלַחְתִּי אֶת הָאַחִים מִתּוֹךְ כַּוָּנָה שֶׁגַּאֲוָתֵנוּ בָּכֶם לֹא תִהְיֶה לָרִיק בָּעִנְיָן הַזֶּה וּכְדֵי שֶׁתִּהְיוּ מוּכָנִים כְּפִי שֶׁאָמַרְתִּי. 4 הֲלֹא אִם יָבוֹאוּ עִמִּי אֲנָשִׁים מִמָּקֶדוֹנְיָה וְיִמְצְאוּ שֶׁאֵינְכֶם מוּכָנִים, אָזַי אֲנַחְנוּ – שֶׁלֹּא לוֹמַר אַתֶּם – נֵבוֹשׁ בְּבִטָּחוֹן הַזֶּה. 5 עַל כֵּן מָצָאתִי לָנָחוּץ לְבַקֵּשׁ מֵהָאַחִים כִּי יַקְדִּימוּ לָבוֹא אֲלֵיכֶם וִיסַדְּרוּ אֶת עִנְיַן הַתְּרוּמָה שֶׁהִבְטַחְתֶּם, לְמַעַן תִּהְיֶה מוּכָנָה מִתּוֹךְ נְדִיבוּת וְלֹא מִתּוֹךְ קַמְצָנוּת. 6 הֵן הַזּוֹרֵעַ בְּצִמְצוּם יִקְצֹר בְּצִמְצוּם, וְהַזּוֹרֵעַ בִּנְדִיבוּת יִקְצֹר בְּשֶׁפַע. 7 כָּל אִישׁ כְּפִי שֶׁיִּדְּבֶנּוּ לִבּוֹ יִתֵּן, לֹא מִתּוֹךְ צַעַר אוֹ הֶכְרֵחַ, שֶׁהֲרֵי אֶת הַנּוֹתֵן בְּשִׂמְחָה אוֹהֵב אֱלֹהִים. 8 וֵאלֹהִים יָכוֹל לְהַשְׁפִּיעַ עֲלֵיכֶם כָּל חֶסֶד, כְּדֵי שֶׁיִּהְיֶה לָכֶם תָּמִיד דֵּי צָרְכְּכֶם בְּכָל דָּבָר, וְהוֹתֵר לְכָל מַעֲשֶׂה טוֹב, 9 כַּכָּתוּב: "פִּזַּר נָתַן לָאֶבְיוֹנִים, צִדְקָתוֹ עוֹמֶדֶת לָעַד." 10 וְהַנּוֹתֵן זֶרַע לַזּוֹרֵעַ וְלֶחֶם לָאֹכֶל, יִתֵּן לָכֶם זֶרַע בְּשֶׁפַע וְיַרְבֶּה פְּרִי צִדְקַתְכֶם, 11 וְתַעֲשִׁירוּ בְּכָל דַּרְכֵי נְדִיבוּת שֶׁתָּבִיא לִידֵי הוֹדָיָה לֵאלֹהִים בִּגְלָלֵנוּ, 12 שֶׁכֵּן עֲשִׂיַּת הַשֵּׁרוּת הַזֶּה לֹא רַק תְּמַלֵּא אֶת מַחְסוֹר הַקְּדוֹשִׁים, אֶלָּא גַּם תְּעוֹרֵר הוֹדָיָה רַבָּה לֵאלֹהִים. 13 בִּגְלַל הַשֵּׁרוּת הַזֶּה שֶׁעָמַד בַּמִּבְחָן יְשַׁבְּחוּ אֶת אֱלֹהִים עַל צִיּוּתְכֶם לִבְשׂוֹרַת הַמָּשִׁיחַ וְהוֹדָאַתְכֶם בָּהּ, וְעַל הִשְׁתַּתְּפוּתְכֶם הַנְּדִיבָה בְּעֶזְרָה לָהֶם וְלַכֹּל. 14 וְהֵם מִתּוֹךְ כִּסּוּפִים אֲלֵיכֶם יִתְפַּלְלוּ בַּעַדְכֶם הוֹדוֹת לְחֶסֶד אֱלֹהִים שֶׁשָּׁפַע בְּקִרְבְּכֶם. 15 לֵאלֹהִים הַתּוֹדָה עַל מַתְּנָתוֹ הָעֲצוּמָה מִסַּפֵּר.

י אֲנִי עַצְמִי, שָׁאוּל, מַפְצִיר בָּכֶם בְּנֹעַם הַמָּשִׁיחַ וּבַעֲנָוָתוֹ – אֲנִי אֲשֶׁר בְּעָמְדִי לִפְנֵיכֶם חַלּוּשׁ אָנֹכִי, אַךְ בְּהֶעָדְרִי מִפְּנֵיכֶם נוֹעָז אֲנִי כְּלַפֵּיכֶם. 2 מְבַקֵּשׁ אֲנִי שֶׁבִּהְיוֹתִי אֶצְלְכֶם לֹא אֶצְטָרֵךְ לִנְהֹג בְּעֹז, בְּאוֹתוֹ בִּטָּחוֹן שֶׁאֲנִי מִתְכַּוֵּן לָצֵאת בּוֹ נֶגֶד כַּמָּה אֲנָשִׁים

which I intend to be bold against some, who think of us as if we walked according to the flesh. ³ For though we walk in the flesh, we do not war according to the flesh. ⁴ For the weapons of our warfare *are* not carnal but mighty in God for pulling down strongholds, ⁵ casting down arguments and every high thing that exalts itself against the knowledge of God, bringing every thought into captivity to the obedience of Christ, ⁶ and being ready to punish all disobedience when your obedience is fulfilled.

⁷ Do you look at things according to the outward appearance? If anyone is convinced in himself that he is Christ's, let him again consider this in himself, that just as he *is* Christ's, even so we *are* Christ's. ⁸ For even if I should boast somewhat more about our authority, which the Lord gave us for edification and not for your destruction, I shall not be ashamed— ⁹ lest I seem to terrify you by letters. ¹⁰ "For *his* letters," they say, "*are* weighty and powerful, but *his* bodily presence *is* weak, and *his* speech contemptible." ¹¹ Let such a person consider this, that what we are in word by letters when we are absent, such we will also *be* in deed when we are present.

¹² For we dare not class ourselves or compare ourselves with those who commend themselves. But they, measuring themselves by themselves, and comparing themselves among themselves, are not wise. ¹³ We, however, will not boast beyond measure, but within the limits of the sphere which God appointed us—a sphere which especially includes you. ¹⁴ For we are not overextending ourselves (as though *our authority* did not extend to you), for it was to you that we came with the gospel of Christ; ¹⁵ not boasting of things beyond measure, *that is,* in other men's labors, but having hope, *that* as your faith is increased, we shall be greatly enlarged by you in our sphere, ¹⁶ to preach the gospel in the *regions* beyond you, *and* not to boast in another man's sphere of accomplishment.

¹⁷ But "he who glories, let him glory in the LORD." ¹⁸ For not he who commends himself is approved, but whom the Lord commends.

11 Oh, that you would bear with me in a little folly—and indeed you do bear with me. ² For I am jealous for you with godly jealousy. For I have betrothed you to one husband, that I may present *you as* a chaste virgin to Christ. ³ But I fear, lest somehow, as the serpent deceived Eve by his craftiness, so your minds may be corrupted from the simplicity that is in Christ. ⁴ For if he who comes preaches another Jesus whom we have not

הַחוֹשְׁבִים אוֹתָנוּ לְמִתְנַהֲגִים עַל־פִּי מַחֲשֶׁבֶת בָּשָׂר וָדָם. ³ אָמְנָם חַיִּים אָנוּ כְּבָשָׂר וָדָם, אַךְ אֵין אָנוּ נִלְחָמִים כְּדֶרֶךְ בָּשָׂר וָדָם; ⁴ שֶׁכֵּן כְּלֵי מִלְחַמְתֵּנוּ עַצְמָתָם אֵינָהּ מִבְּשָׂר וָדָם, אֶלָּא עָצְמַת אֱלֹהִים בָּהֶם לַהֲרֹם מִבְצָרִים. ⁵ אֲנַחְנוּ מְמוֹטְטִים תַּחְבּוּלוֹת וְכָל דָּבָר רָם שֶׁמִּתְנַשֵּׂא נֶגֶד דַּעַת אֱלֹהִים, וּמַכְנִיעִים כָּל מַחֲשָׁבָה לְשֵׁם צִיּוּת לַמָּשִׁיחַ, ⁶ וּמוּכָנִים לְהַעֲנִישׁ עַל כָּל הֲפָרַת מִשְׁמַעַת, כַּאֲשֶׁר תִּשְׁלַם מִשְׁמַעְתְּכֶם אַתֶּם.

⁷ לְפִי מַרְאֶה חִיצוֹנִי בּוֹחֲנִים אַתֶּם אֶת הַדְּבָרִים! אִם מִישֶׁהוּ בָּטוּחַ בְּעַצְמוֹ שֶׁהוּא שַׁיָּךְ לַמָּשִׁיחַ, יַחֲזֹר נָא וְיִתֵּן דַּעְתּוֹ עַל זֹאת: כְּשֵׁם שֶׁהוּא שַׁיָּךְ לַמָּשִׁיחַ, כֵּן גַּם אֲנַחְנוּ. ⁸ וְגַם אִם אֶתְגָּאֶה קְצָת יוֹתֵר מִדַּי בַּסַּמְכוּת אֲשֶׁר נָתַן לָנוּ הָאָדוֹן לִבְנוֹת וְלֹא לַהֲרֹם, לֹא אֵבוֹשׁ. ⁹ אֵין כַּוָּנָתִי לְהַרְאוֹת כְּמֵאַיֵּם עֲלֵיכֶם בָּאִגְּרוֹת. ¹⁰ יֵשׁ אוֹמְרִים: "אִגְּרוֹתָיו אָמְנָם מַרְשִׁימוֹת וְתַקִּיפוֹת, אַךְ בְּעָמְדוֹ לְפָנֵינוּ בְּגוּפוֹ הֲרֵיהוּ חַלָּשׁ וּדְבָרוֹ חֲסַר־עֵרֶךְ." ¹¹ הָאוֹמֵר כָּךְ יֵדַע נָא אֶת זֹאת: כְּדֶרֶךְ שֶׁאֲנַחְנוּ בְּאֹמֶר עַל־יְדֵי אִגְּרוֹת בְּעֵת הֵעָדְרֵנוּ, כֵּן אֲנַחְנוּ גַּם בְּמַעֲשֶׂה בְּעֵת נוֹכְחוּתֵנוּ.

¹² אֵין אָנוּ מֵעֵזִים לְכַלֵּל עַצְמֵנוּ עִם כַּמָּה מֵאוֹתָם אֲנָשִׁים הַמְשַׁבְּחִים אֶת עַצְמָם, גַּם לֹא נָעֵז לְהַשְׁווֹת עַצְמֵנוּ אֲלֵיהֶם. הַלָּלוּ מוֹדְדִים אֶת עַצְמָם כְּשֶׁהֵם מְשַׁמְּשִׁים קְנֵי מִדָּה לְעַצְמָם וּמַשְׁווִים אֶת עַצְמָם לְעַצְמָם, וְאֵינָם אֶלָּא חַסְרֵי בִּינָה. ¹³ אֲנַחְנוּ לֹא נִתְגָּאֶה יוֹתֵר מִן הַמִּדָּה, אֶלָּא בַּמִּדָּה הַהוֹלֶמֶת אֶת הַתְּחוּם שֶׁהִקְצָה לָנוּ אֱלֹהִים, תְּחוּם הַמַּגִּיעַ גַּם עֲדֵיכֶם. ¹⁴ אֵין אָנוּ מַסִּיגִים גְּבוּל, כְּאִלּוּ לֹא הִגַּעְנוּ עֲדֵיכֶם; שֶׁהֲרֵי גַּם אֲלֵיכֶם הִגַּעְנוּ עִם בְּשׂוֹרַת הַמָּשִׁיחַ. ¹⁵ אֵין גַּאֲוָתֵנוּ חוֹרֶגֶת מִן הַמִּדָּה בְּאֹפֶן שֶׁנִּתְגָּאֶה בַּעֲמָלָם שֶׁל אֲחֵרִים. אֲבָל מְקַוִּים אָנוּ כִּי בִּגְדֹל אֱמוּנַתְכֶם נִגְדַּל בְּקִרְבְּכֶם בִּמְלוֹא הַמִּדָּה הַנְּתוּנָה לָנוּ, ¹⁶ עַד כְּדֵי לְבַשֵּׂר אֶת הַבְּשׂוֹרָה בִּמְקוֹמוֹת אֲשֶׁר מֵעֵבֶר לָאֵזוֹרְכֶם, וְלֹא נִתְגָּאֶה בְּמַה שֶּׁכְּבָר נַעֲשָׂה בִּתְחוּמָם שֶׁל אֲחֵרִים. ¹⁷ "הַמִּתְהַלֵּל יִתְהַלֵּל בַּיהוה"; ¹⁸ כִּי לֹא הַמְהַלֵּל אֶת עַצְמוֹ מֵהֵימָן, אֶלָּא מִי שֶׁיהוה מְהַלְלוֹ.

יא מִי יִתֵּן וְתִסְבְּלוּנִי עַל אִוֶּלֶת־מָה! וְאוּלָם אַתֶּם סוֹבְלִים אוֹתִי. ² מְקַנֵּא אֲנִי לָכֶם קִנְאַת אֱלֹהִים, כִּי הֵאֵרַשְׂתִּי אֶתְכֶם לְאִישׁ אֶחָד, לַמָּשִׁיחַ, כְּדֵי לְהַצִּיגְכֶם בְּתוּלָה טְהוֹרָה לְפָנָיו. ³ אַךְ חוֹשְׁשַׁנִי שֶׁמָּא תֻּדַּחְנָה מַחְשְׁבוֹתֵיכֶם מִן הַפַּשְׁטוּת שֶׁבַּמָּשִׁיחַ, כְּמוֹ שֶׁאֶרֶץ לַחַוָּה כַּאֲשֶׁר הֵדִיחַ אוֹתָהּ הַנָּחָשׁ בְּעָרְמָתוֹ; ⁴ שֶׁכֵּן

preached, or *if* you receive a different spirit which you have not received, or a different gospel which you have not accepted—you may well put up with it!

⁵ For I consider that I am not at all inferior to the most eminent apostles. ⁶ Even though *I am* untrained in speech, yet *I am* not in knowledge. But we have been thoroughly manifested among you in all things.

⁷ Did I commit sin in humbling myself that you might be exalted, because I preached the gospel of God to you free of charge? ⁸ I robbed other churches, taking wages *from them* to minister to you. ⁹ And when I was present with you, and in need, I was a burden to no one, for what I lacked the brethren who came from Macedonia supplied. And in everything I kept myself from being burdensome to you, and so I will keep *myself*. ¹⁰ As the truth of Christ is in me, no one shall stop me from this boasting in the regions of Achaia. ¹¹ Why? Because I do not love you? God knows!

¹² But what I do, I will also continue to do, that I may cut off the opportunity from those who desire an opportunity to be regarded just as we are in the things of which they boast. ¹³ For such *are* false apostles, deceitful workers, transforming themselves into apostles of Christ. ¹⁴ And no wonder! For Satan himself transforms himself into an angel of light. ¹⁵ Therefore *it is* no great thing if his ministers also transform themselves into ministers of righteousness, whose end will be according to their works.

¹⁶ I say again, let no one think me a fool. If otherwise, at least receive me as a fool, that I also may boast a little. ¹⁷ What I speak, I speak not according to the Lord, but as it were, foolishly, in this confidence of boasting. ¹⁸ Seeing that many boast according to the flesh, I also will boast. ¹⁹ For you put up with fools gladly, since you *yourselves* are wise! ²⁰ For you put up with it if one brings you into bondage, if one devours *you,* if one takes *from you,* if one exalts himself, if one strikes you on the face. ²¹ To *our* shame I say that we were too weak for that! But in whatever anyone is bold—I speak foolishly—I am bold also.

²² Are they Hebrews? So *am* I. Are they Israelites? So *am* I. Are they the seed of Abraham? So *am* I. ²³ Are they ministers of Christ?—I speak as a fool—I *am* more: in labors more abundant, in stripes above measure, in prisons more frequently, in deaths often. ²⁴ From the Jews five times I received forty *stripes* minus one. ²⁵ Three times I was beaten with rods; once I was stoned; three times I was shipwrecked; a night and a day I have been in the

אִם בָּא מִישֶׁהוּ וּמַכְרִיז לָכֶם עַל יֵשׁוּעַ אַחֵר אֲשֶׁר לֹא הִכְרַזְנוּ, אוֹ בְּקַבֶּלְכֶם רוּחַ שׁוֹנָה מִזּוֹ שֶׁנְּתַנָּה לָכֶם, אוֹ בְּשׂוֹרָה שׁוֹנָה מִזּוֹ שֶׁקִּבַּלְתֶּם, אֲזַי אַתֶּם סוֹבְלִים אוֹתוֹ הֵיטֵב.

⁵ סְבוּרַנִי שֶׁאֵינֶנִּי נוֹפֵל בִּמְאוּמָה מֵאוֹתָם שְׁלִיחִים מְעֻלִּים. ⁶ וְגַם אִם בַּעַר אֲנִי בְּדִבּוּר אֵינֶנִּי בַּעַר בְּדַעַת, אֶלָּא בַּכֹּל, בְּכָל דָּבָר, הֶרְאֵינוּ לָכֶם אֶת זֹאת. ⁷ הֶחָטָאתִי אֶת עַצְמִי כְּדֵי לְרוֹמֵם אֶתְכֶם בְּכַשְּׁרִי לָכֶם אֶת בְּשׂוֹרַת אֱלֹהִים בְּחִנָּם; הַאִם חֵטְא עָשִׂיתִי בְךָ? ⁸ מִקְּהִלּוֹת אֲחֵרוֹת נָטַלְתִּי, מֵהֶם לָקַחְתִּי שָׂכָר כְּדֵי לְשָׁרֵת אֶתְכֶם. ⁹ וְכַאֲשֶׁר הָיִיתִי אֶצְלְכֶם וְחָסַר לִי דְּבַר מָה, לֹא הָיִיתִי לְמַעֲמָסָה עַל אִישׁ, כִּי הָאַחִים שֶׁבָּאוּ מִמַּקֶּדוֹנְיָה נָתְנוּ לִי דֵּי צָרְכִּי. וּבְכָל דָּבָר נִשְׁמַרְתִּי שֶׁלֹּא אֶהְיֶה לְמַשָּׂא עֲלֵיכֶם, וְכֵן אַמְשִׁיךְ וְאֶשָּׁמֵר. ¹⁰ כְּשֵׁם שֶׁאֱמֶת הַמָּשִׁיחַ בִּי, כֵּן הַגַּאֲוָה הַזֹּאת לֹא תִשָּׁלֵל מִמֶּנִּי בְּגָלִילוֹת אֲכָיָה. ¹¹ וּמַדּוּעַ? הַאִם מִשּׁוּם שֶׁאֵינֶנִּי אוֹהֵב אֶתְכֶם? הָאֱלֹהִים יוֹדֵעַ!

¹² אֲבָל אֶת אֲשֶׁר אֲנִי עוֹשֶׂה גַּם אוֹסִיף לַעֲשׂוֹת כְּדֵי לְהָסִיר עִלָּה מִידֵי הַמְבַקְשִׁים עִלָּה לְהִשְׁתַּוּוֹת לָנוּ בַּדָּבָר שֶׁהֵם מִתְגָּאִים בּוֹ. ¹³ הֲרֵי אֲנָשִׁים כָּאֵלֶּה שְׁלִיחֵי שֶׁקֶר הֵם, פּוֹעֲלֵי רְמִיָּה הַמִּתְחַפְּשִׂים לִשְׁלִיחֵי הַמָּשִׁיחַ. ¹⁴ וְאֵין לִתְמֹהַּ עַל כָּךְ, שֶׁהֲרֵי הַשָּׂטָן עַצְמוֹ מִתְחַפֵּשׂ לְמַלְאַךְ אוֹר. ¹⁵ עַל כֵּן אֵין רְבוּתָא בְּכָךְ שֶׁגַּם מְשָׁרְתָיו מִתְחַפְּשִׂים לִמְשָׁרְתֵי הַצֶּדֶק; סוֹפָם יִהְיֶה כְּפִי מַעֲלָלֵיהֶם.

¹⁶ אֲנִי חוֹזֵר וְאוֹמֵר: אַל יַחְשְׁבֵנִי אִישׁ לִכְסִיל. אֲבָל אִם אָכֵן כָּזֶה אֲנִי בְּעֵינֵיכֶם, כִּכְסִיל קַבְּלוּ אוֹתִי, כְּדֵי שֶׁגַּם אֲנִי אֶתְגָּאֶה קִמְעָה. ¹⁷ בְּדַבְּרִי כָּךְ לֹא כְּדֶרֶךְ הָאָדוֹן אֲנִי מְדַבֵּר, אֶלָּא כְּמוֹ בְּאִוֶּלֶת, בְּבִטָּחוֹן הַגַּאֲוָה הַזֹּאת. ¹⁸ וּמֵאַחַר שֶׁרַבִּים מִתְגָּאִים כְּדֶרֶךְ בָּשָׂר וָדָם, אֶתְגָּאֶה גַּם אֲנִי; ¹⁹ שֶׁהֲרֵי בְּשִׂמְחָה אַתֶּם סוֹבְלִים אֶת הָאֱוִילִים, אַתֶּם הַחֲכָמִים! ²⁰ אִם מִישֶׁהוּ מְשַׁעְבֵּד אֶתְכֶם, מְכַרְסֵם בָּכֶם, עוֹשֵׁק אֶתְכֶם, מִתְנַשֵּׂא עֲלֵיכֶם אוֹ סוֹטֵר לָכֶם עַל הַפָּנִים – אַתֶּם סוֹבְלִים זֹאת. ²¹ בִּתְחוּשַׁת בּוּשָׁה אֲנִי אוֹמֵר זֹאת, כְּאִלּוּ הָיִינוּ אֲנַחְנוּ חַלָּשִׁים. וְאוּלָם בְּכָל דָּבָר שֶׁעַז אִישׁ – וַאֲנִי מְדַבֵּר בְּאִוֶּלֶת – אַרְהִיב עֹז גַּם אֲנִי. ²² עִבְרִים הֵם? כֵּן גַּם אֲנִי. יִשְׂרְאֵלִים הֵם? כֵּן גַּם אֲנִי. צֶאֱצָאֵי אַבְרָהָם? כֵּן גַּם אֲנִי. ²³ מְשָׁרְתֵי הַמָּשִׁיחַ הֵם? – כְּאֱוִיל אֲדַבֵּר – אֲנִי עוֹד יוֹתֵר; בֶּעָמָל, אֲנִי יוֹתֵר מֵהֶם; בְּבָתֵּי כֶלֶא, אֲנִי יוֹתֵר; בְּמַלְקוֹת, אֲנִי הַרְבֵּה יוֹתֵר; בְּסַכָּנַת מָוֶת – פְּעָמִים רַבּוֹת. ²⁴ חָמֵשׁ פְּעָמִים הִלְקוּנִי הַיְּהוּדִים אַרְבָּעִים פְּעָמִים חָסֵר אַחַת. ²⁵ שָׁלֹשׁ פְּעָמִים הֻלְקֵיתִי

deep; 26 in journeys often, in perils of waters, in perils of robbers, in perils of my own countrymen, in perils of the Gentiles, in perils in the city, in perils in the wilderness, in perils in the sea, in perils among false brethren; 27 in weariness and toil, in sleeplessness often, in hunger and thirst, in fastings often, in cold and nakedness— 28 besides the other things, what comes upon me daily: my deep concern for all the churches. 29 Who is weak, and I am not weak? Who is made to stumble, and I do not burn with indignation?

30 If I must boast, I will boast in the things which concern my infirmity. 31 The God and Father of our Lord Jesus Christ, who is blessed forever, knows that I am not lying. 32 In Damascus the governor, under Aretas the king, was guarding the city of the Damascenes with a garrison, desiring to arrest me; 33 but I was let down in a basket through a window in the wall, and escaped from his hands.

12 It is doubtless not profitable for me to boast. I will come to visions and revelations of the Lord: 2 I know a man in Christ who fourteen years ago— whether in the body I do not know, or whether out of the body I do not know, God knows—such a one was caught up to the third heaven. 3 And I know such a man—whether in the body or out of the body I do not know, God knows— 4 how he was caught up into Paradise and heard inexpressible words, which it is not lawful for a man to utter. 5 Of such a one I will boast; yet of myself I will not boast, except in my infirmities. 6 For though I might desire to boast, I will not be a fool; for I will speak the truth. But I refrain, lest anyone should think of me above what he sees me to be or hears from me.

7 And lest I should be exalted above measure by the abundance of the revelations, a thorn in the flesh was given to me, a messenger of Satan to buffet me, lest I be exalted above measure. 8 Concerning this thing I pleaded with the Lord three times that it might depart from me. 9 And He said to me, "My grace is sufficient for you, for My strength is made perfect in weakness." Therefore most gladly I will rather boast in my infirmities, that the power of Christ may rest upon me. 10 Therefore I take pleasure in infirmities, in reproaches, in needs, in persecutions, in distresses, for Christ's sake. For when I am weak, then I am strong.

11 I have become a fool in boasting; you have compelled me. For I ought to have been commended by you; for in nothing was I behind the most eminent apostles, though I am nothing. 12 Truly the signs of an apostle were accomplished

בְּשׁוֹטִים; פַּעַם אַחַת נִרְגַּמְתִּי בַּאֲבָנִים; שָׁלֹשׁ פְּעָמִים נִטְרְפָה סְפִינָתִי, וּפַעַם שֶׁהָיִיתִי בַּמַּיִם בִּמְשַׁךְ יְמָמָה. 26 וְנִתְנַסֵּיתִי בְּמַסָּעוֹת רַבִּים, בְּסַכָּנוֹת עַל פְּנֵי נְהָרוֹת, בְּסַכָּנוֹת מִפְּנֵי שׁוֹדְדִים, בְּסַכָּנוֹת מִבְּנֵי עַמִּי, בְּסַכָּנוֹת מִן הַגּוֹיִם, בְּסַכָּנוֹת בָּעִיר וּבַמִּדְבָּר וּבַיָּם, בְּסַכָּנוֹת בְּקֶרֶב אֲחֵי שֶׁקֶר; 27 בְּעָמָל וּבְתִלְאָה, בְּלֵילוֹת רַבִּים לְלֹא שֵׁנָה, בְּרָעָב וּבַצָּמָא, בְּצוֹמוֹת הַרְבֵּה, בְּקֹר וּבְעֵירֹם; 28 וּמִלְּבַד דְּבָרִים אֲחֵרִים, הַטֹּרַח הַבָּא עָלַי יוֹם יוֹם, הַדְּאָגָה לְכָל הַקְּהִלּוֹת. 29 מִי יֶחֱלַשׁ וַאֲנִי לֹא אֶחֱלַשׁ עִמּוֹ? מִי יִכָּשֵׁל וְלִבִּי אֵינוֹ בּוֹעֵר?

30 אִם מִן הָרָאוּי לְהִתְגָּאוֹת, אֶתְגָּאֶה בַּדְּבָרִים הַנּוֹגְעִים לְחֻלְשָׁתִי. 31 הָאֱלֹהִים וַאֲבִי הָאָדוֹן יֵשׁוּעַ, הוּא הַמְבֹרָךְ לְעוֹלָמִים, יוֹדֵעַ שֶׁאֵינֶנִּי מְשַׁקֵּר. 32 בְּדַמֶּשֶׂק הִצִּיב הַמּוֹשֵׁל מִטַּעַם הַמֶּלֶךְ אֲרֵטַס שְׁמִירָה עַל הָעִיר כְּדֵי לְתָפְשֵׂנִי, 33 אֶלָּא שֶׁהוֹרִידוּנִי בְּסַל דֶּרֶךְ חַלּוֹן אֲשֶׁר בַּחוֹמָה וְנִמְלַטְתִּי מִיָּדָיו.

יב אֲנִי נֶאֱלָץ לְהִתְגָּאוֹת; אָמְנָם אֵין בָּזֶה מוֹעִיל, אַךְ אֶפְנֶה לְחֶזְיוֹנוֹת וּלְהִתְגַּלִּיּוֹת אֲשֶׁר מֵאֵת הָאָדוֹן. 2 אֲנִי מַכִּיר אִישׁ בַּמָּשִׁיחַ, אֲשֶׁר לִפְנֵי אַרְבַּע-עֶשְׂרֵה שָׁנִים נִלְקַח אֶל הָרָקִיעַ הַשְּׁלִישִׁי; אֵינֶנִּי יוֹדֵעַ אִם בְּגוּפוֹ אוֹ מְחוּץ לְגוּפוֹ, הָאֱלֹהִים יוֹדֵעַ. 3 אֲנִי מַכִּיר אִישׁ כָּזֶה – אֵינֶנִּי יוֹדֵעַ אִם בְּגוּפוֹ אוֹ מְחוּץ לְגוּפוֹ, הָאֱלֹהִים יוֹדֵעַ – 4 אֲשֶׁר נִלְקַח אֶל גַּן עֵדֶן וְשָׁמַע מִלִּים שֶׁאֵין לְבַטְּאָן, שֶׁאָסוּר לְאָדָם לְמַלְּלָן. 5 בְּאִישׁ כָּזֶה אֶתְגָּאֶה, אַךְ בִּי עַצְמִי לֹא אֶתְגָּאֶה, זוּלָתִי בְּחֻלְשׁוֹתַי. 6 גַּם אִם אֶרְצֶה לְהִתְגָּאוֹת לֹא אֶהְיֶה בְּחֶזְקַת כְּסִיל, שֶׁכֵּן אֲדַבֵּר אֱמֶת. אֲבָל נִמְנָע אֲנִי, פֶּן יַחְשְׁבֵנִי לְיוֹתֵר מִמַּה שֶּׁרוֹאִים בִּי אוֹ שׁוֹמְעִים מִמֶּנִּי. 7 וּכְדֵי שֶׁלֹּא אֶתְנַשֵּׂא בִּגְלַל הַהִתְגַּלִּיּוֹת הַנַּעֲלוֹת, נִתַּן לִי קוֹץ בִּבְשָׂרִי – מַלְאָכוֹ שֶׁל הַשָּׂטָן – לְהַכּוֹתֵנִי כְּדֵי שֶׁלֹּא אֶתְנַשֵּׂא. 8 עַל זֹאת הִתְחַנַּנְתִּי שָׁלֹשׁ פְּעָמִים אֶל הָאָדוֹן לַהֲסִירוֹ מִמֶּנִּי. 9 אַךְ הוּא אָמַר לִי: "דַּי לְךָ חַסְדִּי, כִּי בַּחֻלְשָׁה תֻּשְׁלַם גְּבוּרָתִי." עַל כֵּן בְּשִׂמְחָה רַבָּה אֶתְגָּאֶה בְּחֻלְשׁוֹתַי, כְּדֵי שֶׁתִּשְׁרֶה עָלַי גְּבוּרַת הַמָּשִׁיחַ. 10 מִשּׁוּם כָּךְ מְרֻצֶּה אֲנִי בַּחֻלְשׁוֹת, בַּחֲרָפוֹת, בְּמַצּוּקוֹת מַחְסוֹר, בִּרְדִיפוֹת וּבְצָרוֹת הַבָּאוֹת עָלַי לְמַעַן הַמָּשִׁיחַ; כִּי כַּאֲשֶׁר אֲנִי חַלָּשׁ, דַּוְקָא אָז חָזָק אֲנִי.

11 כְּסִיל נִהְיֵיתִי! אַתֶּם אִלַּצְתֶּם אוֹתִי. הֵן מִן הָרָאוּי הָיָה שֶׁאֲקֻבַּל אֵת שִׁבְחִי מִכֶּם, כִּי אֵינֶנִּי נוֹפֵל בְּשׁוּם דָּבָר מִן הַשְּׁלִיחִים הַמְּעֻלִּים, אַף שֶׁכָּאַן, אַף כְּאַפַס אָנֹכִי. 12 הֲרֵי אוֹתוֹת הַהֶכֵּר שֶׁל הַשָּׁלִיחַ נַעֲשׂוּ בְּקִרְבְּכֶם בִּמְלוֹא סַבְלָנוּת, בְּאוֹתוֹת וּבְמוֹפְתִים

among you with all perseverance, in signs and wonders and mighty deeds. 13 For what is it in which you were inferior to other churches, except that I myself was not burdensome to you? Forgive me this wrong!

14 Now *for* the third time I am ready to come to you. And I will not be burdensome to you; for I do not seek yours, but you. For the children ought not to lay up for the parents, but the parents for the children. 15 And I will very gladly spend and be spent for your souls; though the more abundantly I love you, the less I am loved.

16 But be that *as it may,* I did not burden you. Nevertheless, being crafty, I caught you by cunning! 17 Did I take advantage of you by any of those whom I sent to you? 18 I urged Titus, and sent our brother with *him.* Did Titus take advantage of you? Did we not walk in the same spirit? Did *we* not *walk* in the same steps?

19 Again, do you think that we excuse ourselves to you? We speak before God in Christ. But *we do* all things, beloved, for your edification. 20 For I fear lest, when I come, I shall not find you such as I wish, and *that* I shall be found by you such as you do not wish; lest *there be* contentions, jealousies, outbursts of wrath, selfish ambitions, backbitings, whisperings, conceits, tumults; 21 lest, when I come again, my God will humble me among you, and I shall mourn for many who have sinned before and have not repented of the uncleanness, fornication, and lewdness which they have practiced.

13 This *will be* the third *time* I am coming to you. "*By the mouth of two or three witnesses every word shall be established.*" 2 I have told you before, and foretell as if I were present the second time, and now being absent I write to those who have sinned before, and to all the rest, that if I come again I will not spare— 3 since you seek a proof of Christ speaking in me, who is not weak toward you, but mighty in you. 4 For though He was crucified in weakness, yet He lives by the power of God. For we also are weak in Him, but we shall live with Him by the power of God toward you.

5 Examine yourselves *as to* whether you are in the faith. Test yourselves. Do you not know yourselves, that Jesus Christ is in you?—unless indeed you are disqualified. 6 But I trust that you will know that we are not disqualified.

7 Now I pray to God that you do no evil, not that we should appear approved, but that you should do what is honorable, though we may seem

וּבִגְבוּרוֹת. 13 וּבַמֶּה גָּרַעְתֶּם לְעֻמַּת שְׁאָר הַקְּהִלּוֹת, זוּלָתִי בָּזֶה שֶׁאֲנִי עַצְמִי לֹא הָיִיתִי לָכֶם לְמַעֲמָסָה? סִלְחוּ נָא לִי אֶת הָעָוֶל הַזֶּה! 14 הֲרֵינִי מוּכָן לָבוֹא אֲלֵיכֶם פַּעַם שְׁלִישִׁית; וְלֹא אֶהְיֶה לְטֹרַח עֲלֵיכֶם, שֶׁכֵּן אֵינֶנִּי מְבַקֵּשׁ אֶת אֲשֶׁר לָכֶם, אֶלָּא אֶתְכֶם. הֲלֹא הַבָּנִים אֵינָם חַיָּבִים לֶאֱצֹר אוֹצָרוֹת לְהוֹרֵיהֶם, אֶלָּא הַהוֹרִים לִבְנֵיהֶם. 15 וַאֲנִי בְּשִׂמְחָה אֶתֵּן גַּם אֶת מַה שֶּׁיֵּשׁ לִי וְגַם אֶת עַצְמִי לְמַעַן נַפְשׁוֹתֵיכֶם. אִם אֲנִי אוֹהֵב אֶתְכֶם בְּמִדָּה יְתֵרָה, הֲתֶאֱהֲבוּ אוֹתִי בְּמִדָּה פְּחוּתָה?

16 כֵּן, אֲנִי לֹא הָיִיתִי לְמַעֲמָסָה עֲלֵיכֶם, אַךְ הוֹאִיל וַאֲנִי אִישׁ עָרוּם לָכַדְתִּי אֶתְכֶם בְּעָרְמָה! 17 הַגִּידוּ לִי, הַאִם הוֹנֵיתִי אֶתְכֶם עַל־יְדֵי אִישׁ מֵהָאֲנָשִׁים אֲשֶׁר שָׁלַחְתִּי אֲלֵיכֶם? 18 בִּקַּשְׁתִּי מִטִּיטוֹס וְשָׁלַחְתִּי אִתּוֹ אֶת הָאָח. הַאִם טִיטוֹס הוֹנָה אֶתְכֶם? הַאִם לֹא הִתְהַלַּכְנוּ לְפִי אוֹתָהּ רוּחַ? הַאִם לֹא בְּאוֹתָהּ דֶּרֶךְ? 19 זֶה מִכְּבָר סְבוּרִים אַתֶּם שֶׁאֲנַחְנוּ מְגִנִּים עַל עַצְמֵנוּ לִפְנֵיכֶם. וּבְכֵן לִפְנֵי אֱלֹהִים, בַּמָּשִׁיחַ, אֲנַחְנוּ מְדַבְּרִים; וְהַכֹּל, חֲבִיבַי, כְּדֵי שֶׁתִּבָּנוּ. 20 חוֹשֵׁשׁ אֲנִי שֶׁבְּבוֹאִי לֹא אֶמְצָא אֶתְכֶם כִּלְבָבִי, וְאַתֶּם לֹא תִּמְצָאוּנִי כִּלְבַבְכֶם; שֶׁמָּא אֶמְצָא מְרִיבָה, קִנְאָה, רֹגֶז, תַּחֲרוּת, דִּבָּה רָעָה, רְכִילוּת, יְהִירוּת וְאִי־דְרָלְמוֹסְיָה. 21 וְשֶׁמָּא בְּשׁוּבִי אֲלֵיכֶם יַשְׁפִּילֵנִי אֱלֹהַי אֶצְלְכֶם, וְאֶתְאַבֵּל עַל רַבִּים אֲשֶׁר חָטְאוּ כְּבָר וְלֹא חָזְרוּ בִּתְשׁוּבָה עַל הַטֻּמְאָה וְהַזְּנוּת וְהַזִּמָּה שֶׁעָשׂוּ.

יג זוֹ הַפַּעַם הַשְּׁלִישִׁית אָבוֹא אֲלֵיכֶם. "עַל־פִּי שְׁנֵי עֵדִים אוֹ עַל־פִּי שְׁלֹשָׁה־עֵדִים יָקוּם דָּבָר." 2 בִּהְיוֹתִי אֶצְלְכֶם בַּפַּעַם הַשְּׁנִיָּה כְּבָר אָמַרְתִּי, וְעַתָּה, כְּשֶׁאֵינֶנִּי עִמָּכֶם, אֲנִי מַקְדִּים וְאוֹמֵר לְאוֹתָם אֲנָשִׁים אֲשֶׁר חָטְאוּ בֶּעָבָר, וּלְכָל הַשְּׁאָר – שֶׁאִם אָבוֹא שׁוּב, לֹא אָחוּס; 3 שֶׁכֵּן מְבַקְשִׁים אַתֶּם לְהוֹכָחַ אִם הַמָּשִׁיחַ מְדַבֵּר בִּי, הַמָּשִׁיחַ אֲשֶׁר אֵינוֹ חַלָּשׁ לִפְנֵיכֶם כִּי אִם חָזָק בְּקִרְבְּכֶם. 4 וְאַף כִּי נִצְלַב כְּשֶׁהָיָה חַלָּשׁ, הוּא חַי בִּגְבוּרַת אֱלֹהִים. אָמְנָם גַּם אֲנַחְנוּ חַלָּשִׁים בּוֹ, אַךְ נִחְיֶה אִתּוֹ בִּגְבוּרַת אֱלֹהִים הַמְכֻוֶּנֶת אֲלֵיכֶם.

5 נַסּוּ אֶת עַצְמְכֶם אִם עוֹמְדִים אַתֶּם בָּאֱמוּנָה, בַּחֲנוּ אֶת עַצְמְכֶם; אוֹ שֶׁמָּא אַתֶּם עַצְמְכֶם אֵינְכֶם מַבְחִינִים שֶׁהָאָדוֹן יֵשׁוּעַ בְּקִרְבְּכֶם? – אִם אָמְנָם לֹא נִכְשַׁלְתֶּם אַתֶּם בַּמִּבְחָן. 6 אֲבָל מְקַוֶּה אֲנִי שֶׁתִּוָּכְרוּ כִּי אֲנַחְנוּ לֹא נִכְשַׁלְנוּ. 7 וַאֲנַחְנוּ מִתְפַּלְלִים לֵאלֹהִים שֶׁלֹּא תַּעֲשׂוּ שׁוּם רַע, לֹא כְּדֵי שֶׁאֲנַחְנוּ נֵרָאֶה מְהֵימָנִים, אֶלָּא כְּדֵי שֶׁאַתֶּם תַּעֲשׂוּ אֶת הַטּוֹב וַאֲנַחְנוּ

disqualified. [8] For we can do nothing against the truth, but for the truth. [9] For we are glad when we are weak and you are strong. And this also we pray, that you may be made complete. [10] Therefore I write these things being absent, lest being present I should use sharpness, according to the authority which the Lord has given me for edification and not for destruction.

[11] Finally, brethren, farewell. Become complete. Be of good comfort, be of one mind, live in peace; and the God of love and peace will be with you.

[12] Greet one another with a holy kiss.

[13] All the saints greet you.

[14] The grace of the Lord Jesus Christ, and the love of God, and the communion of the Holy Spirit be with you all. Amen.

נִהְיֶה כִּבְלְתֵּי מְהֵימָנִים. [8] הֲרֵי אֵין אָנוּ יְכוֹלִים לַעֲשׂוֹת מְאוּמָה נֶגֶד הָאֱמֶת, אֶלָּא בְּעַד הָאֱמֶת. [9] אָנוּ שְׂמֵחִים כַּאֲשֶׁר אֲנַחְנוּ חַלָּשִׁים וְאַתֶּם חֲזָקִים; וְזֹהִי גַּם תְּפִלָּתֵנוּ – שֶׁתָּבוֹאוּ לִידֵי תִקּוּן. [10] עַל כֵּן כָּתַבְתִּי אֶת הַדְּבָרִים הָאֵלֶּה בִּהְיוֹתִי רָחוֹק מִכֶּם, כְּדֵי שֶׁבִּהְיוֹתִי אֶצְלְכֶם לֹא אֶצְטָרֵךְ לִנְהֹג בְּחָמְרָה עַל-פִּי הַסַּמְכוּת שֶׁנָּתַן לִי הָאָדוֹן – לִבְנוֹת וְלֹא לַהֲרֹס. [11] סוֹף דָּבָר, אַחַי, שִׂמְחוּ. תַּקְּנוּ אֶת עַצְמְכֶם וְהִתְעוֹדְדוּ. הֱיוּ לֵב אֶחָד, חְיוּ בְּשָׁלוֹם, וֵאלֹהֵי הָאַהֲבָה וְהַשָּׁלוֹם יִהְיֶה עִמָּכֶם. [12] בָּרְכוּ לְשָׁלוֹם אִישׁ אֶת רֵעֵהוּ בִּנְשִׁיקָה קְדוֹשָׁה. [13] כָּל הַקְּדוֹשִׁים דּוֹרְשִׁים בִּשְׁלוֹמְכֶם. [14] חֶסֶד הָאָדוֹן יֵשׁוּעַ הַמָּשִׁיחַ וְאַהֲבַת הָאֱלֹהִים וְהִתְחַבְּרוּת בְּרוּחַ הַקֹּדֶשׁ עִם כֻּלְּכֶם!

The Epistle of Paul to the

GALATIANS

1 Paul, an apostle (not from men nor through man, but through Jesus Christ and God the Father who raised Him from the dead), ²and all the brethren who are with me,

To the churches of Galatia:

³Grace to you and peace from God the Father and our Lord Jesus Christ, ⁴who gave Himself for our sins, that He might deliver us from this present evil age, according to the will of our God and Father, ⁵to whom *be* glory forever and ever. Amen.

⁶I marvel that you are turning away so soon from Him who called you in the grace of Christ, to a different gospel, ⁷which is not another; but there are some who trouble you and want to pervert the gospel of Christ. ⁸But even if we, or an angel from heaven, preach any other gospel to you than what we have preached to you, let him be accursed. ⁹As we have said before, so now I say again, if anyone preaches any other gospel to you than what you have received, let him be accursed.

¹⁰For do I now persuade men, or God? Or do I seek to please men? For if I still pleased men, I would not be a bondservant of Christ.

¹¹But I make known to you, brethren, that the gospel which was preached by me is not according to man. ¹²For I neither received it from man, nor was I taught *it,* but *it came* through the revelation of Jesus Christ.

¹³For you have heard of my former conduct in Judaism, how I persecuted the church of God beyond measure and *tried to* destroy it. ¹⁴And I advanced in Judaism beyond many of my contemporaries in my own nation, being more exceedingly zealous for the traditions of my fathers.

¹⁵But when it pleased God, who separated me from my mother's womb and called *me* through His grace, ¹⁶to reveal His Son in me, that I might preach Him among the Gentiles, I did not immediately confer with flesh and blood, ¹⁷nor did I go up to Jerusalem to those *who were* apostles before me; but I went to Arabia, and returned again to Damascus.

¹⁸Then after three years I went up to Jerusalem to see Peter, and remained with him fifteen days. ¹⁹But I saw none of the other apostles except

אִגֶּרֶת שָׁאוּל אֶל הַגָּלָטִים

א מֵאֵת שָׁאוּל – שָׁלִיחַ שֶׁאֵינוֹ מִטַּעַם בְּנֵי אָדָם אַף לֹא נִתְמַנָּה עַל־יְדֵי אָדָם, אֶלָּא עַל־יְדֵי יֵשׁוּעַ הַמָּשִׁיחַ וֵאלֹהִים הָאָב שֶׁהֱקִימוֹ מִן הַמֵּתִים – ²וּמֵאֵת כָּל הָאַחִים אֲשֶׁר אִתִּי, אֶל קְהִלּוֹת גָּלַטְיָה: ³חֶסֶד וְשָׁלוֹם לָכֶם מֵאֵת הָאֱלֹהִים אָבִינוּ וּמֵאֵת אֲדוֹנֵנוּ יֵשׁוּעַ הַמָּשִׁיחַ ⁴שֶׁנָּתַן אֶת עַצְמוֹ עַל חַטֹּאתֵינוּ כְּדֵי לְחַלְּצֵנוּ מִן הָעוֹלָם הָרָע הַזֶּה, כִּרְצוֹן אֱלֹהִים אָבִינוּ. ⁵לֵאלֹהִים הַכָּבוֹד לְעוֹלְמֵי עוֹלָמִים. אָמֵן.

⁶מִתְפַּלֵּא אֲנִי שֵׂכֶל כָּךְ מַהֵר אַתֶּם סָרִים מִמִּי שֶׁקָּרָא אֶתְכֶם בְּחֶסֶד הַמָּשִׁיחַ וְעוֹבְרִים אֶל בְּשׂוֹרָה אַחֶרֶת. ⁷וְאֵין אַחֶרֶת, אֶלָּא שֶׁיֵּשׁ כַּמָּה אֲנָשִׁים הַמְבַלְבְּלִים אֶתְכֶם וַחֲפֵצִים לַעֲוֵת אֶת בְּשׂוֹרַת הַמָּשִׁיחַ. ⁸אַךְ אִם מִישֶׁהוּ, אֲפִלּוּ אֲנַחְנוּ אוֹ מַלְאָךְ מִן הַשָּׁמַיִם, יְבַשֵּׂר לָכֶם בְּשׂוֹרָה שׁוֹנָה מִזּוֹ שֶׁבִּשַּׂרְנוּ לָכֶם, חֵרֶם יִהְיֶה! ⁹אֲנִי חוֹזֵר וְאוֹמֵר מַה שֶּׁאָמַרְנוּ קֹדֶם לָכֵן: אִם מִישֶׁהוּ יְשַׂמֵּעַ לָכֶם בְּשׂוֹרָה שׁוֹנָה מִזּוֹ שֶׁקִּבַּלְתֶּם, חֵרֶם יִהְיֶה!

¹⁰הַאִם אֶל בְּנֵי אָדָם אֲנִי מִתְרַצֶּה כָּעֵת, אוֹ אֶל אֱלֹהִים? הַאִם מִשְׁתַּדֵּל אֲנִי לִמְצֹא חֵן בְּעֵינֵי בְּנֵי אָדָם? אִלּוּ עֲדַיִן הִשְׁתַּדַּלְתִּי לִמְצֹא חֵן בְּעֵינֵי אָדָם, לֹא הָיִיתִי עֶבֶד הַמָּשִׁיחַ.

¹¹הֲרֵינִי מוֹדִיעַ לָכֶם, אַחַי, כִּי הַבְּשׂוֹרָה שֶׁבִּשַּׂרְתִּי אֵינֶנָּה לְפִי מַחֲשֶׁבֶת אָדָם, ¹²שֶׁכֵּן לֹא קִבַּלְתִּיהָ מֵאָדָם אַף לֹא לֻמַּדְנוּ אוֹתָהּ, אֶלָּא קִבַּלְתִּיהָ בְּהִתְגַּלּוּת שֶׁל יֵשׁוּעַ הַמָּשִׁיחַ.

¹³הֲרֵי שְׁמַעְתֶּם עַל הִתְנַהֲגוּתִי בֶּעָבָר בַּיַּהֲדוּת, שֶׁרָדַפְתִּי נִמְרָצוֹת אֶת קְהִלַּת אֱלֹהִים וְעָשִׂיתִי בָּהּ שַׁמּוֹת ¹⁴וְהִתְעַלֵּיתִי בַּיַּהֲדוּת עַל רַבִּים מִבְּנֵי גִּילִי אֲשֶׁר בְּעַמִּי, מִשּׁוּם קַנָּאתִי הַיְתֵרָה לְמָסוֹרוֹת אֲבוֹתַי. ¹⁵אֲבָל כַּאֲשֶׁר אֱלֹהִים, שֶׁהִקְדִּישַׁנִי מֵרֶחֶם אִמִּי וּקְרָאַנִי בְּחַסְדּוֹ, רָצָה ¹⁶לְגַלּוֹת בִּי אֶת בְּנוֹ כְּדֵי שֶׁאֲבַשְּׂרֶנּוּ בַּגּוֹיִים, לֹא נוֹעַצְתִּי אָז עִם בָּשָׂר וָדָם, ¹⁷גַּם לֹא עָלִיתִי לִירוּשָׁלַיִם אֶל מִי שֶׁהָיוּ שְׁלִיחִים לְפָנַי, אֶלָּא יָצָאתִי לַעֲרָב וְאַחַר כָּךְ חָזַרְתִּי לְדַמֶּשֶׂק. ¹⁸אַחֲרֵי שָׁלוֹשׁ שָׁנִים עָלִיתִי לִירוּשָׁלַיִם לִרְאוֹת אֶת כֵּיפָא וְשָׁהִיתִי אֶצְלוֹ חֲמִשָּׁה־עָשָׂר יָמִים. ¹⁹שְׁלִיחַ

James, the Lord's brother. 20 (Now *concerning* the things which I write to you, indeed, before God, I do not lie.)

21 Afterward I went into the regions of Syria and Cilicia. 22 And I was unknown by face to the churches of Judea which *were* in Christ. 23 But they were hearing only, "He who formerly persecuted us now preaches the faith which he once *tried to* destroy." 24 And they glorified God in me.

2 Then after fourteen years I went up again to Jerusalem with Barnabas, and also took Titus with *me*. 2 And I went up by revelation, and communicated to them that gospel which I preach among the Gentiles, but privately to those who were of reputation, lest by any means I might run, or had run, in vain. 3 Yet not even Titus who *was* with me, being a Greek, was compelled to be circumcised. 4 And *this occurred* because of false brethren secretly brought in (who came in by stealth to spy out our liberty which we have in Christ Jesus, that they might bring us into bondage), 5 to whom we did not yield submission even for an hour, that the truth of the gospel might continue with you.

6 But from those who seemed to be something— whatever they were, it makes no difference to me; God shows personal favoritism to no man—for those who seemed *to be something* added nothing to me. 7 But on the contrary, when they saw that the gospel for the uncircumcised had been committed to me, as *the gospel* for the circumcised *was* to Peter 8 (for He who worked effectively in Peter for the apostleship to the circumcised also worked effectively in me toward the Gentiles), 9 and when James, Cephas, and John, who seemed to be pillars, perceived the grace that had been given to me, they gave me and Barnabas the right hand of fellowship, that we *should go* to the Gentiles and they to the circumcised. 10 *They desired* only that we should remember the poor, the very thing which I also was eager to do.

11 Now when Peter had come to Antioch, I withstood him to his face, because he was to be blamed; 12 for before certain men came from James, he would eat with the Gentiles; but when they came, he withdrew and separated himself, fearing those who were of the circumcision. 13 And the rest of the Jews also played the hypocrite with him, so that even Barnabas was carried away with their hypocrisy.

14 But when I saw that they were not straightforward about the truth of the gospel, I said to Peter before *them* all, "If you, being a Jew, live in the manner of Gentiles and not as the Jews, why do you

אַחֵר לֹא רָאִיתִי, אֶלָּא אֶת יַעֲקֹב אֲחִי אֲדוֹנֵנוּ. 20 וַאֲשֶׁר לַדְּבָרִים שֶׁאֲנִי כּוֹתֵב אֲלֵיכֶם, אֱלֹהִים עֵד שֶׁאֵינֶנִּי מְשַׁקֵּר. 21 אַחֲרֵי כֵן בָּאתִי אֶל גְּלִילוֹת סוּרְיָה וְקִילִיקְיָה. 22 אֲבָל לֹא הָיִיתִי מֻכָּר בְּאֹפֶן אִישִׁי בִּקְהִלּוֹת הַמָּשִׁיחַ אֲשֶׁר בִּיהוּדָה. 23 הֵם רַק שָׁמְעוּ "כִּי הָאִישׁ אֲשֶׁר רָדַף אוֹתָנוּ בְּעָבָר, מַטִּיף עַכְשָׁו אֶת הָאֱמוּנָה אֲשֶׁר בְּעָבָר עָשָׂה בָּהּ שַׁמּוֹת," 24 וְהִלְּלוּ אֶת אֱלֹהִים בַּעֲבוּרִי.

ב אַחֲרֵי אַרְבַּע-עֶשְׂרֵה שָׁנִים עָלִיתִי שׁוּב לִירוּשָׁלַיִם יַחַד עִם בַּר-נַבָּא, וְגַם אֶת טִיטוֹם לָקַחְתִּי אִתִּי. 2 עָלִיתִי לְשָׁם עַל-פִּי הִתְגַּלּוּת שֶׁקִּבַּלְתִּי, וְהִצַּגְתִּי לִפְנֵיהֶם אֶת הַבְּשׂוֹרָה שֶׁאֲנִי מְבַשֵּׂר בַּגּוֹיִים; הַצַּגְתִּיהָ לִפְנֵי הַחֲשׁוּבִים שֶׁבָּהֶם בִּפְגִישָׁה מְיֻחֶדֶת, כְּדֵי שֶׁלֹּא לַשָּׁוְא יִהְיֶה הַמֵּרוֹץ אֲשֶׁר רַצְתִּי וְעוֹדֶנִּי רָץ. 3 אֲפִלּוּ טִיטוֹם שֶׁהָיָה אִתִּי, עַל אַף הֱיוֹתוֹ יְוָנִי, לֹא הֻכְרַח לְהִמּוֹל. 4 וּבִגְלַל אוֹתָם אַחֵי שֶׁקֶר שֶׁהֻסְתַּנְנוּ בַּחֲשַׁאי כְּדֵי לְבַלֵּשׁ אַחַר הַחֵרוּת שֶׁיֵּשׁ לָנוּ בַּמָּשִׁיחַ יֵשׁוּעַ; כָּל כַּוָּנָתָם הָיְתָה לְשַׁעְבֵּד אוֹתָנוּ, 5 אַךְ לֹא נִכְנַעְנוּ לָהֶם אַף לְרֶגַע, וְזֹאת לְמַעַן תַּעֲמֹד בְּקִרְבְּכֶם אֱמֶת הַבְּשׂוֹרָה.

6 בְּרַם, הָאֲנָשִׁים הַנֶּחְשָׁבִים לַחֲשׁוּבִים – בְּעֵינַי לֹא קוֹבֵעַ מַה הָיָה מַעֲמָדָם אָז, שֶׁהֲרֵי אֱלֹהִים אֵינֶנּוּ נוֹשֵׂא פְּנֵי אִישׁ – לֹא הוֹסִיפוּ לִי דָבָר. 7 אַדְּרַבָּא, הֵם הִכִּירוּ שֶׁבִּידֵי הֻפְקְדָה הַבְּשׂוֹרָה אֲשֶׁר לָעֲרֵלִים כְּשֵׁם שֶׁבִּידֵי פֶּטְרוֹס הֻפְקְדָה הַבְּשׂוֹרָה אֲשֶׁר לַנִּמּוֹלִים. 8 הֲרֵי מִי שֶׁעוֹרֵר אֶת פֶּטְרוֹס לִשְׁלִיחוּת אֶל הַנִּמּוֹלִים עוֹרֵר גַּם אוֹתִי אֶל הַגּוֹיִים. 9 וְכַאֲשֶׁר יַעֲקֹב, כֵּיפָא וְיוֹחָנָן, הַנֶּחְשָׁבִים לְעַמּוּדֵי תָּוֶךְ, הִכִּירוּ בַּחֶסֶד שֶׁנִּתַּן לִי, הֵם הוֹשִׁיטוּ לִי וּלְבַר-נַבָּא אֶת יַד יְמִינָם לְאוֹת שֻׁתָּף – שֶׁאָנוּ נֵלֵךְ לַגּוֹיִים וְהֵם לַנִּמּוֹלִים, 10 וּבִלְבַד שֶׁנִּזְכֹּר אֶת הָעֲנִיִּים. וְאָכֵן אֶת זֹאת שָׁקַדְתִּי לַעֲשׂוֹת. 11 כְּשֶׁבָּא כֵּיפָא לְאַנְטְיוֹכְיָה הִתְיַצַּבְתִּי נֶגְדּוֹ מִפְּנֵי שֶׁנִּמְצָא בּוֹ דְּבַר אַשְׁמָה. 12 בְּטֶרֶם בָּאוּ כַּמָּה אֲנָשִׁים מֵאֵת יַעֲקֹב הוּא סָעַר יַחַד עִם הָאַחִים מִן הַגּוֹיִים, אֲבָל כַּאֲשֶׁר בָּאוּ הַלָּלוּ נָסוֹג מֵהֶם בִּגְלַל פַּחְדּוֹ מִן הָאַחִים הַנִּמּוֹלִים. 13 וְיֶתֶר הָאַחִים הַיְּהוּדִים כִּחֲשׁוּ כָּמוֹהוּ, עַד שֶׁאֲפִלּוּ בַּר-נַבָּא נִגְרַר אַחֲרֵיהֶם בְּכַחֲשָׁם. 14 בִּרְאוֹתִי כִּי הֵם סוֹטִים מֵאֱמֶת הַבְּשׂוֹרָה, אָמַרְתִּי לְכֵיפָא לְעֵינֵי כָּל הַנּוֹכְחִים: "אִם אַתָּה הַיְּהוּדִי מִתְנַהֵג כְּגוֹי וְלֹא כִּיהוּדִי, מַדּוּעַ תְּאַלֵּץ אֶת הַגּוֹיִים לִחְיוֹת כִּיהוּדִים?

compel Gentiles to live as Jews? ¹⁵ We *who are* Jews by nature, and not sinners of the Gentiles, ¹⁶ knowing that a man is not justified by the works of the law but by faith in Jesus Christ, even we have believed in Christ Jesus, that we might be justified by faith in Christ and not by the works of the law; for by the works of the law no flesh shall be justified.

¹⁷ "But if, while we seek to be justified by Christ, we ourselves also are found sinners, *is* Christ therefore a minister of sin? Certainly not! ¹⁸ For if I build again those things which I destroyed, I make myself a transgressor. ¹⁹ For I through the law died to the law that I might live to God. ²⁰ I have been crucified with Christ; it is no longer I who live, but Christ lives in me; and the *life* which I now live in the flesh I live by faith in the Son of God, who loved me and gave Himself for me. ²¹ I do not set aside the grace of God; for if righteousness *comes* through the law, then Christ died in vain."

3 O foolish Galatians! Who has bewitched you that you should not obey the truth, before whose eyes Jesus Christ was clearly portrayed among you as crucified? ² This only I want to learn from you: Did you receive the Spirit by the works of the law, or by the hearing of faith? ³ Are you so foolish? Having begun in the Spirit, are you now being made perfect by the flesh? ⁴ Have you suffered so many things in vain—if indeed *it was* in vain?

⁵ Therefore He who supplies the Spirit to you and works miracles among you, *does He do it* by the works of the law, or by the hearing of faith?— ⁶ just as Abraham *"believed God, and it was accounted to him for righteousness."* ⁷ Therefore know that *only* those who are of faith are sons of Abraham. ⁸ And the Scripture, foreseeing that God would justify the Gentiles by faith, preached the gospel to Abraham beforehand, *saying,* "In you all the nations shall be blessed." ⁹ So then those who *are* of faith are blessed with believing Abraham.

¹⁰ For as many as are of the works of the law are under the curse; for it is written, *"Cursed is everyone who does not continue in all things which are written in the book of the law, to do them."* ¹¹ But that no one is justified by the law in the sight of God *is* evident, for *"the just shall live by faith."* ¹² Yet the law is not of faith, but *"the man who does them shall live by them."*

¹³ Christ has redeemed us from the curse of the law, having become a curse for us (for it is written,

15 אָנוּ יְהוּדִים בְּנֵי יְהוּדִים, לֹא ׳אֲנָשִׁים חַטָּאִים מִן הַגּוֹיִם׳. 16 וְכֵיוָן שֶׁיּוֹדְעִים אָנוּ כִּי הָאָדָם אֵינוֹ נִצְדָּק בְּקִיּוּם מִצְווֹת הַתּוֹרָה, אֶלָּא בֶּאֱמוּנַת הַמָּשִׁיחַ יֵשׁוּעַ, הֶאֱמַנּוּ גַּם אֲנַחְנוּ בַּמָּשִׁיחַ יֵשׁוּעַ, לְמַעַן נִצְדַּק מִתּוֹךְ אֱמוּנָה בַּמָּשִׁיחַ וְלֹא בְּקִיּוּם מִצְווֹת הַתּוֹרָה, שֶׁכֵּן בְּקִיּוּם מִצְווֹת הַתּוֹרָה לֹא יִצְדַּק כָּל בָּשָׂר. 17 אֲבָל אִם בְּשָׁעָה שֶׁאֲנַחְנוּ מְבַקְשִׁים לְהִצָּדֵק בַּמָּשִׁיחַ יִמָּצֵא שֶׁגַּם אֲנַחְנוּ אֲנָשִׁים חוֹטְאִים, הַאִם נוֹבֵעַ מִזֶּה שֶׁהַמָּשִׁיחַ מְשָׁרֵת לַחֵטְא? חַס וְחָלִילָה! 18 שֶׁהֲרֵי אִם אֲנִי בּוֹנֶה שׁוּב אֶת מַה שֶּׁהָרַסְתִּי, בְּכָךְ אֲנִי מֵעִיד עַל עַצְמִי שֶׁאֲנִי עֲבַרְיָן. 19 אֲנִי מַתִּי לִבְּנֵי הַתּוֹרָה בִּגְלַל הַתּוֹרָה, כְּדֵי שֶׁאֶחְיֶה לֵאלֹהִים. 20 עִם הַמָּשִׁיחַ נִצְלַבְתִּי וְלֹא עוֹד אֲנִי חַי, אֶלָּא הַמָּשִׁיחַ חַי בִּי. הַחַיִּים שֶׁאֲנִי חַי עַכְשָׁו בַּבָּשָׂר, אֲנִי חַי אוֹתָם בֶּאֱמוּנַת בֶּן־הָאֱלֹהִים אֲשֶׁר אֲהָבַנִי וּמָסַר עַצְמוֹ בַּעֲדִי. 21 אֵינֶנִּי מְבַטֵּל אֶת חֶסֶד אֱלֹהִים. הֲלֹא אִם אֶפְשָׁר לְהִצָּדֵק עַל־יְדֵי הַתּוֹרָה, הֲרֵי שֶׁהַמָּשִׁיחַ מֵת לַשָּׁוְא."

ג הוֹי גָּלָטִים כְּסִילִים! מִי אָחַז אֶת עֵינֵיכֶם אַחֲרֵי שֶׁהוֹדִיעוּכֶם בְּפֵרוּשׁ שֶׁיֵּשׁוּעַ הַמָּשִׁיחַ נִצְלַב? 2 דָּבָר אֶחָד רוֹצֶה אֲנִי שֶׁתּוֹדִיעוּנִי: הַאִם בִּשֶׁל קִיּוּם מִצְווֹת הַתּוֹרָה קִבַּלְתֶּם אֶת הָרוּחַ, אוֹ בִּשֶׁל שְׁמִיעָה שֶׁבָּאֱמוּנָה? 3 הַאִם כְּסִילִים אַתֶּם כָּל כָּךְ? הַאִם לְאַחַר שֶׁהִתְחַלְתֶּם בָּרוּחַ תַּגִּיעוּ כָּעֵת לִשְׁלֵמוּת עַל־ יְדֵי הַבָּשָׂר? 4 הַאִם לַשָּׁוְא הִתְנַסֵּיתֶם בִּדְבָרִים רַבִּים כָּל כָּךְ? הַאֻמְנָם לַשָּׁוְא? 5 הַמֵּאֲצִיל עֲלֵיכֶם אֶת הָרוּחַ וְעוֹשֶׂה בְּקִרְבְּכֶם נִפְלָאוֹת, הַאִם הוּא עוֹשֶׂה זֹאת בִּשֶׁל קִיּוּם מִצְווֹת הַתּוֹרָה, אוֹ בִּשֶׁל שְׁמִיעָה שֶׁבָּאֱמוּנָה? – 6 כְּמוֹ שֶׁאַבְרָהָם הֶאֱמִין בֵּאלֹהִים וְנֶחְשְׁבָה לוֹ צְדָקָה.

7 וּבְכֵן דְּעוּ כִּי בְּנֵי הָאֱמוּנָה הֵם בְּנֵי אַבְרָהָם. 8 וְהַכָּתוּב, בְּיָדְעוֹ מֵרֹאשׁ שֶׁאֱלֹהִים יַצְדִּיק אֶת הַגּוֹיִם עַל־יְדֵי אֱמוּנָה, הִקְדִּים לְבַשֵּׂר לְאַבְרָהָם: "וְנִבְרְכוּ בְךָ כָּל הַגּוֹיִם." 9 מִכָּאן שֶׁהַמַּחֲזִיקִים בָּאֱמוּנָה מְבֹרָכִים יַחַד עִם אַבְרָהָם הַמַּאֲמִין. 10 הַנִּשְׁעָנִים עַל קִיּוּם מִצְווֹת הַתּוֹרָה נְתוּנִים תַּחַת קְלָלָה, שֶׁהֲרֵי כָּתוּב, "אָרוּר כָּל מִי שֶׁלֹּא יָקִים אֶת כָּל הַדְּבָרִים הַכְּתוּבִים בְּסֵפֶר הַתּוֹרָה לַעֲשׂוֹת אוֹתָם." 11 דָּבָר בָּרוּר הוּא שֶׁאִישׁ לֹא יִצְדַּק לִפְנֵי אֱלֹהִים עַל־יְדֵי הַתּוֹרָה, שֶׁכֵּן צַדִּיק בֶּאֱמוּנָתוֹ יִחְיֶה. 12 וְהַתּוֹרָה אֵינֶנָּה נִזְקֶקֶת לָאֱמוּנָה, אֶלָּא שֶׁיַּעֲשֶׂה הָאָדָם אֶת דְּבָרֶיהָ וְחַי בָּהֶם. 13 הַמָּשִׁיחַ פָּדָה אוֹתָנוּ

"Cursed is everyone who hangs on a tree"), [14] that the blessing of Abraham might come upon the Gentiles in Christ Jesus, that we might receive the promise of the Spirit through faith.

[15] Brethren, I speak in the manner of men: Though *it is* only a man's covenant, yet *if it is* confirmed, no one annuls or adds to it. [16] Now to Abraham and his Seed were the promises made. He does not say, "And to seeds," as of many, but as of one, *"And to your Seed,"* who is Christ. [17] And this I say, *that* the law, which was four hundred and thirty years later, cannot annul the covenant that was confirmed before by God in Christ, that it should make the promise of no effect. [18] For if the inheritance *is* of the law, *it is* no longer of promise; but God gave *it* to Abraham by promise.

[19] What purpose then *does* the law serve? It was added because of transgressions, till the Seed should come to whom the promise was made; *and it was* appointed through angels by the hand of a mediator. [20] Now a mediator does not *mediate* for one *only*, but God is one.

[21] *Is* the law then against the promises of God? Certainly not! For if there had been a law given which could have given life, truly righteousness would have been by the law. [22] But the Scripture has confined all under sin, that the promise by faith in Jesus Christ might be given to those who believe. [23] But before faith came, we were kept under guard by the law, kept for the faith which would afterward be revealed. [24] Therefore the law was our tutor *to bring us* to Christ, that we might be justified by faith. [25] But after faith has come, we are no longer under a tutor.

[26] For you are all sons of God through faith in Christ Jesus. [27] For as many of you as were baptized into Christ have put on Christ. [28] There is neither Jew nor Greek, there is neither slave nor free, there is neither male nor female; for you are all one in Christ Jesus. [29] And if you *are* Christ's, then you are Abraham's seed, and heirs according to the promise.

4 Now I say *that* the heir, as long as he is a child, does not differ at all from a slave, though he is master of all, [2] but is under guardians and stewards until the time appointed by the father. [3] Even so we, when we were children, were in bondage under the elements of the world. [4] But when the fullness of the time had come, God sent forth His Son, born of a woman, born under the law, [5] to redeem those who were under the law, that we might receive the adoption as sons.

מִקְלְלַת הַתּוֹרָה בְּךָ שֶׁהָיָה לִקְלָלָה בַּעֲדֵנוּ – שֶׁכֵּן הַכָּתוּב אוֹמֵר, "קִלְלַת אֱלֹהִים תָּלוּי עַל־עֵץ", [14] כְּדֵי שֶׁבְּיֵשׁוּעַ הַמָּשִׁיחַ תַּגִּיעַ בִּרְכַּת אַבְרָהָם אֶל הַגּוֹיִים, לְמַעַן נִנְחַל עַל־יְדֵי הָאֱמוּנָה אֶת הָרוּחַ הַמֻּבְטַחַת.

[15] אַחַי, אֲדַבֵּר מִנְּקֻדַּת רְאוּת אֱנוֹשִׁית: אֲפִלּוּ צַוָּאָה שֶׁל אָדָם, לְאַחַר שֶׁקִּבְּלָה תֹּקֶף, אִישׁ אֵינוֹ יָכוֹל לְבַטְּלָהּ אוֹ לְהוֹסִיף עָלֶיהָ. [16] וְהִנֵּה הַהַבְטָחוֹת נֶאֶמְרוּ לְאַבְרָהָם, וּלְזַרְעוֹ. לֹא נֶאֱמַר "לִזְרָעֶיךָ", כְּמוֹ עַל רַבִּים, אֶלָּא "לְזַרְעֲךָ", כְּמוֹ עַל יָחִיד, וְהוּא הַמָּשִׁיחַ. [17] הֲרֵינִי אוֹמֵר זֹאת: בְּרִית אֲשֶׁר אֱלֹהִים כָּרַת מִקֶּדֶם, הַתּוֹרָה שֶׁנִּתְּנָה אַחֲרֵי אַרְבַּע מֵאוֹת וּשְׁלֹשִׁים שָׁנָה לֹא תּוּכַל לְהָפֵר אוֹתָהּ וּלְבַטֵּל אֶת הַהַבְטָחָה; [18] שֶׁהֲרֵי אִם הַנַּחֲלָה הִיא מִן הַתּוֹרָה, אֲזַי אֵינֶנָּה מְבֻסֶּסֶת עוֹד עַל הַהַבְטָחָה. אֲבָל בְּהַבְטָחָה הֶעֱנִיק אֱלֹהִים לְאַבְרָהָם אֶת הַנַּחֲלָה. [19] אִם כֵּן לְשֵׁם מָה הַתּוֹרָה? הִיא נוֹסְפָה בִּגְלַל הָעֲבֵרוֹת, עַד כִּי יָבוֹא הַזֶּרַע אֲשֶׁר לוֹ מְכֻוֶּנֶת הַהַבְטָחָה. הַתּוֹרָה נִמְסְרָה בְּאֶמְצָעוּת מַלְאָכִים בִּידֵי מְתַוֵּךְ. [20] הַמְתַוֵּךְ אֵינֶנּוּ שֶׁל אֶחָד וֵאלֹהִים הוּא אֶחָד.

[21] הַאִם מִכָּאן שֶׁהַתּוֹרָה נוֹגֶדֶת אֶת הַבְטָחוֹת אֱלֹהִים? חָלִילָה! שֶׁכֵּן אִלּוּ נִתְּנָה תּוֹרָה שֶׁבִּיכָלְתָּהּ לָתֵת חַיִּים, כִּי אָז בֶּאֱמֶת הָיָה אֶפְשָׁר לְהִצָּדֵק עַל־יְדֵי הַתּוֹרָה. [22] אֲבָל הַמִּקְרָא הִסְגִּיר אֶת הַכֹּל בְּיַד הַחֵטְא, כְּדֵי שֶׁעַל סְמַךְ אֱמוּנַת יֵשׁוּעַ הַמָּשִׁיחַ תִּנָּתֵן הַהַבְטָחָה לַמַּאֲמִינִים.

[23] לִפְנֵי בּוֹא הָאֱמוּנָה נִשְׁמַרְנוּ תַּחַת יַד הַתּוֹרָה, כְּלוּאִים הָיִינוּ לִקְרָאת הָאֱמוּנָה הָעֲתִידָה לְהִגָּלוֹת. [24] לְפִיכָךְ הָיְתָה הַתּוֹרָה אוֹמֶנֶת הַמַּדְרִיכָה אוֹתָנוּ אֶל הַמָּשִׁיחַ, לְמַעַן נִצָּדֵק עַל־יְדֵי אֱמוּנָה. [25] אֲבָל לְאַחַר בּוֹא הָאֱמוּנָה אֵינֶנּוּ נְתוּנִים עוֹד לְמָרוּת הָאוֹמֶנֶת. [26] כֻּלְּכֶם בָּנִים־לֵאלֹהִים עַל־יְדֵי הָאֱמוּנָה בַּמָּשִׁיחַ יֵשׁוּעַ; [27] כִּי כֻּלְּכֶם אֲשֶׁר נִטְבַּלְתֶּם לַמָּשִׁיחַ לְבַשְׁתֶּם אֶת הַמָּשִׁיחַ. [28] אֵין יְהוּדִי אַף לֹא גּוֹי, אֵין עֶבֶד אַף לֹא בֶּן חוֹרִין, לֹא זָכָר אַף לֹא נְקֵבָה, מִשּׁוּם שֶׁכֻּלְּכֶם אֶחָד בַּמָּשִׁיחַ יֵשׁוּעַ. [29] וְאִם אַתֶּם שַׁיָּכִים לַמָּשִׁיחַ, אֲזַי זֶרַע אַבְרָהָם אַתֶּם וְיוֹרְשִׁים עַל־פִּי הַהַבְטָחָה.

ד הֲרֵינִי אוֹמֵר זֹאת: כָּל עוֹד הַיּוֹרֵשׁ קָטֹן אֵין הוּא שׁוֹנֶה מֵעֶבֶד, אַף כִּי הוּא אֲדוֹן כָּל הַנַּחֲלָה. [2] וְאוּלָם הוּא נָתוּן לְמָרוּת שֶׁל אֶפִּיטְרוֹפְּסִים וַאֲנָשִׁים הַמֻּפְקָדִים עַל הַבַּיִת עַד לַמּוֹעֵד שֶׁקָּבַע אָבִיו. [3] כֵּן גַּם אֲנַחְנוּ, בְּעֵת הֱיוֹתֵנוּ קְטַנִּים – הָיִינוּ מְשֻׁעְבָּדִים לִיסוֹדוֹת הָעוֹלָם. [4] אֲבָל כַּאֲשֶׁר מָלְאָה הָעֵת שָׁלַח אֱלֹהִים אֶת בְּנוֹ, יְלוּד אִשָּׁה וְכָפוּף לַתּוֹרָה, [5] לִפְדּוֹת

6 And because you are sons, God has sent forth the Spirit of His Son into your hearts, crying out, "Abba, Father!" 7 Therefore you are no longer a slave but a son, and if a son, then an heir of God through Christ.

8 But then, indeed, when you did not know God, you served those which by nature are not gods. 9 But now after you have known God, or rather are known by God, how *is it that* you turn again to the weak and beggarly elements, to which you desire again to be in bondage? 10 You observe days and months and seasons and years. 11 I am afraid for you, lest I have labored for you in vain.

12 Brethren, I urge you to become like me, for I *became* like you. You have not injured me at all. 13 You know that because of physical infirmity I preached the gospel to you at the first. 14 And my trial which was in my flesh you did not despise or reject, but you received me as an angel of God, *even* as Christ Jesus. 15 What then was the blessing you *enjoyed?* For I bear you witness that, if possible, you would have plucked out your own eyes and given them to me. 16 Have I therefore become your enemy because I tell you the truth?

17 They zealously court you, *but* for no good; yes, they want to exclude you, that you may be zealous for them. 18 But it is good to be zealous in a good thing always, and not only when I am present with you. 19 My little children, for whom I labor in birth again until Christ is formed in you, 20 I would like to be present with you now and to change my tone; for I have doubts about you.

21 Tell me, you who desire to be under the law, do you not hear the law? 22 For it is written that Abraham had two sons: the one by a bondwoman, the other by a freewoman. 23 But he *who was* of the bondwoman was born according to the flesh, and he of the freewoman through promise, 24 which things are symbolic. For these are the two covenants: the one from Mount Sinai which gives birth to bondage, which is Hagar— 25 for this Hagar is Mount Sinai in Arabia, and corresponds to Jerusalem which now is, and is in bondage with her children— 26 but the Jerusalem above is free, which is the mother of us all. 27 For it is written:

"Rejoice, O barren,
You who do not bear!
Break forth and shout,
You who are not in labor!
For the desolate has many more children
Than she who has a husband."

אֶת הַפְּסוּפִים לַתּוֹרָה כְּדֵי שֶׁנְּקַבֵּל אֶת מַעֲמַד הַבָּנִים. 6 וְכֵיוָן שֶׁאַתֶּם בָּנִים, אֱלֹהִים נָתַן בִּלְבַבְכֶם אֶת רוּחַ בְּנוֹ הַקּוֹרֵאת "אַבָּא, אָבִינוּ". 7 לְפִיכָךְ אֵינְךָ עֶבֶד עוֹד, כִּי אִם בֵּן; וְאִם בֵּן, אֲזַי גַּם יוֹרֵשׁ מִטַּעַם אֱלֹהִים.

8 בְּעָבָר, בְּעֵת שֶׁלֹּא יְדַעְתֶּם אֶת אֱלֹהִים, עֲבַדְתֶּם אֶת מִי שֶׁבְּמַהוּתָם אֵינָם אֱלֹהִים. 9 אֲבָל כָּעֵת, כְּשֶׁאַתֶּם יוֹדְעִים אֶת אֱלֹהִים – אוֹ לְיֶתֶר דִּיּוּק, כְּשֶׁאֱלֹהִים יוֹדֵעַ אֶתְכֶם – כֵּיצַד זֶה חוֹזְרִים אַתֶּם לִיסוֹדוֹת הַחַלָּשִׁים וְהָעֲלוּבִים שֶׁבִּרְצוֹנְכֶם לַעֲבָדָם מֵחָדָשׁ? 10 הִנֵּה אַתֶּם מְכַבְּדִים יָמִים וַחֳדָשִׁים; מוֹעֲדִים וְשָׁנִים. 11 חוֹשְׁשַׁנִי כִּי לַשָּׁוְא עָמַלְתִּי בָּכֶם.

12 הֱיוּ כָּמוֹנִי, כִּי גַּם אֲנִי נִהְיֵיתִי כְּמוֹכֶם, אַחַי! אֲנִי מְבַקֵּשׁ מִכֶּם! לֹא עֲשִׂיתֶם לִי שׁוּם רַע. 13 אַתֶּם יוֹדְעִים שֶׁבִּנְסִבּוֹת שֶׁל חֻלְשַׁת הַגּוּף בִּשַּׂרְתִּי לָכֶם אֶת הַבְּשׂוֹרָה בַּתְּחִלָּה. 14 וְלֹא בְחַלְתֶּם בַּנִּסָּיוֹן שֶׁבָּא עֲלֵיכֶם בִּשַׂל גּוּפִי, אַף לֹא הִגְבַּתֶּם בְּבוּז, אֶלָּא קִבַּלְתֶּם אוֹתִי כְּמַלְאַךְ אֱלֹהִים, כַּמָּשִׁיחַ יֵשׁוּעַ. 15 אִם כֵּן אֵיפֹה חֶדְוַתְכֶם עַתָּה? הֲרֵינִי מֵעִיד עֲלֵיכֶם שֶׁאִלּוּ יְכָלְתֶּם הֱיִיתֶם עוֹקְרִים אֶת עֵינֵיכֶם כְּדֵי לְתִתָּן לִי. 16 וְעַתָּה הַאִם הָפַכְתִּי לָכֶם לְאוֹיֵב בְּאָמְרִי לָכֶם אֶת הָאֱמֶת? 17 הָאֲנָשִׁים הַלָּלוּ מְקַנְּאִים לָכֶם שֶׁלֹּא לְטוֹבָה; רְצוֹנָם לְהַרְחִיק אֶתְכֶם כְּדֵי שֶׁאַתֶּם תְּקַנְּאוּ לָהֶם. 18 טוֹב הַדָּבָר אִם תָּמִיד מְקַנְּאִים לְטוֹבָה, וְלֹא רַק כְּשֶׁאֲנִי שׁוֹהֶה אֶצְלְכֶם. 19 יְלָדַי, שׁוּב נָתוּן אֲנִי בְּחֶבְלֵי לֵדָה עֲלֵיכֶם עַד אֲשֶׁר יִכּוֹן הַמָּשִׁיחַ בָּכֶם. 20 רְצוֹנִי לִהְיוֹת עִמָּכֶם עַכְשָׁו וּלְשַׁנּוֹת אֶת נִימַת קוֹלִי, שֶׁכֵּן אֲנִי נָבוֹךְ בְּנוֹגֵעַ אֲלֵיכֶם.

21 אִמְרוּ לִי, אַתֶּם הָרוֹצִים לִהְיוֹת כְּפוּפִים לַתּוֹרָה, הַאֵינְכֶם שׁוֹמְעִים אֶת הַתּוֹרָה? 22 הֲלֹא כָּתוּב שֶׁלְּאַבְרָהָם הָיוּ שְׁנֵי בָּנִים, הָאֶחָד מִן הָאָמָה וְהַשֵּׁנִי מֵהָאִשָּׁה הַחָפְשִׁיָּה. 23 אַךְ בֶּן הָאָמָה נוֹלַד לְפִי הַבָּשָׂר, וְאִלּוּ בֶּן הַחָפְשִׁיָּה עַל-פִּי הַהַבְטָחָה. 24 הַדְּבָרִים הָאֵלֶּה הֵם מָשָׁל לִשְׁתֵּי הַבְּרִיתוֹת. הָאַחַת מֵהַר סִינַי, הַיּוֹלֶדֶת לְעַבְדוּת, וְהִיא הָגָר. 25 הָגָר מְסַמֶּלֶת אֶת הַר סִינַי שֶׁבַּעֲרָב וּמַקְבִּילָה לִירוּשָׁלַיִם שֶׁל יָמֵינוּ, כִּי הִיא בְּעַבְדוּת עִם בָּנֶיהָ. 26 אֲבָל יְרוּשָׁלַיִם שֶׁל מַעְלָה בַּת חוֹרִין הִיא, וְהִיא אֵם לָנוּ; 27 שֶׁהֲרֵי כָּתוּב:

"רָנִּי עֲקָרָה לֹא יָלָדָה,
פִּצְחִי רִנָּה וְצַהֲלִי לֹא-חָלָה,
כִּי-רַבִּים בְּנֵי-שׁוֹמֵמָה מִבְּנֵי בְעוּלָה."

²⁸ Now we, brethren, as Isaac *was,* are children of promise. ²⁹ But, as he who was born according to the flesh then persecuted him *who was born according to the Spirit,* even so *it is* now. ³⁰ Nevertheless what does the Scripture say? *"Cast out the bondwoman and her son, for the son of the bondwoman shall not be heir with the son of the freewoman."* ³¹ So then, brethren, we are not children of the bondwoman but of the free.

5 Stand fast therefore in the liberty by which Christ has made us free, and do not be entangled again with a yoke of bondage. ² Indeed I, Paul, say to you that if you become circumcised, Christ will profit you nothing. ³ And I testify again to every man who becomes circumcised that he is a debtor to keep the whole law. ⁴ You have become estranged from Christ, you who *attempt to* be justified by law; you have fallen from grace. ⁵ For we through the Spirit eagerly wait for the hope of righteousness by faith. ⁶ For in Christ Jesus neither circumcision nor uncircumcision avails anything, but faith working through love.

⁷ You ran well. Who hindered you from obeying the truth? ⁸ This persuasion does not *come* from Him who calls you. ⁹ A little leaven leavens the whole lump. ¹⁰ I have confidence in you, in the Lord, that you will have no other mind; but he who troubles you shall bear his judgment, whoever he is.

¹¹ And I, brethren, if I still preach circumcision, why do I still suffer persecution? Then the offense of the cross has ceased. ¹² I could wish that those who trouble you would even cut themselves off!

¹³ For you, brethren, have been called to liberty; only do not *use* liberty as an opportunity for the flesh, but through love serve one another. ¹⁴ For all the law is fulfilled in one word, *even* in this: *"You shall love your neighbor as yourself."* ¹⁵ But if you bite and devour one another, beware lest you be consumed by one another!

¹⁶ I say then: Walk in the Spirit, and you shall not fulfill the lust of the flesh. ¹⁷ For the flesh lusts against the Spirit, and the Spirit against the flesh; and these are contrary to one another, so that you do not do the things that you wish. ¹⁸ But if you are led by the Spirit, you are not under the law.

¹⁹ Now the works of the flesh are evident, which are: adultery, fornication, uncleanness, lewdness, ²⁰ idolatry, sorcery, hatred, contentions, jealousies, outbursts of wrath, selfish ambitions, dissensions, heresies, ²¹ envy, murders, drunkenness, revelries, and the like; of which I tell you beforehand, just as I also told *you* in time past, that those who practice such things will not inherit the kingdom of God.

28 וְאַתֶּם, אַחַי, אַתֶּם בְּנֵי הַהַבְטָחָה כְּיִצְחָק. 29 וּכְשֵׁם שֶׁאָז רָדַף הַבֵּן שֶׁנּוֹלַד לְפִי הַבָּשָׂר אֶת הַבֵּן שֶׁנּוֹלַד לְפִי הָרוּחַ, כֵּן גַּם עַכְשָׁו. 30 אֲבָל מָה אוֹמֵר הַכָּתוּב? "גָּרֵשׁ הָאָמָה וְאֶת-בְּנָהּ, כִּי לֹא יִירַשׁ בֶּן-הָאָמָה עִם-בֵּן הַחָפְשִׁיָּה." 31 לְפִיכָךְ, אַחַי, אֵין אָנוּ בְּנֵי הָאָמָה, אֶלָּא בְּנֵי הַחָפְשִׁיָּה.

ה הַמָּשִׁיחַ שִׁחְרֵר אוֹתָנוּ אֱלֵי חֵרוּת, לָכֵן עִמְדוּ וְאַל תִּכָּנְעוּ שׁוּב לְעֹל הָעַבְדוּת. 2 אֲנִי, שָׁאוּל, אוֹמֵר לָכֶם שֶׁאִם תִּמּוֹלוּ, לֹא יוֹעִיל לָכֶם הַמָּשִׁיחַ. 3 אֲנִי חוֹזֵר וּמֵעִיד בְּכָל אִישׁ אֲשֶׁר יִמּוֹל, כִּי חוֹבָה עָלָיו לִשְׁמֹר אֶת כָּל הַתּוֹרָה. 4 אַתֶּם הַמְבַקְשִׁים לְהִצָּדֵק בַּתּוֹרָה נִתַּקְתֶּם מִן הַמָּשִׁיחַ, נִשְׁמַטְתֶּם מִן הַחֶסֶד. 5 וַאֲנַחְנוּ, בָּרוּחַ, עַל-יְסוֹד אֱמוּנָה, מְיַחֲלִים לְתִקְוָה, פְּרִי הַצִּדְקָתֵנוּ; 6 שֶׁכֵּן בַּמָּשִׁיחַ יֵשׁוּעַ אֵין חֲשִׁיבוּת לֹא לַמִּילָה וְלֹא לָעָרְלָה, אֶלָּא לָאֱמוּנָה הַפּוֹעֶלֶת בְּדֶרֶךְ אַהֲבָה.

7 מְרוּצַתְכֶם הָיְתָה טוֹבָה; מִי הֵנִיא אֶתְכֶם מִלְּצַיֵּת לָאֱמֶת? 8 פִּתּוּי זֶה אֵינוֹ מֵאֵת הַקּוֹרֵא אֶתְכֶם. 9 מְעַט שְׂאוֹר מַחְמִיץ אֶת כָּל הַבָּצֵק. 10 אֲנִי בּוֹטֵחַ בָּאָדוֹן בְּנוֹגֵעַ אֲלֵיכֶם שֶׁלֹּא תַעֲלֶה עַל לְבַבְכֶם שׁוּם מַחֲשָׁבָה זָרָה. וּמִי שֶׁעוֹכֵר אֶתְכֶם יִשָּׂא אֶת עֲווֹנוֹ, יִהְיֶה הָאִישׁ מִי שֶׁיִּהְיֶה. 11 וַאֲנִי, אַחַי, אִם אֲנִי עֲדַיִן מַטִּיף בְּעַד הַמִּילָה, מַדּוּעַ זֶה מוֹסִיפִים לִרְדֹּף אוֹתִי? אִלּוּ הִטַּפְתִּי כָּךְ, הָיָה מִתְבַּטֵּל מִכְשׁוֹל הַצְּלָב. 12 מִי יִתֵּן וְיִכָּרְתוּ הַמַּתְעִים אֶתְכֶם!

13 אַחַי, לְחֵרוּת נִקְרֵאתֶם, רַק שֶׁלֹּא תְהֵא הַחֵרוּת אֶמְצָעִי בִּידֵי הַבָּשָׂר, אֶלָּא שָׁרְתוּ אִישׁ אֶת רֵעֵהוּ בְּאַהֲבָה. 14 הֲרֵי כָּל הַתּוֹרָה כְּלוּלָה בְּמַאֲמָר אֶחָד – "וְאָהַבְתָּ לְרֵעֲךָ כָּמוֹךָ." 15 אַךְ אִם אַתֶּם נוֹשְׁכִים וְטוֹרְפִים זֶה אֶת זֶה, כִּי אָז תִּשָּׁמְדוּ אִישׁ בְּיַד רֵעֵהוּ. 16 אוֹמֵר אֲנִי לָכֶם: הִתְהַלְּכוּ בְּדֶרֶךְ הָרוּחַ וְלֹא תְמַלְּאוּ אֶת תַּאֲוַות הַבָּשָׂר; 17 כִּי הַבָּשָׂר מִתְאַוֶּה לְמַה שֶּׁבְּנֶגֶד לָרוּחַ, וְהָרוּחַ מִתְנַגֶּדֶת לַבָּשָׂר; שְׁנֵיהֶם מִתְנַגְּדִים זֶה לָזֶה וְלָכֵן אֵינְכֶם יְכוֹלִים לַעֲשׂוֹת אֶת מַה שֶּׁבִּרְצוֹנְכֶם. 18 אֲבָל אִם הָרוּחַ מַנְהִיגָה אֶתְכֶם, אֵין אֵינְכֶם כְּפוּפִים לַתּוֹרָה. 19 מַעֲשֵׂי הַבָּשָׂר גְּלוּיִים וְאֵלֶּה הֵם: נִאוּף וּזְנוּת, טֻמְאָה, זִמָּה, 20 עֲבוֹדַת אֱלִילִים, כִּשּׁוּף, שִׂנְאָה, מָדוֹן, צָרוּת עַיִן, כַּעַס, מְרִיבָה, מַחֲלוֹקוֹת, כִּתּוֹת, 21 קִנְאָה, שְׁכָרוֹת, הוֹלְלוּת וְכַדּוֹמֶה. אוֹמֵר אֲנִי לָכֶם מֵרֹאשׁ מַה שֶּׁכְּבָר אָמַרְתִּי: עוֹשֵׂי מַעֲשִׂים כָּאֵלֶּה לֹא יִירְשׁוּ אֶת מַלְכוּת הָאֱלֹהִים.

22 But the fruit of the Spirit is love, joy, peace, longsuffering, kindness, goodness, faithfulness, 23 gentleness, self-control. Against such there is no law. 24 And those *who are* Christ's have crucified the flesh with its passions and desires. 25 If we live in the Spirit, let us also walk in the Spirit. 26 Let us not become conceited, provoking one another, envying one another.

6 Brethren, if a man is overtaken in any trespass, you who *are* spiritual restore such a one in a spirit of gentleness, considering yourself lest you also be tempted. 2 Bear one another's burdens, and so fulfill the law of Christ. 3 For if anyone thinks himself to be something, when he is nothing, he deceives himself. 4 But let each one examine his own work, and then he will have rejoicing in himself alone, and not in another. 5 For each one shall bear his own load.

6 Let him who is taught the word share in all good things with him who teaches.

7 Do not be deceived, God is not mocked; for whatever a man sows, that he will also reap. 8 For he who sows to his flesh will of the flesh reap corruption, but he who sows to the Spirit will of the Spirit reap everlasting life. 9 And let us not grow weary while doing good, for in due season we shall reap if we do not lose heart. 10 Therefore, as we have opportunity, let us do good to all, especially to those who are of the household of faith.

11 See with what large letters I have written to you with my own hand! 12 As many as desire to make a good showing in the flesh, these *would* compel you to be circumcised, only that they may not suffer persecution for the cross of Christ. 13 For not even those who are circumcised keep the law, but they desire to have you circumcised that they may boast in your flesh. 14 But God forbid that I should boast except in the cross of our Lord Jesus Christ, by whom the world has been crucified to me, and I to the world. 15 For in Christ Jesus neither circumcision nor uncircumcision avails anything, but a new creation.

16 And as many as walk according to this rule, peace and mercy *be* upon them, and upon the Israel of God.

17 From now on let no one trouble me, for I bear in my body the marks of the Lord Jesus.

18 Brethren, the grace of our Lord Jesus Christ *be* with your spirit. Amen.

22 לְעֻמַּת זֹאת, פְּרִי הָרוּחַ הוּא אַהֲבָה, שִׂמְחָה, שָׁלוֹם, אֹרֶךְ רוּחַ, נְדִיבוּת, טוּב לֵב, נֶאֱמָנוּת, 23 עֲנָוָה, רִסּוּן עַצְמִי – עַל מִדּוֹת כָּאֵלֶּה אֵין תּוֹרָה חָלָה. 24 הָאֲנָשִׁים הַשַּׁיָּכִים לַמָּשִׁיחַ צָלְבוּ אֶת בְּשָׂרָם עִם תְּשׁוּקוֹתָיו וְתַאֲוֺותָיו. 25 אִם חַיִּינוּ מִן הָרוּחַ, הָבָה גַּם נִתְהַלֵּךְ עַל־פִּי הָרוּחַ. 26 אַל נָא נִהְיֶה שׁוֹאֲפֵי כְּבוֹד שָׁוְא, הַמִּתְגָּרִים וּמְקַנְאִים אִישׁ בְּרֵעֵהוּ.

א אַחַי, אִם יִכָּשֵׁל אִישׁ מִכֶּם בְּאֵיזוֹ עֲבֵרָה, אַתֶּם הָאֲנָשִׁים הָרוּחָנִיִּים תָּקִימוּ אוֹתוֹ בְּרוּחַ שֶׁל עֲנָוָה; וְהִזָּהֵר שֶׁלֹּא תָבוֹא גַם אַתָּה לִידֵי נִסָּיוֹן. 2 שְׂאוּ אִישׁ אֶת מַעֲמָסַת רֵעֵהוּ וְכָךְ תְּקַיְּמוּ אֶת תּוֹרַת הַמָּשִׁיחַ. 3 אִם אָדָם חוֹשֵׁב אֶת עַצְמוֹ לְמַשֶּׁהוּ בְּעוֹד שֶׁאֵינוֹ כְּלוּם, הֲרֵיהוּ מַשְׁלֶה אֶת עַצְמוֹ. 4 יִבְחַן כָּל אֶחָד אֶת מַעֲשָׂיו וְאָז הַסִּבָּה לִתְהִלָּתוֹ תִּהְיֶה בּוֹ עַצְמוֹ בְּלִי תְלוּת בַּזּוּלַת, 5 שֶׁכֵּן כָּל אֶחָד יִשָּׂא אֶת הַנֵּטֶל שֶׁלּוֹ. 6 מִי שֶׁלּוֹמֵד אֶת דְּבַר אֱלֹהִים צָרִיךְ לְשַׁתֵּף בְּכָל הַדְּבָרִים הַטּוֹבִים אֶת מִי שֶׁמְּלַמֵּד אוֹתוֹ. 7 אַל תִּטְעוּ, בֵּאלֹהִים אֵין לְהָתֵל; כִּי מַה שֶּׁאָדָם זוֹרֵעַ, אֶת זֹאת גַּם יִקְצֹר. 8 מִי שֶׁזּוֹרֵעַ בִּשְׂדֵה בְּשָׂרוֹ, מִן הַבָּשָׂר יִקְצֹר כִּלָּיוֹן. אֲבָל הַזּוֹרֵעַ בִּשְׂדֵה הָרוּחַ, מִן הָרוּחַ יִקְצֹר חַיֵּי עוֹלָם. 9 אַל נָא יִרְפּוּ יָדֵינוּ מֵעֲשׂוֹת טוֹב; בְּבוֹא הָעֵת נִקְצֹר, אִם לֹא נִרְפֶּה. 10 לָכֵן בְּעוֹד יֵשׁ לָנוּ הַזְדַּמְּנוּת, נִגְמֹל טוֹב לְכָל אָדָם, וּבְיִחוּד לִבְנֵי אֱמוּנָתֵנוּ. 11 רְאוּ בְּאֵלּוּ אוֹתִיּוֹת גְּדוֹלוֹת כָּתַבְתִּי אֲלֵיכֶם בְּמוֹ יָדִי! 12 הָאֲנָשִׁים הַחֲפֵצִים לְהִתְהַדֵּר בַּבָּשָׂר מַכְרִיחִים אֶתְכֶם לְהִמּוֹל רַק כְּדֵי שֶׁלֹּא יֵרָדְפוּ עַל צְלַב הַמָּשִׁיחַ. 13 הֲרֵי אֲפִלּוּ הַנִּמּוֹלִים עַצְמָם אֵינָם שׁוֹמְרִים אֶת הַתּוֹרָה, אֲבָל רוֹצִים הֵם שֶׁתִּמּוֹלוּ לְמַעַן יִתְהַלְּלוּ בִּבְשַׂרְכֶם. 14 וַאֲנִי חָלִילָה לִי מֵהִתְהַלֵּל בִּלְתִּי אִם בִּצְלַב אֲדוֹנֵנוּ יֵשׁוּעַ הַמָּשִׁיחַ, שֶׁבְּאֶמְצָעוּתוֹ הָעוֹלָם צָלוּב לִי וַאֲנִי צָלוּב לָעוֹלָם; 15 כִּי לֹא הַמִּילָה חֲשׁוּבָה אַף לֹא הָעָרְלָה, אֶלָּא בְּרִיאָה חֲדָשָׁה. 16 כָּל הַנּוֹהֲגִים לְפִי כְּלָל זֶה, שָׁלוֹם וְרַחֲמִים עֲלֵיהֶם וְעַל יִשְׂרָאֵל הַשַּׁיָּכִים לֵאלֹהִים.

17 מֵעַתָּה וְאֵילָךְ אַל נָא יוֹגִיעֵנִי אִישׁ, שֶׁכֵּן אֶת צַלְקוֹת יֵשׁוּעַ אֲנִי נוֹשֵׂא בְּגוּפִי. 18 אַחַי, חֶסֶד אֲדוֹנֵנוּ יֵשׁוּעַ הַמָּשִׁיחַ עִם רוּחֲכֶם. אָמֵן.

The Epistle of Paul to the

EPHESIANS

1 Paul, an apostle of Jesus Christ by the will of God,

To the saints who are in Ephesus, and faithful in Christ Jesus:

[2] Grace to you and peace from God our Father and the Lord Jesus Christ.

[3] Blessed *be* the God and Father of our Lord Jesus Christ, who has blessed us with every spiritual blessing in the heavenly *places* in Christ, [4] just as He chose us in Him before the foundation of the world, that we should be holy and without blame before Him in love, [5] having predestined us to adoption as sons by Jesus Christ to Himself, according to the good pleasure of His will, [6] to the praise of the glory of His grace, by which He made us accepted in the Beloved.

[7] In Him we have redemption through His blood, the forgiveness of sins, according to the riches of His grace [8] which He made to abound toward us in all wisdom and prudence, [9] having made known to us the mystery of His will, according to His good pleasure which He purposed in Himself, [10] that in the dispensation of the fullness of the times He might gather together in one all things in Christ, both which are in heaven and which are on earth— in Him. [11] In Him also we have obtained an inheritance, being predestined according to the purpose of Him who works all things according to the counsel of His will, [12] that we who first trusted in Christ should be to the praise of His glory.

[13] In Him you also *trusted,* after you heard the word of truth, the gospel of your salvation; in whom also, having believed, you were sealed with the Holy Spirit of promise, [14] who is the guarantee of our inheritance until the redemption of the purchased possession, to the praise of His glory.

[15] Therefore I also, after I heard of your faith in the Lord Jesus and your love for all the saints, [16] do not cease to give thanks for you, making mention of you in my prayers: [17] that the God of our Lord Jesus Christ, the Father of glory, may give to you the spirit of wisdom and revelation in the knowledge of Him, [18] the eyes of your understanding being enlightened; that you may know what is the hope of His calling, what are the riches of the glory of His inheritance in the saints, [19] and what *is* the exceeding greatness of His power toward us who

אִגֶּרֶת שָׁאוּל אֶל הָאֶפְסִים

א מֵאֵת שָׁאוּל, שְׁלִיחַ הַמָּשִׁיחַ יֵשׁוּעַ בִּרְצוֹן אֱלֹהִים, אֶל הַקְּדוֹשִׁים אֲשֶׁר [בְּאֶפְסוֹס], הַמַּאֲמִינִים בַּמָּשִׁיחַ יֵשׁוּעַ: [2] חֶסֶד וְשָׁלוֹם לָכֶם מֵאֵת הָאֱלֹהִים אָבִינוּ וְהָאָדוֹן יֵשׁוּעַ הַמָּשִׁיחַ.

[3] בָּרוּךְ הָאֱלֹהִים אֲבִי אֲדוֹנֵנוּ יֵשׁוּעַ הַמָּשִׁיחַ, אֲשֶׁר בֵּרַךְ אוֹתָנוּ בְּכָל בְּרָכָה רוּחָנִית בַּשָּׁמַיִם, בַּמָּשִׁיחַ, [4] כְּשֵׁם שֶׁבָּחַר אוֹתָנוּ בּוֹ בְּטֶרֶם הוּסַד תֵּבֵל, לִהְיוֹת קְדוֹשִׁים וּבְלִי דֹּפִי לְפָנָיו בְּאַהֲבָה. [5] הוּא יָעַד אוֹתָנוּ לִהְיוֹת לוֹ לְבָנִים עַל-יְדֵי יֵשׁוּעַ הַמָּשִׁיחַ, כְּחֵפֶץ רְצוֹנוֹ, [6] לִתְהִלַּת כְּבוֹד עַל חַסְדּוֹ אֲשֶׁר הֶעֱנִיק לָנוּ בְּאָהוּב, [7] שֶׁבְּדָמוֹ יֵשׁ לָנוּ הַפְּדוּת, סְלִיחַת הַחֲטָאִים כְּפִי עֹשֶׁר חֶסֶד הָאֱלֹהִים. [8] אֶת הַחֶסֶד הַזֶּה הוּא הִשְׁפִּיעַ עָלֵינוּ בְּמְלֹא חָכְמָה וּבִינָה, [9] וְהוֹדִיעַ לָנוּ אֶת סוֹד רְצוֹנוֹ כְּפִי חֶפְצוֹ, אֶת הַתָּכְנִית שֶׁהִקְדִּים וְעָרַךְ בּוֹ – [10] הַתָּכְנִית לְקַבֵּץ אֶת הַכֹּל בַּמָּשִׁיחַ בִּמְלֹאת הָעִתִּים, אֶת מַה שֶׁבַּשָּׁמַיִם וְאֶת מַה שֶׁבָּאָרֶץ. [11] וּבוֹ נוֹעֲדָה לָנוּ נַחֲלָה, כִּי נִבְחַרְנוּ מֵרֹאשׁ לְפִי תָּכְנִיתוֹ שֶׁל הַפּוֹעֵל בַּכֹּל בְּהַתְאֵם לְמַחֲשֶׁבֶת רְצוֹנוֹ, [12] כְּדֵי שֶׁנִּהְיֶה לְתִהְלַּת כְּבוֹדוֹ, אָנוּ הַמַּקְדִּימִים לְקַוּוֹת לַמָּשִׁיחַ. [13] וּבוֹ נַחְלְתֶכֶם גַּם אַתֶּם; שֶׁכֵּן בְּשָׁמְעֲכֶם אֶת דְּבַר הָאֱמֶת, אֶת בְּשׂוֹרַת יְשׁוּעַתְכֶם, וּבְהַאֲמִינְכֶם בּוֹ, נֶחְתַּמְתֶּם גַּם אַתֶּם בְּרוּחַ הַהַבְטָחָה, רוּחַ הַקֹּדֶשׁ, [14] אֲשֶׁר הִיא עֵרָבוֹן לְנַחֲלָתֵנוּ עַד לִפְדִיַּת הַקִּנְיָן, לְתִהְלַּת כְּבוֹדוֹ.

[15] מִשּׁוּם כָּךְ גַּם אֲנִי, לְאַחַר שֶׁשָּׁמַעְתִּי עַל אֱמוּנַתְכֶם בָּאָדוֹן יֵשׁוּעַ וְעַל אַהֲבַתְכֶם לְכָל הַקְּדוֹשִׁים, [16] אֵינֶנִּי חָדֵל לְהוֹדוֹת עֲלֵיכֶם וּלְהַזְכִּיר אֶתְכֶם בִּתְפִלּוֹתַי, [17] כְּדֵי שֶׁאֱלֹהֵי אֲדוֹנֵנוּ יֵשׁוּעַ הַמָּשִׁיחַ, אֲבִי הַכָּבוֹד, יִתֵּן לָכֶם רוּחַ שֶׁל חָכְמָה וְהִתְגַּלּוּת שֶׁתֵּיטִיבוּ לָדַעַת אוֹתוֹ, [18] וְיָאִיר עֵינֵי לְבַבְכֶם לָדַעַת מַהִי הַתִּקְוָה הַצְּפוּנָה בִּקְרִיאָתוֹ, מָה עֲתִירַת כָּבוֹד נַחֲלָתוֹ בְּקֶרֶב הַקְּדוֹשִׁים, [19] וּמַה נַּעֲלָה גְּדֻלַּת גְּבוּרָתוֹ הַשּׁוֹפַעַת

believe, according to the working of His mighty power [20] which He worked in Christ when He raised Him from the dead and seated *Him* at His right hand in the heavenly *places,* [21] far above all principality and power and might and dominion, and every name that is named, not only in this age but also in that which is to come.

[22] And He put all *things* under His feet, and gave Him *to be* head over all *things* to the church, [23] which is His body, the fullness of Him who fills all in all.

2 And you *He made alive,* who were dead in trespasses and sins, [2] in which you once walked according to the course of this world, according to the prince of the power of the air, the spirit who now works in the sons of disobedience, [3] among whom also we all once conducted ourselves in the lusts of our flesh, fulfilling the desires of the flesh and of the mind, and were by nature children of wrath, just as the others.

[4] But God, who is rich in mercy, because of His great love with which He loved us, [5] even when we were dead in trespasses, made us alive together with Christ (by grace you have been saved), [6] and raised *us* up together, and made *us* sit together in the heavenly *places* in Christ Jesus, [7] that in the ages to come He might show the exceeding riches of His grace in *His* kindness toward us in Christ Jesus. [8] For by grace you have been saved through faith, and that not of yourselves; *it is* the gift of God, [9] not of works, lest anyone should boast. [10] For we are His workmanship, created in Christ Jesus for good works, which God prepared beforehand that we should walk in them.

[11] Therefore remember that you, once Gentiles in the flesh—who are called Uncircumcision by what is called the Circumcision made in the flesh by hands— [12] that at that time you were without Christ, being aliens from the commonwealth of Israel and strangers from the covenants of promise, having no hope and without God in the world. [13] But now in Christ Jesus you who once were far off have been brought near by the blood of Christ.

[14] For He Himself is our peace, who has made both one, and has broken down the middle wall of separation, [15] having abolished in His flesh the enmity, *that is,* the law of commandments *contained* in ordinances, so as to create in Himself one new man *from* the two, *thus* making peace, [16] and that He might reconcile them both to God in one body through the cross, thereby putting to death the enmity. [17] And He came and preached peace to you

עָלֵינוּ, הַמַּאֲמִינִים, כְּמִדַּת פֹּעַל כֹּחוֹ הֶעָצוּם [20] אֲשֶׁר פָּעַל בַּמָּשִׁיחַ בַּהֲקִימוֹ אוֹתוֹ מִבֵּין הַמֵּתִים וּבְהוֹשִׁיבוֹ אוֹתוֹ לִימִינוֹ בַּשָּׁמַיִם, [21] מֵעַל לְכָל מֶמְשָׁלָה וְשִׁלְטוֹן, גְּבוּרָה וּמִשְׂרָה, וְכָל שֵׁם נִקְרָא – לֹא בָּעוֹלָם הַזֶּה בִּלְבַד, אֶלָּא גַּם בָּעוֹלָם הַבָּא. [22] וְאֶת הַכֹּל שָׁת תַּחַת רַגְלָיו וְנָתַן אוֹתוֹ לַקָּהִלָּה לְרֹאשׁ עַל כֹּל; [23] וְהִיא גוּפוֹ, מְלוֹאוֹ שֶׁל הַמְמַלֵּא אֶת הַכֹּל בַּכֹּל.

ב גַּם אַתֶּם שֶׁהֱיִיתֶם מֵתִים בְּפִשְׁעֵיכֶם וַחֲטָאֵיכֶם, [2] בַּעֲבוּר הִתְהַלַּכְתֶּם בָּהֶם לְפִי עִדָּן הָעוֹלָם הַזֶּה, כִּרְצוֹן הַשַּׂר אֲשֶׁר לוֹ הַשִּׁלְטוֹן בִּסְפֵירַת הַבֵּינַיִם וְהוּא הָרוּחַ הַפּוֹעֶלֶת עַתָּה בִּבְנֵי הַמֶּרִי. [3] וְגַם אֲנַחְנוּ כֻּלָּנוּ הָיִינוּ מְעֹרָבִים עִמָּהֶם בֶּעָבָר; עָסַקְנוּ בְּתַאֲוֹתֵינוּ הַבְּשָׂרִיּוֹת, מִלֵּאנוּ אֶת תְּשׁוּקוֹת הַגּוּף וְאֶת דַּחַף הַמַּחֲשָׁבוֹת, וְהָיִינוּ מִטִּבְעֵנוּ בְּנֵי זַעַם כִּשְׁאָר בְּנֵי אָדָם. [4] אֲבָל אֱלֹהִים הַמָּלֵא רַחֲמִים אָהַב אוֹתָנוּ, וּבְאַהֲבָתוֹ הָרַבָּה, [5] אַף כִּי מֵתִים הָיִינוּ בְּפִשְׁעֵינוּ, הֶחֱיָנוּ עִם הַמָּשִׁיחַ – הֵן בְּחֶסֶד נוֹשַׁעְתֶּם! – [6] וְהֵקִים אוֹתָנוּ עִמּוֹ וְהוֹשִׁיבָנוּ עִמּוֹ בַּשָּׁמַיִם, בַּמָּשִׁיחַ יֵשׁוּעַ, [7] כְּדֵי לְהַרְאוֹת בָּעוֹלָמִים הַבָּאִים אֶת שֶׁפַע עֹשֶׁר חַסְדּוֹ בַּטּוֹבָה שֶׁגָּמַל עָלֵינוּ בַּמָּשִׁיחַ יֵשׁוּעַ. [8] הֵן בְּחֶסֶד נוֹשַׁעְתֶּם עַל-יְדֵי הָאֱמוּנָה; וְזֹאת לֹא מִיֶּדְכֶם, כִּי אִם מַתְּנַת אֱלֹהִים הִיא. [9] אֵין זֶה נוֹבֵעַ מִמַּעֲשִׂים, כְּדֵי שֶׁלֹּא יִתְגָּאֶה אִישׁ; [10] שֶׁהֲרֵי מַעֲשֵׂה יְדֵי אֱלֹהִים אֲנַחְנוּ, בְּרוּאִים בַּמָּשִׁיחַ יֵשׁוּעַ לְמַעֲשִׂים טוֹבִים אֲשֶׁר אֱלֹהִים הֵכִינָם מִקֶּדֶם לְמַעַן נִחְיֶה בָּהֶם.

[11] עַל כֵּן זִכְרוּ אַתֶּם מֶה הָיָה בֶּעָבָר, אַתֶּם, הַגּוֹיִים מִבְּחִינָה גּוּפָנִית, הַנִּקְרָאִים "עֲרֵלִים" בְּפִי הַנִּקְרָאִים "נִמּוֹלִים", אֲשֶׁר מִילָתָם בַּבָּשָׂר וּמַעֲשֵׂה יָדַיִם הִיא. [12] בְּאוֹתָהּ עֵת הֱיִיתֶם בְּלִי מָשִׁיחַ, זָרִים לַעֲדַת יִשְׂרָאֵל וְנָכְרִים לִבְרִיתוֹת הַהַבְטָחָה, מְחֻסְּרֵי תִּקְוָה וּלְלֹא אֱלֹהִים בָּעוֹלָם. [13] אֲבָל כָּעֵת, בַּמָּשִׁיחַ יֵשׁוּעַ, אַתֶּם הָרְחוֹקִים בֶּעָבָר, נִהְיֵיתֶם קְרוֹבִים עַל-יְדֵי דַּם הַמָּשִׁיחַ. [14] הֵן הוּא שְׁלוֹמֵנוּ; הוּא עָשָׂה אֶת הַשְּׁנַיִם לְאֶחָד וְהָרַס אֶת מְחִצַּת הָאֵיבָה. [15] הוּא בִּטֵּל אֶת תּוֹרַת הַמִּצְווֹת שֶׁבַּחֻקִּים, כְּדֵי לִבְרֹא בּוֹ עַצְמוֹ אֶת הַשְּׁנַיִם לְאָדָם חָדָשׁ אֶחָד וּבְכָךְ לַעֲשׂוֹת שָׁלוֹם, [16] וּכְדֵי שֶׁבְּגוּף אֶחָד יְרַצֶּה אֶת שְׁנֵיהֶם לֵאלֹהִים עַל-יְדֵי הַצְּלָב, בַּהֲמִיתוֹ בּוֹ אֶת הָאֵיבָה. [17] הוּא בָּא וּבִשֵּׂר שָׁלוֹם, לָכֶם הָרְחוֹקִים וְגַם

who were afar off and to those who were near.
18 For through Him we both have access by one
Spirit to the Father.

19 Now, therefore, you are no longer strangers
and foreigners, but fellow citizens with the saints
and members of the household of God, 20 having
been built on the foundation of the apostles and
prophets, Jesus Christ Himself being the chief
cornerstone, 21 in whom the whole building, being
fitted together, grows into a holy temple in the
Lord, 22 in whom you also are being built together
for a dwelling place of God in the Spirit.

3 For this reason I, Paul, the prisoner of Christ
Jesus for you Gentiles— 2 if indeed you have heard
of the dispensation of the grace of God which was
given to me for you, 3 how that by revelation He
made known to me the mystery (as I have briefly
written already, 4 by which, when you read, you
may understand my knowledge in the mystery of
Christ), 5 which in other ages was not made known
to the sons of men, as it has now been revealed by
the Spirit to His holy apostles and prophets: 6 that
the Gentiles should be fellow heirs, of the same
body, and partakers of His promise in Christ
through the gospel, 7 of which I became a minister
according to the gift of the grace of God given to
me by the effective working of His power.

8 To me, who am less than the least of all the
saints, this grace was given, that I should preach
among the Gentiles the unsearchable riches of
Christ, 9 and to make all see what is the fellowship
of the mystery, which from the beginning of the
ages has been hidden in God who created all things
through Jesus Christ; 10 to the intent that now the
manifold wisdom of God might be made known by
the church to the principalities and powers in the
heavenly places, 11 according to the eternal purpose
which He accomplished in Christ Jesus our Lord,
12 in whom we have boldness and access with
confidence through faith in Him. 13 Therefore I
ask that you do not lose heart at my tribulations for
you, which is your glory.

14 For this reason I bow my knees to the Father
of our Lord Jesus Christ, 15 from whom the whole
family in heaven and earth is named, 16 that He
would grant you, according to the riches of His
glory, to be strengthened with might through His
Spirit in the inner man, 17 that Christ may dwell in
your hearts through faith; that you, being rooted
and grounded in love, 18 may be able to comprehend
with all the saints what is the width and length and

לַקְּרוֹבִים. 18 דַּרְכּוֹ יֵשׁ לָכֶם וְלָנוּ גִּישָׁה בְּרוּחַ אַחַת
אֶל הָאָב. 19 לָכֵן אֵינְכֶם עוֹד זָרִים אוֹ תּוֹשָׁבִים
נָכְרִים, אֶלָּא בְּנֵי עִירָם שֶׁל הַקְּדוֹשִׁים וּבְנֵי בֵּית
אֱלֹהִים; 20 בְּנוּיִים עַל יְסוֹד הַשְּׁלִיחִים וְהַנְּבִיאִים,
וְהַמָּשִׁיחַ יֵשׁוּעַ עַצְמוֹ הוּא אֶבֶן הַפִּנָּה. 21 בּוֹ כָּל
הַבִּנְיָן מְחֻבָּר יַחַד וְגָדֵל לִהְיוֹת הֵיכַל קֹדֶשׁ לַיהוה;
22 וּבוֹ גַּם אַתֶּם נִבְנִים יַחְדָּיו לִהְיוֹת מִשְׁכַּן אֱלֹהִים
עַל־יְדֵי הָרוּחַ.

ג מִשּׁוּם כָּךְ אֲנִי, שָׁאוּל, אֲסִיר הַמָּשִׁיחַ יֵשׁוּעַ
בַּעֲבוּרְכֶם הַגּוֹיִים... 2 אִם אָמְנָם שְׁמַעְתֶּם עַל
הַתַּפְקִיד הַנּוֹגֵעַ לְחֶסֶד אֱלֹהִים שֶׁנִּתַּן לִי לְמַעַנְכֶם,
3 וְכֵיצַד בְּחָזוֹן נִגְלָה לִי הָרָז, כְּפִי שֶׁכָּתַבְתִּי לְעֵיל
בְּכַמָּה מִלִּים. 4 כְּשֶׁתִּקְרְאוּ תּוּכְלוּ לִרְאוֹת אֶת הֲבָנָתִי
בְּרָז הַמָּשִׁיחַ, 5 הָרָז אֲשֶׁר בַּדּוֹרוֹת הַקּוֹדְמִים לֹא נוֹדַע
לִבְנֵי אָדָם, כְּמוֹ שֶׁנִּגְלָה כָּעֵת לִשְׁלִיחָיו וְלִנְבִיאָיו
הַקְּדוֹשִׁים, בְּדֶרֶךְ הָרוּחַ – 6 שֶׁיִּהְיוּ הַגּוֹיִים שֻׁתָּפֵי
נַחֲלָה, שֻׁתָּפֵי גּוּף וְשֻׁתָּפֵי הַהַבְטָחָה בַּמָּשִׁיחַ יֵשׁוּעַ
עַל־יְדֵי הַבְּשׂוֹרָה; 7 וְלַבְּשׂוֹרָה זֹאת הָיִיתִי לִמְשָׁרֵת
מִתֹּקֶף מַתְּנַת הַחֶסֶד שֶׁאֱלֹהִים נָתַן לִי כְּפִי פְּעֻלַּת
כֹּחוֹ. 8 לִי, הַקָּטֹן מִכָּל הַקְּדוֹשִׁים, נָתַן הַחֶסֶד הַזֶּה
לְבַשֵּׂר לַגּוֹיִים אֶת עֹשֶׁר הַמָּשִׁיחַ, הֶעָצוּם לְאֵין חֵקֶר,
9 וּלְהָאִיר עֵינֵי כֹּל לָדַעַת מַהִי תָּכְנִית הָרָז אֲשֶׁר הָיָה
צָפוּן מֵעוֹלָמִים בֵּאלֹהִים בּוֹרֵא הַכֹּל. 10 וְכָךְ
בְּאֶמְצָעוּת הַקְּהִלָּה תִּוָּדַע עַתָּה לָרָשֻׁיּוֹת
וְלַמֶּמְשָׁלוֹת שֶׁבַּשָּׁמַיִם חָכְמַת אֱלֹהִים הָעֲתִירָה,
11 עַל־פִּי תָּכְנִית הָעוֹלָמִים שֶׁעָשָׂה בַּמָּשִׁיחַ יֵשׁוּעַ
אֲדוֹנֵנוּ, 12 אֲשֶׁר בּוֹ לָנוּ עֹז וְגִישָׁה בְּטוּחָה עַל־יְדֵי
אֱמוּנָתוֹ. 13 לָכֵן אֲנִי מְבַקֵּשׁ שֶׁלֹּא תִּפֹּל רוּחֲכֶם בִּגְלַל
צָרוֹתַי הַבָּאוֹת עָלַי לְמַעַנְכֶם, אֲשֶׁר לִכְבוֹד הֵן לָכֶם.
14 מִשּׁוּם כָּךְ כּוֹרֵעַ אֲנִי עַל בִּרְכַּי לִפְנֵי הָאָב 15 אֲשֶׁר
קָרָא שֵׁם לְכָל מִשְׁפָּחָה בַּשָּׁמַיִם וּבָאָרֶץ; 16 שֶׁיִּתֵּן
לָכֶם כֹּחַ, כְּפִי עֹשֶׁר כְּבוֹדוֹ, לְהִתְחַזֵּק עַל־יְדֵי רוּחוֹ
בָּאָדָם הַפְּנִימִי שֶׁלָּכֶם, 17 כְּדֵי שֶׁיִּשְׁכֹּן הַמָּשִׁיחַ
בִּלְבַבְכֶם עַל־יְדֵי הָאֱמוּנָה וְתִהְיוּ מֻשְׁרָשִׁים וּמְיֻסָּדִים
בְּאַהֲבָה; 18 כָּךְ תּוּכְלוּ לְהָבִין יַחַד עִם כָּל הַקְּדוֹשִׁים

depth and height— ¹⁹to know the love of Christ which passes knowledge; that you may be filled with all the fullness of God.

²⁰Now to Him who is able to do exceedingly abundantly above all that we ask or think, according to the power that works in us, ²¹to Him *be* glory in the church by Christ Jesus to all generations, forever and ever. Amen.

4 I, therefore, the prisoner of the Lord, beseech you to walk worthy of the calling with which you were called, ²with all lowliness and gentleness, with longsuffering, bearing with one another in love, ³endeavoring to keep the unity of the Spirit in the bond of peace. ⁴*There is* one body and one Spirit, just as you were called in one hope of your calling; ⁵one Lord, one faith, one baptism; ⁶one God and Father of all, who *is* above all, and through all, and in you all.

⁷But to each one of us grace was given according to the measure of Christ's gift. ⁸Therefore He says:

"When He ascended on high,
He led captivity captive,
And gave gifts to men."

⁹(Now this, *"He ascended"*—what does it mean but that He also first descended into the lower parts of the earth? ¹⁰He who descended is also the One who ascended far above all the heavens, that He might fill all things.)

¹¹And He Himself gave some *to be* apostles, some prophets, some evangelists, and some pastors and teachers, ¹²for the equipping of the saints for the work of ministry, for the edifying of the body of Christ, ¹³till we all come to the unity of the faith and of the knowledge of the Son of God, to a perfect man, to the measure of the stature of the fullness of Christ; ¹⁴that we should no longer be children, tossed to and fro and carried about with every wind of doctrine, by the trickery of men, in the cunning craftiness of deceitful plotting, ¹⁵but, speaking the truth in love, may grow up in all things into Him who is the head—Christ— ¹⁶from whom the whole body, joined and knit together by what every joint supplies, according to the effective working by which every part does its share, causes growth of the body for the edifying of itself in love.

¹⁷This I say, therefore, and testify in the Lord, that you should no longer walk as the rest of the Gentiles walk, in the futility of their mind, ¹⁸having their understanding darkened, being alienated from the life of God, because of the ignorance that is in them, because of the blindness of their heart;

מָה הָרֹחַב וְהָאֹרֶךְ וְהַגֹּבַהּ וְהָעֹמֶק, ¹⁹וְלָדַעַת אֶת אַהֲבַת הַמָּשִׁיחַ הַנִּשְׂגָּבָה מִדַּעַת, לְמַעַן תִּמָּלְאוּ בְּכָל מְלוֹא הָאֱלֹהִים.

²⁰וְלוֹ אֲשֶׁר יָכוֹל לַעֲשׂוֹת יוֹתֵר מִכָּל מַה שֶּׁאָנוּ מְבַקְשִׁים אוֹ מִמַּה שֶּׁעוֹלֶה עַל דַּעְתֵּנוּ, כְּפִי כֹחוֹ הַפּוֹעֵל בָּנוּ, ²¹לוֹ הַכָּבוֹד בַּקְּהִלָּה וּבַמָּשִׁיחַ יֵשׁוּעַ, בְּכָל הַדּוֹרוֹת לְעוֹלָם וָעֶד. אָמֵן.

ד לְפִיכָךְ אֲנִי, הָאָסִיר לְמַעַן הָאָדוֹן, מַפְצִיר בָּכֶם לְהִתְנַהֵג כַּיָּאֶה לַיִּעוּד שֶׁנִּקְרֵאתֶם אֵלָיו. ²הִתְנַהֲגוּ בְּכָל עֲנָוָה וַעֲנִיכוּת רוּחַ, וּבְאֹרֶךְ אַפַּיִם. סִבְלוּ אִישׁ אֶת רֵעֵהוּ בְּאַהֲבָה. ³שִׁקְדוּ לִשְׁמֹר אֶת אַחְדוּת הָרוּחַ בְּקֶשֶׁר שֶׁל שָׁלוֹם. ⁴הִנֵּה: גּוּף אֶחָד וְרוּחַ אַחַת, כְּשֵׁם שֶׁגַּם אַתֶּם נִקְרֵאתֶם אֶל תִּקְוַת יִעוּדְכֶם הָאֶחָת; ⁵אָדוֹן אֶחָד, אֱמוּנָה אַחַת, טְבִילָה אַחַת, ⁶אֵל וְאָב אֶחָד לַכֹּל, הוּא אֲשֶׁר מֵעַל כֹּל, פּוֹעֵל בַּכֹּל, וּבְתוֹךְ הַכֹּל.

⁷אֲבָל לְכָל אֶחָד וְאֶחָד מֵאִתָּנוּ הָעֳנַק חֶסֶד כְּפִי הַמִּדָּה שֶׁהֶעֱנִיק לוֹ הַמָּשִׁיחַ. ⁸לָכֵן נֶאֱמַר: "עָלָה לַמָּרוֹם, שָׁבָה שֶׁבִי, וַיִּתֵּן מַתָּנוֹת לִבְנֵי אָדָם." ⁹"עָלָה" מַה פֵּרוּשׁוֹ אִם לֹא שֶׁגַּם הִקְדִּים וְיָרַד אֶל תַּחְתִּיּוֹת אָרֶץ. ¹⁰הַיּוֹרֵד הוּא אֲשֶׁר גַּם עָלָה אֶל מֵעַל כָּל הַשָּׁמַיִם, לְמַעַן יְמַלֵּא אֶת הַכֹּל. ¹¹וְהוּא נָתַן אֶת אֵלֶּה לִהְיוֹת שְׁלִיחִים, אֶת אֵלֶּה נְבִיאִים, אֶת אֵלֶּה מְבַשְּׂרִים, וְאֶת אֵלֶּה רוֹעִים וּמוֹרִים, ¹²כְּדֵי לְהַכְשִׁיר אֶת הַקְּדוֹשִׁים לַעֲבוֹדַת הַשָּׁרוּת, לְבִנְיַת גּוּף הַמָּשִׁיחַ, ¹³עַד כִּי נַגִּיעַ כֻּלָּנוּ אֶל אַחְדוּת הָאֱמוּנָה וְאַחְדוּת יְדִיעַת בֶּן־הָאֱלֹהִים, אֶל הָאָדָם הַשָּׁלֵם, אֶל שִׁעוּר קוֹמָתוֹ הַמָּלֵא שֶׁל הַמָּשִׁיחַ. ¹⁴וְכָךְ לֹא נִהְיֶה עוֹד יְלָדִים נִדָּפִים וּמְטֻלְטָלִים בְּרוּחַ שֶׁל כָּל תּוֹרָה הַמּוּפֶצֶת עַל־יְדֵי בְּנֵי אָדָם בְּעָרְמָה וּבְתַרְמִית כְּדֵי לְהַטְעוֹת, ¹⁵אֶלָּא נְדַבֵּר אֶת הָאֱמֶת בְּאַהֲבָה וְנִגְדַּל בְּכָל דָּבָר אֱלֵי הַמָּשִׁיחַ, אֲשֶׁר הוּא הָרֹאשׁ, ¹⁶וְעַל־יָדָיו כָּל הַגּוּף מֻרְכָּב וּמִתְחַבֵּר בְּאֶמְצָעוּת כָּל קֶשֶׁר מְסַיֵּעַ, בְּהֵתְאֵם לַפְּעֻלָּה הַמְיֻעֶדֶת לְכָל אֵיבָר וְאֵיבָר, כְּדֵי שֶׁיִּגְדַּל הַגּוּף וְיִבָּנֶה בְּאַהֲבָה.

¹⁷הִנֵּה זֹאת אֲנִי אוֹמֵר וּמַכְרִיז מִטַּעַם הָאָדוֹן: אַל תֵּלְכוּ עוֹד כַּגּוֹיִים הַהוֹלְכִים בְּהַבְלֵי שִׂכְלָם. ¹⁸חֲשׁוּכֵי דַעַת הֵם, זָרִים לְחַיֵּי אֱלֹהִים בִּגְלַל אֱוִּלְתָּם וּקְשִׁי

[19] who, being past feeling, have given themselves over to lewdness, to work all uncleanness with greediness.

[20] But you have not so learned Christ, [21] if indeed you have heard Him and have been taught by Him, as the truth is in Jesus: [22] that you put off, concerning your former conduct, the old man which grows corrupt according to the deceitful lusts, [23] and be renewed in the spirit of your mind, [24] and that you put on the new man which was created according to God, in true righteousness and holiness.

[25] Therefore, putting away lying, *"Let each one of you speak truth with his neighbor,"* for we are members of one another. [26] *"Be angry, and do not sin"*: do not let the sun go down on your wrath, [27] nor give place to the devil. [28] Let him who stole steal no longer, but rather let him labor, working with *his* hands what is good, that he may have something to give him who has need. [29] Let no corrupt word proceed out of your mouth, but what is good for necessary edification, that it may impart grace to the hearers. [30] And do not grieve the Holy Spirit of God, by whom you were sealed for the day of redemption. [31] Let all bitterness, wrath, anger, clamor, and evil speaking be put away from you, with all malice. [32] And be kind to one another, tenderhearted, forgiving one another, even as God in Christ forgave you.

5 Therefore be imitators of God as dear children. [2] And walk in love, as Christ also has loved us and given Himself for us, an offering and a sacrifice to God for a sweet-smelling aroma.

[3] But fornication and all uncleanness or covetousness, let it not even be named among you, as is fitting for saints; [4] neither filthiness, nor foolish talking, nor coarse jesting, which are not fitting, but rather giving of thanks. [5] For this you know, that no fornicator, unclean person, nor covetous man, who is an idolater, has any inheritance in the kingdom of Christ and God. [6] Let no one deceive you with empty words, for because of these things the wrath of God comes upon the sons of disobedience. [7] Therefore do not be partakers with them.

[8] For you were once darkness, but now *you are* light in the Lord. Walk as children of light [9] (for the fruit of the Spirit *is* in all goodness, righteousness, and truth), [10] finding out what is acceptable to the Lord. [11] And have no fellowship with the unfruitful works of darkness, but rather expose *them.* [12] For it is shameful even to speak of those things which are done by them in secret. [13] But all things that are

לָכֶם; [19] וְכֵיוָן שֶׁהִתְנוּנוּ הִתְמַכְּרוּ בְּתַאֲוָה לְזִמָּה וּלְכָל מַעֲשֵׂה טֻמְאָה. [20] אֲבָל אַתֶּם לֹא בְּדֶרֶךְ זֹאת לְמַדְתֶּם אֶת הַמָּשִׁיחַ, [21] אִם אָמְנָם שְׁמַעְתֶּם אוֹתוֹ וְלֻמַּדְתֶּם בּוֹ אֶת הָאֱמֶת כְּפִי שֶׁהִיא בְּיֵשׁוּעַ – [22] שֶׁעֲלֵיכֶם לִפְשֹׁט אֶת הָאָדָם הַיָּשָׁן אֲשֶׁר הִתְנַהֲגוּתְכֶם הָרִאשׁוֹנָה כְּרוּכָה עִמּוֹ וְהוּא נִשְׁחָת בְּתַאֲווֹת מַתְעוֹת, [23] וּלְהִתְחַדֵּשׁ הִתְחַדְּשׁוּת רוּחָנִית בְּשִׂכְלְכֶם, [24] וְלִלְבֹּשׁ אֶת הָאָדָם הֶחָדָשׁ הַנִּבְרָא כִּדְמוּת אֱלֹהִים בְּצִדְקָה וּקְדֻשָּׁה שֶׁל אֱמֶת.

[25] עַל כֵּן הָסִירוּ אֶת הַשֶּׁקֶר וְדַבְּרוּ אֱמֶת אִישׁ לְרֵעֵהוּ, כִּי אֵיבָרִים אֲנַחְנוּ אִישׁ לְרֵעֵהוּ. [26] רִגְזוּ וְאַל-תֶּחֱטָאוּ; אַל תִּשְׁקַע הַשֶּׁמֶשׁ עַל כַּעַסְכֶם, [27] וְאַל תִּתְּנוּ מָקוֹם לַשָּׂטָן. [28] הַגּוֹנֵב אַל יוֹסִיף לִגְנֹב, כִּי אִם יַעֲמֹל וּבְיָדָיו יַעֲשֶׂה אֶת הַטּוֹב כְּדֵי שֶׁיּוּכַל לָתֵת לְמִי שֶׁשָּׂרוּי בְּמַחְסוֹר. [29] אַל יֵצֵא מִפִּיכֶם כָּל דָּבָר נָבוּל, אֶלָּא דָּבָר שֶׁהוּא טוֹב בְּעִתּוֹ וְיֵשׁ בּוֹ כְּדֵי לִבְנוֹת, לְמַעַן יַשְׁפִּיעַ נֹעַם עַל הַשּׁוֹמְעִים. [30] וְאַל תַּעֲצִיבוּ אֶת רוּחַ הַקֹּדֶשׁ אֲשֶׁר נֶחְתַּמְתֶּם בָּהּ לְיוֹם הַגְּאֻלָּה. [31] הָסִירוּ מִכֶּם כָּל מְרִירוּת וְחֵמָה וְכַעַס וּצְעָקָה וְגִדּוּף וְכָל רִשְׁעָה. [32] הֱיוּ טוֹבִים אִישׁ לְרֵעֵהוּ, הֱיוּ מְלֵאֵי רַחֲמִים וְסִלְחוּ אִישׁ לְרֵעֵהוּ כְּשֵׁם שֶׁאֱלֹהִים סָלַח לָכֶם בַּמָּשִׁיחַ.

ה וּבְכֵן לְכוּ בְּדַרְכֵי אֱלֹהִים כְּבָנִים אֲהוּבִים, [2] וְהִתְהַלְּכוּ בְּאַהֲבָה כְּשֵׁם שֶׁגַּם הַמָּשִׁיחַ אָהַב אוֹתָנוּ וּמָסַר אֶת עַצְמוֹ בַּעֲדֵנוּ כְּמִנְחָה וְקָרְבָּן לֵאלֹהִים, לְרֵיחַ נִיחוֹחַ. [3] וְכִיאֶה לַקְּדוֹשִׁים, אַף לֹא תַּעֲלוּ עַל דַּל שִׂפְתֵיכֶם מַעֲשֵׂי זְנוּת וְכָל טֻמְאָה אוֹ תַּאַוְתָנוּת; [4] גַּם לֹא נִבּוּל פֶּה וְשִׂיחַת סִכְלוּת אוֹ הִתְלוֹצְצוּת, דְּבָרִים שֶׁאֵינָם יָאִים, אֶלָּא קוֹל תּוֹדָה. [5] זֹאת עֲלֵיכֶם לָדַעַת: כָּל זוֹנֶה אוֹ טָמֵא אוֹ בַּעַל תַּאֲווֹת, שֶׁאֵינוֹ אֶלָּא עוֹבֵד אֱלִילִים, אֵין לוֹ נַחֲלָה בְּמַלְכוּת הַמָּשִׁיחַ וְהָאֱלֹהִים. [6] אַל יַתְעֶה אֶתְכֶם אִישׁ בְּדִבְּרֵי הֶבֶל. בִּגְלַל הַדְּבָרִים הַלָּלוּ בָּא וַעַם אֱלֹהִים עַל בְּנֵי הַמֶּרִי. [7] עַל כֵּן אַל תִּהְיוּ שֻׁתָּפִים לָהֶם. [8] בְּעָבַר הֱיִיתֶם חֹשֶׁךְ, אַךְ עַכְשָׁו אוֹר אַתֶּם בָּאָדוֹן. הִתְנַהֲגוּ נָא כִּבְנֵי הָאוֹר, [9] כִּי פְּרִי הָאוֹר הוּא כָּל טוּב וְכָל צְדָקָה וֶאֱמֶת. [10] בַּחֲנוּ וְהוֹכִחוּ מָה רָצוּי בְּעֵינֵי הָאָדוֹן. [11] אַל תִּשְׁתַּתְּפוּ בְּמַעֲשֵׂי הַחֹשֶׁךְ, אֲשֶׁר עֲקָרִים הֵם כֻּלָּם, אֶלָּא הוֹכֵחַ תּוֹכִיחוּ אֶת עוֹשֵׂיהֶם. [12] הֲרֵי מַה שֶּׁהֵם עוֹשִׂים בַּסֵּתֶר, חֶרְפָּה אֲפִלּוּ לְבַטֵּא בְּמִלִּים. [13] אֲבָל כָּל מַה שֶּׁמּוּכָח עַל-יְדֵי הָאוֹר נִרְאֶה

exposed are made manifest by the light, for whatever makes manifest is light. [14] Therefore He says:

> "Awake, you who sleep,
> Arise from the dead,
> And Christ will give you light."

[15] See then that you walk circumspectly, not as fools but as wise, [16] redeeming the time, because the days are evil.

[17] Therefore do not be unwise, but understand what the will of the Lord *is*. [18] And do not be drunk with wine, in which is dissipation; but be filled with the Spirit, [19] speaking to one another in psalms and hymns and spiritual songs, singing and making melody in your heart to the Lord, [20] giving thanks always for all things to God the Father in the name of our Lord Jesus Christ, [21] submitting to one another in the fear of God.

[22] Wives, submit to your own husbands, as to the Lord. [23] For the husband is head of the wife, as also Christ is head of the church; and He is the Savior of the body. [24] Therefore, just as the church is subject to Christ, so *let* the wives *be* to their own husbands in everything.

[25] Husbands, love your wives, just as Christ also loved the church and gave Himself for her, [26] that He might sanctify and cleanse her with the washing of water by the word, [27] that He might present her to Himself a glorious church, not having spot or wrinkle or any such thing, but that she should be holy and without blemish. [28] So husbands ought to love their own wives as their own bodies; he who loves his wife loves himself. [29] For no one ever hated his own flesh, but nourishes and cherishes it, just as the Lord *does* the church. [30] For we are members of His body, of His flesh and of His bones. [31] "For this reason a man shall leave his father and mother and be joined to his wife, and the two shall become one flesh." [32] This is a great mystery, but I speak concerning Christ and the church. [33] Nevertheless let each one of you in particular so love his own wife as himself, and let the wife *see* that she respects *her* husband.

6 Children, obey your parents in the Lord, for this is right. [2] "Honor your father and mother," which is the first commandment with promise: [3] "that it may be well with you and you may live long on the earth."

[4] And you, fathers, do not provoke your children to wrath, but bring them up in the training and admonition of the Lord.

בְּבֵרוּר, שֶׁהֲרֵי כָּל מַה שֶׁנִּרְאֶה בְּבֵרוּר הוּא אוֹר. [14] עַל כֵּן נֶאֱמַר: "עוּרָה הַיָּשֵׁן וְקוּמָה מִן הַמֵּתִים, וְיָאִיר לְךָ הַמָּשִׁיחַ." [15] וְעַתָּה שִׂימוּ לִבְּכֶם לְהִתְהַלֵּךְ בִּזְהִירוּת – לֹא כִּכְסִילִים, אֶלָּא כַּחֲכָמִים [16] הַמְנַצְּלִים כָּל הַהִזְדַּמְּנוּת, שֶׁכֵּן הַיָּמִים רָעִים. [17] לָכֵן אַל תִּהְיוּ חַסְרֵי דַּעַת, אֶלָּא הָבִינוּ לָדַעַת מַה רְצוֹנוֹ שֶׁל הָאָדוֹן. [18] אַל תִּשְׁתַּכְּרוּ מִיַּיִן, שֶׁכֵּן זֶה מֵבִיא לִידֵי פְּרִיצוּת, אֶלָּא הִמָּלְאוּ בְּרוּחַ [19] וְהַשְׁמִיעוּ בֵּינֵיכֶם תְּהִלּוֹת וְתִשְׁבָּחוֹת וְשִׁירוֹת רוּחָנִיּוֹת. שִׁירוּ וְזַמְּרוּ לַאדֹנָי בִּלְבַבְכֶם, [20] וּבְכָל עֵת הוֹדוּ עַל הַכֹּל לֵאלֹהִים אָבִינוּ בְּשֵׁם אֲדוֹנֵנוּ יֵשׁוּעַ הַמָּשִׁיחַ. [21] הִכָּנְעוּ אִישׁ לְרֵעֵהוּ מִתּוֹךְ יִרְאַת הַמָּשִׁיחַ. [22] הַנָּשִׁים, הִכָּנַעְנָה לְבַעֲלֵיכֶן כְּמוֹ לַאֲדוֹנֵנוּ, [23] כִּי הָאִישׁ הוּא רֹאשׁ הָאִשָּׁה כְּפִי שֶׁהַמָּשִׁיחַ הוּא רֹאשׁ הַקְּהִלָּה – הַמּוֹשִׁיעַ שֶׁל הַגּוּף. [24] וּכְשֵׁם שֶׁהַקְּהִלָּה נִכְנַעַת לַמָּשִׁיחַ, כֵּן גַּם הַנָּשִׁים תִּכָּנַעְנָה לְבַעֲלֵיהֶן בְּכָל דָּבָר. [25] הָאֲנָשִׁים, אֶהֱבוּ אֶת נְשֵׁיכֶם כְּשֵׁם שֶׁגַּם הַמָּשִׁיחַ אָהַב אֶת הַקְּהִלָּה וּמָסַר אֶת עַצְמוֹ בַּעֲדָהּ [26] כְּדֵי לְקַדְּשָׁהּ וּלְטַהֲרָהּ עַל־יְדֵי רְחִיצַת מַיִם, בְּלִוּוּי דְּבָרוֹ, [27] לְמַעַן יַעֲמִיד לְפָנָיו אֶת הַקְּהִלָּה כְּשֶׁהִיא מְפֹאֶרֶת בְּכָבוֹד, לְלֹא כֶּתֶם וְקֶמֶט וְכַדּוֹמֶה, לְמַעַן תִּהְיֶה קְדוֹשָׁה וּלְלֹא דֹּפִי. [28] כֵּן חַיָּבִים גַּם הָאֲנָשִׁים לֶאֱהֹב אֶת נְשֵׁיהֶם כְּאַהֲבָתָם אֶת גּוּפָם הֵם. הָאוֹהֵב אֶת אִשְׁתּוֹ אוֹהֵב אֶת עַצְמוֹ. [29] הֵן מֵעוֹלָם לֹא שָׂנֵא אִישׁ אֶת בְּשָׂרוֹ, אֶלָּא הוּא מְכַלְכֵּל וּמְטַפֵּחַ אוֹתוֹ כְּדֶרֶךְ שֶׁגַּם הַמָּשִׁיחַ נוֹהֵג בַּקְּהִלָּה, [30] שֶׁהֲרֵי אֵיבְרֵי גּוּפוֹ אֲנַחְנוּ. [31] "עַל־כֵּן יַעֲזָב־אִישׁ אֶת־אָבִיו וְאֶת־אִמּוֹ וְדָבַק בְּאִשְׁתּוֹ, וְהָיוּ לְבָשָׂר אֶחָד." [32] גָּדוֹל הָרָז הַזֶּה, וַאֲנִי מִתְכַּוֵּן לַמָּשִׁיחַ וְלַקְּהִלָּה. [33] אֲבָל גַּם אַתֶּם, אִישׁ אִישׁ יֹאהַב אֶת אִשְׁתּוֹ כְּאַהֲבָתוֹ אֶת עַצְמוֹ; וְהָאִשָּׁה תִּירָא אֶת בַּעְלָהּ.

ו הַבָּנִים, שִׁמְעוּ בְּקוֹל הוֹרֵיכֶם עַל־פִּי הָאָדוֹן, כִּי כָךְ רָאוּי. [2] "כַּבֵּד אֶת־אָבִיךָ וְאֶת־אִמֶּךָ", הִיא הַמִּצְוָה הָרִאשׁוֹנָה אֲשֶׁר הַבְטָחָה בְּצִדָּהּ: [3] "לְמַעַן יַאֲרִיכֻן יָמֶיךָ וּלְמַעַן יִיטַב לָךְ עַל הָאֲדָמָה." [4] וְאַתֶּם הָאָבוֹת, אַל תַּכְעִיסוּ אֶת בְּנֵיכֶם, אֶלָּא גַּדְּלוּ אוֹתָם

⁵Bondservants, be obedient to those who are your masters according to the flesh, with fear and trembling, in sincerity of heart, as to Christ; ⁶not with eyeservice, as men-pleasers, but as bondservants of Christ, doing the will of God from the heart, ⁷with goodwill doing service, as to the Lord, and not to men, ⁸knowing that whatever good anyone does, he will receive the same from the Lord, whether *he is* a slave or free.

⁹And you, masters, do the same things to them, giving up threatening, knowing that your own Master also is in heaven, and there is no partiality with Him.

¹⁰Finally, my brethren, be strong in the Lord and in the power of His might. ¹¹Put on the whole armor of God, that you may be able to stand against the wiles of the devil. ¹²For we do not wrestle against flesh and blood, but against principalities, against powers, against the rulers of the darkness of this age, against spiritual *hosts* of wickedness in the heavenly *places*. ¹³Therefore take up the whole armor of God, that you may be able to withstand in the evil day, and having done all, to stand.

¹⁴Stand therefore, having girded your waist with truth, having put on the breastplate of righteousness, ¹⁵and having shod your feet with the preparation of the gospel of peace; ¹⁶above all, taking the shield of faith with which you will be able to quench all the fiery darts of the wicked one. ¹⁷And take the helmet of salvation, and the sword of the Spirit, which is the word of God; ¹⁸praying always with all prayer and supplication in the Spirit, being watchful to this end with all perseverance and supplication for all the saints— ¹⁹and for me, that utterance may be given to me, that I may open my mouth boldly to make known the mystery of the gospel, ²⁰for which I am an ambassador in chains; that in it I may speak boldly, as I ought to speak.

²¹But that you also may know my affairs *and* how I am doing, Tychicus, a beloved brother and faithful minister in the Lord, will make all things known to you; ²²whom I have sent to you for this very purpose, that you may know our affairs, and *that* he may comfort your hearts.

²³Peace to the brethren, and love with faith, from God the Father and the Lord Jesus Christ. ²⁴Grace *be* with all those who love our Lord Jesus Christ in sincerity. Amen.

---

⁵ הָעֲבָדִים, הִשָּׁמְעוּ לַאֲדוֹנֵיכֶם שֶׁבָּעוֹלָם הַזֶּה, בְּיִרְאָה וּבִרְתֵת וּבְתָם לֵב, כְּמוֹ לַמָּשִׁיחַ – ⁶ לֹא בְּשֵׁרוּת לְמַרְאִית עַיִן, כִּמְבַקְשִׁים לִמְצֹא חֵן בְּעֵינֵי בְּנֵי אָדָם, אֶלָּא כְּעַבְדֵי הַמָּשִׁיחַ הָעוֹשִׂים אֶת רְצוֹן אֱלֹהִים בְּכָל נַפְשָׁם ⁷ וּמְשָׁרְתִים בְּחֵפֶץ לֵב כַּעֲבָדִים לָאָדוֹן וְלֹא לִבְנֵי אָדָם, ⁸ וְיוֹדְעִים שֶׁכָּל טוֹב אֲשֶׁר יַעֲשֶׂה אָדָם, אֶת זֶה יְקַבֵּל מֵאֵת הָאָדוֹן, אִם עֶבֶד הוּא וְאִם בֶּן חוֹרִין. ⁹ וְאַתֶּם הָאֲדוֹנִים, בְּאוֹתוֹ אֹפֶן הִתְנַהֲגוּ עִמָּהֶם. חִדְלוּ לְאַיֵּם עֲלֵיהֶם, שֶׁכֵּן יוֹדְעִים אַתֶּם כִּי גַם לָהֶם וְגַם לָכֶם הָאָדוֹן בַּשָּׁמַיִם, וְאֵין עִמּוֹ מַשּׂוֹא פָנִים.

¹⁰ סוֹף דָּבָר, חִזְקוּ בָּאָדוֹן וּבְכֹחַ גְּבוּרָתוֹ. ¹¹ לִבְשׁוּ אֶת מְלוֹא נֶשֶׁק הָאֱלֹהִים לְמַעַן תּוּכְלוּ לַעֲמֹד נֶגֶד נִכְלֵי הַשָּׂטָן; ¹² כִּי לֹא עִם בָּשָׂר־וָדָם מִלְחָמָה לָנוּ, אֶלָּא עִם מֶמְשָׁלוֹת וְשָׂרָרוֹת, עִם מוֹשְׁלֵי חֶשְׁכַת הָעוֹלָם הַזֶּה, עִם כֹּחוֹת רוּחָנִיִּים רָעִים בַּשָּׁמַיִם. ¹³ עַל כֵּן קְחוּ אֶת מְלוֹא נֶשֶׁק הָאֱלֹהִים, לְמַעַן תּוּכְלוּ לְהִתְנַגֵּד בְּיוֹם הָרָע, וְלַעֲמֹד לְאַחַר עֲשׂוֹתְכֶם אֶת הַכֹּל. ¹⁴ עִמְדוּ כְּשֶׁהָאֱמֶת חֲגוּרָה עַל מָתְנֵיכֶם וְשִׁרְיוֹן הַצֶּדֶק לְבוּשְׁכֶם, ¹⁵ וּכְשֶׁרַגְלֵיכֶם נְעוּלוֹת נְכוֹנוּת לִבְשׂוֹרַת הַשָּׁלוֹם. ¹⁶ עִם כָּל אֵלֶּה שְׂאוּ אֶת מָגֵן הָאֱמוּנָה אֲשֶׁר תּוּכְלוּ לְכַבּוֹת בּוֹ אֶת כָּל חִצֵּי הַבּוֹעֲרִים שֶׁל הָרָע. ¹⁷ וּקְחוּ אֶת כּוֹבַע הַיְשׁוּעָה וְאֶת חֶרֶב הָרוּחַ, שֶׁהִיא דְּבַר הָאֱלֹהִים. ¹⁸ בְּכָל תְּפִלָּה וּתְחִנָּה הִתְפַּלְלוּ תָּמִיד בָּרוּחַ. שִׁקְדוּ בִּתְפִלַּתְכֶם וְהַתְמִידוּ בִּתְחִנָּה בְּעַד כָּל הַקְּדוֹשִׁים ¹⁹ וְגַם בַּעֲדִי, שֶׁתִּנָּתְנָה לִי מִלִּים וּבְאֹמֶץ לֵב אֶפְתַּח פִּי לְהוֹדִיעַ אֶת סוֹד הַבְּשׂוֹרָה, ²⁰ אֲשֶׁר בִּגְלָלָהּ אֲנִי שַׁגְרִיר אָסוּר בִּכְבָלִים, וַאֲדַבֵּר בְּבִטָּחוֹן כְּפִי שֶׁעָלַי לְדַבֵּר. ²¹ רְצוֹנִי שֶׁתֵּדְעוּ גַם אַתֶּם מַה הַנְּסִבּוֹת שֶׁאֲנִי נָתוּן בָּהֶן וּמָה אֲנִי עוֹשֶׂה; לָכֵן טִיכִיקוֹס, הָאָח הֶחָבִיב וְהַמְשָׁרֵת הַנֶּאֱמָן בָּאָדוֹן, יְסַפֵּר לָכֶם הַכֹּל. ²² שָׁלַחְתִּי אוֹתוֹ אֲלֵיכֶם לְמַטָּרָה זֹאת, כְּדֵי שֶׁתֵּדְעוּ מַה הַמַּצָּב אֶצְלֵנוּ וְהוּא יְעוֹדֵד אֶתְכֶם.

²³ שָׁלוֹם לָאַחִים וְאַהֲבָה עִם אֱמוּנָה מֵאֵת אֱלֹהִים הָאָב וְהָאָדוֹן יֵשׁוּעַ הַמָּשִׁיחַ. ²⁴ חֶסֶד עִם כָּל הָאוֹהֲבִים אֶת אֲדוֹנֵנוּ יֵשׁוּעַ הַמָּשִׁיחַ בְּאַהֲבָה בִּלְתִּי דוֹעֶכֶת.

The Epistle of Paul to the

PHILIPPIANS

1 Paul and Timothy, bondservants of Jesus Christ,
To all the saints in Christ Jesus who are in
Philippi, with the bishops and deacons:

² Grace to you and peace from God our Father
and the Lord Jesus Christ.

³ I thank my God upon every remembrance of
you, ⁴ always in every prayer of mine making
request for you all with joy, ⁵ for your fellowship
in the gospel from the first day until now, ⁶ being
confident of this very thing, that He who has begun
a good work in you will complete *it* until the day of
Jesus Christ; ⁷ just as it is right for me to think this
of you all, because I have you in my heart,
inasmuch as both in my chains and in the defense
and confirmation of the gospel, you all are
partakers with me of grace. ⁸ For God is my
witness, how greatly I long for you all with the
affection of Jesus Christ.

⁹ And this I pray, that your love may abound still
more and more in knowledge and all discernment,
¹⁰ that you may approve the things that are
excellent, that you may be sincere and without
offense till the day of Christ, ¹¹ being filled with the
fruits of righteousness which *are* by Jesus Christ, to
the glory and praise of God.

¹² But I want you to know, brethren, that the
things *which happened* to me have actually turned
out for the furtherance of the gospel, ¹³ so that it has
become evident to the whole palace guard, and to
all the rest, that my chains are in Christ; ¹⁴ and most
of the brethren in the Lord, having become
confident by my chains, are much more bold to
speak the word without fear.

¹⁵ Some indeed preach Christ even from envy and
strife, and some also from goodwill: ¹⁶ The former
preach Christ from selfish ambition, not sincerely,
supposing to add affliction to my chains; ¹⁷ but the
latter out of love, knowing that I am appointed for
the defense of the gospel. ¹⁸ What then? Only *that* in
every way, whether in pretense or in truth, Christ is
preached; and in this I rejoice, yes, and will rejoice.

¹⁹ For I know that this will turn out for my
deliverance through your prayer and the supply of
the Spirit of Jesus Christ, ²⁰ according to my earnest
expectation and hope that in nothing I shall be
ashamed, but with all boldness, as always, so now
also Christ will be magnified in my body, whether

אִגֶּרֶת שָׁאוּל אֶל הַפִילִיפִּים

א מֵאֵת שָׁאוּל וְטִימוֹתִיאוֹס, עַבְדֵי הַמָּשִׁיחַ יֵשׁוּעַ,
אֶל כָּל הַקְּדוֹשִׁים בַּמָּשִׁיחַ יֵשׁוּעַ הַנִּמְצָאִים בְּפִילִיפִּי,
וּמַנְהִיגֵי הַקְּהִלָּה וְהַשַּׁמָּשִׁים בִּכְלָל זֶה: ² חֶסֶד וְשָׁלוֹם
לָכֶם מֵאֵת הָאֱלֹהִים אָבִינוּ וְהָאָדוֹן יֵשׁוּעַ הַמָּשִׁיחַ.
³ מוֹדֶה אֲנִי לֵאלֹהַי מִדֵּי זָכְרִי אֶתְכֶם ⁴ וְתָמִיד, בְּכָל
תְּפִלּוֹתַי בַּעַד כֻּלְּכֶם, מִתְפַּלֵּל אֲנִי מִתּוֹךְ שִׂמְחָה ⁵ עַל
הִשְׁתַּתְּפוּתְכֶם בַּבְּשׂוֹרָה לְמִן הַיּוֹם הָרִאשׁוֹן וְעַד
עָתָּה. ⁶ בָּוֹאת בָּטוּחַ אֲנִי, שֶׁהַמַּתְחִיל בָּכֶם אֶת
הַפְּעֻלָּה הַטּוֹבָה הַשְׁלֵם יַשְׁלִים אוֹתָהּ עַד יוֹם
הַמָּשִׁיחַ יֵשׁוּעַ. ⁷ בְּצֶדֶק אֲנִי חוֹשֵׁב זֹאת עַל כֻּלְּכֶם,
שֶׁכֵּן אֲנִי נוֹשֵׂא אֶתְכֶם בְּלִבִּי בִּגְלַל הֱיוֹתְכֶם שֻׁתָּפִים
לַחֶסֶד שֶׁהוּא מְנָת חֶלְקִי, הֵן בְּמַאֲסָרִי וְהֵן בְּפָעֳלָתִי
לַהֲגֵנַּת הַבְּשׂוֹרָה וְחִזּוּקָהּ. ⁸ הָאֱלֹהִים עֵד לִי, כַּמָּה
נִכְסָף אֲנִי אֶל כֻּלְּכֶם בְּאַהֲבַת הַמָּשִׁיחַ יֵשׁוּעַ.
⁹ תְּפִלָּתִי הִיא שֶׁאַהֲבַתְכֶם תִּרְבֶּה יוֹתֵר וְיוֹתֵר
וְתִלְוֶה בְּדַעַת וּבְכָל תְּבוּנָה, ¹⁰ לְמַעַן תַּבְחִינוּ מַה
הֵם הַדְּבָרִים הַמְצֻיָּנִים וְתִהְיוּ זַכִּים וְלֹא דִּפִי לְיוֹם
הַמָּשִׁיחַ ¹¹ וּמְלֵאִים פְּרִי צְדָקָה שֶׁמֵּנִיב יֵשׁוּעַ הַמָּשִׁיחַ,
לִכְבוֹד אֱלֹהִים וְלִתְהִלָּתוֹ.
¹² אַחַי, רְצוֹנִי שֶׁתֵּדְעוּ כִּי מַה שֶּׁקָּרָה לִי הָיָה דַּוְקָא
לְטוֹבַת הַבְּשׂוֹרָה: ¹³ הָעֻבְדָּה שֶׁאֲנִי חָבוּשׁ בְּמַאֲסָר
לְמַעַן הַמָּשִׁיחַ נִתְפַּרְסְמָה בֵּין כָּל אַנְשֵׁי מִשְׁמַר
הַקֵּיסָר וְנוֹדְעָה לְכָל הַשְּׁאָר; ¹⁴ וְרֹב הָאַחִים בְּבִטְחָם
בָּאָדוֹן הִתְחַזְּקוּ עוֹד יוֹתֵר בִּגְלַל מַאֲסָרִי וְהֵעֵזּוּ לְדַבֵּר
בְּלִי פַּחַד אֶת דְּבַר הָאֱלֹהִים. ¹⁵ אָמְנָם יֵשׁ הַמַּכְרִיזִים
אֶת הַמָּשִׁיחַ מִתּוֹךְ קִנְאָה וְתַחֲרוּת, אַךְ יֵשׁ
הַמַּכְרִיזִים מִתּוֹךְ כַּוָּנָה טוֹבָה. ¹⁶ אֵלֶּה עוֹשִׂים זֹאת
מִתּוֹךְ אַהֲבָה, בְּיָדְעָם כִּי מֻפְקָד אֲנִי עַל הֲגֵנַּת
הַבְּשׂוֹרָה; ¹⁷ וְאֵלֶּה מַכְרִיזִים אֶת הַמָּשִׁיחַ מִתּוֹךְ
תַּחֲרוּת וְלֹא בְּלֵב טָהוֹר, וְכַוָּנָתָם לְהוֹסִיף צָרָה עַל
כְּבָלַי. ¹⁸ אָז מַה? הַתּוֹצָאָה הִיא שֶׁבֵּין כָּךְ וּבֵין כָּךְ,
אִם בְּהַעֲמָדַת פָּנִים וְאִם מִתּוֹךְ כֵּנוּת, הַמָּשִׁיחַ מֻכְרָז,
וּבְזֹאת אֲנִי שָׂמֵחַ וְגַם אוֹסִיף לִשְׂמֹחַ. ¹⁹ כִּי יוֹדֵעַ אֲנִי
שֶׁכָּל זֶה יָבִיא לִידֵי שִׁחְרוּרִי, בְּעֶזְרַת תְּפִלַּתְכֶם
וּבִתְמִיכַת רוּחַ יֵשׁוּעַ הַמָּשִׁיחַ; ²⁰ וְזֹאת בְּהֶתְאֵם
לְצִפִּיָּתִי הָעֲמֻקָּה וְתִקְוָתִי שֶׁלֹּא אֵבוֹשׁ בְּשׁוּם דָּבָר,
אֶלָּא שֶׁבְּכָל עֹז, כְּתָמִיד כֵּן גַּם עַתָּה, יֵרוֹמַם וְיִתְגַּדֵּל

by life or by death. 21 For to me, to live *is* Christ,
and to die *is* gain. 22 But if *I* live on in the flesh, this
will mean fruit from *my* labor; yet what I shall
choose I cannot tell. 23 For I am hard-pressed
between the two, having a desire to depart and be
with Christ, *which is* far better. 24 Nevertheless to
remain in the flesh *is* more needful for you. 25 And
being confident of this, I know that I shall remain
and continue with you all for your progress and joy
of faith, 26 that your rejoicing for me may be more
abundant in Jesus Christ by my coming to you
again.

27 Only let your conduct be worthy of the gospel
of Christ, so that whether I come and see you or am
absent, I may hear of your affairs, that you stand
fast in one spirit, with one mind striving together
for the faith of the gospel, 28 and not in any way
terrified by your adversaries, which is to them a
proof of perdition, but to you of salvation, and that
from God. 29 For to you it has been granted on
behalf of Christ, not only to believe in Him, but
also to suffer for His sake, 30 having the same
conflict which you saw in me and now hear *is* in me.

2 Therefore if *there is* any consolation in Christ, if
any comfort of love, if any fellowship of the Spirit,
if any affection and mercy, 2 fulfill my joy by being
like-minded, having the same love, *being* of one
accord, of one mind. 3 *Let* nothing *be done* through
selfish ambition or conceit, but in lowliness of mind
let each esteem others better than himself. 4 Let each
of you look out not only for his own interests, but
also for the interests of others.

5 Let this mind be in you which was also in Christ
Jesus, 6 who, being in the form of God, did not
consider it robbery to be equal with God, 7 but
made Himself of no reputation, taking the form of a
bondservant, *and* coming in the likeness of men.
8 And being found in appearance as a man, He
humbled Himself and became obedient to *the point*
of death, even the death of the cross. 9 Therefore
God also has highly exalted Him and given Him the
name which is above every name, 10 that at the
name of Jesus every knee should bow, of those in
heaven, and of those on earth, and of those under
the earth, 11 and *that* every tongue should confess
that Jesus Christ *is* Lord, to the glory of God the
Father.

12 Therefore, my beloved, as you have always
obeyed, not as in my presence only, but now much
more in my absence, work out your own salvation
with fear and trembling; 13 for it is God who works
in you both to will and to do for *His* good pleasure.

הַמָּשִׁיחַ בְּגוּפִי, אִם עַל־יְדֵי חַיַּי וְאִם עַל־יְדֵי מוֹתִי.
21 הֵן, לְגַבֵּי דִידִי, לִחְיוֹת פֵּרוּשׁוֹ הַמָּשִׁיחַ, וְלָמוּת
פֵּרוּשׁוֹ רָוַח. 22 אַךְ אִם לִחְיוֹת בַּגּוּף – הֲרֵי זֶה
בִּשְׁבִילִי עֲבוֹדָה פּוֹרִיָּה וְאֵינֶנִּי יוֹדֵעַ בַּמֶּה לִבְחֹר.
23 אֲנִי לָחוּץ עַל־יְדֵי הַשְּׁנַיִם. אֲנִי מִשְׁתּוֹקֵק לְהִסְתַּלֵּק
וְלִהְיוֹת עִם הַמָּשִׁיחַ, שֶׁכֵּן זֶה טוֹב הַרְבֵּה יוֹתֵר.
24 אוּלָם הִשָּׁאֲרוּתִי בַּגּוּף נְחוּצָה יוֹתֵר לְמַעַנְכֶם.
25 וּבְהִיוֹתִי בָּטוּחַ בְּכָךְ אֲנִי יוֹדֵעַ שֶׁאֶשָּׁאֵר וְאַמְשִׁיךְ
עִם כֻּלְּכֶם לְמַעַן הִתְקַדְּמוּתְכֶם וְשִׂמְחַתְכֶם בָּאֱמוּנָה,
26 וְאָז תַּרְבּוּ לְהִתְהַלֵּל בַּמָּשִׁיחַ יֵשׁוּעַ בִּגְלָלִי, בִּגְלַל
נוֹכְחוּתִי שׁוּב עִמָּכֶם.

27 רַק הִתְנַהֲגוּ כָּרָאוּי לִבְשׂוֹרַת הַמָּשִׁיחַ, לְמַעַן
אֶשְׁמַע עֲלֵיכֶם – אִם בְּבוֹאִי לִרְאוֹתְכֶם, אִם בִּהְיוֹתִי
רָחוֹק מִכֶּם – כִּי עוֹמְדִים אַתֶּם בְּרוּחַ אַחַת וְנִלְחָמִים
בְּלֵב אֶחָד בְּעַד אֱמוּנַת הַבְּשׂוֹרָה, 28 וְאֵינְכֶם פּוֹחֲדִים
כְּלָל מִפְּנֵי הַמִּתְנַגְּדִים, דָּבָר אֲשֶׁר לָהֶם הוּא אוֹת
לַאֲבַדּוֹן וְלָכֶם אוֹת לִישׁוּעָה, וְזֹאת מֵאֵת הָאֱלֹהִים.
29 הֵן לָכֶם נִתַּן, לְמַעַן הַמָּשִׁיחַ, לֹא רַק לְהַאֲמִין בּוֹ,
אֶלָּא גַּם לִסְבֹּל לְמַעֲנוֹ, 30 שֶׁהֲרֵי לָכֶם אוֹתוֹ הַמַּאֲבָק
שֶׁבְּעָבָר רְאִיתֶם אוֹתִי נֶאֱבָק בּוֹ וְכָעֵת אַתֶּם שׁוֹמְעִים
כִּי אֲנִי נִמְצָא בּוֹ.

ב לָכֵן אִם יֵשׁ אֵיזֶה עִדּוּד בַּמָּשִׁיחַ, אִם אֵיזוֹ נֶחָמָה
שֶׁל אַהֲבָה, אִם אֵיזוֹ שֻׁתָּפוּת שֶׁל רוּחַ, אִם אֵלּוּ
רַחֲמִים וְחֶמְלָה – 2 אֲזַי מַלְּאוּ נָא אֶת שִׂמְחָתִי בְּזֶה
שֶׁתִּהְיוּ תְּמִימֵי דֵעִים, חַדּוּרֵי אַהֲבָה אַחַת, בַּעֲלֵי
כַּוָּנָה אַחַת וּמַחֲשָׁבָה אַחַת 3 וְאַל תַּעֲשׂוּ דָּבָר מִתּוֹךְ
תַּחֲרוּת, אַף לֹא מִתּוֹךְ כְּבוֹד שָׁוְא, אֶלָּא בַּנְמִיכוּת
רוּחַ יַחֲשֹׁב אִישׁ אִישׁ אֶת רֵעֵהוּ לְנִכְבָּד מִמֶּנּוּ. 4 כָּל
אֶחָד אַל יִדְאַג רַק לְעִנְיָנָיו, אֶלָּא גַּם לְעִנְיָנֵי שֶׁל
זוּלָתוֹ. 5 יְהֵא בָּכֶם הֲלָךְ רוּחַ זֶה אֲשֶׁר הָיָה בַּמָּשִׁיחַ
יֵשׁוּעַ: 6 הוּא אֲשֶׁר הָיָה קַיָּם בִּדְמוּת אֱלֹהִים לֹא
חָשַׁב לְשָׁלָל הֱיוֹת שָׁוֶה לֵאלֹהִים, 7 אֶלָּא הֵרִיק אֶת
עַצְמוֹ, נָטַל דְּמוּת עֶבֶד וְנִהְיָה כִּבְנֵי אָדָם; וְכַאֲשֶׁר
הָיָה בְּצוּרָתוֹ כְּאָדָם, 8 הִשְׁפִּיל עַצְמוֹ וְרָצָה עַד מָוֶת,
עַד מָוֶת בַּצְּלָב. 9 עַל כֵּן הִגְבִּיהוֹ אֱלֹהִים מְאֹד וְנָתַן
לוֹ אֶת הַשֵּׁם הַנַּעֲלֶה עַל כָּל שֵׁם, 10 לְמַעַן תִּכְרַע
בְּשֵׁם יֵשׁוּעַ כָּל בֶּרֶךְ, בַּשָּׁמַיִם וּבָאָרֶץ וּמִתַּחַת לָאָרֶץ,
11 וְכָל לָשׁוֹן תּוֹדֶה כִּי יֵשׁוּעַ הַמָּשִׁיחַ הוּא הָאָדוֹן,
לְתִפְאֶרֶת אֱלֹהִים הָאָב.

12 לָכֵן אֲהוּבַי, כְּשֵׁם שֶׁצִּיַּתֶּם תָּמִיד, לֹא רַק כְּמוֹ
בְּעֵת נוֹכְחוּתִי, אֶלָּא עַל אַחַת כַּמָּה וְכַמָּה כָּעֵת,
בְּהֶעָדְרִי – הִשָּׁמְעוּ עַתָּה, וּבְיִרְאָה וּבַחֲרָדָה פַּעֲלוּ
לְמִמּוּשׁ תְּשׁוּעַתְכֶם; 13 וְאָמְנָם אֱלֹהִים הוּא הַפּוֹעֵל

¹⁴ Do all things without complaining and disput-
ing, ¹⁵ that you may become blameless and harmless, children of God without fault in the midst of a
crooked and perverse generation, among whom you
shine as lights in the world, ¹⁶ holding fast the word
of life, so that I may rejoice in the day of Christ that
I have not run in vain or labored in vain.

¹⁷ Yes, and if I am being poured out *as a drink
offering* on the sacrifice and service of your faith, I
am glad and rejoice with you all. ¹⁸ For the same
reason you also be glad and rejoice with me.

¹⁹ But I trust in the Lord Jesus to send Timothy
to you shortly, that I also may be encouraged when
I know your state. ²⁰ For I have no one like-minded,
who will sincerely care for your state. ²¹ For all seek
their own, not the things which are of Christ Jesus.
²² But you know his proven character, that as a son
with *his* father he served with me in the gospel.
²³ Therefore I hope to send him at once, as soon as I
see how it goes with me. ²⁴ But I trust in the Lord
that I myself shall also come shortly.

²⁵ Yet I considered it necessary to send to you
Epaphroditus, my brother, fellow worker, and
fellow soldier, but your messenger and the one
who ministered to my need; ²⁶ since he was longing
for you all, and was distressed because you had
heard that he was sick. ²⁷ For indeed he was sick
almost unto death; but God had mercy on him, and
not only on him but on me also, lest I should have
sorrow upon sorrow. ²⁸ Therefore I sent him the
more eagerly, that when you see him again you may
rejoice, and I may be less sorrowful. ²⁹ Receive him
therefore in the Lord with all gladness, and hold
such men in esteem; ³⁰ because for the work of
Christ he came close to death, not regarding his life,
to supply what was lacking in your service toward
me.

3 Finally, my brethren, rejoice in the Lord. For me
to write the same things to you *is* not tedious, but
for you *it is* safe.

² Beware of dogs, beware of evil workers, beware
of the mutilation! ³ For we are the circumcision,
who worship God in the Spirit, rejoice in Christ
Jesus, and have no confidence in the flesh, ⁴ though
I also might have confidence in the flesh. If anyone
else thinks he may have confidence in the flesh, I
more so: ⁵ circumcised the eighth day, of the stock
of Israel, *of* the tribe of Benjamin, a Hebrew of the
Hebrews; concerning the law, a Pharisee; ⁶ concerning zeal, persecuting the church; concerning the
righteousness which is in the law, blameless.

בָּכֶם גַּם שֶׁתִּרְצוּ וְגַם שֶׁתִּפְעֲלוּ כַּטּוֹב בְּעֵינָיו. ¹⁴ עֲשׂוּ
כָּל דָּבָר בְּלִי לְהִתְלוֹנֵן וּבְלִי לְהִתְוַכֵּחַ, ¹⁵ לְמַעַן תִּהְיוּ
נְקִיִּים מֵאָשָׁם וּטְהוֹרִים, בָּנִים לֵאלֹהִים אֵין דֹּפִי
בָּהֶם, בְּתוֹךְ דּוֹר עִקֵּשׁ וּפְתַלְתֹּל אֲשֶׁר תּוֹפִיעוּ בּוֹ
כִּמְאוֹרוֹת בָּעוֹלָם, ¹⁶ בְּהַחֲזִיקְכֶם אֶת דְּבַר הַחַיִּים;
זֹאת תִּהְיֶה לִי לִתְהִלָּה בְּיוֹם הַמָּשִׁיחַ, שֶׁלֹּא לַשָּׁוְא
רַצְתִּי וְלֹא לָרִיק עָמַלְתִּי. ¹⁷ אֲבָל גַּם אִם אֶשָּׁפֵךְ
כְּנֶסֶךְ עַל קָרְבַּן עֲבוֹדַת הַקֹּדֶשׁ שֶׁל אֱמוּנַתְכֶם, שָׂמֵחַ
אֲנִי וְשָׂשׂ עִם כֻּלְּכֶם. ¹⁸ כָּךְ שִׂמְחוּ גַם אַתֶּם וְשִׂישׂוּ
עִמִּי.

¹⁹ תִּקְוָתִי בָּאָדוֹן יֵשׁוּעַ שֶׁאֶשְׁלַח אֲלֵיכֶם בִּמְהֵרָה אֶת
טִימוֹתֵיאוֹס, לְמַעַן אֶתְעוֹדֵד גַּם אֲנִי בְּהִוָּדַע לִי מַה
מַּצַּבְכֶם. ²⁰ אֵין לִי אִישׁ תְּמִים דֵּעִים עִמִּי כָּמוֹהוּ,
אֲשֶׁר בְּלֵב שָׁלֵם יִדְאַג לְעִנְיְנֵיכֶם. ²¹ הַכֹּל דּוֹאֲגִים
לְעִנְיְנֵיהֶם, לֹא לַדְּבָרִים אֲשֶׁר לַמָּשִׁיחַ יֵשׁוּעַ. ²² אֲבָל
יוֹדְעִים אַתֶּם אֶת אָפְיוֹ הַבָּחוּן; כְּמוֹ בֵן הָעוֹבֵד עִם
אָבִיו הוּא שֵׁרֵת עִמִּי בַּעֲבוֹדַת הַבְּשׂוֹרָה. ²³ לָכֵן
אוֹתוֹ מְקַוֶּה אֲנִי לִשְׁלֹחַ מִיָּד לְאַחַר שֶׁאֶרְאֶה מַה
יֵּעָשׂוּ בִּי. ²⁴ וּבוֹטֵחַ אֲנִי בָּאָדוֹן שֶׁגַּם אֲנִי אָבוֹא
בִּמְהֵרָה.

²⁵ אֲבָל חָשַׁבְתִּי לְנָחוּץ לִשְׁלֹחַ אֲלֵיכֶם אֶת הָאָח
אֶפַּפְרוֹדִיטוֹס, שֻׁתָּפִי לָעֲבוֹדָה וְלַמַּעֲרָכָה וְגַם
שְׁלִיחֲכֶם הַמְשָׁרֵת בְּמִלּוּי מַחְסוֹרִי, ²⁶ שֶׁכֵּן
הִתְגַּעְגֵּעַ אֶל כֻּלְּכֶם וְאַף נֶעֱצַב מְאֹד עַל שֶׁנּוֹדַע
לָכֶם כִּי חָלָה. ²⁷ אָמְנָם חָלָה וְנָטָה לָמוּת, אַךְ
אֱלֹהִים רִחֵם עָלָיו וְלֹא רַק עָלָיו, אֶלָּא גַּם עָלַי, לְמַעַן
לֹא יָבוֹא עָלַי יָגוֹן עַל יָגוֹן. ²⁸ לָכֵן מִהַרְתִּי לְשָׁלְחוֹ
אֲלֵיכֶם כְּדֵי שֶׁתִּשְׂמְחוּ בִּרְאוֹתְכֶם אוֹתוֹ שׁוּב, וְאָז
יִמְעַט יְגוֹנִי. ²⁹ עַל כֵּן קַבְּלוּהוּ בָּאָדוֹן בִּמְלֹא שִׂמְחָה
וְהוֹקִירוּ אֲנָשִׁים כָּאֵלֶּה, ³⁰ כִּי בִּגְלַל עֲבוֹדַת הַמָּשִׁיחַ
הִגִּיעַ עַד סַף הַמָּוֶת, בְּסַכְּנוֹ אֶת נַפְשׁוֹ כְּדֵי לְמַלֵּא
אֶת מַה שֶׁנִּבְצַר מִכֶּם לַעֲשׂוֹת בְּשֵׁרוּתְכֶם לְמַעֲנִי.

ג וּבְכֵן, אַחַי, שִׂמְחוּ בָּאָדוֹן. לִכְתֹּב לָכֶם שׁוּב אֶת
אוֹתוֹ דָּבָר אֵינֶנּוּ לְטֹרַח עָלַי, אַךְ לָכֶם זֶה מוֹסִיף
לְבִטָּחוֹן. ² הִזָּהֲרוּ מֵהַכְּלָבִים. הִזָּהֲרוּ מִפּוֹעֲלֵי הָרֶשַׁע.
הִזָּהֲרוּ מִן הַחִתּוּךְ. ³ הֲרֵי אֲנַחְנוּ בְּנֵי הַמִּילָה –
הָעוֹבְדִים אֶת אֱלֹהִים בָּרוּחַ וּמִתְגָּאִים בַּמָּשִׁיחַ יֵשׁוּעַ
בְּלִי לִבְטֹחַ בַּבָּשָׂר, ⁴ אַף שֶׁאֲנִי עַצְמִי יָכֹל לִבְטֹחַ גַּם
בַּבָּשָׂר. אִם מִישֶׁהוּ סָבוּר שֶׁיּוּכַל לִבְטֹחַ בַּבָּשָׂר, אֲזַי
אֲנִי יוֹתֵר: ⁵ נִמַּלְתִּי בִּהְיוֹתִי בֶּן שְׁמוֹנַת יָמִים; מִמּוֹצָא
יִשְׂרָאֵל אָנֹכִי, מִשֵּׁבֶט בִּנְיָמִין, עִבְרִי מִן הָעִבְרִים;
אֲשֶׁר לַתּוֹרָה, מִכַּת הַפְּרוּשִׁים אָנִי; ⁶ אֲשֶׁר לַקִּנְאוּת,

7 But what things were gain to me, these I have counted loss for Christ. 8 Yet indeed I also count all things loss for the excellence of the knowledge of Christ Jesus my Lord, for whom I have suffered the loss of all things, and count them as rubbish, that I may gain Christ 9 and be found in Him, not having my own righteousness, which is from the law, but that which is through faith in Christ, the righteousness which is from God by faith; 10 that I may know Him and the power of His resurrection, and the fellowship of His sufferings, being conformed to His death, 11 if, by any means, I may attain to the resurrection from the dead.

12 Not that I have already attained, or am already perfected; but I press on, that I may lay hold of that for which Christ Jesus has also laid hold of me. 13 Brethren, I do not count myself to have apprehended; but one thing I do, forgetting those things which are behind and reaching forward to those things which are ahead, 14 I press toward the goal for the prize of the upward call of God in Christ Jesus.

15 Therefore let us, as many as are mature, have this mind; and if in anything you think otherwise, God will reveal even this to you. 16 Nevertheless, to the degree that we have already attained, let us walk by the same rule, let us be of the same mind.

17 Brethren, join in following my example, and note those who so walk, as you have us for a pattern. 18 For many walk, of whom I have told you often, and now tell you even weeping, that they are the enemies of the cross of Christ: 19 whose end is destruction, whose god is their belly, and whose glory is in their shame—who set their mind on earthly things. 20 For our citizenship is in heaven, from which we also eagerly wait for the Savior, the Lord Jesus Christ, 21 who will transform our lowly body that it may be conformed to His glorious body, according to the working by which He is able even to subdue all things to Himself.

4 Therefore, my beloved and longed-for brethren, my joy and crown, so stand fast in the Lord, beloved.

2 I implore Euodia and I implore Syntyche to be of the same mind in the Lord. 3 And I urge you also, true companion, help these women who labored with me in the gospel, with Clement also, and the rest of my fellow workers, whose names are in the Book of Life.

4 Rejoice in the Lord always. Again I will say, rejoice!

5 Let your gentleness be known to all men. The Lord is at hand.

רוֹדֵף הַקְּהִלָּה אֲנִי; מִבְּחִינַת הַצְּדָקָה הַמְשֻׁתֶּתֶת עַל הַתּוֹרָה, אֵין בִּי דֹּפִי. 7 אֲבָל הַדְּבָרִים שֶׁהָיוּ יִתְרוֹן בְּעֵינַי, אוֹתָם חָשַׁבְתִּי לְהֶפְסֵד בִּגְלַל הַמָּשִׁיחַ; 8 וְלֹא עוֹד אֶלָּא שֶׁאֲנִי חוֹשֵׁב אֶת הַכֹּל לְהֶפְסֵד בִּגְלַל הַיִּתְרוֹן לָדַעַת אֶת הַמָּשִׁיחַ יֵשׁוּעַ אֲדוֹנִי, אֲשֶׁר לְמַעֲנוֹ הִפְסַדְתִּי אֶת כָּל הַדְּבָרִים; וַאֲנִי חוֹשֵׁב לִפְסֹלֶת בִּשְׁאִיפָתִי לְהַרְוִיחַ אֶת הַמָּשִׁיחַ 9 וּלְהִמָּצֵא בּוֹ – בְּאֹפֶן שֶׁצִּדְקָתִי לֹא תִּהְיֶה לִי מִן הַתּוֹרָה, אֶלָּא תִּהְיֶה זוֹ הַצְּדָקָה אֲשֶׁר עַל-יְדֵי אֱמוּנַת הַמָּשִׁיחַ, צְדָקָה אֲשֶׁר מֵאֱלֹהִים הִיא וִיסוֹדָהּ בָּאֱמוּנָה – 10 כְּדֵי לָדַעַת אוֹתוֹ וְאֶת כֹּחַ תְּחִיָּתוֹ וְאֶת הַשֻּׁתָּפוּת בְּיִסּוּרָיו וּלְהִדָּמוֹת לוֹ בְּמוֹתוֹ, 11 בְּתִקְוָה שֶׁאַגִּיעַ לַתְּחִיָּה מִן הַמֵּתִים.

12 לֹא שֶׁכְּבָר הִשַּׂגְתִּי אוֹ שֶׁכְּבָר הִגַּעְתִּי לִשְׁלֵמוּת, אֲבָל רָץ אֲנִי בְּתִקְוָה לְהַשִּׂיג, כִּי מִשּׁוּם כָּךְ גַּם הִשִּׂיגַנִי הַמָּשִׁיחַ יֵשׁוּעַ. 13 אַחַי, עֲדַיִן אֵינֶנִּי חוֹשֵׁב אֶת עַצְמִי לְמִי שֶׁהִשִּׂיג. אֲבָל דָּבָר אֶחָד: אֲנִי שׁוֹכֵחַ אֶת אֲשֶׁר מֵאַחֲרַי וְנֶחְלָץ קָדִימָה אֶל מַה שֶּׁלְּפָנַי. 14 אֲנִי רָץ אֶל הַמַּטָּרָה כְּדֵי לְהַשִּׂיג אֶת הַפְּרָס שֶׁבַּקְּרִיאָה-שֶׁל-מַעְלָה, קְרִיאָתוֹ שֶׁל אֱלֹהִים בַּמָּשִׁיחַ יֵשׁוּעַ. 15 לָכֵן כָּל בּוֹגֵר שֶׁבֵּינֵינוּ יַחְשֹׁב נָא כָּךְ, וְאִם בְּאֵיזֶה עִנְיָן חוֹשְׁבִים אַתֶּם אַחֶרֶת, גַּם אֶת זֹאת יְגַלֶּה לָכֶם אֱלֹהִים. 16 אֲבָל מַה שֶּׁהִגַּעְנוּ אֵלָיו, לְפִי זֶה עָלֵינוּ לְהִתְהַלֵּךְ.

17 אַחַי, הִתְנַהֲגוּ כָּמוֹנִי. שִׂימוּ לְבַבְכֶם אֶל הָאֲנָשִׁים הַמִּתְהַלְּכִים עַל-פִּי הַדֻּגְמָה שֶׁיֵּשׁ לָכֶם בָּנוּ. 18 הֵן רַבִּים הַמִּתְהַלְּכִים אֲשֶׁר פְּעָמִים רַבּוֹת אָמַרְתִּי לָכֶם עֲלֵיהֶם – וְעַתָּה גַּם בִּבְכִי אֲנִי אוֹמֵר – שֶׁהֵם אוֹיְבֵי צְלַב הַמָּשִׁיחַ; 19 אֲנָשִׁים אֲשֶׁר סוֹפָם אֲבַדּוֹן, אֲשֶׁר הַכֶּרֶס הִיא אֱלֹהֵיהֶם; תִּפְאַרְתָּם הִיא בְּמַעֲשֵׂיהֶם הַבְּזוּיִים וְהָאַרְצִיּוּת מְמַלֵּאת אֶת לִבָּם. 20 אֲשֶׁר לָנוּ, אֶזְרָחוּתֵנוּ בַּשָּׁמַיִם הִיא; מִשָּׁם גַּם יָבוֹא מוֹשִׁיעַ אֲשֶׁר מְחַכִּים אָנוּ לוֹ – הָאָדוֹן יֵשׁוּעַ הַמָּשִׁיחַ, 21 אֲשֶׁר יַחֲלִיף אֶת גּוּפֵנוּ הַנָּחוּת וְיַעֲשֵׂהוּ דוֹמֶה לְגוּפוֹ הֶהָדוּר כָּבוֹד, כְּפִי כֹּחַ יְכָלְתּוֹ לְשַׁעְבֵּד אֵלָיו אֶת הַכֹּל.

ד עַל כֵּן, אַחַי, הָאֲהוּבִים וְהַיְקָרִים, שִׂמְחָתִי וַעֲטֶרֶת רֹאשִׁי, בְּדֶרֶךְ זֹאת עִמְדוּ נָא בָּאָדוֹן, אֲהוּבַי. 2 הִנְנִי מַפְצִיר בְּאֶבְהוֹדְיָה וּבְסִינְטִיכִי לִהְיוֹת לֵב אֶחָד בָּאָדוֹן. 3 וְאַתָּה, חֲבֵרִי הָאֲמִתִּי, הַנּוֹשֵׂא עִמִּי בְּעֹל, גַּם מִמְּךָ אֲנִי מְבַקֵּשׁ: עֲזֹר נָא לָהֶן; הֵן הִשְׁתַּתְּפוּ עִמִּי בְּמַאֲבַק הַבְּשׂוֹרָה, יַחַד עִם קְלֵמֶנְטוֹס וְעִם יֶתֶר שֻׁתָּפַי לָעֲבוֹדָה אֲשֶׁר שְׁמוֹתֵיהֶם בְּסֵפֶר הַחַיִּים. 4 שִׂמְחוּ בָּאָדוֹן בְּכָל עֵת; אֹמַר שׁוּב, שִׂמְחוּ. 5 נֹעַם

6 Be anxious for nothing, but in everything by prayer and supplication, with thanksgiving, let your requests be made known to God; 7 and the peace of God, which surpasses all understanding, will guard your hearts and minds through Christ Jesus.

8 Finally, brethren, whatever things are true, whatever things *are* noble, whatever things *are* just, whatever things *are* pure, whatever things *are* lovely, whatever things *are* of good report, if *there is* any virtue and if *there is* anything praiseworthy— meditate on these things. 9 The things which you learned and received and heard and saw in me, these do, and the God of peace will be with you.

10 But I rejoiced in the Lord greatly that now at last your care for me has flourished again; though you surely did care, but you lacked opportunity. 11 Not that I speak in regard to need, for I have learned in whatever state I am, to be content: 12 I know how to be abased, and I know how to abound. Everywhere and in all things I have learned both to be full and to be hungry, both to abound and to suffer need. 13 I can do all things through Christ who strengthens me.

14 Nevertheless you have done well that you shared in my distress. 15 Now you Philippians know also that in the beginning of the gospel, when I departed from Macedonia, no church shared with me concerning giving and receiving but you only. 16 For even in Thessalonica you sent *aid* once and again for my necessities. 17 Not that I seek the gift, but I seek the fruit that abounds to your account. 18 Indeed I have all and abound. I am full, having received from Epaphroditus the things *sent* from you, a sweet-smelling aroma, an acceptable sacrifice, well pleasing to God. 19 And my God shall supply all your need according to His riches in glory by Christ Jesus. 20 Now to our God and Father *be* glory forever and ever. Amen.

21 Greet every saint in Christ Jesus. The brethren who are with me greet you. 22 All the saints greet you, but especially those who are of Caesar's household.

23 The grace of our Lord Jesus Christ be with you all. Amen.

הֲלִיכוֹתֵיכֶם יֻדַּע נָא לְכָל אָדָם. הָאָדוֹן קָרוֹב. 6 אַל תִּדְאֲגוּ לְשׁוּם דָּבָר, כִּי אִם בְּכָל דְּבַר הַצִּיגוּ מִשְׁאֲלוֹתֵיכֶם לֵאלֹהִים בִּתְפִלָּה וּבְתַחֲנוּנִים וּבְהוֹדָיָה. 7 וּשְׁלוֹם אֱלֹהִים הַנִּשְׂגָּב מִכָּל שֵׂכֶל יִנְצֹר אֶת לְבַבְכֶם וְאֶת מַחְשְׁבוֹתֵיכֶם בַּמָּשִׁיחַ יֵשׁוּעַ.

8 סוֹף דָּבָר, אַחַי, כָּל אֲשֶׁר אֱמֶת, כָּל מַה שֶׁנִּכְבָּד, כָּל דָּבָר יָשָׁר, טָהוֹר, מָלֵא נֹעַם, כָּל אֲשֶׁר שִׁמְעוֹ טוֹב, כָּל מַעֲשֶׂה נַעֲלֶה, וְכָל דָּבָר הָרָאוּי לְשֶׁבַח – בְּאֵלֶּה יֶהְגֶּה לְבַבְכֶם. 9 הַדְּבָרִים אֲשֶׁר לְמַדְתֶּם וְקִבַּלְתֶּם וּשְׁמַעְתֶּם מִמֶּנִּי, וַאֲשֶׁר רְאִיתֶם בִּי – אוֹתָם עֲשׂוּ; וֵאלֹהֵי הַשָּׁלוֹם יִהְיֶה עִמָּכֶם.

10 אָכֵן שָׂמַחְתִּי מְאֹד בָּאָדוֹן שֶׁשּׁוּב עוֹרַרְתֶּם אֶת דַּאֲגַתְכֶם לִי; אָמְנָם בַּעֲבָר דְּאַגְתֶּם לִי, אֶלָּא שֶׁלֹּא הָיְתָה לָכֶם הַזְדַּמְּנוּת לִפְעֹל. 11 אֵינֶנִּי מְדַבֵּר מִתּוֹךְ מַחְסוֹר; לָמַדְתִּי לְהִסְתַּפֵּק בְּמַה שֶׁיֵּשׁ לִי, בְּכָל מַצָּב. 12 יוֹדֵעַ אֲנִי לַעֲמֹד בְּעֹנִי, וְיוֹדֵעַ אֲנִי לַעֲמֹד בְּשֶׁפַע. בְּכָל דָּבָר וּבְכָל הַנְּסִבּוֹת מֻרְגָּל אֲנִי גַּם לִשְׂבַּע וְגַם לָרָעֵב, גַּם לְשֶׁפַע גַּם לְמַחְסוֹר. 13 הַכֹּל אֲנִי יָכוֹל בְּעֶזְרָתוֹ שֶׁל הַנּוֹתֵן בִּי כֹחַ. 14 עִם זֹאת טוֹב עֲשִׂיתֶם שֶׁהִשְׁתַּתַּפְתֶּם בְּצָרָתִי.

15 אַתֶּם הַפִּילִיפִּים גַּם יוֹדְעִים שֶׁכַּאֲשֶׁר יָצָאתִי מִמַּקֶדוֹנְיָה בְּרֵאשִׁית יְמֵי הַבְּשׂוֹרָה, שׁוּם קְהִלָּה מִלְּבַדְכֶם לֹא חָבְרָה אֵלַי בְּעִנְיַן מַתַּן עֶזְרָה אוֹ קַבָּלַת עֶזְרָה; 16 הֵן גַּם בִּהְיוֹתִי בְּתֶסָּלוֹנִיקִי שְׁלַחְתֶּם אֵלַי כַּמֶּה פְּעָמִים לְסַפֵּק אֶת צָרְכִּי. 17 לֹא שֶׁאֲנִי שׁוֹאֵף לְמַתָּנוֹת; שׁוֹאֵף אֲנִי לִפְרִי שֶׁיִּרְבֶּה לְזְכוּתְכֶם. 18 יֵשׁ לִי הַכֹּל בְּשֶׁפַע; מָלֵאתִי לְאַחַר שֶׁקִּבַּלְתִּי מִידֵי אֶפַּפְרוֹדִיטוֹס אֶת הַדְּבָרִים אֲשֶׁר שְׁלַחְתֶּם – רֵיחַ נִיחוֹחַ הֵם, מִנְחָה עֲרֵבָה רְצוּיָה לֵאלֹהִים. 19 וֵאלֹהַי יְמַלֵּא אֶת כָּל צָרְכְּכֶם כְּפִי עֹשֶׁר כְּבוֹדוֹ בַּמָּשִׁיחַ יֵשׁוּעַ. 20 לֵאלֹהִים אָבִינוּ הַכָּבוֹד לְעוֹלְמֵי עוֹלָמִים. אָמֵן.

21 דִּרְשׁוּ בְּשָׁלוֹם כָּל קָדוֹשׁ בַּמָּשִׁיחַ יֵשׁוּעַ. הָאַחִים אֲשֶׁר עִמִּי דּוֹרְשִׁים בִּשְׁלוֹמְכֶם. 22 כָּל הַקְּדוֹשִׁים דּוֹרְשִׁים בִּשְׁלוֹמְכֶם, בְּעִקָּר אֵלֶּה אֲשֶׁר מִבֵּית הַקֵּיסָר. 23 חֶסֶד הָאָדוֹן יֵשׁוּעַ הַמָּשִׁיחַ עִם רוּחֲכֶם.

The Epistle of Paul to the

COLOSSIANS

1 Paul, an apostle of Jesus Christ by the will of God, and Timothy our brother,

² To the saints and faithful brethren in Christ *who are* in Colosse:

Grace to you and peace from God our Father and the Lord Jesus Christ.

³ We give thanks to the God and Father of our Lord Jesus Christ, praying always for you, ⁴ since we heard of your faith in Christ Jesus and of your love for all the saints; ⁵ because of the hope which is laid up for you in heaven, of which you heard before in the word of the truth of the gospel, ⁶ which has come to you, as *it has* also in all the world, and is bringing forth fruit, as *it is* also among you since the day you heard and knew the grace of God in truth; ⁷ as you also learned from Epaphras, our dear fellow servant, who is a faithful minister of Christ on your behalf, ⁸ who also declared to us your love in the Spirit.

⁹ For this reason we also, since the day we heard it, do not cease to pray for you, and to ask that you may be filled with the knowledge of His will in all wisdom and spiritual understanding; ¹⁰ that you may walk worthy of the Lord, fully pleasing *Him,* being fruitful in every good work and increasing in the knowledge of God; ¹¹ strengthened with all might, according to His glorious power, for all patience and longsuffering with joy; ¹² giving thanks to the Father who has qualified us to be partakers of the inheritance of the saints in the light. ¹³ He has delivered us from the power of darkness and conveyed *us* into the kingdom of the Son of His love, ¹⁴ in whom we have redemption through His blood, the forgiveness of sins.

¹⁵ He is the image of the invisible God, the firstborn over all creation. ¹⁶ For by Him all things were created that are in heaven and that are on earth, visible and invisible, whether thrones or dominions or principalities or powers. All things were created through Him and for Him. ¹⁷ And He is before all things, and in Him all things consist. ¹⁸ And He is the head of the body, the church, who is the beginning, the firstborn from the dead, that in all things He may have the preeminence.

אִגֶּרֶת שָׁאוּל אֶל הַקּוֹלוֹסִים

א מֵאֵת שָׁאוּל, שְׁלִיחַ הַמָּשִׁיחַ יֵשׁוּעַ בִּרְצוֹן אֱלֹהִים, וּמֵאֵת טִימוֹתֵיאוֹס אָחִינוּ, ²אֶל הַקְּדוֹשִׁים אֲשֶׁר בְּקוֹלוֹסָה, הָאַחִים הַנֶּאֱמָנִים בַּמָּשִׁיחַ: חֶסֶד וְשָׁלוֹם לָכֶם מֵאֵת הָאֱלֹהִים אָבִינוּ וְהָאָדוֹן יֵשׁוּעַ הַמָּשִׁיחַ. ³מוֹדִים אֲנַחְנוּ לֵאלֹהִים אֲבִי אֲדוֹנֵנוּ יֵשׁוּעַ הַמָּשִׁיחַ וּמִתְפַּלְלִים בַּעַדְכֶם תָּמִיד, ⁴כִּי שָׁמַעְנוּ עַל אֱמוּנַתְכֶם בַּמָּשִׁיחַ יֵשׁוּעַ וְעַל אַהֲבַתְכֶם לְכָל הַקְּדוֹשִׁים ⁵לְנֹכַח הַתִּקְוָה הַשְּׁמוּרָה לָכֶם בַּשָּׁמַיִם, תִּקְוָה אֲשֶׁר שְׁמַעְתֶּם עָלֶיהָ קֹדֶם לָכֵן בִּדְבַר הָאֱמֶת שֶׁל הַבְּשׂוֹרָה ⁶שֶׁהִגִּיעָה אֲלֵיכֶם. וּכְשֵׁם שֶׁהַבְּשׂוֹרָה עוֹשָׂה פְּרִי וּמִשְׁגַּשֶּׂגֶת בְּכָל הָעוֹלָם, כֵּן גַּם בְּקִרְבְּכֶם לְמִן הַיּוֹם שֶׁשְּׁמַעְתֶּם וְהִכַּרְתֶּם בֶּאֱמֶת אֶת חֶסֶד אֱלֹהִים, ⁷כְּדֶרֶךְ שֶׁלְּמַדְתֶּם מֵאֵת אֶפַּפְרַס הָאָהוּב, חֲבֵרֵנוּ לַעֲבוֹדָה וּמְשָׁרֵת נֶאֱמָן שֶׁל הַמָּשִׁיחַ לְמַעַנְכֶם, ⁸אֲשֶׁר גַּם סִפֵּר לָנוּ עַל אַהֲבַתְכֶם שֶׁבָּרוּחַ.

⁹מִשּׁוּם כָּךְ גַּם אָנוּ, מִיּוֹם שֶׁשָּׁמַעְנוּ אֶת זֹאת, אֵינֶנּוּ חֲדֵלִים לְהִתְפַּלֵּל בַּעַדְכֶם וּלְבַקֵּשׁ שֶׁתִּתְמַלְאוּ דַּעַת רְצוֹנוֹ, בִּלְוִית כָּל חָכְמָה וּתְבוּנָה רוּחָנִית, ¹⁰לְמַעַן תִּתְהַלְּכוּ כָּיָאוּת לִפְנֵי הָאָדוֹן, בְּכָל חֶפְצוֹ, וּלְמַעַן תָּנִיבוּ פְּרִי בְּכָל מַעֲשֶׂה טוֹב וְתִגְדְּלוּ בְּדַעַת אֱלֹהִים, ¹¹וְתִתְחַזְּקוּ בְּכָל כֹּחַ כְּפִי עֹצֶם כְּבוֹדוֹ, וְתִהְיֶה לָכֶם סַבְלָנוּת וְאֹרֶךְ רוּחַ בַּכֹּל, וּבְשִׂמְחָה ¹²תִּתְּנוּ תוֹדָה לְאָבִינוּ שֶׁהִכְשִׁיר אֶתְכֶם לְהִשְׁתַּתֵּף בְּנַחֲלַת הַקְּדוֹשִׁים בָּאוֹר. ¹³הֵן הָאָב הִצִּילָנוּ מִשִּׁלְטוֹן הַחֹשֶׁךְ וְהֶעֱבִירָנוּ אֶל מַלְכוּת בְּנוֹ אֲהוּבוֹ, ¹⁴אֲשֶׁר בּוֹ לָנוּ הַפְּרוּת, סְלִיחַת הַחֲטָאִים, ¹⁵וְהוּא צֶלֶם שֶׁל הָאֱלֹהִים הַבִּלְתִּי נִרְאֶה, בְּכוֹר כָּל בְּרִיאָה; ¹⁶כִּי בּוֹ נִבְרָא כָּל אֲשֶׁר בַּשָּׁמַיִם וַאֲשֶׁר בָּאָרֶץ, מַה שֶּׁנִּרְאֶה וּמַה שֶּׁבִּלְתִּי נִרְאֶה, גַּם כִּסְאוֹת וְרָשִׁיּוֹת וְגַם מֶמְשָׁלוֹת וְשִׁלְטוֹנוֹת. הַכֹּל נִבְרָא בְּאֶמְצָעוּתוֹ וּלְמַעֲנוֹ, ¹⁷וְהוּא קוֹדֵם לַכֹּל וְהַכֹּל קַיָּם בּוֹ. ¹⁸הוּא הָרֹאשׁ שֶׁל הַגּוּף, כְּלוֹמַר, שֶׁל הַקְּהִלָּה. הוּא הָרֵאשִׁית, בְּכוֹר

19 For it pleased *the Father that* in Him all the fullness should dwell, 20 and by Him to reconcile all things to Himself, by Him, whether things on earth or things in heaven, having made peace through the blood of His cross.

21 And you, who once were alienated and enemies in your mind by wicked works, yet now He has reconciled 22 in the body of His flesh through death, to present you holy, and blameless, and above reproach in His sight— 23 if indeed you continue in the faith, grounded and steadfast, and are not moved away from the hope of the gospel which you heard, which was preached to every creature under heaven, of which I, Paul, became a minister.

24 I now rejoice in my sufferings for you, and fill up in my flesh what is lacking in the afflictions of Christ, for the sake of His body, which is the church, 25 of which I became a minister according to the stewardship from God which was given to me for you, to fulfill the word of God, 26 the mystery which has been hidden from ages and from generations, but now has been revealed to His saints. 27 To them God willed to make known what are the riches of the glory of this mystery among the Gentiles: which is Christ in you, the hope of glory. 28 Him we preach, warning every man and teaching every man in all wisdom, that we may present every man perfect in Christ Jesus. 29 To this *end* I also labor, striving according to His working which works in me mightily.

2 For I want you to know what a great conflict I have for you and those in Laodicea, and *for* as many as have not seen my face in the flesh, 2 that their hearts may be encouraged, being knit together in love, and *attaining* to all riches of the full assurance of understanding, to the knowledge of the mystery of God, both of the Father and of Christ, 3 in whom are hidden all the treasures of wisdom and knowledge.

4 Now this I say lest anyone should deceive you with persuasive words. 5 For though I am absent in the flesh, yet I am with you in spirit, rejoicing to see your *good* order and the steadfastness of your faith in Christ.

6 As you therefore have received Christ Jesus the Lord, so walk in Him, 7 rooted and built up in Him and established in the faith, as you have been taught, abounding in it with thanksgiving.

8 Beware lest anyone cheat you through philosophy and empty deceit, according to the tradition of men, according to the basic principles of the world, and not according to Christ. 9 For in Him dwells all

מִבֵּין הַמֵּתִים, לְמַעַן יִהְיֶה רִאשׁוֹן בַּכֹּל, 19 כִּי כֵן הָיָה רָצוֹן לְשַׁכֵּן בּוֹ אֶת כָּל הַמְלוֹא 20 וּבְאֶמְצָעוּתוֹ לְרַצּוֹת אֶל עַצְמוֹ אֶת הַכֹּל. הֵן מַה שֶׁבַּשָּׁמַיִם וְהֵן מַה שֶׁבָּאָרֶץ, בְּאֶמְצָעוּתוֹ, בַּעֲשׂוֹת שָׁלוֹם בְּדָמוֹ עַל הַצְּלָב.

21 אַתֶּם לְפָנִים הֱיִיתֶם נָכְרִים וְאוֹיְבִים בְּמַחְשְׁבוֹתֵיכֶם וּבְמַעֲשֵׂיכֶם הָרָעִים. 22 אֲבָל כָּעֵת עָשָׂה רָצוּי בְּגוּף בְּשָׂרוֹ עַל-יְדֵי מוֹתוֹ, כְּדֵי לְהַצִּיגְכֶם לְפָנָיו קְדוֹשִׁים, בְּלִי מוּם וּבְלִי דֹּפִי – 23 אִם אָמְנָם עוֹמְדִים אַתֶּם מְבֻסָּסִים וְרִצִיבִים בָּאֱמוּנָה וְאֵינְכֶם מֻרְפִּים מֵהַתִּקְוָה הַכְּלוּלָה בַּבְּשׂוֹרָה שֶׁשְּׁמַעְתֶּם, הִיא הַבְּשׂוֹרָה שֶׁהֻכְרְזָה לְכָל הַבְּרִיאָה מִתַּחַת לַשָּׁמַיִם, וַאֲנִי, שָׁאוּל, הָיִיתִי לָהּ לִמְשָׁרֵת.

24 כָּעֵת אֲנִי שָׂמֵחַ בַּסֵּבֶל שֶׁאֲנִי סוֹבֵל לְמַעַנְכֶם וַאֲנִי מְמַלֵּא בִּבְשָׂרִי אֶת סִבְלוֹת הַמָּשִׁיחַ שֶׁיֵּשׁ עוֹד לִסְבֹּל בַּעֲד גּוּפוֹ – הַקְּהִלָּה; 25 נִהְיֵיתִי לָהּ לִמְשָׁרֵת בְּהֶתְאֵם לְתַפְקִיד שֶׁאֱלֹהִים נָתַן לִי לְמַעַנְכֶם, לְהַשְׁלִים אֶת דְּבַר אֱלֹהִים 26 בְּמִסִירַת הָרָז שֶׁהָיָה צָפוּן מֵעוֹלָמִים וּמִדּוֹרוֹת וְעַתָּה נִגְלָה לִקְדוֹשָׁיו. 27 אָכֵן לָכֶם רָצָה אֱלֹהִים לְהוֹדִיעַ מַהוּ עֹשֶׁר תִּפְאֶרֶת הָרָז הַזֶּה בְּקֶרֶב הַגּוֹיִים, וְהוּא: הַמָּשִׁיחַ בְּקִרְבְּכֶם, הַתִּקְוָה אֶל הַכָּבוֹד. 28 עָלָיו אָנוּ מַכְרִיזִים וּבְכָל בְּזְמַן מַזְהִירִים כָּל אָדָם וּמְלַמְּדִים כָּל אָדָם בְּכָל חָכְמָה, לְמַעַן נוּכַל לְהַצִּיג כָּל אָדָם כְּשֶׁהוּא מֻשְׁלָם בַּמָּשִׁיחַ. 29 לְמַטָּרָה זֹאת אֲנִי גַּם עָמֵל וְנֶאֱבָק, כְּמִדַּת פְּעֻלָּתוֹ שֶׁל הַפּוֹעֵל בִּי בִּגְבוּרָה.

ב רְצוֹנִי שֶׁתֵּדְעוּ מַה גָּדוֹל הַמַּאֲבָק שֶׁאֲנִי נֶאֱבָק בַּעַדְכֶם וּבְעַד אַנְשֵׁי לָאוֹדִיקְאָה, וּבְעַד אֵלֶּה שֶׁלֹּא רָאוּ אוֹתִי פָּנִים אֶל פָּנִים, 2 לְמַעַן יְנֻחַם לְבָבָם וְיִתְקַשְּׁרוּ יַחְדָּיו בְּאַהֲבָה וְיַגִּיעוּ אֶל כָּל הָעֹשֶׁר אֲשֶׁר בַּהֲבָנָה הַשְּׁלֵמָה, אֶל יְדִיעַת רַז הָאֱלֹהִים, הַמָּשִׁיחַ, 3 אֲשֶׁר צְפוּנִים בּוֹ כָּל אוֹצְרוֹת הַחָכְמָה וְהַדַּעַת. 4 זֹאת אֲנִי אוֹמֵר כְּדֵי שֶׁלֹּא יַטְעֶה אֶתְכֶם אִישׁ בְּדִבּוּרִים מְחַכְּמִים. 5 גַּם אִם נֶעְדָּר אֲנִי מִבֵּינֵיכֶם בְּגוּפִי, הֲרֵי בְּרוּחִי אֲנִי נִמְצָא בֵּינֵיכֶם, וְשָׂמֵחַ אֲנִי בִּרְאוֹתִי אֶת הַסֵּדֶר אֲשֶׁר בְּקִרְבְּכֶם וְאֶת אֵיתָנוּת אֱמוּנַתְכֶם בַּמָּשִׁיחַ.

6 לָכֵן כְּשֵׁם שֶׁקִּבַּלְתֶּם אֶת הַמָּשִׁיחַ יֵשׁוּעַ, הָאָדוֹן, כֵּן הִתְהַלְּכוּ בּוֹ 7 כְּשֶׁאַתֶּם מֻשְׁרָשִׁים וְנִבְנִים בּוֹ, מְבֻסָּסִים בָּאֱמוּנָה לְפִי מַה שֶׁלֻּמַּדְתֶּם, וְשׁוֹפְעִים בְּהוֹדָיָה. 8 הִזָּהֲרוּ שֶׁאִישׁ לֹא יוֹלִיךְ אֶתְכֶם שׁוֹלָל בְּפִילוֹסוֹפְיָה וּבְתַעְתּוּעֵי הֶבֶל, עַל-פִּי מָסוֹרוֹת שֶׁל בְּנֵי אָדָם, עַל-פִּי עִקְּרֵי הָעוֹלָם וְלֹא עַל-פִּי הַמָּשִׁיחַ. 9 הֵן בַּמָּשִׁיחַ, בְּגוּפוֹ, שׁוֹכֵן כָּל מְלוֹא הָאֱלֹהוּת;

the fullness of the Godhead bodily; [10] and you are complete in Him, who is the head of all principality and power.

[11] In Him you were also circumcised with the circumcision made without hands, by putting off the body of the sins of the flesh, by the circumcision of Christ, [12] buried with Him in baptism, in which you also were raised with *Him* through faith in the working of God, who raised Him from the dead. [13] And you, being dead in your trespasses and the uncircumcision of your flesh, He has made alive together with Him, having forgiven you all trespasses, [14] having wiped out the handwriting of requirements that was against us, which was contrary to us. And He has taken it out of the way, having nailed it to the cross. [15] Having disarmed principalities and powers, He made a public spectacle of them, triumphing over them in it.

[16] So let no one judge you in food or in drink, or regarding a festival or a new moon or sabbaths, [17] which are a shadow of things to come, but the substance is of Christ. [18] Let no one cheat you of your reward, taking delight in *false* humility and worship of angels, intruding into those things which he has not seen, vainly puffed up by his fleshly mind, [19] and not holding fast to the Head, from whom all the body, nourished and knit together by joints and ligaments, grows with the increase *that is* from God.

[20] Therefore, if you died with Christ from the basic principles of the world, why, as *though* living in the world, do you subject yourselves to regulations— [21] "Do not touch, do not taste, do not handle," [22] which all concern things which perish with the using—according to the commandments and doctrines of men? [23] These things indeed have an appearance of wisdom in self-imposed religion, *false* humility, and neglect of the body, *but are* of no value against the indulgence of the flesh.

3 If then you were raised with Christ, seek those things which are above, where Christ is, sitting at the right hand of God. [2] Set your mind on things above, not on things on the earth. [3] For you died, and your life is hidden with Christ in God. [4] When Christ *who is* our life appears, then you also will appear with Him in glory.

[5] Therefore put to death your members which are on the earth: fornication, uncleanness, passion, evil desire, and covetousness, which is idolatry. [6] Because of these things the wrath of God is coming upon the sons of disobedience, [7] in which you yourselves once walked when you lived in them.

[10] וְאַתֶּם נִמְלֵאתֶם בּוֹ, אֲשֶׁר הוּא רֹאשׁ כָּל רְשׁוּת וְשִׁלְטוֹן. [11] בּוֹ גַּם נִמַּלְתֶּם מִילָה שֶׁאֵינָה מַעֲשֵׂה יָדַיִם, וְזֹאת בְּהַפְשָׁטַת הַגּוּף הַבְּשָׂרִי, בְּמִילַת הַמָּשִׁיחַ; [12] נִקְבַּרְתֶּם אִתּוֹ בַּטְּבִילָה, וְאִתּוֹ גַּם הוּקַמְתֶּם לִתְחִיָּה עַל־יְדֵי אֱמוּנַתְכֶם בְּכֹחַ אֱלֹהִים אֲשֶׁר הֵקִימוֹ מִן הַמֵּתִים. [13] וּבִהְיוֹתְכֶם מֵתִים בְּפִשְׁעֵיכֶם וּבְעָרְלַת בְּשַׂרְכֶם, הֶחֱיָה אֶתְכֶם עִמּוֹ. הוּא סָלַח לָנוּ עַל כָּל פְּשָׁעֵינוּ; [14] בִּטֵּל אֶת שְׁטַר הַחוֹב אֲשֶׁר הָיָה נֶגְדֵּנוּ עַד תֻּמּוֹ וַהֲסִירוֹ בְּתָקְעוֹ אוֹתוֹ בַּצְּלָב. [15] וּבְהַפְשִׁיטוֹ אֶת עָצְמַת הָרָשֻׁיּוֹת וְהַשְּׂרָרוֹת, הִצִּיגָן לְרַאֲוָה בְּתַהֲלוּכַת נִצָּחוֹנוֹ, נִצָּחוֹן שֶׁהִשִּׂיג בּוֹ. [16] לָכֵן אִישׁ אַל יָחֲרֹץ עֲלֵיכֶם מִשְׁפָּט עַל־דְּבַר מַאֲכָל וּמַשְׁקֶה אוֹ עַל־דְּבַר מוֹעֵד, רֹאשׁ חֹדֶשׁ אוֹ שַׁבָּת, [17] אֲשֶׁר הֵם צֵל הַדְּבָרִים הָעֲתִידִים לָבוֹא, אֲבָל הַגּוּף הוּא שֶׁל הַמָּשִׁיחַ. [18] אִישׁ אַל יְבַטֵּל אֶתְכֶם כְּשֶׁהוּא מִתְגַּדֵּר בַּעֲנָוּוּת רוּחַ וּבְפֻלְחָן לַמַּלְאָכִים, כְּשֶׁהוּא נֶאֱחָז בַּמֶּה שֶׁרָאָה וּבְלִבּוֹ גַּאֲוָה רֵיקָה הַנּוֹבַעַת מִשִּׂכְלוֹ הַבִּלְתִּי רוּחָנִי, [19] וְאֵין הוּא נִצְמָד לָרֹאשׁ אֲשֶׁר מִמֶּנּוּ גָּדֵל כָּל הַגּוּף – הַנִּזּוֹן וּמִתְחַבֵּר עַל־יְדֵי פְּרָקִים וְגִידִים – גְּדֵילָה כִּיד הָאֱלֹהִים. [20] אִם מַתֶּם עִם הַמָּשִׁיחַ לְגַבֵּי עִקְּרֵי הָעוֹלָם, לָמָּה אַתֶּם נוֹהֲגִים כְּמוֹ אֲנָשִׁים הַחַיִּים בָּעוֹלָם וְנִכְנָעִים לַחֻקִּים [21] "אַל תֹּאחֵז, אַל תִּטְעַם, אַל תִּגַּע"? [22] וְכֻלָּם דְּבָרִים שֶׁנּוֹעֲדוּ לְכִלָּיוֹן בְּשִׁמּוּשָׁם וְהֵם לְפִי מִצְווֹת וְהוֹרָאוֹת שֶׁל בְּנֵי אָדָם; [23] דְּבָרִים שֶׁאָמְנָם יֵשׁ לָהֶם חֲזוּת שֶׁל חָכְמָה וְהֵם מִתְבַּטְּאִים בְּדָת שֶׁהִיא פְּרִי רְצוֹנָם וּבַעֲנָוּוּת רוּחַ וְסִגּוּף הַגּוּף, אַךְ אֵין זֶה מוֹעִיל נֶגֶד מַאֲוַיֵּי הַבָּשָׂר.

ג לָכֵן אִם הוּקַמְתֶּם עִם הַמָּשִׁיחַ, שַׁאֲפוּ לַדְּבָרִים אֲשֶׁר לְמַעְלָה, אֲשֶׁר שָׁם הַמָּשִׁיחַ יוֹשֵׁב לִימִין אֱלֹהִים. [2] בַּדְּבָרִים אֲשֶׁר לְמַעְלָה יֶהְגֶּה לְבַבְכֶם, לֹא בַּדְּבָרִים אֲשֶׁר בָּאָרֶץ; [3] כִּי מַתֶּם וְחַיֵּיכֶם צְפוּנִים עִם הַמָּשִׁיחַ בֵּאלֹהִים. [4] וְכַאֲשֶׁר יִתְגַּלֶּה הַמָּשִׁיחַ, אֲשֶׁר הוּא חַיֵּינוּ, אָז גַּם אַתֶּם תִּגָּלוּ עִמּוֹ בַּהֲדַר כָּבוֹד. [5] עַל כֵּן מוֹתְתוּ אֶת הָאֵיבָרִים הַשַּׁיָּכִים לָאָרֶץ, אֶת הַזְּנוּת וְהַטֻּמְאָה וְהַזִּמָּה וְהַתַּאֲוָה הָרָעָה, וְאֶת הַחַמְדָנוּת שֶׁאֵינָה אֶלָּא עֲבוֹדַת אֱלִילִים; [6] כִּי בִּגְלַל אֵלֶּה בָּא חֲרוֹן אֱלֹהִים [עַל בְּנֵי הַמֶּרִי]. [7] בַּדְּבָרִים הַלָּלוּ גַּם אַתֶּם הִתְהַלַּכְתֶּם בְּעָבָר, כַּאֲשֶׁר חֱיִיתֶם

8 But now you yourselves are to put off all these:
anger, wrath, malice, blasphemy, filthy language
out of your mouth. 9 Do not lie to one another,
since you have put off the old man with his deeds,
10 and have put on the new *man* who is renewed in
knowledge according to the image of Him who
created him, 11 where there is neither Greek nor
Jew, circumcised nor uncircumcised, barbarian,
Scythian, slave *nor* free, but Christ *is* all and in all.

12 Therefore, as *the* elect of God, holy and
beloved, put on tender mercies, kindness, humility,
meekness, longsuffering; 13 bearing with one another, and forgiving one another, if anyone has a
complaint against another; even as Christ forgave
you, so you also *must do*. 14 But above all these
things put on love, which is the bond of perfection.
15 And let the peace of God rule in your hearts, to
which also you were called in one body; and be
thankful. 16 Let the word of Christ dwell in you
richly in all wisdom, teaching and admonishing one
another in psalms and hymns and spiritual songs,
singing with grace in your hearts to the Lord.
17 And *whatever* you do in word or deed, *do* all in
the name of the Lord Jesus, giving thanks to God
the Father through Him.

18 Wives, submit to your own husbands, as is
fitting in the Lord.

19 Husbands, love your wives and do not be bitter
toward them.

20 Children, obey your parents in all things, for
this is well pleasing to the Lord.

21 Fathers, do not provoke your children, lest
they become discouraged.

22 Bondservants, obey in all things your masters
according to the flesh, not with eyeservice, as men-
pleasers, but in sincerity of heart, fearing God.
23 And whatever you do, do it heartily, as to the
Lord and not to men, 24 knowing that from the
Lord you will receive the reward of the inheritance;
for you serve the Lord Christ. 25 But he who does
wrong will be repaid for what he has done, and
there is no partiality.

4 Masters, give your bondservants what is just and
fair, knowing that you also have a Master in
heaven.

2 Continue earnestly in prayer, being vigilant in it
with thanksgiving; 3 meanwhile praying also for us,
that God would open to us a door for the word, to
speak the mystery of Christ, for which I am also in
chains, 4 that I may make it manifest, as I ought to
speak.

בָּהֶם. 8 אֲבָל כָּעֵת הָסִירוּ גַם אַתֶּם אֶת כָּל אֵלֶּה:
אֶת הָרֹגֶז וְהַכַּעַס וְאֶת הָרֶשַׁע וְהַגִּדּוּף וְאֶת נִבּוּל
הַפֶּה. 9 אַל תְּשַׁקְּרוּ אִישׁ לְרֵעֵהוּ, שֶׁכֵּן פְּשַׁטְתֶּם אֶת
הָאָדָם הַיָּשָׁן עִם מַעֲשָׂיו 10 וּלְבַשְׁתֶּם אֶת הָאָדָם
הֶחָדָשׁ, הַהוֹלֵךְ וּמִתְחַדֵּשׁ בְּדַעַת לְפִי צֶלֶם בּוֹרְאוֹ.
11 בַּמַּצָּב הַזֶּה אֵין יְוָנִי וִיהוּדִי, אֵין מִילָה וְעָרְלָה, אֵין
לוֹעֵז וּסְקִיתִי וְאֵין עֶבֶד וּבֶן חוֹרִין, אֶלָּא הַמָּשִׁיחַ הוּא
הַכֹּל וּבַכֹּל.

12 לָכֵן אַתֶּם, כִּבְחִירֵי אֱלֹהִים קְדוֹשִׁים וַאֲהוּבִים,
לִבְשׁוּ חֶמְלָה וְרַחֲמִים וּנְדִיבוּת לֵב, נְמִיכוּת רוּחַ
וַעֲנָוָה וְאֹרֶךְ אַפַּיִם. 13 נַהֲגוּ בְּסַבְלָנוּת אִישׁ עִם
רֵעֵהוּ, וְסִלְחוּ זֶה לָזֶה כַּאֲשֶׁר לְמִישֶׁהוּ טַעֲנָה עַל
רֵעֵהוּ. כְּשֵׁם שֶׁהָאָדוֹן סָלַח לָכֶם, כֵּן סִלְחוּ גַם אַתֶּם.
14 מֵעַל לְכָל אֵלֶּה תִּשְׂרֹר הָאַהֲבָה, שֶׁהִיא קֶשֶׁר
הַשְּׁלֵמוּת, 15 וְיִשְׁלֹט נָא בִּלְבַבְכֶם שְׁלוֹם הַמָּשִׁיחַ,
שֶׁהֲרֵי לְזֶה נִקְרֵאתֶם בְּגוּף אֶחָד, וֶהֱיוּ מַכִּירֵי טוֹבָה.
16 דְּבַר הַמָּשִׁיחַ יִשְׁכֹּן נָא בְּקִרְבְּכֶם בְּשֶׁפַע; לַמְּדוּ
וְהוֹכִיחוּ זֶה אֶת זֶה בִּמְלוֹא חָכְמָה; שִׁירוּ לֵאלֹהִים
בְּתוֹדָה וְנֹעַם בִּלְבַבְכֶם, בְּמִזְמוֹרִים וְתִשְׁבָּחוֹת
וְשִׁירִים רוּחָנִיִּים. 17 וְכָל מַה שֶּׁתַּעֲשׂוּ, הֵן בְּאֹמֶר
הֵן בְּמַעֲשֶׂה, עֲשׂוּ הַכֹּל בְּשֵׁם הָאָדוֹן יֵשׁוּעַ וְהוֹדוּ
לֵאלֹהִים אָבִינוּ בְּאֶמְצָעוּתוֹ.

18 הַנָּשִׁים, הִכָּנַעְנָה לְבַעֲלֵיכֶן, כְּמוֹ שֶׁיָּאֶה לְנֹכַח
הָאָדוֹן. 19 הָאֲנָשִׁים, אֶהֱבוּ אֶת נְשֵׁיכֶם וְאַל תְּהֵא
בִּלְבַבְכֶם מְרִירוּת נֶגְדָּן. 20 הַבָּנִים, שִׁמְעוּ בְּקוֹל
הַהוֹרִים בְּכָל דָּבָר, כִּי זֶה לְרָצוֹן בְּעֵינֵי הָאָדוֹן.
21 הָאָבוֹת, אַל תַּרְגִּיזוּ אֶת יַלְדֵיכֶם, פֶּן תִּפֹּל רוּחָם.
22 הָעֲבָדִים, הִשָּׁמְעוּ בְּכָל דָּבָר לַאֲדוֹנֵיכֶם אֲשֶׁר
בָּעוֹלָם הַזֶּה, לֹא לְמַרְאִית עַיִן, כְּמִתְרַצִּים אֶל בְּנֵי
אָדָם, אֶלָּא בְּתָם לֵב וּבְיִרְאַת הָאָדוֹן. 23 כָּל מַה
שֶּׁאַתֶּם עוֹשִׂים, עֲשׂוּ בְּכָל נַפְשְׁכֶם, כְּעוֹשִׂים לְמַעַן
הָאָדוֹן וְלֹא לְמַעַן בְּנֵי אָדָם, 24 שֶׁכֵּן יוֹדְעִים אַתֶּם כִּי
תְּקַבְּלוּ מֵאֵת הָאָדוֹן אֶת שְׂכַר הַנַּחֲלָה. אֶת הָאָדוֹן
הַמָּשִׁיחַ אַתֶּם עוֹבְדִים! 25 אַךְ הָעוֹשֶׂה עָוֶל יְקַבֵּל אֶת
גְּמוּל עֲוֺלָתוֹ, וְאֵין מַשּׂוֹא פָּנִים.

ד הָאֲדוֹנִים, הִתְנַהֲגוּ עִם עַבְדֵיכֶם בְּצֶדֶק וּבְיֹשֶׁר,
שֶׁהֲרֵי יוֹדְעִים אַתֶּם כִּי גַם לָכֶם אָדוֹן בַּשָּׁמָיִם.
2 הַתְמִידוּ בִּתְפִלָּה וְשִׁקְדוּ בָּהּ בְּהוֹדָיָה. 3 הִתְפַּלְלוּ
גַם בַּעֲדֵנוּ, כְּדֵי שֶׁאֱלֹהִים יִפְתַּח לָנוּ אֶת שַׁעַר הַדִּבּוּר
לְהַגִּיד אֶת רָז הַמָּשִׁיחַ שֶׁבִּגְלָלוֹ אַף אָסִיר אָנֹכִי,
4 וּכְדֵי שֶׁאֲגַלֶּה אוֹתוֹ כְּפִי שֶׁעָלַי לְדַבֵּר.

⁵Walk in wisdom toward those *who are* outside, redeeming the time. ⁶ *Let* your speech always *be* with grace, seasoned with salt, that you may know how you ought to answer each one.

⁷Tychicus, a beloved brother, faithful minister, and fellow servant in the Lord, will tell you all the news about me. ⁸I am sending him to you for this very purpose, that he may know your circumstances and comfort your hearts, ⁹with Onesimus, a faithful and beloved brother, who is *one* of you. They will make known to you all things which *are happening* here.

¹⁰Aristarchus my fellow prisoner greets you, with Mark the cousin of Barnabas (about whom you received instructions: if he comes to you, welcome him), ¹¹and Jesus who is called Justus. These *are my* only fellow workers for the kingdom of God who are of the circumcision; they have proved to be a comfort to me.

¹²Epaphras, who is *one* of you, a bondservant of Christ, greets you, always laboring fervently for you in prayers, that you may stand perfect and complete in all the will of God. ¹³For I bear him witness that he has a great zeal for you, and those who are in Laodicea, and those in Hierapolis. ¹⁴Luke the beloved physician and Demas greet you. ¹⁵Greet the brethren who are in Laodicea, and Nymphas and the church that *is* in his house.

¹⁶Now when this epistle is read among you, see that it is read also in the church of the Laodiceans, and that you likewise read the epistle from Laodicea. ¹⁷And say to Archippus, "Take heed to the ministry which you have received in the Lord, that you may fulfill it."

¹⁸This salutation by my own hand—Paul. Remember my chains. Grace *be* with you. Amen.

⁵הִתְנַהֲגוּ בְחָכְמָה עִם אֵלֶּה אֲשֶׁר בַּחוּץ, וְנַצְּלוּ אֶת הַהִזְדַּמְּנוּת. ⁶יִהְיוּ נָא דִּבְרֵיכֶם מְלֵאִים תָּמִיד בְּחֵן וּמְתֻבָּלִים בְּמֶלַח, בְּאֹפֶן שֶׁתֵּדְעוּ אֵיךְ לְהָשִׁיב לְכָל שׁוֹאֵל.

⁷אֶת כָּל הַפְּרָטִים עַל־אוֹדוֹת מַצָּבִי יַגִּיד לָכֶם טִיכִיקוֹס, הָאָח הָאָהוּב וְהַמְשָׁרֵת הַנֶּאֱמָן, חֲבֵרִי לָעֲבוֹדָה בָּאָדוֹן. ⁸לְשֵׁם כָּךְ שְׁלַחְתִּיו אֲלֵיכֶם, לְמַעַן יוֹדִיעַ לָכֶם מַה מַּצָּבֵנוּ וִיעוֹדֵד אֶתְכֶם; ⁹וְיַחַד אִתּוֹ אוֹנִיסִימוֹס, הָאָח הַנֶּאֱמָן וְהָאָהוּב שֶׁהוּא אֶחָד מִכֶּם. הֵם יוֹדִיעוּ לָכֶם אֶת כָּל הַנַּעֲשֶׂה כָּאן.

¹⁰אֲרִיסְטַרְכוֹס, חֲבֵרִי לַמַּאֲסָר, דּוֹרֵשׁ בִּשְׁלוֹמְכֶם; כֵּן גַּם מַרְקוֹס, בֶּן אֲחוֹת בַּר־נַבָּא, אֲשֶׁר קִבַּלְתֶּם הוֹרָאוֹת בְּנוֹגֵעַ אֵלָיו – שֶׁאִם יָבוֹא אֲלֵיכֶם תְּקַבְּלוּהוּ; ¹¹וְכֵן גַּם יֵשׁוּעַ הַמְכֻנֶּה יוּסְטוֹס. מִבֵּין הַנִּמּוֹלִים רַק הֵם חֲבֵרַי לָעֲבוֹדָה לְמַעַן מַלְכוּת אֱלֹהִים, וְאָכֵן הָיוּ לִי לְנֶחָמָה. ¹²דְּרִישַׁת שָׁלוֹם מֵאֶפְּרַס, עֶבֶד הַמָּשִׁיחַ יֵשׁוּעַ וְאֶחָד מִכֶּם; בְּכָל עֵת הוּא נֶאֱבָק לְמַעַנְכֶם בִּתְפִלּוֹת, לְמַעַן תַּעַמְדוּ מֻשְׁלָמִים וּמְלֵאֵי בִּטָּחוֹן בְּכָל אֲשֶׁר לִרְצוֹן אֱלֹהִים. ¹³מֵעִיד אֲנִי עָלָיו כִּי הוּא עָמֵל הַרְבֵּה לְמַעַנְכֶם וּלְמַעַן אַנְשֵׁי לָאוֹדִיקֵאָה וְאַנְשֵׁי הִירָפּוֹלִים. ¹⁴לוּקָס, הָרוֹפֵא הָאָהוּב, וְדֵימַס דּוֹרְשִׁים בִּשְׁלוֹמְכֶם. ¹⁵דִּרְשׁוּ בִּשְׁלוֹם הָאַחִים אֲשֶׁר בְּלָאוֹדִיקֵאָה, וּבִשְׁלוֹם נִימְפַס וְהַקְּהִלָּה הַמִּתְאַסֶּפֶת בְּבֵיתוֹ. ¹⁶אַחֲרֵי שֶׁתִּקָּרֵא אִגַּרְתִּי אֶצְלְכֶם, דַּאֲגוּ לְכָךְ שֶׁתִּקָּרֵא גַּם בִּקְהִלַּת לָאוֹדִיקֵאָה, וְאֶת אִגֶּרֶת אֲשֶׁר מִלָּאוֹדִיקֵאָה קִרְאוּ גַּם אַתֶּם. ¹⁷אִמְרוּ לְאַרְכִּיפּוֹס: "שִׂים לִבְּךָ לְמַלֵּא אֶת הַשֵּׁרוּת שֶׁקִּבַּלְתָּ לְמַעַן הָאָדוֹן." ¹⁸דְּרִישַׁת שָׁלוֹם בִּכְתַב יָדִי אֲנִי – שָׁאוּל. זִכְרוּ שִׁבְתִּי בַּמַּאֲסָר. הַחֶסֶד עִמָּכֶם.

THESSALONIANS

1 Paul, Silvanus, and Timothy,

To the church of the Thessalonians in God the Father and the Lord Jesus Christ:

Grace to you and peace from God our Father and the Lord Jesus Christ.

[2] We give thanks to God always for you all, making mention of you in our prayers, [3] remembering without ceasing your work of faith, labor of love, and patience of hope in our Lord Jesus Christ in the sight of our God and Father, [4] knowing, beloved brethren, your election by God. [5] For our gospel did not come to you in word only, but also in power, and in the Holy Spirit and in much assurance, as you know what kind of men we were among you for your sake.

[6] And you became followers of us and of the Lord, having received the word in much affliction, with joy of the Holy Spirit, [7] so that you became examples to all in Macedonia and Achaia who believe. [8] For from you the word of the Lord has sounded forth, not only in Macedonia and Achaia, but also in every place. Your faith toward God has gone out, so that we do not need to say anything. [9] For they themselves declare concerning us what manner of entry we had to you, and how you turned to God from idols to serve the living and true God, [10] and to wait for His Son from heaven, whom He raised from the dead, *even* Jesus who delivers us from the wrath to come.

2 For you yourselves know, brethren, that our coming to you was not in vain. [2] But even after we had suffered before and were spitefully treated at Philippi, as you know, we were bold in our God to speak to you the gospel of God in much conflict. [3] For our exhortation *did* not *come* from error or uncleanness, nor *was it* in deceit.

[4] But as we have been approved by God to be entrusted with the gospel, even so we speak, not as pleasing men, but God who tests our hearts. [5] For neither at any time did we use flattering words, as you know, nor a cloak for covetousness—God *is*

אִגֶּרֶת שָׁאוּל הָרִאשׁוֹנָה אֶל הַתֶּסָּלוֹנִיקִים

א מֵאֵת שָׁאוּל וְסִילְוָנוֹס וְטִימוֹתִיאוֹס, אֶל קְהִלַּת הַתֶּסָּלוֹנִיקִים אֲשֶׁר בֵּאלֹהִים הָאָב וּבָאֲדוֹן יֵשׁוּעַ הַמָּשִׁיחַ: חֶסֶד וְשָׁלוֹם לָכֶם מֵאֵת הָאֱלֹהִים אָבִינוּ וְהָאָדוֹן יֵשׁוּעַ הַמָּשִׁיחַ. [2] אָנוּ מַתְמִידִים לְהוֹדוֹת לֵאלֹהִים עַל כֻּלְּכֶם וּמַזְכִּירִים אֶתְכֶם בִּתְפִלּוֹתֵינוּ, [3] בְּזָכְרֵנוּ תָּמִיד לִפְנֵי אֱלֹהִים אָבִינוּ אֶת פֹּעַל אֱמוּנַתְכֶם, אֶת הֶעָמָל שֶׁעֲמַלְתֶּם בְּאַהֲבָה, וְאֶת הִתְמַדַּתְכֶם בַּתִּקְוָה לְבוֹא אֲדוֹנֵנוּ יֵשׁוּעַ הַמָּשִׁיחַ. [4] אַחִים אֲהוּבֵי אֱלֹהִים, אָנוּ יוֹדְעִים שֶׁנִּבְחַרְתֶּם; [5] שֶׁהֲרֵי בְּשׂוֹרָתֵנוּ לֹא בָּאָה אֲלֵיכֶם רַק בְּמִלִּים, אֶלָּא גַּם בִּגְבוּרָה וּבְרוּחַ הַקֹּדֶשׁ וּבְבִטָּחוֹן רַב – דָּבָר שֶׁאַתֶּם יוֹדְעִים מִשֶּׁנּוֹכַחְתֶּם כֵּיצַד הִתְנַהַגְנוּ לְמַעַנְכֶם כַּאֲשֶׁר הָיִינוּ בֵּינֵיכֶם. [6] וְאַתֶּם הֲלַכְתֶּם בְּעִקְּבוֹתֵינוּ וּבְעִקְּבוֹת אֲדוֹנֵנוּ וְקִבַּלְתֶּם אֶת דְּבַר הַבְּשׂוֹרָה בְּתוֹךְ סֵבֶל רַב, בְּשִׂמְחַת רוּחַ הַקֹּדֶשׁ. [7] בְּכָךְ הֱיִיתֶם לְמוֹפֵת לְכָל הַמַּאֲמִינִים אֲשֶׁר בְּמָקֵדוֹנְיָה וְאָכַיָה. [8] הֵן מִכֶּם יָצָא שֵׁמַע דְּבַר הָאָדוֹן לֹא רַק בְּמָקֵדוֹנְיָה וְאָכַיָה בִּלְבַד, אֶלָּא בְּכָל מָקוֹם נִתְפַּרְסְמָה אֱמוּנַתְכֶם בֵּאלֹהִים עַד כִּי אֵין לָנוּ צֹרֶךְ לְהַגִּיד דָּבָר, [9] שֶׁכֵּן הֵם בְּעַצְמָם מְסַפְּרִים כֵּיצַד קִבַּלְתֶּם אוֹתָנוּ וְכֵיצַד פְּנִיתֶם מִן הָאֱלִילִים לֵאלֹהִים כְּדֵי לַעֲבֹד אֶל חַי וַאֲמִתִּי [10] וּלְחַכּוֹת לִבְנוֹ מִן הַשָּׁמַיִם, אֲשֶׁר הוּא הֵקִימוֹ מִן הַמֵּתִים, לְיֵשׁוּעַ הַמַּצִּיל אוֹתָנוּ מִן הַזַּעַם הַבָּא.

ב אַחַי, הֲרֵי אַתֶּם יוֹדְעִים שֶׁבּוֹאֵנוּ אֲלֵיכֶם לֹא הָיָה לַשָּׁוְא. [2] אָמְנָם קֹדֶם לָכֵן סָבַלְנוּ וְהָיִינוּ לְבוּז בְּפִילִיפִּי, דָּבָר שֶׁיָּדוּעַ לָכֶם, אַךְ הִתְחַזַּקְנוּ בֵּאלֹהֵינוּ לְהַגִּיד לָכֶם אֶת בְּשׂוֹרַת אֱלֹהִים בְּנִסְבּוֹת שֶׁל מַאֲבָקִים רַבִּים. [3] קְרִיאָתֵנוּ אֲלֵיכֶם אֵינָהּ נוֹבַעַת מִתּוֹךְ טָעוּת וְלֹא מִתּוֹךְ מְנִיעִים בִּלְתִּי טְהוֹרִים, אַף אֵינֶנָּה בְּרֶמִיָּה, [4] אֶלָּא כְּפִי שֶׁנִּמְצֵאנוּ נֶאֱמָנִים בְּעֵינֵי אֱלֹהִים לִהְיוֹת מֻפְקָדִים עַל הַבְּשׂוֹרָה, בְּהֶתְאֵם לְכָךְ אֲנַחְנוּ מְדַבְּרִים, לֹא כְּמַשְׂבִּיעִים אֶת רְצוֹן בְּנֵי אָדָם, אֶלָּא אֶת רְצוֹן אֱלֹהִים הַבּוֹחֵן אֶת לְבָבֵנוּ. [5] הֵן יוֹדְעִים

witness. 6 Nor did we seek glory from men, either from you or from others, when we might have made demands as apostles of Christ. 7 But we were gentle among you, just as a nursing *mother* cherishes her own children. 8 So, affectionately longing for you, we were well pleased to impart to you not only the gospel of God, but also our own lives, because you had become dear to us. 9 For you remember, brethren, our labor and toil; for laboring night and day, that we might not be a burden to any of you, we preached to you the gospel of God.

10 You *are* witnesses, and God *also,* how devoutly and justly and blamelessly we behaved ourselves among you who believe; 11 as you know how we exhorted, and comforted, and charged every one of you, as a father *does* his own children, 12 that you would walk worthy of God who calls you into His own kingdom and glory.

13 For this reason we also thank God without ceasing, because when you received the word of God which you heard from us, you welcomed *it* not *as* the word of men, but as it is in truth, the word of God, which also effectively works in you who believe. 14 For you, brethren, became imitators of the churches of God which are in Judea in Christ Jesus. For you also suffered the same things from your own countrymen, just as they *did* from the Judeans, 15 who killed both the Lord Jesus and their own prophets, and have persecuted us; and they do not please God and are contrary to all men, 16 forbidding us to speak to the Gentiles that they may be saved, so as always to fill up *the measure of* their sins; but wrath has come upon them to the uttermost.

17 But we, brethren, having been taken away from you for a short time in presence, not in heart, endeavored more eagerly to see your face with great desire. 18 Therefore we wanted to come to you— even I, Paul, time and again— but Satan hindered us. 19 For what *is* our hope, or joy, or crown of rejoicing? *Is it* not even you in the presence of our Lord Jesus Christ at His coming? 20 For you are our glory and joy.

3 Therefore, when we could no longer endure it, we thought it good to be left in Athens alone, 2 and sent Timothy, our brother and minister of God, and our fellow laborer in the gospel of Christ, to establish you and encourage you concerning your faith, 3 that no one should be shaken by these afflictions; for you yourselves know that we are appointed to this. 4 For, in fact, we told you before when we were with you that we would suffer tribulation, just as it happened, and you know.

אַתֶּם שְׁמַעְתֶּם לֹא בָּאנוּ בִּמְלוֹת חֲנֻפָּה, וְלֹא בְּתֵרוּצִים הַמְכַסִּים עַל שְׁאִיפָה לְבֶצַע – עֵד הָאֱלֹהִים! 6 אַף לֹא בִּקַּשְׁנוּ לָנוּ כָּבוֹד מִבְּנֵי אָדָם, לֹא מִכֶּם וְלֹא מֵאֲחֵרִים, הֲגַם שֶׁבְּתוֹר שְׁלִיחֵי הַמָּשִׁיחַ הָיִינוּ רַשָּׁאִים לְהִתְכַּבֵּד. 7 אֲבָל נָהַגְנוּ בַּעֲדִינוּת כְּשֶׁהָיִינוּ אִתְּכֶם, כְּאִשָּׁה הַמְטַפֶּלֶת בִּילָדֶיהָ. 8 חָבַבְנוּ אֶתְכֶם כָּל כָּךְ, שֶׁבְּחֶפֶץ לֵב שַׁשְׂנוּ לָתֵת לָכֶם לֹא רַק אֶת בְּשׂוֹרַת אֱלֹהִים אֶלָּא גַם אֶת נַפְשֵׁנוּ, שֶׁכֵּן נְהִיֵיתֶם אֲהוּבִים עָלֵינוּ. 9 אַתֶּם זוֹכְרִים, אַחַי, אֶת עֲמָלֵנוּ וִיגִיעָתֵנוּ; עָבַדְנוּ יוֹמָם וָלַיְלָה כְּדֵי שֶׁלֹּא לִהְיוֹת לְמַשָּׂא עַל אִישׁ מִכֶּם בְּעֵת שֶׁבִּשַּׂרְנוּ לָכֶם אֶת בְּשׂוֹרַת אֱלֹהִים. 10 עֵדִים אַתֶּם וְעֵד אֱלֹהִים כִּי בִּקְדֻשָׁה וּבְצֶדֶק וּבְלֹא דֹפִי נָהַגְנוּ עִמָּכֶם הַמַּאֲמִינִים. 11 וְיוֹדְעִים אַתֶּם כִּי כְּאָב אֶל בָּנָיו דִּבַּרְנוּ דִּבְרֵי מוּסָר וְעִדּוּד אֶל כָּל אֶחָד וְאֶחָד מִכֶּם, 12 וְהַעִידוֹנוּ בָּכֶם לְהִתְהַלֵּךְ כָּרָאוּי לִפְנֵי אֱלֹהִים הַקּוֹרֵא אֶתְכֶם לְמַלְכוּתוֹ וּכְבוֹדוֹ.

13 גַּם מִסִּבָּה נוֹסֶפֶת מַתְמִידִים אָנוּ לְהוֹדוֹת לֵאלֹהִים: כַּאֲשֶׁר קִבַּלְתֶּם אֶת דְּבַר אֱלֹהִים שֶׁשְּׁמַעְתֶּם מֵאִתָּנוּ, קִבַּלְתֶּם אוֹתוֹ לֹא כִּדְבַר בְּנֵי אָדָם, אֶלָּא כְּפִי שֶׁהוּא בֶּאֱמֶת – דְּבַר אֱלֹהִים, הַדָּבָר אֲשֶׁר פּוֹעֵל גַּם בָּכֶם הַמַּאֲמִינִים. 14 הֲלֹא אַתֶּם, אַחַי, הֲלַכְתֶּם בְּעִקְבוֹת קְהִלּוֹת אֱלֹהִים שֶׁבִּיהוּדָה הַשַּׁיָּכוֹת לַמָּשִׁיחַ יֵשׁוּעַ; כִּי גַם אַתֶּם סְבַלְתֶּם מִידֵי בְּנֵי עַמְּכֶם כְּמוֹ שֶׁגַּם הֵם סָבְלוּ מִידֵי תּוֹשְׁבֵי יְהוּדָה, 15 אֵלֶּה אֲשֶׁר הֵמִיתוּ גַם אֶת הָאָדוֹן יֵשׁוּעַ וְגַם אֶת הַנְּבִיאִים, וְאוֹתָנוּ רָדְפוּ. אֵין הֵם מַשְׂבִּיעִים אֶת רְצוֹן אֱלֹהִים וּמִתְנַגְּדִים לְכָל בְּנֵי אָדָם, 16 בְּנַסּוֹתָם לִמְנֹעַ אוֹתָנוּ מֵהַגִּיד לַגּוֹיִים אֶת הַדֶּרֶךְ לִישׁוּעָה. בְּזֹאת הֵם מְמַלְּאִים אֶת מְאַת חַטֹּאתֵיהֶם בְּכָל עֵת, וּבָא עֲלֵיהֶם הֶחָרוֹן עַד תֹּם. 17 אֲבָל אֲנַחְנוּ, אַחַי, לְאַחַר זְמַן קָצָר שֶׁהָיִינוּ מְרֻחָקִים מִכֶּם – מְרֻחָקִים בְּמַרְאֵה פָנִים, אַךְ לֹא בַּלֵּב – נִכְסַפְנוּ עַד מְאֹד לִרְאוֹת אֶת פְּנֵיכֶם. 18 לְפִיכָךְ חָפַצְנוּ לָבוֹא אֲלֵיכֶם – אֲנִי שָׁאוּל רָצִיתִי בָּזֶה יוֹתֵר מִפַּעַם אַחַת, אֶלָּא שֶׁהַשָּׂטָן מָנַע בַּעֲדֵנוּ – 19 כִּי מִי תִּקְוָתֵנוּ וְשִׂמְחָתֵנוּ וַעֲטֶרֶת תְּהִלָּתֵנוּ לְנֹכַח אֲדוֹנֵנוּ יֵשׁוּעַ בְּבוֹאוֹ, מִי אִם לֹא אַתֶּם? 20 הֲרֵי אַתֶּם תִּפְאַרְתֵּנוּ וְשִׂמְחָתֵנוּ!

ג וּמֵאַחַר שֶׁלֹּא יָכֹלְנוּ עוֹד לִסְבֹּל זֹאת, הֶחְלַטְנוּ לְהִשָּׁאֵר לְבַדֵּנוּ בְּאַתּוּנָה, 2 שָׁלַחְנוּ אֶת טִימוֹתִיאוֹס אָחִינוּ וַעֲמִיתֵנוּ הַמְשָׁרֵת אֶת אֱלֹהִים בִּבְשׂוֹרַת הַמָּשִׁיחַ. שְׁלַחְנוּהוּ אוֹתוֹ לְחַזֵּק וּלְעוֹדֵד אֶתְכֶם בֶּאֱמוּנַתְכֶם, 3 כְּדֵי שֶׁאִישׁ מִכֶּם לֹא יָמוּט בַּצָּרוֹת הָאֵלֶּה; הֲלֹא יוֹדְעִים אַתֶּם שֶׁלָּזֹאת יֻעַדְנוּ. 4 הֵן גַּם

5 For this reason, when I could no longer endure it, I sent to know your faith, lest by some means the tempter had tempted you, and our labor might be in vain.

6 But now that Timothy has come to us from you, and brought us good news of your faith and love, and that you always have good remembrance of us, greatly desiring to see us, as we also *to see* you— 7 therefore, brethren, in all our affliction and distress we were comforted concerning you by your faith. 8 For now we live, if you stand fast in the Lord.

9 For what thanks can we render to God for you, for all the joy with which we rejoice for your sake before our God, 10 night and day praying exceedingly that we may see your face and perfect what is lacking in your faith?

11 Now may our God and Father Himself, and our Lord Jesus Christ, direct our way to you. 12 And may the Lord make you increase and abound in love to one another and to all, just as we *do* to you, 13 so that He may establish your hearts blameless in holiness before our God and Father at the coming of our Lord Jesus Christ with all His saints.

4 Finally then, brethren, we urge and exhort in the Lord Jesus that you should abound more and more, just as you received from us how you ought to walk and to please God; 2 for you know what commandments we gave you through the Lord Jesus.

3 For this is the will of God, your sanctification: that you should abstain from sexual immorality; 4 that each of you should know how to possess his own vessel in sanctification and honor, 5 not in passion of lust, like the Gentiles who do not know God; 6 that no one should take advantage of and defraud his brother in this matter, because the Lord *is* the avenger of all such, as we also forewarned you and testified. 7 For God did not call us to uncleanness, but in holiness. 8 Therefore he who rejects *this* does not reject man, but God, who has also given us His Holy Spirit.

9 But concerning brotherly love you have no need that I should write to you, for you yourselves are taught by God to love one another; 10 and indeed you do so toward all the brethren who are in all Macedonia. But we urge you, brethren, that you increase more and more; 11 that you also aspire to lead a quiet life, to mind your own business, and to work with your own hands, as we commanded you, 12 that you may walk properly toward those who are outside, and *that* you may lack nothing.

כַּאֲשֶׁר הָיִינוּ אֶצְלְכֶם אָמַרְנוּ לָכֶם מֵרֹאשׁ שֶׁעֲתִידִים אֲנַחְנוּ לִסְבֹּל, מַה שֶּׁאָכֵן קָרָה וְגַם יָדוּעַ לָכֶם. 5 לָכֵן כַּאֲשֶׁר לֹא יָכֹלְתִּי עוֹד לָשֵׂאת זֹאת, שָׁלַחְתִּי לְהִוָּדַע מַה מַּצָּב אֱמוּנַתְכֶם, מֵחֲשָׁשׁ שֶׁמָּא נִסָּה אֶתְכֶם הַמְנַסֶּה וַעֲמָלֵנוּ הָיָה לָרִיק. 6 אֲבָל כָּעֵת טִימוֹתֵיאוֹס בָּא אֵלֵינוּ מִכֶּם וּבִשֵּׂר לָנוּ טוֹבוֹת עַל אֱמוּנַתְכֶם וְאַהֲבַתְכֶם, וְסִפֵּר שֶׁאַתֶּם זוֹכְרִים אוֹתָנוּ לְטוֹבָה בְּכָל עֵת וְנִכְסָפִים לִרְאוֹתֵנוּ, כְּשֵׁם שֶׁגַּם אָנוּ נִכְסָפִים לִרְאוֹת אֶתְכֶם. 7 עַל כֵּן, אַחַי, בְּכָל מְצוּקָתֵנוּ וְצָרָתֵנוּ הִתְעוֹדַדְנוּ בָּכֶם בִּגְלַל אֱמוּנַתְכֶם; 8 וְאָמְנָם עַכְשָׁו חַיִּים אֲנַחְנוּ, אִם אַתֶּם מַחֲזִיקִים מַעֲמָד בָּאָדוֹן. 9 וְאֵילוּ תּוֹדוֹת יְכוֹלִים אָנוּ לְשַׁלֵּם לֵאלֹהִים בַּעֲדְכֶם עַל כָּל הַשִּׂמְחָה שֶׁאָנוּ שְׂמֵחִים בִּגְלַלְכֶם לִפְנֵי אֱלֹהֵינוּ? 10 יוֹמָם וָלַיְלָה אָנוּ מַרְבִּים לְהִתְפַּלֵּל שֶׁנִּרְאֶה אֶת פְּנֵיכֶם וְנַשְׁלִים אֶת הֶחָסֵר לֶאֱמוּנַתְכֶם. 11 יָכֵן אֱלֹהִים אָבִינוּ וַאֲדוֹנֵנוּ יֵשׁוּעַ אֶת דַּרְכֵּנוּ אֲלֵיכֶם. 12 וְהָאָדוֹן יַרְבֶּה וְיַשְׂגֶּה אֶת הָאַהֲבָה בְּקִרְבְּכֶם, לֶאֱהֹב אִישׁ אֶת רֵעֵהוּ וְאֶת כָּל אָדָם כְּשֵׁם שֶׁגַּם אֲנַחְנוּ אוֹהֲבִים אֶתְכֶם; 13 וְכָךְ יְכוֹנֵן אֶת לְבַבְכֶם לִהְיוֹת תְּמִים בַּקְּדֻשָּׁה לִפְנֵי הָאֱלֹהִים אָבִינוּ בְּבוֹא אֲדוֹנֵנוּ יֵשׁוּעַ עִם כָּל קְדוֹשָׁיו.

ד לְבַסּוֹף, אַחַי, אָנוּ מְבַקְשִׁים מִכֶּם בָּאָדוֹן יֵשׁוּעַ וּמְפַצִּירִים בָּכֶם: קִבַּלְתֶּם מֵאִתָּנוּ אֵיךְ עֲלֵיכֶם לְהִתְנַהֵג וְלִמְצֹא חֵן בְּעֵינֵי אֱלֹהִים, וְאָמְנָם כָּךְ אַתֶּם מִתְנַהֲגִים; אָנָּא, הִתְקַדְּמוּ עוֹד יוֹתֵר. 2 אַתֶּם יוֹדְעִים אֵילוּ מִצְווֹת נָתַנּוּ לָכֶם מִטַּעַם הָאָדוֹן יֵשׁוּעַ. 3 וְזֶהוּ רְצוֹן הָאֱלֹהִים: שֶׁתִּתְקַדְּשׁוּ, שֶׁתִּתְרַחֲקוּ מִן הַזְּנוּת, 4 שֶׁכָּל אֶחָד מִכֶּם יֵדַע לָקַחַת אִשָּׁה בִּקְדֻשָּׁה וּבְכָבוֹד, 5 לֹא בְּתַאֲוַת זִמָּה כְּדֶרֶךְ הַגּוֹיִים אֲשֶׁר אֵינָם יוֹדְעִים אֶת אֱלֹהִים. 6 וְאִישׁ אַל יֶחֱטָא וְאַל יַעֲשֶׂה עָוֶל לְאָחִיו בָּעִנְיָן הַזֶּה, כִּי נוֹקֵם יהוה עַל כָּל זֹאת, כְּפִי שֶׁכְּבָר אָמַרְנוּ לָכֶם וְהִזְהַרְנוּ אֶתְכֶם. 7 הֵן אֱלֹהִים לֹא קָרָא אוֹתָנוּ לְטֻמְאָה, כִּי אִם לִקְדֻשָּׁה. 8 עַל כֵּן הַדּוֹחֶה זֹאת, לֹא אָדָם הוּא דּוֹחֶה, אֶלָּא אֶת אֱלֹהִים הַנּוֹתֵן לָכֶם אֶת רוּחַ קָדְשׁוֹ. 9 עַל־דְּבַר אַהֲבַת אַחִים אֵין צֹרֶךְ לִכְתֹּב לָכֶם, שֶׁכֵּן אַתֶּם בְּעַצְמְכֶם לְמוּדֵי אֱלֹהִים וְיוֹדְעִים שֶׁעֲלֵיכֶם לֶאֱהֹב אִישׁ אֶת רֵעֵהוּ, 10 וְאָמְנָם אַתֶּם נוֹהֲגִים כָּךְ כְּלַפֵּי כָּל הָאַחִים אֲשֶׁר בְּכָל מָקְדוֹנְיָה. אֲבָל מְבַקְשִׁים אָנוּ מִכֶּם, אַחַי, שֶׁתִּשְׁפְּעוּ עוֹד יוֹתֵר. 11 הִשְׁתַּדְּלוּ לִחְיוֹת בְּהַשְׁקֵט, לַעֲסֹק בְּעִנְיְנֵי שֶׁלָּכֶם וְלַעֲבֹד בִּידֵיכֶם אַתֶּם, כְּפִי שֶׁצִּוִּינוּ אֶתְכֶם, 12 לְמַעַן תִּתְנַהֲגוּ כַּיָּאוּת עִם אֵלֶּה אֲשֶׁר בַּחוּץ וּלְמַעַן לֹא יֶחְסַר לָכֶם דָּבָר.

13 But I do not want you to be ignorant, brethren, concerning those who have fallen asleep, lest you sorrow as others who have no hope. 14 For if we believe that Jesus died and rose again, even so God will bring with Him those who sleep in Jesus.

15 For this we say to you by the word of the Lord, that we who are alive *and* remain until the coming of the Lord will by no means precede those who are asleep. 16 For the Lord Himself will descend from heaven with a shout, with the voice of an archangel, and with the trumpet of God. And the dead in Christ will rise first. 17 Then we who are alive *and* remain shall be caught up together with them in the clouds to meet the Lord in the air. And thus we shall always be with the Lord. 18 Therefore comfort one another with these words.

5 But concerning the times and the seasons, brethren, you have no need that I should write to you. 2 For you yourselves know perfectly that the day of the Lord so comes as a thief in the night. 3 For when they say, "Peace and safety!" then sudden destruction comes upon them, as labor pains upon a pregnant woman. And they shall not escape. 4 But you, brethren, are not in darkness, so that this Day should overtake you as a thief. 5 You are all sons of light and sons of the day. We are not of the night nor of darkness. 6 Therefore let us not sleep, as others *do*, but let us watch and be sober. 7 For those who sleep, sleep at night, and those who get drunk are drunk at night. 8 But let us who are of the day be sober, putting on the breastplate of faith and love, and *as* a helmet the hope of salvation. 9 For God did not appoint us to wrath, but to obtain salvation through our Lord Jesus Christ, 10 who died for us, that whether we wake or sleep, we should live together with Him.

11 Therefore comfort each other and edify one another, just as you also are doing.

12 And we urge you, brethren, to recognize those who labor among you, and are over you in the Lord and admonish you, 13 and to esteem them very highly in love for their work's sake. Be at peace among yourselves.

14 Now we exhort you, brethren, warn those who are unruly, comfort the fainthearted, uphold the weak, be patient with all. 15 See that no one renders evil for evil to anyone, but always pursue what is good both for yourselves and for all.

16 Rejoice always, 17 pray without ceasing, 18 in everything give thanks; for this is the will of God in Christ Jesus for you.

13 אַחַי, אֵין אָנוּ רוֹצִים שֶׁיַּעֲלֵם מִכֶּם מַה שֶּׁנּוֹגֵעַ לִישֵׁנֵי עָפָר, כְּדֵי שֶׁלֹּא תִּתְעַצְּבוּ כַּאֲחֵרִים אֲשֶׁר אֵין לָהֶם הַתִּקְוָה. 14 אִם אָמְנָם מַאֲמִינִים אָנוּ שֶׁיֵּשׁוּעַ מֵת וְקָם לִתְחִיָּה, כָּךְ גַּם אֶת הַיְשֵׁנִים, בְּאֶמְצָעוּת יֵשׁוּעַ, אֱלֹהִים יָבִיא יַחַד אִתּוֹ. 15 הִנֵּה זֹאת אָנוּ אוֹמְרִים לָכֶם עַל־פִּי דְּבַר הָאָדוֹן: אֲנַחְנוּ הַחַיִּים אֲשֶׁר נִשָּׁאֵר עַד בּוֹא הָאָדוֹן לֹא נַקְדִּים אֶת הַמֵּתִים. 16 שֶׁכֵּן הָאָדוֹן עַצְמוֹ יֵרֵד מִן הַשָּׁמַיִם בִּקְרִיאָה שֶׁל פְּקֻדָּה, בְּקוֹל שַׂר הַמַּלְאָכִים וּבְשׁוֹפָר אֱלֹהִים, וְהַמֵּתִים הַשַּׁיָּכִים לַמָּשִׁיחַ יָקוּמוּ רִאשׁוֹנָה. 17 אַחֲרֵי כֵן אֲנַחְנוּ הַנִּשְׁאָרִים בַּחַיִּים נִלָּקַח יַחַד אִתָּם בָּעֲנָנִים לִפְגֹּשׁ אֶת הָאָדוֹן בָּאֲוִיר, וְכָךְ נִהְיֶה תָּמִיד עִם הָאָדוֹן. 18 עַל כֵּן עוֹדְדוּ זֶה אֶת זֶה בַּדְּבָרִים הָאֵלֶּה.

ה וְעַל־דְּבַר הָעִתִּים וְהַזְּמַנִּים, אַחַי, אֵין צֹרֶךְ לִכְתֹּב לָכֶם. 2 הֲרֵי אַתֶּם יוֹדְעִים הֵיטֵב שֶׁיּוֹם יהוה יָבוֹא כְּגַנָּב בַּלַּיְלָה. 3 כַּאֲשֶׁר יֹאמְרוּ הַבְּרִיּוֹת: "שָׁלוֹם וּבִטָּחוֹן!", אָז יָבוֹא עֲלֵיהֶם שֶׁבֶר פִּתְאֹם, כִּצִירֵי לֵדָה עַל אִשָּׁה הָרָה, וְלֹא יוּכְלוּ לְהִמָּלֵט. 4 אֲבָל אַתֶּם, אַחַי, אֵינְכֶם בַּחֹשֶׁךְ בְּאֹפֶן שֶׁיִּפְתִּיעַ אֶתְכֶם הַיּוֹם כְּגַנָּב. 5 אַתֶּם כֻּלְּכֶם בְּנֵי הָאוֹר וּבְנֵי הַיּוֹם. לֹא בְּנֵי הַלַּיְלָה אֲנַחְנוּ וְלֹא בְּנֵי הַחֹשֶׁךְ. 6 לָכֵן אַל נָא נִישַׁן כַּאֲחֵרִים, אֶלָּא נִהְיֶה עֵרִים וּמְפֻכָּחִים. 7 הֵן הַיְשֵׁנִים יְשֵׁנִים בַּלַּיְלָה, וְהַמִּשְׁתַּכְּרִים מִשְׁתַּכְּרִים בַּלַּיְלָה. 8 אֲבָל אָנוּ, אֲשֶׁר בְּנֵי הַיּוֹם אֲנַחְנוּ, נִהְיֶה נָא מְפֻכָּחִים, נִלְבַּשׁ אֶת שִׁרְיוֹן הָאֱמוּנָה וְהָאַהֲבָה וְנַחְבֹּשׁ כַּכּוֹבַע אֶת תִּקְוַת הַיְשׁוּעָה. 9 כִּי אֱלֹהִים לֹא יְעָדָנוּ לְזַעַם, אֶלָּא לִנְחֹל יְשׁוּעָה עַל־יְדֵי אֲדוֹנֵנוּ יֵשׁוּעַ הַמָּשִׁיחַ 10 אֲשֶׁר מֵת בַּעֲדֵנוּ לְמַעַן נִחְיֶה יַחַד אִתּוֹ, בֵּין שֶׁאָנוּ עֵרִים בֵּין שֶׁאָנוּ יְשֵׁנִים. 11 עַל כֵּן עוֹדְדוּ זֶה אֶת זֶה וּבְנוּ אִישׁ אֶת אָחִיו, כְּפִי שֶׁאַתֶּם גַּם עוֹשִׂים. 12 אָנוּ מְבַקְשִׁים מִכֶּם, אַחַי, לְהַכִּיר בָּאֲנָשִׁים הָעֲמֵלִים בְּקִרְבְּכֶם, הַמַּנְהִיגִים אֶתְכֶם בָּאָדוֹן וּמוֹכִיחִים אֶתְכֶם. 13 הוֹקִירוּ אוֹתָם בְּרֹב אַהֲבָה בַּעֲבוּר עֲבוֹדָתָם. הֱיוּ בְּשָׁלוֹם אִישׁ עִם רֵעֵהוּ. 14 אַחַי, אָנוּ מְבַקְשִׁים מִכֶּם: הוֹכִיחוּ אֶת הַהוֹלְכִים בָּטֵל; עוֹדְדוּ אֶת הַנִּכְאָבִים; תִּמְכוּ בַּחַלָּשִׁים; הֱיוּ סַבְלָנִים כְּלַפֵּי כָּל אָדָם. 15 הִזָּהֲרוּ שֶׁלֹּא יִגְמֹל אִישׁ לְאִישׁ רָעָה תַּחַת רָעָה; בְּכָל עֵת חִתְרוּ לְהֵיטִיב אִישׁ עִם רֵעֵהוּ וְגַם עִם כָּל אָדָם. 16 שִׂמְחוּ תָּמִיד; 17 הִתְמִידוּ לְהִתְפַּלֵּל; 18 הוֹדוּ עַל כָּל דָּבָר, כִּי זֶהוּ

19 Do not quench the Spirit. 20 Do not despise prophecies. 21 Test all things; hold fast what is good. 22 Abstain from every form of evil.

23 Now may the God of peace Himself sanctify you completely; and may your whole spirit, soul, and body be preserved blameless at the coming of our Lord Jesus Christ. 24 He who calls you *is* faithful, who also will do *it*.

25 Brethren, pray for us.

26 Greet all the brethren with a holy kiss.

27 I charge you by the Lord that this epistle be read to all the holy brethren.

28 The grace of our Lord Jesus Christ *be* with you. Amen.

רְצוֹן אֱלֹהִים לְנֶגְדְּכֶם בַּמָּשִׁיחַ יֵשׁוּעַ. 19 אַל תְּכַבּוּ אֶת הָרוּחַ; 20 אַל תְּזַלְזְלוּ בִּנְבוּאוֹת; 21 בַּחֲנוּ כָּל דָּבָר וְהַחֲזִיקוּ בַּטּוֹב. 22 הִתְרַחֲקוּ מִן הָרַע עַל כָּל צוּרוֹתָיו.

23 יְקַדֵּשׁ אֶתְכֶם אֱלֹהֵי הַשָּׁלוֹם קָדְשָׁה שְׁלֵמָה וְתִשָּׁמֵר שְׁלֵמוּת רוּחֲכֶם וְנַפְשְׁכֶם וְגוּפְכֶם, לִהְיוֹת בְּלִי דֹּפִי בְּבוֹא אֲדוֹנֵנוּ יֵשׁוּעַ הַמָּשִׁיחַ. 24 נֶאֱמָן הוּא הַקּוֹרֵא אֶתְכֶם, אֲשֶׁר גַּם יַעֲשֶׂה זֹאת.

25 אַחַי, הִתְפַּלְּלוּ בַּעֲדֵנוּ. 26 דִּרְשׁוּ בְּשָׁלוֹם כָּל הָאַחִים בִּנְשִׁיקָה קְדוֹשָׁה. 27 אֲנִי מַשְׁבִּיעַ אֶתְכֶם בָּאָדוֹן, שֶׁתִּקָּרֵא הָאִגֶּרֶת הַזֹּאת בְּאָזְנֵי כָּל הָאַחִים. 28 חֶסֶד אֲדוֹנֵנוּ יֵשׁוּעַ הַמָּשִׁיחַ עִמָּכֶם.

THESSALONIANS

1 Paul, Silvanus, and Timothy,

To the church of the Thessalonians in God our Father and the Lord Jesus Christ:

² Grace to you and peace from God our Father and the Lord Jesus Christ.

³ We are bound to thank God always for you, brethren, as it is fitting, because your faith grows exceedingly, and the love of every one of you all abounds toward each other, ⁴ so that we ourselves boast of you among the churches of God for your patience and faith in all your persecutions and tribulations that you endure, ⁵ *which is* manifest evidence of the righteous judgment of God, that you may be counted worthy of the kingdom of God, for which you also suffer; ⁶ since *it is a* righteous thing with God to repay with tribulation those who trouble you, ⁷ and to *give* you who are troubled rest with us when the Lord Jesus is revealed from heaven with His mighty angels, ⁸ in flaming fire taking vengeance on those who do not know God, and on those who do not obey the gospel of our Lord Jesus Christ. ⁹ These shall be punished with everlasting destruction from the presence of the Lord and from the glory of His power, ¹⁰ when He comes, in that Day, to be glorified in His saints and to be admired among all those who believe, because our testimony among you was believed.

¹¹ Therefore we also pray always for you that our God would count you worthy of *this* calling, and fulfill all the good pleasure of *His* goodness and the work of faith with power, ¹² that the name of our Lord Jesus Christ may be glorified in you, and you in Him, according to the grace of our God and the Lord Jesus Christ.

2 Now, brethren, concerning the coming of our Lord Jesus Christ and our gathering together to Him, we ask you, ² not to be soon shaken in mind or troubled, either by spirit or by word or by letter, as if from us, as though the day of Christ had come. ³ Let no one deceive you by any means; for *that Day will not come* unless the falling away comes first, and the man of sin is revealed, the son of perdition, ⁴ who opposes and exalts himself above all that is

אִגֶּרֶת שָׁאוּל הַשְּׁנִיָּה אֶל הַתֶּסָּלוֹנִיקִים

א מֵאֵת שָׁאוּל וְסִילְוָנוֹס וְטִימוֹתֵיאוֹס, אֶל קְהִלַּת הַתֶּסָּלוֹנִיקִים אֲשֶׁר בֵּאלֹהִים אָבִינוּ וּבָאָדוֹן יֵשׁוּעַ הַמָּשִׁיחַ: ² חֶסֶד וְשָׁלוֹם לָכֶם מֵאֵת הָאֱלֹהִים אָבִינוּ וְהָאָדוֹן יֵשׁוּעַ הַמָּשִׁיחַ.

³ אַחַי, חַיָּבִים אֲנַחְנוּ לְהוֹדוֹת עֲלֵיכֶם לֵאלֹהִים בְּכָל עֵת; וְרָאוּי הַדָּבָר, מִשּׁוּם שֶׁאֱמוּנַתְכֶם גְּדֵלָה בְּיֶתֶר שְׂאֵת וְאַהֲבַת אִישׁ אֶת רֵעֵהוּ מִתְגַּבֶּרֶת אֵצֶל כֻּלְּכֶם. ⁴ לְפִיכָךְ אֲנַחְנוּ עַצְמֵנוּ מִתְגָּאִים בָּכֶם בִּקְהִלּוֹת אֱלֹהִים עַל אֱמוּנַתְכֶם וְסַבְלָנוּתְכֶם בְּכָל הָרְדִיפוֹת וְהַצָּרוֹת הָעוֹבְרוֹת עֲלֵיכֶם, ⁵ אֲשֶׁר אוֹת הֵן לְמִשְׁפָּטוֹ הַצּוֹדֵק שֶׁל אֱלֹהִים, שֶׁתִּמָּצְאוּ רְאוּיִים לְמַלְכוּת הָאֱלֹהִים אֲשֶׁר בַּעֲבוּרָהּ אַתֶּם גַּם סוֹבְלִים. ⁶ הֲלֹא מִן הַצֶּדֶק הוּא בְּעֵינֵי אֱלֹהִים לִגְמֹל צָרָה לְרוֹדְפֵיכֶם ⁷ וְלָתֵת לָכֶם, הַנִּרְדָּפִים, רְוָחָה יַחַד עִמָּנוּ, כַּאֲשֶׁר יִתְגַּלֶּה הָאָדוֹן יֵשׁוּעַ מִן הַשָּׁמַיִם עִם מַלְאֲכֵי עֻזּוֹ ⁸ בְּאֵשׁ לֶהָבָה, לְהָשִׁיב נָקָם לְאֵלֶּה שֶׁאֵינָם יוֹדְעִים אֶת הָאֱלֹהִים וּלְאֵלֶּה שֶׁאֵינָם נִשְׁמָעִים לִבְשׂוֹרַת אֲדוֹנֵנוּ יֵשׁוּעַ. ⁹ הַלָּלוּ יֻטַּל עֲלֵיהֶם עֹנֶשׁ שֶׁל אֲבַדּוֹן עוֹלָם מִלִּפְנֵי הָאָדוֹן וּמֵהֲדַר עֻזּוֹ, ¹⁰ כְּשֶׁיָּבוֹא בַּיּוֹם הַהוּא לְהִכָּבֵד בִּקְדוֹשָׁיו וְלִהְיוֹת נַעֲרָץ בֵּין כָּל הַמַּאֲמִינִים; וַהֲרֵי אַתֶּם הֶאֱמַנְתֶּם לְעֵדוּתֵנוּ. ¹¹ לְכָךְ אָנוּ גַּם מִתְפַּלְלִים בַּעַדְכֶם בְּכָל עֵת, שֶׁאֱלֹהֵינוּ יַעֲשֶׂה אֶתְכֶם רְאוּיִים לִקְרִיאָתוֹ, וּבִגְבוּרָתוֹ יְמַלֵּא כָּל שְׁאִיפָה טוֹבָה וְיַשְׁלִים כָּל מַעֲשֵׂה אֱמוּנָה, ¹² לְמַעַן יְכֻבַּד שֵׁם אֲדוֹנֵנוּ יֵשׁוּעַ בָּכֶם וְאַתֶּם תְּכֻבְּדוּ בוֹ, כְּפִי חֶסֶד אֱלֹהֵינוּ וְהָאָדוֹן יֵשׁוּעַ הַמָּשִׁיחַ.

ב אֲשֶׁר לְבוֹא אֲדוֹנֵנוּ יֵשׁוּעַ הַמָּשִׁיחַ וַאֲסִיפָתֵנוּ אֵלָיו, אָנוּ מְבַקְשִׁים מִכֶּם, אַחַי: ² אַל תְּמַהֲרוּ לְאַבֵּד אֶת עֶשְׁתּוֹנוֹתֵיכֶם וְאַל תִּבָּהֲלוּ, לֹא בִּגְלַל אֵיזוֹ הִתְבַּטְּאוּת שֶׁל רוּחַ, לֹא בִּגְלַל אֵיזֶה דִּבּוּר, וְלֹא בִּגְלַל אֵיזוֹ אִגֶּרֶת אֲשֶׁר כִּבְיָכוֹל נִשְׁלְחָה מֵאִתָּנוּ – כְּאִלּוּ הִגִּיעַ יוֹם יהוה. ³ אַל יַטְעֶה אֶתְכֶם אִישׁ בְּאֵיזֶה אֹפֶן שֶׁהוּא, שֶׁכֵּן לֹא יַגִּיעַ אִם לֹא תִּהְיֶה בָּרִאשׁוֹנָה הָעֲזִיבָה וְיִתְגַּלֶּה אִישׁ הָרֶשַׁע, בֶּן הָאֲבַדּוֹן, ⁴ הַמִּתְקוֹמֵם וּמְרוֹמֵם עַצְמוֹ עַל כָּל הַנִּקְרָא אֱלֹהַּ

called God or that is worshiped, so that he sits as God in the temple of God, showing himself that he is God.

5 Do you not remember that when I was still with you I told you these things? 6 And now you know what is restraining, that he may be revealed in his own time. 7 For the mystery of lawlessness is already at work; only He who now restrains *will do so* until He is taken out of the way. 8 And then the lawless one will be revealed, whom the Lord will consume with the breath of His mouth and destroy with the brightness of His coming. 9 The coming of the *lawless one* is according to the working of Satan, with all power, signs, and lying wonders, 10 and with all unrighteous deception among those who perish, because they did not receive the love of the truth, that they might be saved. 11 And for this reason God will send them strong delusion, that they should believe the lie, 12 that they all may be condemned who did not believe the truth but had pleasure in unrighteousness.

13 But we are bound to give thanks to God always for you, brethren beloved by the Lord, because God from the beginning chose you for salvation through sanctification by the Spirit and belief in the truth, 14 to which He called you by our gospel, for the obtaining of the glory of our Lord Jesus Christ. 15 Therefore, brethren, stand fast and hold the traditions which you were taught, whether by word or our epistle.

16 Now may our Lord Jesus Christ Himself, and our God and Father, who has loved us and given *us* everlasting consolation and good hope by grace, 17 comfort your hearts and establish you in every good word and work.

3 Finally, brethren, pray for us, that the word of the Lord may run *swiftly* and be glorified, just as *it is* with you, 2 and that we may be delivered from unreasonable and wicked men; for not all have faith.

3 But the Lord is faithful, who will establish you and guard *you* from the evil one. 4 And we have confidence in the Lord concerning you, both that you do and will do the things we command you. 5 Now may the Lord direct your hearts into the love of God and into the patience of Christ.

6 But we command you, brethren, in the name of our Lord Jesus Christ, that you withdraw from every brother who walks disorderly and not according to the tradition which he received from us. 7 For you yourselves know how you ought to follow us, for we were not disorderly among you; 8 nor did we eat anyone's bread free of charge, but

או קֹדֶשׁ, עַד כִּי יֵשֵׁב בְּהֵיכַל הָאֱלֹהִים כְּהַצְהִירוֹ עַל עַצְמוֹ שֶׁהוּא אֱלֹהִים. 5 הַאִם אֵינְכֶם זוֹכְרִים כִּי עוֹד בִּהְיוֹתִי אֶצְלְכֶם אָמַרְתִּי לָכֶם אֶת הַדְּבָרִים הָאֵלֶּה? 6 אַתֶּם יוֹדְעִים מַה מְּעַכֵּב אוֹתוֹ כָּעֵת כְּדֵי שֶׁיִּתְגַּלֶּה בְּעִתּוֹ. 7 הֵן סוֹד הָרֶשַׁע כְּבָר פּוֹעֵל; רַק שֶׁבַּעַת הַמְעַכֵּב נִמְצָא עַד שֶׁיֵּצֵא, 8 וְאָז יִתְגַּלֶּה הָרָשָׁע אֲשֶׁר הָאָדוֹן יָמִית אוֹתוֹ בְּרוּחַ פִּיו וִיכַלֵּהוּ בְּהוֹפָעַת בּוֹאוֹ – 9 אֶת הָרָשָׁע אֲשֶׁר בּוֹאוֹ הוּא בְּהֶתְאֵם לִפְעֻלַּת הַשָּׂטָן, מְלֵוֶה בְּכָל גְּבוּרָה, בְּאוֹתוֹת וּבְמוֹפְתֵי שֶׁקֶר 10 וּבְכָל תַּרְמִית רֶשַׁע הַמְּיֹעָדִים לִבְנֵי הָאֲבַדּוֹן, וְזֹאת מִפְּנֵי שֶׁלֹּא קִבְּלוּ אֶת אַהֲבַת הָאֱמֶת אֲשֶׁר יָכְלוּ לְהִוָּשַׁע בָּהּ; 11 עַל כֵּן אֱלֹהִים שׁוֹלֵחַ לָהֶם מַדּוּחִים לְהַטְעוֹתָם לְהַאֲמִין לַשֶּׁקֶר, 12 לְמַעַן יִדּוֹנוּ כָּל אֲשֶׁר לֹא הֶאֱמִינוּ לָאֱמֶת אֶלָּא חָפְצוּ בָּעַוְלָה.

13 חַיָּבִים אָנוּ לְהוֹדוֹת לֵאלֹהִים עֲלֵיכֶם בְּכָל עֵת, אַחַי אֲהוּבֵי הָאָדוֹן, כִּי מֵרֵאשִׁית בָּחַר בָּכֶם אֱלֹהִים לִישׁוּעָה בְּקִדּוּשׁ עַל-יְדֵי הָרוּחַ וּבֶאֱמוּנָה בָּאֱמֶת; 14 וּבְאֶמְצָעוּת בְּשׂוֹרָתֵנוּ אַף קָרָא אֶתְכֶם לְנַחֲלָה בְּתִפְאַרְתּוֹ שֶׁל אֲדוֹנֵנוּ יֵשׁוּעַ הַמָּשִׁיחַ. 15 לְפִיכָךְ, אַחַי, עִמְדוּ עֲמִידָה אֵיתָנָה וְהַחֲזִיקוּ בַּמְּסוֹרוֹת שֶׁלֻּמַּדְתֶּם הֵן עַל-יְדֵי דְּבָרִים שֶׁאָמַרְנוּ וְהֵן עַל-יְדֵי אִגֶּרֶת שֶׁכָּתַבְנוּ. 16 וְהוּא, אֲדוֹנֵנוּ יֵשׁוּעַ הַמָּשִׁיחַ, וֵאלֹהִים אָבִינוּ, אֲשֶׁר אָהַב אוֹתָנוּ וּבְחַסְדּוֹ נָתַן לָנוּ נֶחָמַת עוֹלָם וְתִקְוָה טוֹבָה, 17 הוּא יְנַחֵם אֶת לְבַבְכֶם וִיכוֹנֵן אֶתְכֶם בְּכָל דִּבּוּר אוֹ מַעֲשֶׂה טוֹב.

ג סוֹף דָּבָר, אַחַי, הִתְפַּלְּלוּ בַּעֲדֵנוּ שֶׁדְּבַר הָאָדוֹן יוּפַץ מַהֵר וִיכֻבַּד, כְּמוֹ אֶצְלְכֶם, 2 וְשֶׁנִּנָּצֵל מֵאֲנָשִׁים רָעִים וּרְשָׁעִים, שֶׁהֲרֵי לֹא לְכָל בְּנֵי אָדָם הָאֱמוּנָה. 3 אֲבָל נֶאֱמָן הָאָדוֹן וְהוּא יְחַזֵּק אֶתְכֶם וְיִשְׁמֹר אֶתְכֶם מִן הָרָע. 4 אֲנַחְנוּ בְּטוּחִים בָּאָדוֹן בְּנוֹגֵעַ אֲלֵיכֶם, שֶׁאַתֶּם עוֹשִׂים וְאַף תּוֹסִיפוּ לַעֲשׂוֹת אֶת מַה שֶׁצִּוִּינוּ. 5 יְכוֹנֵן הָאָדוֹן אֶת לְבַבְכֶם לְאַהֲבַת אֱלֹהִים וּלְסַבְלָנוּת הַמָּשִׁיחַ.

6 אָנוּ מְצַוִּים אֶתְכֶם, אַחִים, בְּשֵׁם הָאָדוֹן יֵשׁוּעַ הַמָּשִׁיחַ, לְהִבָּדֵל מִכָּל אָח שֶׁהוֹלֵךְ בָּטֵל וְאֵינֶנּוּ מִתְנַהֵג לְפִי הַמָּסוֹרוֹת שֶׁקִּבַּלְתֶּם מֵאִתָּנוּ. 7 הֲרֵי אַתֶּם יוֹדְעִים שֶׁמָּן הָרָאוּי לְהִתְנַהֵג כָּמוֹנוּ, שֶׁכֵּן לֹא הוֹלַכְנוּ

worked with labor and toil night and day, that we might not be a burden to any of you, [9] not because we do not have authority, but to make ourselves an example of how you should follow us.

[10] For even when we were with you, we commanded you this: If anyone will not work, neither shall he eat. [11] For we hear that there are some who walk among you in a disorderly manner, not working at all, but are busybodies. [12] Now those who are such we command and exhort through our Lord Jesus Christ that they work in quietness and eat their own bread.

[13] But *as for* you, brethren, do not grow weary *in* doing good. [14] And if anyone does not obey our word in this epistle, note that person and do not keep company with him, that he may be ashamed. [15] Yet do not count *him* as an enemy, but admonish *him* as a brother.

[16] Now may the Lord of peace Himself give you peace always in every way. The Lord *be* with you all.

[17] The salutation of Paul with my own hand, which is a sign in every epistle; so I write.

[18] The grace of our Lord Jesus Christ *be* with you all. Amen.

בָּטֵל הָיִינוּ בְּתוֹכְכֶם. 8 גַּם לֹא אָכַלְנוּ לֶחֶם חִנָּם מִידֵי אִישׁ, אֶלָּא בְּעָמָל וָיֶגַע עָבַדְנוּ יוֹמָם וָלַיְלָה כְּדֵי שֶׁלֹּא נִהְיֶה לְמַשָּׂא עַל אִישׁ מִכֶּם; 9 לֹא שֶׁאֵין לָנוּ זְכוּת לְכָךְ, אֶלָּא כְּדֵי שֶׁאֲנַחְנוּ נִהְיֶה לָכֶם לְמוֹפֵת וְתִתְנַהֲגוּ כָּמוֹנוּ. 10 הֵן גַּם כַּאֲשֶׁר הָיִינוּ אֶצְלְכֶם, זֹאת צִוִּינוּ אֶתְכֶם: מִי שֶׁאֵינוֹ רוֹצֶה לַעֲבֹד, גַּם אַל יֹאכַל; 11 כִּי שָׁמַעְנוּ שֶׁיֵּשׁ הוֹלְכֵי בָּטֵל בֵּינֵיכֶם שֶׁאֵינָם עוֹבְדִים כְּלָל, אֶלָּא מִתְעַסְּקִים בַּהֲבָלִים. 12 אֲנַחְנוּ מְצַוִּים עַל אוֹתָם הָאֲנָשִׁים וְדוֹרְשִׁים מֵהֶם בְּשֵׁם הָאָדוֹן יֵשׁוּעַ הַמָּשִׁיחַ, שֶׁיַּעַבְדוּ בְּנַחַת וְיֹאכְלוּ אֶת לַחְמָם שֶׁלָּהֶם. 13 וְאַתֶּם, אַחַי, אַל יִרְפּוּ יְדֵיכֶם בַּעֲשִׂיַּת הַטּוֹב. 14 אִם מִישֶׁהוּ לֹא יִצַּיֵּת לַדְּבָרִים שֶׁכָּתַבְנוּ בָּאִגֶּרֶת, צַיְּנוּ לָכֶם אֶת הָאִישׁ הַזֶּה וְאַל תִּתְעָרְבוּ עִמּוֹ, לְמַעַן יֵבוֹשׁ. 15 אֲבָל אַל תַּחְשְׁבוּהוּ לְאוֹיֵב, אֶלָּא הוֹכִיחוּ אוֹתוֹ כְּאָח.

16 וַאֲדוֹן הַשָּׁלוֹם יִתֵּן לָכֶם אֶת הַשָּׁלוֹם, תָּמִיד וּבְכָל מָקוֹם. הָאָדוֹן עִם כֻּלְּכֶם. 17 פְּרִיסַת שָׁלוֹם בְּמוֹ כְתַב יָדִי, אֲנִי שָׁאוּל. זֶהוּ הַסִּימָן בְּכָל אִגְּרוֹתַי; כָּךְ אֲנִי כּוֹתֵב. 18 חֶסֶד אֲדוֹנֵנוּ יֵשׁוּעַ הַמָּשִׁיחַ עִם כֻּלְּכֶם.

The First Epistle of Paul to

TIMOTHY

1 Paul, an apostle of Jesus Christ, by the commandment of God our Savior and the Lord Jesus Christ, our hope,

² To Timothy, a true son in the faith:

Grace, mercy, *and* peace from God our Father and Jesus Christ our Lord.

³ As I urged you when I went into Macedonia—remain in Ephesus that you may charge some that they teach no other doctrine, ⁴ nor give heed to fables and endless genealogies, which cause disputes rather than godly edification which is in faith. ⁵ Now the purpose of the commandment is love from a pure heart, *from* a good conscience, and *from* sincere faith, ⁶ from which some, having strayed, have turned aside to idle talk, ⁷ desiring to be teachers of the law, understanding neither what they say nor the things which they affirm.

⁸ But we know that the law *is* good if one uses it lawfully, ⁹ knowing this: that the law is not made for a righteous person, but for *the* lawless and insubordinate, for *the* ungodly and for sinners, for *the* unholy and profane, for murderers of fathers and murderers of mothers, for manslayers, ¹⁰ for fornicators, for sodomites, for kidnappers, for liars, for perjurers, and if there is any other thing that is contrary to sound doctrine, ¹¹ according to the glorious gospel of the blessed God which was committed to my trust.

¹² And I thank Christ Jesus our Lord who has enabled me, because He counted me faithful, putting *me* into the ministry, ¹³ although I was formerly a blasphemer, a persecutor, and an insolent man; but I obtained mercy because I did *it* ignorantly in unbelief. ¹⁴ And the grace of our Lord was exceedingly abundant, with faith and love which are in Christ Jesus. ¹⁵ This *is* a faithful saying and worthy of all acceptance, that Christ Jesus came into the world to save sinners, of whom I am chief. ¹⁶ However, for this reason I obtained mercy, that in me first Jesus Christ might show all longsuffering, as a pattern to those who are going to believe on Him for everlasting life. ¹⁷ Now to the King eternal, immortal, invisible, to God who alone is wise, *be* honor and glory forever and ever. Amen.

¹⁸ This charge I commit to you, son Timothy, according to the prophecies previously made concerning you, that by them you may wage the good

אִגֶּרֶת שָׁאוּל הָרִאשׁוֹנָה אֶל טִימוֹתִיאוֹס

א מֵאֵת שָׁאוּל, שְׁלִיחַ הַמָּשִׁיחַ יֵשׁוּעַ עַל־פִּי מִצְוַת הָאֱלֹהִים מוֹשִׁיעֵנוּ וְהַמָּשִׁיחַ יֵשׁוּעַ תִּקְוָתֵנוּ, ² אֶל טִימוֹתִיאוֹס בְּנִי הָאֲמִתִּי בָּאֱמוּנָה: חֶסֶד וְרַחֲמִים וְשָׁלוֹם מֵאֵת אֱלֹהִים אָבִינוּ וְהַמָּשִׁיחַ יֵשׁוּעַ אֲדוֹנֵנוּ. ³ כַּאֲשֶׁר הָלַכְתִּי לְמַקֶּדוֹנְיָה בִּקַּשְׁתִּי מִמְּךָ לְהִשָּׁאֵר בְּאֶפְסוֹס וּלְצַוּוֹת עַל כַּמָּה אֲנָשִׁים שֶׁלֹּא יוֹרוּ תּוֹרָה אַחֶרֶת, ⁴ וְלֹא יִתְּנוּ לִבָּם לַאֲגָדוֹת וּלְסִפּוּרִים אֵין קֵץ עַל תּוֹלְדוֹת הַדּוֹרוֹת, דְּבָרִים הַנּוֹתְנִים מָקוֹם לְחִטּוּטִים וּכְוּוּחִים יוֹתֵר מֵאֲשֶׁר לְתַכְנִית אֱלֹהִים שֶׁיְּסוֹדָהּ בָּאֱמוּנָה. ⁵ תַּכְלִיתָהּ שֶׁל הַמִּצְוָה הַזֹּאת הִיא הָאַהֲבָה הַנּוֹבַעַת מִלֵּב טָהוֹר, מִמַּצְפּוּן יָשָׁר וּמֵאֱמוּנָה אֲמִתִּית. ⁶ יֵשׁ שֶׁסָּטוּ מִזֶּה וּפָנוּ לְדִבּוּרֵי הֶבֶל; ⁷ רְצוֹנָם לִהְיוֹת מוֹרֵי תּוֹרָה, אַךְ אֵין הֵם מְבִינִים לֹא אֶת מַה שֶּׁהֵם אוֹמְרִים וְלֹא אֶת מַה שֶּׁהֵם טוֹעֲנִים בְּתֹקֶף.

⁸ אֲנַחְנוּ יוֹדְעִים שֶׁהַתּוֹרָה טוֹבָה אִם חַיִּים בָּהּ לְפִי חֻקָּהּ. ⁹ זֹאת יוֹדְעִים אָנוּ, שֶׁחֹק אֵינוֹ נִקְבַּע בִּשְׁבִיל אָדָם צַדִּיק, אֶלָּא מְכֻוָּן הוּא לְמַפְקִרִים וּלְסוֹרְרִים, לִרְשָׁעִים וּלְחַטָּאִים, לִטְמֵאִים וְעוֹשֵׂי תּוֹעֵבָה, לְרוֹצְחֵי אָב וָאֵם וְלִמְרַצְּחִים, ¹⁰ לְזוֹנִים וּלְשׁוֹכְבֵי זָכָר, לְחוֹטְפֵי אָדָם וְשַׁקְרָנִים וְנִשְׁבָּעִים לַשֶּׁקֶר, לְכָל מַה שֶּׁנּוֹגֵד אֶת הַתּוֹרָה הַבְּרִיאָה ¹¹ אֲשֶׁר עַל־פִּי בְּשׂוֹרַת הַכָּבוֹד שֶׁל אֱלֹהִים הַמְבֹרָךְ, הִיא הַבְּשׂוֹרָה שֶׁהֻפְקְדָה בְּיָדִי.

¹² אֲנִי מַכִּיר טוֹבָה לַנּוֹתֵן בִּי כֹּחַ, לַמָּשִׁיחַ יֵשׁוּעַ אֲדוֹנֵנוּ, כִּי חֲשָׁבַנִי נֶאֱמָן וּמִנָּה אוֹתִי לְשֵׁרוּתוֹ, ¹³ אַף שֶׁקֹּדֶם לָכֵן הָיִיתִי מְגַדֵּף, רוֹדֵף וּמְבַזֶּה. אֲבָל רֻחַמְתִּי מִפְּנֵי שֶׁבְּהֱיוֹתִי חֲסַר אֱמוּנָה פָּעַלְתִּי בְּלִי דַעַת, ¹⁴ וְחֶסֶד אֲדוֹנֵנוּ שָׁפַע עָלַי יַחַד עִם אֱמוּנָה וְאַהֲבָה אֲשֶׁר בַּמָּשִׁיחַ יֵשׁוּעַ. ¹⁵ מְהֵימָן הַדָּבָר וְרָאוּי לְהַסְכָּמָה מְלֵאָה, שֶׁהַמָּשִׁיחַ יֵשׁוּעַ בָּא אֶל הָעוֹלָם לְהוֹשִׁיעַ חוֹטְאִים אֲשֶׁר אֲנִי הַגָּדוֹל בָּהֶם. ¹⁶ וְאוּלָם מִשּׁוּם כָּךְ רֻחַמְתִּי, כְּדֵי שֶׁבִּי בָּרִאשׁוֹנָה יַרְאֶה יֵשׁוּעַ הַמָּשִׁיחַ אֶת כָּל אֹרֶךְ רוּחוֹ, כְּמוֹפֵת לָעֲתִידִים לְהַאֲמִין בּוֹ לְשֵׁם חַיֵּי עוֹלָם. ¹⁷ לְמֶלֶךְ הָעוֹלָמִים, הַקַּיָּם לְאֵין קֵץ וְהַבִּלְתִּי נִרְאֶה, אֲשֶׁר הוּא לְבַדּוֹ הָאֱלֹהִים, לוֹ הַכָּבוֹד וְהַתִּפְאֶרֶת לְעוֹלְמֵי עוֹלָמִים. אָמֵן.

¹⁸ אֶת הַמִּצְוָה הַזֹּאת אֲנִי מוֹסֵר לְךָ, טִימוֹתִיאוֹס בְּנִי,

warfare, ¹⁹having faith and a good conscience, which some having rejected, concerning the faith have suffered shipwreck, ²⁰of whom are Hymenaeus and Alexander, whom I delivered to Satan that they may learn not to blaspheme.

2 Therefore I exhort first of all that supplications, prayers, intercessions, *and* giving of thanks be made for all men, ²for kings and all who are in authority, that we may lead a quiet and peaceable life in all godliness and reverence. ³For this *is* good and acceptable in the sight of God our Savior, ⁴who desires all men to be saved and to come to the knowledge of the truth. ⁵For *there is* one God and one Mediator between God and men, *the* Man Christ Jesus, ⁶who gave Himself a ransom for all, to be testified in due time, ⁷for which I was appointed a preacher and an apostle—I am speaking the truth in Christ *and* not lying—a teacher of the Gentiles in faith and truth.

⁸I desire therefore that the men pray everywhere, lifting up holy hands, without wrath and doubting; ⁹in like manner also, that the women adorn themselves in modest apparel, with propriety and moderation, not with braided hair or gold or pearls or costly clothing, ¹⁰but, which is proper for women professing godliness, with good works. ¹¹Let a woman learn in silence with all submission. ¹²And I do not permit a woman to teach or to have authority over a man, but to be in silence. ¹³For Adam was formed first, then Eve. ¹⁴And Adam was not deceived, but the woman being deceived, fell into transgression. ¹⁵Nevertheless she will be saved in childbearing if they continue in faith, love, and holiness, with self-control.

3 This *is* a faithful saying: If a man desires the position of a bishop, he desires a good work. ²A bishop then must be blameless, the husband of one wife, temperate, sober-minded, of good behavior, hospitable, able to teach; ³not given to wine, not violent, not greedy for money, but gentle, not quarrelsome, not covetous; ⁴one who rules his own house well, having *his* children in submission with all reverence ⁵(for if a man does not know how to rule his own house, how will he take care of the church of God?); ⁶not a novice, lest being puffed up with pride he fall into the *same* condemnation as the devil. ⁷Moreover he must have a good testimony among those who are outside, lest he fall into reproach and the snare of the devil.

עַל־פִּי נְבוּאוֹת מִן הֶעָבָר הַנּוֹגְעוֹת אֵלֶיךָ, כְּדֵי שֶׁתִּלָּחֵם בְּעֶזְרָתָן אֶת הַמִּלְחָמָה הַטּוֹבָה, ¹⁹מִתּוֹךְ אֱמוּנָה וּמַצְפּוּן יָשָׁר. יֵשׁ שֶׁהִשְׁלִיכוּ מֵעֲלֵיהֶם אֶת אֵלֶּה וְנִשְׁבְּרָה סְפִינַת אֱמוּנָתָם; ²⁰וּמֵהֶם הִימֶנָאוּס וַאֲלֶכְּסַנְדֶּר אֲשֶׁר מָסַרְתִּי אוֹתָם לַשָּׂטָן לְמַעַן יִחָנְכוּ שֶׁלֹּא לְגַדֵּף.

ב קֹדֶם כֹּל אֲנִי מְבַקֵּשׁ מִכֶּם לָשֵׂאת תְּחִנּוֹת וּתְפִלּוֹת וּבַקָּשׁוֹת וְהוֹדָיוֹת בְּעַד כָּל בְּנֵי אָדָם, ²בְּעַד מְלָכִים וְכָל רָאשֵׁי הַשִּׁלְטוֹן, לְמַעַן נִחְיֶה חַיֵּי שַׁלְוָה וְהַשְׁקֵט בְּמִלּוֹא חֲסִידוּת וְדֶרֶךְ אֶרֶץ. ³טוֹב הַדָּבָר הַזֶּה וְרָצוּי בְּעֵינֵי אֱלֹהִים מוֹשִׁיעֵנוּ, ⁴הֶחָפֵץ שֶׁכָּל בְּנֵי אָדָם יִוָּשְׁעוּ וְיַגִּיעוּ לְהַכָּרַת הָאֱמֶת. ⁵הֵן אֶחָד הָאֱלֹהִים, וְאֶחָד הַמְתַוֵּךְ בֵּין אֱלֹהִים לִבְנֵי אָדָם – הָאָדָם הַמָּשִׁיחַ יֵשׁוּעַ, ⁶אֲשֶׁר נָתַן אֶת עַצְמוֹ כֹּפֶר בְּעַד הַכֹּל. אֶת הָעֵדוּת בְּעִתּוֹתֶיהָ, ⁷אֲשֶׁר אֲנִי נִתְמַנֵּיתִי לָהּ לְכָרוֹז וּלְשָׁלִיחַ – אֱמֶת אֲנִי מְדַבֵּר, אֵינֶנִּי מְשַׁקֵּר – לְמוֹרֶה אֱמוּנָה וֶאֱמֶת לַגּוֹיִים. ⁸רְצוֹנִי שֶׁהָאֲנָשִׁים יִתְפַּלְּלוּ בְּכָל מָקוֹם בִּנְשִׂיאַת יָדַיִם טְהוֹרוֹת, בְּלֹא כַּעַס וּבְלֹא מַחֲלֹקֶת. ⁹כְּמוֹ כֵן תַּעֲטֶינָה הַנָּשִׁים תִּלְבֹּשֶׁת הוֹלֶמֶת, בִּצְנִיעוּת וּבְאִפּוּק; לֹא בְּהִתְנַגְדְרוּת שֵׂעָר, לֹא בְּזָהָב וּפְנִינִים, וְלֹא בְּמַלְבּוּשִׁים יְקָרִים, ¹⁰אֶלָּא בְּמַה שֶׁיָּאֶה לְנָשִׁים הַמַּצְדִּירוֹת עַל יִרְאַת שָׁמַיִם – בְּמַעֲשִׂים טוֹבִים. ¹¹הָאִשָּׁה תִּלְמַד בְּדוּמִיָּה, בְּהִכָּנְעָה שְׁלֵמָה. ¹²אֵינֶנִּי מַרְשֶׁה לָאִשָּׁה לְלַמֵּד, אַף לֹא לְהִשְׁתָּרֵר עַל הָאִישׁ, אֶלָּא לְהִשָּׁאֵר בְּדוּמִיָּה; ¹³כִּי אָדָם נוֹצַר רִאשׁוֹנָה וְאַחֲרָיו כֵּן חַוָּה. ¹⁴אָדָם לֹא נִפְתָּה, אֶלָּא הָאִשָּׁה שָׁמְעָה לְקוֹל הַמְפַתֶּה וּבָאָה לִידֵי עֲבֵרָה. ¹⁵אֲבָל הִיא תִּוָּשַׁע בְּלִדְתָּהּ יְלָדִים, אִם תַּעֲמֹד בָּאֱמוּנָה, בָּאַהֲבָה, בַּקְּדֻשָּׁה וּבַצְּנִיעוּת.

ג מְהֵימָן הַדָּבָר: אִישׁ הַשּׁוֹאֵף לִהְיוֹת מַנְהִיג בַּקְּהִלָּה, הֲרֵיהוּ מִשְׁתּוֹקֵק לַעֲבוֹדָה נַעֲלָה. ²לָכֵן הַמַּנְהִיג צָרִיךְ לִהְיוֹת אִישׁ שֶׁאֵין בּוֹ דֹּפִי, בַּעַל אִשָּׁה אַחַת, אִישׁ מִפֻּכָּח, מָאֻפָּק, מִתְנַהֵג בְּדֶרֶךְ אֶרֶץ, מַכְנִיס אוֹרְחִים, יוֹדֵעַ לְלַמֵּד; ³לֹא מִתְמַכֵּר לְיַיִן, לֹא בַּעַל אֶגְרוֹף אֶלָּא אָדָם הַנּוֹהֵג בְּסוֹבְלָנוּת, לֹא נִמְהָר לָרִיב וְלֹא רוֹדֵף כֶּסֶף; ⁴אָדָם שֶׁמַּנְהִיג הֵיטֵב אֶת בֵּיתוֹ שֶׁלּוֹ וּבָנָיו נִשְׁמָעִים לוֹ בְּמִלּוֹא דֶרֶךְ אֶרֶץ. ⁵הֲרֵי אִם לֹא יֵדַע אִישׁ לְנַהֵל אֶת בֵּיתוֹ שֶׁלּוֹ, כֵּיצַד יוּכַל לִדְאֹג לִקְהִלַּת אֱלֹהִים? ⁶וְאַל יְהֵא צָעִיר בָּאֱמוּנָה, פֶּן יִתְהַר וְיִפֹּל בְּדִין הַשָּׂטָן. ⁷הוּא צָרִיךְ גַּם לְשֵׁם טוֹב

8 Likewise deacons *must be* reverent, not double-tongued, not given to much wine, not greedy for money, 9 holding the mystery of the faith with a pure conscience. 10 But let these also first be tested; then let them serve as deacons, being *found* blameless. 11 Likewise, *their* wives *must be* reverent, not slanderers, temperate, faithful in all things. 12 Let deacons be the husbands of one wife, ruling *their* children and their own houses well. 13 For those who have served well as deacons obtain for themselves a good standing and great boldness in the faith which is in Christ Jesus.

14 These things I write to you, though I hope to come to you shortly; 15 but if I am delayed, *I write* so that you may know how you ought to conduct yourself in the house of God, which is the church of the living God, the pillar and ground of the truth. 16 And without controversy great is the mystery of godliness:

God was manifested in the flesh,
Justified in the Spirit,
Seen by angels,
Preached among the Gentiles,
Believed on in the world,
Received up in glory.

4 Now the Spirit expressly says that in latter times some will depart from the faith, giving heed to deceiving spirits and doctrines of demons, 2 speaking lies in hypocrisy, having their own conscience seared with a hot iron, 3 forbidding to marry, *and commanding* to abstain from foods which God created to be received with thanksgiving by those who believe and know the truth. 4 For every creature of God *is* good, and nothing is to be refused if it is received with thanksgiving; 5 for it is sanctified by the word of God and prayer.

6 If you instruct the brethren in these things, you will be a good minister of Jesus Christ, nourished in the words of faith and of the good doctrine which you have carefully followed. 7 But reject profane and old wives' fables, and exercise yourself toward godliness. 8 For bodily exercise profits a little, but godliness is profitable for all things, having promise of the life that now is and of that which is to come. 9 This *is* a faithful saying and worthy of all acceptance. 10 For to this *end* we both labor and suffer reproach, because we trust in the living God, who is *the* Savior of all men, especially of those who believe. 11 These things command and teach.

12 Let no one despise your youth, but be an example to the believers in word, in conduct, in love, in spirit, in faith, in purity. 13 Till I come, give

בְּפִי אֵלֶּה שֶׁבַּחוּץ, כְּדֵי שֶׁלֹּא יִהְיֶה לְחֶרְפָּה וְלֹא יִפֹּל בְּפַח הַשָּׂטָן. 8 כֵּן גַּם הַשַּׁמָּשִׁים צְרִיכִים לִהְיוֹת אֲנָשִׁים רְצִינִיִּים; לֹא הֲפַכְפְּכָנִים בְּדִבּוּרָם, לֹא מִתְמַכְּרִים לַיַּיִן וְלֹא רוֹדְפֵי בֶּצַע, 9 אֶלָּא אֲנָשִׁים הַמַּחֲזִיקִים אֶת סוֹד הָאֱמוּנָה בְּמַצְפּוּן טָהוֹר. 10 הַלָּלוּ יִבָּחֲנוּ תְּחִלָּה; אַחֲרֵי שֶׁיִּמָּצֵא שֶׁאֵין בָּהֶם דֹּפִי יְשָׁרְתוּ כְּשַׁמָּשִׁים. 11 כְּמוֹ כֵן הַנָּשִׁים; עֲלֵיהֶן לִהְיוֹת רְצִינִיּוֹת, נִמְנָעוֹת מִלְּשׁוֹן הָרָע, מִפֻּכָּחוֹת, נֶאֱמָנוֹת בְּכָל דָּבָר. 12 הַשַּׁמָּשׁ יִהְיֶה בַּעַל אִשָּׁה אַחַת, אָדָם שֶׁמַּנְהִיג הֵיטֵב אֶת בָּנָיו וְאֶת בֵּיתוֹ. 13 הַמֵּיטִיבִים לְשָׁרֵת מַשִּׂיגִים לְעַצְמָם מַעֲמָד טוֹב וּבִטָּחוֹן רַב בָּאֱמוּנָה בַּמָּשִׁיחַ יֵשׁוּעַ.

14 אֲנִי כּוֹתֵב לְךָ אֶת הַדְּבָרִים הָאֵלֶּה בְּתִקְוָה לָבוֹא אֵלֶיךָ בִּמְהֵרָה. 15 אֲבָל אִם אִתְמַהְמֵהַּ, הִנֵּה תֵּדַע כֵּיצַד לְהִתְנַהֵג בְּבֵית אֱלֹהִים, אֲשֶׁר הוּא קְהִלַּת אֱלֹהִים חַיִּים, עַמּוּד הָאֱמֶת וִיסוֹדָהּ. 16 אָכֵן גָּדוֹל סוֹד הַחֲסִידוּת:

הִתְגַּלָּה בַּבָּשָׂר,
הַצֻּדַּק בָּרוּחַ, נִרְאָה לַמַּלְאָכִים,
הֻגַּד בַּגּוֹיִים, הֶאֱמִינוּ בּוֹ בָּעוֹלָם,
הֹעֲלָה לַמָּרוֹם בְּכָבוֹד.

ד הָרוּחַ אוֹמֶרֶת בְּפֵרוּשׁ, שֶׁבְּרַבּוֹת הַיָּמִים יָסֹטוּ אֲנָשִׁים מִן הָאֱמוּנָה וְיִפְנוּ לְרוּחוֹת מַטְעוֹת וּלְתוֹרוֹת שֶׁל שֵׁדִים, 2 בְּאַמְצָעוּת מַטִּיפֵי כָּזָב מִתְחַסְּדִים אֲשֶׁר מַצְפּוּנָם שֶׁלָּהֶם קָהָה כְּחֻשִּׁים שֶׁקָּהוּ בְּבַרְזֶל מְלֻבָּן. 3 הַלָּלוּ יֹאסְרוּ לָשֵׂאת אִשָּׁה וְיִטִּילוּ אִסּוּר עַל מִינֵי מַאֲכָל אֲשֶׁר בְּרָאָם אֱלֹהִים לְמַעַן יֹאכְלוּם בְּתוֹדָה הַמַּאֲמִינִים וְיוֹדְעֵי הָאֱמֶת. 4 הֵן כָּל מַה שֶּׁבָּרָא אֱלֹהִים טוֹב הוּא, וְאֵין לִפְסֹל דָּבָר אִם אוֹכְלִים אוֹתוֹ בִּבְרָכָה, 5 שֶׁכֵּן הוּא מְקֻדָּשׁ בִּדְבַר אֱלֹהִים וּבִתְפִלָּה. 6 אִם תּוֹרֶה אֶת הַדְּבָרִים הָאֵלֶּה לָאַחִים, תִּהְיֶה מְשָׁרֵת טוֹב לַמָּשִׁיחַ יֵשׁוּעַ, מְשָׁרֵת הַנִּזּוֹן מִדִּבְרֵי הָאֱמוּנָה וּמֵהַתּוֹרָה הַטּוֹבָה שֶׁדָּבַקְתָּ בָּהּ. 7 אוּלָם הִתְרַחֵק מֵאַגָּדוֹת טִפְּלוֹת וּנְפָסְדוֹת. אַמֵּן אֶת עַצְמְךָ לַחֲסִידוּת, 8 שֶׁהֲרֵי הִתְאַמְּנוּת הַגּוּפָנִית מוֹעִילָה בְּמִדָּה מְעַטָּה, אֲבָל הַחֲסִידוּת מוֹעִילָה בַּכֹּל וּבָהּ הַבְטָחָה לַחַיִּים שֶׁבַּהֹוֶה וְלַחַיִּים שֶׁלֶּעָתִיד לָבוֹא. 9 מְהֵימָן הַדָּבָר הַזֶּה וְרָאוּי לְהִסָּכְמָה מְלֵאָה — 10 וְאָמְנָם לְשֵׁם כָּךְ אֲנַחְנוּ עֲמֵלִים וְנֶאֱבָקִים — שֶׁתִּקְוָתֵנוּ הִיא בֵּאלֹהִים חַיִּים אֲשֶׁר הוּא הַמּוֹשִׁיעַ שֶׁל כָּל בְּנֵי אָדָם, בְּיִחוּד שֶׁל הַמַּאֲמִינִים. 11 אֶת הַדְּבָרִים הָאֵלֶּה תְּצַוֶּה וּתְלַמֵּד. 12 אַל יָבוּז לְךָ אִישׁ בְּשֶׁל צְעִירוּתְךָ. וְאוּלָם הֱיֵה מוֹפֵת לַמַּאֲמִינִים, בְּדִבּוּר, בְּהִתְנַהֲגוּת, בְּאַהֲבָה, בָּאֱמוּנָה וּבְטָהֳרָה. 13 שְׁקֹד עַל קְרִיאָה בְּצִבּוּר שֶׁל כִּתְבֵי הַקֹּדֶשׁ, עַל

attention to reading, to exhortation, to doctrine.
[14] Do not neglect the gift that is in you, which was
given to you by prophecy with the laying on of the
hands of the eldership. [15] Meditate on these things;
give yourself entirely to them, that your progress
may be evident to all. [16] Take heed to yourself and
to the doctrine. Continue in them, for in doing this
you will save both yourself and those who hear you.

5 Do not rebuke an older man, but exhort *him* as a
father, younger men as brothers, [2] older women as
mothers, younger women as sisters, with all purity.

[3] Honor widows who are really widows. [4] But if
any widow has children or grandchildren, let them
first learn to show piety at home and to repay their
parents; for this is good and acceptable before God.
[5] Now she who is really a widow, and left alone,
trusts in God and continues in supplications and
prayers night and day. [6] But she who lives in
pleasure is dead while she lives. [7] And these things
command, that they may be blameless. [8] But if
anyone does not provide for his own, and especially
for those of his household, he has denied the faith
and is worse than an unbeliever.

[9] Do not let a widow under sixty years old be
taken into the number, *and not unless* she has been
the wife of one man, [10] well reported for good
works: if she has brought up children, if she has
lodged strangers, if she has washed the saints' feet,
if she has relieved the afflicted, if she has diligently
followed every good work.

[11] But refuse *the* younger widows; for when they
have begun to grow wanton against Christ, they
desire to marry, [12] having condemnation because
they have cast off their first faith. [13] And besides
they learn *to be* idle, wandering about from house
to house, and not only idle but also gossips and
busybodies, saying things which they ought not.
[14] Therefore I desire that *the* younger *widows* marry,
bear children, manage the house, give no opportunity to the adversary to speak reproachfully. [15] For
some have already turned aside after Satan. [16] If any
believing man or woman has widows, let them
relieve them, and do not let the church be burdened,
that it may relieve those who are really widows.

[17] Let the elders who rule well be counted worthy
of double honor, especially those who labor in the
word and doctrine. [18] For the Scripture says, *"You
shall not muzzle an ox while it treads out the grain,"*
and, *"The laborer is worthy of his wages."* [19] Do
not receive an accusation against an elder except
from two or three witnesses. [20] Those who are
sinning rebuke in the presence of all, that the rest
also may fear.

הַהַטָּפָה וְעַל הַהוֹרָאָה – עַד שֶׁאָבוֹא. 14 אַל תַּזְנִיחַ
אֶת הַמַּתָּנָה אֲשֶׁר בְּךָ, שֶׁנִּתְּנָה לְךָ עַל-פִּי נְבוּאָה
בִּסְמִיכַת יְדֵיהֶם שֶׁל זִקְנֵי הַקְּהִלָּה. 15 שִׂים לְךָ אֶל
הַדְּבָרִים הָאֵלֶּה, הַתְמֵד בָּהֶם, לְמַעַן תֵּרָאֶה
הִתְקַדְּמוּתְךָ לַכֹּל. 16 הַשְׁגֵּחַ עַל עַצְמְךָ וְשִׂית לִבְּךָ
לַהוֹרָאָה. הַתְמֵד בָּזֶה, כִּי בַּעֲשׂוֹתְךָ כֵּן תּוֹשִׁיעַ גַּם
אֶת עַצְמְךָ וְגַם אֶת הַשּׁוֹמְעִים אֵלֶיךָ.

ה אַל תִּגְעַר בְּזָקֵן, כִּי אִם הַפְצֵר בּוֹ כְּבֵן הַפּוֹנֶה
לְאָבִיו. פְּנֵה אֶל הַצְּעִירִים כְּאֶל אַחִים, 2 אֶל הַזְּקֵנוֹת
כְּאֶל אִמָּהוֹת, וְאֶל הַצְּעִירוֹת כְּאֶל אֲחָיוֹת – בְּמִלּוֹא
הַטֹּהַר. 3 כַּבֵּד אֶת הָאַלְמָנוֹת אֲשֶׁר הֵן אָכֵן אַלְמָנוֹת.
4 וְאִם לְאַלְמָנָה יֵשׁ בָּנִים אוֹ בְּנֵי בָנִים, עֲלֵיהֶם קֹדֶם
כֹּל לִלְמֹד לַעֲשׂוֹת חֶסֶד עִם בֵּיתָם הֵם וּלְהָשִׁיב גְּמוּל
לְהוֹרֵיהֶם, כִּי כֵן רָצוּי לִפְנֵי אֱלֹהִים. 5 הָאִשָּׁה שֶׁהִיא
אָכֵן אַלְמָנָה וְנִשְׁאֲרָה לְבַדָּהּ, מְיַחֶלֶת לֵאלֹהִים
וּמַתְמִידָה בִּתְחִנּוֹת וּתְפִלּוֹת יוֹמָם וָלָיְלָה. 6 אַךְ זוֹ
שֶׁלְּוָה לְתַעֲנוּגוֹת, הֲרֵיהִי בְּבִחִינַת מֵתָה בְּחַיֶּיהָ.
7 אֶת הַדְּבָרִים הָאֵלֶּה תְּצַוֶּה, כְּדֵי שֶׁלֹּא יִמָּצֵא בָּהֶן
דֹּפִי. 8 וּמִי שֶׁאֵינוֹ דּוֹאֵג לִקְרוֹבָיו, בְּיִחוּד לִבְנֵי בֵיתוֹ,
כָּפַר בָּאֱמוּנָה וְהוּא גָּרוּעַ מִמִּי שֶׁאֵינוֹ מַאֲמִין.
9 אַלְמָנָה לֹא תֵרָשֵׁם אֶלָּא אִם מָלְאוּ לָהּ שִׁשִּׁים
שָׁנָה וְהָיְתָה נְשׂוּאָה לְאִישׁ אֶחָד, 10 וְלִזְכוּתָהּ עֵדוּת
עַל מַעֲשִׂים טוֹבִים – שֶׁגִּדְּלָה בָנִים, הִכְנִיסָה
אוֹרְחִים, רָחֲצָה אֶת רַגְלֵי הַקְּדוֹשִׁים, הָיְתָה לְמֵעַד
לַסּוֹבְלִים וְהִתְמַסְּרָה לְכָל מַעֲשֶׂה טוֹב. 11 אַל תְּקַבֵּל
אַלְמָנוֹת צְעִירוֹת, כִּי כַּאֲשֶׁר הַיֵּצֶר שֶׁלָּהֶן נוֹטֶה מֵעִם
הַמָּשִׁיחַ הֵן רוֹצוֹת לְהִנָּשֵׂא, 12 וְנֶחֱרָץ עֲלֵיהֶן מִשְׁפָּט
מִפְּנֵי שֶׁהֵפֵרוּ אֶת הַבְטָחָתָן הָרִאשׁוֹנָה. 13 נוֹסָף עַל
כָּךְ הֵן מְשׁוֹטְטוֹת מִבַּיִת לְבַיִת וּמִתְרַגְּלוֹת לִהְיוֹת
בַּטְלָנִיּוֹת; וְלֹא בַּטְלָנִיּוֹת בִּלְבַד, אֶלָּא גַם רַכְלָנִיּוֹת
וּמִתְעָרְבוֹת בְּעִנְיָנִים לֹא לָהֶן וּמְדַבְּרוֹת דְּבָרִים שֶׁאֵין
צֹרֶךְ לְהַשְׁמִיעָם. 14 לָכֵן רְצוֹנִי שֶׁהָאַלְמָנוֹת הַצְּעִירוֹת
תִּנָּשֶׂאנָה, תֵּלַדְנָה יְלָדִים, תְּנַהֵלְנָה אֶת הַבַּיִת וְלֹא
תִּתֵּנָּה בְּיַד הַמִּתְנַגֵּד שׁוּם תּוֹאֲנָה לַקָּטֵרוּג, 15 כִּי יֵשׁ
מֵהֶן שֶׁכְּבָר סָרוּ אַחֲרֵי הַשָּׂטָן. 16 אִם לְמַאֲמִין אוֹ
לְמַאֲמִינָה יֵשׁ אַלְמָנוֹת בְּמִשְׁפַּחְתָּם, יַעַזְרוּ לָהֶן; אַל
תִּהְיֶינָה לְמַשָּׂא עַל הַקְּהִלָּה; כָּךְ תּוּכַל הַקְּהִלָּה לַעֲזֹר
לָאַלְמָנוֹת הָרְשׁוּמוֹת.

17 הַזְּקֵנִים הַמֵּיטִיבִים לְנַהֵל רְאוּיִים לְמִשְׁנֶה כָּבוֹד,
בְּעִקָּר הָעֲמֵלִים בְּהַטָּפַת הַדָּבָר וּבַהוֹרָאָה. 18 הֵן
הַכָּתוּב אוֹמֵר: "לֹא תַחְסֹם שׁוֹר בְּדִישׁוֹ", וְגַם
"הַפּוֹעֵל רָאוּי לִשְׂכָרוֹ". 19 אַל תְּקַבֵּל דְּבַר קִטְרוּג עַל
זָקֵן, בִּלְתִּי אִם עַל-פִּי שְׁנַיִם אוֹ שְׁלֹשָׁה עֵדִים. 20 אֶת

²¹ I charge *you* before God and the Lord Jesus Christ and the elect angels that you observe these things without prejudice, doing nothing with partiality. ²² Do not lay hands on anyone hastily, nor share in other people's sins; keep yourself pure.

²³ No longer drink only water, but use a little wine for your stomach's sake and your frequent infirmities.

²⁴ Some men's sins are clearly evident, preceding *them* to judgment, but those of some *men* follow later. ²⁵ Likewise, the good works *of some* are clearly evident, and those that are otherwise cannot be hidden.

6 Let as many bondservants as are under the yoke count their own masters worthy of all honor, so that the name of God and *His* doctrine may not be blasphemed. ² And those who have believing masters, let them not despise *them* because they are brethren, but rather serve *them* because those who are benefited are believers and beloved. Teach and exhort these things.

³ If anyone teaches otherwise and does not consent to wholesome words, *even* the words of our Lord Jesus Christ, and to the doctrine which accords with godliness, ⁴ he is proud, knowing nothing, but is obsessed with disputes and arguments over words, from which come envy, strife, reviling, evil suspicions, ⁵ useless wranglings of men of corrupt minds and destitute of the truth, who suppose that godliness is a *means of* gain. From such withdraw yourself.

⁶ Now godliness with contentment is great gain. ⁷ For we brought nothing into *this* world, *and it is* certain we can carry nothing out. ⁸ And having food and clothing, with these we shall be content. ⁹ But those who desire to be rich fall into temptation and a snare, and *into* many foolish and harmful lusts which drown men in destruction and perdition. ¹⁰ For the love of money is a root of all *kinds of* evil, for which some have strayed from the faith in their greediness, and pierced themselves through with many sorrows.

¹¹ But you, O man of God, flee these things and pursue righteousness, godliness, faith, love, patience, gentleness. ¹² Fight the good fight of faith, lay hold on eternal life, to which you were also called and have confessed the good confession in the presence of many witnesses. ¹³ I urge you in the sight of God who gives life to all things, and *before* Christ Jesus who witnessed the good confession before Pontius Pilate, ¹⁴ that you keep *this* commandment without spot, blameless until our Lord Jesus Christ's appearing, ¹⁵ which He will manifest

הַחוֹטְאִים תּוֹכִיחַ לְעֵינֵי כֹל, לְמַעַן תִּהְיֶה יִרְאָה גַּם בְּלֵב הָאֲחֵרִים. ²¹ הִנְנִי מֵעִיד בְּךָ לִפְנֵי אֱלֹהִים וְהַמָּשִׁיחַ יֵשׁוּעַ וְלִפְנֵי הַמַּלְאָכִים הַבְּחִירִים, שֶׁתַּקְפִּיד לְקַיֵּם אֶת הַדְּבָרִים הָאֵלֶּה בְּלִי לַחֲרֹץ מִשְׁפָּט מֵרֹאשׁ, וְאַל תַּעֲשֶׂה דָבָר כְּמַשּׂוֹא פָנִים. ²² אַל תְּמַהֵר לִסְמֹךְ יָדַיִם עַל אִישׁ, וְאַל תְּהֵא שֻׁתָּף לַחֲטָאֵי אֲחֵרִים. הִשָּׁמֵר לִהְיוֹת טָהוֹר. ²³ אַל תּוֹסִיף לִשְׁתּוֹת רַק מַיִם, כִּי אִם שְׁתֵה קְצָת יַיִן בִּגְלַל קֵבָתְךָ וּמַחֲלוֹתֶיךָ הַתְּכוּפוֹת.

²⁴ יֵשׁ בְּנֵי אָדָם שֶׁחֲטָאֵיהֶם גְּלוּיִים עוֹד לִפְנֵי הַמִּשְׁפָּט, אַךְ יֵשׁ שֶׁחֲטָאֵיהֶם מִתְבָּרְרִים אַחֲרֵי כֵן. ²⁵ כָּךְ גְּלוּיִים גַּם הַמַּעֲשִׂים הַטּוֹבִים; וְאֵלֶּה שֶׁאֵינָם גְּלוּיִים לֹא יוּכְלוּ לְהֵחָבֵא.

ו כָּל הַנִּמְצָאִים תַּחַת עֹל הָעַבְדוּת יַחְשְׁבוּ נָא אֶת אֲדוֹנֵיהֶם רְאוּיִים לִמְלוֹא כָּבוֹד, לְמַעַן לֹא יְגֻדַּף שֵׁם אֱלֹהִים וְלֹא תְּגֻדַּף תּוֹרָתֵנוּ. ² וְאֵלֶּה אֲשֶׁר אֲדוֹנֵיהֶם מַאֲמִינִים, אַל יָקֵלּוּ רֹאשׁ כְּנֶגְדָּם בְּשֶׁל הֱיוֹתָם אֲחֵיהֶם לָאֱמוּנָה; אַדְּרַבָּא, יַעַבְדוּ נָא אוֹתָם מִשּׁוּם שֶׁהַנֶּהֱנִים מִשֵּׁרוּתָם מַאֲמִינִים הֵם וַאֲהוּבִים. אֶת הַדְּבָרִים הָאֵלֶּה תְּלַמֵּד וְתַדְרִישׁ. ³ אִישׁ הַמּוֹרֶה תּוֹרָה אַחֶרֶת וְאֵינוֹ מַסְכִּים לְדִבְרָיו הַבְּרִיאִים שֶׁל אֲדוֹנֵנוּ יֵשׁוּעַ הַמָּשִׁיחַ וְלַתּוֹרָה אֲשֶׁר בְּהֶתְאֵם לַחֲסִידוּת, ⁴ אֲזַי הַגַּאֲוָה הֶעֱבִירָה אוֹתוֹ עַל דַּעְתּוֹ וְאֵינוֹ מֵבִין דָּבָר, וְהוּא בַּעַל נְטִיָּה חוֹלָנִית לַחֲקִירוֹת וּוִכּוּחִים הַמְּבִיאִים לִידֵי קִנְאָה, רִיב, גִּדּוּפִים, חֲשָׁדוֹת מַרְשִׁיעִים, ⁵ וּלְדֵי הַתְנַצְּחֻיּוֹת שֶׁל אֲנָשִׁים אֲשֶׁר שִׂכְלָם הֻתְעָן וְהָאֱמֶת נֶעֶדְרָת מֵהֶם, שֶׁבְּעֵינֵיהֶם חַיֵּי חֲסִידוּת פֵּרוּשָׁם לְהַרְוִיחַ רֶוַח. ⁶ וְאָמְנָם חַיֵּי חֲסִידוּת הַמְּלֵאִים הִסְתַּפְּקוּת עַצְמִית רֶוַח גָּדוֹל הֵם; ⁷ שֶׁהֲרֵי מְאוּמָה לֹא הֵבֵאנוּ עִמָּנוּ לָעוֹלָם וְיָדוּעַ שֶׁלֹּא נוּכַל לְהוֹצִיא מִמֶּנּוּ מְאוּמָה. ⁸ וְכַאֲשֶׁר יֵשׁ לָנוּ מָזוֹן וּבְגָדִים, נִסְתַּפֵּק נָא בָּהֶם. ⁹ אֲבָל הַשּׁוֹאֲפִים לְהִתְעַשֵּׁר נִלְכָּדִים בְּנִסָּיוֹן וּבְמַלְכֹּדֶת וּבְרֹב תַּאֲווֹת אֱוִילִיּוֹת וּמַזִּיקוֹת, הַמּוֹרִידוֹת אֶת הָאָדָם אֱלֵי הֶרֶס וַאֲבַדּוֹן. ¹⁰ הֲלֹא שֹׁרֶשׁ כָּל הָרָעוֹת הוּא אַהֲבַת הַכֶּסֶף, וְיֵשׁ לְהוֹטִים אַחֲרָיו שֶׁסָּטוּ מִן הָאֱמוּנָה וְגָרְמוּ לְעַצְמָם מַכְאוֹבִים רַבִּים.

¹¹ אֲבָל אַתָּה, אִישׁ הָאֱלֹהִים, בְּרַח לְךָ מֵאֵלֶּה, רְדֹף צֶדֶק, חֲסִידוּת, אֱמוּנָה, אַהֲבָה, סַבְלָנוּת וַעֲנָוָה. ¹² הֵאָבֵק הַמַּאֲבָק הַטּוֹב לְמַעַן הָאֱמוּנָה. אֱחֹז בְּחַיֵּי עוֹלָם אֲשֶׁר נִקְרֵאתָ אֵלֵיהֶם וַאֲשֶׁר הִצְהַרְתָּ עֲלֵיהֶם אֶת הַהוֹדָאָה הַיָּפָה בְּמַעֲמַד עֵדִים רַבִּים. ¹³ לְנֶגֶד עֵינֵי אֱלֹהִים הַמְּחַיֶּה אֶת הַכֹּל וּלְנֶגֶד עֵינֵי הַמָּשִׁיחַ יֵשׁוּעַ, אֲשֶׁר הֵעִיד לִפְנֵי פּוֹנְטִיּוֹס פִּילָטוֹס בְּהוֹדָאָתוֹ הַיָּפָה, הִנְנִי מְצַוֶּה עָלֶיךָ ¹⁴ לִשְׁמֹר אֶת הַמִּצְוָה בְּטֹהַר וּבְלֹא דֹפִי עַד הוֹפָעַת אֲדוֹנֵנוּ יֵשׁוּעַ הַמָּשִׁיחַ, ¹⁵ אֲשֶׁר

in His own time, *He who is* the blessed and only
Potentate, the King of kings and Lord of lords,
[16]who alone has immortality, dwelling in unap-
proachable light, whom no man has seen or can see,
to whom *be* honor and everlasting power. Amen.

[17]Command those who are rich in this present
age not to be haughty, nor to trust in uncertain
riches but in the living God, who gives us richly all
things to enjoy. [18]*Let them* do good, that they be
rich in good works, ready to give, willing to share,
[19]storing up for themselves a good foundation for
the time to come, that they may lay hold on eternal
life.

[20]O Timothy! Guard what was committed to
your trust, avoiding the profane *and* idle babblings
and contradictions of what is falsely called
knowledge— [21]by professing it some have strayed
concerning the faith.

Grace *be* with you. Amen.

בְּעִתּוֹתָיו יַרְאֶה אוֹתָהּ הַמְבֹרָךְ, הָרִבּוֹן הַיָּחִיד, מֶלֶךְ
הַמְּלָכִים וַאֲדוֹן הָאֲדוֹנִים; 16 לוֹ לְבַדּוֹ הָאַלְמָוֶת וְהוּא
שׁוֹכֵן אוֹר נִשְׂגָּב מִקְּרָב אֵלָיו; אָדָם לֹא רָאָהוּ וְאַף
אֵינוֹ יָכוֹל לִרְאוֹתוֹ. לוֹ הַכָּבוֹד וְהַגְּבוּרָה לְעוֹלָמִים.
אָמֵן.
17 אֶת עֲשִׁירֵי הָעוֹלָם הַזֶּה צַוֵּה שֶׁלֹּא יָרוּם לְבָבָם
וְלֹא יִבְטְחוּ בָּעשֶׁר שֶׁאֵין בּוֹ בִּטָּחוֹן, אֶלָּא בֵּאלֹהִים
הַמַּעֲנִיק לָנוּ אֶת הַכֹּל בְּשֶׁפַע לַהֲנָאָתֵנוּ. 18 אֱמֹר לָהֶם
לַעֲשׂוֹת אֶת הַטּוֹב, לְהַעֲשִׁיר בְּמַעֲשִׂים טוֹבִים,
לִהְיוֹת נְכוֹנִים לָתֵת, לִהְיוֹת נְדִיבִים, 19 לֶאֱצֹר
לְעַצְמָם אוֹצָר טוֹב לֶעָתִיד, כְּדֵי שֶׁיַּשִּׂיגוּ אֶת הַחַיִּים
הָאֲמִתִּיִּים.
20 טִימוֹתֵיאוֹס, שְׁמֹר אֶת הַפִּקָּדוֹן! סוּר מִדִּבּוּרִים
תְּפֵלִים וְחַסְרֵי קְדֻשָּׁה, וּמִטְּעָנוֹת וּפְרָכוֹת שֶׁל מַה
שֶּׁבְּכָזָב מְכֻנֶּה "דַּעַת." 21 יֵשׁ שֶׁהִתְחַיְּמְרוּ בָּהּ וְסָטוּ מִן
הָאֱמוּנָה. הַחֶסֶד עִמָּכֶם. אָמֵן.

The Second Epistle of Paul to

TIMOTHY

1 Paul, an apostle of Jesus Christ by the will of God, according to the promise of life which is in Christ Jesus,

2 To Timothy, a beloved son:

Grace, mercy, *and* peace from God the Father and Christ Jesus our Lord.

3 I thank God, whom I serve with a pure conscience, as *my* forefathers *did,* as without ceasing I remember you in my prayers night and day, 4 greatly desiring to see you, being mindful of your tears, that I may be filled with joy, 5 when I call to remembrance the genuine faith that is in you, which dwelt first in your grandmother Lois and your mother Eunice, and I am persuaded is in you also. 6 Therefore I remind you to stir up the gift of God which is in you through the laying on of my hands. 7 For God has not given us a spirit of fear, but of power and of love and of a sound mind.

8 Therefore do not be ashamed of the testimony of our Lord, nor of me His prisoner, but share with me in the sufferings for the gospel according to the power of God, 9 who has saved us and called *us* with a holy calling, not according to our works, but according to His own purpose and grace which was given to us in Christ Jesus before time began, 10 but has now been revealed by the appearing of our Savior Jesus Christ, *who* has abolished death and brought life and immortality to light through the gospel, 11 to which I was appointed a preacher, an apostle, and a teacher of the Gentiles. 12 For this reason I also suffer these things; nevertheless I am not ashamed, for I know whom I have believed and am persuaded that He is able to keep what I have committed to Him until that Day.

13 Hold fast the pattern of sound words which you have heard from me, in faith and love which are in Christ Jesus. 14 That good thing which was committed to you, keep by the Holy Spirit who dwells in us.

15 This you know, that all those in Asia have turned away from me, among whom are Phygellus and Hermogenes. 16 The Lord grant mercy to the household of Onesiphorus, for he often refreshed me, and was not ashamed of my chain; 17 but when he arrived in Rome, he sought me out very zealously and found *me.* 18 The Lord grant to him

אִגֶּרֶת שָׁאוּל הַשְּׁנִיָּה אֶל טִימוֹתִיאוֹס

א מֵאֵת שָׁאוּל, שְׁלִיחַ הַמָּשִׁיחַ יֵשׁוּעַ בִּרְצוֹן אֱלֹהִים וּבְהַתְאֵם לְהַבְטָחַת הַחַיִּים אֲשֶׁר בַּמָּשִׁיחַ יֵשׁוּעַ, 2 אֶל טִימוֹתִיאוֹס בְּנִי הָאָהוּב: חֶסֶד וְרַחֲמִים וְשָׁלוֹם מֵאֵת אֱלֹהִים הָאָב וְהַמָּשִׁיחַ יֵשׁוּעַ אֲדוֹנֵנוּ.

3 אֲנִי מוֹדֶה לֵאלֹהִים אֲשֶׁר בְּעִקְבוֹת אֲבוֹתַי אֲנִי עוֹבֵד אוֹתוֹ בְּמַצְפּוּן טָהוֹר, וְאֵינֶנִּי חָדֵל לִזְכֹּר אוֹתְךָ בִּתְפִלּוֹתַי יוֹמָם וָלַיְלָה. 4 בְּזָכְרִי לִי דִּמְעוֹתֶיךָ וַאֲנִי נִכְסָף לִרְאוֹתְךָ לְמַעַן אֶמָּלֵא שִׂמְחָה. 5 זוֹכֵר אֲנִי אֶת אֱמוּנָתְךָ הַכֵּנָה, אֱמוּנָה שֶׁשָּׁכְנָה תְּחִלָּה בְּלוֹאִיס סָבָתְךָ וּבְאַבְנִיקָה אִמְּךָ, וּבְטוּחֲנִי שֶׁהִיא שׁוֹכֶנֶת גַּם בְּךָ. 6 עַל כֵּן אֲנִי מַזְכִּירְךָ לְעוֹרֵר אֶת מַתְּנַת אֱלֹהִים אֲשֶׁר הָעֲנָקָה לְךָ בִּסְמִיכַת יָדַי. 7 הֵן הָאֱלֹהִים לֹא נָתַן לָנוּ רוּחַ שֶׁל פַּחַד, אֶלָּא רוּחַ שֶׁל גְּבוּרָה וְאַהֲבָה וְיִשׁוּב הַדַּעַת. 8 לָכֵן אַל תֵּבוֹשׁ לֹא בְּעֵדוּת אֲדוֹנֵנוּ וְלֹא בִּי, אֲסִירוֹ, אֶלָּא סְבֹל אִתִּי אֶת חֶבְלֵי הַבְּשׂוֹרָה כְּפִי כֹּחַ הָאֱלֹהִים 9 הַמּוֹשִׁיעַ אוֹתָנוּ וְקוֹרֵא אוֹתָנוּ בִּקְרִיאָה קְדוֹשָׁה, לֹא לְפִי מַעֲשֵׂינוּ, כִּי אִם לְפִי תָּכְנִיתוֹ וּלְפִי חַסְדּוֹ הַנָּתוּן לָנוּ בַּמָּשִׁיחַ יֵשׁוּעַ מִלִּפְנֵי עִתּוֹת עוֹלָם. 10 אֲבָל כָּעֵת נִגְלָה חַסְדּוֹ בְּהוֹפָעַת מוֹשִׁיעֵנוּ הַמָּשִׁיחַ יֵשׁוּעַ, הַמְבַטֵּל אֶת הַמָּוֶת וּמוֹצִיא לָאוֹר אֶת הַחַיִּים וְהָאַל־כִּלָּיוֹן עַל־יְדֵי הַבְּשׂוֹרָה. 11 בַּשּׂוֹרָה זֹאת – אֲנִי נִתְמַנֵּיתִי לָהּ לִכְרוֹז וְשָׁלִיחַ וּמוֹרֶה, 12 וּבַעֲבוּרָהּ אֲנִי סוֹבֵל גַּם אֶת הַדְּבָרִים הָאֵלֶּה. אַךְ אֵינֶנִּי בּוֹשׁ, כִּי יוֹדֵעַ אֲנִי בְּמִי הֶאֱמַנְתִּי וּבָטוּחַ אֲנִי שֶׁהוּא יָכוֹל לִשְׁמֹר אֶת פִּקְדוֹנִי לַיּוֹם הַהוּא. 13 הַחֲזֵק בְּמַתְכֹּנֶת הַדְּבָרִים הַבְּרִיאִים אֲשֶׁר שָׁמַעְתָּ מִמֶּנִּי, בֶּאֱמוּנָה וּבְאַהֲבָה אֲשֶׁר בַּמָּשִׁיחַ יֵשׁוּעַ. 14 שְׁמֹר אֶת הַפִּקָּדוֹן הַטּוֹב בְּעֶזְרַת רוּחַ הַקֹּדֶשׁ הַשּׁוֹכֶנֶת בָּנוּ.

15 זֹאת אַתָּה יוֹדֵעַ, שֶׁעָזְבוּ אוֹתִי כָּל אֵלֶּה אֲשֶׁר בְּאַסְיָה, וּבִכְלָלָם פִּיגֵלוֹם וְהֶרְמוֹגֶנֶס. 16 יַשְׁפִּיעַ הָאָדוֹן רַחֲמִים עַל בֵּית אוֹנִיסִיפוֹרוֹס, כִּי פְּעָמִים רַבּוֹת עוֹדֵד אֶת נַפְשִׁי וְלֹא בּוֹשׁ בְּכַבְלִי. 17 אַדְרַבָּא, בִּהְיוֹתוֹ בְּרוֹמָא שָׁקַד לְחַפְּשֵׂנִי עַד כִּי מְצָאַנִי. 18 יִתֵּן

that he may find mercy from the Lord in that Day—and you know very well how many ways he ministered *to me* at Ephesus.

2 You therefore, my son, be strong in the grace that is in Christ Jesus. ²And the things that you have heard from me among many witnesses, commit these to faithful men who will be able to teach others also. ³You therefore must endure hardship as a good soldier of Jesus Christ. ⁴No one engaged in warfare entangles himself with the affairs of *this* life, that he may please him who enlisted him as a soldier. ⁵And also if anyone competes in athletics, he is not crowned unless he competes according to the rules. ⁶The hardworking farmer must be first to partake of the crops. ⁷Consider what I say, and may the Lord give you understanding in all things.

⁸Remember that Jesus Christ, of the seed of David, was raised from the dead according to my gospel, ⁹for which I suffer trouble as an evildoer, *even* to the point of chains; but the word of God is not chained. ¹⁰Therefore I endure all things for the sake of the elect, that they also may obtain the salvation which is in Christ Jesus with eternal glory.

¹¹*This is* a faithful saying:

For if we died with *Him*,
  We shall also live with *Him*.
¹² If we endure,
  We shall also reign with *Him*.
If we deny *Him*,
  He also will deny us.
¹³ If we are faithless,
  He remains faithful;
  He cannot deny Himself.

¹⁴Remind *them* of these things, charging *them* before the Lord not to strive about words to no profit, to the ruin of the hearers. ¹⁵Be diligent to present yourself approved to God, a worker who does not need to be ashamed, rightly dividing the word of truth. ¹⁶But shun profane *and* idle babblings, for they will increase to more ungodliness. ¹⁷And their message will spread like cancer. Hymenaeus and Philetus are of this sort, ¹⁸who have strayed concerning the truth, saying that the resurrection is already past; and they overthrow the faith of some. ¹⁹Nevertheless the solid foundation of God stands, having this seal: "The Lord knows those who are His," and, "Let everyone who names the name of Christ depart from iniquity."

לוֹ הָאָדוֹן לִמְצֹא רַחֲמִים מִלִּפְנֵי יהוה בַּיּוֹם הַהוּא. אַתָּה יוֹדֵעַ הֵיטֵב עַד כַּמָּה הִרְבָּה לְשָׁרֵת בְּאֶפְסוֹס.

ב וְאַתָּה, בְּנִי, הִתְחַזֵּק בַּחֶסֶד אֲשֶׁר בַּמָּשִׁיחַ יֵשׁוּעַ. ²וְהַדְּבָרִים שֶׁשָּׁמַעְתָּ מִמֶּנִּי בְּמַעֲמַד עֵדִים רַבִּים, הַפְקֵד אוֹתָם בִּידֵי אֲנָשִׁים נֶאֱמָנִים הַמֻּכְשָׁרִים לְלַמֵּד גַּם אֲנָשִׁים אֲחֵרִים. ³הִשְׁתַּתֵּף בַּסֵּבֶל כְּחַיָּל טוֹב שֶׁל הַמָּשִׁיחַ יֵשׁוּעַ. ⁴אִישׁ הַמְשָׁרֵת בַּצָּבָא לֹא יִתְעָרֵב בְּעִסְקֵי הַחַיִּים, וְזֹאת כְּדֵי לְהַשְׂבִּיעַ אֶת רְצוֹן מְפַקְּדוֹ. ⁵וְגַם הַמִּשְׁתַּתֵּף בַּתַּחֲרוּת לֹא יֻכְתַּר אִם לֹא יִתְחָרֶה לְפִי הַכְּלָלִים. ⁶הָאִכָּר הֶעָמֵל, מִן הַדִּין שֶׁיִּהְיֶה רִאשׁוֹן לָקַחַת חֵלֶק מִן הַפְּרִי. ⁷שִׂים לְבְךָ לְמָה שֶׁאֲנִי אוֹמֵר, וְהָאָדוֹן יִתֵּן לְךָ בִּינָה בַּכֹּל.

⁸זְכֹר אֶת יֵשׁוּעַ הַמָּשִׁיחַ שֶׁנֵּעוֹר מִן הַמֵּתִים, אֲשֶׁר הוּא מִזֶּרַע דָּוִד כְּדִבְרֵי בְּשׂוֹרָתִי, ⁹הִיא הַבְּשׂוֹרָה שֶׁבַּעֲבוּרָהּ אֲנִי סוֹבֵל רָעוֹת עַד כְּדֵי שִׁבְתִּי בִּכְבָלִים כְּעוֹשֵׂה עָוֶל. אוּלָם דְּבַר הָאֱלֹהִים אֵינֶנּוּ בִּכְבָלִים. ¹⁰עַל כֵּן אֲנִי סוֹבֵל הַכֹּל לְמַעַן הַנִּבְחָרִים, כְּדֵי שֶׁגַּם הֵם יַשִּׂיגוּ תְּשׁוּעָה בַּמָּשִׁיחַ יֵשׁוּעַ עִם כְּבוֹד עוֹלָמִים:

¹¹מְהֵימָן הַדָּבָר:

אִם מַתְנוּ אִתּוֹ, גַּם נִחְיֶה אִתּוֹ;
¹²אִם נַחֲזִיק מַעֲמָד, גַּם נִמְלֹךְ אִתּוֹ;
אִם נִתְכַּחֵשׁ, גַּם הוּא יִתְכַּחֵשׁ לָנוּ;
¹³אִם אֵינֶנּוּ נֶאֱמָנִים, הוּא נִשְׁאָר נֶאֱמָן,
כִּי לֹא יוּכַל לְהִתְכַּחֵשׁ לְעַצְמוֹ.

¹⁴הַזְכֵּר לָהֶם אֶת הַדְּבָרִים הָאֵלֶּה וְהַזְהֵר אוֹתָם לִפְנֵי הָאֱלֹהִים, שֶׁלֹּא יִתְוַכְּחוּ עַל דְּבָרִים שֶׁאֵין בָּהֶם מוֹעִיל וְאֵינָם אֶלָּא הוֹרְסִים אֶת הַשּׁוֹמְעִים. ¹⁵הֱיֵה שָׁקוּד לְהִתְיַצֵּב נֶאֱמָן לִפְנֵי אֱלֹהִים – פּוֹעֵל לֹא יֵבוֹשׁ, הַמְחַלֵּק נְכוֹנָה אֶת דְּבַר הָאֱמֶת. ¹⁶רְחַק מִדִּבּוּרִים תְּפֵלִים וְחַסְרֵי קְדֻשָּׁה, כִּי בַּעֲלֵיהֶם יוֹסִיפוּ רֶשַׁע עַל רֶשַׁע, ¹⁷וְדִבְרָם כְּרָקָב יֹאכַל; עִמָּהֶם נִמְנִים הִימֶנָאוֹס וּפִילֵיטוֹס ¹⁸אֲשֶׁר תָּעוּ מִן הָאֱמֶת, בְּאָמְרָם כִּי תְּחִיַּת הַמֵּתִים כְּבָר הָיְתָה, וְהֵם מְמוֹטְטִים אֱמוּנַת כַּמָּה אֲנָשִׁים. ¹⁹אֲבָל הַיְסוֹד הֶחָזָק שֶׁהִנִּיחַ אֱלֹהִים עוֹמֵד אֵיתָן וְיֵשׁ לוֹ הַחוֹתָם הַזֶּה: "יָדַע יהוה אֶת אֲשֶׁר לוֹ", וְגַם "יָסוּר מֵעָוֶל כָּל

²⁰But in a great house there are not only vessels of gold and silver, but also of wood and clay, some for honor and some for dishonor. ²¹Therefore if anyone cleanses himself from the latter, he will be a vessel for honor, sanctified and useful for the Master, prepared for every good work. ²²Flee also youthful lusts; but pursue righteousness, faith, love, peace with those who call on the Lord out of a pure heart. ²³But avoid foolish and ignorant disputes, knowing that they generate strife. ²⁴And a servant of the Lord must not quarrel but be gentle to all, able to teach, patient, ²⁵in humility correcting those who are in opposition, if God perhaps will grant them repentance, so that they may know the truth, ²⁶and *that* they may come to their senses *and escape* the snare of the devil, having been taken captive by him. to *do* his will.

3 But know this, that in the last days perilous times will come: ²For men will be lovers of themselves, lovers of money, boasters, proud, blasphemers, disobedient to parents, unthankful, unholy, ³unloving, unforgiving, slanderers, without self-control, brutal, despisers of good, ⁴traitors, headstrong, haughty, lovers of pleasure rather than lovers of God, ⁵having a form of godliness but denying its power. And from such people turn away! ⁶For of this sort are those who creep into households and make captives of gullible women loaded down with sins, led away by various lusts, ⁷always learning and never able to come to the knowledge of the truth. ⁸Now as Jannes and Jambres resisted Moses, so do these also resist the truth: men of corrupt minds, disapproved concerning the faith; ⁹but they will progress no further, for their folly will be manifest to all, as theirs also was.

¹⁰But you have carefully followed my doctrine, manner of life, purpose, faith, longsuffering, love, perseverance, ¹¹persecutions, afflictions, which happened to me at Antioch, at Iconium, at Lystra—what persecutions I endured. And out of *them* all the Lord delivered me. ¹²Yes, and all who desire to live godly in Christ Jesus will suffer persecution. ¹³But evil men and impostors will grow worse and worse, deceiving and being deceived. ¹⁴But you must continue in the things which you have learned and been assured of, knowing from whom you have learned *them,* ¹⁵and that from childhood you have known the Holy Scriptures, which are able to make you wise for salvation through faith which is in Christ Jesus.

הַקּוֹרֵא בְּשֵׁם יהוה". ²⁰הִנֵּה בְּבַיִת גָּדוֹל לֹא רַק כְּלֵי זָהָב וָכֶסֶף, אֶלָּא גַּם כְּלֵי עֵץ וָחֶרֶס, וּמֵהֶם כַּמָּה לְכָבוֹד וְכַמָּה לְקָלוֹן. ²¹לְפִיכָךְ אִם אִישׁ יְטַהֵר אֶת עַצְמוֹ מֵאֵלֶּה יִהְיֶה כְּלִי לְכָבוֹד, מְקֻדָּשׁ וּמוֹעִיל לְבַעַל הַבַּיִת וּמוּכָן לְכָל מַעֲשֶׂה טוֹב. ²²בְּרַח לְךָ מִתַּאֲווֹת הַנְּעוּרִים וּרְדֹף צֶדֶק, אֱמוּנָה, אַהֲבָה וְשָׁלוֹם, עִם כָּל הַקּוֹרְאִים אֶל יהוה בְּלֵב טָהוֹר. ²³רְחַק מִשְּׁאֵלוֹת אֱוִילִיּוֹת וְנִבְעָרוֹת; אַתָּה יוֹדֵעַ שֶׁהֵן גּוֹרְמוֹת מְרִיבוֹת. ²⁴וְעֶבֶד הָאָדוֹן מִן הַדִּין שֶׁלֹּא יָרִיב, אֶלָּא יְהֵא נֹחַ לַכֹּל, מְכֻשָּׁר לְלַמֵּד, סַבְלָן, ²⁵וּמוֹכִיחַ בַּעֲנָוָה אֶת הַמִּתְנַגְּדִים; אוּלַי יִתֵּן לָהֶם הָאֱלֹהִים לַחֲזֹר בִּתְשׁוּבָה כְּדֵי שֶׁיַּכִּירוּ אֶת הָאֱמֶת ²⁶וְיִתְפַּכְּחוּ וְיֵצְאוּ מִמַּלְכֹּדֶת הַשָּׂטָן אֲשֶׁר לְכָדָם כִּרְצוֹנוֹ.

ג וְזֹאת דַּע לְךָ: בְּאַחֲרִית הַיָּמִים יָבוֹאוּ זְמַנִּים קָשִׁים, ²כִּי יִהְיוּ הָאֲנָשִׁים אוֹהֲבֵי עַצְמָם, אוֹהֲבֵי כֶסֶף, גַּאַוְתָנִים, שַׁחְצָנִים, מְגַדְּפִים, מַמְרִים אֶת פִּי הוֹרֵיהֶם, כְּפוּיֵי טוֹבָה, חַסְרֵי קְדֻשָּׁה, ³קְשׁוּחֵי לֵב, בִּלְתִּי מִתְרַצִּים, מַלְשִׁינִים, הוֹלְלִים, אַכְזָרִים, שׂוֹנְאֵי טוֹב, ⁴בּוֹגְדִים, פּוֹחֲזִים, יְהִירִים, אוֹהֲבִים תַּעֲנוּגוֹת יוֹתֵר מֵשֶּׁהֵם אוֹהֲבִים אֶת אֱלֹהִים, ⁵לְכָאוֹרָה בַּעֲלֵי יִרְאַת שָׁמַיִם, אַךְ כּוֹפְרִים בְּתָקְפָּהּ. הִתְרַחֵק מֵאֵלֶּה. ⁶הֵן מִקִּרְבָּם בָּאִים הָאֲנָשִׁים אֲשֶׁר מִתְנַגְּבִים לְבָתִּים וְלוֹכְדִים נָשִׁים כְּסִילוֹת, עֲמוּסוֹת חֲטָאִים וְנִתְעוֹת בְּכָל מִינֵי תַאֲווֹת, ⁷הַלּוֹמְדוֹת תָּמִיד וְאַף פַּעַם אֵינָן יְכוֹלוֹת לְהַגִּיעַ לִכְלַל יְדִיעַת הָאֱמֶת. ⁸וּכְדֶרֶךְ שֶׁיּוֹחָנָא וּמַמְרֵא הִתְנַגְּדוּ לְמֹשֶׁה, כֵּן גַּם אֵלֶּה מִתְנַגְּדִים לָאֱמֶת, אֲנָשִׁים אֲשֶׁר שְׂכָלָם מְעֻוָּת וְהֵם מְכֻזָּבִים בָּאֱמוּנָה. ⁹אֲבָל לֹא יַצְלִיחוּ עוֹד, כִּי אִוַּלְתָּם תִּגָּלֶה לַכֹּל, כְּמוֹ שֶׁאֵרַע גַּם לָאֲנָשִׁים הָהֵם. ¹⁰אַךְ אַתָּה הָלַכְתָּ בְּעִקְּבוֹתַי בַּהוֹרָאָה, בַּהִתְנַהֲגוּת, בַּתַּכְלִית, בָּאֱמוּנָה, בְּאֹרֶךְ הָרוּחַ, בָּאַהֲבָה, בַּסַּבְלָנוּת, ¹¹בָּרְדִיפוֹת וּבַסֵּבֶל שֶׁבָּאוּ עָלַי בְּאַנְטְיוֹכְיָה, בְּאִיקוֹנְיוֹן וּבְלִיסְטְרָה, וְאֵילוּ רְדִיפוֹת סָבַלְתִּי! וּמִכֻּלָּן הִצִּילַנִי הָאָדוֹן. ¹²וְאָמְנָם כָּל הָרוֹצִים לִחְיוֹת חַיֵּי חֲסִידוּת בַּמָּשִׁיחַ יֵשׁוּעַ, יֵרָדְפוּ. ¹³אַךְ אֲנָשִׁים רָעִים וּמַדִּיחִים יוֹסִיפוּ רָעָתָם, יַתְעוּ וְיִתְעוּ. ¹⁴אֲבָל אַתָּה עֲמֹד בַּדְּבָרִים אֲשֶׁר לָמַדְתָּ וַאֲשֶׁר מְצָאתָם נְכוֹנִים, שֶׁהֲרֵי יוֹדֵעַ אַתָּה מִמִּי לָמַדְתָּ ¹⁵וּמִנְּעוּרֶיךָ אַתָּה יוֹדֵעַ אֶת כִּתְבֵי הַקֹּדֶשׁ הַיְכוֹלִים

16 All Scripture *is* given by inspiration of God, and *is* profitable for doctrine, for reproof, for correction, for instruction in righteousness, 17 that the man of God may be complete, thoroughly equipped for every good work.

4 I charge *you* therefore before God and the Lord Jesus Christ, who will judge the living and the dead at His appearing and His kingdom: 2 Preach the word! Be ready in season *and* out of season. Convince, rebuke, exhort, with all longsuffering and teaching. 3 For the time will come when they will not endure sound doctrine, but according to their own desires, *because* they have itching ears, they will heap up for themselves teachers; 4 and they will turn *their* ears away from the truth, and be turned aside to fables. 5 But you be watchful in all things, endure afflictions, do the work of an evangelist, fulfill your ministry.

6 For I am already being poured out as a drink offering, and the time of my departure is at hand. 7 I have fought the good fight, I have finished the race, I have kept the faith. 8 Finally, there is laid up for me the crown of righteousness, which the Lord, the righteous Judge, will give to me on that Day, and not to me only but also to all who have loved His appearing.

9 Be diligent to come to me quickly; 10 for Demas has forsaken me, having loved this present world, and has departed for Thessalonica—Crescens for Galatia, Titus for Dalmatia. 11 Only Luke is with me. Get Mark and bring him with you, for he is useful to me for ministry. 12 And Tychicus I have sent to Ephesus. 13 Bring the cloak that I left with Carpus at Troas when you come—and the books, especially the parchments.

14 Alexander the coppersmith did me much harm. May the Lord repay him according to his works. 15 You also must beware of him, for he has greatly resisted our words.

16 At my first defense no one stood with me, but all forsook me. May it not be charged against them.

17 But the Lord stood with me and strengthened me, so that the message might be preached fully through me, and *that* all the Gentiles might hear. Also I was delivered out of the mouth of the lion. 18 And the Lord will deliver me from every evil work and preserve *me* for His heavenly kingdom. To Him *be* glory forever and ever. Amen!

19 Greet Prisca and Aquila, and the household of Onesiphorus. 20 Erastus stayed in Corinth, but Trophimus I have left in Miletus sick.

21 Do your utmost to come before winter.

לְהַחְכִּימְךָ לִישׁוּעָה עַל-יְדֵי הָאֱמוּנָה בַּמָּשִׁיחַ יֵשׁוּעַ. 16 כָּל הַכָּתוּב נִכְתַּב בְּרוּחַ אֱלֹהִים, וּמוֹעִיל הוּא לְהוֹרָאָה, לְתוֹכֵחָה, לְתִקּוּן, לְחִנּוּךְ בְּמַעְגְּלֵי צֶדֶק, 17 לְמַעַן יִהְיֶה אִישׁ הָאֱלֹהִים מֻשְׁלָם, וּמֻכְשָׁר לְכָל מַעֲשֶׂה טוֹב.

ד אֲנִי מֵעִיד בְּךָ לִפְנֵי אֱלֹהִים וְלִפְנֵי הַמָּשִׁיחַ יֵשׁוּעַ הֶעָתִיד לִשְׁפֹּט אֶת הַחַיִּים וְאֶת הַמֵּתִים בְּהוֹפָעָתוֹ וּבְמַלְכוּתוֹ: 2 הַכְרֵז אֶת הַדָּבָר, הַתְמֵד בְּעִתּוֹ וְשֶׁלֹּא בְעִתּוֹ, הוֹכֵחַ, גְּעַר, הַפְצֵר, וְזֹאת בְּכָל אֹרֶךְ רוּחַ וְעַל-יְדֵי הַהוֹרָאָה. 3 הֵן יָבוֹא הַזְּמַן שֶׁלֹּא יִסְבְּלוּ אֶת הַלֶּקַח הַבָּרִיא, אֶלָּא יַאַסְפוּ לָהֶם מוֹרִים לְפִי מַאֲוַיֵּיהֶם לְשֵׁם שַׁעֲשׁוּעֵי אָזְנַם, 4 וּמִן הָאֱמֶת יַטּוּ אָזְנֵיהֶם לִפְנוֹת אֶל הָאַגָּדוֹת. 5 אֲבָל אַתָּה עֲמֹד עַל הַמִּשְׁמָר בְּכָל דָּבָר, סְבֹל הָרָעוֹת, עֲשֵׂה אֶת מְלֶאכֶת הַמְבַשֵּׂר, וּמַלֵּא אֶת שֵׁרוּתֶךָ.

6 אֲנִי עַצְמִי כְּבָר מֻסָּךְ כְּנֶסֶךְ וְעֵת פְּטִירָתִי הִגִּיעָה. 7 אֶת הַמִּלְחָמָה הַטּוֹבָה נִלְחַמְתִּי, אֶת הַמֵּרוֹץ הִשְׁלַמְתִּי, אֶת הָאֱמוּנָה שָׁמַרְתִּי. 8 מֵעַתָּה שְׁמוּרָה לִי עֲטֶרֶת הַצְּדָקָה אֲשֶׁר הָאָדוֹן, הַשּׁוֹפֵט הַצַּדִּיק, יִתֵּן לִי בַּיּוֹם הַהוּא; וְלֹא רַק לִי בִּלְבַד, אֶלָּא גַם לְכָל אוֹהֲבֵי הוֹפָעָתוֹ.

9 חוּשָׁה לָבוֹא אֵלַי עַד מְהֵרָה, 10 כִּי דִימָס עֲזָבַנִי בִּגְלַל אַהֲבָתוֹ אֶת הָעוֹלָם הַזֶּה וְהָלַךְ לוֹ לְתֶסָּלוֹנִיקִי; קְרִיסְקִיס הָלַךְ לְגָלַטְיָה וְטִיטוֹס לְדַלְמַטְיָה. 11 רַק לוּקָס לְבַדּוֹ אִתִּי. קַח אֶת מַרְקוֹס וַהֲבִיאֵהוּ אִתְּךָ, כִּי הוּא מוֹעִיל לִי לַשֵּׁרוּת. 12 אֶת טִיכִיקוֹס שָׁלַחְתִּי לְאֶפֶסוֹס. 13 כַּאֲשֶׁר תָּבוֹא, הָבֵא אֶת הַמְּעִיל שֶׁהִשְׁאַרְתִּי בִּטְרוֹאַס אֵצֶל קַרְפּוֹס, כֵּן גַם אֶת הַמְּגִלּוֹת וּבְיִחוּד אֶת יְרִיעוֹת הַקְּלָף. 14 אֲלֶכְּסַנְדֶּר חָרַשׁ הַנְּחֹשֶׁת עָשָׂה לִי רָעוֹת רַבּוֹת, יִגְמֹל לוֹ יהוה כְּמַעֲשָׂיו. 15 גַם אַתָּה הִשָּׁמֵר מִמֶּנּוּ, כִּי הִתְנַגֵּד בְּחָזְקָה לִדְבָרֵינוּ. 16 כְּשֶׁקַּמְתִּי לְהִתְגּוֹנֵן בַּפַּעַם הָרִאשׁוֹנָה, אִישׁ לֹא עָמַד לְצִדִּי, כִּי כֻלָּם עֲזָבוּנִי; אַל יֵחָשֵׁב לָהֶם לַעֲוֹן! 17 אֲבָל הָאָדוֹן עָמַד אִתִּי וְחִזְּקַנִי, כְּדֵי שֶׁתִּכָּרֵז עַל-יְדֵי הַבְּשׂוֹרָה בִּמְלוֹאָהּ וְיִשְׁמְעוּ כָל הַגּוֹיִים, וְאָכֵן נִצַּלְתִּי מִפִּי הָאַרְיֵה. 18 הָאָדוֹן יַצִּילֵנִי מִכָּל מַעֲשֵׂה רַע וְיוֹשִׁיעֵנִי אֶל מַלְכוּתוֹ שֶׁבַּשָּׁמַיִם; לוֹ הַכָּבוֹד לְעוֹלְמֵי עוֹלָמִים. אָמֵן. 19 דְּרֹשׁ בְּשָׁלוֹם פְּרִיסְקָה וַעֲקִילָס וּבֵית אוֹנִיסִיפוֹרוֹס. 20 אֲרַסְטוֹס נִשְׁאַר בְּקוֹרִינְתוֹס. אֶת טְרוֹפִימוֹס הִשְׁאַרְתִּי בְּמִילֶטוֹס כְּשֶׁהוּא חוֹלֶה. 21 חוּשָׁה לָבוֹא

Eubulus greets you, as well as Pudens, Linus, Claudia, and all the brethren.

22 The Lord Jesus Christ be with your spirit. Grace be with you. Amen.

לִפְנֵי הַחֹרֶף. אָבוּלוֹם דּוֹרֵשׁ בִּשְׁלוֹמְךָ, כֵּן גַּם פּוּדִים, לִינוֹם, קְלוֹדְיָה, וְכָל הָאַחִים. ²²הָאָדוֹן עִם רוּחֶךָ. הַחֶסֶד עִמָּכֶם.

The Epistle of Paul to
TITUS

1 Paul, a bondservant of God and an apostle of Jesus Christ, according to the faith of God's elect and the acknowledgment of the truth which accords with godliness, ² in hope of eternal life which God, who cannot lie, promised before time began, ³ but has in due time manifested His word through preaching, which was committed to me according to the commandment of God our Savior;

⁴ To Titus, a true son in *our* common faith:

Grace, mercy, *and* peace from God the Father and the Lord Jesus Christ our Savior.

⁵ For this reason I left you in Crete, that you should set in order the things that are lacking, and appoint elders in every city as I commanded you— ⁶ if a man is blameless, the husband of one wife, having faithful children not accused of dissipation or insubordination. ⁷ For a bishop must be blameless, as a steward of God, not self-willed, not quick-tempered, not given to wine, not violent, not greedy for money, ⁸ but hospitable, a lover of what is good, sober-minded, just, holy, self-controlled, ⁹ holding fast the faithful word as he has been taught, that he may be able, by sound doctrine, both to exhort and convict those who contradict.

¹⁰ For there are many insubordinate, both idle talkers and deceivers, especially those of the circumcision, ¹¹ whose mouths must be stopped, who subvert whole households, teaching things which they ought not, for the sake of dishonest gain. ¹² One of them, a prophet of their own, said, "Cretans *are* always liars, evil beasts, lazy gluttons." ¹³ This testimony is true. Therefore rebuke them sharply, that they may be sound in the faith, ¹⁴ not giving heed to Jewish fables and commandments of men who turn from the truth. ¹⁵ To the pure all things are pure, but to those who are defiled and unbelieving nothing is pure; but even their mind and conscience are defiled. ¹⁶ They profess to know God, but in works they deny Him, being abominable, disobedient, and disqualified for every good work.

אִגֶּרֶת שָׁאוּל אֶל טִיטוֹס

א מֵאֵת שָׁאוּל, עֶבֶד אֱלֹהִים וּשְׁלִיחַ יֵשׁוּעַ הַמָּשִׁיחַ לְמַעַן אֱמוּנָתָם שֶׁל בְּחִירֵי אֱלֹהִים וְהַכָּרָתָם אֶת הָאֱמֶת אֲשֶׁר הִיא בְּהֶתְאֵם לְיִרְאַת שָׁמַיִם, ² בְּתִקְוָה לְחַיֵּי עוֹלָם אֲשֶׁר הָאֱלֹהִים – אֲשֶׁר אֵינוֹ מְכַזֵּב – הִבְטִיחַ לִפְנֵי עִתּוֹת עוֹלָם, ³ וּבְעִתּוֹתָיו גִּלָּה אֶת דְּבָרוֹ בַּהַכְרָזָה שֶׁהֻפְקְדָה בְּיָדִי עַל־פִּי מִצְוַת הָאֱלֹהִים מוֹשִׁיעֵנוּ; ⁴ אֶל טִיטוֹס בְּנִי הָאֲמִתִּי בָּאֱמוּנָה הַמְשֻׁתֶּפֶת: חֶסֶד וְשָׁלוֹם מֵאֵת הָאֱלֹהִים אָבִינוּ וְהַמָּשִׁיחַ יֵשׁוּעַ מוֹשִׁיעֵנוּ.

⁵ הִשְׁאַרְתִּיךָ בִּכְרֵתִים כְּדֵי שֶׁתְּסַדֵּר מַה שֶּׁיֵּשׁ עוֹד לְסַדֵּר וּתְמַנֶּה זְקֵנִים בְּכָל עִיר כְּפִי שֶׁצִּוִּיתִיךָ, כְּלוֹמַר: ⁶ אֶת מִי שֶׁאֵין בּוֹ דֹּפִי וְהוּא בַּעַל אִשָּׁה אַחַת וְיֵשׁ לוֹ בָּנִים מַאֲמִינִים אֲשֶׁר אֵין עֲלֵיהֶם טַעֲנַת הוֹלְלוּת אוֹ סוֹרְרוּת.

⁷ הֲלֹא בְּתוֹר סוֹכֵן עַל בֵּית אֱלֹהִים צָרִיךְ הַמַּנְהִיג לִהְיוֹת אִישׁ שֶׁאֵין בּוֹ דֹּפִי, לֹא עִקֵּשׁ, לֹא רַגְזָן, לֹא מִתְמַכֵּר לְיַיִן, לֹא בַּעַל אֶגְרוֹף, לֹא רוֹדֵף בֶּצַע, ⁸ אֶלָּא מַכְנִיס אוֹרְחִים, אוֹהֵב אֶת הַטּוֹב, מְיֻשָּׁב בְּדַעְתּוֹ, צַדִּיק, קָדוֹשׁ, כּוֹבֵשׁ אֶת יִצְרוֹ ⁹ וּמַחֲזִיק בַּדָּבָר הַמְּהֵימָן אֲשֶׁר עַל־פִּי תּוֹרָתֵנוּ, לְמַעַן יוּכַל גַּם לְעוֹדֵד בְּהוֹרָאַת הַלֶּקַח הַבָּרִיא וְגַם לְהוֹכִיחַ אֶת הַמִּתְנַגְּדִים; ¹⁰ כִּי יֵשׁ רַבִּים הַמְסָרְבִים לְהִשָּׁמַע, דּוֹבְרֵי הֶבֶל וּמַתְעִים, בִּפְרָט מִבֵּין הַנִּמּוֹלִים, ¹¹ אֲשֶׁר מִן הַדִּין שֶׁיִּסָּכֵר פִּיהֶם; מַשְׁחִיתִים הֵם מִשְׁפָּחוֹת שְׁלֵמוֹת בְּלַמְּדָם דְּבָרִים פְּסוּלִים, וְזֹאת לְמַעַן רֶוַח שָׁפָל. ¹² וּכְבָר אָמַר אֶחָד מֵהֶם, שֶׁהוּא נָבִיא מִקִּרְבָּם: "הַכְּרֵתִים מְשַׁקְּרִים תָּמִיד, חַיּוֹת רָעוֹת הֵם וּכְרֵשִׂים עֲצֵלִים."

¹³ הָעֵדוּת הַזֹּאת אֱמֶת הִיא. עַל כֵּן הוֹכַח אוֹתָם תּוֹכֵחָה קָשָׁה, לְמַעַן יִהְיוּ בְּרִיאִים בָּאֱמוּנָה ¹⁴ וְלֹא יָשִׂיתוּ לִבָּם לְאַגָּדוֹת יְהוּדִיּוֹת וּלְמִצְווֹת בְּנֵי אָדָם הַסּוֹטִים מִן הָאֱמֶת. ¹⁵ הַכֹּל טָהוֹר לַטְּהוֹרִים, אֲבָל לַטְּמֵאִים וְלִשְׁאֵינָם מַאֲמִינִים שׁוּם דָּבָר אֵינוֹ טָהוֹר, כִּי גַם שִׂכְלָם וְגַם מַצְפּוּנָם טְמֵאִים. ¹⁶ הֵם מַצְהִירִים שֶׁהֵם יוֹדְעִים אֶת אֱלֹהִים, אַךְ בְּמַעֲשֵׂיהֶם כּוֹפְרִים בּוֹ; נִתְעָבִים הֵם וְסָרְבָנִים, וְלֹא יִצְלְחוּ לְשׁוּם מַעֲשֶׂה טוֹב.

2 But as for you, speak the things which are proper for sound doctrine: ²that the older men be sober, reverent, temperate, sound in faith, in love, in patience; ³the older women likewise, that they be reverent in behavior, not slanderers, not given to much wine, teachers of good things— ⁴that they admonish the young women to love their husbands, to love their children, ⁵to be discreet, chaste, homemakers, good, obedient to their own husbands, that the word of God may not be blasphemed.

⁶Likewise, exhort the young men to be sober-minded, ⁷in all things showing yourself *to be* a pattern of good works; in doctrine *showing* integrity, reverence, incorruptibility, ⁸sound speech that cannot be condemned, that one who is an opponent may be ashamed, having nothing evil to say of you.

⁹*Exhort* bondservants to be obedient to their own masters, to be well pleasing in all *things,* not answering back, ¹⁰not pilfering, but showing all good fidelity, that they may adorn the doctrine of God our Savior in all things.

¹¹For the grace of God that brings salvation has appeared to all men, ¹²teaching us that, denying ungodliness and worldly lusts, we should live soberly, righteously, and godly in the present age, ¹³looking for the blessed hope and glorious appearing of our great God and Savior Jesus Christ, ¹⁴who gave Himself for us, that He might redeem us from every lawless deed and purify for Himself *His* own special people, zealous for good works.

¹⁵Speak these things, exhort, and rebuke with all authority. Let no one despise you.

3 Remind them to be subject to rulers and authorities, to obey, to be ready for every good work, ²to speak evil of no one, to be peaceable, gentle, showing all humility to all men. ³For we ourselves were also once foolish, disobedient, deceived, serving various lusts and pleasures, living in malice and envy, hateful and hating one another. ⁴But when the kindness and the love of God our Savior toward man appeared, ⁵not by works of righteousness which we have done, but according to His mercy He saved us, through the washing of regeneration and renewing of the Holy Spirit, ⁶whom He poured out on us abundantly through Jesus Christ our Savior, ⁷that having been justified by His grace we should become heirs according to the hope of eternal life.

ב וְאַתָּה דַּבֵּר אֶת אֲשֶׁר יָאֶה לְתוֹרָתֵנוּ הַבְּרִיאָה: ²שֶׁיִּהְיוּ הַזְּקֵנִים מְפֻכָּחִים, רְצִינִיִּים, מְאֻפָּקִים, בְּרִיאִים בָּאֱמוּנָה, בָּאַהֲבָה וּבְסַבְלָנוּת. ³וְכֵן גַּם הַזְּקֵנוֹת שֶׁתִּתְנַהֲגֶנָה בִּקְדֻשָּׁה; שֶׁלֹּא תִּהְיֶינָה הוֹלְכוֹת רָכִיל וְלֹא תִּתְמַכֵּרְנָה לַיַּיִן, כִּי אִם תִּהְיֶינָה מְלַמְּדוֹת אֶת הַטּוֹב, ⁴כְּדֵי שֶׁתְּחַנֵּכְנָה אֶת הַנָּשִׁים הַצְּעִירוֹת לֶאֱהֹב אֶת בַּעֲלֵיהֶן וְיַלְדֵיהֶן, ⁵וְלִהְיוֹת צְנוּעוֹת, טְהוֹרוֹת, מַשְׁגִּיחוֹת עַל בֵּיתָן, טוֹבוֹת, נִשְׁמָעוֹת לְבַעֲלֵיהֶן; זֹאת לְמַעַן לֹא יְגֻנֶּה דְבַר הָאֱלֹהִים. ⁶כְּמוֹ כֵן הָאֵץ בַּצְּעִירִים שֶׁיִּהְיוּ מְאֻפָּקִים בַּכֹּל; ⁷הַרְאֵה עַצְמְךָ מוֹפֵת לְמַעֲשִׂים טוֹבִים; תְּהֵא הוֹרָאָתְךָ טְהוֹרָה וּמְכֻבֶּדֶת; ⁸יִהְיוּ דְבָרֶיךָ בְּרִיאִים וּבְלִי דֹפִי, לְמַעַן יֵבוֹשׁ הַמִּתְנַגֵּד בְּאֵין לוֹ שׁוּם דָּבָר רַע לוֹמַר עָלֵינוּ. ⁹עַל הָעֲבָדִים לְהִכָּנַע לַאֲדוֹנֵיהֶם בַּכֹּל, לְהַשְׂבִּיעַ אֶת רְצוֹנָם וְלֹא לְהִתְוַכֵּחַ. ¹⁰אַל יִמְעֲלוּ, אֶלָּא יַרְאוּ נֶאֱמָנוּת מְלֵאָה כְּדֵי שֶׁבְּכָל דָּבָר יָרְבּוּ פְאֵר לְתוֹרַת הָאֱלֹהִים מוֹשִׁיעֵנוּ. ¹¹הֵן חֶסֶד הָאֱלֹהִים הוֹפִיעַ לִישׁוּעַת כָּל בְּנֵי אָדָם, ¹²לְהַדְרִיכֵנוּ לְהִבָּדֵל מֵרֶשַׁע וְתַאֲווֹת הָעוֹלָם כְּדֵי שֶׁנִּחְיֶה בָּעוֹלָם הַזֶּה בִּצְנִיעוּת וּבְצֶדֶק וּבַחֲסִידוּת, ¹³בְּצִפִּיָּה לְמִמּוּשׁ הַתִּקְוָה הַמְבֹרֶכֶת וּלְהוֹפָעַת הֲדַר אֱלֹהֵינוּ הַגָּדוֹל וּמוֹשִׁיעֵנוּ יֵשׁוּעַ הַמָּשִׁיחַ, ¹⁴אֲשֶׁר נָתַן אֶת עַצְמוֹ בַּעֲדֵנוּ כְּדֵי לִפְדּוֹת אוֹתָנוּ מִכָּל עָוֶל וּלְטַהֵר לוֹ עַם סְגֻלָּה שׁוֹקֵד עַל מַעֲשִׂים טוֹבִים. ¹⁵אֶת הַדְּבָרִים הָאֵלֶּה תְּדַבֵּר; הָאֵץ וְהוֹכֵחַ בִּמְלֹא הַסַּמְכוּת. אִישׁ אַל יָבוּז לָךְ.

ג הַזְכֵּר לָהֶם לְהִכָּנַע לְשַׁלִּיטִים וּלְבַעֲלֵי סַמְכֻיּוֹת, לְצַיֵּת, לִהְיוֹת נְכוֹנִים לְכָל מַעֲשֶׂה טוֹב; ²שֶׁלֹּא לְגַדֵּף אִישׁ, לַחְדֹּל מִמְּרִיבוֹת, לִהְיוֹת נוֹחִים לַבְּרִיּוֹת וּלְהִתְנַהֵג בַּעֲנָוָה עִם כָּל אָדָם. ³הֲרֵי לְפָנִים גַּם אֲנַחְנוּ הָיִינוּ חַסְרֵי דַעַת, סוֹרְרִים, תּוֹעִים, עֲבָדִים לְכָל מִינֵי תַאֲווֹת וְתַשׁוּקוֹת, מְבַלִּים זְמַנֵּנוּ בְּרִשְׁעָה וְקִנְאָה, שְׂנוּאִים, וְשׂוֹנְאִים אִישׁ אֶת אָחִיו. ⁴אוּלָם כְּשֶׁנִּגְלָה טוּבוֹ שֶׁל הָאֱלֹהִים מוֹשִׁיעֵנוּ וְאַהֲבָתוֹ אֶת הָאָדָם, ⁵אֲוַי לֹא בִּגְלַל מַעֲשֵׂי צְדָקָה שֶׁעָשִׂינוּ הוּא הוֹשִׁיעַ אוֹתָנוּ, כִּי אִם בְּרַחֲמָיו, עַל־יְדֵי רְחִיצַת הַלֵּדָה הַחֲדָשָׁה וְהִתְחַדְּשׁוּת בְּרוּחַ הַקֹּדֶשׁ ⁶אֲשֶׁר שָׁפַךְ עָלֵינוּ לְמַכְבִּיר עַל־יְדֵי יֵשׁוּעַ הַמָּשִׁיחַ מוֹשִׁיעֵנוּ, ⁷לְמַעַן נִצְדַּק בְּחַסְדּוֹ וְנִהְיֶה לְיוֹרְשֵׁי חַיֵּי עוֹלָם בְּהֶתְאֵם לַתִּקְוָה.

⁸ This is a faithful saying, and these things I want you to affirm constantly, that those who have believed in God should be careful to maintain good works. These things are good and profitable to men.

⁹ But avoid foolish disputes, genealogies, contentions, and strivings about the law; for they are unprofitable and useless. ¹⁰ Reject a divisive man after the first and second admonition, ¹¹ knowing that such a person is warped and sinning, being self-condemned.

¹² When I send Artemas to you, or Tychicus, be diligent to come to me at Nicopolis, for I have decided to spend the winter there. ¹³ Send Zenas the lawyer and Apollos on their journey with haste, that they may lack nothing. ¹⁴ And let our *people* also learn to maintain good works, to *meet* urgent needs, that they may not be unfruitful.

¹⁵ All who *are* with me greet you. Greet those who love us in the faith.

Grace *be* with you all. Amen.

⁸ מְהֵימָן הַדָּבָר, וּרְצוֹנִי שֶׁתַּעֲמֹד עַל כָּךְ בְּתֹקֶף כְּדֵי שֶׁהַמַּאֲמִינִים בֵּאלֹהִים יָשִׂיתוּ לִבָּם לַעֲסֹק בְּמַעֲשִׂים טוֹבִים. דְּבָרִים אֵלֶּה טוֹבִים וּמוֹעִילִים לִבְנֵי אָדָם. ⁹ אֲבָל הִמָּנַע מֵחִקְרֵי שְׁאֵלוֹת תְּפֵלוֹת, מֵחִקְרֵי תוֹלְדוֹת הַדּוֹרוֹת, מִמְּרִיבוֹת, וּמֵהִתְנַצְּחֻיּוֹת עַל הַתּוֹרָה, כִּי אֵין בָּהֶם מוֹעִיל וְהֵמָּה הֶבֶל. ¹⁰ וְאִישׁ הַגּוֹרֵם לְפִלּוּגִים, לְאַחַר שֶׁהוּכַח פַּעַם אַחַת וּפַעַם שְׁנִיָּה, אַל יְהָא לְךָ דָּבָר עִמּוֹ: ¹¹ דַּע לְךָ כִּי אִישׁ כָּזֶה סוֹטֶה מִן הַדֶּרֶךְ וְהוּא חוֹטֵא הַמַּרְשִׁיעַ אֶת עַצְמוֹ. ¹² כַּאֲשֶׁר אֶשְׁלַח אֵלֶיךָ אֶת אַרְטֵמָס אוֹ אֶת טִיכִיקוֹס, תְּמַהֵר לָבוֹא אֵלַי לְנִיקוֹפּוֹלִים, כִּי הֶחְלַטְתִּי לִשְׁהוֹת שָׁם בַּחֹרֶף. ¹³ הִזְדָּרֵז לִשְׁלֹחַ אֶת זֵינָס הַמְלֻמָּד בַּתּוֹרָה וְאֶת אַפּוֹלּוֹס, וּדְאַג שֶׁלֹּא יַחְסְרוּ דָּבָר. ¹⁴ וְיִלְמְדוּ גַּם אַנְשֵׁי קְהָלָתֵנוּ לַעֲסֹק בְּמַעֲשִׂים טוֹבִים לְמִלּוּי צְרָכִים חִיּוּנִיִּים, כְּדֵי שֶׁלֹּא יִהְיוּ חַסְרֵי פְּרִי.

¹⁵ כָּל הַנִּמְצָאִים אִתִּי דּוֹרְשִׁים בִּשְׁלוֹמְךָ. דְּרִישַׁת שָׁלוֹם לְאוֹהֲבֵינוּ הַשֻּׁתָּפִים בָּאֱמוּנָה. הַחֶסֶד עִם כֻּלְּכֶם.

The Epistle of Paul to

PHILEMON

Paul, a prisoner of Christ Jesus, and Timothy *our* brother,

To Philemon our beloved *friend* and fellow laborer, [2] to the beloved Apphia, Archippus our fellow soldier, and to the church in your house:

[3] Grace to you and peace from God our Father and the Lord Jesus Christ.

[4] I thank my God, making mention of you always in my prayers, [5] hearing of your love and faith which you have toward the Lord Jesus and toward all the saints, [6] that the sharing of your faith may become effective by the acknowledgment of every good thing which is in you in Christ Jesus. [7] For we have great joy and consolation in your love, because the hearts of the saints have been refreshed by you, brother.

[8] Therefore, though I might be very bold in Christ to command you what is fitting, [9] yet for love's sake I rather appeal *to you*—being such a one as Paul, the aged, and now also a prisoner of Jesus Christ— [10] I appeal to you for my son Onesimus, whom I have begotten *while* in my chains, [11] who once was unprofitable to you, but now is profitable to you and to me.

[12] I am sending him back. You therefore receive him, that is, my own heart, [13] whom I wished to keep with me, that on your behalf he might minister to me in my chains for the gospel. [14] But without your consent I wanted to do nothing, that your good deed might not be by compulsion, as it were, but voluntary.

[15] For perhaps he departed for a while for this *purpose,* that you might receive him forever, [16] no longer as a slave but more than a slave—a beloved brother, especially to me but how much more to you, both in the flesh and in the Lord.

[17] If then you count me as a partner, receive him as *you would* me. [18] But if he has wronged you or owes anything, put that on my account. [19] I, Paul, am writing with my own hand. I will repay—not to mention to you that you owe me even your own self besides. [20] Yes, brother, let me have joy from you in the Lord; refresh my heart in the Lord.

אִגֶּרֶת שָׁאוּל אֶל פִּילִימוֹן

א מֵאֵת שָׁאוּל, אֲסִיר הַמָּשִׁיחַ יֵשׁוּעַ, וּמֵאֵת טִימוֹתִיאוֹס אָחִינוּ, אֶל פִּילִימוֹן הָאָהוּב חֲבֵרֵנוּ לָעֲבוֹדָה, 2 אֶל אַפְּיָה אֲחוֹתֵנוּ, אֶל אַרְכִיפּוֹס שֶׁתָּפֵנוּ לַמַּעֲרָכָה, וְאֶל הַקְּהִלָּה אֲשֶׁר בְּבֵיתְךָ: 3 חֶסֶד וְשָׁלוֹם לָכֶם מֵאֵת הָאֱלֹהִים אָבִינוּ וְהָאָדוֹן יֵשׁוּעַ הַמָּשִׁיחַ. 4 אֲנִי מוֹדֶה לֵאלֹהַי בְּכָל עֵת שֶׁאֲנִי מַזְכִּיר אוֹתְךָ בִּתְפִלּוֹתַי, 5 לְאַחַר שֶׁשָּׁמַעְתִּי עַל הָאַהֲבָה וְהָאֱמוּנָה אֲשֶׁר אַתָּה רוֹחֵשׁ לָאָדוֹן יֵשׁוּעַ וּלְכָל הַקְּדוֹשִׁים. 6 תְּפִלָּתִי הִיא שֶׁהָאֱמוּנָה אֲשֶׁר אַתָּה שֻׁתָּף לָהּ תִּפְעַל בְּךָ בְּהַכִּירְךָ אֶת כָּל הַטּוֹב הַטָּמוּן בָּנוּ לְתוֹעֶלֶת הַמָּשִׁיחַ. 7 אָחִי, הִנֵּה אַהֲבָתְךָ גָּרְמָה לִי שִׂמְחָה גְּדוֹלָה וְנֶחָמָה, מִשּׁוּם שֶׁהֵיטִיב לְמֵשִׁיב נֶפֶשׁ לַקְּדוֹשִׁים.

8 לָכֵן, אַף שֶׁיֵּשׁ לִי הָעֹז בַּמָּשִׁיחַ לְצַוּוֹתְךָ לַעֲשׂוֹת אֶת מַה שֶׁנָּחוּץ, 9 הֲרֵי בִּגְלַל הָאַהֲבָה אֲנִי מַעֲדִיף לְבַקֵּשׁ, אֲנִי שָׁאוּל הַזָּקֵן, וְעַכְשָׁו גַּם אֲסִיר הַמָּשִׁיחַ יֵשׁוּעַ. 10 אֲנִי מְבַקֵּשׁ מִמְּךָ עַל בְּנִי אוֹנִיסִימוֹס, אֲשֶׁר הוֹלַדְתִּי אוֹתוֹ לָאֱמוּנָה בִּהְיוֹתִי בַּמַּאֲסָר. 11 בֶּעָבָר הוּא לֹא הוֹעִיל לְךָ, אַךְ כָּעֵת יֵשׁ בּוֹ לְהוֹעִיל גַּם לְךָ וְגַם לִי. 12 וַאֲנִי מֵשִׁיב אוֹתוֹ אֵלֶיךָ, אֶת אוֹנִיסִימוֹס אֲשֶׁר לִבִּי הוּא. 13 חָפַצְתִּי לְהַחֲזִיקוֹ אֶצְלִי כְּדֵי שֶׁיְשָׁרֵת אוֹתִי בִּמְקוֹמְךָ בַּמַּאֲסָר שֶׁאֲנִי נָתוּן בּוֹ בִּגְלַל הַבְּשׂוֹרָה. 14 אֲבָל לֹא רָצִיתִי לַעֲשׂוֹת דָּבָר בְּלֹא הַסְכָּמָתְךָ, וְזֹאת כְּדֵי שֶׁלֹּא יִהְיֶה פֹּעַל טוּבְךָ מִתּוֹךְ הֶכְרֵחַ כִּי אִם מֵרָצוֹן. 15 וּבִכְלָל, אוּלַי נִפְרַד מִמְּךָ לְשָׁעָה לְמַעַן יִהְיֶה לְךָ לְעוֹלָם, 16 וְלֹא עוֹד כְּעֶבֶד אֶלָּא לְמַעְלָה מֵעֶבֶד, כְּאָח אָהוּב – בִּמְיֻחָד לִי, וְעַל אַחַת כַּמָּה וְכַמָּה לְךָ, הֵן כְּאָדָם וְהֵן כְּאָח בָּאָדוֹן. 17 לְפִיכָךְ, אִם אַתָּה חוֹשֵׁב אוֹתִי לְחָבֵר לָאֱמוּנָה, קַבֵּל אוֹתוֹ כְּמוֹ שֶׁהָיִיתָ מְקַבֵּל אוֹתִי. 18 וְאִם עָשָׂה לְךָ רָעָה אוֹ חַיָּב הוּא לְךָ דָּבָר, חֲשֹׁב זֹאת לְחוֹבָתִי. 19 אֲנִי, שָׁאוּל, כּוֹתֵב זֹאת בְּמוֹ יָדִי – אֲנִי אֲשַׁלֵּם. וְאֵינֶנִּי צָרִיךְ לוֹמַר לְךָ שֶׁאַתָּה חַיָּב לִי גַּם אֶת נַפְשְׁךָ! 20 כֵּן, אָחִי, הֱיֵה נָא לִי לְמוֹעִיל בָּאָדוֹן; שׁוֹבֵב אֶת נַפְשִׁי בַּמָּשִׁיחַ.

²¹ Having confidence in your obedience, I write
to you, knowing that you will do even more than I
say. ²² But, meanwhile, also prepare a guest room
for me, for I trust that through your prayers I shall
be granted to you.

²³ Epaphras, my fellow prisoner in Christ Jesus,
greets you, ²⁴ *as do* Mark, Aristarchus, Demas,
Luke, my fellow laborers.

²⁵ The grace of our Lord Jesus Christ *be* with
your spirit. Amen.

²¹ כֵּיוָן שֶׁבָּטַחְתִּי בְּהֵעָנוּתְךָ כָּתַבְתִּי לְךָ, וְיוֹדֵעַ אֲנִי כִּי
תַּעֲשֶׂה גַּם יוֹתֵר מִמַּה שֶּׁאָמַרְתִּי. ²² נוֹסָף עַל כָּךְ,
הָכֵן לִי מָקוֹם לִינָה, כִּי אֲנִי מְקַוֶּה שֶׁהוֹדוֹת
לִתְפִלּוֹתֵיכֶם אֲשֻׁחְרַר וְאֶנָּתֵן לָכֶם.
²³ דְּרִישַׁת שָׁלוֹם מֵאֶפָּפְרַס, חֲבֵרִי לַמַּאֲסָר לְמַעַן
הַמָּשִׁיחַ יֵשׁוּעַ. ²⁴ גַּם מַרְקוֹם, אֲרִיסְטַרְכוֹס, דִּימַס
וְלוּקַס, חֲבֵרַי לָעֲבוֹדָה, דּוֹרְשִׁים בִּשְׁלוֹמְךָ. ²⁵ חֶסֶד
הָאָדוֹן יֵשׁוּעַ הַמָּשִׁיחַ עִם רוּחֲכֶם.

The Epistle to the
HEBREWS

1 God, who at various times and in various ways
spoke in time past to the fathers by the prophets,
²has in these last days spoken to us by *His* Son,
whom He has appointed heir of all things, through
whom also He made the worlds; ³who being the
brightness of *His* glory and the express image of His
person, and upholding all things by the word of His
power, when He had by Himself purged our sins,
sat down at the right hand of the Majesty on high,
⁴having become so much better than the angels, as
He has by inheritance obtained a more excellent
name than they.

⁵For to which of the angels did He ever say:

"You are My Son,
Today I have begotten You"?

And again:

"I will be to Him a Father,
And He shall be to Me a Son"?

⁶But when He again brings the firstborn into the
world, He says:

"Let all the angels of God worship Him."

⁷And of the angels He says:

"Who makes His angels spirits
And His ministers a flame of fire."

⁸But to the Son *He* says:

"Your throne, O God, *is* forever and ever;
A scepter of righteousness *is* the scepter of
Your kingdom.
⁹ You have loved righteousness and hated
lawlessness;
Therefore God, Your God, has anointed
You
With the oil of gladness more than Your
companions."

¹⁰And:

"You, LORD, in the beginning laid the
foundation of the earth,
And the heavens are the work of Your
hands.
¹¹ They will perish, but You remain;
And they will all grow old like a garment;
¹² Like a cloak You will fold them up,
And they will be changed.

הָאִגֶּרֶת אֶל הָעִבְרִים

א הָאֱלֹהִים אֲשֶׁר דִּבֶּר מִקֶּדֶם פְּעָמִים רַבּוֹת
וּבִדְרָכִים רַבּוֹת אֶל הָאָבוֹת בְּיַד הַנְּבִיאִים, ²דִּבֶּר
אֵלֵינוּ בְּאַחֲרִית הַיָּמִים הָאֵלֶּה בְּיַד הַבֵּן אֲשֶׁר שָׂם
לְיוֹרֵשׁ כֹּל וּבְיָדוֹ גַּם עָשָׂה שָׁמַיִם וָאָרֶץ; ³הוּא זֹהַר
כְּבוֹדוֹ וְצֶלֶם עַצְמוּתוֹ וְנוֹשֵׂא כֹל בִּדְבָרוֹ רַב־הַגְּבוּרָה,
וּלְאַחַר שֶׁעָשָׂה טָהוּר חֲטָאִים יָשַׁב לִימִין הַגְּדֻלָּה
בַּמְּרוֹמִים ⁴וְהָיָה לְגָדוֹל בִּמְאֹד מִן הַמַּלְאָכִים, כִּהְיוֹת
הַשֵּׁם שֶׁיָּרַשׁ נַעֲלֶה מִשֶּׁלָּהֶם, ⁵כִּי אֶל מִי מֵהַמַּלְאָכִים
אָמַר מֵעוֹלָם,

"בְּנִי אַתָּה
אֲנִי הַיּוֹם יְלִדְתִּיךָ?"

וְעוֹד,

"אֲנִי אֶהְיֶה־לּוֹ לְאָב
וְהוּא יִהְיֶה־לִּי לְבֵן?"

⁶וְעוֹד, כַּאֲשֶׁר הוּא מֵבִיא אֶת הַבְּכוֹר אֶל הָעוֹלָם,
הוּא אוֹמֵר,

"וְהִשְׁתַּחֲווּ לוֹ כָּל אֱלֹהִים."

⁷וְעַל הַמַּלְאָכִים הוּא אוֹמֵר,

"עֹשֶׂה מַלְאָכָיו רוּחוֹת,
מְשָׁרְתָיו אֵשׁ לֹהֵט."

⁸אַךְ עַל הַבֵּן הוּא אוֹמֵר,

"כִּסְאֲךָ אֱלֹהִים, עוֹלָם וָעֶד,
שֵׁבֶט מִישֹׁר שֵׁבֶט מַלְכוּתֶךָ.
⁹אָהַבְתָּ צֶּדֶק וַתִּשְׂנָא רֶשַׁע,
עַל־כֵּן מְשָׁחֲךָ אֱלֹהִים, אֱלֹהֶיךָ,
שֶׁמֶן שָׂשׂוֹן מֵחֲבֵרֶיךָ."

¹⁰וְעוֹד,

"אַתָּה אֲדֹנָי לְפָנִים הָאָרֶץ יָסַדְתָּ,
וּמַעֲשֵׂה יָדֶיךָ שָׁמָיִם;
¹¹הֵמָּה יֹאבֵדוּ וְאַתָּה תַעֲמֹד,
וְכֻלָּם כַּבֶּגֶד יִבְלוּ;
¹²כַּלְּבוּשׁ תַּחֲלִיפֵם וְיַחֲלֹפוּ,
וְאַתָּה הוּא וּשְׁנוֹתֶיךָ לֹא יִתָּמּוּ."

But You are the same,
And Your years will not fail."

13 But to which of the angels has He ever said:

"Sit at My right hand,
Till I make Your enemies Your footstool"?

14 Are they not all ministering spirits sent forth to minister for those who will inherit salvation?

2 Therefore we must give the more earnest heed to the things we have heard, lest we drift away. 2 For if the word spoken through angels proved steadfast, and every transgression and disobedience received a just reward, 3 how shall we escape if we neglect so great a salvation, which at the first began to be spoken by the Lord, and was confirmed to us by those who heard *Him,* 4 God also bearing witness both with signs and wonders, with various miracles, and gifts of the Holy Spirit, according to His own will?

5 For He has not put the world to come, of which we speak, in subjection to angels. 6 But one testified in a certain place, saying:

"What is man that You are mindful of him,
Or the son of man that You take care of him?
7   You have made him a little lower than the angels;
You have crowned him with glory and honor,
And set him over the works of Your hands.
8   You have put all things in subjection under his feet."

For in that He put all in subjection under him, He left nothing *that is* not put under him. But now we do not yet see all things put under him. 9 But we see Jesus, who was made a little lower than the angels, for the suffering of death crowned with glory and honor, that He, by the grace of God, might taste death for everyone.

10 For it was fitting for Him, for whom *are* all things and by whom *are* all things, in bringing many sons to glory, to make the captain of their salvation perfect through sufferings. 11 For both He who sanctifies and those who are being sanctified *are* all of one, for which reason He is not ashamed to call them brethren, 12 saying:

"I will declare Your name to My brethren;
In the midst of the assembly I will sing praise to You."

13 And again:

"I will put My trust in Him."

And again:

13 וְאֶל מִי מִן הַמַּלְאָכִים אָמַר מֵעוֹלָם,
"שֵׁב לִימִינִי עַד אָשִׁית אֹיְבֶיךָ הֲדֹם לְרַגְלֶיךָ?"
14 הֲאֵין כֻּלָּם רוּחוֹת־שָׁרֵת, שְׁלוּחִים לְשָׁרֵת לְמַעַן הָעֲתִידִים לָרֶשֶׁת יְשׁוּעָה?

ב עַל כֵּן חַיָּבִים אָנוּ לָשִׂים לִבֵּנוּ בְּיֶתֶר שְׂאֵת אֶל הַדְּבָרִים שֶׁשָּׁמַעְנוּ, פֶּן נָסוּר מִן הַדֶּרֶךְ. 2 הֲרֵי אִם הַדָּבָר אֲשֶׁר נֶאֱמַר בְּפִי מַלְאָכִים קִבֵּל תֹּקֶף, וְעַל כָּל עֲבֵרָה וּמְרִי נִתַּן גְּמוּל צוֹדֵק, 3 אֵיךְ נִמָּלֵט אֲנַחְנוּ אִם לֹא נָשִׂים לֵב לִישׁוּעָה גְדוֹלָה כָּזֹאת אֲשֶׁר בַּתְּחִלָּה נֶאֶמְרָה בְּפִי הָאָדוֹן וְאֻשְּׁרָה לָנוּ עַל־יְדֵי שׁוֹמְעָיו? 4 וְגַם אֱלֹהִים הֵעִיד עָלֶיהָ בְּאוֹתוֹת וּבְמוֹפְתִים וּבְכָל מִינֵי גְבוּרוֹת, וּבְמַתְּנוֹת רוּחַ הַקֹּדֶשׁ אֲשֶׁר חִלֵּק כִּרְצוֹנוֹ.

5 הֵן לֹא תַּחַת יַד הַמַּלְאָכִים שָׁת אֶת הָעוֹלָם הַבָּא אֲשֶׁר אָנוּ מְדַבְּרִים עָלָיו. 6 אֲבָל בְּמָקוֹם אֶחָד הֵעִיד מִישֶׁהוּ לֵאמֹר:

"מָה־אֱנוֹשׁ כִּי־תִזְכְּרֶנּוּ
וּבֶן־אָדָם כִּי תִפְקְדֶנּוּ?
7 וַתְּחַסְּרֵהוּ מְעַט מֵאֱלֹהִים,
וְכָבוֹד וְהָדָר תְּעַטְּרֵהוּ,
וַתַּמְשִׁילֵהוּ בְּמַעֲשֵׂי יָדֶיךָ;
8 כֹּל שַׁתָּה תַחַת רַגְלָיו."

הִנֵּה בַּהֲשִׁיתוֹ הַכֹּל תַּחְתָּיו לֹא הִשְׁאִיר דָּבָר שֶׁלֹּא הוּשַׁת תַּחְתָּיו. אַךְ כָּעֵת עֲדַיִן אֵין אָנוּ רוֹאִים כִּי הַכֹּל הוּשַׁת תַּחְתָּיו. 9 אֲבָל רוֹאִים אָנוּ אֶת יֵשׁוּעַ מְעֻטָּר בְּכָבוֹד וְהָדָר מִשּׁוּם שֶׁסָּבַל מָוֶת, הוּא אֲשֶׁר חֻסַּר מְעַט מִמַּלְאָכִים, כְּדֵי שֶׁבְּחֶסֶד אֱלֹהִים יִטְעַם מָוֶת בְּעַד הַכֹּל.

10 אָכֵן הוּא אֲשֶׁר הַכֹּל לְמַעֲנוֹ וְהַכֹּל עַל־יָדָיו יָאֶה הָיָה לוֹ, בַּהֲבִיאוֹ בָּנִים רַבִּים לְכָבוֹד, לְהַשְׁלִים עַל־יְדֵי סֵבֶל אֶת מְכוֹנֵן יְשׁוּעָתָם. 11 הֵן גַּם הַמְקַדֵּשׁ גַּם הַמְקֻדָּשִׁים כֻּלָּם מֵאֶחָד הֵמָּה, וְלָכֵן אֵינוּ בּוֹשׁ מִקְּרֹא לָהֶם אַחִים, 12 בְּאָמְרוֹ,

"אֲסַפְּרָה שִׁמְךָ לְאֶחָי
בְּתוֹךְ קָהָל אֲהַלְלֶךָ."

13 וְעוֹד,
"וְקִוֵּיתִי־לוֹ",
וְעוֹד,

"Here am I and the children whom God has given Me."

[14] Inasmuch then as the children have partaken of flesh and blood, He Himself likewise shared in the same, that through death He might destroy him who had the power of death, that is, the devil, [15] and release those who through fear of death were all their lifetime subject to bondage. [16] For indeed He does not give aid to angels, but He does give aid to the seed of Abraham. [17] Therefore, in all things He had to be made like *His* brethren, that He might be a merciful and faithful High Priest in things *pertaining* to God, to make propitiation for the sins of the people. [18] For in that He Himself has suffered, being tempted, He is able to aid those who are tempted.

3 Therefore, holy brethren, partakers of the heavenly calling, consider the Apostle and High Priest of our confession, Christ Jesus, [2] who was faithful to Him who appointed Him, as Moses also *was faithful* in all His house. [3] For this One has been counted worthy of more glory than Moses, inasmuch as He who built the house has more honor than the house. [4] For every house is built by someone, but He who built all things *is* God. [5] And Moses indeed *was* faithful in all His house as a servant, for a testimony of those things which would be spoken *afterward*, [6] but Christ as a Son over His own house, whose house we are if we hold fast the confidence and the rejoicing of the hope firm to the end.

[7] Therefore, as the Holy Spirit says:

"*Today, if you will hear His voice,*
[8]   *Do not harden your hearts as in the rebellion,*
    In the day of trial in the wilderness,
[9]   *Where your fathers tested Me, tried Me,*
    And saw My works forty years.
[10]   *Therefore I was angry with that generation,*
    And said, 'They always go astray in their heart,
    And they have not known My ways.'
[11]   *So I swore in My wrath,*
    'They shall not enter My rest.'"

[12] Beware, brethren, lest there be in any of you an evil heart of unbelief in departing from the living God; [13] but exhort one another daily, while it is called "*Today*," lest any of you be hardened through the deceitfulness of sin. [14] For we have

---

"הִנֵּה אָנֹכִי וְהַיְלָדִים אֲשֶׁר נָתַן לִי יהוה."

[14] וְכֵיוָן שֶׁלַּיְלָדִים הָיְתָה שֻׁתָּפוּת שֶׁל בָּשָׂר וָדָם, כְּמוֹ כֵן גַּם הוּא שִׁתֵּף עַצְמוֹ בְּבָשָׂר וָדָם כְּדֵי שֶׁיַּשְׁבִּית עַל־יְדֵי מוֹתוֹ אֶת זֶה שֶׁבְּיָדוֹ מֶמְשֶׁלֶת הַמָּוֶת – הוּא הַשָּׂטָן, [15] וִישַׁחְרֵר אֶת אֵלֶּה שֶׁבִּגְלַל אֵימַת הַמָּוֶת הָיוּ נְתוּנִים לְעַבְדוּת כָּל יְמֵי חַיֵּיהֶם. [16] הֵן לֹא בְּמַלְאָכִים הוּא תּוֹמֵךְ, אֶלָּא בְּזֶרַע אַבְרָהָם. [17] לְפִיכָךְ הָיָה עָלָיו לְהִדָּמוֹת לְאֶחָיו בְּכָל דָּבָר, לְמַעַן יִהְיֶה כֹּהֵן גָּדוֹל רַחֲמָן וְנֶאֱמָן בְּעִנְיְנֵי אֱלֹהִים לְכַפֵּר עַל חַטָּאֵי הָעָם; [18] כִּי מֵאַחַר שֶׁהוּא עַצְמוֹ סָבַל כַּאֲשֶׁר הִתְנַסָּה, הוּא יָכוֹל לַעֲזֹר לְאֵלֶּה אֲשֶׁר נְתוּנִים בְּנִסָּיוֹן.

ג לָכֵן, אַחַי הַקְּדוֹשִׁים, אֲשֶׁר חֶלְקְכֶם בַּקְּרִיאָה שְׁמֵימִית, הִתְבּוֹנְנוּ אֶל הַשָּׁלִיחַ וְהַכֹּהֵן הַגָּדוֹל שֶׁל הַכְרָזַת אֱמוּנָתֵנוּ, יֵשׁוּעַ, [2] הַנֶּאֱמָן לַמְכוֹנֵן אוֹתוֹ, כְּמוֹ שֶׁהָיָה גַּם מֹשֶׁה בְּכָל בֵּיתוֹ; [3] וַהֲרֵי הוּא נִמְצָא רָאוּי לְכָבוֹד רַב יוֹתֵר מִשֶּׁזָּכָה לוֹ מֹשֶׁה, בְּאוֹתָהּ מִדָּה שֶׁבּוֹנֶה הַבַּיִת נִכְבָּד יוֹתֵר מִן הַבַּיִת. [4] הֵן כָּל בַּיִת יֵשׁ לוֹ בּוֹנֶה, אַךְ בּוֹנֵה הַכֹּל הוּא הָאֱלֹהִים. [5] מֹשֶׁה אָמְנָם הָיָה נֶאֱמָן בְּכָל בֵּיתוֹ, כְּעֶבֶד, לְשֵׁם עֵדוּת עַל הַדְּבָרִים אֲשֶׁר הָיוּ עֲתִידִים לְהֵאָמֵר, [6] אֲבָל הַמָּשִׁיחַ הוּא כְּבֵן עַל בֵּיתוֹ; וַאֲנַחְנוּ בֵּיתוֹ, אִם נַחֲזִיק עַד קֵץ בַּבִּטָּחוֹן וּבַתִּקְוָה שֶׁאָנוּ מִתְהַלְּלִים בָּהּ.

[7] עַל כֵּן, כְּמַאֲמַר רוּחַ הַקֹּדֶשׁ,

"הַיּוֹם אִם־בְּקֹלוֹ תִּשְׁמָעוּ;
[8] אַל־תַּקְשׁוּ לְבַבְכֶם כִּמְרִיבָה,
כְּיוֹם מַסָּה בַּמִּדְבָּר,
[9] אֲשֶׁר נִסּוּנִי אֲבוֹתֵיכֶם,
בְּחָנוּנִי גַּם־רָאוּ פָעֳלִי אַרְבָּעִים שָׁנָה.
[10] לָכֵן אָקוּט בְּדוֹר
וָאֹמַר, עַם תֹּעֵי לֵבָב הֵם,
וְהֵם לֹא־יָדְעוּ דְרָכָי.
[11] אֲשֶׁר־נִשְׁבַּעְתִּי בְאַפִּי
אִם יְבֹאוּן אֶל־מְנוּחָתִי."

[12] הִשָּׁמְרוּ, אַחַי, שֶׁלֹּא יִהְיֶה בְּאִישׁ מִכֶּם לֵב מְרֻשָּׁע וַחֲסַר אֱמוּנָה, הַסּוֹטֶה מֵאֱלֹהִים חַיִּים. [13] עוֹדְדוּ אִישׁ אֶת רֵעֵהוּ יוֹם יוֹם, כָּל עוֹד הַזְּמַן מְכֻנֶּה "הַיּוֹם", לְמַעַן לֹא יִקְשֶׁה לֵב אִישׁ מִכֶּם בְּנִכְלֵי הַחֵטְא. [14] הֵן נִהְיֵינוּ שֻׁתָּפִים לַמָּשִׁיחַ אִם נַחֲזִיק לְלֹא הֶרֶף, עַד

become partakers of Christ if we hold the beginning of our confidence steadfast to the end, 15 while it is said:

"Today, if you will hear His voice,
Do not harden your hearts as in the rebellion."

16 For who, having heard, rebelled? Indeed, *was it* not all who came out of Egypt, *led* by Moses? 17 Now with whom was He angry forty years? *Was it* not with those who sinned, whose corpses fell in the wilderness? 18 And to whom did He swear that they would not enter His rest, but to those who did not obey? 19 So we see that they could not enter in because of unbelief.

4 Therefore, since a promise remains of entering His rest, let us fear lest any of you seem to have come short of it. 2 For indeed the gospel was preached to us as well as to them; but the word which they heard did not profit them, not being mixed with faith in those who heard *it.* 3 For we who have believed do enter that rest, as He has said:

"So I swore in My wrath,
'They shall not enter My rest,' "

although the works were finished from the foundation of the world. 4 For He has spoken in a certain place of the seventh *day* in this way: *"And God rested on the seventh day from all His works";* 5 and again in this *place:* "*They shall not enter My rest.*"

6 Since therefore it remains that some *must* enter it, and those to whom it was first preached did not enter because of disobedience, 7 again He designates a certain day, saying in David, *"Today,"* after such a long time, as it has been said:

"Today, if you will hear His voice,
Do not harden your hearts."

8 For if Joshua had given them rest, then He would not afterward have spoken of another day. 9 There remains therefore a rest for the people of God. 10 For he who has entered His rest has himself also ceased from his works as God *did* from His.

11 Let us therefore be diligent to enter that rest, lest anyone fall according to the same example of disobedience. 12 For the word of God *is* living and powerful, and sharper than any two-edged sword, piercing even to the division of soul and spirit, and of joints and marrow, and is a discerner of the thoughts and intents of the heart. 13 And there is no creature hidden from His sight, but all things *are* naked and open to the eyes of Him to whom we *must give* account.

הַסּוֹף, בַּבִּטָּחוֹן אֲשֶׁר הִתְחַלְנוּ בּוֹ, 15 בְּעוֹד שֶׁנֶּאֱמַר "הַיּוֹם אִם־בְּקֹלוֹ תִשְׁמָעוּ, אַל־תַּקְשׁוּ לְבַבְכֶם כִּמְרִיבָה"; 16 כִּי מִי הַשּׁוֹמְעִים אֲשֶׁר רָבוּ אִם לֹא כָּל יוֹצְאֵי מִצְרַיִם בְּיַד מֹשֶׁה? 17 וּבְמִי נָקְטָה נַפְשׁוֹ אַרְבָּעִים שָׁנָה? הֲלֹא בַּחוֹטְאִים אֲשֶׁר נָפְלוּ פְגָרִים בַּמִּדְבָּר? 18 וּלְמִי נִשְׁבַּע שֶׁלֹּא יָבוֹאוּ אֶל מְנוּחָתוֹ אִם לֹא לַסּוֹרְרִים? 19 אֲנַחְנוּ רוֹאִים כִּי לֹא יָכְלוּ לָבוֹא מִשּׁוּם שֶׁלֹּא הֶאֱמִינוּ.

ד לָכֵן, בְּעוֹד עוֹמֶדֶת הַהַבְטָחָה לְהִכָּנֵס אֶל מְנוּחָתוֹ, רָאוּי לָנוּ לַחֲשֹׁשׁ שֶׁמָּא יִמָּצֵא אִישׁ מִכֶּם מְאַחֵר לְהִכָּנֵס. 2 הֲרֵי גַם אֲנַחְנוּ הִתְבַּשַּׂרְנוּ כְּמוֹהֶם, אַךְ הַדָּבָר שֶׁנִּשְׁמַע לֹא הוֹעִיל לָהֶם מִשּׁוּם שֶׁלֹּא הִתְמַזֵּג עִם אֱמוּנָה בְּקֶרֶב הַשּׁוֹמְעִים. 3 אֲנַחְנוּ הַמַּאֲמִינִים נִכְנָסִים לַמְּנוּחָה, כְּשֵׁם שֶׁאָמַר, "אֲשֶׁר־נִשְׁבַּעְתִּי בְאַפִּי אִם־יְבֹאוּן אֶל־מְנוּחָתִי," אַף כִּי מֵהוּסַד תֵּבֵל הֻשְׁלְמוּ הַמַּעֲשִׂים, 4 שֶׁכֵּן בְּמָקוֹם אֶחָד הוּא אוֹמֵר עַל הַיּוֹם הַשְּׁבִיעִי, "וַיִּשְׁבֹּת אֱלֹהִים בַּיּוֹם הַשְּׁבִיעִי מִכָּל־מְלַאכְתּוֹ." 5 וְכָאן שׁוּב, "אִם־יְבֹאוּן אֶל־מְנוּחָתִי." 6 וּמֵאַחַר שֶׁיֵּשׁ אֲשֶׁר נוֹתַר לָהֶם לְהִכָּנֵס אֵלֶיהָ וְאֵלֶּה שֶׁהִתְבַּשְּׂרוּ בָּרִאשׁוֹנָה לֹא נִכְנְסוּ בִּגְלַל הַמֶּרִי, 7 שׁוּב יִעַד יוֹם מְסֻיָּם – הַיּוֹם – בְּאָמְרוֹ בְּפִי דָוִד כַּנֶּאֱמַר לְעֵיל, וְזֹאת לְאַחַר זְמַן רַב, "הַיּוֹם אִם־בְּקֹלוֹ תִשְׁמָעוּ, אַל־תַּקְשׁוּ לְבַבְכֶם."

8 אִלּוּ הֵבִיאָם יְהוֹשֻׁעַ אֶל הַמְּנוּחָה, לֹא הָיָה מְדַבֵּר אַחֲרֵי כֵן עַל יוֹם אַחֵר. 9 לְפִיכָךְ נוֹתְרָה מְנוּחַת שַׁבָּת לְעַם אֱלֹהִים. 10 הֵן הַנִּכְנָס אֶל מְנוּחָתוֹ גַּם הוּא שָׁבַת מִמְּלַאכְתּוֹ, כְּמוֹ הָאֱלֹהִים מִשֶּׁלּוֹ. 11 לָכֵן נֵחָתֵר נָא לְהִכָּנֵס אֶל הַמְּנוּחָה הַהִיא, פֶּן יִכָּשֵׁל אִישׁ וְיִהְיֶה לְמַמְרֶה כְּמוֹהֶם; 12 שֶׁהֲרֵי דְּבַר הָאֱלֹהִים חַי וּפוֹעֵל, וְחַד הוּא מֵחֶרֶב פִּיפִיּוֹת וְחוֹדֵר עַד לְהַבְדִּיל בֵּין נֶפֶשׁ לְרוּחַ וּבֵין פְּרָקִים לְמֹחַ הָעֲצָמוֹת, וּבוֹחֵן מַחְשְׁבוֹת הַלֵּב וְכַוָּנוֹתָיו. 13 אֵין שׁוּם נִבְרָא נִסְתָּר מֵעֵינָיו; הַכֹּל חָשׂוּף וְגָלוּי לְעֵינֵי מִי שֶׁלְּפָנָיו עָלֵינוּ לָתֵת דִּין וְחֶשְׁבּוֹן.

14 Seeing then that we have a great High Priest who has passed through the heavens, Jesus the Son of God, let us hold fast *our* confession. 15 For we do not have a High Priest who cannot sympathize with our weaknesses, but was in all *points* tempted as *we are, yet* without sin. 16 Let us therefore come boldly to the throne of grace, that we may obtain mercy and find grace to help in time of need.

5 For every high priest taken from among men is appointed for men in things *pertaining* to God, that he may offer both gifts and sacrifices for sins. 2 He can have compassion on those who are ignorant and going astray, since he himself is also subject to weakness. 3 Because of this he is required as for the people, so also for himself, to offer *sacrifices* for sins. 4 And no man takes this honor to himself, but he who is called by God, just as Aaron *was*.

5 So also Christ did not glorify Himself to become High Priest, *but it* was He who said to Him:

"You are My Son,
Today I have begotten You."

6 As *He* also *says* in another *place*:

"You *are* a priest forever
According to the order of Melchizedek";

7 who, in the days of His flesh, when He had offered up prayers and supplications, with vehement cries and tears to Him who was able to save Him from death, and was heard because of His godly fear, 8 though He was a Son, *yet* He learned obedience by the things which He suffered. 9 And having been perfected, He became the author of eternal salvation to all who obey Him, 10 called by God as High Priest "according to the order of Melchizedek," 11 of whom we have much to say, and hard to explain, since you have become dull of hearing.

12 For though by this time you ought to be teachers, you need *someone* to teach you again the first principles of the oracles of God; and you have come to need milk and not solid food. 13 For everyone who partakes *only* of milk *is* unskilled in the word of righteousness, for he is a babe. 14 But solid food belongs to those who are of full age, *that is,* those who by reason of use have their senses exercised to discern both good and evil.

6 Therefore, leaving the discussion of the elementary *principles* of Christ, let us go on to perfection, not laying again the foundation of repentance from dead works and of faith toward God, 2 of the

14 וְכֵיוָן שֶׁיֵּשׁ לָנוּ כֹּהֵן גָּדוֹל עֶלְיוֹן אֲשֶׁר עָבַר דֶּרֶךְ הַשָּׁמַיִם, הֲלֹא הוּא יֵשׁוּעַ בֶּן־הָאֱלֹהִים, נַחֲזִיקָה בְּהַכְרָזַת אֱמוּנָתֵנוּ. 15 כִּי אֵין לָנוּ כֹּהֵן גָּדוֹל שֶׁאֵינוֹ יָכוֹל לָחוּשׁ עִמָּנוּ אֶת חֻלְשׁוֹתֵינוּ, אֶלָּא אֶחָד שֶׁהִתְנַסָּה בַּכֹּל כָּמוֹנוּ מִבְּלִי חֵטְא. 16 עַל כֵּן נִקְרְבָה בְּבִטָּחוֹן אֶל כֵּס הַחֶסֶד לְקַבֵּל רַחֲמִים וְלִמְצֹא חֶסֶד לְעֶזְרָה בְּעִתָּהּ.

ה כָּל כֹּהֵן גָּדוֹל הַלָּקוּחַ מִקֶּרֶב בְּנֵי אָדָם, מְמֻנֶּה לְמַעַן בְּנֵי אָדָם עַל עִנְיְנֵי אֱלֹהִים כְּדֵי לְהַקְרִיב מְנָחוֹת וּזְבָחִים עַל חֲטָאִים. 2 הוּא יָכוֹל לַחְמֹל עַל הַשּׁוֹגְגִים וְהַתּוֹעִים, מִשּׁוּם שֶׁגַּם הוּא מֻקָּף חֻלְשָׁה. 3 מִסִּבָּה זֹאת הוּא חַיָּב לְהַקְרִיב עַל חֲטָאִים גַּם בְּעַד הָעָם וְגַם בְּעַד עַצְמוֹ. 4 וְאֵין אִישׁ לוֹקֵחַ לְעַצְמוֹ אֶת הַכָּבוֹד זוּלָתִי הַנִּקְרָא מִטַּעַם אֱלֹהִים, כְּאַהֲרֹן.

5 כֵּן גַּם הַמָּשִׁיחַ לֹא נָטַל לְעַצְמוֹ אֶת הַכָּבוֹד לִהְיוֹת כֹּהֵן גָּדוֹל, אֶלָּא קִבֵּל זֹאת מֵאֵת הָאוֹמֵר אֵלָיו, "בְּנִי אַתָּה, אֲנִי הַיּוֹם יְלִדְתִּיךָ"; 6 כְּמוֹ שֶׁגַּם בְּמָקוֹם אַחֵר הוּא אוֹמֵר, "אַתָּה־כֹהֵן לְעוֹלָם עַל־דִּבְרָתִי מַלְכִּי־צֶדֶק."

7 וּבִימֵי הֱיוֹתוֹ בְּגוּף בָּשָׂר וָדָם, הִקְרִיב תְּפִלּוֹת וְתַחֲנוּנִים בִּצְעָקָה גְדוֹלָה וּבִדְמָעוֹת אֶל הַיָּכוֹל לְהוֹשִׁיעוֹ מִמָּוֶת, וְאָמְנָם נִשְׁמַע בִּגְלַל יִרְאַת הָאֱלֹהִים שֶׁבּוֹ. 8 וְאַף כִּי הָיָה הַבֵּן, מִסִּבְלוֹתָיו לָמַד לְצַיֵּת. 9 וְכַאֲשֶׁר הֻשְׁלַם הָיָה לִמְקוֹר שֶׁל יְשׁוּעַת עוֹלָמִים לְכָל הַמְצַיְּתִים לוֹ, 10 וֵאלֹהִים קָרָא לוֹ, "כֹּהֵן גָּדוֹל עַל־דִּבְרָתִי מַלְכִּי־צֶדֶק."

11 עַל זֹאת יֵשׁ לָנוּ לוֹמַר דְּבָרִים רַבִּים, אַךְ קָשֶׁה לְהַסְבִּירָם מִפְּנֵי שֶׁכָּבְדוּ אָזְנֵיכֶם. 12 הִנֵּה בִּזְמַן שֶׁעֲלֵיכֶם לִהְיוֹת כְּבָר מוֹרִים, שׁוּב צְרִיכִים אַתֶּם לְמִישֶׁהוּ שֶׁיְּלַמֵּד אֶתְכֶם אֶת רֵאשִׁית יְסוֹדוֹת דִּבְרֵי אֱלֹהִים וְנִהְיֵיתֶם זְקוּקִים לְחָלָב וְלֹא לְמָזוֹן מוּצָק. 13 הֵן כָּל מִי שֶׁמַּאֲכָלוֹ חָלָב אֵינֶנּוּ מֵבִין בְּדִבְרֵי צֶדֶק, כִּי עוֹדֶנּוּ תִינוֹק. 14 אַךְ הַמַּאֲכָל הַמּוּצָק הוּא לַמְבֻגָּרִים, אֵלֶּה אֲשֶׁר חוּשֵׁיהֶם הֻרְגְּלוּ עַל־יְדֵי הַנִּסָּיוֹן הַמַּעֲשִׂי לְהַבְחִין בֵּין טוֹב לְרָע.

ו לָכֵן, לְאַחַר שֶׁעֲזַבְנוּ אֶת הַשָּׁלָב הָרִאשׁוֹן שֶׁל דְּבַר הַמָּשִׁיחַ, נִתְקַדֵּם נָא אֶל הַבַּגְרוּת וְאַל נָשׁוּב לְהַנִּיחַ יְסוֹדוֹת שֶׁל חֲזָרָה בִּתְשׁוּבָה מִמַּעֲשִׂים מֵתִים, אֱמוּנָה בֵּאלֹהִים, 2 תּוֹרַת הַטְּבִילוֹת, סְמִיכַת יָדַיִם, תְּחִיַּת

doctrine of baptisms, of laying on of hands, of resurrection of the dead, and of eternal judgment. [3] And this we will do if God permits.

[4] For *it is* impossible for those who were once enlightened, and have tasted the heavenly gift, and have become partakers of the Holy Spirit, [5] and have tasted the good word of God and the powers of the age to come, [6] if they fall away, to renew them again to repentance, since they crucify again for themselves the Son of God, and put *Him* to an open shame.

[7] For the earth which drinks in the rain that often comes upon it, and bears herbs useful for those by whom it is cultivated, receives blessing from God; [8] but if it bears thorns and briers, *it is* rejected and near to being cursed, whose end *is* to be burned.

[9] But, beloved, we are confident of better things concerning you, yes, things that accompany salvation, though we speak in this manner. [10] For God *is* not unjust to forget your work and labor of love which you have shown toward His name, *in that* you have ministered to the saints, and do minister. [11] And we desire that each one of you show the same diligence to the full assurance of hope until the end, [12] that you do not become sluggish, but imitate those who through faith and patience inherit the promises.

[13] For when God made a promise to Abraham, because He could swear by no one greater, He swore by Himself, [14] saying, "Surely blessing I will bless you, and multiplying I will multiply you." [15] And so, after he had patiently endured, he obtained the promise. [16] For men indeed swear by the greater, and an oath for confirmation *is* for them an end of all dispute. [17] Thus God, determining to show more abundantly to the heirs of promise the immutability of His counsel, confirmed *it* by an oath, [18] that by two immutable things, in which *it is* impossible for God to lie, we might have strong consolation, who have fled for refuge to lay hold of the hope set before *us.*

[19] This *hope* we have as an anchor of the soul, both sure and steadfast, and which enters the Presence *behind* the veil, [20] where the forerunner has entered for us, *even* Jesus, having become High Priest forever according to the order of Melchizedek.

7 For this Melchizedek, king of Salem, priest of the Most High God, who met Abraham returning from the slaughter of the kings and blessed him, [2] to whom also Abraham gave a tenth part of all, first being translated "king of righteousness," and then also king of Salem, meaning "king of peace,"

הַמֵּתִים, וּמִשְׁפַּט עוֹלָם. ‎[3] וְזֹאת נַעֲשֶׂה אִם יִרְצֶה אֱלֹהִים. ‎[4] הֵן אֵלֶּה שֶׁכְּבָר הוּאֲרוּ עֵינֵיהֶם וְטָעֲמוּ מִמַּתְּנַת הַשָּׁמַיִם וְנִתַּן לָהֶם חֶלְקָם בְּרוּחַ הַקֹּדֶשׁ ‎[5] וְטָעֲמוּ אֶת דְּבַר אֱלֹהִים הַטּוֹב וְכֹחוֹת הָעוֹלָם הַבָּא, ‎[6] וְנָסוֹגוּ – אִי אֶפְשָׁר לְחַדֵּשׁ אוֹתָם עוֹד לִתְשׁוּבָה, בִּהְיוֹתָם צוֹלְבִים לָהֶם מֵחָדָשׁ אֶת בֶּן הָאֱלֹהִים וְשָׂמִים אוֹתוֹ לְחֶרְפָּה. ‎[7] הֲרֵי אֲדָמָה הַשּׁוֹתָה אֶת הַגֶּשֶׁם הַיּוֹרֵד עָלֶיהָ פְּעָמִים רַבּוֹת וּמוֹצִיאָה עֵשֶׂב טוֹב לְעוֹבְדִים אוֹתָהּ, נוֹשֵׂאת בְּרָכָה מֵאֵת אֱלֹהִים. ‎[8] אֲבָל אִם תַּצְמִיחַ קוֹצִים וְדַרְדָּרִים, פְּסוּלָה הִיא וּקְרוֹבָה לִקְלָלָה וְסוֹפָהּ לְהִשָּׂרֵף.

‎[9] גַּם בְּדַבְּרֵנוּ כָּךְ בְּטוּחִים אָנוּ בָּכֶם, אֲהוּבַי, בְּנוֹגֵעַ לַדְּבָרִים הַטּוֹבִים יוֹתֵר הַטּוֹמְנִים בְּחֻבָּם יְשׁוּעָה; ‎[10] שֶׁכֵּן אֱלֹהִים לֹא יְעַוֵּת צֶדֶק וְלֹא יִשְׁכַּח אֶת פָּעֳלְכֶם וְאֶת הָאַהֲבָה שֶׁהֶרְאֵיתֶם לְמַעַן שְׁמוֹ בְּכָךְ שֶׁשֵּׁרַתֶּם אֶת הַקְּדוֹשִׁים וְעוֹדְכֶם מְשָׁרְתִים אוֹתָם. ‎[11] חֲפֵצִים אָנוּ שֶׁכָּל אֶחָד מִכֶּם יַרְאֶה אֶת אוֹתָהּ שְׁקִידָה בְּעָמְדוֹ בְּבִטָּחוֹן הַתִּקְוָה עַד הַסּוֹף, ‎[12] כְּדֵי שֶׁלֹּא תִּהְיוּ לִנְרְפִּים, אֶלָּא תֵּלְכוּ בְּעִקְבוֹתָם שֶׁל הַיּוֹרְשִׁים אֶת הַהַבְטָחוֹת עַל־יְדֵי אֱמוּנָה וְאֹרֶךְ רוּחַ. ‎[13] כַּאֲשֶׁר אֱלֹהִים הִבְטִיחַ אֶת הַבְטָחָתוֹ לְאַבְרָהָם הוּא נִשְׁבַּע בְּנַפְשׁוֹ, מִפְּנֵי שֶׁאֵין גָּדוֹל מִמֶּנּוּ אֲשֶׁר בּוֹ הוּא יָכוֹל לְהִשָּׁבַע. ‎[14] הוּא אָמַר, "כִּי־בָרֵךְ אֲבָרֶכְךָ וְהַרְבָּה אַרְבֶּה אוֹתָךְ." ‎[15] וְכָךְ, בְּעָמְדוֹ בְּאֹרֶךְ רוּחַ, הִשִּׂיג אַבְרָהָם אֶת אֲשֶׁר הֻבְטַח. ‎[16] בְּנֵי אָדָם נִשְׁבָּעִים בַּגָּדוֹל מֵהֶם, וְהַשְּׁבוּעָה הִיא לָהֶם חוֹתָם שֶׁל אֱמֶת הַשָּׂם קֵץ לְכָל דִּין וּדְבָרִים. ‎[17] וְכַאֲשֶׁר רָצָה אֱלֹהִים לְהַרְאוֹת בְּיֶתֶר תֹּקֶף לְיוֹרְשֵׁי הַהַבְטָחָה כִּי כַּוָּנָתוֹ אֵינָהּ נְתֻנָה לְשִׁנּוּי, הִתְחַיֵּב בִּשְׁבוּעָה. ‎[18] בְּאֹפֶן זֶה, עַל־סְמַךְ שְׁנֵי דְּבָרִים בִּלְתִּי מִשְׁתַּנִּים שֶׁחֲלִילָה לֵאלֹהִים לְשַׁקֵּר בָּהֶם, אֲנַחְנוּ הַנִּמְלָטִים נְתוֹעַד מְאֹד לֶאֱחֹז בַּתִּקְוָה הַמֻּנַּחַת לְפָנֵינוּ; ‎[19] תִּקְוָה שֶׁהִיא כְּעֹגֶן בָּטוּחַ וְיַצִּיב לְנַפְשֵׁנוּ וּמַגִּיעָה אֶל מִבֵּית לַפָּרֹכֶת, ‎[20] אֶל הַמָּקוֹם אֲשֶׁר יֵשׁוּעַ, הֶחָלוּץ הָעוֹבֵר לְפָנֵינוּ, נִכְנַס בַּעֲדֵנוּ וְהָיָה לְכֹהֵן גָּדוֹל לְעוֹלָם עַל־דִּבְרָתִי מַלְכִּי־צֶדֶק.

ז מַלְכִּי־צֶדֶק זֶה, מֶלֶךְ שָׁלֵם, כֹּהֵן לְאֵל עֶלְיוֹן, אֲשֶׁר יָצָא לִקְרַאת אַבְרָהָם בְּשׁוּב אַבְרָהָם מֵהַכּוֹת אֶת הַמְּלָכִים וּבֵרַךְ אוֹתוֹ, ‎[2] וַאֲשֶׁר אַבְרָהָם חָלַק לוֹ מַעֲשֵׂר מִכֹּל, פֵּרוּשׁ שְׁמוֹ בָּרִאשׁוֹנָה מֶלֶךְ צֶדֶק; וְהוּא

³without father, without mother, without genealogy, having neither beginning of days nor end of
life, but made like the Son of God, remains a priest
continually.

⁴Now consider how great this man *was,* to whom
even the patriarch Abraham gave a tenth of the
spoils. ⁵And indeed those who are of the sons of
Levi, who receive the priesthood, have a commandment to receive tithes from the people according to
the law, that is, from their brethren, though they
have come from the loins of Abraham; ⁶but he
whose genealogy is not derived from them received
tithes from Abraham and blessed him who had the
promises. ⁷Now beyond all contradiction the lesser
is blessed by the better. ⁸Here mortal men receive
tithes, but there he *receives them,* of whom it is
witnessed that he lives. ⁹Even Levi, who receives
tithes, paid tithes through Abraham, so to speak,
¹⁰for he was still in the loins of his father when
Melchizedek met him.

¹¹Therefore, if perfection were through the
Levitical priesthood (for under it the people
received the law), what further need *was there* that
another priest should rise according to the order of
Melchizedek, and not be called according to the
order of Aaron? ¹²For the priesthood being
changed, of necessity there is also a change of the
law. ¹³For He of whom these things are spoken
belongs to another tribe, from which no man has
officiated at the altar.

¹⁴For *it is* evident that our Lord arose from
Judah, of which tribe Moses spoke nothing
concerning priesthood. ¹⁵And it is yet far more
evident if, in the likeness of Melchizedek, there
arises another priest ¹⁶who has come, not according
to the law of a fleshly commandment, but according
to the power of an endless life. ¹⁷For He testifies:

> "You are a priest forever
> According to the order of Melchizedek."

¹⁸For on the one hand there is an annulling of
the former commandment because of its weakness
and unprofitableness, ¹⁹for the law made nothing
perfect; on the other hand, *there is the* bringing in of
a better hope, through which we draw near to God.

²⁰And inasmuch as *He was* not *made priest*
without an oath ²¹(for they have become priests
without an oath, but He with an oath by Him who
said to Him:

> "The LORD has sworn
> And will not relent,
> 'You are a priest forever
> According to the order of Melchizedek'"),

גַּם מֶלֶךְ שָׁלֵם, שֶׁפֵּרוּשׁוֹ מֶלֶךְ הַשָּׁלוֹם; ³ בְּלֹא אָב,
בְּלֹא אֵם, בְּלֹא צִיּוּן יֻחֲסִין, אֵין תְּחִלָּה לְיָמָיו וְגַם לֹא
סוֹף לְחַיָּיו, וּבִהְיוֹתוֹ דּוֹמֶה לְבֶן־הָאֱלֹהִים הוּא נִשְׁאָר
כֹּהֵן לְתָמִיד.

⁴ רְאוּ מַה גָּדוֹל הוּא זֶה אֲשֶׁר אַבְרָהָם אָבִינוּ נָתַן לוֹ
מַעֲשֵׂר מִמֵּיטַב הַשָּׁלָל. ⁵ הֲלֹא בְּנֵי לֵוִי, הַיּוֹרְשִׁים אֶת
הַכְּהֻנָּה, צֻוּוּ עַל־פִּי הַתּוֹרָה לָקַחַת מַעֲשֵׂר מִן הָעָם,
כְּלוֹמַר מֵאֲחֵיהֶם, הֲגַם שֶׁהֵלָּלוּ יוֹצְאֵי יֶרֶךְ אַבְרָהָם.
⁶ אֲבָל הוּא אֲשֶׁר לֹא הִתְיַחֵשׂ עַל מִשְׁפַּחְתָּם לָקַח
מַעֲשֵׂר מֵאַבְרָהָם וּבֵרַךְ אֶת זֶה שֶׁהָיוּ לוֹ הַהַבְטָחוֹת.
⁷ אֵין עוֹרְרִים עַל כָּךְ שֶׁהַקָּטֹן יְבֹרַךְ מִפִּי הַגָּדוֹל מִמֶּנּוּ.
⁸ וְהִנֵּה כָּאן לוֹקְחִים אֶת הַמַּעֲשֵׂר בְּנֵי אָדָם שֶׁסּוֹפָם
לָמוּת, אַךְ שָׁם – מִי שֶׁהוּעַד עָלָיו שֶׁהוּא חַי.
⁹ וְאֶפְשָׁר לוֹמַר שֶׁגַּם לֵוִי, מְקַבֵּל הַמַּעֲשְׂרוֹת, נָתַן
מַעֲשֵׂר עַל־יְדֵי אַבְרָהָם, ¹⁰ כִּי הָיָה בְּחַלְצֵי אָבִיו
אַבְרָהָם בְּצֵאת מַלְכִּי־צֶדֶק לִקְרָאתוֹ.
¹¹ לָכֵן אִלּוּ הֻשְׂגָּה שְׁלֵמוּת עַל־יְדֵי כְּהֻנַּת לֵוִי,
שֶׁבְּזִמָּנָהּ קִבֵּל הָעָם אֶת הַתּוֹרָה, מַה צֹּרֶךְ עוֹד
שֶׁיָּקוּם כֹּהֵן אַחֵר עַל־דִּבְרָתִי מַלְכִּי־צֶדֶק וְלֹא יִקָּרֵא
עַל־דִּבְרָתִי אַהֲרֹן? ¹² אָכֵן כַּאֲשֶׁר מִשְׁתַּנֵּית הַכְּהֻנָּה,
מִן הַהֶכְרֵחַ שֶׁתִּשְׁתַּנֶּה גַּם הַתּוֹרָה. ¹³ וּמִי שֶׁנֶּאֱמַר
עָלָיו הַדָּבָר הַזֶּה שַׁיָּךְ לְשֵׁבֶט אַחֵר אֲשֶׁר אִישׁ מִבָּנָיו
לֹא שֵׁרֵת בַּמִּזְבֵּחַ. ¹⁴ הֵן גָּלוּי וְיָדוּעַ שֶׁאֲדוֹנֵנוּ צָמַח
מִיהוּדָה, שֵׁבֶט אֲשֶׁר מֹשֶׁה לֹא דִּבֵּר עָלָיו דָּבָר בְּעִנְיַן
כְּהֻנָּה. ¹⁵ וְזֶה בָּרוּר עוֹד יוֹתֵר כַּאֲשֶׁר, בִּדְמוּת
לְמַלְכִּי־צֶדֶק, קָם כֹּהֵן אַחֵר ¹⁶ שֶׁהָיָה לְכֹהֵן לֹא עַל־פִּי
תּוֹרַת חֻקִּים הַתְּלוּיָה בְּבָשָׂר וָדָם, אֶלָּא מִתֹּקֶף כֹּחַ
הַחַיִּים שֶׁאֵין לָהֶם הֶפְסֵק. ¹⁷ הֵן הֵעִיד עָלָיו, "אַתָּה־
כֹהֵן לְעוֹלָם עַל־דִּבְרָתִי מַלְכִּי־צֶדֶק." ¹⁸ וְאָכֵן
הַמִּצְוָה שֶׁנִּתְּנָה בֶּעָבָר מִתְבַּטֶּלֶת בִּגְלַל חֻלְשָׁתָהּ
וְאִי יְכָלְתָּהּ לְהוֹעִיל, ¹⁹ שֶׁכֵּן הַתּוֹרָה לֹא הִשְׁלִימָה
דָּבָר; לְעֻמַּת זֹאת בָּאָה תִּקְוָה טוֹבָה יוֹתֵר וְעַל־יָדֶיהָ
אֲנַחְנוּ מִתְקָרְבִים לֵאלֹהִים.
²⁰ וּכְשֵׁם שֶׁזֶּה לֹא הָיָה בְּלִי שְׁבוּעָה – ²¹ אָמְנָם
הַלָּלוּ הָיוּ לְכֹהֲנִים בְּלִי שְׁבוּעָה, אַךְ הוּא בִּשְׁבוּעָה,
עַל־יְדֵי הָאוֹמֵר לוֹ, "נִשְׁבַּע אֱלֹהִים וְלֹא יִנָּחֵם,
אַתָּה־כֹהֵן לְעוֹלָם עַל־דִּבְרָתִי מַלְכִּי־צֶדֶק" –

22 by so much more Jesus has become a surety of a better covenant.

23 Also there were many priests, because they were prevented by death from continuing. 24 But He, because He continues forever, has an unchangeable priesthood. 25 Therefore He is also able to save to the uttermost those who come to God through Him, since He always lives to make intercession for them.

26 For such a High Priest was fitting for us, *who is* holy, harmless, undefiled, separate from sinners, and has become higher than the heavens; 27 who does not need daily, as those high priests, to offer up sacrifices, first for His own sins and then for the people's, for this He did once for all when He offered up Himself. 28 For the law appoints as high priests men who have weakness, but the word of the oath, which came after the law, *appoints* the Son who has been perfected forever.

8 Now *this is* the main point of the things we are saying: We have such a High Priest, who is seated at the right hand of the throne of the Majesty in the heavens, 2 a Minister of the sanctuary and of the true tabernacle which the Lord erected, and not man.

3 For every high priest is appointed to offer both gifts and sacrifices. Therefore *it is* necessary that this One also have something to offer. 4 For if He were on earth, He would not be a priest, since there are priests who offer the gifts according to the law; 5 who serve the copy and shadow of the heavenly things, as Moses was divinely instructed when he was about to make the tabernacle. For He said, *"See that you make all things according to the pattern shown you on the mountain."* 6 But now He has obtained a more excellent ministry, inasmuch as He is also Mediator of a better covenant, which was established on better promises.

7 For if that first *covenant* had been faultless, then no place would have been sought for a second. 8 Because finding fault with them, He says: *"Behold, the days are coming, says the* LORD, *when I will make a new covenant with the house of Israel and with the house of Judah— 9 not according to the covenant that I made with their fathers in the day when I took them by the hand to lead them out of the land of Egypt; because they did not continue in My covenant, and I disregarded them, says the* LORD. 10 For this is the covenant that I will make with the house of Israel after those days, says the LORD: I will put My laws in their mind and write them on their hearts; and I will be their God, and they shall be My people. 11 None of them shall teach

22 כָּךְ גַּם טוֹבָה יוֹתֵר הַבְּרִית אֲשֶׁר יֵשׁוּעַ נִהְיָה עָרֵב לָהּ. 23 וְרַבִּים הָיוּ לְכֹהֲנִים, כִּי הַמָּוֶת מְנָעָם מִלְּהַמְשִׁיךְ בַּכְּהֻנָּה. 24 אֲבָל זֶה, מִכֵּיוָן שֶׁהוּא נִשְׁאָר לְעוֹלָם, יֵשׁ לוֹ כְּהֻנָּה שֶׁאֵינֶנָּה עוֹבֶרֶת. 25 לָכֵן הוּא גַּם יָכוֹל לְהוֹשִׁיעַ לָנֶצַח אֶת הַבָּאִים לֵאלֹהִים דַּרְכּוֹ, כִּי חַי הוּא תָּמִיד כְּדֵי לְהַפְגִּיעַ בַּעֲדָם.

26 אָכֵן כֹּהֵן גָּדוֹל כָּזֶה יָאֶה לָנוּ – קָדוֹשׁ, תָּמִים, טָהוֹר, נִבְדָּל מֵחוֹטְאִים וְנִשָּׂא מֵעַל הַשָּׁמַיִם, 27 אֲשֶׁר אֵינוֹ צָרִיךְ יוֹם יוֹם, כַּכֹּהֲנִים הַגְּדוֹלִים, תְּחִלָּה לְהַקְרִיב קָרְבָּנוֹת עַל חֲטָאָיו וְאַחֲרֵי כֵן עַל חֲטָאֵי הָעָם; כִּי זֹאת עָשָׂה אַחַת וּלְתָמִיד בְּהַקְרִיבוֹ אֶת עַצְמוֹ. 28 הֵן הַתּוֹרָה מְנַתָּה בְּנֵי אָדָם חֲלָשִׁים לְתַפְקִיד שֶׁל כֹּהֲנִים גְּדוֹלִים, אַךְ דְּבַר הַשְּׁבוּעָה שֶׁנֶּאֱמַר לְאַחַר הַתּוֹרָה הֶעֱמִיד אֶת הַבֵּן אֲשֶׁר הֻשְׁלַם לְעוֹלָם.

ח עִקַּר הַדְּבָרִים שֶׁנֶּאֱמְרוּ הוּא: יֵשׁ לָנוּ כֹּהֵן גָּדוֹל הַיּוֹשֵׁב לִימִין כִּסֵּא הַגְּדֻלָּה בַּשָּׁמַיִם, 2 וְהוּא מְשָׁרֵת בַּקֹּדֶשׁ וּבַמִּשְׁכָּן הָאֲמִתִּי אֲשֶׁר כּוֹנֵן אֱלֹהִים וְלֹא אָדָם. 3 כָּל כֹּהֵן גָּדוֹל תִּפְקִידוֹ לְהַקְרִיב מְנָחוֹת וּזְבָחִים; לָכֵן צָרִיךְ שֶׁגַּם זֶה יִהְיֶה לוֹ מַה לְהַקְרִיב. 4 אִלּוּ הָיָה בָּאָרֶץ לֹא הָיָה כֹהֵן, כִּי יֵשׁ פֹּה כֹּהֲנִים הַמַּקְרִיבִים מְנָחוֹת לְפִי הַתּוֹרָה 5 וּמְשָׁרְתִים בַּקֹּדֶשׁ לְפִי תַּבְנִית וְצֵל שֶׁל הַדְּבָרִים הַשְּׁמֵימִיִּים, כְּפִי שֶׁצֻּוָּה מֹשֶׁה בְּבוֹאוֹ לְהָקִים אֶת הַמִּשְׁכָּן; הֵן אָמַר אֵלָיו, "רְאֵה וַעֲשֵׂה הַכֹּל כַּתַּבְנִית אֲשֶׁר־אַתָּה מָרְאֶה בָּהָר." 6 וְהִנֵּה יֵשׁוּעַ הִשִּׂיג כְּהֻנָּה נַעֲלָה יוֹתֵר, מִדָּה שֶׁהוּא מְתַוֵּךְ שֶׁל בְּרִית מְעֻלָּה יוֹתֵר אֲשֶׁר נוֹסְדָה עַל הַבְטָחוֹת טוֹבוֹת יוֹתֵר.

7 אִלּוּ הָיְתָה הַבְּרִית הָרִאשׁוֹנָה בְּלִי חִסָּרוֹן, לֹא הָיָה נִדְרָשׁ מָקוֹם לַשְּׁנִיָּה. 8 הֲלֹא בְּהוֹכִיחוֹ אוֹתָם הוּא אוֹמֵר:

"הִנֵּה יָמִים בָּאִים, נְאֻם־יהוה,
וְכָרַתִּי אֶת־בֵּית יִשְׂרָאֵל וְאֶת־בֵּית יְהוּדָה בְּרִית חֲדָשָׁה;

9 לֹא כַבְּרִית אֲשֶׁר כָּרַתִּי אֶת־אֲבוֹתָם
בְּיוֹם הֶחֱזִיקִי בְיָדָם לְהוֹצִיאָם מֵאֶרֶץ מִצְרָיִם,
אֲשֶׁר־הֵמָּה הֵפֵרוּ אֶת־בְּרִיתִי
וְאָנֹכִי בָּחַלְתִּי בָם, נְאֻם־יהוה.

10 כִּי זֹאת הַבְּרִית אֲשֶׁר אֶכְרֹת אֶת־בֵּית יִשְׂרָאֵל
אַחֲרֵי הַיָּמִים הָהֵם, נְאֻם־יהוה:
נָתַתִּי אֶת־תּוֹרָתִי בְּקִרְבָּם
וְעַל־לִבָּם אֶכְתֳּבֶנָּה,
וְהָיִיתִי לָהֶם לֵאלֹהִים
וְהֵמָּה יִהְיוּ־לִי לְעָם.

11 וְלֹא יְלַמְּדוּ עוֹד אִישׁ אֶת־רֵעֵהוּ

his neighbor, and none his brother, saying, 'Know the LORD,' for all shall know Me, from the least of them to the greatest of them. 12 For I will be merciful to their unrighteousness, and their sins and their lawless deeds I will remember no more."

13 In that He says, "A new *covenant*," He has made the first obsolete. Now what is becoming obsolete and growing old is ready to vanish away.

9 Then indeed, even the first *covenant* had ordinances of divine service and the earthly sanctuary. 2 For a tabernacle was prepared: the first *part,* in which *was* the lampstand, the table, and the showbread, which is called the sanctuary; 3 and behind the second veil, the part of the tabernacle which is called the Holiest of All, 4 which had the golden censer and the ark of the covenant overlaid on all sides with gold, in which *were* the golden pot that had the manna, Aaron's rod that budded, and the tablets of the covenant; 5 and above it were the cherubim of glory overshadowing the mercy seat. Of these things we cannot now speak in detail.

6 Now when these things had been thus prepared, the priests always went into the first part of the tabernacle, performing *the services.* 7 But into the second part the high priest *went* alone once a year, not without blood, which he offered for himself and *for* the people's sins *committed* in ignorance; 8 the Holy Spirit indicating this, that the way into the Holiest of All was not yet made manifest while the first tabernacle was still standing. 9 It *was* symbolic for the present time in which both gifts and sacrifices are offered which cannot make him who performed the service perfect in regard to the conscience— 10 *concerned* only with foods and drinks, various washings, and fleshly ordinances imposed until the time of reformation.

11 But Christ came *as* High Priest of the good things to come, with the greater and more perfect tabernacle not made with hands, that is, not of this creation. 12 Not with the blood of goats and calves, but with His own blood He entered the Most Holy Place once for all, having obtained eternal redemption. 13 For if the blood of bulls and goats and the ashes of a heifer, sprinkling the unclean, sanctifies for the purifying of the flesh, 14 how much more shall the blood of Christ, who through the eternal Spirit offered Himself without spot to God, cleanse your conscience from dead works to serve the living God? 15 And for this reason He is the Mediator of the new covenant, by means of death,

וְאִישׁ אֶת־אָחִיו לֵאמֹר, דְּעוּ אֶת יהוה;
כִּי כוּלָם יֵדְעוּ אוֹתִי
לְמִקְטַנָּם וְעַד־גְּדוֹלָם.
12 כִּי אֶסְלַח לַעֲוֹנָם,
וּלְחַטָּאתָם לֹא אֶזְכָּר־עוֹד."
13 הִנֵּה בְּאָמְרוֹ בְּרִית חֲדָשָׁה יִשֵּׁן אֶת הָרִאשׁוֹנָה וּמַה שֶּׁנּוֹשַׁן וּמִזְקִין קָרוֹב לַחֲלֹף.

ט וּבְכֵן לַבְּרִית הָרִאשׁוֹנָה הָיוּ גַם דִּינֵי עֲבוֹדָה וְגַם מִקְדָּשׁ גַּשְׁמִי בָּאָרֶץ; 2 כִּי הוּקַם מִשְׁכָּן חִיצוֹן אֲשֶׁר בּוֹ הַמְּנוֹרָה וְהַשֻּׁלְחָן וְלֶחֶם הַפָּנִים, וְהוּא נִקְרָא קֹדֶשׁ. 3 וּמִבֵּית לַפָּרֹכֶת הַשְּׁנִיָּה מִשְׁכָּן הַנִּקְרָא קֹדֶשׁ הַקֳּדָשִׁים 4 וּבוֹ מִזְבַּח זָהָב לִקְטֹרֶת וַאֲרוֹן הַבְּרִית הַמְצֻפֶּה זָהָב סָבִיב. וּבָאָרוֹן צִנְצֶנֶת זָהָב אֲשֶׁר הַמָּן בְּתוֹכָהּ, מַטֵּה אַהֲרֹן אֲשֶׁר פָּרַח, וְלֻחוֹת הַבְּרִית; 5 וּמִמַּעַל לוֹ כְּרוּבֵי הַכָּבוֹד הַסּוֹכְכִים עַל הַכַּפֹּרֶת. לֹא נְדַבֵּר כָּעֵת עַל כָּל אֶחָד וְאֶחָד מֵהֶם.
6 בִּהְיוֹת כָּל אֵלֶּה עֲרוּכִים כָּךְ, נִכְנָסִים הַכֹּהֲנִים בִּקְבִיעוּת אֶל הַמִּשְׁכָּן הַחִיצוֹן לְמַלֵּא אֶת שֵׁרוּתָם. 7 אֲבָל אֶל הַמִּשְׁכָּן הַפְּנִימִי נִכְנָס הַכֹּהֵן הַגָּדוֹל לְבַדּוֹ פַּעַם אַחַת בְּשָׁנָה, לֹא בְּלִי דָם אֲשֶׁר הוּא מַקְרִיב בְּעַד עַצְמוֹ וּבְעַד שִׁגְגוֹת הָעָם. 8 בְּזֹאת רוּחַ הַקֹּדֶשׁ מוֹדִיעָה שֶׁהַדֶּרֶךְ אֶל הַקֹּדֶשׁ אֵינֶנָּה נִגְלֵית כָּל עוֹד הַמִּשְׁכָּן הַחִיצוֹן עוֹמֵד עַל מְכוֹנוֹ, 9 וְזֶה מָשָׁל לַזְּמַן הַזֶּה, כַּאֲשֶׁר מַקְרִיבִים מְנָחוֹת וּזְבָחִים שֶׁאֵינָם יְכוֹלִים לְהָבִיא אֶת מְשָׁרֵת הַקֹּדֶשׁ לִידֵי שְׁלֵמוּת בְּמַצְפּוּנוֹ, 10 וְשֶׁאֵינָם אֶלָּא כְּרוּכִים בְּמַאֲכָל וּבְמַשְׁקֶה וּבְמִינֵי טְבִילוֹת – פְּקוּדֵי־תּוֹרָה חִיצוֹנִיִּים אֲשֶׁר נִתְּנוּ עַד עֵת תִּקּוּן.
11 אֲבָל הַמָּשִׁיחַ, בְּבוֹאוֹ לִהְיוֹת כֹּהֵן גָּדוֹל לַטּוֹבוֹת הָעֲתִידוֹת, עָבַר בְּמִשְׁכָּן גָּדוֹל וּמֻשְׁלָם יוֹתֵר שֶׁאֵינוֹ מַעֲשֵׂה יָדַיִם – כְּלוֹמַר, שֶׁאֵינוֹ שַׁיָּךְ לַבְּרִיאָה הַזֹּאת 12 וּבְדָמוֹ הוּא, וְלֹא בְּדַם שְׂעִירִים וַעֲגָלִים, נִכְנַס אַחַת וּלְתָמִיד אֶל הַקֹּדֶשׁ וְהִשִּׂיג פְּדוּת עוֹלָמִים; 13 שֶׁכֵּן אִם דַּם פָּרִים וּשְׂעִירִים וְאֵפֶר הַפָּרָה, בְּהִזָּרְקָם עַל הַטְּמֵאִים, יְקַדְּשׁוּ עַד כְּדֵי לְטַהֵר אֶת הַגּוּף, 14 עַל אַחַת כַּמָּה וְכַמָּה דְּמוֹ שֶׁל הַמָּשִׁיחַ אֲשֶׁר הִקְרִיב עַצְמוֹ לֵאלֹהִים בְּרוּחַ עוֹלָמִים וּבְלֹא מוּם – יְטַהֵר אֶת מַצְפּוּנֵנוּ מִמַּעֲשֵׂי מָוֶת כְּדֵי שֶׁנַּעֲבֹד אֶת אֱלֹהִים חַיִּים.
15 לָכֵן הוּא מְתַוֵּךְ לִבְרִית חֲדָשָׁה, וְעַל־יְדֵי כָּךְ – מֵאַחַר שֶׁמֵּת לִפְדוֹת מִן הַפְּשָׁעִים אֲשֶׁר נַעֲשׂוּ בִּימֵי הַבְּרִית הָרִאשׁוֹנָה – יְקַבְּלוּ הַמְקֹרָאִים אֶת נַחֲלַת

for the redemption of the transgressions under the first covenant, that those who are called may receive the promise of the eternal inheritance.

16 For where there is a testament, there must also of necessity be the death of the testator. 17 For a testament is in force after men are dead, since it has no power at all while the testator lives. 18 Therefore not even the first *covenant* was dedicated without blood. 19 For when Moses had spoken every precept to all the people according to the law, he took the blood of calves and goats, with water, scarlet wool, and hyssop, and sprinkled both the book itself and all the people, 20 saying, *"This is the blood of the covenant which God has commanded you."* 21 Then likewise he sprinkled with blood both the tabernacle and all the vessels of the ministry. 22 And according to the law almost all things are purified with blood, and without shedding of blood there is no remission.

23 Therefore it was necessary that the copies of the things in the heavens should be purified with these, but the heavenly things themselves with better sacrifices than these. 24 For Christ has not entered the holy places made with hands, *which are* copies of the true, but into heaven itself, now to appear in the presence of God for us; 25 not that He should offer Himself often, as the high priest enters the Most Holy Place every year with blood of another— 26 He then would have had to suffer often since the foundation of the world; but now, once at the end of the ages, He has appeared to put away sin by the sacrifice of Himself. 27 And as it is appointed for men to die once, but after this the judgment, 28 so Christ was offered once to bear the sins of many. To those who eagerly wait for Him He will appear a second time, apart from sin, for salvation.

10 For the law, having a shadow of the good things to come, *and* not the very image of the things, can never with these same sacrifices, which they offer continually year by year, make those who approach perfect. 2 For then would they not have ceased to be offered? For the worshipers, once purified, would have had no more consciousness of sins. 3 But in those *sacrifices there is* a reminder of sins every year. 4 For *it is* not possible that the blood of bulls and goats could take away sins.

5 Therefore, when He came into the world, He said:

"Sacrifice and offering You did not desire,
But a body You have prepared for Me.
6   In burnt offerings and *sacrifices for sin*

עוֹלָם הַמְּבֻטַּחַת. 16 הֵן בְּהִמָּצֵא צַוָּאָה צָרִיךְ שֶׁיִּוָּשַׁר דְּבַר מוֹתוֹ שֶׁל בַּעַל הַצַּוָּאָה; 17 כִּי רַק בְּמוֹת הַמֵּת תֹּכֶן הַצַּוָּאָה, וְאֵין לָהּ תֹּקֶף כָּל עוֹד חַי בַּעַל הַצַּוָּאָה. 18 לָכֵן גַּם חֲנֻכַּת הַבְּרִית הָרִאשׁוֹנָה לֹא הָיְתָה בְּלִי דָם; 19 כִּי בְּכַלּוֹת מֹשֶׁה לוֹמַר לְכָל הָעָם כָּל מִצְוָה לְפִי הַתּוֹרָה, לָקַח אֶת דַּם הָעֲגָלִים וְהַשְּׂעִירִים עִם מַיִם וְתוֹלַעַת שָׁנִי וְאֵזוֹב, וְזָרַק אוֹתָם עַל הַסֵּפֶר וְעַל כָּל הָעָם, 20 בְּאָמְרוֹ, "הִנֵּה דַם־הַבְּרִית אֲשֶׁר צִוָּה אֶתְכֶם אֱלֹהִים." 21 וְכֵן גַּם עַל הַמִּשְׁכָּן וְעַל כָּל כְּלֵי הַשָּׁרֵת הִזָּה הַדָּם. 22 אָכֵן עַל־פִּי הַתּוֹרָה כִּמְעַט הַכֹּל מְטֹהָר בְּדָם, וּבְלֹא שְׁפִיכַת דָּם אֵין מְחִילָה.

23 לָכֵן הָיָה צָרִיךְ לְטַהֵר עַל־יְדֵי אֵלֶּה אֶת הַדְּבָרִים אֲשֶׁר הֵם תַּבְנִית הַדְּבָרִים הַנִּמְצָאִים בַּשָּׁמַיִם, אֲבָל הַדְּבָרִים הַשְּׁמֵימִיִּם עַצְמָם דּוֹרְשִׁים זְבָחִים טוֹבִים מֵאֵלֶּה. 24 הֲרֵי הַמָּשִׁיחַ לֹא נִכְנַס אֶל מִקְדָּשׁ אֲשֶׁר נַעֲשָׂה בִּידֵי אָדָם וַאֲשֶׁר הוּא בָּבוּאָה שֶׁל הָאֲמִתִּי, כִּי אִם בָּא אֶל עֶצֶם הַשָּׁמַיִם לְהֵרָאוֹת עַתָּה בַּעֲדֵנוּ לִפְנֵי הָאֱלֹהִים; 25 אַף לֹא בָּא לְהַקְרִיב אֶת עַצְמוֹ פְּעָמִים רַבּוֹת, כַּכֹּהֵן הַגָּדוֹל הַנִּכְנָס שָׁנָה בְּשָׁנָה אֶל הַקֹּדֶשׁ בְּדָם אֲשֶׁר אֵינוֹ דָמוֹ; 26 שֶׁאִם כֵּן, הָיָה צָרִיךְ לִסְבֹּל פְּעָמִים רַבּוֹת מֵאָז הֻסַּד תֵּבֵל. אֲבָל כָּעֵת נִגְלָה פַּעַם אַחַת, בְּקֵץ הָעוֹלָמִים, לְהָסִיר אֶת הַחֵטְא בְּקָרְבַּן עַצְמוֹ. 27 וּכְשֵׁם שֶׁנִּגְזַר עַל בְּנֵי אָדָם לָמוּת פַּעַם אַחַת וְאַחֲרֵי כֵן הַמִּשְׁפָּט, 28 כָּךְ גַּם הַמָּשִׁיחַ, אַחֲרֵי שֶׁהֻקְרַב פַּעַם אַחַת לָשֵׂאת חֲטָאֵי רַבִּים, יוֹפִיעַ שֵׁנִית – שֶׁלֹּא לְעִנְיַן הַחֵטְא – לַמְחַכִּים לוֹ לִישׁוּעָה.

10 הַתּוֹרָה, אֲשֶׁר צֵל הַטּוֹבוֹת הָעֲתִידוֹת בָּהּ וְלֹא עֶצֶם צֶלֶם הַדְּבָרִים, אַף פַּעַם אֵינָהּ יְכוֹלָה לְהָבִיא לִידֵי שְׁלֵמוּת עַל־יְדֵי אוֹתָם הַקָּרְבָּנוֹת אֶת הַבָּאִים לְהַקְרִיבָם בְּהַתְמָדָה שָׁנָה בְּשָׁנָה. 2 אִלּוּ יָכְלָה לַעֲשׂוֹת כֵּן, הָיְתָה מַפְסֶקֶת הַקְרָבָתָם; כִּי לְאַחַר שֶׁהַמְשָׁרְתִים בַּקֹּדֶשׁ הָיוּ נִטְהָרִים פַּעַם אַחַת, לֹא הָיְתָה בָּהֶם עוֹד הַכָּרַת חֵטְא. 3 אֲבָל יֵשׁ בַּקָּרְבָּנוֹת הַלָּלוּ זִכְרוֹן חֲטָאִים מִדֵּי שָׁנָה בְּשָׁנָה, 4 שֶׁכֵּן דַּם פָּרִים וּשְׂעִירִים אֵינוֹ יָכוֹל לְהָסִיר חֲטָאִים. 5 לָכֵן בְּהִכָּנְסוֹ אֶל הָעוֹלָם הוּא אוֹמֵר:

"זֶבַח וּמִנְחָה לֹא־חָפַצְתָּ,
גּוּף כּוֹנַנְתָּ לִי;
6 עוֹלָה וַחֲטָאָה לֹא שָׁאַלְתָּ.

You had no pleasure.

7 Then I said, 'Behold, I have come—
In the volume of the book it is written of
Me—
To do Your will, O God.' "

8 Previously saying, "Sacrifice and offering, burnt offerings, and offerings for sin You did not desire, nor had pleasure in them" (which are offered according to the law), 9 then He said, "Behold, I have come to do Your will, O God." He takes away the first that He may establish the second. 10 By that will we have been sanctified through the offering of the body of Jesus Christ once for all.

11 And every priest stands ministering daily and offering repeatedly the same sacrifices, which can never take away sins. 12 But this Man, after He had offered one sacrifice for sins forever, sat down at the right hand of God, 13 from that time waiting till His enemies are made His footstool. 14 For by one offering He has perfected forever those who are being sanctified.

15 But the Holy Spirit also witnesses to us; for after He had said before,

16 "This is the covenant that I will make with them after those days, says the LORD: I will put My laws into their hearts, and in their minds I will write them," 17 then He adds, "Their sins and their lawless deeds I will remember no more." 18 Now where there is remission of these, there is no longer an offering for sin.

19 Therefore, brethren, having boldness to enter the Holiest by the blood of Jesus, 20 by a new and living way which He consecrated for us, through the veil, that is, His flesh, 21 and having a High Priest over the house of God, 22 let us draw near with a true heart in full assurance of faith, having our hearts sprinkled from an evil conscience and our bodies washed with pure water. 23 Let us hold fast the confession of our hope without wavering, for He who promised is faithful. 24 And let us consider one another in order to stir up love and good works, 25 not forsaking the assembling of ourselves together, as is the manner of some, but exhorting one another, and so much the more as you see the Day approaching.

26 For if we sin willfully after we have received the knowledge of the truth, there no longer remains a sacrifice for sins, 27 but a certain fearful expectation of judgment, and fiery indignation which will devour the adversaries. 28 Anyone who has rejected Moses' law dies without mercy on the testimony of two or three witnesses. 29 Of how much worse punishment, do you suppose, will he be thought

7 אָז אָמַרְתִּי: הִנֵּה־בָאתִי –
בִּמְגִלַּת־סֵפֶר כָּתוּב עָלַי –
לַעֲשׂוֹת־רְצוֹנְךָ, אֱלֹהַי."

8 בְּאָמְרוֹ לְעֵיל, "זֶבַח וּמִנְחָה וְעוֹלָה לֹא חָפַצְתָּ אַף לֹא שָׁאָלְתָּ", אֲשֶׁר מַקְרִיבִים אוֹתָם עַל־פִּי הַתּוֹרָה, 9 וּבְאָמְרוֹ אַחֲרֵי כֵן, "הִנֵּה בָאתִי לַעֲשׂוֹת רְצוֹנֶךָ", מֵסִיר הוּא אֶת הָרִאשׁוֹנָה כְּדֵי לְהָקִים אֶת הַשְּׁנִיָּה. 10 וּבְאוֹתוֹ הָרָצוֹן מְקֻדָּשִׁים אֲנַחְנוּ עַל־יְדֵי הַקְרָבַת גּוּפוֹ שֶׁל יֵשׁוּעַ הַמָּשִׁיחַ פַּעַם אַחַת וּלְתָמִיד. 11 כָּל כֹּהֵן עוֹמֵד יוֹם יוֹם לְשָׁרֵת בַּקֹּדֶשׁ וּמַקְרִיב פְּעָמִים רַבּוֹת אֶת אוֹתָם הַקָּרְבָּנוֹת אֲשֶׁר אַף פַּעַם אֵינָם יְכוֹלִים לְהָסִיר חֲטָאִים. 12 אֲבָל זֶה, לְאַחַר שֶׁהִקְרִיב קָרְבָּן אֶחָד עַל הַחֲטָאִים, יָשַׁב לִימִין הָאֱלֹהִים לְתָמִיד 13 וּמֵאָז הוּא מְחַכֶּה עַד אֲשֶׁר יוּשְׁתוּ אוֹיְבָיו הֲדֹם לְרַגְלָיו, 14 שֶׁכֵּן בְּקָרְבָּן אֶחָד הִשְׁלִים לְתָמִיד אֶת הַמְקֻדָּשִׁים. 15 וְגַם רוּחַ הַקֹּדֶשׁ מְעִידָה לָנוּ עַל זֹאת, כִּי לְאַחַר שֶׁאָמַר,

16 "זֹאת הַבְּרִית אֲשֶׁר אֶכְרֹת אִתָּם אַחֲרֵי הַיָּמִים הָהֵם, נְאֻם־יהוה:
נָתַתִּי אֶת־תּוֹרָתִי בְּקִרְבָּם וְעַל־לִבָּם אֶכְתֳּבֶנָּה",

17 הוּא אוֹמֵר,
"וְלַעֲוֹנָם וּלְחַטֹּאתָם לֹא אֶזְכָּר־עוֹד."

18 וּבְמָקוֹם שֶׁהַלָּלוּ נִסְלָחִים אֵין עוֹד קָרְבָּן עַל חֲטָאִים.

19 לָכֵן, אַחַי, מִכֵּיוָן שֶׁיֵּשׁ לָנוּ בִּטָּחוֹן לְהִכָּנֵס אֶל הַקֹּדֶשׁ בְּדַם יֵשׁוּעַ, 20 בְּדֶרֶךְ חֲדָשָׁה וְחַיָּה אֲשֶׁר הוּא חָנַךְ לָנוּ דֶּרֶךְ הַפָּרֹכֶת, שֶׁהִיא בְּשָׂרוֹ, 21 וּבִהְיוֹת לָנוּ כֹּהֵן גָּדוֹל עַל בֵּית אֱלֹהִים, 22 נִתְקָרְבָה נָא בְּלֵבָב שָׁלֵם וּבִמְלוֹא וַדָּאוּת הָאֱמוּנָה, כְּשֶׁלְּבּוֹתֵינוּ מְטֹהָרִים מֵהַרְשָׁעַת מַצְפּוּן וְהַגּוּף רָחוּץ בְּמַיִם טְהוֹרִים. 23 נַחֲזִיקָה נָא בַּתִּקְוָה שֶׁאָנוּ מַצְהִירִים עָלֶיהָ וְאַל נָמוֹט, שֶׁכֵּן נֶאֱמָן הַמַּבְטִיחַ. 24 נָשִׂים לִבֵּנוּ אִישׁ אֶל רֵעֵהוּ, לְעוֹרֵר זֶה אֶת זֶה לְאַהֲבָה וּלְמַעֲשִׂים טוֹבִים. 25 בַּל נַזְנִיחַ אֶת הִתְכַּנְּסוּתֵנוּ כְּמִנְהַג כַּמָּה אֲנָשִׁים, כִּי אִם נְעוֹדֵד אִישׁ אֶת רֵעֵהוּ, וּבְיִחוּד בִּרְאוֹתְכֶם כִּי קָרֵב הַיּוֹם.

26 הֵן אִם נֶחֱטָא בְּזָדוֹן לְאַחַר שֶׁקִּבַּלְנוּ אֶת יְדִיעַת הָאֱמֶת, לֹא יִשָּׁאֵר עוֹד קָרְבָּן לְכַפֵּר עַל חֲטָאִים, 27 אֶלָּא צִפִּיַּת חֲרָדָה לַדִּין, וְלַהַט אֵשׁ אֲשֶׁר תֹּאכַל אֶת הָאוֹיְבִים. 28 הַמֵּפֵר אֶת תּוֹרַת מֹשֶׁה יוּמַת בְּלִי חֶמְלָה עַל־פִּי שְׁנֵי עֵדִים אוֹ עַל־פִּי שְׁלֹשָׁה־עֵדִים. 29 כַּמָּה וְכַמָּה גָּדוֹל יוֹתֵר יִהְיֶה, לְפִי דַעְתְּכֶם, הָעֹנֶשׁ

worthy who has trampled the Son of God under-
foot, counted the blood of the covenant by which he
was sanctified a common thing, and insulted the
Spirit of grace? ³⁰For we know Him who said,
"Vengeance is Mine, I will repay," says the Lord.
And again, "The LORD will judge His people." ³¹It
is a fearful thing to fall into the hands of the living
God.

³²But recall the former days in which, after you
were illuminated, you endured a great struggle with
sufferings: ³³partly while you were made a spectacle
both by reproaches and tribulations, and partly
while you became companions of those who were so
treated; ³⁴for you had compassion on me in my
chains, and joyfully accepted the plundering of your
goods, knowing that you have a better and an
enduring possession for yourselves in heaven.
³⁵Therefore do not cast away your confidence,
which has great reward. ³⁶For you have need of
endurance, so that after you have done the will of
God, you may receive the promise:

³⁷ "For yet a little while,
And He who is coming will come and will not
    tarry.
³⁸ Now the just shall live by faith;
But if anyone draws back,
My soul has no pleasure in him."

³⁹But we are not of those who draw back to
perdition, but of those who believe to the saving of
the soul.

11 Now faith is the substance of things hoped for,
the evidence of things not seen. ²For by it the elders
obtained a good testimony.

³By faith we understand that the worlds were
framed by the word of God, so that the things
which are seen were not made of things which are
visible.

⁴By faith Abel offered to God a more excellent
sacrifice than Cain, through which he obtained
witness that he was righteous, God testifying of his
gifts; and through it he being dead still speaks.

⁵By faith Enoch was taken away so that he did
not see death, "and was not found, because God
had taken him"; for before he was taken he had this
testimony, that he pleased God. ⁶But without faith
it is impossible to please Him, for he who comes to
God must believe that He is, and that He is a
rewarder of those who diligently seek Him.

הָרָאוּי לְמִי שֶׁרוֹמֵס בְּרַגְלוֹ אֶת בֶּן־הָאֱלֹהִים וּמְזַלְזֵל
בְּדַם הַבְּרִית אֲשֶׁר הוּא מְקֻדָּשׁ בּוֹ וּמְחָרֵף אֶת רוּחַ
הַחֶסֶד? ³⁰הֲרֵי מַכִּירִים אֲנַחְנוּ אֶת מִי שֶׁאָמַר, "לִי
נָקָם וְשִׁלֵּם", וְגַם "יָדִין יהוה עַמּוֹ." ³¹אָכֵן נוֹרָא
לִנְפֹּל בְּיַד אֱלֹהִים חַיִּים!

³²זִכְרוּ אֶת הַיָּמִים הָרִאשׁוֹנִים, כַּאֲשֶׁר אוֹרוּ עֵינֵיכֶם
וַעֲמַדְתֶּם בְּמַאֲבָק קָשֶׁה וּבְצָרוֹת. ³³פְּעָמִים סְבַלְתֶּם
חֲרָפוֹת וְצָרוֹת לְעֵינֵי כֹל, וּפְעָמִים הִשְׁתַּתַּפְתֶּם עִם
אֵלֶּה אֲשֶׁר סָבְלוּ כָּזֹאת; ³⁴כִּי אָכֵן צַר הָיָה לָכֶם עַל
הָאֲסִירִים, וְאֶת גְּזֵלַת רְכוּשְׁכֶם סְבַלְתֶּם בְּשִׂמְחָה,
מִתּוֹךְ יְדִיעָה שֶׁיֵּשׁ לָכֶם בַּשָּׁמַיִם קִנְיָן טוֹב יוֹתֵר, יַצִּיב
וְקַיָּם. ³⁵לָכֵן אַל תַּשְׁלִיכוּ אֶת בִּטְחוֹנְכֶם אֲשֶׁר גָּדוֹל
שְׂכָרוֹ, ³⁶שֶׁהֲרֵי צְרִיכִים אַתֶּם לְסַבְלָנוּת כְּדֵי לְקַבֵּל
אֶת הַמֻּבְטָח לְאַחַר שֶׁתַּעֲשׂוּ אֶת רְצוֹן אֱלֹהִים; ³⁷כִּי

"עוֹד מְעַט קָט וְהַבָּא יָבוֹא, וְלֹא יְאַחֵר.

³⁸ צַדִּיק בֶּאֱמוּנָתוֹ יִחְיֶה;

וְאִם יִסּוֹג לֹא רָצְתָה נַפְשִׁי בּוֹ."

³⁹אֲבָל אֲנַחְנוּ אֵינֶנּוּ מִן הַנְּסוֹגִים אֱלֵי אֲבַדּוֹן, כִּי אִם
בְּנֵי הָאֱמוּנָה לְשֵׁם יְשׁוּעַת הַנֶּפֶשׁ.

יא הָאֱמוּנָה הִיא בִּטָּחוֹן בְּמַמָּשׁוּת הַדְּבָרִים
הַמְקֻוִּים, הוֹכָחַת דְּבָרִים שֶׁאֵינָם נִרְאִים. ²בִּגְלָלָהּ
הוּעַד עַל הַקַּדְמוֹנִים.

³בֶּאֱמוּנָה נָבִין כִּי הָעוֹלָמִים הוּכְנוּ בִּדְבַר אֱלֹהִים,
בְּאֹפֶן שֶׁהַנִּרְאֶה נִתְהַוָּה מִן הַבִּלְתִּי נִרְאֶה.

⁴מִתּוֹךְ אֱמוּנָה הֵבִיא הֶבֶל לֵאלֹהִים קָרְבָּן טוֹב מִזֶּה
שֶׁהֵבִיא קַיִן; בִּגְלָלָהּ הוּעַד עָלָיו כִּי צַדִּיק הוּא, שֶׁכֵּן
אֱלֹהִים הֵעִיד עַל מַתְּנוֹתָיו, וּבִגְלָלָהּ הוּא מְדַבֵּר עֲדַיִן
גַּם לְאַחַר שֶׁמֵּת. ⁵בִּזְכוּת אֱמוּנָה לֻקַּח חֲנוֹךְ בְּלִי
לִרְאוֹת מָוֶת, "וְאֵינֶנּוּ, כִּי־לָקַח אֹתוֹ אֱלֹהִים."
וְהוּעַד עָלָיו לִפְנֵי הִלָּקְחוֹ כִּי "אֶת הָאֱלֹהִים
הִתְהַלֵּךְ." ⁶וּבְלִי אֱמוּנָה אִי אֶפְשָׁר לִהְיוֹת רָצוּי
לֵאלֹהִים, כִּי כָּל הַקָּרֵב אֶל אֱלֹהִים צָרִיךְ לְהַאֲמִין

7 By faith Noah, being divinely warned of things not yet seen, moved with godly fear, prepared an ark for the saving of his household, by which he condemned the world and became heir of the righteousness which is according to faith.

8 By faith Abraham obeyed when he was called to go out to the place which he would receive as an inheritance. And he went out, not knowing where he was going. 9 By faith he dwelt in the land of promise as *in* a foreign country, dwelling in tents with Isaac and Jacob, the heirs with him of the same promise; 10 for he waited for the city which has foundations, whose builder and maker *is* God.

11 By faith Sarah herself also received strength to conceive seed, and she bore a child when she was past the age, because she judged Him faithful who had promised. 12 Therefore from one man, and him as good as dead, were born *as many* as the stars of the sky in multitude—innumerable as the sand which is by the seashore.

13 These all died in faith, not having received the promises, but having seen them afar off were assured of them, embraced *them* and confessed that they were strangers and pilgrims on the earth. 14 For those who say such things declare plainly that they seek a homeland. 15 And truly if they had called to mind that *country* from which they had come out, they would have had opportunity to return. 16 But now they desire a better, that is, a heavenly *country*. Therefore God is not ashamed to be called their God, for He has prepared a city for them.

17 By faith Abraham, when he was tested, offered up Isaac, and he who had received the promises offered up his only begotten *son,* 18 of whom it was said, "*In Isaac your seed shall be called,*" 19 concluding that God *was* able to raise *him* up, even from the dead, from which he also received him in a figurative sense.

20 By faith Isaac blessed Jacob and Esau concerning things to come.

21 By faith Jacob, when he was dying, blessed each of the sons of Joseph, and worshiped, *leaning* on the top of his staff.

22 By faith Joseph, when he was dying, made mention of the departure of the children of Israel, and gave instructions concerning his bones.

23 By faith Moses, when he was born, was hidden three months by his parents, because they saw *he was* a beautiful child; and they were not afraid of the king's command.

24 By faith Moses, when he became of age, refused to be called the son of Pharaoh's daughter, 25 choosing rather to suffer affliction with the people of God than to enjoy the passing pleasures

7 מִתּוֹךְ שֶׁהוּא קַיָּם וְהוּא נוֹתֵן גְּמוּל לְדוֹרְשָׁיו. מִתּוֹךְ אֱמוּנָה בָּנָה נֹחַ תֵּבָה לְהַצָּלַת בֵּיתוֹ, בִּהְיוֹתוֹ יְרֵא אַחֲרֵי שֶׁהֻזְהַר עַל דְּבָרִים אֲשֶׁר עוֹד לֹא נִרְאוּ, וּבֶאֱמוּנָתוֹ הִרְשִׁיעַ אֶת הָעוֹלָם וְהָיָה לְיוֹרֵשׁ הַצְּדָקָה הַמְיֻסֶּדֶת עַל אֱמוּנָה.

8 מִתּוֹךְ אֱמוּנָה צִיֵּת אַבְרָהָם בְּהִקָּרְאוֹ לָצֵאת אֶל מָקוֹם שֶׁהָיָה עָתִיד לְקַבֵּל לְנַחֲלָה, וְהוּא יָצָא מִבְּלִי לָדַעַת לְאָן יֵלֵךְ. 9 מִתּוֹךְ אֱמוּנָה הִתְגּוֹרֵר בְּאֶרֶץ הַהַבְטָחָה כְּגֵר בְּאֶרֶץ זָרָה, בְּשִׁבְתּוֹ בְּאֹהָלִים עִם יִצְחָק וְיַעֲקֹב אֲשֶׁר יָרְשׁוּ עִמּוֹ אֶת אוֹתָהּ הַהַבְטָחָה; 10 כִּי חִכָּה לָעִיר שֶׁיֵּשׁ לָהּ יְסוֹדוֹת, שֶׁאֲדְרִיכָלָהּ וּמְקִימָהּ הוּא הָאֱלֹהִים. 11 מִתּוֹךְ אֱמוּנָה קִבְּלָה גַּם שָׂרָה כֹּחַ לַהֲרוֹת אַף לְאַחַר שֶׁהִזְדַּקְנָה, שֶׁכֵּן חָשְׁבָה אֶת הַמַּבְטִיחַ לְנֶאֱמָן. 12 עַל כֵּן גַּם מֵאֶחָד, שֶׁהָיָה בִּבְחִינַת מֵת, יָצְאוּ כְּכוֹכְבֵי הַשָּׁמַיִם לָרֹב וְכַחוֹל עַל שְׂפַת הַיָּם אֲשֶׁר לֹא יִסָּפֵר.

13 בְּעוֹדָם מַחֲזִיקִים בָּאֱמוּנָה מֵתוּ כָּל אֵלֶּה בְּלִי שֶׁהִשִּׂיגוּ אֶת הַדְּבָרִים הַמֻּבְטָחִים, וְאוּלָם רָאוּ אוֹתָם מֵרָחוֹק וְקִדְּמוּ אוֹתָם בְּבִרְכָה כְּשֶׁהֵם מוֹדִים כִּי זָרִים וְגוֹלִים הֵם בָּאָרֶץ. 14 הֵן הַמְדַבְּרִים כָּךְ מַצְהִירִים שֶׁהֵם מְבַקְשִׁים לָהֶם אֶרֶץ מוֹשָׁב. 15 וְאִלּוּ כִּוְּנוּ דַעְתָּם עַל הָאָרֶץ הַהִיא אֲשֶׁר יָצְאוּ מִמֶּנָּה, הָיָה לָהֶם זְמַן לָשׁוּב אֵלֶיהָ. 16 אַךְ עַתָּה נִכְסָפִים הֵם לְטוֹבָה מִמֶּנָּה, לְאֶרֶץ מוֹשָׁב שְׁמֵימִית. לָכֵן לֹא בּוֹשׁ בָּהֶם הָאֱלֹהִים לְהִקָּרֵא אֱלֹהֵיהֶם, שֶׁהֲרֵי הֵכִין לָהֶם עִיר.

17 מִתּוֹךְ אֱמוּנָה הִקְרִיב אַבְרָהָם אֶת יִצְחָק בְּעֵת שֶׁנִּסָּה; הוּא שֶׁקִּבֵּל אֶת הַהַבְטָחוֹת הִקְרִיב אֶת יְחִידוֹ, 18 הוּא שֶׁנֶּאֱמַר לוֹ, "כִּי בְיִצְחָק יִקָּרֵא לְךָ זָרַע", 19 בְּחָשְׁבוֹ בְּלִבּוֹ כִּי הָאֱלֹהִים יָכוֹל לְהָקִים אֲפִלּוּ מֵעִם הַמֵּתִים; מִשָּׁם, בִּבְחִינַת מָשָׁל, אַף קִבֵּל אוֹתוֹ. 20 מִתּוֹךְ אֱמוּנָה בֵּרַךְ יִצְחָק אֶת יַעֲקֹב וְאֶת עֵשָׂו בְּנוֹגֵעַ לִדְבָרִים עֲתִידִים לָבוֹא. 21 מִתּוֹךְ אֱמוּנָה בֵּרַךְ יַעֲקֹב לִפְנֵי מוֹתוֹ אֶת שְׁנֵי בְּנֵי יוֹסֵף, וְקַד מֵעַל רֹאשׁ הַמַּטֶּה. 22 מִתּוֹךְ אֱמוּנָה הִזְכִּיר יוֹסֵף לִפְנֵי מוֹתוֹ אֶת יְצִיאַת בְּנֵי יִשְׂרָאֵל וְצִוָּה עַל-אוֹדוֹת עַצְמוֹתָיו.

23 כְּשֶׁנּוֹלַד מֹשֶׁה, מִתּוֹךְ אֱמוּנָה הִסְתִּירוּהוּ הוֹרָיו בְּמֶשֶׁךְ שְׁלוֹשָׁה חֳדָשִׁים; כִּי רָאוּ שֶׁנָּאֶה הַיֶּלֶד, וְלֹא פָחֲדוּ מִגְּזֵרַת הַמֶּלֶךְ. 24 כַּאֲשֶׁר גָּדַל מֹשֶׁה, מִתּוֹךְ אֱמוּנָה סֵרֵב לְהִקָּרֵא בֶּן לְבַת פַּרְעֹה 25 וּבָחַר לְהִתְעַנּוֹת עִם עַם אֱלֹהִים מִלְּהִתְעַנֵּג לְשָׁעָה בְּתַעֲנוּגֵי

of sin, 26esteeming the reproach of Christ greater riches than the treasures in Egypt; for he looked to the reward.

27By faith he forsook Egypt, not fearing the wrath of the king; for he endured as seeing Him who is invisible. 28By faith he kept the Passover and the sprinkling of blood, lest he who destroyed the firstborn should touch them.

29By faith they passed through the Red Sea as by dry *land, whereas* the Egyptians, attempting *to do* so, were drowned.

30By faith the walls of Jericho fell down after they were encircled for seven days. 31By faith the harlot Rahab did not perish with those who did not believe, when she had received the spies with peace.

32And what more shall I say? For the time would fail me to tell of Gideon and Barak and Samson and Jephthah, also *of* David and Samuel and the prophets: 33who through faith subdued kingdoms, worked righteousness, obtained promises, stopped the mouths of lions, 34quenched the violence of fire, escaped the edge of the sword, out of weakness were made strong, became valiant in battle, turned to flight the armies of the aliens. 35Women received their dead raised to life again.

Others were tortured, not accepting deliverance, that they might obtain a better resurrection. 36Still others had trial of mockings and scourgings, yes, and of chains and imprisonment. 37They were stoned, they were sawn in two, were tempted, were slain with the sword. They wandered about in sheepskins and goatskins, being destitute, afflicted, tormented— 38of whom the world was not worthy. They wandered in deserts and mountains, *in* dens and caves of the earth.

39And all these, having obtained a good testimony through faith, did not receive the promise, 40God having provided something better for us, that they should not be made perfect apart from us.

12 Therefore we also, since we are surrounded by so great a cloud of witnesses, let us lay aside every weight, and the sin which so easily ensnares *us,* and let us run with endurance the race that is set before us, 2looking unto Jesus, the author and finisher of *our* faith, who for the joy that was set before Him endured the cross, despising the shame, and has sat down at the right hand of the throne of God.

3For consider Him who endured such hostility from sinners against Himself, lest you become weary and discouraged in your souls. 4You have not yet resisted to bloodshed, striving against sin. 5And you have forgotten the exhortation which speaks to you as to sons:

הַחֵטְא. 26הוּא חָשַׁב אֶת חֶרְפַּת הַמָּשִׁיחַ לְעֹשֶׁר גָּדוֹל מֵאוֹצְרוֹת מִצְרַיִם, כִּי נָשָׂא עֵינָיו אֶל הַגְּמוּל. 27בֶּאֱמוּנָה עָזַב אֶת מִצְרַיִם וְלֹא פָחַד מִזַּעַם הַמֶּלֶךְ, כִּי עָמַד בְּעֹז כְּרוֹאֶה אֶת מִי שֶׁאֵינֶנּוּ נִרְאֶה. 28מִתּוֹךְ אֱמוּנָה עָשָׂה אֶת הַפֶּסַח וְאֶת נְתִינַת הַדָּם כְּדֵי שֶׁלֹּא יִגַּע בָּהֶם מַכֵּה הַבְּכוֹרִים. 29בֶּאֱמוּנָה עָבְרוּ בְּיַם סוּף כְּמוֹ בַּיַּבָּשָׁה, דָּבָר שֶׁנִּסּוּ הַמִּצְרִים וְטָבְעוּ. 30בִּגְלַל אֱמוּנָה נָפְלוּ חוֹמוֹת יְרִיחוֹ אַחֲרֵי שֶׁהִקִּיפוּ אוֹתָן שִׁבְעַת יָמִים. 31בִּזְכוּת אֱמוּנָה לֹא נִסְפְּתָה רָחָב הַזּוֹנָה עִם הַסּוֹרְרִים, שֶׁכֵּן קִבְּלָה אֶת הַמְרַגְּלִים בְּשָׁלוֹם.

32וּמַה עוֹד אֹמַר? הֵן תִּקְצַר הָעֵת מִלְּסַפֵּר עַל גִּדְעוֹן וּבָרָק וְשִׁמְשׁוֹן וְיִפְתָּח וְדָוִד וּשְׁמוּאֵל וְהַנְּבִיאִים, 33אֲשֶׁר עַל־יְדֵי אֱמוּנָה הִכְנִיעוּ מַמְלָכוֹת, פָּעֲלוּ צֶדֶק, הִשִּׂיגוּ הַבְטָחוֹת, סָגְרוּ פִּי אֲרָיוֹת, 34כִּבּוּ לַהֲבוֹת אֵשׁ, נִמְלְטוּ מִפִּי חֶרֶב, הִתְחַזְּקוּ מֵחֳלְשָׁה, עָשׂוּ חַיִל בַּמִּלְחָמָה וְהֵבִיסוּ צִבְאוֹת זָרִים. 35נָשִׁים קִבְּלוּ אֶת מֵתֵיהֶן שֶׁקָּמוּ לִתְחִיָּה. אֲחֵרִים עֻנּוּ עַד מָוֶת וְלֹא הִסְכִּימוּ לְהִנָּצֵל, לְמַעַן יִשִּׂיגוּ תְּחִיָּה טוֹבָה יוֹתֵר. 36אֲחֵרִים הִתְנַסּוּ בְּחֶרְפַּת לַעַג וְהַלְקָאוֹת שׁוֹטִים וְגַם בְּכְבָלִים וָכֶלֶא; 37נִסְקְלוּ, נֻסְּרוּ בְּעִנּוּיִים, נִסְּרוּ בַּמַּשּׂוֹר, הוּמְתוּ בְּחֶרֶב, נָעוּ וָנָדוּ עֲטוּפֵי עוֹרוֹת כְּבָשִׂים וְעִזִּים, בְּסָבְלָם מַחְסוֹר, צָרוֹת וְהִתְעַלְּלוּת – 38אֲבָל הָעוֹלָם לֹא הָיָה רָאוּי לַאֲנָשִׁים אֲשֶׁר כָּאֵלֶּה – וְתוֹעִים הָיוּ בְּמִדְבָּרִיּוֹת, בֶּהָרִים, בִּמְעָרוֹת וּבְנִקְיקֵי הָאָרֶץ.

39כָּל אֵלֶּה, אַף כִּי אֲמוּנָתָם הֵעִידָה עֲלֵיהֶם, לֹא רָאוּ בְּקִיּוּם הַהַבְטָחָה. 40וְאוּלָם אֱלֹהִים הֵכִין לָנוּ דָּבָר טוֹב יוֹתֵר, כְּדֵי שֶׁלֹּא יוּבְאוּ לִידֵי שְׁלֵמוּת בִּלְעָדֵינוּ.

יב לָכֵן גַּם אֲנַחְנוּ, אֲשֶׁר עָנָן עֵדִים כָּזֶה אוֹפֵף אוֹתָנוּ, נָסִירָה נָא כָּל מַעֲמָסָה וְגַם אֶת הַחֵטְא הַדּוֹבֵק עַל נְקַלָּה, וּבְסַבְלָנוּת נָרוּצָה אֶת הַמֵּרוֹץ הֶעָרוּךְ לְפָנֵינוּ, 2בְּהַבִּיטֵנוּ אֶל יֵשׁוּעַ מְכוֹן הָאֱמוּנָה וּמַשְׁלִימָהּ, אֲשֶׁר בַּעַד הַשִּׂמְחָה הָעֲרוּכָה לְפָנָיו סָבַל אֶת הַצְּלָב וּבָז לַחֶרְפָּה, וְיָשַׁב לִימִין כִּסֵּא הָאֱלֹהִים. 3הִתְבּוֹנְנוּ אֶל הָאֶחָד שֶׁסָּבַל הִתְנַגְּדוּת כָּזֹאת מֵאֵת הַחוֹטְאִים, כְּדֵי שֶׁלֹּא תִּתְעַיְּפוּ וְלֹא תִרְפֶּה נַפְשְׁכֶם. 4עֲדַיִן לֹא נִלְחַמְתֶּם עַד דָּם בְּמַאֲבַקְכֶם עִם הַחֵטְא, 5וּשְׁכַחְתֶּם אֶת מִלּוֹת הַנֹּחַם הַמְדַבְּרוֹת אֲלֵיכֶם כְּאֶל בָּנִים:

"מוּסַר יְהוָה, בְּנִי, אַל־תִּמְאָס, וְאַל־תָּקֹץ בְּתוֹכַחְתּוֹ;

"*My son, do not despise the chastening of the* LORD,

Nor be discouraged when you are rebuked by Him;

6   *For whom the* LORD *loves He chastens, And scourges every son whom He receives."*

7 If you endure chastening, God deals with you as with sons; for what son is there whom a father does not chasten? 8 But if you are without chastening, of which all have become partakers, then you are illegitimate and not sons. 9 Furthermore, we have had human fathers who corrected *us*, and we paid *them* respect. Shall we not much more readily be in subjection to the Father of spirits and live? 10 For they indeed for a few days chastened *us* as seemed *best* to them, but He for *our* profit, that *we* may be partakers of His holiness. 11 Now no chastening seems to be joyful for the present, but painful; nevertheless, afterward it yields the peaceable fruit of righteousness to those who have been trained by it.

12 Therefore strengthen the hands which hang down, and the feeble knees, 13 and make straight paths for your feet, so that what is lame may not be *dislocated*, but rather be healed.

14 Pursue peace with all *people*, and holiness, without which no one will see the Lord: 15 looking carefully lest anyone fall short of the grace of God; lest any root of bitterness springing up cause trouble, and by this many become defiled; 16 lest there *be* any fornicator or profane person like Esau, who for one morsel of food sold his birthright. 17 For you know that afterward, when he wanted to inherit the blessing, he was rejected, for he found no place for repentance, though he sought it diligently with tears.

18 For you have not come to the mountain that may be touched and that burned with fire, and to blackness and darkness and tempest, 19 and the sound of a trumpet and the voice of words, so that those who heard *it* begged that the word should not be spoken to them anymore. 20 (For they could not endure what was commanded: *"And if so much as a beast touches the mountain, it shall be stoned or shot with an arrow."* 21 And so terrifying was the sight *that* Moses said, *"I am exceedingly afraid and trembling."*)

22 But you have come to Mount Zion and to the city of the living God, the heavenly Jerusalem, to an innumerable company of angels, 23 to the general assembly and church of the firstborn *who are* registered in heaven, to God the Judge of all, to the spirits of just men made perfect, 24 to Jesus the

6 כִּי אֶת אֲשֶׁר יֶאֱהַב יהוה יוֹכִיחַ,
יַכְאִיב אֶת־בֵּן יִרְצֶה."

7 לָשֶׁם מוּסָר סוֹבְלִים אַתֶּם, וֵאלֹהִים נוֹהֵג עִמָּכֶם כְּעַם בָּנִים; כִּי אֵיזֶהוּ הַבֵּן אֲשֶׁר אָבִיו אֵינוֹ מְיַסֵּר אוֹתוֹ? 8 אַךְ אִם אַתֶּם בְּלֹא מוּסָר, אֲשֶׁר הַכֹּל נוֹטְלִים בּוֹ חֶלְקָם, אֲזַי מַמְזֵרִים אַתֶּם וְלֹא בָנִים. 9 וְעוֹד, הָאָבוֹת שֶׁהוֹלִידוּ אֶת גּוּפֵנוּ יִסְּרוּ אוֹתָנוּ וְאָנוּ יְרֵאנוּ מֵהֶם, הֲלֹא כָּל שֶׁכֵּן נִכָּנַע לִפְנֵי אֲבִי הָרוּחוֹת וְנִחְיֶה? 10 הֵם אָמְנָם יִסְּרוּנוּ יָמִים מְעַטִּים עַל־פִּי מַה שֶׁהֵם רָאוּ לְנָכוֹן, אַךְ הוּא לְהוֹעִיל מְיַסֵּר אוֹתָנוּ, לְמַעַן יִהְיֶה לָנוּ חֵלֶק בִּקְדֻשָּׁתוֹ. 11 כָּל מוּסָר בְּעֵת בּוֹאוֹ אֵינוּ נֶחְשָׁב לְשִׂמְחָה כִּי אִם לְעֶצֶב, אֲבָל אַחֲרֵי כֵן יִתֵּן פְּרִי שָׁלוֹם וּצְדָקָה לַמִּתְחַנְּכִים בּוֹ.

12 עַל כֵּן אַמְּצוּ יָדַיִם רָפוֹת וְחַזְּקוּ בִּרְכַּיִם כּוֹשְׁלוֹת; 13 וְכוֹנְנוּ נְתִיבוֹת יְשָׁרוֹת לְרַגְלֵיכֶם, לְמַעַן לֹא יִסְטֶה הַצּוֹלֵעַ כִּי אִם יֵרָפֵא.

14 רִדְפוּ שָׁלוֹם עִם כָּל אָדָם, וְגַם אֶת הַקְּדֻשָּׁה שֶׁבִּלְעָדֶיהָ לֹא יִרְאֶה אִישׁ אֶת הָאָדוֹן. 15 הִשָּׁמְרוּ פֶּן יִגְרַע אִישׁ מֵחֶסֶד אֱלֹהִים; פֶּן יַפְרִיעַ אֶתְכֶם שֹׁרֶשׁ פּוֹרֶה מְרִירוּת וְיִטַּמְאוּ בּוֹ רַבִּים; 16 פֶּן יִהְיֶה אִישׁ זוֹנֶה אוֹ חֲסַר קְדֻשָּׁה כְּעֵשָׂו אֲשֶׁר בִּנְזִיד אֶחָד מָכַר אֶת בְּכוֹרָתוֹ. 17 יוֹדְעִים אַתֶּם כִּי אַחֲרֵי כֵן, כַּאֲשֶׁר רָצָה לָרֶשֶׁת אֶת הַבְּרָכָה, נִדְחָה; הוּא לֹא מָצָא מָקוֹם לַחֲזוֹר בּוֹ, אַף כִּי בִּקֵּשׁ זֹאת בִּדְמָעוֹת. 18 הֵן לֹא בָאתֶם אֶל הַר מוּחָשִׁי וּבוֹעֵר בָּאֵשׁ, וְלֹא אֶל אֲפֵלָה וְחֹשֶׁךְ וּסְעָרָה, 19 וְלֹא לְקוֹל שׁוֹפָר וּלְקוֹל דְּבָרִים אֲשֶׁר שׁוֹמְעָיו בִּקְשׁוּ שֶׁלֹּא יוֹסִיף לְדַבֵּר עִמָּם, 20 כִּי לֹא יָכְלוּ לָשֵׂאת אֶת מַה שֶּׁצֻוָּה, "גַּם אִם בְּהֵמָה תִּגַּע בָּהָר סָקוֹל תִּסָּקֵל"; 21 וְהַמַּרְאֶה הָיָה נוֹרָא מְאֹד עַד כִּי מֹשֶׁה אָמַר, "יָרֵא אֲנִי וְחָרֵד". 22 אַתֶּם בָּאתֶם אֶל הַר צִיּוֹן וְאֶל עִיר אֱלֹהִים חַיִּים, אֶל יְרוּשָׁלַיִם הַשְּׁמֵימִית וְאֶל רִבְבוֹת הַמַּלְאָכִים, אֶל עֲצֶרֶת, 23 אֶל קְהַלַּת הַבְּכוֹרִים הַכְּתוּבִים בַּשָּׁמַיִם, אֶל אֱלֹהִים שׁוֹפֵט הַכֹּל, אֶל רוּחוֹת הַצַּדִּיקִים שֶׁנַּעֲשׂוּ מֻשְׁלָמִים, 24 אֶל יֵשׁוּעַ מְתַוֵּךְ הַבְּרִית הַחֲדָשָׁה וְאֶל דַּם הַהַזָּיָה הַמֵּיטִיב דַּבֵּר מִדַּם הֶבֶל.

Mediator of the new covenant, and to the blood of sprinkling that speaks better things than *that of* Abel.

25 See that you do not refuse Him who speaks. For if they did not escape who refused Him who spoke on earth, much more *shall we not escape* if we turn away from Him who *speaks* from heaven, 26 whose voice then shook the earth; but now He has promised, saying, "Yet once more I shake not only the earth, *but also heaven.*" 27 Now this, "*Yet once more,*" indicates the removal of those things that are being shaken, as of things that are made, that the things which cannot be shaken may remain.

28 Therefore, since we are receiving a kingdom which cannot be shaken, let us have grace, by which we may serve God acceptably with reverence and godly fear. 29 For our God *is* a consuming fire.

13 Let brotherly love continue. 2 Do not forget to entertain strangers, for by so *doing* some have unwittingly entertained angels. 3 Remember the prisoners as if chained with them—those who are mistreated—since you yourselves are in the body also.

4 Marriage *is* honorable among all, and the bed undefiled; but fornicators and adulterers God will judge.

5 *Let your* conduct *be* without covetousness; *be* content with such things as you have. For He Himself has said, "I will never leave you nor forsake you." 6 So we may boldly say:

"The LORD is my helper;
I will not fear.
What can man do to me?"

7 Remember those who rule over you, who have spoken the word of God to you, whose faith follow, considering the outcome of *their* conduct. 8 Jesus Christ *is* the same yesterday, today, and forever. 9 Do not be carried about with various and strange doctrines. For *it is* good that the heart be established by grace, not with foods which have not profited those who have been occupied with them.

10 We have an altar from which those who serve the tabernacle have no right to eat. 11 For the bodies of those animals, whose blood is brought into the sanctuary by the high priest for sin, are burned outside the camp. 12 Therefore Jesus also, that He might sanctify the people with His own blood, suffered outside the gate. 13 Therefore let us go forth to Him, outside the camp, bearing His reproach. 14 For here we have no continuing city, but we seek the one to come. 15 Therefore by Him let us

25 לָכֵן הִזָּהֲרוּ פֶּן תְּסָרְבוּ לַמְדַבֵּר, שֶׁכֵּן אִם לֹא נִמְלְטוּ אֵלֶּה שֶׁסֵּרְבוּ לַמְדַבֵּר עַל הָאָרֶץ, עַל אַחַת כַּמָּה וְכַמָּה לֹא נִמָּלֵט אֲנַחְנוּ אִם נָסוּר מֵהַמְדַבֵּר מִן הַשָּׁמַיִם, 26 אֲשֶׁר קוֹלוֹ הִרְעִישׁ אָז אֶת הָאָרֶץ וְעַתָּה הִבְטִיחַ בְּאָמְרוֹ, "עוֹד אַחַת וַאֲנִי מַרְעִישׁ לֹא אֶת־ הָאָרֶץ בִּלְבַד, אֶלָּא גַּם אֶת־הַשָּׁמַיִם." 27 "עוֹד אַחַת" מְצַיֵּן אֶת הֲסָרַת הַדְּבָרִים הַמִּתְמוֹטְטִים – כְּגוֹן דְּבָרִים שֶׁנַּעֲשׂוּ – לְמַעַן יִשָּׁאֲרוּ הַדְּבָרִים אֲשֶׁר לֹא יָמוֹטוּ. 28 וְכֵיוָן שֶׁאָנוּ מְקַבְּלִים מַלְכוּת אֲשֶׁר לֹא תִּמּוֹט, נִהְיֶה נָא מַכִּירֵי טוֹבָה וּבְהַכָּרָה זֹאת נַעֲבֹד אֶת אֱלֹהִים כִּרְצוֹנוֹ, בַּחֲסִידוּת וּבְיִרְאָה; 29 כִּי אֱלֹהֵינוּ אֵשׁ אוֹכְלָה הוּא.

יג תְּהֵא אַהֲבַת אַחִים קַיֶּמֶת בֵּינֵיכֶם. 2 הַכְנָסַת אוֹרְחִים אַל תִּשְׁכְּחוּ, כִּי יֵשׁ אֲשֶׁר הִכְנִיסוּ אֶל בֵּיתָם מַלְאָכִים מִבְּלִי לָדַעַת זֹאת. 3 זִכְרוּ אֶת הָאֲסוּרִים כְּאִלּוּ הֱיִיתֶם בַּמַּאֲסָר עִמָּהֶם; זִכְרוּ אֶת הַמְעֻנִּים, כְּשֵׁם שֶׁגַּם אַתֶּם חַיִּים בַּגּוּף. 4 חַיֵּי אִישׁוּת יְכֻבְּדוּ אֵצֶל הַכֹּל וִיצוּעֲכֶם אַל יְחֻלָּל. אֶת הַזּוֹנִים וְהַנּוֹאֲפִים יִשְׁפֹּט אֱלֹהִים. 5 רַחֲקוּ מֵאַהֲבַת כֶּסֶף וְשִׂמְחוּ בְּחֶלְקְכֶם, כִּי הוּא אָמַר, "לֹא אַרְפְּךָ וְלֹא אֶעֶזְבֶךָ." 6 עַל כֵּן נִבְטַח וְנֹאמַר, "יהוה לִי בְּעֹזְרָי, לֹא אִירָא מַה־יַּעֲשֶׂה לִי אָדָם."

7 זִכְרוּ אֶת מַנְהִיגֵיכֶם אֲשֶׁר דִּבְּרוּ אֲלֵיכֶם אֶת דְּבַר אֱלֹהִים; הַבִּיטוּ אֶל אַחֲרִית דַּרְכָּם וּלְכוּ בְּעִקְבוֹת אֱמוּנָתָם. 8 יֵשׁוּעַ הַמָּשִׁיחַ הוּא הוּא – אֶתְמוֹל, הַיּוֹם וּלְעוֹלָמִים. 9 אַל תִּפָּחֲפוּ עַל־יְדֵי תּוֹרוֹת שׁוֹנוֹת וְזָרוֹת; הֵן טוֹב לִסְעֹד אֶת הַלֵּב בְּחֶסֶד וְלֹא בְּדִבְרֵי מַאֲכָל אֲשֶׁר לֹא הוֹעִילוּ לְמִי שֶׁחַי עַל־פִּיהֶם. 10 יֵשׁ לָנוּ מִזְבֵּחַ אֲשֶׁר אֵין רְשׁוּת לִמְשָׁרְתֵי הַמִּשְׁכָּן לֶאֱכֹל מֵעָלָיו. 11 הַבְּהֵמוֹת אֲשֶׁר דָּמָן מוּבָא אֶל הַקֹּדֶשׁ בְּיַד הַכֹּהֵן הַגָּדוֹל לְכַפָּרַת הַחֵטְא, גּוּפוֹתֵיהֶן נִשְׂרָפוֹת מִחוּץ לַמַּחֲנֶה. 12 לָכֵן גַּם יֵשׁוּעַ, כְּדֵי לְקַדֵּשׁ אֶת הָעָם בְּדָמוֹ, סָבַל מִחוּץ לַשַּׁעַר. 13 עַל כֵּן נֵצֵא נָא אֵלָיו אֶל מִחוּץ לַמַּחֲנֶה וְנִשָּׂא אֶת חֶרְפָּתוֹ; 14 כִּי אֵין לָנוּ פֹּה עִיר קֶבַע, אֶלָּא אֶת זוֹ שֶׁלֶּעָתִיד לָבוֹא

continually offer the sacrifice of praise to God, that
is, the fruit of *our* lips, giving thanks to His name.
16 But do not forget to do good and to share, for
with such sacrifices God is well pleased.

17 Obey those who rule over you, and be
submissive, for they watch out for your souls, as
those who must give account. Let them do so with
joy and not with grief, for that would be
unprofitable for you.

18 Pray for us; for we are confident that we have a
good conscience, in all things desiring to live
honorably. 19 But I especially urge *you* to do this,
that I may be restored to you the sooner.

20 Now may the God of peace who brought up
our Lord Jesus from the dead, that great Shepherd
of the sheep, through the blood of the everlasting
covenant, 21 make you complete in every good work
to do His will, working in you what is well pleasing
in His sight, through Jesus Christ, to whom *be* glory
forever and ever. Amen.

22 And I appeal to you, brethren, bear with the
word of exhortation, for I have written to you in
few words. 23 Know that *our* brother Timothy has
been set free, with whom I shall see you if he comes
shortly.

24 Greet all those who rule over you, and all the
saints. Those from Italy greet you.

25 Grace *be* with you all. Amen.

מְבַקְשִׁים אָנוּ. 15 לָכֵן בְּכָל עֵת נַקְרִיבָה בְּתוּוכוֹ זֶבַח
תּוֹדָה לֵאלֹהִים, כְּלוֹמַר, פְּרִי שְׂפָתַיִם הַמּוֹדוֹת לִשְׁמוֹ.
16 וְאַל תִּשְׁכְּחוּ לִגְמֹל חֶסֶד וּלְשַׁתֵּף אֶת הַזּוּלַת בְּמַה
שֶּׁיֵּשׁ לָכֶם, כִּי זְבָחִים כָּאֵלֶּה יֶעֶרְבוּ לֵאלֹהִים.
17 שִׁמְעוּ בְּקוֹל מַנְהִיגֵיכֶם וְהִכָּנְעוּ לָהֶם, כִּי מַשְׁגִּיחִים
הֵם עַל נַפְשׁוֹתֵיכֶם כַּעֲתִידִים לָתֵת דִּין וְחֶשְׁבּוֹן; נַהֲגוּ
כָּךְ, לְמַעַן יַעֲשׂוּ זֹאת בְּשִׂמְחָה וְלֹא בַּאֲנָחָה, שֶׁאִם
לֹא כֵן אֵין זֶה לְתוֹעֶלֶת לָכֶם.
18 הִתְפַּלְּלוּ בַּעֲדֵנוּ. בְּטוּחִים אָנוּ כִּי שָׁלֵם מַצְפּוּנֵנוּ;
רְצוֹנֵנוּ לְהִתְנַהֵג בַּיֹּשֶׁר בְּכָל דָּבָר. 19 מַפְצִיר אֲנִי בָּכֶם
מְאֹד לַעֲשׂוֹת זֹאת, לְמַעַן יֻנְתַּן לִי לָשׁוּב אֲלֵיכֶם
בִּמְהֵרָה.
20 וֵאלֹהֵי הַשָּׁלוֹם אֲשֶׁר בְּדַם בְּרִית עוֹלָם הֶעֱלָה מִן
הַמֵּתִים אֶת רוֹעֵה הַצֹּאן הַגָּדוֹל, אֶת אֲדוֹנֵנוּ יֵשׁוּעַ,
21 הוּא יַכְשִׁיר אֶתְכֶם לְכָל דָּבָר טוֹב כְּדֵי שֶׁתַּעֲשׂוּ
אֶת רְצוֹנוֹ, בְּפָעֳלוֹ בָּכֶם אֶת הָרָצוּי לְפָנָיו בְּיַד יֵשׁוּעַ
הַמָּשִׁיחַ, אֲשֶׁר לוֹ הַכָּבוֹד לְעוֹלְמֵי עוֹלָמִים. אָמֵן.
22 וַאֲנִי מְבַקֵּשׁ מִכֶּם, אַחַי, לְקַבֵּל בְּסַבְלָנוּת אֶת דְּבַר
הַהַטָּפָה, שֶׁהֲרֵי בִּקְצָרָה כָּתַבְתִּי אֲלֵיכֶם. 23 דְּעוּ כִּי
טִימוֹתֵיאוֹס אָחִינוּ שֻׁלַּח לַחָפְשִׁי. אִם יַקְדִּים לָבוֹא,
אָבוֹא יַחַד אִתּוֹ לִרְאוֹת אֶתְכֶם.
24 דִּרְשׁוּ בְּשָׁלוֹם כָּל מַנְהִיגֵיכֶם וְכָל הַקְּדוֹשִׁים. בְּנֵי
אֶרֶץ אִיטַלְיָה דוֹרְשִׁים בִּשְׁלוֹמְכֶם. 25 הַחֶסֶד עִם
כֻּלְּכֶם. אָמֵן.

The Epistle of

JAMES

1 James, a bondservant of God and of the Lord Jesus Christ,

To the twelve tribes which are scattered abroad: Greetings:

[2] My brethren, count it all joy when you fall into various trials, [3] knowing that the testing of your faith produces patience. [4] But let patience have *its* perfect work, that you may be perfect and complete, lacking nothing. [5] If any of you lacks wisdom, let him ask of God, who gives to all liberally and without reproach, and it will be given to him. [6] But let him ask in faith, with no doubting, for he who doubts is like a wave of the sea driven and tossed by the wind. [7] For let not that man suppose that he will receive anything from the Lord; [8] *he is* a double-minded man, unstable in all his ways.

[9] Let the lowly brother glory in his exaltation, [10] but the rich in his humiliation, because as a flower of the field he will pass away. [11] For no sooner has the sun risen with a burning heat than it withers the grass; its flower falls, and its beautiful appearance perishes. So the rich man also will fade away in his pursuits.

[12] Blessed *is* the man who endures temptation; for when he has been approved, he will receive the crown of life which the Lord has promised to those who love Him. [13] Let no one say when he is tempted, "I am tempted by God"; for God cannot be tempted by evil, nor does He Himself tempt anyone. [14] But each one is tempted when he is drawn away by his own desires and enticed. [15] Then, when desire has conceived, it gives birth to sin; and sin, when it is full-grown, brings forth death.

[16] Do not be deceived, my beloved brethren. [17] Every good gift and every perfect gift is from above, and comes down from the Father of lights, with whom there is no variation or shadow of turning. [18] Of His own will He brought us forth by the word of truth, that we might be a kind of firstfruits of His creatures.

[19] So then, my beloved brethren, let every man be swift to hear, slow to speak, slow to wrath; [20] for the wrath of man does not produce the righteousness of God.

אִגֶּרֶת יַעֲקֹב

א יַעֲקֹב, עֶבֶד אֱלֹהִים וַאֲדוֹנֵנוּ יֵשׁוּעַ הַמָּשִׁיחַ, דּוֹרֵשׁ בְּשָׁלוֹם שְׁנֵים־עָשָׂר הַשְּׁבָטִים שֶׁבַּגּוֹלָה. [2] לְשִׂמְחָה גְדוֹלָה חִשְׁבוּ זֹאת, אַחַי, כַּאֲשֶׁר אַתֶּם בָּאִים בְּכָל מִינֵי נִסְיוֹנוֹת, [3] שֶׁהֲרֵי יוֹדְעִים אַתֶּם כִּי בְּחִינַת אֱמוּנַתְכֶם מְבִיאָה לִידֵי סַבְלָנוּת. [4] אֲבָל שֶׁתְּהֵא הַסַּבְלָנוּת שְׁלֵמָה בְּפָעֳלָהּ, לְמַעַן תִּהְיוּ שְׁלֵמִים וּבְלֹא דֹּפִי וְלֹא יֶחְסַר לָכֶם דָּבָר. [5] אִישׁ מִכֶּם אִם יֶחְסַר חָכְמָה, יְבַקֵּשׁ מֵאֱלֹהִים הַנּוֹתֵן לַכֹּל בִּנְדִיבוּת וּבְלֹא גְעָרָה, וְתִנָּתֵן לוֹ. [6] אַךְ יְבַקֵּשׁ בֶּאֱמוּנָה וּבְלִי סָפֵק, כִּי בַּעַל־סָפֵק דּוֹמֶה לְגַלֵּי הַיָּם הַנִּדְחָפִים וְסוֹעֲרִים מִפְּנֵי הָרוּחַ. [7] אוֹתוֹ הָאִישׁ אַל יַחְשֹׁב כִּי יְקַבֵּל מַשֶּׁהוּ מֵאֵת יהוה, [8] בִּהְיוֹתוֹ אִישׁ הַפּוֹסֵחַ עַל שְׁתֵּי הַסְּעִפִּים הֲפַכְפַּךְ בְּכָל דְּרָכָיו.

[9] יִתְהַלֵּל הָאָח הַדַּל בְּרוֹמְמוּתוֹ, [10] וְהֶעָשִׁיר שֶׁיִּתְהַלֵּל בְּשִׁפְלוֹ, כִּי כְּצִיץ חָצִיר הוּא יַחֲלֹף. [11] הֵן בַּעֲלוֹת הַשֶּׁמֶשׁ הַלּוֹהֶטֶת יִיבַשׁ הֶחָצִיר וְיִפֹּל צִיצוֹ וְיֹאבַד חֵן מַרְאֵהוּ; כֵּן גַּם הֶעָשִׁיר יִבֹּל בַּהֲלִיכוֹתָיו.

[12] אַשְׁרֵי הָאִישׁ הַמַּחֲזִיק מַעֲמָד בְּנִסָּיוֹן, כִּי לְאַחַר עָמְדוֹ בַּנִּסָּיוֹן יְקַבֵּל אֶת עֲטֶרֶת הַחַיִּים אֲשֶׁר הִבְטִיחַ הָאָדוֹן לְאוֹהֲבָיו. [13] מִי שֶׁמִּתְנַסֶּה אַל יֹאמַר, "אֱלֹהִים מְנַסֶּה אוֹתִי", שֶׁכֵּן אֱלֹהִים לֹא יְנֻסֶּה בְּרָע וְאֵין הוּא מְנַסֶּה אִישׁ. [14] אֶלָּא שֶׁכָּל אִישׁ מִתְנַסֶּה כַּאֲשֶׁר הוּא נִמְשָׁךְ וּמִתְפַּתֶּה בְּתַאֲוָתוֹ שֶׁלּוֹ. [15] אַחֲרֵי כֵן תַּהֲרֶה הַתַּאֲוָה וְתֵלֵד חֵטְא; וְהַחֵטְא כְּשֶׁיִּשְׁלַם יוֹלִיד מָוֶת. [16] אַל נָא תִּטְעוּ, אַחַי אֲהוּבַי. [17] כָּל מַתָּנָה טוֹבָה וְכָל מַתָּנָה שְׁלֵמָה יוֹרֶדֶת מִמַּעַל מֵאֵת אֲבִי הָאוֹרוֹת אֲשֶׁר כָּל שִׁנּוּי וְכָל צֵל חִלּוּף אֵין בּוֹ. [18] הוּא כִּרְצוֹנוֹ הוֹלִיד אוֹתָנוּ בִּדְבַר הָאֱמֶת, לְמַעַן נִהְיֶה בִּכּוּרֵי יְצִירָיו.

[19] עַל כֵּן, אַחַי אֲהוּבַי, יְהֵא כָּל אִישׁ מָהִיר לִשְׁמֹעַ, בִּלְתִּי נֶחְפָּז לְדַבֵּר וְקָשֶׁה לִכְעֹם, [20] שֶׁהֲרֵי כַּעַס אָדָם לֹא יִפְעַל צִדְקַת אֱלֹהִים. [21] לָכֵן הָסִירוּ מֵעֲלֵיכֶם כָּל טִנּוּף וְרֹב רֶשַׁע, וְקַבְּלוּ בַּעֲנָוָה אֶת הַדָּבָר הַנָּטוּעַ אֲשֶׁר יָכוֹל לְהוֹשִׁיעַ אֶת נַפְשׁוֹתֵיכֶם.

²¹ Therefore lay aside all filthiness and overflow of wickedness, and receive with meekness the implanted word, which is able to save your souls.

²² But be doers of the word, and not hearers only, deceiving yourselves. ²³ For if anyone is a hearer of the word and not a doer, he is like a man observing his natural face in a mirror; ²⁴ for he observes himself, goes away, and immediately forgets what kind of man he was. ²⁵ But he who looks into the perfect law of liberty and continues *in it*, and is not a forgetful hearer but a doer of the work, this one will be blessed in what he does.

²⁶ If anyone among you thinks he is religious, and does not bridle his tongue but deceives his own heart, this one's religion *is* useless. ²⁷ Pure and undefiled religion before God and the Father is this: to visit orphans and widows in their trouble, *and to* keep oneself unspotted from the world.

2 My brethren, do not hold the faith of our Lord Jesus Christ, *the Lord* of glory, with partiality. ² For if there should come into your assembly a man with gold rings, in fine apparel, and there should also come in a poor man in filthy clothes, ³ and you pay attention to the one wearing the fine clothes and say to him, "You sit here in a good place," and say to the poor man, "You stand there," or, "Sit here at my footstool," ⁴ have you not shown partiality among yourselves, and become judges with evil thoughts?

⁵ Listen, my beloved brethren: Has God not chosen the poor of this world *to be* rich in faith and heirs of the kingdom which He promised to those who love Him? ⁶ But you have dishonored the poor man. Do not the rich oppress you and drag you into the courts? ⁷ Do they not blaspheme that noble name by which you are called?

⁸ If you really fulfill *the* royal law according to the Scripture, *"You shall love your neighbor as yourself,"* you do well; ⁹ but if you show partiality, you commit sin, and are convicted by the law as transgressors. ¹⁰ For whoever shall keep the whole law, and yet stumble in one *point*, he is guilty of all. ¹¹ For He who said, *"Do not commit adultery,"* also said, *"Do not murder."* Now if you do not commit adultery, but you do murder, you have become a transgressor of the law. ¹² So speak and so do as those who will be judged by the law of liberty. ¹³ For judgment is without mercy to the one who has shown no mercy. Mercy triumphs over judgment.

¹⁴ What *does it* profit, my brethren, if someone says he has faith but does not have works? Can faith save him? ¹⁵ If a brother or sister is naked and

²² הֱיוּ עוֹשֵׂי הַדָּבָר וְלֹא רַק שׁוֹמְעִים, פֶּן תְּרַמּוּ אֶת עַצְמְכֶם; ²³ כִּי מִי שֶׁשּׁוֹמֵעַ אֶת הַדָּבָר וְאֵינוֹ עוֹשֶׂה, כְּמוֹהוּ כְּאִישׁ הַמַּבִּיט עַל תֹּאַר פָּנָיו בַּמַּרְאָה; ²⁴ הוּא הִתְבּוֹנֵן בְּעַצְמוֹ וְהָלַךְ לוֹ, וּמִיָּד שָׁכַח מַה צּוּרָתוֹ. ²⁵ אֲבָל הַמַּשְׁקִיף בְּתוֹרָה הַשְּׁלֵמָה, תּוֹרַת הַחֵרוּת, וְעוֹמֵד בָּהּ מִבְּלִי לִהְיוֹת שׁוֹמֵעַ־וְשׁוֹכֵחַ, אֶלָּא עוֹשֶׂה בְּפֹעַל – אִישׁ זֶה מְבֹרָךְ יִהְיֶה בְּמַעֲשֵׂהוּ.

²⁶ מִי שֶׁסָּבוּר שֶׁהוּא עוֹבֵד אֱלֹהִים, וְאֵינֶנּוּ שָׂם רֶסֶן לִלְשׁוֹנוֹ כִּי אִם מַתְעֶה אֶת לִבּוֹ, עֲבוֹדָתוֹ אֵינָה אֶלָּא הֶבֶל. ²⁷ זֹאת הִיא עֲבוֹדַת אֱלֹהִים טְהוֹרָה וּתְמִימָה לִפְנֵי אֱלֹהִים אָבִינוּ: לִפְקֹד אֶת הַיְתוֹמִים וְהָאַלְמָנוֹת בְּצָרָתָם, וּלְהִשָּׁמֵר נָקִי מִטֻּמְאַת הָעוֹלָם.

ב אַחַי, אַל יְהֵא בָכֶם מַשּׂוֹא פָנִים בֶּאֱמוּנַת אֲדוֹנֵנוּ יֵשׁוּעַ הַמָּשִׁיחַ, אֲדוֹן הַכָּבוֹד. ² אִם יָבוֹא אִישׁ לְבֵית הַכְּנֶסֶת שֶׁלָּכֶם וְטַבַּעַת זָהָב עַל יָדוֹ וּלְבוּשׁוֹ הָדוּר, וּבָא גַם אִישׁ עָנִי לָבוּשׁ בְּגָדִים בָּלִים, ³ וְהִנֵּה פּוֹנִים אַתֶּם אֶל הָאִישׁ אֲשֶׁר לְבוּשׁוֹ הָדוּר וְאוֹמְרִים: "שֵׁב לְךָ פֹּה בְּטוֹב"; וְלֶעָנִי אַתֶּם אוֹמְרִים: "עֲמֹד שָׁם" אוֹ "שֵׁב מִתַּחַת לַהֲדֹם רַגְלַי" – ⁴ הַאִם אֵינְכֶם מַפְלִים בְּקִרְבְּכֶם בֵּין אִישׁ לְאִישׁ וְהוֹפְכִים לִהְיוֹת שׁוֹפְטִים בַּעֲלֵי מַחְשָׁבוֹת רֶשַׁע?

⁵ שִׁמְעוּ, אַחַי אֲהוּבַי, הֲלֹא בַּעֲנִיֵּי הָעוֹלָם הַזֶּה בָּחַר אֱלֹהִים לִהְיוֹת עֲשִׁירֵי אֱמוּנָה וְיוֹרְשֵׁי הַמַּלְכוּת אֲשֶׁר הִבְטִיחַ לְאוֹהֲבָיו. ⁶ וְאַתֶּם בִּזִּיתֶם אֶת הֶעָנִי. הֲלֹא הָעֲשִׁירִים מְדַכְּאִים אֶתְכֶם וְסוֹחֲבִים אֶתְכֶם לְבָתֵּי מִשְׁפָּט. ⁷ הֲלֹא הֵם הַמְגַדְּפִים אֶת הַשֵּׁם הַטּוֹב הַנִּקְרָא עֲלֵיכֶם. ⁸ אִם בֶּאֱמֶת מְקַיְּמִים אַתֶּם אֶת תּוֹרַת הַמַּלְכוּת, כַּכָּתוּב, "וְאָהַבְתָּ לְרֵעֲךָ כָּמוֹךָ", אֲזַי הֵיטַבְתֶּם לַעֲשׂוֹת. ⁹ אֲבָל אִם אַתֶּם נוֹהֲגִים בְּמַשּׂוֹא פָנִים, חוֹטְאִים אַתֶּם וְהַתּוֹרָה תַּאֲשִׁימְכֶם כְּעוֹבְרֵי עֲבֵרָה. ¹⁰ הֲרֵי מִי שֶׁמְּקַיֵּם אֶת כָּל הַתּוֹרָה וְנִכְשָׁל בְּדָבָר אֶחָד, אָשֵׁם הוּא בַּכֹּל; ¹¹ שֶׁכֵּן הָאוֹמֵר "לֹא תִנְאַף" אָמַר גַּם "לֹא תִרְצַח", וְאִם אֵינְךָ נוֹאֵף אֲבָל כֵּן רוֹצֵחַ, עוֹבֵר אַתָּה עַל מִצְווֹת הַתּוֹרָה. ¹² דַּבְּרוּ וַעֲשׂוּ אֶת מַעֲשֵׂיכֶם כַּאֲנָשִׁים הָעֲתִידִים לְהִשָּׁפֵט עַל־פִּי תּוֹרָה שֶׁל חֵרוּת. ¹³ אֵין רַחֲמִים בַּדִּין לְמִי שֶׁלֹּא נָהַג בְּרַחֲמִים; הָרַחֲמִים מִתְנַשְּׂאִים עַל הַדִּין.

¹⁴ אַחַי, מַה תּוֹעֶלֶת בַּדָּבָר אִם יֹאמַר אִישׁ, "יֵשׁ לִי אֱמוּנָה", וְאֵין לוֹ מַעֲשִׂים? הֲתוּכַל הָאֱמוּנָה לְהוֹשִׁיעוֹ? ¹⁵ אָח אוֹ אָחוֹת אִם יִהְיוּ בְּעֵירֹם וְאֵין

destitute of daily food, ¹⁶ and one of you says to them, "Depart in peace, be warmed and filled," but you do not give them the things which are needed for the body, what *does it* profit? ¹⁷ Thus also faith by itself, if it does not have works, is dead.

¹⁸ But someone will say, "You have faith, and I have works." Show me your faith without your works, and I will show you my faith by my works. ¹⁹ You believe that there is one God. You do well. Even the demons believe—and tremble! ²⁰ But do you want to know, O foolish man, that faith without works is dead? ²¹ Was not Abraham our father justified by works when he offered Isaac his son on the altar? ²² Do you see that faith was working together with his works, and by works faith was made perfect? ²³ And the Scripture was fulfilled which says, *"Abraham believed God, and it was accounted to him for righteousness."* And he was called the friend of God. ²⁴ You see then that a man is justified by works, and not by faith only.

²⁵ Likewise, was not Rahab the harlot also justified by works when she received the messengers and sent *them* out another way?

²⁶ For as the body without the spirit is dead, so faith without works is dead also.

3 My brethren, let not many of you become teachers, knowing that we shall receive a stricter judgment. ² For we all stumble in many things. If anyone does not stumble in word, he *is* a perfect man, able also to bridle the whole body. ³ Indeed, we put bits in horses' mouths that they may obey us, and we turn their whole body. ⁴ Look also at ships: although they are so large and are driven by fierce winds, they are turned by a very small rudder wherever the pilot desires. ⁵ Even so the tongue is a little member and boasts great things.

See how great a forest a little fire kindles! ⁶ And the tongue *is* a fire, a world of iniquity. The tongue is so set among our members that it defiles the whole body, and sets on fire the course of nature; and it is set on fire by hell. ⁷ For every kind of beast and bird, of reptile and creature of the sea, is tamed and has been tamed by mankind. ⁸ But no man can tame the tongue. *It is* an unruly evil, full of deadly poison. ⁹ With it we bless our God and Father, and with it we curse men, who have been made in the similitude of God. ¹⁰ Out of the same mouth proceed blessing and cursing. My brethren, these things ought not to be so. ¹¹ Does a spring send forth fresh *water* and bitter from the same opening? ¹² Can a fig tree, my brethren, bear olives, or a grapevine bear figs? Thus no spring yields both salt water and fresh.

לָהֶם לֶחֶם חֻקָּם, ¹⁶ וְאִישׁ מִכֶּם יֹאמַר לָהֶם, "לְכוּ לְשָׁלוֹם, הִתְחַמְּמוּ וְאִכְלוּ לָשֹׂבַע", וְלֹא תִּתְּנוּ לָהֶם צָרְכֵי גּוּפָם – מַה הוֹעַלְתֶּם? ¹⁷ כָּךְ גַּם הָאֱמוּנָה, אִם אֵין בָּהּ מַעֲשִׂים, מֵתָה הִיא כְּשֶׁלְעַצְמָהּ.

¹⁸ וְאוּלָם מִישֶׁהוּ יֹאמַר, "אַתָּה, יֵשׁ לְךָ אֱמוּנָה; וַאֲנִי, יֵשׁ לִי מַעֲשִׂים. הַרְאֵנִי אֶת אֱמוּנָתְךָ בִּבְלִי הַמַּעֲשִׂים, וַאֲנִי אַרְאֶה לְךָ אֶת אֱמוּנָתִי מִתּוֹךְ מַעֲשָׂי. ¹⁹ אַתָּה מַאֲמִין שֶׁהָאֱלֹהִים אֶחָד הוּא. הֵיטַבְתָּ לַעֲשׂוֹת! גַּם הַשֵּׁדִים מַאֲמִינִים וְאַף רוֹעֲדִים." ²⁰ אִישׁ בַּעַר, הַאִם רְצוֹנְךָ לְהִוָּכַח שֶׁאֱמוּנָה בְּלִי מַעֲשִׂים עֲקָרָה הִיא? ²¹ אַבְרָהָם אָבִינוּ, הַאִם לֹא בְּמַעֲשָׂיו נִצְדַּק בְּהַעֲלוֹתוֹ אֶת יִצְחָק בְּנוֹ עַל הַמִּזְבֵּחַ? ²² רוֹאֶה אַתָּה כִּי הָאֱמוּנָה עָזְרָה לְמַעֲשָׂיו וּמִתּוֹךְ הַמַּעֲשִׂים הֻשְׁלְמָה הָאֱמוּנָה, ²³ וְהִתְקַיֵּם הַכָּתוּב הָאוֹמֵר, "וְהֶאֱמִן אַבְרָהָם בַּיהוה וַיַּחְשְׁבֶהָ לּוֹ צְדָקָה", וְגַם נִקְרָא "אוֹהֵב אֱלֹהִים". ²⁴ רוֹאִים אַתֶּם כִּי בְּמַעֲשִׂים יִצְדַּק אִישׁ וְלֹא בֶּאֱמוּנָה לְבַדָּהּ. ²⁵ וְכֵן גַּם רָחָב הַזּוֹנָה, הַאִם לֹא נִצְדְּקָה בְּמַעֲשִׂים כַּאֲשֶׁר אָסְפָה אֶת שְׁלִיחֵי יְהוֹשֻׁעַ אֶל בֵּיתָהּ וְשִׁלְּחָה אוֹתָם בְּדֶרֶךְ אַחֶרֶת? ²⁶ כִּי כְּשֵׁם שֶׁהַגּוּף בְּלֹא הָרוּחַ מֵת הוּא, כֵּן גַּם הָאֱמוּנָה בְּלֹא מַעֲשִׂים מֵתָה הִיא.

3 אַחַי, אַל יִהְיוּ רַבִּים מִכֶּם לְמוֹרִים, שֶׁהֲרֵי יְדַעְתֶּם כִּי עָלֵינוּ יִהְיֶה הַדִּין חָמוּר יוֹתֵר. ² וַהֲלֹא כֻּלָּנוּ מַרְבִּים לְהִכָּשֵׁל. מִי שֶׁאֵינוֹ נִכְשָׁל בְּדִבּוּר, אִישׁ מֻשְׁלָם הוּא וְיָכוֹל לָשִׂים רֶסֶן לְכָל גּוּפוֹ. ³ הִנֵּה כְּפִי הַסּוּסִים שָׂמִים אָנוּ רֶסֶן כְּדֵי שֶׁיִּשְׁמְעוּ לָנוּ, וְכָךְ מְנַהֲגִים אָנוּ אֶת כָּל גּוּפָם. ⁴ וְהִנֵּה גַּם הָאֳנִיּוֹת, אַף שֶׁגְּדוֹלוֹת הֵן וְנֶהְדָּפוֹת בְּרוּחַ עַזָּה, הֶגֶה קָטָן יַנְהַג אוֹתָן אֶל הַמָּקוֹם שֶׁיִּרְצֶה הַחוֹבֵל. ⁵ כֵּן גַּם הַלָּשׁוֹן אֵיבָר קָטָן הִיא, וּמְדַבֶּרֶת גְּדוֹלוֹת.

רְאוּ אֵיזוֹ אֵשׁ קְטַנָּה מַבְעִירָה יַעַר גָּדוֹל! ⁶ גַּם הַלָּשׁוֹן אֵשׁ הִיא, עוֹלָם שֶׁל עַוְלָה. הַלָּשׁוֹן נִצֶּבֶת בֵּין אֵיבָרֵינוּ וּמְטַמֵּאת אֶת כָּל הַגּוּף. הִיא מַצִּיתָה אֶת גַּלְגַּל הֱיוֹתֵנוּ וְנִצֶּתֶת בְּאֵשׁ גֵּיהִנּוֹם. ⁷ כָּל מִין בְּהֵמָה וָעוֹף וָרֶמֶשׂ וְחַיּוֹת הַיָּם, הַמִּין הָאֱנוֹשִׁי יָכוֹל לְהִשְׁתַּלֵּט עָלָיו, וְאָכֵן הִשְׁתַּלֵּט. ⁸ אֲבָל הַלָּשׁוֹן אֵין אָדָם יָכוֹל לְהִשְׁתַּלֵּט עָלֶיהָ; רָעָה הִיא וְחַסְרַת מַעְצוֹר, וּמְלֵאָה אֶרֶס מָוֶת. ⁹ בָּהּ מְבָרְכִים אָנוּ אֶת הָאָדוֹן וְהָאָב, וּבָהּ מְקַלְּלִים אָנוּ אֲנָשִׁים שֶׁנַּעֲשׂוּ בְּצֶלֶם אֱלֹהִים. ¹⁰ מֵאוֹתוֹ הַפֶּה יוֹצֵאת בְּרָכָה וְגַם קְלָלָה. אַחַי, לֹא צָרִיךְ שֶׁיִּהְיֶה כַּדָּבָר הַזֶּה. ¹¹ הֲיַבִּיעַ הַמַּעְיָן מַיִם מְתוּקִים וּמַיִם מָרִים מִמּוֹצָא אֶחָד? ¹² אַחַי, הֲיוּכַל

13 Who *is* wise and understanding among you? Let him show by good conduct *that* his works *are* done in the meekness of wisdom. 14 But if you have bitter envy and self-seeking in your hearts, do not boast and lie against the truth. 15 This wisdom does not descend from above, but *is* earthly, sensual, demonic. 16 For where envy and self-seeking *exist*, confusion and every evil thing *are* there. 17 But the wisdom that is from above is first pure, then peaceable, gentle, willing to yield, full of mercy and good fruits, without partiality and without hypocrisy. 18 Now the fruit of righteousness is sown in peace by those who make peace.

4 Where do wars and fights *come* from among you? Do *they* not *come* from your *desires for* pleasure that war in your members? 2 You lust and do not have. You murder and covet and cannot obtain. You fight and war. Yet you do not have because you do not ask. 3 You ask and do not receive, because you ask amiss, that you may spend *it* on your pleasures. 4 Adulterers and adulteresses! Do you not know that friendship with the world is enmity with God? Whoever therefore wants to be a friend of the world makes himself an enemy of God. 5 Or do you think that the Scripture says in vain, "The Spirit who dwells in us yearns jealously"?

6 But He gives more grace. Therefore He says:

> "God resists the proud,
> But gives grace to the humble."

7 Therefore submit to God. Resist the devil and he will flee from you. 8 Draw near to God and He will draw near to you. Cleanse *your* hands, *you* sinners; and purify *your* hearts, *you* double-minded. 9 Lament and mourn and weep! Let your laughter be turned to mourning and *your* joy to gloom. 10 Humble yourselves in the sight of the Lord, and He will lift you up.

11 Do not speak evil of one another, brethren. He who speaks evil of a brother and judges his brother, speaks evil of the law and judges the law. But if you judge the law, you are not a doer of the law but a judge. 12 There is one Lawgiver, who is able to save and to destroy. Who are you to judge another?

13 Come now, you who say, "Today or tomorrow we will go to such and such a city, spend a year there, buy and sell, and make a profit"; 14 whereas you do not know what *will happen* tomorrow. For what *is* your life? It is even a vapor that appears for a little time and then vanishes away. 15 Instead you *ought* to say, "If the Lord wills, we shall live and do

עֵץ הַתְּאֵנָה לַעֲשׂוֹת זֵיתִים, אוֹ הַתּוּכַל הַגֶּפֶן לַעֲשׂוֹת תְּאֵנִים? כֵּן גַּם מְקוֹר מַיִם מְלוּחִים אֵינֶנּוּ מֵפִיק מַיִם מְתוּקִים.

13 מִי בָכֶם חָכָם וְנָבוֹן? יַרְאֶה נָא מִתּוֹךְ הִתְנַהֲגוּתוֹ הַטּוֹבָה אֶת מַעֲשָׂיו הַנַּעֲשִׂים בַּעֲנָוָה וְחָכְמָה. 14 וְאִם קִנְאָה מָרָה וּמְרִיבָה בִּלְבַבְכֶם, אַל תִּתְגָּאוּ, אַל תְּשַׁקְּרוּ בָאֱמֶת. 15 אֵין זוֹ הַחָכְמָה הַיּוֹרֶדֶת מִמַּעַל, אֶלָּא זוֹ שֶׁהִיא אַרְצִית וְנוֹבַעַת מִן הַיֵּצֶר וְהַשֵּׁדִים. 16 הֵן בִּמְקוֹם שֶׁיֵּשׁ קִנְאָה וּמְרִיבָה, שָׁם מְהוּמָה וְכָל מַעֲשֶׂה רַע. 17 אֲבָל הַחָכְמָה אֲשֶׁר מִמַּעַל, רֵאשִׁית טְהוֹרָה הִיא; לְאַחַר זֹאת אוֹהֶבֶת שָׁלוֹם, סוֹבְלָנִית, נוֹחָה לְהִתְרַצּוֹת, מְלֵאָה רַחֲמִים וּפְרִי טוֹב, וְאֵין עִמָּהּ מַשּׂוֹא פָנִים וּצְבִיעוּת. 18 וּלְעוֹשֵׂי שָׁלוֹם פְּרִי הַצֶּדֶק נִזְרָע בְּשָׁלוֹם.

ד מֵאַיִן הַסִּכְסוּכִים וְהַמְּרִיבוֹת אֲשֶׁר בֵּינֵיכֶם? הַאִם לֹא מִתַּאֲווֹתֵיכֶם הַנִּלְחָמוֹת בְּתוֹךְ אֵיבָרֵיכֶם? 2 אַתֶּם מִתְאַוִּים וְאֵין לָכֶם. אַתֶּם הוֹרְגִים וּמְקַנְּאִים וְאֵינְכֶם יְכוֹלִים לְהַשִּׂיג. אַתֶּם רָבִים וְנִלְחָמִים וְאֵין לָכֶם מִפְּנֵי שֶׁאֵינְכֶם מְבַקְשִׁים. 3 אַתֶּם מְבַקְשִׁים וְאֵינְכֶם מְקַבְּלִים מִפְּנֵי שֶׁאַתֶּם מְבַקְשִׁים מִתּוֹךְ כַּוָּנָה רָעָה, כְּדֵי לְבַזְבֵּז בְּתַאֲווֹתֵיכֶם. 4 מְפִירֵי נֶאֱמָנוּת, הַאֵינְכֶם יוֹדְעִים כִּי יְדִידוּת עִם הָעוֹלָם הִיא אֵיבָה לֵאלֹהִים? לְפִיכָךְ, מִי שֶׁרוֹצֶה לִהְיוֹת יָדִיד לָעוֹלָם הוֹפֵךְ לְאוֹיֵב אֱלֹהִים. 5 הַחוֹשְׁבִים אַתֶּם כִּי לַשָּׁוְא אוֹמֵר הַכָּתוּב: "בְּקִנְאָה מִשְׁתּוֹקֵק אֱלֹהִים לָרוּחַ אֲשֶׁר הִשְׁכִּין בָּנוּ"? 6 וְאוּלָם נוֹתֵן הוּא יֶתֶר חֵן. לָכֵן הַכָּתוּב אוֹמֵר "אֱלֹהִים לַלֵּצִים הוּא־יָלִיץ וְלַעֲנָוִים יִתֶּן־חֵן." 7 עַל כֵּן הִכָּנְעוּ לִפְנֵי אֱלֹהִים. הִתְיַצְּבוּ נֶגֶד הַשָּׂטָן וְיִבְרַח מִפְּנֵיכֶם. 8 קִרְבוּ לֵאלֹהִים וְיִקְרַב אֲלֵיכֶם. הַחוֹטְאִים, רַחֲצוּ יְדֵיכֶם! טַהֲרוּ אֶת לְבַבְכֶם, הַפַּכְפְּכֵי הַלֵּב! 9 הִתְעַנּוּ וְהִתְאַבְּלוּ וּבְכוּ; יֵהָפֵךְ נָא שְׂחוֹקְכֶם לְאֵבֶל וְשִׂמְחַתְכֶם לְיָגוֹן. 10 הַשְׁפִּילוּ עַצְמְכֶם לִפְנֵי יהוה וְהוּא יְרוֹמֵם אֶתְכֶם.

11 אַחַי, אַל תְּדַבְּרוּ רָעוֹת אִישׁ בְּרֵעֵהוּ. הַמְדַבֵּר רָעָה בְּאָחִיו וְדָן אֶת אָחִיו, מְדַבֵּר רָעָה בַּתּוֹרָה וְדָן אֶת הַתּוֹרָה. וְאִם תָּדִין אֶת הַתּוֹרָה, אֵינְךָ מְקַיֵּם הַתּוֹרָה כִּי אִם שׁוֹפֵט. 12 אֶחָד הוּא הַמְחוֹקֵק וְשׁוֹפֵט, הוּא אֲשֶׁר יָכוֹל לְהוֹשִׁיעַ וּלְאַבֵּד. וּמִי אַתָּה כִּי תִשְׁפֹּט אֶת עֲמִיתְךָ?

13 הוֹי הָאוֹמְרִים, "הַיּוֹם אוֹ מָחָר נֵלֵךְ לְעִיר פְּלוֹנִית, נַעֲשֶׂה שָׁם שָׁנָה אַחַת, נִסְחַר וְנַעֲשֶׂה הוֹן", 14 וְאֵינְכֶם יוֹדְעִים מַה יֵּלֶד יוֹם. מַה הֵם חַיֵּיכֶם? הֲלֹא אֵד אַתֶּם, הַנִּרְאֶה לְרֶגַע וְאַחַר כָּךְ נֶעֱלָם. 15 רָאוּי הָיָה שֶׁתֹּאמְרוּ, "אִם יִרְצֶה יהוה, נִחְיֶה

this or that." 16 But now you boast in your arrogance. All such boasting is evil.

17 Therefore, to him who knows to do good and does not do *it*, to him it is sin.

5 Come now, *you* rich, weep and howl for your miseries that are coming upon *you!* 2 Your riches are corrupted, and your garments are moth-eaten. 3 Your gold and silver are corroded, and their corrosion will be a witness against you and will eat your flesh like fire. You have heaped up treasure in the last days. 4 Indeed the wages of the laborers who mowed your fields, which you kept back by fraud, cry out; and the cries of the reapers have reached the ears of the Lord of Sabaoth. 5 You have lived on the earth in pleasure and luxury; you have fattened your hearts as in a day of slaughter. 6 You have condemned, you have murdered the just; he does not resist you.

7 Therefore be patient, brethren, until the coming of the Lord. See *how* the farmer waits for the precious fruit of the earth, waiting patiently for it until it receives the early and latter rain. 8 You also be patient. Establish your hearts, for the coming of the Lord is at hand.

9 Do not grumble against one another, brethren, lest you be condemned. Behold, the Judge is standing at the door! 10 My brethren, take the prophets, who spoke in the name of the Lord, as an example of suffering and patience. 11 Indeed we count them blessed who endure. You have heard of the perseverance of Job and seen the end *intended* *by* the Lord—that the Lord is very compassionate and merciful.

12 But above all, my brethren, do not swear, either by heaven or by earth or with any other oath. But let your "Yes" be "Yes," and *your* "No," "No," lest you fall into judgment.

13 Is anyone among you suffering? Let him pray. Is anyone cheerful? Let him sing psalms. 14 Is anyone among you sick? Let him call for the elders of the church, and let them pray over him, anointing him with oil in the name of the Lord. 15 And the prayer of faith will save the sick, and the Lord will raise him up. And if he has committed sins, he will be forgiven. 16 Confess *your* trespasses to one another, and pray for one another, that you may be healed. The effective, fervent prayer of a righteous man avails much. 17 Elijah was a man with a nature like ours, and he prayed earnestly that it would not rain; and it did not rain on the land for three years and six months. 18 And he prayed again, and the heaven gave rain, and the earth produced its fruit.

וְנַעֲשֶׂה כָּזֹאת וְכָזֹאת". 16 אַךְ הִנֵּה אַתֶּם עוֹד מִתְגָּאִים בְּיָמְרוֹתֵיכֶם. כָּל גַּאֲוָה כָּזֹאת רָעָה הִיא. 17 לָכֵן הַיּוֹדֵעַ לַעֲשׂוֹת טוֹב וְאֵינֶנּוּ עוֹשֶׂה, לְחֵטְא יֵחָשֵׁב לוֹ.

ה הוֹי הָעֲשִׁירִים, בְּכוּ וְהֵילִילוּ עַל הַצָּרוֹת הַבָּאוֹת עֲלֵיכֶם. 2 עָשְׁרְכֶם נִרְקַב, וּבִגְדֵיכֶם הָיוּ לְמַאֲכַל עָשׁ. 3 זְהַבְכֶם וְכַסְפְּכֶם נֶחְלְדוּ, וַחֲלוּדָתָם תִּהְיֶה לְעֵדוּת נֶגְדְּכֶם וְתֹאכַל אֶת בְּשַׂרְכֶם כְּמוֹ אֵשׁ. אוֹצָר אֲצַרְתֶּם לְאַחֲרִית הַיָּמִים! 4 הִנֵּה זוֹעֵק שְׂכַר הַפּוֹעֲלִים קוֹצְרֵי שְׂדוֹתֵיכֶם אֲשֶׁר הֲלִינוֹתֶם אוֹתוֹ, וְצַעֲקַת הַקּוֹצְרִים בָּאָה בְּאָזְנֵי יהוה צְבָאוֹת. 5 חֲיִיתֶם בָּאָרֶץ חַיֵּי תַעֲנוּגוֹת וְהוֹלֵלוּת; סְעַדְתֶּם אֶת לִבְּכֶם כְּמוֹ בְיוֹם זֶבַח. 6 הִרְשַׁעְתֶּם וַהֲרַגְתֶּם אֶת הַצַּדִּיק וְהוּא אֵינוּ קָם עֲלֵיכֶם.

7 לָכֵן, אָחַי, הִתְאָרְכוּ אֶרֶךְ רוּחַ עַד בּוֹא הָאָדוֹן. הִנֵּה הָאִכָּר מְחַכֶּה לִפְרִי הָאֲדָמָה הַיָּקָר וּמְיַחֵל לוֹ בְּסַבְלָנוּת עַד שֶׁיִּזְכֶּה לְיוֹרֶה וּמַלְקוֹשׁ. 8 גַּם אַתֶּם הִתְאָרְכוּ אֶרֶךְ רוּחַ, כּוֹנְנוּ אֶת לְבַבְכֶם, כִּי קָרְבָה בִּיאַת הָאָדוֹן. 9 אַחַי, אַל תִּתְלוֹנְנוּ אִישׁ עַל רֵעֵהוּ, לְמַעַן לֹא תִּשָּׁפֵטוּ. הִנֵּה הַשּׁוֹפֵט עוֹמֵד בַּפֶּתַח. 10 אַחַי, הַנְּבִיאִים אֲשֶׁר דִּבְּרוּ בְּשֵׁם יהוה יִהְיוּ לָכֶם לְדֻגְמָה שֶׁל סֵבֶל וְאֹרֶךְ רוּחַ. 11 הֵן חוֹשְׁבִים אָנוּ לִמְאֻשָּׁרִים אֶת הָעוֹמְדִים בַּסֵּבֶל. שְׁמַעְתֶּם עַל־ אוֹדוֹת עֲמִידָתוֹ שֶׁל אִיּוֹב בַּסֵּבֶל וּרְאִיתֶם אֶת תַּכְלִית יהוה – כִּי רַחוּם וְחַנּוּן יהוה.

12 וְרֵאשִׁית כֹּל, אַחַי, אַל תִּשָּׁבְעוּ לֹא בַּשָּׁמַיִם וְלֹא בָּאָרֶץ וְלֹא כָּל שְׁבוּעָה אַחֶרֶת. יְהֵא הַ"כֵּן" שֶׁלָּכֶם "כֵּן", וְהַ"לֹא" שֶׁלָּכֶם "לֹא", פֶּן תִּפְּלוּ בִּידֵי הַדִּין. 13 אִישׁ מִכֶּם אִם יִסְבֹּל, יִתְפַּלֵּל. אִם שִׂמְחָה בְּלִבּוֹ, יָשִׁיר שִׁירֵי הַלֵּל. 14 אִם יֵשׁ חוֹלֶה בֵּינֵיכֶם, יִקְרָא אֶת זִקְנֵי הַקְּהִלָּה וְיִתְפַּלְלוּ בַּעֲדוֹ בְּמָשְׁחָם אוֹתוֹ שֶׁמֶן בְּשֵׁם יהוה. 15 וּתְפִלַּת הָאֱמוּנָה תּוֹשִׁיעַ אֶת הַחֹלֶה, וַיהוה יָקִים אוֹתוֹ. וְאִם חָטָא יִסָּלַח לוֹ. 16 הִתְוַדּוּ עַל חֲטָאֵיכֶם אִישׁ לִפְנֵי רֵעֵהוּ וְהִתְפַּלְלוּ אִישׁ בְּעַד רֵעֵהוּ, לְמַעַן תֵּרָפְאוּ. גָּדוֹל כֹּחָהּ שֶׁל תְּפִלַּת צַדִּיק בִּפְעֻלָּתָהּ. 17 אֵלִיָּהוּ הָיָה אָדָם אֱנוֹשִׁי כָּמוֹנוּ; הוּא הִתְפַּלֵּל בְּחָזְקָה שֶׁלֹּא יִהְיֶה מָטָר, וְלֹא יָרַד מָטָר עַל הָאָרֶץ שָׁלוֹשׁ שָׁנִים וְשִׁשָּׁה חֳדָשִׁים. 18 הוּא הִתְפַּלֵּל שֵׁנִית, וְהַשָּׁמַיִם נָתְנוּ מָטָר וְהָאָרֶץ הִצְמִיחָה אֶת פִּרְיָהּ.

¹⁹Brethren, if anyone among you wanders from the truth, and someone turns him back, ²⁰let him know that he who turns a sinner from the error of his way will save a soul from death and cover a multitude of sins.

¹⁹ אַחַי, אִם אִישׁ מִכֶּם סוֹטֶה מִן הָאֱמֶת וְאִישׁ אַחֵר מֵשִׁיב אוֹתוֹ, ²⁰ דְּעוּ כִּי הַמֵּשִׁיב אֶת הַחוֹטֵא מִסְּטִיַּת דַּרְכּוֹ יוֹשִׁיעַ אֶת נַפְשׁוֹ מִמָּוֶת וִיכַסֶּה עַל הֲמוֹן פְּשָׁעִים.

The First Epistle of
PETER

1 Peter, an apostle of Jesus Christ,
  To the pilgrims of the Dispersion in Pontus,
Galatia, Cappadocia, Asia, and Bithynia, [2]elect
according to the foreknowledge of God the Father,
in sanctification of the Spirit, for obedience and
sprinkling of the blood of Jesus Christ:
  Grace to you and peace be multiplied.

[3]Blessed be the God and Father of our Lord
Jesus Christ, who according to His abundant mercy
has begotten us again to a living hope through the
resurrection of Jesus Christ from the dead, [4]to an
inheritance incorruptible and undefiled and that
does not fade away, reserved in heaven for you,
[5]who are kept by the power of God through faith
for salvation ready to be revealed in the last time.

[6]In this you greatly rejoice, though now for a
little while, if need be, you have been grieved by
various trials, [7]that the genuineness of your faith,
being much more precious than gold that perishes,
though it is tested by fire, may be found to praise,
honor, and glory at the revelation of Jesus Christ,
[8]whom having not seen you love. Though now you
do not see Him, yet believing, you rejoice with joy
inexpressible and full of glory, [9]receiving the end of
your faith—the salvation of your souls.

[10]Of this salvation the prophets have inquired
and searched carefully, who prophesied of the grace
that would come to you, [11]searching what, or what
manner of time, the Spirit of Christ who was in
them was indicating when He testified beforehand
the sufferings of Christ and the glories that would
follow. [12]To them it was revealed that, not to
themselves, but to us they were ministering the
things which now have been reported to you
through those who have preached the gospel to
you by the Holy Spirit sent from heaven—things
which angels desire to look into.

[13]Therefore gird up the loins of your mind, be
sober, and rest your hope fully upon the grace that
is to be brought to you at the revelation of Jesus
Christ; [14]as obedient children, not conforming
yourselves to the former lusts, as in your ignorance;
[15]but as He who called you is holy, you also be holy
in all your conduct, [16]because it is written, "Be
holy, for I am holy."

[17]And if you call on the Father, who without
partiality judges according to each one's work,
conduct yourselves throughout the time of your

אִגֶּרֶת פֶּטְרוֹם הָרִאשׁוֹנָה

א מֵאֵת פֶּטְרוֹם, שְׁלִיחַ יֵשׁוּעַ הַמָּשִׁיחַ, אֶל תּוֹשְׁבֵי
תְּפוּצוֹת פּוֹנְטוֹם, גָּלַטְיָה, קַפַּדוֹקְיָה, אַסְיָה וּבִיתִינְיָה,
הַנִּבְחָרִים [2]עַל־פִּי יְדִיעָתוֹ מִקֶּדֶם שֶׁל אֱלֹהִים הָאָב,
בִּקְדוּשׁ הָרוּחַ, אֶל צִיּוּת יֵשׁוּעַ הַמָּשִׁיחַ וְהַזָּיַת דָּמוֹ:
חֶסֶד וְשָׁלוֹם יִשְׁפְּעוּ עֲלֵיכֶם לְמַכְבִּיר.

[3]בָּרוּךְ הָאֱלֹהִים אֲבִי אֲדוֹנֵנוּ יֵשׁוּעַ הַמָּשִׁיחַ אֲשֶׁר
בְּרֹב רַחֲמָיו הוֹלִיד אוֹתָנוּ מֵחָדָשׁ לְתִקְוָה חַיָּה
בִּתְחִיַּת יֵשׁוּעַ הַמָּשִׁיחַ מִן הַמֵּתִים, [4]לְנַחֲלָה אֲשֶׁר לֹא
תִשָּׁחֵת, לֹא תִטַּמֵּא וְלֹא תִבֹּל, הַצְּפוּנָה לָכֶם
בַּשָּׁמַיִם, [5]לָכֶם הַשְּׁמוּרִים בִּגְבוּרַת אֱלֹהִים, בִּזְכוּת
אֱמוּנָה, אֱלֵי יְשׁוּעָה הָעֲתִידָה לְהִגָּלוֹת בְּעֵת קֵץ.
[6]וּבָזֶה שְׂמֵחִים אַתֶּם גַּם אִם מִן הַצֹּרֶךְ הוּא
שֶׁתִּתְעַצְּבוּ זְמַן מָה בְּכָל מִינֵי מַסּוֹת [7]כְּדֵי
שֶׁאֱמוּנַתְכֶם הַצְּרוּפָה וְהִיקָרָה הַרְבֵּה יוֹתֵר מִזָּהָב,
הַנִּשְׁחָת עַל אַף הִצָּרְפוֹ בָּאֵשׁ, תֵּצֵא לִתְהִלָּה וְלִכָבוֹד
וּלְתִפְאֶרֶת בְּהִתְגַּלּוֹת יֵשׁוּעַ הַמָּשִׁיחַ; [8]הוּא אֲשֶׁר
אַתֶּם אוֹהֲבִים אוֹתוֹ אַף כִּי לֹא רְאִיתֶם אוֹתוֹ, וַאֲשֶׁר
כָּעֵת אֵינְכֶם רוֹאִים אוֹתוֹ וּבְכָל זֹאת מַאֲמִינִים אַתֶּם
בּוֹ וְשָׂשִׂים בְּשִׂמְחָה מְפֹאָרָה וַעֲצוּמָה מִסַּפֵּר,
[9]בְּהַשִּׂיגְכֶם אֶת תַּכְלִית אֱמוּנַתְכֶם, אֶת יְשׁוּעַת
נַפְשׁוֹתֵיכֶם.

[10]אֶת הַיְשׁוּעָה הַזֹּאת חָקְרוּ וְדָרְשׁוּ הַנְּבִיאִים שֶׁנִּבְּאוּ
עַל הַחֶסֶד הַמֵּיעָד לָכֶם. [11]הֵם חָקְרוּ מָה הָעֵת
וְהַנְּסִבּוֹת שֶׁהוֹדִיעָה רוּחַ הַמָּשִׁיחַ אֲשֶׁר בְּקִרְבָּם,
כְּשֶׁהֵעִידָה מֵרֹאשׁ עַל סִבְלוֹת הַמָּשִׁיחַ וְעַל הַכָּבוֹד
וְהַתִּפְאֶרֶת שֶׁיָּבוֹאוּ אַחֲרֵיהֶם. [12]וְנִגְלָה לָהֶם כִּי לֹא
לְמַעַן עַצְמָם אֶלָּא לְמַעַנְכֶם שֵׁרְתוּ בַּדְּבָרִים הָהֵם,
אֲשֶׁר כָּעֵת הִשְׁמִיעוּ לָכֶם מִפִּי הַמְבַשְּׂרִים אֶת
הַבְּשׂוֹרָה בְּרוּחַ הַקֹּדֶשׁ הַשְּׁלוּחָה מִן הַשָּׁמַיִם, דְּבָרִים
אֲשֶׁר מַלְאָכִים נִכְסָפִים לְהַשְׁקִיף אֶל תּוֹכָם.

[13]לָכֵן חִגְרוּ מָתְנֵי שִׂכְלְכֶם, הֱיוּ עֵרָנִים וְקַוּוּ בְּכָל
לְבַבְכֶם לַחֶסֶד הַבָּא עֲלֵיכֶם בְּהִתְגַּלּוֹת יֵשׁוּעַ
הַמָּשִׁיחַ. [14]כְּבָנִים מְצַיְּתִים, אַל תִּתְנַהֲגוּ לְפִי
הַתַּאֲווֹת שֶׁהָיוּ לָכֶם בְּעָבָר כְּשֶׁהֱיִיתֶם חַסְרֵי דַּעַת,
[15]אֶלָּא הֱיוּ גַּם אַתֶּם קְדוֹשִׁים בְּכָל דַּרְכֵיכֶם כְּמוֹ
שֶׁקָּדוֹשׁ הוּא אֲשֶׁר קָרָא אֶתְכֶם, [16]שֶׁהֲרֵי כָּתוּב,
"קְדוֹשִׁים תִּהְיוּ כִּי קָדוֹשׁ אָנִי."

[17]וְאִם קוֹרְאִים אַתֶּם אֶל הָאָב, הַשּׁוֹפֵט בְּלִי מַשּׂוֹא
פָּנִים לְפִי מַעֲשֵׂי אִישׁ וָאִישׁ, אֲזַי הִתְהַלְּכוּ בְּיִרְאָה

stay *here* in fear; [18] knowing that you were not redeemed with corruptible things, *like* silver or gold, from your aimless conduct *received* by tradition from your fathers, [19] but with the precious blood of Christ, as of a lamb without blemish and without spot. [20] He indeed was foreordained before the foundation of the world, but was manifest in these last times for you [21] who through Him believe in God, who raised Him from the dead and gave Him glory, so that your faith and hope are in God.

[22] Since you have purified your souls in obeying the truth through the Spirit in sincere love of the brethren, love one another fervently with a pure heart, [23] having been born again, not of corruptible seed but incorruptible, through the word of God which lives and abides forever, [24] because

> *All flesh is as grass,*
> *And all the glory of man as the flower of the*
>   *grass.*
> *The grass withers,*
> *And its flower falls away,*
> [25] *But the word of the* LORD *endures forever."*

Now this is the word which by the gospel was preached to you.

2 Therefore, laying aside all malice, all deceit, hypocrisy, envy, and all evil speaking, [2] as newborn babes, desire the pure milk of the word, that you may grow thereby, [3] if indeed you have tasted that the Lord *is* gracious.

[4] Coming to Him *as to* a living stone, rejected indeed by men, but chosen by God *and* precious, [5] you also, as living stones, are being built up a spiritual house, a holy priesthood, to offer up spiritual sacrifices acceptable to God through Jesus Christ. [6] Therefore it is also contained in the Scripture,

> *"Behold, I lay in Zion*
> *A chief cornerstone, elect, precious,*
> *And he who believes on Him will by no means be*
>   *put to shame."*

[7] Therefore, to you who believe, *He is* precious; but to those who are disobedient,

> *"The stone which the builders rejected*
> *Has become the chief cornerstone,"*

[8] and

> *"A stone of stumbling*
> *And a rock of offense."*

They stumble, being disobedient to the word, to which they also were appointed.

בִּימֵי מְגוּרֵיכֶם עֲלֵי אֲדָמוֹת; [18] שֶׁהֲרֵי יוֹדְעִים אַתֶּם כִּי לֹא בְּדָבָר נִשְׁחָת, לֹא בְּכֶסֶף וְלֹא בְּזָהָב, נִפְדֵּיתֶם מִדַּרְכְּכֶם הַתְּפֵלָה שֶׁנַּחֲלְתֶּם מֵאֲבוֹתֵיכֶם, [19] כִּי אִם בְּדַם יָקָר שֶׁל שֶׂה תָמִים שֶׁאֵין בּוֹ מוּם, בְּדָמוֹ שֶׁל הַמָּשִׁיחַ [20] אֲשֶׁר נוֹדַע מִקֶּדֶם, לִפְנֵי הִוָּסֵד תֵּבֵל, וְנִגְלָה בְּאַחֲרִית הַיָּמִים לְמַעַנְכֶם, [21] אַתֶּם אֲשֶׁר הוֹדוֹת לוֹ מַאֲמִינִים בֵּאלֹהִים שֶׁהֱקִימוֹ מִן הַמֵּתִים וְנָתַן לוֹ כָּבוֹד לְמַעַן תִּהְיֶה אֱמוּנַתְכֶם וְתִקְוַתְכֶם בֵּאלֹהִים.

[22] וְכֵיוָן שֶׁטִּהַרְתֶּם אֶת נַפְשׁוֹתֵיכֶם בְּצִיּתְכֶם לָאֱמֶת וְהִגַּעְתֶּם אֱלֵי אַחֲוָה שֶׁאֵין בָּהּ חֲנֻפָּה, אֶהֱבוּ זֶה אֶת זֶה בְּכָל לְבַבְכֶם וּמְאֹדְכֶם; [23] שֶׁהֲרֵי נוֹלַדְתֶּם מֵחָדָשׁ לֹא מִזֶּרַע נִשְׁחָת כִּי אִם מִבִּלְתִּי נִשְׁחָת, בִּדְבַר אֱלֹהִים הַחַי וְקַיָּם.

[24] הֵן "כָּל־הַבָּשָׂר חָצִיר
וְכָל־חַסְדּוֹ כְּצִיץ הַשָּׂדֶה.
יָבֵשׁ חָצִיר, נָבֵל צִיץ,
[25] וּדְבַר־אֱלֹהֵינוּ יָקוּם לְעוֹלָם."
וְהוּא הַדָּבָר אֲשֶׁר בִּשְּׂרוּ לָכֶם.

ב וְעַתָּה הָסִירוּ מֵעֲלֵיכֶם כָּל רֶשַׁע וְכָל מִרְמָה, אֶת הַצְּבִיעוּת וְהַקִּנְאָה וְכָל לָשׁוֹן הָרָע, [2] וּכְעוֹלָלִים אֲשֶׁר זֶה מִקָּרוֹב נוֹלְדוּ הִתְאַוּוּ לֶחָלָב הַזַּךְ שֶׁל הַדָּבָר, לְמַעַן תִּגְדְּלוּ בְּאֶמְצָעוּתוֹ לִישׁוּעָה, [3] אִם אָמְנָם טְעַמְתֶּם כִּי טוֹב הָאָדוֹן [4] אֲשֶׁר אַתֶּם נִגָּשִׁים אֵלָיו – אֶבֶן חַיָּה שֶׁמְּאָסוּהָ בְּנֵי אָדָם, אַךְ נִבְחָרָה וִיקָרָה לֵאלֹהִים. [5] וְגַם אַתֶּם, כַּאֲבָנִים חַיּוֹת, נִבְנִים לְבֵית רוּחָנִי, לִכְהֻנַּת קֹדֶשׁ, כְּדֵי לְהַעֲלוֹת זִבְחֵי רוּחַ רְצוּיִים לֵאלֹהִים בִּזְכוּת יֵשׁוּעַ הַמָּשִׁיחַ. [6] מִשּׁוּם כָּךְ אוֹמֵר הַכָּתוּב: "הִנְנִי יִסַּד בְּצִיּוֹן אֶבֶן פִּנָּה נִבְחָרָה וִיקָרָה, וְהַמַּאֲמִין בָּהּ לֹא יֵבוֹשׁ." [7] עַל כֵּן לָכֶם הַמַּאֲמִינִים הִיא אֶבֶן הַיְקָר, אֲבָל לַסּוֹרְרִים – "אֶבֶן מָאֲסוּ הַבּוֹנִים הָיְתָה לְרֹאשׁ פִּנָּה", [8] וְגַם "אֶבֶן נֶגֶף וְצוּר מִכְשׁוֹל." וְאָמְנָם הֵם נִכְשָׁלִים בִּדְבַר סָרְבָנוּתָם, וּלְכָךְ גַּם נוֹעָדוּ.

9 But you *are* a chosen generation, a royal priesthood, a holy nation, His own special people, that you may proclaim the praises of Him who called you out of darkness into His marvelous light; 10 who once *were* not a people but *are* now the people of God, who had not obtained mercy but now have obtained mercy.

11 Beloved, I beg *you* as sojourners and pilgrims, abstain from fleshly lusts which war against the soul, 12 having your conduct honorable among the Gentiles, that when they speak against you as evildoers, they may, by *your* good works which they observe, glorify God in the day of visitation.

13 Therefore submit yourselves to every ordinance of man for the Lord's sake, whether to the king as supreme, 14 or to governors, as to those who are sent by him for the punishment of evildoers and *for the* praise of those who do good. 15 For this is the will of God, that by doing good you may put to silence the ignorance of foolish men— 16 as free, yet not using liberty as a cloak for vice, but as bondservants of God. 17 Honor all *people*. Love the brotherhood. Fear God. Honor the king.

18 Servants, *be* submissive to *your* masters with all fear, not only to the good and gentle, but also to the harsh. 19 For this *is* commendable, if because of conscience toward God one endures grief, suffering wrongfully. 20 For what credit *is it* if, when you are beaten for your faults, you take it patiently? But when you do good and suffer, if you take it patiently, this *is* commendable before God. 21 For to this you were called, because Christ also suffered for us, leaving us an example, that you should follow His steps:

22   *"Who committed no sin,*
      Nor was deceit found in His mouth";

23 who, when He was reviled, did not revile in return; when He suffered, He did not threaten, but committed *Himself* to Him who judges righteously; 24 who Himself bore our sins in His own body on the tree, that we, having died to sins, might live for righteousness—by whose stripes you were healed. 25 For you were like sheep going astray, but have now returned to the Shepherd and Overseer of your souls.

3 Wives, likewise, *be* submissive to your own husbands, that even if some do not obey the word, they, without a word, may be won by the conduct of their wives, 2 when they observe your chaste conduct *accompanied* by fear. 3 Do not let your adornment be *merely* outward—arranging the hair, wearing gold, or putting on *fine* apparel— 4 rather

9 אֲבָל אַתֶּם עַם נִבְחָר, מַמְלֶכֶת כֹּהֲנִים וְגוֹי קָדוֹשׁ, עַם סְגֻלָּה, לְמַעַן תְּסַפְּרוּ תְהִלּוֹתָיו שֶׁל הַקּוֹרֵא אֶתְכֶם מֵחֹשֶׁךְ אֶל אוֹרוֹ הַנִּפְלָא; 10 אַתֶּם אֲשֶׁר לְפָנִים לֹא עַם הֱיִיתֶם, אַךְ כָּעֵת עַם אֱלֹהִים אַתֶּם; אֲשֶׁר לְפָנִים לֹא רֻחַמְתּוּ, אַךְ כָּעֵת מְרֻחָמִים.

11 אֲהוּבַי, שֶׁבְּחִינַת זָרִים וְגוֹלִים אַתֶּם, מַפְצִיר אֲנִי בָּכֶם לְהִנָּזֵר מִתַּאֲווֹת בְּשָׂרִים הַנִּלְחָמוֹת נֶגֶד הַנָּפֶשׁ. 12 הֵיטִיבוּ אֶת דַּרְכֵּיכֶם בַּגּוֹיִים, כְּדֵי שֶׁיִּתְבּוֹנְנוּ בְמַעֲשֵׂיכֶם הַטּוֹבִים וִיהַלְלוּ אֶת אֱלֹהִים בְּיוֹם פְּקֻדָּה עַל אוֹתָם הַדְּבָרִים שֶׁבִּגְלָלָם הִשְׁמִיצוּ אֶתְכֶם כְּעוֹשֵׂי רָעָה.

13 הִכָּנְעוּ לְכָל מוֹסַד אֱנוֹשִׁי לְמַעַן הָאָדוֹן: אִם לַמֶּלֶךְ, בִּהְיוֹתוֹ הָרֹאשׁ; 14 אִם לַמּוֹשְׁלִים, בִּהְיוֹתָם שְׁלוּחִים מִטַּעֲמוֹ לִנְקָמָה בְּעוֹשֵׂי הָרַע, אַךְ לְמַתַּן שֶׁבַח לְעוֹשֵׂי הַטּוֹב. 15 הֵן זֶהוּ רְצוֹן אֱלֹהִים, שֶׁתַּעַשׂוּ הַטּוֹב וְכָךְ תָּשִׂימוּ מַחְסוֹם לְאִוֶּלֶת הָאֲנָשִׁים אֲשֶׁר אֵין בָּהֶם דַּעַת. 16 הִתְנַהֲגוּ כַּאֲנָשִׁים חָפְשִׁים, לֹא כַּאֲנָשִׁים הַמַּחֲזִיקִים בַּחֹפֶשׁ כִּכְסוּת לָרֶשַׁע, אֶלָּא כְּעַבְדֵי אֱלֹהִים. 17 נַהֲגוּ כָבוֹד בְּכָל אָדָם; אֶהֱבוּ אֶת הָאַחִים; יְראוּ אֶת אֱלֹהִים; כַּבְּדוּ אֶת הַמֶּלֶךְ.

18 הָעֲבָדִים, הִכָּנְעוּ לִפְנֵי אֲדוֹנֵיכֶם בְּכָל יִרְאָה, לֹא רַק לִפְנֵי הַטּוֹבִים וְהַנּוֹחִים לַבְּרִיּוֹת, אֶלָּא גַּם לִפְנֵי הָעִקְּשִׁים. 19 הֵן בִּרְכַּת חֶסֶד בְּכָךְ אִם בִּגְלַל הַכָּרָתוֹ בֵּאלֹהִים יִשָּׂא אָדָם מַכְאוֹב וְיִסְבֹּל שֶׁלֹּא בְּצֶדֶק; 20 שֶׁהֲרֵי מַה תְּהִלָּה בְּכָךְ אִם תַּעַמְדוּ בְּסֵבֶל שֶׁל מַכּוֹת עַל חֲטָאֵיכֶם? אֲבָל אִם בַּעֲשׂוֹתְכֶם אֶת הַטּוֹב תִּסְבְּלוּ וְתַעַמְדוּ בַּסֵּבֶל, בִּרְכַּת חֶסֶד הִיא מִלִּפְנֵי אֱלֹהִים. 21 אָכֵן לְזֹאת נִקְרֵאתֶם, כִּי גַם הַמָּשִׁיחַ סָבַל בַּעֲדְכֶם וְהִשְׁאִיר לָכֶם מוֹפֵת כְּדֵי שֶׁתֵּלְכוּ בְּעִקְּבוֹתָיו – 22 הוּא אֲשֶׁר חֵטְא לֹא עָשָׂה וְלֹא נִמְצְאָה מִרְמָה בְּפִיו; 23 אֲשֶׁר חֵרְפוּהוּ וְלֹא הֵשִׁיב חֵרוּף, סָבַל וְלֹא אִיֵּם, כִּי אִם מָסַר דִּינוֹ לְשׁוֹפֵט הַצֶּדֶק; 24 הוּא אֲשֶׁר אֶת חֲטָאֵינוּ נָשָׂא בְּגוּפוֹ עַל הָעֵץ, כְּדֵי שֶׁנָּמוּת לְגַבֵּי הַחֵטְא וְנִחְיֶה לַצְּדָקָה; אֲשֶׁר בְּחַבּוּרָתוֹ נִרְפָּא לָכֶם, 25 כִּי הֱיִיתֶם כְּצֹאן אוֹבְרוֹת, אַךְ עַתָּה שַׁבְתֶּם אֶל הָרוֹעֶה הַשּׁוֹמֵר אֶת נַפְשׁוֹתֵיכֶם.

ג כֵּן גַּם אַתֶּן, הַנָּשִׁים, הִכָּנַעְנָה לְבַעֲלֵיכֶן; וְכָךְ, אִם יֵשׁ שֶׁאֵינָם מְצַיְּתִים לַדָּבָר, יִקָּנֶה לָכֶם בְּלֹא עַל-יְדֵי דִּבּוּר אֶלָּא עַל-יְדֵי הִתְנַהֲגוּת הַנָּשִׁים, 2 בִּרְאוֹתָם אֶת הִתְנַהֲגוּתְכֶן הַטְּהוֹרָה הַמְּלֵאָה בְּיִרְאָה. 3 וּפְאַרְכֶן אַל יְהֵא פְּאֵר חִיצוֹנִי שֶׁל מַחְלְפוֹת שֵׂעָר וַעֲדִי זָהָב וּבְגָדִים, 4 אֶלָּא הָאָדָם אֲשֶׁר בְּסֵתֶר הַלֵּב, הַפְּאֵר

let it be the hidden person of the heart, with the incorruptible *beauty* of a gentle and quiet spirit, which is very precious in the sight of God. 5 For in this manner, in former times, the holy women who trusted in God also adorned themselves, being submissive to their own husbands, 6 as Sarah obeyed Abraham, calling him lord, whose daughters you are if you do good and are not afraid with any terror.

7 Husbands, likewise, dwell with *them* with understanding, giving honor to the wife, as to the weaker vessel, and as *being* heirs together of the grace of life, that your prayers may not be hindered.

8 Finally, all *of you be* of one mind, having compassion for one another; love as brothers, *be* tenderhearted, *be* courteous; 9 not returning evil for evil or reviling for reviling, but on the contrary blessing, knowing that you were called to this, that you may inherit a blessing. 10 For

"He who would love life
And see good days,
Let him refrain his tongue from evil,
And his lips from speaking deceit.
11 Let him turn away from evil and do good;
Let him seek peace and pursue it.
12 For the eyes of the LORD are on the
righteous,
And His ears *are* open to their prayers;
But the face of the LORD is against those who
do evil."

13 And who *is* he who will harm you if you become followers of what is good? 14 But even if you should suffer for righteousness' sake, *you are* blessed. "And do not be afraid of their threats, nor be troubled." 15 But sanctify the Lord God in your hearts, and always *be* ready *to give* a defense to everyone who asks you a reason for the hope that is in you, with meekness and fear; 16 having a good conscience, that when they defame you as evildoers, those who revile your good conduct in Christ may be ashamed. 17 For *it is* better, if it is the will of God, to suffer for doing good than for doing evil.

18 For Christ also suffered once for sins, the just for the unjust, that He might bring us to God, being put to death in the flesh but made alive by the Spirit, 19 by whom also He went and preached to the spirits in prison, 20 who formerly were disobedient, when once the Divine longsuffering waited in the days of Noah, while *the* ark was being prepared, in which a few, that is, eight souls, were saved through water. 21 There is also an antitype which now saves us—baptism (not the removal of the filth of the flesh, but the answer of a good conscience toward

הִבָּלְתִּי נִשְׁחַת שֶׁל רוּחַ עֲנָוָה וּשְׁקֵטָה אֲשֶׁר יְקָרָה הִיא מְאֹד בְּעֵינֵי אֱלֹהִים. 5 כָּךְ הִתְקַשְּׁטוּ בְּעָבָר גַּם הַנָּשִׁים הַקְּדוֹשׁוֹת וְהַמְיַחֲלוֹת לֵאלֹהִים, בְּהִכָּנְעָן לְבַעֲלֵיהֶן; 6 כְּשָׂרָה אֲשֶׁר שָׁמְעָה בְּקוֹל אַבְרָהָם וְקָרְאָה לוֹ אָדוֹן. וְאַתֶּן נְהִיתֶן בָּנוֹת לָהּ, אִם אַתֶּן עֹשׂוֹת אֶת הַטּוֹב וְאֵינְכֶן פּוֹחֲדוֹת פַּחַד.

7 וְכֵן אַתֶּם, הַבְּעָלִים, חֲיוּ יַחַד עִמָּהֶן בִּידִיעָה שֶׁרִאשָׁה הִיא כְּלִי חַלָּשׁ יוֹתֵר, וּתְנוּ לָהֶן כָּבוֹד כְּשֻׁתָּפוֹת בְּנַחֲלַת חֶסֶד הַחַיִּים, לְמַעַן לֹא תֵּעָכַבְנָה תְּפִלּוֹתֵיכֶם.

8 סוֹף דָּבָר, הֱיוּ כֻּלְּכֶם לֵב אֶחָד, שֻׁתָּפִים לְצַעַר הַזּוּלַת, אוֹהֲבֵי הָאַחִים, רַחֲמָנִים וַעֲנָוִים. 9 אַל תְּשַׁלְּמוּ רָעָה תַּחַת רָעָה וְלֹא חֵרוּף תַּחַת חֵרוּף; אַדְּרַבָּא – תְּבָרְכוּ, שֶׁהֲרֵי לְכָךְ נִקְרֵאתֶם, לְמַעַן תִּירְשׁוּ אֶת הַבְּרָכָה; 10 כִּי

"הָאִישׁ הֶחָפֵץ חַיִּים אֹהֵב יָמִים לִרְאוֹת טוֹב,
יִנְצֹר לְשׁוֹנוֹ מֵרָע, וּשְׂפָתָיו מִדַּבֵּר מִרְמָה.
11 סוּר מֵרָע וַעֲשֵׂה־טוֹב, יְבַקֵּשׁ שָׁלוֹם וְיִרְדְּפֵהוּ",
12 כִּי "עֵינֵי יהוה אֶל־צַדִּיקִים, וְאָזְנָיו אֶל־שַׁוְעָתָם;
וּפְנֵי יהוה בְּעֹשֵׂי רָע."

13 וּמִי יָרַע לָכֶם אִם תִּהְיוּ קַנָּאִים לַטּוֹב? 14 אַךְ גַּם אִם תִּסְבְּלוּ לְמַעַן הַצְּדָקָה – אַשְׁרֵיכֶם. אַל תְּפַחֲדוּ מֵאֵימָתָם וְאַל תִּבָּהֲלוּ. 15 אֶת הָאָדוֹן הַמָּשִׁיחַ הַקְדִּישׁוּ בִּלְבַבְכֶם, וְתָמִיד הֱיוּ מוּכָנִים לְהָשִׁיב בַּעֲנָוָה וְיִרְאָה לְכָל מִי שֶׁמְּבַקֵּשׁ מִכֶּם דִּין וְחֶשְׁבּוֹן בִּדְבַר הַתִּקְוָה שֶׁבְּלִבְּכֶם. 16 יְהֵא מַצְפּוּנְכֶם טָהוֹר, כְּדֵי שֶׁיֵּבוֹשׁוּ הַמַּשְׁמִיצִים מֵאוֹתָם דְּבָרִים שֶׁבִּגְלָלָם הֵם מְגַנִּים אֶת הִתְנַהֲגוּתְכֶם הַטּוֹבָה בַּמָּשִׁיחַ. 17 מוּטָב שֶׁתִּסְבְּלוּ, אִם זֶהוּ רְצוֹן אֱלֹהִים, בַּעֲשׂוֹתְכֶם אֶת הַטּוֹב מִשֶּׁתִּסְבְּלוּ בַּעֲשׂוֹתְכֶם רַע. 18 הֵן גַּם הַמָּשִׁיחַ מֵת לְכַפֵּר חֲטָאִים, אַחַת וּלְתָמִיד, הַצַּדִּיק בְּעַד הָרְשָׁעִים, כְּדֵי לְקָרֵב אוֹתָנוּ אֶל הָאֱלֹהִים. הוּא הוּמַת בַּבָּשָׂר, אַךְ הֶחֱיָה בָּרוּחַ 19 וּבָהּ גַּם הָלַךְ וּבִשֵּׂר לָרוּחוֹת הַכְּלוּאוֹת בַּמַּאֲסָר, 20 לָאֵלֶּה שֶׁלֹּא צִיְּתוּ כַּאֲשֶׁר חִכָּה אֱלֹהִים בְּאֶרֶךְ אַפּוֹ בִּימֵי נֹחַ. בְּאוֹתָם יָמִים נִבְנְתָה הַתֵּבָה אֲשֶׁר מְעַטִּים בְּתוֹכָהּ – שְׁמוֹנָה נְפָשׁוֹת – נוֹשְׁעוּ בַּמַּיִם; 21 וְזֶה מְסַמֵּל אֶת הַטְּבִילָה הַמּוֹשִׁיעָה כָּעֵת גַּם אֶתְכֶם – אֵין הִיא הֲסָרַת זֻהֲמַת הַגּוּף, אֶלָּא הִתְחַיְּבוּת שֶׁל

God), through the resurrection of Jesus Christ,
22 who has gone into heaven and is at the right hand
of God, angels and authorities and powers having
been made subject to Him.

מִצָּפוֹן טָהוֹר כְּלַפֵּי אֱלֹהִים – בְּתַחַת יֵשׁוּעַ הַמָּשִׁיחַ
22 אֲשֶׁר עָלָה הַשָּׁמַיְמָה וְהוּא לִימִין אֱלֹהִים, וּלְפָנָיו
הִכְנְעוּ מַלְאָכִים וְרָשֻׁיּוֹת וּגְבוּרוֹת.

4 Therefore, since Christ suffered for us in the
flesh, arm yourselves also with the same mind, for
he who has suffered in the flesh has ceased from sin,
2 that he no longer should live the rest of *his* time in
the flesh for the lusts of men, but for the will of
God. 3 For we *have spent* enough of our past
lifetime in doing the will of the Gentiles—when we
walked in lewdness, lusts, drunkenness, revelries,
drinking parties, and abominable idolatries. 4 In
regard to these, they think it strange that you do
not run with *them* in the same flood of dissipation,
speaking evil of *you*. 5 They will give an account to
Him who is ready to judge the living and the dead.
6 For this reason the gospel was preached also to
those who are dead, that they might be judged
according to men in the flesh, but live according to
God in the spirit.

7 But the end of all things is at hand; therefore be
serious and watchful in your prayers. 8 And above
all things have fervent love for one another, for
"love will cover a multitude of sins." 9 Be hospitable
to one another without grumbling. 10 As each one
has received a gift, minister it to one another, as
good stewards of the manifold grace of God. 11 If
anyone speaks, *let him speak* as the oracles of God.
If anyone ministers, *let him do it* as with the ability
which God supplies, that in all things God may be
glorified through Jesus Christ, to whom belong the
glory and the dominion forever and ever. Amen.

12 Beloved, do not think it strange concerning the
fiery trial which is to try you, as though some
strange thing happened to you; 13 but rejoice to the
extent that you partake of Christ's sufferings, that
when His glory is revealed, you may also be glad
with exceeding joy. 14 If you are reproached for the
name of Christ, blessed *are you*, for the Spirit of
glory and of God rests upon you. On their part He
is blasphemed, but on your part He is glorified.
15 But let none of you suffer as a murderer, a thief,
an evildoer, or as a busybody in other people's
matters. 16 Yet if *anyone suffers* as a Christian, let
him not be ashamed, but let him glorify God in this
matter.

17 For the time *has come* for judgment to begin at
the house of God; and if *it begins* with us first, what
will *be* the end of those who do not obey the gospel
of God? 18 Now

"If the righteous one is scarcely saved,

ד כֵּיוָן שֶׁהַמָּשִׁיחַ סָבַל בְּעַדֵנוּ בְּגוּפוֹ, גַּם אַתֶּם
הִתְאַזְּרוּ בְּאוֹתוֹ הֶלֶךְ-הָרוּחַ; שֶׁכֵּן הַסּוֹבֵל בְּגוּפוֹ חָדֵל
לַחֲטֹא, 2 לְמַעַן לֹא יִחְיֶה עוֹד לְפִי תַּאֲוֹת בְּנֵי אָדָם
בַּזְּמַן שֶׁנּוֹתַר לוֹ לִחְיוֹת בְּגוּפוֹ, אֶלָּא לְפִי רְצוֹן
אֱלֹהִים. 3 הֵן דֵּי הָיָה הַזְּמַן שֶׁעָבַר עֲלֵיכֶם בַּעֲשִׂיַּת
חֵפֶץ הַגּוֹיִים, כַּאֲשֶׁר הִתְהַלַּכְתֶּם בְּדַרְכֵי זִמָּה
וְתַאֲוֹת, שִׁכְרוּת וְהוֹלְלוּת, נִשְׁפֵּי שְׁתִיָּה וַעֲבוֹדַת
אֱלִילִים אֲסוּרָה. 4 וְכֵיוָן שֶׁאֵינְכֶם רָצִים עִמָּהֶם לְשֶׁטֶף
זִמָּתָם, תְּמֵהִים הֵם עַל כָּךְ וּמְגַדְּפִים. 5 הַלָּלוּ יִתְּנוּ
דִין וְחֶשְׁבּוֹן לִפְנֵי מִי שֶׁעָתִיד לִשְׁפֹּט אֶת הַחַיִּים וְאֶת
הַמֵּתִים. 6 לָכֵן הִתְבַּשְּׂרוּ גַם הַמֵּתִים, כְּדֵי שֶׁיִּשָּׁפְטוּ
כְּדֶרֶךְ בְּנֵי אָדָם בַּבָּשָׂר, אַךְ יִחְיוּ כְּדֶרֶךְ אֱלֹהִים בָּרוּחַ.
7 הִנֵּה קֵץ הַכֹּל קָרֵב. עַל כֵּן הֱיוּ מְפֻכָּחִים, וַהֲיוּ עֵרִים
לְהִתְפַּלֵּל. 8 וּבְרֹאשׁ וּבָרִאשׁוֹנָה אֶהֱבוּ אִישׁ אֶת רֵעֵהוּ
אַהֲבָה עַזָּה, כִּי עַל רֹב פְּשָׁעִים תְּכַסֶּה אַהֲבָה. 9 הֱיוּ
מְאָרְחִים זֶה אֶת זֶה בְּלִי לְהִתְלוֹנֵן. 10 אִישׁ אִישׁ כְּפִי
הַמַּתָּנָה אֲשֶׁר קִבֵּל בָּהּ בְּקִרְבְּכֶם, כְּסוֹכְנִים
טוֹבִים עַל חַסְדּוֹ רַב-הַפָּנִים שֶׁל אֱלֹהִים. 11 אִישׁ כִּי
יְדַבֵּר, אִמְרֵי אֱלֹהִים יְדַבֵּר; אִישׁ כִּי יְשָׁרֵת, יַעֲשֶׂה
זֹאת מִתּוֹךְ הַכֹּחַ שֶׁנָּתַן לוֹ אֱלֹהִים; וְזֹאת לְמַעַן יְכֻבַּד
הָאֱלֹהִים בַּכֹּל דֶּרֶךְ יֵשׁוּעַ הַמָּשִׁיחַ אֲשֶׁר לוֹ הַכָּבוֹד
וְהַגְּבוּרָה לְעוֹלְמֵי עוֹלָמִים. אָמֵן.
12 אֲהוּבַי, בְּבוֹא עֲלֵיכֶם צְרִיפַת אֵשׁ כְּדֵי לִבְחֹן
אֶתְכֶם, אַל תִּתְמְהוּ כְּאִלּוּ מִקְרֶה מוּזָר קָרָה לָכֶם,
13 אֶלָּא שִׂמְחוּ בְּכָל שֶׁחֵלֶק לָכֶם בְּסִבְלוֹת הַמָּשִׁיחַ,
לְמַעַן תִּשְׂמְחוּ וְתַעַלְצוּ גַם בְּהִגָּלוֹת כְּבוֹדוֹ.
14 אַשְׁרֵיכֶם אִם יְחָרְפוּ אֶתְכֶם בַּעֲבוּר שֵׁם
הַמָּשִׁיחַ, כִּי אָז רוּחַ הַכָּבוֹד, רוּחַ אֱלֹהִים, נָחָה
עֲלֵיכֶם. 15 רַק אַל יִסְבֹּל אִישׁ מִכֶּם כְּרוֹצֵחַ אוֹ כְּגַנָּב
אוֹ כְּעוֹשֵׂה רָעָה אוֹ כְּמִתְעָרֵב בְּעִנְיְנֵי אֲחֵרִים. 16 וְאִם
יִסְבֹּל כִּמְשִׁיחִי, אַל יֵבוֹשׁ כִּי אִם יְכַבֵּד אֶת אֱלֹהִים
בַּשֵּׁם הַזֶּה, 17 שֶׁהֲרֵי עֵת לְהַתְחִיל הַמִּשְׁפָּט מִבֵּית
אֱלֹהִים. וְאִם מֵאִתָּנוּ יַתְחִיל, מַה תִּהְיֶה אַחֲרִית
הָאֲנָשִׁים שֶׁאֵינָם נִשְׁמָעִים לִבְשׂוֹרַת אֱלֹהִים? 18 אִם
צַדִּיק בְּקֹשִׁי נוֹשָׁע, חוֹטֵא וְרָשָׁע מַה יִּהְיֶה עָלָיו?

Where will the ungodly and the sinner appear?"

19 Therefore let those who suffer according to the will of God commit their souls *to Him* in doing good, as to a faithful Creator.

5 The elders who are among you I exhort, I who am a fellow elder and a witness of the sufferings of Christ, and also a partaker of the glory that will be revealed: 2 Shepherd the flock of God which is among you, serving as overseers, not by compulsion but willingly, not for dishonest gain but eagerly; 3 nor as being lords over those entrusted to you, but being examples to the flock; 4 and when the Chief Shepherd appears, you will receive the crown of glory that does not fade away.

5 Likewise you younger people, submit yourselves to *your* elders. Yes, all of *you* be submissive to one another, and be clothed with humility, for

> *"God resists the proud,*
> *But gives grace to the humble."*

6 Therefore humble yourselves under the mighty hand of God, that He may exalt you in due time, 7 casting all your care upon Him, for He cares for you.

8 Be sober, be vigilant; because your adversary the devil walks about like a roaring lion, seeking whom he may devour. 9 Resist him, steadfast in the faith, knowing that the same sufferings are experienced by your brotherhood in the world. 10 But may the God of all grace, who called us to His eternal glory by Christ Jesus, after you have suffered a while, perfect, establish, strengthen, and settle *you*. 11 To Him *be* the glory and the dominion forever and ever. Amen.

12 By Silvanus, our faithful brother as I consider him, I have written to you briefly, exhorting and testifying that this is the true grace of God in which you stand.

13 She who is in Babylon, elect together with *you*, greets you; and *so does* Mark my son. 14 Greet one another with a kiss of love.

Peace to you all who are in Christ Jesus. Amen.

---

19 לָכֵן גַּם הַסּוֹבְלִים כִּרְצוֹן אֱלֹהִים יַפְקִידוּ נָא אֶת נַפְשׁוֹתֵיהֶם בְּיַד הַבּוֹרֵא הַנֶּאֱמָן, בַּעֲשׂוֹת הַטּוֹב.

ה מִן הַזְּקֵנִים אֲשֶׁר בְּקִרְבְּכֶם אֲבַקֵּשׁ, אֲנִי הַזָּקֵן עֲמִיתָם וְעֵד סִבְלוֹת הַמָּשִׁיחַ וְגַם שֻׁתָּף לַכָּבוֹד הֶעָתִיד לְהִתְגַּלּוֹת: 2 רְעוּ אֶת עֵדֶר אֱלֹהִים הַנִּמְצָא עִמָּכֶם וְהַשְׁגִּיחוּ עָלָיו לֹא מִתּוֹךְ כְּפִיָּה כִּי אִם בְּרָצוֹן, כִּרְצוּי לֵאלֹהִים; לֹא בְחֶמְדַּת בֶּצַע כִּי אִם בְּנֶפֶשׁ חֲפֵצָה; 3 לֹא כְרוֹדְנִים עַל מַה שֶׁהֻפְקַד בְּיֶדְכֶם, אֶלָּא בִּהְיוֹתְכֶם מוֹפֵת לַצֹּאן. 4 וּבְהוֹפַעַת שַׂר הָרוֹעִים תְּקַבְּלוּ עֲטֶרֶת כָּבוֹד אֲשֶׁר לֹא תִּבֹּל.

5 כְּמוֹ כֵן, הַצְּעִירִים, הִכָּנְעוּ לִפְנֵי הַזְּקֵנִים. וְאוּלָם חִגְרוּ כֻּלְּכֶם גְּמִיכוּת רוּחַ אִישׁ כְּלַפֵּי רֵעֵהוּ, כִּי אֱלֹהִים לַלֵּצִים הוּא־יָלִיץ וְלַעֲנָוִים יִתֶּן־חֵן.

6 הַשְׁפִּילוּ עַצְמְכֶם תַּחַת יַד אֱלֹהִים הַחֲזָקָה, לְמַעַן יְרוֹמֵם אֶתְכֶם בְּעִתּוֹ. 7 הַשְׁלִיכוּ עָלָיו כָּל יְהָבְכֶם, כִּי הוּא דוֹאֵג לָכֶם. 8 הֱיוּ עֵרִים וְעִמְדוּ עַל הַמִּשְׁמָר. אוֹיִבְכֶם הַשָּׂטָן מְשׁוֹטֵט כְּאַרְיֵה שׁוֹאֵג וּמְחַפֵּשׂ לוֹ לִטְרֹף מִישֶׁהוּ. 9 עִמְדוּ נֶגְדּוֹ יַצִּיבִים בָּאֱמוּנָה, בִּידִיעָה שֶׁאוֹתָן הַצָּרוֹת עוֹבְרוֹת עַל אֲחֵיכֶם אֲשֶׁר בָּעוֹלָם. 10 וֵאלֹהֵי כָּל חֶסֶד אֲשֶׁר קָרָא אֶתְכֶם אֶל כְּבוֹדוֹ לְעוֹלָמִים בַּמָּשִׁיחַ יֵשׁוּעַ, אַחֲרֵי סִבְלְכֶם הַמְּעַט הוּא יַשְׁלִים אֶתְכֶם וְגַם יְיַצֵּב וִיחַזֵּק וִיכוֹנֵן אֶתְכֶם. 11 לוֹ הַכָּבוֹד וְהַגְּבוּרָה לְעוֹלְמֵי עוֹלָמִים. אָמֵן.

12 בְּיַד הָאָח סִילְוָנוֹס שֶׁאֲנִי חוֹשֵׁב לְנֶאֱמָן, כָּתַבְתִּי לָכֶם דְּבָרִים מְעַטִּים לְעוֹרֵר וּלְהָעִיד כִּי זֶהוּ חֶסֶד הָאֱלֹהִים, הַחֶסֶד הָאֲמִתִּי; עִמְדוּ בּוֹ. 13 הַקְּהִלָּה אֲשֶׁר בְּבָבֶל, שֶׁנִּבְחֲרָה אִתְּכֶם, דּוֹרֶשֶׁת בִּשְׁלוֹמְכֶם; וְכֵן גַּם מַרְקוֹס בְּנִי. 14 דִּרְשׁוּ אִישׁ בִּשְׁלוֹם רֵעֵהוּ בִּנְשִׁיקַת אַהֲבָה. שָׁלוֹם לְכֻלְּכֶם אֲשֶׁר בַּמָּשִׁיחַ יֵשׁוּעַ.

The Second Epistle of

PETER

1 Simon Peter, a bondservant and apostle of Jesus Christ,

To those who have obtained like precious faith with us by the righteousness of our God and Savior Jesus Christ:

[2] Grace and peace be multiplied to you in the knowledge of God and of Jesus our Lord, [3] as His divine power has given to us all things that *pertain* to life and godliness, through the knowledge of Him who called us by glory and virtue, [4] by which have been given to us exceedingly great and precious promises, that through these you may be partakers of the divine nature, having escaped the corruption *that is* in the world through lust.

[5] But also for this very reason, giving all diligence, add to your faith virtue, to virtue knowledge, [6] to knowledge self-control, to self-control perseverance, to perseverance godliness, [7] to godliness brotherly kindness, and to brotherly kindness love. [8] For if these things are yours and abound, *you will be* neither barren nor unfruitful in the knowledge of our Lord Jesus Christ. [9] For he who lacks these things is shortsighted, even to blindness, and has forgotten that he was cleansed from his old sins.

[10] Therefore, brethren, be even more diligent to make your call and election sure, for if you do these things you will never stumble; [11] for so an entrance will be supplied to you abundantly into the ever-lasting kingdom of our Lord and Savior Jesus Christ.

[12] For this reason I will not be negligent to remind you always of these things, though you know and are established in the present truth. [13] Yes, I think it is right, as long as I am in this tent, to stir you up by reminding *you*, [14] knowing that shortly I *must* put off my tent, just as our Lord Jesus Christ showed me. [15] Moreover I will be careful to ensure that you always have a reminder of these things after my decease.

[16] For we did not follow cunningly devised fables when we made known to you the power and coming of our Lord Jesus Christ, but were eyewitnesses of His majesty. [17] For He received from God the Father honor and glory when such a voice came to Him from the Excellent Glory: "This is My beloved

אִגֶּרֶת פֶּטְרוֹס הַשְּׁנִיָּה

א מֵאֵת שִׁמְעוֹן פֶּטְרוֹס, עֶבֶד יֵשׁוּעַ הַמָּשִׁיחַ וּשְׁלִיחוֹ, לְאֵלֶּה אֲשֶׁר בְּצִדְקַת אֱלֹהֵינוּ וּמוֹשִׁיעֵנוּ יֵשׁוּעַ הַמָּשִׁיחַ קִבְּלוּ אֱמוּנָה יְקָרָה כְּשֶׁלָּנוּ: [2] חֶסֶד וְשָׁלוֹם יִשָּׁפְעוּ עֲלֵיכֶם לְמַכְבִּיר בִּידִיעַתְכֶם אֶת אֱלֹהִים וְיֵשׁוּעַ אֲדוֹנֵנוּ.

[3] הֵן גְּבוּרָתוֹ הָאֱלֹהִית נָתְנָה לָנוּ אֶת כָּל צָרְכֵינוּ לְחַיִּים וְלַחֲסִידוּת, עַל־יְדֵי יְדִיעָתֵנוּ אֶת הַקּוֹרֵא אוֹתָנוּ אֶל כְּבוֹדוֹ וְהוֹדוֹ. [4] בְּדַרְךְ זֹאת נָתַן לָנוּ הַבְטָחוֹת גְּדוֹלוֹת מְאֹד וִיקָרוֹת, לְמַעַן תִּהְיוּ שֻׁתָּפִים עַל־יָדָן בַּטֶּבַע הָאֱלֹהִי בְּהִמָּלֶטְכֶם מֵהַכִּלָּיוֹן הַשּׁוֹרֵר בָּעוֹלָם בְּשֶׁל הַתַּאֲוָה. [5] מִשּׁוּם כָּךְ שִׁקְדוּ בְּכָל מְאֹדְכֶם לְהוֹסִיף עַל אֱמוּנַתְכֶם אֶת הַמַּעֲלָה הַמּוּסָרִית, וְעַל הַמַּעֲלָה הַמּוּסָרִית אֶת הַדַּעַת, [6] וְעַל הַדַּעַת אֶת כִּבּוּשׁ הַיֵּצֶר, וְעַל כִּבּוּשׁ הַיֵּצֶר אֶת הַסַּבְלָנוּת, וְעַל הַסַּבְלָנוּת אֶת הַחֲסִידוּת, [7] וְעַל הַחֲסִידוּת אֶת הָאַחֲוָה, וְעַל הָאַחֲוָה אֶת הָאַהֲבָה; [8] שֶׁהֲרֵי אִם אֵלֶּה יִהְיוּ בָּכֶם וְיִרְבּוּ, לֹא יַנִּיחַ לָכֶם לִהְיוֹת בְּטֵלִים וּבִלְתִּי פּוֹרִים בְּמַה שֶׁנּוֹגֵעַ לִידִיעַת אֲדוֹנֵנוּ יֵשׁוּעַ הַמָּשִׁיחַ. [9] מִי שֶׁאֵין לוֹ הַדְּבָרִים הַלָּלוּ, עִוֵּר הוּא, קְצַר רְאוּת; הוּא שָׁכַח כִּי טֹהַר מֵחֲטָאָיו הָרִאשׁוֹנִים. [10] לָכֵן, אַחַי, שִׁקְדוּ בְּיֶתֶר שְׂאֵת לְחַזֵּק אֶת הַקְּרִיאָה וְהַבְּחִירָה שֶׁהֵן מְנָת חֶלְקְכֶם; שֶׁהֲרֵי אִם כָּךְ תַּעֲשׂוּ לֹא תִּכָּשְׁלוּ אַף פַּעַם, [11] וּבְדֶרֶךְ זֹאת יִפָּתַח לָכֶם לִרְוָחָה הַמָּבוֹא אֶל מַלְכוּת עוֹלָמִים שֶׁל אֲדוֹנֵנוּ וּמוֹשִׁיעֵנוּ יֵשׁוּעַ הַמָּשִׁיחַ.

[12] עַל כֵּן לֹא אֶחְדַּל לְהַזְכִּירְכֶם בְּכָל עֵת אֶת הַדְּבָרִים הַלָּלוּ, אַף עַל פִּי שֶׁאַתֶּם יוֹדְעִים אוֹתָם וְאַתֶּם יַצִּיבִים בָּאֱמֶת הַזֹּאת. [13] וְרוֹאֶה אֲנִי לְנָכוֹן לְהַזְכִּיר וּלְעוֹרֵר אֶתְכֶם כָּל עוֹד אֲנִי נִמְצָא בַּמִּשְׁכָּן הַזֶּה, [14] כִּי יָדוּעַ לִי שֶׁבְּקָרוֹב יוּסַר מִשְׁכָּנִי, כְּפִי שֶׁגִּלָּה לִי אֲדוֹנֵנוּ יֵשׁוּעַ הַמָּשִׁיחַ. [15] אַךְ אֶשְׁתַּדֵּל שֶׁגַּם לְאַחַר פְּטִירָתִי יִהְיֶה לָכֶם תָּמִיד זִכְרוֹן הַדְּבָרִים הָאֵלֶּה.

[16] לֹא אַחֲרֵי אַגָּדוֹת מְחֻכָּמוֹת הָלַכְנוּ כַּאֲשֶׁר הוֹדַעְנוּ לָכֶם אֶת גְּבוּרַת אֲדוֹנֵנוּ יֵשׁוּעַ הַמָּשִׁיחַ וְאֶת בּוֹאוֹ, אֶלָּא כְּמוֹ עֵינֵינוּ רָאִינוּ אֶת גְּדֻלָּתוֹ; [17] שֶׁכֵּן קִבֵּל יְקָר

Son, in whom I am well pleased." [18] And we heard this voice which came from heaven when we were with Him on the holy mountain.

[19] And so we have the prophetic word confirmed, which you do well to heed as a light that shines in a dark place, until the day dawns and the morning star rises in your hearts; [20] knowing this first, that no prophecy of Scripture is of any private interpretation, [21] for prophecy never came by the will of man, but holy men of God spoke *as they were* moved by the Holy Spirit.

2 But there were also false prophets among the people, even as there will be false teachers among you, who will secretly bring in destructive heresies, even denying the Lord who bought them, *and* bring on themselves swift destruction. [2] And many will follow their destructive ways, because of whom the way of truth will be blasphemed. [3] By covetousness they will exploit you with deceptive words; for a long time their judgment has not been idle, and their destruction does not slumber.

[4] For if God did not spare the angels who sinned, but cast *them* down to hell and delivered *them* into chains of darkness, to be reserved for judgment; [5] and did not spare the ancient world, but saved Noah, *one of* eight *people,* a preacher of right-eousness, bringing in the flood on the world of the ungodly; [6] and turning the cities of Sodom and Gomorrah into ashes, condemned *them* to destruction, making *them* an example to those who afterward would live ungodly; [7] and delivered righteous Lot, *who was* oppressed by the filthy conduct of the wicked [8] (for that righteous man, dwelling among them, tormented *his* righteous soul from day to day by seeing and hearing *their* lawless deeds)— [9] *then* the Lord knows how to deliver the godly out of temptations and to reserve the unjust under punishment for the day of judgment, [10] and especially those who walk according to the flesh in the lust of uncleanness and despise authority. *They are* presumptuous, self-willed. They are not afraid to speak evil of dignitaries, [11] whereas angels, who are greater in power and might, do not bring a reviling accusation against them before the Lord.

[12] But these, like natural brute beasts made to be caught and destroyed, speak evil of the things they do not understand, and will utterly perish in their own corruption, [13] *and* will receive the wages of unrighteousness, *as* those who count it pleasure to carouse in the daytime. *They are* spots and blemishes, carousing in their own deceptions while they feast with you, [14] having eyes full of adultery and that cannot cease from sin, enticing unstable

וְכָבוֹד מֵאֵת אֱלֹהִים הָאָב כַּאֲשֶׁר נִשָּׂא אֵלָיו הַקּוֹל הַזֶּה מֵהֲדָרַת הַכָּבוֹד: "זֶה בְּנִי אֲהוּבִי אֲשֶׁר בּוֹ חָפַצְתִּי", [18] וְאֶת הַקּוֹל הַזֶּה שָׁמַעְנוּ בָּא מִן הַשָּׁמַיִם בִּהְיוֹתֵנוּ עִמּוֹ בְּהַר הַקֹּדֶשׁ. [19] אָכֵן נִתְאַשֵּׁר לָנוּ בְּיֶתֶר תֹּקֶף דְּבַר הַנְּבוּאָה, וְתֵיטִיבוּ לַעֲשׂוֹת בְּשִׂימְכֶם לֵב אֵלָיו כְּאֶל נֵר מֵאִיר בְּמָקוֹם אֹפֶל, עַד כִּי יִבְקַע אוֹר הַיּוֹם וְזָרַח וְאֵילַת הַשַּׁחַר תִּזְרַח בִּלְבַבְכֶם. [20] וְזֹאת דְּעוּ רִאשׁוֹנָה, שֶׁכָּל נְבוּאַת הַמִּקְרָא אֵינָהּ עִנְיַן שֶׁל פֵּרוּשׁ אִישִׁי, [21] כִּי מֵעוֹלָם לֹא יָצְאָה נְבוּאָה עַל־פִּי רְצוֹן הָאָדָם, אֶלָּא רוּחַ הַקֹּדֶשׁ הֵנִיעָה בְּנֵי אָדָם לְדַבֵּר מִטַּעַם אֱלֹהִים.

ב אֲבָל גַּם נְבִיאֵי שֶׁקֶר הָיוּ בָעָם, כְּשֵׁם שֶׁגַּם בֵּינֵיכֶם יִהְיוּ מוֹרֵי שֶׁקֶר. הַלָּלוּ יַכְנִיסוּ בַּחֲשַׁאי תּוֹרוֹת הַרְסָנִיּוֹת וִיכַפְּרוּ בָּאָדוֹן אֲשֶׁר קָנָה אוֹתָם, וְיָבִיאוּ עַל עַצְמָם אָבְדָן פִּתְאֹם. [2] רַבִּים יֵלְכוּ אַחֲרֵי תּוֹעֲבוֹתֵיהֶם, וּבִגְלָלָם תִּגָּדֵף דֶּרֶךְ הָאֱמֶת. [3] וּבְתַאֲוָתָם לַבֶּצַע יְדַבְּרוּ כָּזָב וְיִסְחֲרוּ בָכֶם; וְאָמְנָם לֹא יִתְעַכֵּב מִשְׁפָּטָם שֶׁזֶּה מִקֶּדֶם, וְאָבְדָנָם לֹא יָנוּם.

[4] הֵן אֱלֹהִים לֹא חָם עַל הַמַּלְאָכִים הַחוֹטְאִים, אֶלָּא הוֹרִידָם אֶל תַּחְתִּיּוֹת אֶרֶץ וּנְתָנָם בְּכַבְלֵי אֹפֶל לְשָׁמְרָם לַמִּשְׁפָּט. [5] וְגַם עַל הָעוֹלָם הַקֶּדֶם לֹא חָם, אֲבָל בַּהֲבִיאוֹ מַבּוּל עַל עוֹלָם שֶׁל רְשָׁעִים שָׁמַר אֶת נֹחַ, מַטִּיף הַצֶּדֶק, וְהַשִּׁבְעָה אֲשֶׁר עִמּוֹ. [6] אֶת עָרֵי סְדֹם וַעֲמֹרָה שָׂרַף לְאֵפֶר לְאַחַר שֶׁדָּן אוֹתָן לְמַהְפֵּכָה, בְּשִׂימוֹ אוֹתָן לְדֻגְמָה לָעֲתִידִים לַעֲשׂוֹת רִשְׁעָה, [7] וְהִצִּיל אֶת לוֹט הַצַּדִּיק, אֲשֶׁר נִדְכְּאָה נַפְשׁוֹ בִּגְלַל הִתְנַהֲגוּת הָרְשָׁעִים שְׁטוּפֵי זִמָּה; [8] כִּי הַצַּדִּיק הַזֶּה, אֲשֶׁר בְּשִׁבְתּוֹ בְּקִרְבָּם רָאָה וְשָׁמַע אֶת הַנַּעֲשֶׂה, יוֹם יוֹם הִתְעַנָּה בְּנַפְשׁוֹ הַיְשָׁרָה עַל מַעֲשֵׂי רִשְׁעָתָם. [9] אָכֵן יוֹדֵעַ אֲדֹנָי לְהַצִּיל אֶת חֲסִידָיו מִנִּסָּיוֹן וְעִם זֹאת לַחְשֹׁךְ אֶת הָרְשָׁעִים לְיוֹם הַדִּין כְּדֵי לְהַעֲנִישָׁם, [10] בְּיִחוּד אֶת הַהוֹלְכִים אַחַר הַבָּשָׂר בְּתַאֲוֹת טֻמְאָה וּבוֹזִים אֶת הַסַּמְכוּת הָעֶלְיוֹנָה. חֲצוּפִים הֵם, הוֹלְכִים בִּשְׁרִירוּת לִבָּם וְאֵינָם נִרְתָּעִים מֵחָרֵף אֶת נוֹשְׂאֵי הַמִּשְׂרוֹת הַנִּכְבָּדוֹת, [11] אֲשֶׁר אַף הַמַּלְאָכִים, הַגְּדוֹלִים מֵהֶם בְּעָצְמָה וְכֹחַ, אֵינָם מְבִיאִים עֲלֵיהֶם קִטְרוּג שֶׁל גִּדּוּף לִפְנֵי יהוה. [12] אַךְ הַלָּלוּ דּוֹמִים לַחַיּוֹת חַסְרוֹת תְּבוּנָה שֶׁבְּדֶרֶךְ הַטֶּבַע נוֹלְדוֹת כְּדֵי לְהִלָּכֵד וּלְהִשָּׁמֵד. הֵם מְחָרְפִים מַה שֶּׁאֵינָם יוֹדְעִים, וּכְמוֹ שֶׁהֵן נִשְׁמָדוֹת גַּם הֵם יִשָּׁמְדוּ, [13] וּבְזֶה יִסְבְּלוּ אֶת גְּמוּל עַוְלָתָם. אֶת הַהוֹלְלוּת בַּיּוֹם חוֹשְׁבִים הֵם לְתַעֲנוּג; כִּתְמֵי טֻמְאָה וּמוּמִים הֵם, הַסּוֹעֲדִים עִמָּכֶם וּמוֹצְאִים הֲנָאָה בְּתַרְמִיתָם. [14] עֵינַיִם לָהֶם מְלֵאוֹת נִאוּפִים וְאֵינָן מֵרְפּוֹת מִן

souls. *They have* a heart trained in covetous practices, *and are* accursed children. ¹⁵ They have forsaken the right way and gone astray, following the way of Balaam the *son* of Beor, who loved the wages of unrighteousness; ¹⁶ but he was rebuked for his iniquity: a dumb donkey speaking with a man's voice restrained the madness of the prophet.

¹⁷ These are wells without water, clouds carried by a tempest, for whom is reserved the blackness of darkness forever.

¹⁸ For when they speak great swelling *words* of emptiness, they allure through the lusts of the flesh, through lewdness, the ones who have actually escaped from those who live in error. ¹⁹ While they promise them liberty, they themselves are slaves of corruption; for by whom a person is overcome, by him also he is brought into bondage. ²⁰ For if, after they have escaped the pollutions of the world through the knowledge of the Lord and Savior Jesus Christ, they are again entangled in them and overcome, the latter end is worse for them than the beginning. ²¹ For it would have been better for them not to have known the way of righteousness, than having known *it,* to turn from the holy commandment delivered to them. ²² But it has happened to them according to the true proverb: "A dog returns to his own vomit," and, "a sow, having washed, to her wallowing in the mire."

3 Beloved, I now write to you this second epistle (in *both of* which I stir up your pure minds by way of reminder), ² that you may be mindful of the words which were spoken before by the holy prophets, and of the commandment of us, the apostles of the Lord and Savior, ³ knowing this first: that scoffers will come in the last days, walking according to their own lusts, ⁴ and saying, "Where is the promise of His coming? For since the fathers fell asleep, all things continue as *they were* from the beginning of creation." ⁵ For this they willfully forget: that by the word of God the heavens are of old, and the earth standing out of water and in the water, ⁶ by which the world *that* then existed perished, being flooded with water. ⁷ But the heavens and the earth *which* are now preserved by the same word, are reserved for fire until the day of judgment and perdition of ungodly men.

⁸ But, beloved, do not forget this one thing, that with the Lord one day *is* as a thousand years, and a thousand years as one day. ⁹ The Lord is not slack concerning *His* promise, as some count slackness, but is longsuffering toward us, not willing that any should perish but that all should come to repentance.

הַחֵטְא. הֵם לוֹכְדִים נְפָשׁוֹת בִּלְתִּי יַצִּיבוֹת; לָבָּם מֻרְגָּל בְּחַמְדָנוּת; אָכֵן בָּנִים אֲרוּרִים. ¹⁵ בְּעָזְבָם אֶת דֶּרֶךְ הַיָּשָׁר תָּעוּ וַהֵלְכוּ בְּדֶרֶךְ בִּלְעָם בֶּן בְּעוֹר אֲשֶׁר אָהַב אֶת שְׂכַר הָרֶשַׁע, ¹⁶ וְהוּכַח עַל עֲוֹלָתוֹ: אָתוֹן אִלֶּמֶת דִּבְּרָה בְּקוֹל אָדָם וְעָצְרָה אֶת אִוֶּלֶת הַנָּבִיא. ¹⁷ בְּאֵרוֹת בְּלִי מַיִם הֵם, עֲנָנִים נִדָּפִים בִּסְעָרָה, אֲשֶׁר אֲפֵלַת חֹשֶׁךְ שְׁמוּרָה לָהֶם. ¹⁸ בְּדַבְּרָם גְּדוֹלוֹת, דְּבָרִים שֶׁאֵינָם אֶלָּא הֶבֶל, הֵם לוֹכְדִים בְּתַאֲווֹת בְּשָׂרִים וּבְמַעֲשֵׂי זִמָּה אֶת אֵלֶּה אֲשֶׁר אַךְ נִמְלְטוּ מִידֵי הַהֹלְכִים בְּדֶרֶךְ הַתָּעוּת. ¹⁹ הֵם מַבְטִיחִים לָהֶם חֹפֶשׁ בְּשָׁעָה שֶׁהֵם עַצְמָם עֲבָדִים לְכָל אֲשֶׁר מַשְׁחִית; הֲרֵי לְמַה שֶּׁאָדָם נִכְנָע, לָזֶה הוּא מִשְׁתַּעְבֵּד. ²⁰ הֲלֹא אִם אַחֲרֵי שֶׁנִּמְלְטוּ מִטֻּמְאוֹת הָעוֹלָם בִּידִיעָתָם אֶת אֲדוֹנֵנוּ וּמוֹשִׁיעֵנוּ יֵשׁוּעַ הַמָּשִׁיחַ, שׁוּב נִסְתַּבְּכוּ בָּהֶן וְנֻצְּחוּ – כִּי אָז מַצָּבָם הָאַחֲרוֹן גָּרוֹעַ מִן הָרִאשׁוֹן. ²¹ מוּטָב הָיָה לָהֶם שֶׁלֹּא לָדַעַת אֶת דֶּרֶךְ הַצְּדָקָה מֵאֲשֶׁר לָדַעַת אוֹתָהּ וְלָסוּר מִן הַמִּצְוָה הַקְּדוֹשָׁה הַמְּסוּרָה לָהֶם. ²² הִתְקַמֵּשׁ בָּהֶם הַמָּשָׁל הָאֲמִתִּי: "הַכֶּלֶב שָׁב עַל־קֵאוֹ", וְגַם "הַחֲזִיר עוֹלֶה מִן הָרַחֲצָה לְהִתְגּוֹלֵל בָּרֶפֶשׁ".

ג אֲהוּבַי, זֹאת כְּבָר הָאִגֶּרֶת הַשְּׁנִיָּה שֶׁאֲנִי כּוֹתֵב לָכֶם, וּבִשְׁתֵּיהֶן אֲנִי מַזְכִּיר אֶתְכֶם וּמְעוֹרֵר אֶת מַחְשַׁבְתְּכֶם הַתַּמָּה, ² לְמַעַן תִּזְכְּרוּ אֶת הַדְּבָרִים שֶׁנֶּאֶמְרוּ מִקֶּדֶם בְּיַד הַנְּבִיאִים הַקְּדוֹשִׁים, וְאֶת מִצְוַת שְׁלִיחֵיכֶם מִטַּעַם הָאָדוֹן וְהַמּוֹשִׁיעַ. ³ וְקֹדֶם כֹּל דְּעוּ זֹאת, שֶׁבְּאַחֲרִית הַיָּמִים יָבוֹאוּ לֵצִים הַמִּתְהַלְּכִים לְפִי מַאֲוִיֵּיהֶם הָאִישִׁיִּים וְיִתְלוֹצְצוּ לֵאמֹר: ⁴ "אֵיפֹה בּוֹאוֹ הַמֻּבְטָח? הֲרֵי מֵאָז שָׁכְבוּ הָאָבוֹת הַכֹּל מַמְשִׁיךְ כְּמוֹ שֶׁהָיָה מֵרֵאשִׁית הַבְּרִיאָה!" ⁵ מֵרְצוֹן שׁוֹכְחִים הֵם אֶת הַדָּבָר הַזֶּה, שֶׁהַשָּׁמַיִם הָיוּ מִקֶּדֶם וְכִי הָאָרֶץ נִתְהַוְּתָה מִן הַמַּיִם וְעַל־יְדֵי הַמַּיִם בִּדְבַר אֱלֹהִים; ⁶ וְעַל־יְדֵי אֵלֶּה נֶחֱרַם הָעוֹלָם שֶׁהָיָה אָז, בְּהִשָּׁפְטוֹ בַּמַּיִם. ⁷ וְאוּלָם הַשָּׁמַיִם וְהָאָרֶץ הַנּוֹכְחִיִּים אֲצוּרִים עַל־יְדֵי אוֹתוֹ הַדָּבָר לָאֵשׁ, שְׁמוּרִים לְיוֹם הַדִּין, לְאָבְדַן אַנְשֵׁי הָרֶשַׁע. ⁸ אַךְ אַל יֵעָלֵם מִכֶּם הַדָּבָר הַזֶּה, אֲהוּבַי: יוֹם אֶחָד כְּאֶלֶף שָׁנִים בְּעֵינֵי אֲדֹנָי, וְאֶלֶף שָׁנִים כְּיוֹם אֶחָד. ⁹ אֵין אֲדֹנָי מְאַחֵר בַּדָּבָר אֲשֶׁר הִבְטִיחַ, כְּמוֹ שֶׁיֵּשׁ הַחוֹשְׁבִים זֹאת לְאָחוּר,

10 But the day of the Lord will come as a thief in the night, in which the heavens will pass away with a great noise, and the elements will melt with fervent heat; both the earth and the works that are in it will be burned up. 11 Therefore, since all these things will be dissolved, what manner *of persons* ought you to be in holy conduct and godliness, 12 looking for and hastening the coming of the day of God, because of which the heavens will be dissolved, being on fire, and the elements will melt with fervent heat? 13 Nevertheless we, according to His promise, look for new heavens and a new earth in which righteousness dwells.

14 Therefore, beloved, looking forward to these things, be diligent to be found by Him in peace, without spot and blameless; 15 and consider *that* the longsuffering of our Lord *is* salvation—as also our beloved brother Paul, according to the wisdom given to him, has written to you, 16 as also in all his epistles, speaking in them of these things, in which are some things hard to understand, which untaught and unstable *people* twist to their own destruction, as *they do* also the rest of the Scriptures.

17 You therefore, beloved, since you know *this* beforehand, beware lest you also fall from your own steadfastness, being led away with the error of the wicked; 18 but grow in the grace and knowledge of our Lord and Savior Jesus Christ.

To Him *be* the glory both now and forever. Amen.

אֶלָּא שֶׁהוּא מַאֲרִיךְ אַפּוֹ לָנוּ; אֵין הוּא רוֹצֶה שֶׁיֹּאבַד אִישׁ, אֶלָּא שֶׁהַכֹּל יָבוֹאוּ לִידֵי תְּשׁוּבָה. 10 יוֹם יהוה כְּגַנָּב יָבוֹא. אָז הַשָּׁמַיִם בְּשָׁאוֹן יַחְלְפוּ וְהַיְסוֹדוֹת יִבְעֲרוּ וְיִתְפָּרְקוּ, וְהָאָרֶץ וְהַמַּעֲשִׂים אֲשֶׁר עָלֶיהָ. 11 וְכֵיוָן שֶׁכָּל אֵלֶּה יִתְפָּרְקוּ, עַד כַּמָּה עֲלֵיכֶם לִחְיוֹת בִּקְדֻשָּׁה וּבַחֲסִידוּת, 12 לְחַכּוֹת לְבוֹא יוֹם הָאֱלֹהִים וּלְהָחִישׁ אוֹתוֹ, יוֹם שֶׁבְּגִלָּלוֹ הַשָּׁמַיִם יִתְפָּרְקוּ בָּאֵשׁ וְהַיְסוֹדוֹת יִבְעֲרוּ וְיִמַּסּוּ. 13 וַאֲנַחְנוּ מְחַכִּים, עַל־פִּי הַבְטָחָתוֹ, לְשָׁמַיִם חֲדָשִׁים וּלְאֶרֶץ חֲדָשָׁה אֲשֶׁר צֶדֶק יִשְׁכֹּן בָּם.

14 עַל כֵּן, אֲהוּבַי, בְּחַכּוֹתְכֶם לַדְּבָרִים הָאֵלֶּה שִׁקְדוּ לְהִמָּצֵא לְפָנָיו בְּשָׁלוֹם, נְקִיִּים וּבְלֹא דֹפִי. 15 וְאֶת אֹרֶךְ־רוּחַ אֲדוֹנֵנוּ חִשְׁבוּ לִתְשׁוּעָה; כְּמוֹ שֶׁגַּם אָחִינוּ הָאָהוּב שָׁאוּל כָּתַב לָכֶם לְפִי הַחָכְמָה הַנְּתוּנָה לוֹ, 16 וּכְמוֹ שֶׁכָּתוּב בְּכָל אִגְּרוֹתָיו, בְּדַבְּרוֹ עַל הַדְּבָרִים הָאֵלֶּה. יֵשׁ בָּהֶן דְּבָרִים קָשִׁים לַהֲבָנָה אֲשֶׁר הַנִּבְעָרִים וְהַבִּלְתִּי יַצִּיבִים מְעַוְּתִים אוֹתָם – כְּמוֹ שֶׁהֵם עוֹשִׂים בְּיֶתֶר הַכְּתוּבִים – לְאָבְדָנָם הֵם.

17 וְאַתֶּם, אֲהוּבַי, כֵּיוָן שֶׁאַתֶּם יוֹדְעִים זֹאת מֵרֹאשׁ, הִשָּׁמְרוּ פֶּן תִּמָּשְׁכוּ בְּתָעוּתָם שֶׁל אַנְשֵׁי בְּלִיַּעַל וְתִפְּלוּ מִיַּצִּיבוּתְכֶם. 18 גִּדְלוּ בְּחֶסֶד וּבְדַעַת אֲדוֹנֵנוּ וּמוֹשִׁיעֵנוּ יֵשׁוּעַ הַמָּשִׁיחַ. לוֹ הַכָּבוֹד גַּם עַכְשָׁו גַּם לְיוֹם עוֹלָם. אָמֵן.

The First Epistle of

JOHN

אִגֶּרֶת יוֹחָנָן הָרִאשׁוֹנָה

1 That which was from the beginning, which we have heard, which we have seen with our eyes, which we have looked upon, and our hands have handled, concerning the Word of life— 2 the life was manifested, and we have seen, and bear witness, and declare to you that eternal life which was with the Father and was manifested to us— 3 that which we have seen and heard we declare to you, that you also may have fellowship with us; and truly our fellowship *is* with the Father and with His Son Jesus Christ. 4 And these things we write to you that your joy may be full.

5 This is the message which we have heard from Him and declare to you, that God is light and in Him is no darkness at all. 6 If we say that we have fellowship with Him, and walk in darkness, we lie and do not practice the truth. 7 But if we walk in the light as He is in the light, we have fellowship with one another, and the blood of Jesus Christ His Son cleanses us from all sin.

8 If we say that we have no sin, we deceive ourselves, and the truth is not in us. 9 If we confess our sins, He is faithful and just to forgive us *our* sins and to cleanse us from all unrighteousness. 10 If we say that we have not sinned, we make Him a liar, and His word is not in us.

2 My little children, these things I write to you, so that you may not sin. And if anyone sins, we have an Advocate with the Father, Jesus Christ the righteous. 2 And He Himself is the propitiation for our sins, and not for ours only but also for the whole world.

3 Now by this we know that we know Him, if we keep His commandments. 4 He who says, "I know Him," and does not keep His commandments, is a liar, and the truth is not in him. 5 But whoever keeps His word, truly the love of God is perfected in him. By this we know that we are in Him. 6 He who says he abides in Him ought himself also to walk just as He walked.

7 Brethren, I write no new commandment to you, but an old commandment which you have had from the beginning. The old commandment is the word which you heard from the beginning. 8 Again, a new

א אֵת אֲשֶׁר הָיָה מֵרֵאשִׁית, אֵת אֲשֶׁר שָׁמַעְנוּ, אֵת אֲשֶׁר רָאִינוּ בְּעֵינֵינוּ, אֲשֶׁר הִבַּטְנוּ בּוֹ וְיָדֵינוּ מִשְׁשׁוּ אוֹתוֹ, עַל־אוֹדוֹת דְּבַר הַחַיִּים, – 2 וְהַחַיִּים נִגְלוּ וַאֲנַחְנוּ רָאִינוּ, וַהֲרֵינוּ מְעִידִים וּמוֹדִיעִים לָכֶם אֶת חַיֵּי הָעוֹלָמִים אֲשֶׁר הָיוּ אֵצֶל הָאָב וְנִגְלוּ לָנוּ – 3 אֶת אֲשֶׁר רָאִינוּ וְשָׁמַעְנוּ מוֹדִיעִים אָנוּ גַּם לָכֶם, לְמַעַן תִּתְחַבְּרוּ עִמָּנוּ גַּם אַתֶּם. וְאָכֵן הִתְחַבְּרוּתֵנוּ הִיא עִם הָאָב וְעִם בְּנוֹ יֵשׁוּעַ הַמָּשִׁיחַ. 4 זֹאת אֲנַחְנוּ כּוֹתְבִים לְמַעַן תִּהְיֶה שִׂמְחַתְנוּ שְׁלֵמָה.

5 וְזֶה דְּבַר הַבְּשׂוֹרָה אֲשֶׁר שָׁמַעְנוּ מִמֶּנּוּ וַאֲנַחְנוּ מַשְׁמִיעִים לָכֶם, שֶׁהָאֱלֹהִים אוֹר הוּא וְכָל חֹשֶׁךְ אֵין בּוֹ. 6 אִם נֹאמַר שֶׁהִתְחַבְּרוּת לָנוּ אִתּוֹ וְנִתְהַלֵּךְ בַּחֹשֶׁךְ, דּוֹבְרֵי שֶׁקֶר אֲנַחְנוּ וְאֵינֶנּוּ מְקַיְּמִים אֶת הָאֱמֶת. 7 אֲבָל אִם נִתְהַלֵּךְ בָּאוֹר, כְּמוֹ שֶׁהוּא בָּאוֹר, כִּי אָז הִתְחַבַּרְנוּ זֶה עִם זֶה וְדַם יֵשׁוּעַ הַמָּשִׁיחַ בְּנוֹ מְטַהֵר אוֹתָנוּ מִכָּל חֵטְא. 8 אִם נֹאמַר שֶׁאֵין בָּנוּ חֵטְא, מַתְעִים אָנוּ אֶת עַצְמֵנוּ וְהָאֱמֶת אֵינֶנָּה בָּנוּ. 9 אִם נִתְוַדֶּה עַל חֲטָאֵינוּ, נֶאֱמָן הוּא וְצַדִּיק לִסְלֹחַ לָנוּ עַל חֲטָאֵינוּ וּלְטַהֵר אוֹתָנוּ מִכָּל עַוְלָה. 10 אִם נֹאמַר שֶׁלֹּא חָטָאנוּ, לְכוֹזֵב שַׂמְנוּ אוֹתוֹ וּדְבָרוֹ אֵינוֹ בָּנוּ.

ב יְלָדַי, כּוֹתֵב אֲנִי לָכֶם אֶת הַדְּבָרִים הָאֵלֶּה לְמַעַן לֹא תֶחֱטָאוּ; וְאִם יֶחֱטָא אִישׁ יֵשׁ לָנוּ מֵלִיץ לִפְנֵי הָאָב – יֵשׁוּעַ הַמָּשִׁיחַ, הַצַּדִּיק. 2 וְהוּא כַּפָּרָה עַל חֲטָאֵינוּ, וְלֹא עַל חֲטָאֵינוּ בִּלְבָד, אֶלָּא גַּם עַל חֲטָאֵי כָּל הָעוֹלָם. 3 וּבָזֶה נֵדַע שֶׁהִכַּרְנוּ אוֹתוֹ – אִם נִשְׁמֹר אֶת מִצְוֹתָיו. 4 הָאוֹמֵר "אֲנִי מַכִּיר אוֹתוֹ" וְאֵינוֹ שׁוֹמֵר אֶת מִצְוֹתָיו, דּוֹבֵר שֶׁקֶר הוּא וְהָאֱמֶת אֵינֶנָּה בּוֹ. 5 אַךְ הַשּׁוֹמֵר אֶת דְּבָרוֹ, בָּאוֹתוֹ הָאִישׁ נִשְׁלְמָה בֶּאֱמֶת אַהֲבַת אֱלֹהִים. בָּזֶה נֵדַע כִּי בּוֹ אֲנַחְנוּ: 6 הָאוֹמֵר שֶׁהוּא עוֹמֵד בְּיֵשׁוּעַ, כְּדֶרֶךְ שֶׁהִתְהַלֵּךְ יֵשׁוּעַ כֵּן גַּם עָלָיו לְהִתְהַלֵּךְ.

7 אֲהוּבַי, לֹא מִצְוָה חֲדָשָׁה כּוֹתֵב אֲנִי לָכֶם, כִּי אִם מִצְוָה יְשָׁנָה אֲשֶׁר הָיְתָה לָכֶם מֵרֵאשִׁית; הַמִּצְוָה הַיְשָׁנָה הִיא הַדָּבָר אֲשֶׁר שְׁמַעְתֶּם. 8 וּבְכָל זֹאת

commandment I write to you, which thing is true in Him and in you, because the darkness is passing away, and the true light is already shining.

⁹He who says he is in the light, and hates his brother, is in darkness until now. ¹⁰He who loves his brother abides in the light, and there is no cause for stumbling in him. ¹¹But he who hates his brother is in darkness and walks in darkness, and does not know where he is going, because the darkness has blinded his eyes.

12 I write to you, little children,
      Because your sins are forgiven you for His
        name's sake.
13 I write to you, fathers,
      Because you have known Him *who is* from the
        beginning.
    I write to you, young men,
      Because you have overcome the wicked one.
    I write to you, little children,
      Because you have known the Father.
14 I have written to you, fathers,
      Because you have known Him *who is* from the
        beginning.
    I have written to you, young men,
      Because you are strong, and the word of God
        abides in you,
    And you have overcome the wicked one.

¹⁵Do not love the world or the things in the world. If anyone loves the world, the love of the Father is not in him. ¹⁶For all that *is* in the world—the lust of the flesh, the lust of the eyes, and the pride of life—is not of the Father but is of the world. ¹⁷And the world is passing away, and the lust of it; but he who does the will of God abides forever.

¹⁸Little children, it is the last hour; and as you have heard that the Antichrist is coming, even now many antichrists have come, by which we know that it is the last hour. ¹⁹They went out from us, but they were not of us; for if they had been of us, they would have continued with us; but *they went out* that they might be made manifest, that none of them were of us.

²⁰But you have an anointing from the Holy One, and you know all things. ²¹I have not written to you because you do not know the truth, but because you know it, and that no lie is of the truth.

²²Who is a liar but he who denies that Jesus is the Christ? He is antichrist who denies the Father and the Son. ²³Whoever denies the Son does not have the Father either; he who acknowledges the Son has the Father also.

מִצְוָה חֲדָשָׁה כּוֹתֵב אֲנִי לָכֶם, דָּבָר שֶׁנָּכוֹן גַּם בּוֹ וְגַם בָּכֶם, שֶׁהֲרֵי הַחֹשֶׁךְ עוֹבֵר וְהָאוֹר הָאֲמִתִּי כְּבָר זוֹרֵחַ. ⁹הָאוֹמֵר כִּי בָּאוֹר הוּא וְעִם זֹאת שׂוֹנֵא אֶת אָחִיו, עוֹדֶנּוּ בַּחֹשֶׁךְ. ¹⁰הָאוֹהֵב אֶת אָחִיו עוֹמֵד בָּאוֹר וּמִכְשׁוֹל אֵין בּוֹ. ¹¹אֲבָל הַשּׂוֹנֵא אֶת אָחִיו בַּחֹשֶׁךְ הוּא; בַּחֹשֶׁךְ הוּא מִתְהַלֵּךְ וְאֵינוֹ יוֹדֵעַ לְאָן הוּא הוֹלֵךְ, כִּי הַחֹשֶׁךְ עִוֵּר אֶת עֵינָיו.

¹²כּוֹתֵב אֲנִי לָכֶם, יְלָדַי, מִפְּנֵי שֶׁנִּסְלְחוּ לָכֶם חֲטָאֵיכֶם בַּעֲבוּר שְׁמוֹ. ¹³כּוֹתֵב אֲנִי לָכֶם, אָבוֹת, מִפְּנֵי שֶׁהִכַּרְתֶּם אוֹתוֹ אֲשֶׁר הוּא מֵרֵאשִׁית. כּוֹתֵב אֲנִי לָכֶם, בַּחוּרִים, מִפְּנֵי שֶׁנִּצַּחְתֶּם אֶת הָרַע. ¹⁴כָּתַבְתִּי לָכֶם, יְלָדִים, מִפְּנֵי שֶׁהִכַּרְתֶּם אֶת הָאָב. כָּתַבְתִּי לָכֶם, אָבוֹת, מִפְּנֵי שֶׁהִכַּרְתֶּם אוֹתוֹ אֲשֶׁר הוּא מֵרֵאשִׁית. כָּתַבְתִּי לָכֶם, בַּחוּרִים, מִפְּנֵי שֶׁאַתֶּם חֲזָקִים וּדְבַר אֱלֹהִים קַיָּם בְּקִרְבְּכֶם וְנִצַּחְתֶּם אֶת הָרַע.

¹⁵אַל תֹּאהֲבוּ אֶת הָעוֹלָם, אַף לֹא אֶת מַה שֶּׁבָּעוֹלָם. אִישׁ אִם יֹאהַב אֶת הָעוֹלָם אֵין בּוֹ אַהֲבַת הָאָב; ¹⁶כִּי כָּל אֲשֶׁר בָּעוֹלָם – תַּאֲוַת בְּשָׂרִים, תַּאֲוַת הָעֵינַיִם וְגַאֲוַת הַנְּכָסִים – לֹא מִן הָאָב הוּא כִּי אִם מִן הָעוֹלָם. ¹⁷וְהָעוֹלָם עוֹבֵר עִם תַּאֲווֹתָיו, אַךְ הָעוֹשֶׂה אֶת רְצוֹן אֱלֹהִים עוֹמֵד לָעַד.

¹⁸יְלָדַי, זֹאת הַשָּׁעָה הָאַחֲרוֹנָה. וּכְמוֹ שֶׁשְּׁמַעְתֶּם כִּי יָבוֹא צוֹרֵר הַמָּשִׁיחַ, גַּם עַכְשָׁו קָמוּ צוֹרְרֵי מָשִׁיחַ רַבִּים; מִכָּאן יוֹדְעִים אָנוּ שֶׁזּוֹהִי הַשָּׁעָה הָאַחֲרוֹנָה. ¹⁹הַלָּלוּ מִקִּרְבֵּנוּ יָצְאוּ, אֲבָל לֹא מִשֶּׁלָּנוּ הָיוּ; כִּי אִלּוּ הָיוּ מִשֶּׁלָּנוּ, הָיוּ נִשְׁאָרִים אִתָּנוּ, אַךְ הֵם יָצְאוּ לְמַעַן יִוָּדַע שֶׁכֻּלָּם אֵינָם מִשֶּׁלָּנוּ. ²⁰וְאַתֶּם יֵשׁ לָכֶם הַמִּשְׁחָה מֵאֵת הַקָּדוֹשׁ, וְכֻלְּכֶם יוֹדְעִים. ²¹כָּתַבְתִּי אֲלֵיכֶם לֹא מִפְּנֵי שֶׁאֵינְכֶם יוֹדְעִים אֶת הָאֱמֶת, אֶלָּא מִפְּנֵי שֶׁאַתֶּם יוֹדְעִים אוֹתָהּ וְיוֹדְעִים שֶׁכָּל שֶׁקֶר אֵינֶנּוּ מִן הָאֱמֶת. ²²מִי הוּא דּוֹבֵר שֶׁקֶר בִּלְתִּי אִם הַכּוֹפֵר בְּכָךְ שֶׁיֵּשׁוּעַ הוּא הַמָּשִׁיחַ? זֶה הוּא צוֹרֵר הַמָּשִׁיחַ, הַכּוֹפֵר בָּאָב וּבַבֵּן. ²³כָּל הַכּוֹפֵר בַּבֵּן גַּם הָאָב אֵין

²⁴Therefore let that abide in you which you heard from the beginning. If what you heard from the beginning abides in you, you also will abide in the Son and in the Father. ²⁵And this is the promise that He has promised us—eternal life.

²⁶These things I have written to you concerning those who *try to* deceive you. ²⁷But the anointing which you have received from Him abides in you, and you do not need that anyone teach you; but as the same anointing teaches you concerning all things, and is true, and is not a lie, and just as it has taught you, you will abide in Him.

²⁸And now, little children, abide in Him, that when He appears, we may have confidence and not be ashamed before Him at His coming. ²⁹If you know that He is righteous, you know that everyone who practices righteousness is born of Him.

3 Behold what manner of love the Father has bestowed on us, that we should be called children of God! Therefore the world does not know us, because it did not know Him. ²Beloved, now we are children of God; and it has not yet been revealed what we shall be, but we know that when He is revealed, we shall be like Him, for we shall see Him as He is. ³And everyone who has this hope in Him purifies himself, just as He is pure.

⁴Whoever commits sin also commits lawlessness, and sin is lawlessness. ⁵And you know that He was manifested to take away our sins, and in Him there is no sin. ⁶Whoever abides in Him does not sin. Whoever sins has neither seen Him nor known Him.

⁷Little children, let no one deceive you. He who practices righteousness is righteous, just as He is righteous. ⁸He who sins is of the devil, for the devil has sinned from the beginning. For this purpose the Son of God was manifested, that He might destroy the works of the devil. ⁹Whoever has been born of God does not sin, for His seed remains in him; and he cannot sin, because he has been born of God.

¹⁰In this the children of God and the children of the devil are manifest: Whoever does not practice righteousness is not of God, nor *is* he who does not love his brother. ¹¹For this is the message that you heard from the beginning, that we should love one another, ¹²not as Cain *who* was of the wicked one and murdered his brother. And why did he murder him? Because his works were evil and his brother's righteous.

¹³Do not marvel, my brethren, if the world hates you. ¹⁴We know that we have passed from death to life, because we love the brethren. He who does not

לו; הַמּוֹדֶה בַּבֵּן יֶשׁ לוֹ גַּם הָאָב. ²⁴אַתֶּם, מַה שֶּׁשְּׁמַעְתֶּם מֵרֵאשִׁית יִשָּׁאֶר נָא בְּקִרְבְּכֶם. אִם יִשָּׁאֵר בְּקִרְבְּכֶם מַה שֶּׁשְּׁמַעְתֶּם מֵרֵאשִׁית, אֲזַי גַּם אַתֶּם תִּשָּׁאֲרוּ בַּבֵּן וּבָאָב. ²⁵וְזֹּאתִי הַהַבְטָחָה שֶׁהוּא הִבְטִיחַ לָנוּ – חַיֵּי עוֹלָם.

²⁶אֶת הַדְּבָרִים הָאֵלֶּה כָּתַבְתִּי לָכֶם עַל־אוֹדוֹת הַמַּתְעִים אֶתְכֶם. ²⁷וְהַמְּשִׁיחָה שֶׁאַתֶּם קִבַּלְתֶּם מֵאִתּוֹ נִשְׁאֶרֶת בְּקִרְבְּכֶם וְאֵינְכֶם צְרִיכִים לְמִישֶׁהוּ שֶׁיְּלַמֵּד אֶתְכֶם, אֶלָּא כְּמוֹ שֶׁמְּשִׁיחָתוֹ מְלַמֶּדֶת אֶתְכֶם עַל־אוֹדוֹת הַכֹּל – וְהִיא אֱמֶת וְאֵינֶנָּה כָּזָב – לְפִי מַה שֶּׁלִּמְּדָה אֶתְכֶם עִמְדוּ בּוֹ.

²⁸וְעַתָּה, יֶלֶד, עִמְדוּ בּוֹ, כְּדֵי שֶׁיִּהְיֶה לָנוּ עֹז כַּאֲשֶׁר יִתְגַּלֶּה וְלֹא נֵבוֹשׁ מִפָּנָיו בְּבוֹאוֹ. ²⁹אִם יוֹדְעִים אַתֶּם שֶׁהוּא צַדִּיק, יוֹדְעִים אַתֶּם שֶׁגַּם כָּל עוֹשֵׂה צְדָקָה נוֹלַד מִמֶּנּוּ.

ג רְאוּ אֵיזוֹ אַהֲבָה נָתַן לָנוּ הָאָב לְהִקָּרֵא יַלְדֵי אֱלֹהִים! וְאָכֵן כָּךְ אֲנַחְנוּ. מִשּׁוּם כָּךְ הָעוֹלָם אֵינוֹ מַכִּיר אוֹתָנוּ, מִשּׁוּם שֶׁלֹּא הִכִּיר אוֹתוֹ. ²אֲהוּבַי, עַכְשָׁו יַלְדֵי אֱלֹהִים אֲנַחְנוּ, וְעוֹד לֹא נִגְלָה מַה נִּהְיֶה. יוֹדְעִים אָנוּ שֶׁבְּהִגָּלוֹתוֹ נִהְיֶה כָּמוֹהוּ, כִּי נִרְאֵהוּ כְּמוֹ שֶׁהוּא. ³וְכָל מִי שֶׁנִּסְמָךְ עָלָיו בַּתִּקְוָה הַזֹּאת, מְטַהֵר אֶת עַצְמוֹ כְּפִי שֶׁטָּהוֹר הָאֶחָד הַהוּא.

⁴כָּל מִי שֶׁחוֹטֵא גַּם עוֹבֵר עַל הַתּוֹרָה; הַחֵטְא הוּא עֲבֵרָה עַל הַתּוֹרָה. ⁵אַתֶּם יוֹדְעִים שֶׁהוּא נִגְלָה כְּדֵי לָשֵׂאת אֶת חֲטָאֵינוּ, וּבוֹ אֵין חֵטְא. ⁶כָּל הָעוֹמֵד בּוֹ לֹא יֶחֱטָא; כָּל הַחוֹטֵא לֹא רָאָהוּ אַף לֹא יְדָעוֹ. ⁷יְלָדַי, אַל יַתְעֶה אֶתְכֶם אִישׁ: הָעוֹשֶׂה צְדָקָה צַדִּיק, כְּשֵׁם שֶׁהוּא צַדִּיק. ⁸הָעוֹשֶׂה חֵטְא מִן הַשָּׂטָן הוּא, כִּי הַשָּׂטָן חוֹטֵא מֵרֵאשִׁית. לָזֹאת נִגְלָה בֶּן־הָאֱלֹהִים, לְהָפֵר אֶת פְּעֻלּוֹת הַשָּׂטָן. ⁹כָּל הַנּוֹלָד מֵאֱלֹהִים אֵינֶנּוּ חוֹטֵא, כִּי זַרְעוֹ נִשְׁאָר בּוֹ; וְאֵין הוּא יָכוֹל לַחֲטֹא, כִּי מֵאֱלֹהִים נוֹלַד. ¹⁰בָּזֶה יִוָּדְעוּ יַלְדֵי הָאֱלֹהִים וְיַלְדֵי הַשָּׂטָן: כָּל מִי שֶׁאֵינוֹ עוֹשֶׂה צְדָקָה אֵינֶנּוּ מֵאֱלֹהִים, וְכֵן מִי שֶׁאֵינוֹ אוֹהֵב אֶת אָחִיו.

¹¹הֵן זֶהוּ דְּבַר הַבְּשׂוֹרָה אֲשֶׁר שְׁמַעְתֶּם מֵרֵאשִׁית, שֶׁנֶּאֱהַב אִישׁ אֶת רֵעֵהוּ; ¹²לֹא כְּקַיִן אֲשֶׁר הָיָה מִן הָרַע וְהָרַג אֶת אָחִיו. וּמַדּוּעַ הֲרָגוֹ? מִפְּנֵי שֶׁמַּעֲשָׂיו הָיוּ רָעִים, אַךְ מַעֲשֵׂי אָחִיו מַעֲשֵׂי צֶדֶק. ¹³אַחַי, אַל תִּתְמְהוּ אִם הָעוֹלָם שׂוֹנֵא אֶתְכֶם. ¹⁴אֲנַחְנוּ יוֹדְעִים כִּי עָבַרְנוּ מִן הַמָּוֶת אֶל הַחַיִּים, שֶׁכֵּן אוֹהֲבִים אֲנַחְנוּ

love *his* brother abides in death. 15 Whoever hates his brother is a murderer, and you know that no murderer has eternal life abiding in him.

16 By this we know love, because He laid down His life for us. And we also ought to lay down *our* lives for the brethren. 17 But whoever has this world's goods, and sees his brother in need, and shuts up his heart from him, how does the love of God abide in him?

18 My little children, let us not love in word or in tongue, but in deed and in truth. 19 And by this we know that we are of the truth, and shall assure our hearts before Him. 20 For if our heart condemns us, God is greater than our heart, and knows all things. 21 Beloved, if our heart does not condemn us, we have confidence toward God. 22 And whatever we ask we receive from Him, because we keep His commandments and do those things that are pleasing in His sight. 23 And this is His commandment: that we should believe on the name of His Son Jesus Christ and love one another, as He gave us commandment.

24 Now he who keeps His commandments abides in Him, and He in him. And by this we know that He abides in us, by the Spirit whom He has given us.

4 Beloved, do not believe every spirit, but test the spirits, whether they are of God; because many false prophets have gone out into the world. 2 By this you know the Spirit of God: Every spirit that confesses that Jesus Christ has come in the flesh is of God, 3 and every spirit that does not confess that Jesus Christ has come in the flesh is not of God. And this is the *spirit* of the Antichrist, which you have heard was coming, and is now already in the world.

4 You are of God, little children, and have overcome them, because He who is in you is greater than he who is in the world. 5 They are of the world. Therefore they speak *as* of the world, and the world hears them. 6 We are of God. He who knows God hears us; he who is not of God does not hear us. By this we know the spirit of truth and the spirit of error.

7 Beloved, let us love one another, for love is of God; and everyone who loves is born of God and knows God. 8 He who does not love does not know God, for God is love. 9 In this the love of God was manifested toward us, that God has sent His only begotten Son into the world, that we might live through Him. 10 In this is love, not that we loved God, but that He loved us and sent His Son *to be* the propitiation for our sins. 11 Beloved, if God so loved us, we also ought to love one another.

אֶת אָחִינוּ. אִישׁ אֲשֶׁר אֵינוֹ אוֹהֵב נִשְׁאָר בַּמָּוֶת. 15 כָּל הַשּׂוֹנֵא אֶת אָחִיו רוֹצֵחַ הוּא. וְיוֹדְעִים אַתֶּם שֶׁכָּל רוֹצֵחַ אֵין חַיֵּי עוֹלָם מִתְקַיְּמִים בּוֹ. 16 בְּזֹאת הִכַּרְנוּ מַה הִיא אַהֲבָה, בַּעֲבֻדָּה שֶׁהוּא מָסַר אֶת נַפְשׁוֹ בַּעֲדֵנוּ. גַּם אֲנַחְנוּ חַיָּבִים לִמְסֹר אֶת נַפְשֵׁנוּ בְּעַד אַחֵינוּ. 17 מִי שֶׁיֵּשׁ לוֹ נִכְסֵי הָעוֹלָם וְהוּא רוֹאֶה אֶת אָחִיו בְּמַחְסוֹר וּמוֹנֵעַ אֶת רַחֲמָיו מִמֶּנּוּ, אֵיךְ תַּעֲמֹד בּוֹ אַהֲבַת אֱלֹהִים? 18 יְלָדַי, אַל נָא נֶאֱהַב בְּמִלִּים וּבְדִבּוּר, כִּי אִם בְּפֹעַל וּבֶאֱמֶת.

19 בָּזֶה נֵדַע כִּי מִן הָאֱמֶת אֲנַחְנוּ וְנַשְׁקִיט אֶת לְבָבֵנוּ לְפָנָיו, 20 שֶׁכֵּן אִם לִבֵּנוּ יַרְשִׁיעַ אוֹתָנוּ, הָאֱלֹהִים גָּדוֹל מִלִּבֵּנוּ וְהוּא יוֹדֵעַ הַכֹּל. 21 אֲהוּבַי, אִם לִבֵּנוּ אֵינוֹ מַרְשִׁיעַ אוֹתָנוּ, עֹז לָנוּ לִפְנֵי אֱלֹהִים; 22 וְכָל אֲשֶׁר נְבַקֵּשׁ נְקַבֵּל מִמֶּנּוּ, מִפְּנֵי שֶׁשּׁוֹמְרִים אָנוּ אֶת מִצְוֹתָיו וְעוֹשִׂים אֶת הַטּוֹב בְּעֵינָיו. 23 זֹאת מִצְוָתוֹ: לְהַאֲמִין בְּשֵׁם בְּנוֹ יֵשׁוּעַ הַמָּשִׁיחַ וְלֶאֱהֹב זֶה אֶת זֶה כְּפִי שֶׁצִּוָּנוּ. 24 הַשּׁוֹמֵר אֶת מִצְוֹת אֱלֹהִים שׁוֹכֵן בֵּאלֹהִים וֵאלֹהִים בּוֹ. וּבְזֹאת נֵדַע שֶׁהוּא שׁוֹכֵן בָּנוּ: בָּרוּחַ אֲשֶׁר נָתַן לָנוּ.

ד אֲהוּבַי, אַל תַּאֲמִינוּ לְכָל רוּחַ, כִּי אִם בַּחֲנוּ אֶת הָרוּחוֹת אִם מֵאֱלֹהִים הֵן, כִּי נְבִיאֵי שֶׁקֶר רַבִּים יָצְאוּ לָעוֹלָם. 2 בָּזֶה תַּכִּירוּ אֶת רוּחַ אֱלֹהִים: כָּל רוּחַ הַמּוֹדָה כִּי יֵשׁוּעַ הַמָּשִׁיחַ בָּא בִּלְבוּשׁ בָּשָׂר, מֵאֱלֹהִים הִיא; 3 וְכָל רוּחַ אֲשֶׁר אֵינֶנָּה מוֹדָה בְּיֵשׁוּעַ לֹא מֵאֱלֹהִים הִיא. זוֹהִי רוּחַ צוֹרֵר הַמָּשִׁיחַ אֲשֶׁר שְׁמַעְתֶּם כִּי תָבוֹא, וּכְבָר כָּעֵת הִיא בָּעוֹלָם. 4 אַתֶּם, יְלָדַי, מֵאֱלֹהִים אַתֶּם, וְנִצַּחְתֶּם אוֹתָם, שֶׁכֵּן הוּא אֲשֶׁר בָּכֶם גָּדוֹל מִזֶּה אֲשֶׁר בָּעוֹלָם. 5 הֵם מִן הָעוֹלָם; לָכֵן הֵם מְדַבְּרִים דְּבָרִים הַנּוֹבְעִים מִן הָעוֹלָם וְהָעוֹלָם שׁוֹמֵעַ לָהֶם. 6 אֲנַחְנוּ מֵאֱלֹהִים. הַיּוֹדֵעַ אֶת אֱלֹהִים שׁוֹמֵעַ לָנוּ; מִי שֶׁאֵינוֹ מֵאֱלֹהִים אֵינֶנּוּ שׁוֹמֵעַ לָנוּ. מִתּוֹךְ כָּךְ מַכִּירִים אָנוּ אֶת רוּחַ הָאֱמֶת וְאֶת רוּחַ הַתָּעוּת.

7 אֲהוּבַי, נֹאהַב נָא אִישׁ אֶת רֵעֵהוּ, כִּי הָאַהֲבָה מֵאֱלֹהִים הִיא; וְכָל מִי שֶׁאוֹהֵב נוֹלַד מֵאֱלֹהִים וְיוֹדֵעַ אֶת אֱלֹהִים. 8 מִי שֶׁאֵינוֹ אוֹהֵב אֵינוֹ יוֹדֵעַ אֶת אֱלֹהִים, שֶׁכֵּן הָאֱלֹהִים הוּא אַהֲבָה. 9 בְּזֹאת נִגְלְתָה אַהֲבַת הָאֱלֹהִים בָּנוּ, בַּעֲבֻדָּה שֶׁאֱלֹהִים שָׁלַח אֶת בְּנוֹ יְחִידוֹ לָעוֹלָם לְמַעַן נִחְיֶה בְּכוֹחוֹ. 10 בְּזֹאת הִיא הָאַהֲבָה, לֹא שֶׁאֲנַחְנוּ אָהַבְנוּ אֶת אֱלֹהִים, אֶלָּא שֶׁהוּא אָהַב אוֹתָנוּ וְשָׁלַח אֶת בְּנוֹ לִהְיוֹת כַּפָּרָה עַל חֲטָאֵינוּ. 11 אֲהוּבַי, אִם כָּכָה אָהַב אוֹתָנוּ הָאֱלֹהִים,

[12] No one has seen God at any time. If we love one another, God abides in us, and His love has been perfected in us. [13] By this we know that we abide in Him, and He in us, because He has given us of His Spirit. [14] And we have seen and testify that the Father has sent the Son as Savior of the world. [15] Whoever confesses that Jesus is the Son of God, God abides in him, and he in God. [16] And we have known and believed the love that God has for us. God is love, and he who abides in love abides in God, and God in him.

[17] Love has been perfected among us in this: that we may have boldness in the day of judgment; because as He is, so are we in this world. [18] There is no fear in love; but perfect love casts out fear, because fear involves torment. But he who fears has not been made perfect in love. [19] We love Him because He first loved us.

[20] If someone says, "I love God," and hates his brother, he is a liar; for he who does not love his brother whom he has seen, how can he love God whom he has not seen? [21] And this commandment we have from Him: that he who loves God must love his brother also.

5 Whoever believes that Jesus is the Christ is born of God, and everyone who loves Him who begot also loves him who is begotten of Him. [2] By this we know that we love the children of God, when we love God and keep His commandments. [3] For this is the love of God, that we keep His commandments. And His commandments are not burdensome. [4] For whatever is born of God overcomes the world. And this is the victory that has overcome the world—our faith. [5] Who is he who overcomes the world, but he who believes that Jesus is the Son of God?

[6] This is He who came by water and blood—Jesus Christ; not only by water, but by water and blood. And it is the Spirit who bears witness, because the Spirit is truth. [7] For there are three that bear witness in heaven: the Father, the Word, and the Holy Spirit; and these three are one. [8] And there are three that bear witness on earth: the Spirit, the water, and the blood; and these three agree as one.

[9] If we receive the witness of men, the witness of God is greater; for this is the witness of God which He has testified of His Son. [10] He who believes in the Son of God has the witness in himself; he who does not believe God has made Him a liar, because he has not believed the testimony that God has given of His Son. [11] And this is the testimony: that God has given us eternal life, and this life is in His Son. [12] He who has the Son has life; he who does

גַּם אֲנַחְנוּ חַיָּבִים לֶאֱהֹב אִישׁ אֶת רֵעֵהוּ. 12 אֶת הָאֱלֹהִים לֹא רָאָה אִישׁ מֵעוֹלָם. אִם אֲנַחְנוּ אוֹהֲבִים זֶה אֶת זֶה, הָאֱלֹהִים שׁוֹכֵן בְּקִרְבֵּנוּ וְאַהֲבָתוֹ נִשְׁלְמָה בָּנוּ. 13 בָּזֹאת יוֹדְעִים אָנוּ שֶׁעוֹמְדִים אָנוּ בוֹ וְהוּא בָּנוּ, כִּי נָתַן לָנוּ מֵרוּחוֹ. 14 וַאֲנַחְנוּ הִתְבּוֹנַנּוּ וַהֲרֵינוּ מְעִידִים כִּי הָאָב שָׁלַח אֶת הַבֵּן מוֹשִׁיעַ הָעוֹלָם. 15 כָּל הַמּוֹדֶה כִּי יֵשׁוּעַ הוּא בֶּן־הָאֱלֹהִים, אֱלֹהִים שׁוֹכֵן בּוֹ וְהוּא בֵּאלֹהִים. 16 וַאֲנַחְנוּ הִכַּרְנוּ אֶת הָאַהֲבָה שֶׁאֱלֹהִים מְקַיֵּם בָּנוּ וְהֶאֱמַנּוּ בָהּ. הָאֱלֹהִים הוּא אַהֲבָה; הָעוֹמֵד בָּאַהֲבָה עוֹמֵד בֵּאלֹהִים וֵאלֹהִים עוֹמֵד בּוֹ. 17 בָּזֶה נִשְׁלְמָה הָאַהֲבָה אֶצְלֵנוּ בְּאֹפֶן שֶׁיִּהְיֶה לָנוּ בִּטָּחוֹן בְּיוֹם הַדִּין, שֶׁכֵּן כְּדֶרֶךְ שֶׁהָאֶחָד הַהוּא כֵּן גַּם אֲנַחְנוּ בָּעוֹלָם הַזֶּה. 18 אֵין פַּחַד בָּאַהֲבָה. אַדְּרַבָּא, הָאַהֲבָה הַשְּׁלֵמָה מְגָרֶשֶׁת אֶת הַפַּחַד. הֵן הַפַּחַד כָּרוּךְ בְּעֹנֶשׁ, וְהַמְּפַחֵד אֵינֶנּוּ שָׁלֵם בָּאַהֲבָה. 19 אֲנַחְנוּ אוֹהֲבִים מִפְּנֵי שֶׁהוּא אָהַב אוֹתָנוּ תְּחִלָּה. 20 אִישׁ אִם יֹאמַר "אוֹהֵב אֲנִי אֶת אֱלֹהִים" וְהוּא שׂוֹנֵא אֶת אָחִיו, שַׁקְרָן הוּא; כִּי מִי שֶׁאֵינֶנּוּ אוֹהֵב אֶת אָחִיו אֲשֶׁר הוּא רוֹאֶה אוֹתוֹ לֹא יוּכַל לֶאֱהֹב אֶת הָאֱלֹהִים אֲשֶׁר הוּא אֵינֶנּוּ רוֹאֶה אוֹתוֹ. 21 מִצְוָה זֹאת קִבַּלְנוּ מִמֶּנּוּ, שֶׁהָאוֹהֵב אֶת אֱלֹהִים יֹאהַב גַּם אֶת אָחִיו.

ה כָּל הַמַּאֲמִין כִּי יֵשׁוּעַ הוּא הַמָּשִׁיחַ, נוֹלַד מֵאֱלֹהִים. וְכָל הָאוֹהֵב אֶת הַמּוֹלִיד אוֹהֵב גַּם אֶת מִי שֶׁנּוֹלַד מִמֶּנּוּ. 2 בָּזֹאת נֵדַע כִּי אוֹהֲבִים אָנוּ אֶת יַלְדֵי אֱלֹהִים: בִּהְיוֹתֵנוּ אוֹהֲבִים אֶת אֱלֹהִים וּמְקַיְּמִים אֶת מִצְוֹתָיו. 3 הֵן זֹאת הִיא אַהֲבַת אֱלֹהִים, שֶׁנִּשְׁמֹר אֶת מִצְוֹתָיו. וּמִצְוֹתָיו אֵינָן קָשׁוֹת, 4 שֶׁכֵּן כָּל הַנּוֹלָד מֵאֵת אֱלֹהִים מְנַצֵּחַ אֶת הָעוֹלָם. וְזֶהוּ הַנִּצָּחוֹן הַמְנַצֵּחַ אֶת הָעוֹלָם – אֱמוּנָתֵנוּ. 5 מִי הַמְנַצֵּחַ אֶת הָעוֹלָם בִּלְתִּי אִם הַמַּאֲמִין כִּי יֵשׁוּעַ הוּא בֶּן הָאֱלֹהִים? 6 זֶה הוּא אֲשֶׁר בָּא בְּמַיִם וּבְדָם – יֵשׁוּעַ הַמָּשִׁיחַ; לֹא בְּמַיִם בִּלְבַד, כִּי אִם בְּמַיִם וּבְדָם. וְהָרוּחַ הִיא הַמְעִידָה, שֶׁהֲרֵי הָרוּחַ הִיא הָאֱמֶת. 7 הֵן שְׁלוֹשָׁה הֵם הַמְעִידִים: 8 הָרוּחַ וְהַמַּיִם וְהַדָּם, וּשְׁלָשְׁתָּם לְשֵׁם הָאֶחָד הֵם. 9 אִם מְקַבְּלִים אָנוּ עֵדוּת בְּנֵי אָדָם, עֵדוּת אֱלֹהִים גְּדוֹלָה מִמֶּנָּה, שֶׁכֵּן זֹאת עֵדוּת אֱלֹהִים אֲשֶׁר הוּא הֵעִיד עַל בְּנוֹ. 10 הַמַּאֲמִין בְּבֶן־הָאֱלֹהִים הָעֵדוּת נִמְצֵאת בְּקִרְבּוֹ. מִי שֶׁאֵינוֹ מַאֲמִין לֵאלֹהִים שָׂם אוֹתוֹ לְכוֹזֵב, מִפְּנֵי שֶׁלֹּא הֶאֱמִין בָּעֵדוּת אֲשֶׁר הֵעִיד אֱלֹהִים עַל בְּנוֹ. 11 וְזֹאת הִיא הָעֵדוּת: אֱלֹהִים נָתַן לָנוּ חַיֵּי עוֹלָם, וְהַחַיִּים הָאֵלֶּה בִּבְנוֹ הֵם. 12 מִי

not have the Son of God does not have life.
13 These things I have written to you who believe in
the name of the Son of God, that you may know
that you have eternal life, and that you may
continue to believe in the name of the Son of God.

14 Now this is the confidence that we have in
Him, that if we ask anything according to His will,
He hears us. 15 And if we know that He hears us,
whatever we ask, we know that we have the
petitions that we have asked of Him.

16 If anyone sees his brother sinning a sin *which
does* not *lead* to death, he will ask, and He will give
him life for those who commit sin not *leading* to
death. There is sin *leading* to death. I do not say
that he should pray about that. 17 All unrighteousness is sin, and there is sin not *leading* to death.

18 We know that whoever is born of God does
not sin; but he who has been born of God keeps
himself, and the wicked one does not touch him.

19 We know that we are of God, and the whole
world lies *under the sway of* the wicked one.

20 And we know that the Son of God has come
and has given us an understanding, that we may
know Him who is true; and we are in Him who is
true, in His Son Jesus Christ. This is the true God
and eternal life.

21 Little children, keep yourselves from idols.
Amen.

שֶׁיֶּשׁ לוֹ הַבֵּן יֶשׁ לוֹ הַחַיִּים. מִי שֶׁאֵין לוֹ הַבֵּן אֵין לוֹ
הַחַיִּים.

13 זֹאת כָּתַבְתִּי אֲלֵיכֶם, הַמַּאֲמִינִים בְּשֵׁם בֶּן־
הָאֱלֹהִים, לְמַעַן תֵּדְעוּ שֶׁיֶּשׁ לָכֶם חַיֵּי עוֹלָם.
14 וּבְטְחוֹנֵנוּ בוֹ שֶׁאִם נְבַקֵּשׁ דָּבָר כִּרְצוֹנוֹ יִשְׁמַע
אוֹתָנוּ. 15 וְאִם יוֹדְעִים אָנוּ שֶׁהוּא שׁוֹמֵעַ אוֹתָנוּ בְּכָל
אֲשֶׁר נְבַקֵּשׁ, יוֹדְעִים אָנוּ כִּי הַמִּשְׁאָלוֹת שֶׁבִּקַּשְׁנוּ
מִמֶּנּוּ נִתָּנוֹת לָנוּ.

16 אִישׁ אִם יִרְאֶה אֶת אָחִיו חוֹטֵא חֵטְא שֶׁאֵינֶנּוּ
חֵטְא־מָוֶת, יִתְפַּלֵּל, וֵאלֹהִים יִתֵּן לוֹ חַיִּים, לָאֵלֶּה
שֶׁלֹּא חָטְאוּ חֵטְא־מָוֶת. יֶשׁ חֵטְא־מָוֶת; עַל זֶה אֵינֶנִּי
אוֹמֵר שֶׁיִּתְפַּלֵּל. 17 כָּל עַוְלָה חֵטְא הִיא, אַךְ יֶשׁ חֵטְא
שֶׁאֵינוֹ חֵטְא־מָוֶת. 18 יוֹדְעִים אָנוּ כִּי כָּל מִי שֶׁנּוֹלַד
מֵאֱלֹהִים אֵינֶנּוּ חוֹטֵא; הוּא אֲשֶׁר נוֹלַד מֵאֱלֹהִים
שׁוֹמֵר אוֹתוֹ וְהָרַע אֵינוֹ נוֹגֵעַ בּוֹ. 19 יוֹדְעִים אָנוּ כִּי
מֵאֱלֹהִים אֲנַחְנוּ וְכִי הָעוֹלָם כֻּלּוֹ שָׁרוּי בְּרָע.
20 וְיוֹדְעִים אָנוּ שֶׁבֶּן־הָאֱלֹהִים בָּא וְנָתַן לָנוּ בִּינָה
לָדַעַת אֶת הָאֲמִתִּי; וַאֲנַחְנוּ בָּאֲמִתִּי, בִּבְנוֹ יֵשׁוּעַ
הַמָּשִׁיחַ. הוּא הָאֵל הָאֲמִתִּי וְחַיֵּי עוֹלָם. 21 יְלָדַי,
הִשָּׁמְרוּ לָכֶם מִן הָאֱלִילִים.

The Second Epistle of

JOHN

The Elder,

To the elect lady and her children, whom I love in truth, and not only I, but also all those who have known the truth, [2]because of the truth which abides in us and will be with us forever:

[3]Grace, mercy, *and* peace will be with you from God the Father and from the Lord Jesus Christ, the Son of the Father, in truth and love.

[4]I rejoiced greatly that I have found *some* of your children walking in truth, as we received commandment from the Father. [5]And now I plead with you, lady, not as though I wrote a new commandment to you, but that which we have had from the beginning: that we love one another. [6]This is love, that we walk according to His commandments. This is the commandment, that as you have heard from the beginning, you should walk in it.

[7]For many deceivers have gone out into the world who do not confess Jesus Christ *as* coming in the flesh. This is a deceiver and an antichrist. [8]Look to yourselves, that we do not lose those things we worked for, but *that* we may receive a full reward.

[9]Whoever transgresses and does not abide in the doctrine of Christ does not have God. He who abides in the doctrine of Christ has both the Father and the Son. [10]If anyone comes to you and does not bring this doctrine, do not receive him into your house nor greet him; [11]for he who greets him shares in his evil deeds.

[12]Having many things to write to you, I did not wish *to do so* with paper and ink; but I hope to come to you and speak face to face, that our joy may be full.

[13]The children of your elect sister greet you. Amen.

אִגֶּרֶת יוֹחָנָן הַשְּׁנִיָּה

‏1 מֵאֵת הַזָּקֵן אֶל הַגְּבִירָה הַבְּחִירָה וְאֶל יְלָדֶיהָ אֲשֶׁר אֲנִי אוֹהֵב בֶּאֱמֶת, וְלֹא רַק אֲנִי אֶלָּא גַּם כָּל יוֹדְעֵי הָאֱמֶת; ‏2 וְזֹאת הוֹדוֹת לָאֱמֶת הָעוֹמֶדֶת בְּקִרְבֵּנוּ וַאֲשֶׁר תִּהְיֶה עִמָּנוּ לְעוֹלָם. ‏3 חֶסֶד וְרַחֲמִים וְשָׁלוֹם יִהְיוּ עִמָּנוּ מֵאֵת הָאֱלֹהִים הָאָב וּמֵאֵת הָאָדוֹן יֵשׁוּעַ הַמָּשִׁיחַ בֶּן הָאָב, בֶּאֱמֶת וּבְאַהֲבָה.

‏4 שָׂמַחְתִּי מְאֹד כִּי מָצָאתִי מִקֶּרֶב יְלָדַיִךְ מִתְהַלְּכִים בֶּאֱמֶת, כַּמִּצְוָה אֲשֶׁר קִבַּלְנוּ מֵאֵת הָאָב. ‏5 וְעַכְשָׁו מְבַקֵּשׁ אֲנִי מִמֵּךְ, הַגְּבִירָה, לֹא כְּכוֹתֵב אֵלַיִךְ מִצְוָה חֲדָשָׁה, כִּי אִם מִצְוָה שֶׁהָיְתָה לָנוּ מֵרֵאשִׁית – שֶׁנֹּאהַב אִישׁ אֶת רֵעֵהוּ. ‏6 וְזֹאת הִיא הָאַהֲבָה: שֶׁנִּתְהַלֵּךְ עַל־פִּי מִצְווֹתָיו. זֹאת הִיא הַמִּצְוָה כְּפִי שֶׁשְּׁמַעְתֶּם מֵרֵאשִׁית וַעֲלֵיכֶם לְהִתְהַלֵּךְ בָּהּ. ‏7 הֵן מַתְעִים רַבִּים בָּאוּ לָעוֹלָם, אֲשֶׁר אֵינָם מוֹדִים בְּיֵשׁוּעַ הַמָּשִׁיחַ הַבָּא בְּלִבּוּשׁ בָּשָׂר. זֶהוּ הַמַּתְעֶה וְצוֹרֵר הַמָּשִׁיחַ. ‏8 הִזָּהֲרוּ, כְּדֵי שֶׁלֹּא תְּאַבְּדוּ אֶת פְּרִי פָּעֳלְכֶם אֶלָּא שֶׁתְּקַבְּלוּ שָׂכָר מָלֵא. ‏9 כָּל הַמַּרְחִיק לֶכֶת וְאֵינוֹ עוֹמֵד בְּתוֹרַת הַמָּשִׁיחַ, אֵין לוֹ אֱלֹהִים. הָעוֹמֵד בְּתוֹרַת הַמָּשִׁיחַ יֵשׁ לוֹ גַּם הָאָב וְגַם הַבֵּן. ‏10 אִישׁ אִם יָבוֹא אֲלֵיכֶם וְלֹא יָבִיא אֶת הַתּוֹרָה הַזֹּאת, אַל תְּקַבְּלוּ אוֹתוֹ הַבַּיְתָה וְאַל תֹּאמְרוּ לוֹ "שָׁלוֹם"; ‏11 כִּי הַמְבָרֵךְ אוֹתוֹ בְּבִרְכַּת שָׁלוֹם מִשְׁתַּתֵּף בְּמַעֲשָׂיו הָרָעִים.

‏12 הַרְבֵּה יֵשׁ לִי לִכְתֹּב אֲלֵיכֶם, אַךְ לֹא רָצִיתִי בִּנְיָר וּבִדְיוֹ. אֲנִי מְקַוֶּה לָבוֹא אֲלֵיכֶם וּלְדַבֵּר פֶּה אֶל פֶּה כְּדֵי שֶׁתִּהְיֶה שִׂמְחָתֵנוּ שְׁלֵמָה. ‏13 יַלְדֵי אֲחוֹתֵךְ הַבְּחִירָה דּוֹרְשִׁים בִּשְׁלוֹמֵךְ.

The Third Epistle of
JOHN

The Elder,

To the beloved Gaius, whom I love in truth:

[2] Beloved, I pray that you may prosper in all things and be in health, just as your soul prospers. [3] For I rejoiced greatly when brethren came and testified of the truth *that is* in you, just as you walk in the truth. [4] I have no greater joy than to hear that my children walk in truth.

[5] Beloved, you do faithfully whatever you do for the brethren and for strangers, [6] who have borne witness of your love before the church. *If* you send them forward on their journey in a manner worthy of God, you will do well, [7] because they went forth for His name's sake, taking nothing from the Gentiles. [8] We therefore ought to receive such, that we may become fellow workers for the truth.

[9] I wrote to the church, but Diotrephes, who loves to have the preeminence among them, does not receive us. [10] Therefore, if I come, I will call to mind his deeds which he does, prating against us with malicious words. And not content with that, he himself does not receive the brethren, and forbids those who wish to, putting *them* out of the church.

[11] Beloved, do not imitate what is evil, but what is good. He who does good is of God, but he who does evil has not seen God.

[12] Demetrius has a *good* testimony from all, and from the truth itself. And we also bear witness, and you know that our testimony is true.

[13] I had many things to write, but I do not wish to write to you with pen and ink; [14] but I hope to see you shortly, and we shall speak face to face.

Peace to you. Our friends greet you. Greet the friends by name.

אִגֶּרֶת יוֹחָנָן הַשְּׁלִישִׁית

[1] מֵאֵת הַזָּקֵן אֶל גָּיוֹס הָאָהוּב אֲשֶׁר אֲנִי אוֹהֵב בֶּאֱמֶת. [2] חֲבִיבִי, אֲנִי מִתְפַּלֵּל שֶׁיִּהְיֶה לְךָ טוֹב בַּכֹּל וְתִהְיֶה בָּרִיא, כְּשֵׁם שֶׁטּוֹב לְנַפְשְׁךָ. [3] שָׂמַחְתִּי מְאֹד כַּאֲשֶׁר בָּאוּ אַחִים וְהֵעִידוּ עַל הָאֱמֶת אֲשֶׁר בָּךְ, וְאָמְנָם בָּךְ אַתָּה מִתְהַלֵּךְ בֶּאֱמֶת. [4] אֵין לִי שִׂמְחָה גְדוֹלָה מִלִּשְׁמֹעַ שֶׁיְּלָדַי מִתְהַלְּכִים בֶּאֱמֶת.

[5] חֲבִיבִי, אַתָּה נוֹהֵג בְּנֶאֱמָנוּת בְּכָל מַה שֶּׁאַתָּה עוֹשֶׂה לְמַעַן הָאַחִים אֲפִלּוּ כְּשֶׁהֵם זָרִים. [6] הַלָּלוּ הֵעִידוּ עַל אַהֲבָתְךָ לִפְנֵי הַקְּהִלָּה, וְיָפֶה תַעֲשֶׂה אִם תְּשַׁלַּח אוֹתָם כָּיָאֶה לִפְנֵי הָאֱלֹהִים; [7] כִּי לְמַעַן הַשֵּׁם יָצְאוּ לַדֶּרֶךְ, וְלֹא לָקְחוּ דָבָר מִן הַגּוֹיִים. [8] עַל כֵּן חוֹבָה עָלֵינוּ לִתְמֹךְ בַּאֲנָשִׁים כָּאֵלֶּה, כְּדֵי שֶׁנִּהְיֶה שֻׁתָּפִים לָעֲבוֹדָה בִּשְׁרוּת הָאֱמֶת.

[9] כָּתַבְתִּי אֶל הַקְּהִלָּה, אֲבָל דְּיוֹטְרֶפֶם הַמִּתְאַוֶּה לִהְיוֹת לָהֶם לְרֹאשׁ אֵינֶנּוּ מְקַבֵּל אוֹתָנוּ. [10] לָכֵן בְּבוֹאִי אַזְכִּיר אֶת הַמַּעֲשִׂים שֶׁהוּא עוֹשֶׂה. הוּא מַשְׁמִיץ אוֹתָנוּ בְּדִבְרֵי רֶשַׁע וְאֵינוֹ מִסְתַּפֵּק בָּזֶה; גַּם אֵינֶנּוּ מְקַבֵּל אֶת הָאַחִים, וְאֶת הָרוֹצִים לְקַבְּלָם הוּא מוֹנֵעַ וּמְגָרֵשׁ מִן הַקְּהִלָּה.

[11] חֲבִיבִי, אַל תֵּלֵךְ בְּעִקְּבוֹת הָרַע, כִּי אִם בְּעִקְּבוֹת הַטּוֹב. הָעוֹשֶׂה טוֹב מֵאֱלֹהִים הוּא, וְהָעוֹשֶׂה רַע לֹא רָאָה אֶת אֱלֹהִים. [12] עַל דְּמֶטְרִיּוֹס הֵעִידוּ הַכֹּל, גַּם הָאֱמֶת עַצְמָהּ; וְגַם אֲנַחְנוּ מְעִידִים, וְיוֹדֵעַ אַתָּה כִּי עֵדוּתֵנוּ אֱמֶת.

[13] הַרְבֵּה יֵשׁ לִי לִכְתֹּב אֵלֶיךָ, אַךְ אֵינֶנִּי רוֹצֶה לִכְתֹּב אֵלֶיךָ בִּדְיוֹ וָעֵט. [14] אֲנִי מְקַוֶּה לִרְאוֹתְךָ בִּמְהֵרָה וְאָז פֶּה אֶל פֶּה נְדַבֵּר. [15] שָׁלוֹם לָךְ. הַיְדִידִים דּוֹרְשִׁים בִּשְׁלוֹמְךָ. דְּרֹשׁ בִּשְׁלוֹם הַיְדִידִים אִישׁ אִישׁ בִּשְׁמוֹ.

The Epistle of

JUDE

Jude, a bondservant of Jesus Christ, and brother of James,

To those who are called, sanctified by God the Father, and preserved in Jesus Christ:

2 Mercy, peace, and love be multiplied to you.

3 Beloved, while I was very diligent to write to you concerning our common salvation, I found it necessary to write to you exhorting you to contend earnestly for the faith which was once for all delivered to the saints. 4 For certain men have crept in unnoticed, who long ago were marked out for this condemnation, ungodly men, who turn the grace of our God into lewdness and deny the only Lord God and our Lord Jesus Christ.

5 But I want to remind you, though you once knew this, that the Lord, having saved the people out of the land of Egypt, afterward destroyed those who did not believe. 6 And the angels who did not keep their proper domain, but left their own abode, He has reserved in everlasting chains under darkness for the judgment of the great day; 7 as Sodom and Gomorrah, and the cities around them in a similar manner to these, having given themselves over to sexual immorality and gone after strange flesh, are set forth as an example, suffering the vengeance of eternal fire.

8 Likewise also these dreamers defile the flesh, reject authority, and speak evil of dignitaries. 9 Yet Michael the archangel, in contending with the devil, when he disputed about the body of Moses, dared not bring against him a reviling accusation, but said, "The Lord rebuke you!" 10 But these speak evil of whatever they do not know; and whatever they know naturally, like brute beasts, in these things they corrupt themselves. 11 Woe to them! For they have gone in the way of Cain, have run greedily in the error of Balaam for profit, and perished in the rebellion of Korah.

12 These are spots in your love feasts, while they feast with you without fear, serving only themselves. They are clouds without water, carried about by the winds; late autumn trees without fruit, twice dead, pulled up by the roots; 13 raging waves of the sea, foaming up their own shame; wandering stars for whom is reserved the blackness of darkness forever.

אִגֶּרֶת יְהוּדָה

1 מֵאֵת יְהוּדָה, עֶבֶד יֵשׁוּעַ הַמָּשִׁיחַ וְאָחִיו שֶׁל יַעֲקֹב, אֶל הַקְּרוּאִים, הָאֲהוּבִים עַל אֱלֹהִים הָאָב וּשְׁמוּרִים לְיֵשׁוּעַ הַמָּשִׁיחַ: 2 רַחֲמִים וְשָׁלוֹם וְאַהֲבָה יִשָּׁפְעוּ עֲלֵיכֶם לְמַכְבִּיר.

3 אֲהוּבַי, כַּאֲשֶׁר שָׁקַדְתִּי בְּכָל מְאֹדִי לִכְתֹּב לָכֶם עַל־דְּבַר יְשׁוּעָתֵנוּ הַמְשֻׁתֶּפֶת, נֶעוֹר בִּי הַצֹּרֶךְ לִכְתֹּב אֲלֵיכֶם וְלְהַאִיצְכֶם לְהִלָּחֵם לְמַעַן הָאֱמוּנָה שֶׁנִּמְסְרָה אַחַת וּלְתָמִיד לַקְּדוֹשִׁים; 4 כִּי הִתְגַּנְּבוּ אֲנָשִׁים אֲשֶׁר הַמִּשְׁפָּט הַזֶּה נֶחֱרַץ עֲלֵיהֶם מִקֶּדֶם, אַנְשֵׁי רֶשַׁע הַהוֹפְכִים אֶת חֶסֶד אֱלֹהֵינוּ לְזִמָּה וְכוֹפְרִים בְּרִבּוֹנֵנוּ וַאֲדוֹנֵנוּ הַיָּחִיד יֵשׁוּעַ הַמָּשִׁיחַ.

5 בִּרְצוֹנִי לְהַזְכִּיר לָכֶם דְּבָרִים שֶׁפַּעַם יְדַעְתֶּם הֵיטֵב – שֶׁיהוה, אַחֲרֵי הוֹשִׁיעוֹ אֶת הָעָם מֵאֶרֶץ מִצְרַיִם, הִשְׁמִיד אֶת אֲשֶׁר לֹא הֶאֱמִינוּ. 6 וְאֶת הַמַּלְאָכִים, אֲשֶׁר לֹא שָׁמְרוּ אֶת מַעֲמָדָם הָרָם כִּי אִם עָזְבוּ אֶת מְעוֹנָם, שָׁמַר בְּכַבְלֵי עוֹלָם וּבַאֲפֵלָה לְמִשְׁפַּט הַיּוֹם הַגָּדוֹל; 7 כְּשֵׁם שֶׁסְּדוֹם וַעֲמֹרָה וְהֶעָרִים הַקְּרוֹבוֹת, אֲשֶׁר בְּדֶרֶךְ דּוֹמָה לָהֶם הִתְמַכְּרוּ לִזְנוּת וְהָלְכוּ אַחַר יְצוּרִים אֲחֵרִים, מֻצָּגוֹת לְדֻגְמָה בְּסָבְלָן דִּין אֵשׁ עוֹלָם.

8 כְּמוֹ כֵן גַּם בַּעֲלֵי־הַחֲלוֹמוֹת הָאֵלֶּה מְטַמְּאִים אֶת הַגּוּף, דּוֹחִים אֶת הַסַּמְכוּת הָעֶלְיוֹנָה וּמְגַדְּפִים אֶת נוֹשְׂאֵי הַמִּשְׂרוֹת הַנִּכְבָּדוֹת. 9 אַךְ מִיכָאֵל, שַׂר הַמַּלְאָכִים, כַּאֲשֶׁר רָב עִם הַשָּׂטָן וְהִתְוַכֵּחַ עַל גּוּפַת מֹשֶׁה, לֹא הֵעֵז לַחֲרֹץ מִשְׁפַּט גִּדּוּף, כִּי אִם אָמַר, "יִגְעַר יהוה בְּךָ". 10 אֵלֶּה, לְעֻמַּת זֹאת, מְגַדְּפִים אֶת אֲשֶׁר אֵינָם יוֹדְעִים; וּבַדְּבָרִים אֲשֶׁר הֵם מְבִינִים בְּאֹפֶן טִבְעִי, כְּחַיּוֹת חַסְרוֹת דַּעַת, בָּהֶם הֵם נִשְׁחָתִים. 11 אוֹי לָהֶם, כִּי בְּדֶרֶךְ קַיִן הָלְכוּ וּבַעֲבוּר שָׂכָר הִתְמַסְּרוּ לְמָעוּת בִּלְעָם, וְאָבְדוּ בִּמְרַד קֹרַח. 12 אַבְנֵי נֶגֶף הֵם בִּסְעוּדוֹת הָאַהֲבָה שֶׁלָּכֶם, סוֹעֲדִים עִמָּכֶם לְלֹא יִרְאָה וְדוֹאֲגִים רַק לְעַצְמָם; עֲנָנֵי חֶסְרֵי מַיִם הַנִּדָּפִים בָּרוּחַ, עֵצִים בְּשִׁלְהֶכֶת בְּלֹא פְּרִי, אֲשֶׁר מֵתוּ פַּעֲמַיִם וְנֶעְקְרוּ; 13 גַּלֵּי יָם עַזִּים הַמַּעֲלִים כְּקֶצֶף אֶת חֶרְפָּתָם; כּוֹכָבִים תּוֹעִים אֲשֶׁר חֶשְׁכַת אֹפֶל

14 Now Enoch, the seventh from Adam, prophesied about these men also, saying, "Behold, the Lord comes with ten thousands of His saints, 15 to execute judgment on all, to convict all who are ungodly among them of all their ungodly deeds which they have committed in an ungodly way, and of all the harsh things which ungodly sinners have spoken against Him."

16 These are grumblers, complainers, walking according to their own lusts; and they mouth great swelling *words,* flattering people to gain advantage. 17 But you, beloved, remember the words which were spoken before by the apostles of our Lord Jesus Christ: 18 how they told you that there would be mockers in the last time who would walk according to their own ungodly lusts. 19 These are sensual persons, who cause divisions, not having the Spirit.

20 But you, beloved, building yourselves up on your most holy faith, praying in the Holy Spirit, 21 keep yourselves in the love of God, looking for the mercy of our Lord Jesus Christ unto eternal life.

22 And on some have compassion, making a distinction; 23 but others save with fear, pulling *them* out of the fire, hating even the garment defiled by the flesh.

24   Now to Him who is able to keep you from stumbling,
         And to present *you* faultless
         Before the presence of His glory with exceeding joy,
25   To God our Savior,
         Who alone is wise,
         Be glory and majesty,
         Dominion and power,
         Both now and forever.
         Amen.

שְׁמוּרָה לָהֶם לְעוֹלָם. 14 גַּם חֲנוֹךְ, הַשְּׁבִיעִי לְאָדָם, נִבָּא עֲלֵיהֶם לֵאמֹר: "הִנֵּה יהוה בָּא בְּרִבְבוֹת קְדוֹשָׁיו, 15 לַעֲשׂוֹת מִשְׁפָּט בַּכֹּל וּלְהוֹכִיחַ אֶת כָּל הָרְשָׁעִים עַל כָּל מַעֲשֵׂי רִשְׁעָתָם וְעַל כָּל הַקָּשׁוֹת אֲשֶׁר דִּבְּרוּ עָלָיו חוֹטְאִים רְשָׁעִים". 16 הַלָּלוּ רוֹגְנִים הֵם, מִתְלוֹנְנִים, הוֹלְכִים אַחַר תַּאֲווֹתֵיהֶם וּפִיהֶם מְדַבֵּר גְּבוֹהָה, נוֹהֲגִים בְּמַשּׂוֹא פָנִים לְמַעַן רָוַח. 17 אֲבָל אַתֶּם, אֲהוּבַי, זִכְרוּ אֶת הַדְּבָרִים שֶׁנֶּאֶמְרוּ קֹדֶם בְּיַד שְׁלִיחֵי אֲדוֹנֵנוּ יֵשׁוּעַ הַמָּשִׁיחַ. 18 הֲרֵי אָמְרוּ לָכֶם כִּי, "בְּאַחֲרִית הַיָּמִים יָבוֹאוּ לֵצִים הַהוֹלְכִים אַחַר תַּאֲווֹתֵיהֶם הַמְרֻשָּׁעוֹת." 19 אֵלֶּה הֵם הַגּוֹרְמִים פְּלוּגִים; מְשֻׁעְבָּדִים הֵם לַנֶּפֶשׁ, וְרוּחַ אֵין לָהֶם. 20 וְאַתֶּם, אֲהוּבַי, הִבָּנוּ בֶּאֱמוּנַתְכֶם הַנַּעֲלָה מְאֹד בִּקְדֻשָּׁתָהּ וְהִתְפַּלְּלוּ בְּרוּחַ הַקֹּדֶשׁ. 21 שִׁמְרוּ אֶת עַצְמְכֶם בְּאַהֲבַת הָאֱלֹהִים וְחַכּוּ לְרַחֲמֵי אֲדוֹנֵנוּ יֵשׁוּעַ הַמָּשִׁיחַ לְשֵׁם חַיֵּי עוֹלָם. 22 יֵשׁ הַמְהַסְּסִים, הִתְנַהֲגוּ עִמָּהֶם בְּרַחֲמִים; 23 חִטְפוּ אוֹתָם מִן הָאֵשׁ וְהוֹשִׁיעוּ אוֹתָם. עַל אֲחֵרִים רַחֲמוּ בְּיִרְאָה, וְעִם זֹאת שִׂנְאוּ אֶת הַלְּבוּשׁ הַמְגֹאָל בְּטֻמְאַת הַבָּשָׂר. 24 וְהוּא אֲשֶׁר יָכוֹל לִשְׁמֹר אֶתְכֶם מִמִּכְשׁוֹל וּלְהַעֲמִיד אֶתְכֶם לִפְנֵי כְבוֹדוֹ נְקִיִּים מִדֹּפִי וּמְלֵאֵי שִׂמְחָה, 25 הָאֱלֹהִים הַיָּחִיד, מוֹשִׁיעֵנוּ עַל-יְדֵי יֵשׁוּעַ הַמָּשִׁיחַ אֲדוֹנֵנוּ – לוֹ הַכָּבוֹד וְהַגְּדֻלָּה וְהָעֹז וְהַשִּׁלְטוֹן לִפְנֵי כָּל עוֹלָם, גַּם עַתָּה גַּם לְכָל הָעוֹלָמִים. אָמֵן.

THE REVELATION

of Jesus Christ

1 The Revelation of Jesus Christ, which God gave Him to show His servants—things which must shortly take place. And He sent and signified *it* by His angel to His servant John, ²who bore witness to the word of God, and to the testimony of Jesus Christ, to all things that he saw. ³Blessed *is* he who reads and those who hear the words of this prophecy, and keep those things which are written in it; for the time *is* near.

⁴John, to the seven churches which are in Asia:

Grace to you and peace from Him who is and who was and who is to come, and from the seven Spirits who are before His throne, ⁵and from Jesus Christ, the faithful witness, the firstborn from the dead, and the ruler over the kings of the earth.

To Him who loved us and washed us from our sins in His own blood, ⁶and has made us kings and priests to His God and Father, to Him *be* glory and dominion forever and ever. Amen.

⁷Behold, He is coming with clouds, and every eye will see Him, even they who pierced Him. And all the tribes of the earth will mourn because of Him. Even so, Amen.

⁸"I am the Alpha and the Omega, *the* Beginning and *the* End," says the Lord, "who is and who was and who is to come, the Almighty."

⁹I, John, both your brother and companion in the tribulation and kingdom and patience of Jesus Christ, was on the island that is called Patmos for the word of God and for the testimony of Jesus Christ. ¹⁰I was in the Spirit on the Lord's Day, and I heard behind me a loud voice, as of a trumpet, ¹¹saying, "I am the Alpha and the Omega, the First and the Last," and, "What you see, write in a book and send *it* to the seven churches which are in Asia: to Ephesus, to Smyrna, to Pergamos, to Thyatira, to Sardis, to Philadelphia, and to Laodicea."

¹²Then I turned to see the voice that spoke with me. And having turned I saw seven golden lampstands, ¹³and in the midst of the seven lampstands *One* like the Son of Man, clothed with a garment down to the feet and girded about the chest with a golden band. ¹⁴His head and hair *were* white like wool, as white as snow, and His eyes like a flame of fire; ¹⁵His feet *were* like fine brass, as if refined in a furnace, and His voice as the sound of many waters; ¹⁶He had in His right hand seven stars, out of His

הַהִתְגַּלּוּת

א הִתְגַּלּוּת יֵשׁוּעַ הַמָּשִׁיחַ שֶׁנָּתַן לוֹ הָאֱלֹהִים כְּדֵי לְהַרְאוֹת לַעֲבָדָיו אֶת אֲשֶׁר צָרִיךְ לִהְיוֹת בִּמְהֵרָה. וְהוּא שָׁלַח בְּיַד מַלְאָכוֹ וְהוֹדִיעַ לְעַבְדּוֹ יוֹחָנָן ²שֶׁהֵעִיד אֶת דְּבַר אֱלֹהִים וְאֶת עֵדוּת יֵשׁוּעַ הַמָּשִׁיחַ, אֶת כָּל אֲשֶׁר רָאָה. ³אַשְׁרֵי הַקּוֹרֵא וְאַשְׁרֵי הַשּׁוֹמְעִים אֶת דִּבְרֵי הַנְּבוּאָה וְשֹׁמְרִים אֶת הַכָּתוּב בָּהּ, כִּי קְרוֹבָה הָעֵת.

⁴יוֹחָנָן אֶל שֶׁבַע הַקְּהִלּוֹת אֲשֶׁר בְּאַסְיָה: חֶסֶד וְשָׁלוֹם לָכֶם מֵאֵת הַהֹוֶה וְהָיָה וְיָבוֹא, וּמֵאֵת שֶׁבַע הָרוּחוֹת אֲשֶׁר לִפְנֵי כִּסְאוֹ, ⁵וּמֵאֵת יֵשׁוּעַ הַמָּשִׁיחַ הָעֵד הַנֶּאֱמָן, בְּכוֹר הַמֵּתִים וְעֶלְיוֹן לְמַלְכֵי הָאָרֶץ. לָאוֹהֵב אוֹתָנוּ אֲשֶׁר בְּדָמוֹ שִׁחְרֵר אוֹתָנוּ מֵחֲטָאֵינוּ ⁶וְעָשָׂה אוֹתָנוּ מַמְלֶכֶת כֹּהֲנִים לֵאלֹהִים אָבִיו, לוֹ הַכָּבוֹד וְהַגְּבוּרָה לְעוֹלְמֵי עוֹלָמִים. אָמֵן.

⁷הִנֵּה הוּא בָּא עִם הָעֲנָנִים. כָּל עַיִן תִּרְאֶה אוֹתוֹ, גַּם אֵלֶּה שֶׁדְּקָרוּהוּ, וְיִסְפְּדוּ עָלָיו כָּל מִשְׁפְּחוֹת הָאָרֶץ. כֵּן, אָמֵן. ⁸"אֲנִי הָאָלֶף אַף אֲנִי הַתָּו", נְאֻם יהוה אֱלֹהִים, "הַהֹוֶה וְהָיָה וְיָבוֹא, אֱלֹהֵי צְבָאוֹת."

⁹אֲנִי יוֹחָנָן אֲחִיכֶם וְשֻׁתָּף בַּצָּרָה וּבַמַּלְכוּת וּבַסַּבְלָנוּת בְּיֵשׁוּעַ, הָיִיתִי בָּאִי הַקָּרוּי פַּטְמוֹס בַּעֲבוּר דְּבַר אֱלֹהִים וְעֵדוּת יֵשׁוּעַ. ¹⁰הָיִיתִי בְּהִשָּׁרְאַת הָרוּחַ בְּיוֹם הָאָדוֹן וְשָׁמַעְתִּי מֵאַחֲרַי קוֹל גָּדוֹל כְּקוֹל שׁוֹפָר ¹¹אוֹמֵר: "אֶת אֲשֶׁר אַתָּה רֹאֶה כְּתֹב בְּסֵפֶר וּשְׁלַח אֶל שֶׁבַע הַקְּהִלּוֹת: אֶל אֶפְסוֹס, אֶל זְמִירְנָה, אֶל פֶּרְגָמוֹס, אֶל תִּיאָטִירָה, אֶל סַרְדִּיס, אֶל פִילָדֶלְפִיָה וְאֶל לָאוֹדִיקֵאָה." ¹²פָּנִיתִי לִרְאוֹת אֶת הַקּוֹל הַמְדַבֵּר אֵלַי, וּכְשֶׁפָּנִיתִי רָאִיתִי שֶׁבַע מְנוֹרוֹת זָהָב, ¹³וּבֵין שֶׁבַע הַמְנוֹרוֹת כְּמַרְאֵה בֶּן־אָדָם עוֹטֶה מְעִיל עַד מַרְגְּלוֹתָיו וְחָגוּר חֲגוֹרַת זָהָב עַל חָזֵהוּ. ¹⁴רֹאשׁוֹ וְשַׂעֲרוֹ לְבָנִים כְּצֶמֶר לָבָן כַּשֶּׁלֶג, וְעֵינָיו כְּשַׁלְהֶבֶת אֵשׁ; ¹⁵רַגְלָיו כְּמוֹ נְחֹשֶׁת נוֹצֶצֶת שֶׁנִּצְרְפָה בַּכּוּר, וְקוֹלוֹ כְּקוֹל מַיִם רַבִּים. ¹⁶בְּיַד יְמִינוֹ שִׁבְעָה כוֹכָבִים; מִפִּיו יוֹצֵאת חֶרֶב פִּיפִיּוֹת חַדָּה, וּפָנָיו כַּשֶּׁמֶשׁ הַמְּאִירָה בִּגְבוּרָתָהּ.

mouth went a sharp two-edged sword, and His countenance *was* like the sun shining in its strength. [17] And when I saw Him, I fell at His feet as dead. But He laid His right hand on me, saying to me, "Do not be afraid; I am the First and the Last. [18] I *am* He who lives, and was dead, and behold, I am alive forevermore. Amen. And I have the keys of Hades and of Death. [19] Write the things which you have seen, and the things which are, and the things which will take place after this. [20] The mystery of the seven stars which you saw in My right hand, and the seven golden lampstands: The seven stars are the angels of the seven churches, and the seven lampstands which you saw are the seven churches.

2 "To the angel of the church of Ephesus write,

'These things says He who holds the seven stars in His right hand, who walks in the midst of the seven golden lampstands: [2] "I know your works, your labor, your patience, and that you cannot bear those who are evil. And you have tested those who say they are apostles and are not, and have found them liars; [3] and you have persevered and have patience, and have labored for My name's sake and have not become weary. [4] Nevertheless I have *this* against you, that you have left your first love. [5] Remember therefore from where you have fallen; repent and do the first works, or else I will come to you quickly and remove your lampstand from its place—unless you repent. [6] But this you have, that you hate the deeds of the Nicolaitans, which I also hate.

[7] "He who has an ear, let him hear what the Spirit says to the churches. To him who overcomes I will give to eat from the tree of life, which is in the midst of the Paradise of God." '

[8] "And to the angel of the church in Smyrna write,

'These things says the First and the Last, who was dead, and came to life: [9] "I know your works, tribulation, and poverty (but you are rich); and *I know* the blasphemy of those who say they are Jews and are not, but *are* a synagogue of Satan. [10] Do not fear any of those things which you are about to suffer. Indeed, the devil is about to throw *some* of you into prison, that you may be tested, and you will have tribulation ten days. Be faithful until death, and I will give you the crown of life.

[11] "He who has an ear, let him hear what the Spirit says to the churches. He who overcomes shall not be hurt by the second death." '

[12] "And to the angel of the church in Pergamos write,

<hr>

17 כַּאֲשֶׁר רְאִיתִיו נָפַלְתִּי לְרַגְלָיו כַּמֵּת, וְהוּא שָׂם אֶת יַד יְמִינוֹ עָלַי וְאָמַר: "אַל תִּירָא. אֲנִי הָרִאשׁוֹן וְהָאַחֲרוֹן וְהֶחָי. 18 הָיִיתִי מֵת וְהִנֵּה חַי אֲנִי לְעוֹלְמֵי עוֹלָמִים, וְלִי מַפְתְּחוֹת שְׁאוֹל וָמָוֶת. 19 כְּתֹב אֶת אֲשֶׁר רָאִיתָ וְאֶת אֲשֶׁר הֹוֶה וְאֶת אֲשֶׁר עָתִיד לִהְיוֹת אַחֲרֵי כֵן, 20 אֶת סוֹד שִׁבְעַת הַכּוֹכָבִים אֲשֶׁר רָאִיתָ בִּימִינִי וְשֶׁבַע מְנוֹרוֹת הַזָּהָב: שִׁבְעַת הַכּוֹכָבִים הֵם מַלְאֲכֵי שֶׁבַע הַקְּהִלּוֹת, וְשֶׁבַע הַמְּנוֹרוֹת הֵן שֶׁבַע קְהִלּוֹת."

ב "אֶל מַלְאַךְ קְהִלַּת אֶפְסוֹס כְּתֹב:

אֶת אֵלֶּה הַדְּבָרִים אוֹמֵר הָאוֹחֵז בִּימִינוֹ אֶת שִׁבְעַת הַכּוֹכָבִים, הַמִּתְהַלֵּךְ בֵּין שֶׁבַע מְנוֹרוֹת הַזָּהָב: 2 אֲנִי יוֹדֵעַ אֶת מַעֲשֶׂיךָ וְאֶת עֲמָלְךָ וְאֶת סַבְלָנוּתְךָ וְשֶׁאֵינְךָ יָכֹל לָשֵׂאת אַנְשֵׁי רֶשַׁע. בָּחַנְתָּ אֶת הַמְכַנִּים עַצְמָם שְׁלִיחִים וְאֵינָם, וּמְצָאתָ אוֹתָם כּוֹזְבִים. 3 יֵשׁ לְךָ סַבְלָנוּת וְסָבַלְתָּ בִּגְלַל שְׁמִי וְלֹא עָיַפְתָּ. 4 אֲבָל יֵשׁ לִי טַעֲנָה נֶגְדְּךָ, כִּי עָזַבְתָּ אֶת אַהֲבָתְךָ הָרִאשׁוֹנָה. 5 לָכֵן זְכֹר מִנַּיִן נָפַלְתָּ וַחֲזֹר בִּתְשׁוּבָה וַעֲשֵׂה אֶת הַמַּעֲשִׂים הָרִאשׁוֹנִים; שֶׁאִם לֹא כֵן, אָבוֹא אֵלֶיךָ וְאָסִיר אֶת מְנוֹרָתְךָ מִמְּקוֹמָהּ – אִם לֹא תַחֲזֹר בִּתְשׁוּבָה. 6 אַךְ זֹאת לִזְכוּתְךָ: אַתָּה שׂוֹנֵא אֶת מַעֲשֵׂי הַנִּיקוֹלָסִים אֲשֶׁר גַּם אֲנִי שׂוֹנֵא. 7 מִי שֶׁאֹזֶן לוֹ, יִשְׁמַע נָא מַה שֶׁהָרוּחַ אוֹמֶרֶת לַקְּהִלּוֹת. הַמְנַצֵּחַ, אֲנִי אֶתֵּן לוֹ לֶאֱכֹל מֵעֵץ הַחַיִּים אֲשֶׁר בְּגַן אֱלֹהִים.

8 אֶל מַלְאַךְ קְהִלַּת זְמִירְנָה כְּתֹב:

אֶת אֵלֶּה הַדְּבָרִים אוֹמֵר הָרִאשׁוֹן וְהָאַחֲרוֹן, אֲשֶׁר מֵת וַיֶּחִי: 9 אֲנִי יוֹדֵעַ אֶת צָרָתְךָ וְאֶת עָנְיְךָ – אֶלָּא שֶׁעָשִׁיר אַתָּה – וְאֶת גִּדּוּפָם שֶׁל הָאוֹמְרִים 'יְהוּדִים אֲנַחְנוּ' וְאֵינָם אֶלָּא כְּנֶסֶת הַשָּׂטָן. 10 אַל תִּירָא מִפְּנֵי מַה שֶׁאַתָּה עָתִיד לִסְבֹּל. הִנֵּה עָתִיד הַשָּׂטָן לְהַשְׁלִיךְ אֲנָשִׁים מִכֶּם לַכֶּלֶא כְּדֵי שֶׁתְּנֻסּוּ, וְתִהְיֶה לָכֶם צָרָה עֲשֶׂרֶת יָמִים. הֱיֵה נֶאֱמָן עַד מָוֶת וְאֶתֵּן לְךָ עֲטֶרֶת הַחַיִּים. 11 מִי שֶׁאֹזֶן לוֹ, יִשְׁמַע נָא מַה שֶׁהָרוּחַ אוֹמֶרֶת לַקְּהִלּוֹת. הַמְנַצֵּחַ לֹא יֻנַּק בַּמָּוֶת הַשֵּׁנִי.

12 אֶל מַלְאַךְ קְהִלַּת פֶּרְגָמוֹם כְּתֹב:

אֶת אֵלֶּה הַדְּבָרִים אוֹמֵר זֶה אֲשֶׁר לוֹ חֶרֶב הַפִּיפִיּוֹת

'These things says He who has the sharp two-edged sword: [13] "I know your works, and where you dwell, where Satan's throne is. And you hold fast to My name, and did not deny My faith even in the days in which Antipas was My faithful martyr, who was killed among you, where Satan dwells. [14] But I have a few things against you, because you have there those who hold the doctrine of Balaam, who taught Balak to put a stumbling block before the children of Israel, to eat things sacrificed to idols, and to commit sexual immorality. [15] Thus you also have those who hold the doctrine of the Nicolaitans, which thing I hate. [16] Repent, or else I will come to you quickly and will fight against them with the sword of My mouth.

[17] "He who has an ear, let him hear what the Spirit says to the churches. To him who overcomes I will give some of the hidden manna to eat. And I will give him a white stone, and on the stone a new name written which no one knows except him who receives it." '

[18] "And to the angel of the church in Thyatira write,

'These things says the Son of God, who has eyes like a flame of fire, and His feet like fine brass: [19] "I know your works, love, service, faith, and your patience; and as for your works, the last are more than the first. [20] Nevertheless I have a few things against you, because you allow that woman Jezebel, who calls herself a prophetess, to teach and seduce My servants to commit sexual immorality and eat things sacrificed to idols. [21] And I gave her time to repent of her sexual immorality, and she did not repent. [22] Indeed I will cast her into a sickbed, and those who commit adultery with her into great tribulation, unless they repent of their deeds. [23] I will kill her children with death, and all the churches shall know that I am He who searches the minds and hearts. And I will give to each one of you according to your works.

[24] "Now to you I say, and to the rest in Thyatira, as many as do not have this doctrine, who have not known the depths of Satan, as they say, I will put on you no other burden. [25] But hold fast what you have till I come. [26] And he who overcomes, and keeps My works until the end, to him I will give power over the nations—

[27]   'He shall rule them with a rod of iron;
        They shall be dashed to pieces like the potter's
            vessels'—

as I also have received from My Father; [28] and I will give him the morning star.

הַחַדָּה: 13 אֲנִי יוֹדֵעַ אֶת מְקוֹם שִׁבְתְּךָ, אֲשֶׁר שָׁם כִּסֵּא הַשָּׂטָן. אַתָּה מַחֲזִיק בִּשְׁמִי וְלֹא הִתְכַּחַשְׁתָּ לֶאֱמוּנָתִי אֲפִלּוּ בִּימֵי אַנְטִיפַס עֵדִי הַנֶּאֱמָן אֲשֶׁר נֶהֱרַג אֶצְלְכֶם בִּמְקוֹם מוֹשָׁבוֹ שֶׁל הַשָּׂטָן, 14 אַךְ יֵשׁ לִי נֶגְדְּךָ דְּבָרִים מְעַטִּים: יֵשׁ לְךָ שָׁם אֲנָשִׁים הַמַּחֲזִיקִים בְּתוֹרַת בִּלְעָם אֲשֶׁר לִמֵּד אֶת בָּלָק לָשִׂים מִכְשׁוֹל לִפְנֵי בְּנֵי יִשְׂרָאֵל כְּדֵי שֶׁיֹּאכְלוּ מִזִּבְחֵי אֱלִילִים וְיִזְנוּ. 15 כֵּן גַּם נִמְצָאִים אֶצְלְךָ אֲנָשִׁים הַמַּחֲזִיקִים בְּתוֹרַת הַנִּיקוֹלָסִים בְּאֹפֶן דּוֹמֶה. 16 לָכֵן חֲזֹר בִּתְשׁוּבָה; שֶׁאִם לֹא כֵן, אָבוֹא אֵלֶיךָ מַהֵר וְאֶלָּחֵם בָּהֶם בְּחֶרֶב פִּי. 17 מִי שֶׁאָזְנוֹ לוֹ, יִשְׁמַע נָא מַה שֶּׁהָרוּחַ אוֹמֶרֶת לַקְּהִלּוֹת. הַמְנַצֵּחַ, אֲנִי אֶתֵּן לוֹ מִן הַמָּן הַגָּנוּז, וְאֶתֵּן לוֹ אֶבֶן לְבָנָה וְעַל הָאֶבֶן כָּתוּב שֵׁם חָדָשׁ אֲשֶׁר לֹא יְדָעֶנּוּ אִישׁ זוּלָתִי הַמְקַבֵּל.

18 אֶל מַלְאַךְ קְהִלַּת תִּיאָטִירָה כְּתֹב: אֶת אֵלֶּה הַדְּבָרִים אוֹמֵר בֶּן־הָאֱלֹהִים אֲשֶׁר עֵינָיו כְּשַׁלְהֶבֶת אֵשׁ וְרַגְלָיו כְּמוֹ נְחֹשֶׁת נוֹצֶצֶת: 19 אֲנִי יוֹדֵעַ אֶת מַעֲשֶׂיךָ וְאֶת אַהֲבָתְךָ, אֶת אֱמוּנָתְךָ, אֶת שֵׁרוּתְךָ וְסַבְלָנוּתְךָ; וּמַעֲשֶׂיךָ הָאַחֲרוֹנִים רַבִּים מִן הָרִאשׁוֹנִים. 20 אַךְ יֵשׁ לִי טַעֲנָה נֶגְדְּךָ, כִּי אַתָּה מַנִּיחַ לָאִשָּׁה אִיזֶבֶל הַקּוֹרֵאת לְעַצְמָהּ נְבִיאָה וּמְלַמֶּדֶת וּמַדִּיחָה אֶת עֲבָדַי לִזְנוֹת וְלֶאֱכֹל זִבְחֵי אֱלִילִים. 21 נָתַתִּי לָהּ זְמַן לַחֲזֹר בִּתְשׁוּבָה וְהִיא אֵינָהּ רוֹצָה לָשׁוּב מִתַּזְנוּתָהּ. 22 הִנְנִי מַשְׁלִיךְ אוֹתָהּ לְמִטָּה, וְאֶת הַמְנָאֲפִים עִמָּהּ אַשְׁלִיךְ לְצָרָה גְּדוֹלָה אִם לֹא יָשׁוּבוּ מִמַּעֲשֵׂיהֶם. 23 אַהֲרֹג בַּמָּוֶת אֶת בָּנֶיהָ וְיֵדְעוּ כָּל הַקְּהִלּוֹת שֶׁאֲנִי הוּא הַבּוֹחֵן כְּלָיוֹת וָלֵב, וְאֶתֵּן לָכֶם אִישׁ אִישׁ כְּמַעֲשֵׂיכֶם. 24 אֲבָל אוֹמֵר אֲנִי לָכֶם, לִשְׁאָר הַנִּמְצָאִים בְּתִיאָטִירָה, כָּל אֲשֶׁר אֵין לָהֶם הַתּוֹרָה הַזֹּאת וַאֲשֶׁר לֹא יָדְעוּ אֶת עֲמֻקּוֹת הַשָּׂטָן, כְּמוֹ שֶׁנּוֹהֲגִים לוֹמַר – לֹא אָטִיל עֲלֵיכֶם מַשָּׂא אַחֵר. 25 בְּרַם הַחֲזִיקוּ בְּמַה שֶּׁיֵּשׁ לָכֶם עַד אֲשֶׁר אָבוֹא. 26 הַמְנַצֵּחַ וְשׁוֹמֵר אֶת מַעֲשַׂי עַד קֵץ, אֲנִי אֶתֵּן לוֹ סַמְכוּת עַל הַגּוֹיִים 27 וְהוּא יִרְעֶה אוֹתָם בְּשֵׁבֶט בַּרְזֶל, כִּכְלִי חֶרֶס יְנֻפָּצוּ, 28 כְּשֵׁם שֶׁגַּם אֲנִי קִבַּלְתִּי

29"He who has an ear, let him hear what the Spirit says to the churches."'

3 "And to the angel of the church in Sardis write, 'These things says He who has the seven Spirits of God and the seven stars: "I know your works, that you have a name that you are alive, but you are dead. 2Be watchful, and strengthen the things which remain, that are ready to die, for I have not found your works perfect before God. 3Remember therefore how you have received and heard; hold fast and repent. Therefore if you will not watch, I will come upon you as a thief, and you will not know what hour I will come upon you. 4You have a few names even in Sardis who have not defiled their garments; and they shall walk with Me in white, for they are worthy. 5He who overcomes shall be clothed in white garments, and I will not blot out his name from the Book of Life; but I will confess his name before My Father and before His angels.

6"He who has an ear, let him hear what the Spirit says to the churches."'

7"And to the angel of the church in Philadelphia write,

'These things says He who is holy, He who is true, *He who has the key of David, He who opens and no one shuts, and shuts and no one opens*": 8"I know your works. See, I have set before you an open door, and no one can shut it; for you have a little strength, have kept My word, and have not denied My name. 9Indeed I will make *those* of the synagogue of Satan, who say they are Jews and are not, but lie—indeed I will make them come and worship before your feet, and to know that I have loved you. 10Because you have kept My command to persevere, I also will keep you from the hour of trial which shall come upon the whole world, to test those who dwell on the earth. 11Behold, I am coming quickly! Hold fast what you have, that no one may take your crown. 12He who overcomes, I will make him a pillar in the temple of My God, and he shall go out no more. I will write on him the name of My God and the name of the city of My God, the New Jerusalem, which comes down out of heaven from My God. And *I will write on him* My new name.

13"He who has an ear, let him hear what the Spirit says to the churches."'

14"And to the angel of the church of the Laodiceans write,

'These things says the Amen, the Faithful and True Witness, the Beginning of the creation of God: 15"I know your works, that you are neither cold

סַמְכוּת מֵאֵת אָבִי. וְאֶתֶּן לוֹ אֶת כּוֹכַב הַשָּׁחַר. 29 מִי שֶׁאֹזֶן לוֹ, יִשְׁמַע נָא מַה שֶׁהָרוּחַ אוֹמֶרֶת לַקְּהִלּוֹת.

ג אֶל מַלְאַךְ קְהִלַּת סַרְדִּים כְּתֹב: אֶת אֵלֶּה הַדְּבָרִים אוֹמֵר זֶה אֲשֶׁר לוֹ שֶׁבַע רוּחוֹת הָאֱלֹהִים וְשִׁבְעַת הַכּוֹכָבִים: אֲנִי יוֹדֵעַ אֶת מַעֲשֶׂיךָ, יֵשׁ לְךָ שֵׁם שֶׁאַתָּה חַי, וְאַתָּה מֵת. 2 שְׁקֹד וְחַזֵּק אֶת הַשְּׁאֵרִית שֶׁנִּטְתָה לָמוּת, כִּי לֹא מָצָאתִי אֶת מַעֲשֶׂיךָ מֻשְׁלָמִים לִפְנֵי אֱלֹהָי. 3 לָכֵן זְכֹר כֵּיצַד קִבַּלְתָּ וְשָׁמַעְתָּ, וּשְׁמֹר וַחֲזֹר בִּתְשׁוּבָה. אִם לֹא תִשְׁקֹד אָבוֹא כְּגַנָּב וְלֹא תֵדַע בְּאֵיזוֹ שָׁעָה אָבוֹא עָלֶיךָ. 4 וְאוּלָם יֵשׁ אֶצְלְךָ שֵׁמוֹת מְעַטִּים בְּסַרְדִּים אֲשֶׁר לֹא הִכְתִּימוּ אֶת בִּגְדֵיהֶם. הֵמָּה יֵלְכוּ אִתִּי בִּבְגָדִים לְבָנִים, כִּי רְאוּיִים הֵם. 5 הַמְנַצֵּחַ יִלְבַּשׁ בְּגָדִים לְבָנִים וְלֹא אֶמְחֶה אֶת שְׁמוֹ מִסֵּפֶר הַחַיִּים, וְאוֹדֶה אֶת שְׁמוֹ לִפְנֵי אָבִי וְלִפְנֵי מַלְאָכָיו. 6 מִי שֶׁאֹזֶן לוֹ, יִשְׁמַע נָא מַה שֶׁהָרוּחַ אוֹמֶרֶת לַקְּהִלּוֹת.

7 אֶל מַלְאַךְ קְהִלַּת פִילָדֶלְפִיָה כְּתֹב: אֶת אֵלֶּה הַדְּבָרִים אוֹמֵר הַקָּדוֹשׁ, הָאֲמִתִּי, אֲשֶׁר לוֹ מַפְתֵּחַ דָּוִד, הַפּוֹתֵחַ וְאֵין סוֹגֵר וְסוֹגֵר וְאֵין פּוֹתֵחַ: 8 אֲנִי יוֹדֵעַ אֶת מַעֲשֶׂיךָ. הִנֵּה נָתַתִּי לְפָנֶיךָ דֶּלֶת פְּתוּחָה אֲשֶׁר אֵין אִישׁ יָכוֹל לְסָגְרָהּ, כִּי מְעַט כֹּחַ לְךָ וְשָׁמַרְתָּ אֶת דְּבָרִי וְלֹא הִתְכַּחַשְׁתָּ לִשְׁמִי. 9 הִנְנִי נוֹתֵן אֲנָשִׁים מִכְּנֶסֶת הַשָּׂטָן, הָאוֹמְרִים 'יְהוּדִים אֲנַחְנוּ' וְאֵינָם; אֵין הֵם אֶלָּא מְשַׁקְּרִים. רְאֵה, אֲנִי אֶעֱשֶׂה שֶׁהֵם יָבוֹאוּ וְיִשְׁתַּחֲווּ לְרַגְלֶיךָ וְיֵדְעוּ שֶׁאֲנִי אֲהַבְתִּיךָ. 10 מִפְּנֵי שֶׁשָּׁמַרְתָּ אֶת מִצְוָתִי לַעֲמִידָה בְּסַבְלָנוּת, גַּם אֲנִי אֶשְׁמֹר אוֹתְךָ מִשְּׁעַת הַנִּסָּיוֹן הָעֲתִידָה לָבוֹא עַל כָּל תֵּבֵל, לְנַסּוֹת אֶת יוֹשְׁבֵי הָאָרֶץ. 11 אֲנִי בָּא מַהֵר. הַחֲזֵק בַּמֶּה שֶׁיֵּשׁ לְךָ, כְּדֵי שֶׁאִישׁ לֹא יִקַּח אֶת הָעֲטֶרֶת שֶׁלְּךָ. 12 הַמְנַצֵּחַ, אֲנִי אֶעֱשֵׂהוּ עַמּוּד בְּהֵיכַל אֱלֹהַי וְלֹא יֵצֵא עוֹד הַחוּצָה. וְאֶכְתֹּב עָלָיו אֶת שֵׁם אֱלֹהַי וְאֶת שֵׁם עִיר אֱלֹהַי, יְרוּשָׁלַיִם הַחֲדָשָׁה, הַיּוֹרֶדֶת מִשָּׁמַיִם מֵאֵת אֱלֹהַי, וְאֶת שְׁמִי הֶחָדָשׁ. 13 מִי שֶׁאֹזֶן לוֹ, יִשְׁמַע נָא מַה שֶׁהָרוּחַ אוֹמֶרֶת לַקְּהִלּוֹת.

14 אֶל מַלְאַךְ קְהִלַּת לָאוֹדִיקֵאָה כְּתֹב: אֶת אֵלֶּה הַדְּבָרִים אוֹמֵר הָאָמֵן, הָעֵד הַנֶּאֱמָן וְהָאֲמִתִּי, הָרֵאשִׁית שֶׁל בְּרִיאַת אֱלֹהִים: 15 אֲנִי יוֹדֵעַ

nor hot. I could wish you were cold or hot. [16] So then, because you are lukewarm, and neither cold nor hot, I will vomit you out of My mouth. [17] Because you say, 'I am rich, have become wealthy, and have need of nothing'—and do not know that you are wretched, miserable, poor, blind, and naked— [18] I counsel you to buy from Me gold refined in the fire, that you may be rich; and white garments, that you may be clothed, *that* the shame of your nakedness may not be revealed; and anoint your eyes with eye salve, that you may see. [19] As many as I love, I rebuke and chasten. Therefore be zealous and repent. [20] Behold, I stand at the door and knock. If anyone hears My voice and opens the door, I will come in to him and dine with him, and he with Me. [21] To him who overcomes I will grant to sit with Me on My throne, as I also overcame and sat down with My Father on His throne.

[22] "He who has an ear, let him hear what the Spirit says to the churches." ' "

4 After these things I looked, and behold, a door *standing* open in heaven. And the first voice which I heard *was* like a trumpet speaking with me, saying, "Come up here, and I will show you things which must take place after this."

[2] Immediately I was in the Spirit; and behold, a throne set in heaven, and *One* sat on the throne. [3] And He who sat there was like a jasper and a sardius stone in appearance; and *there was* a rainbow around the throne, in appearance like an emerald. [4] Around the throne *were* twenty-four thrones, and on the thrones I saw twenty-four elders sitting, clothed in white robes; and they had crowns of gold on their heads. [5] And from the throne proceeded lightnings, thunderings, and voices. Seven lamps of fire *were* burning before the throne, which are the seven Spirits of God.

[6] Before the throne *there was* a sea of glass, like crystal. And in the midst of the throne, and around the throne, *were* four living creatures full of eyes in front and in back. [7] The first living creature *was* like a lion, the second living creature like a calf, the third living creature had a face like a man, and the fourth living creature *was* like a flying eagle. [8] *The* four living creatures, each having six wings, were full of eyes around and within. And they do not rest day or night, saying:

"Holy, holy, holy,
  Lord God Almighty,
  Who was and is and is to come!"

אֶת מַעֲשֶׂיךָ, שֶׁלֹּא קַר אַתָּה וְלֹא חַם. מִי יִתֵּן וְהָיִיתָ קַר אוֹ חַם. 16 וּבְכֵן, מִפְּנֵי שֶׁאַתָּה פּוֹשֵׁר וְלֹא חַם וְלֹא קַר, אֲנִי עָתִיד לְהָקִיא אוֹתְךָ מִפִּי. 17 מִכֵּיוָן שֶׁאַתָּה אוֹמֵר 'עָשִׁיר אֲנִי', עָשַׁרְתִּי וְלֹא חָסֵר לִי כְּלוּם' וְאֵינְךָ יוֹדֵעַ שֶׁאַתָּה הָאֻמְלָל וְהַמִּסְכֵּן, עָנִי וְעִוֵּר וְעָרוֹם, 18 אָנֹכִי מַצִּיעַ לְךָ לִקְנוֹת מִמֶּנִּי זָהָב צָרוּף בָּאֵשׁ לְמַעַן תַּעֲשִׁיר, וּבְגָדִים לְבָנִים לְמַעַן תִּתְלַבֵּשׁ וְלֹא תֵרָאֶה בֹּשֶׁת עֶרְוָתְךָ, וְקִילוּרִית לִמְשֹׁחַ אֶת עֵינֶיךָ לְמַעַן תִּרְאֶה. 19 אֲנִי אֶת אֲשֶׁר אֹהַב אוֹכִיחַ וַאֲיַסֵּר. לָכֵן הֱיֵה נִמְרָץ וַחֲזֹר בִּתְשׁוּבָה. 20 הִנְנִי עוֹמֵד לְיַד הַדֶּלֶת וְדוֹפֵק. אִישׁ כִּי יִשְׁמַע אֶת קוֹלִי וְיִפְתַּח אֶת הַדֶּלֶת, אָבֹא אֵלָיו וְאֶסְעַד אִתּוֹ וְהוּא אִתִּי. 21 הַמְנַצֵּחַ, אֲנִי אֶתֵּן לוֹ לָשֶׁבֶת אִתִּי עַל כִּסְאִי כְּמוֹ שֶׁגַּם אֲנִי נִצַּחְתִּי וְיָשַׁבְתִּי עִם אָבִי עַל כִּסְאוֹ. 22 מִי שֶׁאֹזֶן לוֹ, יִשְׁמַע נָא מַה שֶׁהָרוּחַ אוֹמֶרֶת לַקְּהִלּוֹת.

ד אַחַר הַדְּבָרִים הָאֵלֶּה רָאִיתִי וְהִנֵּה דֶּלֶת פְּתוּחָה בַּשָּׁמַיִם; וְהַקּוֹל הָרִאשׁוֹן – אֲשֶׁר שָׁמַעְתִּי כְּקוֹל שׁוֹפָר מְדַבֵּר אֵלַי – אוֹמֵר: "עֲלֵה הֵנָּה וְאַרְאֶה לְךָ אֶת אֲשֶׁר צָרִיךְ לִהְיוֹת אַחֲרֵי כֵן." 2 מִיָּד הָיִיתִי בְּהַשְׁרָאַת הָרוּחַ וְהִנֵּה כִּסֵּא מֻצָּב בַּשָּׁמַיִם וְעַל הַכִּסֵּא יוֹשֵׁב. 3 וְהַיּוֹשֵׁב דּוֹמֶה בְּמַרְאֶה לְאֶבֶן יָשְׁפֵה וְאֹדֶם, וְקֶשֶׁת סָבִיב לַכִּסֵּא דּוֹמֶה בְּמַרְאֶה לְבָרֶקֶת. 4 סָבִיב לַכִּסֵּא עֶשְׂרִים וְאַרְבָּעָה כִסְאוֹת, וְעַל הַכִּסְאוֹת יוֹשְׁבִים עֶשְׂרִים וְאַרְבָּעָה זְקֵנִים לְבוּשִׁים בְּגָדִים לְבָנִים וְעַטְרוֹת זָהָב עַל רָאשֵׁיהֶם. 5 וּמִן הַכִּסֵּא יוֹצְאִים בְּרָקִים, קוֹלוֹת וּרְעָמִים; וְשִׁבְעָה לַפִּידֵי אֵשׁ בּוֹעֲרִים לִפְנֵי הַכִּסֵּא, אֲשֶׁר הֵם שֶׁבַע רוּחוֹת הָאֱלֹהִים. 6 לִפְנֵי הַכִּסֵּא כְּיָם זְכוּכִית דּוֹמֶה לִבְדֹלַח, וּבְאֶמְצַע הַכִּסֵּא וְסָבִיב לַכִּסֵּא אַרְבַּע חַיּוֹת מְלֵאוֹת עֵינַיִם מִלְּפָנִים וּמֵאָחוֹר. 7 הַחַיָּה הָרִאשׁוֹנָה דּוֹמָה לְאַרְיֵה; הַחַיָּה הַשְּׁנִיָּה דּוֹמָה לְעֵגֶל; הַחַיָּה הַשְּׁלִישִׁית פָּנִים לָהּ כִּפְנֵי אָדָם; וְהַחַיָּה הָרְבִיעִית דּוֹמָה לְנֶשֶׁר מְעוֹפֵף. 8 וְאַרְבַּע הַחַיּוֹת לְכָל אַחַת מֵהֶן שֵׁשׁ כְּנָפַיִם. מִסָּבִיב וּמִבִּפְנִים הֵן מְלֵאוֹת עֵינַיִם, וְיוֹמָם וָלַיְלָה אֵינָן חֲדֵלוֹת לוֹמַר:

"קָדוֹשׁ, קָדוֹשׁ, קָדוֹשׁ, יהוה אֱלֹהֵי צְבָאוֹת אֲשֶׁר הָיָה וְהֹוֶה וְיָבוֹא."

9 Whenever the living creatures give glory and honor and thanks to Him who sits on the throne, who lives forever and ever, 10 the twenty-four elders fall down before Him who sits on the throne and worship Him who lives forever and ever, and cast their crowns before the throne, saying:

11 "You are worthy, O Lord,
To receive glory and honor and power;
For You created all things,
And by Your will they exist and were created."

5 And I saw in the right *hand* of Him who sat on the throne a scroll written inside and on the back, sealed with seven seals. 2 Then I saw a strong angel proclaiming with a loud voice, "Who is worthy to open the scroll and to loose its seals?" 3 And no one in heaven or on the earth or under the earth was able to open the scroll, or to look at it.

4 So I wept much, because no one was found worthy to open and read the scroll, or to look at it. 5 But one of the elders said to me, "Do not weep. Behold, the Lion of the tribe of Judah, the Root of David, has prevailed to open the scroll and to loose its seven seals."

6 And I looked, and behold, in the midst of the throne and of the four living creatures, and in the midst of the elders, stood a Lamb as though it had been slain, having seven horns and seven eyes, which are the seven Spirits of God sent out into all the earth. 7 Then He came and took the scroll out of the right hand of Him who sat on the throne.

8 Now when He had taken the scroll, the four living creatures and the twenty-four elders fell down before the Lamb, each having a harp, and golden bowls full of incense, which are the prayers of the saints. 9 And they sang a new song, saying:

"You are worthy to take the scroll,
And to open its seals;
For You were slain,
And have redeemed us to God by Your blood
Out of every tribe and tongue and people and nation,
10   And have made us kings and priests to our God;
And we shall reign on the earth."

11 Then I looked, and I heard the voice of many angels around the throne, the living creatures, and the elders; and the number of them was ten thousand times ten thousand, and thousands of thousands, 12 saying with a loud voice:

9 וּבְכָל עֵת שֶׁתִּתֵּנָה הַחַיּוֹת כָּבוֹד וִיקָר וְתוֹדָה לַיּוֹשֵׁב עַל הַכִּסֵּא, הַחַי לְעוֹלְמֵי עוֹלָמִים, 10 יִפְּלוּ עֶשְׂרִים וְאַרְבָּעָה הַזְּקֵנִים לִפְנֵי הַיּוֹשֵׁב עַל הַכִּסֵּא וְיִשְׁתַּחֲווּ לַחַי לְעוֹלְמֵי עוֹלָמִים, וְיַנִּיחוּ אֶת עַטְרוֹתֵיהֶם לִפְנֵי הַכִּסֵּא בְּאָמְרָם:

11 "לְךָ יָאֶה, אֲדוֹנֵנוּ וֵאלֹהֵינוּ, לְקַבֵּל אֶת הַכָּבוֹד וְהַיְקָר וְהַגְּבוּרָה, כִּי אַתָּה בָּרָאתָ הַכֹּל וּבִרְצוֹנְךָ הָיוּ וְנִבְרָאוּ."

ה רָאִיתִי לִימִין הַיּוֹשֵׁב עַל הַכִּסֵּא סֵפֶר כָּתוּב מִפָּנִים וּמֵאָחוֹר, חָתוּם בְּשִׁבְעָה חוֹתָמוֹת. 2 וְרָאִיתִי מַלְאָךְ רַב־כֹּחַ קוֹרֵא בְּקוֹל גָּדוֹל: "מִי רָאוּי לִפְתֹּחַ אֶת הַסֵּפֶר וּלְהַתִּיר אֶת חוֹתָמָיו?" 3 וְלֹא יָכוֹל אִישׁ לֹא בַּשָּׁמַיִם וְלֹא בָּאָרֶץ וְלֹא מִתַּחַת לָאָרֶץ לִפְתֹּחַ אֶת הַסֵּפֶר, אַף לֹא לְהַבִּיט בּוֹ. 4 וַאֲנִי בָּכִיתִי הַרְבֵּה, כִּי אִישׁ לֹא נִמְצָא רָאוּי לִפְתֹּחַ אֶת הַסֵּפֶר, אַף לֹא לְהַבִּיט בּוֹ. 5 אָמַר אֵלַי אַחַד הַזְּקֵנִים: "אַל תִּבְכֶּה. הִנֵּה נִצַּח נְצַח הָאַרְיֵה מִשֵּׁבֶט יְהוּדָה, שֹׁרֶשׁ דָּוִד, לִפְתֹּחַ אֶת הַסֵּפֶר וְאֶת שִׁבְעַת חוֹתָמָיו."

6 וְרָאִיתִי בֵּין הַכִּסֵּא וְאַרְבַּע הַחַיּוֹת וּבֵין הַזְּקֵנִים עוֹמֵד שֶׂה כְּמוֹ שָׁחוּט; שֶׁבַע קְרָנַיִם לוֹ, וְשֶׁבַע עֵינַיִם אֲשֶׁר הֵן שֶׁבַע רוּחוֹת הָאֱלֹהִים הַשְּׁלוּחוֹת אֶל כָּל הָאָרֶץ. 7 הוּא בָּא וְלָקַח אֶת הַסֵּפֶר מִימִין הַיּוֹשֵׁב עַל הַכִּסֵּא. 8 וְכַאֲשֶׁר לָקַח אוֹתוֹ נָפְלוּ אַרְבַּע הַחַיּוֹת וְעֶשְׂרִים וְאַרְבָּעָה הַזְּקֵנִים לִפְנֵי הַשֶּׂה, וּלְכָל אֶחָד נֵבֶל וְקַעֲרוֹת זָהָב מְלֵאוֹת קְטֹרֶת אֲשֶׁר הִיא תְּפִלוֹת הַקְּדוֹשִׁים, 9 וְשָׁרוּ שִׁיר חָדָשׁ:

"רָאוּי אַתָּה לָקַחַת אֶת הַסֵּפֶר וְלִפְתֹּחַ אֶת חוֹתָמָיו,

כִּי אַתָּה נִשְׁחַטְתָּ וּבְדָמְךָ קָנִיתָ לֵאלֹהִים מִבְּנֵי כָּל שֵׁבֶט וְלָשׁוֹן, מִכָּל עַם וְאֻמָּה;

10 וְעָשִׂיתָ אוֹתָם מַמְלֶכֶת כֹּהֲנִים לֵאלֹהֵינוּ, וְיִמְלְכוּ עַל הָאָרֶץ."

11 רָאִיתִי וְשָׁמַעְתִּי קוֹל מַלְאָכִים רַבִּים סָבִיב לַכִּסֵּא וְלַחַיּוֹת וְלַזְּקֵנִים – מִסְפָּרָם רִבְבוֹת רְבָבוֹת וְאַלְפֵי אֲלָפִים – 12 וְהֵם אוֹמְרִים בְּקוֹל גָּדוֹל:

"רָאוּי הַשֶּׂה שֶׁנִּשְׁחַט לְקַבֵּל גְּבוּרָה, עֹשֶׁר וְחָכְמָה וְכֹחַ וִיקָר וְכָבוֹד וּבְרָכָה."

"Worthy is the Lamb who was slain
To receive power and riches and wisdom,
And strength and honor and glory and
blessing!"

[13] And every creature which is in heaven and on
the earth and under the earth and such as are in the
sea, and all that are in them, I heard saying:

"Blessing and honor and glory and power
Be to Him who sits on the throne,
And to the Lamb, forever and ever!"

[14] Then the four living creatures said, "Amen!"
And the twenty-four elders fell down and worshiped Him who lives forever and ever.

6 Now I saw when the Lamb opened one of the
seals; and I heard one of the four living creatures
saying with a voice like thunder, "Come and see."
[2] And I looked, and behold, a white horse. He who
sat on it had a bow; and a crown was given to him,
and he went out conquering and to conquer.

[3] When He opened the second seal, I heard the
second living creature saying, "Come and see."
[4] Another horse, fiery red, went out. And it was
granted to the one who sat on it to take peace from
the earth, and that *people* should kill one another;
and there was given to him a great sword.

[5] When He opened the third seal, I heard the
third living creature say, "Come and see." So I
looked, and behold, a black horse, and he who sat
on it had a pair of scales in his hand. [6] And I heard
a voice in the midst of the four living creatures
saying, "A quart of wheat for a denarius, and three
quarts of barley for a denarius; and do not harm the
oil and the wine."

[7] When He opened the fourth seal, I heard the
voice of the fourth living creature saying, "Come
and see." [8] So I looked, and behold, a pale horse.
And the name of him who sat on it was Death, and
Hades followed with him. And power was given to
them over a fourth of the earth, to kill with sword,
with hunger, with death, and by the beasts of the
earth.

[9] When He opened the fifth seal, I saw under the
altar the souls of those who had been slain for the
word of God and for the testimony which they held.
[10] And they cried with a loud voice, saying, "How
long, O Lord, holy and true, until You judge and
avenge our blood on those who dwell on the earth?"
[11] Then a white robe was given to each of them; and
it was said to them that they should rest a little

13 וְכָל בְּרִיָּה אֲשֶׁר בַּשָּׁמַיִם וּבָאָרֶץ וּמִתַּחַת לָאָרֶץ
וְעַל הַיָּם וְכָל אֲשֶׁר בָּם, שָׁמַעְתִּי אוֹמְרִים:
"לַיּוֹשֵׁב עַל הַכִּסֵּא וְלַשֶּׂה הַבְּרָכָה
וְהַיְקָר וְהַכָּבוֹד וְהָעֹז לְעוֹלְמֵי עוֹלָמִים."
14 וְאַרְבַּע הַחַיּוֹת אָמְרוּ: "אָמֵן!" וְהַזְּקֵנִים נָפְלוּ
וְהִשְׁתַּחֲווּ.

ו רָאִיתִי כַּאֲשֶׁר פָּתַח אֶת אֶחָד מִשִּׁבְעַת
הַחוֹתָמוֹת, וְשָׁמַעְתִּי אַחַת מֵאַרְבַּע הַחַיּוֹת אוֹמֶרֶת
כְּמוֹ בְּקוֹל רַעַם: "בּוֹא!" 2 רָאִיתִי וְהִנֵּה סוּס לָבָן
וְרוֹכְבוֹ נוֹשֵׂא קֶשֶׁת; עֲטֶרֶת נִתְּנָה לוֹ וְהוּא יָצָא
מְנַצֵּחַ וּלְמַעַן יְנַצֵּחַ. 3 כַּאֲשֶׁר פָּתַח אֶת הַחוֹתָם הַשֵּׁנִי
שָׁמַעְתִּי אֶת הַחַיָּה הַשְּׁנִיָּה אוֹמֶרֶת: "בּוֹא!" 4 סוּס
אַחֵר יָצָא, אָדֹם כָּאֵשׁ. לְרוֹכְבוֹ הֻתַּר לְהָסִיר אֶת
הַשָּׁלוֹם מִן הָאָרֶץ כְּדֵי שֶׁיַּהַרְגוּ זֶה אֶת זֶה; וְחֶרֶב
גְּדוֹלָה נִתְּנָה לוֹ.

5 כַּאֲשֶׁר פָּתַח אֶת הַחוֹתָם הַשְּׁלִישִׁי שָׁמַעְתִּי אֶת
הַחַיָּה הַשְּׁלִישִׁית אוֹמֶרֶת: "בּוֹא!" רָאִיתִי וְהִנֵּה סוּס
שָׁחוֹר וְרוֹכְבוֹ מַחֲזִיק מֹאזְנַיִם בְּיָדוֹ. 6 וְשָׁמַעְתִּי כְּמוֹ
קוֹל בֵּין אַרְבַּע הַחַיּוֹת אוֹמֵר: "קַב חִטִּים בְּדִינָר
וּשְׁלוֹשָׁה קַבִּין שְׂעוֹרִים בְּדִינָר, וְלַשֶּׁמֶן וְלַיַּיִן אַל
תַּזִּיק." 7 כַּאֲשֶׁר פָּתַח אֶת הַחוֹתָם הָרְבִיעִי שָׁמַעְתִּי
אֶת קוֹל הַחַיָּה הָרְבִיעִית אוֹמֵר: "בּוֹא!" 8 רָאִיתִי
וְהִנֵּה סוּס יְרַקְרַק וְרוֹכְבוֹ שְׁמוֹ מָוֶת, וּשְׁאוֹל הָלְכָה
אַחֲרָיו. וְנִתְּנָה לָהֶם סַמְכוּת עַל רֶבַע הָאָרֶץ, לַהֲרֹג
בַּחֶרֶב וּבְרָעָב וּבַמָּוֶת וְעַל יְדֵי חַיּוֹת הָאָרֶץ.

9 כַּאֲשֶׁר פָּתַח אֶת הַחוֹתָם הַחֲמִישִׁי רָאִיתִי מִתַּחַת
לַמִּזְבֵּחַ אֶת נַפְשׁוֹת הַטְּבוּחִים עַל דְּבַר הָאֱלֹהִים וְעַל
הָעֵדוּת שֶׁהֶחֱזִיקוּ בָהּ. 10 וְהֵם צָעֲקוּ בְּקוֹל גָּדוֹל: "עַד
מָתַי, אֲדֹנָי הַקָּדוֹשׁ וַאֲמִתִּי, לֹא תִשְׁפֹּט וְתִנְקֹם אֶת
דָּמֵינוּ מִיּוֹשְׁבֵי הָאָרֶץ?" 11 לְכָל אֶחָד מֵהֶם נִתְּנָה
גְּלִימָה לְבָנָה וְנֶאֱמַר לָהֶם לָנוּחַ עוֹד זְמַן מְעַט, עַד
שֶׁיִּמָּלֵא גַם מִסְפַּר חַבְרֵיהֶם הָעֲבָדִים וַאֲחֵיהֶם
הָעֲתִידִים לֵהָרֵג כְּמוֹהֶם.

6 קַב - לִיטֶר; דִּינָר - שְׂכַר יוֹמֵי שֶׁל פֹּעֵל.

while longer, until both *the number of* their fellow servants and their brethren, who would be killed as they *were,* was completed.

¹²I looked when He opened the sixth seal, and behold, there was a great earthquake; and the sun became black as sackcloth of hair, and the moon became like blood. ¹³And the stars of heaven fell to the earth, as a fig tree drops its late figs when it is shaken by a mighty wind. ¹⁴Then the sky receded as a scroll when it is rolled up, and every mountain and island was moved out of its place. ¹⁵And the kings of the earth, the great men, the rich men, the commanders, the mighty men, every slave and every free man, hid themselves in the caves and in the rocks of the mountains, ¹⁶and said to the mountains and rocks, "Fall on us and hide us from the face of Him who sits on the throne and from the wrath of the Lamb! ¹⁷For the great day of His wrath has come, and who is able to stand?"

7 After these things I saw four angels standing at the four corners of the earth, holding the four winds of the earth, that the wind should not blow on the earth, on the sea, or on any tree. ²Then I saw another angel ascending from the east, having the seal of the living God. And he cried with a loud voice to the four angels to whom it was granted to harm the earth and the sea, ³saying, "Do not harm the earth, the sea, or the trees till we have sealed the servants of our God on their foreheads." ⁴And I heard the number of those who were sealed. One hundred *and* forty-four thousand of all the tribes of the children of Israel *were* sealed:

5　of the tribe of Judah twelve thousand *were* sealed;
　of the tribe of Reuben twelve thousand *were* sealed;
　of the tribe of Gad twelve thousand *were* sealed;
6　of the tribe of Asher twelve thousand *were* sealed;
　of the tribe of Naphtali twelve thousand *were* sealed;
　of the tribe of Manasseh twelve thousand *were* sealed;
7　of the tribe of Simeon twelve thousand *were* sealed;
　of the tribe of Levi twelve thousand *were* sealed;
　of the tribe of Issachar twelve thousand *were* sealed;
8　of the tribe of Zebulun twelve thousand *were* sealed;

¹²רָאִיתִי כְּשֶׁפָּתַח אֶת הַחוֹתָם הַשִּׁשִּׁי הִתְחוֹלְלָה רְעִידַת אֲדָמָה גְדוֹלָה; הַשֶּׁמֶשׁ הִשְׁחִירָה כְּשַׂק שֵׂעָר וְהַיָּרֵחַ כֻּלּוֹ הָיָה כַדָּם; ¹³כּוֹכְבֵי הַשָּׁמַיִם נָפְלוּ אַרְצָה, כִּתְאֵנָה הַמַּשְׁלִיכָה אֶת פַּגֶּיהָ כַּאֲשֶׁר הִיא מְטַלְטֶלֶת בְּרוּחַ חֲזָקָה; ¹⁴הַשָּׁמַיִם נָסוֹגוּ כִּמְגִלָּה נִגְלֶלֶת; כָּל הַר וְאִי נֶעְתְּקוּ מִמְּקוֹמָם. ¹⁵וּמַלְכֵי הָאָרֶץ וְהַנִּכְבָּדִים, שָׂרֵי הָאֲלָפִים וְהָעֲשִׁירִים וּבַעֲלֵי הָעָצְמָה, כָּל עֶבֶד וְכָל בֶּן־חוֹרִין, הִתְחַבְּאוּ בַּמְּעָרוֹת וּבְסַלְעֵי הֶהָרִים, ¹⁶וְאָמְרוּ לֶהָרִים וְלַסְּלָעִים: "נִפְלוּ עָלֵינוּ וְהַסְתִּירוּ אוֹתָנוּ מִפְּנֵי הַיּוֹשֵׁב עַל הַכִּסֵּא וּמִזַּעַם הַשֶּׂה, ¹⁷כִּי בָּא הַיּוֹם הַגָּדוֹל, יוֹם חֲרוֹנָם, וּמִי יָכוֹל לַעֲמֹד?"

ז אַחֲרֵי כֵן רָאִיתִי אַרְבָּעָה מַלְאָכִים עוֹמְדִים בְּאַרְבַּע פִּנּוֹת הָאָרֶץ, אוֹחֲזִים אֶת אַרְבַּע רוּחוֹת הָאָרֶץ כְּדֵי שֶׁלֹּא תִשֵּׁב רוּחַ לֹא עַל הָאָרֶץ וְלֹא עַל הַיָּם וְלֹא עַל כָּל עֵץ. ²רָאִיתִי מַלְאָךְ אַחֵר עוֹלֶה מִמִּזְרַח שֶׁמֶשׁ וּבִרְשׁוּתוֹ חוֹתַם אֱלֹהִים חַיִּים. הוּא קָרָא בְּקוֹל גָּדוֹל אֶל אַרְבַּעַת הַמַּלְאָכִים אֲשֶׁר הֻתַּר לָהֶם לְחַבֵּל בָּאָרֶץ וּבַיָּם, ³בְּאָמְרוֹ: "אַל תְּחַבְּלוּ בָּאָרֶץ וּבַיָּם וּבָעֵצִים עַד אֲשֶׁר נַחְתֹּם אֶת עַבְדֵי אֱלֹהֵינוּ עַל מִצְחוֹתֵיהֶם. ⁴וְשָׁמַעְתִּי אֶת מִסְפַּר הַחֲתוּמִים – מֵאָה וְאַרְבָּעִים וְאַרְבָּעָה אֶלֶף חֲתוּמִים מִכָּל שִׁבְטֵי בְּנֵי יִשְׂרָאֵל:

⁵מִשֵּׁבֶט יְהוּדָה שְׁנֵים־עָשָׂר אֶלֶף חֲתוּמִים,
מִשֵּׁבֶט רְאוּבֵן שְׁנֵים־עָשָׂר אֶלֶף,
מִשֵּׁבֶט גָּד שְׁנֵים־עָשָׂר אֶלֶף,
⁶מִשֵּׁבֶט אָשֵׁר שְׁנֵים־עָשָׂר אֶלֶף,
מִשֵּׁבֶט נַפְתָּלִי שְׁנֵים־עָשָׂר אֶלֶף,
מִשֵּׁבֶט מְנַשֶּׁה שְׁנֵים־עָשָׂר אֶלֶף,
⁷מִשֵּׁבֶט שִׁמְעוֹן שְׁנֵים־עָשָׂר אֶלֶף,
מִשֵּׁבֶט לֵוִי שְׁנֵים־עָשָׂר אֶלֶף,
מִשֵּׁבֶט יִשָּׂשכָר שְׁנֵים־עָשָׂר אֶלֶף,
⁸מִשֵּׁבֶט זְבוּלוּן שְׁנֵים־עָשָׂר אֶלֶף,
מִשֵּׁבֶט יוֹסֵף שְׁנֵים־עָשָׂר אֶלֶף,
מִשֵּׁבֶט בִּנְיָמִין שְׁנֵים־עָשָׂר אֶלֶף חֲתוּמִים.

of the tribe of Joseph twelve thousand *were* sealed;
of the tribe of Benjamin twelve thousand *were* sealed.

⁹ After these things I looked, and behold, a great multitude which no one could number, of all nations, tribes, peoples, and tongues, standing before the throne and before the Lamb, clothed with white robes, with palm branches in their hands, ¹⁰ and crying out with a loud voice, saying, "Salvation *belongs* to our God who sits on the throne, and to the Lamb!" ¹¹ All the angels stood around the throne and the elders and the four living creatures, and fell on their faces before the throne and worshiped God, ¹² saying:

"Amen! Blessing and glory and wisdom,
Thanksgiving and honor and power and might,
Be to our God forever and ever.
Amen."

¹³ Then one of the elders answered, saying to me, "Who are these arrayed in white robes, and where did they come from?"

¹⁴ And I said to him, "Sir, you know."

So he said to me, "These are the ones who come out of the great tribulation, and washed their robes and made them white in the blood of the Lamb. ¹⁵ Therefore they are before the throne of God, and serve Him day and night in His temple. And He who sits on the throne will dwell among them. ¹⁶ They shall neither hunger anymore nor thirst anymore; the sun shall not strike them, nor any heat; ¹⁷ for the Lamb who is in the midst of the throne will shepherd them and lead them to living fountains of waters. And God will wipe away every tear from their eyes."

8 When He opened the seventh seal, there was silence in heaven for about half an hour. ² And I saw the seven angels who stand before God, and to them were given seven trumpets. ³ Then another angel, having a golden censer, came and stood at the altar. He was given much incense, that he should offer *it* with the prayers of all the saints upon the golden altar which was before the throne. ⁴ And the smoke of the incense, with the prayers of the saints, ascended before God from the angel's hand. ⁵ Then the angel took the censer, filled it with fire from the altar, and threw *it* to the earth. And there were noises, thunderings, lightnings, and an earthquake.

⁶ So the seven angels who had the seven trumpets prepared themselves to sound.

⁹ אַחֲרֵי כֵן רָאִיתִי וְהִנֵּה הָמוֹן רַב, אֲשֶׁר לֹא יָכוֹל אִישׁ לִמְנוֹתוֹ, מִכָּל הָאֻמּוֹת וְהַשְּׁבָטִים וְהָעַמִּים וְהַלְּשׁוֹנוֹת – עוֹמְדִים לִפְנֵי הַכִּסֵּא וְלִפְנֵי הַשֶּׂה וְהֵם לְבוּשִׁים גְּלִימוֹת לְבָנוֹת וְכַפּוֹת תְּמָרִים בִּידֵיהֶם, ¹⁰ וְקוֹרְאִים בְּקוֹל גָּדוֹל:

"הַיְשׁוּעָה לֵאלֹהֵינוּ הַיּוֹשֵׁב עַל הַכִּסֵּא וְלַשֶּׂה." ¹¹ כָּל הַמַּלְאָכִים עָמְדוּ סָבִיב לַכִּסֵּא וְלַזְּקֵנִים וּלְאַרְבַּע הַחַיּוֹת. הֵם נָפְלוּ עַל פְּנֵיהֶם לִפְנֵי הַכִּסֵּא וְהִשְׁתַּחֲווּ לֵאלֹהִים ¹² בְּאָמְרָם:

"אָמֵן. הַבְּרָכָה וְהַכָּבוֹד, הַחָכְמָה וְהַתּוֹדָה, הַיְקָר וְהַגְּבוּרָה וְהָעֹז לֵאלֹהֵינוּ לְעוֹלְמֵי עוֹלָמִים. אָמֵן." ¹³ דִּבֵּר אַחַד הַזְּקֵנִים וְאָמַר אֵלַי: "אֵלֶּה הַלְּבוּשִׁים גְּלִימוֹת לְבָנוֹת מִי הֵם וּמֵאַיִן בָּאוּ?"

¹⁴ הֵשַׁבְתִּי לוֹ: "אֲדוֹנִי, אַתָּה יוֹדֵעַ."

אָמַר אֵלַי: "אֵלֶּה הֵם הַבָּאִים מִן הַצָּרָה הַגְּדוֹלָה. הֵם כִּבְּסוּ אֶת גְּלִימוֹתֵיהֶם וְהִלְבִּינוּ אוֹתָן בְּדַם הַשֶּׂה. ¹⁵ לָכֵן הֵם נִמְצָאִים לִפְנֵי כִּסֵּא אֱלֹהִים וְעוֹבְדִים אוֹתוֹ יוֹמָם וָלַיְלָה בְּהֵיכָלוֹ, וְהַיּוֹשֵׁב עַל הַכִּסֵּא יִפְרֹשׂ מִשְׁכָּנוֹ עֲלֵיהֶם. ¹⁶ לֹא יִרְעֲבוּ עוֹד וְלֹא יִצְמָאוּ, אַף לֹא תַכֶּה עֲלֵיהֶם הַשֶּׁמֶשׁ וְכָל שָׁרָב, ¹⁷ כִּי הַשֶּׂה אֲשֶׁר בְּאֶמְצַע הַכִּסֵּא יִרְעֶה אוֹתָם וְיַנְהִיגֵם אֶל מַבּוּעֵי מַיִם חַיִּים; וֵאלֹהִים יִמְחֶה כָּל דִּמְעָה מֵעֵינֵיהֶם."

ח כַּאֲשֶׁר פָּתַח אֶת הַחוֹתָם הַשְּׁבִיעִי הָיְתָה דְּמָמָה בַּשָּׁמַיִם כַּחֲצִי שָׁעָה. ² רָאִיתִי אֶת שִׁבְעַת הַמַּלְאָכִים הָעוֹמְדִים לִפְנֵי הָאֱלֹהִים; שִׁבְעָה שׁוֹפָרוֹת נִתְּנוּ לָהֶם.

³ וּמַלְאָךְ אַחֵר בָּא וְעָמַד אֵצֶל הַמִּזְבֵּחַ; בְּיָדוֹ מַחְתַּת זָהָב, וּקְטֹרֶת רַבָּה נִתְּנָה לוֹ כְּדֵי לָשִׂים אוֹתָהּ בִּתְפִלּוֹת כָּל הַקְּדוֹשִׁים עַל מִזְבַּח הַזָּהָב אֲשֶׁר לִפְנֵי הַכִּסֵּא. ⁴ וַעֲשַׁן הַקְּטֹרֶת עָלָה בִּתְפִלּוֹת הַקְּדוֹשִׁים מִיַּד שֶׁל הַמַּלְאָךְ לִפְנֵי הָאֱלֹהִים. ⁵ לָקַח הַמַּלְאָךְ אֶת הַמַּחְתָּה, מִלֵּא אוֹתָהּ אֵשׁ מִן הַמִּזְבֵּחַ וְהִשְׁלִיךְ עַל הָאָרֶץ. אָז הִתְחוֹלְלוּ רְעָמִים וְקוֹלוֹת וּבְרָקִים וּרְעִידוֹת אֲדָמָה.

⁶ שִׁבְעַת הַמַּלְאָכִים אֲשֶׁר בְּיָדָם שִׁבְעַת הַשּׁוֹפָרוֹת הִתְכּוֹנְנוּ לִתְקֹעַ.

7 The first angel sounded: And hail and fire followed, mingled with blood, and they were thrown to the earth. And a third of the trees were burned up, and all green grass was burned up.

8 Then the second angel sounded: And *something* like a great mountain burning with fire was thrown into the sea, and a third of the sea became blood. 9 And a third of the living creatures in the sea died, and a third of the ships were destroyed.

10 Then the third angel sounded: And a great star fell from heaven, burning like a torch, and it fell on a third of the rivers and on the springs of water. 11 The name of the star is Wormwood. A third of the waters became wormwood, and many men died from the water, because it was made bitter.

12 Then the fourth angel sounded: And a third of the sun was struck, a third of the moon, and a third of the stars, so that a third of them were darkened. A third of the day did not shine, and likewise the night.

13 And I looked, and I heard an angel flying through the midst of heaven, saying with a loud voice, "Woe, woe, woe to the inhabitants of the earth, because of the remaining blasts of the trumpet of the three angels who are about to sound!"

9 Then the fifth angel sounded: And I saw a star fallen from heaven to the earth. To him was given the key to the bottomless pit. 2 And he opened the bottomless pit, and smoke arose out of the pit like the smoke of a great furnace. So the sun and the air were darkened because of the smoke of the pit. 3 Then out of the smoke locusts came upon the earth. And to them was given power, as the scorpions of the earth have power. 4 They were commanded not to harm the grass of the earth, or any green thing, or any tree, but only those men who do not have the seal of God on their foreheads. 5 And they were not given *authority* to kill them, but to torment them *for* five months. Their torment *was* like the torment of a scorpion when it strikes a man. 6 In those days men will seek death and will not find it; they will desire to die, and death will flee from them.

7 The shape of the locusts was like horses prepared for battle. On their heads were crowns of something like gold, and their faces *were* like the faces of men. 8 They had hair like women's hair, and their teeth were like lions' *teeth*. 9 And they had breastplates like breastplates of iron, and the sound of their wings *was* like the sound of chariots with many horses running into battle. 10 They had tails like scorpions, and there were stings in their tails.

7 הָרִאשׁוֹן תָּקַע בַּשּׁוֹפָר וְהִנֵּה הִתְהַוּוּ בָרָד וָאֵשׁ מְעֹרָבִים בְּדָם וְהֻשְׁלְכוּ אַרְצָה; שְׁלִישׁ הָאָרֶץ נִשְׂרַף, שְׁלִישׁ הָעֵצִים נִשְׂרַף, וְכָל יֶרֶק עֵשֶׂב נִשְׂרַף.

8 הַמַּלְאָךְ הַשֵּׁנִי תָּקַע בַּשּׁוֹפָר וּכְמוֹ הַר גָּדוֹל בּוֹעֵר בָּאֵשׁ הֻשְׁלַךְ אֶל הַיָּם; שְׁלִישׁ הַיָּם נִהְיָה לְדָם, 9 שְׁלִישׁ הַיְצוּרִים בַּיָּם – אֲשֶׁר נֶפֶשׁ לָהֶם – מֵתוּ, וּשְׁלִישׁ הָאֳנִיּוֹת נִשְׁמְדוּ.

10 הַמַּלְאָךְ הַשְּׁלִישִׁי תָּקַע בַּשּׁוֹפָר וּמִן הַשָּׁמַיִם נָפַל כּוֹכָב גָּדוֹל בּוֹעֵר כְּלַפִּיד. הוּא נָפַל עַל שְׁלִישׁ הַנְּהָרוֹת וְעַל מַעְיְנוֹת הַמַּיִם – 11 שֵׁם הַכּוֹכָב נִקְרָא לַעֲנָה – וּשְׁלִישׁ הַמַּיִם נֶהְפַּךְ לְלַעֲנָה וְרַבִּים מִבְּנֵי אָדָם מֵתוּ מִן הַמַּיִם שֶׁנִּהְיוּ מָרִים.

12 הַמַּלְאָךְ הָרְבִיעִי תָּקַע בַּשּׁוֹפָר וּשְׁלִישִׁית הַשֶּׁמֶשׁ לָקְתָה וְגַם שְׁלִישׁ הַיָּרֵחַ וּשְׁלִישׁ הַכּוֹכָבִים, כְּדֵי שֶׁיֶּחְשַׁךְ שְׁלִישׁ מֵהֶם וְהַיּוֹם לֹא יָאִיר שְׁלִישִׁיתוֹ וְכֵן גַּם הַלַּיְלָה.

13 רָאִיתִי וְשָׁמַעְתִּי נֶשֶׁר אֶחָד מְעוֹפֵף בְּאֶמְצַע הַשָּׁמַיִם וְהוּא אוֹמֵר בְּקוֹל גָּדוֹל: "אוֹי, אוֹי, אוֹי לְיוֹשְׁבֵי הָאָרֶץ מִיֶּתֶר קוֹלוֹת הַשּׁוֹפָר אֲשֶׁר שְׁלֹשֶׁת הַמַּלְאָכִים עֲתִידִים לִתְקֹעַ."

ט הַמַּלְאָךְ הַחֲמִישִׁי תָּקַע בַּשּׁוֹפָר וְרָאִיתִי כּוֹכָב נוֹפֵל מִן הַשָּׁמַיִם אַרְצָה וְנִתַּן לוֹ מַפְתֵּחַ בּוֹר הַתְּהוֹם. 2 הוּא פָּתַח אֶת בּוֹר הַתְּהוֹם וְעָשָׁן עָלָה מִן הַבּוֹר, כֶּעָשָׁן כִּבְשָׁן גָּדוֹל, וְהַשֶּׁמֶשׁ וְהָאֲוִיר חָשְׁכוּ מֵעֲשַׁן הַבּוֹר. 3 מִן הֶעָשָׁן יָצָא אַרְבֶּה עַל הָאָרֶץ וְנִתַּן לָהֶם כֹּחַ כְּכֹחַ אֲשֶׁר לְעַקְרַבֵּי הָאָרֶץ. 4 נֶאֱמַר לָהֶם שֶׁלֹּא לְהַזִּיק לַעֵשֶׂב הָאָרֶץ, אַף לֹא לְכָל יֶרֶק וְכָל עֵץ, אֶלָּא לָאֲנָשִׁים אֲשֶׁר אֵין לָהֶם חוֹתַם אֱלֹהִים עַל מִצְחוֹתֵיהֶם. 5 הֻתַּר לָהֶם לְעַנּוֹתָם חֲמִשָּׁה חֳדָשִׁים אַךְ לֹא לְהָרְגָם; וְעִנּוּיָם הוּא כְּעִנּוּי שֶׁגּוֹרֵם עַקְרָב בְּעָקְצוֹ אָדָם. 6 בַּיָּמִים הָהֵם יְחַפְּשׂוּ בְּנֵי הָאָדָם אֶת הַמָּוֶת וְלֹא יִמְצְאוּ אוֹתוֹ, וְיִתְאַוּוּ לָמוּת וְהַמָּוֶת יִבְרַח מֵהֶם.

7 בְּצוּרָתָם דּוֹמִים חַגְבֵי הָאַרְבֶּה לְסוּסִים עֲרוּכִים לְמִלְחָמָה; עַל רָאשֵׁיהֶם כַּעֲטָרוֹת דּוֹמוֹת לְזָהָב וּפְנֵיהֶם כִּפְנֵי בְּנֵי אָדָם; 8 שֵׂעָר לָהֶם כִּשְׂעַר נָשִׁים וְשִׁנֵּיהֶם כְּשִׁנֵּי אֲרָיֵה; 9 שִׁרְיוֹנִים לָהֶם כְּשִׁרְיוֹנֵי בַּרְזֶל וְקוֹל כַּנְפֵיהֶם כְּקוֹל מֶרְכְּבוֹת סוּסִים רַבִּים הָרָצִים לַמִּלְחָמָה; 10 זְנָבוֹת לָהֶם כְּזַנְבוֹת עַקְרַבִּים, עִם

Their power *was* to hurt men five months. [11] And they had as king over them the angel of the bottomless pit, whose name in Hebrew *is* Abaddon, but in Greek he has the name Apollyon.

[12] One woe is past. Behold, still two more woes are coming after these things.

[13] Then the sixth angel sounded: And I heard a voice from the four horns of the golden altar which is before God, [14] saying to the sixth angel who had the trumpet, "Release the four angels who are bound at the great river Euphrates." [15] So the four angels, who had been prepared for the hour and day and month and year, were released to kill a third of mankind. [16] Now the number of the army of the horsemen *was* two hundred million; I heard the number of them. [17] And thus I saw the horses in the vision: those who sat on them had breastplates of fiery red, hyacinth blue, and sulfur yellow; and the heads of the horses *were* like the heads of lions; and out of their mouths came fire, smoke, and brimstone. [18] By these three *plagues* a third of mankind was killed—by the fire and the smoke and the brimstone which came out of their mouths. [19] For their power is in their mouth and in their tails; for their tails *are* like serpents, having heads; and with them they do harm.

[20] But the rest of mankind, who were not killed by these plagues, did not repent of the works of their hands, that they should not worship demons, and idols of gold, silver, brass, stone, and wood, which can neither see nor hear nor walk. [21] And they did not repent of their murders or their sorceries or their sexual immorality or their thefts.

10

I saw still another mighty angel coming down from heaven, clothed with a cloud. And a rainbow *was* on his head, his face *was* like the sun, and his feet like pillars of fire. [2] He had a little book open in his hand. And he set his right foot on the sea and *his* left *foot* on the land, [3] and cried with a loud voice, as *when* a lion roars. When he cried out, seven thunders uttered their voices. [4] Now when the seven thunders uttered their voices, I was about to write; but I heard a voice from heaven saying to me, "Seal up the things which the seven thunders uttered, and do not write them."

[5] The angel whom I saw standing on the sea and on the land raised up his hand to heaven [6] and swore by Him who lives forever and ever, who created heaven and the things that are in it, the earth and the things that are in it, and the sea and the things that are in it, that there should be delay no longer, [7] but in the days of the sounding of the

עֲקְצִים, וּבְזַנְבוֹתֵיהֶם כֹּחַ לָהֶם לְהַזִּיק לִבְנֵי אָדָם חֲמִשָּׁה חֳדָשִׁים. [11] וְיֵשׁ לָהֶם מֶלֶךְ עֲלֵיהֶם, מַלְאַךְ הַתְּהוֹם, אֲשֶׁר שְׁמוֹ בְּעִבְרִית אֲבַדּוֹן וּבִיוָנִית שְׁמוֹ אַפַּלְיוֹן. [12] אוֹי אֶחָד חָלָף; הִנֵּה עוֹד אוֹי וְעוֹד אוֹי בָּאִים אַחֲרֵי כֵן. [13] הַמַּלְאָךְ הַשִּׁשִּׁי תָּקַע בַּשּׁוֹפָר וְשָׁמַעְתִּי קוֹל אֶחָד מֵאֵת אַרְבַּע קַרְנוֹת מִזְבַּח הַזָּהָב אֲשֶׁר לִפְנֵי הָאֱלֹהִים, [14] אוֹמֵר לַמַּלְאָךְ הַשִּׁשִּׁי הַמַּחֲזִיק בַּשּׁוֹפָר: "הַתֵּר אֶת אַרְבַּעַת הַמַּלְאָכִים הָאֲסוּרִים עַל הַנָּהָר הַגָּדוֹל נְהַר פְּרָת." [15] אָז הֻתְּרוּ אַרְבַּעַת הַמַּלְאָכִים הַמּוּכָנִים לְשָׁעָה וְלַיּוֹם וְלַחֹדֶשׁ וְלַשָּׁנָה, כְּדֵי שֶׁיַּהַרְגוּ שְׁלִישׁ מִבְּנֵי הָאָדָם. [16] וּמִסְפַּר צִבְאוֹת הַפָּרָשִׁים עֶשְׂרִים אֶלֶף רְבָבוֹת; שָׁמַעְתִּי אֶת מִסְפָּרָם. [17] כָּךְ רָאִיתִי אֶת הַסּוּסִים בֶּחָזוֹן: לְרוֹכְבֵיהֶם יֵשׁ שִׁרְיוֹנוֹת שֶׁל אֵשׁ וְלֶשֶׁם וְגָפְרִית; וְרָאשֵׁי הַסּוּסִים כְּרָאשֵׁי אֲרָיוֹת וּמִפִּיהֶם יוֹצְאִים אֵשׁ וְעָשָׁן וְגָפְרִית. [18] שְׁלִישׁ בְּנֵי הָאָדָם מֵתוּ בִּשְׁלוֹשׁ הַמַּכּוֹת הָאֵלֶּה, בָּאֵשׁ וּבֶעָשָׁן וּבַגָּפְרִית הַיּוֹצְאִים מִפִּיהֶם; [19] שֶׁכֵּן כֹּחַ שֶׁל הַסּוּסִים הוּא בְּפִיּוֹתֵיהֶם וְגַם בְּזַנְבוֹתֵיהֶם, כִּי זַנְבוֹתֵיהֶם דּוֹמִים לִנְחָשִׁים בִּהְיוֹת לָהֶם רָאשִׁים, וּבָהֶם יַזִּיקוּ.

[20] שְׁאָר הָאֲנָשִׁים אֲשֶׁר לֹא נֶהֶרְגוּ בַּמַּכּוֹת הָאֵלֶּה, בְּכָל זֹאת לֹא שָׁבוּ מִמַּעֲשֵׂי יְדֵיהֶם וְלֹא נִמְנְעוּ מֵהִשְׁתַּחֲווֹת לַשֵּׁדִים וְלֶאֱלִילֵי זָהָב וָכֶסֶף וּנְחֹשֶׁת וְאֶבֶן וָעֵץ אֲשֶׁר אֵינָם יְכוֹלִים לִרְאוֹת, אַף לֹא לִשְׁמֹעַ וּלְהַלֵּךְ. [21] וְלֹא שָׁבוּ מֵרְצִיחוֹתֵיהֶם, אַף לֹא מִכִּשּׁוּפֵיהֶם, מִתַּזְנוּתָם וּמִגְּנֵבוֹתֵיהֶם.

[י] רָאִיתִי מַלְאָךְ אַחֵר רַב־כֹּחַ יוֹרֵד מִן הַשָּׁמַיִם וְהוּא לָבוּשׁ עָנָן; קֶשֶׁת עַל רֹאשׁוֹ, פָּנָיו כַּשֶּׁמֶשׁ וְרַגְלָיו כְּעַמּוּדֵי אֵשׁ. [2] וּבְיָדוֹ סֵפֶר קָטָן פָּתוּחַ. הוּא שָׂם אֶת רַגְלוֹ הַיְמָנִית עַל הַיָּם וְאֶת הַשְּׂמָאלִית עַל הָאָרֶץ, [3] וְקָרָא בְּקוֹל גָּדוֹל כְּאַרְיֵה שׁוֹאֵג. כַּאֲשֶׁר קָרָא דִּבְּרוּ שִׁבְעַת הָרְעָמִים בְּקוֹלוֹתֵיהֶם; [4] וּכְשֶׁדִּבְּרוּ שִׁבְעַת הָרְעָמִים הִתְכּוֹנַנְתִּי לִכְתֹּב, אַךְ שָׁמַעְתִּי קוֹל מִן הַשָּׁמַיִם אוֹמֵר: "חֲתֹם אֶת אֲשֶׁר דִּבְּרוּ שִׁבְעַת הָרְעָמִים וְאַל תִּכְתֹּב זֹאת." [5] וְהַמַּלְאָךְ שֶׁרְאִיתִיו עוֹמֵד עַל הַיָּם וְעַל הָאָרֶץ הֵרִים אֶת יַד יְמִינוֹ הַשָּׁמַיְמָה [6] וְנִשְׁבַּע בְּחַי לְעוֹלְמֵי עוֹלָמִים, אֲשֶׁר בָּרָא אֶת הַשָּׁמַיִם וְאֶת אֲשֶׁר בָּם וְאֶת הָאָרֶץ וְאֶת אֲשֶׁר בָּהּ וְאֶת הַיָּם וְאֶת אֲשֶׁר בּוֹ – שֶׁלֹּא תִּהְיֶה עוֹד שָׁהוּת. [7] אוּלָם בִּימֵי קוֹל הַמַּלְאָךְ הַשְּׁבִיעִי, בְּעָמְדוֹ לִתְקֹעַ בַּשּׁוֹפָר, גַּם יֻשְׁלַם רָז הָאֱלֹהִים, כְּמוֹ שֶׁבִּשֵּׂר לַעֲבָדָיו הַנְּבִיאִים.

seventh angel, when he is about to sound, the mystery of God would be finished, as He declared to His servants the prophets.

8 Then the voice which I heard from heaven spoke to me again and said, "Go, take the little book which is open in the hand of the angel who stands on the sea and on the earth."

9 So I went to the angel and said to him, "Give me the little book."

And he said to me, "Take and eat it; and it will make your stomach bitter, but it will be as sweet as honey in your mouth."

10 Then I took the little book out of the angel's hand and ate it, and it was as sweet as honey in my mouth. But when I had eaten it, my stomach became bitter. 11 And he said to me, "You must prophesy again about many peoples, nations, tongues, and kings."

11 Then I was given a reed like a measuring rod. And the angel stood, saying, "Rise and measure the temple of God, the altar, and those who worship there. 2 But leave out the court which is outside the temple, and do not measure it, for it has been given to the Gentiles. And they will tread the holy city underfoot *for* forty-two months. 3 And I will give *power* to my two witnesses, and they will prophesy one thousand two hundred and sixty days, clothed in sackcloth."

4 These are the two olive trees and the two lampstands standing before the God of the earth. 5 And if anyone wants to harm them, fire proceeds from their mouth and devours their enemies. And if anyone wants to harm them, he must be killed in this manner. 6 These have power to shut heaven, so that no rain falls in the days of their prophecy; and they have power over waters to turn them to blood, and to strike the earth with all plagues, as often as they desire.

7 When they finish their testimony, the beast that ascends out of the bottomless pit will make war against them, overcome them, and kill them. 8 And their dead bodies *will lie* in the street of the great city which spiritually is called Sodom and Egypt, where also our Lord was crucified. 9 Then *those* from the peoples, tribes, tongues, and nations will see their dead bodies three-and-a-half days, and not allow their dead bodies to be put into graves. 10 And those who dwell on the earth will rejoice over them, make merry, and send gifts to one another, because these two prophets tormented those who dwell on the earth.

8 וְהַקּוֹל אֲשֶׁר שָׁמַעְתִּי מִן הַשָּׁמַיִם דִּבֶּר אֵלַי שׁוּב וְאָמַר: "לֵךְ קַח אֶת הַסֵּפֶר הַפָּתוּחַ שֶׁבְּיַד הַמַּלְאָךְ הָעוֹמֵד עַל הַיָּם וְעַל הָאָרֶץ." 9 הָלַכְתִּי אֶל הַמַּלְאָךְ וְאָמַרְתִּי לוֹ שֶׁיִּתֵּן לִי אֶת הַסֵּפֶר הַקָּטָן. אָמַר אֵלַי: "קַח וֶאֱכָל אוֹתוֹ, הוּא יָמֵר בְּבִטְנְךָ, אַךְ בְּפִיךָ יִהְיֶה מָתוֹק כִּדְבַשׁ." 10 לָקַחְתִּי אֶת הַסֵּפֶר הַקָּטָן מִיָּדוֹ שֶׁל הַמַּלְאָךְ וַאֲכַלְתִּיו; בְּפִי הָיָה מָתוֹק כִּדְבַשׁ, אֲבָל אַחֲרֵי אָכְלִי אוֹתוֹ הֵמַר לְבִטְנִי. 11 אָז אָמְרוּ לִי: "עָלֶיךָ עוֹד לְהִנָּבֵא עַל עַמִּים וְאֻמּוֹת וּלְשׁוֹנוֹת וּמְלָכִים רַבִּים."

יא נָתַן לִי קָנֶה דּוֹמֶה לְמַטֶּה, וְנֶאֱמַר לִי: "קוּם וּמְדֹד אֶת הֵיכַל אֱלֹהִים וְאֶת הַמִּזְבֵּחַ וְאֶת הַמִּשְׁתַּחֲוִים בּוֹ. 2 אֲבָל אֶת הֶחָצֵר אֲשֶׁר מִחוּץ לַהֵיכַל הַשְׁאֵר בַּחוּץ וְאַל תִּמְדֹּד אוֹתָהּ, כִּי נִתְּנָה לַגּוֹיִים וְיִרְמְסוּ אֶת עִיר הַקֹּדֶשׁ אַרְבָּעִים וּשְׁנַיִם חֳדָשִׁים. 3 וְאֶתֵּן לִשְׁנֵי עֵדַי וְיִנָּבְאוּ אֶלֶף וּמָאתַיִם וְשִׁשִּׁים יָמִים וְהֵם לְבוּשֵׁי שַׂקִּים." 4 אֵלֶּה הֵם שְׁנֵי הַזֵּיתִים וּשְׁתֵּי הַמְּנוֹרוֹת הָעוֹמְדִים לִפְנֵי אֲדוֹן הָאָרֶץ. 5 וְאִישׁ אִם יִרְצֶה לְהָרַע לָהֶם, תֵּצֵא אֵשׁ מִפִּיהֶם וְתֹאכַל אֶת אוֹיְבֵיהֶם; מִי שֶׁיִּרְצֶה לְהָרַע לָהֶם, בְּדֶרֶךְ זֹאת מוֹת יוּמָת. 6 יֵשׁ לָהֶם הַסַּמְכוּת לַעֲצֹר אֶת הַשָּׁמַיִם כְּדֵי שֶׁלֹּא יֵרֵד גֶּשֶׁם בִּימֵי נְבוּאָתָם, וְסַמְכוּת לָהֶם עַל הַמַּיִם לַהֲפֹךְ אוֹתָם לְדָם וּלְהַכּוֹת אֶת הָאָרֶץ בְּכָל מַכָּה שֶׁיִּרְצוּ. 7 כַּאֲשֶׁר יִגְמְרוּ אֶת עֵדוּתָם, הַחַיָּה הָעוֹלָה מִן הַתְּהוֹם תַּעֲשֶׂה עִמָּהֶם מִלְחָמָה, תְּנַצַּח אוֹתָם וְתַהַרְגֵם. 8 גְּוִיּוֹתֵיהֶם תִּהְיֶינָה בִּרְחוֹב הָעִיר הַגְּדוֹלָה הַנִּקְרֵאת בְּאֹפֶן רוּחָנִי סְדוֹם וּמִצְרַיִם, אֲשֶׁר שָׁם גַּם נִצְלַב אֲדוֹנֵנוּ. 9 וּמִן הָעַמִּים וְהַשְּׁבָטִים וְהַלְּשׁוֹנוֹת וְהָאֻמּוֹת יִרְאוּ אֶת גְּוִיּוֹתֵיהֶם בְּמֶשֶׁךְ שְׁלֹשָׁה יָמִים וָחֵצִי, וְלֹא יַרְשׁוּ לְהַנִּיחַ אֶת גְּוִיּוֹתֵיהֶם בַּקֶּבֶר. 10 יוֹשְׁבֵי הָאָרֶץ יִשְׂמְחוּ עֲלֵיהֶם וְיַעַלְזוּ, וְיִשְׁלְחוּ מָנוֹת אִישׁ לְרֵעֵהוּ, שֶׁכֵּן שְׁנֵי הַנְּבִיאִים

11 Now after the three-and-a-half days the breath of life from God entered them, and they stood on their feet, and great fear fell on those who saw them. 12 And they heard a loud voice from heaven saying to them, "Come up here." And they ascended to heaven in a cloud, and their enemies saw them. 13 In the same hour there was a great earthquake, and a tenth of the city fell. In the earthquake seven thousand people were killed, and the rest were afraid and gave glory to the God of heaven.

14 The second woe is past. Behold, the third woe is coming quickly.

15 Then the seventh angel sounded: And there were loud voices in heaven, saying, "The kingdoms of this world have become the kingdoms of our Lord and of His Christ, and He shall reign forever and ever!" 16 And the twenty-four elders who sat before God on their thrones fell on their faces and worshiped God, 17 saying:

"We give You thanks, O Lord God Almighty,
The One who is and who was and who is to come,
Because You have taken Your great power and reigned.
18 The nations were angry, and Your wrath has come,
And the time of the dead, that they should be judged,
And that You should reward Your servants the prophets and the saints,
And those who fear Your name, small and great,
And should destroy those who destroy the earth."

19 Then the temple of God was opened in heaven, and the ark of His covenant was seen in His temple. And there were lightnings, noises, thunderings, an earthquake, and great hail.

12 Now a great sign appeared in heaven: a woman clothed with the sun, with the moon under her feet, and on her head a garland of twelve stars. 2 Then being with child, she cried out in labor and in pain to give birth.

3 And another sign appeared in heaven: behold, a great, fiery red dragon having seven heads and ten horns, and seven diadems on his heads. 4 His tail drew a third of the stars of heaven and threw them to the earth. And the dragon stood before the woman who was ready to give birth, to devour her Child as soon as it was born. 5 She bore a male Child who was to rule all nations with a rod of iron.

הָאֵלֶּה הִכְאִיבוּ לְיוֹשְׁבֵי הָאָרֶץ. 11 אַחֲרֵי שְׁלוֹשָׁה יָמִים וָחֵצִי בָּאָה בָהֶם רוּחַ חַיִּים מֵאֵת הָאֱלֹהִים; הֵם קָמוּ עַל רַגְלֵיהֶם וּפַחַד גָּדוֹל נָפַל עַל רוֹאֵיהֶם. 12 אָז שָׁמְעוּ קוֹל גָּדוֹל מִן הַשָּׁמַיִם אוֹמֵר לָהֶם: "עֲלוּ הֵנָּה!", וְהֵם עָלוּ בֶּעָנָן הַשָּׁמַיְמָה לְעֵינֵי אוֹיְבֵיהֶם. 13 אוֹתָהּ שָׁעָה הִתְחוֹלְלָה רְעִידַת אֲדָמָה גְּדוֹלָה; עֲשִׂירִית הָעִיר נָפְלָה וְשִׁבְעַת אֲלָפִים אֲנָשִׁים נֶהֶרְגוּ בִּרְעִידַת הָאֲדָמָה; וְהַנִּשְׁאָרִים נֶחֶרְדוּ וְנָתְנוּ כָּבוֹד לֵאלֹהֵי הַשָּׁמַיִם.

14 אוֹי שֵׁנִי חָלַף; הִנֵּה אוֹי שְׁלִישִׁי בָּא מַהֵר.

15 הַמַּלְאָךְ הַשְּׁבִיעִי תָּקַע בַּשּׁוֹפָר וְקוֹלוֹת גְּדוֹלִים נִשְׁמְעוּ בַּשָּׁמַיִם – אוֹמְרִים: "הָיְתָה מַמְלֶכֶת תֵּבֵל לְמַמְלַכְתּוֹ שֶׁל אֲדוֹנֵנוּ וְשֶׁל מְשִׁיחוֹ וְהוּא יִמְלֹךְ לְעוֹלְמֵי עוֹלָמִים." 16 עֶשְׂרִים וְאַרְבָּעָה הַזְּקֵנִים, הַיּוֹשְׁבִים עַל כִּסְאוֹתֵיהֶם לִפְנֵי הָאֱלֹהִים, נָפְלוּ עַל פְּנֵיהֶם וְהִשְׁתַּחֲווּ לֵאלֹהִים 17 בְּאָמְרָם:

"מוֹדִים אֲנַחְנוּ לְךָ, יהוה אֱלֹהֵי צְבָאוֹת אֲשֶׁר הֹוֶה וְהָיָה,
כִּי לָבַשְׁתָּ עֻזְּךָ הַגָּדוֹל וַתִּמְלֹךְ.
18 הַגּוֹיִים קָצָפוּ, וּבָא קִצְפְּךָ וְעֵת לְשִׁפּוֹט הַמֵּתִים וְלָתֵת
שָׂכָר לַעֲבָדֶיךָ הַנְּבִיאִים וְלַקְּדוֹשִׁים וּלְיִרְאֵי שְׁמֶךָ,
לַקְּטַנִּים וְלַגְּדוֹלִים, וּלְהַשְׁחִית אֶת מַשְׁחִיתֵי הָאָרֶץ."

19 אָז נִפְתַּח הֵיכַל אֱלֹהִים בַּשָּׁמַיִם וַאֲרוֹן בְּרִיתוֹ נִרְאָה בְּהֵיכָלוֹ; בְּרָקִים וְקוֹלוֹת וּרְעָמִים הִתְחוֹלְלוּ, וּרְעִידַת אֲדָמָה וּבָרָד כָּבֵד.

יב אוֹת גָּדוֹל נִרְאָה בַּשָּׁמַיִם: אִשָּׁה אֲשֶׁר הַשֶּׁמֶשׁ לְבוּשָׁהּ, הַיָּרֵחַ תַּחַת רַגְלֶיהָ, וְעַל רֹאשָׁהּ עֲטֶרֶת שֶׁל שְׁנֵים-עָשָׂר כּוֹכָבִים; 2 הָרָה הִיא וְזוֹעֶקֶת מִכְאֵבִים וְצִירֵי לֵדָה. 3 גַּם אוֹת אַחֵר נִרְאָה בַּשָּׁמַיִם: וְהִנֵּה תַּנִּין גָּדוֹל, אָדֹם כָּאֵשׁ, שִׁבְעָה רָאשִׁים לוֹ וְעֶשֶׂר קַרְנַיִם; עַל רָאשָׁיו שִׁבְעָה כְּתָרִים, 4 וּמִנְּבוֹ סָחַב שְׁלִישׁ מִכּוֹכְבֵי הַשָּׁמַיִם וְהִשְׁלִיכָם אַרְצָה. וְהַתַּנִּין עָמַד לִפְנֵי הָאִשָּׁה הַקְּרוֹבָה לָלֶדֶת, כְּדֵי לִבְלֹעַ אֶת בְּנָהּ בְּעֵת הַלֵּדָה. 5 לְאַחַר שֶׁיָּלְדָה בֵּן זָכָר, אֲשֶׁר עָתִיד לִרְעוֹת אֶת כָּל הַגּוֹיִים בְּשֵׁבֶט בַּרְזֶל, נֶחְטַף

And her Child was caught up to God and His throne. ⁶Then the woman fled into the wilderness, where she has a place prepared by God, that they should feed her there one thousand two hundred and sixty days.

⁷And war broke out in heaven: Michael and his angels fought with the dragon; and the dragon and his angels fought, ⁸but they did not prevail, nor was a place found for them in heaven any longer. ⁹So the great dragon was cast out, that serpent of old, called the Devil and Satan, who deceives the whole world; he was cast to the earth, and his angels were cast out with him.

¹⁰Then I heard a loud voice saying in heaven, "Now salvation, and strength, and the kingdom of our God, and the power of His Christ have come, for the accuser of our brethren, who accused them before our God day and night, has been cast down. ¹¹And they overcame him by the blood of the Lamb and by the word of their testimony, and they did not love their lives to the death. ¹²Therefore rejoice, O heavens, and you who dwell in them! Woe to the inhabitants of the earth and the sea! For the devil has come down to you, having great wrath, because he knows that he has a short time."

¹³Now when the dragon saw that he had been cast to the earth, he persecuted the woman who gave birth to the male *Child*. ¹⁴But the woman was given two wings of a great eagle, that she might fly into the wilderness to her place, where she is nourished for a time and times and half a time, from the presence of the serpent. ¹⁵So the serpent spewed water out of his mouth like a flood after the woman, that he might cause her to be carried away by the flood. ¹⁶But the earth helped the woman, and the earth opened its mouth and swallowed up the flood which the dragon had spewed out of his mouth. ¹⁷And the dragon was enraged with the woman, and he went to make war with the rest of her offspring, who keep the commandments of God and have the testimony of Jesus Christ.

13 Then I stood on the sand of the sea. And I saw a beast rising up out of the sea, having seven heads and ten horns, and on his horns ten crowns, and on his heads a blasphemous name. ²Now the beast which I saw was like a leopard, his feet were like *the feet of* a bear, and his mouth like the mouth of a lion. The dragon gave him his power, his throne, and great authority. ³And *I saw* one of his heads as if it had been mortally wounded, and his deadly wound was healed. And all the world marveled and followed the beast. ⁴So they worshiped the dragon

בְּנָהּ אֶל הָאֱלֹהִים וְאֶל כִּסְאוֹ. ⁶וְהָאִשָּׁה בָּרְחָה לַמִּדְבָּר, אֲשֶׁר שָׁם הוּכַן לָהּ מָקוֹם מֵאֵת הָאֱלֹהִים, כְּדֵי שֶׁיְּכַלְכְּלוּהָ שָׁם אֶלֶף וּמָאתַיִם וְשִׁשִּׁים יוֹם. ⁷וּמִלְחָמָה הִתְחוֹלְלָה בַּשָּׁמַיִם; מִיכָאֵל וּמַלְאָכָיו נִלְחָמִים בַּתַּנִּין וְהַתַּנִּין נִלְחָם וּמַלְאָכָיו. ⁸וְהֵם לֹא הִתְגַּבְּרוּ וְגַם מְקוֹמָם לֹא נִמְצָא עוֹד בַּשָּׁמַיִם. ⁹אָז הֻשְׁלַךְ הַתַּנִּין הַגָּדוֹל, הַנָּחָשׁ הַקַּדְמוֹנִי הַנִּקְרָא מַלְשִׁין וְשָׂטָן, הַמַּתְעֶה אֶת תֵּבֵל כֻּלָּהּ; הוּא הֻשְׁלַךְ אַרְצָה וּמַלְאָכָיו הֻשְׁלְכוּ אִתּוֹ. ¹⁰וְשָׁמַעְתִּי קוֹל גָּדוֹל בַּשָּׁמַיִם אוֹמֵר:

"עַתָּה בָּאָה יְשׁוּעַת אֱלֹהֵינוּ, גְּבוּרָתוֹ וּמַלְכוּתוֹ וּמֶמְשֶׁלֶת מְשִׁיחוֹ, כִּי הֻשְׁלַךְ שׂוֹטֵן אַחֵינוּ הַמְקַטְרֵג עֲלֵיהֶם לִפְנֵי אֱלֹהֵינוּ יוֹמָם וָלָיְלָה. ¹¹וְהֵם נִצְּחוּהוּ בְּדַם הַשֶּׂה וּבִדְבַר עֵדוּתָם, וְלֹא אָהֲבוּ אֶת נַפְשָׁם עַד מָוֶת. ¹²עַל זֹאת שִׂמְחוּ שָׁמַיִם וְשׁוֹכְנֵיהֶם.

אוֹי לָאָרֶץ וְלַיָּם,
כִּי יָרַד אֲלֵיכֶם הַשָּׂטָן בְּחֵמָה גְדוֹלָה,
בְּיָדְעוֹ כִּי קְצָרָה עִתּוֹ."

¹³כַּאֲשֶׁר רָאָה הַתַּנִּין כִּי הֻשְׁלַךְ אַרְצָה, רָדַף אֶת הָאִשָּׁה אֲשֶׁר יָלְדָה אֶת הַזָּכָר. ¹⁴אָז נִתְּנוּ לָאִשָּׁה שְׁתֵּי כַּנְפֵי הַנֶּשֶׁר הַגָּדוֹל כְּדֵי לָעוּף לַמִּדְבָּר אֶל מְקוֹמָהּ אֲשֶׁר תְּכֻלְכַּל שָׁם מוֹעֵד מוֹעֲדִים וַחֲצִי מוֹעֵד מִפְּנֵי הַנָּחָשׁ. ¹⁵הֵטִיל הַנָּחָשׁ מִפִּיו נָהָר מַיִם אַחֲרֵי הָאִשָּׁה, לִשְׁטֹפָהּ בַּנָּהָר. ¹⁶אַךְ הָאָרֶץ עָזְרָה לָאִשָּׁה; פָּתְחָה הָאָרֶץ אֶת פִּיהָ וּבָלְעָה אֶת הַנָּהָר שֶׁהֵטִיל הַתַּנִּין מִפִּיו. ¹⁷קָצַף הַתַּנִּין עַל הָאִשָּׁה וְהָלַךְ לַעֲשׂוֹת מִלְחָמָה עִם שְׁאָר זַרְעָהּ הַשּׁוֹמְרִים אֶת מִצְווֹת אֱלֹהִים וְלָהֶם עֵדוּת יֵשׁוּעַ. ¹⁸וְהוּא עָמַד עַל חוֹל הַיָּם.

יג רָאִיתִי חַיָּה עוֹלָה מִן הַיָּם, עֶשֶׂר קַרְנַיִם לָהּ וְשִׁבְעָה רָאשִׁים; עַל קַרְנֶיהָ עֲשָׂרָה כְּתָרִים וְעַל רָאשֶׁיהָ שְׁמוֹת גִּדּוּפִים. ²וְהַחַיָּה אֲשֶׁר רָאִיתִי הָיְתָה דּוֹמָה לְנָמֵר, רַגְלֶיהָ כְּרַגְלֵי דֹב וּפִיהָ כְּפִי אַרְיֵה. וְהַתַּנִּין נָתַן לָהּ אֶת כֹּחוֹ וְאֶת כִּסְאוֹ וְסַמְכוּת רַבָּה. ³אֶחָד מֵרָאשֶׁיהָ הָיָה כְּשָׁחוּט, אַךְ מַכַּת הַמָּוֶת אֲשֶׁר לָהּ נִרְפְּאָה וְכָל הָאָרֶץ הִשְׁתּוֹמְמָה עַל הַחַיָּה. ⁴הֵם

who gave authority to the beast; and they worshiped the beast, saying, "Who *is* like the beast? Who is able to make war with him?"

⁵ And he was given a mouth speaking great things and blasphemies, and he was given authority to continue for forty-two months. ⁶ Then he opened his mouth in blasphemy against God, to blaspheme His name, His tabernacle, and those who dwell in heaven. ⁷ It was granted to him to make war with the saints and to overcome them. And authority was given him over every tribe, tongue, and nation. ⁸ All who dwell on the earth will worship him, whose names have not been written in the Book of Life of the Lamb slain from the foundation of the world.

⁹ If anyone has an ear, let him hear. ¹⁰ He who leads into captivity shall go into captivity; he who kills with the sword must be killed with the sword. Here is the patience and the faith of the saints.

¹¹ Then I saw another beast coming up out of the earth, and he had two horns like a lamb and spoke like a dragon. ¹² And he exercises all the authority of the first beast in his presence, and causes the earth and those who dwell in it to worship the first beast, whose deadly wound was healed. ¹³ He performs great signs, so that he even makes fire come down from heaven on the earth in the sight of men. ¹⁴ And he deceives those who dwell on the earth by those signs which he was granted to do in the sight of the beast, telling those who dwell on the earth to make an image to the beast who was wounded by the sword and lived. ¹⁵ He was granted *power* to give breath to the image of the beast, that the image of the beast should both speak and cause as many as would not worship the image of the beast to be killed. ¹⁶ He causes all, both small and great, rich and poor, free and slave, to receive a mark on their right hand or on their foreheads, ¹⁷ and that no one may buy or sell except one who has the mark or the name of the beast, or the number of his name.

¹⁸ Here is wisdom. Let him who has understanding calculate the number of the beast, for it is the number of a man: His number *is* 666.

14 Then I looked, and behold, a Lamb standing on Mount Zion, and with Him one hundred *and* forty-four thousand, having His Father's name written on their foreheads. ² And I heard a voice from heaven, like the voice of many waters, and like the voice of loud thunder. And I heard the sound of harpists playing their harps. ³ They sang as it were a new song before the throne, before the four living creatures, and the elders; and no one could learn

הִשְׁתַּחֲווּ לַתַּנִּין מִפְּנֵי שֶׁנָּתַן אֶת הַשִּׁלְטוֹן לַחַיָּה, וְהִשְׁתַּחֲווּ לַחַיָּה בְּאָמְרָם: "מִי כְּמוֹ הַחַיָּה? וּמִי יָכוֹל לְהִלָּחֵם עִמָּהּ?"

⁵ נִתַּן לָהּ פֶּה מְדַבֵּר גְּדוֹלוֹת וְנֶאָצוֹת וְנִתְּנָה לָהּ סַמְכוּת לִפְעֹל אַרְבָּעִים וּשְׁנַיִם חֳדָשִׁים. ⁶ הִיא פָּתְחָה אֶת פִּיהָ בִּנְאָצוֹת כְּלַפֵּי הָאֱלֹהִים, לְנָאֵץ אֶת שְׁמוֹ וְאֶת מִשְׁכָּנוֹ, אֶת הַשּׁוֹכְנִים בַּשָּׁמַיִם. ⁷ הֻתַּר לָהּ לַעֲשׂוֹת מִלְחָמָה עִם הַקְּדוֹשִׁים וּלְנַצְּחָם, וְנִתַּן לָהּ שִׁלְטוֹן עַל כָּל שֵׁבֶט וְעַם וְלָשׁוֹן וְאֻמָּה, ⁸ וְיִשְׁתַּחֲווּ לָהּ כָּל יוֹשְׁבֵי הָאָרֶץ אֲשֶׁר לֹא נִכְתְּבוּ שְׁמוֹתֵיהֶם בְּסֵפֶר הַחַיִּים שֶׁל הַשֶּׂה הַשָּׁחוּט מֵהִוָּסֵד תֵּבֵל.

⁹ מִי שֶׁאָזְן לוֹ, יִשְׁמַע נָא! ¹⁰ הַמּוֹעֵד לַשְּׁבִי יֵלֵךְ בַּשְּׁבִי; וְהַמּוֹעֵד לַהֲרֹג בַּחֶרֶב יֵהָרֵג בַּחֶרֶב. בָּזֶה סַבְלָנוּת הַקְּדוֹשִׁים וֶאֱמוּנָתָם.

¹¹ רָאִיתִי חַיָּה אַחֶרֶת עוֹלָה מִן הָאָרֶץ. הָיוּ לָהּ שְׁתֵּי קַרְנַיִם דּוֹמוֹת לְקַרְנֵי שֶׂה וְהִיא דִּבְּרָה כְּתַנִּין. ¹² אֶת סַמְכוּת הַחַיָּה הָרִאשׁוֹנָה הִיא מוֹצִיאָה אֶל הַפֹּעַל לְפָנֶיהָ, וּמְאַלֶּצֶת אֶת הָאָרֶץ וְיוֹשְׁבֶיהָ לְהִשְׁתַּחֲווֹת לַחַיָּה הָרִאשׁוֹנָה אֲשֶׁר מַכַּת הַמָּוֶת שֶׁלָּהּ נִרְפָּאָה. ¹³ הִיא עוֹשָׂה אוֹתוֹת גְּדוֹלִים, אֲפִלּוּ עַד כְּדֵי הוֹרָדַת אֵשׁ מִן הַשָּׁמַיִם אַרְצָה לְעֵינֵי בְּנֵי אָדָם, ¹⁴ וּמַתְעָה אֶת יוֹשְׁבֵי הָאָרֶץ עַל-יְדֵי הָאוֹתוֹת אֲשֶׁר הֻתַּר לָהּ לַעֲשׂוֹת לְנֹכַח הַחַיָּה, בְּאָמְרָהּ לְיוֹשְׁבֵי הָאָרֶץ לַעֲשׂוֹת צֶלֶם לַחַיָּה אֲשֶׁר הֻכְּתָה מַכַּת חֶרֶב וְחָיְתָה. ¹⁵ גַּם הֻתַּר לָהּ לָתֵת רוּחַ לְצֶלֶם הַחַיָּה בְּאֹפֶן שֶׁצֶּלֶם הַחַיָּה גַּם יְדַבֵּר, וְאַף יִגְרֹם לְכָךְ שֶׁיּוּמְתוּ כָּל אֲשֶׁר אֵינָם מִשְׁתַּחֲוִים לְצֶלֶם הַחַיָּה. ¹⁶ וְהִיא גּוֹרֶמֶת לְכָךְ שֶׁהַכֹּל, הַקְּטַנִּים וְהַגְּדוֹלִים, הָעֲשִׁירִים וְהָעֲנִיִּים, הַחָפְשִׁים וְהָעֲבָדִים, יָשִׂימוּ לָהֶם תָּו עַל יַד יְמִינָם אוֹ עַל מִצְחָם, ¹⁷ כְּדֵי שֶׁלֹּא יוּכַל אִישׁ לִקְנוֹת אוֹ לִמְכֹּר – אֶלָּא מִי שֶׁיֵּשׁ לוֹ הַתָּו, שֵׁם הַחַיָּה אוֹ מִסְפַּר שְׁמָהּ. ¹⁸ בָּזֹאת הַחָכְמָה. מִי שֶׁבִּינָה לוֹ, יְחַשֵּׁב נָא אֶת מִסְפַּר הַחַיָּה, כִּי מִסְפַּר אָדָם הוּא וּמִסְפָּרוֹ שֵׁשׁ מֵאוֹת וְשִׁשִּׁים וָשֵׁשׁ.

יד רָאִיתִי וְהִנֵּה הַשֶּׂה עוֹמֵד עַל הַר צִיּוֹן וְאִתּוֹ מֵאָה וְאַרְבָּעִים וְאַרְבָּעָה אֶלֶף אֲשֶׁר שְׁמוֹ וְשֵׁם אָבִיו כְּתוּבִים עַל מִצְחוֹתֵיהֶם. ² שָׁמַעְתִּי קוֹל מִן הַשָּׁמַיִם כְּקוֹל מַיִם רַבִּים וּכְקוֹל רַעַם גָּדוֹל, וְהַקּוֹל אֲשֶׁר שָׁמַעְתִּי הוּא כְּקוֹל מְנַגְּנֵי-נֵבֶל הַפּוֹרְטִים עַל נִבְלֵיהֶם. ³ הֵם שָׁרוּ שִׁיר חָדָשׁ לִפְנֵי הַכִּסֵּא וְלִפְנֵי אַרְבַּע

that song except the hundred *and* forty-four thousand who were redeemed from the earth. [4] These are the ones who were not defiled with women, for they are virgins. These are the ones who follow the Lamb wherever He goes. These were redeemed from *among* men, *being* firstfruits to God and to the Lamb. [5] And in their mouth was found no deceit, for they are without fault before the throne of God.

[6] Then I saw another angel flying in the midst of heaven, having the everlasting gospel to preach to those who dwell on the earth—to every nation, tribe, tongue, and people— [7] saying with a loud voice, "Fear God and give glory to Him, for the hour of His judgment has come; and worship Him who made heaven and earth, the sea and springs of water."

[8] And another angel followed, saying, "Babylon is fallen, is fallen, that great city, because she has made all nations drink of the wine of the wrath of her fornication."

[9] Then a third angel followed them, saying with a loud voice, "If anyone worships the beast and his image, and receives *his* mark on his forehead or on his hand, [10] he himself shall also drink of the wine of the wrath of God, which is poured out full strength into the cup of His indignation. He shall be tormented with fire and brimstone in the presence of the holy angels and in the presence of the Lamb. [11] And the smoke of their torment ascends forever and ever; and they have no rest day or night, who worship the beast and his image, and whoever receives the mark of his name."

[12] Here is the patience of the saints; here *are* those who keep the commandments of God and the faith of Jesus.

[13] Then I heard a voice from heaven saying to me, "Write: 'Blessed *are* the dead who die in the Lord from now on.' "

"Yes," says the Spirit, "that they may rest from their labors, and their works follow them."

[14] Then I looked, and behold, a white cloud, and on the cloud sat *One* like the Son of Man, having on His head a golden crown, and in His hand a sharp sickle. [15] And another angel came out of the temple, crying with a loud voice to Him who sat on the cloud, "Thrust in Your sickle and reap, for the time has come for You to reap, for the harvest of the earth is ripe." [16] So He who sat on the cloud thrust in His sickle on the earth, and the earth was reaped.

[17] Then another angel came out of the temple which is in heaven, he also having a sharp sickle.

הַחַיּוֹת וְהַזְּקֵנִים, וְאֵין אִישׁ יָכוֹל לִלְמֹד אֶת הַשִּׁיר זוּלָתִי מֵאָה וְאַרְבָּעִים וְאַרְבָּעָה אֶלֶף הַפְּדוּיִים מִן הָאָרֶץ. [4] אֵלֶּה הֵם אֲשֶׁר לֹא נִטְמְאוּ בְּנָשִׁים, כִּי בְתוּלִים הֵם. אֵלֶּה הֵם הַהוֹלְכִים אַחֲרֵי הַשֶּׂה לְכָל אֲשֶׁר יֵלֵךְ. אֵלֶּה נִפְדּוּ מִבְּנֵי אָדָם בִּכּוּרִים לֵאלֹהִים וְלַשֶּׂה. [5] מִרְמָה לֹא נִמְצְאָה בְּפִיהֶם, נְקִיִּים הֵם מִדֹּפִי.

[6] רָאִיתִי מַלְאָךְ אַחֵר מְעוֹפֵף בְּאֶמְצַע הַשָּׁמַיִם, אֲשֶׁר לוֹ בְּשׂוֹרַת עוֹלָם לְבַשֵּׂר לְיוֹשְׁבֵי הָאָרֶץ וּלְכָל אֻמָּה וָשֵׁבֶט וְלָשׁוֹן וָעָם, [7] וְהוּא קוֹרֵא בְּקוֹל גָּדוֹל: "יִרְאוּ אֶת אֱלֹהִים וּתְנוּ לוֹ כָבוֹד, כִּי בָּאָה עֵת מִשְׁפָּטוֹ. הִשְׁתַּחֲווּ לְעוֹשֵׂה הַשָּׁמַיִם וְהָאָרֶץ וְהַיָּם וּמַעְיְנוֹת הַמָּיִם."

[8] וּמַלְאָךְ אַחֵר, שֵׁנִי, בָּא אַחֲרָיו וְאָמַר: "נָפְלָה נָפְלָה בָּבֶל הַגְּדוֹלָה אֲשֶׁר הִשְׁקְתָה אֶת כָּל הַגּוֹיִים מִיֵּין חֲרוֹן תַּזְנוּתָהּ."

[9] מַלְאָךְ אַחֵר, שְׁלִישִׁי, בָּא אַחֲרֵיהֶם וְקָרָא בְּקוֹל גָּדוֹל: "כָּל הַמִּשְׁתַּחֲוֶה לַחַיָּה וּלְצַלְמָהּ וּמְקַבֵּל תָּו עַל מִצְחוֹ אוֹ עַל יָדוֹ, [10] גַּם הוּא יִשְׁתֶּה מִיֵּין חֲרוֹן אֱלֹהִים הַמָּזוּג בְּכוֹס זַעְמוֹ וְאֵינֶנּוּ מָהוּל; וְיֻעֻנֶּה בָּאֵשׁ וְגָפְרִית לִפְנֵי הַמַּלְאָכִים הַקְּדוֹשִׁים וְלִפְנֵי הַשֶּׂה. [11] עֲשַׁן עִנּוּיָם יַעֲלֶה לְעוֹלְמֵי עוֹלָמִים וְלֹא תִהְיֶה לָהֶם מְנוּחָה יוֹמָם וָלָיְלָה – לַמִּשְׁתַּחֲוִים לַחַיָּה וּלְצַלְמָהּ וּלְמִי שֶׁמְּקַבֵּל אֶת תָּו שְׁמָהּ.

[12] בָּזֶה סַבְלָנוּתָם שֶׁל הַקְּדוֹשִׁים הַשּׁוֹמְרִים אֶת מִצְווֹת אֱלֹהִים וֶאֱמוּנַת יֵשׁוּעַ.

[13] שָׁמַעְתִּי קוֹל מִן הַשָּׁמַיִם אוֹמֵר: "כְּתֹב: 'אַשְׁרֵי הַמֵּתִים אֲשֶׁר מֵתִים בָּאָדוֹן מֵעַתָּה.'

"כֵּן", אוֹמֶרֶת הָרוּחַ, "שֶׁיָּנוּחוּ מֵעֲמָלָם, כִּי מַעֲשֵׂיהֶם הוֹלְכִים אַחֲרֵיהֶם."

[14] רָאִיתִי וְהִנֵּה עֲנַן לָבָן וְעַל הֶעָנָן יוֹשֵׁב כִּדְמוּת בֶּן אָדָם; עֲטֶרֶת זָהָב עַל רֹאשׁוֹ וּמַגָּל חַד בְּיָדוֹ. [15] וּמַלְאָךְ אַחֵר יָצָא מִן הַהֵיכָל, קוֹרֵא בְּקוֹל גָּדוֹל אֶל הַיּוֹשֵׁב עַל הֶעָנָן: "שְׁלַח אֶת מַגָּלְךָ וּקְצֹר, כִּי בָּאָה הַשָּׁעָה לִקְצֹר, כִּי יָבֵשׁ קְצִיר הָאָרֶץ." [16] הֵטִיל הַיּוֹשֵׁב עַל הֶעָנָן אֶת מַגָּלוֹ עַל הָאָרֶץ וְהָאָרֶץ נִקְצָרָה.

[17] וּמַלְאָךְ אַחֵר יָצָא מִן הַהֵיכָל אֲשֶׁר בַּשָּׁמַיִם וְגַם לוֹ

[18] And another angel came out from the altar, who had power over fire, and he cried with a loud cry to him who had the sharp sickle, saying, "Thrust in your sharp sickle and gather the clusters of the vine of the earth, for her grapes are fully ripe." [19] So the angel thrust his sickle into the earth and gathered the vine of the earth, and threw *it* into the great winepress of the wrath of God. [20] And the winepress was trampled outside the city, and blood came out of the winepress, up to the horses' bridles, for one thousand six hundred furlongs.

15 Then I saw another sign in heaven, great and marvelous: seven angels having the seven last plagues, for in them the wrath of God is complete.

[2] And I saw *something* like a sea of glass mingled with fire, and those who have the victory over the beast, over his image and over his mark *and* over the number of his name, standing on the sea of glass, having harps of God. [3] They sing the song of Moses, the servant of God, and the song of the Lamb, saying:

"Great and marvelous *are* Your works,
Lord God Almighty!
Just and true *are* Your ways,
O King of the saints!
[4]   Who shall not fear You, O Lord, and glorify
       Your name?
For *You* alone *are* holy.
For all nations shall come and worship
       before You,
For Your judgments have been manifested."

[5] After these things I looked, and behold, the temple of the tabernacle of the testimony in heaven was opened. [6] And out of the temple came the seven angels having the seven plagues, clothed in pure bright linen, and having their chests girded with golden bands. [7] Then one of the four living creatures gave to the seven angels seven golden bowls full of the wrath of God who lives forever and ever. [8] The temple was filled with smoke from the glory of God and from His power, and no one was able to enter the temple till the seven plagues of the seven angels were completed.

16 Then I heard a loud voice from the temple saying to the seven angels, "Go and pour out the bowls of the wrath of God on the earth."

[2] So the first went and poured out his bowl upon the earth, and a foul and loathsome sore came upon the men who had the mark of the beast and those who worshiped his image.

מַגָּל חָד. 18 מַלְאָךְ אַחֵר, אֲשֶׁר לוֹ הַשִּׁלְטוֹן עַל הָאֵשׁ, יָצָא מִן הַמִּזְבֵּחַ וּבְקוֹל גָּדוֹל קָרָא אֶל הָאוֹחֵז אֶת הַמַּגָּל הַחַד וְאָמַר: "שְׁלַח אֶת מַגָּלְךָ הַחַד וּבְצֹר אֶת אֶשְׁכְּלוֹת גֶּפֶן הָאָרֶץ, כִּי בָשְׁלוּ עֲנָבֶיהָ." 19 הֵטִיל הַמַּלְאָךְ אֶת מַגָּלוֹ אֶל הָאָרֶץ, בָּצַר אֶת גֶּפֶן הָאָרֶץ וְהִשְׁלִיךְ אֶל הַגַּת הַגְּדוֹלָה שֶׁל חֲרוֹן הָאֱלֹהִים. 20 הַגַּת נִדְרְכָה מִחוּץ לָעִיר וְהַדָּם יָצָא מִן הַגַּת עַד רִסְנֵי הַסּוּסִים לְמֶרְחָק שֶׁל אֶלֶף וְשֵׁשׁ מֵאוֹת רִים.

טו רָאִיתִי אוֹת אַחֵר בַּשָּׁמַיִם, גָּדוֹל וּמַפְלִיא: שִׁבְעָה מַלְאָכִים נוֹשְׂאִים אֶת שֶׁבַע הַמַּכּוֹת הָאַחֲרוֹנוֹת, כִּי בָּהֶן נִשְׁלַם זַעַם אֱלֹהִים. 2 רָאִיתִי כְּמוֹ יָם זְכוּכִית מְעֹרָב בָּאֵשׁ וְאֶת הַמִּתְגַּבְּרִים עַל הַחַיָּה וְעַל צַלְמָהּ וְעַל מִסְפַּר שְׁמָהּ עוֹמְדִים עַל יָם הַזְּכוּכִית; כִּנּוֹרוֹת אֱלֹהִים בְּיָדָם 3 וְהֵם שָׁרִים אֶת שִׁירַת מֹשֶׁה עֶבֶד אֱלֹהִים וְשִׁירַת הַשֶּׂה לֵאמֹר:

"גְּדוֹלִים וְנִפְלָאִים מַעֲשֶׂיךָ, יְהוָה אֱלֹהֵי צְבָאוֹת;
צֶדֶק וֶאֱמֶת דְּרָכֶיךָ, מֶלֶךְ הַגּוֹיִים.
4 מִי לֹא יִירָאֲךָ, יְהוָה, וְלֹא יִתֵּן כָּבוֹד לִשְׁמֶךָ?
כִּי אַתָּה לְבַדְּךָ קָדוֹשׁ;
הֵן כָּל הַגּוֹיִים יָבוֹאוּ וְיִשְׁתַּחֲווּ לְפָנֶיךָ;
כִּי נִגְלוּ מִשְׁפְּטֵי צִדְקֶךָ."

5 אַחֲרֵי כֵן רָאִיתִי כִּי נִפְתַּח הֵיכַל מִשְׁכַּן הָעֵדוּת בַּשָּׁמַיִם 6 וּמִן הַהֵיכָל יָצְאוּ שִׁבְעַת הַמַּלְאָכִים נוֹשְׂאֵי שֶׁבַע הַמַּכּוֹת, לְבוּשִׁים בַּד טָהוֹר וְצַח וַחֲגוּרִים חֲגוֹרוֹת זָהָב עַל חֲזוֹתֵיהֶם. 7 אַחַת מֵאַרְבַּע הַחַיּוֹת נָתְנָה לְשִׁבְעַת הַמַּלְאָכִים שֶׁבַע קְעָרוֹת זָהָב מְלֵאוֹת זַעַם הָאֱלֹהִים הַחַי לְעוֹלְמֵי עוֹלָמִים. 8 וְהַהֵיכָל נִתְמַלֵּא עָשָׁן מִכְּבוֹד אֱלֹהִים וְעֻזּוֹ וְלֹא יָכוֹל אִישׁ לְהִכָּנֵס אֶל הַהֵיכָל עַד אֲשֶׁר יִגָּמְרוּ שֶׁבַע הַמַּכּוֹת שֶׁל שִׁבְעַת הַמַּלְאָכִים.

טז שָׁמַעְתִּי קוֹל גָּדוֹל מִן הַהֵיכָל אוֹמֵר לְשִׁבְעַת הַמַּלְאָכִים: "לְכוּ וְשִׁפְכוּ עַל הָאָרֶץ אֶת שֶׁבַע קְעָרוֹת זַעַם אֱלֹהִים." 2 הָלַךְ הָרִאשׁוֹן וְשָׁפַךְ אֶת קְעָרָתוֹ עַל הָאָרֶץ, וְנִתְהַוָּה שְׁחִין רַע וּמַכְאִיב בָּאֲנָשִׁים הַנּוֹשְׂאִים אֶת תָּו הַחַיָּה וּמִשְׁתַּחֲוִים לְצַלְמָהּ.

20 אלף ושש מאות רים – כמאתיים מילין או כשלוש מאות קילומטרים.

³ Then the second angel poured out his bowl on the sea, and it became blood as of a dead *man;* and every living creature in the sea died.

⁴ Then the third angel poured out his bowl on the rivers and springs of water, and they became blood. ⁵ And I heard the angel of the waters saying:

"You are righteous, O Lord,
The One who is and who was and who is to be,
Because You have judged these things.
6 For they have shed the blood of saints and prophets,
And You have given them blood to drink.
For it is their just due."

⁷ And I heard another from the altar saying, "Even so, Lord God Almighty, true and righteous *are* Your judgments."

⁸ Then the fourth angel poured out his bowl on the sun, and power was given to him to scorch men with fire. ⁹ And men were scorched with great heat, and they blasphemed the name of God who has power over these plagues; and they did not repent and give Him glory.

¹⁰ Then the fifth angel poured out his bowl on the throne of the beast, and his kingdom became full of darkness; and they gnawed their tongues because of the pain. ¹¹ They blasphemed the God of heaven because of their pains and their sores, and did not repent of their deeds.

¹² Then the sixth angel poured out his bowl on the great river Euphrates, and its water was dried up, so that the way of the kings from the east might be prepared. ¹³ And I saw three unclean spirits like frogs *coming* out of the mouth of the dragon, out of the mouth of the beast, and out of the mouth of the false prophet. ¹⁴ For they are spirits of demons, performing signs, *which* go out to the kings of the earth and of the whole world, to gather them to the battle of that great day of God Almighty.

¹⁵ "Behold, I am coming as a thief. Blessed *is* he who watches, and keeps his garments, lest he walk naked and they see his shame."

¹⁶ And they gathered them together to the place called in Hebrew, Armageddon.

¹⁷ Then the seventh angel poured out his bowl into the air, and a loud voice came out of the temple of heaven, from the throne, saying, "It is done!" ¹⁸ And there were noises and thunderings and lightnings; and there was a great earthquake, such a mighty and great earthquake as had not occurred since men were on the earth. ¹⁹ Now the great city was divided into three parts, and the cities of the nations fell. And great Babylon was remembered

³ שָׁפַךְ הַשֵּׁנִי אֶת קַעֲרָתוֹ עַל הַיָּם וְהַיָּם נֶהְפַּךְ לְדָם כְּדָמוֹ שֶׁל מֵת, וְכָל נֶפֶשׁ חַיָּה אֲשֶׁר בַּיָּם מֵתָה.

⁴ שָׁפַךְ הַשְּׁלִישִׁי אֶת קַעֲרָתוֹ בַּנְּהָרוֹת וּבְמַעְיְנוֹת הַמַּיִם, וַיִּהְיוּ לְדָם. ⁵ שָׁמַעְתִּי אֶת מַלְאַךְ הַמַּיִם אוֹמֵר:

"צַדִּיק אַתָּה הַהֹוֶה וְהָיָה, הַקָּדוֹשׁ – שֶׁכָּךְ שָׁפַטְתָּ;

⁶ כִּי דַם קְדוֹשִׁים וּנְבִיאִים שָׁפְכוּ,
וְדָם נָתַתָּ לָהֶם לִשְׁתּוֹת; רְאוּיִים הֵם."

⁷ וְשָׁמַעְתִּי אֶת הַמִּזְבֵּחַ אוֹמֵר:

"כֵּן, יהוה אֱלֹהֵי צְבָאוֹת, אֱמֶת וְצֶדֶק מִשְׁפָּטֶיךָ."

⁸ שָׁפַךְ הָרְבִיעִי אֶת קַעֲרָתוֹ עַל הַשֶּׁמֶשׁ וְהֻתַּר לוֹ לִצְרֹב אֶת הָאֲנָשִׁים בָּאֵשׁ. ⁹ נִצְרְבוּ הָאֲנָשִׁים בְּחֹם גָּדוֹל וְגִדְּפוּ אֶת שֵׁם אֱלֹהִים אֲשֶׁר לוֹ הַשִּׁלְטוֹן עַל הַמַּכּוֹת הָאֵלֶּה, וְלֹא חָזְרוּ בִּתְשׁוּבָה לָתֵת לוֹ כָּבוֹד.

¹⁰ הַחֲמִישִׁי שָׁפַךְ אֶת קַעֲרָתוֹ עַל כִּסֵּא הַחַיָּה וְחָשְׁכָה מַלְכוּתָהּ. הֵם נָשְׁכוּ אֶת לְשׁוֹנָם מִכְּאֵב ¹¹ וְגִדְּפוּ אֶת אֱלֹהֵי הַשָּׁמַיִם מִמַּכְאוֹבָם וּשְׁחִינָם, וְלֹא שָׁבוּ מִמַּעֲשֵׂיהֶם.

¹² הַשִּׁשִּׁי שָׁפַךְ אֶת קַעֲרָתוֹ עַל הַנָּהָר הַגָּדוֹל, נְהַר פְּרָת, וּמֵימָיו יָבְשׁוּ כְּדֵי לְהָכִין אֶת הַדֶּרֶךְ שֶׁל הַמְּלָכִים מִמִּזְרַח שֶׁמֶשׁ. ¹³ רָאִיתִי מִפִּי הַתַּנִּין וּמִפִּי הַחַיָּה וּמִפִּי נְבִיא הַשֶּׁקֶר שָׁלֹשׁ רוּחוֹת טְמֵאוֹת דּוֹמוֹת לִצְפַרְדְּעִים ¹⁴ – כִּי הֵן רוּחוֹת שֶׁל שֵׁדִים עוֹשֵׂי אוֹתוֹת – וְהֵן יוֹצְאוֹת אֶל מַלְכֵי הָאָרֶץ כֻּלָּהּ לֶאֱסֹף אוֹתָם לַמִּלְחֶמֶת הַיּוֹם הַגָּדוֹל אֲשֶׁר לֵאלֹהֵי צְבָאוֹת. ¹⁵ הִנְנִי בָא כְּגַנָּב. אַשְׁרֵי הַשּׁוֹקֵד וְשׁוֹמֵר אֶת בְּגָדָיו, פֶּן יֵלֵךְ עָרֹם וְיִרְאוּ אֶת עֶרְוָתוֹ. ¹⁶ וְהוּא אָסַף אוֹתָם אֶל הַמָּקוֹם הַנִּקְרָא בְּעִבְרִית הַר מְגִדּוֹן.

¹⁷ הַשְּׁבִיעִי שָׁפַךְ אֶת קַעֲרָתוֹ אֶל הָאֲוִיר וְקוֹל גָּדוֹל יָצָא מִן הַהֵיכָל מֵעִם הַכִּסֵּא – אוֹמֵר: "הָיֹה נִהְיְתָה!" ¹⁸ בְּרָקִים וְקוֹלוֹת וּרְעָמִים הִתְחוֹלְלוּ, וּרְעִידַת־אֲדָמָה גְּדוֹלָה אֲשֶׁר לֹא הָיְתָה כָּמוֹהָ מֵאָז הֱיוֹת אָדָם עַל הָאָרֶץ, רְעִידַת־אֲדָמָה גְּדוֹלָה כָּל כָּךְ! ¹⁹ הָעִיר הַגְּדוֹלָה נֶחְלְקָה לִשְׁלוֹשָׁה חֲלָקִים וְעָרֵי הַגּוֹיִים נָפְלוּ, וְזִכָּרוֹן בָּבֶל הַגְּדוֹלָה עָלָה לִפְנֵי

before God, to give her the cup of the wine of the fierceness of His wrath. 20 Then every island fled away, and the mountains were not found. 21 And great hail from heaven fell upon men, *each hailstone* about the weight of a talent. Men blasphemed God because of the plague of the hail, since that plague was exceedingly great.

17 Then one of the seven angels who had the seven bowls came and talked with me, saying to me, "Come, I will show you the judgment of the great harlot who sits on many waters, 2 with whom the kings of the earth committed fornication, and the inhabitants of the earth were made drunk with the wine of her fornication."

3 So he carried me away in the Spirit into the wilderness. And I saw a woman sitting on a scarlet beast *which was* full of names of blasphemy, having seven heads and ten horns. 4 The woman was arrayed in purple and scarlet, and adorned with gold and precious stones and pearls, having in her hand a golden cup full of abominations and the filthiness of her fornication. 5 And on her forehead a name *was* written:

MYSTERY,
BABYLON THE GREAT,
THE MOTHER OF HARLOTS AND OF THE
ABOMINATIONS OF THE EARTH.

6 I saw the woman, drunk with the blood of the saints and with the blood of the martyrs of Jesus. And when I saw her, I marveled with great amazement.

7 But the angel said to me, "Why did you marvel? I will tell you the mystery of the woman and of the beast that carries her, which has the seven heads and the ten horns. 8 The beast that you saw was, and is not, and will ascend out of the bottomless pit and go to perdition. And those who dwell on the earth will marvel, whose names are not written in the Book of Life from the foundation of the world, when they see the beast that was, and is not, and yet is.

9 "Here *is* the mind which has wisdom: The seven heads are seven mountains on which the woman sits. 10 There are also seven kings. Five have fallen, one is, *and* the other has not yet come. And when he comes, he must continue a short time. 11 The beast that was, and is not, is himself also the eighth, and is of the seven, and is going to perdition.

12 "The ten horns which you saw are ten kings who have received no kingdom as yet, but they receive authority for one hour as kings with the

הָאֱלֹהִים לָתֵת לָהּ אֶת כּוֹס יֵין חֲרוֹן אַפּוֹ. 20 כָּל אִי נָסוֹג וְהָרִים לֹא נִמְצָאוּ. 21 אַבְנֵי בָרָד גְּדוֹלוֹת שֶׁמִּשְׁקָלָן כְּמֵאָה וּשְׁלוֹשִׁים לִיטְרָאוֹת יָרְדוּ מִן הַשָּׁמַיִם עַל בְּנֵי אָדָם, וּבְנֵי אָדָם גִּדְּפוּ אֶת אֱלֹהִים בִּגְלַל מַכַּת הַבָּרָד, כִּי גְדוֹלָה מְאֹד מַכָּתוֹ.

יז אֶחָד מִשִּׁבְעַת הַמַּלְאָכִים נוֹשְׂאֵי שֶׁבַע הַקְּעָרוֹת בָּא וְדִבֶּר אִתִּי. "בּוֹא! אַרְאֶה לְךָ אֶת מִשְׁפַּט הַזּוֹנָה הַגְּדוֹלָה הַיּוֹשֶׁבֶת עַל מַיִם רַבִּים, 2 אֲשֶׁר מַלְכֵי הָאָרֶץ זָנוּ עִמָּהּ וְשׁוֹכְנֵי הָאָרֶץ הִשְׁתַּכְּרוּ מִיֵּין תַּזְנוּתָהּ." 3 הוּא נְשָׂאַנִי לַמִּדְבָּר, בָּרוּחַ, וְרָאִיתִי אִשָּׁה יוֹשֶׁבֶת עַל חַיָּה אֲדֻמָּה כְּשָׁנִי וְהַחַיָּה מְלֵאָה שְׁמוֹת גִּדּוּפִים וְהִיא בַּעֲלַת שִׁבְעָה רָאשִׁים וְעֶשֶׂר קַרְנַיִם. 4 הָאִשָּׁה הָיְתָה לְבוּשָׁה אַרְגָּמָן וְשָׁנִי וּמְקֻשֶּׁטֶת בְּזָהָב וְאֶבֶן יְקָרָה וּפְנִינִים; בְּיָדָהּ כּוֹס זָהָב מְלֵאָה תּוֹעֵבוֹת וְטֻמְאוֹת תַּזְנוּתָהּ, 5 וְעַל מִצְחָהּ כָּתוּב שֵׁם, רָז: "בָּבֶל הַגְּדוֹלָה, אֵם לַזּוֹנוֹת וּלְתוֹעֲבוֹת הָאָרֶץ." 6 רָאִיתִי אֶת הָאִשָּׁה שְׁכוּרָה מִדַּם הַקְּדוֹשִׁים וּמִדַּם עֵדֵי יֵשׁוּעַ. כִּרְאוֹתִי אוֹתָהּ הִתְפַּלֵּאתִי פְּלִיאָה גְדוֹלָה. 7 שָׁאַל אוֹתִי הַמַּלְאָךְ: "מַדּוּעַ הִתְפַּלֵּאתָ? אֲנִי אַגִּיד לְךָ אֶת סוֹד הָאִשָּׁה וְהַחַיָּה הַנּוֹשֵׂאת אוֹתָהּ אֲשֶׁר לָהּ שִׁבְעַת הָרָאשִׁים וְעֶשֶׂר הַקְּרָנַיִם. 8 הַחַיָּה אֲשֶׁר רָאִיתָ – הָיְתָה וְאֵינֶנָּה, וְהִיא עֲתִידָה לַעֲלוֹת מִן הַתְּהוֹם וְלָלֶכֶת לָאֲבַדּוֹן. וְיוֹשְׁבֵי הָאָרֶץ אֲשֶׁר שְׁמָם לֹא נִכְתַּב בְּסֵפֶר הַחַיִּים מֵעֵת הֻסַּד תֵּבֵל יִתְפַּלְּאוּ כִּרְאוֹתָם אֶת הַחַיָּה שֶׁהָיְתָה וְאֵינֶנָּה וַעֲתִידָה לָבוֹא. 9 כָּאן הַתְּבוּנָה שֶׁיֵּשׁ עִמָּהּ חָכְמָה! שִׁבְעַת הָרָאשִׁים הֵם שִׁבְעָה הָרִים אֲשֶׁר הָאִשָּׁה יוֹשֶׁבֶת עֲלֵיהֶם. 10 גַּם שִׁבְעָה מְלָכִים הֵם: הַחֲמִשָּׁה נָפְלוּ; הָאֶחָד יֶשְׁנוֹ; הָאַחֵר עוֹד לֹא בָא, וְכַאֲשֶׁר יָבוֹא הוּא צָרִיךְ לְהִשָּׁאֵר זְמַן מְעַט. 11 הַחַיָּה אֲשֶׁר הָיְתָה וְאֵינֶנָּה הוּא הַשְּׁמִינִי; מִן הַשִּׁבְעָה הוּא וְלָאֲבַדּוֹן יֵלֵךְ. 12 עֶשֶׂר הַקְּרָנַיִם אֲשֶׁר רָאִיתָ הֵם עֲשָׂרָה מְלָכִים אֲשֶׁר עֲדַיִן לֹא קִבְּלוּ מַלְכוּת, אַךְ יְקַבְּלוּ סַמְכוּת כִּמְלָכִים לְשָׁעָה אַחַת

beast. ¹³These are of one mind, and they will give their power and authority to the beast. ¹⁴These will make war with the Lamb, and the Lamb will overcome them, for He is Lord of lords and King of kings; and those *who are* with Him *are* called, chosen, and faithful."

¹⁵Then he said to me, "The waters which you saw, where the harlot sits, are peoples, multitudes, nations, and tongues. ¹⁶And the ten horns which you saw on the beast, these will hate the harlot, make her desolate and naked, eat her flesh and burn her with fire. ¹⁷For God has put it into their hearts to fulfill His purpose, to be of one mind, and to give their kingdom to the beast, until the words of God are fulfilled. ¹⁸And the woman whom you saw is that great city which reigns over the kings of the earth."

18 After these things I saw another angel coming down from heaven, having great authority, and the earth was illuminated with his glory. ²And he cried mightily with a loud voice, saying, "Babylon the great is fallen, is fallen, and has become a dwelling place of demons, a prison for every foul spirit, and a cage for every unclean and hated bird! ³For all the nations have drunk of the wine of the wrath of her fornication, the kings of the earth have committed fornication with her, and the merchants of the earth have become rich through the abundance of her luxury."

⁴And I heard another voice from heaven saying, "Come out of her, my people, lest you share in her sins, and lest you receive of her plagues. ⁵For her sins have reached to heaven, and God has remembered her iniquities. ⁶Render to her just as she rendered to you, and repay her double according to her works; in the cup which she has mixed, mix double for her. ⁷In the measure that she glorified herself and lived luxuriously, in the same measure give her torment and sorrow; for she says in her heart, 'I sit *as* queen, and am no widow, and will not see sorrow.' ⁸Therefore her plagues will come in one day—death and mourning and famine. And she will be utterly burned with fire, for strong *is* the Lord God who judges her.

⁹"The kings of the earth who committed fornication and lived luxuriously with her will weep and lament for her, when they see the smoke of her burning, ¹⁰standing at a distance for fear of her torment, saying, 'Alas, alas, that great city Babylon, that mighty city! For in one hour your judgment has come.'

יַחַד עִם הַחַיָּה. ¹³הַלָּלוּ כֻּוָּנָה אַחַת לָהֶם וְיִתְּנוּ אֶת כֹּחָם וְסַמְכוּתָם לַחַיָּה. ¹⁴הֵם יִלָּחֲמוּ בַּשֶּׂה וְהַשֶּׂה יְנַצֵּחַ אוֹתָם מִפְּנֵי שֶׁהוּא אֲדוֹן הָאֲדוֹנִים וּמֶלֶךְ הַמְּלָכִים, וְאִתּוֹ גַּם הַקְּרוּאִים וְהַנִּבְחָרִים וְנֶאֱמָנִים."

¹⁵עוֹד אָמַר אֵלַי: "הַמַּיִם אֲשֶׁר רָאִיתָ, אֲשֶׁר שָׁם הַזּוֹנָה יוֹשֶׁבֶת, עַמִּים וַהֲמוֹנִים הֵם, וְאֻמּוֹת וּלְשׁוֹנוֹת. ¹⁶עֶשֶׂר הַקְּרָנַיִם אֲשֶׁר רָאִיתָ וְהַחַיָּה – הַלָּלוּ יִשְׂנְאוּ אֶת הַזּוֹנָה וְיַעֲשׂוּהָ שׁוֹמֵמָה וַעֲרֻמָּה; גַּם יֹאכְלוּ אֶת בְּשָׂרָהּ וְאוֹתָהּ יִשְׂרְפוּ בָּאֵשׁ, ¹⁷כִּי אֱלֹהִים נָתַן בְּלִבָּם לְהוֹצִיא לְפֹעַל אֶת כַּוָּנָתוֹ, וְלִהְיוֹת עֵצָה אַחַת וְלָתֵת אֶת מַלְכוּתָם לַחַיָּה, עַד אֲשֶׁר יִתְקַיְּמוּ דִּבְרֵי אֱלֹהִים. ¹⁸וְהָאִשָּׁה אֲשֶׁר רָאִיתָ הִיא הָעִיר הַגְּדוֹלָה הַמּוֹלֶכֶת עַל מַלְכֵי הָאָרֶץ."

יח אַחֲרֵי כֵן רָאִיתִי מַלְאָךְ אַחֵר יוֹרֵד מִן הַשָּׁמַיִם; רַבָּה הָיְתָה סַמְכוּתוֹ וְהָאָרֶץ הֵאִירָה מִכְּבוֹדוֹ. ²הוּא קָרָא בְּקוֹל חָזָק וְאָמַר: "נָפְלָה נָפְלָה בָּבֶל הַגְּדוֹלָה וְהָיְתָה לִמְעוֹן שֵׁדִים וּלְבֵית כֶּלֶא לְכָל רוּחַ טְמֵאָה וּבֵית כֶּלֶא לְכָל עוֹף טָמֵא וּמָאוּס, ³כִּי מִיֵּין חֲרוֹן תַּזְנוּתָהּ שָׁתוּ כָל הַגּוֹיִים, וּמַלְכֵי הָאָרֶץ זָנוּ עִמָּהּ וְסוֹחֲרֵי הָאָרֶץ הִתְעַשְּׁרוּ מֵעֹצֶם מוֹתְרוֹתֶיהָ."

⁴שָׁמַעְתִּי קוֹל אַחֵר מִן הַשָּׁמַיִם אוֹמֵר:
"צְאוּ מִמֶּנָּה, עַמִּי, פֶּן תִּשְׁתַּתְּפוּ בְּחַטֹּאתֶיהָ וּפֶן תְּקַבְּלוּ מִמַּכּוֹתֶיהָ,
⁵כִּי הִגִּיעוּ חַטֹּאתֶיהָ עַד הַשָּׁמַיִם וְזָכַר אֱלֹהִים אֶת פְּשָׁעֶיהָ.
⁶שַׁלְּמוּ לָהּ כִּגְמוּל שֶׁשִּׁלְּמָה גַם הִיא וְכִפְלוּ לָהּ כִּפְלַיִם כְּמַעֲלָלֶיהָ;
בַּכּוֹס אֲשֶׁר מָסְכָה מִסְכוּ לָהּ כִּפְלַיִם.
⁷בַּמִּדָּה שֶׁרוֹמְמָה עַצְמָהּ וְהִתְעַנְּגָה כֵּן תְּנוּ לָהּ מַכְאוֹב וָאֵבֶל,
כִּי אָמְרָה בְּלִבָּהּ: 'יוֹשֶׁבֶת אֲנִי, מַלְכָּה; אֵינֶנִּי אַלְמָנָה וְאֵבֶל לֹא אֶרְאֶה.'
⁸עַל כֵּן בְּיוֹם אֶחָד תָּבֹאנָה מַכּוֹתֶיהָ:
מָוֶת, אֵבֶל וְרָעָב, וּבָאֵשׁ תִּשָּׂרֵף;
כִּי חָזָק יהוה אֱלֹהִים הַשּׁוֹפֵט אוֹתָהּ."

⁹וּמַלְכֵי הָאָרֶץ אֲשֶׁר זָנוּ וְהִתְעַנְּגוּ אִתָּהּ יִבְכּוּ וְיִסְפְּדוּ עָלֶיהָ כִּרְאוֹתָם אֶת עֲשַׁן שְׂרֵפָתָהּ. ¹⁰מֵרָחוֹק יַעַמְדוּ מִפְּנֵי אֵימַת עִנּוּיָהּ וְיֹאמְרוּ: "אוֹי, אוֹי, בָּבֶל הָעִיר הַגְּדוֹלָה, הָעִיר הַחֲזָקָה, כִּי בְּשָׁעָה אַחַת בָּא מִשְׁפָּטֵךְ."

11 "And the merchants of the earth will weep and mourn over her, for no one buys their merchandise anymore: 12 merchandise of gold and silver, precious stones and pearls, fine linen and purple, silk and scarlet, every kind of citron wood, every kind of object of ivory, every kind of object of most precious wood, bronze, iron, and marble; 13 and cinnamon and incense, fragrant oil and frankincense, wine and oil, fine flour and wheat, cattle and sheep, horses and chariots, and bodies and souls of men. 14 The fruit that your soul longed for has gone from you, and all the things which are rich and splendid have gone from you, and you shall find them no more at all. 15 The merchants of these things, who became rich by her, will stand at a distance for fear of her torment, weeping and wailing, 16 and saying, 'Alas, alas, that great city that was clothed in fine linen, purple, and scarlet, and adorned with gold and precious stones and pearls! 17 For in one hour such great riches came to nothing.' Every shipmaster, all who travel by ship, sailors, and as many as trade on the sea, stood at a distance 18 and cried out when they saw the smoke of her burning, saying, 'What is like this great city?'

19 "They threw dust on their heads and cried out, weeping and wailing, and saying, 'Alas, alas, that great city, in which all who had ships on the sea became rich by her wealth! For in one hour she is made desolate.'

20 "Rejoice over her, O heaven, and you holy apostles and prophets, for God has avenged you on her!"

21 Then a mighty angel took up a stone like a great millstone and threw it into the sea, saying, "Thus with violence the great city Babylon shall be thrown down, and shall not be found anymore. 22 The sound of harpists, musicians, flutists, and trumpeters shall not be heard in you anymore. No craftsman of any craft shall be found in you anymore, and the sound of a millstone shall not be heard in you anymore. 23 The light of a lamp shall not shine in you anymore, and the voice of bridegroom and bride shall not be heard in you anymore. For your merchants were the great men of the earth, for by your sorcery all the nations were deceived. 24 And in her was found the blood of prophets and saints, and of all who were slain on the earth."

19 After these things I heard a loud voice of a great multitude in heaven, saying, "Alleluia! Salvation and glory and honor and power belong to the Lord our God! 2 For true and righteous are His judgments, because He has judged the great harlot

11 גַּם סוֹחֲרֵי הָאָרֶץ בּוֹכִים וּמִתְאַבְּלִים עָלֶיהָ, כִּי אֵין קוֹנֶה עוֹד אֶת מִטְעַן סְחוֹרָתָם, 12 מִטְעַן שֶׁל זָהָב וָכֶסֶף וְאֶבֶן יְקָרָה וּפְנִינִים וּבוּץ וְאַרְגָּמָן וּמֶשִׁי וְשָׁנִי; כָּל עֵץ בֹּשֶׂם וְכָל כְּלִי שֶׁנְהָב, כָּל כְּלִי מֵעֵץ יָקָר וּמִנְּחֹשֶׁת, מִבַּרְזֶל וּמִשַּׁיִשׁ; 13 קִנָּמוֹן וַאֲמוֹמוֹן, קְטֹרֶת סַמִּים, מֹר וּלְבוֹנָה, יַיִן וְשֶׁמֶן, סֹלֶת וְחִטָּה, בָּקָר וְצֹאן, סוּסִים וּמֶרְכָּבוֹת, עֲבָדִים וְנֶפֶשׁ אָדָם.

14 "סָר מִמֵּךְ הַפְּרִי חֶמְדַּת נַפְשֵׁךְ; כָּל הַמֻּתָרוֹת וְכָל נוֹצֵץ אָבְדוּ מִמֵּךְ; לֹא יִמָּצְאוּם עוֹד."

15 סוֹחֲרֵי הַדְּבָרִים הָאֵלֶּה, אֲשֶׁר הִתְעַשְּׁרוּ מִמֶּנָּה, יַעַמְדוּ מֵרָחוֹק מִפְּנֵי אֵימַת עִנּוּיָהּ, בּוֹכִים וּמִתְאַבְּלִים 16 וְאוֹמְרִים:

"אוֹי, אוֹי, הָעִיר הַגְּדוֹלָה הַלְּבוּשָׁה שֵׁשׁ וְאַרְגָּמָן וְשָׁנִי וּמְקֻשֶּׁטֶת בְּזָהָב וְאֶבֶן יְקָרָה וּפְנִינִים, 17 כִּי בְּשָׁעָה אַחַת הֶחֱרַב עֹשֶׁר גָּדוֹל כָּזֶה!"

וְכָל רַב־חוֹבֵל וְכָל הַנּוֹסֵעַ לִמְחוֹז חֶפְצוֹ, גַּם מַלָּחִים וְכָל אֲשֶׁר מְלַאכְתָּם בַּיָּם, עָמְדוּ מֵרָחוֹק 18 וְצָעֲקוּ בִּרְאוֹתָם אֶת עֲשַׁן שְׂרֵפָתָהּ. "מִי בְּעָרִים כָּעִיר הַגְּדוֹלָה?" אָמְרוּ. 19 הֵם זָרְקוּ עָפָר עַל רָאשֵׁיהֶם וְצָעֲקוּ בִּבְכִי וְיָגוֹן:

"אוֹי, אוֹי, הָעִיר הַגְּדוֹלָה אֲשֶׁר עָשְׁרוּ בָהּ מֵהוֹנָהּ כָּל בַּעֲלֵי הָאֳנִיּוֹת בַּיָּם, כִּי בְּשָׁעָה אַחַת הָחְרְבָה!" 20 גִּילוּ עָלֶיהָ שָׁמַיִם, גַּם קְדוֹשִׁים וּשְׁלִיחִים וּנְבִיאִים, כִּי שָׁפַט אֱלֹהִים אֶת מִשְׁפַּטְכֶם מִמֶּנָּה!

21 וּמַלְאָךְ חָזָק אֶחָד הֵרִים אֶבֶן, כְּאֶבֶן רֵיחַיִם גְּדוֹלָה, וְהִשְׁלִיךְ אוֹתָהּ לַיָּם בְּאָמְרוֹ:

"כָּכָה תֻּשְׁלַךְ בְּשֶׁצֶף בָּבֶל הָעִיר הַגְּדוֹלָה וְלֹא תִמָּצֵא עוֹד. 22 צְלִילֵי פוֹרְטֵי נֵבֶל, צְלִילֵי נוֹגְנִים וּמְחַלְלִים בַּחֲלִילִים,

וּצְלִילֵי תוֹקְעִים בַּחֲצוֹצְרוֹת – לֹא יִשָּׁמְעוּ בָךְ עוֹד. וְכָל אָמָּן מִכָּל אֻמָּנוּת לֹא יִמָּצֵא בָךְ עוֹד, וְלֹא יִשָּׁמַע עוֹד בְּקִרְבֵּךְ קוֹל רֵיחַיִם. 23 אוֹר מְנוֹרָה לֹא יָאִיר בָּךְ עוֹד, וְקוֹל חָתָן וְכַלָּה לֹא יִשָּׁמַע בָּךְ עוֹד; כִּי סוֹחֲרַיִךְ הָיוּ נִכְבַּדֵּי הָאָרֶץ וּבִכְשָׁפַיִךְ הִתְעוּ כָּל הַגּוֹיִם. 24 בָּהּ נִמְצָא דַּם נְבִיאִים וּקְדוֹשִׁים וְדַם כָּל אֲשֶׁר נִטְבְּחוּ עֲלֵי אָרֶץ."

יט אַחֲרֵי כֵן שָׁמַעְתִּי קוֹל גָּדוֹל כְּקוֹל הָמוֹן רַב בַּשָּׁמַיִם אוֹמֵר:

"הַלְלוּיָהּ! הַיְשׁוּעָה וְהַכָּבוֹד וְהַגְּבוּרָה לֵאלֹהֵינוּ, 2 כִּי אֱמֶת וָצֶדֶק מִשְׁפָּטָיו;

who corrupted the earth with her fornication; and He has avenged on her the blood of His servants *shed* by her." ³Again they said, "Alleluia! Her smoke rises up forever and ever!" ⁴And the twenty-four elders and the four living creatures fell down and worshiped God who sat on the throne, saying, "Amen! Alleluia!" ⁵Then a voice came from the throne, saying, "Praise our God, all you His servants and those who fear Him, both small and great!"

⁶And I heard, as it were, the voice of a great multitude, as the sound of many waters and as the sound of mighty thunderings, saying, "Alleluia! For the Lord God Omnipotent reigns! ⁷Let us be glad and rejoice and give Him glory, for the marriage of the Lamb has come, and His wife has made herself ready." ⁸And to her it was granted to be arrayed in fine linen, clean and bright, for the fine linen is the righteous acts of the saints.

⁹Then he said to me, "Write: 'Blessed *are* those who are called to the marriage supper of the Lamb!'" And he said to me, "These are the true sayings of God." ¹⁰And I fell at his feet to worship him. But he said to me, "See *that you do* not *do that!* I am your fellow servant, and of your brethren who have the testimony of Jesus. Worship God! For the testimony of Jesus is the spirit of prophecy."

¹¹Now I saw heaven opened, and behold, a white horse. And He who sat on him *was* called Faithful and True, and in righteousness He judges and makes war. ¹²His eyes *were* like a flame of fire, and on His head *were* many crowns. He had a name written that no one knew except Himself. ¹³He *was* clothed with a robe dipped in blood, and His name is called The Word of God. ¹⁴And the armies in heaven, clothed in fine linen, white and clean, followed Him on white horses. ¹⁵Now out of His mouth goes a sharp sword, that with it He should strike the nations. And He Himself will rule them with a rod of iron. He Himself treads the winepress of the fierceness and wrath of Almighty God. ¹⁶And He has on *His* robe and on His thigh a name written:

KING OF KINGS
AND LORD OF LORDS.

¹⁷Then I saw an angel standing in the sun; and he cried with a loud voice, saying to all the birds that fly in the midst of heaven, "Come and gather together for the supper of the great God, ¹⁸that you may eat the flesh of kings, the flesh of captains, the flesh of mighty men, the flesh of horses and of those who sit on them, and the flesh of all *people,* free and slave, both small and great."

כִּי שָׁפַט אֶת הַזּוֹנָה הַגְּדוֹלָה
אֲשֶׁר הִשְׁחִיתָה אֶת הָאָרֶץ בְּתַזְנוּתָהּ,
וַיִּנְקֹם אֶת דַּם עֲבָדָיו מִיָּדָהּ."
³וְשֵׁנִית אָמְרוּ:
"הַלְלוּיָהּ! עֲשָׁנָהּ עוֹלֶה לְעוֹלְמֵי עוֹלָמִים!"
⁴וְעֶשְׂרִים וְאַרְבָּעָה הַזְּקֵנִים וְאַרְבַּע הַחַיּוֹת נָפְלוּ
וְהִשְׁתַּחֲווּ לֵאלֹהִים הַיּוֹשֵׁב עַל הַכִּסֵּא בְּאָמְרָם:
"אָמֵן, הַלְלוּיָהּ!"
⁵יָצָא קוֹל מִן הַכִּסֵּא – אוֹמֵר:
"הַלְלוּ אֶת אֱלֹהֵינוּ כָּל עֲבָדָיו – הַיְרֵאִים אוֹתוֹ,
הַקְּטַנִּים וְהַגְּדוֹלִים!"
⁶וְשָׁמַעְתִּי קוֹל כְּקוֹל הָמוֹן רַב וּכְקוֹל מַיִם רַבִּים
וּכְקוֹל רְעָמִים חֲזָקִים – אוֹמֵר:
"הַלְלוּיָהּ כִּי מָלַךְ יהוה אֱלֹהֵינוּ, אֱלֹהֵי צְבָאוֹת.
⁷נָגִילָה וְנִשְׂמְחָה וְנִתֵּן לוֹ כָּבוֹד,
כִּי בָּאָה חֲתֻנַּת הַשֶּׂה וְאִשְׁתּוֹ הֵכִינָה עַצְמָהּ;
⁸וְנִתַּן לָהּ לִלְבֹּשׁ בּוּץ טָהוֹר וְצַח,
כִּי הַבּוּץ הוּא צִדְקוֹת הַקְּדוֹשִׁים."
⁹אָמַר אֵלַי: "כְּתֹב: 'אַשְׁרֵי הַקְּרוּאִים אֶל מִשְׁתֵּה
חֲתֻנַּת הַשֶּׂה.'" הוֹסִיף וְאָמַר לִי: "אֵלֶּה הֵם דִּבְרֵי
אֱמֶת שֶׁל אֱלֹהִים."
¹⁰נָפַלְתִּי לְרַגְלָיו לְהִשְׁתַּחֲווֹת לוֹ, אַךְ הוּא אָמַר אֵלַי:
"רְאֵה, אַל נָא. עֶבֶד־חָבֵר אֲנִי לְךָ וּלְאַחֶיךָ אֲשֶׁר יֵשׁ
לָהֶם עֵדוּת יֵשׁוּעַ. לֵאלֹהִים תִּשְׁתַּחֲוֶה! הֵן עֵדוּת
יֵשׁוּעַ הִיא רוּחַ הַנְּבוּאָה."
¹¹רָאִיתִי אֶת הַשָּׁמַיִם פְּתוּחִים וְהִנֵּה סוּס לָבָן
וְהַיּוֹשֵׁב עָלָיו נִקְרָא נֶאֱמָן וַאֲמִתִּי; בְּצֶדֶק הוּא שׁוֹפֵט
וְלוֹחֵם. ¹²עֵינָיו שַׁלְהֶבֶת אֵשׁ, עַל רֹאשׁוֹ עֲטָרוֹת
רַבּוֹת, וְיֵשׁ לוֹ שֵׁם כָּתוּב אֲשֶׁר אֵין אִישׁ יוֹדֵעַ אוֹתוֹ
מִלְּבַדּוֹ. ¹³הוּא לָבוּשׁ בֶּגֶד טָבוּל בְּדָם וּשְׁמוֹ נִקְרָא
דְּבַר הָאֱלֹהִים. ¹⁴צִבְאוֹת הַשָּׁמַיִם יוֹצְאִים אַחֲרָיו,
רֹכְבִים עַל סוּסִים לְבָנִים וּלְבוּשִׁים בּוּץ לָבָן וְטָהוֹר.
¹⁵מִפִּיו יוֹצֵאת חֶרֶב חַדָּה לְהַכּוֹת בָּהּ אֶת הַגּוֹיִים
וְהוּא יִרְעֵם בְּשֵׁבֶט בַּרְזֶל. הוּא דּוֹרֵךְ אֶת גַּת הַיַּיִן שֶׁל
חֲרוֹן אַף אֱלֹהֵי צְבָאוֹת, ¹⁶וְעַל בִּגְדוֹ וְעַל יְרֵכוֹ כָּתוּב
שֵׁם: "מֶלֶךְ הַמְּלָכִים וַאֲדוֹן הָאֲדוֹנִים."
¹⁷רָאִיתִי מַלְאָךְ אֶחָד עוֹמֵד בַּשֶּׁמֶשׁ וְקוֹרֵא בְּקוֹל
גָּדוֹל, בְּאָמְרוֹ לְכָל בַּעֲלֵי כָּנָף הַמְעוֹפְפִים בְּאֶמְצַע
הַשָּׁמַיִם: "בּוֹאוּ, הֵאָסְפוּ אֶל הַסְּעוּדָה הַגְּדוֹלָה אֲשֶׁר
לֵאלֹהִים, ¹⁸לְמַעַן תֹּאכְלוּ בְּשַׂר מְלָכִים וּבְשַׂר שָׂרֵי
אֲלָפִים, בְּשַׂר גִּבּוֹרִים וּבְשַׂר סוּסִים וְרוֹכְבֵיהֶם, וּבְשַׂר
הַכֹּל: גַּם חָפְשִׁים וַעֲבָדִים, גַּם קְטַנִּים וְגַם גְּדוֹלִים."

19 And I saw the beast, the kings of the earth, and their armies, gathered together to make war against Him who sat on the horse and against His army. 20 Then the beast was captured, and with him the false prophet who worked signs in his presence, by which he deceived those who received the mark of the beast and those who worshiped his image. These two were cast alive into the lake of fire burning with brimstone. 21 And the rest were killed with the sword which proceeded from the mouth of Him who sat on the horse. And all the birds were filled with their flesh.

20

Then I saw an angel coming down from heaven, having the key to the bottomless pit and a great chain in his hand. 2 He laid hold of the dragon, that serpent of old, who is *the* Devil and Satan, and bound him for a thousand years; 3 and he cast him into the bottomless pit, and shut him up, and set a seal on him, so that he should deceive the nations no more till the thousand years were finished. But after these things he must be released for a little while.

4 And I saw thrones, and they sat on them, and judgment was committed to them. Then *I saw* the souls of those who had been beheaded for their witness to Jesus and for the word of God, who had not worshiped the beast or his image, and had not received *his* mark on their foreheads or on their hands. And they lived and reigned with Christ for a thousand years. 5 But the rest of the dead did not live again until the thousand years were finished. This *is* the first resurrection. 6 Blessed and holy *is* he who has part in the first resurrection. Over such the second death has no power, but they shall be priests of God and of Christ, and shall reign with Him a thousand years.

7 Now when the thousand years have expired, Satan will be released from his prison 8 and will go out to deceive the nations which are in the four corners of the earth, Gog and Magog, to gather them together to battle, whose number *is* as the sand of the sea. 9 They went up on the breadth of the earth and surrounded the camp of the saints and the beloved city. And fire came down from God out of heaven and devoured them. 10 The devil, who deceived them, was cast into the lake of fire and brimstone where the beast and the false prophet *are*. And they will be tormented day and night forever and ever.

11 Then I saw a great white throne and Him who sat on it, from whose face the earth and the heaven fled away. And there was found no place for them. 12 And I saw the dead, small and great, standing

19 וְרָאִיתִי אֶת הַחַיָּה וְאֶת מַלְכֵי הָאָרֶץ וְצִבְאוֹתֵיהֶם נֶאֱסָפִים לַעֲשׂוֹת מִלְחָמָה בַּיּוֹשֵׁב עַל הַסּוּס וּבִצְבָאוֹ. 20 הַחַיָּה נִתְפְּסָה וְאִתָּהּ נְבִיא הַשֶּׁקֶר שֶׁעָשָׂה אֶת הָאוֹתוֹת לְפָנֶיהָ וְהִתְעָה בְּאֶמְצָעוּתָם אֶת מְקַבְּלֵי תָּו הַחַיָּה וְאֶת הַמִּשְׁתַּחֲוִים לְצַלְמָהּ; הַשְּׁנַיִם הֻשְׁלְכוּ חַיִּים אֶל אֲגַם הָאֵשׁ הַבּוֹעֵר בְּגָפְרִית. 21 וְהַנִּשְׁאָרִים נֶהֶרְגוּ בַּחֶרֶב הַיּוֹצֵאת מִפִּי הַיּוֹשֵׁב עַל הַסּוּס, וְכָל בַּעֲלֵי הַכָּנָף שָׂבְעוּ מִבְּשָׂרָם.

כ רָאִיתִי מַלְאָךְ יוֹרֵד מִן הַשָּׁמַיִם וּבְיָדוֹ מַפְתֵּחַ הַתְּהוֹם וְשַׁרְשֶׁרֶת גְּדוֹלָה. 2 הוּא תָּפַשׂ אֶת הַתַּנִּין, הַנָּחָשׁ הַקַּדְמוֹנִי אֲשֶׁר הוּא הַמַּלְשִׁין וְהַשָּׂטָן, וְקָשַׁר אוֹתוֹ לְאֶלֶף שָׁנִים. 3 הִשְׁלִיךְ אוֹתוֹ אֶל הַתְּהוֹם וְסָגַר וְחָתַם עָלָיו כְּדֵי שֶׁלֹּא יַתְעֶה עוֹד אֶת הַגּוֹיִים עַד תֹּם אֶלֶף הַשָּׁנִים; אַחֲרֵי כֵן צָרִיךְ שֶׁיֻּתַּר לִזְמַן מְעָט. 4 רָאִיתִי כִּסְאוֹת, הִתְיַשְּׁבוּ עֲלֵיהֶם וּמִשְׁפָּט נִתַּן בְּיָדָם. וְנַפְשׁוֹת הַנֶּעֱרָפִים עַל עֵדוּת יֵשׁוּעַ וְעַל דְּבַר אֱלֹהִים, וְאֵלֶּה אֲשֶׁר לֹא הִשְׁתַּחֲווּ לַחַיָּה וּלְצַלְמָהּ וְלֹא קִבְּלוּ אֶת הַתָּו עַל מִצְחָם וְעַל יָדָם – חָיוּ וּמָלְכוּ עִם הַמָּשִׁיחַ אֶלֶף שָׁנִים. 5 שְׁאָר הַמֵּתִים לֹא חָיוּ עַד תֹּם אֶלֶף הַשָּׁנִים. זֹאת הַתְּחִיָּה הָרִאשׁוֹנָה. 6 מְאֻשָּׁר וְקָדוֹשׁ מִי שֶׁחֶלְקוֹ בַּתְּחִיָּה הָרִאשׁוֹנָה; עַל אֵלֶּה אֵין לַמָּוֶת הַשֵּׁנִי שִׁלְטוֹן, כִּי יִהְיוּ כֹּהֲנִים לֵאלֹהִים וְלַמָּשִׁיחַ וְיִמְלְכוּ אִתּוֹ אֶלֶף שָׁנִים. 7 אַחֲרֵי כְּלוֹת אֶלֶף הַשָּׁנִים יֻתַּר הַשָּׂטָן מִכִּלְאוֹ 8 וְיֵצֵא לְהַתְעוֹת אֶת הַגּוֹיִים בְּאַרְבַּע קְצוֹת הָאָרֶץ, אֶת גּוֹג וּמָגוֹג, לֶאֱסֹף אוֹתָם לַמִּלְחָמָה; וּמִסְפָּרָם כְּחוֹל הַיָּם. 9 הֵם עָלוּ עַל מֶרְחַב הָאָרֶץ וְהִקִּיפוּ אֶת מַחֲנֵה הַקְּדוֹשִׁים וְאֶת הָעִיר הָאֲהוּבָה; אֵשׁ יָרְדָה מִן הַשָּׁמַיִם מֵאֵת אֱלֹהִים וְאָכְלָה אוֹתָם. 10 וְהַשָּׂטָן אֲשֶׁר הִדִּיחָם הֻשְׁלַךְ אֶל אֲגַם הָאֵשׁ וְהַגָּפְרִית, אֲשֶׁר שָׁם גַּם הַחַיָּה וּנְבִיא הַשֶּׁקֶר, וְהֵם יְעֻנּוּ יוֹמָם וָלַיְלָה לְעוֹלְמֵי עוֹלָמִים.

11 רָאִיתִי כִּסֵּא לָבָן גָּדוֹל וְאֶת הַיּוֹשֵׁב עָלָיו אֲשֶׁר נָסוּ מִפָּנָיו הָאָרֶץ וְהַשָּׁמַיִם, וּמָקוֹם לֹא נִמְצָא לָהֶם. 12 וְרָאִיתִי אֶת הַמֵּתִים, הַקְּטַנִּים וְהַגְּדוֹלִים, עוֹמְדִים לִפְנֵי הַכִּסֵּא וּסְפָרִים נִפְתָּחוּ. גַּם סֵפֶר אַחֵר נִפְתַּח,

before God, and books were opened. And another book was opened, which is *the Book* of Life. And the dead were judged according to their works, by the things which were written in the books. 13 The sea gave up the dead who were in it, and Death and Hades delivered up the dead who were in them. And they were judged, each one according to his works. 14 Then Death and Hades were cast into the lake of fire. This is the second death. 15 And anyone not found written in the Book of Life was cast into the lake of fire.

21 Now I saw a new heaven and a new earth, for the first heaven and the first earth had passed away. Also there was no more sea. 2 Then I, John, saw the holy city, New Jerusalem, coming down out of heaven from God, prepared as a bride adorned for her husband. 3 And I heard a loud voice from heaven saying, "Behold, the tabernacle of God *is* with men, and He will dwell with them, and they shall be His people. God Himself will be with them *and be* their God. 4 And God will wipe away every tear from their eyes; there shall be no more death, nor sorrow, nor crying. There shall be no more pain, for the former things have passed away."

5 Then He who sat on the throne said, "Behold, I make all things new." And He said to me, "Write, for these words are true and faithful."

6 And He said to me, "It is done! I am the Alpha and the Omega, the Beginning and the End. I will give of the fountain of the water of life freely to him who thirsts. 7 He who overcomes shall inherit all things, and I will be his God and he shall be My son. 8 But the cowardly, unbelieving, abominable, murderers, sexually immoral, sorcerers, idolaters, and all liars shall have their part in the lake which burns with fire and brimstone, which is the second death."

9 Then one of the seven angels who had the seven bowls filled with the seven last plagues came to me and talked with me, saying, "Come, I will show you the bride, the Lamb's wife." 10 And he carried me away in the Spirit to a great and high mountain, and showed me the great city, the holy Jerusalem, descending out of heaven from God, 11 having the glory of God. Her light *was* like a most precious stone, like a jasper stone, clear as crystal. 12 Also she had a great and high wall with twelve gates, and twelve angels at the gates, and names written on them, which are *the names* of the twelve tribes of the children of Israel: 13 three gates on the east, three gates on the north, three gates on the south, and three gates on the west.

סֵפֶר הַחַיִּים. וְהַמֵּתִים נִשְׁפְּטוּ מִתּוֹךְ הַדְּבָרִים הַכְּתוּבִים בַּסְּפָרִים, לְפִי מַעֲשֵׂיהֶם. 13 הַיָּם נָתַן אֶת הַמֵּתִים אֲשֶׁר בּוֹ, מָוֶת וּשְׁאוֹל נָתְנוּ אֶת מֵתֵיהֶם, וְאִישׁ אִישׁ נִשְׁפְּטוּ לְפִי מַעֲשֵׂיהֶם. 14 הַמָּוֶת וְהַשְּׁאוֹל הֻשְׁלְכוּ אֶל אֲגַם הָאֵשׁ. זֶהוּ הַמָּוֶת הַשֵּׁנִי – אֲגַם הָאֵשׁ. 15 וּמִי שֶׁלֹּא נִמְצָא כָּתוּב בְּסֵפֶר הַחַיִּים, הֻשְׁלַךְ אֶל אֲגַם הָאֵשׁ.

כא רָאִיתִי שָׁמַיִם חֲדָשִׁים וְאֶרֶץ חֲדָשָׁה, כִּי הַשָּׁמַיִם הָרִאשׁוֹנִים וְהָאָרֶץ הָרִאשׁוֹנָה עָבְרוּ וְהַיָּם אֵינֶנּוּ עוֹד. 2 רָאִיתִי אֶת עִיר הַקֹּדֶשׁ, יְרוּשָׁלַיִם הַחֲדָשָׁה, יוֹרֶדֶת מִן הַשָּׁמַיִם מֵאֵת הָאֱלֹהִים, מוּכָנָה כְּכַלָּה מְקֻשֶּׁטֶת לְבַעְלָהּ. 3 וְשָׁמַעְתִּי קוֹל גָּדוֹל מִן הַכִּסֵּא – אוֹמֵר:

"הִנֵּה מִשְׁכַּן הָאֱלֹהִים עִם בְּנֵי אָדָם וְיִשְׁכֹּן עִמָּהֶם; הֵמָּה יִהְיוּ לוֹ לְעַם וְהוּא הָאֱלֹהִים יִהְיֶה עִמָּהֶם, 4 וְיִמְחֶה כָּל דִּמְעָה מֵעֵינֵיהֶם וְהַמָּוֶת לֹא יִהְיֶה עוֹד; גַּם אֵבֶל וְזַעֲקָה וּכְאֵב לֹא יִהְיוּ עוֹד, כִּי הָרִאשׁוֹנוֹת עָבְרוּ."

5 אָמַר הַיּוֹשֵׁב עַל הַכִּסֵּא: "הִנְנִי עוֹשֶׂה הַכֹּל חָדָשׁ." אָמַר אֵלַי: "כְּתֹב, כִּי הַדְּבָרִים הָאֵלֶּה נֶאֱמָנִים וַאֲמִתִּיִּים הֵם." 6 הוֹסִיף וְאָמַר אֵלַי: "הָיֹה נִהְיָה. אֲנִי הָאָלֶף וְהַתָּו, הָרֵאשִׁית וְהַתַּכְלִית. אֲנִי אֶתֵּן לַצָּמֵא מִמַּעְיַן הַמַּיִם שֶׁל הַחַיִּים – חִנָּם. 7 הַמְנַצֵּחַ יִירַשׁ אֶת אֵלֶּה וַאֲנִי אֶהְיֶה לוֹ לֵאלֹהִים וְהוּא יִהְיֶה לִי לְבֵן. 8 אֲבָל מוּגֵי הַלֵּב וְהַבִּלְתִּי מַאֲמִינִים, הַמְתֹעָבִים וְהַמְרַצְּחִים, הַזּוֹנִים וְהַמְכַשְּׁפִים, עוֹבְדֵי הָאֱלִילִים וְכָל הַמְשַׁקְּרִים – חֶלְקָם בָּאֲגַם הַבּוֹעֵר בְּאֵשׁ וְגָפְרִית אֲשֶׁר הוּא הַמָּוֶת הַשֵּׁנִי."

9 אֶחָד מִשִּׁבְעַת הַמַּלְאָכִים, אֲשֶׁר לָהֶם שֶׁבַע הַקְּעָרוֹת הַמְּלֵאוֹת בְּשֶׁבַע הַמַּכּוֹת הָאַחֲרוֹנוֹת, בָּא וְדִבֶּר אִתִּי. אָמַר: "בּוֹא אַרְאֶה לְךָ אֶת הַכַּלָּה אֵשֶׁת הַשֶּׂה." 10 הוּא נָשָׂא אוֹתִי, בָּרוּחַ, אֶל הַר גָּדוֹל וְגָבוֹהַּ וְהֶרְאָה לִי אֶת עִיר הַקֹּדֶשׁ, יְרוּשָׁלַיִם, יוֹרֶדֶת מִן הַשָּׁמַיִם מֵאֵת אֱלֹהִים 11 וּכְבוֹד אֱלֹהִים לָהּ. אוֹר נֹגַהּ כְּאֶבֶן יְקָרָה מְאֹד, כְּאֶבֶן יָשְׁפֶה זַכָּה כִּבְדֹלַח. 12 וְיֵשׁ לָהּ חוֹמָה גְּדוֹלָה וּגְבוֹהָה עִם שְׁנֵים-עָשָׂר שְׁעָרִים, וְעַל הַשְּׁעָרִים שְׁנֵים-עָשָׂר מַלְאָכִים וְשֵׁמוֹת כְּתוּבִים עֲלֵיהֶם – שְׁנֵים-עָשָׂר שִׁבְטֵי בְּנֵי יִשְׂרָאֵל; 13 מִמִּזְרָח שְׁלוֹשָׁה שְׁעָרִים, מִצָּפוֹן שְׁלוֹשָׁה שְׁעָרִים, מִדָּרוֹם שְׁלוֹשָׁה שְׁעָרִים, מִמַּעֲרָב שְׁלוֹשָׁה שְׁעָרִים.

14 Now the wall of the city had twelve founda-tions, and on them were the names of the twelve apostles of the Lamb. 15 And he who talked with me had a gold reed to measure the city, its gates, and its wall. 16 The city is laid out as a square; its length is as great as its breadth. And he measured the city with the reed: twelve thousand furlongs. Its length, breadth, and height are equal. 17 Then he measured its wall: one hundred *and* forty-four cubits, *accord-ing* to the measure of a man, that is, of an angel. 18 The construction of its wall was *of* jasper; and the city *was* pure gold, like clear glass. 19 The founda-tions of the wall of the city *were* adorned with all kinds of precious stones: the first foundation *was* jasper, the second sapphire, the third chalcedony, the fourth emerald, 20 the fifth sardonyx, the sixth sardius, the seventh chrysolite, the eighth beryl, the ninth topaz, the tenth chrysoprase, the eleventh jacinth, and the twelfth amethyst. 21 The twelve gates *were* twelve pearls: each individual gate was of one pearl. And the street of the city *was* pure gold, like transparent glass.

22 But I saw no temple in it, for the Lord God Almighty and the Lamb are its temple. 23 The city had no need of the sun or of the moon to shine in it, for the glory of God illuminated it. The Lamb *is* its light. 24 And the nations of those who are saved shall walk in its light, and the kings of the earth bring their glory and honor into it. 25 Its gates shall not be shut at all by day (there shall be no night there). 26 And they shall bring the glory and the honor of the nations into it. 27 But there shall by no means enter it anything that defiles, or causes an abomination or a lie, but only those who are written in the Lamb's Book of Life.

22 And he showed me a pure river of water of life, clear as crystal, proceeding from the throne of God and of the Lamb. 2 In the middle of its street, and on either side of the river, *was* the tree of life, which bore twelve fruits, each *tree* yielding its fruit every month. The leaves of the tree *were* for the healing of the nations. 3 And there shall be no more curse, but the throne of God and of the Lamb shall be in it, and His servants shall serve Him. 4 They shall see His face, and His name *shall be* on their foreheads. 5 There shall be no night there: They need no lamp nor light of the sun, for the Lord God gives them light. And they shall reign forever and ever.

6 Then he said to me, "These words *are* faithful and true." And the Lord God of the holy prophets sent His angel to show His servants the things which must shortly take place.

14 וּלְחוֹמַת הָעִיר שְׁנֵים־עָשָׂר יְסוֹדוֹת וַעֲלֵיהֶם שְׁנֵים־עָשָׂר שֵׁמוֹת שֶׁל שְׁנֵים־עָשָׂר שְׁלִיחֵי הַשֶּׂה. 15 הַמְדַבֵּר אֵלַי הֶחֱזִיק קְנֵה־מִדָּה מִזָּהָב כְּדֵי לִמְדֹּד אֶת הָעִיר וְאֶת שְׁעָרֶיהָ וְאֶת חוֹמָתָהּ. 16 וְהָעִיר מְרֻבַּעַת, אָרְכָּהּ כְּרָחְבָּהּ. הוּא מָדַד אֶת הָעִיר בְּקָנֶה – שְׁנֵים־עָשָׂר אֶלֶף רִיס; אָרְכָּה וְרָחְבָּה וְקוֹמָתָהּ שָׁוִים. 17 גַּם אֶת חוֹמָתָהּ מָדַד, וְהַמִּדָּה מֵאָה וְאַרְבָּעִים וְאַרְבַּע אַמּוֹת לְפִי מִדָּה אֱנוֹשִׁית אֲשֶׁר הִיא מִדָּה שֶׁל מַלְאָךְ. 18 הַחוֹמָה בְּנֻיָה אֶבֶן יָשְׁפֶה, וְהָעִיר זָהָב טָהוֹר כִּזְכוּכִית טְהוֹרָה. 19 יְסוֹדוֹת חוֹמַת הָעִיר מְקֻשָּׁטִים בְּכָל אֶבֶן יְקָרָה; הַיְסוֹד הָרִאשׁוֹן יָשְׁפֶה, הַשֵּׁנִי סַפִּיר, הַשְּׁלִישִׁי שְׁבוֹ, הָרְבִיעִי בָּרֶקֶת, 20 הַחֲמִישִׁי יַהֲלֹם, הַשִּׁשִּׁי אֹדֶם, הַשְּׁבִיעִי תַּרְשִׁישׁ, הַשְּׁמִינִי שֹׁהַם, הַתְּשִׁיעִי פִּטְדָה, הָעֲשִׂירִי נֹפֶךְ, הָאַחַד־עָשָׂר לֶשֶׁם, הַשְּׁנֵים־עָשָׂר אַחְלָמָה. 21 וּשְׁנֵים־עָשָׂר הַשְּׁעָרִים – שְׁתֵּים־עֶשְׂרֵה מַרְגָּלִיּוֹת; כָּל שַׁעַר וְשַׁעַר הָיָה מִמַּרְגָּלִית אַחַת, וּרְחוֹב הָעִיר זָהָב טָהוֹר כִּזְכוּכִית זַכָּה. 22 הֵיכָל לֹא רָאִיתִי בָּהּ, כִּי הֵיכָלָהּ הוּא יְהוָה אֱלֹהֵי צְבָאוֹת וְהַשֶּׂה. 23 וְהָעִיר אֵינֶנָּה צְרִיכָה לַשֶּׁמֶשׁ וְלַיָּרֵחַ שֶׁיָּאִירוּ בָּהּ, כִּי כְּבוֹד אֱלֹהִים הֵאִיר אוֹתָהּ וְהַשֶּׂה הוּא מְנוֹרָתָהּ. 24 הַגּוֹיִים יֵלְכוּ לְאוֹרָהּ וּמַלְכֵי הָאָרֶץ מְבִיאִים אֶת כְּבוֹדָם אֵלֶיהָ. 25 שְׁעָרֶיהָ לֹא יִסָּגְרוּ בַּיּוֹם; וַהֲרֵי לַיְלָה לֹא יִהְיֶה שָׁם. 26 אֶת כְּבוֹד הַגּוֹיִים וִיקָרָם יָבִיאוּ אֵלֶיהָ, 27 וְלֹא יָכֹנֵם אֵלֶיהָ כָּל טָמֵא וְעוֹשֵׂה תוֹעֵבָה וָשֶׁקֶר, כִּי אִם הַכְּתוּבִים בְּסֵפֶר הַחַיִּים שֶׁל הַשֶּׂה.

כב הוּא הֶרְאָה לִי נְהַר מַיִם חַיִּים, מַבְהִיק כִּבְדֹלַח, יוֹצֵא מִכִּסֵּא הָאֱלֹהִים וְהַשֶּׂה. 2 בְּאֶמְצַע רְחוֹב הָעִיר וְעַל שְׂפַת הַנָּהָר מִזֶּה וּמִזֶּה – עֵץ חַיִּים עוֹשֶׂה פֵּרוֹת שְׁתֵּים־עֶשְׂרֵה פְּעָמִים, בִּתְּתוֹ בְּכָל חֹדֶשׁ וְחֹדֶשׁ אֶת פִּרְיוֹ, וַעֲלֵה הָעֵץ לְמִרְפֵּא הַגּוֹיִים. 3 שׁוּם קְלָלָה לֹא תִהְיֶה עוֹד. כִּסֵּא אֱלֹהִים וְהַשֶּׂה יִהְיֶה בָּהּ וַעֲבָדָיו יְשָׁרְתוּהוּ. 4 הֵם יִרְאוּ אֶת פָּנָיו, וּשְׁמוֹ עַל מִצְחוֹתָם. 5 וְלַיְלָה לֹא יִהְיֶה עוֹד וְלֹא יִצְטָרְכוּ לְאוֹר מְנוֹרָה וּלְאוֹר שֶׁמֶשׁ, כִּי יְהוָה אֱלֹהִים יָאִיר עֲלֵיהֶם וְיִמְלְכוּ לְעוֹלְמֵי עוֹלָמִים. 6 עוֹד אָמַר אֵלַי: "הַדְּבָרִים הָאֵלֶּה נֶאֱמָנִים וַאֲמִתִּיִּים וַיהוָה אֱלֹהֵי רוּחוֹת הַנְּבִיאִים שָׁלַח אֶת מַלְאָכוֹ לְהַרְאוֹת אֶת עֲבָדָיו אֶת אֲשֶׁר צָרִיךְ לִהְיוֹת בִּמְהֵרָה."

16 שנים־עשר אלף ריס – אלפים ושלוש מאות קילומטרים.

7 "Behold, I am coming quickly! Blessed *is* he who keeps the words of the prophecy of this book."

8 Now I, John, saw and heard these things. And when I heard and saw, I fell down to worship before the feet of the angel who showed me these things.

9 Then he said to me, "See *that you do* not *do that.* For I am your fellow servant, and of your brethren the prophets, and of those who keep the words of this book. Worship God." 10 And he said to me, "Do not seal the words of the prophecy of this book, for the time is at hand. 11 He who is unjust, let him be unjust still; he who is filthy, let him be filthy still; he who is righteous, let him be righteous still; he who is holy, let him be holy still."

12 "And behold, I am coming quickly, and My reward *is* with Me, to give to every one according to his work. 13 I am the Alpha and the Omega, *the* Beginning and *the* End, the First and the Last."

14 Blessed *are* those who do His commandments, that they may have the right to the tree of life, and may enter through the gates into the city. 15 But outside *are* dogs and sorcerers and sexually immoral and murderers and idolaters, and whoever loves and practices a lie.

16 "I, Jesus, have sent My angel to testify to you these things in the churches. I am the Root and the Offspring of David, the Bright and Morning Star."

17 And the Spirit and the bride say, "Come!" And let him who hears say, "Come!" And let him who thirsts come. Whoever desires, let him take the water of life freely.

18 For I testify to everyone who hears the words of the prophecy of this book: If anyone adds to these things, God will add to him the plagues that are written in this book; 19 and if anyone takes away from the words of the book of this prophecy, God shall take away his part from the Book of Life, from the holy city, and *from* the things which are written in this book.

20 He who testifies to these things says, "Surely I am coming quickly."

Amen. Even so, come, Lord Jesus!

21 The grace of our Lord Jesus Christ *be* with you all. Amen.

7 "הִנְנִי בָּא מַהֵר. אַשְׁרֵי הַשּׁוֹמֵר אֶת דִּבְרֵי הַנְּבוּאָה שֶׁל הַסֵּפֶר הַזֶּה."

8 וַאֲנִי, יוֹחָנָן, הָרוֹאֶה וְשׁוֹמֵעַ אֶת אֵלֶּה. וְכַאֲשֶׁר שָׁמַעְתִּי וְרָאִיתִי, נָפַלְתִּי לְהִשְׁתַּחֲווֹת לְרַגְלֵי הַמַּלְאָךְ אֲשֶׁר הֶרְאַנִי אֶת אֵלֶּה. 9 אָמַר אֵלַי: "רְאֵה, אַל־נָא; עֶבֶד־חָבֵר אֲנִי לְךָ וּלְאַחֶיךָ הַנְּבִיאִים וְלַשּׁוֹמְרִים אֶת דִּבְרֵי הַסֵּפֶר הַזֶּה. לֵאלֹהִים תִּשְׁתַּחֲוֶה!" 10 עוֹד אָמַר אֵלַי: "אַל תַּחְתֹּם אֶת דִּבְרֵי הַנְּבוּאָה שֶׁל הַסֵּפֶר הַזֶּה, כִּי קָרוֹב הַמּוֹעֵד. 11 הַמָּעוּל – שֶׁיּוֹסִיף לַעֲשׂוֹת עָוֶל; הַטָּמֵא – שֶׁיִּטַּמֵּא עוֹד; הַצַּדִּיק – שֶׁיִּצְדַּק עוֹד; הַקָּדוֹשׁ – שֶׁיִּתְקַדֵּשׁ עוֹד."

12 "הִנְנִי בָּא מַהֵר וְאִתִּי הַשָּׂכָר לְשַׁלֵּם לְכָל אִישׁ כְּמַעֲשֵׂהוּ. 13 אֲנִי הָאָלֶף אַף אֲנִי הַתָּו, הָרִאשׁוֹן אַף הָאַחֲרוֹן, הָרֵאשִׁית וְהַתַּכְלִית."

14 אַשְׁרֵי הַמְכַבְּסִים אֶת גְּלִימוֹתֵיהֶם, לְמַעַן תִּהְיֶה לָהֶם זְכוּת עַל עֵץ הַחַיִּים וְיִכָּנְסוּ הָעִירָה דֶּרֶךְ הַשְּׁעָרִים. 15 בַּחוּץ יִהְיוּ הַכְּלָבִים וְהַמְכַשְּׁפִים, הַזּוֹנִים וְהַמְרַצְּחִים, עוֹבְדֵי אֱלִילִים וְכָל אוֹהֵב שֶׁקֶר וְעוֹשֵׂהוּ.

16 "אֲנִי יֵשׁוּעַ שָׁלַחְתִּי אֶת מַלְאָכִי לְהָעִיד לָכֶם אֶת הַדְּבָרִים הָאֵלֶּה בַּקְּהִלּוֹת. אָנֹכִי שֹׁרֶשׁ דָּוִד וְצֶאֱצָאוֹ, אַיֶּלֶת הַשַּׁחַר."

17 הָרוּחַ וְהַכַּלָּה אוֹמְרוֹת: "בּוֹא!", וְהַשּׁוֹמֵעַ יֹאמַר נָא "בּוֹא!"; הַצָּמֵא יָבוֹא נָא, וְהֶחָפֵץ יִקַּח נָא מַיִם חַיִּים חִנָּם.

18 אָנֹכִי מֵעִיד בְּכָל מִי שֶׁשּׁוֹמֵעַ אֶת דִּבְרֵי נְבוּאַת הַסֵּפֶר הַזֶּה: אִישׁ אִם יוֹסִיף עֲלֵיהֶם, יוֹסִיף עָלָיו אֱלֹהִים אֶת הַמַּכּוֹת הַכְּתוּבוֹת בַּסֵּפֶר הַזֶּה. 19 וְאִישׁ אִם יִגְרַע מִדִּבְרֵי סֵפֶר הַנְּבוּאָה הַזֹּאת, יִגְרַע הָאֱלֹהִים אֶת חֶלְקוֹ מֵעֵץ הַחַיִּים וּמֵעִיר הַקֹּדֶשׁ, מִן הַדְּבָרִים הַכְּתוּבִים בַּסֵּפֶר הַזֶּה. 20 הַמֵּעִיד אֶת הַדְּבָרִים הָאֵלֶּה אוֹמֵר: "אָכֵן, אֲנִי בָּא מַהֵר." אָמֵן. בּוֹא נָא הָאָדוֹן יֵשׁוּעַ.

21 חֶסֶד הָאָדוֹן יֵשׁוּעַ עִם כָּל הַקְּדוֹשִׁים. אָמֵן.

G-d

19 And I saw the beast, the kings of the earth, and their armies, gathered together to make war against Him who sat on the horse and against His army. 20 Then the beast was captured, and with him the false prophet who worked signs in his presence, by which he deceived those who received the mark of the beast and those who worshiped his image. These two were cast alive into the lake of fire burning with brimstone. 21 And the rest were killed with the sword which proceeded from the mouth of Him who sat on the horse. And all the birds were filled with their flesh.

20 Then I saw an angel coming down from heaven, having the key to the bottomless pit and a great chain in his hand. 2 He laid hold of the dragon, that serpent of old, who is *the* Devil and Satan, and bound him for a thousand years; 3 and he cast him into the bottomless pit, and shut him up, and set a seal on him, so that he should deceive the nations no more till the thousand years were finished. But after these things he must be released for a little while.

4 And I saw thrones, and they sat on them, and judgment was committed to them. Then *I* saw the souls of those who had been beheaded for their witness to Jesus and for the word of God, who had not worshiped the beast or his image, and had not received *his* mark on their foreheads or on their hands. And they lived and reigned with Christ for a thousand years. 5 But the rest of the dead did not live again until the thousand years were finished. This *is* the first resurrection. 6 Blessed and holy *is* he who has part in the first resurrection. Over such the second death has no power, but they shall be priests of God and of Christ, and shall reign with Him a thousand years.

7 Now when the thousand years have expired, Satan will be released from his prison 8 and will go out to deceive the nations which are in the four corners of the earth, Gog and Magog, to gather them together to battle, whose number *is* as the sand of the sea. 9 They went up on the breadth of the earth and surrounded the camp of the saints and the beloved city. And fire came down from God out of heaven and devoured them. 10 The devil, who deceived them, was cast into the lake of fire and brimstone where the beast and the false prophet *are*. And they will be tormented day and night forever and ever.

11 Then I saw a great white throne and Him who sat on it, from whose face the earth and the heaven fled away. And there was found no place for them. 12 And I saw the dead, small and great, standing

19 וְרָאִיתִי אֶת הַחַיָּה וְאֶת מַלְכֵי הָאָרֶץ וְצִבְאוֹתֵיהֶם נֶאֱסָפִים לַעֲשׂוֹת מִלְחָמָה בַּיּוֹשֵׁב עַל הַסּוּס וּבִצְבָאוֹ. 20 הַחַיָּה נִתְפְּשָׂה וְאִתָּהּ נְבִיא הַשֶּׁקֶר שֶׁעָשָׂה אֶת הָאוֹתוֹת לְפָנֶיהָ וְהִתְעָה בְּאֶמְצָעוּתָם אֶת מְקַבְּלֵי תָּו הַחַיָּה וְאֶת הַמִּשְׁתַּחֲוִים לְצַלְמָהּ; הַשְּׁנַיִם הֻשְׁלְכוּ חַיִּים אֶל אֲגַם הָאֵשׁ הַבּוֹעֵר בְּגָפְרִית. 21 וְהַנִּשְׁאָרִים נֶהֶרְגוּ בַּחֶרֶב הַיּוֹצֵאת מִפִּי הַיּוֹשֵׁב עַל הַסּוּס, וְכָל בַּעֲלֵי הַכָּנָף שָׂבְעוּ מִבְּשָׂרָם.

כ רָאִיתִי מַלְאָךְ יוֹרֵד מִן הַשָּׁמַיִם וּבְיָדוֹ מַפְתֵּחַ הַתְּהוֹם וְשַׁרְשֶׁרֶת גְּדוֹלָה. 2 הוּא תָּפַשׂ אֶת הַתַּנִּין, הַנָּחָשׁ הַקַּדְמוֹנִי אֲשֶׁר הוּא הַמַּלְשִׁין וְהַשָּׂטָן, וְקָשַׁר אוֹתוֹ לְאֶלֶף שָׁנִים. 3 הִשְׁלִיךְ אוֹתוֹ אֶל הַתְּהוֹם וְסָגַר וְחָתַם עָלָיו כְּדֵי שֶׁלֹּא יַתְעֶה עוֹד אֶת הַגּוֹיִים עַד תֹּם אֶלֶף הַשָּׁנִים; אַחֲרֵי כֵן צָרִיךְ שֶׁיֻּתַּר לִזְמַן מְעָט.

4 רָאִיתִי כִּסְאוֹת; הִתְיַשְּׁבוּ עֲלֵיהֶם וּמִשְׁפָּט נִתַּן בְּיָדָם. וְנַפְשׁוֹת הַנֶּעֱרָפִים עַל עֵדוּת יֵשׁוּעַ וְעַל דְּבַר אֱלֹהִים, וְאֵלֶּה אֲשֶׁר לֹא הִשְׁתַּחֲווּ לַחַיָּה וּלְצַלְמָהּ וְלֹא קִבְּלוּ אֶת הַתָּו עַל מִצְחָם וְעַל יָד – חָיוּ וּמָלְכוּ עִם הַמָּשִׁיחַ אֶלֶף שָׁנִים. 5 שְׁאָר הַמֵּתִים לֹא חָיוּ עַד תֹּם אֶלֶף הַשָּׁנִים. זֹאת הַתְּחִיָּה הָרִאשׁוֹנָה. 6 מְאֻשָּׁר וְקָדוֹשׁ מִי שֶׁחֶלְקוֹ בַּתְּחִיָּה הָרִאשׁוֹנָה; עַל אֵלֶּה אֵין לַמָּוֶת הַשֵּׁנִי שִׁלְטוֹן, כִּי יִהְיוּ כֹּהֲנִים לֵאלֹהִים וְלַמָּשִׁיחַ וְיִמְלְכוּ אִתּוֹ אֶלֶף שָׁנִים.

7 אַחֲרֵי כְּלוֹת אֶלֶף הַשָּׁנִים יֻתַּר הַשָּׂטָן מִכִּלְאוֹ 8 וְיֵצֵא לְהַתְעוֹת אֶת הַגּוֹיִים בְּאַרְבַּע קְצוֹת הָאָרֶץ, אֶת גּוֹג וּמָגוֹג, לֶאֱסֹף אוֹתָם לַמִּלְחָמָה; וּמִסְפָּרָם כְּחוֹל הַיָּם. 9 הֵם עָלוּ עַל מֶרְחַב הָאָרֶץ וְהִקִּיפוּ אֶת מַחֲנֵה הַקְּדוֹשִׁים וְאֶת הָעִיר הָאֲהוּבָה; אֵשׁ יָרְדָה מִן הַשָּׁמַיִם מֵאֵת אֱלֹהִים וְאָכְלָה אוֹתָם. 10 וְהַשָּׂטָן אֲשֶׁר הִדִּיחָם הֻשְׁלַךְ אֶל אֲגַם הָאֵשׁ וְהַגָּפְרִית, אֲשֶׁר שָׁם גַּם הַחַיָּה וּנְבִיא הַשֶּׁקֶר, וְהֵם יְעֻנּוּ יוֹמָם וָלַיְלָה לְעוֹלְמֵי עוֹלָמִים.

11 רָאִיתִי כִּסֵּא לָבָן גָּדוֹל וְאֶת הַיּוֹשֵׁב עָלָיו אֲשֶׁר נָסוּ מִפָּנָיו הָאָרֶץ וְהַשָּׁמַיִם, וּמָקוֹם לֹא נִמְצָא לָהֶם. 12 וְרָאִיתִי אֶת הַמֵּתִים, הַקְּטַנִּים וְהַגְּדוֹלִים, עוֹמְדִים לִפְנֵי הַכִּסֵּא וּסְפָרִים נִפְתָּחוּ. גַּם סֵפֶר אַחֵר נִפְתַּח,

before God, and books were opened. And another
book was opened, which is *the Book* of Life. And
the dead were judged according to their works, by
the things which were written in the books. ¹³ The
sea gave up the dead who were in it, and Death and
Hades delivered up the dead who were in them.
And they were judged, each one according to his
works. ¹⁴ Then Death and Hades were cast into the
lake of fire. This is the second death. ¹⁵ And anyone
not found written in the Book of Life was cast into
the lake of fire.

21 Now I saw a new heaven and a new earth, for
the first heaven and the first earth had passed away.
Also there was no more sea. ² Then I, John, saw the
holy city, New Jerusalem, coming down out of
heaven from God, prepared as a bride adorned for
her husband. ³ And I heard a loud voice from
heaven saying, "Behold, the tabernacle of God *is*
with men, and He will dwell with them, and they
shall be His people. God Himself will be with them
and be their God. ⁴ And God will wipe away every
tear from their eyes; there shall be no more death,
nor sorrow, nor crying. There shall be no more
pain, for the former things have passed away."

⁵ Then He who sat on the throne said, "Behold, I
make all things new." And He said to me, "Write,
for these words are true and faithful."

⁶ And He said to me, "It is done! I am the Alpha
and the Omega, the Beginning and the End. I will
give of the fountain of the water of life freely to him
who thirsts. ⁷ He who overcomes shall inherit all
things, and I will be his God and he shall be My
son. ⁸ But the cowardly, unbelieving, abominable,
murderers, sexually immoral, sorcerers, idolaters,
and all liars shall have their part in the lake which
burns with fire and brimstone, which is the second
death."

⁹ Then one of the seven angels who had the seven
bowls filled with the seven last plagues came to me
and talked with me, saying, "Come, I will show you
the bride, the Lamb's wife." ¹⁰ And he carried me
away in the Spirit to a great and high mountain,
and showed me the great city, the holy Jerusalem,
descending out of heaven from God, ¹¹ having the
glory of God. Her light *was* like a most precious
stone, like a jasper stone, clear as crystal. ¹² Also she
had a great and high wall with twelve gates, and
twelve angels at the gates, and names written on
them, which are *the names* of the twelve tribes of the
children of Israel: ¹³ three gates on the east, three
gates on the north, three gates on the south, and
three gates on the west.

סֵפֶר הַחַיִּים. וְהַמֵּתִים נִשְׁפְּטוּ מִתּוֹךְ הַדְּבָרִים
הַכְּתוּבִים בַּסְּפָרִים, לְפִי מַעֲשֵׂיהֶם. ¹³ הַיָּם נָתַן אֶת
הַמֵּתִים אֲשֶׁר בּוֹ, מָוֶת וּשְׁאוֹל נָתְנוּ אֶת מֵתֵיהֶם,
וְאִישׁ אִישׁ נִשְׁפְּטוּ לְפִי מַעֲשָׂיו. ¹⁴ הַמָּוֶת וְהַשְּׁאוֹל
הֻשְׁלְכוּ אֶל אֲגַם הָאֵשׁ. זֶהוּ הַמָּוֶת הַשֵּׁנִי – אֲגַם
הָאֵשׁ. ¹⁵ וּמִי שֶׁלֹּא נִמְצָא כָּתוּב בְּסֵפֶר הַחַיִּים,
הֻשְׁלַךְ אֶל אֲגַם הָאֵשׁ.

כא רָאִיתִי שָׁמַיִם חֲדָשִׁים וְאֶרֶץ חֲדָשָׁה, כִּי
הַשָּׁמַיִם הָרִאשׁוֹנִים וְהָאָרֶץ הָרִאשׁוֹנָה עָבְרוּ וְהַיָּם
אֵינֶנּוּ עוֹד. ² רָאִיתִי אֶת עִיר הַקֹּדֶשׁ, יְרוּשָׁלַיִם
הַחֲדָשָׁה, יוֹרֶדֶת מִן הַשָּׁמַיִם מֵאֵת הָאֱלֹהִים, מוּכָנָה
כְּכַלָּה מְקֻשֶּׁטֶת לְבַעֲלָהּ. ³ וְשָׁמַעְתִּי קוֹל גָּדוֹל מִן
הַכִּסֵּא – אוֹמֵר:

"הִנֵּה מִשְׁכַּן הָאֱלֹהִים עִם בְּנֵי אָדָם וְיִשְׁכֹּן עִמָּהֶם;
הֵמָּה יִהְיוּ לוֹ לְעָם וְהוּא הָאֱלֹהִים יִהְיֶה עִמָּהֶם,
⁴ וְיִמְחֶה כָּל דִּמְעָה מֵעֵינֵיהֶם וְהַמָּוֶת לֹא יִהְיֶה עוֹד;
גַּם אֵבֶל וְזַעֲקָה וּכְאֵב לֹא יִהְיוּ עוֹד,
כִּי הָרִאשׁוֹנוֹת עָבְרוּ."

⁵ אָמַר הַיּוֹשֵׁב עַל הַכִּסֵּא: "הִנְנִי עוֹשֶׂה הַכֹּל חָדָשׁ."
אָמַר אֵלַי: "כְּתֹב, כִּי הַדְּבָרִים הָאֵלֶּה נֶאֱמָנִים
וַאֲמִתִּיִּים הֵם." ⁶ הוֹסִיף וְאָמַר אֵלַי: "הָיֹה נִהְיָה. אֲנִי
הָאָלֶף וְהַתָּו, הָרֵאשִׁית וְהַתַּכְלִית. אֲנִי אֶתֵּן לַצָּמֵא
מִמַּעְיַן הַמַּיִם שֶׁל הַחַיִּים – חִנָּם. ⁷ הַמְנַצֵּחַ יִירַשׁ אֶת
אֵלֶּה וַאֲנִי אֶהְיֶה לּוֹ לֵאלֹהִים וְהוּא יִהְיֶה לִי לְבֵן.
⁸ אֲבָל מוּגֵי הַלֵּב וְהַבִּלְתִּי מַאֲמִינִים, הַמְתֹעָבִים
וְהַמְרַצְּחִים, הַזּוֹנִים וְהַמְכַשְּׁפִים, עוֹבְדֵי הָאֱלִילִים
וְכָל הַמְשַׁקְּרִים – חֶלְקָם בָּאֲגַם הַבּוֹעֵר בְּאֵשׁ וְגָפְרִית
אֲשֶׁר הוּא הַמָּוֶת הַשֵּׁנִי."

⁹ אֶחָד מִשִּׁבְעַת הַמַּלְאָכִים, אֲשֶׁר לָהֶם שֶׁבַע
הַקְּעָרוֹת הַמְלֵאוֹת בְּשֶׁבַע הַמַּכּוֹת הָאַחֲרוֹנוֹת, בָּא
וְדִבֶּר אִתִּי. אָמַר: "בּוֹא אַרְאֶה לְךָ אֶת הַכַּלָּה אֵשֶׁת
הַשֶּׂה." ¹⁰ הוּא נָשָׂא אוֹתִי, בָּרוּחַ, אֶל הַר גָּדוֹל
וְגָבֹהַּ וְהֶרְאָה לִי אֶת עִיר הַקֹּדֶשׁ, יְרוּשָׁלַיִם, יוֹרֶדֶת
מִן הַשָּׁמַיִם מֵאֵת אֱלֹהִים ¹¹ וּכְבוֹד אֱלֹהִים לָהּ. אוֹר
נָגְהָהּ כְּאֶבֶן יְקָרָה מְאֹד, כְּאֶבֶן יָשְׁפֵה זַכָּה כִּבְדֹלַח.
¹² וְיֵשׁ לָהּ חוֹמָה גְּדוֹלָה וּגְבוֹהָה עִם שְׁנֵים-עָשָׂר
שְׁעָרִים, וְעַל הַשְּׁעָרִים שְׁנֵים-עָשָׂר מַלְאָכִים וְשֵׁמוֹת
כְּתוּבִים עֲלֵיהֶם – שְׁנֵים-עָשָׂר שִׁבְטֵי בְּנֵי יִשְׂרָאֵל;
¹³ מִמִּזְרָח שְׁלוֹשָׁה שְׁעָרִים, מִצָּפוֹן שְׁלוֹשָׁה שְׁעָרִים,
מִדָּרוֹם שְׁלוֹשָׁה שְׁעָרִים, מִמַּעֲרָב שְׁלוֹשָׁה שְׁעָרִים.